Profiles
of
New York State

2019-2020
Fifteenth Edition

Profiles
of
New York State

A UNIVERSAL REFERENCE BOOK

Grey House
Publishing

PRESIDENT: Richard Gottlieb
PUBLISHER: Leslie Mackenzie
EDITORIAL DIRECTOR: Laura Mars
SENIOR EDITOR: David Garoogian
MARKETING DIRECTOR: Jessica Moody

Grey House Publishing, Inc.
4919 Route 22
Amenia, NY 12501
(518) 789-8700
Fax: (845) 373-6390
www.greyhouse.com
e-mail: books@greyhouse.com

Profiles of New York State
2 Volume Set (*New York State Directory* and *Profiles of New York State*)

ISBN: 978-1-64265-073-0
ISBN: 978-1-64265-075-4

Table of Contents

Introduction

This is the fifteenth edition of *Profiles of New York State—Facts, Figures & Statistics for 2,565 Populated Places in New York.* As with the other titles in our *State Profiles* series, it was built with content from Grey House Publishing's award-winning *Profiles of America*—a 4-volume compilation of data on more than 43,000 places in the United States. We have included the New York chapter from *Profiles of America,* and added several new chapters of demographic information and ranking sections, so that *Profiles of New York State* is the most comprehensive portrait of the state of New York ever published.

Profiles of New York State provides data on all populated communities and counties in the state of New York for which the US Census provides individual statistics. This edition also includes profiles of 440 unincorporated places and neighborhoods (i.e. Flushing, Queens) based on US Census data by zip code.

This premier reference work includes five major sections that cover everything from **Education** to **Ethnic Backgrounds** to **Climate.** All sections include **Comparative Statistics** or **Rankings.** A section called **About New York** at the front of the book includes detailed narrative and colorful photos and maps. Here is an overview of each section:

1. About New York
This 4-color section gives the researcher a real sense of the state and its history. It includes a Photo Gallery, and comprehensive sections on New York's Government, Timeline of New York History, Land and Natural Resources, New York State Energy Profile and Demographic Maps. These 46 pages, with the help of photos, maps and charts, anchor the researcher to the state, both physically and politically.

2. Profiles
This section, organized by county, gives detailed profiles of 2,565 places plus 62 counties, based on Census 2010 and data from the 2013-2017 American Community Survey. In addition, we have added current government statistics and original research, so that these profiles pull together statistical and descriptive information on every Census-recognized place in the state. Major fields of information include:

Geography	*Housing*	*Education*	*Religion*
Ancestry	*Transportation*	*Population*	*Climate*
Economy	*Industry*	*Health*	

In addition to place and county profiles, this section includes a **Place Name Index.**

3. Comparative Statistics
This section includes tables that compare New York's 100 largest communities by dozens of data points.

4. Community Rankings
This section includes tables that rank the top 150 and bottom 150 incorporated communities with population over 2,500, in dozens of categories.

5. Education
This section begins with an **Educational State Profile,** summarizing number of schools, students, diplomas granted and educational dollars spent. Following the state profile are **School District Rankings** on 16 topics ranging from *Teacher/Student Ratios* to *High School Drop-Out Rates.* Following these rankings are statewide *National Assessment of Educational Progress (NAEP)* results and data from the *New York State Report Card*—an overview of student performance by subject, including easy-to-read charts and graphs.

6. Ancestry and Ethnicity
This section provides a detailed look at the ancestral, Hispanic and racial makeup of New York's 200+ ethnic categories. Data is ranked three ways: 1) by number, based on all places regardless of population; 2) by percent, based on all places regardless of population; 3) by percent, based on places with populations of 50,000 or more. You will discover, for example, that Rochester has the greatest number of *Laotians* in the state (668), and that 13.5% of the population of Harbor Hills are of *Armenian* ancestry.

7. Climate

This section includes a State Summary, colorful maps, and profiles of both National and Cooperative Weather Stations. In addition, you'll find Weather Station Rankings with hundreds of interesting details, such as Boonville 2 SSW reporting the highest annual snowfall with 197.5 inches.

This section also includes Significant Storm Event data from January 2000 through December 2009. Here you will learn that a flash flood caused $250 million in property damage in Delaware County in June 2006 and that excessive heat was responsible for 42 deaths in Southeast New York state in August 2006.

Note: The extensive **User Guide** that precedes **About New York** is segmented into four sections and examines, in some detail, each data field in the individual profiles and comparative sections for all chapters. It provides sources for all data points and statistical definitions as necessary.

User Guide

Profile Section

Places Covered

All 62 counties.

607 incorporated municipalities. Comprised of 62 cities and 545 villages.

941 Minor Civil Divisions (MCD). Comprise of 924 towns, 5 boroughs, and 12 reservations. These communities are included for states where the Census Bureau has determined that they serve as general-purpose governments. Those states are Connecticut, Maine, Massachusetts, Michigan, Minnesota, New Hampshire, New Jersey, New York, Pennsylvania, Rhode Island, Vermont, and Wisconsin. In some states incorporated municipalities are part of minor civil divisions and in some states they are independent of them.

572 Census Designated Places (CDP). The U.S. Bureau of the Census defines a CDP as "a statistical entity, defined for each decennial census according to Census Bureau guidelines, comprising a densely settled concentration of population that is not within an incorporated place, but is locally identified by a name. CDPs are delineated cooperatively by state and local officials and the Census Bureau, following Census Bureau guidelines.

440 unincorporated communities. The communities included have statistics for their ZIP Code Tabulation Area (ZCTA) available from the Census Bureau. They are referred to as "postal areas." "Postal areas" can span multiple ZCTAs. A ZCTA is a statistical entity developed by the Census Bureau to approximate the delivery area for a US Postal Service 5-digit or 3-digit ZIP Code in the US and Puerto Rico. A ZCTA is an aggregation of census blocks that have the same predominant ZIP Code associated with the mailing addresses in the Census Bureau's Master Address File. Thus, the Postal Service's delivery areas have been adjusted to encompass whole census blocks so that the Census Bureau can tabulate census data for the ZCTAs. ZCTAs do not include all ZIP Codes used for mail delivery and therefore do not precisely depict the area within which mail deliveries associated with that ZIP Code occur. Additionally, some areas that are known by a unique name, although they are part of a larger incorporated place, are also included as "postal areas."

Five communities have a mixed designation of town/village.

For a more in-depth discussion of geographic areas, please refer to the Census Bureau's Geographic Areas Reference Manual at http://www.census.gov/geo/www/garm.html.

IMPORTANT NOTES

- Since the last decennial census, the U.S. Census replaced the long-form sample with the American Community Survey (ACS), which uses a series of monthly samples to produce annually updated estimates for the same areas. ACS estimates are based on data from a sample of housing units and people in the population, not the full population. ACS sampling error (uncertainty of data) is greater for those areas with smaller populations.

- *Profiles of New York State* uses the term "community" to refer to all places except counties. The term "county" is used to refer to counties and county-equivalents. All places are defined as of the 2010 Census.

- If a community spans multiple counties, the community will be shown in the county that contains its largest population.

- Several states, including New York, have incorporated municipalities and minor civil divisions in the same county with the same name. Those communities are given separate entries (e.g. Adams, New York, in Jefferson County will be listed under both the village and town of Adams).

- The city of New York (composed of five coextensive counties/boroughs) has a unique format. Statistical information for the individual counties/boroughs can be found within the New York City entry. The five counties/boroughs are: Bronx County and Borough, Kings County and Brooklyn Borough, New York County and Manhattan Borough, Queens County and Borough, and Richmond County and Staten Island Borough.

- When a county and city are coextensive (occupying the same geographic area and sharing the same government), they are given a single entry.

- In each community profile, only school districts that have schools that are physically located within the community are shown. In addition, statistics for each school district cover the entire district, regardless of the physical location of the schools within the district.

- Special care should be taken when interpreting certain statistics for communities containing large colleges or universities. College students were counted as residents of the area in which they were living while attending college (as they have been since the 1950 census). One effect this may have is skewing the figures for population, income, housing, and educational attainment.

- Some information (e.g. income) is available for both counties and individual communities. Other information is available for just counties (e.g. election results), or just individual communities (e.g. local newspapers). Refer to the "Data Explanation and Sources" section for a complete listing.

- Some statistical information is available only for larger communities. In addition, the larger places are more apt to have services such as newspapers, airports, school districts, etc.

- For the most complete information on any community, users should also check the entry for the county in which the community is located. In addition, more information and services will be listed under the larger places in the county.

Data Explanation and Sources—County Profiles

PHYSICAL AND GEOGRAPHICAL CHARACTERISTICS

Physical Location: Describes the physical location of the county. *Source: Columbia University Press, The Columbia Gazetteer of North America and original research.*

Land and Water Area: Land and water area in square miles. *Source: U.S. Census Bureau, Census 2010*

Latitude and Longitude: Latitude and longitude in degrees. *Source: U.S. Census Bureau, Census 2010*

Time Zone: Lists the time zone. *Source: Original research*

Year Organized: Year the county government was organized. *Source: National Association of Counties*

County Seat: Lists the county seat. If a county has more than one seat, then both are listed. *Source: National Association of Counties*

Metropolitan Area: Indicates the metropolitan area the county is located in. Also lists all the component counties of that metropolitan area. The Office of Management and Budget (OMB) defines metropolitan and micropolitan statistical areas. The most current definitions are as of September 2018. *Source: U.S. Census Bureau*

Climate: Includes all weather stations located within the county. Indicates the station name and elevation as well as the monthly average high and low temperatures, average precipitation, and average snowfall. The period of record is generally 1980-2009, however, certain weather stations contain averages going back as far as 1900. *Source: Grey House Publishing, Weather America: A Thirty-Year Summary of Statistical Weather Data and Rankings, 2010*

POPULATION

Population: Current population. *Source: U.S. Census Bureau, American Community Survey, 2013-2017 Five-Year Estimates*

Population Growth: The increase or decrease in population since 2000. *Source: U.S. Census Bureau, Census 2000; U.S. Census Bureau, American Community Survey, 2013-2017 Five-Year Estimates*

Population Density: Total current population divided by the land area in square miles. *Source: U.S. Census Bureau, Census 2010; U.S. Census Bureau, American Community Survey, 2013-2017 Five-Year Estimates*

Race/Hispanic Origin: Figures include the U.S. Census Bureau categories of White alone; Black/African American alone; Asian alone; American Indian/Alaska Native alone; Native Hawaiian/Other Pacific Islander alone; two or more races; and Hispanic of any race. Alone refers to the fact that these figures are not in combination with any other race. *Source: U.S. Census Bureau, American Community Survey, 2013-2017 Five-Year Estimates*

The concept of race, as used by the Census Bureau, reflects self-identification by people according to the race or races with which they most closely identify. These categories are socio-political constructs and should not be interpreted as being scientific or anthropological in nature. Furthermore, the race categories include both racial and national-origin groups.

- **White.** A person having origins in any of the original peoples of Europe, the Middle East, or North Africa. It includes people who indicated their race(s) as "White" or reported entries such as Irish, German, Italian, Lebanese, Arab, Moroccan, or Caucasian.
- **Black/African American.** A person having origins in any of the Black racial groups of Africa. It includes people who indicated their race(s) as "Black, African Am., or Negro" or reported entries such as African American, Kenyan, Nigerian, or Haitian.
- **Asian.** A person having origins in any of the original peoples of the Far East, Southeast Asia, or the Indian subcontinent, including, for example, Cambodia, China, India, Japan, Korea, Malaysia, Pakistan, the Philippine Islands, Thailand, and Vietnam. It includes people who indicated their race(s) as "Asian" or reported entries such as "Asian Indian," "Chinese," "Filipino," "Korean," "Japanese," "Vietnamese," and "Other Asian" or provided other detailed Asian responses.
- **American Indian/Alaska Native.** A person having origins in any of the original peoples of North and South America (including Central America) and who maintains tribal affiliation or community attachment. This category includes people who indicated their race(s) as "American Indian or Alaska Native" or

reported their enrolled or principal tribe, such as Navajo, Blackfeet, Inupiat, Yup'ik, or Central American Indian groups or South American Indian groups.

- **Native Hawaiian/Other Pacific Islander.** A person having origins in any of the original peoples of Hawaii, Guam, Samoa, or other Pacific Islands. It includes people who indicated their race(s) as "Pacific Islander" or reported entries such as "Native Hawaiian," "Guamanian or Chamorro," "Samoan," and "Other Pacific Islander" or provided other detailed Pacific Islander responses..

- **Two or More Races.** People may choose to provide two or more races either by checking two or more race response check boxes, by providing multiple responses, or by some combination of check boxes and other responses. The race response categories shown on the questionnaire are collapsed into the five minimum race groups identified by OMB, and the Census Bureau's "Some Other Race" category.

- **Hispanic.** The data on the Hispanic or Latino population were derived from answers to a question that was asked of all people. The terms "Spanish," "Hispanic origin," and "Latino" are used interchangeably. Some respondents identify with all three terms while others may identify with only one of these three specific terms. Hispanics or Latinos who identify with the terms "Spanish," "Hispanic," or "Latino" are those who classify themselves in one of the specific Spanish, Hispanic, or Latino categories listed on the questionnaire ("Mexican," "Puerto Rican," or "Cuban") as well as those who indicate that they are "other Spanish/Hispanic/Latino." People who do not identify with one of the specific origins listed on the questionnaire but indicate that they are "other Spanish/Hispanic/Latino" are those whose origins are from Spain, the Spanish-speaking countries of Central or South America, the Dominican Republic, or people identifying themselves generally as Spanish, Spanish-American, Hispanic, Hispano, Latino, and so on. All write-in responses to the "other Spanish/Hispanic/Latino" category were coded. Origin can be viewed as the heritage, nationality group, lineage, or country of birth of the person or the person's parents or ancestors before their arrival in the United States. People who identify their origin as Spanish, Hispanic, or Latino may be of any race.

Average Household Size: Number of persons in the average household. *Source: U.S. Census Bureau, American Community Survey, 2013-2017 Five-Year Estimates*

Median Age: Median age of the population. *Source: U.S. Census Bureau, American Community Survey, 2013-2017 Five-Year Estimates*

Age Under 18: Percent of the total population under 18 years old. *Source: U.S. Census Bureau, American Community Survey, 2013-2017 Five-Year Estimates*

Age 65 and Over: Percent of the total population age 65 and over. *Source: U.S. Census Bureau, American Community Survey, 2013-2017 Five-Year Estimates*

Males per 100 Females: Number of males per 100 females. *Source: U.S. Census Bureau, American Community Survey, 2013-2017 Five-Year Estimates*

Marital Status: Percentage of population never married, now married, separated, widowed, or divorced. *Source: U.S. Census Bureau, American Community Survey, 2013-2017 Five-Year Estimates*

The marital status classification refers to the status at the time of enumeration. Data on marital status are tabulated only for the population 15 years old and over. Each person was asked whether they were "Now married," "Widowed," "Separated," "Divorced," or "Never married." Couples who live together (for example, people in common-law marriages) were able to report the marital status they considered to be the most appropriate.

- **Never married.** Never married includes all people who have never been married, including people whose only marriage(s) was annulled.

- **Now married.** All people whose current marriage has not ended by widowhood or divorce. This category includes people defined as "separated."

- **Separated.** Includes people legally separated or otherwise absent from their spouse because of marital discord. Those without a final divorce decree are classified as "separated." This category also includes people who have been deserted or who have parted because they no longer want to live together, but who have not obtained a divorce.

- **Widowed.** This category includes widows and widowers who have not remarried.

- **Divorced.** This category includes people who are legally divorced and who have not remarried.

Foreign Born: Percentage of population who were not U.S. citizens at birth. Foreign-born people are those who indicated they were either a U.S. citizen by naturalization or they were not a citizen of the United States. *Source: U.S. Census Bureau, American Community Survey, 2013-2017 Five-Year Estimates*

Speak English Only: Percent of population that reported speaking only English at home. *Source: U.S. Census Bureau, American Community Survey, 2013-2017 Five-Year Estimates*

With Disability: Percent of the civilian noninstitutionalized population that reported having a disability. Disability status is determined from from six types of difficulty: vision, hearing, cognitive, ambulatory, self-care, and independent living. For children under 5 years old, hearing and vision difficulty are used to determine disability status. For children between the ages of 5 and 14, disability status is determined from hearing, vision, cognitive, ambulatory, and self-care difficulties. For people aged 15 years and older, they are considered to have a disability if they have difficulty with any one of the six difficulty types. *Source: U.S. Census Bureau, American Community Survey, 2013-2017 Five-Year Estimates*

Veterans: Percent of the civilian population 18 years and over who have served (even for a short time), but are not currently serving, on active duty in the U.S. Army, Navy, Air Force, Marine Corps, or the Coast Guard, or who served in the U.S. Merchant Marine during World War II. People who served in the National Guard or Reserves are classified as veterans only if they were ever called or ordered to active duty, not counting the 4-6 months for initial training or yearly summer camps. All other civilians are classified as nonveterans. Note: While it is possible for 17 year olds to be veterans of the Armed Forces, ACS data products are restricted to the population 18 years and older. *Source: U.S. Census Bureau, American Community Survey, 2013-2017 Five-Year Estimates*

Ancestry: Largest ancestry groups reported (up to five). The data includes persons who report multiple ancestries. For example, if a person reported being Irish and Italian, they would be included in both categories. Thus, the sum of the percentages may be greater than 100%. *Source: U.S. Census Bureau, American Community Survey, 2013-2017 Five-Year Estimates*

The data represent self-classification by people according to the ancestry group or groups with which they most closely identify. Ancestry refers to a person's ethnic origin or descent, "roots," heritage, or the place of birth of the person, the person's parents, or their ancestors before their arrival in the United States. Some ethnic identities, such as Egyptian or Polish, can be traced to geographic areas outside the United States, while other ethnicities such as Pennsylvania German or Cajun evolved in the United States.

The ancestry question was intended to provide data for groups that were not included in the Hispanic origin and race questions. Therefore, although data on all groups are collected, the ancestry data shown in these tabulations are for non-Hispanic and non-race groups. *See* Race/Hispanic Origin for information on Hispanic and race groups.

RELIGION

Religion: Lists the largest religious groups (up to six) based on the number of adherents divided by the population of the county. Adherents are defined as "all members, including full members, their children and the estimated number of other regular participants who are not considered as communicant, confirmed or full members." *Source: American Religious Bodies, 2010 U.S. Religion Census: Religious Congregations & Membership Study*

ECONOMY

Unemployment Rate: Unemployment rate as of September 2018. Includes all civilians age 16 or over who were unemployed and looking for work. *Source: U.S. Department of Labor, Bureau of Labor Statistics, Local Area Unemployment Statistics*

Leading Industries: Lists the three leading industries (excluding government) based on the number of establishments. *Source: U.S. Census Bureau, County Business Patterns 2016*

Farms: The total number of farms and the total acreage they occupy. *Source: U.S. Department of Agriculture, National Agricultural Statistics Service, 2012 Census of Agriculture*

Company Size: The numbers of companies at various employee headcounts. Includes private employers only. *Source: U.S. Census Bureau, County Business Patterns 2016*

- **Employ 1,000 or more persons.** The numbers of companies that employ 1,000 or more persons.
- **Employ 500-999 persons.** The numbers of companies that employ 500 to 999 persons.

- **Employ 100-499 persons.** The numbers of companies that employ 100 to 499 persons.
- **Employ 1-99 persons.** The numbers of companies that employ 1 to 99 persons.

Business Ownership: Number of businesses that are majority-owned by women or various minority groups. *Source: U.S. Census Bureau, 2012 Economic Census, Survey of Business Owners*

- **Women-Owned.** Number of businesses that are majority-owned by a woman. Majority ownership is defined as having 51 percent or more of the stock or equity in the business.
- **Black-Owned.** Number of businesses that are majority-owned by a Black or African American person(s). Majority ownership is defined as having 51 percent or more of the stock or equity in the business. Black or African American is defined as a person having origins in any of the black racial groups of Africa, including those who consider themselves to be "Haitian."
- **Asian-Owned.** Number of businesses that are majority-owned by an Asian person(s). Majority ownership is defined as having 51 percent or more of the stock or equity in the business.
- **American Indian/Alaska Native-Owned.** Number of businesses that are majority-owned by an American Indian or Alaska Native person(s). Majority ownership is defined as having 51 percent or more of the stock or equity in the business.
- **Hispanic-Owned.** Number of businesses that are majority-owned by a person(s) of Hispanic or Latino origin. Majority ownership is defined as having 51 percent or more of the stock or equity in the business. Hispanic or Latino origin is defined as a person of Cuban, Mexican, Puerto Rican, South or Central American, or other Spanish culture or origin, regardless of race.

EMPLOYMENT

Employment by Occupation: Percentage of the employed civilian population 16 years and over in management, professional, service, sales, farming, construction, and production occupations. *Source: U.S. Census Bureau, American Community Survey, 2013-2017 Five-Year Estimates*

- Management, business, and financial occupations include:
    Management occupations
    Business and financial operations occupations

- Computer, engineering, and science occupations include:
    Computer and mathematical occupations
    Architecture and engineering occupations
    Life, physical, and social science occupations

- Education, legal, community service, arts, and media occupations include:
    Community and social service occupations
    Legal occupations
    Education, training, and library occupations
    Arts, design, entertainment, sports, and media occupations

- Healthcare practitioners and technical occupations include:
    Health diagnosing and treating practitioners and other technical occupations
    Health technologists and technicians

- Service occupations include:
    Healthcare support occupations
    Protective service occupations:
        Fire fighting and prevention, and other protective service workers including supervisors
        Law enforcement workers including supervisors
    Food preparation and serving related occupations
    Building and grounds cleaning and maintenance occupations
    Personal care and service occupations

- Sales and office occupations include:
    Sales and related occupations
    Office and administrative support occupations

- Natural resources, construction, and maintenance occupations include:
    Farming, fishing, and forestry occupations
    Construction and extraction occupations
    Installation, maintenance, and repair occupations

- Production, transportation, and material moving occupations include:
    Production occupations
    Transportation occupations
    Material moving occupations

INCOME

Per Capita Income: Per capita income is the mean income computed for every man, woman, and child in a particular group. It is derived by dividing the total income of a particular group by the total population in that group. Per capita income is rounded to the nearest whole dollar. *Source: U.S. Census Bureau, American Community Survey, 2013-2017 Five-Year Estimates*

Median Household Income: Includes the income of the householder and all other individuals 15 years old and over in the household, whether they are related to the householder or not. The median divides the income distribution into two equal parts: one-half of the cases falling below the median income and one-half above the median. For households, the median income is based on the distribution of the total number of households including those with no income. Median income for households is computed on the basis of a standard distribution and is rounded to the nearest whole dollar. *Source: U.S. Census Bureau, American Community Survey, 2013-2017 Five-Year Estimates*

Average Household Income: Average household income is obtained by dividing total household income by the total number of households. *Source: U.S. Census Bureau, American Community Survey, 2013-2017 Five-Year Estimates*

Percent of Households with Income of $100,000 or more: Percent of households with income of $100,000 or more. *Source: U.S. Census Bureau, American Community Survey, 2013-2017 Five-Year Estimates*

Poverty Rate: Percentage of population with income below the poverty level. Based on individuals for whom poverty status is determined. Poverty status was determined for all people except institutionalized people, people in military group quarters, people in college dormitories, and unrelated individuals under 15 years old. *Source: U.S. Census Bureau, American Community Survey, 2013-2017 Five-Year Estimates*

EDUCATIONAL ATTAINMENT

Figures show the percent of population age 25 and over with the following levels of educational attainment. *Source: U.S. Census Bureau, American Community Survey, 2013-2017 Five-Year Estimates*

- **High school diploma or higher.** Includes people whose highest degree is a high school diploma or its equivalent (GED), people who attended college but did not receive a degree, and people who received a college, university, or professional degree.
- **Bachelor's degree or higher.** Includes people who received a bachelor's, master's, doctorate, or professional degree.
- **Graduate/professional degree or higher.** Includes people who received a master's, doctorate, or professional degree.

HOUSING

Homeownership Rate: Percentage of housing units that are owner-occupied. *Source: U.S. Census Bureau, American Community Survey, 2013-2017 Five-Year Estimates*

Median Home Value: Median value in dollars of all owner-occupied housing units as reported by the owner. *Source: U.S. Census Bureau, American Community Survey, 2013-2017 Five-Year Estimates*

Median Year Structure Built: Year structure built refers to when the building was first constructed, not when it was remodeled, added to, or converted. For mobile homes, houseboats, RVs, etc, the manufacturer's model year was assumed to be the year built. The data relate to the number of units built during the specified periods that were still in existence at the time of enumeration. *Source: U.S. Census Bureau, American Community Survey, 2013-2017 Five-Year Estimates*

Homeowner Vacancy Rate: Proportion of the homeowner inventory that is vacant "for sale." It is computed by dividing the number of vacant units "for sale only" by the sum of the owner-occupied units, vacant units that are "for sale only," and vacant units that have been sold but not yet occupied, and then multiplying by 100. This measure is rounded to the nearest tenth. *Source: U.S. Census Bureau, American Community Survey, 2013-2017 Five-Year Estimates*

Median Selected Monthly Owner Costs: Selected monthly owner costs are the sum of payments for mortgages, deeds of trust, contracts to purchase, or similar debts on the property (including payments for the first mortgage, second mortgages, home equity loans, and other junior mortgages); real estate taxes; fire, hazard, and flood insurance on the property; utilities (electricity, gas, and water and sewer); and fuels (oil, coal, kerosene, wood, etc.). It also includes, where appropriate, the monthly condominium fee for condominiums and mobile home costs (personal property taxes, site rent, registration fees, and license fees). Selected monthly owner costs were tabulated for all owner-occupied units, and are shown separately for units "with a mortgage" and for units "not mortgaged." *Source: U.S. Census Bureau, American Community Survey, 2013-2017 Five-Year Estimates*

Median Gross Rent: Median monthly gross rent in dollars on specified renter-occupied and specified vacant-for-rent units. Specified renter-occupied and specified vacant-for-rent units exclude 1-family houses on 10 acres or more. Gross rent is the contract rent plus the estimated average monthly cost of utilities (electricity, gas, and water and sewer) and fuels (oil, coal, kerosene, wood, etc.) if these are paid by the renter (or paid for the renter by someone else). Gross rent is intended to eliminate differentials that result from varying practices with respect to the inclusion of utilities and fuels as part of the rental payment. Contract rent is the monthly rent agreed to or contracted for, regardless of any furnishings, utilities, fees, meals, or services that may be included. For vacant units, it is the monthly rent asked for the rental unit at the time of enumeration. *Source: U.S. Census Bureau, American Community Survey, 2013-2017 Five-Year Estimates*

Rental Vacancy Rate: Proportion of the rental inventory that is vacant "for rent." It is computed by dividing the number of vacant units "for rent" by the sum of the renter-occupied units, vacant units that are "for rent," and vacant units that have been rented but not yet occupied, and then multiplying by 100. This measure is rounded to the nearest tenth. *Source: U.S. Census Bureau, American Community Survey, 2013-2017 Five-Year Estimates*

VITAL STATISTICS

Birth Rate: Estimated number of births per 10,000 population in 2017. *Source: U.S. Census Bureau, Annual Components of Population Change, July 1, 2010 - July 1, 2017*

Death Rate: Estimated number of deaths per 10,000 population in 2017. *Source: U.S. Census Bureau, Annual Components of Population Change, July 1, 2010 - July 1, 2017*

Age-adjusted Cancer Mortality Rate: Number of age-adjusted deaths from cancer per 100,000 population in 2017. Cancer is defined as International Classification of Disease (ICD) codes C00–D48.9 Neoplasms. *Source: Centers for Disease Control, CDC Wonder, 2017*

Age-adjusted death rates are weighted averages of the age-specific death rates, where the weights represent a fixed population by age. They are used because the rates of almost all causes of death vary by age. Age adjustment is a technique for "removing" the effects of age from crude rates, so as to allow meaningful comparisons across populations with different underlying age structures. For example, comparing the crude rate of heart disease in Virginia to that of California is misleading, because the relatively older population in Virginia will lead to a higher crude death rate, even if the age-specific rates of heart disease in Virginia and California are the same. For such a comparison, age-adjusted rates would be preferable. Age-adjusted rates should be viewed as relative indexes rather than as direct or actual measures of mortality risk.

Death rates based on counts of twenty or less ($\leq$ 20) are flagged as "Unreliable". Death rates based on fewer than three years of data for counties with populations of less than 100,000 in the 2000 Census counts, are also flagged as "Unreliable" if the number of deaths is five or less ($\leq$ 5).

HEALTH INSURANCE

Health insurance coverage in the ACS and other Census Bureau surveys define coverage to include plans and programs that provide comprehensive health coverage. Plans that provide insurance for specific conditions or situations such as cancer and long-term care policies are not considered coverage. Likewise, other types of insurance like dental, vision, life, and disability insurance are not considered health insurance coverage.

For reporting purposes, the Census Bureau broadly classifies health insurance coverage as private health insurance or public coverage. Private health insurance is a plan provided through an employer or union, a plan purchased by an individual from a private company, or TRICARE or other military health care. Public health coverage includes the federal programs Medicare, Medicaid, and VA Health Care (provided through the Department of Veterans Affairs); the Children's Health Insurance Program (CHIP); and individual state health plans. The types of health insurance are not mutually exclusive; people may be covered by more than one at the same time. People who had no reported health coverage, or those whose only health coverage was Indian Health Service, were considered uninsured. *Source: U.S. Census Bureau, American Community Survey, 2013-2017 Five-Year Estimates*

- **Have Insurance:** Percent of the civilian noninstitutionalized population with any type of comprehensive health insurance.
- **Have Private Insurance.** Percent of the civilian noninstitutionalized population with private health insurance. A person may report that they have both public and private health insurance, thus, the sum of the percentages may be greater than 100%.
- **Have Public Insurance.** Percent of the civilian noninstitutionalized population with public health insurance. A person may report that they have both public and private health insurance, thus, the sum of the percentages may be greater than 100%.
- **Do Not Have Insurance.** Percent of the civilian noninstitutionalized population with no health insurance.
- **Children Under 19 With No Insurance.** Percent of the civilian noninstitutionalized population under age 19 with no health insurance.

HEALTH CARE

Number of physicians, hospital beds and hospital admission per 10,000 population. *Source: Area Health Resource File (AHRF) 2017-2018. U.S. Department of Health and Human Services, Health Resources and Services Administration, Bureau of Health Professions, Rockville, MD.*

- **Number of Physicians.** The number of active, non-federal physicians (MDs and DOs) per 10,000 population in 2016.
- **Number of Dentists.** The number of dentists per 10,000 population in 2017.
- **Number of Hospital Beds.** The number of hospital beds per 10,000 population in 2016.
- **Number of Hospital Admissions.** The number of hospital admissions per 10,000 population in 2016.

AIR QUALITY INDEX

The percentage of days in 2017 the AQI fell into the Good (0-50), Moderate (51-100), Unhealthy for Sensitive Groups (101-150), Unhealthy (151-200), Very Unhealthy (201-300), and Hazardous (300+) ranges. If a range does not appear, its value is zero. Data covers January 2016 through December 2016 and only includes counties for which air quality data was available for 100 days or more. *Source: AirData: Access to Air Pollution Data, U.S. Environmental Protection Agency, Office of Air and Radiation*

The AQI is an index for reporting daily air quality. It tells you how clean or polluted your air is, and what associated health concerns you should be aware of. The AQI focuses on health effects that can happen within a few hours or days after breathing polluted air. EPA uses the AQI for five major air pollutants regulated by the Clean Air Act: ground-level ozone, particulate matter, carbon monoxide, sulfur dioxide, and nitrogen dioxide. For each of these pollutants, EPA has established national air quality standards to protect against harmful health effects.

The AQI runs from 0 to 500. The higher the AQI value, the greater the level of air pollution and the greater the health danger. For example, an AQI value of 50 represents good air quality and little potential to affect public health, while an AQI value over 300 represents hazardous air quality. An AQI value of 100 generally corresponds to the national air quality standard for the pollutant, which is the level EPA has set to protect public health. So, AQI values below 100 are generally thought of as satisfactory. When AQI values are above 100, air quality is considered to be unhealthy—at first for certain sensitive groups of people, then for everyone as AQI values get higher. Each category corresponds to a different level of health concern. For example, when the AQI for a pollutant is between 51 and 100, the health concern is "Moderate." Here are the six levels of health concern and what they mean:

- "Good" The AQI value for your community is between 0 and 50. Air quality is considered satisfactory and air pollution poses little or no risk.

- "Moderate" The AQI for your community is between 51 and 100. Air quality is acceptable; however, for some pollutants there may be a moderate health concern for a very small number of individuals. For example, people who are unusually sensitive to ozone may experience respiratory symptoms.
- "Unhealthy for Sensitive Groups" Certain groups of people are particularly sensitive to the harmful effects of certain air pollutants. This means they are likely to be affected at lower levels than the general public. For example, children and adults who are active outdoors and people with respiratory disease are at greater risk from exposure to ozone, while people with heart disease are at greater risk from carbon monoxide. Some people may be sensitive to more than one pollutant. When AQI values are between 101 and 150, members of sensitive groups may experience health effects. The general public is not likely to be affected when the AQI is in this range.
- "Unhealthy" AQI values are between 151 and 200. Everyone may begin to experience health effects. Members of sensitive groups may experience more serious health effects.
- "Very Unhealthy" AQI values between 201 and 300 trigger a health alert, meaning everyone may experience more serious health effects.
- "Hazardous" AQI values over 300 trigger health warnings of emergency conditions. The entire population is more likely to be affected.

TRANSPORTATION

Commute to Work: Percentage of workers 16 years old and over that use the following means of transportation to commute to work: car; public transportation; walk; work from home. The means of transportation data for some areas may show workers using modes of public transportation that are not available in those areas (e.g. subway or elevated riders in a metropolitan area where there actually is no subway or elevated service). This result is largely due to people who worked during the reference week at a location that was different from their usual place of work (such as people away from home on business in an area where subway service was available) and people who used more than one means of transportation each day but whose principal means was unavailable where they lived (e.g. residents of non-metropolitan areas who drove to the fringe of a metropolitan area and took the commuter railroad most of the distance to work). *Source: U.S. Census Bureau, American Community Survey, 2013-2017 Five-Year Estimates*

Mean Travel Time to Work: Mean travel time to work for workers 16 years old and over. Travel time to work refers to the total number of minutes that it usually took the person to get from home to work each day during the reference week. The elapsed time includes time spent waiting for public transportation, picking up passengers in carpools, and time spent in other activities related to getting to work. *Source: U.S. Census Bureau, American Community Survey, 2013-2017 Five-Year Estimates*

PRESIDENTIAL ELECTION

2016 Presidential election results. *Source: Dave Leip's Atlas of U.S. Presidential Elections*

NATIONAL AND STATE PARKS

Lists National/State parks located in the area. *Source: U.S. Geological Survey, Geographic Names Information System*

ADDITIONAL INFORMATION CONTACTS

General telephone number and website address (if available) of local government.

Data Explanation and Sources—Community Profiles

PHYSICAL AND GEOGRAPHICAL CHARACTERISTICS

Place Type: Lists the type of place (city, town, village, borough, Census-Designated Place (CDP), township, charter township, plantation, gore, district, grant, location, purchase, municipality, reservation, unorganized territory, or unincorporated postal area). *Source: U.S. Census Bureau, American Community Survey, 2013-2017 Five-Year Estimates and U.S. Postal Service, City State File*

ZCTA: *This only appears within unincorporated postal areas.* The statistics that follow cover the corresponding ZIP Code Tabulation Area (ZCTA). A ZCTA is a statistical entity developed by the Census Bureau to approximate the delivery area for a US Postal Service 5-digit or 3-digit ZIP Code in the US and Puerto Rico. A ZCTA is an aggregation of census blocks that have the same predominant ZIP Code associated with the mailing addresses in the Census Bureau's Master Address File. Thus, the Postal Service's delivery areas have been adjusted to encompass whole census blocks so that the Census Bureau can tabulate census data for the ZCTAs. ZCTAs do not include all ZIP Codes used for mail delivery and therefore do not precisely depict the area within which mail deliveries associated with that ZIP Code occur. Additionally, some areas that are known by a unique name, although they are part of a larger incorporated place, are also included as "postal areas."

Land and Water Area: Land and water area in square miles. *Source: U.S. Census Bureau, Census 2010*

Latitude and Longitude: Latitude and longitude in degrees. *Source: U.S. Census Bureau, Census 2010*

Elevation: Elevation in feet. *Source: U.S. Geological Survey, Geographic Names Information System (GNIS)*

HISTORY

Historical information. *Source: Columbia University Press, The Columbia Gazetteer of North America; Original research*

POPULATION

Population: Current population. *Source: U.S. Census Bureau, American Community Survey, 2013-2017 Five-Year Estimates*

Population Growth: The increase or decrease in population since 2000. *Source: U.S. Census Bureau, Census 2000; U.S. Census Bureau, American Community Survey, 2013-2017 Five-Year Estimates*

Population Density: Total current population divided by the land area in square miles. *Source: U.S. Census Bureau, Census 2010; U.S. Census Bureau, American Community Survey, 2013-2017 Five-Year Estimates*

Race/Hispanic Origin: Figures include the U.S. Census Bureau categories of White alone; Black/African American alone; Asian alone; American Indian/Alaska Native alone; Native Hawaiian/Other Pacific Islander alone; two or more races; and Hispanic of any race. Alone refers to the fact that these figures are not in combination with any other race. *Source: U.S. Census Bureau, American Community Survey, 2013-2017 Five-Year Estimates*

The concept of race, as used by the Census Bureau, reflects self-identification by people according to the race or races with which they most closely identify. These categories are socio-political constructs and should not be interpreted as being scientific or anthropological in nature. Furthermore, the race categories include both racial and national-origin groups.

- **White.** A person having origins in any of the original peoples of Europe, the Middle East, or North Africa. It includes people who indicated their race(s) as "White" or reported entries such as Irish, German, Italian, Lebanese, Arab, Moroccan, or Caucasian.
- **Black/African American.** A person having origins in any of the Black racial groups of Africa. It includes people who indicated their race(s) as "Black, African Am., or Negro" or reported entries such as African American, Kenyan, Nigerian, or Haitian.
- **Asian.** A person having origins in any of the original peoples of the Far East, Southeast Asia, or the Indian subcontinent, including, for example, Cambodia, China, India, Japan, Korea, Malaysia, Pakistan, the Philippine Islands, Thailand, and Vietnam. It includes people who indicated their race(s) as "Asian" or reported entries such as "Asian Indian," "Chinese," "Filipino," "Korean," "Japanese," "Vietnamese," and "Other Asian" or provided other detailed Asian responses.

- **American Indian/Alaska Native.** A person having origins in any of the original peoples of North and South America (including Central America) and who maintains tribal affiliation or community attachment. This category includes people who indicated their race(s) as "American Indian or Alaska Native" or reported their enrolled or principal tribe, such as Navajo, Blackfeet, Inupiat, Yup'ik, or Central American Indian groups or South American Indian groups.

- **Native Hawaiian/Other Pacific Islander.** A person having origins in any of the original peoples of Hawaii, Guam, Samoa, or other Pacific Islands. It includes people who indicated their race(s) as "Pacific Islander" or reported entries such as "Native Hawaiian," "Guamanian or Chamorro," "Samoan," and "Other Pacific Islander" or provided other detailed Pacific Islander responses..

- **Two or More Races.** People may choose to provide two or more races either by checking two or more race response check boxes, by providing multiple responses, or by some combination of check boxes and other responses. The race response categories shown on the questionnaire are collapsed into the five minimum race groups identified by OMB, and the Census Bureau's "Some Other Race" category.

- **Hispanic.** The data on the Hispanic or Latino population were derived from answers to a question that was asked of all people. The terms "Spanish," "Hispanic origin," and "Latino" are used interchangeably. Some respondents identify with all three terms while others may identify with only one of these three specific terms. Hispanics or Latinos who identify with the terms "Spanish," "Hispanic," or "Latino" are those who classify themselves in one of the specific Spanish, Hispanic, or Latino categories listed on the questionnaire ("Mexican," "Puerto Rican," or "Cuban") as well as those who indicate that they are "other Spanish/Hispanic/Latino." People who do not identify with one of the specific origins listed on the questionnaire but indicate that they are "other Spanish/Hispanic/Latino" are those whose origins are from Spain, the Spanish-speaking countries of Central or South America, the Dominican Republic, or people identifying themselves generally as Spanish, Spanish-American, Hispanic, Hispano, Latino, and so on. All write-in responses to the "other Spanish/Hispanic/Latino" category were coded. Origin can be viewed as the heritage, nationality group, lineage, or country of birth of the person or the person's parents or ancestors before their arrival in the United States. People who identify their origin as Spanish, Hispanic, or Latino may be of any race.

Average Household Size: Number of persons in the average household. *Source: U.S. Census Bureau, American Community Survey, 2013-2017 Five-Year Estimates*

Median Age: Median age of the population. *Source: U.S. Census Bureau, American Community Survey, 2013-2017 Five-Year Estimates*

Age Under 18: Percent of the total population under 18 years old. *Source: U.S. Census Bureau, American Community Survey, 2013-2017 Five-Year Estimates*

Age 65 and Over: Percent of the total population age 65 and over. *Source: U.S. Census Bureau, American Community Survey, 2013-2017 Five-Year Estimates*

Males per 100 Females: Number of males per 100 females. *Source: U.S. Census Bureau, American Community Survey, 2013-2017 Five-Year Estimates*

Marital Status: Percentage of population never married, now married, separated, widowed, or divorced. *Source: U.S. Census Bureau, American Community Survey, 2013-2017 Five-Year Estimates*

The marital status classification refers to the status at the time of enumeration. Data on marital status are tabulated only for the population 15 years old and over. Each person was asked whether they were "Now married," "Widowed," "Separated," "Divorced," or "Never married." Couples who live together (for example, people in common-law marriages) were able to report the marital status they considered to be the most appropriate.

- **Never married.** Never married includes all people who have never been married, including people whose only marriage(s) was annulled.

- **Now married.** All people whose current marriage has not ended by widowhood or divorce. This category includes people defined as "separated."

- **Separated.** Includes people legally separated or otherwise absent from their spouse because of marital discord. Those without a final divorce decree are classified as "separated." This category also includes people who have been deserted or who have parted because they no longer want to live together, but who have not obtained a divorce.

- **Widowed.** This category includes widows and widowers who have not remarried.

- **Divorced.** This category includes people who are legally divorced and who have not remarried.

Foreign Born: Percentage of population who were not U.S. citizens at birth. Foreign-born people are those who indicated they were either a U.S. citizen by naturalization or they were not a citizen of the United States. *Source: U.S. Census Bureau, American Community Survey, 2013-2017 Five-Year Estimates*

Speak English Only: Percent of population that reported speaking only English at home. *Source: U.S. Census Bureau, American Community Survey, 2013-2017 Five-Year Estimates*

With Disability: Percent of the civilian noninstitutionalized population that reported having a disability. Disability status is determined from from six types of difficulty: vision, hearing, cognitive, ambulatory, self-care, and independent living. For children under 5 years old, hearing and vision difficulty are used to determine disability status. For children between the ages of 5 and 14, disability status is determined from hearing, vision, cognitive, ambulatory, and self-care difficulties. For people aged 15 years and older, they are considered to have a disability if they have difficulty with any one of the six difficulty types. *Source: U.S. Census Bureau, American Community Survey, 2013-2017 Five-Year Estimates*

Veterans: Percent of the civilian population 18 years and over who have served (even for a short time), but are not currently serving, on active duty in the U.S. Army, Navy, Air Force, Marine Corps, or the Coast Guard, or who served in the U.S. Merchant Marine during World War II. People who served in the National Guard or Reserves are classified as veterans only if they were ever called or ordered to active duty, not counting the 4-6 months for initial training or yearly summer camps. All other civilians are classified as nonveterans. Note: While it is possible for 17 year olds to be veterans of the Armed Forces, ACS data products are restricted to the population 18 years and older. *Source: U.S. Census Bureau, American Community Survey, 2013-2017 Five-Year Estimates*

Ancestry: Largest ancestry groups reported (up to five). The data includes persons who report multiple ancestries. For example, if a person reported being Irish and Italian, they would be included in both categories. Thus, the sum of the percentages may be greater than 100%. *Source: U.S. Census Bureau, American Community Survey, 2013-2017 Five-Year Estimates*

The data represent self-classification by people according to the ancestry group or groups with which they most closely identify. Ancestry refers to a person's ethnic origin or descent, "roots," heritage, or the place of birth of the person, the person's parents, or their ancestors before their arrival in the United States. Some ethnic identities, such as Egyptian or Polish, can be traced to geographic areas outside the United States, while other ethnicities such as Pennsylvania German or Cajun evolved in the United States.

The ancestry question was intended to provide data for groups that were not included in the Hispanic origin and race questions. Therefore, although data on all groups are collected, the ancestry data shown in these tabulations are for non-Hispanic and non-race groups. *See* Race/Hispanic Origin for information on Hispanic and race groups.

EMPLOYMENT

Employment by Occupation: Percentage of the employed civilian population 16 years and over in management, professional, service, sales, farming, construction, and production occupations. *Source: U.S. Census Bureau, American Community Survey, 2013-2017 Five-Year Estimates*

- Management, business, and financial occupations include:
    - Management occupations
    - Business and financial operations occupations

- Computer, engineering, and science occupations include:
    - Computer and mathematical occupations
    - Architecture and engineering occupations
    - Life, physical, and social science occupations

- Education, legal, community service, arts, and media occupations include:
    - Community and social service occupations
    - Legal occupations
    - Education, training, and library occupations
    - Arts, design, entertainment, sports, and media occupations

- Healthcare practitioners and technical occupations include:
    - Health diagnosing and treating practitioners and other technical occupations
    - Health technologists and technicians

- Service occupations include:
    - Healthcare support occupations
    - Protective service occupations:
        - Fire fighting and prevention, and other protective service workers including supervisors
        - Law enforcement workers including supervisors
    - Food preparation and serving related occupations
    - Building and grounds cleaning and maintenance occupations
    - Personal care and service occupations

- Sales and office occupations include:
    - Sales and related occupations
    - Office and administrative support occupations

- Natural resources, construction, and maintenance occupations include;
    - Farming, fishing, and forestry occupations
    - Construction and extraction occupations
    - Installation, maintenance, and repair occupations

- Production, transportation, and material moving occupations include:
    - Production occupations
    - Transportation occupations
    - Material moving occupations

INCOME

Per Capita Income: Per capita income is the mean income computed for every man, woman, and child in a particular group. It is derived by dividing the total income of a particular group by the total population in that group. Per capita income is rounded to the nearest whole dollar. *Source: U.S. Census Bureau, American Community Survey, 2013-2017 Five-Year Estimates*

Median Household Income: Includes the income of the householder and all other individuals 15 years old and over in the household, whether they are related to the householder or not. The median divides the income distribution into two equal parts: one-half of the cases falling below the median income and one-half above the median. For households, the median income is based on the distribution of the total number of households including those with no income. Median income for households is computed on the basis of a standard distribution and is rounded to the nearest whole dollar. *Source: U.S. Census Bureau, American Community Survey, 2013-2017 Five-Year Estimates*

Average Household Income: Average household income is obtained by dividing total household income by the total number of households. *Source: U.S. Census Bureau, American Community Survey, 2013-2017 Five-Year Estimates*

Percent of Households with Income of $100,000 or more: Percent of households with income of $100,000 or more. *Source: U.S. Census Bureau, American Community Survey, 2013-2017 Five-Year Estimates*

Poverty Rate: Percentage of population with income below the poverty level. Based on individuals for whom poverty status is determined. Poverty status was determined for all people except institutionalized people, people in military group quarters, people in college dormitories, and unrelated individuals under 15 years old. *Source: U.S. Census Bureau, American Community Survey, 2013-2017 Five-Year Estimates*

EDUCATIONAL ATTAINMENT

Figures show the percent of population age 25 and over with the following levels of educational attainment. *Source: U.S. Census Bureau, American Community Survey, 2013-2017 Five-Year Estimates*

- **High school diploma or higher.** Includes people whose highest degree is a high school diploma or its equivalent (GED), people who attended college but did not receive a degree, and people who received a college, university, or professional degree.
- **Bachelor's degree or higher.** Includes people who received a bachelor's, master's, doctorate, or professional degree.
- **Graduate/professional degree or higher.** Includes people who received a master's, doctorate, or professional degree.

SCHOOL DISTRICTS

Lists the name of each school district, the grade range (PK=pre-kindergarten; KG=kindergarten), the student enrollment, and the district headquarters' phone number. In each community profile, only school districts that have schools that are physically located within the community are shown. In addition, statistics for each school district cover the entire district, regardless of the physical location of the schools within the district. *Source: U.S. Department of Education, National Center for Educational Statistics, Directory of Public Elementary and Secondary Education Agencies, 2017-18*

COLLEGES

Four-year Colleges: Lists the name of each four-year college, the type of institution (private or public; for-profit or non-profit; religious affiliation; historically black), the total estimated student enrollment in Fall 2017, the general telephone number, and the annual tuition and fees for full-time, first-time undergraduate students (in-state and out-of-state). *Source: U.S. Department of Education, National Center for Educational Statistics, IPEDS College Data, 2017-18*

Two-year Colleges: Lists the name of each two-year college, the type of institution (private or public; for-profit or non-profit; religious affiliation; historically black), the total estimated student enrollment in Fall 2017, the general telephone number, and the annual tuition and fees for full-time, first-time undergraduate students (in-state and out-of-state). *Source: U.S. Department of Education, National Center for Educational Statistics, IPEDS College Data, 2017-18*

Vocational/Technical Schools: Lists the name of each vocational/technical school, the type of institution (private or public; for-profit or non-profit; religious affiliation; historically black), the total estimated student enrollment in Fall 2017, the general telephone number, and the annual tuition and fees for full-time students. *Source: U.S. Department of Education, National Center for Educational Statistics, IPEDS College Data, 2017-18*

HOUSING

Homeownership Rate: Percentage of housing units that are owner-occupied. *Source: U.S. Census Bureau, American Community Survey, 2013-2017 Five-Year Estimates*

Median Home Value: Median value in dollars of all owner-occupied housing units as reported by the owner. *Source: U.S. Census Bureau, American Community Survey, 2013-2017 Five-Year Estimates*

Median Year Structure Built: Year structure built refers to when the building was first constructed, not when it was remodeled, added to, or converted. For mobile homes, houseboats, RVs, etc, the manufacturer's model year was assumed to be the year built. The data relate to the number of units built during the specified periods that were still in existence at the time of enumeration. *Source: U.S. Census Bureau, American Community Survey, 2013-2017 Five-Year Estimates*

Homeowner Vacancy Rate: Proportion of the homeowner inventory that is vacant "for sale." It is computed by dividing the number of vacant units "for sale only" by the sum of the owner-occupied units, vacant units that are "for sale only," and vacant units that have been sold but not yet occupied, and then multiplying by 100. This measure is rounded to the nearest tenth. *Source: U.S. Census Bureau, American Community Survey, 2013-2017 Five-Year Estimates*

Median Selected Monthly Owner Costs: Selected monthly owner costs are the sum of payments for mortgages, deeds of trust, contracts to purchase, or similar debts on the property (including payments for the first mortgage, second mortgages, home equity loans, and other junior mortgages); real estate taxes; fire, hazard, and flood insurance on the property; utilities (electricity, gas, and water and sewer); and fuels (oil, coal, kerosene, wood, etc.). It also includes, where appropriate, the monthly condominium fee for condominiums and mobile home costs (personal property taxes, site rent, registration fees, and license fees). Selected monthly owner costs were tabulated for all owner-occupied units, and are shown separately for units "with a mortgage" and for units "not mortgaged." *Source: U.S. Census Bureau, American Community Survey, 2013-2017 Five-Year Estimates*

Median Gross Rent: Median monthly gross rent in dollars on specified renter-occupied and specified vacant-for-rent units. Specified renter-occupied and specified vacant-for-rent units exclude 1-family houses on 10 acres or more. Gross rent is the contract rent plus the estimated average monthly cost of utilities (electricity, gas, and water and sewer) and fuels (oil, coal, kerosene, wood, etc.) if these are paid by the renter (or paid for the renter by someone else). Gross rent is intended to eliminate differentials that result from varying practices with respect to the inclusion of utilities and fuels as part of the rental payment. Contract rent is the monthly rent agreed to or contracted for, regardless of any furnishings, utilities, fees, meals, or services that may be included. For vacant units, it is the monthly rent asked for the rental unit at the time of enumeration. *Source: U.S. Census Bureau, American Community Survey, 2013-2017 Five-Year Estimates*

Rental Vacancy Rate: Proportion of the rental inventory that is vacant "for rent." It is computed by dividing the number of vacant units "for rent" by the sum of the renter-occupied units, vacant units that are "for rent," and vacant units that have been rented but not yet occupied, and then multiplying by 100. This measure is rounded to the nearest tenth. *Source: U.S. Census Bureau, American Community Survey, 2013-2017 Five-Year Estimates*

HEALTH INSURANCE

Health insurance coverage in the ACS and other Census Bureau surveys define coverage to include plans and programs that provide comprehensive health coverage. Plans that provide insurance for specific conditions or situations such as cancer and long-term care policies are not considered coverage. Likewise, other types of insurance like dental, vision, life, and disability insurance are not considered health insurance coverage.

For reporting purposes, the Census Bureau broadly classifies health insurance coverage as private health insurance or public coverage. Private health insurance is a plan provided through an employer or union, a plan purchased by an individual from a private company, or TRICARE or other military health care. Public health coverage includes the federal programs Medicare, Medicaid, and VA Health Care (provided through the Department of Veterans Affairs); the Children's Health Insurance Program (CHIP); and individual state health plans. The types of health insurance are not mutually exclusive; people may be covered by more than one at the same time. People who had no reported health coverage, or those whose only health coverage was Indian Health Service, were considered uninsured. *Source: U.S. Census Bureau, American Community Survey, 2013-2017 Five-Year Estimates*

- **Have Insurance:** Percent of the civilian noninstitutionalized population with any type of comprehensive health insurance.
- **Have Private Insurance.** Percent of the civilian noninstitutionalized population with private health insurance. A person may report that they have both public and private health insurance, thus, the sum of the percentages may be greater than 100%.
- **Have Public Insurance.** Percent of the civilian noninstitutionalized population with public health insurance. A person may report that they have both public and private health insurance, thus, the sum of the percentages may be greater than 100%.
- **Do Not Have Insurance.** Percent of the civilian noninstitutionalized population with no health insurance.
- **Children Under 19 With No Insurance.** Percent of the civilian noninstitutionalized population under age 19 with no health insurance.

HOSPITALS

Lists the hospital name and the number of licensed beds. *Source: Grey House Publishing, The Comparative Guide to American Hospitals, 2014*; Original research

NEWSPAPERS

List of daily and weekly newspapers with circulation figures. *Source: Gebbie Press, 2015 All-In-One Media Directory*

SAFETY

Violent Crime Rate: Number of violent crimes reported per 10,000 population. Violent crimes include murder, forcible rape, robbery, and aggravated assault. Statistics include the revised definition of forcible rate if available. Otherwise statistics using the legacy definition are used. *Source: Federal Bureau of Investigation, Uniform Crime Reports 2017*

Property Crime Rate: Number of property crimes reported per 10,000 population. Property crimes include burglary, larceny-theft, and motor vehicle theft. *Source: Federal Bureau of Investigation, Uniform Crime Reports 2017*

TRANSPORTATION

Commute to Work: Percentage of workers 16 years old and over that use the following means of transportation to commute to work: car; public transportation; walk; work from home. The means of transportation data for some areas may show workers using modes of public transportation that are not available in those areas (e.g. subway or elevated riders in a metropolitan area where there actually is no subway or elevated service). This result is largely due to people who worked during the reference week at a location that was different from their usual place of work (such as people away from home on business in an area where subway service was available) and people who used more than one means of transportation each day but whose principal means was unavailable where they lived (e.g. residents of non-metropolitan areas who drove to the fringe of a metropolitan area and took the commuter railroad most of the distance to work). *Source: U.S. Census Bureau, American Community Survey, 2013-2017 Five-Year Estimates*

Mean Travel Time to Work: Mean travel time to work for workers 16 years old and over. Travel time to work refers to the total number of minutes that it usually took the person to get from home to work each day during the reference week. The elapsed time includes time spent waiting for public transportation, picking up passengers in carpools, and time spent in other activities related to getting to work. *Source: U.S. Census Bureau, American Community Survey, 2013-2017 Five-Year Estimates*

Amtrak: Indicates if Amtrak rail or bus service is available. Please note that the cities being served continually change. *Source: National Railroad Passenger Corporation, Amtrak National Timetable, 2019*

AIRPORTS

Lists the local airport(s) along with type of service and hub size. *Source: U.S. Department of Transportation, Bureau of Transportation Statistics*

ADDITIONAL INFORMATION CONTACTS

General telephone number and website address (if available) of local government.

xxvi   User Guide: Education Section

Profiles of New York State

Education Section

State Public School Educational Profile

Schools: Total number of schools in the district. Figures exclude schools with the following status codes: 2 (school has closed since the time of the last report) and 6 (school is temporarily closed and may reopen within three years). *Source: U.S. Department of Education, National Center for Education Statistics, Common Core of Data, Public Elementary/Secondary School Universe Survey: School Year 2015-2016.*

Instructional Level

Primary: Low grade—prekindergarten through 3; high grade—prekindergarten through 8
Middle: Low grade—4 through 7; high grade—4 through 9
High: Low grade—7 through 12; high grade—12 only
Other/Not Reported: Any configuration not falling within the previous three, including ungraded schools

Curriculum

Regular: A regular school is defined as a public elementary/secondary school that does not focus primarily on vocational, special, or alternative education.

Special Education: A special education school is defined as a public elementary/secondary school that focuses primarily on special education, including instruction for any of the following: autism, deaf-blindness, developmental delay, hearing impairment, mental retardation, multiple disabilities, orthopedic impairment, serious emotional disturbance, specific learning disability, speech or language impairment, traumatic brain injury, visual impairment, and other health impairments. These schools adapt curriculum, materials or instruction for students served.

Vocational: A vocational educational school is defined as a public elementary/secondary school that focuses primarily on providing formal preparation for semi-skilled, skilled, technical, or professional occupations for high school-aged students who have opted to develop or expand their employment opportunities, often in lieu of preparing for college entry.

Alternative: A public elementary/secondary school that addresses needs of students which typically cannot be met in a regular school; provides nontraditional education; serves as an adjunct to a regular school; and falls outside of the categories of regular, special education, or vocational education.

Type

Magnet: A special school or program designed to attract students of different racial/ethnic backgrounds for the purpose of reducing, preventing or eliminating racial isolation (50 percent or more minority enrollment); and/or to provide an academic or social focus on a particular theme (e.g., science/math, performing arts, gifted/talented, or foreign language).

Charter: A school providing free public elementary and/or secondary education to eligible students under a specific charter granted by the state legislature or other appropriate authority, and designated by such authority to be a charter school.

Title I Eligible: A school designated under appropriate state and federal regulations as being eligible for participation in programs authorized by Title I of Public Law 103-382.

School-wide Title I: A school in which all the pupils in a school are designated under appropriate state and federal regulations as being eligible for participation in programs authorized by Title I of Public Law 103-382.

Students: A student is an individual for whom instruction is provided in an elementary or secondary education program that is not an adult education program and is under the jurisdiction of a school, school system, or other education institution. *Sources: U.S. Department of Education, National Center for Education Statistics, Common Core of Data, Local Education Agency (School District) Universe Survey: School Year 2015-2016; U.S. Department of Education, National Center for Education Statistics, Common Core of Data, Public Elementary/Secondary School Universe Survey: School Year 2015-2016*

Gender: Percentage of male and female students.

Race/Ethnicity

White: A person having origins in any of the original peoples of Europe, North Africa, or the Middle East. Figures include non-Hispanic whites only.

Black: A person having origins in any of the black racial groups of Africa. Figures include non-Hispanic blacks only.

Asian: A person having origins in any of the original peoples of the Far east, Southeast Asia, and the Indian subcontinent. This includes, for example, China, India, Japan, Korea, and the Philippines. Figures include non-Hispanic Asians only.

American Indian/Alaska Native: A person having origins in any of the original peoples of North America, and who maintains cultural identification through tribal affiliation or community recognition. Figures include non-Hispanic American Indian/Alaska Natives only.

Hawaiian Native/Pacific Islander: A person having origins in any of the original peoples of Hawaii, Guam, Samoa, or other Pacific Islands. Figures include non-Hispanic Hawaiian Native/Pacific Islanders only.

Two or More Races: A person identifying himself or herself as of two or more of the following race groups: White, Black, Asian, Native Hawaiian/Pacific Islander, or American Indian/Alaska Native. Some, but not all, reporting districts use this category. Figures include non-Hispanics, multiple-race students only.

Hispanic: A person of Mexican, Puerto Rican, Cuban, Central or South American, or other Spanish culture or origin, regardless of race.

Special Programs

Individual Education Program (IEP): A written instructional plan for students with disabilities designated as special education students under IDEA-Part B. The written instructional plan includes a statement of present levels of educational performance of a child; statement of annual goals, including short-term instructional objectives; statement of specific educational services to be provided and the extent to which the child will be able to participate in regular educational programs; the projected date for initiation and anticipated duration of services; the appropriate objectives, criteria and evaluation procedures; and the schedules for determining, on at least an annual basis, whether instructional objectives are being achieved. *Source: U.S. Department of Education, National Center for Education Statistics, Common Core of Data, Local Education Agency (School District) Universe Survey: School Year 2015-2016*

English Language Learner (ELL): Formerly referred to as Limited English Proficient (LEP). Students being served in appropriate programs of language assistance (e.g., English as a Second Language, High Intensity Language Training, bilingual education). Does not include pupils enrolled in a class to learn a language other than English. Also Limited-English-Proficient students are individuals who were not born in the United States or whose native language is a language other than English; or individuals who come from environments where a language other than English is dominant; or individuals who are American Indians and Alaskan Natives and who come from environments where a language other than English has had a significant impact on their level of English language proficiency; and who, by reason thereof, have sufficient difficulty speaking, reading, writing, or understanding the English language, to deny such individuals the opportunity to learn successfully in classrooms where the language of instruction is English or to participate fully in our society. *Source: U.S. Department of Education, National Center for Education Statistics, Common Core of Data, Local Education Agency (School District) Universe Survey: School Year 2015-2016*

Eligible for Free Lunch Program: The free lunch program is defined as a program under the National School Lunch Act that provides cash subsidies for free lunches to students based on family size and income criteria. *Source: U.S. Department of Education, National Center for Education Statistics, Common Core of Data, Public Elementary/Secondary School Universe Survey: School Year 2015-2016*

Eligible for Reduced-Price Lunch Program: A student who is eligible to participate in the Reduced-Price Lunch Program under the National School Lunch Act. *Source: U.S. Department of Education, National Center for Education Statistics, Common Core of Data, Public Elementary/Secondary School Universe Survey: School Year 2015-2016*

Adjusted Cohort Graduation Rate (ACGR): The 4-year ACGR is the number of students who graduate in 4 years with a regular high school diploma divided by the number of students who form the adjusted cohort for the graduating class. From the beginning of 9th grade (or the earliest high school grade), students who are entering that grade for the first time form a cohort that is "adjusted" by adding any students who subsequently transfer into the cohort and subtracting any students who subsequently transfer out, emigrate to another country, or die. There are some differences in how states implemented the requirements for the ACGR, leading to the potential for differences across states in how the rates are calculated. This is particularly applicable to the population of children with disabilities. Black includes African American, Hispanic includes Latino, Asian/Pacific Islander includes Native Hawaiian or Other Pacific Islander, and American Indian includes Alaska Native. Race categories exclude Hispanic origin unless specified. Variances of +/- 5% from year-to-year for any subgroup over 50 in cohort size were addressed with states through ED's Coordinated Data Quality Review. With one exception, West Virginia, states provided explanations for the increase/decrease. The state comment was not accepted by the data steward (OESE) for California, Illinois, Louisiana, New Mexico, Texas, Utah and the District of Columbia. Those seven states and West Virginia received a letter from OESE to the state's Chief State School Officer outlining data quality concerns that are expected to be addressed in future submissions. *Source: EDFacts Data Groups 695 and 696, School Year 2015–16, October 25, 2017.*

Status Dropout Rate: "Status" dropouts are 16- to 24-year-olds who are not enrolled in school and who have not completed a high school program, regardless of when they left school. People who have received GED credentials are counted as high school completers. Data are based on a sample survey of the noninstitutionalized and institutionalized populations. The noninstitutionalized population includes persons living in households as well as persons living in college and university housing, military quarters, facilities for workers and religious groups, and temporary shelters for the homeless. The institutionalized population includes persons living in adult and juvenile correctional facilities, nursing facilities, and other healthcare facilities. Totals include other racial/ethnic groups not separately shown. Race categories exclude persons of Hispanic ethnicity. *Source: Trends in High School Dropout and Completion Rates in the United States: 2014, March 2018*

Note: Drop-out rates are no longer available to the general public disaggregated by grade, race/ethnicity, and gender at the school district level.

Staff

Teachers: Teachers are defined as individuals who provide instruction to pre-kindergarten, kindergarten, grades 1 through 12, or ungraded classes, or individuals who teach in an environment other than a classroom setting, and who maintain daily student attendance records. Numbers reported are full-time equivalents (FTE). The students per teacher ratio is shown in parentheses. *Source: U.S. Department of Education, National Center for Education Statistics, Common Core of Data, Local Education Agency (School District) Universe Survey: School Year 2015-2016.*

Teacher Salary: The average classroom teacher salary in 2015-2016. *Source: National Education Association, Rankings of the States 2017 and Estimates of School Statistics 2018*

Librarians/Media Specialists: Library and media support staff are defined as staff members who render other professional library and media services; also includes library aides and those involved in library/media support. Their duties include selecting, preparing, caring for, and making available to instructional staff, equipment, films, filmstrips, transparencies, tapes, TV programs, and similar materials maintained separately or as part of an instructional materials center. Also included are activities in the audio-visual center, TV studio, related-work-study areas, and services provided by audio-visual personnel. Numbers reported are full-time equivalents (FTE). The students per librarian/media specialist ratio is shown in parentheses. *Source: U.S. Department of Education, National Center for Education Statistics, Common Core of Data, Local Education Agency (School District) Universe Survey: School Year 2015-2016.*

Guidance Counselors: Professional staff assigned specific duties and school time for any of the following activities in an elementary or secondary setting: counseling with students and parents; consulting with other staff members on learning problems; evaluating student abilities; assisting students in making educational and career choices; assisting students in personal and social development; providing referral assistance; and/or working with other staff members in planning and conducting guidance programs for students. The state applies its own standards in apportioning the aggregate of guidance counselors/directors into the elementary and secondary level components. Numbers reported are full-time equivalents (FTE). The students per guidance counselor ratio is shown in parentheses. *Source: U.S. Department of Education, National Center for Education Statistics, Common Core of Data, Local Education Agency (School District) Universe Survey: School Year 2015-2016.*

Ratios

Number of Students per Teacher: The number of students divided by the number of teachers (FTE). See Number of Students and Number of Teachers above for more information. *Source: U.S. Department of*

Education, National Center for Education Statistics, Common Core of Data, Local Education Agency (School District) Universe Survey: School Year 2015-2016.

Number of Students per Librarian: The number of students divided by the number of library and media support staff. Library and media support staff are defined as staff members who render other professional library and media services; also includes library aides and those involved in library/media support. Their duties include selecting, preparing, caring for, and making available to instructional staff, equipment, films, filmstrips, transparencies, tapes, TV programs, and similar materials maintained separately or as part of an instructional materials center. Also included are activities in the audio-visual center, TV studio, related-work-study areas, and services provided by audio-visual personnel. Numbers are based on full-time equivalents. *Source: U.S. Department of Education, National Center for Education Statistics, Common Core of Data, Local Education Agency (School District) Universe Survey: School Year 2015-2016.*

Number of Students per Counselor: The number of students divided by the number of guidance counselors. Guidance counselors are professional staff assigned specific duties and school time for any of the following activities in an elementary or secondary setting: counseling with students and parents; consulting with other staff members on learning problems; evaluating student abilities; assisting students in making educational and career choices; assisting students in personal and social development; providing referral assistance; and/or working with other staff members in planning and conducting guidance programs for students. The state applies its own standards in apportioning the aggregate of guidance counselors/directors into the elementary and secondary level components. Numbers reported are full-time equivalents. *Source: U.S. Department of Education, National Center for Education Statistics, Common Core of Data, Local Education Agency (School District) Universe Survey: School Year 2015-2016.*

Finances

Total Expenditures per Pupil: This is the total expenditures divided by the fall membership as reported in the state finance file. The total expenditures is the subtotal of direct state support expenditures for private schools, debt services expenditures—interest and total expenditures for education.

Total Current Expenditures per Pupil: This is the total current expenditures for public elementary and secondary education divided by the fall membership as reported in the state finance file. The expenditures for equipment, non-public education, school construction, debt financing and community services are excluded from this data item.

Instruction Expenditures per Pupil: This is the total of instructional expenditures divided by the fall membership as reported in the state finance file. Instruction expenditures are for services and materials directly related to classroom instruction and the interaction between teachers and students. Teacher salaries and benefits, textbooks, classroom supplies and extra curricular activities are included in Instruction. Expenditures for the library and in-service teacher training are reported as instruction support services. Guidance counselors and nurses are reported under student support services.

Support Services Expenditures per Pupil: This is the total of support services expenditures divided by the fall membership as reported in the state finance file.

Non-Instruction Expenditures per Pupil: This is the total for food services operations expenditures and enterprise operations expenditures divided by the fall membership as reported in the state finance file. This does not include property or community services expenditures.

Net Current Expenditures per Attendance for Title I: Net current expenditures per average daily attendance (ADA) are calculated by NCES. Net current expenditures are calculated by NCES and are equal to current expenditures minus total exclusions. Computation of ADA is defined by state laws or regulations or by NCES. Net current expenditures per ADA (or state per public expenditures—SPPE) are used to calculate allocations for certain federal education programs, including Title I, impact aid, Indian education and individuals with disabilities.

Total Revenues per Pupil: Total revenues per student are the total revenues from all sources divided by the fall membership as reported in the state finance file.

Federal Revenues per Pupil: Federal revenues per student are federal revenues divided by the fall membership as reported in the state finance file.

State Revenues per Pupil: State revenues per student are revenues received by the LEAs from the state, divided by the fall membership as reported in the state finance file.

Local Revenues per Pupil: Local revenues per student are the total of all local revenue categories divided by the fall membership as reported in the state finance file. Local revenues are raised and allocated by local governments.

Intermediate Revenue per Pupil: Intermediate revenue per pupil are intermediate sources of revenue divided by the student membership as reported on the state finance file. Intermediate sources of revenue are from educational agencies that possess independent fund-raising capabilities and that operate between the state and local government levels. *Source: U.S. Department of Education, National Center for Education Statistics, Common Core of Data (CCD), National Public Education Financial Survey (State Fiscal), 2014-15 (FY 2015) v.1a*

College Entrance Exam Scores

Scholastic Aptitude Test (SAT). On March 5, 2014, the College Board announced its plan to redesign the SAT in order to link the exam more closely to the work high school students encounter in the classroom. The new exam was administered for the first time in March 2016. Some of the major changes are: an emphasis on the use of evidence to support answers, a shift away from obscure vocabulary to words that students are more likely to encounter in college and career, a math section that is focused on fewer areas, a return to the 1600-point score scale, an optional essay, and the removal of penalty for wrong answers (rights-only scoring). Note: The College Board strongly discourages the comparison or ranking of states on the basis of SAT scores alone. *Source: The College Board, SAT, 2017 College-Bound Seniors, State Profile Reports*

American College Testing Program (ACT). *Source: ACT, Inc., 2017 ACT National and State Scores*

Note: n/a indicates data not available.

School District Rankings

Number of Schools: Total number of schools in the district. *Source: U.S. Department of Education, National Center for Education Statistics, Common Core of Data, Public Elementary/Secondary School Universe Survey: School Year 2015-2016.*

Number of Teachers: Teachers are defined as individuals who provide instruction to pre-kindergarten, kindergarten, grades 1 through 12, or ungraded classes, or individuals who teach in an environment other than a classroom setting, and who maintain daily student attendance records. Numbers reported are full-time equivalents (FTE). *Source: U.S. Department of Education, National Center for Education Statistics, Common Core of Data, Local Education Agency (School District) Universe Survey: School Year 2015-2016.*

Number of Students: A student is an individual for whom instruction is provided in an elementary or secondary education program that is not an adult education program and is under the jurisdiction of a school, school system, or other education institution. *Source: U.S. Department of Education, National Center for Education Statistics, Common Core of Data, Local Education Agency (School District) Universe Survey: School Year 2015-2016*

Male Students: Percentage of students who are male. *Source: U.S. Department of Education, National Center for Education Statistics, Common Core of Data, Local Education Agency (School District) Universe Survey: School Year 2015-2016*

Female Students: Percentage of students who are female. *Source: U.S. Department of Education, National Center for Education Statistics, Common Core of Data, Local Education Agency (School District) Universe Survey: School Year 2015-2016*

White Students: Percentage of students who are white (a person having origins in any of the original peoples of Europe, North Africa, or the Middle East). Figures include non-Hispanic whites only. *Source: U.S. Department of Education, National Center for Education Statistics, Common Core of Data, Local Education Agency (School District) Universe Survey: School Year 2015-2016*

Black Students: Percentage of students who are black (a person having origins in any of the black racial groups of Africa). Figures include non-Hispanic blacks only. *Source: U.S. Department of Education, National Center for Education Statistics, Common Core of Data, Local Education Agency (School District) Universe Survey: School Year 2015-2016*

Asian Students: Percentage of students who are Asian (a person having origins in any of the original peoples of the Far east, Southeast Asia, and the Indian subcontinent. This includes, for example, China, India, Japan, Korea, and the Philippines). Figures include non-Hispanic Asians only. *Source: U.S. Department of Education, National Center* *for Education Statistics, Common Core of Data, Local Education Agency (School District) Universe Survey: School Year 2015-2016*

American Indian/Alaska Native Students: Percentage of students who are American Indian/Alaska Native Students (a person having origins in any of the original peoples of North America, and who maintains cultural identification through tribal affiliation or community recognition). Figures include non-Hispanic American Indian/Alaska Natives only. *Source: U.S. Department of Education, National Center for Education Statistics, Common Core of Data, Local Education Agency (School District) Universe Survey: School Year 2015-2016*

Hawaiian Native/Pacific Islander Students: Percentage of students who are Hawaiian Native/Pacific Islander (a person having origins in any of the original peoples of Hawaii, Guam, Samoa, or other Pacific Islands). Figures include non-Hispanic Hawaiian Native/Pacific Islanders only. *Source: U.S. Department of Education, National Center for Education Statistics, Common Core of Data, Local Education Agency (School District) Universe Survey: School Year 2015-2016*

Students who are Two or More Races: Percentage of students who are two or more races (a person identifying himself or herself as of two or more of the following race groups: White, Black, Asian, Native Hawaiian/Pacific Islander, or American Indian/Alaska Native). Some, but not all, reporting districts use this category. Figures include non-Hispanic, multiple-race students only. *Source: U.S. Department of Education, National Center for Education Statistics, Common Core of Data, Local Education Agency (School District) Universe Survey: School Year 2015-2016*

Hispanic Students: Percentage of students who are Hispanic (a person of Mexican, Puerto Rican, Cuban, Central or South American, or other Spanish culture or origin, regardless of race). *Source: U.S. Department of Education, National Center for Education Statistics, Common Core of Data, Local Education Agency (School District) Universe Survey: School Year 2015-2016*

Individual Education Program (IEP) Students: Percentage of students who have an Individual Education Program (IEP) which is a written instructional plan for students with disabilities designated as special education students under IDEA-Part B. The written instructional plan includes a statement of present levels of educational performance of a child; statement of annual goals, including short-term instructional objectives; statement of specific educational services to be provided and the extent to which the child will be able to participate in regular educational programs; the projected date for initiation and anticipated duration of services; the appropriate objectives, criteria and evaluation procedures; and the schedules for determining, on at least an annual basis, whether instructional objectives are being achieved. *Source: U.S. Department of Education, National Center for Education Statistics, Common Core of Data, Local Education Agency (School District) Universe Survey: School Year 2015-2016*

English Language Learner (ELL) Students: Percentage of students who are English Language Learners (ELL). Formerly referred to as Limited English Proficient (LEP). Students being served in appropriate programs of language assistance (e.g., English as a Second Language, High Intensity Language Training, bilingual education). Does not include pupils enrolled in a class to learn a language other than English. Also Limited-English-Proficient students are individuals who were not born in the United States or whose native language is a language other than English; or individuals who come from environments where a language other than English is dominant; or individuals who are American Indians and Alaskan Natives and who come from environments where a language other than English has had a significant impact on their level of English language proficiency; and who, by reason thereof, have sufficient difficulty speaking, reading, writing, or understanding the English language, to deny such individuals the opportunity to learn successfully in classrooms where the language of instruction is English or to participate fully in our society. *Source: U.S. Department of Education, National Center for Education Statistics, Common Core of Data, Local Education Agency (School District) Universe Survey: School Year 2015-2016*

Students Eligible for Free Lunch Program: Percentage of students that are eligible for the free lunch program. The free lunch program is defined as a program under the National School Lunch Act that provides cash subsidies for free lunches to students based on family size and income criteria. *Source: U.S. Department of Education, National Center for Education Statistics, Common Core of Data, Public Elementary/Secondary School Universe Survey: School Year 2015-2016*

Students Eligible for Reduced-Price Lunch Program: Percentage of students that are eligible for the reduced-price lunch program. A student who is eligible to participate in the reduced-price lunch program under the National School Lunch Act. *Source: U.S. Department of Education, National Center for Education Statistics, Common Core of Data, Public Elementary/Secondary School Universe Survey: School Year 2015-2016*

Student/Teacher Ratio: The number of students divided by the number of teachers (FTE). See Number of Students and Number of Teachers above for for information. *Source: U.S. Department of Education, National Center for Education Statistics, Common Core of Data, Local Education Agency (School District) Universe Survey: School Year 2015-2016*

Student/Librarian Ratio: The number of students divided by the number of library and media support staff. Library and media support staff are defined as staff members who render other professional library and media services; also includes library aides and those involved in library/media support. Their duties include selecting, preparing, caring for, and making available to instructional staff, equipment, films, filmstrips, transparencies, tapes, TV programs, and similar materials maintained separately or as part of an instructional materials center. Also included are activities in the audio-visual center, TV studio, related-work-study areas, and services provided by audio-visual personnel. Numbers are based on full-time equivalents. *Source: U.S. Department of Education, National Center for Education Statistics, Common Core of Data, Local Education Agency (School District) Universe Survey: School Year 2015-2016.*

Student/Counselor Ratio: The number of students divided by the number of guidance counselors. Guidance counselors are professional staff assigned specific duties and school time for any of the following activities in an elementary or secondary setting: counseling with students and parents; consulting with other staff members on learning problems; evaluating student abilities; assisting students in making educational and career choices; assisting students in personal and social development; providing referral assistance; and/or working with other staff members in planning and conducting guidance programs for students. The state applies its own standards in apportioning the aggregate of guidance counselors/directors into the elementary and secondary level components. Numbers reported are full-time equivalents. *Source: U.S. Department of Education, National Center for Education Statistics, Common Core of Data, Local Education Agency (School District) Universe Survey: School Year 2015-2016.*

Current Spending per Student: Expenditure for Instruction, Support Services, and Other Elementary/Secondary Programs. Includes salaries, employee benefits, purchased services, and supplies, as well as payments made by states on behalf of school districts. Also includes transfers made by school districts into their own retirement system. Excludes expenditure for Non-Elementary/Secondary Programs, debt service, capital outlay, and transfers to other governments or school districts. This item is formally called "Current Expenditures for Public Elementary/Secondary Education."

Values shown are dollars per pupil per year. They were calculated by dividing the total dollar amounts by the fall membership. Fall membership is comprised of the total student enrollment on October 1 (or the closest school day to October 1) for all grade levels (including prekindergarten and kindergarten) and ungraded pupils. Membership includes students both present and absent on the measurement day. *Source: U.S. Department of Education, National Center for Education Statistics, Common Core of Data, School District Finance Survey (F-33), Fiscal Year 2014.*

Total General Revenue per Student: The sum of revenue contributions emerging from local, state, and federal sources as reported in the district finance file.

Values shown are dollars per pupil per year. They were calculated by dividing the total dollar amounts by the fall membership. Fall membership is comprised of the total student enrollment on October 1 (or the closest school day to October 1) for all grade levels (including prekindergarten and kindergarten) and ungraded pupils. Membership includes students both present and absent on the measurement day. *Source: U.S. Department of Education, National Center for Education Statistics, Common Core of Data, School District Finance Survey (F-33), Fiscal Year 2014.*

Long-Term Debt per Student (end of FY): Includes long-term credit obligations of the school system or its parent government and all interest-bearing short-term (repayable within 1 year) credit obligations. Excludes non-interest bearing short-term obligations, interfund obligations, amounts owed in a trust agency capacity, advances and contingent loans from other governments, and rights of individuals to benefits from school system employee retirement funds.

Values shown are dollars per pupil per year. They were calculated by dividing the total dollar amounts at the end of the fiscal year by the fall membership. Fall membership is comprised of the total student enrollment on October 1 (or the closest school day to October 1) for all grade levels (including prekindergarten and kindergarten) and ungraded pupils. Membership includes students both present and absent on the measurement day. *Source: U.S. Department of Education, National Center for Education Statistics, Common Core of Data, School District Finance Survey (F-33), Fiscal Year 2014.*

Note: n/a indicates data not available.

National Assessment of Educational Progress (NAEP)

The National Assessment of Educational Progress (NAEP), also known as "The Nation's Report Card," is the only nationally representative and continuing assessment of what America's students know and can do in various subject areas. As a result of the "No Child Left Behind" legislation, all states are required to participate in NAEP.

For more information, visit the U.S. Department of Education, National Center for Education Statistics at http://nces.ed.gov/nationsreportcard.

Ancestry and Ethnicity Section

Places Covered

The ancestry and ethnicity profile section of this book covers the state and all counties and places with populations of 50,000 or more. Places included fall into one of the following categories:

Incorporated Places. Depending on the state, places are incorporated as either cities, towns, villages, boroughs, municipalities, independent cities, or corporations. A few municipalities have a form of government combined with another entity (e.g. county) and are listed as special cities or consolidated, unified, or metropolitan governments.

Census Designated Places (CDP). The U.S. Census Bureau defines a CDP as "a statistical entity," defined for each decennial census according to Census Bureau guidelines, comprising a densely settled concentration of population that is not within an incorporated place, but is locally identified by a name. CDPs are delineated cooperatively by state and local officials and the Census Bureau, following Census Bureau guidelines.

Minor Civil Divisions (called charter townships, districts, gores, grants, locations, plantations, purchases, reservations, towns, townships, and unorganized territories) for the states where the Census Bureau has determined that they serve as general-purpose governments. Those states are Connecticut, Maine, Massachusetts, Michigan, Minnesota, New Hampshire, New Jersey, New York, Pennsylvania, Rhode Island, Vermont, and Wisconsin. In some states incorporated municipalities are part of minor civil divisions and in some states they are independent of them.

Note: Several states have incorporated municipalities and minor civil divisions in the same county with the same name. Those communities are given separate entries (e.g. Burlington, New Jersey, in Burlington County will be listed under both the city and township of Burlington). A few states have Census Designated Places and minor civil divisions in the same county with the same name. Those communities are given separate entries (e.g. Bridgewater, Massachusetts, in Plymouth County will be listed under both the CDP and town of Bridgewater).

Source of Data

The ethnicities shown in this book were compiled from two different sources. Data for Race and Hispanic Origin was taken from Census 2010 Summary File 1 (SF1) while Ancestry data was taken from the American Community Survey (ACS) 2006-2010 Five-Year Estimate. The distinction is important because SF1 contains 100-percent data, which is the information compiled from the questions asked of all people and about every housing unit. ACS estimates are compiled from a sampling of households. The 2006-2010 Five-Year Estimate is based on data collected from January 1, 2006 to December 31, 2010.

The American Community Survey (ACS) is a relatively new survey conducted by the U.S. Census Bureau. It uses a series of monthly samples to produce annually updated data for the same small areas (census tracts and block groups) formerly surveyed via the decennial census long-form sample. While some version of this survey has been in the field since 1999, it was not fully implemented in terms of coverage until 2006. In 2005 it was expanded to cover all counties in the country and the 1-in-40 households sampling rate was first applied. The full implementation of the (household) sampling strategy for ACS entails having the survey mailed to about 250,000 households nationwide every month of every year and was begun in January 2005. In January 2006 sampling of group quarters was added to complete the sample as planned. In any given year about 2.5% (1 in 40) of U.S. households will receive the survey. Over any 5-year period about 1 in 8 households should receive the survey (as compared to about 1 in 6 that received the census long form in the 2000 census). Since receiving the survey is not the same as responding to it, the Bureau has adopted a strategy of sampling for non-response, resulting in something closer to 1 in 11 households actually participating in the survey over any 5-year period. For more information about the American Community Survey visit http://www.census.gov/acs/www.

Ancestry

Ancestry refers to a person's ethnic origin, heritage, descent, or "roots," which may reflect their place of birth or that of previous generations of their family. Some ethnic identities, such as "Egyptian" or "Polish" can be traced to geographic areas outside the United States, while other ethnicities such as "Pennsylvania German" or "Cajun" evolved in the United States.

The intent of the ancestry question in the ACS was not to measure the degree of attachment the respondent had to a particular ethnicity, but simply to establish that the respondent had a connection to and self-identified with a particular ethnic group. For example, a response of "Irish" might reflect total involvement in an Irish community or only a memory of ancestors several generations removed from the respondent.

The Census Bureau coded the responses into a numeric representation of over 1,000 categories. Responses initially were processed through an automated coding system; then, those that were not automatically assigned a code were coded by individuals trained in coding ancestry responses. The code list reflects the results of the Census Bureau's own research and consultations with many ethnic experts. Many decisions were made to determine the classification of responses. These decisions affected the grouping of the tabulated data. For example, the "Indonesian" category includes the responses of "Indonesian," "Celebesian," "Moluccan," and a number of other responses.

Ancestries Covered

Afghan	Palestinian	French, ex. Basque	Scottish
African, Sub-Saharan	Syrian	French Canadian	Serbian
African	Other Arab	German	Slavic
Cape Verdean	Armenian	German Russian	Slovak
Ethiopian	Assyrian/Chaldean/Syriac	Greek	Slovene
Ghanaian	Australian	Guyanese	Soviet Union
Kenyan	Austrian	Hungarian	Swedish
Liberian	Basque	Icelander	Swiss
Nigerian	Belgian	Iranian	Turkish
Senegalese	Brazilian	Irish	Ukrainian
Sierra Leonean	British	Israeli	Welsh
Somalian	Bulgarian	Italian	West Indian, ex.
South African	Cajun	Latvian	Hispanic
Sudanese	Canadian	Lithuanian	Bahamian
Ugandan	Carpatho Rusyn	Luxemburger	Barbadian
Zimbabwean	Celtic	Macedonian	Belizean
Other Sub-Saharan African	Croatian	Maltese	Bermudan
Albanian	Cypriot	New Zealander	British West Indian
Alsatian	Czech	Northern European	Dutch West Indian
American	Czechoslovakian	Norwegian	Haitian
Arab	Danish	Pennsylvania German	Jamaican
Arab	Dutch	Polish	Trinidadian/
Egyptian	Eastern European	Portuguese	Tobagonian
Iraqi	English	Romanian	U.S. Virgin Islander
Jordanian	Estonian	Russian	West Indian
Lebanese	European	Scandinavian	Other West Indian
Moroccan	Finnish	Scotch-Irish	Yugoslavian

The ancestry question allowed respondents to report one or more ancestry groups. Generally, only the first two responses reported were coded. If a response was in terms of a dual ancestry, for example, "Irish English," the person was assigned two codes, in this case one for Irish and another for English. However, in certain cases, multiple responses such as "French Canadian," "Scotch-Irish," "Greek Cypriot," and "Black Dutch" were assigned a single code reflecting their status as unique groups. If a person reported one of these unique groups in addition to another group, for example, "Scotch-Irish English," resulting in three terms, that person received one code for the unique group (Scotch-Irish) and another one for the remaining group (English). If a person reported "English Irish French," only English and Irish were coded. If there were more than two ancestries listed and one of the ancestries was a part of another, such as "German Bavarian Hawaiian," the responses were coded using the more detailed groups (Bavarian and Hawaiian).

The Census Bureau accepted "American" as a unique ethnicity if it was given alone or with one other ancestry. There were some groups such as "American Indian," "Mexican American," and "African American" that were coded and identified separately.

The ancestry question is asked for every person in the American Community Survey, regardless of age, place of birth, Hispanic origin, or race.

Although some people consider religious affiliation a component of ethnic identity, the ancestry question was not designed to collect any information concerning religion. Thus, if a religion was given as an answer to the ancestry question, it was listed in the "Other groups" category which is not shown in this book.

Ancestry should not be confused with a person's place of birth, although a person's place of birth and ancestry may be the same.

Hispanic Origin

The data on the Hispanic or Latino population were derived from answers to a Census 2010 question that was asked of all people. The terms "Spanish," "Hispanic origin," and "Latino" are used interchangeably. Some respondents identify with all three terms while others may identify with only one of these three specific terms. Hispanics or Latinos who identify with the terms "Spanish," "Hispanic," or "Latino" are those who classify themselves in one of the specific Spanish, Hispanic, or Latino categories listed on the questionnaire ("Mexican," "Puerto Rican," or "Cuban") as well as those who indicate that they are "other Spanish/Hispanic/Latino." People who do not identify with one of the specific origins listed on the questionnaire but indicate that they are "other Spanish/Hispanic/Latino" are those whose origins are from Spain, the Spanish-speaking countries of Central or South America, the Dominican Republic, or people identifying themselves generally as Spanish, Spanish-American, Hispanic, Hispano, Latino, and so on. All write-in responses to the "other Spanish/Hispanic/Latino" category were coded.

Hispanic Origins Covered

Hispanic or Latino	Salvadoran	Argentinean	Uruguayan
Central American, ex. Mexican	Other Central American	Bolivian	Venezuelan
Costa Rican	Cuban	Chilean	Other South American
Guatemalan	Dominican Republic	Colombian	Other Hispanic or Latino
Honduran	Mexican	Ecuadorian	
Nicaraguan	Puerto Rican	Paraguayan	
Panamanian	South American	Peruvian	

Origin can be viewed as the heritage, nationality group, lineage, or country of birth of the person or the person's parents or ancestors before their arrival in the United States. People who identify their origin as Hispanic, Latino, or Spanish may be of any race.

Ethnicities Based on Race

The data on race were derived from answers to the Census 2010 question on race that was asked of individuals in the United States. The Census Bureau collects racial data in accordance with guidelines provided by the U.S. Office of Management and Budget (OMB), and these data are based on self-identification.

The racial categories included in the census questionnaire generally reflect a social definition of race recognized in this country and not an attempt to define race biologically, anthropologically, or genetically. In addition, it is recognized that the categories of the race item include racial and national origin or sociocultural groups. People may choose to report more than one race to indicate their racial mixture, such as "American Indian" and "White." People who identify their origin as Hispanic, Latino, or Spanish may be of any race.

Racial Groups Covered

African-American/Black	Crow	Spanish American Indian	Korean
Not Hispanic	Delaware	Tlingit-Haida *(Alaska Native)*	Laotian
Hispanic	Hopi	Tohono O'Odham	Malaysian
American Indian/Alaska Native	Houma	Tsimshian *(Alaska Native)*	Nepalese
Not Hispanic	Inupiat *(Alaska Native)*	Ute	Pakistani
Hispanic	Iroquois	Yakama	Sri Lankan
Alaska Athabascan *(Ala. Nat.)*	Kiowa	Yaqui	Taiwanese
Aleut *(Alaska Native)*	Lumbee	Yuman	Thai
Apache	Menominee	Yup'ik *(Alaska Native)*	Vietnamese
Arapaho	Mexican American Indian	**Asian**	**Hawaii Native/Pacific Islander**
Blackfeet	Navajo	*Not Hispanic*	*Not Hispanic*
Canadian/French Am. Indian	Osage	*Hispanic*	*Hispanic*
Central American Indian	Ottawa	Bangladeshi	Fijian
Cherokee	Paiute	Bhutanese	Guamanian/Chamorro
Cheyenne	Pima	Burmese	Marshallese
Chickasaw	Potawatomi	Cambodian	Native Hawaiian
Chippewa	Pueblo	Chinese, ex. Taiwanese	Samoan
Choctaw	Puget Sound Salish	Filipino	Tongan
Colville	Seminole	Hmong	**White**
Comanche	Shoshone	Indian	*Not Hispanic*
Cree	Sioux	Indonesian	*Hispanic*
Creek	South American Indian	Japanese	

African American or Black: A person having origins in any of the Black racial groups of Africa. It includes people who indicated their race(s) as "Black, African Am., or Negro" or reported entries such as African American, Kenyan, Nigerian, or Haitian.

American Indian or Alaska Native: A person having origins in any of the original peoples of North and South America (including Central America) and who maintains tribal affiliation or community attachment. This category includes people who indicated their race(s) as "American Indian or Alaska Native" or reported their enrolled or principal tribe, such as Navajo, Blackfeet, Inupiat, Yup'ik, or Central American Indian groups or South American Indian groups.

Asian: A person having origins in any of the original peoples of the Far East, Southeast Asia, or the Indian subcontinent, including, for example, Cambodia, China, India, Japan, Korea, Malaysia, Pakistan, the Philippine Islands, Thailand, and Vietnam. It includes people who indicated their race(s) as "Asian" or reported entries such as "Asian Indian," "Chinese," "Filipino," "Korean," "Japanese," "Vietnamese," and "Other Asian" or provided other detailed Asian responses.

Native Hawaiian or Other Pacific Islander: A person having origins in any of the original peoples of Hawaii, Guam, Samoa, or other Pacific Islands. It includes people who indicated their race(s) as "Pacific Islander" or reported entries such as "Native Hawaiian," "Guamanian or Chamorro," "Samoan," and "Other Pacific Islander" or provided other detailed Pacific Islander responses.

White: A person having origins in any of the original peoples of Europe, the Middle East, or North Africa. It includes people who indicated their race(s) as "White" or reported entries such as Irish, German, Italian, Lebanese, Arab, Moroccan, or Caucasian.

Profiles

Each profile shows the name of the place, the county (if a place spans more than one county, the county that holds the majority of the population is shown), and the 2010 population (based on 100-percent data from Census 2010 Summary File 1). The rest of each profile is comprised of all 218 ethnicities grouped into three sections: ancestry; Hispanic origin; and race.

Column one displays the ancestry/Hispanic origin/race name, column two displays the number of people reporting each ancestry/Hispanic origin/race, and column three is the percent of the total population reporting each ancestry/Hispanic origin/race. The population figure shown is used to calculate the value in the "%" column for ethnicities based on race and Hispanic origin. The 2006-2010 estimated population figure from the American Community Survey (not shown) is used to calculate the value in the "%" column for all other ancestries.

For ethnicities in the ancestries group, the value in the "Number" column includes multiple ancestries reported. For example, if a person reported a multiple ancestry such as "French Danish," that response was counted twice in the tabulations, once in the French category and again in the Danish category. Thus, the sum of the counts is not the total population but the total of all responses. Numbers in parentheses indicate the number of people reporting a single ancestry. People reporting a single ancestry includes all people who reported only one ethnic group such as "German." Also included in this category are people with only a multiple-term response such as "Scotch-Irish" who are assigned a single code because they represent one distinct group. For example, the count for German would be interpreted as "The number of people who reported that German was their only ancestry."

For ethnicities based on Hispanic origin, the value in the "Number" column represents the number of people who reported being Mexican, Puerto Rican, Cuban or other Spanish/Hispanic/ Latino (all written-in responses were coded). All ethnicities based on Hispanic origin can be of any race.

For ethnicities based on race data the value in the "Number" column represents the total number of people who reported each category alone or in combination with one or more other race categories. This number represents the maximum number of people reporting and therefore the individual race categories may add up to more than the total population because people may be included in more than one category. The figures in parentheses show the number of people that reported that particular ethnicity alone, not in combination with any other race. For example, in Alabama, the entry for Korean shows 8,320 in parentheses and 10,624 in the "Number" column. This means that 8,320 people reported being Korean alone and 10,624 people reported being Korean alone or in combination with one or more other races.

Rankings

In the rankings section, each ethnicity has three tables. The first table shows the top 10 places sorted by ethnic population (based on all places, regardless of total population), the second table shows the top 10 places sorted by percent of the total population (based on all places, regardless of total population), the third table shows the top 10 places sorted by percent of the total population (based on places with total population of 50,000 or more).

Within each table, column one displays the place name, the state, and the county (if a place spans more than one county, the county that holds the majority of the population is shown). Column one in the first table displays the state only. Column two displays the number of people reporting each ancestry (includes people reporting multiple ancestries), Hispanic origin, or race (alone or in combination with any other race). Column three is the percent of the total population reporting each ancestry, Hispanic origin or race. For tables representing ethnicities based on race or Hispanic origin, the 100-percent population figure from SF1 is used to calculate the value in the "%" column. For all other ancestries, the 2006-2010 five-year estimated population figure from the American Community Survey is used to calculate the value in the "%" column.

Alphabetical Ethnicity Cross-Reference Guide

Afghan *see* Ancestry–Afghan
African *see* Ancestry–African, Sub-Saharan: African
African-American *see* Race–African-American/Black
African-American: Hispanic *see* Race–African-American/Black: Hispanic
African-American: Not Hispanic *see* Race–African-American/Black: Not Hispanic
Alaska Athabascan *see* Race–Alaska Native: Alaska Athabascan
Alaska Native *see* Race–American Indian/Alaska Native
Alaska Native: Hispanic *see* Race–American Indian/Alaska Native: Hispanic
Alaska Native: Not Hispanic *see* Race–American Indian/Alaska Native: Not Hispanic
Albanian *see* Ancestry–Albanian
Aleut *see* Race–Alaska Native: Aleut
Alsatian *see* Ancestry–Alsatian
American *see* Ancestry–American
American Indian *see* Race–American Indian/Alaska Native
American Indian: Hispanic *see* Race–American Indian/Alaska Native: Hispanic
American Indian: Not Hispanic *see* Race–American Indian/Alaska Native: Not Hispanic
Apache *see* Race–American Indian: Apache
Arab *see* Ancestry–Arab: Arab
Arab: Other *see* Ancestry–Arab: Other
Arapaho *see* Race–American Indian: Arapaho
Argentinean *see* Hispanic Origin–South American: Argentinean
Armenian *see* Ancestry–Armenian
Asian *see* Race–Asian
Asian Indian *see* Race–Asian: Indian
Asian: Hispanic *see* Race–Asian: Hispanic
Asian: Not Hispanic *see* Race–Asian: Not Hispanic
Assyrian *see* Ancestry–Assyrian/Chaldean/Syriac
Australian *see* Ancestry–Australian
Austrian *see* Ancestry–Austrian
Bahamian *see* Ancestry–West Indian: Bahamian, except Hispanic
Bangladeshi *see* Race–Asian: Bangladeshi
Barbadian *see* Ancestry–West Indian: Barbadian, except Hispanic
Basque *see* Ancestry–Basque
Belgian *see* Ancestry–Belgian
Belizean *see* Ancestry–West Indian: Belizean, except Hispanic
Bermudan *see* Ancestry–West Indian: Bermudan, except Hispanic
Bhutanese *see* Race–Asian: Bhutanese
Black *see* Race–African-American/Black
Black: Hispanic *see* Race–African-American/Black: Hispanic
Black: Not Hispanic *see* Race–African-American/Black: Not Hispanic
Blackfeet *see* Race–American Indian: Blackfeet
Bolivian *see* Hispanic Origin–South American: Bolivian
Brazilian *see* Ancestry–Brazilian
British *see* Ancestry–British

British West Indian *see* Ancestry–West Indian: British West Indian, except Hispanic
Bulgarian *see* Ancestry–Bulgarian
Burmese *see* Race–Asian: Burmese
Cajun *see* Ancestry–Cajun
Cambodian *see* Race–Asian: Cambodian
Canadian *see* Ancestry–Canadian
Canadian/French American Indian *see* Race–American Indian: Canadian/French American Indian
Cape Verdean *see* Ancestry–African, Sub-Saharan: Cape Verdean
Carpatho Rusyn *see* Ancestry–Carpatho Rusyn
Celtic *see* Ancestry–Celtic
Central American *see* Hispanic Origin–Central American, except Mexican
Central American Indian *see* Race–American Indian: Central American Indian
Central American: Other *see* Hispanic Origin–Central American: Other Central American
Chaldean *see* Ancestry–Assyrian/Chaldean/Syriac
Chamorro *see* Race–Hawaii Native/Pacific Islander: Guamanian or Chamorro
Cherokee *see* Race–American Indian: Cherokee
Cheyenne *see* Race–American Indian: Cheyenne
Chickasaw *see* Race–American Indian: Chickasaw
Chilean *see* Hispanic Origin–South American: Chilean
Chinese (except Taiwanese) *see* Race–Asian: Chinese, except Taiwanese
Chippewa *see* Race–American Indian: Chippewa
Choctaw *see* Race–American Indian: Choctaw
Colombian *see* Hispanic Origin–South American: Colombian
Colville *see* Race–American Indian: Colville
Comanche *see* Race–American Indian: Comanche
Costa Rican *see* Hispanic Origin–Central American: Costa Rican
Cree *see* Race–American Indian: Cree
Creek *see* Race–American Indian: Creek
Croatian *see* Ancestry–Croatian
Crow *see* Race–American Indian: Crow
Cuban *see* Hispanic Origin–Cuban
Cypriot *see* Ancestry–Cypriot
Czech *see* Ancestry–Czech
Czechoslovakian *see* Ancestry–Czechoslovakian
Danish *see* Ancestry–Danish
Delaware *see* Race–American Indian: Delaware
Dominican Republic *see* Hispanic Origin–Dominican Republic
Dutch *see* Ancestry–Dutch
Dutch West Indian *see* Ancestry–West Indian: Dutch West Indian, except Hispanic
Eastern European *see* Ancestry–Eastern European
Ecuadorian *see* Hispanic Origin–South American: Ecuadorian
Egyptian *see* Ancestry–Arab: Egyptian
English *see* Ancestry–English
Eskimo *see* Race–Alaska Native: Inupiat
Estonian *see* Ancestry–Estonian
Ethiopian *see* Ancestry–African, Sub-Saharan: Ethiopian
European *see* Ancestry–European
Fijian *see* Race–Hawaii Native/Pacific Islander: Fijian
Filipino *see* Race–Asian: Filipino
Finnish *see* Ancestry–Finnish
French (except Basque) *see* Ancestry–French, except Basque
French Canadian *see* Ancestry–French Canadian
German *see* Ancestry–German
German Russian *see* Ancestry–German Russian
Ghanaian *see* Ancestry–African, Sub-Saharan: Ghanaian
Greek *see* Ancestry–Greek
Guamanian *see* Race–Hawaii Native/Pacific Islander: Guamanian or Chamorro
Guatemalan *see* Hispanic Origin–Central American: Guatemalan
Guyanese *see* Ancestry–Guyanese
Haitian *see* Ancestry–West Indian: Haitian, except Hispanic
Hawaii Native *see* Race–Hawaii Native/Pacific Islander
Hawaii Native: Hispanic *see* Race–Hawaii Native/Pacific Islander: Hispanic

Hawaii Native: Not Hispanic *see* Race–Hawaii Native/Pacific Islander: Not Hispanic
Hispanic or Latino: *see* Hispanic Origin–Hispanic or Latino (of any race)
Hispanic or Latino: Other *see* Hispanic Origin–Other Hispanic or Latino
Hmong *see* Race–Asian: Hmong
Honduran *see* Hispanic Origin–Central American: Honduran
Hopi *see* Race–American Indian: Hopi
Houma *see* Race–American Indian: Houma
Hungarian *see* Ancestry–Hungarian
Icelander *see* Ancestry–Icelander
Indonesian *see* Race–Asian: Indonesian
Inupiat *see* Race–Alaska Native: Inupiat
Iranian *see* Ancestry–Iranian
Iraqi *see* Ancestry–Arab: Iraqi
Irish *see* Ancestry–Irish
Iroquois *see* Race–American Indian: Iroquois
Israeli *see* Ancestry–Israeli
Italian *see* Ancestry–Italian
Jamaican *see* Ancestry–West Indian: Jamaican, except Hispanic
Japanese *see* Race–Asian: Japanese
Jordanian *see* Ancestry–Arab: Jordanian
Kenyan *see* Ancestry–African, Sub-Saharan: Kenyan
Kiowa *see* Race–American Indian: Kiowa
Korean *see* Race–Asian: Korean
Laotian *see* Race–Asian: Laotian
Latvian *see* Ancestry–Latvian
Lebanese *see* Ancestry–Arab: Lebanese
Liberian *see* Ancestry–African, Sub-Saharan: Liberian
Lithuanian *see* Ancestry–Lithuanian
Lumbee *see* Race–American Indian: Lumbee
Luxemburger *see* Ancestry–Luxemburger
Macedonian *see* Ancestry–Macedonian
Malaysian *see* Race–Asian: Malaysian
Maltese *see* Ancestry–Maltese
Marshallese *see* Race–Hawaii Native/Pacific Islander: Marshallese
Menominee *see* Race–American Indian: Menominee
Mexican *see* Hispanic Origin–Mexican
Mexican American Indian *see* Race–American Indian: Mexican American Indian
Moroccan *see* Ancestry–Arab: Moroccan
Native Hawaiian *see* Race–Hawaii Native/Pacific Islander: Native Hawaiian
Navajo *see* Race–American Indian: Navajo
Nepalese *see* Race–Asian: Nepalese
New Zealander *see* Ancestry–New Zealander
Nicaraguan *see* Hispanic Origin–Central American: Nicaraguan
Nigerian *see* Ancestry–African, Sub-Saharan: Nigerian
Northern European *see* Ancestry–Northern European
Norwegian *see* Ancestry–Norwegian
Osage *see* Race–American Indian: Osage
Ottawa *see* Race–American Indian: Ottawa
Pacific Islander *see* Race–Hawaii Native/Pacific Islander
Pacific Islander: Hispanic *see* Race–Hawaii Native/Pacific Islander: Hispanic
Pacific Islander: Not Hispanic *see* Race–Hawaii Native/Pacific Islander: Not Hispanic
Paiute *see* Race–American Indian: Paiute
Pakistani *see* Race–Asian: Pakistani
Palestinian *see* Ancestry–Arab: Palestinian
Panamanian *see* Hispanic Origin–Central American: Panamanian
Paraguayan *see* Hispanic Origin–South American: Paraguayan
Pennsylvania German *see* Ancestry–Pennsylvania German
Peruvian *see* Hispanic Origin–South American: Peruvian
Pima *see* Race–American Indian: Pima
Polish *see* Ancestry–Polish
Portuguese *see* Ancestry–Portuguese
Potawatomi *see* Race–American Indian: Potawatomi

Pueblo *see* Race–American Indian: Pueblo
Puerto Rican *see* Hispanic Origin–Puerto Rican
Puget Sound Salish *see* Race–American Indian: Puget Sound Salish
Romanian *see* Ancestry–Romanian
Russian *see* Ancestry–Russian
Salvadoran *see* Hispanic Origin–Central American: Salvadoran
Samoan *see* Race–Hawaii Native/Pacific Islander: Samoan
Scandinavian *see* Ancestry–Scandinavian
Scotch-Irish *see* Ancestry–Scotch-Irish
Scottish *see* Ancestry–Scottish
Seminole *see* Race–American Indian: Seminole
Senegalese *see* Ancestry–African, Sub-Saharan: Senegalese
Serbian *see* Ancestry–Serbian
Shoshone *see* Race–American Indian: Shoshone
Sierra Leonean *see* Ancestry–African, Sub-Saharan: Sierra Leonean
Sioux *see* Race–American Indian: Sioux
Slavic *see* Ancestry–Slavic
Slovak *see* Ancestry–Slovak
Slovene *see* Ancestry–Slovene
Somalian *see* Ancestry–African, Sub-Saharan: Somalian
South African *see* Ancestry–African, Sub-Saharan: South African
South American *see* Hispanic Origin–South American
South American Indian *see* Race–American Indian: South American Indian
South American: Other *see* Hispanic Origin–South American: Other South American
Soviet Union *see* Ancestry–Soviet Union
Spanish American Indian *see* Race–American Indian: Spanish American Indian
Sri Lankan *see* Race–Asian: Sri Lankan
Sub-Saharan African *see* Ancestry–African, Sub-Saharan
Sub-Saharan African: Other *see* Ancestry–African, Sub-Saharan: Other
Sudanese *see* Ancestry–African, Sub-Saharan: Sudanese
Swedish *see* Ancestry–Swedish
Swiss *see* Ancestry–Swiss
Syriac *see* Ancestry–Assyrian/Chaldean/Syriac
Syrian *see* Ancestry–Arab: Syrian
Taiwanese *see* Race–Asian: Taiwanese
Thai *see* Race–Asian: Thai
Tlingit-Haida *see* Race–Alaska Native: Tlingit-Haida
Tohono O'Odham *see* Race–American Indian: Tohono O'Odham
Tongan *see* Race–Hawaii Native/Pacific Islander: Tongan
Trinidadian and Tobagonian *see* Ancestry–West Indian: Trinidadian and Tobagonian, except Hispanic
Tsimshian *see* Race–Alaska Native: Tsimshian
Turkish *see* Ancestry–Turkish
U.S. Virgin Islander *see* Ancestry–West Indian: U.S. Virgin Islander, except Hispanic
Ugandan *see* Ancestry–African, Sub-Saharan: Ugandan
Ukrainian *see* Ancestry–Ukrainian
Uruguayan *see* Hispanic Origin–South American: Uruguayan
Ute *see* Race–American Indian: Ute
Venezuelan *see* Hispanic Origin–South American: Venezuelan
Vietnamese *see* Race–Asian: Vietnamese
Welsh *see* Ancestry–Welsh
West Indian *see* Ancestry–West Indian: West Indian, except Hispanic
West Indian (except Hispanic) *see* Ancestry–West Indian, except Hispanic
West Indian: Other *see* Ancestry–West Indian: Other, except Hispanic
White *see* Race–White
White: Hispanic *see* Race–White: Hispanic
White: Not Hispanic *see* Race–White: Not Hispanic
Yakama *see* Race–American Indian: Yakama
Yaqui *see* Race–American Indian: Yaqui
Yugoslavian *see* Ancestry–Yugoslavian
Yuman *see* Race–American Indian: Yuman
Yup'ik *see* Race–Alaska Native: Yup'ik
Zimbabwean *see* Ancestry–African, Sub-Saharan: Zimbabwean

Climate Section

SOURCES OF THE DATA

The National Climactic Data Center (NCDC) has two main classes or types of weather stations; first-order stations which are staffed by professional meteorologists and cooperative stations which are staffed by volunteers. All National Weather Service (NWS) stations included in this book are first-order stations.

The data in the climate section is compiled from several sources. The majority comes from the original NCDC computer tapes (DSI-3220 Summary of Month Cooperative). This data was used to create the entire table for each cooperative station and part of each National Weather Service station. The remainder of the data for each NWS station comes from the International Station Meteorological Climate Summary, Version 4.0, September 1996, which is also available from the NCDC.

Storm events come from the NCDC Storm Events Database which is accessible over the Internet at https://www.ncdc.noaa.gov/stormevents.

WEATHER STATION TABLES

The weather station tables are grouped by type (National Weather Service and Cooperative) and then arranged alphabetically. The station name is almost always a place name, and is shown here just as it appears in NCDC data. The station name is followed by the county in which the station is located (or by county equivalent name), the elevation of the station (at the time beginning of the thirty year period) and the latitude and longitude.

The National Weather Service Station tables contain 32 data elements which were compiled from two different sources, the International Station Meteorological Climate Summary (ISMCS) and NCDC DSI-3220 data tapes. The following 13 elements are from the ISMCS: maximum precipitation, minimum precipitation, maximum snowfall, maximum 24-hour snowfall, thunderstorm days, foggy days, predominant sky cover, relative humidity (morning and afternoon), dewpoint, wind speed and direction, and maximum wind gust. The remaining 19 elements come from the DSI-3220 data tapes. The period of record (POR) for data from the DSI-3220 data tapes is 1980-2009. The POR for ISMCS data varies from station to station and appears in a note below each station.

The Cooperative Station tables contain 19 data elements which were all compiled from the DSI-3220 data tapes with a POR of 1980-2009.

WEATHER ELEMENTS (NWS AND COOPERATIVE STATIONS)

The following elements were compiled by the editor from the NCDC DSI-3220 data tapes using a period of record of 1980-2009.

The average temperatures (maximum, minimum, and mean) are the average (see Methodology below) of those temperatures for all available values for a given month. For example, for a given station the average maximum temperature for July is the arithmetic average of all available maximum July temperatures for that station. (Maximum means the highest recorded temperature, minimum means the lowest recorded temperature, and mean means an arithmetic average temperature.)

The extreme maximum temperature is the highest temperature recorded in each month over the period 1980-2009. The extreme minimum temperature is the lowest temperature recorded in each month over the same time period. The extreme maximum daily precipitation is the largest amount of precipitation recorded over a 24-hour period in each month from 1980-2009. The maximum snow depth is the maximum snow depth recorded in each month over the period 1980-2009.

The days for maximum temperature and minimum temperature are the average number of days those criteria were met for all available instances. The symbol ≥ means greater than or equal to, the symbol ≤ means less than or equal to. For example, for a given station, the number of days the maximum temperature was greater than or equal to 90°F in July, is just an arithmetic average of the number of days in all the available Julys for that station.

Heating and cooling degree days are based on the median temperature for a given day and its variance from 65°F. For example, for a given station if the day's high temperature was 50°F and the day's low temperature was 30°F, the median (midpoint) temperature was 40°F. 40°F is 25 degrees below 65°F, hence on this day there would be 25 heating degree days. This also applies for cooling degree days. For example, for a given station if the day's high temperature was 80°F and the day's low temperature was 70°F, the median (midpoint) temperature was 75°F. 75°F is 10 degrees above 65°F, hence on this day there would be 10 cooling degree days. All heating and/or cooling degree days in a month are summed for the month giving respective totals for each element for that month. These sums for a given month for a given station over the past thirty years are again summed and then arithmetically averaged. It should be noted that the heating and cooling degree days do not cancel each other out. It is possible to have both for a given station in the same month.

Precipitation data is computed the same as heating and cooling degree days. Mean precipitation and mean snowfall are arithmetic averages of cumulative totals for the month. All available values for the thirty year period for a given month for a given station are summed and then divided by the number of values. The same is true for days of greater than or equal to 0.1", 0.5",and 1.0" of precipitation, and days of greater than or equal to 1.0" of snow depth on the ground. The word trace appears for precipitation and snowfall amounts that are too small to measure.

Finally, remember that all values presented in the tables and the rankings are averages, maximums, or minimums of available data (see Methodology below) for that specific data element for the last thirty years (1980-2009).

WEATHER ELEMENTS (NWS STATIONS ONLY)

The following elements were taken directly from the International Station Meteorological Climate Summary. The periods of records vary per station and are noted at the bottom of each table.

Maximum precipitation, minimum precipitation, maximum snowfall, maximum snow depth, maximum 24-hour snowfall, thunderstorm days, foggy days, relative humidity (morning and afternoon), dewpoint, prevailing wind speed and direction, and maximum wind gust are all self-explanatory.

The word trace appears for precipitation and snowfall amounts that are too small to measure.

Predominant sky cover contains four possible entries: CLR (clear); SCT (scattered); BRK (broken); and OVR (overcast).

INCLUSION CRITERIA—HOW STATIONS WERE SELECTED

The basic criteria is that a station must have data for temperature, precipitation, heating and cooling degree days of sufficient quantity in order to create a meaningful average. More specifically, the definition of sufficiency here has two parts. First, there must be 22 values for a given data element, and second, ten of the nineteen elements included in the table must pass this sufficiency test. For example, in regard to mean maximum temperature (the first element on every data table), a given station needs to have a value for every month of at least 22 of the last thirty years in order to meet the criteria, and, in addition, every station included must have at least ten of the nineteen elements with at least this minimal level of completeness in order to fulfill the criteria. We then removed stations that were geographically close together, giving preference to stations with better data quality.

METHODOLOGY

The following discussion applies only to data compiled from the NCDC DSI-3220 data tapes and excludes weather elements that are extreme maximums or minimums.

The data is based on an arithmetic average of all available data for a specific data element at a given station. For example, the average maximum daily high temperature during July for any given station was abstracted from NCDC source tapes for the thirty Julys, starting in July, 1980 and ending in July, 2009. These thirty figures were then summed and divided by thirty to produce an arithmetic average. As might be expected, there were not thirty values for every data element on every table. For a variety of reasons, NCDC data is sometimes incomplete. Thus the following standards were established.

For those data elements where there were 26-30 values, the data was taken to be essentially complete and an average was computed. For data elements where there were 22-25 values, the data was taken as being partly complete but still valid enough to use to compute an average. Such averages are shown in *bold italic* type to indicate that there was less than 26 values. For the few data elements where there were not even 22 values, no average was computed and 'na' appears in the space. If any of the twelve months for a given data element reported a value of 'na', no annual average was computed and the annual average was reported as 'na' as well.

Thus the basic computational methodology used is designed to provide an arithmetic average. Because of this, such a pure arithmetic average is somewhat different from the special type of average (called a "normal") which NCDC procedures produces and appears in federal publications.

Perhaps the best outline of the contrasting normalization methodology is found in the following paragraph (which appears as part of an NCDC technical document titled, CLIM81 1961-1990 NORMALS TD-9641 prepared by Lewis France of NCDC in May, 1992):

Normals have been defined as the arithmetic mean of a climatological element computed over a long time period. International agreements eventually led to the decision that the appropriate time period would be three consecutive decades (Guttman, 1989). The data record should be consistent (have no changes in location, instruments, observation practices, etc.; these are identified here as "exposure changes") and have no missing values so a normal will reflect the actual average climatic conditions. If any significant exposure changes have occurred, the data record is said to be "inhomogeneous," and the normal may not reflect a true climatic average. Such data need to be adjusted to remove the nonclimatic inhomogeneities. The resulting (adjusted) record is then said to be "homogeneous." If no exposure changes have occurred at a station, the normal is calculated simply by averaging the appropriate 30 values from the 1961-1990 record.

In the main, there are two "inhomogeneities" that NCDC is correcting for with normalization: adjusting for variances in time of day of observation (at the so-called First Order stations data is based on midnight to midnight observation times and this practice is not necessarily followed at cooperative stations which are staffed by volunteers), and second, estimating data that is either missing or incongruent.

The editors had some concerns regarding the comparative results of the two methodologies. Would our methodology produce strikingly different results than NCDC's? To allay concerns, results of the two processes were compared for the time period normalized results are available (1971-2000). In short, what was found was that the answer to this question is no. Never the less, users should be aware that because of both the time period covered (1980-2009) and the methodology used, data is not compatible with data from other sources.

POTENTIAL CAUTIONS

First, as with any statistical reference work of this type, users need to be aware of the source of the data. The information here comes from NOAA, and it is the most comprehensive and reliable core data available. Although it is the best, it is not perfect. Most weather stations are staffed by volunteers, times of observation sometimes vary, stations occasionally are moved (especially over a thirty year period), equipment is changed or upgraded, and all of these factors affect the uniformity of the data. The editors do not attempt to correct for these factors, and this data is not intended for either climatologists or atmospheric scientists. Users with concerns about data collection and reporting protocols are both referred to NCDC technical documentation.

Second, users need to be aware of the methodology here which is described above. Although this methodology has produced fully satisfactory results, it is not directly compatible with other methodologies, hence variances in the results published here and those which appear in other publications will doubtlessly arise.

Third, is the trap of that informal logical fallacy known as "hasty generalization," and its corollaries. This may involve presuming the future will be like the past (specifically, next year will be an average year), or it may involve misunderstanding the limitations of an arithmetic average, but more interestingly, it may involve those mistakes made most innocently by generalizing informally on too broad a basis. As weather is highly localized, the data should be taken in that context. A weather station collects data about climatic conditions at that spot, and that spot may or may not be an effective paradigm for an entire town or area.

About New York State

Governor	**Andrew M. Cuomo (D)**
Lt Governor	**Kathleen Courtney "Kathy" Hochul (D)**
State Capital	Albany
Date of Statehood	July 26, 1788 (11th state)
State Nickname	The Empire State
Demonym	New Yorker
Largest City	New York
Highest Point	Mount Marcy (5,344 feet)
Lowest Point	Atlantic Ocean (sea level)
Time Zone	Eastern
State Beverage	2% Milk
State Bird	Eastern bluebird *(sialia sialis)*
State Bush	Lilac bush *(syringa vulgaris)*
State Butterfly	Red-spotted purple/White admiral *(limenitis arthemis)*
State Fish, fresh water	Brook trout *(salvelinus fontinalis)*
State Fish, salt water	Striped bass *(morone saxatilis)*
State Flower	Rose
State Fossil	Sea scorpion *(eurypterus remipes)*
State Fruit	Apple
State Gem	Garnet
State Insect	Nine-spotted ladybug *(coccinella novemnotata)*
State Mammal	Beaver *(castor canadensis)*
State Motto	Excelsior *(Ever upward)*
State Muffin	Apple *(genus malus)*
State Reptile	Common snapping turtle *(chelydra serpentina)*
State Shell	Bay scallop *(argopecten irradians)*
State Slogan	I ♥ NY®
State Song	I Love New York (words and music by Steve Karmen)
State Tree	Sugar maple *(acer saccharum)*

The Metropolitan Museum of Art of New York City, top photo, is the largest art museum in the United States. It was founded in 1870, and the number of visitors in 2016 topped 7 million. The Met's permanent collection includes works of art from classical antiquity to American and modern art. Liberty Island in New York Harbor, bottom photo, comprises 14.7 acres and is best known as the location of the Statue of Liberty. Visitors in recent years to Liberty Island have reached nearly 5 million.

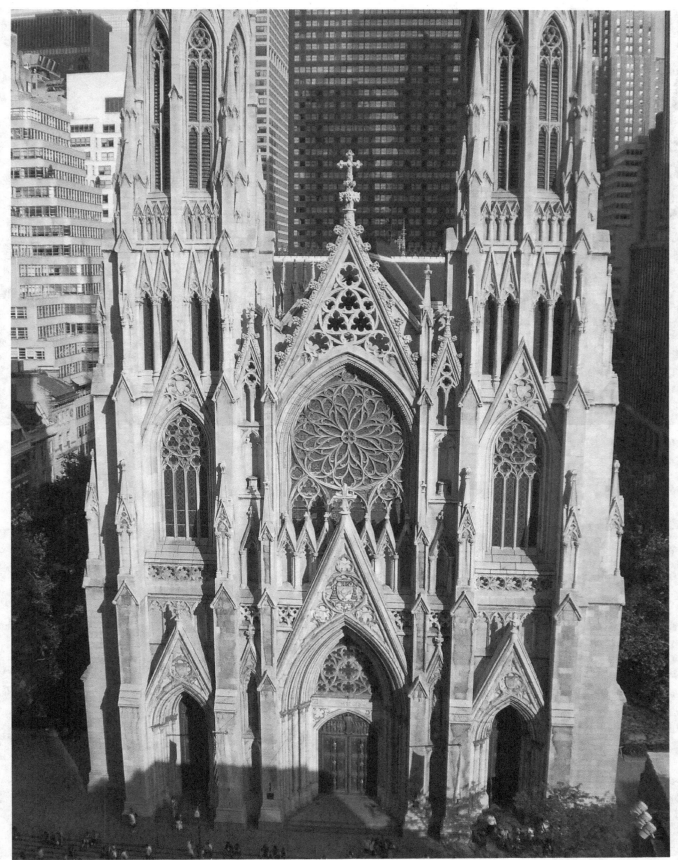

St. Patrick's Cathedral is a prominent landmark of New York City, located in Midtown Manhattan on Fifth Avenue. It is a decorated Neo-Gothic-style Roman Catholic cathedral church, and the seat of the archbishop of the Roman Catholic Archdiocese of New York as well as a parish church. Built in 1878, it was declared a National Historic Landmark in 1976. The cathedral sits on a two-acre site, and underwent an extensive renovation from 2012-2015.

Long Island, New York, is the longest and largest island in the contiguous United States, with over 400 miles of coastline, from the New York Harbor to Montauk Point. The top photo pictures one of its hundreds of beautiful beaches. Long Island is also home to top wine producing vineyards. The bottom photo shows a vineyard along the north shore of Long Island's eastern end.

Times Square, pictured above, is a major commercial intersection and neighborhood in Midtown Manhattan, New York City. At the junction of Broadway and Seventh Avenue, it's brightly adorned by billboards and advertisements. As one of the world's most visited tourist attractions, Times Square is passed through by approximately 330,000 people daily, many of them tourists.

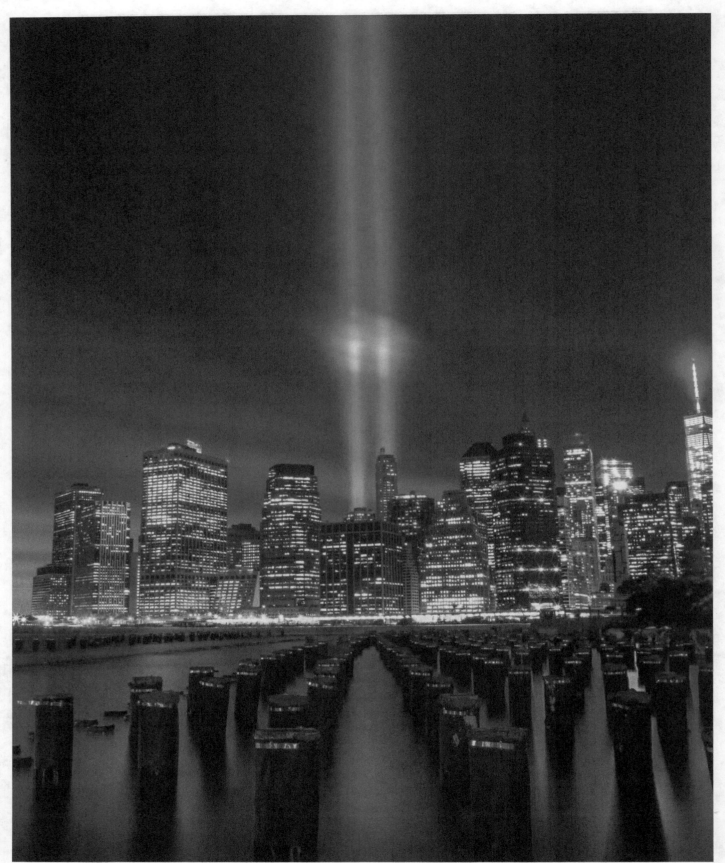

Restoration of the site of the 9/11 New York City terrorist attack is nearly complete. Pictured above is Tribute of Light, 88 high-powered light bulbs assembled in two 48-foot squares to echo the footprints of the original towers, illuminated from a nearby parking garage roof. The beams have lit the sky annually on September 11, reaching four miles into the sky. At 7,000 watts, they are the most powerful shafts of light ever projected from Earth.

Niagara Falls comprise three waterfalls on the border between Ontario, Canada and New York State, United States. American Falls are shown, top; the others are Horseshoe Falls and Bridal Veil Falls. Famed for both its beauty and its valuable hydroelectric power, Niagara Falls is a popular tourist destination. The Rush Rhees Library, bottom, is the main academic library of the University of Rochester in Rochester, N.Y. Construction started in 1927, and the building is one of the most recognizable landmarks on the university's campus.

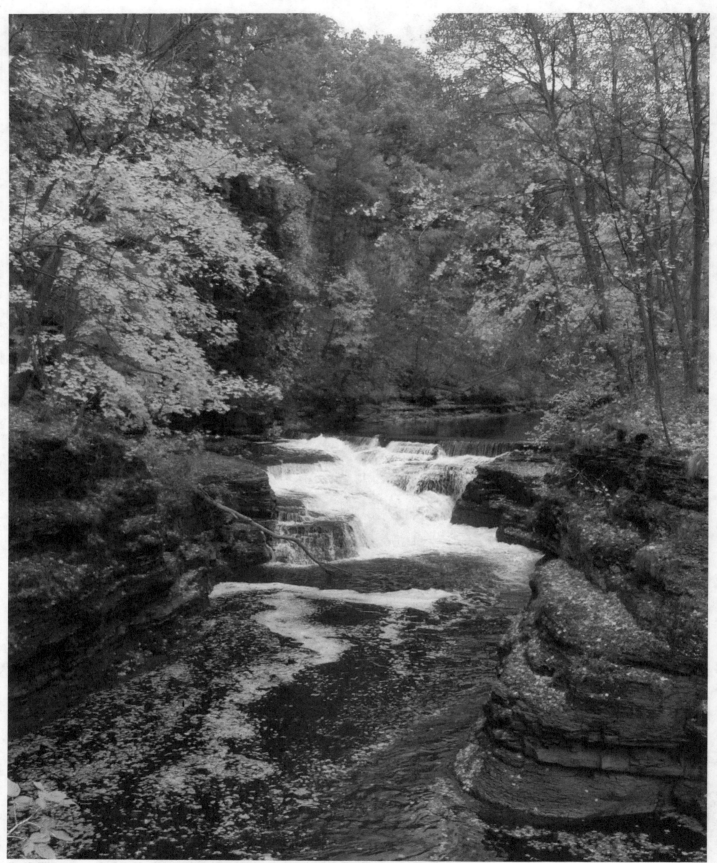

Hemlock Gorge, pictured here, is part of the Cornell University campus in Ithaca, New York. In addition to scenic views and recreational trails, the gorge provides hydroelectric power and drinking water for the university, as well as research and teaching opportunities. Ithaca, with a population of just over 30,000, is located in the Southern Tier-Finger Lakes region of New York, and home to Cornell University, Ithaca College and Tompkins Cortland Community College.

Syracuse, shown in the top photo, is a city in and the county seat of Onondaga County in upstate New York, and the fifth most populous city in the state. The city of Buffalo is the second most populous city in New York, after New York City. The bottom photo shows Buffalo's downtown and surrounding area; it's located on the eastern shore of Lake Erie, across from Ontario, Canada.

The top photo is Kykuit, aka the John D. Rockefeller Estate, in Mount Pleasant, N.Y. The 40-room mansion, built in 1913, was home to four generations of the family. Tours of the National Historic Landmark are given by Historic Hudson Valley. The New York State Capitol, bottom photo, located in Albany, was completed in 1899 at a cost of $25 million. The Romanesque Revival, Neo-Renaissance building was the most expensive government building of its time and declared a National Historic Landmark in 1979.

Seneca Lake, top photo, is the largest of the glacial Finger Lakes in upstate New York with 66.9 miles of surface area and an average depth of 291 feet. It is considered the lake trout capital of the world and, due to its unique macro-climate, the region is home to over 50 wineries. Whiteface Mountain, bottom photo, is one of the High Peaks of the Adirondack Mountains, just northeast of Lake Placid. The mountain, with an elevation of 4,867 feet, is home to a major ski area that hosted the alpine skiing competitions of the 1980 Winter Olympics.

A Brief History of New York State

New York harbor was visited by Verrazano in 1524, and the Hudson River was first explored by Henry Hudson in 1609. The Dutch settled here permanently in 1624 and for 40 years they ruled over the colony of New Netherland. It was conquered by the English in 1664 and was then named New York in honor of the Duke of York.

Existing as a colony of Great Britain for over a century, New York declared its independence on July 9, 1776, becoming one of the original 13 states of the Federal Union. The next year, on April 20, 1777, New York's first constitution was adopted.

In many ways, New York State was the principal battleground of the Revolutionary War. The Battle of Saratoga was the turning point of the Revolution leading to the French alliance and eventual victory. New York City, long occupied by British troops, was evacuated on November 25, 1783 where, on December 4 at Fraunces Tavern, General George Washington bade farewell to his officers.

During the Revolutionary War, an election for the first governor took place and George Clinton was inaugurated as Governor at Kingston, July 30, 1777. New York City became the first capital of the new nation, where President George Washington was inaugurated on April 30, 1789. Albany became the capital of the State in January 1797.

In following years, New York's economic and industrial growth encouraged the title "The Empire State," an expression possibly originated by George Washington in 1784.

The Erie Canal, completed in 1825, greatly enhanced the importance of the port of New York and caused populous towns and cities to spring up across the state. The Erie Canal was replaced by the Barge Canal in 1918, and the system of waterways was further expanded by the construction of the St. Lawrence Seaway.

Overland transportation grew rapidly from a system of turnpikes established in the early 1880s to the modern day Governor Thomas E. Dewey New York State Thruway. By 1853, railroads crossed the state in systems like the Erie and New York Central.

Located in New York harbor, the Statue of Liberty was formally presented to the U.S. Minister to France, Levi Parsons on July 4, 1884 by Ferdinand Lesseps, representing the Franco-American Union. President Grover Cleveland dedicated the Statue of Liberty on October 28, 1886, when the last rivet was put into place. Its famous inscription, "Give me your tired, your poor, your huddled masses yearning to breathe free," was the first symbol of America's mission.

The international character of New York City, the principal port for overseas commerce, and later for transcontinental and international airways, has been further enhanced by becoming the home of the United Nations, capital of the free world. Here the people of all nations and races come to discuss and try to solve the world's problems in a free and democratic climate.

As one of the wealthiest states, New York made tremendous strides in industry and commerce. The New York Stock Exchange, founded in 1792, has become the center of world finance. New York City also became a leading national center for art, music and literature, as exemplified by the Metropolitan Museum of Art, The Metropolitan Opera Company, and large publishing houses.

New York State Timeline

1524
Explorer Giovanni da Verrazzano, commissioned by the King of France, sailed to the New World, and into what is now New York Harbor; probably accompanied by Jacques Cartier.

1609
After sailing to the New World on the Halve Maen, Henry Hudson explored the mighty river that would later be named for him. Samuel de Champlain explored the northeastern region of the area now called New York and discovered his namesake, Lake Champlain.

1624
The first Dutch settlement was established; for 40 years the Dutch ruled over the colony of New Netherland.

1664
The British army conquered the colony of New Netherland, which was then re-named New York, in honor of the Duke of York.

1754-1763
The French and Indian War, a fierce contest to gain control of the New World, changed the course of history. The British and American colonists fought against the French and Canadians, with Native American allies on both sides. By uniting the colonies and building their military strength and confidence, this war set the stage for the American Revolution.

1765
New York City hosted the first Colonial Congress, a conference called to discuss the King of England's Stamp Act.

1775-1783
The Revolutionary War. On May 10, 1775, Ethan Allen, Benedict Arnold and 83 "Green Mountain Boys" surprised the sleeping British garrison at Fort Ticonderoga and took the fort called the Key to a Continent without firing a shot. This was the first American victory of the Revolutionary War.

1776
After serving as a colony of Great Britain for over a century, New York declared its independence on July 9, becoming one of the original 13 states of the Federal Union.

1777
New York's first constitution was adopted on April 20. George Clinton was elected as New York's first Governor in June. On October 17, the Americans defeated the British at the Battle of Saratoga, one of the decisive battles of the world. This victory marked the turning point of the Revolution, leading to the Americans' alliance with the French and eventual victory.

1783
On November 25, the last British troops evacuated New York City, which had been occupied by the British since September 1776. This was the last British military position in the US. After they departed, US General George Washington entered the city in triumph to the cheers of New Yorkers.

1785-1790
New York City became the first capital of the United States. In 1789, it was the site of George Washington's inauguration as the first US President; it remained the nation's capital until 1790.

1792
The New York Stock Exchange was founded in New York City.

1797
In January, Albany became the capital of New York State.

1802
The US Military Academy opened at West Point.

1807
Robert Fulton's North River Steamboat traveled from New York to Albany. This first voyage of significant distance made by a steamboat began a new era in transportation.

1825
The Erie Canal opened in 1825, linking the Hudson River to the Great Lakes and leading to greater development in the western part of the state.

1827
New York outlawed slavery. At the forefront of the Underground Railroad movement, New York had more anti-slavery organizations than any other state and strong abolitionist leaders such as Harriet Tubman, Frederick Douglass and John Brown. From the early 1800s until the end of the Civil War in 1865, thousands of people passed through New York as they traveled to freedom in Canada.

1837
Martin Van Buren, born in Kinderhook, became the eighth President of the US.

1848
Elizabeth Cady Stanton, Lucretia Mott, and more than 300 women and men gathered in Seneca Falls, for the nation's first women's rights convention.

1850
Millard Fillmore, born in Cayuga County, became the 13th President of the US.

1860s
The State of New York supplied almost one-sixth of all Union forces during the Civil War, which began in 1861.

1883
The Brooklyn Bridge, a wonder of design and engineering, opened. P.T. Barnum led a parade of 21 elephants back and forth across the bridge, to demonstrate its sturdiness to skeptics.

1886
The Statue of Liberty, a gift from France to the United States in honor of the Centennial of the American Declaration of Independence, was dedicated on October 28 in New York Harbor.

1890s-1954
Between 1892 and 1954, more than 12 million immigrants passed through Ellis Island, an immigration facility that is now part of the Statue of Liberty National Monument.

1899
The State Capitol at Albany was completed.

1901
When President William McKinley was assassinated in Buffalo, Theodore Roosevelt (born in New York City), was hurriedly sworn in as the 26th president of the US. Not quite 43 years old, TR became the youngest president in the nation's history.

1902
New York City's first skyscraper was built: the 21-story Flatiron building at 23rd Street and Fifth Avenue.

1904
New York City's first subway line, called the IRT, opened.

1920
On August 26, the 19th Amendment to the US Constitution extended the right to vote to women. After a long struggle, women could vote in the fall elections, including the Presidential election.

1932
Lake Placid hosted the Olympic Winter Games. The Whiteface Lake Placid Olympic Center at the site features an Olympic Museum and Sports Complex.

1931
The Empire State Building and the Chrysler Building were completed, and the George Washington Bridge opened, all adding to the New York City's burgeoning skyline.

1933
Franklin D. Roosevelt, born near Hyde Park, became the 32nd President of the US.

1939
The World's Fair opened in New York City, corresponding to the 150th anniversary of George Washington's inauguration as first President of the US. Many countries around the world participated; over 44 million people attended over two seasons.

1941-1945
World War II. Three WWII ships on display at the Buffalo/Erie County Naval and Military Park include the Destroyer USS The Sullivans, named for five brothers who lost their lives on November 13, 1942 following the Naval Battle of Guadalcanal; the guided missile cruiser USS Little Rock; and the submarine USS Croaker.

1952
New York City became the permanent headquarters of the United Nations.

1956
New York City hosted a Subway Series; a Major League baseball championship between the New York Yankees and the Brooklyn Dodgers.

1961-1975
The Vietnam War. The New York State Vietnam Memorial at the Empire State Plaza in Albany commemorates the military service of New York State residents who served their country in Southeast Asia between 1961 and 1975, including more than 4,000 who lost their lives or were declared missing in action.

1964
The World's Fair opened (again) in New York City.

1969
The three-day Woodstock Music & Art Fair was held on a former dairy farm in Bethel. The open-air festival featured icons of rock music and attracted half a million fans. Today the Bethel Woods Center for the Arts features a1960s museum and presents concerts at the site. The New York Mets won the 1969 World Series.

1973
The World Trade Center was completed. Each of the twin towers measured 1,368 feet in height. Lieutenant Governor Malcom Wilson became Governor of NY upon the resignation of Nelson Rockefeller.

1974 and 1978
Hugh Carey was elected Governor of NY.

1977
The I LOVE NEW YORK tourism campaign was created. Amid a nationwide recession, Governor Hugh Carey and the NY Department of Commerce made a strategic decision—to market tourism as a means to improve the state's economy. It started with four little words. I LOVE NEW YORK—slogan, logo and jingle—created an overall theme that was an instant hit. The clear simple message has endured for more than 35 years, reflecting its universal appeal and New York's cultural and natural wonders.

1977 and 1978
The New York Yankees won the World Series.

1980
Lake Placid hosted the Olympic Winter Games for a second time. The Whiteface Lake Placid Olympic Center at the site features an Olympic Museum and Sports Complex.

1982, 1986, and 1990
Mario Cuomo was elected Governor of NY.

1982
The musical Cats opened on Broadway, beginning a run of nearly 20 years. Winner of the 1983 Tony for Best Musical, this show charmed audiences with spectacular choreography and songs by Andrew Lloyd Webber.

1984
The New York State Vietnam Memorial was dedicated at the Empire State Plaza in Albany. Commemorating the military service of New York State residents who served their country in Southeast Asia between 1961 and 1975, including more than 4,000 who lost their lives or were declared missing in action, the memorial was the first such state effort in the nation.

1986
The New York Mets won the World Series.

1988
The musical Phantom of the Opera, now a multi-Tony Award winner and the longest running show on Broadway, opened.

1989
David Dinkins was elected Mayor of New York City. He was the City's first African-American mayor.

1992
On May 17, the New York Stock Exchange Bicentennial celebrated its 200th anniversary as one of the world's most vital and enduring financial institutions.

1993
On February 26, a terrorist attack at the World Trade Center killed six people and injured over 1000. In 1995, militant Sheik Omar Abdel Rahman and nine others were convicted of conspiracy charges, and in 1998, Ramzi Yousef, believed to have been the mastermind, was convicted of the bombing. Al-Qaeda involvement was suspected.

1994
On January 1, Rudolph Giuliani was sworn in as the 107th Mayor of New York City. He was the City's first Republican mayor in two decades. Among other things, he set out to reduce crime and reinvent the Times Square area as a family-friendly tourist destination.

1994, 1998, and 2002
George Pataki was elected Governor of NY.

1996, 1998, 1999 and 2000
The New York Yankees won the World Series.

2000
Former first lady Hillary Clinton was elected to the US Senate. She was the first female senator to represent New York.

2001
On September 11, terrorist attacks destroyed the World Trade Center. Nearly 3,000 people were killed. The NY Stock Exchange closed for four days—its longest closure since 1933. Symbolizing our nation's strength and resilience, it reopened on September 17, setting a record volume of 2.37 billion shares. Today, the National September 11 Memorial & Museum honors the nearly 3,000 people killed in the terror attacks of September 11, 2001 at the World Trade Center site; near Shanksville, Pennsylvania; and at the Pentagon; as well as the six people killed in the World Trade Center bombing in February 1993.

2006
The National Purple Heart Hall of Honor opened in November at the New Windsor Cantonment State Historic Site in the Hudson Valley. The facility commemorates the extraordinary sacrifices of America's servicemen and servicewomen who were killed or wounded in combat, and shares the stories of America's combat wounded

veterans and those who never returned, all recipients of the Purple Heart. The first beam of the new Freedom Tower was placed at the World Trade Center Memorial Site, now the National September 11 Memorial & Museum.

2007
Eliot Spitzer was sworn in as Governor of NY on January 11.

2008
In March, Lieutenant Governor David Paterson became Governor of NY, upon the resignation of Eliot Spitzer. He is New York's first African-American governor and first legally blind governor, as well as the fourth African-American governor in the US. Governor Paterson is nationally recognized as a leading advocate for the visually and physically impaired.

2009
In January, NY Senator Hilary Clinton was sworn in as US Secretary of State. Appointed by President Barack Obama, she is the first former First Lady to serve in a president's cabinet.

In May, Pedestrian Malls were created at Times Square and Herald Square on Broadway. Beginning on May 22, New York City's Broadway was closed to vehicle traffic for five blocks at Times Square, turning part of the "Crossroads of the World" into a pedestrian mall with cafe tables and benches. A second promenade was created at Herald Square where Macy's, the world's largest store, dominates the intersection. The plan is part of an experiment to create open spaces for tourists and make the city even more pedestrian friendly. The first section of the High Line, from Gansevoort Street to West 20th Street, opened June 9. The unique public park, built on an historic freight rail line elevated above the streets on Manhattan's West Side, offers spectacular views.

2010
Andrew Cuomo was elected Governor of New York on November 2. Governor Andrew Cuomo's father, Mario Cuomo, was New York governor from 1983 to 1994.

2011
On June 24, New York became the sixth state in the nation to legalize same-sex marriage. New adventure parks opened at ski mountains across New York, including the Outdoor Adventure Center at Greek Peak, featuring an Alpine Mountain coaster; the Sky High Adventure Park, Aerial Adventure and Mountain Coaster at Holiday Valley; and the New York Zipline at Hunter Mountain, the longest and highest in North America. On September 22, Jane's Carousel was installed in Brooklyn Bridge Park. The first carousel to be listed on the National Register of Historic Places, it was painstakingly restored by Jane Walentas at her studio in Brooklyn's DUMBO neighborhood. Set beside the East River between the Brooklyn and Manhattan bridges, the elegant 1922 carousel has 48 hand-carved horses and 1200 brilliant lights. Housed in a spectacular Pavilion designed by renowned architect Jean Nouvel, it delights local children and visitors from around the world. The Carousel and Pavilion were a gift from the Walentas family to the people of the City of New York.

2012
Destiny USA, one of the nation's largest shopping centers, opened in Syracuse. The 2.4-million-square-foot tourist destination features luxury retailers, premium outlets, diverse restaurants and unique entertainment like an Ice Museum, WonderWorks and Canyon Climb Adventure. Hurricane Sandy hit New York City on October 29. It was the deadliest and most destructive tropical cyclone of the 2012 Atlantic hurricane season, as well as the second-costliest hurricane in US history. New Yorkers and many other volunteers pulled together to help clean up, supply food, and provide overall assistance in the City's recovery. Volun-tourism focused on the areas hardest hit by Hurricane Sandy. Jane's Carousel (see 2011) survived Hurricane Sandy.

Raging waters engulfed the carousel, set on a three-foot-high pavilion that usually stands 30 feet from the river. From seven stories above and a block away, neighbors took a photo of the still-lit pavilion—surrounded by surging tides that threatened to wash it away. Amazingly it survived. The photo of the illuminated carousel surrounded by darkness and crashing waves spread across the Internet, as a symbol of New York City's resilience.

2013
Historic Saratoga Race Course celebrates its 150th Anniversary.

2014
IBM says it's teaming up with the New York Genome Center to help fight brain cancer. Its Watson cloud computing system will be used in partnership with the genetic research center to help sequence DNA for the treatment of glioblastoma, the most common type of brain cancer in US adults.

On June 6, Karen DeCrow (b.1937), former head of NOW (1974-1977), the National Organization for Women, died at her home in Jamesville, NY.

A freakish storm swept off the Great Lakes on November 18 and after 3 days deposited 7 feet of snow and more and left at least 12 people dead.

2015
David Letterman retires as the longest-serving talk show host in history, broadcasting from New York City's Ed Sullivan Theater for 33 years.

NYS Assembly Speaker Sheldon Silver is arrested on Federal corruption charges, the 41st elected New York state official to be accused of misdeeds in the past 12 years.

After thirty-seven years, thoroughbred racehorse American Pharoah joined the elite list of Triple Crown winners with a resounding victory in the Belmont in New York. He is the twelfth Triple Crown winner in American racing history.

2016
A massive snowstorm, January 22-23 broke a snowfall record in Central Park with 27.5 inches of snow, the most seen in New York City since recordkeeping began in 1869. More still—34 inches—fell in Jackson Heights, Queens.

Despite losing the New York State primary to Democratic presidential candidate Hillary Clinton, Donald Trump defeated Clinton to win the White House. Throughout the campaign billionaire Trump appealed to white, working-class Americans and others who felt left behind by the economic recovery following the 2008 recession, and he took traditional Democratic stronghold states such as Michigan, Wisconsin and Pennsylvania. Since taking office, the Trump Towers in New York City has been the scene of much Presidential business.

2017
The first phase of a new New York City subway line—the Second Avenue Subway (SAS) opened in January with three new stations under Second Avenue on the East Side of Manhattan. It will serve an estimated 200,000 riders daily. The full Second Avenue Line, is planned in three additional phases, between 125th Street and Hanover Square, for a total of 8.5 miles, 16 stations, a projected daily ridership of 560,000, and a cost of more than $17 billion.

A rented pickup truck was driven into cyclists and runners for about one mile of the Hudson River Park's bike path in lower Manhattan, New York City, killing eight and injuring eleven. Material found in the truck indicated allegiance to the terrorist group ISIS.

The New York State Board of Regents adopted the newly revised English Language Arts and Mathematics Learning Standards, the result of a two-year collaboration.

Simone Askew (20) became the first black woman to captain the 4,400 member Corps of Cadets at West Point.

New York state's Court of Appeals ruled that state lawmakers had a rational reason for passing a ban on assisted suicide and that the ban does not violate the state Constitution.

2018
Joseph Percoco, a former aide to New York Governor Andrew Cuomo, took more than $300,000 in bribes from executives at two companies that did business with the state government in the highest-profile federal corruption case in New York since former state Assembly Speaker Democrat Sheldon Silver, and former state Senate leader Republican Dean Skelos, were convicted of corruption in 2015.

A Catskills casino promoted as economic boost to this old resort area opened with more than 150 table games and 2,150 slot machines about 80 miles northwest of New York City. The $1.2 billion resort complex features a hotel and golf course and is the fourth Las Vegas-style upstate casino to open under a voter-approved amendment to the state constitution.

The 2018 Olympic Winter Games in South Korea included a number of athletes from upstate New York—Remsen native Erin Hamlin, Saranac Lake native Andrew Weibrecht, Codie Bascue of Whitehall, and Rochester native Morgan Schild. The U.S. Ice Hockey team included Brian Gionta (Rochester), Jordan Greenway (Canton), David Leggio (Buffalo), and Emily Pfalzer (Buffalo).

New York Supreme Court Judge Saliann Scarpulla ruled that allegations "sufficiently support a claim that President Trump intentionally used [Trump] Foundation assets for his private interests knowing that it may not be in the Foundation's best interest," clearing the way for a civil lawsuit against the Trump Foundation. The lawsuit spurred an investigation of the organization's tax practices by the state Tax Department, and the Trump Foundation agreed to dissolve in December.

2019

New York State increased its minimum wage effective December 31, 2018. In New York City, employers with 10 employees or less saw the minimum wage rise to $13.50/hour, and employers with 11 employees or more saw the minimum wage rise to $15.00/hour. The minimum wage increased to $12.00/hour for workers in Long Island and Westchester, and $11.10/hour for workers in the remainder of New York State. Fast food workers in New York City saw their wages rise to $15.00/hour; fast food workers elsewhere in the state saw an increase to $12.75/hour.

New York began phasing in its landmark Paid Family Leave law. Currently, eligible employees may take up to eight weeks of leave to care for a family member with a serious health condition, to bond with a child's first year after birth, for adoption or foster care placement, or for any qualified exigency arising from a family member's call to active military service, with wage replacement benefits of 50 percent of the employee's average weekly wage, up to a maximum of 50 percent of the current statewide Average Weekly Wage. Starting January 1, 2019, the number of weeks increased to 10 weeks, and the wage replacement benefits increased to 55 percent, up to a cap of 55 percent of the state Average Weekly Wage.

Source: New York Department of Economic Development; Original research.

An Introduction to New York State Government

Organization

New York's state government contains three branches: legislative, judicial and executive.

The Legislative Branch

The legislative branch consists of a bicameral (two chamber) Legislature—a 62 member Senate and 150 member Assembly that, together, represent the 18 million citizens of the State. All members are elected for two-year terms.

The Judicial Branch

The judicial branch comprises a range of courts (from trial to appellate) with various jurisdictions (from village and town courts to the State's highest court—the Court of Appeals). The State assumes the cost for all but the town and village courts.

The Judiciary functions under a Unified Court System whose organization, administration and financing are prescribed by the State Constitution and the Unified Court Budget Act. The Unified Court System has responsibility for peacefully and fairly resolving civil claims, family disputes, and criminal accusations, as well as providing legal protection for children, mentally-ill persons and others entitled to special protections.

The Executive Branch

The executive branch of New York State government consists of 20 departments—the maximum number allowed by the State Constitution. This limitation came about as a result of constitutional reforms from the 1920s that were designed to make State government more manageable by eliminating many of the independently elected executive officers and curbing the creation of new departments. The 20 departments are:

- **Agriculture and Markets:** Serves agricultural producers and the consuming public. Promotes agriculture through various industry and export development programs; enforces food safety laws.
- **Audit and Control:** Maintains the State's accounts; pays the State's payrolls and bills; invests State funds; audits State agencies and local governments; and administers the State employee retirement system.
- **Banking:** Primary regulator for State-licensed and State-chartered financial entities operating in New York, including: domestic banks, foreign agencies, branch and representative offices, savings institutions and trust companies, mortgage bankers and brokers, check cashers and money transmitters. Ensures the safe and sound conduct of these businesses, maintains public confidence in the banking system and protects the public interest as well as the interests of depositors, creditors and shareholders.
- **Civil Service:** The central personnel agency for the Executive branch of State government. Provides the State of New York with a trained workforce; administers health, dental and insurance programs covering State employees and retirees as well as some local government employees; and provides technical services to the State's 102 municipal service agencies, covering approximately 392,000 local government employees.
- **Correctional Services:** Operates facilities for the custody and rehabilitation of inmates.
- **Economic Development:** Creates jobs and encourages economic prosperity by providing technical and financial assistance to businesses.
- **Education:** Supervises all educational institutions in the State, operates certain educational and cultural institutions, certifies teachers and certifies/licenses 44 other professions.
- **Environmental Conservation:** Administers programs designed to protect and improve the State's natural resources.
- **Executive:** Since the 1920s constitutional reforms, numerous agencies have been created within the Executive Department to accommodate various governmental functions. These include the Division of Veterans' Affairs (which advises veterans on services, benefits and entitlements, and administers payments of bonuses and annuities to blind veterans) and the Office of General Services (which provides centralized data processing, construction, maintenance and design services as well as printing, transportation and communication systems).

- **Family Assistance:** Promotes greater self-sufficiency by providing support services for needy families and adults that lead to self-reliance.
- **Health:** Protects and promotes the health of New Yorkers through enforcement of public health and related laws, and assurance of quality health care delivery.
- **Insurance:** Supervises and regulates all insurance business in New York State. Issues licenses to agents, brokers and consultants; conducts examinations of insurers; reviews complaints from policyholders; and approves corporate formations, mergers and consolidations.
- **Labor:** Helps New York work by preparing individuals for jobs; administering unemployment insurance, disability benefits and workers' compensation; and ensuring workplace safety.
- **Law:** Protects the rights of New Yorkers; represents the State in legal matters; and prosecutes violations of State law.
- **Mental Hygiene:** Provides services for individuals suffering from mental illness, developmental disabilities and/or substance abuse.
- **Motor Vehicles:** Registers vehicles, licenses drivers and promotes highway safety.
- **Public Service:** Ensures that all New Yorkers have access to reliable and low-cost utility services by promoting competition and reliability in utility services.
- **State:** Known as the keeper of records, the Department of State issues business licenses, enforces building codes, provides technical assistance to local governments and administers fire prevention and control services.
- **Taxation and Finance:** Collects taxes and administers the State's tax laws.
- **Transportation:** Coordinates and assists in the development and operation of highway, railroad, mass transit, port, waterway and aviation facilities.

Elected Officers and Appointed Officials

Only four statewide government officers are directly elected:

- The Governor, who heads the Executive Department, and Lieutenant Governor (who are elected on a joint ballot).
- The State Comptroller, who heads the Department of Audit and Control.
- The Attorney General, who heads the Department of Law.

With a few exceptions, the Governor appoints the heads of all State departments and agencies of the executive branch. The exceptions include:

- The Commissioner of the State Education Department, who is appointed by and serves at the pleasure of the State Board of Regents.
- The Chancellor of the State University of New York, who is appointed by a Board of Trustees.
- The Chancellor of the City University of New York, who is appointed by a Board of Trustees.

Local Governments

Geographically, New York State is divided into 62 counties (five of which are boroughs of New York City). Within these counties are 62 cities (including New York City), 932 towns, 555 villages and 697 school districts (including New York City). In addition to counties, cities, towns and villages, "special districts" meet local needs for fire and police protection, sewer and water systems or other services.

Local governments are granted the power to adopt local laws that are not inconsistent with the provisions of the State Constitution or other general law. The Legislature, in turn, may not pass any law that affects only one locality unless the governing body of that locality has first approved the bill—referred to as a home rule request—or unless a State interest exists.

Source: New York State Division of the Budget, June 2012

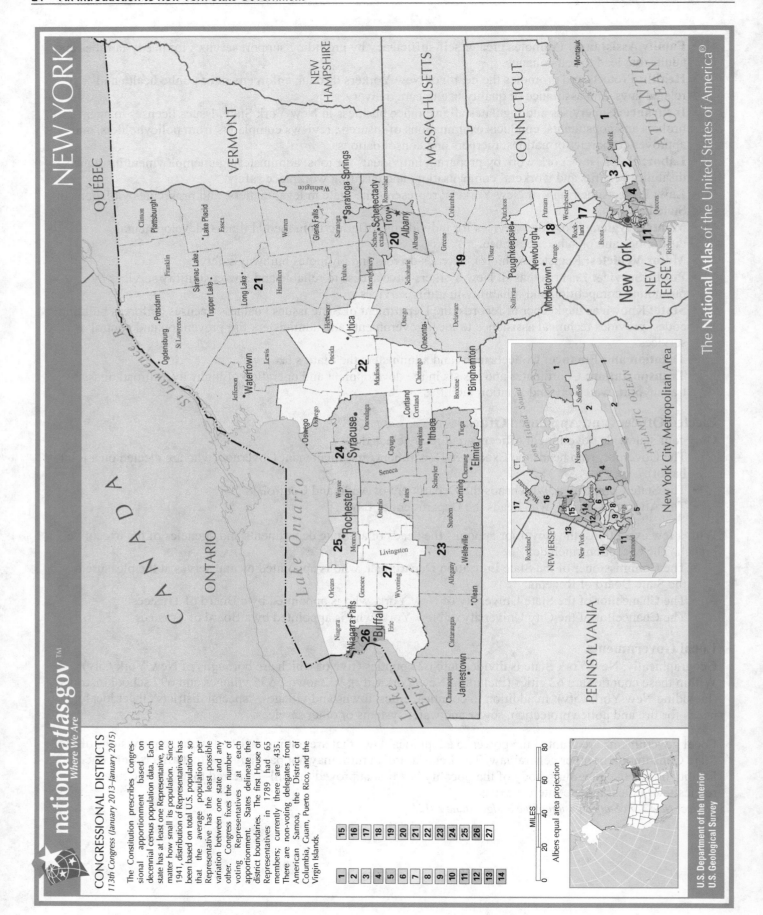

NEW YORK

CONGRESSIONAL DISTRICTS
113th Congress (January 2013–January 2015)

The Constitution prescribes Congressional apportionment based on decennial census population data. Each state has at least one Representative, no matter how small its population. Since 1941, distribution of Representatives has been based on total U.S. population, so that the average population per Representative has the least possible variation between one state and any other. Congress fixes the number of voting Representatives at each apportionment. States delineate the district boundaries. The first House of Representatives in 1789 had 65 members; currently there are 435. There are non-voting delegates from American Samoa, the District of Columbia, Guam, Puerto Rico, and the Virgin Islands.

nationalatlas.gov™
Where We Are

The National Atlas of the United States of America®

New York City Metropolitan Area

MILES
Albers equal area projection

U.S. Department of the Interior
U.S. Geological Survey

Percent of Population Who Voted for Donald Trump in 2016

Legend
- 60.0 and Over
- 55.0 to 59.9
- 50.0 to 54.9
- 45.0 to 49.9
- 40.0 to 44.9
- Under 40.0

Land and Natural Resources

Topic	Value	Time Period
Total Surface Area (acres)	31,409,100	2012
Land	29,985,600	2012
Federal Land	212,500	2012
Owned	180,903	FY 2016
Leased	1,867	FY 2016
Otherwise Managed	2,761	FY 2016
National Wilderness	1,380	October 15, 2017
Non-Federal Land, Developed	3,844,200	2012
Non-Federal Land, Rural	25,928,900	2012
Cropland	5,122,600	2012
CRP Land	28,200	2012
Pastureland	2,509,700	2012
Rangeland	0	2012
Forest Land	17,486,000	2012
Other Rural Land	782,400	2012
Water	1,423,500	2012
World Heritage Sites	1	September 30, 2016
National Heritage Areas	4	September 30, 2016
National Natural Landmarks	28	September 30, 2016
National Historic Landmarks	268	September 30, 2016
National Register of Historic Places	5,895	September 30, 2016
National Parks	23	September 30, 2016
Wild and Scenic Rivers Managed by the NPS	1	September 30, 2016
Archeological Sites in National Parks	310	September 30, 2016
Visitors to National Parks	17,907,433	September 30, 2016
Economic Benefit from National Park Tourism (dollars)	697,900,000	September 30, 2016
Land and Water Conservation Fund Grants (dollars)	241,303,695	Since 1965
Community Conservation and Recreation Projects	95	Since 1987
Federal Acres Transferred for Local Parks and Recreation	6,449	Since 1948
Crude Oil Production (thousand barrels per year)	222	2016
Crude Oil Reserves, Proved (million barrels)	0	December 31, 2016
Natural Gas Marketed Production (million cubic feet per year)	13,446	2016
Natural Gas Reserves, Dry (billion cubic feet)	120	December 31, 2016
Coal Production (thousand short tons per year)	0	2016
Coal Reserves, Recoverable (million short tons)	0	2016

Sources: *U.S. Department of the Interior, National Park Service, State Profiles, September 30, 2016; United States Department of Agriculture, Natural Resources Conservation Service, 2012 National Resources Inventory; U.S. General Services Administration, Federal Real Property Profile, FY 2016; University of Montana, Wilderness Connect (www.wilderness.net), October 15, 2017; Department of Energy, Energy Information Administration (www.eia.gov), Coal, Natural Gas, Petroleum and Other Liquids*

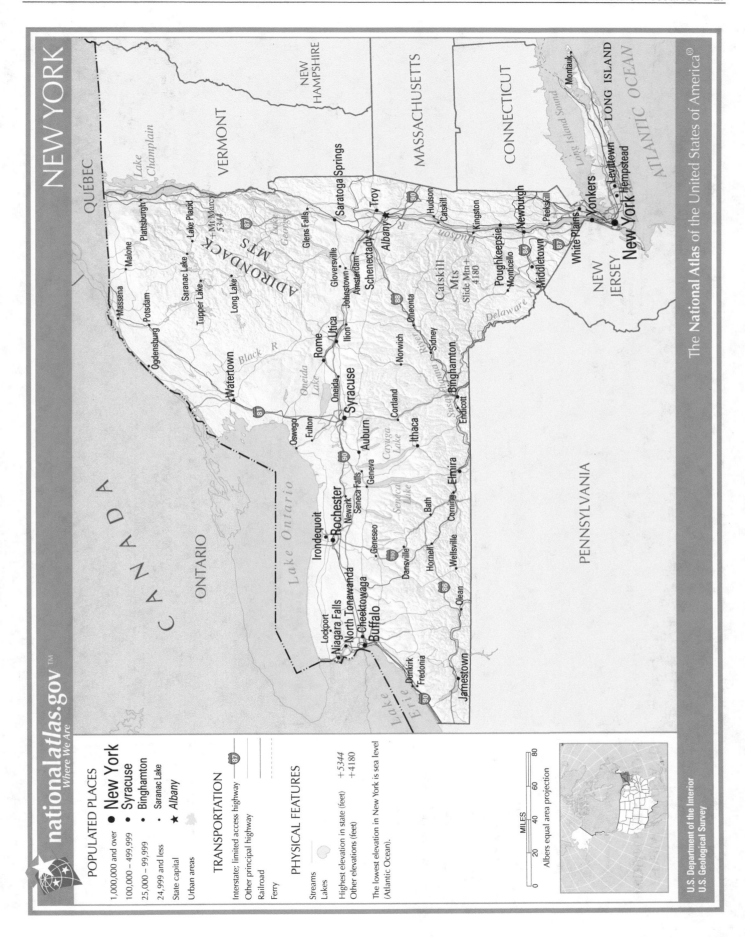

NEW YORK

POPULATED PLACES

- New York — 1,000,000 and over
- Syracuse — 100,000 – 499,999
- Binghamton — 25,000 – 99,999
- Saranac Lake — 24,999 and less
- ★ Albany — State capital
- Urban areas

TRANSPORTATION

- 87 — Interstate; limited access highway
- Other principal highway
- Railroad
- Ferry

PHYSICAL FEATURES

- Streams
- Lakes
- +5344 — Highest elevation in state (feet)
- +4180 — Other elevations (feet)

The lowest elevation in New York is sea level (Atlantic Ocean).

MILES
0 20 40 60 80

Albers equal area projection

U.S. Department of the Interior
U.S. Geological Survey

QUÉBEC

NEW HAMPSHIRE

VERMONT

MASSACHUSETTS

CONNECTICUT

CANADA

ONTARIO

PENNSYLVANIA

NEW JERSEY

LONG ISLAND

ATLANTIC OCEAN

Long Island Sound

Lake Champlain

Lake George

ADIRONDACK MTS

+Mt Marcy 5344

Catskill Mts

Slide Mtn + 4180

Black R.

Oneida Lake

Lake Ontario

Lake Erie

Hudson

Delaware R.

Susquehanna River

Seneca Lake

Cayuga Lake

Plattsburgh
Malone
Massena
Potsdam
Ogdensburg
Lake Placid
Saranac Lake
Tupper Lake
Long Lake
Watertown
Glens Falls
Saratoga Springs
Troy
Gloversville
Amsterdam
Johnstown
Schenectady
Albany
Hudson
Catskill
Kingston
Newburgh
Peekskill
White Plains
Yonkers
New York
Levittown
Hempstead
Montauk
Poughkeepsie
Monticello
Middletown
Rome
Utica
Ilion
Oneonta
Sidney
Binghamton
Endicott
Norwich
Cortland
Syracuse
Oswego
Fulton
Oneida
Auburn
Ithaca
Elmira
Geneva
Corning
Bath
Rochester
Irondequoit
Newark
Seneca Falls
Geneseo
Dansville
Hornell
Wellsville
Olean
Lockport
Niagara Falls
North Tonawanda
Cheektowaga
Buffalo
Dunkirk
Fredonia
Jamestown

87
81
90
88
86
390

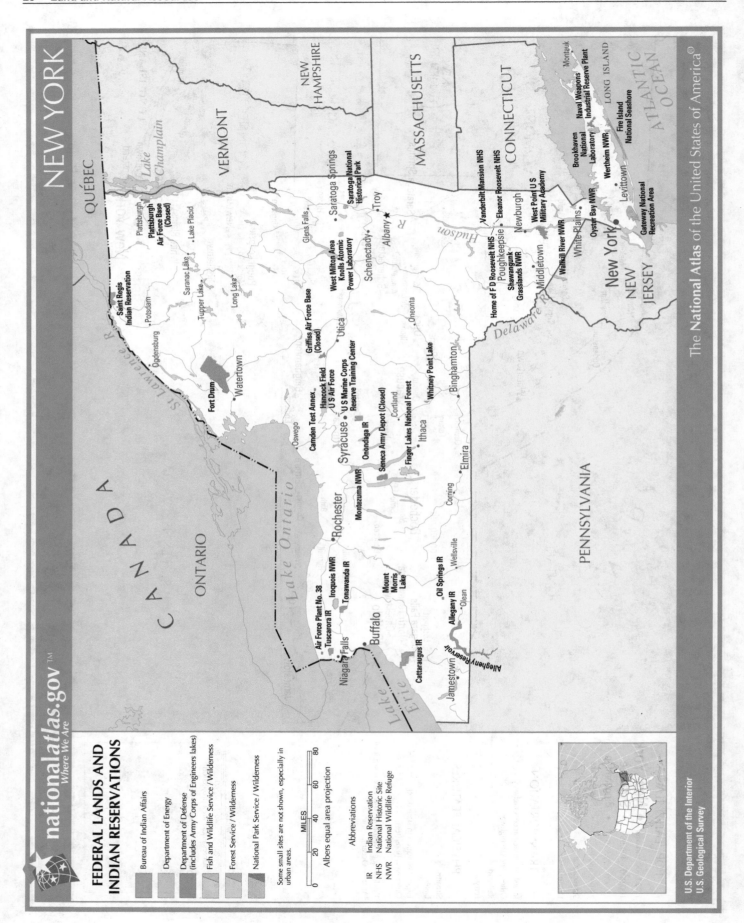

NEW YORK

FEDERAL LANDS AND
INDIAN RESERVATIONS

Bureau of Indian Affairs

Department of Energy

Department of Defense
(includes Army Corps of Engineers lakes)

Fish and Wildlife Service / Wilderness

Forest Service / Wilderness

National Park Service / Wilderness

Some small sites are not shown, especially in
urban areas.

MILES

0   20   40   60   80

Albers equal area projection

Abbreviations

IR   Indian Reservation
NHS   National Historic Site
NWR   National Wildlife Refuge

The **National Atlas** of the United States of America®

U.S. Department of the Interior
U.S. Geological Survey

QUÉBEC

CANADA

ONTARIO

NEW HAMPSHIRE

VERMONT

MASSACHUSETTS

CONNECTICUT

PENNSYLVANIA

NEW JERSEY

Lake Champlain

Lake Ontario

Lake Erie

ATLANTIC OCEAN

LONG ISLAND

Montauk

Plattsburgh
Plattsburgh
Air Force Base
(Closed)

Lake Placid

Saint Regis
Indian Reservation

Potsdam

Ogdensburg

Saranac Lake

Tupper Lake

Long Lake

Glens Falls

Saratoga Springs

Saratoga National
Historical Park

Troy

Albany ★

Schenectady

West Milton Area
Knolls Atomic
Power Laboratory

Griffiss Air Force Base
(Closed)

Utica

Hancock Field
U S Air Force

Camden Test Annex

U S Marine Corps
Reserve Training Center

Onondaga IR

Syracuse

Seneca Army Depot (Closed)

Cortland

Finger Lakes National Forest

Ithaca

Oneonta

Whitney Point Lake

Binghamton

Elmira

Corning

Wellsville

Olean

Jamestown

Allegheny Reservoir

Allegany IR

Oil Springs IR

Mount
Morris
Lake

Iroquois NWR

Tonawanda IR

Air Force Plant No. 38

Tuscarora IR

Niagara Falls

Buffalo

Cattaraugus IR

Rochester

Oswego

Watertown

Fort Drum

St Lawrence R

Vanderbilt Mansion NHS

Eleanor Roosevelt NHS

Home of F D Roosevelt NHS

Poughkeepsie

Shawangunk
Grasslands NWR

Middletown

Wallkill River NWR

Newburgh

West Point U S
Military Academy

White Plains

New York

Montezuma NWR

Naval Weapons
Industrial Reserve Plant

Brookhaven
National
Laboratory

Wertheim NWR

Oyster Bay NWR

Levittown

Fire Island
National Seashore

Gateway National
Recreation Area

Hudson

Delaware R

Mohawk R

NEW YORK

SATELLITE VIEW

In 1972, Landsat began transmitting views of our planet back to Earth. The first Landsat and its five successors (two of them are in operation now) have delivered millions of images from a satellite orbiting 438 miles above the Earth. Landsat's orbit enables a new image to be recorded every sixteen days of any area on the Earth's surface. The satellite view on this map was created from a mosaic of many Landsat images joined together. Colors were selected to better show variations in the landscape. Relief shading was added to enhance the terrain and make the landforms of each state more apparent.

QUÉBEC · VERMONT · NEW HAMPSHIRE · MASSACHUSETTS · CONNECTICUT · LONG ISLAND · ATLANTIC OCEAN · Long Island Sound · NEW JERSEY · PENNSYLVANIA · ONTARIO · CANADA · Lake Ontario · Lake Erie

MILES 0 20 40 60 80
Albers equal area projection

New York State Energy Profile

Quick Facts

- New York's Clean Energy Standard requires that the contribution to in-state electricity generation from renewable resources rise to 50% by 2030, and, in 2017, 28% of New York's in-state generation came from renewable sources.
- New York generates about one-third of its electricity from nuclear power plants, and the state includes nuclear power as a zero emissions resource that counts toward New York's 2030 emissions reduction goals.
- In 2017, New York produced more hydroelectric power than any other state east of the Rocky Mountains and was the fourth-largest producer of hydroelectricity among all 50 states.
- New York State was the fifth-largest natural gas consumer for electric power generation among the states in 2017, and more than one-third of New York's electricity-generating capacity is in units that can burn either natural gas or fuel oil, switching between fuels when needed.
- New York State is the fifth-largest consumer of petroleum among the states, but has the lowest petroleum consumption per capita in the nation.

Overview

New York, the largest of the northeastern states, is the fourth most populous state in the nation and has the third-largest economy.[1,2,3] Dependent on supplies from out of state for more than three-fourths of its energy, New York has developed one of the most energy-efficient state economies in the nation, and the state consumes less total energy per capita than all other states except Rhode Island.[4,5] The state's energy efficiency results in part from the New York City metropolitan region's widely used mass transportation systems. Two-fifths of New York City's workers use public transit. Overall, almost three-tenths of state residents use public transit, which is more than five times the U.S. average.[6]

Although New York produces only small amounts of natural gas and oil, the state has many renewable resources.[7] New York is a leading producer of hydroelectric power. In addition to the Niagara Falls, the state includes parts of 2 Great Lakes to the north and west, 9 major rivers, and 8,000 lakes, many of which were carved out by the glaciers during the Ice Ages more than 10,000 years ago.[8,9] The densely populated metropolitan areas downstate include the nation's largest city, New York, but much of the state is rolling agricultural land and rugged mountains with plentiful wind, solar, and biomass resources.[10,11] The state climate ranges from humid continental upstate, where Arctic winds and lake-effect snows sweep in from Canada across the Great Lakes in winter, to the temperate, ocean-moderated southeast along the Atlantic Ocean shores of Long Island downstate.[12] The Great Lakes and Atlantic Ocean shorelines have some of the state's best wind resources.[13]

The transportation sector leads energy demand in New York, followed by the commercial sector and the residential sector.[14] Most of New York's key industries—finance and real estate; professional and business services; and government—are not energy-intensive industries, and the industrial sector consumes just one-tenth of the energy used in the state, a smaller share than in all other states except Maryland.[15,16,17]

Electricity

Natural gas, nuclear power, and hydroelectricity typically provide more than nine-tenths of New York State's net electricity generation; other renewable resources provide most of the rest.[18] In 2017, almost two-fifths of the state's net electricity generation came from natural gas, about one-third from nuclear power, and almost one-fourth from hydropower.[19] More than half of New York's generating capacity is at natural gas-fired power plants, and more than one-third of state capacity is at units with dual-fuel capability that can use either natural gas or fuel oil.[20] To increase reliability, especially during the winter months when natural gas pipelines are highly congested, New York regulators require the electricity generating units with dual-fuel capability to be ready to switch to fuel oil in the event of a natural gas supply disruption.[21]

New York's statewide grid is managed by a single independent system operator called the NYISO. The NYISO manages state wholesale electricity markets and transmission. Electricity usually flows east and south because two-thirds of the state's power demand is in the New York City and Long Island region, but only about half of net electricity generation originates there.[22,23] New York has long imported some electricity from neighboring states and Canada, with amounts peaking at almost 20 million megawatthours in 2004. Maintaining the capability to exchange electricity with neighboring grids remains vital to power reliability and system efficiency.[24]

The commercial sector leads consumption of electricity in New York, using more than half of all retail electricity sold in the state. The residential sector accounts for more than one-third of retail electricity sales, and the industrial and transportation sectors use the rest.[25] About one in nine New York households use electricity for heating, and, in terms of electricity consumption per capita, New York ranks among the lowest in the nation.[26,27,28]

Renewable energy

New York obtains almost three-tenths of its net electricity generation from renewable sources, including hydroelectric, wind, biomass, and solar photovoltaic (PV) generation. Most of that renewable generation comes from hydroelectricity, but increasing amounts come from wind, biomass, and solar sources.[29] The state is home to the 2.4-gigawatt Robert Moses Niagara hydroelectric power plant at Lewiston, New York, near Niagara Falls. It was the largest hydroelectric power plant in the Western hemisphere when it began operating in 1961. The Robert Moses Niagara plant is now the third-largest conventional hydroelectric power plant in the United States and, when hydroelectric pumped storage facilities are included, it is the nation's fourth-largest hydropower facility.[30,31,32] New York produces more hydroelectric power than any other state east of the Rocky Mountains, and in 2017, hydroelectricity provided almost one-fourth of in-state power generation.[33]

More than three-fifths of New York's nonhydroelectric utility-scale renewable generation was provided by wind in 2017.[34] Wind first contributed to the state's utility-scale electricity generation in 2000.[35] Currently, more than two dozen wind farms operate around the state, and more are in development.[36] In early 2018, New York committed funding for three new wind farms.[37] New York has an estimated potential for nearly 140,000 megawatts of onshore wind energy, primarily to the east of Lake Erie and Lake Ontario, along the Long Island shoreline, and on peaks of the Adirondack Mountains and the Catskill Mountains. However, the state's highest peaks are in state parks.[38,39] Some areas off the Long Island coast are also considered suitable for large-scale offshore wind farms, and one is under development.[40,41]

Biomass fuels more than one-third of New York's nonhydroelectric renewable generation and the state is among the top one-fourth of states in the amount of electricity generated from biomass.[42] Municipal solid waste facilities account for the largest share of the state's biomass electricity generation capacity, followed by New York's four utility-scale wood- and wood waste-fueled generating facilities.[43] Wood contributes more than one-fourth of state biomass-fueled generation.[44] New York has many smaller landfill gas electricity generating facilities at locations across the state.[45]

In 2014, as part of the state's NY-Sun initiative, New York set as a target the installation of 3,000 megawatts of solar photovoltaic (PV) systems by 2023, including community, school, and lower-income housing solar projects. By the end of 2017, 972 megawatts of solar PV capacity were installed in New York under NY-Sun, and 1,119 megawatts more were in development.[46] New York also encourages distributed (customer-sited, small-scale) solar installations, such as rooftop solar, through net metering and a variety of financial support programs. The state had nearly 1,400 megawatts of installed solar capacity by the end of 2017, ranking it 12th in the nation. By early 2018, the state's rank had risen to 11th.[47] In 2017, solar PV systems provided more than 1% of New York's net electricity generation, most of which was distributed generation.[48] The 32-megawatt Long Island Solar Farm is currently the largest solar PV generator in the state, but most solar installations in New York are small.[49] Five-sixths of the state's 2017 solar generation came from distributed installations of less than 1-megawatt each, and New York was fifth nationally in the amount of generation from distributed solar facilities.[50] In 2018, New York committed $1.4 billion to the development of 26 renewable projects chosen by the New York State Energy Research and Development Authority (NYSERDA). Twenty-two of those projects are solar farms that range in size from 1.53 to 100 megawatts.[51]

New York adopted its first renewable portfolio standard (RPS) in 2004. The 2004 RPS was modified in 2010, and the state set a renewable energy target of 29% of electricity sales by 2015.[52] New York reached the target, and, when its RPS expired in 2016, it was superseded by the state's Clean Energy Standard (CES), which requires utilities and other retail electricity suppliers to acquire 50% of the electricity sold in the state from clean energy resources by 2030. In addition to renewable resources, the CES identifies existing nuclear power plants in the state as zero emission resources that will contribute to New York's additional goal to reduce greenhouse gas emissions by 40% from 1990 levels by 2030.[53] State emissions from electricity generation have declined since 2000 because of increased use of renewable resources and natural gas, retirements of petroleum- and coal-fired power plants, and compliance with the Regional Greenhouse Gas Initiative, a program to reduce power plant emissions in nine northeastern states.[54,55,56] In 2015, New York's per capita carbon dioxide emissions were lower than any other state in the nation.[57,58] The CES is part of a larger program called Reforming the Energy Vision (REV) that offers electric utilities increased financial incentives for renewable and distributed energy resources as well as consumer incentives for efficiency and distributed generation. In addition to New York's CES goals for 2030, the REV also has a goal to reduce energy consumption in buildings by 23% from 2012 levels by 2030.[59]

Petroleum

New York is one of the nation's five largest consumers of petroleum, but the state consumes less petroleum per capita than any other state.[60,61] New York has few proved crude oil reserves and produces only small amounts of crude oil from wells in the southwestern part of the state.[62,63,64] In the 19th century, New York was an important center for crude oil production and processing with more than 50 oil refineries, including one of the world's largest. By the end of the 20th century, all the refineries in the state were closed, and now the small amount of crude oil produced in New York is shipped to out-of-state refineries.[65]

Petroleum products consumed in New York are supplied by refineries in New Jersey and Pennsylvania, by pipelines from the Gulf Coast and the Midwest, and by imports, mostly from Canada. New York Harbor, which includes terminals on both the New York and New Jersey shorelines, is the largest petroleum products hub in the Northeast, with bulk storage capacity exceeding 75 million barrels. Petroleum products delivered to the harbor are redistributed by truck or by barge to smaller ports on Long Island and upstate along the Hudson River, as well as to western New England. Western New York receives refined products from Pennsylvania through pipelines and from Canada through the Port of Buffalo.[66,67]

About four-fifths of the petroleum consumed in New York is used in the transportation sector, and much of the rest is used for heating.[68,69] About one-fourth of New York households are heated with petroleum products, primarily fuel oil.[70] In 2000, the federal government created the Northeast Home Heating Oil Reserve to avert shortages of home heating oil in the Northeast. In 2011, the federal government converted the reserve to ultra-low sulfur diesel (ULSD), in part because of New York's decision to require consumers heating with petroleum to use ULSD starting in 2012.[71] New York's decision led to a substantial increase in demand for ULSD, and almost all the other northeastern states phased in ULSD as of July 2018.[72]

To reduce ozone formation, reformulated motor gasoline blended with ethanol is required year-round in New York City and the surrounding metropolitan area. The rest of the state is required to use a low volatility blend in the summer.[73] New York Harbor is the primary Northeast distribution hub for ethanol supplies. Although some ethanol is produced in New York, ethanol produced in the Midwest and marine imports from overseas arrive through New York Harbor for distribution throughout the Northeast. A large storage facility at Albany, New York, also receives ethanol for distribution throughout the Northeast.[74,75]

Natural gas

Natural gas has been produced in western New York for almost 200 years, but annual production has never exceeded the 2006 peak of nearly 56 billion cubic feet.[76,77] The state holds less than 0.05% of the nation's total natural gas reserves.[78] Most of the natural gas consumed in the state is supplied by pipelines from other states and Canada. An increasing share of New York's natural gas comes from Pennsylvania.[79] The Marcellus Shale, named for a town in central New York where the shale is visible at the surface, is a natural gas-bearing formation extending under parts of New York, Pennsylvania, Ohio, West Virginia, and Maryland. It is currently the most prolific natural gas area in the United States.[80] Because of environmental concerns, New York has banned hydraulic fracturing, a technique used to produce natural gas from shales.[81] There has been no recent development of the Marcellus Shale natural gas resources in New York, and the total amount of retrievable natural gas under the state is unclear.[82,83]

New York was the sixth-largest natural gas consumer among the states in 2016.[84] The residential sector, the electric power sector, and the commercial sector consume almost all the natural gas used in New York. The industrial sector consumes less than 7% of the natural gas used in the state.[85] Natural gas fuels two-fifths of the state's net electricity generation, and nearly three-fifths of state households heat with natural gas.[86,87] New York has 26 natural gas underground storage facilities.[88] Along with storage in other nearby states, those facilities are key to meeting northeastern winter heating demand.[89] Virtually all major interstate pipelines from the Gulf Coast and Canada reach

New York, both to supply in-state customers and to ship supplies onward to New England.[90] Several pipeline companies are expanding their systems to increase natural gas deliveries to customers in New York.[91]

Coal

New York has no coal reserves or coal mining.[92] About three-fifths of the domestically-mined coal consumed in New York is used by industrial plants and coking facilities. Since 2000, coal has been providing progressively less of New York's net electricity generation.[93] The coal that is used to fuel the small amount of in-state power generation, less than 1% in 2017, is transported to New York electricity generating plants from nearby states.[94,95] U.S. coal exports that travel through New York primarily leave the state through the Port of Buffalo, although some coal also leaves the state through the ports at New York City and at Ogdensburg in northern New York. Small amounts of imported coal also enter the state at those three ports.[96]

Source: U.S. Energy Information Administration, State Profile and Energy Estimates, August 16, 2018

Endnotes

[1] U.S. Geological Survey, The USGS Water Science School, How much of your state is wet?, updated March 29, 2018.
[2] U.S. Census Bureau, Data, State Population Totals and Components of Change: 2010-2017, Annual Estimates of the Resident Population for the United States, Regions, States, and Puerto Rico: April 1, 2010 to July 1, 2017 (NST-EST2017-01).
[3] U.S. Energy Information Administration (EIA), State Energy Consumption Estimates 1960 Through 2016, DOE/EIA-0214(2016), June 2018, Table C12, Total Energy Consumption Estimates, Real Gross Domestic Product (GDP), Energy Consumption Estimates per Real Dollar of GDP, Ranked by State, 2016.
[4] U.S. EIA, State Energy Production Estimates 1960 Through 2016, Table P3, Energy Production and Consumption Estimates in Trillion Btu, 2016.
[5] U.S. EIA, State Energy Consumption Estimates 1960 Through 2016, DOE/EIA-0214(2016), Table C13, Energy Consumption Estimates per Capita by End-Use Sector, Ranked by State, 2016.
[6] U.S. Census Bureau, American FactFinder, B08124 Means of Transportation to Work by Occupation, Workers 16 years and over, 2012-2016 American Community Survey 5-Year Estimates, Geographies: United States, New York State, and New York City Metro Area.
[7] U.S. EIA, State Energy Production Estimates 1960 Through 2016, Table PT2, Primary Energy Production Estimates in Trillion Btu, New York, 1960-2016.
[8] Campbell, Alan K., and Paul Joseph Scudiere, "New York," *Encyclopædia Britannica*, accessed July 19, 2018.
[9] Geography of New York State, Physical Geography of New York, accessed July 31, 2018.
[10] World Population Review, US City Populations 2018, accessed July 19, 2018.
[11] Campbell, Alan K., and Paul Joseph Scudiere, "New York," *Encyclopædia Britannica*, accessed July 19, 2018.
[12] "Climate of New York facts," *Kiddle Encyclopedia*, accessed July 19, 2018.
[13] U.S. Department of Energy, Energy Efficiency and Renewable Energy, WINDExchange, Wind Energy in New York, accessed July 15, 2018.
[14] U.S. EIA, State Energy Consumption Estimates 1960 Through 2016, DOE/EIA-0214(2016), June 2018, Table C10, Energy Consumption Estimates by End-Use Sector, Ranked by State, 2016.
[15] NETSTATE, New York Economy, updated December 19, 2017.
[16] U.S. Bureau of Economic Analysis, Interactive Data, Regional Data, GDP & Personal Income, Annual Gross Domestic Product (GDP) by State, GDP in Current Dollars, NAICS, All Industries, New York, 2017.
[17] U.S. EIA, State Energy Consumption Estimates 1960 Through 2016, DOE/EIA-0214(2016) (June 2018), Table C10, Energy Consumption Estimates by End-Use Sector, Ranked by State, 2016.
[18] U.S. EIA, New York Electricity Profile 2016, Table 5, Electric power industry generation by primary energy source, 1990 through 2016.
[19] U.S. EIA, Electric Power Monthly (February 2018), Tables 1.3.B, 1.7.B, 1.9.B, 1.10.B.
[20] U.S. EIA, Electricity, Form EIA-860 detailed data, 2017 Early Release, Form EIA-860 Data, Schedule 3, 'Generator Data' (Operable Units Only).
[21] New York Independent System Operator, Power Trends 2017, p. 35.
[22] U.S. Federal Energy Regulatory Commission, Electric Power Markets: New York (NYISO), accessed July 31, 2018.
[23] New York Independent System Operator, Power Trends 2017, p. 11.
[24] U.S. EIA, State Electricity Profiles, New York Electricity Profile 2016, Table 10, Supply and disposition of electricity, 1990 through 2016.
[25] U.S. EIA, Electric Power Monthly (February 2018), Table 5.4.B.
[26] U.S. Census Bureau, American FactFinder, New York, Table B25040, House Heating Fuel, 2016 American Community Survey 1-Year Estimates.
[27] U.S. EIA, Electric Power Monthly (February 2018), Table 5.4.B.
[28] U.S. Census Bureau, Data, State Population Totals and Components of Change: 2010-2017, Annual Estimates of the Resident Population for the United States, Regions, States, and Puerto Rico: April 1, 2010 to July 1, 2017 (NST-EST2017-01).
[29] U.S. EIA, Electric Power Monthly (February 2018), Tables 1.3.B, 1.10.B, 1.11.B, 1.14.B, 1.15.B, 1.17.B.
[30] "A Powerful 50 Years at Niagara," *International Water Power & Dam Construction* (April 15, 2011).
[31] New York State, NY Power Authority, Niagara Power Project, accessed July 14, 2018.
[32] U.S. EIA, Electricity, Form EIA-860 detailed data, 2017 Early Release, Form EIA-860 Data, Schedule 3, 'Generator Data' (Operable Units Only).
[33] U.S. EIA, Electric Power Monthly (February 2018), Tables 1.3.B, 1.10.B.
[34] U.S. EIA, Electric Power Monthly (February 2018), Tables 1.11.B, 1.14.B.
[35] U.S. EIA, New York Electricity Profile 2016, Table 5, Electric power industry generation by primary energy source, 1990 through 2016.
[36] American Wind Energy Association, Wind Energy in New York, accessed July 15, 2018.
[37] Geuss, Megan, "New York commits $1.4 billion to renewable energy projects," *Ars Technica* (March 12, 2018).
[38] American Wind Energy Association, Wind Energy in New York, accessed July 15, 2018.
[39] U.S. Department of Energy, Energy Efficiency and Renewable Energy, WINDExchange, Wind Energy in New York, accessed July 15, 2018.
[40] New York State Energy Research and Development Authority, Offshore Wind in New York State (May 2018).
[41] Deepwater Wind, Southfork Wind Farm, accessed July 15, 2018.
[42] U.S. EIA, Electric Power Monthly (February 2018), Tables 1.11.B, 1.15.B.
[43] U.S. EIA, Electricity, Form EIA-860 detailed data, 2017 Early Release, Form EIA-860 Data, Schedule 3, 'Generator Data' (Operable Units Only).
[44] U.S. EIA, Electricity, Detailed State Data, Annual Data, 1990-2016 Net Generation by State by Type of Producer by Energy Source (EIA-906, EIA-920, and EIA-923).
[45] U.S. EIA, New York Profile Overview, Biomass Power Plant Map Layer, accessed July 14, 2018.
[46] New York State Energy Research and Development Authority, NY-Sun Annual Performance Report Through December 31, 2017, Final Report (March 2018), p. 1.
[47] Solar Energy Industries Association, Solar Spotlight-New York (June 2018).
[48] U.S. EIA, Electric Power Monthly (February 2018), Tables 1.17.B.
[49] U.S. EIA, Electricity, Form EIA-860 detailed data, 2017 Early Release, Form EIA-860 Data, Schedule 3, 'Generator Data' (Operable Units Only).
[50] U.S. EIA, Electric Power Monthly (February 2018), Table 1.17.B.
[51] Geuss, Megan, "New York commits $1.4 billion to renewable energy projects," *Ars Technica* (March 12, 2018).
[52] NC Clean Energy Technology Center, DSIRE, New York, Renewable Portfolio Standard, updated June 26, 2018.
[53] NC Clean Energy Technology Center, DSIRE, New York, Clean Energy Standard, updated June 26, 2018.
[54] New York Independent System Operator (NYISO), Power Trends 2016, p. 2-4.
[55] Regional Greenhouse Gas Initiative, Welcome, accessed July 17, 2018.
[56] U.S. EIA, Electricity, Form EIA-860 detailed data, 2017 Early Release, Form EIA-860 Data, Schedule 3, 'Generator Data' (Retired & Canceled Units Only).
[57] U.S. EIA, U.S. States, Rankings: Total Carbon Dioxide Emissions, 2015.

[58] U.S. Census Bureau, Data, State Population Totals and Components of Change: 2010-2017, Annual Estimates of the Resident Population for the United States, Regions, States, and Puerto Rico: April 1, 2010 to July 1, 2017 (NST-EST2017-01).

[59] New York State, Department of Public Service, Reforming the Energy Vision, About the Initiative, updated May 9, 2018.

[60] U.S. EIA, State Energy Data System, Table F15, Total Petroleum Consumption Estimates, 2016.

[61] U.S. Census Bureau, Data, State Population Totals and Components of Change: 2010-2017, Annual Estimates of the Resident Population for the United States, Regions, States, and Puerto Rico: April 1, 2010 to July 1, 2017 (NST-EST2017-01).

[62] U.S. EIA, U.S. Crude Oil and Natural Gas Proved Reserves, Year-end 2016 (February 2018), Table 7, Crude oil proved reserves, reserves changes, and production, 2016.

[63] U.S. EIA, Crude Oil Production, Annual-Thousand Barrels, 2012-17.

[64] New York State Department of Environmental Conservation, New York State Oil, Gas and Mineral Resources, 2015, Oil and Gas Production by Town in Each County.

[65] New York State Energy Research and Development Authority, New York's Natural Gas and Oil Resource Endowment: Past, Present and Potential, New York's Oil and Natural Gas History, A Long Story, But Not The Final Chapter, p. 10, accessed July 3, 2018.

[66] New York State Energy Research and Development Authority, Energy Infrastructure Reports, New York State Transportation Fuels Infrastructure Study (September 2012) p. 87-91.

[67] New York State Energy Research and Development Authority, Energy Infrastructure Reports, New York State Energy Assurance Plan (September 14, 2012) p. IV-6.

[68] U.S. EIA, State Energy Data System, Table F15, Total Petroleum Consumption Estimates, 2016.

[69] U.S. EIA, State Energy Consumption Estimates 1960 Through 2016, DOE/EIA-0214(2016) (June 2018), Table C4, Total End-Use Energy Consumption Estimates, 2016.

[70] U.S. Census Bureau, American FactFinder, New York, Table B25040, House Heating Fuel, 2016 American Community Survey 1-Year Estimates.

[71] U.S. Department of Energy, Office of Fossil Energy, Northeast Home Heating Oil Reserve (NEHHOR) History, accessed July 4, 2018.

[72] Brown, Elizabeth, "Feature: Six US states ready for July transition to ultra-low sulfur heating oil," Platts S&P Global (June 27, 2018).

[73] U.S. Environmental Protection Agency, Gasoline Standards, Gasoline Programs, Reformulated gasoline, Reid vapor pressure, accessed July 4, 2018.

[74] Ethanol Producer Magazine, U.S. Ethanol Plants, RINs, All Plants, updated July 1, 2018.

[75] New York State Energy Research and Development Authority, Energy Infrastructure Reports, New York State Energy Assurance Plan (September 14, 2012), p. IV-7.

[76] New York State Department of Environmental Conservation, New York's Oil and Natural Gas History, accessed July 5, 2018, p. 8, 9.

[77] U.S. EIA, New York Natural Gas Gross Withdrawals, 1967-2016.

[78] U.S. EIA, Natural Gas Reserves Summary as of December 31, Dry Natural Gas, Annual, 2016.

[79] U.S. EIA, International and Interstate Movements of Natural Gas by State, New York, Annual, 2011-16.

[80] U.S. EIA, Top 100 U.S. Oil and Gas Fields (March 2015), p. 4, 8.

[81] Kaplan, Thomas, "Citing Health Risks, Cuomo Bans Fracking in New York State," *New York Times* (December 17, 2014).

[82] U.S. EIA, Marcellus Shale Play Geology review, Updates to the Marcellus Shale Play Maps (January 2017), p. 3.

[83] Berman, Arthur, and Lyndon Pittinger, Resource Assessment of Potentially Producible Natural Gas Volumes from the Marcellus Shale, State of New York, Labyrinth Consulting (April 10, 2014), p. 3-4.

[84] U.S. EIA, Natural Gas Consumption by End Use, Total Consumption, Annual, 2012-17.

[85] U.S. EIA, Natural Gas Consumption by End Use, New York, Annual, 2012-17.

[86] U.S. EIA, Electric Power Monthly (February 2018), Tables 1.3.B, 1.7.B.

[87] U.S. Census Bureau, American FactFinder, New York, Table B25040, House Heating Fuel, 2016 American Community Survey 1-Year Estimates.

[88] U.S. EIA, Underground Natural Gas Storage Capacity, New York, Annual, 2011-16.

[89] U.S. EIA, Underground Natural Gas Storage Capacity, Total Storage Capacity, Annual, 2011-16.

[90] U.S. EIA, Natural Gas Pipelines in the Northeast Region, accessed July 6, 2018.

[91] Northeast Gas Association, Planned Enhancements, Northeast Natural Gas Pipeline Systems (as of April 23, 2018).

[92] U.S. EIA, Annual Coal Report 2016 (November 2017), Table 1, Coal Production and Number of Mines by State and Mine Type, 2016 and 2015, and Table 14, Recoverable Coal Reserves and Average Recovery Percentage at Producing Mines by State, 2016 and 2015.

[93] U.S. EIA, New York Electricity Profile 2016, Table 5, Electric power industry generation by primary energy source, 1990 through 2016.

[94] U.S. EIA, Annual Coal Distribution Report 2016 (November 2017), New York, Table DS-31, Domestic Coal Distribution, by Destination State, 2016.

[95] U.S. EIA, Electric Power Monthly (February 2018), Tables 1.3.B, 1.4.B.

[96] U.S. EIA, Quarterly Coal Report, October-December 2017 (April 2018), Table 13, Coal Exports by Customs District, and Table 20, Coal Imports by Customs District.

Household Energy Use in New York

A closer look at residential energy consumption

All data from EIA's 2009 Residential Energy Consumption Survey
www.eia.gov/consumption/residential/

- New York households consume an average of 103 million Btu per year, 15% more than the U.S. average.
- Electricity consumption in New York homes is much lower than the U.S. average, because many households use other fuels for major energy end uses like space heating, water heating, and cooking. Electricity costs are closer to the national average due to higher than average electricity prices in the state.
- New York homes are typically older and, with a higher percentage of apartments, are smaller on average than homes in other parts of the country.

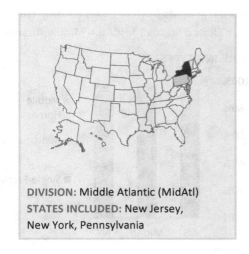

DIVISION: Middle Atlantic (MidAtl)
STATES INCLUDED: New Jersey, New York, Pennsylvania

ALL ENERGY *average per household (excl. transportation)*

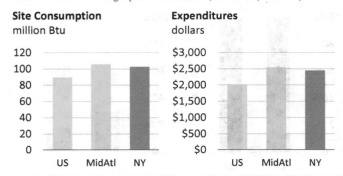

ELECTRICITY ONLY *average per household*

CONSUMPTION BY END USE

Since the weather in New York is cooler than most other areas of the United States, space heating (56%) makes up a greater portion of energy use in homes compared to the U.S. average, and air conditioning makes up only 1% of energy use.

MAIN HEATING FUEL USED

Natural gas provides space heating for 57% of New York households. Fuel oil (29%) is still a popular choice, despite declining usage nationwide.

COOLING EQUIPMENT USED

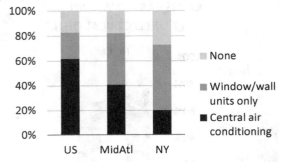

More than half of New York households (53%) use individual window/wall air conditioning units, while only 20% have a central system.

More highlights from RECS on housing characteristics and energy-related features per household...
US = United States | MidAtl = Middle Atlantic | NY = New York

About the Residential Energy Consumption Survey (RECS) Program

The RECS gathers energy characteristics through personal interviews from a nationwide sample of homes, and cost and consumption from energy suppliers.

The 2009 RECS is the thirteenth edition of the survey, which was first conducted in 1978.

Resulting products include:
- Home energy characteristics
- Average consumption & cost
- Detailed energy end-use statistics
- Reports highlighting key findings
- Microdata file for in-depth analysis

www.eia.gov/consumption/residential/

Population

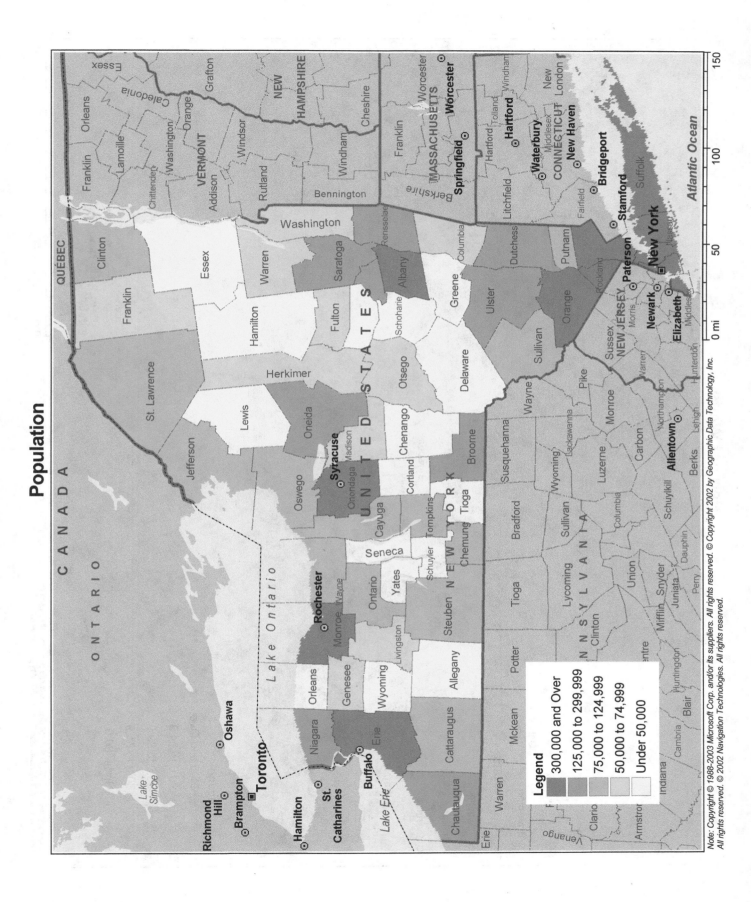

Legend

- 300,000 and Over
- 125,000 to 299,999
- 75,000 to 124,999
- 50,000 to 74,999
- Under 50,000

Percent White

Percent Black

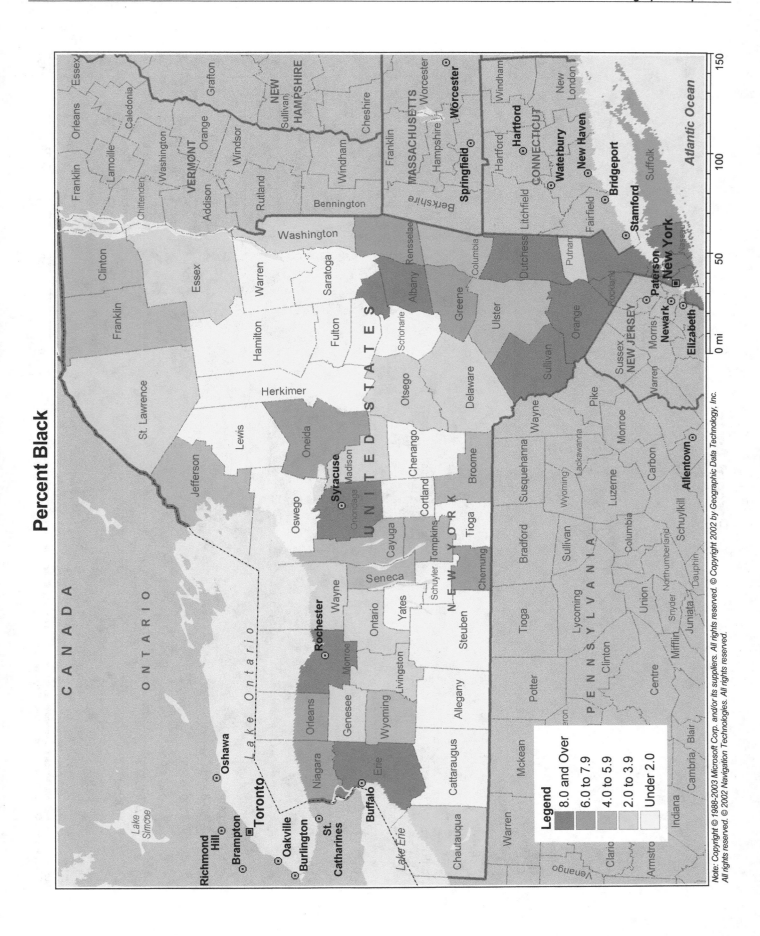

Legend

- 8.0 and Over
- 6.0 to 7.9
- 4.0 to 5.9
- 2.0 to 3.9
- Under 2.0

Percent Asian

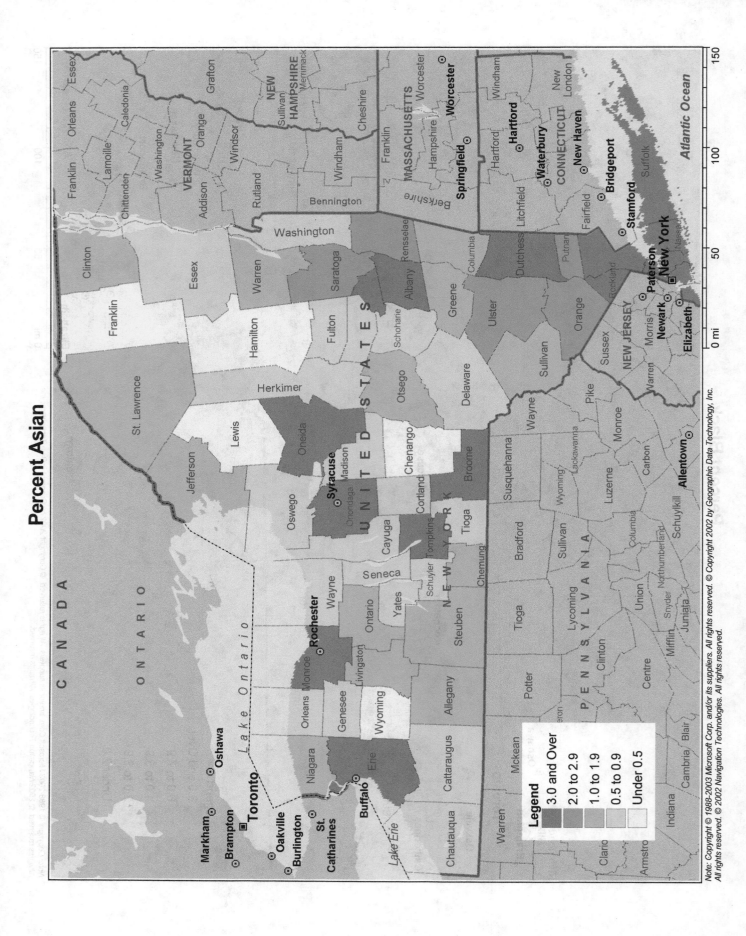

Legend

- 3.0 and Over
- 2.0 to 2.9
- 1.0 to 1.9
- 0.5 to 0.9
- Under 0.5

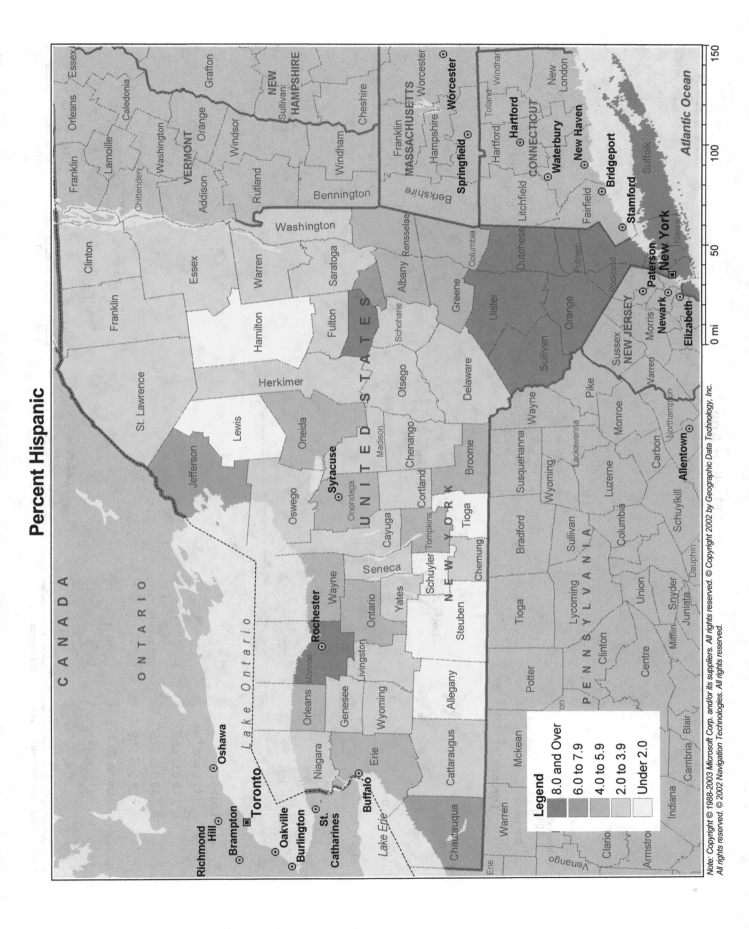

Percent Hispanic

Legend
- 8.0 and Over
- 6.0 to 7.9
- 4.0 to 5.9
- 2.0 to 3.9
- Under 2.0

Median Age

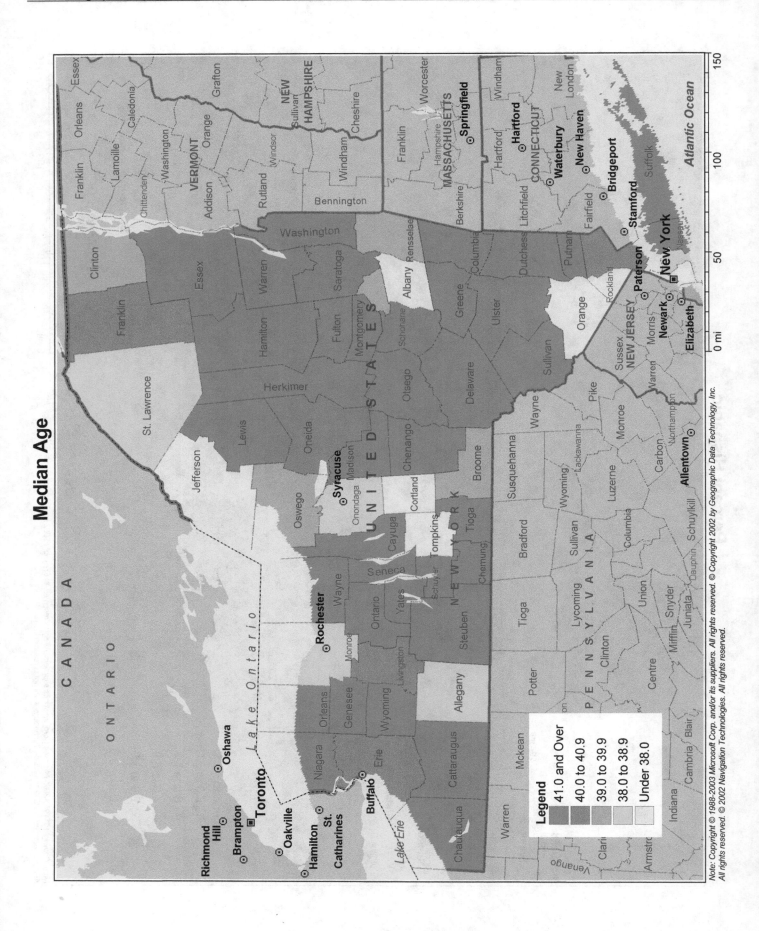

Legend

- 41.0 and Over
- 40.0 to 40.9
- 39.0 to 39.9
- 38.0 to 38.9
- Under 38.0

Median Household Income

Legend

- 57,000 and Over
- 53,000 to 56,999
- 50,000 to 52,999
- 47,000 to 49,999
- Under 47,000

Median Home Value

Legend
- 200,000 and Over
- 175,000 to 199,999
- 150,000 to 174,999
- 125,000 to 149,999
- 100,000 to 124,999
- Under 100,000

High School Graduates*

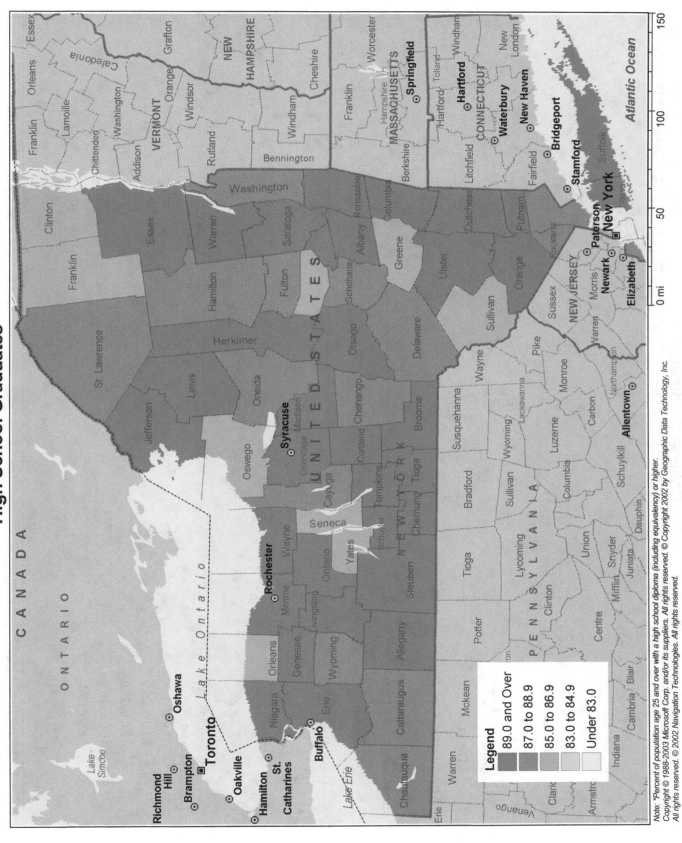

Legend
- 89.0 and Over
- 87.0 to 88.9
- 85.0 to 86.9
- 83.0 to 84.9
- Under 83.0

College Graduates*

Legend

- 27.0 and Over
- 23.0 to 26.9
- 19.0 to 22.9
- 15.0 to 18.9
- Under 15.0

Profiles

Albany County

Located in eastern New York; bounded on the east by the Hudson River; includes the Helderbergs and part of the Catskills. Covers a land area of 522.804 square miles, a water area of 10.498 square miles, and is located in the Eastern Time Zone at 42.59° N. Lat., 73.97° W. Long. The county was founded in 1683. County seat is Albany.

Albany County is part of the Albany-Schenectady-Troy, NY Metropolitan Statistical Area. The entire metro area includes: Albany County, NY; Rensselaer County, NY; Saratoga County, NY; Schenectady County, NY; Schoharie County, NY

Weather Station: Albany County Arpt   Elevation: 274 feet

	Jan	Feb	Mar	Apr	May	Jun	Jul	Aug	Sep	Oct	Nov	Dec
High	31	35	44	58	70	78	82	81	72	60	48	36
Low	14	17	25	37	47	56	61	60	51	39	31	21
Precip	2.5	2.1	3.3	3.2	3.6	3.8	4.1	3.6	3.3	3.5	3.3	2.9
Snow	17.7	11.5	11.4	2.3	0.1	tr	tr	0.0	tr	0.3	3.2	13.7

High and Low temperatures in degrees Fahrenheit; Precipitation and Snow in inches

Weather Station: Alcove Dam   Elevation: 606 feet

	Jan	Feb	Mar	Apr	May	Jun	Jul	Aug	Sep	Oct	Nov	Dec
High	31	35	42	56	68	76	80	79	71	59	47	36
Low	12	14	22	34	44	53	58	57	49	37	29	19
Precip	2.4	2.1	3.5	3.8	3.5	4.5	3.8	3.5	3.7	3.5	3.5	2.8
Snow	na	na	na	0.4	tr	0.0	0.0	0.0	0.0	0.1	0.4	na

High and Low temperatures in degrees Fahrenheit; Precipitation and Snow in inches

Population: 308,580; Growth (since 2000): 4.8%; Density: 590.2 persons per square mile; Race: 76.0% White, 12.3% Black/African American, 6.4% Asian, 0.2% American Indian/Alaska Native, 0.0% Native Hawaiian/Other Pacific Islander, 3.7% two or more races, 5.7% Hispanic of any race; Average household size: 2.32; Median age: 37.8; Age under 18: 18.8%; Age 65 and over: 15.6%; Males per 100 females: 93.6; Marriage status: 42.3% never married, 42.8% now married, 1.8% separated, 5.9% widowed, 9.0% divorced; Foreign born: 9.8%; Speak English only: 87.3%; With disability: 11.3%; Veterans: 6.1%; Ancestry: 20.9% Irish, 16.1% Italian, 14.0% German, 7.8% English, 5.7% Polish
Religion: Six largest groups: 28.0% Catholicism, 3.1% Non-denominational Protestant, 2.1% Presbyterian-Reformed, 2.0% Methodist/Pietist, 1.7% Judaism, 1.5% Muslim Estimate
Economy: Unemployment rate: 3.4%; Leading industries: 13.9 % retail trade; 12.8 % professional, scientific, and technical services; 11.3 % other services (except public administration); Farms: 494 totaling 63,394 acres; Company size: 10 employ 1,000 or more persons, 21 employs 500 to 999 persons, 271 employs 100 to 499 persons, 9,229 employ less than 100 persons; Business ownership: 7,125 women-owned, 1,179 Black-owned, 821 Hispanic-owned, 1,229 Asian-owned, 75 American Indian/Alaska Native-owned
Employment: 16.9% management, business, and financial, 7.7% computer, engineering, and science, 13.4% education, legal, community service, arts, and media, 6.7% healthcare practitioners, 17.3% service, 25.1% sales and office, 5.5% natural resources, construction, and maintenance, 7.5% production, transportation, and material moving
Income: Per capita: $35,278; Median household: $62,293; Average household: $84,568; Households with income of $100,000 or more: 29.4%; Poverty rate: 12.4%
Educational Attainment: High school diploma or higher: 92.6%; Bachelor's degree or higher: 40.5%; Graduate/professional degree or higher: 19.5%
Housing: Homeownership rate: 56.8%; Median home value: $214,400; Median year structure built: 1959; Homeowner vacancy rate: 1.4%; Median selected monthly owner costs: $1,688 with a mortgage, $624 without a mortgage; Median gross rent: $969 per month; Rental vacancy rate: 4.4%
Vital Statistics: Birth rate: 99.4 per 10,000 population; Death rate: 88.1 per 10,000 population; Age-adjusted cancer mortality rate: 169.9 deaths per 100,000 population
Health Insurance: 95.3% have insurance; 78.0% have private insurance; 31.9% have public insurance; 4.7% do not have insurance; 1.9% of children under 18 do not have insurance
Health Care: Physicians: 62.0 per 10,000 population; Dentists: 9.0 per 10,000 population; Hospital beds: 50.8 per 10,000 population; Hospital admissions: 2,281.3 per 10,000 population

Air Quality Index (AQI): Percent of Days: 84.9% good, 15.1% moderate, 0.0% unhealthy for sensitive individuals, 0.0% unhealthy, 0.0% very unhealthy; Annual median: 37; Annual maximum: 84
Transportation: Commute: 84.4% car, 5.9% public transportation, 4.6% walk, 3.5% work from home; Mean travel time to work: 20.4 minutes
2016 Presidential Election: 34.2% Trump, 59.4% Clinton, 3.4% Johnson, 1.8% Stein
National and State Parks: Thacher State Park
Additional Information Contacts
Albany Government. . . . . (518) 447-7300
   http://www.albanycounty.com

Albany County Communities

ALBANY (city). State capital. County seat. Covers a land area of 21.388 square miles and a water area of 0.548 square miles. Located at 42.67° N. Lat; 73.80° W. Long. Elevation is 148 feet.
History: Native American trails running in all directions crossed at the site of Albany. Several ship captains, including Henry Hudson, dropped anchor in the shallows near the present city, and made friends with the inhabitants. The next settlers, who came in 1624, were mostly Walloons from Holland. They built a fort and called it Fort Orange. Dutch, Norwegians, Danes, Germans, and Scots all settled on this land. In 1652, Peter Stuyvesant was sent out by the West India Company to set up a court and he laid out space around Fort Orange for a new village called Beverwyck. In 1685, control was relinquished to the English. The town became a mixture of Dutch and British people and cultures. It was chartered as Albany in 1686. Early fur trade made Albany residents wealthy, but wars plagued the area for almost a century. At the end of the wars, Albany found itself at the crossroad of a developing nation, with travelers coming by land, water, and rail. Lumbering and manufacturing also became important in the 19th century.
Population: 98,498; Growth (since 2000): 3.0%; Density: 4,605.2 persons per square mile; Race: 55.1% White, 28.7% Black/African American, 7.4% Asian, 0.3% American Indian/Alaska Native, 0.0% Native Hawaiian/Other Pacific Islander, 5.6% Two or more races, 9.8% Hispanic of any race; Average household size: 2.14; Median age: 30.9; Age under 18: 17.3%; Age 65 and over: 12.6%; Males per 100 females: 93.6; Marriage status: 59.4% never married, 26.5% now married, 1.9% separated, 5.5% widowed, 8.5% divorced; Foreign born: 12.7%; Speak English only: 83.3%; With disability: 12.1%; Veterans: 4.2%; Ancestry: 14.8% Irish, 12.3% Italian, 10.2% German, 5.2% English, 3.9% Polish
Employment: 13.2% management, business, and financial, 7.2% computer, engineering, and science, 13.5% education, legal, community service, arts, and media, 6.8% healthcare practitioners, 23.6% service, 24.9% sales and office, 4.4% natural resources, construction, and maintenance, 6.4% production, transportation, and material moving
Income: Per capita: $27,632; Median household: $43,790; Average household: $63,120; Households with income of $100,000 or more: 18.6%; Poverty rate: 24.5%
Educational Attainment: High school diploma or higher: 89.6%; Bachelor's degree or higher: 38.1%; Graduate/professional degree or higher: 18.4%

School District(s)
Albany City SD (PK-12)
   Enrollment: 9,788 . . . . (518) 475-6010
Albany Community Charter School (KG-08)
   Enrollment: 682. . . . . (518) 433-1500
Albany Leadership Charter High School for Girls (09-12)
   Enrollment: 394. . . . . (518) 694-5300
Albany-Schoharie-Schenectady-Saratoga Boces
   Enrollment: n/a . . . . (518) 862-4901
Brighter Choice Charter School for Boys (KG-04)
   Enrollment: 311. . . . . (518) 694-8200
Brighter Choice Charter School for Girls (KG-04)
   Enrollment: 317. . . . . (518) 694-4100
Green Tech High Charter School (09-12)
   Enrollment: 353. . . . . (518) 694-3400
Guilderland Central SD (KG-12)
   Enrollment: 4,879 . . . . (518) 456-6200
Henry Johnson Charter School (KG-04)
   Enrollment: 380. . . . . (518) 432-4300
Kipp Tech Valley Charter School (05-08)
   Enrollment: 415. . . . . (518) 694-9494

New York State Department of Corrections
  Enrollment: 1,124 . . . . (518) 457-8126
New York State Omh (01-12)
  Enrollment: 281 . . . . (518) 474-3619
Nys Office for People With Developmental Disabilit
  Enrollment: 7 . . . . (518) 473-5436
South Colonie Central SD (PK-12)
  Enrollment: 4,911 . . . . (518) 869-3576

Four-year College(s)
Albany College of Pharmacy and Health Sciences (Private, Not-for-profit)
  Enrollment: 1,384 . . . . (518) 694-7200
  Tuition: In-state $33,621; Out-of-state $33,621
Albany Law School (Private, Not-for-profit)
  Enrollment: 435 . . . . (518) 445-2311
Albany Medical College (Private, Not-for-profit)
  Enrollment: 840 . . . . (518) 262-3125
Bryant & Stratton College-Albany (Private, For-profit)
  Enrollment: 371 . . . . (518) 437-1802
  Tuition: In-state $16,694; Out-of-state $16,694
Excelsior College (Private, Not-for-profit)
  Enrollment: 34,022 . . . . (518) 464-8500
Maria College of Albany (Private, Not-for-profit)
  Enrollment: 855 . . . . (518) 438-3111
  Tuition: In-state $14,610; Out-of-state $14,610
SUNY at Albany (Public)
  Enrollment: 17,743 . . . . (518) 442-3300
  Tuition: In-state $9,490; Out-of-state $24,370
The College of Saint Rose (Private, Not-for-profit)
  Enrollment: 3,929 . . . . (518) 454-5111
  Tuition: In-state $31,612; Out-of-state $31,612

Two-year College(s)
Memorial College of Nursing (Private, Not-for-profit)
  Enrollment: 124 . . . . (518) 471-3260
  Tuition: In-state $12,595; Out-of-state $12,595
Mildred Elley School-Albany Campus (Private, For-profit)
  Enrollment: 521 . . . . (518) 786-0855
  Tuition: In-state $12,285; Out-of-state $12,285

Vocational/Technical School(s)
Albany BOCES-Adult Practical Nursing Program (Public)
  Enrollment: 142 . . . . (518) 862-4800
  Tuition: $15,060
Austin's School of Spa Technology (Private, For-profit)
  Enrollment: n/a . . . . (518) 438-7879
  Tuition: $10,375
Branford Hall Career Institute-Albany Campus (Private, For-profit)
  Enrollment: 140 . . . . (518) 456-4464
  Tuition: $14,666
Center for Natural Wellness School of Massage Therapy (Private, For-profit)
  Enrollment: 69 . . . . (518) 489-4026
  Tuition: $16,600
New School of Radio and Television (Private, For-profit)
  Enrollment: 48 . . . . (518) 438-7682
  Tuition: $11,410
Orlo School of Hair Design and Cosmetology (Private, For-profit)
  Enrollment: 58 . . . . (518) 459-7832
  Tuition: $11,500
Housing: Homeownership rate: 37.2%; Median home value: $171,900; Median year structure built: Before 1940; Homeowner vacancy rate: 2.7%; Median selected monthly owner costs: $1,597 with a mortgage, $634 without a mortgage; Median gross rent: $924 per month; Rental vacancy rate: 4.8%
Health Insurance: 92.8% have insurance; 66.8% have private insurance; 38.1% have public insurance; 7.2% do not have insurance; 2.4% of children under 18 do not have insurance
Hospitals: Albany Medical Center Hospital (651 beds); Albany Memorial Hospital (165 beds); Albany VA Medical Center (156 beds); Saint Peter's Hospital (442 beds)
Safety: Violent crime rate: 89.2 per 10,000 population; Property crime rate: 345.7 per 10,000 population
Newspapers: Metroland (weekly circulation 40,000); Times Union (daily circulation 95,500)
Transportation: Commute: 70.6% car, 14.3% public transportation, 10.6% walk, 2.5% work from home; Mean travel time to work: 18.6 minutes; Amtrak: Train service available.

Airports: Albany International (primary service/small hub)
Additional Information Contacts
City of Albany . . . . (518) 434-5075
  http://www.albanyny.org/home.aspx

ALTAMONT (village).
Covers a land area of 1.186 square miles and a water area of <.001 square miles. Located at 42.71° N. Lat; 74.03° W. Long. Elevation is 463 feet.
Population: 1,742; Growth (since 2000): 0.3%; Density: 1,468.3 persons per square mile; Race: 91.6% White, 1.1% Black/African American, 3.7% Asian, 0.0% American Indian/Alaska Native, 0.2% Native Hawaiian/Other Pacific Islander, 2.2% Two or more races, 5.0% Hispanic of any race; Average household size: 2.48; Median age: 44.7; Age under 18: 22.1%; Age 65 and over: 17.4%; Males per 100 females: 94.4; Marriage status: 27.6% never married, 56.8% now married, 0.8% separated, 8.0% widowed, 7.6% divorced; Foreign born: 6.2%; Speak English only: 94.5%; With disability: 12.5%; Veterans: 4.1%; Ancestry: 22.8% Irish, 19.3% English, 16.7% Italian, 14.4% German, 8.4% Polish
Employment: 17.7% management, business, and financial, 7.8% computer, engineering, and science, 20.7% education, legal, community service, arts, and media, 6.3% healthcare practitioners, 12.5% service, 25.8% sales and office, 6.2% natural resources, construction, and maintenance, 3.0% production, transportation, and material moving
Income: Per capita: $41,237; Median household: $87,917; Average household: $103,702; Households with income of $100,000 or more: 48.0%; Poverty rate: 7.9%
Educational Attainment: High school diploma or higher: 94.8%; Bachelor's degree or higher: 49.8%; Graduate/professional degree or higher: 25.4%

School District(s)
Guilderland Central SD (KG-12)
  Enrollment: 4,879 . . . . (518) 456-6200
Housing: Homeownership rate: 72.7%; Median home value: $255,500; Median year structure built: 1958; Homeowner vacancy rate: 0.0%; Median selected monthly owner costs: $1,912 with a mortgage, $737 without a mortgage; Median gross rent: $948 per month; Rental vacancy rate: 4.8%
Health Insurance: 98.9% have insurance; 88.1% have private insurance; 27.6% have public insurance; 1.1% do not have insurance; 0.0% of children under 18 do not have insurance
Newspapers: Altamont Enterprise (weekly circulation 6,300)
Transportation: Commute: 91.5% car, 0.9% public transportation, 2.4% walk, 4.0% work from home; Mean travel time to work: 26.8 minutes

BERNE (town).
Covers a land area of 64.030 square miles and a water area of 0.704 square miles. Located at 42.60° N. Lat; 74.13° W. Long. Elevation is 971 feet.
Population: 2,811; Growth (since 2000): -1.2%; Density: 43.9 persons per square mile; Race: 96.1% White, 0.1% Black/African American, 0.6% Asian, 0.0% American Indian/Alaska Native, 0.6% Native Hawaiian/Other Pacific Islander, 2.2% Two or more races, 1.8% Hispanic of any race; Average household size: 2.53; Median age: 47.7; Age under 18: 20.3%; Age 65 and over: 16.5%; Males per 100 females: 102.3; Marriage status: 26.2% never married, 61.1% now married, 2.7% separated, 4.8% widowed, 7.9% divorced; Foreign born: 2.0%; Speak English only: 98.0%; With disability: 11.0%; Veterans: 7.0%; Ancestry: 20.4% Irish, 18.1% German, 13.3% American, 11.8% Italian, 9.9% English
Employment: 15.6% management, business, and financial, 5.2% computer, engineering, and science, 10.9% education, legal, community service, arts, and media, 8.5% healthcare practitioners, 9.3% service, 22.8% sales and office, 18.9% natural resources, construction, and maintenance, 8.9% production, transportation, and material moving
Income: Per capita: $35,326; Median household: $73,385; Average household: $88,553; Households with income of $100,000 or more: 38.5%; Poverty rate: 7.5%
Educational Attainment: High school diploma or higher: 95.7%; Bachelor's degree or higher: 29.9%; Graduate/professional degree or higher: 13.5%

School District(s)
Berne-Knox-Westerlo Central SD (KG-12)
  Enrollment: 789 . . . . (518) 872-1293
Housing: Homeownership rate: 92.1%; Median home value: $195,400; Median year structure built: 1972; Homeowner vacancy rate: 4.8%; Median selected monthly owner costs: $1,681 with a mortgage, $581 without a mortgage; Median gross rent: $779 per month; Rental vacancy rate: 15.7%

Health Insurance: 97.3% have insurance; 81.5% have private insurance; 31.2% have public insurance; 2.7% do not have insurance; 0.9% of children under 18 do not have insurance
Transportation: Commute: 91.1% car, 0.0% public transportation, 0.9% walk, 3.9% work from home; Mean travel time to work: 32.8 minutes

BETHLEHEM (town). Covers a land area of 49.030 square miles and a water area of 0.834 square miles. Located at 42.59° N. Lat; 73.83° W. Long. Elevation is 210 feet.

Population: 34,912; Growth (since 2000): 11.5%; Density: 712.1 persons per square mile; Race: 91.6% White, 2.1% Black/African American, 4.1% Asian, 0.0% American Indian/Alaska Native, 0.0% Native Hawaiian/Other Pacific Islander, 1.9% Two or more races, 1.5% Hispanic of any race; Average household size: 2.51; Median age: 42.8; Age under 18: 22.8%; Age 65 and over: 17.2%; Males per 100 females: 92.2; Marriage status: 27.9% never married, 58.1% now married, 0.7% separated, 6.6% widowed, 7.5% divorced; Foreign born: 6.6%; Speak English only: 92.3%; With disability: 8.9%; Veterans: 6.4%; Ancestry: 25.7% Irish, 18.7% German, 17.0% Italian, 12.8% English, 6.5% Polish
Employment: 21.5% management, business, and financial, 8.8% computer, engineering, and science, 20.6% education, legal, community service, arts, and media, 7.4% healthcare practitioners, 10.6% service, 21.4% sales and office, 4.7% natural resources, construction, and maintenance, 5.0% production, transportation, and material moving
Income: Per capita: $49,794; Median household: $96,384; Average household: $125,738; Households with income of $100,000 or more: 48.2%; Poverty rate: 5.0%
Educational Attainment: High school diploma or higher: 97.0%; Bachelor's degree or higher: 58.6%; Graduate/professional degree or higher: 33.0%
Housing: Homeownership rate: 75.8%; Median home value: $275,000; Median year structure built: 1975; Homeowner vacancy rate: 1.4%; Median selected monthly owner costs: $2,025 with a mortgage, $797 without a mortgage; Median gross rent: $1,122 per month; Rental vacancy rate: 5.1%
Health Insurance: 97.6% have insurance; 91.4% have private insurance; 22.3% have public insurance; 2.4% do not have insurance; 1.4% of children under 18 do not have insurance
Safety: Violent crime rate: 5.3 per 10,000 population; Property crime rate: 136.8 per 10,000 population
Transportation: Commute: 90.4% car, 1.3% public transportation, 1.7% walk, 5.7% work from home; Mean travel time to work: 21.4 minutes
Additional Information Contacts
Town of Bethlehem . . . . (518) 439-4955
　http://www.townofbethlehem.org

COEYMANS (town). Covers a land area of 50.129 square miles and a water area of 3.038 square miles. Located at 42.49° N. Lat; 73.88° W. Long. Elevation is 59 feet.

History: Coeymans is named after an early settler, who was the patent-holder for the area.
Population: 7,433; Growth (since 2000): -8.8%; Density: 148.3 persons per square mile; Race: 95.9% White, 3.0% Black/African American, 0.1% Asian, 0.1% American Indian/Alaska Native, 0.0% Native Hawaiian/Other Pacific Islander, 0.7% Two or more races, 1.1% Hispanic of any race; Average household size: 2.43; Median age: 42.4; Age under 18: 19.6%; Age 65 and over: 18.3%; Males per 100 females: 99.3; Marriage status: 31.6% never married, 51.8% now married, 1.1% separated, 6.8% widowed, 9.8% divorced; Foreign born: 1.3%; Speak English only: 97.5%; With disability: 10.7%; Veterans: 9.0%; Ancestry: 22.1% Irish, 20.1% American, 18.1% German, 15.0% Italian, 7.8% English
Employment: 13.5% management, business, and financial, 7.4% computer, engineering, and science, 9.7% education, legal, community service, arts, and media, 4.1% healthcare practitioners, 12.9% service, 24.9% sales and office, 8.4% natural resources, construction, and maintenance, 19.1% production, transportation, and material moving
Income: Per capita: $29,581; Median household: $60,812; Average household: $70,187; Households with income of $100,000 or more: 20.8%; Poverty rate: 7.9%
Educational Attainment: High school diploma or higher: 91.1%; Bachelor's degree or higher: 21.8%; Graduate/professional degree or higher: 7.1%

School District(s)
Ravena-Coeymans-Selkirk Central SD (PK-12)
　Enrollment: 1,884 . . . . (518) 756-5200

Housing: Homeownership rate: 69.3%; Median home value: $168,600; Median year structure built: 1956; Homeowner vacancy rate: 2.7%; Median selected monthly owner costs: $1,613 with a mortgage, $611 without a mortgage; Median gross rent: $840 per month; Rental vacancy rate: 8.3%
Health Insurance: 93.6% have insurance; 78.4% have private insurance; 30.9% have public insurance; 6.4% do not have insurance; 2.8% of children under 18 do not have insurance
Safety: Violent crime rate: 6.8 per 10,000 population; Property crime rate: 111.3 per 10,000 population
Transportation: Commute: 95.1% car, 0.3% public transportation, 0.2% walk, 2.3% work from home; Mean travel time to work: 25.6 minutes
Additional Information Contacts
Town of Coeymans . . . . (518) 756-6006
　http://www.coeymans.org

COEYMANS HOLLOW (unincorporated postal area)
ZCTA: 12046
　Covers a land area of 15.349 square miles and a water area of 2.081 square miles. Located at 42.51° N. Lat; 73.92° W. Long. Elevation is 413 feet.
Population: 1,069; Growth (since 2000): 14.5%; Density: 69.6 persons per square mile; Race: 100.0% White, 0.0% Black/African American, 0.0% Asian, 0.0% American Indian/Alaska Native, 0.0% Native Hawaiian/Other Pacific Islander, 0.0% Two or more races, 0.0% Hispanic of any race; Average household size: 2.74; Median age: 36.3; Age under 18: 31.3%; Age 65 and over: 14.5%; Males per 100 females: 97.8; Marriage status: 33.0% never married, 45.4% now married, 0.0% separated, 6.0% widowed, 15.6% divorced; Foreign born: 1.4%; Speak English only: 98.4%; With disability: 7.9%; Veterans: 12.7%; Ancestry: 35.3% Irish, 29.4% German, 13.8% American, 11.6% English, 8.4% Italian
Employment: 6.7% management, business, and financial, 12.9% computer, engineering, and science, 6.0% education, legal, community service, arts, and media, 0.0% healthcare practitioners, 18.2% service, 22.7% sales and office, 5.8% natural resources, construction, and maintenance, 27.7% production, transportation, and material moving
Income: Per capita: $33,845; Median household: $82,692; Average household: $90,004; Households with income of $100,000 or more: 39.0%; Poverty rate: n/a
Educational Attainment: High school diploma or higher: 90.9%; Bachelor's degree or higher: 27.0%; Graduate/professional degree or higher: 4.2%
Housing: Homeownership rate: 90.5%; Median home value: $148,100; Median year structure built: 1951; Homeowner vacancy rate: 0.0%; Median selected monthly owner costs: $1,660 with a mortgage, $594 without a mortgage; Median gross rent: n/a per month; Rental vacancy rate: 0.0%
Health Insurance: 100.0% have insurance; 86.0% have private insurance; 25.0% have public insurance; 0.0% do not have insurance; 0.0% of children under 18 do not have insurance
Transportation: Commute: 86.3% car, 0.0% public transportation, 0.0% walk, 10.2% work from home; Mean travel time to work: 29.5 minutes

COHOES (city). Covers a land area of 3.774 square miles and a water area of 0.463 square miles. Located at 42.77° N. Lat; 73.71° W. Long. Elevation is 98 feet.

History: The world's first power-operated knitting mill was opened here in 1832. Van Schaick Mansion (1735), now a Museum, was used as headquarters by General Horatio Gates during the American Revolution. Settled by Dutch 1665, Incorporated 1869.
Population: 16,574; Growth (since 2000): 6.8%; Density: 4,392.2 persons per square mile; Race: 88.2% White, 5.5% Black/African American, 1.1% Asian, 0.4% American Indian/Alaska Native, 0.0% Native Hawaiian/Other Pacific Islander, 4.1% Two or more races, 4.8% Hispanic of any race; Average household size: 2.12; Median age: 39.8; Age under 18: 16.5%; Age 65 and over: 19.3%; Males per 100 females: 89.7; Marriage status: 39.9% never married, 40.3% now married, 1.6% separated, 8.5% widowed, 11.4% divorced; Foreign born: 4.1%; Speak English only: 94.7%; With disability: 17.6%; Veterans: 9.0%; Ancestry: 22.6% Irish, 15.2% Italian, 14.4% French, 10.4% German, 10.1% Polish
Employment: 12.9% management, business, and financial, 6.3% computer, engineering, and science, 9.4% education, legal, community service, arts, and media, 4.1% healthcare practitioners, 20.2% service, 26.9% sales and office, 8.3% natural resources, construction, and maintenance, 12.0% production, transportation, and material moving

Income: Per capita: $27,866; Median household: $50,065; Average household: $58,816; Households with income of $100,000 or more: 14.8%; Poverty rate: 14.9%
Educational Attainment: High school diploma or higher: 87.8%; Bachelor's degree or higher: 21.8%; Graduate/professional degree or higher: 8.0%

School District(s)
Cohoes City SD (PK-12)
 Enrollment: 1,961 . . . . (518) 237-0100
North Colonie CSD (KG-12)
 Enrollment: 5,562 . . . . (518) 785-8591
Housing: Homeownership rate: 42.0%; Median home value: $158,400; Median year structure built: Before 1940; Homeowner vacancy rate: 0.0%; Median selected monthly owner costs: $1,437 with a mortgage, $543 without a mortgage; Median gross rent: $859 per month; Rental vacancy rate: 5.7%
Health Insurance: 93.9% have insurance; 68.6% have private insurance; 41.9% have public insurance; 6.1% do not have insurance; 2.7% of children under 18 do not have insurance
Safety: Violent crime rate: 24.1 per 10,000 population; Property crime rate: 117.6 per 10,000 population
Transportation: Commute: 92.2% car, 2.6% public transportation, 1.5% walk, 1.9% work from home; Mean travel time to work: 20.5 minutes
Additional Information Contacts
City of Cohoes. . . . . (518) 233-2121
 http://www.cohoes.com

COLONIE (town).
Covers a land area of 55.943 square miles and a water area of 1.900 square miles. Located at 42.74° N. Lat; 73.79° W. Long. Elevation is 312 feet.
History: Incorporated 1921.
Population: 83,051; Growth (since 2000): 4.8%; Density: 1,484.6 persons per square mile; Race: 80.9% White, 5.9% Black/African American, 8.6% Asian, 0.2% American Indian/Alaska Native, 0.1% Native Hawaiian/Other Pacific Islander, 3.5% Two or more races, 4.5% Hispanic of any race; Average household size: 2.45; Median age: 41.1; Age under 18: 18.6%; Age 65 and over: 17.2%; Males per 100 females: 92.8; Marriage status: 35.3% never married, 49.4% now married, 1.8% separated, 5.8% widowed, 9.5% divorced; Foreign born: 12.0%; Speak English only: 84.9%; With disability: 10.5%; Veterans: 6.8%; Ancestry: 23.8% Irish, 19.1% Italian, 14.8% German, 7.3% English, 6.5% Polish
Employment: 19.3% management, business, and financial, 8.1% computer, engineering, and science, 11.6% education, legal, community service, arts, and media, 7.3% healthcare practitioners, 15.4% service, 26.0% sales and office, 5.0% natural resources, construction, and maintenance, 7.2% production, transportation, and material moving
Income: Per capita: $37,295; Median household: $74,244; Average household: $93,422; Households with income of $100,000 or more: 34.7%; Poverty rate: 6.6%
Educational Attainment: High school diploma or higher: 92.8%; Bachelor's degree or higher: 41.0%; Graduate/professional degree or higher: 18.2%

Four-year College(s)
Siena College (Private, Not-for-profit, Roman Catholic)
 Enrollment: 3,226 . . . . (518) 783-2300
 Tuition: In-state $35,735; Out-of-state $35,735
Housing: Homeownership rate: 68.8%; Median home value: $226,600; Median year structure built: 1968; Homeowner vacancy rate: 0.7%; Median selected monthly owner costs: $1,649 with a mortgage, $571 without a mortgage; Median gross rent: $1,089 per month; Rental vacancy rate: 1.6%
Health Insurance: 96.6% have insurance; 83.5% have private insurance; 29.6% have public insurance; 3.4% do not have insurance; 1.8% of children under 18 do not have insurance
Safety: Violent crime rate: 10.6 per 10,000 population; Property crime rate: 239.2 per 10,000 population
Transportation: Commute: 89.8% car, 2.8% public transportation, 2.2% walk, 3.7% work from home; Mean travel time to work: 19.6 minutes
Additional Information Contacts
Town of Colonie . . . . (518) 783-2700
 http://www.colonie.org

COLONIE (village).
Covers a land area of 3.242 square miles and a water area of 0.003 square miles. Located at 42.72° N. Lat; 73.83° W. Long. Elevation is 312 feet.
Population: 7,856; Growth (since 2000): -0.8%; Density: 2,423.5 persons per square mile; Race: 82.9% White, 2.8% Black/African American, 8.4% Asian, 0.2% American Indian/Alaska Native, 0.0% Native Hawaiian/Other Pacific Islander, 3.9% Two or more races, 4.0% Hispanic of any race; Average household size: 2.55; Median age: 44.5; Age under 18: 16.7%; Age 65 and over: 20.3%; Males per 100 females: 91.4; Marriage status: 31.9% never married, 50.0% now married, 0.8% separated, 7.6% widowed, 10.5% divorced; Foreign born: 10.2%; Speak English only: 85.8%; With disability: 10.2%; Veterans: 5.4%; Ancestry: 21.2% Irish, 19.3% Italian, 16.1% German, 8.8% English, 8.4% Polish
Employment: 12.8% management, business, and financial, 9.0% computer, engineering, and science, 7.9% education, legal, community service, arts, and media, 5.0% healthcare practitioners, 14.0% service, 34.6% sales and office, 6.2% natural resources, construction, and maintenance, 10.6% production, transportation, and material moving
Income: Per capita: $33,128; Median household: $78,431; Average household: $81,485; Households with income of $100,000 or more: 31.7%; Poverty rate: 4.0%
Educational Attainment: High school diploma or higher: 91.8%; Bachelor's degree or higher: 34.2%; Graduate/professional degree or higher: 14.4%

Four-year College(s)
Siena College (Private, Not-for-profit, Roman Catholic)
 Enrollment: 3,226 . . . . (518) 783-2300
 Tuition: In-state $35,735; Out-of-state $35,735
Housing: Homeownership rate: 77.3%; Median home value: $206,900; Median year structure built: 1961; Homeowner vacancy rate: 2.5%; Median selected monthly owner costs: $1,451 with a mortgage, $536 without a mortgage; Median gross rent: $1,170 per month; Rental vacancy rate: 0.0%
Health Insurance: 97.7% have insurance; 80.0% have private insurance; 38.2% have public insurance; 2.3% do not have insurance; 1.0% of children under 18 do not have insurance
Transportation: Commute: 93.2% car, 1.5% public transportation, 2.4% walk, 1.3% work from home; Mean travel time to work: 17.2 minutes
Additional Information Contacts
Village of Colonie . . . . (518) 869-7562
 http://www.colonievillage.org

DELMAR (unincorporated postal area)
ZCTA: 12054
 Covers a land area of 15.447 square miles and a water area of 0.030 square miles. Located at 42.61° N. Lat; 73.86° W. Long. Elevation is 223 feet.
Population: 17,100; Growth (since 2000): 4.1%; Density: 1,107.0 persons per square mile; Race: 92.2% White, 2.8% Black/African American, 2.8% Asian, 0.0% American Indian/Alaska Native, 0.0% Native Hawaiian/Other Pacific Islander, 1.9% Two or more races, 1.5% Hispanic of any race; Average household size: 2.46; Median age: 42.3; Age under 18: 23.4%; Age 65 and over: 16.8%; Males per 100 females: 91.3; Marriage status: 26.8% never married, 57.9% now married, 0.8% separated, 7.4% widowed, 8.0% divorced; Foreign born: 6.0%; Speak English only: 95.9%; With disability: 7.9%; Veterans: 5.6%; Ancestry: 27.5% Irish, 19.5% German, 15.4% Italian, 13.2% English, 7.0% Polish
Employment: 22.1% management, business, and financial, 9.2% computer, engineering, and science, 24.6% education, legal, community service, arts, and media, 8.0% healthcare practitioners, 8.6% service, 19.8% sales and office, 3.6% natural resources, construction, and maintenance, 4.0% production, transportation, and material moving
Income: Per capita: $50,729; Median household: $100,677; Average household: $125,375; Households with income of $100,000 or more: 50.3%; Poverty rate: 4.4%
Educational Attainment: High school diploma or higher: 97.4%; Bachelor's degree or higher: 67.7%; Graduate/professional degree or higher: 38.1%

School District(s)
Bethlehem Central SD (KG-12)
 Enrollment: 4,624 . . . . (518) 439-7098
Housing: Homeownership rate: 73.9%; Median home value: $271,600; Median year structure built: 1962; Homeowner vacancy rate: 1.9%; Median selected monthly owner costs: $2,060 with a mortgage, $832

without a mortgage; Median gross rent: $1,138 per month; Rental vacancy rate: 5.2%

Health Insurance: 98.8% have insurance; 93.4% have private insurance; 21.5% have public insurance; 1.2% do not have insurance; 0.6% of children under 18 do not have insurance

Newspapers: Spotlight LLC (weekly circulation 53,000)

Transportation: Commute: 90.2% car, 1.4% public transportation, 1.0% walk, 6.6% work from home; Mean travel time to work: 20.1 minutes

EAST BERNE (unincorporated postal area)
ZCTA: 12059

Covers a land area of 25.950 square miles and a water area of 0.699 square miles. Located at 42.62° N. Lat; 74.06° W. Long. Elevation is 1,178 feet.

Population: 1,657; Growth (since 2000): -10.1%; Density: 63.9 persons per square mile; Race: 98.4% White, 0.3% Black/African American, 0.5% Asian, 0.0% American Indian/Alaska Native, 0.0% Native Hawaiian/Other Pacific Islander, 0.3% Two or more races, 0.8% Hispanic of any race; Average household size: 2.57; Median age: 48.6; Age under 18: 18.1%; Age 65 and over: 16.1%; Males per 100 females: 105.5; Marriage status: 28.0% never married, 60.4% now married, 2.5% separated, 3.6% widowed, 7.9% divorced; Foreign born: 2.4%; Speak English only: 98.5%; With disability: 10.0%; Veterans: 7.2%; Ancestry: 21.0% German, 19.6% Irish, 16.5% American, 14.7% Italian, 11.7% English

Employment: 19.5% management, business, and financial, 6.1% computer, engineering, and science, 6.4% education, legal, community service, arts, and media, 9.2% healthcare practitioners, 8.9% service, 22.4% sales and office, 19.0% natural resources, construction, and maintenance, 8.6% production, transportation, and material moving

Income: Per capita: $37,010; Median household: $84,091; Average household: $94,543; Households with income of $100,000 or more: 41.4%; Poverty rate: 7.2%

Educational Attainment: High school diploma or higher: 96.4%; Bachelor's degree or higher: 32.2%; Graduate/professional degree or higher: 14.0%

Housing: Homeownership rate: 91.3%; Median home value: $221,100; Median year structure built: 1978; Homeowner vacancy rate: 7.3%; Median selected monthly owner costs: $1,723 with a mortgage, $600 without a mortgage; Median gross rent: $803 per month; Rental vacancy rate: 20.2%

Health Insurance: 96.4% have insurance; 83.5% have private insurance; 28.3% have public insurance; 3.6% do not have insurance; 6.4% of children under 18 do not have insurance

Transportation: Commute: 95.0% car, 0.0% public transportation, 0.7% walk, 1.7% work from home; Mean travel time to work: 35.3 minutes

FEURA BUSH (unincorporated postal area)
ZCTA: 12067

Covers a land area of 21.411 square miles and a water area of 0.197 square miles. Located at 42.56° N. Lat; 73.92° W. Long. Elevation is 266 feet.

Population: 1,619; Growth (since 2000): -12.7%; Density: 75.6 persons per square mile; Race: 99.3% White, 0.0% Black/African American, 0.0% Asian, 0.0% American Indian/Alaska Native, 0.0% Native Hawaiian/Other Pacific Islander, 0.7% Two or more races, 1.5% Hispanic of any race; Average household size: 2.71; Median age: 49.1; Age under 18: 18.1%; Age 65 and over: 20.3%; Males per 100 females: 100.5; Marriage status: 28.6% never married, 56.4% now married, 0.8% separated, 7.8% widowed, 7.3% divorced; Foreign born: 0.0%; Speak English only: 96.0%; With disability: 5.7%; Veterans: 6.9%; Ancestry: 19.8% American, 14.5% Irish, 14.1% Italian, 11.6% German, 11.6% French

Employment: 14.8% management, business, and financial, 5.8% computer, engineering, and science, 18.6% education, legal, community service, arts, and media, 4.4% healthcare practitioners, 9.6% service, 33.1% sales and office, 6.5% natural resources, construction, and maintenance, 7.3% production, transportation, and material moving

Income: Per capita: $32,224; Median household: $75,909; Average household: $83,209; Households with income of $100,000 or more: 29.1%; Poverty rate: 3.7%

Educational Attainment: High school diploma or higher: 97.2%; Bachelor's degree or higher: 29.9%; Graduate/professional degree or higher: 17.6%

Housing: Homeownership rate: 93.3%; Median home value: $238,000; Median year structure built: 1976; Homeowner vacancy rate: 0.0%; Median selected monthly owner costs: $1,844 with a mortgage, $744 without a mortgage; Median gross rent: $1,045 per month; Rental vacancy rate: 0.0%

Health Insurance: 99.3% have insurance; 90.1% have private insurance; 23.8% have public insurance; 0.7% do not have insurance; 0.0% of children under 18 do not have insurance

Transportation: Commute: 93.9% car, 0.0% public transportation, 3.0% walk, 2.2% work from home; Mean travel time to work: 24.2 minutes

GLENMONT (unincorporated postal area)
ZCTA: 12077

Covers a land area of 10.086 square miles and a water area of 0.396 square miles. Located at 42.59° N. Lat; 73.78° W. Long. Elevation is 46 feet.

Population: 6,701; Growth (since 2000): 17.2%; Density: 664.4 persons per square mile; Race: 88.5% White, 2.5% Black/African American, 5.8% Asian, 0.0% American Indian/Alaska Native, 0.0% Native Hawaiian/Other Pacific Islander, 3.2% Two or more races, 1.7% Hispanic of any race; Average household size: 2.61; Median age: 43.2; Age under 18: 23.4%; Age 65 and over: 16.3%; Males per 100 females: 95.4; Marriage status: 30.4% never married, 55.7% now married, 0.8% separated, 5.5% widowed, 8.4% divorced; Foreign born: 7.1%; Speak English only: 88.3%; With disability: 10.8%; Veterans: 7.7%; Ancestry: 24.3% Irish, 16.7% German, 13.2% Italian, 10.8% English, 7.0% American

Employment: 18.5% management, business, and financial, 14.2% computer, engineering, and science, 16.3% education, legal, community service, arts, and media, 7.1% healthcare practitioners, 11.6% service, 23.4% sales and office, 5.4% natural resources, construction, and maintenance, 3.6% production, transportation, and material moving

Income: Per capita: $49,883; Median household: $98,716; Average household: $133,068; Households with income of $100,000 or more: 48.5%; Poverty rate: 7.3%

Educational Attainment: High school diploma or higher: 96.1%; Bachelor's degree or higher: 54.2%; Graduate/professional degree or higher: 32.5%

School District(s)
Bethlehem Central SD (KG-12)
    Enrollment: 4,624 . . . . (518) 439-7098

Housing: Homeownership rate: 76.2%; Median home value: $290,400; Median year structure built: 1987; Homeowner vacancy rate: 2.7%; Median selected monthly owner costs: $2,112 with a mortgage, $949 without a mortgage; Median gross rent: $1,023 per month; Rental vacancy rate: 6.6%

Health Insurance: 94.0% have insurance; 84.0% have private insurance; 24.0% have public insurance; 6.0% do not have insurance; 3.9% of children under 18 do not have insurance

Transportation: Commute: 91.1% car, 0.2% public transportation, 2.2% walk, 6.3% work from home; Mean travel time to work: 22.5 minutes

GREEN ISLAND (town/village). Covers a land area of 0.747 square miles and a water area of 0.186 square miles. Located at 42.75° N. Lat; 73.69° W. Long. Elevation is 23 feet.

Population: 2,621; Growth (since 2000): 15.1%; Density: 3,508.1 persons per square mile; Race: 89.9% White, 4.0% Black/African American, 4.3% Asian, 0.0% American Indian/Alaska Native, 0.0% Native Hawaiian/Other Pacific Islander, 1.9% Two or more races, 9.7% Hispanic of any race; Average household size: 2.17; Median age: 39.4; Age under 18: 16.9%; Age 65 and over: 16.8%; Males per 100 females: 89.7; Marriage status: 46.4% never married, 34.8% now married, 5.1% separated, 4.8% widowed, 14.1% divorced; Foreign born: 5.2%; Speak English only: 89.4%; With disability: 13.0%; Veterans: 8.2%; Ancestry: 26.1% Irish, 18.7% Italian, 13.8% French, 10.0% German, 6.9% Polish

Employment: 13.3% management, business, and financial, 4.9% computer, engineering, and science, 11.8% education, legal, community service, arts, and media, 7.9% healthcare practitioners, 19.7% service, 24.9% sales and office, 9.8% natural resources, construction, and maintenance, 7.7% production, transportation, and material moving

Income: Per capita: $28,686; Median household: $49,875; Average household: $60,806; Households with income of $100,000 or more: 14.3%; Poverty rate: 8.5%

Educational Attainment: High school diploma or higher: 94.2%; Bachelor's degree or higher: 20.3%; Graduate/professional degree or higher: 3.5%

School District(s)

Green Island Union Free SD (PK-12)
Enrollment: 332 . . . . (518) 273-1422

Housing: Homeownership rate: 32.4%; Median home value: $120,800; Median year structure built: Before 1940; Homeowner vacancy rate: 0.0%; Median selected monthly owner costs: $1,365 with a mortgage, $501 without a mortgage; Median gross rent: $825 per month; Rental vacancy rate: 1.6%

Health Insurance: 92.2% have insurance; 69.7% have private insurance; 39.2% have public insurance; 7.8% do not have insurance; 1.8% of children under 18 do not have insurance

Safety: Violent crime rate: 15.4 per 10,000 population; Property crime rate: 115.6 per 10,000 population

Transportation: Commute: 92.4% car, 0.9% public transportation, 4.0% walk, 2.7% work from home; Mean travel time to work: 16.9 minutes

GUILDERLAND (town). Covers a land area of 57.902 square miles and a water area of 0.885 square miles. Located at 42.71° N. Lat; 73.96° W. Long. Elevation is 207 feet.

History: Guilderland is a town in Albany County, New York, named for the Gelderland province in the Netherlands.

Population: 35,745; Growth (since 2000): 9.4%; Density: 617.3 persons per square mile; Race: 84.3% White, 4.5% Black/African American, 8.2% Asian, 0.0% American Indian/Alaska Native, 0.0% Native Hawaiian/Other Pacific Islander, 1.8% Two or more races, 4.0% Hispanic of any race; Average household size: 2.36; Median age: 40.0; Age under 18: 20.0%; Age 65 and over: 16.2%; Males per 100 females: 94.0; Marriage status: 34.9% never married, 50.3% now married, 1.7% separated, 6.0% widowed, 8.7% divorced; Foreign born: 9.0%; Speak English only: 88.8%; With disability: 8.9%; Veterans: 6.1%; Ancestry: 23.1% Irish, 19.4% Italian, 15.6% German, 10.5% English, 6.3% Polish

Employment: 18.7% management, business, and financial, 10.1% computer, engineering, and science, 15.1% education, legal, community service, arts, and media, 7.2% healthcare practitioners, 12.9% service, 25.9% sales and office, 4.5% natural resources, construction, and maintenance, 5.6% production, transportation, and material moving

Income: Per capita: $43,336; Median household: $78,194; Average household: $106,519; Households with income of $100,000 or more: 41.5%; Poverty rate: 4.9%

Educational Attainment: High school diploma or higher: 97.8%; Bachelor's degree or higher: 50.3%; Graduate/professional degree or higher: 26.5%

School District(s)

Guilderland Central SD (KG-12)
Enrollment: 4,879 . . . . (518) 456-6200

Housing: Homeownership rate: 65.8%; Median home value: $251,500; Median year structure built: 1976; Homeowner vacancy rate: 0.7%; Median selected monthly owner costs: $1,876 with a mortgage, $657 without a mortgage; Median gross rent: $1,145 per month; Rental vacancy rate: 6.6%

Health Insurance: 96.8% have insurance; 86.9% have private insurance; 25.1% have public insurance; 3.2% do not have insurance; 0.9% of children under 18 do not have insurance

Safety: Violent crime rate: 7.9 per 10,000 population; Property crime rate: 200.9 per 10,000 population

Transportation: Commute: 89.9% car, 1.4% public transportation, 2.2% walk, 4.6% work from home; Mean travel time to work: 21.4 minutes

Additional Information Contacts

Town of Guilderland . . . . (518) 356-1980
http://www.townofguilderland.org

GUILDERLAND CENTER (unincorporated postal area)
ZCTA: 12085

Covers a land area of 0.176 square miles and a water area of 0 square miles. Located at 42.70° N. Lat; 73.96° W. Long. Elevation is 318 feet.

Population: 448; Growth (since 2000): n/a; Density: 2,551.7 persons per square mile; Race: 82.8% White, 2.7% Black/African American, 0.0% Asian, 0.0% American Indian/Alaska Native, 0.0% Native Hawaiian/Other Pacific Islander, 7.6% Two or more races, 9.6% Hispanic of any race; Average household size: 2.54; Median age: 32.9; Age under 18: 27.0%; Age 65 and over: 20.8%; Males per 100 females: 59.1; Marriage status: 33.3% never married, 31.9% now married, 8.0%

separated, 26.3% widowed, 8.6% divorced; Foreign born: 12.5%; Speak English only: 86.8%; With disability: 11.5%; Veterans: 1.5%; Ancestry: 13.8% German, 13.8% Irish, 13.4% Italian, 9.6% English, 5.8% Dutch

Employment: 4.2% management, business, and financial, 3.7% computer, engineering, and science, 6.3% education, legal, community service, arts, and media, 4.2% healthcare practitioners, 22.8% service, 58.7% sales and office, 0.0% natural resources, construction, and maintenance, 0.0% production, transportation, and material moving

Income: Per capita: $17,054; Median household: $43,710; Average household: $46,736; Households with income of $100,000 or more: 7.1%; Poverty rate: 7.3%

Educational Attainment: High school diploma or higher: 98.2%; Bachelor's degree or higher: 20.0%; Graduate/professional degree or higher: 2.1%

School District(s)

Guilderland Central SD (KG-12)
Enrollment: 4,879 . . . . (518) 456-6200

Housing: Homeownership rate: 10.7%; Median home value: n/a; Median year structure built: 1965; Homeowner vacancy rate: 0.0%; Median selected monthly owner costs: $0 with a mortgage, $0 without a mortgage; Median gross rent: $1,098 per month; Rental vacancy rate: 19.9%

Health Insurance: 90.7% have insurance; 66.5% have private insurance; 24.2% have public insurance; 9.3% do not have insurance; 0.0% of children under 18 do not have insurance

Transportation: Commute: 100.0% car, 0.0% public transportation, 0.0% walk, 0.0% work from home; Mean travel time to work: 22.0 minutes

KNOX (town). Covers a land area of 41.762 square miles and a water area of 0.174 square miles. Located at 42.69° N. Lat; 74.11° W. Long. Elevation is 1,234 feet.

Population: 2,818; Growth (since 2000): 6.5%; Density: 67.5 persons per square mile; Race: 98.9% White, 0.5% Black/African American, 0.2% Asian, 0.2% American Indian/Alaska Native, 0.0% Native Hawaiian/Other Pacific Islander, 0.1% Two or more races, 0.0% Hispanic of any race; Average household size: 2.87; Median age: 41.0; Age under 18: 21.1%; Age 65 and over: 11.7%; Males per 100 females: 103.2; Marriage status: 30.4% never married, 58.8% now married, 1.3% separated, 1.9% widowed, 8.9% divorced; Foreign born: 2.1%; Speak English only: 96.5%; With disability: 10.6%; Veterans: 7.7%; Ancestry: 22.2% Irish, 20.5% German, 18.9% Italian, 13.6% English, 10.5% Dutch

Employment: 19.1% management, business, and financial, 6.7% computer, engineering, and science, 12.3% education, legal, community service, arts, and media, 5.2% healthcare practitioners, 14.8% service, 22.1% sales and office, 11.2% natural resources, construction, and maintenance, 8.7% production, transportation, and material moving

Income: Per capita: $33,480; Median household: $82,056; Average household: $95,032; Households with income of $100,000 or more: 41.0%; Poverty rate: 3.8%

Educational Attainment: High school diploma or higher: 95.7%; Bachelor's degree or higher: 33.4%; Graduate/professional degree or higher: 13.7%

Housing: Homeownership rate: 89.7%; Median home value: $229,700; Median year structure built: 1972; Homeowner vacancy rate: 2.2%; Median selected monthly owner costs: $1,603 with a mortgage, $719 without a mortgage; Median gross rent: $1,006 per month; Rental vacancy rate: 12.2%

Health Insurance: 93.6% have insurance; 82.9% have private insurance; 22.8% have public insurance; 6.4% do not have insurance; 4.8% of children under 18 do not have insurance

Transportation: Commute: 92.5% car, 0.0% public transportation, 4.0% walk, 3.1% work from home; Mean travel time to work: 31.3 minutes

Additional Information Contacts

Town of Knox . . . . (518) 872-2551
http://www.knoxny.org

LATHAM (unincorporated postal area)
ZCTA: 12110

Covers a land area of 14.686 square miles and a water area of 0.450 square miles. Located at 42.75° N. Lat; 73.78° W. Long. Elevation is 354 feet.

Population: 22,684; Growth (since 2000): 10.9%; Density: 1,544.6 persons per square mile; Race: 81.0% White, 4.6% Black/African American, 9.2% Asian, 0.2% American Indian/Alaska Native, 0.3%

Native Hawaiian/Other Pacific Islander, 3.2% Two or more races, 6.5% Hispanic of any race; Average household size: 2.56; Median age: 37.9; Age under 18: 17.1%; Age 65 and over: 15.2%; Males per 100 females: 94.3; Marriage status: 41.0% never married, 46.6% now married, 2.4% separated, 4.3% widowed, 8.1% divorced; Foreign born: 12.5%; Speak English only: 82.3%; With disability: 9.4%; Veterans: 6.4%; Ancestry: 26.4% Irish, 21.0% Italian, 13.7% German, 6.6% English, 5.8% Polish
Employment: 18.9% management, business, and financial, 7.5% computer, engineering, and science, 12.3% education, legal, community service, arts, and media, 14.7% healthcare practitioners, 8.2% service, 27.0% sales and office, 5.6% natural resources, construction, and maintenance, 5.7% production, transportation, and material moving
Income: Per capita: $32,198; Median household: $76,652; Average household: $91,838; Households with income of $100,000 or more: 36.0%; Poverty rate: 6.9%
Educational Attainment: High school diploma or higher: 94.4%; Bachelor's degree or higher: 41.0%; Graduate/professional degree or higher: 19.3%

School District(s)
North Colonie CSD (KG-12)
    Enrollment: 5,562 . . . . (518) 785-8591

Four-year College(s)
Aesthetic Science Institute (Private, For-profit)
    Enrollment: 70 . . . . (518) 786-0760
John Paolo's Xtreme Beauty Institute-Goldwell Product Artistry (Private, For-profit)
    Enrollment: n/a . . . . (518) 783-0808

Two-year College(s)
Aesthetic Science Institute (Private, For-profit)
    Enrollment: 70 . . . . (518) 786-0760
John Paolo's Xtreme Beauty Institute-Goldwell Product Artistry (Private, For-profit)
    Enrollment: n/a . . . . (518) 783-0808

Vocational/Technical School(s)
Aesthetic Science Institute (Private, For-profit)
    Enrollment: 70 . . . . (518) 786-0760
    2016-17 Tuition: $8,500
John Paolo's Xtreme Beauty Institute-Goldwell Product Artistry (Private, For-profit)
    Enrollment: n/a . . . . (518) 783-0808
    2016-17 Tuition: $13,500
Housing: Homeownership rate: 69.9%; Median home value: $239,200; Median year structure built: 1968; Homeowner vacancy rate: 0.2%; Median selected monthly owner costs: $1,692 with a mortgage, $559 without a mortgage; Median gross rent: $1,202 per month; Rental vacancy rate: 0.0%
Health Insurance: 95.6% have insurance; 84.6% have private insurance; 26.6% have public insurance; 4.4% do not have insurance; 2.9% of children under 18 do not have insurance
Transportation: Commute: 88.6% car, 1.3% public transportation, 4.2% walk, 3.0% work from home; Mean travel time to work: 18.5 minutes

MEDUSA (unincorporated postal area)
ZCTA: 12120
    Covers a land area of 17.511 square miles and a water area of 0.063 square miles. Located at 42.45° N. Lat; 74.15° W. Long. Elevation is 804 feet.
Population: 587; Growth (since 2000): 8.9%; Density: 33.5 persons per square mile; Race: 97.3% White, 0.7% Black/African American, 0.0% Asian, 0.0% American Indian/Alaska Native, 0.0% Native Hawaiian/Other Pacific Islander, 2.0% Two or more races, 2.7% Hispanic of any race; Average household size: 2.46; Median age: 49.6; Age under 18: 18.2%; Age 65 and over: 25.2%; Males per 100 females: 103.7; Marriage status: 29.2% never married, 51.9% now married, 0.0% separated, 7.8% widowed, 11.1% divorced; Foreign born: 1.5%; Speak English only: 97.2%; With disability: 11.1%; Veterans: 10.8%; Ancestry: 28.6% American, 18.7% Irish, 15.8% German, 14.3% Italian, 7.2% Dutch
Employment: 27.9% management, business, and financial, 7.3% computer, engineering, and science, 4.2% education, legal, community service, arts, and media, 10.7% healthcare practitioners, 9.9% service, 14.5% sales and office, 12.2% natural resources, construction, and maintenance, 13.4% production, transportation, and material moving

Income: Per capita: $32,615; Median household: $49,732; Average household: $76,634; Households with income of $100,000 or more: 30.6%; Poverty rate: 13.1%
Educational Attainment: High school diploma or higher: 90.6%; Bachelor's degree or higher: 19.2%; Graduate/professional degree or higher: 12.7%
Housing: Homeownership rate: 83.7%; Median home value: $170,800; Median year structure built: 1979; Homeowner vacancy rate: 0.0%; Median selected monthly owner costs: $1,569 with a mortgage, $618 without a mortgage; Median gross rent: $863 per month; Rental vacancy rate: 0.0%
Health Insurance: 96.9% have insurance; 79.9% have private insurance; 34.4% have public insurance; 3.1% do not have insurance; 0.0% of children under 18 do not have insurance
Transportation: Commute: 90.4% car, 1.7% public transportation, 1.7% walk, 6.1% work from home; Mean travel time to work: 31.9 minutes

MENANDS (village). Covers a land area of 3.058 square miles and a water area of 0.251 square miles. Located at 42.69° N. Lat; 73.73° W. Long. Elevation is 36 feet.
History: Incorporated 1924.
Population: 3,977; Growth (since 2000): 1.7%; Density: 1,300.5 persons per square mile; Race: 57.4% White, 16.0% Black/African American, 17.2% Asian, 0.0% American Indian/Alaska Native, 0.0% Native Hawaiian/Other Pacific Islander, 8.7% Two or more races, 8.8% Hispanic of any race; Average household size: 2.34; Median age: 34.2; Age under 18: 26.1%; Age 65 and over: 12.0%; Males per 100 females: 91.1; Marriage status: 37.4% never married, 47.4% now married, 2.8% separated, 2.8% widowed, 12.4% divorced; Foreign born: 22.2%; Speak English only: 81.6%; With disability: 9.0%; Veterans: 4.7%; Ancestry: 26.6% Irish, 13.8% Italian, 9.6% German, 5.4% English, 4.1% American
Employment: 21.0% management, business, and financial, 15.9% computer, engineering, and science, 15.6% education, legal, community service, arts, and media, 3.9% healthcare practitioners, 10.2% service, 30.0% sales and office, 1.9% natural resources, construction, and maintenance, 1.5% production, transportation, and material moving
Income: Per capita: $38,545; Median household: $65,297; Average household: $90,530; Households with income of $100,000 or more: 23.8%; Poverty rate: 14.6%
Educational Attainment: High school diploma or higher: 96.5%; Bachelor's degree or higher: 67.9%; Graduate/professional degree or higher: 32.1%

School District(s)
Menands Union Free SD (KG-08)
    Enrollment: 264 . . . . (518) 465-4561
Housing: Homeownership rate: 37.3%; Median home value: $204,100; Median year structure built: 1966; Homeowner vacancy rate: 0.0%; Median selected monthly owner costs: $1,626 with a mortgage, $721 without a mortgage; Median gross rent: $1,159 per month; Rental vacancy rate: 0.0%
Health Insurance: 98.6% have insurance; 84.6% have private insurance; 25.7% have public insurance; 1.4% do not have insurance; 0.0% of children under 18 do not have insurance
Safety: Violent crime rate: 25.3 per 10,000 population; Property crime rate: 381.3 per 10,000 population
Transportation: Commute: 84.2% car, 5.3% public transportation, 5.7% walk, 4.8% work from home; Mean travel time to work: 16.5 minutes
Additional Information Contacts
Village of Menands . . . . (518) 434-2922
    http://www.villageofmenands.com

NEW SCOTLAND (town). Covers a land area of 57.499 square miles and a water area of 0.470 square miles. Located at 42.60° N. Lat; 73.94° W. Long. Elevation is 282 feet.
Population: 8,783; Growth (since 2000): 1.8%; Density: 152.8 persons per square mile; Race: 96.1% White, 0.2% Black/African American, 1.7% Asian, 0.0% American Indian/Alaska Native, 0.0% Native Hawaiian/Other Pacific Islander, 1.9% Two or more races, 3.3% Hispanic of any race; Average household size: 2.62; Median age: 46.2; Age under 18: 21.2%; Age 65 and over: 16.6%; Males per 100 females: 98.4; Marriage status: 27.7% never married, 60.4% now married, 1.2% separated, 4.0% widowed, 7.9% divorced; Foreign born: 4.3%; Speak English only: 93.5%; With disability: 8.0%; Veterans: 6.5%; Ancestry: 25.2% Irish, 23.0% German, 18.3% Italian, 8.5% English, 6.7% American

Employment: 22.7% management, business, and financial, 6.0% computer, engineering, and science, 14.4% education, legal, community service, arts, and media, 3.9% healthcare practitioners, 10.5% service, 26.5% sales and office, 7.5% natural resources, construction, and maintenance, 8.4% production, transportation, and material moving
Income: Per capita: $42,961; Median household: $90,370; Average household: $111,029; Households with income of $100,000 or more: 43.0%; Poverty rate: 3.7%
Educational Attainment: High school diploma or higher: 95.5%; Bachelor's degree or higher: 45.1%; Graduate/professional degree or higher: 22.7%
Housing: Homeownership rate: 86.7%; Median home value: $247,000; Median year structure built: 1967; Homeowner vacancy rate: 1.4%; Median selected monthly owner costs: $1,843 with a mortgage, $716 without a mortgage; Median gross rent: $964 per month; Rental vacancy rate: 0.0%
Health Insurance: 98.6% have insurance; 89.7% have private insurance; 24.3% have public insurance; 1.4% do not have insurance; 0.0% of children under 18 do not have insurance
Transportation: Commute: 92.8% car, 0.8% public transportation, 1.5% walk, 4.2% work from home; Mean travel time to work: 23.6 minutes
Additional Information Contacts
Town of New Scotland . . . . (518) 439-4865
  http://www.townofnewscotland.com

PRESTON HOLLOW (unincorporated postal area)
ZCTA: 12469
Covers a land area of 33.905 square miles and a water area of 0.020 square miles. Located at 42.45° N. Lat; 74.24° W. Long. Elevation is 846 feet.
Population: 627; Growth (since 2000): -19.9%; Density: 18.5 persons per square mile; Race: 98.6% White, 0.0% Black/African American, 0.0% Asian, 0.0% American Indian/Alaska Native, 0.0% Native Hawaiian/Other Pacific Islander, 1.0% Two or more races, 4.0% Hispanic of any race; Average household size: 2.32; Median age: 49.6; Age under 18: 16.3%; Age 65 and over: 21.5%; Males per 100 females: 102.7; Marriage status: 27.2% never married, 53.4% now married, 3.5% separated, 4.2% widowed, 15.2% divorced; Foreign born: 14.2%; Speak English only: 83.5%; With disability: 11.6%; Veterans: 10.9%; Ancestry: 18.0% American, 17.2% Irish, 13.4% German, 13.1% Italian, 9.9% English
Employment: 13.5% management, business, and financial, 2.0% computer, engineering, and science, 5.0% education, legal, community service, arts, and media, 2.3% healthcare practitioners, 6.3% service, 24.8% sales and office, 28.1% natural resources, construction, and maintenance, 18.2% production, transportation, and material moving
Income: Per capita: $27,646; Median household: $49,500; Average household: $62,107; Households with income of $100,000 or more: 17.8%; Poverty rate: 4.6%
Educational Attainment: High school diploma or higher: 84.6%; Bachelor's degree or higher: 15.8%; Graduate/professional degree or higher: 7.3%
Housing: Homeownership rate: 92.6%; Median home value: $153,400; Median year structure built: 1969; Homeowner vacancy rate: 15.3%; Median selected monthly owner costs: $1,449 with a mortgage, $417 without a mortgage; Median gross rent: n/a per month; Rental vacancy rate: 0.0%
Health Insurance: 92.3% have insurance; 68.6% have private insurance; 39.9% have public insurance; 7.7% do not have insurance; 0.0% of children under 18 do not have insurance
Transportation: Commute: 83.5% car, 2.3% public transportation, 3.6% walk, 5.6% work from home; Mean travel time to work: 34.2 minutes

PRESTON-POTTER HOLLOW (CDP). Covers a land area of 10.134 square miles and a water area of 0 square miles. Located at 42.43° N. Lat; 74.23° W. Long. Elevation is 860 feet.
Population: 340; Growth (since 2000): -9.1%; Density: 33.5 persons per square mile; Race: 98.8% White, 0.0% Black/African American, 0.0% Asian, 0.0% American Indian/Alaska Native, 0.0% Native Hawaiian/Other Pacific Islander, 1.2% Two or more races, 0.0% Hispanic of any race; Average household size: 2.43; Median age: 49.4; Age under 18: 16.5%; Age 65 and over: 23.5%; Males per 100 females: 95.7; Marriage status: 29.4% never married, 58.4% now married, 1.4% separated, 3.7% widowed, 8.4% divorced; Foreign born: 12.4%; Speak English only: 86.0%; With disability: 11.5%; Veterans: 14.4%; Ancestry: 22.1% American, 12.9% Irish, 10.9% German, 9.1% English, 7.1% Other Arab

Employment: 19.4% management, business, and financial, 0.0% computer, engineering, and science, 5.2% education, legal, community service, arts, and media, 0.0% healthcare practitioners, 0.0% service, 23.2% sales and office, 34.8% natural resources, construction, and maintenance, 17.4% production, transportation, and material moving
Income: Per capita: $26,709; Median household: $49,000; Average household: $61,849; Households with income of $100,000 or more: 20.7%; Poverty rate: 7.1%
Educational Attainment: High school diploma or higher: 85.6%; Bachelor's degree or higher: 14.4%; Graduate/professional degree or higher: 7.2%
Housing: Homeownership rate: 89.3%; Median home value: $143,800; Median year structure built: 1961; Homeowner vacancy rate: 12.0%; Median selected monthly owner costs: $1,563 with a mortgage, $378 without a mortgage; Median gross rent: n/a per month; Rental vacancy rate: 0.0%
Health Insurance: 90.3% have insurance; 67.6% have private insurance; 40.9% have public insurance; 9.7% do not have insurance; 0.0% of children under 18 do not have insurance
Transportation: Commute: 79.4% car, 4.5% public transportation, 5.2% walk, 7.1% work from home; Mean travel time to work: 33.3 minutes

RAVENA (village). Covers a land area of 1.467 square miles and a water area of 0.005 square miles. Located at 42.48° N. Lat; 73.81° W. Long. Elevation is 230 feet.
History: Incorporated 1914.
Population: 3,266; Growth (since 2000): -3.1%; Density: 2,226.2 persons per square mile; Race: 91.9% White, 6.8% Black/African American, 0.0% Asian, 0.0% American Indian/Alaska Native, 0.0% Native Hawaiian/Other Pacific Islander, 1.3% Two or more races, 1.3% Hispanic of any race; Average household size: 2.40; Median age: 40.8; Age under 18: 20.7%; Age 65 and over: 15.1%; Males per 100 females: 94.2; Marriage status: 36.5% never married, 47.1% now married, 2.1% separated, 6.3% widowed, 10.1% divorced; Foreign born: 0.9%; Speak English only: 98.2%; With disability: 11.8%; Veterans: 7.3%; Ancestry: 24.2% American, 20.6% Irish, 17.8% Italian, 13.6% German, 5.8% English
Employment: 14.8% management, business, and financial, 7.4% computer, engineering, and science, 10.8% education, legal, community service, arts, and media, 3.4% healthcare practitioners, 14.9% service, 25.4% sales and office, 3.9% natural resources, construction, and maintenance, 19.5% production, transportation, and material moving
Income: Per capita: $26,838; Median household: $52,500; Average household: $62,691; Households with income of $100,000 or more: 14.0%; Poverty rate: 9.5%
Educational Attainment: High school diploma or higher: 90.7%; Bachelor's degree or higher: 21.1%; Graduate/professional degree or higher: 5.9%
School District(s)
Ravena-Coeymans-Selkirk Central SD (PK-12)
  Enrollment: 1,884 . . . . (518) 756-5200
Housing: Homeownership rate: 61.0%; Median home value: $162,200; Median year structure built: 1958; Homeowner vacancy rate: 3.0%; Median selected monthly owner costs: $1,441 with a mortgage, $555 without a mortgage; Median gross rent: $869 per month; Rental vacancy rate: 10.3%
Health Insurance: 90.0% have insurance; 72.8% have private insurance; 31.4% have public insurance; 10.0% do not have insurance; 4.8% of children under 18 do not have insurance
Transportation: Commute: 95.3% car, 0.0% public transportation, 0.5% walk, 1.0% work from home; Mean travel time to work: 26.8 minutes

RENSSELAERVILLE (town). Covers a land area of 61.464 square miles and a water area of 0.420 square miles. Located at 42.48° N. Lat; 74.18° W. Long. Elevation is 1,365 feet.
Population: 1,752; Growth (since 2000): -8.5%; Density: 28.5 persons per square mile; Race: 97.1% White, 1.0% Black/African American, 0.0% Asian, 0.0% American Indian/Alaska Native, 0.0% Native Hawaiian/Other Pacific Islander, 1.9% Two or more races, 2.2% Hispanic of any race; Average household size: 2.41; Median age: 49.2; Age under 18: 19.6%; Age 65 and over: 24.7%; Males per 100 females: 103.6; Marriage status: 27.5% never married, 56.9% now married, 1.7% separated, 7.0% widowed, 8.5% divorced; Foreign born: 5.1%; Speak English only: 93.8%; With disability: 13.5%; Veterans: 11.0%; Ancestry: 24.9% American, 15.9% Irish, 14.8% German, 9.9% Italian, 8.0% Dutch
Employment: 21.0% management, business, and financial, 6.1% computer, engineering, and science, 8.0% education, legal, community

service, arts, and media, 5.2% healthcare practitioners, 9.7% service, 15.9% sales and office, 17.4% natural resources, construction, and maintenance, 16.8% production, transportation, and material moving
Income: Per capita: $32,538; Median household: $57,375; Average household: $76,559; Households with income of $100,000 or more: 30.9%; Poverty rate: 11.3%
Educational Attainment: High school diploma or higher: 91.0%; Bachelor's degree or higher: 24.8%; Graduate/professional degree or higher: 15.3%
Housing: Homeownership rate: 88.6%; Median home value: $180,000; Median year structure built: 1967; Homeowner vacancy rate: 5.8%; Median selected monthly owner costs: $1,607 with a mortgage, $581 without a mortgage; Median gross rent: $907 per month; Rental vacancy rate: 0.0%
Health Insurance: 95.6% have insurance; 78.4% have private insurance; 35.0% have public insurance; 4.4% do not have insurance; 1.9% of children under 18 do not have insurance
Transportation: Commute: 85.6% car, 1.4% public transportation, 1.6% walk, 5.4% work from home; Mean travel time to work: 34.3 minutes

SELKIRK (unincorporated postal area)
ZCTA: 12158
Covers a land area of 30.595 square miles and a water area of 0.943 square miles. Located at 42.54° N. Lat; 73.82° W. Long. Elevation is 161 feet.
Population: 7,116; Growth (since 2000): 23.1%; Density: 232.6 persons per square mile; Race: 95.0% White, 0.8% Black/African American, 2.1% Asian, 0.1% American Indian/Alaska Native, 0.0% Native Hawaiian/Other Pacific Islander, 1.7% Two or more races, 1.3% Hispanic of any race; Average household size: 2.74; Median age: 40.0; Age under 18: 22.2%; Age 65 and over: 11.4%; Males per 100 females: 98.3; Marriage status: 32.6% never married, 56.7% now married, 0.5% separated, 4.0% widowed, 6.8% divorced; Foreign born: 3.2%; Speak English only: 94.3%; With disability: 8.7%; Veterans: 7.1%; Ancestry: 21.4% German, 21.2% Irish, 18.8% Italian, 11.2% American, 9.4% English
Employment: 16.3% management, business, and financial, 5.3% computer, engineering, and science, 13.6% education, legal, community service, arts, and media, 6.3% healthcare practitioners, 14.2% service, 25.7% sales and office, 7.6% natural resources, construction, and maintenance, 11.0% production, transportation, and material moving
Income: Per capita: $37,901; Median household: $85,458; Average household: $101,773; Households with income of $100,000 or more: 42.0%; Poverty rate: 8.4%
Educational Attainment: High school diploma or higher: 95.8%; Bachelor's degree or higher: 32.2%; Graduate/professional degree or higher: 17.1%
School District(s)
Ravena-Coeymans-Selkirk Central SD (PK-12)
    Enrollment: 1,884 . . . . (518) 756-5200
Housing: Homeownership rate: 80.4%; Median home value: $220,400; Median year structure built: 1981; Homeowner vacancy rate: 0.0%; Median selected monthly owner costs: $1,713 with a mortgage, $618 without a mortgage; Median gross rent: $1,062 per month; Rental vacancy rate: 11.4%
Health Insurance: 98.5% have insurance; 91.0% have private insurance; 18.2% have public insurance; 1.5% do not have insurance; 0.0% of children under 18 do not have insurance
Transportation: Commute: 91.5% car, 0.9% public transportation, 3.5% walk, 1.9% work from home; Mean travel time to work: 23.7 minutes

SLINGERLANDS (unincorporated postal area)
ZCTA: 12159
Covers a land area of 14.088 square miles and a water area of 0.044 square miles. Located at 42.65° N. Lat; 73.89° W. Long. Elevation is 220 feet.
Population: 7,614; Growth (since 2000): -0.4%; Density: 540.4 persons per square mile; Race: 88.7% White, 0.9% Black/African American, 8.3% Asian, 0.1% American Indian/Alaska Native, 0.0% Native Hawaiian/Other Pacific Islander, 2.0% Two or more races, 1.8% Hispanic of any race; Average household size: 2.28; Median age: 48.6; Age under 18: 20.5%; Age 65 and over: 23.6%; Males per 100 females: 89.1; Marriage status: 24.7% never married, 59.0% now married, 0.9% separated, 8.4% widowed, 7.9% divorced; Foreign born: 10.2%; Speak English only: 88.1%; With disability: 11.8%; Veterans: 5.1%; Ancestry:

27.6% Irish, 17.5% Italian, 14.6% German, 14.0% English, 5.9% American
Employment: 29.1% management, business, and financial, 6.0% computer, engineering, and science, 18.9% education, legal, community service, arts, and media, 8.4% healthcare practitioners, 10.8% service, 20.9% sales and office, 2.4% natural resources, construction, and maintenance, 3.3% production, transportation, and material moving
Income: Per capita: $60,495; Median household: $86,991; Average household: $138,821; Households with income of $100,000 or more: 45.7%; Poverty rate: 2.5%
Educational Attainment: High school diploma or higher: 97.2%; Bachelor's degree or higher: 62.6%; Graduate/professional degree or higher: 36.6%
Housing: Homeownership rate: 74.0%; Median home value: $342,200; Median year structure built: 1988; Homeowner vacancy rate: 0.4%; Median selected monthly owner costs: $2,331 with a mortgage, $1,070 without a mortgage; Median gross rent: $1,093 per month; Rental vacancy rate: 0.0%
Health Insurance: 97.8% have insurance; 91.3% have private insurance; 27.9% have public insurance; 2.2% do not have insurance; 0.0% of children under 18 do not have insurance
Transportation: Commute: 91.6% car, 1.5% public transportation, 1.2% walk, 4.6% work from home; Mean travel time to work: 21.0 minutes

SOUTH BETHLEHEM (unincorporated postal area)
ZCTA: 12161
Covers a land area of 0.409 square miles and a water area of 0.006 square miles. Located at 42.53° N. Lat; 73.85° W. Long. Elevation is 213 feet.
Population: 187; Growth (since 2000): n/a; Density: 456.9 persons per square mile; Race: 100.0% White, 0.0% Black/African American, 0.0% Asian, 0.0% American Indian/Alaska Native, 0.0% Native Hawaiian/Other Pacific Islander, 0.0% Two or more races, 0.0% Hispanic of any race; Average household size: 2.28; Median age: 34.0; Age under 18: 15.5%; Age 65 and over: 0.0%; Males per 100 females: 102.5; Marriage status: 79.1% never married, 13.9% now married, 0.0% separated, 0.0% widowed, 7.0% divorced; Foreign born: 0.0%; Speak English only: 100.0%; With disability: 0.0%; Veterans: 0.0%; Ancestry: 49.2% Italian, 33.7% Norwegian, 29.9% German, 20.9% English, 15.5% French
Employment: 9.0% management, business, and financial, 0.0% computer, engineering, and science, 0.0% education, legal, community service, arts, and media, 9.0% healthcare practitioners, 0.0% service, 0.0% sales and office, 82.1% natural resources, construction, and maintenance, 0.0% production, transportation, and material moving
Income: Per capita: $37,228; Median household: $78,750; Average household: $82,283; Households with income of $100,000 or more: 15.9%; Poverty rate: n/a
Educational Attainment: High school diploma or higher: 100.0%; Bachelor's degree or higher: 16.5%; Graduate/professional degree or higher: n/a
Housing: Homeownership rate: 84.1%; Median home value: n/a; Median year structure built: 1983; Homeowner vacancy rate: 0.0%; Median selected monthly owner costs: $0 with a mortgage, $0 without a mortgage; Median gross rent: n/a per month; Rental vacancy rate: 0.0%
Health Insurance: 59.4% have insurance; 59.4% have private insurance; 8.6% have public insurance; 40.6% do not have insurance; 0.0% of children under 18 do not have insurance
Transportation: Commute: 100.0% car, 0.0% public transportation, 0.0% walk, 0.0% work from home; Mean travel time to work: 0.0 minutes

VOORHEESVILLE (village). Covers a land area of 2.139 square miles and a water area of 0.005 square miles. Located at 42.65° N. Lat; 73.93° W. Long. Elevation is 338 feet.
Population: 2,829; Growth (since 2000): 4.6%; Density: 1,322.7 persons per square mile; Race: 95.9% White, 0.7% Black/African American, 2.3% Asian, 0.0% American Indian/Alaska Native, 0.0% Native Hawaiian/Other Pacific Islander, 1.1% Two or more races, 4.0% Hispanic of any race; Average household size: 2.54; Median age: 44.6; Age under 18: 24.0%; Age 65 and over: 17.9%; Males per 100 females: 94.8; Marriage status: 24.1% never married, 61.2% now married, 1.4% separated, 5.5% widowed, 9.2% divorced; Foreign born: 5.7%; Speak English only: 91.7%; With disability: 8.3%; Veterans: 7.5%; Ancestry: 28.8% Irish, 22.5% German, 21.8% Italian, 9.9% English, 6.5% Polish

Employment: 23.5% management, business, and financial, 6.6% computer, engineering, and science, 16.2% education, legal, community service, arts, and media, 2.9% healthcare practitioners, 9.9% service, 27.5% sales and office, 6.3% natural resources, construction, and maintenance, 7.0% production, transportation, and material moving
Income: Per capita: $41,628; Median household: $90,888; Average household: $105,800; Households with income of $100,000 or more: 40.8%; Poverty rate: 3.7%
Educational Attainment: High school diploma or higher: 97.9%; Bachelor's degree or higher: 54.1%; Graduate/professional degree or higher: 24.4%

School District(s)
Voorheesville Central SD (KG-12)
    Enrollment: 1,194 . . . . (518) 765-3313
Housing: Homeownership rate: 82.1%; Median home value: $230,100; Median year structure built: 1968; Homeowner vacancy rate: 0.0%; Median selected monthly owner costs: $1,794 with a mortgage, $739 without a mortgage; Median gross rent: $958 per month; Rental vacancy rate: 0.0%
Health Insurance: 98.4% have insurance; 89.1% have private insurance; 25.7% have public insurance; 1.6% do not have insurance; 0.0% of children under 18 do not have insurance
Transportation: Commute: 93.4% car, 1.0% public transportation, 1.3% walk, 4.1% work from home; Mean travel time to work: 24.8 minutes

WATERVLIET (city).
Covers a land area of 1.345 square miles and a water area of 0.130 square miles. Located at 42.72° N. Lat; 73.71° W. Long. Elevation is 30 feet.
History: The U.S. Watervliet Arsenal here, which specializes in the production of heavy ordnance, was established 1813. In 1776, Ann Lee founded the first American community of Shakers (United Society of Believers) in Watervliet. Founded by the Dutch 1735, Incorporated as a city 1896.
Population: 10,201; Growth (since 2000): -0.1%; Density: 7,581.6 persons per square mile; Race: 78.6% White, 10.6% Black/African American, 3.7% Asian, 0.0% American Indian/Alaska Native, 0.0% Native Hawaiian/Other Pacific Islander, 5.8% Two or more races, 5.5% Hispanic of any race; Average household size: 2.22; Median age: 37.6; Age under 18: 19.7%; Age 65 and over: 12.5%; Males per 100 females: 92.9; Marriage status: 45.8% never married, 38.2% now married, 3.7% separated, 5.7% widowed, 10.3% divorced; Foreign born: 7.7%; Speak English only: 89.6%; With disability: 17.6%; Veterans: 7.6%; Ancestry: 25.7% Irish, 16.5% Italian, 11.8% German, 6.7% English, 5.9% Polish
Employment: 11.4% management, business, and financial, 4.6% computer, engineering, and science, 7.6% education, legal, community service, arts, and media, 5.3% healthcare practitioners, 22.5% service, 28.0% sales and office, 4.7% natural resources, construction, and maintenance, 15.8% production, transportation, and material moving
Income: Per capita: $26,308; Median household: $49,887; Average household: $57,549; Households with income of $100,000 or more: 11.4%; Poverty rate: 16.2%
Educational Attainment: High school diploma or higher: 87.6%; Bachelor's degree or higher: 23.8%; Graduate/professional degree or higher: 7.7%

School District(s)
Watervliet City SD (PK-12)
    Enrollment: 1,316 . . . . (518) 629-3201
Housing: Homeownership rate: 35.7%; Median home value: $142,800; Median year structure built: Before 1940; Homeowner vacancy rate: 0.0%; Median selected monthly owner costs: $1,349 with a mortgage, $567 without a mortgage; Median gross rent: $861 per month; Rental vacancy rate: 3.6%
Health Insurance: 93.7% have insurance; 65.5% have private insurance; 40.0% have public insurance; 6.3% do not have insurance; 2.3% of children under 18 do not have insurance
Safety: Violent crime rate: 41.6 per 10,000 population; Property crime rate: 203.0 per 10,000 population
Transportation: Commute: 87.3% car, 7.6% public transportation, 2.8% walk, 1.7% work from home; Mean travel time to work: 18.5 minutes
Additional Information Contacts
City of Watervliet . . . . (518) 270-3800
    http://www.watervliet.com

WESTERLO (town).
Covers a land area of 57.791 square miles and a water area of 0.746 square miles. Located at 42.50° N. Lat; 74.05° W. Long. Elevation is 1,165 feet.
Population: 3,381; Growth (since 2000): -2.5%; Density: 58.5 persons per square mile; Race: 97.6% White, 0.3% Black/African American, 0.9% Asian, 0.0% American Indian/Alaska Native, 0.0% Native Hawaiian/Other Pacific Islander, 0.0% Two or more races, 3.3% Hispanic of any race; Average household size: 2.55; Median age: 48.6; Age under 18: 16.3%; Age 65 and over: 19.9%; Males per 100 females: 102.7; Marriage status: 22.5% never married, 60.3% now married, 0.0% separated, 9.8% widowed, 7.4% divorced; Foreign born: 2.8%; Speak English only: 95.7%; With disability: 14.3%; Veterans: 7.9%; Ancestry: 22.1% German, 21.5% Irish, 18.0% American, 14.6% English, 11.0% Italian
Employment: 15.2% management, business, and financial, 4.1% computer, engineering, and science, 7.9% education, legal, community service, arts, and media, 9.4% healthcare practitioners, 12.6% service, 22.5% sales and office, 15.0% natural resources, construction, and maintenance, 13.2% production, transportation, and material moving
Income: Per capita: $37,314; Median household: $79,974; Average household: $92,494; Households with income of $100,000 or more: 40.3%; Poverty rate: 5.4%
Educational Attainment: High school diploma or higher: 92.5%; Bachelor's degree or higher: 22.8%; Graduate/professional degree or higher: 7.3%
Housing: Homeownership rate: 89.1%; Median home value: $191,500; Median year structure built: 1977; Homeowner vacancy rate: 2.4%; Median selected monthly owner costs: $1,645 with a mortgage, $631 without a mortgage; Median gross rent: n/a per month; Rental vacancy rate: 0.0%
Health Insurance: 98.8% have insurance; 87.3% have private insurance; 30.4% have public insurance; 1.2% do not have insurance; 0.0% of children under 18 do not have insurance
Transportation: Commute: 94.4% car, 0.6% public transportation, 1.9% walk, 3.1% work from home; Mean travel time to work: 32.3 minutes

WESTMERE (CDP).
Covers a land area of 3.171 square miles and a water area of 0.010 square miles. Located at 42.69° N. Lat; 73.87° W. Long. Elevation is 292 feet.
Population: 6,950; Growth (since 2000): -3.3%; Density: 2,191.7 persons per square mile; Race: 78.3% White, 5.2% Black/African American, 12.6% Asian, 0.0% American Indian/Alaska Native, 0.0% Native Hawaiian/Other Pacific Islander, 1.2% Two or more races, 6.1% Hispanic of any race; Average household size: 2.22; Median age: 37.6; Age under 18: 18.5%; Age 65 and over: 17.2%; Males per 100 females: 94.8; Marriage status: 35.9% never married, 47.4% now married, 2.8% separated, 6.8% widowed, 9.9% divorced; Foreign born: 14.0%; Speak English only: 82.5%; With disability: 8.6%; Veterans: 7.4%; Ancestry: 19.8% Irish, 18.7% Italian, 13.9% German, 10.1% English, 5.3% Polish
Employment: 18.2% management, business, and financial, 8.0% computer, engineering, and science, 13.6% education, legal, community service, arts, and media, 9.1% healthcare practitioners, 14.1% service, 23.3% sales and office, 5.2% natural resources, construction, and maintenance, 8.5% production, transportation, and material moving
Income: Per capita: $42,517; Median household: $69,119; Average household: $93,743; Households with income of $100,000 or more: 36.4%; Poverty rate: 6.6%
Educational Attainment: High school diploma or higher: 97.7%; Bachelor's degree or higher: 43.5%; Graduate/professional degree or higher: 23.9%
Housing: Homeownership rate: 56.0%; Median home value: $235,800; Median year structure built: 1971; Homeowner vacancy rate: 1.4%; Median selected monthly owner costs: $1,752 with a mortgage, $530 without a mortgage; Median gross rent: $1,174 per month; Rental vacancy rate: 6.8%
Health Insurance: 95.9% have insurance; 87.2% have private insurance; 24.9% have public insurance; 4.1% do not have insurance; 1.2% of children under 18 do not have insurance
Transportation: Commute: 91.1% car, 0.7% public transportation, 1.4% walk, 5.6% work from home; Mean travel time to work: 20.4 minutes

Allegany County

Located in western New York; bounded on the south by Pennsylvania. Covers a land area of 1,029.308 square miles, a water area of 5.079

square miles, and is located in the Eastern Time Zone at 42.25° N. Lat., 78.03° W. Long. The county was founded in 1806. County seat is Belmont.

Weather Station: Alfred   Elevation: 1,770 feet

	Jan	Feb	Mar	Apr	May	Jun	Jul	Aug	Sep	Oct	Nov	Dec
High	31	35	44	57	68	76	80	79	71	59	47	36
Low	13	13	20	31	40	50	54	52	46	35	28	19
Precip	2.2	1.7	2.7	3.0	3.3	4.3	3.9	3.6	3.7	3.3	3.3	2.6
Snow	20.8	16.7	17.1	4.0	0.3	0.0	0.0	0.0	0.0	0.5	8.6	19.6

High and Low temperatures in degrees Fahrenheit; Precipitation and Snow in inches

Weather Station: Angelica   Elevation: 1,444 feet

	Jan	Feb	Mar	Apr	May	Jun	Jul	Aug	Sep	Oct	Nov	Dec
High	32	34	43	56	67	75	79	78	71	59	47	36
Low	13	13	20	31	39	49	53	52	45	35	28	19
Precip	2.2	1.9	2.6	3.1	3.3	4.5	3.9	4.1	3.7	3.3	3.2	2.5
Snow	15.8	11.3	11.8	3.2	0.2	0.0	0.0	0.0	0.0	0.2	7.1	14.1

High and Low temperatures in degrees Fahrenheit; Precipitation and Snow in inches

Population: 47,400; Growth (since 2000): -5.1%; Density: 46.1 persons per square mile; Race: 95.5% White, 1.4% Black/African American, 1.2% Asian, 0.3% American Indian/Alaska Native, 0.0% Native Hawaiian/Other Pacific Islander, 1.1% two or more races, 1.5% Hispanic of any race; Average household size: 2.34; Median age: 38.6; Age under 18: 20.4%; Age 65 and over: 17.4%; Males per 100 females: 101.8; Marriage status: 33.2% never married, 49.7% now married, 2.0% separated, 6.8% widowed, 10.3% divorced; Foreign born: 2.4%; Speak English only: 94.9%; With disability: 15.6%; Veterans: 10.1%; Ancestry: 24.3% German, 17.0% Irish, 15.7% English, 6.8% Italian, 5.8% American

Religion: Six largest groups: 8.8% Catholicism, 6.9% Methodist/Pietist, 3.8% Holiness, 2.8% Non-denominational Protestant, 2.6% Baptist, 1.4% European Free-Church

Economy: Unemployment rate: 4.5%; Leading industries: 17.5 % retail trade; 15.3 % other services (except public administration); 12.3 % health care and social assistance; Farms: 784 totaling 150,383 acres; Company size: 1 employs 1,000 or more persons, 4 employ 500 to 999 persons, 10 employ 100 to 499 persons, 764 employ less than 100 persons; Business ownership: 920 women-owned, n/a Black-owned, 27 Hispanic-owned, 129 Asian-owned, 28 American Indian/Alaska Native-owned

Employment: 9.9% management, business, and financial, 2.9% computer, engineering, and science, 13.5% education, legal, community service, arts, and media, 5.1% healthcare practitioners, 22.2% service, 19.2% sales and office, 10.5% natural resources, construction, and maintenance, 16.6% production, transportation, and material moving

Income: Per capita: $22,377; Median household: $45,359; Average household: $56,806; Households with income of $100,000 or more: 12.4%; Poverty rate: 16.5%

Educational Attainment: High school diploma or higher: 89.4%; Bachelor's degree or higher: 19.8%; Graduate/professional degree or higher: 9.9%

Housing: Homeownership rate: 74.3%; Median home value: $73,300; Median year structure built: 1964; Homeowner vacancy rate: 2.0%; Median selected monthly owner costs: $987 with a mortgage, $448 without a mortgage; Median gross rent: $633 per month; Rental vacancy rate: 6.2%

Vital Statistics: Birth rate: 103.9 per 10,000 population; Death rate: 94.0 per 10,000 population; Age-adjusted cancer mortality rate: 182.6 deaths per 100,000 population

Health Insurance: 91.9% have insurance; 68.4% have private insurance; 39.7% have public insurance; 8.1% do not have insurance; 9.9% of children under 18 do not have insurance

Health Care: Physicians: 6.8 per 10,000 population; Dentists: 3.0 per 10,000 population; Hospital beds: 24.2 per 10,000 population; Hospital admissions: 479.7 per 10,000 population

Transportation: Commute: 82.8% car, 0.6% public transportation, 12.4% walk, 2.8% work from home; Mean travel time to work: 21.4 minutes

2016 Presidential Election: 67.0% Trump, 26.1% Clinton, 3.9% Johnson, 1.5% Stein

Additional Information Contacts

Allegany Government . . . . (585) 268-9222
    http://www.alleganyco.com

Allegany County Communities

ALFRED (town). Covers a land area of 31.476 square miles and a water area of 0.149 square miles. Located at 42.23° N. Lat; 77.80° W. Long. Elevation is 1,765 feet.

History: Alfred is a town in Allegany County, New York, and includes a village of the same name. Alfred University and Alfred State College are located in the Village of Alfred.

Population: 5,073; Growth (since 2000): -1.3%; Density: 161.2 persons per square mile; Race: 84.5% White, 8.2% Black/African American, 3.9% Asian, 0.4% American Indian/Alaska Native, 0.0% Native Hawaiian/Other Pacific Islander, 0.9% Two or more races, 6.2% Hispanic of any race; Average household size: 2.12; Median age: 20.3; Age under 18: 6.2%; Age 65 and over: 4.3%; Males per 100 females: 143.2; Marriage status: 84.3% never married, 13.0% now married, 0.1% separated, 1.1% widowed, 1.7% divorced; Foreign born: 6.6%; Speak English only: 88.7%; With disability: 4.0%; Veterans: 1.7%; Ancestry: 12.8% Irish, 12.2% German, 11.0% Italian, 6.6% English, 3.7% Polish

Employment: 6.3% management, business, and financial, 4.8% computer, engineering, and science, 19.8% education, legal, community service, arts, and media, 0.6% healthcare practitioners, 36.0% service, 22.4% sales and office, 5.6% natural resources, construction, and maintenance, 4.4% production, transportation, and material moving

Income: Per capita: $11,507; Median household: $39,375; Average household: $58,714; Households with income of $100,000 or more: 18.3%; Poverty rate: 28.8%

Educational Attainment: High school diploma or higher: 93.5%; Bachelor's degree or higher: 55.4%; Graduate/professional degree or higher: 35.5%

Four-year College(s)
Alfred University (Private, Not-for-profit)
    Enrollment: 2,354 . . . . (607) 871-2111
    Tuition: In-state $28,114; Out-of-state $28,114
SUNY College of Technology at Alfred (Public)
    Enrollment: 3,686 . . . . (800) 425-3733
    Tuition: In-state $8,327; Out-of-state $8,327

Housing: Homeownership rate: 49.8%; Median home value: $109,600; Median year structure built: 1966; Homeowner vacancy rate: 3.7%; Median selected monthly owner costs: $1,316 with a mortgage, $623 without a mortgage; Median gross rent: $704 per month; Rental vacancy rate: 15.6%

Health Insurance: 95.7% have insurance; 84.9% have private insurance; 18.5% have public insurance; 4.3% do not have insurance; 7.0% of children under 18 do not have insurance

Newspapers: Alfred Sun (weekly circulation 1,000)

Transportation: Commute: 37.3% car, 0.1% public transportation, 59.8% walk, 2.2% work from home; Mean travel time to work: 10.9 minutes

Additional Information Contacts

Town of Alfred . . . . (607) 587-8524
    http://townofalfred.com

ALFRED (village). Covers a land area of 1.190 square miles and a water area of 0 square miles. Located at 42.25° N. Lat; 77.79° W. Long. Elevation is 1,765 feet.

History: Alfred is a town in Allegany County, New York. The Town of Alfred has a village named Alfred in the center of the town. Alfred University and Alfred State College are located in the Village of Alfred.

Population: 4,275; Growth (since 2000): 8.1%; Density: 3,592.9 persons per square mile; Race: 81.7% White, 9.7% Black/African American, 4.7% Asian, 0.5% American Indian/Alaska Native, 0.0% Native Hawaiian/Other Pacific Islander, 1.0% Two or more races, 7.3% Hispanic of any race; Average household size: 1.96; Median age: 20.1; Age under 18: 2.5%; Age 65 and over: 2.1%; Males per 100 females: 154.7; Marriage status: 93.4% never married, 5.8% now married, 0.1% separated, 0.5% widowed, 0.3% divorced; Foreign born: 7.4%; Speak English only: 88.7%; With disability: 3.4%; Veterans: 0.5%; Ancestry: 13.1% Irish, 11.3% German, 10.6% Italian, 4.8% English, 4.2% Polish

Employment: 3.6% management, business, and financial, 5.0% computer, engineering, and science, 17.1% education, legal, community service, arts, and media, 0.4% healthcare practitioners, 40.9% service, 25.8% sales and office, 5.2% natural resources, construction, and maintenance, 2.2% production, transportation, and material moving

Income: Per capita: $8,376; Median household: $31,875; Average household: $53,987; Households with income of $100,000 or more: 18.6%; Poverty rate: 38.1%

Educational Attainment: High school diploma or higher: 100.0%; Bachelor's degree or higher: 73.3%; Graduate/professional degree or higher: 46.9%

Four-year College(s)
Alfred University (Private, Not-for-profit)
  Enrollment: 2,354 . . . . (607) 871-2111
  Tuition: In-state $28,114; Out-of-state $28,114
SUNY College of Technology at Alfred (Public)
  Enrollment: 3,686 . . . . (800) 425-3733
  Tuition: In-state $8,327; Out-of-state $8,327
Housing: Homeownership rate: 28.9%; Median home value: $114,200; Median year structure built: 1966; Homeowner vacancy rate: 7.6%; Median selected monthly owner costs: $1,317 with a mortgage, $708 without a mortgage; Median gross rent: $806 per month; Rental vacancy rate: 11.1%
Health Insurance: 97.6% have insurance; 87.6% have private insurance; 15.2% have public insurance; 2.4% do not have insurance; 2.1% of children under 18 do not have insurance
Newspapers: Alfred Sun (weekly circulation 1,000)
Transportation: Commute: 26.4% car, 0.0% public transportation, 71.2% walk, 1.9% work from home; Mean travel time to work: 9.7 minutes
Additional Information Contacts
Village of Alfred . . . . (607) 587-9188
  http://www.alfredny.org

ALFRED STATION (unincorporated postal area)
ZCTA: 14803
  Covers a land area of 24.924 square miles and a water area of 0.097 square miles. Located at 42.27° N. Lat; 77.75° W. Long. Elevation is 1,644 feet.
Population: 918; Growth (since 2000): -26.0%; Density: 36.8 persons per square mile; Race: 94.6% White, 1.5% Black/African American, 3.5% Asian, 0.0% American Indian/Alaska Native, 0.0% Native Hawaiian/Other Pacific Islander, 0.4% Two or more races, 0.1% Hispanic of any race; Average household size: 2.07; Median age: 44.7; Age under 18: 18.6%; Age 65 and over: 16.3%; Males per 100 females: 110.0; Marriage status: 31.0% never married, 53.2% now married, 0.4% separated, 3.9% widowed, 11.8% divorced; Foreign born: 6.0%; Speak English only: 97.8%; With disability: 7.4%; Veterans: 7.4%; Ancestry: 20.0% German, 18.8% English, 14.6% Irish, 13.7% Italian, 7.0% American
Employment: 12.7% management, business, and financial, 3.3% computer, engineering, and science, 29.4% education, legal, community service, arts, and media, 3.3% healthcare practitioners, 17.4% service, 12.3% sales and office, 8.6% natural resources, construction, and maintenance, 12.9% production, transportation, and material moving
Income: Per capita: $28,428; Median household: $45,000; Average household: $58,488; Households with income of $100,000 or more: 16.7%; Poverty rate: 15.7%
Educational Attainment: High school diploma or higher: 92.0%; Bachelor's degree or higher: 44.2%; Graduate/professional degree or higher: 24.3%
Housing: Homeownership rate: 65.5%; Median home value: $104,900; Median year structure built: 1972; Homeowner vacancy rate: 1.7%; Median selected monthly owner costs: $1,214 with a mortgage, $557 without a mortgage; Median gross rent: $705 per month; Rental vacancy rate: 18.6%
Health Insurance: 96.1% have insurance; 75.9% have private insurance; 40.2% have public insurance; 3.9% do not have insurance; 0.0% of children under 18 do not have insurance
Transportation: Commute: 87.0% car, 0.0% public transportation, 10.4% walk, 2.6% work from home; Mean travel time to work: 18.1 minutes

ALLEN (town). Covers a land area of 36.377 square miles and a water area of 0.203 square miles. Located at 42.40° N. Lat; 78.00° W. Long.
Population: 586; Growth (since 2000): 26.8%; Density: 16.1 persons per square mile; Race: 97.4% White, 0.0% Black/African American, 0.0% Asian, 0.0% American Indian/Alaska Native, 0.0% Native Hawaiian/Other Pacific Islander, 2.4% Two or more races, 1.7% Hispanic of any race; Average household size: 3.10; Median age: 32.5; Age under 18: 38.9%; Age 65 and over: 12.3%; Males per 100 females: 111.3; Marriage status: 29.0% never married, 57.7% now married, 1.0% separated, 4.8% widowed, 8.5% divorced; Foreign born: 0.5%; Speak English only: 70.9%; With disability: 11.1%; Veterans: 7.5%; Ancestry: 16.2% German, 16.0% Dutch, 11.9% Pennsylvania German, 9.0% Swiss, 8.5% Irish

Employment: 8.5% management, business, and financial, 5.6% computer, engineering, and science, 7.9% education, legal, community service, arts, and media, 2.3% healthcare practitioners, 21.5% service, 16.9% sales and office, 15.8% natural resources, construction, and maintenance, 21.5% production, transportation, and material moving
Income: Per capita: $17,597; Median household: $46,750; Average household: $61,060; Households with income of $100,000 or more: 9.0%; Poverty rate: 29.9%
Educational Attainment: High school diploma or higher: 79.6%; Bachelor's degree or higher: 7.1%; Graduate/professional degree or higher: 3.4%
Housing: Homeownership rate: 93.7%; Median home value: $76,800; Median year structure built: 1981; Homeowner vacancy rate: 2.2%; Median selected monthly owner costs: $1,183 with a mortgage, $356 without a mortgage; Median gross rent: $479 per month; Rental vacancy rate: 0.0%
Health Insurance: 54.8% have insurance; 43.0% have private insurance; 23.5% have public insurance; 45.2% do not have insurance; 76.5% of children under 18 do not have insurance
Transportation: Commute: 85.7% car, 0.0% public transportation, 9.7% walk, 2.3% work from home; Mean travel time to work: 31.7 minutes

ALLENTOWN (unincorporated postal area)
ZCTA: 14707
  Covers a land area of 1.987 square miles and a water area of 0 square miles. Located at 42.08° N. Lat; 78.06° W. Long. Elevation is 1,847 feet.
Population: 216; Growth (since 2000): n/a; Density: 108.7 persons per square mile; Race: 98.6% White, 0.0% Black/African American, 0.0% Asian, 0.0% American Indian/Alaska Native, 0.0% Native Hawaiian/Other Pacific Islander, 1.4% Two or more races, 2.8% Hispanic of any race; Average household size: 2.14; Median age: 54.9; Age under 18: 15.7%; Age 65 and over: 20.4%; Males per 100 females: 123.4; Marriage status: 25.6% never married, 53.3% now married, 4.5% separated, 3.0% widowed, 18.1% divorced; Foreign born: 0.9%; Speak English only: 100.0%; With disability: 17.6%; Veterans: 20.9%; Ancestry: 23.1% German, 16.7% Irish, 13.0% American, 9.3% English, 7.4% Canadian
Employment: 5.5% management, business, and financial, 0.0% computer, engineering, and science, 9.9% education, legal, community service, arts, and media, 3.3% healthcare practitioners, 37.4% service, 1.1% sales and office, 12.1% natural resources, construction, and maintenance, 30.8% production, transportation, and material moving
Income: Per capita: $33,168; Median household: $80,417; Average household: $75,304; Households with income of $100,000 or more: 25.7%; Poverty rate: 2.8%
Educational Attainment: High school diploma or higher: 94.1%; Bachelor's degree or higher: 14.1%; Graduate/professional degree or higher: 9.4%
Housing: Homeownership rate: 90.1%; Median home value: $59,400; Median year structure built: Before 1940; Homeowner vacancy rate: 9.9%; Median selected monthly owner costs: $1,172 with a mortgage, $592 without a mortgage; Median gross rent: n/a per month; Rental vacancy rate: 0.0%
Health Insurance: 90.7% have insurance; 65.3% have private insurance; 45.8% have public insurance; 9.3% do not have insurance; 0.0% of children under 18 do not have insurance
Transportation: Commute: 90.8% car, 0.0% public transportation, 3.4% walk, 2.3% work from home; Mean travel time to work: 14.8 minutes

ALMA (town). Covers a land area of 36.215 square miles and a water area of 0.301 square miles. Located at 42.05° N. Lat; 78.02° W. Long. Elevation is 1,549 feet.
Population: 777; Growth (since 2000): -8.3%; Density: 21.5 persons per square mile; Race: 96.1% White, 0.0% Black/African American, 1.0% Asian, 0.0% American Indian/Alaska Native, 0.9% Native Hawaiian/Other Pacific Islander, 1.9% Two or more races, 0.9% Hispanic of any race; Average household size: 2.32; Median age: 48.2; Age under 18: 22.0%; Age 65 and over: 16.6%; Males per 100 females: 113.7; Marriage status: 18.4% never married, 60.5% now married, 3.5% separated, 5.4% widowed, 15.7% divorced; Foreign born: 1.5%; Speak English only: 97.6%; With disability: 15.3%; Veterans: 16.2%; Ancestry: 26.9% German, 16.5% Irish, 13.3% English, 7.2% Italian, 6.2% American
Employment: 14.0% management, business, and financial, 4.4% computer, engineering, and science, 9.6% education, legal, community service, arts, and media, 8.0% healthcare practitioners, 15.2% service,

11.0% sales and office, 10.5% natural resources, construction, and maintenance, 27.3% production, transportation, and material moving
Income: Per capita: $30,565; Median household: $57,679; Average household: $68,339; Households with income of $100,000 or more: 17.9%; Poverty rate: 7.4%
Educational Attainment: High school diploma or higher: 89.0%; Bachelor's degree or higher: 13.4%; Graduate/professional degree or higher: 7.9%
Housing: Homeownership rate: 91.6%; Median home value: $61,500; Median year structure built: 1973; Homeowner vacancy rate: 5.4%; Median selected monthly owner costs: $1,043 with a mortgage, $507 without a mortgage; Median gross rent: $700 per month; Rental vacancy rate: 0.0%
Health Insurance: 93.2% have insurance; 70.0% have private insurance; 38.9% have public insurance; 6.8% do not have insurance; 1.2% of children under 18 do not have insurance
Transportation: Commute: 94.7% car, 0.0% public transportation, 3.1% walk, 1.4% work from home; Mean travel time to work: 24.4 minutes

ALMOND (town). Covers a land area of 45.717 square miles and a water area of 0.067 square miles. Located at 42.34° N. Lat; 77.78° W. Long. Elevation is 1,335 feet.
Population: 1,530; Growth (since 2000): -4.6%; Density: 33.5 persons per square mile; Race: 95.8% White, 0.2% Black/African American, 2.5% Asian, 0.0% American Indian/Alaska Native, 0.0% Native Hawaiian/Other Pacific Islander, 0.6% Two or more races, 0.5% Hispanic of any race; Average household size: 2.46; Median age: 40.6; Age under 18: 25.1%; Age 65 and over: 15.4%; Males per 100 females: 99.6; Marriage status: 19.7% never married, 64.9% now married, 1.7% separated, 5.8% widowed, 9.6% divorced; Foreign born: 3.5%; Speak English only: 96.8%; With disability: 14.5%; Veterans: 9.8%; Ancestry: 21.6% German, 17.1% Irish, 12.9% American, 10.5% English, 6.3% Polish
Employment: 11.9% management, business, and financial, 4.6% computer, engineering, and science, 16.9% education, legal, community service, arts, and media, 5.2% healthcare practitioners, 21.4% service, 18.4% sales and office, 9.3% natural resources, construction, and maintenance, 12.3% production, transportation, and material moving
Income: Per capita: $26,448; Median household: $57,759; Average household: $64,949; Households with income of $100,000 or more: 17.3%; Poverty rate: 13.6%
Educational Attainment: High school diploma or higher: 95.9%; Bachelor's degree or higher: 31.5%; Graduate/professional degree or higher: 16.6%

School District(s)
Alfred-Almond Central SD (PK-12)
    Enrollment: 633 . . . . (607) 276-6500
Housing: Homeownership rate: 78.0%; Median home value: $84,000; Median year structure built: 1974; Homeowner vacancy rate: 1.8%; Median selected monthly owner costs: $1,168 with a mortgage, $490 without a mortgage; Median gross rent: $705 per month; Rental vacancy rate: 3.5%
Health Insurance: 97.4% have insurance; 78.7% have private insurance; 35.8% have public insurance; 2.6% do not have insurance; 3.0% of children under 18 do not have insurance
Transportation: Commute: 96.7% car, 0.4% public transportation, 1.1% walk, 1.4% work from home; Mean travel time to work: 21.2 minutes

ALMOND (village). Covers a land area of 0.564 square miles and a water area of 0 square miles. Located at 42.32° N. Lat; 77.74° W. Long. Elevation is 1,335 feet.
Population: 443; Growth (since 2000): -3.9%; Density: 785.0 persons per square mile; Race: 94.8% White, 0.2% Black/African American, 1.8% Asian, 0.0% American Indian/Alaska Native, 0.0% Native Hawaiian/Other Pacific Islander, 3.2% Two or more races, 0.0% Hispanic of any race; Average household size: 2.64; Median age: 40.1; Age under 18: 28.4%; Age 65 and over: 16.0%; Males per 100 females: 104.4; Marriage status: 15.9% never married, 65.2% now married, 3.3% separated, 6.3% widowed, 12.6% divorced; Foreign born: 2.3%; Speak English only: 98.3%; With disability: 17.8%; Veterans: 13.6%; Ancestry: 27.3% German, 18.5% Irish, 14.4% English, 10.8% Italian, 5.6% American
Employment: 12.6% management, business, and financial, 7.4% computer, engineering, and science, 18.3% education, legal, community service, arts, and media, 2.9% healthcare practitioners, 16.0% service, 21.1% sales and office, 5.7% natural resources, construction, and maintenance, 16.0% production, transportation, and material moving

Income: Per capita: $22,075; Median household: $56,250; Average household: $57,374; Households with income of $100,000 or more: 11.9%; Poverty rate: 22.3%
Educational Attainment: High school diploma or higher: 96.9%; Bachelor's degree or higher: 27.3%; Graduate/professional degree or higher: 17.6%
School District(s)
Alfred-Almond Central SD (PK-12)
    Enrollment: 633 . . . . (607) 276-6500
Housing: Homeownership rate: 73.2%; Median home value: $69,200; Median year structure built: Before 1940; Homeowner vacancy rate: 0.0%; Median selected monthly owner costs: $968 with a mortgage, $437 without a mortgage; Median gross rent: $681 per month; Rental vacancy rate: 10.0%
Health Insurance: 98.2% have insurance; 75.4% have private insurance; 43.1% have public insurance; 1.8% do not have insurance; 0.0% of children under 18 do not have insurance
Transportation: Commute: 94.2% car, 1.7% public transportation, 2.3% walk, 1.7% work from home; Mean travel time to work: 22.8 minutes

AMITY (town). Covers a land area of 34.442 square miles and a water area of 0.123 square miles. Located at 42.23° N. Lat; 78.00° W. Long. Elevation is 1,391 feet.
Population: 2,238; Growth (since 2000): -0.3%; Density: 65.0 persons per square mile; Race: 92.9% White, 2.7% Black/African American, 0.8% Asian, 0.4% American Indian/Alaska Native, 0.0% Native Hawaiian/Other Pacific Islander, 2.6% Two or more races, 1.5% Hispanic of any race; Average household size: 2.23; Median age: 39.9; Age under 18: 20.6%; Age 65 and over: 19.5%; Males per 100 females: 102.6; Marriage status: 32.8% never married, 46.9% now married, 3.8% separated, 6.5% widowed, 13.8% divorced; Foreign born: 2.3%; Speak English only: 96.2%; With disability: 21.0%; Veterans: 12.5%; Ancestry: 31.0% German, 20.6% Irish, 15.2% English, 10.1% Italian, 4.6% American
Employment: 11.6% management, business, and financial, 1.3% computer, engineering, and science, 14.4% education, legal, community service, arts, and media, 7.9% healthcare practitioners, 18.7% service, 22.1% sales and office, 10.2% natural resources, construction, and maintenance, 13.8% production, transportation, and material moving
Income: Per capita: $23,426; Median household: $47,697; Average household: $54,898; Households with income of $100,000 or more: 10.5%; Poverty rate: 18.3%
Educational Attainment: High school diploma or higher: 90.0%; Bachelor's degree or higher: 15.3%; Graduate/professional degree or higher: 6.1%
Housing: Homeownership rate: 72.9%; Median home value: $61,900; Median year structure built: 1960; Homeowner vacancy rate: 0.0%; Median selected monthly owner costs: $900 with a mortgage, $433 without a mortgage; Median gross rent: $589 per month; Rental vacancy rate: 3.6%
Health Insurance: 94.4% have insurance; 65.2% have private insurance; 46.7% have public insurance; 5.6% do not have insurance; 5.5% of children under 18 do not have insurance
Safety: Violent crime rate: 0.0 per 10,000 population; Property crime rate: 0.0 per 10,000 population
Transportation: Commute: 92.0% car, 1.8% public transportation, 0.2% walk, 5.0% work from home; Mean travel time to work: 25.8 minutes

ANDOVER (town). Covers a land area of 39.430 square miles and a water area of 0.066 square miles. Located at 42.15° N. Lat; 77.81° W. Long. Elevation is 1,660 feet.
History: Incorporated 1892.
Population: 1,610; Growth (since 2000): -17.2%; Density: 40.8 persons per square mile; Race: 98.7% White, 0.0% Black/African American, 1.2% Asian, 0.0% American Indian/Alaska Native, 0.0% Native Hawaiian/Other Pacific Islander, 0.0% Two or more races, 1.6% Hispanic of any race; Average household size: 2.24; Median age: 43.9; Age under 18: 22.6%; Age 65 and over: 16.6%; Males per 100 females: 96.8; Marriage status: 26.0% never married, 56.4% now married, 2.5% separated, 8.5% widowed, 9.1% divorced; Foreign born: 3.0%; Speak English only: 98.3%; With disability: 15.8%; Veterans: 13.2%; Ancestry: 25.8% German, 20.9% English, 19.4% Irish, 4.4% American, 3.5% Scottish
Employment: 8.1% management, business, and financial, 3.5% computer, engineering, and science, 11.6% education, legal, community service, arts, and media, 4.7% healthcare practitioners, 19.6% service, 20.9% sales and office, 13.9% natural resources, construction, and maintenance, 17.6% production, transportation, and material moving

Income: Per capita: $25,509; Median household: $52,639; Average household: $57,910; Households with income of $100,000 or more: 11.6%; Poverty rate: 10.7%
Educational Attainment: High school diploma or higher: 92.1%; Bachelor's degree or higher: 16.7%; Graduate/professional degree or higher: 6.6%

School District(s)
Andover Central SD (PK-12)
  Enrollment: 340. . . . . (607) 478-8491
Housing: Homeownership rate: 72.4%; Median home value: $65,200; Median year structure built: 1953; Homeowner vacancy rate: 5.3%; Median selected monthly owner costs: $1,007 with a mortgage, $393 without a mortgage; Median gross rent: $631 per month; Rental vacancy rate: 11.2%
Health Insurance: 94.8% have insurance; 68.1% have private insurance; 46.1% have public insurance; 5.2% do not have insurance; 3.2% of children under 18 do not have insurance
Transportation: Commute: 89.7% car, 1.7% public transportation, 4.7% walk, 3.2% work from home; Mean travel time to work: 20.9 minutes

ANDOVER (village). Covers a land area of 1.001 square miles and a water area of 0.015 square miles. Located at 42.16° N. Lat; 77.80° W. Long. Elevation is 1,660 feet.
Population: 833; Growth (since 2000): -22.4%; Density: 832.2 persons per square mile; Race: 97.6% White, 0.0% Black/African American, 2.4% Asian, 0.0% American Indian/Alaska Native, 0.0% Native Hawaiian/Other Pacific Islander, 0.0% Two or more races, 0.1% Hispanic of any race; Average household size: 2.25; Median age: 42.2; Age under 18: 22.2%; Age 65 and over: 16.0%; Males per 100 females: 91.2; Marriage status: 26.8% never married, 56.7% now married, 1.6% separated, 7.8% widowed, 8.7% divorced; Foreign born: 2.9%; Speak English only: 100.0%; With disability: 15.7%; Veterans: 13.1%; Ancestry: 33.4% German, 20.6% Irish, 20.4% English, 5.6% Scottish, 4.1% Dutch
Employment: 8.1% management, business, and financial, 3.0% computer, engineering, and science, 12.2% education, legal, community service, arts, and media, 3.8% healthcare practitioners, 23.3% service, 19.5% sales and office, 10.1% natural resources, construction, and maintenance, 20.0% production, transportation, and material moving
Income: Per capita: $23,706; Median household: $52,667; Average household: $53,728; Households with income of $100,000 or more: 5.1%; Poverty rate: 9.1%
Educational Attainment: High school diploma or higher: 94.3%; Bachelor's degree or higher: 18.5%; Graduate/professional degree or higher: 4.9%

School District(s)
Andover Central SD (PK-12)
  Enrollment: 340. . . . . (607) 478-8491
Housing: Homeownership rate: 67.3%; Median home value: $59,600; Median year structure built: Before 1940; Homeowner vacancy rate: 4.2%; Median selected monthly owner costs: $1,026 with a mortgage, $349 without a mortgage; Median gross rent: $665 per month; Rental vacancy rate: 11.0%
Health Insurance: 96.3% have insurance; 67.5% have private insurance; 50.7% have public insurance; 3.7% do not have insurance; 0.0% of children under 18 do not have insurance
Safety: Violent crime rate: 0.0 per 10,000 population; Property crime rate: 0.0 per 10,000 population
Transportation: Commute: 86.8% car, 3.1% public transportation, 6.5% walk, 3.6% work from home; Mean travel time to work: 17.7 minutes

ANGELICA (town). Covers a land area of 36.394 square miles and a water area of 0.038 square miles. Located at 42.30° N. Lat; 78.02° W. Long. Elevation is 1,434 feet.
History: Oldest village in the county; founded in 1800 by Captain Philip Church, nephew of Alexander Hamilton. Church is buried with his wife at Until the Day Dawns Cemetery. Contingent of French royalists settled here in 1806; one of them became the French ambassador to U.S; another was Victor Marie du Pont de Nemours.
Population: 1,358; Growth (since 2000): -3.8%; Density: 37.3 persons per square mile; Race: 97.9% White, 0.2% Black/African American, 1.7% Asian, 0.0% American Indian/Alaska Native, 0.0% Native Hawaiian/Other Pacific Islander, 0.2% Two or more races, 0.7% Hispanic of any race; Average household size: 2.40; Median age: 43.3; Age under 18: 25.1%; Age 65 and over: 18.2%; Males per 100 females: 111.9; Marriage status: 23.7% never married, 56.1% now married, 1.4% separated, 5.7% widowed, 14.5% divorced; Foreign born: 1.8%; Speak English only: 94.7%;

With disability: 17.4%; Veterans: 13.2%; Ancestry: 27.2% German, 18.2% Irish, 13.8% English, 9.4% American, 8.6% Italian
Employment: 14.8% management, business, and financial, 0.4% computer, engineering, and science, 12.7% education, legal, community service, arts, and media, 6.0% healthcare practitioners, 19.7% service, 15.8% sales and office, 12.8% natural resources, construction, and maintenance, 17.9% production, transportation, and material moving
Income: Per capita: $28,169; Median household: $46,071; Average household: $68,014; Households with income of $100,000 or more: 16.9%; Poverty rate: 16.8%
Educational Attainment: High school diploma or higher: 93.3%; Bachelor's degree or higher: 20.9%; Graduate/professional degree or higher: 8.7%
Housing: Homeownership rate: 78.3%; Median home value: $86,000; Median year structure built: 1962; Homeowner vacancy rate: 1.1%; Median selected monthly owner costs: $1,064 with a mortgage, $399 without a mortgage; Median gross rent: $635 per month; Rental vacancy rate: 7.0%
Health Insurance: 92.9% have insurance; 68.5% have private insurance; 42.6% have public insurance; 7.1% do not have insurance; 10.9% of children under 18 do not have insurance
Transportation: Commute: 91.4% car, 0.0% public transportation, 5.5% walk, 2.0% work from home; Mean travel time to work: 24.4 minutes

ANGELICA (village). Covers a land area of 2.152 square miles and a water area of 0 square miles. Located at 42.31° N. Lat; 78.02° W. Long. Elevation is 1,434 feet.
Population: 783; Growth (since 2000): -13.3%; Density: 363.9 persons per square mile; Race: 99.6% White, 0.0% Black/African American, 0.0% Asian, 0.0% American Indian/Alaska Native, 0.0% Native Hawaiian/Other Pacific Islander, 0.4% Two or more races, 1.3% Hispanic of any race; Average household size: 2.28; Median age: 41.7; Age under 18: 20.8%; Age 65 and over: 20.6%; Males per 100 females: 104.5; Marriage status: 23.4% never married, 58.7% now married, 1.9% separated, 6.1% widowed, 11.9% divorced; Foreign born: 0.1%; Speak English only: 99.6%; With disability: 15.3%; Veterans: 14.4%; Ancestry: 27.5% German, 21.5% Irish, 19.3% English, 13.7% Italian, 7.9% American
Employment: 18.7% management, business, and financial, 0.5% computer, engineering, and science, 12.5% education, legal, community service, arts, and media, 3.7% healthcare practitioners, 17.1% service, 14.4% sales and office, 10.7% natural resources, construction, and maintenance, 22.4% production, transportation, and material moving
Income: Per capita: $33,826; Median household: $57,143; Average household: $77,273; Households with income of $100,000 or more: 16.6%; Poverty rate: 7.7%
Educational Attainment: High school diploma or higher: 91.9%; Bachelor's degree or higher: 20.4%; Graduate/professional degree or higher: 7.4%
Housing: Homeownership rate: 75.0%; Median home value: $80,700; Median year structure built: Before 1940; Homeowner vacancy rate: 1.9%; Median selected monthly owner costs: $977 with a mortgage, $386 without a mortgage; Median gross rent: $615 per month; Rental vacancy rate: 0.0%
Health Insurance: 96.7% have insurance; 78.7% have private insurance; 41.4% have public insurance; 3.3% do not have insurance; 0.0% of children under 18 do not have insurance
Safety: Violent crime rate: 0.0 per 10,000 population; Property crime rate: 12.1 per 10,000 population
Transportation: Commute: 90.3% car, 0.0% public transportation, 7.5% walk, 2.2% work from home; Mean travel time to work: 23.6 minutes

BELFAST (CDP). Covers a land area of 1.385 square miles and a water area of 0.027 square miles. Located at 42.34° N. Lat; 78.12° W. Long. Elevation is 1,309 feet.
Population: 823; Growth (since 2000): n/a; Density: 594.2 persons per square mile; Race: 99.0% White, 0.0% Black/African American, 0.0% Asian, 0.0% American Indian/Alaska Native, 0.0% Native Hawaiian/Other Pacific Islander, 0.7% Two or more races, 6.0% Hispanic of any race; Average household size: 2.46; Median age: 32.4; Age under 18: 31.7%; Age 65 and over: 20.8%; Males per 100 females: 87.7; Marriage status: 19.6% never married, 60.5% now married, 2.7% separated, 8.6% widowed, 11.3% divorced; Foreign born: 0.6%; Speak English only: 99.3%; With disability: 15.6%; Veterans: 16.7%; Ancestry: 25.4% German, 21.6% Irish, 13.6% English, 8.7% American, 7.2% Dutch
Employment: 5.0% management, business, and financial, 3.7% computer, engineering, and science, 28.2% education, legal, community service, arts,

and media, 1.7% healthcare practitioners, 19.5% service, 17.1% sales and office, 5.0% natural resources, construction, and maintenance, 19.8% production, transportation, and material moving
Income: Per capita: $19,110; Median household: $44,022; Average household: $48,145; Households with income of $100,000 or more: 9.3%; Poverty rate: 12.4%
Educational Attainment: High school diploma or higher: 87.5%; Bachelor's degree or higher: 19.5%; Graduate/professional degree or higher: 11.4%

School District(s)
Belfast Central SD (PK-12)
    Enrollment: 363 . . . . (585) 365-2646
Housing: Homeownership rate: 58.1%; Median home value: $64,600; Median year structure built: 1950; Homeowner vacancy rate: 0.0%; Median selected monthly owner costs: $862 with a mortgage, $442 without a mortgage; Median gross rent: $620 per month; Rental vacancy rate: 5.4%
Health Insurance: 93.0% have insurance; 67.8% have private insurance; 40.0% have public insurance; 7.0% do not have insurance; 10.0% of children under 18 do not have insurance
Transportation: Commute: 87.2% car, 0.0% public transportation, 10.4% walk, 1.7% work from home; Mean travel time to work: 18.1 minutes

---

BELFAST (town). Covers a land area of 36.295 square miles and a water area of 0.249 square miles. Located at 42.30° N. Lat; 78.14° W. Long. Elevation is 1,309 feet.
Population: 1,880; Growth (since 2000): 9.7%; Density: 51.8 persons per square mile; Race: 99.1% White, 0.0% Black/African American, 0.0% Asian, 0.0% American Indian/Alaska Native, 0.0% Native Hawaiian/Other Pacific Islander, 0.3% Two or more races, 3.0% Hispanic of any race; Average household size: 2.60; Median age: 31.8; Age under 18: 31.0%; Age 65 and over: 16.6%; Males per 100 females: 98.0; Marriage status: 17.3% never married, 62.9% now married, 1.5% separated, 5.8% widowed, 14.0% divorced; Foreign born: 1.1%; Speak English only: 83.4%; With disability: 15.0%; Veterans: 11.7%; Ancestry: 33.5% German, 16.7% Irish, 13.2% English, 6.1% American, 5.5% Dutch
Employment: 11.9% management, business, and financial, 3.3% computer, engineering, and science, 18.7% education, legal, community service, arts, and media, 2.2% healthcare practitioners, 15.5% service, 16.8% sales and office, 11.3% natural resources, construction, and maintenance, 20.4% production, transportation, and material moving
Income: Per capita: $20,087; Median household: $48,947; Average household: $52,590; Households with income of $100,000 or more: 7.9%; Poverty rate: 14.8%
Educational Attainment: High school diploma or higher: 81.3%; Bachelor's degree or higher: 15.7%; Graduate/professional degree or higher: 10.1%

School District(s)
Belfast Central SD (PK-12)
    Enrollment: 363 . . . . (585) 365-2646
Housing: Homeownership rate: 76.2%; Median home value: $77,800; Median year structure built: 1974; Homeowner vacancy rate: 0.5%; Median selected monthly owner costs: $958 with a mortgage, $421 without a mortgage; Median gross rent: $626 per month; Rental vacancy rate: 4.4%
Health Insurance: 77.8% have insurance; 59.5% have private insurance; 31.2% have public insurance; 22.2% do not have insurance; 36.8% of children under 18 do not have insurance
Transportation: Commute: 84.4% car, 0.0% public transportation, 8.9% walk, 5.8% work from home; Mean travel time to work: 21.6 minutes

---

BELMONT (village). County seat. Covers a land area of 0.996 square miles and a water area of 0.002 square miles. Located at 42.22° N. Lat; 78.03° W. Long. Elevation is 1,391 feet.
History: Incorporated 1871.
Population: 902; Growth (since 2000): -5.3%; Density: 905.8 persons per square mile; Race: 99.7% White, 0.3% Black/African American, 0.0% Asian, 0.0% American Indian/Alaska Native, 0.0% Native Hawaiian/Other Pacific Islander, 0.0% Two or more races, 0.1% Hispanic of any race; Average household size: 2.20; Median age: 35.6; Age under 18: 27.1%; Age 65 and over: 16.5%; Males per 100 females: 94.2; Marriage status: 25.1% never married, 53.0% now married, 2.2% separated, 6.2% widowed, 15.6% divorced; Foreign born: 0.3%; Speak English only: 97.7%; With disability: 18.2%; Veterans: 5.2%; Ancestry: 28.7% German, 19.6% Italian, 19.0% Irish, 11.8% English, 5.4% American
Employment: 10.8% management, business, and financial, 1.6% computer, engineering, and science, 15.9% education, legal, community

service, arts, and media, 10.2% healthcare practitioners, 23.7% service, 10.2% sales and office, 9.4% natural resources, construction, and maintenance, 18.1% production, transportation, and material moving
Income: Per capita: $21,951; Median household: $39,205; Average household: $48,691; Households with income of $100,000 or more: 11.4%; Poverty rate: 14.1%
Educational Attainment: High school diploma or higher: 91.9%; Bachelor's degree or higher: 22.7%; Graduate/professional degree or higher: 12.2%

School District(s)
Genesee Valley Central SD At Angelica-Belmont (PK-12)
    Enrollment: 544 . . . . (585) 268-7900
Housing: Homeownership rate: 62.3%; Median home value: $63,600; Median year structure built: Before 1940; Homeowner vacancy rate: 0.0%; Median selected monthly owner costs: $927 with a mortgage, $452 without a mortgage; Median gross rent: $561 per month; Rental vacancy rate: 6.2%
Health Insurance: 98.8% have insurance; 68.0% have private insurance; 48.2% have public insurance; 1.2% do not have insurance; 0.0% of children under 18 do not have insurance
Transportation: Commute: 93.5% car, 1.1% public transportation, 0.5% walk, 3.8% work from home; Mean travel time to work: 28.4 minutes

---

BIRDSALL (town). Covers a land area of 35.889 square miles and a water area of 0.171 square miles. Located at 42.40° N. Lat; 77.89° W. Long. Elevation is 1,693 feet.
Population: 179; Growth (since 2000): -33.2%; Density: 5.0 persons per square mile; Race: 100.0% White, 0.0% Black/African American, 0.0% Asian, 0.0% American Indian/Alaska Native, 0.0% Native Hawaiian/Other Pacific Islander, 0.0% Two or more races, 1.1% Hispanic of any race; Average household size: 2.18; Median age: 52.4; Age under 18: 14.0%; Age 65 and over: 26.8%; Males per 100 females: 104.6; Marriage status: 17.8% never married, 56.7% now married, 5.7% separated, 7.0% widowed, 18.5% divorced; Foreign born: 0.0%; Speak English only: 100.0%; With disability: 23.5%; Veterans: 13.6%; Ancestry: 17.9% German, 16.2% Irish, 14.5% English, 5.6% American, 5.0% Dutch
Employment: 6.3% management, business, and financial, 6.3% computer, engineering, and science, 7.5% education, legal, community service, arts, and media, 1.3% healthcare practitioners, 16.3% service, 16.3% sales and office, 16.3% natural resources, construction, and maintenance, 30.0% production, transportation, and material moving
Income: Per capita: $22,522; Median household: $42,778; Average household: $46,552; Households with income of $100,000 or more: 9.8%; Poverty rate: 16.4%
Educational Attainment: High school diploma or higher: 79.3%; Bachelor's degree or higher: 13.8%; Graduate/professional degree or higher: 6.2%
Housing: Homeownership rate: 89.0%; Median home value: $67,100; Median year structure built: 1981; Homeowner vacancy rate: 0.0%; Median selected monthly owner costs: $975 with a mortgage, $429 without a mortgage; Median gross rent: n/a per month; Rental vacancy rate: 0.0%
Health Insurance: 96.1% have insurance; 76.5% have private insurance; 46.4% have public insurance; 3.9% do not have insurance; 0.0% of children under 18 do not have insurance
Transportation: Commute: 90.8% car, 0.0% public transportation, 1.3% walk, 5.3% work from home; Mean travel time to work: 50.8 minutes

---

BLACK CREEK (unincorporated postal area)
ZCTA: 14714
    Covers a land area of 18.175 square miles and a water area of 0.081 square miles. Located at 42.30° N. Lat; 78.23° W. Long. Elevation is 1,509 feet.
    Population: 512; Growth (since 2000): 48.4%; Density: 28.2 persons per square mile; Race: 98.2% White, 0.0% Black/African American, 0.0% Asian, 0.0% American Indian/Alaska Native, 0.0% Native Hawaiian/Other Pacific Islander, 1.8% Two or more races, 0.0% Hispanic of any race; Average household size: 2.46; Median age: 42.5; Age under 18: 22.7%; Age 65 and over: 18.9%; Males per 100 females: 107.2; Marriage status: 28.7% never married, 54.5% now married, 0.5% separated, 8.0% widowed, 8.8% divorced; Foreign born: 0.4%; Speak English only: 92.9%; With disability: 17.8%; Veterans: 11.1%; Ancestry: 21.9% German, 18.9% English, 11.9% Irish, 8.4% American, 6.1% Polish
    Employment: 10.0% management, business, and financial, 1.4% computer, engineering, and science, 14.2% education, legal, community

service, arts, and media, 9.0% healthcare practitioners, 12.3% service, 11.8% sales and office, 17.1% natural resources, construction, and maintenance, 24.2% production, transportation, and material moving
Income: Per capita: $23,340; Median household: $48,409; Average household: $56,961; Households with income of $100,000 or more: 11.5%; Poverty rate: 14.3%
Educational Attainment: High school diploma or higher: 87.6%; Bachelor's degree or higher: 18.2%; Graduate/professional degree or higher: 12.1%
Housing: Homeownership rate: 84.6%; Median home value: $86,900; Median year structure built: 1980; Homeowner vacancy rate: 1.1%; Median selected monthly owner costs: $1,097 with a mortgage, $515 without a mortgage; Median gross rent: $980 per month; Rental vacancy rate: 0.0%
Health Insurance: 87.5% have insurance; 71.7% have private insurance; 45.1% have public insurance; 12.5% do not have insurance; 11.8% of children under 18 do not have insurance
Transportation: Commute: 86.4% car, 3.0% public transportation, 3.0% walk, 4.5% work from home; Mean travel time to work: 30.9 minutes

BOLIVAR (town). Covers a land area of 35.863 square miles and a water area of 0.010 square miles. Located at 42.03° N. Lat; 78.14° W. Long. Elevation is 1,594 feet.
History: Surrounding region was prominent early petroleum-producing area from late 19th to early 20th century. Incorporated 1882.
Population: 2,246; Growth (since 2000): 1.0%; Density: 62.6 persons per square mile; Race: 96.7% White, 0.4% Black/African American, 0.7% Asian, 1.6% American Indian/Alaska Native, 0.0% Native Hawaiian/Other Pacific Islander, 0.7% Two or more races, 0.6% Hispanic of any race; Average household size: 2.65; Median age: 36.9; Age under 18: 29.4%; Age 65 and over: 14.4%; Males per 100 females: 96.5; Marriage status: 27.4% never married, 54.0% now married, 2.2% separated, 7.3% widowed, 11.3% divorced; Foreign born: 2.1%; Speak English only: 98.3%; With disability: 16.2%; Veterans: 11.5%; Ancestry: 20.6% German, 19.7% English, 18.6% Irish, 9.0% Italian, 5.7% American
Employment: 11.7% management, business, and financial, 2.2% computer, engineering, and science, 15.3% education, legal, community service, arts, and media, 5.6% healthcare practitioners, 15.9% service, 16.0% sales and office, 11.6% natural resources, construction, and maintenance, 21.9% production, transportation, and material moving
Income: Per capita: $20,235; Median household: $41,042; Average household: $52,893; Households with income of $100,000 or more: 8.1%; Poverty rate: 19.7%
Educational Attainment: High school diploma or higher: 86.7%; Bachelor's degree or higher: 13.6%; Graduate/professional degree or higher: 6.0%

School District(s)
Bolivar-Richburg Central SD (PK-12)
    Enrollment: 788 . . . . (585) 928-2561
Housing: Homeownership rate: 67.1%; Median home value: $68,200; Median year structure built: 1949; Homeowner vacancy rate: 2.2%; Median selected monthly owner costs: $1,069 with a mortgage, $515 without a mortgage; Median gross rent: $634 per month; Rental vacancy rate: 10.3%
Health Insurance: 97.0% have insurance; 70.2% have private insurance; 41.4% have public insurance; 3.0% do not have insurance; 2.9% of children under 18 do not have insurance
Transportation: Commute: 88.4% car, 0.0% public transportation, 5.8% walk, 4.4% work from home; Mean travel time to work: 25.9 minutes

BOLIVAR (village). Covers a land area of 0.798 square miles and a water area of 0 square miles. Located at 42.07° N. Lat; 78.17° W. Long. Elevation is 1,594 feet.
Population: 1,122; Growth (since 2000): -4.3%; Density: 1,405.4 persons per square mile; Race: 95.7% White, 0.3% Black/African American, 1.3% Asian, 1.3% American Indian/Alaska Native, 0.0% Native Hawaiian/Other Pacific Islander, 1.3% Two or more races, 0.0% Hispanic of any race; Average household size: 2.35; Median age: 37.7; Age under 18: 24.5%; Age 65 and over: 16.6%; Males per 100 females: 96.8; Marriage status: 30.6% never married, 50.2% now married, 3.6% separated, 7.7% widowed, 11.5% divorced; Foreign born: 2.4%; Speak English only: 98.9%; With disability: 18.9%; Veterans: 12.4%; Ancestry: 25.0% German, 18.5% English, 13.1% Irish, 7.7% Scottish, 5.6% Italian
Employment: 7.5% management, business, and financial, 4.4% computer, engineering, and science, 15.7% education, legal, community service, arts, and media, 10.1% healthcare practitioners, 19.2% service, 14.3% sales

and office, 15.7% natural resources, construction, and maintenance, 13.1% production, transportation, and material moving
Income: Per capita: $22,162; Median household: $38,207; Average household: $51,832; Households with income of $100,000 or more: 4.6%; Poverty rate: 18.6%
Educational Attainment: High school diploma or higher: 85.8%; Bachelor's degree or higher: 16.4%; Graduate/professional degree or higher: 8.5%

School District(s)
Bolivar-Richburg Central SD (PK-12)
    Enrollment: 788 . . . . (585) 928-2561
Housing: Homeownership rate: 59.7%; Median home value: $64,700; Median year structure built: Before 1940; Homeowner vacancy rate: 4.3%; Median selected monthly owner costs: $979 with a mortgage, $527 without a mortgage; Median gross rent: $589 per month; Rental vacancy rate: 5.0%
Health Insurance: 97.9% have insurance; 71.7% have private insurance; 47.0% have public insurance; 2.1% do not have insurance; 0.0% of children under 18 do not have insurance
Transportation: Commute: 84.8% car, 0.0% public transportation, 7.3% walk, 7.3% work from home; Mean travel time to work: 22.2 minutes

BURNS (town). Covers a land area of 27.220 square miles and a water area of 0.036 square miles. Located at 42.44° N. Lat; 77.78° W. Long. Elevation is 1,197 feet.
Population: 1,391; Growth (since 2000): 11.5%; Density: 51.1 persons per square mile; Race: 96.3% White, 0.0% Black/African American, 1.7% Asian, 0.0% American Indian/Alaska Native, 0.0% Native Hawaiian/Other Pacific Islander, 0.0% Two or more races, 2.0% Hispanic of any race; Average household size: 2.75; Median age: 41.5; Age under 18: 28.7%; Age 65 and over: 14.5%; Males per 100 females: 104.2; Marriage status: 22.4% never married, 64.0% now married, 0.2% separated, 6.0% widowed, 7.5% divorced; Foreign born: 2.4%; Speak English only: 96.5%; With disability: 14.8%; Veterans: 6.4%; Ancestry: 31.5% German, 17.6% Irish, 13.0% English, 5.7% American, 3.8% Italian
Employment: 12.3% management, business, and financial, 1.2% computer, engineering, and science, 5.7% education, legal, community service, arts, and media, 10.3% healthcare practitioners, 19.9% service, 21.2% sales and office, 20.5% natural resources, construction, and maintenance, 8.9% production, transportation, and material moving
Income: Per capita: $20,887; Median household: $47,375; Average household: $56,221; Households with income of $100,000 or more: 11.9%; Poverty rate: 12.2%
Educational Attainment: High school diploma or higher: 95.3%; Bachelor's degree or higher: 13.3%; Graduate/professional degree or higher: 5.9%
Housing: Homeownership rate: 79.6%; Median home value: $74,500; Median year structure built: 1952; Homeowner vacancy rate: 1.9%; Median selected monthly owner costs: $1,088 with a mortgage, $492 without a mortgage; Median gross rent: $774 per month; Rental vacancy rate: 5.5%
Health Insurance: 97.8% have insurance; 77.3% have private insurance; 38.7% have public insurance; 2.2% do not have insurance; 0.0% of children under 18 do not have insurance
Transportation: Commute: 96.6% car, 1.1% public transportation, 1.3% walk, 1.1% work from home; Mean travel time to work: 26.9 minutes

CANASERAGA (village). Covers a land area of 1.062 square miles and a water area of 0 square miles. Located at 42.46° N. Lat; 77.78° W. Long. Elevation is 1,250 feet.
Population: 541; Growth (since 2000): -8.9%; Density: 509.3 persons per square mile; Race: 97.4% White, 0.0% Black/African American, 2.6% Asian, 0.0% American Indian/Alaska Native, 0.0% Native Hawaiian/Other Pacific Islander, 0.0% Two or more races, 0.6% Hispanic of any race; Average household size: 2.63; Median age: 41.8; Age under 18: 24.4%; Age 65 and over: 14.2%; Males per 100 females: 101.5; Marriage status: 26.4% never married, 55.1% now married, 0.5% separated, 6.6% widowed, 11.8% divorced; Foreign born: 2.6%; Speak English only: 94.9%; With disability: 18.7%; Veterans: 7.3%; Ancestry: 44.4% German, 23.1% Irish, 14.6% English, 8.3% American, 7.4% Italian
Employment: 17.8% management, business, and financial, 1.6% computer, engineering, and science, 4.3% education, legal, community service, arts, and media, 3.8% healthcare practitioners, 15.7% service, 22.7% sales and office, 18.4% natural resources, construction, and maintenance, 15.7% production, transportation, and material moving

Income: Per capita: $18,109; Median household: $37,500; Average household: $46,619; Households with income of $100,000 or more: 10.7%; Poverty rate: 25.3%
Educational Attainment: High school diploma or higher: 90.9%; Bachelor's degree or higher: 12.5%; Graduate/professional degree or higher: 4.7%

School District(s)
Canaseraga Central SD (PK-12)
   Enrollment: 255 . . . . (607) 545-6421
Housing: Homeownership rate: 74.8%; Median home value: $52,000; Median year structure built: Before 1940; Homeowner vacancy rate: 4.9%; Median selected monthly owner costs: $857 with a mortgage, $472 without a mortgage; Median gross rent: $694 per month; Rental vacancy rate: 10.3%
Health Insurance: 94.8% have insurance; 56.7% have private insurance; 58.4% have public insurance; 5.2% do not have insurance; 0.0% of children under 18 do not have insurance
Transportation: Commute: 94.0% car, 3.3% public transportation, 1.6% walk, 1.1% work from home; Mean travel time to work: 27.8 minutes

---

CANEADEA (town). Covers a land area of 35.649 square miles and a water area of 0.693 square miles. Located at 42.39° N. Lat; 78.13° W. Long. Elevation is 1,253 feet.
Population: 2,454; Growth (since 2000): -8.9%; Density: 68.8 persons per square mile; Race: 87.3% White, 4.4% Black/African American, 4.8% Asian, 0.5% American Indian/Alaska Native, 0.0% Native Hawaiian/Other Pacific Islander, 2.2% Two or more races, 3.3% Hispanic of any race; Average household size: 2.42; Median age: 22.0; Age under 18: 14.1%; Age 65 and over: 16.0%; Males per 100 females: 79.6; Marriage status: 53.6% never married, 35.5% now married, 1.6% separated, 7.0% widowed, 3.9% divorced; Foreign born: 6.1%; Speak English only: 90.9%; With disability: 10.4%; Veterans: 5.8%; Ancestry: 21.8% German, 18.1% English, 14.6% Irish, 5.7% Polish, 4.0% Italian
Employment: 5.5% management, business, and financial, 2.0% computer, engineering, and science, 24.1% education, legal, community service, arts, and media, 4.5% healthcare practitioners, 33.9% service, 15.0% sales and office, 7.3% natural resources, construction, and maintenance, 7.7% production, transportation, and material moving
Income: Per capita: $16,434; Median household: $44,196; Average household: $56,437; Households with income of $100,000 or more: 12.7%; Poverty rate: 10.2%
Educational Attainment: High school diploma or higher: 95.5%; Bachelor's degree or higher: 42.2%; Graduate/professional degree or higher: 24.6%
Housing: Homeownership rate: 66.1%; Median home value: $100,800; Median year structure built: 1965; Homeowner vacancy rate: 2.9%; Median selected monthly owner costs: $1,028 with a mortgage, $473 without a mortgage; Median gross rent: $658 per month; Rental vacancy rate: 0.0%
Health Insurance: 93.6% have insurance; 76.4% have private insurance; 29.5% have public insurance; 6.4% do not have insurance; 2.8% of children under 18 do not have insurance
Transportation: Commute: 49.9% car, 0.0% public transportation, 46.6% walk, 3.6% work from home; Mean travel time to work: 15.8 minutes

---

CENTERVILLE (town). Covers a land area of 35.435 square miles and a water area of 0.047 square miles. Located at 42.47° N. Lat; 78.27° W. Long. Elevation is 1,759 feet.
Population: 750; Growth (since 2000): -1.6%; Density: 21.2 persons per square mile; Race: 99.7% White, 0.0% Black/African American, 0.0% Asian, 0.3% American Indian/Alaska Native, 0.0% Native Hawaiian/Other Pacific Islander, 0.0% Two or more races, 0.0% Hispanic of any race; Average household size: 2.68; Median age: 31.2; Age under 18: 31.7%; Age 65 and over: 13.2%; Males per 100 females: 98.1; Marriage status: 25.1% never married, 59.3% now married, 4.0% separated, 4.4% widowed, 11.2% divorced; Foreign born: 0.5%; Speak English only: 87.5%; With disability: 12.3%; Veterans: 5.9%; Ancestry: 29.9% German, 16.0% English, 10.5% Polish, 10.3% Irish, 4.5% Italian
Employment: 12.2% management, business, and financial, 1.0% computer, engineering, and science, 8.7% education, legal, community service, arts, and media, 4.2% healthcare practitioners, 10.5% service, 17.8% sales and office, 21.6% natural resources, construction, and maintenance, 24.0% production, transportation, and material moving
Income: Per capita: $18,011; Median household: $41,346; Average household: $48,846; Households with income of $100,000 or more: 5.8%; Poverty rate: 21.7%

Educational Attainment: High school diploma or higher: 76.3%; Bachelor's degree or higher: 10.2%; Graduate/professional degree or higher: 5.7%
Housing: Homeownership rate: 79.6%; Median home value: $79,800; Median year structure built: 1980; Homeowner vacancy rate: 0.0%; Median selected monthly owner costs: $891 with a mortgage, $420 without a mortgage; Median gross rent: $697 per month; Rental vacancy rate: 0.0%
Health Insurance: 70.7% have insurance; 41.7% have private insurance; 39.3% have public insurance; 29.3% do not have insurance; 39.7% of children under 18 do not have insurance
Transportation: Commute: 80.4% car, 0.0% public transportation, 7.3% walk, 8.0% work from home; Mean travel time to work: 30.7 minutes

---

CERES (unincorporated postal area)
ZCTA: 14721
   Covers a land area of 3.732 square miles and a water area of 0 square miles. Located at 42.01° N. Lat; 78.27° W. Long. Elevation is 1,453 feet.
Population: 130; Growth (since 2000): 27.5%; Density: 34.8 persons per square mile; Race: 100.0% White, 0.0% Black/African American, 0.0% Asian, 0.0% American Indian/Alaska Native, 0.0% Native Hawaiian/Other Pacific Islander, 0.0% Two or more races, 0.0% Hispanic of any race; Average household size: 1.78; Median age: 27.5; Age under 18: 14.6%; Age 65 and over: 16.9%; Males per 100 females: 98.3; Marriage status: 41.9% never married, 46.2% now married, 0.0% separated, 8.5% widowed, 3.4% divorced; Foreign born: 0.0%; Speak English only: 100.0%; With disability: 6.9%; Veterans: 9.0%; Ancestry: 25.4% Polish, 20.8% German, 13.1% English, 10.8% Ukrainian, 5.4% Irish
Employment: 4.7% management, business, and financial, 0.0% computer, engineering, and science, 16.5% education, legal, community service, arts, and media, 0.0% healthcare practitioners, 12.9% service, 7.1% sales and office, 12.9% natural resources, construction, and maintenance, 45.9% production, transportation, and material moving
Income: Per capita: $19,936; Median household: $39,063; Average household: $37,027; Households with income of $100,000 or more: n/a; Poverty rate: 10.0%
Educational Attainment: High school diploma or higher: 100.0%; Bachelor's degree or higher: 7.9%; Graduate/professional degree or higher: 3.4%
Housing: Homeownership rate: 65.8%; Median home value: $47,500; Median year structure built: 1972; Homeowner vacancy rate: 0.0%; Median selected monthly owner costs: $1,125 with a mortgage, $325 without a mortgage; Median gross rent: $475 per month; Rental vacancy rate: 0.0%
Health Insurance: 77.7% have insurance; 68.5% have private insurance; 26.2% have public insurance; 22.3% do not have insurance; 0.0% of children under 18 do not have insurance
Transportation: Commute: 87.1% car, 0.0% public transportation, 9.4% walk, 3.5% work from home; Mean travel time to work: 27.5 minutes

---

CLARKSVILLE (town). Covers a land area of 36.276 square miles and a water area of 0.020 square miles. Located at 42.14° N. Lat; 78.25° W. Long.
Population: 963; Growth (since 2000): -16.0%; Density: 26.5 persons per square mile; Race: 99.7% White, 0.3% Black/African American, 0.0% Asian, 0.0% American Indian/Alaska Native, 0.0% Native Hawaiian/Other Pacific Islander, 0.0% Two or more races, 1.2% Hispanic of any race; Average household size: 2.27; Median age: 49.6; Age under 18: 18.3%; Age 65 and over: 25.4%; Males per 100 females: 101.6; Marriage status: 19.2% never married, 67.6% now married, 2.2% separated, 6.6% widowed, 6.6% divorced; Foreign born: 1.3%; Speak English only: 96.6%; With disability: 21.0%; Veterans: 14.9%; Ancestry: 26.9% German, 21.7% Irish, 18.0% English, 11.8% Polish, 8.1% Italian
Employment: 5.7% management, business, and financial, 5.0% computer, engineering, and science, 15.5% education, legal, community service, arts, and media, 3.9% healthcare practitioners, 13.9% service, 20.7% sales and office, 7.5% natural resources, construction, and maintenance, 27.8% production, transportation, and material moving
Income: Per capita: $22,412; Median household: $44,375; Average household: $49,027; Households with income of $100,000 or more: 9.9%; Poverty rate: 6.9%
Educational Attainment: High school diploma or higher: 87.4%; Bachelor's degree or higher: 17.5%; Graduate/professional degree or higher: 9.5%

Housing: Homeownership rate: 88.2%; Median home value: $62,600; Median year structure built: 1973; Homeowner vacancy rate: 0.0%; Median selected monthly owner costs: $816 with a mortgage, $411 without a mortgage; Median gross rent: $731 per month; Rental vacancy rate: 0.0%
Health Insurance: 95.2% have insurance; 72.4% have private insurance; 45.3% have public insurance; 4.8% do not have insurance; 0.0% of children under 18 do not have insurance
Transportation: Commute: 95.3% car, 2.6% public transportation, 0.5% walk, 1.6% work from home; Mean travel time to work: 28.8 minutes

CUBA (town).
Covers a land area of 35.129 square miles and a water area of 0.763 square miles. Located at 42.21° N. Lat; 78.24° W. Long. Elevation is 1,496 feet.
History: Seneca Oil Spring, where oil was first noted by Jesuit missionaries in early 17th century, is nearby; the spring was the precursor of the "Pennsylvania field," the first oil field in the U.S. Incorporated 1850.
Population: 3,167; Growth (since 2000): -6.6%; Density: 90.2 persons per square mile; Race: 97.0% White, 0.3% Black/African American, 0.0% Asian, 0.0% American Indian/Alaska Native, 0.0% Native Hawaiian/Other Pacific Islander, 2.7% Two or more races, 0.9% Hispanic of any race; Average household size: 2.39; Median age: 46.6; Age under 18: 20.7%; Age 65 and over: 21.1%; Males per 100 females: 91.7; Marriage status: 26.8% never married, 53.7% now married, 2.0% separated, 6.5% widowed, 13.0% divorced; Foreign born: 1.0%; Speak English only: 97.7%; With disability: 16.5%; Veterans: 14.2%; Ancestry: 22.3% German, 14.4% English, 14.0% Irish, 9.6% Polish, 7.3% Italian
Employment: 12.4% management, business, and financial, 4.0% computer, engineering, and science, 13.2% education, legal, community service, arts, and media, 6.3% healthcare practitioners, 15.9% service, 28.0% sales and office, 4.5% natural resources, construction, and maintenance, 15.6% production, transportation, and material moving
Income: Per capita: $30,223; Median household: $54,088; Average household: $71,798; Households with income of $100,000 or more: 19.1%; Poverty rate: 16.1%
Educational Attainment: High school diploma or higher: 94.0%; Bachelor's degree or higher: 21.5%; Graduate/professional degree or higher: 11.2%
School District(s)
Cuba-Rushford Central SD (PK-12)
    Enrollment: 847 . . . . (585) 968-2650
Housing: Homeownership rate: 82.0%; Median home value: $75,100; Median year structure built: 1958; Homeowner vacancy rate: 0.8%; Median selected monthly owner costs: $1,086 with a mortgage, $493 without a mortgage; Median gross rent: $565 per month; Rental vacancy rate: 8.6%
Health Insurance: 93.1% have insurance; 72.2% have private insurance; 39.2% have public insurance; 6.9% do not have insurance; 7.4% of children under 18 do not have insurance
Hospitals: Cuba Memorial Hospital
Safety: Violent crime rate: 19.6 per 10,000 population; Property crime rate: 150.3 per 10,000 population
Newspapers: Patriot & Free Press (weekly circulation 5,000)
Transportation: Commute: 92.1% car, 0.3% public transportation, 3.9% walk, 2.3% work from home; Mean travel time to work: 19.4 minutes

CUBA (village).
Covers a land area of 1.216 square miles and a water area of 0 square miles. Located at 42.22° N. Lat; 78.28° W. Long. Elevation is 1,496 feet.
Population: 1,487; Growth (since 2000): -8.9%; Density: 1,222.4 persons per square mile; Race: 97.2% White, 0.6% Black/African American, 0.0% Asian, 0.0% American Indian/Alaska Native, 0.0% Native Hawaiian/Other Pacific Islander, 2.2% Two or more races, 1.9% Hispanic of any race; Average household size: 2.43; Median age: 41.0; Age under 18: 22.3%; Age 65 and over: 17.6%; Males per 100 females: 85.5; Marriage status: 28.1% never married, 47.4% now married, 2.4% separated, 7.1% widowed, 17.4% divorced; Foreign born: 0.8%; Speak English only: 97.8%; With disability: 17.3%; Veterans: 12.5%; Ancestry: 19.2% German, 17.7% Irish, 14.6% English, 11.1% Polish, 7.3% Italian
Employment: 9.8% management, business, and financial, 5.9% computer, engineering, and science, 15.7% education, legal, community service, arts, and media, 5.1% healthcare practitioners, 21.4% service, 18.1% sales and office, 3.0% natural resources, construction, and maintenance, 21.1% production, transportation, and material moving
Income: Per capita: $23,799; Median household: $51,641; Average household: $58,776; Households with income of $100,000 or more: 17.2%; Poverty rate: 20.8%

Educational Attainment: High school diploma or higher: 94.4%; Bachelor's degree or higher: 24.4%; Graduate/professional degree or higher: 8.7%
School District(s)
Cuba-Rushford Central SD (PK-12)
    Enrollment: 847 . . . . (585) 968-2650
Housing: Homeownership rate: 67.1%; Median home value: $66,900; Median year structure built: Before 1940; Homeowner vacancy rate: 2.2%; Median selected monthly owner costs: $989 with a mortgage, $470 without a mortgage; Median gross rent: $500 per month; Rental vacancy rate: 10.2%
Health Insurance: 91.7% have insurance; 66.1% have private insurance; 39.7% have public insurance; 8.3% do not have insurance; 7.3% of children under 18 do not have insurance
Hospitals: Cuba Memorial Hospital
Newspapers: Patriot & Free Press (weekly circulation 5,000)
Transportation: Commute: 86.3% car, 0.7% public transportation, 5.4% walk, 4.7% work from home; Mean travel time to work: 19.5 minutes

FARMERSVILLE STATION (unincorporated postal area)
ZCTA: 14060
Covers a land area of 17.740 square miles and a water area of 0.149 square miles. Located at 42.45° N. Lat; 78.30° W. Long..
Population: 303; Growth (since 2000): -31.3%; Density: 17.1 persons per square mile; Race: 100.0% White, 0.0% Black/African American, 0.0% Asian, 0.0% American Indian/Alaska Native, 0.0% Native Hawaiian/Other Pacific Islander, 0.0% Two or more races, 3.6% Hispanic of any race; Average household size: 1.97; Median age: 58.1; Age under 18: 12.2%; Age 65 and over: 32.0%; Males per 100 females: 113.0; Marriage status: 13.2% never married, 63.7% now married, 5.1% separated, 7.3% widowed, 15.8% divorced; Foreign born: 0.0%; Speak English only: 100.0%; With disability: 18.2%; Veterans: 9.0%; Ancestry: 33.3% English, 18.5% German, 12.9% Irish, 12.5% Polish, 5.6% Scottish
Employment: 14.2% management, business, and financial, 0.0% computer, engineering, and science, 5.8% education, legal, community service, arts, and media, 8.3% healthcare practitioners, 10.8% service, 29.2% sales and office, 11.7% natural resources, construction, and maintenance, 20.0% production, transportation, and material moving
Income: Per capita: $29,925; Median household: $46,250; Average household: $58,589; Households with income of $100,000 or more: 16.9%; Poverty rate: 4.0%
Educational Attainment: High school diploma or higher: 76.0%; Bachelor's degree or higher: 6.5%; Graduate/professional degree or higher: 3.0%
Housing: Homeownership rate: 94.8%; Median home value: $75,400; Median year structure built: 1970; Homeowner vacancy rate: 0.0%; Median selected monthly owner costs: $938 with a mortgage, $453 without a mortgage; Median gross rent: n/a per month; Rental vacancy rate: 0.0%
Health Insurance: 91.1% have insurance; 63.4% have private insurance; 49.8% have public insurance; 8.9% do not have insurance; 0.0% of children under 18 do not have insurance
Transportation: Commute: 100.0% car, 0.0% public transportation, 0.0% walk, 0.0% work from home; Mean travel time to work: 30.0 minutes

FILLMORE (CDP).
Covers a land area of 0.816 square miles and a water area of 0 square miles. Located at 42.47° N. Lat; 78.11° W. Long. Elevation is 1,197 feet.
Population: 404; Growth (since 2000): n/a; Density: 495.2 persons per square mile; Race: 97.0% White, 0.0% Black/African American, 0.0% Asian, 0.0% American Indian/Alaska Native, 0.0% Native Hawaiian/Other Pacific Islander, 0.0% Two or more races, 3.0% Hispanic of any race; Average household size: 2.20; Median age: 45.8; Age under 18: 27.0%; Age 65 and over: 15.1%; Males per 100 females: 91.4; Marriage status: 26.9% never married, 54.4% now married, 0.0% separated, 10.9% widowed, 7.8% divorced; Foreign born: 0.7%; Speak English only: 100.0%; With disability: 16.6%; Veterans: 5.1%; Ancestry: 37.6% German, 11.9% English, 11.4% American, 10.6% Irish, 7.7% British
Employment: 5.6% management, business, and financial, 1.1% computer, engineering, and science, 35.8% education, legal, community service, arts, and media, 2.2% healthcare practitioners, 14.5% service, 20.7% sales and office, 7.3% natural resources, construction, and maintenance, 12.8% production, transportation, and material moving

Income: Per capita: $20,945; Median household: $36,625; Average household: $46,193; Households with income of $100,000 or more: 6.5%; Poverty rate: 14.9%
Educational Attainment: High school diploma or higher: 95.8%; Bachelor's degree or higher: 26.7%; Graduate/professional degree or higher: 20.5%

School District(s)
Fillmore Central SD (PK-12)
    Enrollment: 671 . . . . (585) 567-2251
Housing: Homeownership rate: 71.2%; Median home value: $76,900; Median year structure built: Before 1940; Homeowner vacancy rate: 0.0%; Median selected monthly owner costs: $879 with a mortgage, $466 without a mortgage; Median gross rent: $658 per month; Rental vacancy rate: 30.8%
Health Insurance: 96.0% have insurance; 79.7% have private insurance; 32.9% have public insurance; 4.0% do not have insurance; 0.0% of children under 18 do not have insurance
Transportation: Commute: 75.6% car, 0.0% public transportation, 15.9% walk, 6.8% work from home; Mean travel time to work: 23.4 minutes

FRIENDSHIP (CDP). Covers a land area of 2.889 square miles and a water area of 0 square miles. Located at 42.21° N. Lat; 78.14° W. Long. Elevation is 1,506 feet.
Population: 1,158; Growth (since 2000): -1.5%; Density: 400.9 persons per square mile; Race: 97.1% White, 0.0% Black/African American, 0.0% Asian, 0.0% American Indian/Alaska Native, 0.0% Native Hawaiian/Other Pacific Islander, 2.9% Two or more races, 0.0% Hispanic of any race; Average household size: 2.36; Median age: 34.5; Age under 18: 25.8%; Age 65 and over: 17.4%; Males per 100 females: 93.3; Marriage status: 29.4% never married, 51.6% now married, 3.1% separated, 7.3% widowed, 11.7% divorced; Foreign born: 4.5%; Speak English only: 97.7%; With disability: 19.7%; Veterans: 13.5%; Ancestry: 27.9% Irish, 21.8% English, 19.3% German, 11.0% Dutch, 9.1% American
Employment: 9.3% management, business, and financial, 6.7% computer, engineering, and science, 2.8% education, legal, community service, arts, and media, 2.8% healthcare practitioners, 15.2% service, 36.5% sales and office, 11.0% natural resources, construction, and maintenance, 15.7% production, transportation, and material moving
Income: Per capita: $17,838; Median household: $36,027; Average household: $41,420; Households with income of $100,000 or more: 4.3%; Poverty rate: 23.3%
Educational Attainment: High school diploma or higher: 92.6%; Bachelor's degree or higher: 14.2%; Graduate/professional degree or higher: 6.2%

School District(s)
Friendship Central SD (PK-12)
    Enrollment: 360 . . . . (585) 973-3534
Housing: Homeownership rate: 70.1%; Median home value: $44,100; Median year structure built: Before 1940; Homeowner vacancy rate: 0.0%; Median selected monthly owner costs: $920 with a mortgage, $447 without a mortgage; Median gross rent: $634 per month; Rental vacancy rate: 0.0%
Health Insurance: 94.1% have insurance; 52.4% have private insurance; 54.9% have public insurance; 5.9% do not have insurance; 1.6% of children under 18 do not have insurance
Transportation: Commute: 100.0% car, 0.0% public transportation, 0.0% walk, 0.0% work from home; Mean travel time to work: 24.4 minutes

FRIENDSHIP (town). Covers a land area of 36.215 square miles and a water area of 0.013 square miles. Located at 42.21° N. Lat; 78.13° W. Long. Elevation is 1,506 feet.
History: Incorporated 1898.
Population: 1,819; Growth (since 2000): -5.6%; Density: 50.2 persons per square mile; Race: 97.1% White, 0.0% Black/African American, 0.0% Asian, 0.0% American Indian/Alaska Native, 0.0% Native Hawaiian/Other Pacific Islander, 2.9% Two or more races, 0.0% Hispanic of any race; Average household size: 2.22; Median age: 38.2; Age under 18: 22.8%; Age 65 and over: 19.0%; Males per 100 females: 99.8; Marriage status: 28.0% never married, 51.0% now married, 3.3% separated, 7.5% widowed, 13.6% divorced; Foreign born: 2.9%; Speak English only: 98.0%; With disability: 21.2%; Veterans: 14.1%; Ancestry: 23.9% Irish, 20.1% German, 15.4% English, 11.4% American, 7.2% Dutch
Employment: 6.4% management, business, and financial, 4.6% computer, engineering, and science, 4.2% education, legal, community service, arts, and media, 4.4% healthcare practitioners, 19.4% service, 28.4% sales and

office, 11.7% natural resources, construction, and maintenance, 20.9% production, transportation, and material moving
Income: Per capita: $19,654; Median household: $35,917; Average household: $43,193; Households with income of $100,000 or more: 4.6%; Poverty rate: 23.1%
Educational Attainment: High school diploma or higher: 91.1%; Bachelor's degree or higher: 12.2%; Graduate/professional degree or higher: 5.3%

School District(s)
Friendship Central SD (PK-12)
    Enrollment: 360 . . . . (585) 973-3534
Housing: Homeownership rate: 74.9%; Median home value: $45,000; Median year structure built: 1952; Homeowner vacancy rate: 1.0%; Median selected monthly owner costs: $892 with a mortgage, $406 without a mortgage; Median gross rent: $622 per month; Rental vacancy rate: 0.0%
Health Insurance: 94.9% have insurance; 53.3% have private insurance; 57.3% have public insurance; 5.1% do not have insurance; 1.2% of children under 18 do not have insurance
Safety: Violent crime rate: 10.5 per 10,000 population; Property crime rate: 15.8 per 10,000 population
Transportation: Commute: 100.0% car, 0.0% public transportation, 0.0% walk, 0.0% work from home; Mean travel time to work: 26.0 minutes

GENESEE (town). Covers a land area of 36.239 square miles and a water area of 0.048 square miles. Located at 42.05° N. Lat; 78.25° W. Long.
Population: 1,508; Growth (since 2000): -16.4%; Density: 41.6 persons per square mile; Race: 98.1% White, 0.0% Black/African American, 0.6% Asian, 0.0% American Indian/Alaska Native, 0.0% Native Hawaiian/Other Pacific Islander, 1.3% Two or more races, 0.1% Hispanic of any race; Average household size: 2.35; Median age: 47.1; Age under 18: 20.8%; Age 65 and over: 20.0%; Males per 100 females: 99.6; Marriage status: 28.6% never married, 56.8% now married, 2.5% separated, 6.4% widowed, 8.2% divorced; Foreign born: 1.4%; Speak English only: 99.5%; With disability: 16.0%; Veterans: 13.2%; Ancestry: 37.1% German, 18.9% Irish, 14.1% English, 7.9% Polish, 7.6% Italian
Employment: 9.5% management, business, and financial, 2.9% computer, engineering, and science, 9.7% education, legal, community service, arts, and media, 2.7% healthcare practitioners, 23.2% service, 20.0% sales and office, 11.7% natural resources, construction, and maintenance, 20.3% production, transportation, and material moving
Income: Per capita: $24,661; Median household: $49,457; Average household: $57,323; Households with income of $100,000 or more: 13.9%; Poverty rate: 16.6%
Educational Attainment: High school diploma or higher: 89.0%; Bachelor's degree or higher: 15.7%; Graduate/professional degree or higher: 6.9%
Housing: Homeownership rate: 83.0%; Median home value: $80,100; Median year structure built: 1973; Homeowner vacancy rate: 1.1%; Median selected monthly owner costs: $1,051 with a mortgage, $424 without a mortgage; Median gross rent: $525 per month; Rental vacancy rate: 0.0%
Health Insurance: 94.0% have insurance; 72.3% have private insurance; 39.7% have public insurance; 6.0% do not have insurance; 0.0% of children under 18 do not have insurance
Transportation: Commute: 90.3% car, 0.0% public transportation, 5.0% walk, 3.2% work from home; Mean travel time to work: 27.9 minutes

GRANGER (town). Covers a land area of 31.938 square miles and a water area of 0.100 square miles. Located at 42.48° N. Lat; 78.01° W. Long.
Population: 646; Growth (since 2000): 12.0%; Density: 20.2 persons per square mile; Race: 99.8% White, 0.0% Black/African American, 0.0% Asian, 0.0% American Indian/Alaska Native, 0.0% Native Hawaiian/Other Pacific Islander, 0.0% Two or more races, 0.2% Hispanic of any race; Average household size: 2.56; Median age: 38.9; Age under 18: 22.8%; Age 65 and over: 18.9%; Males per 100 females: 116.1; Marriage status: 22.2% never married, 62.1% now married, 0.4% separated, 5.5% widowed, 10.2% divorced; Foreign born: 0.9%; Speak English only: 94.3%; With disability: 16.3%; Veterans: 12.6%; Ancestry: 26.2% German, 25.4% English, 13.2% Irish, 12.8% French, 8.4% Polish
Employment: 13.3% management, business, and financial, 2.2% computer, engineering, and science, 9.7% education, legal, community service, arts, and media, 10.0% healthcare practitioners, 10.0% service, 11.8% sales and office, 25.1% natural resources, construction, and maintenance, 17.9% production, transportation, and material moving

Income: Per capita: $24,349; Median household: $52,955; Average household: $62,746; Households with income of $100,000 or more: 12.7%; Poverty rate: 11.5%
Educational Attainment: High school diploma or higher: 85.4%; Bachelor's degree or higher: 11.5%; Graduate/professional degree or higher: 6.6%
Housing: Homeownership rate: 91.3%; Median home value: $78,800; Median year structure built: 1978; Homeowner vacancy rate: 6.9%; Median selected monthly owner costs: $1,083 with a mortgage, $408 without a mortgage; Median gross rent: $725 per month; Rental vacancy rate: 0.0%
Health Insurance: 90.1% have insurance; 64.1% have private insurance; 44.0% have public insurance; 9.9% do not have insurance; 9.3% of children under 18 do not have insurance
Transportation: Commute: 94.5% car, 0.0% public transportation, 1.8% walk, 3.6% work from home; Mean travel time to work: 31.7 minutes

GROVE (town). Covers a land area of 33.366 square miles and a water area of 0.335 square miles. Located at 42.48° N. Lat; 77.89° W. Long. Elevation is 1,627 feet.
Population: 441; Growth (since 2000): -17.3%; Density: 13.2 persons per square mile; Race: 99.1% White, 0.0% Black/African American, 0.0% Asian, 0.0% American Indian/Alaska Native, 0.0% Native Hawaiian/Other Pacific Islander, 0.9% Two or more races, 0.2% Hispanic of any race; Average household size: 2.04; Median age: 55.9; Age under 18: 9.3%; Age 65 and over: 28.3%; Males per 100 females: 113.2; Marriage status: 21.5% never married, 47.6% now married, 2.9% separated, 10.7% widowed, 20.2% divorced; Foreign born: 0.0%; Speak English only: 99.8%; With disability: 20.0%; Veterans: 9.0%; Ancestry: 32.4% German, 24.5% English, 23.6% Irish, 7.3% Italian, 5.0% American
Employment: 16.8% management, business, and financial, 2.5% computer, engineering, and science, 7.6% education, legal, community service, arts, and media, 8.6% healthcare practitioners, 19.3% service, 23.9% sales and office, 9.6% natural resources, construction, and maintenance, 11.7% production, transportation, and material moving
Income: Per capita: $30,945; Median household: $53,333; Average household: $63,590; Households with income of $100,000 or more: 14.3%; Poverty rate: 8.8%
Educational Attainment: High school diploma or higher: 91.7%; Bachelor's degree or higher: 16.3%; Graduate/professional degree or higher: 6.7%
Housing: Homeownership rate: 94.4%; Median home value: $83,300; Median year structure built: 1976; Homeowner vacancy rate: 4.2%; Median selected monthly owner costs: $975 with a mortgage, $500 without a mortgage; Median gross rent: $665 per month; Rental vacancy rate: 20.0%
Health Insurance: 96.1% have insurance; 70.1% have private insurance; 43.1% have public insurance; 3.9% do not have insurance; 0.0% of children under 18 do not have insurance
Transportation: Commute: 90.7% car, 1.0% public transportation, 5.7% walk, 2.6% work from home; Mean travel time to work: 29.1 minutes

HOUGHTON (CDP). Covers a land area of 2.479 square miles and a water area of 0.010 square miles. Located at 42.43° N. Lat; 78.17° W. Long. Elevation is 1,207 feet.
History: Seat of Houghton College (1923).
Population: 1,734; Growth (since 2000): -0.8%; Density: 699.5 persons per square mile; Race: 84.1% White, 6.3% Black/African American, 6.7% Asian, 0.3% American Indian/Alaska Native, 0.0% Native Hawaiian/Other Pacific Islander, 1.3% Two or more races, 4.6% Hispanic of any race; Average household size: 2.67; Median age: 20.9; Age under 18: 13.1%; Age 65 and over: 11.6%; Males per 100 females: 67.5; Marriage status: 66.5% never married, 27.2% now married, 0.8% separated, 4.7% widowed, 1.5% divorced; Foreign born: 8.4%; Speak English only: 87.4%; With disability: 6.5%; Veterans: 2.3%; Ancestry: 16.2% German, 15.7% English, 12.9% Irish, 4.6% European, 4.4% Swedish
Employment: 5.0% management, business, and financial, 2.3% computer, engineering, and science, 27.5% education, legal, community service, arts, and media, 3.4% healthcare practitioners, 35.5% service, 16.8% sales and office, 3.7% natural resources, construction, and maintenance, 5.8% production, transportation, and material moving
Income: Per capita: $14,025; Median household: $57,045; Average household: $64,634; Households with income of $100,000 or more: 19.9%; Poverty rate: 10.9%
Educational Attainment: High school diploma or higher: 96.4%; Bachelor's degree or higher: 65.4%; Graduate/professional degree or higher: 40.1%

Four-year College(s)
Houghton College (Private, Not-for-profit, Wesleyan)
  Enrollment: 1,043 . . . . (585) 567-9200
  Tuition: In-state $31,540; Out-of-state $31,540
Housing: Homeownership rate: 59.4%; Median home value: $112,200; Median year structure built: 1963; Homeowner vacancy rate: 6.6%; Median selected monthly owner costs: $982 with a mortgage, $566 without a mortgage; Median gross rent: $646 per month; Rental vacancy rate: 0.0%
Health Insurance: 95.1% have insurance; 85.5% have private insurance; 18.6% have public insurance; 4.9% do not have insurance; 3.6% of children under 18 do not have insurance
Transportation: Commute: 35.9% car, 0.0% public transportation, 59.6% walk, 4.4% work from home; Mean travel time to work: 10.1 minutes

HUME (town). Covers a land area of 37.890 square miles and a water area of 0.431 square miles. Located at 42.48° N. Lat; 78.12° W. Long. Elevation is 1,273 feet.
Population: 2,042; Growth (since 2000): 2.8%; Density: 53.9 persons per square mile; Race: 98.6% White, 0.0% Black/African American, 0.0% Asian, 0.1% American Indian/Alaska Native, 0.0% Native Hawaiian/Other Pacific Islander, 0.6% Two or more races, 0.8% Hispanic of any race; Average household size: 2.38; Median age: 40.1; Age under 18: 26.8%; Age 65 and over: 15.9%; Males per 100 females: 100.7; Marriage status: 21.5% never married, 56.2% now married, 0.7% separated, 5.8% widowed, 16.5% divorced; Foreign born: 1.1%; Speak English only: 96.3%; With disability: 18.9%; Veterans: 9.9%; Ancestry: 29.1% German, 16.3% English, 11.6% Irish, 8.4% Polish, 7.0% American
Employment: 6.6% management, business, and financial, 0.2% computer, engineering, and science, 14.7% education, legal, community service, arts, and media, 2.3% healthcare practitioners, 21.6% service, 18.4% sales and office, 16.4% natural resources, construction, and maintenance, 19.7% production, transportation, and material moving
Income: Per capita: $19,446; Median household: $36,964; Average household: $45,628; Households with income of $100,000 or more: 6.7%; Poverty rate: 23.6%
Educational Attainment: High school diploma or higher: 84.4%; Bachelor's degree or higher: 19.4%; Graduate/professional degree or higher: 11.0%
Housing: Homeownership rate: 70.8%; Median home value: $73,800; Median year structure built: Before 1940; Homeowner vacancy rate: 1.1%; Median selected monthly owner costs: $880 with a mortgage, $469 without a mortgage; Median gross rent: $574 per month; Rental vacancy rate: 9.4%
Health Insurance: 93.8% have insurance; 58.0% have private insurance; 49.4% have public insurance; 6.2% do not have insurance; 0.9% of children under 18 do not have insurance
Transportation: Commute: 89.3% car, 0.0% public transportation, 4.6% walk, 3.6% work from home; Mean travel time to work: 29.5 minutes
Additional Information Contacts
Town of Hume . . . . (585) 567-2666
  http://www.humetown.org

INDEPENDENCE (town). Covers a land area of 34.484 square miles and a water area of 0.005 square miles. Located at 42.04° N. Lat; 77.79° W. Long. Elevation is 2,057 feet.
Population: 1,064; Growth (since 2000): -0.9%; Density: 30.9 persons per square mile; Race: 100.0% White, 0.0% Black/African American, 0.0% Asian, 0.0% American Indian/Alaska Native, 0.0% Native Hawaiian/Other Pacific Islander, 0.0% Two or more races, 0.8% Hispanic of any race; Average household size: 2.42; Median age: 42.0; Age under 18: 25.6%; Age 65 and over: 19.7%; Males per 100 females: 105.5; Marriage status: 16.1% never married, 62.7% now married, 2.2% separated, 6.6% widowed, 14.6% divorced; Foreign born: 1.0%; Speak English only: 99.4%; With disability: 10.2%; Veterans: 8.6%; Ancestry: 32.0% German, 20.6% Irish, 18.9% English, 7.5% American, 4.3% Italian
Employment: 14.0% management, business, and financial, 5.2% computer, engineering, and science, 11.9% education, legal, community service, arts, and media, 3.8% healthcare practitioners, 14.6% service, 17.3% sales and office, 16.9% natural resources, construction, and maintenance, 16.5% production, transportation, and material moving
Income: Per capita: $23,421; Median household: $48,088; Average household: $56,003; Households with income of $100,000 or more: 14.5%; Poverty rate: 22.5%

Educational Attainment: High school diploma or higher: 90.0%; Bachelor's degree or higher: 12.2%; Graduate/professional degree or higher: 3.8%
Housing: Homeownership rate: 89.3%; Median home value: $74,200; Median year structure built: 1953; Homeowner vacancy rate: 2.0%; Median selected monthly owner costs: $944 with a mortgage, $419 without a mortgage; Median gross rent: $677 per month; Rental vacancy rate: 39.7%
Health Insurance: 95.7% have insurance; 69.5% have private insurance; 42.1% have public insurance; 4.3% do not have insurance; 0.0% of children under 18 do not have insurance
Safety: Violent crime rate: 0.0 per 10,000 population; Property crime rate: 26.0 per 10,000 population
Transportation: Commute: 86.1% car, 0.9% public transportation, 4.5% walk, 7.7% work from home; Mean travel time to work: 22.5 minutes

LITTLE GENESEE (unincorporated postal area)
ZCTA: 14754

Covers a land area of 16.613 square miles and a water area of 0.014 square miles. Located at 42.02° N. Lat; 78.20° W. Long. Elevation is 1,552 feet.
Population: 624; Growth (since 2000): 14.5%; Density: 37.6 persons per square mile; Race: 99.5% White, 0.0% Black/African American, 0.0% Asian, 0.0% American Indian/Alaska Native, 0.0% Native Hawaiian/Other Pacific Islander, 0.5% Two or more races, 0.2% Hispanic of any race; Average household size: 2.25; Median age: 46.8; Age under 18: 19.2%; Age 65 and over: 21.3%; Males per 100 females: 102.1; Marriage status: 25.0% never married, 61.5% now married, 3.6% separated, 7.4% widowed, 6.1% divorced; Foreign born: 2.2%; Speak English only: 99.3%; With disability: 14.6%; Veterans: 19.2%; Ancestry: 30.0% German, 23.9% Irish, 16.7% English, 8.8% American, 5.1% Dutch
Employment: 8.4% management, business, and financial, 5.1% computer, engineering, and science, 7.7% education, legal, community service, arts, and media, 0.7% healthcare practitioners, 18.2% service, 29.6% sales and office, 15.8% natural resources, construction, and maintenance, 14.5% production, transportation, and material moving
Income: Per capita: $23,938; Median household: $46,550; Average household: $53,618; Households with income of $100,000 or more: 15.2%; Poverty rate: 15.2%
Educational Attainment: High school diploma or higher: 85.7%; Bachelor's degree or higher: 6.4%; Graduate/professional degree or higher: 3.6%
Housing: Homeownership rate: 78.3%; Median home value: $75,800; Median year structure built: 1970; Homeowner vacancy rate: 0.0%; Median selected monthly owner costs: $1,071 with a mortgage, $406 without a mortgage; Median gross rent: $571 per month; Rental vacancy rate: 0.0%
Health Insurance: 94.4% have insurance; 72.6% have private insurance; 41.0% have public insurance; 5.6% do not have insurance; 0.0% of children under 18 do not have insurance
Transportation: Commute: 94.9% car, 0.0% public transportation, 0.0% walk, 5.1% work from home; Mean travel time to work: 29.4 minutes

NEW HUDSON (town). Covers a land area of 36.195 square miles and a water area of 0.124 square miles. Located at 42.29° N. Lat; 78.25° W. Long.
Population: 822; Growth (since 2000): 11.7%; Density: 22.7 persons per square mile; Race: 93.8% White, 0.0% Black/African American, 1.7% Asian, 0.0% American Indian/Alaska Native, 0.0% Native Hawaiian/Other Pacific Islander, 4.5% Two or more races, 0.1% Hispanic of any race; Average household size: 2.64; Median age: 39.6; Age under 18: 27.0%; Age 65 and over: 15.8%; Males per 100 females: 111.1; Marriage status: 22.2% never married, 61.2% now married, 1.0% separated, 6.3% widowed, 10.3% divorced; Foreign born: 1.5%; Speak English only: 94.8%; With disability: 16.4%; Veterans: 14.1%; Ancestry: 22.4% German, 15.5% English, 15.2% Irish, 9.2% Italian, 6.7% Polish
Employment: 6.3% management, business, and financial, 3.7% computer, engineering, and science, 10.7% education, legal, community service, arts, and media, 11.0% healthcare practitioners, 13.8% service, 18.2% sales and office, 12.7% natural resources, construction, and maintenance, 23.6% production, transportation, and material moving
Income: Per capita: $21,850; Median household: $46,750; Average household: $57,470; Households with income of $100,000 or more: 16.1%; Poverty rate: 12.4%

Educational Attainment: High school diploma or higher: 89.4%; Bachelor's degree or higher: 16.9%; Graduate/professional degree or higher: 8.7%
Housing: Homeownership rate: 83.3%; Median home value: $80,300; Median year structure built: 1980; Homeowner vacancy rate: 0.8%; Median selected monthly owner costs: $1,185 with a mortgage, $526 without a mortgage; Median gross rent: $980 per month; Rental vacancy rate: 0.0%
Health Insurance: 88.6% have insurance; 66.9% have private insurance; 42.9% have public insurance; 11.4% do not have insurance; 8.8% of children under 18 do not have insurance
Transportation: Commute: 90.4% car, 1.7% public transportation, 1.7% walk, 3.2% work from home; Mean travel time to work: 29.5 minutes

OIL SPRINGS RESERVATION (reservation). Covers a land area of 0.590 square miles and a water area of 0.010 square miles. Located at 42.23° N. Lat; 78.30° W. Long.
Population: 2; Growth (since 2000): n/a; Density: 3.4 persons per square mile; Race: 50.0% White, 0.0% Black/African American, 0.0% Asian, 0.0% American Indian/Alaska Native, 0.0% Native Hawaiian/Other Pacific Islander, 50.0% Two or more races, 0.0% Hispanic of any race; Average household size: 2.00; Median age: n/a; Age under 18: 0.0%; Age 65 and over: 0.0%; Males per 100 females: All males; Marriage status: 0.0% never married, 100.0% now married, 0.0% separated, 0.0% widowed, 0.0% divorced; Foreign born: 0.0%; Speak English only: 100.0%; With disability: 50.0%; Veterans: 0.0%; Ancestry: 50.0% Irish
Employment: 0.0% management, business, and financial, 0.0% computer, engineering, and science, 50.0% education, legal, community service, arts, and media, 0.0% healthcare practitioners, 50.0% service, 0.0% sales and office, 0.0% natural resources, construction, and maintenance, 0.0% production, transportation, and material moving
Income: Per capita: n/a; Median household: n/a; Average household: n/a; Households with income of $100,000 or more: n/a; Poverty rate: n/a
Educational Attainment: High school diploma or higher: n/a; Bachelor's degree or higher: n/a; Graduate/professional degree or higher: n/a
Housing: Homeownership rate: 100.0%; Median home value: n/a; Median year structure built: Before 1940; Homeowner vacancy rate: 0.0%; Median selected monthly owner costs: n/a with a mortgage, n/a without a mortgage; Median gross rent: n/a per month; Rental vacancy rate: 0.0%
Health Insurance: 100.0% have insurance; 100.0% have private insurance; 0.0% have public insurance; 0.0% do not have insurance; 0.0% of children under 18 do not have insurance
Transportation: Commute: 100.0% car, 0.0% public transportation, 0.0% walk, 0.0% work from home; Mean travel time to work: 0.0 minutes

RICHBURG (village). Covers a land area of 0.900 square miles and a water area of 0 square miles. Located at 42.09° N. Lat; 78.16° W. Long. Elevation is 1,660 feet.
Population: 475; Growth (since 2000): 6.0%; Density: 527.7 persons per square mile; Race: 100.0% White, 0.0% Black/African American, 0.0% Asian, 0.0% American Indian/Alaska Native, 0.0% Native Hawaiian/Other Pacific Islander, 0.0% Two or more races, 0.8% Hispanic of any race; Average household size: 2.79; Median age: 36.1; Age under 18: 32.8%; Age 65 and over: 10.5%; Males per 100 females: 89.1; Marriage status: 26.3% never married, 57.4% now married, 0.0% separated, 6.2% widowed, 10.1% divorced; Foreign born: 0.4%; Speak English only: 99.5%; With disability: 17.7%; Veterans: 12.2%; Ancestry: 20.8% Irish, 19.4% German, 16.6% English, 14.7% Italian, 5.7% American
Employment: 8.2% management, business, and financial, 2.6% computer, engineering, and science, 5.2% education, legal, community service, arts, and media, 9.3% healthcare practitioners, 17.0% service, 24.7% sales and office, 9.8% natural resources, construction, and maintenance, 23.2% production, transportation, and material moving
Income: Per capita: $16,013; Median household: $37,500; Average household: $46,024; Households with income of $100,000 or more: 10.0%; Poverty rate: 17.3%
Educational Attainment: High school diploma or higher: 88.3%; Bachelor's degree or higher: 10.7%; Graduate/professional degree or higher: 6.5%

School District(s)
Bolivar-Richburg Central SD (PK-12)
    Enrollment: 788. . . . . (585) 928-2561
Housing: Homeownership rate: 70.0%; Median home value: $53,200; Median year structure built: 1946; Homeowner vacancy rate: 3.3%; Median selected monthly owner costs: $904 with a mortgage, $443 without a mortgage; Median gross rent: $705 per month; Rental vacancy rate: 16.4%

Health Insurance: 96.2% have insurance; 58.1% have private insurance; 49.3% have public insurance; 3.8% do not have insurance; 2.5% of children under 18 do not have insurance
Transportation: Commute: 95.4% car, 0.5% public transportation, 4.1% walk, 0.0% work from home; Mean travel time to work: 23.1 minutes

RUSHFORD (CDP).
Covers a land area of 0.559 square miles and a water area of 0 square miles. Located at 42.39° N. Lat; 78.25° W. Long. Elevation is 1,499 feet.
Population: 359; Growth (since 2000): n/a; Density: 642.7 persons per square mile; Race: 87.7% White, 0.0% Black/African American, 0.0% Asian, 0.0% American Indian/Alaska Native, 0.0% Native Hawaiian/Other Pacific Islander, 12.3% Two or more races, 0.0% Hispanic of any race; Average household size: 2.72; Median age: 44.9; Age under 18: 24.2%; Age 65 and over: 10.9%; Males per 100 females: 81.5; Marriage status: 29.7% never married, 41.0% now married, 1.4% separated, 9.9% widowed, 19.5% divorced; Foreign born: 3.6%; Speak English only: 99.7%; With disability: 23.4%; Veterans: 13.6%; Ancestry: 37.6% German, 20.9% Irish, 6.1% American, 6.1% English, 6.1% Italian
Employment: 8.3% management, business, and financial, 0.0% computer, engineering, and science, 7.1% education, legal, community service, arts, and media, 0.0% healthcare practitioners, 32.1% service, 11.9% sales and office, 4.8% natural resources, construction, and maintenance, 35.7% production, transportation, and material moving
Income: Per capita: $20,224; Median household: $46,667; Average household: $55,192; Households with income of $100,000 or more: 9.8%; Poverty rate: 12.3%
Educational Attainment: High school diploma or higher: 86.0%; Bachelor's degree or higher: 11.9%; Graduate/professional degree or higher: 7.0%
School District(s)
Cuba-Rushford Central SD (PK-12)
    Enrollment: 847 . . . . (585) 968-2650
Housing: Homeownership rate: 68.2%; Median home value: $51,300; Median year structure built: Before 1940; Homeowner vacancy rate: 10.0%; Median selected monthly owner costs: $920 with a mortgage, $358 without a mortgage; Median gross rent: $535 per month; Rental vacancy rate: 0.0%
Health Insurance: 88.0% have insurance; 66.0% have private insurance; 38.2% have public insurance; 12.0% do not have insurance; 4.4% of children under 18 do not have insurance
Transportation: Commute: 90.5% car, 6.0% public transportation, 2.4% walk, 1.2% work from home; Mean travel time to work: 28.8 minutes

RUSHFORD (town).
Covers a land area of 35.294 square miles and a water area of 0.790 square miles. Located at 42.39° N. Lat; 78.25° W. Long. Elevation is 1,499 feet.
Population: 1,057; Growth (since 2000): -16.0%; Density: 29.9 persons per square mile; Race: 95.8% White, 0.0% Black/African American, 0.0% Asian, 0.0% American Indian/Alaska Native, 0.0% Native Hawaiian/Other Pacific Islander, 4.2% Two or more races, 0.0% Hispanic of any race; Average household size: 2.17; Median age: 50.8; Age under 18: 16.4%; Age 65 and over: 23.2%; Males per 100 females: 104.6; Marriage status: 22.6% never married, 54.1% now married, 2.0% separated, 10.5% widowed, 12.8% divorced; Foreign born: 1.2%; Speak English only: 98.9%; With disability: 16.3%; Veterans: 14.5%; Ancestry: 32.3% German, 22.3% Irish, 15.5% English, 8.3% Polish, 6.8% American
Employment: 10.4% management, business, and financial, 0.9% computer, engineering, and science, 7.4% education, legal, community service, arts, and media, 7.0% healthcare practitioners, 25.3% service, 10.6% sales and office, 10.2% natural resources, construction, and maintenance, 28.1% production, transportation, and material moving
Income: Per capita: $26,557; Median household: $44,531; Average household: $57,700; Households with income of $100,000 or more: 15.1%; Poverty rate: 11.3%
Educational Attainment: High school diploma or higher: 89.7%; Bachelor's degree or higher: 22.5%; Graduate/professional degree or higher: 11.6%
School District(s)
Cuba-Rushford Central SD (PK-12)
    Enrollment: 847 . . . . (585) 968-2650
Housing: Homeownership rate: 83.1%; Median home value: $76,200; Median year structure built: 1968; Homeowner vacancy rate: 6.3%; Median selected monthly owner costs: $916 with a mortgage, $509 without a mortgage; Median gross rent: $542 per month; Rental vacancy rate: 0.0%

Health Insurance: 91.9% have insurance; 69.2% have private insurance; 47.3% have public insurance; 8.1% do not have insurance; 2.2% of children under 18 do not have insurance
Transportation: Commute: 86.2% car, 3.1% public transportation, 2.2% walk, 7.1% work from home; Mean travel time to work: 24.4 minutes

SCIO (CDP).
Covers a land area of 1.352 square miles and a water area of 0 square miles. Located at 42.17° N. Lat; 77.98° W. Long. Elevation is 1,457 feet.
Population: 572; Growth (since 2000): n/a; Density: 423.1 persons per square mile; Race: 96.3% White, 0.9% Black/African American, 0.0% Asian, 0.0% American Indian/Alaska Native, 0.0% Native Hawaiian/Other Pacific Islander, 2.4% Two or more races, 1.4% Hispanic of any race; Average household size: 2.29; Median age: 43.9; Age under 18: 24.1%; Age 65 and over: 15.0%; Males per 100 females: 102.3; Marriage status: 20.5% never married, 61.8% now married, 3.1% separated, 11.3% widowed, 6.5% divorced; Foreign born: 1.6%; Speak English only: 95.2%; With disability: 11.9%; Veterans: 12.0%; Ancestry: 23.4% English, 16.3% Irish, 12.6% German, 6.3% American, 3.8% Italian
Employment: 7.1% management, business, and financial, 2.1% computer, engineering, and science, 17.8% education, legal, community service, arts, and media, 9.6% healthcare practitioners, 13.9% service, 21.7% sales and office, 5.7% natural resources, construction, and maintenance, 22.1% production, transportation, and material moving
Income: Per capita: $25,599; Median household: $57,188; Average household: $58,994; Households with income of $100,000 or more: 9.6%; Poverty rate: 12.7%
Educational Attainment: High school diploma or higher: 94.6%; Bachelor's degree or higher: 22.2%; Graduate/professional degree or higher: 13.1%
School District(s)
Scio Central SD (PK-12)
    Enrollment: 358 . . . . (585) 593-5076
Housing: Homeownership rate: 82.0%; Median home value: $66,300; Median year structure built: 1957; Homeowner vacancy rate: 0.0%; Median selected monthly owner costs: $948 with a mortgage, $457 without a mortgage; Median gross rent: $706 per month; Rental vacancy rate: 0.0%
Health Insurance: 98.4% have insurance; 80.2% have private insurance; 39.0% have public insurance; 1.6% do not have insurance; 0.0% of children under 18 do not have insurance
Transportation: Commute: 87.1% car, 5.4% public transportation, 3.2% walk, 4.3% work from home; Mean travel time to work: 13.4 minutes

SCIO (town).
Covers a land area of 35.295 square miles and a water area of 0.039 square miles. Located at 42.15° N. Lat; 77.99° W. Long. Elevation is 1,457 feet.
Population: 1,511; Growth (since 2000): -21.1%; Density: 42.8 persons per square mile; Race: 97.6% White, 1.0% Black/African American, 0.0% Asian, 0.0% American Indian/Alaska Native, 0.0% Native Hawaiian/Other Pacific Islander, 1.3% Two or more races, 0.5% Hispanic of any race; Average household size: 2.25; Median age: 49.1; Age under 18: 18.1%; Age 65 and over: 20.8%; Males per 100 females: 103.7; Marriage status: 22.3% never married, 57.7% now married, 2.6% separated, 9.2% widowed, 10.8% divorced; Foreign born: 1.3%; Speak English only: 97.2%; With disability: 16.8%; Veterans: 10.1%; Ancestry: 19.9% English, 16.1% Irish, 15.2% German, 10.7% American, 4.2% Italian
Employment: 7.9% management, business, and financial, 2.3% computer, engineering, and science, 11.7% education, legal, community service, arts, and media, 6.6% healthcare practitioners, 18.2% service, 24.2% sales and office, 7.7% natural resources, construction, and maintenance, 21.5% production, transportation, and material moving
Income: Per capita: $24,581; Median household: $44,688; Average household: $55,542; Households with income of $100,000 or more: 11.5%; Poverty rate: 14.7%
Educational Attainment: High school diploma or higher: 89.4%; Bachelor's degree or higher: 19.6%; Graduate/professional degree or higher: 10.5%
School District(s)
Scio Central SD (PK-12)
    Enrollment: 358 . . . . (585) 593-5076
Housing: Homeownership rate: 78.3%; Median home value: $66,700; Median year structure built: 1966; Homeowner vacancy rate: 1.1%; Median selected monthly owner costs: $941 with a mortgage, $460 without a mortgage; Median gross rent: $667 per month; Rental vacancy rate: 6.5%

Health Insurance: 95.8% have insurance; 75.1% have private insurance; 44.8% have public insurance; 4.2% do not have insurance; 0.0% of children under 18 do not have insurance
Transportation: Commute: 91.4% car, 2.2% public transportation, 1.9% walk, 3.6% work from home; Mean travel time to work: 16.7 minutes

STANNARDS (CDP).
Covers a land area of 2.797 square miles and a water area of 0 square miles. Located at 42.07° N. Lat; 77.91° W. Long. Elevation is 1,549 feet.
Population: 563; Growth (since 2000): -35.1%; Density: 201.3 persons per square mile; Race: 100.0% White, 0.0% Black/African American, 0.0% Asian, 0.0% American Indian/Alaska Native, 0.0% Native Hawaiian/Other Pacific Islander, 0.0% Two or more races, 0.0% Hispanic of any race; Average household size: 2.25; Median age: 51.3; Age under 18: 13.1%; Age 65 and over: 26.3%; Males per 100 females: 89.5; Marriage status: 19.2% never married, 65.6% now married, 1.8% separated, 7.3% widowed, 7.9% divorced; Foreign born: 1.1%; Speak English only: 100.0%; With disability: 14.6%; Veterans: 7.6%; Ancestry: 23.8% English, 22.6% German, 22.6% Irish, 5.3% Italian, 5.2% Dutch
Employment: 14.1% management, business, and financial, 3.1% computer, engineering, and science, 26.5% education, legal, community service, arts, and media, 4.8% healthcare practitioners, 19.6% service, 14.4% sales and office, 2.4% natural resources, construction, and maintenance, 15.1% production, transportation, and material moving
Income: Per capita: $34,612; Median household: $50,625; Average household: $76,580; Households with income of $100,000 or more: 26.0%; Poverty rate: 14.4%
Educational Attainment: High school diploma or higher: 94.3%; Bachelor's degree or higher: 35.4%; Graduate/professional degree or higher: 20.2%
Housing: Homeownership rate: 78.0%; Median home value: $77,200; Median year structure built: 1961; Homeowner vacancy rate: 0.0%; Median selected monthly owner costs: $950 with a mortgage, $476 without a mortgage; Median gross rent: $564 per month; Rental vacancy rate: 0.0%
Health Insurance: 91.3% have insurance; 70.0% have private insurance; 43.9% have public insurance; 8.7% do not have insurance; 6.6% of children under 18 do not have insurance
Transportation: Commute: 96.2% car, 0.0% public transportation, 0.0% walk, 3.8% work from home; Mean travel time to work: 20.7 minutes

SWAIN (unincorporated postal area)
ZCTA: 14884
Covers a land area of 19.162 square miles and a water area of 0.324 square miles. Located at 42.48° N. Lat; 77.89° W. Long. Elevation is 1,316 feet.
Population: 219; Growth (since 2000): -29.1%; Density: 11.4 persons per square mile; Race: 100.0% White, 0.0% Black/African American, 0.0% Asian, 0.0% American Indian/Alaska Native, 0.0% Native Hawaiian/Other Pacific Islander, 0.0% Two or more races, 0.5% Hispanic of any race; Average household size: 1.89; Median age: 55.0; Age under 18: 11.9%; Age 65 and over: 23.7%; Males per 100 females: 108.4; Marriage status: 18.2% never married, 41.9% now married, 5.9% separated, 8.9% widowed, 31.0% divorced; Foreign born: 0.0%; Speak English only: 99.5%; With disability: 18.7%; Veterans: 9.3%; Ancestry: 24.2% German, 22.8% Irish, 19.6% English, 7.8% Italian, 7.3% American
Employment: 19.4% management, business, and financial, 1.9% computer, engineering, and science, 7.4% education, legal, community service, arts, and media, 10.2% healthcare practitioners, 25.0% service, 18.5% sales and office, 10.2% natural resources, construction, and maintenance, 7.4% production, transportation, and material moving
Income: Per capita: $33,714; Median household: $55,000; Average household: $64,459; Households with income of $100,000 or more: 16.4%; Poverty rate: 12.3%
Educational Attainment: High school diploma or higher: 94.0%; Bachelor's degree or higher: 19.7%; Graduate/professional degree or higher: 10.4%
Housing: Homeownership rate: 93.1%; Median home value: $84,400; Median year structure built: 1976; Homeowner vacancy rate: 7.7%; Median selected monthly owner costs: $988 with a mortgage, $459 without a mortgage; Median gross rent: n/a per month; Rental vacancy rate: 27.3%
Health Insurance: 98.6% have insurance; 70.3% have private insurance; 43.8% have public insurance; 1.4% do not have insurance; 0.0% of children under 18 do not have insurance

Transportation: Commute: 93.5% car, 0.0% public transportation, 1.9% walk, 4.6% work from home; Mean travel time to work: 31.5 minutes

WARD (town).
Covers a land area of 29.175 square miles and a water area of 0.017 square miles. Located at 42.23° N. Lat; 77.90° W. Long.
Population: 423; Growth (since 2000): 8.5%; Density: 14.5 persons per square mile; Race: 97.6% White, 0.0% Black/African American, 0.0% Asian, 0.0% American Indian/Alaska Native, 0.0% Native Hawaiian/Other Pacific Islander, 1.2% Two or more races, 1.7% Hispanic of any race; Average household size: 2.84; Median age: 39.9; Age under 18: 27.4%; Age 65 and over: 17.7%; Males per 100 females: 106.7; Marriage status: 18.6% never married, 54.7% now married, 3.5% separated, 8.5% widowed, 18.2% divorced; Foreign born: 1.7%; Speak English only: 99.5%; With disability: 16.1%; Veterans: 12.4%; Ancestry: 35.0% German, 19.1% English, 15.1% Irish, 7.6% American, 4.0% Scottish
Employment: 13.1% management, business, and financial, 3.4% computer, engineering, and science, 14.9% education, legal, community service, arts, and media, 4.0% healthcare practitioners, 13.1% service, 12.6% sales and office, 16.6% natural resources, construction, and maintenance, 22.3% production, transportation, and material moving
Income: Per capita: $24,370; Median household: $52,188; Average household: $66,023; Households with income of $100,000 or more: 21.5%; Poverty rate: 10.6%
Educational Attainment: High school diploma or higher: 94.3%; Bachelor's degree or higher: 16.0%; Graduate/professional degree or higher: 8.7%
Housing: Homeownership rate: 87.2%; Median home value: $79,300; Median year structure built: 1985; Homeowner vacancy rate: 4.4%; Median selected monthly owner costs: $1,080 with a mortgage, $528 without a mortgage; Median gross rent: n/a per month; Rental vacancy rate: 0.0%
Health Insurance: 95.0% have insurance; 64.1% have private insurance; 47.8% have public insurance; 5.0% do not have insurance; 0.0% of children under 18 do not have insurance
Transportation: Commute: 91.4% car, 1.1% public transportation, 1.1% walk, 2.3% work from home; Mean travel time to work: 24.6 minutes

WELLSVILLE (town).
Covers a land area of 36.646 square miles and a water area of 0.037 square miles. Located at 42.12° N. Lat; 77.93° W. Long. Elevation is 1,512 feet.
History: Wellsville was settled in 1795 and named for Gardiner Wells, early settler and chief landowner. Site of David A. Howe Library (1937), with museum and theater. Special museum, Mather Homestead, for visually impaired. Incorporated in 1871.
Population: 7,145; Growth (since 2000): -6.9%; Density: 195.0 persons per square mile; Race: 96.9% White, 0.8% Black/African American, 1.0% Asian, 0.7% American Indian/Alaska Native, 0.0% Native Hawaiian/Other Pacific Islander, 0.3% Two or more races, 0.7% Hispanic of any race; Average household size: 2.12; Median age: 47.5; Age under 18: 17.4%; Age 65 and over: 22.3%; Males per 100 females: 89.8; Marriage status: 25.9% never married, 51.5% now married, 3.4% separated, 10.9% widowed, 11.6% divorced; Foreign born: 2.0%; Speak English only: 97.1%; With disability: 20.2%; Veterans: 10.8%; Ancestry: 23.2% German, 19.2% English, 19.1% Irish, 6.6% Italian, 5.2% American
Employment: 9.4% management, business, and financial, 2.4% computer, engineering, and science, 12.3% education, legal, community service, arts, and media, 6.2% healthcare practitioners, 27.4% service, 16.2% sales and office, 8.1% natural resources, construction, and maintenance, 18.0% production, transportation, and material moving
Income: Per capita: $25,972; Median household: $43,756; Average household: $55,932; Households with income of $100,000 or more: 11.3%; Poverty rate: 15.1%
Educational Attainment: High school diploma or higher: 88.2%; Bachelor's degree or higher: 20.9%; Graduate/professional degree or higher: 9.1%
School District(s)
Wellsville Central SD (PK-12)
    Enrollment: 1,306 . . . . (585) 596-2170
Housing: Homeownership rate: 60.6%; Median home value: $68,700; Median year structure built: 1945; Homeowner vacancy rate: 1.9%; Median selected monthly owner costs: $954 with a mortgage, $417 without a mortgage; Median gross rent: $622 per month; Rental vacancy rate: 2.5%
Health Insurance: 89.2% have insurance; 61.1% have private insurance; 46.1% have public insurance; 10.8% do not have insurance; 13.1% of children under 18 do not have insurance
Hospitals: Jones Memorial Hospital (70 beds)

Newspapers: Daily Reporter (daily circulation 4,500)
Transportation: Commute: 87.7% car, 0.7% public transportation, 7.7% walk, 0.9% work from home; Mean travel time to work: 15.9 minutes
Additional Information Contacts
Town of Wellsville . . . . (585) 593-1780
http://www.townofwellsvilleny.org

WELLSVILLE (village).
Covers a land area of 2.424 square miles and a water area of 0 square miles. Located at 42.12° N. Lat; 77.95° W. Long. Elevation is 1,512 feet.
Population: 4,514; Growth (since 2000): -12.7%; Density: 1,862.1 persons per square mile; Race: 98.1% White, 0.9% Black/African American, 0.0% Asian, 0.0% American Indian/Alaska Native, 0.0% Native Hawaiian/Other Pacific Islander, 0.5% Two or more races, 0.7% Hispanic of any race; Average household size: 2.09; Median age: 45.3; Age under 18: 18.4%; Age 65 and over: 19.4%; Males per 100 females: 88.9; Marriage status: 31.3% never married, 44.4% now married, 3.9% separated, 9.9% widowed, 14.4% divorced; Foreign born: 1.5%; Speak English only: 98.5%; With disability: 21.9%; Veterans: 10.3%; Ancestry: 26.8% German, 20.3% English, 19.5% Irish, 5.6% Italian, 4.9% American
Employment: 8.4% management, business, and financial, 1.9% computer, engineering, and science, 12.5% education, legal, community service, arts, and media, 6.4% healthcare practitioners, 31.6% service, 16.0% sales and office, 7.4% natural resources, construction, and maintenance, 15.9% production, transportation, and material moving
Income: Per capita: $26,053; Median household: $43,152; Average household: $55,310; Households with income of $100,000 or more: 10.8%; Poverty rate: 19.6%
Educational Attainment: High school diploma or higher: 87.2%; Bachelor's degree or higher: 20.5%; Graduate/professional degree or higher: 8.6%

School District(s)
Wellsville Central SD (PK-12)
    Enrollment: 1,306 . . . . (585) 596-2170
Housing: Homeownership rate: 50.3%; Median home value: $60,500; Median year structure built: Before 1940; Homeowner vacancy rate: 3.5%; Median selected monthly owner costs: $841 with a mortgage, $435 without a mortgage; Median gross rent: $611 per month; Rental vacancy rate: 3.0%
Health Insurance: 87.5% have insurance; 53.0% have private insurance; 49.2% have public insurance; 12.5% do not have insurance; 16.2% of children under 18 do not have insurance
Hospitals: Jones Memorial Hospital (70 beds)
Safety: Violent crime rate: 24.7 per 10,000 population; Property crime rate: 154.9 per 10,000 population
Newspapers: Daily Reporter (daily circulation 4,500)
Transportation: Commute: 83.0% car, 0.9% public transportation, 10.4% walk, 1.0% work from home; Mean travel time to work: 15.5 minutes
Additional Information Contacts
Village of Wellsville . . . . (585) 593-1121
http://www.wellsvilleny.com

WEST ALMOND (town).
Covers a land area of 35.995 square miles and a water area of 0.095 square miles. Located at 42.31° N. Lat; 77.91° W. Long. Elevation is 1,854 feet.
Population: 299; Growth (since 2000): -15.3%; Density: 8.3 persons per square mile; Race: 97.7% White, 0.0% Black/African American, 0.0% Asian, 0.0% American Indian/Alaska Native, 0.0% Native Hawaiian/Other Pacific Islander, 2.3% Two or more races, 1.7% Hispanic of any race; Average household size: 2.41; Median age: 45.4; Age under 18: 27.4%; Age 65 and over: 21.7%; Males per 100 females: 115.5; Marriage status: 23.7% never married, 57.8% now married, 0.4% separated, 10.3% widowed, 8.2% divorced; Foreign born: 1.3%; Speak English only: 84.1%; With disability: 15.7%; Veterans: 19.8%; Ancestry: 27.1% German, 23.1% Irish, 18.7% English, 13.0% Pennsylvania German, 11.7% Dutch
Employment: 17.4% management, business, and financial, 1.7% computer, engineering, and science, 6.6% education, legal, community service, arts, and media, 3.3% healthcare practitioners, 11.6% service, 19.8% sales and office, 20.7% natural resources, construction, and maintenance, 19.0% production, transportation, and material moving
Income: Per capita: $24,763; Median household: $58,125; Average household: $62,506; Households with income of $100,000 or more: 14.5%; Poverty rate: 9.6%

Educational Attainment: High school diploma or higher: 90.0%; Bachelor's degree or higher: 17.9%; Graduate/professional degree or higher: 2.0%
Housing: Homeownership rate: 88.7%; Median home value: $84,700; Median year structure built: 1973; Homeowner vacancy rate: 0.0%; Median selected monthly owner costs: $1,100 with a mortgage, $500 without a mortgage; Median gross rent: $325 per month; Rental vacancy rate: 0.0%
Health Insurance: 77.3% have insurance; 65.9% have private insurance; 36.1% have public insurance; 22.7% do not have insurance; 41.2% of children under 18 do not have insurance
Transportation: Commute: 86.8% car, 0.0% public transportation, 11.6% walk, 1.7% work from home; Mean travel time to work: 24.4 minutes

WHITESVILLE (unincorporated postal area)
ZCTA: 14897
    Covers a land area of 25.532 square miles and a water area of 0.002 square miles. Located at 42.02° N. Lat; 77.79° W. Long. Elevation is 1,716 feet.
Population: 766; Growth (since 2000): -13.9%; Density: 30.0 persons per square mile; Race: 100.0% White, 0.0% Black/African American, 0.0% Asian, 0.0% American Indian/Alaska Native, 0.0% Native Hawaiian/Other Pacific Islander, 0.0% Two or more races, 0.3% Hispanic of any race; Average household size: 2.33; Median age: 43.7; Age under 18: 22.8%; Age 65 and over: 19.1%; Males per 100 females: 103.3; Marriage status: 16.5% never married, 65.8% now married, 0.8% separated, 6.5% widowed, 11.1% divorced; Foreign born: 0.3%; Speak English only: 99.2%; With disability: 11.9%; Veterans: 9.6%; Ancestry: 28.7% German, 19.3% Irish, 16.2% English, 9.0% American, 4.2% European
Employment: 10.3% management, business, and financial, 6.8% computer, engineering, and science, 9.2% education, legal, community service, arts, and media, 1.9% healthcare practitioners, 18.2% service, 19.0% sales and office, 17.1% natural resources, construction, and maintenance, 17.4% production, transportation, and material moving
Income: Per capita: $22,172; Median household: $46,016; Average household: $50,926; Households with income of $100,000 or more: 8.8%; Poverty rate: 14.0%
Educational Attainment: High school diploma or higher: 90.0%; Bachelor's degree or higher: 10.2%; Graduate/professional degree or higher: 3.9%

School District(s)
Whitesville Central SD (PK-12)
    Enrollment: 241 . . . . (607) 356-3301
Housing: Homeownership rate: 88.1%; Median home value: $66,300; Median year structure built: 1946; Homeowner vacancy rate: 2.7%; Median selected monthly owner costs: $878 with a mortgage, $397 without a mortgage; Median gross rent: $679 per month; Rental vacancy rate: 35.0%
Health Insurance: 94.9% have insurance; 73.5% have private insurance; 39.3% have public insurance; 5.1% do not have insurance; 3.3% of children under 18 do not have insurance
Transportation: Commute: 87.6% car, 1.1% public transportation, 3.1% walk, 7.0% work from home; Mean travel time to work: 22.7 minutes

WILLING (town).
Covers a land area of 36.240 square miles and a water area of 0.030 square miles. Located at 42.04° N. Lat; 77.89° W. Long.
Population: 1,422; Growth (since 2000): 3.7%; Density: 39.2 persons per square mile; Race: 100.0% White, 0.0% Black/African American, 0.0% Asian, 0.0% American Indian/Alaska Native, 0.0% Native Hawaiian/Other Pacific Islander, 0.0% Two or more races, 0.0% Hispanic of any race; Average household size: 2.41; Median age: 44.2; Age under 18: 22.2%; Age 65 and over: 19.9%; Males per 100 females: 99.7; Marriage status: 22.4% never married, 62.2% now married, 2.1% separated, 4.8% widowed, 10.5% divorced; Foreign born: 0.4%; Speak English only: 95.2%; With disability: 14.2%; Veterans: 7.1%; Ancestry: 29.5% German, 17.2% Irish, 16.0% English, 8.8% Pennsylvania German, 6.1% Italian
Employment: 14.9% management, business, and financial, 2.0% computer, engineering, and science, 10.8% education, legal, community service, arts, and media, 8.2% healthcare practitioners, 19.2% service, 19.7% sales and office, 11.2% natural resources, construction, and maintenance, 14.0% production, transportation, and material moving
Income: Per capita: $24,233; Median household: $42,596; Average household: $58,887; Households with income of $100,000 or more: 17.7%; Poverty rate: 22.2%

Educational Attainment: High school diploma or higher: 87.2%; Bachelor's degree or higher: 18.7%; Graduate/professional degree or higher: 8.7%

Housing: Homeownership rate: 78.3%; Median home value: $83,700; Median year structure built: 1963; Homeowner vacancy rate: 4.2%; Median selected monthly owner costs: $981 with a mortgage, $405 without a mortgage; Median gross rent: $585 per month; Rental vacancy rate: 0.0%

Health Insurance: 87.0% have insurance; 67.4% have private insurance; 37.3% have public insurance; 13.0% do not have insurance; 25.2% of children under 18 do not have insurance

Transportation: Commute: 96.0% car, 0.0% public transportation, 1.8% walk, 2.2% work from home; Mean travel time to work: 24.7 minutes

---

WIRT (town). Covers a land area of 35.938 square miles and a water area of 0.066 square miles. Located at 42.12° N. Lat; 78.13° W. Long. Elevation is 1,877 feet.

Population: 997; Growth (since 2000): -17.9%; Density: 27.7 persons per square mile; Race: 100.0% White, 0.0% Black/African American, 0.0% Asian, 0.0% American Indian/Alaska Native, 0.0% Native Hawaiian/Other Pacific Islander, 0.0% Two or more races, 0.4% Hispanic of any race; Average household size: 2.17; Median age: 50.0; Age under 18: 18.8%; Age 65 and over: 19.7%; Males per 100 females: 94.9; Marriage status: 18.5% never married, 58.2% now married, 1.3% separated, 9.1% widowed, 14.2% divorced; Foreign born: 1.1%; Speak English only: 99.5%; With disability: 22.6%; Veterans: 15.9%; Ancestry: 25.6% German, 19.9% English, 16.4% Irish, 10.5% American, 7.3% Italian

Employment: 11.5% management, business, and financial, 3.1% computer, engineering, and science, 5.5% education, legal, community service, arts, and media, 4.7% healthcare practitioners, 17.3% service, 17.8% sales and office, 15.7% natural resources, construction, and maintenance, 24.3% production, transportation, and material moving

Income: Per capita: $20,741; Median household: $33,250; Average household: $45,541; Households with income of $100,000 or more: 11.1%; Poverty rate: 15.3%

Educational Attainment: High school diploma or higher: 84.5%; Bachelor's degree or higher: 6.0%; Graduate/professional degree or higher: 2.9%

Housing: Homeownership rate: 84.8%; Median home value: $56,100; Median year structure built: 1967; Homeowner vacancy rate: 1.0%; Median selected monthly owner costs: $969 with a mortgage, $360 without a mortgage; Median gross rent: $625 per month; Rental vacancy rate: 19.5%

Health Insurance: 92.2% have insurance; 64.9% have private insurance; 47.6% have public insurance; 7.8% do not have insurance; 4.1% of children under 18 do not have insurance

Transportation: Commute: 92.3% car, 0.3% public transportation, 3.7% walk, 2.6% work from home; Mean travel time to work: 26.9 minutes

Bronx County and Borough

See New York City

Brooklyn Borough

See New York City

Broome County

Located in southern New York; bounded on the south by Pennsylvania. Covers a land area of 705.766 square miles, a water area of 9.749 square miles, and is located in the Eastern Time Zone at 42.16° N. Lat., 75.83° W. Long. The county was founded in 1806. County seat is Binghamton.

Broome County is part of the Binghamton, NY Metropolitan Statistical Area. The entire metro area includes: Broome County, NY; Tioga County, NY

Weather Station: Binghamton Edwin A Link Field   Elevation: 1,600 feet

	Jan	Feb	Mar	Apr	May	Jun	Jul	Aug	Sep	Oct	Nov	Dec
High	29	33	41	55	66	74	78	77	69	57	45	34
Low	16	17	25	36	46	55	60	58	51	40	31	21
Precip	2.4	2.3	3.1	3.5	3.5	4.3	3.7	3.4	3.6	3.3	3.3	2.8
Snow	21.7	15.9	15.5	4.3	0.1	tr	0.0	tr	tr	1.1	7.0	17.2

High and Low temperatures in degrees Fahrenheit; Precipitation and Snow in inches

Population: 196,124; Growth (since 2000): -2.2%; Density: 277.9 persons per square mile; Race: 86.1% White, 5.8% Black/African American, 4.2% Asian, 0.2% American Indian/Alaska Native, 0.0% Native Hawaiian/Other Pacific Islander, 2.8% two or more races, 4.0% Hispanic of any race; Average household size: 2.36; Median age: 39.6; Age under 18: 19.6%; Age 65 and over: 17.9%; Males per 100 females: 96.2; Marriage status: 36.7% never married, 45.6% now married, 2.1% separated, 6.6% widowed, 11.1% divorced; Foreign born: 6.7%; Speak English only: 90.5%; With disability: 15.4%; Veterans: 7.7%; Ancestry: 18.8% Irish, 15.7% German, 12.3% Italian, 11.7% English, 6.1% Polish

Religion: Six largest groups: 31.0% Catholicism, 7.1% Methodist/Pietist, 3.0% Non-denominational Protestant, 1.9% Holiness, 1.5% Presbyterian-Reformed, 1.4% Lutheran

Economy: Unemployment rate: 4.1%; Leading industries: 16.6 % retail trade; 12.2 % accommodation and food services; 12.1 % other services (except public administration); Farms: 563 totaling 79,676 acres; Company size: 4 employ 1,000 or more persons, 8 employ 500 to 999 persons, 100 employ 100 to 499 persons, 4,135 employ less than 100 persons; Business ownership: 4,461 women-owned, 583 Black-owned, 226 Hispanic-owned, 434 Asian-owned, 98 American Indian/Alaska Native-owned

Employment: 11.9% management, business, and financial, 5.7% computer, engineering, and science, 13.2% education, legal, community service, arts, and media, 6.8% healthcare practitioners, 19.5% service, 24.5% sales and office, 6.9% natural resources, construction, and maintenance, 11.4% production, transportation, and material moving

Income: Per capita: $26,790; Median household: $49,064; Average household: $65,202; Households with income of $100,000 or more: 18.7%; Poverty rate: 17.1%

Educational Attainment: High school diploma or higher: 90.4%; Bachelor's degree or higher: 28.0%; Graduate/professional degree or higher: 12.4%

Housing: Homeownership rate: 65.7%; Median home value: $113,100; Median year structure built: 1956; Homeowner vacancy rate: 1.7%; Median selected monthly owner costs: $1,185 with a mortgage, $495 without a mortgage; Median gross rent: $734 per month; Rental vacancy rate: 8.0%

Vital Statistics: Birth rate: 99.5 per 10,000 population; Death rate: 109.2 per 10,000 population; Age-adjusted cancer mortality rate: 151.8 deaths per 100,000 population

Health Insurance: 95.1% have insurance; 69.2% have private insurance; 41.7% have public insurance; 4.9% do not have insurance; 3.0% of children under 18 do not have insurance

Health Care: Physicians: 31.0 per 10,000 population; Dentists: 7.1 per 10,000 population; Hospital beds: 36.3 per 10,000 population; Hospital admissions: 1,396.8 per 10,000 population

Transportation: Commute: 88.8% car, 3.1% public transportation, 3.9% walk, 3.1% work from home; Mean travel time to work: 19.7 minutes

2016 Presidential Election: 47.6% Trump, 45.6% Clinton, 3.8% Johnson, 1.8% Stein

National and State Parks: Broome State Forest; Chenango Valley State Park; Tracy Creek State Forest

Additional Information Contacts
Broome Government . . . . (607) 778-2109
  http://www.gobroomecounty.com/legis

Broome County Communities

BARKER (town). Covers a land area of 41.403 square miles and a water area of 0.376 square miles. Located at 42.27° N. Lat; 75.91° W. Long.

Population: 2,678; Growth (since 2000): -2.2%; Density: 64.7 persons per square mile; Race: 98.4% White, 0.0% Black/African American, 0.4% Asian, 0.0% American Indian/Alaska Native, 0.0% Native Hawaiian/Other Pacific Islander, 0.3% Two or more races, 1.5% Hispanic of any race; Average household size: 2.67; Median age: 46.2; Age under 18: 20.0%; Age 65 and over: 15.2%; Males per 100 females: 104.6; Marriage status: 23.3% never married, 62.1% now married, 1.6% separated, 4.6% widowed, 9.9% divorced; Foreign born: 1.8%; Speak English only: 95.8%; With disability: 17.0%; Veterans: 9.4%; Ancestry: 15.4% German, 15.0% Irish, 12.9% American, 11.0% English, 7.6% Italian

Employment: 15.4% management, business, and financial, 3.4% computer, engineering, and science, 6.2% education, legal, community service, arts, and media, 5.7% healthcare practitioners, 12.7% service, 26.6% sales and office, 12.2% natural resources, construction, and maintenance, 17.8% production, transportation, and material moving

Income: Per capita: $27,356; Median household: $63,015; Average household: $72,767; Households with income of $100,000 or more: 24.6%; Poverty rate: 8.4%
Educational Attainment: High school diploma or higher: 91.3%; Bachelor's degree or higher: 17.1%; Graduate/professional degree or higher: 6.3%
Housing: Homeownership rate: 95.6%; Median home value: $109,500; Median year structure built: 1973; Homeowner vacancy rate: 0.0%; Median selected monthly owner costs: $1,258 with a mortgage, $522 without a mortgage; Median gross rent: $850 per month; Rental vacancy rate: 15.9%
Health Insurance: 94.0% have insurance; 72.9% have private insurance; 35.3% have public insurance; 6.0% do not have insurance; 0.0% of children under 18 do not have insurance
Transportation: Commute: 94.3% car, 0.0% public transportation, 1.6% walk, 4.1% work from home; Mean travel time to work: 24.8 minutes

BINGHAMTON (city). County seat. Covers a land area of 10.489 square miles and a water area of 0.647 square miles. Located at 42.10° N. Lat; 75.91° W. Long. Elevation is 866 feet.

History: Little is known of the Binghamton area before the Revolution. The site was purchased in 1786 by William Bingham, a Philadelphia merchant. Joseph Leonard, first permanent settler, built his log cabin nearby in 1787 and was soon joined by other pioneers, who called the new settlement Chenango. It was later renamed in honor of Bingham, who made liberal donations of land to the settlement. It was incorporated as a village in 1834 and as a city in 1867.
Population: 45,964; Growth (since 2000): -3.0%; Density: 4,382.1 persons per square mile; Race: 75.0% White, 13.3% Black/African American, 4.6% Asian, 0.4% American Indian/Alaska Native, 0.0% Native Hawaiian/Other Pacific Islander, 4.9% Two or more races, 7.1% Hispanic of any race; Average household size: 2.21; Median age: 36.4; Age under 18: 19.3%; Age 65 and over: 17.0%; Males per 100 females: 96.1; Marriage status: 46.4% never married, 32.6% now married, 2.6% separated, 7.8% widowed, 13.2% divorced; Foreign born: 9.5%; Speak English only: 86.5%; With disability: 20.3%; Veterans: 6.3%; Ancestry: 19.2% Irish, 13.8% German, 11.5% Italian, 8.9% English, 4.8% Polish
Employment: 10.2% management, business, and financial, 3.9% computer, engineering, and science, 14.8% education, legal, community service, arts, and media, 4.6% healthcare practitioners, 25.1% service, 27.1% sales and office, 4.7% natural resources, construction, and maintenance, 9.6% production, transportation, and material moving
Income: Per capita: $21,710; Median household: $31,103; Average household: $48,530; Households with income of $100,000 or more: 10.1%; Poverty rate: 33.3%
Educational Attainment: High school diploma or higher: 85.1%; Bachelor's degree or higher: 23.5%; Graduate/professional degree or higher: 10.7%

School District(s)
Binghamton City SD (PK-12)
    Enrollment: 5,696 . . . . (607) 762-8100
Broome-Delaware-Tioga Boces
    Enrollment: n/a . . . . (607) 766-3802
Chenango Forks Central SD (PK-12)
    Enrollment: 1,601 . . . . (607) 648-7543
Chenango Valley Central SD (PK-12)
    Enrollment: 1,794 . . . . (607) 762-6801
Susquehanna Valley Central SD (KG-12)
    Enrollment: 1,514 . . . . (607) 775-0170
Two-year College(s)
SUNY Broome Community College (Public)
    Enrollment: 5,624 . . . . (607) 778-5000
    Tuition: In-state $5,165; Out-of-state $9,747
Vocational/Technical School(s)
Broome Delaware Tioga BOCES-Practical Nursing Program (Public)
    Enrollment: 66 . . . . (607) 763-3465
    Tuition: $12,800
Ridley-Lowell Business & Technical Institute-Binghamton (Private, For-profit)
    Enrollment: n/a . . . . (607) 724-2941
    Tuition: $13,000
Housing: Homeownership rate: 45.0%; Median home value: $87,500; Median year structure built: 1941; Homeowner vacancy rate: 3.7%; Median selected monthly owner costs: $1,073 with a mortgage, $477 without a mortgage; Median gross rent: $702 per month; Rental vacancy rate: 8.5%

Health Insurance: 93.7% have insurance; 52.7% have private insurance; 54.7% have public insurance; 6.3% do not have insurance; 1.3% of children under 18 do not have insurance
Hospitals: Our Lady of Lourdes Memorial Hospital (161 beds)
Safety: Violent crime rate: 79.7 per 10,000 population; Property crime rate: 436.8 per 10,000 population
Newspapers: Press & Sun-Bulletin (daily circulation 52,000)
Transportation: Commute: 80.7% car, 7.9% public transportation, 6.2% walk, 2.8% work from home; Mean travel time to work: 17.0 minutes
Airports: Greater Binghamton/Edwin A Link Field (primary service/non-hub)
Additional Information Contacts
City of Binghamton . . . . (607) 772-7001
    http://www.cityofbinghamton.com

BINGHAMTON (town). Covers a land area of 25.251 square miles and a water area of 0.088 square miles. Located at 42.04° N. Lat; 75.91° W. Long. Elevation is 866 feet.

History: Grew mainly after the Chenango Canal connected it with Utica in 1837. First railroad service began in 1869. State University of N.Y. at Binghamton in the vicinity. Settled 1787, Incorporated as a city 1867.
Population: 4,826; Growth (since 2000): -2.9%; Density: 191.1 persons per square mile; Race: 94.4% White, 0.6% Black/African American, 2.4% Asian, 0.0% American Indian/Alaska Native, 0.0% Native Hawaiian/Other Pacific Islander, 2.6% Two or more races, 1.1% Hispanic of any race; Average household size: 2.58; Median age: 47.8; Age under 18: 19.0%; Age 65 and over: 18.5%; Males per 100 females: 101.6; Marriage status: 28.2% never married, 60.8% now married, 1.0% separated, 3.5% widowed, 7.4% divorced; Foreign born: 5.5%; Speak English only: 92.9%; With disability: 9.0%; Veterans: 7.3%; Ancestry: 25.5% Irish, 15.2% German, 14.4% Italian, 14.3% English, 6.3% Polish
Employment: 16.7% management, business, and financial, 8.4% computer, engineering, and science, 15.1% education, legal, community service, arts, and media, 4.8% healthcare practitioners, 13.2% service, 24.3% sales and office, 6.8% natural resources, construction, and maintenance, 10.7% production, transportation, and material moving
Income: Per capita: $39,428; Median household: $73,723; Average household: $101,435; Households with income of $100,000 or more: 40.0%; Poverty rate: 5.2%
Educational Attainment: High school diploma or higher: 93.6%; Bachelor's degree or higher: 38.4%; Graduate/professional degree or higher: 21.6%

School District(s)
Binghamton City SD (PK-12)
    Enrollment: 5,696 . . . . (607) 762-8100
Broome-Delaware-Tioga Boces
    Enrollment: n/a . . . . (607) 766-3802
Chenango Forks Central SD (PK-12)
    Enrollment: 1,601 . . . . (607) 648-7543
Chenango Valley Central SD (PK-12)
    Enrollment: 1,794 . . . . (607) 762-6801
Susquehanna Valley Central SD (KG-12)
    Enrollment: 1,514 . . . . (607) 775-0170
Two-year College(s)
SUNY Broome Community College (Public)
    Enrollment: 5,624 . . . . (607) 778-5000
    Tuition: In-state $5,165; Out-of-state $9,747
Vocational/Technical School(s)
Broome Delaware Tioga BOCES-Practical Nursing Program (Public)
    Enrollment: 66 . . . . (607) 763-3465
    Tuition: $12,800
Ridley-Lowell Business & Technical Institute-Binghamton (Private, For-profit)
    Enrollment: n/a . . . . (607) 724-2941
    Tuition: $13,000
Housing: Homeownership rate: 91.6%; Median home value: $154,500; Median year structure built: 1967; Homeowner vacancy rate: 2.5%; Median selected monthly owner costs: $1,420 with a mortgage, $585 without a mortgage; Median gross rent: $776 per month; Rental vacancy rate: 0.0%
Health Insurance: 97.2% have insurance; 77.1% have private insurance; 35.6% have public insurance; 2.8% do not have insurance; 0.0% of children under 18 do not have insurance
Hospitals: Our Lady of Lourdes Memorial Hospital (161 beds)
Newspapers: Press & Sun-Bulletin (daily circulation 52,000)

Transportation: Commute: 96.4% car, 0.8% public transportation, 0.0% walk, 2.4% work from home; Mean travel time to work: 20.2 minutes
Airports: Greater Binghamton/Edwin A Link Field (primary service/non-hub)
Additional Information Contacts
Town of Binghamton . . . . (607) 772-0357
  http://www.townofbinghamton.com

BINGHAMTON UNIVERSITY (CDP). Covers a land area of 0.775 square miles and a water area of 0 square miles. Located at 42.09° N. Lat; 75.97° W. Long.

History: Binghamton is a city in, and the county seat of, Broome County, New York. It is the home of Binghamton University, a state university of New York.
Population: 6,240; Growth (since 2000): n/a; Density: 8,046.5 persons per square mile; Race: 64.0% White, 6.4% Black/African American, 23.2% Asian, 0.0% American Indian/Alaska Native, 0.0% Native Hawaiian/Other Pacific Islander, 4.9% Two or more races, 10.2% Hispanic of any race; Average household size: 1.88; Median age: 19.6; Age under 18: 1.6%; Age 65 and over: 0.2%; Males per 100 females: 109.1; Marriage status: 99.4% never married, 0.6% now married, 0.0% separated, 0.0% widowed, 0.0% divorced; Foreign born: 9.7%; Speak English only: 70.1%; With disability: 4.6%; Veterans: 0.0%; Ancestry: 13.2% Irish, 13.0% Italian, 9.8% German, 6.1% Polish, 4.5% Russian
Employment: 4.5% management, business, and financial, 5.4% computer, engineering, and science, 13.8% education, legal, community service, arts, and media, 0.0% healthcare practitioners, 40.0% service, 30.0% sales and office, 0.0% natural resources, construction, and maintenance, 6.3% production, transportation, and material moving
Income: Per capita: $3,100; Median household: n/a; Average household: n/a; Households with income of $100,000 or more: n/a; Poverty rate: n/a
Educational Attainment: High school diploma or higher: n/a; Bachelor's degree or higher: n/a; Graduate/professional degree or higher: n/a
Housing: Homeownership rate: n/a; Median home value: n/a; Median year structure built: n/a; Homeowner vacancy rate: n/a; Median selected monthly owner costs: n/a with a mortgage, n/a without a mortgage; Median gross rent: n/a per month; Rental vacancy rate: n/a
Health Insurance: 94.9% have insurance; 85.9% have private insurance; 11.7% have public insurance; 5.1% do not have insurance; 3.1% of children under 18 do not have insurance
Transportation: Commute: 32.7% car, 4.8% public transportation, 47.5% walk, 13.3% work from home; Mean travel time to work: 12.6 minutes

CASTLE CREEK (unincorporated postal area)
ZCTA: 13744
  Covers a land area of 11.587 square miles and a water area of 0.004 square miles. Located at 42.24° N. Lat; 75.91° W. Long. Elevation is 1,050 feet.
  Population: 1,193; Growth (since 2000): -0.7%; Density: 103.0 persons per square mile; Race: 98.6% White, 0.0% Black/African American, 0.0% Asian, 0.0% American Indian/Alaska Native, 0.1% Native Hawaiian/Other Pacific Islander, 1.3% Two or more races, 0.8% Hispanic of any race; Average household size: 2.50; Median age: 47.3; Age under 18: 19.0%; Age 65 and over: 16.8%; Males per 100 females: 105.2; Marriage status: 21.0% never married, 64.6% now married, 0.5% separated, 5.3% widowed, 9.2% divorced; Foreign born: 4.1%; Speak English only: 93.9%; With disability: 14.6%; Veterans: 10.0%; Ancestry: 25.1% German, 13.6% American, 11.3% Irish, 10.1% Polish, 7.7% English
  Employment: 16.1% management, business, and financial, 5.4% computer, engineering, and science, 11.5% education, legal, community service, arts, and media, 6.7% healthcare practitioners, 13.0% service, 23.9% sales and office, 9.1% natural resources, construction, and maintenance, 14.3% production, transportation, and material moving
  Income: Per capita: $28,720; Median household: $59,853; Average household: $71,771; Households with income of $100,000 or more: 21.8%; Poverty rate: 11.4%
  Educational Attainment: High school diploma or higher: 92.9%; Bachelor's degree or higher: 28.6%; Graduate/professional degree or higher: 9.3%
  Housing: Homeownership rate: 93.5%; Median home value: $116,000; Median year structure built: 1973; Homeowner vacancy rate: 0.0%; Median selected monthly owner costs: $1,171 with a mortgage, $516 without a mortgage; Median gross rent: n/a per month; Rental vacancy rate: 37.5%

Health Insurance: 94.8% have insurance; 78.0% have private insurance; 36.7% have public insurance; 5.2% do not have insurance; 0.0% of children under 18 do not have insurance
Transportation: Commute: 91.8% car, 0.0% public transportation, 3.0% walk, 5.2% work from home; Mean travel time to work: 19.4 minutes

CHENANGO (town). Covers a land area of 33.834 square miles and a water area of 0.434 square miles. Located at 42.22° N. Lat; 75.90° W. Long.

Population: 10,896; Growth (since 2000): -4.9%; Density: 322.0 persons per square mile; Race: 95.7% White, 1.0% Black/African American, 1.1% Asian, 0.1% American Indian/Alaska Native, 0.0% Native Hawaiian/Other Pacific Islander, 2.0% Two or more races, 0.5% Hispanic of any race; Average household size: 2.50; Median age: 44.4; Age under 18: 20.0%; Age 65 and over: 18.3%; Males per 100 females: 96.5; Marriage status: 29.6% never married, 55.8% now married, 1.5% separated, 5.4% widowed, 9.1% divorced; Foreign born: 3.7%; Speak English only: 94.0%; With disability: 14.8%; Veterans: 8.1%; Ancestry: 20.8% Irish, 19.7% German, 14.2% English, 11.2% Italian, 8.6% Polish
Employment: 15.4% management, business, and financial, 5.8% computer, engineering, and science, 14.8% education, legal, community service, arts, and media, 9.2% healthcare practitioners, 12.4% service, 23.2% sales and office, 9.3% natural resources, construction, and maintenance, 9.9% production, transportation, and material moving
Income: Per capita: $34,339; Median household: $68,935; Average household: $84,343; Households with income of $100,000 or more: 26.5%; Poverty rate: 8.9%
Educational Attainment: High school diploma or higher: 94.3%; Bachelor's degree or higher: 33.3%; Graduate/professional degree or higher: 13.2%
Housing: Homeownership rate: 83.1%; Median home value: $139,600; Median year structure built: 1964; Homeowner vacancy rate: 1.0%; Median selected monthly owner costs: $1,317 with a mortgage, $512 without a mortgage; Median gross rent: $759 per month; Rental vacancy rate: 14.4%
Health Insurance: 96.5% have insurance; 76.9% have private insurance; 35.0% have public insurance; 3.5% do not have insurance; 2.1% of children under 18 do not have insurance
Transportation: Commute: 95.6% car, 1.0% public transportation, 0.4% walk, 2.1% work from home; Mean travel time to work: 20.4 minutes
Additional Information Contacts
Town of Chenango . . . . (607) 648-4809
  http://www.townofchenango.com

CHENANGO BRIDGE (CDP). Covers a land area of 2.448 square miles and a water area of 0.144 square miles. Located at 42.17° N. Lat; 75.86° W. Long. Elevation is 896 feet.

Population: 2,934; Growth (since 2000): n/a; Density: 1,198.3 persons per square mile; Race: 98.2% White, 0.3% Black/African American, 0.9% Asian, 0.0% American Indian/Alaska Native, 0.0% Native Hawaiian/Other Pacific Islander, 0.3% Two or more races, 0.3% Hispanic of any race; Average household size: 2.59; Median age: 45.5; Age under 18: 18.3%; Age 65 and over: 19.3%; Males per 100 females: 96.0; Marriage status: 29.4% never married, 58.4% now married, 0.6% separated, 5.1% widowed, 7.1% divorced; Foreign born: 3.0%; Speak English only: 97.6%; With disability: 12.2%; Veterans: 5.9%; Ancestry: 20.0% Irish, 15.0% German, 14.5% English, 12.7% Italian, 8.0% Polish
Employment: 19.1% management, business, and financial, 7.8% computer, engineering, and science, 18.2% education, legal, community service, arts, and media, 9.2% healthcare practitioners, 9.8% service, 19.0% sales and office, 5.5% natural resources, construction, and maintenance, 11.5% production, transportation, and material moving
Income: Per capita: $41,323; Median household: $70,508; Average household: $104,613; Households with income of $100,000 or more: 30.2%; Poverty rate: 8.6%
Educational Attainment: High school diploma or higher: 94.4%; Bachelor's degree or higher: 38.7%; Graduate/professional degree or higher: 17.6%
Housing: Homeownership rate: 87.9%; Median home value: $136,100; Median year structure built: 1958; Homeowner vacancy rate: 0.0%; Median selected monthly owner costs: $1,328 with a mortgage, $503 without a mortgage; Median gross rent: $699 per month; Rental vacancy rate: 16.0%
Health Insurance: 96.2% have insurance; 81.5% have private insurance; 31.2% have public insurance; 3.8% do not have insurance; 3.0% of children under 18 do not have insurance

Transportation: Commute: 96.8% car, 0.0% public transportation, 0.7% walk, 2.5% work from home; Mean travel time to work: 18.9 minutes

CHENANGO FORKS (unincorporated postal area)
ZCTA: 13746

Covers a land area of 27.735 square miles and a water area of 0.483 square miles. Located at 42.27° N. Lat; 75.88° W. Long. Elevation is 915 feet.

Population: 2,027; Growth (since 2000): -8.0%; Density: 73.1 persons per square mile; Race: 94.9% White, 0.0% Black/African American, 0.2% Asian, 1.2% American Indian/Alaska Native, 0.0% Native Hawaiian/Other Pacific Islander, 2.5% Two or more races, 0.8% Hispanic of any race; Average household size: 2.40; Median age: 50.2; Age under 18: 21.4%; Age 65 and over: 21.0%; Males per 100 females: 104.9; Marriage status: 19.8% never married, 66.9% now married, 1.3% separated, 6.0% widowed, 7.3% divorced; Foreign born: 2.0%; Speak English only: 96.9%; With disability: 12.6%; Veterans: 7.4%; Ancestry: 20.4% English, 19.3% Irish, 17.0% German, 11.2% Italian, 10.7% American

Employment: 10.9% management, business, and financial, 4.1% computer, engineering, and science, 14.1% education, legal, community service, arts, and media, 12.2% healthcare practitioners, 16.4% service, 21.7% sales and office, 8.7% natural resources, construction, and maintenance, 11.9% production, transportation, and material moving

Income: Per capita: $27,227; Median household: $51,667; Average household: $65,932; Households with income of $100,000 or more: 18.9%; Poverty rate: 9.3%

Educational Attainment: High school diploma or higher: 92.3%; Bachelor's degree or higher: 25.0%; Graduate/professional degree or higher: 11.5%

Housing: Homeownership rate: 92.7%; Median home value: $118,100; Median year structure built: 1972; Homeowner vacancy rate: 0.8%; Median selected monthly owner costs: $1,285 with a mortgage, $586 without a mortgage; Median gross rent: $693 per month; Rental vacancy rate: 15.1%

Health Insurance: 99.1% have insurance; 78.6% have private insurance; 37.5% have public insurance; 0.9% do not have insurance; 0.0% of children under 18 do not have insurance

Transportation: Commute: 98.9% car, 0.0% public transportation, 0.0% walk, 1.1% work from home; Mean travel time to work: 25.0 minutes

COLESVILLE (town). Covers a land area of 78.347 square miles and a water area of 0.824 square miles. Located at 42.18° N. Lat; 75.65° W. Long.

Population: 5,135; Growth (since 2000): -5.6%; Density: 65.5 persons per square mile; Race: 95.3% White, 1.1% Black/African American, 0.0% Asian, 1.2% American Indian/Alaska Native, 0.0% Native Hawaiian/Other Pacific Islander, 2.3% Two or more races, 0.5% Hispanic of any race; Average household size: 2.62; Median age: 41.7; Age under 18: 22.5%; Age 65 and over: 15.5%; Males per 100 females: 107.3; Marriage status: 19.9% never married, 62.1% now married, 1.6% separated, 7.7% widowed, 10.2% divorced; Foreign born: 2.3%; Speak English only: 92.7%; With disability: 19.9%; Veterans: 12.6%; Ancestry: 25.8% Irish, 23.2% German, 12.1% English, 10.2% American, 5.5% Dutch

Employment: 6.2% management, business, and financial, 1.4% computer, engineering, and science, 15.2% education, legal, community service, arts, and media, 4.8% healthcare practitioners, 19.1% service, 15.9% sales and office, 10.9% natural resources, construction, and maintenance, 26.6% production, transportation, and material moving

Income: Per capita: $22,133; Median household: $48,175; Average household: $56,980; Households with income of $100,000 or more: 11.5%; Poverty rate: 16.6%

Educational Attainment: High school diploma or higher: 83.1%; Bachelor's degree or higher: 15.3%; Graduate/professional degree or higher: 7.5%

Housing: Homeownership rate: 75.3%; Median home value: $88,500; Median year structure built: 1972; Homeowner vacancy rate: 2.6%; Median selected monthly owner costs: $1,166 with a mortgage, $453 without a mortgage; Median gross rent: $677 per month; Rental vacancy rate: 7.6%

Health Insurance: 95.3% have insurance; 63.4% have private insurance; 45.6% have public insurance; 4.7% do not have insurance; 3.5% of children under 18 do not have insurance

Transportation: Commute: 97.9% car, 0.0% public transportation, 1.2% walk, 0.9% work from home; Mean travel time to work: 26.8 minutes

CONKLIN (town). Covers a land area of 24.385 square miles and a water area of 0.504 square miles. Located at 42.04° N. Lat; 75.84° W. Long. Elevation is 869 feet.

Population: 5,291; Growth (since 2000): -10.9%; Density: 217.0 persons per square mile; Race: 98.2% White, 1.3% Black/African American, 0.0% Asian, 0.1% American Indian/Alaska Native, 0.0% Native Hawaiian/Other Pacific Islander, 0.4% Two or more races, 3.2% Hispanic of any race; Average household size: 2.61; Median age: 43.4; Age under 18: 23.8%; Age 65 and over: 15.7%; Males per 100 females: 97.2; Marriage status: 26.8% never married, 54.2% now married, 2.5% separated, 2.8% widowed, 16.2% divorced; Foreign born: 0.7%; Speak English only: 97.6%; With disability: 10.8%; Veterans: 7.6%; Ancestry: 26.8% Irish, 24.0% English, 20.2% German, 15.1% Italian, 4.8% Polish

Employment: 10.2% management, business, and financial, 2.6% computer, engineering, and science, 11.5% education, legal, community service, arts, and media, 6.7% healthcare practitioners, 24.9% service, 17.8% sales and office, 6.7% natural resources, construction, and maintenance, 19.7% production, transportation, and material moving

Income: Per capita: $27,213; Median household: $55,699; Average household: $69,437; Households with income of $100,000 or more: 20.1%; Poverty rate: 11.9%

Educational Attainment: High school diploma or higher: 92.8%; Bachelor's degree or higher: 23.1%; Graduate/professional degree or higher: 10.5%

School District(s)
Susquehanna Valley Central SD (KG-12)
    Enrollment: 1,514 . . . . (607) 775-0170
Housing: Homeownership rate: 84.1%; Median home value: $118,400; Median year structure built: 1973; Homeowner vacancy rate: 0.0%; Median selected monthly owner costs: $1,144 with a mortgage, $495 without a mortgage; Median gross rent: $596 per month; Rental vacancy rate: 0.0%

Health Insurance: 91.4% have insurance; 74.7% have private insurance; 30.8% have public insurance; 8.6% do not have insurance; 21.7% of children under 18 do not have insurance

Newspapers: Country Courier (weekly circulation 1,300); Windsor Standard (weekly circulation 1,300)

Transportation: Commute: 99.5% car, 0.0% public transportation, 0.0% walk, 0.5% work from home; Mean travel time to work: 24.2 minutes

DICKINSON (town). Covers a land area of 4.772 square miles and a water area of 0.105 square miles. Located at 42.13° N. Lat; 75.92° W. Long.

History: Incorporated 1876.

Population: 5,174; Growth (since 2000): -3.0%; Density: 1,084.3 persons per square mile; Race: 91.6% White, 5.4% Black/African American, 0.3% Asian, 0.0% American Indian/Alaska Native, 0.0% Native Hawaiian/Other Pacific Islander, 2.7% Two or more races, 2.5% Hispanic of any race; Average household size: 2.16; Median age: 41.2; Age under 18: 15.3%; Age 65 and over: 18.9%; Males per 100 females: 103.8; Marriage status: 43.4% never married, 36.9% now married, 2.7% separated, 6.7% widowed, 13.0% divorced; Foreign born: 2.6%; Speak English only: 94.9%; With disability: 14.3%; Veterans: 9.7%; Ancestry: 19.8% Irish, 17.9% German, 13.7% Italian, 11.9% English, 7.0% Polish

Employment: 10.0% management, business, and financial, 3.9% computer, engineering, and science, 12.0% education, legal, community service, arts, and media, 7.6% healthcare practitioners, 25.7% service, 28.6% sales and office, 5.0% natural resources, construction, and maintenance, 7.2% production, transportation, and material moving

Income: Per capita: $26,629; Median household: $54,838; Average household: $62,823; Households with income of $100,000 or more: 16.9%; Poverty rate: 11.4%

Educational Attainment: High school diploma or higher: 91.6%; Bachelor's degree or higher: 26.3%; Graduate/professional degree or higher: 10.5%

Housing: Homeownership rate: 72.3%; Median home value: $108,000; Median year structure built: 1950; Homeowner vacancy rate: 0.0%; Median selected monthly owner costs: $1,174 with a mortgage, $436 without a mortgage; Median gross rent: $733 per month; Rental vacancy rate: 7.0%

Health Insurance: 96.2% have insurance; 77.3% have private insurance; 37.9% have public insurance; 3.8% do not have insurance; 2.7% of children under 18 do not have insurance
Transportation: Commute: 94.1% car, 2.0% public transportation, 1.3% walk, 2.5% work from home; Mean travel time to work: 16.3 minutes
Additional Information Contacts
Town of Dickinson . . . . (607) 723-9401
http://www.townofdickinson.com

ENDICOTT (village). Covers a land area of 3.194 square miles and a water area of 0.004 square miles. Located at 42.10° N. Lat; 76.06° W. Long. Elevation is 840 feet.
History: Settled c.1795; incorporated 1906.
Population: 12,980; Growth (since 2000): -0.4%; Density: 4,064.0 persons per square mile; Race: 83.5% White, 8.4% Black/African American, 1.2% Asian, 0.3% American Indian/Alaska Native, 0.0% Native Hawaiian/Other Pacific Islander, 4.2% Two or more races, 6.7% Hispanic of any race; Average household size: 2.14; Median age: 39.5; Age under 18: 20.2%; Age 65 and over: 18.2%; Males per 100 females: 93.4; Marriage status: 38.3% never married, 40.1% now married, 3.6% separated, 7.0% widowed, 14.7% divorced; Foreign born: 6.7%; Speak English only: 91.8%; With disability: 18.1%; Veterans: 8.9%; Ancestry: 15.6% Italian, 14.0% Irish, 10.5% German, 10.4% English, 5.9% American
Employment: 10.9% management, business, and financial, 4.7% computer, engineering, and science, 8.2% education, legal, community service, arts, and media, 4.3% healthcare practitioners, 22.9% service, 27.5% sales and office, 6.8% natural resources, construction, and maintenance, 14.6% production, transportation, and material moving
Income: Per capita: $21,704; Median household: $35,371; Average household: $46,981; Households with income of $100,000 or more: 9.5%; Poverty rate: 19.6%
Educational Attainment: High school diploma or higher: 88.2%; Bachelor's degree or higher: 20.0%; Graduate/professional degree or higher: 6.7%
School District(s)
Union-Endicott Central SD (KG-12)
    Enrollment: 3,872 . . . . (607) 757-2103
Housing: Homeownership rate: 43.7%; Median home value: $89,800; Median year structure built: Before 1940; Homeowner vacancy rate: 3.3%; Median selected monthly owner costs: $1,051 with a mortgage, $480 without a mortgage; Median gross rent: $686 per month; Rental vacancy rate: 10.3%
Health Insurance: 91.4% have insurance; 56.6% have private insurance; 48.2% have public insurance; 8.6% do not have insurance; 1.5% of children under 18 do not have insurance
Safety: Violent crime rate: 57.2 per 10,000 population; Property crime rate: 331.0 per 10,000 population
Transportation: Commute: 83.5% car, 3.6% public transportation, 8.6% walk, 2.9% work from home; Mean travel time to work: 20.3 minutes
Additional Information Contacts
Village of Endicott . . . . (607) 757-5337
http://www.endicottny.com

ENDWELL (CDP). Covers a land area of 3.744 square miles and a water area of 0.032 square miles. Located at 42.12° N. Lat; 76.02° W. Long. Elevation is 846 feet.
History: Also called Hooper.
Population: 11,412; Growth (since 2000): -2.5%; Density: 3,048.4 persons per square mile; Race: 92.8% White, 3.0% Black/African American, 2.3% Asian, 0.0% American Indian/Alaska Native, 0.0% Native Hawaiian/Other Pacific Islander, 1.2% Two or more races, 3.4% Hispanic of any race; Average household size: 2.25; Median age: 45.6; Age under 18: 19.4%; Age 65 and over: 21.2%; Males per 100 females: 91.2; Marriage status: 29.2% never married, 52.7% now married, 0.9% separated, 6.1% widowed, 12.0% divorced; Foreign born: 5.3%; Speak English only: 93.7%; With disability: 13.5%; Veterans: 8.3%; Ancestry: 19.3% Irish, 18.0% Italian, 16.5% German, 11.6% English, 8.1% Polish
Employment: 13.7% management, business, and financial, 8.5% computer, engineering, and science, 13.0% education, legal, community service, arts, and media, 6.5% healthcare practitioners, 19.0% service, 24.3% sales and office, 5.6% natural resources, construction, and maintenance, 9.4% production, transportation, and material moving
Income: Per capita: $32,288; Median household: $55,800; Average household: $72,455; Households with income of $100,000 or more: 26.1%; Poverty rate: 8.5%

Educational Attainment: High school diploma or higher: 93.7%; Bachelor's degree or higher: 36.9%; Graduate/professional degree or higher: 14.1%
School District(s)
Maine-Endwell Central SD (PK-12)
    Enrollment: 2,478 . . . . (607) 754-1400
Housing: Homeownership rate: 72.1%; Median home value: $132,700; Median year structure built: 1957; Homeowner vacancy rate: 0.6%; Median selected monthly owner costs: $1,192 with a mortgage, $482 without a mortgage; Median gross rent: $640 per month; Rental vacancy rate: 6.7%
Health Insurance: 96.4% have insurance; 79.4% have private insurance; 35.5% have public insurance; 3.6% do not have insurance; 1.7% of children under 18 do not have insurance
Transportation: Commute: 88.4% car, 0.9% public transportation, 3.3% walk, 5.9% work from home; Mean travel time to work: 18.1 minutes

FENTON (town). Covers a land area of 32.773 square miles and a water area of 0.592 square miles. Located at 42.20° N. Lat; 75.80° W. Long.
Population: 6,486; Growth (since 2000): -6.1%; Density: 197.9 persons per square mile; Race: 96.8% White, 0.3% Black/African American, 0.3% Asian, 1.2% American Indian/Alaska Native, 0.0% Native Hawaiian/Other Pacific Islander, 1.4% Two or more races, 0.0% Hispanic of any race; Average household size: 2.41; Median age: 44.7; Age under 18: 19.9%; Age 65 and over: 17.5%; Males per 100 females: 97.6; Marriage status: 29.6% never married, 52.3% now married, 1.4% separated, 6.3% widowed, 11.8% divorced; Foreign born: 1.2%; Speak English only: 98.7%; With disability: 12.9%; Veterans: 6.4%; Ancestry: 24.3% Irish, 21.5% German, 18.7% English, 10.8% Italian, 9.2% Polish
Employment: 10.1% management, business, and financial, 4.2% computer, engineering, and science, 12.8% education, legal, community service, arts, and media, 7.5% healthcare practitioners, 18.8% service, 21.6% sales and office, 10.3% natural resources, construction, and maintenance, 14.7% production, transportation, and material moving
Income: Per capita: $28,711; Median household: $49,241; Average household: $68,812; Households with income of $100,000 or more: 21.5%; Poverty rate: 13.0%
Educational Attainment: High school diploma or higher: 91.1%; Bachelor's degree or higher: 25.3%; Graduate/professional degree or higher: 9.3%
Housing: Homeownership rate: 86.3%; Median home value: $108,900; Median year structure built: 1960; Homeowner vacancy rate: 1.0%; Median selected monthly owner costs: $1,223 with a mortgage, $467 without a mortgage; Median gross rent: $698 per month; Rental vacancy rate: 6.6%
Health Insurance: 96.7% have insurance; 76.9% have private insurance; 36.4% have public insurance; 3.3% do not have insurance; 6.2% of children under 18 do not have insurance
Transportation: Commute: 97.8% car, 0.4% public transportation, 0.0% walk, 1.8% work from home; Mean travel time to work: 20.6 minutes
Additional Information Contacts
Town of Fenton . . . . (607) 648-4800
http://www.townoffenton.com

GLEN AUBREY (CDP). Covers a land area of 0.986 square miles and a water area of 0 square miles. Located at 42.26° N. Lat; 76.00° W. Long. Elevation is 991 feet.
Population: 289; Growth (since 2000): n/a; Density: 293.0 persons per square mile; Race: 96.5% White, 1.7% Black/African American, 0.0% Asian, 0.0% American Indian/Alaska Native, 0.0% Native Hawaiian/Other Pacific Islander, 1.7% Two or more races, 0.0% Hispanic of any race; Average household size: 2.43; Median age: 47.4; Age under 18: 10.4%; Age 65 and over: 39.8%; Males per 100 females: 84.4; Marriage status: 36.1% never married, 41.1% now married, 1.1% separated, 11.0% widowed, 11.8% divorced; Foreign born: 0.0%; Speak English only: 100.0%; With disability: 19.7%; Veterans: 6.6%; Ancestry: 24.2% German, 14.2% American, 10.0% English, 5.5% Irish, 3.5% Dutch
Employment: 6.7% management, business, and financial, 2.2% computer, engineering, and science, 4.5% education, legal, community service, arts, and media, 0.0% healthcare practitioners, 34.3% service, 11.9% sales and office, 8.2% natural resources, construction, and maintenance, 32.1% production, transportation, and material moving
Income: Per capita: $24,929; Median household: $52,361; Average household: $61,427; Households with income of $100,000 or more: 11.0%; Poverty rate: 16.3%

Educational Attainment: High school diploma or higher: 95.1%; Bachelor's degree or higher: 3.4%; Graduate/professional degree or higher: n/a
Housing: Homeownership rate: 72.3%; Median home value: $126,200; Median year structure built: 1980; Homeowner vacancy rate: 0.0%; Median selected monthly owner costs: $1,131 with a mortgage, $383 without a mortgage; Median gross rent: $586 per month; Rental vacancy rate: 25.0%
Health Insurance: 93.8% have insurance; 62.6% have private insurance; 52.6% have public insurance; 6.2% do not have insurance; 0.0% of children under 18 do not have insurance
Transportation: Commute: 100.0% car, 0.0% public transportation, 0.0% walk, 0.0% work from home; Mean travel time to work: 28.0 minutes

HARPURSVILLE (unincorporated postal area)
ZCTA: 13787
Covers a land area of 63.639 square miles and a water area of 0.465 square miles. Located at 42.21° N. Lat; 75.67° W. Long. Elevation is 1,024 feet.
Population: 3,609; Growth (since 2000): -0.9%; Density: 56.7 persons per square mile; Race: 97.1% White, 1.1% Black/African American, 0.0% Asian, 1.8% American Indian/Alaska Native, 0.0% Native Hawaiian/Other Pacific Islander, 0.0% Two or more races, 0.7% Hispanic of any race; Average household size: 2.62; Median age: 41.4; Age under 18: 24.9%; Age 65 and over: 14.7%; Males per 100 females: 103.9; Marriage status: 17.2% never married, 61.4% now married, 2.9% separated, 9.5% widowed, 11.9% divorced; Foreign born: 0.0%; Speak English only: 94.6%; With disability: 21.9%; Veterans: 12.5%; Ancestry: 25.7% Irish, 20.9% German, 12.2% English, 8.9% American, 7.2% Italian
Employment: 9.9% management, business, and financial, 4.1% computer, engineering, and science, 16.7% education, legal, community service, arts, and media, 2.0% healthcare practitioners, 14.1% service, 17.2% sales and office, 12.3% natural resources, construction, and maintenance, 23.9% production, transportation, and material moving
Income: Per capita: $20,989; Median household: $44,177; Average household: $53,894; Households with income of $100,000 or more: 11.9%; Poverty rate: 20.4%
Educational Attainment: High school diploma or higher: 78.8%; Bachelor's degree or higher: 15.4%; Graduate/professional degree or higher: 8.4%
School District(s)
Harpursville Central SD (PK-12)
    Enrollment: 852 . . . . (607) 693-8112
Housing: Homeownership rate: 66.8%; Median home value: $84,800; Median year structure built: 1980; Homeowner vacancy rate: 4.2%; Median selected monthly owner costs: $1,338 with a mortgage, $429 without a mortgage; Median gross rent: $682 per month; Rental vacancy rate: 8.0%
Health Insurance: 94.2% have insurance; 63.6% have private insurance; 42.9% have public insurance; 5.8% do not have insurance; 1.9% of children under 18 do not have insurance
Transportation: Commute: 97.4% car, 0.0% public transportation, 1.2% walk, 1.5% work from home; Mean travel time to work: 24.7 minutes

JOHNSON CITY (village). Covers a land area of 4.536 square miles and a water area of 0.099 square miles. Located at 42.13° N. Lat; 75.96° W. Long. Elevation is 873 feet.
History: Originally called Lestershire, the area remained rural until a shoe company built a factory here in 1890. The name was changed in 1916. Incorporated 1892.
Population: 14,728; Growth (since 2000): -5.2%; Density: 3,246.6 persons per square mile; Race: 78.4% White, 7.3% Black/African American, 8.8% Asian, 0.2% American Indian/Alaska Native, 0.2% Native Hawaiian/Other Pacific Islander, 4.0% Two or more races, 4.0% Hispanic of any race; Average household size: 2.24; Median age: 35.5; Age under 18: 22.3%; Age 65 and over: 16.2%; Males per 100 females: 92.1; Marriage status: 37.6% never married, 41.0% now married, 3.4% separated, 9.2% widowed, 12.2% divorced; Foreign born: 9.6%; Speak English only: 88.9%; With disability: 16.0%; Veterans: 6.2%; Ancestry: 18.0% Irish, 13.4% German, 13.3% Italian, 8.6% English, 7.9% Polish
Employment: 7.3% management, business, and financial, 4.7% computer, engineering, and science, 13.5% education, legal, community service, arts, and media, 10.9% healthcare practitioners, 21.7% service, 29.0% sales and office, 3.7% natural resources, construction, and maintenance, 9.1% production, transportation, and material moving

Income: Per capita: $23,904; Median household: $39,992; Average household: $54,147; Households with income of $100,000 or more: 13.8%; Poverty rate: 18.6%
Educational Attainment: High school diploma or higher: 88.9%; Bachelor's degree or higher: 24.5%; Graduate/professional degree or higher: 8.9%
School District(s)
Johnson City Central SD (KG-12)
    Enrollment: 2,530 . . . . (607) 763-1230
Four-year College(s)
Davis College (Private, Not-for-profit, Undenominational)
    Enrollment: 288. . . . . (607) 729-1581
    Tuition: In-state $16,800; Out-of-state $16,800
Housing: Homeownership rate: 54.8%; Median home value: $85,800; Median year structure built: 1946; Homeowner vacancy rate: 1.7%; Median selected monthly owner costs: $1,064 with a mortgage, $504 without a mortgage; Median gross rent: $752 per month; Rental vacancy rate: 5.4%
Health Insurance: 93.6% have insurance; 63.3% have private insurance; 46.7% have public insurance; 6.4% do not have insurance; 3.2% of children under 18 do not have insurance
Hospitals: United Health Services Hospitals (516 beds)
Safety: Violent crime rate: 62.4 per 10,000 population; Property crime rate: 518.0 per 10,000 population
Transportation: Commute: 82.3% car, 6.5% public transportation, 7.0% walk, 2.4% work from home; Mean travel time to work: 16.0 minutes
Additional Information Contacts
Village of Johnson City . . . . (607) 798-7861
    http://www.villageofjc.com

KILLAWOG (unincorporated postal area)
ZCTA: 13794
Covers a land area of 0.717 square miles and a water area of 0 square miles. Located at 42.39° N. Lat; 76.01° W. Long. Elevation is 1,007 feet.
Population: 71; Growth (since 2000): n/a; Density: 99.0 persons per square mile; Race: 100.0% White, 0.0% Black/African American, 0.0% Asian, 0.0% American Indian/Alaska Native, 0.0% Native Hawaiian/Other Pacific Islander, 0.0% Two or more races, 0.0% Hispanic of any race; Average household size: 2.96; Median age: 30.6; Age under 18: 33.8%; Age 65 and over: 0.0%; Males per 100 females: 114.3; Marriage status: 42.6% never married, 57.4% now married, 0.0% separated, 0.0% widowed, 0.0% divorced; Foreign born: 0.0%; Speak English only: 100.0%; With disability: 0.0%; Veterans: 0.0%; Ancestry: 23.9% German, 11.3% Italian, 8.5% Armenian, 8.5% Scotch-Irish, 7.0% Irish
Employment: 0.0% management, business, and financial, 0.0% computer, engineering, and science, 0.0% education, legal, community service, arts, and media, 0.0% healthcare practitioners, 37.2% service, 25.6% sales and office, 0.0% natural resources, construction, and maintenance, 37.2% production, transportation, and material moving
Income: Per capita: $18,151; Median household: $57,500; Average household: $56,292; Households with income of $100,000 or more: n/a; Poverty rate: n/a
Educational Attainment: High school diploma or higher: 100.0%; Bachelor's degree or higher: 14.9%; Graduate/professional degree or higher: n/a
Housing: Homeownership rate: 100.0%; Median home value: n/a; Median year structure built: 1943; Homeowner vacancy rate: 0.0%; Median selected monthly owner costs: $700 with a mortgage, $0 without a mortgage; Median gross rent: n/a per month; Rental vacancy rate: 0.0%
Health Insurance: 100.0% have insurance; 69.0% have private insurance; 31.0% have public insurance; 0.0% do not have insurance; 0.0% of children under 18 do not have insurance
Transportation: Commute: 86.0% car, 0.0% public transportation, 0.0% walk, 14.0% work from home; Mean travel time to work: 35.1 minutes

KIRKWOOD (town). Covers a land area of 30.795 square miles and a water area of 0.397 square miles. Located at 42.09° N. Lat; 75.80° W. Long. Elevation is 892 feet.
Population: 5,680; Growth (since 2000): 0.5%; Density: 184.4 persons per square mile; Race: 95.2% White, 3.3% Black/African American, 0.0% Asian, 0.0% American Indian/Alaska Native, 0.0% Native Hawaiian/Other Pacific Islander, 0.9% Two or more races, 7.0% Hispanic of any race; Average household size: 2.53; Median age: 44.8; Age under 18: 23.2%; Age 65 and over: 20.0%; Males per 100 females: 97.9; Marriage status:

29.3% never married, 52.4% now married, 3.7% separated, 6.6% widowed, 11.7% divorced; Foreign born: 2.8%; Speak English only: 94.2%; With disability: 21.1%; Veterans: 9.8%; Ancestry: 19.3% German, 18.9% Irish, 14.9% English, 7.7% Italian, 6.2% Polish

Employment: 8.6% management, business, and financial, 6.2% computer, engineering, and science, 7.9% education, legal, community service, arts, and media, 8.6% healthcare practitioners, 15.2% service, 22.5% sales and office, 12.7% natural resources, construction, and maintenance, 18.3% production, transportation, and material moving

Income: Per capita: $30,224; Median household: $53,861; Average household: $75,726; Households with income of $100,000 or more: 23.1%; Poverty rate: 13.9%

Educational Attainment: High school diploma or higher: 89.4%; Bachelor's degree or higher: 18.8%; Graduate/professional degree or higher: 8.6%

School District(s)

Windsor Central SD (PK-12)

   Enrollment: 1,698 . . . . (607) 655-8216

Housing: Homeownership rate: 67.3%; Median home value: $102,500; Median year structure built: 1964; Homeowner vacancy rate: 0.0%; Median selected monthly owner costs: $1,135 with a mortgage, $469 without a mortgage; Median gross rent: $763 per month; Rental vacancy rate: 0.0%

Health Insurance: 94.2% have insurance; 71.0% have private insurance; 42.2% have public insurance; 5.8% do not have insurance; 8.8% of children under 18 do not have insurance

Transportation: Commute: 95.5% car, 0.5% public transportation, 0.0% walk, 4.1% work from home; Mean travel time to work: 21.8 minutes

Additional Information Contacts

Town of Kirkwood . . . . (607) 775-1370

   http://www.townofkirkwood.org

LISLE (town). Covers a land area of 46.894 square miles and a water area of 0.090 square miles. Located at 42.38° N. Lat; 76.06° W. Long. Elevation is 974 feet.

Population: 2,707; Growth (since 2000): 0.0%; Density: 57.7 persons per square mile; Race: 97.8% White, 0.0% Black/African American, 0.0% Asian, 0.0% American Indian/Alaska Native, 0.0% Native Hawaiian/Other Pacific Islander, 2.2% Two or more races, 0.1% Hispanic of any race; Average household size: 2.78; Median age: 40.2; Age under 18: 24.4%; Age 65 and over: 15.6%; Males per 100 females: 94.6; Marriage status: 32.4% never married, 51.5% now married, 2.3% separated, 6.1% widowed, 10.1% divorced; Foreign born: 0.6%; Speak English only: 98.0%; With disability: 18.4%; Veterans: 6.5%; Ancestry: 15.9% German, 15.8% English, 14.5% American, 12.0% Irish, 5.4% Polish

Employment: 8.3% management, business, and financial, 2.8% computer, engineering, and science, 9.5% education, legal, community service, arts, and media, 3.7% healthcare practitioners, 16.2% service, 27.6% sales and office, 17.8% natural resources, construction, and maintenance, 14.1% production, transportation, and material moving

Income: Per capita: $23,495; Median household: $52,188; Average household: $64,743; Households with income of $100,000 or more: 14.8%; Poverty rate: 13.4%

Educational Attainment: High school diploma or higher: 87.2%; Bachelor's degree or higher: 10.3%; Graduate/professional degree or higher: 4.2%

Housing: Homeownership rate: 85.3%; Median home value: $88,800; Median year structure built: 1976; Homeowner vacancy rate: 0.8%; Median selected monthly owner costs: $1,111 with a mortgage, $463 without a mortgage; Median gross rent: $747 per month; Rental vacancy rate: 0.0%

Health Insurance: 93.4% have insurance; 67.6% have private insurance; 41.2% have public insurance; 6.6% do not have insurance; 5.8% of children under 18 do not have insurance

Transportation: Commute: 92.3% car, 0.2% public transportation, 1.1% walk, 5.0% work from home; Mean travel time to work: 28.4 minutes

LISLE (village). Covers a land area of 0.936 square miles and a water area of 0 square miles. Located at 42.35° N. Lat; 76.01° W. Long. Elevation is 974 feet.

Population: 263; Growth (since 2000): -12.9%; Density: 280.9 persons per square mile; Race: 95.4% White, 0.0% Black/African American, 0.0% Asian, 0.0% American Indian/Alaska Native, 0.0% Native Hawaiian/Other Pacific Islander, 4.6% Two or more races, 1.5% Hispanic of any race; Average household size: 2.35; Median age: 44.3; Age under 18: 23.6%; Age 65 and over: 19.4%; Males per 100 females: 93.9; Marriage status: 38.9% never married, 39.9% now married, 1.9% separated, 6.3%

widowed, 14.9% divorced; Foreign born: 0.0%; Speak English only: 98.4%; With disability: 27.0%; Veterans: 5.0%; Ancestry: 17.9% Irish, 12.2% American, 11.8% German, 11.0% Dutch, 7.6% Italian

Employment: 5.8% management, business, and financial, 1.9% computer, engineering, and science, 7.7% education, legal, community service, arts, and media, 1.9% healthcare practitioners, 27.9% service, 21.2% sales and office, 14.4% natural resources, construction, and maintenance, 19.2% production, transportation, and material moving

Income: Per capita: $27,832; Median household: $51,111; Average household: $63,777; Households with income of $100,000 or more: 10.7%; Poverty rate: 27.4%

Educational Attainment: High school diploma or higher: 90.5%; Bachelor's degree or higher: 6.9%; Graduate/professional degree or higher: 4.2%

Housing: Homeownership rate: 66.1%; Median home value: $90,000; Median year structure built: Before 1940; Homeowner vacancy rate: 8.1%; Median selected monthly owner costs: $1,031 with a mortgage, $508 without a mortgage; Median gross rent: $655 per month; Rental vacancy rate: 0.0%

Health Insurance: 92.8% have insurance; 51.0% have private insurance; 67.7% have public insurance; 7.2% do not have insurance; 3.2% of children under 18 do not have insurance

Transportation: Commute: 86.1% car, 2.0% public transportation, 2.0% walk, 5.9% work from home; Mean travel time to work: 25.7 minutes

MAINE (town). Covers a land area of 45.643 square miles and a water area of 0.117 square miles. Located at 42.20° N. Lat; 76.02° W. Long. Elevation is 912 feet.

Population: 5,265; Growth (since 2000): -3.6%; Density: 115.4 persons per square mile; Race: 97.1% White, 0.8% Black/African American, 0.2% Asian, 0.0% American Indian/Alaska Native, 0.0% Native Hawaiian/Other Pacific Islander, 1.6% Two or more races, 1.9% Hispanic of any race; Average household size: 2.58; Median age: 45.0; Age under 18: 20.7%; Age 65 and over: 19.5%; Males per 100 females: 98.0; Marriage status: 26.9% never married, 54.5% now married, 1.6% separated, 8.2% widowed, 10.3% divorced; Foreign born: 1.6%; Speak English only: 97.1%; With disability: 13.9%; Veterans: 7.6%; Ancestry: 22.6% Irish, 17.0% German, 16.2% English, 10.5% Italian, 7.9% Polish

Employment: 13.5% management, business, and financial, 5.2% computer, engineering, and science, 12.7% education, legal, community service, arts, and media, 7.5% healthcare practitioners, 19.4% service, 23.9% sales and office, 10.9% natural resources, construction, and maintenance, 6.9% production, transportation, and material moving

Income: Per capita: $27,799; Median household: $59,375; Average household: $71,319; Households with income of $100,000 or more: 21.6%; Poverty rate: 8.6%

Educational Attainment: High school diploma or higher: 92.9%; Bachelor's degree or higher: 27.6%; Graduate/professional degree or higher: 12.2%

School District(s)

Maine-Endwell Central SD (PK-12)

   Enrollment: 2,478 . . . . (607) 754-1400

Housing: Homeownership rate: 81.2%; Median home value: $121,800; Median year structure built: 1965; Homeowner vacancy rate: 1.8%; Median selected monthly owner costs: $1,277 with a mortgage, $581 without a mortgage; Median gross rent: $689 per month; Rental vacancy rate: 0.0%

Health Insurance: 95.2% have insurance; 79.0% have private insurance; 37.8% have public insurance; 4.8% do not have insurance; 0.8% of children under 18 do not have insurance

Transportation: Commute: 92.8% car, 0.0% public transportation, 1.9% walk, 5.3% work from home; Mean travel time to work: 29.0 minutes

Additional Information Contacts

Town of Maine. . . . . (607) 862-3334

   http://townofmaine.org/content

NANTICOKE (town). Covers a land area of 24.270 square miles and a water area of 0.089 square miles. Located at 42.28° N. Lat; 76.03° W. Long. Elevation is 1,089 feet.

Population: 1,631; Growth (since 2000): -8.9%; Density: 67.2 persons per square mile; Race: 98.5% White, 0.9% Black/African American, 0.0% Asian, 0.0% American Indian/Alaska Native, 0.0% Native Hawaiian/Other Pacific Islander, 0.6% Two or more races, 0.6% Hispanic of any race; Average household size: 2.76; Median age: 45.4; Age under 18: 20.6%; Age 65 and over: 21.7%; Males per 100 females: 102.2; Marriage status: 25.4% never married, 63.2% now married, 1.2% separated, 4.7%

widowed, 6.7% divorced; Foreign born: 1.2%; Speak English only: 99.8%; With disability: 18.8%; Veterans: 9.4%; Ancestry: 21.9% German, 15.1% Irish, 12.3% English, 11.2% American, 6.5% Italian

Employment: 9.2% management, business, and financial, 6.5% computer, engineering, and science, 3.6% education, legal, community service, arts, and media, 4.2% healthcare practitioners, 19.2% service, 21.6% sales and office, 12.3% natural resources, construction, and maintenance, 23.4% production, transportation, and material moving

Income: Per capita: $23,577; Median household: $55,167; Average household: $64,092; Households with income of $100,000 or more: 17.6%; Poverty rate: 9.5%

Educational Attainment: High school diploma or higher: 89.3%; Bachelor's degree or higher: 10.4%; Graduate/professional degree or higher: 1.7%

Housing: Homeownership rate: 89.2%; Median home value: $123,200; Median year structure built: 1981; Homeowner vacancy rate: 1.6%; Median selected monthly owner costs: $1,168 with a mortgage, $415 without a mortgage; Median gross rent: $600 per month; Rental vacancy rate: 14.7%

Health Insurance: 96.0% have insurance; 63.7% have private insurance; 49.2% have public insurance; 4.0% do not have insurance; 0.0% of children under 18 do not have insurance

Transportation: Commute: 98.3% car, 0.0% public transportation, 0.7% walk, 1.0% work from home; Mean travel time to work: 28.2 minutes

NINEVEH (unincorporated postal area)
ZCTA: 13813

Covers a land area of 27.856 square miles and a water area of 0.665 square miles. Located at 42.16° N. Lat; 75.55° W. Long. Elevation is 965 feet.

Population: 510; Growth (since 2000): -44.3%; Density: 18.3 persons per square mile; Race: 79.8% White, 0.0% Black/African American, 0.0% Asian, 0.0% American Indian/Alaska Native, 0.0% Native Hawaiian/Other Pacific Islander, 20.2% Two or more races, 0.0% Hispanic of any race; Average household size: 2.74; Median age: 59.2; Age under 18: 25.5%; Age 65 and over: 30.6%; Males per 100 females: 105.3; Marriage status: 18.8% never married, 66.4% now married, 0.0% separated, 4.7% widowed, 10.1% divorced; Foreign born: 2.7%; Speak English only: 94.1%; With disability: 15.5%; Veterans: 20.3%; Ancestry: 24.3% German, 20.6% Scottish, 19.4% English, 17.5% American, 9.0% Italian

Employment: 0.0% management, business, and financial, 0.0% computer, engineering, and science, 19.0% education, legal, community service, arts, and media, 17.2% healthcare practitioners, 6.1% service, 8.0% sales and office, 27.0% natural resources, construction, and maintenance, 22.7% production, transportation, and material moving

Income: Per capita: $23,047; Median household: $50,375; Average household: $62,471; Households with income of $100,000 or more: 8.8%; Poverty rate: 24.1%

Educational Attainment: High school diploma or higher: 92.2%; Bachelor's degree or higher: 31.1%; Graduate/professional degree or higher: 15.6%

Housing: Homeownership rate: 100.0%; Median home value: $120,500; Median year structure built: 1976; Homeowner vacancy rate: 4.2%; Median selected monthly owner costs: $740 with a mortgage, $537 without a mortgage; Median gross rent: n/a per month; Rental vacancy rate: 0.0%

Health Insurance: 96.1% have insurance; 60.8% have private insurance; 56.5% have public insurance; 3.9% do not have insurance; 0.0% of children under 18 do not have insurance

Transportation: Commute: 100.0% car, 0.0% public transportation, 0.0% walk, 0.0% work from home; Mean travel time to work: 21.5 minutes

PORT CRANE (unincorporated postal area)
ZCTA: 13833

Covers a land area of 35.734 square miles and a water area of 0.150 square miles. Located at 42.20° N. Lat; 75.77° W. Long. Elevation is 889 feet.

Population: 4,131; Growth (since 2000): -7.4%; Density: 115.6 persons per square mile; Race: 97.3% White, 0.0% Black/African American, 0.5% Asian, 1.8% American Indian/Alaska Native, 0.0% Native Hawaiian/Other Pacific Islander, 0.4% Two or more races, 0.0% Hispanic of any race; Average household size: 2.41; Median age: 45.8; Age under 18: 14.5%; Age 65 and over: 15.7%; Males per 100 females: 104.3; Marriage status: 29.4% never married, 53.2% now married, 1.8%

separated, 5.6% widowed, 11.8% divorced; Foreign born: 1.1%; Speak English only: 98.4%; With disability: 12.6%; Veterans: 8.3%; Ancestry: 25.0% German, 22.5% Irish, 19.5% English, 7.6% Dutch, 5.4% Polish

Employment: 8.6% management, business, and financial, 4.2% computer, engineering, and science, 7.5% education, legal, community service, arts, and media, 2.9% healthcare practitioners, 21.2% service, 19.9% sales and office, 10.7% natural resources, construction, and maintenance, 25.2% production, transportation, and material moving

Income: Per capita: $27,184; Median household: $55,013; Average household: $64,199; Households with income of $100,000 or more: 19.3%; Poverty rate: 13.3%

Educational Attainment: High school diploma or higher: 85.2%; Bachelor's degree or higher: 14.4%; Graduate/professional degree or higher: 2.9%

Housing: Homeownership rate: 88.0%; Median home value: $87,200; Median year structure built: 1972; Homeowner vacancy rate: 1.6%; Median selected monthly owner costs: $1,145 with a mortgage, $457 without a mortgage; Median gross rent: $740 per month; Rental vacancy rate: 11.2%

Health Insurance: 93.4% have insurance; 70.0% have private insurance; 42.1% have public insurance; 6.6% do not have insurance; 14.6% of children under 18 do not have insurance

Transportation: Commute: 98.3% car, 0.0% public transportation, 0.5% walk, 1.2% work from home; Mean travel time to work: 24.3 minutes

PORT DICKINSON (village). Covers a land area of 0.637 square miles and a water area of 0.078 square miles. Located at 42.14° N. Lat; 75.89° W. Long. Elevation is 863 feet.

Population: 1,909; Growth (since 2000): 12.5%; Density: 2,994.6 persons per square mile; Race: 92.4% White, 3.6% Black/African American, 0.5% Asian, 0.0% American Indian/Alaska Native, 0.0% Native Hawaiian/Other Pacific Islander, 3.4% Two or more races, 0.4% Hispanic of any race; Average household size: 2.41; Median age: 36.6; Age under 18: 23.7%; Age 65 and over: 12.1%; Males per 100 females: 83.8; Marriage status: 34.9% never married, 47.8% now married, 4.2% separated, 3.0% widowed, 14.3% divorced; Foreign born: 1.2%; Speak English only: 97.1%; With disability: 8.2%; Veterans: 11.7%; Ancestry: 21.9% Irish, 21.1% German, 14.2% English, 13.8% Italian, 7.4% American

Employment: 15.1% management, business, and financial, 2.8% computer, engineering, and science, 12.6% education, legal, community service, arts, and media, 10.2% healthcare practitioners, 24.7% service, 21.4% sales and office, 4.6% natural resources, construction, and maintenance, 8.7% production, transportation, and material moving

Income: Per capita: $27,620; Median household: $58,190; Average household: $65,724; Households with income of $100,000 or more: 18.0%; Poverty rate: 11.9%

Educational Attainment: High school diploma or higher: 97.8%; Bachelor's degree or higher: 29.9%; Graduate/professional degree or higher: 12.7%

Housing: Homeownership rate: 67.9%; Median home value: $110,200; Median year structure built: Before 1940; Homeowner vacancy rate: 0.0%; Median selected monthly owner costs: $1,268 with a mortgage, $508 without a mortgage; Median gross rent: $731 per month; Rental vacancy rate: 0.0%

Health Insurance: 94.1% have insurance; 75.6% have private insurance; 29.9% have public insurance; 5.9% do not have insurance; 4.9% of children under 18 do not have insurance

Safety: Violent crime rate: 0.0 per 10,000 population; Property crime rate: 101.7 per 10,000 population

Transportation: Commute: 94.6% car, 1.8% public transportation, 0.9% walk, 2.7% work from home; Mean travel time to work: 17.8 minutes

SANFORD (town). Covers a land area of 90.098 square miles and a water area of 0.924 square miles. Located at 42.09° N. Lat; 75.50° W. Long. Elevation is 1,178 feet.

Population: 2,360; Growth (since 2000): -4.7%; Density: 26.2 persons per square mile; Race: 95.6% White, 0.9% Black/African American, 0.9% Asian, 0.0% American Indian/Alaska Native, 0.3% Native Hawaiian/Other Pacific Islander, 2.1% Two or more races, 3.4% Hispanic of any race; Average household size: 2.41; Median age: 49.3; Age under 18: 18.6%; Age 65 and over: 25.2%; Males per 100 females: 101.1; Marriage status: 24.4% never married, 58.5% now married, 1.6% separated, 6.5% widowed, 10.6% divorced; Foreign born: 3.4%; Speak English only: 94.6%; With disability: 19.2%; Veterans: 14.5%; Ancestry: 16.1% German, 15.1% Irish, 12.0% Italian, 11.4% English, 11.4% American

Employment: 4.2% management, business, and financial, 3.4% computer, engineering, and science, 12.2% education, legal, community service, arts, and media, 3.4% healthcare practitioners, 22.4% service, 21.3% sales and office, 16.5% natural resources, construction, and maintenance, 16.6% production, transportation, and material moving
Income: Per capita: $24,165; Median household: $42,708; Average household: $57,178; Households with income of $100,000 or more: 15.8%; Poverty rate: 9.6%
Educational Attainment: High school diploma or higher: 87.4%; Bachelor's degree or higher: 16.2%; Graduate/professional degree or higher: 4.8%
Housing: Homeownership rate: 77.9%; Median home value: $125,000; Median year structure built: 1962; Homeowner vacancy rate: 4.6%; Median selected monthly owner costs: $1,161 with a mortgage, $518 without a mortgage; Median gross rent: $690 per month; Rental vacancy rate: 0.0%
Health Insurance: 92.8% have insurance; 61.4% have private insurance; 49.6% have public insurance; 7.2% do not have insurance; 0.0% of children under 18 do not have insurance
Transportation: Commute: 83.4% car, 0.0% public transportation, 7.3% walk, 8.0% work from home; Mean travel time to work: 28.0 minutes

---

TRIANGLE (town). Covers a land area of 37.875 square miles and a water area of 1.907 square miles. Located at 42.36° N. Lat; 75.93° W. Long. Elevation is 1,070 feet.
Population: 2,868; Growth (since 2000): -5.4%; Density: 75.7 persons per square mile; Race: 97.9% White, 0.6% Black/African American, 0.1% Asian, 0.0% American Indian/Alaska Native, 0.2% Native Hawaiian/Other Pacific Islander, 0.5% Two or more races, 2.7% Hispanic of any race; Average household size: 2.57; Median age: 39.6; Age under 18: 25.3%; Age 65 and over: 15.6%; Males per 100 females: 96.4; Marriage status: 26.4% never married, 58.8% now married, 3.2% separated, 6.0% widowed, 8.8% divorced; Foreign born: 1.9%; Speak English only: 96.3%; With disability: 13.7%; Veterans: 8.8%; Ancestry: 18.7% German, 13.0% Irish, 11.3% English, 10.2% American, 5.6% Italian
Employment: 11.5% management, business, and financial, 9.7% computer, engineering, and science, 8.2% education, legal, community service, arts, and media, 5.1% healthcare practitioners, 13.9% service, 25.1% sales and office, 10.6% natural resources, construction, and maintenance, 15.9% production, transportation, and material moving
Income: Per capita: $25,960; Median household: $61,150; Average household: $66,450; Households with income of $100,000 or more: 22.1%; Poverty rate: 10.5%
Educational Attainment: High school diploma or higher: 90.2%; Bachelor's degree or higher: 18.7%; Graduate/professional degree or higher: 8.0%
Housing: Homeownership rate: 76.5%; Median home value: $107,300; Median year structure built: 1971; Homeowner vacancy rate: 0.7%; Median selected monthly owner costs: $1,230 with a mortgage, $524 without a mortgage; Median gross rent: $658 per month; Rental vacancy rate: 10.0%
Health Insurance: 99.4% have insurance; 78.2% have private insurance; 36.4% have public insurance; 0.6% do not have insurance; 0.0% of children under 18 do not have insurance
Transportation: Commute: 91.8% car, 0.0% public transportation, 5.5% walk, 2.4% work from home; Mean travel time to work: 28.0 minutes

---

UNION (town). Covers a land area of 35.452 square miles and a water area of 0.538 square miles. Located at 42.13° N. Lat; 76.03° W. Long. Elevation is 846 feet.
Population: 54,817; Growth (since 2000): -2.6%; Density: 1,546.2 persons per square mile; Race: 86.2% White, 5.7% Black/African American, 3.9% Asian, 0.1% American Indian/Alaska Native, 0.1% Native Hawaiian/Other Pacific Islander, 3.0% Two or more races, 3.6% Hispanic of any race; Average household size: 2.23; Median age: 41.6; Age under 18: 20.0%; Age 65 and over: 19.7%; Males per 100 females: 92.3; Marriage status: 33.0% never married, 47.3% now married, 2.4% separated, 7.4% widowed, 12.3% divorced; Foreign born: 7.0%; Speak English only: 91.8%; With disability: 15.0%; Veterans: 8.2%; Ancestry: 17.1% Irish, 15.6% Italian, 13.9% German, 10.6% English, 6.9% Polish
Employment: 11.8% management, business, and financial, 7.2% computer, engineering, and science, 11.9% education, legal, community service, arts, and media, 8.1% healthcare practitioners, 19.1% service, 26.0% sales and office, 5.2% natural resources, construction, and maintenance, 10.7% production, transportation, and material moving

Income: Per capita: $28,166; Median household: $47,824; Average household: $63,147; Households with income of $100,000 or more: 19.4%; Poverty rate: 13.4%
Educational Attainment: High school diploma or higher: 91.6%; Bachelor's degree or higher: 30.3%; Graduate/professional degree or higher: 11.9%
Housing: Homeownership rate: 60.7%; Median home value: $110,500; Median year structure built: 1954; Homeowner vacancy rate: 1.5%; Median selected monthly owner costs: $1,142 with a mortgage, $495 without a mortgage; Median gross rent: $733 per month; Rental vacancy rate: 8.6%
Health Insurance: 94.6% have insurance; 68.8% have private insurance; 42.6% have public insurance; 5.4% do not have insurance; 2.7% of children under 18 do not have insurance
Transportation: Commute: 87.4% car, 2.8% public transportation, 4.9% walk, 3.7% work from home; Mean travel time to work: 18.1 minutes
Additional Information Contacts
Town of Union . . . . (607) 786-2900
   http://www.townofunion.com

VESTAL (town). Covers a land area of 51.742 square miles and a water area of 0.854 square miles. Located at 42.05° N. Lat; 76.02° W. Long. Elevation is 830 feet.
History: Vestal is home to Binghamton University, which employs more than 3,000 faculty and staff.
Population: 28,232; Growth (since 2000): 6.4%; Density: 545.6 persons per square mile; Race: 79.5% White, 4.3% Black/African American, 13.3% Asian, 0.2% American Indian/Alaska Native, 0.0% Native Hawaiian/Other Pacific Islander, 2.0% Two or more races, 4.7% Hispanic of any race; Average household size: 2.49; Median age: 26.4; Age under 18: 15.9%; Age 65 and over: 16.1%; Males per 100 females: 96.2; Marriage status: 47.6% never married, 40.6% now married, 0.6% separated, 4.8% widowed, 6.9% divorced; Foreign born: 12.3%; Speak English only: 82.3%; With disability: 9.3%; Veterans: 6.3%; Ancestry: 15.6% Irish, 13.7% German, 12.1% Italian, 10.1% English, 5.7% Polish
Employment: 15.1% management, business, and financial, 7.9% computer, engineering, and science, 16.4% education, legal, community service, arts, and media, 8.3% healthcare practitioners, 18.1% service, 22.6% sales and office, 4.8% natural resources, construction, and maintenance, 6.7% production, transportation, and material moving
Income: Per capita: $27,106; Median household: $61,993; Average household: $84,950; Households with income of $100,000 or more: 25.2%; Poverty rate: 13.4%
Educational Attainment: High school diploma or higher: 95.6%; Bachelor's degree or higher: 44.0%; Graduate/professional degree or higher: 23.2%

School District(s)
Vestal Central SD (KG-12)
   Enrollment: 3,373 . . . . (607) 757-2241
Four-year College(s)
Binghamton University (Public)
   Enrollment: 17,351 . . . . (607) 777-2000
   Tuition: In-state $9,523; Out-of-state $24,403
Housing: Homeownership rate: 77.4%; Median home value: $145,300; Median year structure built: 1965; Homeowner vacancy rate: 1.2%; Median selected monthly owner costs: $1,410 with a mortgage, $570 without a mortgage; Median gross rent: $930 per month; Rental vacancy rate: 7.6%
Health Insurance: 97.4% have insurance; 84.6% have private insurance; 27.8% have public insurance; 2.6% do not have insurance; 2.0% of children under 18 do not have insurance
Safety: Violent crime rate: 7.8 per 10,000 population; Property crime rate: 204.0 per 10,000 population
Newspapers: The Reporter (weekly circulation 2,400)
Transportation: Commute: 86.5% car, 3.4% public transportation, 5.9% walk, 3.3% work from home; Mean travel time to work: 18.4 minutes
Additional Information Contacts
Town of Vestal . . . . (607) 748-1514
   http://www.vestalny.com

WHITNEY POINT (village). Covers a land area of 1.043 square miles and a water area of 0.070 square miles. Located at 42.33° N. Lat; 75.97° W. Long. Elevation is 958 feet.
Population: 934; Growth (since 2000): -3.2%; Density: 895.9 persons per square mile; Race: 96.8% White, 1.2% Black/African American, 0.2% Asian, 0.0% American Indian/Alaska Native, 0.0% Native Hawaiian/Other Pacific Islander, 0.0% Two or more races, 6.5% Hispanic of any race;

Average household size: 2.39; Median age: 31.9; Age under 18: 29.4%; Age 65 and over: 20.4%; Males per 100 females: 90.9; Marriage status: 32.2% never married, 45.4% now married, 1.9% separated, 9.0% widowed, 13.5% divorced; Foreign born: 3.3%; Speak English only: 93.1%; With disability: 18.1%; Veterans: 4.7%; Ancestry: 13.9% English, 13.2% German, 13.0% Irish, 11.6% American, 4.4% Italian

Employment: 11.6% management, business, and financial, 9.3% computer, engineering, and science, 10.9% education, legal, community service, arts, and media, 2.8% healthcare practitioners, 23.5% service, 34.1% sales and office, 4.7% natural resources, construction, and maintenance, 3.1% production, transportation, and material moving

Income: Per capita: $20,664; Median household: $34,318; Average household: $49,451; Households with income of $100,000 or more: 13.9%; Poverty rate: 21.5%

Educational Attainment: High school diploma or higher: 86.9%; Bachelor's degree or higher: 24.6%; Graduate/professional degree or higher: 10.7%

School District(s)
Whitney Point Central SD (PK-12)
    Enrollment: 1,453 . . . . (607) 692-8313
Housing: Homeownership rate: 49.5%; Median home value: $103,500; Median year structure built: Before 1940; Homeowner vacancy rate: 0.0%; Median selected monthly owner costs: $1,189 with a mortgage, $538 without a mortgage; Median gross rent: $560 per month; Rental vacancy rate: 12.8%
Health Insurance: 98.8% have insurance; 73.6% have private insurance; 42.5% have public insurance; 1.2% do not have insurance; 0.0% of children under 18 do not have insurance
Transportation: Commute: 81.9% car, 0.0% public transportation, 16.3% walk, 1.8% work from home; Mean travel time to work: 25.0 minutes

WINDSOR (town). Covers a land area of 91.743 square miles and a water area of 1.264 square miles. Located at 42.06° N. Lat; 75.67° W. Long. Elevation is 948 feet.

History: Windsor is a town in Broome County, New York. The town is on the south border of the county, east of Binghamton, and includes the village of Windsor, located on the Susquehanna River.

Population: 6,114; Growth (since 2000): -4.8%; Density: 66.6 persons per square mile; Race: 99.3% White, 0.1% Black/African American, 0.4% Asian, 0.0% American Indian/Alaska Native, 0.0% Native Hawaiian/Other Pacific Islander, 0.2% Two or more races, 1.9% Hispanic of any race; Average household size: 2.70; Median age: 42.4; Age under 18: 24.7%; Age 65 and over: 14.4%; Males per 100 females: 102.8; Marriage status: 22.6% never married, 62.5% now married, 4.8% separated, 4.8% widowed, 10.0% divorced; Foreign born: 1.0%; Speak English only: 98.4%; With disability: 12.7%; Veterans: 9.5%; Ancestry: 22.2% German, 22.0% Irish, 16.3% English, 11.1% Italian, 6.5% American

Employment: 15.2% management, business, and financial, 4.0% computer, engineering, and science, 12.5% education, legal, community service, arts, and media, 3.8% healthcare practitioners, 14.7% service, 17.2% sales and office, 13.8% natural resources, construction, and maintenance, 18.9% production, transportation, and material moving

Income: Per capita: $28,811; Median household: $68,438; Average household: $77,168; Households with income of $100,000 or more: 24.6%; Poverty rate: 6.6%

Educational Attainment: High school diploma or higher: 92.9%; Bachelor's degree or higher: 20.4%; Graduate/professional degree or higher: 9.7%

School District(s)
Windsor Central SD (PK-12)
    Enrollment: 1,698 . . . . (607) 655-8216
Housing: Homeownership rate: 92.6%; Median home value: $114,800; Median year structure built: 1975; Homeowner vacancy rate: 0.4%; Median selected monthly owner costs: $1,213 with a mortgage, $426 without a mortgage; Median gross rent: $632 per month; Rental vacancy rate: 0.9%
Health Insurance: 94.6% have insurance; 78.5% have private insurance; 35.3% have public insurance; 5.4% do not have insurance; 2.6% of children under 18 do not have insurance
Transportation: Commute: 97.0% car, 0.0% public transportation, 0.9% walk, 2.0% work from home; Mean travel time to work: 22.2 minutes
Additional Information Contacts
Town of Windsor . . . . (607) 655-2023
    http://www.windsorny.org

WINDSOR (village). Covers a land area of 1.095 square miles and a water area of 0.072 square miles. Located at 42.08° N. Lat; 75.64° W. Long. Elevation is 948 feet.

Population: 963; Growth (since 2000): 6.9%; Density: 879.5 persons per square mile; Race: 98.0% White, 0.7% Black/African American, 0.0% Asian, 0.0% American Indian/Alaska Native, 0.0% Native Hawaiian/Other Pacific Islander, 1.2% Two or more races, 0.9% Hispanic of any race; Average household size: 2.63; Median age: 38.2; Age under 18: 23.1%; Age 65 and over: 14.3%; Males per 100 females: 92.4; Marriage status: 21.8% never married, 67.0% now married, 2.6% separated, 4.0% widowed, 7.1% divorced; Foreign born: 0.6%; Speak English only: 97.4%; With disability: 11.0%; Veterans: 11.1%; Ancestry: 21.1% German, 19.8% Italian, 19.1% Irish, 18.3% English, 7.7% American

Employment: 11.2% management, business, and financial, 7.7% computer, engineering, and science, 12.0% education, legal, community service, arts, and media, 2.6% healthcare practitioners, 16.1% service, 27.7% sales and office, 6.7% natural resources, construction, and maintenance, 15.9% production, transportation, and material moving

Income: Per capita: $27,150; Median household: $62,045; Average household: $69,384; Households with income of $100,000 or more: 18.8%; Poverty rate: 11.6%

Educational Attainment: High school diploma or higher: 92.3%; Bachelor's degree or higher: 22.4%; Graduate/professional degree or higher: 9.4%

School District(s)
Windsor Central SD (PK-12)
    Enrollment: 1,698 . . . . (607) 655-8216
Housing: Homeownership rate: 74.0%; Median home value: $105,400; Median year structure built: Before 1940; Homeowner vacancy rate: 2.7%; Median selected monthly owner costs: $1,186 with a mortgage, $552 without a mortgage; Median gross rent: $641 per month; Rental vacancy rate: 1.9%
Health Insurance: 92.7% have insurance; 72.1% have private insurance; 34.1% have public insurance; 7.3% do not have insurance; 4.5% of children under 18 do not have insurance
Transportation: Commute: 89.5% car, 0.0% public transportation, 5.5% walk, 4.6% work from home; Mean travel time to work: 22.6 minutes

Cattaraugus County

Located in western New York; bounded on the south by Pennsylvania; crossed by the Allegheny River. Covers a land area of 1,308.350 square miles, a water area of 14.135 square miles, and is located in the Eastern Time Zone at 42.24° N. Lat., 78.68° W. Long. The county was founded in 1808. County seat is Little Valley.

Cattaraugus County is part of the Olean, NY Micropolitan Statistical Area. The entire metro area includes: Cattaraugus County, NY

Weather Station: Allegany State Park										Elevation: 1,500 feet		
	Jan	Feb	Mar	Apr	May	Jun	Jul	Aug	Sep	Oct	Nov	Dec
High	30	33	42	55	67	75	78	76	69	57	46	35
Low	13	14	20	32	41	50	54	53	47	36	29	19
Precip	3.0	2.3	3.1	3.5	3.8	4.9	4.6	4.1	4.1	3.8	3.9	3.4
Snow	na	na	10.5	2.1	tr	0.0	0.0	0.0	0.0	0.1	4.3	na

High and Low temperatures in degrees Fahrenheit; Precipitation and Snow in inches

Weather Station: Franklinville										Elevation: 1,549 feet		
	Jan	Feb	Mar	Apr	May	Jun	Jul	Aug	Sep	Oct	Nov	Dec
High	30	32	40	54	66	74	78	77	70	58	46	34
Low	12	12	18	31	39	49	54	53	46	35	28	18
Precip	2.6	2.1	2.9	3.3	3.7	4.4	4.5	4.0	4.4	3.8	3.6	3.1
Snow	27.8	17.7	16.7	4.0	0.2	0.0	0.0	0.0	0.0	0.6	10.2	25.6

High and Low temperatures in degrees Fahrenheit; Precipitation and Snow in inches

Weather Station: Little Valley										Elevation: 1,625 feet		
	Jan	Feb	Mar	Apr	May	Jun	Jul	Aug	Sep	Oct	Nov	Dec
High	30	33	41	54	66	74	78	77	70	58	46	34
Low	13	14	20	32	41	50	55	54	47	37	30	19
Precip	3.2	2.5	3.1	3.6	3.6	4.4	4.5	4.0	4.5	4.3	4.3	3.8
Snow	28.2	19.8	16.7	4.5	0.3	0.0	0.0	0.0	0.0	0.8	12.9	30.3

High and Low temperatures in degrees Fahrenheit; Precipitation and Snow in inches

Population: 78,175; Growth (since 2000): -6.9%; Density: 59.8 persons per square mile; Race: 92.1% White, 1.7% Black/African American, 0.9% Asian, 3.0% American Indian/Alaska Native, 0.0% Native Hawaiian/Other

Pacific Islander, 2.0% two or more races, 2.0% Hispanic of any race; Average household size: 2.38; Median age: 41.7; Age under 18: 22.6%; Age 65 and over: 17.7%; Males per 100 females: 97.9; Marriage status: 30.3% never married, 50.7% now married, 2.0% separated, 6.9% widowed, 12.1% divorced; Foreign born: 2.0%; Speak English only: 95.3%; With disability: 15.7%; Veterans: 10.6%; Ancestry: 29.2% German, 18.2% Irish, 11.6% English, 9.8% Polish, 9.6% Italian
Religion: Six largest groups: 15.4% Catholicism, 5.4% Methodist/Pietist, 2.5% Lutheran, 2.2% Holiness, 1.9% Non-denominational Protestant, 1.9% Muslim Estimate
Economy: Unemployment rate: 4.3%; Leading industries: 20.2 % retail trade; 12.6 % other services (except public administration); 12.0 % accommodation and food services; Farms: 1,038 totaling 197,257 acres; Company size: 2 employ 1,000 or more persons, 4 employ 500 to 999 persons, 22 employ 100 to 499 persons, 1,599 employ less than 100 persons; Business ownership: 1,554 women-owned, n/a Black-owned, n/a Hispanic-owned, 161 Asian-owned, 84 American Indian/Alaska Native-owned
Employment: 11.7% management, business, and financial, 3.0% computer, engineering, and science, 10.6% education, legal, community service, arts, and media, 5.2% healthcare practitioners, 19.1% service, 24.3% sales and office, 10.8% natural resources, construction, and maintenance, 15.3% production, transportation, and material moving
Income: Per capita: $23,984; Median household: $45,571; Average household: $58,197; Households with income of $100,000 or more: 15.2%; Poverty rate: 16.9%
Educational Attainment: High school diploma or higher: 88.4%; Bachelor's degree or higher: 18.9%; Graduate/professional degree or higher: 8.2%
Housing: Homeownership rate: 71.3%; Median home value: $86,500; Median year structure built: 1959; Homeowner vacancy rate: 2.3%; Median selected monthly owner costs: $1,053 with a mortgage, $465 without a mortgage; Median gross rent: $626 per month; Rental vacancy rate: 5.9%
Vital Statistics: Birth rate: 109.4 per 10,000 population; Death rate: 106.5 per 10,000 population; Age-adjusted cancer mortality rate: 160.0 deaths per 100,000 population
Health Insurance: 92.5% have insurance; 67.6% have private insurance; 42.5% have public insurance; 7.5% do not have insurance; 7.6% of children under 18 do not have insurance
Health Care: Physicians: 12.7 per 10,000 population; Dentists: 4.5 per 10,000 population; Hospital beds: 23.9 per 10,000 population; Hospital admissions: 724.9 per 10,000 population
Transportation: Commute: 90.5% car, 0.4% public transportation, 4.7% walk, 3.0% work from home; Mean travel time to work: 21.9 minutes
2016 Presidential Election: 63.2% Trump, 30.5% Clinton, 4.0% Johnson, 1.4% Stein
National and State Parks: Allegany State Park; Harry E Dobbins Memorial State Forest
Additional Information Contacts
Cattaraugus Government . . . . (716) 938-9111
  http://www.cattco.org

Cattaraugus County Communities

ALLEGANY (town). Covers a land area of 70.923 square miles and a water area of 0.658 square miles. Located at 42.09° N. Lat; 78.53° W. Long. Elevation is 1,421 feet.
History: Incorporated 1906.
Population: 7,715; Growth (since 2000): -6.3%; Density: 108.8 persons per square mile; Race: 93.1% White, 2.0% Black/African American, 2.1% Asian, 0.3% American Indian/Alaska Native, 0.0% Native Hawaiian/Other Pacific Islander, 1.0% Two or more races, 2.7% Hispanic of any race; Average household size: 2.22; Median age: 39.5; Age under 18: 15.1%; Age 65 and over: 19.7%; Males per 100 females: 90.8; Marriage status: 41.3% never married, 44.5% now married, 0.9% separated, 5.7% widowed, 8.6% divorced; Foreign born: 4.3%; Speak English only: 95.3%; With disability: 13.2%; Veterans: 9.6%; Ancestry: 28.4% German, 21.2% Irish, 13.1% Italian, 11.4% English, 10.6% Polish
Employment: 12.2% management, business, and financial, 4.0% computer, engineering, and science, 11.4% education, legal, community service, arts, and media, 6.9% healthcare practitioners, 17.5% service, 29.8% sales and office, 4.4% natural resources, construction, and maintenance, 13.8% production, transportation, and material moving

Income: Per capita: $23,694; Median household: $50,262; Average household: $63,712; Households with income of $100,000 or more: 19.1%; Poverty rate: 13.7%
Educational Attainment: High school diploma or higher: 93.3%; Bachelor's degree or higher: 28.6%; Graduate/professional degree or higher: 13.8%
School District(s)
Allegany-Limestone Central SD (PK-12)
  Enrollment: 1,161 . . . . (716) 375-6600
Housing: Homeownership rate: 76.7%; Median home value: $94,300; Median year structure built: 1967; Homeowner vacancy rate: 0.5%; Median selected monthly owner costs: $1,085 with a mortgage, $538 without a mortgage; Median gross rent: $658 per month; Rental vacancy rate: 0.9%
Health Insurance: 97.4% have insurance; 79.4% have private insurance; 36.2% have public insurance; 2.6% do not have insurance; 0.0% of children under 18 do not have insurance
Transportation: Commute: 86.1% car, 0.0% public transportation, 9.2% walk, 4.0% work from home; Mean travel time to work: 17.9 minutes
Additional Information Contacts
Town of Allegany. . . . . (716) 373-0120
  http://www.allegany.org

ALLEGANY (village). Covers a land area of 0.705 square miles and a water area of 0.007 square miles. Located at 42.09° N. Lat; 78.49° W. Long. Elevation is 1,421 feet.
Population: 2,011; Growth (since 2000): 6.8%; Density: 2,850.7 persons per square mile; Race: 94.7% White, 1.8% Black/African American, 0.8% Asian, 0.0% American Indian/Alaska Native, 0.0% Native Hawaiian/Other Pacific Islander, 1.8% Two or more races, 1.7% Hispanic of any race; Average household size: 2.50; Median age: 32.7; Age under 18: 19.2%; Age 65 and over: 12.6%; Males per 100 females: 90.8; Marriage status: 41.0% never married, 45.5% now married, 1.5% separated, 4.0% widowed, 9.4% divorced; Foreign born: 3.0%; Speak English only: 96.8%; With disability: 8.9%; Veterans: 9.5%; Ancestry: 29.5% German, 21.0% Irish, 15.2% Italian, 9.4% Polish, 8.2% English
Employment: 15.0% management, business, and financial, 4.7% computer, engineering, and science, 16.4% education, legal, community service, arts, and media, 6.7% healthcare practitioners, 16.2% service, 31.3% sales and office, 5.5% natural resources, construction, and maintenance, 4.3% production, transportation, and material moving
Income: Per capita: $25,685; Median household: $49,539; Average household: $64,361; Households with income of $100,000 or more: 19.8%; Poverty rate: 24.4%
Educational Attainment: High school diploma or higher: 96.5%; Bachelor's degree or higher: 42.5%; Graduate/professional degree or higher: 22.3%
School District(s)
Allegany-Limestone Central SD (PK-12)
  Enrollment: 1,161 . . . . (716) 375-6600
Housing: Homeownership rate: 58.5%; Median home value: $102,500; Median year structure built: 1950; Homeowner vacancy rate: 2.1%; Median selected monthly owner costs: $1,163 with a mortgage, $566 without a mortgage; Median gross rent: $740 per month; Rental vacancy rate: 1.7%
Health Insurance: 94.1% have insurance; 74.0% have private insurance; 32.8% have public insurance; 5.9% do not have insurance; 0.0% of children under 18 do not have insurance
Safety: Violent crime rate: 5.8 per 10,000 population; Property crime rate: 69.9 per 10,000 population
Transportation: Commute: 94.1% car, 0.0% public transportation, 1.7% walk, 3.3% work from home; Mean travel time to work: 17.1 minutes
Additional Information Contacts
Village of Allegany. . . . . (716) 373-1460
  http://www.allegany.org

ALLEGANY RESERVATION (reservation). Covers a land area of 36.288 square miles and a water area of 7.380 square miles. Located at 42.12° N. Lat; 78.67° W. Long.
Population: 989; Growth (since 2000): -10.0%; Density: 27.3 persons per square mile; Race: 30.4% White, 2.0% Black/African American, 4.7% Asian, 60.4% American Indian/Alaska Native, 0.0% Native Hawaiian/Other Pacific Islander, 2.5% Two or more races, 0.7% Hispanic of any race; Average household size: 2.53; Median age: 37.3; Age under 18: 25.3%; Age 65 and over: 14.3%; Males per 100 females: 92.8; Marriage status: 38.9% never married, 35.2% now married, 2.9% separated, 8.4% widowed, 17.6% divorced; Foreign born: 3.5%; Speak English only: 90.1%;

With disability: 16.2%; Veterans: 5.4%; Ancestry: 9.6% German, 5.9% Irish, 3.5% Trinidadian and Tobagonian, 3.1% Polish, 3.0% Italian

Employment: 8.6% management, business, and financial, 1.9% computer, engineering, and science, 7.8% education, legal, community service, arts, and media, 0.0% healthcare practitioners, 22.4% service, 32.4% sales and office, 10.8% natural resources, construction, and maintenance, 16.1% production, transportation, and material moving

Income: Per capita: $16,210; Median household: $31,164; Average household: $40,858; Households with income of $100,000 or more: 5.6%; Poverty rate: 27.8%

Educational Attainment: High school diploma or higher: 90.1%; Bachelor's degree or higher: 6.8%; Graduate/professional degree or higher: 2.9%

Housing: Homeownership rate: 72.6%; Median home value: $67,900; Median year structure built: 1980; Homeowner vacancy rate: 1.0%; Median selected monthly owner costs: $950 with a mortgage, $248 without a mortgage; Median gross rent: $566 per month; Rental vacancy rate: 5.0%

Health Insurance: 86.0% have insurance; 40.6% have private insurance; 56.5% have public insurance; 14.0% do not have insurance; 13.1% of children under 18 do not have insurance

Transportation: Commute: 96.6% car, 1.4% public transportation, 2.0% walk, 0.0% work from home; Mean travel time to work: 21.6 minutes

ASHFORD (town). Covers a land area of 51.737 square miles and a water area of 0.164 square miles. Located at 42.44° N. Lat; 78.65° W. Long. Elevation is 1,634 feet.

Population: 2,266; Growth (since 2000): 1.9%; Density: 43.8 persons per square mile; Race: 93.9% White, 0.0% Black/African American, 0.1% Asian, 0.5% American Indian/Alaska Native, 0.0% Native Hawaiian/Other Pacific Islander, 5.4% Two or more races, 0.9% Hispanic of any race; Average household size: 2.53; Median age: 41.1; Age under 18: 23.9%; Age 65 and over: 17.5%; Males per 100 females: 106.4; Marriage status: 26.8% never married, 57.7% now married, 2.1% separated, 5.9% widowed, 9.6% divorced; Foreign born: 1.3%; Speak English only: 96.9%; With disability: 12.4%; Veterans: 13.9%; Ancestry: 45.3% German, 17.5% Irish, 12.2% English, 11.0% Polish, 5.2% Italian

Employment: 11.2% management, business, and financial, 3.5% computer, engineering, and science, 3.7% education, legal, community service, arts, and media, 3.0% healthcare practitioners, 23.8% service, 27.0% sales and office, 13.8% natural resources, construction, and maintenance, 14.0% production, transportation, and material moving

Income: Per capita: $24,002; Median household: $48,750; Average household: $61,217; Households with income of $100,000 or more: 19.8%; Poverty rate: 14.2%

Educational Attainment: High school diploma or higher: 91.9%; Bachelor's degree or higher: 14.7%; Graduate/professional degree or higher: 4.9%

Housing: Homeownership rate: 82.7%; Median home value: $111,600; Median year structure built: 1971; Homeowner vacancy rate: 0.9%; Median selected monthly owner costs: $1,193 with a mortgage, $664 without a mortgage; Median gross rent: $860 per month; Rental vacancy rate: 3.1%

Health Insurance: 97.0% have insurance; 70.9% have private insurance; 44.6% have public insurance; 3.0% do not have insurance; 0.0% of children under 18 do not have insurance

Transportation: Commute: 94.5% car, 0.9% public transportation, 0.6% walk, 3.3% work from home; Mean travel time to work: 31.3 minutes

CARROLLTON (town). Covers a land area of 42.299 square miles and a water area of 0.041 square miles. Located at 42.06° N. Lat; 78.64° W. Long. Elevation is 1,398 feet.

Population: 1,395; Growth (since 2000): -1.1%; Density: 33.0 persons per square mile; Race: 98.1% White, 0.3% Black/African American, 0.0% Asian, 1.6% American Indian/Alaska Native, 0.0% Native Hawaiian/Other Pacific Islander, 0.0% Two or more races, 1.6% Hispanic of any race; Average household size: 2.32; Median age: 44.4; Age under 18: 24.4%; Age 65 and over: 18.0%; Males per 100 females: 95.3; Marriage status: 24.3% never married, 55.1% now married, 1.2% separated, 9.6% widowed, 11.0% divorced; Foreign born: 1.2%; Speak English only: 97.9%; With disability: 16.5%; Veterans: 16.0%; Ancestry: 35.4% German, 18.3% Irish, 10.8% English, 8.3% Polish, 6.5% Swedish

Employment: 7.2% management, business, and financial, 0.5% computer, engineering, and science, 11.2% education, legal, community service, arts, and media, 4.3% healthcare practitioners, 16.1% service, 28.3% sales and office, 15.6% natural resources, construction, and maintenance, 16.9% production, transportation, and material moving

Income: Per capita: $23,145; Median household: $40,750; Average household: $53,265; Households with income of $100,000 or more: 12.2%; Poverty rate: 13.9%

Educational Attainment: High school diploma or higher: 90.9%; Bachelor's degree or higher: 13.5%; Graduate/professional degree or higher: 4.5%

Housing: Homeownership rate: 82.8%; Median home value: $67,300; Median year structure built: 1963; Homeowner vacancy rate: 0.0%; Median selected monthly owner costs: $914 with a mortgage, $375 without a mortgage; Median gross rent: $631 per month; Rental vacancy rate: 0.0%

Health Insurance: 92.5% have insurance; 73.2% have private insurance; 40.3% have public insurance; 7.5% do not have insurance; 5.8% of children under 18 do not have insurance

Transportation: Commute: 93.4% car, 0.0% public transportation, 0.0% walk, 5.6% work from home; Mean travel time to work: 25.4 minutes

CATTARAUGUS (village). Covers a land area of 1.117 square miles and a water area of 0.002 square miles. Located at 42.33° N. Lat; 78.87° W. Long. Elevation is 1,375 feet.

History: Settled 1851 during construction of Erie Railroad; incorporated 1882.

Population: 933; Growth (since 2000): -13.2%; Density: 835.0 persons per square mile; Race: 97.6% White, 0.1% Black/African American, 0.0% Asian, 0.5% American Indian/Alaska Native, 0.0% Native Hawaiian/Other Pacific Islander, 1.7% Two or more races, 0.0% Hispanic of any race; Average household size: 2.15; Median age: 46.6; Age under 18: 18.8%; Age 65 and over: 23.2%; Males per 100 females: 94.2; Marriage status: 29.9% never married, 49.3% now married, 2.9% separated, 7.1% widowed, 13.8% divorced; Foreign born: 1.3%; Speak English only: 97.7%; With disability: 20.8%; Veterans: 13.6%; Ancestry: 49.5% German, 20.6% Irish, 14.9% English, 10.2% Polish, 8.3% Italian

Employment: 8.1% management, business, and financial, 0.9% computer, engineering, and science, 9.5% education, legal, community service, arts, and media, 7.4% healthcare practitioners, 24.2% service, 22.1% sales and office, 12.8% natural resources, construction, and maintenance, 14.9% production, transportation, and material moving

Income: Per capita: $22,539; Median household: $44,018; Average household: $47,827; Households with income of $100,000 or more: 10.0%; Poverty rate: 13.6%

Educational Attainment: High school diploma or higher: 86.6%; Bachelor's degree or higher: 22.4%; Graduate/professional degree or higher: 9.9%

School District(s)
Cattaraugus-Little Valley Central SD (PK-12)
    Enrollment: 939 . . . . (716) 257-5292

Housing: Homeownership rate: 67.5%; Median home value: $67,600; Median year structure built: Before 1940; Homeowner vacancy rate: 3.0%; Median selected monthly owner costs: $1,037 with a mortgage, $519 without a mortgage; Median gross rent: $484 per month; Rental vacancy rate: 2.1%

Health Insurance: 95.8% have insurance; 76.0% have private insurance; 42.9% have public insurance; 4.2% do not have insurance; 0.0% of children under 18 do not have insurance

Safety: Violent crime rate: 0.0 per 10,000 population; Property crime rate: 10.8 per 10,000 population

Transportation: Commute: 94.8% car, 0.0% public transportation, 4.5% walk, 0.7% work from home; Mean travel time to work: 23.2 minutes

CATTARAUGUS RESERVATION (reservation). Covers a land area of 5.845 square miles and a water area of 0.194 square miles. Located at 42.53° N. Lat; 79.03° W. Long.

Population: 350; Growth (since 2000): n/a; Density: 59.9 persons per square mile; Race: 2.6% White, 0.0% Black/African American, 20.6% Asian, 70.9% American Indian/Alaska Native, 0.0% Native Hawaiian/Other Pacific Islander, 6.0% Two or more races, 0.0% Hispanic of any race; Average household size: 3.33; Median age: 27.4; Age under 18: 41.1%; Age 65 and over: 10.0%; Males per 100 females: 84.7; Marriage status: 50.4% never married, 32.6% now married, 0.0% separated, 12.1% widowed, 4.9% divorced; Foreign born: 10.9%; Speak English only: 48.4%; With disability: 8.0%; Veterans: 3.4%; Ancestry: 8.6% Swiss, 2.6% Greek

Employment: 0.0% management, business, and financial, 0.0% computer, engineering, and science, 23.6% education, legal, community service, arts, and media, 0.0% healthcare practitioners, 53.9% service, 0.0% sales and office, 0.0% natural resources, construction, and maintenance, 22.5% production, transportation, and material moving

Income: Per capita: $10,935; Median household: $35,489; Average household: $34,433; Households with income of $100,000 or more: n/a; Poverty rate: 24.3%
Educational Attainment: High school diploma or higher: 86.2%; Bachelor's degree or higher: 13.8%; Graduate/professional degree or higher: 9.0%
Housing: Homeownership rate: 82.9%; Median home value: $63,900; Median year structure built: 1975; Homeowner vacancy rate: 0.0%; Median selected monthly owner costs: $1,386 with a mortgage, $430 without a mortgage; Median gross rent: n/a per month; Rental vacancy rate: 0.0%
Health Insurance: 58.0% have insurance; 45.7% have private insurance; 12.3% have public insurance; 42.0% do not have insurance; 28.0% of children under 18 do not have insurance
Transportation: Commute: 100.0% car, 0.0% public transportation, 0.0% walk, 0.0% work from home; Mean travel time to work: 8.3 minutes

COLDSPRING (town).
Covers a land area of 51.464 square miles and a water area of 0.554 square miles. Located at 42.06° N. Lat; 78.84° W. Long. Elevation is 1,407 feet.
Population: 679; Growth (since 2000): -9.6%; Density: 13.2 persons per square mile; Race: 98.4% White, 0.0% Black/African American, 0.0% Asian, 1.6% American Indian/Alaska Native, 0.0% Native Hawaiian/Other Pacific Islander, 0.0% Two or more races, 0.7% Hispanic of any race; Average household size: 2.50; Median age: 40.4; Age under 18: 25.2%; Age 65 and over: 13.0%; Males per 100 females: 108.5; Marriage status: 17.3% never married, 62.9% now married, 2.1% separated, 5.1% widowed, 14.7% divorced; Foreign born: 0.3%; Speak English only: 99.1%; With disability: 16.1%; Veterans: 11.6%; Ancestry: 25.2% German, 23.7% Irish, 20.8% English, 9.9% Swedish, 5.2% Italian
Employment: 7.4% management, business, and financial, 1.2% computer, engineering, and science, 3.4% education, legal, community service, arts, and media, 8.3% healthcare practitioners, 22.1% service, 11.0% sales and office, 21.8% natural resources, construction, and maintenance, 24.8% production, transportation, and material moving
Income: Per capita: $26,832; Median household: $45,156; Average household: $67,711; Households with income of $100,000 or more: 13.9%; Poverty rate: 16.9%
Educational Attainment: High school diploma or higher: 85.9%; Bachelor's degree or higher: 9.5%; Graduate/professional degree or higher: 4.8%
Housing: Homeownership rate: 82.0%; Median home value: $76,100; Median year structure built: 1961; Homeowner vacancy rate: 0.0%; Median selected monthly owner costs: $961 with a mortgage, $504 without a mortgage; Median gross rent: $900 per month; Rental vacancy rate: 0.0%
Health Insurance: 84.8% have insurance; 57.9% have private insurance; 41.2% have public insurance; 15.2% do not have insurance; 14.6% of children under 18 do not have insurance
Transportation: Commute: 91.5% car, 0.9% public transportation, 0.9% walk, 3.2% work from home; Mean travel time to work: 25.7 minutes

CONEWANGO (town).
Covers a land area of 36.114 square miles and a water area of 0.022 square miles. Located at 42.23° N. Lat; 79.01° W. Long. Elevation is 1,293 feet.
Population: 1,627; Growth (since 2000): -6.1%; Density: 45.1 persons per square mile; Race: 99.4% White, 0.0% Black/African American, 0.0% Asian, 0.4% American Indian/Alaska Native, 0.0% Native Hawaiian/Other Pacific Islander, 0.2% Two or more races, 0.8% Hispanic of any race; Average household size: 3.22; Median age: 28.1; Age under 18: 38.3%; Age 65 and over: 14.3%; Males per 100 females: 100.8; Marriage status: 24.7% never married, 59.6% now married, 1.6% separated, 6.0% widowed, 9.7% divorced; Foreign born: 0.8%; Speak English only: 66.7%; With disability: 8.8%; Veterans: 7.4%; Ancestry: 19.3% German, 14.3% Pennsylvania German, 11.1% Dutch, 8.7% English, 7.3% Irish
Employment: 16.0% management, business, and financial, 1.7% computer, engineering, and science, 10.8% education, legal, community service, arts, and media, 1.9% healthcare practitioners, 17.6% service, 19.5% sales and office, 16.2% natural resources, construction, and maintenance, 16.3% production, transportation, and material moving
Income: Per capita: $15,637; Median household: $38,274; Average household: $49,542; Households with income of $100,000 or more: 10.5%; Poverty rate: 28.6%
Educational Attainment: High school diploma or higher: 69.7%; Bachelor's degree or higher: 14.0%; Graduate/professional degree or higher: 6.1%

Housing: Homeownership rate: 79.2%; Median home value: $78,500; Median year structure built: 1974; Homeowner vacancy rate: 2.7%; Median selected monthly owner costs: $926 with a mortgage, $335 without a mortgage; Median gross rent: $588 per month; Rental vacancy rate: 0.0%
Health Insurance: 56.9% have insurance; 37.7% have private insurance; 29.4% have public insurance; 43.1% do not have insurance; 57.4% of children under 18 do not have insurance
Transportation: Commute: 80.3% car, 0.0% public transportation, 3.5% walk, 11.8% work from home; Mean travel time to work: 26.1 minutes

CONEWANGO VALLEY (unincorporated postal area)
ZCTA: 14726
Covers a land area of 40.668 square miles and a water area of <.001 square miles. Located at 42.25° N. Lat; 79.02° W. Long..
Population: 1,902; Growth (since 2000): -11.3%; Density: 46.8 persons per square mile; Race: 99.7% White, 0.0% Black/African American, 0.0% Asian, 0.1% American Indian/Alaska Native, 0.0% Native Hawaiian/Other Pacific Islander, 0.2% Two or more races, 1.0% Hispanic of any race; Average household size: 3.25; Median age: 26.2; Age under 18: 36.8%; Age 65 and over: 10.5%; Males per 100 females: 103.0; Marriage status: 23.1% never married, 65.4% now married, 2.2% separated, 3.6% widowed, 7.9% divorced; Foreign born: 1.3%; Speak English only: 65.9%; With disability: 9.2%; Veterans: 4.9%; Ancestry: 20.8% Pennsylvania German, 16.9% German, 8.4% Irish, 7.0% English, 5.5% Italian
Employment: 13.8% management, business, and financial, 1.4% computer, engineering, and science, 8.7% education, legal, community service, arts, and media, 5.1% healthcare practitioners, 16.4% service, 10.5% sales and office, 22.7% natural resources, construction, and maintenance, 21.5% production, transportation, and material moving
Income: Per capita: $14,156; Median household: $37,569; Average household: $45,226; Households with income of $100,000 or more: 6.6%; Poverty rate: 32.8%
Educational Attainment: High school diploma or higher: 69.0%; Bachelor's degree or higher: 10.2%; Graduate/professional degree or higher: 1.9%
Housing: Homeownership rate: 72.6%; Median home value: $70,700; Median year structure built: 1975; Homeowner vacancy rate: 5.3%; Median selected monthly owner costs: $858 with a mortgage, $381 without a mortgage; Median gross rent: $613 per month; Rental vacancy rate: 5.9%
Health Insurance: 52.6% have insurance; 31.2% have private insurance; 27.1% have public insurance; 47.4% do not have insurance; 58.7% of children under 18 do not have insurance
Transportation: Commute: 74.0% car, 0.0% public transportation, 4.2% walk, 15.5% work from home; Mean travel time to work: 28.5 minutes

DAYTON (town).
Covers a land area of 35.527 square miles and a water area of 0.618 square miles. Located at 42.38° N. Lat; 79.00° W. Long. Elevation is 1,339 feet.
Population: 1,853; Growth (since 2000): -4.7%; Density: 52.2 persons per square mile; Race: 98.8% White, 0.0% Black/African American, 0.0% Asian, 0.4% American Indian/Alaska Native, 0.0% Native Hawaiian/Other Pacific Islander, 0.2% Two or more races, 3.5% Hispanic of any race; Average household size: 2.54; Median age: 36.5; Age under 18: 25.3%; Age 65 and over: 16.5%; Males per 100 females: 102.6; Marriage status: 29.9% never married, 52.8% now married, 1.9% separated, 6.9% widowed, 10.3% divorced; Foreign born: 0.4%; Speak English only: 93.4%; With disability: 16.5%; Veterans: 9.0%; Ancestry: 33.6% German, 16.3% English, 9.8% Irish, 9.6% Polish, 7.3% Italian
Employment: 7.1% management, business, and financial, 1.0% computer, engineering, and science, 7.6% education, legal, community service, arts, and media, 8.9% healthcare practitioners, 23.9% service, 14.4% sales and office, 19.6% natural resources, construction, and maintenance, 17.5% production, transportation, and material moving
Income: Per capita: $21,659; Median household: $49,750; Average household: $54,972; Households with income of $100,000 or more: 11.2%; Poverty rate: 20.7%
Educational Attainment: High school diploma or higher: 80.9%; Bachelor's degree or higher: 11.0%; Graduate/professional degree or higher: 3.6%
Housing: Homeownership rate: 77.7%; Median home value: $74,900; Median year structure built: Before 1940; Homeowner vacancy rate: 0.7%; Median selected monthly owner costs: $982 with a mortgage, $441 without

a mortgage; Median gross rent: $618 per month; Rental vacancy rate: 0.0%
Health Insurance: 87.3% have insurance; 62.8% have private insurance; 37.0% have public insurance; 12.7% do not have insurance; 22.0% of children under 18 do not have insurance
Transportation: Commute: 89.4% car, 0.1% public transportation, 4.8% walk, 3.0% work from home; Mean travel time to work: 27.0 minutes

DELEVAN (village).
Covers a land area of 0.994 square miles and a water area of 0 square miles. Located at 42.49° N. Lat; 78.48° W. Long. Elevation is 1,424 feet.
Population: 1,080; Growth (since 2000): -0.8%; Density: 1,086.5 persons per square mile; Race: 99.9% White, 0.0% Black/African American, 0.1% Asian, 0.0% American Indian/Alaska Native, 0.0% Native Hawaiian/Other Pacific Islander, 0.0% Two or more races, 0.0% Hispanic of any race; Average household size: 2.54; Median age: 40.5; Age under 18: 26.3%; Age 65 and over: 13.0%; Males per 100 females: 98.7; Marriage status: 36.3% never married, 49.1% now married, 5.8% separated, 6.1% widowed, 8.4% divorced; Foreign born: 0.1%; Speak English only: 99.9%; With disability: 18.0%; Veterans: 8.5%; Ancestry: 43.4% German, 26.5% Irish, 15.6% Polish, 9.6% English, 8.9% Italian
Employment: 8.3% management, business, and financial, 1.7% computer, engineering, and science, 10.4% education, legal, community service, arts, and media, 4.3% healthcare practitioners, 23.5% service, 23.0% sales and office, 13.6% natural resources, construction, and maintenance, 15.1% production, transportation, and material moving
Income: Per capita: $19,331; Median household: $39,722; Average household: $49,664; Households with income of $100,000 or more: 9.1%; Poverty rate: 21.5%
Educational Attainment: High school diploma or higher: 87.7%; Bachelor's degree or higher: 11.5%; Graduate/professional degree or higher: 2.2%

School District(s)
Yorkshire-Pioneer Central SD (PK-12)
    Enrollment: 2,544 . . . . (716) 492-9304
Housing: Homeownership rate: 53.8%; Median home value: $95,500; Median year structure built: 1955; Homeowner vacancy rate: 0.0%; Median selected monthly owner costs: $1,143 with a mortgage, $442 without a mortgage; Median gross rent: $583 per month; Rental vacancy rate: 12.8%
Health Insurance: 89.9% have insurance; 59.5% have private insurance; 48.8% have public insurance; 10.1% do not have insurance; 9.9% of children under 18 do not have insurance
Transportation: Commute: 94.6% car, 0.0% public transportation, 3.5% walk, 1.9% work from home; Mean travel time to work: 24.1 minutes

EAST OTTO (town).
Covers a land area of 40.070 square miles and a water area of 0.326 square miles. Located at 42.41° N. Lat; 78.74° W. Long. Elevation is 1,427 feet.
Population: 1,022; Growth (since 2000): -7.5%; Density: 25.5 persons per square mile; Race: 98.4% White, 0.0% Black/African American, 0.5% Asian, 0.0% American Indian/Alaska Native, 0.0% Native Hawaiian/Other Pacific Islander, 1.0% Two or more races, 0.2% Hispanic of any race; Average household size: 2.21; Median age: 49.8; Age under 18: 16.0%; Age 65 and over: 15.1%; Males per 100 females: 113.7; Marriage status: 24.6% never married, 53.3% now married, 0.7% separated, 7.7% widowed, 14.4% divorced; Foreign born: 1.1%; Speak English only: 94.9%; With disability: 15.0%; Veterans: 10.3%; Ancestry: 38.7% German, 11.6% Irish, 9.5% Italian, 9.4% English, 6.4% Polish
Employment: 18.0% management, business, and financial, 1.2% computer, engineering, and science, 4.8% education, legal, community service, arts, and media, 5.9% healthcare practitioners, 22.3% service, 17.1% sales and office, 20.7% natural resources, construction, and maintenance, 10.0% production, transportation, and material moving
Income: Per capita: $34,428; Median household: $63,750; Average household: $75,978; Households with income of $100,000 or more: 14.5%; Poverty rate: 12.7%
Educational Attainment: High school diploma or higher: 93.9%; Bachelor's degree or higher: 17.4%; Graduate/professional degree or higher: 8.6%
Housing: Homeownership rate: 84.6%; Median home value: $103,400; Median year structure built: 1973; Homeowner vacancy rate: 0.0%; Median selected monthly owner costs: $1,270 with a mortgage, $606 without a mortgage; Median gross rent: $669 per month; Rental vacancy rate: 4.1%

Health Insurance: 88.8% have insurance; 71.9% have private insurance; 31.1% have public insurance; 11.2% do not have insurance; 17.1% of children under 18 do not have insurance
Transportation: Commute: 93.0% car, 0.0% public transportation, 2.6% walk, 3.9% work from home; Mean travel time to work: 32.0 minutes

EAST RANDOLPH (CDP).
Covers a land area of 1.088 square miles and a water area of <.001 square miles. Located at 42.17° N. Lat; 78.96° W. Long. Elevation is 1,325 feet.
Population: 588; Growth (since 2000): -6.7%; Density: 540.2 persons per square mile; Race: 95.1% White, 1.9% Black/African American, 0.5% Asian, 0.0% American Indian/Alaska Native, 0.0% Native Hawaiian/Other Pacific Islander, 2.6% Two or more races, 1.0% Hispanic of any race; Average household size: 2.60; Median age: 31.0; Age under 18: 37.1%; Age 65 and over: 16.2%; Males per 100 females: 112.3; Marriage status: 39.4% never married, 40.8% now married, 3.7% separated, 5.3% widowed, 14.4% divorced; Foreign born: 1.0%; Speak English only: 100.0%; With disability: 17.6%; Veterans: 15.7%; Ancestry: 31.6% German, 22.6% Irish, 20.1% English, 5.3% Swedish, 4.6% Italian
Employment: 11.1% management, business, and financial, 3.4% computer, engineering, and science, 8.7% education, legal, community service, arts, and media, 12.6% healthcare practitioners, 9.2% service, 28.0% sales and office, 10.1% natural resources, construction, and maintenance, 16.9% production, transportation, and material moving
Income: Per capita: $15,049; Median household: $32,721; Average household: $40,943; Households with income of $100,000 or more: 5.9%; Poverty rate: 22.7%
Educational Attainment: High school diploma or higher: 89.0%; Bachelor's degree or higher: 8.1%; Graduate/professional degree or higher: 5.8%
Housing: Homeownership rate: 52.2%; Median home value: $81,500; Median year structure built: Before 1940; Homeowner vacancy rate: 0.0%; Median selected monthly owner costs: $983 with a mortgage, $422 without a mortgage; Median gross rent: $595 per month; Rental vacancy rate: 0.0%
Health Insurance: 90.7% have insurance; 57.1% have private insurance; 50.2% have public insurance; 9.3% do not have insurance; 3.2% of children under 18 do not have insurance
Transportation: Commute: 86.2% car, 0.0% public transportation, 10.1% walk, 3.7% work from home; Mean travel time to work: 21.5 minutes

ELLICOTTVILLE (town).
Covers a land area of 45.095 square miles and a water area of 0.093 square miles. Located at 42.31° N. Lat; 78.64° W. Long. Elevation is 1,549 feet.
History: Incorporated 1881.
Population: 1,306; Growth (since 2000): -24.9%; Density: 29.0 persons per square mile; Race: 95.5% White, 1.4% Black/African American, 0.0% Asian, 0.9% American Indian/Alaska Native, 0.0% Native Hawaiian/Other Pacific Islander, 1.5% Two or more races, 2.1% Hispanic of any race; Average household size: 2.16; Median age: 49.7; Age under 18: 17.7%; Age 65 and over: 26.3%; Males per 100 females: 104.9; Marriage status: 25.5% never married, 58.8% now married, 2.0% separated, 6.0% widowed, 9.7% divorced; Foreign born: 3.9%; Speak English only: 97.1%; With disability: 14.5%; Veterans: 8.3%; Ancestry: 39.2% German, 17.5% Irish, 15.8% English, 8.2% Italian, 8.1% Polish
Employment: 17.4% management, business, and financial, 2.4% computer, engineering, and science, 10.9% education, legal, community service, arts, and media, 4.3% healthcare practitioners, 15.3% service, 22.5% sales and office, 19.8% natural resources, construction, and maintenance, 7.4% production, transportation, and material moving
Income: Per capita: $35,806; Median household: $61,364; Average household: $78,313; Households with income of $100,000 or more: 26.6%; Poverty rate: 8.5%
Educational Attainment: High school diploma or higher: 91.3%; Bachelor's degree or higher: 30.4%; Graduate/professional degree or higher: 13.2%

School District(s)
Ellicottville Central SD (PK-12)
    Enrollment: 645 . . . . (716) 699-2368
Housing: Homeownership rate: 81.5%; Median home value: $184,500; Median year structure built: 1985; Homeowner vacancy rate: 8.0%; Median selected monthly owner costs: $1,452 with a mortgage, $578 without a mortgage; Median gross rent: $678 per month; Rental vacancy rate: 2.4%

Health Insurance: 94.9% have insurance; 84.5% have private insurance; 34.4% have public insurance; 5.1% do not have insurance; 0.8% of children under 18 do not have insurance
Safety: Violent crime rate: 6.3 per 10,000 population; Property crime rate: 62.5 per 10,000 population
Transportation: Commute: 90.2% car, 0.0% public transportation, 4.9% walk, 2.5% work from home; Mean travel time to work: 26.0 minutes

---

ELLICOTTVILLE (village). Covers a land area of 0.820 square miles and a water area of 0.014 square miles. Located at 42.27° N. Lat; 78.67° W. Long. Elevation is 1,549 feet.

Population: 278; Growth (since 2000): -41.1%; Density: 338.8 persons per square mile; Race: 92.8% White, 0.0% Black/African American, 0.0% Asian, 0.0% American Indian/Alaska Native, 0.0% Native Hawaiian/Other Pacific Islander, 7.2% Two or more races, 0.0% Hispanic of any race; Average household size: 1.92; Median age: 55.6; Age under 18: 12.9%; Age 65 and over: 41.0%; Males per 100 females: 106.6; Marriage status: 34.2% never married, 54.1% now married, 0.8% separated, 8.6% widowed, 3.1% divorced; Foreign born: 5.8%; Speak English only: 94.1%; With disability: 23.1%; Veterans: 7.2%; Ancestry: 37.1% German, 29.9% English, 15.8% Irish, 8.3% French Canadian, 7.6% Polish
Employment: 25.4% management, business, and financial, 3.3% computer, engineering, and science, 14.8% education, legal, community service, arts, and media, 4.1% healthcare practitioners, 17.2% service, 17.2% sales and office, 11.5% natural resources, construction, and maintenance, 6.6% production, transportation, and material moving
Income: Per capita: $30,766; Median household: $43,125; Average household: $59,114; Households with income of $100,000 or more: 15.9%; Poverty rate: 12.9%
Educational Attainment: High school diploma or higher: 90.5%; Bachelor's degree or higher: 31.2%; Graduate/professional degree or higher: 13.1%

School District(s)
Ellicottville Central SD (PK-12)
   Enrollment: 645 . . . . (716) 699-2368
Housing: Homeownership rate: 79.3%; Median home value: $186,000; Median year structure built: Before 1940; Homeowner vacancy rate: 1.6%; Median selected monthly owner costs: $1,522 with a mortgage, $544 without a mortgage; Median gross rent: $775 per month; Rental vacancy rate: 0.0%
Health Insurance: 94.5% have insurance; 77.7% have private insurance; 53.8% have public insurance; 5.5% do not have insurance; 5.3% of children under 18 do not have insurance
Transportation: Commute: 74.8% car, 0.0% public transportation, 23.6% walk, 1.6% work from home; Mean travel time to work: 19.5 minutes

---

FARMERSVILLE (town). Covers a land area of 47.833 square miles and a water area of 0.138 square miles. Located at 42.38° N. Lat; 78.41° W. Long. Elevation is 1,837 feet.

Population: 1,075; Growth (since 2000): 4.6%; Density: 22.5 persons per square mile; Race: 99.0% White, 0.0% Black/African American, 0.2% Asian, 0.0% American Indian/Alaska Native, 0.0% Native Hawaiian/Other Pacific Islander, 0.8% Two or more races, 2.5% Hispanic of any race; Average household size: 2.27; Median age: 50.6; Age under 18: 16.0%; Age 65 and over: 20.8%; Males per 100 females: 97.5; Marriage status: 21.5% never married, 62.4% now married, 3.2% separated, 6.6% widowed, 9.6% divorced; Foreign born: 1.0%; Speak English only: 95.8%; With disability: 14.9%; Veterans: 9.6%; Ancestry: 29.2% German, 15.8% English, 13.3% Irish, 7.7% Polish, 7.3% Italian
Employment: 11.9% management, business, and financial, 0.4% computer, engineering, and science, 8.2% education, legal, community service, arts, and media, 9.4% healthcare practitioners, 13.8% service, 19.1% sales and office, 13.1% natural resources, construction, and maintenance, 24.0% production, transportation, and material moving
Income: Per capita: $23,754; Median household: $46,875; Average household: $53,932; Households with income of $100,000 or more: 14.3%; Poverty rate: 12.6%
Educational Attainment: High school diploma or higher: 81.0%; Bachelor's degree or higher: 15.1%; Graduate/professional degree or higher: 6.1%
Housing: Homeownership rate: 88.4%; Median home value: $97,900; Median year structure built: 1984; Homeowner vacancy rate: 0.0%; Median selected monthly owner costs: $1,287 with a mortgage, $437 without a mortgage; Median gross rent: $602 per month; Rental vacancy rate: 0.0%

Health Insurance: 86.1% have insurance; 60.1% have private insurance; 41.7% have public insurance; 13.9% do not have insurance; 35.2% of children under 18 do not have insurance
Transportation: Commute: 91.5% car, 0.0% public transportation, 3.3% walk, 1.2% work from home; Mean travel time to work: 27.2 minutes

---

FRANKLINVILLE (town). Covers a land area of 51.812 square miles and a water area of 0.173 square miles. Located at 42.30° N. Lat; 78.50° W. Long. Elevation is 1,591 feet.

History: Settled 1806, incorporated 1874.
Population: 2,889; Growth (since 2000): -7.6%; Density: 55.8 persons per square mile; Race: 97.3% White, 0.1% Black/African American, 0.4% Asian, 0.2% American Indian/Alaska Native, 0.0% Native Hawaiian/Other Pacific Islander, 1.8% Two or more races, 3.0% Hispanic of any race; Average household size: 2.48; Median age: 39.0; Age under 18: 24.5%; Age 65 and over: 17.0%; Males per 100 females: 98.9; Marriage status: 27.3% never married, 53.3% now married, 0.8% separated, 7.4% widowed, 11.9% divorced; Foreign born: 0.8%; Speak English only: 98.8%; With disability: 16.2%; Veterans: 14.7%; Ancestry: 35.2% German, 17.8% Polish, 15.5% Irish, 14.0% English, 7.3% Italian
Employment: 11.5% management, business, and financial, 2.4% computer, engineering, and science, 15.2% education, legal, community service, arts, and media, 2.6% healthcare practitioners, 19.6% service, 23.2% sales and office, 11.8% natural resources, construction, and maintenance, 13.6% production, transportation, and material moving
Income: Per capita: $23,483; Median household: $48,648; Average household: $57,974; Households with income of $100,000 or more: 15.1%; Poverty rate: 15.8%
Educational Attainment: High school diploma or higher: 90.8%; Bachelor's degree or higher: 21.4%; Graduate/professional degree or higher: 12.6%

School District(s)
Franklinville Central SD (PK-12)
   Enrollment: 717 . . . . (716) 676-8029
Housing: Homeownership rate: 76.5%; Median home value: $70,900; Median year structure built: 1950; Homeowner vacancy rate: 4.6%; Median selected monthly owner costs: $986 with a mortgage, $528 without a mortgage; Median gross rent: $617 per month; Rental vacancy rate: 3.5%
Health Insurance: 93.1% have insurance; 63.9% have private insurance; 42.9% have public insurance; 6.9% do not have insurance; 4.2% of children under 18 do not have insurance
Transportation: Commute: 95.5% car, 0.3% public transportation, 1.7% walk, 1.7% work from home; Mean travel time to work: 26.6 minutes
Additional Information Contacts
Town of Franklinville . . . . (716) 676-3077
   http://www.franklinvilleny.org

FRANKLINVILLE (village). Covers a land area of 1.100 square miles and a water area of 0 square miles. Located at 42.33° N. Lat; 78.45° W. Long. Elevation is 1,591 feet.

Population: 1,703; Growth (since 2000): -8.2%; Density: 1,548.2 persons per square mile; Race: 95.5% White, 0.2% Black/African American, 0.7% Asian, 0.3% American Indian/Alaska Native, 0.0% Native Hawaiian/Other Pacific Islander, 3.1% Two or more races, 5.0% Hispanic of any race; Average household size: 2.48; Median age: 35.5; Age under 18: 28.9%; Age 65 and over: 15.4%; Males per 100 females: 95.5; Marriage status: 27.5% never married, 53.2% now married, 1.5% separated, 9.5% widowed, 9.8% divorced; Foreign born: 1.4%; Speak English only: 98.0%; With disability: 17.9%; Veterans: 12.3%; Ancestry: 41.0% German, 17.4% Irish, 15.0% English, 11.3% Polish, 5.5% French
Employment: 11.1% management, business, and financial, 3.1% computer, engineering, and science, 7.6% education, legal, community service, arts, and media, 4.9% healthcare practitioners, 23.7% service, 23.8% sales and office, 8.7% natural resources, construction, and maintenance, 17.1% production, transportation, and material moving
Income: Per capita: $20,210; Median household: $42,650; Average household: $50,251; Households with income of $100,000 or more: 11.1%; Poverty rate: 19.7%
Educational Attainment: High school diploma or higher: 85.7%; Bachelor's degree or higher: 15.4%; Graduate/professional degree or higher: 6.7%

School District(s)
Franklinville Central SD (PK-12)
   Enrollment: 717 . . . . (716) 676-8029

Housing: Homeownership rate: 61.3%; Median home value: $66,600; Median year structure built: Before 1940; Homeowner vacancy rate: 3.4%; Median selected monthly owner costs: $963 with a mortgage, $491 without a mortgage; Median gross rent: $617 per month; Rental vacancy rate: 3.7%

Health Insurance: 91.5% have insurance; 55.5% have private insurance; 53.0% have public insurance; 8.5% do not have insurance; 6.3% of children under 18 do not have insurance

Safety: Violent crime rate: 6.0 per 10,000 population; Property crime rate: 120.4 per 10,000 population

Transportation: Commute: 91.9% car, 0.6% public transportation, 3.1% walk, 3.1% work from home; Mean travel time to work: 26.9 minutes

Additional Information Contacts

Village of Franklinville . . . . (716) 676-3010
http://www.franklinvilleny.org

FREEDOM (town). Covers a land area of 40.987 square miles and a water area of 0.329 square miles. Located at 42.47° N. Lat; 78.38° W. Long. Elevation is 1,801 feet.

Population: 2,319; Growth (since 2000): -7.0%; Density: 56.6 persons per square mile; Race: 97.2% White, 0.3% Black/African American, 1.6% Asian, 0.0% American Indian/Alaska Native, 0.0% Native Hawaiian/Other Pacific Islander, 0.9% Two or more races, 0.0% Hispanic of any race; Average household size: 2.61; Median age: 42.6; Age under 18: 25.3%; Age 65 and over: 20.6%; Males per 100 females: 106.1; Marriage status: 13.0% never married, 71.2% now married, 1.2% separated, 6.7% widowed, 9.1% divorced; Foreign born: 5.5%; Speak English only: 92.8%; With disability: 10.5%; Veterans: 11.1%; Ancestry: 29.5% German, 17.0% Irish, 12.8% English, 10.8% Polish, 5.8% American

Employment: 10.7% management, business, and financial, 2.3% computer, engineering, and science, 4.9% education, legal, community service, arts, and media, 1.8% healthcare practitioners, 16.1% service, 20.9% sales and office, 14.9% natural resources, construction, and maintenance, 28.5% production, transportation, and material moving

Income: Per capita: $22,814; Median household: $51,571; Average household: $58,810; Households with income of $100,000 or more: 15.8%; Poverty rate: 8.2%

Educational Attainment: High school diploma or higher: 86.6%; Bachelor's degree or higher: 12.2%; Graduate/professional degree or higher: 5.8%

Housing: Homeownership rate: 91.2%; Median home value: $110,500; Median year structure built: 1978; Homeowner vacancy rate: 1.6%; Median selected monthly owner costs: $1,029 with a mortgage, $442 without a mortgage; Median gross rent: $792 per month; Rental vacancy rate: 0.0%

Health Insurance: 96.5% have insurance; 69.9% have private insurance; 46.2% have public insurance; 3.5% do not have insurance; 2.0% of children under 18 do not have insurance

Transportation: Commute: 92.9% car, 0.0% public transportation, 3.6% walk, 2.9% work from home; Mean travel time to work: 26.3 minutes

GOWANDA (village). Covers a land area of 1.593 square miles and a water area of 0.016 square miles. Located at 42.46° N. Lat; 78.93° W. Long. Elevation is 761 feet.

Population: 2,864; Growth (since 2000): 0.8%; Density: 1,797.6 persons per square mile; Race: 87.8% White, 0.7% Black/African American, 2.1% Asian, 2.7% American Indian/Alaska Native, 0.1% Native Hawaiian/Other Pacific Islander, 6.3% Two or more races, 1.2% Hispanic of any race; Average household size: 2.10; Median age: 41.0; Age under 18: 20.8%; Age 65 and over: 20.2%; Males per 100 females: 91.7; Marriage status: 38.5% never married, 36.1% now married, 2.8% separated, 10.1% widowed, 15.3% divorced; Foreign born: 2.0%; Speak English only: 95.8%; With disability: 19.5%; Veterans: 8.3%; Ancestry: 32.8% German, 15.1% Irish, 13.7% Italian, 13.3% English, 13.1% Polish

Employment: 9.3% management, business, and financial, 2.2% computer, engineering, and science, 10.1% education, legal, community service, arts, and media, 8.5% healthcare practitioners, 29.2% service, 16.2% sales and office, 12.6% natural resources, construction, and maintenance, 11.8% production, transportation, and material moving

Income: Per capita: $27,468; Median household: $35,616; Average household: $58,965; Households with income of $100,000 or more: 11.6%; Poverty rate: 23.7%

Educational Attainment: High school diploma or higher: 86.4%; Bachelor's degree or higher: 15.0%; Graduate/professional degree or higher: 8.1%

Gowanda Central SD (PK-12)
    Enrollment: 1,214 . . . . (716) 532-3325

Housing: Homeownership rate: 59.5%; Median home value: $77,200; Median year structure built: Before 1940; Homeowner vacancy rate: 0.0%; Median selected monthly owner costs: $883 with a mortgage, $395 without a mortgage; Median gross rent: $612 per month; Rental vacancy rate: 2.4%

Health Insurance: 89.8% have insurance; 64.2% have private insurance; 42.2% have public insurance; 10.2% do not have insurance; 7.3% of children under 18 do not have insurance

Hospitals: TLC Health Network (65 beds)

Transportation: Commute: 90.8% car, 0.0% public transportation, 5.1% walk, 2.5% work from home; Mean travel time to work: 30.0 minutes

GREAT VALLEY (town). Covers a land area of 49.635 square miles and a water area of 0.036 square miles. Located at 42.20° N. Lat; 78.64° W. Long. Elevation is 1,460 feet.

Population: 1,999; Growth (since 2000): -6.8%; Density: 40.3 persons per square mile; Race: 96.4% White, 0.2% Black/African American, 0.4% Asian, 2.1% American Indian/Alaska Native, 0.0% Native Hawaiian/Other Pacific Islander, 0.9% Two or more races, 0.1% Hispanic of any race; Average household size: 2.23; Median age: 51.4; Age under 18: 17.7%; Age 65 and over: 23.5%; Males per 100 females: 97.6; Marriage status: 27.5% never married, 54.0% now married, 3.2% separated, 4.5% widowed, 14.0% divorced; Foreign born: 1.1%; Speak English only: 98.5%; With disability: 17.9%; Veterans: 14.1%; Ancestry: 30.2% German, 25.4% Irish, 13.3% English, 10.3% Polish, 6.8% Italian

Employment: 12.6% management, business, and financial, 5.1% computer, engineering, and science, 12.0% education, legal, community service, arts, and media, 4.1% healthcare practitioners, 22.9% service, 19.6% sales and office, 16.6% natural resources, construction, and maintenance, 7.0% production, transportation, and material moving

Income: Per capita: $27,243; Median household: $50,956; Average household: $60,960; Households with income of $100,000 or more: 21.5%; Poverty rate: 9.7%

Educational Attainment: High school diploma or higher: 89.3%; Bachelor's degree or higher: 20.6%; Graduate/professional degree or higher: 7.2%

Housing: Homeownership rate: 85.7%; Median home value: $118,200; Median year structure built: 1983; Homeowner vacancy rate: 1.9%; Median selected monthly owner costs: $1,088 with a mortgage, $513 without a mortgage; Median gross rent: $578 per month; Rental vacancy rate: 19.0%

Health Insurance: 90.3% have insurance; 72.4% have private insurance; 38.7% have public insurance; 9.7% do not have insurance; 1.4% of children under 18 do not have insurance

Transportation: Commute: 94.1% car, 0.5% public transportation, 0.3% walk, 4.8% work from home; Mean travel time to work: 22.9 minutes

HINSDALE (town). Covers a land area of 38.731 square miles and a water area of 0.042 square miles. Located at 42.17° N. Lat; 78.37° W. Long. Elevation is 1,480 feet.

Population: 1,897; Growth (since 2000): -16.4%; Density: 49.0 persons per square mile; Race: 93.7% White, 2.3% Black/African American, 1.5% Asian, 0.0% American Indian/Alaska Native, 0.0% Native Hawaiian/Other Pacific Islander, 1.5% Two or more races, 0.6% Hispanic of any race; Average household size: 2.31; Median age: 44.7; Age under 18: 20.6%; Age 65 and over: 18.7%; Males per 100 females: 98.2; Marriage status: 25.3% never married, 57.6% now married, 4.5% separated, 9.9% widowed, 7.2% divorced; Foreign born: 2.3%; Speak English only: 99.0%; With disability: 23.2%; Veterans: 11.1%; Ancestry: 31.0% German, 17.9% Irish, 14.3% Polish, 13.2% Italian, 11.9% English

Employment: 7.3% management, business, and financial, 3.4% computer, engineering, and science, 13.5% education, legal, community service, arts, and media, 8.7% healthcare practitioners, 13.6% service, 23.8% sales and office, 11.4% natural resources, construction, and maintenance, 18.4% production, transportation, and material moving

Income: Per capita: $23,986; Median household: $46,471; Average household: $55,371; Households with income of $100,000 or more: 10.8%; Poverty rate: 14.3%

Educational Attainment: High school diploma or higher: 87.6%; Bachelor's degree or higher: 16.2%; Graduate/professional degree or higher: 6.6%

School District(s)

Hinsdale Central SD (PK-12)

    Enrollment: 444 . . . . (716) 557-2227

Housing: Homeownership rate: 86.8%; Median home value: $71,600; Median year structure built: 1976; Homeowner vacancy rate: 1.7%; Median selected monthly owner costs: $1,036 with a mortgage, $427 without a mortgage; Median gross rent: $715 per month; Rental vacancy rate: 0.0%

Health Insurance: 94.6% have insurance; 69.9% have private insurance; 43.4% have public insurance; 5.4% do not have insurance; 4.3% of children under 18 do not have insurance

Transportation: Commute: 94.5% car, 0.0% public transportation, 1.7% walk, 2.8% work from home; Mean travel time to work: 20.9 minutes

---

HUMPHREY (town). Covers a land area of 37.136 square miles and a water area of 0.017 square miles. Located at 42.23° N. Lat; 78.50° W. Long. Elevation is 1,617 feet.

Population: 828; Growth (since 2000): 14.8%; Density: 22.3 persons per square mile; Race: 97.9% White, 0.0% Black/African American, 0.0% Asian, 0.0% American Indian/Alaska Native, 0.0% Native Hawaiian/Other Pacific Islander, 2.1% Two or more races, 0.0% Hispanic of any race; Average household size: 2.60; Median age: 38.3; Age under 18: 27.8%; Age 65 and over: 10.4%; Males per 100 females: 113.4; Marriage status: 27.6% never married, 51.5% now married, 3.7% separated, 5.5% widowed, 15.4% divorced; Foreign born: 0.5%; Speak English only: 99.6%; With disability: 16.5%; Veterans: 6.7%; Ancestry: 30.7% Irish, 26.7% German, 10.6% American, 6.5% Italian, 5.7% Polish

Employment: 15.1% management, business, and financial, 3.0% computer, engineering, and science, 10.8% education, legal, community service, arts, and media, 6.5% healthcare practitioners, 9.1% service, 25.4% sales and office, 10.3% natural resources, construction, and maintenance, 19.6% production, transportation, and material moving

Income: Per capita: $27,548; Median household: $60,000; Average household: $72,037; Households with income of $100,000 or more: 20.2%; Poverty rate: 21.7%

Educational Attainment: High school diploma or higher: 81.0%; Bachelor's degree or higher: 16.1%; Graduate/professional degree or higher: 7.3%

Housing: Homeownership rate: 88.4%; Median home value: $111,100; Median year structure built: 1984; Homeowner vacancy rate: 0.0%; Median selected monthly owner costs: $1,191 with a mortgage, $518 without a mortgage; Median gross rent: $756 per month; Rental vacancy rate: 0.0%

Health Insurance: 95.5% have insurance; 77.3% have private insurance; 34.9% have public insurance; 4.5% do not have insurance; 0.0% of children under 18 do not have insurance

Transportation: Commute: 90.9% car, 0.0% public transportation, 0.8% walk, 7.8% work from home; Mean travel time to work: 25.6 minutes

---

ISCHUA (town). Covers a land area of 32.377 square miles and a water area of 0.021 square miles. Located at 42.24° N. Lat; 78.38° W. Long. Elevation is 1,542 feet.

Population: 770; Growth (since 2000): -14.0%; Density: 23.8 persons per square mile; Race: 98.8% White, 0.3% Black/African American, 0.0% Asian, 0.0% American Indian/Alaska Native, 0.0% Native Hawaiian/Other Pacific Islander, 0.9% Two or more races, 1.6% Hispanic of any race; Average household size: 2.08; Median age: 52.3; Age under 18: 16.9%; Age 65 and over: 24.2%; Males per 100 females: 116.4; Marriage status: 18.7% never married, 61.3% now married, 1.2% separated, 8.9% widowed, 11.2% divorced; Foreign born: 0.6%; Speak English only: 95.7%; With disability: 20.9%; Veterans: 12.8%; Ancestry: 26.5% German, 15.3% English, 13.8% American, 10.8% Polish, 10.1% Irish

Employment: 15.6% management, business, and financial, 3.5% computer, engineering, and science, 4.1% education, legal, community service, arts, and media, 5.4% healthcare practitioners, 14.3% service, 25.5% sales and office, 11.1% natural resources, construction, and maintenance, 20.4% production, transportation, and material moving

Income: Per capita: $25,454; Median household: $42,813; Average household: $52,775; Households with income of $100,000 or more: 14.5%; Poverty rate: 14.7%

Educational Attainment: High school diploma or higher: 84.9%; Bachelor's degree or higher: 13.9%; Graduate/professional degree or higher: 3.1%

Housing: Homeownership rate: 89.8%; Median home value: $81,000; Median year structure built: 1972; Homeowner vacancy rate: 0.0%; Median selected monthly owner costs: $1,196 with a mortgage, $441 without a mortgage; Median gross rent: $664 per month; Rental vacancy rate: 0.0%

Health Insurance: 95.8% have insurance; 68.2% have private insurance; 46.1% have public insurance; 4.2% do not have insurance; 4.0% of children under 18 do not have insurance

Transportation: Commute: 95.5% car, 0.0% public transportation, 1.9% walk, 2.6% work from home; Mean travel time to work: 19.3 minutes

---

KILL BUCK (unincorporated postal area)

ZCTA: 14748

Covers a land area of 17.902 square miles and a water area of 0.376 square miles. Located at 42.16° N. Lat; 78.64° W. Long. Elevation is 1,407 feet.

Population: 664; Growth (since 2000): 0.6%; Density: 37.1 persons per square mile; Race: 70.9% White, 0.0% Black/African American, 0.3% Asian, 27.6% American Indian/Alaska Native, 0.0% Native Hawaiian/Other Pacific Islander, 1.2% Two or more races, 1.1% Hispanic of any race; Average household size: 2.40; Median age: 33.7; Age under 18: 24.2%; Age 65 and over: 19.0%; Males per 100 females: 95.8; Marriage status: 41.8% never married, 40.1% now married, 6.8% separated, 4.2% widowed, 13.9% divorced; Foreign born: 0.3%; Speak English only: 97.8%; With disability: 15.5%; Veterans: 10.7%; Ancestry: 29.8% German, 17.5% Irish, 15.4% Polish, 8.1% Italian, 6.3% Dutch

Employment: 8.8% management, business, and financial, 1.5% computer, engineering, and science, 7.7% education, legal, community service, arts, and media, 2.3% healthcare practitioners, 19.9% service, 26.4% sales and office, 22.2% natural resources, construction, and maintenance, 11.1% production, transportation, and material moving

Income: Per capita: $17,097; Median household: $26,563; Average household: $42,193; Households with income of $100,000 or more: 5.8%; Poverty rate: 36.9%

Educational Attainment: High school diploma or higher: 78.3%; Bachelor's degree or higher: 11.1%; Graduate/professional degree or higher: 5.7%

Housing: Homeownership rate: 65.7%; Median home value: $65,900; Median year structure built: 1976; Homeowner vacancy rate: 0.0%; Median selected monthly owner costs: $1,094 with a mortgage, $322 without a mortgage; Median gross rent: $565 per month; Rental vacancy rate: 5.9%

Health Insurance: 89.5% have insurance; 46.7% have private insurance; 57.5% have public insurance; 10.5% do not have insurance; 1.7% of children under 18 do not have insurance

Transportation: Commute: 86.2% car, 2.0% public transportation, 2.8% walk, 9.1% work from home; Mean travel time to work: 18.7 minutes

---

LEON (town). Covers a land area of 36.182 square miles and a water area of 0.027 square miles. Located at 42.30° N. Lat; 79.00° W. Long. Elevation is 1,375 feet.

Population: 1,194; Growth (since 2000): -13.5%; Density: 33.0 persons per square mile; Race: 95.4% White, 0.3% Black/African American, 0.0% Asian, 0.0% American Indian/Alaska Native, 0.0% Native Hawaiian/Other Pacific Islander, 4.3% Two or more races, 0.0% Hispanic of any race; Average household size: 3.01; Median age: 25.9; Age under 18: 35.5%; Age 65 and over: 11.4%; Males per 100 females: 103.1; Marriage status: 21.7% never married, 66.0% now married, 3.4% separated, 3.8% widowed, 8.5% divorced; Foreign born: 0.3%; Speak English only: 72.8%; With disability: 15.5%; Veterans: 5.9%; Ancestry: 24.3% German, 15.5% Pennsylvania German, 10.5% Irish, 7.6% English, 6.9% Italian

Employment: 10.1% management, business, and financial, 3.0% computer, engineering, and science, 4.5% education, legal, community service, arts, and media, 3.8% healthcare practitioners, 18.6% service, 17.3% sales and office, 26.9% natural resources, construction, and maintenance, 15.8% production, transportation, and material moving

Income: Per capita: $18,289; Median household: $38,839; Average household: $54,949; Households with income of $100,000 or more: 7.8%; Poverty rate: 23.6%

Educational Attainment: High school diploma or higher: 76.7%; Bachelor's degree or higher: 9.7%; Graduate/professional degree or higher: 2.4%

Housing: Homeownership rate: 70.3%; Median home value: $76,500; Median year structure built: 1974; Homeowner vacancy rate: 6.4%; Median selected monthly owner costs: $873 with a mortgage, $455 without a mortgage; Median gross rent: $539 per month; Rental vacancy rate: 7.8%

Health Insurance: 64.2% have insurance; 40.4% have private insurance; 33.1% have public insurance; 35.8% do not have insurance; 42.6% of children under 18 do not have insurance

Transportation: Commute: 73.4% car, 0.0% public transportation, 2.8% walk, 15.4% work from home; Mean travel time to work: 31.7 minutes

LIME LAKE (CDP). Covers a land area of 2.378 square miles and a water area of 0.266 square miles. Located at 42.43° N. Lat; 78.48° W. Long. Elevation is 1,660 feet.

Population: 785; Growth (since 2000): n/a; Density: 330.1 persons per square mile; Race: 100.0% White, 0.0% Black/African American, 0.0% Asian, 0.0% American Indian/Alaska Native, 0.0% Native Hawaiian/Other Pacific Islander, 0.0% Two or more races, 0.0% Hispanic of any race; Average household size: 2.54; Median age: 50.5; Age under 18: 25.2%; Age 65 and over: 25.6%; Males per 100 females: 91.8; Marriage status: 21.0% never married, 55.1% now married, 0.0% separated, 12.3% widowed, 11.6% divorced; Foreign born: 0.0%; Speak English only: 99.4%; With disability: 12.6%; Veterans: 8.0%; Ancestry: 36.4% German, 14.8% English, 10.7% Polish, 10.3% Irish, 7.6% Italian

Employment: 14.1% management, business, and financial, 2.0% computer, engineering, and science, 4.6% education, legal, community service, arts, and media, 10.8% healthcare practitioners, 14.1% service, 19.9% sales and office, 15.7% natural resources, construction, and maintenance, 19.0% production, transportation, and material moving

Income: Per capita: $24,499; Median household: $52,019; Average household: $65,095; Households with income of $100,000 or more: 12.2%; Poverty rate: 16.8%

Educational Attainment: High school diploma or higher: 88.0%; Bachelor's degree or higher: 14.8%; Graduate/professional degree or higher: 4.5%

Housing: Homeownership rate: 71.6%; Median home value: $114,400; Median year structure built: 1959; Homeowner vacancy rate: 3.1%; Median selected monthly owner costs: $1,153 with a mortgage, $448 without a mortgage; Median gross rent: $1,000 per month; Rental vacancy rate: 21.3%

Health Insurance: 95.1% have insurance; 74.4% have private insurance; 48.7% have public insurance; 4.9% do not have insurance; 5.6% of children under 18 do not have insurance

Transportation: Commute: 97.1% car, 0.0% public transportation, 2.9% walk, 0.0% work from home; Mean travel time to work: 24.3 minutes

LIMESTONE (CDP). Covers a land area of 1.623 square miles and a water area of 0.010 square miles. Located at 42.02° N. Lat; 78.63° W. Long. Elevation is 1,407 feet.

History: The field was the first major oil-producing region in the U.S. When the first well was successfully drilled near Titusville, Pennsylvania, in 1859, Allegany, Cattaraugus, and Chautauqua counties all shared in the prosperity.

Population: 432; Growth (since 2000): 5.1%; Density: 266.2 persons per square mile; Race: 98.1% White, 0.9% Black/African American, 0.0% Asian, 0.9% American Indian/Alaska Native, 0.0% Native Hawaiian/Other Pacific Islander, 0.0% Two or more races, 0.2% Hispanic of any race; Average household size: 2.56; Median age: 34.7; Age under 18: 32.4%; Age 65 and over: 13.7%; Males per 100 females: 87.9; Marriage status: 28.0% never married, 54.7% now married, 0.0% separated, 6.9% widowed, 10.4% divorced; Foreign born: 0.0%; Speak English only: 100.0%; With disability: 10.4%; Veterans: 7.9%; Ancestry: 42.8% German, 15.3% Irish, 12.7% Swedish, 11.8% English, 7.6% Welsh

Employment: 2.8% management, business, and financial, 1.4% computer, engineering, and science, 12.3% education, legal, community service, arts, and media, 4.7% healthcare practitioners, 18.4% service, 27.4% sales and office, 13.7% natural resources, construction, and maintenance, 19.3% production, transportation, and material moving

Income: Per capita: $23,214; Median household: $49,625; Average household: $59,705; Households with income of $100,000 or more: 21.2%; Poverty rate: 8.8%

Educational Attainment: High school diploma or higher: 91.6%; Bachelor's degree or higher: 11.0%; Graduate/professional degree or higher: 1.1%

Housing: Homeownership rate: 63.0%; Median home value: $63,500; Median year structure built: 1950; Homeowner vacancy rate: 0.0%; Median selected monthly owner costs: $892 with a mortgage, $363 without a mortgage; Median gross rent: $769 per month; Rental vacancy rate: 0.0%

Health Insurance: 88.9% have insurance; 75.6% have private insurance; 37.4% have public insurance; 11.1% do not have insurance; 5.2% of children under 18 do not have insurance

Transportation: Commute: 92.5% car, 0.0% public transportation, 0.0% walk, 6.1% work from home; Mean travel time to work: 21.0 minutes

LITTLE VALLEY (town). Covers a land area of 29.787 square miles and a water area of 0.006 square miles. Located at 42.22° N. Lat; 78.76° W. Long. Elevation is 1,598 feet.

History: Incorporated 1876.

Population: 1,937; Growth (since 2000): 8.3%; Density: 65.0 persons per square mile; Race: 91.9% White, 3.1% Black/African American, 0.1% Asian, 1.9% American Indian/Alaska Native, 0.0% Native Hawaiian/Other Pacific Islander, 1.4% Two or more races, 4.5% Hispanic of any race; Average household size: 2.46; Median age: 35.4; Age under 18: 24.9%; Age 65 and over: 15.7%; Males per 100 females: 111.7; Marriage status: 32.8% never married, 47.4% now married, 3.3% separated, 6.5% widowed, 13.3% divorced; Foreign born: 0.8%; Speak English only: 97.1%; With disability: 13.3%; Veterans: 9.9%; Ancestry: 30.1% German, 19.2% Irish, 16.7% English, 7.0% Polish, 4.1% American

Employment: 6.1% management, business, and financial, 1.6% computer, engineering, and science, 12.7% education, legal, community service, arts, and media, 4.6% healthcare practitioners, 28.6% service, 16.2% sales and office, 11.3% natural resources, construction, and maintenance, 18.9% production, transportation, and material moving

Income: Per capita: $18,813; Median household: $40,579; Average household: $47,668; Households with income of $100,000 or more: 10.0%; Poverty rate: 21.2%

Educational Attainment: High school diploma or higher: 88.3%; Bachelor's degree or higher: 12.8%; Graduate/professional degree or higher: 4.6%

School District(s)
Cattaraugus-Little Valley Central SD (PK-12)
    Enrollment: 939. . . . . (716) 257-5292

Housing: Homeownership rate: 64.3%; Median home value: $91,200; Median year structure built: 1950; Homeowner vacancy rate: 3.3%; Median selected monthly owner costs: $943 with a mortgage, $458 without a mortgage; Median gross rent: $541 per month; Rental vacancy rate: 3.9%

Health Insurance: 93.9% have insurance; 64.2% have private insurance; 46.1% have public insurance; 6.1% do not have insurance; 0.0% of children under 18 do not have insurance

Transportation: Commute: 92.7% car, 0.0% public transportation, 6.9% walk, 0.3% work from home; Mean travel time to work: 22.6 minutes

LITTLE VALLEY (village). County seat. Covers a land area of 1.002 square miles and a water area of 0 square miles. Located at 42.25° N. Lat; 78.80° W. Long. Elevation is 1,598 feet.

Population: 1,268; Growth (since 2000): 12.2%; Density: 1,265.4 persons per square mile; Race: 87.8% White, 4.8% Black/African American, 0.0% Asian, 2.9% American Indian/Alaska Native, 0.0% Native Hawaiian/Other Pacific Islander, 2.2% Two or more races, 6.9% Hispanic of any race; Average household size: 2.43; Median age: 34.5; Age under 18: 24.8%; Age 65 and over: 14.3%; Males per 100 females: 112.8; Marriage status: 39.5% never married, 39.5% now married, 2.4% separated, 7.7% widowed, 13.4% divorced; Foreign born: 1.1%; Speak English only: 95.7%; With disability: 15.1%; Veterans: 9.8%; Ancestry: 28.0% German, 18.4% English, 16.9% Irish, 6.2% Polish, 5.4% American

Employment: 5.9% management, business, and financial, 1.8% computer, engineering, and science, 11.2% education, legal, community service, arts, and media, 1.2% healthcare practitioners, 32.3% service, 15.9% sales and office, 11.6% natural resources, construction, and maintenance, 20.1% production, transportation, and material moving

Income: Per capita: $16,835; Median household: $33,553; Average household: $43,035; Households with income of $100,000 or more: 9.3%; Poverty rate: 19.9%

Educational Attainment: High school diploma or higher: 85.5%; Bachelor's degree or higher: 11.7%; Graduate/professional degree or higher: 2.1%

School District(s)
Cattaraugus-Little Valley Central SD (PK-12)
    Enrollment: 939. . . . . (716) 257-5292

Housing: Homeownership rate: 56.3%; Median home value: $74,100; Median year structure built: Before 1940; Homeowner vacancy rate: 0.8%; Median selected monthly owner costs: $906 with a mortgage, $418 without a mortgage; Median gross rent: $535 per month; Rental vacancy rate: 5.2%

Health Insurance: 91.5% have insurance; 62.1% have private insurance; 45.5% have public insurance; 8.5% do not have insurance; 0.0% of children under 18 do not have insurance

Transportation: Commute: 89.2% car, 0.0% public transportation, 10.6% walk, 0.0% work from home; Mean travel time to work: 22.0 minutes

LYNDON (town). Covers a land area of 33.231 square miles and a water area of 0.036 square miles. Located at 42.31° N. Lat; 78.38° W. Long. Elevation is 2,064 feet.
Population: 696; Growth (since 2000): 5.3%; Density: 20.9 persons per square mile; Race: 97.8% White, 0.0% Black/African American, 0.0% Asian, 0.3% American Indian/Alaska Native, 0.0% Native Hawaiian/Other Pacific Islander, 1.0% Two or more races, 0.9% Hispanic of any race; Average household size: 2.44; Median age: 44.5; Age under 18: 24.1%; Age 65 and over: 15.9%; Males per 100 females: 115.5; Marriage status: 24.1% never married, 61.7% now married, 1.5% separated, 3.1% widowed, 11.1% divorced; Foreign born: 1.1%; Speak English only: 98.6%; With disability: 16.1%; Veterans: 15.2%; Ancestry: 30.3% German, 19.5% Irish, 9.2% Polish, 8.3% English, 6.5% Italian
Employment: 16.0% management, business, and financial, 0.0% computer, engineering, and science, 1.5% education, legal, community service, arts, and media, 8.0% healthcare practitioners, 23.3% service, 16.0% sales and office, 18.2% natural resources, construction, and maintenance, 17.1% production, transportation, and material moving
Income: Per capita: $22,120; Median household: $47,868; Average household: $54,010; Households with income of $100,000 or more: 10.6%; Poverty rate: 17.2%
Educational Attainment: High school diploma or higher: 87.3%; Bachelor's degree or higher: 12.3%; Graduate/professional degree or higher: 4.5%
Housing: Homeownership rate: 88.1%; Median home value: $96,300; Median year structure built: 1987; Homeowner vacancy rate: 2.7%; Median selected monthly owner costs: $1,243 with a mortgage, $547 without a mortgage; Median gross rent: $616 per month; Rental vacancy rate: 0.0%
Health Insurance: 92.8% have insurance; 70.5% have private insurance; 35.6% have public insurance; 7.2% do not have insurance; 2.3% of children under 18 do not have insurance
Transportation: Commute: 98.9% car, 0.0% public transportation, 0.0% walk, 1.1% work from home; Mean travel time to work: 32.4 minutes

MACHIAS (CDP). Covers a land area of 0.865 square miles and a water area of 0.167 square miles. Located at 42.41° N. Lat; 78.49° W. Long. Elevation is 1,680 feet.
Population: 469; Growth (since 2000): n/a; Density: 542.0 persons per square mile; Race: 100.0% White, 0.0% Black/African American, 0.0% Asian, 0.0% American Indian/Alaska Native, 0.0% Native Hawaiian/Other Pacific Islander, 0.0% Two or more races, 11.9% Hispanic of any race; Average household size: 2.44; Median age: 35.2; Age under 18: 27.7%; Age 65 and over: 14.9%; Males per 100 females: 89.9; Marriage status: 33.8% never married, 48.8% now married, 0.0% separated, 3.8% widowed, 13.6% divorced; Foreign born: 0.0%; Speak English only: 100.0%; With disability: 19.6%; Veterans: 13.0%; Ancestry: 26.4% German, 18.1% Irish, 15.4% Italian, 13.4% English, 11.5% American
Employment: 7.6% management, business, and financial, 0.0% computer, engineering, and science, 6.1% education, legal, community service, arts, and media, 13.1% healthcare practitioners, 12.1% service, 33.8% sales and office, 8.6% natural resources, construction, and maintenance, 18.7% production, transportation, and material moving
Income: Per capita: $20,690; Median household: $39,881; Average household: $50,082; Households with income of $100,000 or more: 9.9%; Poverty rate: 8.4%
Educational Attainment: High school diploma or higher: 94.4%; Bachelor's degree or higher: 10.3%; Graduate/professional degree or higher: 7.6%
Housing: Homeownership rate: 70.8%; Median home value: $93,300; Median year structure built: 1969; Homeowner vacancy rate: 0.0%; Median selected monthly owner costs: $1,000 with a mortgage, $573 without a mortgage; Median gross rent: $758 per month; Rental vacancy rate: 18.8%
Health Insurance: 100.0% have insurance; 85.9% have private insurance; 46.9% have public insurance; 0.0% do not have insurance; 0.0% of children under 18 do not have insurance
Transportation: Commute: 97.0% car, 0.0% public transportation, 3.0% walk, 0.0% work from home; Mean travel time to work: 27.9 minutes

MACHIAS (town). Covers a land area of 40.429 square miles and a water area of 0.649 square miles. Located at 42.40° N. Lat; 78.51° W. Long. Elevation is 1,680 feet.
Population: 2,358; Growth (since 2000): -5.0%; Density: 58.3 persons per square mile; Race: 99.8% White, 0.0% Black/African American, 0.0% Asian, 0.0% American Indian/Alaska Native, 0.0% Native Hawaiian/Other Pacific Islander, 0.2% Two or more races, 2.4% Hispanic of any race;

Average household size: 2.70; Median age: 42.9; Age under 18: 26.2%; Age 65 and over: 18.5%; Males per 100 females: 94.4; Marriage status: 29.2% never married, 55.4% now married, 0.6% separated, 6.6% widowed, 8.9% divorced; Foreign born: 0.7%; Speak English only: 99.4%; With disability: 16.6%; Veterans: 10.9%; Ancestry: 31.8% German, 18.7% Irish, 13.6% English, 10.8% Polish, 6.9% American
Employment: 9.4% management, business, and financial, 2.9% computer, engineering, and science, 6.8% education, legal, community service, arts, and media, 7.0% healthcare practitioners, 16.7% service, 21.3% sales and office, 16.7% natural resources, construction, and maintenance, 19.2% production, transportation, and material moving
Income: Per capita: $22,431; Median household: $50,956; Average household: $61,118; Households with income of $100,000 or more: 14.2%; Poverty rate: 11.6%
Educational Attainment: High school diploma or higher: 87.5%; Bachelor's degree or higher: 12.7%; Graduate/professional degree or higher: 5.8%
Housing: Homeownership rate: 79.6%; Median home value: $100,200; Median year structure built: 1972; Homeowner vacancy rate: 0.9%; Median selected monthly owner costs: $1,078 with a mortgage, $550 without a mortgage; Median gross rent: $779 per month; Rental vacancy rate: 16.5%
Health Insurance: 97.5% have insurance; 71.9% have private insurance; 48.6% have public insurance; 2.5% do not have insurance; 2.4% of children under 18 do not have insurance
Transportation: Commute: 96.0% car, 0.0% public transportation, 2.2% walk, 1.8% work from home; Mean travel time to work: 28.1 minutes

MANSFIELD (town). Covers a land area of 40.126 square miles and a water area of 0.031 square miles. Located at 42.30° N. Lat; 78.77° W. Long.
Population: 809; Growth (since 2000): 1.1%; Density: 20.2 persons per square mile; Race: 98.3% White, 0.0% Black/African American, 0.0% Asian, 0.0% American Indian/Alaska Native, 0.0% Native Hawaiian/Other Pacific Islander, 0.9% Two or more races, 2.5% Hispanic of any race; Average household size: 2.45; Median age: 48.0; Age under 18: 20.6%; Age 65 and over: 16.3%; Males per 100 females: 101.5; Marriage status: 21.4% never married, 61.2% now married, 0.9% separated, 7.5% widowed, 9.8% divorced; Foreign born: 6.1%; Speak English only: 92.8%; With disability: 9.5%; Veterans: 10.0%; Ancestry: 34.1% German, 16.9% Irish, 8.2% English, 7.4% Italian, 4.8% French
Employment: 15.3% management, business, and financial, 0.7% computer, engineering, and science, 7.7% education, legal, community service, arts, and media, 6.7% healthcare practitioners, 19.7% service, 23.9% sales and office, 17.4% natural resources, construction, and maintenance, 8.6% production, transportation, and material moving
Income: Per capita: $32,694; Median household: $65,625; Average household: $78,133; Households with income of $100,000 or more: 24.0%; Poverty rate: 10.5%
Educational Attainment: High school diploma or higher: 92.0%; Bachelor's degree or higher: 25.8%; Graduate/professional degree or higher: 11.5%
Housing: Homeownership rate: 89.7%; Median home value: $145,600; Median year structure built: 1976; Homeowner vacancy rate: 1.3%; Median selected monthly owner costs: $1,240 with a mortgage, $588 without a mortgage; Median gross rent: $738 per month; Rental vacancy rate: 0.0%
Health Insurance: 86.0% have insurance; 75.2% have private insurance; 27.8% have public insurance; 14.0% do not have insurance; 23.8% of children under 18 do not have insurance
Transportation: Commute: 92.9% car, 0.0% public transportation, 1.4% walk, 5.7% work from home; Mean travel time to work: 22.0 minutes

NAPOLI (town). Covers a land area of 36.375 square miles and a water area of 0.170 square miles. Located at 42.21° N. Lat; 78.88° W. Long. Elevation is 1,732 feet.
Population: 1,133; Growth (since 2000): -2.2%; Density: 31.1 persons per square mile; Race: 96.2% White, 0.2% Black/African American, 0.0% Asian, 2.4% American Indian/Alaska Native, 0.0% Native Hawaiian/Other Pacific Islander, 1.2% Two or more races, 0.0% Hispanic of any race; Average household size: 2.57; Median age: 42.9; Age under 18: 25.9%; Age 65 and over: 13.9%; Males per 100 females: 112.2; Marriage status: 29.4% never married, 50.8% now married, 3.2% separated, 4.2% widowed, 15.7% divorced; Foreign born: 0.0%; Speak English only: 90.7%; With disability: 16.2%; Veterans: 10.3%; Ancestry: 33.0% German, 17.7% English, 14.9% Irish, 8.6% American, 6.4% Polish

Employment: 5.1% management, business, and financial, 4.7% computer, engineering, and science, 9.6% education, legal, community service, arts, and media, 8.3% healthcare practitioners, 23.2% service, 14.1% sales and office, 20.4% natural resources, construction, and maintenance, 14.5% production, transportation, and material moving

Income: Per capita: $21,852; Median household: $51,500; Average household: $56,624; Households with income of $100,000 or more: 12.5%; Poverty rate: 17.8%

Educational Attainment: High school diploma or higher: 84.6%; Bachelor's degree or higher: 16.8%; Graduate/professional degree or higher: 7.8%

Housing: Homeownership rate: 87.9%; Median home value: $78,800; Median year structure built: 1974; Homeowner vacancy rate: 0.0%; Median selected monthly owner costs: $1,064 with a mortgage, $439 without a mortgage; Median gross rent: $516 per month; Rental vacancy rate: 0.0%

Health Insurance: 86.8% have insurance; 59.8% have private insurance; 40.3% have public insurance; 13.2% do not have insurance; 22.8% of children under 18 do not have insurance

Transportation: Commute: 89.8% car, 0.0% public transportation, 0.0% walk, 6.1% work from home; Mean travel time to work: 26.7 minutes

---

NEW ALBION (town). Covers a land area of 35.629 square miles and a water area of 0.194 square miles. Located at 42.31° N. Lat; 78.89° W. Long. Elevation is 1,417 feet.

Population: 1,875; Growth (since 2000): -9.3%; Density: 52.6 persons per square mile; Race: 98.7% White, 0.1% Black/African American, 0.2% Asian, 0.3% American Indian/Alaska Native, 0.0% Native Hawaiian/Other Pacific Islander, 0.9% Two or more races, 0.0% Hispanic of any race; Average household size: 2.27; Median age: 47.5; Age under 18: 19.8%; Age 65 and over: 19.1%; Males per 100 females: 98.4; Marriage status: 24.9% never married, 55.4% now married, 3.7% separated, 6.7% widowed, 13.1% divorced; Foreign born: 0.6%; Speak English only: 98.8%; With disability: 19.2%; Veterans: 11.8%; Ancestry: 45.2% German, 20.6% Irish, 13.1% English, 11.9% Polish, 7.3% Italian

Employment: 6.5% management, business, and financial, 1.0% computer, engineering, and science, 8.0% education, legal, community service, arts, and media, 5.3% healthcare practitioners, 23.2% service, 23.4% sales and office, 15.3% natural resources, construction, and maintenance, 17.3% production, transportation, and material moving

Income: Per capita: $22,465; Median household: $45,284; Average household: $50,633; Households with income of $100,000 or more: 11.3%; Poverty rate: 13.8%

Educational Attainment: High school diploma or higher: 85.9%; Bachelor's degree or higher: 15.6%; Graduate/professional degree or higher: 8.4%

Housing: Homeownership rate: 75.8%; Median home value: $68,800; Median year structure built: Before 1940; Homeowner vacancy rate: 2.0%; Median selected monthly owner costs: $983 with a mortgage, $465 without a mortgage; Median gross rent: $536 per month; Rental vacancy rate: 1.5%

Health Insurance: 95.9% have insurance; 75.8% have private insurance; 39.3% have public insurance; 4.1% do not have insurance; 3.6% of children under 18 do not have insurance

Transportation: Commute: 93.8% car, 0.4% public transportation, 3.3% walk, 1.9% work from home; Mean travel time to work: 24.9 minutes

---

OLEAN (city). Covers a land area of 5.908 square miles and a water area of 0.258 square miles. Located at 42.08° N. Lat; 78.44° W. Long. Elevation is 1,447 feet.

History: Olean came to life as a lumber camp. From their lumber, settlers built rafts to sell to emigrants who gathered to await the spring flood which would float them down the Allegheny and Ohio Rivers to the western frontier.

Population: 13,911; Growth (since 2000): -9.4%; Density: 2,354.7 persons per square mile; Race: 91.1% White, 5.2% Black/African American, 1.5% Asian, 0.6% American Indian/Alaska Native, 0.0% Native Hawaiian/Other Pacific Islander, 1.7% Two or more races, 1.2% Hispanic of any race; Average household size: 2.22; Median age: 40.8; Age under 18: 21.0%; Age 65 and over: 16.3%; Males per 100 females: 92.2; Marriage status: 35.3% never married, 41.9% now married, 2.0% separated, 6.8% widowed, 16.0% divorced; Foreign born: 2.4%; Speak English only: 96.7%; With disability: 16.9%; Veterans: 9.7%; Ancestry: 23.5% German, 20.6% Irish, 18.0% Italian, 10.5% English, 10.3% Polish

Employment: 14.4% management, business, and financial, 4.5% computer, engineering, and science, 16.1% education, legal, community

service, arts, and media, 3.9% healthcare practitioners, 16.8% service, 29.4% sales and office, 3.6% natural resources, construction, and maintenance, 11.3% production, transportation, and material moving

Income: Per capita: $25,924; Median household: $40,291; Average household: $57,802; Households with income of $100,000 or more: 16.0%; Poverty rate: 22.8%

Educational Attainment: High school diploma or higher: 90.0%; Bachelor's degree or higher: 26.2%; Graduate/professional degree or higher: 11.5%

School District(s)

Cattaraugus-Allegany-Erie-Wyoming Boces
    Enrollment: n/a . . . . (716) 376-8223
Olean City SD (PK-12)
    Enrollment: 2,173 . . . . (716) 375-8055

Vocational/Technical School(s)

Cattaraugus Allegany BOCES-Practical Nursing Program (Public)
    Enrollment: 68 . . . . (716) 376-8268
Continental School of Beauty Culture-Olean (Private, For-profit)
    Enrollment: 56 . . . . (716) 372-5095
    Tuition: $12,690

Housing: Homeownership rate: 50.0%; Median home value: $77,600; Median year structure built: Before 1940; Homeowner vacancy rate: 5.8%; Median selected monthly owner costs: $1,025 with a mortgage, $475 without a mortgage; Median gross rent: $623 per month; Rental vacancy rate: 7.3%

Health Insurance: 96.3% have insurance; 67.2% have private insurance; 47.7% have public insurance; 3.7% do not have insurance; 0.0% of children under 18 do not have insurance

Hospitals: Olean General Hospital (217 beds)

Safety: Violent crime rate: 22.6 per 10,000 population; Property crime rate: 278.2 per 10,000 population

Newspapers: Times-Herald (daily circulation 14,000)

Transportation: Commute: 84.5% car, 1.1% public transportation, 9.3% walk, 2.5% work from home; Mean travel time to work: 16.0 minutes

Airports: Cattaraugus County-Olean (general aviation)

Additional Information Contacts
City of Olean . . . . (716) 376-5604
    http://www.cityofolean.com

OLEAN (town). Covers a land area of 29.609 square miles and a water area of 0.127 square miles. Located at 42.06° N. Lat; 78.42° W. Long. Elevation is 1,447 feet.

History: Once an oil-based economy emanating from nearby Pennsylvania oil fields. St. Bonaventure University nearby. Major outfitting post for settlers moving west down the Allegheny and Ohio rivers in early 1800s. In 1972 a severe flood associated with Hurricane Agnes flooded large areas and damaged more than 2,900 homes. Settled 1804, Incorporated 1893.

Population: 2,074; Growth (since 2000): 2.2%; Density: 70.0 persons per square mile; Race: 94.9% White, 0.6% Black/African American, 2.6% Asian, 0.8% American Indian/Alaska Native, 0.0% Native Hawaiian/Other Pacific Islander, 1.1% Two or more races, 0.0% Hispanic of any race; Average household size: 2.41; Median age: 44.6; Age under 18: 21.0%; Age 65 and over: 17.6%; Males per 100 females: 103.0; Marriage status: 27.1% never married, 59.9% now married, 0.7% separated, 5.8% widowed, 7.1% divorced; Foreign born: 1.9%; Speak English only: 98.4%; With disability: 14.9%; Veterans: 8.2%; Ancestry: 21.4% German, 18.1% Irish, 14.5% Italian, 14.4% Polish, 9.1% English

Employment: 17.2% management, business, and financial, 3.2% computer, engineering, and science, 11.3% education, legal, community service, arts, and media, 5.1% healthcare practitioners, 16.0% service, 24.8% sales and office, 7.8% natural resources, construction, and maintenance, 14.7% production, transportation, and material moving

Income: Per capita: $29,090; Median household: $52,431; Average household: $69,930; Households with income of $100,000 or more: 26.5%; Poverty rate: 14.3%

Educational Attainment: High school diploma or higher: 92.8%; Bachelor's degree or higher: 24.3%; Graduate/professional degree or higher: 9.3%

School District(s)

Cattaraugus-Allegany-Erie-Wyoming Boces
    Enrollment: n/a . . . . (716) 376-8223
Olean City SD (PK-12)
    Enrollment: 2,173 . . . . (716) 375-8055

Vocational/Technical School(s)
Cattaraugus Allegany BOCES-Practical Nursing Program (Public)
Enrollment: 68 . . . . (716) 376-8268
Continental School of Beauty Culture-Olean (Private, For-profit)
Enrollment: 56 . . . . (716) 372-5095
Tuition: $12,690
Housing: Homeownership rate: 82.6%; Median home value: $101,900; Median year structure built: 1960; Homeowner vacancy rate: 2.0%; Median selected monthly owner costs: $1,339 with a mortgage, $516 without a mortgage; Median gross rent: $700 per month; Rental vacancy rate: 0.0%
Health Insurance: 94.3% have insurance; 69.8% have private insurance; 41.0% have public insurance; 5.7% do not have insurance; 5.7% of children under 18 do not have insurance
Hospitals: Olean General Hospital (217 beds)
Newspapers: Times-Herald (daily circulation 14,000)
Transportation: Commute: 96.8% car, 0.9% public transportation, 0.0% walk, 1.3% work from home; Mean travel time to work: 13.4 minutes
Airports: Cattaraugus County-Olean (general aviation)

OTTO (town). Covers a land area of 32.730 square miles and a water area of 0.117 square miles. Located at 42.40° N. Lat; 78.84° W. Long. Elevation is 1,260 feet.
Population: 823; Growth (since 2000): -1.0%; Density: 25.1 persons per square mile; Race: 97.6% White, 2.2% Black/African American, 0.0% Asian, 0.0% American Indian/Alaska Native, 0.0% Native Hawaiian/Other Pacific Islander, 0.2% Two or more races, 1.2% Hispanic of any race; Average household size: 2.51; Median age: 43.7; Age under 18: 24.4%; Age 65 and over: 16.2%; Males per 100 females: 106.1; Marriage status: 26.6% never married, 64.8% now married, 1.3% separated, 3.6% widowed, 5.0% divorced; Foreign born: 1.5%; Speak English only: 93.4%; With disability: 14.2%; Veterans: 15.1%; Ancestry: 40.1% German, 11.9% Irish, 8.7% English, 8.4% Polish, 7.9% Italian
Employment: 13.6% management, business, and financial, 1.4% computer, engineering, and science, 6.8% education, legal, community service, arts, and media, 6.5% healthcare practitioners, 21.5% service, 21.2% sales and office, 18.7% natural resources, construction, and maintenance, 10.2% production, transportation, and material moving
Income: Per capita: $27,474; Median household: $53,750; Average household: $70,069; Households with income of $100,000 or more: 19.7%; Poverty rate: 17.1%
Educational Attainment: High school diploma or higher: 87.8%; Bachelor's degree or higher: 13.9%; Graduate/professional degree or higher: 5.7%
Housing: Homeownership rate: 86.4%; Median home value: $120,400; Median year structure built: 1961; Homeowner vacancy rate: 4.8%; Median selected monthly owner costs: $1,263 with a mortgage, $563 without a mortgage; Median gross rent: $900 per month; Rental vacancy rate: 0.0%
Health Insurance: 86.4% have insurance; 67.7% have private insurance; 38.0% have public insurance; 13.6% do not have insurance; 23.4% of children under 18 do not have insurance
Transportation: Commute: 88.0% car, 0.0% public transportation, 2.3% walk, 9.7% work from home; Mean travel time to work: 29.6 minutes

PERRYSBURG (town). Covers a land area of 28.421 square miles and a water area of 0.126 square miles. Located at 42.48° N. Lat; 79.02° W. Long. Elevation is 1,322 feet.
Population: 1,665; Growth (since 2000): -6.0%; Density: 58.6 persons per square mile; Race: 97.8% White, 0.3% Black/African American, 0.0% Asian, 0.7% American Indian/Alaska Native, 0.0% Native Hawaiian/Other Pacific Islander, 0.9% Two or more races, 4.5% Hispanic of any race; Average household size: 2.43; Median age: 45.9; Age under 18: 21.5%; Age 65 and over: 17.8%; Males per 100 females: 97.3; Marriage status: 28.5% never married, 56.2% now married, 0.6% separated, 5.9% widowed, 9.4% divorced; Foreign born: 1.6%; Speak English only: 97.5%; With disability: 16.2%; Veterans: 9.5%; Ancestry: 32.1% German, 16.5% Irish, 14.4% Italian, 11.4% Polish, 10.5% English
Employment: 12.1% management, business, and financial, 3.0% computer, engineering, and science, 9.7% education, legal, community service, arts, and media, 3.0% healthcare practitioners, 25.9% service, 21.1% sales and office, 11.8% natural resources, construction, and maintenance, 13.4% production, transportation, and material moving
Income: Per capita: $27,502; Median household: $55,000; Average household: $68,195; Households with income of $100,000 or more: 19.6%; Poverty rate: 12.1%

Educational Attainment: High school diploma or higher: 88.0%; Bachelor's degree or higher: 12.8%; Graduate/professional degree or higher: 5.9%
Housing: Homeownership rate: 77.3%; Median home value: $109,700; Median year structure built: 1952; Homeowner vacancy rate: 2.1%; Median selected monthly owner costs: $1,149 with a mortgage, $524 without a mortgage; Median gross rent: $631 per month; Rental vacancy rate: 0.0%
Health Insurance: 95.0% have insurance; 72.9% have private insurance; 39.9% have public insurance; 5.0% do not have insurance; 0.8% of children under 18 do not have insurance
Transportation: Commute: 95.4% car, 0.0% public transportation, 1.6% walk, 3.0% work from home; Mean travel time to work: 22.3 minutes

PERRYSBURG (CDP). Covers a land area of 0.984 square miles and a water area of 0.003 square miles. Located at 42.46° N. Lat; 79.00° W. Long. Elevation is 1,322 feet.
Population: 417; Growth (since 2000): 2.2%; Density: 423.6 persons per square mile; Race: 95.9% White, 1.2% Black/African American, 0.0% Asian, 1.2% American Indian/Alaska Native, 0.0% Native Hawaiian/Other Pacific Islander, 0.5% Two or more races, 1.7% Hispanic of any race; Average household size: 2.40; Median age: 48.5; Age under 18: 22.3%; Age 65 and over: 22.8%; Males per 100 females: 95.6; Marriage status: 37.2% never married, 45.8% now married, 1.7% separated, 7.7% widowed, 9.2% divorced; Foreign born: 2.9%; Speak English only: 97.7%; With disability: 22.5%; Veterans: 3.1%; Ancestry: 31.2% German, 21.8% Italian, 21.3% Irish, 9.8% American, 8.4% French
Employment: 16.4% management, business, and financial, 1.5% computer, engineering, and science, 8.2% education, legal, community service, arts, and media, 0.0% healthcare practitioners, 22.4% service, 25.4% sales and office, 7.5% natural resources, construction, and maintenance, 18.7% production, transportation, and material moving
Income: Per capita: $25,112; Median household: $44,688; Average household: $63,918; Households with income of $100,000 or more: 18.9%; Poverty rate: 13.9%
Educational Attainment: High school diploma or higher: 78.1%; Bachelor's degree or higher: 3.5%; Graduate/professional degree or higher: 2.1%
Housing: Homeownership rate: 66.2%; Median home value: $102,600; Median year structure built: Before 1940; Homeowner vacancy rate: 0.0%; Median selected monthly owner costs: $1,265 with a mortgage, $507 without a mortgage; Median gross rent: $619 per month; Rental vacancy rate: 0.0%
Health Insurance: 97.6% have insurance; 67.6% have private insurance; 45.3% have public insurance; 2.4% do not have insurance; 3.2% of children under 18 do not have insurance
Transportation: Commute: 100.0% car, 0.0% public transportation, 0.0% walk, 0.0% work from home; Mean travel time to work: 23.2 minutes

PERSIA (town). Covers a land area of 20.893 square miles and a water area of 0.097 square miles. Located at 42.42° N. Lat; 78.92° W. Long. Elevation is 1,342 feet.
Population: 2,310; Growth (since 2000): -8.0%; Density: 110.6 persons per square mile; Race: 92.0% White, 0.4% Black/African American, 0.8% Asian, 2.1% American Indian/Alaska Native, 0.0% Native Hawaiian/Other Pacific Islander, 4.2% Two or more races, 0.7% Hispanic of any race; Average household size: 2.10; Median age: 45.4; Age under 18: 19.3%; Age 65 and over: 23.5%; Males per 100 females: 96.1; Marriage status: 32.7% never married, 39.1% now married, 2.4% separated, 11.1% widowed, 17.2% divorced; Foreign born: 1.2%; Speak English only: 96.1%; With disability: 17.9%; Veterans: 11.9%; Ancestry: 33.7% German, 17.8% Irish, 15.8% English, 14.4% Polish, 12.9% Italian
Employment: 8.9% management, business, and financial, 3.7% computer, engineering, and science, 8.6% education, legal, community service, arts, and media, 8.6% healthcare practitioners, 26.0% service, 17.0% sales and office, 11.7% natural resources, construction, and maintenance, 15.5% production, transportation, and material moving
Income: Per capita: $24,147; Median household: $38,561; Average household: $52,195; Households with income of $100,000 or more: 13.3%; Poverty rate: 17.3%
Educational Attainment: High school diploma or higher: 89.9%; Bachelor's degree or higher: 13.3%; Graduate/professional degree or higher: 5.1%
Housing: Homeownership rate: 67.8%; Median home value: $76,000; Median year structure built: Before 1940; Homeowner vacancy rate: 0.0%; Median selected monthly owner costs: $919 with a mortgage, $394 without

a mortgage; Median gross rent: $655 per month; Rental vacancy rate: 3.8%

Health Insurance: 91.7% have insurance; 69.8% have private insurance; 40.8% have public insurance; 8.3% do not have insurance; 8.4% of children under 18 do not have insurance

Transportation: Commute: 90.7% car, 0.0% public transportation, 5.5% walk, 1.9% work from home; Mean travel time to work: 29.1 minutes

---

PORTVILLE (town).
Covers a land area of 35.580 square miles and a water area of 0.448 square miles. Located at 42.06° N. Lat; 78.35° W. Long. Elevation is 1,430 feet.

History: Incorporated 1895.

Population: 3,613; Growth (since 2000): -8.6%; Density: 101.5 persons per square mile; Race: 98.8% White, 0.0% Black/African American, 0.0% Asian, 0.2% American Indian/Alaska Native, 0.0% Native Hawaiian/Other Pacific Islander, 0.8% Two or more races, 1.6% Hispanic of any race; Average household size: 2.34; Median age: 45.7; Age under 18: 19.4%; Age 65 and over: 22.0%; Males per 100 females: 94.9; Marriage status: 24.3% never married, 56.0% now married, 0.8% separated, 8.7% widowed, 11.0% divorced; Foreign born: 0.8%; Speak English only: 96.8%; With disability: 16.4%; Veterans: 12.1%; Ancestry: 28.9% German, 20.7% Irish, 14.8% English, 7.5% Polish, 6.4% Italian

Employment: 12.1% management, business, and financial, 5.7% computer, engineering, and science, 8.7% education, legal, community service, arts, and media, 9.2% healthcare practitioners, 14.0% service, 24.0% sales and office, 10.2% natural resources, construction, and maintenance, 16.1% production, transportation, and material moving

Income: Per capita: $32,221; Median household: $63,411; Average household: $75,486; Households with income of $100,000 or more: 23.9%; Poverty rate: 7.6%

Educational Attainment: High school diploma or higher: 93.3%; Bachelor's degree or higher: 21.2%; Graduate/professional degree or higher: 9.8%

School District(s)
Portville Central SD (PK-12)
    Enrollment: 1,014 . . . . (716) 933-7140

Housing: Homeownership rate: 76.3%; Median home value: $89,000; Median year structure built: 1957; Homeowner vacancy rate: 0.8%; Median selected monthly owner costs: $1,160 with a mortgage, $436 without a mortgage; Median gross rent: $493 per month; Rental vacancy rate: 5.0%

Health Insurance: 95.8% have insurance; 80.3% have private insurance; 39.4% have public insurance; 4.2% do not have insurance; 2.4% of children under 18 do not have insurance

Transportation: Commute: 95.8% car, 0.1% public transportation, 0.8% walk, 1.5% work from home; Mean travel time to work: 19.4 minutes

---

PORTVILLE (village).
Covers a land area of 0.802 square miles and a water area of 0 square miles. Located at 42.04° N. Lat; 78.34° W. Long. Elevation is 1,430 feet.

Population: 1,007; Growth (since 2000): -1.7%; Density: 1,255.5 persons per square mile; Race: 97.6% White, 0.0% Black/African American, 0.0% Asian, 0.0% American Indian/Alaska Native, 0.0% Native Hawaiian/Other Pacific Islander, 1.6% Two or more races, 1.8% Hispanic of any race; Average household size: 2.39; Median age: 39.8; Age under 18: 27.8%; Age 65 and over: 19.6%; Males per 100 females: 86.4; Marriage status: 26.1% never married, 50.1% now married, 1.8% separated, 9.7% widowed, 14.1% divorced; Foreign born: 0.8%; Speak English only: 99.0%; With disability: 15.3%; Veterans: 12.4%; Ancestry: 31.8% German, 25.7% Irish, 14.9% English, 8.8% Italian, 5.8% Polish

Employment: 12.0% management, business, and financial, 1.7% computer, engineering, and science, 21.1% education, legal, community service, arts, and media, 5.6% healthcare practitioners, 16.1% service, 27.3% sales and office, 4.6% natural resources, construction, and maintenance, 11.6% production, transportation, and material moving

Income: Per capita: $25,807; Median household: $50,179; Average household: $63,028; Households with income of $100,000 or more: 15.0%; Poverty rate: 13.6%

Educational Attainment: High school diploma or higher: 92.8%; Bachelor's degree or higher: 31.2%; Graduate/professional degree or higher: 13.3%

School District(s)
Portville Central SD (PK-12)
    Enrollment: 1,014 . . . . (716) 933-7140

Housing: Homeownership rate: 66.0%; Median home value: $82,400; Median year structure built: 1942; Homeowner vacancy rate: 3.1%; Median

---

selected monthly owner costs: $980 with a mortgage, $421 without a mortgage; Median gross rent: $532 per month; Rental vacancy rate: 0.0%

Health Insurance: 95.1% have insurance; 73.2% have private insurance; 39.6% have public insurance; 4.9% do not have insurance; 6.2% of children under 18 do not have insurance

Safety: Violent crime rate: 0.0 per 10,000 population; Property crime rate: 0.0 per 10,000 population

Transportation: Commute: 93.4% car, 0.0% public transportation, 3.0% walk, 1.7% work from home; Mean travel time to work: 17.2 minutes

---

RANDOLPH (town).
Covers a land area of 36.064 square miles and a water area of 0.223 square miles. Located at 42.13° N. Lat; 79.00° W. Long. Elevation is 1,276 feet.

Population: 2,535; Growth (since 2000): -5.4%; Density: 70.3 persons per square mile; Race: 95.0% White, 0.4% Black/African American, 0.2% Asian, 0.2% American Indian/Alaska Native, 0.0% Native Hawaiian/Other Pacific Islander, 4.2% Two or more races, 4.1% Hispanic of any race; Average household size: 2.52; Median age: 41.0; Age under 18: 29.7%; Age 65 and over: 14.6%; Males per 100 females: 103.6; Marriage status: 25.9% never married, 57.3% now married, 3.9% separated, 6.6% widowed, 10.2% divorced; Foreign born: 1.9%; Speak English only: 96.5%; With disability: 10.8%; Veterans: 9.9%; Ancestry: 25.2% German, 16.4% English, 15.7% Irish, 7.8% Italian, 6.4% Swedish

Employment: 10.5% management, business, and financial, 2.1% computer, engineering, and science, 11.4% education, legal, community service, arts, and media, 6.6% healthcare practitioners, 15.9% service, 27.2% sales and office, 6.0% natural resources, construction, and maintenance, 20.3% production, transportation, and material moving

Income: Per capita: $21,163; Median household: $38,859; Average household: $54,455; Households with income of $100,000 or more: 16.1%; Poverty rate: 14.8%

Educational Attainment: High school diploma or higher: 89.6%; Bachelor's degree or higher: 15.9%; Graduate/professional degree or higher: 8.4%

School District(s)
Randolph Academy Union Free SD (KG-12)
    Enrollment: 31 . . . . (716) 358-6866
Randolph Central SD (PK-12)
    Enrollment: 963 . . . . (716) 358-7005

Housing: Homeownership rate: 62.3%; Median home value: $83,800; Median year structure built: 1945; Homeowner vacancy rate: 0.0%; Median selected monthly owner costs: $979 with a mortgage, $460 without a mortgage; Median gross rent: $558 per month; Rental vacancy rate: 7.3%

Health Insurance: 94.5% have insurance; 66.8% have private insurance; 45.2% have public insurance; 5.5% do not have insurance; 2.0% of children under 18 do not have insurance

Transportation: Commute: 92.7% car, 0.0% public transportation, 5.3% walk, 1.5% work from home; Mean travel time to work: 19.4 minutes

---

RED HOUSE (town).
Covers a land area of 55.668 square miles and a water area of 0.188 square miles. Located at 42.07° N. Lat; 78.74° W. Long. Elevation is 1,339 feet.

Population: 53; Growth (since 2000): 39.5%; Density: 1.0 persons per square mile; Race: 100.0% White, 0.0% Black/African American, 0.0% Asian, 0.0% American Indian/Alaska Native, 0.0% Native Hawaiian/Other Pacific Islander, 0.0% Two or more races, 0.0% Hispanic of any race; Average household size: 3.12; Median age: 32.3; Age under 18: 35.8%; Age 65 and over: 11.3%; Males per 100 females: 123.5; Marriage status: 50.0% never married, 29.4% now married, 5.9% separated, 5.9% widowed, 14.7% divorced; Foreign born: 0.0%; Speak English only: 97.8%; With disability: 5.7%; Veterans: 8.8%; Ancestry: 13.2% Irish, 9.4% German, 7.5% American, 7.5% Italian, 7.5% Polish

Employment: 15.4% management, business, and financial, 7.7% computer, engineering, and science, 0.0% education, legal, community service, arts, and media, 0.0% healthcare practitioners, 15.4% service, 0.0% sales and office, 46.2% natural resources, construction, and maintenance, 15.4% production, transportation, and material moving

Income: Per capita: $16,106; Median household: $34,063; Average household: $43,165; Households with income of $100,000 or more: n/a; Poverty rate: 47.2%

Educational Attainment: High school diploma or higher: 66.7%; Bachelor's degree or higher: 27.3%; Graduate/professional degree or higher: 6.1%

Housing: Homeownership rate: 52.9%; Median home value: n/a; Median year structure built: Before 1940; Homeowner vacancy rate: 0.0%; Median

selected monthly owner costs: n/a with a mortgage, $420 without a mortgage; Median gross rent: $585 per month; Rental vacancy rate: 0.0%
Health Insurance: 100.0% have insurance; 75.5% have private insurance; 37.7% have public insurance; 0.0% do not have insurance; 0.0% of children under 18 do not have insurance
Transportation: Commute: 76.9% car, 0.0% public transportation, 23.1% walk, 0.0% work from home; Mean travel time to work: 15.8 minutes

SAINT BONAVENTURE (CDP).

Covers a land area of 1.976 square miles and a water area of 0.152 square miles. Located at 42.08° N. Lat; 78.47° W. Long. Elevation is 1,427 feet.
Population: 1,988; Growth (since 2000): -6.5%; Density: 1,006.0 persons per square mile; Race: 85.1% White, 5.5% Black/African American, 2.7% Asian, 0.2% American Indian/Alaska Native, 0.0% Native Hawaiian/Other Pacific Islander, 1.7% Two or more races, 7.2% Hispanic of any race; Average household size: 1.59; Median age: 20.5; Age under 18: 2.3%; Age 65 and over: 12.0%; Males per 100 females: 85.3; Marriage status: 79.5% never married, 15.2% now married, 0.5% separated, 2.0% widowed, 3.3% divorced; Foreign born: 10.9%; Speak English only: 89.4%; With disability: 11.0%; Veterans: 4.6%; Ancestry: 21.2% Irish, 17.8% German, 14.2% Italian, 10.3% Polish, 4.5% English
Employment: 3.0% management, business, and financial, 1.2% computer, engineering, and science, 16.9% education, legal, community service, arts, and media, 7.5% healthcare practitioners, 27.8% service, 32.1% sales and office, 2.7% natural resources, construction, and maintenance, 8.9% production, transportation, and material moving
Income: Per capita: $13,655; Median household: $36,331; Average household: $70,630; Households with income of $100,000 or more: 24.1%; Poverty rate: 25.3%
Educational Attainment: High school diploma or higher: 86.6%; Bachelor's degree or higher: 29.5%; Graduate/professional degree or higher: 17.4%

Four-year College(s)

St Bonaventure University (Private, Not-for-profit, Roman Catholic)
Enrollment: 2,084 . . . . (716) 375-2000
Tuition: In-state $33,331; Out-of-state $33,331
Housing: Homeownership rate: 70.8%; Median home value: $92,800; Median year structure built: 1959; Homeowner vacancy rate: 0.0%; Median selected monthly owner costs: $825 with a mortgage, $483 without a mortgage; Median gross rent: n/a per month; Rental vacancy rate: 0.0%
Health Insurance: 99.3% have insurance; 91.0% have private insurance; 20.1% have public insurance; 0.7% do not have insurance; 0.0% of children under 18 do not have insurance
Transportation: Commute: 51.7% car, 0.0% public transportation, 41.2% walk, 7.1% work from home; Mean travel time to work: 10.6 minutes

SALAMANCA (city).

Covers a land area of 5.994 square miles and a water area of 0.242 square miles. Located at 42.16° N. Lat; 78.74° W. Long. Elevation is 1,381 feet.
Population: 5,594; Growth (since 2000): -8.2%; Density: 933.3 persons per square mile; Race: 67.9% White, 3.7% Black/African American, 0.5% Asian, 17.6% American Indian/Alaska Native, 0.0% Native Hawaiian/Other Pacific Islander, 8.6% Two or more races, 7.1% Hispanic of any race; Average household size: 2.47; Median age: 33.3; Age under 18: 30.2%; Age 65 and over: 14.4%; Males per 100 females: 91.0; Marriage status: 36.2% never married, 39.9% now married, 2.6% separated, 8.5% widowed, 15.4% divorced; Foreign born: 2.0%; Speak English only: 93.1%; With disability: 15.9%; Veterans: 9.6%; Ancestry: 19.6% German, 17.2% Irish, 9.1% Polish, 6.4% English, 5.7% Italian
Employment: 11.0% management, business, and financial, 1.4% computer, engineering, and science, 10.1% education, legal, community service, arts, and media, 3.2% healthcare practitioners, 27.0% service, 26.4% sales and office, 8.7% natural resources, construction, and maintenance, 12.1% production, transportation, and material moving
Income: Per capita: $16,839; Median household: $30,319; Average household: $41,114; Households with income of $100,000 or more: 6.8%; Poverty rate: 27.2%
Educational Attainment: High school diploma or higher: 84.2%; Bachelor's degree or higher: 13.9%; Graduate/professional degree or higher: 4.2%

School District(s)

Salamanca City SD (PK-12)
Enrollment: 1,255 . . . . (716) 945-2400
Housing: Homeownership rate: 52.3%; Median home value: $65,700; Median year structure built: Before 1940; Homeowner vacancy rate: 1.0%;

Median selected monthly owner costs: $810 with a mortgage, $333 without a mortgage; Median gross rent: $620 per month; Rental vacancy rate: 10.4%
Health Insurance: 90.6% have insurance; 53.5% have private insurance; 49.8% have public insurance; 9.4% do not have insurance; 7.2% of children under 18 do not have insurance
Safety: Violent crime rate: 16.3 per 10,000 population; Property crime rate: 168.7 per 10,000 population
Newspapers: County Chronicle (weekly circulation 5,000); Salamanca Press (daily circulation 2,000)
Transportation: Commute: 90.6% car, 0.2% public transportation, 6.1% walk, 1.7% work from home; Mean travel time to work: 18.1 minutes
Additional Information Contacts
City of Salamanca . . . . (716) 945-4620
http://www.salmun.com

SALAMANCA (town).

Covers a land area of 18.391 square miles and a water area of <.001 square miles. Located at 42.17° N. Lat; 78.81° W. Long. Elevation is 1,381 feet.
History: In Allegany Indian Reservation. Allegany State Park is just S. Furniture, plastic and wood prods; printing. Most of the city is built on land that is leased from the Seneca Nation's Allegany Indian Reservation. Settled in 1860s; inc. as city 1913.
Population: 556; Growth (since 2000): 2.2%; Density: 30.2 persons per square mile; Race: 80.4% White, 0.0% Black/African American, 0.0% Asian, 17.3% American Indian/Alaska Native, 0.0% Native Hawaiian/Other Pacific Islander, 1.8% Two or more races, 1.3% Hispanic of any race; Average household size: 2.74; Median age: 45.7; Age under 18: 27.0%; Age 65 and over: 24.3%; Males per 100 females: 114.7; Marriage status: 24.5% never married, 59.1% now married, 1.9% separated, 8.9% widowed, 7.5% divorced; Foreign born: 0.7%; Speak English only: 96.0%; With disability: 12.6%; Veterans: 14.8%; Ancestry: 24.1% Irish, 21.4% German, 11.3% Polish, 7.6% Italian, 6.5% English
Employment: 10.1% management, business, and financial, 4.5% computer, engineering, and science, 8.5% education, legal, community service, arts, and media, 6.0% healthcare practitioners, 22.1% service, 18.6% sales and office, 12.1% natural resources, construction, and maintenance, 18.1% production, transportation, and material moving
Income: Per capita: $23,581; Median household: $61,250; Average household: $65,495; Households with income of $100,000 or more: 16.8%; Poverty rate: 7.1%
Educational Attainment: High school diploma or higher: 87.6%; Bachelor's degree or higher: 13.7%; Graduate/professional degree or higher: 4.9%

School District(s)

Salamanca City SD (PK-12)
Enrollment: 1,255 . . . . (716) 945-2400
Housing: Homeownership rate: 89.2%; Median home value: $92,300; Median year structure built: 1967; Homeowner vacancy rate: 0.0%; Median selected monthly owner costs: $1,125 with a mortgage, $423 without a mortgage; Median gross rent: $1,094 per month; Rental vacancy rate: 18.5%
Health Insurance: 93.3% have insurance; 71.9% have private insurance; 48.6% have public insurance; 6.7% do not have insurance; 3.9% of children under 18 do not have insurance
Newspapers: County Chronicle (weekly circulation 5,000); Salamanca Press (daily circulation 2,000)
Transportation: Commute: 99.5% car, 0.0% public transportation, 0.5% walk, 0.0% work from home; Mean travel time to work: 18.1 minutes

SOUTH DAYTON (village).

Covers a land area of 1.006 square miles and a water area of 0 square miles. Located at 42.36° N. Lat; 79.05° W. Long. Elevation is 1,306 feet.
Population: 638; Growth (since 2000): -3.6%; Density: 634.4 persons per square mile; Race: 98.0% White, 0.0% Black/African American, 0.0% Asian, 0.0% American Indian/Alaska Native, 0.0% Native Hawaiian/Other Pacific Islander, 0.0% Two or more races, 4.9% Hispanic of any race; Average household size: 2.29; Median age: 36.1; Age under 18: 27.3%; Age 65 and over: 13.5%; Males per 100 females: 94.4; Marriage status: 30.4% never married, 49.2% now married, 2.8% separated, 8.9% widowed, 11.5% divorced; Foreign born: 0.6%; Speak English only: 97.9%; With disability: 20.2%; Veterans: 8.8%; Ancestry: 37.1% German, 21.9% English, 13.6% Irish, 12.4% Polish, 5.5% Italian
Employment: 10.9% management, business, and financial, 0.7% computer, engineering, and science, 7.7% education, legal, community

service, arts, and media, 14.1% healthcare practitioners, 20.1% service, 15.8% sales and office, 11.6% natural resources, construction, and maintenance, 19.0% production, transportation, and material moving
Income: Per capita: $19,900; Median household: $42,083; Average household: $45,234; Households with income of $100,000 or more: 2.9%; Poverty rate: 16.5%
Educational Attainment: High school diploma or higher: 86.2%; Bachelor's degree or higher: 14.3%; Graduate/professional degree or higher: 5.6%

School District(s)
Pine Valley Central SD (South Dayton) (PK-12)
    Enrollment: 583 . . . . (716) 988-3293
Housing: Homeownership rate: 74.9%; Median home value: $59,500; Median year structure built: Before 1940; Homeowner vacancy rate: 1.8%; Median selected monthly owner costs: $991 with a mortgage, $494 without a mortgage; Median gross rent: $604 per month; Rental vacancy rate: 0.0%
Health Insurance: 95.1% have insurance; 75.1% have private insurance; 37.3% have public insurance; 4.9% do not have insurance; 1.1% of children under 18 do not have insurance
Transportation: Commute: 88.5% car, 0.0% public transportation, 10.0% walk, 1.5% work from home; Mean travel time to work: 23.2 minutes

SOUTH VALLEY (town). Covers a land area of 36.840 square miles and a water area of 0.247 square miles. Located at 42.05° N. Lat; 79.00° W. Long.
Population: 266; Growth (since 2000): -11.9%; Density: 7.2 persons per square mile; Race: 100.0% White, 0.0% Black/African American, 0.0% Asian, 0.0% American Indian/Alaska Native, 0.0% Native Hawaiian/Other Pacific Islander, 0.0% Two or more races, 0.0% Hispanic of any race; Average household size: 1.71; Median age: 58.5; Age under 18: 4.5%; Age 65 and over: 31.6%; Males per 100 females: 123.7; Marriage status: 27.7% never married, 50.8% now married, 0.8% separated, 7.4% widowed, 14.1% divorced; Foreign born: 0.0%; Speak English only: 100.0%; With disability: 18.8%; Veterans: 15.4%; Ancestry: 36.5% German, 11.7% Irish, 10.5% American, 9.8% Swedish, 6.8% Polish
Employment: 12.6% management, business, and financial, 0.9% computer, engineering, and science, 10.8% education, legal, community service, arts, and media, 9.0% healthcare practitioners, 10.8% service, 21.6% sales and office, 11.7% natural resources, construction, and maintenance, 22.5% production, transportation, and material moving
Income: Per capita: $31,743; Median household: $42,500; Average household: $52,826; Households with income of $100,000 or more: 14.1%; Poverty rate: 9.0%
Educational Attainment: High school diploma or higher: 89.3%; Bachelor's degree or higher: 18.1%; Graduate/professional degree or higher: 12.3%
Housing: Homeownership rate: 93.6%; Median home value: $78,800; Median year structure built: 1987; Homeowner vacancy rate: 0.0%; Median selected monthly owner costs: $1,025 with a mortgage, $514 without a mortgage; Median gross rent: $725 per month; Rental vacancy rate: 0.0%
Health Insurance: 94.0% have insurance; 74.4% have private insurance; 51.5% have public insurance; 6.0% do not have insurance; 0.0% of children under 18 do not have insurance
Transportation: Commute: 94.2% car, 0.0% public transportation, 1.0% walk, 1.0% work from home; Mean travel time to work: 39.9 minutes

STEAMBURG (unincorporated postal area)
ZCTA: 14783
    Covers a land area of 24.917 square miles and a water area of 6.425 square miles. Located at 42.08° N. Lat; 78.89° W. Long. Elevation is 1,407 feet.
Population: 396; Growth (since 2000): -3.9%; Density: 15.9 persons per square mile; Race: 43.2% White, 1.3% Black/African American, 11.6% Asian, 43.9% American Indian/Alaska Native, 0.0% Native Hawaiian/Other Pacific Islander, 0.0% Two or more races, 0.0% Hispanic of any race; Average household size: 2.77; Median age: 38.8; Age under 18: 32.1%; Age 65 and over: 8.1%; Males per 100 females: 113.3; Marriage status: 15.8% never married, 54.2% now married, 1.4% separated, 4.9% widowed, 25.0% divorced; Foreign born: 7.1%; Speak English only: 93.8%; With disability: 12.1%; Veterans: 3.7%; Ancestry: 16.2% German, 15.7% Irish, 10.1% English, 8.8% Trinidadian and Tobagonian, 1.8% French
Employment: 4.5% management, business, and financial, 0.0% computer, engineering, and science, 12.8% education, legal, community

service, arts, and media, 1.3% healthcare practitioners, 19.9% service, 26.3% sales and office, 23.7% natural resources, construction, and maintenance, 11.5% production, transportation, and material moving
Income: Per capita: $23,229; Median household: $31,458; Average household: $62,969; Households with income of $100,000 or more: 3.5%; Poverty rate: 24.0%
Educational Attainment: High school diploma or higher: 89.8%; Bachelor's degree or higher: 7.5%; Graduate/professional degree or higher: 6.0%
Housing: Homeownership rate: 81.8%; Median home value: $81,900; Median year structure built: 1975; Homeowner vacancy rate: 0.0%; Median selected monthly owner costs: $993 with a mortgage, $297 without a mortgage; Median gross rent: n/a per month; Rental vacancy rate: 0.0%
Health Insurance: 79.5% have insurance; 51.5% have private insurance; 43.2% have public insurance; 20.5% do not have insurance; 8.7% of children under 18 do not have insurance
Transportation: Commute: 100.0% car, 0.0% public transportation, 0.0% walk, 0.0% work from home; Mean travel time to work: 20.2 minutes

VERSAILLES (unincorporated postal area)
ZCTA: 14168
    Covers a land area of 0.040 square miles and a water area of 0 square miles. Located at 42.52° N. Lat; 78.99° W. Long. Elevation is 764 feet.
Population: 79; Growth (since 2000): n/a; Density: 1,993.3 persons per square mile; Race: 100.0% White, 0.0% Black/African American, 0.0% Asian, 0.0% American Indian/Alaska Native, 0.0% Native Hawaiian/Other Pacific Islander, 0.0% Two or more races, 55.7% Hispanic of any race; Average household size: 6.08; Median age: 13.6; Age under 18: 55.7%; Age 65 and over: 0.0%; Males per 100 females: 111.8; Marriage status: 0.0% never married, 100.0% now married, 0.0% separated, 0.0% widowed, 0.0% divorced; Foreign born: 0.0%; Speak English only: 100.0%; With disability: 25.3%; Veterans: 8.6%; Ancestry: 32.9% Swedish, 27.8% French, 27.8% Italian, 22.8% German, 20.3% Scottish
Employment: 0.0% management, business, and financial, 0.0% computer, engineering, and science, 0.0% education, legal, community service, arts, and media, 0.0% healthcare practitioners, 26.7% service, 10.0% sales and office, 63.3% natural resources, construction, and maintenance, 0.0% production, transportation, and material moving
Income: Per capita: $6,053; Median household: n/a; Average household: $24,885; Households with income of $100,000 or more: n/a; Poverty rate: 93.7%
Educational Attainment: High school diploma or higher: 100.0%; Bachelor's degree or higher: 22.9%; Graduate/professional degree or higher: n/a
Housing: Homeownership rate: 38.5%; Median home value: n/a; Median year structure built: Before 1940; Homeowner vacancy rate: 0.0%; Median selected monthly owner costs: $0 with a mortgage, $0 without a mortgage; Median gross rent: n/a per month; Rental vacancy rate: 0.0%
Health Insurance: 63.3% have insurance; 3.8% have private insurance; 63.3% have public insurance; 36.7% do not have insurance; 0.0% of children under 18 do not have insurance
Transportation: Commute: 100.0% car, 0.0% public transportation, 0.0% walk, 0.0% work from home; Mean travel time to work: 0.0 minutes

WEST VALLEY (CDP). Covers a land area of 1.532 square miles and a water area of 0.003 square miles. Located at 42.40° N. Lat; 78.61° W. Long. Elevation is 1,522 feet.
Population: 670; Growth (since 2000): n/a; Density: 437.3 persons per square mile; Race: 90.4% White, 0.0% Black/African American, 0.0% Asian, 0.0% American Indian/Alaska Native, 0.0% Native Hawaiian/Other Pacific Islander, 9.6% Two or more races, 3.1% Hispanic of any race; Average household size: 2.78; Median age: 35.5; Age under 18: 28.7%; Age 65 and over: 17.2%; Males per 100 females: 103.9; Marriage status: 28.8% never married, 59.9% now married, 5.2% separated, 1.0% widowed, 10.3% divorced; Foreign born: 0.0%; Speak English only: 95.8%; With disability: 7.0%; Veterans: 13.6%; Ancestry: 54.2% German, 11.3% Irish, 10.4% Scottish, 7.2% Italian, 5.8% French
Employment: 6.7% management, business, and financial, 1.8% computer, engineering, and science, 5.5% education, legal, community service, arts, and media, 3.4% healthcare practitioners, 33.5% service, 20.4% sales and

office, 9.8% natural resources, construction, and maintenance, 18.9% production, transportation, and material moving
Income: Per capita: $20,682; Median household: $59,250; Average household: $57,527; Households with income of $100,000 or more: 17.0%; Poverty rate: 26.4%
Educational Attainment: High school diploma or higher: 96.0%; Bachelor's degree or higher: 16.6%; Graduate/professional degree or higher: 6.9%

School District(s)
West Valley Central SD (PK-12)
    Enrollment: 240. . . . . (716) 942-3293
Housing: Homeownership rate: 70.1%; Median home value: $93,600; Median year structure built: 1954; Homeowner vacancy rate: 0.0%; Median selected monthly owner costs: $1,147 with a mortgage, $587 without a mortgage; Median gross rent: $811 per month; Rental vacancy rate: 0.0%
Health Insurance: 98.2% have insurance; 80.1% have private insurance; 43.0% have public insurance; 1.8% do not have insurance; 0.0% of children under 18 do not have insurance
Transportation: Commute: 90.5% car, 0.0% public transportation, 1.8% walk, 7.6% work from home; Mean travel time to work: 32.9 minutes

WESTON MILLS (CDP). Covers a land area of 6.669 square miles and a water area of 0.073 square miles. Located at 42.08° N. Lat; 78.37° W. Long. Elevation is 1,463 feet.
Population: 1,511; Growth (since 2000): -6.0%; Density: 226.6 persons per square mile; Race: 97.2% White, 0.0% Black/African American, 0.9% Asian, 1.1% American Indian/Alaska Native, 0.0% Native Hawaiian/Other Pacific Islander, 0.8% Two or more races, 1.9% Hispanic of any race; Average household size: 2.33; Median age: 49.5; Age under 18: 15.7%; Age 65 and over: 23.6%; Males per 100 females: 96.3; Marriage status: 33.7% never married, 47.3% now married, 0.4% separated, 8.7% widowed, 10.2% divorced; Foreign born: 0.4%; Speak English only: 98.9%; With disability: 22.8%; Veterans: 11.5%; Ancestry: 26.9% German, 23.9% Irish, 12.8% English, 10.3% Italian, 5.2% Ukrainian
Employment: 10.8% management, business, and financial, 2.7% computer, engineering, and science, 9.4% education, legal, community service, arts, and media, 14.1% healthcare practitioners, 12.4% service, 23.5% sales and office, 5.8% natural resources, construction, and maintenance, 21.1% production, transportation, and material moving
Income: Per capita: $30,989; Median household: $58,355; Average household: $72,116; Households with income of $100,000 or more: 21.8%; Poverty rate: 7.7%
Educational Attainment: High school diploma or higher: 92.2%; Bachelor's degree or higher: 17.7%; Graduate/professional degree or higher: 8.6%
Housing: Homeownership rate: 70.9%; Median home value: $85,700; Median year structure built: 1959; Homeowner vacancy rate: 3.1%; Median selected monthly owner costs: $1,168 with a mortgage, $428 without a mortgage; Median gross rent: $480 per month; Rental vacancy rate: 0.0%
Health Insurance: 95.2% have insurance; 74.5% have private insurance; 45.6% have public insurance; 4.8% do not have insurance; 0.0% of children under 18 do not have insurance
Transportation: Commute: 97.7% car, 1.5% public transportation, 0.0% walk, 0.9% work from home; Mean travel time to work: 19.4 minutes

WESTONS MILLS (unincorporated postal area)
ZCTA: 14788
    Covers a land area of 0.210 square miles and a water area of 0 square miles. Located at 42.06° N. Lat; 78.38° W. Long. Elevation is 1,440 feet.
    Population: 152; Growth (since 2000): n/a; Density: 722.3 persons per square mile; Race: 100.0% White, 0.0% Black/African American, 0.0% Asian, 0.0% American Indian/Alaska Native, 0.0% Native Hawaiian/Other Pacific Islander, 0.0% Two or more races, 10.5% Hispanic of any race; Average household size: 1.47; Median age: 57.0; Age under 18: 2.6%; Age 65 and over: 46.1%; Males per 100 females: 123.3; Marriage status: 29.1% never married, 46.4% now married, 0.0% separated, 17.2% widowed, 7.3% divorced; Foreign born: 0.0%; Speak English only: 100.0%; With disability: 49.7%; Veterans: 0.0%; Ancestry: 32.2% German, 27.0% Irish, 17.1% Polish, 10.5% Hungarian, 6.6% Italian
    Employment: 0.0% management, business, and financial, 0.0% computer, engineering, and science, 0.0% education, legal, community service, arts, and media, 71.4% healthcare practitioners, 0.0% service, 3.6% sales and office, 23.2% natural resources, construction, and maintenance, 1.8% production, transportation, and material moving

Income: Per capita: $34,778; Median household: n/a; Average household: $56,104; Households with income of $100,000 or more: 14.3%; Poverty rate: 21.1%
Educational Attainment: High school diploma or higher: 79.6%; Bachelor's degree or higher: 18.4%; Graduate/professional degree or higher: 18.4%
Housing: Homeownership rate: 41.8%; Median home value: n/a; Median year structure built: Before 1940; Homeowner vacancy rate: 0.0%; Median selected monthly owner costs: $0 with a mortgage, $0 without a mortgage; Median gross rent: n/a per month; Rental vacancy rate: 0.0%
Health Insurance: 81.6% have insurance; 53.1% have private insurance; 63.9% have public insurance; 18.4% do not have insurance; 0.0% of children under 18 do not have insurance
Transportation: Commute: 98.2% car, 1.8% public transportation, 0.0% walk, 0.0% work from home; Mean travel time to work: 0.0 minutes

YORKSHIRE (CDP). Covers a land area of 1.845 square miles and a water area of 0.010 square miles. Located at 42.52° N. Lat; 78.48° W. Long. Elevation is 1,434 feet.
Population: 1,190; Growth (since 2000): -15.2%; Density: 645.0 persons per square mile; Race: 100.0% White, 0.0% Black/African American, 0.0% Asian, 0.0% American Indian/Alaska Native, 0.0% Native Hawaiian/Other Pacific Islander, 0.0% Two or more races, 0.0% Hispanic of any race; Average household size: 1.95; Median age: 49.5; Age under 18: 11.9%; Age 65 and over: 22.3%; Males per 100 females: 85.8; Marriage status: 21.2% never married, 47.3% now married, 0.0% separated, 11.9% widowed, 19.6% divorced; Foreign born: 0.0%; Speak English only: 100.0%; With disability: 28.8%; Veterans: 12.4%; Ancestry: 45.3% German, 24.1% Irish, 17.0% English, 13.3% Polish, 6.9% French
Employment: 2.7% management, business, and financial, 0.0% computer, engineering, and science, 3.5% education, legal, community service, arts, and media, 0.0% healthcare practitioners, 14.5% service, 27.0% sales and office, 11.6% natural resources, construction, and maintenance, 40.7% production, transportation, and material moving
Income: Per capita: $21,905; Median household: $37,800; Average household: $43,446; Households with income of $100,000 or more: 1.0%; Poverty rate: 9.1%
Educational Attainment: High school diploma or higher: 79.6%; Bachelor's degree or higher: 11.5%; Graduate/professional degree or higher: 6.4%

School District(s)
Yorkshire-Pioneer Central SD (PK-12)
    Enrollment: 2,544 . . . . (716) 492-9304
Housing: Homeownership rate: 76.7%; Median home value: $22,300; Median year structure built: 1981; Homeowner vacancy rate: 10.5%; Median selected monthly owner costs: $797 with a mortgage, $289 without a mortgage; Median gross rent: $669 per month; Rental vacancy rate: 0.0%
Health Insurance: 91.5% have insurance; 59.0% have private insurance; 54.7% have public insurance; 8.5% do not have insurance; 0.0% of children under 18 do not have insurance
Transportation: Commute: 92.8% car, 0.0% public transportation, 7.2% walk, 0.0% work from home; Mean travel time to work: 22.4 minutes

YORKSHIRE (town). Covers a land area of 36.249 square miles and a water area of 0.145 square miles. Located at 42.48° N. Lat; 78.52° W. Long. Elevation is 1,434 feet.
Population: 3,794; Growth (since 2000): -9.9%; Density: 104.7 persons per square mile; Race: 100.0% White, 0.0% Black/African American, 0.0% Asian, 0.0% American Indian/Alaska Native, 0.0% Native Hawaiian/Other Pacific Islander, 0.0% Two or more races, 1.6% Hispanic of any race; Average household size: 2.41; Median age: 43.3; Age under 18: 21.0%; Age 65 and over: 16.0%; Males per 100 females: 99.7; Marriage status: 29.0% never married, 51.4% now married, 2.8% separated, 7.1% widowed, 12.5% divorced; Foreign born: 0.2%; Speak English only: 99.7%; With disability: 20.7%; Veterans: 11.9%; Ancestry: 43.4% German, 23.0% Irish, 12.7% Polish, 11.0% English, 5.5% Italian
Employment: 6.8% management, business, and financial, 0.5% computer, engineering, and science, 6.2% education, legal, community service, arts, and media, 5.0% healthcare practitioners, 17.2% service, 25.6% sales and office, 14.4% natural resources, construction, and maintenance, 24.3% production, transportation, and material moving

Income: Per capita: $20,951; Median household: $42,031; Average household: $50,513; Households with income of $100,000 or more: 6.5%; Poverty rate: 10.9%
Educational Attainment: High school diploma or higher: 83.3%; Bachelor's degree or higher: 13.6%; Graduate/professional degree or higher: 5.0%

School District(s)
Yorkshire-Pioneer Central SD (PK-12)
Enrollment: 2,544 . . . . (716) 492-9304
Housing: Homeownership rate: 72.5%; Median home value: $89,300; Median year structure built: 1974; Homeowner vacancy rate: 4.5%; Median selected monthly owner costs: $1,053 with a mortgage, $381 without a mortgage; Median gross rent: $641 per month; Rental vacancy rate: 6.3%
Health Insurance: 91.6% have insurance; 64.8% have private insurance; 46.9% have public insurance; 8.4% do not have insurance; 6.8% of children under 18 do not have insurance
Transportation: Commute: 93.2% car, 0.0% public transportation, 5.0% walk, 1.1% work from home; Mean travel time to work: 24.2 minutes

Cayuga County

Located in west central New York; bounded on the north by Lake Ontario; drained by the Seneca River. Covers a land area of 691.582 square miles, a water area of 172.089 square miles, and is located in the Eastern Time Zone at 43.01° N. Lat., 76.57° W. Long. The county was founded in 1799. County seat is Auburn.

Cayuga County is part of the Auburn, NY Micropolitan Statistical Area. The entire metro area includes: Cayuga County, NY

Weather Station: Aurora Research Farm										Elevation: 830 feet		
	Jan	Feb	Mar	Apr	May	Jun	Jul	Aug	Sep	Oct	Nov	Dec
High	32	34	42	56	68	77	81	80	73	60	48	37
Low	17	18	25	36	46	56	61	59	52	41	33	23
Precip	1.9	1.7	2.6	3.3	3.2	3.8	3.5	3.1	4.1	3.4	3.2	2.3
Snow	14.5	11.8	12.1	4.0	0.2	0.0	0.0	0.0	0.0	0.2	4.9	11.3

High and Low temperatures in degrees Fahrenheit; Precipitation and Snow in inches

Population: 78,319; Growth (since 2000): -4.4%; Density: 113.2 persons per square mile; Race: 92.0% White, 4.1% Black/African American, 0.5% Asian, 0.3% American Indian/Alaska Native, 0.0% Native Hawaiian/Other Pacific Islander, 2.5% two or more races, 2.8% Hispanic of any race; Average household size: 2.36; Median age: 42.5; Age under 18: 20.3%; Age 65 and over: 17.4%; Males per 100 females: 104.2; Marriage status: 31.1% never married, 49.8% now married, 2.7% separated, 7.3% widowed, 11.8% divorced; Foreign born: 2.2%; Speak English only: 95.4%; With disability: 14.1%; Veterans: 9.2%; Ancestry: 21.6% Irish, 18.4% German, 15.3% English, 14.2% Italian, 5.9% Polish
Religion: Six largest groups: 29.9% Catholicism, 4.2% Methodist/Pietist, 2.0% Baptist, 1.6% Presbyterian-Reformed, 1.4% Non-denominational Protestant, 1.0% Holiness
Economy: Unemployment rate: 3.6%; Leading industries: 14.9 % construction; 14.7 % retail trade; 12.4 % health care and social assistance; Farms: 891 totaling 238,444 acres; Company size: 0 employ 1,000 or more persons, 1 employs 500 to 999 persons, 29 employ 100 to 499 persons, 1,589 employ less than 100 persons; Business ownership: 1,511 women-owned, 50 Black-owned, 25 Hispanic-owned, 79 Asian-owned, 38 American Indian/Alaska Native-owned
Employment: 12.5% management, business, and financial, 3.8% computer, engineering, and science, 11.4% education, legal, community service, arts, and media, 6.1% healthcare practitioners, 18.8% service, 22.2% sales and office, 11.0% natural resources, construction, and maintenance, 14.2% production, transportation, and material moving
Income: Per capita: $27,957; Median household: $54,664; Average household: $68,362; Households with income of $100,000 or more: 21.0%; Poverty rate: 11.6%
Educational Attainment: High school diploma or higher: 87.6%; Bachelor's degree or higher: 22.4%; Graduate/professional degree or higher: 8.9%
Housing: Homeownership rate: 70.8%; Median home value: $120,000; Median year structure built: 1955; Homeowner vacancy rate: 1.6%; Median selected monthly owner costs: $1,231 with a mortgage, $521 without a mortgage; Median gross rent: $715 per month; Rental vacancy rate: 4.8%
Vital Statistics: Birth rate: 89.9 per 10,000 population; Death rate: 88.7 per 10,000 population; Age-adjusted cancer mortality rate: 161.9 deaths per 100,000 population

Health Insurance: 93.5% have insurance; 72.4% have private insurance; 37.9% have public insurance; 6.5% do not have insurance; 5.2% of children under 18 do not have insurance
Health Care: Physicians: 9.6 per 10,000 population; Dentists: 4.6 per 10,000 population; Hospital beds: 23.0 per 10,000 population; Hospital admissions: 674.4 per 10,000 population
Transportation: Commute: 89.9% car, 1.0% public transportation, 4.3% walk, 3.4% work from home; Mean travel time to work: 23.0 minutes
2016 Presidential Election: 52.4% Trump, 40.8% Clinton, 4.1% Johnson, 1.5% Stein
National and State Parks: Bear Swamp State Forest; Fair Haven Beach State Park; Fillmore Glen State Park; Howland Island State Wildlife Management Area; Long Point State Park; Summer Hill State Forest
Additional Information Contacts
Cayuga Government . . . . (315) 253-1211
　http://www.co.cayuga.ny.us

Cayuga County Communities

AUBURN (city). County seat. Covers a land area of 8.336 square miles and a water area of 0.075 square miles. Located at 42.93° N. Lat; 76.57° W. Long. Elevation is 686 feet.
History: In 1793, Colonel John Hardenbergh, surveyor and Revolutionary veteran, built the first cabin on the present site of Auburn and a year later erected the first gristmill on the Owasco Outlet. At a meeting in 1805 the present name was taken from Goldsmith's "The Deserted Village." Transportation facilities and abundant water power attracted industry. A scythe factory, a carpet factory, and the D. M. Osborne Company, which was later absorbed by International Harvester, were among its industries. The Auburn Theological Seminary, chartered by the Presbyterian General Assembly in 1819, was merged with the Union Theological Seminary in New York City 120 years later.
Population: 26,962; Growth (since 2000): -5.6%; Density: 3,234.3 persons per square mile; Race: 85.5% White, 8.7% Black/African American, 0.7% Asian, 0.5% American Indian/Alaska Native, 0.0% Native Hawaiian/Other Pacific Islander, 4.0% Two or more races, 3.7% Hispanic of any race; Average household size: 2.13; Median age: 38.6; Age under 18: 19.8%; Age 65 and over: 16.8%; Males per 100 females: 102.9; Marriage status: 37.3% never married, 38.9% now married, 3.7% separated, 8.8% widowed, 14.9% divorced; Foreign born: 2.7%; Speak English only: 92.8%; With disability: 14.9%; Veterans: 7.7%; Ancestry: 22.5% Irish, 18.2% Italian, 15.8% German, 10.8% English, 7.1% Polish
Employment: 10.7% management, business, and financial, 4.1% computer, engineering, and science, 14.0% education, legal, community service, arts, and media, 7.6% healthcare practitioners, 22.1% service, 21.8% sales and office, 6.6% natural resources, construction, and maintenance, 13.0% production, transportation, and material moving
Income: Per capita: $23,187; Median household: $40,708; Average household: $52,687; Households with income of $100,000 or more: 12.2%; Poverty rate: 17.6%
Educational Attainment: High school diploma or higher: 84.6%; Bachelor's degree or higher: 20.7%; Graduate/professional degree or higher: 7.5%

School District(s)
Auburn City SD (KG-12)
Enrollment: 4,281 . . . . (315) 255-8835
Cayuga-Onondaga Boces
Enrollment: n/a . . . . (315) 253-0361
Two-year College(s)
Cayuga County Community College (Public)
Enrollment: 3,784 . . . . (315) 255-1743
Tuition: In-state $5,116; Out-of-state $9,660
Vocational/Technical School(s)
Cayuga Onondaga BOCES-Practical Nursing Program (Public)
Enrollment: 31 . . . . (315) 253-0361
Tuition: In-state $10,240; Out-of-state $10,240
Housing: Homeownership rate: 46.9%; Median home value: $97,800; Median year structure built: Before 1940; Homeowner vacancy rate: 2.4%; Median selected monthly owner costs: $1,131 with a mortgage, $493 without a mortgage; Median gross rent: $696 per month; Rental vacancy rate: 5.3%
Health Insurance: 93.6% have insurance; 67.7% have private insurance; 43.2% have public insurance; 6.4% do not have insurance; 2.8% of children under 18 do not have insurance
Hospitals: Auburn Community Hospital (99 beds)

Newspapers: Skaneateles Journal (weekly circulation 5,500); The Citizen (daily circulation 11,600)
Transportation: Commute: 85.0% car, 2.8% public transportation, 8.1% walk, 2.1% work from home; Mean travel time to work: 18.0 minutes
Additional Information Contacts
City of Auburn . . . . (315) 255-4104
  http://www.auburnny.gov

AURELIUS (town). Covers a land area of 30.245 square miles and a water area of 1.749 square miles. Located at 42.93° N. Lat; 76.67° W. Long.
Population: 2,718; Growth (since 2000): -7.4%; Density: 89.9 persons per square mile; Race: 98.2% White, 1.1% Black/African American, 0.1% Asian, 0.2% American Indian/Alaska Native, 0.0% Native Hawaiian/Other Pacific Islander, 0.3% Two or more races, 0.1% Hispanic of any race; Average household size: 2.39; Median age: 47.1; Age under 18: 16.9%; Age 65 and over: 20.8%; Males per 100 females: 100.6; Marriage status: 24.6% never married, 59.4% now married, 2.6% separated, 6.3% widowed, 9.7% divorced; Foreign born: 1.8%; Speak English only: 98.1%; With disability: 13.6%; Veterans: 8.9%; Ancestry: 24.4% Irish, 20.9% Italian, 20.3% English, 14.9% German, 8.2% Polish
Employment: 11.2% management, business, and financial, 4.3% computer, engineering, and science, 10.3% education, legal, community service, arts, and media, 6.3% healthcare practitioners, 16.2% service, 22.6% sales and office, 13.0% natural resources, construction, and maintenance, 16.2% production, transportation, and material moving
Income: Per capita: $29,521; Median household: $58,417; Average household: $70,105; Households with income of $100,000 or more: 26.2%; Poverty rate: 6.1%
Educational Attainment: High school diploma or higher: 87.9%; Bachelor's degree or higher: 19.4%; Graduate/professional degree or higher: 9.7%
Housing: Homeownership rate: 83.8%; Median home value: $120,900; Median year structure built: 1961; Homeowner vacancy rate: 2.7%; Median selected monthly owner costs: $1,234 with a mortgage, $480 without a mortgage; Median gross rent: $725 per month; Rental vacancy rate: 0.0%
Health Insurance: 92.9% have insurance; 75.2% have private insurance; 36.3% have public insurance; 7.1% do not have insurance; 9.6% of children under 18 do not have insurance
Transportation: Commute: 93.6% car, 0.0% public transportation, 3.5% walk, 2.9% work from home; Mean travel time to work: 22.4 minutes
Additional Information Contacts
Town of Aurelius . . . . (315) 255-1894
  http://co.cayuga.ny.us/aurelius/index.html

AURORA (village). Covers a land area of 0.919 square miles and a water area of <.001 square miles. Located at 42.75° N. Lat; 76.70° W. Long. Elevation is 413 feet.
History: Seat of Wells College (1869).
Population: 687; Growth (since 2000): -4.6%; Density: 747.5 persons per square mile; Race: 72.2% White, 7.1% Black/African American, 2.8% Asian, 0.0% American Indian/Alaska Native, 0.0% Native Hawaiian/Other Pacific Islander, 10.3% Two or more races, 12.4% Hispanic of any race; Average household size: 1.96; Median age: 21.5; Age under 18: 8.3%; Age 65 and over: 11.6%; Males per 100 females: 60.5; Marriage status: 69.1% never married, 25.1% now married, 0.4% separated, 0.9% widowed, 4.9% divorced; Foreign born: 10.2%; Speak English only: 81.4%; With disability: 10.8%; Veterans: 3.3%; Ancestry: 27.8% Irish, 21.8% German, 18.8% Italian, 13.7% English, 4.8% French
Employment: 10.4% management, business, and financial, 4.4% computer, engineering, and science, 27.4% education, legal, community service, arts, and media, 0.8% healthcare practitioners, 19.8% service, 27.9% sales and office, 4.7% natural resources, construction, and maintenance, 4.4% production, transportation, and material moving
Income: Per capita: $26,322; Median household: $75,288; Average household: $86,244; Households with income of $100,000 or more: 36.3%; Poverty rate: 1.5%
Educational Attainment: High school diploma or higher: 93.2%; Bachelor's degree or higher: 51.0%; Graduate/professional degree or higher: 31.9%

School District(s)
Southern Cayuga Central SD (PK-12)
  Enrollment: 663 . . . . (315) 364-7211

Four-year College(s)
Wells College (Private, Not-for-profit)
  Enrollment: 488 . . . . (315) 364-3266
  Tuition: In-state $39,600; Out-of-state $39,600
Housing: Homeownership rate: 70.4%; Median home value: $197,500; Median year structure built: Before 1940; Homeowner vacancy rate: 4.0%; Median selected monthly owner costs: $1,688 with a mortgage, $632 without a mortgage; Median gross rent: $877 per month; Rental vacancy rate: 0.0%
Health Insurance: 96.8% have insurance; 74.7% have private insurance; 32.6% have public insurance; 3.2% do not have insurance; 1.0% of children under 18 do not have insurance
Transportation: Commute: 38.7% car, 1.7% public transportation, 43.3% walk, 16.3% work from home; Mean travel time to work: 14.6 minutes

---

BRUTUS (town). Covers a land area of 22.106 square miles and a water area of 0.394 square miles. Located at 43.05° N. Lat; 76.55° W. Long.
Population: 4,357; Growth (since 2000): -8.8%; Density: 197.1 persons per square mile; Race: 97.0% White, 0.5% Black/African American, 1.1% Asian, 0.2% American Indian/Alaska Native, 0.0% Native Hawaiian/Other Pacific Islander, 1.2% Two or more races, 0.7% Hispanic of any race; Average household size: 2.42; Median age: 43.2; Age under 18: 22.9%; Age 65 and over: 15.6%; Males per 100 females: 94.6; Marriage status: 30.2% never married, 50.4% now married, 2.0% separated, 6.7% widowed, 12.6% divorced; Foreign born: 1.9%; Speak English only: 98.0%; With disability: 16.1%; Veterans: 12.6%; Ancestry: 24.1% German, 20.6% Irish, 20.3% English, 15.4% Italian, 8.5% Polish
Employment: 14.0% management, business, and financial, 2.7% computer, engineering, and science, 6.2% education, legal, community service, arts, and media, 5.0% healthcare practitioners, 16.9% service, 31.6% sales and office, 11.4% natural resources, construction, and maintenance, 12.2% production, transportation, and material moving
Income: Per capita: $29,547; Median household: $56,940; Average household: $70,796; Households with income of $100,000 or more: 24.0%; Poverty rate: 6.2%
Educational Attainment: High school diploma or higher: 90.3%; Bachelor's degree or higher: 22.0%; Graduate/professional degree or higher: 7.4%
Housing: Homeownership rate: 76.1%; Median home value: $121,900; Median year structure built: 1973; Homeowner vacancy rate: 1.4%; Median selected monthly owner costs: $1,351 with a mortgage, $510 without a mortgage; Median gross rent: $758 per month; Rental vacancy rate: 4.6%
Health Insurance: 98.3% have insurance; 83.0% have private insurance; 33.5% have public insurance; 1.7% do not have insurance; 0.3% of children under 18 do not have insurance
Transportation: Commute: 95.3% car, 0.0% public transportation, 1.1% walk, 1.2% work from home; Mean travel time to work: 25.1 minutes
Additional Information Contacts
Town of Brutus . . . . (315) 834-9398
  http://www.townofbrutus.org

CATO (town). Covers a land area of 33.643 square miles and a water area of 2.544 square miles. Located at 43.12° N. Lat; 76.54° W. Long. Elevation is 459 feet.
Population: 2,473; Growth (since 2000): -9.9%; Density: 73.5 persons per square mile; Race: 97.6% White, 0.6% Black/African American, 1.0% Asian, 0.4% American Indian/Alaska Native, 0.0% Native Hawaiian/Other Pacific Islander, 0.4% Two or more races, 0.3% Hispanic of any race; Average household size: 2.70; Median age: 43.1; Age under 18: 24.1%; Age 65 and over: 15.6%; Males per 100 females: 104.3; Marriage status: 24.0% never married, 61.1% now married, 1.1% separated, 5.7% widowed, 9.3% divorced; Foreign born: 2.5%; Speak English only: 95.8%; With disability: 14.3%; Veterans: 11.5%; Ancestry: 21.0% German, 20.7% Irish, 14.6% English, 8.3% Italian, 7.8% American
Employment: 14.8% management, business, and financial, 5.7% computer, engineering, and science, 5.6% education, legal, community service, arts, and media, 8.4% healthcare practitioners, 15.7% service, 24.3% sales and office, 11.8% natural resources, construction, and maintenance, 13.7% production, transportation, and material moving
Income: Per capita: $29,103; Median household: $63,750; Average household: $77,216; Households with income of $100,000 or more: 31.4%; Poverty rate: 8.7%

Educational Attainment: High school diploma or higher: 89.5%; Bachelor's degree or higher: 27.1%; Graduate/professional degree or higher: 7.8%

School District(s)
Cato-Meridian Central SD (PK-12)
  Enrollment: 985....................................(315) 626-3439
Housing: Homeownership rate: 86.4%; Median home value: $138,600; Median year structure built: 1978; Homeowner vacancy rate: 1.5%; Median selected monthly owner costs: $1,386 with a mortgage, $514 without a mortgage; Median gross rent: $763 per month; Rental vacancy rate: 11.3%
Health Insurance: 92.6% have insurance; 75.7% have private insurance; 30.7% have public insurance; 7.4% do not have insurance; 7.6% of children under 18 do not have insurance
Transportation: Commute: 93.6% car, 0.3% public transportation, 1.0% walk, 5.1% work from home; Mean travel time to work: 29.6 minutes

CATO (village). Covers a land area of 0.989 square miles and a water area of 0.025 square miles. Located at 43.17° N. Lat; 76.57° W. Long. Elevation is 459 feet.
Population: 695; Growth (since 2000): 15.6%; Density: 703.1 persons per square mile; Race: 91.9% White, 0.0% Black/African American, 0.0% Asian, 1.6% American Indian/Alaska Native, 0.0% Native Hawaiian/Other Pacific Islander, 0.0% Two or more races, 0.0% Hispanic of any race; Average household size: 2.77; Median age: 30.6; Age under 18: 33.1%; Age 65 and over: 9.6%; Males per 100 females: 90.0; Marriage status: 36.3% never married, 47.0% now married, 4.3% separated, 4.7% widowed, 12.0% divorced; Foreign born: 0.3%; Speak English only: 98.8%; With disability: 14.7%; Veterans: 12.7%; Ancestry: 26.8% Irish, 14.7% German, 13.1% English, 10.2% Polish, 6.6% Italian
Employment: 15.2% management, business, and financial, 0.6% computer, engineering, and science, 6.1% education, legal, community service, arts, and media, 7.6% healthcare practitioners, 15.5% service, 28.0% sales and office, 10.7% natural resources, construction, and maintenance, 16.2% production, transportation, and material moving
Income: Per capita: $21,292; Median household: $50,208; Average household: $58,666; Households with income of $100,000 or more: 17.9%; Poverty rate: 12.3%
Educational Attainment: High school diploma or higher: 93.3%; Bachelor's degree or higher: 12.5%; Graduate/professional degree or higher: 6.0%

School District(s)
Cato-Meridian Central SD (PK-12)
  Enrollment: 985....................................(315) 626-3439
Housing: Homeownership rate: 61.0%; Median home value: $105,500; Median year structure built: Before 1940; Homeowner vacancy rate: 7.5%; Median selected monthly owner costs: $1,099 with a mortgage, $538 without a mortgage; Median gross rent: $748 per month; Rental vacancy rate: 0.0%
Health Insurance: 91.2% have insurance; 74.2% have private insurance; 26.5% have public insurance; 8.8% do not have insurance; 0.0% of children under 18 do not have insurance
Transportation: Commute: 84.8% car, 0.0% public transportation, 11.5% walk, 3.7% work from home; Mean travel time to work: 26.8 minutes

CAYUGA (village). Covers a land area of 0.904 square miles and a water area of 0.462 square miles. Located at 42.92° N. Lat; 76.73° W. Long. Elevation is 482 feet.
Population: 512; Growth (since 2000): 0.6%; Density: 566.5 persons per square mile; Race: 96.9% White, 1.8% Black/African American, 0.0% Asian, 0.8% American Indian/Alaska Native, 0.0% Native Hawaiian/Other Pacific Islander, 0.4% Two or more races, 0.8% Hispanic of any race; Average household size: 2.33; Median age: 48.1; Age under 18: 22.9%; Age 65 and over: 21.3%; Males per 100 females: 94.7; Marriage status: 28.1% never married, 53.0% now married, 1.6% separated, 7.6% widowed, 11.3% divorced; Foreign born: 0.0%; Speak English only: 97.7%; With disability: 15.4%; Veterans: 7.3%; Ancestry: 25.4% Irish, 23.6% English, 17.2% German, 13.3% Italian, 7.8% Polish
Employment: 8.2% management, business, and financial, 3.7% computer, engineering, and science, 16.8% education, legal, community service, arts, and media, 5.3% healthcare practitioners, 26.6% service, 17.2% sales and office, 9.4% natural resources, construction, and maintenance, 12.7% production, transportation, and material moving
Income: Per capita: $30,534; Median household: $54,167; Average household: $71,555; Households with income of $100,000 or more: 27.8%; Poverty rate: 2.7%

Educational Attainment: High school diploma or higher: 92.0%; Bachelor's degree or higher: 29.1%; Graduate/professional degree or higher: 10.8%

School District(s)
Union Springs Central SD (PK-12)
  Enrollment: 863....................................(315) 889-4101
Housing: Homeownership rate: 76.4%; Median home value: $111,800; Median year structure built: Before 1940; Homeowner vacancy rate: 13.4%; Median selected monthly owner costs: $1,238 with a mortgage, $511 without a mortgage; Median gross rent: $478 per month; Rental vacancy rate: 0.0%
Health Insurance: 99.6% have insurance; 83.4% have private insurance; 35.4% have public insurance; 0.4% do not have insurance; 0.0% of children under 18 do not have insurance
Transportation: Commute: 99.6% car, 0.0% public transportation, 0.0% walk, 0.4% work from home; Mean travel time to work: 26.7 minutes
Additional Information Contacts
Village of Cayuga ....(315) 252-1707
  http://co.cayuga.ny.us/cayugavil

CONQUEST (town). Covers a land area of 35.222 square miles and a water area of 1.096 square miles. Located at 43.12° N. Lat; 76.66° W. Long. Elevation is 440 feet.
Population: 1,720; Growth (since 2000): -10.6%; Density: 48.8 persons per square mile; Race: 97.0% White, 0.6% Black/African American, 0.0% Asian, 0.1% American Indian/Alaska Native, 0.0% Native Hawaiian/Other Pacific Islander, 2.1% Two or more races, 2.0% Hispanic of any race; Average household size: 2.43; Median age: 45.8; Age under 18: 19.3%; Age 65 and over: 15.9%; Males per 100 females: 106.7; Marriage status: 26.2% never married, 57.6% now married, 1.9% separated, 4.8% widowed, 11.4% divorced; Foreign born: 0.8%; Speak English only: 97.8%; With disability: 14.5%; Veterans: 7.2%; Ancestry: 22.2% Irish, 19.0% English, 16.2% German, 9.2% Dutch, 8.4% American
Employment: 8.2% management, business, and financial, 4.2% computer, engineering, and science, 5.3% education, legal, community service, arts, and media, 4.6% healthcare practitioners, 19.6% service, 23.6% sales and office, 11.5% natural resources, construction, and maintenance, 23.0% production, transportation, and material moving
Income: Per capita: $28,211; Median household: $54,766; Average household: $69,082; Households with income of $100,000 or more: 16.0%; Poverty rate: 9.7%
Educational Attainment: High school diploma or higher: 82.5%; Bachelor's degree or higher: 12.5%; Graduate/professional degree or higher: 5.3%
Housing: Homeownership rate: 88.3%; Median home value: $93,100; Median year structure built: 1977; Homeowner vacancy rate: 0.0%; Median selected monthly owner costs: $1,083 with a mortgage, $462 without a mortgage; Median gross rent: $790 per month; Rental vacancy rate: 0.0%
Health Insurance: 90.5% have insurance; 69.1% have private insurance; 36.7% have public insurance; 9.5% do not have insurance; 10.5% of children under 18 do not have insurance
Transportation: Commute: 96.4% car, 0.6% public transportation, 0.0% walk, 2.3% work from home; Mean travel time to work: 25.6 minutes
Additional Information Contacts
Town of Conquest ....(315) 776-4539
  http://co.cayuga.ny.us/conquest

FAIR HAVEN (village). Covers a land area of 1.755 square miles and a water area of 1.168 square miles. Located at 43.32° N. Lat; 76.71° W. Long. Elevation is 285 feet.
Population: 810; Growth (since 2000): -8.4%; Density: 461.6 persons per square mile; Race: 97.4% White, 0.0% Black/African American, 0.6% Asian, 0.1% American Indian/Alaska Native, 0.0% Native Hawaiian/Other Pacific Islander, 0.9% Two or more races, 1.0% Hispanic of any race; Average household size: 2.08; Median age: 50.4; Age under 18: 13.5%; Age 65 and over: 22.5%; Males per 100 females: 94.0; Marriage status: 26.5% never married, 47.2% now married, 3.1% separated, 6.5% widowed, 19.8% divorced; Foreign born: 4.0%; Speak English only: 96.7%; With disability: 18.7%; Veterans: 9.1%; Ancestry: 24.7% German, 17.3% Irish, 14.7% English, 12.2% French, 6.3% Dutch
Employment: 9.8% management, business, and financial, 5.3% computer, engineering, and science, 13.5% education, legal, community service, arts, and media, 4.3% healthcare practitioners, 20.3% service, 16.5% sales and office, 8.3% natural resources, construction, and maintenance, 22.1% production, transportation, and material moving

Income: Per capita: $38,394; Median household: $58,438; Average household: $80,495; Households with income of $100,000 or more: 23.2%; Poverty rate: 12.6%
Educational Attainment: High school diploma or higher: 93.6%; Bachelor's degree or higher: 30.2%; Graduate/professional degree or higher: 12.3%
Housing: Homeownership rate: 79.0%; Median home value: $99,800; Median year structure built: 1948; Homeowner vacancy rate: 2.0%; Median selected monthly owner costs: $1,109 with a mortgage, $540 without a mortgage; Median gross rent: $718 per month; Rental vacancy rate: 6.0%
Health Insurance: 90.7% have insurance; 68.2% have private insurance; 43.9% have public insurance; 9.3% do not have insurance; 14.4% of children under 18 do not have insurance
Transportation: Commute: 93.8% car, 0.0% public transportation, 2.7% walk, 3.5% work from home; Mean travel time to work: 32.0 minutes
Additional Information Contacts
Village of Fair Haven . . . . (315) 947-5112
  http://co.cayuga.ny.us/fairhaven

FLEMING (town). Covers a land area of 21.819 square miles and a water area of 2.480 square miles. Located at 42.87° N. Lat; 76.58° W. Long. Elevation is 902 feet.
Population: 2,597; Growth (since 2000): -1.9%; Density: 119.0 persons per square mile; Race: 97.7% White, 0.2% Black/African American, 0.3% Asian, 0.3% American Indian/Alaska Native, 0.0% Native Hawaiian/Other Pacific Islander, 0.3% Two or more races, 2.2% Hispanic of any race; Average household size: 2.39; Median age: 52.4; Age under 18: 14.7%; Age 65 and over: 22.8%; Males per 100 females: 102.6; Marriage status: 22.6% never married, 63.1% now married, 0.7% separated, 3.7% widowed, 10.6% divorced; Foreign born: 3.2%; Speak English only: 97.0%; With disability: 8.8%; Veterans: 8.8%; Ancestry: 27.0% Irish, 19.0% German, 18.5% English, 15.1% Italian, 7.9% Polish
Employment: 13.2% management, business, and financial, 4.8% computer, engineering, and science, 11.5% education, legal, community service, arts, and media, 4.7% healthcare practitioners, 19.3% service, 19.7% sales and office, 15.2% natural resources, construction, and maintenance, 11.7% production, transportation, and material moving
Income: Per capita: $40,661; Median household: $79,444; Average household: $96,543; Households with income of $100,000 or more: 37.2%; Poverty rate: 2.4%
Educational Attainment: High school diploma or higher: 93.3%; Bachelor's degree or higher: 29.1%; Graduate/professional degree or higher: 15.2%
Housing: Homeownership rate: 88.5%; Median home value: $186,400; Median year structure built: 1961; Homeowner vacancy rate: 0.0%; Median selected monthly owner costs: $1,424 with a mortgage, $716 without a mortgage; Median gross rent: $792 per month; Rental vacancy rate: 0.0%
Health Insurance: 97.9% have insurance; 88.8% have private insurance; 27.3% have public insurance; 2.1% do not have insurance; 0.0% of children under 18 do not have insurance
Transportation: Commute: 91.6% car, 0.1% public transportation, 1.6% walk, 6.2% work from home; Mean travel time to work: 22.8 minutes
Additional Information Contacts
Town of Fleming . . . . (315) 252-8988
  http://co.cayuga.ny.us/fleming

GENOA (town). Covers a land area of 39.598 square miles and a water area of 3.565 square miles. Located at 42.65° N. Lat; 76.57° W. Long. Elevation is 853 feet.
Population: 1,714; Growth (since 2000): -10.4%; Density: 43.3 persons per square mile; Race: 98.9% White, 0.0% Black/African American, 0.0% Asian, 0.6% American Indian/Alaska Native, 0.0% Native Hawaiian/Other Pacific Islander, 0.5% Two or more races, 2.8% Hispanic of any race; Average household size: 2.48; Median age: 45.8; Age under 18: 20.8%; Age 65 and over: 17.6%; Males per 100 females: 105.6; Marriage status: 24.8% never married, 60.9% now married, 3.1% separated, 5.4% widowed, 8.9% divorced; Foreign born: 1.5%; Speak English only: 96.0%; With disability: 14.1%; Veterans: 10.4%; Ancestry: 19.3% German, 19.1% English, 19.0% Irish, 9.0% Italian, 4.4% Polish
Employment: 16.2% management, business, and financial, 3.7% computer, engineering, and science, 11.5% education, legal, community service, arts, and media, 7.3% healthcare practitioners, 14.7% service, 18.8% sales and office, 14.1% natural resources, construction, and maintenance, 13.6% production, transportation, and material moving

Income: Per capita: $35,197; Median household: $67,228; Average household: $86,660; Households with income of $100,000 or more: 26.9%; Poverty rate: 8.7%
Educational Attainment: High school diploma or higher: 94.7%; Bachelor's degree or higher: 29.8%; Graduate/professional degree or higher: 11.4%
Housing: Homeownership rate: 83.1%; Median home value: $143,000; Median year structure built: 1957; Homeowner vacancy rate: 1.8%; Median selected monthly owner costs: $1,377 with a mortgage, $468 without a mortgage; Median gross rent: $658 per month; Rental vacancy rate: 14.0%
Health Insurance: 96.4% have insurance; 77.5% have private insurance; 33.1% have public insurance; 3.6% do not have insurance; 0.0% of children under 18 do not have insurance
Transportation: Commute: 89.8% car, 0.4% public transportation, 3.2% walk, 6.1% work from home; Mean travel time to work: 25.1 minutes
Additional Information Contacts
Town of Genoa . . . . (315) 364-5505
  http://co.cayuga.ny.us/genoa

IRA (town). Covers a land area of 34.795 square miles and a water area of 0.103 square miles. Located at 43.21° N. Lat; 76.53° W. Long. Elevation is 489 feet.
Population: 2,360; Growth (since 2000): -2.7%; Density: 67.8 persons per square mile; Race: 95.1% White, 1.0% Black/African American, 0.0% Asian, 0.5% American Indian/Alaska Native, 0.0% Native Hawaiian/Other Pacific Islander, 1.5% Two or more races, 0.3% Hispanic of any race; Average household size: 2.73; Median age: 37.3; Age under 18: 24.8%; Age 65 and over: 12.6%; Males per 100 females: 103.1; Marriage status: 31.0% never married, 56.0% now married, 4.9% separated, 5.3% widowed, 7.7% divorced; Foreign born: 0.9%; Speak English only: 99.9%; With disability: 14.7%; Veterans: 11.3%; Ancestry: 18.4% Irish, 17.0% German, 14.3% English, 10.9% French, 6.7% Polish
Employment: 14.7% management, business, and financial, 4.2% computer, engineering, and science, 10.4% education, legal, community service, arts, and media, 4.7% healthcare practitioners, 12.1% service, 22.5% sales and office, 16.4% natural resources, construction, and maintenance, 15.0% production, transportation, and material moving
Income: Per capita: $27,567; Median household: $57,422; Average household: $75,051; Households with income of $100,000 or more: 22.3%; Poverty rate: 6.3%
Educational Attainment: High school diploma or higher: 91.2%; Bachelor's degree or higher: 23.1%; Graduate/professional degree or higher: 9.4%
Housing: Homeownership rate: 89.5%; Median home value: $117,800; Median year structure built: 1976; Homeowner vacancy rate: 0.8%; Median selected monthly owner costs: $1,109 with a mortgage, $487 without a mortgage; Median gross rent: $739 per month; Rental vacancy rate: 0.0%
Health Insurance: 92.7% have insurance; 74.3% have private insurance; 30.5% have public insurance; 7.3% do not have insurance; 5.4% of children under 18 do not have insurance
Transportation: Commute: 93.3% car, 0.0% public transportation, 3.6% walk, 3.1% work from home; Mean travel time to work: 29.6 minutes
Additional Information Contacts
Town of Ira . . . . (315) 626-6905
  http://co.cayuga.ny.us/ira

KING FERRY (unincorporated postal area)
ZCTA: 13081
  Covers a land area of 28.958 square miles and a water area of 0.012 square miles. Located at 42.67° N. Lat; 76.63° W. Long. Elevation is 955 feet.
  Population: 1,068; Growth (since 2000): -10.2%; Density: 36.9 persons per square mile; Race: 98.5% White, 0.0% Black/African American, 0.0% Asian, 0.8% American Indian/Alaska Native, 0.0% Native Hawaiian/Other Pacific Islander, 0.7% Two or more races, 1.2% Hispanic of any race; Average household size: 2.39; Median age: 50.3; Age under 18: 17.1%; Age 65 and over: 17.6%; Males per 100 females: 101.6; Marriage status: 21.4% never married, 65.1% now married, 1.6% separated, 4.7% widowed, 8.8% divorced; Foreign born: 2.2%; Speak English only: 96.1%; With disability: 14.3%; Veterans: 9.5%; Ancestry: 21.9% Irish, 20.6% English, 16.0% German, 6.7% Italian, 4.8% Polish
  Employment: 15.4% management, business, and financial, 5.0% computer, engineering, and science, 13.7% education, legal, community service, arts, and media, 5.0% healthcare practitioners, 17.6% service,

20.8% sales and office, 10.4% natural resources, construction, and maintenance, 12.0% production, transportation, and material moving
Income: Per capita: $41,657; Median household: $74,250; Average household: $99,500; Households with income of $100,000 or more: 35.0%; Poverty rate: 11.6%
Educational Attainment: High school diploma or higher: 95.1%; Bachelor's degree or higher: 36.7%; Graduate/professional degree or higher: 17.8%
Housing: Homeownership rate: 86.8%; Median home value: $163,400; Median year structure built: 1955; Homeowner vacancy rate: 2.0%; Median selected monthly owner costs: $1,438 with a mortgage, $478 without a mortgage; Median gross rent: $764 per month; Rental vacancy rate: 14.5%
Health Insurance: 97.0% have insurance; 77.8% have private insurance; 35.5% have public insurance; 3.0% do not have insurance; 1.5% of children under 18 do not have insurance
Transportation: Commute: 95.7% car, 0.0% public transportation, 0.7% walk, 3.1% work from home; Mean travel time to work: 28.4 minutes

LEDYARD (town). Covers a land area of 36.112 square miles and a water area of 12.469 square miles. Located at 42.75° N. Lat; 76.67° W. Long. Elevation is 984 feet.
Population: 1,747; Growth (since 2000): -4.6%; Density: 48.4 persons per square mile; Race: 85.3% White, 2.8% Black/African American, 1.4% Asian, 0.0% American Indian/Alaska Native, 0.0% Native Hawaiian/Other Pacific Islander, 4.3% Two or more races, 8.4% Hispanic of any race; Average household size: 2.22; Median age: 40.5; Age under 18: 13.2%; Age 65 and over: 17.8%; Males per 100 females: 84.0; Marriage status: 42.3% never married, 46.2% now married, 1.4% separated, 3.2% widowed, 8.3% divorced; Foreign born: 7.0%; Speak English only: 88.0%; With disability: 11.7%; Veterans: 6.5%; Ancestry: 26.7% Irish, 24.1% German, 18.1% English, 10.5% Italian, 4.9% Dutch
Employment: 16.2% management, business, and financial, 3.7% computer, engineering, and science, 20.0% education, legal, community service, arts, and media, 1.7% healthcare practitioners, 16.0% service, 22.2% sales and office, 11.2% natural resources, construction, and maintenance, 9.1% production, transportation, and material moving
Income: Per capita: $30,204; Median household: $67,188; Average household: $77,560; Households with income of $100,000 or more: 24.1%; Poverty rate: 12.1%
Educational Attainment: High school diploma or higher: 90.5%; Bachelor's degree or higher: 42.6%; Graduate/professional degree or higher: 21.9%
Housing: Homeownership rate: 79.8%; Median home value: $175,800; Median year structure built: 1966; Homeowner vacancy rate: 0.8%; Median selected monthly owner costs: $1,429 with a mortgage, $558 without a mortgage; Median gross rent: $867 per month; Rental vacancy rate: 0.0%
Health Insurance: 92.7% have insurance; 70.6% have private insurance; 36.5% have public insurance; 7.3% do not have insurance; 4.9% of children under 18 do not have insurance
Transportation: Commute: 74.4% car, 0.6% public transportation, 16.2% walk, 7.8% work from home; Mean travel time to work: 24.6 minutes
Additional Information Contacts
Town of Ledyard . . . . (315) 364-5707
http://co.cayuga.ny.us/ledyard

LOCKE (town). Covers a land area of 24.305 square miles and a water area of 0.105 square miles. Located at 42.65° N. Lat; 76.42° W. Long. Elevation is 791 feet.
History: President Millard Fillmore born here.
Population: 1,751; Growth (since 2000): -7.8%; Density: 72.0 persons per square mile; Race: 97.4% White, 0.3% Black/African American, 0.0% Asian, 0.1% American Indian/Alaska Native, 0.0% Native Hawaiian/Other Pacific Islander, 0.0% Two or more races, 5.5% Hispanic of any race; Average household size: 2.39; Median age: 44.6; Age under 18: 18.9%; Age 65 and over: 16.6%; Males per 100 females: 100.5; Marriage status: 32.6% never married, 49.4% now married, 0.9% separated, 3.9% widowed, 14.1% divorced; Foreign born: 1.9%; Speak English only: 94.1%; With disability: 14.3%; Veterans: 11.0%; Ancestry: 20.6% German, 17.8% Irish, 17.2% English, 8.9% American, 6.1% Italian
Employment: 13.8% management, business, and financial, 5.2% computer, engineering, and science, 10.1% education, legal, community service, arts, and media, 4.3% healthcare practitioners, 15.4% service, 23.6% sales and office, 13.0% natural resources, construction, and maintenance, 14.5% production, transportation, and material moving

Income: Per capita: $28,328; Median household: $57,232; Average household: $66,822; Households with income of $100,000 or more: 20.0%; Poverty rate: 10.9%
Educational Attainment: High school diploma or higher: 86.2%; Bachelor's degree or higher: 21.4%; Graduate/professional degree or higher: 9.5%
Housing: Homeownership rate: 84.3%; Median home value: $110,800; Median year structure built: 1977; Homeowner vacancy rate: 3.2%; Median selected monthly owner costs: $1,159 with a mortgage, $493 without a mortgage; Median gross rent: $842 per month; Rental vacancy rate: 0.0%
Health Insurance: 92.4% have insurance; 69.8% have private insurance; 38.9% have public insurance; 7.6% do not have insurance; 2.4% of children under 18 do not have insurance
Transportation: Commute: 90.2% car, 0.2% public transportation, 2.3% walk, 3.2% work from home; Mean travel time to work: 25.6 minutes
Additional Information Contacts
Town of Locke . . . . (315) 497-9338
http://co.cayuga.ny.us/locke

MARTVILLE (unincorporated postal area)
ZCTA: 13111
Covers a land area of 26.607 square miles and a water area of 0.091 square miles. Located at 43.26° N. Lat; 76.61° W. Long. Elevation is 354 feet.
Population: 1,619; Growth (since 2000): -7.4%; Density: 60.8 persons per square mile; Race: 99.3% White, 0.0% Black/African American, 0.0% Asian, 0.0% American Indian/Alaska Native, 0.0% Native Hawaiian/Other Pacific Islander, 0.7% Two or more races, 0.0% Hispanic of any race; Average household size: 2.62; Median age: 48.3; Age under 18: 24.0%; Age 65 and over: 13.8%; Males per 100 females: 109.6; Marriage status: 17.1% never married, 64.6% now married, 1.7% separated, 10.8% widowed, 7.5% divorced; Foreign born: 0.6%; Speak English only: 99.6%; With disability: 16.4%; Veterans: 13.2%; Ancestry: 15.6% Irish, 13.0% German, 9.0% Italian, 7.1% English, 6.5% American
Employment: 20.6% management, business, and financial, 4.7% computer, engineering, and science, 10.9% education, legal, community service, arts, and media, 0.4% healthcare practitioners, 11.5% service, 16.9% sales and office, 17.5% natural resources, construction, and maintenance, 17.5% production, transportation, and material moving
Income: Per capita: $19,709; Median household: $46,685; Average household: $51,785; Households with income of $100,000 or more: 10.2%; Poverty rate: 33.1%
Educational Attainment: High school diploma or higher: 87.1%; Bachelor's degree or higher: 11.3%; Graduate/professional degree or higher: 4.4%
Housing: Homeownership rate: 93.2%; Median home value: $98,400; Median year structure built: 1984; Homeowner vacancy rate: 0.0%; Median selected monthly owner costs: $994 with a mortgage, $460 without a mortgage; Median gross rent: $663 per month; Rental vacancy rate: 0.0%
Health Insurance: 92.6% have insurance; 60.4% have private insurance; 51.0% have public insurance; 7.4% do not have insurance; 5.3% of children under 18 do not have insurance
Transportation: Commute: 90.7% car, 0.6% public transportation, 1.4% walk, 7.3% work from home; Mean travel time to work: 30.9 minutes

MELROSE PARK (CDP). Covers a land area of 3.732 square miles and a water area of 0.584 square miles. Located at 42.91° N. Lat; 76.51° W. Long. Elevation is 732 feet.
Population: 2,331; Growth (since 2000): -1.2%; Density: 624.7 persons per square mile; Race: 99.8% White, 0.0% Black/African American, 0.1% Asian, 0.0% American Indian/Alaska Native, 0.0% Native Hawaiian/Other Pacific Islander, 0.0% Two or more races, 0.1% Hispanic of any race; Average household size: 2.67; Median age: 48.4; Age under 18: 21.5%; Age 65 and over: 17.8%; Males per 100 females: 93.8; Marriage status: 21.4% never married, 64.8% now married, 1.2% separated, 6.1% widowed, 7.6% divorced; Foreign born: 1.9%; Speak English only: 93.7%; With disability: 9.7%; Veterans: 9.1%; Ancestry: 32.4% Italian, 22.8% Irish, 22.4% German, 15.6% English, 10.2% Pennsylvania German
Employment: 18.1% management, business, and financial, 4.8% computer, engineering, and science, 12.2% education, legal, community service, arts, and media, 7.4% healthcare practitioners, 20.6% service, 20.4% sales and office, 7.3% natural resources, construction, and maintenance, 9.2% production, transportation, and material moving

Income: Per capita: $39,163; Median household: $87,917; Average household: $104,242; Households with income of $100,000 or more: 43.1%; Poverty rate: 5.2%
Educational Attainment: High school diploma or higher: 91.7%; Bachelor's degree or higher: 39.8%; Graduate/professional degree or higher: 15.8%
Housing: Homeownership rate: 91.6%; Median home value: $155,400; Median year structure built: 1957; Homeowner vacancy rate: 0.0%; Median selected monthly owner costs: $1,477 with a mortgage, $592 without a mortgage; Median gross rent: $823 per month; Rental vacancy rate: 0.0%
Health Insurance: 88.6% have insurance; 83.2% have private insurance; 21.6% have public insurance; 11.4% do not have insurance; 32.5% of children under 18 do not have insurance
Transportation: Commute: 95.5% car, 0.1% public transportation, 0.6% walk, 1.6% work from home; Mean travel time to work: 23.3 minutes

MENTZ (town). Covers a land area of 16.922 square miles and a water area of 0.260 square miles. Located at 43.04° N. Lat; 76.63° W. Long.
Population: 2,309; Growth (since 2000): -5.6%; Density: 136.5 persons per square mile; Race: 96.1% White, 1.1% Black/African American, 0.2% Asian, 0.0% American Indian/Alaska Native, 0.0% Native Hawaiian/Other Pacific Islander, 2.6% Two or more races, 2.1% Hispanic of any race; Average household size: 2.52; Median age: 39.0; Age under 18: 21.7%; Age 65 and over: 16.3%; Males per 100 females: 95.6; Marriage status: 32.0% never married, 53.3% now married, 3.2% separated, 6.6% widowed, 8.1% divorced; Foreign born: 0.7%; Speak English only: 98.7%; With disability: 16.1%; Veterans: 8.2%; Ancestry: 22.3% Irish, 19.7% German, 18.7% English, 10.6% Italian, 7.1% Dutch
Employment: 8.0% management, business, and financial, 2.1% computer, engineering, and science, 5.9% education, legal, community service, arts, and media, 5.3% healthcare practitioners, 19.0% service, 24.8% sales and office, 13.9% natural resources, construction, and maintenance, 21.1% production, transportation, and material moving
Income: Per capita: $22,935; Median household: $53,289; Average household: $57,201; Households with income of $100,000 or more: 13.5%; Poverty rate: 10.8%
Educational Attainment: High school diploma or higher: 86.1%; Bachelor's degree or higher: 11.0%; Graduate/professional degree or higher: 3.0%
Housing: Homeownership rate: 82.9%; Median home value: $75,900; Median year structure built: 1960; Homeowner vacancy rate: 0.5%; Median selected monthly owner costs: $1,086 with a mortgage, $449 without a mortgage; Median gross rent: $777 per month; Rental vacancy rate: 4.7%
Health Insurance: 92.4% have insurance; 67.3% have private insurance; 37.5% have public insurance; 7.6% do not have insurance; 1.3% of children under 18 do not have insurance
Transportation: Commute: 93.9% car, 0.0% public transportation, 1.2% walk, 2.0% work from home; Mean travel time to work: 22.3 minutes
Additional Information Contacts
Town of Mentz . . . . (315) 776-8692
  http://www.townofmentz.com

MERIDIAN (village). Covers a land area of 0.691 square miles and a water area of 0 square miles. Located at 43.16° N. Lat; 76.54° W. Long. Elevation is 453 feet.
Population: 296; Growth (since 2000): -15.4%; Density: 428.5 persons per square mile; Race: 96.6% White, 0.0% Black/African American, 0.0% Asian, 0.3% American Indian/Alaska Native, 0.0% Native Hawaiian/Other Pacific Islander, 3.0% Two or more races, 2.4% Hispanic of any race; Average household size: 3.12; Median age: 34.5; Age under 18: 34.8%; Age 65 and over: 8.1%; Males per 100 females: 103.3; Marriage status: 27.3% never married, 58.3% now married, 0.0% separated, 6.0% widowed, 8.3% divorced; Foreign born: 0.0%; Speak English only: 96.7%; With disability: 11.8%; Veterans: 13.0%; Ancestry: 26.0% Irish, 18.2% German, 11.5% English, 6.8% Italian, 6.1% Polish
Employment: 17.4% management, business, and financial, 1.4% computer, engineering, and science, 10.9% education, legal, community service, arts, and media, 2.2% healthcare practitioners, 10.1% service, 20.3% sales and office, 21.0% natural resources, construction, and maintenance, 16.7% production, transportation, and material moving
Income: Per capita: $24,608; Median household: $70,469; Average household: $73,234; Households with income of $100,000 or more: 23.2%; Poverty rate: 18.4%

Educational Attainment: High school diploma or higher: 90.7%; Bachelor's degree or higher: 19.7%; Graduate/professional degree or higher: 5.5%
Housing: Homeownership rate: 72.6%; Median home value: $100,600; Median year structure built: Before 1940; Homeowner vacancy rate: 6.8%; Median selected monthly owner costs: $1,338 with a mortgage, $505 without a mortgage; Median gross rent: $755 per month; Rental vacancy rate: 0.0%
Health Insurance: 95.3% have insurance; 73.0% have private insurance; 32.1% have public insurance; 4.7% do not have insurance; 3.9% of children under 18 do not have insurance
Transportation: Commute: 93.8% car, 2.3% public transportation, 0.0% walk, 3.1% work from home; Mean travel time to work: 26.3 minutes

MONTEZUMA (town). Covers a land area of 18.242 square miles and a water area of 0.473 square miles. Located at 43.01° N. Lat; 76.70° W. Long. Elevation is 397 feet.
Population: 1,457; Growth (since 2000): 1.8%; Density: 79.9 persons per square mile; Race: 97.6% White, 0.3% Black/African American, 0.9% Asian, 0.3% American Indian/Alaska Native, 0.0% Native Hawaiian/Other Pacific Islander, 0.1% Two or more races, 2.4% Hispanic of any race; Average household size: 2.76; Median age: 42.4; Age under 18: 21.1%; Age 65 and over: 13.3%; Males per 100 females: 102.7; Marriage status: 27.7% never married, 56.0% now married, 2.2% separated, 5.2% widowed, 11.1% divorced; Foreign born: 1.4%; Speak English only: 97.8%; With disability: 19.2%; Veterans: 12.3%; Ancestry: 23.0% English, 21.6% German, 19.1% Irish, 9.5% Italian, 5.8% French
Employment: 11.0% management, business, and financial, 2.0% computer, engineering, and science, 7.3% education, legal, community service, arts, and media, 2.9% healthcare practitioners, 20.5% service, 21.9% sales and office, 12.9% natural resources, construction, and maintenance, 21.5% production, transportation, and material moving
Income: Per capita: $24,401; Median household: $54,875; Average household: $66,939; Households with income of $100,000 or more: 19.5%; Poverty rate: 11.8%
Educational Attainment: High school diploma or higher: 84.3%; Bachelor's degree or higher: 8.2%; Graduate/professional degree or higher: 2.6%
Housing: Homeownership rate: 79.7%; Median home value: $92,200; Median year structure built: 1975; Homeowner vacancy rate: 0.0%; Median selected monthly owner costs: $1,144 with a mortgage, $448 without a mortgage; Median gross rent: $800 per month; Rental vacancy rate: 0.0%
Health Insurance: 94.0% have insurance; 67.7% have private insurance; 44.5% have public insurance; 6.0% do not have insurance; 0.0% of children under 18 do not have insurance
Transportation: Commute: 96.5% car, 0.0% public transportation, 0.0% walk, 3.5% work from home; Mean travel time to work: 26.6 minutes
Additional Information Contacts
Town of Montezuma . . . . (315) 776-8844
  http://co.cayuga.ny.us/montezuma

MORAVIA (town). Covers a land area of 28.884 square miles and a water area of 0.753 square miles. Located at 42.73° N. Lat; 76.41° W. Long. Elevation is 735 feet.
History: Fillmore Glen State Park and the birthplace of President Millard Fillmore are nearby. Incorporated 1837.
Population: 3,498; Growth (since 2000): -13.4%; Density: 121.1 persons per square mile; Race: 81.2% White, 13.2% Black/African American, 0.4% Asian, 0.0% American Indian/Alaska Native, 0.0% Native Hawaiian/Other Pacific Islander, 3.5% Two or more races, 4.1% Hispanic of any race; Average household size: 2.41; Median age: 41.1; Age under 18: 16.6%; Age 65 and over: 14.9%; Males per 100 females: 173.7; Marriage status: 38.9% never married, 43.2% now married, 4.1% separated, 6.0% widowed, 11.9% divorced; Foreign born: 1.0%; Speak English only: 95.0%; With disability: 15.8%; Veterans: 8.8%; Ancestry: 19.0% Irish, 15.3% German, 13.0% English, 6.6% Italian, 4.2% American
Employment: 12.7% management, business, and financial, 3.8% computer, engineering, and science, 8.6% education, legal, community service, arts, and media, 3.9% healthcare practitioners, 16.6% service, 24.0% sales and office, 11.6% natural resources, construction, and maintenance, 18.8% production, transportation, and material moving
Income: Per capita: $20,120; Median household: $56,364; Average household: $64,353; Households with income of $100,000 or more: 20.6%; Poverty rate: 12.2%

Educational Attainment: High school diploma or higher: 81.9%; Bachelor's degree or higher: 12.4%; Graduate/professional degree or higher: 5.0%

School District(s)
Moravia Central SD (PK-12)
 Enrollment: 1,022 . . . . (315) 497-2670
Housing: Homeownership rate: 70.3%; Median home value: $117,300; Median year structure built: 1947; Homeowner vacancy rate: 2.1%; Median selected monthly owner costs: $1,138 with a mortgage, $526 without a mortgage; Median gross rent: $627 per month; Rental vacancy rate: 8.1%
Health Insurance: 96.3% have insurance; 68.9% have private insurance; 44.0% have public insurance; 3.7% do not have insurance; 0.7% of children under 18 do not have insurance
Newspapers: Republican-Register (weekly circulation 1,000)
Transportation: Commute: 94.2% car, 0.0% public transportation, 2.6% walk, 3.2% work from home; Mean travel time to work: 27.8 minutes
Additional Information Contacts
Town of Moravia . . . . (315) 497-1972
 http://co.cayuga.ny.us/townofmoravia

MORAVIA (village).
Covers a land area of 1.703 square miles and a water area of 0.021 square miles. Located at 42.71° N. Lat; 76.42° W. Long. Elevation is 735 feet.
Population: 1,469; Growth (since 2000): 7.8%; Density: 862.5 persons per square mile; Race: 94.5% White, 0.0% Black/African American, 1.0% Asian, 0.0% American Indian/Alaska Native, 0.0% Native Hawaiian/Other Pacific Islander, 3.9% Two or more races, 0.6% Hispanic of any race; Average household size: 2.31; Median age: 44.9; Age under 18: 21.4%; Age 65 and over: 21.1%; Males per 100 females: 92.8; Marriage status: 27.8% never married, 48.4% now married, 2.1% separated, 10.5% widowed, 13.3% divorced; Foreign born: 1.2%; Speak English only: 98.9%; With disability: 19.8%; Veterans: 11.1%; Ancestry: 25.8% Irish, 21.2% German, 20.6% English, 8.5% Italian, 5.8% Dutch
Employment: 11.2% management, business, and financial, 4.8% computer, engineering, and science, 9.8% education, legal, community service, arts, and media, 5.2% healthcare practitioners, 18.8% service, 24.9% sales and office, 6.3% natural resources, construction, and maintenance, 19.1% production, transportation, and material moving
Income: Per capita: $24,583; Median household: $52,083; Average household: $56,875; Households with income of $100,000 or more: 15.1%; Poverty rate: 10.8%
Educational Attainment: High school diploma or higher: 90.2%; Bachelor's degree or higher: 19.2%; Graduate/professional degree or higher: 8.8%

School District(s)
Moravia Central SD (PK-12)
 Enrollment: 1,022 . . . . (315) 497-2670
Housing: Homeownership rate: 62.8%; Median home value: $103,600; Median year structure built: Before 1940; Homeowner vacancy rate: 0.0%; Median selected monthly owner costs: $1,170 with a mortgage, $471 without a mortgage; Median gross rent: $603 per month; Rental vacancy rate: 6.1%
Health Insurance: 97.1% have insurance; 72.9% have private insurance; 43.5% have public insurance; 2.9% do not have insurance; 1.3% of children under 18 do not have insurance
Newspapers: Republican-Register (weekly circulation 1,000)
Transportation: Commute: 93.2% car, 0.0% public transportation, 4.0% walk, 2.8% work from home; Mean travel time to work: 23.1 minutes
Additional Information Contacts
Village of Moravia . . . . (315) 497-1820
 http://co.cayuga.ny.us/villageofmoravia

NILES (town).
Covers a land area of 38.975 square miles and a water area of 4.376 square miles. Located at 42.82° N. Lat; 76.40° W. Long. Elevation is 915 feet.
Population: 1,311; Growth (since 2000): 8.5%; Density: 33.6 persons per square mile; Race: 96.2% White, 1.8% Black/African American, 0.4% Asian, 0.0% American Indian/Alaska Native, 0.0% Native Hawaiian/Other Pacific Islander, 1.1% Two or more races, 1.4% Hispanic of any race; Average household size: 2.66; Median age: 44.1; Age under 18: 24.9%; Age 65 and over: 20.0%; Males per 100 females: 111.7; Marriage status: 22.9% never married, 64.5% now married, 1.2% separated, 5.2% widowed, 7.5% divorced; Foreign born: 1.4%; Speak English only: 98.6%; With disability: 13.0%; Veterans: 9.4%; Ancestry: 21.3% English, 21.1% German, 18.3% Irish, 7.6% American, 7.1% French Canadian

Employment: 17.2% management, business, and financial, 2.8% computer, engineering, and science, 11.4% education, legal, community service, arts, and media, 3.3% healthcare practitioners, 13.7% service, 16.7% sales and office, 10.9% natural resources, construction, and maintenance, 24.1% production, transportation, and material moving
Income: Per capita: $31,979; Median household: $64,318; Average household: $83,366; Households with income of $100,000 or more: 26.5%; Poverty rate: 4.1%
Educational Attainment: High school diploma or higher: 93.2%; Bachelor's degree or higher: 28.0%; Graduate/professional degree or higher: 11.4%
Housing: Homeownership rate: 94.7%; Median home value: $168,900; Median year structure built: 1973; Homeowner vacancy rate: 0.0%; Median selected monthly owner costs: $1,356 with a mortgage, $676 without a mortgage; Median gross rent: $817 per month; Rental vacancy rate: 0.0%
Health Insurance: 92.2% have insurance; 78.4% have private insurance; 34.6% have public insurance; 7.8% do not have insurance; 13.3% of children under 18 do not have insurance
Transportation: Commute: 91.8% car, 0.0% public transportation, 1.0% walk, 6.6% work from home; Mean travel time to work: 25.6 minutes
Additional Information Contacts
Town of Niles. . . . . (315) 497-0066
 http://co.cayuga.ny.us/niles

OWASCO (town).
Covers a land area of 20.881 square miles and a water area of 2.594 square miles. Located at 42.89° N. Lat; 76.49° W. Long. Elevation is 892 feet.
Population: 3,696; Growth (since 2000): -1.6%; Density: 177.0 persons per square mile; Race: 99.6% White, 0.0% Black/African American, 0.1% Asian, 0.0% American Indian/Alaska Native, 0.0% Native Hawaiian/Other Pacific Islander, 0.3% Two or more races, 0.2% Hispanic of any race; Average household size: 2.43; Median age: 50.5; Age under 18: 18.7%; Age 65 and over: 22.2%; Males per 100 females: 97.9; Marriage status: 22.8% never married, 60.2% now married, 1.2% separated, 8.2% widowed, 8.8% divorced; Foreign born: 2.2%; Speak English only: 93.2%; With disability: 8.2%; Veterans: 8.9%; Ancestry: 29.0% Italian, 24.1% Irish, 18.8% German, 17.1% English, 6.7% Pennsylvania German
Employment: 16.0% management, business, and financial, 4.9% computer, engineering, and science, 15.3% education, legal, community service, arts, and media, 8.9% healthcare practitioners, 19.7% service, 19.6% sales and office, 7.9% natural resources, construction, and maintenance, 7.7% production, transportation, and material moving
Income: Per capita: $42,317; Median household: $85,430; Average household: $102,498; Households with income of $100,000 or more: 41.7%; Poverty rate: 3.8%
Educational Attainment: High school diploma or higher: 91.6%; Bachelor's degree or higher: 42.7%; Graduate/professional degree or higher: 18.5%
Housing: Homeownership rate: 93.3%; Median home value: $179,700; Median year structure built: 1961; Homeowner vacancy rate: 0.0%; Median selected monthly owner costs: $1,564 with a mortgage, $604 without a mortgage; Median gross rent: $837 per month; Rental vacancy rate: 0.0%
Health Insurance: 92.8% have insurance; 86.6% have private insurance; 26.6% have public insurance; 7.2% do not have insurance; 23.4% of children under 18 do not have insurance
Transportation: Commute: 96.5% car, 0.1% public transportation, 0.9% walk, 1.1% work from home; Mean travel time to work: 22.4 minutes
Additional Information Contacts
Town of Owasco . . . . (315) 253-9021
 http://co.cayuga.ny.us/owasco

PORT BYRON (village).
Covers a land area of 0.979 square miles and a water area of 0.029 square miles. Located at 43.04° N. Lat; 76.63° W. Long. Elevation is 407 feet.
Population: 1,141; Growth (since 2000): -12.0%; Density: 1,165.7 persons per square mile; Race: 95.9% White, 1.0% Black/African American, 0.4% Asian, 0.0% American Indian/Alaska Native, 0.0% Native Hawaiian/Other Pacific Islander, 2.6% Two or more races, 4.0% Hispanic of any race; Average household size: 2.55; Median age: 39.5; Age under 18: 20.6%; Age 65 and over: 15.5%; Males per 100 females: 90.3; Marriage status: 38.5% never married, 46.3% now married, 3.9% separated, 5.2% widowed, 10.0% divorced; Foreign born: 1.1%; Speak English only: 98.2%; With disability: 15.0%; Veterans: 9.4%; Ancestry: 28.2% Irish, 23.3% English, 15.1% German, 11.1% Italian, 6.7% Polish

Employment: 7.6% management, business, and financial, 1.5% computer, engineering, and science, 7.5% education, legal, community service, arts, and media, 8.1% healthcare practitioners, 19.9% service, 24.5% sales and office, 12.1% natural resources, construction, and maintenance, 18.7% production, transportation, and material moving
Income: Per capita: $22,287; Median household: $47,368; Average household: $55,673; Households with income of $100,000 or more: 16.1%; Poverty rate: 14.4%
Educational Attainment: High school diploma or higher: 87.4%; Bachelor's degree or higher: 9.9%; Graduate/professional degree or higher: 2.7%

School District(s)

Port Byron Central SD (PK-12)
    Enrollment: 965. . . . . (315) 776-5728
Housing: Homeownership rate: 69.2%; Median home value: $79,700; Median year structure built: 1952; Homeowner vacancy rate: 1.3%; Median selected monthly owner costs: $1,055 with a mortgage, $473 without a mortgage; Median gross rent: $772 per month; Rental vacancy rate: 5.8%
Health Insurance: 91.0% have insurance; 65.6% have private insurance; 37.5% have public insurance; 9.0% do not have insurance; 3.0% of children under 18 do not have insurance
Safety: Violent crime rate: 0.0 per 10,000 population; Property crime rate: 8.2 per 10,000 population
Transportation: Commute: 96.2% car, 0.0% public transportation, 1.4% walk, 0.5% work from home; Mean travel time to work: 22.0 minutes
Additional Information Contacts
Village of Port Byron . . . . (315) 776-4321
    http://www.villageofportbyron.com

SCIPIO (town). Covers a land area of 36.558 square miles and a water area of 2.751 square miles. Located at 42.79° N. Lat; 76.57° W. Long.
Population: 1,734; Growth (since 2000): 12.8%; Density: 47.4 persons per square mile; Race: 99.2% White, 0.2% Black/African American, 0.0% Asian, 0.0% American Indian/Alaska Native, 0.0% Native Hawaiian/Other Pacific Islander, 0.6% Two or more races, 2.7% Hispanic of any race; Average household size: 2.66; Median age: 37.4; Age under 18: 24.2%; Age 65 and over: 15.2%; Males per 100 females: 106.4; Marriage status: 26.6% never married, 59.0% now married, 1.1% separated, 6.0% widowed, 8.3% divorced; Foreign born: 2.0%; Speak English only: 95.7%; With disability: 10.0%; Veterans: 8.0%; Ancestry: 19.2% Irish, 19.0% German, 13.7% English, 8.2% Italian, 5.4% Dutch
Employment: 12.3% management, business, and financial, 3.5% computer, engineering, and science, 13.7% education, legal, community service, arts, and media, 5.4% healthcare practitioners, 16.2% service, 20.5% sales and office, 13.5% natural resources, construction, and maintenance, 14.8% production, transportation, and material moving
Income: Per capita: $30,680; Median household: $59,250; Average household: $80,400; Households with income of $100,000 or more: 25.8%; Poverty rate: 7.8%
Educational Attainment: High school diploma or higher: 85.4%; Bachelor's degree or higher: 21.4%; Graduate/professional degree or higher: 9.4%
Housing: Homeownership rate: 75.7%; Median home value: $135,300; Median year structure built: 1957; Homeowner vacancy rate: 3.7%; Median selected monthly owner costs: $1,169 with a mortgage, $525 without a mortgage; Median gross rent: $900 per month; Rental vacancy rate: 0.0%
Health Insurance: 86.0% have insurance; 67.9% have private insurance; 32.6% have public insurance; 14.0% do not have insurance; 17.8% of children under 18 do not have insurance
Transportation: Commute: 83.9% car, 0.3% public transportation, 6.6% walk, 8.2% work from home; Mean travel time to work: 22.2 minutes
Additional Information Contacts
Town of Scipio. . . . . (315) 364-5740
    http://co.cayuga.ny.us/scipio

SCIPIO CENTER (unincorporated postal area)
ZCTA: 13147
    Covers a land area of 35.885 square miles and a water area of 0.007 square miles. Located at 42.78° N. Lat; 76.57° W. Long. Elevation is 1,191 feet.
Population: 1,316; Growth (since 2000): 9.3%; Density: 36.7 persons per square mile; Race: 97.5% White, 0.7% Black/African American, 0.0% Asian, 0.0% American Indian/Alaska Native, 0.0% Native Hawaiian/Other Pacific Islander, 0.5% Two or more races, 7.9% Hispanic of any race; Average household size: 2.60; Median age: 40.1;

Age under 18: 20.2%; Age 65 and over: 14.0%; Males per 100 females: 113.1; Marriage status: 27.1% never married, 56.5% now married, 1.6% separated, 6.3% widowed, 10.1% divorced; Foreign born: 4.3%; Speak English only: 92.0%; With disability: 10.3%; Veterans: 8.1%; Ancestry: 19.8% Irish, 15.4% German, 14.0% English, 5.9% Italian, 5.1% French
Employment: 9.5% management, business, and financial, 2.1% computer, engineering, and science, 13.3% education, legal, community service, arts, and media, 4.5% healthcare practitioners, 20.0% service, 19.5% sales and office, 15.2% natural resources, construction, and maintenance, 15.9% production, transportation, and material moving
Income: Per capita: $30,650; Median household: $54,792; Average household: $79,011; Households with income of $100,000 or more: 22.9%; Poverty rate: 9.7%
Educational Attainment: High school diploma or higher: 81.1%; Bachelor's degree or higher: 15.5%; Graduate/professional degree or higher: 6.3%
Housing: Homeownership rate: 72.2%; Median home value: $109,100; Median year structure built: Before 1940; Homeowner vacancy rate: 0.0%; Median selected monthly owner costs: $1,003 with a mortgage, $534 without a mortgage; Median gross rent: $911 per month; Rental vacancy rate: 0.0%
Health Insurance: 87.0% have insurance; 63.6% have private insurance; 35.3% have public insurance; 13.0% do not have insurance; 9.8% of children under 18 do not have insurance
Transportation: Commute: 89.3% car, 0.0% public transportation, 1.1% walk, 9.1% work from home; Mean travel time to work: 25.0 minutes

SEMPRONIUS (town). Covers a land area of 29.339 square miles and a water area of 0.379 square miles. Located at 42.74° N. Lat; 76.33° W. Long. Elevation is 1,598 feet.
Population: 862; Growth (since 2000): -3.5%; Density: 29.4 persons per square mile; Race: 98.1% White, 0.2% Black/African American, 0.0% Asian, 1.2% American Indian/Alaska Native, 0.0% Native Hawaiian/Other Pacific Islander, 0.5% Two or more races, 0.1% Hispanic of any race; Average household size: 2.43; Median age: 43.1; Age under 18: 23.3%; Age 65 and over: 16.1%; Males per 100 females: 114.6; Marriage status: 27.1% never married, 51.7% now married, 3.1% separated, 5.8% widowed, 15.4% divorced; Foreign born: 0.2%; Speak English only: 98.7%; With disability: 13.9%; Veterans: 9.5%; Ancestry: 23.3% German, 20.8% Irish, 15.0% English, 11.1% American, 4.5% French
Employment: 8.8% management, business, and financial, 1.0% computer, engineering, and science, 6.6% education, legal, community service, arts, and media, 6.6% healthcare practitioners, 17.1% service, 14.9% sales and office, 16.8% natural resources, construction, and maintenance, 28.3% production, transportation, and material moving
Income: Per capita: $24,308; Median household: $49,306; Average household: $58,978; Households with income of $100,000 or more: 17.5%; Poverty rate: 14.2%
Educational Attainment: High school diploma or higher: 91.2%; Bachelor's degree or higher: 12.9%; Graduate/professional degree or higher: 6.0%
Housing: Homeownership rate: 86.8%; Median home value: $106,800; Median year structure built: 1980; Homeowner vacancy rate: 0.0%; Median selected monthly owner costs: $1,088 with a mortgage, $502 without a mortgage; Median gross rent: $736 per month; Rental vacancy rate: 0.0%
Health Insurance: 96.1% have insurance; 66.1% have private insurance; 41.3% have public insurance; 3.9% do not have insurance; 1.0% of children under 18 do not have insurance
Transportation: Commute: 92.1% car, 0.0% public transportation, 0.5% walk, 4.7% work from home; Mean travel time to work: 28.4 minutes
Additional Information Contacts
Town of Sempronius . . . . (315) 496-2376
    http://co.cayuga.ny.us/sempronius

SENNETT (town). Covers a land area of 28.820 square miles and a water area of 0.024 square miles. Located at 42.98° N. Lat; 76.52° W. Long. Elevation is 594 feet.
Population: 3,518; Growth (since 2000): 8.4%; Density: 122.1 persons per square mile; Race: 94.5% White, 2.7% Black/African American, 1.0% Asian, 0.0% American Indian/Alaska Native, 0.0% Native Hawaiian/Other Pacific Islander, 1.6% Two or more races, 1.3% Hispanic of any race; Average household size: 2.47; Median age: 47.5; Age under 18: 20.8%; Age 65 and over: 19.6%; Males per 100 females: 102.8; Marriage status: 26.4% never married, 55.0% now married, 1.2% separated, 10.3% widowed, 8.3% divorced; Foreign born: 1.4%; Speak English only: 98.5%;

With disability: 13.7%; Veterans: 10.5%; Ancestry: 24.9% Irish, 22.3% German, 17.4% Italian, 16.5% English, 6.1% French
Employment: 16.2% management, business, and financial, 4.9% computer, engineering, and science, 11.9% education, legal, community service, arts, and media, 7.4% healthcare practitioners, 18.3% service, 25.5% sales and office, 7.6% natural resources, construction, and maintenance, 8.3% production, transportation, and material moving
Income: Per capita: $36,838; Median household: $81,750; Average household: $98,081; Households with income of $100,000 or more: 40.2%; Poverty rate: 3.1%
Educational Attainment: High school diploma or higher: 92.1%; Bachelor's degree or higher: 33.6%; Graduate/professional degree or higher: 12.3%
Housing: Homeownership rate: 93.1%; Median home value: $180,200; Median year structure built: 1969; Homeowner vacancy rate: 0.0%; Median selected monthly owner costs: $1,675 with a mortgage, $598 without a mortgage; Median gross rent: $923 per month; Rental vacancy rate: 22.6%
Health Insurance: 97.1% have insurance; 84.8% have private insurance; 30.5% have public insurance; 2.9% do not have insurance; 3.9% of children under 18 do not have insurance
Transportation: Commute: 92.0% car, 0.4% public transportation, 1.0% walk, 5.7% work from home; Mean travel time to work: 25.2 minutes
Additional Information Contacts
Town of Sennett . . . . (315) 253-3712
    http://co.cayuga.ny.us/sennett

SPRINGPORT (town). Covers a land area of 21.399 square miles and a water area of 5.431 square miles. Located at 42.85° N. Lat; 76.67° W. Long.
Population: 2,357; Growth (since 2000): 4.5%; Density: 110.1 persons per square mile; Race: 89.0% White, 0.5% Black/African American, 0.6% Asian, 0.2% American Indian/Alaska Native, 0.0% Native Hawaiian/Other Pacific Islander, 8.4% Two or more races, 8.5% Hispanic of any race; Average household size: 2.51; Median age: 43.7; Age under 18: 21.2%; Age 65 and over: 19.2%; Males per 100 females: 98.9; Marriage status: 28.8% never married, 55.6% now married, 4.0% separated, 7.5% widowed, 8.1% divorced; Foreign born: 2.7%; Speak English only: 96.3%; With disability: 11.5%; Veterans: 8.7%; Ancestry: 23.9% Irish, 21.9% English, 18.9% German, 10.8% Italian, 5.5% Polish
Employment: 14.4% management, business, and financial, 1.9% computer, engineering, and science, 13.3% education, legal, community service, arts, and media, 4.1% healthcare practitioners, 24.1% service, 18.6% sales and office, 8.5% natural resources, construction, and maintenance, 15.1% production, transportation, and material moving
Income: Per capita: $30,221; Median household: $66,458; Average household: $76,767; Households with income of $100,000 or more: 28.2%; Poverty rate: 10.4%
Educational Attainment: High school diploma or higher: 90.2%; Bachelor's degree or higher: 23.4%; Graduate/professional degree or higher: 9.2%
Housing: Homeownership rate: 77.8%; Median home value: $123,800; Median year structure built: 1968; Homeowner vacancy rate: 2.5%; Median selected monthly owner costs: $1,295 with a mortgage, $506 without a mortgage; Median gross rent: n/a per month; Rental vacancy rate: 0.0%
Health Insurance: 91.9% have insurance; 70.3% have private insurance; 39.2% have public insurance; 8.1% do not have insurance; 5.9% of children under 18 do not have insurance
Transportation: Commute: 89.1% car, 0.0% public transportation, 6.5% walk, 3.3% work from home; Mean travel time to work: 22.2 minutes
Additional Information Contacts
Town of Springport . . . . (315) 889-7717
    http://co.cayuga.ny.us/springport

STERLING (town). Covers a land area of 45.454 square miles and a water area of 1.661 square miles. Located at 43.32° N. Lat; 76.66° W. Long. Elevation is 315 feet.
Population: 3,042; Growth (since 2000): -11.4%; Density: 66.9 persons per square mile; Race: 98.9% White, 0.0% Black/African American, 0.2% Asian, 0.0% American Indian/Alaska Native, 0.0% Native Hawaiian/Other Pacific Islander, 0.7% Two or more races, 0.3% Hispanic of any race; Average household size: 2.44; Median age: 47.4; Age under 18: 20.6%; Age 65 and over: 20.9%; Males per 100 females: 102.9; Marriage status: 24.5% never married, 53.7% now married, 1.5% separated, 8.6% widowed, 13.2% divorced; Foreign born: 1.2%; Speak English only: 99.0%;

With disability: 16.6%; Veterans: 12.5%; Ancestry: 20.6% German, 14.6% English, 14.0% Irish, 7.7% French, 7.3% Italian
Employment: 12.0% management, business, and financial, 3.0% computer, engineering, and science, 10.7% education, legal, community service, arts, and media, 5.6% healthcare practitioners, 10.4% service, 21.5% sales and office, 19.6% natural resources, construction, and maintenance, 17.3% production, transportation, and material moving
Income: Per capita: $31,104; Median household: $57,528; Average household: $75,222; Households with income of $100,000 or more: 20.6%; Poverty rate: 16.6%
Educational Attainment: High school diploma or higher: 91.9%; Bachelor's degree or higher: 18.5%; Graduate/professional degree or higher: 7.9%
Housing: Homeownership rate: 87.6%; Median home value: $99,000; Median year structure built: 1973; Homeowner vacancy rate: 4.0%; Median selected monthly owner costs: $1,136 with a mortgage, $520 without a mortgage; Median gross rent: $705 per month; Rental vacancy rate: 3.1%
Health Insurance: 90.7% have insurance; 62.6% have private insurance; 44.2% have public insurance; 9.3% do not have insurance; 5.1% of children under 18 do not have insurance
Transportation: Commute: 95.0% car, 1.1% public transportation, 0.8% walk, 3.0% work from home; Mean travel time to work: 31.9 minutes
Additional Information Contacts
Town of Sterling . . . . (315) 947-5666
    http://co.cayuga.ny.us/sterling

SUMMERHILL (town). Covers a land area of 25.861 square miles and a water area of 0.123 square miles. Located at 42.65° N. Lat; 76.32° W. Long.
Population: 1,268; Growth (since 2000): 15.5%; Density: 49.0 persons per square mile; Race: 99.0% White, 0.4% Black/African American, 0.0% Asian, 0.2% American Indian/Alaska Native, 0.0% Native Hawaiian/Other Pacific Islander, 0.0% Two or more races, 1.3% Hispanic of any race; Average household size: 2.74; Median age: 42.7; Age under 18: 22.1%; Age 65 and over: 15.2%; Males per 100 females: 104.2; Marriage status: 30.9% never married, 51.9% now married, 2.4% separated, 8.6% widowed, 8.7% divorced; Foreign born: 0.5%; Speak English only: 98.0%; With disability: 10.7%; Veterans: 11.2%; Ancestry: 17.7% German, 15.5% English, 13.6% Irish, 7.3% French, 6.9% American
Employment: 11.7% management, business, and financial, 5.8% computer, engineering, and science, 8.3% education, legal, community service, arts, and media, 7.2% healthcare practitioners, 13.2% service, 24.0% sales and office, 17.3% natural resources, construction, and maintenance, 12.6% production, transportation, and material moving
Income: Per capita: $27,612; Median household: $60,662; Average household: $76,621; Households with income of $100,000 or more: 19.1%; Poverty rate: 18.1%
Educational Attainment: High school diploma or higher: 89.7%; Bachelor's degree or higher: 19.6%; Graduate/professional degree or higher: 6.4%
Housing: Homeownership rate: 89.6%; Median home value: $116,000; Median year structure built: 1976; Homeowner vacancy rate: 1.0%; Median selected monthly owner costs: $1,325 with a mortgage, $514 without a mortgage; Median gross rent: $833 per month; Rental vacancy rate: 0.0%
Health Insurance: 90.1% have insurance; 65.9% have private insurance; 37.8% have public insurance; 9.9% do not have insurance; 6.8% of children under 18 do not have insurance
Transportation: Commute: 93.1% car, 0.0% public transportation, 3.7% walk, 1.8% work from home; Mean travel time to work: 23.0 minutes
Additional Information Contacts
Town of Summerhill . . . . (315) 497-3494
    http://co.cayuga.ny.us/summerhill

THROOP (town). Covers a land area of 18.586 square miles and a water area of 0.111 square miles. Located at 42.98° N. Lat; 76.62° W. Long. Elevation is 548 feet.
Population: 1,956; Growth (since 2000): 7.2%; Density: 105.2 persons per square mile; Race: 95.9% White, 1.8% Black/African American, 0.2% Asian, 0.0% American Indian/Alaska Native, 0.0% Native Hawaiian/Other Pacific Islander, 1.9% Two or more races, 1.9% Hispanic of any race; Average household size: 2.40; Median age: 47.6; Age under 18: 20.4%; Age 65 and over: 19.4%; Males per 100 females: 99.0; Marriage status: 22.2% never married, 58.2% now married, 1.7% separated, 8.9% widowed, 10.7% divorced; Foreign born: 0.9%; Speak English only: 98.5%;

With disability: 13.4%; Veterans: 11.0%; Ancestry: 27.9% Irish, 21.4% Italian, 19.0% German, 16.9% English, 11.1% Polish
Employment: 14.7% management, business, and financial, 1.6% computer, engineering, and science, 9.8% education, legal, community service, arts, and media, 5.5% healthcare practitioners, 23.3% service, 22.8% sales and office, 11.6% natural resources, construction, and maintenance, 10.8% production, transportation, and material moving
Income: Per capita: $32,028; Median household: $65,417; Average household: $76,962; Households with income of $100,000 or more: 27.6%; Poverty rate: 9.5%
Educational Attainment: High school diploma or higher: 91.5%; Bachelor's degree or higher: 19.8%; Graduate/professional degree or higher: 8.9%
Housing: Homeownership rate: 91.4%; Median home value: $144,800; Median year structure built: 1963; Homeowner vacancy rate: 1.3%; Median selected monthly owner costs: $1,422 with a mortgage, $590 without a mortgage; Median gross rent: $838 per month; Rental vacancy rate: 0.0%
Health Insurance: 96.8% have insurance; 82.6% have private insurance; 34.6% have public insurance; 3.2% do not have insurance; 0.7% of children under 18 do not have insurance
Transportation: Commute: 92.2% car, 0.0% public transportation, 1.1% walk, 5.8% work from home; Mean travel time to work: 23.9 minutes
Additional Information Contacts
Town of Throop . . . . (315) 252-7373
    http://co.cayuga.ny.us/throop

UNION SPRINGS (village). Covers a land area of 1.737 square miles and a water area of 0.015 square miles. Located at 42.85° N. Lat; 76.69° W. Long. Elevation is 410 feet.

Population: 1,195; Growth (since 2000): 11.3%; Density: 687.9 persons per square mile; Race: 79.7% White, 1.0% Black/African American, 1.1% Asian, 0.4% American Indian/Alaska Native, 0.0% Native Hawaiian/Other Pacific Islander, 15.1% Two or more races, 15.5% Hispanic of any race; Average household size: 2.42; Median age: 39.0; Age under 18: 23.6%; Age 65 and over: 17.5%; Males per 100 females: 97.5; Marriage status: 29.9% never married, 54.7% now married, 5.7% separated, 7.2% widowed, 8.1% divorced; Foreign born: 3.4%; Speak English only: 94.8%; With disability: 12.1%; Veterans: 8.9%; Ancestry: 19.8% German, 18.4% Irish, 18.3% English, 8.3% Italian, 4.4% French
Employment: 13.1% management, business, and financial, 3.1% computer, engineering, and science, 14.3% education, legal, community service, arts, and media, 3.3% healthcare practitioners, 27.6% service, 20.5% sales and office, 4.4% natural resources, construction, and maintenance, 13.7% production, transportation, and material moving
Income: Per capita: $26,513; Median household: $61,875; Average household: $65,936; Households with income of $100,000 or more: 21.4%; Poverty rate: 16.8%
Educational Attainment: High school diploma or higher: 93.4%; Bachelor's degree or higher: 22.1%; Graduate/professional degree or higher: 8.8%

School District(s)
Union Springs Central SD (PK-12)
    Enrollment: 863 . . . . (315) 889-4101
Housing: Homeownership rate: 69.3%; Median home value: $125,000; Median year structure built: 1943; Homeowner vacancy rate: 5.2%; Median selected monthly owner costs: $1,071 with a mortgage, $470 without a mortgage; Median gross rent: $482 per month; Rental vacancy rate: 0.0%
Health Insurance: 91.0% have insurance; 64.8% have private insurance; 42.8% have public insurance; 9.0% do not have insurance; 5.4% of children under 18 do not have insurance
Transportation: Commute: 80.8% car, 0.0% public transportation, 12.9% walk, 4.0% work from home; Mean travel time to work: 19.9 minutes
Additional Information Contacts
Village of Union Springs . . . . (315) 889-7341
    http://unionspringsny.com

VENICE (town). Covers a land area of 41.088 square miles and a water area of 0.200 square miles. Located at 42.72° N. Lat; 76.54° W. Long.

Population: 1,315; Growth (since 2000): 2.3%; Density: 32.0 persons per square mile; Race: 92.0% White, 0.7% Black/African American, 0.0% Asian, 0.0% American Indian/Alaska Native, 0.0% Native Hawaiian/Other Pacific Islander, 5.5% Two or more races, 10.6% Hispanic of any race; Average household size: 2.54; Median age: 40.5; Age under 18: 22.2%; Age 65 and over: 15.7%; Males per 100 females: 112.8; Marriage status: 25.9% never married, 59.4% now married, 1.9% separated, 4.9%

widowed, 9.8% divorced; Foreign born: 5.7%; Speak English only: 92.6%; With disability: 13.6%; Veterans: 9.9%; Ancestry: 20.4% English, 19.5% Irish, 14.4% German, 5.6% Italian, 3.9% Polish
Employment: 13.5% management, business, and financial, 2.9% computer, engineering, and science, 8.4% education, legal, community service, arts, and media, 3.4% healthcare practitioners, 20.5% service, 16.9% sales and office, 23.1% natural resources, construction, and maintenance, 11.2% production, transportation, and material moving
Income: Per capita: $30,908; Median household: $53,203; Average household: $77,915; Households with income of $100,000 or more: 22.2%; Poverty rate: 10.2%
Educational Attainment: High school diploma or higher: 85.8%; Bachelor's degree or higher: 25.1%; Graduate/professional degree or higher: 12.9%
Housing: Homeownership rate: 78.0%; Median home value: $119,300; Median year structure built: Before 1940; Homeowner vacancy rate: 0.0%; Median selected monthly owner costs: $1,228 with a mortgage, $502 without a mortgage; Median gross rent: $713 per month; Rental vacancy rate: 0.0%
Health Insurance: 89.6% have insurance; 61.7% have private insurance; 42.7% have public insurance; 10.4% do not have insurance; 4.0% of children under 18 do not have insurance
Transportation: Commute: 89.7% car, 0.0% public transportation, 1.8% walk, 8.0% work from home; Mean travel time to work: 26.5 minutes
Additional Information Contacts
Town of Venice . . . . (315) 364-9512
    http://co.cayuga.ny.us/venice

VICTORY (town). Covers a land area of 34.394 square miles and a water area of 0.058 square miles. Located at 43.21° N. Lat; 76.65° W. Long. Elevation is 423 feet.

Population: 1,597; Growth (since 2000): -13.1%; Density: 46.4 persons per square mile; Race: 99.0% White, 0.3% Black/African American, 0.0% Asian, 0.8% American Indian/Alaska Native, 0.0% Native Hawaiian/Other Pacific Islander, 0.0% Two or more races, 0.4% Hispanic of any race; Average household size: 2.61; Median age: 43.5; Age under 18: 24.5%; Age 65 and over: 15.9%; Males per 100 females: 103.7; Marriage status: 21.4% never married, 60.0% now married, 4.3% separated, 6.4% widowed, 12.2% divorced; Foreign born: 1.0%; Speak English only: 98.4%; With disability: 19.2%; Veterans: 10.1%; Ancestry: 27.8% German, 20.6% English, 14.7% Irish, 7.3% American, 7.2% Italian
Employment: 11.8% management, business, and financial, 4.8% computer, engineering, and science, 7.9% education, legal, community service, arts, and media, 1.7% healthcare practitioners, 16.9% service, 10.8% sales and office, 21.2% natural resources, construction, and maintenance, 24.9% production, transportation, and material moving
Income: Per capita: $22,822; Median household: $50,486; Average household: $59,682; Households with income of $100,000 or more: 14.6%; Poverty rate: 12.0%
Educational Attainment: High school diploma or higher: 86.3%; Bachelor's degree or higher: 13.0%; Graduate/professional degree or higher: 4.0%
Housing: Homeownership rate: 91.5%; Median home value: $99,500; Median year structure built: 1975; Homeowner vacancy rate: 0.0%; Median selected monthly owner costs: $959 with a mortgage, $481 without a mortgage; Median gross rent: $681 per month; Rental vacancy rate: 0.0%
Health Insurance: 86.0% have insurance; 65.3% have private insurance; 36.8% have public insurance; 14.0% do not have insurance; 18.4% of children under 18 do not have insurance
Transportation: Commute: 90.2% car, 0.6% public transportation, 0.8% walk, 6.2% work from home; Mean travel time to work: 30.4 minutes

WEEDSPORT (village). Covers a land area of 0.976 square miles and a water area of 0 square miles. Located at 43.05° N. Lat; 76.56° W. Long. Elevation is 413 feet.

History: Incorporated 1831.
Population: 2,040; Growth (since 2000): 1.1%; Density: 2,090.9 persons per square mile; Race: 95.1% White, 0.6% Black/African American, 2.1% Asian, 0.4% American Indian/Alaska Native, 0.0% Native Hawaiian/Other Pacific Islander, 1.8% Two or more races, 0.3% Hispanic of any race; Average household size: 2.40; Median age: 41.8; Age under 18: 22.5%; Age 65 and over: 20.3%; Males per 100 females: 89.9; Marriage status: 30.8% never married, 48.1% now married, 2.2% separated, 7.1% widowed, 14.0% divorced; Foreign born: 1.5%; Speak English only: 97.5%;

With disability: 17.2%; Veterans: 13.0%; Ancestry: 26.3% English, 26.3% German, 25.3% Irish, 11.8% Italian, 5.3% Polish
Employment: 10.7% management, business, and financial, 0.9% computer, engineering, and science, 12.1% education, legal, community service, arts, and media, 7.1% healthcare practitioners, 14.0% service, 28.4% sales and office, 12.9% natural resources, construction, and maintenance, 14.0% production, transportation, and material moving
Income: Per capita: $27,678; Median household: $54,620; Average household: $66,808; Households with income of $100,000 or more: 21.7%; Poverty rate: 6.1%
Educational Attainment: High school diploma or higher: 89.8%; Bachelor's degree or higher: 20.5%; Graduate/professional degree or higher: 8.0%

School District(s)
Weedsport Central SD (KG-12)
    Enrollment: 820 . . . . (315) 834-6637
Housing: Homeownership rate: 61.5%; Median home value: $118,000; Median year structure built: 1943; Homeowner vacancy rate: 0.0%; Median selected monthly owner costs: $1,267 with a mortgage, $467 without a mortgage; Median gross rent: $682 per month; Rental vacancy rate: 0.0%
Health Insurance: 97.5% have insurance; 79.7% have private insurance; 37.6% have public insurance; 2.5% do not have insurance; 0.6% of children under 18 do not have insurance
Safety: Violent crime rate: 0.0 per 10,000 population; Property crime rate: 86.4 per 10,000 population
Transportation: Commute: 95.7% car, 0.0% public transportation, 1.2% walk, 1.1% work from home; Mean travel time to work: 21.0 minutes
Additional Information Contacts
Village of Weedsport . . . . (315) 834-6634
   http://villageofweedsport.org

Chautauqua County

Located in western New York; bounded on the northwest by Lake Erie, and on the west and south by Pennsylvania. Covers a land area of 1,060.226 square miles, a water area of 439.957 square miles, and is located in the Eastern Time Zone at 42.30° N. Lat., 79.41° W. Long. The county was founded in 1808. County seat is Mayville.

Chautauqua County is part of the Jamestown-Dunkirk-Fredonia, NY Micropolitan Statistical Area. The entire metro area includes: Chautauqua County, NY

Weather Station: Fredonia										Elevation: 759 feet	
	Jan	Feb	Mar	Apr	May	Jun	Jul	Aug	Sep	Oct	Nov	Dec
High	33	36	44	57	68	77	80	79	73	61	50	38
Low	20	20	27	38	48	58	63	62	55	45	36	26
Precip	2.6	2.1	2.7	3.3	3.5	3.7	4.1	3.7	4.6	4.3	4.0	3.4
Snow	25.4	13.3	11.1	2.7	0.3	0.0	0.0	0.0	0.0	0.2	5.9	20.3

High and Low temperatures in degrees Fahrenheit; Precipitation and Snow in inches

Weather Station: Jamestown 4 NE										Elevation: 1,250 feet	
	Jan	Feb	Mar	Apr	May	Jun	Jul	Aug	Sep	Oct	Nov	Dec
High	32	35	43	57	67	76	80	79	72	59	48	36
Low	15	15	22	33	42	52	56	55	48	37	31	21
Precip	3.1	2.5	3.0	3.6	3.9	4.8	4.8	4.1	4.4	3.8	4.1	3.5
Snow	24.9	15.6	13.1	2.9	tr	0.0	0.0	0.0	0.0	0.4	8.3	21.4

High and Low temperatures in degrees Fahrenheit; Precipitation and Snow in inches

Weather Station: Westfield 2 SSE										Elevation: 707 feet	
	Jan	Feb	Mar	Apr	May	Jun	Jul	Aug	Sep	Oct	Nov	Dec
High	33	35	43	56	67	76	80	78	71	60	48	37
Low	20	21	27	38	49	58	63	62	55	45	35	26
Precip	2.5	2.2	2.9	3.4	3.8	4.1	4.2	4.0	4.9	4.9	4.3	3.4
Snow	21.2	14.0	12.7	2.7	0.4	0.0	0.0	0.0	tr	0.4	8.7	24.4

High and Low temperatures in degrees Fahrenheit; Precipitation and Snow in inches

Population: 130,846; Growth (since 2000): -6.4%; Density: 123.4 persons per square mile; Race: 92.7% White, 2.6% Black/African American, 0.6% Asian, 0.3% American Indian/Alaska Native, 0.0% Native Hawaiian/Other Pacific Islander, 2.0% two or more races, 7.2% Hispanic of any race; Average household size: 2.35; Median age: 42.3; Age under 18: 20.8%; Age 65 and over: 18.5%; Males per 100 females: 97.2; Marriage status: 31.6% never married, 49.6% now married, 2.7% separated, 6.9% widowed, 12.0% divorced; Foreign born: 2.1%; Speak English only: 92.2%; With disability: 15.8%; Veterans: 9.0%; Ancestry: 21.0% German, 14.8% Italian, 13.9% Irish, 12.2% English, 11.7% Swedish

Religion: Six largest groups: 15.5% Catholicism, 8.4% Methodist/Pietist, 3.3% Lutheran, 2.2% Presbyterian-Reformed, 2.1% Holiness, 2.1% Non-denominational Protestant
Economy: Unemployment rate: 4.2%; Leading industries: 16.7 % retail trade; 13.6 % other services (except public administration); 12.2 % accommodation and food services; Farms: 1,515 totaling 236,546 acres; Company size: 3 employ 1,000 or more persons, 4 employ 500 to 999 persons, 56 employ 100 to 499 persons, 2,817 employ less than 100 persons; Business ownership: 2,757 women-owned, 56 Black-owned, 259 Hispanic-owned, 101 Asian-owned, n/a American Indian/Alaska Native-owned
Employment: 10.6% management, business, and financial, 2.5% computer, engineering, and science, 11.4% education, legal, community service, arts, and media, 5.4% healthcare practitioners, 19.4% service, 22.0% sales and office, 9.8% natural resources, construction, and maintenance, 18.8% production, transportation, and material moving
Income: Per capita: $23,962; Median household: $44,304; Average household: $57,231; Households with income of $100,000 or more: 13.8%; Poverty rate: 18.5%
Educational Attainment: High school diploma or higher: 88.5%; Bachelor's degree or higher: 21.2%; Graduate/professional degree or higher: 9.5%
Housing: Homeownership rate: 70.0%; Median home value: $85,800; Median year structure built: 1950; Homeowner vacancy rate: 2.7%; Median selected monthly owner costs: $975 with a mortgage, $444 without a mortgage; Median gross rent: $631 per month; Rental vacancy rate: 7.7%
Vital Statistics: Birth rate: 106.0 per 10,000 population; Death rate: 105.5 per 10,000 population; Age-adjusted cancer mortality rate: 169.2 deaths per 100,000 population
Health Insurance: 93.4% have insurance; 65.6% have private insurance; 43.8% have public insurance; 6.6% do not have insurance; 7.3% of children under 18 do not have insurance
Health Care: Physicians: 12.4 per 10,000 population; Dentists: 5.7 per 10,000 population; Hospital beds: 20.5 per 10,000 population; Hospital admissions: 686.6 per 10,000 population
Air Quality Index (AQI): Percent of Days: 90.1% good, 9.3% moderate, 0.6% unhealthy for sensitive individuals, 0.0% unhealthy, 0.0% very unhealthy; Annual median: 37; Annual maximum: 129
Transportation: Commute: 90.2% car, 0.4% public transportation, 4.7% walk, 3.7% work from home; Mean travel time to work: 18.0 minutes
2016 Presidential Election: 58.3% Trump, 35.2% Clinton, 4.1% Johnson, 1.4% Stein
National and State Parks: Lake Erie State Park
Additional Information Contacts
Chautauqua Government . . . . (716) 753-4211
   http://www.co.chautauqua.ny.us

Chautauqua County Communities

ARKWRIGHT (town). Covers a land area of 35.670 square miles and a water area of 0.060 square miles. Located at 42.39° N. Lat; 79.24° W. Long. Elevation is 1,634 feet.
Population: 1,161; Growth (since 2000): 3.1%; Density: 32.5 persons per square mile; Race: 98.8% White, 0.3% Black/African American, 0.3% Asian, 0.0% American Indian/Alaska Native, 0.0% Native Hawaiian/Other Pacific Islander, 0.5% Two or more races, 5.3% Hispanic of any race; Average household size: 2.47; Median age: 44.5; Age under 18: 20.2%; Age 65 and over: 16.7%; Males per 100 females: 108.4; Marriage status: 34.6% never married, 55.2% now married, 1.7% separated, 4.1% widowed, 6.1% divorced; Foreign born: 0.3%; Speak English only: 97.3%; With disability: 16.3%; Veterans: 7.3%; Ancestry: 19.9% German, 18.9% Polish, 14.0% Irish, 13.0% English, 8.5% American
Employment: 8.3% management, business, and financial, 7.8% computer, engineering, and science, 9.8% education, legal, community service, arts, and media, 5.1% healthcare practitioners, 18.1% service, 25.3% sales and office, 12.7% natural resources, construction, and maintenance, 12.9% production, transportation, and material moving
Income: Per capita: $26,787; Median household: $59,167; Average household: $66,448; Households with income of $100,000 or more: 21.8%; Poverty rate: 12.1%
Educational Attainment: High school diploma or higher: 85.9%; Bachelor's degree or higher: 24.7%; Graduate/professional degree or higher: 10.7%
Housing: Homeownership rate: 85.5%; Median home value: $95,000; Median year structure built: 1981; Homeowner vacancy rate: 0.0%; Median

selected monthly owner costs: $1,394 with a mortgage, $416 without a mortgage; Median gross rent: $692 per month; Rental vacancy rate: 0.0%
Health Insurance: 96.1% have insurance; 69.9% have private insurance; 41.7% have public insurance; 3.9% do not have insurance; 1.3% of children under 18 do not have insurance
Transportation: Commute: 94.1% car, 0.0% public transportation, 1.1% walk, 2.7% work from home; Mean travel time to work: 23.4 minutes

ASHVILLE (unincorporated postal area)
ZCTA: 14710
Covers a land area of 48.365 square miles and a water area of 0.057 square miles. Located at 42.09° N. Lat; 79.42° W. Long. Elevation is 1,358 feet.
Population: 3,233; Growth (since 2000): -18.4%; Density: 66.8 persons per square mile; Race: 98.4% White, 0.0% Black/African American, 0.9% Asian, 0.0% American Indian/Alaska Native, 0.0% Native Hawaiian/Other Pacific Islander, 0.4% Two or more races, 1.5% Hispanic of any race; Average household size: 2.41; Median age: 49.8; Age under 18: 17.4%; Age 65 and over: 23.6%; Males per 100 females: 100.0; Marriage status: 19.8% never married, 60.1% now married, 2.3% separated, 6.1% widowed, 14.0% divorced; Foreign born: 2.1%; Speak English only: 97.2%; With disability: 12.4%; Veterans: 8.9%; Ancestry: 20.0% German, 19.5% Swedish, 16.2% English, 14.5% Irish, 8.3% Italian
Employment: 10.7% management, business, and financial, 1.4% computer, engineering, and science, 11.8% education, legal, community service, arts, and media, 5.8% healthcare practitioners, 14.0% service, 23.0% sales and office, 12.3% natural resources, construction, and maintenance, 21.0% production, transportation, and material moving
Income: Per capita: $28,048; Median household: $54,314; Average household: $66,452; Households with income of $100,000 or more: 18.0%; Poverty rate: 10.5%
Educational Attainment: High school diploma or higher: 91.6%; Bachelor's degree or higher: 21.3%; Graduate/professional degree or higher: 12.7%
Housing: Homeownership rate: 88.4%; Median home value: $97,600; Median year structure built: 1958; Homeowner vacancy rate: 2.8%; Median selected monthly owner costs: $1,031 with a mortgage, $456 without a mortgage; Median gross rent: $896 per month; Rental vacancy rate: 0.0%
Health Insurance: 93.8% have insurance; 71.7% have private insurance; 40.7% have public insurance; 6.2% do not have insurance; 2.7% of children under 18 do not have insurance
Transportation: Commute: 92.6% car, 0.3% public transportation, 0.3% walk, 6.1% work from home; Mean travel time to work: 21.8 minutes

BEMUS POINT (village). Covers a land area of 0.436 square miles and a water area of 0 square miles. Located at 42.16° N. Lat; 79.39° W. Long. Elevation is 1,322 feet.
Population: 314; Growth (since 2000): -7.6%; Density: 720.1 persons per square mile; Race: 99.0% White, 1.0% Black/African American, 0.0% Asian, 0.0% American Indian/Alaska Native, 0.0% Native Hawaiian/Other Pacific Islander, 0.0% Two or more races, 0.0% Hispanic of any race; Average household size: 1.88; Median age: 56.8; Age under 18: 19.7%; Age 65 and over: 32.2%; Males per 100 females: 86.7; Marriage status: 24.9% never married, 43.9% now married, 4.3% separated, 20.6% widowed, 10.7% divorced; Foreign born: 1.0%; Speak English only: 99.0%; With disability: 20.1%; Veterans: 7.9%; Ancestry: 23.9% Irish, 18.8% German, 18.8% Swedish, 17.2% Italian, 16.6% English
Employment: 27.9% management, business, and financial, 1.8% computer, engineering, and science, 10.8% education, legal, community service, arts, and media, 10.8% healthcare practitioners, 18.9% service, 12.6% sales and office, 1.8% natural resources, construction, and maintenance, 15.3% production, transportation, and material moving
Income: Per capita: $50,502; Median household: $35,729; Average household: $90,849; Households with income of $100,000 or more: 19.2%; Poverty rate: 25.8%
Educational Attainment: High school diploma or higher: 90.7%; Bachelor's degree or higher: 30.6%; Graduate/professional degree or higher: 13.3%
School District(s)
Bemus Point Central SD (PK-12)
    Enrollment: 735 . . . . (716) 386-2375
Housing: Homeownership rate: 41.9%; Median home value: $203,600; Median year structure built: 1941; Homeowner vacancy rate: 23.9%;

Median selected monthly owner costs: $1,531 with a mortgage, $531 without a mortgage; Median gross rent: $544 per month; Rental vacancy rate: 7.6%
Health Insurance: 98.4% have insurance; 66.9% have private insurance; 52.2% have public insurance; 1.6% do not have insurance; 0.0% of children under 18 do not have insurance
Transportation: Commute: 83.2% car, 0.0% public transportation, 6.5% walk, 10.3% work from home; Mean travel time to work: 17.0 minutes

BROCTON (village). Covers a land area of 1.710 square miles and a water area of 0 square miles. Located at 42.39° N. Lat; 79.44° W. Long. Elevation is 735 feet.
History: A short-lived community of the Brotherhood of the New Life was founded here in 1867 by Thomas L. Harris. Incorporated 1894.
Population: 1,384; Growth (since 2000): -10.5%; Density: 809.5 persons per square mile; Race: 98.5% White, 0.4% Black/African American, 0.0% Asian, 0.0% American Indian/Alaska Native, 0.0% Native Hawaiian/Other Pacific Islander, 1.1% Two or more races, 0.4% Hispanic of any race; Average household size: 2.18; Median age: 44.6; Age under 18: 22.5%; Age 65 and over: 20.7%; Males per 100 females: 91.5; Marriage status: 30.5% never married, 39.9% now married, 1.9% separated, 11.4% widowed, 18.2% divorced; Foreign born: 0.0%; Speak English only: 99.3%; With disability: 20.1%; Veterans: 7.6%; Ancestry: 30.2% German, 19.1% Italian, 18.4% Irish, 11.6% Polish, 10.6% English
Employment: 10.9% management, business, and financial, 2.4% computer, engineering, and science, 8.8% education, legal, community service, arts, and media, 3.3% healthcare practitioners, 24.4% service, 16.3% sales and office, 5.4% natural resources, construction, and maintenance, 28.6% production, transportation, and material moving
Income: Per capita: $21,309; Median household: $38,900; Average household: $45,256; Households with income of $100,000 or more: 3.7%; Poverty rate: 18.0%
Educational Attainment: High school diploma or higher: 87.8%; Bachelor's degree or higher: 15.7%; Graduate/professional degree or higher: 7.3%
School District(s)
Brocton Central SD (PK-12)
    Enrollment: 587 . . . . (716) 792-2173
Housing: Homeownership rate: 63.4%; Median home value: $71,500; Median year structure built: 1942; Homeowner vacancy rate: 0.7%; Median selected monthly owner costs: $898 with a mortgage, $414 without a mortgage; Median gross rent: $564 per month; Rental vacancy rate: 0.0%
Health Insurance: 94.9% have insurance; 65.6% have private insurance; 43.6% have public insurance; 5.1% do not have insurance; 0.0% of children under 18 do not have insurance
Transportation: Commute: 94.2% car, 0.0% public transportation, 3.6% walk, 0.5% work from home; Mean travel time to work: 18.8 minutes

BUSTI (CDP). Covers a land area of 2.264 square miles and a water area of 0 square miles. Located at 42.04° N. Lat; 79.28° W. Long. Elevation is 1,365 feet.
Population: 330; Growth (since 2000): n/a; Density: 145.8 persons per square mile; Race: 100.0% White, 0.0% Black/African American, 0.0% Asian, 0.0% American Indian/Alaska Native, 0.0% Native Hawaiian/Other Pacific Islander, 0.0% Two or more races, 0.0% Hispanic of any race; Average household size: 3.75; Median age: 25.6; Age under 18: 35.2%; Age 65 and over: 4.2%; Males per 100 females: 100.5; Marriage status: 29.9% never married, 56.1% now married, 0.0% separated, 0.0% widowed, 14.0% divorced; Foreign born: 2.7%; Speak English only: 97.5%; With disability: 12.7%; Veterans: 12.1%; Ancestry: 33.3% English, 12.4% Swedish, 12.1% American, 11.8% Irish, 9.1% Italian
Employment: 0.0% management, business, and financial, 15.4% computer, engineering, and science, 4.1% education, legal, community service, arts, and media, 0.0% healthcare practitioners, 20.3% service, 20.3% sales and office, 19.5% natural resources, construction, and maintenance, 20.3% production, transportation, and material moving
Income: Per capita: $16,566; Median household: $60,625; Average household: $60,326; Households with income of $100,000 or more: 13.6%; Poverty rate: 5.5%
Educational Attainment: High school diploma or higher: 100.0%; Bachelor's degree or higher: 23.4%; Graduate/professional degree or higher: 2.9%
Housing: Homeownership rate: 80.7%; Median home value: $127,700; Median year structure built: 1971; Homeowner vacancy rate: 0.0%; Median

selected monthly owner costs: n/a with a mortgage, n/a without a mortgage; Median gross rent: n/a per month; Rental vacancy rate: 0.0%
Health Insurance: 93.6% have insurance; 43.3% have private insurance; 62.1% have public insurance; 6.4% do not have insurance; 0.0% of children under 18 do not have insurance
Transportation: Commute: 94.6% car, 0.0% public transportation, 0.0% walk, 5.4% work from home; Mean travel time to work: 14.5 minutes

BUSTI (town). Covers a land area of 47.825 square miles and a water area of 0.014 square miles. Located at 42.05° N. Lat; 79.33° W. Long. Elevation is 1,365 feet.
Population: 7,289; Growth (since 2000): -6.1%; Density: 152.4 persons per square mile; Race: 97.3% White, 0.5% Black/African American, 0.8% Asian, 0.0% American Indian/Alaska Native, 0.0% Native Hawaiian/Other Pacific Islander, 1.3% Two or more races, 1.2% Hispanic of any race; Average household size: 2.25; Median age: 49.0; Age under 18: 19.1%; Age 65 and over: 24.6%; Males per 100 females: 98.4; Marriage status: 22.3% never married, 56.8% now married, 1.5% separated, 8.9% widowed, 12.0% divorced; Foreign born: 1.4%; Speak English only: 97.4%; With disability: 12.7%; Veterans: 9.5%; Ancestry: 20.7% German, 19.9% Swedish, 15.0% English, 13.1% Irish, 12.4% Italian
Employment: 12.9% management, business, and financial, 4.7% computer, engineering, and science, 9.5% education, legal, community service, arts, and media, 8.5% healthcare practitioners, 18.3% service, 20.1% sales and office, 9.8% natural resources, construction, and maintenance, 16.2% production, transportation, and material moving
Income: Per capita: $32,429; Median household: $54,020; Average household: $72,544; Households with income of $100,000 or more: 20.9%; Poverty rate: 10.4%
Educational Attainment: High school diploma or higher: 94.7%; Bachelor's degree or higher: 30.0%; Graduate/professional degree or higher: 12.8%
Housing: Homeownership rate: 79.7%; Median home value: $119,000; Median year structure built: 1959; Homeowner vacancy rate: 2.7%; Median selected monthly owner costs: $1,197 with a mortgage, $480 without a mortgage; Median gross rent: $672 per month; Rental vacancy rate: 4.0%
Health Insurance: 96.0% have insurance; 75.2% have private insurance; 42.7% have public insurance; 4.0% do not have insurance; 4.1% of children under 18 do not have insurance
Transportation: Commute: 94.6% car, 0.2% public transportation, 1.5% walk, 3.3% work from home; Mean travel time to work: 16.4 minutes
Additional Information Contacts
Town of Busti . . . . (716) 763-8561
　http://www.townofbusti.com

CARROLL (town). Covers a land area of 33.320 square miles and a water area of 0.023 square miles. Located at 42.04° N. Lat; 79.10° W. Long.
Population: 3,413; Growth (since 2000): -6.1%; Density: 102.4 persons per square mile; Race: 98.2% White, 1.3% Black/African American, 0.0% Asian, 0.0% American Indian/Alaska Native, 0.0% Native Hawaiian/Other Pacific Islander, 0.0% Two or more races, 0.5% Hispanic of any race; Average household size: 2.32; Median age: 54.0; Age under 18: 17.1%; Age 65 and over: 23.6%; Males per 100 females: 95.5; Marriage status: 23.3% never married, 53.6% now married, 3.3% separated, 11.3% widowed, 11.8% divorced; Foreign born: 0.0%; Speak English only: 100.0%; With disability: 17.7%; Veterans: 12.1%; Ancestry: 33.1% Swedish, 18.3% Italian, 12.3% English, 12.2% Irish, 10.7% German
Employment: 7.0% management, business, and financial, 0.0% computer, engineering, and science, 13.7% education, legal, community service, arts, and media, 6.1% healthcare practitioners, 11.9% service, 28.7% sales and office, 10.7% natural resources, construction, and maintenance, 22.0% production, transportation, and material moving
Income: Per capita: $26,526; Median household: $43,899; Average household: $59,464; Households with income of $100,000 or more: 16.2%; Poverty rate: 6.1%
Educational Attainment: High school diploma or higher: 87.3%; Bachelor's degree or higher: 15.1%; Graduate/professional degree or higher: 5.4%
Housing: Homeownership rate: 82.9%; Median home value: $85,300; Median year structure built: 1961; Homeowner vacancy rate: 3.5%; Median selected monthly owner costs: $989 with a mortgage, $499 without a mortgage; Median gross rent: $757 per month; Rental vacancy rate: 0.0%

Health Insurance: 99.1% have insurance; 69.8% have private insurance; 49.4% have public insurance; 0.9% do not have insurance; 0.0% of children under 18 do not have insurance
Safety: Violent crime rate: 0.0 per 10,000 population; Property crime rate: 0.0 per 10,000 population
Transportation: Commute: 94.1% car, 0.0% public transportation, 3.0% walk, 1.9% work from home; Mean travel time to work: 22.1 minutes

CASSADAGA (village). Covers a land area of 0.839 square miles and a water area of 0.217 square miles. Located at 42.34° N. Lat; 79.32° W. Long. Elevation is 1,339 feet.
Population: 548; Growth (since 2000): -18.9%; Density: 653.5 persons per square mile; Race: 96.7% White, 0.0% Black/African American, 2.4% Asian, 0.0% American Indian/Alaska Native, 0.0% Native Hawaiian/Other Pacific Islander, 0.9% Two or more races, 0.5% Hispanic of any race; Average household size: 2.18; Median age: 48.2; Age under 18: 18.2%; Age 65 and over: 26.3%; Males per 100 females: 100.6; Marriage status: 25.5% never married, 53.5% now married, 1.5% separated, 8.9% widowed, 12.0% divorced; Foreign born: 1.5%; Speak English only: 98.9%; With disability: 16.2%; Veterans: 13.6%; Ancestry: 26.5% German, 24.1% English, 10.8% Irish, 7.8% Swedish, 7.1% Italian
Employment: 9.3% management, business, and financial, 0.0% computer, engineering, and science, 11.4% education, legal, community service, arts, and media, 7.2% healthcare practitioners, 24.1% service, 16.9% sales and office, 8.9% natural resources, construction, and maintenance, 22.4% production, transportation, and material moving
Income: Per capita: $25,592; Median household: $45,536; Average household: $54,392; Households with income of $100,000 or more: 8.0%; Poverty rate: 6.6%
Educational Attainment: High school diploma or higher: 93.0%; Bachelor's degree or higher: 19.7%; Graduate/professional degree or higher: 10.5%
School District(s)
Cassadaga Valley Central SD (PK-12)
　Enrollment: 892 . . . . (716) 962-5155
Housing: Homeownership rate: 69.7%; Median home value: $102,000; Median year structure built: Before 1940; Homeowner vacancy rate: 5.2%; Median selected monthly owner costs: $889 with a mortgage, $391 without a mortgage; Median gross rent: $663 per month; Rental vacancy rate: 0.0%
Health Insurance: 93.6% have insurance; 77.2% have private insurance; 39.8% have public insurance; 6.4% do not have insurance; 2.7% of children under 18 do not have insurance
Transportation: Commute: 82.6% car, 0.9% public transportation, 8.5% walk, 7.1% work from home; Mean travel time to work: 23.2 minutes

CATTARAUGUS RESERVATION (reservation). Covers a land area of 2.446 square miles and a water area of 0.328 square miles. Located at 42.54° N. Lat; 79.09° W. Long.
Population: 28; Growth (since 2000): n/a; Density: 11.4 persons per square mile; Race: 0.0% White, 0.0% Black/African American, 0.0% Asian, 100.0% American Indian/Alaska Native, 0.0% Native Hawaiian/Other Pacific Islander, 0.0% Two or more races, 0.0% Hispanic of any race; Average household size: 2.00; Median age: 29.7; Age under 18: 35.7%; Age 65 and over: 28.6%; Males per 100 females: 123.5; Marriage status: 100.0% never married, 0.0% now married, 0.0% separated, 0.0% widowed, 0.0% divorced; Foreign born: 0.0%; Speak English only: 68.0%; With disability: 28.6%; Veterans: 44.4%; Ancestry: n/a.
Employment: 0.0% management, business, and financial, 0.0% computer, engineering, and science, 100.0% education, legal, community service, arts, and media, 0.0% healthcare practitioners, 0.0% service, 0.0% sales and office, 0.0% natural resources, construction, and maintenance, 0.0% production, transportation, and material moving
Income: Per capita: n/a; Median household: n/a; Average household: n/a; Households with income of $100,000 or more: n/a; Poverty rate: 100.0%
Educational Attainment: High school diploma or higher: 33.3%; Bachelor's degree or higher: n/a; Graduate/professional degree or higher: n/a
Housing: Homeownership rate: 57.1%; Median home value: n/a; Median year structure built: n/a; Homeowner vacancy rate: 0.0%; Median selected monthly owner costs: n/a with a mortgage, n/a without a mortgage; Median gross rent: n/a per month; Rental vacancy rate: 0.0%
Health Insurance: 100.0% have insurance; 21.4% have private insurance; 78.6% have public insurance; 0.0% do not have insurance; 0.0% of children under 18 do not have insurance

Transportation: Commute: 100.0% car, 0.0% public transportation, 0.0% walk, 0.0% work from home; Mean travel time to work: 0.0 minutes

CELORON (village).
Covers a land area of 0.747 square miles and a water area of <.001 square miles. Located at 42.11° N. Lat; 79.28° W. Long. Elevation is 1,319 feet.

History: Incorporated 1896.

Population: 1,161; Growth (since 2000): -10.3%; Density: 1,553.3 persons per square mile; Race: 98.0% White, 0.0% Black/African American, 1.4% Asian, 0.0% American Indian/Alaska Native, 0.0% Native Hawaiian/Other Pacific Islander, 0.6% Two or more races, 5.0% Hispanic of any race; Average household size: 2.12; Median age: 43.1; Age under 18: 17.1%; Age 65 and over: 18.8%; Males per 100 females: 98.6; Marriage status: 33.3% never married, 39.5% now married, 6.4% separated, 6.0% widowed, 21.2% divorced; Foreign born: 0.9%; Speak English only: 96.6%; With disability: 15.5%; Veterans: 5.3%; Ancestry: 26.9% Swedish, 16.7% German, 13.8% Irish, 9.6% English, 9.3% Italian

Employment: 8.6% management, business, and financial, 0.9% computer, engineering, and science, 7.2% education, legal, community service, arts, and media, 4.6% healthcare practitioners, 23.3% service, 24.9% sales and office, 9.0% natural resources, construction, and maintenance, 21.5% production, transportation, and material moving

Income: Per capita: $23,561; Median household: $41,622; Average household: $48,914; Households with income of $100,000 or more: 9.0%; Poverty rate: 16.9%

Educational Attainment: High school diploma or higher: 84.4%; Bachelor's degree or higher: 11.0%; Graduate/professional degree or higher: 3.3%

Housing: Homeownership rate: 58.7%; Median home value: $53,500; Median year structure built: 1941; Homeowner vacancy rate: 3.1%; Median selected monthly owner costs: $816 with a mortgage, $368 without a mortgage; Median gross rent: $648 per month; Rental vacancy rate: 12.6%

Health Insurance: 92.2% have insurance; 60.2% have private insurance; 48.7% have public insurance; 7.8% do not have insurance; 0.0% of children under 18 do not have insurance

Transportation: Commute: 98.9% car, 0.5% public transportation, 0.0% walk, 0.0% work from home; Mean travel time to work: 14.6 minutes

CHARLOTTE (town).
Covers a land area of 36.432 square miles and a water area of 0 square miles. Located at 42.30° N. Lat; 79.24° W. Long. Elevation is 1,532 feet.

Population: 1,835; Growth (since 2000): 7.1%; Density: 50.4 persons per square mile; Race: 98.5% White, 0.0% Black/African American, 0.2% Asian, 0.3% American Indian/Alaska Native, 0.0% Native Hawaiian/Other Pacific Islander, 0.9% Two or more races, 1.6% Hispanic of any race; Average household size: 2.76; Median age: 42.3; Age under 18: 26.3%; Age 65 and over: 14.0%; Males per 100 females: 105.3; Marriage status: 24.9% never married, 59.8% now married, 1.4% separated, 6.6% widowed, 8.6% divorced; Foreign born: 0.5%; Speak English only: 98.3%; With disability: 13.7%; Veterans: 9.1%; Ancestry: 21.0% German, 16.6% English, 15.5% Swedish, 14.9% Irish, 11.8% Italian

Employment: 11.6% management, business, and financial, 0.6% computer, engineering, and science, 11.2% education, legal, community service, arts, and media, 3.0% healthcare practitioners, 26.8% service, 16.2% sales and office, 8.9% natural resources, construction, and maintenance, 21.7% production, transportation, and material moving

Income: Per capita: $20,217; Median household: $47,689; Average household: $54,599; Households with income of $100,000 or more: 13.7%; Poverty rate: 22.2%

Educational Attainment: High school diploma or higher: 83.2%; Bachelor's degree or higher: 14.3%; Graduate/professional degree or higher: 6.8%

Housing: Homeownership rate: 84.8%; Median home value: $81,600; Median year structure built: 1973; Homeowner vacancy rate: 1.4%; Median selected monthly owner costs: $1,064 with a mortgage, $513 without a mortgage; Median gross rent: $613 per month; Rental vacancy rate: 0.0%

Health Insurance: 94.9% have insurance; 62.5% have private insurance; 41.3% have public insurance; 5.1% do not have insurance; 0.0% of children under 18 do not have insurance

Transportation: Commute: 91.7% car, 0.5% public transportation, 2.7% walk, 3.3% work from home; Mean travel time to work: 24.9 minutes

CHAUTAUQUA (CDP).
Covers a land area of 0.427 square miles and a water area of 0 square miles. Located at 42.21° N. Lat; 79.47° W. Long. Elevation is 1,362 feet.

Population: 471; Growth (since 2000): n/a; Density: 1,103.0 persons per square mile; Race: 81.5% White, 6.4% Black/African American, 3.0% Asian, 0.0% American Indian/Alaska Native, 0.0% Native Hawaiian/Other Pacific Islander, 5.3% Two or more races, 5.1% Hispanic of any race; Average household size: 1.75; Median age: 23.8; Age under 18: 3.2%; Age 65 and over: 35.2%; Males per 100 females: 83.7; Marriage status: 53.5% never married, 36.8% now married, 0.0% separated, 2.2% widowed, 7.5% divorced; Foreign born: 7.0%; Speak English only: 90.9%; With disability: 8.9%; Veterans: 0.0%; Ancestry: 18.3% Italian, 11.7% Swedish, 11.0% British, 10.6% Irish, 8.1% German

Employment: 13.8% management, business, and financial, 0.0% computer, engineering, and science, 16.1% education, legal, community service, arts, and media, 0.0% healthcare practitioners, 37.9% service, 29.9% sales and office, 2.3% natural resources, construction, and maintenance, 0.0% production, transportation, and material moving

Income: Per capita: $34,906; Median household: $115,577; Average household: $113,370; Households with income of $100,000 or more: 61.9%; Poverty rate: 2.0%

Educational Attainment: High school diploma or higher: 99.1%; Bachelor's degree or higher: 85.9%; Graduate/professional degree or higher: 60.7%

Housing: Homeownership rate: 88.8%; Median home value: $640,900; Median year structure built: 1964; Homeowner vacancy rate: 0.0%; Median selected monthly owner costs: $1,673 with a mortgage, $1,106 without a mortgage; Median gross rent: n/a per month; Rental vacancy rate: 0.0%

Health Insurance: 91.1% have insurance; 84.3% have private insurance; 41.4% have public insurance; 8.9% do not have insurance; 5.6% of children under 18 do not have insurance

Transportation: Commute: 39.7% car, 6.8% public transportation, 34.2% walk, 19.2% work from home; Mean travel time to work: 13.7 minutes

CHAUTAUQUA (town).
Covers a land area of 67.099 square miles and a water area of 0.094 square miles. Located at 42.24° N. Lat; 79.51° W. Long. Elevation is 1,362 feet.

History: Founded as meeting place for Methodist ministers and laity. Chautauqua Institute, founded in 1864, is located here. Famous people connected with the school include U.S. Presidents Garfield, Grant, McKinley, Harding, and both Roosevelts; explorers Admiral Richard Byrd and Amelia Earhart; inventors Henry Ford and Thomas Edison; Senator Robert Kennedy, William Jennings Bryan, Jane Addams, Ida Tarbell and N.Y. governor Al Smith. Village formerly known as Fair Point.

Population: 4,362; Growth (since 2000): -6.5%; Density: 65.0 persons per square mile; Race: 93.7% White, 2.5% Black/African American, 0.5% Asian, 0.0% American Indian/Alaska Native, 0.2% Native Hawaiian/Other Pacific Islander, 1.9% Two or more races, 1.6% Hispanic of any race; Average household size: 2.28; Median age: 45.7; Age under 18: 17.1%; Age 65 and over: 23.1%; Males per 100 females: 108.3; Marriage status: 29.4% never married, 55.8% now married, 2.7% separated, 5.7% widowed, 9.1% divorced; Foreign born: 2.7%; Speak English only: 89.6%; With disability: 10.9%; Veterans: 7.0%; Ancestry: 25.1% German, 19.4% English, 10.3% Swedish, 9.9% Irish, 8.6% Italian

Employment: 15.1% management, business, and financial, 3.1% computer, engineering, and science, 9.9% education, legal, community service, arts, and media, 5.3% healthcare practitioners, 22.3% service, 20.7% sales and office, 12.0% natural resources, construction, and maintenance, 11.5% production, transportation, and material moving

Income: Per capita: $27,522; Median household: $55,625; Average household: $68,262; Households with income of $100,000 or more: 21.1%; Poverty rate: 13.0%

Educational Attainment: High school diploma or higher: 91.0%; Bachelor's degree or higher: 30.7%; Graduate/professional degree or higher: 14.5%

Housing: Homeownership rate: 82.5%; Median home value: $106,700; Median year structure built: 1962; Homeowner vacancy rate: 4.5%; Median selected monthly owner costs: $985 with a mortgage, $421 without a mortgage; Median gross rent: $563 per month; Rental vacancy rate: 2.9%

Health Insurance: 89.2% have insurance; 71.6% have private insurance; 39.7% have public insurance; 10.8% do not have insurance; 18.2% of children under 18 do not have insurance

Transportation: Commute: 81.3% car, 0.3% public transportation, 5.2% walk, 11.6% work from home; Mean travel time to work: 20.9 minutes

Additional Information Contacts
Town of Chautauqua . . . . (716) 753-7342
http://www.townofchautauqua.com

CHERRY CREEK (town). Covers a land area of 36.632 square miles and a water area of 0.013 square miles. Located at 42.30° N. Lat; 79.12° W. Long. Elevation is 1,302 feet.

Population: 1,004; Growth (since 2000): -12.8%; Density: 27.4 persons per square mile; Race: 99.0% White, 0.2% Black/African American, 0.2% Asian, 0.0% American Indian/Alaska Native, 0.0% Native Hawaiian/Other Pacific Islander, 0.6% Two or more races, 0.3% Hispanic of any race; Average household size: 2.76; Median age: 39.4; Age under 18: 25.9%; Age 65 and over: 16.9%; Males per 100 females: 101.8; Marriage status: 26.7% never married, 59.6% now married, 2.5% separated, 4.3% widowed, 9.4% divorced; Foreign born: 0.9%; Speak English only: 93.3%; With disability: 14.3%; Veterans: 7.8%; Ancestry: 33.7% German, 18.2% Irish, 14.1% English, 11.0% Italian, 7.8% Polish
Employment: 8.3% management, business, and financial, 0.0% computer, engineering, and science, 9.0% education, legal, community service, arts, and media, 7.9% healthcare practitioners, 20.3% service, 18.2% sales and office, 15.1% natural resources, construction, and maintenance, 21.2% production, transportation, and material moving
Income: Per capita: $22,774; Median household: $52,969; Average household: $60,146; Households with income of $100,000 or more: 15.0%; Poverty rate: 22.2%
Educational Attainment: High school diploma or higher: 84.7%; Bachelor's degree or higher: 15.7%; Graduate/professional degree or higher: 8.2%
Housing: Homeownership rate: 82.1%; Median home value: $79,900; Median year structure built: 1951; Homeowner vacancy rate: 3.1%; Median selected monthly owner costs: $1,115 with a mortgage, $476 without a mortgage; Median gross rent: $764 per month; Rental vacancy rate: 0.0%
Health Insurance: 92.9% have insurance; 67.2% have private insurance; 39.5% have public insurance; 7.1% do not have insurance; 5.2% of children under 18 do not have insurance
Transportation: Commute: 95.1% car, 0.0% public transportation, 4.9% walk, 0.0% work from home; Mean travel time to work: 24.6 minutes

CHERRY CREEK (village). Covers a land area of 1.362 square miles and a water area of 0 square miles. Located at 42.30° N. Lat; 79.10° W. Long. Elevation is 1,302 feet.

Population: 493; Growth (since 2000): -10.5%; Density: 361.9 persons per square mile; Race: 99.6% White, 0.0% Black/African American, 0.4% Asian, 0.0% American Indian/Alaska Native, 0.0% Native Hawaiian/Other Pacific Islander, 0.0% Two or more races, 0.6% Hispanic of any race; Average household size: 2.97; Median age: 36.2; Age under 18: 29.4%; Age 65 and over: 11.8%; Males per 100 females: 97.9; Marriage status: 25.1% never married, 62.0% now married, 2.5% separated, 6.1% widowed, 6.9% divorced; Foreign born: 0.8%; Speak English only: 98.2%; With disability: 13.6%; Veterans: 6.9%; Ancestry: 45.0% German, 22.9% Irish, 16.2% Italian, 14.2% English, 10.1% Polish
Employment: 6.4% management, business, and financial, 0.0% computer, engineering, and science, 7.8% education, legal, community service, arts, and media, 13.3% healthcare practitioners, 19.3% service, 16.5% sales and office, 16.1% natural resources, construction, and maintenance, 20.6% production, transportation, and material moving
Income: Per capita: $21,144; Median household: $52,857; Average household: $58,712; Households with income of $100,000 or more: 13.8%; Poverty rate: 20.8%
Educational Attainment: High school diploma or higher: 89.3%; Bachelor's degree or higher: 13.0%; Graduate/professional degree or higher: 5.7%
Housing: Homeownership rate: 73.5%; Median home value: $67,000; Median year structure built: Before 1940; Homeowner vacancy rate: 3.9%; Median selected monthly owner costs: $1,013 with a mortgage, $507 without a mortgage; Median gross rent: $773 per month; Rental vacancy rate: 0.0%
Health Insurance: 93.5% have insurance; 73.4% have private insurance; 31.0% have public insurance; 6.5% do not have insurance; 7.2% of children under 18 do not have insurance
Transportation: Commute: 98.1% car, 0.0% public transportation, 1.9% walk, 0.0% work from home; Mean travel time to work: 27.8 minutes

CLYMER (town). Covers a land area of 36.070 square miles and a water area of 0.093 square miles. Located at 42.05° N. Lat; 79.58° W. Long. Elevation is 1,457 feet.

Population: 1,556; Growth (since 2000): 3.7%; Density: 43.1 persons per square mile; Race: 98.7% White, 0.4% Black/African American, 0.4% Asian, 0.0% American Indian/Alaska Native, 0.0% Native Hawaiian/Other Pacific Islander, 0.6% Two or more races, 0.0% Hispanic of any race; Average household size: 2.98; Median age: 32.6; Age under 18: 31.9%; Age 65 and over: 13.0%; Males per 100 females: 100.0; Marriage status: 29.5% never married, 57.4% now married, 1.5% separated, 5.5% widowed, 7.6% divorced; Foreign born: 0.8%; Speak English only: 60.4%; With disability: 8.3%; Veterans: 6.2%; Ancestry: 23.8% German, 20.2% Dutch, 12.5% Pennsylvania German, 11.2% English, 6.9% Irish
Employment: 15.4% management, business, and financial, 2.1% computer, engineering, and science, 9.5% education, legal, community service, arts, and media, 3.9% healthcare practitioners, 21.8% service, 16.5% sales and office, 13.0% natural resources, construction, and maintenance, 17.8% production, transportation, and material moving
Income: Per capita: $22,262; Median household: $49,542; Average household: $64,743; Households with income of $100,000 or more: 17.4%; Poverty rate: 11.8%
Educational Attainment: High school diploma or higher: 76.2%; Bachelor's degree or higher: 13.6%; Graduate/professional degree or higher: 7.6%

School District(s)
Clymer Central SD (PK-12)
   Enrollment: 478 . . . . (716) 355-4444
Housing: Homeownership rate: 83.7%; Median home value: $108,200; Median year structure built: 1963; Homeowner vacancy rate: 0.0%; Median selected monthly owner costs: $924 with a mortgage, $393 without a mortgage; Median gross rent: $755 per month; Rental vacancy rate: 0.0%
Health Insurance: 62.5% have insurance; 46.1% have private insurance; 27.6% have public insurance; 37.5% do not have insurance; 60.2% of children under 18 do not have insurance
Transportation: Commute: 71.8% car, 2.8% public transportation, 10.1% walk, 9.9% work from home; Mean travel time to work: 22.3 minutes

DEWITTVILLE (unincorporated postal area)
ZCTA: 14728
  Covers a land area of 26.795 square miles and a water area of 0.047 square miles. Located at 42.26° N. Long; 79.42° W. Long. Elevation is 1,325 feet.

Population: 866; Growth (since 2000): -19.1%; Density: 32.3 persons per square mile; Race: 96.7% White, 0.0% Black/African American, 0.0% Asian, 0.0% American Indian/Alaska Native, 0.0% Native Hawaiian/Other Pacific Islander, 3.3% Two or more races, 0.0% Hispanic of any race; Average household size: 2.05; Median age: 60.5; Age under 18: 12.8%; Age 65 and over: 38.3%; Males per 100 females: 105.8; Marriage status: 13.6% never married, 70.5% now married, 2.5% separated, 9.7% widowed, 6.2% divorced; Foreign born: 1.6%; Speak English only: 99.0%; With disability: 15.1%; Veterans: 12.8%; Ancestry: 21.4% German, 17.6% English, 11.7% Irish, 10.3% American, 7.3% Swedish
Employment: 9.8% management, business, and financial, 7.3% computer, engineering, and science, 13.3% education, legal, community service, arts, and media, 2.2% healthcare practitioners, 18.0% service, 14.2% sales and office, 8.5% natural resources, construction, and maintenance, 26.6% production, transportation, and material moving
Income: Per capita: $31,285; Median household: $42,404; Average household: $61,970; Households with income of $100,000 or more: 16.2%; Poverty rate: 9.1%
Educational Attainment: High school diploma or higher: 91.5%; Bachelor's degree or higher: 26.6%; Graduate/professional degree or higher: 12.9%
Housing: Homeownership rate: 91.3%; Median home value: $93,300; Median year structure built: 1973; Homeowner vacancy rate: 0.0%; Median selected monthly owner costs: $898 with a mortgage, $428 without a mortgage; Median gross rent: n/a per month; Rental vacancy rate: 0.0%
Health Insurance: 97.9% have insurance; 70.7% have private insurance; 62.5% have public insurance; 2.1% do not have insurance; 0.0% of children under 18 do not have insurance
Transportation: Commute: 86.7% car, 0.0% public transportation, 5.1% walk, 2.0% work from home; Mean travel time to work: 19.3 minutes

DUNKIRK (city).

DUNKIRK (city). Covers a land area of 4.502 square miles and a water area of 0.050 square miles. Located at 42.48° N. Lat; 79.33° W. Long. Elevation is 617 feet.

History: In 1946, it developed a program to help Dunkerque, France (for which it was named), recover from World War II. Other U.S. cities followed, and established a program, called the One World Plan, to aid war-damaged European cities. Founded c.1800, Incorporated as city 1880.

Population: 12,064; Growth (since 2000): -8.1%; Density: 2,679.8 persons per square mile; Race: 87.9% White, 4.2% Black/African American, 0.4% Asian, 0.5% American Indian/Alaska Native, 0.0% Native Hawaiian/Other Pacific Islander, 3.3% Two or more races, 30.9% Hispanic of any race; Average household size: 2.30; Median age: 39.1; Age under 18: 21.2%; Age 65 and over: 15.8%; Males per 100 females: 96.2; Marriage status: 38.1% never married, 43.8% now married, 4.1% separated, 5.0% widowed, 13.1% divorced; Foreign born: 4.6%; Speak English only: 79.6%; With disability: 19.8%; Veterans: 9.4%; Ancestry: 21.2% Polish, 16.2% German, 13.4% Italian, 10.7% Irish, 5.2% English

Employment: 7.3% management, business, and financial, 2.2% computer, engineering, and science, 9.7% education, legal, community service, arts, and media, 4.5% healthcare practitioners, 25.4% service, 21.3% sales and office, 9.4% natural resources, construction, and maintenance, 20.3% production, transportation, and material moving

Income: Per capita: $20,052; Median household: $34,707; Average household: $44,791; Households with income of $100,000 or more: 8.2%; Poverty rate: 22.7%

Educational Attainment: High school diploma or higher: 85.2%; Bachelor's degree or higher: 13.9%; Graduate/professional degree or higher: 6.3%

School District(s)

Dunkirk City SD (PK-12)
    Enrollment: 2,065 . . . . (716) 366-9300

Housing: Homeownership rate: 60.0%; Median home value: $64,300; Median year structure built: Before 1940; Homeowner vacancy rate: 6.2%; Median selected monthly owner costs: $835 with a mortgage, $426 without a mortgage; Median gross rent: $640 per month; Rental vacancy rate: 3.0%

Health Insurance: 95.0% have insurance; 56.0% have private insurance; 53.3% have public insurance; 5.0% do not have insurance; 4.0% of children under 18 do not have insurance

Hospitals: Brooks Memorial Hospital (99 beds)

Safety: Violent crime rate: 36.3 per 10,000 population; Property crime rate: 165.5 per 10,000 population

Newspapers: The Observer (daily circulation 9,100)

Transportation: Commute: 93.0% car, 0.5% public transportation, 3.7% walk, 1.5% work from home; Mean travel time to work: 13.1 minutes; Amtrak: Bus service available.

Additional Information Contacts
City of Dunkirk . . . . (716) 366-3967
    http://www.dunkirkny.org

DUNKIRK (town).

DUNKIRK (town). Covers a land area of 6.228 square miles and a water area of 0.054 square miles. Located at 42.47° N. Lat; 79.32° W. Long. Elevation is 617 feet.

Population: 1,247; Growth (since 2000): -10.1%; Density: 200.2 persons per square mile; Race: 92.9% White, 1.5% Black/African American, 1.8% Asian, 1.0% American Indian/Alaska Native, 0.0% Native Hawaiian/Other Pacific Islander, 1.3% Two or more races, 21.3% Hispanic of any race; Average household size: 2.06; Median age: 57.7; Age under 18: 10.6%; Age 65 and over: 37.4%; Males per 100 females: 83.8; Marriage status: 26.4% never married, 45.0% now married, 3.4% separated, 16.5% widowed, 12.1% divorced; Foreign born: 5.0%; Speak English only: 80.6%; With disability: 24.3%; Veterans: 12.7%; Ancestry: 15.6% Polish, 14.3% German, 12.3% Italian, 9.3% Irish, 8.7% English

Employment: 9.2% management, business, and financial, 0.6% computer, engineering, and science, 11.9% education, legal, community service, arts, and media, 5.5% healthcare practitioners, 12.8% service, 23.1% sales and office, 5.9% natural resources, construction, and maintenance, 31.0% production, transportation, and material moving

Income: Per capita: $31,746; Median household: $38,984; Average household: $72,608; Households with income of $100,000 or more: 20.1%; Poverty rate: 15.5%

Educational Attainment: High school diploma or higher: 84.9%; Bachelor's degree or higher: 25.5%; Graduate/professional degree or higher: 11.8%

School District(s)

Dunkirk City SD (PK-12)
    Enrollment: 2,065 . . . . (716) 366-9300

Housing: Homeownership rate: 75.7%; Median home value: $99,700; Median year structure built: 1957; Homeowner vacancy rate: 4.3%; Median selected monthly owner costs: $1,086 with a mortgage, $446 without a mortgage; Median gross rent: $641 per month; Rental vacancy rate: 2.4%

Health Insurance: 98.0% have insurance; 66.2% have private insurance; 51.2% have public insurance; 2.0% do not have insurance; 0.0% of children under 18 do not have insurance

Hospitals: Brooks Memorial Hospital (99 beds)

Newspapers: The Observer (daily circulation 9,100)

Transportation: Commute: 96.3% car, 0.0% public transportation, 0.7% walk, 2.4% work from home; Mean travel time to work: 18.7 minutes; Amtrak: Bus service available.

ELLERY (town).

ELLERY (town). Covers a land area of 47.454 square miles and a water area of 0.117 square miles. Located at 42.19° N. Lat; 79.35° W. Long.

Population: 4,418; Growth (since 2000): -3.5%; Density: 93.1 persons per square mile; Race: 97.6% White, 1.4% Black/African American, 0.0% Asian, 0.1% American Indian/Alaska Native, 0.0% Native Hawaiian/Other Pacific Islander, 0.9% Two or more races, 0.2% Hispanic of any race; Average household size: 2.29; Median age: 49.5; Age under 18: 17.2%; Age 65 and over: 25.9%; Males per 100 females: 95.9; Marriage status: 24.8% never married, 59.1% now married, 0.6% separated, 6.8% widowed, 9.3% divorced; Foreign born: 0.2%; Speak English only: 99.3%; With disability: 9.7%; Veterans: 11.3%; Ancestry: 26.6% Swedish, 18.6% English, 18.6% German, 14.7% Italian, 14.1% Irish

Employment: 15.7% management, business, and financial, 3.2% computer, engineering, and science, 13.0% education, legal, community service, arts, and media, 5.0% healthcare practitioners, 23.2% service, 23.5% sales and office, 7.1% natural resources, construction, and maintenance, 9.3% production, transportation, and material moving

Income: Per capita: $32,855; Median household: $50,298; Average household: $76,307; Households with income of $100,000 or more: 24.8%; Poverty rate: 9.6%

Educational Attainment: High school diploma or higher: 95.5%; Bachelor's degree or higher: 29.5%; Graduate/professional degree or higher: 13.9%

Housing: Homeownership rate: 84.2%; Median home value: $128,500; Median year structure built: 1962; Homeowner vacancy rate: 1.4%; Median selected monthly owner costs: $1,232 with a mortgage, $447 without a mortgage; Median gross rent: $671 per month; Rental vacancy rate: 2.6%

Health Insurance: 94.1% have insurance; 80.0% have private insurance; 33.1% have public insurance; 5.9% do not have insurance; 4.7% of children under 18 do not have insurance

Transportation: Commute: 92.6% car, 0.0% public transportation, 2.7% walk, 4.2% work from home; Mean travel time to work: 18.6 minutes

Additional Information Contacts
Town of Ellery . . . . (716) 386-3465
    http://www.elleryny.org

ELLICOTT (town).

ELLICOTT (town). Covers a land area of 30.449 square miles and a water area of 0.024 square miles. Located at 42.13° N. Lat; 79.23° W. Long.

Population: 8,503; Growth (since 2000): -8.4%; Density: 279.2 persons per square mile; Race: 96.9% White, 0.8% Black/African American, 0.8% Asian, 0.0% American Indian/Alaska Native, 0.0% Native Hawaiian/Other Pacific Islander, 1.5% Two or more races, 1.8% Hispanic of any race; Average household size: 2.26; Median age: 46.0; Age under 18: 18.8%; Age 65 and over: 20.5%; Males per 100 females: 94.5; Marriage status: 25.7% never married, 53.6% now married, 2.9% separated, 8.5% widowed, 12.2% divorced; Foreign born: 1.5%; Speak English only: 96.1%; With disability: 13.9%; Veterans: 9.0%; Ancestry: 21.0% Italian, 20.9% Swedish, 17.0% German, 14.3% Irish, 13.3% English

Employment: 10.5% management, business, and financial, 3.5% computer, engineering, and science, 9.7% education, legal, community service, arts, and media, 6.2% healthcare practitioners, 17.4% service, 19.7% sales and office, 7.1% natural resources, construction, and maintenance, 25.9% production, transportation, and material moving

Income: Per capita: $26,859; Median household: $51,333; Average household: $60,335; Households with income of $100,000 or more: 18.2%; Poverty rate: 13.2%

Educational Attainment: High school diploma or higher: 91.0%; Bachelor's degree or higher: 21.4%; Graduate/professional degree or higher: 9.2%
Housing: Homeownership rate: 73.0%; Median home value: $87,600; Median year structure built: 1951; Homeowner vacancy rate: 3.0%; Median selected monthly owner costs: $971 with a mortgage, $433 without a mortgage; Median gross rent: $634 per month; Rental vacancy rate: 11.3%
Health Insurance: 94.6% have insurance; 73.3% have private insurance; 39.0% have public insurance; 5.4% do not have insurance; 6.8% of children under 18 do not have insurance
Safety: Violent crime rate: 17.7 per 10,000 population; Property crime rate: 363.2 per 10,000 population
Transportation: Commute: 93.4% car, 0.3% public transportation, 3.0% walk, 2.4% work from home; Mean travel time to work: 13.6 minutes
Additional Information Contacts
Town of Ellicott . . . . (716) 665-5317
    http://www.townofellicott.com

ELLINGTON (town). Covers a land area of 36.545 square miles and a water area of 0.014 square miles. Located at 42.22° N. Lat; 79.12° W. Long. Elevation is 1,371 feet.
Population: 1,711; Growth (since 2000): 4.4%; Density: 46.8 persons per square mile; Race: 97.7% White, 0.0% Black/African American, 0.5% Asian, 0.8% American Indian/Alaska Native, 0.0% Native Hawaiian/Other Pacific Islander, 1.0% Two or more races, 3.2% Hispanic of any race; Average household size: 2.83; Median age: 40.6; Age under 18: 25.4%; Age 65 and over: 13.4%; Males per 100 females: 105.6; Marriage status: 26.6% never married, 59.6% now married, 0.2% separated, 6.1% widowed, 7.7% divorced; Foreign born: 1.4%; Speak English only: 91.2%; With disability: 10.8%; Veterans: 8.6%; Ancestry: 20.7% German, 18.7% English, 12.9% Irish, 11.0% Swedish, 9.8% French
Employment: 17.2% management, business, and financial, 2.6% computer, engineering, and science, 7.9% education, legal, community service, arts, and media, 5.5% healthcare practitioners, 13.1% service, 18.6% sales and office, 11.4% natural resources, construction, and maintenance, 23.7% production, transportation, and material moving
Income: Per capita: $27,654; Median household: $53,558; Average household: $75,936; Households with income of $100,000 or more: 14.6%; Poverty rate: 12.7%
Educational Attainment: High school diploma or higher: 84.6%; Bachelor's degree or higher: 11.5%; Graduate/professional degree or higher: 3.2%
Housing: Homeownership rate: 84.8%; Median home value: $87,700; Median year structure built: 1971; Homeowner vacancy rate: 0.0%; Median selected monthly owner costs: $1,044 with a mortgage, $494 without a mortgage; Median gross rent: $613 per month; Rental vacancy rate: 0.0%
Health Insurance: 81.2% have insurance; 57.3% have private insurance; 34.5% have public insurance; 18.8% do not have insurance; 24.7% of children under 18 do not have insurance
Transportation: Commute: 90.5% car, 1.1% public transportation, 0.5% walk, 6.5% work from home; Mean travel time to work: 24.1 minutes

FALCONER (village). Covers a land area of 1.093 square miles and a water area of 0 square miles. Located at 42.12° N. Lat; 79.20° W. Long. Elevation is 1,263 feet.
History: Settled 1807, incorporated 1891.
Population: 2,430; Growth (since 2000): -4.3%; Density: 2,223.6 persons per square mile; Race: 96.7% White, 0.6% Black/African American, 1.2% Asian, 0.0% American Indian/Alaska Native, 0.0% Native Hawaiian/Other Pacific Islander, 1.6% Two or more races, 1.8% Hispanic of any race; Average household size: 2.29; Median age: 38.6; Age under 18: 24.1%; Age 65 and over: 17.9%; Males per 100 females: 100.2; Marriage status: 32.0% never married, 44.6% now married, 4.0% separated, 9.0% widowed, 14.6% divorced; Foreign born: 1.2%; Speak English only: 98.2%; With disability: 13.2%; Veterans: 10.1%; Ancestry: 25.6% Swedish, 25.5% Italian, 16.0% German, 13.5% English, 11.3% Irish
Employment: 7.4% management, business, and financial, 1.9% computer, engineering, and science, 8.7% education, legal, community service, arts, and media, 6.9% healthcare practitioners, 16.3% service, 25.5% sales and office, 3.2% natural resources, construction, and maintenance, 30.1% production, transportation, and material moving
Income: Per capita: $21,496; Median household: $41,028; Average household: $47,834; Households with income of $100,000 or more: 7.9%; Poverty rate: 14.4%

Educational Attainment: High school diploma or higher: 92.6%; Bachelor's degree or higher: 14.7%; Graduate/professional degree or higher: 6.5%
School District(s)
Falconer Central SD (PK-12)
    Enrollment: 1,183 . . . . (716) 665-6624
Housing: Homeownership rate: 57.8%; Median home value: $67,700; Median year structure built: Before 1940; Homeowner vacancy rate: 2.7%; Median selected monthly owner costs: $875 with a mortgage, $390 without a mortgage; Median gross rent: $597 per month; Rental vacancy rate: 8.4%
Health Insurance: 95.8% have insurance; 69.9% have private insurance; 46.7% have public insurance; 4.2% do not have insurance; 0.0% of children under 18 do not have insurance
Transportation: Commute: 89.3% car, 0.0% public transportation, 7.0% walk, 1.7% work from home; Mean travel time to work: 11.2 minutes

FINDLEY LAKE (unincorporated postal area)
ZCTA: 14736
    Covers a land area of 5.226 square miles and a water area of 0 square miles. Located at 42.14° N. Lat; 79.75° W. Long. Elevation is 1,440 feet.
Population: 245; Growth (since 2000): -15.2%; Density: 46.9 persons per square mile; Race: 100.0% White, 0.0% Black/African American, 0.0% Asian, 0.0% American Indian/Alaska Native, 0.0% Native Hawaiian/Other Pacific Islander, 0.0% Two or more races, 0.0% Hispanic of any race; Average household size: 2.31; Median age: 53.2; Age under 18: 21.6%; Age 65 and over: 9.4%; Males per 100 females: 100.0; Marriage status: 14.9% never married, 75.7% now married, 2.0% separated, 3.0% widowed, 6.4% divorced; Foreign born: 1.2%; Speak English only: 100.0%; With disability: 14.7%; Veterans: 8.3%; Ancestry: 29.4% German, 16.7% Irish, 10.6% English, 9.0% Italian, 8.2% European
Employment: 8.4% management, business, and financial, 0.0% computer, engineering, and science, 8.4% education, legal, community service, arts, and media, 3.1% healthcare practitioners, 20.6% service, 38.2% sales and office, 5.3% natural resources, construction, and maintenance, 16.0% production, transportation, and material moving
Income: Per capita: $27,832; Median household: $46,111; Average household: $64,570; Households with income of $100,000 or more: 18.9%; Poverty rate: 14.7%
Educational Attainment: High school diploma or higher: 98.4%; Bachelor's degree or higher: 20.2%; Graduate/professional degree or higher: 13.7%
Housing: Homeownership rate: 70.8%; Median home value: $155,700; Median year structure built: 1976; Homeowner vacancy rate: 0.0%; Median selected monthly owner costs: $1,375 with a mortgage, $0 without a mortgage; Median gross rent: $913 per month; Rental vacancy rate: 0.0%
Health Insurance: 89.8% have insurance; 74.3% have private insurance; 25.7% have public insurance; 10.2% do not have insurance; 0.0% of children under 18 do not have insurance
Transportation: Commute: 89.3% car, 0.0% public transportation, 7.6% walk, 3.1% work from home; Mean travel time to work: 18.9 minutes

FORESTVILLE (village). Covers a land area of 0.979 square miles and a water area of 0 square miles. Located at 42.47° N. Lat; 79.18° W. Long. Elevation is 932 feet.
Population: 746; Growth (since 2000): -3.1%; Density: 761.7 persons per square mile; Race: 95.3% White, 1.7% Black/African American, 0.0% Asian, 0.3% American Indian/Alaska Native, 0.0% Native Hawaiian/Other Pacific Islander, 2.7% Two or more races, 7.2% Hispanic of any race; Average household size: 2.66; Median age: 36.0; Age under 18: 26.4%; Age 65 and over: 11.9%; Males per 100 females: 112.5; Marriage status: 35.6% never married, 43.1% now married, 3.4% separated, 4.1% widowed, 17.3% divorced; Foreign born: 0.1%; Speak English only: 98.3%; With disability: 19.8%; Veterans: 11.5%; Ancestry: 26.8% German, 24.7% Irish, 22.7% Italian, 14.1% English, 13.1% Polish
Employment: 11.9% management, business, and financial, 2.8% computer, engineering, and science, 2.2% education, legal, community service, arts, and media, 6.3% healthcare practitioners, 19.7% service, 26.6% sales and office, 6.3% natural resources, construction, and maintenance, 24.1% production, transportation, and material moving
Income: Per capita: $20,525; Median household: $51,083; Average household: $54,654; Households with income of $100,000 or more: 9.8%; Poverty rate: 18.9%

Educational Attainment: High school diploma or higher: 94.0%; Bachelor's degree or higher: 11.7%; Graduate/professional degree or higher: 2.2%

School District(s)

Forestville Central SD (PK-12)
  Enrollment: 505 . . . . (716) 965-2742

Housing: Homeownership rate: 74.5%; Median home value: $80,400; Median year structure built: Before 1940; Homeowner vacancy rate: 0.0%; Median selected monthly owner costs: $938 with a mortgage, $417 without a mortgage; Median gross rent: $641 per month; Rental vacancy rate: 0.0%

Health Insurance: 95.4% have insurance; 61.1% have private insurance; 45.7% have public insurance; 4.6% do not have insurance; 0.0% of children under 18 do not have insurance

Transportation: Commute: 94.6% car, 0.0% public transportation, 2.0% walk, 3.4% work from home; Mean travel time to work: 16.3 minutes

FREDONIA (village).
Covers a land area of 5.189 square miles and a water area of 0 square miles. Located at 42.44° N. Lat; 79.33° W. Long. Elevation is 722 feet.

History: Incorporated 1829. Was the site of the first gas well in the U.S. The first local unit of the Natioanl Grange (Patrons of Husbandry) Movement was also founded here. State University of N.Y. at Fredonia here.

Population: 10,695; Growth (since 2000): -0.1%; Density: 2,061.1 persons per square mile; Race: 89.3% White, 3.9% Black/African American, 1.8% Asian, 0.0% American Indian/Alaska Native, 0.2% Native Hawaiian/Other Pacific Islander, 2.6% Two or more races, 6.6% Hispanic of any race; Average household size: 2.34; Median age: 25.4; Age under 18: 15.6%; Age 65 and over: 13.8%; Males per 100 females: 88.1; Marriage status: 50.6% never married, 39.2% now married, 1.8% separated, 4.9% widowed, 5.2% divorced; Foreign born: 4.8%; Speak English only: 92.9%; With disability: 9.1%; Veterans: 5.0%; Ancestry: 25.6% Italian, 24.8% German, 19.6% Irish, 13.9% Polish, 13.1% English

Employment: 10.9% management, business, and financial, 2.5% computer, engineering, and science, 21.9% education, legal, community service, arts, and media, 2.8% healthcare practitioners, 21.8% service, 22.9% sales and office, 7.5% natural resources, construction, and maintenance, 9.7% production, transportation, and material moving

Income: Per capita: $24,285; Median household: $49,826; Average household: $70,171; Households with income of $100,000 or more: 20.5%; Poverty rate: 20.8%

Educational Attainment: High school diploma or higher: 97.9%; Bachelor's degree or higher: 44.4%; Graduate/professional degree or higher: 23.6%

School District(s)

Fredonia Central SD (PK-12)
  Enrollment: 1,548 . . . . (716) 679-1581

Four-year College(s)

SUNY at Fredonia (Public)
  Enrollment: 4,630 . . . . (716) 673-3111
  Tuition: In-state $8,286; Out-of-state $17,936

Housing: Homeownership rate: 65.1%; Median home value: $133,200; Median year structure built: 1945; Homeowner vacancy rate: 5.0%; Median selected monthly owner costs: $1,224 with a mortgage, $612 without a mortgage; Median gross rent: $645 per month; Rental vacancy rate: 12.6%

Health Insurance: 97.1% have insurance; 78.4% have private insurance; 31.6% have public insurance; 2.9% do not have insurance; 1.2% of children under 18 do not have insurance

Safety: Violent crime rate: 12.3 per 10,000 population; Property crime rate: 148.9 per 10,000 population

Transportation: Commute: 79.7% car, 0.3% public transportation, 12.7% walk, 6.0% work from home; Mean travel time to work: 13.9 minutes; Amtrak: Train service available.

FRENCH CREEK (town).
Covers a land area of 36.259 square miles and a water area of 0.020 square miles. Located at 42.04° N. Lat; 79.71° W. Long. Elevation is 1,417 feet.

Population: 977; Growth (since 2000): 4.5%; Density: 26.9 persons per square mile; Race: 99.6% White, 0.0% Black/African American, 0.0% Asian, 0.0% American Indian/Alaska Native, 0.0% Native Hawaiian/Other Pacific Islander, 0.4% Two or more races, 0.0% Hispanic of any race; Average household size: 2.83; Median age: 35.4; Age under 18: 27.6%; Age 65 and over: 12.8%; Males per 100 females: 106.4; Marriage status: 29.3% never married, 57.3% now married, 1.8% separated, 3.6%

widowed, 9.8% divorced; Foreign born: 0.0%; Speak English only: 96.7%; With disability: 14.5%; Veterans: 9.6%; Ancestry: 30.5% German, 11.9% English, 11.7% Irish, 9.1% Polish, 7.8% Dutch

Employment: 11.1% management, business, and financial, 2.8% computer, engineering, and science, 8.9% education, legal, community service, arts, and media, 5.6% healthcare practitioners, 13.2% service, 13.2% sales and office, 16.9% natural resources, construction, and maintenance, 28.2% production, transportation, and material moving

Income: Per capita: $21,152; Median household: $51,563; Average household: $58,606; Households with income of $100,000 or more: 13.0%; Poverty rate: 19.3%

Educational Attainment: High school diploma or higher: 87.0%; Bachelor's degree or higher: 14.0%; Graduate/professional degree or higher: 5.0%

Housing: Homeownership rate: 83.8%; Median home value: $96,200; Median year structure built: 1985; Homeowner vacancy rate: 3.0%; Median selected monthly owner costs: $892 with a mortgage, $453 without a mortgage; Median gross rent: $680 per month; Rental vacancy rate: 20.0%

Health Insurance: 87.9% have insurance; 70.7% have private insurance; 30.7% have public insurance; 12.1% do not have insurance; 24.5% of children under 18 do not have insurance

Transportation: Commute: 95.9% car, 0.0% public transportation, 2.6% walk, 1.0% work from home; Mean travel time to work: 27.4 minutes

FREWSBURG (CDP).
Covers a land area of 3.373 square miles and a water area of 0.015 square miles. Located at 42.06° N. Lat; 79.13° W. Long. Elevation is 1,299 feet.

Population: 2,057; Growth (since 2000): 4.7%; Density: 609.9 persons per square mile; Race: 98.4% White, 1.5% Black/African American, 0.0% Asian, 0.0% American Indian/Alaska Native, 0.0% Native Hawaiian/Other Pacific Islander, 0.0% Two or more races, 0.0% Hispanic of any race; Average household size: 2.46; Median age: 53.4; Age under 18: 19.2%; Age 65 and over: 23.8%; Males per 100 females: 90.0; Marriage status: 23.9% never married, 55.0% now married, 0.8% separated, 14.1% widowed, 7.0% divorced; Foreign born: 0.0%; Speak English only: 100.0%; With disability: 16.5%; Veterans: 12.3%; Ancestry: 33.0% Swedish, 15.5% Italian, 15.2% Irish, 10.8% Polish, 8.7% English

Employment: 5.0% management, business, and financial, 0.0% computer, engineering, and science, 9.9% education, legal, community service, arts, and media, 8.7% healthcare practitioners, 13.6% service, 30.0% sales and office, 6.9% natural resources, construction, and maintenance, 25.9% production, transportation, and material moving

Income: Per capita: $27,234; Median household: $49,146; Average household: $65,530; Households with income of $100,000 or more: 21.4%; Poverty rate: 2.6%

Educational Attainment: High school diploma or higher: 90.4%; Bachelor's degree or higher: 20.8%; Graduate/professional degree or higher: 8.3%

School District(s)

Frewsburg Central SD (PK-12)
  Enrollment: 836 . . . . (716) 569-7041

Housing: Homeownership rate: 84.9%; Median home value: $87,400; Median year structure built: 1953; Homeowner vacancy rate: 0.0%; Median selected monthly owner costs: $957 with a mortgage, $513 without a mortgage; Median gross rent: n/a per month; Rental vacancy rate: 0.0%

Health Insurance: 99.3% have insurance; 70.0% have private insurance; 47.8% have public insurance; 0.7% do not have insurance; 0.0% of children under 18 do not have insurance

Transportation: Commute: 95.1% car, 0.0% public transportation, 0.0% walk, 3.2% work from home; Mean travel time to work: 16.8 minutes

GERRY (town).
Covers a land area of 36.125 square miles and a water area of 0.018 square miles. Located at 42.22° N. Lat; 79.24° W. Long. Elevation is 1,302 feet.

Population: 1,871; Growth (since 2000): -8.9%; Density: 51.8 persons per square mile; Race: 96.8% White, 1.3% Black/African American, 0.0% Asian, 0.0% American Indian/Alaska Native, 0.0% Native Hawaiian/Other Pacific Islander, 1.7% Two or more races, 0.3% Hispanic of any race; Average household size: 2.39; Median age: 51.6; Age under 18: 16.6%; Age 65 and over: 25.2%; Males per 100 females: 91.8; Marriage status: 22.3% never married, 57.5% now married, 1.7% separated, 9.5% widowed, 10.7% divorced; Foreign born: 1.3%; Speak English only: 98.6%; With disability: 15.6%; Veterans: 12.8%; Ancestry: 19.1% Swedish, 17.2% German, 16.2% English, 13.2% Irish, 8.0% American

Employment: 13.2% management, business, and financial, 1.9% computer, engineering, and science, 3.1% education, legal, community service, arts, and media, 5.3% healthcare practitioners, 19.0% service, 25.6% sales and office, 12.9% natural resources, construction, and maintenance, 19.0% production, transportation, and material moving
Income: Per capita: $24,055; Median household: $50,263; Average household: $57,959; Households with income of $100,000 or more: 13.5%; Poverty rate: 7.1%
Educational Attainment: High school diploma or higher: 88.0%; Bachelor's degree or higher: 12.6%; Graduate/professional degree or higher: 4.2%
Housing: Homeownership rate: 78.0%; Median home value: $86,400; Median year structure built: 1973; Homeowner vacancy rate: 4.0%; Median selected monthly owner costs: $976 with a mortgage, $404 without a mortgage; Median gross rent: $633 per month; Rental vacancy rate: 12.0%
Health Insurance: 92.8% have insurance; 70.0% have private insurance; 40.7% have public insurance; 7.2% do not have insurance; 9.1% of children under 18 do not have insurance
Transportation: Commute: 91.4% car, 0.0% public transportation, 0.0% walk, 7.4% work from home; Mean travel time to work: 22.1 minutes

GREENHURST (unincorporated postal area)
ZCTA: 14742

Covers a land area of 0.225 square miles and a water area of 0 square miles. Located at 42.12° N. Lat; 79.31° W. Long. Elevation is 1,319 feet.
Population: 301; Growth (since 2000): n/a; Density: 1,340.4 persons per square mile; Race: 75.1% White, 10.0% Black/African American, 0.0% Asian, 2.0% American Indian/Alaska Native, 0.0% Native Hawaiian/Other Pacific Islander, 13.0% Two or more races, 0.0% Hispanic of any race; Average household size: 2.04; Median age: 62.8; Age under 18: 0.0%; Age 65 and over: 46.2%; Males per 100 females: 67.9; Marriage status: 20.6% never married, 46.2% now married, 0.0% separated, 27.2% widowed, 6.0% divorced; Foreign born: 2.3%; Speak English only: 96.7%; With disability: 4.6%; Veterans: 14.0%; Ancestry: 42.5% Swedish, 12.6% German, 7.3% English, 5.6% Irish, 4.7% American
Employment: 25.6% management, business, and financial, 0.0% computer, engineering, and science, 8.3% education, legal, community service, arts, and media, 0.0% healthcare practitioners, 32.2% service, 8.3% sales and office, 0.0% natural resources, construction, and maintenance, 25.6% production, transportation, and material moving
Income: Per capita: $25,747; Median household: n/a; Average household: $73,045; Households with income of $100,000 or more: 10.6%; Poverty rate: 4.0%
Educational Attainment: High school diploma or higher: 95.2%; Bachelor's degree or higher: 9.7%; Graduate/professional degree or higher: 7.6%
Housing: Homeownership rate: 78.8%; Median home value: $95,800; Median year structure built: 1944; Homeowner vacancy rate: 0.0%; Median selected monthly owner costs: $0 with a mortgage, $347 without a mortgage; Median gross rent: n/a per month; Rental vacancy rate: 0.0%
Health Insurance: 100.0% have insurance; 87.3% have private insurance; 28.9% have public insurance; 0.0% do not have insurance; 0.0% of children under 18 do not have insurance
Transportation: Commute: 100.0% car, 0.0% public transportation, 0.0% walk, 0.0% work from home; Mean travel time to work: 14.5 minutes

HANOVER (town). Covers a land area of 49.178 square miles and a water area of 0.284 square miles. Located at 42.49° N. Lat; 79.12° W. Long.
Population: 6,904; Growth (since 2000): -9.6%; Density: 140.4 persons per square mile; Race: 94.2% White, 1.6% Black/African American, 0.0% Asian, 1.4% American Indian/Alaska Native, 0.0% Native Hawaiian/Other Pacific Islander, 2.0% Two or more races, 4.1% Hispanic of any race; Average household size: 2.34; Median age: 44.9; Age under 18: 19.9%; Age 65 and over: 19.5%; Males per 100 females: 97.3; Marriage status: 28.7% never married, 50.8% now married, 3.3% separated, 7.1% widowed, 13.4% divorced; Foreign born: 1.7%; Speak English only: 97.4%; With disability: 18.3%; Veterans: 11.0%; Ancestry: 29.7% German, 19.0% Italian, 19.0% Irish, 17.3% Polish, 12.9% English
Employment: 9.4% management, business, and financial, 1.7% computer, engineering, and science, 9.7% education, legal, community service, arts, and media, 5.0% healthcare practitioners, 23.3% service, 20.9% sales and

office, 13.1% natural resources, construction, and maintenance, 16.9% production, transportation, and material moving
Income: Per capita: $25,774; Median household: $56,143; Average household: $60,344; Households with income of $100,000 or more: 11.9%; Poverty rate: 12.4%
Educational Attainment: High school diploma or higher: 89.3%; Bachelor's degree or higher: 19.9%; Graduate/professional degree or higher: 7.6%
Housing: Homeownership rate: 79.8%; Median home value: $88,700; Median year structure built: 1951; Homeowner vacancy rate: 1.1%; Median selected monthly owner costs: $976 with a mortgage, $473 without a mortgage; Median gross rent: $719 per month; Rental vacancy rate: 10.2%
Health Insurance: 94.9% have insurance; 71.1% have private insurance; 41.1% have public insurance; 5.1% do not have insurance; 1.7% of children under 18 do not have insurance
Transportation: Commute: 95.5% car, 0.0% public transportation, 2.3% walk, 1.9% work from home; Mean travel time to work: 24.0 minutes
Additional Information Contacts
Town of Hanover . . . . (716) 934-2273
    http://townofhanover.org/content

HARMONY (town). Covers a land area of 45.400 square miles and a water area of 0.161 square miles. Located at 42.05° N. Lat; 79.46° W. Long.
Population: 2,128; Growth (since 2000): -9.0%; Density: 46.9 persons per square mile; Race: 98.5% White, 0.0% Black/African American, 0.0% Asian, 0.0% American Indian/Alaska Native, 0.0% Native Hawaiian/Other Pacific Islander, 0.5% Two or more races, 1.7% Hispanic of any race; Average household size: 2.57; Median age: 43.4; Age under 18: 24.5%; Age 65 and over: 18.4%; Males per 100 females: 97.3; Marriage status: 24.7% never married, 58.1% now married, 4.2% separated, 5.4% widowed, 11.8% divorced; Foreign born: 0.4%; Speak English only: 93.9%; With disability: 14.2%; Veterans: 8.0%; Ancestry: 23.7% German, 19.9% Swedish, 14.3% English, 10.1% Irish, 9.9% Italian
Employment: 9.0% management, business, and financial, 1.5% computer, engineering, and science, 9.6% education, legal, community service, arts, and media, 7.2% healthcare practitioners, 11.9% service, 26.2% sales and office, 14.2% natural resources, construction, and maintenance, 20.5% production, transportation, and material moving
Income: Per capita: $24,261; Median household: $50,417; Average household: $60,814; Households with income of $100,000 or more: 12.3%; Poverty rate: 9.6%
Educational Attainment: High school diploma or higher: 89.4%; Bachelor's degree or higher: 15.9%; Graduate/professional degree or higher: 6.9%
Housing: Homeownership rate: 81.8%; Median home value: $82,600; Median year structure built: 1963; Homeowner vacancy rate: 2.1%; Median selected monthly owner costs: $1,015 with a mortgage, $369 without a mortgage; Median gross rent: $622 per month; Rental vacancy rate: 3.2%
Health Insurance: 93.0% have insurance; 70.5% have private insurance; 37.1% have public insurance; 7.0% do not have insurance; 4.2% of children under 18 do not have insurance
Transportation: Commute: 93.2% car, 0.5% public transportation, 1.8% walk, 3.3% work from home; Mean travel time to work: 22.5 minutes

JAMESTOWN (city). Covers a land area of 8.935 square miles and a water area of 0.128 square miles. Located at 42.10° N. Lat; 79.24° W. Long. Elevation is 1,378 feet.
History: The founder of the Jamestown settlement was James Prendergast, who purchased 1,000 acres of land his brother had earlier bought from the Holland Land Company. Among the early settlers were a number of skilled woodworkers, who began to make furniture to supply the needs of the pioneers of the region. In 1849, some Swedish immigrants appeared. After the close of the Civil War, many others joined them. Most of them were cabinet makers attracted by the furniture factories. In 1888, two years after Jamestown had become officially a city, construction of metal furniture had begun.
Population: 30,094; Growth (since 2000): -5.2%; Density: 3,368.3 persons per square mile; Race: 86.9% White, 5.2% Black/African American, 0.5% Asian, 0.4% American Indian/Alaska Native, 0.0% Native Hawaiian/Other Pacific Islander, 3.7% Two or more races, 8.6% Hispanic of any race; Average household size: 2.29; Median age: 38.1; Age under 18: 23.9%; Age 65 and over: 16.3%; Males per 100 females: 94.6; Marriage status: 35.4% never married, 41.7% now married, 3.7% separated, 6.8% widowed, 16.1% divorced; Foreign born: 1.8%; Speak English only: 91.2%;

With disability: 20.5%; Veterans: 8.5%; Ancestry: 16.4% Italian, 15.6% German, 15.5% Swedish, 13.4% Irish, 9.4% English
Employment: 9.4% management, business, and financial, 2.6% computer, engineering, and science, 10.9% education, legal, community service, arts, and media, 4.6% healthcare practitioners, 18.6% service, 26.1% sales and office, 7.5% natural resources, construction, and maintenance, 20.3% production, transportation, and material moving
Income: Per capita: $18,983; Median household: $31,875; Average household: $43,076; Households with income of $100,000 or more: 6.8%; Poverty rate: 29.7%
Educational Attainment: High school diploma or higher: 86.3%; Bachelor's degree or higher: 17.5%; Graduate/professional degree or higher: 7.3%

School District(s)
Jamestown City SD (PK-12)
  Enrollment: 5,013 . . . . (716) 483-4420
Southwestern Central SD At Jamestown (PK-12)
  Enrollment: 1,376 . . . . (716) 484-1136
Four-year College(s)
Jamestown Business College (Private, For-profit)
  Enrollment: 323 . . . . (716) 664-5100
  Tuition: In-state $12,600; Out-of-state $12,600
Two-year College(s)
Jamestown Community College (Public)
  Enrollment: 4,463 . . . . (716) 338-1000
  Tuition: In-state $5,670; Out-of-state $10,420
Housing: Homeownership rate: 50.3%; Median home value: $63,900; Median year structure built: Before 1940; Homeowner vacancy rate: 2.2%; Median selected monthly owner costs: $850 with a mortgage, $395 without a mortgage; Median gross rent: $593 per month; Rental vacancy rate: 10.3%
Health Insurance: 93.4% have insurance; 53.6% have private insurance; 54.2% have public insurance; 6.6% do not have insurance; 6.1% of children under 18 do not have insurance
Hospitals: Woman's Christian Association (342 beds)
Safety: Violent crime rate: 66.3 per 10,000 population; Property crime rate: 297.3 per 10,000 population
Newspapers: Post-Journal (daily circulation 18,600)
Transportation: Commute: 88.1% car, 0.8% public transportation, 7.2% walk, 2.2% work from home; Mean travel time to work: 14.7 minutes; Amtrak: Bus service available.
Airports: Chautauqua County/Jamestown (commercial service–non-primary)
Additional Information Contacts
City of Jamestown . . . . (716) 483-7612
  http://www.jamestownny.net

JAMESTOWN WEST (CDP).
Covers a land area of 2.517 square miles and a water area of 0 square miles. Located at 42.09° N. Lat; 79.28° W. Long.
Population: 2,334; Growth (since 2000): -7.9%; Density: 927.4 persons per square mile; Race: 94.9% White, 1.7% Black/African American, 0.3% Asian, 0.0% American Indian/Alaska Native, 0.0% Native Hawaiian/Other Pacific Islander, 2.7% Two or more races, 2.1% Hispanic of any race; Average household size: 2.17; Median age: 52.4; Age under 18: 15.6%; Age 65 and over: 28.1%; Males per 100 females: 86.7; Marriage status: 25.1% never married, 52.8% now married, 1.9% separated, 12.7% widowed, 9.4% divorced; Foreign born: 3.3%; Speak English only: 94.9%; With disability: 19.8%; Veterans: 5.6%; Ancestry: 17.4% English, 17.2% Italian, 16.6% German, 16.2% Irish, 15.4% Swedish
Employment: 11.4% management, business, and financial, 8.9% computer, engineering, and science, 13.5% education, legal, community service, arts, and media, 4.5% healthcare practitioners, 12.3% service, 23.3% sales and office, 5.3% natural resources, construction, and maintenance, 20.8% production, transportation, and material moving
Income: Per capita: $30,881; Median household: $64,901; Average household: $68,655; Households with income of $100,000 or more: 22.4%; Poverty rate: 6.0%
Educational Attainment: High school diploma or higher: 87.9%; Bachelor's degree or higher: 32.7%; Graduate/professional degree or higher: 14.0%
Housing: Homeownership rate: 81.9%; Median home value: $100,000; Median year structure built: 1956; Homeowner vacancy rate: 0.0%; Median selected monthly owner costs: $981 with a mortgage, $466 without a mortgage; Median gross rent: $721 per month; Rental vacancy rate: 0.0%

Health Insurance: 98.1% have insurance; 73.9% have private insurance; 42.9% have public insurance; 1.9% do not have insurance; 1.6% of children under 18 do not have insurance
Transportation: Commute: 92.2% car, 0.8% public transportation, 2.1% walk, 3.9% work from home; Mean travel time to work: 16.7 minutes

KENNEDY (CDP).
Covers a land area of 2.035 square miles and a water area of 0 square miles. Located at 42.16° N. Lat; 79.10° W. Long. Elevation is 1,266 feet.
Population: 429; Growth (since 2000): n/a; Density: 210.8 persons per square mile; Race: 100.0% White, 0.0% Black/African American, 0.0% Asian, 0.0% American Indian/Alaska Native, 0.0% Native Hawaiian/Other Pacific Islander, 0.0% Two or more races, 0.0% Hispanic of any race; Average household size: 2.27; Median age: 54.4; Age under 18: 14.2%; Age 65 and over: 27.5%; Males per 100 females: 97.0; Marriage status: 17.6% never married, 60.2% now married, 2.1% separated, 7.8% widowed, 14.4% divorced; Foreign born: 0.0%; Speak English only: 98.8%; With disability: 11.9%; Veterans: 11.7%; Ancestry: 28.7% Swedish, 18.6% English, 14.9% German, 14.2% American, 12.8% Italian
Employment: 11.2% management, business, and financial, 2.9% computer, engineering, and science, 11.2% education, legal, community service, arts, and media, 3.4% healthcare practitioners, 6.8% service, 30.7% sales and office, 9.8% natural resources, construction, and maintenance, 23.9% production, transportation, and material moving
Income: Per capita: $24,846; Median household: $41,583; Average household: $56,003; Households with income of $100,000 or more: 9.0%; Poverty rate: 15.4%
Educational Attainment: High school diploma or higher: 82.1%; Bachelor's degree or higher: 8.8%; Graduate/professional degree or higher: 7.3%

School District(s)
Falconer Central SD (PK-12)
  Enrollment: 1,183 . . . . (716) 665-6624
Housing: Homeownership rate: 75.7%; Median home value: $67,100; Median year structure built: Before 1940; Homeowner vacancy rate: 0.0%; Median selected monthly owner costs: $833 with a mortgage, $443 without a mortgage; Median gross rent: n/a per month; Rental vacancy rate: 23.3%
Health Insurance: 98.6% have insurance; 75.5% have private insurance; 44.1% have public insurance; 1.4% do not have insurance; 0.0% of children under 18 do not have insurance
Transportation: Commute: 94.0% car, 0.0% public transportation, 6.0% walk, 0.0% work from home; Mean travel time to work: 19.0 minutes

KIANTONE (town).
Covers a land area of 18.397 square miles and a water area of 0.140 square miles. Located at 42.03° N. Lat; 79.19° W. Long. Elevation is 1,503 feet.
Population: 1,378; Growth (since 2000): -0.5%; Density: 74.9 persons per square mile; Race: 99.7% White, 0.3% Black/African American, 0.0% Asian, 0.0% American Indian/Alaska Native, 0.0% Native Hawaiian/Other Pacific Islander, 0.0% Two or more races, 2.0% Hispanic of any race; Average household size: 2.59; Median age: 44.0; Age under 18: 26.9%; Age 65 and over: 18.1%; Males per 100 females: 96.8; Marriage status: 21.3% never married, 61.1% now married, 1.2% separated, 7.8% widowed, 9.7% divorced; Foreign born: 1.5%; Speak English only: 97.4%; With disability: 12.0%; Veterans: 10.9%; Ancestry: 27.3% Swedish, 16.4% German, 13.1% Irish, 12.7% Italian, 10.9% English
Employment: 12.9% management, business, and financial, 0.8% computer, engineering, and science, 13.1% education, legal, community service, arts, and media, 6.5% healthcare practitioners, 15.4% service, 25.6% sales and office, 8.1% natural resources, construction, and maintenance, 17.6% production, transportation, and material moving
Income: Per capita: $28,138; Median household: $58,889; Average household: $72,019; Households with income of $100,000 or more: 22.5%; Poverty rate: 5.2%
Educational Attainment: High school diploma or higher: 92.3%; Bachelor's degree or higher: 26.0%; Graduate/professional degree or higher: 13.5%
Housing: Homeownership rate: 92.5%; Median home value: $118,500; Median year structure built: 1966; Homeowner vacancy rate: 0.0%; Median selected monthly owner costs: $1,110 with a mortgage, $415 without a mortgage; Median gross rent: $775 per month; Rental vacancy rate: 0.0%
Health Insurance: 98.1% have insurance; 81.1% have private insurance; 29.2% have public insurance; 1.9% do not have insurance; 3.2% of children under 18 do not have insurance

Transportation: Commute: 95.4% car, 0.0% public transportation, 2.0% walk, 2.7% work from home; Mean travel time to work: 14.4 minutes

LAKEWOOD (village). Covers a land area of 1.976 square miles and a water area of 0 square miles. Located at 42.10° N. Lat; 79.32° W. Long. Elevation is 1,325 feet.

History: Settled 1809, incorporated 1893.

Population: 2,888; Growth (since 2000): -11.4%; Density: 1,461.4 persons per square mile; Race: 98.5% White, 0.6% Black/African American, 0.9% Asian, 0.0% American Indian/Alaska Native, 0.0% Native Hawaiian/Other Pacific Islander, 0.0% Two or more races, 1.0% Hispanic of any race; Average household size: 2.03; Median age: 47.9; Age under 18: 21.1%; Age 65 and over: 27.1%; Males per 100 females: 92.4; Marriage status: 24.9% never married, 48.7% now married, 1.8% separated, 12.8% widowed, 13.6% divorced; Foreign born: 1.4%; Speak English only: 97.4%; With disability: 13.9%; Veterans: 9.6%; Ancestry: 26.2% German, 15.0% Swedish, 14.7% Irish, 13.0% Italian, 12.3% English

Employment: 15.3% management, business, and financial, 5.8% computer, engineering, and science, 12.6% education, legal, community service, arts, and media, 9.5% healthcare practitioners, 16.3% service, 21.1% sales and office, 6.2% natural resources, construction, and maintenance, 13.1% production, transportation, and material moving

Income: Per capita: $33,221; Median household: $49,180; Average household: $67,703; Households with income of $100,000 or more: 20.3%; Poverty rate: 11.5%

Educational Attainment: High school diploma or higher: 94.7%; Bachelor's degree or higher: 34.3%; Graduate/professional degree or higher: 15.3%

Housing: Homeownership rate: 64.5%; Median home value: $114,900; Median year structure built: 1958; Homeowner vacancy rate: 7.4%; Median selected monthly owner costs: $1,366 with a mortgage, $469 without a mortgage; Median gross rent: $680 per month; Rental vacancy rate: 5.1%

Health Insurance: 95.6% have insurance; 74.4% have private insurance; 42.5% have public insurance; 4.4% do not have insurance; 0.0% of children under 18 do not have insurance

Transportation: Commute: 95.7% car, 0.0% public transportation, 1.6% walk, 2.0% work from home; Mean travel time to work: 15.0 minutes

LILY DALE (unincorporated postal area)
ZCTA: 14752

Covers a land area of 0.251 square miles and a water area of 0 square miles. Located at 42.35° N. Lat; 79.32° W. Long. Elevation is 1,332 feet.

Population: 221; Growth (since 2000): n/a; Density: 881.3 persons per square mile; Race: 100.0% White, 0.0% Black/African American, 0.0% Asian, 0.0% American Indian/Alaska Native, 0.0% Native Hawaiian/Other Pacific Islander, 0.0% Two or more races, 0.0% Hispanic of any race; Average household size: 1.53; Median age: 54.6; Age under 18: 13.6%; Age 65 and over: 40.3%; Males per 100 females: 65.7; Marriage status: 35.1% never married, 35.6% now married, 0.0% separated, 4.7% widowed, 24.6% divorced; Foreign born: 11.8%; Speak English only: 95.8%; With disability: 31.7%; Veterans: 0.0%; Ancestry: 38.5% Irish, 13.6% German, 12.2% Czech, 12.2% English, 7.7% French

Employment: 48.6% management, business, and financial, 25.7% computer, engineering, and science, 0.0% education, legal, community service, arts, and media, 0.0% healthcare practitioners, 0.0% service, 25.7% sales and office, 0.0% natural resources, construction, and maintenance, 0.0% production, transportation, and material moving

Income: Per capita: $24,106; Median household: n/a; Average household: $35,638; Households with income of $100,000 or more: 5.6%; Poverty rate: 48.9%

Educational Attainment: High school diploma or higher: 88.7%; Bachelor's degree or higher: 29.1%; Graduate/professional degree or higher: 17.9%

Housing: Homeownership rate: 80.6%; Median home value: $83,300; Median year structure built: Before 1940; Homeowner vacancy rate: 0.0%; Median selected monthly owner costs: $0 with a mortgage, $369 without a mortgage; Median gross rent: n/a per month; Rental vacancy rate: 0.0%

Health Insurance: 100.0% have insurance; 45.7% have private insurance; 82.8% have public insurance; 0.0% do not have insurance; 0.0% of children under 18 do not have insurance

Transportation: Commute: 77.1% car, 0.0% public transportation, 0.0% walk, 22.9% work from home; Mean travel time to work: 0.0 minutes

MAPLE SPRINGS (unincorporated postal area)
ZCTA: 14756

Covers a land area of 0.137 square miles and a water area of 0 square miles. Located at 42.20° N. Lat; 79.42° W. Long. Elevation is 1,312 feet.

Population: 81; Growth (since 2000): n/a; Density: 590.7 persons per square mile; Race: 100.0% White, 0.0% Black/African American, 0.0% Asian, 0.0% American Indian/Alaska Native, 0.0% Native Hawaiian/Other Pacific Islander, 0.0% Two or more races, 0.0% Hispanic of any race; Average household size: 1.69; Median age: 45.9; Age under 18: 0.0%; Age 65 and over: 22.2%; Males per 100 females: 89.7; Marriage status: 40.7% never married, 45.7% now married, 0.0% separated, 0.0% widowed, 13.6% divorced; Foreign born: 0.0%; Speak English only: 100.0%; With disability: 21.0%; Veterans: 22.2%; Ancestry: 35.8% Italian, 28.4% Swedish, 27.2% German, 24.7% Irish, 21.0% English

Employment: 0.0% management, business, and financial, 0.0% computer, engineering, and science, 57.6% education, legal, community service, arts, and media, 0.0% healthcare practitioners, 42.4% service, 0.0% sales and office, 0.0% natural resources, construction, and maintenance, 0.0% production, transportation, and material moving

Income: Per capita: $31,904; Median household: $39,211; Average household: $51,400; Households with income of $100,000 or more: 16.7%; Poverty rate: 13.6%

Educational Attainment: High school diploma or higher: 100.0%; Bachelor's degree or higher: 59.3%; Graduate/professional degree or higher: n/a

Housing: Homeownership rate: 100.0%; Median home value: n/a; Median year structure built: 1950; Homeowner vacancy rate: 0.0%; Median selected monthly owner costs: $0 with a mortgage, $0 without a mortgage; Median gross rent: n/a per month; Rental vacancy rate: 0.0%

Health Insurance: 100.0% have insurance; 86.4% have private insurance; 35.8% have public insurance; 0.0% do not have insurance; 0.0% of children under 18 do not have insurance

Transportation: Commute: 100.0% car, 0.0% public transportation, 0.0% walk, 0.0% work from home; Mean travel time to work: 0.0 minutes

MAYVILLE (village). County seat. Covers a land area of 1.991 square miles and a water area of 0.002 square miles. Located at 42.25° N. Lat; 79.50° W. Long. Elevation is 1,453 feet.

History: Incorporated 1830.

Population: 1,331; Growth (since 2000): -24.2%; Density: 668.4 persons per square mile; Race: 91.7% White, 5.9% Black/African American, 0.0% Asian, 0.0% American Indian/Alaska Native, 0.0% Native Hawaiian/Other Pacific Islander, 0.2% Two or more races, 3.0% Hispanic of any race; Average household size: 2.19; Median age: 38.3; Age under 18: 18.2%; Age 65 and over: 15.6%; Males per 100 females: 116.3; Marriage status: 37.5% never married, 43.2% now married, 4.0% separated, 5.9% widowed, 13.5% divorced; Foreign born: 0.8%; Speak English only: 96.4%; With disability: 15.2%; Veterans: 6.9%; Ancestry: 27.9% German, 15.8% Swedish, 14.4% English, 10.6% Irish, 8.7% Italian

Employment: 9.6% management, business, and financial, 2.4% computer, engineering, and science, 9.3% education, legal, community service, arts, and media, 8.2% healthcare practitioners, 24.5% service, 23.9% sales and office, 14.8% natural resources, construction, and maintenance, 7.2% production, transportation, and material moving

Income: Per capita: $22,650; Median household: $51,635; Average household: $58,798; Households with income of $100,000 or more: 13.7%; Poverty rate: 16.2%

Educational Attainment: High school diploma or higher: 90.9%; Bachelor's degree or higher: 19.0%; Graduate/professional degree or higher: 8.7%

School District(s)
Chautauqua Lake Central SD (PK-12)
    Enrollment: 907 . . . . (716) 753-5808

Housing: Homeownership rate: 66.5%; Median home value: $101,200; Median year structure built: 1948; Homeowner vacancy rate: 3.8%; Median selected monthly owner costs: $985 with a mortgage, $465 without a mortgage; Median gross rent: $471 per month; Rental vacancy rate: 5.1%

Health Insurance: 96.3% have insurance; 69.7% have private insurance; 43.8% have public insurance; 3.7% do not have insurance; 0.0% of children under 18 do not have insurance

Transportation: Commute: 88.6% car, 0.0% public transportation, 5.1% walk, 4.9% work from home; Mean travel time to work: 20.6 minutes

MINA (town). Covers a land area of 35.817 square miles and a water area of 0.511 square miles. Located at 42.12° N. Lat; 79.70° W. Long. Elevation is 1,594 feet.
Population: 983; Growth (since 2000): -16.4%; Density: 27.4 persons per square mile; Race: 95.4% White, 0.0% Black/African American, 0.0% Asian, 0.0% American Indian/Alaska Native, 0.0% Native Hawaiian/Other Pacific Islander, 4.6% Two or more races, 0.0% Hispanic of any race; Average household size: 2.49; Median age: 46.0; Age under 18: 21.6%; Age 65 and over: 11.1%; Males per 100 females: 97.9; Marriage status: 23.0% never married, 63.5% now married, 1.6% separated, 4.7% widowed, 8.8% divorced; Foreign born: 0.3%; Speak English only: 98.8%; With disability: 11.3%; Veterans: 9.6%; Ancestry: 23.7% German, 15.8% English, 9.1% American, 8.9% Irish, 7.5% Polish
Employment: 14.8% management, business, and financial, 3.9% computer, engineering, and science, 9.8% education, legal, community service, arts, and media, 10.6% healthcare practitioners, 13.6% service, 19.3% sales and office, 10.0% natural resources, construction, and maintenance, 18.1% production, transportation, and material moving
Income: Per capita: $25,539; Median household: $46,321; Average household: $62,948; Households with income of $100,000 or more: 19.2%; Poverty rate: 6.8%
Educational Attainment: High school diploma or higher: 89.7%; Bachelor's degree or higher: 20.8%; Graduate/professional degree or higher: 11.4%
Housing: Homeownership rate: 86.6%; Median home value: $139,500; Median year structure built: 1969; Homeowner vacancy rate: 2.8%; Median selected monthly owner costs: $1,150 with a mortgage, $496 without a mortgage; Median gross rent: $773 per month; Rental vacancy rate: 15.9%
Health Insurance: 92.9% have insurance; 72.0% have private insurance; 29.5% have public insurance; 7.1% do not have insurance; 0.0% of children under 18 do not have insurance
Transportation: Commute: 92.2% car, 0.0% public transportation, 5.5% walk, 2.2% work from home; Mean travel time to work: 27.2 minutes

NORTH HARMONY (town). Covers a land area of 42.133 square miles and a water area of 0.023 square miles. Located at 42.13° N. Lat; 79.46° W. Long.
Population: 2,167; Growth (since 2000): -14.0%; Density: 51.4 persons per square mile; Race: 98.0% White, 0.0% Black/African American, 1.6% Asian, 0.0% American Indian/Alaska Native, 0.0% Native Hawaiian/Other Pacific Islander, 0.0% Two or more races, 3.2% Hispanic of any race; Average household size: 2.37; Median age: 49.4; Age under 18: 18.4%; Age 65 and over: 23.4%; Males per 100 females: 104.1; Marriage status: 19.6% never married, 64.4% now married, 1.3% separated, 5.5% widowed, 10.5% divorced; Foreign born: 4.5%; Speak English only: 95.7%; With disability: 13.8%; Veterans: 8.7%; Ancestry: 22.4% German, 18.9% Swedish, 18.4% English, 18.0% Irish, 8.1% Italian
Employment: 13.0% management, business, and financial, 3.8% computer, engineering, and science, 14.0% education, legal, community service, arts, and media, 3.7% healthcare practitioners, 17.7% service, 19.4% sales and office, 12.0% natural resources, construction, and maintenance, 16.4% production, transportation, and material moving
Income: Per capita: $30,597; Median household: $56,136; Average household: $71,564; Households with income of $100,000 or more: 24.0%; Poverty rate: 11.6%
Educational Attainment: High school diploma or higher: 95.0%; Bachelor's degree or higher: 28.7%; Graduate/professional degree or higher: 17.3%
Housing: Homeownership rate: 87.1%; Median home value: $124,000; Median year structure built: 1961; Homeowner vacancy rate: 2.3%; Median selected monthly owner costs: $1,130 with a mortgage, $455 without a mortgage; Median gross rent: $924 per month; Rental vacancy rate: 10.6%
Health Insurance: 91.3% have insurance; 73.2% have private insurance; 37.1% have public insurance; 8.7% do not have insurance; 9.1% of children under 18 do not have insurance
Transportation: Commute: 88.7% car, 0.0% public transportation, 0.4% walk, 9.9% work from home; Mean travel time to work: 22.1 minutes

PANAMA (village). Covers a land area of 2.200 square miles and a water area of 0.006 square miles. Located at 42.07° N. Lat; 79.49° W. Long. Elevation is 1,552 feet.
History: Panama Rocks, a 25-acre park with a 60-foot high rock outcropping containing abundant early Paleozoic marine fossils, is 1 mile West Southwest.

Population: 449; Growth (since 2000): -8.6%; Density: 204.1 persons per square mile; Race: 100.0% White, 0.0% Black/African American, 0.0% Asian, 0.0% American Indian/Alaska Native, 0.0% Native Hawaiian/Other Pacific Islander, 0.0% Two or more races, 0.7% Hispanic of any race; Average household size: 2.41; Median age: 37.5; Age under 18: 25.2%; Age 65 and over: 21.6%; Males per 100 females: 94.7; Marriage status: 24.0% never married, 57.6% now married, 4.0% separated, 8.5% widowed, 9.9% divorced; Foreign born: 0.0%; Speak English only: 97.5%; With disability: 18.7%; Veterans: 8.6%; Ancestry: 19.6% German, 18.3% English, 16.5% Irish, 12.0% Swedish, 9.1% Dutch
Employment: 16.2% management, business, and financial, 2.2% computer, engineering, and science, 6.1% education, legal, community service, arts, and media, 6.7% healthcare practitioners, 21.8% service, 19.6% sales and office, 10.6% natural resources, construction, and maintenance, 16.8% production, transportation, and material moving
Income: Per capita: $20,703; Median household: $40,000; Average household: $49,703; Households with income of $100,000 or more: 10.2%; Poverty rate: 9.2%
Educational Attainment: High school diploma or higher: 92.0%; Bachelor's degree or higher: 13.0%; Graduate/professional degree or higher: 5.6%

School District(s)
Panama Central SD (PK-12)
    Enrollment: 503 . . . . (716) 782-4445
Housing: Homeownership rate: 66.1%; Median home value: $83,000; Median year structure built: 1941; Homeowner vacancy rate: 0.0%; Median selected monthly owner costs: $1,018 with a mortgage, $339 without a mortgage; Median gross rent: $610 per month; Rental vacancy rate: 7.4%
Health Insurance: 88.4% have insurance; 65.9% have private insurance; 44.5% have public insurance; 11.6% do not have insurance; 9.2% of children under 18 do not have insurance
Transportation: Commute: 87.1% car, 0.0% public transportation, 5.1% walk, 7.9% work from home; Mean travel time to work: 24.3 minutes

POLAND (town). Covers a land area of 36.617 square miles and a water area of 0.266 square miles. Located at 42.13° N. Lat; 79.12° W. Long.
Population: 2,252; Growth (since 2000): -8.7%; Density: 61.5 persons per square mile; Race: 97.5% White, 0.2% Black/African American, 0.2% Asian, 0.4% American Indian/Alaska Native, 0.0% Native Hawaiian/Other Pacific Islander, 0.4% Two or more races, 1.6% Hispanic of any race; Average household size: 2.53; Median age: 40.6; Age under 18: 24.5%; Age 65 and over: 18.2%; Males per 100 females: 102.6; Marriage status: 20.2% never married, 64.8% now married, 2.4% separated, 6.4% widowed, 8.6% divorced; Foreign born: 0.5%; Speak English only: 94.5%; With disability: 10.2%; Veterans: 12.0%; Ancestry: 19.7% Swedish, 16.1% German, 15.9% English, 14.9% Italian, 13.7% Irish
Employment: 18.9% management, business, and financial, 2.3% computer, engineering, and science, 10.6% education, legal, community service, arts, and media, 10.2% healthcare practitioners, 11.7% service, 17.4% sales and office, 11.5% natural resources, construction, and maintenance, 17.4% production, transportation, and material moving
Income: Per capita: $23,025; Median household: $45,469; Average household: $56,787; Households with income of $100,000 or more: 14.3%; Poverty rate: 13.7%
Educational Attainment: High school diploma or higher: 86.3%; Bachelor's degree or higher: 13.3%; Graduate/professional degree or higher: 5.3%
Housing: Homeownership rate: 85.1%; Median home value: $81,100; Median year structure built: 1965; Homeowner vacancy rate: 0.0%; Median selected monthly owner costs: $915 with a mortgage, $423 without a mortgage; Median gross rent: $564 per month; Rental vacancy rate: 9.3%
Health Insurance: 91.8% have insurance; 69.2% have private insurance; 37.0% have public insurance; 8.2% do not have insurance; 18.4% of children under 18 do not have insurance
Transportation: Commute: 93.7% car, 0.0% public transportation, 2.8% walk, 3.5% work from home; Mean travel time to work: 20.3 minutes

POMFRET (town). Covers a land area of 43.855 square miles and a water area of 0.334 square miles. Located at 42.41° N. Lat; 79.33° W. Long.
Population: 14,357; Growth (since 2000): -2.4%; Density: 327.4 persons per square mile; Race: 89.9% White, 3.9% Black/African American, 1.5% Asian, 0.0% American Indian/Alaska Native, 0.1% Native Hawaiian/Other Pacific Islander, 2.2% Two or more races, 7.3% Hispanic of any race;

Average household size: 2.33; Median age: 31.3; Age under 18: 17.0%; Age 65 and over: 15.4%; Males per 100 females: 90.5; Marriage status: 45.4% never married, 42.8% now married, 1.6% separated, 4.7% widowed, 7.0% divorced; Foreign born: 4.3%; Speak English only: 93.3%; With disability: 11.2%; Veterans: 7.2%; Ancestry: 24.9% German, 22.4% Italian, 18.5% Irish, 16.9% Polish, 12.0% English

Employment: 9.4% management, business, and financial, 2.3% computer, engineering, and science, 19.0% education, legal, community service, arts, and media, 5.1% healthcare practitioners, 21.7% service, 23.4% sales and office, 6.8% natural resources, construction, and maintenance, 12.3% production, transportation, and material moving

Income: Per capita: $25,090; Median household: $50,405; Average household: $68,872; Households with income of $100,000 or more: 19.3%; Poverty rate: 18.7%

Educational Attainment: High school diploma or higher: 95.4%; Bachelor's degree or higher: 38.6%; Graduate/professional degree or higher: 20.0%

Housing: Homeownership rate: 69.6%; Median home value: $124,800; Median year structure built: 1948; Homeowner vacancy rate: 3.9%; Median selected monthly owner costs: $1,209 with a mortgage, $549 without a mortgage; Median gross rent: $702 per month; Rental vacancy rate: 10.6%

Health Insurance: 96.3% have insurance; 76.1% have private insurance; 34.8% have public insurance; 3.7% do not have insurance; 1.6% of children under 18 do not have insurance

Transportation: Commute: 83.7% car, 0.2% public transportation, 9.8% walk, 5.1% work from home; Mean travel time to work: 14.9 minutes

Additional Information Contacts
Town of Pomfret . . . . (716) 672-7496
  http://townofpomfretny.org/content

PORTLAND (town). Covers a land area of 34.116 square miles and a water area of 0.064 square miles. Located at 42.37° N. Lat; 79.46° W. Long. Elevation is 761 feet.

Population: 4,778; Growth (since 2000): -13.2%; Density: 140.0 persons per square mile; Race: 90.1% White, 6.5% Black/African American, 0.1% Asian, 0.0% American Indian/Alaska Native, 0.0% Native Hawaiian/Other Pacific Islander, 0.4% Two or more races, 5.4% Hispanic of any race; Average household size: 2.38; Median age: 38.0; Age under 18: 17.5%; Age 65 and over: 16.5%; Males per 100 females: 126.6; Marriage status: 42.0% never married, 35.4% now married, 2.3% separated, 7.1% widowed, 15.6% divorced; Foreign born: 1.5%; Speak English only: 93.2%; With disability: 17.3%; Veterans: 6.8%; Ancestry: 27.5% German, 15.9% Italian, 14.6% Irish, 10.0% English, 7.3% Polish

Employment: 11.0% management, business, and financial, 0.9% computer, engineering, and science, 10.4% education, legal, community service, arts, and media, 2.9% healthcare practitioners, 27.3% service, 19.9% sales and office, 7.5% natural resources, construction, and maintenance, 20.0% production, transportation, and material moving

Income: Per capita: $20,443; Median household: $43,472; Average household: $54,742; Households with income of $100,000 or more: 9.9%; Poverty rate: 23.7%

Educational Attainment: High school diploma or higher: 80.5%; Bachelor's degree or higher: 15.9%; Graduate/professional degree or higher: 7.0%

Housing: Homeownership rate: 71.8%; Median home value: $84,200; Median year structure built: 1955; Homeowner vacancy rate: 2.5%; Median selected monthly owner costs: $1,048 with a mortgage, $450 without a mortgage; Median gross rent: $611 per month; Rental vacancy rate: 0.0%

Health Insurance: 91.7% have insurance; 63.7% have private insurance; 47.3% have public insurance; 8.3% do not have insurance; 2.4% of children under 18 do not have insurance

Transportation: Commute: 93.0% car, 0.1% public transportation, 2.6% walk, 3.7% work from home; Mean travel time to work: 20.6 minutes

Additional Information Contacts
Town of Portland . . . . (716) 792-9614
  http://www.town.portland.ny.us

RIPLEY (CDP). Covers a land area of 1.372 square miles and a water area of 0 square miles. Located at 42.27° N. Lat; 79.71° W. Long. Elevation is 735 feet.

Population: 928; Growth (since 2000): -9.9%; Density: 676.4 persons per square mile; Race: 97.8% White, 0.8% Black/African American, 0.0% Asian, 0.0% American Indian/Alaska Native, 0.0% Native Hawaiian/Other Pacific Islander, 1.4% Two or more races, 0.5% Hispanic of any race; Average household size: 2.41; Median age: 41.4; Age under 18: 22.7%;

Age 65 and over: 16.2%; Males per 100 females: 95.1; Marriage status: 26.3% never married, 51.2% now married, 0.7% separated, 8.0% widowed, 14.5% divorced; Foreign born: 0.0%; Speak English only: 100.0%; With disability: 16.5%; Veterans: 14.8%; Ancestry: 32.8% German, 23.9% Irish, 18.0% Italian, 17.6% English, 12.1% Polish

Employment: 3.6% management, business, and financial, 2.8% computer, engineering, and science, 6.9% education, legal, community service, arts, and media, 1.3% healthcare practitioners, 25.7% service, 20.6% sales and office, 13.1% natural resources, construction, and maintenance, 26.0% production, transportation, and material moving

Income: Per capita: $17,910; Median household: $29,813; Average household: $42,097; Households with income of $100,000 or more: 4.7%; Poverty rate: 22.0%

Educational Attainment: High school diploma or higher: 88.8%; Bachelor's degree or higher: 14.0%; Graduate/professional degree or higher: 5.2%

School District(s)
Ripley Central SD (PK-06)
  Enrollment: 165 . . . . (716) 736-2631
Housing: Homeownership rate: 75.1%; Median home value: $60,400; Median year structure built: Before 1940; Homeowner vacancy rate: 14.2%; Median selected monthly owner costs: $843 with a mortgage, $407 without a mortgage; Median gross rent: $662 per month; Rental vacancy rate: 0.0%

Health Insurance: 92.2% have insurance; 53.2% have private insurance; 52.8% have public insurance; 7.8% do not have insurance; 2.8% of children under 18 do not have insurance

Transportation: Commute: 93.1% car, 0.0% public transportation, 6.9% walk, 0.0% work from home; Mean travel time to work: 28.3 minutes

RIPLEY (town). Covers a land area of 48.763 square miles and a water area of 0.104 square miles. Located at 42.23° N. Lat; 79.70° W. Long. Elevation is 735 feet.

Population: 2,376; Growth (since 2000): -9.9%; Density: 48.7 persons per square mile; Race: 97.9% White, 0.8% Black/African American, 0.0% Asian, 0.0% American Indian/Alaska Native, 0.0% Native Hawaiian/Other Pacific Islander, 0.5% Two or more races, 1.9% Hispanic of any race; Average household size: 2.45; Median age: 43.9; Age under 18: 21.0%; Age 65 and over: 18.1%; Males per 100 females: 101.6; Marriage status: 22.8% never married, 60.4% now married, 1.1% separated, 6.4% widowed, 10.4% divorced; Foreign born: 1.3%; Speak English only: 98.6%; With disability: 15.5%; Veterans: 14.6%; Ancestry: 27.6% German, 15.4% Irish, 14.5% English, 9.8% Italian, 8.2% Polish

Employment: 10.0% management, business, and financial, 2.6% computer, engineering, and science, 7.1% education, legal, community service, arts, and media, 5.3% healthcare practitioners, 19.0% service, 20.7% sales and office, 14.5% natural resources, construction, and maintenance, 20.8% production, transportation, and material moving

Income: Per capita: $27,123; Median household: $44,688; Average household: $65,314; Households with income of $100,000 or more: 10.3%; Poverty rate: 13.4%

Educational Attainment: High school diploma or higher: 87.4%; Bachelor's degree or higher: 13.4%; Graduate/professional degree or higher: 3.1%

School District(s)
Ripley Central SD (PK-06)
  Enrollment: 165 . . . . (716) 736-2631
Housing: Homeownership rate: 83.7%; Median home value: $80,100; Median year structure built: 1952; Homeowner vacancy rate: 5.6%; Median selected monthly owner costs: $890 with a mortgage, $424 without a mortgage; Median gross rent: $583 per month; Rental vacancy rate: 0.0%

Health Insurance: 91.5% have insurance; 60.4% have private insurance; 46.8% have public insurance; 8.5% do not have insurance; 9.2% of children under 18 do not have insurance

Transportation: Commute: 92.7% car, 0.0% public transportation, 3.5% walk, 3.2% work from home; Mean travel time to work: 26.6 minutes

SHERIDAN (town). Covers a land area of 37.252 square miles and a water area of 0.051 square miles. Located at 42.49° N. Lat; 79.23° W. Long. Elevation is 748 feet.

Population: 2,590; Growth (since 2000): -8.7%; Density: 69.5 persons per square mile; Race: 94.2% White, 0.3% Black/African American, 2.2% Asian, 0.6% American Indian/Alaska Native, 0.0% Native Hawaiian/Other Pacific Islander, 1.0% Two or more races, 5.8% Hispanic of any race; Average household size: 2.32; Median age: 50.0; Age under 18: 18.0%;

Age 65 and over: 19.2%; Males per 100 females: 98.9; Marriage status: 23.8% never married, 53.3% now married, 3.9% separated, 8.6% widowed, 14.4% divorced; Foreign born: 3.0%; Speak English only: 93.3%; With disability: 19.0%; Veterans: 8.5%; Ancestry: 26.0% German, 23.3% Polish, 17.2% English, 12.2% Irish, 11.5% Italian
Employment: 10.6% management, business, and financial, 3.8% computer, engineering, and science, 12.2% education, legal, community service, arts, and media, 7.1% healthcare practitioners, 16.8% service, 17.5% sales and office, 15.2% natural resources, construction, and maintenance, 16.8% production, transportation, and material moving
Income: Per capita: $28,641; Median household: $53,500; Average household: $66,210; Households with income of $100,000 or more: 24.5%; Poverty rate: 9.8%
Educational Attainment: High school diploma or higher: 92.0%; Bachelor's degree or higher: 20.2%; Graduate/professional degree or higher: 8.9%
Housing: Homeownership rate: 88.2%; Median home value: $118,200; Median year structure built: 1956; Homeowner vacancy rate: 0.0%; Median selected monthly owner costs: $1,114 with a mortgage, $501 without a mortgage; Median gross rent: $725 per month; Rental vacancy rate: 0.0%
Health Insurance: 94.8% have insurance; 75.1% have private insurance; 35.0% have public insurance; 5.2% do not have insurance; 3.5% of children under 18 do not have insurance
Transportation: Commute: 92.8% car, 0.5% public transportation, 1.1% walk, 4.3% work from home; Mean travel time to work: 22.0 minutes

SHERMAN (town). Covers a land area of 36.271 square miles and a water area of 0.130 square miles. Located at 42.14° N. Lat; 79.58° W. Long. Elevation is 1,539 feet.
Population: 1,751; Growth (since 2000): 12.7%; Density: 48.3 persons per square mile; Race: 99.7% White, 0.0% Black/African American, 0.1% Asian, 0.0% American Indian/Alaska Native, 0.0% Native Hawaiian/Other Pacific Islander, 0.2% Two or more races, 1.0% Hispanic of any race; Average household size: 3.22; Median age: 29.0; Age under 18: 33.2%; Age 65 and over: 13.1%; Males per 100 females: 100.1; Marriage status: 29.3% never married, 55.7% now married, 1.7% separated, 5.0% widowed, 10.0% divorced; Foreign born: 0.4%; Speak English only: 71.6%; With disability: 9.3%; Veterans: 5.0%; Ancestry: 41.4% German, 10.5% English, 9.4% Irish, 9.2% Dutch, 7.4% Italian
Employment: 15.1% management, business, and financial, 0.0% computer, engineering, and science, 6.9% education, legal, community service, arts, and media, 2.8% healthcare practitioners, 14.8% service, 16.6% sales and office, 30.3% natural resources, construction, and maintenance, 13.4% production, transportation, and material moving
Income: Per capita: $18,063; Median household: $42,738; Average household: $55,956; Households with income of $100,000 or more: 12.2%; Poverty rate: 17.4%
Educational Attainment: High school diploma or higher: 77.3%; Bachelor's degree or higher: 16.8%; Graduate/professional degree or higher: 6.3%
School District(s)
Sherman Central SD (PK-12)
    Enrollment: 442 . . . . (716) 761-6122
Housing: Homeownership rate: 81.4%; Median home value: $83,900; Median year structure built: Before 1940; Homeowner vacancy rate: 0.0%; Median selected monthly owner costs: $1,021 with a mortgage, $407 without a mortgage; Median gross rent: $613 per month; Rental vacancy rate: 0.0%
Health Insurance: 67.7% have insurance; 48.9% have private insurance; 29.6% have public insurance; 32.3% do not have insurance; 50.2% of children under 18 do not have insurance
Transportation: Commute: 86.6% car, 0.6% public transportation, 5.3% walk, 7.1% work from home; Mean travel time to work: 22.0 minutes

SHERMAN (village). Covers a land area of 0.854 square miles and a water area of 0 square miles. Located at 42.16° N. Lat; 79.59° W. Long. Elevation is 1,539 feet.
Population: 680; Growth (since 2000): -4.8%; Density: 796.5 persons per square mile; Race: 99.3% White, 0.0% Black/African American, 0.3% Asian, 0.0% American Indian/Alaska Native, 0.0% Native Hawaiian/Other Pacific Islander, 0.4% Two or more races, 1.9% Hispanic of any race; Average household size: 2.36; Median age: 34.9; Age under 18: 23.7%; Age 65 and over: 21.0%; Males per 100 females: 97.3; Marriage status: 23.5% never married, 58.5% now married, 2.8% separated, 8.6% widowed, 9.5% divorced; Foreign born: 0.6%; Speak English only: 96.5%;

With disability: 12.9%; Veterans: 7.9%; Ancestry: 40.6% German, 19.7% English, 9.4% Dutch, 9.0% Irish, 5.9% Scottish
Employment: 11.0% management, business, and financial, 0.0% computer, engineering, and science, 11.3% education, legal, community service, arts, and media, 2.7% healthcare practitioners, 19.6% service, 19.3% sales and office, 23.6% natural resources, construction, and maintenance, 12.6% production, transportation, and material moving
Income: Per capita: $21,743; Median household: $38,750; Average household: $49,403; Households with income of $100,000 or more: 8.0%; Poverty rate: 14.6%
Educational Attainment: High school diploma or higher: 85.8%; Bachelor's degree or higher: 25.1%; Graduate/professional degree or higher: 8.9%
School District(s)
Sherman Central SD (PK-12)
    Enrollment: 442 . . . . (716) 761-6122
Housing: Homeownership rate: 68.4%; Median home value: $72,400; Median year structure built: Before 1940; Homeowner vacancy rate: 0.0%; Median selected monthly owner costs: $963 with a mortgage, $429 without a mortgage; Median gross rent: $606 per month; Rental vacancy rate: 0.0%
Health Insurance: 90.9% have insurance; 62.4% have private insurance; 46.0% have public insurance; 9.1% do not have insurance; 10.5% of children under 18 do not have insurance
Transportation: Commute: 90.1% car, 0.0% public transportation, 4.9% walk, 4.9% work from home; Mean travel time to work: 19.8 minutes

SILVER CREEK (village). Covers a land area of 1.160 square miles and a water area of 0 square miles. Located at 42.54° N. Lat; 79.17° W. Long. Elevation is 587 feet.
History: Annual grape festival held here in October. Incorporated 1848.
Population: 2,557; Growth (since 2000): -11.7%; Density: 2,204.0 persons per square mile; Race: 95.4% White, 1.4% Black/African American, 0.0% Asian, 0.8% American Indian/Alaska Native, 0.0% Native Hawaiian/Other Pacific Islander, 1.9% Two or more races, 1.9% Hispanic of any race; Average household size: 2.32; Median age: 38.8; Age under 18: 24.9%; Age 65 and over: 15.2%; Males per 100 females: 95.9; Marriage status: 25.4% never married, 54.5% now married, 3.3% separated, 7.7% widowed, 12.4% divorced; Foreign born: 2.9%; Speak English only: 97.8%; With disability: 17.8%; Veterans: 10.0%; Ancestry: 26.7% German, 24.8% Italian, 21.0% Polish, 18.6% Irish, 13.0% English
Employment: 11.1% management, business, and financial, 3.1% computer, engineering, and science, 10.3% education, legal, community service, arts, and media, 4.6% healthcare practitioners, 23.3% service, 20.1% sales and office, 11.9% natural resources, construction, and maintenance, 15.6% production, transportation, and material moving
Income: Per capita: $24,523; Median household: $53,029; Average household: $56,283; Households with income of $100,000 or more: 11.8%; Poverty rate: 16.6%
Educational Attainment: High school diploma or higher: 90.8%; Bachelor's degree or higher: 25.2%; Graduate/professional degree or higher: 8.3%
School District(s)
Silver Creek Central SD (PK-12)
    Enrollment: 1,107 . . . . (716) 934-2603
Housing: Homeownership rate: 75.3%; Median home value: $82,100; Median year structure built: Before 1940; Homeowner vacancy rate: 3.1%; Median selected monthly owner costs: $981 with a mortgage, $500 without a mortgage; Median gross rent: $792 per month; Rental vacancy rate: 13.0%
Health Insurance: 94.2% have insurance; 71.5% have private insurance; 38.9% have public insurance; 5.8% do not have insurance; 2.8% of children under 18 do not have insurance
Transportation: Commute: 93.9% car, 0.0% public transportation, 3.8% walk, 1.8% work from home; Mean travel time to work: 24.2 minutes

SINCLAIRVILLE (village). Covers a land area of 1.612 square miles and a water area of 0 square miles. Located at 42.27° N. Lat; 79.26° W. Long. Elevation is 1,401 feet.
Population: 799; Growth (since 2000): 20.2%; Density: 495.6 persons per square mile; Race: 95.9% White, 2.6% Black/African American, 0.0% Asian, 0.4% American Indian/Alaska Native, 0.0% Native Hawaiian/Other Pacific Islander, 1.1% Two or more races, 0.8% Hispanic of any race; Average household size: 2.91; Median age: 35.9; Age under 18: 33.5%; Age 65 and over: 13.3%; Males per 100 females: 102.1; Marriage status:

22.0% never married, 63.4% now married, 3.0% separated, 5.3% widowed, 9.3% divorced; Foreign born: 0.6%; Speak English only: 98.9%; With disability: 16.3%; Veterans: 9.0%; Ancestry: 21.2% German, 20.3% Swedish, 17.1% Irish, 11.4% English, 10.4% Italian
Employment: 10.6% management, business, and financial, 0.0% computer, engineering, and science, 8.3% education, legal, community service, arts, and media, 4.0% healthcare practitioners, 24.3% service, 22.9% sales and office, 8.3% natural resources, construction, and maintenance, 21.6% production, transportation, and material moving
Income: Per capita: $17,322; Median household: $41,771; Average household: $49,540; Households with income of $100,000 or more: 8.4%; Poverty rate: 18.9%
Educational Attainment: High school diploma or higher: 88.9%; Bachelor's degree or higher: 16.9%; Graduate/professional degree or higher: 8.0%

School District(s)

Cassadaga Valley Central SD (PK-12)
    Enrollment: 892 . . . . (716) 962-5155
Housing: Homeownership rate: 77.8%; Median home value: $76,700; Median year structure built: Before 1940; Homeowner vacancy rate: 0.0%; Median selected monthly owner costs: $931 with a mortgage, $513 without a mortgage; Median gross rent: $473 per month; Rental vacancy rate: 0.0%
Health Insurance: 96.1% have insurance; 55.3% have private insurance; 49.6% have public insurance; 3.9% do not have insurance; 0.0% of children under 18 do not have insurance
Transportation: Commute: 92.4% car, 1.3% public transportation, 1.3% walk, 3.3% work from home; Mean travel time to work: 21.1 minutes

STOCKTON (town). Covers a land area of 47.160 square miles and a water area of 0.489 square miles. Located at 42.30° N. Lat; 79.36° W. Long. Elevation is 1,325 feet.
Population: 2,080; Growth (since 2000): -10.8%; Density: 44.1 persons per square mile; Race: 97.7% White, 0.0% Black/African American, 0.6% Asian, 0.0% American Indian/Alaska Native, 0.0% Native Hawaiian/Other Pacific Islander, 1.6% Two or more races, 1.2% Hispanic of any race; Average household size: 2.52; Median age: 40.6; Age under 18: 23.0%; Age 65 and over: 16.8%; Males per 100 females: 98.4; Marriage status: 27.9% never married, 54.3% now married, 1.7% separated, 6.5% widowed, 11.3% divorced; Foreign born: 0.6%; Speak English only: 99.3%; With disability: 17.7%; Veterans: 9.5%; Ancestry: 32.5% German, 15.7% English, 15.5% Irish, 11.1% Italian, 8.0% Polish
Employment: 8.4% management, business, and financial, 4.8% computer, engineering, and science, 11.0% education, legal, community service, arts, and media, 3.7% healthcare practitioners, 20.6% service, 20.2% sales and office, 9.8% natural resources, construction, and maintenance, 21.5% production, transportation, and material moving
Income: Per capita: $23,573; Median household: $51,713; Average household: $58,007; Households with income of $100,000 or more: 15.1%; Poverty rate: 22.0%
Educational Attainment: High school diploma or higher: 89.0%; Bachelor's degree or higher: 19.9%; Graduate/professional degree or higher: 6.8%
Housing: Homeownership rate: 69.2%; Median home value: $95,900; Median year structure built: 1960; Homeowner vacancy rate: 4.5%; Median selected monthly owner costs: $939 with a mortgage, $452 without a mortgage; Median gross rent: $771 per month; Rental vacancy rate: 0.0%
Health Insurance: 96.0% have insurance; 67.5% have private insurance; 42.9% have public insurance; 4.0% do not have insurance; 0.6% of children under 18 do not have insurance
Transportation: Commute: 94.5% car, 0.2% public transportation, 2.7% walk, 1.8% work from home; Mean travel time to work: 23.8 minutes

SUNSET BAY (CDP). Covers a land area of 0.661 square miles and a water area of 0.044 square miles. Located at 42.56° N. Lat; 79.13° W. Long. Elevation is 577 feet.
Population: 786; Growth (since 2000): n/a; Density: 1,189.7 persons per square mile; Race: 82.3% White, 2.7% Black/African American, 0.0% Asian, 6.7% American Indian/Alaska Native, 0.0% Native Hawaiian/Other Pacific Islander, 4.1% Two or more races, 4.8% Hispanic of any race; Average household size: 2.13; Median age: 52.7; Age under 18: 16.4%; Age 65 and over: 20.5%; Males per 100 females: 91.9; Marriage status: 38.3% never married, 38.9% now married, 0.4% separated, 6.1% widowed, 16.6% divorced; Foreign born: 0.0%; Speak English only:

100.0%; With disability: 17.6%; Veterans: 10.4%; Ancestry: 30.8% German, 26.6% Polish, 16.4% Irish, 14.5% Italian, 7.9% English
Employment: 13.6% management, business, and financial, 0.0% computer, engineering, and science, 0.0% education, legal, community service, arts, and media, 0.0% healthcare practitioners, 37.9% service, 29.1% sales and office, 11.3% natural resources, construction, and maintenance, 8.1% production, transportation, and material moving
Income: Per capita: $28,915; Median household: $77,826; Average household: $69,965; Households with income of $100,000 or more: 17.3%; Poverty rate: 2.8%
Educational Attainment: High school diploma or higher: 86.4%; Bachelor's degree or higher: 12.5%; Graduate/professional degree or higher: 3.3%
Housing: Homeownership rate: 76.1%; Median home value: $96,600; Median year structure built: 1953; Homeowner vacancy rate: 0.0%; Median selected monthly owner costs: $882 with a mortgage, $629 without a mortgage; Median gross rent: n/a per month; Rental vacancy rate: 0.0%
Health Insurance: 95.0% have insurance; 78.6% have private insurance; 24.5% have public insurance; 5.0% do not have insurance; 0.0% of children under 18 do not have insurance
Transportation: Commute: 97.2% car, 0.0% public transportation, 2.8% walk, 0.0% work from home; Mean travel time to work: 21.2 minutes

VILLENOVA (town). Covers a land area of 36.093 square miles and a water area of 0.111 square miles. Located at 42.39° N. Lat; 79.12° W. Long.
Population: 849; Growth (since 2000): -24.3%; Density: 23.5 persons per square mile; Race: 94.1% White, 0.0% Black/African American, 0.0% Asian, 2.6% American Indian/Alaska Native, 0.0% Native Hawaiian/Other Pacific Islander, 2.2% Two or more races, 2.6% Hispanic of any race; Average household size: 2.21; Median age: 52.7; Age under 18: 11.8%; Age 65 and over: 23.8%; Males per 100 females: 97.5; Marriage status: 22.5% never married, 60.5% now married, 2.1% separated, 4.1% widowed, 13.0% divorced; Foreign born: 1.2%; Speak English only: 98.0%; With disability: 14.5%; Veterans: 11.3%; Ancestry: 39.0% German, 16.0% Irish, 14.0% English, 13.1% Polish, 7.4% Italian
Employment: 4.8% management, business, and financial, 2.0% computer, engineering, and science, 5.6% education, legal, community service, arts, and media, 5.1% healthcare practitioners, 16.5% service, 16.8% sales and office, 23.6% natural resources, construction, and maintenance, 25.6% production, transportation, and material moving
Income: Per capita: $23,906; Median household: $42,232; Average household: $51,202; Households with income of $100,000 or more: 9.2%; Poverty rate: 10.8%
Educational Attainment: High school diploma or higher: 88.1%; Bachelor's degree or higher: 9.3%; Graduate/professional degree or higher: 3.5%
Housing: Homeownership rate: 86.2%; Median home value: $82,300; Median year structure built: 1976; Homeowner vacancy rate: 0.0%; Median selected monthly owner costs: $1,163 with a mortgage, $426 without a mortgage; Median gross rent: $557 per month; Rental vacancy rate: 0.0%
Health Insurance: 94.2% have insurance; 70.1% have private insurance; 46.5% have public insurance; 5.8% do not have insurance; 0.0% of children under 18 do not have insurance
Transportation: Commute: 95.6% car, 0.0% public transportation, 0.8% walk, 3.6% work from home; Mean travel time to work: 28.7 minutes

WESTFIELD (town). Covers a land area of 47.185 square miles and a water area of 0.066 square miles. Located at 42.27° N. Lat; 79.60° W. Long. Elevation is 745 feet.
History: In 1873 Thomas and Charles Bradwell Welch, ardent Prohibitionists, devised method of pressing Concord grapes into unfermented wine. Settled 1800, incorporated 1833.
Population: 4,720; Growth (since 2000): -9.8%; Density: 100.0 persons per square mile; Race: 98.3% White, 0.0% Black/African American, 1.4% Asian, 0.0% American Indian/Alaska Native, 0.0% Native Hawaiian/Other Pacific Islander, 0.0% Two or more races, 6.9% Hispanic of any race; Average household size: 2.29; Median age: 49.2; Age under 18: 17.9%; Age 65 and over: 23.2%; Males per 100 females: 93.8; Marriage status: 23.0% never married, 56.9% now married, 3.8% separated, 11.0% widowed, 9.1% divorced; Foreign born: 2.2%; Speak English only: 92.9%; With disability: 11.7%; Veterans: 7.3%; Ancestry: 27.5% German, 15.1% English, 12.4% Irish, 10.2% Polish, 8.8% American
Employment: 12.3% management, business, and financial, 1.7% computer, engineering, and science, 13.4% education, legal, community

service, arts, and media, 5.9% healthcare practitioners, 13.6% service, 15.6% sales and office, 11.3% natural resources, construction, and maintenance, 26.2% production, transportation, and material moving
Income: Per capita: $24,196; Median household: $46,125; Average household: $55,279; Households with income of $100,000 or more: 13.3%; Poverty rate: 16.2%
Educational Attainment: High school diploma or higher: 85.9%; Bachelor's degree or higher: 23.2%; Graduate/professional degree or higher: 11.3%

School District(s)
Westfield Central SD (KG-12)
   Enrollment: 672. . . . . (716) 326-2151
Housing: Homeownership rate: 76.8%; Median home value: $89,900; Median year structure built: 1952; Homeowner vacancy rate: 0.0%; Median selected monthly owner costs: $974 with a mortgage, $415 without a mortgage; Median gross rent: $650 per month; Rental vacancy rate: 8.9%
Health Insurance: 96.3% have insurance; 74.8% have private insurance; 38.5% have public insurance; 3.7% do not have insurance; 0.0% of children under 18 do not have insurance
Hospitals: Westfield Memorial Hospital (32 beds)
Newspapers: Westfield Republican (weekly circulation 1,400)
Transportation: Commute: 82.8% car, 0.0% public transportation, 8.1% walk, 9.1% work from home; Mean travel time to work: 20.9 minutes
Additional Information Contacts
Town of Westfield . . . . (716) 326-3211
  http://www.townofwestfield.org

WESTFIELD (village). Covers a land area of 3.822 square miles and a water area of 0 square miles. Located at 42.32° N. Lat; 79.57° W. Long. Elevation is 745 feet.
Population: 3,224; Growth (since 2000): -7.4%; Density: 843.5 persons per square mile; Race: 97.5% White, 0.0% Black/African American, 2.1% Asian, 0.0% American Indian/Alaska Native, 0.0% Native Hawaiian/Other Pacific Islander, 0.0% Two or more races, 10.1% Hispanic of any race; Average household size: 2.37; Median age: 43.5; Age under 18: 21.2%; Age 65 and over: 22.3%; Males per 100 females: 89.3; Marriage status: 26.0% never married, 48.9% now married, 2.0% separated, 13.2% widowed, 11.9% divorced; Foreign born: 3.2%; Speak English only: 89.8%; With disability: 12.3%; Veterans: 6.9%; Ancestry: 25.5% German, 14.3% English, 11.9% American, 9.8% Irish, 9.2% Polish
Employment: 9.6% management, business, and financial, 1.3% computer, engineering, and science, 11.3% education, legal, community service, arts, and media, 9.4% healthcare practitioners, 18.9% service, 13.5% sales and office, 12.4% natural resources, construction, and maintenance, 23.7% production, transportation, and material moving
Income: Per capita: $23,981; Median household: $41,199; Average household: $56,998; Households with income of $100,000 or more: 14.8%; Poverty rate: 20.5%
Educational Attainment: High school diploma or higher: 85.2%; Bachelor's degree or higher: 23.3%; Graduate/professional degree or higher: 12.8%

School District(s)
Westfield Central SD (KG-12)
   Enrollment: 672. . . . . (716) 326-2151
Housing: Homeownership rate: 68.3%; Median home value: $85,900; Median year structure built: 1941; Homeowner vacancy rate: 0.0%; Median selected monthly owner costs: $877 with a mortgage, $417 without a mortgage; Median gross rent: $684 per month; Rental vacancy rate: 10.7%
Health Insurance: 95.9% have insurance; 72.3% have private insurance; 37.8% have public insurance; 4.1% do not have insurance; 0.0% of children under 18 do not have insurance
Hospitals: Westfield Memorial Hospital (32 beds)
Safety: Violent crime rate: 9.9 per 10,000 population; Property crime rate: 33.0 per 10,000 population
Newspapers: Westfield Republican (weekly circulation 1,400)
Transportation: Commute: 89.2% car, 0.0% public transportation, 8.4% walk, 2.4% work from home; Mean travel time to work: 20.5 minutes

Chemung County

Located in southern New York; hilly area bounded on the south by Pennsylvania; cut by the Chemung River Valley. Covers a land area of 407.352 square miles, a water area of 3.427 square miles, and is located in the Eastern Time Zone at 42.16° N. Lat., 76.75° W. Long. The county was founded in 1836. County seat is Elmira.

Chemung County is part of the Elmira, NY Metropolitan Statistical Area. The entire metro area includes: Chemung County, NY

Weather Station: Elmira										Elevation: 844 feet		
	Jan	Feb	Mar	Apr	May	Jun	Jul	Aug	Sep	Oct	Nov	Dec
High	33	36	44	58	70	78	82	81	73	61	49	37
Low	16	17	23	34	44	53	58	57	49	38	31	21
Precip	1.9	1.8	2.9	3.2	3.0	4.2	3.7	3.6	3.5	2.8	3.0	2.3
Snow	10.6	8.2	9.4	1.3	0.0	0.0	0.0	0.0	0.0	0.2	2.7	7.8

High and Low temperatures in degrees Fahrenheit; Precipitation and Snow in inches

Population: 86,883; Growth (since 2000): -4.6%; Density: 213.3 persons per square mile; Race: 88.3% White, 6.0% Black/African American, 1.6% Asian, 0.5% American Indian/Alaska Native, 0.0% Native Hawaiian/Other Pacific Islander, 3.2% two or more races, 3.0% Hispanic of any race; Average household size: 2.37; Median age: 41.2; Age under 18: 21.8%; Age 65 and over: 17.3%; Males per 100 females: 98.9; Marriage status: 31.8% never married, 51.1% now married, 2.9% separated, 6.7% widowed, 10.3% divorced; Foreign born: 2.8%; Speak English only: 96.3%; With disability: 14.9%; Veterans: 8.8%; Ancestry: 17.8% Irish, 17.4% German, 12.6% American, 11.8% Italian, 10.7% English
Religion: Six largest groups: 16.4% Catholicism, 5.3% Methodist/Pietist, 2.4% Non-denominational Protestant, 1.9% Holiness, 1.9% Baptist, 1.9% Muslim Estimate
Economy: Unemployment rate: 4.2%; Leading industries: 18.3 % retail trade; 11.7 % health care and social assistance; 11.4 % accommodation and food services; Farms: 372 totaling 58,114 acres; Company size: 1 employs 1,000 or more persons, 2 employ 500 to 999 persons, 40 employ 100 to 499 persons, 1,748 employ less than 100 persons; Business ownership: 1,877 women-owned, 213 Black-owned, 105 Hispanic-owned, 171 Asian-owned, n/a American Indian/Alaska Native-owned
Employment: 12.1% management, business, and financial, 4.1% computer, engineering, and science, 11.7% education, legal, community service, arts, and media, 7.8% healthcare practitioners, 20.2% service, 23.2% sales and office, 8.1% natural resources, construction, and maintenance, 12.8% production, transportation, and material moving
Income: Per capita: $27,209; Median household: $51,251; Average household: $67,055; Households with income of $100,000 or more: 19.8%; Poverty rate: 15.8%
Educational Attainment: High school diploma or higher: 90.4%; Bachelor's degree or higher: 25.1%; Graduate/professional degree or higher: 11.6%
Housing: Homeownership rate: 68.1%; Median home value: $105,500; Median year structure built: 1953; Homeowner vacancy rate: 1.7%; Median selected monthly owner costs: $1,134 with a mortgage, $462 without a mortgage; Median gross rent: $764 per month; Rental vacancy rate: 7.6%
Vital Statistics: Birth rate: 109.5 per 10,000 population; Death rate: 108.9 per 10,000 population; Age-adjusted cancer mortality rate: 193.8 deaths per 100,000 population
Health Insurance: 94.5% have insurance; 67.4% have private insurance; 42.3% have public insurance; 5.5% do not have insurance; 3.8% of children under 18 do not have insurance
Health Care: Physicians: 26.3 per 10,000 population; Dentists: 5.6 per 10,000 population; Hospital beds: 47.3 per 10,000 population; Hospital admissions: 1,798.7 per 10,000 population
Transportation: Commute: 91.4% car, 2.0% public transportation, 3.2% walk, 2.3% work from home; Mean travel time to work: 19.6 minutes
2016 Presidential Election: 55.6% Trump, 38.1% Clinton, 4.0% Johnson, 1.3% Stein
Additional Information Contacts
Chemung Government . . . . (607) 737-2920
  http://www.chemungcounty.com

Chemung County Communities

ASHLAND (town). Covers a land area of 14.182 square miles and a water area of 0.355 square miles. Located at 42.02° N. Lat; 76.75° W. Long.
Population: 1,460; Growth (since 2000): -25.2%; Density: 102.9 persons per square mile; Race: 97.4% White, 0.5% Black/African American, 0.0% Asian, 0.1% American Indian/Alaska Native, 0.2% Native Hawaiian/Other Pacific Islander, 1.8% Two or more races, 0.7% Hispanic of any race; Average household size: 2.29; Median age: 50.4; Age under 18: 16.8%; Age 65 and over: 23.5%; Males per 100 females: 98.9; Marriage status: 22.6% never married, 56.0% now married, 2.7% separated, 8.2% widowed, 13.2% divorced; Foreign born: 1.8%; Speak English only: 98.0%;

With disability: 15.5%; Veterans: 10.6%; Ancestry: 19.3% German, 19.3% Irish, 16.8% American, 9.9% English, 8.9% Italian
Employment: 8.5% management, business, and financial, 2.2% computer, engineering, and science, 4.4% education, legal, community service, arts, and media, 7.2% healthcare practitioners, 27.5% service, 16.2% sales and office, 13.1% natural resources, construction, and maintenance, 20.9% production, transportation, and material moving
Income: Per capita: $23,906; Median household: $43,393; Average household: $54,192; Households with income of $100,000 or more: 10.2%; Poverty rate: 18.7%
Educational Attainment: High school diploma or higher: 86.1%; Bachelor's degree or higher: 11.3%; Graduate/professional degree or higher: 3.9%
Housing: Homeownership rate: 88.7%; Median home value: $81,200; Median year structure built: 1967; Homeowner vacancy rate: 5.4%; Median selected monthly owner costs: $994 with a mortgage, $451 without a mortgage; Median gross rent: $761 per month; Rental vacancy rate: 13.2%
Health Insurance: 95.7% have insurance; 62.3% have private insurance; 57.0% have public insurance; 4.3% do not have insurance; 3.5% of children under 18 do not have insurance
Transportation: Commute: 96.4% car, 0.3% public transportation, 0.5% walk, 2.2% work from home; Mean travel time to work: 23.1 minutes

BALDWIN (town). Covers a land area of 25.716 square miles and a water area of 0.020 square miles. Located at 42.10° N. Lat; 76.66° W. Long.
Population: 869; Growth (since 2000): 1.9%; Density: 33.8 persons per square mile; Race: 99.5% White, 0.0% Black/African American, 0.0% Asian, 0.0% American Indian/Alaska Native, 0.0% Native Hawaiian/Other Pacific Islander, 0.5% Two or more races, 0.3% Hispanic of any race; Average household size: 2.19; Median age: 48.7; Age under 18: 17.6%; Age 65 and over: 22.3%; Males per 100 females: 108.5; Marriage status: 23.4% never married, 55.3% now married, 3.1% separated, 8.5% widowed, 12.8% divorced; Foreign born: 1.0%; Speak English only: 98.1%; With disability: 18.1%; Veterans: 10.3%; Ancestry: 24.9% Irish, 20.8% German, 12.8% American, 7.7% English, 7.6% Italian
Employment: 15.2% management, business, and financial, 1.2% computer, engineering, and science, 11.2% education, legal, community service, arts, and media, 4.2% healthcare practitioners, 20.6% service, 16.4% sales and office, 11.2% natural resources, construction, and maintenance, 19.9% production, transportation, and material moving
Income: Per capita: $27,254; Median household: $50,625; Average household: $60,177; Households with income of $100,000 or more: 16.7%; Poverty rate: 7.7%
Educational Attainment: High school diploma or higher: 91.2%; Bachelor's degree or higher: 11.4%; Graduate/professional degree or higher: 3.5%
Housing: Homeownership rate: 85.1%; Median home value: $100,200; Median year structure built: 1974; Homeowner vacancy rate: 2.0%; Median selected monthly owner costs: $1,090 with a mortgage, $443 without a mortgage; Median gross rent: $648 per month; Rental vacancy rate: 0.0%
Health Insurance: 97.0% have insurance; 76.6% have private insurance; 41.1% have public insurance; 3.0% do not have insurance; 0.0% of children under 18 do not have insurance
Transportation: Commute: 98.5% car, 0.0% public transportation, 0.0% walk, 1.5% work from home; Mean travel time to work: 24.9 minutes

BIG FLATS (CDP). Covers a land area of 16.300 square miles and a water area of 0.077 square miles. Located at 42.16° N. Lat; 76.91° W. Long. Elevation is 902 feet.
Population: 5,463; Growth (since 2000): 120.1%; Density: 335.1 persons per square mile; Race: 96.7% White, 1.0% Black/African American, 2.3% Asian, 0.0% American Indian/Alaska Native, 0.0% Native Hawaiian/Other Pacific Islander, 0.0% Two or more races, 1.2% Hispanic of any race; Average household size: 2.43; Median age: 45.2; Age under 18: 20.7%; Age 65 and over: 19.5%; Males per 100 females: 97.6; Marriage status: 23.9% never married, 62.1% now married, 2.1% separated, 5.5% widowed, 8.5% divorced; Foreign born: 1.8%; Speak English only: 97.7%; With disability: 11.3%; Veterans: 10.1%; Ancestry: 26.0% German, 19.5% Irish, 14.1% English, 10.5% Italian, 9.7% American
Employment: 20.4% management, business, and financial, 5.6% computer, engineering, and science, 14.0% education, legal, community service, arts, and media, 7.8% healthcare practitioners, 13.5% service, 23.4% sales and office, 7.3% natural resources, construction, and maintenance, 8.0% production, transportation, and material moving

Income: Per capita: $36,174; Median household: $75,645; Average household: $86,829; Households with income of $100,000 or more: 35.0%; Poverty rate: 5.0%
Educational Attainment: High school diploma or higher: 95.5%; Bachelor's degree or higher: 39.1%; Graduate/professional degree or higher: 16.7%

School District(s)
Horseheads Central SD (PK-12)
    Enrollment: 4,237 . . . . (607) 739-5601
Housing: Homeownership rate: 82.7%; Median home value: $161,000; Median year structure built: 1971; Homeowner vacancy rate: 4.3%; Median selected monthly owner costs: $1,369 with a mortgage, $493 without a mortgage; Median gross rent: $975 per month; Rental vacancy rate: 10.4%
Health Insurance: 96.9% have insurance; 84.0% have private insurance; 29.3% have public insurance; 3.1% do not have insurance; 3.3% of children under 18 do not have insurance
Transportation: Commute: 95.7% car, 1.2% public transportation, 1.8% walk, 1.3% work from home; Mean travel time to work: 19.6 minutes

BIG FLATS (town). Covers a land area of 44.484 square miles and a water area of 0.581 square miles. Located at 42.14° N. Lat; 76.91° W. Long. Elevation is 902 feet.
Population: 7,742; Growth (since 2000): 7.2%; Density: 174.0 persons per square mile; Race: 97.4% White, 0.9% Black/African American, 1.7% Asian, 0.0% American Indian/Alaska Native, 0.0% Native Hawaiian/Other Pacific Islander, 0.0% Two or more races, 1.0% Hispanic of any race; Average household size: 2.42; Median age: 45.0; Age under 18: 21.5%; Age 65 and over: 18.1%; Males per 100 females: 97.9; Marriage status: 26.0% never married, 62.6% now married, 2.6% separated, 4.6% widowed, 6.8% divorced; Foreign born: 1.8%; Speak English only: 97.2%; With disability: 10.4%; Veterans: 10.3%; Ancestry: 22.6% German, 18.8% Irish, 13.9% English, 10.9% Italian, 9.8% American
Employment: 20.7% management, business, and financial, 5.6% computer, engineering, and science, 15.1% education, legal, community service, arts, and media, 8.8% healthcare practitioners, 13.7% service, 21.0% sales and office, 8.0% natural resources, construction, and maintenance, 7.2% production, transportation, and material moving
Income: Per capita: $38,034; Median household: $75,625; Average household: $91,095; Households with income of $100,000 or more: 34.1%; Poverty rate: 5.7%
Educational Attainment: High school diploma or higher: 95.0%; Bachelor's degree or higher: 40.2%; Graduate/professional degree or higher: 19.4%

School District(s)
Horseheads Central SD (PK-12)
    Enrollment: 4,237 . . . . (607) 739-5601
Housing: Homeownership rate: 85.2%; Median home value: $155,100; Median year structure built: 1970; Homeowner vacancy rate: 3.0%; Median selected monthly owner costs: $1,420 with a mortgage, $478 without a mortgage; Median gross rent: $1,019 per month; Rental vacancy rate: 8.7%
Health Insurance: 97.4% have insurance; 84.7% have private insurance; 28.4% have public insurance; 2.6% do not have insurance; 3.0% of children under 18 do not have insurance
Transportation: Commute: 95.9% car, 0.9% public transportation, 1.4% walk, 1.9% work from home; Mean travel time to work: 19.6 minutes
Additional Information Contacts
Town of Big Flats. . . . . (607) 562-8443
    http://www.bigflatsny.gov/pmwiki.php

BREESPORT (CDP). Covers a land area of 1.628 square miles and a water area of 0.012 square miles. Located at 42.18° N. Lat; 76.74° W. Long. Elevation is 1,099 feet.
Population: 483; Growth (since 2000): n/a; Density: 296.6 persons per square mile; Race: 92.1% White, 0.0% Black/African American, 0.0% Asian, 0.0% American Indian/Alaska Native, 0.0% Native Hawaiian/Other Pacific Islander, 7.9% Two or more races, 10.6% Hispanic of any race; Average household size: 2.53; Median age: 46.3; Age under 18: 24.6%; Age 65 and over: 9.7%; Males per 100 females: 108.0; Marriage status: 19.9% never married, 76.6% now married, 4.5% separated, 3.5% widowed, 0.0% divorced; Foreign born: 2.7%; Speak English only: 82.0%; With disability: 3.7%; Veterans: 12.9%; Ancestry: 23.0% Italian, 19.3% English, 12.0% Polish, 9.3% Irish, 6.8% German
Employment: 12.4% management, business, and financial, 0.0% computer, engineering, and science, 12.9% education, legal, community

service, arts, and media, 11.2% healthcare practitioners, 13.3% service, 19.3% sales and office, 8.0% natural resources, construction, and maintenance, 22.9% production, transportation, and material moving
Income: Per capita: $30,936; Median household: $62,284; Average household: $80,165; Households with income of $100,000 or more: 17.3%; Poverty rate: n/a
Educational Attainment: High school diploma or higher: 95.7%; Bachelor's degree or higher: 26.1%; Graduate/professional degree or higher: 10.3%
Housing: Homeownership rate: 100.0%; Median home value: $103,500; Median year structure built: 1966; Homeowner vacancy rate: 0.0%; Median selected monthly owner costs: $1,055 with a mortgage, $294 without a mortgage; Median gross rent: n/a per month; Rental vacancy rate: 0.0%
Health Insurance: 100.0% have insurance; 93.2% have private insurance; 27.5% have public insurance; 0.0% do not have insurance; 0.0% of children under 18 do not have insurance
Transportation: Commute: 100.0% car, 0.0% public transportation, 0.0% walk, 0.0% work from home; Mean travel time to work: 31.6 minutes

CATLIN (town). Covers a land area of 37.989 square miles and a water area of 0.027 square miles. Located at 42.23° N. Lat; 76.90° W. Long.
Population: 2,578; Growth (since 2000): -2.7%; Density: 67.9 persons per square mile; Race: 96.5% White, 1.5% Black/African American, 0.7% Asian, 0.1% American Indian/Alaska Native, 0.0% Native Hawaiian/Other Pacific Islander, 0.4% Two or more races, 2.0% Hispanic of any race; Average household size: 2.59; Median age: 38.9; Age under 18: 25.8%; Age 65 and over: 10.5%; Males per 100 females: 101.7; Marriage status: 24.6% never married, 61.9% now married, 3.1% separated, 4.5% widowed, 8.9% divorced; Foreign born: 2.2%; Speak English only: 97.2%; With disability: 9.4%; Veterans: 8.0%; Ancestry: 22.1% American, 21.8% German, 16.5% Irish, 12.2% Italian, 10.6% English
Employment: 11.3% management, business, and financial, 5.8% computer, engineering, and science, 9.4% education, legal, community service, arts, and media, 3.5% healthcare practitioners, 15.5% service, 24.5% sales and office, 9.2% natural resources, construction, and maintenance, 20.8% production, transportation, and material moving
Income: Per capita: $30,423; Median household: $64,219; Average household: $78,421; Households with income of $100,000 or more: 27.7%; Poverty rate: 10.9%
Educational Attainment: High school diploma or higher: 90.9%; Bachelor's degree or higher: 20.0%; Graduate/professional degree or higher: 9.4%
Housing: Homeownership rate: 86.5%; Median home value: $111,900; Median year structure built: 1974; Homeowner vacancy rate: 0.0%; Median selected monthly owner costs: $1,250 with a mortgage, $537 without a mortgage; Median gross rent: $708 per month; Rental vacancy rate: 0.0%
Health Insurance: 96.8% have insurance; 76.6% have private insurance; 30.1% have public insurance; 3.2% do not have insurance; 2.8% of children under 18 do not have insurance
Transportation: Commute: 94.2% car, 0.0% public transportation, 1.2% walk, 3.5% work from home; Mean travel time to work: 22.2 minutes

CHEMUNG (town). Covers a land area of 49.479 square miles and a water area of 0.562 square miles. Located at 42.06° N. Lat; 76.61° W. Long. Elevation is 846 feet.
Population: 2,340; Growth (since 2000): -12.2%; Density: 47.3 persons per square mile; Race: 99.2% White, 0.0% Black/African American, 0.0% Asian, 0.0% American Indian/Alaska Native, 0.0% Native Hawaiian/Other Pacific Islander, 0.8% Two or more races, 2.4% Hispanic of any race; Average household size: 2.53; Median age: 47.5; Age under 18: 19.5%; Age 65 and over: 18.6%; Males per 100 females: 98.8; Marriage status: 22.8% never married, 66.0% now married, 1.1% separated, 5.1% widowed, 6.1% divorced; Foreign born: 2.9%; Speak English only: 99.8%; With disability: 15.2%; Veterans: 10.1%; Ancestry: 19.7% German, 12.7% Italian, 12.6% American, 11.8% Irish, 10.2% English
Employment: 11.1% management, business, and financial, 3.2% computer, engineering, and science, 11.0% education, legal, community service, arts, and media, 5.3% healthcare practitioners, 18.4% service, 25.7% sales and office, 13.4% natural resources, construction, and maintenance, 11.8% production, transportation, and material moving
Income: Per capita: $27,659; Median household: $61,912; Average household: $70,382; Households with income of $100,000 or more: 23.3%; Poverty rate: 8.9%

Educational Attainment: High school diploma or higher: 93.9%; Bachelor's degree or higher: 21.2%; Graduate/professional degree or higher: 8.8%
School District(s)
Waverly Central SD (PK-12)
    Enrollment: 1,593 . . . . (607) 565-2841
Housing: Homeownership rate: 86.8%; Median home value: $116,400; Median year structure built: 1972; Homeowner vacancy rate: 0.0%; Median selected monthly owner costs: $1,190 with a mortgage, $429 without a mortgage; Median gross rent: $752 per month; Rental vacancy rate: 0.0%
Health Insurance: 96.0% have insurance; 74.2% have private insurance; 34.4% have public insurance; 4.0% do not have insurance; 0.0% of children under 18 do not have insurance
Transportation: Commute: 94.0% car, 0.5% public transportation, 1.8% walk, 3.3% work from home; Mean travel time to work: 21.3 minutes
Additional Information Contacts
Town of Chemung . . . . (607) 529-3532
    http://townofchemung.com

ELMIRA (city). County seat. Covers a land area of 7.249 square miles and a water area of 0.326 square miles. Located at 42.09° N. Lat; 76.81° W. Long. Elevation is 853 feet.
History: The Sullivan-Clinton Expedition entered the region of Elmira in 1779. Most of the early settlers were emigrants from Wyoming and Wilkes-Barre, Pennsylvania. In 1789 a famine struck the valley as the result of a frost. The only deaths that occurred resulted not from starvation but from overeating when food was finally obtained. The present name was adopted in 1828. According to local tradition, Nathan Teall, an early settler, had a daughter named Elmira, for whom her mother called in a shrill, far-reaching voice. When it was decided to adopt a new name, several people suggested the one they had heard so often when Elmira was a child.
Population: 28,302; Growth (since 2000): -8.5%; Density: 3,904.4 persons per square mile; Race: 76.7% White, 15.0% Black/African American, 0.4% Asian, 0.2% American Indian/Alaska Native, 0.0% Native Hawaiian/Other Pacific Islander, 6.5% Two or more races, 5.2% Hispanic of any race; Average household size: 2.42; Median age: 33.4; Age under 18: 23.9%; Age 65 and over: 11.5%; Males per 100 females: 102.4; Marriage status: 46.8% never married, 35.7% now married, 3.6% separated, 6.0% widowed, 11.5% divorced; Foreign born: 2.5%; Speak English only: 96.0%; With disability: 18.1%; Veterans: 5.9%; Ancestry: 17.9% Irish, 14.5% German, 13.4% American, 11.6% Italian, 7.2% English
Employment: 6.2% management, business, and financial, 3.2% computer, engineering, and science, 11.0% education, legal, community service, arts, and media, 5.9% healthcare practitioners, 28.4% service, 23.3% sales and office, 8.4% natural resources, construction, and maintenance, 13.6% production, transportation, and material moving
Income: Per capita: $17,288; Median household: $32,646; Average household: $46,074; Households with income of $100,000 or more: 10.0%; Poverty rate: 30.9%
Educational Attainment: High school diploma or higher: 84.2%; Bachelor's degree or higher: 15.5%; Graduate/professional degree or higher: 6.8%
School District(s)
Elmira City SD (PK-12)
    Enrollment: 6,115 . . . . (607) 735-3010
Finn Academy - An Elmira Charter School (KG-04)
    Enrollment: 249 . . . . (607) 737-8040
Four-year College(s)
Elmira College (Private, Not-for-profit)
    Enrollment: 1,012 . . . . (607) 735-1800
    Tuition: In-state $41,900; Out-of-state $41,900
Two-year College(s)
Arnot Ogden Medical Center (Private, Not-for-profit)
    Enrollment: 68 . . . . (607) 737-4153
Elmira Business Institute (Private, For-profit)
    Enrollment: 205 . . . . (607) 733-7177
    Tuition: In-state $21,700; Out-of-state $21,700
Vocational/Technical School(s)
Schuyler Steuben Chemung Tioga Allegany BOCES (Public)
    Enrollment: 155 . . . . (607) 739-3581
    Tuition: $12,595
Housing: Homeownership rate: 45.1%; Median home value: $72,800; Median year structure built: Before 1940; Homeowner vacancy rate: 1.4%; Median selected monthly owner costs: $932 with a mortgage, $427 without

a mortgage; Median gross rent: $710 per month; Rental vacancy rate: 8.1%
Health Insurance: 93.8% have insurance; 48.9% have private insurance; 54.9% have public insurance; 6.2% do not have insurance; 3.5% of children under 18 do not have insurance
Hospitals: Arnot Ogden Medical Center (256 beds); Saint Joseph's Hospital (295 beds)
Safety: Violent crime rate: 28.8 per 10,000 population; Property crime rate: 311.1 per 10,000 population
Newspapers: Star-Gazette (daily circulation 26,300)
Transportation: Commute: 82.7% car, 5.8% public transportation, 7.5% walk, 2.6% work from home; Mean travel time to work: 18.5 minutes
Airports: Elmira/Corning Regional (primary service/non-hub)
Additional Information Contacts
City of Elmira . . . . (607) 737-5672
   http://www.cityofelmira.net

ELMIRA (town). Covers a land area of 22.212 square miles and a water area of 0.329 square miles. Located at 42.09° N. Lat; 76.78° W. Long. Elevation is 853 feet.
History: Formerly Newtown, renamed for Elmira Teall, an innkeeper's daughter. The Treaty of Painted Post, ending warfare between settlers and the Iroquois confederation, was signed here in 1791. Site of a Confederate prison camp in 1864-1865 and 3,000 Confederate prisoners are buried here. The well-known Elmira Correctional Facility (est. 1876) led the way in prison reform. Mark Twain spent many summers in Elmira and is buried here. Settled 1788, Incorporated 1864.
Population: 6,729; Growth (since 2000): -6.5%; Density: 302.9 persons per square mile; Race: 96.9% White, 0.6% Black/African American, 0.9% Asian, 0.0% American Indian/Alaska Native, 0.0% Native Hawaiian/Other Pacific Islander, 1.4% Two or more races, 0.6% Hispanic of any race; Average household size: 2.24; Median age: 47.7; Age under 18: 22.9%; Age 65 and over: 24.0%; Males per 100 females: 90.0; Marriage status: 19.2% never married, 65.6% now married, 2.2% separated, 8.7% widowed, 6.5% divorced; Foreign born: 3.4%; Speak English only: 97.2%; With disability: 10.0%; Veterans: 10.5%; Ancestry: 24.8% Irish, 15.8% German, 14.7% Italian, 12.0% American, 9.6% English
Employment: 18.2% management, business, and financial, 1.5% computer, engineering, and science, 21.0% education, legal, community service, arts, and media, 8.8% healthcare practitioners, 11.4% service, 25.5% sales and office, 6.2% natural resources, construction, and maintenance, 7.3% production, transportation, and material moving
Income: Per capita: $44,736; Median household: $64,896; Average household: $101,070; Households with income of $100,000 or more: 29.4%; Poverty rate: 7.3%
Educational Attainment: High school diploma or higher: 97.3%; Bachelor's degree or higher: 46.5%; Graduate/professional degree or higher: 22.5%

School District(s)
Elmira City SD (PK-12)
   Enrollment: 6,115 . . . . (607) 735-3010
Finn Academy - An Elmira Charter School (KG-04)
   Enrollment: 249 . . . . (607) 737-8040
Four-year College(s)
Elmira College (Private, Not-for-profit)
   Enrollment: 1,012 . . . . (607) 735-1800
   Tuition: In-state $41,900; Out-of-state $41,900
Two-year College(s)
Arnot Ogden Medical Center (Private, Not-for-profit)
   Enrollment: 68 . . . . (607) 737-4153
Elmira Business Institute (Private, For-profit)
   Enrollment: 205 . . . . (607) 733-7177
   Tuition: In-state $21,700; Out-of-state $21,700
Vocational/Technical School(s)
Schuyler Steuben Chemung Tioga Allegany BOCES (Public)
   Enrollment: 155 . . . . (607) 739-3581
   Tuition: $12,595
Housing: Homeownership rate: 86.2%; Median home value: $121,700; Median year structure built: 1950; Homeowner vacancy rate: 0.0%; Median selected monthly owner costs: $1,171 with a mortgage, $532 without a mortgage; Median gross rent: $918 per month; Rental vacancy rate: 0.0%
Health Insurance: 92.0% have insurance; 74.5% have private insurance; 37.3% have public insurance; 8.0% do not have insurance; 10.1% of children under 18 do not have insurance

Hospitals: Arnot Ogden Medical Center (256 beds); Saint Joseph's Hospital (295 beds)
Safety: Violent crime rate: 1.8 per 10,000 population; Property crime rate: 1.8 per 10,000 population
Newspapers: Star-Gazette (daily circulation 26,300)
Transportation: Commute: 93.4% car, 0.5% public transportation, 3.2% walk, 1.9% work from home; Mean travel time to work: 16.2 minutes
Airports: Elmira/Corning Regional (primary service/non-hub)
Additional Information Contacts
Town of Elmira . . . . (607) 734-2031
   http://www.townofelmira.com

ELMIRA HEIGHTS (village). Covers a land area of 1.146 square miles and a water area of 0 square miles. Located at 42.13° N. Lat; 76.83° W. Long. Elevation is 879 feet.
Population: 3,999; Growth (since 2000): -4.1%; Density: 3,488.2 persons per square mile; Race: 88.0% White, 2.2% Black/African American, 3.6% Asian, 0.0% American Indian/Alaska Native, 0.0% Native Hawaiian/Other Pacific Islander, 5.7% Two or more races, 0.5% Hispanic of any race; Average household size: 2.28; Median age: 35.2; Age under 18: 25.3%; Age 65 and over: 15.5%; Males per 100 females: 93.3; Marriage status: 35.8% never married, 46.4% now married, 3.2% separated, 8.3% widowed, 9.6% divorced; Foreign born: 2.1%; Speak English only: 96.0%; With disability: 17.0%; Veterans: 8.8%; Ancestry: 19.3% Irish, 16.3% German, 15.1% Italian, 9.1% American, 4.9% Polish
Employment: 6.7% management, business, and financial, 4.2% computer, engineering, and science, 14.6% education, legal, community service, arts, and media, 6.3% healthcare practitioners, 20.3% service, 26.0% sales and office, 4.9% natural resources, construction, and maintenance, 17.0% production, transportation, and material moving
Income: Per capita: $23,026; Median household: $43,533; Average household: $52,119; Households with income of $100,000 or more: 11.6%; Poverty rate: 14.4%
Educational Attainment: High school diploma or higher: 90.1%; Bachelor's degree or higher: 19.8%; Graduate/professional degree or higher: 9.0%

School District(s)
Elmira Heights Central SD (PK-12)
   Enrollment: 1,063 . . . . (607) 734-7114
Housing: Homeownership rate: 49.4%; Median home value: $83,400; Median year structure built: 1946; Homeowner vacancy rate: 3.3%; Median selected monthly owner costs: $1,035 with a mortgage, $485 without a mortgage; Median gross rent: $665 per month; Rental vacancy rate: 2.5%
Health Insurance: 94.2% have insurance; 69.6% have private insurance; 38.4% have public insurance; 5.8% do not have insurance; 1.8% of children under 18 do not have insurance
Safety: Violent crime rate: 7.7 per 10,000 population; Property crime rate: 143.3 per 10,000 population
Transportation: Commute: 89.2% car, 1.8% public transportation, 3.6% walk, 1.7% work from home; Mean travel time to work: 18.6 minutes
Additional Information Contacts
Village of Elmira Heights . . . . (607) 734-7156
   http://www.elmiraheights.org

ERIN (CDP). Covers a land area of 0.747 square miles and a water area of 0.010 square miles. Located at 42.18° N. Lat; 76.67° W. Long. Elevation is 1,263 feet.
Population: 395; Growth (since 2000): n/a; Density: 528.5 persons per square mile; Race: 93.9% White, 2.3% Black/African American, 2.5% Asian, 0.5% American Indian/Alaska Native, 0.0% Native Hawaiian/Other Pacific Islander, 0.8% Two or more races, 0.0% Hispanic of any race; Average household size: 2.28; Median age: 44.8; Age under 18: 18.7%; Age 65 and over: 12.9%; Males per 100 females: 104.7; Marriage status: 22.8% never married, 56.0% now married, 6.3% separated, 6.9% widowed, 14.4% divorced; Foreign born: 3.5%; Speak English only: 97.3%; With disability: 24.8%; Veterans: 15.6%; Ancestry: 24.8% German, 24.6% Irish, 16.7% American, 8.4% Italian, 3.8% English
Employment: 6.0% management, business, and financial, 2.4% computer, engineering, and science, 2.4% education, legal, community service, arts, and media, 6.6% healthcare practitioners, 20.4% service, 24.0% sales and office, 16.2% natural resources, construction, and maintenance, 22.2% production, transportation, and material moving
Income: Per capita: $18,160; Median household: $32,153; Average household: $40,895; Households with income of $100,000 or more: 4.0%; Poverty rate: 18.3%

Educational Attainment: High school diploma or higher: 88.6%; Bachelor's degree or higher: 6.4%; Graduate/professional degree or higher: 4.7%
Housing: Homeownership rate: 98.3%; Median home value: $46,700; Median year structure built: 1974; Homeowner vacancy rate: 0.0%; Median selected monthly owner costs: $1,025 with a mortgage, $407 without a mortgage; Median gross rent: n/a per month; Rental vacancy rate: 0.0%
Health Insurance: 93.4% have insurance; 51.4% have private insurance; 61.3% have public insurance; 6.6% do not have insurance; 0.0% of children under 18 do not have insurance
Transportation: Commute: 97.5% car, 0.0% public transportation, 0.0% walk, 0.0% work from home; Mean travel time to work: 29.2 minutes

ERIN (town). Covers a land area of 44.247 square miles and a water area of 0.221 square miles. Located at 42.18° N. Lat; 76.67° W. Long. Elevation is 1,263 feet.
Population: 2,050; Growth (since 2000): -0.2%; Density: 46.3 persons per square mile; Race: 97.9% White, 0.4% Black/African American, 0.5% Asian, 0.4% American Indian/Alaska Native, 0.0% Native Hawaiian/Other Pacific Islander, 0.4% Two or more races, 0.3% Hispanic of any race; Average household size: 2.41; Median age: 43.3; Age under 18: 21.4%; Age 65 and over: 16.6%; Males per 100 females: 106.5; Marriage status: 22.2% never married, 60.1% now married, 1.8% separated, 5.9% widowed, 11.8% divorced; Foreign born: 1.6%; Speak English only: 98.1%; With disability: 13.6%; Veterans: 12.0%; Ancestry: 20.6% American, 20.1% German, 16.5% Irish, 10.4% Italian, 8.7% English
Employment: 11.8% management, business, and financial, 2.5% computer, engineering, and science, 5.5% education, legal, community service, arts, and media, 6.6% healthcare practitioners, 21.9% service, 19.7% sales and office, 11.5% natural resources, construction, and maintenance, 20.4% production, transportation, and material moving
Income: Per capita: $27,864; Median household: $56,809; Average household: $66,367; Households with income of $100,000 or more: 17.3%; Poverty rate: 10.6%
Educational Attainment: High school diploma or higher: 90.6%; Bachelor's degree or higher: 14.3%; Graduate/professional degree or higher: 3.8%
Housing: Homeownership rate: 93.7%; Median home value: $93,400; Median year structure built: 1977; Homeowner vacancy rate: 3.4%; Median selected monthly owner costs: $1,164 with a mortgage, $448 without a mortgage; Median gross rent: $925 per month; Rental vacancy rate: 0.0%
Health Insurance: 95.5% have insurance; 76.4% have private insurance; 35.1% have public insurance; 4.5% do not have insurance; 0.0% of children under 18 do not have insurance
Transportation: Commute: 96.4% car, 0.0% public transportation, 0.0% walk, 2.2% work from home; Mean travel time to work: 25.8 minutes

HORSEHEADS (town). Covers a land area of 35.606 square miles and a water area of 0.314 square miles. Located at 42.16° N. Lat; 76.78° W. Long. Elevation is 896 feet.
History: Settled 1789, incorporated 1837.
Population: 19,442; Growth (since 2000): -0.6%; Density: 546.0 persons per square mile; Race: 90.9% White, 1.3% Black/African American, 5.0% Asian, 0.0% American Indian/Alaska Native, 0.0% Native Hawaiian/Other Pacific Islander, 2.6% Two or more races, 1.6% Hispanic of any race; Average household size: 2.31; Median age: 43.5; Age under 18: 21.5%; Age 65 and over: 20.6%; Males per 100 females: 90.3; Marriage status: 26.8% never married, 55.2% now married, 2.7% separated, 8.6% widowed, 9.4% divorced; Foreign born: 4.9%; Speak English only: 93.7%; With disability: 13.3%; Veterans: 9.0%; Ancestry: 16.6% Irish, 16.4% German, 13.2% Italian, 12.0% English, 11.0% American
Employment: 15.1% management, business, and financial, 4.5% computer, engineering, and science, 11.5% education, legal, community service, arts, and media, 11.4% healthcare practitioners, 16.3% service, 23.9% sales and office, 6.5% natural resources, construction, and maintenance, 10.8% production, transportation, and material moving
Income: Per capita: $30,592; Median household: $55,992; Average household: $71,263; Households with income of $100,000 or more: 22.3%; Poverty rate: 9.6%
Educational Attainment: High school diploma or higher: 92.9%; Bachelor's degree or higher: 30.4%; Graduate/professional degree or higher: 14.1%

School District(s)
Horseheads Central SD (PK-12)
    Enrollment: 4,237 . . . . (607) 739-5601

Housing: Homeownership rate: 65.5%; Median home value: $122,300; Median year structure built: 1961; Homeowner vacancy rate: 1.8%; Median selected monthly owner costs: $1,217 with a mortgage, $471 without a mortgage; Median gross rent: $871 per month; Rental vacancy rate: 5.8%
Health Insurance: 95.1% have insurance; 76.7% have private insurance; 35.2% have public insurance; 4.9% do not have insurance; 4.2% of children under 18 do not have insurance
Transportation: Commute: 94.7% car, 0.6% public transportation, 0.8% walk, 2.6% work from home; Mean travel time to work: 18.5 minutes
Additional Information Contacts
Town of Horseheads . . . . (607) 739-8783
    http://townofhorseheads.org

HORSEHEADS (village). Covers a land area of 3.887 square miles and a water area of 0.015 square miles. Located at 42.17° N. Lat; 76.83° W. Long. Elevation is 896 feet.
Population: 6,561; Growth (since 2000): 1.7%; Density: 1,687.9 persons per square mile; Race: 93.0% White, 0.8% Black/African American, 3.5% Asian, 0.0% American Indian/Alaska Native, 0.0% Native Hawaiian/Other Pacific Islander, 2.6% Two or more races, 2.0% Hispanic of any race; Average household size: 2.13; Median age: 42.5; Age under 18: 21.2%; Age 65 and over: 24.0%; Males per 100 females: 82.8; Marriage status: 31.4% never married, 48.1% now married, 2.9% separated, 11.5% widowed, 8.9% divorced; Foreign born: 4.7%; Speak English only: 95.0%; With disability: 14.8%; Veterans: 10.2%; Ancestry: 17.2% German, 17.0% Irish, 15.5% English, 14.1% American, 12.8% Italian
Employment: 18.0% management, business, and financial, 5.0% computer, engineering, and science, 9.8% education, legal, community service, arts, and media, 11.7% healthcare practitioners, 15.1% service, 23.5% sales and office, 8.5% natural resources, construction, and maintenance, 8.5% production, transportation, and material moving
Income: Per capita: $29,998; Median household: $47,377; Average household: $64,178; Households with income of $100,000 or more: 17.3%; Poverty rate: 10.5%
Educational Attainment: High school diploma or higher: 92.7%; Bachelor's degree or higher: 30.3%; Graduate/professional degree or higher: 12.8%

School District(s)
Horseheads Central SD (PK-12)
    Enrollment: 4,237 . . . . (607) 739-5601
Housing: Homeownership rate: 56.3%; Median home value: $106,300; Median year structure built: 1959; Homeowner vacancy rate: 0.0%; Median selected monthly owner costs: $1,092 with a mortgage, $445 without a mortgage; Median gross rent: $908 per month; Rental vacancy rate: 3.3%
Health Insurance: 95.1% have insurance; 73.8% have private insurance; 41.8% have public insurance; 4.9% do not have insurance; 4.2% of children under 18 do not have insurance
Safety: Violent crime rate: 0.0 per 10,000 population; Property crime rate: 65.6 per 10,000 population
Transportation: Commute: 96.6% car, 0.9% public transportation, 0.9% walk, 1.4% work from home; Mean travel time to work: 16.6 minutes
Additional Information Contacts
Village of Horseheads . . . . (607) 739-5691
    http://www.horseheads.org

HORSEHEADS NORTH (CDP). Covers a land area of 2.211 square miles and a water area of 0.029 square miles. Located at 42.20° N. Lat; 76.80° W. Long.
Population: 2,655; Growth (since 2000): -6.9%; Density: 1,200.6 persons per square mile; Race: 96.6% White, 0.0% Black/African American, 2.3% Asian, 0.0% American Indian/Alaska Native, 0.0% Native Hawaiian/Other Pacific Islander, 0.6% Two or more races, 3.2% Hispanic of any race; Average household size: 2.54; Median age: 40.5; Age under 18: 19.5%; Age 65 and over: 12.0%; Males per 100 females: 89.3; Marriage status: 24.2% never married, 68.2% now married, 1.6% separated, 1.3% widowed, 6.2% divorced; Foreign born: 3.5%; Speak English only: 95.8%; With disability: 11.2%; Veterans: 7.1%; Ancestry: 19.8% Irish, 19.7% German, 15.3% Italian, 13.6% Polish, 13.1% English
Employment: 15.7% management, business, and financial, 5.7% computer, engineering, and science, 13.4% education, legal, community service, arts, and media, 12.1% healthcare practitioners, 17.3% service, 22.9% sales and office, 7.8% natural resources, construction, and maintenance, 5.2% production, transportation, and material moving

Income: Per capita: $31,845; Median household: $73,516; Average household: $80,400; Households with income of $100,000 or more: 31.3%; Poverty rate: 4.6%
Educational Attainment: High school diploma or higher: 99.7%; Bachelor's degree or higher: 38.9%; Graduate/professional degree or higher: 14.7%
Housing: Homeownership rate: 76.8%; Median home value: $167,200; Median year structure built: 1967; Homeowner vacancy rate: 4.4%; Median selected monthly owner costs: $1,330 with a mortgage, $550 without a mortgage; Median gross rent: $937 per month; Rental vacancy rate: 13.3%
Health Insurance: 97.3% have insurance; 85.2% have private insurance; 22.1% have public insurance; 2.7% do not have insurance; 0.0% of children under 18 do not have insurance
Transportation: Commute: 98.9% car, 0.0% public transportation, 0.0% walk, 1.1% work from home; Mean travel time to work: 20.2 minutes

LOWMAN (unincorporated postal area)
ZCTA: 14861
Covers a land area of 34.223 square miles and a water area of 0.261 square miles. Located at 42.09° N. Lat; 76.69° W. Long. Elevation is 840 feet.
Population: 1,245; Growth (since 2000): -14.7%; Density: 36.4 persons per square mile; Race: 100.0% White, 0.0% Black/African American, 0.0% Asian, 0.0% American Indian/Alaska Native, 0.0% Native Hawaiian/Other Pacific Islander, 0.0% Two or more races, 0.0% Hispanic of any race; Average household size: 2.11; Median age: 48.7; Age under 18: 17.6%; Age 65 and over: 23.5%; Males per 100 females: 100.6; Marriage status: 17.7% never married, 62.0% now married, 4.7% separated, 9.2% widowed, 11.2% divorced; Foreign born: 1.5%; Speak English only: 98.6%; With disability: 18.5%; Veterans: 10.7%; Ancestry: 20.9% American, 17.4% Irish, 15.7% German, 7.1% Italian, 5.3% English
Employment: 17.0% management, business, and financial, 0.5% computer, engineering, and science, 10.0% education, legal, community service, arts, and media, 5.4% healthcare practitioners, 22.0% service, 19.6% sales and office, 8.8% natural resources, construction, and maintenance, 16.8% production, transportation, and material moving
Income: Per capita: $26,346; Median household: $44,808; Average household: $55,750; Households with income of $100,000 or more: 10.8%; Poverty rate: 11.9%
Educational Attainment: High school diploma or higher: 87.6%; Bachelor's degree or higher: 12.0%; Graduate/professional degree or higher: 5.4%
Housing: Homeownership rate: 89.2%; Median home value: $103,400; Median year structure built: 1973; Homeowner vacancy rate: 1.8%; Median selected monthly owner costs: $1,119 with a mortgage, $444 without a mortgage; Median gross rent: $645 per month; Rental vacancy rate: 0.0%
Health Insurance: 97.1% have insurance; 73.3% have private insurance; 44.3% have public insurance; 2.9% do not have insurance; 0.0% of children under 18 do not have insurance
Transportation: Commute: 93.0% car, 0.0% public transportation, 1.3% walk, 5.7% work from home; Mean travel time to work: 22.2 minutes

MILLPORT (village). Covers a land area of 0.348 square miles and a water area of 0 square miles. Located at 42.27° N. Lat; 76.84° W. Long. Elevation is 718 feet.
Population: 434; Growth (since 2000): 46.1%; Density: 1,247.0 persons per square mile; Race: 95.6% White, 0.0% Black/African American, 0.5% Asian, 0.0% American Indian/Alaska Native, 0.0% Native Hawaiian/Other Pacific Islander, 3.9% Two or more races, 0.0% Hispanic of any race; Average household size: 2.73; Median age: 34.5; Age under 18: 22.4%; Age 65 and over: 13.1%; Males per 100 females: 98.7; Marriage status: 39.3% never married, 42.7% now married, 2.6% separated, 3.4% widowed, 14.5% divorced; Foreign born: 1.2%; Speak English only: 99.7%; With disability: 13.4%; Veterans: 11.0%; Ancestry: 26.7% Irish, 22.8% English, 15.0% American, 12.4% German, 10.6% Italian
Employment: 3.2% management, business, and financial, 3.2% computer, engineering, and science, 10.1% education, legal, community service, arts, and media, 3.7% healthcare practitioners, 26.6% service, 22.3% sales and office, 5.3% natural resources, construction, and maintenance, 25.5% production, transportation, and material moving
Income: Per capita: $18,091; Median household: $39,792; Average household: $48,807; Households with income of $100,000 or more: 5.7%; Poverty rate: 20.5%

Educational Attainment: High school diploma or higher: 87.3%; Bachelor's degree or higher: 7.5%; Graduate/professional degree or higher: 5.5%
Housing: Homeownership rate: 78.6%; Median home value: $66,400; Median year structure built: Before 1940; Homeowner vacancy rate: 3.8%; Median selected monthly owner costs: $1,016 with a mortgage, $368 without a mortgage; Median gross rent: $825 per month; Rental vacancy rate: 0.0%
Health Insurance: 92.6% have insurance; 48.4% have private insurance; 52.3% have public insurance; 7.4% do not have insurance; 3.7% of children under 18 do not have insurance
Transportation: Commute: 94.1% car, 0.0% public transportation, 1.1% walk, 2.7% work from home; Mean travel time to work: 24.6 minutes

PINE CITY (unincorporated postal area)
ZCTA: 14871
Covers a land area of 57.175 square miles and a water area of 0.499 square miles. Located at 42.04° N. Lat; 76.91° W. Long. Elevation is 1,001 feet.
Population: 5,135; Growth (since 2000): 4.6%; Density: 89.8 persons per square mile; Race: 92.9% White, 5.5% Black/African American, 0.1% Asian, 0.0% American Indian/Alaska Native, 0.0% Native Hawaiian/Other Pacific Islander, 1.0% Two or more races, 4.3% Hispanic of any race; Average household size: 2.39; Median age: 45.9; Age under 18: 18.2%; Age 65 and over: 21.5%; Males per 100 females: 131.8; Marriage status: 26.4% never married, 56.3% now married, 1.8% separated, 6.9% widowed, 10.5% divorced; Foreign born: 1.4%; Speak English only: 97.5%; With disability: 15.8%; Veterans: 11.5%; Ancestry: 16.8% English, 16.0% German, 13.6% Irish, 12.6% American, 10.3% Italian
Employment: 11.2% management, business, and financial, 4.3% computer, engineering, and science, 10.1% education, legal, community service, arts, and media, 8.6% healthcare practitioners, 16.7% service, 22.0% sales and office, 13.0% natural resources, construction, and maintenance, 14.2% production, transportation, and material moving
Income: Per capita: $29,784; Median household: $65,700; Average household: $79,791; Households with income of $100,000 or more: 29.1%; Poverty rate: 5.6%
Educational Attainment: High school diploma or higher: 90.4%; Bachelor's degree or higher: 23.5%; Graduate/professional degree or higher: 11.7%
School District(s)
Elmira City SD (PK-12)
    Enrollment: 6,115 . . . . (607) 735-3010
Housing: Homeownership rate: 84.7%; Median home value: $144,300; Median year structure built: 1958; Homeowner vacancy rate: 1.9%; Median selected monthly owner costs: $1,335 with a mortgage, $425 without a mortgage; Median gross rent: $772 per month; Rental vacancy rate: 8.2%
Health Insurance: 97.7% have insurance; 81.6% have private insurance; 37.9% have public insurance; 2.3% do not have insurance; 4.6% of children under 18 do not have insurance
Transportation: Commute: 96.4% car, 0.5% public transportation, 0.6% walk, 1.7% work from home; Mean travel time to work: 22.8 minutes

PINE VALLEY (CDP). Covers a land area of 1.204 square miles and a water area of 0.014 square miles. Located at 42.23° N. Lat; 76.85° W. Long. Elevation is 932 feet.
Population: 733; Growth (since 2000): n/a; Density: 608.6 persons per square mile; Race: 85.7% White, 5.0% Black/African American, 0.0% Asian, 0.0% American Indian/Alaska Native, 0.0% Native Hawaiian/Other Pacific Islander, 3.3% Two or more races, 10.0% Hispanic of any race; Average household size: 2.09; Median age: 51.4; Age under 18: 4.5%; Age 65 and over: 23.3%; Males per 100 females: 96.9; Marriage status: 30.9% never married, 53.5% now married, 1.3% separated, 2.7% widowed, 12.9% divorced; Foreign born: 10.1%; Speak English only: 93.3%; With disability: 17.3%; Veterans: 11.9%; Ancestry: 22.8% Italian, 21.4% German, 10.5% American, 7.1% English, 7.1% Irish
Employment: 10.0% management, business, and financial, 1.5% computer, engineering, and science, 3.3% education, legal, community service, arts, and media, 0.9% healthcare practitioners, 16.9% service, 26.9% sales and office, 7.9% natural resources, construction, and maintenance, 32.6% production, transportation, and material moving

Income: Per capita: $25,746; Median household: $49,500; Average household: $53,580; Households with income of $100,000 or more: 12.8%; Poverty rate: 23.2%

Educational Attainment: High school diploma or higher: 79.7%; Bachelor's degree or higher: 4.7%; Graduate/professional degree or higher: 2.0%

Housing: Homeownership rate: 85.7%; Median home value: $97,900; Median year structure built: 1972; Homeowner vacancy rate: 0.0%; Median selected monthly owner costs: $1,285 with a mortgage, $442 without a mortgage; Median gross rent: $663 per month; Rental vacancy rate: 0.0%

Health Insurance: 99.5% have insurance; 82.4% have private insurance; 47.1% have public insurance; 0.5% do not have insurance; 0.0% of children under 18 do not have insurance

Transportation: Commute: 100.0% car, 0.0% public transportation, 0.0% walk, 0.0% work from home; Mean travel time to work: 20.5 minutes

SOUTHPORT (CDP).

Covers a land area of 6.377 square miles and a water area of 0.239 square miles. Located at 42.06° N. Lat; 76.82° W. Long. Elevation is 889 feet.

History: Southport is a town in Chemung County, New York, first settled around 1788. The town of Southport was formed from the town of Elmira in 1822.

Population: 6,832; Growth (since 2000): -7.6%; Density: 1,071.4 persons per square mile; Race: 92.0% White, 1.9% Black/African American, 0.2% Asian, 4.6% American Indian/Alaska Native, 0.0% Native Hawaiian/Other Pacific Islander, 1.2% Two or more races, 3.3% Hispanic of any race; Average household size: 2.18; Median age: 45.5; Age under 18: 19.5%; Age 65 and over: 18.6%; Males per 100 females: 93.4; Marriage status: 25.9% never married, 49.5% now married, 3.7% separated, 8.1% widowed, 16.4% divorced; Foreign born: 0.4%; Speak English only: 99.2%; With disability: 19.2%; Veterans: 11.4%; Ancestry: 19.5% German, 18.0% Irish, 17.0% English, 13.0% American, 11.6% Italian

Employment: 8.8% management, business, and financial, 4.2% computer, engineering, and science, 5.6% education, legal, community service, arts, and media, 5.5% healthcare practitioners, 27.9% service, 22.1% sales and office, 9.8% natural resources, construction, and maintenance, 16.1% production, transportation, and material moving

Income: Per capita: $26,463; Median household: $45,813; Average household: $57,698; Households with income of $100,000 or more: 12.7%; Poverty rate: 15.0%

Educational Attainment: High school diploma or higher: 91.8%; Bachelor's degree or higher: 15.4%; Graduate/professional degree or higher: 6.0%

Housing: Homeownership rate: 70.1%; Median home value: $84,000; Median year structure built: 1952; Homeowner vacancy rate: 2.4%; Median selected monthly owner costs: $900 with a mortgage, $419 without a mortgage; Median gross rent: $726 per month; Rental vacancy rate: 14.2%

Health Insurance: 91.4% have insurance; 64.2% have private insurance; 43.9% have public insurance; 8.6% do not have insurance; 0.0% of children under 18 do not have insurance

Transportation: Commute: 92.4% car, 1.2% public transportation, 2.9% walk, 1.6% work from home; Mean travel time to work: 17.7 minutes

SOUTHPORT (town).

Covers a land area of 46.414 square miles and a water area of 0.426 square miles. Located at 42.05° N. Lat; 76.88° W. Long. Elevation is 889 feet.

Population: 10,457; Growth (since 2000): -6.5%; Density: 225.3 persons per square mile; Race: 91.4% White, 4.0% Black/African American, 0.1% Asian, 3.1% American Indian/Alaska Native, 0.0% Native Hawaiian/Other Pacific Islander, 1.2% Two or more races, 4.3% Hispanic of any race; Average household size: 2.30; Median age: 45.2; Age under 18: 18.7%; Age 65 and over: 18.4%; Males per 100 females: 111.5; Marriage status: 26.9% never married, 52.8% now married, 3.3% separated, 6.7% widowed, 13.6% divorced; Foreign born: 0.8%; Speak English only: 98.5%; With disability: 17.4%; Veterans: 10.9%; Ancestry: 19.0% German, 16.8% Irish, 15.3% English, 13.0% American, 10.7% Italian

Employment: 9.1% management, business, and financial, 4.3% computer, engineering, and science, 7.1% education, legal, community service, arts, and media, 6.6% healthcare practitioners, 24.6% service, 22.9% sales and office, 9.5% natural resources, construction, and maintenance, 15.9% production, transportation, and material moving

Income: Per capita: $27,151; Median household: $51,902; Average household: $65,819; Households with income of $100,000 or more: 19.0%; Poverty rate: 11.1%

Educational Attainment: High school diploma or higher: 91.4%; Bachelor's degree or higher: 19.5%; Graduate/professional degree or higher: 7.8%

Housing: Homeownership rate: 74.2%; Median home value: $91,800; Median year structure built: 1953; Homeowner vacancy rate: 2.6%; Median selected monthly owner costs: $1,024 with a mortgage, $429 without a mortgage; Median gross rent: $743 per month; Rental vacancy rate: 14.0%

Health Insurance: 93.1% have insurance; 70.0% have private insurance; 41.0% have public insurance; 6.9% do not have insurance; 2.2% of children under 18 do not have insurance

Transportation: Commute: 93.7% car, 1.0% public transportation, 2.3% walk, 1.3% work from home; Mean travel time to work: 18.9 minutes

Additional Information Contacts

Town of Southport . . . . (607) 734-1548
  http://www.townofsouthport.com

VAN ETTEN (town).

Covers a land area of 41.446 square miles and a water area of 0.124 square miles. Located at 42.23° N. Lat; 76.58° W. Long. Elevation is 1,017 feet.

Population: 1,666; Growth (since 2000): 9.7%; Density: 40.2 persons per square mile; Race: 98.3% White, 0.4% Black/African American, 0.0% Asian, 0.2% American Indian/Alaska Native, 0.0% Native Hawaiian/Other Pacific Islander, 1.1% Two or more races, 1.7% Hispanic of any race; Average household size: 2.68; Median age: 43.8; Age under 18: 23.7%; Age 65 and over: 15.8%; Males per 100 females: 99.4; Marriage status: 23.9% never married, 54.6% now married, 1.7% separated, 7.4% widowed, 14.1% divorced; Foreign born: 0.9%; Speak English only: 98.3%; With disability: 13.3%; Veterans: 11.5%; Ancestry: 21.3% German, 18.5% Irish, 15.7% American, 10.0% English, 7.3% Polish

Employment: 12.0% management, business, and financial, 3.8% computer, engineering, and science, 9.8% education, legal, community service, arts, and media, 2.4% healthcare practitioners, 18.3% service, 17.8% sales and office, 12.7% natural resources, construction, and maintenance, 23.2% production, transportation, and material moving

Income: Per capita: $24,183; Median household: $51,591; Average household: $63,202; Households with income of $100,000 or more: 17.5%; Poverty rate: 9.2%

Educational Attainment: High school diploma or higher: 91.3%; Bachelor's degree or higher: 17.5%; Graduate/professional degree or higher: 5.1%

School District(s)

Spencer-Van Etten Central SD (PK-12)
  Enrollment 933 . . . . (607) 589-7100

Housing: Homeownership rate: 83.3%; Median home value: $103,400; Median year structure built: 1966; Homeowner vacancy rate: 0.6%; Median selected monthly owner costs: $1,175 with a mortgage, $523 without a mortgage; Median gross rent: $800 per month; Rental vacancy rate: 0.0%

Health Insurance: 94.1% have insurance; 61.1% have private insurance; 44.6% have public insurance; 5.9% do not have insurance; 1.7% of children under 18 do not have insurance

Transportation: Commute: 90.9% car, 0.5% public transportation, 5.3% walk, 2.3% work from home; Mean travel time to work: 32.3 minutes

VAN ETTEN (village).

Covers a land area of 0.869 square miles and a water area of <.001 square miles. Located at 42.20° N. Lat; 76.55° W. Long. Elevation is 1,017 feet.

Population: 721; Growth (since 2000): 24.1%; Density: 829.4 persons per square mile; Race: 98.9% White, 0.0% Black/African American, 0.0% Asian, 0.0% American Indian/Alaska Native, 0.0% Native Hawaiian/Other Pacific Islander, 1.1% Two or more races, 1.1% Hispanic of any race; Average household size: 2.85; Median age: 36.7; Age under 18: 27.9%; Age 65 and over: 11.4%; Males per 100 females: 96.7; Marriage status: 30.4% never married, 47.3% now married, 0.9% separated, 5.0% widowed, 17.3% divorced; Foreign born: 1.0%; Speak English only: 100.0%; With disability: 14.7%; Veterans: 13.8%; Ancestry: 27.0% German, 22.2% Irish, 14.4% Polish, 13.0% American, 8.3% English

Employment: 13.8% management, business, and financial, 2.6% computer, engineering, and science, 11.2% education, legal, community service, arts, and media, 4.2% healthcare practitioners, 22.8% service, 15.4% sales and office, 11.5% natural resources, construction, and maintenance, 18.6% production, transportation, and material moving

Income: Per capita: $21,269; Median household: $49,911; Average household: $61,670; Households with income of $100,000 or more: 18.6%; Poverty rate: 10.5%

Educational Attainment: High school diploma or higher: 91.4%; Bachelor's degree or higher: 12.2%; Graduate/professional degree or higher: 2.0%

School District(s)

Spencer-Van Etten Central SD (PK-12)

    Enrollment: 933 . . . . (607) 589-7100

Housing: Homeownership rate: 70.0%; Median home value: $95,500; Median year structure built: Before 1940; Homeowner vacancy rate: 1.7%; Median selected monthly owner costs: $1,180 with a mortgage, $529 without a mortgage; Median gross rent: $738 per month; Rental vacancy rate: 0.0%

Health Insurance: 95.8% have insurance; 55.5% have private insurance; 51.5% have public insurance; 4.2% do not have insurance; 0.0% of children under 18 do not have insurance

Transportation: Commute: 91.8% car, 0.7% public transportation, 5.6% walk, 1.0% work from home; Mean travel time to work: 30.1 minutes

VETERAN (town).

Covers a land area of 38.327 square miles and a water area of 0.143 square miles. Located at 42.25° N. Lat; 76.79° W. Long.

Population: 3,248; Growth (since 2000): -0.7%; Density: 84.7 persons per square mile; Race: 90.4% White, 3.6% Black/African American, 1.8% Asian, 0.0% American Indian/Alaska Native, 0.0% Native Hawaiian/Other Pacific Islander, 2.8% Two or more races, 2.2% Hispanic of any race; Average household size: 2.32; Median age: 51.9; Age under 18: 15.4%; Age 65 and over: 28.9%; Males per 100 females: 95.5; Marriage status: 21.5% never married, 63.7% now married, 1.1% separated, 5.2% widowed, 9.5% divorced; Foreign born: 3.2%; Speak English only: 96.8%; With disability: 16.1%; Veterans: 12.7%; Ancestry: 23.0% German, 16.4% English, 13.3% Irish, 10.2% Italian, 5.7% American

Employment: 11.8% management, business, and financial, 10.3% computer, engineering, and science, 14.3% education, legal, community service, arts, and media, 8.1% healthcare practitioners, 12.2% service, 25.7% sales and office, 2.8% natural resources, construction, and maintenance, 14.8% production, transportation, and material moving

Income: Per capita: $31,223; Median household: $62,112; Average household: $72,082; Households with income of $100,000 or more: 25.6%; Poverty rate: 9.2%

Educational Attainment: High school diploma or higher: 92.9%; Bachelor's degree or higher: 31.0%; Graduate/professional degree or higher: 19.8%

Housing: Homeownership rate: 94.0%; Median home value: $135,800; Median year structure built: 1970; Homeowner vacancy rate: 0.4%; Median selected monthly owner costs: $1,306 with a mortgage, $509 without a mortgage; Median gross rent: $593 per month; Rental vacancy rate: 0.0%

Health Insurance: 94.9% have insurance; 81.7% have private insurance; 42.0% have public insurance; 5.1% do not have insurance; 4.3% of children under 18 do not have insurance

Transportation: Commute: 98.2% car, 0.0% public transportation, 1.2% walk, 0.3% work from home; Mean travel time to work: 25.3 minutes

WELLSBURG (village).

Covers a land area of 0.568 square miles and a water area of 0.009 square miles. Located at 42.01° N. Lat; 76.73° W. Long. Elevation is 827 feet.

Population: 513; Growth (since 2000): -18.7%; Density: 903.0 persons per square mile; Race: 94.9% White, 0.4% Black/African American, 0.0% Asian, 0.0% American Indian/Alaska Native, 0.0% Native Hawaiian/Other Pacific Islander, 4.7% Two or more races, 0.0% Hispanic of any race; Average household size: 2.66; Median age: 37.9; Age under 18: 23.0%; Age 65 and over: 15.4%; Males per 100 females: 106.4; Marriage status: 37.5% never married, 45.0% now married, 1.5% separated, 3.6% widowed, 13.9% divorced; Foreign born: 4.3%; Speak English only: 95.1%; With disability: 16.8%; Veterans: 6.8%; Ancestry: 23.2% German, 20.9% American, 14.4% Irish, 11.3% Italian, 7.4% English

Employment: 7.3% management, business, and financial, 1.0% computer, engineering, and science, 0.0% education, legal, community service, arts, and media, 10.7% healthcare practitioners, 41.3% service, 18.9% sales and office, 11.2% natural resources, construction, and maintenance, 9.7% production, transportation, and material moving

Income: Per capita: $21,007; Median household: $39,063; Average household: $55,757; Households with income of $100,000 or more: 11.1%; Poverty rate: 28.8%

Educational Attainment: High school diploma or higher: 90.2%; Bachelor's degree or higher: 14.5%; Graduate/professional degree or higher: 0.6%

Housing: Homeownership rate: 85.2%; Median home value: $81,200; Median year structure built: 1954; Homeowner vacancy rate: 5.8%; Median selected monthly owner costs: $875 with a mortgage, $448 without a mortgage; Median gross rent: $597 per month; Rental vacancy rate: 12.2%

Health Insurance: 95.9% have insurance; 62.2% have private insurance; 58.9% have public insurance; 4.1% do not have insurance; 3.1% of children under 18 do not have insurance

Transportation: Commute: 96.1% car, 1.0% public transportation, 0.0% walk, 2.9% work from home; Mean travel time to work: 26.1 minutes

WEST ELMIRA (CDP).

Covers a land area of 3.038 square miles and a water area of 0.116 square miles. Located at 42.09° N. Lat; 76.84° W. Long. Elevation is 886 feet.

Population: 4,991; Growth (since 2000): -2.8%; Density: 1,642.7 persons per square mile; Race: 97.4% White, 0.8% Black/African American, 1.0% Asian, 0.0% American Indian/Alaska Native, 0.0% Native Hawaiian/Other Pacific Islander, 0.6% Two or more races, 0.7% Hispanic of any race; Average household size: 2.28; Median age: 49.7; Age under 18: 23.2%; Age 65 and over: 28.6%; Males per 100 females: 89.4; Marriage status: 15.1% never married, 68.0% now married, 0.9% separated, 9.5% widowed, 7.3% divorced; Foreign born: 4.2%; Speak English only: 96.3%; With disability: 9.9%; Veterans: 9.8%; Ancestry: 23.1% Irish, 14.8% Italian, 13.9% German, 10.7% American, 9.6% Polish

Employment: 20.2% management, business, and financial, 1.4% computer, engineering, and science, 22.5% education, legal, community service, arts, and media, 9.9% healthcare practitioners, 10.2% service, 25.1% sales and office, 5.6% natural resources, construction, and maintenance, 5.2% production, transportation, and material moving

Income: Per capita: $46,577; Median household: $70,508; Average household: $106,185; Households with income of $100,000 or more: 29.7%; Poverty rate: 7.4%

Educational Attainment: High school diploma or higher: 98.3%; Bachelor's degree or higher: 51.9%; Graduate/professional degree or higher: 25.8%

Housing: Homeownership rate: 89.5%; Median home value: $124,400; Median year structure built: 1950; Homeowner vacancy rate: 0.0%; Median selected monthly owner costs: $1,130 with a mortgage, $546 without a mortgage; Median gross rent: $963 per month; Rental vacancy rate: 0.0%

Health Insurance: 91.4% have insurance; 73.7% have private insurance; 40.2% have public insurance; 8.6% do not have insurance; 13.4% of children under 18 do not have insurance

Transportation: Commute: 94.8% car, 0.1% public transportation, 1.9% walk, 1.8% work from home; Mean travel time to work: 16.3 minutes

Chenango County

Located in central New York; bounded on the east by the Unadilla River; drained by the Susquehanna, Otselic, and Chenango Rivers. Covers a land area of 893.548 square miles, a water area of 5.082 square miles, and is located in the Eastern Time Zone at 42.49° N. Lat., 75.60° W. Long. The county was founded in 1798. County seat is Norwich.

Weather Station: Norwich										Elevation: 1,020 feet		
	Jan	Feb	Mar	Apr	May	Jun	Jul	Aug	Sep	Oct	Nov	Dec
High	32	35	44	57	69	77	81	79	72	60	48	36
Low	13	14	22	33	43	52	57	56	48	37	29	19
Precip	2.9	2.6	3.3	3.6	3.7	4.3	3.8	3.8	4.0	3.6	3.6	3.3
Snow	17.9	14.1	11.5	2.7	tr	0.0	0.0	0.0	0.0	0.5	5.6	15.4

High and Low temperatures in degrees Fahrenheit; Precipitation and Snow in inches

Weather Station: Sherburne 2 S										Elevation: 1,080 feet		
	Jan	Feb	Mar	Apr	May	Jun	Jul	Aug	Sep	Oct	Nov	Dec
High	32	34	42	56	68	77	81	80	72	60	48	36
Low	13	12	20	32	42	53	56	55	47	37	29	19
Precip	2.2	2.0	2.9	3.3	3.5	4.5	3.8	3.4	3.8	3.5	3.3	2.6
Snow	16.9	14.1	13.1	2.9	tr	0.0	0.0	0.0	tr	0.5	6.0	14.5

High and Low temperatures in degrees Fahrenheit; Precipitation and Snow in inches

Population: 48,763; Growth (since 2000): -5.1%; Density: 54.6 persons per square mile; Race: 96.1% White, 0.9% Black/African American, 0.4% Asian, 0.3% American Indian/Alaska Native, 0.0% Native Hawaiian/Other Pacific Islander, 1.9% two or more races, 2.1% Hispanic of any race; Average household size: 2.36; Median age: 44.4; Age under 18: 21.2%; Age 65 and over: 19.2%; Males per 100 females: 99.2; Marriage status: 27.3% never married, 52.7% now married, 2.8% separated, 7.0% widowed, 13.1% divorced; Foreign born: 1.7%; Speak English only: 96.7%;

With disability: 18.5%; Veterans: 9.3%; Ancestry: 18.3% German, 17.1% English, 16.8% Irish, 10.5% Italian, 10.4% American
Religion: Six largest groups: 11.0% Catholicism, 5.7% Methodist/Pietist, 2.9% Episcopalianism/Anglicanism, 2.1% Baptist, 2.1% Presbyterian-Reformed, 2.0% Non-denominational Protestant
Economy: Unemployment rate: 3.6%; Leading industries: 16.6 % retail trade; 12.9 % other services (except public administration); 11.8 % health care and social assistance; Farms: 828 totaling 167,226 acres; Company size: 2 employ 1,000 or more persons, 3 employ 500 to 999 persons, 17 employ 100 to 499 persons, 902 employ less than 100 persons; Business ownership: 1,075 women-owned, n/a Black-owned, 57 Hispanic-owned, n/a Asian-owned, n/a American Indian/Alaska Native-owned
Employment: 13.5% management, business, and financial, 3.8% computer, engineering, and science, 10.5% education, legal, community service, arts, and media, 4.8% healthcare practitioners, 17.6% service, 20.9% sales and office, 10.8% natural resources, construction, and maintenance, 18.0% production, transportation, and material moving
Income: Per capita: $25,233; Median household: $48,567; Average household: $60,495; Households with income of $100,000 or more: 15.7%; Poverty rate: 14.5%
Educational Attainment: High school diploma or higher: 87.8%; Bachelor's degree or higher: 18.6%; Graduate/professional degree or higher: 8.3%
Housing: Homeownership rate: 74.9%; Median home value: $95,900; Median year structure built: 1964; Homeowner vacancy rate: 2.0%; Median selected monthly owner costs: $1,141 with a mortgage, $464 without a mortgage; Median gross rent: $645 per month; Rental vacancy rate: 4.9%
Vital Statistics: Birth rate: 99.9 per 10,000 population; Death rate: 114.3 per 10,000 population; Age-adjusted cancer mortality rate: 147.1 deaths per 100,000 population
Health Insurance: 94.7% have insurance; 68.3% have private insurance; 43.9% have public insurance; 5.3% do not have insurance; 4.0% of children under 18 do not have insurance
Health Care: Physicians: 8.9 per 10,000 population; Dentists: 3.6 per 10,000 population; Hospital beds: 28.6 per 10,000 population; Hospital admissions: 299.9 per 10,000 population
Transportation: Commute: 88.6% car, 0.4% public transportation, 4.9% walk, 5.0% work from home; Mean travel time to work: 24.1 minutes
2016 Presidential Election: 59.1% Trump, 33.6% Clinton, 4.5% Johnson, 1.8% Stein
National and State Parks: Chenango State Forest; Hunt's Pond State Park
Additional Information Contacts
Chenango Government . . . . (607) 337-1470
    http://www.co.chenango.ny.us

Chenango County Communities

AFTON (town). Covers a land area of 45.836 square miles and a water area of 0.679 square miles. Located at 42.23° N. Lat; 75.53° W. Long. Elevation is 1,001 feet.
Population: 2,773; Growth (since 2000): -6.9%; Density: 60.5 persons per square mile; Race: 97.2% White, 1.3% Black/African American, 0.3% Asian, 0.5% American Indian/Alaska Native, 0.0% Native Hawaiian/Other Pacific Islander, 0.8% Two or more races, 1.1% Hispanic of any race; Average household size: 2.35; Median age: 49.4; Age under 18: 16.0%; Age 65 and over: 19.0%; Males per 100 females: 97.0; Marriage status: 30.7% never married, 45.3% now married, 1.6% separated, 5.8% widowed, 18.2% divorced; Foreign born: 2.3%; Speak English only: 99.1%; With disability: 20.3%; Veterans: 10.6%; Ancestry: 20.4% German, 18.2% Irish, 13.9% American, 12.4% English, 11.4% Italian
Employment: 9.2% management, business, and financial, 3.3% computer, engineering, and science, 14.4% education, legal, community service, arts, and media, 5.8% healthcare practitioners, 11.9% service, 25.7% sales and office, 8.5% natural resources, construction, and maintenance, 21.3% production, transportation, and material moving
Income: Per capita: $28,273; Median household: $51,839; Average household: $73,938; Households with income of $100,000 or more: 20.3%; Poverty rate: 12.0%
Educational Attainment: High school diploma or higher: 90.4%; Bachelor's degree or higher: 14.4%; Graduate/professional degree or higher: 5.3%

School District(s)
Afton Central SD (PK-12)
    Enrollment: 536 . . . . (607) 639-8229

Housing: Homeownership rate: 82.5%; Median home value: $116,400; Median year structure built: 1976; Homeowner vacancy rate: 4.6%; Median selected monthly owner costs: $1,379 with a mortgage, $612 without a mortgage; Median gross rent: $564 per month; Rental vacancy rate: 3.3%
Health Insurance: 91.7% have insurance; 63.1% have private insurance; 46.6% have public insurance; 8.3% do not have insurance; 1.3% of children under 18 do not have insurance
Transportation: Commute: 82.5% car, 0.0% public transportation, 1.9% walk, 15.6% work from home; Mean travel time to work: 27.4 minutes

AFTON (village). Covers a land area of 1.527 square miles and a water area of 0.073 square miles. Located at 42.23° N. Lat; 75.52° W. Long. Elevation is 1,001 feet.
Population: 991; Growth (since 2000): 18.5%; Density: 649.2 persons per square mile; Race: 95.5% White, 0.2% Black/African American, 0.8% Asian, 1.4% American Indian/Alaska Native, 0.0% Native Hawaiian/Other Pacific Islander, 2.1% Two or more races, 3.1% Hispanic of any race; Average household size: 2.27; Median age: 46.2; Age under 18: 18.4%; Age 65 and over: 24.1%; Males per 100 females: 86.4; Marriage status: 30.0% never married, 43.4% now married, 2.9% separated, 9.3% widowed, 17.3% divorced; Foreign born: 0.9%; Speak English only: 97.6%; With disability: 23.2%; Veterans: 9.6%; Ancestry: 17.4% Irish, 15.2% English, 14.9% German, 10.6% American, 8.4% Italian
Employment: 7.6% management, business, and financial, 6.0% computer, engineering, and science, 16.2% education, legal, community service, arts, and media, 6.0% healthcare practitioners, 16.5% service, 20.4% sales and office, 8.4% natural resources, construction, and maintenance, 18.8% production, transportation, and material moving
Income: Per capita: $24,615; Median household: $41,750; Average household: $57,630; Households with income of $100,000 or more: 19.4%; Poverty rate: 18.4%
Educational Attainment: High school diploma or higher: 87.1%; Bachelor's degree or higher: 14.7%; Graduate/professional degree or higher: 8.2%

School District(s)
Afton Central SD (PK-12)
    Enrollment: 536 . . . . (607) 639-8229
Housing: Homeownership rate: 68.9%; Median home value: $92,700; Median year structure built: Before 1940; Homeowner vacancy rate: 0.0%; Median selected monthly owner costs: $1,274 with a mortgage, $503 without a mortgage; Median gross rent: $541 per month; Rental vacancy rate: 4.9%
Health Insurance: 95.2% have insurance; 64.5% have private insurance; 51.1% have public insurance; 4.8% do not have insurance; 3.0% of children under 18 do not have insurance
Safety: Violent crime rate: 0.0 per 10,000 population; Property crime rate: 24.8 per 10,000 population
Transportation: Commute: 93.4% car, 0.0% public transportation, 5.8% walk, 0.8% work from home; Mean travel time to work: 28.5 minutes

BAINBRIDGE (town). Covers a land area of 34.323 square miles and a water area of 0.433 square miles. Located at 42.30° N. Lat; 75.48° W. Long. Elevation is 994 feet.
History: Settled before 1790, incorporated 1829.
Population: 3,220; Growth (since 2000): -5.3%; Density: 93.8 persons per square mile; Race: 98.0% White, 0.2% Black/African American, 0.2% Asian, 0.2% American Indian/Alaska Native, 0.0% Native Hawaiian/Other Pacific Islander, 1.3% Two or more races, 0.5% Hispanic of any race; Average household size: 2.37; Median age: 40.3; Age under 18: 27.0%; Age 65 and over: 24.1%; Males per 100 females: 99.6; Marriage status: 25.2% never married, 53.2% now married, 3.1% separated, 6.9% widowed, 14.6% divorced; Foreign born: 1.8%; Speak English only: 94.6%; With disability: 13.4%; Veterans: 11.1%; Ancestry: 21.2% German, 13.8% Irish, 13.8% English, 12.2% Italian, 10.7% Swedish
Employment: 13.8% management, business, and financial, 0.7% computer, engineering, and science, 11.9% education, legal, community service, arts, and media, 4.6% healthcare practitioners, 18.3% service, 20.8% sales and office, 8.9% natural resources, construction, and maintenance, 21.1% production, transportation, and material moving
Income: Per capita: $25,377; Median household: $47,364; Average household: $60,316; Households with income of $100,000 or more: 13.2%; Poverty rate: 7.4%
Educational Attainment: High school diploma or higher: 90.1%; Bachelor's degree or higher: 26.5%; Graduate/professional degree or higher: 11.5%

School District(s)
Bainbridge-Guilford Central SD (PK-12)
Enrollment: 831. . . . . (607) 967-6321
Housing: Homeownership rate: 73.5%; Median home value: $95,300; Median year structure built: 1958; Homeowner vacancy rate: 1.2%; Median selected monthly owner costs: $1,170 with a mortgage, $488 without a mortgage; Median gross rent: $811 per month; Rental vacancy rate: 3.0%
Health Insurance: 87.1% have insurance; 65.7% have private insurance; 41.3% have public insurance; 12.9% do not have insurance; 24.9% of children under 18 do not have insurance
Transportation: Commute: 96.7% car, 0.0% public transportation, 1.9% walk, 0.2% work from home; Mean travel time to work: 28.4 minutes

---

BAINBRIDGE (village). Covers a land area of 1.239 square miles and a water area of 0.035 square miles. Located at 42.30° N. Lat; 75.48° W. Long. Elevation is 994 feet.
Population: 1,345; Growth (since 2000): -1.5%; Density: 1,085.7 persons per square mile; Race: 96.4% White, 0.4% Black/African American, 0.6% Asian, 0.6% American Indian/Alaska Native, 0.0% Native Hawaiian/Other Pacific Islander, 2.0% Two or more races, 0.7% Hispanic of any race; Average household size: 2.25; Median age: 37.9; Age under 18: 27.0%; Age 65 and over: 20.8%; Males per 100 females: 93.3; Marriage status: 30.9% never married, 43.1% now married, 3.8% separated, 7.6% widowed, 18.4% divorced; Foreign born: 2.3%; Speak English only: 97.0%; With disability: 14.9%; Veterans: 10.6%; Ancestry: 26.9% German, 23.5% Irish, 15.8% English, 15.8% Italian, 5.9% American
Employment: 14.4% management, business, and financial, 1.6% computer, engineering, and science, 18.7% education, legal, community service, arts, and media, 5.6% healthcare practitioners, 14.7% service, 16.7% sales and office, 6.5% natural resources, construction, and maintenance, 21.8% production, transportation, and material moving
Income: Per capita: $24,020; Median household: $47,443; Average household: $54,999; Households with income of $100,000 or more: 10.9%; Poverty rate: 13.3%
Educational Attainment: High school diploma or higher: 90.0%; Bachelor's degree or higher: 25.5%; Graduate/professional degree or higher: 10.8%

School District(s)
Bainbridge-Guilford Central SD (PK-12)
Enrollment: 831. . . . . (607) 967-6321
Housing: Homeownership rate: 64.7%; Median home value: $89,400; Median year structure built: Before 1940; Homeowner vacancy rate: 3.3%; Median selected monthly owner costs: $1,156 with a mortgage, $471 without a mortgage; Median gross rent: $727 per month; Rental vacancy rate: 5.0%
Health Insurance: 93.8% have insurance; 68.4% have private insurance; 47.0% have public insurance; 6.2% do not have insurance; 0.0% of children under 18 do not have insurance
Safety: Violent crime rate: 0.0 per 10,000 population; Property crime rate: 30.2 per 10,000 population
Transportation: Commute: 92.3% car, 0.0% public transportation, 4.4% walk, 0.6% work from home; Mean travel time to work: 25.2 minutes

---

COLUMBUS (town). Covers a land area of 37.368 square miles and a water area of 0.124 square miles. Located at 42.69° N. Lat; 75.37° W. Long. Elevation is 1,296 feet.
Population: 814; Growth (since 2000): -12.6%; Density: 21.8 persons per square mile; Race: 99.1% White, 0.7% Black/African American, 0.0% Asian, 0.1% American Indian/Alaska Native, 0.0% Native Hawaiian/Other Pacific Islander, 0.0% Two or more races, 3.7% Hispanic of any race; Average household size: 2.29; Median age: 49.1; Age under 18: 14.3%; Age 65 and over: 19.4%; Males per 100 females: 109.7; Marriage status: 24.3% never married, 57.9% now married, 1.1% separated, 5.2% widowed, 12.6% divorced; Foreign born: 3.1%; Speak English only: 98.9%; With disability: 16.6%; Veterans: 9.3%; Ancestry: 22.6% English, 20.5% German, 15.5% Irish, 13.4% Italian, 7.4% American
Employment: 10.4% management, business, and financial, 4.6% computer, engineering, and science, 10.9% education, legal, community service, arts, and media, 3.3% healthcare practitioners, 17.8% service, 27.2% sales and office, 13.7% natural resources, construction, and maintenance, 12.2% production, transportation, and material moving
Income: Per capita: $25,030; Median household: $49,063; Average household: $55,586; Households with income of $100,000 or more: 10.9%; Poverty rate: 9.1%

Educational Attainment: High school diploma or higher: 78.6%; Bachelor's degree or higher: 12.4%; Graduate/professional degree or higher: 3.8%
Housing: Homeownership rate: 90.4%; Median home value: $100,000; Median year structure built: 1974; Homeowner vacancy rate: 1.4%; Median selected monthly owner costs: $1,171 with a mortgage, $434 without a mortgage; Median gross rent: $561 per month; Rental vacancy rate: 0.0%
Health Insurance: 90.7% have insurance; 68.6% have private insurance; 39.1% have public insurance; 9.3% do not have insurance; 7.7% of children under 18 do not have insurance
Transportation: Commute: 87.6% car, 0.0% public transportation, 4.1% walk, 8.2% work from home; Mean travel time to work: 23.0 minutes

---

COVENTRY (town). Covers a land area of 48.697 square miles and a water area of 0.167 square miles. Located at 42.29° N. Lat; 75.63° W. Long. Elevation is 1,660 feet.
Population: 1,494; Growth (since 2000): -6.0%; Density: 30.7 persons per square mile; Race: 99.7% White, 0.3% Black/African American, 0.0% Asian, 0.0% American Indian/Alaska Native, 0.0% Native Hawaiian/Other Pacific Islander, 0.0% Two or more races, 1.7% Hispanic of any race; Average household size: 2.50; Median age: 46.1; Age under 18: 22.1%; Age 65 and over: 18.7%; Males per 100 females: 106.6; Marriage status: 26.8% never married, 57.1% now married, 1.7% separated, 4.4% widowed, 11.6% divorced; Foreign born: 1.5%; Speak English only: 98.3%; With disability: 16.7%; Veterans: 8.4%; Ancestry: 22.6% German, 16.7% Irish, 14.7% English, 9.8% American, 9.7% Italian
Employment: 10.8% management, business, and financial, 2.5% computer, engineering, and science, 12.4% education, legal, community service, arts, and media, 3.8% healthcare practitioners, 23.2% service, 16.5% sales and office, 13.4% natural resources, construction, and maintenance, 17.4% production, transportation, and material moving
Income: Per capita: $23,659; Median household: $45,417; Average household: $58,950; Households with income of $100,000 or more: 14.4%; Poverty rate: 12.9%
Educational Attainment: High school diploma or higher: 84.6%; Bachelor's degree or higher: 12.8%; Graduate/professional degree or higher: 6.4%
Housing: Homeownership rate: 84.4%; Median home value: $111,300; Median year structure built: 1983; Homeowner vacancy rate: 2.8%; Median selected monthly owner costs: $1,272 with a mortgage, $508 without a mortgage; Median gross rent: $661 per month; Rental vacancy rate: 0.0%
Health Insurance: 97.0% have insurance; 60.6% have private insurance; 50.8% have public insurance; 3.0% do not have insurance; 3.2% of children under 18 do not have insurance
Transportation: Commute: 93.5% car, 0.0% public transportation, 2.4% walk, 3.6% work from home; Mean travel time to work: 26.9 minutes

---

GERMAN (town). Covers a land area of 28.408 square miles and a water area of 0.031 square miles. Located at 42.50° N. Lat; 75.82° W. Long.
Population: 360; Growth (since 2000): -4.8%; Density: 12.7 persons per square mile; Race: 98.3% White, 0.0% Black/African American, 0.0% Asian, 0.3% American Indian/Alaska Native, 0.0% Native Hawaiian/Other Pacific Islander, 0.6% Two or more races, 0.8% Hispanic of any race; Average household size: 2.16; Median age: 45.0; Age under 18: 18.9%; Age 65 and over: 19.7%; Males per 100 females: 105.6; Marriage status: 21.4% never married, 59.5% now married, 1.7% separated, 7.4% widowed, 11.7% divorced; Foreign born: 0.6%; Speak English only: 97.1%; With disability: 18.9%; Veterans: 9.9%; Ancestry: 20.3% English, 16.4% Irish, 9.7% American, 9.2% German, 8.6% Italian
Employment: 13.9% management, business, and financial, 1.4% computer, engineering, and science, 5.6% education, legal, community service, arts, and media, 3.5% healthcare practitioners, 11.1% service, 25.0% sales and office, 10.4% natural resources, construction, and maintenance, 29.2% production, transportation, and material moving
Income: Per capita: $24,600; Median household: $39,375; Average household: $55,478; Households with income of $100,000 or more: 10.8%; Poverty rate: 11.9%
Educational Attainment: High school diploma or higher: 88.3%; Bachelor's degree or higher: 11.0%; Graduate/professional degree or higher: 4.4%
Housing: Homeownership rate: 85.6%; Median home value: $84,600; Median year structure built: 1978; Homeowner vacancy rate: 1.9%; Median selected monthly owner costs: $818 with a mortgage, $481 without a mortgage; Median gross rent: $750 per month; Rental vacancy rate: 0.0%

Health Insurance: 98.1% have insurance; 71.9% have private insurance; 42.5% have public insurance; 1.9% do not have insurance; 0.0% of children under 18 do not have insurance
Transportation: Commute: 93.6% car, 0.0% public transportation, 2.1% walk, 4.3% work from home; Mean travel time to work: 36.5 minutes

GREENE (town).
Covers a land area of 75.077 square miles and a water area of 0.542 square miles. Located at 42.31° N. Lat; 75.75° W. Long. Elevation is 919 feet.
History: Settled 1792, incorporated 1842.
Population: 5,297; Growth (since 2000): -7.5%; Density: 70.6 persons per square mile; Race: 96.8% White, 1.1% Black/African American, 0.4% Asian, 0.5% American Indian/Alaska Native, 0.0% Native Hawaiian/Other Pacific Islander, 1.0% Two or more races, 1.6% Hispanic of any race; Average household size: 2.45; Median age: 45.5; Age under 18: 20.9%; Age 65 and over: 18.7%; Males per 100 females: 98.1; Marriage status: 27.8% never married, 56.2% now married, 1.7% separated, 6.2% widowed, 9.9% divorced; Foreign born: 1.2%; Speak English only: 97.7%; With disability: 13.9%; Veterans: 6.6%; Ancestry: 21.7% English, 18.2% Irish, 15.2% American, 13.5% German, 6.8% Italian
Employment: 12.5% management, business, and financial, 4.9% computer, engineering, and science, 12.5% education, legal, community service, arts, and media, 6.0% healthcare practitioners, 16.0% service, 23.4% sales and office, 7.3% natural resources, construction, and maintenance, 17.5% production, transportation, and material moving
Income: Per capita: $28,254; Median household: $58,147; Average household: $68,672; Households with income of $100,000 or more: 21.0%; Poverty rate: 12.4%
Educational Attainment: High school diploma or higher: 94.2%; Bachelor's degree or higher: 25.0%; Graduate/professional degree or higher: 11.2%

School District(s)
Greene Central SD (PK-12)
    Enrollment: 993. . . . . (607) 656-4161
Housing: Homeownership rate: 77.5%; Median home value: $127,000; Median year structure built: 1960; Homeowner vacancy rate: 0.5%; Median selected monthly owner costs: $1,242 with a mortgage, $538 without a mortgage; Median gross rent: $582 per month; Rental vacancy rate: 7.5%
Health Insurance: 95.3% have insurance; 76.1% have private insurance; 36.4% have public insurance; 4.7% do not have insurance; 0.4% of children under 18 do not have insurance
Newspapers: Paden Publishing (weekly circulation 3,500)
Transportation: Commute: 88.5% car, 0.1% public transportation, 5.0% walk, 5.0% work from home; Mean travel time to work: 26.7 minutes
Additional Information Contacts
Town of Greene. . . . . (607) 656-4191
    http://www.nygreene.com/townofgreene.htm

GREENE (village).
Covers a land area of 1.068 square miles and a water area of 0.038 square miles. Located at 42.33° N. Lat; 75.77° W. Long. Elevation is 919 feet.
Population: 1,624; Growth (since 2000): -4.5%; Density: 1,521.0 persons per square mile; Race: 95.0% White, 1.5% Black/African American, 0.7% Asian, 0.0% American Indian/Alaska Native, 0.0% Native Hawaiian/Other Pacific Islander, 2.8% Two or more races, 2.3% Hispanic of any race; Average household size: 2.21; Median age: 40.0; Age under 18: 23.5%; Age 65 and over: 17.7%; Males per 100 females: 87.4; Marriage status: 30.3% never married, 47.6% now married, 1.6% separated, 10.9% widowed, 11.3% divorced; Foreign born: 2.5%; Speak English only: 96.0%; With disability: 19.7%; Veterans: 6.1%; Ancestry: 18.3% English, 16.9% Irish, 12.6% German, 12.4% American, 7.3% Italian
Employment: 5.6% management, business, and financial, 5.5% computer, engineering, and science, 16.5% education, legal, community service, arts, and media, 9.4% healthcare practitioners, 17.8% service, 21.6% sales and office, 7.4% natural resources, construction, and maintenance, 16.3% production, transportation, and material moving
Income: Per capita: $27,491; Median household: $52,660; Average household: $60,359; Households with income of $100,000 or more: 19.4%; Poverty rate: 10.0%
Educational Attainment: High school diploma or higher: 92.7%; Bachelor's degree or higher: 29.9%; Graduate/professional degree or higher: 13.7%

School District(s)
Greene Central SD (PK-12)
    Enrollment: 993. . . . . (607) 656-4161

Housing: Homeownership rate: 57.4%; Median home value: $110,600; Median year structure built: Before 1940; Homeowner vacancy rate: 1.9%; Median selected monthly owner costs: $1,138 with a mortgage, $487 without a mortgage; Median gross rent: $598 per month; Rental vacancy rate: 4.4%
Health Insurance: 92.8% have insurance; 72.9% have private insurance; 38.3% have public insurance; 7.2% do not have insurance; 1.0% of children under 18 do not have insurance
Safety: Violent crime rate: 0.0 per 10,000 population; Property crime rate: 88.9 per 10,000 population
Newspapers: Paden Publishing (weekly circulation 3,500)
Transportation: Commute: 83.4% car, 0.0% public transportation, 10.7% walk, 2.9% work from home; Mean travel time to work: 22.4 minutes

GUILFORD (CDP).
Covers a land area of 1.336 square miles and a water area of 0.118 square miles. Located at 42.41° N. Lat; 75.49° W. Long. Elevation is 1,486 feet.
Population: 329; Growth (since 2000): n/a; Density: 246.3 persons per square mile; Race: 100.0% White, 0.0% Black/African American, 0.0% Asian, 0.0% American Indian/Alaska Native, 0.0% Native Hawaiian/Other Pacific Islander, 0.0% Two or more races, 0.0% Hispanic of any race; Average household size: 1.77; Median age: 54.6; Age under 18: 15.5%; Age 65 and over: 24.3%; Males per 100 females: 101.1; Marriage status: 16.9% never married, 59.4% now married, 0.0% separated, 15.8% widowed, 7.9% divorced; Foreign born: 0.0%; Speak English only: 96.1%; With disability: 27.7%; Veterans: 32.7%; Ancestry: 26.4% Italian, 21.0% Irish, 20.1% German, 9.7% English, 8.2% American
Employment: 0.0% management, business, and financial, 0.0% computer, engineering, and science, 0.0% education, legal, community service, arts, and media, 31.8% healthcare practitioners, 0.0% service, 0.0% sales and office, 17.3% natural resources, construction, and maintenance, 50.9% production, transportation, and material moving
Income: Per capita: $26,583; Median household: n/a; Average household: $46,154; Households with income of $100,000 or more: 14.0%; Poverty rate: 11.2%
Educational Attainment: High school diploma or higher: 82.4%; Bachelor's degree or higher: 3.2%; Graduate/professional degree or higher: n/a

School District(s)
Bainbridge-Guilford Central SD (PK-12)
    Enrollment: 831. . . . . (607) 967-6321
Housing: Homeownership rate: 74.7%; Median home value: $109,200; Median year structure built: Before 1940; Homeowner vacancy rate: 0.0%; Median selected monthly owner costs: $1,307 with a mortgage, $563 without a mortgage; Median gross rent: n/a per month; Rental vacancy rate: 0.0%
Health Insurance: 100.0% have insurance; 79.3% have private insurance; 62.6% have public insurance; 0.0% do not have insurance; 0.0% of children under 18 do not have insurance
Transportation: Commute: 91.8% car, 0.0% public transportation, 8.2% walk, 0.0% work from home; Mean travel time to work: 33.6 minutes

GUILFORD (town).
Covers a land area of 61.716 square miles and a water area of 0.244 square miles. Located at 42.40° N. Lat; 75.45° W. Long. Elevation is 1,486 feet.
Population: 2,847; Growth (since 2000): -6.5%; Density: 46.1 persons per square mile; Race: 97.4% White, 0.3% Black/African American, 0.0% Asian, 0.0% American Indian/Alaska Native, 0.0% Native Hawaiian/Other Pacific Islander, 2.3% Two or more races, 2.4% Hispanic of any race; Average household size: 2.15; Median age: 48.9; Age under 18: 16.0%; Age 65 and over: 19.0%; Males per 100 females: 101.5; Marriage status: 25.9% never married, 48.5% now married, 1.9% separated, 11.4% widowed, 14.2% divorced; Foreign born: 1.0%; Speak English only: 97.7%; With disability: 17.6%; Veterans: 10.8%; Ancestry: 18.9% Irish, 15.8% American, 14.7% German, 13.3% English, 12.4% Italian
Employment: 12.2% management, business, and financial, 4.0% computer, engineering, and science, 5.8% education, legal, community service, arts, and media, 5.3% healthcare practitioners, 11.5% service, 16.3% sales and office, 17.2% natural resources, construction, and maintenance, 27.7% production, transportation, and material moving
Income: Per capita: $27,940; Median household: $50,736; Average household: $60,529; Households with income of $100,000 or more: 13.4%; Poverty rate: 13.9%

Educational Attainment: High school diploma or higher: 88.6%; Bachelor's degree or higher: 15.8%; Graduate/professional degree or higher: 5.6%

School District(s)
Bainbridge-Guilford Central SD (PK-12)
 Enrollment: 831 . . . . (607) 967-6321
Housing: Homeownership rate: 83.0%; Median home value: $95,300; Median year structure built: 1970; Homeowner vacancy rate: 4.8%; Median selected monthly owner costs: $1,151 with a mortgage, $471 without a mortgage; Median gross rent: $544 per month; Rental vacancy rate: 0.0%
Health Insurance: 96.7% have insurance; 74.0% have private insurance; 40.7% have public insurance; 3.3% do not have insurance; 0.0% of children under 18 do not have insurance
Transportation: Commute: 85.2% car, 3.1% public transportation, 4.3% walk, 7.3% work from home; Mean travel time to work: 32.4 minutes

LINCKLAEN (town). Covers a land area of 26.263 square miles and a water area of 0.011 square miles. Located at 42.68° N. Lat; 75.84° W. Long. Elevation is 1,191 feet.
Population: 361; Growth (since 2000): -13.2%; Density: 13.7 persons per square mile; Race: 97.5% White, 0.0% Black/African American, 0.0% Asian, 1.1% American Indian/Alaska Native, 0.0% Native Hawaiian/Other Pacific Islander, 1.4% Two or more races, 1.7% Hispanic of any race; Average household size: 2.42; Median age: 47.9; Age under 18: 15.8%; Age 65 and over: 22.4%; Males per 100 females: 106.3; Marriage status: 24.8% never married, 58.1% now married, 1.0% separated, 3.8% widowed, 13.3% divorced; Foreign born: 0.0%; Speak English only: 95.7%; With disability: 18.8%; Veterans: 10.2%; Ancestry: 21.3% German, 13.3% English, 12.5% American, 8.6% Dutch, 4.7% Italian
Employment: 7.7% management, business, and financial, 0.0% computer, engineering, and science, 13.7% education, legal, community service, arts, and media, 2.2% healthcare practitioners, 9.8% service, 2.7% sales and office, 31.1% natural resources, construction, and maintenance, 32.8% production, transportation, and material moving
Income: Per capita: $25,329; Median household: $60,341; Average household: $59,996; Households with income of $100,000 or more: 16.7%; Poverty rate: 16.3%
Educational Attainment: High school diploma or higher: 86.0%; Bachelor's degree or higher: 14.0%; Graduate/professional degree or higher: 9.1%
Housing: Homeownership rate: 86.6%; Median home value: $70,500; Median year structure built: 1977; Homeowner vacancy rate: 0.0%; Median selected monthly owner costs: $946 with a mortgage, $429 without a mortgage; Median gross rent: $821 per month; Rental vacancy rate: 20.0%
Health Insurance: 94.7% have insurance; 64.0% have private insurance; 47.4% have public insurance; 5.3% do not have insurance; 0.0% of children under 18 do not have insurance
Transportation: Commute: 94.2% car, 0.0% public transportation, 2.9% walk, 1.7% work from home; Mean travel time to work: 27.7 minutes

MCDONOUGH (town). Covers a land area of 39.038 square miles and a water area of 0.593 square miles. Located at 42.50° N. Lat; 75.73° W. Long. Elevation is 1,430 feet.
Population: 782; Growth (since 2000): -10.1%; Density: 20.0 persons per square mile; Race: 96.8% White, 1.7% Black/African American, 0.0% Asian, 0.0% American Indian/Alaska Native, 0.0% Native Hawaiian/Other Pacific Islander, 1.5% Two or more races, 4.2% Hispanic of any race; Average household size: 2.20; Median age: 49.5; Age under 18: 17.6%; Age 65 and over: 21.9%; Males per 100 females: 111.5; Marriage status: 21.2% never married, 52.6% now married, 0.4% separated, 9.3% widowed, 16.9% divorced; Foreign born: 4.2%; Speak English only: 97.4%; With disability: 17.5%; Veterans: 13.7%; Ancestry: 24.6% German, 21.7% English, 19.8% Irish, 11.0% Italian, 6.5% American
Employment: 15.6% management, business, and financial, 2.2% computer, engineering, and science, 15.0% education, legal, community service, arts, and media, 7.2% healthcare practitioners, 20.3% service, 15.0% sales and office, 10.8% natural resources, construction, and maintenance, 13.9% production, transportation, and material moving
Income: Per capita: $23,052; Median household: $40,000; Average household: $50,475; Households with income of $100,000 or more: 11.6%; Poverty rate: 15.0%
Educational Attainment: High school diploma or higher: 87.9%; Bachelor's degree or higher: 16.3%; Graduate/professional degree or higher: 6.9%

Housing: Homeownership rate: 91.0%; Median home value: $85,700; Median year structure built: 1974; Homeowner vacancy rate: 4.5%; Median selected monthly owner costs: $1,023 with a mortgage, $383 without a mortgage; Median gross rent: $654 per month; Rental vacancy rate: 0.0%
Health Insurance: 94.5% have insurance; 66.4% have private insurance; 49.0% have public insurance; 5.5% do not have insurance; 0.0% of children under 18 do not have insurance
Transportation: Commute: 86.6% car, 0.6% public transportation, 4.9% walk, 5.8% work from home; Mean travel time to work: 30.6 minutes

MOUNT UPTON (unincorporated postal area)
ZCTA: 13809
 Covers a land area of 30.076 square miles and a water area of 0 square miles. Located at 42.40° N. Lat; 75.40° W. Long. Elevation is 1,030 feet.
Population: 1,729; Growth (since 2000): 26.0%; Density: 57.5 persons per square mile; Race: 96.6% White, 0.5% Black/African American, 0.0% Asian, 0.0% American Indian/Alaska Native, 0.0% Native Hawaiian/Other Pacific Islander, 0.5% Two or more races, 4.6% Hispanic of any race; Average household size: 2.46; Median age: 44.0; Age under 18: 22.8%; Age 65 and over: 18.4%; Males per 100 females: 101.5; Marriage status: 21.8% never married, 65.1% now married, 0.7% separated, 8.8% widowed, 4.3% divorced; Foreign born: 0.6%; Speak English only: 98.6%; With disability: 15.2%; Veterans: 4.3%; Ancestry: 21.7% American, 20.6% German, 16.1% English, 14.1% Irish, 5.7% Norwegian
Employment: 16.8% management, business, and financial, 0.0% computer, engineering, and science, 6.0% education, legal, community service, arts, and media, 2.6% healthcare practitioners, 12.0% service, 25.5% sales and office, 5.1% natural resources, construction, and maintenance, 32.0% production, transportation, and material moving
Income: Per capita: $24,776; Median household: $52,734; Average household: $61,158; Households with income of $100,000 or more: 10.4%; Poverty rate: 20.7%
Educational Attainment: High school diploma or higher: 86.3%; Bachelor's degree or higher: 13.4%; Graduate/professional degree or higher: 7.7%
Housing: Homeownership rate: 79.2%; Median home value: $68,800; Median year structure built: 1964; Homeowner vacancy rate: 0.0%; Median selected monthly owner costs: $1,067 with a mortgage, $483 without a mortgage; Median gross rent: $783 per month; Rental vacancy rate: 0.0%
Health Insurance: 96.9% have insurance; 74.9% have private insurance; 42.9% have public insurance; 3.1% do not have insurance; 0.0% of children under 18 do not have insurance
Transportation: Commute: 89.4% car, 5.5% public transportation, 0.0% walk, 5.1% work from home; Mean travel time to work: 26.0 minutes

NEW BERLIN (town). Covers a land area of 46.134 square miles and a water area of 0.440 square miles. Located at 42.59° N. Lat; 75.39° W. Long. Elevation is 1,112 feet.
History: Incorporated 1819.
Population: 2,570; Growth (since 2000): -8.3%; Density: 55.7 persons per square mile; Race: 97.4% White, 0.0% Black/African American, 1.0% Asian, 0.2% American Indian/Alaska Native, 0.0% Native Hawaiian/Other Pacific Islander, 1.4% Two or more races, 1.0% Hispanic of any race; Average household size: 2.24; Median age: 47.9; Age under 18: 19.4%; Age 65 and over: 25.1%; Males per 100 females: 92.5; Marriage status: 21.7% never married, 57.8% now married, 3.6% separated, 7.6% widowed, 12.9% divorced; Foreign born: 2.1%; Speak English only: 97.8%; With disability: 23.3%; Veterans: 12.0%; Ancestry: 20.7% English, 18.7% German, 17.6% Irish, 8.8% American, 8.1% Italian
Employment: 15.7% management, business, and financial, 6.0% computer, engineering, and science, 8.3% education, legal, community service, arts, and media, 4.0% healthcare practitioners, 19.6% service, 20.7% sales and office, 8.1% natural resources, construction, and maintenance, 17.6% production, transportation, and material moving
Income: Per capita: $26,123; Median household: $47,122; Average household: $59,502; Households with income of $100,000 or more: 13.6%; Poverty rate: 9.1%
Educational Attainment: High school diploma or higher: 84.0%; Bachelor's degree or higher: 16.1%; Graduate/professional degree or higher: 7.4%

School District(s)
Unadilla Valley Central SD (PK-12)
 Enrollment: 810 . . . . (607) 847-7500

Housing: Homeownership rate: 79.9%; Median home value: $84,700; Median year structure built: 1947; Homeowner vacancy rate: 1.5%; Median selected monthly owner costs: $1,036 with a mortgage, $503 without a mortgage; Median gross rent: $682 per month; Rental vacancy rate: 10.7%
Health Insurance: 91.9% have insurance; 62.4% have private insurance; 49.4% have public insurance; 8.1% do not have insurance; 6.1% of children under 18 do not have insurance
Safety: Violent crime rate: 0.0 per 10,000 population; Property crime rate: 111.7 per 10,000 population
Transportation: Commute: 93.8% car, 0.0% public transportation, 3.4% walk, 2.8% work from home; Mean travel time to work: 24.0 minutes

NEW BERLIN (village). Covers a land area of 1.066 square miles and a water area of 0 square miles. Located at 42.62° N. Lat; 75.34° W. Long. Elevation is 1,112 feet.
Population: 1,089; Growth (since 2000): -3.5%; Density: 1,022.0 persons per square mile; Race: 97.2% White, 0.0% Black/African American, 1.7% Asian, 0.0% American Indian/Alaska Native, 0.0% Native Hawaiian/Other Pacific Islander, 1.2% Two or more races, 0.7% Hispanic of any race; Average household size: 2.10; Median age: 48.2; Age under 18: 17.9%; Age 65 and over: 27.8%; Males per 100 females: 85.6; Marriage status: 28.0% never married, 49.2% now married, 1.7% separated, 10.6% widowed, 12.2% divorced; Foreign born: 3.6%; Speak English only: 96.4%; With disability: 26.0%; Veterans: 12.1%; Ancestry: 23.8% English, 19.7% German, 17.9% Irish, 12.1% American, 9.9% Scottish
Employment: 10.6% management, business, and financial, 10.4% computer, engineering, and science, 9.9% education, legal, community service, arts, and media, 4.2% healthcare practitioners, 19.3% service, 21.7% sales and office, 5.7% natural resources, construction, and maintenance, 18.3% production, transportation, and material moving
Income: Per capita: $21,134; Median household: $40,705; Average household: $45,517; Households with income of $100,000 or more: 7.8%; Poverty rate: 12.0%
Educational Attainment: High school diploma or higher: 81.7%; Bachelor's degree or higher: 16.0%; Graduate/professional degree or higher: 7.9%

School District(s)
Unadilla Valley Central SD (PK-12)
    Enrollment: 810 . . . . (607) 847-7500
Housing: Homeownership rate: 67.1%; Median home value: $82,600; Median year structure built: Before 1940; Homeowner vacancy rate: 1.8%; Median selected monthly owner costs: $1,055 with a mortgage, $604 without a mortgage; Median gross rent: $598 per month; Rental vacancy rate: 14.2%
Health Insurance: 91.4% have insurance; 58.4% have private insurance; 48.6% have public insurance; 8.6% do not have insurance; 4.7% of children under 18 do not have insurance
Transportation: Commute: 90.4% car, 0.0% public transportation, 5.8% walk, 3.8% work from home; Mean travel time to work: 21.7 minutes

NORTH NORWICH (town). Covers a land area of 28.142 square miles and a water area of 0.102 square miles. Located at 42.59° N. Lat; 75.51° W. Long. Elevation is 1,037 feet.
Population: 1,707; Growth (since 2000): -13.2%; Density: 60.7 persons per square mile; Race: 96.4% White, 1.1% Black/African American, 0.5% Asian, 0.5% American Indian/Alaska Native, 0.0% Native Hawaiian/Other Pacific Islander, 1.5% Two or more races, 0.5% Hispanic of any race; Average household size: 2.34; Median age: 46.9; Age under 18: 18.2%; Age 65 and over: 19.4%; Males per 100 females: 99.2; Marriage status: 25.7% never married, 57.3% now married, 2.2% separated, 5.5% widowed, 11.5% divorced; Foreign born: 2.2%; Speak English only: 97.2%; With disability: 17.9%; Veterans: 8.7%; Ancestry: 16.1% Irish, 15.3% German, 12.5% English, 11.5% Italian, 8.5% American
Employment: 19.2% management, business, and financial, 4.4% computer, engineering, and science, 5.4% education, legal, community service, arts, and media, 5.9% healthcare practitioners, 11.7% service, 22.5% sales and office, 13.8% natural resources, construction, and maintenance, 17.1% production, transportation, and material moving
Income: Per capita: $29,602; Median household: $51,875; Average household: $69,571; Households with income of $100,000 or more: 17.1%; Poverty rate: 10.0%
Educational Attainment: High school diploma or higher: 86.6%; Bachelor's degree or higher: 15.0%; Graduate/professional degree or higher: 6.9%

Housing: Homeownership rate: 87.1%; Median home value: $96,900; Median year structure built: 1972; Homeowner vacancy rate: 2.3%; Median selected monthly owner costs: $1,075 with a mortgage, $460 without a mortgage; Median gross rent: $787 per month; Rental vacancy rate: 0.0%
Health Insurance: 92.7% have insurance; 64.1% have private insurance; 41.6% have public insurance; 7.3% do not have insurance; 9.9% of children under 18 do not have insurance
Transportation: Commute: 89.2% car, 0.0% public transportation, 5.1% walk, 5.7% work from home; Mean travel time to work: 17.9 minutes

NORTH PITCHER (unincorporated postal area)
ZCTA: 13124
    Covers a land area of 4.685 square miles and a water area of 0.005 square miles. Located at 42.66° N. Lat; 75.82° W. Long. Elevation is 1,161 feet.
Population: 86; Growth (since 2000): -36.3%; Density: 18.4 persons per square mile; Race: 100.0% White, 0.0% Black/African American, 0.0% Asian, 0.0% American Indian/Alaska Native, 0.0% Native Hawaiian/Other Pacific Islander, 0.0% Two or more races, 9.3% Hispanic of any race; Average household size: 2.21; Median age: 47.6; Age under 18: 18.6%; Age 65 and over: 15.1%; Males per 100 females: 138.5; Marriage status: 20.3% never married, 55.4% now married, 1.4% separated, 9.5% widowed, 14.9% divorced; Foreign born: 0.0%; Speak English only: 100.0%; With disability: 27.9%; Veterans: 15.7%; Ancestry: 20.9% American, 11.6% English, 9.3% Irish, 8.1% German, 7.0% Czech
Employment: 8.3% management, business, and financial, 0.0% computer, engineering, and science, 0.0% education, legal, community service, arts, and media, 6.3% healthcare practitioners, 27.1% service, 8.3% sales and office, 29.2% natural resources, construction, and maintenance, 20.8% production, transportation, and material moving
Income: Per capita: $25,588; Median household: $46,250; Average household: $52,413; Households with income of $100,000 or more: 10.2%; Poverty rate: 5.8%
Educational Attainment: High school diploma or higher: 91.4%; Bachelor's degree or higher: 7.1%; Graduate/professional degree or higher: n/a
Housing: Homeownership rate: 87.2%; Median home value: $82,500; Median year structure built: 1964; Homeowner vacancy rate: 0.0%; Median selected monthly owner costs: $963 with a mortgage, $442 without a mortgage; Median gross rent: n/a per month; Rental vacancy rate: 0.0%
Health Insurance: 94.2% have insurance; 58.1% have private insurance; 47.7% have public insurance; 5.8% do not have insurance; 0.0% of children under 18 do not have insurance
Transportation: Commute: 95.8% car, 0.0% public transportation, 0.0% walk, 0.0% work from home; Mean travel time to work: 22.0 minutes

NORWICH (city). County seat. Covers a land area of 2.124 square miles and a water area of 0 square miles. Located at 42.53° N. Lat; 75.52° W. Long. Elevation is 1,014 feet.
Population: 6,890; Growth (since 2000): -6.3%; Density: 3,243.3 persons per square mile; Race: 93.4% White, 1.4% Black/African American, 0.7% Asian, 0.0% American Indian/Alaska Native, 0.1% Native Hawaiian/Other Pacific Islander, 4.0% Two or more races, 4.2% Hispanic of any race; Average household size: 2.35; Median age: 34.8; Age under 18: 24.3%; Age 65 and over: 18.4%; Males per 100 females: 84.5; Marriage status: 35.4% never married, 42.7% now married, 5.2% separated, 8.2% widowed, 13.7% divorced; Foreign born: 2.2%; Speak English only: 95.4%; With disability: 20.0%; Veterans: 6.1%; Ancestry: 19.8% German, 19.1% Irish, 18.0% English, 16.6% Italian, 9.9% American
Employment: 13.9% management, business, and financial, 6.8% computer, engineering, and science, 12.5% education, legal, community service, arts, and media, 3.7% healthcare practitioners, 20.2% service, 23.2% sales and office, 5.5% natural resources, construction, and maintenance, 14.3% production, transportation, and material moving
Income: Per capita: $22,683; Median household: $40,614; Average household: $53,775; Households with income of $100,000 or more: 15.4%; Poverty rate: 24.2%
Educational Attainment: High school diploma or higher: 86.7%; Bachelor's degree or higher: 25.1%; Graduate/professional degree or higher: 11.9%

School District(s)
Delaware-Chenango-Madison-Otsego Boces
    Enrollment: n/a . . . . (607) 335-1233

Norwich City SD (PK-12)
    Enrollment: 1,834 . . . . (607) 334-1600
Housing: Homeownership rate: 46.1%; Median home value: $86,100;
Median year structure built: Before 1940; Homeowner vacancy rate: 2.6%;
Median selected monthly owner costs: $1,144 with a mortgage, $489
without a mortgage; Median gross rent: $648 per month; Rental vacancy
rate: 10.1%
Health Insurance: 97.3% have insurance; 65.8% have private insurance;
47.4% have public insurance; 2.7% do not have insurance; 0.0% of
children under 18 do not have insurance
Hospitals: Chenango Memorial Hospital (139 beds)
Safety: Violent crime rate: 38.2 per 10,000 population; Property crime rate:
277.8 per 10,000 population
Newspapers: Evening Sun (daily circulation 5,000); The Gazette (weekly
circulation 2,400)
Transportation: Commute: 79.6% car, 0.6% public transportation, 11.6%
walk, 4.8% work from home; Mean travel time to work: 16.1 minutes
Additional Information Contacts
City of Norwich . . . . (607) 334-1230
    http://www.norwichnewyork.net

NORWICH (town). Covers a land area of 41.963 square miles and a
water area of 0.075 square miles. Located at 42.51° N. Lat; 75.49° W.
Long. Elevation is 1,014 feet.
History: Gail Borden born here. Settled 1788. Incorporated 1915.
Population: 3,857; Growth (since 2000): 0.5%; Density: 91.9 persons per
square mile; Race: 96.3% White, 1.0% Black/African American, 1.7%
Asian, 0.0% American Indian/Alaska Native, 0.0% Native Hawaiian/Other
Pacific Islander, 0.9% Two or more races, 0.4% Hispanic of any race;
Average household size: 2.40; Median age: 42.6; Age under 18: 20.4%;
Age 65 and over: 16.6%; Males per 100 females: 103.3; Marriage status:
28.6% never married, 48.0% now married, 0.5% separated, 7.2%
widowed, 16.2% divorced; Foreign born: 1.6%; Speak English only: 96.7%;
With disability: 19.9%; Veterans: 10.9%; Ancestry: 17.0% English, 16.8%
Irish, 12.9% German, 12.8% Italian, 11.1% American
Employment: 14.0% management, business, and financial, 3.1%
computer, engineering, and science, 8.5% education, legal, community
service, arts, and media, 2.8% healthcare practitioners, 24.6% service,
16.3% sales and office, 10.7% natural resources, construction, and
maintenance, 20.1% production, transportation, and material moving
Income: Per capita: $25,436; Median household: $55,341; Average
household: $64,948; Households with income of $100,000 or more: 19.9%;
Poverty rate: 9.7%
Educational Attainment: High school diploma or higher: 84.6%;
Bachelor's degree or higher: 15.1%; Graduate/professional degree or
higher: 6.5%
School District(s)
Delaware-Chenango-Madison-Otsego Boces
    Enrollment: n/a . . . . (607) 335-1233
Norwich City SD (PK-12)
    Enrollment: 1,834 . . . . (607) 334-1600
Housing: Homeownership rate: 83.4%; Median home value: $83,000;
Median year structure built: 1972; Homeowner vacancy rate: 2.2%; Median
selected monthly owner costs: $1,103 with a mortgage, $384 without a
mortgage; Median gross rent: $631 per month; Rental vacancy rate: 0.0%
Health Insurance: 98.3% have insurance; 73.1% have private insurance;
42.5% have public insurance; 1.7% do not have insurance; 1.3% of
children under 18 do not have insurance
Hospitals: Chenango Memorial Hospital (139 beds)
Newspapers: Evening Sun (daily circulation 5,000); The Gazette (weekly
circulation 2,400)
Transportation: Commute: 96.0% car, 0.0% public transportation, 1.2%
walk, 1.4% work from home; Mean travel time to work: 20.3 minutes

OTSELIC (town). Covers a land area of 37.977 square miles and a
water area of 0.067 square miles. Located at 42.68° N. Lat; 75.74° W.
Long. Elevation is 1,355 feet.
Population: 897; Growth (since 2000): -10.4%; Density: 23.6 persons per
square mile; Race: 97.0% White, 0.0% Black/African American, 0.0%
Asian, 0.8% American Indian/Alaska Native, 0.0% Native Hawaiian/Other
Pacific Islander, 2.2% Two or more races, 4.0% Hispanic of any race;
Average household size: 2.42; Median age: 42.6; Age under 18: 19.8%;
Age 65 and over: 17.7%; Males per 100 females: 116.0; Marriage status:
29.6% never married, 55.4% now married, 3.3% separated, 4.1%
widowed, 10.8% divorced; Foreign born: 1.0%; Speak English only: 95.6%;

With disability: 15.7%; Veterans: 10.2%; Ancestry: 21.4% English, 17.8%
German, 13.9% Irish, 10.7% American, 5.2% Dutch
Employment: 10.2% management, business, and financial, 4.8%
computer, engineering, and science, 15.0% education, legal, community
service, arts, and media, 9.3% healthcare practitioners, 13.6% service,
15.5% sales and office, 15.2% natural resources, construction, and
maintenance, 16.4% production, transportation, and material moving
Income: Per capita: $27,591; Median household: $54,896; Average
household: $66,013; Households with income of $100,000 or more: 19.4%;
Poverty rate: 13.0%
Educational Attainment: High school diploma or higher: 84.4%;
Bachelor's degree or higher: 16.2%; Graduate/professional degree or
higher: 5.2%
Housing: Homeownership rate: 77.6%; Median home value: $76,800;
Median year structure built: 1953; Homeowner vacancy rate: 0.0%; Median
selected monthly owner costs: $825 with a mortgage, $453 without a
mortgage; Median gross rent: $605 per month; Rental vacancy rate: 0.0%
Health Insurance: 95.2% have insurance; 69.3% have private insurance;
41.7% have public insurance; 4.8% do not have insurance; 2.7% of
children under 18 do not have insurance
Transportation: Commute: 87.0% car, 0.0% public transportation, 10.4%
walk, 2.6% work from home; Mean travel time to work: 31.2 minutes

OXFORD (town). Covers a land area of 60.063 square miles and a
water area of 0.352 square miles. Located at 42.40° N. Lat; 75.60° W.
Long. Elevation is 971 feet.
History: Site of N.Y. State Women's Relief Corps Home built in 1896 and
now operated as the N.Y. State Veterans' Home. Settled 1788;
incorporated 1808.
Population: 3,804; Growth (since 2000): -4.7%; Density: 63.3 persons per
square mile; Race: 94.2% White, 1.2% Black/African American, 0.0%
Asian, 0.2% American Indian/Alaska Native, 0.0% Native Hawaiian/Other
Pacific Islander, 1.1% Two or more races, 4.9% Hispanic of any race;
Average household size: 2.23; Median age: 52.6; Age under 18: 16.5%;
Age 65 and over: 22.5%; Males per 100 females: 105.7; Marriage status:
22.3% never married, 56.9% now married, 2.9% separated, 9.5%
widowed, 11.3% divorced; Foreign born: 2.0%; Speak English only: 93.4%;
With disability: 24.2%; Veterans: 13.2%; Ancestry: 25.4% German, 19.7%
Irish, 17.1% English, 8.8% American, 8.3% Italian
Employment: 14.6% management, business, and financial, 4.4%
computer, engineering, and science, 13.1% education, legal, community
service, arts, and media, 2.7% healthcare practitioners, 17.4% service,
25.5% sales and office, 10.2% natural resources, construction, and
maintenance, 12.1% production, transportation, and material moving
Income: Per capita: $26,124; Median household: $45,733; Average
household: $59,098; Households with income of $100,000 or more: 15.6%;
Poverty rate: 10.7%
Educational Attainment: High school diploma or higher: 90.0%;
Bachelor's degree or higher: 19.4%; Graduate/professional degree or
higher: 10.2%
School District(s)
Oxford Academy and Central SD (PK-12)
    Enrollment: 773 . . . . (607) 843-2025
Housing: Homeownership rate: 78.7%; Median home value: $96,900;
Median year structure built: 1960; Homeowner vacancy rate: 2.0%; Median
selected monthly owner costs: $1,149 with a mortgage, $453 without a
mortgage; Median gross rent: $674 per month; Rental vacancy rate: 0.8%
Health Insurance: 97.3% have insurance; 72.1% have private insurance;
46.0% have public insurance; 2.7% do not have insurance; 0.0% of
children under 18 do not have insurance
Transportation: Commute: 88.2% car, 0.6% public transportation, 2.3%
walk, 6.9% work from home; Mean travel time to work: 23.1 minutes

OXFORD (village). Covers a land area of 1.785 square miles and a
water area of 0 square miles. Located at 42.44° N. Lat; 75.60° W. Long.
Elevation is 971 feet.
Population: 1,392; Growth (since 2000): -12.1%; Density: 779.9 persons
per square mile; Race: 93.6% White, 2.7% Black/African American, 0.0%
Asian, 0.6% American Indian/Alaska Native, 0.0% Native Hawaiian/Other
Pacific Islander, 0.8% Two or more races, 6.6% Hispanic of any race;
Average household size: 2.29; Median age: 40.5; Age under 18: 21.0%;
Age 65 and over: 14.4%; Males per 100 females: 90.0; Marriage status:
29.4% never married, 47.4% now married, 5.5% separated, 6.7%
widowed, 16.6% divorced; Foreign born: 3.7%; Speak English only: 93.3%;

With disability: 18.5%; Veterans: 9.6%; Ancestry: 27.6% German, 18.8% Irish, 15.9% English, 7.5% Italian, 6.4% Dutch
Employment: 11.5% management, business, and financial, 2.4% computer, engineering, and science, 12.1% education, legal, community service, arts, and media, 4.0% healthcare practitioners, 17.9% service, 29.7% sales and office, 8.4% natural resources, construction, and maintenance, 13.9% production, transportation, and material moving
Income: Per capita: $25,476; Median household: $43,869; Average household: $57,416; Households with income of $100,000 or more: 15.6%; Poverty rate: 15.9%
Educational Attainment: High school diploma or higher: 92.3%; Bachelor's degree or higher: 26.2%; Graduate/professional degree or higher: 13.3%
School District(s)
Oxford Academy and Central SD (PK-12)
    Enrollment: 773 . . . . (607) 843-2025
Housing: Homeownership rate: 61.7%; Median home value: $100,400; Median year structure built: Before 1940; Homeowner vacancy rate: 0.0%; Median selected monthly owner costs: $1,088 with a mortgage, $566 without a mortgage; Median gross rent: $643 per month; Rental vacancy rate: 1.2%
Health Insurance: 94.8% have insurance; 69.0% have private insurance; 44.0% have public insurance; 5.2% do not have insurance; 0.0% of children under 18 do not have insurance
Transportation: Commute: 88.7% car, 1.4% public transportation, 5.6% walk, 3.9% work from home; Mean travel time to work: 22.6 minutes

PHARSALIA (town). Covers a land area of 38.816 square miles and a water area of 0.292 square miles. Located at 42.60° N. Lat; 75.73° W. Long. Elevation is 1,562 feet.
Population: 674; Growth (since 2000): 24.4%; Density: 17.4 persons per square mile; Race: 91.2% White, 0.0% Black/African American, 0.0% Asian, 7.3% American Indian/Alaska Native, 0.0% Native Hawaiian/Other Pacific Islander, 1.5% Two or more races, 0.9% Hispanic of any race; Average household size: 2.29; Median age: 49.3; Age under 18: 19.3%; Age 65 and over: 13.6%; Males per 100 females: 99.7; Marriage status: 27.6% never married, 55.6% now married, 1.4% separated, 1.9% widowed, 14.9% divorced; Foreign born: 0.0%; Speak English only: 97.0%; With disability: 16.6%; Veterans: 8.1%; Ancestry: 18.2% German, 14.4% Irish, 14.2% Italian, 13.9% English, 8.5% American
Employment: 14.9% management, business, and financial, 2.2% computer, engineering, and science, 1.9% education, legal, community service, arts, and media, 1.9% healthcare practitioners, 18.4% service, 23.1% sales and office, 18.0% natural resources, construction, and maintenance, 19.6% production, transportation, and material moving
Income: Per capita: $19,984; Median household: $37,344; Average household: $46,862; Households with income of $100,000 or more: 7.1%; Poverty rate: 12.6%
Educational Attainment: High school diploma or higher: 88.3%; Bachelor's degree or higher: 9.5%; Graduate/professional degree or higher: 4.1%
Housing: Homeownership rate: 88.1%; Median home value: $61,200; Median year structure built: 1975; Homeowner vacancy rate: 0.0%; Median selected monthly owner costs: $829 with a mortgage, $309 without a mortgage; Median gross rent: $437 per month; Rental vacancy rate: 0.0%
Health Insurance: 96.4% have insurance; 60.1% have private insurance; 49.7% have public insurance; 3.6% do not have insurance; 0.0% of children under 18 do not have insurance
Transportation: Commute: 92.7% car, 0.0% public transportation, 6.7% walk, 0.6% work from home; Mean travel time to work: 30.4 minutes

PITCHER (town). Covers a land area of 28.465 square miles and a water area of 0.014 square miles. Located at 42.59° N. Lat; 75.83° W. Long. Elevation is 1,135 feet.
Population: 673; Growth (since 2000): -20.6%; Density: 23.6 persons per square mile; Race: 96.1% White, 0.0% Black/African American, 0.0% Asian, 0.0% American Indian/Alaska Native, 0.0% Native Hawaiian/Other Pacific Islander, 0.6% Two or more races, 6.1% Hispanic of any race; Average household size: 2.25; Median age: 46.2; Age under 18: 21.7%; Age 65 and over: 19.3%; Males per 100 females: 111.3; Marriage status: 26.1% never married, 51.2% now married, 1.8% separated, 6.4% widowed, 16.3% divorced; Foreign born: 0.9%; Speak English only: 97.8%; With disability: 22.6%; Veterans: 16.5%; Ancestry: 18.3% English, 15.0% Irish, 13.1% American, 10.0% German, 5.3% Dutch

Employment: 9.2% management, business, and financial, 1.5% computer, engineering, and science, 10.4% education, legal, community service, arts, and media, 1.9% healthcare practitioners, 23.5% service, 12.7% sales and office, 15.4% natural resources, construction, and maintenance, 25.4% production, transportation, and material moving
Income: Per capita: $22,305; Median household: $41,188; Average household: $50,166; Households with income of $100,000 or more: 6.3%; Poverty rate: 18.6%
Educational Attainment: High school diploma or higher: 90.1%; Bachelor's degree or higher: 14.1%; Graduate/professional degree or higher: 5.8%
Housing: Homeownership rate: 76.6%; Median home value: $73,400; Median year structure built: 1975; Homeowner vacancy rate: 5.1%; Median selected monthly owner costs: $1,046 with a mortgage, $425 without a mortgage; Median gross rent: $652 per month; Rental vacancy rate: 0.0%
Health Insurance: 92.4% have insurance; 59.1% have private insurance; 54.4% have public insurance; 7.6% do not have insurance; 7.3% of children under 18 do not have insurance
Transportation: Commute: 91.2% car, 0.0% public transportation, 4.8% walk, 3.2% work from home; Mean travel time to work: 37.8 minutes

PLYMOUTH (town). Covers a land area of 42.177 square miles and a water area of 0.169 square miles. Located at 42.61° N. Lat; 75.60° W. Long. Elevation is 1,243 feet.
Population: 1,949; Growth (since 2000): -4.9%; Density: 46.2 persons per square mile; Race: 96.1% White, 0.8% Black/African American, 0.3% Asian, 0.6% American Indian/Alaska Native, 0.0% Native Hawaiian/Other Pacific Islander, 2.2% Two or more races, 0.9% Hispanic of any race; Average household size: 2.67; Median age: 45.1; Age under 18: 23.4%; Age 65 and over: 19.1%; Males per 100 females: 101.3; Marriage status: 24.7% never married, 55.7% now married, 5.8% separated, 5.9% widowed, 13.7% divorced; Foreign born: 0.9%; Speak English only: 97.5%; With disability: 16.8%; Veterans: 9.3%; Ancestry: 18.5% German, 14.2% Irish, 12.5% English, 9.1% American, 6.9% Italian
Employment: 11.3% management, business, and financial, 4.6% computer, engineering, and science, 6.6% education, legal, community service, arts, and media, 5.4% healthcare practitioners, 23.7% service, 24.9% sales and office, 8.3% natural resources, construction, and maintenance, 15.2% production, transportation, and material moving
Income: Per capita: $23,646; Median household: $50,607; Average household: $63,632; Households with income of $100,000 or more: 20.5%; Poverty rate: 19.1%
Educational Attainment: High school diploma or higher: 86.3%; Bachelor's degree or higher: 13.7%; Graduate/professional degree or higher: 4.0%
Housing: Homeownership rate: 88.2%; Median home value: $104,500; Median year structure built: 1973; Homeowner vacancy rate: 0.0%; Median selected monthly owner costs: $1,238 with a mortgage, $507 without a mortgage; Median gross rent: $676 per month; Rental vacancy rate: 0.0%
Health Insurance: 93.7% have insurance; 62.2% have private insurance; 48.0% have public insurance; 6.3% do not have insurance; 1.3% of children under 18 do not have insurance
Transportation: Commute: 91.3% car, 1.0% public transportation, 4.0% walk, 3.4% work from home; Mean travel time to work: 19.8 minutes

PRESTON (town). Covers a land area of 34.876 square miles and a water area of 0.171 square miles. Located at 42.50° N. Lat; 75.61° W. Long. Elevation is 1,470 feet.
Population: 1,028; Growth (since 2000): 10.8%; Density: 29.5 persons per square mile; Race: 98.3% White, 0.0% Black/African American, 0.3% Asian, 0.0% American Indian/Alaska Native, 0.4% Native Hawaiian/Other Pacific Islander, 0.3% Two or more races, 0.4% Hispanic of any race; Average household size: 2.50; Median age: 42.7; Age under 18: 23.3%; Age 65 and over: 13.8%; Males per 100 females: 114.4; Marriage status: 19.2% never married, 63.9% now married, 3.8% separated, 4.7% widowed, 12.3% divorced; Foreign born: 1.8%; Speak English only: 97.7%; With disability: 19.9%; Veterans: 6.2%; Ancestry: 21.3% English, 17.1% German, 16.1% Irish, 11.5% Italian, 10.7% American
Employment: 12.2% management, business, and financial, 2.2% computer, engineering, and science, 7.0% education, legal, community service, arts, and media, 4.0% healthcare practitioners, 19.1% service, 24.1% sales and office, 19.3% natural resources, construction, and maintenance, 12.0% production, transportation, and material moving

Income: Per capita: $23,790; Median household: $51,587; Average household: $58,972; Households with income of $100,000 or more: 12.4%; Poverty rate: 9.6%
Educational Attainment: High school diploma or higher: 86.8%; Bachelor's degree or higher: 13.6%; Graduate/professional degree or higher: 9.4%
Housing: Homeownership rate: 83.9%; Median home value: $90,400; Median year structure built: 1979; Homeowner vacancy rate: 0.0%; Median selected monthly owner costs: $1,063 with a mortgage, $398 without a mortgage; Median gross rent: $717 per month; Rental vacancy rate: 0.0%
Health Insurance: 95.6% have insurance; 76.7% have private insurance; 33.4% have public insurance; 4.4% do not have insurance; 3.8% of children under 18 do not have insurance
Transportation: Commute: 90.0% car, 0.0% public transportation, 3.7% walk, 6.3% work from home; Mean travel time to work: 25.8 minutes

SHERBURNE (town). Covers a land area of 43.554 square miles and a water area of 0.020 square miles. Located at 42.69° N. Lat; 75.48° W. Long. Elevation is 1,047 feet.
History: Former summer resort. Settled 1793, incorporated 1830.
Population: 3,925; Growth (since 2000): -1.4%; Density: 90.1 persons per square mile; Race: 96.2% White, 1.0% Black/African American, 0.2% Asian, 0.2% American Indian/Alaska Native, 0.0% Native Hawaiian/Other Pacific Islander, 2.5% Two or more races, 0.8% Hispanic of any race; Average household size: 2.29; Median age: 39.5; Age under 18: 24.6%; Age 65 and over: 16.9%; Males per 100 females: 94.0; Marriage status: 25.5% never married, 55.9% now married, 3.1% separated, 4.7% widowed, 14.0% divorced; Foreign born: 1.7%; Speak English only: 96.5%; With disability: 18.6%; Veterans: 5.6%; Ancestry: 22.9% German, 20.7% English, 13.4% Irish, 6.8% French, 6.1% Italian
Employment: 17.0% management, business, and financial, 2.1% computer, engineering, and science, 10.9% education, legal, community service, arts, and media, 10.0% healthcare practitioners, 13.9% service, 19.0% sales and office, 14.0% natural resources, construction, and maintenance, 13.2% production, transportation, and material moving
Income: Per capita: $24,541; Median household: $43,013; Average household: $56,689; Households with income of $100,000 or more: 14.6%; Poverty rate: 16.4%
Educational Attainment: High school diploma or higher: 87.1%; Bachelor's degree or higher: 19.4%; Graduate/professional degree or higher: 9.2%

School District(s)
Sherburne-Earlville Central SD (PK-12)
    Enrollment: 1,371 . . . . (607) 674-7300
Housing: Homeownership rate: 64.6%; Median home value: $106,300; Median year structure built: 1961; Homeowner vacancy rate: 0.8%; Median selected monthly owner costs: $1,172 with a mortgage, $412 without a mortgage; Median gross rent: $628 per month; Rental vacancy rate: 0.0%
Health Insurance: 95.5% have insurance; 69.5% have private insurance; 45.4% have public insurance; 4.5% do not have insurance; 2.3% of children under 18 do not have insurance
Newspapers: Sherburne News (weekly circulation 1,900)
Transportation: Commute: 86.9% car, 0.0% public transportation, 7.6% walk, 5.4% work from home; Mean travel time to work: 20.1 minutes
Additional Information Contacts
Town of Sherburne . . . . (607) 674-4481
    http://www.sherburne.org

SHERBURNE (village). Covers a land area of 1.519 square miles and a water area of 0 square miles. Located at 42.68° N. Lat; 75.50° W. Long. Elevation is 1,047 feet.
Population: 1,366; Growth (since 2000): -6.1%; Density: 899.1 persons per square mile; Race: 96.4% White, 2.9% Black/African American, 0.5% Asian, 0.0% American Indian/Alaska Native, 0.0% Native Hawaiian/Other Pacific Islander, 0.2% Two or more races, 2.3% Hispanic of any race; Average household size: 2.01; Median age: 50.6; Age under 18: 17.5%; Age 65 and over: 21.0%; Males per 100 females: 83.7; Marriage status: 30.6% never married, 41.7% now married, 3.4% separated, 8.1% widowed, 19.7% divorced; Foreign born: 3.4%; Speak English only: 91.9%; With disability: 22.6%; Veterans: 8.1%; Ancestry: 22.1% English, 19.5% German, 13.6% Irish, 10.6% American, 6.8% Dutch
Employment: 17.6% management, business, and financial, 5.0% computer, engineering, and science, 15.9% education, legal, community service, arts, and media, 4.2% healthcare practitioners, 17.6% service,

20.1% sales and office, 6.6% natural resources, construction, and maintenance, 13.1% production, transportation, and material moving
Income: Per capita: $27,130; Median household: $37,768; Average household: $55,690; Households with income of $100,000 or more: 16.3%; Poverty rate: 16.2%
Educational Attainment: High school diploma or higher: 86.7%; Bachelor's degree or higher: 27.8%; Graduate/professional degree or higher: 11.7%

School District(s)
Sherburne-Earlville Central SD (PK-12)
    Enrollment: 1,371 . . . . (607) 674-7300
Housing: Homeownership rate: 43.5%; Median home value: $112,500; Median year structure built: 1952; Homeowner vacancy rate: 0.0%; Median selected monthly owner costs: $1,051 with a mortgage, $477 without a mortgage; Median gross rent: $567 per month; Rental vacancy rate: 0.0%
Health Insurance: 95.5% have insurance; 64.3% have private insurance; 50.0% have public insurance; 4.5% do not have insurance; 8.5% of children under 18 do not have insurance
Safety: Violent crime rate: 7.5 per 10,000 population; Property crime rate: 60.4 per 10,000 population
Newspapers: Sherburne News (weekly circulation 1,900)
Transportation: Commute: 74.2% car, 0.0% public transportation, 17.3% walk, 8.5% work from home; Mean travel time to work: 17.2 minutes

SMITHVILLE (town). Covers a land area of 50.445 square miles and a water area of 0.481 square miles. Located at 42.41° N. Lat; 75.76° W. Long.
Population: 1,474; Growth (since 2000): 9.4%; Density: 29.2 persons per square mile; Race: 91.0% White, 0.9% Black/African American, 0.5% Asian, 0.0% American Indian/Alaska Native, 0.6% Native Hawaiian/Other Pacific Islander, 7.1% Two or more races, 4.9% Hispanic of any race; Average household size: 2.79; Median age: 37.1; Age under 18: 26.8%; Age 65 and over: 14.3%; Males per 100 females: 115.2; Marriage status: 32.3% never married, 55.8% now married, 3.4% separated, 5.1% widowed, 6.7% divorced; Foreign born: 1.4%; Speak English only: 95.7%; With disability: 16.8%; Veterans: 10.1%; Ancestry: 16.6% Irish, 12.5% German, 12.0% Italian, 11.0% English, 8.5% American
Employment: 13.6% management, business, and financial, 1.3% computer, engineering, and science, 11.8% education, legal, community service, arts, and media, 1.8% healthcare practitioners, 17.4% service, 16.1% sales and office, 15.6% natural resources, construction, and maintenance, 22.5% production, transportation, and material moving
Income: Per capita: $21,474; Median household: $47,083; Average household: $59,580; Households with income of $100,000 or more: 13.7%; Poverty rate: 25.8%
Educational Attainment: High school diploma or higher: 88.5%; Bachelor's degree or higher: 18.9%; Graduate/professional degree or higher: 9.4%
Housing: Homeownership rate: 80.2%; Median home value: $98,500; Median year structure built: 1965; Homeowner vacancy rate: 2.9%; Median selected monthly owner costs: $1,112 with a mortgage, $481 without a mortgage; Median gross rent: $724 per month; Rental vacancy rate: 0.0%
Health Insurance: 93.3% have insurance; 70.7% have private insurance; 36.2% have public insurance; 6.7% do not have insurance; 2.0% of children under 18 do not have insurance
Transportation: Commute: 91.3% car, 0.5% public transportation, 3.4% walk, 4.8% work from home; Mean travel time to work: 30.2 minutes

SMITHVILLE FLATS (CDP). Covers a land area of 1.422 square miles and a water area of 0 square miles. Located at 42.39° N. Lat; 75.81° W. Long. Elevation is 1,024 feet.
Population: 380; Growth (since 2000): n/a; Density: 267.2 persons per square mile; Race: 86.1% White, 0.0% Black/African American, 0.0% Asian, 0.0% American Indian/Alaska Native, 2.4% Native Hawaiian/Other Pacific Islander, 11.6% Two or more races, 0.0% Hispanic of any race; Average household size: 2.48; Median age: 41.6; Age under 18: 26.1%; Age 65 and over: 15.5%; Males per 100 females: 123.6; Marriage status: 25.0% never married, 60.1% now married, 8.3% separated, 8.3% widowed, 6.6% divorced; Foreign born: 2.4%; Speak English only: 98.6%; With disability: 15.3%; Veterans: 10.7%; Ancestry: 32.1% Italian, 22.6% German, 13.4% English, 13.2% Irish, 5.5% French
Employment: 20.1% management, business, and financial, 0.0% computer, engineering, and science, 8.2% education, legal, community service, arts, and media, 0.0% healthcare practitioners, 6.0% service,

17.9% sales and office, 20.1% natural resources, construction, and maintenance, 27.6% production, transportation, and material moving
Income: Per capita: $21,006; Median household: $38,523; Average household: $52,229; Households with income of $100,000 or more: 15.0%; Poverty rate: 34.5%
Educational Attainment: High school diploma or higher: 91.6%; Bachelor's degree or higher: 14.1%; Graduate/professional degree or higher: 3.6%
Housing: Homeownership rate: 79.1%; Median home value: $100,500; Median year structure built: 1954; Homeowner vacancy rate: 9.2%; Median selected monthly owner costs: $1,066 with a mortgage, $550 without a mortgage; Median gross rent: n/a per month; Rental vacancy rate: 0.0%
Health Insurance: 87.4% have insurance; 76.8% have private insurance; 24.7% have public insurance; 12.6% do not have insurance; 0.0% of children under 18 do not have insurance
Transportation: Commute: 84.7% car, 0.0% public transportation, 1.5% walk, 13.7% work from home; Mean travel time to work: 42.1 minutes

SMYRNA (town). Covers a land area of 42.087 square miles and a water area of 0.076 square miles. Located at 42.69° N. Lat; 75.62° W. Long. Elevation is 1,204 feet.
Population: 1,367; Growth (since 2000): -3.6%; Density: 32.5 persons per square mile; Race: 97.1% White, 1.5% Black/African American, 0.0% Asian, 0.3% American Indian/Alaska Native, 0.0% Native Hawaiian/Other Pacific Islander, 0.7% Two or more races, 1.2% Hispanic of any race; Average household size: 2.52; Median age: 40.9; Age under 18: 23.8%; Age 65 and over: 17.7%; Males per 100 females: 113.0; Marriage status: 26.8% never married, 56.3% now married, 5.4% separated, 8.2% widowed, 8.8% divorced; Foreign born: 0.4%; Speak English only: 98.5%; With disability: 18.6%; Veterans: 9.7%; Ancestry: 17.8% American, 14.6% English, 14.0% German, 10.8% Irish, 9.5% Italian
Employment: 13.0% management, business, and financial, 0.9% computer, engineering, and science, 5.1% education, legal, community service, arts, and media, 3.7% healthcare practitioners, 16.9% service, 16.3% sales and office, 11.1% natural resources, construction, and maintenance, 33.0% production, transportation, and material moving
Income: Per capita: $19,168; Median household: $43,700; Average household: $48,020; Households with income of $100,000 or more: 7.9%; Poverty rate: 22.6%
Educational Attainment: High school diploma or higher: 83.2%; Bachelor's degree or higher: 12.6%; Graduate/professional degree or higher: 3.8%
Housing: Homeownership rate: 75.3%; Median home value: $80,600; Median year structure built: 1966; Homeowner vacancy rate: 0.0%; Median selected monthly owner costs: $1,067 with a mortgage, $408 without a mortgage; Median gross rent: $515 per month; Rental vacancy rate: 2.7%
Health Insurance: 91.1% have insurance; 60.2% have private insurance; 46.5% have public insurance; 8.9% do not have insurance; 12.8% of children under 18 do not have insurance
Transportation: Commute: 94.1% car, 0.0% public transportation, 1.8% walk, 2.1% work from home; Mean travel time to work: 25.6 minutes

SMYRNA (village). Covers a land area of 0.244 square miles and a water area of 0 square miles. Located at 42.69° N. Lat; 75.57° W. Long. Elevation is 1,204 feet.
Population: 253; Growth (since 2000): 5.0%; Density: 1,036.2 persons per square mile; Race: 94.1% White, 5.9% Black/African American, 0.0% Asian, 0.0% American Indian/Alaska Native, 0.0% Native Hawaiian/Other Pacific Islander, 0.0% Two or more races, 0.0% Hispanic of any race; Average household size: 2.69; Median age: 39.6; Age under 18: 28.1%; Age 65 and over: 16.2%; Males per 100 females: 95.4; Marriage status: 38.3% never married, 45.3% now married, 5.0% separated, 9.5% widowed, 7.0% divorced; Foreign born: 0.0%; Speak English only: 99.1%; With disability: 14.2%; Veterans: 8.2%; Ancestry: 28.5% German, 21.3% Irish, 8.3% American, 7.1% Italian, 6.7% English
Employment: 17.3% management, business, and financial, 0.0% computer, engineering, and science, 1.0% education, legal, community service, arts, and media, 1.9% healthcare practitioners, 19.2% service, 26.9% sales and office, 8.7% natural resources, construction, and maintenance, 25.0% production, transportation, and material moving
Income: Per capita: $15,741; Median household: $28,750; Average household: $40,385; Households with income of $100,000 or more: 9.6%; Poverty rate: 24.5%

Educational Attainment: High school diploma or higher: 88.6%; Bachelor's degree or higher: 15.6%; Graduate/professional degree or higher: 6.0%
Housing: Homeownership rate: 57.4%; Median home value: $67,100; Median year structure built: Before 1940; Homeowner vacancy rate: 0.0%; Median selected monthly owner costs: $950 with a mortgage, $384 without a mortgage; Median gross rent: $535 per month; Rental vacancy rate: 9.1%
Health Insurance: 86.2% have insurance; 52.6% have private insurance; 47.8% have public insurance; 13.8% do not have insurance; 20.0% of children under 18 do not have insurance
Transportation: Commute: 86.5% car, 0.0% public transportation, 9.6% walk, 3.8% work from home; Mean travel time to work: 32.4 minutes

SOUTH NEW BERLIN (unincorporated postal area)
ZCTA: 13843
Covers a land area of 54.416 square miles and a water area of 0.079 square miles. Located at 42.51° N. Lat; 75.38° W. Long. Elevation is 1,053 feet.
Population: 2,198; Growth (since 2000): 27.8%; Density: 40.4 persons per square mile; Race: 98.3% White, 0.0% Black/African American, 0.2% Asian, 0.0% American Indian/Alaska Native, 0.0% Native Hawaiian/Other Pacific Islander, 1.5% Two or more races, 0.8% Hispanic of any race; Average household size: 2.55; Median age: 44.7; Age under 18: 22.1%; Age 65 and over: 20.3%; Males per 100 females: 102.1; Marriage status: 22.3% never married, 63.8% now married, 2.9% separated, 4.6% widowed, 9.3% divorced; Foreign born: 1.7%; Speak English only: 98.1%; With disability: 20.7%; Veterans: 9.8%; Ancestry: 23.2% English, 18.5% Irish, 16.6% German, 11.0% Italian, 7.5% American
Employment: 13.3% management, business, and financial, 5.1% computer, engineering, and science, 11.0% education, legal, community service, arts, and media, 3.6% healthcare practitioners, 14.8% service, 24.5% sales and office, 12.4% natural resources, construction, and maintenance, 15.3% production, transportation, and material moving
Income: Per capita: $23,240; Median household: $50,927; Average household: $59,694; Households with income of $100,000 or more: 16.1%; Poverty rate: 14.0%
Educational Attainment: High school diploma or higher: 89.2%; Bachelor's degree or higher: 19.3%; Graduate/professional degree or higher: 7.3%
Housing: Homeownership rate: 88.5%; Median home value: $106,400; Median year structure built: 1954; Homeowner vacancy rate: 1.4%; Median selected monthly owner costs: $1,309 with a mortgage, $408 without a mortgage; Median gross rent: $714 per month; Rental vacancy rate: 0.0%
Health Insurance: 94.7% have insurance; 66.2% have private insurance; 45.4% have public insurance; 5.3% do not have insurance; 4.4% of children under 18 do not have insurance
Transportation: Commute: 92.2% car, 0.0% public transportation, 2.5% walk, 5.3% work from home; Mean travel time to work: 24.3 minutes

SOUTH OTSELIC (unincorporated postal area)
ZCTA: 13155
Covers a land area of 20.452 square miles and a water area of 0.054 square miles. Located at 42.67° N. Lat; 75.78° W. Long. Elevation is 1,227 feet.
Population: 662; Growth (since 2000): -2.2%; Density: 32.4 persons per square mile; Race: 95.9% White, 0.0% Black/African American, 0.0% Asian, 1.1% American Indian/Alaska Native, 0.0% Native Hawaiian/Other Pacific Islander, 3.0% Two or more races, 3.6% Hispanic of any race; Average household size: 2.27; Median age: 45.3; Age under 18: 16.6%; Age 65 and over: 22.2%; Males per 100 females: 110.5; Marriage status: 33.0% never married, 53.6% now married, 2.4% separated, 1.2% widowed, 12.2% divorced; Foreign born: 1.4%; Speak English only: 95.8%; With disability: 15.3%; Veterans: 9.4%; Ancestry: 26.9% English, 16.8% German, 13.6% Irish, 5.4% American, 4.5% Dutch
Employment: 10.5% management, business, and financial, 2.5% computer, engineering, and science, 18.6% education, legal, community service, arts, and media, 9.3% healthcare practitioners, 13.0% service, 16.4% sales and office, 13.8% natural resources, construction, and maintenance, 15.8% production, transportation, and material moving

Income: Per capita: $27,703; Median household: $51,750; Average household: $63,205; Households with income of $100,000 or more: 15.5%; Poverty rate: 10.9%

Educational Attainment: High school diploma or higher: 90.1%; Bachelor's degree or higher: 21.5%; Graduate/professional degree or higher: 9.0%

School District(s)

Georgetown-South Otselic Central SD (PK-12)

  Enrollment: 356 . . . . (315) 653-7218

Housing: Homeownership rate: 76.6%; Median home value: $74,800; Median year structure built: 1961; Homeowner vacancy rate: 0.0%; Median selected monthly owner costs: $828 with a mortgage, $406 without a mortgage; Median gross rent: $618 per month; Rental vacancy rate: 0.0%

Health Insurance: 94.4% have insurance; 70.2% have private insurance; 43.4% have public insurance; 5.6% do not have insurance; 1.7% of children under 18 do not have insurance

Transportation: Commute: 88.6% car, 0.0% public transportation, 11.1% walk, 0.3% work from home; Mean travel time to work: 27.3 minutes

SOUTH PLYMOUTH (unincorporated postal area)

ZCTA: 13844

Covers a land area of 23.991 square miles and a water area of 0.041 square miles. Located at 42.61° N. Lat; 75.67° W. Long. Elevation is 1,138 feet.

Population: 852; Growth (since 2000): -17.6%; Density: 35.5 persons per square mile; Race: 94.7% White, 1.9% Black/African American, 0.0% Asian, 0.0% American Indian/Alaska Native, 0.0% Native Hawaiian/Other Pacific Islander, 3.4% Two or more races, 0.6% Hispanic of any race; Average household size: 2.84; Median age: 40.0; Age under 18: 27.7%; Age 65 and over: 17.3%; Males per 100 females: 102.2; Marriage status: 31.5% never married, 52.7% now married, 6.2% separated, 3.8% widowed, 12.0% divorced; Foreign born: 1.6%; Speak English only: 94.1%; With disability: 16.4%; Veterans: 9.7%; Ancestry: 18.9% German, 13.6% English, 10.8% Irish, 9.6% Italian, 8.0% French

Employment: 11.9% management, business, and financial, 3.1% computer, engineering, and science, 2.1% education, legal, community service, arts, and media, 3.6% healthcare practitioners, 25.6% service, 24.3% sales and office, 8.3% natural resources, construction, and maintenance, 21.2% production, transportation, and material moving

Income: Per capita: $19,606; Median household: $47,188; Average household: $54,683; Households with income of $100,000 or more: 12.7%; Poverty rate: 19.0%

Educational Attainment: High school diploma or higher: 81.7%; Bachelor's degree or higher: 7.5%; Graduate/professional degree or higher: 0.2%

Housing: Homeownership rate: 81.7%; Median home value: $86,700; Median year structure built: 1968; Homeowner vacancy rate: 0.0%; Median selected monthly owner costs: $1,090 with a mortgage, $409 without a mortgage; Median gross rent: $678 per month; Rental vacancy rate: 0.0%

Health Insurance: 94.7% have insurance; 56.0% have private insurance; 54.2% have public insurance; 5.3% do not have insurance; 1.2% of children under 18 do not have insurance

Transportation: Commute: 95.9% car, 0.0% public transportation, 1.1% walk, 3.0% work from home; Mean travel time to work: 23.8 minutes

Clinton County

Located in northeastern New York; bounded on the north by the Canadian province of Quebec, and on the east by Lake Champlain and the Vermont border; includes the North Adirondacks. Covers a land area of 1,037.852 square miles, a water area of 79.674 square miles, and is located in the Eastern Time Zone at 44.75° N. Lat., 73.71° W. Long. The county was founded in 1788. County seat is Plattsburgh.

Clinton County is part of the Plattsburgh, NY Micropolitan Statistical Area. The entire metro area includes: Clinton County, NY

Weather Station: Chazy									Elevation: 169 feet		
	Jan	Feb	Mar	Apr	May	Jun	Jul	Aug	Sep	Oct	Nov	Dec
High	27	30	40	55	68	76	80	79	70	57	45	33
Low	8	10	20	34	45	54	59	57	49	39	29	16
Precip	0.8	na	0.9	2.3	2.9	3.5	3.5	3.8	3.2	3.1	2.2	0.8
Snow	13.7	12.7	11.1	2.9	0.1	0.0	0.0	0.0	0.0	0.3	4.6	11.2

High and Low temperatures in degrees Fahrenheit; Precipitation and Snow in inches

Weather Station: Dannemora									Elevation: 1,339 feet		
	Jan	Feb	Mar	Apr	May	Jun	Jul	Aug	Sep	Oct	Nov	Dec
High	26	30	38	53	65	74	78	76	68	56	43	31
Low	8	11	20	33	45	54	58	57	49	38	28	15
Precip	2.5	2.1	2.5	3.3	3.6	4.0	4.2	4.4	3.9	3.9	3.6	2.9
Snow	na	na	na	tr	0.0	0.0	0.0	0.0	0.0	tr	1.0	na

High and Low temperatures in degrees Fahrenheit; Precipitation and Snow in inches

Weather Station: Peru 2 WSW									Elevation: 509 feet		
	Jan	Feb	Mar	Apr	May	Jun	Jul	Aug	Sep	Oct	Nov	Dec
High	28	32	41	56	68	77	81	79	71	58	45	33
Low	9	12	21	34	45	54	59	57	49	38	29	17
Precip	1.4	1.3	1.7	2.6	2.7	3.6	3.5	3.5	2.8	3.0	2.7	2.0
Snow	11.3	10.4	11.1	2.9	0.0	0.0	0.0	0.0	0.0	0.5	3.2	12.6

High and Low temperatures in degrees Fahrenheit; Precipitation and Snow in inches

Population: 81,224; Growth (since 2000): 1.7%; Density: 78.3 persons per square mile; Race: 91.0% White, 4.2% Black/African American, 1.5% Asian, 0.2% American Indian/Alaska Native, 0.0% Native Hawaiian/Other Pacific Islander, 1.5% two or more races, 2.8% Hispanic of any race; Average household size: 2.32; Median age: 39.4; Age under 18: 18.2%; Age 65 and over: 15.4%; Males per 100 females: 105.2; Marriage status: 35.3% never married, 48.6% now married, 2.1% separated, 6.0% widowed, 10.1% divorced; Foreign born: 4.4%; Speak English only: 94.5%; With disability: 15.7%; Veterans: 9.1%; Ancestry: 20.9% French, 16.3% Irish, 8.6% French Canadian, 8.2% German, 8.1% English

Religion: Six largest groups: 33.7% Catholicism, 2.2% Methodist/Pietist, 1.9% Muslim Estimate, 1.4% Holiness, 0.8% Presbyterian-Reformed, 0.7% Non-denominational Protestant

Economy: Unemployment rate: 3.6%; Leading industries: 19.7 % retail trade; 12.7 % health care and social assistance; 10.7 % accommodation and food services; Farms: 603 totaling 147,229 acres; Company size: 1 employs 1,000 or more persons, 0 employ 500 to 999 persons, 30 employ 100 to 499 persons, 1,795 employ less than 100 persons; Business ownership: 1,528 women-owned, 60 Black-owned, 73 Hispanic-owned, n/a Asian-owned, n/a American Indian/Alaska Native-owned

Employment: 11.0% management, business, and financial, 3.1% computer, engineering, and science, 11.3% education, legal, community service, arts, and media, 6.3% healthcare practitioners, 22.1% service, 23.0% sales and office, 9.2% natural resources, construction, and maintenance, 14.1% production, transportation, and material moving

Income: Per capita: $25,833; Median household: $52,759; Average household: $65,435; Households with income of $100,000 or more: 19.2%; Poverty rate: 15.7%

Educational Attainment: High school diploma or higher: 86.8%; Bachelor's degree or higher: 21.9%; Graduate/professional degree or higher: 10.6%

Housing: Homeownership rate: 68.0%; Median home value: $129,000; Median year structure built: 1973; Homeowner vacancy rate: 1.7%; Median selected monthly owner costs: $1,235 with a mortgage, $466 without a mortgage; Median gross rent: $762 per month; Rental vacancy rate: 3.6%

Vital Statistics: Birth rate: 94.7 per 10,000 population; Death rate: 88.7 per 10,000 population; Age-adjusted cancer mortality rate: 157.1 deaths per 100,000 population

Health Insurance: 95.1% have insurance; 72.9% have private insurance; 38.6% have public insurance; 4.9% do not have insurance; 1.6% of children under 18 do not have insurance

Health Care: Physicians: 24.1 per 10,000 population; Dentists: 5.9 per 10,000 population; Hospital beds: 30.5 per 10,000 population; Hospital admissions: 1,109.9 per 10,000 population

Transportation: Commute: 89.6% car, 0.8% public transportation, 4.0% walk, 2.7% work from home; Mean travel time to work: 19.8 minutes

2016 Presidential Election: 45.0% Trump, 46.9% Clinton, 4.1% Johnson, 1.9% Stein

National and State Parks: Ausable Marsh State Game Management Area; Clinton State Forest; Cumberland Bay State Park; King Bay State Wetland Game Management Area; Lake Alice State Game Management Area; Miner Lake State Park; New York State Game Management Area

Additional Information Contacts
Clinton Government . . . . (518) 565-4700
  http://www.clintoncountygov.com

Clinton County Communities

ALTONA (CDP). Covers a land area of 1.709 square miles and a water area of 0 square miles. Located at 44.89° N. Lat; 73.66° W. Long. Elevation is 636 feet.
Population: 771; Growth (since 2000): -27.0%; Density: 451.1 persons per square mile; Race: 56.0% White, 29.3% Black/African American, 0.5% Asian, 0.5% American Indian/Alaska Native, 0.0% Native Hawaiian/Other Pacific Islander, 2.7% Two or more races, 15.3% Hispanic of any race; Average household size: 2.19; Median age: 36.8; Age under 18: 7.5%; Age 65 and over: 9.6%; Males per 100 females: 371.0; Marriage status: 50.6% never married, 35.7% now married, 2.4% separated, 4.0% widowed, 9.7% divorced; Foreign born: 5.1%; Speak English only: 92.5%; With disability: 24.2%; Veterans: 4.8%; Ancestry: 19.6% French, 11.8% Irish, 6.0% American, 5.3% Italian, 5.1% German
Employment: 6.1% management, business, and financial, 0.0% computer, engineering, and science, 0.0% education, legal, community service, arts, and media, 4.9% healthcare practitioners, 26.8% service, 36.6% sales and office, 13.4% natural resources, construction, and maintenance, 12.2% production, transportation, and material moving
Income: Per capita: $6,785; Median household: $31,413; Average household: $34,046; Households with income of $100,000 or more: n/a; Poverty rate: 13.8%
Educational Attainment: High school diploma or higher: 72.0%; Bachelor's degree or higher: 3.6%; Graduate/professional degree or higher: 1.1%
Housing: Homeownership rate: 63.6%; Median home value: $67,100; Median year structure built: 1951; Homeowner vacancy rate: 0.0%; Median selected monthly owner costs: $760 with a mortgage, $430 without a mortgage; Median gross rent: $646 per month; Rental vacancy rate: 0.0%
Health Insurance: 96.5% have insurance; 51.9% have private insurance; 74.0% have public insurance; 3.5% do not have insurance; 0.0% of children under 18 do not have insurance
Transportation: Commute: 100.0% car, 0.0% public transportation, 0.0% walk, 0.0% work from home; Mean travel time to work: 27.7 minutes

ALTONA (town). Covers a land area of 100.983 square miles and a water area of 0.357 square miles. Located at 44.84° N. Lat; 73.67° W. Long. Elevation is 636 feet.
Population: 2,915; Growth (since 2000): -7.8%; Density: 28.9 persons per square mile; Race: 86.6% White, 7.8% Black/African American, 0.1% Asian, 0.1% American Indian/Alaska Native, 0.1% Native Hawaiian/Other Pacific Islander, 2.2% Two or more races, 5.4% Hispanic of any race; Average household size: 2.37; Median age: 41.4; Age under 18: 19.5%; Age 65 and over: 13.7%; Males per 100 females: 134.7; Marriage status: 30.5% never married, 53.4% now married, 2.3% separated, 7.1% widowed, 9.0% divorced; Foreign born: 2.1%; Speak English only: 95.7%; With disability: 21.3%; Veterans: 8.3%; Ancestry: 22.8% French, 12.7% Irish, 12.3% French Canadian, 8.6% American, 7.4% German
Employment: 10.7% management, business, and financial, 3.4% computer, engineering, and science, 7.3% education, legal, community service, arts, and media, 8.2% healthcare practitioners, 20.0% service, 20.3% sales and office, 11.3% natural resources, construction, and maintenance, 18.8% production, transportation, and material moving
Income: Per capita: $19,899; Median household: $40,875; Average household: $55,651; Households with income of $100,000 or more: 13.2%; Poverty rate: 15.9%
Educational Attainment: High school diploma or higher: 81.9%; Bachelor's degree or higher: 11.6%; Graduate/professional degree or higher: 4.6%
Housing: Homeownership rate: 78.9%; Median home value: $88,600; Median year structure built: 1984; Homeowner vacancy rate: 0.0%; Median selected monthly owner costs: $1,011 with a mortgage, $351 without a mortgage; Median gross rent: $771 per month; Rental vacancy rate: 0.0%
Health Insurance: 95.1% have insurance; 63.2% have private insurance; 48.1% have public insurance; 4.9% do not have insurance; 0.8% of children under 18 do not have insurance
Transportation: Commute: 95.5% car, 0.5% public transportation, 0.0% walk, 1.8% work from home; Mean travel time to work: 29.9 minutes

AU SABLE (town). Covers a land area of 39.109 square miles and a water area of 4.740 square miles. Located at 44.50° N. Lat; 73.53° W. Long.
Population: 3,085; Growth (since 2000): 2.3%; Density: 78.9 persons per square mile; Race: 94.9% White, 1.5% Black/African American, 1.6% Asian, 0.2% American Indian/Alaska Native, 0.0% Native Hawaiian/Other Pacific Islander, 1.3% Two or more races, 2.1% Hispanic of any race; Average household size: 2.49; Median age: 43.4; Age under 18: 21.7%; Age 65 and over: 16.9%; Males per 100 females: 99.9; Marriage status: 33.9% never married, 47.6% now married, 3.6% separated, 6.1% widowed, 12.4% divorced; Foreign born: 1.7%; Speak English only: 95.6%; With disability: 20.0%; Veterans: 13.7%; Ancestry: 22.5% Irish, 22.1% French, 10.7% English, 6.8% German, 5.7% American
Employment: 7.0% management, business, and financial, 2.8% computer, engineering, and science, 8.3% education, legal, community service, arts, and media, 4.6% healthcare practitioners, 27.1% service, 20.9% sales and office, 7.5% natural resources, construction, and maintenance, 21.8% production, transportation, and material moving
Income: Per capita: $22,113; Median household: $43,182; Average household: $55,496; Households with income of $100,000 or more: 12.6%; Poverty rate: 16.3%
Educational Attainment: High school diploma or higher: 85.7%; Bachelor's degree or higher: 12.8%; Graduate/professional degree or higher: 6.0%
School District(s)
Ausable Valley Central SD (KG-12)
    Enrollment: 1,143 . . . . (518) 834-2845
Housing: Homeownership rate: 70.6%; Median home value: $93,600; Median year structure built: 1976; Homeowner vacancy rate: 2.3%; Median selected monthly owner costs: $994 with a mortgage, $348 without a mortgage; Median gross rent: $646 per month; Rental vacancy rate: 5.5%
Health Insurance: 93.1% have insurance; 65.3% have private insurance; 41.3% have public insurance; 6.9% do not have insurance; 2.8% of children under 18 do not have insurance
Transportation: Commute: 93.6% car, 0.0% public transportation, 0.9% walk, 1.5% work from home; Mean travel time to work: 20.9 minutes

AU SABLE FORKS (CDP). Covers a land area of 2.520 square miles and a water area of 0.023 square miles. Located at 44.45° N. Lat; 73.67° W. Long.
Population: 435; Growth (since 2000): -35.1%; Density: 172.6 persons per square mile; Race: 100.0% White, 0.0% Black/African American, 0.0% Asian, 0.0% American Indian/Alaska Native, 0.0% Native Hawaiian/Other Pacific Islander, 0.0% Two or more races, 0.0% Hispanic of any race; Average household size: 2.39; Median age: 47.8; Age under 18: 21.4%; Age 65 and over: 19.8%; Males per 100 females: 103.3; Marriage status: 24.7% never married, 56.3% now married, 2.7% separated, 9.2% widowed, 9.8% divorced; Foreign born: 0.0%; Speak English only: 100.0%; With disability: 15.2%; Veterans: 13.2%; Ancestry: 28.3% French, 20.2% Irish, 10.1% American, 9.2% German, 7.1% Italian
Employment: 11.4% management, business, and financial, 5.7% computer, engineering, and science, 10.5% education, legal, community service, arts, and media, 0.0% healthcare practitioners, 17.6% service, 14.8% sales and office, 14.3% natural resources, construction, and maintenance, 25.7% production, transportation, and material moving
Income: Per capita: $25,592; Median household: $48,333; Average household: $62,302; Households with income of $100,000 or more: 18.6%; Poverty rate: 11.5%
Educational Attainment: High school diploma or higher: 81.3%; Bachelor's degree or higher: 7.9%; Graduate/professional degree or higher: 4.2%
School District(s)
Ausable Valley Central SD (KG-12)
    Enrollment: 1,143 . . . . (518) 834-2845
Housing: Homeownership rate: 60.4%; Median home value: $113,200; Median year structure built: 1967; Homeowner vacancy rate: 0.0%; Median selected monthly owner costs: $1,031 with a mortgage, n/a without a mortgage; Median gross rent: $683 per month; Rental vacancy rate: 10.0%
Health Insurance: 95.6% have insurance; 62.5% have private insurance; 50.1% have public insurance; 4.4% do not have insurance; 0.0% of children under 18 do not have insurance
Transportation: Commute: 94.7% car, 0.0% public transportation, 0.0% walk, 5.3% work from home; Mean travel time to work: 25.8 minutes

BEEKMANTOWN (town). Covers a land area of 60.425 square miles and a water area of 9.202 square miles. Located at 44.79° N. Lat; 73.50° W. Long. Elevation is 253 feet.

Population: 5,498; Growth (since 2000): 3.2%; Density: 91.0 persons per square mile; Race: 96.7% White, 1.0% Black/African American, 0.9% Asian, 0.0% American Indian/Alaska Native, 0.0% Native Hawaiian/Other Pacific Islander, 1.4% Two or more races, 0.0% Hispanic of any race; Average household size: 2.27; Median age: 42.6; Age under 18: 19.0%; Age 65 and over: 17.2%; Males per 100 females: 99.5; Marriage status: 26.6% never married, 58.0% now married, 0.4% separated, 5.9% widowed, 9.5% divorced; Foreign born: 2.3%; Speak English only: 96.8%; With disability: 17.8%; Veterans: 13.6%; Ancestry: 25.0% French, 16.7% Irish, 12.4% French Canadian, 11.2% American, 7.8% Italian

Employment: 12.9% management, business, and financial, 1.6% computer, engineering, and science, 11.6% education, legal, community service, arts, and media, 8.2% healthcare practitioners, 26.5% service, 17.5% sales and office, 9.6% natural resources, construction, and maintenance, 11.9% production, transportation, and material moving

Income: Per capita: $33,925; Median household: $63,708; Average household: $77,556; Households with income of $100,000 or more: 22.7%; Poverty rate: 11.6%

Educational Attainment: High school diploma or higher: 91.5%; Bachelor's degree or higher: 23.7%; Graduate/professional degree or higher: 14.3%

Housing: Homeownership rate: 83.5%; Median home value: $135,400; Median year structure built: 1984; Homeowner vacancy rate: 0.0%; Median selected monthly owner costs: $1,267 with a mortgage, $453 without a mortgage; Median gross rent: $735 per month; Rental vacancy rate: 7.6%

Health Insurance: 97.4% have insurance; 78.7% have private insurance; 39.1% have public insurance; 2.6% do not have insurance; 0.0% of children under 18 do not have insurance

Transportation: Commute: 89.9% car, 2.4% public transportation, 2.8% walk, 2.8% work from home; Mean travel time to work: 21.1 minutes

Additional Information Contacts

Town of Beekmantown . . . . (518) 563-4650
    http://townofbeekmantown.com

BLACK BROOK (town). Covers a land area of 129.974 square miles and a water area of 4.361 square miles. Located at 44.52° N. Lat; 73.82° W. Long. Elevation is 974 feet.

Population: 1,385; Growth (since 2000): -16.6%; Density: 10.7 persons per square mile; Race: 99.3% White, 0.3% Black/African American, 0.0% Asian, 0.0% American Indian/Alaska Native, 0.0% Native Hawaiian/Other Pacific Islander, 0.4% Two or more races, 0.1% Hispanic of any race; Average household size: 2.28; Median age: 47.6; Age under 18: 17.3%; Age 65 and over: 23.7%; Males per 100 females: 105.1; Marriage status: 24.1% never married, 59.6% now married, 2.3% separated, 6.3% widowed, 10.0% divorced; Foreign born: 2.0%; Speak English only: 96.9%; With disability: 17.5%; Veterans: 12.8%; Ancestry: 26.4% French, 13.5% Irish, 11.0% German, 8.1% American, 6.8% English

Employment: 12.9% management, business, and financial, 2.2% computer, engineering, and science, 9.3% education, legal, community service, arts, and media, 2.8% healthcare practitioners, 15.1% service, 17.0% sales and office, 16.7% natural resources, construction, and maintenance, 23.8% production, transportation, and material moving

Income: Per capita: $28,287; Median household: $55,313; Average household: $64,595; Households with income of $100,000 or more: 18.8%; Poverty rate: 12.7%

Educational Attainment: High school diploma or higher: 87.0%; Bachelor's degree or higher: 16.1%; Graduate/professional degree or higher: 7.4%

Housing: Homeownership rate: 74.8%; Median home value: $116,500; Median year structure built: 1967; Homeowner vacancy rate: 0.0%; Median selected monthly owner costs: $1,097 with a mortgage, $472 without a mortgage; Median gross rent: $712 per month; Rental vacancy rate: 5.0%

Health Insurance: 94.9% have insurance; 67.9% have private insurance; 48.6% have public insurance; 5.1% do not have insurance; 1.3% of children under 18 do not have insurance

Transportation: Commute: 95.2% car, 0.0% public transportation, 1.3% walk, 3.0% work from home; Mean travel time to work: 28.3 minutes

CADYVILLE (unincorporated postal area)
ZCTA: 12918

Covers a land area of 39.293 square miles and a water area of 0.415 square miles. Located at 44.70° N. Lat; 73.68° W. Long. Elevation is 745 feet.

Population: 2,293; Growth (since 2000): -17.5%; Density: 58.4 persons per square mile; Race: 93.4% White, 0.7% Black/African American, 3.8% Asian, 1.7% American Indian/Alaska Native, 0.0% Native Hawaiian/Other Pacific Islander, 0.5% Two or more races, 0.3% Hispanic of any race; Average household size: 2.58; Median age: 39.3; Age under 18: 24.1%; Age 65 and over: 19.5%; Males per 100 females: 96.8; Marriage status: 19.5% never married, 63.3% now married, 1.4% separated, 10.6% widowed, 6.7% divorced; Foreign born: 5.9%; Speak English only: 98.3%; With disability: 8.5%; Veterans: 10.0%; Ancestry: 28.0% French, 15.3% Irish, 10.7% German, 9.9% American, 5.6% French Canadian

Employment: 11.3% management, business, and financial, 0.0% computer, engineering, and science, 18.1% education, legal, community service, arts, and media, 10.7% healthcare practitioners, 24.2% service, 15.9% sales and office, 10.6% natural resources, construction, and maintenance, 9.2% production, transportation, and material moving

Income: Per capita: $27,595; Median household: $61,886; Average household: $71,457; Households with income of $100,000 or more: 28.0%; Poverty rate: 4.1%

Educational Attainment: High school diploma or higher: 92.0%; Bachelor's degree or higher: 29.6%; Graduate/professional degree or higher: 7.4%

Housing: Homeownership rate: 89.4%; Median home value: $137,500; Median year structure built: 1966; Homeowner vacancy rate: 5.7%; Median selected monthly owner costs: $1,283 with a mortgage, $409 without a mortgage; Median gross rent: $797 per month; Rental vacancy rate: 0.0%

Health Insurance: 96.9% have insurance; 80.6% have private insurance; 31.7% have public insurance; 3.1% do not have insurance; 0.0% of children under 18 do not have insurance

Transportation: Commute: 98.5% car, 0.0% public transportation, 0.0% walk, 1.5% work from home; Mean travel time to work: 24.8 minutes

CHAMPLAIN (town). Covers a land area of 51.231 square miles and a water area of 7.585 square miles. Located at 44.97° N. Lat; 73.44° W. Long. Elevation is 105 feet.

History: Settled 1789, incorporated 1873.

Population: 5,676; Growth (since 2000): -2.0%; Density: 110.8 persons per square mile; Race: 97.4% White, 0.3% Black/African American, 0.4% Asian, 0.0% American Indian/Alaska Native, 0.1% Native Hawaiian/Other Pacific Islander, 1.7% Two or more races, 0.9% Hispanic of any race; Average household size: 2.32; Median age: 42.5; Age under 18: 22.3%; Age 65 and over: 15.8%; Males per 100 females: 95.8; Marriage status: 27.3% never married, 54.8% now married, 3.8% separated, 9.0% widowed, 8.8% divorced; Foreign born: 5.0%; Speak English only: 94.2%; With disability: 15.2%; Veterans: 7.5%; Ancestry: 25.5% French, 15.0% French Canadian, 11.5% Irish, 6.9% American, 6.6% English

Employment: 14.2% management, business, and financial, 4.1% computer, engineering, and science, 5.6% education, legal, community service, arts, and media, 4.4% healthcare practitioners, 17.3% service, 20.3% sales and office, 12.6% natural resources, construction, and maintenance, 21.4% production, transportation, and material moving

Income: Per capita: $25,760; Median household: $46,140; Average household: $60,224; Households with income of $100,000 or more: 15.7%; Poverty rate: 17.8%

Educational Attainment: High school diploma or higher: 84.4%; Bachelor's degree or higher: 14.9%; Graduate/professional degree or higher: 5.3%

School District(s)

Northeastern Clinton Central SD (PK-12)
    Enrollment: 1,382 . . . . (518) 298-8242

Housing: Homeownership rate: 69.5%; Median home value: $113,800; Median year structure built: 1969; Homeowner vacancy rate: 1.0%; Median selected monthly owner costs: $1,076 with a mortgage, $479 without a mortgage; Median gross rent: $673 per month; Rental vacancy rate: 4.4%

Health Insurance: 94.4% have insurance; 68.9% have private insurance; 42.6% have public insurance; 5.6% do not have insurance; 4.2% of children under 18 do not have insurance

Transportation: Commute: 93.5% car, 0.0% public transportation, 3.1% walk, 3.2% work from home; Mean travel time to work: 20.9 minutes

Additional Information Contacts
Town of Champlain . . . . (518) 298-8160
http://www.townofchamplain-ny.com

CHAMPLAIN (village). Covers a land area of 1.390 square miles and a water area of 0.039 square miles. Located at 44.99° N. Lat; 73.44° W. Long. Elevation is 105 feet.

Population: 977; Growth (since 2000): -16.7%; Density: 703.1 persons per square mile; Race: 98.1% White, 0.4% Black/African American, 0.3% Asian, 0.2% American Indian/Alaska Native, 0.0% Native Hawaiian/Other Pacific Islander, 1.0% Two or more races, 1.0% Hispanic of any race; Average household size: 2.25; Median age: 34.1; Age under 18: 25.2%; Age 65 and over: 14.1%; Males per 100 females: 89.5; Marriage status: 25.6% never married, 50.5% now married, 2.7% separated, 9.7% widowed, 14.2% divorced; Foreign born: 1.0%; Speak English only: 96.3%; With disability: 17.1%; Veterans: 10.9%; Ancestry: 28.4% French, 20.6% Irish, 16.8% French Canadian, 8.9% American, 5.9% English

Employment: 9.9% management, business, and financial, 6.6% computer, engineering, and science, 6.9% education, legal, community service, arts, and media, 6.9% healthcare practitioners, 16.8% service, 30.0% sales and office, 7.2% natural resources, construction, and maintenance, 15.7% production, transportation, and material moving

Income: Per capita: $21,753; Median household: $31,938; Average household: $49,391; Households with income of $100,000 or more: 13.8%; Poverty rate: 17.3%

Educational Attainment: High school diploma or higher: 85.4%; Bachelor's degree or higher: 20.6%; Graduate/professional degree or higher: 5.5%

School District(s)
Northeastern Clinton Central SD (PK-12)
    Enrollment: 1,382 . . . . (518) 298-8242
Housing: Homeownership rate: 52.1%; Median home value: $110,700; Median year structure built: 1942; Homeowner vacancy rate: 0.0%; Median selected monthly owner costs: $1,063 with a mortgage, $506 without a mortgage; Median gross rent: $698 per month; Rental vacancy rate: 2.8%
Health Insurance: 92.1% have insurance; 60.9% have private insurance; 50.5% have public insurance; 7.9% do not have insurance; 18.3% of children under 18 do not have insurance
Transportation: Commute: 94.3% car, 0.0% public transportation, 2.6% walk, 3.1% work from home; Mean travel time to work: 17.6 minutes

CHAZY (CDP). Covers a land area of 1.696 square miles and a water area of 0.018 square miles. Located at 44.89° N. Lat; 73.43° W. Long. Elevation is 148 feet.

Population: 532; Growth (since 2000): n/a; Density: 313.7 persons per square mile; Race: 100.0% White, 0.0% Black/African American, 0.0% Asian, 0.0% American Indian/Alaska Native, 0.0% Native Hawaiian/Other Pacific Islander, 0.0% Two or more races, 0.0% Hispanic of any race; Average household size: 2.84; Median age: 41.3; Age under 18: 25.4%; Age 65 and over: 10.3%; Males per 100 females: 89.6; Marriage status: 50.1% never married, 39.4% now married, 5.7% separated, 3.1% widowed, 7.4% divorced; Foreign born: 4.9%; Speak English only: 97.8%; With disability: 21.4%; Veterans: 10.6%; Ancestry: 41.4% French, 16.5% Irish, 12.8% French Canadian, 6.2% Canadian, 6.2% Welsh

Employment: 12.8% management, business, and financial, 4.8% computer, engineering, and science, 3.5% education, legal, community service, arts, and media, 9.3% healthcare practitioners, 6.2% service, 58.6% sales and office, 4.8% natural resources, construction, and maintenance, 0.0% production, transportation, and material moving

Income: Per capita: $29,854; Median household: n/a; Average household: $87,688; Households with income of $100,000 or more: 43.8%; Poverty rate: 14.5%

Educational Attainment: High school diploma or higher: 97.9%; Bachelor's degree or higher: 20.6%; Graduate/professional degree or higher: 11.5%

School District(s)
Chazy Union Free SD (KG-12)
    Enrollment: 458 . . . . (518) 846-7135
Housing: Homeownership rate: 79.1%; Median home value: $118,100; Median year structure built: Before 1940; Homeowner vacancy rate: 0.0%; Median selected monthly owner costs: $1,015 with a mortgage, n/a without a mortgage; Median gross rent: $773 per month; Rental vacancy rate: 40.0%

Health Insurance: 94.5% have insurance; 75.2% have private insurance; 34.0% have public insurance; 5.5% do not have insurance; 0.0% of children under 18 do not have insurance
Transportation: Commute: 100.0% car, 0.0% public transportation, 0.0% walk, 0.0% work from home; Mean travel time to work: 25.8 minutes

CHAZY (town). Covers a land area of 54.153 square miles and a water area of 7.163 square miles. Located at 44.86° N. Lat; 73.46° W. Long. Elevation is 148 feet.

History: Miner Institute, agricultural and environmental research center, founded by William Miner, Railroad industrialist and philanthropist, in the 19th century.

Population: 4,212; Growth (since 2000): 0.7%; Density: 77.8 persons per square mile; Race: 95.6% White, 0.6% Black/African American, 1.5% Asian, 0.0% American Indian/Alaska Native, 0.0% Native Hawaiian/Other Pacific Islander, 0.2% Two or more races, 0.6% Hispanic of any race; Average household size: 2.42; Median age: 44.1; Age under 18: 20.8%; Age 65 and over: 14.6%; Males per 100 females: 101.9; Marriage status: 28.7% never married, 56.8% now married, 2.8% separated, 5.3% widowed, 9.1% divorced; Foreign born: 4.9%; Speak English only: 97.2%; With disability: 11.8%; Veterans: 10.9%; Ancestry: 23.9% French, 14.6% Irish, 8.7% German, 8.3% French Canadian, 7.3% American

Employment: 11.7% management, business, and financial, 4.2% computer, engineering, and science, 9.9% education, legal, community service, arts, and media, 5.6% healthcare practitioners, 14.7% service, 21.6% sales and office, 17.9% natural resources, construction, and maintenance, 14.5% production, transportation, and material moving

Income: Per capita: $29,609; Median household: $62,029; Average household: $73,572; Households with income of $100,000 or more: 23.1%; Poverty rate: 11.4%

Educational Attainment: High school diploma or higher: 86.0%; Bachelor's degree or higher: 21.1%; Graduate/professional degree or higher: 9.9%

School District(s)
Chazy Union Free SD (KG-12)
    Enrollment: 458 . . . . (518) 846-7135
Housing: Homeownership rate: 78.3%; Median home value: $128,300; Median year structure built: 1971; Homeowner vacancy rate: 0.0%; Median selected monthly owner costs: $1,232 with a mortgage, $440 without a mortgage; Median gross rent: $797 per month; Rental vacancy rate: 9.7%
Health Insurance: 94.1% have insurance; 77.4% have private insurance; 31.2% have public insurance; 5.9% do not have insurance; 1.0% of children under 18 do not have insurance
Transportation: Commute: 94.1% car, 0.0% public transportation, 1.9% walk, 2.4% work from home; Mean travel time to work: 20.0 minutes
Additional Information Contacts
Town of Chazy . . . . (518) 846-7544
http://www.townofchazy.com

CHURUBUSCO (unincorporated postal area)
ZCTA: 12923
    Covers a land area of 52.386 square miles and a water area of 0.029 square miles. Located at 44.96° N. Lat; 73.94° W. Long. Elevation is 1,191 feet.

Population: 606; Growth (since 2000): -7.8%; Density: 11.6 persons per square mile; Race: 98.3% White, 0.7% Black/African American, 0.7% Asian, 0.0% American Indian/Alaska Native, 0.0% Native Hawaiian/Other Pacific Islander, 0.3% Two or more races, 0.2% Hispanic of any race; Average household size: 2.37; Median age: 50.8; Age under 18: 14.9%; Age 65 and over: 23.3%; Males per 100 females: 107.2; Marriage status: 28.1% never married, 58.4% now married, 4.1% separated, 6.0% widowed, 7.5% divorced; Foreign born: 0.8%; Speak English only: 97.3%; With disability: 22.4%; Veterans: 7.9%; Ancestry: 26.7% French, 10.6% Irish, 8.9% English, 8.4% French Canadian, 5.3% American

Employment: 12.7% management, business, and financial, 1.1% computer, engineering, and science, 9.4% education, legal, community service, arts, and media, 4.5% healthcare practitioners, 20.6% service, 19.1% sales and office, 14.6% natural resources, construction, and maintenance, 18.0% production, transportation, and material moving

Income: Per capita: $25,060; Median household: $41,667; Average household: $60,725; Households with income of $100,000 or more: 17.9%; Poverty rate: 17.5%

Educational Attainment: High school diploma or higher: 84.4%; Bachelor's degree or higher: 14.1%; Graduate/professional degree or higher: 5.9%
Housing: Homeownership rate: 80.9%; Median home value: $79,800; Median year structure built: 1967; Homeowner vacancy rate: 0.0%; Median selected monthly owner costs: $992 with a mortgage, $317 without a mortgage; Median gross rent: $394 per month; Rental vacancy rate: 0.0%
Health Insurance: 93.7% have insurance; 58.4% have private insurance; 52.1% have public insurance; 6.3% do not have insurance; 0.0% of children under 18 do not have insurance
Transportation: Commute: 86.8% car, 1.9% public transportation, 3.8% walk, 5.3% work from home; Mean travel time to work: 25.6 minutes

CLINTON (town). Covers a land area of 67.070 square miles and a water area of 0.030 square miles. Located at 44.94° N. Lat; 73.92° W. Long.
Population: 671; Growth (since 2000): -7.7%; Density: 10.0 persons per square mile; Race: 98.5% White, 0.6% Black/African American, 0.6% Asian, 0.0% American Indian/Alaska Native, 0.0% Native Hawaiian/Other Pacific Islander, 0.3% Two or more races, 0.1% Hispanic of any race; Average household size: 2.37; Median age: 49.6; Age under 18: 15.2%; Age 65 and over: 21.9%; Males per 100 females: 104.2; Marriage status: 27.3% never married, 59.3% now married, 3.7% separated, 5.8% widowed, 7.6% divorced; Foreign born: 1.2%; Speak English only: 97.1%; With disability: 21.3%; Veterans: 7.6%; Ancestry: 27.0% French, 13.0% Irish, 8.8% English, 7.9% French Canadian, 4.9% American
Employment: 11.9% management, business, and financial, 1.0% computer, engineering, and science, 8.9% education, legal, community service, arts, and media, 4.3% healthcare practitioners, 22.1% service, 17.8% sales and office, 16.5% natural resources, construction, and maintenance, 17.5% production, transportation, and material moving
Income: Per capita: $25,404; Median household: $42,188; Average household: $61,712; Households with income of $100,000 or more: 20.8%; Poverty rate: 16.8%
Educational Attainment: High school diploma or higher: 83.4%; Bachelor's degree or higher: 12.8%; Graduate/professional degree or higher: 5.3%
Housing: Homeownership rate: 82.0%; Median home value: $80,500; Median year structure built: 1972; Homeowner vacancy rate: 0.0%; Median selected monthly owner costs: $1,029 with a mortgage, $306 without a mortgage; Median gross rent: $475 per month; Rental vacancy rate: 0.0%
Health Insurance: 94.2% have insurance; 61.7% have private insurance; 48.6% have public insurance; 5.8% do not have insurance; 0.0% of children under 18 do not have insurance
Transportation: Commute: 85.0% car, 1.7% public transportation, 4.0% walk, 7.3% work from home; Mean travel time to work: 25.5 minutes

CUMBERLAND HEAD (CDP). Covers a land area of 3.591 square miles and a water area of 0 square miles. Located at 44.72° N. Lat; 73.40° W. Long. Elevation is 144 feet.
Population: 1,388; Growth (since 2000): -9.4%; Density: 386.5 persons per square mile; Race: 97.8% White, 1.4% Black/African American, 0.0% Asian, 0.0% American Indian/Alaska Native, 0.7% Native Hawaiian/Other Pacific Islander, 0.1% Two or more races, 1.7% Hispanic of any race; Average household size: 2.08; Median age: 55.2; Age under 18: 11.4%; Age 65 and over: 22.5%; Males per 100 females: 99.9; Marriage status: 18.0% never married, 65.2% now married, 0.0% separated, 5.5% widowed, 11.3% divorced; Foreign born: 6.0%; Speak English only: 97.7%; With disability: 12.4%; Veterans: 8.8%; Ancestry: 26.1% Irish, 16.4% English, 14.0% French, 10.2% French Canadian, 8.7% German
Employment: 17.7% management, business, and financial, 3.8% computer, engineering, and science, 12.6% education, legal, community service, arts, and media, 13.5% healthcare practitioners, 16.7% service, 20.7% sales and office, 7.9% natural resources, construction, and maintenance, 7.1% production, transportation, and material moving
Income: Per capita: $44,941; Median household: $58,472; Average household: $96,606; Households with income of $100,000 or more: 25.1%; Poverty rate: 6.3%
Educational Attainment: High school diploma or higher: 93.7%; Bachelor's degree or higher: 43.4%; Graduate/professional degree or higher: 25.5%
Housing: Homeownership rate: 85.9%; Median home value: $156,800; Median year structure built: 1957; Homeowner vacancy rate: 7.5%; Median

selected monthly owner costs: $1,229 with a mortgage, $592 without a mortgage; Median gross rent: $805 per month; Rental vacancy rate: 0.0%
Health Insurance: 96.8% have insurance; 80.8% have private insurance; 28.5% have public insurance; 3.2% do not have insurance; 0.0% of children under 18 do not have insurance
Transportation: Commute: 85.3% car, 3.4% public transportation, 2.0% walk, 8.3% work from home; Mean travel time to work: 19.6 minutes

DANNEMORA (town). Covers a land area of 59.080 square miles and a water area of 6.759 square miles. Located at 44.75° N. Lat; 73.81° W. Long. Elevation is 1,414 feet.
History: Incorporated 1881.
Population: 4,649; Growth (since 2000): -9.7%; Density: 78.7 persons per square mile; Race: 52.4% White, 35.8% Black/African American, 0.3% Asian, 0.0% American Indian/Alaska Native, 0.0% Native Hawaiian/Other Pacific Islander, 0.6% Two or more races, 13.6% Hispanic of any race; Average household size: 2.37; Median age: 37.3; Age under 18: 5.6%; Age 65 and over: 6.5%; Males per 100 females: 380.2; Marriage status: 54.7% never married, 34.2% now married, 4.0% separated, 2.2% widowed, 8.9% divorced; Foreign born: 7.6%; Speak English only: 90.2%; With disability: 16.3%; Veterans: 5.3%; Ancestry: 11.3% French, 7.1% Irish, 4.3% Italian, 3.9% German, 3.1% French Canadian
Employment: 7.3% management, business, and financial, 1.0% computer, engineering, and science, 9.9% education, legal, community service, arts, and media, 6.4% healthcare practitioners, 29.3% service, 22.9% sales and office, 10.4% natural resources, construction, and maintenance, 12.8% production, transportation, and material moving
Income: Per capita: $9,445; Median household: $53,667; Average household: $66,395; Households with income of $100,000 or more: 16.0%; Poverty rate: 17.9%
Educational Attainment: High school diploma or higher: 77.5%; Bachelor's degree or higher: 4.4%; Graduate/professional degree or higher: 2.0%
Housing: Homeownership rate: 71.5%; Median home value: $114,000; Median year structure built: 1959; Homeowner vacancy rate: 0.0%; Median selected monthly owner costs: $1,120 with a mortgage, $446 without a mortgage; Median gross rent: $715 per month; Rental vacancy rate: 5.0%
Health Insurance: 95.7% have insurance; 68.9% have private insurance; 43.3% have public insurance; 4.3% do not have insurance; 0.0% of children under 18 do not have insurance
Transportation: Commute: 92.8% car, 0.0% public transportation, 1.7% walk, 1.7% work from home; Mean travel time to work: 28.2 minutes
Additional Information Contacts
Town of Dannemora . . . . (518) 492-7541
  http://www.townofdannemora.org

DANNEMORA (village). Covers a land area of 1.148 square miles and a water area of 0 square miles. Located at 44.72° N. Lat; 73.72° W. Long. Elevation is 1,414 feet.
Population: 3,942; Growth (since 2000): -4.5%; Density: 3,434.6 persons per square mile; Race: 44.5% White, 42.1% Black/African American, 0.0% Asian, 0.0% American Indian/Alaska Native, 0.0% Native Hawaiian/Other Pacific Islander, 0.6% Two or more races, 16.4% Hispanic of any race; Average household size: 2.57; Median age: 36.1; Age under 18: 5.1%; Age 65 and over: 4.2%; Males per 100 females: 578.6; Marriage status: 61.4% never married, 28.4% now married, 4.4% separated, 2.1% widowed, 8.2% divorced; Foreign born: 7.7%; Speak English only: 89.7%; With disability: 19.9%; Veterans: 4.2%; Ancestry: 8.0% French, 6.3% Irish, 3.7% Italian, 2.1% English, 2.1% German
Employment: 1.0% management, business, and financial, 0.0% computer, engineering, and science, 7.7% education, legal, community service, arts, and media, 3.2% healthcare practitioners, 34.5% service, 24.5% sales and office, 13.9% natural resources, construction, and maintenance, 15.2% production, transportation, and material moving
Income: Per capita: $4,639; Median household: $48,958; Average household: $54,565; Households with income of $100,000 or more: 8.1%; Poverty rate: 13.5%
Educational Attainment: High school diploma or higher: 75.3%; Bachelor's degree or higher: 2.9%; Graduate/professional degree or higher: 1.3%
Housing: Homeownership rate: 70.6%; Median home value: $102,300; Median year structure built: Before 1940; Homeowner vacancy rate: 3.5%; Median selected monthly owner costs: $1,128 with a mortgage, $466 without a mortgage; Median gross rent: $750 per month; Rental vacancy rate: 9.0%

Health Insurance: 97.2% have insurance; 66.4% have private insurance; 46.1% have public insurance; 2.8% do not have insurance; 0.0% of children under 18 do not have insurance

Transportation: Commute: 84.9% car, 0.0% public transportation, 7.5% walk, 3.9% work from home; Mean travel time to work: 24.6 minutes

ELLENBURG (town). Covers a land area of 106.567 square miles and a water area of 0.890 square miles. Located at 44.81° N. Lat; 73.86° W. Long. Elevation is 961 feet.

Population: 1,852; Growth (since 2000): 2.2%; Density: 17.4 persons per square mile; Race: 92.7% White, 0.2% Black/African American, 4.7% Asian, 0.8% American Indian/Alaska Native, 0.0% Native Hawaiian/Other Pacific Islander, 1.1% Two or more races, 2.5% Hispanic of any race; Average household size: 2.51; Median age: 42.8; Age under 18: 23.0%; Age 65 and over: 17.2%; Males per 100 females: 102.2; Marriage status: 25.6% never married, 59.7% now married, 4.3% separated, 6.8% widowed, 8.0% divorced; Foreign born: 2.9%; Speak English only: 96.7%; With disability: 14.1%; Veterans: 8.8%; Ancestry: 28.9% French, 22.6% Irish, 9.2% German, 7.5% English, 6.0% French Canadian

Employment: 12.9% management, business, and financial, 1.7% computer, engineering, and science, 7.0% education, legal, community service, arts, and media, 5.5% healthcare practitioners, 24.0% service, 15.2% sales and office, 16.4% natural resources, construction, and maintenance, 17.2% production, transportation, and material moving

Income: Per capita: $23,480; Median household: $52,150; Average household: $59,093; Households with income of $100,000 or more: 16.9%; Poverty rate: 14.4%

Educational Attainment: High school diploma or higher: 81.5%; Bachelor's degree or higher: 11.3%; Graduate/professional degree or higher: 2.9%

Housing: Homeownership rate: 77.3%; Median home value: $100,800; Median year structure built: 1971; Homeowner vacancy rate: 1.4%; Median selected monthly owner costs: $1,116 with a mortgage, $386 without a mortgage; Median gross rent: $722 per month; Rental vacancy rate: 0.0%

Health Insurance: 92.0% have insurance; 67.8% have private insurance; 38.8% have public insurance; 8.0% do not have insurance; 6.7% of children under 18 do not have insurance

Transportation: Commute: 87.8% car, 0.0% public transportation, 4.1% walk, 7.9% work from home; Mean travel time to work: 32.6 minutes

ELLENBURG CENTER (unincorporated postal area)
ZCTA: 12934

Covers a land area of 58.851 square miles and a water area of 0.021 square miles. Located at 44.88° N. Lat; 73.87° W. Long. Elevation is 1,220 feet.

Population: 955; Growth (since 2000): -15.2%; Density: 16.2 persons per square mile; Race: 98.4% White, 0.1% Black/African American, 0.8% Asian, 0.0% American Indian/Alaska Native, 0.0% Native Hawaiian/Other Pacific Islander, 0.6% Two or more races, 0.8% Hispanic of any race; Average household size: 2.41; Median age: 44.9; Age under 18: 20.4%; Age 65 and over: 21.0%; Males per 100 females: 102.6; Marriage status: 24.3% never married, 60.6% now married, 4.8% separated, 5.8% widowed, 9.2% divorced; Foreign born: 2.2%; Speak English only: 96.7%; With disability: 17.2%; Veterans: 9.9%; Ancestry: 27.5% French, 18.0% Irish, 12.3% German, 6.8% English, 6.0% Italian

Employment: 5.4% management, business, and financial, 2.4% computer, engineering, and science, 5.4% education, legal, community service, arts, and media, 5.9% healthcare practitioners, 32.3% service, 14.6% sales and office, 17.5% natural resources, construction, and maintenance, 16.4% production, transportation, and material moving

Income: Per capita: $22,055; Median household: $43,036; Average household: $54,120; Households with income of $100,000 or more: 14.7%; Poverty rate: 16.8%

Educational Attainment: High school diploma or higher: 79.3%; Bachelor's degree or higher: 6.4%; Graduate/professional degree or higher: 1.9%

Housing: Homeownership rate: 74.7%; Median home value: $102,300; Median year structure built: 1977; Homeowner vacancy rate: 0.0%; Median selected monthly owner costs: $1,129 with a mortgage, $403 without a mortgage; Median gross rent: $712 per month; Rental vacancy rate: 0.0%

Health Insurance: 89.3% have insurance; 62.7% have private insurance; 42.3% have public insurance; 10.7% do not have insurance; 14.7% of children under 18 do not have insurance

Transportation: Commute: 89.2% car, 0.0% public transportation, 0.6% walk, 10.2% work from home; Mean travel time to work: 30.7 minutes

ELLENBURG DEPOT (unincorporated postal area)
ZCTA: 12935

Covers a land area of 98.613 square miles and a water area of 3.514 square miles. Located at 44.84° N. Lat; 73.80° W. Long. Elevation is 873 feet.

Population: 1,530; Growth (since 2000): -72.2%; Density: 15.5 persons per square mile; Race: 97.1% White, 0.4% Black/African American, 0.0% Asian, 0.9% American Indian/Alaska Native, 0.0% Native Hawaiian/Other Pacific Islander, 1.6% Two or more races, 1.8% Hispanic of any race; Average household size: 2.36; Median age: 45.4; Age under 18: 17.2%; Age 65 and over: 16.3%; Males per 100 females: 109.1; Marriage status: 24.0% never married, 57.4% now married, 2.8% separated, 7.1% widowed, 11.5% divorced; Foreign born: 1.0%; Speak English only: 99.0%; With disability: 17.6%; Veterans: 12.4%; Ancestry: 28.0% French, 16.0% Irish, 10.7% French Canadian, 7.9% American, 7.4% German

Employment: 11.7% management, business, and financial, 0.5% computer, engineering, and science, 8.7% education, legal, community service, arts, and media, 6.2% healthcare practitioners, 25.3% service, 17.4% sales and office, 11.1% natural resources, construction, and maintenance, 19.2% production, transportation, and material moving

Income: Per capita: $25,148; Median household: $49,563; Average household: $59,062; Households with income of $100,000 or more: 17.1%; Poverty rate: 12.2%

Educational Attainment: High school diploma or higher: 83.4%; Bachelor's degree or higher: 10.4%; Graduate/professional degree or higher: 3.3%

School District(s)
Northern Adirondack Central SD (KG-12)
    Enrollment: 819 . . . . (518) 594-7060

Housing: Homeownership rate: 71.5%; Median home value: $113,200; Median year structure built: 1983; Homeowner vacancy rate: 0.0%; Median selected monthly owner costs: $1,078 with a mortgage, $376 without a mortgage; Median gross rent: $682 per month; Rental vacancy rate: 0.0%

Health Insurance: 95.8% have insurance; 65.6% have private insurance; 41.6% have public insurance; 4.2% do not have insurance; 1.8% of children under 18 do not have insurance

Transportation: Commute: 92.7% car, 0.8% public transportation, 3.3% walk, 3.0% work from home; Mean travel time to work: 32.1 minutes

KEESEVILLE (village). Covers a land area of 1.173 square miles and a water area of 0.055 square miles. Located at 44.50° N. Lat; 73.48° W. Long. Elevation is 417 feet.

Population: 2,987; Growth (since 2000): 61.5%; Density: 2,545.6 persons per square mile; Race: 93.1% White, 1.5% Black/African American, 1.6% Asian, 0.2% American Indian/Alaska Native, 0.1% Native Hawaiian/Other Pacific Islander, 2.8% Two or more races, 2.9% Hispanic of any race; Average household size: 2.51; Median age: 42.4; Age under 18: 22.8%; Age 65 and over: 16.1%; Males per 100 females: 98.6; Marriage status: 31.9% never married, 49.7% now married, 4.1% separated, 5.9% widowed, 12.5% divorced; Foreign born: 2.2%; Speak English only: 94.8%; With disability: 21.8%; Veterans: 10.9%; Ancestry: 23.7% French, 15.7% Irish, 12.2% English, 9.4% German, 6.9% French Canadian

Employment: 10.8% management, business, and financial, 2.9% computer, engineering, and science, 6.6% education, legal, community service, arts, and media, 6.5% healthcare practitioners, 27.5% service, 22.2% sales and office, 10.1% natural resources, construction, and maintenance, 13.2% production, transportation, and material moving

Income: Per capita: $21,252; Median household: $41,906; Average household: $51,459; Households with income of $100,000 or more: 9.8%; Poverty rate: 18.6%

Educational Attainment: High school diploma or higher: 84.0%; Bachelor's degree or higher: 15.1%; Graduate/professional degree or higher: 4.8%

School District(s)
Ausable Valley Central SD (KG-12)
    Enrollment: 1,143 . . . . (518) 834-2845

Housing: Homeownership rate: 65.1%; Median home value: $92,200; Median year structure built: 1960; Homeowner vacancy rate: 4.1%; Median selected monthly owner costs: $1,017 with a mortgage, $362 without a mortgage; Median gross rent: $802 per month; Rental vacancy rate: 14.2%

Health Insurance: 94.0% have insurance; 60.1% have private insurance; 49.2% have public insurance; 6.0% do not have insurance; 5.3% of children under 18 do not have insurance
Transportation: Commute: 91.8% car, 0.0% public transportation, 0.5% walk, 2.5% work from home; Mean travel time to work: 23.1 minutes

LYON MOUNTAIN (CDP).
Covers a land area of 10.147 square miles and a water area of 0 square miles. Located at 44.72° N. Lat; 73.88° W. Long. Elevation is 1,798 feet.
Population: 341; Growth (since 2000): -25.5%; Density: 33.6 persons per square mile; Race: 95.0% White, 0.0% Black/African American, 4.4% Asian, 0.6% American Indian/Alaska Native, 0.0% Native Hawaiian/Other Pacific Islander, 0.0% Two or more races, 0.0% Hispanic of any race; Average household size: 2.10; Median age: 45.6; Age under 18: 11.4%; Age 65 and over: 16.4%; Males per 100 females: 88.0; Marriage status: 20.2% never married, 61.6% now married, 4.6% separated, 6.0% widowed, 12.3% divorced; Foreign born: 10.9%; Speak English only: 91.6%; With disability: 21.4%; Veterans: 7.9%; Ancestry: 39.9% French, 29.0% Irish, 12.3% Italian, 10.3% German, 7.3% Portuguese
Employment: 10.7% management, business, and financial, 0.0% computer, engineering, and science, 14.5% education, legal, community service, arts, and media, 2.3% healthcare practitioners, 19.8% service, 26.0% sales and office, 0.0% natural resources, construction, and maintenance, 26.7% production, transportation, and material moving
Income: Per capita: $20,035; Median household: n/a; Average household: $40,377; Households with income of $100,000 or more: 9.9%; Poverty rate: 40.8%
Educational Attainment: High school diploma or higher: 84.0%; Bachelor's degree or higher: 9.8%; Graduate/professional degree or higher: 9.8%
Housing: Homeownership rate: 76.5%; Median home value: $65,500; Median year structure built: Before 1940; Homeowner vacancy rate: 0.0%; Median selected monthly owner costs: $850 with a mortgage, $420 without a mortgage; Median gross rent: $739 per month; Rental vacancy rate: 0.0%
Health Insurance: 93.0% have insurance; 63.9% have private insurance; 48.4% have public insurance; 7.0% do not have insurance; 0.0% of children under 18 do not have insurance
Transportation: Commute: 94.7% car, 0.0% public transportation, 0.0% walk, 0.0% work from home; Mean travel time to work: 30.3 minutes

MOOERS (CDP).
Covers a land area of 1.193 square miles and a water area of 0.038 square miles. Located at 44.96° N. Lat; 73.60° W. Long. Elevation is 282 feet.
Population: 315; Growth (since 2000): -28.4%; Density: 264.0 persons per square mile; Race: 100.0% White, 0.0% Black/African American, 0.0% Asian, 0.0% American Indian/Alaska Native, 0.0% Native Hawaiian/Other Pacific Islander, 0.0% Two or more races, 6.0% Hispanic of any race; Average household size: 1.62; Median age: 60.4; Age under 18: 6.0%; Age 65 and over: 22.9%; Males per 100 females: 90.5; Marriage status: 33.3% never married, 49.5% now married, 5.7% separated, 17.1% widowed, 0.0% divorced; Foreign born: 0.0%; Speak English only: 100.0%; With disability: 44.8%; Veterans: 12.5%; Ancestry: 27.3% English, 21.3% French Canadian, 18.7% French, 10.8% Irish, 10.2% Scottish
Employment: 0.0% management, business, and financial, 0.0% computer, engineering, and science, 26.1% education, legal, community service, arts, and media, 14.3% healthcare practitioners, 15.1% service, 30.3% sales and office, 0.0% natural resources, construction, and maintenance, 14.3% production, transportation, and material moving
Income: Per capita: $30,831; Median household: $41,679; Average household: $49,831; Households with income of $100,000 or more: 8.2%; Poverty rate: 5.4%
Educational Attainment: High school diploma or higher: 88.5%; Bachelor's degree or higher: 22.3%; Graduate/professional degree or higher: 11.1%
School District(s)
Northeastern Clinton Central SD (PK-12)
   Enrollment: 1,382 . . . . (518) 298-8242
Housing: Homeownership rate: 83.1%; Median home value: $120,500; Median year structure built: 1959; Homeowner vacancy rate: 0.0%; Median selected monthly owner costs: n/a with a mortgage, $553 without a mortgage; Median gross rent: n/a per month; Rental vacancy rate: 0.0%
Health Insurance: 100.0% have insurance; 82.2% have private insurance; 55.9% have public insurance; 0.0% do not have insurance; 0.0% of children under 18 do not have insurance

Transportation: Commute: 86.6% car, 0.0% public transportation, 13.4% walk, 0.0% work from home; Mean travel time to work: 26.4 minutes

MOOERS (town).
Covers a land area of 87.632 square miles and a water area of 0.290 square miles. Located at 44.96° N. Lat; 73.66° W. Long. Elevation is 282 feet.
Population: 3,601; Growth (since 2000): 5.8%; Density: 41.1 persons per square mile; Race: 98.0% White, 0.0% Black/African American, 0.0% Asian, 0.0% American Indian/Alaska Native, 0.0% Native Hawaiian/Other Pacific Islander, 0.9% Two or more races, 2.6% Hispanic of any race; Average household size: 2.15; Median age: 47.5; Age under 18: 17.9%; Age 65 and over: 15.0%; Males per 100 females: 101.5; Marriage status: 30.0% never married, 55.9% now married, 0.6% separated, 5.3% widowed, 8.7% divorced; Foreign born: 1.1%; Speak English only: 97.5%; With disability: 22.7%; Veterans: 7.5%; Ancestry: 24.9% Irish, 23.2% French, 14.8% English, 12.7% American, 12.6% French Canadian
Employment: 9.9% management, business, and financial, 3.5% computer, engineering, and science, 7.9% education, legal, community service, arts, and media, 1.0% healthcare practitioners, 25.0% service, 25.0% sales and office, 15.0% natural resources, construction, and maintenance, 12.8% production, transportation, and material moving
Income: Per capita: $26,734; Median household: $42,115; Average household: $58,242; Households with income of $100,000 or more: 19.9%; Poverty rate: 16.2%
Educational Attainment: High school diploma or higher: 85.4%; Bachelor's degree or higher: 17.8%; Graduate/professional degree or higher: 5.5%
School District(s)
Northeastern Clinton Central SD (PK-12)
   Enrollment: 1,382 . . . . (518) 298-8242
Housing: Homeownership rate: 82.0%; Median home value: $97,400; Median year structure built: 1980; Homeowner vacancy rate: 3.5%; Median selected monthly owner costs: $933 with a mortgage, $428 without a mortgage; Median gross rent: $563 per month; Rental vacancy rate: 0.0%
Health Insurance: 95.3% have insurance; 68.5% have private insurance; 47.8% have public insurance; 4.7% do not have insurance; 0.0% of children under 18 do not have insurance
Transportation: Commute: 94.3% car, 0.0% public transportation, 1.0% walk, 4.7% work from home; Mean travel time to work: 25.3 minutes

MOOERS FORKS (unincorporated postal area)
ZCTA: 12959
Covers a land area of 38.629 square miles and a water area of 0.101 square miles. Located at 44.95° N. Lat; 73.72° W. Long. Elevation is 374 feet.
Population: 1,321; Growth (since 2000): -10.0%; Density: 34.2 persons per square mile; Race: 100.0% White, 0.0% Black/African American, 0.0% Asian, 0.0% American Indian/Alaska Native, 0.0% Native Hawaiian/Other Pacific Islander, 0.0% Two or more races, 0.7% Hispanic of any race; Average household size: 2.06; Median age: 49.1; Age under 18: 17.9%; Age 65 and over: 20.1%; Males per 100 females: 99.9; Marriage status: 19.3% never married, 62.8% now married, 0.0% separated, 6.8% widowed, 11.1% divorced; Foreign born: 1.4%; Speak English only: 97.7%; With disability: 24.4%; Veterans: 8.6%; Ancestry: 18.0% American, 17.1% French Canadian, 16.7% Irish, 14.6% French, 13.6% English
Employment: 2.7% management, business, and financial, 0.0% computer, engineering, and science, 0.0% education, legal, community service, arts, and media, 0.0% healthcare practitioners, 31.9% service, 39.3% sales and office, 17.3% natural resources, construction, and maintenance, 8.7% production, transportation, and material moving
Income: Per capita: $21,674; Median household: $37,601; Average household: $45,221; Households with income of $100,000 or more: 14.0%; Poverty rate: 22.6%
Educational Attainment: High school diploma or higher: 85.5%; Bachelor's degree or higher: 10.5%; Graduate/professional degree or higher: 1.6%
Housing: Homeownership rate: 91.2%; Median home value: $89,900; Median year structure built: 1981; Homeowner vacancy rate: 7.8%; Median selected monthly owner costs: $763 with a mortgage, $413 without a mortgage; Median gross rent: n/a per month; Rental vacancy rate: 0.0%
Health Insurance: 95.3% have insurance; 77.3% have private insurance; 42.2% have public insurance; 4.7% do not have insurance; 0.0% of children under 18 do not have insurance

Transportation: Commute: 95.3% car, 0.0% public transportation, 0.0% walk, 4.7% work from home; Mean travel time to work: 25.4 minutes

MORRISONVILLE (CDP). Covers a land area of 2.611 square miles and a water area of 0.090 square miles. Located at 44.69° N. Lat; 73.55° W. Long. Elevation is 361 feet.

Population: 1,338; Growth (since 2000): -21.4%; Density: 512.4 persons per square mile; Race: 89.5% White, 2.2% Black/African American, 2.5% Asian, 0.7% American Indian/Alaska Native, 0.0% Native Hawaiian/Other Pacific Islander, 4.6% Two or more races, 2.3% Hispanic of any race; Average household size: 2.31; Median age: 45.4; Age under 18: 22.1%; Age 65 and over: 23.9%; Males per 100 females: 92.4; Marriage status: 22.0% never married, 59.8% now married, 0.7% separated, 8.0% widowed, 10.1% divorced; Foreign born: 2.9%; Speak English only: 96.5%; With disability: 22.5%; Veterans: 12.0%; Ancestry: 26.7% French, 18.1% Irish, 12.3% American, 11.4% German, 6.7% Italian
Employment: 11.6% management, business, and financial, 5.1% computer, engineering, and science, 10.2% education, legal, community service, arts, and media, 4.4% healthcare practitioners, 15.2% service, 28.4% sales and office, 0.0% natural resources, construction, and maintenance, 25.0% production, transportation, and material moving
Income: Per capita: $27,093; Median household: $46,324; Average household: $62,855; Households with income of $100,000 or more: 13.6%; Poverty rate: 11.6%
Educational Attainment: High school diploma or higher: 95.3%; Bachelor's degree or higher: 24.5%; Graduate/professional degree or higher: 14.8%

School District(s)
Saranac Central SD (KG-12)
    Enrollment: 1,459 . . . . (518) 565-5600
Housing: Homeownership rate: 86.6%; Median home value: $120,100; Median year structure built: 1967; Homeowner vacancy rate: 0.0%; Median selected monthly owner costs: $986 with a mortgage, $414 without a mortgage; Median gross rent: $914 per month; Rental vacancy rate: 0.0%
Health Insurance: 97.7% have insurance; 81.2% have private insurance; 37.4% have public insurance; 2.3% do not have insurance; 5.2% of children under 18 do not have insurance
Transportation: Commute: 94.4% car, 0.0% public transportation, 1.6% walk, 4.1% work from home; Mean travel time to work: 11.9 minutes

PARC (CDP). Covers a land area of 1.231 square miles and a water area of 0 square miles. Located at 44.66° N. Lat; 73.45° W. Long. Elevation is 180 feet.

Population: 250; Growth (since 2000): 363.0%; Density: 203.0 persons per square mile; Race: 72.4% White, 14.4% Black/African American, 3.2% Asian, 0.0% American Indian/Alaska Native, 0.0% Native Hawaiian/Other Pacific Islander, 3.6% Two or more races, 10.0% Hispanic of any race; Average household size: 1.58; Median age: 19.6; Age under 18: 2.4%; Age 65 and over: 0.0%; Males per 100 females: 91.0; Marriage status: 95.6% never married, 0.0% now married, 0.0% separated, 2.0% widowed, 2.4% divorced; Foreign born: 3.2%; Speak English only: 90.4%; With disability: 10.8%; Veterans: 0.0%; Ancestry: 22.8% Irish, 18.0% German, 12.4% Italian, 10.0% French, 5.6% Jamaican
Employment: 0.0% management, business, and financial, 0.0% computer, engineering, and science, 0.0% education, legal, community service, arts, and media, 8.6% healthcare practitioners, 23.5% service, 54.3% sales and office, 0.0% natural resources, construction, and maintenance, 13.6% production, transportation, and material moving
Income: Per capita: $7,805; Median household: $41,607; Average household: $42,816; Households with income of $100,000 or more: n/a; Poverty rate: n/a
Educational Attainment: High school diploma or higher: 80.6%; Bachelor's degree or higher: 22.6%; Graduate/professional degree or higher: 22.6%
Housing: Homeownership rate: 35.5%; Median home value: n/a; Median year structure built: 1968; Homeowner vacancy rate: 0.0%; Median selected monthly owner costs: n/a with a mortgage, n/a without a mortgage; Median gross rent: $1,058 per month; Rental vacancy rate: 0.0%
Health Insurance: 96.8% have insurance; 96.8% have private insurance; 9.2% have public insurance; 3.2% do not have insurance; 0.0% of children under 18 do not have insurance
Transportation: Commute: 81.8% car, 0.0% public transportation, 18.2% walk, 0.0% work from home; Mean travel time to work: 0.0 minutes

PERU (CDP). Covers a land area of 1.590 square miles and a water area of 0 square miles. Located at 44.58° N. Lat; 73.53° W. Long. Elevation is 335 feet.

Population: 1,526; Growth (since 2000): 0.8%; Density: 959.9 persons per square mile; Race: 99.0% White, 1.0% Black/African American, 0.0% Asian, 0.0% American Indian/Alaska Native, 0.0% Native Hawaiian/Other Pacific Islander, 0.0% Two or more races, 0.0% Hispanic of any race; Average household size: 2.08; Median age: 51.5; Age under 18: 14.2%; Age 65 and over: 28.6%; Males per 100 females: 96.9; Marriage status: 32.4% never married, 47.6% now married, 1.6% separated, 10.9% widowed, 9.1% divorced; Foreign born: 0.9%; Speak English only: 99.1%; With disability: 13.9%; Veterans: 15.5%; Ancestry: 18.8% French, 16.1% French Canadian, 11.7% Irish, 8.2% German, 7.5% Norwegian
Employment: 29.5% management, business, and financial, 6.8% computer, engineering, and science, 29.2% education, legal, community service, arts, and media, 0.0% healthcare practitioners, 15.8% service, 7.8% sales and office, 1.8% natural resources, construction, and maintenance, 9.2% production, transportation, and material moving
Income: Per capita: $34,702; Median household: $61,471; Average household: $75,758; Households with income of $100,000 or more: 30.0%; Poverty rate: 9.5%
Educational Attainment: High school diploma or higher: 95.7%; Bachelor's degree or higher: 31.5%; Graduate/professional degree or higher: 15.8%

School District(s)
Peru Central SD (KG-12)
    Enrollment: 1,925 . . . . (518) 643-6002
Housing: Homeownership rate: 80.2%; Median home value: $146,000; Median year structure built: 1965; Homeowner vacancy rate: 0.0%; Median selected monthly owner costs: $1,448 with a mortgage, $606 without a mortgage; Median gross rent: $701 per month; Rental vacancy rate: 32.3%
Health Insurance: 96.9% have insurance; 77.4% have private insurance; 37.0% have public insurance; 3.1% do not have insurance; 0.0% of children under 18 do not have insurance
Transportation: Commute: 89.3% car, 0.0% public transportation, 2.1% walk, 6.2% work from home; Mean travel time to work: 21.1 minutes

PERU (town). Covers a land area of 78.887 square miles and a water area of 13.492 square miles. Located at 44.58° N. Lat; 73.56° W. Long. Elevation is 335 feet.

Population: 6,975; Growth (since 2000): 9.5%; Density: 88.4 persons per square mile; Race: 98.3% White, 0.3% Black/African American, 0.0% Asian, 0.2% American Indian/Alaska Native, 0.0% Native Hawaiian/Other Pacific Islander, 1.0% Two or more races, 1.4% Hispanic of any race; Average household size: 2.61; Median age: 40.8; Age under 18: 23.1%; Age 65 and over: 15.9%; Males per 100 females: 100.5; Marriage status: 24.8% never married, 59.2% now married, 0.7% separated, 5.9% widowed, 10.1% divorced; Foreign born: 3.3%; Speak English only: 95.1%; With disability: 15.6%; Veterans: 10.9%; Ancestry: 22.7% French, 13.4% Irish, 10.5% Italian, 8.2% French Canadian, 6.9% German
Employment: 13.6% management, business, and financial, 4.5% computer, engineering, and science, 10.7% education, legal, community service, arts, and media, 5.2% healthcare practitioners, 20.5% service, 22.0% sales and office, 9.2% natural resources, construction, and maintenance, 14.2% production, transportation, and material moving
Income: Per capita: $30,196; Median household: $62,281; Average household: $78,311; Households with income of $100,000 or more: 21.3%; Poverty rate: 13.3%
Educational Attainment: High school diploma or higher: 87.2%; Bachelor's degree or higher: 25.4%; Graduate/professional degree or higher: 13.5%

School District(s)
Peru Central SD (KG-12)
    Enrollment: 1,925 . . . . (518) 643-6002
Housing: Homeownership rate: 76.2%; Median home value: $149,000; Median year structure built: 1982; Homeowner vacancy rate: 0.0%; Median selected monthly owner costs: $1,420 with a mortgage, $573 without a mortgage; Median gross rent: $925 per month; Rental vacancy rate: 9.3%
Health Insurance: 97.4% have insurance; 77.0% have private insurance; 33.9% have public insurance; 2.6% do not have insurance; 0.6% of children under 18 do not have insurance
Transportation: Commute: 93.0% car, 0.0% public transportation, 1.6% walk, 3.9% work from home; Mean travel time to work: 21.8 minutes

Additional Information Contacts
Town of Peru. . . . . (518) 643-2745
http://www.perutown.com

PLATTSBURGH (city). County seat. Covers a land area of 5.019 square miles and a water area of 1.556 square miles. Located at 44.69° N. Lat; 73.46° W. Long. Elevation is 138 feet.

History: Plattsburg was established at the mouth of the Saranac River, which began to provide water power for manufacturing in 1785. The first mills ground corn and cut lumber for the settlers.

Population: 19,734; Growth (since 2000): 4.9%; Density: 3,932.2 persons per square mile; Race: 87.3% White, 4.4% Black/African American, 3.1% Asian, 0.2% American Indian/Alaska Native, 0.0% Native Hawaiian/Other Pacific Islander, 3.0% Two or more races, 3.9% Hispanic of any race; Average household size: 2.12; Median age: 28.4; Age under 18: 14.2%; Age 65 and over: 14.8%; Males per 100 females: 89.1; Marriage status: 53.4% never married, 30.4% now married, 1.6% separated, 5.8% widowed, 10.4% divorced; Foreign born: 6.4%; Speak English only: 91.5%; With disability: 14.8%; Veterans: 7.5%; Ancestry: 18.8% Irish, 16.5% French, 13.5% German, 9.6% Italian, 9.0% English

Employment: 9.6% management, business, and financial, 2.4% computer, engineering, and science, 14.3% education, legal, community service, arts, and media, 5.3% healthcare practitioners, 24.7% service, 28.4% sales and office, 4.2% natural resources, construction, and maintenance, 11.1% production, transportation, and material moving

Income: Per capita: $23,341; Median household: $43,477; Average household: $56,613; Households with income of $100,000 or more: 16.1%; Poverty rate: 24.3%

Educational Attainment: High school diploma or higher: 88.8%; Bachelor's degree or higher: 31.3%; Graduate/professional degree or higher: 16.4%

School District(s)
Clinton-Essex-Warren-Washington Boces
  Enrollment: n/a . . . . (518) 561-0100
Plattsburgh City SD (PK-12)
  Enrollment: 1,847 . . . . (518) 957-6002
Four-year College(s)
SUNY College at Plattsburgh (Public)
  Enrollment: 5,719 . . . . (518) 564-2000
  Tuition: In-state $8,148; Out-of-state $17,798
Two-year College(s)
CVPH Medical Center School of Radiologic Technology (Private, Not-for-profit)
  Enrollment: 12. . . . . (518) 562-7510
Clinton Community College (Public)
  Enrollment: 1,547 . . . . (518) 562-4200
  Tuition: In-state $5,782; Out-of-state $11,038
Clinton Essex Warren Washington BOCES (Public)
  Enrollment: 70. . . . . (518) 561-0100

Housing: Homeownership rate: 37.4%; Median home value: $148,400; Median year structure built: 1961; Homeowner vacancy rate: 3.6%; Median selected monthly owner costs: $1,370 with a mortgage, $537 without a mortgage; Median gross rent: $778 per month; Rental vacancy rate: 2.3%

Health Insurance: 94.7% have insurance; 72.4% have private insurance; 38.1% have public insurance; 5.3% do not have insurance; 1.5% of children under 18 do not have insurance

Hospitals: Champlain Valley Physicians Hospital Medical Center (405 beds)

Safety: Violent crime rate: 15.7 per 10,000 population; Property crime rate: 179.8 per 10,000 population

Newspapers: Press Republican (daily circulation 20,000)

Transportation: Commute: 79.0% car, 2.1% public transportation, 10.4% walk, 2.4% work from home; Mean travel time to work: 14.1 minutes; Amtrak: Train service available.

Airports: Plattsburgh International (primary service/non-hub)

Additional Information Contacts
City of Plattsburgh. . . . . (518) 563-7702
http://www.cityofplattsburgh.com

PLATTSBURGH (town). Covers a land area of 45.920 square miles and a water area of 22.288 square miles. Located at 44.69° N. Lat; 73.52° W. Long. Elevation is 138 feet.

History: During the War of 1812 a makeshift American fleet under Thomas Macdonough defeated the British in a pitched battle on Lake Champlain near Plattsburgh, compelling an accompanying land-invasion force under

Sir George Prevost to return to Canada. Seat of the State University of N.Y. College at Plattsburgh. Settled 1767, Incorporated 1902.

Population: 11,860; Growth (since 2000): 6.0%; Density: 258.3 persons per square mile; Race: 94.8% White, 2.3% Black/African American, 1.3% Asian, 0.2% American Indian/Alaska Native, 0.1% Native Hawaiian/Other Pacific Islander, 0.6% Two or more races, 1.7% Hispanic of any race; Average household size: 2.36; Median age: 44.3; Age under 18: 19.5%; Age 65 and over: 18.0%; Males per 100 females: 98.6; Marriage status: 26.0% never married, 55.7% now married, 2.7% separated, 6.1% widowed, 12.1% divorced; Foreign born: 4.6%; Speak English only: 95.3%; With disability: 14.4%; Veterans: 10.4%; Ancestry: 21.4% French, 17.4% Irish, 10.9% English, 8.8% French Canadian, 7.1% German

Employment: 12.0% management, business, and financial, 3.5% computer, engineering, and science, 11.3% education, legal, community service, arts, and media, 8.1% healthcare practitioners, 18.2% service, 24.3% sales and office, 8.5% natural resources, construction, and maintenance, 14.0% production, transportation, and material moving

Income: Per capita: $28,909; Median household: $56,417; Average household: $71,208; Households with income of $100,000 or more: 20.6%; Poverty rate: 10.7%

Educational Attainment: High school diploma or higher: 87.7%; Bachelor's degree or higher: 26.8%; Graduate/professional degree or higher: 13.6%

School District(s)
Clinton-Essex-Warren-Washington Boces
  Enrollment: n/a . . . . (518) 561-0100
Plattsburgh City SD (PK-12)
  Enrollment: 1,847 . . . . (518) 957-6002
Four-year College(s)
SUNY College at Plattsburgh (Public)
  Enrollment: 5,719 . . . . (518) 564-2000
  Tuition: In-state $8,148; Out-of-state $17,798
Two-year College(s)
CVPH Medical Center School of Radiologic Technology (Private, Not-for-profit)
  Enrollment: 12. . . . . (518) 562-7510
Clinton Community College (Public)
  Enrollment: 1,547 . . . . (518) 562-4200
  Tuition: In-state $5,782; Out-of-state $11,038
Clinton Essex Warren Washington BOCES (Public)
  Enrollment: 70. . . . . (518) 561-0100

Housing: Homeownership rate: 77.5%; Median home value: $138,700; Median year structure built: 1979; Homeowner vacancy rate: 2.7%; Median selected monthly owner costs: $1,298 with a mortgage, $470 without a mortgage; Median gross rent: $742 per month; Rental vacancy rate: 5.2%

Health Insurance: 93.8% have insurance; 73.9% have private insurance; 37.7% have public insurance; 6.2% do not have insurance; 2.4% of children under 18 do not have insurance

Hospitals: Champlain Valley Physicians Hospital Medical Center (405 beds)

Newspapers: Press Republican (daily circulation 20,000)

Transportation: Commute: 94.3% car, 0.6% public transportation, 1.7% walk, 2.4% work from home; Mean travel time to work: 17.8 minutes; Amtrak: Train service available.

Airports: Plattsburgh International (primary service/non-hub)

Additional Information Contacts
Town of Plattsburgh . . . . (518) 562-6800
http://townofplattsburgh.com

PLATTSBURGH WEST (CDP). Covers a land area of 1.774 square miles and a water area of 0.055 square miles. Located at 44.68° N. Lat; 73.50° W. Long.

Population: 1,428; Growth (since 2000): 10.8%; Density: 805.1 persons per square mile; Race: 98.0% White, 1.1% Black/African American, 0.0% Asian, 0.3% American Indian/Alaska Native, 0.0% Native Hawaiian/Other Pacific Islander, 0.4% Two or more races, 0.5% Hispanic of any race; Average household size: 2.42; Median age: 40.5; Age under 18: 24.2%; Age 65 and over: 12.6%; Males per 100 females: 92.7; Marriage status: 32.7% never married, 49.8% now married, 2.5% separated, 6.5% widowed, 11.0% divorced; Foreign born: 1.3%; Speak English only: 98.0%; With disability: 16.2%; Veterans: 8.9%; Ancestry: 23.5% French, 17.2% Irish, 6.7% French Canadian, 6.4% Dutch, 6.1% American

Employment: 4.9% management, business, and financial, 0.9% computer, engineering, and science, 2.6% education, legal, community service, arts, and media, 5.9% healthcare practitioners, 23.9% service, 31.5% sales and

office, 15.8% natural resources, construction, and maintenance, 14.5% production, transportation, and material moving

Income: Per capita: $20,496; Median household: $40,000; Average household: $49,820; Households with income of $100,000 or more: 8.7%; Poverty rate: 20.7%

Educational Attainment: High school diploma or higher: 79.6%; Bachelor's degree or higher: 8.7%; Graduate/professional degree or higher: 3.4%

Housing: Homeownership rate: 78.8%; Median home value: $77,200; Median year structure built: 1991; Homeowner vacancy rate: 2.5%; Median selected monthly owner costs: $1,093 with a mortgage, $466 without a mortgage; Median gross rent: $688 per month; Rental vacancy rate: 0.0%

Health Insurance: 80.7% have insurance; 48.4% have private insurance; 42.1% have public insurance; 19.3% do not have insurance; 14.5% of children under 18 do not have insurance

Transportation: Commute: 90.6% car, 0.0% public transportation, 6.0% walk, 0.0% work from home; Mean travel time to work: 13.9 minutes

REDFORD (CDP). Covers a land area of 1.347 square miles and a water area of 0.108 square miles. Located at 44.61° N. Lat; 73.81° W. Long. Elevation is 1,171 feet.

Population: 426; Growth (since 2000): -16.8%; Density: 316.3 persons per square mile; Race: 94.8% White, 0.0% Black/African American, 0.0% Asian, 0.0% American Indian/Alaska Native, 0.0% Native Hawaiian/Other Pacific Islander, 0.0% Two or more races, 5.2% Hispanic of any race; Average household size: 2.60; Median age: 33.4; Age under 18: 34.3%; Age 65 and over: 24.4%; Males per 100 females: 107.4; Marriage status: 23.6% never married, 69.6% now married, 17.2% separated, 0.0% widowed, 6.8% divorced; Foreign born: 0.0%; Speak English only: 88.3%; With disability: 28.2%; Veterans: 4.6%; Ancestry: 44.4% French Canadian, 10.8% French, 10.8% German, 9.4% American, 6.8% Russian

Employment: 0.0% management, business, and financial, 11.0% computer, engineering, and science, 10.3% education, legal, community service, arts, and media, 0.0% healthcare practitioners, 30.1% service, 33.1% sales and office, 0.0% natural resources, construction, and maintenance, 15.4% production, transportation, and material moving

Income: Per capita: $17,326; Median household: n/a; Average household: $43,135; Households with income of $100,000 or more: 8.5%; Poverty rate: 54.2%

Educational Attainment: High school diploma or higher: 94.2%; Bachelor's degree or higher: 21.3%; Graduate/professional degree or higher: 12.1%

Housing: Homeownership rate: 48.2%; Median home value: $131,000; Median year structure built: 1975; Homeowner vacancy rate: 0.0%; Median selected monthly owner costs: $1,140 with a mortgage, n/a without a mortgage; Median gross rent: n/a per month; Rental vacancy rate: 0.0%

Health Insurance: 93.4% have insurance; 39.4% have private insurance; 75.4% have public insurance; 6.6% do not have insurance; 0.0% of children under 18 do not have insurance

Transportation: Commute: 100.0% car, 0.0% public transportation, 0.0% walk, 0.0% work from home; Mean travel time to work: 0.0 minutes

ROUSES POINT (village). Covers a land area of 1.761 square miles and a water area of 0.726 square miles. Located at 44.99° N. Lat; 73.36° W. Long. Elevation is 112 feet.

History: Incorporated 1877.

Population: 2,106; Growth (since 2000): -7.5%; Density: 1,196.0 persons per square mile; Race: 97.3% White, 0.7% Black/African American, 1.0% Asian, 0.0% American Indian/Alaska Native, 0.1% Native Hawaiian/Other Pacific Islander, 0.8% Two or more races, 0.8% Hispanic of any race; Average household size: 2.18; Median age: 42.6; Age under 18: 20.0%; Age 65 and over: 18.4%; Males per 100 females: 92.3; Marriage status: 33.0% never married, 50.1% now married, 2.4% separated, 9.1% widowed, 7.8% divorced; Foreign born: 9.8%; Speak English only: 89.2%; With disability: 13.6%; Veterans: 10.4%; Ancestry: 16.4% French, 15.9% French Canadian, 10.3% Irish, 8.2% American, 7.6% English

Employment: 15.3% management, business, and financial, 2.9% computer, engineering, and science, 9.3% education, legal, community service, arts, and media, 3.1% healthcare practitioners, 19.9% service, 22.5% sales and office, 10.6% natural resources, construction, and maintenance, 16.3% production, transportation, and material moving

Income: Per capita: $31,032; Median household: $56,779; Average household: $67,916; Households with income of $100,000 or more: 19.0%; Poverty rate: 13.8%

Educational Attainment: High school diploma or higher: 89.9%; Bachelor's degree or higher: 20.6%; Graduate/professional degree or higher: 8.6%

School District(s)

Northeastern Clinton Central SD (PK-12)

    Enrollment: 1,382 . . . . (518) 298-8242

Housing: Homeownership rate: 56.8%; Median home value: $149,300; Median year structure built: 1968; Homeowner vacancy rate: 3.0%; Median selected monthly owner costs: $1,286 with a mortgage, $500 without a mortgage; Median gross rent: $594 per month; Rental vacancy rate: 6.3%

Health Insurance: 94.9% have insurance; 71.9% have private insurance; 38.0% have public insurance; 5.1% do not have insurance; 2.0% of children under 18 do not have insurance

Transportation: Commute: 91.9% car, 0.0% public transportation, 3.9% walk, 3.7% work from home; Mean travel time to work: 21.5 minutes; Amtrak: Train service available.

SARANAC (town). Covers a land area of 115.286 square miles and a water area of 0.661 square miles. Located at 44.65° N. Lat; 73.81° W. Long. Elevation is 797 feet.

History: Saranac is a town in Clinton County, New York, and was first settled around 1802. The town of Saranac was established from the western part of the town of Plattsburgh in 1824, when the iron industry was important to its economy.

Population: 3,961; Growth (since 2000): -4.9%; Density: 34.4 persons per square mile; Race: 92.6% White, 5.5% Black/African American, 0.8% Asian, 0.3% American Indian/Alaska Native, 0.0% Native Hawaiian/Other Pacific Islander, 0.3% Two or more races, 1.9% Hispanic of any race; Average household size: 2.49; Median age: 37.0; Age under 18: 24.9%; Age 65 and over: 14.5%; Males per 100 females: 100.5; Marriage status: 22.2% never married, 61.1% now married, 1.9% separated, 6.9% widowed, 9.7% divorced; Foreign born: 3.3%; Speak English only: 98.4%; With disability: 12.7%; Veterans: 7.7%; Ancestry: 21.4% French, 12.0% Irish, 9.3% American, 8.8% French Canadian, 6.3% English

Employment: 6.7% management, business, and financial, 1.9% computer, engineering, and science, 17.1% education, legal, community service, arts, and media, 9.4% healthcare practitioners, 24.5% service, 19.9% sales and office, 9.1% natural resources, construction, and maintenance, 11.4% production, transportation, and material moving

Income: Per capita: $27,038; Median household: $61,596; Average household: $66,940; Households with income of $100,000 or more: 26.8%; Poverty rate: 13.8%

Educational Attainment: High school diploma or higher: 93.0%; Bachelor's degree or higher: 23.1%; Graduate/professional degree or higher: 7.9%

School District(s)

Saranac Central SD (KG-12)

    Enrollment: 1,459 . . . . (518) 565-5600

Housing: Homeownership rate: 83.0%; Median home value: $119,100; Median year structure built: 1971; Homeowner vacancy rate: 4.1%; Median selected monthly owner costs: $1,237 with a mortgage, $522 without a mortgage; Median gross rent: $756 per month; Rental vacancy rate: 0.0%

Health Insurance: 95.7% have insurance; 70.5% have private insurance; 38.1% have public insurance; 4.3% do not have insurance; 0.0% of children under 18 do not have insurance

Transportation: Commute: 97.6% car, 0.0% public transportation, 0.7% walk, 1.7% work from home; Mean travel time to work: 28.4 minutes

Additional Information Contacts

Town of Saranac . . . . (518) 293-6666

    http://www.townofsaranac.com

SCHUYLER FALLS (town). Covers a land area of 36.517 square miles and a water area of 0.302 square miles. Located at 44.66° N. Lat; 73.58° W. Long. Elevation is 430 feet.

Population: 5,150; Growth (since 2000): 0.4%; Density: 141.0 persons per square mile; Race: 95.3% White, 0.3% Black/African American, 2.4% Asian, 0.6% American Indian/Alaska Native, 0.0% Native Hawaiian/Other Pacific Islander, 1.2% Two or more races, 1.2% Hispanic of any race; Average household size: 2.42; Median age: 41.7; Age under 18: 19.3%; Age 65 and over: 15.5%; Males per 100 females: 99.7; Marriage status: 25.5% never married, 57.3% now married, 1.9% separated, 7.6% widowed, 9.6% divorced; Foreign born: 3.6%; Speak English only: 95.6%; With disability: 15.0%; Veterans: 8.9%; Ancestry: 21.4% French, 16.8% Irish, 14.9% American, 8.9% German, 8.2% English

Employment: 10.2% management, business, and financial, 4.7% computer, engineering, and science, 11.0% education, legal, community service, arts, and media, 9.8% healthcare practitioners, 22.4% service, 19.7% sales and office, 8.5% natural resources, construction, and maintenance, 13.7% production, transportation, and material moving
Income: Per capita: $29,797; Median household: $65,319; Average household: $72,080; Households with income of $100,000 or more: 24.4%; Poverty rate: 9.0%
Educational Attainment: High school diploma or higher: 88.4%; Bachelor's degree or higher: 22.2%; Graduate/professional degree or higher: 10.1%
Housing: Homeownership rate: 83.9%; Median home value: $137,800; Median year structure built: 1979; Homeowner vacancy rate: 0.0%; Median selected monthly owner costs: $1,250 with a mortgage, $485 without a mortgage; Median gross rent: $753 per month; Rental vacancy rate: 0.0%
Health Insurance: 97.8% have insurance; 81.1% have private insurance; 32.7% have public insurance; 2.2% do not have insurance; 1.5% of children under 18 do not have insurance
Transportation: Commute: 92.3% car, 0.0% public transportation, 1.7% walk, 1.6% work from home; Mean travel time to work: 17.8 minutes
Additional Information Contacts
Town of Schuyler Falls . . . . (518) 563-1129
  http://www.schuylerfallsny.com

WEST CHAZY (CDP). Covers a land area of 1.877 square miles and a water area of 0 square miles. Located at 44.82° N. Lat; 73.51° W. Long. Elevation is 302 feet.
Population: 556; Growth (since 2000): n/a; Density: 296.2 persons per square mile; Race: 99.1% White, 0.0% Black/African American, 0.0% Asian, 0.0% American Indian/Alaska Native, 0.0% Native Hawaiian/Other Pacific Islander, 0.9% Two or more races, 0.0% Hispanic of any race; Average household size: 2.02; Median age: 44.3; Age under 18: 14.6%; Age 65 and over: 20.0%; Males per 100 females: 101.9; Marriage status: 38.7% never married, 51.8% now married, 0.8% separated, 4.0% widowed, 5.6% divorced; Foreign born: 6.7%; Speak English only: 100.0%; With disability: 8.1%; Veterans: 17.3%; Ancestry: 25.4% Irish, 19.4% German, 12.2% English, 8.3% French Canadian, 8.1% French
Employment: 0.0% management, business, and financial, 0.0% computer, engineering, and science, 5.5% education, legal, community service, arts, and media, 14.1% healthcare practitioners, 13.5% service, 30.5% sales and office, 17.0% natural resources, construction, and maintenance, 19.3% production, transportation, and material moving
Income: Per capita: $24,337; Median household: $36,975; Average household: $50,647; Households with income of $100,000 or more: 8.4%; Poverty rate: 11.9%
Educational Attainment: High school diploma or higher: 90.7%; Bachelor's degree or higher: 16.7%; Graduate/professional degree or higher: 4.4%

School District(s)
Beekmantown Central SD (PK-12)
  Enrollment: 1,921 . . . . (518) 324-2999
Housing: Homeownership rate: 60.7%; Median home value: $111,900; Median year structure built: Before 1940; Homeowner vacancy rate: 0.0%; Median selected monthly owner costs: $983 with a mortgage, $293 without a mortgage; Median gross rent: $783 per month; Rental vacancy rate: 0.0%
Health Insurance: 91.4% have insurance; 69.2% have private insurance; 37.2% have public insurance; 8.6% do not have insurance; 0.0% of children under 18 do not have insurance
Transportation: Commute: 95.4% car, 0.0% public transportation, 0.0% walk, 2.3% work from home; Mean travel time to work: 18.7 minutes

Columbia County

Located in southeastern New York; bounded on the east by Massachusetts, and on the west by the Hudson River. Covers a land area of 634.705 square miles, a water area of 13.560 square miles, and is located in the Eastern Time Zone at 42.25° N. Lat., 73.63° W. Long. The county was founded in 1786. County seat is Hudson.

Columbia County is part of the Hudson, NY Micropolitan Statistical Area. The entire metro area includes: Columbia County, NY

Weather Station: Hudson Correctionl Fac | | | | | | | | | | Elevation: 60 feet

	Jan	Feb	Mar	Apr	May	Jun	Jul	Aug	Sep	Oct	Nov	Dec
High	34	38	48	62	73	81	84	82	74	63	51	39
Low	16	19	27	37	47	57	61	60	53	41	33	23
Precip	2.6	2.3	3.4	3.7	3.8	4.3	3.9	3.8	4.0	4.0	3.2	3.0
Snow	11.0	7.4	4.8	1.1	0.0	0.0	0.0	0.0	0.0	0.1	1.0	6.2

High and Low temperatures in degrees Fahrenheit; Precipitation and Snow in inches

Weather Station: Valatie 1 N | | | | | | | | | | Elevation: 299 feet

	Jan	Feb	Mar	Apr	May	Jun	Jul	Aug	Sep	Oct	Nov	Dec
High	32	36	44	58	69	78	82	81	73	61	49	37
Low	13	16	24	35	46	55	59	58	50	38	31	19
Precip	2.1	1.9	2.8	3.7	4.1	4.5	4.1	4.1	4.0	3.9	3.3	2.6
Snow	10.8	8.2	6.4	2.2	0.0	0.0	0.0	0.0	0.0	0.3	2.4	11.1

High and Low temperatures in degrees Fahrenheit; Precipitation and Snow in inches

Population: 61,481; Growth (since 2000): -2.6%; Density: 96.9 persons per square mile; Race: 89.6% White, 4.5% Black/African American, 1.7% Asian, 0.0% American Indian/Alaska Native, 0.0% Native Hawaiian/Other Pacific Islander, 2.8% two or more races, 4.5% Hispanic of any race; Average household size: 2.32; Median age: 47.4; Age under 18: 18.3%; Age 65 and over: 21.6%; Males per 100 females: 101.4; Marriage status: 30.4% never married, 51.1% now married, 2.2% separated, 6.6% widowed, 11.9% divorced; Foreign born: 6.8%; Speak English only: 93.2%; With disability: 16.3%; Veterans: 8.4%; Ancestry: 21.8% Irish, 21.4% German, 16.3% Italian, 9.3% English, 6.8% Polish
Religion: Six largest groups: 24.4% Catholicism, 3.5% Methodist/Pietist, 3.1% Lutheran, 3.0% Presbyterian-Reformed, 1.3% Episcopalianism/Anglicanism, 1.2% Non-denominational Protestant
Economy: Unemployment rate: 2.8%; Leading industries: 15.8 % retail trade; 14.5 % construction; 10.4 % accommodation and food services; Farms: 494 totaling 95,378 acres; Company size: 1 employs 1,000 or more persons, 0 employ 500 to 999 persons, 18 employ 100 to 499 persons, 1,764 employ less than 100 persons; Business ownership: 2,155 women-owned, 139 Black-owned, 125 Hispanic-owned, 190 Asian-owned, n/a American Indian/Alaska Native-owned
Employment: 16.3% management, business, and financial, 3.1% computer, engineering, and science, 13.3% education, legal, community service, arts, and media, 5.7% healthcare practitioners, 21.0% service, 19.9% sales and office, 10.9% natural resources, construction, and maintenance, 9.8% production, transportation, and material moving
Income: Per capita: $34,737; Median household: $61,093; Average household: $82,281; Households with income of $100,000 or more: 26.1%; Poverty rate: 11.4%
Educational Attainment: High school diploma or higher: 89.4%; Bachelor's degree or higher: 30.1%; Graduate/professional degree or higher: 14.6%
Housing: Homeownership rate: 72.4%; Median home value: $224,600; Median year structure built: 1966; Homeowner vacancy rate: 3.1%; Median selected monthly owner costs: $1,675 with a mortgage, $654 without a mortgage; Median gross rent: $886 per month; Rental vacancy rate: 5.2%
Vital Statistics: Birth rate: 83.3 per 10,000 population; Death rate: 107.7 per 10,000 population; Age-adjusted cancer mortality rate: 165.2 deaths per 100,000 population
Health Insurance: 94.8% have insurance; 72.9% have private insurance; 38.6% have public insurance; 5.2% do not have insurance; 2.1% of children under 18 do not have insurance
Health Care: Physicians: 18.0 per 10,000 population; Dentists: 4.1 per 10,000 population; Hospital beds: 31.5 per 10,000 population; Hospital admissions: 901.5 per 10,000 population
Transportation: Commute: 85.7% car, 2.6% public transportation, 4.0% walk, 6.3% work from home; Mean travel time to work: 25.8 minutes
2016 Presidential Election: 44.5% Trump, 49.5% Clinton, 3.1% Johnson, 1.9% Stein
National and State Parks: Beebe Hill State Forest; Clermont State Historic Site; Clermont State Park; Lake Taghkanic State Park; Martin Van Buren National Historic Site; Taconic State Park
Additional Information Contacts
Columbia Government . . . . (518) 828-3339
  http://www.columbiacountyny.com

Columbia County Communities

ANCRAM (town). Covers a land area of 42.478 square miles and a water area of 0.259 square miles. Located at 42.04° N. Lat; 73.58° W. Long. Elevation is 518 feet.
Population: 1,330; Growth (since 2000): -12.1%; Density: 31.3 persons per square mile; Race: 90.5% White, 3.1% Black/African American, 2.9% Asian, 0.0% American Indian/Alaska Native, 0.0% Native Hawaiian/Other Pacific Islander, 3.2% Two or more races, 3.2% Hispanic of any race; Average household size: 2.26; Median age: 54.4; Age under 18: 13.9%; Age 65 and over: 25.0%; Males per 100 females: 105.9; Marriage status: 24.9% never married, 59.4% now married, 2.0% separated, 3.1% widowed, 12.6% divorced; Foreign born: 7.4%; Speak English only: 95.2%; With disability: 13.5%; Veterans: 9.6%; Ancestry: 30.4% Irish, 19.7% German, 11.1% English, 7.1% Italian, 5.4% American
Employment: 12.1% management, business, and financial, 4.8% computer, engineering, and science, 9.7% education, legal, community service, arts, and media, 4.3% healthcare practitioners, 17.3% service, 18.9% sales and office, 17.8% natural resources, construction, and maintenance, 15.2% production, transportation, and material moving
Income: Per capita: $49,779; Median household: $67,031; Average household: $117,799; Households with income of $100,000 or more: 32.7%; Poverty rate: 13.8%
Educational Attainment: High school diploma or higher: 86.0%; Bachelor's degree or higher: 31.1%; Graduate/professional degree or higher: 18.4%
Housing: Homeownership rate: 73.6%; Median home value: $275,000; Median year structure built: 1970; Homeowner vacancy rate: 1.8%; Median selected monthly owner costs: $1,859 with a mortgage, $768 without a mortgage; Median gross rent: $1,328 per month; Rental vacancy rate: 5.7%
Health Insurance: 91.8% have insurance; 74.4% have private insurance; 36.5% have public insurance; 8.2% do not have insurance; 2.1% of children under 18 do not have insurance
Transportation: Commute: 80.9% car, 5.5% public transportation, 3.3% walk, 8.2% work from home; Mean travel time to work: 36.3 minutes

ANCRAMDALE (unincorporated postal area)
ZCTA: 12503
Covers a land area of 21.030 square miles and a water area of 0.158 square miles. Located at 42.04° N. Lat; 73.58° W. Long. Elevation is 548 feet.
Population: 587; Growth (since 2000): -29.3%; Density: 27.9 persons per square mile; Race: 96.4% White, 1.7% Black/African American, 0.5% Asian, 0.0% American Indian/Alaska Native, 0.0% Native Hawaiian/Other Pacific Islander, 0.5% Two or more races, 4.3% Hispanic of any race; Average household size: 2.15; Median age: 55.7; Age under 18: 11.1%; Age 65 and over: 27.4%; Males per 100 females: 107.2; Marriage status: 30.4% never married, 48.0% now married, 1.5% separated, 3.2% widowed, 18.3% divorced; Foreign born: 8.7%; Speak English only: 91.4%; With disability: 14.7%; Veterans: 13.2%; Ancestry: 23.7% Irish, 19.1% German, 10.7% English, 6.0% Italian, 5.6% French
Employment: 14.7% management, business, and financial, 8.6% computer, engineering, and science, 9.3% education, legal, community service, arts, and media, 4.5% healthcare practitioners, 16.6% service, 18.2% sales and office, 20.8% natural resources, construction, and maintenance, 7.3% production, transportation, and material moving
Income: Per capita: $60,466; Median household: $65,104; Average household: $133,360; Households with income of $100,000 or more: 34.7%; Poverty rate: 8.9%
Educational Attainment: High school diploma or higher: 85.0%; Bachelor's degree or higher: 36.8%; Graduate/professional degree or higher: 23.3%
Housing: Homeownership rate: 71.7%; Median home value: $285,700; Median year structure built: 1972; Homeowner vacancy rate: 4.0%; Median selected monthly owner costs: $2,393 with a mortgage, $713 without a mortgage; Median gross rent: $1,339 per month; Rental vacancy rate: 0.0%
Health Insurance: 91.7% have insurance; 73.9% have private insurance; 38.7% have public insurance; 8.3% do not have insurance; 0.0% of children under 18 do not have insurance
Transportation: Commute: 82.6% car, 8.0% public transportation, 2.7% walk, 6.7% work from home; Mean travel time to work: 40.6 minutes

AUSTERLITZ (town). Covers a land area of 48.722 square miles and a water area of 0.092 square miles. Located at 42.32° N. Lat; 73.52° W. Long. Elevation is 1,129 feet.
Population: 1,490; Growth (since 2000): 2.5%; Density: 30.6 persons per square mile; Race: 94.6% White, 1.7% Black/African American, 2.0% Asian, 0.0% American Indian/Alaska Native, 0.0% Native Hawaiian/Other Pacific Islander, 0.3% Two or more races, 1.5% Hispanic of any race; Average household size: 2.24; Median age: 52.6; Age under 18: 18.5%; Age 65 and over: 28.0%; Males per 100 females: 102.4; Marriage status: 24.5% never married, 57.5% now married, 1.6% separated, 4.1% widowed, 13.9% divorced; Foreign born: 5.1%; Speak English only: 95.8%; With disability: 8.5%; Veterans: 8.7%; Ancestry: 23.7% Irish, 19.6% German, 13.9% English, 13.2% Italian, 7.9% Russian
Employment: 17.1% management, business, and financial, 2.6% computer, engineering, and science, 19.2% education, legal, community service, arts, and media, 7.4% healthcare practitioners, 19.4% service, 16.6% sales and office, 13.6% natural resources, construction, and maintenance, 4.0% production, transportation, and material moving
Income: Per capita: $43,728; Median household: $70,125; Average household: $95,355; Households with income of $100,000 or more: 36.1%; Poverty rate: 14.9%
Educational Attainment: High school diploma or higher: 96.8%; Bachelor's degree or higher: 50.8%; Graduate/professional degree or higher: 32.4%
Housing: Homeownership rate: 80.6%; Median home value: $288,900; Median year structure built: 1976; Homeowner vacancy rate: 3.8%; Median selected monthly owner costs: $1,910 with a mortgage, $676 without a mortgage; Median gross rent: $960 per month; Rental vacancy rate: 7.2%
Health Insurance: 96.4% have insurance; 77.7% have private insurance; 45.6% have public insurance; 3.6% do not have insurance; 6.4% of children under 18 do not have insurance
Transportation: Commute: 80.7% car, 5.4% public transportation, 3.1% walk, 10.8% work from home; Mean travel time to work: 26.9 minutes

CANAAN (town). Covers a land area of 36.676 square miles and a water area of 0.280 square miles. Located at 42.41° N. Lat; 73.46° W. Long. Elevation is 850 feet.
Population: 1,751; Growth (since 2000): -3.8%; Density: 47.7 persons per square mile; Race: 94.1% White, 1.5% Black/African American, 1.0% Asian, 0.2% American Indian/Alaska Native, 0.0% Native Hawaiian/Other Pacific Islander, 2.6% Two or more races, 3.4% Hispanic of any race; Average household size: 2.35; Median age: 48.3; Age under 18: 21.1%; Age 65 and over: 23.6%; Males per 100 females: 110.9; Marriage status: 33.6% never married, 52.2% now married, 1.7% separated, 5.5% widowed, 8.8% divorced; Foreign born: 2.9%; Speak English only: 96.1%; With disability: 13.9%; Veterans: 7.5%; Ancestry: 22.4% German, 19.4% Irish, 11.5% English, 10.3% Italian, 8.3% Polish
Employment: 16.2% management, business, and financial, 5.6% computer, engineering, and science, 15.3% education, legal, community service, arts, and media, 5.7% healthcare practitioners, 21.4% service, 16.7% sales and office, 15.2% natural resources, construction, and maintenance, 3.8% production, transportation, and material moving
Income: Per capita: $39,486; Median household: $76,667; Average household: $102,541; Households with income of $100,000 or more: 33.3%; Poverty rate: 10.8%
Educational Attainment: High school diploma or higher: 91.2%; Bachelor's degree or higher: 42.0%; Graduate/professional degree or higher: 24.6%

School District(s)
Berkshire Union Free SD (07-12)
    Enrollment: 41 . . . . (518) 781-3500
Housing: Homeownership rate: 85.3%; Median home value: $308,000; Median year structure built: 1969; Homeowner vacancy rate: 7.8%; Median selected monthly owner costs: $1,981 with a mortgage, $729 without a mortgage; Median gross rent: $1,173 per month; Rental vacancy rate: 0.0%
Health Insurance: 92.1% have insurance; 73.4% have private insurance; 36.9% have public insurance; 7.9% do not have insurance; 6.7% of children under 18 do not have insurance
Transportation: Commute: 82.0% car, 2.9% public transportation, 3.2% walk, 11.1% work from home; Mean travel time to work: 27.9 minutes

CHATHAM (town).
Covers a land area of 53.227 square miles and a water area of 0.316 square miles. Located at 42.43° N. Lat; 73.58° W. Long. Elevation is 463 feet.

History: Incorporated 1869.

Population: 3,978; Growth (since 2000): -6.4%; Density: 74.7 persons per square mile; Race: 87.1% White, 4.7% Black/African American, 0.5% Asian, 0.1% American Indian/Alaska Native, 0.0% Native Hawaiian/Other Pacific Islander, 5.5% Two or more races, 5.1% Hispanic of any race; Average household size: 2.29; Median age: 47.7; Age under 18: 19.6%; Age 65 and over: 24.0%; Males per 100 females: 99.7; Marriage status: 26.4% never married, 59.3% now married, 1.6% separated, 5.2% widowed, 9.2% divorced; Foreign born: 5.0%; Speak English only: 94.8%; With disability: 15.4%; Veterans: 6.5%; Ancestry: 27.7% German, 20.4% Irish, 16.2% Italian, 11.0% English, 7.7% French

Employment: 18.2% management, business, and financial, 3.8% computer, engineering, and science, 17.3% education, legal, community service, arts, and media, 6.8% healthcare practitioners, 15.9% service, 16.8% sales and office, 10.3% natural resources, construction, and maintenance, 10.8% production, transportation, and material moving

Income: Per capita: $42,480; Median household: $71,673; Average household: $97,841; Households with income of $100,000 or more: 30.8%; Poverty rate: 6.5%

Educational Attainment: High school diploma or higher: 94.7%; Bachelor's degree or higher: 39.8%; Graduate/professional degree or higher: 21.9%

School District(s)
Chatham Central SD (PK-12)
    Enrollment: 1,059 . . . . (518) 392-1501

Housing: Homeownership rate: 74.9%; Median home value: $262,900; Median year structure built: 1947; Homeowner vacancy rate: 7.2%; Median selected monthly owner costs: $1,677 with a mortgage, $758 without a mortgage; Median gross rent: $971 per month; Rental vacancy rate: 2.4%

Health Insurance: 93.9% have insurance; 75.1% have private insurance; 38.9% have public insurance; 6.1% do not have insurance; 2.6% of children under 18 do not have insurance

Transportation: Commute: 80.6% car, 3.0% public transportation, 2.9% walk, 12.3% work from home; Mean travel time to work: 27.3 minutes

Additional Information Contacts
Town of Chatham . . . . (518) 392-1655
    http://chathamnewyork.us

CHATHAM (village).
Covers a land area of 1.237 square miles and a water area of 0.004 square miles. Located at 42.36° N. Lat; 73.60° W. Long. Elevation is 463 feet.

Population: 1,531; Growth (since 2000): -12.9%; Density: 1,237.8 persons per square mile; Race: 92.5% White, 3.6% Black/African American, 1.1% Asian, 0.0% American Indian/Alaska Native, 0.0% Native Hawaiian/Other Pacific Islander, 0.9% Two or more races, 3.0% Hispanic of any race; Average household size: 2.20; Median age: 44.8; Age under 18: 14.0%; Age 65 and over: 19.9%; Males per 100 females: 96.4; Marriage status: 36.1% never married, 44.8% now married, 2.8% separated, 6.6% widowed, 12.5% divorced; Foreign born: 4.1%; Speak English only: 93.9%; With disability: 12.3%; Veterans: 6.2%; Ancestry: 26.6% Irish, 24.9% Italian, 20.5% German, 7.8% English, 6.5% French

Employment: 10.1% management, business, and financial, 1.1% computer, engineering, and science, 18.4% education, legal, community service, arts, and media, 5.2% healthcare practitioners, 14.4% service, 15.9% sales and office, 20.1% natural resources, construction, and maintenance, 14.8% production, transportation, and material moving

Income: Per capita: $29,976; Median household: $50,682; Average household: $66,005; Households with income of $100,000 or more: 23.5%; Poverty rate: 9.8%

Educational Attainment: High school diploma or higher: 90.3%; Bachelor's degree or higher: 30.4%; Graduate/professional degree or higher: 16.4%

School District(s)
Chatham Central SD (PK-12)
    Enrollment: 1,059 . . . . (518) 392-1501

Housing: Homeownership rate: 52.5%; Median home value: $214,000; Median year structure built: Before 1940; Homeowner vacancy rate: 8.0%; Median selected monthly owner costs: $1,643 with a mortgage, $873 without a mortgage; Median gross rent: $816 per month; Rental vacancy rate: 18.8%

Health Insurance: 96.6% have insurance; 81.7% have private insurance; 30.4% have public insurance; 3.4% do not have insurance; 0.0% of children under 18 do not have insurance

Safety: Violent crime rate: 0.0 per 10,000 population; Property crime rate: 18.2 per 10,000 population

Transportation: Commute: 87.5% car, 1.2% public transportation, 6.7% walk, 4.6% work from home; Mean travel time to work: 27.0 minutes

CLAVERACK (town).
Covers a land area of 47.559 square miles and a water area of 0.390 square miles. Located at 42.22° N. Lat; 73.69° W. Long. Elevation is 203 feet.

History: Fine old buildings include Van Rensselaer manor house; former county courthouse (built 1786).

Population: 5,824; Growth (since 2000): -9.0%; Density: 122.5 persons per square mile; Race: 96.2% White, 1.9% Black/African American, 0.4% Asian, 0.0% American Indian/Alaska Native, 0.0% Native Hawaiian/Other Pacific Islander, 1.2% Two or more races, 1.3% Hispanic of any race; Average household size: 2.05; Median age: 50.6; Age under 18: 17.6%; Age 65 and over: 24.8%; Males per 100 females: 99.0; Marriage status: 22.3% never married, 53.7% now married, 3.6% separated, 9.7% widowed, 14.3% divorced; Foreign born: 4.7%; Speak English only: 97.6%; With disability: 19.6%; Veterans: 11.0%; Ancestry: 33.5% German, 20.8% Irish, 14.8% Italian, 10.7% English, 8.9% Dutch

Employment: 17.2% management, business, and financial, 2.4% computer, engineering, and science, 8.9% education, legal, community service, arts, and media, 5.9% healthcare practitioners, 19.0% service, 23.6% sales and office, 9.6% natural resources, construction, and maintenance, 13.4% production, transportation, and material moving

Income: Per capita: $32,890; Median household: $52,879; Average household: $68,981; Households with income of $100,000 or more: 15.0%; Poverty rate: 12.5%

Educational Attainment: High school diploma or higher: 85.4%; Bachelor's degree or higher: 24.0%; Graduate/professional degree or higher: 11.3%

Housing: Homeownership rate: 78.2%; Median home value: $202,200; Median year structure built: 1966; Homeowner vacancy rate: 0.9%; Median selected monthly owner costs: $1,697 with a mortgage, $618 without a mortgage; Median gross rent: $882 per month; Rental vacancy rate: 1.7%

Health Insurance: 97.3% have insurance; 74.5% have private insurance; 44.7% have public insurance; 2.7% do not have insurance; 0.9% of children under 18 do not have insurance

Transportation: Commute: 93.9% car, 1.8% public transportation, 1.1% walk, 2.7% work from home; Mean travel time to work: 22.1 minutes

Additional Information Contacts
Town of Claverack. . . . . (518) 672-7911
    http://www.townofclaverack.com

CLAVERACK-RED MILLS (CDP).
Covers a land area of 2.978 square miles and a water area of 0.018 square miles. Located at 42.23° N. Lat; 73.72° W. Long.

Population: 646; Growth (since 2000): -39.1%; Density: 216.9 persons per square mile; Race: 100.0% White, 0.0% Black/African American, 0.0% Asian, 0.0% American Indian/Alaska Native, 0.0% Native Hawaiian/Other Pacific Islander, 0.0% Two or more races, 0.0% Hispanic of any race; Average household size: 2.15; Median age: 49.7; Age under 18: 21.4%; Age 65 and over: 25.1%; Males per 100 females: 98.5; Marriage status: 18.0% never married, 65.5% now married, 3.0% separated, 6.6% widowed, 9.8% divorced; Foreign born: 8.8%; Speak English only: 94.3%; With disability: 15.8%; Veterans: 6.3%; Ancestry: 42.7% German, 31.1% Irish, 23.2% Italian, 13.5% Polish, 10.2% English

Employment: 23.7% management, business, and financial, 0.0% computer, engineering, and science, 21.1% education, legal, community service, arts, and media, 13.0% healthcare practitioners, 14.4% service, 17.2% sales and office, 10.7% natural resources, construction, and maintenance, 0.0% production, transportation, and material moving

Income: Per capita: $34,940; Median household: $62,188; Average household: $74,610; Households with income of $100,000 or more: 26.0%; Poverty rate: n/a

Educational Attainment: High school diploma or higher: 83.1%; Bachelor's degree or higher: 41.1%; Graduate/professional degree or higher: 27.4%

Housing: Homeownership rate: 93.0%; Median home value: $217,300; Median year structure built: 1955; Homeowner vacancy rate: 0.0%; Median selected monthly owner costs: $1,509 with a mortgage, $762 without a mortgage; Median gross rent: n/a per month; Rental vacancy rate: 0.0%

Health Insurance: 100.0% have insurance; 84.2% have private insurance; 35.8% have public insurance; 0.0% do not have insurance; 0.0% of children under 18 do not have insurance
Transportation: Commute: 94.9% car, 0.0% public transportation, 0.0% walk, 5.1% work from home; Mean travel time to work: 14.8 minutes

CLERMONT (town). Covers a land area of 17.996 square miles and a water area of 1.197 square miles. Located at 42.09° N. Lat; 73.85° W. Long. Elevation is 223 feet.

Population: 2,028; Growth (since 2000): 17.5%; Density: 112.7 persons per square mile; Race: 91.8% White, 1.2% Black/African American, 2.7% Asian, 0.0% American Indian/Alaska Native, 0.0% Native Hawaiian/Other Pacific Islander, 2.7% Two or more races, 5.5% Hispanic of any race; Average household size: 2.77; Median age: 44.7; Age under 18: 22.6%; Age 65 and over: 16.4%; Males per 100 females: 103.2; Marriage status: 29.6% never married, 59.2% now married, 0.8% separated, 3.5% widowed, 7.7% divorced; Foreign born: 5.6%; Speak English only: 93.6%; With disability: 13.1%; Veterans: 8.9%; Ancestry: 28.8% Irish, 23.0% German, 19.4% Italian, 12.0% English, 5.4% Polish
Employment: 12.9% management, business, and financial, 2.8% computer, engineering, and science, 13.6% education, legal, community service, arts, and media, 9.6% healthcare practitioners, 17.0% service, 17.3% sales and office, 15.2% natural resources, construction, and maintenance, 11.6% production, transportation, and material moving
Income: Per capita: $36,726; Median household: $79,306; Average household: $104,842; Households with income of $100,000 or more: 34.7%; Poverty rate: 13.2%
Educational Attainment: High school diploma or higher: 89.2%; Bachelor's degree or higher: 34.0%; Graduate/professional degree or higher: 18.5%
Housing: Homeownership rate: 83.7%; Median home value: $280,100; Median year structure built: 1976; Homeowner vacancy rate: 1.8%; Median selected monthly owner costs: $2,052 with a mortgage, $873 without a mortgage; Median gross rent: $1,109 per month; Rental vacancy rate: 4.2%
Health Insurance: 94.6% have insurance; 75.1% have private insurance; 32.1% have public insurance; 5.4% do not have insurance; 5.1% of children under 18 do not have insurance
Transportation: Commute: 86.1% car, 2.9% public transportation, 5.6% walk, 5.0% work from home; Mean travel time to work: 32.6 minutes

COPAKE (town). Covers a land area of 40.762 square miles and a water area of 1.280 square miles. Located at 42.13° N. Lat; 73.55° W. Long. Elevation is 545 feet.

Population: 3,522; Growth (since 2000): 7.4%; Density: 86.4 persons per square mile; Race: 92.1% White, 0.3% Black/African American, 2.3% Asian, 0.0% American Indian/Alaska Native, 0.0% Native Hawaiian/Other Pacific Islander, 4.6% Two or more races, 5.7% Hispanic of any race; Average household size: 2.35; Median age: 48.8; Age under 18: 17.3%; Age 65 and over: 22.1%; Males per 100 females: 99.2; Marriage status: 26.0% never married, 54.9% now married, 1.3% separated, 7.4% widowed, 11.7% divorced; Foreign born: 4.1%; Speak English only: 89.8%; With disability: 21.9%; Veterans: 5.9%; Ancestry: 16.4% German, 15.6% Irish, 14.7% American, 10.0% Italian, 9.4% English
Employment: 15.2% management, business, and financial, 2.6% computer, engineering, and science, 11.9% education, legal, community service, arts, and media, 2.9% healthcare practitioners, 21.8% service, 17.7% sales and office, 18.6% natural resources, construction, and maintenance, 9.4% production, transportation, and material moving
Income: Per capita: $33,632; Median household: $69,333; Average household: $85,058; Households with income of $100,000 or more: 21.5%; Poverty rate: 12.6%
Educational Attainment: High school diploma or higher: 90.0%; Bachelor's degree or higher: 26.1%; Graduate/professional degree or higher: 14.8%
Housing: Homeownership rate: 76.0%; Median home value: $253,200; Median year structure built: 1969; Homeowner vacancy rate: 13.2%; Median selected monthly owner costs: $1,568 with a mortgage, $501 without a mortgage; Median gross rent: $1,079 per month; Rental vacancy rate: 2.4%
Health Insurance: 98.0% have insurance; 73.9% have private insurance; 40.9% have public insurance; 2.0% do not have insurance; 0.0% of children under 18 do not have insurance
Transportation: Commute: 87.4% car, 4.9% public transportation, 4.2% walk, 3.5% work from home; Mean travel time to work: 25.6 minutes

COPAKE FALLS (unincorporated postal area)
ZCTA: 12517

Covers a land area of 10.459 square miles and a water area of 0.016 square miles. Located at 42.11° N. Lat; 73.51° W. Long. Elevation is 643 feet.
Population: 445; Growth (since 2000): 40.4%; Density: 42.5 persons per square mile; Race: 80.0% White, 0.0% Black/African American, 0.0% Asian, 0.0% American Indian/Alaska Native, 0.0% Native Hawaiian/Other Pacific Islander, 20.0% Two or more races, 0.0% Hispanic of any race; Average household size: 1.94; Median age: 39.0; Age under 18: 18.7%; Age 65 and over: 14.4%; Males per 100 females: 104.4; Marriage status: 26.1% never married, 43.3% now married, 3.0% separated, 16.1% widowed, 14.5% divorced; Foreign born: 2.0%; Speak English only: 95.8%; With disability: 25.8%; Veterans: 8.3%; Ancestry: 13.7% Irish, 11.7% English, 11.0% German, 10.8% American, 6.5% Italian
Employment: 4.9% management, business, and financial, 0.0% computer, engineering, and science, 0.0% education, legal, community service, arts, and media, 0.0% healthcare practitioners, 41.9% service, 30.9% sales and office, 11.4% natural resources, construction, and maintenance, 11.0% production, transportation, and material moving
Income: Per capita: $31,697; Median household: $44,833; Average household: $64,429; Households with income of $100,000 or more: 9.8%; Poverty rate: 5.8%
Educational Attainment: High school diploma or higher: 92.0%; Bachelor's degree or higher: 24.6%; Graduate/professional degree or higher: 14.6%
Housing: Homeownership rate: 69.0%; Median home value: $238,800; Median year structure built: 1966; Homeowner vacancy rate: 0.0%; Median selected monthly owner costs: $1,633 with a mortgage, $0 without a mortgage; Median gross rent: $548 per month; Rental vacancy rate: 0.0%
Health Insurance: 97.1% have insurance; 73.7% have private insurance; 40.7% have public insurance; 2.9% do not have insurance; 0.0% of children under 18 do not have insurance
Transportation: Commute: 87.2% car, 12.8% public transportation, 0.0% walk, 0.0% work from home; Mean travel time to work: 25.3 minutes

COPAKE LAKE (CDP). Covers a land area of 9.509 square miles and a water area of 0.805 square miles. Located at 42.14° N. Lat; 73.60° W. Long. Elevation is 718 feet.

Population: 527; Growth (since 2000): -30.8%; Density: 55.4 persons per square mile; Race: 98.3% White, 0.0% Black/African American, 0.0% Asian, 0.0% American Indian/Alaska Native, 0.0% Native Hawaiian/Other Pacific Islander, 1.7% Two or more races, 2.3% Hispanic of any race; Average household size: 2.73; Median age: 50.8; Age under 18: 19.9%; Age 65 and over: 26.8%; Males per 100 females: 105.2; Marriage status: 27.5% never married, 61.3% now married, 4.2% separated, 2.6% widowed, 8.6% divorced; Foreign born: 4.6%; Speak English only: 97.9%; With disability: 25.4%; Veterans: 2.6%; Ancestry: 19.9% Irish, 18.2% American, 14.6% German, 12.0% English, 10.1% Scottish
Employment: 9.1% management, business, and financial, 0.0% computer, engineering, and science, 18.8% education, legal, community service, arts, and media, 5.1% healthcare practitioners, 25.6% service, 11.9% sales and office, 8.5% natural resources, construction, and maintenance, 21.0% production, transportation, and material moving
Income: Per capita: $26,612; Median household: $54,583; Average household: $77,829; Households with income of $100,000 or more: 24.8%; Poverty rate: 20.1%
Educational Attainment: High school diploma or higher: 85.9%; Bachelor's degree or higher: 31.3%; Graduate/professional degree or higher: 23.4%
Housing: Homeownership rate: 88.6%; Median home value: $260,200; Median year structure built: 1972; Homeowner vacancy rate: 26.9%; Median selected monthly owner costs: $1,130 with a mortgage, $805 without a mortgage; Median gross rent: $830 per month; Rental vacancy rate: 26.7%
Health Insurance: 95.8% have insurance; 63.8% have private insurance; 49.5% have public insurance; 4.2% do not have insurance; 0.0% of children under 18 do not have insurance
Transportation: Commute: 80.3% car, 0.0% public transportation, 15.0% walk, 4.6% work from home; Mean travel time to work: 21.6 minutes

CRARYVILLE (unincorporated postal area)
ZCTA: 12521

Covers a land area of 32.889 square miles and a water area of 0.314 square miles. Located at 42.17° N. Lat; 73.65° W. Long. Elevation is 636 feet.

Population: 1,248; Growth (since 2000): -16.7%; Density: 37.9 persons per square mile; Race: 97.0% White, 0.0% Black/African American, 0.7% Asian, 0.0% American Indian/Alaska Native, 0.0% Native Hawaiian/Other Pacific Islander, 2.3% Two or more races, 1.3% Hispanic of any race; Average household size: 2.02; Median age: 53.9; Age under 18: 8.7%; Age 65 and over: 26.9%; Males per 100 females: 104.7; Marriage status: 20.6% never married, 59.6% now married, 1.8% separated, 6.0% widowed, 13.8% divorced; Foreign born: 4.2%; Speak English only: 95.9%; With disability: 25.2%; Veterans: 14.1%; Ancestry: 28.0% Irish, 17.7% Italian, 11.6% English, 11.5% German, 7.3% Scottish

Employment: 21.7% management, business, and financial, 8.5% computer, engineering, and science, 8.2% education, legal, community service, arts, and media, 3.2% healthcare practitioners, 26.1% service, 12.4% sales and office, 11.4% natural resources, construction, and maintenance, 8.6% production, transportation, and material moving

Income: Per capita: $57,842; Median household: $90,046; Average household: $110,962; Households with income of $100,000 or more: 30.3%; Poverty rate: 8.6%

Educational Attainment: High school diploma or higher: 94.6%; Bachelor's degree or higher: 33.1%; Graduate/professional degree or higher: 20.3%

School District(s)
Taconic Hills Central SD (PK-12)

 Enrollment: 1,430 . . . . (518) 325-2891

Housing: Homeownership rate: 94.6%; Median home value: $236,000; Median year structure built: 1975; Homeowner vacancy rate: 4.8%; Median selected monthly owner costs: $1,792 with a mortgage, $660 without a mortgage; Median gross rent: $875 per month; Rental vacancy rate: 19.5%

Health Insurance: 96.3% have insurance; 78.9% have private insurance; 43.3% have public insurance; 3.7% do not have insurance; 7.4% of children under 18 do not have insurance

Transportation: Commute: 86.7% car, 6.2% public transportation, 3.3% walk, 3.6% work from home; Mean travel time to work: 31.3 minutes

EAST CHATHAM (unincorporated postal area)
ZCTA: 12060

Covers a land area of 34.504 square miles and a water area of 0.132 square miles. Located at 42.41° N. Lat; 73.51° W. Long. Elevation is 702 feet.

Population: 1,478; Growth (since 2000): 5.9%; Density: 42.8 persons per square mile; Race: 98.3% White, 0.0% Black/African American, 1.4% Asian, 0.1% American Indian/Alaska Native, 0.0% Native Hawaiian/Other Pacific Islander, 0.2% Two or more races, 1.1% Hispanic of any race; Average household size: 2.32; Median age: 49.4; Age under 18: 18.3%; Age 65 and over: 20.4%; Males per 100 females: 102.0; Marriage status: 25.9% never married, 61.4% now married, 1.8% separated, 4.6% widowed, 8.1% divorced; Foreign born: 1.8%; Speak English only: 95.9%; With disability: 12.9%; Veterans: 7.0%; Ancestry: 30.0% Irish, 25.5% German, 13.3% Italian, 9.8% English, 8.6% Polish

Employment: 14.0% management, business, and financial, 3.4% computer, engineering, and science, 21.6% education, legal, community service, arts, and media, 7.1% healthcare practitioners, 20.9% service, 14.4% sales and office, 15.4% natural resources, construction, and maintenance, 3.2% production, transportation, and material moving

Income: Per capita: $43,088; Median household: $71,500; Average household: $101,311; Households with income of $100,000 or more: 28.8%; Poverty rate: 9.4%

Educational Attainment: High school diploma or higher: 97.7%; Bachelor's degree or higher: 41.4%; Graduate/professional degree or higher: 25.3%

Housing: Homeownership rate: 87.4%; Median home value: $252,300; Median year structure built: 1966; Homeowner vacancy rate: 7.5%; Median selected monthly owner costs: $1,872 with a mortgage, $792 without a mortgage; Median gross rent: n/a per month; Rental vacancy rate: 0.0%

Health Insurance: 93.1% have insurance; 78.6% have private insurance; 30.3% have public insurance; 6.9% do not have insurance; 3.1% of children under 18 do not have insurance

Transportation: Commute: 83.0% car, 3.3% public transportation, 4.0% walk, 7.7% work from home; Mean travel time to work: 29.4 minutes

ELIZAVILLE (unincorporated postal area)
ZCTA: 12523

Covers a land area of 21.889 square miles and a water area of 0.185 square miles. Located at 42.09° N. Lat; 73.76° W. Long. Elevation is 289 feet.

Population: 1,586; Growth (since 2000): -19.7%; Density: 72.5 persons per square mile; Race: 96.3% White, 0.4% Black/African American, 1.6% Asian, 0.0% American Indian/Alaska Native, 0.0% Native Hawaiian/Other Pacific Islander, 1.7% Two or more races, 4.0% Hispanic of any race; Average household size: 2.25; Median age: 48.8; Age under 18: 12.6%; Age 65 and over: 18.5%; Males per 100 females: 100.4; Marriage status: 41.0% never married, 38.2% now married, 2.0% separated, 6.7% widowed, 14.1% divorced; Foreign born: 5.4%; Speak English only: 92.6%; With disability: 17.7%; Veterans: 9.4%; Ancestry: 24.0% German, 21.4% Irish, 20.9% Italian, 8.6% Dutch, 6.3% Polish

Employment: 7.9% management, business, and financial, 3.0% computer, engineering, and science, 14.1% education, legal, community service, arts, and media, 8.7% healthcare practitioners, 23.3% service, 24.7% sales and office, 7.9% natural resources, construction, and maintenance, 10.4% production, transportation, and material moving

Income: Per capita: $41,119; Median household: $75,263; Average household: $92,775; Households with income of $100,000 or more: 24.7%; Poverty rate: 7.6%

Educational Attainment: High school diploma or higher: 86.0%; Bachelor's degree or higher: 26.1%; Graduate/professional degree or higher: 16.0%

Housing: Homeownership rate: 76.8%; Median home value: $252,600; Median year structure built: 1978; Homeowner vacancy rate: 1.7%; Median selected monthly owner costs: $1,589 with a mortgage, $643 without a mortgage; Median gross rent: $831 per month; Rental vacancy rate: 0.0%

Health Insurance: 92.5% have insurance; 76.4% have private insurance; 29.8% have public insurance; 7.5% do not have insurance; 7.7% of children under 18 do not have insurance

Transportation: Commute: 90.6% car, 2.7% public transportation, 0.8% walk, 4.0% work from home; Mean travel time to work: 31.8 minutes

GALLATIN (town).
Covers a land area of 39.111 square miles and a water area of 0.521 square miles. Located at 42.06° N. Lat; 73.71° W. Long.

Population: 1,685; Growth (since 2000): 12.4%; Density: 43.1 persons per square mile; Race: 91.7% White, 2.9% Black/African American, 2.8% Asian, 0.0% American Indian/Alaska Native, 0.0% Native Hawaiian/Other Pacific Islander, 2.6% Two or more races, 2.6% Hispanic of any race; Average household size: 2.43; Median age: 50.2; Age under 18: 19.8%; Age 65 and over: 20.4%; Males per 100 females: 105.7; Marriage status: 33.2% never married, 53.7% now married, 2.1% separated, 6.8% widowed, 6.3% divorced; Foreign born: 7.2%; Speak English only: 94.5%; With disability: 17.7%; Veterans: 11.7%; Ancestry: 27.2% Irish, 25.6% German, 16.5% Italian, 7.6% Polish, 6.6% Dutch

Employment: 19.9% management, business, and financial, 3.1% computer, engineering, and science, 9.9% education, legal, community service, arts, and media, 7.8% healthcare practitioners, 20.9% service, 20.4% sales and office, 14.1% natural resources, construction, and maintenance, 3.9% production, transportation, and material moving

Income: Per capita: $38,187; Median household: $71,250; Average household: $92,041; Households with income of $100,000 or more: 33.5%; Poverty rate: 9.7%

Educational Attainment: High school diploma or higher: 88.4%; Bachelor's degree or higher: 31.7%; Graduate/professional degree or higher: 17.1%

Housing: Homeownership rate: 84.4%; Median home value: $297,500; Median year structure built: 1970; Homeowner vacancy rate: 0.5%; Median selected monthly owner costs: $1,809 with a mortgage, $762 without a mortgage; Median gross rent: $1,265 per month; Rental vacancy rate: 7.7%

Health Insurance: 92.3% have insurance; 74.1% have private insurance; 35.4% have public insurance; 7.7% do not have insurance; 4.7% of children under 18 do not have insurance

Transportation: Commute: 88.5% car, 4.7% public transportation, 0.9% walk, 5.1% work from home; Mean travel time to work: 35.7 minutes

GERMANTOWN (CDP).

Covers a land area of 2.679 square miles and a water area of 0.016 square miles. Located at 42.14° N. Lat; 73.89° W. Long. Elevation is 135 feet.

Population: 833; Growth (since 2000): -3.4%; Density: 311.0 persons per square mile; Race: 90.3% White, 0.0% Black/African American, 1.2% Asian, 0.0% American Indian/Alaska Native, 0.0% Native Hawaiian/Other Pacific Islander, 6.4% Two or more races, 14.9% Hispanic of any race; Average household size: 2.51; Median age: 43.4; Age under 18: 20.2%; Age 65 and over: 17.2%; Males per 100 females: 96.1; Marriage status: 23.3% never married, 57.0% now married, 2.6% separated, 7.3% widowed, 12.4% divorced; Foreign born: 9.5%; Speak English only: 90.8%; With disability: 14.5%; Veterans: 12.2%; Ancestry: 22.0% German, 17.8% Italian, 10.9% Irish, 6.8% English, 5.5% American

Employment: 7.9% management, business, and financial, 2.5% computer, engineering, and science, 13.4% education, legal, community service, arts, and media, 3.0% healthcare practitioners, 14.6% service, 28.2% sales and office, 24.3% natural resources, construction, and maintenance, 6.2% production, transportation, and material moving

Income: Per capita: $33,695; Median household: $66,944; Average household: $85,934; Households with income of $100,000 or more: 39.6%; Poverty rate: 5.5%

Educational Attainment: High school diploma or higher: 94.6%; Bachelor's degree or higher: 27.1%; Graduate/professional degree or higher: 9.8%

School District(s)
Germantown Central SD (PK-12)

    Enrollment: 564 . . . . (518) 537-6280

Housing: Homeownership rate: 76.2%; Median home value: $238,400; Median year structure built: Before 1940; Homeowner vacancy rate: 0.0%; Median selected monthly owner costs: $1,559 with a mortgage, $627 without a mortgage; Median gross rent: $1,529 per month; Rental vacancy rate: 0.0%

Health Insurance: 97.1% have insurance; 80.0% have private insurance; 33.6% have public insurance; 2.9% do not have insurance; 0.0% of children under 18 do not have insurance

Transportation: Commute: 91.4% car, 5.6% public transportation, 2.3% walk, 0.8% work from home; Mean travel time to work: 31.6 minutes

GERMANTOWN (town).

Covers a land area of 12.103 square miles and a water area of 1.819 square miles. Located at 42.14° N. Lat; 73.87° W. Long. Elevation is 135 feet.

Population: 1,883; Growth (since 2000): -6.7%; Density: 155.6 persons per square mile; Race: 93.8% White, 1.3% Black/African American, 0.9% Asian, 0.0% American Indian/Alaska Native, 0.0% Native Hawaiian/Other Pacific Islander, 3.0% Two or more races, 8.1% Hispanic of any race; Average household size: 2.32; Median age: 48.1; Age under 18: 18.8%; Age 65 and over: 22.3%; Males per 100 females: 96.8; Marriage status: 18.6% never married, 62.1% now married, 2.2% separated, 9.8% widowed, 9.5% divorced; Foreign born: 6.9%; Speak English only: 93.7%; With disability: 15.7%; Veterans: 9.9%; Ancestry: 21.8% Italian, 19.4% German, 15.2% Irish, 7.5% English, 6.3% Polish

Employment: 18.2% management, business, and financial, 1.8% computer, engineering, and science, 16.5% education, legal, community service, arts, and media, 5.4% healthcare practitioners, 10.7% service, 23.7% sales and office, 18.3% natural resources, construction, and maintenance, 5.4% production, transportation, and material moving

Income: Per capita: $38,176; Median household: $67,917; Average household: $89,911; Households with income of $100,000 or more: 35.2%; Poverty rate: 5.5%

Educational Attainment: High school diploma or higher: 93.3%; Bachelor's degree or higher: 33.7%; Graduate/professional degree or higher: 17.6%

School District(s)
Germantown Central SD (PK-12)

    Enrollment: 564 . . . . (518) 537-6280

Housing: Homeownership rate: 76.1%; Median home value: $276,900; Median year structure built: 1952; Homeowner vacancy rate: 1.9%; Median selected monthly owner costs: $1,808 with a mortgage, $721 without a mortgage; Median gross rent: $870 per month; Rental vacancy rate: 0.0%

Health Insurance: 97.9% have insurance; 82.4% have private insurance; 33.9% have public insurance; 2.1% do not have insurance; 0.0% of children under 18 do not have insurance

Safety: Violent crime rate: 0.0 per 10,000 population; Property crime rate: 5.4 per 10,000 population

Transportation: Commute: 76.6% car, 4.4% public transportation, 5.7% walk, 12.7% work from home; Mean travel time to work: 30.1 minutes

GHENT (CDP).

Covers a land area of 1.538 square miles and a water area of 0.011 square miles. Located at 42.33° N. Lat; 73.62° W. Long. Elevation is 407 feet.

Population: 510; Growth (since 2000): -13.0%; Density: 331.6 persons per square mile; Race: 86.9% White, 8.6% Black/African American, 0.0% Asian, 0.0% American Indian/Alaska Native, 0.0% Native Hawaiian/Other Pacific Islander, 0.0% Two or more races, 4.7% Hispanic of any race; Average household size: 3.70; Median age: 24.7; Age under 18: 34.7%; Age 65 and over: 5.1%; Males per 100 females: 105.8; Marriage status: 30.1% never married, 59.3% now married, 4.7% separated, 0.0% widowed, 10.6% divorced; Foreign born: 8.8%; Speak English only: 90.6%; With disability: 2.5%; Veterans: 12.0%; Ancestry: 26.7% Irish, 24.5% German, 21.4% Italian, 13.5% English, 9.6% European

Employment: 0.5% management, business, and financial, 0.0% computer, engineering, and science, 35.0% education, legal, community service, arts, and media, 0.0% healthcare practitioners, 51.0% service, 0.5% sales and office, 0.5% natural resources, construction, and maintenance, 12.5% production, transportation, and material moving

Income: Per capita: $23,737; Median household: $80,268; Average household: $87,426; Households with income of $100,000 or more: 40.9%; Poverty rate: 39.7%

Educational Attainment: High school diploma or higher: 93.6%; Bachelor's degree or higher: 39.6%; Graduate/professional degree or higher: 20.8%

Housing: Homeownership rate: 90.5%; Median home value: $233,900; Median year structure built: 1942; Homeowner vacancy rate: 0.0%; Median selected monthly owner costs: $1,817 with a mortgage, n/a without a mortgage; Median gross rent: n/a per month; Rental vacancy rate: 0.0%

Health Insurance: 93.7% have insurance; 55.3% have private insurance; 43.3% have public insurance; 6.3% do not have insurance; 0.0% of children under 18 do not have insurance

Newspapers: The Columbia Paper (weekly circulation 5,000)

Transportation: Commute: 91.0% car, 0.5% public transportation, 0.5% walk, 8.0% work from home; Mean travel time to work: 28.5 minutes

GHENT (town).

Covers a land area of 45.132 square miles and a water area of 0.268 square miles. Located at 42.31° N. Lat; 73.65° W. Long. Elevation is 407 feet.

History: 1818, the town of Ghent was founded from parts of the towns of Chatham, Claverack, and Kinderhook. Its name is from the Flemish city Ghent, in Flanders, Belgium. Ghent is home to the historic Van Valkenburgh-Isbister Farm, which in on the National Register of Historic Places.

Population: 5,255; Growth (since 2000): -0.4%; Density: 116.4 persons per square mile; Race: 93.1% White, 4.8% Black/African American, 0.5% Asian, 0.0% American Indian/Alaska Native, 0.0% Native Hawaiian/Other Pacific Islander, 0.0% Two or more races, 2.8% Hispanic of any race; Average household size: 2.52; Median age: 47.8; Age under 18: 15.1%; Age 65 and over: 24.5%; Males per 100 females: 99.4; Marriage status: 32.7% never married, 46.8% now married, 2.0% separated, 6.6% widowed, 13.9% divorced; Foreign born: 6.8%; Speak English only: 93.2%; With disability: 12.8%; Veterans: 9.7%; Ancestry: 25.7% Irish, 21.6% German, 16.0% Italian, 10.9% English, 8.8% Polish

Employment: 10.7% management, business, and financial, 5.2% computer, engineering, and science, 15.4% education, legal, community service, arts, and media, 1.7% healthcare practitioners, 24.6% service, 18.1% sales and office, 13.1% natural resources, construction, and maintenance, 11.2% production, transportation, and material moving

Income: Per capita: $30,870; Median household: $63,509; Average household: $78,093; Households with income of $100,000 or more: 29.2%; Poverty rate: 10.4%

Educational Attainment: High school diploma or higher: 90.0%; Bachelor's degree or higher: 24.8%; Graduate/professional degree or higher: 10.7%

Housing: Homeownership rate: 78.1%; Median home value: $220,300; Median year structure built: 1965; Homeowner vacancy rate: 1.3%; Median selected monthly owner costs: $1,608 with a mortgage, $663 without a mortgage; Median gross rent: $1,033 per month; Rental vacancy rate: 13.6%

Health Insurance: 91.4% have insurance; 74.1% have private insurance; 33.8% have public insurance; 8.6% do not have insurance; 1.0% of children under 18 do not have insurance

Newspapers: The Columbia Paper (weekly circulation 5,000)
Transportation: Commute: 88.9% car, 2.0% public transportation, 1.0% walk, 7.0% work from home; Mean travel time to work: 21.8 minutes
Additional Information Contacts
Town of Ghent . . . . (518) 392-4644
  http://www.townofghent.org

GREENPORT (town).

GREENPORT (town). Covers a land area of 18.607 square miles and a water area of 1.880 square miles. Located at 42.23° N. Lat; 73.80° W. Long.
Population: 4,167; Growth (since 2000): -0.3%; Density: 223.9 persons per square mile; Race: 82.3% White, 8.2% Black/African American, 2.5% Asian, 0.0% American Indian/Alaska Native, 0.0% Native Hawaiian/Other Pacific Islander, 6.9% Two or more races, 4.5% Hispanic of any race; Average household size: 2.18; Median age: 49.4; Age under 18: 15.4%; Age 65 and over: 24.1%; Males per 100 females: 101.0; Marriage status: 34.8% never married, 46.7% now married, 2.2% separated, 8.6% widowed, 9.9% divorced; Foreign born: 7.1%; Speak English only: 92.9%; With disability: 18.2%; Veterans: 8.2%; Ancestry: 24.4% Italian, 21.0% Irish, 18.2% German, 6.7% Dutch, 6.6% English
Employment: 15.4% management, business, and financial, 0.3% computer, engineering, and science, 11.8% education, legal, community service, arts, and media, 7.4% healthcare practitioners, 31.5% service, 19.2% sales and office, 6.2% natural resources, construction, and maintenance, 8.1% production, transportation, and material moving
Income: Per capita: $30,383; Median household: $56,504; Average household: $67,130; Households with income of $100,000 or more: 19.9%; Poverty rate: 13.2%
Educational Attainment: High school diploma or higher: 88.2%; Bachelor's degree or higher: 25.7%; Graduate/professional degree or higher: 12.2%
Housing: Homeownership rate: 68.1%; Median home value: $158,400; Median year structure built: 1967; Homeowner vacancy rate: 0.0%; Median selected monthly owner costs: $1,509 with a mortgage, $519 without a mortgage; Median gross rent: $884 per month; Rental vacancy rate: 3.6%
Health Insurance: 95.9% have insurance; 72.1% have private insurance; 44.7% have public insurance; 4.1% do not have insurance; 2.3% of children under 18 do not have insurance
Safety: Violent crime rate: 0.0 per 10,000 population; Property crime rate: 271.2 per 10,000 population
Transportation: Commute: 92.8% car, 1.7% public transportation, 2.3% walk, 2.8% work from home; Mean travel time to work: 22.8 minutes
Additional Information Contacts
Town of Greenport . . . . (518) 828-4656
  http://www.townofgreenport.com

HILLSDALE (town).

HILLSDALE (town). Covers a land area of 47.724 square miles and a water area of 0.164 square miles. Located at 42.23° N. Lat; 73.52° W. Long. Elevation is 709 feet.
Population: 1,682; Growth (since 2000): -3.6%; Density: 35.2 persons per square mile; Race: 97.0% White, 0.0% Black/African American, 1.2% Asian, 0.0% American Indian/Alaska Native, 0.0% Native Hawaiian/Other Pacific Islander, 1.5% Two or more races, 2.0% Hispanic of any race; Average household size: 2.46; Median age: 48.8; Age under 18: 18.7%; Age 65 and over: 27.8%; Males per 100 females: 107.4; Marriage status: 25.3% never married, 62.2% now married, 3.7% separated, 2.8% widowed, 9.7% divorced; Foreign born: 8.6%; Speak English only: 94.6%; With disability: 16.4%; Veterans: 8.5%; Ancestry: 24.7% German, 19.9% Irish, 14.5% Italian, 9.6% English, 5.6% Polish
Employment: 15.4% management, business, and financial, 3.2% computer, engineering, and science, 18.4% education, legal, community service, arts, and media, 4.0% healthcare practitioners, 14.7% service, 27.5% sales and office, 10.8% natural resources, construction, and maintenance, 6.0% production, transportation, and material moving
Income: Per capita: $52,769; Median household: $66,000; Average household: $125,566; Households with income of $100,000 or more: 36.2%; Poverty rate: 9.6%
Educational Attainment: High school diploma or higher: 93.6%; Bachelor's degree or higher: 39.6%; Graduate/professional degree or higher: 19.9%
Housing: Homeownership rate: 73.8%; Median home value: $283,900; Median year structure built: 1961; Homeowner vacancy rate: 6.7%; Median selected monthly owner costs: $1,517 with a mortgage, $670 without a mortgage; Median gross rent: $1,009 per month; Rental vacancy rate: 7.7%

Health Insurance: 93.9% have insurance; 65.4% have private insurance; 46.3% have public insurance; 6.1% do not have insurance; 2.8% of children under 18 do not have insurance
Transportation: Commute: 71.5% car, 10.1% public transportation, 6.4% walk, 12.0% work from home; Mean travel time to work: 25.0 minutes

HOLLOWVILLE (unincorporated postal area)

ZCTA: 12530
  Covers a land area of 0.348 square miles and a water area of 0 square miles. Located at 42.21° N. Lat; 73.69° W. Long. Elevation is 325 feet.
Population: 111; Growth (since 2000): n/a; Density: 319.3 persons per square mile; Race: 100.0% White, 0.0% Black/African American, 0.0% Asian, 0.0% American Indian/Alaska Native, 0.0% Native Hawaiian/Other Pacific Islander, 0.0% Two or more races, 0.0% Hispanic of any race; Average household size: 1.25; Median age: 61.1; Age under 18: 0.0%; Age 65 and over: 0.0%; Males per 100 females: 110.2; Marriage status: 58.6% never married, 41.4% now married, 0.0% separated, 0.0% widowed, 0.0% divorced; Foreign born: 0.0%; Speak English only: 100.0%; With disability: 44.1%; Veterans: 0.0%; Ancestry: 44.1% Dutch, 44.1% German, 21.6% Polish, 21.6% Russian, 14.4% Italian
Employment: 0.0% management, business, and financial, 0.0% computer, engineering, and science, 47.8% education, legal, community service, arts, and media, 0.0% healthcare practitioners, 0.0% service, 0.0% sales and office, 52.2% natural resources, construction, and maintenance, 0.0% production, transportation, and material moving
Income: Per capita: $28,770; Median household: n/a; Average household: $36,245; Households with income of $100,000 or more: n/a; Poverty rate: n/a
Educational Attainment: High school diploma or higher: 55.9%; Bachelor's degree or higher: 55.9%; Graduate/professional degree or higher: 34.2%
Housing: Homeownership rate: 44.9%; Median home value: n/a; Median year structure built: Before 1940; Homeowner vacancy rate: 0.0%; Median selected monthly owner costs: $0 with a mortgage, $0 without a mortgage; Median gross rent: n/a per month; Rental vacancy rate: 0.0%
Health Insurance: 100.0% have insurance; 41.4% have private insurance; 58.6% have public insurance; 0.0% do not have insurance; 0.0% of children under 18 do not have insurance
Transportation: Commute: 100.0% car, 0.0% public transportation, 0.0% walk, 0.0% work from home; Mean travel time to work: 0.0 minutes

HUDSON (city).

HUDSON (city). County seat. Covers a land area of 2.158 square miles and a water area of 0.172 square miles. Located at 42.25° N. Lat; 73.79° W. Long. Elevation is 82 feet.
History: The city was a whaling and trading port until 1812. Its industries included textiles, furniture, cement, and metal products, but these are largely gone. Many colonial and Revolutionary era homes are in the area. Olana, estate of Frederic E. Church, 2.5 miles South of city. Settled c.1622 by the Dutch and later in 1783 by English whalers; incorporated 1785.
Population: 6,452; Growth (since 2000): -14.2%; Density: 2,990.0 persons per square mile; Race: 62.9% White, 22.2% Black/African American, 7.8% Asian, 0.1% American Indian/Alaska Native, 0.2% Native Hawaiian/Other Pacific Islander, 6.0% Two or more races, 7.5% Hispanic of any race; Average household size: 2.06; Median age: 38.0; Age under 18: 18.8%; Age 65 and over: 12.8%; Males per 100 females: 106.7; Marriage status: 46.6% never married, 32.9% now married, 3.0% separated, 4.1% widowed, 16.4% divorced; Foreign born: 18.8%; Speak English only: 83.8%; With disability: 17.1%; Veterans: 4.4%; Ancestry: 15.3% Italian, 12.9% Irish, 11.8% German, 7.5% Polish, 5.3% American
Employment: 14.9% management, business, and financial, 3.2% computer, engineering, and science, 11.6% education, legal, community service, arts, and media, 3.8% healthcare practitioners, 30.2% service, 21.5% sales and office, 3.7% natural resources, construction, and maintenance, 11.0% production, transportation, and material moving
Income: Per capita: $23,313; Median household: $35,439; Average household: $52,356; Households with income of $100,000 or more: 11.5%; Poverty rate: 19.2%
Educational Attainment: High school diploma or higher: 85.0%; Bachelor's degree or higher: 26.1%; Graduate/professional degree or higher: 10.7%

School District(s)
Hudson City SD (PK-12)
  Enrollment: 1,863 . . . . (518) 828-4360

Two-year College(s)

Columbia-Greene Community College (Public)

　　Enrollment: 1,620 . . . . (518) 828-4181

　　Tuition: In-state $4,888; Out-of-state $9,424

Housing: Homeownership rate: 34.1%; Median home value: $189,400; Median year structure built: Before 1940; Homeowner vacancy rate: 2.5%; Median selected monthly owner costs: $1,424 with a mortgage, $606 without a mortgage; Median gross rent: $768 per month; Rental vacancy rate: 6.9%

Health Insurance: 93.8% have insurance; 59.0% have private insurance; 45.4% have public insurance; 6.2% do not have insurance; 2.5% of children under 18 do not have insurance

Hospitals: Columbia Memorial Hospital (103 beds)

Safety: Violent crime rate: 72.4 per 10,000 population; Property crime rate: 318.0 per 10,000 population

Newspapers: Bleezarde Publishing (weekly circulation 4,200); Register-Star (daily circulation 5,200)

Transportation: Commute: 70.9% car, 3.1% public transportation, 18.1% walk, 4.6% work from home; Mean travel time to work: 21.2 minutes; Amtrak: Train service available.

Airports: Columbia County (general aviation)

Additional Information Contacts

City of Hudson. . . . . (518) 828-1030

　　http://cityofhudson.org/content

KINDERHOOK (town). Covers a land area of 31.806 square miles and a water area of 0.607 square miles. Located at 42.41° N. Lat; 73.68° W. Long. Elevation is 253 feet.

History: Kinderhook (Dutch for "children's corner") was named by its Dutch settlers. President Martin Van Buren was born and buried in Kinderhook. Settled before the American Revolution. Richard Upjohn designed St. Paul's Church (1851) here. The Van Buren homestead, "Lindenwald," is South of the village. The House of History, maintained by the county historical society, occupies an early-19th-century mansion. Incorporated 1838.

Population: 8,393; Growth (since 2000): 1.2%; Density: 263.9 persons per square mile; Race: 95.4% White, 0.9% Black/African American, 0.3% Asian, 0.1% American Indian/Alaska Native, 0.0% Native Hawaiian/Other Pacific Islander, 0.9% Two or more races, 5.0% Hispanic of any race; Average household size: 2.47; Median age: 48.2; Age under 18: 20.8%; Age 65 and over: 21.1%; Males per 100 females: 96.6; Marriage status: 24.5% never married, 57.7% now married, 2.6% separated, 6.9% widowed, 10.9% divorced; Foreign born: 4.3%; Speak English only: 95.3%; With disability: 12.5%; Veterans: 8.2%; Ancestry: 27.9% Irish, 20.6% German, 15.4% Italian, 11.7% English, 8.0% Polish

Employment: 22.6% management, business, and financial, 4.0% computer, engineering, and science, 15.2% education, legal, community service, arts, and media, 6.8% healthcare practitioners, 18.4% service, 17.8% sales and office, 6.5% natural resources, construction, and maintenance, 8.6% production, transportation, and material moving

Income: Per capita: $36,185; Median household: $80,118; Average household: $90,139; Households with income of $100,000 or more: 36.0%; Poverty rate: 8.4%

Educational Attainment: High school diploma or higher: 92.9%; Bachelor's degree or higher: 38.2%; Graduate/professional degree or higher: 16.9%

Housing: Homeownership rate: 80.7%; Median home value: $229,600; Median year structure built: 1974; Homeowner vacancy rate: 0.3%; Median selected monthly owner costs: $1,746 with a mortgage, $690 without a mortgage; Median gross rent: $838 per month; Rental vacancy rate: 7.5%

Health Insurance: 96.3% have insurance; 80.6% have private insurance; 29.4% have public insurance; 3.7% do not have insurance; 2.9% of children under 18 do not have insurance

Transportation: Commute: 90.2% car, 0.7% public transportation, 1.2% walk, 5.8% work from home; Mean travel time to work: 25.3 minutes

Additional Information Contacts

Town of Kinderhook . . . . (518) 784-2233

　　http://www.kinderhook-ny.gov

KINDERHOOK (village). Covers a land area of 2.104 square miles and a water area of 0 square miles. Located at 42.39° N. Lat; 73.70° W. Long. Elevation is 253 feet.

Population: 1,359; Growth (since 2000): 6.6%; Density: 646.0 persons per square mile; Race: 99.0% White, 0.0% Black/African American, 0.4% Asian, 0.0% American Indian/Alaska Native, 0.0% Native Hawaiian/Other

Pacific Islander, 0.5% Two or more races, 1.0% Hispanic of any race; Average household size: 2.10; Median age: 53.3; Age under 18: 17.2%; Age 65 and over: 26.6%; Males per 100 females: 89.5; Marriage status: 21.9% never married, 61.5% now married, 2.1% separated, 9.6% widowed, 7.1% divorced; Foreign born: 5.7%; Speak English only: 97.7%; With disability: 17.6%; Veterans: 8.5%; Ancestry: 36.4% Irish, 20.8% German, 19.9% English, 13.4% Italian, 9.9% Polish

Employment: 21.7% management, business, and financial, 2.6% computer, engineering, and science, 18.9% education, legal, community service, arts, and media, 6.0% healthcare practitioners, 11.3% service, 22.2% sales and office, 8.1% natural resources, construction, and maintenance, 9.2% production, transportation, and material moving

Income: Per capita: $48,756; Median household: $81,375; Average household: $100,640; Households with income of $100,000 or more: 38.6%; Poverty rate: 2.3%

Educational Attainment: High school diploma or higher: 96.2%; Bachelor's degree or higher: 51.7%; Graduate/professional degree or higher: 29.5%

Housing: Homeownership rate: 85.8%; Median home value: $242,000; Median year structure built: 1948; Homeowner vacancy rate: 0.0%; Median selected monthly owner costs: $1,813 with a mortgage, $666 without a mortgage; Median gross rent: $860 per month; Rental vacancy rate: 0.0%

Health Insurance: 98.0% have insurance; 93.1% have private insurance; 26.7% have public insurance; 2.0% do not have insurance; 0.0% of children under 18 do not have insurance

Transportation: Commute: 82.8% car, 2.8% public transportation, 1.2% walk, 12.0% work from home; Mean travel time to work: 31.0 minutes

---

LIVINGSTON (town). Covers a land area of 38.163 square miles and a water area of 0.784 square miles. Located at 42.14° N. Lat; 73.80° W. Long. Elevation is 200 feet.

Population: 3,563; Growth (since 2000): 4.1%; Density: 93.4 persons per square mile; Race: 95.2% White, 1.0% Black/African American, 0.5% Asian, 0.0% American Indian/Alaska Native, 0.0% Native Hawaiian/Other Pacific Islander, 2.3% Two or more races, 6.8% Hispanic of any race; Average household size: 2.35; Median age: 49.8; Age under 18: 16.6%; Age 65 and over: 26.1%; Males per 100 females: 97.7; Marriage status: 32.9% never married, 43.6% now married, 1.1% separated, 11.2% widowed, 12.3% divorced; Foreign born: 4.8%; Speak English only: 93.2%; With disability: 21.1%; Veterans: 8.7%; Ancestry: 21.7% Irish, 20.3% German, 16.2% Italian, 6.5% Polish, 6.4% English

Employment: 14.2% management, business, and financial, 1.2% computer, engineering, and science, 8.4% education, legal, community service, arts, and media, 7.7% healthcare practitioners, 20.3% service, 26.2% sales and office, 10.5% natural resources, construction, and maintenance, 11.5% production, transportation, and material moving

Income: Per capita: $35,558; Median household: $64,612; Average household: $86,803; Households with income of $100,000 or more: 26.2%; Poverty rate: 6.8%

Educational Attainment: High school diploma or higher: 86.3%; Bachelor's degree or higher: 19.8%; Graduate/professional degree or higher: 6.8%

Housing: Homeownership rate: 78.3%; Median home value: $224,300; Median year structure built: 1976; Homeowner vacancy rate: 0.0%; Median selected monthly owner costs: $1,611 with a mortgage, $607 without a mortgage; Median gross rent: $863 per month; Rental vacancy rate: 0.0%

Health Insurance: 95.8% have insurance; 75.2% have private insurance; 40.6% have public insurance; 4.2% do not have insurance; 0.0% of children under 18 do not have insurance

Transportation: Commute: 88.1% car, 0.4% public transportation, 2.0% walk, 6.5% work from home; Mean travel time to work: 30.2 minutes

---

LORENZ PARK (CDP). Covers a land area of 1.784 square miles and a water area of 0.163 square miles. Located at 42.27° N. Lat; 73.78° W. Long. Elevation is 180 feet.

Population: 2,213; Growth (since 2000): 11.7%; Density: 1,240.2 persons per square mile; Race: 83.1% White, 6.4% Black/African American, 2.8% Asian, 0.0% American Indian/Alaska Native, 0.0% Native Hawaiian/Other Pacific Islander, 7.7% Two or more races, 6.3% Hispanic of any race; Average household size: 2.33; Median age: 43.4; Age under 18: 19.5%; Age 65 and over: 18.8%; Males per 100 females: 93.0; Marriage status: 38.1% never married, 44.6% now married, 0.8% separated, 8.9% widowed, 8.4% divorced; Foreign born: 4.9%; Speak English only: 91.0%; With disability: 21.1%; Veterans: 8.6%; Ancestry: 28.2% Italian, 25.2% Irish, 17.1% German, 8.1% Dutch, 5.7% American

Employment: 15.7% management, business, and financial, 0.6% computer, engineering, and science, 11.3% education, legal, community service, arts, and media, 7.9% healthcare practitioners, 35.6% service, 16.2% sales and office, 7.2% natural resources, construction, and maintenance, 5.6% production, transportation, and material moving
Income: Per capita: $29,054; Median household: $56,964; Average household: $67,257; Households with income of $100,000 or more: 18.5%; Poverty rate: 14.6%
Educational Attainment: High school diploma or higher: 89.4%; Bachelor's degree or higher: 19.0%; Graduate/professional degree or higher: 9.0%
Housing: Homeownership rate: 73.4%; Median home value: $151,000; Median year structure built: 1974; Homeowner vacancy rate: 0.0%; Median selected monthly owner costs: $1,614 with a mortgage, $480 without a mortgage; Median gross rent: $830 per month; Rental vacancy rate: 8.1%
Health Insurance: 95.7% have insurance; 68.1% have private insurance; 44.1% have public insurance; 4.3% do not have insurance; 0.0% of children under 18 do not have insurance
Transportation: Commute: 98.1% car, 0.3% public transportation, 1.6% walk, 0.0% work from home; Mean travel time to work: 20.1 minutes

MALDEN BRIDGE (unincorporated postal area)
ZCTA: 12115

Covers a land area of 5.183 square miles and a water area of 0.034 square miles. Located at 42.48° N. Lat; 73.58° W. Long. Elevation is 387 feet.
Population: 144; Growth (since 2000): -40.5%; Density: 27.8 persons per square mile; Race: 100.0% White, 0.0% Black/African American, 0.0% Asian, 0.0% American Indian/Alaska Native, 0.0% Native Hawaiian/Other Pacific Islander, 0.0% Two or more races, 20.8% Hispanic of any race; Average household size: 2.00; Median age: 70.1; Age under 18: 0.0%; Age 65 and over: 52.8%; Males per 100 females: 90.9; Marriage status: 59.7% never married, 33.3% now married, 0.0% separated, 6.9% widowed, 0.0% divorced; Foreign born: 6.9%; Speak English only: 97.2%; With disability: 2.8%; Veterans: 0.0%; Ancestry: 34.7% Italian, 23.6% German, 22.2% English, 8.3% Scotch-Irish, 6.9% French
Employment: 6.5% management, business, and financial, 6.5% computer, engineering, and science, 51.6% education, legal, community service, arts, and media, 35.5% healthcare practitioners, 0.0% service, 0.0% sales and office, 0.0% natural resources, construction, and maintenance, 0.0% production, transportation, and material moving
Income: Per capita: $51,062; Median household: $85,682; Average household: $98,056; Households with income of $100,000 or more: 27.8%; Poverty rate: n/a
Educational Attainment: High school diploma or higher: 100.0%; Bachelor's degree or higher: 55.4%; Graduate/professional degree or higher: 23.1%
Housing: Homeownership rate: 61.1%; Median home value: n/a; Median year structure built: Before 1940; Homeowner vacancy rate: 0.0%; Median selected monthly owner costs: $0 with a mortgage, $0 without a mortgage; Median gross rent: n/a per month; Rental vacancy rate: 0.0%
Health Insurance: 94.4% have insurance; 94.4% have private insurance; 52.8% have public insurance; 5.6% do not have insurance; 0.0% of children under 18 do not have insurance
Transportation: Commute: 35.5% car, 0.0% public transportation, 0.0% walk, 64.5% work from home; Mean travel time to work: 0.0 minutes

NEW LEBANON (town). Covers a land area of 35.857 square miles and a water area of 0.116 square miles. Located at 42.47° N. Lat; 73.44° W. Long. Elevation is 696 feet.
History: Samuel Tilden was born here. Site of Roman Catholic Shrine of Our Lady of Lourdes.
Population: 2,367; Growth (since 2000): -3.5%; Density: 66.0 persons per square mile; Race: 93.6% White, 1.6% Black/African American, 1.3% Asian, 0.0% American Indian/Alaska Native, 0.0% Native Hawaiian/Other Pacific Islander, 1.0% Two or more races, 2.8% Hispanic of any race; Average household size: 2.27; Median age: 47.4; Age under 18: 15.7%; Age 65 and over: 21.4%; Males per 100 females: 105.8; Marriage status: 31.3% never married, 50.4% now married, 1.8% separated, 6.7% widowed, 11.6% divorced; Foreign born: 6.0%; Speak English only: 92.5%; With disability: 12.3%; Veterans: 9.1%; Ancestry: 25.1% Irish, 17.0% German, 14.8% English, 12.7% Italian, 7.9% American

Employment: 15.0% management, business, and financial, 4.2% computer, engineering, and science, 13.9% education, legal, community service, arts, and media, 6.4% healthcare practitioners, 21.2% service, 14.9% sales and office, 17.2% natural resources, construction, and maintenance, 7.2% production, transportation, and material moving
Income: Per capita: $37,826; Median household: $54,315; Average household: $83,234; Households with income of $100,000 or more: 24.0%; Poverty rate: 8.0%
Educational Attainment: High school diploma or higher: 89.5%; Bachelor's degree or higher: 32.9%; Graduate/professional degree or higher: 15.3%

School District(s)
New Lebanon Central SD (PK-12)
　　Enrollment: 416 . . . . (518) 794-7600
Housing: Homeownership rate: 75.4%; Median home value: $202,200; Median year structure built: 1961; Homeowner vacancy rate: 6.2%; Median selected monthly owner costs: $1,784 with a mortgage, $714 without a mortgage; Median gross rent: $920 per month; Rental vacancy rate: 7.3%
Health Insurance: 92.6% have insurance; 72.5% have private insurance; 37.2% have public insurance; 7.4% do not have insurance; 1.2% of children under 18 do not have insurance
Transportation: Commute: 86.8% car, 2.5% public transportation, 5.6% walk, 4.1% work from home; Mean travel time to work: 26.1 minutes

NIVERVILLE (CDP). Covers a land area of 2.874 square miles and a water area of 0.545 square miles. Located at 42.45° N. Lat; 73.65° W. Long. Elevation is 318 feet.
Population: 1,390; Growth (since 2000): -20.0%; Density: 483.6 persons per square mile; Race: 96.8% White, 1.0% Black/African American, 0.0% Asian, 0.0% American Indian/Alaska Native, 0.0% Native Hawaiian/Other Pacific Islander, 1.8% Two or more races, 0.4% Hispanic of any race; Average household size: 2.54; Median age: 48.3; Age under 18: 21.9%; Age 65 and over: 19.4%; Males per 100 females: 104.2; Marriage status: 27.0% never married, 56.5% now married, 4.3% separated, 7.1% widowed, 9.4% divorced; Foreign born: 1.0%; Speak English only: 98.9%; With disability: 11.0%; Veterans: 2.6%; Ancestry: 34.8% Irish, 28.6% German, 17.1% English, 10.0% Italian, 4.7% French
Employment: 23.7% management, business, and financial, 5.3% computer, engineering, and science, 17.7% education, legal, community service, arts, and media, 4.6% healthcare practitioners, 9.1% service, 23.1% sales and office, 3.9% natural resources, construction, and maintenance, 12.7% production, transportation, and material moving
Income: Per capita: $44,720; Median household: $98,462; Average household: $112,617; Households with income of $100,000 or more: 48.6%; Poverty rate: 4.9%
Educational Attainment: High school diploma or higher: 96.1%; Bachelor's degree or higher: 37.4%; Graduate/professional degree or higher: 13.1%
Housing: Homeownership rate: 82.8%; Median home value: $230,500; Median year structure built: 1971; Homeowner vacancy rate: 4.2%; Median selected monthly owner costs: $1,791 with a mortgage, $812 without a mortgage; Median gross rent: $893 per month; Rental vacancy rate: 0.0%
Health Insurance: 99.1% have insurance; 77.5% have private insurance; 36.4% have public insurance; 0.9% do not have insurance; 0.0% of children under 18 do not have insurance
Transportation: Commute: 94.7% car, 0.0% public transportation, 0.8% walk, 4.5% work from home; Mean travel time to work: 29.7 minutes

NORTH CHATHAM (unincorporated postal area)
ZCTA: 12132

Covers a land area of 1.859 square miles and a water area of 0 square miles. Located at 42.47° N. Lat; 73.63° W. Long. Elevation is 351 feet.
Population: 312; Growth (since 2000): n/a; Density: 167.8 persons per square mile; Race: 70.8% White, 0.0% Black/African American, 0.0% Asian, 1.3% American Indian/Alaska Native, 0.0% Native Hawaiian/Other Pacific Islander, 3.2% Two or more races, 24.7% Hispanic of any race; Average household size: 2.46; Median age: 43.6; Age under 18: 28.2%; Age 65 and over: 25.0%; Males per 100 females: 87.8; Marriage status: 36.9% never married, 63.1% now married, 0.0% separated, 0.0% widowed, 0.0% divorced; Foreign born: 19.6%; Speak English only: 88.7%; With disability: 19.9%; Veterans: 8.5%; Ancestry: 20.5% German, 17.6% Irish, 13.5% Italian, 11.2% French, 5.8% Polish
Employment: 25.0% management, business, and financial, 0.0% computer, engineering, and science, 10.5% education, legal, community service, arts, and media, 25.8% healthcare practitioners, 16.9% service,

21.8% sales and office, 0.0% natural resources, construction, and maintenance, 0.0% production, transportation, and material moving
Income: Per capita: $19,676; Median household: $49,395; Average household: $54,149; Households with income of $100,000 or more: 10.2%; Poverty rate: 26.6%
Educational Attainment: High school diploma or higher: 90.6%; Bachelor's degree or higher: 8.9%; Graduate/professional degree or higher: 8.9%
Housing: Homeownership rate: 59.1%; Median home value: n/a; Median year structure built: Before 1940; Homeowner vacancy rate: 8.5%; Median selected monthly owner costs: $1,490 with a mortgage, $0 without a mortgage; Median gross rent: n/a per month; Rental vacancy rate: 0.0%
Health Insurance: 79.2% have insurance; 54.5% have private insurance; 42.9% have public insurance; 20.8% do not have insurance; 25.0% of children under 18 do not have insurance
Transportation: Commute: 86.3% car, 3.2% public transportation, 0.0% walk, 10.5% work from home; Mean travel time to work: 0.0 minutes

OLD CHATHAM (unincorporated postal area)
ZCTA: 12136

Covers a land area of 18.151 square miles and a water area of 0.019 square miles. Located at 42.43° N. Lat; 73.56° W. Long. Elevation is 535 feet.
Population: 772; Growth (since 2000): -11.8%; Density: 42.5 persons per square mile; Race: 94.8% White, 2.2% Black/African American, 0.0% Asian, 0.0% American Indian/Alaska Native, 0.0% Native Hawaiian/Other Pacific Islander, 3.0% Two or more races, 9.3% Hispanic of any race; Average household size: 2.23; Median age: 51.9; Age under 18: 14.9%; Age 65 and over: 28.1%; Males per 100 females: 100.0; Marriage status: 13.9% never married, 75.3% now married, 0.0% separated, 4.3% widowed, 6.4% divorced; Foreign born: 7.8%; Speak English only: 87.9%; With disability: 11.1%; Veterans: 7.8%; Ancestry: 23.8% Irish, 22.0% German, 13.5% English, 12.6% French Canadian, 11.8% Italian
Employment: 32.5% management, business, and financial, 3.7% computer, engineering, and science, 12.3% education, legal, community service, arts, and media, 7.1% healthcare practitioners, 5.2% service, 24.7% sales and office, 10.0% natural resources, construction, and maintenance, 4.5% production, transportation, and material moving
Income: Per capita: $55,071; Median household: $102,829; Average household: $123,538; Households with income of $100,000 or more: 51.5%; Poverty rate: 0.9%
Educational Attainment: High school diploma or higher: 96.4%; Bachelor's degree or higher: 59.3%; Graduate/professional degree or higher: 36.9%
Housing: Homeownership rate: 93.4%; Median home value: $361,300; Median year structure built: 1962; Homeowner vacancy rate: 0.0%; Median selected monthly owner costs: $2,083 with a mortgage, $1,032 without a mortgage; Median gross rent: n/a per month; Rental vacancy rate: 0.0%
Health Insurance: 96.2% have insurance; 79.1% have private insurance; 38.3% have public insurance; 3.8% do not have insurance; 0.0% of children under 18 do not have insurance
Transportation: Commute: 68.2% car, 4.5% public transportation, 3.4% walk, 21.0% work from home; Mean travel time to work: 28.9 minutes

PHILMONT (village). Covers a land area of 1.187 square miles and a water area of 0.039 square miles. Located at 42.25° N. Lat; 73.65° W. Long. Elevation is 407 feet.
Population: 1,238; Growth (since 2000): -16.4%; Density: 1,042.6 persons per square mile; Race: 93.5% White, 0.9% Black/African American, 1.9% Asian, 0.0% American Indian/Alaska Native, 0.0% Native Hawaiian/Other Pacific Islander, 3.8% Two or more races, 1.8% Hispanic of any race; Average household size: 2.16; Median age: 35.6; Age under 18: 25.0%; Age 65 and over: 16.6%; Males per 100 females: 93.4; Marriage status: 30.2% never married, 45.6% now married, 7.0% separated, 7.1% widowed, 17.0% divorced; Foreign born: 3.0%; Speak English only: 97.6%; With disability: 18.1%; Veterans: 4.3%; Ancestry: 31.3% Irish, 27.4% German, 12.6% Italian, 9.9% Dutch, 6.4% English
Employment: 10.8% management, business, and financial, 0.0% computer, engineering, and science, 9.3% education, legal, community service, arts, and media, 2.3% healthcare practitioners, 20.8% service, 35.4% sales and office, 9.2% natural resources, construction, and maintenance, 12.2% production, transportation, and material moving

Income: Per capita: $25,258; Median household: $39,891; Average household: $54,590; Households with income of $100,000 or more: 5.6%; Poverty rate: 24.6%
Educational Attainment: High school diploma or higher: 86.7%; Bachelor's degree or higher: 26.3%; Graduate/professional degree or higher: 10.6%
Housing: Homeownership rate: 43.2%; Median home value: $168,500; Median year structure built: Before 1940; Homeowner vacancy rate: 7.1%; Median selected monthly owner costs: $1,656 with a mortgage, $806 without a mortgage; Median gross rent: $773 per month; Rental vacancy rate: 3.0%
Health Insurance: 95.0% have insurance; 48.9% have private insurance; 57.8% have public insurance; 5.0% do not have insurance; 2.8% of children under 18 do not have insurance
Transportation: Commute: 88.5% car, 1.3% public transportation, 4.2% walk, 3.5% work from home; Mean travel time to work: 18.3 minutes

SPENCERTOWN (unincorporated postal area)
ZCTA: 12165

Covers a land area of 3.227 square miles and a water area of 0.002 square miles. Located at 42.31° N. Lat; 73.51° W. Long. Elevation is 686 feet.
Population: 174; Growth (since 2000): -26.3%; Density: 53.9 persons per square mile; Race: 100.0% White, 0.0% Black/African American, 0.0% Asian, 0.0% American Indian/Alaska Native, 0.0% Native Hawaiian/Other Pacific Islander, 0.0% Two or more races, 0.0% Hispanic of any race; Average household size: 2.20; Median age: 51.7; Age under 18: 13.8%; Age 65 and over: 32.8%; Males per 100 females: 110.8; Marriage status: 29.1% never married, 57.0% now married, 0.0% separated, 1.9% widowed, 12.0% divorced; Foreign born: 3.4%; Speak English only: 97.7%; With disability: 15.5%; Veterans: 9.3%; Ancestry: 26.4% Irish, 21.3% English, 11.5% German, 9.8% American, 9.2% Greek
Employment: 8.8% management, business, and financial, 0.0% computer, engineering, and science, 26.4% education, legal, community service, arts, and media, 6.6% healthcare practitioners, 27.5% service, 9.9% sales and office, 13.2% natural resources, construction, and maintenance, 7.7% production, transportation, and material moving
Income: Per capita: $37,501; Median household: n/a; Average household: $83,290; Households with income of $100,000 or more: 43.0%; Poverty rate: 32.4%
Educational Attainment: High school diploma or higher: 98.5%; Bachelor's degree or higher: 35.4%; Graduate/professional degree or higher: 27.7%
Housing: Homeownership rate: 69.6%; Median home value: n/a; Median year structure built: 1987; Homeowner vacancy rate: 0.0%; Median selected monthly owner costs: $2,250 with a mortgage, $855 without a mortgage; Median gross rent: $683 per month; Rental vacancy rate: 0.0%
Health Insurance: 89.1% have insurance; 78.2% have private insurance; 44.3% have public insurance; 10.9% do not have insurance; 0.0% of children under 18 do not have insurance
Transportation: Commute: 73.6% car, 18.7% public transportation, 4.4% walk, 3.3% work from home; Mean travel time to work: 29.5 minutes

STOCKPORT (town). Covers a land area of 11.648 square miles and a water area of 1.505 square miles. Located at 42.32° N. Lat; 73.76° W. Long. Elevation is 135 feet.
Population: 2,725; Growth (since 2000): -7.1%; Density: 233.9 persons per square mile; Race: 92.2% White, 2.6% Black/African American, 0.0% Asian, 0.1% American Indian/Alaska Native, 0.0% Native Hawaiian/Other Pacific Islander, 0.6% Two or more races, 6.0% Hispanic of any race; Average household size: 2.46; Median age: 40.3; Age under 18: 19.5%; Age 65 and over: 15.0%; Males per 100 females: 106.2; Marriage status: 39.8% never married, 44.4% now married, 2.7% separated, 4.3% widowed, 11.4% divorced; Foreign born: 3.5%; Speak English only: 94.6%; With disability: 15.5%; Veterans: 10.7%; Ancestry: 23.2% Irish, 22.5% Italian, 21.6% German, 7.0% English, 7.0% Polish
Employment: 14.5% management, business, and financial, 1.5% computer, engineering, and science, 6.5% education, legal, community service, arts, and media, 6.6% healthcare practitioners, 23.5% service, 22.0% sales and office, 11.4% natural resources, construction, and maintenance, 13.9% production, transportation, and material moving

Income: Per capita: $26,363; Median household: $50,224; Average household: $64,489; Households with income of $100,000 or more: 16.1%; Poverty rate: 9.9%

Educational Attainment: High school diploma or higher: 85.1%; Bachelor's degree or higher: 15.1%; Graduate/professional degree or higher: 4.0%

Housing: Homeownership rate: 68.7%; Median home value: $151,200; Median year structure built: 1965; Homeowner vacancy rate: 2.3%; Median selected monthly owner costs: $1,441 with a mortgage, $556 without a mortgage; Median gross rent: $946 per month; Rental vacancy rate: 0.0%

Health Insurance: 93.7% have insurance; 62.2% have private insurance; 41.5% have public insurance; 6.3% do not have insurance; 2.2% of children under 18 do not have insurance

Transportation: Commute: 93.6% car, 0.0% public transportation, 0.8% walk, 3.3% work from home; Mean travel time to work: 24.3 minutes

STOTTVILLE (CDP).
Covers a land area of 4.179 square miles and a water area of 0.030 square miles. Located at 42.29° N. Lat; 73.76° W. Long. Elevation is 115 feet.

Population: 1,483; Growth (since 2000): 9.4%; Density: 354.8 persons per square mile; Race: 80.0% White, 5.1% Black/African American, 0.0% Asian, 0.0% American Indian/Alaska Native, 0.0% Native Hawaiian/Other Pacific Islander, 6.4% Two or more races, 8.5% Hispanic of any race; Average household size: 2.47; Median age: 38.4; Age under 18: 24.0%; Age 65 and over: 17.3%; Males per 100 females: 100.4; Marriage status: 37.9% never married, 43.9% now married, 5.5% separated, 4.3% widowed, 13.9% divorced; Foreign born: 7.9%; Speak English only: 91.9%; With disability: 15.6%; Veterans: 12.4%; Ancestry: 21.8% Irish, 17.2% Italian, 15.0% German, 6.9% Polish, 4.2% French Canadian

Employment: 17.3% management, business, and financial, 0.0% computer, engineering, and science, 4.9% education, legal, community service, arts, and media, 6.2% healthcare practitioners, 28.4% service, 13.7% sales and office, 9.5% natural resources, construction, and maintenance, 20.1% production, transportation, and material moving

Income: Per capita: $22,686; Median household: $46,326; Average household: $56,577; Households with income of $100,000 or more: 6.0%; Poverty rate: 19.8%

Educational Attainment: High school diploma or higher: 75.5%; Bachelor's degree or higher: 15.8%; Graduate/professional degree or higher: 7.6%

Housing: Homeownership rate: 48.9%; Median home value: $160,300; Median year structure built: 1959; Homeowner vacancy rate: 4.6%; Median selected monthly owner costs: $1,382 with a mortgage, $487 without a mortgage; Median gross rent: $984 per month; Rental vacancy rate: 0.0%

Health Insurance: 88.7% have insurance; 51.9% have private insurance; 51.8% have public insurance; 11.3% do not have insurance; 4.3% of children under 18 do not have insurance

Transportation: Commute: 90.2% car, 0.0% public transportation, 1.4% walk, 7.0% work from home; Mean travel time to work: 24.7 minutes

STUYVESANT (town).
Covers a land area of 25.004 square miles and a water area of 1.745 square miles. Located at 42.40° N. Lat; 73.75° W. Long. Elevation is 105 feet.

Population: 2,280; Growth (since 2000): 4.2%; Density: 91.2 persons per square mile; Race: 94.4% White, 0.8% Black/African American, 0.0% Asian, 0.0% American Indian/Alaska Native, 0.0% Native Hawaiian/Other Pacific Islander, 4.5% Two or more races, 3.4% Hispanic of any race; Average household size: 2.62; Median age: 40.2; Age under 18: 24.0%; Age 65 and over: 13.2%; Males per 100 females: 101.1; Marriage status: 30.5% never married, 51.6% now married, 1.2% separated, 3.9% widowed, 14.0% divorced; Foreign born: 6.2%; Speak English only: 94.0%; With disability: 14.4%; Veterans: 10.8%; Ancestry: 26.6% Italian, 22.1% German, 18.9% Irish, 8.6% Polish, 7.6% English

Employment: 15.8% management, business, and financial, 3.9% computer, engineering, and science, 16.7% education, legal, community service, arts, and media, 6.0% healthcare practitioners, 12.9% service, 18.1% sales and office, 14.9% natural resources, construction, and maintenance, 11.8% production, transportation, and material moving

Income: Per capita: $32,055; Median household: $74,659; Average household: $82,317; Households with income of $100,000 or more: 37.5%; Poverty rate: 17.1%

Educational Attainment: High school diploma or higher: 93.7%; Bachelor's degree or higher: 28.9%; Graduate/professional degree or higher: 12.1%

Housing: Homeownership rate: 73.6%; Median home value: $215,500; Median year structure built: 1972; Homeowner vacancy rate: 2.4%; Median selected monthly owner costs: $1,690 with a mortgage, $647 without a mortgage; Median gross rent: $1,060 per month; Rental vacancy rate: 0.0%

Health Insurance: 92.5% have insurance; 71.0% have private insurance; 32.5% have public insurance; 7.5% do not have insurance; 0.5% of children under 18 do not have insurance

Transportation: Commute: 89.6% car, 1.0% public transportation, 2.5% walk, 4.9% work from home; Mean travel time to work: 31.3 minutes

STUYVESANT FALLS (unincorporated postal area)
ZCTA: 12174

Covers a land area of 1.149 square miles and a water area of 0 square miles. Located at 42.35° N. Lat; 73.73° W. Long. Elevation is 210 feet.

Population: 342; Growth (since 2000): n/a; Density: 297.5 persons per square mile; Race: 93.9% White, 0.0% Black/African American, 0.0% Asian, 0.0% American Indian/Alaska Native, 0.0% Native Hawaiian/Other Pacific Islander, 6.1% Two or more races, 1.5% Hispanic of any race; Average household size: 3.11; Median age: 33.5; Age under 18: 31.9%; Age 65 and over: 6.1%; Males per 100 females: 99.4; Marriage status: 30.9% never married, 50.4% now married, 0.0% separated, 5.0% widowed, 13.7% divorced; Foreign born: 2.3%; Speak English only: 97.2%; With disability: 2.3%; Veterans: 10.7%; Ancestry: 38.9% Italian, 16.1% Polish, 11.7% English, 5.8% German, 4.4% Ukrainian

Employment: 19.2% management, business, and financial, 11.5% computer, engineering, and science, 17.9% education, legal, community service, arts, and media, 0.6% healthcare practitioners, 24.4% service, 15.4% sales and office, 0.6% natural resources, construction, and maintenance, 10.3% production, transportation, and material moving

Income: Per capita: $27,282; Median household: n/a; Average household: $75,340; Households with income of $100,000 or more: 43.7%; Poverty rate: 12.9%

Educational Attainment: High school diploma or higher: 88.9%; Bachelor's degree or higher: 34.2%; Graduate/professional degree or higher: 13.6%

Housing: Homeownership rate: 62.7%; Median home value: $218,800; Median year structure built: Before 1940; Homeowner vacancy rate: 0.0%; Median selected monthly owner costs: $1,050 with a mortgage, $770 without a mortgage; Median gross rent: $1,006 per month; Rental vacancy rate: 0.0%

Health Insurance: 95.6% have insurance; 59.4% have private insurance; 38.0% have public insurance; 4.4% do not have insurance; 0.0% of children under 18 do not have insurance

Transportation: Commute: 100.0% car, 0.0% public transportation, 0.0% walk, 0.0% work from home; Mean travel time to work: 23.1 minutes

TAGHKANIC (town).
Covers a land area of 39.972 square miles and a water area of 0.166 square miles. Located at 42.13° N. Lat; 73.68° W. Long. Elevation is 725 feet.

Population: 1,106; Growth (since 2000): -1.1%; Density: 27.7 persons per square mile; Race: 97.0% White, 1.1% Black/African American, 0.6% Asian, 0.0% American Indian/Alaska Native, 0.0% Native Hawaiian/Other Pacific Islander, 1.3% Two or more races, 4.3% Hispanic of any race; Average household size: 2.19; Median age: 54.4; Age under 18: 10.5%; Age 65 and over: 29.3%; Males per 100 females: 102.5; Marriage status: 25.2% never married, 57.4% now married, 1.2% separated, 5.1% widowed, 12.2% divorced; Foreign born: 5.3%; Speak English only: 94.7%; With disability: 17.6%; Veterans: 6.3%; Ancestry: 25.2% German, 20.4% Irish, 13.5% Italian, 9.1% English, 8.6% Polish

Employment: 15.9% management, business, and financial, 1.5% computer, engineering, and science, 19.9% education, legal, community service, arts, and media, 7.7% healthcare practitioners, 17.9% service, 24.5% sales and office, 7.9% natural resources, construction, and maintenance, 4.8% production, transportation, and material moving

Income: Per capita: $47,541; Median household: $72,813; Average household: $104,923; Households with income of $100,000 or more: 35.0%; Poverty rate: 17.3%

Educational Attainment: High school diploma or higher: 85.0%; Bachelor's degree or higher: 34.1%; Graduate/professional degree or higher: 21.7%

Housing: Homeownership rate: 87.9%; Median home value: $297,000; Median year structure built: 1975; Homeowner vacancy rate: 8.2%; Median

selected monthly owner costs: $1,939 with a mortgage, $738 without a mortgage; Median gross rent: $895 per month; Rental vacancy rate: 13.0%
Health Insurance: 96.1% have insurance; 73.9% have private insurance; 41.5% have public insurance; 3.9% do not have insurance; 0.0% of children under 18 do not have insurance
Transportation: Commute: 70.4% car, 6.1% public transportation, 7.2% walk, 13.5% work from home; Mean travel time to work: 30.6 minutes

VALATIE (village).
Covers a land area of 1.254 square miles and a water area of 0.012 square miles. Located at 42.41° N. Lat; 73.68° W. Long. Elevation is 239 feet.
History: Incorporated 1856.
Population: 1,585; Growth (since 2000): -7.4%; Density: 1,263.7 persons per square mile; Race: 93.9% White, 1.3% Black/African American, 1.5% Asian, 0.1% American Indian/Alaska Native, 0.0% Native Hawaiian/Other Pacific Islander, 0.7% Two or more races, 5.0% Hispanic of any race; Average household size: 2.62; Median age: 44.7; Age under 18: 20.9%; Age 65 and over: 26.6%; Males per 100 females: 93.1; Marriage status: 34.5% never married, 44.0% now married, 2.7% separated, 11.3% widowed, 10.1% divorced; Foreign born: 5.1%; Speak English only: 94.7%; With disability: 13.7%; Veterans: 9.4%; Ancestry: 22.6% Irish, 17.2% German, 10.2% Italian, 9.2% Polish, 8.6% English
Employment: 11.5% management, business, and financial, 4.3% computer, engineering, and science, 13.3% education, legal, community service, arts, and media, 9.2% healthcare practitioners, 19.4% service, 27.5% sales and office, 9.2% natural resources, construction, and maintenance, 5.6% production, transportation, and material moving
Income: Per capita: $28,702; Median household: $66,607; Average household: $80,009; Households with income of $100,000 or more: 26.1%; Poverty rate: 10.4%
Educational Attainment: High school diploma or higher: 90.2%; Bachelor's degree or higher: 29.1%; Graduate/professional degree or higher: 12.2%
School District(s)
Kinderhook Central SD (PK-12)
    Enrollment: 1,814 . . . . (518) 758-7575
Housing: Homeownership rate: 69.7%; Median home value: $206,300; Median year structure built: 1954; Homeowner vacancy rate: 1.9%; Median selected monthly owner costs: $1,859 with a mortgage, $657 without a mortgage; Median gross rent: $716 per month; Rental vacancy rate: 9.9%
Health Insurance: 94.1% have insurance; 78.2% have private insurance; 28.9% have public insurance; 5.9% do not have insurance; 1.2% of children under 18 do not have insurance
Transportation: Commute: 91.9% car, 1.7% public transportation, 3.8% walk, 2.6% work from home; Mean travel time to work: 22.3 minutes

WEST LEBANON (unincorporated postal area)
ZCTA: 12195
    Covers a land area of 1.955 square miles and a water area of 0 square miles. Located at 42.48° N. Lat; 73.48° W. Long. Elevation is 623 feet.
Population: 136; Growth (since 2000): n/a; Density: 69.6 persons per square mile; Race: 100.0% White, 0.0% Black/African American, 0.0% Asian, 0.0% American Indian/Alaska Native, 0.0% Native Hawaiian/Other Pacific Islander, 0.0% Two or more races, 0.0% Hispanic of any race; Average household size: 1.48; Median age: 68.1; Age under 18: 0.0%; Age 65 and over: 56.6%; Males per 100 females: 97.4; Marriage status: 11.0% never married, 41.2% now married, 0.0% separated, 27.2% widowed, 20.6% divorced; Foreign born: 35.3%; Speak English only: 75.7%; With disability: 49.3%; Veterans: 17.6%; Ancestry: 35.3% Italian, 30.9% German, 17.6% English, 12.5% Polish, 11.8% French Canadian
Employment: 43.4% management, business, and financial, 0.0% computer, engineering, and science, 9.4% education, legal, community service, arts, and media, 0.0% healthcare practitioners, 0.0% service, 26.4% sales and office, 0.0% natural resources, construction, and maintenance, 20.8% production, transportation, and material moving
Income: Per capita: $22,338; Median household: $19,359; Average household: $32,110; Households with income of $100,000 or more: 5.4%; Poverty rate: 12.5%
Educational Attainment: High school diploma or higher: 90.9%; Bachelor's degree or higher: 35.5%; Graduate/professional degree or higher: 4.1%
Housing: Homeownership rate: 81.5%; Median home value: $233,500; Median year structure built: 1969; Homeowner vacancy rate: 0.0%; Median selected monthly owner costs: $2,517 with a mortgage, $859

without a mortgage; Median gross rent: n/a per month; Rental vacancy rate: 0.0%
Health Insurance: 91.9% have insurance; 63.2% have private insurance; 80.1% have public insurance; 8.1% do not have insurance; 0.0% of children under 18 do not have insurance
Transportation: Commute: 59.5% car, 0.0% public transportation, 40.5% walk, 0.0% work from home; Mean travel time to work: 0.0 minutes

Cortland County

Located in central New York; drained by the Tioughnioga River. Covers a land area of 498.760 square miles, a water area of 2.758 square miles, and is located in the Eastern Time Zone at 42.59° N. Lat., 76.08° W. Long. The county was founded in 1808. County seat is Cortland.

Cortland County is part of the Cortland, NY Micropolitan Statistical Area. The entire metro area includes: Cortland County, NY

Weather Station: Tully Heiberg Forest   Elevation: 1,898 feet

	Jan	Feb	Mar	Apr	May	Jun	Jul	Aug	Sep	Oct	Nov	Dec
High	27	30	37	51	63	72	76	75	67	55	43	32
Low	12	13	20	32	43	52	57	56	48	37	28	18
Precip	2.9	2.7	3.3	4.0	4.0	4.9	4.0	4.0	4.8	4.0	4.0	3.3
Snow	26.3	23.3	21.1	7.6	0.4	tr	0.0	0.0	tr	1.8	11.9	23.4

High and Low temperatures in degrees Fahrenheit; Precipitation and Snow in inches

Population: 48,334; Growth (since 2000): -0.5%; Density: 96.9 persons per square mile; Race: 94.7% White, 1.8% Black/African American, 0.8% Asian, 0.2% American Indian/Alaska Native, 0.0% Native Hawaiian/Other Pacific Islander, 2.0% two or more races, 2.6% Hispanic of any race; Average household size: 2.50; Median age: 36.2; Age under 18: 19.6%; Age 65 and over: 15.4%; Males per 100 females: 95.4; Marriage status: 40.1% never married, 45.0% now married, 2.1% separated, 5.8% widowed, 9.0% divorced; Foreign born: 2.0%; Speak English only: 96.9%; With disability: 13.1%; Veterans: 7.4%; Ancestry: 19.5% English, 12.0% Irish, 9.4% German, 7.4% Italian, 6.8% American
Religion: Six largest groups: 12.9% Catholicism, 5.6% Methodist/Pietist, 2.5% Non-denominational Protestant, 2.4% Presbyterian-Reformed, 1.1% Baptist, 0.8% Latter-day Saints
Economy: Unemployment rate: 3.9%; Leading industries: 17.5 % retail trade; 13.4 % accommodation and food services; 12.5 % other services (except public administration); Farms: 518 totaling 115,024 acres; Company size: 0 employ 1,000 or more persons, 3 employ 500 to 999 persons, 18 employ 100 to 499 persons, 984 employ less than 100 persons; Business ownership: 821 women-owned, n/a Black-owned, 31 Hispanic-owned, 47 Asian-owned, 42 American Indian/Alaska Native-owned
Employment: 10.6% management, business, and financial, 5.2% computer, engineering, and science, 13.5% education, legal, community service, arts, and media, 5.2% healthcare practitioners, 20.9% service, 23.0% sales and office, 9.4% natural resources, construction, and maintenance, 12.3% production, transportation, and material moving
Income: Per capita: $26,271; Median household: $52,451; Average household: $68,452; Households with income of $100,000 or more: 19.1%; Poverty rate: 14.7%
Educational Attainment: High school diploma or higher: 90.6%; Bachelor's degree or higher: 26.0%; Graduate/professional degree or higher: 11.2%
Housing: Homeownership rate: 64.7%; Median home value: $113,900; Median year structure built: 1948; Homeowner vacancy rate: 1.4%; Median selected monthly owner costs: $1,229 with a mortgage, $557 without a mortgage; Median gross rent: $742 per month; Rental vacancy rate: 3.1%
Vital Statistics: Birth rate: 94.8 per 10,000 population; Death rate: 86.8 per 10,000 population; Age-adjusted cancer mortality rate: 152.4 deaths per 100,000 population
Health Insurance: 95.2% have insurance; 76.1% have private insurance; 32.5% have public insurance; 4.8% do not have insurance; 4.1% of children under 18 do not have insurance
Health Care: Physicians: 10.6 per 10,000 population; Dentists: 3.3 per 10,000 population; Hospital beds: 35.9 per 10,000 population; Hospital admissions: 762.3 per 10,000 population
Transportation: Commute: 87.6% car, 0.6% public transportation, 6.2% walk, 4.7% work from home; Mean travel time to work: 20.5 minutes
2016 Presidential Election: 48.9% Trump, 43.3% Clinton, 4.7% Johnson, 1.8% Stein

Additional Information Contacts
Cortland Government . . . . (607) 753-5021
http://www.cortland-co.org

Cortland County Communities

BLODGETT MILLS (CDP). Covers a land area of 2.174 square
miles and a water area of 0 square miles. Located at 42.57° N. Lat; 76.13°
W. Long. Elevation is 1,102 feet.
Population: 240; Growth (since 2000): n/a; Density: 110.4 persons per
square mile; Race: 100.0% White, 0.0% Black/African American, 0.0%
Asian, 0.0% American Indian/Alaska Native, 0.0% Native Hawaiian/Other
Pacific Islander, 0.0% Two or more races, 0.0% Hispanic of any race;
Average household size: 2.29; Median age: 54.4; Age under 18: 6.2%;
Age 65 and over: 10.8%; Males per 100 females: 104.7; Marriage status:
21.8% never married, 75.1% now married, 13.3% separated, 0.0%
widowed, 3.1% divorced; Foreign born: 6.7%; Speak English only: 93.1%;
With disability: 19.2%; Veterans: 2.7%; Ancestry: 34.2% American, 30.8%
Irish, 22.9% Italian, 15.0% English, 8.8% German
Employment: 0.0% management, business, and financial, 2.3% computer,
engineering, and science, 18.1% education, legal, community service, arts,
and media, 3.4% healthcare practitioners, 24.9% service, 23.2% sales and
office, 17.5% natural resources, construction, and maintenance, 10.7%
production, transportation, and material moving
Income: Per capita: $34,036; Median household: $54,063; Average
household: $75,719; Households with income of $100,000 or more: 30.5%;
Poverty rate: n/a
Educational Attainment: High school diploma or higher: 78.5%;
Bachelor's degree or higher: 22.6%; Graduate/professional degree or
higher: 7.0%
Housing: Homeownership rate: 93.3%; Median home value: $78,000;
Median year structure built: 1954; Homeowner vacancy rate: 0.0%; Median
selected monthly owner costs: $1,177 with a mortgage, $432 without a
mortgage; Median gross rent: n/a per month; Rental vacancy rate: 0.0%
Health Insurance: 100.0% have insurance; 80.8% have private insurance;
32.1% have public insurance; 0.0% do not have insurance; 0.0% of
children under 18 do not have insurance
Transportation: Commute: 83.5% car, 4.7% public transportation, 0.0%
walk, 7.6% work from home; Mean travel time to work: 20.4 minutes

CINCINNATUS (town). Covers a land area of 25.356 square miles
and a water area of 0.129 square miles. Located at 42.53° N. Lat; 75.91°
W. Long. Elevation is 1,050 feet.
Population: 892; Growth (since 2000): -15.1%; Density: 35.2 persons per
square mile; Race: 99.3% White, 0.0% Black/African American, 0.0%
Asian, 0.0% American Indian/Alaska Native, 0.0% Native Hawaiian/Other
Pacific Islander, 0.7% Two or more races, 1.2% Hispanic of any race;
Average household size: 2.44; Median age: 42.9; Age under 18: 22.8%;
Age 65 and over: 19.8%; Males per 100 females: 98.9; Marriage status:
24.8% never married, 54.8% now married, 5.6% separated, 11.0%
widowed, 9.4% divorced; Foreign born: 0.9%; Speak English only: 99.6%;
With disability: 20.7%; Veterans: 9.3%; Ancestry: 28.0% English, 13.5%
German, 13.3% American, 5.9% Irish, 4.4% Italian
Employment: 7.7% management, business, and financial, 4.9% computer,
engineering, and science, 7.5% education, legal, community service, arts,
and media, 4.1% healthcare practitioners, 25.4% service, 19.8% sales and
office, 22.4% natural resources, construction, and maintenance, 8.2%
production, transportation, and material moving
Income: Per capita: $22,657; Median household: $44,886; Average
household: $55,216; Households with income of $100,000 or more: 13.4%;
Poverty rate: 14.8%
Educational Attainment: High school diploma or higher: 92.4%;
Bachelor's degree or higher: 9.7%; Graduate/professional degree or
higher: 5.4%
School District(s)
Cincinnatus Central SD (PK-12)
    Enrollment: 602. . . . . (607) 863-4069
Housing: Homeownership rate: 77.3%; Median home value: $97,400;
Median year structure built: 1942; Homeowner vacancy rate: 3.2%; Median
selected monthly owner costs: $1,279 with a mortgage, $467 without a
mortgage; Median gross rent: $679 per month; Rental vacancy rate: 4.2%
Health Insurance: 94.3% have insurance; 70.7% have private insurance;
43.4% have public insurance; 5.7% do not have insurance; 1.5% of
children under 18 do not have insurance

Transportation: Commute: 86.3% car, 0.0% public transportation, 4.3%
walk, 3.2% work from home; Mean travel time to work: 34.8 minutes

CORTLAND (city). County seat. Covers a land area of 3.894 square
miles and a water area of 0.020 square miles. Located at 42.60° N. Lat;
76.18° W. Long. Elevation is 1,129 feet.
History: Elmer Ambrose Sperry (1860-1030), inventor, was born in
Cortland. Sperry is credited with 400 patents.
Population: 18,914; Growth (since 2000): 0.9%; Density: 4,857.2 persons
per square mile; Race: 92.9% White, 3.0% Black/African American, 0.6%
Asian, 0.0% American Indian/Alaska Native, 0.0% Native Hawaiian/Other
Pacific Islander, 2.6% Two or more races, 2.8% Hispanic of any race;
Average household size: 2.36; Median age: 27.9; Age under 18: 16.5%;
Age 65 and over: 13.6%; Males per 100 females: 90.7; Marriage status:
56.0% never married, 30.0% now married, 1.6% separated, 5.2%
widowed, 8.8% divorced; Foreign born: 2.1%; Speak English only: 96.3%;
With disability: 13.4%; Veterans: 6.2%; Ancestry: 15.8% English, 12.5%
Irish, 9.4% Italian, 8.0% German, 6.6% American
Employment: 8.0% management, business, and financial, 3.7% computer,
engineering, and science, 16.3% education, legal, community service, arts,
and media, 4.6% healthcare practitioners, 24.5% service, 25.6% sales and
office, 6.4% natural resources, construction, and maintenance, 10.9%
production, transportation, and material moving
Income: Per capita: $20,953; Median household: $42,976; Average
household: $55,229; Households with income of $100,000 or more: 12.2%;
Poverty rate: 24.4%
Educational Attainment: High school diploma or higher: 89.9%;
Bachelor's degree or higher: 26.7%; Graduate/professional degree or
higher: 12.0%
School District(s)
Cortland City SD (KG-12)
    Enrollment: 2,455 . . . . (607) 758-4100
Four-year College(s)
SUNY Cortland (Public)
    Enrollment: 6,913 . . . . (607) 753-2011
    Tuition: In-state $8,300; Out-of-state $17,950
Housing: Homeownership rate: 47.7%; Median home value: $98,200;
Median year structure built: Before 1940; Homeowner vacancy rate: 3.3%;
Median selected monthly owner costs: $1,154 with a mortgage, $540
without a mortgage; Median gross rent: $727 per month; Rental vacancy
rate: 4.0%
Health Insurance: 96.8% have insurance; 76.3% have private insurance;
31.3% have public insurance; 3.2% do not have insurance; 1.8% of
children under 18 do not have insurance
Hospitals: Cortland Regional Medical Center (181 beds)
Safety: Violent crime rate: 8.5 per 10,000 population; Property crime rate:
170.3 per 10,000 population
Newspapers: Cortland Standard (daily circulation 10,300)
Transportation: Commute: 80.3% car, 0.7% public transportation, 14.0%
walk, 4.0% work from home; Mean travel time to work: 16.7 minutes
Additional Information Contacts
City of Cortland . . . . (607) 756-6521
    http://www.cortland.org

CORTLAND WEST (CDP). Covers a land area of 5.166 square
miles and a water area of 0 square miles. Located at 42.59° N. Lat; 76.23°
W. Long.
Population: 1,235; Growth (since 2000): -8.2%; Density: 239.1 persons
per square mile; Race: 97.4% White, 2.6% Black/African American, 0.0%
Asian, 0.0% American Indian/Alaska Native, 0.0% Native Hawaiian/Other
Pacific Islander, 0.0% Two or more races, 0.0% Hispanic of any race;
Average household size: 2.34; Median age: 57.2; Age under 18: 19.0%;
Age 65 and over: 26.4%; Males per 100 females: 95.1; Marriage status:
12.3% never married, 79.0% now married, 0.0% separated, 3.3%
widowed, 5.5% divorced; Foreign born: 0.0%; Speak English only: 100.0%;
With disability: 8.2%; Veterans: 11.9%; Ancestry: 17.2% German, 16.0%
English, 14.5% Irish, 12.1% Italian, 5.7% Canadian
Employment: 14.1% management, business, and financial, 12.8%
computer, engineering, and science, 11.5% education, legal, community
service, arts, and media, 2.7% healthcare practitioners, 18.8% service,
26.6% sales and office, 2.9% natural resources, construction, and
maintenance, 10.5% production, transportation, and material moving
Income: Per capita: $40,889; Median household: $88,125; Average
household: $96,357; Households with income of $100,000 or more: 28.7%;
Poverty rate: 1.3%

Educational Attainment: High school diploma or higher: 90.5%; Bachelor's degree or higher: 33.9%; Graduate/professional degree or higher: 15.7%

Housing: Homeownership rate: 100.0%; Median home value: $168,200; Median year structure built: 1971; Homeowner vacancy rate: 0.0%; Median selected monthly owner costs: $1,243 with a mortgage, $707 without a mortgage; Median gross rent: n/a per month; Rental vacancy rate: 0.0%

Health Insurance: 100.0% have insurance; 88.6% have private insurance; 32.1% have public insurance; 0.0% do not have insurance; 0.0% of children under 18 do not have insurance

Transportation: Commute: 95.3% car, 0.0% public transportation, 0.0% walk, 4.7% work from home; Mean travel time to work: 16.0 minutes

CORTLANDVILLE (town). Covers a land area of 49.720 square miles and a water area of 0.180 square miles. Located at 42.60° N. Lat; 76.12° W. Long.

Population: 8,261; Growth (since 2000): 4.3%; Density: 166.2 persons per square mile; Race: 95.6% White, 1.2% Black/African American, 0.9% Asian, 0.0% American Indian/Alaska Native, 0.0% Native Hawaiian/Other Pacific Islander, 1.7% Two or more races, 5.4% Hispanic of any race; Average household size: 2.41; Median age: 42.4; Age under 18: 17.9%; Age 65 and over: 18.8%; Males per 100 females: 94.4; Marriage status: 30.8% never married, 54.4% now married, 2.2% separated, 7.3% widowed, 7.5% divorced; Foreign born: 2.0%; Speak English only: 97.6%; With disability: 14.0%; Veterans: 7.5%; Ancestry: 20.6% English, 10.6% German, 9.9% Irish, 8.5% Italian, 4.5% American

Employment: 8.9% management, business, and financial, 8.2% computer, engineering, and science, 15.0% education, legal, community service, arts, and media, 4.9% healthcare practitioners, 22.5% service, 20.7% sales and office, 10.9% natural resources, construction, and maintenance, 8.7% production, transportation, and material moving

Income: Per capita: $31,529; Median household: $65,071; Average household: $78,300; Households with income of $100,000 or more: 23.3%; Poverty rate: 8.0%

Educational Attainment: High school diploma or higher: 91.7%; Bachelor's degree or higher: 33.1%; Graduate/professional degree or higher: 14.0%

Housing: Homeownership rate: 72.5%; Median home value: $133,300; Median year structure built: 1961; Homeowner vacancy rate: 0.0%; Median selected monthly owner costs: $1,327 with a mortgage, $556 without a mortgage; Median gross rent: $773 per month; Rental vacancy rate: 4.4%

Health Insurance: 96.9% have insurance; 81.7% have private insurance; 32.3% have public insurance; 3.1% do not have insurance; 0.7% of children under 18 do not have insurance

Transportation: Commute: 92.7% car, 1.2% public transportation, 1.2% walk, 4.3% work from home; Mean travel time to work: 17.8 minutes

Additional Information Contacts

Town of Cortlandville . . . . (607) 756-5725
http://www.cortlandville.org

CUYLER (town). Covers a land area of 43.477 square miles and a water area of 0.032 square miles. Located at 42.73° N. Lat; 75.94° W. Long. Elevation is 1,214 feet.

Population: 853; Growth (since 2000): -17.7%; Density: 19.6 persons per square mile; Race: 97.9% White, 0.0% Black/African American, 0.0% Asian, 0.0% American Indian/Alaska Native, 0.0% Native Hawaiian/Other Pacific Islander, 2.1% Two or more races, 1.6% Hispanic of any race; Average household size: 2.68; Median age: 48.4; Age under 18: 20.9%; Age 65 and over: 17.8%; Males per 100 females: 105.5; Marriage status: 26.1% never married, 51.5% now married, 3.5% separated, 9.1% widowed, 13.3% divorced; Foreign born: 0.5%; Speak English only: 98.2%; With disability: 17.9%; Veterans: 10.2%; Ancestry: 25.9% English, 10.6% Irish, 9.4% American, 7.3% German, 4.8% Italian

Employment: 5.1% management, business, and financial, 4.2% computer, engineering, and science, 11.0% education, legal, community service, arts, and media, 6.5% healthcare practitioners, 22.0% service, 9.9% sales and office, 18.0% natural resources, construction, and maintenance, 23.4% production, transportation, and material moving

Income: Per capita: $25,592; Median household: $52,500; Average household: $66,653; Households with income of $100,000 or more: 17.6%; Poverty rate: 18.3%

Educational Attainment: High school diploma or higher: 83.7%; Bachelor's degree or higher: 13.8%; Graduate/professional degree or higher: 5.6%

Housing: Homeownership rate: 74.2%; Median home value: $90,000; Median year structure built: 1976; Homeowner vacancy rate: 0.0%; Median selected monthly owner costs: $1,250 with a mortgage, $500 without a mortgage; Median gross rent: $683 per month; Rental vacancy rate: 0.0%

Health Insurance: 94.5% have insurance; 60.5% have private insurance; 50.1% have public insurance; 5.5% do not have insurance; 3.8% of children under 18 do not have insurance

Transportation: Commute: 98.0% car, 0.0% public transportation, 0.0% walk, 2.0% work from home; Mean travel time to work: 32.0 minutes

FREETOWN (town). Covers a land area of 25.486 square miles and a water area of 0.142 square miles. Located at 42.52° N. Lat; 76.02° W. Long.

Population: 635; Growth (since 2000): -19.5%; Density: 24.9 persons per square mile; Race: 97.0% White, 1.4% Black/African American, 0.0% Asian, 1.6% American Indian/Alaska Native, 0.0% Native Hawaiian/Other Pacific Islander, 0.0% Two or more races, 0.0% Hispanic of any race; Average household size: 2.49; Median age: 42.2; Age under 18: 22.2%; Age 65 and over: 10.7%; Males per 100 females: 96.1; Marriage status: 28.1% never married, 51.7% now married, 2.4% separated, 4.1% widowed, 16.1% divorced; Foreign born: 0.2%; Speak English only: 99.0%; With disability: 16.7%; Veterans: 10.1%; Ancestry: 13.5% English, 11.7% German, 10.6% American, 6.9% Irish, 6.3% Italian

Employment: 11.0% management, business, and financial, 1.3% computer, engineering, and science, 14.8% education, legal, community service, arts, and media, 4.7% healthcare practitioners, 17.6% service, 15.4% sales and office, 18.6% natural resources, construction, and maintenance, 16.7% production, transportation, and material moving

Income: Per capita: $22,685; Median household: $48,942; Average household: $57,301; Households with income of $100,000 or more: 11.4%; Poverty rate: 13.4%

Educational Attainment: High school diploma or higher: 85.7%; Bachelor's degree or higher: 12.5%; Graduate/professional degree or higher: 5.9%

Housing: Homeownership rate: 79.6%; Median home value: $87,900; Median year structure built: 1985; Homeowner vacancy rate: 1.4%; Median selected monthly owner costs: $1,101 with a mortgage, $508 without a mortgage; Median gross rent: $756 per month; Rental vacancy rate: 0.0%

Health Insurance: 92.4% have insurance; 63.9% have private insurance; 39.1% have public insurance; 7.6% do not have insurance; 11.3% of children under 18 do not have insurance

Transportation: Commute: 94.0% car, 0.0% public transportation, 0.3% walk, 5.4% work from home; Mean travel time to work: 27.2 minutes

HARFORD (town). Covers a land area of 24.152 square miles and a water area of 0.023 square miles. Located at 42.44° N. Lat; 76.21° W. Long. Elevation is 1,197 feet.

Population: 872; Growth (since 2000): -5.2%; Density: 36.1 persons per square mile; Race: 94.4% White, 0.0% Black/African American, 0.0% Asian, 3.0% American Indian/Alaska Native, 0.0% Native Hawaiian/Other Pacific Islander, 2.6% Two or more races, 0.0% Hispanic of any race; Average household size: 2.53; Median age: 41.7; Age under 18: 23.2%; Age 65 and over: 16.5%; Males per 100 females: 107.7; Marriage status: 31.8% never married, 48.6% now married, 1.6% separated, 9.3% widowed, 10.3% divorced; Foreign born: 1.5%; Speak English only: 99.8%; With disability: 16.7%; Veterans: 11.3%; Ancestry: 19.8% English, 11.7% American, 7.2% Irish, 7.0% German, 4.0% Italian

Employment: 18.2% management, business, and financial, 5.4% computer, engineering, and science, 5.4% education, legal, community service, arts, and media, 10.1% healthcare practitioners, 9.8% service, 14.0% sales and office, 8.6% natural resources, construction, and maintenance, 28.5% production, transportation, and material moving

Income: Per capita: $31,765; Median household: $60,294; Average household: $79,390; Households with income of $100,000 or more: 19.8%; Poverty rate: 5.6%

Educational Attainment: High school diploma or higher: 92.0%; Bachelor's degree or higher: 17.8%; Graduate/professional degree or higher: 7.2%

Housing: Homeownership rate: 78.5%; Median home value: $101,000; Median year structure built: 1972; Homeowner vacancy rate: 5.1%; Median selected monthly owner costs: $1,208 with a mortgage, $478 without a mortgage; Median gross rent: $800 per month; Rental vacancy rate: 0.0%

Health Insurance: 92.0% have insurance; 72.2% have private insurance; 31.4% have public insurance; 8.0% do not have insurance; 2.8% of children under 18 do not have insurance

Transportation: Commute: 85.6% car, 0.0% public transportation, 1.8% walk, 10.1% work from home; Mean travel time to work: 29.5 minutes

HOMER (town).
Covers a land area of 50.195 square miles and a water area of 0.461 square miles. Located at 42.66° N. Lat; 76.17° W. Long. Elevation is 1,125 feet.
History: Old Homer Village Historic District here. Settled 1791, incorporated 1835.
Population: 6,313; Growth (since 2000): -0.8%; Density: 125.8 persons per square mile; Race: 93.7% White, 0.7% Black/African American, 2.9% Asian, 0.0% American Indian/Alaska Native, 0.0% Native Hawaiian/Other Pacific Islander, 2.5% Two or more races, 1.3% Hispanic of any race; Average household size: 2.65; Median age: 40.6; Age under 18: 21.4%; Age 65 and over: 17.8%; Males per 100 females: 93.7; Marriage status: 30.5% never married, 53.9% now married, 2.8% separated, 6.0% widowed, 9.6% divorced; Foreign born: 3.2%; Speak English only: 95.6%; With disability: 12.2%; Veterans: 6.6%; Ancestry: 21.3% English, 17.1% Irish, 10.2% German, 6.0% Italian, 4.9% American
Employment: 15.4% management, business, and financial, 7.8% computer, engineering, and science, 13.5% education, legal, community service, arts, and media, 4.3% healthcare practitioners, 15.2% service, 28.5% sales and office, 6.0% natural resources, construction, and maintenance, 9.2% production, transportation, and material moving
Income: Per capita: $32,821; Median household: $62,860; Average household: $86,027; Households with income of $100,000 or more: 27.6%; Poverty rate: 7.9%
Educational Attainment: High school diploma or higher: 90.6%; Bachelor's degree or higher: 32.1%; Graduate/professional degree or higher: 14.3%

School District(s)
Homer Central SD (KG-12)
    Enrollment: 1,969 . . . . (607) 749-7241
Housing: Homeownership rate: 67.3%; Median home value: $140,500; Median year structure built: Before 1940; Homeowner vacancy rate: 0.0%; Median selected monthly owner costs: $1,371 with a mortgage, $711 without a mortgage; Median gross rent: $742 per month; Rental vacancy rate: 0.0%
Health Insurance: 94.1% have insurance; 75.0% have private insurance; 35.2% have public insurance; 5.9% do not have insurance; 7.6% of children under 18 do not have insurance
Transportation: Commute: 93.9% car, 0.6% public transportation, 1.4% walk, 4.0% work from home; Mean travel time to work: 21.0 minutes
Additional Information Contacts
Town of Homer . . . . (607) 749-4581
    http://www.cortland-co.org/Towns/Homer.htm

HOMER (village).
Covers a land area of 1.925 square miles and a water area of 0.013 square miles. Located at 42.64° N. Lat; 76.19° W. Long. Elevation is 1,125 feet.
Population: 3,200; Growth (since 2000): -5.0%; Density: 1,662.0 persons per square mile; Race: 91.4% White, 1.4% Black/African American, 2.8% Asian, 0.0% American Indian/Alaska Native, 0.0% Native Hawaiian/Other Pacific Islander, 4.1% Two or more races, 2.6% Hispanic of any race; Average household size: 2.42; Median age: 39.3; Age under 18: 23.2%; Age 65 and over: 19.6%; Males per 100 females: 86.1; Marriage status: 32.3% never married, 46.6% now married, 1.8% separated, 7.7% widowed, 13.4% divorced; Foreign born: 3.3%; Speak English only: 95.0%; With disability: 15.3%; Veterans: 7.1%; Ancestry: 17.9% English, 15.3% Irish, 14.3% German, 6.4% Italian, 5.1% American
Employment: 10.8% management, business, and financial, 4.6% computer, engineering, and science, 20.3% education, legal, community service, arts, and media, 5.2% healthcare practitioners, 16.9% service, 28.0% sales and office, 5.2% natural resources, construction, and maintenance, 9.0% production, transportation, and material moving
Income: Per capita: $33,293; Median household: $52,417; Average household: $79,850; Households with income of $100,000 or more: 23.4%; Poverty rate: 7.8%
Educational Attainment: High school diploma or higher: 90.2%; Bachelor's degree or higher: 33.8%; Graduate/professional degree or higher: 12.4%

School District(s)
Homer Central SD (KG-12)
    Enrollment: 1,969 . . . . (607) 749-7241
Housing: Homeownership rate: 57.2%; Median home value: $120,900; Median year structure built: Before 1940; Homeowner vacancy rate: 0.0%;

Median selected monthly owner costs: $1,239 with a mortgage, $579 without a mortgage; Median gross rent: $726 per month; Rental vacancy rate: 0.0%
Health Insurance: 95.7% have insurance; 72.2% have private insurance; 40.7% have public insurance; 4.3% do not have insurance; 0.0% of children under 18 do not have insurance
Safety: Violent crime rate: 0.0 per 10,000 population; Property crime rate: 25.6 per 10,000 population
Transportation: Commute: 94.7% car, 0.3% public transportation, 1.0% walk, 3.8% work from home; Mean travel time to work: 21.1 minutes

LAPEER (town).
Covers a land area of 25.039 square miles and a water area of 0.143 square miles. Located at 42.46° N. Lat; 76.11° W. Long. Elevation is 1,329 feet.
Population: 837; Growth (since 2000): 22.0%; Density: 33.4 persons per square mile; Race: 95.7% White, 1.3% Black/African American, 0.8% Asian, 0.0% American Indian/Alaska Native, 0.0% Native Hawaiian/Other Pacific Islander, 2.2% Two or more races, 2.4% Hispanic of any race; Average household size: 3.11; Median age: 32.8; Age under 18: 33.5%; Age 65 and over: 13.7%; Males per 100 females: 100.3; Marriage status: 24.9% never married, 64.3% now married, 2.3% separated, 3.7% widowed, 7.2% divorced; Foreign born: 1.1%; Speak English only: 84.5%; With disability: 6.6%; Veterans: 7.7%; Ancestry: 18.9% Pennsylvania German, 13.5% English, 11.9% German, 9.1% Irish, 5.9% American
Employment: 17.2% management, business, and financial, 3.3% computer, engineering, and science, 7.9% education, legal, community service, arts, and media, 4.4% healthcare practitioners, 16.7% service, 18.9% sales and office, 15.0% natural resources, construction, and maintenance, 16.7% production, transportation, and material moving
Income: Per capita: $23,966; Median household: $62,292; Average household: $73,273; Households with income of $100,000 or more: 20.5%; Poverty rate: 12.0%
Educational Attainment: High school diploma or higher: 94.3%; Bachelor's degree or higher: 13.4%; Graduate/professional degree or higher: 2.0%
Housing: Homeownership rate: 87.4%; Median home value: $129,500; Median year structure built: 1974; Homeowner vacancy rate: 2.9%; Median selected monthly owner costs: $1,073 with a mortgage, $552 without a mortgage; Median gross rent: $1,000 per month; Rental vacancy rate: 0.0%
Health Insurance: 74.2% have insurance; 58.9% have private insurance; 25.7% have public insurance; 25.8% do not have insurance; 52.8% of children under 18 do not have insurance
Transportation: Commute: 84.1% car, 0.0% public transportation, 0.0% walk, 15.9% work from home; Mean travel time to work: 22.9 minutes

LITTLE YORK (unincorporated postal area)
ZCTA: 13087
Covers a land area of 0.204 square miles and a water area of 0.169 square miles. Located at 42.71° N. Lat; 76.15° W. Long. Elevation is 1,161 feet.
Population: 152; Growth (since 2000): n/a; Density: 743.7 persons per square mile; Race: 100.0% White, 0.0% Black/African American, 0.0% Asian, 0.0% American Indian/Alaska Native, 0.0% Native Hawaiian/Other Pacific Islander, 0.0% Two or more races, 0.0% Hispanic of any race; Average household size: 1.95; Median age: 58.7; Age under 18: 7.2%; Age 65 and over: 37.5%; Males per 100 females: 90.9; Marriage status: 14.2% never married, 80.9% now married, 4.3% separated, 2.1% widowed, 2.8% divorced; Foreign born: 1.3%; Speak English only: 100.0%; With disability: 6.6%; Veterans: 4.3%; Ancestry: 53.3% English, 19.1% German, 14.5% American, 10.5% Dutch, 3.9% Irish
Employment: 3.3% management, business, and financial, 0.0% computer, engineering, and science, 38.9% education, legal, community service, arts, and media, 2.2% healthcare practitioners, 0.0% service, 52.2% sales and office, 0.0% natural resources, construction, and maintenance, 3.3% production, transportation, and material moving
Income: Per capita: $56,422; Median household: $147,907; Average household: $114,346; Households with income of $100,000 or more: 70.5%; Poverty rate: 6.6%
Educational Attainment: High school diploma or higher: 100.0%; Bachelor's degree or higher: 71.9%; Graduate/professional degree or higher: 33.6%
Housing: Homeownership rate: 100.0%; Median home value: $316,300; Median year structure built: Before 1940; Homeowner

vacancy rate: 0.0%; Median selected monthly owner costs: $2,063 with a mortgage, $766 without a mortgage; Median gross rent: n/a per month; Rental vacancy rate: 0.0%

Health Insurance: 100.0% have insurance; 90.1% have private insurance; 45.4% have public insurance; 0.0% do not have insurance; 0.0% of children under 18 do not have insurance

Transportation: Commute: 100.0% car, 0.0% public transportation, 0.0% walk, 0.0% work from home; Mean travel time to work: 0.0 minutes

MARATHON (town).
Covers a land area of 24.937 square miles and a water area of 0.133 square miles. Located at 42.43° N. Lat; 76.00° W. Long. Elevation is 1,024 feet.

Population: 2,028; Growth (since 2000): -7.4%; Density: 81.3 persons per square mile; Race: 95.8% White, 2.0% Black/African American, 0.7% Asian, 0.7% American Indian/Alaska Native, 0.0% Native Hawaiian/Other Pacific Islander, 0.7% Two or more races, 1.8% Hispanic of any race; Average household size: 2.63; Median age: 39.3; Age under 18: 22.1%; Age 65 and over: 15.6%; Males per 100 females: 102.4; Marriage status: 28.6% never married, 59.8% now married, 4.2% separated, 3.9% widowed, 7.7% divorced; Foreign born: 1.3%; Speak English only: 98.6%; With disability: 11.1%; Veterans: 11.0%; Ancestry: 34.7% English, 10.1% Irish, 8.7% German, 6.2% American, 3.0% Italian

Employment: 10.1% management, business, and financial, 1.5% computer, engineering, and science, 9.1% education, legal, community service, arts, and media, 4.7% healthcare practitioners, 22.5% service, 19.6% sales and office, 11.8% natural resources, construction, and maintenance, 20.7% production, transportation, and material moving

Income: Per capita: $27,452; Median household: $59,821; Average household: $71,298; Households with income of $100,000 or more: 22.2%; Poverty rate: 9.8%

Educational Attainment: High school diploma or higher: 91.6%; Bachelor's degree or higher: 15.1%; Graduate/professional degree or higher: 5.4%

School District(s)
Marathon Central SD (PK-12)
 Enrollment: 746 . . . . (607) 849-3117

Housing: Homeownership rate: 78.4%; Median home value: $110,600; Median year structure built: Before 1940; Homeowner vacancy rate: 0.0%; Median selected monthly owner costs: $1,250 with a mortgage, $589 without a mortgage; Median gross rent: $597 per month; Rental vacancy rate: 5.6%

Health Insurance: 93.2% have insurance; 74.9% have private insurance; 33.5% have public insurance; 6.8% do not have insurance; 3.9% of children under 18 do not have insurance

Transportation: Commute: 88.1% car, 0.4% public transportation, 2.0% walk, 9.3% work from home; Mean travel time to work: 24.3 minutes

MARATHON (village).
Covers a land area of 1.130 square miles and a water area of 0.002 square miles. Located at 42.44° N. Lat; 76.04° W. Long. Elevation is 1,024 feet.

Population: 866; Growth (since 2000): -18.5%; Density: 766.6 persons per square mile; Race: 98.2% White, 0.0% Black/African American, 0.8% Asian, 0.0% American Indian/Alaska Native, 0.0% Native Hawaiian/Other Pacific Islander, 0.6% Two or more races, 0.5% Hispanic of any race; Average household size: 2.37; Median age: 40.5; Age under 18: 17.2%; Age 65 and over: 18.2%; Males per 100 females: 90.7; Marriage status: 35.2% never married, 49.3% now married, 3.5% separated, 5.2% widowed, 10.4% divorced; Foreign born: 1.8%; Speak English only: 99.1%; With disability: 15.9%; Veterans: 10.5%; Ancestry: 36.8% English, 8.7% American, 8.0% Irish, 7.7% German, 2.5% Italian

Employment: 9.1% management, business, and financial, 0.7% computer, engineering, and science, 12.9% education, legal, community service, arts, and media, 7.0% healthcare practitioners, 19.9% service, 16.9% sales and office, 7.5% natural resources, construction, and maintenance, 26.0% production, transportation, and material moving

Income: Per capita: $23,717; Median household: $46,681; Average household: $56,611; Households with income of $100,000 or more: 14.5%; Poverty rate: 15.4%

Educational Attainment: High school diploma or higher: 91.5%; Bachelor's degree or higher: 13.7%; Graduate/professional degree or higher: 6.4%

School District(s)
Marathon Central SD (PK-12)
 Enrollment: 746 . . . . (607) 849-3117

Housing: Homeownership rate: 61.9%; Median home value: $96,300; Median year structure built: Before 1940; Homeowner vacancy rate: 0.0%; Median selected monthly owner costs: $1,084 with a mortgage, $602 without a mortgage; Median gross rent: $548 per month; Rental vacancy rate: 6.7%

Health Insurance: 90.2% have insurance; 69.7% have private insurance; 40.9% have public insurance; 9.8% do not have insurance; 2.4% of children under 18 do not have insurance

Transportation: Commute: 85.8% car, 0.0% public transportation, 4.3% walk, 9.9% work from home; Mean travel time to work: 22.9 minutes

MCGRAW (village).
Covers a land area of 0.987 square miles and a water area of 0 square miles. Located at 42.59° N. Lat; 76.10° W. Long. Elevation is 1,158 feet.

History: Incorporated 1869.

Population: 928; Growth (since 2000): -7.2%; Density: 940.2 persons per square mile; Race: 95.6% White, 0.3% Black/African American, 0.0% Asian, 0.0% American Indian/Alaska Native, 0.0% Native Hawaiian/Other Pacific Islander, 2.8% Two or more races, 7.0% Hispanic of any race; Average household size: 2.46; Median age: 36.8; Age under 18: 21.8%; Age 65 and over: 19.9%; Males per 100 females: 98.7; Marriage status: 26.2% never married, 62.2% now married, 2.6% separated, 5.1% widowed, 6.5% divorced; Foreign born: 0.1%; Speak English only: 94.6%; With disability: 14.3%; Veterans: 14.0%; Ancestry: 24.7% English, 8.1% American, 8.1% Irish, 5.6% German, 3.4% Polish

Employment: 7.6% management, business, and financial, 2.4% computer, engineering, and science, 16.9% education, legal, community service, arts, and media, 3.0% healthcare practitioners, 20.5% service, 22.5% sales and office, 14.9% natural resources, construction, and maintenance, 12.1% production, transportation, and material moving

Income: Per capita: $25,763; Median household: $62,625; Average household: $61,182; Households with income of $100,000 or more: 10.5%; Poverty rate: 3.3%

Educational Attainment: High school diploma or higher: 89.0%; Bachelor's degree or higher: 11.0%; Graduate/professional degree or higher: 6.6%

School District(s)
Mcgraw Central SD (KG-12)
 Enrollment: 529 . . . . (607) 836-3636

Housing: Homeownership rate: 56.8%; Median home value: $92,200; Median year structure built: Before 1940; Homeowner vacancy rate: 0.0%; Median selected monthly owner costs: $1,057 with a mortgage, $554 without a mortgage; Median gross rent: $653 per month; Rental vacancy rate: 0.0%

Health Insurance: 95.6% have insurance; 75.6% have private insurance; 33.6% have public insurance; 4.4% do not have insurance; 2.3% of children under 18 do not have insurance

Transportation: Commute: 96.6% car, 0.8% public transportation, 0.0% walk, 2.0% work from home; Mean travel time to work: 20.1 minutes

MUNSONS CORNERS (CDP).
Covers a land area of 2.219 square miles and a water area of 0.010 square miles. Located at 42.57° N. Lat; 76.20° W. Long. Elevation is 1,178 feet.

Population: 2,890; Growth (since 2000): 19.1%; Density: 1,302.4 persons per square mile; Race: 97.1% White, 2.4% Black/African American, 0.2% Asian, 0.0% American Indian/Alaska Native, 0.0% Native Hawaiian/Other Pacific Islander, 0.3% Two or more races, 7.1% Hispanic of any race; Average household size: 2.24; Median age: 31.0; Age under 18: 16.9%; Age 65 and over: 17.0%; Males per 100 females: 87.0; Marriage status: 46.5% never married, 34.5% now married, 2.6% separated, 11.5% widowed, 7.5% divorced; Foreign born: 1.8%; Speak English only: 98.6%; With disability: 15.2%; Veterans: 3.9%; Ancestry: 27.3% English, 8.2% Irish, 7.9% Italian, 7.1% German, 3.7% Polish

Employment: 6.9% management, business, and financial, 6.5% computer, engineering, and science, 18.4% education, legal, community service, arts, and media, 2.4% healthcare practitioners, 31.8% service, 17.0% sales and office, 8.8% natural resources, construction, and maintenance, 8.2% production, transportation, and material moving

Income: Per capita: $21,321; Median household: $40,914; Average household: $51,779; Households with income of $100,000 or more: 9.7%; Poverty rate: 19.4%

Educational Attainment: High school diploma or higher: 92.4%; Bachelor's degree or higher: 37.1%; Graduate/professional degree or higher: 14.8%

Housing: Homeownership rate: 47.3%; Median home value: $121,600; Median year structure built: 1973; Homeowner vacancy rate: 0.0%; Median selected monthly owner costs: $1,259 with a mortgage, $559 without a mortgage; Median gross rent: $788 per month; Rental vacancy rate: 6.6%
Health Insurance: 94.5% have insurance; 73.2% have private insurance; 39.3% have public insurance; 5.5% do not have insurance; 1.1% of children under 18 do not have insurance
Transportation: Commute: 86.5% car, 2.8% public transportation, 4.5% walk, 6.2% work from home; Mean travel time to work: 17.4 minutes

PREBLE (town). Covers a land area of 26.845 square miles and a water area of 0.715 square miles. Located at 42.74° N. Lat; 76.13° W. Long. Elevation is 1,224 feet.
Population: 1,455; Growth (since 2000): -8.0%; Density: 54.2 persons per square mile; Race: 100.0% White, 0.0% Black/African American, 0.0% Asian, 0.0% American Indian/Alaska Native, 0.0% Native Hawaiian/Other Pacific Islander, 0.0% Two or more races, 0.0% Hispanic of any race; Average household size: 2.61; Median age: 45.2; Age under 18: 24.7%; Age 65 and over: 15.9%; Males per 100 females: 107.0; Marriage status: 32.6% never married, 51.5% now married, 2.3% separated, 5.2% widowed, 10.8% divorced; Foreign born: 0.5%; Speak English only: 98.8%; With disability: 11.3%; Veterans: 10.5%; Ancestry: 23.4% English, 15.1% Irish, 13.1% German, 7.4% Italian, 6.2% American
Employment: 12.9% management, business, and financial, 6.6% computer, engineering, and science, 8.6% education, legal, community service, arts, and media, 12.5% healthcare practitioners, 11.1% service, 19.4% sales and office, 10.5% natural resources, construction, and maintenance, 18.4% production, transportation, and material moving
Income: Per capita: $28,014; Median household: $55,313; Average household: $71,120; Households with income of $100,000 or more: 26.4%; Poverty rate: 13.2%
Educational Attainment: High school diploma or higher: 93.6%; Bachelor's degree or higher: 25.0%; Graduate/professional degree or higher: 10.1%
Housing: Homeownership rate: 82.3%; Median home value: $119,700; Median year structure built: 1965; Homeowner vacancy rate: 2.5%; Median selected monthly owner costs: $1,234 with a mortgage, $567 without a mortgage; Median gross rent: $878 per month; Rental vacancy rate: 0.0%
Health Insurance: 94.0% have insurance; 78.8% have private insurance; 28.9% have public insurance; 6.0% do not have insurance; 0.0% of children under 18 do not have insurance
Transportation: Commute: 92.2% car, 0.3% public transportation, 1.6% walk, 5.1% work from home; Mean travel time to work: 26.1 minutes
Additional Information Contacts
Town of Preble . . . . (607) 749-3199
    http://www.preble-ny.org

SCOTT (town). Covers a land area of 22.267 square miles and a water area of 0.147 square miles. Located at 42.74° N. Lat; 76.24° W. Long. Elevation is 1,411 feet.
Population: 1,039; Growth (since 2000): -12.9%; Density: 46.7 persons per square mile; Race: 98.7% White, 0.0% Black/African American, 0.7% Asian, 0.0% American Indian/Alaska Native, 0.6% Native Hawaiian/Other Pacific Islander, 0.0% Two or more races, 1.0% Hispanic of any race; Average household size: 2.74; Median age: 43.1; Age under 18: 28.7%; Age 65 and over: 16.0%; Males per 100 females: 108.1; Marriage status: 20.4% never married, 67.5% now married, 3.3% separated, 5.1% widowed, 7.0% divorced; Foreign born: 2.5%; Speak English only: 98.2%; With disability: 12.4%; Veterans: 10.8%; Ancestry: 20.7% English, 14.1% American, 13.3% German, 10.3% Irish, 5.6% Italian
Employment: 11.0% management, business, and financial, 2.5% computer, engineering, and science, 4.9% education, legal, community service, arts, and media, 6.6% healthcare practitioners, 18.6% service, 24.5% sales and office, 11.6% natural resources, construction, and maintenance, 20.3% production, transportation, and material moving
Income: Per capita: $26,026; Median household: $65,694; Average household: $71,520; Households with income of $100,000 or more: 19.3%; Poverty rate: 9.1%
Educational Attainment: High school diploma or higher: 87.4%; Bachelor's degree or higher: 22.9%; Graduate/professional degree or higher: 8.0%
Housing: Homeownership rate: 86.5%; Median home value: $106,200; Median year structure built: 1971; Homeowner vacancy rate: 0.9%; Median selected monthly owner costs: $1,336 with a mortgage, $528 without a mortgage; Median gross rent: $689 per month; Rental vacancy rate: 0.0%

Health Insurance: 96.3% have insurance; 79.2% have private insurance; 30.5% have public insurance; 3.7% do not have insurance; 1.3% of children under 18 do not have insurance
Transportation: Commute: 95.0% car, 1.3% public transportation, 0.0% walk, 3.7% work from home; Mean travel time to work: 28.0 minutes

SOLON (town). Covers a land area of 29.651 square miles and a water area of 0.076 square miles. Located at 42.61° N. Lat; 76.02° W. Long. Elevation is 1,312 feet.
Population: 1,170; Growth (since 2000): 5.6%; Density: 39.5 persons per square mile; Race: 98.4% White, 0.0% Black/African American, 0.0% Asian, 0.0% American Indian/Alaska Native, 0.0% Native Hawaiian/Other Pacific Islander, 1.6% Two or more races, 1.0% Hispanic of any race; Average household size: 2.81; Median age: 39.8; Age under 18: 24.2%; Age 65 and over: 12.1%; Males per 100 females: 100.6; Marriage status: 28.5% never married, 56.6% now married, 1.5% separated, 3.5% widowed, 11.4% divorced; Foreign born: 0.5%; Speak English only: 100.0%; With disability: 11.7%; Veterans: 11.3%; Ancestry: 22.6% English, 14.4% Irish, 9.4% American, 6.6% German, 3.3% Pennsylvania German
Employment: 13.4% management, business, and financial, 2.3% computer, engineering, and science, 5.4% education, legal, community service, arts, and media, 2.6% healthcare practitioners, 21.0% service, 20.7% sales and office, 13.5% natural resources, construction, and maintenance, 21.0% production, transportation, and material moving
Income: Per capita: $24,902; Median household: $63,750; Average household: $69,601; Households with income of $100,000 or more: 21.2%; Poverty rate: 10.2%
Educational Attainment: High school diploma or higher: 90.4%; Bachelor's degree or higher: 11.5%; Graduate/professional degree or higher: 5.6%
Housing: Homeownership rate: 82.2%; Median home value: $96,700; Median year structure built: 1976; Homeowner vacancy rate: 0.0%; Median selected monthly owner costs: $1,074 with a mortgage, $514 without a mortgage; Median gross rent: $800 per month; Rental vacancy rate: 0.0%
Health Insurance: 90.7% have insurance; 72.9% have private insurance; 27.9% have public insurance; 9.3% do not have insurance; 9.0% of children under 18 do not have insurance
Transportation: Commute: 95.4% car, 0.0% public transportation, 0.0% walk, 2.6% work from home; Mean travel time to work: 23.6 minutes

TAYLOR (town). Covers a land area of 29.995 square miles and a water area of 0.124 square miles. Located at 42.60° N. Lat; 75.92° W. Long. Elevation is 1,109 feet.
Population: 499; Growth (since 2000): -0.2%; Density: 16.6 persons per square mile; Race: 95.0% White, 2.8% Black/African American, 0.8% Asian, 0.0% American Indian/Alaska Native, 0.0% Native Hawaiian/Other Pacific Islander, 1.4% Two or more races, 7.0% Hispanic of any race; Average household size: 2.57; Median age: 40.9; Age under 18: 26.3%; Age 65 and over: 14.6%; Males per 100 females: 99.6; Marriage status: 27.0% never married, 58.9% now married, 3.1% separated, 3.9% widowed, 10.3% divorced; Foreign born: 2.2%; Speak English only: 99.1%; With disability: 14.0%; Veterans: 7.1%; Ancestry: 19.4% English, 12.8% American, 8.2% German, 3.4% Dutch, 3.2% European
Employment: 17.0% management, business, and financial, 5.3% computer, engineering, and science, 11.7% education, legal, community service, arts, and media, 4.5% healthcare practitioners, 19.8% service, 16.2% sales and office, 12.1% natural resources, construction, and maintenance, 13.4% production, transportation, and material moving
Income: Per capita: $25,368; Median household: $51,667; Average household: $67,937; Households with income of $100,000 or more: 18.0%; Poverty rate: 6.4%
Educational Attainment: High school diploma or higher: 89.2%; Bachelor's degree or higher: 20.8%; Graduate/professional degree or higher: 9.3%
Housing: Homeownership rate: 67.5%; Median home value: $98,600; Median year structure built: 1973; Homeowner vacancy rate: 0.0%; Median selected monthly owner costs: $1,102 with a mortgage, $482 without a mortgage; Median gross rent: $835 per month; Rental vacancy rate: 0.0%
Health Insurance: 98.2% have insurance; 72.1% have private insurance; 37.9% have public insurance; 1.8% do not have insurance; 0.0% of children under 18 do not have insurance
Transportation: Commute: 95.8% car, 0.0% public transportation, 0.8% walk, 3.4% work from home; Mean travel time to work: 27.6 minutes

TRUXTON (town). Covers a land area of 44.649 square miles and a water area of 0.078 square miles. Located at 42.71° N. Lat; 76.02° W. Long. Elevation is 1,152 feet.

Population: 995; Growth (since 2000): -18.8%; Density: 22.3 persons per square mile; Race: 99.0% White, 0.0% Black/African American, 0.0% Asian, 0.0% American Indian/Alaska Native, 0.0% Native Hawaiian/Other Pacific Islander, 0.8% Two or more races, 0.6% Hispanic of any race; Average household size: 2.46; Median age: 45.9; Age under 18: 19.6%; Age 65 and over: 15.4%; Males per 100 females: 103.4; Marriage status: 30.4% never married, 53.5% now married, 3.6% separated, 6.9% widowed, 9.2% divorced; Foreign born: 0.8%; Speak English only: 98.1%; With disability: 7.2%; Veterans: 8.6%; Ancestry: 26.9% English, 13.6% Irish, 12.3% German, 7.6% American, 4.5% Scottish

Employment: 16.5% management, business, and financial, 3.1% computer, engineering, and science, 11.3% education, legal, community service, arts, and media, 4.9% healthcare practitioners, 17.1% service, 24.7% sales and office, 10.3% natural resources, construction, and maintenance, 12.2% production, transportation, and material moving

Income: Per capita: $31,902; Median household: $56,786; Average household: $76,912; Households with income of $100,000 or more: 26.3%; Poverty rate: 9.4%

Educational Attainment: High school diploma or higher: 91.2%; Bachelor's degree or higher: 23.8%; Graduate/professional degree or higher: 11.3%

School District(s)

Homer Central SD (KG-12)

    Enrollment: 1,969 . . . . (607) 749-7241

Housing: Homeownership rate: 75.4%; Median home value: $118,800; Median year structure built: 1975; Homeowner vacancy rate: 1.0%; Median selected monthly owner costs: $1,244 with a mortgage, $486 without a mortgage; Median gross rent: $708 per month; Rental vacancy rate: 0.0%

Health Insurance: 91.4% have insurance; 73.8% have private insurance; 33.5% have public insurance; 8.6% do not have insurance; 6.8% of children under 18 do not have insurance

Transportation: Commute: 89.7% car, 0.0% public transportation, 4.1% walk, 6.2% work from home; Mean travel time to work: 28.2 minutes

VIRGIL (town). Covers a land area of 47.363 square miles and a water area of 0.036 square miles. Located at 42.52° N. Lat; 76.16° W. Long. Elevation is 1,404 feet.

Population: 2,537; Growth (since 2000): 10.9%; Density: 53.6 persons per square mile; Race: 95.4% White, 2.5% Black/African American, 0.0% Asian, 1.1% American Indian/Alaska Native, 0.0% Native Hawaiian/Other Pacific Islander, 1.0% Two or more races, 0.9% Hispanic of any race; Average household size: 2.70; Median age: 43.8; Age under 18: 21.4%; Age 65 and over: 14.6%; Males per 100 females: 103.0; Marriage status: 28.3% never married, 55.5% now married, 0.7% separated, 7.4% widowed, 8.8% divorced; Foreign born: 2.7%; Speak English only: 97.2%; With disability: 12.1%; Veterans: 6.7%; Ancestry: 19.2% English, 10.8% Irish, 10.5% German, 9.9% American, 6.9% Italian

Employment: 12.9% management, business, and financial, 6.9% computer, engineering, and science, 11.4% education, legal, community service, arts, and media, 7.9% healthcare practitioners, 15.8% service, 15.2% sales and office, 14.0% natural resources, construction, and maintenance, 15.8% production, transportation, and material moving

Income: Per capita: $32,352; Median household: $70,789; Average household: $81,989; Households with income of $100,000 or more: 28.5%; Poverty rate: 8.4%

Educational Attainment: High school diploma or higher: 90.2%; Bachelor's degree or higher: 28.5%; Graduate/professional degree or higher: 12.5%

Housing: Homeownership rate: 79.6%; Median home value: $154,100; Median year structure built: 1974; Homeowner vacancy rate: 0.0%; Median selected monthly owner costs: $1,417 with a mortgage, $594 without a mortgage; Median gross rent: $839 per month; Rental vacancy rate: 0.0%

Health Insurance: 97.1% have insurance; 79.4% have private insurance; 31.7% have public insurance; 2.9% do not have insurance; 0.0% of children under 18 do not have insurance

Transportation: Commute: 89.6% car, 0.0% public transportation, 2.4% walk, 5.9% work from home; Mean travel time to work: 24.9 minutes

WILLET (town). Covers a land area of 25.733 square miles and a water area of 0.321 square miles. Located at 42.45° N. Lat; 75.92° W. Long. Elevation is 1,040 feet.

Population: 1,034; Growth (since 2000): 2.3%; Density: 40.2 persons per square mile; Race: 94.9% White, 1.8% Black/African American, 0.0% Asian, 0.6% American Indian/Alaska Native, 0.0% Native Hawaiian/Other Pacific Islander, 2.7% Two or more races, 4.2% Hispanic of any race; Average household size: 2.75; Median age: 35.8; Age under 18: 27.1%; Age 65 and over: 9.5%; Males per 100 females: 106.1; Marriage status: 30.4% never married, 56.7% now married, 0.9% separated, 1.9% widowed, 11.1% divorced; Foreign born: 0.2%; Speak English only: 98.8%; With disability: 10.6%; Veterans: 6.8%; Ancestry: 17.9% English, 11.6% Irish, 7.4% German, 7.1% American, 5.4% French

Employment: 9.9% management, business, and financial, 0.4% computer, engineering, and science, 8.5% education, legal, community service, arts, and media, 10.4% healthcare practitioners, 18.8% service, 20.9% sales and office, 21.5% natural resources, construction, and maintenance, 9.5% production, transportation, and material moving

Income: Per capita: $21,799; Median household: $56,786; Average household: $60,078; Households with income of $100,000 or more: 14.9%; Poverty rate: 13.5%

Educational Attainment: High school diploma or higher: 92.9%; Bachelor's degree or higher: 10.3%; Graduate/professional degree or higher: 2.5%

Housing: Homeownership rate: 79.5%; Median home value: $79,100; Median year structure built: 1968; Homeowner vacancy rate: 0.0%; Median selected monthly owner costs: $1,145 with a mortgage, $443 without a mortgage; Median gross rent: $819 per month; Rental vacancy rate: 0.0%

Health Insurance: 92.4% have insurance; 71.9% have private insurance; 28.7% have public insurance; 7.6% do not have insurance; 1.0% of children under 18 do not have insurance

Transportation: Commute: 91.8% car, 0.4% public transportation, 1.9% walk, 5.9% work from home; Mean travel time to work: 30.0 minutes

Delaware County

Located in southern New York, in the west Catskills; bounded on the northwest by the Susquehanna River, and on the southwest by the Delaware River and the Pennsylvania border. Covers a land area of 1,442.440 square miles, a water area of 25.006 square miles, and is located in the Eastern Time Zone at 42.19° N. Lat., 74.97° W. Long. The county was founded in 1797. County seat is Delhi.

Weather Station: Delhi 2 SE										Elevation: 1,439 feet		
	Jan	Feb	Mar	Apr	May	Jun	Jul	Aug	Sep	Oct	Nov	Dec
High	31	34	42	55	67	75	79	78	71	59	47	36
Low	11	12	20	32	41	50	54	53	46	35	28	18
Precip	3.2	2.5	3.5	3.9	4.2	4.6	4.6	3.6	4.4	4.0	3.9	3.5
Snow	18.2	12.4	11.2	3.8	0.1	0.0	0.0	0.0	0.0	0.6	4.3	14.8

High and Low temperatures in degrees Fahrenheit; Precipitation and Snow in inches

Weather Station: Deposit										Elevation: 1,000 feet		
	Jan	Feb	Mar	Apr	May	Jun	Jul	Aug	Sep	Oct	Nov	Dec
High	32	36	45	59	70	77	81	80	72	60	48	36
Low	14	16	23	34	44	53	57	56	50	38	30	20
Precip	2.8	2.5	3.2	3.9	3.9	4.2	4.1	3.8	4.0	3.7	3.8	3.1
Snow	na	na	na	1.7	0.0	0.0	0.0	0.0	0.0	tr	1.7	na

High and Low temperatures in degrees Fahrenheit; Precipitation and Snow in inches

Population: 45,950; Growth (since 2000): -4.4%; Density: 31.9 persons per square mile; Race: 95.0% White, 2.0% Black/African American, 0.7% Asian, 0.1% American Indian/Alaska Native, 0.0% Native Hawaiian/Other Pacific Islander, 1.4% two or more races, 3.7% Hispanic of any race; Average household size: 2.28; Median age: 47.0; Age under 18: 17.6%; Age 65 and over: 22.8%; Males per 100 females: 100.9; Marriage status: 30.3% never married, 50.8% now married, 2.6% separated, 7.7% widowed, 11.3% divorced; Foreign born: 4.6%; Speak English only: 93.8%; With disability: 16.3%; Veterans: 8.7%; Ancestry: 22.3% German, 19.6% Irish, 12.2% English, 11.4% Italian, 5.6% American

Religion: Six largest groups: 17.8% Catholicism, 8.7% Methodist/Pietist, 3.9% Presbyterian-Reformed, 3.5% Holiness, 3.2% Muslim Estimate, 1.3% Episcopalianism/Anglicanism

Economy: Unemployment rate: 3.9%; Leading industries: 18.0 % retail trade; 11.7 % accommodation and food services; 11.5 % other services (except public administration); Farms: 704 totaling 145,608 acres; Company size: 1 employs 1,000 or more persons, 1 employs 500 to 999

persons, 14 employ 100 to 499 persons, 1,042 employ less than 100 persons; Business ownership: 1,302 women-owned, 26 Black-owned, 31 Hispanic-owned, 48 Asian-owned, 33 American Indian/Alaska Native-owned

Employment: 11.5% management, business, and financial, 3.2% computer, engineering, and science, 11.9% education, legal, community service, arts, and media, 5.4% healthcare practitioners, 20.3% service, 21.4% sales and office, 11.5% natural resources, construction, and maintenance, 14.9% production, transportation, and material moving

Income: Per capita: $26,016; Median household: $47,921; Average household: $60,360; Households with income of $100,000 or more: 15.9%; Poverty rate: 16.5%

Educational Attainment: High school diploma or higher: 87.7%; Bachelor's degree or higher: 21.6%; Graduate/professional degree or higher: 9.5%

Housing: Homeownership rate: 73.3%; Median home value: $138,000; Median year structure built: 1971; Homeowner vacancy rate: 2.6%; Median selected monthly owner costs: $1,194 with a mortgage, $507 without a mortgage; Median gross rent: $696 per month; Rental vacancy rate: 6.2%

Vital Statistics: Birth rate: 74.9 per 10,000 population; Death rate: 124.2 per 10,000 population; Age-adjusted cancer mortality rate: 134.7 deaths per 100,000 population

Health Insurance: 92.9% have insurance; 66.2% have private insurance; 45.6% have public insurance; 7.1% do not have insurance; 5.4% of children under 18 do not have insurance

Health Care: Physicians: 5.7 per 10,000 population; Dentists: 2.4 per 10,000 population; Hospital beds: 12.3 per 10,000 population; Hospital admissions: 251.6 per 10,000 population

Transportation: Commute: 84.3% car, 1.5% public transportation, 6.2% walk, 6.5% work from home; Mean travel time to work: 24.4 minutes

2016 Presidential Election: 60.3% Trump, 33.5% Clinton, 3.3% Johnson, 1.9% Stein

National and State Parks: Delaware State Forest

Additional Information Contacts

Delaware Government . . . . (607) 746-2123
  http://www.co.delaware.ny.us

Delaware County Communities

ANDES (CDP). Covers a land area of 1.193 square miles and a water area of <.001 square miles. Located at 42.19° N. Lat; 74.78° W. Long. Elevation is 1,598 feet.

Population: 245; Growth (since 2000): -15.2%; Density: 205.3 persons per square mile; Race: 97.6% White, 0.0% Black/African American, 1.6% Asian, 0.8% American Indian/Alaska Native, 0.0% Native Hawaiian/Other Pacific Islander, 0.0% Two or more races, 0.0% Hispanic of any race; Average household size: 2.11; Median age: 50.1; Age under 18: 10.2%; Age 65 and over: 31.8%; Males per 100 females: 96.9; Marriage status: 24.3% never married, 57.4% now married, 4.3% separated, 8.3% widowed, 10.0% divorced; Foreign born: 8.6%; Speak English only: 93.4%; With disability: 16.3%; Veterans: 4.5%; Ancestry: 44.9% German, 15.9% Irish, 11.4% English, 8.2% Italian, 5.7% Scottish

Employment: 9.2% management, business, and financial, 2.8% computer, engineering, and science, 17.6% education, legal, community service, arts, and media, 10.6% healthcare practitioners, 22.5% service, 24.6% sales and office, 7.7% natural resources, construction, and maintenance, 4.9% production, transportation, and material moving

Income: Per capita: $31,466; Median household: $56,042; Average household: $67,639; Households with income of $100,000 or more: 25.0%; Poverty rate: 4.2%

Educational Attainment: High school diploma or higher: 97.1%; Bachelor's degree or higher: 44.7%; Graduate/professional degree or higher: 14.6%

School District(s)

Andes Central SD (PK-12)
  Enrollment: 111 . . . . (845) 676-3167

Housing: Homeownership rate: 79.3%; Median home value: $200,000; Median year structure built: Before 1940; Homeowner vacancy rate: 0.0%; Median selected monthly owner costs: $1,554 with a mortgage, $457 without a mortgage; Median gross rent: $1,075 per month; Rental vacancy rate: 0.0%

Health Insurance: 86.9% have insurance; 64.9% have private insurance; 44.5% have public insurance; 13.1% do not have insurance; 0.0% of children under 18 do not have insurance

Transportation: Commute: 76.3% car, 2.2% public transportation, 12.2% walk, 9.4% work from home; Mean travel time to work: 31.4 minutes

ANDES (town). Covers a land area of 108.592 square miles and a water area of 3.694 square miles. Located at 42.13° N. Lat; 74.79° W. Long. Elevation is 1,598 feet.

Population: 1,050; Growth (since 2000): -22.6%; Density: 9.7 persons per square mile; Race: 98.2% White, 0.0% Black/African American, 0.8% Asian, 0.5% American Indian/Alaska Native, 0.0% Native Hawaiian/Other Pacific Islander, 0.3% Two or more races, 1.3% Hispanic of any race; Average household size: 2.03; Median age: 58.5; Age under 18: 8.6%; Age 65 and over: 37.3%; Males per 100 females: 107.8; Marriage status: 22.9% never married, 56.9% now married, 2.1% separated, 10.2% widowed, 10.0% divorced; Foreign born: 7.9%; Speak English only: 90.7%; With disability: 18.7%; Veterans: 10.2%; Ancestry: 26.5% German, 17.0% English, 14.0% Irish, 8.7% Italian, 7.4% Scottish

Employment: 14.7% management, business, and financial, 4.3% computer, engineering, and science, 12.3% education, legal, community service, arts, and media, 6.5% healthcare practitioners, 20.2% service, 20.0% sales and office, 20.2% natural resources, construction, and maintenance, 1.7% production, transportation, and material moving

Income: Per capita: $28,364; Median household: $41,908; Average household: $56,061; Households with income of $100,000 or more: 13.7%; Poverty rate: 14.0%

Educational Attainment: High school diploma or higher: 89.4%; Bachelor's degree or higher: 29.7%; Graduate/professional degree or higher: 9.2%

School District(s)

Andes Central SD (PK-12)
  Enrollment: 111 . . . . (845) 676-3167

Housing: Homeownership rate: 88.2%; Median home value: $217,300; Median year structure built: 1976; Homeowner vacancy rate: 0.7%; Median selected monthly owner costs: $1,435 with a mortgage, $536 without a mortgage; Median gross rent: $1,020 per month; Rental vacancy rate: 0.0%

Health Insurance: 90.9% have insurance; 66.3% have private insurance; 51.9% have public insurance; 9.1% do not have insurance; 0.0% of children under 18 do not have insurance

Transportation: Commute: 81.1% car, 4.1% public transportation, 4.1% walk, 10.2% work from home; Mean travel time to work: 29.3 minutes

ARKVILLE (unincorporated postal area)
ZCTA: 12406

Covers a land area of 43.232 square miles and a water area of 0.080 square miles. Located at 42.08° N. Lat; 74.52° W. Long. Elevation is 1,365 feet.

Population: 877; Growth (since 2000): -1.7%; Density: 20.3 persons per square mile; Race: 98.5% White, 0.0% Black/African American, 0.0% Asian, 0.0% American Indian/Alaska Native, 0.0% Native Hawaiian/Other Pacific Islander, 1.5% Two or more races, 13.1% Hispanic of any race; Average household size: 1.92; Median age: 47.7; Age under 18: 12.3%; Age 65 and over: 20.2%; Males per 100 females: 94.6; Marriage status: 29.4% never married, 41.0% now married, 0.5% separated, 5.0% widowed, 24.6% divorced; Foreign born: 7.8%; Speak English only: 85.1%; With disability: 12.1%; Veterans: 7.5%; Ancestry: 42.9% German, 17.6% Italian, 17.1% Irish, 9.5% French, 7.1% English

Employment: 8.2% management, business, and financial, 0.0% computer, engineering, and science, 11.3% education, legal, community service, arts, and media, 7.3% healthcare practitioners, 29.2% service, 12.5% sales and office, 8.9% natural resources, construction, and maintenance, 22.6% production, transportation, and material moving

Income: Per capita: $40,555; Median household: $42,153; Average household: $77,404; Households with income of $100,000 or more: 17.5%; Poverty rate: 17.0%

Educational Attainment: High school diploma or higher: 92.1%; Bachelor's degree or higher: 26.6%; Graduate/professional degree or higher: 8.2%

Housing: Homeownership rate: 57.8%; Median home value: $174,500; Median year structure built: 1970; Homeowner vacancy rate: 2.2%; Median selected monthly owner costs: $1,011 with a mortgage, $517 without a mortgage; Median gross rent: $764 per month; Rental vacancy rate: 0.0%

Health Insurance: 88.6% have insurance; 58.6% have private insurance; 43.1% have public insurance; 11.4% do not have insurance; 18.5% of children under 18 do not have insurance

Newspapers: Catskill Mountain News (weekly circulation 4,000)
Transportation: Commute: 81.8% car, 0.0% public transportation, 12.5% walk, 3.2% work from home; Mean travel time to work: 21.4 minutes

BLOOMVILLE (CDP). Covers a land area of 1.317 square miles and a water area of 0.002 square miles. Located at 42.33° N. Lat; 74.82° W. Long. Elevation is 1,457 feet.

Population: 132; Growth (since 2000): n/a; Density: 100.2 persons per square mile; Race: 97.0% White, 0.0% Black/African American, 3.0% Asian, 0.0% American Indian/Alaska Native, 0.0% Native Hawaiian/Other Pacific Islander, 0.0% Two or more races, 0.0% Hispanic of any race; Average household size: 2.59; Median age: 35.9; Age under 18: 9.1%; Age 65 and over: 6.1%; Males per 100 females: 104.8; Marriage status: 48.4% never married, 43.5% now married, 4.8% separated, 0.0% widowed, 8.1% divorced; Foreign born: 3.0%; Speak English only: 97.0%; With disability: 21.2%; Veterans: 5.8%; Ancestry: 28.0% European, 12.9% German, 12.1% American, 7.6% English, 7.6% Scottish
Employment: 0.0% management, business, and financial, 10.3% computer, engineering, and science, 20.5% education, legal, community service, arts, and media, 0.0% healthcare practitioners, 17.9% service, 28.2% sales and office, 14.1% natural resources, construction, and maintenance, 9.0% production, transportation, and material moving
Income: Per capita: $24,111; Median household: $55,469; Average household: $59,998; Households with income of $100,000 or more: 15.7%; Poverty rate: 16.7%
Educational Attainment: High school diploma or higher: 100.0%; Bachelor's degree or higher: 34.5%; Graduate/professional degree or higher: 10.3%
Housing: Homeownership rate: 66.7%; Median home value: $97,500; Median year structure built: Before 1940; Homeowner vacancy rate: 0.0%; Median selected monthly owner costs: $938 with a mortgage, $350 without a mortgage; Median gross rent: $531 per month; Rental vacancy rate: 0.0%
Health Insurance: 97.0% have insurance; 82.6% have private insurance; 27.3% have public insurance; 3.0% do not have insurance; 0.0% of children under 18 do not have insurance
Transportation: Commute: 100.0% car, 0.0% public transportation, 0.0% walk, 0.0% work from home; Mean travel time to work: 17.4 minutes

BOVINA (town). Covers a land area of 44.263 square miles and a water area of 0.232 square miles. Located at 42.27° N. Lat; 74.76° W. Long. Elevation is 1,844 feet.

Population: 673; Growth (since 2000): 1.4%; Density: 15.2 persons per square mile; Race: 95.1% White, 0.0% Black/African American, 2.4% Asian, 0.1% American Indian/Alaska Native, 0.0% Native Hawaiian/Other Pacific Islander, 1.5% Two or more races, 1.8% Hispanic of any race; Average household size: 2.47; Median age: 48.2; Age under 18: 18.9%; Age 65 and over: 22.0%; Males per 100 females: 109.6; Marriage status: 29.3% never married, 61.1% now married, 3.3% separated, 5.5% widowed, 4.1% divorced; Foreign born: 8.3%; Speak English only: 91.2%; With disability: 15.3%; Veterans: 9.5%; Ancestry: 25.1% German, 19.6% Irish, 15.2% English, 8.6% Scottish, 7.1% Dutch
Employment: 8.6% management, business, and financial, 4.3% computer, engineering, and science, 20.1% education, legal, community service, arts, and media, 2.6% healthcare practitioners, 15.2% service, 22.7% sales and office, 17.2% natural resources, construction, and maintenance, 9.2% production, transportation, and material moving
Income: Per capita: $41,779; Median household: $67,500; Average household: $100,875; Households with income of $100,000 or more: 31.3%; Poverty rate: 8.8%
Educational Attainment: High school diploma or higher: 94.8%; Bachelor's degree or higher: 40.2%; Graduate/professional degree or higher: 19.1%
Housing: Homeownership rate: 83.8%; Median home value: $219,400; Median year structure built: 1975; Homeowner vacancy rate: 0.9%; Median selected monthly owner costs: $1,405 with a mortgage, $732 without a mortgage; Median gross rent: $775 per month; Rental vacancy rate: 0.0%
Health Insurance: 94.1% have insurance; 72.7% have private insurance; 41.8% have public insurance; 5.9% do not have insurance; 0.8% of children under 18 do not have insurance
Transportation: Commute: 74.9% car, 4.8% public transportation, 9.0% walk, 11.3% work from home; Mean travel time to work: 32.0 minutes

BOVINA CENTER (unincorporated postal area)
ZCTA: 13740
Covers a land area of 39.569 square miles and a water area of 0.050 square miles. Located at 42.27° N. Lat; 74.76° W. Long. Elevation is 1,660 feet.
Population: 551; Growth (since 2000): -3.0%; Density: 13.9 persons per square mile; Race: 94.0% White, 0.0% Black/African American, 2.9% Asian, 0.2% American Indian/Alaska Native, 0.0% Native Hawaiian/Other Pacific Islander, 1.8% Two or more races, 1.8% Hispanic of any race; Average household size: 2.40; Median age: 51.7; Age under 18: 17.1%; Age 65 and over: 24.9%; Males per 100 females: 109.8; Marriage status: 29.0% never married, 62.7% now married, 3.9% separated, 5.0% widowed, 3.3% divorced; Foreign born: 9.8%; Speak English only: 91.5%; With disability: 18.0%; Veterans: 10.3%; Ancestry: 23.6% German, 20.5% Irish, 17.4% English, 10.5% Scottish, 4.0% American
Employment: 10.4% management, business, and financial, 5.2% computer, engineering, and science, 23.6% education, legal, community service, arts, and media, 1.4% healthcare practitioners, 11.8% service, 20.8% sales and office, 17.7% natural resources, construction, and maintenance, 9.0% production, transportation, and material moving
Income: Per capita: $45,003; Median household: $72,500; Average household: $105,450; Households with income of $100,000 or more: 33.1%; Poverty rate: 9.8%
Educational Attainment: High school diploma or higher: 95.0%; Bachelor's degree or higher: 44.0%; Graduate/professional degree or higher: 22.6%
Housing: Homeownership rate: 81.7%; Median home value: $224,200; Median year structure built: 1977; Homeowner vacancy rate: 1.1%; Median selected monthly owner costs: $1,450 with a mortgage, $718 without a mortgage; Median gross rent: $758 per month; Rental vacancy rate: 0.0%
Health Insurance: 94.4% have insurance; 75.1% have private insurance; 40.7% have public insurance; 5.6% do not have insurance; 0.0% of children under 18 do not have insurance
Transportation: Commute: 75.3% car, 5.8% public transportation, 6.9% walk, 12.0% work from home; Mean travel time to work: 36.3 minutes

COLCHESTER (town). Covers a land area of 136.778 square miles and a water area of 5.398 square miles. Located at 42.04° N. Lat; 74.95° W. Long. Elevation is 1,280 feet.

Population: 1,956; Growth (since 2000): -4.2%; Density: 14.3 persons per square mile; Race: 95.3% White, 2.5% Black/African American, 0.0% Asian, 0.6% American Indian/Alaska Native, 0.0% Native Hawaiian/Other Pacific Islander, 1.3% Two or more races, 3.9% Hispanic of any race; Average household size: 2.21; Median age: 52.8; Age under 18: 15.0%; Age 65 and over: 26.7%; Males per 100 females: 103.6; Marriage status: 27.1% never married, 53.3% now married, 1.1% separated, 7.6% widowed, 12.0% divorced; Foreign born: 3.4%; Speak English only: 92.9%; With disability: 12.4%; Veterans: 12.0%; Ancestry: 32.1% German, 21.6% Irish, 15.5% Italian, 6.7% Dutch, 6.0% English
Employment: 13.6% management, business, and financial, 0.5% computer, engineering, and science, 14.8% education, legal, community service, arts, and media, 4.5% healthcare practitioners, 16.6% service, 25.4% sales and office, 14.8% natural resources, construction, and maintenance, 9.7% production, transportation, and material moving
Income: Per capita: $28,938; Median household: $49,327; Average household: $64,036; Households with income of $100,000 or more: 17.6%; Poverty rate: 15.4%
Educational Attainment: High school diploma or higher: 88.5%; Bachelor's degree or higher: 19.4%; Graduate/professional degree or higher: 10.6%
Housing: Homeownership rate: 80.7%; Median home value: $121,200; Median year structure built: 1975; Homeowner vacancy rate: 2.0%; Median selected monthly owner costs: $914 with a mortgage, $410 without a mortgage; Median gross rent: $636 per month; Rental vacancy rate: 4.7%
Health Insurance: 93.3% have insurance; 68.2% have private insurance; 41.5% have public insurance; 6.7% do not have insurance; 4.7% of children under 18 do not have insurance
Safety: Violent crime rate: 0.0 per 10,000 population; Property crime rate: 50.3 per 10,000 population
Transportation: Commute: 88.0% car, 1.3% public transportation, 6.7% walk, 1.8% work from home; Mean travel time to work: 28.6 minutes

DAVENPORT (town). Covers a land area of 51.563 square miles and a water area of 0.350 square miles. Located at 42.45° N. Lat; 74.90° W. Long. Elevation is 1,306 feet.
Population: 2,805; Growth (since 2000): 1.1%; Density: 54.4 persons per square mile; Race: 97.0% White, 1.1% Black/African American, 1.1% Asian, 0.0% American Indian/Alaska Native, 0.0% Native Hawaiian/Other Pacific Islander, 0.7% Two or more races, 2.5% Hispanic of any race; Average household size: 2.36; Median age: 46.1; Age under 18: 15.2%; Age 65 and over: 21.3%; Males per 100 females: 94.7; Marriage status: 23.5% never married, 57.2% now married, 4.4% separated, 7.6% widowed, 11.8% divorced; Foreign born: 3.4%; Speak English only: 95.5%; With disability: 13.7%; Veterans: 7.4%; Ancestry: 27.1% Irish, 25.7% German, 13.7% Italian, 11.6% English, 4.2% American
Employment: 11.7% management, business, and financial, 1.2% computer, engineering, and science, 16.5% education, legal, community service, arts, and media, 7.4% healthcare practitioners, 18.0% service, 23.7% sales and office, 12.4% natural resources, construction, and maintenance, 9.1% production, transportation, and material moving
Income: Per capita: $26,654; Median household: $47,014; Average household: $61,505; Households with income of $100,000 or more: 13.1%; Poverty rate: 12.4%
Educational Attainment: High school diploma or higher: 85.7%; Bachelor's degree or higher: 19.9%; Graduate/professional degree or higher: 9.6%

School District(s)
Charlotte Valley Central SD (PK-12)
    Enrollment: 400 . . . . (607) 278-5511
Housing: Homeownership rate: 66.2%; Median home value: $118,800; Median year structure built: 1983; Homeowner vacancy rate: 0.0%; Median selected monthly owner costs: $1,133 with a mortgage, $524 without a mortgage; Median gross rent: $845 per month; Rental vacancy rate: 10.6%
Health Insurance: 92.5% have insurance; 67.0% have private insurance; 50.8% have public insurance; 7.5% do not have insurance; 9.4% of children under 18 do not have insurance
Transportation: Commute: 86.3% car, 0.0% public transportation, 6.5% walk, 7.3% work from home; Mean travel time to work: 27.4 minutes

DAVENPORT CENTER (CDP). Covers a land area of 3.102 square miles and a water area of 0.040 square miles. Located at 42.45° N. Lat; 74.90° W. Long. Elevation is 1,217 feet.
Population: 226; Growth (since 2000): n/a; Density: 72.8 persons per square mile; Race: 100.0% White, 0.0% Black/African American, 0.0% Asian, 0.0% American Indian/Alaska Native, 0.0% Native Hawaiian/Other Pacific Islander, 0.0% Two or more races, 0.0% Hispanic of any race; Average household size: 2.15; Median age: 32.4; Age under 18: 21.7%; Age 65 and over: 7.5%; Males per 100 females: 90.7; Marriage status: 0.0% never married, 77.4% now married, 27.1% separated, 0.0% widowed, 22.6% divorced; Foreign born: 0.0%; Speak English only: 100.0%; With disability: 17.7%; Veterans: 6.2%; Ancestry: 50.4% German, 14.2% Dutch, 12.8% American, 12.8% English, 8.8% Irish
Employment: 0.0% management, business, and financial, 0.0% computer, engineering, and science, 12.5% education, legal, community service, arts, and media, 0.0% healthcare practitioners, 47.3% service, 23.2% sales and office, 0.0% natural resources, construction, and maintenance, 17.0% production, transportation, and material moving
Income: Per capita: $27,081; Median household: n/a; Average household: $59,770; Households with income of $100,000 or more: 8.6%; Poverty rate: 4.4%
Educational Attainment: High school diploma or higher: 79.1%; Bachelor's degree or higher: 5.1%; Graduate/professional degree or higher: n/a
Housing: Homeownership rate: 46.7%; Median home value: n/a; Median year structure built: 1988; Homeowner vacancy rate: 0.0%; Median selected monthly owner costs: n/a with a mortgage, <$100 without a mortgage; Median gross rent: $889 per month; Rental vacancy rate: 0.0%
Health Insurance: 56.2% have insurance; 38.5% have private insurance; 34.1% have public insurance; 43.8% do not have insurance; 81.6% of children under 18 do not have insurance
Transportation: Commute: 81.7% car, 0.0% public transportation, 0.0% walk, 18.3% work from home; Mean travel time to work: 0.0 minutes

DELANCEY (unincorporated postal area)
ZCTA: 13752
    Covers a land area of 48.520 square miles and a water area of 1.402 square miles. Located at 42.19° N. Lat; 74.90° W. Long..

Population: 832; Growth (since 2000): 16.4%; Density: 17.1 persons per square mile; Race: 99.3% White, 0.0% Black/African American, 0.0% Asian, 0.0% American Indian/Alaska Native, 0.0% Native Hawaiian/Other Pacific Islander, 0.7% Two or more races, 6.0% Hispanic of any race; Average household size: 2.43; Median age: 52.4; Age under 18: 20.4%; Age 65 and over: 24.9%; Males per 100 females: 108.5; Marriage status: 26.7% never married, 40.6% now married, 2.6% separated, 11.0% widowed, 21.7% divorced; Foreign born: 5.8%; Speak English only: 93.0%; With disability: 13.2%; Veterans: 13.1%; Ancestry: 23.1% Irish, 20.3% German, 15.7% Scottish, 9.4% Italian, 7.8% English
Employment: 5.7% management, business, and financial, 0.0% computer, engineering, and science, 13.7% education, legal, community service, arts, and media, 4.2% healthcare practitioners, 28.2% service, 17.7% sales and office, 20.2% natural resources, construction, and maintenance, 10.2% production, transportation, and material moving
Income: Per capita: $41,300; Median household: $54,583; Average household: $94,403; Households with income of $100,000 or more: 24.3%; Poverty rate: 22.1%
Educational Attainment: High school diploma or higher: 87.5%; Bachelor's degree or higher: 25.2%; Graduate/professional degree or higher: 11.2%
Housing: Homeownership rate: 85.4%; Median home value: $165,900; Median year structure built: 1971; Homeowner vacancy rate: 4.9%; Median selected monthly owner costs: $1,449 with a mortgage, $530 without a mortgage; Median gross rent: $831 per month; Rental vacancy rate: 0.0%
Health Insurance: 93.3% have insurance; 67.7% have private insurance; 48.0% have public insurance; 6.7% do not have insurance; 2.4% of children under 18 do not have insurance
Transportation: Commute: 84.3% car, 0.0% public transportation, 7.7% walk, 8.0% work from home; Mean travel time to work: 20.9 minutes

DELHI (town). Covers a land area of 64.198 square miles and a water area of 0.401 square miles. Located at 42.27° N. Lat; 74.91° W. Long. Elevation is 1,371 feet.
History: Shortly after the Revolutionary War, Ebenezer Foote was so influential locally and as a member of the state legislature that he was nicknamed "the Great Mogul." At the suggestions of facetious citizens the community was named for Delhi, India, the capital city of the real Great Mogul.
Population: 4,938; Growth (since 2000): 6.7%; Density: 76.9 persons per square mile; Race: 84.4% White, 9.9% Black/African American, 1.0% Asian, 0.2% American Indian/Alaska Native, 0.0% Native Hawaiian/Other Pacific Islander, 2.5% Two or more races, 7.8% Hispanic of any race; Average household size: 2.15; Median age: 25.2; Age under 18: 12.6%; Age 65 and over: 13.9%; Males per 100 females: 109.8; Marriage status: 53.6% never married, 31.7% now married, 0.9% separated, 5.0% widowed, 9.7% divorced; Foreign born: 4.1%; Speak English only: 92.8%; With disability: 13.9%; Veterans: 6.1%; Ancestry: 21.5% German, 20.6% Irish, 9.3% Italian, 8.1% English, 4.8% American
Employment: 10.8% management, business, and financial, 7.4% computer, engineering, and science, 10.1% education, legal, community service, arts, and media, 4.3% healthcare practitioners, 24.6% service, 21.8% sales and office, 9.2% natural resources, construction, and maintenance, 11.8% production, transportation, and material moving
Income: Per capita: $24,214; Median household: $51,269; Average household: $74,813; Households with income of $100,000 or more: 25.0%; Poverty rate: 15.4%
Educational Attainment: High school diploma or higher: 93.1%; Bachelor's degree or higher: 31.2%; Graduate/professional degree or higher: 16.9%

School District(s)
Delaware Academy Central School District at Delhi (KG-12)
    Enrollment: 728 . . . . (607) 746-1300
Four-year College(s)
SUNY College of Technology at Delhi (Public)
    Enrollment: 3,511 . . . . (607) 746-4000
    Tuition: In-state $8,120; Out-of-state $12,290
Housing: Homeownership rate: 69.2%; Median home value: $167,800; Median year structure built: 1965; Homeowner vacancy rate: 3.8%; Median selected monthly owner costs: $1,291 with a mortgage, $573 without a mortgage; Median gross rent: $729 per month; Rental vacancy rate: 13.3%
Health Insurance: 95.9% have insurance; 76.0% have private insurance; 33.7% have public insurance; 4.1% do not have insurance; 2.7% of children under 18 do not have insurance

Hospitals: O'Connor Hospital (28 beds)
Newspapers: Delaware County Times (weekly circulation 1,700)
Transportation: Commute: 75.8% car, 1.4% public transportation, 16.1% walk, 5.4% work from home; Mean travel time to work: 20.8 minutes
Additional Information Contacts
Town of Delhi . . . . (607) 746-8696
   http://townofdelhiny.com

DELHI (village). County seat. Covers a land area of 3.142 square miles and a water area of 0.050 square miles. Located at 42.28° N. Lat; 74.91° W. Long. Elevation is 1,371 feet.
Population: 3,176; Growth (since 2000): 23.0%; Density: 1,010.8 persons per square mile; Race: 77.2% White, 14.5% Black/African American, 1.1% Asian, 0.4% American Indian/Alaska Native, 0.0% Native Hawaiian/Other Pacific Islander, 3.7% Two or more races, 11.0% Hispanic of any race; Average household size: 2.10; Median age: 20.6; Age under 18: 10.4%; Age 65 and over: 10.8%; Males per 100 females: 119.1; Marriage status: 68.8% never married, 20.5% now married, 1.1% separated, 3.2% widowed, 7.4% divorced; Foreign born: 4.3%; Speak English only: 90.4%; With disability: 14.4%; Veterans: 3.4%; Ancestry: 16.8% Irish, 16.2% German, 11.9% Italian, 5.7% English, 3.8% Dutch
Employment: 11.9% management, business, and financial, 5.7% computer, engineering, and science, 9.6% education, legal, community service, arts, and media, 3.4% healthcare practitioners, 27.4% service, 24.5% sales and office, 6.7% natural resources, construction, and maintenance, 10.8% production, transportation, and material moving
Income: Per capita: $15,755; Median household: $40,795; Average household: $59,406; Households with income of $100,000 or more: 17.6%; Poverty rate: 26.4%
Educational Attainment: High school diploma or higher: 90.9%; Bachelor's degree or higher: 35.2%; Graduate/professional degree or higher: 19.7%
School District(s)
Delaware Academy Central School District at Delhi (KG-12)
   Enrollment: 728 . . . . (607) 746-1300
Four-year College(s)
SUNY College of Technology at Delhi (Public)
   Enrollment: 3,511 . . . . (607) 746-4000
   Tuition: In-state $8,120; Out-of-state $12,290
Housing: Homeownership rate: 53.1%; Median home value: $156,100; Median year structure built: Before 1940; Homeowner vacancy rate: 7.5%; Median selected monthly owner costs: $1,156 with a mortgage, $624 without a mortgage; Median gross rent: $697 per month; Rental vacancy rate: 9.6%
Health Insurance: 94.6% have insurance; 71.9% have private insurance; 34.0% have public insurance; 5.4% do not have insurance; 3.7% of children under 18 do not have insurance
Hospitals: O'Connor Hospital (28 beds)
Safety: Violent crime rate: 15.9 per 10,000 population; Property crime rate: 76.3 per 10,000 population
Newspapers: Delaware County Times (weekly circulation 1,700)
Transportation: Commute: 65.0% car, 1.9% public transportation, 22.3% walk, 10.0% work from home; Mean travel time to work: 16.9 minutes

DENVER (unincorporated postal area)
ZCTA: 12421
   Covers a land area of 19.606 square miles and a water area of 0.009 square miles. Located at 42.25° N. Lat; 74.55° W. Long. Elevation is 1,631 feet.
   Population: 268; Growth (since 2000): -65.5%; Density: 13.7 persons per square mile; Race: 97.4% White, 0.0% Black/African American, 2.6% Asian, 0.0% American Indian/Alaska Native, 0.0% Native Hawaiian/Other Pacific Islander, 0.0% Two or more races, 2.2% Hispanic of any race; Average household size: 1.69; Median age: 61.6; Age under 18: 0.0%; Age 65 and over: 40.3%; Males per 100 females: 103.5; Marriage status: 14.6% never married, 64.9% now married, 0.0% separated, 1.9% widowed, 18.7% divorced; Foreign born: 10.1%; Speak English only: 88.4%; With disability: 14.9%; Veterans: 5.6%; Ancestry: 26.5% Italian, 21.3% Irish, 19.0% German, 17.5% English, 8.2% Scottish
   Employment: 4.6% management, business, and financial, 15.1% computer, engineering, and science, 15.1% education, legal, community service, arts, and media, 0.0% healthcare practitioners, 36.8% service, 11.2% sales and office, 6.6% natural resources, construction, and maintenance, 10.5% production, transportation, and material moving

Income: Per capita: $43,473; Median household: $53,942; Average household: $73,794; Households with income of $100,000 or more: 16.4%; Poverty rate: 1.9%
Educational Attainment: High school diploma or higher: 78.7%; Bachelor's degree or higher: 26.9%; Graduate/professional degree or higher: 5.2%
Housing: Homeownership rate: 100.0%; Median home value: $159,300; Median year structure built: 1979; Homeowner vacancy rate: 8.1%; Median selected monthly owner costs: $1,340 with a mortgage, $720 without a mortgage; Median gross rent: n/a per month; Rental vacancy rate: 0.0%
Health Insurance: 98.9% have insurance; 69.4% have private insurance; 60.1% have public insurance; 1.1% do not have insurance; 0.0% of children under 18 do not have insurance
Transportation: Commute: 75.0% car, 7.2% public transportation, 4.6% walk, 13.2% work from home; Mean travel time to work: 51.6 minutes

DEPOSIT (town). Covers a land area of 43.015 square miles and a water area of 1.564 square miles. Located at 42.10° N. Lat; 75.37° W. Long.
Population: 1,762; Growth (since 2000): 4.4%; Density: 41.0 persons per square mile; Race: 93.6% White, 2.5% Black/African American, 0.0% Asian, 0.3% American Indian/Alaska Native, 0.0% Native Hawaiian/Other Pacific Islander, 3.2% Two or more races, 1.5% Hispanic of any race; Average household size: 2.41; Median age: 46.4; Age under 18: 21.1%; Age 65 and over: 23.4%; Males per 100 females: 91.9; Marriage status: 25.8% never married, 52.4% now married, 1.5% separated, 10.9% widowed, 10.8% divorced; Foreign born: 2.8%; Speak English only: 96.5%; With disability: 19.5%; Veterans: 10.4%; Ancestry: 26.4% German, 16.1% English, 14.4% Irish, 13.5% Italian, 6.5% Dutch
Employment: 9.1% management, business, and financial, 3.5% computer, engineering, and science, 11.0% education, legal, community service, arts, and media, 4.6% healthcare practitioners, 14.1% service, 21.9% sales and office, 13.9% natural resources, construction, and maintenance, 21.9% production, transportation, and material moving
Income: Per capita: $23,625; Median household: $45,913; Average household: $54,597; Households with income of $100,000 or more: 15.9%; Poverty rate: 16.3%
Educational Attainment: High school diploma or higher: 89.6%; Bachelor's degree or higher: 14.9%; Graduate/professional degree or higher: 7.8%
School District(s)
Deposit Central SD (PK-12)
   Enrollment: 543 . . . . (607) 467-5380
Housing: Homeownership rate: 72.6%; Median home value: $105,500; Median year structure built: 1966; Homeowner vacancy rate: 2.7%; Median selected monthly owner costs: $1,192 with a mortgage, $509 without a mortgage; Median gross rent: $653 per month; Rental vacancy rate: 0.0%
Health Insurance: 88.3% have insurance; 64.4% have private insurance; 46.1% have public insurance; 11.7% do not have insurance; 7.3% of children under 18 do not have insurance
Newspapers: Deposit Courier (weekly circulation 2,200)
Transportation: Commute: 90.4% car, 1.0% public transportation, 2.6% walk, 3.4% work from home; Mean travel time to work: 22.5 minutes

DEPOSIT (village). Covers a land area of 1.263 square miles and a water area of 0.053 square miles. Located at 42.06° N. Lat; 75.42° W. Long. Elevation is 991 feet.
Population: 1,696; Growth (since 2000): -0.2%; Density: 1,343.0 persons per square mile; Race: 91.6% White, 2.9% Black/African American, 0.5% Asian, 0.0% American Indian/Alaska Native, 0.5% Native Hawaiian/Other Pacific Islander, 4.2% Two or more races, 5.5% Hispanic of any race; Average household size: 2.42; Median age: 44.5; Age under 18: 19.5%; Age 65 and over: 21.3%; Males per 100 females: 87.7; Marriage status: 28.3% never married, 51.8% now married, 1.8% separated, 8.9% widowed, 10.9% divorced; Foreign born: 2.2%; Speak English only: 93.7%; With disability: 19.5%; Veterans: 12.7%; Ancestry: 25.5% German, 15.8% Irish, 15.5% Italian, 11.4% English, 5.3% American
Employment: 5.2% management, business, and financial, 2.3% computer, engineering, and science, 6.7% education, legal, community service, arts, and media, 3.0% healthcare practitioners, 21.9% service, 25.6% sales and office, 12.7% natural resources, construction, and maintenance, 22.7% production, transportation, and material moving

Income: Per capita: $18,750; Median household: $34,722; Average household: $44,564; Households with income of $100,000 or more: 7.7%; Poverty rate: 20.3%

Educational Attainment: High school diploma or higher: 88.8%; Bachelor's degree or higher: 10.2%; Graduate/professional degree or higher: 3.3%

School District(s)

Deposit Central SD (PK-12)

  Enrollment: 543 . . . . (607) 467-5380

Housing: Homeownership rate: 61.1%; Median home value: $85,600; Median year structure built: 1943; Homeowner vacancy rate: 7.2%; Median selected monthly owner costs: $1,107 with a mortgage, $526 without a mortgage; Median gross rent: $687 per month; Rental vacancy rate: 0.0%

Health Insurance: 89.1% have insurance; 57.7% have private insurance; 51.8% have public insurance; 10.9% do not have insurance; 6.2% of children under 18 do not have insurance

Newspapers: Deposit Courier (weekly circulation 2,200)

Transportation: Commute: 83.0% car, 0.0% public transportation, 12.7% walk, 2.1% work from home; Mean travel time to work: 21.6 minutes

DOWNSVILLE (CDP). Covers a land area of 3.953 square miles and a water area of 0.079 square miles. Located at 42.08° N. Lat; 75.00° W. Long. Elevation is 1,125 feet.

Population: 466; Growth (since 2000): n/a; Density: 117.9 persons per square mile; Race: 97.0% White, 0.0% Black/African American, 0.0% Asian, 0.0% American Indian/Alaska Native, 0.0% Native Hawaiian/Other Pacific Islander, 3.0% Two or more races, 0.0% Hispanic of any race; Average household size: 2.03; Median age: 54.7; Age under 18: 13.7%; Age 65 and over: 20.2%; Males per 100 females: 91.6; Marriage status: 40.7% never married, 38.8% now married, 0.0% separated, 4.9% widowed, 15.5% divorced; Foreign born: 2.4%; Speak English only: 97.6%; With disability: 22.3%; Veterans: 9.7%; Ancestry: 44.4% German, 25.1% Irish, 21.7% Dutch, 7.5% Scotch-Irish, 7.3% Scottish

Employment: 16.7% management, business, and financial, 0.0% computer, engineering, and science, 8.6% education, legal, community service, arts, and media, 7.2% healthcare practitioners, 10.9% service, 22.6% sales and office, 21.3% natural resources, construction, and maintenance, 12.7% production, transportation, and material moving

Income: Per capita: $19,590; Median household: $35,179; Average household: $39,076; Households with income of $100,000 or more: 3.0%; Poverty rate: 33.0%

Educational Attainment: High school diploma or higher: 75.7%; Bachelor's degree or higher: 3.6%; Graduate/professional degree or higher: 0.8%

School District(s)

Downsville Central SD (PK-12)

  Enrollment: 262 . . . . (607) 363-2101

Housing: Homeownership rate: 61.6%; Median home value: $106,300; Median year structure built: 1948; Homeowner vacancy rate: 9.0%; Median selected monthly owner costs: $498 with a mortgage, $272 without a mortgage; Median gross rent: $525 per month; Rental vacancy rate: 8.3%

Health Insurance: 91.6% have insurance; 59.2% have private insurance; 43.6% have public insurance; 8.4% do not have insurance; 10.8% of children under 18 do not have insurance

Transportation: Commute: 92.3% car, 2.3% public transportation, 1.8% walk, 3.6% work from home; Mean travel time to work: 18.5 minutes

EAST BRANCH (unincorporated postal area)
ZCTA: 13756

  Covers a land area of 45.879 square miles and a water area of 0.645 square miles. Located at 42.00° N. Lat; 75.10° W. Long. Elevation is 1,007 feet.

Population: 412; Growth (since 2000): -20.5%; Density: 9.0 persons per square mile; Race: 100.0% White, 0.0% Black/African American, 0.0% Asian, 0.0% American Indian/Alaska Native, 0.0% Native Hawaiian/Other Pacific Islander, 0.0% Two or more races, 0.0% Hispanic of any race; Average household size: 2.26; Median age: 49.3; Age under 18: 19.7%; Age 65 and over: 23.3%; Males per 100 females: 108.5; Marriage status: 29.3% never married, 48.9% now married, 2.4% separated, 16.3% widowed, 5.4% divorced; Foreign born: 1.2%; Speak English only: 100.0%; With disability: 14.3%; Veterans: 8.2%; Ancestry: 30.1% Irish, 25.5% German, 20.9% English, 20.9% Italian, 9.5% Swedish

Employment: 9.8% management, business, and financial, 3.5% computer, engineering, and science, 0.0% education, legal, community

service, arts, and media, 0.0% healthcare practitioners, 9.1% service, 34.3% sales and office, 11.9% natural resources, construction, and maintenance, 31.5% production, transportation, and material moving

Income: Per capita: $28,130; Median household: $51,250; Average household: $62,153; Households with income of $100,000 or more: 14.2%; Poverty rate: 18.4%

Educational Attainment: High school diploma or higher: 76.4%; Bachelor's degree or higher: 6.9%; Graduate/professional degree or higher: 6.9%

Housing: Homeownership rate: 66.5%; Median home value: $102,500; Median year structure built: 1970; Homeowner vacancy rate: 0.0%; Median selected monthly owner costs: $1,288 with a mortgage, $381 without a mortgage; Median gross rent: $699 per month; Rental vacancy rate: 0.0%

Health Insurance: 90.8% have insurance; 47.6% have private insurance; 62.6% have public insurance; 9.2% do not have insurance; 0.0% of children under 18 do not have insurance

Transportation: Commute: 89.5% car, 0.0% public transportation, 10.5% walk, 0.0% work from home; Mean travel time to work: 35.8 minutes

EAST MEREDITH (unincorporated postal area)
ZCTA: 13757

  Covers a land area of 37.199 square miles and a water area of 0.087 square miles. Located at 42.41° N. Lat; 74.89° W. Long. Elevation is 1,401 feet.

Population: 1,294; Growth (since 2000): 16.9%; Density: 34.8 persons per square mile; Race: 99.2% White, 0.1% Black/African American, 0.0% Asian, 0.0% American Indian/Alaska Native, 0.0% Native Hawaiian/Other Pacific Islander, 0.5% Two or more races, 2.5% Hispanic of any race; Average household size: 2.47; Median age: 45.8; Age under 18: 18.3%; Age 65 and over: 19.9%; Males per 100 females: 96.1; Marriage status: 22.9% never married, 57.1% now married, 3.0% separated, 5.8% widowed, 14.2% divorced; Foreign born: 2.3%; Speak English only: 97.3%; With disability: 12.2%; Veterans: 8.0%; Ancestry: 26.8% Irish, 24.6% German, 20.9% Italian, 16.0% English, 12.2% Dutch

Employment: 13.5% management, business, and financial, 2.8% computer, engineering, and science, 11.3% education, legal, community service, arts, and media, 3.6% healthcare practitioners, 17.0% service, 17.5% sales and office, 19.6% natural resources, construction, and maintenance, 14.8% production, transportation, and material moving

Income: Per capita: $27,394; Median household: $54,123; Average household: $65,618; Households with income of $100,000 or more: 18.4%; Poverty rate: 12.9%

Educational Attainment: High school diploma or higher: 85.6%; Bachelor's degree or higher: 28.6%; Graduate/professional degree or higher: 14.7%

Housing: Homeownership rate: 83.4%; Median home value: $141,700; Median year structure built: 1987; Homeowner vacancy rate: 0.0%; Median selected monthly owner costs: $1,280 with a mortgage, $607 without a mortgage; Median gross rent: $846 per month; Rental vacancy rate: 0.0%

Health Insurance: 86.2% have insurance; 68.2% have private insurance; 46.1% have public insurance; 13.8% do not have insurance; 9.7% of children under 18 do not have insurance

Transportation: Commute: 83.7% car, 0.0% public transportation, 0.6% walk, 14.7% work from home; Mean travel time to work: 26.3 minutes

FISHS EDDY (unincorporated postal area)
ZCTA: 13774

  Covers a land area of 2.844 square miles and a water area of 0.149 square miles. Located at 41.96° N. Lat; 75.15° W. Long. Elevation is 984 feet.

Population: 168; Growth (since 2000): -41.3%; Density: 59.1 persons per square mile; Race: 100.0% White, 0.0% Black/African American, 0.0% Asian, 0.0% American Indian/Alaska Native, 0.0% Native Hawaiian/Other Pacific Islander, 0.0% Two or more races, 0.0% Hispanic of any race; Average household size: 2.80; Median age: 28.8; Age under 18: 30.4%; Age 65 and over: 6.0%; Males per 100 females: 123.3; Marriage status: 32.5% never married, 59.0% now married, 0.0% separated, 8.5% widowed, 0.0% divorced; Foreign born: 0.0%; Speak English only: 100.0%; With disability: 17.9%; Veterans: 0.0%; Ancestry: 19.0% American, 19.0% European, 10.1% Dutch, 10.1% Polish, 4.8% German

Employment: 0.0% management, business, and financial, 13.2% computer, engineering, and science, 22.1% education, legal, community service, arts, and media, 0.0% healthcare practitioners, 11.8% service, 0.0% sales and office, 0.0% natural resources, construction, and maintenance, 52.9% production, transportation, and material moving
Income: Per capita: $14,305; Median household: $33,750; Average household: $38,347; Households with income of $100,000 or more: n/a; Poverty rate: 14.9%
Educational Attainment: High school diploma or higher: 88.9%; Bachelor's degree or higher: n/a; Graduate/professional degree or higher: n/a
Housing: Homeownership rate: 71.7%; Median home value: $78,300; Median year structure built: 1949; Homeowner vacancy rate: 37.7%; Median selected monthly owner costs: $0 with a mortgage, $377 without a mortgage; Median gross rent: n/a per month; Rental vacancy rate: 0.0%
Health Insurance: 100.0% have insurance; 61.3% have private insurance; 38.7% have public insurance; 0.0% do not have insurance; 0.0% of children under 18 do not have insurance
Transportation: Commute: 100.0% car, 0.0% public transportation, 0.0% walk, 0.0% work from home; Mean travel time to work: 20.8 minutes

FLEISCHMANNS (village). Covers a land area of 0.655 square miles and a water area of 0.015 square miles. Located at 42.15° N. Lat; 74.53° W. Long. Elevation is 1,499 feet.
Population: 375; Growth (since 2000): 6.8%; Density: 572.4 persons per square mile; Race: 89.3% White, 0.5% Black/African American, 0.0% Asian, 0.0% American Indian/Alaska Native, 0.0% Native Hawaiian/Other Pacific Islander, 3.5% Two or more races, 22.4% Hispanic of any race; Average household size: 2.64; Median age: 42.4; Age under 18: 26.1%; Age 65 and over: 13.6%; Males per 100 females: 102.9; Marriage status: 18.3% never married, 51.5% now married, 10.8% separated, 14.6% widowed, 15.6% divorced; Foreign born: 39.2%; Speak English only: 51.5%; With disability: 12.5%; Veterans: 3.2%; Ancestry: 29.3% German, 17.3% Irish, 9.1% Czech, 6.7% Italian, 3.2% English
Employment: 15.8% management, business, and financial, 0.0% computer, engineering, and science, 23.3% education, legal, community service, arts, and media, 0.0% healthcare practitioners, 19.5% service, 31.6% sales and office, 6.0% natural resources, construction, and maintenance, 3.8% production, transportation, and material moving
Income: Per capita: $23,502; Median household: $39,688; Average household: $60,694; Households with income of $100,000 or more: 28.9%; Poverty rate: 8.5%
Educational Attainment: High school diploma or higher: 89.2%; Bachelor's degree or higher: 42.8%; Graduate/professional degree or higher: 26.0%
Housing: Homeownership rate: 77.5%; Median home value: $137,000; Median year structure built: Before 1940; Homeowner vacancy rate: 3.5%; Median selected monthly owner costs: $1,135 with a mortgage, $590 without a mortgage; Median gross rent: $679 per month; Rental vacancy rate: 20.0%
Health Insurance: 77.9% have insurance; 38.7% have private insurance; 48.0% have public insurance; 22.1% do not have insurance; 0.0% of children under 18 do not have insurance
Transportation: Commute: 91.7% car, 0.0% public transportation, 8.3% walk, 0.0% work from home; Mean travel time to work: 34.2 minutes

FRANKLIN (town). Covers a land area of 81.249 square miles and a water area of 0.278 square miles. Located at 42.33° N. Lat; 75.11° W. Long. Elevation is 1,234 feet.
Population: 2,358; Growth (since 2000): -10.0%; Density: 29.0 persons per square mile; Race: 96.9% White, 1.1% Black/African American, 0.6% Asian, 0.2% American Indian/Alaska Native, 0.0% Native Hawaiian/Other Pacific Islander, 1.2% Two or more races, 1.4% Hispanic of any race; Average household size: 2.43; Median age: 52.1; Age under 18: 17.0%; Age 65 and over: 25.6%; Males per 100 females: 102.3; Marriage status: 18.3% never married, 64.4% now married, 2.3% separated, 6.1% widowed, 11.2% divorced; Foreign born: 3.3%; Speak English only: 96.6%; With disability: 11.9%; Veterans: 11.0%; Ancestry: 21.1% Irish, 20.8% German, 16.6% English, 10.0% Italian, 7.3% American
Employment: 14.4% management, business, and financial, 1.8% computer, engineering, and science, 14.1% education, legal, community service, arts, and media, 8.5% healthcare practitioners, 14.8% service,

23.3% sales and office, 10.0% natural resources, construction, and maintenance, 13.1% production, transportation, and material moving
Income: Per capita: $29,693; Median household: $55,294; Average household: $69,962; Households with income of $100,000 or more: 24.2%; Poverty rate: 9.2%
Educational Attainment: High school diploma or higher: 93.3%; Bachelor's degree or higher: 29.1%; Graduate/professional degree or higher: 13.0%

School District(s)
Franklin Central SD (PK-12)
    Enrollment: 279 . . . . (607) 829-3551
Housing: Homeownership rate: 84.5%; Median home value: $147,300; Median year structure built: 1950; Homeowner vacancy rate: 1.2%; Median selected monthly owner costs: $1,182 with a mortgage, $535 without a mortgage; Median gross rent: $698 per month; Rental vacancy rate: 7.6%
Health Insurance: 91.9% have insurance; 65.9% have private insurance; 46.6% have public insurance; 8.1% do not have insurance; 14.8% of children under 18 do not have insurance
Transportation: Commute: 82.7% car, 0.0% public transportation, 4.3% walk, 10.9% work from home; Mean travel time to work: 31.8 minutes
Additional Information Contacts
Town of Franklin . . . . (518) 891-2189
    http://townoffranklin.com

FRANKLIN (village). Covers a land area of 0.339 square miles and a water area of 0.007 square miles. Located at 42.34° N. Lat; 75.17° W. Long. Elevation is 1,234 feet.
Population: 455; Growth (since 2000): 13.2%; Density: 1,342.7 persons per square mile; Race: 97.4% White, 2.6% Black/African American, 0.0% Asian, 0.0% American Indian/Alaska Native, 0.0% Native Hawaiian/Other Pacific Islander, 0.0% Two or more races, 0.0% Hispanic of any race; Average household size: 2.59; Median age: 39.6; Age under 18: 20.4%; Age 65 and over: 22.6%; Males per 100 females: 93.8; Marriage status: 30.9% never married, 53.0% now married, 2.6% separated, 3.1% widowed, 13.0% divorced; Foreign born: 2.9%; Speak English only: 97.5%; With disability: 12.7%; Veterans: 12.7%; Ancestry: 27.0% Irish, 23.5% German, 22.4% English, 9.7% Italian, 6.2% French Canadian
Employment: 12.8% management, business, and financial, 5.6% computer, engineering, and science, 15.9% education, legal, community service, arts, and media, 8.7% healthcare practitioners, 27.2% service, 14.4% sales and office, 11.3% natural resources, construction, and maintenance, 4.1% production, transportation, and material moving
Income: Per capita: $25,122; Median household: $48,889; Average household: $63,354; Households with income of $100,000 or more: 14.8%; Poverty rate: 10.0%
Educational Attainment: High school diploma or higher: 94.9%; Bachelor's degree or higher: 35.6%; Graduate/professional degree or higher: 20.3%

School District(s)
Franklin Central SD (PK-12)
    Enrollment: 279 . . . . (607) 829-3551
Housing: Homeownership rate: 68.2%; Median home value: $135,700; Median year structure built: Before 1940; Homeowner vacancy rate: 7.7%; Median selected monthly owner costs: $1,078 with a mortgage, $631 without a mortgage; Median gross rent: $769 per month; Rental vacancy rate: 16.9%
Health Insurance: 86.6% have insurance; 50.5% have private insurance; 56.7% have public insurance; 13.4% do not have insurance; 6.8% of children under 18 do not have insurance
Transportation: Commute: 82.0% car, 0.0% public transportation, 9.5% walk, 7.4% work from home; Mean travel time to work: 27.9 minutes

GRAND GORGE (unincorporated postal area)
ZCTA: 12434
    Covers a land area of 13.769 square miles and a water area of 0.427 square miles. Located at 42.36° N. Lat; 74.50° W. Long. Elevation is 1,401 feet.
    Population: 617; Growth (since 2000): -6.9%; Density: 44.8 persons per square mile; Race: 84.8% White, 10.7% Black/African American, 0.0% Asian, 0.0% American Indian/Alaska Native, 0.0% Native Hawaiian/Other Pacific Islander, 4.5% Two or more races, 0.0% Hispanic of any race; Average household size: 2.02; Median age: 52.4; Age under 18: 5.3%; Age 65 and over: 30.5%; Males per 100 females: 96.1; Marriage status: 34.1% never married, 45.3% now married, 4.5% separated, 10.6% widowed, 10.0% divorced; Foreign born: 4.4%; Speak

English only: 100.0%; With disability: 29.7%; Veterans: 11.8%; Ancestry: 24.6% German, 22.0% Italian, 16.0% Dutch, 15.9% Irish, 11.5% American
Employment: 4.1% management, business, and financial, 3.0% computer, engineering, and science, 13.3% education, legal, community service, arts, and media, 0.0% healthcare practitioners, 16.2% service, 11.4% sales and office, 10.7% natural resources, construction, and maintenance, 41.3% production, transportation, and material moving
Income: Per capita: $23,823; Median household: $31,905; Average household: $43,795; Households with income of $100,000 or more: 16.7%; Poverty rate: 12.3%
Educational Attainment: High school diploma or higher: 83.4%; Bachelor's degree or higher: 11.1%; Graduate/professional degree or higher: 7.7%

School District(s)
Otsego-Delaware-Schoharie-Greene Boces
   Enrollment: n/a .... (607) 588-6291
Housing: Homeownership rate: 62.4%; Median home value: $131,600; Median year structure built: 1964; Homeowner vacancy rate: 12.8%; Median selected monthly owner costs: $1,229 with a mortgage, $475 without a mortgage; Median gross rent: $494 per month; Rental vacancy rate: 0.0%
Health Insurance: 96.9% have insurance; 60.1% have private insurance; 56.9% have public insurance; 3.1% do not have insurance; 0.0% of children under 18 do not have insurance
Transportation: Commute: 80.8% car, 5.9% public transportation, 2.2% walk, 11.1% work from home; Mean travel time to work: 27.9 minutes

HALCOTTSVILLE (unincorporated postal area)
ZCTA: 12438
Covers a land area of 0.439 square miles and a water area of 0.041 square miles. Located at 42.21° N. Lat; 74.60° W. Long. Elevation is 1,401 feet.
Population: 48; Growth (since 2000): n/a; Density: 109.3 persons per square mile; Race: 54.2% White, 0.0% Black/African American, 25.0% Asian, 0.0% American Indian/Alaska Native, 0.0% Native Hawaiian/Other Pacific Islander, 20.8% Two or more races, 0.0% Hispanic of any race; Average household size: 2.67; Median age: 37.2; Age under 18: 20.8%; Age 65 and over: 35.4%; Males per 100 females: 84.4; Marriage status: 0.0% never married, 100.0% now married, 0.0% separated, 0.0% widowed, 0.0% divorced; Foreign born: 43.8%; Speak English only: 56.3%; With disability: 0.0%; Veterans: 0.0%; Ancestry: 35.4% German, 18.8% Dutch, 18.8% Russian, 16.7% Italian
Employment: 27.6% management, business, and financial, 31.0% computer, engineering, and science, 0.0% education, legal, community service, arts, and media, 0.0% healthcare practitioners, 0.0% service, 41.4% sales and office, 0.0% natural resources, construction, and maintenance, 0.0% production, transportation, and material moving
Income: Per capita: $30,308; Median household: n/a; Average household: n/a; Households with income of $100,000 or more: 50.0%; Poverty rate: n/a
Educational Attainment: High school diploma or higher: 68.4%; Bachelor's degree or higher: 44.7%; Graduate/professional degree or higher: 21.1%
Housing: Homeownership rate: 100.0%; Median home value: n/a; Median year structure built: Before 1940; Homeowner vacancy rate: 0.0%; Median selected monthly owner costs: $0 with a mortgage, $0 without a mortgage; Median gross rent: n/a per month; Rental vacancy rate: 0.0%
Health Insurance: 81.3% have insurance; 81.3% have private insurance; 18.8% have public insurance; 18.8% do not have insurance; 0.0% of children under 18 do not have insurance
Transportation: Commute: 69.0% car, 31.0% public transportation, 0.0% walk, 0.0% work from home; Mean travel time to work: 0.0 minutes

HAMDEN (town). Covers a land area of 59.930 square miles and a water area of 0.269 square miles. Located at 42.20° N. Lat; 74.98° W. Long. Elevation is 1,286 feet.
Population: 1,238; Growth (since 2000): -3.3%; Density: 20.7 persons per square mile; Race: 97.7% White, 0.5% Black/African American, 0.8% Asian, 0.1% American Indian/Alaska Native, 0.0% Native Hawaiian/Other Pacific Islander, 0.7% Two or more races, 3.3% Hispanic of any race; Average household size: 2.38; Median age: 52.3; Age under 18: 19.0%; Age 65 and over: 28.2%; Males per 100 females: 100.2; Marriage status: 26.5% never married, 50.1% now married, 2.4% separated, 10.3%

widowed, 13.0% divorced; Foreign born: 3.1%; Speak English only: 95.8%; With disability: 18.4%; Veterans: 10.6%; Ancestry: 26.3% Irish, 20.0% German, 10.4% Scottish, 10.1% English, 10.1% Italian
Employment: 14.1% management, business, and financial, 4.1% computer, engineering, and science, 8.6% education, legal, community service, arts, and media, 7.1% healthcare practitioners, 23.3% service, 17.5% sales and office, 11.5% natural resources, construction, and maintenance, 13.7% production, transportation, and material moving
Income: Per capita: $29,352; Median household: $53,958; Average household: $66,731; Households with income of $100,000 or more: 20.1%; Poverty rate: 17.3%
Educational Attainment: High school diploma or higher: 89.4%; Bachelor's degree or higher: 26.8%; Graduate/professional degree or higher: 13.8%
Housing: Homeownership rate: 80.9%; Median home value: $161,200; Median year structure built: 1971; Homeowner vacancy rate: 5.4%; Median selected monthly owner costs: $1,354 with a mortgage, $523 without a mortgage; Median gross rent: $863 per month; Rental vacancy rate: 7.6%
Health Insurance: 96.1% have insurance; 69.5% have private insurance; 50.3% have public insurance; 3.9% do not have insurance; 1.7% of children under 18 do not have insurance
Transportation: Commute: 80.7% car, 4.0% public transportation, 4.6% walk, 10.7% work from home; Mean travel time to work: 20.6 minutes

HANCOCK (town). Covers a land area of 158.822 square miles and a water area of 2.994 square miles. Located at 41.96° N. Lat; 75.18° W. Long. Elevation is 922 feet.
Population: 3,092; Growth (since 2000): -10.4%; Density: 19.5 persons per square mile; Race: 96.6% White, 0.9% Black/African American, 0.3% Asian, 0.8% American Indian/Alaska Native, 0.0% Native Hawaiian/Other Pacific Islander, 0.7% Two or more races, 1.7% Hispanic of any race; Average household size: 2.36; Median age: 47.9; Age under 18: 20.1%; Age 65 and over: 21.0%; Males per 100 females: 110.3; Marriage status: 28.1% never married, 52.7% now married, 4.1% separated, 8.3% widowed, 10.9% divorced; Foreign born: 5.2%; Speak English only: 96.1%; With disability: 17.6%; Veterans: 9.1%; Ancestry: 25.8% German, 22.9% Irish, 12.3% English, 11.7% Italian, 6.9% American
Employment: 11.3% management, business, and financial, 1.4% computer, engineering, and science, 8.8% education, legal, community service, arts, and media, 3.6% healthcare practitioners, 30.5% service, 19.1% sales and office, 8.4% natural resources, construction, and maintenance, 16.9% production, transportation, and material moving
Income: Per capita: $23,958; Median household: $45,542; Average household: $55,733; Households with income of $100,000 or more: 12.8%; Poverty rate: 13.5%
Educational Attainment: High school diploma or higher: 83.7%; Bachelor's degree or higher: 11.5%; Graduate/professional degree or higher: 7.1%

School District(s)
Hancock Central SD (PK-12)
   Enrollment: 364 .... (607) 637-1301
Housing: Homeownership rate: 73.2%; Median home value: $108,900; Median year structure built: 1963; Homeowner vacancy rate: 4.4%; Median selected monthly owner costs: $1,240 with a mortgage, $459 without a mortgage; Median gross rent: $644 per month; Rental vacancy rate: 2.3%
Health Insurance: 91.1% have insurance; 62.5% have private insurance; 43.9% have public insurance; 8.9% do not have insurance; 1.3% of children under 18 do not have insurance
Newspapers: Hancock Herald (weekly circulation 2,400)
Transportation: Commute: 85.8% car, 0.8% public transportation, 7.9% walk, 4.2% work from home; Mean travel time to work: 22.4 minutes

HANCOCK (village). Covers a land area of 1.502 square miles and a water area of 0.141 square miles. Located at 41.95° N. Lat; 75.28° W. Long. Elevation is 922 feet.
Population: 1,085; Growth (since 2000): -8.7%; Density: 722.5 persons per square mile; Race: 94.0% White, 1.0% Black/African American, 0.0% Asian, 2.3% American Indian/Alaska Native, 0.0% Native Hawaiian/Other Pacific Islander, 1.1% Two or more races, 3.8% Hispanic of any race; Average household size: 2.12; Median age: 45.0; Age under 18: 18.2%; Age 65 and over: 21.5%; Males per 100 females: 97.5; Marriage status: 31.5% never married, 45.5% now married, 6.0% separated, 9.1% widowed, 13.8% divorced; Foreign born: 6.0%; Speak English only: 93.7%; With disability: 21.6%; Veterans: 9.3%; Ancestry: 20.7% German, 17.8% Irish, 11.5% English, 11.1% Italian, 9.6% American

Employment: 5.7% management, business, and financial, 1.0% computer, engineering, and science, 7.1% education, legal, community service, arts, and media, 3.1% healthcare practitioners, 40.9% service, 21.6% sales and office, 8.1% natural resources, construction, and maintenance, 12.6% production, transportation, and material moving
Income: Per capita: $17,473; Median household: $29,000; Average household: $36,114; Households with income of $100,000 or more: 3.4%; Poverty rate: 21.9%
Educational Attainment: High school diploma or higher: 83.3%; Bachelor's degree or higher: 9.2%; Graduate/professional degree or higher: 3.9%

School District(s)
Hancock Central SD (PK-12)
   Enrollment: 364 . . . . (607) 637-1301
Housing: Homeownership rate: 59.4%; Median home value: $105,300; Median year structure built: Before 1940; Homeowner vacancy rate: 5.6%; Median selected monthly owner costs: $1,044 with a mortgage, $518 without a mortgage; Median gross rent: $577 per month; Rental vacancy rate: 3.7%
Health Insurance: 93.4% have insurance; 51.2% have private insurance; 56.3% have public insurance; 6.6% do not have insurance; 0.0% of children under 18 do not have insurance
Safety: Violent crime rate: 0.0 per 10,000 population; Property crime rate: 147.2 per 10,000 population
Newspapers: Hancock Herald (weekly circulation 2,400)
Transportation: Commute: 81.0% car, 0.0% public transportation, 16.3% walk, 1.7% work from home; Mean travel time to work: 20.2 minutes

HARPERSFIELD (town).
Covers a land area of 42.021 square miles and a water area of 0.267 square miles. Located at 42.45° N. Lat; 74.70° W. Long. Elevation is 1,667 feet.
Population: 1,660; Growth (since 2000): 3.6%; Density: 39.5 persons per square mile; Race: 94.8% White, 0.7% Black/African American, 1.9% Asian, 0.1% American Indian/Alaska Native, 0.0% Native Hawaiian/Other Pacific Islander, 2.0% Two or more races, 2.8% Hispanic of any race; Average household size: 2.36; Median age: 50.6; Age under 18: 15.2%; Age 65 and over: 29.2%; Males per 100 females: 96.4; Marriage status: 31.3% never married, 47.5% now married, 0.8% separated, 13.3% widowed, 7.9% divorced; Foreign born: 4.5%; Speak English only: 93.9%; With disability: 17.4%; Veterans: 12.2%; Ancestry: 31.1% German, 20.8% Irish, 13.7% English, 13.6% Italian, 8.5% Dutch
Employment: 12.1% management, business, and financial, 3.7% computer, engineering, and science, 5.9% education, legal, community service, arts, and media, 6.0% healthcare practitioners, 22.9% service, 16.5% sales and office, 11.7% natural resources, construction, and maintenance, 21.2% production, transportation, and material moving
Income: Per capita: $25,508; Median household: $51,250; Average household: $59,960; Households with income of $100,000 or more: 17.3%; Poverty rate: 11.3%
Educational Attainment: High school diploma or higher: 86.3%; Bachelor's degree or higher: 17.6%; Graduate/professional degree or higher: 6.7%
Housing: Homeownership rate: 82.1%; Median home value: $146,900; Median year structure built: 1972; Homeowner vacancy rate: 4.0%; Median selected monthly owner costs: $1,325 with a mortgage, $538 without a mortgage; Median gross rent: $645 per month; Rental vacancy rate: 0.0%
Health Insurance: 92.1% have insurance; 66.8% have private insurance; 44.8% have public insurance; 7.9% do not have insurance; 2.3% of children under 18 do not have insurance
Transportation: Commute: 88.1% car, 2.5% public transportation, 2.3% walk, 6.0% work from home; Mean travel time to work: 22.0 minutes

HOBART (village).
Covers a land area of 0.498 square miles and a water area of 0.007 square miles. Located at 42.37° N. Lat; 74.67° W. Long. Elevation is 1,650 feet.
Population: 474; Growth (since 2000): 21.5%; Density: 952.1 persons per square mile; Race: 96.4% White, 1.7% Black/African American, 1.3% Asian, 0.0% American Indian/Alaska Native, 0.0% Native Hawaiian/Other Pacific Islander, 0.6% Two or more races, 0.0% Hispanic of any race; Average household size: 2.49; Median age: 41.2; Age under 18: 19.0%; Age 65 and over: 18.4%; Males per 100 females: 106.1; Marriage status: 23.8% never married, 62.4% now married, 4.1% separated, 5.4% widowed, 8.4% divorced; Foreign born: 0.8%; Speak English only: 94.4%; With disability: 20.3%; Veterans: 13.0%; Ancestry: 22.4% Irish, 21.9% German, 19.2% English, 15.2% Italian, 11.0% Dutch

Employment: 2.8% management, business, and financial, 6.0% computer, engineering, and science, 9.7% education, legal, community service, arts, and media, 3.2% healthcare practitioners, 14.4% service, 21.8% sales and office, 13.9% natural resources, construction, and maintenance, 28.2% production, transportation, and material moving
Income: Per capita: $25,286; Median household: $49,100; Average household: $61,207; Households with income of $100,000 or more: 13.2%; Poverty rate: 18.8%
Educational Attainment: High school diploma or higher: 91.5%; Bachelor's degree or higher: 27.9%; Graduate/professional degree or higher: 9.6%
Housing: Homeownership rate: 65.8%; Median home value: $137,500; Median year structure built: Before 1940; Homeowner vacancy rate: 2.3%; Median selected monthly owner costs: $1,347 with a mortgage, $645 without a mortgage; Median gross rent: $650 per month; Rental vacancy rate: 0.0%
Health Insurance: 97.9% have insurance; 63.3% have private insurance; 50.4% have public insurance; 2.1% do not have insurance; 0.0% of children under 18 do not have insurance
Transportation: Commute: 75.5% car, 3.2% public transportation, 14.8% walk, 6.0% work from home; Mean travel time to work: 20.3 minutes

KORTRIGHT (town).
Covers a land area of 62.451 square miles and a water area of 0.182 square miles. Located at 42.40° N. Lat; 74.78° W. Long.
Population: 1,425; Growth (since 2000): -12.7%; Density: 22.8 persons per square mile; Race: 94.7% White, 2.3% Black/African American, 0.6% Asian, 0.0% American Indian/Alaska Native, 0.0% Native Hawaiian/Other Pacific Islander, 1.7% Two or more races, 1.5% Hispanic of any race; Average household size: 2.42; Median age: 46.7; Age under 18: 19.9%; Age 65 and over: 24.9%; Males per 100 females: 107.8; Marriage status: 31.3% never married, 51.9% now married, 3.3% separated, 7.0% widowed, 9.8% divorced; Foreign born: 3.5%; Speak English only: 93.2%; With disability: 15.3%; Veterans: 9.3%; Ancestry: 27.5% German, 20.4% Irish, 9.3% Polish, 8.8% English, 8.6% Italian
Employment: 14.1% management, business, and financial, 3.4% computer, engineering, and science, 16.1% education, legal, community service, arts, and media, 2.1% healthcare practitioners, 19.1% service, 15.6% sales and office, 12.7% natural resources, construction, and maintenance, 17.0% production, transportation, and material moving
Income: Per capita: $28,138; Median household: $59,250; Average household: $69,432; Households with income of $100,000 or more: 23.2%; Poverty rate: 17.6%
Educational Attainment: High school diploma or higher: 86.7%; Bachelor's degree or higher: 22.9%; Graduate/professional degree or higher: 9.3%
Housing: Homeownership rate: 86.5%; Median home value: $165,600; Median year structure built: 1981; Homeowner vacancy rate: 0.6%; Median selected monthly owner costs: $1,213 with a mortgage, $503 without a mortgage; Median gross rent: $677 per month; Rental vacancy rate: 10.6%
Health Insurance: 93.7% have insurance; 70.1% have private insurance; 46.1% have public insurance; 6.3% do not have insurance; 3.8% of children under 18 do not have insurance
Transportation: Commute: 89.2% car, 3.8% public transportation, 0.8% walk, 5.2% work from home; Mean travel time to work: 25.1 minutes

LONG EDDY (unincorporated postal area)
ZCTA: 12760
   Covers a land area of 42.316 square miles and a water area of 0.403 square miles. Located at 41.90° N. Lat; 75.11° W. Long..
Population: 405; Growth (since 2000): -44.4%; Density: 9.6 persons per square mile; Race: 97.8% White, 1.0% Black/African American, 0.0% Asian, 0.0% American Indian/Alaska Native, 0.0% Native Hawaiian/Other Pacific Islander, 1.2% Two or more races, 1.7% Hispanic of any race; Average household size: 1.90; Median age: 64.9; Age under 18: 6.4%; Age 65 and over: 49.1%; Males per 100 females: 115.2; Marriage status: 8.8% never married, 57.8% now married, 0.0% separated, 15.8% widowed, 17.6% divorced; Foreign born: 7.9%; Speak English only: 97.7%; With disability: 32.8%; Veterans: 16.1%; Ancestry: 31.6% Irish, 28.4% German, 16.8% Italian, 14.1% English, 13.1% Scottish
Employment: 12.2% management, business, and financial, 0.0% computer, engineering, and science, 2.6% education, legal, community service, arts, and media, 2.6% healthcare practitioners, 35.7% service,

33.0% sales and office, 4.3% natural resources, construction, and maintenance, 9.6% production, transportation, and material moving
Income: Per capita: $35,547; Median household: $57,560; Average household: $67,260; Households with income of $100,000 or more: 17.8%; Poverty rate: 10.6%
Educational Attainment: High school diploma or higher: 81.0%; Bachelor's degree or higher: 15.2%; Graduate/professional degree or higher: 6.7%
Housing: Homeownership rate: 86.9%; Median home value: $94,200; Median year structure built: 1965; Homeowner vacancy rate: 2.6%; Median selected monthly owner costs: $1,472 with a mortgage, $411 without a mortgage; Median gross rent: $910 per month; Rental vacancy rate: 0.0%
Health Insurance: 87.2% have insurance; 66.7% have private insurance; 53.3% have public insurance; 12.8% do not have insurance; 0.0% of children under 18 do not have insurance
Transportation: Commute: 95.5% car, 0.0% public transportation, 4.5% walk, 0.0% work from home; Mean travel time to work: 34.6 minutes

MARGARETVILLE (village). Covers a land area of 0.684 square miles and a water area of 0.018 square miles. Located at 42.15° N. Lat; 74.65° W. Long. Elevation is 1,316 feet.
Population: 621; Growth (since 2000): -3.4%; Density: 907.5 persons per square mile; Race: 93.4% White, 1.9% Black/African American, 0.0% Asian, 0.0% American Indian/Alaska Native, 0.0% Native Hawaiian/Other Pacific Islander, 4.7% Two or more races, 1.1% Hispanic of any race; Average household size: 1.87; Median age: 62.6; Age under 18: 11.0%; Age 65 and over: 44.1%; Males per 100 females: 86.8; Marriage status: 23.5% never married, 42.0% now married, 1.7% separated, 19.9% widowed, 14.5% divorced; Foreign born: 5.2%; Speak English only: 96.1%; With disability: 24.2%; Veterans: 7.2%; Ancestry: 29.3% Irish, 17.4% German, 14.5% Italian, 12.7% English, 10.0% Dutch
Employment: 12.9% management, business, and financial, 0.0% computer, engineering, and science, 14.2% education, legal, community service, arts, and media, 1.8% healthcare practitioners, 24.4% service, 18.2% sales and office, 12.4% natural resources, construction, and maintenance, 16.0% production, transportation, and material moving
Income: Per capita: $21,707; Median household: $35,938; Average household: $42,526; Households with income of $100,000 or more: 7.9%; Poverty rate: 16.5%
Educational Attainment: High school diploma or higher: 80.7%; Bachelor's degree or higher: 16.9%; Graduate/professional degree or higher: 7.3%

School District(s)
Margaretville Central SD (PK-12)
    Enrollment: 382. . . . . (845) 586-2647
Housing: Homeownership rate: 54.8%; Median home value: $173,500; Median year structure built: Before 1940; Homeowner vacancy rate: 0.0%; Median selected monthly owner costs: $1,625 with a mortgage, $634 without a mortgage; Median gross rent: $759 per month; Rental vacancy rate: 10.8%
Health Insurance: 85.3% have insurance; 55.3% have private insurance; 60.4% have public insurance; 14.7% do not have insurance; 25.0% of children under 18 do not have insurance
Hospitals: Margaretville Memorial Hospital (15 beds)
Transportation: Commute: 83.2% car, 0.0% public transportation, 10.6% walk, 3.4% work from home; Mean travel time to work: 19.0 minutes

MASONVILLE (town). Covers a land area of 54.264 square miles and a water area of 0.179 square miles. Located at 42.23° N. Lat; 75.34° W. Long. Elevation is 1,293 feet.
Population: 1,155; Growth (since 2000): -17.8%; Density: 21.3 persons per square mile; Race: 97.4% White, 0.0% Black/African American, 1.8% Asian, 0.0% American Indian/Alaska Native, 0.0% Native Hawaiian/Other Pacific Islander, 0.8% Two or more races, 0.3% Hispanic of any race; Average household size: 2.35; Median age: 48.4; Age under 18: 15.9%; Age 65 and over: 21.2%; Males per 100 females: 107.9; Marriage status: 28.3% never married, 53.3% now married, 1.9% separated, 10.2% widowed, 8.2% divorced; Foreign born: 5.5%; Speak English only: 94.4%; With disability: 18.4%; Veterans: 6.9%; Ancestry: 19.1% German, 14.9% Irish, 11.4% Italian, 10.1% English, 9.8% Polish
Employment: 12.3% management, business, and financial, 0.7% computer, engineering, and science, 6.7% education, legal, community service, arts, and media, 2.5% healthcare practitioners, 18.5% service,

26.1% sales and office, 8.5% natural resources, construction, and maintenance, 24.7% production, transportation, and material moving
Income: Per capita: $29,921; Median household: $53,125; Average household: $69,197; Households with income of $100,000 or more: 16.8%; Poverty rate: 8.8%
Educational Attainment: High school diploma or higher: 81.8%; Bachelor's degree or higher: 12.9%; Graduate/professional degree or higher: 4.2%
Housing: Homeownership rate: 85.1%; Median home value: $122,300; Median year structure built: 1978; Homeowner vacancy rate: 3.6%; Median selected monthly owner costs: $1,167 with a mortgage, $441 without a mortgage; Median gross rent: $665 per month; Rental vacancy rate: 0.0%
Health Insurance: 96.5% have insurance; 75.0% have private insurance; 40.9% have public insurance; 3.5% do not have insurance; 0.0% of children under 18 do not have insurance
Transportation: Commute: 85.5% car, 1.3% public transportation, 4.3% walk, 7.7% work from home; Mean travel time to work: 24.6 minutes

MEREDITH (town). Covers a land area of 58.102 square miles and a water area of 0.214 square miles. Located at 42.37° N. Lat; 74.94° W. Long. Elevation is 2,169 feet.
Population: 1,759; Growth (since 2000): 10.8%; Density: 30.3 persons per square mile; Race: 96.4% White, 0.1% Black/African American, 2.8% Asian, 0.0% American Indian/Alaska Native, 0.0% Native Hawaiian/Other Pacific Islander, 0.5% Two or more races, 5.9% Hispanic of any race; Average household size: 2.34; Median age: 48.8; Age under 18: 13.2%; Age 65 and over: 19.4%; Males per 100 females: 99.6; Marriage status: 29.4% never married, 53.4% now married, 3.2% separated, 5.1% widowed, 12.0% divorced; Foreign born: 7.0%; Speak English only: 91.1%; With disability: 12.9%; Veterans: 7.7%; Ancestry: 20.4% German, 16.9% Irish, 11.5% English, 9.0% Italian, 6.7% Dutch
Employment: 14.2% management, business, and financial, 1.5% computer, engineering, and science, 13.9% education, legal, community service, arts, and media, 4.6% healthcare practitioners, 19.4% service, 17.5% sales and office, 14.1% natural resources, construction, and maintenance, 14.7% production, transportation, and material moving
Income: Per capita: $33,752; Median household: $55,268; Average household: $77,490; Households with income of $100,000 or more: 18.1%; Poverty rate: 9.6%
Educational Attainment: High school diploma or higher: 90.8%; Bachelor's degree or higher: 29.3%; Graduate/professional degree or higher: 12.6%
Housing: Homeownership rate: 73.7%; Median home value: $166,100; Median year structure built: 1974; Homeowner vacancy rate: 0.0%; Median selected monthly owner costs: $1,409 with a mortgage, $573 without a mortgage; Median gross rent: $817 per month; Rental vacancy rate: 0.0%
Health Insurance: 85.6% have insurance; 63.8% have private insurance; 37.8% have public insurance; 14.4% do not have insurance; 8.9% of children under 18 do not have insurance
Transportation: Commute: 85.2% car, 0.0% public transportation, 3.3% walk, 9.9% work from home; Mean travel time to work: 24.1 minutes

MERIDALE (unincorporated postal area)
ZCTA: 13806
    Covers a land area of 3.095 square miles and a water area of 0.004 square miles. Located at 42.38° N. Lat; 74.96° W. Long. Elevation is 1,778 feet.
Population: 282; Growth (since 2000): n/a; Density: 91.1 persons per square mile; Race: 87.6% White, 0.0% Black/African American, 11.0% Asian, 0.0% American Indian/Alaska Native, 0.0% Native Hawaiian/Other Pacific Islander, 1.4% Two or more races, 0.7% Hispanic of any race; Average household size: 2.33; Median age: 49.4; Age under 18: 13.8%; Age 65 and over: 15.6%; Males per 100 females: 97.1; Marriage status: 29.0% never married, 43.5% now married, 4.8% separated, 2.4% widowed, 25.0% divorced; Foreign born: 14.5%; Speak English only: 84.5%; With disability: 12.4%; Veterans: 15.2%; Ancestry: 9.2% Irish, 6.7% Russian, 5.7% English, 5.3% Scottish, 5.0% Italian
Employment: 10.6% management, business, and financial, 2.4% computer, engineering, and science, 22.0% education, legal, community service, arts, and media, 0.0% healthcare practitioners, 30.9% service, 13.0% sales and office, 7.3% natural resources, construction, and maintenance, 13.8% production, transportation, and material moving
Income: Per capita: $25,626; Median household: $40,313; Average household: $59,771; Households with income of $100,000 or more: 14.0%; Poverty rate: 4.6%

Educational Attainment: High school diploma or higher: 86.6%; Bachelor's degree or higher: 23.7%; Graduate/professional degree or higher: 6.3%

Housing: Homeownership rate: 71.1%; Median home value: $150,000; Median year structure built: 1954; Homeowner vacancy rate: 0.0%; Median selected monthly owner costs: $0 with a mortgage, $484 without a mortgage; Median gross rent: $567 per month; Rental vacancy rate: 0.0%

Health Insurance: 95.7% have insurance; 71.6% have private insurance; 38.7% have public insurance; 4.3% do not have insurance; 0.0% of children under 18 do not have insurance

Transportation: Commute: 97.3% car, 0.0% public transportation, 0.0% walk, 0.0% work from home; Mean travel time to work: 20.0 minutes

---

MIDDLETOWN (town). Covers a land area of 96.674 square miles and a water area of 0.620 square miles. Located at 42.16° N. Lat; 74.63° W. Long.

Population: 3,580; Growth (since 2000): -11.6%; Density: 37.0 persons per square mile; Race: 95.8% White, 0.4% Black/African American, 0.6% Asian, 0.0% American Indian/Alaska Native, 0.0% Native Hawaiian/Other Pacific Islander, 2.2% Two or more races, 10.7% Hispanic of any race; Average household size: 1.97; Median age: 55.8; Age under 18: 11.8%; Age 65 and over: 33.2%; Males per 100 females: 96.7; Marriage status: 21.5% never married, 50.7% now married, 2.6% separated, 12.7% widowed, 15.2% divorced; Foreign born: 10.7%; Speak English only: 84.5%; With disability: 20.0%; Veterans: 5.4%; Ancestry: 21.9% German, 21.5% Irish, 14.7% Italian, 10.9% English, 6.2% Russian

Employment: 15.9% management, business, and financial, 3.4% computer, engineering, and science, 8.7% education, legal, community service, arts, and media, 7.2% healthcare practitioners, 20.9% service, 22.5% sales and office, 9.4% natural resources, construction, and maintenance, 12.1% production, transportation, and material moving

Income: Per capita: $30,604; Median household: $45,326; Average household: $60,165; Households with income of $100,000 or more: 15.0%; Poverty rate: 12.3%

Educational Attainment: High school diploma or higher: 86.1%; Bachelor's degree or higher: 27.1%; Graduate/professional degree or higher: 13.3%

Housing: Homeownership rate: 75.2%; Median home value: $202,000; Median year structure built: 1975; Homeowner vacancy rate: 2.1%; Median selected monthly owner costs: $1,233 with a mortgage, $550 without a mortgage; Median gross rent: $784 per month; Rental vacancy rate: 9.7%

Health Insurance: 89.6% have insurance; 60.1% have private insurance; 53.0% have public insurance; 10.4% do not have insurance; 9.5% of children under 18 do not have insurance

Transportation: Commute: 77.2% car, 2.7% public transportation, 3.6% walk, 11.0% work from home; Mean travel time to work: 24.9 minutes

---

NEW KINGSTON (unincorporated postal area)

ZCTA: 12459

Covers a land area of 7.609 square miles and a water area of 0.006 square miles. Located at 42.24° N. Lat; 74.68° W. Long. Elevation is 1,686 feet.

Population: 158; Growth (since 2000): -55.4%; Density: 20.8 persons per square mile; Race: 100.0% White, 0.0% Black/African American, 0.0% Asian, 0.0% American Indian/Alaska Native, 0.0% Native Hawaiian/Other Pacific Islander, 0.0% Two or more races, 7.6% Hispanic of any race; Average household size: 1.40; Median age: 63.7; Age under 18: 0.0%; Age 65 and over: 48.7%; Males per 100 females: 103.8; Marriage status: 0.0% never married, 65.2% now married, 6.3% separated, 17.7% widowed, 17.1% divorced; Foreign born: 0.0%; Speak English only: 100.0%; With disability: 34.8%; Veterans: 7.6%; Ancestry: 34.2% Polish, 21.5% German, 17.7% Dutch, 13.9% Italian, 12.0% Irish

Employment: 16.1% management, business, and financial, 0.0% computer, engineering, and science, 30.6% education, legal, community service, arts, and media, 16.1% healthcare practitioners, 0.0% service, 0.0% sales and office, 0.0% natural resources, construction, and maintenance, 37.1% production, transportation, and material moving

Income: Per capita: $42,863; Median household: $39,213; Average household: $60,113; Households with income of $100,000 or more: 19.4%; Poverty rate: n/a

Educational Attainment: High school diploma or higher: 82.3%; Bachelor's degree or higher: 27.8%; Graduate/professional degree or higher: 27.8%

Housing: Homeownership rate: 100.0%; Median home value: $212,500; Median year structure built: 1980; Homeowner vacancy rate: 0.0%; Median selected monthly owner costs: $1,289 with a mortgage, $454 without a mortgage; Median gross rent: n/a per month; Rental vacancy rate: 0.0%

Health Insurance: 100.0% have insurance; 77.2% have private insurance; 71.5% have public insurance; 0.0% do not have insurance; 0.0% of children under 18 do not have insurance

Transportation: Commute: 25.0% car, 38.5% public transportation, 0.0% walk, 36.5% work from home; Mean travel time to work: 0.0 minutes

---

ROXBURY (town). Covers a land area of 87.114 square miles and a water area of 0.490 square miles. Located at 42.31° N. Lat; 74.53° W. Long. Elevation is 1,493 feet.

Population: 2,288; Growth (since 2000): -8.8%; Density: 26.3 persons per square mile; Race: 93.9% White, 4.6% Black/African American, 0.3% Asian, 0.0% American Indian/Alaska Native, 0.0% Native Hawaiian/Other Pacific Islander, 1.2% Two or more races, 0.7% Hispanic of any race; Average household size: 2.28; Median age: 49.6; Age under 18: 13.9%; Age 65 and over: 26.7%; Males per 100 females: 98.7; Marriage status: 30.9% never married, 52.0% now married, 1.3% separated, 7.8% widowed, 9.4% divorced; Foreign born: 8.3%; Speak English only: 93.1%; With disability: 21.3%; Veterans: 8.8%; Ancestry: 29.5% German, 19.1% Irish, 14.0% Italian, 10.2% Dutch, 9.8% English

Employment: 6.8% management, business, and financial, 8.3% computer, engineering, and science, 12.6% education, legal, community service, arts, and media, 2.5% healthcare practitioners, 25.6% service, 14.3% sales and office, 13.4% natural resources, construction, and maintenance, 16.5% production, transportation, and material moving

Income: Per capita: $26,444; Median household: $39,016; Average household: $55,430; Households with income of $100,000 or more: 14.3%; Poverty rate: 15.1%

Educational Attainment: High school diploma or higher: 88.6%; Bachelor's degree or higher: 24.1%; Graduate/professional degree or higher: 9.2%

School District(s)

Roxbury Central SD (PK-12)

    Enrollment: 298 . . . . (607) 326-4151

Housing: Homeownership rate: 78.5%; Median home value: $148,400; Median year structure built: 1973; Homeowner vacancy rate: 5.5%; Median selected monthly owner costs: $1,289 with a mortgage, $568 without a mortgage; Median gross rent: $594 per month; Rental vacancy rate: 14.9%

Health Insurance: 93.3% have insurance; 71.0% have private insurance; 50.4% have public insurance; 6.7% do not have insurance; 4.6% of children under 18 do not have insurance

Transportation: Commute: 81.9% car, 7.5% public transportation, 1.2% walk, 8.0% work from home; Mean travel time to work: 25.9 minutes

---

SIDNEY (town). Covers a land area of 49.928 square miles and a water area of 0.675 square miles. Located at 42.31° N. Lat; 75.28° W. Long. Elevation is 991 feet.

Population: 5,549; Growth (since 2000): -9.2%; Density: 111.1 persons per square mile; Race: 95.3% White, 0.2% Black/African American, 0.3% Asian, 0.0% American Indian/Alaska Native, 0.0% Native Hawaiian/Other Pacific Islander, 1.8% Two or more races, 3.0% Hispanic of any race; Average household size: 2.29; Median age: 44.7; Age under 18: 23.0%; Age 65 and over: 21.0%; Males per 100 females: 94.8; Marriage status: 30.2% never married, 48.0% now married, 2.0% separated, 7.9% widowed, 14.0% divorced; Foreign born: 3.3%; Speak English only: 95.7%; With disability: 18.0%; Veterans: 10.3%; Ancestry: 21.7% Irish, 19.0% German, 15.9% English, 9.0% Italian, 8.9% American

Employment: 8.9% management, business, and financial, 1.0% computer, engineering, and science, 13.4% education, legal, community service, arts, and media, 7.9% healthcare practitioners, 19.3% service, 27.5% sales and office, 8.3% natural resources, construction, and maintenance, 13.7% production, transportation, and material moving

Income: Per capita: $22,100; Median household: $36,250; Average household: $50,081; Households with income of $100,000 or more: 12.5%; Poverty rate: 21.4%

Educational Attainment: High school diploma or higher: 85.6%; Bachelor's degree or higher: 16.4%; Graduate/professional degree or higher: 5.8%

School District(s)
Sidney Central SD (PK-12)
    Enrollment: 1,089 . . . . (607) 561-7700
Housing: Homeownership rate: 64.1%; Median home value: $85,200; Median year structure built: 1955; Homeowner vacancy rate: 2.5%; Median selected monthly owner costs: $1,176 with a mortgage, $398 without a mortgage; Median gross rent: $675 per month; Rental vacancy rate: 8.1%
Health Insurance: 95.9% have insurance; 64.1% have private insurance; 48.0% have public insurance; 4.1% do not have insurance; 3.8% of children under 18 do not have insurance
Newspapers: Tri-Town News (weekly circulation 5,000)
Transportation: Commute: 86.9% car, 0.0% public transportation, 9.2% walk, 3.4% work from home; Mean travel time to work: 24.3 minutes

SIDNEY (village).
Covers a land area of 2.374 square miles and a water area of 0.015 square miles. Located at 42.30° N. Lat; 75.40° W. Long. Elevation is 991 feet.
Population: 4,160; Growth (since 2000): 2.3%; Density: 1,752.1 persons per square mile; Race: 94.1% White, 0.3% Black/African American, 0.4% Asian, 0.0% American Indian/Alaska Native, 0.0% Native Hawaiian/Other Pacific Islander, 2.0% Two or more races, 3.8% Hispanic of any race; Average household size: 2.41; Median age: 36.1; Age under 18: 27.5%; Age 65 and over: 13.8%; Males per 100 females: 88.9; Marriage status: 35.0% never married, 41.0% now married, 2.4% separated, 7.5% widowed, 16.4% divorced; Foreign born: 3.7%; Speak English only: 95.5%; With disability: 15.0%; Veterans: 7.9%; Ancestry: 24.4% Irish, 21.3% German, 16.2% English, 9.5% Italian, 6.4% American
Employment: 9.9% management, business, and financial, 0.2% computer, engineering, and science, 12.0% education, legal, community service, arts, and media, 6.9% healthcare practitioners, 21.3% service, 26.8% sales and office, 8.0% natural resources, construction, and maintenance, 14.8% production, transportation, and material moving
Income: Per capita: $21,359; Median household: $36,424; Average household: $50,785; Households with income of $100,000 or more: 12.6%; Poverty rate: 24.1%
Educational Attainment: High school diploma or higher: 86.2%; Bachelor's degree or higher: 19.0%; Graduate/professional degree or higher: 7.0%

School District(s)
Sidney Central SD (PK-12)
    Enrollment: 1,089 . . . . (607) 561-7700
Housing: Homeownership rate: 52.0%; Median home value: $85,800; Median year structure built: 1951; Homeowner vacancy rate: 4.1%; Median selected monthly owner costs: $1,213 with a mortgage, $541 without a mortgage; Median gross rent: $674 per month; Rental vacancy rate: 8.4%
Health Insurance: 94.8% have insurance; 62.7% have private insurance; 44.0% have public insurance; 5.2% do not have insurance; 4.2% of children under 18 do not have insurance
Safety: Violent crime rate: 19.1 per 10,000 population; Property crime rate: 253.3 per 10,000 population
Newspapers: Tri-Town News (weekly circulation 5,000)
Transportation: Commute: 87.5% car, 0.0% public transportation, 11.7% walk, 0.8% work from home; Mean travel time to work: 20.0 minutes

SIDNEY CENTER (unincorporated postal area)
ZCTA: 13839
Covers a land area of 39.754 square miles and a water area of 0.155 square miles. Located at 42.26° N. Lat; 75.25° W. Long. Elevation is 1,299 feet.
Population: 1,092; Growth (since 2000): -34.5%; Density: 27.5 persons per square mile; Race: 93.3% White, 1.1% Black/African American, 2.4% Asian, 0.0% American Indian/Alaska Native, 0.0% Native Hawaiian/Other Pacific Islander, 3.2% Two or more races, 3.5% Hispanic of any race; Average household size: 2.19; Median age: 56.3; Age under 18: 10.3%; Age 65 and over: 32.6%; Males per 100 females: 103.3; Marriage status: 25.8% never married, 60.3% now married, 3.2% separated, 5.7% widowed, 8.2% divorced; Foreign born: 5.0%; Speak English only: 94.2%; With disability: 20.5%; Veterans: 14.6%; Ancestry: 15.9% Irish, 15.0% English, 13.7% German, 13.7% Italian, 8.6% Polish
Employment: 5.4% management, business, and financial, 0.0% computer, engineering, and science, 12.1% education, legal, community service, arts, and media, 5.8% healthcare practitioners, 13.1% service, 28.3% sales and office, 8.7% natural resources, construction, and maintenance, 26.6% production, transportation, and material moving

Income: Per capita: $22,933; Median household: $44,792; Average household: $50,156; Households with income of $100,000 or more: 9.8%; Poverty rate: 15.5%
Educational Attainment: High school diploma or higher: 88.4%; Bachelor's degree or higher: 10.6%; Graduate/professional degree or higher: 7.8%
Housing: Homeownership rate: 93.1%; Median home value: $109,500; Median year structure built: 1974; Homeowner vacancy rate: 2.0%; Median selected monthly owner costs: $1,008 with a mortgage, $361 without a mortgage; Median gross rent: $708 per month; Rental vacancy rate: 0.0%
Health Insurance: 97.9% have insurance; 74.4% have private insurance; 50.3% have public insurance; 2.1% do not have insurance; 0.0% of children under 18 do not have insurance
Transportation: Commute: 85.9% car, 0.0% public transportation, 3.3% walk, 9.5% work from home; Mean travel time to work: 26.3 minutes

SOUTH KORTRIGHT (unincorporated postal area)
ZCTA: 13842
Covers a land area of 12.491 square miles and a water area of 0.129 square miles. Located at 42.38° N. Lat; 74.72° W. Long. Elevation is 1,509 feet.
Population: 524; Growth (since 2000): -2.6%; Density: 42.0 persons per square mile; Race: 88.7% White, 7.3% Black/African American, 1.0% Asian, 0.0% American Indian/Alaska Native, 0.0% Native Hawaiian/Other Pacific Islander, 1.9% Two or more races, 2.9% Hispanic of any race; Average household size: 2.26; Median age: 45.9; Age under 18: 18.1%; Age 65 and over: 21.6%; Males per 100 females: 155.5; Marriage status: 44.2% never married, 49.1% now married, 2.6% separated, 4.2% widowed, 2.6% divorced; Foreign born: 4.6%; Speak English only: 93.3%; With disability: 19.9%; Veterans: 8.2%; Ancestry: 17.7% Irish, 17.2% German, 10.7% English, 10.3% Italian, 7.4% Polish
Employment: 26.1% management, business, and financial, 10.2% computer, engineering, and science, 20.4% education, legal, community service, arts, and media, 8.9% healthcare practitioners, 13.4% service, 5.1% sales and office, 4.5% natural resources, construction, and maintenance, 11.5% production, transportation, and material moving
Income: Per capita: $26,219; Median household: $66,964; Average household: $81,739; Households with income of $100,000 or more: 34.1%; Poverty rate: 24.3%
Educational Attainment: High school diploma or higher: 90.2%; Bachelor's degree or higher: 21.2%; Graduate/professional degree or higher: 7.9%

School District(s)
South Kortright Central SD (PK-12)
    Enrollment: 391 . . . . (607) 538-9111
Housing: Homeownership rate: 94.4%; Median home value: $186,100; Median year structure built: 1981; Homeowner vacancy rate: 0.0%; Median selected monthly owner costs: $1,500 with a mortgage, $517 without a mortgage; Median gross rent: n/a per month; Rental vacancy rate: 0.0%
Health Insurance: 98.0% have insurance; 75.9% have private insurance; 43.8% have public insurance; 2.0% do not have insurance; 0.0% of children under 18 do not have insurance
Transportation: Commute: 75.2% car, 5.9% public transportation, 3.3% walk, 9.2% work from home; Mean travel time to work: 33.6 minutes

STAMFORD (town).
Covers a land area of 48.505 square miles and a water area of 0.106 square miles. Located at 42.34° N. Lat; 74.67° W. Long. Elevation is 1,818 feet.
Population: 2,375; Growth (since 2000): 22.2%; Density: 49.0 persons per square mile; Race: 97.3% White, 0.8% Black/African American, 1.1% Asian, 0.0% American Indian/Alaska Native, 0.0% Native Hawaiian/Other Pacific Islander, 0.6% Two or more races, 1.8% Hispanic of any race; Average household size: 2.28; Median age: 47.1; Age under 18: 14.5%; Age 65 and over: 22.7%; Males per 100 females: 99.9; Marriage status: 36.6% never married, 48.7% now married, 3.5% separated, 6.1% widowed, 8.6% divorced; Foreign born: 4.1%; Speak English only: 93.5%; With disability: 19.9%; Veterans: 8.8%; Ancestry: 20.5% German, 17.9% Irish, 13.7% Italian, 12.7% English, 8.0% Dutch
Employment: 10.4% management, business, and financial, 3.9% computer, engineering, and science, 10.2% education, legal, community service, arts, and media, 3.7% healthcare practitioners, 27.9% service, 18.4% sales and office, 7.4% natural resources, construction, and maintenance, 18.1% production, transportation, and material moving

Income: Per capita: $23,697; Median household: $42,679; Average household: $54,743; Households with income of $100,000 or more: 13.2%; Poverty rate: 22.9%
Educational Attainment: High school diploma or higher: 86.1%; Bachelor's degree or higher: 24.3%; Graduate/professional degree or higher: 6.5%

School District(s)

Stamford Central SD (PK-12)
    Enrollment: 320 . . . . (607) 652-7301
Housing: Homeownership rate: 57.5%; Median home value: $132,000; Median year structure built: 1971; Homeowner vacancy rate: 3.3%; Median selected monthly owner costs: $1,201 with a mortgage, $529 without a mortgage; Median gross rent: $624 per month; Rental vacancy rate: 1.8%
Health Insurance: 91.9% have insurance; 55.3% have private insurance; 55.8% have public insurance; 8.1% do not have insurance; 1.9% of children under 18 do not have insurance
Newspapers: Mountain Eagle (weekly circulation 3,000)
Transportation: Commute: 84.0% car, 2.3% public transportation, 5.2% walk, 5.6% work from home; Mean travel time to work: 22.4 minutes

---

STAMFORD (village). Covers a land area of 1.333 square miles and a water area of 0.009 square miles. Located at 42.41° N. Lat; 74.62° W. Long. Elevation is 1,818 feet.
Population: 1,476; Growth (since 2000): 16.7%; Density: 1,107.6 persons per square mile; Race: 96.7% White, 0.9% Black/African American, 1.5% Asian, 0.0% American Indian/Alaska Native, 0.0% Native Hawaiian/Other Pacific Islander, 0.2% Two or more races, 2.9% Hispanic of any race; Average household size: 2.16; Median age: 46.0; Age under 18: 16.5%; Age 65 and over: 25.9%; Males per 100 females: 82.5; Marriage status: 37.7% never married, 36.8% now married, 2.5% separated, 14.2% widowed, 11.4% divorced; Foreign born: 5.5%; Speak English only: 92.7%; With disability: 20.4%; Veterans: 9.9%; Ancestry: 23.9% German, 15.9% Irish, 12.6% Italian, 10.2% English, 6.6% Polish
Employment: 8.5% management, business, and financial, 5.1% computer, engineering, and science, 8.5% education, legal, community service, arts, and media, 1.4% healthcare practitioners, 36.5% service, 18.1% sales and office, 4.4% natural resources, construction, and maintenance, 17.4% production, transportation, and material moving
Income: Per capita: $22,401; Median household: $38,000; Average household: $49,019; Households with income of $100,000 or more: 14.0%; Poverty rate: 22.3%
Educational Attainment: High school diploma or higher: 84.8%; Bachelor's degree or higher: 17.6%; Graduate/professional degree or higher: 5.9%

School District(s)

Stamford Central SD (PK-12)
    Enrollment: 320 . . . . (607) 652-7301
Housing: Homeownership rate: 51.4%; Median home value: $117,400; Median year structure built: 1942; Homeowner vacancy rate: 5.1%; Median selected monthly owner costs: $1,327 with a mortgage, $558 without a mortgage; Median gross rent: $602 per month; Rental vacancy rate: 2.6%
Health Insurance: 92.1% have insurance; 56.4% have private insurance; 53.6% have public insurance; 7.9% do not have insurance; 2.5% of children under 18 do not have insurance
Newspapers: Mountain Eagle (weekly circulation 3,000)
Transportation: Commute: 85.9% car, 0.9% public transportation, 3.5% walk, 7.6% work from home; Mean travel time to work: 21.2 minutes
Additional Information Contacts
Village of Stamford . . . . (607) 652-6671
    http://www.stamfordny.com/villagewebsite

TOMPKINS (town). Covers a land area of 98.133 square miles and a water area of 6.314 square miles. Located at 42.12° N. Lat; 75.27° W. Long.
Population: 989; Growth (since 2000): -10.5%; Density: 10.1 persons per square mile; Race: 96.5% White, 2.1% Black/African American, 0.5% Asian, 0.0% American Indian/Alaska Native, 0.0% Native Hawaiian/Other Pacific Islander, 0.9% Two or more races, 0.5% Hispanic of any race; Average household size: 2.36; Median age: 50.7; Age under 18: 14.9%; Age 65 and over: 23.8%; Males per 100 females: 104.4; Marriage status: 28.1% never married, 56.8% now married, 5.0% separated, 4.2% widowed, 10.9% divorced; Foreign born: 2.1%; Speak English only: 96.2%; With disability: 17.4%; Veterans: 8.1%; Ancestry: 24.4% German, 16.0% Irish, 11.4% Italian, 9.1% French, 8.6% English

Employment: 6.5% management, business, and financial, 0.9% computer, engineering, and science, 6.5% education, legal, community service, arts, and media, 3.8% healthcare practitioners, 10.1% service, 27.4% sales and office, 16.4% natural resources, construction, and maintenance, 28.5% production, transportation, and material moving
Income: Per capita: $23,459; Median household: $57,083; Average household: $54,443; Households with income of $100,000 or more: 11.4%; Poverty rate: 15.7%
Educational Attainment: High school diploma or higher: 88.6%; Bachelor's degree or higher: 7.2%; Graduate/professional degree or higher: 3.9%
Housing: Homeownership rate: 84.7%; Median home value: $107,900; Median year structure built: 1976; Homeowner vacancy rate: 9.4%; Median selected monthly owner costs: $936 with a mortgage, $413 without a mortgage; Median gross rent: $630 per month; Rental vacancy rate: 0.0%
Health Insurance: 93.6% have insurance; 79.1% have private insurance; 35.0% have public insurance; 6.4% do not have insurance; 12.6% of children under 18 do not have insurance
Transportation: Commute: 92.2% car, 0.7% public transportation, 3.4% walk, 0.7% work from home; Mean travel time to work: 26.1 minutes

---

TREADWELL (unincorporated postal area)
ZCTA: 13846
    Covers a land area of 8.131 square miles and a water area of 0.034 square miles. Located at 42.36° N. Lat; 75.05° W. Long. Elevation is 1,529 feet.
    Population: 331; Growth (since 2000): -3.2%; Density: 40.7 persons per square mile; Race: 94.6% White, 0.9% Black/African American, 4.5% Asian, 0.0% American Indian/Alaska Native, 0.0% Native Hawaiian/Other Pacific Islander, 0.0% Two or more races, 0.0% Hispanic of any race; Average household size: 2.28; Median age: 59.2; Age under 18: 21.8%; Age 65 and over: 30.5%; Males per 100 females: 90.6; Marriage status: 8.3% never married, 80.8% now married, 0.0% separated, 5.6% widowed, 5.3% divorced; Foreign born: 4.5%; Speak English only: 91.7%; With disability: 10.6%; Veterans: 10.4%; Ancestry: 26.0% Irish, 23.9% German, 10.9% English, 7.3% Italian, 6.9% Dutch
    Employment: 20.5% management, business, and financial, 0.0% computer, engineering, and science, 9.0% education, legal, community service, arts, and media, 0.0% healthcare practitioners, 15.6% service, 30.3% sales and office, 3.3% natural resources, construction, and maintenance, 21.3% production, transportation, and material moving
    Income: Per capita: $19,079; Median household: $31,250; Average household: $43,399; Households with income of $100,000 or more: 6.9%; Poverty rate: 31.4%
    Educational Attainment: High school diploma or higher: 93.4%; Bachelor's degree or higher: 32.0%; Graduate/professional degree or higher: 11.2%
    Housing: Homeownership rate: 95.2%; Median home value: $151,000; Median year structure built: Before 1940; Homeowner vacancy rate: 0.0%; Median selected monthly owner costs: $1,005 with a mortgage, $559 without a mortgage; Median gross rent: n/a per month; Rental vacancy rate: 0.0%
    Health Insurance: 97.6% have insurance; 51.4% have private insurance; 75.5% have public insurance; 2.4% do not have insurance; 0.0% of children under 18 do not have insurance
    Transportation: Commute: 100.0% car, 0.0% public transportation, 0.0% walk, 0.0% work from home; Mean travel time to work: 27.0 minutes

---

TROUT CREEK (unincorporated postal area)
ZCTA: 13847
    Covers a land area of 3.260 square miles and a water area of 0.023 square miles. Located at 42.18° N. Lat; 75.29° W. Long. Elevation is 1,289 feet.
    Population: 71; Growth (since 2000): n/a; Density: 21.8 persons per square mile; Race: 100.0% White, 0.0% Black/African American, 0.0% Asian, 0.0% American Indian/Alaska Native, 0.0% Native Hawaiian/Other Pacific Islander, 0.0% Two or more races, 0.0% Hispanic of any race; Average household size: 3.23; Median age: 27.8; Age under 18: 32.4%; Age 65 and over: 16.9%; Males per 100 females: 86.1; Marriage status: 21.6% never married, 51.0% now married, 23.5% separated, 0.0% widowed, 27.5% divorced; Foreign born: 0.0%; Speak English only: 100.0%; With disability: 21.1%; Veterans: 0.0%; Ancestry: 36.6% Russian, 32.4% German, 21.1% Polish, 16.9% Irish, 14.1% Italian

Employment: 21.6% management, business, and financial, 10.8% computer, engineering, and science, 0.0% education, legal, community service, arts, and media, 16.2% healthcare practitioners, 32.4% service, 10.8% sales and office, 0.0% natural resources, construction, and maintenance, 8.1% production, transportation, and material moving
Income: Per capita: $24,386; Median household: n/a; Average household: $70,414; Households with income of $100,000 or more: 27.3%; Poverty rate: 14.1%
Educational Attainment: High school diploma or higher: 100.0%; Bachelor's degree or higher: 35.0%; Graduate/professional degree or higher: n/a
Housing: Homeownership rate: 72.7%; Median home value: n/a; Median year structure built: 1984; Homeowner vacancy rate: 48.4%; Median selected monthly owner costs: $0 with a mortgage, $0 without a mortgage; Median gross rent: n/a per month; Rental vacancy rate: 0.0%
Health Insurance: 100.0% have insurance; 85.9% have private insurance; 31.0% have public insurance; 0.0% do not have insurance; 0.0% of children under 18 do not have insurance
Transportation: Commute: 100.0% car, 0.0% public transportation, 0.0% walk, 0.0% work from home; Mean travel time to work: 39.5 minutes

WALTON (town).
Covers a land area of 96.837 square miles and a water area of 0.780 square miles. Located at 42.17° N. Lat; 75.13° W. Long. Elevation is 1,207 feet.
Population: 5,298; Growth (since 2000): -5.5%; Density: 54.7 persons per square mile; Race: 98.7% White, 0.2% Black/African American, 0.0% Asian, 0.0% American Indian/Alaska Native, 0.0% Native Hawaiian/Other Pacific Islander, 1.1% Two or more races, 3.7% Hispanic of any race; Average household size: 2.33; Median age: 40.9; Age under 18: 26.8%; Age 65 and over: 17.7%; Males per 100 females: 98.2; Marriage status: 26.4% never married, 57.1% now married, 4.8% separated, 4.5% widowed, 12.0% divorced; Foreign born: 1.9%; Speak English only: 96.2%; With disability: 12.9%; Veterans: 8.8%; Ancestry: 14.0% English, 12.6% German, 11.9% Irish, 11.2% Italian, 9.4% American
Employment: 10.6% management, business, and financial, 3.8% computer, engineering, and science, 13.4% education, legal, community service, arts, and media, 5.0% healthcare practitioners, 15.4% service, 19.2% sales and office, 14.6% natural resources, construction, and maintenance, 18.1% production, transportation, and material moving
Income: Per capita: $21,897; Median household: $48,300; Average household: $51,092; Households with income of $100,000 or more: 10.8%; Poverty rate: 27.0%
Educational Attainment: High school diploma or higher: 86.7%; Bachelor's degree or higher: 17.3%; Graduate/professional degree or higher: 6.5%
School District(s)
Walton Central SD (PK-12)
    Enrollment: 1,027 . . . . (607) 865-4116
Housing: Homeownership rate: 68.7%; Median home value: $114,900; Median year structure built: 1963; Homeowner vacancy rate: 1.0%; Median selected monthly owner costs: $1,120 with a mortgage, $517 without a mortgage; Median gross rent: $705 per month; Rental vacancy rate: 0.0%
Health Insurance: 93.3% have insurance; 61.9% have private insurance; 45.3% have public insurance; 6.7% do not have insurance; 8.2% of children under 18 do not have insurance
Hospitals: Delaware Valley Hospital (25 beds)
Newspapers: Walton Reporter (weekly circulation 5,100)
Transportation: Commute: 88.5% car, 0.0% public transportation, 4.9% walk, 6.5% work from home; Mean travel time to work: 21.1 minutes

WALTON (village).
Covers a land area of 1.541 square miles and a water area of 0.060 square miles. Located at 42.17° N. Lat; 75.13° W. Long. Elevation is 1,207 feet.
Population: 2,947; Growth (since 2000): -4.0%; Density: 1,912.5 persons per square mile; Race: 99.4% White, 0.0% Black/African American, 0.0% Asian, 0.0% American Indian/Alaska Native, 0.0% Native Hawaiian/Other Pacific Islander, 0.6% Two or more races, 5.0% Hispanic of any race; Average household size: 2.49; Median age: 35.8; Age under 18: 30.9%; Age 65 and over: 19.5%; Males per 100 females: 92.0; Marriage status: 25.7% never married, 56.5% now married, 7.6% separated, 3.3% widowed, 14.5% divorced; Foreign born: 1.1%; Speak English only: 97.2%; With disability: 13.0%; Veterans: 10.7%; Ancestry: 16.4% Irish, 15.1% Italian, 14.3% German, 11.8% English, 9.9% American

Employment: 14.3% management, business, and financial, 0.0% computer, engineering, and science, 16.5% education, legal, community service, arts, and media, 5.2% healthcare practitioners, 20.9% service, 17.4% sales and office, 8.5% natural resources, construction, and maintenance, 17.2% production, transportation, and material moving
Income: Per capita: $17,712; Median household: $30,907; Average household: $43,518; Households with income of $100,000 or more: 8.0%; Poverty rate: 31.3%
Educational Attainment: High school diploma or higher: 82.8%; Bachelor's degree or higher: 16.3%; Graduate/professional degree or higher: 8.6%
School District(s)
Walton Central SD (PK-12)
    Enrollment: 1,027 . . . . (607) 865-4116
Housing: Homeownership rate: 53.8%; Median home value: $96,200; Median year structure built: Before 1940; Homeowner vacancy rate: 0.0%; Median selected monthly owner costs: $1,299 with a mortgage, $533 without a mortgage; Median gross rent: $699 per month; Rental vacancy rate: 0.0%
Health Insurance: 96.6% have insurance; 56.9% have private insurance; 57.1% have public insurance; 3.4% do not have insurance; 0.0% of children under 18 do not have insurance
Hospitals: Delaware Valley Hospital (25 beds)
Newspapers: Walton Reporter (weekly circulation 5,100)
Transportation: Commute: 84.9% car, 0.0% public transportation, 8.5% walk, 6.7% work from home; Mean travel time to work: 19.2 minutes

WEST DAVENPORT (unincorporated postal area)
ZCTA: 13860
    Covers a land area of 0.916 square miles and a water area of 0.002 square miles. Located at 42.45° N. Lat; 74.94° W. Long. Elevation is 1,181 feet.
Population: 80; Growth (since 2000): n/a; Density: 87.4 persons per square mile; Race: 100.0% White, 0.0% Black/African American, 0.0% Asian, 0.0% American Indian/Alaska Native, 0.0% Native Hawaiian/Other Pacific Islander, 0.0% Two or more races, 0.0% Hispanic of any race; Average household size: 3.08; Median age: 28.2; Age under 18: 40.0%; Age 65 and over: 0.0%; Males per 100 females: 91.8; Marriage status: 44.8% never married, 55.2% now married, 0.0% separated, 0.0% widowed, 0.0% divorced; Foreign born: 0.0%; Speak English only: 100.0%; With disability: 0.0%; Veterans: 12.5%; Ancestry: 48.8% Irish, 31.3% Polish, 25.0% German, 22.5% American, 12.5% Scottish
Employment: 0.0% management, business, and financial, 0.0% computer, engineering, and science, 0.0% education, legal, community service, arts, and media, 22.0% healthcare practitioners, 14.6% service, 39.0% sales and office, 0.0% natural resources, construction, and maintenance, 24.4% production, transportation, and material moving
Income: Per capita: $23,859; Median household: $83,250; Average household: $79,196; Households with income of $100,000 or more: n/a; Poverty rate: n/a
Educational Attainment: High school diploma or higher: 100.0%; Bachelor's degree or higher: 24.4%; Graduate/professional degree or higher: n/a
Housing: Homeownership rate: 61.5%; Median home value: n/a; Median year structure built: Before 1940; Homeowner vacancy rate: 0.0%; Median selected monthly owner costs: $0 with a mortgage, $0 without a mortgage; Median gross rent: n/a per month; Rental vacancy rate: 0.0%
Health Insurance: 100.0% have insurance; 77.5% have private insurance; 31.3% have public insurance; 0.0% do not have insurance; 0.0% of children under 18 do not have insurance
Transportation: Commute: 85.4% car, 0.0% public transportation, 14.6% walk, 0.0% work from home; Mean travel time to work: 0.0 minutes

Dutchess County

Located in southeastern New York; bounded on the west by the Hudson River, and on the east by Connecticut; includes part of the Taconic Mountains. Covers a land area of 795.630 square miles, a water area of 29.718 square miles, and is located in the Eastern Time Zone at 41.76° N. Lat., 73.74° W. Long. The county was founded in 1683. County seat is Poughkeepsie.

Dutchess County is part of the New York-Newark-Jersey City, NY-NJ-PA Metropolitan Statistical Area. The entire metro area includes: Dutchess County-Putnam County, NY Metropolitan Division (Dutchess County, NY; Putnam County, NY); Nassau County-Suffolk County, NY Metropolitan Division (Nassau County, NY; Suffolk County, NY); Newark, NJ-PA Metropolitan Division (Essex County, NJ; Hunterdon County, NJ; Morris County, NJ; Somerset County, NJ; Sussex County, NJ; Union County, NJ; Pike County, PA); New York-Jersey City-White Plains, NY-NJ Metropolitan Division (Bergen County, NJ; Hudson County, NJ; Middlesex County, NJ; Monmouth County, NJ; Ocean County, NJ; Passaic County, NJ; Bronx County, NY; Kings County, NY; New York County, NY; Orange County, NY; Queens County, NY; Richmond County, NY; Rockland County, NY; Westchester County, NY)

Weather Station: Poughkeepsie Dutchess Co Arpt   Elevation: 154 feet

	Jan	Feb	Mar	Apr	May	Jun	Jul	Aug	Sep	Oct	Nov	Dec
High	35	39	48	60	71	79	84	82	74	62	51	40
Low	16	19	26	37	47	56	61	60	51	40	31	22
Precip	3.0	2.5	3.4	3.8	4.4	4.2	4.6	4.0	3.9	4.1	3.5	3.4
Snow	10.8	7.9	4.9	1.4	0.0	0.0	0.0	0.0	0.0	tr	1.8	7.4

High and Low temperatures in degrees Fahrenheit; Precipitation and Snow in inches

Population: 295,685; Growth (since 2000): 5.5%; Density: 371.6 persons per square mile; Race: 78.6% White, 10.5% Black/African American, 3.7% Asian, 0.4% American Indian/Alaska Native, 0.0% Native Hawaiian/Other Pacific Islander, 3.0% two or more races, 11.7% Hispanic of any race; Average household size: 2.58; Median age: 41.8; Age under 18: 19.8%; Age 65 and over: 16.0%; Males per 100 females: 99.2; Marriage status: 34.1% never married, 51.0% now married, 2.2% separated, 5.7% widowed, 9.1% divorced; Foreign born: 11.3%; Speak English only: 84.3%; With disability: 13.0%; Veterans: 6.5%; Ancestry: 20.5% Italian, 19.9% Irish, 13.6% German, 6.9% English, 5.2% American
Religion: Six largest groups: 37.4% Catholicism, 2.6% Methodist/Pietist, 2.4% Muslim Estimate, 1.9% Presbyterian-Reformed, 1.7% Episcopalianism/Anglicanism, 1.6% Non-denominational Protestant
Economy: Unemployment rate: 3.4%; Leading industries: 14.3 % retail trade; 13.2 % construction; 11.5 % health care and social assistance; Farms: 678 totaling 112,482 acres; Company size: 9 employ 1,000 or more persons, 6 employ 500 to 999 persons, 113 employ 100 to 499 persons, 7,453 employ less than 100 persons; Business ownership: 8,193 women-owned, 1,240 Black-owned, 1,424 Hispanic-owned, 1,027 Asian-owned, 183 American Indian/Alaska Native-owned
Employment: 14.3% management, business, and financial, 6.2% computer, engineering, and science, 13.6% education, legal, community service, arts, and media, 5.7% healthcare practitioners, 19.4% service, 23.5% sales and office, 9.0% natural resources, construction, and maintenance, 8.4% production, transportation, and material moving
Income: Per capita: $36,704; Median household: $75,585; Average household: $97,278; Households with income of $100,000 or more: 36.7%; Poverty rate: 9.1%
Educational Attainment: High school diploma or higher: 90.5%; Bachelor's degree or higher: 34.6%; Graduate/professional degree or higher: 15.5%
Housing: Homeownership rate: 69.2%; Median home value: $275,200; Median year structure built: 1970; Homeowner vacancy rate: 2.4%; Median selected monthly owner costs: $2,228 with a mortgage, $853 without a mortgage; Median gross rent: $1,174 per month; Rental vacancy rate: 5.3%
Vital Statistics: Birth rate: 87.2 per 10,000 population; Death rate: 88.3 per 10,000 population; Age-adjusted cancer mortality rate: 133.3 deaths per 100,000 population
Health Insurance: 94.4% have insurance; 76.7% have private insurance; 31.4% have public insurance; 5.6% do not have insurance; 2.5% of children under 18 do not have insurance
Health Care: Physicians: 27.2 per 10,000 population; Dentists: 7.1 per 10,000 population; Hospital beds: 14.7 per 10,000 population; Hospital admissions: 870.2 per 10,000 population
Air Quality Index (AQI): Percent of Days: 95.3% good, 4.4% moderate, 0.3% unhealthy for sensitive individuals, 0.0% unhealthy, 0.0% very unhealthy; Annual median: 32; Annual maximum: 101
Transportation: Commute: 83.5% car, 5.3% public transportation, 4.7% walk, 5.6% work from home; Mean travel time to work: 32.2 minutes
2016 Presidential Election: 47.2% Trump, 47.6% Clinton, 2.7% Johnson, 1.5% Stein
National and State Parks: Eleanor Roosevelt National Historic Site; Home of Franklin D Roosevelt National Historic Site; James Baird State Park; Lafayetteville State Multiple Use Area; Margaret Lewis Norrie State Park; Mills Memorial State Park; Roeliff Jansen Kill State Multiple Use Area; Taconic-Hereford State Multiple Use Area; Tivoli Bay State Unique Area; Vanderbilt Mansion National Historic Site; Walkway Over the Hudson State Historic Park; Wassaic State Multiple Use Area
Additional Information Contacts
Dutchess Government. . . . . (845) 486-2120
http://www.dutchessny.gov

Dutchess County Communities

AMENIA (CDP). Covers a land area of 1.218 square miles and a water area of 0.027 square miles. Located at 41.85° N. Lat; 73.56° W. Long. Elevation is 568 feet.
Population: 1,134; Growth (since 2000): 1.7%; Density: 931.3 persons per square mile; Race: 84.0% White, 12.2% Black/African American, 0.0% Asian, 0.7% American Indian/Alaska Native, 0.0% Native Hawaiian/Other Pacific Islander, 3.2% Two or more races, 6.2% Hispanic of any race; Average household size: 2.63; Median age: 49.0; Age under 18: 19.9%; Age 65 and over: 10.5%; Males per 100 females: 97.3; Marriage status: 23.3% never married, 61.0% now married, 4.0% separated, 4.9% widowed, 10.8% divorced; Foreign born: 3.7%; Speak English only: 93.8%; With disability: 13.3%; Veterans: 6.8%; Ancestry: 39.2% Irish, 19.8% German, 13.8% English, 13.5% French, 12.8% Italian
Employment: 7.9% management, business, and financial, 1.0% computer, engineering, and science, 1.9% education, legal, community service, arts, and media, 11.0% healthcare practitioners, 16.0% service, 31.0% sales and office, 17.2% natural resources, construction, and maintenance, 13.8% production, transportation, and material moving
Income: Per capita: $34,486; Median household: $69,375; Average household: $87,341; Households with income of $100,000 or more: 35.0%; Poverty rate: 5.4%
Educational Attainment: High school diploma or higher: 89.9%; Bachelor's degree or higher: 28.2%; Graduate/professional degree or higher: 8.4%

School District(s)
Northeast Central SD (PK-12)
    Enrollment: 748. . . . . (845) 373-4100
Housing: Homeownership rate: 81.0%; Median home value: $248,400; Median year structure built: Before 1940; Homeowner vacancy rate: 0.0%; Median selected monthly owner costs: $2,531 with a mortgage, $740 without a mortgage; Median gross rent: $860 per month; Rental vacancy rate: 0.0%
Health Insurance: 100.0% have insurance; 83.4% have private insurance; 28.8% have public insurance; 0.0% do not have insurance; 0.0% of children under 18 do not have insurance
Transportation: Commute: 94.7% car, 0.0% public transportation, 0.0% walk, 5.3% work from home; Mean travel time to work: 23.0 minutes

AMENIA (town). Covers a land area of 43.220 square miles and a water area of 0.396 square miles. Located at 41.83° N. Lat; 73.53° W. Long. Elevation is 568 feet.
History: Thomas L. Harris had his Brotherhood of the New Life sect here, 1863—1867.
Population: 4,314; Growth (since 2000): 6.6%; Density: 99.8 persons per square mile; Race: 91.7% White, 5.6% Black/African American, 0.4% Asian, 0.2% American Indian/Alaska Native, 0.0% Native Hawaiian/Other Pacific Islander, 1.5% Two or more races, 5.4% Hispanic of any race; Average household size: 2.45; Median age: 45.8; Age under 18: 17.0%; Age 65 and over: 17.7%; Males per 100 females: 97.9; Marriage status: 36.3% never married, 52.6% now married, 2.3% separated, 5.5% widowed, 5.7% divorced; Foreign born: 2.8%; Speak English only: 93.8%; With disability: 18.0%; Veterans: 7.5%; Ancestry: 27.2% Irish, 16.7% German, 13.6% Italian, 13.0% English, 8.6% French
Employment: 12.1% management, business, and financial, 1.4% computer, engineering, and science, 10.3% education, legal, community service, arts, and media, 4.5% healthcare practitioners, 22.2% service, 23.8% sales and office, 10.2% natural resources, construction, and maintenance, 15.7% production, transportation, and material moving
Income: Per capita: $37,158; Median household: $53,736; Average household: $93,531; Households with income of $100,000 or more: 23.7%; Poverty rate: 10.0%
Educational Attainment: High school diploma or higher: 83.8%; Bachelor's degree or higher: 23.7%; Graduate/professional degree or higher: 9.8%

Northeast Central SD (PK-12)
    Enrollment: 748 . . . . (845) 373-4100
Housing: Homeownership rate: 68.7%; Median home value: $247,500;
Median year structure built: 1961; Homeowner vacancy rate: 0.0%; Median
selected monthly owner costs: $1,742 with a mortgage, $669 without a
mortgage; Median gross rent: $1,060 per month; Rental vacancy rate:
0.0%
Health Insurance: 98.5% have insurance; 79.0% have private insurance;
33.2% have public insurance; 1.5% do not have insurance; 0.0% of
children under 18 do not have insurance
Transportation: Commute: 84.4% car, 5.8% public transportation, 3.9%
walk, 6.0% work from home; Mean travel time to work: 25.6 minutes
Additional Information Contacts

Town of Amenia . . . . (845) 373-8118
    http://ameniany.gov

ANNANDALE ON HUDSON (unincorporated postal area)
ZCTA: 12504
    Covers a land area of 1.471 square miles and a water area of 0.813
    square miles. Located at 42.03° N. Lat; 73.91° W. Long..
    Population: 1,495; Growth (since 2000): n/a; Density: 1,016.3 persons
    per square mile; Race: 77.7% White, 3.1% Black/African American,
    11.2% Asian, 0.7% American Indian/Alaska Native, 0.0% Native
    Hawaiian/Other Pacific Islander, 5.7% Two or more races, 9.0%
    Hispanic of any race; Average household size: 2.24; Median age: 19.8;
    Age under 18: 1.7%; Age 65 and over: 1.3%; Males per 100 females:
    76.8; Marriage status: 94.6% never married, 4.8% now married, 0.0%
    separated, 0.0% widowed, 0.6% divorced; Foreign born: 15.9%; Speak
    English only: 78.6%; With disability: 9.0%; Veterans: 1.4%; Ancestry:
    17.2% Italian, 16.5% Irish, 9.7% German, 5.7% English, 4.0% Polish
    Employment: 8.0% management, business, and financial, 7.3%
    computer, engineering, and science, 21.7% education, legal, community
    service, arts, and media, 0.0% healthcare practitioners, 34.8% service,
    27.7% sales and office, 0.0% natural resources, construction, and
    maintenance, 0.5% production, transportation, and material moving
    Income: Per capita: $8,510; Median household: $145,833; Average
    household: $151,859; Households with income of $100,000 or more:
    65.2%; Poverty rate: n/a
    Educational Attainment: High school diploma or higher: 100.0%;
    Bachelor's degree or higher: 59.6%; Graduate/professional degree or
    higher: 51.8%

Four-year College(s)
Bard College (Private, Not-for-profit)
    Enrollment: 2,293 . . . . (845) 758-6822
    Tuition: In-state $52,906; Out-of-state $52,906
Two-year College(s)
Bard College (Private, Not-for-profit)
    Enrollment: 2,293 . . . . (845) 758-6822
    Tuition: In-state $52,906; Out-of-state $52,906
Vocational/Technical School(s)
Bard College (Private, Not-for-profit)
    Enrollment: 2,293 . . . . (845) 758-6822
    2016-17 Tuition: In-state $52,906; Out-of-state $52,906
    Housing: Homeownership rate: 34.8%; Median home value: n/a;
    Median year structure built: Before 1940; Homeowner vacancy rate:
    0.0%; Median selected monthly owner costs: $0 with a mortgage, $0
    without a mortgage; Median gross rent: $1,450 per month; Rental
    vacancy rate: 0.0%
    Health Insurance: 95.8% have insurance; 92.6% have private
    insurance; 7.4% have public insurance; 4.2% do not have insurance;
    5.0% of children under 18 do not have insurance
    Transportation: Commute: 18.1% car, 0.4% public transportation,
    56.0% walk, 16.6% work from home; Mean travel time to work: 11.2
    minutes

ARLINGTON (CDP). Covers a land area of 0.668 square miles and a
water area of 0 square miles. Located at 41.70° N. Lat; 73.90° W. Long.
Elevation is 187 feet.
History: Seat of Vassar College.
Population: 3,765; Growth (since 2000): -69.8%; Density: 5,639.0 persons
per square mile; Race: 52.7% White, 26.1% Black/African American, 9.5%
Asian, 0.2% American Indian/Alaska Native, 0.0% Native Hawaiian/Other
Pacific Islander, 4.1% Two or more races, 21.0% Hispanic of any race;
Average household size: 2.26; Median age: 22.5; Age under 18: 20.6%;

Age 65 and over: 11.7%; Males per 100 females: 83.3; Marriage status:
64.0% never married, 24.8% now married, 6.0% separated, 5.2%
widowed, 6.0% divorced; Foreign born: 19.0%; Speak English only: 75.5%;
With disability: 11.6%; Veterans: 8.4%; Ancestry: 15.1% Italian, 13.1%
Irish, 7.1% German, 6.9% Polish, 5.3% English
Employment: 5.9% management, business, and financial, 5.7% computer,
engineering, and science, 15.3% education, legal, community service, arts,
and media, 7.9% healthcare practitioners, 35.0% service, 18.9% sales and
office, 1.6% natural resources, construction, and maintenance, 9.6%
production, transportation, and material moving
Income: Per capita: $19,588; Median household: $45,750; Average
household: $58,242; Households with income of $100,000 or more: 12.9%;
Poverty rate: 16.5%
Educational Attainment: High school diploma or higher: 90.5%;
Bachelor's degree or higher: 32.5%; Graduate/professional degree or
higher: 11.5%
Housing: Homeownership rate: 27.1%; Median home value: $192,100;
Median year structure built: 1974; Homeowner vacancy rate: 0.0%; Median
selected monthly owner costs: $1,814 with a mortgage, $540 without a
mortgage; Median gross rent: $1,087 per month; Rental vacancy rate:
0.7%
Health Insurance: 91.6% have insurance; 68.2% have private insurance;
30.7% have public insurance; 8.4% do not have insurance; 12.5% of
children under 18 do not have insurance
Transportation: Commute: 57.2% car, 4.5% public transportation, 28.4%
walk, 7.5% work from home; Mean travel time to work: 24.0 minutes

BARRYTOWN (unincorporated postal area)
ZCTA: 12507
    Covers a land area of 1.393 square miles and a water area of 0.118
    square miles. Located at 42.01° N. Lat; 73.92° W. Long. Elevation is
    121 feet.
    Population: 250; Growth (since 2000): 131.5%; Density: 179.4 persons
    per square mile; Race: 92.0% White, 3.6% Black/African American,
    4.4% Asian, 0.0% American Indian/Alaska Native, 0.0% Native
    Hawaiian/Other Pacific Islander, 0.0% Two or more races, 0.0%
    Hispanic of any race; Average household size: 2.56; Median age: 25.9;
    Age under 18: 11.2%; Age 65 and over: 17.6%; Males per 100 females:
    111.4; Marriage status: 57.2% never married, 29.7% now married, 5.0%
    separated, 5.0% widowed, 8.1% divorced; Foreign born: 10.0%; Speak
    English only: 93.5%; With disability: 15.2%; Veterans: 10.4%; Ancestry:
    20.8% German, 13.2% English, 9.6% Italian, 9.2% American, 7.2% Irish
    Employment: 20.4% management, business, and financial, 10.9%
    computer, engineering, and science, 20.4% education, legal, community
    service, arts, and media, 0.0% healthcare practitioners, 14.6% service,
    25.5% sales and office, 8.0% natural resources, construction, and
    maintenance, 0.0% production, transportation, and material moving
    Income: Per capita: $35,251; Median household: $73,250; Average
    household: $107,943; Households with income of $100,000 or more:
    38.7%; Poverty rate: 7.7%
    Educational Attainment: High school diploma or higher: 84.1%;
    Bachelor's degree or higher: 46.4%; Graduate/professional degree or
    higher: 18.1%

Four-year College(s)
Unification Theological Seminary (Private, Not-for-profit, Other (none of the
above))
    Enrollment: 133 . . . . (845) 752-3000
Two-year College(s)
Unification Theological Seminary (Private, Not-for-profit, Other (none of the
above))
    Enrollment: 133 . . . . (845) 752-3000
Vocational/Technical School(s)
Unification Theological Seminary (Private, Not-for-profit, Other (none of the
above))
    Enrollment: 133 . . . . (845) 752-3000
    Housing: Homeownership rate: 78.7%; Median home value: $448,200;
    Median year structure built: Before 1940; Homeowner vacancy rate:
    0.0%; Median selected monthly owner costs: $2,214 with a mortgage,
    $1,501 without a mortgage; Median gross rent: n/a per month; Rental
    vacancy rate: 0.0%
    Health Insurance: 81.6% have insurance; 71.2% have private
    insurance; 27.6% have public insurance; 18.4% do not have insurance;
    40.5% of children under 18 do not have insurance

Transportation: Commute: 58.4% car, 2.9% public transportation, 20.4% walk, 18.2% work from home; Mean travel time to work: 21.5 minutes

BEACON (city). Covers a land area of 4.739 square miles and a water area of 0.137 square miles. Located at 41.50° N. Lat; 73.96° W. Long. Elevation is 135 feet.

History: An incline railroad ascends Mt. Beacon, site of a towering monument to American Revolutionary soldiers who built signal fires there to warn of the coming of the British. Beacon's historic buildings include the Madam Brett homestead (1709) and the Van Wyck homestead (1732). Settled 1663, Incorporated as a city in 1913.

Population: 14,279; Growth (since 2000): 3.4%; Density: 3,013.3 persons per square mile; Race: 66.7% White, 18.1% Black/African American, 2.6% Asian, 1.1% American Indian/Alaska Native, 0.1% Native Hawaiian/Other Pacific Islander, 6.0% Two or more races, 21.6% Hispanic of any race; Average household size: 2.56; Median age: 40.6; Age under 18: 18.8%; Age 65 and over: 13.9%; Males per 100 females: 113.5; Marriage status: 38.0% never married, 46.3% now married, 3.1% separated, 5.7% widowed, 9.9% divorced; Foreign born: 13.0%; Speak English only: 78.1%; With disability: 14.5%; Veterans: 8.4%; Ancestry: 13.4% Italian, 13.0% Irish, 8.9% German, 5.7% English, 4.7% American

Employment: 14.7% management, business, and financial, 6.8% computer, engineering, and science, 15.8% education, legal, community service, arts, and media, 4.2% healthcare practitioners, 21.0% service, 21.9% sales and office, 7.6% natural resources, construction, and maintenance, 7.9% production, transportation, and material moving

Income: Per capita: $34,955; Median household: $68,561; Average household: $90,627; Households with income of $100,000 or more: 34.8%; Poverty rate: 9.4%

Educational Attainment: High school diploma or higher: 91.0%; Bachelor's degree or higher: 34.2%; Graduate/professional degree or higher: 13.4%

School District(s)
Beacon City SD (PK-12)
   Enrollment: 2,988 . . . . (845) 838-6900

Housing: Homeownership rate: 59.3%; Median home value: $251,600; Median year structure built: 1950; Homeowner vacancy rate: 1.9%; Median selected monthly owner costs: $2,224 with a mortgage, $791 without a mortgage; Median gross rent: $1,069 per month; Rental vacancy rate: 6.8%

Health Insurance: 92.4% have insurance; 68.1% have private insurance; 35.0% have public insurance; 7.6% do not have insurance; 3.0% of children under 18 do not have insurance

Safety: Violent crime rate: 31.0 per 10,000 population; Property crime rate: 168.9 per 10,000 population

Transportation: Commute: 78.2% car, 10.0% public transportation, 4.0% walk, 6.4% work from home; Mean travel time to work: 36.3 minutes

Additional Information Contacts
City of Beacon . . . . (845) 838-5000
   http://www.cityofbeacon.org

BEEKMAN (town). Covers a land area of 29.838 square miles and a water area of 0.517 square miles. Located at 41.60° N. Lat; 73.70° W. Long. Elevation is 377 feet.

History: Beekman was named in 1697 for Kingston native Henry Beekman, who had numerous land stakes in Dutchess County. The town was also occupied by the Wappinger Indians before European settlers arrived around 1710.

Population: 14,433; Growth (since 2000): 26.0%; Density: 483.7 persons per square mile; Race: 82.8% White, 9.8% Black/African American, 1.7% Asian, 1.0% American Indian/Alaska Native, 0.0% Native Hawaiian/Other Pacific Islander, 2.2% Two or more races, 10.8% Hispanic of any race; Average household size: 2.84; Median age: 44.2; Age under 18: 20.1%; Age 65 and over: 12.0%; Males per 100 females: 131.0; Marriage status: 31.6% never married, 55.0% now married, 1.6% separated, 5.1% widowed, 8.3% divorced; Foreign born: 9.2%; Speak English only: 86.0%; With disability: 10.9%; Veterans: 6.5%; Ancestry: 26.6% Italian, 25.1% Irish, 16.5% German, 6.5% American, 6.4% English

Employment: 14.9% management, business, and financial, 6.3% computer, engineering, and science, 14.1% education, legal, community service, arts, and media, 7.0% healthcare practitioners, 12.9% service, 23.2% sales and office, 12.9% natural resources, construction, and maintenance, 8.7% production, transportation, and material moving

Income: Per capita: $36,052; Median household: $96,042; Average household: $112,689; Households with income of $100,000 or more: 47.8%; Poverty rate: 5.9%

Educational Attainment: High school diploma or higher: 90.0%; Bachelor's degree or higher: 31.1%; Graduate/professional degree or higher: 13.5%

Housing: Homeownership rate: 89.0%; Median home value: $305,300; Median year structure built: 1984; Homeowner vacancy rate: 2.0%; Median selected monthly owner costs: $2,533 with a mortgage, $925 without a mortgage; Median gross rent: $1,259 per month; Rental vacancy rate: 1.6%

Health Insurance: 96.0% have insurance; 85.2% have private insurance; 23.7% have public insurance; 4.0% do not have insurance; 2.9% of children under 18 do not have insurance

Transportation: Commute: 90.4% car, 3.1% public transportation, 0.6% walk, 4.9% work from home; Mean travel time to work: 38.4 minutes

Additional Information Contacts
Town of Beekman . . . . (845) 724-5300
   http://www.townofbeekman.com

BRINCKERHOFF (CDP). Covers a land area of 1.120 square miles and a water area of 0.005 square miles. Located at 41.55° N. Lat; 73.87° W. Long. Elevation is 220 feet.

Population: 2,486; Growth (since 2000): -9.1%; Density: 2,219.7 persons per square mile; Race: 78.6% White, 9.7% Black/African American, 6.2% Asian, 0.0% American Indian/Alaska Native, 0.0% Native Hawaiian/Other Pacific Islander, 5.2% Two or more races, 9.5% Hispanic of any race; Average household size: 2.68; Median age: 50.6; Age under 18: 11.9%; Age 65 and over: 21.8%; Males per 100 females: 93.2; Marriage status: 26.0% never married, 56.6% now married, 1.5% separated, 7.0% widowed, 10.3% divorced; Foreign born: 11.0%; Speak English only: 81.6%; With disability: 8.6%; Veterans: 9.9%; Ancestry: 24.6% Italian, 15.3% Irish, 11.6% German, 5.0% English, 4.1% American

Employment: 13.8% management, business, and financial, 10.3% computer, engineering, and science, 15.7% education, legal, community service, arts, and media, 4.5% healthcare practitioners, 16.7% service, 22.1% sales and office, 8.0% natural resources, construction, and maintenance, 8.9% production, transportation, and material moving

Income: Per capita: $42,672; Median household: $100,317; Average household: $109,262; Households with income of $100,000 or more: 50.9%; Poverty rate: 6.0%

Educational Attainment: High school diploma or higher: 92.5%; Bachelor's degree or higher: 36.3%; Graduate/professional degree or higher: 15.2%

Housing: Homeownership rate: 83.2%; Median home value: $276,000; Median year structure built: 1971; Homeowner vacancy rate: 0.0%; Median selected monthly owner costs: $2,019 with a mortgage, $811 without a mortgage; Median gross rent: $1,515 per month; Rental vacancy rate: 0.0%

Health Insurance: 93.7% have insurance; 83.7% have private insurance; 27.6% have public insurance; 6.3% do not have insurance; 6.5% of children under 18 do not have insurance

Transportation: Commute: 86.3% car, 4.2% public transportation, 2.6% walk, 5.9% work from home; Mean travel time to work: 34.4 minutes

CHELSEA (unincorporated postal area)
ZCTA: 12512
   Covers a land area of 0.446 square miles and a water area of <.001 square miles. Located at 41.55° N. Lat; 73.97° W. Long. Elevation is 39 feet.

Population: 143; Growth (since 2000): n/a; Density: 320.5 persons per square mile; Race: 100.0% White, 0.0% Black/African American, 0.0% Asian, 0.0% American Indian/Alaska Native, 0.0% Native Hawaiian/Other Pacific Islander, 0.0% Two or more races, 0.0% Hispanic of any race; Average household size: 2.38; Median age: 58.9; Age under 18: 0.0%; Age 65 and over: 49.0%; Males per 100 females: 104.8; Marriage status: 33.6% never married, 49.0% now married, 0.0% separated, 0.0% widowed, 17.5% divorced; Foreign born: 0.0%; Speak English only: 100.0%; With disability: 49.0%; Veterans: 24.5%; Ancestry: 66.4% Irish, 51.0% English, 33.6% German

Employment: 0.0% management, business, and financial, 34.2% computer, engineering, and science, 0.0% education, legal, community service, arts, and media, 0.0% healthcare practitioners, 0.0% service, 31.5% sales and office, 0.0% natural resources, construction, and maintenance, 34.2% production, transportation, and material moving

Income: Per capita: $38,801; Median household: n/a; Average household: n/a; Households with income of $100,000 or more: 41.7%; Poverty rate: n/a

Educational Attainment: High school diploma or higher: 100.0%; Bachelor's degree or higher: n/a; Graduate/professional degree or higher: n/a

Housing: Homeownership rate: 100.0%; Median home value: n/a; Median year structure built: n/a; Homeowner vacancy rate: 0.0%; Median selected monthly owner costs: $0 with a mortgage, $0 without a mortgage; Median gross rent: n/a per month; Rental vacancy rate: 0.0%

Health Insurance: 100.0% have insurance; 100.0% have private insurance; 49.0% have public insurance; 0.0% do not have insurance; 0.0% of children under 18 do not have insurance

Transportation: Commute: 100.0% car, 0.0% public transportation, 0.0% walk, 0.0% work from home; Mean travel time to work: 0.0 minutes

---

CLINTON (town). Covers a land area of 38.143 square miles and a water area of 0.642 square miles. Located at 41.86° N. Lat; 73.82° W. Long.

Population: 4,270; Growth (since 2000): 6.5%; Density: 111.9 persons per square mile; Race: 94.4% White, 1.7% Black/African American, 1.3% Asian, 0.0% American Indian/Alaska Native, 0.0% Native Hawaiian/Other Pacific Islander, 1.8% Two or more races, 3.9% Hispanic of any race; Average household size: 2.67; Median age: 45.9; Age under 18: 21.1%; Age 65 and over: 17.5%; Males per 100 females: 103.2; Marriage status: 29.5% never married, 60.0% now married, 0.4% separated, 4.5% widowed, 6.0% divorced; Foreign born: 5.0%; Speak English only: 94.7%; With disability: 13.6%; Veterans: 8.5%; Ancestry: 31.8% Irish, 20.3% German, 15.8% Italian, 9.7% English, 4.5% Polish

Employment: 11.1% management, business, and financial, 6.3% computer, engineering, and science, 12.6% education, legal, community service, arts, and media, 9.1% healthcare practitioners, 14.6% service, 21.4% sales and office, 14.6% natural resources, construction, and maintenance, 10.3% production, transportation, and material moving

Income: Per capita: $44,011; Median household: $98,094; Average household: $120,035; Households with income of $100,000 or more: 48.0%; Poverty rate: 6.5%

Educational Attainment: High school diploma or higher: 91.6%; Bachelor's degree or higher: 41.1%; Graduate/professional degree or higher: 16.6%

Housing: Homeownership rate: 81.3%; Median home value: $344,400; Median year structure built: 1976; Homeowner vacancy rate: 0.0%; Median selected monthly owner costs: $2,453 with a mortgage, $812 without a mortgage; Median gross rent: $1,218 per month; Rental vacancy rate: 11.7%

Health Insurance: 94.4% have insurance; 78.1% have private insurance; 31.8% have public insurance; 5.6% do not have insurance; 3.4% of children under 18 do not have insurance

Transportation: Commute: 82.1% car, 3.7% public transportation, 1.2% walk, 12.1% work from home; Mean travel time to work: 35.5 minutes

Additional Information Contacts

Town of Clinton . . . . (845) 266-5721
http://www.townofclinton.com

CLINTON CORNERS (unincorporated postal area)
ZCTA: 12514

Covers a land area of 26.646 square miles and a water area of 0.275 square miles. Located at 41.88° N. Lat; 73.76° W. Long. Elevation is 302 feet.

Population: 3,168; Growth (since 2000): 11.0%; Density: 118.9 persons per square mile; Race: 94.0% White, 1.3% Black/African American, 2.7% Asian, 0.0% American Indian/Alaska Native, 0.0% Native Hawaiian/Other Pacific Islander, 0.7% Two or more races, 2.1% Hispanic of any race; Average household size: 2.63; Median age: 48.8; Age under 18: 19.5%; Age 65 and over: 21.9%; Males per 100 females: 101.5; Marriage status: 26.6% never married, 59.7% now married, 0.9% separated, 5.0% widowed, 8.7% divorced; Foreign born: 4.9%; Speak English only: 93.8%; With disability: 13.0%; Veterans: 10.2%; Ancestry: 32.3% Irish, 19.4% German, 18.4% Italian, 12.0% English, 4.3% Dutch

Employment: 16.3% management, business, and financial, 8.6% computer, engineering, and science, 19.8% education, legal, community service, arts, and media, 6.6% healthcare practitioners, 16.9% service, 12.0% sales and office, 9.6% natural resources, construction, and maintenance, 10.0% production, transportation, and material moving

Income: Per capita: $53,885; Median household: $104,621; Average household: $140,142; Households with income of $100,000 or more: 53.2%; Poverty rate: 3.6%

Educational Attainment: High school diploma or higher: 96.1%; Bachelor's degree or higher: 47.4%; Graduate/professional degree or higher: 21.6%

Housing: Homeownership rate: 90.8%; Median home value: $340,600; Median year structure built: 1976; Homeowner vacancy rate: 1.0%; Median selected monthly owner costs: $2,418 with a mortgage, $770 without a mortgage; Median gross rent: $1,341 per month; Rental vacancy rate: 0.0%

Health Insurance: 98.7% have insurance; 81.5% have private insurance; 33.7% have public insurance; 1.3% do not have insurance; 0.0% of children under 18 do not have insurance

Transportation: Commute: 83.3% car, 3.0% public transportation, 1.1% walk, 11.4% work from home; Mean travel time to work: 33.4 minutes

---

CROWN HEIGHTS (CDP). Covers a land area of 0.844 square miles and a water area of 0 square miles. Located at 41.64° N. Lat; 73.93° W. Long. Elevation is 112 feet.

Population: 2,877; Growth (since 2000): -3.8%; Density: 3,410.2 persons per square mile; Race: 79.7% White, 5.6% Black/African American, 4.7% Asian, 0.0% American Indian/Alaska Native, 0.0% Native Hawaiian/Other Pacific Islander, 5.9% Two or more races, 15.7% Hispanic of any race; Average household size: 2.69; Median age: 41.1; Age under 18: 23.5%; Age 65 and over: 13.9%; Males per 100 females: 91.5; Marriage status: 36.4% never married, 48.7% now married, 1.7% separated, 8.4% widowed, 6.5% divorced; Foreign born: 7.0%; Speak English only: 83.0%; With disability: 7.1%; Veterans: 7.9%; Ancestry: 20.0% Italian, 13.6% Irish, 12.7% German, 6.7% American, 5.8% Polish

Employment: 11.6% management, business, and financial, 4.7% computer, engineering, and science, 9.6% education, legal, community service, arts, and media, 7.0% healthcare practitioners, 21.7% service, 30.4% sales and office, 6.5% natural resources, construction, and maintenance, 8.5% production, transportation, and material moving

Income: Per capita: $33,719; Median household: $81,875; Average household: $87,557; Households with income of $100,000 or more: 34.4%; Poverty rate: 11.2%

Educational Attainment: High school diploma or higher: 93.8%; Bachelor's degree or higher: 31.9%; Graduate/professional degree or higher: 9.9%

Housing: Homeownership rate: 85.6%; Median home value: $224,800; Median year structure built: 1963; Homeowner vacancy rate: 0.0%; Median selected monthly owner costs: $2,019 with a mortgage, $882 without a mortgage; Median gross rent: $1,368 per month; Rental vacancy rate: 0.0%

Health Insurance: 97.2% have insurance; 86.5% have private insurance; 25.3% have public insurance; 2.8% do not have insurance; 0.0% of children under 18 do not have insurance

Transportation: Commute: 86.7% car, 7.1% public transportation, 2.0% walk, 4.2% work from home; Mean travel time to work: 23.8 minutes

---

DOVER (town). Covers a land area of 55.190 square miles and a water area of 1.149 square miles. Located at 41.68° N. Lat; 73.57° W. Long.

Population: 8,509; Growth (since 2000): -0.7%; Density: 154.2 persons per square mile; Race: 87.2% White, 3.9% Black/African American, 1.5% Asian, 0.0% American Indian/Alaska Native, 0.0% Native Hawaiian/Other Pacific Islander, 2.7% Two or more races, 15.5% Hispanic of any race; Average household size: 2.64; Median age: 43.4; Age under 18: 20.9%; Age 65 and over: 14.4%; Males per 100 females: 102.8; Marriage status: 33.7% never married, 49.8% now married, 2.1% separated, 4.2% widowed, 12.3% divorced; Foreign born: 11.2%; Speak English only: 84.6%; With disability: 19.5%; Veterans: 6.2%; Ancestry: 22.8% Italian, 22.2% Irish, 18.1% German, 10.0% American, 6.0% Polish

Employment: 13.0% management, business, and financial, 4.0% computer, engineering, and science, 8.6% education, legal, community service, arts, and media, 5.1% healthcare practitioners, 25.3% service, 22.5% sales and office, 11.3% natural resources, construction, and maintenance, 10.3% production, transportation, and material moving

Income: Per capita: $28,085; Median household: $53,617; Average household: $72,665; Households with income of $100,000 or more: 25.9%; Poverty rate: 14.6%

Educational Attainment: High school diploma or higher: 84.7%; Bachelor's degree or higher: 19.7%; Graduate/professional degree or higher: 7.4%

Housing: Homeownership rate: 66.9%; Median home value: $248,300; Median year structure built: 1975; Homeowner vacancy rate: 0.0%; Median selected monthly owner costs: $1,962 with a mortgage, $811 without a mortgage; Median gross rent: $924 per month; Rental vacancy rate: 7.0%
Health Insurance: 91.4% have insurance; 70.6% have private insurance; 35.2% have public insurance; 8.6% do not have insurance; 5.2% of children under 18 do not have insurance
Transportation: Commute: 90.2% car, 2.4% public transportation, 3.6% walk, 3.9% work from home; Mean travel time to work: 39.3 minutes
Additional Information Contacts
Town of Dover . . . . (845) 832-6111
  http://townofdoverny.us

DOVER PLAINS (CDP).
Covers a land area of 0.677 square miles and a water area of 0.015 square miles. Located at 41.74° N. Lat; 73.57° W. Long. Elevation is 400 feet.
Population: 1,057; Growth (since 2000): -47.0%; Density: 1,561.9 persons per square mile; Race: 84.3% White, 0.9% Black/African American, 3.7% Asian, 0.0% American Indian/Alaska Native, 0.0% Native Hawaiian/Other Pacific Islander, 0.0% Two or more races, 21.6% Hispanic of any race; Average household size: 1.79; Median age: 44.3; Age under 18: 17.4%; Age 65 and over: 18.2%; Males per 100 females: 110.7; Marriage status: 42.0% never married, 28.1% now married, 6.0% separated, 5.8% widowed, 24.1% divorced; Foreign born: 14.8%; Speak English only: 79.1%; With disability: 16.4%; Veterans: 4.1%; Ancestry: 21.1% Irish, 12.8% American, 10.3% Italian, 9.9% English, 9.1% German
Employment: 9.3% management, business, and financial, 8.7% computer, engineering, and science, 1.7% education, legal, community service, arts, and media, 4.9% healthcare practitioners, 43.1% service, 9.7% sales and office, 5.3% natural resources, construction, and maintenance, 17.3% production, transportation, and material moving
Income: Per capita: $27,019; Median household: $43,273; Average household: $47,975; Households with income of $100,000 or more: 6.8%; Poverty rate: 17.7%
Educational Attainment: High school diploma or higher: 69.4%; Bachelor's degree or higher: 13.3%; Graduate/professional degree or higher: 2.4%
School District(s)
Dover Union Free SD (KG-12)
  Enrollment: 1,360 . . . . (845) 877-5700
Housing: Homeownership rate: 36.3%; Median home value: n/a; Median year structure built: 1962; Homeowner vacancy rate: 0.0%; Median selected monthly owner costs: $1,911 with a mortgage, $799 without a mortgage; Median gross rent: $728 per month; Rental vacancy rate: 0.0%
Health Insurance: 93.9% have insurance; 68.2% have private insurance; 43.0% have public insurance; 6.1% do not have insurance; 0.0% of children under 18 do not have insurance
Transportation: Commute: 90.3% car, 0.0% public transportation, 5.4% walk, 4.2% work from home; Mean travel time to work: 33.7 minutes

EAST FISHKILL (town).
Covers a land area of 56.503 square miles and a water area of 0.883 square miles. Located at 41.56° N. Lat; 73.79° W. Long. Elevation is 276 feet.
History: Fishkill is famous as home to Hudson Valley Research Park (formerly known as IBM East Fishkill). While IBM produced microchips, new owner GlobalFoundries owned the automated processor facility where IBM's "Cell" processor was co-developed.
Population: 29,312; Growth (since 2000): 14.5%; Density: 518.8 persons per square mile; Race: 87.5% White, 2.1% Black/African American, 3.9% Asian, 0.2% American Indian/Alaska Native, 0.0% Native Hawaiian/Other Pacific Islander, 3.7% Two or more races, 7.2% Hispanic of any race; Average household size: 3.05; Median age: 43.7; Age under 18: 23.2%; Age 65 and over: 15.1%; Males per 100 females: 99.9; Marriage status: 24.9% never married, 62.9% now married, 0.8% separated, 4.5% widowed, 7.7% divorced; Foreign born: 10.1%; Speak English only: 86.1%; With disability: 10.9%; Veterans: 6.9%; Ancestry: 29.2% Italian, 22.5% Irish, 12.9% German, 5.7% English, 5.4% Polish
Employment: 19.7% management, business, and financial, 6.3% computer, engineering, and science, 13.5% education, legal, community service, arts, and media, 6.3% healthcare practitioners, 16.8% service, 22.6% sales and office, 9.9% natural resources, construction, and maintenance, 4.9% production, transportation, and material moving
Income: Per capita: $43,858; Median household: $105,882; Average household: $130,238; Households with income of $100,000 or more: 53.0%; Poverty rate: 3.8%

Educational Attainment: High school diploma or higher: 94.4%; Bachelor's degree or higher: 43.3%; Graduate/professional degree or higher: 18.2%
Housing: Homeownership rate: 89.9%; Median home value: $355,700; Median year structure built: 1980; Homeowner vacancy rate: 0.9%; Median selected monthly owner costs: $2,611 with a mortgage, $948 without a mortgage; Median gross rent: $1,204 per month; Rental vacancy rate: 7.9%
Health Insurance: 96.0% have insurance; 82.7% have private insurance; 25.7% have public insurance; 4.0% do not have insurance; 2.7% of children under 18 do not have insurance
Safety: Violent crime rate: 6.8 per 10,000 population; Property crime rate: 48.5 per 10,000 population
Transportation: Commute: 89.9% car, 3.7% public transportation, 0.5% walk, 5.5% work from home; Mean travel time to work: 37.6 minutes
Additional Information Contacts
Town of East Fishkill . . . . (845) 221-9191
  http://www.eastfishkillny.org

FAIRVIEW (CDP).
Covers a land area of 3.477 square miles and a water area of 0.076 square miles. Located at 41.73° N. Lat; 73.91° W. Long. Elevation is 217 feet.
Population: 5,440; Growth (since 2000): 0.4%; Density: 1,564.5 persons per square mile; Race: 73.0% White, 16.0% Black/African American, 2.5% Asian, 1.3% American Indian/Alaska Native, 0.0% Native Hawaiian/Other Pacific Islander, 4.0% Two or more races, 13.5% Hispanic of any race; Average household size: 2.65; Median age: 31.4; Age under 18: 17.8%; Age 65 and over: 11.2%; Males per 100 females: 102.4; Marriage status: 47.0% never married, 39.6% now married, 1.4% separated, 5.3% widowed, 8.1% divorced; Foreign born: 10.1%; Speak English only: 85.1%; With disability: 11.8%; Veterans: 3.9%; Ancestry: 19.3% Irish, 17.2% German, 15.4% Italian, 7.8% English, 4.8% Jamaican
Employment: 9.7% management, business, and financial, 8.0% computer, engineering, and science, 12.7% education, legal, community service, arts, and media, 4.0% healthcare practitioners, 21.7% service, 30.0% sales and office, 6.2% natural resources, construction, and maintenance, 7.8% production, transportation, and material moving
Income: Per capita: $28,332; Median household: $77,604; Average household: $84,383; Households with income of $100,000 or more: 40.7%; Poverty rate: 18.3%
Educational Attainment: High school diploma or higher: 86.9%; Bachelor's degree or higher: 26.6%; Graduate/professional degree or higher: 12.9%
Housing: Homeownership rate: 71.7%; Median home value: $198,800; Median year structure built: 1958; Homeowner vacancy rate: 6.3%; Median selected monthly owner costs: $1,903 with a mortgage, $877 without a mortgage; Median gross rent: $1,189 per month; Rental vacancy rate: 9.0%
Health Insurance: 94.4% have insurance; 75.8% have private insurance; 30.2% have public insurance; 5.6% do not have insurance; 1.3% of children under 18 do not have insurance
Transportation: Commute: 81.7% car, 2.5% public transportation, 7.0% walk, 6.3% work from home; Mean travel time to work: 26.9 minutes

FISHKILL (town).
Covers a land area of 27.336 square miles and a water area of 4.655 square miles. Located at 41.52° N. Lat; 73.92° W. Long. Elevation is 220 feet.
History: Nearby village of Fishkill Landing joined Matteawan (1913) to form Beacon city.
Population: 23,508; Growth (since 2000): 16.0%; Density: 860.0 persons per square mile; Race: 69.7% White, 12.9% Black/African American, 6.9% Asian, 0.2% American Indian/Alaska Native, 0.1% Native Hawaiian/Other Pacific Islander, 4.3% Two or more races, 16.1% Hispanic of any race; Average household size: 2.45; Median age: 41.6; Age under 18: 17.6%; Age 65 and over: 16.4%; Males per 100 females: 103.5; Marriage status: 32.7% never married, 50.8% now married, 3.3% separated, 5.9% widowed, 10.6% divorced; Foreign born: 13.0%; Speak English only: 79.2%; With disability: 10.1%; Veterans: 6.0%; Ancestry: 22.2% Italian, 16.7% Irish, 10.3% German, 4.8% American, 4.0% English
Employment: 16.2% management, business, and financial, 8.5% computer, engineering, and science, 13.5% education, legal, community service, arts, and media, 4.1% healthcare practitioners, 17.3% service, 23.3% sales and office, 7.1% natural resources, construction, and maintenance, 10.0% production, transportation, and material moving

Income: Per capita: $38,148; Median household: $82,946; Average household: $99,252; Households with income of $100,000 or more: 41.0%; Poverty rate: 8.8%

Educational Attainment: High school diploma or higher: 90.2%; Bachelor's degree or higher: 35.7%; Graduate/professional degree or higher: 16.3%

School District(s)

Beacon City SD (PK-12)
    Enrollment: 2,988 . . . . (845) 838-6900
Wappingers Central SD (PK-12)
    Enrollment: 11,091 . . . . (845) 298-5000

Housing: Homeownership rate: 66.8%; Median home value: $283,400; Median year structure built: 1980; Homeowner vacancy rate: 2.9%; Median selected monthly owner costs: $2,178 with a mortgage, $846 without a mortgage; Median gross rent: $1,503 per month; Rental vacancy rate: 2.0%

Health Insurance: 97.1% have insurance; 81.0% have private insurance; 29.8% have public insurance; 2.9% do not have insurance; 0.7% of children under 18 do not have insurance

Safety: Violent crime rate: 3.3 per 10,000 population; Property crime rate: 56.2 per 10,000 population

Transportation: Commute: 83.9% car, 8.9% public transportation, 2.0% walk, 4.6% work from home; Mean travel time to work: 37.4 minutes

Additional Information Contacts

Town of Fishkill . . . . (845) 831-7800
    http://www.fishkill-ny.gov

FISHKILL (village). Covers a land area of 0.820 square miles and a water area of 0.004 square miles. Located at 41.53° N. Lat; 73.89° W. Long. Elevation is 220 feet.

Population: 2,127; Growth (since 2000): 22.6%; Density: 2,592.7 persons per square mile; Race: 81.4% White, 8.2% Black/African American, 5.2% Asian, 0.0% American Indian/Alaska Native, 0.0% Native Hawaiian/Other Pacific Islander, 2.3% Two or more races, 14.1% Hispanic of any race; Average household size: 2.10; Median age: 42.0; Age under 18: 20.5%; Age 65 and over: 15.3%; Males per 100 females: 87.8; Marriage status: 32.5% never married, 48.7% now married, 4.5% separated, 6.9% widowed, 11.9% divorced; Foreign born: 10.8%; Speak English only: 80.8%; With disability: 8.8%; Veterans: 5.4%; Ancestry: 27.8% Italian, 21.9% Irish, 8.6% American, 6.9% German, 6.4% English

Employment: 16.9% management, business, and financial, 11.7% computer, engineering, and science, 19.4% education, legal, community service, arts, and media, 5.2% healthcare practitioners, 15.8% service, 23.8% sales and office, 3.0% natural resources, construction, and maintenance, 4.2% production, transportation, and material moving

Income: Per capita: $36,481; Median household: $62,917; Average household: $75,748; Households with income of $100,000 or more: 30.4%; Poverty rate: 15.7%

Educational Attainment: High school diploma or higher: 93.8%; Bachelor's degree or higher: 47.6%; Graduate/professional degree or higher: 21.4%

School District(s)

Beacon City SD (PK-12)
    Enrollment: 2,988 . . . . (845) 838-6900
Wappingers Central SD (PK-12)
    Enrollment: 11,091 . . . . (845) 298-5000

Housing: Homeownership rate: 34.9%; Median home value: $220,500; Median year structure built: 1975; Homeowner vacancy rate: 4.1%; Median selected monthly owner costs: $1,692 with a mortgage, $649 without a mortgage; Median gross rent: $1,576 per month; Rental vacancy rate: 6.2%

Health Insurance: 94.8% have insurance; 77.1% have private insurance; 33.6% have public insurance; 5.2% do not have insurance; 3.1% of children under 18 do not have insurance

Safety: Violent crime rate: 9.5 per 10,000 population; Property crime rate: 128.1 per 10,000 population

Transportation: Commute: 83.1% car, 2.6% public transportation, 7.3% walk, 7.0% work from home; Mean travel time to work: 35.3 minutes

---

FREEDOM PLAINS (CDP). Covers a land area of 1.290 square miles and a water area of 0.044 square miles. Located at 41.67° N. Lat; 73.80° W. Long. Elevation is 315 feet.

Population: 379; Growth (since 2000): n/a; Density: 293.9 persons per square mile; Race: 95.5% White, 4.5% Black/African American, 0.0% Asian, 0.0% American Indian/Alaska Native, 0.0% Native Hawaiian/Other

Pacific Islander, 0.0% Two or more races, 5.5% Hispanic of any race; Average household size: 1.96; Median age: 49.3; Age under 18: 19.0%; Age 65 and over: 26.6%; Males per 100 females: 72.5; Marriage status: 34.7% never married, 32.9% now married, 4.9% separated, 13.0% widowed, 19.4% divorced; Foreign born: 3.2%; Speak English only: 89.7%; With disability: 15.0%; Veterans: 8.8%; Ancestry: 26.4% Irish, 25.1% Italian, 13.5% French Canadian, 12.1% English, 10.3% German

Employment: 2.8% management, business, and financial, 0.0% computer, engineering, and science, 9.0% education, legal, community service, arts, and media, 9.7% healthcare practitioners, 15.3% service, 27.1% sales and office, 11.8% natural resources, construction, and maintenance, 24.3% production, transportation, and material moving

Income: Per capita: $40,808; Median household: n/a; Average household: $79,568; Households with income of $100,000 or more: 39.9%; Poverty rate: 1.6%

Educational Attainment: High school diploma or higher: 95.4%; Bachelor's degree or higher: 36.0%; Graduate/professional degree or higher: 6.9%

Housing: Homeownership rate: 60.6%; Median home value: $207,500; Median year structure built: 1986; Homeowner vacancy rate: 12.7%; Median selected monthly owner costs: $1,853 with a mortgage, $917 without a mortgage; Median gross rent: $1,227 per month; Rental vacancy rate: 0.0%

Health Insurance: 100.0% have insurance; 88.1% have private insurance; 31.1% have public insurance; 0.0% do not have insurance; 0.0% of children under 18 do not have insurance

Transportation: Commute: 100.0% car, 0.0% public transportation, 0.0% walk, 0.0% work from home; Mean travel time to work: 33.8 minutes

---

HAVILAND (CDP). Covers a land area of 3.863 square miles and a water area of 0.035 square miles. Located at 41.77° N. Lat; 73.90° W. Long. Elevation is 233 feet.

Population: 3,354; Growth (since 2000): -9.6%; Density: 868.2 persons per square mile; Race: 87.4% White, 3.6% Black/African American, 1.6% Asian, 0.0% American Indian/Alaska Native, 0.0% Native Hawaiian/Other Pacific Islander, 0.4% Two or more races, 9.3% Hispanic of any race; Average household size: 2.58; Median age: 45.4; Age under 18: 20.7%; Age 65 and over: 21.1%; Males per 100 females: 93.3; Marriage status: 23.1% never married, 64.0% now married, 1.1% separated, 4.1% widowed, 8.9% divorced; Foreign born: 2.4%; Speak English only: 90.0%; With disability: 10.0%; Veterans: 6.9%; Ancestry: 25.7% Irish, 20.2% German, 20.0% Italian, 9.3% Polish, 7.5% English

Employment: 11.2% management, business, and financial, 6.4% computer, engineering, and science, 12.4% education, legal, community service, arts, and media, 6.9% healthcare practitioners, 15.8% service, 32.5% sales and office, 6.8% natural resources, construction, and maintenance, 8.1% production, transportation, and material moving

Income: Per capita: $35,542; Median household: $87,260; Average household: $90,599; Households with income of $100,000 or more: 41.3%; Poverty rate: 4.5%

Educational Attainment: High school diploma or higher: 94.6%; Bachelor's degree or higher: 29.9%; Graduate/professional degree or higher: 12.8%

Housing: Homeownership rate: 90.6%; Median home value: $211,500; Median year structure built: 1965; Homeowner vacancy rate: 0.0%; Median selected monthly owner costs: $1,935 with a mortgage, $763 without a mortgage; Median gross rent: $1,357 per month; Rental vacancy rate: 0.0%

Health Insurance: 97.3% have insurance; 88.7% have private insurance; 22.8% have public insurance; 2.7% do not have insurance; 0.0% of children under 18 do not have insurance

Transportation: Commute: 95.2% car, 1.7% public transportation, 0.0% walk, 2.5% work from home; Mean travel time to work: 26.2 minutes

---

HILLSIDE LAKE (CDP). Covers a land area of 0.523 square miles and a water area of 0.040 square miles. Located at 41.62° N. Lat; 73.80° W. Long. Elevation is 374 feet.

Population: 1,170; Growth (since 2000): -42.1%; Density: 2,238.0 persons per square mile; Race: 90.1% White, 0.0% Black/African American, 1.3% Asian, 0.0% American Indian/Alaska Native, 0.0% Native Hawaiian/Other Pacific Islander, 3.9% Two or more races, 11.9% Hispanic of any race; Average household size: 3.31; Median age: 43.7; Age under 18: 23.2%; Age 65 and over: 9.7%; Males per 100 females: 89.5; Marriage status: 31.0% never married, 57.5% now married, 2.3% separated, 7.0% widowed, 4.4% divorced; Foreign born: 7.7%; Speak English only: 89.3%;

With disability: 12.6%; Veterans: 6.8%; Ancestry: 37.8% Italian, 29.7% Irish, 15.8% German, 10.5% Polish, 7.8% Russian
Employment: 14.8% management, business, and financial, 1.7% computer, engineering, and science, 13.0% education, legal, community service, arts, and media, 7.8% healthcare practitioners, 11.5% service, 35.8% sales and office, 9.7% natural resources, construction, and maintenance, 5.8% production, transportation, and material moving
Income: Per capita: $41,892; Median household: $106,771; Average household: $133,272; Households with income of $100,000 or more: 52.3%; Poverty rate: 12.4%
Educational Attainment: High school diploma or higher: 96.5%; Bachelor's degree or higher: 27.2%; Graduate/professional degree or higher: 14.1%
Housing: Homeownership rate: 87.8%; Median home value: $237,100; Median year structure built: 1963; Homeowner vacancy rate: 9.4%; Median selected monthly owner costs: $1,881 with a mortgage, $829 without a mortgage; Median gross rent: n/a per month; Rental vacancy rate: 0.0%
Health Insurance: 95.7% have insurance; 80.7% have private insurance; 23.3% have public insurance; 4.3% do not have insurance; 2.6% of children under 18 do not have insurance
Transportation: Commute: 91.7% car, 6.8% public transportation, 0.0% walk, 1.5% work from home; Mean travel time to work: 42.4 minutes

HOLMES (unincorporated postal area)
ZCTA: 12531

Covers a land area of 17.495 square miles and a water area of 1.007 square miles. Located at 41.54° N. Lat; 73.67° W. Long. Elevation is 692 feet.
Population: 3,132; Growth (since 2000): 2.7%; Density: 179.0 persons per square mile; Race: 93.1% White, 1.8% Black/African American, 1.8% Asian, 0.0% American Indian/Alaska Native, 0.0% Native Hawaiian/Other Pacific Islander, 3.3% Two or more races, 1.4% Hispanic of any race; Average household size: 2.80; Median age: 47.8; Age under 18: 24.9%; Age 65 and over: 17.2%; Males per 100 females: 104.4; Marriage status: 27.9% never married, 56.3% now married, 0.7% separated, 4.3% widowed, 11.4% divorced; Foreign born: 4.6%; Speak English only: 94.3%; With disability: 6.0%; Veterans: 5.7%; Ancestry: 26.5% Irish, 23.6% Italian, 18.1% German, 7.7% American, 6.7% English
Employment: 15.9% management, business, and financial, 1.2% computer, engineering, and science, 16.0% education, legal, community service, arts, and media, 6.3% healthcare practitioners, 14.0% service, 19.6% sales and office, 17.3% natural resources, construction, and maintenance, 9.8% production, transportation, and material moving
Income: Per capita: $39,259; Median household: $81,860; Average household: $110,342; Households with income of $100,000 or more: 43.7%; Poverty rate: 1.1%
Educational Attainment: High school diploma or higher: 93.8%; Bachelor's degree or higher: 30.8%; Graduate/professional degree or higher: 10.3%
Housing: Homeownership rate: 80.0%; Median home value: $277,900; Median year structure built: 1966; Homeowner vacancy rate: 5.3%; Median selected monthly owner costs: $2,465 with a mortgage, $1,041 without a mortgage; Median gross rent: $1,246 per month; Rental vacancy rate: 8.5%
Health Insurance: 92.6% have insurance; 81.9% have private insurance; 24.1% have public insurance; 7.4% do not have insurance; 0.0% of children under 18 do not have insurance
Transportation: Commute: 82.4% car, 7.3% public transportation, 4.2% walk, 5.1% work from home; Mean travel time to work: 41.1 minutes

HOPEWELL JUNCTION (CDP). Covers a land area of 0.474 square miles and a water area of <.001 square miles. Located at 41.58° N. Lat; 73.80° W. Long. Elevation is 246 feet.
Population: 442; Growth (since 2000): -83.1%; Density: 933.3 persons per square mile; Race: 85.1% White, 2.7% Black/African American, 0.0% Asian, 7.2% American Indian/Alaska Native, 0.0% Native Hawaiian/Other Pacific Islander, 5.0% Two or more races, 45.5% Hispanic of any race; Average household size: 3.09; Median age: 39.0; Age under 18: 41.6%; Age 65 and over: 10.4%; Males per 100 females: 100.0; Marriage status: 34.9% never married, 56.3% now married, 0.0% separated, 3.5% widowed, 5.3% divorced; Foreign born: 15.4%; Speak English only: 61.9%; With disability: 12.2%; Veterans: 7.8%; Ancestry: 24.0% German, 23.5% Irish, 7.7% Albanian, 7.2% French, 7.2% West Indian

Employment: 28.1% management, business, and financial, 0.0% computer, engineering, and science, 5.9% education, legal, community service, arts, and media, 9.7% healthcare practitioners, 4.3% service, 27.0% sales and office, 21.6% natural resources, construction, and maintenance, 3.2% production, transportation, and material moving
Income: Per capita: $27,810; Median household: $76,635; Average household: $82,208; Households with income of $100,000 or more: 27.3%; Poverty rate: 7.2%
Educational Attainment: High school diploma or higher: 92.3%; Bachelor's degree or higher: 37.2%; Graduate/professional degree or higher: 18.6%

School District(s)
Wappingers Central SD (PK-12)
    Enrollment: 11,091 . . . . (845) 298-5000
Housing: Homeownership rate: 83.9%; Median home value: $265,100; Median year structure built: 1941; Homeowner vacancy rate: 0.0%; Median selected monthly owner costs: $2,306 with a mortgage, $688 without a mortgage; Median gross rent: n/a per month; Rental vacancy rate: 0.0%
Health Insurance: 100.0% have insurance; 96.4% have private insurance; 12.2% have public insurance; 0.0% do not have insurance; 0.0% of children under 18 do not have insurance
Transportation: Commute: 100.0% car, 0.0% public transportation, 0.0% walk, 0.0% work from home; Mean travel time to work: 39.0 minutes

HYDE PARK (CDP). Covers a land area of 1.206 square miles and a water area of 0.001 square miles. Located at 41.78° N. Lat; 73.93° W. Long. Elevation is 187 feet.
Population: 2,025; Growth (since 2000): n/a; Density: 1,679.6 persons per square mile; Race: 93.3% White, 4.0% Black/African American, 0.3% Asian, 0.8% American Indian/Alaska Native, 0.0% Native Hawaiian/Other Pacific Islander, 0.0% Two or more races, 5.6% Hispanic of any race; Average household size: 2.43; Median age: 44.6; Age under 18: 17.6%; Age 65 and over: 16.2%; Males per 100 females: 95.5; Marriage status: 31.5% never married, 48.0% now married, 0.2% separated, 9.8% widowed, 10.7% divorced; Foreign born: 2.3%; Speak English only: 93.6%; With disability: 13.0%; Veterans: 2.9%; Ancestry: 29.3% Irish, 21.4% Italian, 15.4% English, 14.6% German, 6.6% American
Employment: 11.2% management, business, and financial, 8.2% computer, engineering, and science, 16.1% education, legal, community service, arts, and media, 5.7% healthcare practitioners, 21.8% service, 30.9% sales and office, 0.0% natural resources, construction, and maintenance, 6.3% production, transportation, and material moving
Income: Per capita: $34,316; Median household: $78,333; Average household: $82,049; Households with income of $100,000 or more: 34.9%; Poverty rate: 9.7%
Educational Attainment: High school diploma or higher: 95.6%; Bachelor's degree or higher: 36.8%; Graduate/professional degree or higher: 18.2%

School District(s)
Hyde Park Central SD (KG-12)
    Enrollment: 3,734 . . . . (845) 229-4005
Four-year College(s)
Culinary Institute of America (Private, Not-for-profit)
    Enrollment: 3,131 . . . . (845) 452-9600
    Tuition: In-state $31,616; Out-of-state $31,616
Housing: Homeownership rate: 77.2%; Median home value: $229,300; Median year structure built: 1956; Homeowner vacancy rate: 0.0%; Median selected monthly owner costs: $1,895 with a mortgage, $714 without a mortgage; Median gross rent: $1,095 per month; Rental vacancy rate: 4.6%
Health Insurance: 98.0% have insurance; 82.2% have private insurance; 35.6% have public insurance; 2.0% do not have insurance; 0.0% of children under 18 do not have insurance
Transportation: Commute: 83.9% car, 7.8% public transportation, 2.6% walk, 5.7% work from home; Mean travel time to work: 27.5 minutes

HYDE PARK (town). Covers a land area of 36.663 square miles and a water area of 3.195 square miles. Located at 41.81° N. Lat; 73.90° W. Long. Elevation is 187 feet.
History: Site of Roosevelt estate, part of FDR National Historic Site where President Franklin D. Roosevelt was born and is buried. Roosevelt Library contains historical material dating from 1910 until Roosevelt's death. Adjacent is the Eleanor Roosevelt National Historic Site (Val-Kill), an estate built for Mrs. Roosevelt by her husband. Frederick W. Vanderbilt

mansion also here. All three homes are national historic sites. Seat of Culinary Institute of America. Settled c.1740.

Population: 21,215; Growth (since 2000): 1.7%; Density: 578.7 persons per square mile; Race: 85.8% White, 5.9% Black/African American, 3.9% Asian, 0.2% American Indian/Alaska Native, 0.0% Native Hawaiian/Other Pacific Islander, 2.1% Two or more races, 8.6% Hispanic of any race; Average household size: 2.58; Median age: 39.6; Age under 18: 17.8%; Age 65 and over: 16.9%; Males per 100 females: 98.9; Marriage status: 36.7% never married, 47.8% now married, 2.0% separated, 5.8% widowed, 9.7% divorced; Foreign born: 7.3%; Speak English only: 88.3%; With disability: 13.4%; Veterans: 6.0%; Ancestry: 22.8% Irish, 19.1% Italian, 17.9% German, 7.8% English, 6.0% Polish

Employment: 11.2% management, business, and financial, 6.2% computer, engineering, and science, 10.5% education, legal, community service, arts, and media, 5.4% healthcare practitioners, 21.4% service, 27.8% sales and office, 8.7% natural resources, construction, and maintenance, 8.7% production, transportation, and material moving

Income: Per capita: $32,512; Median household: $75,620; Average household: $89,226; Households with income of $100,000 or more: 34.1%; Poverty rate: 8.7%

Educational Attainment: High school diploma or higher: 91.2%; Bachelor's degree or higher: 28.3%; Graduate/professional degree or higher: 13.4%

School District(s)
Hyde Park Central SD (KG-12)
    Enrollment: 3,734 . . . . (845) 229-4005

Four-year College(s)
Culinary Institute of America (Private, Not-for-profit)
    Enrollment: 3,131 . . . . (845) 452-9600
    Tuition: In-state $31,616; Out-of-state $31,616

Housing: Homeownership rate: 73.6%; Median home value: $219,800; Median year structure built: 1966; Homeowner vacancy rate: 1.3%; Median selected monthly owner costs: $1,898 with a mortgage, $782 without a mortgage; Median gross rent: $1,078 per month; Rental vacancy rate: 4.6%

Health Insurance: 94.9% have insurance; 79.8% have private insurance; 29.5% have public insurance; 5.1% do not have insurance; 3.6% of children under 18 do not have insurance

Safety: Violent crime rate: 4.8 per 10,000 population; Property crime rate: 50.6 per 10,000 population

Transportation: Commute: 87.4% car, 2.9% public transportation, 4.4% walk, 4.6% work from home; Mean travel time to work: 27.7 minutes

Additional Information Contacts
Town of Hyde Park . . . . (845) 229-5111
    http://www.hydeparkny.us

LA GRANGE (town). Covers a land area of 39.879 square miles and a water area of 0.470 square miles. Located at 41.68° N. Lat; 73.80° W. Long.

History: The town was established in 1821 as "Freedom" from parts of the Towns of Beekman and Fishkill. Its name was changed to "LaGrange" in 1828.

Population: 15,680; Growth (since 2000): 5.0%; Density: 393.2 persons per square mile; Race: 89.3% White, 3.7% Black/African American, 5.5% Asian, 0.4% American Indian/Alaska Native, 0.0% Native Hawaiian/Other Pacific Islander, 0.6% Two or more races, 7.7% Hispanic of any race; Average household size: 2.89; Median age: 44.1; Age under 18: 23.4%; Age 65 and over: 15.1%; Males per 100 females: 98.6; Marriage status: 23.8% never married, 62.8% now married, 2.1% separated, 5.8% widowed, 7.5% divorced; Foreign born: 8.0%; Speak English only: 89.5%; With disability: 10.3%; Veterans: 7.7%; Ancestry: 23.6% Irish, 23.1% Italian, 15.2% German, 8.1% English, 6.3% Polish

Employment: 18.8% management, business, and financial, 7.6% computer, engineering, and science, 13.2% education, legal, community service, arts, and media, 6.9% healthcare practitioners, 14.4% service, 22.7% sales and office, 10.7% natural resources, construction, and maintenance, 5.8% production, transportation, and material moving

Income: Per capita: $46,480; Median household: $109,232; Average household: $133,153; Households with income of $100,000 or more: 57.2%; Poverty rate: 2.9%

Educational Attainment: High school diploma or higher: 93.9%; Bachelor's degree or higher: 44.4%; Graduate/professional degree or higher: 23.1%

Housing: Homeownership rate: 94.4%; Median home value: $297,100; Median year structure built: 1974; Homeowner vacancy rate: 1.5%; Median

selected monthly owner costs: $2,452 with a mortgage, $919 without a mortgage; Median gross rent: $1,401 per month; Rental vacancy rate: 5.6%

Health Insurance: 97.1% have insurance; 86.6% have private insurance; 25.4% have public insurance; 2.9% do not have insurance; 1.0% of children under 18 do not have insurance

Transportation: Commute: 90.3% car, 2.8% public transportation, 0.2% walk, 6.5% work from home; Mean travel time to work: 34.2 minutes

Additional Information Contacts
Town of La Grange . . . . (845) 452-1830
    http://www.lagrangeny.org

LAGRANGEVILLE (unincorporated postal area)
ZCTA: 12540

Covers a land area of 34.115 square miles and a water area of 0.300 square miles. Located at 41.67° N. Lat; 73.72° W. Long. Elevation is 358 feet.

Population: 7,940; Growth (since 2000): 19.7%; Density: 232.7 persons per square mile; Race: 92.3% White, 1.8% Black/African American, 4.1% Asian, 0.0% American Indian/Alaska Native, 0.0% Native Hawaiian/Other Pacific Islander, 1.6% Two or more races, 5.3% Hispanic of any race; Average household size: 2.92; Median age: 44.0; Age under 18: 24.0%; Age 65 and over: 14.5%; Males per 100 females: 101.0; Marriage status: 23.9% never married, 65.2% now married, 1.8% separated, 4.3% widowed, 6.6% divorced; Foreign born: 9.8%; Speak English only: 89.2%; With disability: 7.8%; Veterans: 8.4%; Ancestry: 25.9% Italian, 25.7% Irish, 18.3% German, 7.0% English, 6.3% Polish

Employment: 16.0% management, business, and financial, 8.7% computer, engineering, and science, 13.3% education, legal, community service, arts, and media, 6.5% healthcare practitioners, 12.4% service, 22.1% sales and office, 13.8% natural resources, construction, and maintenance, 7.2% production, transportation, and material moving

Income: Per capita: $44,244; Median household: $109,444; Average household: $127,632; Households with income of $100,000 or more: 55.7%; Poverty rate: 3.5%

Educational Attainment: High school diploma or higher: 95.5%; Bachelor's degree or higher: 44.4%; Graduate/professional degree or higher: 21.0%

School District(s)
Arlington Central SD (KG-12)
    Enrollment: 8,398 . . . . (845) 486-4460

Housing: Homeownership rate: 90.9%; Median home value: $332,200; Median year structure built: 1982; Homeowner vacancy rate: 1.6%; Median selected monthly owner costs: $2,477 with a mortgage, $1,070 without a mortgage; Median gross rent: $1,395 per month; Rental vacancy rate: 0.0%

Health Insurance: 97.2% have insurance; 86.9% have private insurance; 23.4% have public insurance; 2.8% do not have insurance; 0.2% of children under 18 do not have insurance

Transportation: Commute: 89.3% car, 1.9% public transportation, 0.7% walk, 6.7% work from home; Mean travel time to work: 37.9 minutes

MERRITT PARK (CDP). Covers a land area of 0.444 square miles and a water area of 0 square miles. Located at 41.54° N. Lat; 73.87° W. Long. Elevation is 220 feet.

Population: 1,654; Growth (since 2000): n/a; Density: 3,724.1 persons per square mile; Race: 46.4% White, 8.3% Black/African American, 42.2% Asian, 0.0% American Indian/Alaska Native, 0.0% Native Hawaiian/Other Pacific Islander, 2.7% Two or more races, 7.1% Hispanic of any race; Average household size: 2.92; Median age: 40.3; Age under 18: 30.1%; Age 65 and over: 10.7%; Males per 100 females: 90.3; Marriage status: 19.5% never married, 69.3% now married, 0.6% separated, 4.8% widowed, 6.4% divorced; Foreign born: 37.5%; Speak English only: 61.0%; With disability: 6.5%; Veterans: 5.1%; Ancestry: 14.2% Italian, 13.7% Irish, 4.5% German, 3.6% American, 3.1% Polish

Employment: 17.6% management, business, and financial, 26.1% computer, engineering, and science, 18.6% education, legal, community service, arts, and media, 5.7% healthcare practitioners, 6.0% service, 16.2% sales and office, 3.8% natural resources, construction, and maintenance, 5.9% production, transportation, and material moving

Income: Per capita: $51,147; Median household: $133,393; Average household: $148,072; Households with income of $100,000 or more: 74.0%; Poverty rate: 4.0%

Educational Attainment: High school diploma or higher: 99.6%; Bachelor's degree or higher: 66.8%; Graduate/professional degree or higher: 33.2%

Housing: Homeownership rate: 83.1%; Median home value: $391,200; Median year structure built: 2006; Homeowner vacancy rate: 0.0%; Median selected monthly owner costs: $3,109 with a mortgage, $1,283 without a mortgage; Median gross rent: $2,488 per month; Rental vacancy rate: 0.0%

Health Insurance: 98.8% have insurance; 90.3% have private insurance; 15.1% have public insurance; 1.2% do not have insurance; 3.2% of children under 18 do not have insurance

Transportation: Commute: 71.5% car, 18.3% public transportation, 1.7% walk, 8.5% work from home; Mean travel time to work: 46.6 minutes

MILAN (town). Covers a land area of 36.109 square miles and a water area of 0.468 square miles. Located at 41.98° N. Lat; 73.78° W. Long. Elevation is 433 feet.

Population: 2,308; Growth (since 2000): -49.4%; Density: 63.9 persons per square mile; Race: 91.4% White, 1.8% Black/African American, 0.9% Asian, 0.0% American Indian/Alaska Native, 0.0% Native Hawaiian/Other Pacific Islander, 4.7% Two or more races, 3.1% Hispanic of any race; Average household size: 2.34; Median age: 48.9; Age under 18: 19.8%; Age 65 and over: 20.6%; Males per 100 females: 106.4; Marriage status: 23.0% never married, 62.9% now married, 2.1% separated, 5.1% widowed, 9.0% divorced; Foreign born: 7.0%; Speak English only: 92.5%; With disability: 12.5%; Veterans: 7.8%; Ancestry: 23.1% German, 22.4% Irish, 14.4% Italian, 11.0% English, 8.6% American

Employment: 17.9% management, business, and financial, 5.5% computer, engineering, and science, 19.2% education, legal, community service, arts, and media, 6.0% healthcare practitioners, 12.3% service, 20.0% sales and office, 12.3% natural resources, construction, and maintenance, 6.8% production, transportation, and material moving

Income: Per capita: $45,006; Median household: $64,239; Average household: $105,326; Households with income of $100,000 or more: 33.3%; Poverty rate: 4.7%

Educational Attainment: High school diploma or higher: 95.9%; Bachelor's degree or higher: 43.5%; Graduate/professional degree or higher: 14.0%

Housing: Homeownership rate: 84.4%; Median home value: $330,500; Median year structure built: 1969; Homeowner vacancy rate: 2.5%; Median selected monthly owner costs: $2,144 with a mortgage, $814 without a mortgage; Median gross rent: $1,283 per month; Rental vacancy rate: 5.6%

Health Insurance: 97.5% have insurance; 86.4% have private insurance; 26.8% have public insurance; 2.5% do not have insurance; 1.3% of children under 18 do not have insurance

Transportation: Commute: 81.0% car, 7.3% public transportation, 3.7% walk, 8.0% work from home; Mean travel time to work: 35.9 minutes

MILLBROOK (village). Covers a land area of 1.931 square miles and a water area of 0.056 square miles. Located at 41.78° N. Lat; 73.69° W. Long. Elevation is 574 feet.

History: Seat of Institute of Ecosystem Studies— N.Y. Botanical Gardens; Millbrook Preparatory School. Many estates and second homes for New Yorkers. Noted for polo playing. Incorporated 1896.

Population: 1,515; Growth (since 2000): 6.0%; Density: 784.7 persons per square mile; Race: 89.2% White, 0.7% Black/African American, 1.5% Asian, 3.4% American Indian/Alaska Native, 0.0% Native Hawaiian/Other Pacific Islander, 4.0% Two or more races, 7.7% Hispanic of any race; Average household size: 2.12; Median age: 45.8; Age under 18: 17.4%; Age 65 and over: 25.0%; Males per 100 females: 87.1; Marriage status: 30.6% never married, 48.0% now married, 4.1% separated, 11.8% widowed, 9.5% divorced; Foreign born: 5.8%; Speak English only: 90.4%; With disability: 13.1%; Veterans: 5.8%; Ancestry: 35.1% Irish, 25.5% Italian, 15.8% English, 15.4% German, 7.5% American

Employment: 19.9% management, business, and financial, 5.1% computer, engineering, and science, 11.4% education, legal, community service, arts, and media, 9.3% healthcare practitioners, 20.6% service, 19.6% sales and office, 6.2% natural resources, construction, and maintenance, 8.0% production, transportation, and material moving

Income: Per capita: $46,374; Median household: $79,167; Average household: $97,378; Households with income of $100,000 or more: 34.7%; Poverty rate: 11.5%

Educational Attainment: High school diploma or higher: 93.0%; Bachelor's degree or higher: 43.3%; Graduate/professional degree or higher: 20.7%

School District(s)
Millbrook Central SD (KG-12)

   Enrollment: 1,008 . . . . (845) 677-4200

Housing: Homeownership rate: 50.3%; Median home value: $356,400; Median year structure built: 1963; Homeowner vacancy rate: 5.3%; Median selected monthly owner costs: $2,235 with a mortgage, $979 without a mortgage; Median gross rent: $1,138 per month; Rental vacancy rate: 2.2%

Health Insurance: 92.3% have insurance; 77.9% have private insurance; 31.1% have public insurance; 7.7% do not have insurance; 8.8% of children under 18 do not have insurance

Transportation: Commute: 79.1% car, 1.8% public transportation, 12.3% walk, 6.9% work from home; Mean travel time to work: 23.9 minutes

MILLERTON (village). Covers a land area of 0.618 square miles and a water area of 0.003 square miles. Located at 41.95° N. Lat; 73.51° W. Long. Elevation is 709 feet.

Population: 888; Growth (since 2000): -4.0%; Density: 1,435.8 persons per square mile; Race: 79.6% White, 2.6% Black/African American, 9.6% Asian, 0.0% American Indian/Alaska Native, 0.0% Native Hawaiian/Other Pacific Islander, 5.6% Two or more races, 9.5% Hispanic of any race; Average household size: 2.12; Median age: 40.6; Age under 18: 14.3%; Age 65 and over: 16.8%; Males per 100 females: 100.4; Marriage status: 42.3% never married, 45.8% now married, 2.2% separated, 6.2% widowed, 5.7% divorced; Foreign born: 13.7%; Speak English only: 85.7%; With disability: 19.9%; Veterans: 6.8%; Ancestry: 32.1% Irish, 18.8% Italian, 15.4% German, 7.3% English, 4.3% French

Employment: 13.1% management, business, and financial, 1.6% computer, engineering, and science, 9.1% education, legal, community service, arts, and media, 2.8% healthcare practitioners, 31.7% service, 20.0% sales and office, 9.1% natural resources, construction, and maintenance, 12.7% production, transportation, and material moving

Income: Per capita: $29,213; Median household: $46,667; Average household: $60,856; Households with income of $100,000 or more: 14.6%; Poverty rate: 16.9%

Educational Attainment: High school diploma or higher: 82.2%; Bachelor's degree or higher: 21.4%; Graduate/professional degree or higher: 2.3%

Housing: Homeownership rate: 55.4%; Median home value: $219,500; Median year structure built: Before 1940; Homeowner vacancy rate: 3.4%; Median selected monthly owner costs: $1,630 with a mortgage, $764 without a mortgage; Median gross rent: $885 per month; Rental vacancy rate: 0.0%

Health Insurance: 81.1% have insurance; 54.1% have private insurance; 39.2% have public insurance; 18.9% do not have insurance; 7.4% of children under 18 do not have insurance

Newspapers: Millerton News (weekly circulation 2,000)

Transportation: Commute: 83.1% car, 0.0% public transportation, 12.0% walk, 5.0% work from home; Mean travel time to work: 15.6 minutes

MYERS CORNER (CDP). Covers a land area of 5.017 square miles and a water area of 0.039 square miles. Located at 41.60° N. Lat; 73.87° W. Long. Elevation is 217 feet.

Population: 6,715; Growth (since 2000): 21.1%; Density: 1,338.5 persons per square mile; Race: 84.8% White, 1.0% Black/African American, 12.6% Asian, 0.2% American Indian/Alaska Native, 0.0% Native Hawaiian/Other Pacific Islander, 0.7% Two or more races, 10.5% Hispanic of any race; Average household size: 2.87; Median age: 43.4; Age under 18: 22.5%; Age 65 and over: 15.1%; Males per 100 females: 96.8; Marriage status: 22.0% never married, 67.3% now married, 0.7% separated, 4.7% widowed, 5.9% divorced; Foreign born: 10.7%; Speak English only: 80.6%; With disability: 9.3%; Veterans: 6.0%; Ancestry: 20.7% Italian, 17.6% Irish, 12.6% German, 6.6% English, 4.6% Polish

Employment: 21.7% management, business, and financial, 5.5% computer, engineering, and science, 11.8% education, legal, community service, arts, and media, 5.8% healthcare practitioners, 13.3% service, 26.9% sales and office, 7.7% natural resources, construction, and maintenance, 7.3% production, transportation, and material moving

Income: Per capita: $41,697; Median household: $100,125; Average household: $118,335; Households with income of $100,000 or more: 50.0%; Poverty rate: 2.4%

Educational Attainment: High school diploma or higher: 94.9%; Bachelor's degree or higher: 44.3%; Graduate/professional degree or higher: 20.1%

Housing: Homeownership rate: 93.1%; Median home value: $307,400; Median year structure built: 1975; Homeowner vacancy rate: 6.6%; Median selected monthly owner costs: $2,267 with a mortgage, $897 without a mortgage; Median gross rent: $1,913 per month; Rental vacancy rate: 23.7%

Health Insurance: 95.8% have insurance; 86.7% have private insurance; 23.0% have public insurance; 4.2% do not have insurance; 4.0% of children under 18 do not have insurance

Transportation: Commute: 86.0% car, 5.8% public transportation, 1.1% walk, 5.4% work from home; Mean travel time to work: 37.6 minutes

NORTH EAST (town).
Covers a land area of 43.163 square miles and a water area of 0.559 square miles. Located at 41.95° N. Lat; 73.55° W. Long.

Population: 2,997; Growth (since 2000): -0.2%; Density: 69.4 persons per square mile; Race: 89.4% White, 3.6% Black/African American, 3.1% Asian, 0.0% American Indian/Alaska Native, 0.0% Native Hawaiian/Other Pacific Islander, 3.2% Two or more races, 16.2% Hispanic of any race; Average household size: 2.46; Median age: 44.1; Age under 18: 16.4%; Age 65 and over: 18.3%; Males per 100 females: 103.3; Marriage status: 35.0% never married, 47.9% now married, 2.2% separated, 7.6% widowed, 9.5% divorced; Foreign born: 12.4%; Speak English only: 82.5%; With disability: 16.0%; Veterans: 7.2%; Ancestry: 26.5% Irish, 14.3% German, 10.6% English, 10.4% Italian, 4.9% American

Employment: 10.3% management, business, and financial, 4.1% computer, engineering, and science, 8.7% education, legal, community service, arts, and media, 2.1% healthcare practitioners, 35.8% service, 13.4% sales and office, 17.0% natural resources, construction, and maintenance, 8.5% production, transportation, and material moving

Income: Per capita: $30,175; Median household: $60,536; Average household: $72,030; Households with income of $100,000 or more: 20.6%; Poverty rate: 8.4%

Educational Attainment: High school diploma or higher: 83.7%; Bachelor's degree or higher: 27.4%; Graduate/professional degree or higher: 8.5%

Housing: Homeownership rate: 61.4%; Median home value: $250,300; Median year structure built: 1959; Homeowner vacancy rate: 3.4%; Median selected monthly owner costs: $1,728 with a mortgage, $762 without a mortgage; Median gross rent: $1,057 per month; Rental vacancy rate: 4.1%

Health Insurance: 87.7% have insurance; 64.3% have private insurance; 36.9% have public insurance; 12.3% do not have insurance; 2.8% of children under 18 do not have insurance

Transportation: Commute: 84.5% car, 3.7% public transportation, 7.4% walk, 4.4% work from home; Mean travel time to work: 25.9 minutes

PAWLING (town).
Covers a land area of 43.835 square miles and a water area of 1.187 square miles. Located at 41.57° N. Lat; 73.60° W. Long. Elevation is 463 feet.

History: In 1937, Thomas E. Dewey, three-term governor and two-time nominee for U.S. president, purchased a 486-acre farm here, although his legal address was the Roosevelt Hotel in N.Y. city. When he returned to legal practice after being governor, he resided at the World Trade Center. He and his wife are buried in Pawling Cemetery. Settled by Quakers c.1740; Incorporated 1893.

Population: 8,336; Growth (since 2000): 10.8%; Density: 190.2 persons per square mile; Race: 90.9% White, 2.6% Black/African American, 1.2% Asian, 0.0% American Indian/Alaska Native, 0.0% Native Hawaiian/Other Pacific Islander, 1.8% Two or more races, 10.0% Hispanic of any race; Average household size: 2.57; Median age: 45.9; Age under 18: 20.8%; Age 65 and over: 17.6%; Males per 100 females: 105.9; Marriage status: 31.0% never married, 51.6% now married, 0.7% separated, 6.4% widowed, 10.9% divorced; Foreign born: 9.1%; Speak English only: 86.1%; With disability: 12.1%; Veterans: 6.5%; Ancestry: 26.3% Italian, 22.5% Irish, 14.4% German, 8.6% English, 6.0% American

Employment: 16.7% management, business, and financial, 3.4% computer, engineering, and science, 14.7% education, legal, community service, arts, and media, 3.9% healthcare practitioners, 18.7% service, 22.9% sales and office, 12.2% natural resources, construction, and maintenance, 7.5% production, transportation, and material moving

Income: Per capita: $40,892; Median household: $82,328; Average household: $104,949; Households with income of $100,000 or more: 41.5%; Poverty rate: 7.6%

Educational Attainment: High school diploma or higher: 93.5%; Bachelor's degree or higher: 34.6%; Graduate/professional degree or higher: 13.8%

School District(s)
Pawling Central SD (KG-12)
    Enrollment: 1,179 . . . . (845) 855-4600

Housing: Homeownership rate: 73.2%; Median home value: $297,300; Median year structure built: 1967; Homeowner vacancy rate: 1.4%; Median selected monthly owner costs: $2,434 with a mortgage, $1,116 without a mortgage; Median gross rent: $1,081 per month; Rental vacancy rate: 4.0%

Health Insurance: 92.4% have insurance; 78.4% have private insurance; 26.6% have public insurance; 7.6% do not have insurance; 1.7% of children under 18 do not have insurance

Transportation: Commute: 83.2% car, 9.3% public transportation, 3.0% walk, 4.1% work from home; Mean travel time to work: 41.2 minutes

Additional Information Contacts

Town of Pawling . . . . (845) 855-5040
    http://www.pawling.org/Pages/index

PAWLING (village).
Covers a land area of 1.997 square miles and a water area of <.001 square miles. Located at 41.56° N. Lat; 73.60° W. Long. Elevation is 463 feet.

Population: 2,053; Growth (since 2000): -8.1%; Density: 1,028.3 persons per square mile; Race: 89.9% White, 4.5% Black/African American, 0.9% Asian, 0.0% American Indian/Alaska Native, 0.0% Native Hawaiian/Other Pacific Islander, 1.1% Two or more races, 13.2% Hispanic of any race; Average household size: 2.23; Median age: 46.3; Age under 18: 17.9%; Age 65 and over: 20.9%; Males per 100 females: 119.6; Marriage status: 36.7% never married, 37.4% now married, 0.3% separated, 9.0% widowed, 16.9% divorced; Foreign born: 11.1%; Speak English only: 83.1%; With disability: 18.5%; Veterans: 7.7%; Ancestry: 27.9% Italian, 20.1% Irish, 10.8% English, 9.8% German, 5.1% American

Employment: 16.2% management, business, and financial, 2.9% computer, engineering, and science, 12.0% education, legal, community service, arts, and media, 6.6% healthcare practitioners, 22.6% service, 24.4% sales and office, 8.3% natural resources, construction, and maintenance, 6.9% production, transportation, and material moving

Income: Per capita: $34,125; Median household: $62,852; Average household: $74,170; Households with income of $100,000 or more: 26.8%; Poverty rate: 9.1%

Educational Attainment: High school diploma or higher: 92.5%; Bachelor's degree or higher: 34.3%; Graduate/professional degree or higher: 16.8%

School District(s)
Pawling Central SD (KG-12)
    Enrollment: 1,179 . . . . (845) 855-4600

Housing: Homeownership rate: 53.9%; Median home value: $273,600; Median year structure built: 1953; Homeowner vacancy rate: 0.0%; Median selected monthly owner costs: $2,416 with a mortgage, $909 without a mortgage; Median gross rent: $876 per month; Rental vacancy rate: 2.9%

Health Insurance: 89.2% have insurance; 70.5% have private insurance; 33.2% have public insurance; 10.8% do not have insurance; 0.0% of children under 18 do not have insurance

Transportation: Commute: 83.4% car, 8.1% public transportation, 5.8% walk, 2.6% work from home; Mean travel time to work: 38.6 minutes

PINE PLAINS (CDP).
Covers a land area of 2.078 square miles and a water area of 0.224 square miles. Located at 41.98° N. Lat; 73.66° W. Long. Elevation is 469 feet.

Population: 1,430; Growth (since 2000): 1.3%; Density: 688.1 persons per square mile; Race: 99.2% White, 0.0% Black/African American, 0.0% Asian, 0.0% American Indian/Alaska Native, 0.0% Native Hawaiian/Other Pacific Islander, 0.8% Two or more races, 7.2% Hispanic of any race; Average household size: 2.50; Median age: 41.6; Age under 18: 22.6%; Age 65 and over: 20.3%; Males per 100 females: 92.2; Marriage status: 27.8% never married, 53.8% now married, 2.5% separated, 12.7% widowed, 5.7% divorced; Foreign born: 6.2%; Speak English only: 92.7%; With disability: 20.7%; Veterans: 4.6%; Ancestry: 23.4% Italian, 23.3% German, 23.1% Irish, 14.7% English, 9.7% Dutch

Employment: 13.5% management, business, and financial, 3.2% computer, engineering, and science, 13.3% education, legal, community

service, arts, and media, 4.4% healthcare practitioners, 22.2% service, 21.1% sales and office, 12.7% natural resources, construction, and maintenance, 9.5% production, transportation, and material moving
Income: Per capita: $32,001; Median household: $53,317; Average household: $78,673; Households with income of $100,000 or more: 20.4%; Poverty rate: 10.1%
Educational Attainment: High school diploma or higher: 92.6%; Bachelor's degree or higher: 15.9%; Graduate/professional degree or higher: 10.1%

School District(s)
Pine Plains Central SD (PK-12)
    Enrollment: 993. . . . . (518) 398-7181
Housing: Homeownership rate: 69.7%; Median home value: $221,300; Median year structure built: 1958; Homeowner vacancy rate: 0.0%; Median selected monthly owner costs: $1,632 with a mortgage, $560 without a mortgage; Median gross rent: $1,426 per month; Rental vacancy rate: 0.0%
Health Insurance: 98.6% have insurance; 70.8% have private insurance; 45.9% have public insurance; 1.4% do not have insurance; 0.0% of children under 18 do not have insurance
Transportation: Commute: 89.2% car, 1.0% public transportation, 5.9% walk, 3.9% work from home; Mean travel time to work: 23.9 minutes

PINE PLAINS (town). Covers a land area of 30.583 square miles and a water area of 0.589 square miles. Located at 41.97° N. Lat; 73.65° W. Long. Elevation is 469 feet.
Population: 2,504; Growth (since 2000): -2.5%; Density: 81.9 persons per square mile; Race: 98.0% White, 0.6% Black/African American, 0.2% Asian, 0.0% American Indian/Alaska Native, 0.0% Native Hawaiian/Other Pacific Islander, 0.5% Two or more races, 5.0% Hispanic of any race; Average household size: 2.37; Median age: 46.2; Age under 18: 17.8%; Age 65 and over: 19.5%; Males per 100 females: 94.7; Marriage status: 27.8% never married, 54.3% now married, 2.2% separated, 10.9% widowed, 7.1% divorced; Foreign born: 7.3%; Speak English only: 91.2%; With disability: 19.1%; Veterans: 7.5%; Ancestry: 22.1% Irish, 19.7% German, 19.5% Italian, 11.9% English, 8.7% American
Employment: 17.4% management, business, and financial, 4.3% computer, engineering, and science, 10.6% education, legal, community service, arts, and media, 4.6% healthcare practitioners, 21.7% service, 20.0% sales and office, 11.3% natural resources, construction, and maintenance, 10.1% production, transportation, and material moving
Income: Per capita: $35,920; Median household: $56,912; Average household: $83,586; Households with income of $100,000 or more: 24.2%; Poverty rate: 13.6%
Educational Attainment: High school diploma or higher: 86.2%; Bachelor's degree or higher: 20.8%; Graduate/professional degree or higher: 8.2%

School District(s)
Pine Plains Central SD (PK-12)
    Enrollment: 993. . . . . (518) 398-7181
Housing: Homeownership rate: 73.4%; Median home value: $240,400; Median year structure built: 1969; Homeowner vacancy rate: 2.4%; Median selected monthly owner costs: $1,742 with a mortgage, $663 without a mortgage; Median gross rent: $1,159 per month; Rental vacancy rate: 0.0%
Health Insurance: 96.4% have insurance; 70.1% have private insurance; 42.8% have public insurance; 3.6% do not have insurance; 0.0% of children under 18 do not have insurance
Safety: Violent crime rate: 0.0 per 10,000 population; Property crime rate: 0.0 per 10,000 population
Transportation: Commute: 82.3% car, 1.3% public transportation, 7.2% walk, 9.3% work from home; Mean travel time to work: 24.6 minutes
Additional Information Contacts
Town of Pine Plains. . . . . (518) 398-7155
    http://pineplains-ny.gov/content

PLEASANT VALLEY (CDP). Covers a land area of 0.934 square miles and a water area of 0.025 square miles. Located at 41.75° N. Lat; 73.83° W. Long. Elevation is 187 feet.
Population: 1,599; Growth (since 2000): -13.1%; Density: 1,711.2 persons per square mile; Race: 87.6% White, 9.3% Black/African American, 0.0% Asian, 0.0% American Indian/Alaska Native, 0.0% Native Hawaiian/Other Pacific Islander, 3.1% Two or more races, 1.7% Hispanic of any race; Average household size: 2.20; Median age: 39.6; Age under 18: 14.7%; Age 65 and over: 14.7%; Males per 100 females: 90.2; Marriage status:

30.2% never married, 50.2% now married, 0.0% separated, 9.1% widowed, 10.5% divorced; Foreign born: 7.8%; Speak English only: 97.5%; With disability: 16.5%; Veterans: 6.7%; Ancestry: 29.9% Italian, 16.6% German, 9.8% English, 9.1% Irish, 7.1% American
Employment: 13.0% management, business, and financial, 1.2% computer, engineering, and science, 18.5% education, legal, community service, arts, and media, 5.3% healthcare practitioners, 22.3% service, 26.0% sales and office, 11.4% natural resources, construction, and maintenance, 2.3% production, transportation, and material moving
Income: Per capita: $30,621; Median household: $65,046; Average household: $67,059; Households with income of $100,000 or more: 20.0%; Poverty rate: 14.1%
Educational Attainment: High school diploma or higher: 91.7%; Bachelor's degree or higher: 35.4%; Graduate/professional degree or higher: 18.9%

School District(s)
Arlington Central SD (KG-12)
    Enrollment: 8,398 . . . . (845) 486-4460
Housing: Homeownership rate: 38.9%; Median home value: $235,900; Median year structure built: 1976; Homeowner vacancy rate: 0.0%; Median selected monthly owner costs: $1,726 with a mortgage, $905 without a mortgage; Median gross rent: $1,547 per month; Rental vacancy rate: 0.0%
Health Insurance: 94.0% have insurance; 80.2% have private insurance; 29.5% have public insurance; 6.0% do not have insurance; 0.0% of children under 18 do not have insurance
Transportation: Commute: 97.5% car, 0.0% public transportation, 0.0% walk, 2.5% work from home; Mean travel time to work: 26.7 minutes

PLEASANT VALLEY (town). Covers a land area of 32.576 square miles and a water area of 0.564 square miles. Located at 41.77° N. Lat; 73.80° W. Long. Elevation is 187 feet.
History: Settlers arrived to the area after 1735. The town was part of the Great Nine Partners Patent of 1697, a land grant whose legality was questioned due to extortion and threats of violence.
Population: 9,769; Growth (since 2000): 7.8%; Density: 299.9 persons per square mile; Race: 86.9% White, 5.7% Black/African American, 1.8% Asian, 0.0% American Indian/Alaska Native, 0.0% Native Hawaiian/Other Pacific Islander, 2.2% Two or more races, 6.9% Hispanic of any race; Average household size: 2.43; Median age: 42.1; Age under 18: 20.1%; Age 65 and over: 13.1%; Males per 100 females: 95.6; Marriage status: 26.9% never married, 57.2% now married, 2.8% separated, 5.2% widowed, 10.7% divorced; Foreign born: 9.0%; Speak English only: 90.3%; With disability: 13.6%; Veterans: 6.7%; Ancestry: 25.0% Italian, 21.7% Irish, 17.9% German, 9.2% English, 6.1% American
Employment: 16.4% management, business, and financial, 5.4% computer, engineering, and science, 13.4% education, legal, community service, arts, and media, 4.5% healthcare practitioners, 14.4% service, 24.2% sales and office, 13.4% natural resources, construction, and maintenance, 8.4% production, transportation, and material moving
Income: Per capita: $36,929; Median household: $77,750; Average household: $88,630; Households with income of $100,000 or more: 34.2%; Poverty rate: 8.2%
Educational Attainment: High school diploma or higher: 91.7%; Bachelor's degree or higher: 30.0%; Graduate/professional degree or higher: 13.6%

School District(s)
Arlington Central SD (KG-12)
    Enrollment: 8,398 . . . . (845) 486-4460
Housing: Homeownership rate: 65.9%; Median home value: $244,600; Median year structure built: 1971; Homeowner vacancy rate: 3.6%; Median selected monthly owner costs: $2,107 with a mortgage, $859 without a mortgage; Median gross rent: $1,328 per month; Rental vacancy rate: 3.9%
Health Insurance: 92.8% have insurance; 75.7% have private insurance; 29.1% have public insurance; 7.2% do not have insurance; 1.9% of children under 18 do not have insurance
Transportation: Commute: 92.3% car, 1.6% public transportation, 0.9% walk, 4.8% work from home; Mean travel time to work: 31.3 minutes
Additional Information Contacts
Town of Pleasant Valley . . . . (845) 635-3274
    http://pleasantvalley-ny.gov

POUGHKEEPSIE (city). County seat. Covers a land area of 5.144 square miles and a water area of 0.575 square miles. Located at 41.69° N. Lat; 73.92° W. Long. Elevation is 200 feet.

History: It became the temporary state capital in 1777, and the U.S. Constitution was ratified (1788) here. Seat of Vassar and Marist Colleges and a community college. Several historic 18th-century buildings still stand. Hyde Park lies just north. Settled 1687 by the Dutch, Incorporated as a city 1854.

Population: 30,505; Growth (since 2000): 2.1%; Density: 5,930.4 persons per square mile; Race: 48.1% White, 37.6% Black/African American, 1.3% Asian, 0.4% American Indian/Alaska Native, 0.0% Native Hawaiian/Other Pacific Islander, 5.2% Two or more races, 17.8% Hispanic of any race; Average household size: 2.34; Median age: 37.7; Age under 18: 20.8%; Age 65 and over: 15.0%; Males per 100 females: 92.4; Marriage status: 47.6% never married, 36.2% now married, 3.7% separated, 5.8% widowed, 10.3% divorced; Foreign born: 19.1%; Speak English only: 78.8%; With disability: 16.2%; Veterans: 5.4%; Ancestry: 12.4% Irish, 11.8% Italian, 7.3% German, 6.8% Jamaican, 5.3% American

Employment: 7.8% management, business, and financial, 4.3% computer, engineering, and science, 11.9% education, legal, community service, arts, and media, 5.3% healthcare practitioners, 29.0% service, 24.2% sales and office, 8.0% natural resources, construction, and maintenance, 9.5% production, transportation, and material moving

Income: Per capita: $26,105; Median household: $40,840; Average household: $59,148; Households with income of $100,000 or more: 14.6%; Poverty rate: 22.4%

Educational Attainment: High school diploma or higher: 81.7%; Bachelor's degree or higher: 23.6%; Graduate/professional degree or higher: 9.7%

School District(s)
Arlington Central SD (KG-12)
   Enrollment: 8,398 . . . . (845) 486-4460
Dutchess Boces
   Enrollment: n/a . . . . (845) 486-4800
Hyde Park Central SD (KG-12)
   Enrollment: 3,734 . . . . (845) 229-4005
Poughkeepsie City SD (PK-12)
   Enrollment: 4,491 . . . . (845) 451-4950
Spackenkill Union Free SD (KG-12)
   Enrollment: 1,439 . . . . (845) 463-7800
Wappingers Central SD (PK-12)
   Enrollment: 11,091 . . . . (845) 298-5000

Four-year College(s)
Marist College (Private, Not-for-profit)
   Enrollment: 6,657 . . . . (845) 575-3000
   Tuition: In-state $36,780; Out-of-state $36,780
Vassar College (Private, Not-for-profit)
   Enrollment: 2,353 . . . . (845) 437-7000
   Tuition: In-state $55,210; Out-of-state $55,210

Two-year College(s)
Dutchess Community College (Public)
   Enrollment: 9,061 . . . . (845) 431-8000
   Tuition: In-state $4,236; Out-of-state $7,932

Vocational/Technical School(s)
Dutchess BOCES-Practical Nursing Program (Public)
   Enrollment: 132 . . . . (845) 486-8001
   Tuition: $10,175
Ridley-Lowell Business & Technical Institute-Poughkeepsie (Private, For-profit)
   Enrollment: n/a . . . . (845) 471-0330
   Tuition: $15,500

Housing: Homeownership rate: 35.2%; Median home value: $190,400; Median year structure built: 1954; Homeowner vacancy rate: 5.5%; Median selected monthly owner costs: $1,904 with a mortgage, $803 without a mortgage; Median gross rent: $1,095 per month; Rental vacancy rate: 6.0%

Health Insurance: 89.0% have insurance; 52.9% have private insurance; 49.2% have public insurance; 11.0% do not have insurance; 2.8% of children under 18 do not have insurance

Hospitals: Saint Francis Hospital (400 beds); Vassar Brothers Medical Center (365 beds)

Safety: Violent crime rate: 70.6 per 10,000 population; Property crime rate: 199.9 per 10,000 population

Newspapers: Poughkeepsie Journal (daily circulation 37,700)

Transportation: Commute: 75.1% car, 9.7% public transportation, 10.8% walk, 1.6% work from home; Mean travel time to work: 25.8 minutes; Amtrak: Train service available.

Airports: Dutchess County (general aviation)

Additional Information Contacts
City of Poughkeepsie . . . . (845) 451-4276
   http://www.cityofpoughkeepsie.com

POUGHKEEPSIE (town). Covers a land area of 28.514 square miles and a water area of 2.630 square miles. Located at 41.67° N. Lat; 73.91° W. Long. Elevation is 200 feet.

History: The name of Poughkeepsie had its origins in a Native American name, the original probably meaning "reed-covered lodge by the little water place." The first record of European settlement dates from 1683. Growth at first was slow, but in 1777 Poughkeepsie was made the capital of the state. The chief event in the history of the town was the ratification of the Federal Constitution by the State on July 26, 1788. Early in the 19th century, Poughkeepsie became prominent as a river port. With the opening of the Erie Canal in 1825, however, competition caused a decline in the value of Dutchess County produce. Poughkeepsie turned to industry and trade. It also acquired a reputation as an educational center, with the most important advance being the founding of Vassar College in 1861.

Population: 44,513; Growth (since 2000): 4.1%; Density: 1,561.1 persons per square mile; Race: 72.9% White, 13.3% Black/African American, 6.0% Asian, 0.3% American Indian/Alaska Native, 0.1% Native Hawaiian/Other Pacific Islander, 3.4% Two or more races, 12.7% Hispanic of any race; Average household size: 2.57; Median age: 36.9; Age under 18: 19.3%; Age 65 and over: 15.7%; Males per 100 females: 91.4; Marriage status: 40.1% never married, 46.0% now married, 2.2% separated, 6.0% widowed, 7.9% divorced; Foreign born: 13.3%; Speak English only: 81.2%; With disability: 12.0%; Veterans: 5.4%; Ancestry: 20.0% Italian, 17.0% Irish, 12.4% German, 6.6% English, 5.3% Polish

Employment: 12.2% management, business, and financial, 7.7% computer, engineering, and science, 15.3% education, legal, community service, arts, and media, 5.7% healthcare practitioners, 19.4% service, 24.9% sales and office, 5.7% natural resources, construction, and maintenance, 9.2% production, transportation, and material moving

Income: Per capita: $33,498; Median household: $74,349; Average household: $94,389; Households with income of $100,000 or more: 35.7%; Poverty rate: 8.5%

Educational Attainment: High school diploma or higher: 91.5%; Bachelor's degree or higher: 37.2%; Graduate/professional degree or higher: 18.3%

School District(s)
Arlington Central SD (KG-12)
   Enrollment: 8,398 . . . . (845) 486-4460
Dutchess Boces
   Enrollment: n/a . . . . (845) 486-4800
Hyde Park Central SD (KG-12)
   Enrollment: 3,734 . . . . (845) 229-4005
Poughkeepsie City SD (PK-12)
   Enrollment: 4,491 . . . . (845) 451-4950
Spackenkill Union Free SD (KG-12)
   Enrollment: 1,439 . . . . (845) 463-7800
Wappingers Central SD (PK-12)
   Enrollment: 11,091 . . . . (845) 298-5000

Four-year College(s)
Marist College (Private, Not-for-profit)
   Enrollment: 6,657 . . . . (845) 575-3000
   Tuition: In-state $36,780; Out-of-state $36,780
Vassar College (Private, Not-for-profit)
   Enrollment: 2,353 . . . . (845) 437-7000
   Tuition: In-state $55,210; Out-of-state $55,210

Two-year College(s)
Dutchess Community College (Public)
   Enrollment: 9,061 . . . . (845) 431-8000
   Tuition: In-state $4,236; Out-of-state $7,932

Vocational/Technical School(s)
Dutchess BOCES-Practical Nursing Program (Public)
   Enrollment: 132 . . . . (845) 486-8001
   Tuition: $10,175
Ridley-Lowell Business & Technical Institute-Poughkeepsie (Private, For-profit)
   Enrollment: n/a . . . . (845) 471-0330
   Tuition: $15,500

Housing: Homeownership rate: 69.3%; Median home value: $241,900; Median year structure built: 1966; Homeowner vacancy rate: 3.0%; Median selected monthly owner costs: $2,143 with a mortgage, $900 without a mortgage; Median gross rent: $1,158 per month; Rental vacancy rate: 4.2%

Health Insurance: 96.2% have insurance; 80.1% have private insurance; 29.3% have public insurance; 3.8% do not have insurance; 2.4% of children under 18 do not have insurance

Hospitals: Saint Francis Hospital (400 beds); Vassar Brothers Medical Center (365 beds)

Newspapers: Poughkeepsie Journal (daily circulation 37,700)

Transportation: Commute: 78.6% car, 4.8% public transportation, 9.7% walk, 5.6% work from home; Mean travel time to work: 26.4 minutes; Amtrak: Train service available.

Airports: Dutchess County (general aviation)

Additional Information Contacts

Town of Poughkeepsie . . . . (845) 485-3600
http://www.townofpoughkeepsie.com

POUGHQUAG (unincorporated postal area)

ZCTA: 12570

Covers a land area of 21.510 square miles and a water area of 0.266 square miles. Located at 41.63° N. Lat; 73.68° W. Long. Elevation is 436 feet.

Population: 7,463; Growth (since 2000): 26.8%; Density: 346.9 persons per square mile; Race: 93.6% White, 1.5% Black/African American, 1.7% Asian, 0.7% American Indian/Alaska Native, 0.0% Native Hawaiian/Other Pacific Islander, 2.2% Two or more races, 10.5% Hispanic of any race; Average household size: 2.90; Median age: 44.4; Age under 18: 22.1%; Age 65 and over: 14.2%; Males per 100 females: 98.7; Marriage status: 28.5% never married, 63.1% now married, 1.0% separated, 4.8% widowed, 3.6% divorced; Foreign born: 5.3%; Speak English only: 90.5%; With disability: 10.8%; Veterans: 4.9%; Ancestry: 30.3% Italian, 27.6% Irish, 18.7% German, 8.8% English, 7.2% American

Employment: 18.8% management, business, and financial, 6.0% computer, engineering, and science, 14.6% education, legal, community service, arts, and media, 6.2% healthcare practitioners, 13.6% service, 22.8% sales and office, 11.0% natural resources, construction, and maintenance, 7.1% production, transportation, and material moving

Income: Per capita: $43,822; Median household: $102,835; Average household: $125,436; Households with income of $100,000 or more: 50.9%; Poverty rate: 1.6%

Educational Attainment: High school diploma or higher: 95.2%; Bachelor's degree or higher: 40.7%; Graduate/professional degree or higher: 19.7%

School District(s)

Arlington Central SD (KG-12)

Enrollment: 8,398 . . . . (845) 486-4460

Housing: Homeownership rate: 90.4%; Median home value: $341,900; Median year structure built: 1989; Homeowner vacancy rate: 0.5%; Median selected monthly owner costs: $2,748 with a mortgage, $925 without a mortgage; Median gross rent: $1,582 per month; Rental vacancy rate: 0.0%

Health Insurance: 94.9% have insurance; 88.5% have private insurance; 20.5% have public insurance; 5.1% do not have insurance; 5.6% of children under 18 do not have insurance

Transportation: Commute: 87.9% car, 3.6% public transportation, 0.2% walk, 6.7% work from home; Mean travel time to work: 37.7 minutes

---

RED HOOK (town). Covers a land area of 36.169 square miles and a water area of 3.871 square miles. Located at 42.02° N. Lat; 73.89° W. Long. Elevation is 220 feet.

History: The region was settled in the late 17th century under the Schuyler Patent. Prior to 1812, Red Hook was part of the Town of Rhinebeck, but because its population was over 5,000, the Albany Legislature authorized the separation of the two precincts to encourage public attendance at town meetings via horseback or carriage.

Population: 11,238; Growth (since 2000): 8.0%; Density: 310.7 persons per square mile; Race: 90.1% White, 2.4% Black/African American, 3.3% Asian, 0.5% American Indian/Alaska Native, 0.0% Native Hawaiian/Other Pacific Islander, 1.6% Two or more races, 6.7% Hispanic of any race; Average household size: 2.46; Median age: 36.7; Age under 18: 18.4%; Age 65 and over: 16.0%; Males per 100 females: 94.5; Marriage status: 42.3% never married, 44.9% now married, 1.4% separated, 4.7%

widowed, 8.2% divorced; Foreign born: 8.5%; Speak English only: 90.0%; With disability: 12.1%; Veterans: 5.9%; Ancestry: 21.1% Irish, 20.3% German, 14.0% Italian, 8.3% English, 6.6% American

Employment: 13.8% management, business, and financial, 7.7% computer, engineering, and science, 19.3% education, legal, community service, arts, and media, 4.8% healthcare practitioners, 21.1% service, 20.5% sales and office, 6.3% natural resources, construction, and maintenance, 6.6% production, transportation, and material moving

Income: Per capita: $33,982; Median household: $75,963; Average household: $94,981; Households with income of $100,000 or more: 35.3%; Poverty rate: 10.1%

Educational Attainment: High school diploma or higher: 93.3%; Bachelor's degree or higher: 43.9%; Graduate/professional degree or higher: 23.5%

School District(s)

Red Hook Central SD (PK-12)

Enrollment: 1,936 . . . . (845) 758-2241

Housing: Homeownership rate: 70.0%; Median home value: $279,100; Median year structure built: 1969; Homeowner vacancy rate: 1.1%; Median selected monthly owner costs: $2,238 with a mortgage, $827 without a mortgage; Median gross rent: $1,157 per month; Rental vacancy rate: 6.2%

Health Insurance: 95.9% have insurance; 82.8% have private insurance; 27.3% have public insurance; 4.1% do not have insurance; 3.5% of children under 18 do not have insurance

Transportation: Commute: 71.7% car, 4.9% public transportation, 10.0% walk, 12.0% work from home; Mean travel time to work: 24.7 minutes

Additional Information Contacts

Town of Red Hook . . . . (845) 758-4606
http://www.redhook.org

RED HOOK (village). Covers a land area of 1.102 square miles and a water area of 0.012 square miles. Located at 42.00° N. Lat; 73.88° W. Long. Elevation is 220 feet.

Population: 2,021; Growth (since 2000): 12.0%; Density: 1,833.3 persons per square mile; Race: 87.4% White, 2.1% Black/African American, 4.9% Asian, 0.0% American Indian/Alaska Native, 0.0% Native Hawaiian/Other Pacific Islander, 2.6% Two or more races, 7.0% Hispanic of any race; Average household size: 2.43; Median age: 39.5; Age under 18: 18.5%; Age 65 and over: 18.4%; Males per 100 females: 87.5; Marriage status: 40.3% never married, 42.8% now married, 1.3% separated, 5.3% widowed, 11.7% divorced; Foreign born: 12.9%; Speak English only: 86.8%; With disability: 14.1%; Veterans: 5.6%; Ancestry: 22.8% German, 20.2% Irish, 8.2% Italian, 7.8% Dutch, 6.3% English

Employment: 13.0% management, business, and financial, 6.2% computer, engineering, and science, 18.6% education, legal, community service, arts, and media, 5.3% healthcare practitioners, 21.6% service, 21.4% sales and office, 6.8% natural resources, construction, and maintenance, 7.0% production, transportation, and material moving

Income: Per capita: $37,002; Median household: $55,938; Average household: $87,297; Households with income of $100,000 or more: 29.6%; Poverty rate: 19.0%

Educational Attainment: High school diploma or higher: 86.5%; Bachelor's degree or higher: 42.5%; Graduate/professional degree or higher: 24.1%

School District(s)

Red Hook Central SD (PK-12)

Enrollment: 1,936 . . . . (845) 758-2241

Housing: Homeownership rate: 50.8%; Median home value: $266,700; Median year structure built: 1962; Homeowner vacancy rate: 2.5%; Median selected monthly owner costs: $2,177 with a mortgage, $768 without a mortgage; Median gross rent: $970 per month; Rental vacancy rate: 8.6%

Health Insurance: 94.6% have insurance; 74.0% have private insurance; 34.2% have public insurance; 5.4% do not have insurance; 0.0% of children under 18 do not have insurance

Transportation: Commute: 75.2% car, 7.8% public transportation, 10.4% walk, 4.4% work from home; Mean travel time to work: 24.1 minutes

---

RED OAKS MILL (CDP). Covers a land area of 2.276 square miles and a water area of 0.031 square miles. Located at 41.65° N. Lat; 73.87° W. Long. Elevation is 164 feet.

Population: 3,516; Growth (since 2000): -28.7%; Density: 1,544.7 persons per square mile; Race: 83.4% White, 9.0% Black/African American, 2.6% Asian, 0.0% American Indian/Alaska Native, 0.0% Native Hawaiian/Other Pacific Islander, 1.1% Two or more races, 12.7% Hispanic of any race;

Average household size: 2.62; Median age: 44.0; Age under 18: 22.1%; Age 65 and over: 17.3%; Males per 100 females: 97.4; Marriage status: 20.8% never married, 65.8% now married, 2.4% separated, 6.0% widowed, 7.4% divorced; Foreign born: 11.0%; Speak English only: 87.4%; With disability: 10.1%; Veterans: 8.2%; Ancestry: 22.5% Italian, 17.3% Irish, 13.5% German, 6.6% English, 5.6% Polish

Employment: 19.6% management, business, and financial, 4.8% computer, engineering, and science, 17.4% education, legal, community service, arts, and media, 9.5% healthcare practitioners, 14.4% service, 21.0% sales and office, 7.9% natural resources, construction, and maintenance, 5.5% production, transportation, and material moving

Income: Per capita: $40,809; Median household: $98,906; Average household: $106,557; Households with income of $100,000 or more: 49.7%; Poverty rate: 1.0%

Educational Attainment: High school diploma or higher: 97.1%; Bachelor's degree or higher: 38.0%; Graduate/professional degree or higher: 21.5%

Housing: Homeownership rate: 98.5%; Median home value: $260,800; Median year structure built: 1961; Homeowner vacancy rate: 0.0%; Median selected monthly owner costs: $2,202 with a mortgage, $800 without a mortgage; Median gross rent: n/a per month; Rental vacancy rate: 0.0%

Health Insurance: 98.1% have insurance; 88.0% have private insurance; 23.4% have public insurance; 1.9% do not have insurance; 0.0% of children under 18 do not have insurance

Transportation: Commute: 85.8% car, 3.0% public transportation, 0.1% walk, 10.7% work from home; Mean travel time to work: 34.2 minutes

RHINEBECK (town).
Covers a land area of 35.682 square miles and a water area of 4.068 square miles. Located at 41.93° N. Lat; 73.90° W. Long. Elevation is 200 feet.

History: It is the site of Beekman Arms, said to be the oldest hotel in the U.S., and of a pre-Revolutionary Dutch Reformed church and cemetery. Unique collection of aircraft from before and during World War I at Old Rhinebeck Aerodrome. Settled before 1700, incorporated 1834.

Population: 7,777; Growth (since 2000): 0.2%; Density: 218.0 persons per square mile; Race: 91.3% White, 3.1% Black/African American, 2.3% Asian, 0.0% American Indian/Alaska Native, 0.0% Native Hawaiian/Other Pacific Islander, 1.2% Two or more races, 4.8% Hispanic of any race; Average household size: 2.17; Median age: 53.5; Age under 18: 16.8%; Age 65 and over: 30.3%; Males per 100 females: 83.3; Marriage status: 25.0% never married, 54.7% now married, 2.0% separated, 9.2% widowed, 11.0% divorced; Foreign born: 10.6%; Speak English only: 89.7%; With disability: 15.0%; Veterans: 7.2%; Ancestry: 19.7% Irish, 15.6% German, 14.3% Italian, 13.8% English, 7.7% American

Employment: 17.1% management, business, and financial, 3.4% computer, engineering, and science, 19.6% education, legal, community service, arts, and media, 13.5% healthcare practitioners, 14.0% service, 21.6% sales and office, 4.6% natural resources, construction, and maintenance, 6.2% production, transportation, and material moving

Income: Per capita: $50,696; Median household: $80,938; Average household: $117,842; Households with income of $100,000 or more: 39.0%; Poverty rate: 8.3%

Educational Attainment: High school diploma or higher: 92.3%; Bachelor's degree or higher: 50.1%; Graduate/professional degree or higher: 28.1%

School District(s)
Rhinebeck Central SD (KG-12)
    Enrollment: 1,072 . . . . (845) 871-5520

Housing: Homeownership rate: 66.8%; Median home value: $377,400; Median year structure built: 1970; Homeowner vacancy rate: 2.4%; Median selected monthly owner costs: $2,224 with a mortgage, $984 without a mortgage; Median gross rent: $1,174 per month; Rental vacancy rate: 4.1%

Health Insurance: 95.0% have insurance; 77.3% have private insurance; 36.0% have public insurance; 5.0% do not have insurance; 3.3% of children under 18 do not have insurance

Hospitals: Northern Dutchess Hospital (68 beds)

Transportation: Commute: 75.8% car, 3.8% public transportation, 8.8% walk, 10.8% work from home; Mean travel time to work: 27.3 minutes

Additional Information Contacts

Town of Rhinebeck . . . . (845) 876-3409
    http://www.rhinebeck-ny.gov

RHINEBECK (village).
Covers a land area of 1.523 square miles and a water area of 0.020 square miles. Located at 41.93° N. Lat; 73.91° W. Long. Elevation is 200 feet.

Population: 2,608; Growth (since 2000): -15.2%; Density: 1,712.0 persons per square mile; Race: 87.8% White, 4.6% Black/African American, 4.3% Asian, 0.0% American Indian/Alaska Native, 0.0% Native Hawaiian/Other Pacific Islander, 2.0% Two or more races, 4.9% Hispanic of any race; Average household size: 1.97; Median age: 54.2; Age under 18: 15.2%; Age 65 and over: 32.6%; Males per 100 females: 80.5; Marriage status: 24.8% never married, 53.6% now married, 2.5% separated, 8.4% widowed, 13.2% divorced; Foreign born: 15.1%; Speak English only: 87.4%; With disability: 14.8%; Veterans: 7.9%; Ancestry: 17.1% Irish, 16.2% German, 15.6% English, 14.0% Italian, 6.4% Russian

Employment: 16.1% management, business, and financial, 2.5% computer, engineering, and science, 23.0% education, legal, community service, arts, and media, 14.2% healthcare practitioners, 18.4% service, 20.4% sales and office, 0.6% natural resources, construction, and maintenance, 4.7% production, transportation, and material moving

Income: Per capita: $42,347; Median household: $65,238; Average household: $86,905; Households with income of $100,000 or more: 30.8%; Poverty rate: 12.3%

Educational Attainment: High school diploma or higher: 93.4%; Bachelor's degree or higher: 55.5%; Graduate/professional degree or higher: 32.9%

School District(s)
Rhinebeck Central SD (KG-12)
    Enrollment: 1,072 . . . . (845) 871-5520

Housing: Homeownership rate: 51.0%; Median home value: $366,200; Median year structure built: 1958; Homeowner vacancy rate: 4.5%; Median selected monthly owner costs: $2,237 with a mortgage, $1,129 without a mortgage; Median gross rent: $1,212 per month; Rental vacancy rate: 0.0%

Health Insurance: 95.5% have insurance; 78.7% have private insurance; 41.2% have public insurance; 4.5% do not have insurance; 2.1% of children under 18 do not have insurance

Hospitals: Northern Dutchess Hospital (68 beds)

Safety: Violent crime rate: 7.7 per 10,000 population; Property crime rate: 151.0 per 10,000 population

Transportation: Commute: 73.9% car, 5.4% public transportation, 12.8% walk, 7.4% work from home; Mean travel time to work: 29.4 minutes

RHINECLIFF (CDP).
Covers a land area of 0.994 square miles and a water area of 0.014 square miles. Located at 41.92° N. Lat; 73.94° W. Long. Elevation is 46 feet.

Population: 420; Growth (since 2000): n/a; Density: 422.3 persons per square mile; Race: 82.1% White, 1.9% Black/African American, 11.0% Asian, 0.0% American Indian/Alaska Native, 0.0% Native Hawaiian/Other Pacific Islander, 0.5% Two or more races, 8.1% Hispanic of any race; Average household size: 3.38; Median age: 40.0; Age under 18: 47.4%; Age 65 and over: 11.4%; Males per 100 females: 120.2; Marriage status: 36.7% never married, 52.2% now married, 3.6% separated, 2.2% widowed, 9.0% divorced; Foreign born: 13.1%; Speak English only: 98.0%; With disability: 22.1%; Veterans: 4.1%; Ancestry: 22.9% Swedish, 20.2% German, 20.0% American, 8.8% Irish, 7.6% English

Employment: 26.2% management, business, and financial, 9.2% computer, engineering, and science, 39.0% education, legal, community service, arts, and media, 4.3% healthcare practitioners, 5.0% service, 4.3% sales and office, 0.0% natural resources, construction, and maintenance, 12.1% production, transportation, and material moving

Income: Per capita: $40,821; Median household: $112,679; Average household: $145,760; Households with income of $100,000 or more: 50.4%; Poverty rate: 1.2%

Educational Attainment: High school diploma or higher: 91.4%; Bachelor's degree or higher: 59.7%; Graduate/professional degree or higher: 35.3%

Housing: Homeownership rate: 78.6%; Median home value: $363,600; Median year structure built: 1951; Homeowner vacancy rate: 0.0%; Median selected monthly owner costs: $1,826 with a mortgage, $1,501 without a mortgage; Median gross rent: $1,632 per month; Rental vacancy rate: 39.0%

Health Insurance: 100.0% have insurance; 92.4% have private insurance; 17.4% have public insurance; 0.0% do not have insurance; 0.0% of children under 18 do not have insurance

Transportation: Commute: 57.8% car, 0.0% public transportation, 28.9% walk, 13.3% work from home; Mean travel time to work: 21.0 minutes; Amtrak: Train service available.

SALT POINT (CDP). Covers a land area of 0.829 square miles and a water area of 0.004 square miles. Located at 41.81° N. Lat; 73.79° W. Long. Elevation is 236 feet.

Population: 84; Growth (since 2000): n/a; Density: 101.3 persons per square mile; Race: 97.6% White, 0.0% Black/African American, 0.0% Asian, 2.4% American Indian/Alaska Native, 0.0% Native Hawaiian/Other Pacific Islander, 0.0% Two or more races, 0.0% Hispanic of any race; Average household size: 1.91; Median age: 54.1; Age under 18: 4.8%; Age 65 and over: 36.9%; Males per 100 females: 91.9; Marriage status: 12.5% never married, 61.3% now married, 0.0% separated, 26.3% widowed, 0.0% divorced; Foreign born: 4.8%; Speak English only: 100.0%; With disability: 19.0%; Veterans: 3.8%; Ancestry: 39.3% English, 39.3% German, 19.0% American, 15.5% Irish, 11.9% Italian

Employment: 0.0% management, business, and financial, 0.0% computer, engineering, and science, 36.4% education, legal, community service, arts, and media, 0.0% healthcare practitioners, 22.7% service, 13.6% sales and office, 27.3% natural resources, construction, and maintenance, 0.0% production, transportation, and material moving

Income: Per capita: $36,823; Median household: n/a; Average household: $67,711; Households with income of $100,000 or more: 31.8%; Poverty rate: 6.0%

Educational Attainment: High school diploma or higher: 80.0%; Bachelor's degree or higher: 31.3%; Graduate/professional degree or higher: 17.5%

Housing: Homeownership rate: 100.0%; Median home value: $220,000; Median year structure built: 1973; Homeowner vacancy rate: 17.0%; Median selected monthly owner costs: n/a with a mortgage, n/a without a mortgage; Median gross rent: n/a per month; Rental vacancy rate: 0.0%

Health Insurance: 88.1% have insurance; 75.0% have private insurance; 44.0% have public insurance; 11.9% do not have insurance; 0.0% of children under 18 do not have insurance

Transportation: Commute: 81.8% car, 0.0% public transportation, 0.0% walk, 18.2% work from home; Mean travel time to work: 0.0 minutes

SPACKENKILL (CDP). Covers a land area of 1.775 square miles and a water area of <.001 square miles. Located at 41.65° N. Lat; 73.91° W. Long. Elevation is 151 feet.

History: Spackenkill is a hamlet Dutchess County, New York and home to an IBM plant and many of its employees. Spackenkill neighborhoods include Hagantown, Nassau, King George, Beechwood, and Crown Heights.

Population: 4,258; Growth (since 2000): -10.5%; Density: 2,399.1 persons per square mile; Race: 77.4% White, 6.4% Black/African American, 7.3% Asian, 0.2% American Indian/Alaska Native, 0.0% Native Hawaiian/Other Pacific Islander, 1.7% Two or more races, 10.7% Hispanic of any race; Average household size: 3.09; Median age: 43.8; Age under 18: 26.2%; Age 65 and over: 18.4%; Males per 100 females: 95.5; Marriage status: 24.0% never married, 62.8% now married, 1.5% separated, 5.9% widowed, 7.2% divorced; Foreign born: 13.6%; Speak English only: 75.6%; With disability: 11.3%; Veterans: 5.0%; Ancestry: 18.7% Italian, 15.7% Irish, 13.0% German, 7.0% English, 6.2% Polish

Employment: 18.5% management, business, and financial, 12.3% computer, engineering, and science, 17.4% education, legal, community service, arts, and media, 9.2% healthcare practitioners, 11.2% service, 18.5% sales and office, 6.2% natural resources, construction, and maintenance, 6.8% production, transportation, and material moving

Income: Per capita: $45,073; Median household: $119,833; Average household: $135,853; Households with income of $100,000 or more: 60.0%; Poverty rate: 2.0%

Educational Attainment: High school diploma or higher: 97.1%; Bachelor's degree or higher: 53.9%; Graduate/professional degree or higher: 25.7%

Housing: Homeownership rate: 94.4%; Median home value: $278,600; Median year structure built: 1964; Homeowner vacancy rate: 0.8%; Median selected monthly owner costs: $2,585 with a mortgage, $1,087 without a mortgage; Median gross rent: $2,161 per month; Rental vacancy rate: 0.0%

Health Insurance: 98.6% have insurance; 87.5% have private insurance; 28.0% have public insurance; 1.4% do not have insurance; 0.6% of children under 18 do not have insurance

Transportation: Commute: 89.9% car, 3.8% public transportation, 1.4% walk, 4.3% work from home; Mean travel time to work: 24.9 minutes

STAATSBURG (CDP). Covers a land area of 1.065 square miles and a water area of 0.001 square miles. Located at 41.85° N. Lat; 73.92° W. Long. Elevation is 30 feet.

Population: 383; Growth (since 2000): -58.0%; Density: 359.5 persons per square mile; Race: 91.6% White, 0.0% Black/African American, 2.9% Asian, 0.0% American Indian/Alaska Native, 0.0% Native Hawaiian/Other Pacific Islander, 0.0% Two or more races, 4.7% Hispanic of any race; Average household size: 2.55; Median age: 58.9; Age under 18: 5.0%; Age 65 and over: 18.8%; Males per 100 females: 99.5; Marriage status: 22.3% never married, 68.1% now married, 4.9% separated, 7.1% widowed, 2.5% divorced; Foreign born: 4.7%; Speak English only: 81.2%; With disability: 14.6%; Veterans: 4.9%; Ancestry: 31.6% German, 15.1% Dutch, 12.8% Austrian, 9.7% Irish, 9.1% French

Employment: 33.3% management, business, and financial, 5.2% computer, engineering, and science, 6.3% education, legal, community service, arts, and media, 0.0% healthcare practitioners, 44.3% service, 5.2% sales and office, 5.7% natural resources, construction, and maintenance, 0.0% production, transportation, and material moving

Income: Per capita: $40,000; Median household: $94,750; Average household: $94,880; Households with income of $100,000 or more: 43.4%; Poverty rate: 9.7%

Educational Attainment: High school diploma or higher: 100.0%; Bachelor's degree or higher: 48.0%; Graduate/professional degree or higher: 20.1%

Housing: Homeownership rate: 82.7%; Median home value: $264,100; Median year structure built: Before 1940; Homeowner vacancy rate: 0.0%; Median selected monthly owner costs: $1,781 with a mortgage, $984 without a mortgage; Median gross rent: n/a per month; Rental vacancy rate: 0.0%

Health Insurance: 90.3% have insurance; 78.3% have private insurance; 25.8% have public insurance; 9.7% do not have insurance; 0.0% of children under 18 do not have insurance

Transportation: Commute: 61.5% car, 0.0% public transportation, 22.4% walk, 16.1% work from home; Mean travel time to work: 17.0 minutes

STANFORD (town). Covers a land area of 49.637 square miles and a water area of 0.649 square miles. Located at 41.90° N. Lat; 73.67° W. Long.

Population: 3,784; Growth (since 2000): 6.8%; Density: 76.2 persons per square mile; Race: 92.6% White, 2.7% Black/African American, 2.3% Asian, 0.0% American Indian/Alaska Native, 0.0% Native Hawaiian/Other Pacific Islander, 1.7% Two or more races, 6.0% Hispanic of any race; Average household size: 2.38; Median age: 50.9; Age under 18: 15.2%; Age 65 and over: 20.2%; Males per 100 females: 101.0; Marriage status: 27.2% never married, 56.3% now married, 1.0% separated, 3.3% widowed, 13.2% divorced; Foreign born: 7.2%; Speak English only: 88.9%; With disability: 13.9%; Veterans: 10.7%; Ancestry: 22.3% Irish, 21.1% German, 13.9% Italian, 11.9% English, 6.6% American

Employment: 19.1% management, business, and financial, 4.0% computer, engineering, and science, 19.3% education, legal, community service, arts, and media, 5.3% healthcare practitioners, 13.7% service, 18.6% sales and office, 10.9% natural resources, construction, and maintenance, 9.1% production, transportation, and material moving

Income: Per capita: $52,369; Median household: $85,536; Average household: $126,290; Households with income of $100,000 or more: 45.5%; Poverty rate: 6.3%

Educational Attainment: High school diploma or higher: 95.1%; Bachelor's degree or higher: 38.1%; Graduate/professional degree or higher: 19.0%

Housing: Homeownership rate: 78.9%; Median home value: $299,900; Median year structure built: 1971; Homeowner vacancy rate: 2.6%; Median selected monthly owner costs: $1,960 with a mortgage, $728 without a mortgage; Median gross rent: $978 per month; Rental vacancy rate: 8.5%

Health Insurance: 97.3% have insurance; 82.4% have private insurance; 32.9% have public insurance; 2.7% do not have insurance; 0.0% of children under 18 do not have insurance

Transportation: Commute: 71.4% car, 4.4% public transportation, 7.1% walk, 16.5% work from home; Mean travel time to work: 29.3 minutes

STANFORDVILLE (unincorporated postal area)
ZCTA: 12581

Covers a land area of 40.432 square miles and a water area of 0.394 square miles. Located at 41.90° N. Lat; 73.70° W. Long. Elevation is 358 feet.

Population: 2,206; Growth (since 2000): -1.1%; Density: 54.6 persons per square mile; Race: 96.4% White, 1.9% Black/African American, 0.0% Asian, 0.0% American Indian/Alaska Native, 0.0% Native Hawaiian/Other Pacific Islander, 1.8% Two or more races, 7.1% Hispanic of any race; Average household size: 2.33; Median age: 50.8; Age under 18: 15.9%; Age 65 and over: 18.3%; Males per 100 females: 98.6; Marriage status: 26.9% never married, 56.5% now married, 0.9% separated, 2.2% widowed, 14.4% divorced; Foreign born: 7.5%; Speak English only: 90.1%; With disability: 10.7%; Veterans: 12.0%; Ancestry: 25.2% Irish, 24.6% German, 14.8% Italian, 13.4% English, 8.0% American

Employment: 19.7% management, business, and financial, 3.4% computer, engineering, and science, 11.8% education, legal, community service, arts, and media, 7.1% healthcare practitioners, 15.1% service, 20.3% sales and office, 15.4% natural resources, construction, and maintenance, 7.3% production, transportation, and material moving

Income: Per capita: $48,235; Median household: $76,750; Average household: $111,158; Households with income of $100,000 or more: 38.0%; Poverty rate: 4.7%

Educational Attainment: High school diploma or higher: 93.1%; Bachelor's degree or higher: 29.5%; Graduate/professional degree or higher: 13.3%

School District(s)
Pine Plains Central SD (PK-12)
   Enrollment: 993 . . . . (518) 398-7181

Housing: Homeownership rate: 77.4%; Median home value: $289,100; Median year structure built: 1969; Homeowner vacancy rate: 5.0%; Median selected monthly owner costs: $1,766 with a mortgage, $708 without a mortgage; Median gross rent: $1,021 per month; Rental vacancy rate: 0.0%

Health Insurance: 97.1% have insurance; 87.2% have private insurance; 30.7% have public insurance; 2.9% do not have insurance; 0.0% of children under 18 do not have insurance

Transportation: Commute: 76.7% car, 4.0% public transportation, 3.5% walk, 15.6% work from home; Mean travel time to work: 32.2 minutes

STORMVILLE (unincorporated postal area)
ZCTA: 12582

Covers a land area of 12.782 square miles and a water area of 0.403 square miles. Located at 41.54° N. Lat; 73.74° W. Long. Elevation is 328 feet.

Population: 6,413; Growth (since 2000): 40.9%; Density: 501.7 persons per square mile; Race: 66.5% White, 19.3% Black/African American, 0.5% Asian, 0.5% American Indian/Alaska Native, 0.0% Native Hawaiian/Other Pacific Islander, 3.1% Two or more races, 12.8% Hispanic of any race; Average household size: 3.10; Median age: 44.0; Age under 18: 14.5%; Age 65 and over: 11.4%; Males per 100 females: 209.2; Marriage status: 37.4% never married, 45.3% now married, 1.8% separated, 5.1% widowed, 12.2% divorced; Foreign born: 9.0%; Speak English only: 79.7%; With disability: 13.1%; Veterans: 9.0%; Ancestry: 15.8% Italian, 12.8% Irish, 10.2% German, 7.6% American, 4.2% English

Employment: 16.1% management, business, and financial, 2.3% computer, engineering, and science, 16.2% education, legal, community service, arts, and media, 6.3% healthcare practitioners, 24.4% service, 17.7% sales and office, 9.1% natural resources, construction, and maintenance, 8.1% production, transportation, and material moving

Income: Per capita: $32,419; Median household: $103,771; Average household: $126,572; Households with income of $100,000 or more: 54.3%; Poverty rate: 4.1%

Educational Attainment: High school diploma or higher: 83.9%; Bachelor's degree or higher: 25.8%; Graduate/professional degree or higher: 9.6%

Housing: Homeownership rate: 85.0%; Median home value: $358,900; Median year structure built: 1979; Homeowner vacancy rate: 0.0%; Median selected monthly owner costs: $2,563 with a mortgage, $1,123 without a mortgage; Median gross rent: $1,326 per month; Rental vacancy rate: 0.0%

Health Insurance: 98.3% have insurance; 87.4% have private insurance; 24.6% have public insurance; 1.7% do not have insurance; 0.6% of children under 18 do not have insurance

Transportation: Commute: 88.9% car, 1.6% public transportation, 0.5% walk, 6.7% work from home; Mean travel time to work: 32.5 minutes

TITUSVILLE (CDP).
Covers a land area of 0.691 square miles and a water area of <.001 square miles. Located at 41.67° N. Lat; 73.87° W. Long. Elevation is 151 feet.

Population: 569; Growth (since 2000): n/a; Density: 823.9 persons per square mile; Race: 95.8% White, 0.0% Black/African American, 1.9% Asian, 0.0% American Indian/Alaska Native, 0.0% Native Hawaiian/Other Pacific Islander, 2.3% Two or more races, 27.4% Hispanic of any race; Average household size: 2.24; Median age: 56.5; Age under 18: 13.9%; Age 65 and over: 23.9%; Males per 100 females: 96.8; Marriage status: 12.2% never married, 64.7% now married, 1.3% separated, 15.1% widowed, 8.0% divorced; Foreign born: 3.3%; Speak English only: 75.9%; With disability: 16.0%; Veterans: 4.5%; Ancestry: 23.9% Irish, 13.2% German, 11.6% Italian, 7.6% English, 7.0% Polish

Employment: 8.2% management, business, and financial, 8.8% computer, engineering, and science, 16.2% education, legal, community service, arts, and media, 7.1% healthcare practitioners, 0.0% service, 32.1% sales and office, 20.9% natural resources, construction, and maintenance, 6.8% production, transportation, and material moving

Income: Per capita: $48,364; Median household: $103,056; Average household: $102,741; Households with income of $100,000 or more: 51.5%; Poverty rate: 3.2%

Educational Attainment: High school diploma or higher: 91.4%; Bachelor's degree or higher: 44.5%; Graduate/professional degree or higher: 14.5%

Housing: Homeownership rate: 90.6%; Median home value: $237,600; Median year structure built: 1960; Homeowner vacancy rate: 13.9%; Median selected monthly owner costs: $1,875 with a mortgage, $777 without a mortgage; Median gross rent: n/a per month; Rental vacancy rate: 0.0%

Health Insurance: 100.0% have insurance; 94.6% have private insurance; 29.3% have public insurance; 0.0% do not have insurance; 0.0% of children under 18 do not have insurance

Transportation: Commute: 100.0% car, 0.0% public transportation, 0.0% walk, 0.0% work from home; Mean travel time to work: 28.1 minutes

TIVOLI (village).
Covers a land area of 1.610 square miles and a water area of 0.028 square miles. Located at 42.05° N. Lat; 73.92° W. Long. Elevation is 151 feet.

Population: 1,018; Growth (since 2000): -12.5%; Density: 632.3 persons per square mile; Race: 97.7% White, 0.4% Black/African American, 1.5% Asian, 0.0% American Indian/Alaska Native, 0.0% Native Hawaiian/Other Pacific Islander, 0.4% Two or more races, 5.8% Hispanic of any race; Average household size: 2.23; Median age: 31.3; Age under 18: 12.1%; Age 65 and over: 15.2%; Males per 100 females: 89.2; Marriage status: 48.7% never married, 37.6% now married, 1.5% separated, 3.9% widowed, 9.8% divorced; Foreign born: 5.7%; Speak English only: 91.8%; With disability: 12.9%; Veterans: 6.6%; Ancestry: 24.0% Irish, 16.5% Italian, 15.4% German, 8.0% English, 6.6% American

Employment: 11.2% management, business, and financial, 4.6% computer, engineering, and science, 26.8% education, legal, community service, arts, and media, 4.4% healthcare practitioners, 21.8% service, 16.2% sales and office, 5.0% natural resources, construction, and maintenance, 9.9% production, transportation, and material moving

Income: Per capita: $29,013; Median household: $45,294; Average household: $63,107; Households with income of $100,000 or more: 24.8%; Poverty rate: 24.1%

Educational Attainment: High school diploma or higher: 87.7%; Bachelor's degree or higher: 43.4%; Graduate/professional degree or higher: 22.7%

Housing: Homeownership rate: 52.4%; Median home value: $216,700; Median year structure built: 1962; Homeowner vacancy rate: 0.0%; Median selected monthly owner costs: $1,770 with a mortgage, $671 without a mortgage; Median gross rent: $1,355 per month; Rental vacancy rate: 7.8%

Health Insurance: 92.5% have insurance; 75.5% have private insurance; 29.1% have public insurance; 7.5% do not have insurance; 2.4% of children under 18 do not have insurance

Transportation: Commute: 73.8% car, 10.3% public transportation, 6.2% walk, 8.8% work from home; Mean travel time to work: 27.0 minutes

UNION VALE (town).
Covers a land area of 37.482 square miles and a water area of 0.324 square miles. Located at 41.70° N. Lat; 73.69° W. Long.

History: Union Vale is a town in Dutchess County, New York. The region was originally part of the Beekman Patent. The town was first settled around 1716, and formed in 1827 from the towns of Beekman and LaGrange.

Population: 4,833; Growth (since 2000): 6.3%; Density: 128.9 persons per square mile; Race: 94.3% White, 1.8% Black/African American, 1.8% Asian, 0.5% American Indian/Alaska Native, 0.0% Native Hawaiian/Other Pacific Islander, 1.6% Two or more races, 3.9% Hispanic of any race; Average household size: 2.63; Median age: 47.8; Age under 18: 18.5%; Age 65 and over: 18.0%; Males per 100 females: 98.2; Marriage status: 24.8% never married, 65.1% now married, 0.9% separated, 4.7% widowed, 5.5% divorced; Foreign born: 10.5%; Speak English only: 87.4%; With disability: 13.2%; Veterans: 5.7%; Ancestry: 28.1% Italian, 20.7% Irish, 15.4% German, 5.7% English, 5.3% American

Employment: 11.1% management, business, and financial, 7.3% computer, engineering, and science, 16.0% education, legal, community service, arts, and media, 7.5% healthcare practitioners, 13.4% service, 26.6% sales and office, 10.8% natural resources, construction, and maintenance, 7.2% production, transportation, and material moving

Income: Per capita: $42,007; Median household: $93,559; Average household: $109,709; Households with income of $100,000 or more: 47.0%; Poverty rate: 5.0%

Educational Attainment: High school diploma or higher: 92.3%; Bachelor's degree or higher: 38.2%; Graduate/professional degree or higher: 18.5%

Housing: Homeownership rate: 80.1%; Median home value: $336,400; Median year structure built: 1979; Homeowner vacancy rate: 1.6%; Median selected monthly owner costs: $2,245 with a mortgage, $1,018 without a mortgage; Median gross rent: $1,128 per month; Rental vacancy rate: 12.5%

Health Insurance: 96.3% have insurance; 82.2% have private insurance; 28.1% have public insurance; 3.7% do not have insurance; 1.8% of children under 18 do not have insurance

Transportation: Commute: 88.5% car, 2.1% public transportation, 1.3% walk, 5.3% work from home; Mean travel time to work: 35.9 minutes

Additional Information Contacts
Town of Union Vale . . . . (845) 724-5600
  http://www2.marist.edu/unionvale

VERBANK (unincorporated postal area)
ZCTA: 12585

Covers a land area of 4.922 square miles and a water area of 0.079 square miles. Located at 41.73° N. Lat; 73.69° W. Long. Elevation is 591 feet.

Population: 856; Growth (since 2000): -10.5%; Density: 173.9 persons per square mile; Race: 86.4% White, 10.4% Black/African American, 1.2% Asian, 0.0% American Indian/Alaska Native, 0.0% Native Hawaiian/Other Pacific Islander, 2.0% Two or more races, 0.0% Hispanic of any race; Average household size: 2.68; Median age: 41.0; Age under 18: 26.3%; Age 65 and over: 14.7%; Males per 100 females: 103.9; Marriage status: 29.3% never married, 65.1% now married, 3.6% separated, 0.0% widowed, 5.7% divorced; Foreign born: 15.4%; Speak English only: 86.1%; With disability: 13.2%; Veterans: 2.2%; Ancestry: 22.1% Italian, 14.7% Irish, 13.9% German, 10.4% American, 9.6% African

Employment: 3.9% management, business, and financial, 2.7% computer, engineering, and science, 21.4% education, legal, community service, arts, and media, 9.3% healthcare practitioners, 23.4% service, 16.4% sales and office, 5.0% natural resources, construction, and maintenance, 18.0% production, transportation, and material moving

Income: Per capita: $41,061; Median household: $110,114; Average household: $114,783; Households with income of $100,000 or more: 52.5%; Poverty rate: 13.3%

Educational Attainment: High school diploma or higher: 84.1%; Bachelor's degree or higher: 31.5%; Graduate/professional degree or higher: 23.0%

Housing: Homeownership rate: 72.4%; Median home value: $346,800; Median year structure built: 1971; Homeowner vacancy rate: 0.0%; Median selected monthly owner costs: $2,441 with a mortgage, $0 without a mortgage; Median gross rent: $958 per month; Rental vacancy rate: 21.7%

Health Insurance: 100.0% have insurance; 74.5% have private insurance; 35.7% have public insurance; 0.0% do not have insurance; 0.0% of children under 18 do not have insurance

Transportation: Commute: 90.5% car, 3.6% public transportation, 0.0% walk, 5.9% work from home; Mean travel time to work: 27.9 minutes

WAPPINGER (town).
Covers a land area of 27.054 square miles and a water area of 1.477 square miles. Located at 41.59° N. Lat; 73.89° W. Long.

History: Society of the Cincinnati founded here in 1783. Incorporated 1871.

Population: 26,906; Growth (since 2000): 2.4%; Density: 994.5 persons per square mile; Race: 79.7% White, 6.4% Black/African American, 5.7% Asian, 0.7% American Indian/Alaska Native, 0.1% Native Hawaiian/Other Pacific Islander, 2.2% Two or more races, 15.5% Hispanic of any race; Average household size: 2.66; Median age: 40.6; Age under 18: 19.7%; Age 65 and over: 15.1%; Males per 100 females: 98.0; Marriage status: 31.6% never married, 53.4% now married, 1.5% separated, 6.3% widowed, 8.7% divorced; Foreign born: 11.9%; Speak English only: 80.7%; With disability: 13.0%; Veterans: 7.2%; Ancestry: 24.5% Italian, 20.0% Irish, 12.1% German, 6.2% English, 4.3% American

Employment: 14.0% management, business, and financial, 5.8% computer, engineering, and science, 10.7% education, legal, community service, arts, and media, 5.7% healthcare practitioners, 19.7% service, 25.0% sales and office, 9.5% natural resources, construction, and maintenance, 9.6% production, transportation, and material moving

Income: Per capita: $36,968; Median household: $78,945; Average household: $96,394; Households with income of $100,000 or more: 36.5%; Poverty rate: 6.5%

Educational Attainment: High school diploma or higher: 91.0%; Bachelor's degree or higher: 32.2%; Graduate/professional degree or higher: 12.3%

Housing: Homeownership rate: 69.1%; Median home value: $278,500; Median year structure built: 1969; Homeowner vacancy rate: 3.9%; Median selected monthly owner costs: $2,226 with a mortgage, $759 without a mortgage; Median gross rent: $1,321 per month; Rental vacancy rate: 7.7%

Health Insurance: 93.1% have insurance; 78.6% have private insurance; 28.8% have public insurance; 6.9% do not have insurance; 3.4% of children under 18 do not have insurance

Transportation: Commute: 88.3% car, 5.5% public transportation, 1.0% walk, 4.2% work from home; Mean travel time to work: 36.3 minutes

Additional Information Contacts
Town of Wappinger . . . . (845) 297-4158
  http://www.townofwappinger.us

WAPPINGERS FALLS (village).
Covers a land area of 1.108 square miles and a water area of 0.076 square miles. Located at 41.60° N. Lat; 73.92° W. Long. Elevation is 157 feet.

History: The Village of Wappingers Falls was named for the cascade in Wappinger Creek, which forms the boundary between Wappinger and Poughkeepsie. The Wappinger were Native Americans whose territory in the 17th century spread along the eastern bank of the Hudson River.

Population: 5,416; Growth (since 2000): 9.9%; Density: 4,887.5 persons per square mile; Race: 63.7% White, 10.3% Black/African American, 5.9% Asian, 3.0% American Indian/Alaska Native, 0.4% Native Hawaiian/Other Pacific Islander, 2.2% Two or more races, 28.1% Hispanic of any race; Average household size: 2.69; Median age: 34.6; Age under 18: 17.0%; Age 65 and over: 15.7%; Males per 100 females: 93.6; Marriage status: 39.8% never married, 42.0% now married, 1.8% separated, 8.5% widowed, 9.7% divorced; Foreign born: 20.4%; Speak English only: 63.8%; With disability: 19.8%; Veterans: 5.8%; Ancestry: 25.0% Italian, 18.6% Irish, 10.5% German, 4.5% English, 2.8% Jordanian

Employment: 6.1% management, business, and financial, 6.8% computer, engineering, and science, 6.6% education, legal, community service, arts, and media, 3.5% healthcare practitioners, 35.1% service, 26.8% sales and office, 8.0% natural resources, construction, and maintenance, 7.0% production, transportation, and material moving

Income: Per capita: $27,960; Median household: $53,654; Average household: $72,988; Households with income of $100,000 or more: 22.0%; Poverty rate: 11.9%

Educational Attainment: High school diploma or higher: 80.8%; Bachelor's degree or higher: 19.4%; Graduate/professional degree or higher: 7.0%

School District(s)

Wappingers Central SD (PK-12)

Enrollment: 11,091 .... (845) 298-5000

Housing: Homeownership rate: 36.7%; Median home value: $211,900; Median year structure built: 1959; Homeowner vacancy rate: 0.0%; Median selected monthly owner costs: $2,404 with a mortgage, $688 without a mortgage; Median gross rent: $1,327 per month; Rental vacancy rate: 11.0%

Health Insurance: 89.7% have insurance; 64.4% have private insurance; 42.9% have public insurance; 10.3% do not have insurance; 0.0% of children under 18 do not have insurance

Newspapers: Beacon Free Press (weekly circulation 7,500); Southern Dutchess News (weekly circulation 7,500)

Transportation: Commute: 83.4% car, 7.2% public transportation, 1.8% walk, 6.2% work from home; Mean travel time to work: 32.6 minutes

Additional Information Contacts

Village of Wappingers Falls........................ (845) 297-8773
http://www.wappingersfallsny.gov

WASHINGTON (town). Covers a land area of 58.170 square miles and a water area of 0.714 square miles. Located at 41.79° N. Lat; 73.68° W. Long.

Population: 4,695; Growth (since 2000): -1.0%; Density: 80.7 persons per square mile; Race: 91.1% White, 3.3% Black/African American, 0.5% Asian, 1.1% American Indian/Alaska Native, 0.0% Native Hawaiian/Other Pacific Islander, 1.3% Two or more races, 7.2% Hispanic of any race; Average household size: 2.37; Median age: 48.5; Age under 18: 19.8%; Age 65 and over: 22.4%; Males per 100 females: 99.4; Marriage status: 26.7% never married, 53.6% now married, 4.5% separated, 7.9% widowed, 11.8% divorced; Foreign born: 7.3%; Speak English only: 93.2%; With disability: 13.0%; Veterans: 7.1%; Ancestry: 30.1% Irish, 19.1% Italian, 13.6% English, 13.0% German, 5.8% American

Employment: 21.4% management, business, and financial, 4.1% computer, engineering, and science, 14.5% education, legal, community service, arts, and media, 5.5% healthcare practitioners, 17.4% service, 14.7% sales and office, 13.0% natural resources, construction, and maintenance, 9.6% production, transportation, and material moving

Income: Per capita: $42,581; Median household: $86,806; Average household: $102,548; Households with income of $100,000 or more: 40.4%; Poverty rate: 10.1%

Educational Attainment: High school diploma or higher: 92.6%; Bachelor's degree or higher: 39.3%; Graduate/professional degree or higher: 16.2%

Housing: Homeownership rate: 65.9%; Median home value: $385,400; Median year structure built: 1960; Homeowner vacancy rate: 5.5%; Median selected monthly owner costs: $2,402 with a mortgage, $878 without a mortgage; Median gross rent: $1,161 per month; Rental vacancy rate: 4.6%

Health Insurance: 92.1% have insurance; 72.6% have private insurance; 33.6% have public insurance; 7.9% do not have insurance; 2.8% of children under 18 do not have insurance

Transportation: Commute: 82.0% car, 2.0% public transportation, 5.8% walk, 9.2% work from home; Mean travel time to work: 31.9 minutes

Additional Information Contacts

Town of Washington .... (845) 677-3419
http://www.washingtonny.org

WASSAIC (unincorporated postal area)
ZCTA: 12592

Covers a land area of 18.704 square miles and a water area of 0.231 square miles. Located at 41.80° N. Lat; 73.58° W. Long. Elevation is 456 feet.

Population: 1,131; Growth (since 2000): -6.8%; Density: 60.5 persons per square mile; Race: 93.2% White, 5.9% Black/African American, 0.9% Asian, 0.0% American Indian/Alaska Native, 0.0% Native Hawaiian/Other Pacific Islander, 0.0% Two or more races, 1.1% Hispanic of any race; Average household size: 2.43; Median age: 53.2; Age under 18: 4.9%; Age 65 and over: 21.7%; Males per 100 females: 96.8; Marriage status: 39.9% never married, 50.5% now married, 3.4% separated, 9.6% widowed, 0.0% divorced; Foreign born: 4.2%; Speak English only: 94.8%; With disability: 26.3%; Veterans: 8.0%; Ancestry: 24.0% Italian, 17.5% English, 14.9% Irish, 11.6% Scottish, 9.1% French

Employment: 10.0% management, business, and financial, 3.5% computer, engineering, and science, 9.5% education, legal, community service, arts, and media, 1.3% healthcare practitioners, 33.3% service,

15.4% sales and office, 5.0% natural resources, construction, and maintenance, 22.1% production, transportation, and material moving

Income: Per capita: $34,491; Median household: $53,906; Average household: $88,926; Households with income of $100,000 or more: 28.4%; Poverty rate: 12.5%

Educational Attainment: High school diploma or higher: 81.6%; Bachelor's degree or higher: 20.1%; Graduate/professional degree or higher: 7.6%

Housing: Homeownership rate: 72.4%; Median home value: $261,400; Median year structure built: 1957; Homeowner vacancy rate: 0.0%; Median selected monthly owner costs: $1,675 with a mortgage, $551 without a mortgage; Median gross rent: $634 per month; Rental vacancy rate: 0.0%

Health Insurance: 95.4% have insurance; 73.7% have private insurance; 33.3% have public insurance; 4.6% do not have insurance; 0.0% of children under 18 do not have insurance

Transportation: Commute: 91.5% car, 3.6% public transportation, 1.2% walk, 3.6% work from home; Mean travel time to work: 23.7 minutes

WINGDALE (unincorporated postal area)
ZCTA: 12594

Covers a land area of 24.063 square miles and a water area of 0.618 square miles. Located at 41.68° N. Lat; 73.56° W. Long. Elevation is 420 feet.

Population: 4,205; Growth (since 2000): 16.2%; Density: 174.7 persons per square mile; Race: 84.4% White, 7.0% Black/African American, 0.4% Asian, 0.0% American Indian/Alaska Native, 0.0% Native Hawaiian/Other Pacific Islander, 3.2% Two or more races, 19.7% Hispanic of any race; Average household size: 2.76; Median age: 40.7; Age under 18: 22.1%; Age 65 and over: 9.9%; Males per 100 females: 99.4; Marriage status: 34.3% never married, 50.8% now married, 1.1% separated, 3.6% widowed, 11.2% divorced; Foreign born: 13.5%; Speak English only: 79.5%; With disability: 15.4%; Veterans: 5.3%; Ancestry: 23.9% Italian, 18.3% Irish, 12.9% German, 6.9% American, 5.9% Polish

Employment: 13.1% management, business, and financial, 4.2% computer, engineering, and science, 10.6% education, legal, community service, arts, and media, 3.1% healthcare practitioners, 21.5% service, 26.8% sales and office, 12.9% natural resources, construction, and maintenance, 7.9% production, transportation, and material moving

Income: Per capita: $30,291; Median household: $62,953; Average household: $82,719; Households with income of $100,000 or more: 33.6%; Poverty rate: 18.0%

Educational Attainment: High school diploma or higher: 89.6%; Bachelor's degree or higher: 23.4%; Graduate/professional degree or higher: 6.9%

School District(s)

Dover Union Free SD (KG-12)

Enrollment: 1,360 .... (845) 877-5700

Housing: Homeownership rate: 70.7%; Median home value: $243,800; Median year structure built: 1977; Homeowner vacancy rate: 0.0%; Median selected monthly owner costs: $1,990 with a mortgage, $912 without a mortgage; Median gross rent: $913 per month; Rental vacancy rate: 10.4%

Health Insurance: 87.4% have insurance; 68.5% have private insurance; 31.9% have public insurance; 12.6% do not have insurance; 10.3% of children under 18 do not have insurance

Transportation: Commute: 89.5% car, 3.4% public transportation, 4.9% walk, 2.2% work from home; Mean travel time to work: 40.8 minutes

Erie County

Located in western New York; bounded on the west by Lake Erie; drained by the Cattaraugus and Tonawanda Creeks. Covers a land area of 1,042.693 square miles, a water area of 184.161 square miles, and is located in the Eastern Time Zone at 42.75° N. Lat., 78.78° W. Long. The county was founded in 1821. County seat is Buffalo.

Erie County is part of the Buffalo-Cheektowaga-Niagara Falls, NY Metropolitan Statistical Area. The entire metro area includes: Erie County, NY; Niagara County, NY

Weather Station: Buffalo Greater Buffalo Int'l   Elevation: 705 feet

	Jan	Feb	Mar	Apr	May	Jun	Jul	Aug	Sep	Oct	Nov	Dec
High	32	34	42	55	67	75	80	79	71	59	48	36
Low	19	19	26	37	47	57	62	61	54	43	34	24
Precip	3.1	2.5	2.9	3.0	3.4	3.6	3.2	3.3	4.0	3.6	4.0	3.9
Snow	24.4	17.2	13.4	2.8	0.3	tr	tr	tr	tr	0.9	8.1	26.9

High and Low temperatures in degrees Fahrenheit; Precipitation and Snow in inches

Weather Station: Wales   Elevation: 1,089 feet

	Jan	Feb	Mar	Apr	May	Jun	Jul	Aug	Sep	Oct	Nov	Dec
High	31	32	41	55	65	74	77	76	70	58	47	35
Low	16	15	22	33	43	54	57	56	49	39	31	21
Precip	3.5	2.6	3.0	3.4	3.4	4.2	3.9	3.7	4.3	3.7	3.7	3.8
Snow	32.8	19.0	15.9	4.8	0.3	0.0	0.0	0.0	0.0	0.3	10.1	27.7

High and Low temperatures in degrees Fahrenheit; Precipitation and Snow in inches

Population: 923,995; Growth (since 2000): -2.8%; Density: 886.2 persons per square mile; Race: 78.0% White, 13.4% Black/African American, 3.5% Asian, 0.5% American Indian/Alaska Native, 0.0% Native Hawaiian/Other Pacific Islander, 2.3% two or more races, 5.2% Hispanic of any race; Average household size: 2.32; Median age: 40.3; Age under 18: 20.6%; Age 65 and over: 16.9%; Males per 100 females: 93.0; Marriage status: 36.6% never married, 46.2% now married, 1.9% separated, 6.9% widowed, 10.2% divorced; Foreign born: 6.8%; Speak English only: 89.7%; With disability: 13.2%; Veterans: 7.5%; Ancestry: 24.4% German, 17.5% Polish, 16.9% Irish, 16.2% Italian, 6.7% English
Religion: Six largest groups: 38.4% Catholicism, 3.1% Baptist, 2.7% Lutheran, 2.1% Non-denominational Protestant, 2.0% Methodist/Pietist, 2.0% Presbyterian-Reformed
Economy: Unemployment rate: 3.7%; Leading industries: 14.6 % retail trade; 11.7 % health care and social assistance; 10.6 % other services (except public administration); Farms: 1,044 totaling 142,679 acres; Company size: 27 employ 1,000 or more persons, 47 employ 500 to 999 persons, 588 employ 100 to 499 persons, 22,133 employ less than 100 persons; Business ownership: 19,041 women-owned, 4,254 Black-owned, 1,316 Hispanic-owned, 2,429 Asian-owned, 291 American Indian/Alaska Native-owned
Employment: 14.5% management, business, and financial, 4.8% computer, engineering, and science, 12.3% education, legal, community service, arts, and media, 7.0% healthcare practitioners, 18.5% service, 25.4% sales and office, 6.3% natural resources, construction, and maintenance, 11.2% production, transportation, and material moving
Income: Per capita: $31,083; Median household: $54,006; Average household: $72,672; Households with income of $100,000 or more: 23.3%; Poverty rate: 14.9%
Educational Attainment: High school diploma or higher: 91.1%; Bachelor's degree or higher: 32.9%; Graduate/professional degree or higher: 14.6%
Housing: Homeownership rate: 65.0%; Median home value: $139,900; Median year structure built: 1955; Homeowner vacancy rate: 0.7%; Median selected monthly owner costs: $1,274 with a mortgage, $517 without a mortgage; Median gross rent: $778 per month; Rental vacancy rate: 4.3%
Vital Statistics: Birth rate: 108.9 per 10,000 population; Death rate: 104.1 per 10,000 population; Age-adjusted cancer mortality rate: 172.0 deaths per 100,000 population
Health Insurance: 95.7% have insurance; 71.6% have private insurance; 38.5% have public insurance; 4.3% do not have insurance; 2.0% of children under 18 do not have insurance
Health Care: Physicians: 41.0 per 10,000 population; Dentists: 8.2 per 10,000 population; Hospital beds: 46.4 per 10,000 population; Hospital admissions: 1,528.5 per 10,000 population
Air Quality Index (AQI): Percent of Days: 79.7% good, 20.0% moderate, 0.3% unhealthy for sensitive individuals, 0.0% unhealthy, 0.0% very unhealthy; Annual median: 39; Annual maximum: 119
Transportation: Commute: 89.6% car, 3.8% public transportation, 2.7% walk, 2.8% work from home; Mean travel time to work: 21.3 minutes
2016 Presidential Election: 44.5% Trump, 50.9% Clinton, 3.0% Johnson, 1.5% Stein
National and State Parks: Beaver Island State Park; Buckhorn Island State Park; Evangola State Park; Theodore Roosevelt Inaugural National Historic Site
Additional Information Contacts
Erie Government. . . . . (716) 858-8865
   http://www.erie.gov

Erie County Communities

AKRON (village). Covers a land area of 1.976 square miles and a water area of 0 square miles. Located at 43.02° N. Lat; 78.50° W. Long. Elevation is 741 feet.
History: Nearby is Tonawanda Indian Reservation. Incorporated 1849.
Population: 2,893; Growth (since 2000): -6.2%; Density: 1,464.2 persons per square mile; Race: 93.3% White, 0.9% Black/African American, 1.6% Asian, 0.0% American Indian/Alaska Native, 0.0% Native Hawaiian/Other Pacific Islander, 2.9% Two or more races, 1.3% Hispanic of any race; Average household size: 2.24; Median age: 42.2; Age under 18: 23.6%; Age 65 and over: 18.0%; Males per 100 females: 93.1; Marriage status: 33.0% never married, 41.2% now married, 0.0% separated, 10.4% widowed, 15.3% divorced; Foreign born: 5.8%; Speak English only: 92.7%; With disability: 12.9%; Veterans: 7.4%; Ancestry: 40.9% German, 19.9% Irish, 14.8% Polish, 11.2% English, 8.8% Italian
Employment: 8.2% management, business, and financial, 5.8% computer, engineering, and science, 7.6% education, legal, community service, arts, and media, 3.4% healthcare practitioners, 20.8% service, 25.1% sales and office, 11.6% natural resources, construction, and maintenance, 17.5% production, transportation, and material moving
Income: Per capita: $29,336; Median household: $51,900; Average household: $65,513; Households with income of $100,000 or more: 16.6%; Poverty rate: 4.8%
Educational Attainment: High school diploma or higher: 92.4%; Bachelor's degree or higher: 25.3%; Graduate/professional degree or higher: 12.2%

School District(s)
Akron Central SD (KG-12)
   Enrollment: 1,394 . . . . (716) 542-5006
Housing: Homeownership rate: 58.7%; Median home value: $115,800; Median year structure built: 1951; Homeowner vacancy rate: 0.0%; Median selected monthly owner costs: $1,121 with a mortgage, $428 without a mortgage; Median gross rent: $635 per month; Rental vacancy rate: 0.0%
Health Insurance: 95.6% have insurance; 77.2% have private insurance; 32.4% have public insurance; 4.4% do not have insurance; 4.2% of children under 18 do not have insurance
Safety: Violent crime rate: 14.0 per 10,000 population; Property crime rate: 24.6 per 10,000 population
Newspapers: Akron Bugle (weekly circulation 1,900)
Transportation: Commute: 89.9% car, 1.9% public transportation, 5.8% walk, 2.4% work from home; Mean travel time to work: 19.8 minutes
Additional Information Contacts
Village of Akron. . . . . (716) 542-9636
   http://www.erie.gov/akron

ALDEN (town). Covers a land area of 34.308 square miles and a water area of 0.201 square miles. Located at 42.91° N. Lat; 78.52° W. Long. Elevation is 863 feet.
History: Incorporated 1869.
Population: 10,135; Growth (since 2000): -3.2%; Density: 295.4 persons per square mile; Race: 83.4% White, 12.3% Black/African American, 0.0% Asian, 0.7% American Indian/Alaska Native, 0.2% Native Hawaiian/Other Pacific Islander, 2.2% Two or more races, 3.3% Hispanic of any race; Average household size: 2.52; Median age: 42.0; Age under 18: 17.8%; Age 65 and over: 15.5%; Males per 100 females: 135.8; Marriage status: 34.8% never married, 49.3% now married, 2.2% separated, 6.9% widowed, 9.1% divorced; Foreign born: 2.7%; Speak English only: 96.0%; With disability: 13.9%; Veterans: 7.6%; Ancestry: 35.3% German, 19.3% Polish, 13.6% Irish, 10.6% Italian, 7.3% English
Employment: 13.1% management, business, and financial, 4.5% computer, engineering, and science, 11.1% education, legal, community service, arts, and media, 5.8% healthcare practitioners, 17.9% service, 26.2% sales and office, 8.7% natural resources, construction, and maintenance, 12.7% production, transportation, and material moving
Income: Per capita: $26,140; Median household: $70,689; Average household: $76,856; Households with income of $100,000 or more: 27.3%; Poverty rate: 5.3%
Educational Attainment: High school diploma or higher: 90.2%; Bachelor's degree or higher: 23.3%; Graduate/professional degree or higher: 7.5%

School District(s)
Alden Central SD (PK-12)
   Enrollment: 1,625 . . . . (716) 937-9116

Housing: Homeownership rate: 80.2%; Median home value: $163,900; Median year structure built: 1962; Homeowner vacancy rate: 0.0%; Median selected monthly owner costs: $1,414 with a mortgage, $552 without a mortgage; Median gross rent: $771 per month; Rental vacancy rate: 0.0%
Health Insurance: 96.1% have insurance; 84.1% have private insurance; 29.9% have public insurance; 3.9% do not have insurance; 3.5% of children under 18 do not have insurance
Newspapers: Alden Advertiser (weekly circulation 3,700)
Transportation: Commute: 97.2% car, 0.0% public transportation, 1.0% walk, 1.6% work from home; Mean travel time to work: 27.0 minutes
Additional Information Contacts
Town of Alden . . . . (716) 937-6969
  http://alden.erie.gov

ALDEN (village).
Covers a land area of 2.718 square miles and a water area of 0 square miles. Located at 42.90° N. Lat; 78.49° W. Long. Elevation is 863 feet.
Population: 2,587; Growth (since 2000): -3.0%; Density: 951.7 persons per square mile; Race: 96.4% White, 0.9% Black/African American, 0.0% Asian, 1.0% American Indian/Alaska Native, 0.7% Native Hawaiian/Other Pacific Islander, 0.9% Two or more races, 0.2% Hispanic of any race; Average household size: 2.16; Median age: 44.1; Age under 18: 19.4%; Age 65 and over: 16.7%; Males per 100 females: 98.4; Marriage status: 29.4% never married, 48.0% now married, 1.9% separated, 8.3% widowed, 14.3% divorced; Foreign born: 2.6%; Speak English only: 98.7%; With disability: 18.1%; Veterans: 8.7%; Ancestry: 44.1% German, 22.9% Polish, 18.0% Irish, 13.1% Italian, 6.6% English
Employment: 12.2% management, business, and financial, 5.1% computer, engineering, and science, 10.2% education, legal, community service, arts, and media, 4.4% healthcare practitioners, 20.3% service, 24.6% sales and office, 5.8% natural resources, construction, and maintenance, 17.3% production, transportation, and material moving
Income: Per capita: $30,516; Median household: $53,558; Average household: $65,267; Households with income of $100,000 or more: 21.6%; Poverty rate: 9.4%
Educational Attainment: High school diploma or higher: 96.9%; Bachelor's degree or higher: 24.4%; Graduate/professional degree or higher: 10.6%
School District(s)
Alden Central SD (PK-12)
  Enrollment: 1,625 . . . . (716) 937-9116
Housing: Homeownership rate: 67.5%; Median home value: $136,800; Median year structure built: 1963; Homeowner vacancy rate: 0.0%; Median selected monthly owner costs: $1,215 with a mortgage, $530 without a mortgage; Median gross rent: $737 per month; Rental vacancy rate: 0.0%
Health Insurance: 94.2% have insurance; 79.7% have private insurance; 33.7% have public insurance; 5.8% do not have insurance; 12.5% of children under 18 do not have insurance
Newspapers: Alden Advertiser (weekly circulation 3,700)
Transportation: Commute: 93.2% car, 0.0% public transportation, 3.0% walk, 3.1% work from home; Mean travel time to work: 27.0 minutes

AMHERST (town).
Covers a land area of 53.203 square miles and a water area of 0.391 square miles. Located at 43.01° N. Lat; 78.76° W. Long. Elevation is 597 feet.
History: Amherst is home of the Amherst campus of the University at Buffalo.
Population: 125,024; Growth (since 2000): 7.3%; Density: 2,350.0 persons per square mile; Race: 80.6% White, 6.5% Black/African American, 8.9% Asian, 0.2% American Indian/Alaska Native, 0.0% Native Hawaiian/Other Pacific Islander, 2.6% Two or more races, 3.7% Hispanic of any race; Average household size: 2.34; Median age: 40.1; Age under 18: 19.3%; Age 65 and over: 19.2%; Males per 100 females: 89.9; Marriage status: 35.0% never married, 49.9% now married, 1.4% separated, 6.6% widowed, 8.4% divorced; Foreign born: 13.1%; Speak English only: 84.2%; With disability: 10.5%; Veterans: 6.5%; Ancestry: 24.7% German, 19.0% Italian, 15.9% Irish, 13.8% Polish, 8.1% English
Employment: 18.8% management, business, and financial, 7.2% computer, engineering, and science, 17.1% education, legal, community service, arts, and media, 9.2% healthcare practitioners, 14.8% service, 23.4% sales and office, 4.2% natural resources, construction, and maintenance, 5.3% production, transportation, and material moving
Income: Per capita: $40,124; Median household: $72,459; Average household: $98,705; Households with income of $100,000 or more: 35.8%; Poverty rate: 10.8%

Educational Attainment: High school diploma or higher: 95.4%; Bachelor's degree or higher: 55.3%; Graduate/professional degree or higher: 28.6%
School District(s)
Amherst Central SD (PK-12)
  Enrollment: 2,944 . . . . (716) 362-3051
Sweet Home Central SD (KG-12)
  Enrollment: 3,193 . . . . (716) 250-1402
Four-year College(s)
Daemen College (Private, Not-for-profit)
  Enrollment: 2,635 . . . . (716) 839-3600
  Tuition: In-state $27,990; Out-of-state $27,990
Housing: Homeownership rate: 70.6%; Median home value: $186,600; Median year structure built: 1970; Homeowner vacancy rate: 1.0%; Median selected monthly owner costs: $1,524 with a mortgage, $630 without a mortgage; Median gross rent: $1,020 per month; Rental vacancy rate: 3.0%
Health Insurance: 97.6% have insurance; 83.5% have private insurance; 30.2% have public insurance; 2.4% do not have insurance; 1.4% of children under 18 do not have insurance
Safety: Violent crime rate: 10.2 per 10,000 population; Property crime rate: 154.2 per 10,000 population
Transportation: Commute: 90.1% car, 1.9% public transportation, 2.9% walk, 4.2% work from home; Mean travel time to work: 19.2 minutes
Additional Information Contacts
Town of Amherst . . . . (716) 631-7000
  http://www.amherst.ny.us

ANGOLA (village).
Covers a land area of 1.417 square miles and a water area of 0 square miles. Located at 42.64° N. Lat; 79.03° W. Long. Elevation is 686 feet.
History: Incorporated 1873.
Population: 2,002; Growth (since 2000): -11.7%; Density: 1,413.2 persons per square mile; Race: 87.9% White, 2.0% Black/African American, 0.2% Asian, 4.9% American Indian/Alaska Native, 0.0% Native Hawaiian/Other Pacific Islander, 2.3% Two or more races, 5.7% Hispanic of any race; Average household size: 2.43; Median age: 40.9; Age under 18: 22.5%; Age 65 and over: 16.3%; Males per 100 females: 87.7; Marriage status: 33.1% never married, 46.8% now married, 2.6% separated, 6.8% widowed, 13.2% divorced; Foreign born: 1.0%; Speak English only: 98.5%; With disability: 15.2%; Veterans: 11.3%; Ancestry: 31.5% German, 25.2% Italian, 21.4% Polish, 18.6% Irish, 9.0% English
Employment: 8.9% management, business, and financial, 3.5% computer, engineering, and science, 7.0% education, legal, community service, arts, and media, 5.2% healthcare practitioners, 16.3% service, 29.6% sales and office, 9.7% natural resources, construction, and maintenance, 19.8% production, transportation, and material moving
Income: Per capita: $27,879; Median household: $56,411; Average household: $66,806; Households with income of $100,000 or more: 18.5%; Poverty rate: 10.7%
Educational Attainment: High school diploma or higher: 93.0%; Bachelor's degree or higher: 21.4%; Graduate/professional degree or higher: 7.9%
School District(s)
Erie 2-Chautauqua-Cattaraugus Boces
  Enrollment: n/a . . . . (716) 549-4454
Evans-Brant Central SD (Lake Shore) (KG-12)
  Enrollment: 2,394 . . . . (716) 926-2201
Vocational/Technical School(s)
Erie 2 Chautauqua Cattaraugus BOCES-Practical Nursing Program (Public)
  Enrollment: 131 . . . . (716) 549-4454
  Tuition: $10,000
Housing: Homeownership rate: 68.7%; Median home value: $113,400; Median year structure built: 1941; Homeowner vacancy rate: 0.2%; Median selected monthly owner costs: $1,281 with a mortgage, $503 without a mortgage; Median gross rent: $636 per month; Rental vacancy rate: 20.3%
Health Insurance: 89.1% have insurance; 67.4% have private insurance; 38.1% have public insurance; 10.9% do not have insurance; 16.5% of children under 18 do not have insurance
Transportation: Commute: 95.7% car, 0.8% public transportation, 3.4% walk, 0.0% work from home; Mean travel time to work: 28.8 minutes

ANGOLA ON THE LAKE (CDP). Covers a land area of 2.546 square miles and a water area of 0 square miles. Located at 42.65° N. Lat; 79.05° W. Long. Elevation is 600 feet.

Population: 1,788; Growth (since 2000): 1.0%; Density: 702.4 persons per square mile; Race: 94.8% White, 0.0% Black/African American, 1.4% Asian, 0.0% American Indian/Alaska Native, 0.0% Native Hawaiian/Other Pacific Islander, 3.8% Two or more races, 0.6% Hispanic of any race; Average household size: 2.18; Median age: 48.0; Age under 18: 17.1%; Age 65 and over: 24.4%; Males per 100 females: 93.4; Marriage status: 34.0% never married, 47.0% now married, 1.6% separated, 8.5% widowed, 10.5% divorced; Foreign born: 4.9%; Speak English only: 98.9%; With disability: 10.0%; Veterans: 8.8%; Ancestry: 28.4% German, 26.6% Irish, 26.3% Polish, 19.8% Italian, 7.9% English

Employment: 16.4% management, business, and financial, 6.9% computer, engineering, and science, 6.3% education, legal, community service, arts, and media, 5.3% healthcare practitioners, 20.7% service, 17.8% sales and office, 3.8% natural resources, construction, and maintenance, 22.7% production, transportation, and material moving

Income: Per capita: $34,058; Median household: $47,008; Average household: $74,258; Households with income of $100,000 or more: 23.3%; Poverty rate: 12.0%

Educational Attainment: High school diploma or higher: 90.4%; Bachelor's degree or higher: 16.9%; Graduate/professional degree or higher: 6.6%

Housing: Homeownership rate: 78.0%; Median home value: $97,500; Median year structure built: 1955; Homeowner vacancy rate: 0.0%; Median selected monthly owner costs: $1,398 with a mortgage, $543 without a mortgage; Median gross rent: $881 per month; Rental vacancy rate: 0.0%

Health Insurance: 92.8% have insurance; 67.8% have private insurance; 43.1% have public insurance; 7.2% do not have insurance; 2.4% of children under 18 do not have insurance

Transportation: Commute: 97.5% car, 0.0% public transportation, 0.0% walk, 2.5% work from home; Mean travel time to work: 29.2 minutes

AURORA (town). Covers a land area of 36.393 square miles and a water area of 0.046 square miles. Located at 42.74° N. Lat; 78.64° W. Long.

History: Seat of Christ the King Seminary. Site (1895-1939) of the Roycroft Shops, founded by Elbert Hubbard. Restored home of Millard and Abigail Fillmore as a National Historic Landmark. Incorporated 1874.

Population: 13,857; Growth (since 2000): -1.0%; Density: 380.8 persons per square mile; Race: 97.2% White, 0.7% Black/African American, 0.6% Asian, 0.1% American Indian/Alaska Native, 0.0% Native Hawaiian/Other Pacific Islander, 1.4% Two or more races, 1.4% Hispanic of any race; Average household size: 2.46; Median age: 45.8; Age under 18: 20.9%; Age 65 and over: 18.5%; Males per 100 females: 92.7; Marriage status: 26.0% never married, 57.6% now married, 1.5% separated, 5.4% widowed, 10.9% divorced; Foreign born: 2.6%; Speak English only: 98.0%; With disability: 10.6%; Veterans: 5.7%; Ancestry: 33.1% German, 21.3% Irish, 17.3% Polish, 15.2% English, 14.0% Italian

Employment: 18.5% management, business, and financial, 6.4% computer, engineering, and science, 15.3% education, legal, community service, arts, and media, 8.0% healthcare practitioners, 13.7% service, 21.7% sales and office, 8.1% natural resources, construction, and maintenance, 8.4% production, transportation, and material moving

Income: Per capita: $41,033; Median household: $76,453; Average household: $101,561; Households with income of $100,000 or more: 37.0%; Poverty rate: 7.4%

Educational Attainment: High school diploma or higher: 95.7%; Bachelor's degree or higher: 46.3%; Graduate/professional degree or higher: 19.1%

Housing: Homeownership rate: 80.7%; Median home value: $201,100; Median year structure built: 1953; Homeowner vacancy rate: 0.6%; Median selected monthly owner costs: $1,672 with a mortgage, $659 without a mortgage; Median gross rent: $734 per month; Rental vacancy rate: 4.0%

Health Insurance: 95.7% have insurance; 82.2% have private insurance; 26.6% have public insurance; 4.3% do not have insurance; 2.4% of children under 18 do not have insurance

Transportation: Commute: 89.1% car, 0.8% public transportation, 2.5% walk, 6.3% work from home; Mean travel time to work: 22.6 minutes

Additional Information Contacts

Town of Aurora . . . . (716) 652-3280
http://www.townofaurora.com

BILLINGTON HEIGHTS (CDP). Covers a land area of 3.193 square miles and a water area of 0.007 square miles. Located at 42.79° N. Lat; 78.63° W. Long. Elevation is 951 feet.

Population: 1,259; Growth (since 2000): -25.5%; Density: 394.3 persons per square mile; Race: 100.0% White, 0.0% Black/African American, 0.0% Asian, 0.0% American Indian/Alaska Native, 0.0% Native Hawaiian/Other Pacific Islander, 0.0% Two or more races, 0.0% Hispanic of any race; Average household size: 2.00; Median age: 52.1; Age under 18: 15.6%; Age 65 and over: 26.1%; Males per 100 females: 95.9; Marriage status: 32.2% never married, 48.6% now married, 1.3% separated, 6.7% widowed, 12.5% divorced; Foreign born: 1.3%; Speak English only: 98.7%; With disability: 10.4%; Veterans: 12.4%; Ancestry: 35.4% German, 17.6% English, 16.4% Irish, 16.2% Polish, 12.6% Italian

Employment: 21.3% management, business, and financial, 13.0% computer, engineering, and science, 9.9% education, legal, community service, arts, and media, 9.4% healthcare practitioners, 18.3% service, 15.5% sales and office, 12.2% natural resources, construction, and maintenance, 0.5% production, transportation, and material moving

Income: Per capita: $39,510; Median household: $67,961; Average household: $78,570; Households with income of $100,000 or more: 38.0%; Poverty rate: 6.4%

Educational Attainment: High school diploma or higher: 96.3%; Bachelor's degree or higher: 63.1%; Graduate/professional degree or higher: 21.3%

Housing: Homeownership rate: 85.1%; Median home value: $217,300; Median year structure built: 1960; Homeowner vacancy rate: 0.0%; Median selected monthly owner costs: $1,755 with a mortgage, $649 without a mortgage; Median gross rent: n/a per month; Rental vacancy rate: 0.0%

Health Insurance: 94.6% have insurance; 78.2% have private insurance; 34.0% have public insurance; 5.4% do not have insurance; 0.0% of children under 18 do not have insurance

Transportation: Commute: 92.3% car, 1.7% public transportation, 0.0% walk, 5.9% work from home; Mean travel time to work: 28.5 minutes

BLASDELL (village). Covers a land area of 1.123 square miles and a water area of 0 square miles. Located at 42.80° N. Lat; 78.83° W. Long. Elevation is 610 feet.

History: Incorporated 1898.

Population: 2,631; Growth (since 2000): -3.2%; Density: 2,343.7 persons per square mile; Race: 94.8% White, 1.5% Black/African American, 0.0% Asian, 1.6% American Indian/Alaska Native, 0.0% Native Hawaiian/Other Pacific Islander, 1.4% Two or more races, 4.0% Hispanic of any race; Average household size: 2.22; Median age: 40.7; Age under 18: 18.9%; Age 65 and over: 15.1%; Males per 100 females: 89.4; Marriage status: 38.3% never married, 35.7% now married, 1.5% separated, 9.6% widowed, 16.5% divorced; Foreign born: 1.9%; Speak English only: 97.5%; With disability: 13.6%; Veterans: 6.7%; Ancestry: 31.6% German, 30.9% Irish, 20.2% Polish, 15.8% Italian, 6.3% English

Employment: 12.2% management, business, and financial, 4.2% computer, engineering, and science, 7.7% education, legal, community service, arts, and media, 5.2% healthcare practitioners, 27.1% service, 20.3% sales and office, 10.9% natural resources, construction, and maintenance, 12.4% production, transportation, and material moving

Income: Per capita: $24,855; Median household: $43,472; Average household: $54,275; Households with income of $100,000 or more: 10.6%; Poverty rate: 12.8%

Educational Attainment: High school diploma or higher: 90.2%; Bachelor's degree or higher: 15.2%; Graduate/professional degree or higher: 4.8%

School District(s)

Frontier Central SD (PK-12)
　　Enrollment: 4,907 . . . . (716) 926-1711

Housing: Homeownership rate: 55.0%; Median home value: $94,000; Median year structure built: 1947; Homeowner vacancy rate: 0.0%; Median selected monthly owner costs: $1,069 with a mortgage, $413 without a mortgage; Median gross rent: $704 per month; Rental vacancy rate: 2.5%

Health Insurance: 92.3% have insurance; 70.2% have private insurance; 35.1% have public insurance; 7.7% do not have insurance; 6.9% of children under 18 do not have insurance

Transportation: Commute: 93.9% car, 0.7% public transportation, 3.5% walk, 0.7% work from home; Mean travel time to work: 18.6 minutes

BOSTON (town). Covers a land area of 35.820 square miles and a water area of 0 square miles. Located at 42.65° N. Lat; 78.76° W. Long. Elevation is 942 feet.

Population: 8,068; Growth (since 2000): 2.2%; Density: 225.2 persons per square mile; Race: 98.6% White, 0.7% Black/African American, 0.0% Asian, 0.0% American Indian/Alaska Native, 0.0% Native Hawaiian/Other Pacific Islander, 0.4% Two or more races, 1.0% Hispanic of any race; Average household size: 2.34; Median age: 49.0; Age under 18: 18.1%; Age 65 and over: 21.7%; Males per 100 females: 101.0; Marriage status: 24.4% never married, 56.9% now married, 0.7% separated, 7.9% widowed, 10.7% divorced; Foreign born: 2.0%; Speak English only: 97.9%; With disability: 9.6%; Veterans: 4.8%; Ancestry: 34.9% German, 24.9% Polish, 23.8% Irish, 17.1% Italian, 11.4% English

Employment: 12.3% management, business, and financial, 7.6% computer, engineering, and science, 13.1% education, legal, community service, arts, and media, 8.5% healthcare practitioners, 16.5% service, 21.5% sales and office, 10.9% natural resources, construction, and maintenance, 9.5% production, transportation, and material moving

Income: Per capita: $34,057; Median household: $65,417; Average household: $78,567; Households with income of $100,000 or more: 29.0%; Poverty rate: 3.5%

Educational Attainment: High school diploma or higher: 96.2%; Bachelor's degree or higher: 30.2%; Graduate/professional degree or higher: 13.2%

Housing: Homeownership rate: 83.6%; Median home value: $183,300; Median year structure built: 1968; Homeowner vacancy rate: 1.0%; Median selected monthly owner costs: $1,405 with a mortgage, $624 without a mortgage; Median gross rent: $782 per month; Rental vacancy rate: 0.0%

Health Insurance: 95.7% have insurance; 84.1% have private insurance; 32.7% have public insurance; 4.3% do not have insurance; 0.0% of children under 18 do not have insurance

Transportation: Commute: 96.2% car, 0.4% public transportation, 0.4% walk, 2.5% work from home; Mean travel time to work: 25.7 minutes

Additional Information Contacts

Town of Boston . . . . (716) 941-6113
http://www.townofboston.com

BOWMANSVILLE (unincorporated postal area)
ZCTA: 14026

Covers a land area of 0.753 square miles and a water area of 0 square miles. Located at 42.94° N. Lat; 78.69° W. Long. Elevation is 709 feet.

Population: 641; Growth (since 2000): -11.2%; Density: 851.4 persons per square mile; Race: 98.3% White, 1.7% Black/African American, 0.0% Asian, 0.0% American Indian/Alaska Native, 0.0% Native Hawaiian/Other Pacific Islander, 0.0% Two or more races, 0.0% Hispanic of any race; Average household size: 1.83; Median age: 52.5; Age under 18: 9.0%; Age 65 and over: 14.0%; Males per 100 females: 103.0; Marriage status: 22.7% never married, 47.5% now married, 0.0% separated, 3.4% widowed, 26.4% divorced; Foreign born: 0.0%; Speak English only: 98.0%; With disability: 11.7%; Veterans: 6.7%; Ancestry: 42.9% German, 26.4% Irish, 17.0% Polish, 10.8% English, 8.7% Italian

Employment: 15.8% management, business, and financial, 8.8% computer, engineering, and science, 6.7% education, legal, community service, arts, and media, 0.0% healthcare practitioners, 24.8% service, 28.5% sales and office, 3.2% natural resources, construction, and maintenance, 12.1% production, transportation, and material moving

Income: Per capita: $50,388; Median household: $81,375; Average household: $89,834; Households with income of $100,000 or more: 33.7%; Poverty rate: 14.7%

Educational Attainment: High school diploma or higher: 97.7%; Bachelor's degree or higher: 15.6%; Graduate/professional degree or higher: 3.5%

Housing: Homeownership rate: 67.1%; Median home value: $172,300; Median year structure built: 1962; Homeowner vacancy rate: 0.0%; Median selected monthly owner costs: $1,566 with a mortgage, $0 without a mortgage; Median gross rent: $643 per month; Rental vacancy rate: 0.0%

Health Insurance: 96.6% have insurance; 72.4% have private insurance; 30.3% have public insurance; 3.4% do not have insurance; 0.0% of children under 18 do not have insurance

Transportation: Commute: 89.8% car, 0.0% public transportation, 0.0% walk, 8.1% work from home; Mean travel time to work: 15.5 minutes

BRANT (town). Covers a land area of 24.314 square miles and a water area of 0.424 square miles. Located at 42.59° N. Lat; 79.02° W. Long. Elevation is 745 feet.

Population: 2,117; Growth (since 2000): 11.1%; Density: 87.1 persons per square mile; Race: 92.8% White, 0.6% Black/African American, 0.0% Asian, 5.1% American Indian/Alaska Native, 0.0% Native Hawaiian/Other Pacific Islander, 1.1% Two or more races, 1.5% Hispanic of any race; Average household size: 2.18; Median age: 46.6; Age under 18: 20.2%; Age 65 and over: 18.8%; Males per 100 females: 101.5; Marriage status: 29.7% never married, 47.8% now married, 3.1% separated, 5.2% widowed, 17.3% divorced; Foreign born: 0.9%; Speak English only: 97.9%; With disability: 12.0%; Veterans: 10.8%; Ancestry: 35.2% German, 25.8% Italian, 22.5% Polish, 13.2% Irish, 12.7% English

Employment: 15.1% management, business, and financial, 1.4% computer, engineering, and science, 7.0% education, legal, community service, arts, and media, 6.6% healthcare practitioners, 20.0% service, 22.2% sales and office, 13.5% natural resources, construction, and maintenance, 14.1% production, transportation, and material moving

Income: Per capita: $31,212; Median household: $49,583; Average household: $67,924; Households with income of $100,000 or more: 18.8%; Poverty rate: 10.3%

Educational Attainment: High school diploma or higher: 94.4%; Bachelor's degree or higher: 22.5%; Graduate/professional degree or higher: 9.9%

Housing: Homeownership rate: 77.8%; Median home value: $129,200; Median year structure built: 1950; Homeowner vacancy rate: 0.0%; Median selected monthly owner costs: $1,361 with a mortgage, $465 without a mortgage; Median gross rent: $648 per month; Rental vacancy rate: 0.0%

Health Insurance: 90.1% have insurance; 66.8% have private insurance; 37.1% have public insurance; 9.9% do not have insurance; 7.7% of children under 18 do not have insurance

Safety: Violent crime rate: 9.7 per 10,000 population; Property crime rate: 73.0 per 10,000 population

Transportation: Commute: 93.3% car, 0.0% public transportation, 1.0% walk, 5.3% work from home; Mean travel time to work: 27.1 minutes

BUFFALO (city). County seat. Covers a land area of 40.384 square miles and a water area of 12.110 square miles. Located at 42.89° N. Lat; 78.86° W. Long. Elevation is 600 feet.

History: Although Joseph Ellicott chose and mapped the site of Buffalo for the Holland Land Company in 1799, it was not until 1804 that he divided the land into lots and offered them for sale. He modeled the city plan after that of Washington, D.C. He called the place New Amsterdam, but settlers preferred to name it after Buffalo Creek. Buffalo was incorporated as a village in 1816. The early welfare of the settlement depended on its function as a trading center. The Erie Canal, opened in 1825, brought trade and prosperity. Buffalo stood at the transportation break in the great east-west route. In 1832, Buffalo was incorporated into a city. Steam engine manufacturers and other industries sprang up. After the Civil War, Buffalo became a railroad center.

Population: 259,574; Growth (since 2000): -11.3%; Density: 6,427.6 persons per square mile; Race: 47.6% White, 37.1% Black/African American, 5.2% Asian, 0.4% American Indian/Alaska Native, 0.0% Native Hawaiian/Other Pacific Islander, 3.8% Two or more races, 11.3% Hispanic of any race; Average household size: 2.26; Median age: 32.8; Age under 18: 22.9%; Age 65 and over: 12.2%; Males per 100 females: 92.0; Marriage status: 51.5% never married, 31.9% now married, 3.1% separated, 6.3% widowed, 10.3% divorced; Foreign born: 9.5%; Speak English only: 82.4%; With disability: 16.2%; Veterans: 6.0%; Ancestry: 12.1% Irish, 12.0% German, 10.7% Italian, 9.0% Polish, 3.6% English

Employment: 11.1% management, business, and financial, 3.3% computer, engineering, and science, 12.9% education, legal, community service, arts, and media, 5.5% healthcare practitioners, 24.1% service, 25.3% sales and office, 5.2% natural resources, construction, and maintenance, 12.7% production, transportation, and material moving

Income: Per capita: $22,294; Median household: $34,268; Average household: $50,456; Households with income of $100,000 or more: 12.1%; Poverty rate: 30.9%

Educational Attainment: High school diploma or higher: 83.9%; Bachelor's degree or higher: 25.8%; Graduate/professional degree or higher: 11.0%

School District(s)

Aloma D Johnson Community Charter School (KG-04)
    Enrollment: 288 . . . . (716) 856-4390

Buffalo Academy of Science Charter School (07-12)
  Enrollment: 460. . . . . (716) 854-2490
Buffalo City SD (PK-12)
  Enrollment: 34,293 . . . . (716) 816-3575
Buffalo United Charter School (KG-08)
  Enrollment: 660. . . . . (716) 835-9862
Charter School for Applied Technologies (KG-12)
  Enrollment: 2,084 . . . . (716) 876-7505
Charter School of Inquiry (KG-03)
  Enrollment: 160. . . . . (716) 833-3250
Cheektowaga Central SD (PK-12)
  Enrollment: 2,190 . . . . (716) 686-3606
Elmwood Village Charter School (KG-08)
  Enrollment: 399. . . . . (716) 886-4581
Elmwood Village Charter School Hertel
  Enrollment: n/a . . . . (716) 982-3421
Enterprise Charter School (KG-08)
  Enrollment: 402. . . . . (716) 855-2114
Health Sciences Charter School (09-12)
  Enrollment: 456. . . . . (716) 888-4080
Kenmore-Tonawanda Union Free SD (KG-12)
  Enrollment: 6,913 . . . . (716) 874-8400
King Center Charter School (KG-08)
  Enrollment: 425. . . . . (716) 891-7912
Oracle Charter School (09-12)
  Enrollment: 357. . . . . (716) 362-3188
South Buffalo Charter School (KG-08)
  Enrollment: 914. . . . . (716) 826-7213
Tapestry Charter School (KG-12)
  Enrollment: 820. . . . . (716) 204-5883
West Buffalo Charter School (KG-05)
  Enrollment: 349. . . . . (716) 923-1534
Western New York Maritime Charter School (09-12)
  Enrollment: 411. . . . . (716) 842-6289
Westminster Community Charter School (KG-08)
  Enrollment: 551. . . . . (716) 816-3450

Four-year College(s)
Bryant & Stratton College-Buffalo (Private, For-profit)
  Enrollment: 491. . . . . (716) 884-9120
  Tuition: In-state $16,995; Out-of-state $16,995
Canisius College (Private, Not-for-profit, Roman Catholic)
  Enrollment: 3,464 . . . . (716) 883-7000
  Tuition: In-state $36,454; Out-of-state $36,454
D'Youville College (Private, Not-for-profit)
  Enrollment: 3,021 . . . . (716) 829-8000
  Tuition: In-state $25,870; Out-of-state $25,870
Medaille College (Private, Not-for-profit)
  Enrollment: 2,198 . . . . (716) 880-2000
  Tuition: In-state $28,360; Out-of-state $28,360
SUNY Buffalo State (Public)
  Enrollment: 9,516 . . . . (716) 878-4000
  Tuition: In-state $7,976; Out-of-state $17,626
Trocaire College (Private, Not-for-profit, Roman Catholic)
  Enrollment: 1,399 . . . . (716) 826-1200
  Tuition: In-state $17,110; Out-of-state $17,110
University at Buffalo (Public)
  Enrollment: 30,648 . . . . (716) 645-2000
  Tuition: In-state $9,828; Out-of-state $27,068
Villa Maria College (Private, Not-for-profit, Roman Catholic)
  Enrollment: 596. . . . . (716) 896-0700
  Tuition: In-state $22,080; Out-of-state $22,080

Two-year College(s)
Erie Community College (Public)
  Enrollment: 11,135 . . . . (716) 851-1322
  Tuition: In-state $5,575; Out-of-state $10,141

Vocational/Technical School(s)
Continental School of Beauty Culture-Buffalo (Private, For-profit)
  Enrollment: 39. . . . . (716) 833-5016
  Tuition: $12,690
National Tractor Trailer School Inc-Buffalo (Private, For-profit)
  Enrollment: 91. . . . . (716) 849-6887
  Tuition: $10,248
Housing: Homeownership rate: 41.0%; Median home value: $77,800; Median year structure built: Before 1940; Homeowner vacancy rate: 0.9%; Median selected monthly owner costs: $947 with a mortgage, $378 without

a mortgage; Median gross rent: $735 per month; Rental vacancy rate: 4.9%
Health Insurance: 93.7% have insurance; 49.5% have private insurance; 54.1% have public insurance; 6.3% do not have insurance; 1.9% of children under 18 do not have insurance
Hospitals: Erie County Medical Center (550 beds); Kaleida Health; Mercy Hospital (349 beds); Sisters of Charity Hospital (413 beds); Upstate New York VA Healthcare System - Western NY (288 beds)
Safety: Violent crime rate: 101.9 per 10,000 population; Property crime rate: 383.6 per 10,000 population
Newspapers: Bee Publications (weekly circulation 37,000); Buffalo News (daily circulation 145,000); Riverside Review (weekly circulation 14,500); Rocket Publications (weekly circulation 34,000); Southtowns Citizen (weekly circulation 6,500)
Transportation: Commute: 78.3% car, 11.5% public transportation, 5.7% walk, 2.5% work from home; Mean travel time to work: 20.9 minutes; Amtrak: Train service available.
Airports: Buffalo Niagara International (primary service/medium hub)
Additional Information Contacts
City of Buffalo . . . . (716) 851-5431
  http://www.ci.buffalo.ny.us

CATTARAUGUS RESERVATION (reservation). Covers a land area of 25.263 square miles and a water area of 0.337 square miles. Located at 42.55° N. Lat; 79.01° W. Long.
Population: 1,910; Growth (since 2000): n/a; Density: 75.6 persons per square mile; Race: 7.5% White, 0.0% Black/African American, 2.0% Asian, 80.9% American Indian/Alaska Native, 0.5% Native Hawaiian/Other Pacific Islander, 7.5% Two or more races, 1.5% Hispanic of any race; Average household size: 2.43; Median age: 35.6; Age under 18: 25.7%; Age 65 and over: 14.0%; Males per 100 females: 89.6; Marriage status: 44.8% never married, 28.8% now married, 0.0% separated, 10.0% widowed, 16.4% divorced; Foreign born: 5.0%; Speak English only: 88.3%; With disability: 19.4%; Veterans: 10.1%; Ancestry: 4.5% Polish, 3.6% German, 2.6% Irish, 2.0% English, 1.4% American
Employment: 15.4% management, business, and financial, 3.0% computer, engineering, and science, 10.1% education, legal, community service, arts, and media, 9.4% healthcare practitioners, 17.5% service, 25.5% sales and office, 6.1% natural resources, construction, and maintenance, 12.9% production, transportation, and material moving
Income: Per capita: $18,574; Median household: $30,031; Average household: $44,466; Households with income of $100,000 or more: 8.9%; Poverty rate: 33.8%
Educational Attainment: High school diploma or higher: 83.5%; Bachelor's degree or higher: 16.0%; Graduate/professional degree or higher: 3.1%
Housing: Homeownership rate: 76.2%; Median home value: $87,600; Median year structure built: 1986; Homeowner vacancy rate: 0.0%; Median selected monthly owner costs: $1,032 with a mortgage, $358 without a mortgage; Median gross rent: $566 per month; Rental vacancy rate: 2.6%
Health Insurance: 78.2% have insurance; 42.4% have private insurance; 41.3% have public insurance; 21.8% do not have insurance; 28.6% of children under 18 do not have insurance
Transportation: Commute: 95.9% car, 0.0% public transportation, 4.1% walk, 0.0% work from home; Mean travel time to work: 19.9 minutes

CHAFFEE (unincorporated postal area)
ZCTA: 14030
Covers a land area of 19.866 square miles and a water area of 0.216 square miles. Located at 42.56° N. Lat; 78.51° W. Long. Elevation is 1,460 feet.
Population: 1,830; Growth (since 2000): 13.2%; Density: 92.1 persons per square mile; Race: 99.6% White, 0.0% Black/African American, 0.0% Asian, 0.0% American Indian/Alaska Native, 0.0% Native Hawaiian/Other Pacific Islander, 0.2% Two or more races, 3.0% Hispanic of any race; Average household size: 2.74; Median age: 44.0; Age under 18: 23.4%; Age 65 and over: 17.0%; Males per 100 females: 107.0; Marriage status: 27.6% never married, 57.6% now married, 0.2% separated, 4.0% widowed, 10.8% divorced; Foreign born: 0.0%; Speak English only: 98.1%; With disability: 13.8%; Veterans: 9.4%; Ancestry: 43.8% German, 16.1% Irish, 14.9% Italian, 13.4% Polish, 12.8% English
Employment: 9.9% management, business, and financial, 2.2% computer, engineering, and science, 6.8% education, legal, community service, arts, and media, 8.2% healthcare practitioners, 15.5% service,

26.2% sales and office, 13.9% natural resources, construction, and maintenance, 17.2% production, transportation, and material moving
Income: Per capita: $27,000; Median household: $63,421; Average household: $74,197; Households with income of $100,000 or more: 27.2%; Poverty rate: 8.2%
Educational Attainment: High school diploma or higher: 90.2%; Bachelor's degree or higher: 10.9%; Graduate/professional degree or higher: 2.6%
Housing: Homeownership rate: 84.0%; Median home value: $134,600; Median year structure built: 1964; Homeowner vacancy rate: 4.9%; Median selected monthly owner costs: $1,156 with a mortgage, $344 without a mortgage; Median gross rent: $830 per month; Rental vacancy rate: 0.0%
Health Insurance: 95.6% have insurance; 81.3% have private insurance; 30.9% have public insurance; 4.4% do not have insurance; 7.5% of children under 18 do not have insurance
Transportation: Commute: 92.8% car, 0.4% public transportation, 1.5% walk, 3.8% work from home; Mean travel time to work: 29.4 minutes

CHEEKTOWAGA (CDP). Covers a land area of 25.343 square miles and a water area of 0.057 square miles. Located at 42.91° N. Lat; 78.75° W. Long. Elevation is 650 feet.
Population: 74,597; Growth (since 2000): -6.7%; Density: 2,943.5 persons per square mile; Race: 82.6% White, 11.8% Black/African American, 2.5% Asian, 0.2% American Indian/Alaska Native, 0.1% Native Hawaiian/Other Pacific Islander, 2.1% Two or more races, 2.8% Hispanic of any race; Average household size: 2.19; Median age: 42.5; Age under 18: 17.5%; Age 65 and over: 19.1%; Males per 100 females: 88.5; Marriage status: 35.8% never married, 44.8% now married, 1.2% separated, 7.7% widowed, 11.7% divorced; Foreign born: 5.2%; Speak English only: 92.6%; With disability: 13.9%; Veterans: 8.8%; Ancestry: 30.2% Polish, 25.7% German, 15.4% Italian, 14.2% Irish, 5.4% English
Employment: 12.0% management, business, and financial, 4.3% computer, engineering, and science, 9.0% education, legal, community service, arts, and media, 6.9% healthcare practitioners, 17.4% service, 29.5% sales and office, 6.9% natural resources, construction, and maintenance, 14.1% production, transportation, and material moving
Income: Per capita: $28,160; Median household: $50,698; Average household: $61,169; Households with income of $100,000 or more: 16.4%; Poverty rate: 11.0%
Educational Attainment: High school diploma or higher: 91.5%; Bachelor's degree or higher: 22.7%; Graduate/professional degree or higher: 8.4%

School District(s)
Cheektowaga Central SD (PK-12)
    Enrollment: 2,190 . . . . (716) 686-3606
Cheektowaga-Maryvale Union Free SD (PK-12)
    Enrollment: 2,246 . . . . (716) 631-7407
Cheektowaga-Sloan Union Free SD (PK-12)
    Enrollment: 1,415 . . . . (716) 891-6402
Cleveland Hill Union Free SD (PK-12)
    Enrollment: 1,285 . . . . (716) 836-7200

Vocational/Technical School(s)
Empire Beauty School-Buffalo (Private, For-profit)
    Enrollment: 75 . . . . (800) 920-4593
    Tuition: $12,750
Housing: Homeownership rate: 69.6%; Median home value: $104,900; Median year structure built: 1960; Homeowner vacancy rate: 1.0%; Median selected monthly owner costs: $1,120 with a mortgage, $479 without a mortgage; Median gross rent: $809 per month; Rental vacancy rate: 5.0%
Health Insurance: 95.2% have insurance; 75.0% have private insurance; 37.3% have public insurance; 4.8% do not have insurance; 2.6% of children under 18 do not have insurance
Newspapers: Cheektowaga Times (weekly circulation 4,000)
Transportation: Commute: 94.9% car, 1.6% public transportation, 1.0% walk, 1.8% work from home; Mean travel time to work: 19.4 minutes

CHEEKTOWAGA (town). Covers a land area of 29.423 square miles and a water area of 0.063 square miles. Located at 42.91° N. Lat; 78.74° W. Long. Elevation is 650 feet.
History: Named for the Indian translation of "place of the crab apple tree". Population grew significantly after World War II. Settled 1809. Incorporated 1834.
Population: 87,484; Growth (since 2000): -7.0%; Density: 2,973.4 persons per square mile; Race: 84.4% White, 10.4% Black/African American, 2.3%

Asian, 0.2% American Indian/Alaska Native, 0.1% Native Hawaiian/Other Pacific Islander, 2.0% Two or more races, 2.6% Hispanic of any race; Average household size: 2.20; Median age: 42.7; Age under 18: 17.7%; Age 65 and over: 19.1%; Males per 100 females: 88.9; Marriage status: 35.4% never married, 45.3% now married, 1.4% separated, 7.8% widowed, 11.5% divorced; Foreign born: 5.0%; Speak English only: 93.0%; With disability: 13.6%; Veterans: 8.9%; Ancestry: 31.3% Polish, 26.4% German, 15.5% Italian, 14.7% Irish, 5.3% English
Employment: 12.3% management, business, and financial, 4.1% computer, engineering, and science, 8.7% education, legal, community service, arts, and media, 6.6% healthcare practitioners, 17.7% service, 29.1% sales and office, 6.9% natural resources, construction, and maintenance, 14.7% production, transportation, and material moving
Income: Per capita: $28,100; Median household: $50,868; Average household: $61,361; Households with income of $100,000 or more: 16.0%; Poverty rate: 10.7%
Educational Attainment: High school diploma or higher: 91.5%; Bachelor's degree or higher: 22.2%; Graduate/professional degree or higher: 8.0%

School District(s)
Cheektowaga Central SD (PK-12)
    Enrollment: 2,190 . . . . (716) 686-3606
Cheektowaga-Maryvale Union Free SD (PK-12)
    Enrollment: 2,246 . . . . (716) 631-7407
Cheektowaga-Sloan Union Free SD (PK-12)
    Enrollment: 1,415 . . . . (716) 891-6402
Cleveland Hill Union Free SD (PK-12)
    Enrollment: 1,285 . . . . (716) 836-7200

Vocational/Technical School(s)
Empire Beauty School-Buffalo (Private, For-profit)
    Enrollment: 75 . . . . (800) 920-4593
    Tuition: $12,750
Housing: Homeownership rate: 70.2%; Median home value: $104,800; Median year structure built: 1959; Homeowner vacancy rate: 1.0%; Median selected monthly owner costs: $1,112 with a mortgage, $479 without a mortgage; Median gross rent: $802 per month; Rental vacancy rate: 4.7%
Health Insurance: 95.3% have insurance; 75.4% have private insurance; 37.1% have public insurance; 4.7% do not have insurance; 2.5% of children under 18 do not have insurance
Safety: Violent crime rate: 24.1 per 10,000 population; Property crime rate: 296.0 per 10,000 population
Newspapers: Cheektowaga Times (weekly circulation 4,000)
Transportation: Commute: 94.9% car, 1.5% public transportation, 1.1% walk, 1.7% work from home; Mean travel time to work: 19.5 minutes
Additional Information Contacts
Town of Cheektowaga. . . . . (716) 686-3400
    http://tocny.org

CLARENCE (CDP). Covers a land area of 2.845 square miles and a water area of 0.065 square miles. Located at 42.98° N. Lat; 78.60° W. Long. Elevation is 738 feet.
Population: 2,740; Growth (since 2000): n/a; Density: 963.0 persons per square mile; Race: 97.6% White, 1.1% Black/African American, 1.3% Asian, 0.0% American Indian/Alaska Native, 0.0% Native Hawaiian/Other Pacific Islander, 0.0% Two or more races, 0.8% Hispanic of any race; Average household size: 2.40; Median age: 47.4; Age under 18: 20.2%; Age 65 and over: 29.2%; Males per 100 females: 79.4; Marriage status: 24.8% never married, 54.1% now married, 3.3% separated, 13.4% widowed, 7.6% divorced; Foreign born: 4.6%; Speak English only: 92.9%; With disability: 14.2%; Veterans: 5.8%; Ancestry: 31.4% German, 21.0% Italian, 16.6% Polish, 14.8% Irish, 7.5% English
Employment: 28.7% management, business, and financial, 2.2% computer, engineering, and science, 15.9% education, legal, community service, arts, and media, 12.4% healthcare practitioners, 10.8% service, 21.1% sales and office, 6.0% natural resources, construction, and maintenance, 3.0% production, transportation, and material moving
Income: Per capita: $33,139; Median household: $87,308; Average household: $84,042; Households with income of $100,000 or more: 45.2%; Poverty rate: 11.3%
Educational Attainment: High school diploma or higher: 93.9%; Bachelor's degree or higher: 45.5%; Graduate/professional degree or higher: 24.2%

School District(s)
Clarence Central SD (KG-12)
    Enrollment: 4,510 . . . . (716) 407-9102

Housing: Homeownership rate: 67.9%; Median home value: $224,800; Median year structure built: 1962; Homeowner vacancy rate: 0.0%; Median selected monthly owner costs: $1,581 with a mortgage, $770 without a mortgage; Median gross rent: $530 per month; Rental vacancy rate: 0.0%
Health Insurance: 96.2% have insurance; 88.8% have private insurance; 27.3% have public insurance; 3.8% do not have insurance; 3.4% of children under 18 do not have insurance
Transportation: Commute: 91.2% car, 1.2% public transportation, 1.1% walk, 6.4% work from home; Mean travel time to work: 25.4 minutes

CLARENCE (town). Covers a land area of 53.503 square miles and a water area of 0.132 square miles. Located at 43.02° N. Lat; 78.65° W. Long. Elevation is 738 feet.

Population: 31,954; Growth (since 2000): 22.3%; Density: 597.2 persons per square mile; Race: 93.0% White, 0.7% Black/African American, 4.4% Asian, 0.0% American Indian/Alaska Native, 0.1% Native Hawaiian/Other Pacific Islander, 1.6% Two or more races, 1.8% Hispanic of any race; Average household size: 2.65; Median age: 44.8; Age under 18: 24.3%; Age 65 and over: 16.9%; Males per 100 females: 94.2; Marriage status: 24.4% never married, 61.5% now married, 1.4% separated, 6.9% widowed, 7.3% divorced; Foreign born: 6.5%; Speak English only: 92.3%; With disability: 8.5%; Veterans: 6.5%; Ancestry: 33.9% German, 25.0% Italian, 18.2% Irish, 15.8% Polish, 8.9% English
Employment: 22.8% management, business, and financial, 5.2% computer, engineering, and science, 16.6% education, legal, community service, arts, and media, 7.7% healthcare practitioners, 12.6% service, 22.2% sales and office, 6.8% natural resources, construction, and maintenance, 5.9% production, transportation, and material moving
Income: Per capita: $46,960; Median household: $95,315; Average household: $124,321; Households with income of $100,000 or more: 47.6%; Poverty rate: 3.9%
Educational Attainment: High school diploma or higher: 96.3%; Bachelor's degree or higher: 50.1%; Graduate/professional degree or higher: 25.3%

School District(s)
Clarence Central SD (KG-12)
    Enrollment: 4,510 . . . . (716) 407-9102
Housing: Homeownership rate: 84.7%; Median home value: $271,300; Median year structure built: 1985; Homeowner vacancy rate: 0.0%; Median selected monthly owner costs: $1,900 with a mortgage, $689 without a mortgage; Median gross rent: $942 per month; Rental vacancy rate: 0.7%
Health Insurance: 97.7% have insurance; 88.9% have private insurance; 22.4% have public insurance; 2.3% do not have insurance; 2.6% of children under 18 do not have insurance
Transportation: Commute: 92.6% car, 0.4% public transportation, 0.6% walk, 6.0% work from home; Mean travel time to work: 22.0 minutes
Additional Information Contacts
Town of Clarence . . . . (716) 741-4715
    http://clarence.ny.us

CLARENCE CENTER (CDP). Covers a land area of 2.258 square miles and a water area of 0 square miles. Located at 43.01° N. Lat; 78.63° W. Long. Elevation is 633 feet.

Population: 2,671; Growth (since 2000): 52.9%; Density: 1,182.9 persons per square mile; Race: 96.1% White, 0.0% Black/African American, 3.9% Asian, 0.0% American Indian/Alaska Native, 0.0% Native Hawaiian/Other Pacific Islander, 0.0% Two or more races, 0.0% Hispanic of any race; Average household size: 3.06; Median age: 37.6; Age under 18: 30.1%; Age 65 and over: 7.0%; Males per 100 females: 96.4; Marriage status: 26.9% never married, 64.5% now married, 0.4% separated, 5.1% widowed, 3.4% divorced; Foreign born: 6.1%; Speak English only: 90.1%; With disability: 3.3%; Veterans: 2.6%; Ancestry: 34.7% German, 28.8% Irish, 23.5% Italian, 15.3% English, 10.1% Polish
Employment: 23.1% management, business, and financial, 5.8% computer, engineering, and science, 31.3% education, legal, community service, arts, and media, 2.9% healthcare practitioners, 11.5% service, 20.4% sales and office, 3.5% natural resources, construction, and maintenance, 1.5% production, transportation, and material moving
Income: Per capita: $39,980; Median household: $107,222; Average household: $121,196; Households with income of $100,000 or more: 55.3%; Poverty rate: 0.5%
Educational Attainment: High school diploma or higher: 99.5%; Bachelor's degree or higher: 69.3%; Graduate/professional degree or higher: 31.0%

School District(s)
Clarence Central SD (KG-12)
    Enrollment: 4,510 . . . . (716) 407-9102
Housing: Homeownership rate: 99.0%; Median home value: $265,500; Median year structure built: 1982; Homeowner vacancy rate: 0.0%; Median selected monthly owner costs: $1,646 with a mortgage, $723 without a mortgage; Median gross rent: n/a per month; Rental vacancy rate: 0.0%
Health Insurance: 100.0% have insurance; 97.4% have private insurance; 7.9% have public insurance; 0.0% do not have insurance; 0.0% of children under 18 do not have insurance
Transportation: Commute: 90.0% car, 0.7% public transportation, 0.7% walk, 7.0% work from home; Mean travel time to work: 22.6 minutes

COLDEN (town). Covers a land area of 35.633 square miles and a water area of 0.089 square miles. Located at 42.65° N. Lat; 78.65° W. Long. Elevation is 1,079 feet.

Population: 3,310; Growth (since 2000): -0.4%; Density: 92.9 persons per square mile; Race: 98.7% White, 0.8% Black/African American, 0.5% Asian, 0.0% American Indian/Alaska Native, 0.0% Native Hawaiian/Other Pacific Islander, 0.0% Two or more races, 3.3% Hispanic of any race; Average household size: 2.47; Median age: 48.3; Age under 18: 20.1%; Age 65 and over: 17.1%; Males per 100 females: 98.2; Marriage status: 24.7% never married, 61.9% now married, 1.3% separated, 4.9% widowed, 8.5% divorced; Foreign born: 2.8%; Speak English only: 96.9%; With disability: 8.6%; Veterans: 7.3%; Ancestry: 37.1% German, 17.4% Irish, 16.3% Polish, 15.6% English, 9.7% Italian
Employment: 15.8% management, business, and financial, 7.8% computer, engineering, and science, 8.1% education, legal, community service, arts, and media, 7.5% healthcare practitioners, 17.2% service, 14.4% sales and office, 14.6% natural resources, construction, and maintenance, 14.6% production, transportation, and material moving
Income: Per capita: $33,217; Median household: $67,052; Average household: $80,969; Households with income of $100,000 or more: 27.7%; Poverty rate: 5.6%
Educational Attainment: High school diploma or higher: 94.3%; Bachelor's degree or higher: 27.0%; Graduate/professional degree or higher: 10.6%

School District(s)
Springville-Griffith Institute Central SD (KG-12)
    Enrollment: 1,757 . . . . (716) 592-3230
Housing: Homeownership rate: 81.6%; Median home value: $194,300; Median year structure built: 1958; Homeowner vacancy rate: 0.6%; Median selected monthly owner costs: $1,383 with a mortgage, $518 without a mortgage; Median gross rent: $626 per month; Rental vacancy rate: 10.2%
Health Insurance: 94.2% have insurance; 76.8% have private insurance; 29.9% have public insurance; 5.8% do not have insurance; 4.0% of children under 18 do not have insurance
Transportation: Commute: 93.5% car, 0.0% public transportation, 1.3% walk, 5.1% work from home; Mean travel time to work: 27.8 minutes

COLLINS (town). Covers a land area of 47.966 square miles and a water area of 0.174 square miles. Located at 42.49° N. Lat; 78.87° W. Long. Elevation is 879 feet.

Population: 6,583; Growth (since 2000): -20.8%; Density: 137.2 persons per square mile; Race: 72.5% White, 16.3% Black/African American, 0.9% Asian, 1.3% American Indian/Alaska Native, 0.1% Native Hawaiian/Other Pacific Islander, 2.8% Two or more races, 8.4% Hispanic of any race; Average household size: 2.34; Median age: 40.5; Age under 18: 11.3%; Age 65 and over: 12.9%; Males per 100 females: 228.6; Marriage status: 44.6% never married, 37.9% now married, 3.4% separated, 5.5% widowed, 12.0% divorced; Foreign born: 4.2%; Speak English only: 89.2%; With disability: 21.4%; Veterans: 7.9%; Ancestry: 28.3% German, 12.3% Irish, 10.3% Italian, 9.9% English, 7.0% Polish
Employment: 7.0% management, business, and financial, 4.3% computer, engineering, and science, 8.7% education, legal, community service, arts, and media, 7.9% healthcare practitioners, 26.4% service, 20.6% sales and office, 13.1% natural resources, construction, and maintenance, 12.0% production, transportation, and material moving
Income: Per capita: $18,643; Median household: $49,698; Average household: $70,193; Households with income of $100,000 or more: 17.0%; Poverty rate: 14.5%
Educational Attainment: High school diploma or higher: 82.4%; Bachelor's degree or higher: 11.5%; Graduate/professional degree or higher: 4.7%

Housing: Homeownership rate: 76.5%; Median home value: $101,600; Median year structure built: 1950; Homeowner vacancy rate: 0.0%; Median selected monthly owner costs: $1,085 with a mortgage, $416 without a mortgage; Median gross rent: $583 per month; Rental vacancy rate: 4.0%
Health Insurance: 94.1% have insurance; 65.7% have private insurance; 46.0% have public insurance; 5.9% do not have insurance; 0.8% of children under 18 do not have insurance
Transportation: Commute: 94.4% car, 0.1% public transportation, 1.9% walk, 3.2% work from home; Mean travel time to work: 26.1 minutes
Additional Information Contacts
Town of Collins . . . . (716) 532-4887
　http://www.townofcollins.com

COLLINS CENTER (unincorporated postal area)
ZCTA: 14035

Covers a land area of 0.228 square miles and a water area of 0 square miles. Located at 42.49° N. Lat; 78.85° W. Long. Elevation is 1,102 feet.
Population: 101; Growth (since 2000): n/a; Density: 442.1 persons per square mile; Race: 100.0% White, 0.0% Black/African American, 0.0% Asian, 0.0% American Indian/Alaska Native, 0.0% Native Hawaiian/Other Pacific Islander, 0.0% Two or more races, 0.0% Hispanic of any race; Average household size: 3.06; Median age: 38.8; Age under 18: 37.6%; Age 65 and over: 16.8%; Males per 100 females: 98.4; Marriage status: 0.0% never married, 66.7% now married, 30.2% separated, 7.9% widowed, 25.4% divorced; Foreign born: 0.0%; Speak English only: 90.5%; With disability: 5.0%; Veterans: 9.5%; Ancestry: 15.8% Polish, 11.9% English, 10.9% Irish, 5.0% French
Employment: 0.0% management, business, and financial, 18.5% computer, engineering, and science, 22.2% education, legal, community service, arts, and media, 59.3% healthcare practitioners, 0.0% service, 0.0% sales and office, 0.0% natural resources, construction, and maintenance, 0.0% production, transportation, and material moving
Income: Per capita: $37,127; Median household: $70,859; Average household: $119,933; Households with income of $100,000 or more: 18.2%; Poverty rate: 5.0%
Educational Attainment: High school diploma or higher: 100.0%; Bachelor's degree or higher: 17.5%; Graduate/professional degree or higher: 9.5%
Housing: Homeownership rate: 51.5%; Median home value: n/a; Median year structure built: Before 1940; Homeowner vacancy rate: 0.0%; Median selected monthly owner costs: $0 with a mortgage, $0 without a mortgage; Median gross rent: n/a per month; Rental vacancy rate: 0.0%
Health Insurance: 81.2% have insurance; 27.7% have private insurance; 65.3% have public insurance; 18.8% do not have insurance; 0.0% of children under 18 do not have insurance
Transportation: Commute: 100.0% car, 0.0% public transportation, 0.0% walk, 0.0% work from home; Mean travel time to work: 0.0 minutes

CONCORD (town). Covers a land area of 69.934 square miles and a water area of 0.160 square miles. Located at 42.55° N. Lat; 78.70° W. Long. Elevation is 1,352 feet.
Population: 8,550; Growth (since 2000): 0.3%; Density: 122.3 persons per square mile; Race: 96.8% White, 0.8% Black/African American, 0.3% Asian, 1.0% American Indian/Alaska Native, 0.0% Native Hawaiian/Other Pacific Islander, 0.9% Two or more races, 1.2% Hispanic of any race; Average household size: 2.32; Median age: 46.4; Age under 18: 21.7%; Age 65 and over: 19.2%; Males per 100 females: 98.0; Marriage status: 24.3% never married, 58.1% now married, 1.9% separated, 7.1% widowed, 10.4% divorced; Foreign born: 2.7%; Speak English only: 97.2%; With disability: 12.5%; Veterans: 11.3%; Ancestry: 39.1% German, 19.6% Polish, 18.6% Irish, 13.1% English, 8.3% Italian
Employment: 12.0% management, business, and financial, 3.9% computer, engineering, and science, 8.9% education, legal, community service, arts, and media, 6.9% healthcare practitioners, 21.0% service, 21.8% sales and office, 12.1% natural resources, construction, and maintenance, 13.5% production, transportation, and material moving
Income: Per capita: $28,850; Median household: $54,832; Average household: $67,239; Households with income of $100,000 or more: 20.3%; Poverty rate: 8.5%
Educational Attainment: High school diploma or higher: 93.6%; Bachelor's degree or higher: 22.8%; Graduate/professional degree or higher: 9.6%
Housing: Homeownership rate: 73.1%; Median home value: $137,700; Median year structure built: 1961; Homeowner vacancy rate: 0.3%; Median

selected monthly owner costs: $1,172 with a mortgage, $497 without a mortgage; Median gross rent: $605 per month; Rental vacancy rate: 2.8%
Health Insurance: 96.9% have insurance; 77.2% have private insurance; 38.2% have public insurance; 3.1% do not have insurance; 1.7% of children under 18 do not have insurance
Transportation: Commute: 95.1% car, 0.0% public transportation, 2.7% walk, 2.2% work from home; Mean travel time to work: 21.9 minutes
Additional Information Contacts
Town of Concord . . . . (716) 592-4948
　http://www.townofconcordny.com

DEPEW (village). Covers a land area of 5.074 square miles and a water area of 0 square miles. Located at 42.91° N. Lat; 78.70° W. Long. Elevation is 673 feet.
History: Founded in 1892 as a village, it was named for Chauncey M. Depew (1834-1928), a Railroad executive and later a U.S. senator. Incorporated 1894.
Population: 15,283; Growth (since 2000): -8.1%; Density: 3,012.1 persons per square mile; Race: 95.1% White, 1.1% Black/African American, 0.8% Asian, 0.8% American Indian/Alaska Native, 0.0% Native Hawaiian/Other Pacific Islander, 1.3% Two or more races, 2.7% Hispanic of any race; Average household size: 2.30; Median age: 41.1; Age under 18: 18.6%; Age 65 and over: 18.2%; Males per 100 females: 92.8; Marriage status: 32.7% never married, 50.5% now married, 2.2% separated, 7.1% widowed, 9.7% divorced; Foreign born: 2.9%; Speak English only: 95.9%; With disability: 11.0%; Veterans: 8.2%; Ancestry: 33.5% German, 32.6% Polish, 18.5% Irish, 16.2% Italian, 5.3% English
Employment: 14.5% management, business, and financial, 3.3% computer, engineering, and science, 7.0% education, legal, community service, arts, and media, 5.6% healthcare practitioners, 20.7% service, 26.5% sales and office, 7.2% natural resources, construction, and maintenance, 15.0% production, transportation, and material moving
Income: Per capita: $28,162; Median household: $54,967; Average household: $63,918; Households with income of $100,000 or more: 16.4%; Poverty rate: 8.2%
Educational Attainment: High school diploma or higher: 94.3%; Bachelor's degree or higher: 21.0%; Graduate/professional degree or higher: 6.6%

School District(s)
Depew Union Free SD (KG-12)
　Enrollment: 1,857 . . . . (716) 686-5105
Lancaster Central SD (KG-12)
　Enrollment: 5,724 . . . . (716) 686-3201
Housing: Homeownership rate: 71.3%; Median home value: $114,600; Median year structure built: 1959; Homeowner vacancy rate: 1.0%; Median selected monthly owner costs: $1,155 with a mortgage, $518 without a mortgage; Median gross rent: $764 per month; Rental vacancy rate: 5.1%
Health Insurance: 96.0% have insurance; 78.7% have private insurance; 35.2% have public insurance; 4.0% do not have insurance; 2.1% of children under 18 do not have insurance
Safety: Violent crime rate: 11.2 per 10,000 population; Property crime rate: 162.4 per 10,000 population
Transportation: Commute: 95.9% car, 0.7% public transportation, 0.7% walk, 1.5% work from home; Mean travel time to work: 20.0 minutes; Amtrak: Train service available.
Additional Information Contacts
Village of Depew . . . . (716) 683-1400
　http://www.villageofdepew.org

DERBY (unincorporated postal area)
ZCTA: 14047

Covers a land area of 13.137 square miles and a water area of 1.001 square miles. Located at 42.69° N. Lat; 78.99° W. Long. Elevation is 702 feet.
Population: 6,430; Growth (since 2000): -5.9%; Density: 489.4 persons per square mile; Race: 97.9% White, 0.5% Black/African American, 0.0% Asian, 0.0% American Indian/Alaska Native, 0.0% Native Hawaiian/Other Pacific Islander, 0.9% Two or more races, 2.3% Hispanic of any race; Average household size: 2.45; Median age: 45.5; Age under 18: 18.3%; Age 65 and over: 17.0%; Males per 100 females: 98.4; Marriage status: 33.2% never married, 52.1% now married, 1.0% separated, 7.2% widowed, 7.6% divorced; Foreign born: 3.6%; Speak English only: 93.7%; With disability: 13.6%; Veterans: 9.4%; Ancestry: 29.7% German, 23.0% Irish, 22.8% Italian, 20.7% Polish, 7.4% English

Employment: 11.2% management, business, and financial, 1.3% computer, engineering, and science, 5.4% education, legal, community service, arts, and media, 8.8% healthcare practitioners, 25.9% service, 23.7% sales and office, 7.2% natural resources, construction, and maintenance, 16.6% production, transportation, and material moving
Income: Per capita: $29,617; Median household: $64,485; Average household: $72,352; Households with income of $100,000 or more: 23.3%; Poverty rate: 11.7%
Educational Attainment: High school diploma or higher: 92.2%; Bachelor's degree or higher: 25.2%; Graduate/professional degree or higher: 10.2%

School District(s)
Evans-Brant Central SD (Lake Shore) (KG-12)
    Enrollment: 2,394 . . . . (716) 926-2201
Housing: Homeownership rate: 85.3%; Median home value: $128,700; Median year structure built: 1970; Homeowner vacancy rate: 0.0%; Median selected monthly owner costs: $1,269 with a mortgage, $563 without a mortgage; Median gross rent: $767 per month; Rental vacancy rate: 0.0%
Health Insurance: 92.3% have insurance; 77.0% have private insurance; 31.2% have public insurance; 7.7% do not have insurance; 10.5% of children under 18 do not have insurance
Transportation: Commute: 95.4% car, 0.4% public transportation, 2.1% walk, 1.7% work from home; Mean travel time to work: 24.4 minutes

EAST AMHERST (unincorporated postal area)
ZCTA: 14051
    Covers a land area of 16.336 square miles and a water area of 0.070 square miles. Located at 43.04° N. Lat; 78.70° W. Long. Elevation is 594 feet.
Population: 19,820; Growth (since 2000): 10.2%; Density: 1,213.3 persons per square mile; Race: 86.0% White, 2.2% Black/African American, 8.7% Asian, 0.1% American Indian/Alaska Native, 0.2% Native Hawaiian/Other Pacific Islander, 2.4% Two or more races, 2.5% Hispanic of any race; Average household size: 2.62; Median age: 45.6; Age under 18: 24.0%; Age 65 and over: 16.4%; Males per 100 females: 95.1; Marriage status: 21.7% never married, 66.7% now married, 1.7% separated, 5.3% widowed, 6.3% divorced; Foreign born: 11.4%; Speak English only: 86.4%; With disability: 7.8%; Veterans: 7.0%; Ancestry: 29.5% German, 23.1% Italian, 16.6% Irish, 12.8% Polish, 7.3% English
Employment: 20.5% management, business, and financial, 8.4% computer, engineering, and science, 15.6% education, legal, community service, arts, and media, 10.3% healthcare practitioners, 12.3% service, 24.2% sales and office, 4.9% natural resources, construction, and maintenance, 3.9% production, transportation, and material moving
Income: Per capita: $51,064; Median household: $113,750; Average household: $132,965; Households with income of $100,000 or more: 55.6%; Poverty rate: 3.5%
Educational Attainment: High school diploma or higher: 96.2%; Bachelor's degree or higher: 62.2%; Graduate/professional degree or higher: 34.7%

School District(s)
Williamsville Central SD (KG-12)
    Enrollment: 10,037 . . . . (716) 626-8005
Housing: Homeownership rate: 85.5%; Median home value: $266,600; Median year structure built: 1985; Homeowner vacancy rate: 0.5%; Median selected monthly owner costs: $1,962 with a mortgage, $775 without a mortgage; Median gross rent: $1,507 per month; Rental vacancy rate: 0.0%
Health Insurance: 97.9% have insurance; 89.4% have private insurance; 22.9% have public insurance; 2.1% do not have insurance; 3.9% of children under 18 do not have insurance
Transportation: Commute: 92.5% car, 0.8% public transportation, 0.6% walk, 5.8% work from home; Mean travel time to work: 22.2 minutes

EAST AURORA (village). Covers a land area of 2.512 square miles and a water area of 0.011 square miles. Located at 42.77° N. Lat; 78.62° W. Long. Elevation is 919 feet.
Population: 6,230; Growth (since 2000): -6.6%; Density: 2,480.6 persons per square mile; Race: 96.6% White, 1.5% Black/African American, 0.3% Asian, 0.1% American Indian/Alaska Native, 0.0% Native Hawaiian/Other Pacific Islander, 1.5% Two or more races, 1.2% Hispanic of any race; Average household size: 2.31; Median age: 44.9; Age under 18: 22.9%; Age 65 and over: 20.6%; Males per 100 females: 85.7; Marriage status: 23.6% never married, 54.5% now married, 1.7% separated, 6.5%

widowed, 15.3% divorced; Foreign born: 1.9%; Speak English only: 98.0%; With disability: 8.5%; Veterans: 6.7%; Ancestry: 35.5% German, 20.6% Irish, 19.5% English, 14.8% Italian, 11.7% Polish
Employment: 25.1% management, business, and financial, 6.0% computer, engineering, and science, 19.2% education, legal, community service, arts, and media, 5.3% healthcare practitioners, 10.9% service, 21.0% sales and office, 7.4% natural resources, construction, and maintenance, 5.1% production, transportation, and material moving
Income: Per capita: $37,255; Median household: $69,554; Average household: $87,535; Households with income of $100,000 or more: 29.9%; Poverty rate: 7.8%
Educational Attainment: High school diploma or higher: 96.1%; Bachelor's degree or higher: 50.8%; Graduate/professional degree or higher: 22.5%

School District(s)
East Aurora Union Free SD (KG-12)
    Enrollment: 1,823 . . . . (716) 687-2302
Iroquois Central SD (KG-12)
    Enrollment: 2,259 . . . . (716) 652-3000
Four-year College(s)
Christ the King Seminary (Private, Not-for-profit, Roman Catholic)
    Enrollment: 78 . . . . (716) 652-8900
Housing: Homeownership rate: 71.1%; Median home value: $189,500; Median year structure built: Before 1940; Homeowner vacancy rate: 0.0%; Median selected monthly owner costs: $1,633 with a mortgage, $605 without a mortgage; Median gross rent: $791 per month; Rental vacancy rate: 5.6%
Health Insurance: 97.0% have insurance; 83.4% have private insurance; 27.7% have public insurance; 3.0% do not have insurance; 1.1% of children under 18 do not have insurance
Newspapers: East Aurora Advertiser (weekly circulation 4,400); Elma Review (weekly circulation 1,200)
Transportation: Commute: 88.3% car, 0.2% public transportation, 4.0% walk, 5.9% work from home; Mean travel time to work: 22.6 minutes
Additional Information Contacts
Village of East Aurora . . . . (716) 652-6000
    http://www.east-aurora.ny.us

EAST CONCORD (unincorporated postal area)
ZCTA: 14055
    Covers a land area of 32.337 square miles and a water area of 0.034 square miles. Located at 42.56° N. Lat; 78.60° W. Long. Elevation is 1,457 feet.
Population: 1,419; Growth (since 2000): -3.4%; Density: 43.9 persons per square mile; Race: 97.0% White, 0.0% Black/African American, 0.0% Asian, 0.0% American Indian/Alaska Native, 0.0% Native Hawaiian/Other Pacific Islander, 3.0% Two or more races, 1.1% Hispanic of any race; Average household size: 2.50; Median age: 47.8; Age under 18: 18.5%; Age 65 and over: 17.2%; Males per 100 females: 100.1; Marriage status: 28.3% never married, 63.1% now married, 0.3% separated, 6.3% widowed, 2.4% divorced; Foreign born: 1.8%; Speak English only: 98.1%; With disability: 11.1%; Veterans: 15.1%; Ancestry: 30.6% German, 19.5% Irish, 16.7% Polish, 13.7% English, 11.5% Italian
Employment: 17.3% management, business, and financial, 3.5% computer, engineering, and science, 11.2% education, legal, community service, arts, and media, 7.4% healthcare practitioners, 12.5% service, 18.2% sales and office, 10.8% natural resources, construction, and maintenance, 19.2% production, transportation, and material moving
Income: Per capita: $29,364; Median household: $65,321; Average household: $72,430; Households with income of $100,000 or more: 26.8%; Poverty rate: 5.5%
Educational Attainment: High school diploma or higher: 92.2%; Bachelor's degree or higher: 20.1%; Graduate/professional degree or higher: 9.5%
Housing: Homeownership rate: 82.9%; Median home value: $173,000; Median year structure built: 1982; Homeowner vacancy rate: 0.0%; Median selected monthly owner costs: $1,284 with a mortgage, $540 without a mortgage; Median gross rent: $497 per month; Rental vacancy rate: 0.0%
Health Insurance: 98.0% have insurance; 71.9% have private insurance; 39.6% have public insurance; 2.0% do not have insurance; 0.9% of children under 18 do not have insurance
Transportation: Commute: 92.3% car, 0.0% public transportation, 1.6% walk, 4.9% work from home; Mean travel time to work: 23.1 minutes

EDEN (CDP). Covers a land area of 5.594 square miles and a water area of 0 square miles. Located at 42.65° N. Lat; 78.90° W. Long. Elevation is 820 feet.

Population: 3,176; Growth (since 2000): -11.3%; Density: 567.7 persons per square mile; Race: 99.6% White, 0.1% Black/African American, 0.0% Asian, 0.0% American Indian/Alaska Native, 0.0% Native Hawaiian/Other Pacific Islander, 0.0% Two or more races, 1.9% Hispanic of any race; Average household size: 2.53; Median age: 47.2; Age under 18: 18.7%; Age 65 and over: 14.1%; Males per 100 females: 100.5; Marriage status: 27.6% never married, 58.5% now married, 2.7% separated, 4.6% widowed, 9.3% divorced; Foreign born: 2.0%; Speak English only: 99.1%; With disability: 9.3%; Veterans: 10.6%; Ancestry: 37.0% German, 24.3% Irish, 13.5% Polish, 13.1% Italian, 10.5% English

Employment: 18.2% management, business, and financial, 5.1% computer, engineering, and science, 9.6% education, legal, community service, arts, and media, 7.3% healthcare practitioners, 15.7% service, 21.2% sales and office, 13.3% natural resources, construction, and maintenance, 9.6% production, transportation, and material moving

Income: Per capita: $34,532; Median household: $79,531; Average household: $86,671; Households with income of $100,000 or more: 40.6%; Poverty rate: 4.3%

Educational Attainment: High school diploma or higher: 98.0%; Bachelor's degree or higher: 36.5%; Graduate/professional degree or higher: 13.3%

School District(s)
Eden Central SD (PK-12)
    Enrollment: 1,396 . . . . (716) 992-3629
Housing: Homeownership rate: 87.4%; Median home value: $171,300; Median year structure built: 1958; Homeowner vacancy rate: 2.2%; Median selected monthly owner costs: $1,528 with a mortgage, $708 without a mortgage; Median gross rent: $574 per month; Rental vacancy rate: 0.0%
Health Insurance: 96.4% have insurance; 85.7% have private insurance; 22.4% have public insurance; 3.6% do not have insurance; 0.0% of children under 18 do not have insurance
Transportation: Commute: 94.0% car, 0.0% public transportation, 2.7% walk, 2.1% work from home; Mean travel time to work: 26.0 minutes

EDEN (town). Covers a land area of 39.790 square miles and a water area of 0.069 square miles. Located at 42.66° N. Lat; 78.88° W. Long. Elevation is 820 feet.

History: The "Original American Kazoo" is still made here, and though the factory itself may no longer be toured, there is still a visitors center that explains modern production methods as well as West African origins of the instrument. Established in 1916, this is now the world's only metal kazoo factory.

Population: 7,692; Growth (since 2000): -4.8%; Density: 193.3 persons per square mile; Race: 99.2% White, 0.1% Black/African American, 0.1% Asian, 0.0% American Indian/Alaska Native, 0.0% Native Hawaiian/Other Pacific Islander, 0.2% Two or more races, 1.8% Hispanic of any race; Average household size: 2.44; Median age: 48.4; Age under 18: 16.7%; Age 65 and over: 17.8%; Males per 100 females: 100.4; Marriage status: 27.7% never married, 54.7% now married, 1.9% separated, 7.0% widowed, 10.6% divorced; Foreign born: 1.7%; Speak English only: 98.2%; With disability: 12.4%; Veterans: 9.4%; Ancestry: 37.5% German, 21.4% Irish, 16.7% Polish, 15.7% Italian, 8.7% English

Employment: 17.3% management, business, and financial, 4.6% computer, engineering, and science, 6.5% education, legal, community service, arts, and media, 7.7% healthcare practitioners, 14.3% service, 21.5% sales and office, 15.1% natural resources, construction, and maintenance, 13.0% production, transportation, and material moving

Income: Per capita: $34,507; Median household: $69,557; Average household: $83,133; Households with income of $100,000 or more: 30.3%; Poverty rate: 4.5%

Educational Attainment: High school diploma or higher: 94.7%; Bachelor's degree or higher: 28.0%; Graduate/professional degree or higher: 10.4%

School District(s)
Eden Central SD (PK-12)
    Enrollment: 1,396 . . . . (716) 992-3629
Housing: Homeownership rate: 84.3%; Median home value: $167,700; Median year structure built: 1957; Homeowner vacancy rate: 1.3%; Median selected monthly owner costs: $1,454 with a mortgage, $616 without a mortgage; Median gross rent: $703 per month; Rental vacancy rate: 0.0%

Health Insurance: 95.6% have insurance; 82.8% have private insurance; 28.1% have public insurance; 4.4% do not have insurance; 0.9% of children under 18 do not have insurance
Safety: Violent crime rate: 6.5 per 10,000 population; Property crime rate: 48.4 per 10,000 population
Transportation: Commute: 94.2% car, 0.1% public transportation, 2.0% walk, 2.6% work from home; Mean travel time to work: 29.7 minutes
Additional Information Contacts
Town of Eden . . . . (716) 992-3408
    http://www.edenny.org

EGGERTSVILLE (CDP). Covers a land area of 2.851 square miles and a water area of 0.001 square miles. Located at 42.97° N. Lat; 78.81° W. Long. Elevation is 653 feet.

Population: 15,364; Growth (since 2000): n/a; Density: 5,388.3 persons per square mile; Race: 72.7% White, 14.9% Black/African American, 8.7% Asian, 0.3% American Indian/Alaska Native, 0.0% Native Hawaiian/Other Pacific Islander, 3.0% Two or more races, 2.9% Hispanic of any race; Average household size: 2.41; Median age: 37.6; Age under 18: 21.6%; Age 65 and over: 14.9%; Males per 100 females: 92.2; Marriage status: 34.1% never married, 51.7% now married, 2.1% separated, 4.9% widowed, 9.2% divorced; Foreign born: 13.6%; Speak English only: 86.1%; With disability: 10.0%; Veterans: 5.6%; Ancestry: 22.6% German, 19.1% Italian, 16.6% Irish, 10.2% Polish, 4.0% American

Employment: 16.7% management, business, and financial, 6.8% computer, engineering, and science, 17.3% education, legal, community service, arts, and media, 8.4% healthcare practitioners, 14.4% service, 23.5% sales and office, 4.3% natural resources, construction, and maintenance, 8.5% production, transportation, and material moving

Income: Per capita: $40,299; Median household: $69,726; Average household: $96,744; Households with income of $100,000 or more: 32.7%; Poverty rate: 13.8%

Educational Attainment: High school diploma or higher: 94.6%; Bachelor's degree or higher: 51.7%; Graduate/professional degree or higher: 26.5%

Housing: Homeownership rate: 75.9%; Median home value: $137,200; Median year structure built: 1952; Homeowner vacancy rate: 1.7%; Median selected monthly owner costs: $1,280 with a mortgage, $533 without a mortgage; Median gross rent: $837 per month; Rental vacancy rate: 2.7%
Health Insurance: 97.7% have insurance; 77.8% have private insurance; 34.1% have public insurance; 2.3% do not have insurance; 1.0% of children under 18 do not have insurance
Transportation: Commute: 89.1% car, 2.4% public transportation, 3.2% walk, 3.6% work from home; Mean travel time to work: 16.8 minutes

ELMA (town). Covers a land area of 34.517 square miles and a water area of 0.011 square miles. Located at 42.83° N. Lat; 78.65° W. Long. Elevation is 712 feet.

Population: 11,735; Growth (since 2000): 3.8%; Density: 340.0 persons per square mile; Race: 99.6% White, 0.0% Black/African American, 0.2% Asian, 0.1% American Indian/Alaska Native, 0.0% Native Hawaiian/Other Pacific Islander, 0.1% Two or more races, 0.1% Hispanic of any race; Average household size: 2.38; Median age: 50.4; Age under 18: 17.2%; Age 65 and over: 21.9%; Males per 100 females: 98.8; Marriage status: 24.0% never married, 60.4% now married, 0.2% separated, 7.2% widowed, 8.3% divorced; Foreign born: 1.9%; Speak English only: 96.3%; With disability: 9.9%; Veterans: 11.1%; Ancestry: 36.9% German, 23.7% Polish, 20.7% Irish, 15.1% Italian, 8.0% English

Employment: 19.3% management, business, and financial, 5.0% computer, engineering, and science, 12.9% education, legal, community service, arts, and media, 7.7% healthcare practitioners, 18.3% service, 18.2% sales and office, 8.0% natural resources, construction, and maintenance, 10.5% production, transportation, and material moving

Income: Per capita: $39,657; Median household: $78,180; Average household: $93,430; Households with income of $100,000 or more: 37.4%; Poverty rate: 4.2%

Educational Attainment: High school diploma or higher: 97.1%; Bachelor's degree or higher: 39.3%; Graduate/professional degree or higher: 17.1%

School District(s)
Iroquois Central SD (KG-12)
    Enrollment: 2,259 . . . . (716) 652-3000
Housing: Homeownership rate: 86.3%; Median home value: $228,900; Median year structure built: 1967; Homeowner vacancy rate: 0.0%; Median

selected monthly owner costs: $1,498 with a mortgage, $635 without a mortgage; Median gross rent: $932 per month; Rental vacancy rate: 0.0%
Health Insurance: 96.8% have insurance; 85.7% have private insurance; 28.2% have public insurance; 3.2% do not have insurance; 1.5% of children under 18 do not have insurance
Transportation: Commute: 93.5% car, 0.0% public transportation, 1.0% walk, 5.3% work from home; Mean travel time to work: 23.1 minutes
Additional Information Contacts
Town of Elma . . . . (716) 652-3260
    http://www.elmanewyork.com

ELMA CENTER (CDP).
Covers a land area of 6.253 square miles and a water area of 0 square miles. Located at 42.83° N. Lat; 78.63° W. Long. Elevation is 804 feet.
Population: 2,835; Growth (since 2000): 13.8%; Density: 453.3 persons per square mile; Race: 98.8% White, 0.0% Black/African American, 0.7% Asian, 0.0% American Indian/Alaska Native, 0.0% Native Hawaiian/Other Pacific Islander, 0.4% Two or more races, 0.4% Hispanic of any race; Average household size: 2.34; Median age: 55.2; Age under 18: 15.4%; Age 65 and over: 27.2%; Males per 100 females: 93.9; Marriage status: 18.5% never married, 59.7% now married, 0.0% separated, 12.7% widowed, 9.0% divorced; Foreign born: 2.8%; Speak English only: 98.2%; With disability: 8.6%; Veterans: 13.7%; Ancestry: 40.5% German, 22.6% Polish, 21.0% Italian, 20.3% Irish, 6.2% English
Employment: 25.3% management, business, and financial, 2.8% computer, engineering, and science, 17.9% education, legal, community service, arts, and media, 9.4% healthcare practitioners, 6.6% service, 19.8% sales and office, 10.2% natural resources, construction, and maintenance, 8.1% production, transportation, and material moving
Income: Per capita: $43,094; Median household: $90,801; Average household: $100,250; Households with income of $100,000 or more: 41.2%; Poverty rate: 1.9%
Educational Attainment: High school diploma or higher: 97.1%; Bachelor's degree or higher: 39.1%; Graduate/professional degree or higher: 16.9%
Housing: Homeownership rate: 92.2%; Median home value: $250,700; Median year structure built: 1969; Homeowner vacancy rate: 0.0%; Median selected monthly owner costs: $1,467 with a mortgage, $664 without a mortgage; Median gross rent: $1,056 per month; Rental vacancy rate: 0.0%
Health Insurance: 99.0% have insurance; 86.8% have private insurance; 31.8% have public insurance; 1.0% do not have insurance; 0.0% of children under 18 do not have insurance
Transportation: Commute: 95.2% car, 0.0% public transportation, 0.0% walk, 3.7% work from home; Mean travel time to work: 21.3 minutes

EVANS (town).
Covers a land area of 41.530 square miles and a water area of 0.032 square miles. Located at 42.65° N. Lat; 79.00° W. Long.
Population: 16,284; Growth (since 2000): -7.4%; Density: 392.1 persons per square mile; Race: 95.7% White, 0.6% Black/African American, 0.4% Asian, 0.7% American Indian/Alaska Native, 0.0% Native Hawaiian/Other Pacific Islander, 1.9% Two or more races, 2.7% Hispanic of any race; Average household size: 2.36; Median age: 47.1; Age under 18: 17.9%; Age 65 and over: 18.8%; Males per 100 females: 96.6; Marriage status: 31.0% never married, 51.2% now married, 1.4% separated, 7.5% widowed, 10.3% divorced; Foreign born: 2.9%; Speak English only: 96.3%; With disability: 14.6%; Veterans: 9.9%; Ancestry: 30.6% German, 21.9% Irish, 21.2% Polish, 20.7% Italian, 7.5% English
Employment: 10.6% management, business, and financial, 3.1% computer, engineering, and science, 7.2% education, legal, community service, arts, and media, 8.0% healthcare practitioners, 21.0% service, 24.7% sales and office, 7.9% natural resources, construction, and maintenance, 17.6% production, transportation, and material moving
Income: Per capita: $30,735; Median household: $60,911; Average household: $72,216; Households with income of $100,000 or more: 23.3%; Poverty rate: 11.1%
Educational Attainment: High school diploma or higher: 93.1%; Bachelor's degree or higher: 22.8%; Graduate/professional degree or higher: 9.4%
Housing: Homeownership rate: 84.0%; Median home value: $116,500; Median year structure built: 1957; Homeowner vacancy rate: 0.0%; Median selected monthly owner costs: $1,245 with a mortgage, $543 without a mortgage; Median gross rent: $768 per month; Rental vacancy rate: 8.4%

Health Insurance: 91.7% have insurance; 73.4% have private insurance; 34.1% have public insurance; 8.3% do not have insurance; 12.0% of children under 18 do not have insurance
Safety: Violent crime rate: 11.1 per 10,000 population; Property crime rate: 133.0 per 10,000 population
Transportation: Commute: 96.4% car, 0.3% public transportation, 1.5% walk, 1.4% work from home; Mean travel time to work: 27.5 minutes
Additional Information Contacts
Town of Evans. . . . . (716) 549-8787
    http://www.townofevans.org

FARNHAM (village).
Covers a land area of 1.207 square miles and a water area of 0 square miles. Located at 42.60° N. Lat; 79.08° W. Long. Elevation is 640 feet.
Population: 422; Growth (since 2000): 31.1%; Density: 349.7 persons per square mile; Race: 93.6% White, 1.2% Black/African American, 0.2% Asian, 0.0% American Indian/Alaska Native, 0.0% Native Hawaiian/Other Pacific Islander, 5.0% Two or more races, 1.7% Hispanic of any race; Average household size: 2.58; Median age: 39.5; Age under 18: 24.2%; Age 65 and over: 13.3%; Males per 100 females: 94.9; Marriage status: 28.7% never married, 55.7% now married, 0.0% separated, 2.9% widowed, 12.8% divorced; Foreign born: 1.4%; Speak English only: 99.7%; With disability: 15.2%; Veterans: 7.8%; Ancestry: 48.1% German, 16.8% Italian, 16.6% Irish, 14.9% English, 13.3% Polish
Employment: 11.0% management, business, and financial, 6.7% computer, engineering, and science, 4.3% education, legal, community service, arts, and media, 7.1% healthcare practitioners, 18.1% service, 16.7% sales and office, 11.4% natural resources, construction, and maintenance, 24.8% production, transportation, and material moving
Income: Per capita: $23,658; Median household: $59,583; Average household: $60,989; Households with income of $100,000 or more: 16.0%; Poverty rate: 13.7%
Educational Attainment: High school diploma or higher: 91.8%; Bachelor's degree or higher: 13.3%; Graduate/professional degree or higher: 5.5%
Housing: Homeownership rate: 82.1%; Median home value: $105,000; Median year structure built: Before 1940; Homeowner vacancy rate: 0.0%; Median selected monthly owner costs: $1,105 with a mortgage, $485 without a mortgage; Median gross rent: $790 per month; Rental vacancy rate: 0.0%
Health Insurance: 92.4% have insurance; 70.9% have private insurance; 35.8% have public insurance; 7.6% do not have insurance; 0.0% of children under 18 do not have insurance
Transportation: Commute: 92.6% car, 0.0% public transportation, 1.0% walk, 4.9% work from home; Mean travel time to work: 28.4 minutes

GETZVILLE (unincorporated postal area)
ZCTA: 14068
Covers a land area of 3.460 square miles and a water area of 0 square miles. Located at 43.03° N. Lat; 78.76° W. Long. Elevation is 584 feet.
Population: 7,066; Growth (since 2000): -29.5%; Density: 2,042.4 persons per square mile; Race: 88.5% White, 3.1% Black/African American, 7.3% Asian, 0.0% American Indian/Alaska Native, 0.0% Native Hawaiian/Other Pacific Islander, 0.8% Two or more races, 3.3% Hispanic of any race; Average household size: 2.37; Median age: 52.1; Age under 18: 18.9%; Age 65 and over: 29.2%; Males per 100 females: 81.7; Marriage status: 25.3% never married, 54.2% now married, 1.2% separated, 10.9% widowed, 9.6% divorced; Foreign born: 14.2%; Speak English only: 84.2%; With disability: 14.9%; Veterans: 9.4%; Ancestry: 25.7% German, 22.5% Italian, 17.7% Polish, 12.1% Irish, 10.3% English
Employment: 23.6% management, business, and financial, 5.1% computer, engineering, and science, 15.4% education, legal, community service, arts, and media, 12.4% healthcare practitioners, 13.1% service, 24.4% sales and office, 2.4% natural resources, construction, and maintenance, 3.6% production, transportation, and material moving
Income: Per capita: $42,324; Median household: $76,579; Average household: $104,406; Households with income of $100,000 or more: 40.5%; Poverty rate: 8.4%
Educational Attainment: High school diploma or higher: 93.1%; Bachelor's degree or higher: 46.5%; Graduate/professional degree or higher: 28.7%

Four-year College(s)
Bryant & Stratton College-Amherst (Private, For-profit)
    Enrollment: 282. . . . . (716) 625-6300
    Tuition: In-state $16,601; Out-of-state $16,601

Two-year College(s)
Bryant & Stratton College-Amherst (Private, For-profit)
 Enrollment: 282. . . . . (716) 625-6300
 Tuition: In-state $16,601; Out-of-state $16,601
Vocational/Technical School(s)
Bryant & Stratton College-Amherst (Private, For-profit)
 Enrollment: 282. . . . . (716) 625-6300
 2016-17 Tuition: In-state $16,601; Out-of-state $16,601
Housing: Homeownership rate: 75.2%; Median home value: $224,600; Median year structure built: 1984; Homeowner vacancy rate: 0.0%; Median selected monthly owner costs: $1,715 with a mortgage, $738 without a mortgage; Median gross rent: $1,011 per month; Rental vacancy rate: 4.3%
Health Insurance: 97.9% have insurance; 79.8% have private insurance; 35.6% have public insurance; 2.1% do not have insurance; 1.3% of children under 18 do not have insurance
Transportation: Commute: 93.8% car, 0.7% public transportation, 1.2% walk, 3.7% work from home; Mean travel time to work: 19.7 minutes

GLENWOOD (unincorporated postal area)
ZCTA: 14069
 Covers a land area of 8.515 square miles and a water area of 0.012 square miles. Located at 42.62° N. Lat; 78.64° W. Long. Elevation is 1,191 feet.
Population: 913; Growth (since 2000): 16.3%; Density: 107.2 persons per square mile; Race: 99.0% White, 0.1% Black/African American, 0.0% Asian, 0.9% American Indian/Alaska Native, 0.0% Native Hawaiian/Other Pacific Islander, 0.0% Two or more races, 0.0% Hispanic of any race; Average household size: 2.50; Median age: 53.8; Age under 18: 19.2%; Age 65 and over: 13.8%; Males per 100 females: 105.9; Marriage status: 13.8% never married, 71.6% now married, 3.2% separated, 4.1% widowed, 10.4% divorced; Foreign born: 1.1%; Speak English only: 98.8%; With disability: 12.0%; Veterans: 8.1%; Ancestry: 34.0% German, 21.4% Irish, 19.4% Italian, 17.9% Polish, 9.5% English
Employment: 5.9% management, business, and financial; 3.6% computer, engineering, and science, 11.6% education, legal, community service, arts, and media, 5.0% healthcare practitioners, 15.0% service, 20.9% sales and office, 21.5% natural resources, construction, and maintenance, 16.6% production, transportation, and material moving
Income: Per capita: $27,596; Median household: $55,278; Average household: $68,080; Households with income of $100,000 or more: 22.1%; Poverty rate: 2.1%
Educational Attainment: High school diploma or higher: 89.8%; Bachelor's degree or higher: 23.8%; Graduate/professional degree or higher: 10.3%
Housing: Homeownership rate: 85.4%; Median home value: $172,600; Median year structure built: 1971; Homeowner vacancy rate: 2.8%; Median selected monthly owner costs: $1,412 with a mortgage, $625 without a mortgage; Median gross rent: $397 per month; Rental vacancy rate: 0.0%
Health Insurance: 100.0% have insurance; 79.0% have private insurance; 35.7% have public insurance; 0.0% do not have insurance; 0.0% of children under 18 do not have insurance
Transportation: Commute: 100.0% car, 0.0% public transportation, 0.0% walk, 0.0% work from home; Mean travel time to work: 29.0 minutes

GRAND ISLAND (town). Covers a land area of 28.273 square miles and a water area of 5.020 square miles. Located at 43.02° N. Lat; 78.96° W. Long.
Population: 20,855; Growth (since 2000): 12.0%; Density: 737.6 persons per square mile; Race: 94.9% White, 1.3% Black/African American, 1.6% Asian, 0.1% American Indian/Alaska Native, 0.0% Native Hawaiian/Other Pacific Islander, 0.9% Two or more races, 2.8% Hispanic of any race; Average household size: 2.58; Median age: 41.9; Age under 18: 22.7%; Age 65 and over: 15.7%; Males per 100 females: 97.3; Marriage status: 25.4% never married, 61.4% now married, 1.9% separated, 4.7% widowed, 8.6% divorced; Foreign born: 6.0%; Speak English only: 94.0%; With disability: 10.0%; Veterans: 8.6%; Ancestry: 27.3% German, 21.8% Italian, 18.0% Irish, 15.2% Polish, 11.2% English
Employment: 18.1% management, business, and financial, 5.5% computer, engineering, and science, 11.8% education, legal, community service, arts, and media, 7.8% healthcare practitioners, 16.5% service, 25.1% sales and office, 5.2% natural resources, construction, and maintenance, 10.0% production, transportation, and material moving

Income: Per capita: $37,646; Median household: $81,818; Average household: $96,350; Households with income of $100,000 or more: 41.0%; Poverty rate: 6.3%
Educational Attainment: High school diploma or higher: 95.7%; Bachelor's degree or higher: 42.3%; Graduate/professional degree or higher: 20.1%
School District(s)
Grand Island Central SD (PK-12)
 Enrollment: 2,931 . . . . (716) 773-8800
Housing: Homeownership rate: 81.3%; Median home value: $193,700; Median year structure built: 1974; Homeowner vacancy rate: 0.8%; Median selected monthly owner costs: $1,546 with a mortgage, $692 without a mortgage; Median gross rent: $942 per month; Rental vacancy rate: 3.9%
Health Insurance: 96.5% have insurance; 84.9% have private insurance; 26.5% have public insurance; 3.5% do not have insurance; 1.9% of children under 18 do not have insurance
Newspapers: Island Dispatch (weekly circulation 1,200)
Transportation: Commute: 94.7% car, 0.2% public transportation, 0.0% walk, 3.5% work from home; Mean travel time to work: 21.7 minutes
Additional Information Contacts
Town of Grand Island . . . . (716) 773-9600
 http://www.gigov.com

GRANDYLE VILLAGE (CDP). Covers a land area of 1.883 square miles and a water area of 0 square miles. Located at 42.99° N. Lat; 78.95° W. Long. Elevation is 594 feet.
Population: 5,324; Growth (since 2000): n/a; Density: 2,827.5 persons per square mile; Race: 93.4% White, 1.4% Black/African American, 1.1% Asian, 0.0% American Indian/Alaska Native, 0.0% Native Hawaiian/Other Pacific Islander, 0.0% Two or more races, 4.8% Hispanic of any race; Average household size: 2.58; Median age: 38.0; Age under 18: 27.2%; Age 65 and over: 12.5%; Males per 100 females: 93.7; Marriage status: 25.7% never married, 60.1% now married, 2.1% separated, 4.0% widowed, 10.1% divorced; Foreign born: 4.8%; Speak English only: 93.6%; With disability: 7.6%; Veterans: 5.7%; Ancestry: 26.1% German, 19.9% Irish, 18.8% Italian, 14.4% Polish, 13.4% English
Employment: 17.4% management, business, and financial, 4.2% computer, engineering, and science, 12.1% education, legal, community service, arts, and media, 8.8% healthcare practitioners, 13.9% service, 23.0% sales and office, 6.7% natural resources, construction, and maintenance, 13.9% production, transportation, and material moving
Income: Per capita: $34,768; Median household: $72,102; Average household: $89,867; Households with income of $100,000 or more: 34.1%; Poverty rate: 8.9%
Educational Attainment: High school diploma or higher: 95.6%; Bachelor's degree or higher: 41.9%; Graduate/professional degree or higher: 16.9%
Housing: Homeownership rate: 89.8%; Median home value: $146,900; Median year structure built: 1959; Homeowner vacancy rate: 2.9%; Median selected monthly owner costs: $1,225 with a mortgage, $510 without a mortgage; Median gross rent: $995 per month; Rental vacancy rate: 0.0%
Health Insurance: 95.7% have insurance; 80.2% have private insurance; 25.4% have public insurance; 4.3% do not have insurance; 1.9% of children under 18 do not have insurance
Transportation: Commute: 94.6% car, 0.0% public transportation, 0.0% walk, 4.9% work from home; Mean travel time to work: 19.7 minutes

HAMBURG (town). Covers a land area of 41.321 square miles and a water area of 0.028 square miles. Located at 42.74° N. Lat; 78.86° W. Long. Elevation is 820 feet.
History: Seat of Hilbert College. Settled c.1808, incorporated 1874.
Population: 58,147; Growth (since 2000): 3.4%; Density: 1,407.2 persons per square mile; Race: 96.3% White, 1.1% Black/African American, 0.4% Asian, 0.3% American Indian/Alaska Native, 0.0% Native Hawaiian/Other Pacific Islander, 1.2% Two or more races, 1.9% Hispanic of any race; Average household size: 2.37; Median age: 43.5; Age under 18: 20.4%; Age 65 and over: 18.6%; Males per 100 females: 92.1; Marriage status: 28.5% never married, 52.0% now married, 1.1% separated, 7.1% widowed, 12.4% divorced; Foreign born: 2.6%; Speak English only: 96.7%; With disability: 11.2%; Veterans: 8.4%; Ancestry: 31.5% German, 25.7% Irish, 22.6% Polish, 17.4% Italian, 7.8% English
Employment: 13.5% management, business, and financial, 4.7% computer, engineering, and science, 12.3% education, legal, community service, arts, and media, 7.6% healthcare practitioners, 18.4% service,

25.1% sales and office, 7.2% natural resources, construction, and maintenance, 11.2% production, transportation, and material moving
Income: Per capita: $34,327; Median household: $65,349; Average household: $80,594; Households with income of $100,000 or more: 27.9%; Poverty rate: 6.8%
Educational Attainment: High school diploma or higher: 94.5%; Bachelor's degree or higher: 32.6%; Graduate/professional degree or higher: 13.7%

School District(s)
Frontier Central SD (PK-12)
  Enrollment: 4,907 . . . . (716) 926-1711
Hamburg Central SD (PK-12)
  Enrollment: 3,634 . . . . (716) 646-3200
Randolph Academy Union Free SD (KG-12)
  Enrollment: 31 . . . . (716) 358-6866

Four-year College(s)
Hilbert College (Private, Not-for-profit, Roman Catholic)
  Enrollment: 792 . . . . (716) 649-7900
  Tuition: In-state $21,800; Out-of-state $21,800
Housing: Homeownership rate: 74.6%; Median home value: $153,200; Median year structure built: 1969; Homeowner vacancy rate: 0.6%; Median selected monthly owner costs: $1,348 with a mortgage, $558 without a mortgage; Median gross rent: $809 per month; Rental vacancy rate: 3.1%
Health Insurance: 96.7% have insurance; 82.8% have private insurance; 29.4% have public insurance; 3.3% do not have insurance; 1.9% of children under 18 do not have insurance
Safety: Violent crime rate: 8.0 per 10,000 population; Property crime rate: 189.8 per 10,000 population
Newspapers: Sun & Erie Co. Independent (weekly circulation 10,000)
Transportation: Commute: 94.6% car, 1.1% public transportation, 1.5% walk, 2.3% work from home; Mean travel time to work: 22.8 minutes
Additional Information Contacts
Town of Hamburg . . . . (716) 649-6111
  http://www.townofhamburgny.com

HAMBURG (village).
Covers a land area of 2.486 square miles and a water area of 0 square miles. Located at 42.72° N. Lat; 78.83° W. Long. Elevation is 820 feet.
Population: 9,603; Growth (since 2000): -5.1%; Density: 3,862.8 persons per square mile; Race: 96.7% White, 0.7% Black/African American, 0.8% Asian, 0.0% American Indian/Alaska Native, 0.0% Native Hawaiian/Other Pacific Islander, 1.6% Two or more races, 0.6% Hispanic of any race; Average household size: 2.38; Median age: 41.3; Age under 18: 23.6%; Age 65 and over: 18.3%; Males per 100 females: 90.1; Marriage status: 23.7% never married, 56.9% now married, 1.1% separated, 7.3% widowed, 12.1% divorced; Foreign born: 1.7%; Speak English only: 96.4%; With disability: 9.2%; Veterans: 9.5%; Ancestry: 33.9% German, 25.4% Irish, 24.0% Polish, 15.1% Italian, 10.7% English
Employment: 15.5% management, business, and financial, 5.9% computer, engineering, and science, 18.0% education, legal, community service, arts, and media, 10.0% healthcare practitioners, 13.1% service, 23.3% sales and office, 4.8% natural resources, construction, and maintenance, 9.3% production, transportation, and material moving
Income: Per capita: $40,837; Median household: $75,459; Average household: $95,763; Households with income of $100,000 or more: 33.2%; Poverty rate: 5.9%
Educational Attainment: High school diploma or higher: 97.6%; Bachelor's degree or higher: 47.0%; Graduate/professional degree or higher: 21.9%

School District(s)
Frontier Central SD (PK-12)
  Enrollment: 4,907 . . . . (716) 926-1711
Hamburg Central SD (PK-12)
  Enrollment: 3,634 . . . . (716) 646-3200
Randolph Academy Union Free SD (KG-12)
  Enrollment: 31 . . . . (716) 358-6866

Four-year College(s)
Hilbert College (Private, Not-for-profit, Roman Catholic)
  Enrollment: 792 . . . . (716) 649-7900
  Tuition: In-state $21,800; Out-of-state $21,800
Housing: Homeownership rate: 72.8%; Median home value: $159,500; Median year structure built: 1954; Homeowner vacancy rate: 0.0%; Median selected monthly owner costs: $1,408 with a mortgage, $655 without a mortgage; Median gross rent: $792 per month; Rental vacancy rate: 0.0%

Health Insurance: 97.7% have insurance; 85.7% have private insurance; 29.4% have public insurance; 2.3% do not have insurance; 0.8% of children under 18 do not have insurance
Newspapers: Sun & Erie Co. Independent (weekly circulation 10,000)
Transportation: Commute: 94.7% car, 1.0% public transportation, 2.8% walk, 0.4% work from home; Mean travel time to work: 23.5 minutes
Additional Information Contacts
Village of Hamburg . . . . (716) 649-0200
  http://www.villagehamburg.com

HARRIS HILL (CDP).
Covers a land area of 4.041 square miles and a water area of 0 square miles. Located at 42.97° N. Lat; 78.68° W. Long. Elevation is 728 feet.
Population: 5,618; Growth (since 2000): 15.1%; Density: 1,390.4 persons per square mile; Race: 94.7% White, 1.2% Black/African American, 2.8% Asian, 0.2% American Indian/Alaska Native, 0.0% Native Hawaiian/Other Pacific Islander, 0.6% Two or more races, 1.7% Hispanic of any race; Average household size: 2.49; Median age: 43.5; Age under 18: 20.7%; Age 65 and over: 18.0%; Males per 100 females: 93.2; Marriage status: 28.5% never married, 56.6% now married, 0.5% separated, 5.8% widowed, 9.2% divorced; Foreign born: 5.6%; Speak English only: 95.1%; With disability: 10.0%; Veterans: 6.0%; Ancestry: 41.8% German, 26.3% Italian, 24.8% Irish, 14.9% Polish, 6.7% English
Employment: 27.8% management, business, and financial, 4.5% computer, engineering, and science, 15.9% education, legal, community service, arts, and media, 6.5% healthcare practitioners, 16.7% service, 17.5% sales and office, 5.3% natural resources, construction, and maintenance, 5.8% production, transportation, and material moving
Income: Per capita: $46,579; Median household: $88,159; Average household: $114,886; Households with income of $100,000 or more: 40.8%; Poverty rate: 2.5%
Educational Attainment: High school diploma or higher: 96.9%; Bachelor's degree or higher: 44.5%; Graduate/professional degree or higher: 20.4%
Housing: Homeownership rate: 83.2%; Median home value: $211,200; Median year structure built: 1962; Homeowner vacancy rate: 0.0%; Median selected monthly owner costs: $1,586 with a mortgage, $587 without a mortgage; Median gross rent: $1,362 per month; Rental vacancy rate: 3.1%
Health Insurance: 97.2% have insurance; 89.4% have private insurance; 24.7% have public insurance; 2.8% do not have insurance; 1.2% of children under 18 do not have insurance
Transportation: Commute: 91.6% car, 0.0% public transportation, 0.6% walk, 7.1% work from home; Mean travel time to work: 19.8 minutes

HOLLAND (CDP).
Covers a land area of 4.004 square miles and a water area of 0 square miles. Located at 42.64° N. Lat; 78.55° W. Long. Elevation is 1,106 feet.
Population: 1,016; Growth (since 2000): -19.4%; Density: 253.7 persons per square mile; Race: 98.8% White, 0.0% Black/African American, 0.0% Asian, 0.0% American Indian/Alaska Native, 0.0% Native Hawaiian/Other Pacific Islander, 1.2% Two or more races, 3.1% Hispanic of any race; Average household size: 2.15; Median age: 48.5; Age under 18: 17.5%; Age 65 and over: 28.0%; Males per 100 females: 95.1; Marriage status: 28.6% never married, 51.4% now married, 0.0% separated, 10.1% widowed, 9.9% divorced; Foreign born: 0.0%; Speak English only: 98.4%; With disability: 13.9%; Veterans: 11.5%; Ancestry: 36.3% German, 15.8% Polish, 14.0% Italian, 10.1% English, 8.5% Irish
Employment: 17.0% management, business, and financial, 3.2% computer, engineering, and science, 7.4% education, legal, community service, arts, and media, 3.6% healthcare practitioners, 15.5% service, 25.7% sales and office, 8.1% natural resources, construction, and maintenance, 19.5% production, transportation, and material moving
Income: Per capita: $28,008; Median household: $62,670; Average household: $59,430; Households with income of $100,000 or more: 16.8%; Poverty rate: 9.9%
Educational Attainment: High school diploma or higher: 90.2%; Bachelor's degree or higher: 19.8%; Graduate/professional degree or higher: n/a

School District(s)
Holland Central SD (PK-12)
  Enrollment: 907 . . . . (716) 537-8222
Housing: Homeownership rate: 71.6%; Median home value: $121,200; Median year structure built: 1954; Homeowner vacancy rate: 0.0%; Median

selected monthly owner costs: $1,118 with a mortgage, $465 without a mortgage; Median gross rent: n/a per month; Rental vacancy rate: 0.0%
Health Insurance: 92.7% have insurance; 69.6% have private insurance; 42.2% have public insurance; 7.3% do not have insurance; 0.0% of children under 18 do not have insurance
Transportation: Commute: 90.6% car, 0.2% public transportation, 6.3% walk, 1.3% work from home; Mean travel time to work: 23.0 minutes

HOLLAND (town).
Covers a land area of 35.790 square miles and a water area of 0.036 square miles. Located at 42.67° N. Lat; 78.52° W. Long. Elevation is 1,106 feet.
Population: 3,382; Growth (since 2000): -6.1%; Density: 94.5 persons per square mile; Race: 98.2% White, 0.0% Black/African American, 0.0% Asian, 0.0% American Indian/Alaska Native, 0.0% Native Hawaiian/Other Pacific Islander, 1.8% Two or more races, 0.9% Hispanic of any race; Average household size: 2.30; Median age: 45.0; Age under 18: 20.0%; Age 65 and over: 15.4%; Males per 100 females: 101.6; Marriage status: 32.3% never married, 52.0% now married, 0.6% separated, 6.5% widowed, 9.2% divorced; Foreign born: 0.7%; Speak English only: 97.5%; With disability: 11.6%; Veterans: 7.7%; Ancestry: 33.2% German, 24.3% Polish, 15.6% Irish, 9.4% English, 9.4% Italian
Employment: 12.9% management, business, and financial, 4.4% computer, engineering, and science, 4.7% education, legal, community service, arts, and media, 5.7% healthcare practitioners, 15.2% service, 27.1% sales and office, 15.8% natural resources, construction, and maintenance, 14.2% production, transportation, and material moving
Income: Per capita: $31,999; Median household: $59,271; Average household: $72,596; Households with income of $100,000 or more: 23.4%; Poverty rate: 8.7%
Educational Attainment: High school diploma or higher: 93.6%; Bachelor's degree or higher: 20.0%; Graduate/professional degree or higher: 7.4%

School District(s)
Holland Central SD (PK-12)
    Enrollment: 907 . . . . (716) 537-8222
Housing: Homeownership rate: 79.3%; Median home value: $149,400; Median year structure built: 1962; Homeowner vacancy rate: 0.0%; Median selected monthly owner costs: $1,260 with a mortgage, $546 without a mortgage; Median gross rent: $537 per month; Rental vacancy rate: 0.0%
Health Insurance: 94.6% have insurance; 78.7% have private insurance; 31.9% have public insurance; 5.4% do not have insurance; 0.0% of children under 18 do not have insurance
Transportation: Commute: 89.0% car, 0.1% public transportation, 3.6% walk, 6.9% work from home; Mean travel time to work: 26.5 minutes

IRVING (unincorporated postal area)
ZCTA: 14081
    Covers a land area of 35.169 square miles and a water area of 0.905 square miles. Located at 42.56° N. Lat; 79.07° W. Long..
Population: 3,097; Growth (since 2000): -9.4%; Density: 88.1 persons per square mile; Race: 57.9% White, 0.8% Black/African American, 0.9% Asian, 33.6% American Indian/Alaska Native, 0.3% Native Hawaiian/Other Pacific Islander, 4.9% Two or more races, 3.5% Hispanic of any race; Average household size: 2.21; Median age: 49.1; Age under 18: 18.9%; Age 65 and over: 19.2%; Males per 100 females: 92.7; Marriage status: 34.1% never married, 39.9% now married, 2.4% separated, 8.3% widowed, 17.7% divorced; Foreign born: 1.9%; Speak English only: 96.5%; With disability: 17.1%; Veterans: 9.9%; Ancestry: 19.2% German, 15.9% Polish, 13.0% Italian, 9.7% Irish, 7.9% English
Employment: 13.3% management, business, and financial, 1.5% computer, engineering, and science, 7.0% education, legal, community service, arts, and media, 6.4% healthcare practitioners, 21.9% service, 26.3% sales and office, 11.4% natural resources, construction, and maintenance, 12.0% production, transportation, and material moving
Income: Per capita: $27,835; Median household: $47,805; Average household: $62,905; Households with income of $100,000 or more: 16.4%; Poverty rate: 16.2%
Educational Attainment: High school diploma or higher: 89.2%; Bachelor's degree or higher: 16.5%; Graduate/professional degree or higher: 6.4%
Housing: Homeownership rate: 70.0%; Median home value: $112,200; Median year structure built: 1964; Homeowner vacancy rate: 0.0%; Median selected monthly owner costs: $1,162 with a mortgage, $429 without a mortgage; Median gross rent: $653 per month; Rental vacancy rate: 0.0%

Health Insurance: 89.1% have insurance; 62.4% have private insurance; 36.7% have public insurance; 10.9% do not have insurance; 13.3% of children under 18 do not have insurance
Transportation: Commute: 94.9% car, 0.0% public transportation, 2.6% walk, 2.5% work from home; Mean travel time to work: 24.1 minutes

KENMORE (village).
Covers a land area of 1.435 square miles and a water area of 0 square miles. Located at 42.96° N. Lat; 78.87° W. Long. Elevation is 614 feet.
History: Named for a prominent citizen. Incorporated 1899.
Population: 15,319; Growth (since 2000): -6.7%; Density: 10,672.5 persons per square mile; Race: 92.3% White, 5.8% Black/African American, 0.4% Asian, 0.2% American Indian/Alaska Native, 0.0% Native Hawaiian/Other Pacific Islander, 1.2% Two or more races, 2.7% Hispanic of any race; Average household size: 2.16; Median age: 42.2; Age under 18: 17.5%; Age 65 and over: 18.1%; Males per 100 females: 87.4; Marriage status: 31.1% never married, 52.7% now married, 1.2% separated, 6.0% widowed, 10.2% divorced; Foreign born: 4.2%; Speak English only: 93.6%; With disability: 13.1%; Veterans: 8.6%; Ancestry: 30.4% German, 27.3% Italian, 21.6% Irish, 13.0% Polish, 8.3% English
Employment: 16.4% management, business, and financial, 3.7% computer, engineering, and science, 14.6% education, legal, community service, arts, and media, 6.3% healthcare practitioners, 15.6% service, 30.5% sales and office, 4.2% natural resources, construction, and maintenance, 8.7% production, transportation, and material moving
Income: Per capita: $32,430; Median household: $59,785; Average household: $69,006; Households with income of $100,000 or more: 24.8%; Poverty rate: 7.9%
Educational Attainment: High school diploma or higher: 94.8%; Bachelor's degree or higher: 35.1%; Graduate/professional degree or higher: 16.6%

School District(s)
Kenmore-Tonawanda Union Free SD (KG-12)
    Enrollment: 6,913 . . . . (716) 874-8400
Housing: Homeownership rate: 68.5%; Median home value: $119,900; Median year structure built: Before 1940; Homeowner vacancy rate: 0.3%; Median selected monthly owner costs: $1,241 with a mortgage, $564 without a mortgage; Median gross rent: $733 per month; Rental vacancy rate: 4.9%
Health Insurance: 97.6% have insurance; 79.7% have private insurance; 34.6% have public insurance; 2.4% do not have insurance; 0.0% of children under 18 do not have insurance
Hospitals: Kenmore Mercy Hospital (184 beds)
Safety: Violent crime rate: 8.6 per 10,000 population; Property crime rate: 153.1 per 10,000 population
Transportation: Commute: 91.9% car, 2.3% public transportation, 2.5% walk, 1.9% work from home; Mean travel time to work: 21.0 minutes
Additional Information Contacts
Village of Kenmore . . . . (716) 873-5700
    http://www.villageofkenmore.org

LACKAWANNA (city).
Covers a land area of 6.571 square miles and a water area of 0.050 square miles. Located at 42.82° N. Lat; 78.83° W. Long. Elevation is 623 feet.
History: Named for the Lackawanna Steel Company. Formerly a major steel-making center, Lackawanna experienced the total decline of its foremost industry in the 1970s and 1980s. A distinguished city landmark is the elaborate Basilica of Our Lady of Victory, a Roman Catholic shrine. Incorporated 1909.
Population: 18,012; Growth (since 2000): -5.5%; Density: 2,741.1 persons per square mile; Race: 80.7% White, 8.5% Black/African American, 0.7% Asian, 0.1% American Indian/Alaska Native, 0.1% Native Hawaiian/Other Pacific Islander, 5.3% Two or more races, 9.5% Hispanic of any race; Average household size: 2.38; Median age: 37.3; Age under 18: 24.6%; Age 65 and over: 15.7%; Males per 100 females: 91.8; Marriage status: 43.4% never married, 36.8% now married, 2.4% separated, 8.9% widowed, 10.9% divorced; Foreign born: 10.3%; Speak English only: 81.0%; With disability: 17.5%; Veterans: 8.1%; Ancestry: 23.4% Polish, 17.2% Irish, 16.6% German, 12.8% Italian, 7.3% Other Arab
Employment: 9.5% management, business, and financial, 2.0% computer, engineering, and science, 8.8% education, legal, community service, arts, and media, 4.5% healthcare practitioners, 26.3% service, 25.6% sales and office, 4.9% natural resources, construction, and maintenance, 18.4% production, transportation, and material moving

Income: Per capita: $19,871; Median household: $35,482; Average household: $46,616; Households with income of $100,000 or more: 7.9%; Poverty rate: 25.4%

Educational Attainment: High school diploma or higher: 80.4%; Bachelor's degree or higher: 13.7%; Graduate/professional degree or higher: 5.6%

School District(s)
Global Concepts Charter School (KG-12)
   Enrollment: 964 . . . . (716) 821-1903
Lackawanna City SD (PK-12)
   Enrollment: 2,003 . . . . (716) 827-6767

Housing: Homeownership rate: 52.4%; Median home value: $90,100; Median year structure built: 1950; Homeowner vacancy rate: 0.0%; Median selected monthly owner costs: $1,003 with a mortgage, $436 without a mortgage; Median gross rent: $621 per month; Rental vacancy rate: 3.8%

Health Insurance: 94.5% have insurance; 54.9% have private insurance; 53.7% have public insurance; 5.5% do not have insurance; 1.5% of children under 18 do not have insurance

Safety: Violent crime rate: 42.1 per 10,000 population; Property crime rate: 200.3 per 10,000 population

Newspapers: Front Page Group (weekly circulation 15,000)

Transportation: Commute: 90.1% car, 5.2% public transportation, 1.8% walk, 0.3% work from home; Mean travel time to work: 20.3 minutes

Additional Information Contacts
City of Lackawanna . . . . (716) 827-6452
   http://www.lackawannany.gov

LAKE ERIE BEACH (CDP). Covers a land area of 3.820 square miles and a water area of 0 square miles. Located at 42.62° N. Lat; 79.08° W. Long. Elevation is 627 feet.

Population: 3,942; Growth (since 2000): -12.4%; Density: 1,031.9 persons per square mile; Race: 95.2% White, 0.4% Black/African American, 0.9% Asian, 0.2% American Indian/Alaska Native, 0.0% Native Hawaiian/Other Pacific Islander, 2.6% Two or more races, 2.4% Hispanic of any race; Average household size: 2.32; Median age: 48.2; Age under 18: 17.6%; Age 65 and over: 19.1%; Males per 100 females: 98.3; Marriage status: 28.5% never married, 52.5% now married, 1.3% separated, 6.9% widowed, 12.1% divorced; Foreign born: 2.7%; Speak English only: 98.1%; With disability: 16.4%; Veterans: 9.7%; Ancestry: 28.1% German, 20.0% Irish, 17.9% Polish, 14.8% Italian, 6.8% English

Employment: 8.1% management, business, and financial, 3.3% computer, engineering, and science, 10.3% education, legal, community service, arts, and media, 7.2% healthcare practitioners, 22.5% service, 20.6% sales and office, 9.3% natural resources, construction, and maintenance, 18.7% production, transportation, and material moving

Income: Per capita: $28,411; Median household: $59,360; Average household: $65,300; Households with income of $100,000 or more: 21.4%; Poverty rate: 10.4%

Educational Attainment: High school diploma or higher: 93.7%; Bachelor's degree or higher: 20.1%; Graduate/professional degree or higher: 8.8%

Housing: Homeownership rate: 88.9%; Median home value: $98,600; Median year structure built: 1952; Homeowner vacancy rate: 0.0%; Median selected monthly owner costs: $1,122 with a mortgage, $503 without a mortgage; Median gross rent: $784 per month; Rental vacancy rate: 0.0%

Health Insurance: 90.4% have insurance; 71.5% have private insurance; 34.1% have public insurance; 9.6% do not have insurance; 13.7% of children under 18 do not have insurance

Transportation: Commute: 97.1% car, 0.3% public transportation, 0.6% walk, 1.6% work from home; Mean travel time to work: 29.2 minutes

LAKE VIEW (unincorporated postal area)
ZCTA: 14085
   Covers a land area of 6.968 square miles and a water area of 0.345 square miles. Located at 42.72° N. Lat; 78.92° W. Long. Elevation is 718 feet.

Population: 7,245; Growth (since 2000): 30.2%; Density: 1,039.7 persons per square mile; Race: 98.3% White, 0.5% Black/African American, 0.8% Asian, 0.0% American Indian/Alaska Native, 0.2% Native Hawaiian/Other Pacific Islander, 0.0% Two or more races, 1.4% Hispanic of any race; Average household size: 2.81; Median age: 39.8; Age under 18: 26.2%; Age 65 and over: 13.1%; Males per 100 females: 101.9; Marriage status: 28.4% never married, 57.2% now married, 0.3% separated, 3.6% widowed, 10.8% divorced; Foreign born: 2.8%; Speak

English only: 95.2%; With disability: 10.2%; Veterans: 12.1%; Ancestry: 28.4% Italian, 28.2% Polish, 28.1% German, 19.9% Irish, 7.1% English

Employment: 10.2% management, business, and financial, 6.3% computer, engineering, and science, 12.6% education, legal, community service, arts, and media, 9.5% healthcare practitioners, 19.3% service, 25.6% sales and office, 8.1% natural resources, construction, and maintenance, 8.4% production, transportation, and material moving

Income: Per capita: $34,818; Median household: $82,351; Average household: $97,290; Households with income of $100,000 or more: 37.5%; Poverty rate: 1.3%

Educational Attainment: High school diploma or higher: 96.3%; Bachelor's degree or higher: 35.2%; Graduate/professional degree or higher: 15.6%

School District(s)
Frontier Central SD (PK-12)
   Enrollment: 4,907 . . . . (716) 926-1711

Housing: Homeownership rate: 97.2%; Median home value: $183,600; Median year structure built: 1981; Homeowner vacancy rate: 2.5%; Median selected monthly owner costs: $1,504 with a mortgage, $540 without a mortgage; Median gross rent: $777 per month; Rental vacancy rate: 37.2%

Health Insurance: 97.4% have insurance; 88.6% have private insurance; 22.4% have public insurance; 2.6% do not have insurance; 2.2% of children under 18 do not have insurance

Transportation: Commute: 96.6% car, 1.0% public transportation, 0.0% walk, 2.4% work from home; Mean travel time to work: 26.3 minutes

LANCASTER (town). Covers a land area of 37.703 square miles and a water area of 0.234 square miles. Located at 42.91° N. Lat; 78.63° W. Long. Elevation is 669 feet.

History: Incorporated 1849.

Population: 42,942; Growth (since 2000): 10.1%; Density: 1,139.0 persons per square mile; Race: 96.6% White, 1.3% Black/African American, 0.6% Asian, 0.4% American Indian/Alaska Native, 0.0% Native Hawaiian/Other Pacific Islander, 0.7% Two or more races, 2.1% Hispanic of any race; Average household size: 2.39; Median age: 42.8; Age under 18: 21.4%; Age 65 and over: 16.2%; Males per 100 females: 93.8; Marriage status: 27.7% never married, 56.6% now married, 2.0% separated, 6.4% widowed, 9.3% divorced; Foreign born: 3.4%; Speak English only: 94.9%; With disability: 9.2%; Veterans: 8.3%; Ancestry: 32.0% Polish, 31.3% German, 19.9% Italian, 15.0% Irish, 6.6% English

Employment: 17.4% management, business, and financial, 4.5% computer, engineering, and science, 9.7% education, legal, community service, arts, and media, 7.4% healthcare practitioners, 16.5% service, 26.8% sales and office, 5.3% natural resources, construction, and maintenance, 12.3% production, transportation, and material moving

Income: Per capita: $35,588; Median household: $68,647; Average household: $84,713; Households with income of $100,000 or more: 32.9%; Poverty rate: 5.7%

Educational Attainment: High school diploma or higher: 95.1%; Bachelor's degree or higher: 33.4%; Graduate/professional degree or higher: 12.9%

School District(s)
Lancaster Central SD (KG-12)
   Enrollment: 5,724 . . . . (716) 686-3201

Housing: Homeownership rate: 77.0%; Median home value: $176,300; Median year structure built: 1974; Homeowner vacancy rate: 0.7%; Median selected monthly owner costs: $1,438 with a mortgage, $574 without a mortgage; Median gross rent: $742 per month; Rental vacancy rate: 1.5%

Health Insurance: 97.1% have insurance; 84.4% have private insurance; 27.8% have public insurance; 2.9% do not have insurance; 1.7% of children under 18 do not have insurance

Safety: Violent crime rate: 6.1 per 10,000 population; Property crime rate: 108.4 per 10,000 population

Transportation: Commute: 95.6% car, 0.6% public transportation, 0.4% walk, 2.9% work from home; Mean travel time to work: 21.9 minutes

Additional Information Contacts
Town of Lancaster . . . . (716) 683-9028
   http://www.lancasterny.gov

LANCASTER (village). Covers a land area of 2.698 square miles and a water area of 0.034 square miles. Located at 42.90° N. Lat; 78.67° W. Long. Elevation is 669 feet.

Population: 10,207; Growth (since 2000): -8.8%; Density: 3,783.8 persons per square mile; Race: 96.9% White, 0.5% Black/African American, 1.1%

Asian, 0.3% American Indian/Alaska Native, 0.0% Native Hawaiian/Other Pacific Islander, 1.3% Two or more races, 2.5% Hispanic of any race; Average household size: 2.25; Median age: 40.9; Age under 18: 20.8%; Age 65 and over: 17.5%; Males per 100 females: 91.5; Marriage status: 35.6% never married, 45.6% now married, 1.5% separated, 6.1% widowed, 12.7% divorced; Foreign born: 2.2%; Speak English only: 94.8%; With disability: 12.6%; Veterans: 8.5%; Ancestry: 35.5% German, 32.4% Polish, 15.4% Italian, 12.6% Irish, 7.3% English

Employment: 10.6% management, business, and financial, 4.9% computer, engineering, and science, 10.3% education, legal, community service, arts, and media, 5.0% healthcare practitioners, 21.0% service, 28.1% sales and office, 6.7% natural resources, construction, and maintenance, 13.3% production, transportation, and material moving

Income: Per capita: $29,509; Median household: $51,338; Average household: $65,515; Households with income of $100,000 or more: 22.9%; Poverty rate: 9.5%

Educational Attainment: High school diploma or higher: 93.5%; Bachelor's degree or higher: 26.0%; Graduate/professional degree or higher: 9.3%

School District(s)
Lancaster Central SD (KG-12)
    Enrollment: 5,724 . . . . (716) 686-3201

Housing: Homeownership rate: 71.5%; Median home value: $122,900; Median year structure built: 1951; Homeowner vacancy rate: 1.1%; Median selected monthly owner costs: $1,218 with a mortgage, $498 without a mortgage; Median gross rent: $649 per month; Rental vacancy rate: 0.0%

Health Insurance: 96.7% have insurance; 76.9% have private insurance; 37.5% have public insurance; 3.3% do not have insurance; 3.4% of children under 18 do not have insurance

Transportation: Commute: 95.7% car, 0.6% public transportation, 0.2% walk, 3.4% work from home; Mean travel time to work: 21.1 minutes

Additional Information Contacts
Village of Lancaster . . . . (716) 683-2105
    http://www.lancastervillage.org

LAWTONS (unincorporated postal area)
ZCTA: 14091

Covers a land area of 21.261 square miles and a water area of 0.008 square miles. Located at 42.54° N. Lat; 78.89° W. Long. Elevation is 850 feet.

Population: 1,043; Growth (since 2000): -8.1%; Density: 49.1 persons per square mile; Race: 75.6% White, 0.0% Black/African American, 0.0% Asian, 23.8% American Indian/Alaska Native, 0.0% Native Hawaiian/Other Pacific Islander, 0.0% Two or more races, 1.7% Hispanic of any race; Average household size: 2.54; Median age: 41.7; Age under 18: 23.9%; Age 65 and over: 18.6%; Males per 100 females: 105.5; Marriage status: 30.7% never married, 56.9% now married, 0.0% separated, 7.3% widowed, 5.1% divorced; Foreign born: 2.7%; Speak English only: 89.0%; With disability: 10.4%; Veterans: 13.6%; Ancestry: 25.6% German, 10.1% Irish, 8.0% Polish, 6.2% Italian, 5.6% English

Employment: 10.4% management, business, and financial, 0.0% computer, engineering, and science, 12.8% education, legal, community service, arts, and media, 11.7% healthcare practitioners, 14.5% service, 24.2% sales and office, 11.5% natural resources, construction, and maintenance, 14.9% production, transportation, and material moving

Income: Per capita: $24,572; Median household: $52,232; Average household: $62,151; Households with income of $100,000 or more: 17.6%; Poverty rate: 15.8%

Educational Attainment: High school diploma or higher: 90.7%; Bachelor's degree or higher: 16.9%; Graduate/professional degree or higher: 5.9%

Housing: Homeownership rate: 84.9%; Median home value: $110,800; Median year structure built: 1972; Homeowner vacancy rate: 0.0%; Median selected monthly owner costs: $1,088 with a mortgage, $413 without a mortgage; Median gross rent: $550 per month; Rental vacancy rate: 0.0%

Health Insurance: 91.4% have insurance; 59.9% have private insurance; 43.6% have public insurance; 8.6% do not have insurance; 13.8% of children under 18 do not have insurance

Transportation: Commute: 100.0% car, 0.0% public transportation, 0.0% walk, 0.0% work from home; Mean travel time to work: 25.8 minutes

MARILLA (town). Covers a land area of 27.505 square miles and a water area of 0.038 square miles. Located at 42.82° N. Lat; 78.53° W. Long. Elevation is 846 feet.

Population: 5,389; Growth (since 2000): -5.6%; Density: 195.9 persons per square mile; Race: 98.9% White, 0.2% Black/African American, 0.0% Asian, 0.8% American Indian/Alaska Native, 0.0% Native Hawaiian/Other Pacific Islander, 0.0% Two or more races, 2.1% Hispanic of any race; Average household size: 2.52; Median age: 49.5; Age under 18: 19.0%; Age 65 and over: 23.4%; Males per 100 females: 96.6; Marriage status: 21.1% never married, 67.0% now married, 0.3% separated, 2.7% widowed, 9.2% divorced; Foreign born: 2.2%; Speak English only: 95.8%; With disability: 10.2%; Veterans: 10.8%; Ancestry: 33.9% German, 33.9% Polish, 17.1% Irish, 10.7% English, 10.5% Italian

Employment: 8.1% management, business, and financial, 3.1% computer, engineering, and science, 15.1% education, legal, community service, arts, and media, 6.5% healthcare practitioners, 12.1% service, 26.7% sales and office, 10.0% natural resources, construction, and maintenance, 18.4% production, transportation, and material moving

Income: Per capita: $35,672; Median household: $80,057; Average household: $88,897; Households with income of $100,000 or more: 33.9%; Poverty rate: 3.9%

Educational Attainment: High school diploma or higher: 92.6%; Bachelor's degree or higher: 29.3%; Graduate/professional degree or higher: 13.1%

School District(s)
Iroquois Central SD (KG-12)
    Enrollment: 2,259 . . . . (716) 652-3000

Housing: Homeownership rate: 94.0%; Median home value: $197,000; Median year structure built: 1972; Homeowner vacancy rate: 2.2%; Median selected monthly owner costs: $1,495 with a mortgage, $575 without a mortgage; Median gross rent: $653 per month; Rental vacancy rate: 23.7%

Health Insurance: 95.8% have insurance; 85.3% have private insurance; 29.5% have public insurance; 4.2% do not have insurance; 1.3% of children under 18 do not have insurance

Transportation: Commute: 94.5% car, 0.0% public transportation, 0.6% walk, 2.0% work from home; Mean travel time to work: 29.7 minutes

Additional Information Contacts
Town of Marilla . . . . (716) 652-5350
    http://townofmarilla.com

NEWSTEAD (town). Covers a land area of 50.759 square miles and a water area of 0.286 square miles. Located at 43.02° N. Lat; 78.52° W. Long.

Population: 8,722; Growth (since 2000): 3.8%; Density: 171.8 persons per square mile; Race: 96.4% White, 1.1% Black/African American, 0.7% Asian, 0.0% American Indian/Alaska Native, 0.0% Native Hawaiian/Other Pacific Islander, 1.2% Two or more races, 0.7% Hispanic of any race; Average household size: 2.31; Median age: 45.7; Age under 18: 19.9%; Age 65 and over: 18.9%; Males per 100 females: 97.4; Marriage status: 28.6% never married, 52.9% now married, 0.9% separated, 7.5% widowed, 11.0% divorced; Foreign born: 3.4%; Speak English only: 97.2%; With disability: 14.8%; Veterans: 8.5%; Ancestry: 43.9% German, 13.8% Polish, 13.5% Irish, 11.5% Italian, 8.4% English

Employment: 10.7% management, business, and financial, 5.9% computer, engineering, and science, 9.1% education, legal, community service, arts, and media, 6.2% healthcare practitioners, 17.6% service, 22.5% sales and office, 11.7% natural resources, construction, and maintenance, 16.4% production, transportation, and material moving

Income: Per capita: $32,939; Median household: $60,387; Average household: $75,016; Households with income of $100,000 or more: 23.1%; Poverty rate: 4.0%

Educational Attainment: High school diploma or higher: 91.5%; Bachelor's degree or higher: 26.0%; Graduate/professional degree or higher: 10.6%

Housing: Homeownership rate: 77.6%; Median home value: $134,000; Median year structure built: 1969; Homeowner vacancy rate: 0.0%; Median selected monthly owner costs: $1,326 with a mortgage, $531 without a mortgage; Median gross rent: $727 per month; Rental vacancy rate: 0.0%

Health Insurance: 95.6% have insurance; 80.0% have private insurance; 30.8% have public insurance; 4.4% do not have insurance; 5.2% of children under 18 do not have insurance

Transportation: Commute: 90.7% car, 1.1% public transportation, 4.3% walk, 3.1% work from home; Mean travel time to work: 26.0 minutes

Additional Information Contacts
Town of Newstead. . . . . (716) 542-4573
   http://www.erie.gov/newstead

NORTH BOSTON (CDP). Covers a land area of 4.074 square miles and a water area of 0 square miles. Located at 42.68° N. Lat; 78.78° W. Long. Elevation is 823 feet.

Population: 2,870; Growth (since 2000): 7.1%; Density: 704.4 persons per square mile; Race: 99.6% White, 0.0% Black/African American, 0.0% Asian, 0.0% American Indian/Alaska Native, 0.0% Native Hawaiian/Other Pacific Islander, 0.4% Two or more races, 0.0% Hispanic of any race; Average household size: 2.45; Median age: 50.3; Age under 18: 17.5%; Age 65 and over: 20.1%; Males per 100 females: 95.7; Marriage status: 22.6% never married, 58.2% now married, 0.7% separated, 6.8% widowed, 12.4% divorced; Foreign born: 2.6%; Speak English only: 97.7%; With disability: 7.0%; Veterans: 4.0%; Ancestry: 34.5% German, 21.4% Polish, 18.6% Irish, 17.7% Italian, 13.8% English
Employment: 9.9% management, business, and financial, 3.7% computer, engineering, and science, 18.0% education, legal, community service, arts, and media, 5.9% healthcare practitioners, 18.6% service, 20.6% sales and office, 11.6% natural resources, construction, and maintenance, 11.6% production, transportation, and material moving
Income: Per capita: $29,585; Median household: $63,125; Average household: $71,500; Households with income of $100,000 or more: 26.9%; Poverty rate: 2.0%
Educational Attainment: High school diploma or higher: 98.6%; Bachelor's degree or higher: 25.0%; Graduate/professional degree or higher: 11.1%
Housing: Homeownership rate: 75.0%; Median home value: $161,500; Median year structure built: 1964; Homeowner vacancy rate: 0.0%; Median selected monthly owner costs: $1,192 with a mortgage, $607 without a mortgage; Median gross rent: $756 per month; Rental vacancy rate: 0.0%
Health Insurance: 90.7% have insurance; 75.3% have private insurance; 32.2% have public insurance; 9.3% do not have insurance; 0.0% of children under 18 do not have insurance
Transportation: Commute: 100.0% car, 0.0% public transportation, 0.0% walk, 0.0% work from home; Mean travel time to work: 21.3 minutes

NORTH COLLINS (town). Covers a land area of 42.854 square miles and a water area of 0.173 square miles. Located at 42.57° N. Lat; 78.86° W. Long. Elevation is 827 feet.

History: Settled c.1810, incorporated 1911.
Population: 3,520; Growth (since 2000): 4.3%; Density: 82.1 persons per square mile; Race: 96.6% White, 0.7% Black/African American, 0.7% Asian, 1.0% American Indian/Alaska Native, 0.0% Native Hawaiian/Other Pacific Islander, 1.0% Two or more races, 1.3% Hispanic of any race; Average household size: 2.70; Median age: 42.2; Age under 18: 25.2%; Age 65 and over: 13.8%; Males per 100 females: 98.5; Marriage status: 26.5% never married, 60.0% now married, 1.6% separated, 5.9% widowed, 7.6% divorced; Foreign born: 2.5%; Speak English only: 97.8%; With disability: 14.5%; Veterans: 7.6%; Ancestry: 39.9% German, 19.1% Italian, 15.2% Irish, 13.5% Polish, 11.8% English
Employment: 8.1% management, business, and financial, 2.6% computer, engineering, and science, 9.2% education, legal, community service, arts, and media, 8.9% healthcare practitioners, 14.1% service, 25.6% sales and office, 15.1% natural resources, construction, and maintenance, 16.3% production, transportation, and material moving
Income: Per capita: $25,919; Median household: $61,854; Average household: $69,862; Households with income of $100,000 or more: 21.0%; Poverty rate: 5.2%
Educational Attainment: High school diploma or higher: 90.0%; Bachelor's degree or higher: 22.7%; Graduate/professional degree or higher: 9.9%

School District(s)
North Collins Central SD (PK-12)
   Enrollment: 643. . . . . (716) 337-0101
Housing: Homeownership rate: 84.7%; Median home value: $125,700; Median year structure built: 1953; Homeowner vacancy rate: 1.5%; Median selected monthly owner costs: $1,222 with a mortgage, $573 without a mortgage; Median gross rent: $624 per month; Rental vacancy rate: 8.8%
Health Insurance: 93.3% have insurance; 70.3% have private insurance; 34.6% have public insurance; 6.7% do not have insurance; 7.1% of children under 18 do not have insurance
Transportation: Commute: 89.6% car, 0.8% public transportation, 4.4% walk, 4.7% work from home; Mean travel time to work: 26.6 minutes

NORTH COLLINS (village). Covers a land area of 0.801 square miles and a water area of 0 square miles. Located at 42.59° N. Lat; 78.94° W. Long. Elevation is 827 feet.

Population: 1,303; Growth (since 2000): 20.8%; Density: 1,626.6 persons per square mile; Race: 92.2% White, 0.5% Black/African American, 1.8% Asian, 2.8% American Indian/Alaska Native, 0.0% Native Hawaiian/Other Pacific Islander, 2.7% Two or more races, 2.9% Hispanic of any race; Average household size: 2.78; Median age: 33.2; Age under 18: 32.9%; Age 65 and over: 13.1%; Males per 100 females: 94.6; Marriage status: 26.6% never married, 55.6% now married, 4.1% separated, 6.3% widowed, 11.5% divorced; Foreign born: 4.5%; Speak English only: 97.3%; With disability: 9.9%; Veterans: 8.4%; Ancestry: 37.7% German, 24.9% Italian, 14.5% Irish, 13.2% Polish, 8.4% English
Employment: 7.8% management, business, and financial, 2.2% computer, engineering, and science, 8.2% education, legal, community service, arts, and media, 6.4% healthcare practitioners, 23.3% service, 32.2% sales and office, 5.1% natural resources, construction, and maintenance, 14.8% production, transportation, and material moving
Income: Per capita: $22,553; Median household: $53,850; Average household: $62,420; Households with income of $100,000 or more: 16.7%; Poverty rate: 6.9%
Educational Attainment: High school diploma or higher: 86.8%; Bachelor's degree or higher: 25.7%; Graduate/professional degree or higher: 9.7%

School District(s)
North Collins Central SD (PK-12)
   Enrollment: 643. . . . . (716) 337-0101
Housing: Homeownership rate: 68.0%; Median home value: $87,000; Median year structure built: Before 1940; Homeowner vacancy rate: 5.1%; Median selected monthly owner costs: $1,107 with a mortgage, $495 without a mortgage; Median gross rent: $614 per month; Rental vacancy rate: 4.5%
Health Insurance: 96.1% have insurance; 73.7% have private insurance; 30.2% have public insurance; 3.9% do not have insurance; 3.0% of children under 18 do not have insurance
Transportation: Commute: 88.8% car, 0.7% public transportation, 8.8% walk, 1.7% work from home; Mean travel time to work: 23.8 minutes

ORCHARD PARK (town). Covers a land area of 38.440 square miles and a water area of 0.079 square miles. Located at 42.75° N. Lat; 78.74° W. Long. Elevation is 863 feet.

History: Until 1934, called East Hamburg. Incorporated 1921.
Population: 29,545; Growth (since 2000): 6.9%; Density: 768.6 persons per square mile; Race: 96.2% White, 0.7% Black/African American, 1.9% Asian, 0.1% American Indian/Alaska Native, 0.0% Native Hawaiian/Other Pacific Islander, 0.6% Two or more races, 2.6% Hispanic of any race; Average household size: 2.54; Median age: 45.6; Age under 18: 21.6%; Age 65 and over: 20.3%; Males per 100 females: 92.1; Marriage status: 25.9% never married, 59.6% now married, 1.4% separated, 5.9% widowed, 8.6% divorced; Foreign born: 3.9%; Speak English only: 95.8%; With disability: 9.6%; Veterans: 8.3%; Ancestry: 27.8% German, 27.6% Irish, 20.4% Polish, 17.0% Italian, 8.5% English
Employment: 19.9% management, business, and financial, 6.5% computer, engineering, and science, 13.8% education, legal, community service, arts, and media, 8.5% healthcare practitioners, 14.6% service, 22.7% sales and office, 5.2% natural resources, construction, and maintenance, 8.7% production, transportation, and material moving
Income: Per capita: $45,698; Median household: $89,955; Average household: $115,888; Households with income of $100,000 or more: 43.3%; Poverty rate: 4.0%
Educational Attainment: High school diploma or higher: 96.2%; Bachelor's degree or higher: 45.8%; Graduate/professional degree or higher: 21.1%

School District(s)
Orchard Park Central SD (KG-12)
   Enrollment: 4,785 . . . . (716) 209-6280
Four-year College(s)
Bryant & Stratton College-Online (Private, For-profit)
   Enrollment: 4,114 . . . . (800) 836-5627
   Tuition: In-state $14,383; Out-of-state $14,383
Bryant & Stratton College-Southtowns (Private, For-profit)
   Enrollment: 418. . . . . (716) 677-9500
   Tuition: In-state $17,288; Out-of-state $17,288
Housing: Homeownership rate: 76.9%; Median home value: $228,100; Median year structure built: 1973; Homeowner vacancy rate: 0.0%; Median

selected monthly owner costs: $1,746 with a mortgage, $672 without a mortgage; Median gross rent: $947 per month; Rental vacancy rate: 8.9%
Health Insurance: 98.1% have insurance; 87.4% have private insurance; 27.4% have public insurance; 1.9% do not have insurance; 0.7% of children under 18 do not have insurance
Safety: Violent crime rate: 9.8 per 10,000 population; Property crime rate: 85.8 per 10,000 population
Transportation: Commute: 94.4% car, 0.4% public transportation, 1.1% walk, 3.4% work from home; Mean travel time to work: 21.8 minutes
Additional Information Contacts
Town of Orchard Park . . . . (716) 662-6410
    http://www.orchardparkny.org

ORCHARD PARK (village). Covers a land area of 1.346 square miles and a water area of 0.041 square miles. Located at 42.76° N. Lat; 78.74° W. Long. Elevation is 863 feet.
Population: 3,177; Growth (since 2000): -3.6%; Density: 2,359.7 persons per square mile; Race: 96.8% White, 0.8% Black/African American, 1.2% Asian, 0.0% American Indian/Alaska Native, 0.0% Native Hawaiian/Other Pacific Islander, 0.3% Two or more races, 4.0% Hispanic of any race; Average household size: 2.43; Median age: 43.8; Age under 18: 23.4%; Age 65 and over: 18.9%; Males per 100 females: 93.0; Marriage status: 29.0% never married, 55.0% now married, 0.9% separated, 4.8% widowed, 11.2% divorced; Foreign born: 1.7%; Speak English only: 97.1%; With disability: 8.0%; Veterans: 7.3%; Ancestry: 34.1% Irish, 25.7% German, 16.2% Italian, 16.0% Polish, 13.8% English
Employment: 19.4% management, business, and financial, 3.5% computer, engineering, and science, 15.1% education, legal, community service, arts, and media, 9.9% healthcare practitioners, 10.9% service, 28.9% sales and office, 4.8% natural resources, construction, and maintenance, 7.5% production, transportation, and material moving
Income: Per capita: $42,757; Median household: $89,679; Average household: $103,042; Households with income of $100,000 or more: 40.7%; Poverty rate: 1.4%
Educational Attainment: High school diploma or higher: 98.9%; Bachelor's degree or higher: 61.9%; Graduate/professional degree or higher: 30.8%

School District(s)
Orchard Park Central SD (KG-12)
    Enrollment: 4,785 . . . . (716) 209-6280
Four-year College(s)
Bryant & Stratton College-Online (Private, For-profit)
    Enrollment: 4,114 . . . . (800) 836-5627
    Tuition: In-state $14,383; Out-of-state $14,383
Bryant & Stratton College-Southtowns (Private, For-profit)
    Enrollment: 418 . . . . (716) 677-9500
    Tuition: In-state $17,288; Out-of-state $17,288
Housing: Homeownership rate: 70.6%; Median home value: $225,800; Median year structure built: 1958; Homeowner vacancy rate: 0.0%; Median selected monthly owner costs: $1,663 with a mortgage, $802 without a mortgage; Median gross rent: $907 per month; Rental vacancy rate: 11.5%
Health Insurance: 98.2% have insurance; 88.2% have private insurance; 26.3% have public insurance; 1.8% do not have insurance; 0.0% of children under 18 do not have insurance
Transportation: Commute: 91.6% car, 0.0% public transportation, 3.8% walk, 3.6% work from home; Mean travel time to work: 19.2 minutes

SARDINIA (town). Covers a land area of 50.175 square miles and a water area of 0.233 square miles. Located at 42.56° N. Lat; 78.53° W. Long. Elevation is 1,394 feet.
Population: 2,792; Growth (since 2000): 3.7%; Density: 55.6 persons per square mile; Race: 99.5% White, 0.0% Black/African American, 0.0% Asian, 0.0% American Indian/Alaska Native, 0.0% Native Hawaiian/Other Pacific Islander, 0.3% Two or more races, 2.5% Hispanic of any race; Average household size: 2.75; Median age: 43.9; Age under 18: 24.9%; Age 65 and over: 17.0%; Males per 100 females: 103.9; Marriage status: 26.3% never married, 58.2% now married, 0.5% separated, 5.5% widowed, 10.0% divorced; Foreign born: 0.2%; Speak English only: 97.5%; With disability: 12.5%; Veterans: 8.5%; Ancestry: 40.9% German, 16.3% Irish, 15.2% Polish, 14.1% Italian, 11.9% English
Employment: 13.0% management, business, and financial, 2.5% computer, engineering, and science, 8.0% education, legal, community service, arts, and media, 8.6% healthcare practitioners, 13.7% service, 22.6% sales and office, 16.1% natural resources, construction, and maintenance, 15.5% production, transportation, and material moving

Income: Per capita: $28,316; Median household: $67,313; Average household: $77,153; Households with income of $100,000 or more: 31.3%; Poverty rate: 7.6%
Educational Attainment: High school diploma or higher: 89.1%; Bachelor's degree or higher: 15.2%; Graduate/professional degree or higher: 6.2%
Housing: Homeownership rate: 85.7%; Median home value: $158,100; Median year structure built: 1969; Homeowner vacancy rate: 0.0%; Median selected monthly owner costs: $1,313 with a mortgage, $467 without a mortgage; Median gross rent: $749 per month; Rental vacancy rate: 0.0%
Health Insurance: 95.9% have insurance; 80.6% have private insurance; 32.2% have public insurance; 4.1% do not have insurance; 5.0% of children under 18 do not have insurance
Transportation: Commute: 93.4% car, 0.2% public transportation, 1.4% walk, 2.9% work from home; Mean travel time to work: 29.7 minutes

SLOAN (village). Covers a land area of 0.786 square miles and a water area of 0.006 square miles. Located at 42.89° N. Lat; 78.79° W. Long. Elevation is 614 feet.
History: Incorporated 1896.
Population: 3,615; Growth (since 2000): -4.2%; Density: 4,598.9 persons per square mile; Race: 91.9% White, 3.7% Black/African American, 2.5% Asian, 0.0% American Indian/Alaska Native, 0.0% Native Hawaiian/Other Pacific Islander, 1.6% Two or more races, 2.6% Hispanic of any race; Average household size: 2.23; Median age: 43.3; Age under 18: 20.1%; Age 65 and over: 14.4%; Males per 100 females: 92.4; Marriage status: 38.3% never married, 40.8% now married, 2.4% separated, 8.5% widowed, 12.4% divorced; Foreign born: 6.5%; Speak English only: 91.1%; With disability: 11.6%; Veterans: 10.0%; Ancestry: 49.5% Polish, 18.9% German, 14.1% Irish, 13.9% Italian, 5.1% English
Employment: 8.7% management, business, and financial, 0.7% computer, engineering, and science, 5.3% education, legal, community service, arts, and media, 2.9% healthcare practitioners, 20.4% service, 29.4% sales and office, 8.0% natural resources, construction, and maintenance, 24.5% production, transportation, and material moving
Income: Per capita: $25,645; Median household: $45,644; Average household: $55,766; Households with income of $100,000 or more: 8.9%; Poverty rate: 13.2%
Educational Attainment: High school diploma or higher: 85.1%; Bachelor's degree or higher: 12.8%; Graduate/professional degree or higher: 2.5%

School District(s)
Cheektowaga-Sloan Union Free SD (PK-12)
    Enrollment: 1,415 . . . . (716) 891-6402
Housing: Homeownership rate: 66.5%; Median home value: $74,900; Median year structure built: 1948; Homeowner vacancy rate: 0.0%; Median selected monthly owner costs: $908 with a mortgage, $381 without a mortgage; Median gross rent: $636 per month; Rental vacancy rate: 0.0%
Health Insurance: 94.7% have insurance; 70.5% have private insurance; 37.9% have public insurance; 5.3% do not have insurance; 0.9% of children under 18 do not have insurance
Transportation: Commute: 93.5% car, 0.3% public transportation, 2.8% walk, 1.1% work from home; Mean travel time to work: 19.1 minutes

SOUTH WALES (unincorporated postal area)
ZCTA: 14139
    Covers a land area of 23.860 square miles and a water area of 0.032 square miles. Located at 42.72° N. Lat; 78.54° W. Long. Elevation is 932 feet.
Population: 2,496; Growth (since 2000): 22.9%; Density: 104.6 persons per square mile; Race: 92.7% White, 0.0% Black/African American, 6.9% Asian, 0.0% American Indian/Alaska Native, 0.0% Native Hawaiian/Other Pacific Islander, 0.0% Two or more races, 1.2% Hispanic of any race; Average household size: 2.49; Median age: 42.7; Age under 18: 23.7%; Age 65 and over: 16.6%; Males per 100 females: 99.7; Marriage status: 17.6% never married, 67.7% now married, 0.0% separated, 7.4% widowed, 7.3% divorced; Foreign born: 5.2%; Speak English only: 98.4%; With disability: 11.5%; Veterans: 6.0%; Ancestry: 27.8% German, 24.8% Polish, 15.3% Irish, 10.3% English, 8.2% Italian
Employment: 17.1% management, business, and financial, 2.7% computer, engineering, and science, 17.4% education, legal, community service, arts, and media, 8.0% healthcare practitioners, 20.2% service, 17.7% sales and office, 5.9% natural resources, construction, and maintenance, 11.1% production, transportation, and material moving

Income: Per capita: $36,179; Median household: $82,993; Average household: $89,411; Households with income of $100,000 or more: 33.7%; Poverty rate: 5.8%

Educational Attainment: High school diploma or higher: 94.3%; Bachelor's degree or higher: 39.7%; Graduate/professional degree or higher: 15.2%

Housing: Homeownership rate: 86.6%; Median home value: $188,700; Median year structure built: 1954; Homeowner vacancy rate: 0.0%; Median selected monthly owner costs: $1,590 with a mortgage, $536 without a mortgage; Median gross rent: $724 per month; Rental vacancy rate: 0.0%

Health Insurance: 97.0% have insurance; 83.3% have private insurance; 26.6% have public insurance; 3.0% do not have insurance; 0.0% of children under 18 do not have insurance

Transportation: Commute: 92.8% car, 0.5% public transportation, 2.7% walk, 1.9% work from home; Mean travel time to work: 25.0 minutes

SPRINGVILLE (village).
Covers a land area of 3.672 square miles and a water area of 0.009 square miles. Located at 42.51° N. Lat; 78.67° W. Long. Elevation is 1,329 feet.

History: Settled 1807, incorporated 1834.

Population: 4,333; Growth (since 2000): 1.9%; Density: 1,180.0 persons per square mile; Race: 95.1% White, 1.4% Black/African American, 0.6% Asian, 1.6% American Indian/Alaska Native, 0.0% Native Hawaiian/Other Pacific Islander, 1.0% Two or more races, 2.3% Hispanic of any race; Average household size: 2.25; Median age: 43.7; Age under 18: 23.6%; Age 65 and over: 18.6%; Males per 100 females: 91.6; Marriage status: 22.3% never married, 53.1% now married, 2.1% separated, 9.3% widowed, 15.3% divorced; Foreign born: 4.2%; Speak English only: 96.6%; With disability: 14.6%; Veterans: 11.7%; Ancestry: 39.6% German, 19.1% Irish, 17.7% Polish, 15.6% English, 6.7% Italian

Employment: 10.9% management, business, and financial, 5.7% computer, engineering, and science, 9.9% education, legal, community service, arts, and media, 8.9% healthcare practitioners, 21.5% service, 21.0% sales and office, 11.3% natural resources, construction, and maintenance, 10.8% production, transportation, and material moving

Income: Per capita: $30,523; Median household: $53,250; Average household: $69,981; Households with income of $100,000 or more: 20.7%; Poverty rate: 11.1%

Educational Attainment: High school diploma or higher: 94.3%; Bachelor's degree or higher: 25.8%; Graduate/professional degree or higher: 9.8%

School District(s)
Springville-Griffith Institute Central SD (KG-12)
    Enrollment: 1,757 .... (716) 592-3230

Housing: Homeownership rate: 60.7%; Median home value: $118,400; Median year structure built: 1947; Homeowner vacancy rate: 0.0%; Median selected monthly owner costs: $1,055 with a mortgage, $546 without a mortgage; Median gross rent: $612 per month; Rental vacancy rate: 3.8%

Health Insurance: 96.1% have insurance; 74.5% have private insurance; 40.2% have public insurance; 3.9% do not have insurance; 2.2% of children under 18 do not have insurance

Hospitals: Bertrand Chaffee Hospital (49 beds)

Newspapers: Springville Journal (weekly circulation 10,000)

Transportation: Commute: 93.9% car, 0.0% public transportation, 5.0% walk, 1.2% work from home; Mean travel time to work: 21.2 minutes

Additional Information Contacts
Village of Springville .... (716) 592-4936
    http://www.villageofspringvilleny.com

TONAWANDA (CDP).
Covers a land area of 17.300 square miles and a water area of 1.336 square miles. Located at 42.99° N. Lat; 78.88° W. Long. Elevation is 574 feet.

Population: 57,725; Growth (since 2000): -6.5%; Density: 3,336.8 persons per square mile; Race: 89.4% White, 4.3% Black/African American, 2.4% Asian, 0.3% American Indian/Alaska Native, 0.0% Native Hawaiian/Other Pacific Islander, 2.4% Two or more races, 4.0% Hispanic of any race; Average household size: 2.20; Median age: 43.8; Age under 18: 19.3%; Age 65 and over: 20.8%; Males per 100 females: 89.1; Marriage status: 29.6% never married, 49.0% now married, 1.7% separated, 9.2% widowed, 12.2% divorced; Foreign born: 5.7%; Speak English only: 92.3%; With disability: 14.8%; Veterans: 8.1%; Ancestry: 28.2% German, 23.3% Italian, 19.1% Irish, 15.8% Polish, 8.9% English

Employment: 14.8% management, business, and financial, 5.5% computer, engineering, and science, 12.3% education, legal, community service, arts, and media, 6.6% healthcare practitioners, 17.5% service, 28.1% sales and office, 6.0% natural resources, construction, and maintenance, 9.2% production, transportation, and material moving

Income: Per capita: $30,794; Median household: $55,247; Average household: $67,042; Households with income of $100,000 or more: 20.0%; Poverty rate: 8.7%

Educational Attainment: High school diploma or higher: 93.4%; Bachelor's degree or higher: 35.5%; Graduate/professional degree or higher: 15.3%

School District(s)
Kenmore-Tonawanda Union Free SD (KG-12)
    Enrollment: 6,913 .... (716) 874-8400
Sweet Home Central SD (KG-12)
    Enrollment: 3,193 .... (716) 250-1402
Tonawanda City SD (PK-12)
    Enrollment: 1,795 .... (716) 694-7784

Vocational/Technical School(s)
The Salon Professional Academy-Tonawanda (Private, For-profit)
    Enrollment: 131 .... (716) 833-8772
    Tuition: $8,150

Housing: Homeownership rate: 74.0%; Median home value: $125,500; Median year structure built: 1955; Homeowner vacancy rate: 0.5%; Median selected monthly owner costs: $1,177 with a mortgage, $483 without a mortgage; Median gross rent: $810 per month; Rental vacancy rate: 4.8%

Health Insurance: 97.3% have insurance; 77.1% have private insurance; 38.0% have public insurance; 2.7% do not have insurance; 0.9% of children under 18 do not have insurance

Transportation: Commute: 93.3% car, 2.1% public transportation, 1.8% walk, 2.0% work from home; Mean travel time to work: 19.7 minutes

TONAWANDA (city).
Covers a land area of 3.803 square miles and a water area of 0.288 square miles. Located at 43.01° N. Lat; 78.88° W. Long. Elevation is 574 feet.

Population: 14,992; Growth (since 2000): -7.1%; Density: 3,941.9 persons per square mile; Race: 94.9% White, 0.3% Black/African American, 0.3% Asian, 0.8% American Indian/Alaska Native, 0.0% Native Hawaiian/Other Pacific Islander, 3.4% Two or more races, 2.3% Hispanic of any race; Average household size: 2.15; Median age: 46.2; Age under 18: 17.3%; Age 65 and over: 18.4%; Males per 100 females: 94.5; Marriage status: 33.5% never married, 45.2% now married, 1.0% separated, 7.1% widowed, 14.1% divorced; Foreign born: 3.1%; Speak English only: 96.3%; With disability: 17.4%; Veterans: 10.5%; Ancestry: 34.5% German, 20.4% Italian, 19.4% Irish, 14.4% Polish, 10.6% English

Employment: 11.8% management, business, and financial, 4.6% computer, engineering, and science, 8.4% education, legal, community service, arts, and media, 6.5% healthcare practitioners, 18.1% service, 29.8% sales and office, 7.1% natural resources, construction, and maintenance, 13.7% production, transportation, and material moving

Income: Per capita: $27,375; Median household: $46,728; Average household: $57,793; Households with income of $100,000 or more: 14.9%; Poverty rate: 13.4%

Educational Attainment: High school diploma or higher: 93.0%; Bachelor's degree or higher: 22.3%; Graduate/professional degree or higher: 8.6%

School District(s)
Kenmore-Tonawanda Union Free SD (KG-12)
    Enrollment: 6,913 .... (716) 874-8400
Sweet Home Central SD (KG-12)
    Enrollment: 3,193 .... (716) 250-1402
Tonawanda City SD (PK-12)
    Enrollment: 1,795 .... (716) 694-7784

Vocational/Technical School(s)
The Salon Professional Academy-Tonawanda (Private, For-profit)
    Enrollment: 131 .... (716) 833-8772
    Tuition: $8,150

Housing: Homeownership rate: 69.4%; Median home value: $98,200; Median year structure built: 1947; Homeowner vacancy rate: 0.3%; Median selected monthly owner costs: $1,101 with a mortgage, $467 without a mortgage; Median gross rent: $693 per month; Rental vacancy rate: 4.9%

Health Insurance: 95.9% have insurance; 77.2% have private insurance; 37.8% have public insurance; 4.1% do not have insurance; 1.2% of children under 18 do not have insurance

Safety: Violent crime rate: 30.4 per 10,000 population; Property crime rate: 210.0 per 10,000 population

Transportation: Commute: 88.8% car, 1.4% public transportation, 4.9% walk, 2.1% work from home; Mean travel time to work: 19.8 minutes
Additional Information Contacts
City of Tonawanda . . . . (716) 695-1800
    http://www.ci.tonawanda.ny.us

TONAWANDA (town).
Covers a land area of 18.735 square miles and a water area of 1.544 square miles. Located at 42.98° N. Lat; 78.88° W. Long. Elevation is 574 feet.
History: Named for the Iroquois translation of "swift water". Incorporated as a village 1854, and as a city in 1903.
Population: 73,044; Growth (since 2000): -6.5%; Density: 3,898.8 persons per square mile; Race: 90.0% White, 4.6% Black/African American, 2.0% Asian, 0.3% American Indian/Alaska Native, 0.0% Native Hawaiian/Other Pacific Islander, 2.2% Two or more races, 3.7% Hispanic of any race; Average household size: 2.19; Median age: 43.4; Age under 18: 18.9%; Age 65 and over: 20.2%; Males per 100 females: 88.8; Marriage status: 29.9% never married, 49.8% now married, 1.6% separated, 8.5% widowed, 11.8% divorced; Foreign born: 5.4%; Speak English only: 92.6%; With disability: 14.4%; Veterans: 8.2%; Ancestry: 28.6% German, 24.1% Italian, 19.6% Irish, 15.2% Polish, 8.8% English
Employment: 15.2% management, business, and financial, 5.1% computer, engineering, and science, 12.8% education, legal, community service, arts, and media, 6.5% healthcare practitioners, 17.1% service, 28.6% sales and office, 5.6% natural resources, construction, and maintenance, 9.1% production, transportation, and material moving
Income: Per capita: $31,137; Median household: $55,936; Average household: $67,462; Households with income of $100,000 or more: 21.1%; Poverty rate: 8.5%
Educational Attainment: High school diploma or higher: 93.7%; Bachelor's degree or higher: 35.4%; Graduate/professional degree or higher: 15.6%
Housing: Homeownership rate: 72.8%; Median home value: $124,200; Median year structure built: 1953; Homeowner vacancy rate: 0.5%; Median selected monthly owner costs: $1,190 with a mortgage, $497 without a mortgage; Median gross rent: $792 per month; Rental vacancy rate: 4.8%
Health Insurance: 97.4% have insurance; 77.6% have private insurance; 37.3% have public insurance; 2.6% do not have insurance; 0.7% of children under 18 do not have insurance
Safety: Violent crime rate: 17.5 per 10,000 population; Property crime rate: 159.4 per 10,000 population
Transportation: Commute: 93.0% car, 2.1% public transportation, 1.9% walk, 1.9% work from home; Mean travel time to work: 20.0 minutes
Additional Information Contacts
Town of Tonawanda . . . . (716) 877-8800
    http://www.tonawanda.ny.us

TONAWANDA RESERVATION (reservation).
Covers a land area of 1.839 square miles and a water area of 0 square miles. Located at 43.08° N. Lat; 78.48° W. Long.
Population: 4; Growth (since 2000): n/a; Density: 2.2 persons per square mile; Race: 0.0% White, 0.0% Black/African American, 0.0% Asian, 100.0% American Indian/Alaska Native, 0.0% Native Hawaiian/Other Pacific Islander, 0.0% Two or more races, 0.0% Hispanic of any race; Average household size: 4.00; Median age: n/a; Age under 18: 75.0%; Age 65 and over: 0.0%; Males per 100 females: 78.9; Marriage status: 75.0% never married, 0.0% now married, 0.0% separated, 25.0% widowed, 0.0% divorced; Foreign born: 0.0%; Speak English only: 100.0%; With disability: 0.0%; Veterans: 0.0%; Ancestry: n/a.
Employment: 0.0% management, business, and financial, 0.0% computer, engineering, and science, 0.0% education, legal, community service, arts, and media, 0.0% healthcare practitioners, 0.0% service, 0.0% sales and office, 100.0% natural resources, construction, and maintenance, 0.0% production, transportation, and material moving
Income: Per capita: n/a; Median household: n/a; Average household: n/a; Households with income of $100,000 or more: 100.0%; Poverty rate: n/a
Educational Attainment: High school diploma or higher: 100.0%; Bachelor's degree or higher: n/a; Graduate/professional degree or higher: n/a
Housing: Homeownership rate: 100.0%; Median home value: n/a; Median year structure built: n/a; Homeowner vacancy rate: 0.0%; Median selected monthly owner costs: n/a with a mortgage, n/a without a mortgage; Median gross rent: n/a per month; Rental vacancy rate: 0.0%

Health Insurance: 100.0% have insurance; 100.0% have private insurance; 0.0% have public insurance; 0.0% do not have insurance; 0.0% of children under 18 do not have insurance
Transportation: Commute: 0.0% car, 0.0% public transportation, 0.0% walk, 100.0% work from home; Mean travel time to work: 0.0 minutes

TOWN LINE (CDP).
Covers a land area of 4.622 square miles and a water area of 0.004 square miles. Located at 42.89° N. Lat; 78.57° W. Long. Elevation is 751 feet.
Population: 1,884; Growth (since 2000): -25.3%; Density: 407.6 persons per square mile; Race: 96.8% White, 0.0% Black/African American, 0.0% Asian, 0.0% American Indian/Alaska Native, 0.0% Native Hawaiian/Other Pacific Islander, 3.2% Two or more races, 0.7% Hispanic of any race; Average household size: 2.73; Median age: 41.6; Age under 18: 24.5%; Age 65 and over: 16.5%; Males per 100 females: 98.1; Marriage status: 24.7% never married, 58.5% now married, 0.6% separated, 9.9% widowed, 6.9% divorced; Foreign born: 0.7%; Speak English only: 98.6%; With disability: 15.1%; Veterans: 11.3%; Ancestry: 49.2% German, 23.2% Polish, 15.6% Irish, 7.4% English, 7.1% Italian
Employment: 17.6% management, business, and financial, 6.9% computer, engineering, and science, 13.6% education, legal, community service, arts, and media, 3.9% healthcare practitioners, 19.5% service, 22.6% sales and office, 3.1% natural resources, construction, and maintenance, 12.7% production, transportation, and material moving
Income: Per capita: $30,244; Median household: $78,333; Average household: $80,514; Households with income of $100,000 or more: 27.5%; Poverty rate: 3.3%
Educational Attainment: High school diploma or higher: 96.5%; Bachelor's degree or higher: 27.3%; Graduate/professional degree or higher: 6.2%
Housing: Homeownership rate: 96.2%; Median home value: $179,500; Median year structure built: 1964; Homeowner vacancy rate: 0.0%; Median selected monthly owner costs: $1,389 with a mortgage, $465 without a mortgage; Median gross rent: n/a per month; Rental vacancy rate: 0.0%
Health Insurance: 98.5% have insurance; 89.8% have private insurance; 30.6% have public insurance; 1.5% do not have insurance; 0.0% of children under 18 do not have insurance
Transportation: Commute: 100.0% car, 0.0% public transportation, 0.0% walk, 0.0% work from home; Mean travel time to work: 25.7 minutes

UNIVERSITY AT BUFFALO (CDP).
Covers a land area of 1.373 square miles and a water area of 0.089 square miles. Located at 43.00° N. Lat; 78.79° W. Long.
History: University at Buffalo, The State University of New York, is a public research university with multiple campuses located in Buffalo and Amherst, New York. The university is the largest in the SUNY system, and also the largest public university in the northeastern United States (comprising New York state and the New England region). It is also the largest of one of SUNY's four comprehensive university centers.
Population: 6,294; Growth (since 2000): n/a; Density: 4,584.9 persons per square mile; Race: 53.4% White, 11.3% Black/African American, 25.6% Asian, 0.0% American Indian/Alaska Native, 0.1% Native Hawaiian/Other Pacific Islander, 4.2% Two or more races, 11.0% Hispanic of any race; Average household size: 2.71; Median age: 19.7; Age under 18: 2.0%; Age 65 and over: 0.0%; Males per 100 females: 104.1; Marriage status: 98.7% never married, 1.2% now married, 0.0% separated, 0.0% widowed, 0.1% divorced; Foreign born: 18.9%; Speak English only: 66.0%; With disability: 3.6%; Veterans: 0.3%; Ancestry: 17.0% Italian, 14.3% German, 12.6% Irish, 8.9% Polish, 5.6% English
Employment: 5.7% management, business, and financial, 4.4% computer, engineering, and science, 10.6% education, legal, community service, arts, and media, 1.4% healthcare practitioners, 27.7% service, 45.3% sales and office, 0.9% natural resources, construction, and maintenance, 4.1% production, transportation, and material moving
Income: Per capita: $3,638; Median household: n/a; Average household: $14,650; Households with income of $100,000 or more: n/a; Poverty rate: n/a
Educational Attainment: High school diploma or higher: 100.0%; Bachelor's degree or higher: 74.0%; Graduate/professional degree or higher: 28.8%
Housing: Homeownership rate: n/a; Median home value: n/a; Median year structure built: 1994; Homeowner vacancy rate: n/a; Median selected monthly owner costs: n/a with a mortgage, n/a without a mortgage; Median gross rent: $1,216 per month; Rental vacancy rate: n/a

Health Insurance: 99.4% have insurance; 88.3% have private insurance; 12.5% have public insurance; 0.6% do not have insurance; 0.7% of children under 18 do not have insurance
Transportation: Commute: 43.8% car, 15.7% public transportation, 33.0% walk, 5.6% work from home; Mean travel time to work: 13.6 minutes

WALES (town).

Covers a land area of 35.588 square miles and a water area of 0.051 square miles. Located at 42.74° N. Lat; 78.52° W. Long.
Population: 3,032; Growth (since 2000): 2.4%; Density: 85.2 persons per square mile; Race: 94.0% White, 0.0% Black/African American, 4.4% Asian, 0.0% American Indian/Alaska Native, 0.0% Native Hawaiian/Other Pacific Islander, 1.3% Two or more races, 0.9% Hispanic of any race; Average household size: 2.58; Median age: 44.1; Age under 18: 22.2%; Age 65 and over: 14.4%; Males per 100 females: 98.0; Marriage status: 18.9% never married, 62.1% now married, 0.8% separated, 6.4% widowed, 12.6% divorced; Foreign born: 1.4%; Speak English only: 98.5%; With disability: 8.5%; Veterans: 5.2%; Ancestry: 39.8% German, 24.3% Polish, 14.4% Irish, 9.4% English, 7.8% Italian
Employment: 21.9% management, business, and financial, 4.5% computer, engineering, and science, 8.5% education, legal, community service, arts, and media, 7.2% healthcare practitioners, 17.9% service, 20.8% sales and office, 11.0% natural resources, construction, and maintenance, 8.3% production, transportation, and material moving
Income: Per capita: $35,629; Median household: $72,150; Average household: $89,604; Households with income of $100,000 or more: 40.6%; Poverty rate: 6.3%
Educational Attainment: High school diploma or higher: 93.5%; Bachelor's degree or higher: 29.1%; Graduate/professional degree or higher: 9.7%
Housing: Homeownership rate: 91.6%; Median home value: $175,600; Median year structure built: 1969; Homeowner vacancy rate: 2.1%; Median selected monthly owner costs: $1,469 with a mortgage, $495 without a mortgage; Median gross rent: $783 per month; Rental vacancy rate: 0.0%
Health Insurance: 97.6% have insurance; 79.1% have private insurance; 29.1% have public insurance; 2.4% do not have insurance; 1.3% of children under 18 do not have insurance
Transportation: Commute: 92.6% car, 0.4% public transportation, 2.3% walk, 3.1% work from home; Mean travel time to work: 26.4 minutes

WALES CENTER (unincorporated postal area)
ZCTA: 14169

Covers a land area of 0.308 square miles and a water area of 0 square miles. Located at 42.77° N. Lat; 78.52° W. Long. Elevation is 889 feet.
Population: 132; Growth (since 2000): n/a; Density: 428.2 persons per square mile; Race: 100.0% White, 0.0% Black/African American, 0.0% Asian, 0.0% American Indian/Alaska Native, 0.0% Native Hawaiian/Other Pacific Islander, 0.0% Two or more races, 0.0% Hispanic of any race; Average household size: 1.97; Median age: 42.8; Age under 18: 34.1%; Age 65 and over: 22.7%; Males per 100 females: 86.4; Marriage status: 20.9% never married, 27.3% now married, 0.0% separated, 0.0% widowed, 51.8% divorced; Foreign born: 0.0%; Speak English only: 100.0%; With disability: 45.5%; Veterans: 8.0%; Ancestry: 37.9% Polish, 34.8% German, 17.4% French, 16.7% Irish, 16.7% Italian
Employment: 0.0% management, business, and financial, 0.0% computer, engineering, and science, 0.0% education, legal, community service, arts, and media, 0.0% healthcare practitioners, 82.1% service, 0.0% sales and office, 0.0% natural resources, construction, and maintenance, 17.9% production, transportation, and material moving
Income: Per capita: $14,301; Median household: $30,875; Average household: $28,609; Households with income of $100,000 or more: n/a; Poverty rate: 34.8%
Educational Attainment: High school diploma or higher: 93.1%; Bachelor's degree or higher: 9.2%; Graduate/professional degree or higher: 9.2%
Housing: Homeownership rate: 65.7%; Median home value: <$10,000; Median year structure built: 1996; Homeowner vacancy rate: 0.0%; Median selected monthly owner costs: $0 with a mortgage, $0 without a mortgage; Median gross rent: n/a per month; Rental vacancy rate: 0.0%
Health Insurance: 100.0% have insurance; 15.2% have private insurance; 96.2% have public insurance; 0.0% do not have insurance; 0.0% of children under 18 do not have insurance
Transportation: Commute: 100.0% car, 0.0% public transportation, 0.0% walk, 0.0% work from home; Mean travel time to work: 0.0 minutes

WANAKAH (CDP).

Covers a land area of 1.204 square miles and a water area of 0 square miles. Located at 42.74° N. Lat; 78.90° W. Long. Elevation is 591 feet.
Population: 2,902; Growth (since 2000): n/a; Density: 2,409.5 persons per square mile; Race: 93.7% White, 0.0% Black/African American, 2.9% Asian, 2.8% American Indian/Alaska Native, 0.0% Native Hawaiian/Other Pacific Islander, 0.6% Two or more races, 1.1% Hispanic of any race; Average household size: 2.24; Median age: 49.2; Age under 18: 18.3%; Age 65 and over: 23.7%; Males per 100 females: 92.2; Marriage status: 17.3% never married, 61.2% now married, 0.4% separated, 11.2% widowed, 10.3% divorced; Foreign born: 2.6%; Speak English only: 97.1%; With disability: 10.4%; Veterans: 10.7%; Ancestry: 30.9% Irish, 30.6% German, 15.6% Italian, 11.1% Polish, 5.1% English
Employment: 14.1% management, business, and financial, 3.1% computer, engineering, and science, 12.6% education, legal, community service, arts, and media, 5.5% healthcare practitioners, 21.3% service, 22.9% sales and office, 6.8% natural resources, construction, and maintenance, 13.7% production, transportation, and material moving
Income: Per capita: $37,699; Median household: $73,041; Average household: $83,704; Households with income of $100,000 or more: 29.5%; Poverty rate: 3.2%
Educational Attainment: High school diploma or higher: 94.3%; Bachelor's degree or higher: 31.6%; Graduate/professional degree or higher: 12.5%
Housing: Homeownership rate: 91.8%; Median home value: $146,300; Median year structure built: 1955; Homeowner vacancy rate: 0.0%; Median selected monthly owner costs: $1,258 with a mortgage, $515 without a mortgage; Median gross rent: $840 per month; Rental vacancy rate: 0.0%
Health Insurance: 97.8% have insurance; 89.8% have private insurance; 29.0% have public insurance; 2.2% do not have insurance; 0.0% of children under 18 do not have insurance
Transportation: Commute: 95.1% car, 2.7% public transportation, 0.0% walk, 2.2% work from home; Mean travel time to work: 21.9 minutes

WEST FALLS (unincorporated postal area)
ZCTA: 14170

Covers a land area of 12.326 square miles and a water area of 0.054 square miles. Located at 42.70° N. Lat; 78.67° W. Long. Elevation is 925 feet.
Population: 2,681; Growth (since 2000): 1.8%; Density: 217.5 persons per square mile; Race: 97.9% White, 0.0% Black/African American, 0.0% Asian, 0.0% American Indian/Alaska Native, 0.0% Native Hawaiian/Other Pacific Islander, 2.1% Two or more races, 4.3% Hispanic of any race; Average household size: 2.60; Median age: 43.8; Age under 18: 23.3%; Age 65 and over: 12.9%; Males per 100 females: 102.3; Marriage status: 25.1% never married, 57.4% now married, 0.0% separated, 3.4% widowed, 14.1% divorced; Foreign born: 2.4%; Speak English only: 97.4%; With disability: 10.8%; Veterans: 7.5%; Ancestry: 36.0% German, 24.9% Irish, 18.7% Polish, 18.1% Italian, 15.4% English
Employment: 11.5% management, business, and financial, 4.6% computer, engineering, and science, 7.5% education, legal, community service, arts, and media, 12.7% healthcare practitioners, 16.7% service, 18.8% sales and office, 14.6% natural resources, construction, and maintenance, 13.6% production, transportation, and material moving
Income: Per capita: $45,920; Median household: $73,873; Average household: $117,759; Households with income of $100,000 or more: 32.0%; Poverty rate: 7.6%
Educational Attainment: High school diploma or higher: 97.3%; Bachelor's degree or higher: 22.8%; Graduate/professional degree or higher: 11.2%
Housing: Homeownership rate: 83.0%; Median home value: $171,500; Median year structure built: 1955; Homeowner vacancy rate: 0.0%; Median selected monthly owner costs: $1,427 with a mortgage, $552 without a mortgage; Median gross rent: $706 per month; Rental vacancy rate: 0.0%
Health Insurance: 91.4% have insurance; 78.8% have private insurance; 25.1% have public insurance; 8.6% do not have insurance; 6.0% of children under 18 do not have insurance
Transportation: Commute: 94.5% car, 0.0% public transportation, 0.0% walk, 5.5% work from home; Mean travel time to work: 26.7 minutes

WEST SENECA (CDP). Covers a land area of 21.357 square miles and a water area of 0.057 square miles. Located at 42.84° N. Lat; 78.75° W. Long. Elevation is 597 feet.
Population: 45,340; Growth (since 2000): -1.3%; Density: 2,122.9 persons per square mile; Race: 96.3% White, 1.7% Black/African American, 0.3% Asian, 0.1% American Indian/Alaska Native, 0.0% Native Hawaiian/Other Pacific Islander, 0.8% Two or more races, 1.9% Hispanic of any race; Average household size: 2.29; Median age: 45.0; Age under 18: 18.4%; Age 65 and over: 20.3%; Males per 100 females: 91.7; Marriage status: 30.7% never married, 51.0% now married, 0.9% separated, 8.3% widowed, 10.0% divorced; Foreign born: 2.5%; Speak English only: 96.0%; With disability: 12.7%; Veterans: 8.5%; Ancestry: 30.3% German, 27.1% Polish, 24.7% Irish, 19.4% Italian, 5.2% English
Employment: 14.0% management, business, and financial, 5.6% computer, engineering, and science, 10.1% education, legal, community service, arts, and media, 7.7% healthcare practitioners, 15.4% service, 27.0% sales and office, 6.6% natural resources, construction, and maintenance, 13.6% production, transportation, and material moving
Income: Per capita: $32,413; Median household: $62,705; Average household: $73,617; Households with income of $100,000 or more: 23.2%; Poverty rate: 7.0%
Educational Attainment: High school diploma or higher: 93.9%; Bachelor's degree or higher: 28.3%; Graduate/professional degree or higher: 11.1%

School District(s)
Erie 1 Boces
   Enrollment: n/a . . . . (716) 821-7001
West Seneca Central SD (PK-12)
   Enrollment: 6,715 . . . . (716) 677-3101
Vocational/Technical School(s)
Continental School of Beauty Culture-West Seneca (Private, For-profit)
   Enrollment: 117 . . . . (716) 675-8205
   Tuition: $12,690
Erie 1 BOCES (Public)
   Enrollment: 420 . . . . (716) 821-7500
   Tuition: $9,800
Housing: Homeownership rate: 76.9%; Median home value: $141,500; Median year structure built: 1964; Homeowner vacancy rate: 0.2%; Median selected monthly owner costs: $1,275 with a mortgage, $578 without a mortgage; Median gross rent: $780 per month; Rental vacancy rate: 2.2%
Health Insurance: 96.6% have insurance; 80.5% have private insurance; 34.0% have public insurance; 3.4% do not have insurance; 0.5% of children under 18 do not have insurance
Safety: Violent crime rate: 9.7 per 10,000 population; Property crime rate: 123.5 per 10,000 population
Transportation: Commute: 95.7% car, 1.0% public transportation, 1.2% walk, 1.8% work from home; Mean travel time to work: 20.9 minutes
Additional Information Contacts
Town of West Seneca . . . . (716) 674-5600
   http://www.westseneca.net

WILLIAMSVILLE (village). Covers a land area of 1.260 square miles and a water area of 0.010 square miles. Located at 42.96° N. Lat; 78.74° W. Long. Elevation is 676 feet.
History: Settled c.1800, incorporated 1869.
Population: 5,263; Growth (since 2000): -5.6%; Density: 4,176.4 persons per square mile; Race: 90.9% White, 4.3% Black/African American, 3.4% Asian, 0.6% American Indian/Alaska Native, 0.0% Native Hawaiian/Other Pacific Islander, 0.7% Two or more races, 1.9% Hispanic of any race; Average household size: 2.08; Median age: 48.3; Age under 18: 15.6%; Age 65 and over: 24.0%; Males per 100 females: 77.7; Marriage status: 34.4% never married, 41.8% now married, 1.3% separated, 7.2% widowed, 16.6% divorced; Foreign born: 6.4%; Speak English only: 92.6%; With disability: 11.8%; Veterans: 9.1%; Ancestry: 29.1% German, 21.7% Irish, 17.4% Italian, 14.9% Polish, 11.8% English
Employment: 17.2% management, business, and financial, 7.2% computer, engineering, and science, 22.2% education, legal, community service, arts, and media, 7.2% healthcare practitioners, 17.7% service, 19.7% sales and office, 2.8% natural resources, construction, and maintenance, 6.2% production, transportation, and material moving
Income: Per capita: $38,194; Median household: $63,600; Average household: $80,440; Households with income of $100,000 or more: 28.1%; Poverty rate: 8.9%

Educational Attainment: High school diploma or higher: 97.9%; Bachelor's degree or higher: 60.4%; Graduate/professional degree or higher: 28.3%
School District(s)
Clarence Central SD (KG-12)
   Enrollment: 4,510 . . . . (716) 407-9102
Williamsville Central SD (KG-12)
   Enrollment: 10,037 . . . . (716) 626-8005
Vocational/Technical School(s)
Leon Studio One School of Beauty Knowledge (Private, For-profit)
   Enrollment: 32 . . . . (716) 631-3878
   Tuition: $11,900
New York Institute of Massage Inc (Private, For-profit)
   Enrollment: 46 . . . . (716) 633-0355
   Tuition: $17,500
Housing: Homeownership rate: 59.4%; Median home value: $164,600; Median year structure built: 1950; Homeowner vacancy rate: 0.3%; Median selected monthly owner costs: $1,403 with a mortgage, $620 without a mortgage; Median gross rent: $932 per month; Rental vacancy rate: 0.0%
Health Insurance: 97.6% have insurance; 85.7% have private insurance; 31.1% have public insurance; 2.4% do not have insurance; 7.4% of children under 18 do not have insurance
Transportation: Commute: 89.0% car, 1.6% public transportation, 5.3% walk, 2.6% work from home; Mean travel time to work: 17.5 minutes
Additional Information Contacts
Village of Williamsville . . . . (716) 632-4120
   http://village.williamsville.ny.us

Essex County

Located in northeastern New York, in the Adirondacks; bounded on the east by Lake Champlain; drained by the Hudson and Ausable Rivers; includes Lake Placid and Saranac Lake, and Mt. Marcy, the highest point in the state (5,344 ft). Covers a land area of 1,794.228 square miles, a water area of 122.000 square miles, and is located in the Eastern Time Zone at 44.11° N. Lat., 73.78° W. Long. The county was founded in 1799. County seat is Elizabethtown.

Weather Station: Lake Placid 2 S								Elevation: 1,938 feet			
	Jan	Feb	Mar	Apr	May	Jun	Jul	Aug	Sep	Oct	Nov	Dec
High	27	31	40	53	65	73	77	75	68	56	43	32
Low	6	8	16	29	39	48	53	51	44	34	24	12
Precip	2.5	2.1	2.6	2.8	3.5	4.3	4.4	4.2	3.9	3.9	3.5	3.0
Snow	na	na	18.8	7.2	0.3	0.0	0.0	0.0	tr	2.5	10.8	22.7

High and Low temperatures in degrees Fahrenheit; Precipitation and Snow in inches

Weather Station: Newcomb								Elevation: 1,620 feet			
	Jan	Feb	Mar	Apr	May	Jun	Jul	Aug	Sep	Oct	Nov	Dec
High	25	28	38	51	64	72	76	74	66	55	41	29
Low	5	4	14	28	39	49	53	52	45	34	25	11
Precip	3.0	2.7	2.9	3.2	3.8	3.7	3.9	3.9	3.9	4.0	3.8	3.4
Snow	24.3	22.6	18.7	5.7	0.2	tr	0.0	0.0	tr	1.1	8.9	24.2

High and Low temperatures in degrees Fahrenheit; Precipitation and Snow in inches

Weather Station: Ray Brook								Elevation: 1,620 feet			
	Jan	Feb	Mar	Apr	May	Jun	Jul	Aug	Sep	Oct	Nov	Dec
High	25	29	38	51	64	72	77	75	67	54	41	30
Low	3	5	14	28	39	48	52	51	43	33	25	12
Precip	na	na	2.5	2.7	3.1	3.8	3.7	3.8	4.1	3.4	3.4	na
Snow	23.5	19.6	19.9	9.2	0.8	tr	0.0	tr	0.1	1.6	14.6	22.4

High and Low temperatures in degrees Fahrenheit; Precipitation and Snow in inches

Population: 38,233; Growth (since 2000): -1.6%; Density: 21.3 persons per square mile; Race: 92.8% White, 3.2% Black/African American, 0.5% Asian, 0.2% American Indian/Alaska Native, 0.0% Native Hawaiian/Other Pacific Islander, 2.1% two or more races, 3.2% Hispanic of any race; Average household size: 2.32; Median age: 46.7; Age under 18: 16.9%; Age 65 and over: 21.4%; Males per 100 females: 107.4; Marriage status: 30.2% never married, 51.4% now married, 1.8% separated, 7.9% widowed, 10.6% divorced; Foreign born: 3.0%; Speak English only: 94.1%; With disability: 17.4%; Veterans: 9.7%; Ancestry: 23.2% Irish, 16.1% French, 12.8% English, 12.4% German, 8.1% Italian
Religion: Six largest groups: 21.5% Catholicism, 5.6% Methodist/Pietist, 2.0% Non-denominational Protestant, 1.3% Presbyterian-Reformed, 1.1% Episcopalianism/Anglicanism, 1.1% Baptist

Economy: Unemployment rate: 3.6%; Leading industries: 18.2 % accommodation and food services; 17.2 % retail trade; 12.7 % health care and social assistance; Farms: 261 totaling 54,837 acres; Company size: 0 employ 1,000 or more persons, 1 employs 500 to 999 persons, 13 employ 100 to 499 persons, 1,163 employ less than 100 persons; Business ownership: 1,164 women-owned, n/a Black-owned, 33 Hispanic-owned, 36 Asian-owned, n/a American Indian/Alaska Native-owned

Employment: 11.8% management, business, and financial, 2.5% computer, engineering, and science, 12.1% education, legal, community service, arts, and media, 5.8% healthcare practitioners, 23.7% service, 22.0% sales and office, 11.3% natural resources, construction, and maintenance, 10.8% production, transportation, and material moving

Income: Per capita: $29,008; Median household: $55,294; Average household: $69,488; Households with income of $100,000 or more: 20.1%; Poverty rate: 8.9%

Educational Attainment: High school diploma or higher: 90.9%; Bachelor's degree or higher: 26.7%; Graduate/professional degree or higher: 12.2%

Housing: Homeownership rate: 76.0%; Median home value: $146,900; Median year structure built: 1960; Homeowner vacancy rate: 3.7%; Median selected monthly owner costs: $1,230 with a mortgage, $515 without a mortgage; Median gross rent: $798 per month; Rental vacancy rate: 7.1%

Vital Statistics: Birth rate: 84.8 per 10,000 population; Death rate: 109.3 per 10,000 population; Age-adjusted cancer mortality rate: 162.6 deaths per 100,000 population

Health Insurance: 94.8% have insurance; 72.5% have private insurance; 41.8% have public insurance; 5.2% do not have insurance; 3.4% of children under 18 do not have insurance

Health Care: Physicians: 8.2 per 10,000 population; Dentists: 3.2 per 10,000 population; Hospital beds: 10.5 per 10,000 population; Hospital admissions: 149.4 per 10,000 population

Air Quality Index (AQI): Percent of Days: 85.5% good, 14.5% moderate, 0.0% unhealthy for sensitive individuals, 0.0% unhealthy, 0.0% very unhealthy; Annual median: 39; Annual maximum: 90

Transportation: Commute: 88.2% car, 0.4% public transportation, 2.7% walk, 6.1% work from home; Mean travel time to work: 21.9 minutes

2016 Presidential Election: 46.2% Trump, 45.1% Clinton, 4.2% Johnson, 2.4% Stein

National and State Parks: Wickham Marsh State Game Management Area

Additional Information Contacts

Essex Government . . . . (518) 873-3601
   http://www.co.essex.ny.us

Essex County Communities

BLOOMINGDALE (unincorporated postal area)

ZCTA: 12913

Covers a land area of 27.122 square miles and a water area of 2.224 square miles. Located at 44.43° N. Lat; 74.00° W. Long. Elevation is 1,572 feet.

Population: 1,297; Growth (since 2000): 8.6%; Density: 47.8 persons per square mile; Race: 99.4% White, 0.0% Black/African American, 0.0% Asian, 0.0% American Indian/Alaska Native, 0.0% Native Hawaiian/Other Pacific Islander, 0.2% Two or more races, 1.5% Hispanic of any race; Average household size: 2.40; Median age: 45.2; Age under 18: 24.6%; Age 65 and over: 16.5%; Males per 100 females: 102.3; Marriage status: 17.7% never married, 66.6% now married, 0.7% separated, 7.4% widowed, 8.3% divorced; Foreign born: 2.5%; Speak English only: 94.1%; With disability: 14.9%; Veterans: 9.0%; Ancestry: 26.2% Irish, 20.1% French, 12.2% English, 11.0% German, 9.9% Italian

Employment: 14.2% management, business, and financial, 5.7% computer, engineering, and science, 13.8% education, legal, community service, arts, and media, 7.4% healthcare practitioners, 20.3% service, 19.0% sales and office, 15.9% natural resources, construction, and maintenance, 3.8% production, transportation, and material moving

Income: Per capita: $32,612; Median household: $57,813; Average household: $76,363; Households with income of $100,000 or more: 23.7%; Poverty rate: 8.2%

Educational Attainment: High school diploma or higher: 93.0%; Bachelor's degree or higher: 32.8%; Graduate/professional degree or higher: 11.7%

Housing: Homeownership rate: 82.4%; Median home value: $161,600; Median year structure built: 1982; Homeowner vacancy rate: 0.0%; Median selected monthly owner costs: $1,287 with a mortgage, $469

without a mortgage; Median gross rent: $648 per month; Rental vacancy rate: 0.0%

Health Insurance: 96.1% have insurance; 81.8% have private insurance; 28.1% have public insurance; 3.9% do not have insurance; 3.9% of children under 18 do not have insurance

Transportation: Commute: 93.2% car, 0.0% public transportation, 1.0% walk, 4.2% work from home; Mean travel time to work: 19.1 minutes

CHESTERFIELD (town). Covers a land area of 79.036 square miles and a water area of 26.336 square miles. Located at 44.45° N. Lat; 73.45° W. Long.

Population: 2,633; Growth (since 2000): 9.3%; Density: 33.3 persons per square mile; Race: 96.5% White, 0.4% Black/African American, 0.0% Asian, 0.0% American Indian/Alaska Native, 0.1% Native Hawaiian/Other Pacific Islander, 2.6% Two or more races, 2.1% Hispanic of any race; Average household size: 2.56; Median age: 47.4; Age under 18: 18.5%; Age 65 and over: 19.3%; Males per 100 females: 101.7; Marriage status: 25.5% never married, 55.4% now married, 2.0% separated, 8.6% widowed, 10.5% divorced; Foreign born: 2.0%; Speak English only: 96.0%; With disability: 15.9%; Veterans: 12.4%; Ancestry: 25.3% French, 15.4% Irish, 11.0% English, 10.8% German, 9.5% American

Employment: 14.5% management, business, and financial, 1.1% computer, engineering, and science, 15.0% education, legal, community service, arts, and media, 6.6% healthcare practitioners, 21.4% service, 19.8% sales and office, 9.6% natural resources, construction, and maintenance, 11.8% production, transportation, and material moving

Income: Per capita: $32,291; Median household: $59,667; Average household: $79,187; Households with income of $100,000 or more: 23.2%; Poverty rate: 7.7%

Educational Attainment: High school diploma or higher: 91.1%; Bachelor's degree or higher: 28.2%; Graduate/professional degree or higher: 13.8%

Housing: Homeownership rate: 81.5%; Median home value: $116,400; Median year structure built: 1958; Homeowner vacancy rate: 2.7%; Median selected monthly owner costs: $1,154 with a mortgage, $466 without a mortgage; Median gross rent: $795 per month; Rental vacancy rate: 19.9%

Health Insurance: 91.5% have insurance; 66.7% have private insurance; 40.8% have public insurance; 8.5% do not have insurance; 12.1% of children under 18 do not have insurance

Transportation: Commute: 87.2% car, 0.0% public transportation, 0.0% walk, 8.4% work from home; Mean travel time to work: 23.3 minutes

CROWN POINT (town). Covers a land area of 76.121 square miles and a water area of 5.724 square miles. Located at 43.96° N. Lat; 73.58° W. Long. Elevation is 223 feet.

History: The French began building Fort St. Frederic in 1731. In the French and Indian Wars the fort resisted early English attacks but was demolished (1759) before the advance of Jeffrey Amherst. The British began building a new fort, Fort Amherst (renamed Crown Point), in 1759. Early in the Revolution, Crown Point was captured by Seth Warner and the Green Mt. Boys. Abandoned (1777) to Gen. John Burgoyne. Crown Point Reservation, with bathing and fishing, a Museum and ruins of colonial forts, is nearby.

Population: 1,834; Growth (since 2000): -13.4%; Density: 24.1 persons per square mile; Race: 98.1% White, 0.1% Black/African American, 0.6% Asian, 0.7% American Indian/Alaska Native, 0.0% Native Hawaiian/Other Pacific Islander, 0.5% Two or more races, 0.1% Hispanic of any race; Average household size: 2.46; Median age: 44.9; Age under 18: 17.6%; Age 65 and over: 22.0%; Males per 100 females: 104.0; Marriage status: 29.6% never married, 53.4% now married, 2.9% separated, 6.0% widowed, 11.0% divorced; Foreign born: 1.9%; Speak English only: 99.3%; With disability: 22.4%; Veterans: 12.6%; Ancestry: 24.8% Irish, 22.8% French, 16.6% English, 10.8% German, 6.3% Polish

Employment: 12.4% management, business, and financial, 6.1% computer, engineering, and science, 9.6% education, legal, community service, arts, and media, 1.3% healthcare practitioners, 24.6% service, 9.4% sales and office, 15.4% natural resources, construction, and maintenance, 21.2% production, transportation, and material moving

Income: Per capita: $26,732; Median household: $52,878; Average household: $64,924; Households with income of $100,000 or more: 15.9%; Poverty rate: 13.2%

Educational Attainment: High school diploma or higher: 91.4%; Bachelor's degree or higher: 12.2%; Graduate/professional degree or higher: 5.5%

Crown Point Central SD (PK-12)
    Enrollment: 290. . . . . (518) 597-4200
Housing: Homeownership rate: 80.6%; Median home value: $120,800;
Median year structure built: 1969; Homeowner vacancy rate: 4.2%; Median
selected monthly owner costs: $1,175 with a mortgage, $445 without a
mortgage; Median gross rent: $867 per month; Rental vacancy rate: 9.4%
Health Insurance: 95.0% have insurance; 68.8% have private insurance;
46.3% have public insurance; 5.0% do not have insurance; 0.0% of
children under 18 do not have insurance
Transportation: Commute: 86.8% car, 0.7% public transportation, 0.4%
walk, 4.9% work from home; Mean travel time to work: 30.5 minutes

ELIZABETHTOWN (CDP). Covers a land area of 3.307 square
miles and a water area of 0.004 square miles. Located at 44.23° N. Lat;
73.59° W. Long. Elevation is 564 feet.
Population: 739; Growth (since 2000): n/a; Density: 223.4 persons per
square mile; Race: 90.9% White, 3.4% Black/African American, 0.7%
Asian, 0.0% American Indian/Alaska Native, 0.0% Native Hawaiian/Other
Pacific Islander, 4.7% Two or more races, 5.4% Hispanic of any race;
Average household size: 2.24; Median age: 55.0; Age under 18: 16.0%;
Age 65 and over: 30.3%; Males per 100 females: 87.1; Marriage status:
29.1% never married, 39.7% now married, 3.0% separated, 13.6%
widowed, 17.6% divorced; Foreign born: 1.8%; Speak English only: 95.8%;
With disability: 10.8%; Veterans: 9.0%; Ancestry: 25.3% Irish, 17.7%
English, 11.6% French, 10.0% Danish, 7.2% German
Employment: 11.5% management, business, and financial, 3.0%
computer, engineering, and science, 10.8% education, legal, community
service, arts, and media, 7.2% healthcare practitioners, 20.0% service,
19.0% sales and office, 16.4% natural resources, construction, and
maintenance, 12.1% production, transportation, and material moving
Income: Per capita: $26,480; Median household: $48,229; Average
household: $65,109; Households with income of $100,000 or more: 15.5%;
Poverty rate: 12.8%
Educational Attainment: High school diploma or higher: 89.8%;
Bachelor's degree or higher: 23.5%; Graduate/professional degree or
higher: 11.4%

Elizabethtown-Lewis Central SD (KG-12)
    Enrollment: 241. . . . . (518) 873-6371
Housing: Homeownership rate: 68.8%; Median home value: $155,100;
Median year structure built: 1942; Homeowner vacancy rate: 4.9%; Median
selected monthly owner costs: $1,132 with a mortgage, $564 without a
mortgage; Median gross rent: $766 per month; Rental vacancy rate: 0.0%
Health Insurance: 97.0% have insurance; 65.8% have private insurance;
53.6% have public insurance; 3.0% do not have insurance; 0.0% of
children under 18 do not have insurance
Hospitals: Elizabethtown Community Hospital (25 beds)
Newspapers: Denton Publications (weekly circulation 80,000)
Transportation: Commute: 82.1% car, 0.0% public transportation, 9.6%
walk, 8.3% work from home; Mean travel time to work: 11.3 minutes

ELIZABETHTOWN (town). County seat. Covers a land area of
81.633 square miles and a water area of 1.477 square miles. Located at
44.19° N. Lat; 73.65° W. Long. Elevation is 564 feet.
Population: 1,200; Growth (since 2000): -8.7%; Density: 14.7 persons per
square mile; Race: 93.1% White, 2.1% Black/African American, 0.4%
Asian, 0.0% American Indian/Alaska Native, 0.0% Native Hawaiian/Other
Pacific Islander, 3.3% Two or more races, 4.3% Hispanic of any race;
Average household size: 2.21; Median age: 54.7; Age under 18: 15.3%;
Age 65 and over: 28.6%; Males per 100 females: 92.9; Marriage status:
26.3% never married, 48.7% now married, 1.8% separated, 11.5%
widowed, 13.4% divorced; Foreign born: 1.9%; Speak English only: 96.3%;
With disability: 11.9%; Veterans: 10.9%; Ancestry: 26.8% Irish, 21.0%
English, 12.2% French, 6.4% Danish, 5.9% German
Employment: 12.6% management, business, and financial, 3.1%
computer, engineering, and science, 11.7% education, legal, community
service, arts, and media, 9.1% healthcare practitioners, 20.2% service,
18.3% sales and office, 13.4% natural resources, construction, and
maintenance, 11.7% production, transportation, and material moving
Income: Per capita: $29,198; Median household: $49,200; Average
household: $67,365; Households with income of $100,000 or more: 21.0%;
Poverty rate: 12.0%

Educational Attainment: High school diploma or higher: 92.3%;
Bachelor's degree or higher: 27.9%; Graduate/professional degree or
higher: 12.6%

Elizabethtown-Lewis Central SD (KG-12)
    Enrollment: 241. . . . . (518) 873-6371
Housing: Homeownership rate: 69.9%; Median home value: $167,500;
Median year structure built: 1952; Homeowner vacancy rate: 5.2%; Median
selected monthly owner costs: $1,135 with a mortgage, $556 without a
mortgage; Median gross rent: $768 per month; Rental vacancy rate: 0.0%
Health Insurance: 94.8% have insurance; 70.2% have private insurance;
47.2% have public insurance; 5.2% do not have insurance; 0.0% of
children under 18 do not have insurance
Hospitals: Elizabethtown Community Hospital (25 beds)
Newspapers: Denton Publications (weekly circulation 80,000)
Transportation: Commute: 86.8% car, 0.0% public transportation, 5.7%
walk, 7.5% work from home; Mean travel time to work: 14.2 minutes

ESSEX (town). Covers a land area of 31.631 square miles and a water
area of 5.969 square miles. Located at 44.28° N. Lat; 73.40° W. Long.
Elevation is 125 feet.
Population: 569; Growth (since 2000): -20.2%; Density: 18.0 persons per
square mile; Race: 98.8% White, 0.2% Black/African American, 1.1%
Asian, 0.0% American Indian/Alaska Native, 0.0% Native Hawaiian/Other
Pacific Islander, 0.0% Two or more races, 0.0% Hispanic of any race;
Average household size: 2.14; Median age: 55.1; Age under 18: 11.6%;
Age 65 and over: 26.0%; Males per 100 females: 104.0; Marriage status:
23.5% never married, 58.6% now married, 2.7% separated, 9.9%
widowed, 8.0% divorced; Foreign born: 3.0%; Speak English only: 98.7%;
With disability: 15.1%; Veterans: 9.1%; Ancestry: 17.2% English, 17.0%
Irish, 11.2% German, 10.7% French, 8.1% American
Employment: 20.4% management, business, and financial, 1.1%
computer, engineering, and science, 22.9% education, legal, community
service, arts, and media, 3.2% healthcare practitioners, 13.7% service,
15.5% sales and office, 12.3% natural resources, construction, and
maintenance, 10.9% production, transportation, and material moving
Income: Per capita: $33,018; Median household: $62,000; Average
household: $67,620; Households with income of $100,000 or more: 22.2%;
Poverty rate: 11.6%
Educational Attainment: High school diploma or higher: 91.7%;
Bachelor's degree or higher: 43.3%; Graduate/professional degree or
higher: 23.9%
Housing: Homeownership rate: 82.3%; Median home value: $176,300;
Median year structure built: Before 1940; Homeowner vacancy rate: 9.2%;
Median selected monthly owner costs: $1,164 with a mortgage, $642
without a mortgage; Median gross rent: $633 per month; Rental vacancy
rate: 21.7%
Health Insurance: 94.7% have insurance; 75.4% have private insurance;
43.6% have public insurance; 5.3% do not have insurance; 0.0% of
children under 18 do not have insurance
Transportation: Commute: 87.1% car, 2.7% public transportation, 0.0%
walk, 8.0% work from home; Mean travel time to work: 24.8 minutes

JAY (town). Covers a land area of 67.688 square miles and a water area
of 0.421 square miles. Located at 44.38° N. Lat; 73.70° W. Long. Elevation
is 712 feet.
Population: 2,709; Growth (since 2000): 17.5%; Density: 40.0 persons per
square mile; Race: 98.0% White, 0.3% Black/African American, 0.1%
Asian, 0.1% American Indian/Alaska Native, 0.0% Native Hawaiian/Other
Pacific Islander, 1.6% Two or more races, 0.1% Hispanic of any race;
Average household size: 2.50; Median age: 46.2; Age under 18: 22.7%;
Age 65 and over: 19.6%; Males per 100 females: 98.4; Marriage status:
21.6% never married, 60.1% now married, 1.1% separated, 8.6%
widowed, 9.7% divorced; Foreign born: 1.3%; Speak English only: 98.8%;
With disability: 13.7%; Veterans: 9.9%; Ancestry: 20.0% Irish, 19.2%
French, 14.2% English, 10.3% Italian, 10.2% German
Employment: 11.2% management, business, and financial, 0.9%
computer, engineering, and science, 14.5% education, legal, community
service, arts, and media, 6.3% healthcare practitioners, 32.9% service,
16.5% sales and office, 8.1% natural resources, construction, and
maintenance, 9.6% production, transportation, and material moving
Income: Per capita: $29,953; Median household: $58,728; Average
household: $73,260; Households with income of $100,000 or more: 21.3%;
Poverty rate: 3.6%

Educational Attainment: High school diploma or higher: 94.5%; Bachelor's degree or higher: 32.0%; Graduate/professional degree or higher: 17.0%
Housing: Homeownership rate: 81.0%; Median home value: $151,400; Median year structure built: 1975; Homeowner vacancy rate: 2.0%; Median selected monthly owner costs: $1,176 with a mortgage, $473 without a mortgage; Median gross rent: $847 per month; Rental vacancy rate: 0.0%
Health Insurance: 95.1% have insurance; 78.1% have private insurance; 32.0% have public insurance; 4.9% do not have insurance; 1.0% of children under 18 do not have insurance
Transportation: Commute: 87.3% car, 0.3% public transportation, 0.8% walk, 7.7% work from home; Mean travel time to work: 28.9 minutes

---

KEENE (town).
Covers a land area of 155.941 square miles and a water area of 0.676 square miles. Located at 44.12° N. Lat; 73.88° W. Long. Elevation is 840 feet.
Population: 1,156; Growth (since 2000): 8.7%; Density: 7.4 persons per square mile; Race: 96.0% White, 0.0% Black/African American, 0.5% Asian, 0.0% American Indian/Alaska Native, 0.5% Native Hawaiian/Other Pacific Islander, 1.1% Two or more races, 0.0% Hispanic of any race; Average household size: 2.09; Median age: 50.7; Age under 18: 13.3%; Age 65 and over: 24.6%; Males per 100 females: 90.8; Marriage status: 25.8% never married, 56.1% now married, 3.1% separated, 6.1% widowed, 12.0% divorced; Foreign born: 3.5%; Speak English only: 97.3%; With disability: 12.8%; Veterans: 5.9%; Ancestry: 28.4% English, 23.4% Irish, 19.2% German, 12.0% French, 12.0% Italian
Employment: 8.2% management, business, and financial, 3.2% computer, engineering, and science, 15.8% education, legal, community service, arts, and media, 3.9% healthcare practitioners, 18.0% service, 30.3% sales and office, 11.9% natural resources, construction, and maintenance, 8.7% production, transportation, and material moving
Income: Per capita: $36,561; Median household: $54,519; Average household: $75,367; Households with income of $100,000 or more: 25.4%; Poverty rate: 4.1%
Educational Attainment: High school diploma or higher: 98.1%; Bachelor's degree or higher: 49.3%; Graduate/professional degree or higher: 21.0%
Housing: Homeownership rate: 78.5%; Median home value: $235,900; Median year structure built: 1970; Homeowner vacancy rate: 4.2%; Median selected monthly owner costs: $1,389 with a mortgage, $574 without a mortgage; Median gross rent: $950 per month; Rental vacancy rate: 2.5%
Health Insurance: 97.5% have insurance; 77.2% have private insurance; 41.2% have public insurance; 2.5% do not have insurance; 0.0% of children under 18 do not have insurance
Transportation: Commute: 81.9% car, 0.0% public transportation, 5.5% walk, 10.7% work from home; Mean travel time to work: 19.6 minutes

---

KEENE VALLEY (unincorporated postal area)
ZCTA: 12943
Covers a land area of 103.005 square miles and a water area of 0.554 square miles. Located at 44.12° N. Lat; 73.88° W. Long. Elevation is 1,024 feet.
Population: 320; Growth (since 2000): -18.2%; Density: 3.1 persons per square mile; Race: 99.4% White, 0.0% Black/African American, 0.0% Asian, 0.0% American Indian/Alaska Native, 0.6% Native Hawaiian/Other Pacific Islander, 0.0% Two or more races, 0.0% Hispanic of any race; Average household size: 1.93; Median age: 45.6; Age under 18: 15.3%; Age 65 and over: 21.9%; Males per 100 females: 92.1; Marriage status: 23.1% never married, 56.0% now married, 5.1% separated, 10.5% widowed, 10.5% divorced; Foreign born: 1.3%; Speak English only: 96.0%; With disability: 24.7%; Veterans: 4.1%; Ancestry: 20.3% Irish, 11.6% German, 10.9% English, 8.4% Romanian, 8.4% Russian
Employment: 5.5% management, business, and financial, 5.5% computer, engineering, and science, 16.9% education, legal, community service, arts, and media, 0.0% healthcare practitioners, 21.9% service, 23.5% sales and office, 9.3% natural resources, construction, and maintenance, 17.5% production, transportation, and material moving
Income: Per capita: $25,297; Median household: $41,667; Average household: $49,069; Households with income of $100,000 or more: 10.8%; Poverty rate: 7.2%
Educational Attainment: High school diploma or higher: 98.5%; Bachelor's degree or higher: 54.6%; Graduate/professional degree or higher: 18.5%

School District(s)
Keene Central SD (KG-12)
    Enrollment: 169 . . . . (518) 576-4555
Housing: Homeownership rate: 53.0%; Median home value: $207,700; Median year structure built: 1957; Homeowner vacancy rate: 10.2%; Median selected monthly owner costs: $1,203 with a mortgage, $294 without a mortgage; Median gross rent: $1,058 per month; Rental vacancy rate: 0.0%
Health Insurance: 97.2% have insurance; 58.4% have private insurance; 49.4% have public insurance; 2.8% do not have insurance; 0.0% of children under 18 do not have insurance
Transportation: Commute: 68.0% car, 0.0% public transportation, 9.3% walk, 17.4% work from home; Mean travel time to work: 15.3 minutes

---

LAKE PLACID (village).
Covers a land area of 1.371 square miles and a water area of 0.166 square miles. Located at 44.28° N. Lat; 73.99° W. Long. Elevation is 1,801 feet.
History: Winter Olympics (1932, 1980) and the World Bobsled Championships (1969) were held here. The farm and burial place of the abolitionist John Brown are nearby. Terminus of 133-mile Northville—Lake Placid trail connecting Adirondack foothills and High Peaks region. Settled 1850, Incorporated 1900.
Population: 2,606; Growth (since 2000): -1.2%; Density: 1,900.6 persons per square mile; Race: 90.8% White, 0.3% Black/African American, 0.8% Asian, 0.2% American Indian/Alaska Native, 0.0% Native Hawaiian/Other Pacific Islander, 5.8% Two or more races, 8.7% Hispanic of any race; Average household size: 2.30; Median age: 37.5; Age under 18: 20.6%; Age 65 and over: 12.3%; Males per 100 females: 99.6; Marriage status: 36.5% never married, 43.3% now married, 2.1% separated, 4.8% widowed, 15.3% divorced; Foreign born: 4.0%; Speak English only: 84.8%; With disability: 14.1%; Veterans: 8.0%; Ancestry: 18.8% German, 17.0% Irish, 11.4% American, 8.5% French, 6.6% Italian
Employment: 14.5% management, business, and financial, 1.6% computer, engineering, and science, 5.6% education, legal, community service, arts, and media, 6.1% healthcare practitioners, 16.9% service, 39.8% sales and office, 8.1% natural resources, construction, and maintenance, 7.5% production, transportation, and material moving
Income: Per capita: $28,995; Median household: $53,487; Average household: $65,135; Households with income of $100,000 or more: 15.9%; Poverty rate: 7.7%
Educational Attainment: High school diploma or higher: 88.2%; Bachelor's degree or higher: 29.5%; Graduate/professional degree or higher: 9.4%

School District(s)
Lake Placid Central SD (KG-12)
    Enrollment: 687 . . . . (518) 523-2475
Housing: Homeownership rate: 38.0%; Median home value: $211,500; Median year structure built: 1969; Homeowner vacancy rate: 7.1%; Median selected monthly owner costs: $1,162 with a mortgage, $531 without a mortgage; Median gross rent: $833 per month; Rental vacancy rate: 8.0%
Health Insurance: 89.0% have insurance; 70.5% have private insurance; 32.2% have public insurance; 11.0% do not have insurance; 12.6% of children under 18 do not have insurance
Safety: Violent crime rate: 8.3 per 10,000 population; Property crime rate: 132.0 per 10,000 population
Newspapers: Lake Placid News (weekly circulation 4,200)
Transportation: Commute: 88.6% car, 1.4% public transportation, 3.1% walk, 6.8% work from home; Mean travel time to work: 16.2 minutes; Amtrak: Bus service available.
Airports: Lake Placid (general aviation)

LEWIS (town).
Covers a land area of 84.790 square miles and a water area of 0.210 square miles. Located at 44.32° N. Lat; 73.58° W. Long. Elevation is 666 feet.
Population: 1,232; Growth (since 2000): 2.7%; Density: 14.5 persons per square mile; Race: 91.7% White, 3.4% Black/African American, 0.2% Asian, 0.2% American Indian/Alaska Native, 0.0% Native Hawaiian/Other Pacific Islander, 2.9% Two or more races, 2.4% Hispanic of any race; Average household size: 2.37; Median age: 50.2; Age under 18: 16.1%; Age 65 and over: 20.5%; Males per 100 females: 107.2; Marriage status: 18.4% never married, 65.2% now married, 2.7% separated, 6.9% widowed, 9.5% divorced; Foreign born: 2.8%; Speak English only: 96.1%; With disability: 13.3%; Veterans: 11.8%; Ancestry: 22.7% French, 21.6% Irish, 10.9% English, 7.7% Italian, 7.1% American

Employment: 9.7% management, business, and financial, 0.0% computer, engineering, and science, 3.6% education, legal, community service, arts, and media, 4.9% healthcare practitioners, 19.7% service, 28.1% sales and office, 23.2% natural resources, construction, and maintenance, 10.8% production, transportation, and material moving
Income: Per capita: $27,736; Median household: $57,019; Average household: $67,059; Households with income of $100,000 or more: 21.0%; Poverty rate: 6.0%
Educational Attainment: High school diploma or higher: 91.8%; Bachelor's degree or higher: 12.2%; Graduate/professional degree or higher: 5.3%
Housing: Homeownership rate: 87.6%; Median home value: $113,500; Median year structure built: 1972; Homeowner vacancy rate: 0.0%; Median selected monthly owner costs: $992 with a mortgage, $426 without a mortgage; Median gross rent: $732 per month; Rental vacancy rate: 0.0%
Health Insurance: 92.6% have insurance; 72.5% have private insurance; 39.7% have public insurance; 7.4% do not have insurance; 4.0% of children under 18 do not have insurance
Transportation: Commute: 91.7% car, 1.1% public transportation, 0.6% walk, 4.7% work from home; Mean travel time to work: 22.9 minutes

MINERVA (town). Covers a land area of 156.766 square miles and a water area of 3.508 square miles. Located at 43.86° N. Lat; 74.12° W. Long. Elevation is 1,388 feet.
Population: 686; Growth (since 2000): -13.8%; Density: 4.4 persons per square mile; Race: 99.1% White, 0.0% Black/African American, 0.0% Asian, 0.0% American Indian/Alaska Native, 0.0% Native Hawaiian/Other Pacific Islander, 0.9% Two or more races, 0.0% Hispanic of any race; Average household size: 2.29; Median age: 54.2; Age under 18: 16.2%; Age 65 and over: 33.7%; Males per 100 females: 104.8; Marriage status: 18.8% never married, 66.8% now married, 0.5% separated, 5.2% widowed, 9.1% divorced; Foreign born: 1.6%; Speak English only: 99.2%; With disability: 14.7%; Veterans: 16.2%; Ancestry: 30.8% Irish, 17.6% French, 13.7% English, 13.4% German, 8.3% American
Employment: 10.0% management, business, and financial, 1.4% computer, engineering, and science, 9.3% education, legal, community service, arts, and media, 8.6% healthcare practitioners, 23.8% service, 15.9% sales and office, 16.9% natural resources, construction, and maintenance, 14.1% production, transportation, and material moving
Income: Per capita: $26,744; Median household: $51,938; Average household: $59,863; Households with income of $100,000 or more: 15.8%; Poverty rate: 9.5%
Educational Attainment: High school diploma or higher: 79.3%; Bachelor's degree or higher: 20.9%; Graduate/professional degree or higher: 10.1%
Housing: Homeownership rate: 88.9%; Median home value: $134,200; Median year structure built: 1969; Homeowner vacancy rate: 1.1%; Median selected monthly owner costs: $1,118 with a mortgage, $460 without a mortgage; Median gross rent: $1,000 per month; Rental vacancy rate: 0.0%
Health Insurance: 98.3% have insurance; 68.4% have private insurance; 59.9% have public insurance; 1.7% do not have insurance; 0.0% of children under 18 do not have insurance
Transportation: Commute: 89.4% car, 0.0% public transportation, 2.9% walk, 7.7% work from home; Mean travel time to work: 24.3 minutes

MINEVILLE (CDP). Covers a land area of 3.702 square miles and a water area of 0.006 square miles. Located at 44.09° N. Lat; 73.52° W. Long. Elevation is 1,296 feet.
Population: 1,288; Growth (since 2000): n/a; Density: 347.9 persons per square mile; Race: 89.8% White, 6.9% Black/African American, 0.3% Asian, 0.5% American Indian/Alaska Native, 0.0% Native Hawaiian/Other Pacific Islander, 0.0% Two or more races, 2.5% Hispanic of any race; Average household size: 3.08; Median age: 31.0; Age under 18: 17.9%; Age 65 and over: 12.9%; Males per 100 females: 111.9; Marriage status: 46.9% never married, 31.2% now married, 4.0% separated, 4.2% widowed, 17.6% divorced; Foreign born: 0.7%; Speak English only: 96.4%; With disability: 26.1%; Veterans: 3.6%; Ancestry: 36.6% Irish, 19.5% Italian, 12.7% French, 7.6% Polish, 7.2% Dutch
Employment: 6.9% management, business, and financial, 1.8% computer, engineering, and science, 13.7% education, legal, community service, arts, and media, 8.4% healthcare practitioners, 30.4% service, 13.8% sales and office, 8.7% natural resources, construction, and maintenance, 16.3% production, transportation, and material moving

Income: Per capita: $21,309; Median household: $49,667; Average household: $64,129; Households with income of $100,000 or more: 18.6%; Poverty rate: 11.1%
Educational Attainment: High school diploma or higher: 80.5%; Bachelor's degree or higher: 19.2%; Graduate/professional degree or higher: 8.3%
Housing: Homeownership rate: 78.7%; Median home value: $77,100; Median year structure built: 1948; Homeowner vacancy rate: 9.4%; Median selected monthly owner costs: $2,023 with a mortgage, $592 without a mortgage; Median gross rent: n/a per month; Rental vacancy rate: 0.0%
Health Insurance: 98.2% have insurance; 62.4% have private insurance; 48.2% have public insurance; 1.8% do not have insurance; 0.0% of children under 18 do not have insurance
Transportation: Commute: 80.1% car, 0.0% public transportation, 0.0% walk, 0.0% work from home; Mean travel time to work: 35.4 minutes

MORIAH (town). Covers a land area of 64.491 square miles and a water area of 6.619 square miles. Located at 44.05° N. Lat; 73.53° W. Long. Elevation is 850 feet.
Population: 4,707; Growth (since 2000): -3.5%; Density: 73.0 persons per square mile; Race: 93.1% White, 2.1% Black/African American, 0.2% Asian, 0.2% American Indian/Alaska Native, 0.0% Native Hawaiian/Other Pacific Islander, 3.1% Two or more races, 2.7% Hispanic of any race; Average household size: 2.50; Median age: 46.4; Age under 18: 18.8%; Age 65 and over: 19.6%; Males per 100 females: 105.3; Marriage status: 29.2% never married, 48.8% now married, 2.3% separated, 7.4% widowed, 14.6% divorced; Foreign born: 0.5%; Speak English only: 96.2%; With disability: 21.5%; Veterans: 9.1%; Ancestry: 28.5% Irish, 18.8% French, 12.4% Italian, 8.3% Polish, 7.5% German
Employment: 8.5% management, business, and financial, 1.5% computer, engineering, and science, 11.6% education, legal, community service, arts, and media, 6.0% healthcare practitioners, 27.5% service, 15.0% sales and office, 14.2% natural resources, construction, and maintenance, 15.6% production, transportation, and material moving
Income: Per capita: $26,248; Median household: $54,833; Average household: $65,061; Households with income of $100,000 or more: 17.8%; Poverty rate: 10.1%
Educational Attainment: High school diploma or higher: 89.4%; Bachelor's degree or higher: 15.5%; Graduate/professional degree or higher: 5.3%
Housing: Homeownership rate: 76.7%; Median home value: $104,300; Median year structure built: 1944; Homeowner vacancy rate: 4.3%; Median selected monthly owner costs: $1,168 with a mortgage, $539 without a mortgage; Median gross rent: $669 per month; Rental vacancy rate: 3.2%
Health Insurance: 96.9% have insurance; 70.2% have private insurance; 43.6% have public insurance; 3.1% do not have insurance; 3.0% of children under 18 do not have insurance
Safety: Violent crime rate: 5.7 per 10,000 population; Property crime rate: 0.0 per 10,000 population
Transportation: Commute: 90.1% car, 0.0% public transportation, 0.2% walk, 2.0% work from home; Mean travel time to work: 30.1 minutes

MORIAH CENTER (unincorporated postal area)
ZCTA: 12961
Covers a land area of 4.001 square miles and a water area of 0 square miles. Located at 44.06° N. Lat; 73.55° W. Long. Elevation is 791 feet.
Population: 294; Growth (since 2000): 71.9%; Density: 73.5 persons per square mile; Race: 86.4% White, 0.0% Black/African American, 0.0% Asian, 0.0% American Indian/Alaska Native, 0.0% Native Hawaiian/Other Pacific Islander, 6.5% Two or more races, 13.6% Hispanic of any race; Average household size: 1.99; Median age: 53.1; Age under 18: 16.3%; Age 65 and over: 20.7%; Males per 100 females: 133.8; Marriage status: 24.9% never married, 42.1% now married, 0.0% separated, 0.0% widowed, 33.0% divorced; Foreign born: 0.0%; Speak English only: 92.9%; With disability: 37.4%; Veterans: 9.8%; Ancestry: 22.8% Irish, 20.7% Italian, 20.1% Polish, 14.3% French, 8.2% German
Employment: 67.6% management, business, and financial, 0.0% computer, engineering, and science, 0.0% education, legal, community service, arts, and media, 0.0% healthcare practitioners, 32.4% service, 0.0% sales and office, 0.0% natural resources, construction, and maintenance, 0.0% production, transportation, and material moving
Income: Per capita: $16,676; Median household: $28,980; Average household: $32,657; Households with income of $100,000 or more: n/a; Poverty rate: 28.9%

Educational Attainment: High school diploma or higher: 94.8%; Bachelor's degree or higher: n/a; Graduate/professional degree or higher: n/a

Housing: Homeownership rate: 59.5%; Median home value: $112,500; Median year structure built: 1942; Homeowner vacancy rate: 0.0%; Median selected monthly owner costs: $0 with a mortgage, $477 without a mortgage; Median gross rent: n/a per month; Rental vacancy rate: 0.0%

Health Insurance: 100.0% have insurance; 59.2% have private insurance; 67.7% have public insurance; 0.0% do not have insurance; 0.0% of children under 18 do not have insurance

Transportation: Commute: 32.4% car, 0.0% public transportation, 0.0% walk, 67.6% work from home; Mean travel time to work: 0.0 minutes

NEW RUSSIA (unincorporated postal area)
ZCTA: 12964

Covers a land area of 34.498 square miles and a water area of 0.709 square miles. Located at 44.13° N. Lat; 73.63° W. Long. Elevation is 627 feet.

Population: 125; Growth (since 2000): -12.0%; Density: 3.6 persons per square mile; Race: 96.8% White, 0.0% Black/African American, 0.0% Asian, 0.0% American Indian/Alaska Native, 0.0% Native Hawaiian/Other Pacific Islander, 3.2% Two or more races, 0.0% Hispanic of any race; Average household size: 3.38; Median age: 38.2; Age under 18: 40.0%; Age 65 and over: 14.4%; Males per 100 females: 91.7; Marriage status: 19.0% never married, 62.0% now married, 0.0% separated, 7.6% widowed, 11.4% divorced; Foreign born: 0.0%; Speak English only: 100.0%; With disability: 8.0%; Veterans: 17.3%; Ancestry: 44.0% Irish, 18.4% French, 12.0% English, 8.8% Polish, 3.2% German

Employment: 18.9% management, business, and financial, 13.2% computer, engineering, and science, 18.9% education, legal, community service, arts, and media, 11.3% healthcare practitioners, 26.4% service, 7.5% sales and office, 3.8% natural resources, construction, and maintenance, 0.0% production, transportation, and material moving

Income: Per capita: $37,974; Median household: $158,438; Average household: $126,249; Households with income of $100,000 or more: 62.1%; Poverty rate: 3.2%

Educational Attainment: High school diploma or higher: 89.3%; Bachelor's degree or higher: 42.7%; Graduate/professional degree or higher: 28.0%

Housing: Homeownership rate: 51.4%; Median home value: n/a; Median year structure built: 1953; Homeowner vacancy rate: 0.0%; Median selected monthly owner costs: $1,188 with a mortgage, $0 without a mortgage; Median gross rent: $1,591 per month; Rental vacancy rate: 0.0%

Health Insurance: 92.8% have insurance; 89.6% have private insurance; 19.2% have public insurance; 7.2% do not have insurance; 0.0% of children under 18 do not have insurance

Transportation: Commute: 79.2% car, 0.0% public transportation, 0.0% walk, 20.8% work from home; Mean travel time to work: 29.6 minutes

NEWCOMB (town). Covers a land area of 226.271 square miles and a water area of 6.898 square miles. Located at 44.01° N. Lat; 74.10° W. Long. Elevation is 1,555 feet.

Population: 444; Growth (since 2000): -7.7%; Density: 2.0 persons per square mile; Race: 96.2% White, 0.5% Black/African American, 0.5% Asian, 0.9% American Indian/Alaska Native, 0.0% Native Hawaiian/Other Pacific Islander, 2.0% Two or more races, 1.4% Hispanic of any race; Average household size: 1.95; Median age: 60.4; Age under 18: 11.0%; Age 65 and over: 41.4%; Males per 100 females: 102.8; Marriage status: 21.9% never married, 51.4% now married, 5.9% separated, 17.4% widowed, 9.3% divorced; Foreign born: 2.7%; Speak English only: 97.5%; With disability: 20.5%; Veterans: 15.4%; Ancestry: 19.1% French, 18.9% Irish, 16.2% German, 15.1% English, 12.4% American

Employment: 12.1% management, business, and financial, 8.4% computer, engineering, and science, 10.5% education, legal, community service, arts, and media, 1.1% healthcare practitioners, 19.5% service, 23.2% sales and office, 13.7% natural resources, construction, and maintenance, 11.6% production, transportation, and material moving

Income: Per capita: $29,386; Median household: $46,500; Average household: $56,897; Households with income of $100,000 or more: 18.3%; Poverty rate: 8.0%

Educational Attainment: High school diploma or higher: 88.4%; Bachelor's degree or higher: 22.3%; Graduate/professional degree or higher: 12.1%

Newcomb Central SD (PK-12)
    Enrollment: 88 . . . . (518) 582-3341

Housing: Homeownership rate: 94.6%; Median home value: $158,800; Median year structure built: 1961; Homeowner vacancy rate: 2.3%; Median selected monthly owner costs: $1,063 with a mortgage, $426 without a mortgage; Median gross rent: $610 per month; Rental vacancy rate: 0.0%

Health Insurance: 93.7% have insurance; 79.5% have private insurance; 54.7% have public insurance; 6.3% do not have insurance; 0.0% of children under 18 do not have insurance

Transportation: Commute: 97.3% car, 0.0% public transportation, 1.6% walk, 1.1% work from home; Mean travel time to work: 15.8 minutes

Additional Information Contacts
Town of Newcomb . . . . (518) 582-3211
    http://www.newcombny.com/ParkitinNewcomb/Welcome.html

NORTH ELBA (town). Covers a land area of 151.654 square miles and a water area of 4.737 square miles. Located at 44.21° N. Lat; 74.05° W. Long. Elevation is 1,965 feet.

History: Here are the farm, home (now a museum), and grave of John Brown.

Population: 8,484; Growth (since 2000): -2.0%; Density: 55.9 persons per square mile; Race: 81.0% White, 11.4% Black/African American, 0.8% Asian, 0.4% American Indian/Alaska Native, 0.0% Native Hawaiian/Other Pacific Islander, 2.9% Two or more races, 9.7% Hispanic of any race; Average household size: 2.18; Median age: 39.9; Age under 18: 12.6%; Age 65 and over: 16.5%; Males per 100 females: 139.9; Marriage status: 42.6% never married, 41.1% now married, 2.0% separated, 5.4% widowed, 10.9% divorced; Foreign born: 5.9%; Speak English only: 84.9%; With disability: 14.2%; Veterans: 6.5%; Ancestry: 20.9% Irish, 15.7% German, 9.0% English, 7.2% French, 7.1% Italian

Employment: 15.0% management, business, and financial, 3.4% computer, engineering, and science, 10.2% education, legal, community service, arts, and media, 5.8% healthcare practitioners, 23.7% service, 30.2% sales and office, 5.7% natural resources, construction, and maintenance, 6.0% production, transportation, and material moving

Income: Per capita: $27,965; Median household: $60,651; Average household: $75,407; Households with income of $100,000 or more: 23.8%; Poverty rate: 7.5%

Educational Attainment: High school diploma or higher: 90.2%; Bachelor's degree or higher: 33.8%; Graduate/professional degree or higher: 15.3%

Housing: Homeownership rate: 59.1%; Median home value: $194,200; Median year structure built: 1967; Homeowner vacancy rate: 1.9%; Median selected monthly owner costs: $1,379 with a mortgage, $543 without a mortgage; Median gross rent: $857 per month; Rental vacancy rate: 6.4%

Health Insurance: 92.9% have insurance; 77.9% have private insurance; 34.1% have public insurance; 7.1% do not have insurance; 8.5% of children under 18 do not have insurance

Transportation: Commute: 86.6% car, 1.0% public transportation, 5.6% walk, 6.6% work from home; Mean travel time to work: 16.3 minutes

Additional Information Contacts
Town of North Elba . . . . (518) 523-9516
    http://www.northelba.org

NORTH HUDSON (town). Covers a land area of 181.452 square miles and a water area of 3.218 square miles. Located at 44.03° N. Lat; 73.76° W. Long. Elevation is 883 feet.

Population: 224; Growth (since 2000): -15.8%; Density: 1.2 persons per square mile; Race: 98.7% White, 0.0% Black/African American, 0.0% Asian, 0.4% American Indian/Alaska Native, 0.0% Native Hawaiian/Other Pacific Islander, 0.0% Two or more races, 2.7% Hispanic of any race; Average household size: 1.93; Median age: 54.5; Age under 18: 8.5%; Age 65 and over: 23.7%; Males per 100 females: 95.1; Marriage status: 22.9% never married, 62.4% now married, 0.0% separated, 11.4% widowed, 3.3% divorced; Foreign born: 0.9%; Speak English only: 97.3%; With disability: 23.7%; Veterans: 13.7%; Ancestry: 22.8% Irish, 20.1% Italian, 14.3% French, 12.9% American, 8.5% English

Employment: 11.8% management, business, and financial, 1.8% computer, engineering, and science, 5.5% education, legal, community service, arts, and media, 5.5% healthcare practitioners, 23.6% service, 23.6% sales and office, 12.7% natural resources, construction, and maintenance, 15.5% production, transportation, and material moving

Income: Per capita: $26,740; Median household: $45,000; Average household: $51,447; Households with income of $100,000 or more: 7.8%; Poverty rate: 11.6%
Educational Attainment: High school diploma or higher: 83.4%; Bachelor's degree or higher: 9.8%; Graduate/professional degree or higher: 2.6%
Housing: Homeownership rate: 79.3%; Median home value: $131,700; Median year structure built: 1969; Homeowner vacancy rate: 0.0%; Median selected monthly owner costs: $1,091 with a mortgage, $370 without a mortgage; Median gross rent: $645 per month; Rental vacancy rate: 0.0%
Health Insurance: 96.9% have insurance; 79.5% have private insurance; 43.8% have public insurance; 3.1% do not have insurance; 0.0% of children under 18 do not have insurance
Transportation: Commute: 97.1% car, 0.0% public transportation, 1.9% walk, 1.0% work from home; Mean travel time to work: 27.2 minutes

OLMSTEDVILLE (unincorporated postal area)
ZCTA: 12857
Covers a land area of 42.932 square miles and a water area of 0.551 square miles. Located at 43.82° N. Lat; 73.89° W. Long. Elevation is 1,181 feet.
Population: 587; Growth (since 2000): 16.9%; Density: 13.7 persons per square mile; Race: 100.0% White, 0.0% Black/African American, 0.0% Asian, 0.0% American Indian/Alaska Native, 0.0% Native Hawaiian/Other Pacific Islander, 0.0% Two or more races, 0.0% Hispanic of any race; Average household size: 2.95; Median age: 42.1; Age under 18: 29.1%; Age 65 and over: 22.0%; Males per 100 females: 100.8; Marriage status: 17.4% never married, 71.0% now married, 0.7% separated, 6.5% widowed, 5.1% divorced; Foreign born: 5.5%; Speak English only: 92.5%; With disability: 10.1%; Veterans: 13.5%; Ancestry: 40.4% Irish, 27.1% German, 15.5% French, 11.1% English, 7.2% Scottish
Employment: 9.2% management, business, and financial, 0.9% computer, engineering, and science, 18.3% education, legal, community service, arts, and media, 9.6% healthcare practitioners, 24.5% service, 10.0% sales and office, 16.6% natural resources, construction, and maintenance, 10.9% production, transportation, and material moving
Income: Per capita: $25,156; Median household: $56,875; Average household: $71,922; Households with income of $100,000 or more: 23.1%; Poverty rate: 3.4%
Educational Attainment: High school diploma or higher: 85.2%; Bachelor's degree or higher: 27.5%; Graduate/professional degree or higher: 12.2%

School District(s)
Minerva Central SD (PK-12)
    Enrollment: 113 . . . . (518) 251-2000
Housing: Homeownership rate: 80.4%; Median home value: $137,500; Median year structure built: 1961; Homeowner vacancy rate: 0.0%; Median selected monthly owner costs: $1,170 with a mortgage, $475 without a mortgage; Median gross rent: $967 per month; Rental vacancy rate: 0.0%
Health Insurance: 97.3% have insurance; 62.5% have private insurance; 52.5% have public insurance; 2.7% do not have insurance; 0.0% of children under 18 do not have insurance
Transportation: Commute: 83.5% car, 0.0% public transportation, 2.3% walk, 14.2% work from home; Mean travel time to work: 21.0 minutes

PARADOX (unincorporated postal area)
ZCTA: 12858
Covers a land area of 9.785 square miles and a water area of 1.447 square miles. Located at 43.91° N. Lat; 73.68° W. Long. Elevation is 873 feet.
Population: 76; Growth (since 2000): 58.3%; Density: 7.8 persons per square mile; Race: 100.0% White, 0.0% Black/African American, 0.0% Asian, 0.0% American Indian/Alaska Native, 0.0% Native Hawaiian/Other Pacific Islander, 0.0% Two or more races, 0.0% Hispanic of any race; Average household size: 1.85; Median age: 77.0; Age under 18: 0.0%; Age 65 and over: 85.5%; Males per 100 females: 73.5; Marriage status: 5.3% never married, 81.6% now married, 0.0% separated, 7.9% widowed, 5.3% divorced; Foreign born: 0.0%; Speak English only: 100.0%; With disability: 14.5%; Veterans: 19.7%; Ancestry: 46.1% German, 31.6% Irish, 30.3% English, 14.5% Italian, 5.3% French
Employment: 25.0% management, business, and financial, 0.0% computer, engineering, and science, 0.0% education, legal, community

service, arts, and media, 18.8% healthcare practitioners, 18.8% service, 0.0% sales and office, 0.0% natural resources, construction, and maintenance, 37.5% production, transportation, and material moving
Income: Per capita: $33,303; Median household: $72,188; Average household: $62,529; Households with income of $100,000 or more: 9.8%; Poverty rate: 34.2%
Educational Attainment: High school diploma or higher: 93.4%; Bachelor's degree or higher: 59.2%; Graduate/professional degree or higher: 31.6%
Housing: Homeownership rate: 100.0%; Median home value: $316,700; Median year structure built: 1946; Homeowner vacancy rate: 18.0%; Median selected monthly owner costs: $0 with a mortgage, $239 without a mortgage; Median gross rent: n/a per month; Rental vacancy rate: 100.0%
Health Insurance: 100.0% have insurance; 86.8% have private insurance; 89.5% have public insurance; 0.0% do not have insurance; 0.0% of children under 18 do not have insurance
Transportation: Commute: 81.3% car, 0.0% public transportation, 0.0% walk, 18.8% work from home; Mean travel time to work: 0.0 minutes

PORT HENRY (village). Covers a land area of 1.177 square miles and a water area of 0.300 square miles. Located at 44.05° N. Lat; 73.46° W. Long. Elevation is 243 feet.
History: Incorporated 1869.
Population: 1,104; Growth (since 2000): -4.2%; Density: 938.4 persons per square mile; Race: 97.2% White, 0.7% Black/African American, 0.0% Asian, 0.4% American Indian/Alaska Native, 0.0% Native Hawaiian/Other Pacific Islander, 1.4% Two or more races, 0.5% Hispanic of any race; Average household size: 2.27; Median age: 48.2; Age under 18: 20.7%; Age 65 and over: 29.3%; Males per 100 females: 98.7; Marriage status: 25.3% never married, 54.7% now married, 1.2% separated, 8.1% widowed, 11.9% divorced; Foreign born: 1.0%; Speak English only: 95.8%; With disability: 25.7%; Veterans: 10.5%; Ancestry: 21.6% Irish, 19.4% French, 11.8% Italian, 8.3% Polish, 7.2% English
Employment: 6.3% management, business, and financial, 5.2% computer, engineering, and science, 9.9% education, legal, community service, arts, and media, 8.2% healthcare practitioners, 32.3% service, 16.4% sales and office, 14.8% natural resources, construction, and maintenance, 6.8% production, transportation, and material moving
Income: Per capita: $27,011; Median household: $35,221; Average household: $60,070; Households with income of $100,000 or more: 17.3%; Poverty rate: 13.5%
Educational Attainment: High school diploma or higher: 85.9%; Bachelor's degree or higher: 16.8%; Graduate/professional degree or higher: 7.9%

School District(s)
Moriah Central SD (PK-12)
    Enrollment: 734 . . . . (518) 546-3301
Housing: Homeownership rate: 69.9%; Median home value: $94,700; Median year structure built: Before 1940; Homeowner vacancy rate: 8.7%; Median selected monthly owner costs: $1,169 with a mortgage, $514 without a mortgage; Median gross rent: $588 per month; Rental vacancy rate: 8.8%
Health Insurance: 93.2% have insurance; 61.4% have private insurance; 52.1% have public insurance; 6.8% do not have insurance; 11.8% of children under 18 do not have insurance
Transportation: Commute: 86.8% car, 0.0% public transportation, 1.1% walk, 4.2% work from home; Mean travel time to work: 30.0 minutes; Amtrak: Train service available.

PORT KENT (unincorporated postal area)
ZCTA: 12975
Covers a land area of 2.852 square miles and a water area of 0 square miles. Located at 44.53° N. Lat; 73.43° W. Long. Elevation is 154 feet.
Population: 277; Growth (since 2000): n/a; Density: 97.1 persons per square mile; Race: 96.8% White, 0.0% Black/African American, 0.0% Asian, 0.0% American Indian/Alaska Native, 0.0% Native Hawaiian/Other Pacific Islander, 3.2% Two or more races, 0.0% Hispanic of any race; Average household size: 1.91; Median age: 48.2; Age under 18: 18.8%; Age 65 and over: 7.9%; Males per 100 females: 86.6; Marriage status: 23.5% never married, 49.0% now married, 2.4% separated, 4.4% widowed, 23.1% divorced; Foreign born: 0.0%; Speak English only: 91.8%; With disability: 16.2%; Veterans: 0.0%; Ancestry: 24.5% French, 23.1% Irish, 20.6% English, 16.6% Italian, 13.7% Scottish

Employment: 13.3% management, business, and financial, 0.0% computer, engineering, and science, 39.4% education, legal, community service, arts, and media, 3.0% healthcare practitioners, 22.2% service, 16.7% sales and office, 3.0% natural resources, construction, and maintenance, 2.5% production, transportation, and material moving
Income: Per capita: $36,992; Median household: n/a; Average household: $68,457; Households with income of $100,000 or more: 17.9%; Poverty rate: 8.3%
Educational Attainment: High school diploma or higher: 97.7%; Bachelor's degree or higher: 47.9%; Graduate/professional degree or higher: 34.7%
Housing: Homeownership rate: 69.0%; Median home value: $131,300; Median year structure built: 1951; Homeowner vacancy rate: 3.8%; Median selected monthly owner costs: $1,375 with a mortgage, $383 without a mortgage; Median gross rent: $767 per month; Rental vacancy rate: 0.0%
Health Insurance: 94.2% have insurance; 83.4% have private insurance; 18.8% have public insurance; 5.8% do not have insurance; 0.0% of children under 18 do not have insurance
Transportation: Commute: 76.5% car, 0.0% public transportation, 0.0% walk, 7.5% work from home; Mean travel time to work: 16.4 minutes; Amtrak: Train service available.

RAY BROOK (unincorporated postal area)
ZCTA: 12977
Covers a land area of 8.945 square miles and a water area of 0.112 square miles. Located at 44.28° N. Lat; 74.07° W. Long. Elevation is 1,591 feet.
Population: 1,810; Growth (since 2000): n/a; Density: 202.4 persons per square mile; Race: 35.6% White, 46.5% Black/African American, 1.3% Asian, 0.9% American Indian/Alaska Native, 0.0% Native Hawaiian/Other Pacific Islander, 4.1% Two or more races, 28.0% Hispanic of any race; Average household size: 2.11; Median age: 35.2; Age under 18: 0.0%; Age 65 and over: 5.0%; Males per 100 females: ***.*; Marriage status: 68.8% never married, 25.1% now married, 4.6% separated, 0.4% widowed, 5.6% divorced; Foreign born: 12.2%; Speak English only: 67.1%; With disability: 47.4%; Veterans: 2.7%; Ancestry: 6.2% Italian, 6.1% Irish, 5.4% French, 3.3% African, 3.0% Polish
Employment: 52.6% management, business, and financial, 0.0% computer, engineering, and science, 0.0% education, legal, community service, arts, and media, 0.0% healthcare practitioners, 0.0% service, 47.4% sales and office, 0.0% natural resources, construction, and maintenance, 0.0% production, transportation, and material moving
Income: Per capita: $7,418; Median household: n/a; Average household: n/a; Households with income of $100,000 or more: n/a; Poverty rate: n/a
Educational Attainment: High school diploma or higher: 80.5%; Bachelor's degree or higher: 2.4%; Graduate/professional degree or higher: 2.4%
Housing: Homeownership rate: 100.0%; Median home value: n/a; Median year structure built: n/a; Homeowner vacancy rate: 0.0%; Median selected monthly owner costs: $0 with a mortgage, $0 without a mortgage; Median gross rent: n/a per month; Rental vacancy rate: 0.0%
Health Insurance: 100.0% have insurance; 100.0% have private insurance; 100.0% have public insurance; 0.0% do not have insurance; 0.0% of children under 18 do not have insurance
Transportation: Commute: 47.4% car, 0.0% public transportation, 0.0% walk, 52.6% work from home; Mean travel time to work: 0.0 minutes

SAINT ARMAND (town). Covers a land area of 56.511 square miles and a water area of 0.934 square miles. Located at 44.37° N. Lat; 74.01° W. Long.
Population: 1,651; Growth (since 2000): 25.0%; Density: 29.2 persons per square mile; Race: 99.0% White, 0.0% Black/African American, 0.0% Asian, 0.0% American Indian/Alaska Native, 0.0% Native Hawaiian/Other Pacific Islander, 0.6% Two or more races, 1.2% Hispanic of any race; Average household size: 2.31; Median age: 49.3; Age under 18: 21.9%; Age 65 and over: 20.5%; Males per 100 females: 96.7; Marriage status: 18.1% never married, 68.4% now married, 0.4% separated, 6.0% widowed, 7.6% divorced; Foreign born: 2.8%; Speak English only: 95.0%; With disability: 15.1%; Veterans: 8.9%; Ancestry: 29.2% Irish, 20.7% French, 16.1% English, 12.8% German, 9.7% Italian
Employment: 18.2% management, business, and financial, 4.3% computer, engineering, and science, 15.2% education, legal, community service, arts, and media, 7.7% healthcare practitioners, 18.2% service,

19.6% sales and office, 13.7% natural resources, construction, and maintenance, 3.1% production, transportation, and material moving
Income: Per capita: $33,314; Median household: $57,708; Average household: $74,407; Households with income of $100,000 or more: 24.5%; Poverty rate: 8.4%
Educational Attainment: High school diploma or higher: 93.9%; Bachelor's degree or higher: 34.6%; Graduate/professional degree or higher: 15.0%
Housing: Homeownership rate: 77.3%; Median home value: $188,700; Median year structure built: 1974; Homeowner vacancy rate: 0.0%; Median selected monthly owner costs: $1,366 with a mortgage, $588 without a mortgage; Median gross rent: $743 per month; Rental vacancy rate: 4.1%
Health Insurance: 96.7% have insurance; 81.3% have private insurance; 32.0% have public insurance; 3.3% do not have insurance; 3.5% of children under 18 do not have insurance
Transportation: Commute: 89.9% car, 0.9% public transportation, 1.2% walk, 6.2% work from home; Mean travel time to work: 16.8 minutes

SCHROON (town). Covers a land area of 132.678 square miles and a water area of 8.732 square miles. Located at 43.86° N. Lat; 73.76° W. Long.
Population: 1,066; Growth (since 2000): -39.4%; Density: 8.0 persons per square mile; Race: 97.4% White, 0.5% Black/African American, 0.4% Asian, 0.6% American Indian/Alaska Native, 0.0% Native Hawaiian/Other Pacific Islander, 1.2% Two or more races, 0.2% Hispanic of any race; Average household size: 2.08; Median age: 57.3; Age under 18: 12.1%; Age 65 and over: 31.1%; Males per 100 females: 91.2; Marriage status: 27.6% never married, 51.3% now married, 0.6% separated, 13.7% widowed, 7.4% divorced; Foreign born: 3.0%; Speak English only: 99.6%; With disability: 23.6%; Veterans: 11.7%; Ancestry: 32.3% English, 24.5% German, 22.2% Irish, 12.6% French, 12.4% Italian
Employment: 3.7% management, business, and financial, 2.1% computer, engineering, and science, 18.4% education, legal, community service, arts, and media, 3.4% healthcare practitioners, 32.9% service, 26.0% sales and office, 3.9% natural resources, construction, and maintenance, 9.7% production, transportation, and material moving
Income: Per capita: $28,163; Median household: $33,929; Average household: $58,175; Households with income of $100,000 or more: 17.8%; Poverty rate: 7.7%
Educational Attainment: High school diploma or higher: 93.0%; Bachelor's degree or higher: 34.7%; Graduate/professional degree or higher: 22.9%
Housing: Homeownership rate: 79.1%; Median home value: $197,800; Median year structure built: 1965; Homeowner vacancy rate: 8.3%; Median selected monthly owner costs: $1,426 with a mortgage, $535 without a mortgage; Median gross rent: $674 per month; Rental vacancy rate: 12.5%
Health Insurance: 93.6% have insurance; 67.8% have private insurance; 59.3% have public insurance; 6.4% do not have insurance; 0.0% of children under 18 do not have insurance
Transportation: Commute: 77.6% car, 0.0% public transportation, 3.3% walk, 16.0% work from home; Mean travel time to work: 16.3 minutes

SCHROON LAKE (CDP). Covers a land area of 2.886 square miles and a water area of 0.799 square miles. Located at 43.84° N. Lat; 73.77° W. Long. Elevation is 869 feet.
Population: 511; Growth (since 2000): n/a; Density: 177.1 persons per square mile; Race: 99.4% White, 0.0% Black/African American, 0.0% Asian, 0.6% American Indian/Alaska Native, 0.0% Native Hawaiian/Other Pacific Islander, 0.0% Two or more races, 0.0% Hispanic of any race; Average household size: 2.04; Median age: 54.8; Age under 18: 17.0%; Age 65 and over: 24.7%; Males per 100 females: 86.8; Marriage status: 28.0% never married, 44.5% now married, 0.0% separated, 20.6% widowed, 6.9% divorced; Foreign born: 2.9%; Speak English only: 100.0%; With disability: 32.9%; Veterans: 9.4%; Ancestry: 35.0% English, 27.0% German, 20.9% Irish, 13.7% French, 9.4% Italian
Employment: 4.6% management, business, and financial, 4.6% computer, engineering, and science, 19.1% education, legal, community service, arts, and media, 3.1% healthcare practitioners, 36.6% service, 19.1% sales and office, 6.7% natural resources, construction, and maintenance, 6.2% production, transportation, and material moving
Income: Per capita: $30,703; Median household: $35,000; Average household: $60,166; Households with income of $100,000 or more: 14.8%; Poverty rate: 6.8%

Educational Attainment: High school diploma or higher: 96.5%; Bachelor's degree or higher: 35.1%; Graduate/professional degree or higher: 22.6%

School District(s)
Schroon Lake Central SD (PK-12)
    Enrollment: 225. . . . . (518) 532-7164
Housing: Homeownership rate: 67.6%; Median home value: $169,900; Median year structure built: 1965; Homeowner vacancy rate: 12.0%; Median selected monthly owner costs: $1,438 with a mortgage, $527 without a mortgage; Median gross rent: $575 per month; Rental vacancy rate: 0.0%
Health Insurance: 99.4% have insurance; 66.3% have private insurance; 66.3% have public insurance; 0.6% do not have insurance; 0.0% of children under 18 do not have insurance
Transportation: Commute: 90.8% car, 0.0% public transportation, 7.6% walk, 0.0% work from home; Mean travel time to work: 17.7 minutes

SEVERANCE (unincorporated postal area)
ZCTA: 12872
    Covers a land area of 0.305 square miles and a water area of 0 square miles. Located at 43.87° N. Lat; 73.73° W. Long. Elevation is 840 feet.
    Population: 42; Growth (since 2000): n/a; Density: 137.6 persons per square mile; Race: 100.0% White, 0.0% Black/African American, 0.0% Asian, 0.0% American Indian/Alaska Native, 0.0% Native Hawaiian/Other Pacific Islander, 0.0% Two or more races, 0.0% Hispanic of any race; Average household size: 2.47; Median age: 49.7; Age under 18: 26.2%; Age 65 and over: 16.7%; Males per 100 females: 82.4; Marriage status: 26.2% never married, 66.7% now married, 0.0% separated, 0.0% widowed, 7.1% divorced; Foreign born: 0.0%; Speak English only: 100.0%; With disability: 0.0%; Veterans: 0.0%; Ancestry: 76.2% Dutch, 57.1% English, 35.7% German, 7.1% Norwegian
    Employment: 9.7% management, business, and financial, 0.0% computer, engineering, and science, 9.7% education, legal, community service, arts, and media, 0.0% healthcare practitioners, 32.3% service, 0.0% sales and office, 12.9% natural resources, construction, and maintenance, 35.5% production, transportation, and material moving
    Income: Per capita: $12,933; Median household: $29,625; Average household: $31,118; Households with income of $100,000 or more: n/a; Poverty rate: n/a
    Educational Attainment: High school diploma or higher: 100.0%; Bachelor's degree or higher: 22.6%; Graduate/professional degree or higher: 22.6%
    Housing: Homeownership rate: 82.4%; Median home value: n/a; Median year structure built: 1964; Homeowner vacancy rate: 0.0%; Median selected monthly owner costs: $0 with a mortgage, $0 without a mortgage; Median gross rent: n/a per month; Rental vacancy rate: 0.0%
    Health Insurance: 100.0% have insurance; 100.0% have private insurance; 16.7% have public insurance; 0.0% do not have insurance; 0.0% of children under 18 do not have insurance
    Transportation: Commute: 90.3% car, 0.0% public transportation, 0.0% walk, 9.7% work from home; Mean travel time to work: 0.0 minutes

TICONDEROGA (CDP). Covers a land area of 4.272 square miles and a water area of 0.079 square miles. Located at 43.84° N. Lat; 73.42° W. Long. Elevation is 151 feet.
Population: 3,084; Growth (since 2000): n/a; Density: 721.9 persons per square mile; Race: 97.3% White, 0.9% Black/African American, 1.1% Asian, 0.0% American Indian/Alaska Native, 0.0% Native Hawaiian/Other Pacific Islander, 0.6% Two or more races, 0.2% Hispanic of any race; Average household size: 2.47; Median age: 37.9; Age under 18: 24.0%; Age 65 and over: 14.0%; Males per 100 females: 94.4; Marriage status: 40.6% never married, 45.1% now married, 1.9% separated, 7.7% widowed, 6.6% divorced; Foreign born: 2.3%; Speak English only: 97.6%; With disability: 21.3%; Veterans: 14.9%; Ancestry: 24.1% Irish, 19.9% French, 15.6% English, 10.7% German, 10.0% American
Employment: 5.8% management, business, and financial, 3.3% computer, engineering, and science, 10.5% education, legal, community service, arts, and media, 8.0% healthcare practitioners, 21.2% service, 22.3% sales and office, 12.8% natural resources, construction, and maintenance, 16.1% production, transportation, and material moving
Income: Per capita: $24,681; Median household: $52,981; Average household: $60,766; Households with income of $100,000 or more: 18.7%; Poverty rate: 15.5%

Educational Attainment: High school diploma or higher: 91.5%; Bachelor's degree or higher: 21.3%; Graduate/professional degree or higher: 9.8%

School District(s)
Ticonderoga Central SD (PK-12)
    Enrollment: 822. . . . . (518) 585-7400
Housing: Homeownership rate: 72.3%; Median home value: $114,300; Median year structure built: Before 1940; Homeowner vacancy rate: 7.8%; Median selected monthly owner costs: $1,185 with a mortgage, $614 without a mortgage; Median gross rent: $766 per month; Rental vacancy rate: 9.5%
Health Insurance: 95.3% have insurance; 59.9% have private insurance; 50.1% have public insurance; 4.7% do not have insurance; 0.0% of children under 18 do not have insurance
Hospitals: Moses - Ludington Hospital (99 beds)
Transportation: Commute: 93.5% car, 0.0% public transportation, 3.8% walk, 2.7% work from home; Mean travel time to work: 19.4 minutes

TICONDEROGA (town). Covers a land area of 81.433 square miles and a water area of 7.012 square miles. Located at 43.84° N. Lat; 73.55° W. Long. Elevation is 151 feet.
History: Ticonderoga is a variation of the Native American "Cheonderoga," meaning "between two waters." The French built a military road at the site and in 1755 they constructed Fort Carillon, later called Fort Ticonderoga.
Population: 4,929; Growth (since 2000): -4.6%; Density: 60.5 persons per square mile; Race: 97.8% White, 0.8% Black/African American, 0.8% Asian, 0.1% American Indian/Alaska Native, 0.0% Native Hawaiian/Other Pacific Islander, 0.5% Two or more races, 0.3% Hispanic of any race; Average household size: 2.34; Median age: 44.7; Age under 18: 20.8%; Age 65 and over: 20.6%; Males per 100 females: 97.9; Marriage status: 34.0% never married, 46.5% now married, 1.1% separated, 10.7% widowed, 8.8% divorced; Foreign born: 2.9%; Speak English only: 96.2%; With disability: 21.2%; Veterans: 12.8%; Ancestry: 25.0% Irish, 22.5% French, 13.7% English, 9.6% German, 7.5% American
Employment: 6.1% management, business, and financial, 2.0% computer, engineering, and science, 10.5% education, legal, community service, arts, and media, 7.0% healthcare practitioners, 23.0% service, 24.0% sales and office, 12.7% natural resources, construction, and maintenance, 14.6% production, transportation, and material moving
Income: Per capita: $25,865; Median household: $48,750; Average household: $60,389; Households with income of $100,000 or more: 17.8%; Poverty rate: 11.6%
Educational Attainment: High school diploma or higher: 91.6%; Bachelor's degree or higher: 22.2%; Graduate/professional degree or higher: 9.6%

School District(s)
Ticonderoga Central SD (PK-12)
    Enrollment: 822. . . . . (518) 585-7400
Housing: Homeownership rate: 78.5%; Median home value: $120,700; Median year structure built: 1955; Homeowner vacancy rate: 6.8%; Median selected monthly owner costs: $1,243 with a mortgage, $596 without a mortgage; Median gross rent: $736 per month; Rental vacancy rate: 7.3%
Health Insurance: 97.1% have insurance; 65.0% have private insurance; 48.4% have public insurance; 2.9% do not have insurance; 0.0% of children under 18 do not have insurance
Hospitals: Moses - Ludington Hospital (99 beds)
Safety: Violent crime rate: 20.5 per 10,000 population; Property crime rate: 77.7 per 10,000 population
Transportation: Commute: 94.2% car, 0.0% public transportation, 2.3% walk, 3.0% work from home; Mean travel time to work: 21.5 minutes; Amtrak: Train service available.
Additional Information Contacts
Town of Ticonderoga. . . . . (518) 585-6265
    http://townofticonderoga.org

UPPER JAY (unincorporated postal area)
ZCTA: 12987
    Covers a land area of 6.199 square miles and a water area of 0.015 square miles. Located at 44.32° N. Lat; 73.75° W. Long. Elevation is 673 feet.
    Population: 217; Growth (since 2000): -33.4%; Density: 35.0 persons per square mile; Race: 100.0% White, 0.0% Black/African American, 0.0% Asian, 0.0% American Indian/Alaska Native, 0.0% Native Hawaiian/Other Pacific Islander, 0.0% Two or more races, 0.0% Hispanic of any race; Average household size: 1.67; Median age: 57.7;

Age under 18: 8.8%; Age 65 and over: 28.6%; Males per 100 females: 95.1; Marriage status: 22.7% never married, 49.8% now married, 0.0% separated, 15.8% widowed, 11.8% divorced; Foreign born: 1.8%; Speak English only: 100.0%; With disability: 14.3%; Veterans: 2.0%; Ancestry: 31.3% Irish, 30.0% English, 21.2% French, 8.8% German, 7.4% Scotch-Irish

Employment: 34.2% management, business, and financial, 0.0% computer, engineering, and science, 4.5% education, legal, community service, arts, and media, 12.6% healthcare practitioners, 26.1% service, 9.9% sales and office, 5.4% natural resources, construction, and maintenance, 7.2% production, transportation, and material moving

Income: Per capita: $31,214; Median household: $32,500; Average household: $51,053; Households with income of $100,000 or more: 15.4%; Poverty rate: 20.7%

Educational Attainment: High school diploma or higher: 85.3%; Bachelor's degree or higher: 44.0%; Graduate/professional degree or higher: 23.6%

Housing: Homeownership rate: 84.6%; Median home value: $135,000; Median year structure built: 1995; Homeowner vacancy rate: 0.0%; Median selected monthly owner costs: $1,500 with a mortgage, $556 without a mortgage; Median gross rent: n/a per month; Rental vacancy rate: 0.0%

Health Insurance: 93.5% have insurance; 86.2% have private insurance; 28.6% have public insurance; 6.5% do not have insurance; 0.0% of children under 18 do not have insurance

Transportation: Commute: 65.0% car, 0.0% public transportation, 4.9% walk, 30.1% work from home; Mean travel time to work: 22.2 minutes

WESTPORT (CDP). Covers a land area of 2.361 square miles and a water area of 0 square miles. Located at 44.18° N. Lat; 73.44° W. Long. Elevation is 121 feet.

Population: 452; Growth (since 2000): n/a; Density: 191.4 persons per square mile; Race: 89.8% White, 4.4% Black/African American, 0.0% Asian, 0.0% American Indian/Alaska Native, 0.0% Native Hawaiian/Other Pacific Islander, 5.8% Two or more races, 0.0% Hispanic of any race; Average household size: 2.14; Median age: 49.0; Age under 18: 15.0%; Age 65 and over: 34.1%; Males per 100 females: 81.8; Marriage status: 23.6% never married, 53.1% now married, 2.6% separated, 10.1% widowed, 13.2% divorced; Foreign born: 3.1%; Speak English only: 96.9%; With disability: 23.5%; Veterans: 7.8%; Ancestry: 21.0% Irish, 15.0% English, 12.4% Italian, 11.3% German, 9.3% French

Employment: 12.1% management, business, and financial, 8.4% computer, engineering, and science, 23.2% education, legal, community service, arts, and media, 4.2% healthcare practitioners, 12.6% service, 18.9% sales and office, 4.7% natural resources, construction, and maintenance, 15.8% production, transportation, and material moving

Income: Per capita: $38,918; Median household: $50,625; Average household: $87,563; Households with income of $100,000 or more: 25.7%; Poverty rate: 13.9%

Educational Attainment: High school diploma or higher: 86.2%; Bachelor's degree or higher: 37.3%; Graduate/professional degree or higher: 16.4%

School District(s)
Westport Central SD (KG-12)
    Enrollment: 228 . . . . (518) 962-8244
Housing: Homeownership rate: 74.3%; Median home value: $129,200; Median year structure built: Before 1940; Homeowner vacancy rate: 12.0%; Median selected monthly owner costs: $1,432 with a mortgage, $525 without a mortgage; Median gross rent: $833 per month; Rental vacancy rate: 31.4%
Health Insurance: 96.5% have insurance; 53.8% have private insurance; 64.4% have public insurance; 3.5% do not have insurance; 0.0% of children under 18 do not have insurance
Transportation: Commute: 87.4% car, 0.0% public transportation, 1.6% walk, 5.8% work from home; Mean travel time to work: 23.8 minutes

WESTPORT (town). Covers a land area of 58.171 square miles and a water area of 8.636 square miles. Located at 44.18° N. Lat; 73.45° W. Long. Elevation is 121 feet.
Population: 1,244; Growth (since 2000): -8.7%; Density: 21.4 persons per square mile; Race: 95.3% White, 1.6% Black/African American, 0.1% Asian, 0.0% American Indian/Alaska Native, 0.0% Native Hawaiian/Other Pacific Islander, 3.0% Two or more races, 0.0% Hispanic of any race; Average household size: 2.16; Median age: 55.0; Age under 18: 16.7%; Age 65 and over: 33.5%; Males per 100 females: 92.4; Marriage status:

19.6% never married, 55.8% now married, 1.9% separated, 10.6% widowed, 14.0% divorced; Foreign born: 2.5%; Speak English only: 97.4%; With disability: 18.2%; Veterans: 9.1%; Ancestry: 20.3% Irish, 14.2% English, 13.9% French, 10.8% German, 8.9% Italian
Employment: 10.4% management, business, and financial, 3.1% computer, engineering, and science, 18.5% education, legal, community service, arts, and media, 4.4% healthcare practitioners, 18.1% service, 18.5% sales and office, 11.8% natural resources, construction, and maintenance, 15.2% production, transportation, and material moving
Income: Per capita: $31,493; Median household: $47,727; Average household: $68,234; Households with income of $100,000 or more: 17.2%; Poverty rate: 13.4%
Educational Attainment: High school diploma or higher: 85.8%; Bachelor's degree or higher: 29.2%; Graduate/professional degree or higher: 13.6%

School District(s)
Westport Central SD (KG-12)
    Enrollment: 228 . . . . (518) 962-8244
Housing: Homeownership rate: 82.1%; Median home value: $150,400; Median year structure built: 1942; Homeowner vacancy rate: 7.2%; Median selected monthly owner costs: $1,378 with a mortgage, $560 without a mortgage; Median gross rent: $758 per month; Rental vacancy rate: 20.9%
Health Insurance: 93.1% have insurance; 66.6% have private insurance; 54.6% have public insurance; 6.9% do not have insurance; 5.1% of children under 18 do not have insurance
Transportation: Commute: 90.3% car, 0.0% public transportation, 0.6% walk, 7.2% work from home; Mean travel time to work: 18.5 minutes; Amtrak: Train service available.
Additional Information Contacts
Town of Westport . . . . (518) 962-4419
    http://www.westportny.net

WILLSBORO (CDP). Covers a land area of 1.924 square miles and a water area of 0.033 square miles. Located at 44.36° N. Lat; 73.39° W. Long. Elevation is 223 feet.
Population: 816; Growth (since 2000): n/a; Density: 424.2 persons per square mile; Race: 94.7% White, 0.0% Black/African American, 0.0% Asian, 0.0% American Indian/Alaska Native, 0.0% Native Hawaiian/Other Pacific Islander, 5.3% Two or more races, 2.1% Hispanic of any race; Average household size: 2.44; Median age: 45.3; Age under 18: 20.5%; Age 65 and over: 15.7%; Males per 100 females: 98.2; Marriage status: 34.4% never married, 41.3% now married, 0.9% separated, 5.8% widowed, 18.6% divorced; Foreign born: 0.0%; Speak English only: 100.0%; With disability: 23.9%; Veterans: 4.9%; Ancestry: 30.3% German, 21.1% French, 20.0% Irish, 9.7% English, 7.1% Dutch
Employment: 8.3% management, business, and financial, 3.2% computer, engineering, and science, 24.1% education, legal, community service, arts, and media, 1.1% healthcare practitioners, 21.6% service, 20.4% sales and office, 11.7% natural resources, construction, and maintenance, 9.6% production, transportation, and material moving
Income: Per capita: $30,502; Median household: $44,417; Average household: $70,961; Households with income of $100,000 or more: 10.2%; Poverty rate: 17.8%
Educational Attainment: High school diploma or higher: 88.3%; Bachelor's degree or higher: 19.0%; Graduate/professional degree or higher: 14.1%

School District(s)
Willsboro Central SD (PK-12)
    Enrollment: 259 . . . . (518) 963-4456
Housing: Homeownership rate: 76.4%; Median home value: $94,600; Median year structure built: 1949; Homeowner vacancy rate: 0.0%; Median selected monthly owner costs: $1,003 with a mortgage, $402 without a mortgage; Median gross rent: $798 per month; Rental vacancy rate: 0.0%
Health Insurance: 94.9% have insurance; 58.5% have private insurance; 46.6% have public insurance; 5.1% do not have insurance; 0.0% of children under 18 do not have insurance
Transportation: Commute: 68.9% car, 0.0% public transportation, 11.6% walk, 12.8% work from home; Mean travel time to work: 18.4 minutes

WILLSBORO (town). Covers a land area of 42.723 square miles and a water area of 30.661 square miles. Located at 44.39° N. Lat; 73.40° W. Long. Elevation is 223 feet.
Population: 2,143; Growth (since 2000): 12.6%; Density: 50.2 persons per square mile; Race: 95.7% White, 0.0% Black/African American, 0.5% Asian, 0.0% American Indian/Alaska Native, 0.0% Native Hawaiian/Other

Pacific Islander, 2.2% Two or more races, 1.8% Hispanic of any race; Average household size: 2.31; Median age: 52.4; Age under 18: 14.6%; Age 65 and over: 27.3%; Males per 100 females: 97.4; Marriage status: 27.6% never married, 56.2% now married, 0.6% separated, 6.1% widowed, 10.0% divorced; Foreign born: 1.7%; Speak English only: 96.4%; With disability: 22.4%; Veterans: 8.0%; Ancestry: 26.0% Irish, 20.6% German, 15.3% French, 12.1% English, 6.2% French Canadian

Employment: 15.8% management, business, and financial, 3.2% computer, engineering, and science, 13.0% education, legal, community service, arts, and media, 5.0% healthcare practitioners, 16.3% service, 22.8% sales and office, 13.4% natural resources, construction, and maintenance, 10.5% production, transportation, and material moving

Income: Per capita: $33,872; Median household: $64,219; Average household: $75,963; Households with income of $100,000 or more: 13.1%; Poverty rate: 8.4%

Educational Attainment: High school diploma or higher: 91.0%; Bachelor's degree or higher: 17.2%; Graduate/professional degree or higher: 7.5%

School District(s)

Willsboro Central SD (PK-12)
  Enrollment: 259. . . . . (518) 963-4456

Housing: Homeownership rate: 83.0%; Median home value: $121,100; Median year structure built: 1960; Homeowner vacancy rate: 1.9%; Median selected monthly owner costs: $1,112 with a mortgage, $474 without a mortgage; Median gross rent: $820 per month; Rental vacancy rate: 4.1%

Health Insurance: 94.3% have insurance; 75.2% have private insurance; 44.0% have public insurance; 5.7% do not have insurance; 0.0% of children under 18 do not have insurance

Transportation: Commute: 82.4% car, 0.5% public transportation, 4.5% walk, 9.2% work from home; Mean travel time to work: 20.0 minutes

WILMINGTON (CDP).

Covers a land area of 8.252 square miles and a water area of 0.088 square miles. Located at 44.39° N. Lat; 73.82° W. Long. Elevation is 1,014 feet.

Population: 955; Growth (since 2000): n/a; Density: 115.7 persons per square mile; Race: 96.2% White, 0.0% Black/African American, 0.0% Asian, 0.0% American Indian/Alaska Native, 0.0% Native Hawaiian/Other Pacific Islander, 3.7% Two or more races, 2.6% Hispanic of any race; Average household size: 2.50; Median age: 45.0; Age under 18: 19.7%; Age 65 and over: 15.4%; Males per 100 females: 96.0; Marriage status: 27.6% never married, 59.6% now married, 0.9% separated, 8.8% widowed, 4.0% divorced; Foreign born: 2.1%; Speak English only: 97.0%; With disability: 9.9%; Veterans: 7.2%; Ancestry: 25.4% Irish, 15.3% English, 12.1% German, 10.9% Italian, 9.3% American

Employment: 13.4% management, business, and financial, 1.2% computer, engineering, and science, 12.8% education, legal, community service, arts, and media, 5.4% healthcare practitioners, 33.6% service, 15.6% sales and office, 12.2% natural resources, construction, and maintenance, 5.8% production, transportation, and material moving

Income: Per capita: $29,709; Median household: $58,385; Average household: $73,934; Households with income of $100,000 or more: 23.3%; Poverty rate: 11.8%

Educational Attainment: High school diploma or higher: 89.6%; Bachelor's degree or higher: 28.6%; Graduate/professional degree or higher: 11.5%

Housing: Homeownership rate: 77.7%; Median home value: $221,400; Median year structure built: 1971; Homeowner vacancy rate: 5.0%; Median selected monthly owner costs: $1,250 with a mortgage, $588 without a mortgage; Median gross rent: $895 per month; Rental vacancy rate: 15.8%

Health Insurance: 92.5% have insurance; 71.5% have private insurance; 34.5% have public insurance; 7.5% do not have insurance; 2.4% of children under 18 do not have insurance

Transportation: Commute: 86.1% car, 0.8% public transportation, 6.1% walk, 4.6% work from home; Mean travel time to work: 24.2 minutes

WILMINGTON (town).

Covers a land area of 65.240 square miles and a water area of 0.233 square miles. Located at 44.37° N. Lat; 73.89° W. Long. Elevation is 1,014 feet.

Population: 1,322; Growth (since 2000): 16.9%; Density: 20.3 persons per square mile; Race: 95.5% White, 0.1% Black/African American, 0.2% Asian, 0.0% American Indian/Alaska Native, 0.1% Native Hawaiian/Other Pacific Islander, 4.0% Two or more races, 3.9% Hispanic of any race; Average household size: 2.39; Median age: 45.0; Age under 18: 19.5%; Age 65 and over: 17.2%; Males per 100 females: 101.1; Marriage status: 25.5% never married, 59.4% now married, 0.8% separated, 9.1%

widowed, 6.1% divorced; Foreign born: 4.5%; Speak English only: 94.1%; With disability: 10.7%; Veterans: 9.5%; Ancestry: 22.7% Irish, 13.2% English, 11.1% Italian, 10.7% German, 8.1% French

Employment: 12.9% management, business, and financial, 1.9% computer, engineering, and science, 11.0% education, legal, community service, arts, and media, 5.9% healthcare practitioners, 34.4% service, 15.9% sales and office, 12.6% natural resources, construction, and maintenance, 5.4% production, transportation, and material moving

Income: Per capita: $31,114; Median household: $57,604; Average household: $75,298; Households with income of $100,000 or more: 23.5%; Poverty rate: 9.6%

Educational Attainment: High school diploma or higher: 88.1%; Bachelor's degree or higher: 29.2%; Graduate/professional degree or higher: 10.8%

Housing: Homeownership rate: 79.1%; Median home value: $204,900; Median year structure built: 1974; Homeowner vacancy rate: 3.5%; Median selected monthly owner costs: $1,310 with a mortgage, $557 without a mortgage; Median gross rent: $879 per month; Rental vacancy rate: 11.9%

Health Insurance: 93.0% have insurance; 74.4% have private insurance; 32.7% have public insurance; 7.0% do not have insurance; 1.8% of children under 18 do not have insurance

Transportation: Commute: 87.0% car, 0.6% public transportation, 5.1% walk, 5.6% work from home; Mean travel time to work: 23.4 minutes

WITHERBEE (CDP).

Covers a land area of 0.734 square miles and a water area of 0 square miles. Located at 44.08° N. Lat; 73.54° W. Long. Elevation is 1,257 feet.

Population: 250; Growth (since 2000): n/a; Density: 340.5 persons per square mile; Race: 78.0% White, 0.0% Black/African American, 2.8% Asian, 0.0% American Indian/Alaska Native, 0.0% Native Hawaiian/Other Pacific Islander, 19.2% Two or more races, 0.0% Hispanic of any race; Average household size: 1.97; Median age: 47.8; Age under 18: 24.8%; Age 65 and over: 10.0%; Males per 100 females: 94.9; Marriage status: 14.2% never married, 58.8% now married, 0.0% separated, 6.6% widowed, 20.4% divorced; Foreign born: 0.0%; Speak English only: 100.0%; With disability: 9.2%; Veterans: 18.1%; Ancestry: 41.6% Irish, 36.8% Hungarian, 13.6% German, 11.6% French, 6.4% Polish

Employment: 6.0% management, business, and financial, 0.0% computer, engineering, and science, 14.5% education, legal, community service, arts, and media, 0.0% healthcare practitioners, 12.0% service, 15.4% sales and office, 0.0% natural resources, construction, and maintenance, 52.1% production, transportation, and material moving

Income: Per capita: $21,650; Median household: $43,828; Average household: $43,363; Households with income of $100,000 or more: n/a; Poverty rate: n/a

Educational Attainment: High school diploma or higher: 92.0%; Bachelor's degree or higher: n/a; Graduate/professional degree or higher: n/a

Housing: Homeownership rate: 87.4%; Median home value: $55,700; Median year structure built: Before 1940; Homeowner vacancy rate: 0.0%; Median selected monthly owner costs: n/a with a mortgage, $422 without a mortgage; Median gross rent: n/a per month; Rental vacancy rate: 0.0%

Health Insurance: 100.0% have insurance; 69.6% have private insurance; 40.4% have public insurance; 0.0% do not have insurance; 0.0% of children under 18 do not have insurance

Transportation: Commute: 100.0% car, 0.0% public transportation, 0.0% walk, 0.0% work from home; Mean travel time to work: 19.2 minutes

Franklin County

Located in northeastern New York, partly in the Adirondacks; bounded on the north by the Canadian province of Quebec; drained by the Saranac, Saint Regis, Salmon, Little Salmon, Chateaugay, and Raquette Rivers; includes many lakes, including Saranac ke and Tupper Lake. Covers a land area of 1,629.119 square miles, a water area of 68.353 square miles, and is located in the Eastern Time Zone at 44.59° N. Lat., 74.31° W. Long. The county was founded in 1808. County seat is Malone.

Franklin County is part of the Malone, NY Micropolitan Statistical Area. The entire metro area includes: Franklin County, NY

Weather Station: Malone | | | | | | | | | | Elevation: 879 feet

	Jan	Feb	Mar	Apr	May	Jun	Jul	Aug	Sep	Oct	Nov	Dec
High	24	26	35	51	63	72	76	75	67	54	42	30
Low	6	7	17	32	44	54	58	56	48	37	27	13
Precip	2.3	1.8	2.2	3.0	3.2	4.0	4.3	4.3	3.8	3.8	3.3	2.7
Snow	22.1	18.1	16.3	7.0	0.6	0.0	0.0	0.0	tr	2.0	9.3	20.2

High and Low temperatures in degrees Fahrenheit; Precipitation and Snow in inches

Weather Station: Tupper Lake Sunmount | | | | | | | | | | Elevation: 1,680 feet

	Jan	Feb	Mar	Apr	May	Jun	Jul	Aug	Sep	Oct	Nov	Dec
High	25	29	36	51	64	72	76	75	68	55	42	30
Low	3	5	13	29	40	49	53	52	44	34	25	11
Precip	3.1	2.6	3.0	3.3	3.7	4.0	4.6	4.6	4.1	4.0	3.9	3.3
Snow	24.6	22.7	16.8	5.1	0.2	tr	0.0	0.0	tr	1.1	7.9	22.6

High and Low temperatures in degrees Fahrenheit; Precipitation and Snow in inches

Population: 51,054; Growth (since 2000): -0.2%; Density: 31.3 persons per square mile; Race: 82.5% White, 5.9% Black/African American, 0.4% Asian, 6.9% American Indian/Alaska Native, 0.2% Native Hawaiian/Other Pacific Islander, 1.9% two or more races, 3.4% Hispanic of any race; Average household size: 2.38; Median age: 40.5; Age under 18: 19.6%; Age 65 and over: 15.5%; Males per 100 females: 121.8; Marriage status: 35.8% never married, 47.6% now married, 3.2% separated, 5.7% widowed, 10.9% divorced; Foreign born: 4.5%; Speak English only: 92.5%; With disability: 15.5%; Veterans: 8.6%; Ancestry: 17.8% French, 17.0% Irish, 8.6% English, 8.0% German, 6.4% French Canadian
Religion: Six largest groups: 35.7% Catholicism, 3.6% Methodist/Pietist, 1.0% Presbyterian-Reformed, 0.9% Baptist, 0.8% Episcopalianism/Anglicanism, 0.8% Non-denominational Protestant
Economy: Unemployment rate: 3.9%; Leading industries: 17.4 % health care and social assistance; 17.3 % retail trade; 12.0 % accommodation and food services; Farms: 688 totaling 145,023 acres; Company size: 0 employ 1,000 or more persons, 3 employ 500 to 999 persons, 7 employ 100 to 499 persons, 949 employ less than 100 persons; Business ownership: 1,084 women-owned, n/a Black-owned, n/a Hispanic-owned, 45 Asian-owned, 118 American Indian/Alaska Native-owned
Employment: 10.0% management, business, and financial, 2.1% computer, engineering, and science, 13.5% education, legal, community service, arts, and media, 6.0% healthcare practitioners, 27.3% service, 19.5% sales and office, 10.1% natural resources, construction, and maintenance, 11.5% production, transportation, and material moving
Income: Per capita: $24,294; Median household: $50,733; Average household: $62,870; Households with income of $100,000 or more: 16.7%; Poverty rate: 19.4%
Educational Attainment: High school diploma or higher: 86.2%; Bachelor's degree or higher: 18.7%; Graduate/professional degree or higher: 9.6%
Housing: Homeownership rate: 72.9%; Median home value: $102,200; Median year structure built: 1964; Homeowner vacancy rate: 1.3%; Median selected monthly owner costs: $1,140 with a mortgage, $440 without a mortgage; Median gross rent: $670 per month; Rental vacancy rate: 4.3%
Vital Statistics: Birth rate: 93.1 per 10,000 population; Death rate: 96.3 per 10,000 population; Age-adjusted cancer mortality rate: 174.8 deaths per 100,000 population
Health Insurance: 92.7% have insurance; 67.0% have private insurance; 42.1% have public insurance; 7.3% do not have insurance; 8.2% of children under 18 do not have insurance
Health Care: Physicians: 14.9 per 10,000 population; Dentists: 4.3 per 10,000 population; Hospital beds: 67.5 per 10,000 population; Hospital admissions: 863.5 per 10,000 population
Air Quality Index (AQI): Percent of Days: 97.8% good, 2.2% moderate, 0.0% unhealthy for sensitive individuals, 0.0% unhealthy, 0.0% very unhealthy; Annual median: 25; Annual maximum: 93
Transportation: Commute: 87.3% car, 0.8% public transportation, 4.3% walk, 5.8% work from home; Mean travel time to work: 20.9 minutes
2016 Presidential Election: 48.5% Trump, 43.0% Clinton, 4.2% Johnson, 2.1% Stein
National and State Parks: Franklin State Forest
Additional Information Contacts
Franklin Government . . . . (518) 481-1681
     http://www.franklincony.org

Franklin County Communities

BANGOR (town). Covers a land area of 43.118 square miles and a water area of 0 square miles. Located at 44.84° N. Lat; 74.43° W. Long. Elevation is 768 feet.
Population: 2,141; Growth (since 2000): -0.3%; Density: 49.7 persons per square mile; Race: 95.8% White, 0.0% Black/African American, 0.0% Asian, 4.2% American Indian/Alaska Native, 0.0% Native Hawaiian/Other Pacific Islander, 0.0% Two or more races, 0.2% Hispanic of any race; Average household size: 2.66; Median age: 34.5; Age under 18: 25.3%; Age 65 and over: 11.3%; Males per 100 females: 102.6; Marriage status: 29.4% never married, 57.0% now married, 3.5% separated, 3.1% widowed, 10.5% divorced; Foreign born: 1.4%; Speak English only: 93.9%; With disability: 14.4%; Veterans: 5.7%; Ancestry: 25.3% French, 11.7% English, 9.5% Irish, 6.1% German, 5.7% Italian
Employment: 7.2% management, business, and financial, 3.5% computer, engineering, and science, 14.6% education, legal, community service, arts, and media, 9.3% healthcare practitioners, 26.9% service, 15.3% sales and office, 10.4% natural resources, construction, and maintenance, 12.9% production, transportation, and material moving
Income: Per capita: $21,926; Median household: $48,056; Average household: $57,547; Households with income of $100,000 or more: 14.9%; Poverty rate: 25.2%
Educational Attainment: High school diploma or higher: 90.1%; Bachelor's degree or higher: 12.1%; Graduate/professional degree or higher: 6.7%
Housing: Homeownership rate: 72.8%; Median home value: $82,100; Median year structure built: 1972; Homeowner vacancy rate: 2.4%; Median selected monthly owner costs: $1,101 with a mortgage, $436 without a mortgage; Median gross rent: $748 per month; Rental vacancy rate: 5.6%
Health Insurance: 88.2% have insurance; 61.2% have private insurance; 45.3% have public insurance; 11.8% do not have insurance; 7.8% of children under 18 do not have insurance
Transportation: Commute: 91.6% car, 2.6% public transportation, 0.0% walk, 5.8% work from home; Mean travel time to work: 23.5 minutes

BELLMONT (town). Covers a land area of 164.141 square miles and a water area of 3.019 square miles. Located at 44.76° N. Lat; 74.13° W. Long.
Population: 1,588; Growth (since 2000): 11.6%; Density: 9.7 persons per square mile; Race: 95.4% White, 0.4% Black/African American, 0.0% Asian, 0.4% American Indian/Alaska Native, 0.1% Native Hawaiian/Other Pacific Islander, 3.0% Two or more races, 1.8% Hispanic of any race; Average household size: 2.36; Median age: 45.7; Age under 18: 20.0%; Age 65 and over: 19.0%; Males per 100 females: 109.3; Marriage status: 29.9% never married, 55.2% now married, 1.5% separated, 4.5% widowed, 10.4% divorced; Foreign born: 2.1%; Speak English only: 96.9%; With disability: 16.2%; Veterans: 11.9%; Ancestry: 24.9% Irish, 23.6% French, 13.2% English, 9.6% French Canadian, 7.5% American
Employment: 14.1% management, business, and financial, 1.0% computer, engineering, and science, 14.6% education, legal, community service, arts, and media, 5.9% healthcare practitioners, 31.5% service, 12.1% sales and office, 11.2% natural resources, construction, and maintenance, 9.6% production, transportation, and material moving
Income: Per capita: $34,085; Median household: $57,150; Average household: $79,174; Households with income of $100,000 or more: 18.1%; Poverty rate: 15.1%
Educational Attainment: High school diploma or higher: 88.5%; Bachelor's degree or higher: 15.8%; Graduate/professional degree or higher: 8.3%
Housing: Homeownership rate: 87.7%; Median home value: $91,100; Median year structure built: 1964; Homeowner vacancy rate: 0.6%; Median selected monthly owner costs: $1,094 with a mortgage, $421 without a mortgage; Median gross rent: $941 per month; Rental vacancy rate: 0.0%
Health Insurance: 92.4% have insurance; 66.6% have private insurance; 43.9% have public insurance; 7.6% do not have insurance; 10.5% of children under 18 do not have insurance
Transportation: Commute: 87.7% car, 0.9% public transportation, 0.9% walk, 10.6% work from home; Mean travel time to work: 27.7 minutes

BOMBAY (town). Covers a land area of 35.743 square miles and a water area of 0.125 square miles. Located at 44.91° N. Lat; 74.59° W. Long. Elevation is 194 feet.

Population: 1,309; Growth (since 2000): 9.8%; Density: 36.6 persons per square mile; Race: 75.0% White, 0.0% Black/African American, 0.1% Asian, 21.8% American Indian/Alaska Native, 0.0% Native Hawaiian/Other Pacific Islander, 3.0% Two or more races, 1.6% Hispanic of any race; Average household size: 2.68; Median age: 31.9; Age under 18: 36.1%; Age 65 and over: 14.1%; Males per 100 females: 99.6; Marriage status: 32.3% never married, 48.2% now married, 3.9% separated, 7.6% widowed, 11.9% divorced; Foreign born: 1.5%; Speak English only: 97.4%; With disability: 13.2%; Veterans: 10.0%; Ancestry: 18.6% Irish, 16.7% French, 14.7% German, 8.0% English, 7.3% Italian

Employment: 13.4% management, business, and financial, 0.0% computer, engineering, and science, 8.0% education, legal, community service, arts, and media, 4.0% healthcare practitioners, 23.1% service, 24.6% sales and office, 14.5% natural resources, construction, and maintenance, 12.4% production, transportation, and material moving

Income: Per capita: $19,219; Median household: $38,452; Average household: $52,513; Households with income of $100,000 or more: 12.6%; Poverty rate: 25.1%

Educational Attainment: High school diploma or higher: 84.6%; Bachelor's degree or higher: 12.8%; Graduate/professional degree or higher: 6.9%

Housing: Homeownership rate: 69.8%; Median home value: $74,400; Median year structure built: 1975; Homeowner vacancy rate: 0.0%; Median selected monthly owner costs: $1,033 with a mortgage, $377 without a mortgage; Median gross rent: $692 per month; Rental vacancy rate: 6.4%

Health Insurance: 83.8% have insurance; 50.6% have private insurance; 44.2% have public insurance; 16.2% do not have insurance; 23.0% of children under 18 do not have insurance

Transportation: Commute: 90.5% car, 0.0% public transportation, 2.5% walk, 5.9% work from home; Mean travel time to work: 21.7 minutes

BRANDON (town). Covers a land area of 41.255 square miles and a water area of 0.067 square miles. Located at 44.74° N. Lat; 74.41° W. Long.

Population: 497; Growth (since 2000): -8.3%; Density: 12.0 persons per square mile; Race: 99.8% White, 0.0% Black/African American, 0.0% Asian, 0.0% American Indian/Alaska Native, 0.0% Native Hawaiian/Other Pacific Islander, 0.2% Two or more races, 0.0% Hispanic of any race; Average household size: 2.19; Median age: 45.9; Age under 18: 17.5%; Age 65 and over: 14.9%; Males per 100 females: 113.7; Marriage status: 23.9% never married, 57.1% now married, 2.6% separated, 11.4% widowed, 7.6% divorced; Foreign born: 2.8%; Speak English only: 97.7%; With disability: 24.5%; Veterans: 9.3%; Ancestry: 15.1% French, 12.1% Irish, 10.9% French Canadian, 9.3% American, 8.2% English

Employment: 10.2% management, business, and financial, 1.9% computer, engineering, and science, 8.3% education, legal, community service, arts, and media, 2.8% healthcare practitioners, 29.6% service, 25.0% sales and office, 15.3% natural resources, construction, and maintenance, 6.9% production, transportation, and material moving

Income: Per capita: $19,897; Median household: $33,083; Average household: $42,263; Households with income of $100,000 or more: 4.4%; Poverty rate: 25.4%

Educational Attainment: High school diploma or higher: 87.4%; Bachelor's degree or higher: 10.2%; Graduate/professional degree or higher: 5.1%

Housing: Homeownership rate: 92.5%; Median home value: $60,000; Median year structure built: 1981; Homeowner vacancy rate: 0.0%; Median selected monthly owner costs: $798 with a mortgage, $305 without a mortgage; Median gross rent: $505 per month; Rental vacancy rate: 0.0%

Health Insurance: 89.9% have insurance; 55.7% have private insurance; 46.1% have public insurance; 10.1% do not have insurance; 5.7% of children under 18 do not have insurance

Transportation: Commute: 99.5% car, 0.0% public transportation, 0.5% walk, 0.0% work from home; Mean travel time to work: 22.0 minutes

BRIGHTON (town). Covers a land area of 77.896 square miles and a water area of 5.100 square miles. Located at 44.47° N. Lat; 74.25° W. Long.

Population: 1,460; Growth (since 2000): -13.2%; Density: 18.7 persons per square mile; Race: 91.4% White, 4.2% Black/African American, 1.4% Asian, 1.6% American Indian/Alaska Native, 0.2% Native Hawaiian/Other Pacific Islander, 0.5% Two or more races, 1.1% Hispanic of any race;

Average household size: 2.20; Median age: 21.7; Age under 18: 6.9%; Age 65 and over: 9.8%; Males per 100 females: 146.1; Marriage status: 67.5% never married, 26.0% now married, 2.0% separated, 1.3% widowed, 5.2% divorced; Foreign born: 2.4%; Speak English only: 93.7%; With disability: 11.1%; Veterans: 1.8%; Ancestry: 18.0% Irish, 14.3% Italian, 12.1% German, 10.4% English, 10.1% French

Employment: 13.9% management, business, and financial, 6.3% computer, engineering, and science, 12.9% education, legal, community service, arts, and media, 3.2% healthcare practitioners, 26.8% service, 20.4% sales and office, 12.4% natural resources, construction, and maintenance, 4.1% production, transportation, and material moving

Income: Per capita: $20,787; Median household: $56,042; Average household: $70,040; Households with income of $100,000 or more: 21.3%; Poverty rate: 13.0%

Educational Attainment: High school diploma or higher: 96.1%; Bachelor's degree or higher: 48.7%; Graduate/professional degree or higher: 21.4%

Housing: Homeownership rate: 80.1%; Median home value: $178,300; Median year structure built: 1956; Homeowner vacancy rate: 1.3%; Median selected monthly owner costs: $1,368 with a mortgage, $521 without a mortgage; Median gross rent: $1,140 per month; Rental vacancy rate: 0.0%

Health Insurance: 95.1% have insurance; 82.3% have private insurance; 21.8% have public insurance; 4.9% do not have insurance; 4.9% of children under 18 do not have insurance

Transportation: Commute: 66.2% car, 0.3% public transportation, 19.6% walk, 13.6% work from home; Mean travel time to work: 20.5 minutes

Additional Information Contacts

Town of Brighton . . . . (585) 784-5250
  http://www.townofbrighton.org

BRUSHTON (village). Covers a land area of 0.276 square miles and a water area of 0 square miles. Located at 44.83° N. Lat; 74.51° W. Long. Elevation is 420 feet.

Population: 538; Growth (since 2000): 12.3%; Density: 1,946.5 persons per square mile; Race: 93.9% White, 0.9% Black/African American, 0.0% Asian, 0.6% American Indian/Alaska Native, 0.0% Native Hawaiian/Other Pacific Islander, 0.7% Two or more races, 2.0% Hispanic of any race; Average household size: 2.47; Median age: 38.5; Age under 18: 22.9%; Age 65 and over: 8.7%; Males per 100 females: 95.9; Marriage status: 29.2% never married, 51.3% now married, 3.4% separated, 7.4% widowed, 12.2% divorced; Foreign born: 3.2%; Speak English only: 93.6%; With disability: 16.5%; Veterans: 4.8%; Ancestry: 20.8% French, 13.2% Irish, 11.0% French Canadian, 10.8% English, 7.6% Pennsylvania German

Employment: 9.8% management, business, and financial, 8.3% computer, engineering, and science, 9.8% education, legal, community service, arts, and media, 0.0% healthcare practitioners, 28.3% service, 19.5% sales and office, 16.6% natural resources, construction, and maintenance, 7.8% production, transportation, and material moving

Income: Per capita: $25,187; Median household: $55,278; Average household: $60,463; Households with income of $100,000 or more: 20.7%; Poverty rate: 22.5%

Educational Attainment: High school diploma or higher: 85.4%; Bachelor's degree or higher: 17.2%; Graduate/professional degree or higher: 6.3%

School District(s)

Brushton-Moira Central SD (PK-12)
  Enrollment: 819 . . . . (518) 529-8942

Housing: Homeownership rate: 64.7%; Median home value: $86,000; Median year structure built: Before 1940; Homeowner vacancy rate: 0.0%; Median selected monthly owner costs: $980 with a mortgage, $476 without a mortgage; Median gross rent: $583 per month; Rental vacancy rate: 8.3%

Health Insurance: 73.8% have insurance; 54.1% have private insurance; 31.6% have public insurance; 26.2% do not have insurance; 29.3% of children under 18 do not have insurance

Transportation: Commute: 98.0% car, 0.0% public transportation, 0.0% walk, 2.0% work from home; Mean travel time to work: 23.0 minutes

BURKE (town). Covers a land area of 44.405 square miles and a water area of 0 square miles. Located at 44.93° N. Lat; 74.18° W. Long. Elevation is 863 feet.

Population: 1,409; Growth (since 2000): 3.7%; Density: 31.7 persons per square mile; Race: 95.3% White, 1.7% Black/African American, 1.1% Asian, 0.0% American Indian/Alaska Native, 0.0% Native Hawaiian/Other

Pacific Islander, 1.3% Two or more races, 1.8% Hispanic of any race; Average household size: 2.42; Median age: 46.3; Age under 18: 20.2%; Age 65 and over: 16.1%; Males per 100 females: 109.9; Marriage status: 27.2% never married, 53.5% now married, 2.4% separated, 5.0% widowed, 14.2% divorced; Foreign born: 3.2%; Speak English only: 87.9%; With disability: 10.5%; Veterans: 8.2%; Ancestry: 18.6% French, 14.6% Irish, 13.4% English, 9.9% American, 6.4% French Canadian

Employment: 11.9% management, business, and financial, 0.9% computer, engineering, and science, 11.8% education, legal, community service, arts, and media, 7.0% healthcare practitioners, 19.6% service, 14.8% sales and office, 18.4% natural resources, construction, and maintenance, 15.7% production, transportation, and material moving

Income: Per capita: $26,575; Median household: $52,788; Average household: $63,829; Households with income of $100,000 or more: 17.4%; Poverty rate: 18.1%

Educational Attainment: High school diploma or higher: 84.3%; Bachelor's degree or higher: 12.7%; Graduate/professional degree or higher: 3.9%

Housing: Homeownership rate: 80.7%; Median home value: $105,600; Median year structure built: 1976; Homeowner vacancy rate: 0.0%; Median selected monthly owner costs: $1,130 with a mortgage, $402 without a mortgage; Median gross rent: $678 per month; Rental vacancy rate: 0.0%

Health Insurance: 87.8% have insurance; 63.4% have private insurance; 38.5% have public insurance; 12.2% do not have insurance; 20.0% of children under 18 do not have insurance

Transportation: Commute: 83.5% car, 0.0% public transportation, 3.2% walk, 10.8% work from home; Mean travel time to work: 22.0 minutes

BURKE (village). Covers a land area of 0.290 square miles and a water area of 0 square miles. Located at 44.90° N. Lat; 74.17° W. Long. Elevation is 863 feet.

Population: 212; Growth (since 2000): -0.5%; Density: 731.4 persons per square mile; Race: 89.6% White, 0.0% Black/African American, 0.0% Asian, 0.0% American Indian/Alaska Native, 0.0% Native Hawaiian/Other Pacific Islander, 7.1% Two or more races, 10.8% Hispanic of any race; Average household size: 2.48; Median age: 36.3; Age under 18: 27.8%; Age 65 and over: 20.3%; Males per 100 females: 106.9; Marriage status: 23.9% never married, 49.0% now married, 0.0% separated, 10.3% widowed, 16.8% divorced; Foreign born: 1.9%; Speak English only: 95.9%; With disability: 18.4%; Veterans: 9.2%; Ancestry: 22.6% French, 20.3% Irish, 12.3% English, 10.8% German, 9.9% American

Employment: 3.9% management, business, and financial, 2.6% computer, engineering, and science, 16.9% education, legal, community service, arts, and media, 10.4% healthcare practitioners, 19.5% service, 9.1% sales and office, 32.5% natural resources, construction, and maintenance, 5.2% production, transportation, and material moving

Income: Per capita: $19,678; Median household: $41,875; Average household: $45,946; Households with income of $100,000 or more: 7.1%; Poverty rate: 32.5%

Educational Attainment: High school diploma or higher: 85.5%; Bachelor's degree or higher: 21.4%; Graduate/professional degree or higher: 11.0%

Housing: Homeownership rate: 64.7%; Median home value: $88,100; Median year structure built: Before 1940; Homeowner vacancy rate: 0.0%; Median selected monthly owner costs: $1,071 with a mortgage, $323 without a mortgage; Median gross rent: $760 per month; Rental vacancy rate: 0.0%

Health Insurance: 97.6% have insurance; 67.0% have private insurance; 49.1% have public insurance; 2.4% do not have insurance; 0.0% of children under 18 do not have insurance

Transportation: Commute: 97.3% car, 0.0% public transportation, 0.0% walk, 1.4% work from home; Mean travel time to work: 24.0 minutes

CHATEAUGAY (town). Covers a land area of 49.789 square miles and a water area of 0.012 square miles. Located at 44.93° N. Lat; 74.08° W. Long. Elevation is 945 feet.

History: Settled 1796, incorporated 1869.

Population: 1,629; Growth (since 2000): -20.0%; Density: 32.7 persons per square mile; Race: 92.5% White, 5.9% Black/African American, 0.4% Asian, 0.2% American Indian/Alaska Native, 0.0% Native Hawaiian/Other Pacific Islander, 0.4% Two or more races, 1.4% Hispanic of any race; Average household size: 2.15; Median age: 44.0; Age under 18: 18.5%; Age 65 and over: 18.0%; Males per 100 females: 116.1; Marriage status: 28.3% never married, 55.4% now married, 1.2% separated, 11.3% widowed, 5.1% divorced; Foreign born: 2.2%; Speak English only: 96.9%;

With disability: 17.4%; Veterans: 10.6%; Ancestry: 17.9% French, 16.3% Irish, 8.8% English, 7.9% American, 7.4% German

Employment: 8.5% management, business, and financial, 2.6% computer, engineering, and science, 12.6% education, legal, community service, arts, and media, 4.5% healthcare practitioners, 20.5% service, 16.3% sales and office, 15.3% natural resources, construction, and maintenance, 19.7% production, transportation, and material moving

Income: Per capita: $22,750; Median household: $44,063; Average household: $53,698; Households with income of $100,000 or more: 15.5%; Poverty rate: 25.2%

Educational Attainment: High school diploma or higher: 83.1%; Bachelor's degree or higher: 13.2%; Graduate/professional degree or higher: 6.6%

School District(s)
Chateaugay Central SD (PK-12)
 Enrollment: 525 . . . . (518) 497-6420

Housing: Homeownership rate: 68.2%; Median home value: $82,100; Median year structure built: 1945; Homeowner vacancy rate: 2.5%; Median selected monthly owner costs: $959 with a mortgage, $403 without a mortgage; Median gross rent: $599 per month; Rental vacancy rate: 3.0%

Health Insurance: 93.9% have insurance; 62.3% have private insurance; 49.4% have public insurance; 6.1% do not have insurance; 5.5% of children under 18 do not have insurance

Transportation: Commute: 93.8% car, 0.8% public transportation, 2.1% walk, 2.0% work from home; Mean travel time to work: 25.4 minutes

CHATEAUGAY (village). Covers a land area of 1.083 square miles and a water area of 0 square miles. Located at 44.93° N. Lat; 74.08° W. Long. Elevation is 945 feet.

Population: 644; Growth (since 2000): -19.3%; Density: 594.4 persons per square mile; Race: 98.1% White, 0.0% Black/African American, 1.1% Asian, 0.0% American Indian/Alaska Native, 0.0% Native Hawaiian/Other Pacific Islander, 0.8% Two or more races, 1.1% Hispanic of any race; Average household size: 2.13; Median age: 50.6; Age under 18: 16.9%; Age 65 and over: 26.2%; Males per 100 females: 87.2; Marriage status: 20.0% never married, 57.5% now married, 0.9% separated, 13.6% widowed, 8.9% divorced; Foreign born: 5.6%; Speak English only: 96.2%; With disability: 21.4%; Veterans: 11.2%; Ancestry: 21.3% Irish, 18.0% French, 12.4% German, 12.1% English, 6.5% Italian

Employment: 8.5% management, business, and financial, 3.6% computer, engineering, and science, 14.5% education, legal, community service, arts, and media, 2.4% healthcare practitioners, 26.2% service, 19.4% sales and office, 5.2% natural resources, construction, and maintenance, 20.2% production, transportation, and material moving

Income: Per capita: $24,420; Median household: $41,250; Average household: $51,190; Households with income of $100,000 or more: 12.9%; Poverty rate: 27.2%

Educational Attainment: High school diploma or higher: 90.7%; Bachelor's degree or higher: 18.4%; Graduate/professional degree or higher: 10.7%

School District(s)
Chateaugay Central SD (PK-12)
 Enrollment: 525 . . . . (518) 497-6420

Housing: Homeownership rate: 64.2%; Median home value: $83,500; Median year structure built: Before 1940; Homeowner vacancy rate: 5.9%; Median selected monthly owner costs: $981 with a mortgage, $465 without a mortgage; Median gross rent: $567 per month; Rental vacancy rate: 5.9%

Health Insurance: 93.2% have insurance; 62.9% have private insurance; 55.1% have public insurance; 6.8% do not have insurance; 13.7% of children under 18 do not have insurance

Transportation: Commute: 90.7% car, 0.8% public transportation, 5.2% walk, 0.0% work from home; Mean travel time to work: 25.1 minutes

CONSTABLE (town). Covers a land area of 32.806 square miles and a water area of 0.012 square miles. Located at 44.97° N. Lat; 74.28° W. Long. Elevation is 354 feet.

Population: 1,491; Growth (since 2000): 4.4%; Density: 45.4 persons per square mile; Race: 96.7% White, 2.0% Black/African American, 0.1% Asian, 0.1% American Indian/Alaska Native, 0.0% Native Hawaiian/Other Pacific Islander, 0.9% Two or more races, 1.7% Hispanic of any race; Average household size: 2.33; Median age: 43.6; Age under 18: 21.2%; Age 65 and over: 13.1%; Males per 100 females: 109.1; Marriage status: 24.3% never married, 57.5% now married, 3.8% separated, 7.0% widowed, 11.2% divorced; Foreign born: 1.7%; Speak English only: 98.1%;

With disability: 17.3%; Veterans: 15.9%; Ancestry: 27.4% French, 18.6% Irish, 10.6% American, 9.7% German, 8.0% English
Employment: 7.8% management, business, and financial, 0.4% computer, engineering, and science, 6.4% education, legal, community service, arts, and media, 9.6% healthcare practitioners, 30.9% service, 20.0% sales and office, 9.5% natural resources, construction, and maintenance, 15.4% production, transportation, and material moving
Income: Per capita: $28,039; Median household: $57,065; Average household: $66,131; Households with income of $100,000 or more: 22.1%; Poverty rate: 10.5%
Educational Attainment: High school diploma or higher: 90.7%; Bachelor's degree or higher: 12.5%; Graduate/professional degree or higher: 5.4%
Housing: Homeownership rate: 83.7%; Median home value: $91,300; Median year structure built: 1978; Homeowner vacancy rate: 0.8%; Median selected monthly owner costs: $1,098 with a mortgage, $371 without a mortgage; Median gross rent: $580 per month; Rental vacancy rate: 0.0%
Health Insurance: 93.7% have insurance; 73.0% have private insurance; 35.3% have public insurance; 6.3% do not have insurance; 4.9% of children under 18 do not have insurance
Transportation: Commute: 93.4% car, 0.6% public transportation, 3.6% walk, 2.3% work from home; Mean travel time to work: 20.7 minutes

DICKINSON (town).
Covers a land area of 44.224 square miles and a water area of 0.089 square miles. Located at 44.73° N. Lat; 74.54° W. Long. Elevation is 722 feet.
Population: 998; Growth (since 2000): 35.0%; Density: 22.6 persons per square mile; Race: 90.0% White, 0.4% Black/African American, 1.3% Asian, 0.6% American Indian/Alaska Native, 4.4% Native Hawaiian/Other Pacific Islander, 3.3% Two or more races, 0.9% Hispanic of any race; Average household size: 2.76; Median age: 43.7; Age under 18: 25.9%; Age 65 and over: 18.3%; Males per 100 females: 103.7; Marriage status: 27.4% never married, 60.0% now married, 0.9% separated, 4.8% widowed, 7.9% divorced; Foreign born: 2.8%; Speak English only: 90.8%; With disability: 12.6%; Veterans: 11.4%; Ancestry: 16.7% French, 11.0% German, 10.4% Irish, 8.8% English, 7.7% American
Employment: 11.0% management, business, and financial, 1.3% computer, engineering, and science, 12.3% education, legal, community service, arts, and media, 5.0% healthcare practitioners, 28.0% service, 17.5% sales and office, 14.3% natural resources, construction, and maintenance, 10.8% production, transportation, and material moving
Income: Per capita: $21,946; Median household: $58,021; Average household: $59,095; Households with income of $100,000 or more: 13.6%; Poverty rate: 22.9%
Educational Attainment: High school diploma or higher: 86.3%; Bachelor's degree or higher: 13.7%; Graduate/professional degree or higher: 5.5%
Housing: Homeownership rate: 89.2%; Median home value: $86,300; Median year structure built: 1966; Homeowner vacancy rate: 2.1%; Median selected monthly owner costs: $1,029 with a mortgage, $410 without a mortgage; Median gross rent: $775 per month; Rental vacancy rate: 0.0%
Health Insurance: 87.4% have insurance; 61.9% have private insurance; 40.2% have public insurance; 12.6% do not have insurance; 18.8% of children under 18 do not have insurance
Transportation: Commute: 83.8% car, 0.0% public transportation, 5.3% walk, 9.6% work from home; Mean travel time to work: 30.9 minutes

DICKINSON CENTER (unincorporated postal area)
ZCTA: 12930
Covers a land area of 36.166 square miles and a water area of 0.076 square miles. Located at 44.72° N. Lat; 74.54° W. Long. Elevation is 955 feet.
Population: 786; Growth (since 2000): 37.7%; Density: 21.7 persons per square mile; Race: 87.9% White, 0.5% Black/African American, 1.5% Asian, 0.6% American Indian/Alaska Native, 5.6% Native Hawaiian/Other Pacific Islander, 3.8% Two or more races, 1.1% Hispanic of any race; Average household size: 2.76; Median age: 38.1; Age under 18: 30.3%; Age 65 and over: 14.8%; Males per 100 females: 103.2; Marriage status: 31.3% never married, 54.5% now married, 1.2% separated, 5.1% widowed, 9.1% divorced; Foreign born: 2.2%; Speak English only: 93.7%; With disability: 11.0%; Veterans: 11.5%; Ancestry: 15.4% French, 12.6% Irish, 10.6% German, 9.3% English, 6.5% American
Employment: 8.4% management, business, and financial, 0.3% computer, engineering, and science, 13.1% education, legal, community

service, arts, and media, 6.7% healthcare practitioners, 27.9% service, 17.1% sales and office, 14.1% natural resources, construction, and maintenance, 12.4% production, transportation, and material moving
Income: Per capita: $21,265; Median household: $48,750; Average household: $56,916; Households with income of $100,000 or more: 14.4%; Poverty rate: 23.0%
Educational Attainment: High school diploma or higher: 89.3%; Bachelor's degree or higher: 15.1%; Graduate/professional degree or higher: 6.2%
Housing: Homeownership rate: 82.8%; Median home value: $89,200; Median year structure built: 1973; Homeowner vacancy rate: 2.9%; Median selected monthly owner costs: $1,095 with a mortgage, $412 without a mortgage; Median gross rent: $775 per month; Rental vacancy rate: 0.0%
Health Insurance: 92.9% have insurance; 64.0% have private insurance; 40.6% have public insurance; 7.1% do not have insurance; 0.0% of children under 18 do not have insurance
Transportation: Commute: 88.1% car, 0.0% public transportation, 3.7% walk, 6.4% work from home; Mean travel time to work: 27.9 minutes

DUANE (town).
Covers a land area of 74.952 square miles and a water area of 3.032 square miles. Located at 44.60° N. Lat; 74.23° W. Long.
Population: 182; Growth (since 2000): 14.5%; Density: 2.4 persons per square mile; Race: 98.9% White, 0.0% Black/African American, 0.0% Asian, 0.0% American Indian/Alaska Native, 0.0% Native Hawaiian/Other Pacific Islander, 1.1% Two or more races, 0.0% Hispanic of any race; Average household size: 2.02; Median age: 56.0; Age under 18: 8.2%; Age 65 and over: 30.8%; Males per 100 females: 123.1; Marriage status: 15.0% never married, 68.3% now married, 1.2% separated, 7.2% widowed, 9.6% divorced; Foreign born: 1.1%; Speak English only: 98.9%; With disability: 13.7%; Veterans: 15.6%; Ancestry: 22.5% Irish, 18.1% French, 14.8% English, 13.2% American, 11.5% German
Employment: 7.7% management, business, and financial, 0.0% computer, engineering, and science, 25.6% education, legal, community service, arts, and media, 2.6% healthcare practitioners, 19.2% service, 19.2% sales and office, 15.4% natural resources, construction, and maintenance, 10.3% production, transportation, and material moving
Income: Per capita: $45,497; Median household: $61,250; Average household: $90,751; Households with income of $100,000 or more: 7.7%; Poverty rate: 8.2%
Educational Attainment: High school diploma or higher: 93.0%; Bachelor's degree or higher: 28.7%; Graduate/professional degree or higher: 14.0%
Housing: Homeownership rate: 75.6%; Median home value: $100,000; Median year structure built: 1971; Homeowner vacancy rate: 0.0%; Median selected monthly owner costs: $990 with a mortgage, $298 without a mortgage; Median gross rent: $888 per month; Rental vacancy rate: 0.0%
Health Insurance: 95.1% have insurance; 82.4% have private insurance; 45.6% have public insurance; 4.9% do not have insurance; 0.0% of children under 18 do not have insurance
Transportation: Commute: 84.0% car, 2.7% public transportation, 2.7% walk, 10.7% work from home; Mean travel time to work: 29.6 minutes

FORT COVINGTON (town).
Covers a land area of 36.734 square miles and a water area of 0 square miles. Located at 44.95° N. Lat; 74.49° W. Long. Elevation is 180 feet.
Population: 2,060; Growth (since 2000): 25.2%; Density: 56.1 persons per square mile; Race: 71.6% White, 4.2% Black/African American, 0.1% Asian, 15.0% American Indian/Alaska Native, 0.0% Native Hawaiian/Other Pacific Islander, 8.3% Two or more races, 1.2% Hispanic of any race; Average household size: 2.87; Median age: 36.6; Age under 18: 31.3%; Age 65 and over: 11.4%; Males per 100 females: 100.7; Marriage status: 38.7% never married, 47.6% now married, 0.4% separated, 4.7% widowed, 9.0% divorced; Foreign born: 2.3%; Speak English only: 93.7%; With disability: 13.9%; Veterans: 10.5%; Ancestry: 24.0% French, 14.4% Irish, 7.1% English, 6.1% German, 5.4% Italian
Employment: 10.8% management, business, and financial, 0.5% computer, engineering, and science, 13.3% education, legal, community service, arts, and media, 4.1% healthcare practitioners, 26.4% service, 16.0% sales and office, 15.0% natural resources, construction, and maintenance, 14.0% production, transportation, and material moving
Income: Per capita: $18,896; Median household: $44,236; Average household: $53,160; Households with income of $100,000 or more: 14.9%; Poverty rate: 17.1%

Educational Attainment: High school diploma or higher: 89.9%; Bachelor's degree or higher: 16.4%; Graduate/professional degree or higher: 7.2%

School District(s)
Salmon River Central SD (PK-12)
    Enrollment: 1,540 . . . . (518) 358-6610
Housing: Homeownership rate: 81.5%; Median home value: $86,500; Median year structure built: 1965; Homeowner vacancy rate: 0.8%; Median selected monthly owner costs: $1,021 with a mortgage, $440 without a mortgage; Median gross rent: $771 per month; Rental vacancy rate: 6.3%
Health Insurance: 90.5% have insurance; 64.1% have private insurance; 41.3% have public insurance; 9.5% do not have insurance; 16.0% of children under 18 do not have insurance
Transportation: Commute: 86.5% car, 0.0% public transportation, 3.3% walk, 9.2% work from home; Mean travel time to work: 18.7 minutes

FORT COVINGTON HAMLET (CDP).
Covers a land area of 19.322 square miles and a water area of 0.010 square miles. Located at 44.97° N. Lat; 74.51° W. Long.
Population: 1,501; Growth (since 2000): n/a; Density: 77.7 persons per square mile; Race: 68.8% White, 1.8% Black/African American, 0.2% Asian, 18.7% American Indian/Alaska Native, 0.0% Native Hawaiian/Other Pacific Islander, 9.3% Two or more races, 1.7% Hispanic of any race; Average household size: 2.94; Median age: 37.2; Age under 18: 30.6%; Age 65 and over: 12.7%; Males per 100 females: 99.4; Marriage status: 37.2% never married, 48.5% now married, 0.2% separated, 5.3% widowed, 9.0% divorced; Foreign born: 3.0%; Speak English only: 96.8%; With disability: 14.1%; Veterans: 11.0%; Ancestry: 27.5% French, 14.4% Irish, 7.1% German, 5.1% French Canadian, 5.1% Italian
Employment: 9.9% management, business, and financial, 0.7% computer, engineering, and science, 12.8% education, legal, community service, arts, and media, 4.8% healthcare practitioners, 27.2% service, 17.5% sales and office, 12.3% natural resources, construction, and maintenance, 14.7% production, transportation, and material moving
Income: Per capita: $19,477; Median household: $45,759; Average household: $54,795; Households with income of $100,000 or more: 13.8%; Poverty rate: 12.1%
Educational Attainment: High school diploma or higher: 92.4%; Bachelor's degree or higher: 17.9%; Graduate/professional degree or higher: 7.5%
Housing: Homeownership rate: 84.9%; Median home value: $77,200; Median year structure built: 1955; Homeowner vacancy rate: 1.1%; Median selected monthly owner costs: $889 with a mortgage, $438 without a mortgage; Median gross rent: $725 per month; Rental vacancy rate: 10.5%
Health Insurance: 94.3% have insurance; 71.6% have private insurance; 38.9% have public insurance; 5.7% do not have insurance; 4.1% of children under 18 do not have insurance
Transportation: Commute: 88.1% car, 0.0% public transportation, 3.8% walk, 7.2% work from home; Mean travel time to work: 17.3 minutes

FRANKLIN (town).
Covers a land area of 169.827 square miles and a water area of 5.395 square miles. Located at 44.52° N. Lat; 74.07° W. Long.
Population: 1,114; Growth (since 2000): -6.9%; Density: 6.6 persons per square mile; Race: 94.0% White, 0.0% Black/African American, 3.7% Asian, 0.0% American Indian/Alaska Native, 0.6% Native Hawaiian/Other Pacific Islander, 1.7% Two or more races, 0.8% Hispanic of any race; Average household size: 2.15; Median age: 51.8; Age under 18: 15.5%; Age 65 and over: 22.4%; Males per 100 females: 102.5; Marriage status: 19.7% never married, 64.9% now married, 2.7% separated, 6.0% widowed, 9.4% divorced; Foreign born: 5.4%; Speak English only: 95.5%; With disability: 9.9%; Veterans: 15.6%; Ancestry: 18.1% German, 17.3% Irish, 13.7% French, 9.8% English, 6.6% French Canadian
Employment: 13.2% management, business, and financial, 3.1% computer, engineering, and science, 16.8% education, legal, community service, arts, and media, 6.7% healthcare practitioners, 21.1% service, 24.5% sales and office, 10.1% natural resources, construction, and maintenance, 4.5% production, transportation, and material moving
Income: Per capita: $36,358; Median household: $67,857; Average household: $78,438; Households with income of $100,000 or more: 32.7%; Poverty rate: 9.2%
Educational Attainment: High school diploma or higher: 94.4%; Bachelor's degree or higher: 39.7%; Graduate/professional degree or higher: 19.4%

Housing: Homeownership rate: 87.6%; Median home value: $182,200; Median year structure built: 1974; Homeowner vacancy rate: 1.1%; Median selected monthly owner costs: $1,239 with a mortgage, $479 without a mortgage; Median gross rent: $744 per month; Rental vacancy rate: 0.0%
Health Insurance: 96.8% have insurance; 82.9% have private insurance; 34.2% have public insurance; 3.2% do not have insurance; 1.2% of children under 18 do not have insurance
Transportation: Commute: 95.1% car, 0.9% public transportation, 0.5% walk, 3.5% work from home; Mean travel time to work: 27.2 minutes

GABRIELS (unincorporated postal area)
ZCTA: 12939
Covers a land area of 4.136 square miles and a water area of 0.022 square miles. Located at 44.43° N. Lat; 74.16° W. Long. Elevation is 1,699 feet.
Population: 233; Growth (since 2000): n/a; Density: 56.3 persons per square mile; Race: 100.0% White, 0.0% Black/African American, 0.0% Asian, 0.0% American Indian/Alaska Native, 0.0% Native Hawaiian/Other Pacific Islander, 0.0% Two or more races, 0.0% Hispanic of any race; Average household size: 2.20; Median age: 37.7; Age under 18: 12.4%; Age 65 and over: 4.7%; Males per 100 females: 97.1; Marriage status: 50.9% never married, 37.2% now married, 5.5% separated, 1.4% widowed, 10.6% divorced; Foreign born: 5.6%; Speak English only: 95.6%; With disability: 11.6%; Veterans: 0.0%; Ancestry: 24.0% Irish, 18.5% Italian, 14.2% French, 10.3% English, 9.9% German
Employment: 12.4% management, business, and financial, 8.8% computer, engineering, and science, 2.2% education, legal, community service, arts, and media, 2.9% healthcare practitioners, 23.4% service, 16.1% sales and office, 26.3% natural resources, construction, and maintenance, 8.0% production, transportation, and material moving
Income: Per capita: $32,674; Median household: $56,389; Average household: $68,028; Households with income of $100,000 or more: 17.9%; Poverty rate: 13.3%
Educational Attainment: High school diploma or higher: 98.6%; Bachelor's degree or higher: 31.5%; Graduate/professional degree or higher: 18.5%
Housing: Homeownership rate: 68.9%; Median home value: $138,800; Median year structure built: 1952; Homeowner vacancy rate: 0.0%; Median selected monthly owner costs: $1,188 with a mortgage, $517 without a mortgage; Median gross rent: $1,117 per month; Rental vacancy rate: 0.0%
Health Insurance: 97.4% have insurance; 79.4% have private insurance; 22.7% have public insurance; 2.6% do not have insurance; 0.0% of children under 18 do not have insurance
Transportation: Commute: 97.7% car, 0.0% public transportation, 2.3% walk, 0.0% work from home; Mean travel time to work: 21.6 minutes

HARRIETSTOWN (town).
Covers a land area of 196.866 square miles and a water area of 16.814 square miles. Located at 44.22° N. Lat; 74.21° W. Long. Elevation is 1,854 feet.
Population: 5,609; Growth (since 2000): 0.6%; Density: 28.5 persons per square mile; Race: 94.5% White, 3.2% Black/African American, 0.0% Asian, 0.6% American Indian/Alaska Native, 0.0% Native Hawaiian/Other Pacific Islander, 1.0% Two or more races, 0.8% Hispanic of any race; Average household size: 2.27; Median age: 42.5; Age under 18: 22.4%; Age 65 and over: 19.1%; Males per 100 females: 103.9; Marriage status: 32.6% never married, 51.5% now married, 2.9% separated, 6.3% widowed, 9.6% divorced; Foreign born: 1.7%; Speak English only: 97.4%; With disability: 14.0%; Veterans: 10.7%; Ancestry: 22.0% Irish, 12.7% French, 12.4% English, 11.6% German, 7.9% Italian
Employment: 11.5% management, business, and financial, 3.1% computer, engineering, and science, 13.6% education, legal, community service, arts, and media, 9.1% healthcare practitioners, 25.0% service, 23.2% sales and office, 7.2% natural resources, construction, and maintenance, 7.3% production, transportation, and material moving
Income: Per capita: $30,401; Median household: $52,629; Average household: $69,531; Households with income of $100,000 or more: 18.7%; Poverty rate: 19.4%
Educational Attainment: High school diploma or higher: 93.2%; Bachelor's degree or higher: 31.1%; Graduate/professional degree or higher: 16.9%
Housing: Homeownership rate: 60.9%; Median home value: $171,900; Median year structure built: Before 1940; Homeowner vacancy rate: 1.3%; Median selected monthly owner costs: $1,422 with a mortgage, $658

without a mortgage; Median gross rent: $701 per month; Rental vacancy rate: 9.2%

Health Insurance: 95.3% have insurance; 66.1% have private insurance; 46.6% have public insurance; 4.7% do not have insurance; 3.9% of children under 18 do not have insurance

Transportation: Commute: 80.8% car, 2.2% public transportation, 9.2% walk, 5.8% work from home; Mean travel time to work: 17.0 minutes

Additional Information Contacts

Town of Harrietstown . . . . (518) 891-1470
    http://www.harrietstown.org

HOGANSBURG (unincorporated postal area)
ZCTA: 13655

Covers a land area of 20.221 square miles and a water area of 2.252 square miles. Located at 44.98° N. Lat; 74.65° W. Long. Elevation is 171 feet.

Population: 3,398; Growth (since 2000): 32.8%; Density: 168.0 persons per square mile; Race: 5.4% White, 0.1% Black/African American, 1.6% Asian, 81.0% American Indian/Alaska Native, 2.0% Native Hawaiian/Other Pacific Islander, 5.4% Two or more races, 8.0% Hispanic of any race; Average household size: 2.70; Median age: 45.7; Age under 18: 18.1%; Age 65 and over: 15.0%; Males per 100 females: 96.4; Marriage status: 45.6% never married, 32.1% now married, 5.4% separated, 1.6% widowed, 20.7% divorced; Foreign born: 24.9%; Speak English only: 64.7%; With disability: 18.7%; Veterans: 5.5%; Ancestry: 2.4% Greek, 1.6% Polish, 1.5% English, 0.1% Israeli

Employment: 10.4% management, business, and financial, 6.4% computer, engineering, and science, 28.0% education, legal, community service, arts, and media, 3.5% healthcare practitioners, 22.3% service, 1.2% sales and office, 8.9% natural resources, construction, and maintenance, 19.3% production, transportation, and material moving

Income: Per capita: $25,066; Median household: $36,712; Average household: $49,828; Households with income of $100,000 or more: 11.7%; Poverty rate: 19.7%

Educational Attainment: High school diploma or higher: 93.0%; Bachelor's degree or higher: 25.5%; Graduate/professional degree or higher: 18.5%

School District(s)
Salmon River Central SD (PK-12)
    Enrollment: 1,540 . . . . (518) 358-6610

Housing: Homeownership rate: 73.8%; Median home value: $114,200; Median year structure built: 1989; Homeowner vacancy rate: 0.0%; Median selected monthly owner costs: $943 with a mortgage, $251 without a mortgage; Median gross rent: $443 per month; Rental vacancy rate: 0.0%

Health Insurance: 81.3% have insurance; 57.9% have private insurance; 28.3% have public insurance; 18.7% do not have insurance; 28.9% of children under 18 do not have insurance

Transportation: Commute: 85.5% car, 0.0% public transportation, 0.0% walk, 0.0% work from home; Mean travel time to work: 34.8 minutes

LAKE CLEAR (unincorporated postal area)
ZCTA: 12945

Covers a land area of 33.208 square miles and a water area of 7.218 square miles. Located at 44.31° N. Lat; 74.24° W. Long. Elevation is 1,640 feet.

Population: 523; Growth (since 2000): -28.9%; Density: 15.7 persons per square mile; Race: 100.0% White, 0.0% Black/African American, 0.0% Asian, 0.0% American Indian/Alaska Native, 0.0% Native Hawaiian/Other Pacific Islander, 0.0% Two or more races, 0.0% Hispanic of any race; Average household size: 2.50; Median age: 41.0; Age under 18: 21.4%; Age 65 and over: 34.6%; Males per 100 females: 98.8; Marriage status: 15.7% never married, 70.5% now married, 0.0% separated, 6.3% widowed, 7.5% divorced; Foreign born: 0.0%; Speak English only: 96.5%; With disability: 14.0%; Veterans: 7.8%; Ancestry: 30.8% Irish, 20.7% English, 19.3% French, 18.0% Italian, 12.8% German

Employment: 9.6% management, business, and financial, 0.0% computer, engineering, and science, 16.3% education, legal, community service, arts, and media, 12.6% healthcare practitioners, 29.3% service, 23.0% sales and office, 0.4% natural resources, construction, and maintenance, 8.8% production, transportation, and material moving

Income: Per capita: $26,405; Median household: $62,303; Average household: $66,937; Households with income of $100,000 or more: 20.1%; Poverty rate: 14.5%

Educational Attainment: High school diploma or higher: 100.0%; Bachelor's degree or higher: 31.7%; Graduate/professional degree or higher: 24.3%

Housing: Homeownership rate: 96.2%; Median home value: $187,100; Median year structure built: Before 1940; Homeowner vacancy rate: 1.0%; Median selected monthly owner costs: $1,330 with a mortgage, $495 without a mortgage; Median gross rent: n/a per month; Rental vacancy rate: 72.4%

Health Insurance: 99.6% have insurance; 88.5% have private insurance; 48.6% have public insurance; 0.4% do not have insurance; 0.0% of children under 18 do not have insurance

Transportation: Commute: 99.1% car, 0.0% public transportation, 0.0% walk, 0.0% work from home; Mean travel time to work: 26.1 minutes

MALONE (town). Covers a land area of 101.519 square miles and a water area of 1.283 square miles. Located at 44.80° N. Lat; 74.29° W. Long. Elevation is 712 feet.

History: Malone was settled by Vermonters in 1802. The name was bestowed by William Constable, an early landowner, in honor of his friend, Edmund Malone, Shakespearian scholar.

Population: 14,526; Growth (since 2000): -3.0%; Density: 143.1 persons per square mile; Race: 76.3% White, 16.5% Black/African American, 0.4% Asian, 0.5% American Indian/Alaska Native, 0.0% Native Hawaiian/Other Pacific Islander, 1.8% Two or more races, 6.8% Hispanic of any race; Average household size: 2.34; Median age: 36.3; Age under 18: 17.3%; Age 65 and over: 12.1%; Males per 100 females: 175.8; Marriage status: 44.2% never married, 39.9% now married, 4.0% separated, 5.8% widowed, 10.1% divorced; Foreign born: 5.0%; Speak English only: 91.8%; With disability: 16.1%; Veterans: 6.8%; Ancestry: 19.3% French, 16.7% Irish, 6.4% American, 6.2% German, 5.9% English

Employment: 9.8% management, business, and financial, 1.7% computer, engineering, and science, 14.6% education, legal, community service, arts, and media, 6.2% healthcare practitioners, 26.2% service, 23.5% sales and office, 7.7% natural resources, construction, and maintenance, 10.2% production, transportation, and material moving

Income: Per capita: $18,235; Median household: $46,801; Average household: $59,863; Households with income of $100,000 or more: 15.8%; Poverty rate: 24.0%

Educational Attainment: High school diploma or higher: 79.0%; Bachelor's degree or higher: 14.6%; Graduate/professional degree or higher: 7.8%

School District(s)
Franklin-Essex-Hamilton Boces
    Enrollment: n/a . . . . (518) 483-6420
Malone Central SD (PK-12)
    Enrollment: 2,357 . . . . (518) 483-7800

Housing: Homeownership rate: 68.3%; Median home value: $96,100; Median year structure built: 1955; Homeowner vacancy rate: 0.6%; Median selected monthly owner costs: $1,258 with a mortgage, $476 without a mortgage; Median gross rent: $658 per month; Rental vacancy rate: 3.2%

Health Insurance: 96.8% have insurance; 67.4% have private insurance; 48.2% have public insurance; 3.2% do not have insurance; 1.9% of children under 18 do not have insurance

Hospitals: Alice Hyde Medical Center (151 beds)

Newspapers: Malone Telegram (daily circulation 5,600)

Transportation: Commute: 87.2% car, 0.9% public transportation, 4.6% walk, 5.6% work from home; Mean travel time to work: 17.8 minutes

Additional Information Contacts

Town of Malone . . . . (518) 483-4740
    http://www.malonetown.com

MALONE (village). County seat. Covers a land area of 3.111 square miles and a water area of 0.066 square miles. Located at 44.85° N. Lat; 74.29° W. Long. Elevation is 712 feet.

History: Was gathering point for the Fenians, who raided Canada in 1866. Settled c.1800, Incorporated 1833.

Population: 5,752; Growth (since 2000): -5.3%; Density: 1,849.1 persons per square mile; Race: 97.3% White, 0.3% Black/African American, 0.0% Asian, 0.4% American Indian/Alaska Native, 0.0% Native Hawaiian/Other Pacific Islander, 1.8% Two or more races, 2.3% Hispanic of any race; Average household size: 2.20; Median age: 41.3; Age under 18: 21.3%; Age 65 and over: 17.1%; Males per 100 females: 85.0; Marriage status: 34.2% never married, 42.8% now married, 4.8% separated, 8.4% widowed, 14.6% divorced; Foreign born: 1.6%; Speak English only: 98.0%;

With disability: 18.9%; Veterans: 8.7%; Ancestry: 20.7% French, 16.5% Irish, 9.5% English, 8.0% American, 7.8% German

Employment: 7.6% management, business, and financial, 1.5% computer, engineering, and science, 13.8% education, legal, community service, arts, and media, 5.2% healthcare practitioners, 28.1% service, 22.1% sales and office, 6.2% natural resources, construction, and maintenance, 15.5% production, transportation, and material moving

Income: Per capita: $23,428; Median household: $36,621; Average household: $52,746; Households with income of $100,000 or more: 14.3%; Poverty rate: 32.3%

Educational Attainment: High school diploma or higher: 81.3%; Bachelor's degree or higher: 20.8%; Graduate/professional degree or higher: 9.4%

School District(s)
Franklin-Essex-Hamilton Boces
    Enrollment: n/a . . . . (518) 483-6420
Malone Central SD (PK-12)
    Enrollment: 2,357 . . . . (518) 483-7800

Housing: Homeownership rate: 53.1%; Median home value: $82,200; Median year structure built: 1941; Homeowner vacancy rate: 0.0%; Median selected monthly owner costs: $1,052 with a mortgage, $540 without a mortgage; Median gross rent: $674 per month; Rental vacancy rate: 0.0%

Health Insurance: 97.2% have insurance; 61.2% have private insurance; 57.0% have public insurance; 2.8% do not have insurance; 0.0% of children under 18 do not have insurance

Hospitals: Alice Hyde Medical Center (151 beds)

Safety: Violent crime rate: 47.8 per 10,000 population; Property crime rate: 238.9 per 10,000 population

Newspapers: Malone Telegram (daily circulation 5,600)

Transportation: Commute: 82.8% car, 1.7% public transportation, 8.1% walk, 4.4% work from home; Mean travel time to work: 16.8 minutes

Additional Information Contacts
Village of Malone. . . . . (518) 483-4570
    http://www.malonevillage.com

MOIRA (town). Covers a land area of 45.228 square miles and a water area of 0 square miles. Located at 44.83° N. Lat; 74.56° W. Long. Elevation is 420 feet.

Population: 2,861; Growth (since 2000): 0.1%; Density: 63.3 persons per square mile; Race: 97.9% White, 0.3% Black/African American, 0.0% Asian, 0.3% American Indian/Alaska Native, 0.0% Native Hawaiian/Other Pacific Islander, 0.7% Two or more races, 0.4% Hispanic of any race; Average household size: 2.42; Median age: 44.4; Age under 18: 18.2%; Age 65 and over: 21.7%; Males per 100 females: 96.5; Marriage status: 26.1% never married, 57.5% now married, 2.3% separated, 6.1% widowed, 10.3% divorced; Foreign born: 2.2%; Speak English only: 97.9%; With disability: 16.4%; Veterans: 8.6%; Ancestry: 21.3% Irish, 20.0% French, 12.0% German, 11.6% English, 9.3% French Canadian

Employment: 5.7% management, business, and financial, 1.5% computer, engineering, and science, 12.8% education, legal, community service, arts, and media, 6.7% healthcare practitioners, 30.9% service, 23.1% sales and office, 5.0% natural resources, construction, and maintenance, 14.3% production, transportation, and material moving

Income: Per capita: $29,983; Median household: $53,750; Average household: $72,334; Households with income of $100,000 or more: 15.8%; Poverty rate: 24.9%

Educational Attainment: High school diploma or higher: 85.8%; Bachelor's degree or higher: 14.8%; Graduate/professional degree or higher: 6.8%

Housing: Homeownership rate: 75.4%; Median home value: $90,400; Median year structure built: 1969; Homeowner vacancy rate: 0.0%; Median selected monthly owner costs: $1,129 with a mortgage, $396 without a mortgage; Median gross rent: $712 per month; Rental vacancy rate: 2.3%

Health Insurance: 93.0% have insurance; 67.3% have private insurance; 49.2% have public insurance; 7.0% do not have insurance; 5.8% of children under 18 do not have insurance

Transportation: Commute: 93.4% car, 0.0% public transportation, 0.0% walk, 6.6% work from home; Mean travel time to work: 26.8 minutes

NORTH BANGOR (unincorporated postal area)
ZCTA: 12966
    Covers a land area of 86.158 square miles and a water area of 0.067 square miles. Located at 44.80° N. Lat; 74.42° W. Long. Elevation is 666 feet.

Population: 2,717; Growth (since 2000): -4.2%; Density: 31.5 persons per square mile; Race: 97.4% White, 0.0% Black/African American, 0.0% Asian, 2.3% American Indian/Alaska Native, 0.0% Native Hawaiian/Other Pacific Islander, 0.2% Two or more races, 0.3% Hispanic of any race; Average household size: 2.54; Median age: 37.3; Age under 18: 22.6%; Age 65 and over: 11.7%; Males per 100 females: 105.1; Marriage status: 28.2% never married, 56.7% now married, 4.1% separated, 4.4% widowed, 10.7% divorced; Foreign born: 1.3%; Speak English only: 96.5%; With disability: 16.8%; Veterans: 5.7%; Ancestry: 23.1% French, 11.3% English, 10.4% Irish, 8.1% American, 6.1% French Canadian

Employment: 7.4% management, business, and financial, 2.9% computer, engineering, and science, 10.1% education, legal, community service, arts, and media, 7.2% healthcare practitioners, 30.2% service, 18.6% sales and office, 11.3% natural resources, construction, and maintenance, 12.2% production, transportation, and material moving

Income: Per capita: $21,742; Median household: $47,500; Average household: $54,473; Households with income of $100,000 or more: 11.5%; Poverty rate: 24.4%

Educational Attainment: High school diploma or higher: 87.8%; Bachelor's degree or higher: 10.2%; Graduate/professional degree or higher: 4.8%

Housing: Homeownership rate: 79.4%; Median home value: $72,300; Median year structure built: 1975; Homeowner vacancy rate: 0.0%; Median selected monthly owner costs: $997 with a mortgage, $402 without a mortgage; Median gross rent: $737 per month; Rental vacancy rate: 5.6%

Health Insurance: 90.1% have insurance; 61.4% have private insurance; 46.3% have public insurance; 9.9% do not have insurance; 7.7% of children under 18 do not have insurance

Transportation: Commute: 93.0% car, 1.9% public transportation, 0.1% walk, 5.0% work from home; Mean travel time to work: 22.7 minutes

OWLS HEAD (unincorporated postal area)
ZCTA: 12969
    Covers a land area of 98.651 square miles and a water area of 1.857 square miles. Located at 44.71° N. Lat; 74.10° W. Long. Elevation is 1,532 feet.

Population: 497; Growth (since 2000): -10.3%; Density: 5.0 persons per square mile; Race: 95.2% White, 0.0% Black/African American, 0.0% Asian, 1.2% American Indian/Alaska Native, 0.0% Native Hawaiian/Other Pacific Islander, 3.6% Two or more races, 2.0% Hispanic of any race; Average household size: 2.13; Median age: 49.1; Age under 18: 22.5%; Age 65 and over: 27.2%; Males per 100 females: 119.2; Marriage status: 26.2% never married, 54.6% now married, 0.7% separated, 5.7% widowed, 13.5% divorced; Foreign born: 2.8%; Speak English only: 95.0%; With disability: 9.7%; Veterans: 14.8%; Ancestry: 36.8% Irish, 35.6% French, 15.3% English, 9.5% French Canadian, 8.0% German

Employment: 14.3% management, business, and financial, 0.0% computer, engineering, and science, 8.1% education, legal, community service, arts, and media, 5.6% healthcare practitioners, 31.7% service, 23.6% sales and office, 11.8% natural resources, construction, and maintenance, 5.0% production, transportation, and material moving

Income: Per capita: $23,927; Median household: $41,058; Average household: $52,242; Households with income of $100,000 or more: 8.2%; Poverty rate: 20.1%

Educational Attainment: High school diploma or higher: 92.8%; Bachelor's degree or higher: 19.8%; Graduate/professional degree or higher: 9.4%

Housing: Homeownership rate: 96.6%; Median home value: $86,100; Median year structure built: 1957; Homeowner vacancy rate: 0.0%; Median selected monthly owner costs: $1,083 with a mortgage, $353 without a mortgage; Median gross rent: n/a per month; Rental vacancy rate: 0.0%

Health Insurance: 94.6% have insurance; 62.2% have private insurance; 61.8% have public insurance; 5.4% do not have insurance; 4.3% of children under 18 do not have insurance

Transportation: Commute: 93.5% car, 0.0% public transportation, 0.0% walk, 6.5% work from home; Mean travel time to work: 31.2 minutes

PAUL SMITHS (CDP).
Covers a land area of 0.255 square miles and a water area of 0.135 square miles. Located at 44.43° N. Lat; 74.25° W. Long. Elevation is 1,673 feet.

Population: 653; Growth (since 2000): n/a; Density: 2,558.3 persons per square mile; Race: 87.4% White, 7.8% Black/African American, 1.4% Asian, 1.7% American Indian/Alaska Native, 0.0% Native Hawaiian/Other Pacific Islander, 0.3% Two or more races, 1.4% Hispanic of any race; Average household size: 0.00; Median age: 19.5; Age under 18: 0.0%; Age 65 and over: 0.0%; Males per 100 females: 238.9; Marriage status: 99.4% never married, 0.6% now married, 0.0% separated, 0.0% widowed, 0.0% divorced; Foreign born: 0.0%; Speak English only: 91.1%; With disability: 10.9%; Veterans: 0.0%; Ancestry: 14.2% Irish, 13.5% Italian, 10.0% German, 6.3% French, 4.7% French Canadian

Employment: 6.4% management, business, and financial, 6.1% computer, engineering, and science, 11.7% education, legal, community service, arts, and media, 0.0% healthcare practitioners, 40.1% service, 25.1% sales and office, 7.3% natural resources, construction, and maintenance, 3.2% production, transportation, and material moving

Income: Per capita: $5,565; Median household: n/a; Average household: n/a; Households with income of $100,000 or more: n/a; Poverty rate: n/a

Educational Attainment: High school diploma or higher: n/a; Bachelor's degree or higher: n/a; Graduate/professional degree or higher: n/a

Four-year College(s)
Paul Smiths College of Arts and Science (Private, Not-for-profit)
Enrollment: 771 . . . . (518) 327-6000
Tuition: In-state $27,621; Out-of-state $27,621

Housing: Homeownership rate: n/a; Median home value: n/a; Median year structure built: n/a; Homeowner vacancy rate: 0.0%; Median selected monthly owner costs: n/a with a mortgage, n/a without a mortgage; Median gross rent: n/a per month; Rental vacancy rate: 0.0%

Health Insurance: 95.4% have insurance; 90.2% have private insurance; 7.2% have public insurance; 4.6% do not have insurance; 6.8% of children under 18 do not have insurance

Transportation: Commute: 35.4% car, 0.0% public transportation, 45.2% walk, 19.4% work from home; Mean travel time to work: 16.9 minutes

RAINBOW LAKE (unincorporated postal area)
ZCTA: 12976

Covers a land area of 38.370 square miles and a water area of 1.198 square miles. Located at 44.52° N. Lat; 74.21° W. Long. Elevation is 1,690 feet.

Population: 213; Growth (since 2000): n/a; Density: 5.6 persons per square mile; Race: 98.1% White, 0.0% Black/African American, 0.0% Asian, 0.0% American Indian/Alaska Native, 1.4% Native Hawaiian/Other Pacific Islander, 0.5% Two or more races, 1.4% Hispanic of any race; Average household size: 2.09; Median age: 51.9; Age under 18: 7.5%; Age 65 and over: 20.7%; Males per 100 females: 100.0; Marriage status: 35.5% never married, 58.1% now married, 2.5% separated, 2.0% widowed, 4.4% divorced; Foreign born: 3.3%; Speak English only: 97.6%; With disability: 13.1%; Veterans: 2.0%; Ancestry: 23.0% English, 20.7% Italian, 19.2% German, 11.3% Irish, 10.3% French

Employment: 30.7% management, business, and financial, 1.8% computer, engineering, and science, 17.5% education, legal, community service, arts, and media, 8.8% healthcare practitioners, 7.0% service, 19.3% sales and office, 11.4% natural resources, construction, and maintenance, 3.5% production, transportation, and material moving

Income: Per capita: $38,664; Median household: $68,750; Average household: $80,592; Households with income of $100,000 or more: 32.4%; Poverty rate: 16.1%

Educational Attainment: High school diploma or higher: 100.0%; Bachelor's degree or higher: 56.6%; Graduate/professional degree or higher: 27.7%

Housing: Homeownership rate: 91.2%; Median home value: $213,500; Median year structure built: 1975; Homeowner vacancy rate: 2.1%; Median selected monthly owner costs: $1,455 with a mortgage, $621 without a mortgage; Median gross rent: n/a per month; Rental vacancy rate: 0.0%

Health Insurance: 95.3% have insurance; 87.3% have private insurance; 26.8% have public insurance; 4.7% do not have insurance; 0.0% of children under 18 do not have insurance

Transportation: Commute: 68.4% car, 1.8% public transportation, 1.8% walk, 28.1% work from home; Mean travel time to work: 20.3 minutes

SAINT REGIS FALLS (CDP).
Covers a land area of 1.292 square miles and a water area of 0 square miles. Located at 44.68° N. Lat; 74.53° W. Long. Elevation is 1,266 feet.

Population: 462; Growth (since 2000): n/a; Density: 357.7 persons per square mile; Race: 100.0% White, 0.0% Black/African American, 0.0% Asian, 0.0% American Indian/Alaska Native, 0.0% Native Hawaiian/Other Pacific Islander, 0.0% Two or more races, 4.5% Hispanic of any race; Average household size: 2.50; Median age: 40.4; Age under 18: 22.7%; Age 65 and over: 12.1%; Males per 100 females: 89.4; Marriage status: 41.2% never married, 36.1% now married, 2.4% separated, 8.6% widowed, 14.2% divorced; Foreign born: 0.9%; Speak English only: 96.7%; With disability: 18.6%; Veterans: 11.5%; Ancestry: 23.2% French, 19.3% German, 18.4% English, 8.9% Irish, 8.7% Scottish

Employment: 9.6% management, business, and financial, 0.0% computer, engineering, and science, 1.8% education, legal, community service, arts, and media, 1.8% healthcare practitioners, 37.3% service, 18.1% sales and office, 28.9% natural resources, construction, and maintenance, 2.4% production, transportation, and material moving

Income: Per capita: $19,627; Median household: $32,386; Average household: $48,123; Households with income of $100,000 or more: 8.1%; Poverty rate: 33.1%

Educational Attainment: High school diploma or higher: 86.3%; Bachelor's degree or higher: 9.2%; Graduate/professional degree or higher: 2.9%

School District(s)
Saint Regis Falls Central SD (PK-12)
Enrollment: 271 . . . . (518) 856-9421

Housing: Homeownership rate: 80.0%; Median home value: $47,900; Median year structure built: 1942; Homeowner vacancy rate: 6.0%; Median selected monthly owner costs: $832 with a mortgage, $458 without a mortgage; Median gross rent: $816 per month; Rental vacancy rate: 0.0%

Health Insurance: 80.7% have insurance; 33.1% have private insurance; 56.3% have public insurance; 19.3% do not have insurance; 11.6% of children under 18 do not have insurance

Transportation: Commute: 91.0% car, 5.4% public transportation, 2.4% walk, 1.2% work from home; Mean travel time to work: 38.0 minutes

SAINT REGIS MOHAWK RESERVATION (reservation).
Covers a land area of 18.940 square miles and a water area of 2.049 square miles. Located at 44.98° N. Lat; 74.64° W. Long.

Population: 3,292; Growth (since 2000): 22.0%; Density: 173.8 persons per square mile; Race: 5.3% White, 0.1% Black/African American, 1.1% Asian, 81.2% American Indian/Alaska Native, 2.1% Native Hawaiian/Other Pacific Islander, 5.6% Two or more races, 8.2% Hispanic of any race; Average household size: 2.77; Median age: 45.8; Age under 18: 18.1%; Age 65 and over: 14.7%; Males per 100 females: 94.8; Marriage status: 44.5% never married, 33.0% now married, 5.6% separated, 1.7% widowed, 20.8% divorced; Foreign born: 25.2%; Speak English only: 64.7%; With disability: 18.6%; Veterans: 5.7%; Ancestry: 2.5% Greek, 1.7% Polish, 1.6% English, 0.1% Israeli

Employment: 10.2% management, business, and financial, 6.6% computer, engineering, and science, 28.9% education, legal, community service, arts, and media, 3.7% healthcare practitioners, 21.9% service, 0.0% sales and office, 8.5% natural resources, construction, and maintenance, 20.1% production, transportation, and material moving

Income: Per capita: $25,297; Median household: $40,331; Average household: $51,170; Households with income of $100,000 or more: 12.1%; Poverty rate: 19.6%

Educational Attainment: High school diploma or higher: 94.4%; Bachelor's degree or higher: 25.8%; Graduate/professional degree or higher: 19.1%

Housing: Homeownership rate: 77.1%; Median home value: $114,500; Median year structure built: 1990; Homeowner vacancy rate: 0.0%; Median selected monthly owner costs: $941 with a mortgage, $251 without a mortgage; Median gross rent: $446 per month; Rental vacancy rate: 0.0%

Health Insurance: 81.4% have insurance; 59.0% have private insurance; 27.3% have public insurance; 18.6% do not have insurance; 26.7% of children under 18 do not have insurance

Transportation: Commute: 84.9% car, 0.0% public transportation, 0.0% walk, 0.0% work from home; Mean travel time to work: 35.9 minutes

SANTA CLARA (town). Covers a land area of 174.417 square miles and a water area of 17.292 square miles. Located at 44.50° N. Lat; 74.36° W. Long. Elevation is 1,339 feet.

Population: 410; Growth (since 2000): 3.8%; Density: 2.4 persons per square mile; Race: 91.7% White, 6.3% Black/African American, 0.0% Asian, 0.0% American Indian/Alaska Native, 0.0% Native Hawaiian/Other Pacific Islander, 0.0% Two or more races, 2.0% Hispanic of any race; Average household size: 2.11; Median age: 57.8; Age under 18: 6.6%; Age 65 and over: 33.7%; Males per 100 females: 113.0; Marriage status: 20.4% never married, 69.3% now married, 0.3% separated, 3.9% widowed, 6.4% divorced; Foreign born: 1.2%; Speak English only: 98.5%; With disability: 6.7%; Veterans: 11.2%; Ancestry: 24.4% Irish, 22.2% English, 22.2% German, 11.0% French, 6.3% Scottish

Employment: 23.4% management, business, and financial, 4.1% computer, engineering, and science, 20.3% education, legal, community service, arts, and media, 6.6% healthcare practitioners, 16.8% service, 18.3% sales and office, 5.1% natural resources, construction, and maintenance, 5.6% production, transportation, and material moving

Income: Per capita: $42,962; Median household: $85,625; Average household: $100,627; Households with income of $100,000 or more: 33.3%; Poverty rate: 7.0%

Educational Attainment: High school diploma or higher: 95.2%; Bachelor's degree or higher: 54.4%; Graduate/professional degree or higher: 24.8%

Housing: Homeownership rate: 74.7%; Median home value: $283,300; Median year structure built: 1973; Homeowner vacancy rate: 7.3%; Median selected monthly owner costs: $1,750 with a mortgage, $647 without a mortgage; Median gross rent: $1,300 per month; Rental vacancy rate: 2.2%

Health Insurance: 99.0% have insurance; 85.9% have private insurance; 44.0% have public insurance; 1.0% do not have insurance; 0.0% of children under 18 do not have insurance

Transportation: Commute: 77.4% car, 0.0% public transportation, 5.6% walk, 15.4% work from home; Mean travel time to work: 21.7 minutes

SARANAC LAKE (village). Covers a land area of 2.779 square miles and a water area of 0.249 square miles. Located at 44.32° N. Lat; 74.13° W. Long. Elevation is 1,545 feet.

History: The village is named after the nearby Upper, Middle and Lower Saranac Lakes.

Population: 5,670; Growth (since 2000): 12.5%; Density: 2,040.3 persons per square mile; Race: 94.3% White, 3.2% Black/African American, 0.2% Asian, 0.7% American Indian/Alaska Native, 0.0% Native Hawaiian/Other Pacific Islander, 1.0% Two or more races, 0.8% Hispanic of any race; Average household size: 2.16; Median age: 43.6; Age under 18: 19.2%; Age 65 and over: 19.0%; Males per 100 females: 98.1; Marriage status: 36.7% never married, 45.8% now married, 2.9% separated, 6.8% widowed, 10.6% divorced; Foreign born: 1.6%; Speak English only: 98.1%; With disability: 16.0%; Veterans: 9.4%; Ancestry: 26.4% Irish, 13.1% German, 11.8% English, 10.4% French, 7.1% Italian

Employment: 11.7% management, business, and financial, 4.4% computer, engineering, and science, 13.7% education, legal, community service, arts, and media, 9.7% healthcare practitioners, 22.9% service, 24.7% sales and office, 5.2% natural resources, construction, and maintenance, 7.7% production, transportation, and material moving

Income: Per capita: $28,040; Median household: $48,605; Average household: $61,389; Households with income of $100,000 or more: 16.1%; Poverty rate: 18.5%

Educational Attainment: High school diploma or higher: 92.9%; Bachelor's degree or higher: 34.7%; Graduate/professional degree or higher: 16.9%

School District(s)
Saranac Lake Central SD (KG-12)
    Enrollment: 1,192 . . . . (518) 891-5460

Two-year College(s)
North Country Community College (Public)
    Enrollment: 2,006 . . . . (518) 891-2915
    Tuition: In-state $5,614; Out-of-state $11,990

Housing: Homeownership rate: 54.8%; Median home value: $163,100; Median year structure built: Before 1940; Homeowner vacancy rate: 1.4%; Median selected monthly owner costs: $1,435 with a mortgage, $625 without a mortgage; Median gross rent: $714 per month; Rental vacancy rate: 7.7%

Health Insurance: 93.6% have insurance; 63.9% have private insurance; 46.8% have public insurance; 6.4% do not have insurance; 5.3% of children under 18 do not have insurance

Hospitals: Adirondack Medical Center (97 beds)

Safety: Violent crime rate: 30.4 per 10,000 population; Property crime rate: 87.3 per 10,000 population

Newspapers: Adirondack Daily Enterprise (daily circulation 4,100)

Transportation: Commute: 79.6% car, 2.2% public transportation, 10.7% walk, 5.8% work from home; Mean travel time to work: 16.1 minutes

Airports: Adirondack Regional (commercial service–non-primary)

Additional Information Contacts
Village of Saranac Lake . . . . (518) 891-4150
    http://www.saranaclakeny.gov

TUPPER LAKE (town). Covers a land area of 117.348 square miles and a water area of 12.754 square miles. Located at 44.24° N. Lat; 74.47° W. Long. Elevation is 1,598 feet.

Population: 5,860; Growth (since 2000): n/a; Density: 49.9 persons per square mile; Race: 94.6% White, 1.7% Black/African American, 0.5% Asian, 0.1% American Indian/Alaska Native, 0.0% Native Hawaiian/Other Pacific Islander, 1.5% Two or more races, 2.7% Hispanic of any race; Average household size: 2.25; Median age: 42.4; Age under 18: 19.7%; Age 65 and over: 16.8%; Males per 100 females: 111.2; Marriage status: 29.3% never married, 52.4% now married, 2.9% separated, 6.7% widowed, 11.6% divorced; Foreign born: 2.2%; Speak English only: 95.9%; With disability: 14.1%; Veterans: 7.2%; Ancestry: 23.0% Irish, 21.8% French, 16.2% French Canadian, 8.6% German, 8.5% English

Employment: 8.7% management, business, and financial, 1.1% computer, engineering, and science, 11.8% education, legal, community service, arts, and media, 3.8% healthcare practitioners, 34.9% service, 17.9% sales and office, 10.0% natural resources, construction, and maintenance, 11.8% production, transportation, and material moving

Income: Per capita: $27,861; Median household: $54,618; Average household: $65,111; Households with income of $100,000 or more: 18.8%; Poverty rate: 11.0%

Educational Attainment: High school diploma or higher: 87.6%; Bachelor's degree or higher: 19.4%; Graduate/professional degree or higher: 9.2%

School District(s)
Tupper Lake Central SD (PK-12)
    Enrollment: 793 . . . . (518) 359-3371

Housing: Homeownership rate: 69.1%; Median home value: $119,300; Median year structure built: 1955; Homeowner vacancy rate: 3.9%; Median selected monthly owner costs: $1,071 with a mortgage, $470 without a mortgage; Median gross rent: $652 per month; Rental vacancy rate: 5.3%

Health Insurance: 94.4% have insurance; 74.9% have private insurance; 34.8% have public insurance; 5.6% do not have insurance; 5.4% of children under 18 do not have insurance

Newspapers: Free Press & Herald (weekly circulation 4,000)

Transportation: Commute: 90.0% car, 0.1% public transportation, 4.4% walk, 4.9% work from home; Mean travel time to work: 13.8 minutes

TUPPER LAKE (village). Covers a land area of 2.090 square miles and a water area of 0.044 square miles. Located at 44.23° N. Lat; 74.46° W. Long. Elevation is 1,598 feet.

History: Settled 1890, incorporated 1902.

Population: 3,670; Growth (since 2000): -6.7%; Density: 1,755.7 persons per square mile; Race: 95.2% White, 0.5% Black/African American, 0.0% Asian, 0.0% American Indian/Alaska Native, 0.0% Native Hawaiian/Other Pacific Islander, 2.1% Two or more races, 3.1% Hispanic of any race; Average household size: 2.19; Median age: 39.4; Age under 18: 21.2%; Age 65 and over: 14.4%; Males per 100 females: 97.7; Marriage status: 26.4% never married, 55.3% now married, 4.1% separated, 7.4% widowed, 11.0% divorced; Foreign born: 1.5%; Speak English only: 95.7%; With disability: 12.8%; Veterans: 7.7%; Ancestry: 25.2% French, 24.0% Irish, 15.4% French Canadian, 7.9% German, 7.2% English

Employment: 5.5% management, business, and financial, 0.8% computer, engineering, and science, 11.5% education, legal, community service, arts, and media, 4.0% healthcare practitioners, 36.9% service, 17.0% sales and office, 10.5% natural resources, construction, and maintenance, 13.9% production, transportation, and material moving

Income: Per capita: $27,930; Median household: $52,775; Average household: $60,593; Households with income of $100,000 or more: 17.2%; Poverty rate: 11.7%

Educational Attainment: High school diploma or higher: 88.7%; Bachelor's degree or higher: 14.4%; Graduate/professional degree or higher: 6.5%

School District(s)
Tupper Lake Central SD (PK-12)
    Enrollment: 793 . . . . (518) 359-3371
Housing: Homeownership rate: 62.7%; Median home value: $95,600; Median year structure built: 1946; Homeowner vacancy rate: 6.1%; Median selected monthly owner costs: $974 with a mortgage, $442 without a mortgage; Median gross rent: $620 per month; Rental vacancy rate: 6.4%
Health Insurance: 93.4% have insurance; 73.4% have private insurance; 34.2% have public insurance; 6.6% do not have insurance; 5.7% of children under 18 do not have insurance
Safety: Violent crime rate: 14.2 per 10,000 population; Property crime rate: 249.9 per 10,000 population
Newspapers: Free Press & Herald (weekly circulation 4,000)
Transportation: Commute: 90.9% car, 0.1% public transportation, 4.3% walk, 4.7% work from home; Mean travel time to work: 13.1 minutes

VERMONTVILLE (unincorporated postal area)
ZCTA: 12989
    Covers a land area of 147.752 square miles and a water area of 2.814 square miles. Located at 44.52° N. Lat; 74.07° W. Long. Elevation is 1,644 feet.
Population: 945; Growth (since 2000): 10.8%; Density: 6.4 persons per square mile; Race: 93.1% White, 0.0% Black/African American, 4.3% Asian, 0.0% American Indian/Alaska Native, 0.7% Native Hawaiian/Other Pacific Islander, 1.8% Two or more races, 1.0% Hispanic of any race; Average household size: 2.18; Median age: 52.3; Age under 18: 16.4%; Age 65 and over: 24.0%; Males per 100 females: 103.6; Marriage status: 19.6% never married, 64.2% now married, 3.1% separated, 6.4% widowed, 9.8% divorced; Foreign born: 6.0%; Speak English only: 95.0%; With disability: 10.5%; Veterans: 15.4%; Ancestry: 19.7% Irish, 18.5% German, 13.3% French, 9.0% English, 7.2% French Canadian
Employment: 13.3% management, business, and financial, 1.7% computer, engineering, and science, 17.1% education, legal, community service, arts, and media, 7.6% healthcare practitioners, 23.7% service, 24.7% sales and office, 8.9% natural resources, construction, and maintenance, 3.0% production, transportation, and material moving
Income: Per capita: $33,711; Median household: $66,167; Average household: $73,460; Households with income of $100,000 or more: 30.6%; Poverty rate: 10.6%
Educational Attainment: High school diploma or higher: 93.4%; Bachelor's degree or higher: 35.2%; Graduate/professional degree or higher: 16.5%
Housing: Homeownership rate: 86.6%; Median home value: $175,600; Median year structure built: 1972; Homeowner vacancy rate: 1.3%; Median selected monthly owner costs: $1,349 with a mortgage, $485 without a mortgage; Median gross rent: $825 per month; Rental vacancy rate: 0.0%
Health Insurance: 97.4% have insurance; 84.4% have private insurance; 35.6% have public insurance; 2.6% do not have insurance; 1.3% of children under 18 do not have insurance
Transportation: Commute: 94.8% car, 1.1% public transportation, 0.6% walk, 3.5% work from home; Mean travel time to work: 27.9 minutes

WAVERLY (town). Covers a land area of 125.112 square miles and a water area of 1.294 square miles. Located at 44.53° N. Lat; 74.55° W. Long.
Population: 920; Growth (since 2000): -17.7%; Density: 7.4 persons per square mile; Race: 100.0% White, 0.0% Black/African American, 0.0% Asian, 0.0% American Indian/Alaska Native, 0.0% Native Hawaiian/Other Pacific Islander, 0.0% Two or more races, 2.3% Hispanic of any race; Average household size: 2.23; Median age: 45.3; Age under 18: 18.8%; Age 65 and over: 18.7%; Males per 100 females: 92.5; Marriage status: 32.1% never married, 47.7% now married, 4.6% separated, 8.5% widowed, 11.7% divorced; Foreign born: 1.8%; Speak English only: 98.4%; With disability: 24.7%; Veterans: 12.6%; Ancestry: 22.3% French, 16.0% Irish, 13.6% German, 12.0% English, 5.5% French Canadian
Employment: 5.6% management, business, and financial, 0.0% computer, engineering, and science, 1.7% education, legal, community service, arts, and media, 4.8% healthcare practitioners, 33.1% service, 22.9% sales and office, 21.5% natural resources, construction, and maintenance, 10.5% production, transportation, and material moving

Income: Per capita: $21,998; Median household: $41,705; Average household: $48,889; Households with income of $100,000 or more: 11.4%; Poverty rate: 26.7%
Educational Attainment: High school diploma or higher: 83.2%; Bachelor's degree or higher: 7.6%; Graduate/professional degree or higher: 1.7%
Housing: Homeownership rate: 83.3%; Median home value: $60,600; Median year structure built: 1970; Homeowner vacancy rate: 4.0%; Median selected monthly owner costs: $1,042 with a mortgage, $404 without a mortgage; Median gross rent: $632 per month; Rental vacancy rate: 0.0%
Health Insurance: 85.4% have insurance; 50.3% have private insurance; 50.1% have public insurance; 14.6% do not have insurance; 10.9% of children under 18 do not have insurance
Transportation: Commute: 92.3% car, 2.6% public transportation, 2.3% walk, 2.8% work from home; Mean travel time to work: 30.2 minutes

WESTVILLE (town). Covers a land area of 34.798 square miles and a water area of 0.014 square miles. Located at 44.94° N. Lat; 74.38° W. Long. Elevation is 200 feet.
Population: 1,698; Growth (since 2000): -6.9%; Density: 48.8 persons per square mile; Race: 97.9% White, 0.4% Black/African American, 0.3% Asian, 0.6% American Indian/Alaska Native, 0.0% Native Hawaiian/Other Pacific Islander, 0.2% Two or more races, 2.7% Hispanic of any race; Average household size: 2.26; Median age: 47.9; Age under 18: 15.2%; Age 65 and over: 17.9%; Males per 100 females: 106.7; Marriage status: 26.8% never married, 52.0% now married, 4.0% separated, 6.9% widowed, 14.3% divorced; Foreign born: 3.0%; Speak English only: 93.6%; With disability: 21.8%; Veterans: 12.4%; Ancestry: 18.4% French, 15.8% Irish, 10.1% English, 7.2% American, 6.4% French Canadian
Employment: 5.5% management, business, and financial, 1.4% computer, engineering, and science, 8.1% education, legal, community service, arts, and media, 4.7% healthcare practitioners, 30.7% service, 21.9% sales and office, 11.5% natural resources, construction, and maintenance, 16.3% production, transportation, and material moving
Income: Per capita: $24,941; Median household: $48,958; Average household: $56,384; Households with income of $100,000 or more: 10.7%; Poverty rate: 14.0%
Educational Attainment: High school diploma or higher: 85.5%; Bachelor's degree or higher: 7.9%; Graduate/professional degree or higher: 2.1%
Housing: Homeownership rate: 75.5%; Median home value: $78,800; Median year structure built: 1981; Homeowner vacancy rate: 0.0%; Median selected monthly owner costs: $945 with a mortgage, $361 without a mortgage; Median gross rent: $693 per month; Rental vacancy rate: 0.0%
Health Insurance: 93.5% have insurance; 68.3% have private insurance; 45.9% have public insurance; 6.5% do not have insurance; 9.9% of children under 18 do not have insurance
Transportation: Commute: 94.1% car, 0.5% public transportation, 1.1% walk, 3.3% work from home; Mean travel time to work: 18.9 minutes

Fulton County

Located in east central New York, in the Adirondacks; drained by East Canada Creek and the Sacandaga River; includes several lakes. Covers a land area of 495.469 square miles, a water area of 37.411 square miles, and is located in the Eastern Time Zone at 43.12° N. Lat., 74.42° W. Long. The county was founded in 1838. County seat is Johnstown.

Fulton County is part of the Gloversville, NY Micropolitan Statistical Area. The entire metro area includes: Fulton County, NY

Weather Station: Gloversville | | | | | | | | | | Elevation: 898 feet
	Jan	Feb	Mar	Apr	May	Jun	Jul	Aug	Sep	Oct	Nov	Dec
High	29	32	41	56	68	76	80	79	71	58	46	33
Low	10	12	21	33	44	54	59	57	49	36	29	17
Precip	3.1	2.7	3.5	4.1	4.3	4.3	4.2	4.5	3.9	4.1	3.4	3.4
Snow	20.9	14.2	14.6	1.6	tr	0.0	0.0	0.0	0.0	0.1	4.3	17.0

High and Low temperatures in degrees Fahrenheit; Precipitation and Snow in inches

Population: 53,955; Growth (since 2000): -2.0%; Density: 108.9 persons per square mile; Race: 94.7% White, 1.8% Black/African American, 0.7% Asian, 0.3% American Indian/Alaska Native, 0.0% Native Hawaiian/Other Pacific Islander, 1.5% two or more races, 2.8% Hispanic of any race; Average household size: 2.34; Median age: 43.4; Age under 18: 20.6%; Age 65 and over: 18.2%; Males per 100 females: 97.9; Marriage status: 28.2% never married, 52.5% now married, 3.3% separated, 8.1%

widowed, 11.2% divorced; Foreign born: 2.0%; Speak English only: 96.7%; With disability: 16.2%; Veterans: 8.7%; Ancestry: 18.3% German, 17.8% American, 16.0% Italian, 15.7% Irish, 9.7% English

Religion: Six largest groups: 14.3% Catholicism, 5.1% Methodist/Pietist, 1.9% Presbyterian-Reformed, 1.4% Non-denominational Protestant, 0.8% Latter-day Saints, 0.7% Episcopalianism/Anglicanism

Economy: Unemployment rate: 4.2%; Leading industries: 17.8 % retail trade; 15.6 % health care and social assistance; 11.7 % construction; Farms: 211 totaling 31,869 acres; Company size: 0 employ 1,000 or more persons, 2 employ 500 to 999 persons, 21 employs 100 to 499 persons, 1,171 employs less than 100 persons; Business ownership: 1,291 women-owned, n/a Black-owned, n/a Hispanic-owned, n/a Asian-owned, n/a American Indian/Alaska Native-owned

Employment: 11.5% management, business, and financial, 3.3% computer, engineering, and science, 10.0% education, legal, community service, arts, and media, 5.9% healthcare practitioners, 20.5% service, 23.3% sales and office, 9.5% natural resources, construction, and maintenance, 16.1% production, transportation, and material moving

Income: Per capita: $26,298; Median household: $48,033; Average household: $61,941; Households with income of $100,000 or more: 18.2%; Poverty rate: 16.0%

Educational Attainment: High school diploma or higher: 87.0%; Bachelor's degree or higher: 17.7%; Graduate/professional degree or higher: 7.9%

Housing: Homeownership rate: 71.4%; Median home value: $107,600; Median year structure built: 1954; Homeowner vacancy rate: 2.3%; Median selected monthly owner costs: $1,134 with a mortgage, $483 without a mortgage; Median gross rent: $734 per month; Rental vacancy rate: 4.7%

Vital Statistics: Birth rate: 95.0 per 10,000 population; Death rate: 106.5 per 10,000 population; Age-adjusted cancer mortality rate: 156.8 deaths per 100,000 population

Health Insurance: 92.8% have insurance; 65.1% have private insurance; 44.0% have public insurance; 7.2% do not have insurance; 5.4% of children under 18 do not have insurance

Health Care: Physicians: 8.8 per 10,000 population; Dentists: 2.8 per 10,000 population; Hospital beds: 29.4 per 10,000 population; Hospital admissions: 429.6 per 10,000 population

Transportation: Commute: 92.5% car, 0.6% public transportation, 2.7% walk, 2.1% work from home; Mean travel time to work: 25.0 minutes

2016 Presidential Election: 63.5% Trump, 30.6% Clinton, 3.7% Johnson, 1.5% Stein

National and State Parks: Adirondack State Park; Sir William Johnson State Park

Additional Information Contacts

Fulton Government . . . . (518) 725-0641
  http://www.fultoncountyny.gov

Fulton County Communities

BLEECKER (town). Covers a land area of 57.127 square miles and a water area of 2.285 square miles. Located at 43.17° N. Lat; 74.38° W. Long. Elevation is 1,503 feet.

Population: 678; Growth (since 2000): 18.3%; Density: 11.9 persons per square mile; Race: 98.7% White, 0.0% Black/African American, 0.0% Asian, 0.0% American Indian/Alaska Native, 0.0% Native Hawaiian/Other Pacific Islander, 1.3% Two or more races, 0.0% Hispanic of any race; Average household size: 2.25; Median age: 52.1; Age under 18: 17.3%; Age 65 and over: 25.1%; Males per 100 females: 109.8; Marriage status: 19.7% never married, 63.0% now married, 3.7% separated, 8.5% widowed, 8.8% divorced; Foreign born: 0.7%; Speak English only: 98.6%; With disability: 17.6%; Veterans: 11.9%; Ancestry: 21.5% American, 14.5% German, 12.2% Irish, 8.6% Italian, 7.4% English

Employment: 16.4% management, business, and financial, 0.7% computer, engineering, and science, 16.7% education, legal, community service, arts, and media, 2.1% healthcare practitioners, 11.4% service, 22.1% sales and office, 11.4% natural resources, construction, and maintenance, 19.2% production, transportation, and material moving

Income: Per capita: $28,631; Median household: $50,625; Average household: $66,180; Households with income of $100,000 or more: 19.7%; Poverty rate: 6.7%

Educational Attainment: High school diploma or higher: 83.3%; Bachelor's degree or higher: 24.4%; Graduate/professional degree or higher: 14.3%

Housing: Homeownership rate: 77.7%; Median home value: $140,800; Median year structure built: 1976; Homeowner vacancy rate: 0.0%; Median

selected monthly owner costs: $1,411 with a mortgage, $547 without a mortgage; Median gross rent: $813 per month; Rental vacancy rate: 0.0%

Health Insurance: 93.1% have insurance; 65.0% have private insurance; 47.8% have public insurance; 6.9% do not have insurance; 0.0% of children under 18 do not have insurance

Transportation: Commute: 98.9% car, 0.0% public transportation, 0.0% walk, 1.1% work from home; Mean travel time to work: 32.3 minutes

BROADALBIN (town). Covers a land area of 31.722 square miles and a water area of 8.059 square miles. Located at 43.08° N. Lat; 74.15° W. Long. Elevation is 804 feet.

History: Settled 1770, incorporated 1924.

Population: 5,166; Growth (since 2000): 2.0%; Density: 162.9 persons per square mile; Race: 98.3% White, 0.8% Black/African American, 0.3% Asian, 0.0% American Indian/Alaska Native, 0.0% Native Hawaiian/Other Pacific Islander, 0.2% Two or more races, 1.4% Hispanic of any race; Average household size: 2.36; Median age: 42.8; Age under 18: 19.6%; Age 65 and over: 15.6%; Males per 100 females: 98.1; Marriage status: 23.6% never married, 56.7% now married, 1.9% separated, 7.8% widowed, 11.8% divorced; Foreign born: 1.5%; Speak English only: 97.6%; With disability: 9.9%; Veterans: 10.8%; Ancestry: 21.8% Irish, 18.7% American, 17.1% German, 16.4% Italian, 10.1% Polish

Employment: 9.9% management, business, and financial, 8.2% computer, engineering, and science, 10.4% education, legal, community service, arts, and media, 9.3% healthcare practitioners, 19.2% service, 19.6% sales and office, 11.4% natural resources, construction, and maintenance, 12.1% production, transportation, and material moving

Income: Per capita: $32,101; Median household: $67,617; Average household: $75,803; Households with income of $100,000 or more: 26.5%; Poverty rate: 7.0%

Educational Attainment: High school diploma or higher: 94.8%; Bachelor's degree or higher: 17.9%; Graduate/professional degree or higher: 5.8%

School District(s)

Broadalbin-Perth Central SD (PK-12)
  Enrollment: 1,826 . . . . (518) 954-2500

Housing: Homeownership rate: 85.4%; Median home value: $157,300; Median year structure built: 1974; Homeowner vacancy rate: 0.4%; Median selected monthly owner costs: $1,292 with a mortgage, $493 without a mortgage; Median gross rent: $801 per month; Rental vacancy rate: 5.9%

Health Insurance: 94.5% have insurance; 78.8% have private insurance; 28.8% have public insurance; 5.5% do not have insurance; 1.6% of children under 18 do not have insurance

Transportation: Commute: 97.7% car, 1.0% public transportation, 0.1% walk, 1.0% work from home; Mean travel time to work: 26.9 minutes

Additional Information Contacts

Town of Broadalbin . . . . (518) 883-4657
  http://www.townofbroadalbin.org

BROADALBIN (village). Covers a land area of 1.122 square miles and a water area of 0.004 square miles. Located at 43.06° N. Lat; 74.20° W. Long. Elevation is 804 feet.

Population: 1,388; Growth (since 2000): -1.6%; Density: 1,237.6 persons per square mile; Race: 96.5% White, 1.5% Black/African American, 0.0% Asian, 0.0% American Indian/Alaska Native, 0.0% Native Hawaiian/Other Pacific Islander, 0.3% Two or more races, 2.4% Hispanic of any race; Average household size: 2.40; Median age: 36.6; Age under 18: 24.3%; Age 65 and over: 14.5%; Males per 100 females: 92.3; Marriage status: 35.8% never married, 38.8% now married, 1.1% separated, 10.2% widowed, 15.3% divorced; Foreign born: 1.6%; Speak English only: 96.8%; With disability: 6.7%; Veterans: 6.3%; Ancestry: 22.8% Irish, 17.4% German, 17.4% Italian, 15.9% American, 8.4% English

Employment: 9.8% management, business, and financial, 1.9% computer, engineering, and science, 10.8% education, legal, community service, arts, and media, 9.8% healthcare practitioners, 23.1% service, 18.6% sales and office, 14.4% natural resources, construction, and maintenance, 11.6% production, transportation, and material moving

Income: Per capita: $27,478; Median household: $58,654; Average household: $64,684; Households with income of $100,000 or more: 18.3%; Poverty rate: 11.5%

Educational Attainment: High school diploma or higher: 92.8%; Bachelor's degree or higher: 18.1%; Graduate/professional degree or higher: 4.5%

Broadalbin-Perth Central SD (PK-12)
    Enrollment: 1,826 . . . . (518) 954-2500
Housing: Homeownership rate: 61.4%; Median home value: $118,200;
Median year structure built: 1940; Homeowner vacancy rate: 2.1%; Median
selected monthly owner costs: $1,329 with a mortgage, $495 without a
mortgage; Median gross rent: $771 per month; Rental vacancy rate: 8.2%
Health Insurance: 90.5% have insurance; 72.1% have private insurance;
29.7% have public insurance; 9.5% do not have insurance; 5.0% of
children under 18 do not have insurance
Transportation: Commute: 97.4% car, 0.8% public transportation, 0.8%
walk, 0.4% work from home; Mean travel time to work: 26.3 minutes

CAROGA (town). Covers a land area of 50.627 square miles and a
water area of 3.651 square miles. Located at 43.12° N. Lat; 74.53° W.
Long.
Population: 1,206; Growth (since 2000): -14.3%; Density: 23.8 persons
per square mile; Race: 89.1% White, 0.0% Black/African American, 4.4%
Asian, 2.2% American Indian/Alaska Native, 0.0% Native Hawaiian/Other
Pacific Islander, 4.4% Two or more races, 0.0% Hispanic of any race;
Average household size: 2.19; Median age: 54.6; Age under 18: 13.3%;
Age 65 and over: 28.1%; Males per 100 females: 113.3; Marriage status:
14.2% never married, 69.4% now married, 1.6% separated, 5.4%
widowed, 11.1% divorced; Foreign born: 3.2%; Speak English only: 94.2%;
With disability: 11.1%; Veterans: 15.6%; Ancestry: 26.0% American, 15.5%
German, 13.3% Irish, 12.4% Italian, 7.8% English
Employment: 12.6% management, business, and financial, 7.7%
computer, engineering, and science, 15.7% education, legal, community
service, arts, and media, 2.4% healthcare practitioners, 15.2% service,
19.7% sales and office, 14.1% natural resources, construction, and
maintenance, 12.6% production, transportation, and material moving
Income: Per capita: $30,681; Median household: $48,798; Average
household: $66,389; Households with income of $100,000 or more: 21.3%;
Poverty rate: 6.4%
Educational Attainment: High school diploma or higher: 93.1%;
Bachelor's degree or higher: 22.7%; Graduate/professional degree or
higher: 11.6%
Housing: Homeownership rate: 89.7%; Median home value: $132,900;
Median year structure built: 1952; Homeowner vacancy rate: 3.1%; Median
selected monthly owner costs: $1,150 with a mortgage, $493 without a
mortgage; Median gross rent: $817 per month; Rental vacancy rate: 9.5%
Health Insurance: 93.7% have insurance; 75.0% have private insurance;
46.5% have public insurance; 6.3% do not have insurance; 0.0% of
children under 18 do not have insurance
Transportation: Commute: 91.6% car, 0.0% public transportation, 0.7%
walk, 5.9% work from home; Mean travel time to work: 29.0 minutes

CAROGA LAKE (CDP). Covers a land area of 2.500 square miles
and a water area of 0.873 square miles. Located at 43.13° N. Lat; 74.48°
W. Long. Elevation is 1,480 feet.
Population: 519; Growth (since 2000): n/a; Density: 207.6 persons per
square mile; Race: 88.4% White, 0.0% Black/African American, 0.0%
Asian, 5.0% American Indian/Alaska Native, 0.0% Native Hawaiian/Other
Pacific Islander, 6.6% Two or more races, 0.0% Hispanic of any race;
Average household size: 2.08; Median age: 58.9; Age under 18: 13.1%;
Age 65 and over: 30.3%; Males per 100 females: 112.3; Marriage status:
13.9% never married, 58.4% now married, 1.5% separated, 12.6%
widowed, 15.2% divorced; Foreign born: 1.9%; Speak English only: 98.2%;
With disability: 14.3%; Veterans: 11.5%; Ancestry: 22.0% German, 19.5%
American, 18.5% Irish, 8.1% Italian, 4.8% French
Employment: 9.5% management, business, and financial, 7.0% computer,
engineering, and science, 20.2% education, legal, community service, arts,
and media, 5.8% healthcare practitioners, 13.2% service, 12.8% sales and
office, 9.5% natural resources, construction, and maintenance, 22.2%
production, transportation, and material moving
Income: Per capita: $33,091; Median household: $47,228; Average
household: $67,144; Households with income of $100,000 or more: 24.5%;
Poverty rate: 8.9%
Educational Attainment: High school diploma or higher: 98.6%;
Bachelor's degree or higher: 32.1%; Graduate/professional degree or
higher: 16.7%

Wheelerville Union Free SD (PK-08)
    Enrollment: 133 . . . . (518) 835-2171

Housing: Homeownership rate: 88.8%; Median home value: $133,500;
Median year structure built: 1951; Homeowner vacancy rate: 3.4%; Median
selected monthly owner costs: $1,375 with a mortgage, $527 without a
mortgage; Median gross rent: $756 per month; Rental vacancy rate: 20.0%
Health Insurance: 93.4% have insurance; 76.5% have private insurance;
48.9% have public insurance; 6.6% do not have insurance; 0.0% of
children under 18 do not have insurance
Transportation: Commute: 89.7% car, 0.0% public transportation, 0.0%
walk, 6.2% work from home; Mean travel time to work: 27.6 minutes

EPHRATAH (town). Covers a land area of 39.170 square miles and a
water area of 0.277 square miles. Located at 43.04° N. Lat; 74.56° W.
Long. Elevation is 682 feet.
Population: 1,528; Growth (since 2000): -9.7%; Density: 39.0 persons per
square mile; Race: 97.8% White, 0.9% Black/African American, 0.2%
Asian, 0.0% American Indian/Alaska Native, 0.0% Native Hawaiian/Other
Pacific Islander, 1.1% Two or more races, 0.0% Hispanic of any race;
Average household size: 2.37; Median age: 48.6; Age under 18: 16.8%;
Age 65 and over: 18.0%; Males per 100 females: 108.2; Marriage status:
24.3% never married, 57.4% now married, 3.9% separated, 7.4%
widowed, 11.0% divorced; Foreign born: 0.2%; Speak English only: 98.6%;
With disability: 15.3%; Veterans: 10.5%; Ancestry: 26.3% American, 17.1%
German, 13.0% English, 7.7% Irish, 5.1% Italian
Employment: 4.6% management, business, and financial, 2.6% computer,
engineering, and science, 6.8% education, legal, community service, arts,
and media, 4.8% healthcare practitioners, 17.9% service, 23.7% sales and
office, 15.9% natural resources, construction, and maintenance, 23.6%
production, transportation, and material moving
Income: Per capita: $25,252; Median household: $48,125; Average
household: $59,684; Households with income of $100,000 or more: 16.0%;
Poverty rate: 12.0%
Educational Attainment: High school diploma or higher: 81.7%;
Bachelor's degree or higher: 14.5%; Graduate/professional degree or
higher: 4.1%
Housing: Homeownership rate: 88.3%; Median home value: $92,300;
Median year structure built: 1973; Homeowner vacancy rate: 5.7%; Median
selected monthly owner costs: $1,089 with a mortgage, $446 without a
mortgage; Median gross rent: $756 per month; Rental vacancy rate: 0.0%
Health Insurance: 93.7% have insurance; 64.6% have private insurance;
44.9% have public insurance; 6.3% do not have insurance; 4.1% of
children under 18 do not have insurance
Transportation: Commute: 95.3% car, 0.9% public transportation, 0.5%
walk, 2.1% work from home; Mean travel time to work: 36.0 minutes

GLOVERSVILLE (city). Covers a land area of 5.139 square miles
and a water area of 0.009 square miles. Located at 43.05° N. Lat; 74.35°
W. Long. Elevation is 820 feet.
History: Gloversville was named for its outstanding industry. The making
of fine kid gloves became a Fulton County specialty. The beginnings of the
industry in the county have been traced back to the 1760's when Sir
William Johnson brought over as settlers a group of glovers from
Perthshire, Scotland, who made gloves for local sale.
Population: 15,052; Growth (since 2000): -2.3%; Density: 2,928.8 persons
per square mile; Race: 93.3% White, 1.9% Black/African American, 1.0%
Asian, 0.7% American Indian/Alaska Native, 0.0% Native Hawaiian/Other
Pacific Islander, 1.7% Two or more races, 4.5% Hispanic of any race;
Average household size: 2.35; Median age: 40.1; Age under 18: 23.1%;
Age 65 and over: 15.5%; Males per 100 females: 92.5; Marriage status:
34.8% never married, 44.4% now married, 4.2% separated, 8.7%
widowed, 12.2% divorced; Foreign born: 1.9%; Speak English only: 97.1%;
With disability: 19.2%; Veterans: 8.8%; Ancestry: 20.9% American, 17.6%
Italian, 14.0% German, 13.6% Irish, 7.5% English
Employment: 10.2% management, business, and financial, 1.7%
computer, engineering, and science, 8.1% education, legal, community
service, arts, and media, 3.1% healthcare practitioners, 24.6% service,
23.9% sales and office, 8.5% natural resources, construction, and
maintenance, 19.8% production, transportation, and material moving
Income: Per capita: $20,353; Median household: $35,397; Average
household: $47,954; Households with income of $100,000 or more: 10.2%;
Poverty rate: 28.4%
Educational Attainment: High school diploma or higher: 81.7%;
Bachelor's degree or higher: 13.2%; Graduate/professional degree or
higher: 6.2%

School District(s)

Gloversville City SD (PK-12)

Enrollment: 2,877 . . . . (518) 775-5791

Housing: Homeownership rate: 51.0%; Median home value: $77,400; Median year structure built: Before 1940; Homeowner vacancy rate: 5.7%; Median selected monthly owner costs: $992 with a mortgage, $509 without a mortgage; Median gross rent: $699 per month; Rental vacancy rate: 5.2%

Health Insurance: 92.3% have insurance; 50.2% have private insurance; 54.3% have public insurance; 7.7% do not have insurance; 6.7% of children under 18 do not have insurance

Hospitals: Nathan Littauer Hospital (208 beds)

Safety: Violent crime rate: 43.2 per 10,000 population; Property crime rate: 244.1 per 10,000 population

Newspapers: Leader-Herald (daily circulation 10,200)

Transportation: Commute: 88.7% car, 0.5% public transportation, 4.6% walk, 0.9% work from home; Mean travel time to work: 22.5 minutes

Additional Information Contacts

City of Gloversville. . . . . (518) 773-4542
  http://www.cityofgloversville.com

JOHNSTOWN (city). County seat. Covers a land area of 4.875 square miles and a water area of 0.008 square miles. Located at 43.01° N. Lat; 74.38° W. Long. Elevation is 673 feet.

History: Its leather-glove industry dates back to 1800. Notable buildings include the county courthouse (1774) and Fort Johnstown (1771) and the county jail. The last American Revolutionary battle in N.Y. state was fought in Johnstown on Oct. 25, 1781. Elizabeth Cady Stanton born here. Founded 1772, Incorporated 1895.

Population: 8,358; Growth (since 2000): -1.8%; Density: 1,714.4 persons per square mile; Race: 90.6% White, 4.5% Black/African American, 1.0% Asian, 0.0% American Indian/Alaska Native, 0.0% Native Hawaiian/Other Pacific Islander, 2.4% Two or more races, 4.9% Hispanic of any race; Average household size: 2.38; Median age: 38.7; Age under 18: 22.2%; Age 65 and over: 16.5%; Males per 100 females: 89.4; Marriage status: 27.7% never married, 53.9% now married, 3.2% separated, 6.0% widowed, 12.4% divorced; Foreign born: 3.4%; Speak English only: 94.4%; With disability: 17.3%; Veterans: 7.1%; Ancestry: 20.8% German, 19.2% Irish, 17.8% Italian, 12.8% American, 7.3% English

Employment: 15.0% management, business, and financial, 3.8% computer, engineering, and science, 11.0% education, legal, community service, arts, and media, 3.8% healthcare practitioners, 20.6% service, 26.9% sales and office, 4.5% natural resources, construction, and maintenance, 14.3% production, transportation, and material moving

Income: Per capita: $25,991; Median household: $47,071; Average household: $61,235; Households with income of $100,000 or more: 18.4%; Poverty rate: 15.8%

Educational Attainment: High school diploma or higher: 89.5%; Bachelor's degree or higher: 24.4%; Graduate/professional degree or higher: 9.4%

School District(s)

Hamilton-Fulton-Montgomery Boces

Enrollment: n/a . . . . (518) 736-4300

Johnstown City SD (PK-12)

Enrollment: 1,734 . . . . (518) 762-4611

Two-year College(s)

Fulton-Montgomery Community College (Public)

Enrollment: 2,403 . . . . (518) 762-3622
  Tuition: In-state $5,020; Out-of-state $9,470

Vocational/Technical School(s)

Hamilton Fulton Montgomery BOCES-Practical Nursing Program (Public)

Enrollment: n/a . . . . (518) 736-4305

Housing: Homeownership rate: 60.9%; Median home value: $88,600; Median year structure built: Before 1940; Homeowner vacancy rate: 3.5%; Median selected monthly owner costs: $1,077 with a mortgage, $483 without a mortgage; Median gross rent: $782 per month; Rental vacancy rate: 3.3%

Health Insurance: 93.2% have insurance; 66.9% have private insurance; 41.2% have public insurance; 6.8% do not have insurance; 3.7% of children under 18 do not have insurance

Safety: Violent crime rate: 13.3 per 10,000 population; Property crime rate: 254.5 per 10,000 population

Transportation: Commute: 93.1% car, 0.4% public transportation, 3.3% walk, 2.1% work from home; Mean travel time to work: 18.6 minutes

Additional Information Contacts

City of Johnstown . . . . (518) 736-4011
  http://www.cityofjohnstown-ny.com

JOHNSTOWN (town). Covers a land area of 70.214 square miles and a water area of 1.082 square miles. Located at 43.04° N. Lat; 74.40° W. Long. Elevation is 673 feet.

Population: 7,278; Growth (since 2000): 1.6%; Density: 103.7 persons per square mile; Race: 95.4% White, 2.3% Black/African American, 0.2% Asian, 0.0% American Indian/Alaska Native, 0.0% Native Hawaiian/Other Pacific Islander, 1.0% Two or more races, 2.0% Hispanic of any race; Average household size: 2.31; Median age: 46.8; Age under 18: 18.0%; Age 65 and over: 22.7%; Males per 100 females: 111.3; Marriage status: 26.0% never married, 53.2% now married, 3.7% separated, 10.1% widowed, 10.6% divorced; Foreign born: 1.5%; Speak English only: 97.7%; With disability: 17.3%; Veterans: 7.5%; Ancestry: 25.7% German, 17.3% Irish, 14.6% English, 14.6% Italian, 11.7% American

Employment: 12.4% management, business, and financial, 2.5% computer, engineering, and science, 14.7% education, legal, community service, arts, and media, 12.2% healthcare practitioners, 21.7% service, 14.9% sales and office, 10.4% natural resources, construction, and maintenance, 11.2% production, transportation, and material moving

Income: Per capita: $31,050; Median household: $55,634; Average household: $74,543; Households with income of $100,000 or more: 26.4%; Poverty rate: 13.4%

Educational Attainment: High school diploma or higher: 87.1%; Bachelor's degree or higher: 20.4%; Graduate/professional degree or higher: 11.1%

School District(s)

Hamilton-Fulton-Montgomery Boces

Enrollment: n/a . . . . (518) 736-4300

Johnstown City SD (PK-12)

Enrollment: 1,734 . . . . (518) 762-4611

Two-year College(s)

Fulton-Montgomery Community College (Public)

Enrollment: 2,403 . . . . (518) 762-3622
  Tuition: In-state $5,020; Out-of-state $9,470

Vocational/Technical School(s)

Hamilton Fulton Montgomery BOCES-Practical Nursing Program (Public)

Enrollment: n/a . . . . (518) 736-4305

Housing: Homeownership rate: 90.1%; Median home value: $114,900; Median year structure built: 1963; Homeowner vacancy rate: 0.0%; Median selected monthly owner costs: $1,110 with a mortgage, $421 without a mortgage; Median gross rent: $970 per month; Rental vacancy rate: 0.0%

Health Insurance: 90.7% have insurance; 69.4% have private insurance; 40.6% have public insurance; 9.3% do not have insurance; 10.0% of children under 18 do not have insurance

Transportation: Commute: 94.3% car, 0.0% public transportation, 0.0% walk, 5.7% work from home; Mean travel time to work: 27.4 minutes

Additional Information Contacts

Town of Johnstown . . . . (518) 762-7070
  http://townofjohnstown.org/content

MAYFIELD (town). Covers a land area of 58.385 square miles and a water area of 6.299 square miles. Located at 43.12° N. Lat; 74.26° W. Long. Elevation is 850 feet.

Population: 6,283; Growth (since 2000): -2.3%; Density: 107.6 persons per square mile; Race: 97.5% White, 0.2% Black/African American, 0.1% Asian, 0.2% American Indian/Alaska Native, 0.0% Native Hawaiian/Other Pacific Islander, 2.1% Two or more races, 1.4% Hispanic of any race; Average household size: 2.29; Median age: 47.9; Age under 18: 17.0%; Age 65 and over: 20.3%; Males per 100 females: 98.3; Marriage status: 26.8% never married, 55.9% now married, 3.1% separated, 8.7% widowed, 8.6% divorced; Foreign born: 0.9%; Speak English only: 97.8%; With disability: 16.0%; Veterans: 8.5%; Ancestry: 21.1% German, 17.7% American, 15.6% Irish, 15.0% Italian, 12.8% English

Employment: 12.0% management, business, and financial, 2.0% computer, engineering, and science, 8.0% education, legal, community service, arts, and media, 5.2% healthcare practitioners, 19.7% service, 23.9% sales and office, 9.5% natural resources, construction, and maintenance, 19.6% production, transportation, and material moving

Income: Per capita: $27,271; Median household: $51,451; Average household: $62,065; Households with income of $100,000 or more: 16.0%; Poverty rate: 8.8%

Educational Attainment: High school diploma or higher: 88.4%; Bachelor's degree or higher: 12.7%; Graduate/professional degree or higher: 6.1%

School District(s)
Mayfield Central SD (PK-12)
    Enrollment: 967. . . . . (518) 661-8222
Housing: Homeownership rate: 76.9%; Median home value: $130,600; Median year structure built: 1974; Homeowner vacancy rate: 0.0%; Median selected monthly owner costs: $1,206 with a mortgage, $538 without a mortgage; Median gross rent: $726 per month; Rental vacancy rate: 0.0%
Health Insurance: 94.3% have insurance; 74.5% have private insurance; 41.4% have public insurance; 5.7% do not have insurance; 0.3% of children under 18 do not have insurance
Transportation: Commute: 94.9% car, 0.0% public transportation, 2.3% walk, 1.7% work from home; Mean travel time to work: 24.4 minutes
Additional Information Contacts
Town of Mayfield. . . . . (518) 661-5414
    http://mayfieldny.org/content

MAYFIELD (village). Covers a land area of 0.907 square miles and a water area of 0.177 square miles. Located at 43.10° N. Lat; 74.27° W. Long. Elevation is 850 feet.
Population: 785; Growth (since 2000): -1.9%; Density: 865.7 persons per square mile; Race: 99.7% White, 0.0% Black/African American, 0.0% Asian, 0.0% American Indian/Alaska Native, 0.0% Native Hawaiian/Other Pacific Islander, 0.3% Two or more races, 3.6% Hispanic of any race; Average household size: 2.45; Median age: 38.7; Age under 18: 16.7%; Age 65 and over: 6.9%; Males per 100 females: 90.4; Marriage status: 36.0% never married, 53.2% now married, 0.3% separated, 3.1% widowed, 7.6% divorced; Foreign born: 1.4%; Speak English only: 94.7%; With disability: 7.4%; Veterans: 9.2%; Ancestry: 17.7% American, 16.7% Italian, 16.6% German, 13.2% Irish, 9.9% English
Employment: 8.9% management, business, and financial, 1.6% computer, engineering, and science, 8.9% education, legal, community service, arts, and media, 7.5% healthcare practitioners, 20.0% service, 37.6% sales and office, 6.9% natural resources, construction, and maintenance, 8.7% production, transportation, and material moving
Income: Per capita: $25,828; Median household: $58,125; Average household: $62,928; Households with income of $100,000 or more: 19.0%; Poverty rate: 7.9%
Educational Attainment: High school diploma or higher: 93.4%; Bachelor's degree or higher: 21.5%; Graduate/professional degree or higher: 9.9%

School District(s)
Mayfield Central SD (PK-12)
    Enrollment: 967. . . . . (518) 661-8222
Housing: Homeownership rate: 83.8%; Median home value: $105,800; Median year structure built: 1946; Homeowner vacancy rate: 0.0%; Median selected monthly owner costs: $1,260 with a mortgage, $559 without a mortgage; Median gross rent: $725 per month; Rental vacancy rate: 0.0%
Health Insurance: 93.8% have insurance; 75.7% have private insurance; 26.2% have public insurance; 6.2% do not have insurance; 2.1% of children under 18 do not have insurance
Transportation: Commute: 89.1% car, 0.0% public transportation, 4.9% walk, 4.7% work from home; Mean travel time to work: 25.9 minutes

NORTHAMPTON (town). Covers a land area of 21.116 square miles and a water area of 13.613 square miles. Located at 43.16° N. Lat; 74.17° W. Long.
Population: 2,584; Growth (since 2000): -6.4%; Density: 122.4 persons per square mile; Race: 98.7% White, 0.2% Black/African American, 0.0% Asian, 0.0% American Indian/Alaska Native, 0.3% Native Hawaiian/Other Pacific Islander, 0.7% Two or more races, 0.4% Hispanic of any race; Average household size: 2.35; Median age: 44.5; Age under 18: 23.1%; Age 65 and over: 19.3%; Males per 100 females: 100.6; Marriage status: 27.4% never married, 52.3% now married, 4.1% separated, 7.7% widowed, 12.6% divorced; Foreign born: 1.8%; Speak English only: 98.7%; With disability: 11.0%; Veterans: 8.9%; Ancestry: 28.1% American, 19.9% German, 14.9% Irish, 13.2% English, 9.1% Italian
Employment: 9.9% management, business, and financial, 2.7% computer, engineering, and science, 10.9% education, legal, community service, arts, and media, 9.0% healthcare practitioners, 22.6% service, 22.8% sales and office, 8.3% natural resources, construction, and maintenance, 13.7% production, transportation, and material moving

Income: Per capita: $28,804; Median household: $58,452; Average household: $68,000; Households with income of $100,000 or more: 22.6%; Poverty rate: 11.3%
Educational Attainment: High school diploma or higher: 92.8%; Bachelor's degree or higher: 23.3%; Graduate/professional degree or higher: 10.0%
Housing: Homeownership rate: 75.0%; Median home value: $161,500; Median year structure built: 1963; Homeowner vacancy rate: 4.4%; Median selected monthly owner costs: $1,195 with a mortgage, $480 without a mortgage; Median gross rent: $780 per month; Rental vacancy rate: 7.4%
Health Insurance: 91.7% have insurance; 70.8% have private insurance; 39.2% have public insurance; 8.3% do not have insurance; 5.5% of children under 18 do not have insurance
Transportation: Commute: 90.2% car, 0.0% public transportation, 4.9% walk, 2.2% work from home; Mean travel time to work: 25.6 minutes

NORTHVILLE (village). Covers a land area of 1.039 square miles and a water area of 0.344 square miles. Located at 43.22° N. Lat; 74.17° W. Long. Elevation is 807 feet.
History: Incorporated 1873.
Population: 1,195; Growth (since 2000): 4.9%; Density: 1,150.2 persons per square mile; Race: 99.6% White, 0.3% Black/African American, 0.1% Asian, 0.0% American Indian/Alaska Native, 0.0% Native Hawaiian/Other Pacific Islander, 0.0% Two or more races, 0.0% Hispanic of any race; Average household size: 2.56; Median age: 32.8; Age under 18: 29.5%; Age 65 and over: 16.2%; Males per 100 females: 86.0; Marriage status: 34.1% never married, 48.6% now married, 8.4% separated, 8.2% widowed, 9.1% divorced; Foreign born: 2.2%; Speak English only: 98.5%; With disability: 11.7%; Veterans: 8.7%; Ancestry: 34.6% American, 22.8% German, 13.1% English, 13.0% Irish, 10.7% Italian
Employment: 4.1% management, business, and financial, 0.6% computer, engineering, and science, 9.8% education, legal, community service, arts, and media, 9.0% healthcare practitioners, 27.6% service, 29.5% sales and office, 8.3% natural resources, construction, and maintenance, 11.2% production, transportation, and material moving
Income: Per capita: $21,745; Median household: $50,064; Average household: $54,976; Households with income of $100,000 or more: 14.1%; Poverty rate: 12.6%
Educational Attainment: High school diploma or higher: 95.1%; Bachelor's degree or higher: 17.7%; Graduate/professional degree or higher: 7.1%

School District(s)
Northville Central SD (PK-12)
    Enrollment: 478. . . . . (518) 863-7000
Housing: Homeownership rate: 60.4%; Median home value: $134,200; Median year structure built: Before 1940; Homeowner vacancy rate: 7.6%; Median selected monthly owner costs: $1,147 with a mortgage, $453 without a mortgage; Median gross rent: $818 per month; Rental vacancy rate: 10.7%
Health Insurance: 91.8% have insurance; 70.8% have private insurance; 40.0% have public insurance; 8.2% do not have insurance; 4.3% of children under 18 do not have insurance
Safety: Violent crime rate: 0.0 per 10,000 population; Property crime rate: 47.5 per 10,000 population
Transportation: Commute: 87.2% car, 0.0% public transportation, 8.3% walk, 1.3% work from home; Mean travel time to work: 26.5 minutes

OPPENHEIM (town). Covers a land area of 56.134 square miles and a water area of 0.306 square miles. Located at 43.08° N. Lat; 74.67° W. Long. Elevation is 1,096 feet.
Population: 1,823; Growth (since 2000): 2.8%; Density: 32.5 persons per square mile; Race: 97.9% White, 0.9% Black/African American, 0.1% Asian, 0.0% American Indian/Alaska Native, 0.0% Native Hawaiian/Other Pacific Islander, 0.9% Two or more races, 1.1% Hispanic of any race; Average household size: 2.39; Median age: 43.4; Age under 18: 21.0%; Age 65 and over: 18.7%; Males per 100 females: 108.7; Marriage status: 23.8% never married, 59.0% now married, 2.1% separated, 6.1% widowed, 11.1% divorced; Foreign born: 1.4%; Speak English only: 93.5%; With disability: 18.7%; Veterans: 7.4%; Ancestry: 23.6% German, 20.3% American, 12.7% Irish, 9.9% Italian, 8.3% English
Employment: 8.8% management, business, and financial, 0.9% computer, engineering, and science, 2.5% education, legal, community service, arts, and media, 7.2% healthcare practitioners, 16.2% service, 20.8% sales and office, 18.7% natural resources, construction, and maintenance, 24.9% production, transportation, and material moving

Income: Per capita: $23,531; Median household: $44,853; Average household: $57,301; Households with income of $100,000 or more: 12.3%; Poverty rate: 13.8%

Educational Attainment: High school diploma or higher: 80.2%; Bachelor's degree or higher: 11.9%; Graduate/professional degree or higher: 5.8%

Housing: Homeownership rate: 87.8%; Median home value: $88,900; Median year structure built: 1977; Homeowner vacancy rate: 0.6%; Median selected monthly owner costs: $1,070 with a mortgage, $393 without a mortgage; Median gross rent: $669 per month; Rental vacancy rate: 0.0%

Health Insurance: 89.3% have insurance; 64.2% have private insurance; 41.5% have public insurance; 10.7% do not have insurance; 20.1% of children under 18 do not have insurance

Transportation: Commute: 86.2% car, 0.0% public transportation, 7.8% walk, 3.0% work from home; Mean travel time to work: 30.5 minutes

PERTH (town). Covers a land area of 26.083 square miles and a water area of 0.027 square miles. Located at 43.01° N. Lat; 74.20° W. Long. Elevation is 869 feet.

Population: 3,496; Growth (since 2000): -3.9%; Density: 134.0 persons per square mile; Race: 93.8% White, 2.4% Black/African American, 1.7% Asian, 0.0% American Indian/Alaska Native, 0.0% Native Hawaiian/Other Pacific Islander, 1.3% Two or more races, 2.5% Hispanic of any race; Average household size: 2.50; Median age: 44.6; Age under 18: 23.1%; Age 65 and over: 18.1%; Males per 100 females: 98.3; Marriage status: 30.1% never married, 53.1% now married, 0.9% separated, 8.2% widowed, 8.5% divorced; Foreign born: 4.6%; Speak English only: 94.8%; With disability: 12.2%; Veterans: 8.9%; Ancestry: 24.4% Italian, 18.0% Polish, 12.7% Irish, 11.7% German, 11.0% American

Employment: 11.6% management, business, and financial, 5.3% computer, engineering, and science, 10.8% education, legal, community service, arts, and media, 3.4% healthcare practitioners, 12.2% service, 36.0% sales and office, 11.8% natural resources, construction, and maintenance, 8.9% production, transportation, and material moving

Income: Per capita: $30,519; Median household: $59,313; Average household: $77,173; Households with income of $100,000 or more: 27.8%; Poverty rate: 6.9%

Educational Attainment: High school diploma or higher: 88.2%; Bachelor's degree or higher: 20.3%; Graduate/professional degree or higher: 9.2%

Housing: Homeownership rate: 85.6%; Median home value: $160,300; Median year structure built: 1981; Homeowner vacancy rate: 0.8%; Median selected monthly owner costs: $1,464 with a mortgage, $544 without a mortgage; Median gross rent: $743 per month; Rental vacancy rate: 21.4%

Health Insurance: 95.0% have insurance; 72.1% have private insurance; 42.3% have public insurance; 5.0% do not have insurance; 2.7% of children under 18 do not have insurance

Transportation: Commute: 90.9% car, 3.4% public transportation, 3.4% walk, 0.6% work from home; Mean travel time to work: 31.2 minutes

STRATFORD (town). Covers a land area of 74.876 square miles and a water area of 1.795 square miles. Located at 43.21° N. Lat; 74.61° W. Long. Elevation is 1,066 feet.

Population: 503; Growth (since 2000): -21.4%; Density: 6.7 persons per square mile; Race: 100.0% White, 0.0% Black/African American, 0.0% Asian, 0.0% American Indian/Alaska Native, 0.0% Native Hawaiian/Other Pacific Islander, 0.0% Two or more races, 3.6% Hispanic of any race; Average household size: 1.91; Median age: 56.3; Age under 18: 11.1%; Age 65 and over: 19.7%; Males per 100 females: 99.3; Marriage status: 14.7% never married, 64.8% now married, 4.8% separated, 9.0% widowed, 11.6% divorced; Foreign born: 3.2%; Speak English only: 97.9%; With disability: 14.9%; Veterans: 9.2%; Ancestry: 26.4% American, 11.3% German, 8.9% Irish, 8.3% Italian, 5.6% English

Employment: 11.9% management, business, and financial, 1.0% computer, engineering, and science, 8.1% education, legal, community service, arts, and media, 11.4% healthcare practitioners, 14.8% service, 20.0% sales and office, 6.2% natural resources, construction, and maintenance, 26.7% production, transportation, and material moving

Income: Per capita: $26,132; Median household: $38,594; Average household: $50,921; Households with income of $100,000 or more: 12.5%; Poverty rate: 18.5%

Educational Attainment: High school diploma or higher: 85.3%; Bachelor's degree or higher: 18.2%; Graduate/professional degree or higher: 9.3%

Housing: Homeownership rate: 95.1%; Median home value: $96,300; Median year structure built: 1969; Homeowner vacancy rate: 0.0%; Median selected monthly owner costs: $978 with a mortgage, $368 without a mortgage; Median gross rent: $514 per month; Rental vacancy rate: 0.0%

Health Insurance: 97.4% have insurance; 66.8% have private insurance; 51.1% have public insurance; 2.6% do not have insurance; 0.0% of children under 18 do not have insurance

Transportation: Commute: 96.6% car, 0.0% public transportation, 1.0% walk, 2.4% work from home; Mean travel time to work: 34.9 minutes

Genesee County

Located in western New York; drained by Tonawanda and Oak Orchard Creeks. Covers a land area of 492.936 square miles, a water area of 2.372 square miles, and is located in the Eastern Time Zone at 43.00° N. Lat., 78.19° W. Long. The county was founded in 1802. County seat is Batavia.

Genesee County is part of the Batavia, NY Micropolitan Statistical Area. The entire metro area includes: Genesee County, NY

Weather Station: Batavia   Elevation: 899 feet

	Jan	Feb	Mar	Apr	May	Jun	Jul	Aug	Sep	Oct	Nov	Dec
High	32	35	44	57	69	78	81	80	73	61	49	37
Low	17	18	25	37	47	57	61	60	53	42	33	22
Precip	2.0	1.8	2.2	3.0	3.3	3.7	3.3	3.2	3.8	3.2	2.8	2.4
Snow	19.6	13.2	11.9	2.2	0.3	0.0	0.0	0.0	0.0	0.4	5.0	16.2

High and Low temperatures in degrees Fahrenheit; Precipitation and Snow in inches

Population: 58,537; Growth (since 2000): -3.0%; Density: 118.8 persons per square mile; Race: 92.1% White, 2.5% Black/African American, 0.7% Asian, 1.0% American Indian/Alaska Native, 0.0% Native Hawaiian/Other Pacific Islander, 2.2% two or more races, 3.1% Hispanic of any race; Average household size: 2.41; Median age: 43.2; Age under 18: 20.8%; Age 65 and over: 17.6%; Males per 100 females: 98.1; Marriage status: 28.0% never married, 54.9% now married, 2.3% separated, 6.0% widowed, 11.1% divorced; Foreign born: 1.9%; Speak English only: 96.5%; With disability: 14.8%; Veterans: 9.0%; Ancestry: 27.8% German, 17.8% Irish, 15.8% Italian, 15.2% English, 10.3% Polish

Religion: Six largest groups: 25.7% Catholicism, 5.0% Methodist/Pietist, 2.8% Presbyterian-Reformed, 2.6% Holiness, 2.4% Non-denominational Protestant, 2.2% Baptist

Economy: Unemployment rate: 3.3%; Leading industries: 16.7 % retail trade; 12.7 % construction; 11.7 % other services (except public administration); Farms: 549 totaling 187,317 acres; Company size: 0 employ 1,000 or more persons, 1 employs 500 to 999 persons, 23 employ 100 to 499 persons, 1,270 employ less than 100 persons; Business ownership: 1,238 women-owned, n/a Black-owned, 48 Hispanic-owned, 56 Asian-owned, n/a American Indian/Alaska Native-owned

Employment: 12.2% management, business, and financial, 3.0% computer, engineering, and science, 9.8% education, legal, community service, arts, and media, 6.0% healthcare practitioners, 18.2% service, 22.1% sales and office, 11.1% natural resources, construction, and maintenance, 17.6% production, transportation, and material moving

Income: Per capita: $27,499; Median household: $54,033; Average household: $66,534; Households with income of $100,000 or more: 20.1%; Poverty rate: 12.8%

Educational Attainment: High school diploma or higher: 91.1%; Bachelor's degree or higher: 21.4%; Graduate/professional degree or higher: 8.8%

Housing: Homeownership rate: 72.5%; Median home value: $111,900; Median year structure built: 1956; Homeowner vacancy rate: 0.8%; Median selected monthly owner costs: $1,194 with a mortgage, $493 without a mortgage; Median gross rent: $748 per month; Rental vacancy rate: 3.0%

Vital Statistics: Birth rate: 96.5 per 10,000 population; Death rate: 107.7 per 10,000 population; Age-adjusted cancer mortality rate: 178.4 deaths per 100,000 population

Health Insurance: 94.9% have insurance; 74.1% have private insurance; 37.6% have public insurance; 5.1% do not have insurance; 2.1% of children under 18 do not have insurance

Health Care: Physicians: 9.8 per 10,000 population; Dentists: 4.0 per 10,000 population; Hospital beds: 44.5 per 10,000 population; Hospital admissions: 1,386.4 per 10,000 population

Transportation: Commute: 91.7% car, 0.4% public transportation, 3.6% walk, 2.6% work from home; Mean travel time to work: 22.2 minutes

2016 Presidential Election: 64.0% Trump, 28.9% Clinton, 5.0% Johnson, 1.2% Stein

National and State Parks: Oak Orchard Creek State Game Refuge; White Memorial State Game Farm
Additional Information Contacts
Genesee Government . . . . (585) 344-2550
http://www.co.genesee.ny.us

Genesee County Communities

ALABAMA (town). Covers a land area of 42.370 square miles and a water area of 0.406 square miles. Located at 43.09° N. Lat; 78.37° W. Long. Elevation is 643 feet.
Population: 1,783; Growth (since 2000): -5.2%; Density: 42.1 persons per square mile; Race: 96.4% White, 1.1% Black/African American, 0.0% Asian, 0.5% American Indian/Alaska Native, 0.0% Native Hawaiian/Other Pacific Islander, 1.4% Two or more races, 2.4% Hispanic of any race; Average household size: 2.59; Median age: 42.2; Age under 18: 20.0%; Age 65 and over: 11.4%; Males per 100 females: 101.4; Marriage status: 29.5% never married, 58.1% now married, 3.8% separated, 4.3% widowed, 8.1% divorced; Foreign born: 1.2%; Speak English only: 97.7%; With disability: 10.3%; Veterans: 7.5%; Ancestry: 35.7% German, 16.7% Irish, 14.6% English, 13.4% Polish, 11.9% Italian
Employment: 8.0% management, business, and financial, 3.0% computer, engineering, and science, 5.2% education, legal, community service, arts, and media, 4.0% healthcare practitioners, 19.7% service, 18.3% sales and office, 18.0% natural resources, construction, and maintenance, 23.8% production, transportation, and material moving
Income: Per capita: $25,543; Median household: $57,273; Average household: $65,355; Households with income of $100,000 or more: 19.8%; Poverty rate: 10.8%
Educational Attainment: High school diploma or higher: 90.7%; Bachelor's degree or higher: 10.9%; Graduate/professional degree or higher: 4.1%
Housing: Homeownership rate: 82.7%; Median home value: $105,300; Median year structure built: 1951; Homeowner vacancy rate: 0.0%; Median selected monthly owner costs: $1,083 with a mortgage, $491 without a mortgage; Median gross rent: $540 per month; Rental vacancy rate: 0.0%
Health Insurance: 93.4% have insurance; 73.4% have private insurance; 32.5% have public insurance; 6.6% do not have insurance; 4.3% of children under 18 do not have insurance
Transportation: Commute: 93.9% car, 0.0% public transportation, 3.3% walk, 0.6% work from home; Mean travel time to work: 22.7 minutes

ALEXANDER (town). Covers a land area of 35.467 square miles and a water area of 0.096 square miles. Located at 42.92° N. Lat; 78.25° W. Long. Elevation is 932 feet.
Population: 2,611; Growth (since 2000): 6.5%; Density: 73.6 persons per square mile; Race: 99.4% White, 0.5% Black/African American, 0.0% Asian, 0.0% American Indian/Alaska Native, 0.0% Native Hawaiian/Other Pacific Islander, 0.2% Two or more races, 0.2% Hispanic of any race; Average household size: 2.61; Median age: 44.3; Age under 18: 21.5%; Age 65 and over: 16.4%; Males per 100 females: 97.2; Marriage status: 24.2% never married, 58.9% now married, 1.8% separated, 3.9% widowed, 12.9% divorced; Foreign born: 0.7%; Speak English only: 99.2%; With disability: 15.1%; Veterans: 7.8%; Ancestry: 42.1% German, 19.5% Irish, 17.3% Polish, 12.8% English, 10.3% Italian
Employment: 9.0% management, business, and financial, 3.5% computer, engineering, and science, 6.2% education, legal, community service, arts, and media, 6.4% healthcare practitioners, 20.5% service, 24.3% sales and office, 13.5% natural resources, construction, and maintenance, 16.6% production, transportation, and material moving
Income: Per capita: $28,602; Median household: $60,188; Average household: $73,682; Households with income of $100,000 or more: 21.2%; Poverty rate: 12.6%
Educational Attainment: High school diploma or higher: 90.7%; Bachelor's degree or higher: 17.0%; Graduate/professional degree or higher: 6.6%

School District(s)
Alexander Central SD (PK-12)
    Enrollment: 848 . . . . (585) 591-1551
Housing: Homeownership rate: 82.9%; Median home value: $121,800; Median year structure built: 1952; Homeowner vacancy rate: 0.5%; Median selected monthly owner costs: $1,212 with a mortgage, $505 without a mortgage; Median gross rent: $788 per month; Rental vacancy rate: 0.0%

Health Insurance: 94.6% have insurance; 80.0% have private insurance; 34.4% have public insurance; 5.4% do not have insurance; 2.7% of children under 18 do not have insurance
Transportation: Commute: 93.8% car, 0.4% public transportation, 0.4% walk, 4.5% work from home; Mean travel time to work: 26.3 minutes

ALEXANDER (village). Covers a land area of 0.437 square miles and a water area of 0 square miles. Located at 42.90° N. Lat; 78.26° W. Long. Elevation is 932 feet.
Population: 560; Growth (since 2000): 16.4%; Density: 1,280.7 persons per square mile; Race: 98.9% White, 1.1% Black/African American, 0.0% Asian, 0.0% American Indian/Alaska Native, 0.0% Native Hawaiian/Other Pacific Islander, 0.0% Two or more races, 0.0% Hispanic of any race; Average household size: 2.83; Median age: 36.6; Age under 18: 29.1%; Age 65 and over: 13.6%; Males per 100 females: 89.2; Marriage status: 32.3% never married, 48.6% now married, 3.4% separated, 2.3% widowed, 16.8% divorced; Foreign born: 0.5%; Speak English only: 97.9%; With disability: 10.9%; Veterans: 7.6%; Ancestry: 34.8% German, 21.3% Irish, 14.8% English, 14.3% Italian, 8.2% Polish
Employment: 6.9% management, business, and financial, 2.8% computer, engineering, and science, 7.2% education, legal, community service, arts, and media, 9.3% healthcare practitioners, 29.7% service, 17.6% sales and office, 7.2% natural resources, construction, and maintenance, 19.3% production, transportation, and material moving
Income: Per capita: $22,647; Median household: $54,167; Average household: $62,268; Households with income of $100,000 or more: 16.6%; Poverty rate: 12.4%
Educational Attainment: High school diploma or higher: 96.1%; Bachelor's degree or higher: 20.9%; Graduate/professional degree or higher: 9.3%

School District(s)
Alexander Central SD (PK-12)
    Enrollment: 848 . . . . (585) 591-1551
Housing: Homeownership rate: 70.7%; Median home value: $109,700; Median year structure built: 1943; Homeowner vacancy rate: 2.8%; Median selected monthly owner costs: $1,143 with a mortgage, $537 without a mortgage; Median gross rent: $750 per month; Rental vacancy rate: 0.0%
Health Insurance: 98.2% have insurance; 83.0% have private insurance; 32.5% have public insurance; 1.8% do not have insurance; 2.9% of children under 18 do not have insurance
Transportation: Commute: 89.3% car, 1.8% public transportation, 1.8% walk, 2.8% work from home; Mean travel time to work: 25.1 minutes

BASOM (unincorporated postal area)
ZCTA: 14013
    Covers a land area of 40.497 square miles and a water area of 0.365 square miles. Located at 43.09° N. Lat; 78.40° W. Long. Elevation is 715 feet.
Population: 1,630; Growth (since 2000): -10.5%; Density: 40.3 persons per square mile; Race: 71.3% White, 0.7% Black/African American, 1.7% Asian, 22.9% American Indian/Alaska Native, 0.0% Native Hawaiian/Other Pacific Islander, 2.0% Two or more races, 1.3% Hispanic of any race; Average household size: 2.23; Median age: 47.4; Age under 18: 17.1%; Age 65 and over: 16.5%; Males per 100 females: 99.7; Marriage status: 32.7% never married, 55.2% now married, 2.9% separated, 4.2% widowed, 7.8% divorced; Foreign born: 0.7%; Speak English only: 95.0%; With disability: 12.4%; Veterans: 9.8%; Ancestry: 25.1% German, 11.8% Irish, 11.0% Polish, 9.1% Italian, 8.8% English
Employment: 11.0% management, business, and financial, 2.4% computer, engineering, and science, 3.7% education, legal, community service, arts, and media, 2.7% healthcare practitioners, 20.4% service, 18.5% sales and office, 11.5% natural resources, construction, and maintenance, 29.8% production, transportation, and material moving
Income: Per capita: $25,574; Median household: $53,272; Average household: $57,845; Households with income of $100,000 or more: 14.9%; Poverty rate: 13.4%
Educational Attainment: High school diploma or higher: 89.9%; Bachelor's degree or higher: 10.7%; Graduate/professional degree or higher: 4.3%
Housing: Homeownership rate: 87.7%; Median home value: $93,100; Median year structure built: 1956; Homeowner vacancy rate: 0.0%; Median selected monthly owner costs: $1,095 with a mortgage, $440 without a mortgage; Median gross rent: $782 per month; Rental vacancy rate: 0.0%

Health Insurance: 94.2% have insurance; 72.0% have private insurance; 37.0% have public insurance; 5.8% do not have insurance; 5.6% of children under 18 do not have insurance
Transportation: Commute: 88.3% car, 1.6% public transportation, 5.1% walk, 2.6% work from home; Mean travel time to work: 23.4 minutes

BATAVIA (city). County seat. Covers a land area of 5.196 square miles and a water area of 0.081 square miles. Located at 43.00° N. Lat; 78.18° W. Long. Elevation is 892 feet.
History: Batavia is noteworthy as the "capital" of the Holland Land Purchase. In 1801, Joseph Ellicott, surveyor and subagent for the company, built a land office on the site. Ellicott proposed naming the place Bustia or Bustiville, for Paul Busti, the company's general agent. The latter objected and proposed Batavia, the name of the Dutch republic to which the proprietors belonged.
Population: 14,868; Growth (since 2000): -8.5%; Density: 2,861.5 persons per square mile; Race: 87.4% White, 6.8% Black/African American, 0.6% Asian, 0.6% American Indian/Alaska Native, 0.0% Native Hawaiian/Other Pacific Islander, 2.9% Two or more races, 4.4% Hispanic of any race; Average household size: 2.35; Median age: 38.5; Age under 18: 22.0%; Age 65 and over: 18.6%; Males per 100 females: 89.9; Marriage status: 32.4% never married, 46.0% now married, 2.5% separated, 7.7% widowed, 13.8% divorced; Foreign born: 1.9%; Speak English only: 95.7%; With disability: 16.2%; Veterans: 10.1%; Ancestry: 23.4% German, 20.1% Italian, 17.3% Irish, 9.3% English, 8.2% Polish
Employment: 11.5% management, business, and financial, 2.8% computer, engineering, and science, 13.4% education, legal, community service, arts, and media, 7.1% healthcare practitioners, 22.8% service, 22.0% sales and office, 5.9% natural resources, construction, and maintenance, 14.6% production, transportation, and material moving
Income: Per capita: $23,700; Median household: $44,342; Average household: $56,902; Households with income of $100,000 or more: 14.3%; Poverty rate: 21.8%
Educational Attainment: High school diploma or higher: 88.7%; Bachelor's degree or higher: 23.5%; Graduate/professional degree or higher: 9.4%

School District(s)
Batavia City SD (PK-12)
    Enrollment: 2,291 . . . . (585) 343-2480
New York State School for the Blind (02-12)
    Enrollment: 54 . . . . (585) 343-5384
Two-year College(s)
Genesee Community College (Public)
    Enrollment: 5,906 . . . . (585) 343-0055
    Tuition: In-state $4,580; Out-of-state $5,180
Vocational/Technical School(s)
Continental School of Beauty Culture-Batavia (Private, For-profit)
    Enrollment: 26 . . . . (585) 344-0886
    Tuition: $12,690
Genesee Valley BOCES-Practical Nursing Program (Public)
    Enrollment: 86 . . . . (585) 344-7720
    Tuition: $13,368
Housing: Homeownership rate: 49.7%; Median home value: $94,200; Median year structure built: Before 1940; Homeowner vacancy rate: 3.7%; Median selected monthly owner costs: $1,082 with a mortgage, $455 without a mortgage; Median gross rent: $757 per month; Rental vacancy rate: 4.3%
Health Insurance: 95.1% have insurance; 64.8% have private insurance; 46.9% have public insurance; 4.9% do not have insurance; 2.4% of children under 18 do not have insurance
Hospitals: United Memorial Medical Center (126 beds)
Safety: Violent crime rate: 63.9 per 10,000 population; Property crime rate: 329.0 per 10,000 population
Newspapers: Daily News (daily circulation 12,500)
Transportation: Commute: 85.8% car, 0.7% public transportation, 7.6% walk, 1.6% work from home; Mean travel time to work: 18.5 minutes
Airports: Genesee County (general aviation)
Additional Information Contacts
City of Batavia . . . . (585) 345-6305
    http://www.batavianewyork.com

BATAVIA (town). Covers a land area of 48.187 square miles and a water area of 0.218 square miles. Located at 43.00° N. Lat; 78.23° W. Long. Elevation is 892 feet.
History: Laid out in 1801 by Joseph Ellicott, agent for the Holland Land Company, the city was a center of the Anti-Masonic movement in the 19th century. Attica prison, site of the 1971 riots, is nearby. Incorporated 1915.
Population: 6,865; Growth (since 2000): 16.1%; Density: 142.5 persons per square mile; Race: 95.8% White, 0.1% Black/African American, 1.6% Asian, 0.7% American Indian/Alaska Native, 0.0% Native Hawaiian/Other Pacific Islander, 0.5% Two or more races, 3.3% Hispanic of any race; Average age: 2.17; Median age: 51.5; Age under 18: 15.6%; Age 65 and over: 20.1%; Males per 100 females: 112.0; Marriage status: 26.0% never married, 58.5% now married, 3.2% separated, 4.7% widowed, 10.8% divorced; Foreign born: 2.3%; Speak English only: 95.7%; With disability: 16.5%; Veterans: 11.7%; Ancestry: 29.3% German, 23.8% Italian, 19.7% English, 18.6% Irish, 8.6% Polish
Employment: 15.2% management, business, and financial, 1.8% computer, engineering, and science, 9.5% education, legal, community service, arts, and media, 8.5% healthcare practitioners, 18.0% service, 20.3% sales and office, 9.7% natural resources, construction, and maintenance, 16.9% production, transportation, and material moving
Income: Per capita: $34,755; Median household: $62,633; Average household: $76,487; Households with income of $100,000 or more: 24.6%; Poverty rate: 6.2%
Educational Attainment: High school diploma or higher: 94.3%; Bachelor's degree or higher: 23.9%; Graduate/professional degree or higher: 12.6%

School District(s)
Batavia City SD (PK-12)
    Enrollment: 2,291 . . . . (585) 343-2480
New York State School for the Blind (02-12)
    Enrollment: 54 . . . . (585) 343-5384
Two-year College(s)
Genesee Community College (Public)
    Enrollment: 5,906 . . . . (585) 343-0055
    Tuition: In-state $4,580; Out-of-state $5,180
Vocational/Technical School(s)
Continental School of Beauty Culture-Batavia (Private, For-profit)
    Enrollment: 26 . . . . (585) 344-0886
    Tuition: $12,690
Genesee Valley BOCES-Practical Nursing Program (Public)
    Enrollment: 86 . . . . (585) 344-7720
    Tuition: $13,368
Housing: Homeownership rate: 85.6%; Median home value: $120,800; Median year structure built: 1974; Homeowner vacancy rate: 0.0%; Median selected monthly owner costs: $1,346 with a mortgage, $505 without a mortgage; Median gross rent: $624 per month; Rental vacancy rate: 7.6%
Health Insurance: 93.5% have insurance; 75.8% have private insurance; 36.9% have public insurance; 6.5% do not have insurance; 0.0% of children under 18 do not have insurance
Hospitals: United Memorial Medical Center (126 beds)
Newspapers: Daily News (daily circulation 12,500)
Transportation: Commute: 92.6% car, 0.1% public transportation, 3.0% walk, 4.0% work from home; Mean travel time to work: 19.7 minutes
Airports: Genesee County (general aviation)
Additional Information Contacts
Town of Batavia . . . . (585) 343-1729
    http://www.townofbatavia.com

BERGEN (town). Covers a land area of 27.559 square miles and a water area of 0.036 square miles. Located at 43.10° N. Lat; 77.96° W. Long. Elevation is 607 feet.
Population: 3,010; Growth (since 2000): -5.4%; Density: 109.2 persons per square mile; Race: 89.7% White, 0.0% Black/African American, 2.0% Asian, 0.2% American Indian/Alaska Native, 0.0% Native Hawaiian/Other Pacific Islander, 7.5% Two or more races, 0.9% Hispanic of any race; Average household size: 2.61; Median age: 43.9; Age under 18: 23.4%; Age 65 and over: 14.5%; Males per 100 females: 98.7; Marriage status: 32.4% never married, 50.1% now married, 0.3% separated, 8.4% widowed, 9.0% divorced; Foreign born: 3.4%; Speak English only: 96.3%; With disability: 18.4%; Veterans: 4.6%; Ancestry: 23.8% German, 22.9% English, 15.4% Irish, 8.9% Dutch, 8.4% Italian
Employment: 8.6% management, business, and financial, 3.5% computer, engineering, and science, 11.0% education, legal, community service, arts, and media, 5.3% healthcare practitioners, 13.7% service, 25.2% sales and

office, 14.8% natural resources, construction, and maintenance, 18.0% production, transportation, and material moving
Income: Per capita: $23,843; Median household: $45,735; Average household: $61,551; Households with income of $100,000 or more: 21.6%; Poverty rate: 13.9%
Educational Attainment: High school diploma or higher: 94.1%; Bachelor's degree or higher: 21.9%; Graduate/professional degree or higher: 8.7%
School District(s)
Byron-Bergen Central SD (PK-12)
    Enrollment: 965. . . . . (585) 494-1220
Housing: Homeownership rate: 74.0%; Median home value: $120,100; Median year structure built: 1971; Homeowner vacancy rate: 0.0%; Median selected monthly owner costs: $1,385 with a mortgage, $621 without a mortgage; Median gross rent: $753 per month; Rental vacancy rate: 0.0%
Health Insurance: 94.8% have insurance; 73.9% have private insurance; 36.3% have public insurance; 5.2% do not have insurance; 4.1% of children under 18 do not have insurance
Transportation: Commute: 93.1% car, 0.0% public transportation, 3.0% walk, 3.0% work from home; Mean travel time to work: 21.7 minutes

BERGEN (village). Covers a land area of 0.737 square miles and a water area of 0 square miles. Located at 43.08° N. Lat; 77.94° W. Long. Elevation is 607 feet.
Population: 1,150; Growth (since 2000): -7.3%; Density: 1,561.3 persons per square mile; Race: 94.5% White, 0.0% Black/African American, 1.8% Asian, 0.5% American Indian/Alaska Native, 0.0% Native Hawaiian/Other Pacific Islander, 1.5% Two or more races, 2.4% Hispanic of any race; Average household size: 2.73; Median age: 35.5; Age under 18: 24.3%; Age 65 and over: 12.5%; Males per 100 females: 94.4; Marriage status: 37.4% never married, 49.3% now married, 0.8% separated, 5.6% widowed, 7.6% divorced; Foreign born: 3.0%; Speak English only: 94.6%; With disability: 14.5%; Veterans: 5.5%; Ancestry: 26.9% German, 15.9% Irish, 13.4% English, 9.9% European, 9.0% Italian
Employment: 10.2% management, business, and financial, 5.8% computer, engineering, and science, 14.0% education, legal, community service, arts, and media, 3.8% healthcare practitioners, 13.2% service, 24.9% sales and office, 9.2% natural resources, construction, and maintenance, 18.9% production, transportation, and material moving
Income: Per capita: $25,413; Median household: $61,125; Average household: $67,795; Households with income of $100,000 or more: 20.6%; Poverty rate: 10.6%
Educational Attainment: High school diploma or higher: 96.4%; Bachelor's degree or higher: 27.7%; Graduate/professional degree or higher: 9.6%
School District(s)
Byron-Bergen Central SD (PK-12)
    Enrollment: 965. . . . . (585) 494-1220
Housing: Homeownership rate: 80.4%; Median home value: $107,400; Median year structure built: Before 1940; Homeowner vacancy rate: 0.0%; Median selected monthly owner costs: $1,179 with a mortgage, $557 without a mortgage; Median gross rent: $706 per month; Rental vacancy rate: 0.0%
Health Insurance: 90.3% have insurance; 74.1% have private insurance; 32.0% have public insurance; 9.7% do not have insurance; 9.7% of children under 18 do not have insurance
Transportation: Commute: 88.1% car, 0.0% public transportation, 6.8% walk, 2.9% work from home; Mean travel time to work: 21.4 minutes

BETHANY (town). Covers a land area of 36.035 square miles and a water area of 0.035 square miles. Located at 42.92° N. Lat; 78.13° W. Long.
Population: 1,751; Growth (since 2000): -0.5%; Density: 48.6 persons per square mile; Race: 89.9% White, 1.5% Black/African American, 0.0% Asian, 0.8% American Indian/Alaska Native, 0.0% Native Hawaiian/Other Pacific Islander, 0.9% Two or more races, 6.7% Hispanic of any race; Average household size: 2.37; Median age: 44.5; Age under 18: 21.1%; Age 65 and over: 18.0%; Males per 100 females: 103.6; Marriage status: 18.3% never married, 66.7% now married, 1.3% separated, 8.3% widowed, 6.7% divorced; Foreign born: 3.4%; Speak English only: 94.7%; With disability: 11.9%; Veterans: 8.5%; Ancestry: 27.9% German, 16.8% Irish, 16.6% English, 10.9% Italian, 9.0% American
Employment: 15.3% management, business, and financial, 3.7% computer, engineering, and science, 7.9% education, legal, community service, arts, and media, 4.0% healthcare practitioners, 15.3% service,

22.5% sales and office, 17.1% natural resources, construction, and maintenance, 14.1% production, transportation, and material moving
Income: Per capita: $28,721; Median household: $58,571; Average household: $67,409; Households with income of $100,000 or more: 18.3%; Poverty rate: 3.5%
Educational Attainment: High school diploma or higher: 94.5%; Bachelor's degree or higher: 22.8%; Graduate/professional degree or higher: 10.1%
Housing: Homeownership rate: 79.1%; Median home value: $119,000; Median year structure built: 1957; Homeowner vacancy rate: 0.0%; Median selected monthly owner costs: $1,252 with a mortgage, $470 without a mortgage; Median gross rent: $719 per month; Rental vacancy rate: 0.0%
Health Insurance: 94.2% have insurance; 77.2% have private insurance; 35.0% have public insurance; 5.8% do not have insurance; 5.2% of children under 18 do not have insurance
Transportation: Commute: 91.5% car, 0.0% public transportation, 2.9% walk, 4.8% work from home; Mean travel time to work: 21.2 minutes

BYRON (town). Covers a land area of 32.212 square miles and a water area of 0.079 square miles. Located at 43.08° N. Lat; 78.07° W. Long. Elevation is 620 feet.
Population: 2,282; Growth (since 2000): -8.5%; Density: 70.8 persons per square mile; Race: 98.6% White, 0.3% Black/African American, 0.6% Asian, 0.2% American Indian/Alaska Native, 0.0% Native Hawaiian/Other Pacific Islander, 0.3% Two or more races, 0.7% Hispanic of any race; Average household size: 2.61; Median age: 42.9; Age under 18: 20.0%; Age 65 and over: 17.5%; Males per 100 females: 104.6; Marriage status: 28.8% never married, 57.3% now married, 2.2% separated, 5.0% widowed, 8.9% divorced; Foreign born: 1.5%; Speak English only: 98.7%; With disability: 14.4%; Veterans: 12.5%; Ancestry: 28.1% German, 25.6% English, 15.6% Irish, 9.7% Italian, 7.1% Polish
Employment: 11.9% management, business, and financial, 4.4% computer, engineering, and science, 4.4% education, legal, community service, arts, and media, 6.3% healthcare practitioners, 15.4% service, 24.8% sales and office, 17.4% natural resources, construction, and maintenance, 15.5% production, transportation, and material moving
Income: Per capita: $30,426; Median household: $65,282; Average household: $77,568; Households with income of $100,000 or more: 22.3%; Poverty rate: 10.1%
Educational Attainment: High school diploma or higher: 91.0%; Bachelor's degree or higher: 20.4%; Graduate/professional degree or higher: 6.1%
Housing: Homeownership rate: 85.3%; Median home value: $114,800; Median year structure built: 1970; Homeowner vacancy rate: 0.0%; Median selected monthly owner costs: $1,163 with a mortgage, $486 without a mortgage; Median gross rent: $1,038 per month; Rental vacancy rate: 0.0%
Health Insurance: 94.7% have insurance; 78.0% have private insurance; 34.2% have public insurance; 5.3% do not have insurance; 4.9% of children under 18 do not have insurance
Transportation: Commute: 95.8% car, 0.5% public transportation, 1.4% walk, 2.2% work from home; Mean travel time to work: 25.3 minutes

CORFU (village). Covers a land area of 0.995 square miles and a water area of 0 square miles. Located at 42.96° N. Lat; 78.40° W. Long. Elevation is 863 feet.
Population: 685; Growth (since 2000): -13.8%; Density: 688.4 persons per square mile; Race: 95.2% White, 3.8% Black/African American, 0.4% Asian, 0.0% American Indian/Alaska Native, 0.0% Native Hawaiian/Other Pacific Islander, 0.6% Two or more races, 0.7% Hispanic of any race; Average household size: 2.16; Median age: 44.3; Age under 18: 15.3%; Age 65 and over: 18.1%; Males per 100 females: 92.1; Marriage status: 34.8% never married, 49.3% now married, 4.2% separated, 5.4% widowed, 10.5% divorced; Foreign born: 0.7%; Speak English only: 98.5%; With disability: 14.0%; Veterans: 10.0%; Ancestry: 37.8% German, 17.8% Polish, 17.4% Irish, 13.4% English, 13.1% Italian
Employment: 11.4% management, business, and financial, 1.7% computer, engineering, and science, 12.4% education, legal, community service, arts, and media, 10.0% healthcare practitioners, 8.5% service, 17.4% sales and office, 9.0% natural resources, construction, and maintenance, 29.6% production, transportation, and material moving
Income: Per capita: $26,241; Median household: $48,750; Average household: $56,177; Households with income of $100,000 or more: 13.3%; Poverty rate: 10.8%

Educational Attainment: High school diploma or higher: 94.9%; Bachelor's degree or higher: 23.5%; Graduate/professional degree or higher: 11.7%

School District(s)
Pembroke Central SD (KG-12)
   Enrollment: 951 . . . . (585) 599-4525
Housing: Homeownership rate: 63.7%; Median home value: $113,700; Median year structure built: 1952; Homeowner vacancy rate: 0.0%; Median selected monthly owner costs: $1,095 with a mortgage, $494 without a mortgage; Median gross rent: $676 per month; Rental vacancy rate: 4.2%
Health Insurance: 96.2% have insurance; 78.5% have private insurance; 33.1% have public insurance; 3.8% do not have insurance; 0.0% of children under 18 do not have insurance
Transportation: Commute: 92.5% car, 0.0% public transportation, 2.4% walk, 4.3% work from home; Mean travel time to work: 23.3 minutes

DARIEN (town).
Covers a land area of 47.371 square miles and a water area of 0.219 square miles. Located at 42.91° N. Lat; 78.38° W. Long. Elevation is 1,001 feet.
Population: 3,072; Growth (since 2000): 0.4%; Density: 64.8 persons per square mile; Race: 99.6% White, 0.0% Black/African American, 0.0% Asian, 0.2% American Indian/Alaska Native, 0.0% Native Hawaiian/Other Pacific Islander, 0.3% Two or more races, 3.6% Hispanic of any race; Average household size: 2.73; Median age: 43.8; Age under 18: 22.4%; Age 65 and over: 16.1%; Males per 100 females: 105.7; Marriage status: 29.4% never married, 60.2% now married, 1.6% separated, 3.6% widowed, 6.7% divorced; Foreign born: 1.0%; Speak English only: 97.4%; With disability: 12.9%; Veterans: 7.8%; Ancestry: 39.1% German, 22.9% Polish, 17.1% Irish, 13.7% Italian, 11.5% English
Employment: 4.9% management, business, and financial, 3.2% computer, engineering, and science, 8.6% education, legal, community service, arts, and media, 6.5% healthcare practitioners, 18.6% service, 17.4% sales and office, 18.0% natural resources, construction, and maintenance, 22.9% production, transportation, and material moving
Income: Per capita: $27,886; Median household: $70,353; Average household: $74,631; Households with income of $100,000 or more: 29.0%; Poverty rate: 9.6%
Educational Attainment: High school diploma or higher: 95.7%; Bachelor's degree or higher: 15.6%; Graduate/professional degree or higher: 7.4%
Housing: Homeownership rate: 86.3%; Median home value: $154,100; Median year structure built: 1967; Homeowner vacancy rate: 0.0%; Median selected monthly owner costs: $1,287 with a mortgage, $571 without a mortgage; Median gross rent: $814 per month; Rental vacancy rate: 0.0%
Health Insurance: 95.2% have insurance; 78.3% have private insurance; 33.6% have public insurance; 4.8% do not have insurance; 2.5% of children under 18 do not have insurance
Transportation: Commute: 95.7% car, 0.1% public transportation, 1.0% walk, 1.5% work from home; Mean travel time to work: 26.2 minutes

DARIEN CENTER (unincorporated postal area)
ZCTA: 14040
   Covers a land area of 29.227 square miles and a water area of 0.191 square miles. Located at 42.89° N. Lat; 78.38° W. Long. Elevation is 1,017 feet.
Population: 2,021; Growth (since 2000): -13.3%; Density: 69.1 persons per square mile; Race: 99.4% White, 0.0% Black/African American, 0.0% Asian, 0.2% American Indian/Alaska Native, 0.0% Native Hawaiian/Other Pacific Islander, 0.4% Two or more races, 2.3% Hispanic of any race; Average household size: 2.40; Median age: 48.2; Age under 18: 16.1%; Age 65 and over: 17.7%; Males per 100 females: 108.2; Marriage status: 32.6% never married, 56.5% now married, 1.8% separated, 6.0% widowed, 4.9% divorced; Foreign born: 1.6%; Speak English only: 97.1%; With disability: 13.3%; Veterans: 6.1%; Ancestry: 40.9% German, 27.8% Polish, 13.5% Irish, 13.3% English, 12.8% Italian
Employment: 6.0% management, business, and financial, 1.5% computer, engineering, and science, 11.6% education, legal, community service, arts, and media, 4.0% healthcare practitioners, 19.0% service, 19.5% sales and office, 11.7% natural resources, construction, and maintenance, 26.7% production, transportation, and material moving
Income: Per capita: $31,192; Median household: $54,119; Average household: $72,268; Households with income of $100,000 or more: 22.9%; Poverty rate: 5.6%

Educational Attainment: High school diploma or higher: 92.8%; Bachelor's degree or higher: 13.3%; Graduate/professional degree or higher: 7.7%
Housing: Homeownership rate: 83.8%; Median home value: $155,000; Median year structure built: 1964; Homeowner vacancy rate: 0.0%; Median selected monthly owner costs: $1,352 with a mortgage, $538 without a mortgage; Median gross rent: $826 per month; Rental vacancy rate: 0.0%
Health Insurance: 95.5% have insurance; 79.4% have private insurance; 32.2% have public insurance; 4.5% do not have insurance; 4.9% of children under 18 do not have insurance
Transportation: Commute: 95.1% car, 0.2% public transportation, 1.0% walk, 2.8% work from home; Mean travel time to work: 29.3 minutes

EAST BETHANY (unincorporated postal area)
ZCTA: 14054
   Covers a land area of 24.858 square miles and a water area of 0.024 square miles. Located at 42.92° N. Lat; 78.13° W. Long. Elevation is 1,001 feet.
Population: 1,291; Growth (since 2000): -5.1%; Density: 51.9 persons per square mile; Race: 86.3% White, 2.0% Black/African American, 0.0% Asian, 1.1% American Indian/Alaska Native, 0.0% Native Hawaiian/Other Pacific Islander, 1.2% Two or more races, 9.1% Hispanic of any race; Average household size: 2.30; Median age: 43.1; Age under 18: 21.5%; Age 65 and over: 16.0%; Males per 100 females: 103.3; Marriage status: 19.0% never married, 66.7% now married, 1.7% separated, 7.0% widowed, 7.3% divorced; Foreign born: 4.3%; Speak English only: 92.9%; With disability: 12.1%; Veterans: 8.6%; Ancestry: 25.7% German, 16.7% Irish, 15.3% English, 11.3% Italian, 9.5% American
Employment: 14.5% management, business, and financial, 2.9% computer, engineering, and science, 7.2% education, legal, community service, arts, and media, 5.2% healthcare practitioners, 18.9% service, 18.0% sales and office, 18.9% natural resources, construction, and maintenance, 14.5% production, transportation, and material moving
Income: Per capita: $29,564; Median household: $57,679; Average household: $68,249; Households with income of $100,000 or more: 18.0%; Poverty rate: 3.4%
Educational Attainment: High school diploma or higher: 94.6%; Bachelor's degree or higher: 20.6%; Graduate/professional degree or higher: 9.3%
Housing: Homeownership rate: 77.4%; Median home value: $115,900; Median year structure built: 1956; Homeowner vacancy rate: 0.0%; Median selected monthly owner costs: $1,210 with a mortgage, $454 without a mortgage; Median gross rent: $671 per month; Rental vacancy rate: 0.0%
Health Insurance: 95.4% have insurance; 75.6% have private insurance; 35.8% have public insurance; 4.6% do not have insurance; 0.0% of children under 18 do not have insurance
Transportation: Commute: 91.7% car, 0.0% public transportation, 2.5% walk, 5.2% work from home; Mean travel time to work: 21.0 minutes

ELBA (town).
Covers a land area of 35.649 square miles and a water area of 0.043 square miles. Located at 43.09° N. Lat; 78.17° W. Long. Elevation is 761 feet.
Population: 2,164; Growth (since 2000): -11.3%; Density: 60.7 persons per square mile; Race: 87.2% White, 1.1% Black/African American, 0.1% Asian, 0.0% American Indian/Alaska Native, 0.0% Native Hawaiian/Other Pacific Islander, 1.8% Two or more races, 13.3% Hispanic of any race; Average household size: 2.68; Median age: 41.0; Age under 18: 23.2%; Age 65 and over: 16.3%; Males per 100 females: 100.3; Marriage status: 20.6% never married, 66.2% now married, 1.1% separated, 5.3% widowed, 7.9% divorced; Foreign born: 5.0%; Speak English only: 88.9%; With disability: 10.7%; Veterans: 7.7%; Ancestry: 27.2% German, 18.0% English, 13.4% Irish, 13.3% Italian, 8.4% Polish
Employment: 13.7% management, business, and financial, 2.3% computer, engineering, and science, 9.4% education, legal, community service, arts, and media, 6.8% healthcare practitioners, 17.0% service, 20.4% sales and office, 18.0% natural resources, construction, and maintenance, 12.5% production, transportation, and material moving
Income: Per capita: $26,827; Median household: $63,690; Average household: $70,773; Households with income of $100,000 or more: 21.7%; Poverty rate: 7.8%

Educational Attainment: High school diploma or higher: 85.8%; Bachelor's degree or higher: 21.7%; Graduate/professional degree or higher: 7.9%

School District(s)
Elba Central SD (PK-12)
  Enrollment: 407 . . . . (585) 757-9967
Housing: Homeownership rate: 81.7%; Median home value: $112,300; Median year structure built: 1955; Homeowner vacancy rate: 1.4%; Median selected monthly owner costs: $1,214 with a mortgage, $500 without a mortgage; Median gross rent: $731 per month; Rental vacancy rate: 4.5%
Health Insurance: 94.4% have insurance; 74.9% have private insurance; 38.1% have public insurance; 5.6% do not have insurance; 0.4% of children under 18 do not have insurance
Transportation: Commute: 88.5% car, 0.0% public transportation, 7.3% walk, 3.8% work from home; Mean travel time to work: 20.2 minutes

ELBA (village). Covers a land area of 1.017 square miles and a water area of 0 square miles. Located at 43.08° N. Lat; 78.19° W. Long. Elevation is 761 feet.
Population: 610; Growth (since 2000): -12.4%; Density: 600.0 persons per square mile; Race: 95.4% White, 1.6% Black/African American, 0.0% Asian, 0.0% American Indian/Alaska Native, 0.0% Native Hawaiian/Other Pacific Islander, 2.6% Two or more races, 8.4% Hispanic of any race; Average household size: 2.70; Median age: 43.2; Age under 18: 22.0%; Age 65 and over: 13.3%; Males per 100 females: 104.2; Marriage status: 25.6% never married, 61.9% now married, 0.0% separated, 4.4% widowed, 8.1% divorced; Foreign born: 0.5%; Speak English only: 94.6%; With disability: 8.4%; Veterans: 10.1%; Ancestry: 27.7% German, 22.3% Irish, 18.2% English, 17.9% Italian, 9.7% Polish
Employment: 17.3% management, business, and financial, 6.1% computer, engineering, and science, 9.4% education, legal, community service, arts, and media, 7.0% healthcare practitioners, 20.9% service, 17.6% sales and office, 8.8% natural resources, construction, and maintenance, 13.0% production, transportation, and material moving
Income: Per capita: $28,655; Median household: $66,875; Average household: $75,189; Households with income of $100,000 or more: 22.6%; Poverty rate: 7.4%
Educational Attainment: High school diploma or higher: 95.8%; Bachelor's degree or higher: 23.2%; Graduate/professional degree or higher: 9.6%

School District(s)
Elba Central SD (PK-12)
  Enrollment: 407 . . . . (585) 757-9967
Housing: Homeownership rate: 85.0%; Median home value: $118,000; Median year structure built: Before 1940; Homeowner vacancy rate: 1.0%; Median selected monthly owner costs: $1,314 with a mortgage, $567 without a mortgage; Median gross rent: $733 per month; Rental vacancy rate: 17.1%
Health Insurance: 97.7% have insurance; 84.8% have private insurance; 25.9% have public insurance; 2.3% do not have insurance; 1.4% of children under 18 do not have insurance
Transportation: Commute: 95.4% car, 0.0% public transportation, 2.6% walk, 0.7% work from home; Mean travel time to work: 26.2 minutes

LE ROY (town). Covers a land area of 42.084 square miles and a water area of 0.090 square miles. Located at 42.99° N. Lat; 77.97° W. Long. Elevation is 896 feet.
History: In 1897, Pearl Bixby Wait, a local carpenter, perfected the formula for Jello gelatin dessert, then sold it for $450. Until 1964, General Foods had a plant that produced Jello in the village. Jello Museum is housed in the Historical Society Building. Settled 1793, Incorporated 1834.
Population: 7,445; Growth (since 2000): -4.4%; Density: 176.9 persons per square mile; Race: 92.7% White, 2.9% Black/African American, 0.0% Asian, 0.0% American Indian/Alaska Native, 0.0% Native Hawaiian/Other Pacific Islander, 3.9% Two or more races, 2.2% Hispanic of any race; Average household size: 2.33; Median age: 40.1; Age under 18: 22.4%; Age 65 and over: 17.4%; Males per 100 females: 95.6; Marriage status: 29.6% never married, 52.1% now married, 2.4% separated, 4.6% widowed, 13.8% divorced; Foreign born: 1.2%; Speak English only: 98.3%; With disability: 12.7%; Veterans: 8.2%; Ancestry: 22.5% German, 19.8% Italian, 19.5% Irish, 14.6% English, 8.5% Polish
Employment: 15.6% management, business, and financial, 3.1% computer, engineering, and science, 10.0% education, legal, community service, arts, and media, 4.4% healthcare practitioners, 19.5% service,

22.9% sales and office, 7.9% natural resources, construction, and maintenance, 16.6% production, transportation, and material moving
Income: Per capita: $28,033; Median household: $53,882; Average household: $65,491; Households with income of $100,000 or more: 20.2%; Poverty rate: 10.1%
Educational Attainment: High school diploma or higher: 93.0%; Bachelor's degree or higher: 24.5%; Graduate/professional degree or higher: 9.4%

School District(s)
Genesee Valley Boces
  Enrollment: n/a . . . . (585) 658-7905
Le Roy Central SD (PK-12)
  Enrollment: 1,255 . . . . (585) 768-8133
Housing: Homeownership rate: 71.3%; Median home value: $102,600; Median year structure built: 1953; Homeowner vacancy rate: 0.0%; Median selected monthly owner costs: $1,206 with a mortgage, $482 without a mortgage; Median gross rent: $751 per month; Rental vacancy rate: 0.0%
Health Insurance: 94.1% have insurance; 77.8% have private insurance; 33.0% have public insurance; 5.9% do not have insurance; 3.1% of children under 18 do not have insurance
Transportation: Commute: 94.3% car, 0.1% public transportation, 2.5% walk, 2.9% work from home; Mean travel time to work: 23.6 minutes
Additional Information Contacts
Town of Le Roy . . . . (585) 768-6910
  http://www.leroyny.org

LE ROY (village). Covers a land area of 2.688 square miles and a water area of 0.003 square miles. Located at 42.98° N. Lat; 77.99° W. Long. Elevation is 896 feet.
Population: 4,260; Growth (since 2000): -4.5%; Density: 1,584.6 persons per square mile; Race: 91.1% White, 2.4% Black/African American, 0.0% Asian, 0.0% American Indian/Alaska Native, 0.0% Native Hawaiian/Other Pacific Islander, 5.5% Two or more races, 3.8% Hispanic of any race; Average household size: 2.28; Median age: 36.7; Age under 18: 23.9%; Age 65 and over: 15.5%; Males per 100 females: 93.5; Marriage status: 33.1% never married, 47.9% now married, 4.3% separated, 5.7% widowed, 13.4% divorced; Foreign born: 1.4%; Speak English only: 97.5%; With disability: 14.0%; Veterans: 7.6%; Ancestry: 26.5% German, 18.2% Italian, 16.4% Irish, 15.7% English, 9.5% Polish
Employment: 14.3% management, business, and financial, 1.8% computer, engineering, and science, 8.3% education, legal, community service, arts, and media, 4.8% healthcare practitioners, 25.3% service, 22.9% sales and office, 6.3% natural resources, construction, and maintenance, 16.3% production, transportation, and material moving
Income: Per capita: $26,821; Median household: $44,408; Average household: $61,365; Households with income of $100,000 or more: 14.7%; Poverty rate: 11.3%
Educational Attainment: High school diploma or higher: 92.2%; Bachelor's degree or higher: 23.7%; Graduate/professional degree or higher: 10.0%

School District(s)
Genesee Valley Boces
  Enrollment: n/a . . . . (585) 658-7905
Le Roy Central SD (PK-12)
  Enrollment: 1,255 . . . . (585) 768-8133
Housing: Homeownership rate: 60.5%; Median home value: $93,100; Median year structure built: Before 1940; Homeowner vacancy rate: 0.0%; Median selected monthly owner costs: $1,130 with a mortgage, $455 without a mortgage; Median gross rent: $677 per month; Rental vacancy rate: 0.0%
Health Insurance: 95.5% have insurance; 74.6% have private insurance; 34.9% have public insurance; 4.5% do not have insurance; 5.0% of children under 18 do not have insurance
Safety: Violent crime rate: 14.2 per 10,000 population; Property crime rate: 113.6 per 10,000 population
Transportation: Commute: 91.9% car, 0.1% public transportation, 4.5% walk, 3.2% work from home; Mean travel time to work: 22.5 minutes
Additional Information Contacts
Village of Le Roy . . . . (585) 768-6910
  http://www.leroyny.org

OAKFIELD (town). Covers a land area of 23.309 square miles and a water area of 0.624 square miles. Located at 43.08° N. Lat; 78.27° W. Long. Elevation is 755 feet.
History: Settled 1850, incorporated 1858.

Population: 3,151; Growth (since 2000): -1.6%; Density: 135.2 persons per square mile; Race: 95.7% White, 1.3% Black/African American, 0.6% Asian, 0.7% American Indian/Alaska Native, 0.0% Native Hawaiian/Other Pacific Islander, 1.2% Two or more races, 1.3% Hispanic of any race; Average household size: 2.62; Median age: 39.2; Age under 18: 22.8%; Age 65 and over: 15.3%; Males per 100 females: 94.6; Marriage status: 27.5% never married, 59.0% now married, 2.1% separated, 5.4% widowed, 8.1% divorced; Foreign born: 2.3%; Speak English only: 97.3%; With disability: 13.7%; Veterans: 10.4%; Ancestry: 33.9% German, 20.8% Irish, 14.4% English, 11.5% Polish, 9.6% Italian

Employment: 14.3% management, business, and financial, 1.3% computer, engineering, and science, 6.7% education, legal, community service, arts, and media, 3.9% healthcare practitioners, 12.4% service, 26.5% sales and office, 16.1% natural resources, construction, and maintenance, 18.7% production, transportation, and material moving

Income: Per capita: $26,219; Median household: $54,911; Average household: $68,990; Households with income of $100,000 or more: 24.1%; Poverty rate: 10.3%

Educational Attainment: High school diploma or higher: 86.3%; Bachelor's degree or higher: 13.8%; Graduate/professional degree or higher: 6.4%

School District(s)
Oakfield-Alabama Central SD (PK-12)
    Enrollment: 833 . . . . (585) 948-5211

Housing: Homeownership rate: 80.4%; Median home value: $94,100; Median year structure built: Before 1940; Homeowner vacancy rate: 0.0%; Median selected monthly owner costs: $1,116 with a mortgage, $507 without a mortgage; Median gross rent: $707 per month; Rental vacancy rate: 3.6%

Health Insurance: 94.9% have insurance; 72.0% have private insurance; 38.4% have public insurance; 5.1% do not have insurance; 1.5% of children under 18 do not have insurance

Transportation: Commute: 94.0% car, 1.0% public transportation, 1.7% walk, 1.6% work from home; Mean travel time to work: 24.7 minutes

OAKFIELD (village). Covers a land area of 0.661 square miles and a water area of 0 square miles. Located at 43.06° N. Lat; 78.27° W. Long. Elevation is 755 feet.

Population: 1,714; Growth (since 2000): -5.0%; Density: 2,595.0 persons per square mile; Race: 92.5% White, 2.3% Black/African American, 1.1% Asian, 1.2% American Indian/Alaska Native, 0.0% Native Hawaiian/Other Pacific Islander, 2.2% Two or more races, 1.9% Hispanic of any race; Average household size: 2.63; Median age: 39.6; Age under 18: 23.5%; Age 65 and over: 16.2%; Males per 100 females: 90.8; Marriage status: 28.5% never married, 54.7% now married, 1.6% separated, 6.3% widowed, 10.5% divorced; Foreign born: 3.9%; Speak English only: 95.6%; With disability: 17.0%; Veterans: 13.0%; Ancestry: 32.0% German, 19.0% Irish, 14.5% Italian, 12.4% English, 12.4% Polish

Employment: 9.4% management, business, and financial, 2.4% computer, engineering, and science, 8.3% education, legal, community service, arts, and media, 3.2% healthcare practitioners, 16.1% service, 29.3% sales and office, 14.3% natural resources, construction, and maintenance, 17.0% production, transportation, and material moving

Income: Per capita: $24,142; Median household: $53,170; Average household: $63,410; Households with income of $100,000 or more: 19.4%; Poverty rate: 10.8%

Educational Attainment: High school diploma or higher: 89.2%; Bachelor's degree or higher: 13.1%; Graduate/professional degree or higher: 5.0%

School District(s)
Oakfield-Alabama Central SD (PK-12)
    Enrollment: 833 . . . . (585) 948-5211

Housing: Homeownership rate: 77.0%; Median home value: $89,600; Median year structure built: Before 1940; Homeowner vacancy rate: 0.0%; Median selected monthly owner costs: $1,069 with a mortgage, $485 without a mortgage; Median gross rent: $729 per month; Rental vacancy rate: 5.5%

Health Insurance: 96.4% have insurance; 75.8% have private insurance; 40.5% have public insurance; 3.6% do not have insurance; 2.6% of children under 18 do not have insurance

Transportation: Commute: 89.8% car, 1.8% public transportation, 3.2% walk, 1.8% work from home; Mean travel time to work: 21.9 minutes

Additional Information Contacts
Village of Oakfield . . . . (585) 948-5862
    http://www.oakfield.govoffice.com

PAVILION (CDP). Covers a land area of 3.312 square miles and a water area of 0 square miles. Located at 42.88° N. Lat; 78.02° W. Long. Elevation is 955 feet.

Population: 509; Growth (since 2000): n/a; Density: 153.7 persons per square mile; Race: 100.0% White, 0.0% Black/African American, 0.0% Asian, 0.0% American Indian/Alaska Native, 0.0% Native Hawaiian/Other Pacific Islander, 0.0% Two or more races, 0.0% Hispanic of any race; Average household size: 2.56; Median age: 44.7; Age under 18: 16.7%; Age 65 and over: 22.4%; Males per 100 females: 104.4; Marriage status: 26.8% never married, 57.8% now married, 1.1% separated, 6.0% widowed, 9.4% divorced; Foreign born: 1.0%; Speak English only: 100.0%; With disability: 8.8%; Veterans: 11.3%; Ancestry: 37.1% German, 14.1% English, 12.8% Irish, 9.4% Italian, 5.1% Polish

Employment: 7.1% management, business, and financial, 7.7% computer, engineering, and science, 2.7% education, legal, community service, arts, and media, 3.4% healthcare practitioners, 24.6% service, 24.2% sales and office, 11.1% natural resources, construction, and maintenance, 19.2% production, transportation, and material moving

Income: Per capita: $40,004; Median household: $84,250; Average household: $104,115; Households with income of $100,000 or more: 36.2%; Poverty rate: 2.8%

Educational Attainment: High school diploma or higher: 97.3%; Bachelor's degree or higher: 26.3%; Graduate/professional degree or higher: 5.7%

School District(s)
Pavilion Central SD (PK-12)
    Enrollment: 731 . . . . (585) 584-3115

Housing: Homeownership rate: 80.9%; Median home value: $101,900; Median year structure built: Before 1940; Homeowner vacancy rate: 3.0%; Median selected monthly owner costs: $1,006 with a mortgage, $450 without a mortgage; Median gross rent: $717 per month; Rental vacancy rate: 0.0%

Health Insurance: 100.0% have insurance; 84.5% have private insurance; 35.4% have public insurance; 0.0% do not have insurance; 0.0% of children under 18 do not have insurance

Transportation: Commute: 85.5% car, 2.8% public transportation, 11.7% walk, 0.0% work from home; Mean travel time to work: 23.7 minutes

PAVILION (town). Covers a land area of 35.612 square miles and a water area of 0.108 square miles. Located at 42.91° N. Lat; 78.01° W. Long. Elevation is 955 feet.

Population: 2,540; Growth (since 2000): 3.0%; Density: 71.3 persons per square mile; Race: 95.1% White, 1.7% Black/African American, 0.0% Asian, 0.0% American Indian/Alaska Native, 0.0% Native Hawaiian/Other Pacific Islander, 0.5% Two or more races, 2.8% Hispanic of any race; Average household size: 2.58; Median age: 46.1; Age under 18: 20.5%; Age 65 and over: 15.7%; Males per 100 females: 108.1; Marriage status: 23.1% never married, 61.0% now married, 2.1% separated, 6.0% widowed, 10.0% divorced; Foreign born: 0.9%; Speak English only: 97.3%; With disability: 11.0%; Veterans: 7.7%; Ancestry: 23.6% German, 20.8% Irish, 20.4% English, 8.5% Italian, 6.0% Polish

Employment: 13.3% management, business, and financial, 3.5% computer, engineering, and science, 5.7% education, legal, community service, arts, and media, 5.4% healthcare practitioners, 14.8% service, 21.8% sales and office, 15.4% natural resources, construction, and maintenance, 20.1% production, transportation, and material moving

Income: Per capita: $29,840; Median household: $73,043; Average household: $77,084; Households with income of $100,000 or more: 25.2%; Poverty rate: 4.8%

Educational Attainment: High school diploma or higher: 93.7%; Bachelor's degree or higher: 21.2%; Graduate/professional degree or higher: 9.4%

School District(s)
Pavilion Central SD (PK-12)
    Enrollment: 731 . . . . (585) 584-3115

Housing: Homeownership rate: 85.6%; Median home value: $119,000; Median year structure built: 1975; Homeowner vacancy rate: 1.2%; Median selected monthly owner costs: $1,171 with a mortgage, $414 without a mortgage; Median gross rent: $640 per month; Rental vacancy rate: 0.0%

Health Insurance: 96.7% have insurance; 81.0% have private insurance; 30.1% have public insurance; 3.3% do not have insurance; 0.0% of children under 18 do not have insurance

Transportation: Commute: 92.6% car, 0.6% public transportation, 4.2% walk, 2.3% work from home; Mean travel time to work: 24.7 minutes

PEMBROKE (town). Covers a land area of 41.627 square miles and a water area of 0.090 square miles. Located at 43.00° N. Lat; 78.39° W. Long. Elevation is 843 feet.

Population: 4,241; Growth (since 2000): -6.4%; Density: 101.9 persons per square mile; Race: 93.9% White, 1.2% Black/African American, 1.4% Asian, 0.0% American Indian/Alaska Native, 0.0% Native Hawaiian/Other Pacific Islander, 2.9% Two or more races, 1.1% Hispanic of any race; Average household size: 2.51; Median age: 45.6; Age under 18: 19.8%; Age 65 and over: 18.5%; Males per 100 females: 95.4; Marriage status: 23.6% never married, 60.9% now married, 2.8% separated, 6.1% widowed, 9.4% divorced; Foreign born: 1.3%; Speak English only: 98.2%; With disability: 16.7%; Veterans: 5.7%; Ancestry: 31.7% German, 19.5% Polish, 18.2% English, 16.5% Irish, 11.7% Italian

Employment: 11.2% management, business, and financial, 5.2% computer, engineering, and science, 12.8% education, legal, community service, arts, and media, 2.7% healthcare practitioners, 11.8% service, 20.0% sales and office, 10.2% natural resources, construction, and maintenance, 26.1% production, transportation, and material moving

Income: Per capita: $27,944; Median household: $56,771; Average household: $69,288; Households with income of $100,000 or more: 19.8%; Poverty rate: 13.2%

Educational Attainment: High school diploma or higher: 89.3%; Bachelor's degree or higher: 23.3%; Graduate/professional degree or higher: 6.8%

Housing: Homeownership rate: 79.7%; Median home value: $149,300; Median year structure built: 1962; Homeowner vacancy rate: 0.0%; Median selected monthly owner costs: $1,163 with a mortgage, $526 without a mortgage; Median gross rent: $789 per month; Rental vacancy rate: 1.3%

Health Insurance: 96.6% have insurance; 81.0% have private insurance; 31.5% have public insurance; 3.4% do not have insurance; 0.0% of children under 18 do not have insurance

Transportation: Commute: 95.2% car, 0.0% public transportation, 0.4% walk, 2.3% work from home; Mean travel time to work: 27.1 minutes

Additional Information Contacts

Town of Pembroke . . . . (585) 599-4892
http://www.townofpembroke.org

STAFFORD (town). Covers a land area of 31.097 square miles and a water area of 0.179 square miles. Located at 42.99° N. Lat; 78.08° W. Long. Elevation is 892 feet.

Population: 2,294; Growth (since 2000): -4.8%; Density: 73.8 persons per square mile; Race: 96.8% White, 0.9% Black/African American, 0.7% Asian, 0.2% American Indian/Alaska Native, 0.0% Native Hawaiian/Other Pacific Islander, 1.5% Two or more races, 0.2% Hispanic of any race; Average household size: 2.14; Median age: 49.0; Age under 18: 15.8%; Age 65 and over: 20.9%; Males per 100 females: 101.7; Marriage status: 21.1% never married, 59.3% now married, 0.6% separated, 8.2% widowed, 11.4% divorced; Foreign born: 1.1%; Speak English only: 97.9%; With disability: 15.1%; Veterans: 8.4%; Ancestry: 29.6% German, 20.9% Irish, 17.6% English, 13.2% Italian, 8.8% American

Employment: 11.2% management, business, and financial, 3.5% computer, engineering, and science, 9.6% education, legal, community service, arts, and media, 8.2% healthcare practitioners, 17.3% service, 25.9% sales and office, 8.9% natural resources, construction, and maintenance, 15.3% production, transportation, and material moving

Income: Per capita: $29,362; Median household: $50,781; Average household: $62,434; Households with income of $100,000 or more: 19.7%; Poverty rate: 10.9%

Educational Attainment: High school diploma or higher: 92.0%; Bachelor's degree or higher: 21.1%; Graduate/professional degree or higher: 8.4%

Housing: Homeownership rate: 79.5%; Median home value: $119,400; Median year structure built: 1957; Homeowner vacancy rate: 0.0%; Median selected monthly owner costs: $1,154 with a mortgage, $521 without a mortgage; Median gross rent: $695 per month; Rental vacancy rate: 5.6%

Health Insurance: 97.0% have insurance; 82.9% have private insurance; 32.3% have public insurance; 3.0% do not have insurance; 0.0% of children under 18 do not have insurance

Transportation: Commute: 95.9% car, 0.4% public transportation, 0.4% walk, 2.5% work from home; Mean travel time to work: 22.8 minutes

TONAWANDA RESERVATION (reservation). Covers a land area of 9.161 square miles and a water area of 0.070 square miles. Located at 43.07° N. Lat; 78.44° W. Long.

Population: 460; Growth (since 2000): n/a; Density: 50.2 persons per square mile; Race: 6.5% White, 0.0% Black/African American, 5.9% Asian, 79.3% American Indian/Alaska Native, 0.0% Native Hawaiian/Other Pacific Islander, 3.5% Two or more races, 1.5% Hispanic of any race; Average household size: 1.76; Median age: 52.6; Age under 18: 16.5%; Age 65 and over: 18.9%; Males per 100 females: 92.4; Marriage status: 45.4% never married, 42.1% now married, 4.0% separated, 5.3% widowed, 7.3% divorced; Foreign born: 2.4%; Speak English only: 85.8%; With disability: 20.4%; Veterans: 13.3%; Ancestry: 5.0% Irish, 3.7% German, 1.5% Polish

Employment: 17.8% management, business, and financial, 0.0% computer, engineering, and science, 0.0% education, legal, community service, arts, and media, 0.0% healthcare practitioners, 17.8% service, 14.6% sales and office, 7.3% natural resources, construction, and maintenance, 42.5% production, transportation, and material moving

Income: Per capita: $22,464; Median household: $27,143; Average household: $42,240; Households with income of $100,000 or more: 6.5%; Poverty rate: 27.2%

Educational Attainment: High school diploma or higher: 86.7%; Bachelor's degree or higher: 7.6%; Graduate/professional degree or higher: 2.9%

Housing: Homeownership rate: 80.5%; Median home value: n/a; Median year structure built: 1980; Homeowner vacancy rate: 0.0%; Median selected monthly owner costs: $1,402 with a mortgage, $373 without a mortgage; Median gross rent: n/a per month; Rental vacancy rate: 0.0%

Health Insurance: 93.5% have insurance; 57.8% have private insurance; 48.5% have public insurance; 6.5% do not have insurance; 0.0% of children under 18 do not have insurance

Transportation: Commute: 78.1% car, 7.3% public transportation, 6.3% walk, 8.3% work from home; Mean travel time to work: 27.5 minutes

Greene County

Located in southeastern New York, mainly in the Catskills; bounded on the east by the Hudson River; includes many small lakes. Covers a land area of 647.161 square miles, a water area of 10.888 square miles, and is located in the Eastern Time Zone at 42.29° N. Lat., 74.15° W. Long. The county was founded in 1800. County seat is Catskill.

Weather Station: Cairo 4 NW — Elevation: 490 feet

	Jan	Feb	Mar	Apr	May	Jun	Jul	Aug	Sep	Oct	Nov	Dec
High	32	36	45	58	69	78	82	81	73	61	49	38
Low	13	15	24	35	45	54	59	57	49	38	30	20
Precip	2.8	2.4	3.6	3.8	3.4	3.9	3.3	3.0	3.9	3.8	3.8	3.1
Snow	13.3	9.8	9.9	2.0	0.0	0.0	0.0	0.0	0.0	0.1	2.2	10.7

High and Low temperatures in degrees Fahrenheit; Precipitation and Snow in inches

Population: 47,791; Growth (since 2000): -0.8%; Density: 73.8 persons per square mile; Race: 89.6% White, 6.2% Black/African American, 1.1% Asian, 0.3% American Indian/Alaska Native, 0.0% Native Hawaiian/Other Pacific Islander, 1.7% two or more races, 5.5% Hispanic of any race; Average household size: 2.60; Median age: 45.6; Age under 18: 17.1%; Age 65 and over: 20.3%; Males per 100 females: 109.1; Marriage status: 35.1% never married, 49.0% now married, 2.0% separated, 7.0% widowed, 9.0% divorced; Foreign born: 6.1%; Speak English only: 92.3%; With disability: 14.3%; Veterans: 8.5%; Ancestry: 18.7% Irish, 18.1% German, 15.4% Italian, 15.2% American, 6.8% English

Religion: Six largest groups: 20.2% Catholicism, 7.4% Methodist/Pietist, 2.3% Presbyterian-Reformed, 2.1% Non-denominational Protestant, 2.0% Lutheran, 0.8% Episcopalianism/Anglicanism

Economy: Unemployment rate: 3.7%; Leading industries: 16.7 % retail trade; 16.5 % accommodation and food services; 13.4 % construction; Farms: 273 totaling 42,986 acres; Company size: 0 employ 1,000 or more persons, 1 employs 500 to 999 persons, 14 employ 100 to 499 persons, 1,132 employ less than 100 persons; Business ownership: 1,170 women-owned, 58 Black-owned, 104 Hispanic-owned, 54 Asian-owned, 30 American Indian/Alaska Native-owned

Employment: 12.5% management, business, and financial, 3.3% computer, engineering, and science, 13.6% education, legal, community service, arts, and media, 6.1% healthcare practitioners, 18.8% service, 21.9% sales and office, 9.8% natural resources, construction, and maintenance, 14.0% production, transportation, and material moving

Income: Per capita: $27,402; Median household: $53,214; Average household: $69,417; Households with income of $100,000 or more: 21.7%; Poverty rate: 12.4%

Educational Attainment: High school diploma or higher: 85.9%; Bachelor's degree or higher: 22.0%; Graduate/professional degree or higher: 9.6%

Housing: Homeownership rate: 75.8%; Median home value: $176,100; Median year structure built: 1969; Homeowner vacancy rate: 3.2%; Median selected monthly owner costs: $1,532 with a mortgage, $580 without a mortgage; Median gross rent: $876 per month; Rental vacancy rate: 10.5%

Vital Statistics: Birth rate: 79.8 per 10,000 population; Death rate: 110.8 per 10,000 population; Age-adjusted cancer mortality rate: 189.6 deaths per 100,000 population

Health Insurance: 94.3% have insurance; 70.5% have private insurance; 40.8% have public insurance; 5.7% do not have insurance; 3.3% of children under 18 do not have insurance

Health Care: Physicians: 7.4 per 10,000 population; Dentists: 3.6 per 10,000 population; Hospital beds: 0.0 per 10,000 population; Hospital admissions: 0.0 per 10,000 population

Transportation: Commute: 90.4% car, 1.2% public transportation, 2.5% walk, 4.3% work from home; Mean travel time to work: 27.6 minutes

2016 Presidential Election: 59.3% Trump, 33.6% Clinton, 2.9% Johnson, 2.0% Stein

National and State Parks: Catskill State Park

Additional Information Contacts

Greene Government . . . . (518) 719-3270
   http://www.greenegovernment.com

Greene County Communities

ACRA (unincorporated postal area)

ZCTA: 12405

Covers a land area of 7.145 square miles and a water area of 0.029 square miles. Located at 42.32° N. Lat; 74.09° W. Long. Elevation is 653 feet.

Population: 529; Growth (since 2000): 16.5%; Density: 74.0 persons per square mile; Race: 94.1% White, 0.0% Black/African American, 2.3% Asian, 0.0% American Indian/Alaska Native, 0.0% Native Hawaiian/Other Pacific Islander, 0.0% Two or more races, 3.6% Hispanic of any race; Average household size: 3.15; Median age: 56.1; Age under 18: 7.9%; Age 65 and over: 31.9%; Males per 100 females: 94.0; Marriage status: 24.1% never married, 56.4% now married, 0.0% separated, 7.0% widowed, 12.4% divorced; Foreign born: 9.3%; Speak English only: 80.9%; With disability: 14.0%; Veterans: 7.4%; Ancestry: 30.8% Italian, 19.1% Irish, 16.8% German, 7.9% French Canadian, 6.0% English

Employment: 19.5% management, business, and financial, 13.6% computer, engineering, and science, 1.5% education, legal, community service, arts, and media, 8.5% healthcare practitioners, 26.5% service, 19.1% sales and office, 5.1% natural resources, construction, and maintenance, 6.3% production, transportation, and material moving

Income: Per capita: $24,411; Median household: $48,750; Average household: $60,477; Households with income of $100,000 or more: 14.9%; Poverty rate: 6.2%

Educational Attainment: High school diploma or higher: 97.2%; Bachelor's degree or higher: 25.8%; Graduate/professional degree or higher: 3.5%

Housing: Homeownership rate: 70.8%; Median home value: $226,700; Median year structure built: 1953; Homeowner vacancy rate: 0.0%; Median selected monthly owner costs: $1,614 with a mortgage, $661 without a mortgage; Median gross rent: n/a per month; Rental vacancy rate: 0.0%

Health Insurance: 91.1% have insurance; 47.8% have private insurance; 52.9% have public insurance; 8.9% do not have insurance; 0.0% of children under 18 do not have insurance

Transportation: Commute: 98.5% car, 0.0% public transportation, 1.5% walk, 0.0% work from home; Mean travel time to work: 26.9 minutes

ASHLAND (town).

Covers a land area of 25.958 square miles and a water area of 0 square miles. Located at 42.32° N. Lat; 74.34° W. Long. Elevation is 1,421 feet.

Population: 789; Growth (since 2000): 4.9%; Density: 30.4 persons per square mile; Race: 97.5% White, 0.0% Black/African American, 1.9% Asian, 0.0% American Indian/Alaska Native, 0.0% Native Hawaiian/Other Pacific Islander, 0.0% Two or more races, 2.3% Hispanic of any race;

Average household size: 2.38; Median age: 55.6; Age under 18: 14.4%; Age 65 and over: 31.8%; Males per 100 females: 99.0; Marriage status: 27.4% never married, 55.3% now married, 2.7% separated, 9.1% widowed, 8.2% divorced; Foreign born: 6.7%; Speak English only: 95.0%; With disability: 14.3%; Veterans: 10.7%; Ancestry: 16.3% Italian, 15.7% German, 15.5% Irish, 10.9% American, 10.4% English

Employment: 14.2% management, business, and financial, 3.5% computer, engineering, and science, 19.2% education, legal, community service, arts, and media, 0.9% healthcare practitioners, 12.3% service, 29.9% sales and office, 11.0% natural resources, construction, and maintenance, 9.1% production, transportation, and material moving

Income: Per capita: $36,682; Median household: $46,250; Average household: $82,727; Households with income of $100,000 or more: 19.8%; Poverty rate: 14.2%

Educational Attainment: High school diploma or higher: 91.1%; Bachelor's degree or higher: 30.7%; Graduate/professional degree or higher: 14.9%

Housing: Homeownership rate: 92.5%; Median home value: $238,000; Median year structure built: 1980; Homeowner vacancy rate: 1.9%; Median selected monthly owner costs: $1,302 with a mortgage, $550 without a mortgage; Median gross rent: $844 per month; Rental vacancy rate: 0.0%

Health Insurance: 95.1% have insurance; 65.1% have private insurance; 46.1% have public insurance; 4.9% do not have insurance; 4.4% of children under 18 do not have insurance

Transportation: Commute: 89.8% car, 4.8% public transportation, 1.3% walk, 3.5% work from home; Mean travel time to work: 26.0 minutes

ATHENS (town).

Covers a land area of 26.246 square miles and a water area of 2.622 square miles. Located at 42.28° N. Lat; 73.86° W. Long. Elevation is 26 feet.

History: Settled 1686, incorporated 1805.

Population: 3,951; Growth (since 2000): -1.0%; Density: 150.5 persons per square mile; Race: 94.3% White, 1.2% Black/African American, 1.5% Asian, 0.0% American Indian/Alaska Native, 0.0% Native Hawaiian/Other Pacific Islander, 2.9% Two or more races, 5.4% Hispanic of any race; Average household size: 2.71; Median age: 48.5; Age under 18: 15.5%; Age 65 and over: 19.2%; Males per 100 females: 97.6; Marriage status: 30.0% never married, 51.0% now married, 5.0% separated, 7.1% widowed, 11.9% divorced; Foreign born: 2.8%; Speak English only: 97.9%; With disability: 18.9%; Veterans: 7.3%; Ancestry: 23.3% German, 19.9% Irish, 15.7% American, 15.5% Italian, 7.2% Polish

Employment: 8.8% management, business, and financial, 2.6% computer, engineering, and science, 18.3% education, legal, community service, arts, and media, 5.3% healthcare practitioners, 20.0% service, 26.3% sales and office, 7.8% natural resources, construction, and maintenance, 10.9% production, transportation, and material moving

Income: Per capita: $27,521; Median household: $51,066; Average household: $65,183; Households with income of $100,000 or more: 19.5%; Poverty rate: 13.0%

Educational Attainment: High school diploma or higher: 86.1%; Bachelor's degree or higher: 18.7%; Graduate/professional degree or higher: 8.6%

School District(s)

Coxsackie-Athens Central SD (KG-12)
   Enrollment: 1,357 . . . . (518) 731-1710

Housing: Homeownership rate: 78.3%; Median home value: $180,100; Median year structure built: 1972; Homeowner vacancy rate: 1.5%; Median selected monthly owner costs: $1,472 with a mortgage, $626 without a mortgage; Median gross rent: $924 per month; Rental vacancy rate: 0.0%

Health Insurance: 95.0% have insurance; 70.4% have private insurance; 40.4% have public insurance; 5.0% do not have insurance; 2.2% of children under 18 do not have insurance

Transportation: Commute: 93.7% car, 0.5% public transportation, 1.7% walk, 3.4% work from home; Mean travel time to work: 24.3 minutes

Additional Information Contacts

Town of Athens . . . . (518) 945-1052
   http://www.townofathensny.com

ATHENS (village).

Covers a land area of 3.420 square miles and a water area of 1.185 square miles. Located at 42.27° N. Lat; 73.82° W. Long. Elevation is 26 feet.

Population: 1,465; Growth (since 2000): -13.6%; Density: 428.4 persons per square mile; Race: 95.0% White, 2.6% Black/African American, 1.5% Asian, 0.1% American Indian/Alaska Native, 0.0% Native Hawaiian/Other Pacific Islander, 0.5% Two or more races, 0.3% Hispanic of any race;

Average household size: 2.41; Median age: 48.4; Age under 18: 13.4%; Age 65 and over: 22.7%; Males per 100 females: 91.9; Marriage status: 36.5% never married, 41.8% now married, 5.9% separated, 11.0% widowed, 10.8% divorced; Foreign born: 2.7%; Speak English only: 97.5%; With disability: 16.5%; Veterans: 7.1%; Ancestry: 21.4% German, 19.2% Irish, 14.4% Italian, 14.3% American, 6.8% Dutch
Employment: 9.3% management, business, and financial, 1.9% computer, engineering, and science, 16.0% education, legal, community service, arts, and media, 6.0% healthcare practitioners, 22.8% service, 25.4% sales and office, 5.1% natural resources, construction, and maintenance, 13.7% production, transportation, and material moving
Income: Per capita: $28,703; Median household: $49,602; Average household: $64,058; Households with income of $100,000 or more: 16.9%; Poverty rate: 13.8%
Educational Attainment: High school diploma or higher: 90.9%; Bachelor's degree or higher: 23.2%; Graduate/professional degree or higher: 11.8%

School District(s)
Coxsackie-Athens Central SD (KG-12)
　　Enrollment: 1,357 . . . . (518) 731-1710
Housing: Homeownership rate: 65.3%; Median home value: $179,900; Median year structure built: Before 1940; Homeowner vacancy rate: 4.1%; Median selected monthly owner costs: $1,611 with a mortgage, $648 without a mortgage; Median gross rent: $777 per month; Rental vacancy rate: 0.0%
Health Insurance: 96.6% have insurance; 72.7% have private insurance; 42.8% have public insurance; 3.4% do not have insurance; 2.5% of children under 18 do not have insurance
Transportation: Commute: 89.6% car, 1.2% public transportation, 3.4% walk, 4.2% work from home; Mean travel time to work: 22.1 minutes

CAIRO (CDP). Covers a land area of 4.227 square miles and a water area of 0.006 square miles. Located at 42.31° N. Lat; 74.01° W. Long. Elevation is 374 feet.
Population: 1,194; Growth (since 2000): -14.1%; Density: 282.5 persons per square mile; Race: 94.4% White, 0.3% Black/African American, 1.4% Asian, 0.0% American Indian/Alaska Native, 0.0% Native Hawaiian/Other Pacific Islander, 3.2% Two or more races, 0.7% Hispanic of any race; Average household size: 2.43; Median age: 48.8; Age under 18: 14.6%; Age 65 and over: 11.5%; Males per 100 females: 87.9; Marriage status: 36.1% never married, 36.9% now married, 2.2% separated, 3.6% widowed, 23.4% divorced; Foreign born: 3.3%; Speak English only: 94.9%; With disability: 21.7%; Veterans: 6.9%; Ancestry: 28.4% Irish, 21.4% German, 15.3% Italian, 6.5% Polish, 4.0% Norwegian
Employment: 9.8% management, business, and financial, 0.0% computer, engineering, and science, 7.9% education, legal, community service, arts, and media, 0.0% healthcare practitioners, 29.4% service, 27.8% sales and office, 17.5% natural resources, construction, and maintenance, 7.5% production, transportation, and material moving
Income: Per capita: $20,428; Median household: $24,663; Average household: $42,846; Households with income of $100,000 or more: 4.0%; Poverty rate: 15.1%
Educational Attainment: High school diploma or higher: 75.7%; Bachelor's degree or higher: 9.5%; Graduate/professional degree or higher: 2.8%

School District(s)
Cairo-Durham Central SD (KG-12)
　　Enrollment: 1,239 . . . . (518) 622-8534
Housing: Homeownership rate: 59.4%; Median home value: $140,500; Median year structure built: 1957; Homeowner vacancy rate: 13.6%; Median selected monthly owner costs: $1,210 with a mortgage, $413 without a mortgage; Median gross rent: $930 per month; Rental vacancy rate: 0.0%
Health Insurance: 93.0% have insurance; 57.0% have private insurance; 42.5% have public insurance; 7.0% do not have insurance; 0.0% of children under 18 do not have insurance
Transportation: Commute: 100.0% car, 0.0% public transportation, 0.0% walk, 0.0% work from home; Mean travel time to work: 22.7 minutes

CAIRO (town). Covers a land area of 59.828 square miles and a water area of 0.254 square miles. Located at 42.30° N. Lat; 74.02° W. Long. Elevation is 374 feet.
Population: 6,483; Growth (since 2000): 2.0%; Density: 108.4 persons per square mile; Race: 89.9% White, 2.2% Black/African American, 3.1% Asian, 0.0% American Indian/Alaska Native, 0.0% Native Hawaiian/Other

Pacific Islander, 1.7% Two or more races, 6.9% Hispanic of any race; Average household size: 2.81; Median age: 45.1; Age under 18: 17.3%; Age 65 and over: 16.9%; Males per 100 females: 95.0; Marriage status: 34.1% never married, 50.3% now married, 1.4% separated, 4.7% widowed, 10.9% divorced; Foreign born: 8.3%; Speak English only: 86.4%; With disability: 12.7%; Veterans: 7.3%; Ancestry: 22.7% German, 18.6% Irish, 15.7% American, 13.6% Italian, 3.7% English
Employment: 14.2% management, business, and financial, 2.4% computer, engineering, and science, 13.3% education, legal, community service, arts, and media, 6.0% healthcare practitioners, 19.6% service, 19.5% sales and office, 8.3% natural resources, construction, and maintenance, 16.8% production, transportation, and material moving
Income: Per capita: $25,801; Median household: $55,036; Average household: $64,211; Households with income of $100,000 or more: 20.3%; Poverty rate: 8.3%
Educational Attainment: High school diploma or higher: 85.4%; Bachelor's degree or higher: 22.1%; Graduate/professional degree or higher: 8.4%

School District(s)
Cairo-Durham Central SD (KG-12)
　　Enrollment: 1,239 . . . . (518) 622-8534
Housing: Homeownership rate: 75.0%; Median home value: $170,500; Median year structure built: 1972; Homeowner vacancy rate: 7.2%; Median selected monthly owner costs: $1,425 with a mortgage, $495 without a mortgage; Median gross rent: $952 per month; Rental vacancy rate: 3.6%
Health Insurance: 95.4% have insurance; 72.2% have private insurance; 35.2% have public insurance; 4.6% do not have insurance; 0.0% of children under 18 do not have insurance
Safety: Violent crime rate: 6.2 per 10,000 population; Property crime rate: 54.5 per 10,000 population
Transportation: Commute: 94.2% car, 0.6% public transportation, 1.8% walk, 3.5% work from home; Mean travel time to work: 30.0 minutes
Additional Information Contacts
Town of Cairo . . . . (518) 622-3120
　　http://www.townofcairo.com/Pages/index

CATSKILL (town). Covers a land area of 60.439 square miles and a water area of 3.726 square miles. Located at 42.21° N. Lat; 73.94° W. Long. Elevation is 43 feet.
History: Originally known as Catskill Landing, the settlement of Catskill was subsidiary to the old Dutch hamlet of Kaatskill, in the hills to the west. Mountains, creeks, and village were named by the Dutch for the wildcats that occasionally came down from the hills, where they roamed in large numbers. In the heyday of turnpike and river transportation, the place bustled with prosperity. Thomas Cole lived and painted in the village. Settled 17th, incorporated in 1806.
Population: 11,439; Growth (since 2000): -3.5%; Density: 189.3 persons per square mile; Race: 84.3% White, 8.9% Black/African American, 0.6% Asian, 1.4% American Indian/Alaska Native, 0.0% Native Hawaiian/Other Pacific Islander, 3.8% Two or more races, 5.4% Hispanic of any race; Average household size: 2.59; Median age: 44.7; Age under 18: 19.8%; Age 65 and over: 21.5%; Males per 100 females: 95.5; Marriage status: 37.7% never married, 45.0% now married, 1.7% separated, 8.2% widowed, 9.1% divorced; Foreign born: 4.8%; Speak English only: 93.8%; With disability: 20.1%; Veterans: 8.7%; Ancestry: 22.1% Italian, 22.1% Irish, 16.3% German, 8.1% American, 4.9% English
Employment: 13.0% management, business, and financial, 2.7% computer, engineering, and science, 15.6% education, legal, community service, arts, and media, 6.0% healthcare practitioners, 18.1% service, 22.1% sales and office, 8.3% natural resources, construction, and maintenance, 14.3% production, transportation, and material moving
Income: Per capita: $25,881; Median household: $43,981; Average household: $62,410; Households with income of $100,000 or more: 17.0%; Poverty rate: 17.5%
Educational Attainment: High school diploma or higher: 85.1%; Bachelor's degree or higher: 21.2%; Graduate/professional degree or higher: 8.0%

School District(s)
Catskill Central SD (PK-12)
　　Enrollment: 1,526 . . . . (518) 943-4696
Housing: Homeownership rate: 62.8%; Median home value: $169,600; Median year structure built: 1953; Homeowner vacancy rate: 3.7%; Median selected monthly owner costs: $1,609 with a mortgage, $627 without a mortgage; Median gross rent: $853 per month; Rental vacancy rate: 17.0%

Health Insurance: 93.4% have insurance; 69.7% have private insurance; 45.0% have public insurance; 6.6% do not have insurance; 2.3% of children under 18 do not have insurance
Newspapers: Daily Mail (daily circulation 3,400)
Transportation: Commute: 86.4% car, 2.6% public transportation, 5.1% walk, 3.4% work from home; Mean travel time to work: 25.8 minutes
Additional Information Contacts
Town of Catskill. . . . . (518) 943-2141
  http://www.townofcatskillny.gov/Public_Documents/index

CATSKILL (village). County seat. Covers a land area of 2.280 square miles and a water area of 0.579 square miles. Located at 42.21° N. Lat; 73.86° W. Long. Elevation is 43 feet.

Population: 3,894; Growth (since 2000): -11.3%; Density: 1,708.2 persons per square mile; Race: 74.9% White, 21.5% Black/African American, 0.4% Asian, 3.1% American Indian/Alaska Native, 0.0% Native Hawaiian/Other Pacific Islander, 0.0% Two or more races, 4.1% Hispanic of any race; Average household size: 2.85; Median age: 37.4; Age under 18: 19.6%; Age 65 and over: 16.0%; Males per 100 females: 98.9; Marriage status: 47.8% never married, 34.8% now married, 2.7% separated, 6.1% widowed, 11.3% divorced; Foreign born: 3.9%; Speak English only: 96.7%; With disability: 23.1%; Veterans: 10.4%; Ancestry: 23.6% Irish, 16.5% Italian, 11.6% American, 10.9% German, 5.3% Jamaican
Employment: 7.4% management, business, and financial, 3.6% computer, engineering, and science, 19.4% education, legal, community service, arts, and media, 9.8% healthcare practitioners, 21.5% service, 23.0% sales and office, 5.2% natural resources, construction, and maintenance, 10.1% production, transportation, and material moving
Income: Per capita: $22,001; Median household: $35,024; Average household: $55,369; Households with income of $100,000 or more: 11.1%; Poverty rate: 29.2%
Educational Attainment: High school diploma or higher: 85.7%; Bachelor's degree or higher: 20.6%; Graduate/professional degree or higher: 6.9%

School District(s)
Catskill Central SD (PK-12)
  Enrollment: 1,526 . . . . (518) 943-4696
Housing: Homeownership rate: 49.2%; Median home value: $176,600; Median year structure built: Before 1940; Homeowner vacancy rate: 5.5%; Median selected monthly owner costs: $1,945 with a mortgage, $787 without a mortgage; Median gross rent: $740 per month; Rental vacancy rate: 20.2%
Health Insurance: 95.5% have insurance; 64.9% have private insurance; 50.7% have public insurance; 4.5% do not have insurance; 1.8% of children under 18 do not have insurance
Newspapers: Daily Mail (daily circulation 3,400)
Transportation: Commute: 79.2% car, 4.6% public transportation, 8.6% walk, 1.6% work from home; Mean travel time to work: 20.3 minutes
Additional Information Contacts
Village of Catskill. . . . . (518) 943-3830
  http://www.villageofcatskill.net

CLIMAX (unincorporated postal area)
ZCTA: 12042
  Covers a land area of 4.344 square miles and a water area of 0.012 square miles. Located at 42.42° N. Lat; 73.94° W. Long. Elevation is 246 feet.
Population: 217; Growth (since 2000): -73.3%; Density: 49.9 persons per square mile; Race: 100.0% White, 0.0% Black/African American, 0.0% Asian, 0.0% American Indian/Alaska Native, 0.0% Native Hawaiian/Other Pacific Islander, 0.0% Two or more races, 0.0% Hispanic of any race; Average household size: 1.84; Median age: 54.7; Age under 18: 0.0%; Age 65 and over: 25.8%; Males per 100 females: 108.5; Marriage status: 17.1% never married, 62.2% now married, 0.0% separated, 0.0% widowed, 20.7% divorced; Foreign born: 2.8%; Speak English only: 94.9%; With disability: 12.9%; Veterans: 4.6%; Ancestry: 35.9% German, 35.5% Irish, 32.3% English, 14.3% French Canadian, 9.2% French
Employment: 15.6% management, business, and financial, 15.6% computer, engineering, and science, 13.8% education, legal, community service, arts, and media, 0.0% healthcare practitioners, 23.9% service, 12.8% sales and office, 9.2% natural resources, construction, and maintenance, 9.2% production, transportation, and material moving

Income: Per capita: $31,073; Median household: $44,583; Average household: $56,742; Households with income of $100,000 or more: 11.9%; Poverty rate: 9.7%
Educational Attainment: High school diploma or higher: 100.0%; Bachelor's degree or higher: 20.9%; Graduate/professional degree or higher: 13.4%
Housing: Homeownership rate: 72.0%; Median home value: $145,600; Median year structure built: 1965; Homeowner vacancy rate: 21.3%; Median selected monthly owner costs: $1,344 with a mortgage, $660 without a mortgage; Median gross rent: n/a per month; Rental vacancy rate: 0.0%
Health Insurance: 87.1% have insurance; 73.3% have private insurance; 25.8% have public insurance; 12.9% do not have insurance; 0.0% of children under 18 do not have insurance
Transportation: Commute: 90.1% car, 0.0% public transportation, 0.0% walk, 9.9% work from home; Mean travel time to work: 0.0 minutes

CORNWALLVILLE (unincorporated postal area)
ZCTA: 12418
  Covers a land area of 13.815 square miles and a water area of 0 square miles. Located at 42.36° N. Lat; 74.16° W. Long. Elevation is 958 feet.
Population: 400; Growth (since 2000): -34.6%; Density: 29.0 persons per square mile; Race: 91.8% White, 8.3% Black/African American, 0.0% Asian, 0.0% American Indian/Alaska Native, 0.0% Native Hawaiian/Other Pacific Islander, 0.0% Two or more races, 0.0% Hispanic of any race; Average household size: 3.70; Median age: 38.3; Age under 18: 22.0%; Age 65 and over: 11.8%; Males per 100 females: 94.6; Marriage status: 46.9% never married, 46.6% now married, 1.5% separated, 1.5% widowed, 4.9% divorced; Foreign born: 1.3%; Speak English only: 100.0%; With disability: 11.5%; Veterans: 3.2%; Ancestry: 26.3% Italian, 21.0% German, 15.8% Irish, 7.3% American, 6.5% English
Employment: 9.0% management, business, and financial, 0.0% computer, engineering, and science, 7.5% education, legal, community service, arts, and media, 2.5% healthcare practitioners, 24.6% service, 24.6% sales and office, 6.0% natural resources, construction, and maintenance, 25.6% production, transportation, and material moving
Income: Per capita: $28,101; Median household: $72,727; Average household: $80,559; Households with income of $100,000 or more: 16.6%; Poverty rate: 23.3%
Educational Attainment: High school diploma or higher: 93.1%; Bachelor's degree or higher: 22.6%; Graduate/professional degree or higher: 6.9%
Housing: Homeownership rate: 100.0%; Median home value: $182,900; Median year structure built: 1974; Homeowner vacancy rate: 0.0%; Median selected monthly owner costs: $1,817 with a mortgage, $0 without a mortgage; Median gross rent: n/a per month; Rental vacancy rate: 100.0%
Health Insurance: 75.3% have insurance; 66.5% have private insurance; 22.5% have public insurance; 24.8% do not have insurance; 33.0% of children under 18 do not have insurance
Transportation: Commute: 86.9% car, 0.0% public transportation, 2.5% walk, 10.6% work from home; Mean travel time to work: 32.4 minutes

COXSACKIE (town). Covers a land area of 36.865 square miles and a water area of 1.548 square miles. Located at 42.35° N. Lat; 73.86° W. Long. Elevation is 141 feet.
History: Franklin air-cooled automobile engine invented here. Settled by the Dutch before 1700; incorporated 1867.
Population: 8,594; Growth (since 2000): -3.3%; Density: 233.1 persons per square mile; Race: 79.4% White, 19.5% Black/African American, 0.8% Asian, 0.0% American Indian/Alaska Native, 0.0% Native Hawaiian/Other Pacific Islander, 0.2% Two or more races, 11.8% Hispanic of any race; Average household size: 2.73; Median age: 37.9; Age under 18: 17.6%; Age 65 and over: 13.8%; Males per 100 females: 184.3; Marriage status: 47.3% never married, 41.4% now married, 2.3% separated, 4.5% widowed, 6.8% divorced; Foreign born: 6.4%; Speak English only: 87.6%; With disability: 12.4%; Veterans: 6.1%; Ancestry: 16.4% American, 12.5% Irish, 12.2% German, 9.1% Italian, 7.2% English
Employment: 11.9% management, business, and financial, 2.7% computer, engineering, and science, 12.3% education, legal, community service, arts, and media, 8.2% healthcare practitioners, 19.7% service, 23.5% sales and office, 6.6% natural resources, construction, and maintenance, 15.1% production, transportation, and material moving

Income: Per capita: $23,487; Median household: $68,218; Average household: $83,279; Households with income of $100,000 or more: 28.4%; Poverty rate: 7.7%

Educational Attainment: High school diploma or higher: 73.6%; Bachelor's degree or higher: 16.5%; Graduate/professional degree or higher: 7.7%

School District(s)

Coxsackie-Athens Central SD (KG-12)

    Enrollment: 1,357 . . . . (518) 731-1710

Housing: Homeownership rate: 72.5%; Median home value: $161,300; Median year structure built: 1971; Homeowner vacancy rate: 2.7%; Median selected monthly owner costs: $1,640 with a mortgage, $626 without a mortgage; Median gross rent: $814 per month; Rental vacancy rate: 0.0%

Health Insurance: 96.1% have insurance; 72.5% have private insurance; 36.3% have public insurance; 3.9% do not have insurance; 7.4% of children under 18 do not have insurance

Transportation: Commute: 95.4% car, 1.0% public transportation, 0.1% walk, 1.4% work from home; Mean travel time to work: 29.5 minutes

Additional Information Contacts

Town of Coxsackie . . . . (518) 731-2727

    http://www.coxsackie.org

COXSACKIE (village). Covers a land area of 2.172 square miles and a water area of 0.423 square miles. Located at 42.36° N. Lat; 73.81° W. Long. Elevation is 141 feet.

Population: 2,705; Growth (since 2000): -6.6%; Density: 1,245.6 persons per square mile; Race: 95.4% White, 3.7% Black/African American, 0.6% Asian, 0.0% American Indian/Alaska Native, 0.0% Native Hawaiian/Other Pacific Islander, 0.3% Two or more races, 1.0% Hispanic of any race; Average household size: 2.56; Median age: 44.4; Age under 18: 23.2%; Age 65 and over: 21.9%; Males per 100 females: 89.9; Marriage status: 35.0% never married, 43.8% now married, 0.3% separated, 8.8% widowed, 12.5% divorced; Foreign born: 5.2%; Speak English only: 98.1%; With disability: 16.2%; Veterans: 9.1%; Ancestry: 28.5% American, 20.7% German, 20.4% Irish, 12.6% Italian, 11.7% English

Employment: 13.6% management, business, and financial, 4.2% computer, engineering, and science, 11.1% education, legal, community service, arts, and media, 5.8% healthcare practitioners, 23.0% service, 19.3% sales and office, 9.4% natural resources, construction, and maintenance, 13.6% production, transportation, and material moving

Income: Per capita: $30,843; Median household: $57,422; Average household: $74,008; Households with income of $100,000 or more: 24.1%; Poverty rate: 7.9%

Educational Attainment: High school diploma or higher: 88.7%; Bachelor's degree or higher: 18.2%; Graduate/professional degree or higher: 7.1%

School District(s)

Coxsackie-Athens Central SD (KG-12)

    Enrollment: 1,357 . . . . (518) 731-1710

Housing: Homeownership rate: 64.5%; Median home value: $155,500; Median year structure built: 1951; Homeowner vacancy rate: 4.1%; Median selected monthly owner costs: $1,684 with a mortgage, $573 without a mortgage; Median gross rent: $722 per month; Rental vacancy rate: 0.0%

Health Insurance: 99.0% have insurance; 65.8% have private insurance; 47.1% have public insurance; 1.0% do not have insurance; 0.0% of children under 18 do not have insurance

Transportation: Commute: 96.3% car, 0.0% public transportation, 0.0% walk, 1.5% work from home; Mean travel time to work: 24.8 minutes

DURHAM (town). Covers a land area of 49.314 square miles and a water area of 0.041 square miles. Located at 42.37° N. Lat; 74.15° W. Long. Elevation is 771 feet.

Population: 2,681; Growth (since 2000): 3.4%; Density: 54.4 persons per square mile; Race: 95.2% White, 2.4% Black/African American, 1.4% Asian, 0.0% American Indian/Alaska Native, 0.0% Native Hawaiian/Other Pacific Islander, 0.0% Two or more races, 1.9% Hispanic of any race; Average household size: 2.90; Median age: 43.9; Age under 18: 20.5%; Age 65 and over: 16.4%; Males per 100 females: 101.9; Marriage status: 35.6% never married, 50.8% now married, 3.3% separated, 5.3% widowed, 8.3% divorced; Foreign born: 4.8%; Speak English only: 95.7%; With disability: 9.9%; Veterans: 6.6%; Ancestry: 25.1% Irish, 16.7% American, 14.5% German, 11.6% Italian, 7.5% English

Employment: 9.6% management, business, and financial, 3.3% computer, engineering, and science, 11.2% education, legal, community service, arts, and media, 4.3% healthcare practitioners, 18.3% service, 25.9% sales and

office, 10.3% natural resources, construction, and maintenance, 17.1% production, transportation, and material moving

Income: Per capita: $28,066; Median household: $52,738; Average household: $70,791; Households with income of $100,000 or more: 21.4%; Poverty rate: 19.4%

Educational Attainment: High school diploma or higher: 93.1%; Bachelor's degree or higher: 22.7%; Graduate/professional degree or higher: 10.1%

School District(s)

Cairo-Durham Central SD (KG-12)

    Enrollment: 1,239 . . . . (518) 622-8534

Housing: Homeownership rate: 81.9%; Median home value: $179,200; Median year structure built: 1964; Homeowner vacancy rate: 0.7%; Median selected monthly owner costs: $1,497 with a mortgage, $588 without a mortgage; Median gross rent: $793 per month; Rental vacancy rate: 17.6%

Health Insurance: 92.1% have insurance; 63.7% have private insurance; 40.5% have public insurance; 7.9% do not have insurance; 10.0% of children under 18 do not have insurance

Safety: Violent crime rate: 0.0 per 10,000 population; Property crime rate: 33.8 per 10,000 population

Transportation: Commute: 88.7% car, 1.1% public transportation, 2.0% walk, 5.4% work from home; Mean travel time to work: 31.8 minutes

EARLTON (unincorporated postal area)

ZCTA: 12058

    Covers a land area of 19.232 square miles and a water area of 0.306 square miles. Located at 42.35° N. Lat; 73.92° W. Long. Elevation is 417 feet.

Population: 1,741; Growth (since 2000): 24.4%; Density: 90.5 persons per square mile; Race: 91.2% White, 6.0% Black/African American, 1.0% Asian, 0.0% American Indian/Alaska Native, 0.0% Native Hawaiian/Other Pacific Islander, 1.8% Two or more races, 6.5% Hispanic of any race; Average household size: 2.95; Median age: 36.9; Age under 18: 29.6%; Age 65 and over: 9.6%; Males per 100 females: 106.7; Marriage status: 23.3% never married, 70.9% now married, 2.1% separated, 2.1% widowed, 3.7% divorced; Foreign born: 0.5%; Speak English only: 97.3%; With disability: 6.7%; Veterans: 9.1%; Ancestry: 23.7% American, 21.1% Irish, 11.3% Italian, 11.3% German, 7.4% English

Employment: 10.9% management, business, and financial, 5.4% computer, engineering, and science, 8.0% education, legal, community service, arts, and media, 6.3% healthcare practitioners, 22.5% service, 20.9% sales and office, 6.2% natural resources, construction, and maintenance, 19.8% production, transportation, and material moving

Income: Per capita: $28,312; Median household: $82,768; Average household: $80,354; Households with income of $100,000 or more: 27.8%; Poverty rate: 7.0%

Educational Attainment: High school diploma or higher: 95.4%; Bachelor's degree or higher: 22.0%; Graduate/professional degree or higher: 9.7%

Housing: Homeownership rate: 83.6%; Median home value: $196,000; Median year structure built: 1980; Homeowner vacancy rate: 0.0%; Median selected monthly owner costs: $1,551 with a mortgage, $782 without a mortgage; Median gross rent: $865 per month; Rental vacancy rate: 0.0%

Health Insurance: 97.4% have insurance; 76.1% have private insurance; 26.6% have public insurance; 2.6% do not have insurance; 1.2% of children under 18 do not have insurance

Transportation: Commute: 92.9% car, 1.1% public transportation, 0.0% walk, 3.2% work from home; Mean travel time to work: 37.3 minutes

EAST DURHAM (unincorporated postal area)

ZCTA: 12423

    Covers a land area of 12.716 square miles and a water area of 0 square miles. Located at 42.38° N. Lat; 74.11° W. Long. Elevation is 535 feet.

Population: 1,108; Growth (since 2000): 6.4%; Density: 87.1 persons per square mile; Race: 93.1% White, 2.9% Black/African American, 3.4% Asian, 0.0% American Indian/Alaska Native, 0.0% Native Hawaiian/Other Pacific Islander, 0.0% Two or more races, 1.4% Hispanic of any race; Average household size: 2.63; Median age: 44.6; Age under 18: 23.1%; Age 65 and over: 19.1%; Males per 100 females: 106.6; Marriage status: 32.0% never married, 49.4% now married, 5.9% separated, 6.8% widowed, 11.8% divorced; Foreign born: 8.2%; Speak English only: 95.0%; With disability: 7.9%; Veterans: 2.6%; Ancestry:

32.0% Irish, 23.0% American, 16.6% German, 9.6% Italian, 5.9% French

Employment: 13.8% management, business, and financial, 7.3% computer, engineering, and science, 16.9% education, legal, community service, arts, and media, 2.2% healthcare practitioners, 18.7% service, 26.1% sales and office, 9.4% natural resources, construction, and maintenance, 5.7% production, transportation, and material moving

Income: Per capita: $28,759; Median household: $43,789; Average household: $66,818; Households with income of $100,000 or more: 21.9%; Poverty rate: 21.8%

Educational Attainment: High school diploma or higher: 92.1%; Bachelor's degree or higher: 22.0%; Graduate/professional degree or higher: 10.9%

Housing: Homeownership rate: 75.8%; Median home value: $197,200; Median year structure built: 1965; Homeowner vacancy rate: 0.0%; Median selected monthly owner costs: $1,411 with a mortgage, $618 without a mortgage; Median gross rent: $930 per month; Rental vacancy rate: 22.1%

Health Insurance: 97.0% have insurance; 58.8% have private insurance; 47.4% have public insurance; 3.0% do not have insurance; 1.8% of children under 18 do not have insurance

Transportation: Commute: 91.7% car, 0.0% public transportation, 1.2% walk, 4.4% work from home; Mean travel time to work: 33.6 minutes

EAST JEWETT (unincorporated postal area)
ZCTA: 12424

Covers a land area of 17.771 square miles and a water area of 0.115 square miles. Located at 42.25° N. Lat; 74.12° W. Long. Elevation is 1,965 feet.

Population: 226; Growth (since 2000): -25.4%; Density: 12.7 persons per square mile; Race: 100.0% White, 0.0% Black/African American, 0.0% Asian, 0.0% American Indian/Alaska Native, 0.0% Native Hawaiian/Other Pacific Islander, 0.0% Two or more races, 0.0% Hispanic of any race; Average household size: 2.13; Median age: 65.0; Age under 18: 0.0%; Age 65 and over: 50.0%; Males per 100 females: 111.9; Marriage status: 19.5% never married, 50.9% now married, 0.0% separated, 22.6% widowed, 7.1% divorced; Foreign born: 8.0%; Speak English only: 98.2%; With disability: 19.9%; Veterans: 10.6%; Ancestry: 22.1% Irish, 14.2% English, 11.1% German, 3.5% American, 3.5% Scottish

Employment: 0.0% management, business, and financial, 12.9% computer, engineering, and science, 26.7% education, legal, community service, arts, and media, 26.7% healthcare practitioners, 11.9% service, 0.0% sales and office, 17.8% natural resources, construction, and maintenance, 4.0% production, transportation, and material moving

Income: Per capita: $43,561; Median household: $68,750; Average household: $75,188; Households with income of $100,000 or more: 37.7%; Poverty rate: 5.3%

Educational Attainment: High school diploma or higher: 94.9%; Bachelor's degree or higher: 47.9%; Graduate/professional degree or higher: 18.9%

Housing: Homeownership rate: 90.6%; Median home value: $207,600; Median year structure built: 1983; Homeowner vacancy rate: 0.0%; Median selected monthly owner costs: $1,156 with a mortgage, $431 without a mortgage; Median gross rent: n/a per month; Rental vacancy rate: 0.0%

Health Insurance: 92.9% have insurance; 61.1% have private insurance; 53.5% have public insurance; 7.1% do not have insurance; 0.0% of children under 18 do not have insurance

Transportation: Commute: 77.2% car, 0.0% public transportation, 0.0% walk, 9.9% work from home; Mean travel time to work: 33.5 minutes

ELKA PARK (unincorporated postal area)
ZCTA: 12427

Covers a land area of 41.000 square miles and a water area of 0.037 square miles. Located at 42.13° N. Lat; 74.14° W. Long. Elevation is 2,178 feet.

Population: 532; Growth (since 2000): 39.6%; Density: 13.0 persons per square mile; Race: 94.9% White, 0.0% Black/African American, 3.6% Asian, 0.0% American Indian/Alaska Native, 0.0% Native Hawaiian/Other Pacific Islander, 0.0% Two or more races, 1.5% Hispanic of any race; Average household size: 2.10; Median age: 34.9; Age under 18: 23.3%; Age 65 and over: 20.3%; Males per 100 females: 82.9; Marriage status: 47.9% never married, 46.1% now married, 0.0% separated, 4.6% widowed, 1.4% divorced; Foreign born: 12.2%; Speak

English only: 91.4%; With disability: 9.8%; Veterans: 6.6%; Ancestry: 33.1% American, 15.2% Eastern European, 12.0% Italian, 10.2% German, 9.6% Irish

Employment: 31.1% management, business, and financial, 21.7% computer, engineering, and science, 10.6% education, legal, community service, arts, and media, 0.0% healthcare practitioners, 7.9% service, 0.0% sales and office, 0.0% natural resources, construction, and maintenance, 28.7% production, transportation, and material moving

Income: Per capita: $41,400; Median household: $92,262; Average household: $134,799; Households with income of $100,000 or more: 48.6%; Poverty rate: 25.2%

Educational Attainment: High school diploma or higher: 100.0%; Bachelor's degree or higher: 43.1%; Graduate/professional degree or higher: 15.3%

Housing: Homeownership rate: 89.0%; Median home value: n/a; Median year structure built: Before 1940; Homeowner vacancy rate: 0.0%; Median selected monthly owner costs: $0 with a mortgage, $490 without a mortgage; Median gross rent: n/a per month; Rental vacancy rate: 0.0%

Health Insurance: 95.9% have insurance; 50.2% have private insurance; 54.9% have public insurance; 4.1% do not have insurance; 0.0% of children under 18 do not have insurance

Transportation: Commute: 65.0% car, 0.0% public transportation, 28.7% walk, 6.3% work from home; Mean travel time to work: 21.1 minutes

FREEHOLD (unincorporated postal area)
ZCTA: 12431

Covers a land area of 15.466 square miles and a water area of 0.027 square miles. Located at 42.36° N. Lat; 74.02° W. Long. Elevation is 423 feet.

Population: 1,088; Growth (since 2000): -25.6%; Density: 70.3 persons per square mile; Race: 100.0% White, 0.0% Black/African American, 0.0% Asian, 0.0% American Indian/Alaska Native, 0.0% Native Hawaiian/Other Pacific Islander, 0.0% Two or more races, 3.2% Hispanic of any race; Average household size: 2.62; Median age: 39.8; Age under 18: 22.7%; Age 65 and over: 20.9%; Males per 100 females: 105.5; Marriage status: 33.3% never married, 50.1% now married, 0.0% separated, 6.3% widowed, 10.4% divorced; Foreign born: 1.7%; Speak English only: 100.0%; With disability: 13.6%; Veterans: 12.2%; Ancestry: 37.9% American, 20.4% Italian, 15.4% German, 14.6% English, 9.5% Irish

Employment: 11.5% management, business, and financial, 3.1% computer, engineering, and science, 23.8% education, legal, community service, arts, and media, 7.5% healthcare practitioners, 18.5% service, 18.0% sales and office, 9.1% natural resources, construction, and maintenance, 8.4% production, transportation, and material moving

Income: Per capita: $21,609; Median household: $38,605; Average household: $51,594; Households with income of $100,000 or more: 13.1%; Poverty rate: 26.8%

Educational Attainment: High school diploma or higher: 97.5%; Bachelor's degree or higher: 35.4%; Graduate/professional degree or higher: 24.9%

Housing: Homeownership rate: 65.8%; Median home value: $194,000; Median year structure built: 1973; Homeowner vacancy rate: 0.0%; Median selected monthly owner costs: $1,875 with a mortgage, $601 without a mortgage; Median gross rent: $1,096 per month; Rental vacancy rate: 0.0%

Health Insurance: 88.8% have insurance; 66.5% have private insurance; 42.0% have public insurance; 11.2% do not have insurance; 0.0% of children under 18 do not have insurance

Transportation: Commute: 90.1% car, 0.0% public transportation, 0.0% walk, 9.9% work from home; Mean travel time to work: 20.9 minutes

GREENVILLE (CDP).
Covers a land area of 3.432 square miles and a water area of 0.020 square miles. Located at 42.41° N. Lat; 74.02° W. Long. Elevation is 709 feet.

Population: 573; Growth (since 2000): 16.2%; Density: 167.0 persons per square mile; Race: 98.3% White, 0.0% Black/African American, 1.7% Asian, 0.0% American Indian/Alaska Native, 0.0% Native Hawaiian/Other Pacific Islander, 0.0% Two or more races, 0.0% Hispanic of any race; Average household size: 2.16; Median age: 47.3; Age under 18: 16.6%; Age 65 and over: 24.8%; Males per 100 females: 89.5; Marriage status: 23.7% never married, 43.7% now married, 0.0% separated, 12.3% widowed, 20.3% divorced; Foreign born: 7.5%; Speak English only: 97.0%;

With disability: 8.7%; Veterans: 14.0%; Ancestry: 24.8% Irish, 18.7% American, 15.4% German, 10.3% English, 8.9% Polish
Employment: 15.0% management, business, and financial, 0.0% computer, engineering, and science, 15.4% education, legal, community service, arts, and media, 2.6% healthcare practitioners, 19.4% service, 18.7% sales and office, 11.4% natural resources, construction, and maintenance, 17.6% production, transportation, and material moving
Income: Per capita: $27,671; Median household: $48,583; Average household: $57,736; Households with income of $100,000 or more: 23.0%; Poverty rate: 12.4%
Educational Attainment: High school diploma or higher: 72.7%; Bachelor's degree or higher: 16.6%; Graduate/professional degree or higher: 9.8%

School District(s)
Greenville Central SD (KG-12)
    Enrollment: 1,170 . . . . (518) 966-5070
Housing: Homeownership rate: 81.9%; Median home value: $157,200; Median year structure built: 1969; Homeowner vacancy rate: 0.0%; Median selected monthly owner costs: $1,672 with a mortgage, $485 without a mortgage; Median gross rent: $950 per month; Rental vacancy rate: 0.0%
Health Insurance: 95.1% have insurance; 75.0% have private insurance; 42.4% have public insurance; 4.9% do not have insurance; 0.0% of children under 18 do not have insurance
Transportation: Commute: 92.8% car, 0.0% public transportation, 2.6% walk, 4.5% work from home; Mean travel time to work: 27.8 minutes

GREENVILLE (town).
Covers a land area of 38.788 square miles and a water area of 0.296 square miles. Located at 42.40° N. Lat; 74.01° W. Long. Elevation is 709 feet.
Population: 3,613; Growth (since 2000): 9.0%; Density: 93.1 persons per square mile; Race: 97.2% White, 0.4% Black/African American, 0.4% Asian, 0.0% American Indian/Alaska Native, 0.0% Native Hawaiian/Other Pacific Islander, 0.8% Two or more races, 1.5% Hispanic of any race; Average household size: 2.67; Median age: 44.3; Age under 18: 21.1%; Age 65 and over: 17.2%; Males per 100 females: 97.0; Marriage status: 32.9% never married, 50.9% now married, 0.7% separated, 6.2% widowed, 10.0% divorced; Foreign born: 4.8%; Speak English only: 97.1%; With disability: 7.2%; Veterans: 10.7%; Ancestry: 27.1% American, 16.9% Irish, 15.6% German, 15.2% Italian, 9.1% English
Employment: 8.9% management, business, and financial, 3.9% computer, engineering, and science, 12.4% education, legal, community service, arts, and media, 9.5% healthcare practitioners, 17.6% service, 16.1% sales and office, 15.0% natural resources, construction, and maintenance, 16.5% production, transportation, and material moving
Income: Per capita: $26,019; Median household: $49,750; Average household: $65,797; Households with income of $100,000 or more: 21.6%; Poverty rate: 12.8%
Educational Attainment: High school diploma or higher: 92.5%; Bachelor's degree or higher: 26.9%; Graduate/professional degree or higher: 14.9%

School District(s)
Greenville Central SD (KG-12)
    Enrollment: 1,170 . . . . (518) 966-5070
Housing: Homeownership rate: 82.3%; Median home value: $169,000; Median year structure built: 1972; Homeowner vacancy rate: 0.0%; Median selected monthly owner costs: $1,643 with a mortgage, $542 without a mortgage; Median gross rent: $975 per month; Rental vacancy rate: 0.0%
Health Insurance: 95.7% have insurance; 78.8% have private insurance; 34.0% have public insurance; 4.3% do not have insurance; 0.0% of children under 18 do not have insurance
Transportation: Commute: 94.0% car, 0.8% public transportation, 1.3% walk, 3.9% work from home; Mean travel time to work: 27.5 minutes

HAINES FALLS (unincorporated postal area)
ZCTA: 12436
    Covers a land area of 15.353 square miles and a water area of 0.138 square miles. Located at 42.20° N. Lat; 74.08° W. Long. Elevation is 1,903 feet.
Population: 78; Growth (since 2000): n/a; Density: 5.1 persons per square mile; Race: 100.0% White, 0.0% Black/African American, 0.0% Asian, 0.0% American Indian/Alaska Native, 0.0% Native Hawaiian/Other Pacific Islander, 0.0% Two or more races, 0.0% Hispanic of any race; Average household size: 0.00; Median age: 52.9; Age under 18: 0.0%; Age 65 and over: 42.3%; Males per 100 females: 99.5; Marriage status: 57.7% never married, 0.0% now married, 0.0%

separated, 17.9% widowed, 24.4% divorced; Foreign born: 0.0%; Speak English only: 100.0%; With disability: 0.0%; Veterans: 17.9%; Ancestry: 75.6% Irish
Employment: 0.0% management, business, and financial, 0.0% computer, engineering, and science, 0.0% education, legal, community service, arts, and media, 0.0% healthcare practitioners, 0.0% service, 29.7% sales and office, 70.3% natural resources, construction, and maintenance, 0.0% production, transportation, and material moving
Income: Per capita: $76,618; Median household: n/a; Average household: $76,618; Households with income of $100,000 or more: 57.7%; Poverty rate: n/a
Educational Attainment: High school diploma or higher: 100.0%; Bachelor's degree or higher: 17.9%; Graduate/professional degree or higher: 17.9%
Housing: Homeownership rate: 75.6%; Median home value: n/a; Median year structure built: Before 1940; Homeowner vacancy rate: 0.0%; Median selected monthly owner costs: $0 with a mortgage, $0 without a mortgage; Median gross rent: n/a per month; Rental vacancy rate: 0.0%
Health Insurance: 100.0% have insurance; 100.0% have private insurance; 42.3% have public insurance; 0.0% do not have insurance; 0.0% of children under 18 do not have insurance
Transportation: Commute: 100.0% car, 0.0% public transportation, 0.0% walk, 0.0% work from home; Mean travel time to work: 0.0 minutes

HALCOTT (town).
Covers a land area of 23.041 square miles and a water area of 0 square miles. Located at 42.22° N. Lat; 74.48° W. Long.
Population: 293; Growth (since 2000): 51.8%; Density: 12.7 persons per square mile; Race: 88.4% White, 0.0% Black/African American, 0.0% Asian, 0.7% American Indian/Alaska Native, 0.0% Native Hawaiian/Other Pacific Islander, 10.9% Two or more races, 7.8% Hispanic of any race; Average household size: 2.14; Median age: 57.8; Age under 18: 12.6%; Age 65 and over: 22.2%; Males per 100 females: 100.0; Marriage status: 13.9% never married, 72.9% now married, 2.3% separated, 5.6% widowed, 7.5% divorced; Foreign born: 8.9%; Speak English only: 89.4%; With disability: 13.7%; Veterans: 10.9%; Ancestry: 17.4% Irish, 17.1% German, 16.7% Italian, 13.0% English, 7.8% American
Employment: 20.9% management, business, and financial, 5.2% computer, engineering, and science, 6.1% education, legal, community service, arts, and media, 6.1% healthcare practitioners, 31.3% service, 18.3% sales and office, 6.1% natural resources, construction, and maintenance, 6.1% production, transportation, and material moving
Income: Per capita: $37,478; Median household: $73,594; Average household: $74,494; Households with income of $100,000 or more: 23.3%; Poverty rate: 6.1%
Educational Attainment: High school diploma or higher: 92.9%; Bachelor's degree or higher: 29.0%; Graduate/professional degree or higher: 16.3%
Housing: Homeownership rate: 83.2%; Median home value: $182,100; Median year structure built: 1978; Homeowner vacancy rate: 4.0%; Median selected monthly owner costs: $1,083 with a mortgage, $405 without a mortgage; Median gross rent: $636 per month; Rental vacancy rate: 0.0%
Health Insurance: 93.9% have insurance; 75.8% have private insurance; 31.7% have public insurance; 6.1% do not have insurance; 0.0% of children under 18 do not have insurance
Transportation: Commute: 81.6% car, 1.8% public transportation, 0.0% walk, 16.7% work from home; Mean travel time to work: 51.9 minutes
Additional Information Contacts
Town of Halcott . . . . (845) 901-2625
    http://halcottcenter.wordpress.com

HANNACROIX (unincorporated postal area)
ZCTA: 12087
    Covers a land area of 19.689 square miles and a water area of 0.255 square miles. Located at 42.43° N. Lat; 73.89° W. Long. Elevation is 190 feet.
Population: 1,138; Growth (since 2000): 125.8%; Density: 57.8 persons per square mile; Race: 98.8% White, 1.2% Black/African American, 0.0% Asian, 0.0% American Indian/Alaska Native, 0.0% Native Hawaiian/Other Pacific Islander, 0.0% Two or more races, 0.0% Hispanic of any race; Average household size: 3.40; Median age: 31.9; Age under 18: 19.2%; Age 65 and over: 10.5%; Males per 100 females: 105.6; Marriage status: 27.8% never married, 58.6% now married, 4.3% separated, 2.6% widowed, 11.0% divorced; Foreign born: 0.7%; Speak English only: 100.0%; With disability: 12.7%; Veterans: 7.3%; Ancestry:

29.1% German, 24.3% Irish, 15.4% American, 7.8% English, 6.9% Italian

Employment: 14.5% management, business, and financial, 4.0% computer, engineering, and science, 9.0% education, legal, community service, arts, and media, 3.2% healthcare practitioners, 17.7% service, 12.2% sales and office, 17.5% natural resources, construction, and maintenance, 21.9% production, transportation, and material moving

Income: Per capita: $23,168; Median household: $73,720; Average household: $69,384; Households with income of $100,000 or more: 20.6%; Poverty rate: 2.4%

Educational Attainment: High school diploma or higher: 95.8%; Bachelor's degree or higher: 6.0%; Graduate/professional degree or higher: 3.5%

Housing: Homeownership rate: 90.7%; Median home value: $113,400; Median year structure built: 1955; Homeowner vacancy rate: 0.0%; Median selected monthly owner costs: $1,152 with a mortgage, $0 without a mortgage; Median gross rent: n/a per month; Rental vacancy rate: 0.0%

Health Insurance: 95.7% have insurance; 82.8% have private insurance; 23.6% have public insurance; 4.3% do not have insurance; 0.0% of children under 18 do not have insurance

Transportation: Commute: 95.8% car, 3.0% public transportation, 0.0% walk, 1.2% work from home; Mean travel time to work: 29.1 minutes

HENSONVILLE (unincorporated postal area)
ZCTA: 12439

Covers a land area of 7.832 square miles and a water area of 0.023 square miles. Located at 42.28° N. Lat; 74.21° W. Long. Elevation is 1,637 feet.

Population: 292; Growth (since 2000): 172.9%; Density: 37.3 persons per square mile; Race: 100.0% White, 0.0% Black/African American, 0.0% Asian, 0.0% American Indian/Alaska Native, 0.0% Native Hawaiian/Other Pacific Islander, 0.0% Two or more races, 0.0% Hispanic of any race; Average household size: 2.34; Median age: 53.7; Age under 18: 3.4%; Age 65 and over: 36.0%; Males per 100 females: 117.9; Marriage status: 34.4% never married, 47.2% now married, 1.4% separated, 14.9% widowed, 3.5% divorced; Foreign born: 11.6%; Speak English only: 88.4%; With disability: 11.3%; Veterans: 8.5%; Ancestry: 49.0% Irish, 16.4% Italian, 12.7% German, 11.0% American, 8.9% Polish

Employment: 0.0% management, business, and financial, 2.8% computer, engineering, and science, 2.8% education, legal, community service, arts, and media, 12.7% healthcare practitioners, 61.3% service, 12.7% sales and office, 7.7% natural resources, construction, and maintenance, 0.0% production, transportation, and material moving

Income: Per capita: $28,068; Median household: $41,705; Average household: $55,278; Households with income of $100,000 or more: 9.6%; Poverty rate: 1.0%

Educational Attainment: High school diploma or higher: 89.5%; Bachelor's degree or higher: 19.1%; Graduate/professional degree or higher: 9.4%

Housing: Homeownership rate: 86.4%; Median home value: $185,400; Median year structure built: 1982; Homeowner vacancy rate: 7.7%; Median selected monthly owner costs: $1,193 with a mortgage, $478 without a mortgage; Median gross rent: $939 per month; Rental vacancy rate: 0.0%

Health Insurance: 86.3% have insurance; 67.8% have private insurance; 46.9% have public insurance; 13.7% do not have insurance; 0.0% of children under 18 do not have insurance

Transportation: Commute: 100.0% car, 0.0% public transportation, 0.0% walk, 0.0% work from home; Mean travel time to work: 29.4 minutes

HUNTER (town). Covers a land area of 90.419 square miles and a water area of 0.322 square miles. Located at 42.17° N. Lat; 74.15° W. Long. Elevation is 1,588 feet.

Population: 2,650; Growth (since 2000): -2.6%; Density: 29.3 persons per square mile; Race: 95.9% White, 0.3% Black/African American, 1.1% Asian, 0.0% American Indian/Alaska Native, 0.0% Native Hawaiian/Other Pacific Islander, 2.4% Two or more races, 2.6% Hispanic of any race; Average household size: 2.01; Median age: 52.4; Age under 18: 14.0%; Age 65 and over: 29.6%; Males per 100 females: 102.4; Marriage status: 35.6% never married, 46.3% now married, 1.7% separated, 11.7% widowed, 6.4% divorced; Foreign born: 12.3%; Speak English only: 92.9%;

With disability: 5.4%; Veterans: 10.1%; Ancestry: 21.0% American, 19.2% Irish, 15.8% Italian, 13.8% German, 5.5% Polish

Employment: 15.2% management, business, and financial, 7.2% computer, engineering, and science, 11.8% education, legal, community service, arts, and media, 3.4% healthcare practitioners, 18.6% service, 19.9% sales and office, 11.1% natural resources, construction, and maintenance, 12.8% production, transportation, and material moving

Income: Per capita: $35,077; Median household: $51,642; Average household: $71,907; Households with income of $100,000 or more: 20.8%; Poverty rate: 12.8%

Educational Attainment: High school diploma or higher: 97.1%; Bachelor's degree or higher: 33.0%; Graduate/professional degree or higher: 12.6%

School District(s)
Hunter-Tannersville Central SD (PK-12)
    Enrollment: 367. . . . . (518) 589-5400

Housing: Homeownership rate: 71.1%; Median home value: $216,200; Median year structure built: 1965; Homeowner vacancy rate: 0.2%; Median selected monthly owner costs: $1,765 with a mortgage, $641 without a mortgage; Median gross rent: $880 per month; Rental vacancy rate: 13.5%

Health Insurance: 95.5% have insurance; 68.6% have private insurance; 45.0% have public insurance; 4.5% do not have insurance; 2.8% of children under 18 do not have insurance

Transportation: Commute: 79.0% car, 0.0% public transportation, 8.5% walk, 11.7% work from home; Mean travel time to work: 21.3 minutes

HUNTER (village). Covers a land area of 1.735 square miles and a water area of 0.032 square miles. Located at 42.21° N. Lat; 74.22° W. Long. Elevation is 1,588 feet.

Population: 404; Growth (since 2000): -17.6%; Density: 232.8 persons per square mile; Race: 97.3% White, 1.7% Black/African American, 0.0% Asian, 0.0% American Indian/Alaska Native, 0.0% Native Hawaiian/Other Pacific Islander, 1.0% Two or more races, 0.0% Hispanic of any race; Average household size: 1.60; Median age: 54.8; Age under 18: 8.9%; Age 65 and over: 36.4%; Males per 100 females: 111.8; Marriage status: 42.9% never married, 20.7% now married, 4.1% separated, 32.1% widowed, 4.3% divorced; Foreign born: 3.0%; Speak English only: 89.7%; With disability: 14.6%; Veterans: 10.9%; Ancestry: 40.1% Italian, 11.6% Irish, 7.9% German, 6.2% French Canadian, 5.4% American

Employment: 20.5% management, business, and financial, 0.0% computer, engineering, and science, 26.2% education, legal, community service, arts, and media, 4.8% healthcare practitioners, 14.4% service, 17.9% sales and office, 5.2% natural resources, construction, and maintenance, 10.9% production, transportation, and material moving

Income: Per capita: $20,782; Median household: $26,518; Average household: $31,065; Households with income of $100,000 or more: n/a; Poverty rate: 28.0%

Educational Attainment: High school diploma or higher: 93.6%; Bachelor's degree or higher: 37.1%; Graduate/professional degree or higher: 14.4%

School District(s)
Hunter-Tannersville Central SD (PK-12)
    Enrollment: 367. . . . . (518) 589-5400

Housing: Homeownership rate: 53.0%; Median home value: $170,800; Median year structure built: 1976; Homeowner vacancy rate: 0.0%; Median selected monthly owner costs: $2,068 with a mortgage, $431 without a mortgage; Median gross rent: $814 per month; Rental vacancy rate: 5.6%

Health Insurance: 93.1% have insurance; 65.6% have private insurance; 55.9% have public insurance; 6.9% do not have insurance; 0.0% of children under 18 do not have insurance

Transportation: Commute: 83.8% car, 0.0% public transportation, 4.8% walk, 6.1% work from home; Mean travel time to work: 13.5 minutes

JEFFERSON HEIGHTS (CDP). Covers a land area of 1.476 square miles and a water area of 0.021 square miles. Located at 42.24° N. Lat; 73.88° W. Long. Elevation is 177 feet.

Population: 982; Growth (since 2000): -11.1%; Density: 665.3 persons per square mile; Race: 77.3% White, 9.0% Black/African American, 0.8% Asian, 0.0% American Indian/Alaska Native, 0.0% Native Hawaiian/Other Pacific Islander, 11.5% Two or more races, 2.5% Hispanic of any race; Average household size: 2.17; Median age: 59.6; Age under 18: 11.4%; Age 65 and over: 36.7%; Males per 100 females: 73.7; Marriage status: 26.3% never married, 41.9% now married, 3.0% separated, 18.9% widowed, 13.0% divorced; Foreign born: 6.9%; Speak English only: 94.7%;

With disability: 12.6%; Veterans: 5.3%; Ancestry: 17.9% Irish, 15.3% Italian, 14.6% Polish, 9.9% American, 5.2% West Indian
Employment: 24.0% management, business, and financial, 0.0% computer, engineering, and science, 5.2% education, legal, community service, arts, and media, 2.2% healthcare practitioners, 14.4% service, 28.8% sales and office, 2.6% natural resources, construction, and maintenance, 22.9% production, transportation, and material moving
Income: Per capita: $27,361; Median household: $45,679; Average household: $70,250; Households with income of $100,000 or more: 29.3%; Poverty rate: 13.9%
Educational Attainment: High school diploma or higher: 89.6%; Bachelor's degree or higher: 22.5%; Graduate/professional degree or higher: 5.3%
Housing: Homeownership rate: 66.9%; Median home value: $167,200; Median year structure built: 1959; Homeowner vacancy rate: 0.0%; Median selected monthly owner costs: $1,936 with a mortgage, $573 without a mortgage; Median gross rent: $1,169 per month; Rental vacancy rate: 44.3%
Health Insurance: 100.0% have insurance; 81.4% have private insurance; 51.1% have public insurance; 0.0% do not have insurance; 0.0% of children under 18 do not have insurance
Transportation: Commute: 97.0% car, 0.0% public transportation, 3.0% walk, 0.0% work from home; Mean travel time to work: 25.7 minutes

JEWETT (town). Covers a land area of 50.323 square miles and a water area of 0.199 square miles. Located at 42.24° N. Lat; 74.23° W. Long. Elevation is 1,801 feet.
Population: 913; Growth (since 2000): -5.9%; Density: 18.1 persons per square mile; Race: 98.6% White, 0.0% Black/African American, 0.9% Asian, 0.5% American Indian/Alaska Native, 0.0% Native Hawaiian/Other Pacific Islander, 0.0% Two or more races, 0.9% Hispanic of any race; Average household size: 2.11; Median age: 60.8; Age under 18: 7.7%; Age 65 and over: 41.0%; Males per 100 females: 107.6; Marriage status: 22.3% never married, 53.2% now married, 0.5% separated, 17.0% widowed, 7.5% divorced; Foreign born: 11.4%; Speak English only: 91.0%; With disability: 12.5%; Veterans: 11.6%; Ancestry: 23.3% Irish, 14.1% Italian, 13.3% American, 10.8% English, 10.3% German
Employment: 14.2% management, business, and financial, 3.4% computer, engineering, and science, 21.6% education, legal, community service, arts, and media, 12.4% healthcare practitioners, 19.6% service, 16.8% sales and office, 6.7% natural resources, construction, and maintenance, 5.4% production, transportation, and material moving
Income: Per capita: $35,384; Median household: $53,889; Average household: $66,911; Households with income of $100,000 or more: 23.5%; Poverty rate: 5.2%
Educational Attainment: High school diploma or higher: 97.6%; Bachelor's degree or higher: 32.6%; Graduate/professional degree or higher: 17.3%
Housing: Homeownership rate: 93.5%; Median home value: $221,100; Median year structure built: 1982; Homeowner vacancy rate: 5.1%; Median selected monthly owner costs: $1,331 with a mortgage, $404 without a mortgage; Median gross rent: $850 per month; Rental vacancy rate: 0.0%
Health Insurance: 94.0% have insurance; 68.1% have private insurance; 48.3% have public insurance; 6.0% do not have insurance; 0.0% of children under 18 do not have insurance
Transportation: Commute: 88.9% car, 0.0% public transportation, 0.3% walk, 3.9% work from home; Mean travel time to work: 38.1 minutes

LANESVILLE (unincorporated postal area)
ZCTA: 12450
Covers a land area of 9.898 square miles and a water area of 0 square miles. Located at 42.13° N. Lat; 74.24° W. Long. Elevation is 1,280 feet.
Population: 141; Growth (since 2000): -67.2%; Density: 14.2 persons per square mile; Race: 100.0% White, 0.0% Black/African American, 0.0% Asian, 0.0% American Indian/Alaska Native, 0.0% Native Hawaiian/Other Pacific Islander, 0.0% Two or more races, 0.0% Hispanic of any race; Average household size: 1.99; Median age: 75.0; Age under 18: 0.0%; Age 65 and over: 100.0%; Males per 100 females: 105.6; Marriage status: 0.0% never married, 100.0% now married, 0.0% separated, 0.0% widowed, 0.0% divorced; Foreign born: 40.4%; Speak English only: 100.0%; With disability: 0.0%; Veterans: 39.7%; Ancestry: 40.4% English, 39.7% Norwegian, 9.9% Dutch, 9.9% Irish
Employment: n/a management, business, and financial, n/a computer, engineering, and science, n/a education, legal, community service, arts, and media, n/a healthcare practitioners, n/a service, n/a sales and

office, n/a natural resources, construction, and maintenance, n/a production, transportation, and material moving
Income: Per capita: $26,137; Median household: n/a; Average household: n/a; Households with income of $100,000 or more: n/a; Poverty rate: n/a
Educational Attainment: High school diploma or higher: 100.0%; Bachelor's degree or higher: 40.4%; Graduate/professional degree or higher: n/a
Housing: Homeownership rate: 100.0%; Median home value: n/a; Median year structure built: 1984; Homeowner vacancy rate: 0.0%; Median selected monthly owner costs: $0 with a mortgage, $0 without a mortgage; Median gross rent: n/a per month; Rental vacancy rate: 0.0%
Health Insurance: 100.0% have insurance; 60.3% have private insurance; 100.0% have public insurance; 0.0% do not have insurance; 0.0% of children under 18 do not have insurance
Transportation: Commute: n/a car, n/a public transportation, n/a walk, n/a work from home; Mean travel time to work: 0.0 minutes

LEEDS (CDP). Covers a land area of 0.529 square miles and a water area of 0.009 square miles. Located at 42.25° N. Lat; 73.89° W. Long. Elevation is 157 feet.
Population: 285; Growth (since 2000): -22.8%; Density: 538.6 persons per square mile; Race: 100.0% White, 0.0% Black/African American, 0.0% Asian, 0.0% American Indian/Alaska Native, 0.0% Native Hawaiian/Other Pacific Islander, 0.0% Two or more races, 0.0% Hispanic of any race; Average household size: 5.09; Median age: 15.4; Age under 18: 51.9%; Age 65 and over: 0.0%; Males per 100 females: 84.8; Marriage status: 24.7% never married, 75.3% now married, 0.0% separated, 0.0% widowed, 0.0% divorced; Foreign born: 0.0%; Speak English only: 100.0%; With disability: 3.5%; Veterans: 0.0%; Ancestry: 48.8% Irish, 46.7% Italian, 10.9% French, 10.2% German, 5.3% American
Employment: 9.7% management, business, and financial, 14.6% computer, engineering, and science, 10.7% education, legal, community service, arts, and media, 0.0% healthcare practitioners, 47.6% service, 8.7% sales and office, 0.0% natural resources, construction, and maintenance, 8.7% production, transportation, and material moving
Income: Per capita: $19,083; Median household: $84,750; Average household: $88,866; Households with income of $100,000 or more: 21.4%; Poverty rate: n/a
Educational Attainment: High school diploma or higher: 73.7%; Bachelor's degree or higher: 29.9%; Graduate/professional degree or higher: 8.0%
Housing: Homeownership rate: 83.9%; Median home value: $177,500; Median year structure built: 1944; Homeowner vacancy rate: 0.0%; Median selected monthly owner costs: $1,608 with a mortgage, n/a without a mortgage; Median gross rent: n/a per month; Rental vacancy rate: 87.5%
Health Insurance: 100.0% have insurance; 93.3% have private insurance; 6.7% have public insurance; 0.0% do not have insurance; 0.0% of children under 18 do not have insurance
Transportation: Commute: 90.3% car, 0.0% public transportation, 0.0% walk, 9.7% work from home; Mean travel time to work: 0.0 minutes

LEXINGTON (town). Covers a land area of 79.686 square miles and a water area of 0.037 square miles. Located at 42.21° N. Lat; 74.33° W. Long. Elevation is 1,322 feet.
Population: 909; Growth (since 2000): 9.5%; Density: 11.4 persons per square mile; Race: 100.0% White, 0.0% Black/African American, 0.0% Asian, 0.0% American Indian/Alaska Native, 0.0% Native Hawaiian/Other Pacific Islander, 0.0% Two or more races, 2.6% Hispanic of any race; Average household size: 2.13; Median age: 60.3; Age under 18: 8.4%; Age 65 and over: 32.6%; Males per 100 females: 82.1; Marriage status: 25.3% never married, 58.4% now married, 0.3% separated, 11.0% widowed, 5.2% divorced; Foreign born: 5.1%; Speak English only: 92.6%; With disability: 15.6%; Veterans: 13.6%; Ancestry: 19.9% German, 18.2% American, 15.5% Italian, 12.1% English, 11.2% Irish
Employment: 20.4% management, business, and financial, 2.4% computer, engineering, and science, 14.9% education, legal, community service, arts, and media, 6.7% healthcare practitioners, 17.4% service, 12.5% sales and office, 10.4% natural resources, construction, and maintenance, 15.2% production, transportation, and material moving
Income: Per capita: $32,065; Median household: $46,528; Average household: $67,626; Households with income of $100,000 or more: 17.8%; Poverty rate: 9.7%

Educational Attainment: High school diploma or higher: 88.7%; Bachelor's degree or higher: 24.6%; Graduate/professional degree or higher: 10.4%

Housing: Homeownership rate: 93.0%; Median home value: $208,800; Median year structure built: 1974; Homeowner vacancy rate: 0.8%; Median selected monthly owner costs: $1,228 with a mortgage, $477 without a mortgage; Median gross rent: $850 per month; Rental vacancy rate: 11.8%

Health Insurance: 85.5% have insurance; 60.8% have private insurance; 48.2% have public insurance; 14.5% do not have insurance; 18.4% of children under 18 do not have insurance

Transportation: Commute: 83.2% car, 1.2% public transportation, 0.0% walk, 8.2% work from home; Mean travel time to work: 29.4 minutes

---

MAPLECREST (unincorporated postal area)
ZCTA: 12454

Covers a land area of 11.135 square miles and a water area of 0.044 square miles. Located at 42.29° N. Lat; 74.15° W. Long. Elevation is 1,762 feet.

Population: 299; Growth (since 2000): -45.8%; Density: 26.9 persons per square mile; Race: 89.0% White, 0.0% Black/African American, 0.0% Asian, 0.0% American Indian/Alaska Native, 0.0% Native Hawaiian/Other Pacific Islander, 0.0% Two or more races, 0.0% Hispanic of any race; Average household size: 2.79; Median age: 46.5; Age under 18: 13.0%; Age 65 and over: 17.4%; Males per 100 females: 106.3; Marriage status: 39.8% never married, 50.6% now married, 3.3% separated, 5.9% widowed, 3.7% divorced; Foreign born: 2.3%; Speak English only: 100.0%; With disability: 15.3%; Veterans: 4.8%; Ancestry: 32.4% American, 30.8% German, 25.4% English, 17.1% Irish, 13.0% Dutch

Employment: 12.2% management, business, and financial, 2.4% computer, engineering, and science, 7.9% education, legal, community service, arts, and media, 3.0% healthcare practitioners, 12.2% service, 30.5% sales and office, 19.5% natural resources, construction, and maintenance, 12.2% production, transportation, and material moving

Income: Per capita: $31,022; Median household: $70,313; Average household: $72,374; Households with income of $100,000 or more: 21.5%; Poverty rate: 6.7%

Educational Attainment: High school diploma or higher: 88.8%; Bachelor's degree or higher: 19.5%; Graduate/professional degree or higher: 8.3%

Housing: Homeownership rate: 88.8%; Median home value: $257,600; Median year structure built: 1968; Homeowner vacancy rate: 0.0%; Median selected monthly owner costs: $1,601 with a mortgage, $469 without a mortgage; Median gross rent: n/a per month; Rental vacancy rate: 0.0%

Health Insurance: 95.1% have insurance; 76.0% have private insurance; 49.0% have public insurance; 4.9% do not have insurance; 0.0% of children under 18 do not have insurance

Transportation: Commute: 92.3% car, 0.0% public transportation, 0.0% walk, 7.7% work from home; Mean travel time to work: 24.0 minutes

---

NEW BALTIMORE (town).
Covers a land area of 41.427 square miles and a water area of 1.601 square miles. Located at 42.42° N. Lat; 73.86° W. Long. Elevation is 82 feet.

Population: 3,279; Growth (since 2000): -4.0%; Density: 79.2 persons per square mile; Race: 98.0% White, 0.5% Black/African American, 0.0% Asian, 0.0% American Indian/Alaska Native, 0.0% Native Hawaiian/Other Pacific Islander, 0.7% Two or more races, 2.0% Hispanic of any race; Average household size: 2.78; Median age: 48.5; Age under 18: 14.3%; Age 65 and over: 19.1%; Males per 100 females: 99.6; Marriage status: 21.7% never married, 63.4% now married, 1.4% separated, 6.6% widowed, 8.3% divorced; Foreign born: 3.5%; Speak English only: 97.4%; With disability: 14.3%; Veterans: 10.4%; Ancestry: 31.0% German, 21.2% Irish, 18.4% American, 12.7% Italian, 10.6% English

Employment: 15.2% management, business, and financial, 5.3% computer, engineering, and science, 9.9% education, legal, community service, arts, and media, 5.4% healthcare practitioners, 14.5% service, 23.1% sales and office, 14.4% natural resources, construction, and maintenance, 12.2% production, transportation, and material moving

Income: Per capita: $33,169; Median household: $76,229; Average household: $87,639; Households with income of $100,000 or more: 36.7%; Poverty rate: 7.4%

Educational Attainment: High school diploma or higher: 88.2%; Bachelor's degree or higher: 22.8%; Graduate/professional degree or higher: 11.2%

Housing: Homeownership rate: 95.8%; Median home value: $183,000; Median year structure built: 1963; Homeowner vacancy rate: 3.9%; Median selected monthly owner costs: $1,537 with a mortgage, $472 without a mortgage; Median gross rent: $1,063 per month; Rental vacancy rate: 0.0%

Health Insurance: 95.5% have insurance; 76.7% have private insurance; 38.2% have public insurance; 4.5% do not have insurance; 0.0% of children under 18 do not have insurance

Transportation: Commute: 91.4% car, 1.2% public transportation, 0.0% walk, 5.9% work from home; Mean travel time to work: 28.2 minutes

---

OAK HILL (unincorporated postal area)
ZCTA: 12460

Covers a land area of 2.063 square miles and a water area of 0 square miles. Located at 42.42° N. Lat; 74.15° W. Long. Elevation is 643 feet.

Population: 324; Growth (since 2000): -13.8%; Density: 157.0 persons per square mile; Race: 100.0% White, 0.0% Black/African American, 0.0% Asian, 0.0% American Indian/Alaska Native, 0.0% Native Hawaiian/Other Pacific Islander, 0.0% Two or more races, 5.2% Hispanic of any race; Average household size: 2.87; Median age: 39.1; Age under 18: 17.9%; Age 65 and over: 7.4%; Males per 100 females: 97.9; Marriage status: 60.5% never married, 31.3% now married, 1.7% separated, 1.7% widowed, 6.5% divorced; Foreign born: 1.5%; Speak English only: 100.0%; With disability: 9.6%; Veterans: 10.2%; Ancestry: 19.4% American, 17.0% Italian, 15.1% Irish, 11.7% English, 8.6% German

Employment: 0.0% management, business, and financial, 0.0% computer, engineering, and science, 0.0% education, legal, community service, arts, and media, 0.0% healthcare practitioners, 31.5% service, 23.1% sales and office, 3.7% natural resources, construction, and maintenance, 41.7% production, transportation, and material moving

Income: Per capita: $12,774; Median household: $25,809; Average household: $36,453; Households with income of $100,000 or more: 4.4%; Poverty rate: 40.7%

Educational Attainment: High school diploma or higher: 91.6%; Bachelor's degree or higher: n/a; Graduate/professional degree or higher: n/a

Housing: Homeownership rate: 65.5%; Median home value: $137,500; Median year structure built: 1946; Homeowner vacancy rate: 0.0%; Median selected monthly owner costs: $1,021 with a mortgage, $0 without a mortgage; Median gross rent: $694 per month; Rental vacancy rate: 0.0%

Health Insurance: 88.3% have insurance; 38.0% have private insurance; 56.2% have public insurance; 11.7% do not have insurance; 36.2% of children under 18 do not have insurance

Transportation: Commute: 100.0% car, 0.0% public transportation, 0.0% walk, 0.0% work from home; Mean travel time to work: 36.6 minutes

---

PALENVILLE (CDP).
Covers a land area of 3.325 square miles and a water area of 0.009 square miles. Located at 42.19° N. Lat; 74.03° W. Long. Elevation is 568 feet.

History: Legendary home of Rip Van Winkle; Sleepy Hollow, where he reputedly slept for 20 years, is nearby.

Population: 946; Growth (since 2000): -15.5%; Density: 284.5 persons per square mile; Race: 90.2% White, 3.8% Black/African American, 0.0% Asian, 0.0% American Indian/Alaska Native, 0.0% Native Hawaiian/Other Pacific Islander, 6.0% Two or more races, 0.0% Hispanic of any race; Average household size: 2.53; Median age: 44.1; Age under 18: 14.9%; Age 65 and over: 7.1%; Males per 100 females: 91.3; Marriage status: 32.3% never married, 58.4% now married, 1.6% separated, 3.1% widowed, 6.2% divorced; Foreign born: 3.9%; Speak English only: 93.6%; With disability: 10.3%; Veterans: 13.4%; Ancestry: 25.6% Italian, 24.2% Irish, 14.5% German, 8.5% American, 7.4% Polish

Employment: 16.5% management, business, and financial, 0.0% computer, engineering, and science, 18.7% education, legal, community service, arts, and media, 7.1% healthcare practitioners, 20.1% service, 19.5% sales and office, 11.4% natural resources, construction, and maintenance, 6.7% production, transportation, and material moving

Income: Per capita: $38,580; Median household: $83,750; Average household: $95,439; Households with income of $100,000 or more: 33.4%; Poverty rate: 7.8%

Educational Attainment: High school diploma or higher: 96.2%; Bachelor's degree or higher: 35.8%; Graduate/professional degree or higher: 16.9%

Housing: Homeownership rate: 86.1%; Median home value: $186,500; Median year structure built: 1963; Homeowner vacancy rate: 0.0%; Median selected monthly owner costs: $1,490 with a mortgage, $710 without a mortgage; Median gross rent: $870 per month; Rental vacancy rate: 0.0%
Health Insurance: 89.7% have insurance; 76.8% have private insurance; 27.8% have public insurance; 10.3% do not have insurance; 0.0% of children under 18 do not have insurance
Transportation: Commute: 91.6% car, 4.8% public transportation, 0.0% walk, 3.7% work from home; Mean travel time to work: 29.0 minutes

PRATTSVILLE (CDP). Covers a land area of 4.038 square miles and a water area of 0 square miles. Located at 42.35° N. Lat; 74.43° W. Long. Elevation is 1,161 feet.
Population: 294; Growth (since 2000): n/a; Density: 72.8 persons per square mile; Race: 100.0% White, 0.0% Black/African American, 0.0% Asian, 0.0% American Indian/Alaska Native, 0.0% Native Hawaiian/Other Pacific Islander, 0.0% Two or more races, 0.0% Hispanic of any race; Average household size: 2.47; Median age: 53.6; Age under 18: 18.0%; Age 65 and over: 40.1%; Males per 100 females: 101.7; Marriage status: 31.7% never married, 44.8% now married, 0.0% separated, 14.7% widowed, 8.7% divorced; Foreign born: 5.8%; Speak English only: 91.5%; With disability: 12.6%; Veterans: 4.1%; Ancestry: 27.6% German, 18.7% American, 17.7% Dutch, 15.3% Italian, 11.9% Irish
Employment: 4.2% management, business, and financial, 0.0% computer, engineering, and science, 16.9% education, legal, community service, arts, and media, 0.0% healthcare practitioners, 25.4% service, 11.3% sales and office, 26.8% natural resources, construction, and maintenance, 15.5% production, transportation, and material moving
Income: Per capita: $17,858; Median household: $35,625; Average household: $39,891; Households with income of $100,000 or more: 6.7%; Poverty rate: 29.9%
Educational Attainment: High school diploma or higher: 80.8%; Bachelor's degree or higher: 9.1%; Graduate/professional degree or higher: 2.0%
Housing: Homeownership rate: 70.6%; Median home value: $112,500; Median year structure built: 1958; Homeowner vacancy rate: 7.7%; Median selected monthly owner costs: $1,297 with a mortgage, $469 without a mortgage; Median gross rent: $393 per month; Rental vacancy rate: 0.0%
Health Insurance: 95.6% have insurance; 53.7% have private insurance; 68.0% have public insurance; 4.4% do not have insurance; 13.2% of children under 18 do not have insurance
Transportation: Commute: 89.9% car, 0.0% public transportation, 10.1% walk, 0.0% work from home; Mean travel time to work: 21.4 minutes

PRATTSVILLE (town). Covers a land area of 19.627 square miles and a water area of 0.106 square miles. Located at 42.32° N. Lat; 74.41° W. Long. Elevation is 1,161 feet.
Population: 730; Growth (since 2000): 9.8%; Density: 37.2 persons per square mile; Race: 100.0% White, 0.0% Black/African American, 0.0% Asian, 0.0% American Indian/Alaska Native, 0.0% Native Hawaiian/Other Pacific Islander, 0.0% Two or more races, 0.0% Hispanic of any race; Average household size: 2.50; Median age: 53.4; Age under 18: 11.0%; Age 65 and over: 30.1%; Males per 100 females: 101.7; Marriage status: 25.4% never married, 58.9% now married, 0.5% separated, 8.6% widowed, 7.1% divorced; Foreign born: 8.1%; Speak English only: 90.6%; With disability: 12.3%; Veterans: 8.3%; Ancestry: 25.3% German, 19.3% American, 13.8% Italian, 10.4% Dutch, 9.7% English
Employment: 6.9% management, business, and financial, 0.0% computer, engineering, and science, 9.3% education, legal, community service, arts, and media, 0.0% healthcare practitioners, 18.2% service, 22.7% sales and office, 26.5% natural resources, construction, and maintenance, 16.5% production, transportation, and material moving
Income: Per capita: $22,136; Median household: $37,250; Average household: $47,140; Households with income of $100,000 or more: 8.9%; Poverty rate: 22.1%
Educational Attainment: High school diploma or higher: 92.2%; Bachelor's degree or higher: 16.2%; Graduate/professional degree or higher: 8.5%
Housing: Homeownership rate: 81.8%; Median home value: $139,900; Median year structure built: 1976; Homeowner vacancy rate: 2.8%; Median selected monthly owner costs: $1,231 with a mortgage, $471 without a mortgage; Median gross rent: $596 per month; Rental vacancy rate: 0.0%
Health Insurance: 86.8% have insurance; 57.5% have private insurance; 47.8% have public insurance; 13.2% do not have insurance; 16.1% of children under 18 do not have insurance

Transportation: Commute: 92.0% car, 0.0% public transportation, 2.4% walk, 3.8% work from home; Mean travel time to work: 32.0 minutes

PURLING (unincorporated postal area)
ZCTA: 12470
Covers a land area of 9.786 square miles and a water area of 0.039 square miles. Located at 42.30° N. Lat; 74.10° W. Long. Elevation is 482 feet.
Population: 391; Growth (since 2000): -46.4%; Density: 40.0 persons per square mile; Race: 56.0% White, 0.0% Black/African American, 44.0% Asian, 0.0% American Indian/Alaska Native, 0.0% Native Hawaiian/Other Pacific Islander, 0.0% Two or more races, 0.0% Hispanic of any race; Average household size: 2.66; Median age: 37.8; Age under 18: 17.1%; Age 65 and over: 22.0%; Males per 100 females: 92.8; Marriage status: 41.4% never married, 41.4% now married, 0.0% separated, 4.8% widowed, 12.3% divorced; Foreign born: 41.2%; Speak English only: 51.4%; With disability: 33.8%; Veterans: 5.2%; Ancestry: 16.6% German, 12.0% Italian, 10.2% Irish, 9.5% American, 3.8% Swedish
Employment: 52.6% management, business, and financial, 0.0% computer, engineering, and science, 5.2% education, legal, community service, arts, and media, 0.0% healthcare practitioners, 12.9% service, 8.6% sales and office, 6.0% natural resources, construction, and maintenance, 14.7% production, transportation, and material moving
Income: Per capita: $20,865; Median household: $47,375; Average household: $55,923; Households with income of $100,000 or more: 21.8%; Poverty rate: 5.1%
Educational Attainment: High school diploma or higher: 98.2%; Bachelor's degree or higher: 51.6%; Graduate/professional degree or higher: 32.0%
Housing: Homeownership rate: 57.1%; Median home value: $158,300; Median year structure built: 1964; Homeowner vacancy rate: 22.2%; Median selected monthly owner costs: $1,538 with a mortgage, $0 without a mortgage; Median gross rent: n/a per month; Rental vacancy rate: 0.0%
Health Insurance: 96.4% have insurance; 77.0% have private insurance; 33.5% have public insurance; 3.6% do not have insurance; 0.0% of children under 18 do not have insurance
Transportation: Commute: 73.3% car, 9.5% public transportation, 5.2% walk, 12.1% work from home; Mean travel time to work: 39.5 minutes

ROUND TOP (unincorporated postal area)
ZCTA: 12473
Covers a land area of 15.016 square miles and a water area of 0 square miles. Located at 42.26° N. Lat; 74.04° W. Long. Elevation is 604 feet.
Population: 1,184; Growth (since 2000): 60.9%; Density: 78.8 persons per square mile; Race: 99.8% White, 0.2% Black/African American, 0.0% Asian, 0.0% American Indian/Alaska Native, 0.0% Native Hawaiian/Other Pacific Islander, 0.0% Two or more races, 0.0% Hispanic of any race; Average household size: 2.75; Median age: 40.4; Age under 18: 24.2%; Age 65 and over: 11.7%; Males per 100 females: 97.9; Marriage status: 33.0% never married, 57.5% now married, 1.9% separated, 7.5% widowed, 2.0% divorced; Foreign born: 2.1%; Speak English only: 100.0%; With disability: 2.6%; Veterans: 11.4%; Ancestry: 48.1% German, 25.5% American, 16.0% Irish, 8.1% Dutch, 5.2% Russian
Employment: 21.0% management, business, and financial, 0.0% computer, engineering, and science, 33.3% education, legal, community service, arts, and media, 3.1% healthcare practitioners, 13.5% service, 3.5% sales and office, 8.1% natural resources, construction, and maintenance, 17.4% production, transportation, and material moving
Income: Per capita: $27,626; Median household: $75,125; Average household: $73,928; Households with income of $100,000 or more: 23.9%; Poverty rate: 5.1%
Educational Attainment: High school diploma or higher: 100.0%; Bachelor's degree or higher: 40.4%; Graduate/professional degree or higher: 16.5%
Housing: Homeownership rate: 100.0%; Median home value: $185,100; Median year structure built: 1981; Homeowner vacancy rate: 1.4%; Median selected monthly owner costs: $1,294 with a mortgage, $417 without a mortgage; Median gross rent: n/a per month; Rental vacancy rate: 0.0%
Health Insurance: 100.0% have insurance; 95.8% have private insurance; 13.9% have public insurance; 0.0% do not have insurance; 0.0% of children under 18 do not have insurance

Transportation: Commute: 89.6% car, 0.0% public transportation, 6.8% walk, 3.5% work from home; Mean travel time to work: 20.0 minutes

SOUTH CAIRO (unincorporated postal area)
ZCTA: 12482

Covers a land area of 2.211 square miles and a water area of 0 square miles. Located at 42.27° N. Lat; 73.96° W. Long. Elevation is 200 feet.

Population: 475; Growth (since 2000): 5.1%; Density: 214.8 persons per square mile; Race: 92.8% White, 0.0% Black/African American, 0.0% Asian, 0.0% American Indian/Alaska Native, 0.0% Native Hawaiian/Other Pacific Islander, 7.2% Two or more races, 6.3% Hispanic of any race; Average household size: 2.29; Median age: 53.0; Age under 18: 10.7%; Age 65 and over: 47.6%; Males per 100 females: 98.3; Marriage status: 33.7% never married, 37.5% now married, 0.0% separated, 20.3% widowed, 8.5% divorced; Foreign born: 1.9%; Speak English only: 100.0%; With disability: 38.3%; Veterans: 11.3%; Ancestry: 38.1% German, 16.6% Irish, 16.4% Italian, 11.2% English, 8.2% French

Employment: 0.0% management, business, and financial, 13.8% computer, engineering, and science, 4.9% education, legal, community service, arts, and media, 8.1% healthcare practitioners, 42.3% service, 15.4% sales and office, 8.1% natural resources, construction, and maintenance, 7.3% production, transportation, and material moving

Income: Per capita: $23,355; Median household: $41,220; Average household: $47,620; Households with income of $100,000 or more: 2.9%; Poverty rate: 3.4%

Educational Attainment: High school diploma or higher: 63.2%; Bachelor's degree or higher: 2.5%; Graduate/professional degree or higher: n/a

Housing: Homeownership rate: 76.3%; Median home value: $33,900; Median year structure built: 1984; Homeowner vacancy rate: 15.5%; Median selected monthly owner costs: $1,208 with a mortgage, $657 without a mortgage; Median gross rent: n/a per month; Rental vacancy rate: 0.0%

Health Insurance: 100.0% have insurance; 64.0% have private insurance; 64.2% have public insurance; 0.0% do not have insurance; 0.0% of children under 18 do not have insurance

Transportation: Commute: 100.0% car, 0.0% public transportation, 0.0% walk, 0.0% work from home; Mean travel time to work: 18.6 minutes

SURPRISE (unincorporated postal area)
ZCTA: 12176

Covers a land area of 3.326 square miles and a water area of 0.099 square miles. Located at 42.38° N. Lat; 73.98° W. Long. Elevation is 548 feet.

Population: 478; Growth (since 2000): 173.1%; Density: 143.7 persons per square mile; Race: 90.2% White, 0.0% Black/African American, 0.0% Asian, 0.0% American Indian/Alaska Native, 0.0% Native Hawaiian/Other Pacific Islander, 1.0% Two or more races, 0.0% Hispanic of any race; Average household size: 3.54; Median age: 48.2; Age under 18: 15.5%; Age 65 and over: 4.0%; Males per 100 females: 108.4; Marriage status: 43.4% never married, 33.9% now married, 0.0% separated, 5.9% widowed, 16.8% divorced; Foreign born: 0.0%; Speak English only: 97.8%; With disability: 14.4%; Veterans: 9.9%; Ancestry: 29.3% American, 16.9% Irish, 13.4% German, 11.7% Italian, 8.2% Polish

Employment: 6.1% management, business, and financial, 0.0% computer, engineering, and science, 5.7% education, legal, community service, arts, and media, 24.0% healthcare practitioners, 12.5% service, 5.1% sales and office, 28.4% natural resources, construction, and maintenance, 18.2% production, transportation, and material moving

Income: Per capita: $27,371; Median household: $75,846; Average household: $76,703; Households with income of $100,000 or more: 28.9%; Poverty rate: 16.3%

Educational Attainment: High school diploma or higher: 92.7%; Bachelor's degree or higher: 23.6%; Graduate/professional degree or higher: 11.8%

Housing: Homeownership rate: 94.8%; Median home value: $184,500; Median year structure built: 1970; Homeowner vacancy rate: 0.0%; Median selected monthly owner costs: $1,238 with a mortgage, $565 without a mortgage; Median gross rent: n/a per month; Rental vacancy rate: 0.0%

Health Insurance: 100.0% have insurance; 83.1% have private insurance; 32.4% have public insurance; 0.0% do not have insurance; 0.0% of children under 18 do not have insurance

Transportation: Commute: 92.9% car, 0.0% public transportation, 4.7% walk, 2.4% work from home; Mean travel time to work: 34.8 minutes

TANNERSVILLE (village).
Covers a land area of 1.164 square miles and a water area of 0.033 square miles. Located at 42.19° N. Lat; 74.14° W. Long. Elevation is 1,900 feet.

Population: 950; Growth (since 2000): 112.1%; Density: 815.9 persons per square mile; Race: 92.5% White, 0.0% Black/African American, 1.2% Asian, 0.0% American Indian/Alaska Native, 0.0% Native Hawaiian/Other Pacific Islander, 6.3% Two or more races, 6.3% Hispanic of any race; Average household size: 2.84; Median age: 36.2; Age under 18: 22.3%; Age 65 and over: 11.4%; Males per 100 females: 117.3; Marriage status: 48.9% never married, 39.2% now married, 3.3% separated, 7.4% widowed, 4.5% divorced; Foreign born: 0.7%; Speak English only: 98.6%; With disability: 1.7%; Veterans: 6.6%; Ancestry: 32.5% Irish, 26.5% American, 24.7% German, 18.4% Italian, 5.8% Norwegian

Employment: 7.2% management, business, and financial, 0.0% computer, engineering, and science, 7.0% education, legal, community service, arts, and media, 4.6% healthcare practitioners, 19.5% service, 36.1% sales and office, 10.1% natural resources, construction, and maintenance, 15.6% production, transportation, and material moving

Income: Per capita: $24,555; Median household: $52,578; Average household: $60,016; Households with income of $100,000 or more: 17.3%; Poverty rate: 8.7%

Educational Attainment: High school diploma or higher: 94.0%; Bachelor's degree or higher: 30.6%; Graduate/professional degree or higher: 12.0%

School District(s)
Hunter-Tannersville Central SD (PK-12)
    Enrollment: 367 . . . . (518) 589-5400

Housing: Homeownership rate: 57.6%; Median home value: $164,300; Median year structure built: 1947; Homeowner vacancy rate: 1.0%; Median selected monthly owner costs: $1,477 with a mortgage, $581 without a mortgage; Median gross rent: $927 per month; Rental vacancy rate: 12.9%

Health Insurance: 92.8% have insurance; 75.8% have private insurance; 26.9% have public insurance; 7.2% do not have insurance; 4.6% of children under 18 do not have insurance

Transportation: Commute: 92.3% car, 0.0% public transportation, 0.0% walk, 7.7% work from home; Mean travel time to work: 20.1 minutes

WEST COXSACKIE (unincorporated postal area)
ZCTA: 12192

Covers a land area of 17.165 square miles and a water area of 0.043 square miles. Located at 42.41° N. Lat; 73.83° W. Long. Elevation is 131 feet.

Population: 1,968; Growth (since 2000): -13.3%; Density: 114.6 persons per square mile; Race: 97.7% White, 0.2% Black/African American, 0.0% Asian, 0.0% American Indian/Alaska Native, 0.0% Native Hawaiian/Other Pacific Islander, 1.1% Two or more races, 10.3% Hispanic of any race; Average household size: 2.77; Median age: 51.7; Age under 18: 17.6%; Age 65 and over: 25.5%; Males per 100 females: 95.9; Marriage status: 32.6% never married, 53.5% now married, 0.9% separated, 6.0% widowed, 8.0% divorced; Foreign born: 4.6%; Speak English only: 90.4%; With disability: 10.7%; Veterans: 10.9%; Ancestry: 25.7% German, 19.3% Irish, 17.3% American, 15.4% Italian, 11.8% English

Employment: 10.6% management, business, and financial, 0.9% computer, engineering, and science, 11.2% education, legal, community service, arts, and media, 3.4% healthcare practitioners, 18.5% service, 32.1% sales and office, 11.7% natural resources, construction, and maintenance, 11.6% production, transportation, and material moving

Income: Per capita: $39,970; Median household: $83,533; Average household: $101,661; Households with income of $100,000 or more: 43.1%; Poverty rate: 6.1%

Educational Attainment: High school diploma or higher: 85.1%; Bachelor's degree or higher: 23.8%; Graduate/professional degree or higher: 12.6%

Housing: Homeownership rate: 88.7%; Median home value: $170,000; Median year structure built: 1972; Homeowner vacancy rate: 0.0%; Median selected monthly owner costs: $1,717 with a mortgage, $675 without a mortgage; Median gross rent: $1,048 per month; Rental vacancy rate: 0.0%

Health Insurance: 93.3% have insurance; 69.5% have private insurance; 46.9% have public insurance; 6.7% do not have insurance; 27.7% of children under 18 do not have insurance
Transportation: Commute: 96.6% car, 0.0% public transportation, 0.0% walk, 0.8% work from home; Mean travel time to work: 28.9 minutes

WEST KILL (unincorporated postal area)
ZCTA: 12492
Covers a land area of 38.463 square miles and a water area of 0 square miles. Located at 42.18° N. Lat; 74.34° W. Long. Elevation is 1,470 feet.
Population: 248; Growth (since 2000): -11.7%; Density: 6.4 persons per square mile; Race: 100.0% White, 0.0% Black/African American, 0.0% Asian, 0.0% American Indian/Alaska Native, 0.0% Native Hawaiian/Other Pacific Islander, 0.0% Two or more races, 4.4% Hispanic of any race; Average household size: 1.88; Median age: 62.8; Age under 18: 0.0%; Age 65 and over: 35.1%; Males per 100 females: 81.9; Marriage status: 19.0% never married, 71.4% now married, 0.0% separated, 1.2% widowed, 8.5% divorced; Foreign born: 1.6%; Speak English only: 98.4%; With disability: 5.2%; Veterans: 8.5%; Ancestry: 30.6% English, 23.0% Irish, 21.4% German, 18.1% Italian, 7.3% Dutch
Employment: 11.7% management, business, and financial, 0.0% computer, engineering, and science, 10.4% education, legal, community service, arts, and media, 13.0% healthcare practitioners, 14.3% service, 6.5% sales and office, 23.4% natural resources, construction, and maintenance, 20.8% production, transportation, and material moving
Income: Per capita: $31,404; Median household: $50,455; Average household: $60,277; Households with income of $100,000 or more: 18.2%; Poverty rate: n/a
Educational Attainment: High school diploma or higher: 96.7%; Bachelor's degree or higher: 23.1%; Graduate/professional degree or higher: 3.7%
Housing: Homeownership rate: 96.2%; Median home value: $254,000; Median year structure built: 1962; Homeowner vacancy rate: 0.0%; Median selected monthly owner costs: $1,889 with a mortgage, $733 without a mortgage; Median gross rent: n/a per month; Rental vacancy rate: 44.4%
Health Insurance: 98.8% have insurance; 77.4% have private insurance; 45.2% have public insurance; 1.2% do not have insurance; 0.0% of children under 18 do not have insurance
Transportation: Commute: 81.8% car, 0.0% public transportation, 0.0% walk, 0.0% work from home; Mean travel time to work: 45.5 minutes

WINDHAM (CDP).
Covers a land area of 1.877 square miles and a water area of 0 square miles. Located at 42.31° N. Lat; 74.25° W. Long. Elevation is 1,516 feet.
Population: 294; Growth (since 2000): -18.1%; Density: 156.6 persons per square mile; Race: 100.0% White, 0.0% Black/African American, 0.0% Asian, 0.0% American Indian/Alaska Native, 0.0% Native Hawaiian/Other Pacific Islander, 0.0% Two or more races, 1.7% Hispanic of any race; Average household size: 1.86; Median age: 69.3; Age under 18: 4.4%; Age 65 and over: 52.0%; Males per 100 females: 107.3; Marriage status: 16.9% never married, 58.5% now married, 1.4% separated, 10.6% widowed, 14.1% divorced; Foreign born: 0.0%; Speak English only: 95.2%; With disability: 18.0%; Veterans: 29.5%; Ancestry: 23.5% Italian, 17.3% German, 15.6% Irish, 7.8% American, 6.1% Dutch
Employment: 12.4% management, business, and financial, 0.0% computer, engineering, and science, 18.6% education, legal, community service, arts, and media, 8.5% healthcare practitioners, 23.3% service, 23.3% sales and office, 11.6% natural resources, construction, and maintenance, 2.3% production, transportation, and material moving
Income: Per capita: $38,613; Median household: $60,833; Average household: $68,058; Households with income of $100,000 or more: 26.0%; Poverty rate: 11.6%
Educational Attainment: High school diploma or higher: 93.5%; Bachelor's degree or higher: 16.0%; Graduate/professional degree or higher: 9.1%

School District(s)
Windham-Ashland-Jewett Central SD (KG-12)
    Enrollment: 296. . . . . (518) 734-3400
Housing: Homeownership rate: 65.8%; Median home value: $232,600; Median year structure built: 1984; Homeowner vacancy rate: 11.9%; Median selected monthly owner costs: $1,847 with a mortgage, $534 without a mortgage; Median gross rent: $553 per month; Rental vacancy rate: 26.0%

Health Insurance: 98.3% have insurance; 56.8% have private insurance; 65.0% have public insurance; 1.7% do not have insurance; 0.0% of children under 18 do not have insurance
Newspapers: Windham Journal (weekly circulation 1,700)
Transportation: Commute: 92.6% car, 0.0% public transportation, 7.4% walk, 0.0% work from home; Mean travel time to work: 16.4 minutes

WINDHAM (town).
Covers a land area of 45.200 square miles and a water area of 0.137 square miles. Located at 42.32° N. Lat; 74.22° W. Long. Elevation is 1,516 feet.
Population: 1,467; Growth (since 2000): -11.6%; Density: 32.5 persons per square mile; Race: 97.5% White, 0.0% Black/African American, 0.0% Asian, 0.0% American Indian/Alaska Native, 0.0% Native Hawaiian/Other Pacific Islander, 0.3% Two or more races, 3.3% Hispanic of any race; Average household size: 2.39; Median age: 55.0; Age under 18: 8.9%; Age 65 and over: 35.6%; Males per 100 females: 104.2; Marriage status: 24.6% never married, 52.6% now married, 1.2% separated, 7.8% widowed, 15.1% divorced; Foreign born: 7.6%; Speak English only: 91.0%; With disability: 15.5%; Veterans: 12.7%; Ancestry: 25.2% German, 21.5% Irish, 20.2% Italian, 12.3% English, 10.8% American
Employment: 12.6% management, business, and financial, 2.4% computer, engineering, and science, 9.3% education, legal, community service, arts, and media, 4.2% healthcare practitioners, 27.8% service, 25.0% sales and office, 12.3% natural resources, construction, and maintenance, 6.4% production, transportation, and material moving
Income: Per capita: $32,169; Median household: $54,375; Average household: $69,428; Households with income of $100,000 or more: 22.7%; Poverty rate: 8.4%
Educational Attainment: High school diploma or higher: 87.8%; Bachelor's degree or higher: 18.7%; Graduate/professional degree or higher: 6.8%

School District(s)
Windham-Ashland-Jewett Central SD (KG-12)
    Enrollment: 296. . . . . (518) 734-3400
Housing: Homeownership rate: 83.6%; Median home value: $217,400; Median year structure built: 1983; Homeowner vacancy rate: 7.2%; Median selected monthly owner costs: $1,463 with a mortgage, $471 without a mortgage; Median gross rent: $758 per month; Rental vacancy rate: 29.4%
Health Insurance: 91.1% have insurance; 59.5% have private insurance; 53.3% have public insurance; 8.9% do not have insurance; 0.0% of children under 18 do not have insurance
Safety: Violent crime rate: 0.0 per 10,000 population; Property crime rate: 77.4 per 10,000 population
Newspapers: Windham Journal (weekly circulation 1,700)
Transportation: Commute: 92.5% car, 0.0% public transportation, 1.4% walk, 4.5% work from home; Mean travel time to work: 20.6 minutes

Hamilton County

Located in north central New York, in the Adirondacks; drained by tributaries of the Hudson, and by the Raquette, Black, and Sacandaga Rivers; includes many lakes. Covers a land area of 1,717.373 square miles, a water area of 90.431 square miles, and is located in the Eastern Time Zone at 43.66° N. Lat., 74.50° W. Long. The county was founded in 1816. County seat is Lake Pleasant.

Weather Station: Indian Lake 2 SW — Elevation: 1,660 feet

	Jan	Feb	Mar	Apr	May	Jun	Jul	Aug	Sep	Oct	Nov	Dec
High	25	29	37	50	63	71	74	73	66	54	42	30
Low	5	6	15	28	39	49	53	52	45	34	25	13
Precip	2.8	2.3	2.9	3.2	3.6	3.7	3.9	3.6	3.7	4.2	3.3	2.9
Snow	na	na	na	3.0	0.1	0.0	0.0	0.0	0.0	0.7	na	na

High and Low temperatures in degrees Fahrenheit; Precipitation and Snow in inches

Population: 4,646; Growth (since 2000): -13.6%; Density: 2.7 persons per square mile; Race: 96.7% White, 0.8% Black/African American, 0.0% Asian, 0.0% American Indian/Alaska Native, 0.0% Native Hawaiian/Other Pacific Islander, 2.2% two or more races, 1.5% Hispanic of any race; Average household size: 4.13; Median age: 53.7; Age under 18: 14.1%; Age 65 and over: 27.6%; Males per 100 females: 102.3; Marriage status: 38.8% never married, 38.5% now married, 3.2% separated, 13.1% widowed, 9.5% divorced; Foreign born: 2.8%; Speak English only: 94.4%; With disability: 22.6%; Veterans: 7.8%; Ancestry: 19.8% English, 15.8% American, 15.3% German, 13.3% Irish, 9.3% Italian

Religion: Six largest groups: 33.7% Catholicism, 15.7% Muslim Estimate, 8.0% Methodist/Pietist, 3.3% Presbyterian-Reformed, 2.3% Holiness, 0.8% Episcopalianism/Anglicanism

Economy: Unemployment rate: 3.5%; Leading industries: 30.2 % accommodation and food services; 16.6 % retail trade; 15.1 % construction; Farms: 26 totaling 2,078 acres; Company size: 0 employ 1,000 or more persons, 0 employ 500 to 999 persons, 1 employs 100 to 499 persons, 198 employ less than 100 persons; Business ownership: 227 women-owned, n/a Black-owned, n/a Hispanic-owned, n/a Asian-owned, n/a American Indian/Alaska Native-owned

Employment: 9.8% management, business, and financial, 2.0% computer, engineering, and science, 10.6% education, legal, community service, arts, and media, 3.0% healthcare practitioners, 26.2% service, 19.1% sales and office, 23.0% natural resources, construction, and maintenance, 6.4% production, transportation, and material moving

Income: Per capita: $24,891; Median household: $55,587; Average household: $64,039; Households with income of $100,000 or more: 17.9%; Poverty rate: 9.7%

Educational Attainment: High school diploma or higher: 87.8%; Bachelor's degree or higher: 20.0%; Graduate/professional degree or higher: 11.3%

Housing: Homeownership rate: 84.7%; Median home value: $164,000; Median year structure built: 1965; Homeowner vacancy rate: 5.6%; Median selected monthly owner costs: $1,189 with a mortgage, $467 without a mortgage; Median gross rent: $713 per month; Rental vacancy rate: 11.1%

Vital Statistics: Birth rate: 64.7 per 10,000 population; Death rate: 149.4 per 10,000 population; Age-adjusted cancer mortality rate: 295.5 deaths per 100,000 population

Health Insurance: 88.4% have insurance; 62.0% have private insurance; 43.4% have public insurance; 11.6% do not have insurance; 1.5% of children under 18 do not have insurance

Health Care: Physicians: 2.2 per 10,000 population; Dentists: 0.0 per 10,000 population; Hospital beds: 0.0 per 10,000 population; Hospital admissions: 0.0 per 10,000 population

Air Quality Index (AQI): Percent of Days: 95.3% good, 4.7% moderate, 0.0% unhealthy for sensitive individuals, 0.0% unhealthy, 0.0% very unhealthy; Annual median: 34; Annual maximum: 87

Transportation: Commute: 87.7% car, 0.3% public transportation, 4.2% walk, 2.4% work from home; Mean travel time to work: 25.3 minutes

2016 Presidential Election: 64.0% Trump, 29.4% Clinton, 3.7% Johnson, 1.4% Stein

Additional Information Contacts

Hamilton Government . . . . (518) 548-3076
   http://www.hamiltoncounty.com

Hamilton County Communities

ARIETTA (town). Covers a land area of 317.178 square miles and a water area of 12.229 square miles. Located at 43.50° N. Lat; 74.58° W. Long. Elevation is 1,693 feet.

Population: 309; Growth (since 2000): 5.5%; Density: 1.0 persons per square mile; Race: 99.7% White, 0.0% Black/African American, 0.0% Asian, 0.0% American Indian/Alaska Native, 0.0% Native Hawaiian/Other Pacific Islander, 0.3% Two or more races, 0.0% Hispanic of any race; Average household size: 5.24; Median age: 63.2; Age under 18: 4.2%; Age 65 and over: 12.0%; Males per 100 females: 93.6; Marriage status: 73.5% never married, 21.5% now married, 0.7% separated, 3.4% widowed, 1.7% divorced; Foreign born: 0.0%; Speak English only: 99.3%; With disability: 8.4%; Veterans: 3.4%; Ancestry: 50.5% Dutch, 23.3% Irish, 18.4% English, 13.3% German, 2.9% French

Employment: 21.1% management, business, and financial, 0.0% computer, engineering, and science, 5.6% education, legal, community service, arts, and media, 0.0% healthcare practitioners, 38.0% service, 19.7% sales and office, 11.3% natural resources, construction, and maintenance, 4.2% production, transportation, and material moving

Income: Per capita: $24,503; Median household: $57,750; Average household: $71,227; Households with income of $100,000 or more: 18.7%; Poverty rate: 1.9%

Educational Attainment: High school diploma or higher: 91.6%; Bachelor's degree or higher: 9.1%; Graduate/professional degree or higher: 4.0%

Housing: Homeownership rate: 91.5%; Median home value: $183,300; Median year structure built: 1971; Homeowner vacancy rate: 6.3%; Median selected monthly owner costs: $1,275 with a mortgage, $388 without a mortgage; Median gross rent: n/a per month; Rental vacancy rate: 0.0%

Health Insurance: 54.7% have insurance; 46.9% have private insurance; 17.5% have public insurance; 45.3% do not have insurance; 0.0% of children under 18 do not have insurance

Transportation: Commute: 77.1% car, 0.0% public transportation, 0.0% walk, 1.4% work from home; Mean travel time to work: 20.7 minutes

BENSON (town). Covers a land area of 82.617 square miles and a water area of 0.580 square miles. Located at 43.29° N. Lat; 74.37° W. Long. Elevation is 1,165 feet.

Population: 349; Growth (since 2000): 73.6%; Density: 4.2 persons per square mile; Race: 98.3% White, 0.0% Black/African American, 0.0% Asian, 0.0% American Indian/Alaska Native, 0.0% Native Hawaiian/Other Pacific Islander, 0.0% Two or more races, 2.3% Hispanic of any race; Average household size: 4.47; Median age: 40.5; Age under 18: 22.3%; Age 65 and over: 12.0%; Males per 100 females: 102.1; Marriage status: 19.9% never married, 69.9% now married, 2.1% separated, 2.1% widowed, 8.0% divorced; Foreign born: 26.9%; Speak English only: 70.0%; With disability: 15.8%; Veterans: 12.5%; Ancestry: 23.2% German, 12.9% Irish, 12.0% American, 8.9% English, 7.2% Italian

Employment: 11.1% management, business, and financial, 1.0% computer, engineering, and science, 2.0% education, legal, community service, arts, and media, 7.1% healthcare practitioners, 10.6% service, 63.6% sales and office, 3.5% natural resources, construction, and maintenance, 1.0% production, transportation, and material moving

Income: Per capita: $20,035; Median household: $72,500; Average household: $72,500; Households with income of $100,000 or more: 30.8%; Poverty rate: 2.6%

Educational Attainment: High school diploma or higher: 95.4%; Bachelor's degree or higher: 50.4%; Graduate/professional degree or higher: 46.9%

Housing: Homeownership rate: 88.5%; Median home value: $164,800; Median year structure built: 1974; Homeowner vacancy rate: 2.8%; Median selected monthly owner costs: $1,531 with a mortgage, $450 without a mortgage; Median gross rent: $642 per month; Rental vacancy rate: 18.2%

Health Insurance: 100.0% have insurance; 83.7% have private insurance; 52.1% have public insurance; 0.0% do not have insurance; 0.0% of children under 18 do not have insurance

Transportation: Commute: 92.4% car, 0.0% public transportation, 3.0% walk, 0.5% work from home; Mean travel time to work: 33.4 minutes

BLUE MOUNTAIN LAKE (unincorporated postal area)
ZCTA: 12812

Covers a land area of 61.949 square miles and a water area of 4.534 square miles. Located at 43.88° N. Lat; 74.39° W. Long. Elevation is 1,824 feet.

Population: 89; Growth (since 2000): -29.4%; Density: 1.4 persons per square mile; Race: 100.0% White, 0.0% Black/African American, 0.0% Asian, 0.0% American Indian/Alaska Native, 0.0% Native Hawaiian/Other Pacific Islander, 0.0% Two or more races, 0.0% Hispanic of any race; Average household size: 2.41; Median age: 36.1; Age under 18: 44.9%; Age 65 and over: 11.2%; Males per 100 females: 80.7; Marriage status: 7.5% never married, 60.4% now married, 1.9% separated, 11.3% widowed, 20.8% divorced; Foreign born: 0.0%; Speak English only: 100.0%; With disability: 0.0%; Veterans: 0.0%; Ancestry: 24.7% Irish, 22.5% French, 19.1% Italian, 16.9% German, 6.7% European

Employment: 44.4% management, business, and financial, 0.0% computer, engineering, and science, 0.0% education, legal, community service, arts, and media, 0.0% healthcare practitioners, 37.8% service, 0.0% sales and office, 17.8% natural resources, construction, and maintenance, 0.0% production, transportation, and material moving

Income: Per capita: $23,775; Median household: $71,042; Average household: $70,214; Households with income of $100,000 or more: 16.2%; Poverty rate: n/a

Educational Attainment: High school diploma or higher: 91.8%; Bachelor's degree or higher: 44.9%; Graduate/professional degree or higher: 34.7%

Housing: Homeownership rate: 91.9%; Median home value: $137,500; Median year structure built: 1948; Homeowner vacancy rate: 12.8%; Median selected monthly owner costs: $1,056 with a mortgage, $0 without a mortgage; Median gross rent: n/a per month; Rental vacancy rate: 0.0%

Health Insurance: 100.0% have insurance; 93.3% have private insurance; 22.5% have public insurance; 0.0% do not have insurance; 0.0% of children under 18 do not have insurance

Transportation: Commute: 95.6% car, 0.0% public transportation, 4.4% walk, 0.0% work from home; Mean travel time to work: 32.3 minutes

HOFFMEISTER (unincorporated postal area)
ZCTA: 13353

Covers a land area of 197.914 square miles and a water area of 3.716 square miles. Located at 43.45° N. Lat; 74.69° W. Long. Elevation is 1,857 feet.

Population: 15; Growth (since 2000): -90.1%; Density: 0.1 persons per square mile; Race: 100.0% White, 0.0% Black/African American, 0.0% Asian, 0.0% American Indian/Alaska Native, 0.0% Native Hawaiian/Other Pacific Islander, 0.0% Two or more races, 0.0% Hispanic of any race; Average household size: 1.67; Median age: 65.2; Age under 18: 0.0%; Age 65 and over: 53.3%; Males per 100 females: 138.9; Marriage status: 0.0% never married, 73.3% now married, 0.0% separated, 26.7% widowed, 0.0% divorced; Foreign born: 0.0%; Speak English only: 100.0%; With disability: 6.7%; Veterans: 6.7%; Ancestry: 60.0% German, 33.3% Polish, 6.7% American, 6.7% Dutch

Employment: 20.0% management, business, and financial, 0.0% computer, engineering, and science, 20.0% education, legal, community service, arts, and media, 0.0% healthcare practitioners, 0.0% service, 0.0% sales and office, 60.0% natural resources, construction, and maintenance, 0.0% production, transportation, and material moving

Income: Per capita: $17,953; Median household: $35,625; Average household: $28,733; Households with income of $100,000 or more: n/a; Poverty rate: 20.0%

Educational Attainment: High school diploma or higher: 100.0%; Bachelor's degree or higher: n/a; Graduate/professional degree or higher: n/a

Housing: Homeownership rate: 55.6%; Median home value: $258,300; Median year structure built: 1965; Homeowner vacancy rate: 0.0%; Median selected monthly owner costs: $0 with a mortgage, $650 without a mortgage; Median gross rent: n/a per month; Rental vacancy rate: 0.0%

Health Insurance: 100.0% have insurance; 33.3% have private insurance; 100.0% have public insurance; 0.0% do not have insurance; 0.0% of children under 18 do not have insurance

Transportation: Commute: 100.0% car, 0.0% public transportation, 0.0% walk, 0.0% work from home; Mean travel time to work: 0.0 minutes

HOPE (town).
Covers a land area of 40.703 square miles and a water area of 0.933 square miles. Located at 43.32° N. Lat; 74.23° W. Long. Elevation is 810 feet.

Population: 759; Growth (since 2000): 93.6%; Density: 18.6 persons per square mile; Race: 98.4% White, 0.0% Black/African American, 0.0% Asian, 0.0% American Indian/Alaska Native, 0.1% Native Hawaiian/Other Pacific Islander, 1.4% Two or more races, 4.0% Hispanic of any race; Average household size: 5.88; Median age: 39.7; Age under 18: 14.8%; Age 65 and over: 20.6%; Males per 100 females: 98.5; Marriage status: 67.7% never married, 28.7% now married, 0.9% separated, 1.8% widowed, 1.8% divorced; Foreign born: 1.7%; Speak English only: 99.4%; With disability: 23.5%; Veterans: 4.8%; Ancestry: 24.5% American, 21.3% German, 15.8% Irish, 9.5% Italian, 5.5% French

Employment: 6.4% management, business, and financial, 0.4% computer, engineering, and science, 11.4% education, legal, community service, arts, and media, 1.8% healthcare practitioners, 32.5% service, 13.2% sales and office, 30.4% natural resources, construction, and maintenance, 3.9% production, transportation, and material moving

Income: Per capita: $25,969; Median household: $42,917; Average household: $64,270; Households with income of $100,000 or more: 20.9%; Poverty rate: 8.2%

Educational Attainment: High school diploma or higher: 93.5%; Bachelor's degree or higher: 6.3%; Graduate/professional degree or higher: 2.7%

Housing: Homeownership rate: 79.1%; Median home value: $113,100; Median year structure built: 1974; Homeowner vacancy rate: 0.0%; Median selected monthly owner costs: $878 with a mortgage, $450 without a mortgage; Median gross rent: $917 per month; Rental vacancy rate: 0.0%

Health Insurance: 93.9% have insurance; 53.2% have private insurance; 44.7% have public insurance; 6.1% do not have insurance; 0.0% of children under 18 do not have insurance

Transportation: Commute: 96.0% car, 1.4% public transportation, 0.7% walk, 1.1% work from home; Mean travel time to work: 56.7 minutes

INDIAN LAKE (town).
Covers a land area of 251.800 square miles and a water area of 14.439 square miles. Located at 43.81° N. Lat; 74.42° W. Long. Elevation is 1,742 feet.

History: Dr. Thomas Durant and William West Durant, father and son, were early promoters of the Indian Lake section of the Adirondacks. The father, financier and railroad builder, constructed a railroad from Saratoga to Blue Mountain Lake, and the son expanded his father's promotional activities by building elaborate camps and selling them to the wealthy.

Population: 901; Growth (since 2000): -38.7%; Density: 3.6 persons per square mile; Race: 89.2% White, 0.8% Black/African American, 0.1% Asian, 0.1% American Indian/Alaska Native, 0.0% Native Hawaiian/Other Pacific Islander, 9.8% Two or more races, 0.0% Hispanic of any race; Average household size: 2.99; Median age: 54.1; Age under 18: 15.0%; Age 65 and over: 37.2%; Males per 100 females: 99.7; Marriage status: 27.9% never married, 32.0% now married, 3.0% separated, 27.9% widowed, 12.3% divorced; Foreign born: 0.2%; Speak English only: 99.5%; With disability: 33.5%; Veterans: 7.0%; Ancestry: 39.1% English, 18.1% Irish, 12.7% French, 10.3% German, 9.9% American

Employment: 9.4% management, business, and financial, 3.0% computer, engineering, and science, 2.3% education, legal, community service, arts, and media, 3.6% healthcare practitioners, 36.3% service, 14.5% sales and office, 24.1% natural resources, construction, and maintenance, 6.9% production, transportation, and material moving

Income: Per capita: $21,717; Median household: $55,719; Average household: $55,328; Households with income of $100,000 or more: 10.5%; Poverty rate: 10.3%

Educational Attainment: High school diploma or higher: 88.5%; Bachelor's degree or higher: 15.8%; Graduate/professional degree or higher: 7.0%

School District(s)

Indian Lake Central SD (PK-12)

    Enrollment: 117 . . . . (518) 648-5024

Housing: Homeownership rate: 82.6%; Median home value: $124,100; Median year structure built: 1962; Homeowner vacancy rate: 6.6%; Median selected monthly owner costs: $1,047 with a mortgage, $433 without a mortgage; Median gross rent: $563 per month; Rental vacancy rate: 22.7%

Health Insurance: 95.7% have insurance; 59.5% have private insurance; 50.3% have public insurance; 4.3% do not have insurance; 0.0% of children under 18 do not have insurance

Transportation: Commute: 76.2% car, 0.0% public transportation, 13.5% walk, 5.3% work from home; Mean travel time to work: 14.2 minutes

INLET (town).
Covers a land area of 62.195 square miles and a water area of 4.176 square miles. Located at 43.72° N. Lat; 74.71° W. Long. Elevation is 1,749 feet.

Population: 246; Growth (since 2000): -39.4%; Density: 4.0 persons per square mile; Race: 100.0% White, 0.0% Black/African American, 0.0% Asian, 0.0% American Indian/Alaska Native, 0.0% Native Hawaiian/Other Pacific Islander, 0.0% Two or more races, 0.0% Hispanic of any race; Average household size: 6.00; Median age: 36.8; Age under 18: 13.4%; Age 65 and over: 29.3%; Males per 100 females: 106.8; Marriage status: 33.3% never married, 39.4% now married, 0.9% separated, 25.9% widowed, 1.4% divorced; Foreign born: 0.4%; Speak English only: 99.2%; With disability: 25.6%; Veterans: 3.8%; Ancestry: 40.7% German, 20.7% Polish, 19.5% Scottish, 16.7% English, 15.0% American

Employment: 7.8% management, business, and financial, 0.0% computer, engineering, and science, 40.4% education, legal, community service, arts, and media, 0.0% healthcare practitioners, 9.9% service, 10.6% sales and office, 29.1% natural resources, construction, and maintenance, 2.1% production, transportation, and material moving

Income: Per capita: $24,896; Median household: $54,375; Average household: $80,093; Households with income of $100,000 or more: 14.7%; Poverty rate: 1.6%

Educational Attainment: High school diploma or higher: 74.6%; Bachelor's degree or higher: 35.0%; Graduate/professional degree or higher: 4.1%

School District(s)

Inlet Common SD (PK-06)

    Enrollment: 15 . . . . (315) 357-3305

Housing: Homeownership rate: 92.7%; Median home value: $307,700; Median year structure built: 1956; Homeowner vacancy rate: 0.0%; Median selected monthly owner costs: $1,750 with a mortgage, $525 without a mortgage; Median gross rent: n/a per month; Rental vacancy rate: 40.0%

Health Insurance: 99.2% have insurance; 66.7% have private insurance; 41.1% have public insurance; 0.8% do not have insurance; 0.0% of children under 18 do not have insurance
Safety: Violent crime rate: 0.0 per 10,000 population; Property crime rate: 97.1 per 10,000 population
Transportation: Commute: 50.0% car, 0.0% public transportation, 6.8% walk, 6.8% work from home; Mean travel time to work: 7.4 minutes

LAKE PLEASANT (town). County seat. Covers a land area of 187.984 square miles and a water area of 10.000 square miles. Located at 43.58° N. Lat; 74.42° W. Long. Elevation is 1,785 feet.

Population: 599; Growth (since 2000): -31.6%; Density: 3.2 persons per square mile; Race: 97.2% White, 1.7% Black/African American, 0.0% Asian, 0.0% American Indian/Alaska Native, 0.0% Native Hawaiian/Other Pacific Islander, 0.0% Two or more races, 1.3% Hispanic of any race; Average household size: 3.39; Median age: 59.7; Age under 18: 9.5%; Age 65 and over: 40.7%; Males per 100 females: 98.7; Marriage status: 10.7% never married, 54.7% now married, 0.2% separated, 10.8% widowed, 23.8% divorced; Foreign born: 0.2%; Speak English only: 99.3%; With disability: 30.3%; Veterans: 8.1%; Ancestry: 27.5% English, 14.7% French Canadian, 14.5% German, 10.0% French, 9.0% Irish
Employment: 9.0% management, business, and financial, 2.3% computer, engineering, and science, 9.0% education, legal, community service, arts, and media, 1.7% healthcare practitioners, 39.8% service, 23.7% sales and office, 7.4% natural resources, construction, and maintenance, 7.0% production, transportation, and material moving
Income: Per capita: $30,792; Median household: $66,250; Average household: $68,719; Households with income of $100,000 or more: 19.9%; Poverty rate: 9.6%
Educational Attainment: High school diploma or higher: 83.8%; Bachelor's degree or higher: 12.6%; Graduate/professional degree or higher: 4.2%
Housing: Homeownership rate: 80.0%; Median home value: $191,700; Median year structure built: 1970; Homeowner vacancy rate: 10.8%; Median selected monthly owner costs: $1,000 with a mortgage, $586 without a mortgage; Median gross rent: $810 per month; Rental vacancy rate: 5.7%
Health Insurance: 97.5% have insurance; 72.9% have private insurance; 50.8% have public insurance; 2.5% do not have insurance; 0.0% of children under 18 do not have insurance
Transportation: Commute: 92.9% car, 0.0% public transportation, 2.7% walk, 1.4% work from home; Mean travel time to work: 11.3 minutes

LONG LAKE (CDP). Covers a land area of 11.721 square miles and a water area of 2.209 square miles. Located at 43.96° N. Lat; 74.45° W. Long. Elevation is 1,673 feet.

Population: 332; Growth (since 2000): n/a; Density: 28.3 persons per square mile; Race: 94.6% White, 5.4% Black/African American, 0.0% Asian, 0.0% American Indian/Alaska Native, 0.0% Native Hawaiian/Other Pacific Islander, 0.0% Two or more races, 6.0% Hispanic of any race; Average household size: 3.16; Median age: 53.6; Age under 18: 16.6%; Age 65 and over: 25.0%; Males per 100 females: 109.6; Marriage status: 39.9% never married, 50.5% now married, 1.4% separated, 5.1% widowed, 4.4% divorced; Foreign born: 6.3%; Speak English only: 76.7%; With disability: 17.4%; Veterans: 13.0%; Ancestry: 32.8% English, 16.6% Irish, 9.3% French, 6.9% American, 5.4% German
Employment: 12.1% management, business, and financial, 0.0% computer, engineering, and science, 38.3% education, legal, community service, arts, and media, 4.3% healthcare practitioners, 14.9% service, 15.6% sales and office, 1.4% natural resources, construction, and maintenance, 13.5% production, transportation, and material moving
Income: Per capita: $21,323; Median household: $55,556; Average household: $71,516; Households with income of $100,000 or more: 25.0%; Poverty rate: 17.8%
Educational Attainment: High school diploma or higher: 93.6%; Bachelor's degree or higher: 30.8%; Graduate/professional degree or higher: 12.8%
School District(s)
Long Lake Central SD (PK-12)
    Enrollment: 63 . . . . (518) 624-2147
Housing: Homeownership rate: 89.1%; Median home value: $250,000; Median year structure built: 1963; Homeowner vacancy rate: 0.0%; Median selected monthly owner costs: $1,681 with a mortgage, $521 without a mortgage; Median gross rent: $1,042 per month; Rental vacancy rate: 0.0%

Health Insurance: 99.0% have insurance; 74.3% have private insurance; 48.0% have public insurance; 1.0% do not have insurance; 0.0% of children under 18 do not have insurance
Transportation: Commute: 90.6% car, 0.7% public transportation, 1.4% walk, 5.1% work from home; Mean travel time to work: 24.1 minutes

LONG LAKE (town). Covers a land area of 407.033 square miles and a water area of 42.804 square miles. Located at 43.96° N. Lat; 74.65° W. Long. Elevation is 1,673 feet.

Population: 473; Growth (since 2000): -44.5%; Density: 1.2 persons per square mile; Race: 96.2% White, 3.8% Black/African American, 0.0% Asian, 0.0% American Indian/Alaska Native, 0.0% Native Hawaiian/Other Pacific Islander, 0.0% Two or more races, 4.2% Hispanic of any race; Average household size: 3.30; Median age: 57.7; Age under 18: 11.6%; Age 65 and over: 34.7%; Males per 100 females: 112.9; Marriage status: 32.9% never married, 46.3% now married, 0.9% separated, 15.7% widowed, 5.1% divorced; Foreign born: 4.4%; Speak English only: 83.6%; With disability: 15.5%; Veterans: 22.0%; Ancestry: 24.1% English, 13.3% Irish, 12.1% Welsh, 7.4% French, 6.8% German
Employment: 22.7% management, business, and financial, 1.5% computer, engineering, and science, 30.8% education, legal, community service, arts, and media, 3.0% healthcare practitioners, 14.1% service, 15.7% sales and office, 2.5% natural resources, construction, and maintenance, 9.6% production, transportation, and material moving
Income: Per capita: $27,825; Median household: $55,795; Average household: $70,114; Households with income of $100,000 or more: 25.1%; Poverty rate: 12.4%
Educational Attainment: High school diploma or higher: 88.9%; Bachelor's degree or higher: 26.4%; Graduate/professional degree or higher: 11.6%
School District(s)
Long Lake Central SD (PK-12)
    Enrollment: 63 . . . . (518) 624-2147
Housing: Homeownership rate: 87.0%; Median home value: $250,000; Median year structure built: 1965; Homeowner vacancy rate: 0.0%; Median selected monthly owner costs: $1,625 with a mortgage, $462 without a mortgage; Median gross rent: $1,069 per month; Rental vacancy rate: 0.0%
Health Insurance: 98.7% have insurance; 78.4% have private insurance; 53.3% have public insurance; 1.3% do not have insurance; 0.0% of children under 18 do not have insurance
Transportation: Commute: 93.3% car, 0.5% public transportation, 1.0% walk, 3.6% work from home; Mean travel time to work: 24.9 minutes

MOREHOUSE (town). Covers a land area of 191.064 square miles and a water area of 3.705 square miles. Located at 43.45° N. Lat; 74.69° W. Long.

Population: 15; Growth (since 2000): -90.1%; Density: 0.1 persons per square mile; Race: 100.0% White, 0.0% Black/African American, 0.0% Asian, 0.0% American Indian/Alaska Native, 0.0% Native Hawaiian/Other Pacific Islander, 0.0% Two or more races, 0.0% Hispanic of any race; Average household size: 1.67; Median age: 65.2; Age under 18: 0.0%; Age 65 and over: 53.3%; Males per 100 females: 138.9; Marriage status: 0.0% never married, 73.3% now married, 0.0% separated, 26.7% widowed, 0.0% divorced; Foreign born: 0.0%; Speak English only: 100.0%; With disability: 6.7%; Veterans: 6.7%; Ancestry: 60.0% German, 33.3% Polish, 6.7% American, 6.7% Dutch
Employment: 20.0% management, business, and financial, 0.0% computer, engineering, and science, 20.0% education, legal, community service, arts, and media, 0.0% healthcare practitioners, 0.0% service, 0.0% sales and office, 60.0% natural resources, construction, and maintenance, 0.0% production, transportation, and material moving
Income: Per capita: $17,953; Median household: $35,625; Average household: $28,733; Households with income of $100,000 or more: n/a; Poverty rate: 20.0%
Educational Attainment: High school diploma or higher: 100.0%; Bachelor's degree or higher: n/a; Graduate/professional degree or higher: n/a
Housing: Homeownership rate: 55.6%; Median home value: $258,300; Median year structure built: 1965; Homeowner vacancy rate: 0.0%; Median selected monthly owner costs: n/a with a mortgage, $650 without a mortgage; Median gross rent: n/a per month; Rental vacancy rate: 0.0%
Health Insurance: 100.0% have insurance; 33.3% have private insurance; 100.0% have public insurance; 0.0% do not have insurance; 0.0% of children under 18 do not have insurance

Transportation: Commute: 100.0% car, 0.0% public transportation, 0.0% walk, 0.0% work from home; Mean travel time to work: 0.0 minutes

PISECO (unincorporated postal area)
ZCTA: 12139

Covers a land area of 239.085 square miles and a water area of 10.023 square miles. Located at 43.50° N. Lat; 74.58° W. Long. Elevation is 1,676 feet.

Population: 309; Growth (since 2000): 13.6%; Density: 1.3 persons per square mile; Race: 99.7% White, 0.0% Black/African American, 0.0% Asian, 0.0% American Indian/Alaska Native, 0.0% Native Hawaiian/Other Pacific Islander, 0.3% Two or more races, 0.0% Hispanic of any race; Average household size: 5.24; Median age: 63.2; Age under 18: 4.2%; Age 65 and over: 12.0%; Males per 100 females: 94.1; Marriage status: 73.5% never married, 21.5% now married, 0.7% separated, 3.4% widowed, 1.7% divorced; Foreign born: 0.0%; Speak English only: 99.3%; With disability: 8.4%; Veterans: 3.4%; Ancestry: 50.5% Dutch, 23.3% Irish, 18.4% English, 13.3% German, 2.9% French

Employment: 21.1% management, business, and financial, 0.0% computer, engineering, and science, 5.6% education, legal, community service, arts, and media, 0.0% healthcare practitioners, 38.0% service, 19.7% sales and office, 11.3% natural resources, construction, and maintenance, 4.2% production, transportation, and material moving

Income: Per capita: $24,503; Median household: $57,750; Average household: $71,227; Households with income of $100,000 or more: 18.7%; Poverty rate: 1.9%

Educational Attainment: High school diploma or higher: 91.6%; Bachelor's degree or higher: 9.1%; Graduate/professional degree or higher: 4.0%

Housing: Homeownership rate: 91.5%; Median home value: $183,300; Median year structure built: 1971; Homeowner vacancy rate: 6.3%; Median selected monthly owner costs: $1,275 with a mortgage, $388 without a mortgage; Median gross rent: n/a per month; Rental vacancy rate: 0.0%

Health Insurance: 54.7% have insurance; 46.9% have private insurance; 17.5% have public insurance; 45.3% do not have insurance; 0.0% of children under 18 do not have insurance

Transportation: Commute: 77.1% car, 0.0% public transportation, 0.0% walk, 1.4% work from home; Mean travel time to work: 20.7 minutes

RAQUETTE LAKE (unincorporated postal area)
ZCTA: 13436

Covers a land area of 38.337 square miles and a water area of 9.611 square miles. Located at 43.81° N. Lat; 74.67° W. Long. Elevation is 1,765 feet.

Population: 125; Growth (since 2000): 1.6%; Density: 3.3 persons per square mile; Race: 100.0% White, 0.0% Black/African American, 0.0% Asian, 0.0% American Indian/Alaska Native, 0.0% Native Hawaiian/Other Pacific Islander, 0.0% Two or more races, 0.0% Hispanic of any race; Average household size: 4.17; Median age: 73.1; Age under 18: 0.0%; Age 65 and over: 56.8%; Males per 100 females: 129.8; Marriage status: 20.8% never married, 30.4% now married, 0.0% separated, 41.6% widowed, 7.2% divorced; Foreign born: 0.0%; Speak English only: 99.2%; With disability: 11.2%; Veterans: 43.2%; Ancestry: 41.6% Welsh, 7.2% German, 6.4% French Canadian, 6.4% Irish, 3.2% French

Employment: 57.1% management, business, and financial, 0.0% computer, engineering, and science, 4.1% education, legal, community service, arts, and media, 0.0% healthcare practitioners, 14.3% service, 18.4% sales and office, 6.1% natural resources, construction, and maintenance, 0.0% production, transportation, and material moving

Income: Per capita: $43,835; Median household: $56,250; Average household: $65,323; Households with income of $100,000 or more: 26.7%; Poverty rate: 0.8%

Educational Attainment: High school diploma or higher: 77.7%; Bachelor's degree or higher: 12.4%; Graduate/professional degree or higher: 3.3%

Housing: Homeownership rate: 76.7%; Median home value: $255,000; Median year structure built: 1968; Homeowner vacancy rate: 0.0%; Median selected monthly owner costs: $0 with a mortgage, $308 without a mortgage; Median gross rent: n/a per month; Rental vacancy rate: 0.0%

Health Insurance: 97.6% have insurance; 88.0% have private insurance; 64.8% have public insurance; 2.4% do not have insurance; 0.0% of children under 18 do not have insurance

Transportation: Commute: 100.0% car, 0.0% public transportation, 0.0% walk, 0.0% work from home; Mean travel time to work: 25.0 minutes

SABAEL (unincorporated postal area)
ZCTA: 12864

Covers a land area of 0.209 square miles and a water area of 0 square miles. Located at 43.73° N. Lat; 74.31° W. Long. Elevation is 1,745 feet.

Population: 30; Growth (since 2000): n/a; Density: 143.7 persons per square mile; Race: 100.0% White, 0.0% Black/African American, 0.0% Asian, 0.0% American Indian/Alaska Native, 0.0% Native Hawaiian/Other Pacific Islander, 0.0% Two or more races, 0.0% Hispanic of any race; Average household size: 1.15; Median age: 49.8; Age under 18: 0.0%; Age 65 and over: 43.3%; Males per 100 females: 100.0; Marriage status: 0.0% never married, 56.7% now married, 33.3% separated, 43.3% widowed, 0.0% divorced; Foreign born: 0.0%; Speak English only: 100.0%; With disability: 43.3%; Veterans: 0.0%; Ancestry: 100.0% English, 56.7% German, 33.3% French, 10.0% Scottish

Employment: 0.0% management, business, and financial, 0.0% computer, engineering, and science, 0.0% education, legal, community service, arts, and media, 0.0% healthcare practitioners, 0.0% service, 100.0% sales and office, 0.0% natural resources, construction, and maintenance, 0.0% production, transportation, and material moving

Income: Per capita: $21,593; Median household: n/a; Average household: $24,246; Households with income of $100,000 or more: n/a; Poverty rate: 33.3%

Educational Attainment: High school diploma or higher: 100.0%; Bachelor's degree or higher: 10.0%; Graduate/professional degree or higher: n/a

Housing: Homeownership rate: 88.5%; Median home value: n/a; Median year structure built: 1962; Homeowner vacancy rate: 0.0%; Median selected monthly owner costs: $0 with a mortgage, $0 without a mortgage; Median gross rent: n/a per month; Rental vacancy rate: 0.0%

Health Insurance: 86.7% have insurance; 43.3% have private insurance; 86.7% have public insurance; 13.3% do not have insurance; 0.0% of children under 18 do not have insurance

Transportation: Commute: 100.0% car, 0.0% public transportation, 0.0% walk, 0.0% work from home; Mean travel time to work: 0.0 minutes

SPECULATOR (village). Covers a land area of 44.571 square miles and a water area of 2.595 square miles. Located at 43.59° N. Lat; 74.36° W. Long. Elevation is 1,739 feet.

Population: 357; Growth (since 2000): 2.6%; Density: 8.0 persons per square mile; Race: 97.8% White, 2.2% Black/African American, 0.0% Asian, 0.0% American Indian/Alaska Native, 0.0% Native Hawaiian/Other Pacific Islander, 0.0% Two or more races, 0.0% Hispanic of any race; Average household size: 5.74; Median age: 62.4; Age under 18: 2.5%; Age 65 and over: 44.8%; Males per 100 females: 97.6; Marriage status: 8.5% never married, 42.5% now married, 0.0% separated, 13.7% widowed, 35.3% divorced; Foreign born: 0.0%; Speak English only: 99.2%; With disability: 33.9%; Veterans: 4.9%; Ancestry: 41.5% English, 24.4% French Canadian, 18.8% German, 12.9% French, 8.1% American

Employment: 2.5% management, business, and financial, 0.0% computer, engineering, and science, 8.6% education, legal, community service, arts, and media, 2.5% healthcare practitioners, 50.0% service, 26.8% sales and office, 1.5% natural resources, construction, and maintenance, 8.1% production, transportation, and material moving

Income: Per capita: $34,346; Median household: $68,958; Average household: $94,168; Households with income of $100,000 or more: 26.3%; Poverty rate: 0.3%

Educational Attainment: High school diploma or higher: 78.3%; Bachelor's degree or higher: 9.1%; Graduate/professional degree or higher: 3.8%

School District(s)

Lake Pleasant Central SD (PK-09)

    Enrollment: 86. . . . . (518) 548-7571

Housing: Homeownership rate: 94.7%; Median home value: $145,800; Median year structure built: 1965; Homeowner vacancy rate: 6.9%; Median selected monthly owner costs: $1,350 with a mortgage, $622 without a mortgage; Median gross rent: n/a per month; Rental vacancy rate: 40.0%

Health Insurance: 99.4% have insurance; 77.0% have private insurance; 51.0% have public insurance; 0.6% do not have insurance; 0.0% of children under 18 do not have insurance

Newspapers: Hamilton Co. Express (weekly circulation 3,300)

Transportation: Commute: 98.0% car, 0.0% public transportation, 1.5% walk, 0.5% work from home; Mean travel time to work: 8.4 minutes

WELLS (town). Covers a land area of 176.800 square miles and a water area of 1.564 square miles. Located at 43.48° N. Lat; 74.29° W. Long. Elevation is 1,010 feet.
Population: 995; Growth (since 2000): 35.0%; Density: 5.6 persons per square mile; Race: 99.9% White, 0.1% Black/African American, 0.0% Asian, 0.0% American Indian/Alaska Native, 0.0% Native Hawaiian/Other Pacific Islander, 0.0% Two or more races, 0.3% Hispanic of any race; Average household size: 5.11; Median age: 51.8; Age under 18: 17.4%; Age 65 and over: 22.5%; Males per 100 females: 101.8; Marriage status: 44.7% never married, 32.3% now married, 10.2% separated, 11.9% widowed, 11.2% divorced; Foreign born: 0.0%; Speak English only: 93.8%; With disability: 16.8%; Veterans: 4.7%; Ancestry: 32.0% American, 24.1% Italian, 14.0% English, 14.0% French, 10.8% German
Employment: 4.7% management, business, and financial, 3.5% computer, engineering, and science, 4.0% education, legal, community service, arts, and media, 3.7% healthcare practitioners, 19.3% service, 7.4% sales and office, 47.2% natural resources, construction, and maintenance, 10.4% production, transportation, and material moving
Income: Per capita: $23,922; Median household: $53,125; Average household: $61,565; Households with income of $100,000 or more: 16.4%; Poverty rate: 15.9%
Educational Attainment: High school diploma or higher: 84.9%; Bachelor's degree or higher: 24.1%; Graduate/professional degree or higher: 17.6%

School District(s)
Wells Central SD (PK-12)
    Enrollment: 153 . . . . (518) 924-6000
Housing: Homeownership rate: 90.0%; Median home value: $158,700; Median year structure built: 1964; Homeowner vacancy rate: 8.4%; Median selected monthly owner costs: $1,340 with a mortgage, $445 without a mortgage; Median gross rent: $857 per month; Rental vacancy rate: 0.0%
Health Insurance: 71.1% have insurance; 53.7% have private insurance; 31.9% have public insurance; 28.9% do not have insurance; 6.4% of children under 18 do not have insurance
Transportation: Commute: 98.2% car, 0.3% public transportation, 1.0% walk, 0.5% work from home; Mean travel time to work: 26.9 minutes

Herkimer County

Located in central and north central New York, extending north into the Adirondacks and south into the Mohawk Valley; drained by the Mohawk, Unadilla, Black, and Moose Rivers. Covers a land area of 1,411.470 square miles, a water area of 46.487 square miles, and is located in the Eastern Time Zone at 43.46° N. Lat., 74.89° W. Long. The county was founded in 1791. County seat is Herkimer.

Herkimer County is part of the Utica-Rome, NY Metropolitan Statistical Area. The entire metro area includes: Herkimer County, NY; Oneida County, NY

Weather Station: Old Forge   Elevation: 1,720 feet

	Jan	Feb	Mar	Apr	May	Jun	Jul	Aug	Sep	Oct	Nov	Dec
High	25	29	37	50	63	71	75	74	66	54	41	30
Low	3	6	15	28	39	49	53	52	44	33	24	11
Precip	3.9	2.9	3.4	3.7	4.2	4.1	4.4	4.4	4.7	4.7	4.6	4.3
Snow	48.4	31.6	27.4	9.2	0.8	tr	0.0	0.0	tr	3.1	19.3	41.4

High and Low temperatures in degrees Fahrenheit; Precipitation and Snow in inches

Population: 62,943; Growth (since 2000): -2.3%; Density: 44.6 persons per square mile; Race: 96.0% White, 1.2% Black/African American, 0.5% Asian, 0.3% American Indian/Alaska Native, 0.1% Native Hawaiian/Other Pacific Islander, 1.4% two or more races, 2.1% Hispanic of any race; Average household size: 2.45; Median age: 43.7; Age under 18: 21.1%; Age 65 and over: 19.0%; Males per 100 females: 95.9; Marriage status: 30.1% never married, 50.6% now married, 2.3% separated, 7.2% widowed, 12.1% divorced; Foreign born: 2.5%; Speak English only: 95.2%; With disability: 15.8%; Veterans: 10.0%; Ancestry: 19.9% German, 18.8% Irish, 18.0% Italian, 10.7% English, 8.3% Polish
Religion: Six largest groups: 23.9% Catholicism, 4.5% Methodist/Pietist, 2.0% Baptist, 1.9% Presbyterian-Reformed, 1.6% Lutheran, 1.1% Episcopalianism/Anglicanism
Economy: Unemployment rate: 3.8%; Leading industries: 15.6 % retail trade; 14.5 % accommodation and food services; 13.7 % construction;

Farms: 687 totaling 140,270 acres; Company size: 1 employs 1,000 or more persons, 0 employ 500 to 999 persons, 14 employ 100 to 499 persons, 1,097 employ less than 100 persons; Business ownership: 1,070 women-owned, n/a Black-owned, n/a Hispanic-owned, 38 Asian-owned, n/a American Indian/Alaska Native-owned
Employment: 10.8% management, business, and financial, 3.1% computer, engineering, and science, 10.7% education, legal, community service, arts, and media, 6.8% healthcare practitioners, 20.6% service, 23.4% sales and office, 10.1% natural resources, construction, and maintenance, 14.5% production, transportation, and material moving
Income: Per capita: $24,932; Median household: $49,077; Average household: $60,652; Households with income of $100,000 or more: 15.9%; Poverty rate: 14.9%
Educational Attainment: High school diploma or higher: 89.8%; Bachelor's degree or higher: 20.7%; Graduate/professional degree or higher: 8.8%
Housing: Homeownership rate: 71.7%; Median home value: $95,800; Median year structure built: 1954; Homeowner vacancy rate: 2.4%; Median selected monthly owner costs: $1,112 with a mortgage, $464 without a mortgage; Median gross rent: $657 per month; Rental vacancy rate: 6.6%
Vital Statistics: Birth rate: 96.2 per 10,000 population; Death rate: 105.4 per 10,000 population; Age-adjusted cancer mortality rate: 163.6 deaths per 100,000 population
Health Insurance: 93.4% have insurance; 64.3% have private insurance; 44.4% have public insurance; 6.6% do not have insurance; 5.2% of children under 18 do not have insurance
Health Care: Physicians: 5.6 per 10,000 population; Dentists: 3.5 per 10,000 population; Hospital beds: 4.0 per 10,000 population; Hospital admissions: 120.8 per 10,000 population
Air Quality Index (AQI): Percent of Days: 98.7% good, 1.3% moderate, 0.0% unhealthy for sensitive individuals, 0.0% unhealthy, 0.0% very unhealthy; Annual median: 31; Annual maximum: 77
Transportation: Commute: 89.3% car, 1.1% public transportation, 4.5% walk, 4.1% work from home; Mean travel time to work: 23.1 minutes
2016 Presidential Election: 63.6% Trump, 30.8% Clinton, 3.8% Johnson, 1.5% Stein
National and State Parks: Black Creek State Forest
Additional Information Contacts
Herkimer Government . . . . (315) 867-1129
    http://www.herkimercounty.org

Herkimer County Communities

COLD BROOK (village). Covers a land area of 0.439 square miles and a water area of 0 square miles. Located at 43.24° N. Lat; 75.04° W. Long. Elevation is 945 feet.
Population: 315; Growth (since 2000): -6.3%; Density: 717.2 persons per square mile; Race: 96.5% White, 0.0% Black/African American, 0.0% Asian, 0.0% American Indian/Alaska Native, 0.0% Native Hawaiian/Other Pacific Islander, 1.9% Two or more races, 3.5% Hispanic of any race; Average household size: 2.86; Median age: 29.9; Age under 18: 32.4%; Age 65 and over: 11.1%; Males per 100 females: 105.6; Marriage status: 41.0% never married, 32.4% now married, 1.8% separated, 9.0% widowed, 17.6% divorced; Foreign born: 0.0%; Speak English only: 98.0%; With disability: 19.0%; Veterans: 6.1%; Ancestry: 30.5% Irish, 27.3% German, 15.6% English, 14.9% French, 13.3% Italian
Employment: 11.3% management, business, and financial, 0.0% computer, engineering, and science, 6.0% education, legal, community service, arts, and media, 9.0% healthcare practitioners, 11.3% service, 26.3% sales and office, 11.3% natural resources, construction, and maintenance, 24.8% production, transportation, and material moving
Income: Per capita: $17,662; Median household: $29,643; Average household: $47,843; Households with income of $100,000 or more: 13.6%; Poverty rate: 30.8%
Educational Attainment: High school diploma or higher: 90.2%; Bachelor's degree or higher: 9.8%; Graduate/professional degree or higher: 4.3%
Housing: Homeownership rate: 77.3%; Median home value: $78,200; Median year structure built: Before 1940; Homeowner vacancy rate: 0.0%; Median selected monthly owner costs: $930 with a mortgage, $389 without a mortgage; Median gross rent: $525 per month; Rental vacancy rate: 0.0%
Health Insurance: 94.6% have insurance; 57.5% have private insurance; 47.9% have public insurance; 5.4% do not have insurance; 0.0% of children under 18 do not have insurance

Transportation: Commute: 92.9% car, 4.0% public transportation, 0.8% walk, 0.8% work from home; Mean travel time to work: 30.8 minutes

COLUMBIA (town). Covers a land area of 35.073 square miles and a water area of 0.030 square miles. Located at 42.93° N. Lat; 75.05° W. Long.

Population: 1,555; Growth (since 2000): -4.6%; Density: 44.3 persons per square mile; Race: 99.7% White, 0.0% Black/African American, 0.0% Asian, 0.0% American Indian/Alaska Native, 0.0% Native Hawaiian/Other Pacific Islander, 0.2% Two or more races, 1.1% Hispanic of any race; Average household size: 2.63; Median age: 45.5; Age under 18: 22.8%; Age 65 and over: 19.8%; Males per 100 females: 107.1; Marriage status: 18.4% never married, 67.0% now married, 0.9% separated, 6.7% widowed, 7.9% divorced; Foreign born: 0.3%; Speak English only: 97.3%; With disability: 12.7%; Veterans: 8.3%; Ancestry: 22.2% German, 13.4% Irish, 8.8% Polish, 8.6% English, 8.5% Dutch
Employment: 12.9% management, business, and financial, 3.4% computer, engineering, and science, 8.8% education, legal, community service, arts, and media, 6.4% healthcare practitioners, 15.3% service, 20.9% sales and office, 12.5% natural resources, construction, and maintenance, 19.9% production, transportation, and material moving
Income: Per capita: $24,484; Median household: $53,125; Average household: $63,400; Households with income of $100,000 or more: 19.8%; Poverty rate: 14.4%
Educational Attainment: High school diploma or higher: 90.2%; Bachelor's degree or higher: 14.7%; Graduate/professional degree or higher: 7.4%
Housing: Homeownership rate: 92.0%; Median home value: $100,900; Median year structure built: 1975; Homeowner vacancy rate: 0.0%; Median selected monthly owner costs: $1,155 with a mortgage, $394 without a mortgage; Median gross rent: $745 per month; Rental vacancy rate: 0.0%
Health Insurance: 89.8% have insurance; 63.6% have private insurance; 39.7% have public insurance; 10.2% do not have insurance; 13.9% of children under 18 do not have insurance
Transportation: Commute: 87.8% car, 0.4% public transportation, 6.7% walk, 3.4% work from home; Mean travel time to work: 28.6 minutes

DANUBE (town). Covers a land area of 29.354 square miles and a water area of 0.259 square miles. Located at 42.98° N. Lat; 74.80° W. Long.

Population: 910; Growth (since 2000): -17.1%; Density: 31.0 persons per square mile; Race: 99.1% White, 0.0% Black/African American, 0.0% Asian, 0.0% American Indian/Alaska Native, 0.0% Native Hawaiian/Other Pacific Islander, 0.9% Two or more races, 0.0% Hispanic of any race; Average household size: 2.61; Median age: 44.1; Age under 18: 17.1%; Age 65 and over: 20.2%; Males per 100 females: 115.6; Marriage status: 27.5% never married, 59.5% now married, 0.9% separated, 6.4% widowed, 6.6% divorced; Foreign born: 0.0%; Speak English only: 99.2%; With disability: 12.7%; Veterans: 9.4%; Ancestry: 24.6% German, 16.4% Irish, 11.8% Italian, 9.3% American, 7.5% English
Employment: 15.8% management, business, and financial, 3.0% computer, engineering, and science, 4.3% education, legal, community service, arts, and media, 4.7% healthcare practitioners, 14.3% service, 22.0% sales and office, 17.3% natural resources, construction, and maintenance, 18.6% production, transportation, and material moving
Income: Per capita: $26,755; Median household: $63,523; Average household: $67,152; Households with income of $100,000 or more: 23.2%; Poverty rate: 12.9%
Educational Attainment: High school diploma or higher: 91.8%; Bachelor's degree or higher: 17.2%; Graduate/professional degree or higher: 2.9%
Housing: Homeownership rate: 87.4%; Median home value: $100,300; Median year structure built: 1973; Homeowner vacancy rate: 0.0%; Median selected monthly owner costs: $1,155 with a mortgage, $500 without a mortgage; Median gross rent: $660 per month; Rental vacancy rate: 17.0%
Health Insurance: 89.2% have insurance; 66.7% have private insurance; 35.4% have public insurance; 10.8% do not have insurance; 6.7% of children under 18 do not have insurance
Transportation: Commute: 85.9% car, 0.0% public transportation, 7.6% walk, 5.4% work from home; Mean travel time to work: 24.9 minutes
Additional Information Contacts
Town of Danube . . . . (315) 868-6368
  http://town.danube.ny.us

DOLGEVILLE (village). Covers a land area of 1.791 square miles and a water area of 0.044 square miles. Located at 43.11° N. Lat; 74.78° W. Long. Elevation is 791 feet.

History: Incorporated 1891.
Population: 2,544; Growth (since 2000): 17.5%; Density: 1,420.8 persons per square mile; Race: 98.2% White, 0.4% Black/African American, 0.0% Asian, 0.6% American Indian/Alaska Native, 0.0% Native Hawaiian/Other Pacific Islander, 0.8% Two or more races, 1.3% Hispanic of any race; Average household size: 2.51; Median age: 35.8; Age under 18: 28.3%; Age 65 and over: 15.1%; Males per 100 females: 91.8; Marriage status: 29.6% never married, 53.3% now married, 3.7% separated, 8.3% widowed, 8.8% divorced; Foreign born: 1.2%; Speak English only: 97.3%; With disability: 11.4%; Veterans: 10.1%; Ancestry: 21.8% German, 14.7% Irish, 13.1% Italian, 11.7% English, 10.1% French
Employment: 7.6% management, business, and financial, 1.6% computer, engineering, and science, 18.2% education, legal, community service, arts, and media, 8.6% healthcare practitioners, 15.7% service, 19.3% sales and office, 10.1% natural resources, construction, and maintenance, 18.9% production, transportation, and material moving
Income: Per capita: $22,263; Median household: $45,313; Average household: $55,933; Households with income of $100,000 or more: 16.2%; Poverty rate: 20.3%
Educational Attainment: High school diploma or higher: 88.1%; Bachelor's degree or higher: 18.5%; Graduate/professional degree or higher: 13.4%

School District(s)
Dolgeville Central SD (PK-12)
  Enrollment: 962 . . . . (315) 429-3155
Housing: Homeownership rate: 67.7%; Median home value: $82,000; Median year structure built: Before 1940; Homeowner vacancy rate: 2.0%; Median selected monthly owner costs: $1,016 with a mortgage, $489 without a mortgage; Median gross rent: $625 per month; Rental vacancy rate: 4.4%
Health Insurance: 96.6% have insurance; 57.5% have private insurance; 51.5% have public insurance; 3.4% do not have insurance; 1.9% of children under 18 do not have insurance
Safety: Violent crime rate: 9.5 per 10,000 population; Property crime rate: 76.2 per 10,000 population
Transportation: Commute: 89.6% car, 0.0% public transportation, 5.1% walk, 1.6% work from home; Mean travel time to work: 23.0 minutes

EAGLE BAY (unincorporated postal area)
ZCTA: 13331
  Covers a land area of 80.667 square miles and a water area of 4.673 square miles. Located at 43.87° N. Lat; 74.88° W. Long. Elevation is 1,778 feet.
Population: 144; Growth (since 2000): -50.9%; Density: 1.8 persons per square mile; Race: 100.0% White, 0.0% Black/African American, 0.0% Asian, 0.0% American Indian/Alaska Native, 0.0% Native Hawaiian/Other Pacific Islander, 0.0% Two or more races, 0.0% Hispanic of any race; Average household size: 1.66; Median age: 67.2; Age under 18: 0.0%; Age 65 and over: 64.6%; Males per 100 females: 110.0; Marriage status: 3.5% never married, 72.9% now married, 0.0% separated, 18.8% widowed, 4.9% divorced; Foreign born: 0.0%; Speak English only: 96.5%; With disability: 3.5%; Veterans: 16.7%; Ancestry: 26.4% Italian, 26.4% Polish, 18.8% English, 11.8% Irish, 9.7% German
Employment: 16.4% management, business, and financial, 0.0% computer, engineering, and science, 0.0% education, legal, community service, arts, and media, 18.2% healthcare practitioners, 21.8% service, 34.5% sales and office, 9.1% natural resources, construction, and maintenance, 0.0% production, transportation, and material moving
Income: Per capita: $42,237; Median household: $45,250; Average household: $71,115; Households with income of $100,000 or more: 26.4%; Poverty rate: 3.5%
Educational Attainment: High school diploma or higher: 96.5%; Bachelor's degree or higher: 43.1%; Graduate/professional degree or higher: 14.6%
Housing: Homeownership rate: 100.0%; Median home value: $321,400; Median year structure built: 1958; Homeowner vacancy rate: 0.0%; Median selected monthly owner costs: $0 with a mortgage, $542 without a mortgage; Median gross rent: n/a per month; Rental vacancy rate: 0.0%
Health Insurance: 100.0% have insurance; 88.9% have private insurance; 65.3% have public insurance; 0.0% do not have insurance; 0.0% of children under 18 do not have insurance

Transportation: Commute: 83.6% car, 0.0% public transportation, 16.4% walk, 0.0% work from home; Mean travel time to work: 19.1 minutes

FAIRFIELD (town). Covers a land area of 41.296 square miles and a water area of 0.162 square miles. Located at 43.13° N. Lat; 74.94° W. Long. Elevation is 1,266 feet.
Population: 1,458; Growth (since 2000): -9.3%; Density: 35.3 persons per square mile; Race: 97.7% White, 0.0% Black/African American, 0.2% Asian, 0.0% American Indian/Alaska Native, 0.0% Native Hawaiian/Other Pacific Islander, 2.1% Two or more races, 0.5% Hispanic of any race; Average household size: 2.54; Median age: 44.9; Age under 18: 23.3%; Age 65 and over: 19.1%; Males per 100 females: 102.6; Marriage status: 22.5% never married, 59.8% now married, 0.5% separated, 6.6% widowed, 11.2% divorced; Foreign born: 3.2%; Speak English only: 92.8%; With disability: 13.7%; Veterans: 9.1%; Ancestry: 29.8% German, 13.1% Irish, 13.0% American, 9.9% English, 9.8% Italian
Employment: 17.1% management, business, and financial, 4.8% computer, engineering, and science, 10.5% education, legal, community service, arts, and media, 5.2% healthcare practitioners, 9.7% service, 16.2% sales and office, 20.6% natural resources, construction, and maintenance, 16.0% production, transportation, and material moving
Income: Per capita: $30,355; Median household: $50,781; Average household: $76,646; Households with income of $100,000 or more: 22.7%; Poverty rate: 6.4%
Educational Attainment: High school diploma or higher: 89.2%; Bachelor's degree or higher: 19.5%; Graduate/professional degree or higher: 8.6%
Housing: Homeownership rate: 91.1%; Median home value: $114,000; Median year structure built: 1969; Homeowner vacancy rate: 1.5%; Median selected monthly owner costs: $1,237 with a mortgage, $498 without a mortgage; Median gross rent: n/a per month; Rental vacancy rate: 13.6%
Health Insurance: 92.6% have insurance; 69.4% have private insurance; 38.9% have public insurance; 7.4% do not have insurance; 4.7% of children under 18 do not have insurance
Transportation: Commute: 86.5% car, 0.0% public transportation, 4.8% walk, 8.7% work from home; Mean travel time to work: 28.5 minutes

FRANKFORT (town). Covers a land area of 36.421 square miles and a water area of 0.106 square miles. Located at 43.04° N. Lat; 75.14° W. Long. Elevation is 407 feet.
History: Settled 1723, incorporated 1863.
Population: 7,449; Growth (since 2000): -0.4%; Density: 204.5 persons per square mile; Race: 97.0% White, 0.6% Black/African American, 0.1% Asian, 0.9% American Indian/Alaska Native, 0.3% Native Hawaiian/Other Pacific Islander, 0.5% Two or more races, 1.7% Hispanic of any race; Average household size: 2.44; Median age: 45.1; Age under 18: 17.9%; Age 65 and over: 20.6%; Males per 100 females: 94.1; Marriage status: 28.8% never married, 51.8% now married, 2.1% separated, 6.7% widowed, 12.8% divorced; Foreign born: 3.9%; Speak English only: 94.0%; With disability: 14.4%; Veterans: 10.1%; Ancestry: 32.9% Italian, 19.9% German, 15.2% Irish, 8.1% American, 7.6% English
Employment: 10.8% management, business, and financial, 2.3% computer, engineering, and science, 8.9% education, legal, community service, arts, and media, 8.3% healthcare practitioners, 24.4% service, 25.4% sales and office, 7.0% natural resources, construction, and maintenance, 13.0% production, transportation, and material moving
Income: Per capita: $25,494; Median household: $53,104; Average household: $60,823; Households with income of $100,000 or more: 14.9%; Poverty rate: 11.7%
Educational Attainment: High school diploma or higher: 92.7%; Bachelor's degree or higher: 21.0%; Graduate/professional degree or higher: 7.5%
School District(s)
Frankfort-Schuyler Central SD (PK-12)
    Enrollment: 970 . . . . (315) 894-5083
Housing: Homeownership rate: 75.8%; Median home value: $109,600; Median year structure built: 1954; Homeowner vacancy rate: 2.3%; Median selected monthly owner costs: $1,179 with a mortgage, $486 without a mortgage; Median gross rent: $674 per month; Rental vacancy rate: 3.7%
Health Insurance: 95.4% have insurance; 73.5% have private insurance; 39.5% have public insurance; 4.6% do not have insurance; 0.0% of children under 18 do not have insurance
Transportation: Commute: 95.3% car, 0.0% public transportation, 2.6% walk, 1.7% work from home; Mean travel time to work: 20.6 minutes

Additional Information Contacts
Town of Frankfort . . . . (315) 894-8737
    http://www.townoffrankfort.com

FRANKFORT (village). Covers a land area of 1.014 square miles and a water area of 0.017 square miles. Located at 43.04° N. Lat; 75.07° W. Long. Elevation is 407 feet.
Population: 2,502; Growth (since 2000): -1.4%; Density: 2,468.1 persons per square mile; Race: 94.0% White, 1.0% Black/African American, 0.2% Asian, 0.8% American Indian/Alaska Native, 0.8% Native Hawaiian/Other Pacific Islander, 1.1% Two or more races, 3.0% Hispanic of any race; Average household size: 2.49; Median age: 41.5; Age under 18: 20.6%; Age 65 and over: 16.5%; Males per 100 females: 91.5; Marriage status: 35.3% never married, 43.7% now married, 2.0% separated, 5.1% widowed, 15.9% divorced; Foreign born: 3.0%; Speak English only: 94.5%; With disability: 14.3%; Veterans: 7.6%; Ancestry: 42.9% Italian, 14.4% German, 11.9% Irish, 10.7% Polish, 8.1% American
Employment: 10.8% management, business, and financial, 1.8% computer, engineering, and science, 13.5% education, legal, community service, arts, and media, 7.7% healthcare practitioners, 27.4% service, 21.2% sales and office, 4.8% natural resources, construction, and maintenance, 12.8% production, transportation, and material moving
Income: Per capita: $23,192; Median household: $47,000; Average household: $55,494; Households with income of $100,000 or more: 14.1%; Poverty rate: 14.6%
Educational Attainment: High school diploma or higher: 91.1%; Bachelor's degree or higher: 20.3%; Graduate/professional degree or higher: 8.3%
School District(s)
Frankfort-Schuyler Central SD (PK-12)
    Enrollment: 970 . . . . (315) 894-5083
Housing: Homeownership rate: 64.2%; Median home value: $89,300; Median year structure built: Before 1940; Homeowner vacancy rate: 3.2%; Median selected monthly owner costs: $1,086 with a mortgage, $428 without a mortgage; Median gross rent: $596 per month; Rental vacancy rate: 7.2%
Health Insurance: 96.3% have insurance; 71.2% have private insurance; 37.8% have public insurance; 3.7% do not have insurance; 0.0% of children under 18 do not have insurance
Transportation: Commute: 94.0% car, 0.0% public transportation, 2.5% walk, 2.5% work from home; Mean travel time to work: 19.7 minutes

GERMAN FLATTS (town). Covers a land area of 33.695 square miles and a water area of 0.499 square miles. Located at 42.99° N. Lat; 74.98° W. Long.
Population: 12,806; Growth (since 2000): -6.0%; Density: 380.1 persons per square mile; Race: 93.6% White, 2.5% Black/African American, 0.8% Asian, 0.1% American Indian/Alaska Native, 0.5% Native Hawaiian/Other Pacific Islander, 2.0% Two or more races, 3.7% Hispanic of any race; Average household size: 2.48; Median age: 39.9; Age under 18: 23.5%; Age 65 and over: 17.6%; Males per 100 females: 93.2; Marriage status: 34.7% never married, 46.3% now married, 3.0% separated, 6.1% widowed, 12.9% divorced; Foreign born: 1.9%; Speak English only: 98.4%; With disability: 16.4%; Veterans: 9.4%; Ancestry: 23.0% Irish, 20.1% Italian, 20.1% German, 12.0% English, 6.1% Polish
Employment: 11.2% management, business, and financial, 4.7% computer, engineering, and science, 10.8% education, legal, community service, arts, and media, 7.5% healthcare practitioners, 20.2% service, 24.1% sales and office, 7.9% natural resources, construction, and maintenance, 13.6% production, transportation, and material moving
Income: Per capita: $23,732; Median household: $45,726; Average household: $57,728; Households with income of $100,000 or more: 16.5%; Poverty rate: 18.9%
Educational Attainment: High school diploma or higher: 90.8%; Bachelor's degree or higher: 22.9%; Graduate/professional degree or higher: 10.6%
Housing: Homeownership rate: 64.8%; Median home value: $82,500; Median year structure built: Before 1940; Homeowner vacancy rate: 1.1%; Median selected monthly owner costs: $1,028 with a mortgage, $414 without a mortgage; Median gross rent: $622 per month; Rental vacancy rate: 5.2%
Health Insurance: 93.4% have insurance; 57.1% have private insurance; 49.7% have public insurance; 6.6% do not have insurance; 4.2% of children under 18 do not have insurance

Transportation: Commute: 92.2% car, 1.3% public transportation, 2.2% walk, 2.9% work from home; Mean travel time to work: 21.1 minutes

HERKIMER (town). Covers a land area of 31.662 square miles and a water area of 0.566 square miles. Located at 43.06° N. Lat; 75.00° W. Long. Elevation is 384 feet.

History: Herkimer was settled by a group of Palatines in 1725 and was long known as German Flats. In 1776 Fort Dayton, a wooden structure surrounded by a stockade, was built on a plot now at the center of town. From that fort on August 4, 1777, General Nicholas Herkimer marched to the Battle of Oriskany. The town was named for him.

Population: 9,866; Growth (since 2000): -1.0%; Density: 311.6 persons per square mile; Race: 93.3% White, 2.4% Black/African American, 1.0% Asian, 0.2% American Indian/Alaska Native, 0.0% Native Hawaiian/Other Pacific Islander, 2.2% Two or more races, 1.5% Hispanic of any race; Average household size: 2.20; Median age: 44.1; Age under 18: 16.2%; Age 65 and over: 22.0%; Males per 100 females: 90.5; Marriage status: 32.1% never married, 45.8% now married, 2.3% separated, 9.2% widowed, 13.0% divorced; Foreign born: 2.9%; Speak English only: 95.0%; With disability: 21.4%; Veterans: 11.8%; Ancestry: 21.8% Italian, 19.7% German, 18.8% Irish, 9.6% Polish, 8.2% American

Employment: 8.5% management, business, and financial, 2.6% computer, engineering, and science, 12.0% education, legal, community service, arts, and media, 4.7% healthcare practitioners, 24.5% service, 28.9% sales and office, 4.6% natural resources, construction, and maintenance, 14.1% production, transportation, and material moving

Income: Per capita: $24,868; Median household: $46,399; Average household: $56,504; Households with income of $100,000 or more: 13.6%; Poverty rate: 16.9%

Educational Attainment: High school diploma or higher: 88.9%; Bachelor's degree or higher: 19.5%; Graduate/professional degree or higher: 7.5%

School District(s)
Herkimer Central SD (PK-12)
    Enrollment: 1,182 . . . . (315) 866-2230
Herkimer-Fulton-Hamilton-Otsego Boces
    Enrollment: n/a . . . . (315) 867-2023
Two-year College(s)
Herkimer County Community College (Public)
    Enrollment: 2,632 . . . . (315) 866-0300
    Tuition: In-state $5,120; Out-of-state $8,250

Housing: Homeownership rate: 51.9%; Median home value: $89,400; Median year structure built: Before 1940; Homeowner vacancy rate: 4.7%; Median selected monthly owner costs: $1,140 with a mortgage, $509 without a mortgage; Median gross rent: $741 per month; Rental vacancy rate: 5.0%

Health Insurance: 94.7% have insurance; 64.0% have private insurance; 49.6% have public insurance; 5.3% do not have insurance; 1.7% of children under 18 do not have insurance

Newspapers: Evening Telegram (daily circulation 6,700); The Times (daily circulation 4,000)

Transportation: Commute: 83.5% car, 2.2% public transportation, 10.5% walk, 3.0% work from home; Mean travel time to work: 18.8 minutes

Additional Information Contacts
Town of Herkimer . . . . (315) 866-2690
    http://www.townofherkimer.org

HERKIMER (village). County seat. Covers a land area of 2.588 square miles and a water area of 0.115 square miles. Located at 43.03° N. Lat; 74.99° W. Long. Elevation is 384 feet.

History: Formerly shipping, commercial and trade center for surrounding Mohawk valley Agriculture and industrial area that stretched west through village of Mohawk to Ilion and Frankfort. Herkimer County Historical Society has important documents and exhibits here. World-renowned Herkimer diamonds (actually a clear quartz) are to be found along West Canada Creek Valley north of the village. Settled c.1725, Incorporated 1807.

Population: 7,361; Growth (since 2000): -1.8%; Density: 2,843.8 persons per square mile; Race: 91.0% White, 3.2% Black/African American, 1.4% Asian, 0.3% American Indian/Alaska Native, 0.0% Native Hawaiian/Other Pacific Islander, 3.0% Two or more races, 2.0% Hispanic of any race; Average household size: 2.17; Median age: 40.5; Age under 18: 16.2%; Age 65 and over: 22.1%; Males per 100 females: 88.6; Marriage status: 32.3% never married, 43.5% now married, 2.6% separated, 10.7% widowed, 13.6% divorced; Foreign born: 3.6%; Speak English only: 94.5%;

With disability: 20.9%; Veterans: 11.3%; Ancestry: 20.4% Irish, 20.4% Italian, 14.6% German, 9.6% American, 8.7% Polish

Employment: 6.0% management, business, and financial, 3.1% computer, engineering, and science, 10.3% education, legal, community service, arts, and media, 4.2% healthcare practitioners, 27.6% service, 32.4% sales and office, 1.6% natural resources, construction, and maintenance, 14.8% production, transportation, and material moving

Income: Per capita: $21,917; Median household: $41,227; Average household: $50,031; Households with income of $100,000 or more: 10.6%; Poverty rate: 18.8%

Educational Attainment: High school diploma or higher: 87.3%; Bachelor's degree or higher: 17.5%; Graduate/professional degree or higher: 7.1%

School District(s)
Herkimer Central SD (PK-12)
    Enrollment: 1,182 . . . . (315) 866-2230
Herkimer-Fulton-Hamilton-Otsego Boces
    Enrollment: n/a . . . . (315) 867-2023
Two-year College(s)
Herkimer County Community College (Public)
    Enrollment: 2,632 . . . . (315) 866-0300
    Tuition: In-state $5,120; Out-of-state $8,250

Housing: Homeownership rate: 41.6%; Median home value: $81,900; Median year structure built: Before 1940; Homeowner vacancy rate: 5.8%; Median selected monthly owner costs: $1,089 with a mortgage, $507 without a mortgage; Median gross rent: $719 per month; Rental vacancy rate: 5.5%

Health Insurance: 93.9% have insurance; 60.4% have private insurance; 51.6% have public insurance; 6.1% do not have insurance; 1.5% of children under 18 do not have insurance

Safety: Violent crime rate: 67.5 per 10,000 population; Property crime rate: 437.2 per 10,000 population

Newspapers: Evening Telegram (daily circulation 6,700); The Times (daily circulation 4,000)

Transportation: Commute: 81.9% car, 3.1% public transportation, 10.6% walk, 3.6% work from home; Mean travel time to work: 18.6 minutes

Additional Information Contacts
Village of Herkimer . . . . (315) 866-3303
    http://village.herkimer.ny.us/content

ILION (village). Covers a land area of 2.493 square miles and a water area of 0.059 square miles. Located at 43.01° N. Lat; 75.04° W. Long. Elevation is 407 feet.

History: Part of the former Herkimer (village). Remington Arms Museum. Incorporated 1852.

Population: 7,930; Growth (since 2000): -7.9%; Density: 3,181.0 persons per square mile; Race: 92.6% White, 3.1% Black/African American, 0.3% Asian, 0.1% American Indian/Alaska Native, 0.8% Native Hawaiian/Other Pacific Islander, 2.2% Two or more races, 4.6% Hispanic of any race; Average household size: 2.50; Median age: 38.5; Age under 18: 25.9%; Age 65 and over: 16.4%; Males per 100 females: 91.8; Marriage status: 34.5% never married, 46.0% now married, 3.6% separated, 7.0% widowed, 12.6% divorced; Foreign born: 0.6%; Speak English only: 98.9%; With disability: 13.8%; Veterans: 9.8%; Ancestry: 22.2% Irish, 21.5% Italian, 17.9% German, 11.4% English, 5.5% Polish

Employment: 13.1% management, business, and financial, 5.7% computer, engineering, and science, 12.1% education, legal, community service, arts, and media, 6.4% healthcare practitioners, 17.1% service, 24.6% sales and office, 6.2% natural resources, construction, and maintenance, 14.8% production, transportation, and material moving

Income: Per capita: $22,810; Median household: $44,813; Average household: $56,280; Households with income of $100,000 or more: 17.8%; Poverty rate: 20.9%

Educational Attainment: High school diploma or higher: 91.8%; Bachelor's degree or higher: 23.4%; Graduate/professional degree or higher: 12.1%

School District(s)
Central Valley CSD at Ilion-Mohawk (PK-12)
    Enrollment: 2,412 . . . . (315) 894-9934
Vocational/Technical School(s)
Herkimer County BOCES-Practical Nursing Program (Public)
    Enrollment: 97 . . . . (315) 895-2210
    Tuition: $13,500

Housing: Homeownership rate: 61.8%; Median home value: $77,800; Median year structure built: Before 1940; Homeowner vacancy rate: 1.8%;

Median selected monthly owner costs: $975 with a mortgage, $450 without a mortgage; Median gross rent: $629 per month; Rental vacancy rate: 7.7%
Health Insurance: 93.5% have insurance; 54.1% have private insurance; 51.6% have public insurance; 6.5% do not have insurance; 3.4% of children under 18 do not have insurance
Safety: Violent crime rate: 41.0 per 10,000 population; Property crime rate: 324.3 per 10,000 population
Transportation: Commute: 91.0% car, 0.4% public transportation, 3.0% walk, 3.6% work from home; Mean travel time to work: 21.1 minutes
Additional Information Contacts
Village of Ilion . . . . (315) 895-7449
http://www.ilionny.com

JORDANVILLE (unincorporated postal area)
ZCTA: 13361
Covers a land area of 28.325 square miles and a water area of 0.003 square miles. Located at 42.90° N. Lat; 74.87° W. Long. Elevation is 1,499 feet.
Population: 900; Growth (since 2000): 24.3%; Density: 31.8 persons per square mile; Race: 96.7% White, 0.3% Black/African American, 1.9% Asian, 0.0% American Indian/Alaska Native, 0.0% Native Hawaiian/Other Pacific Islander, 0.7% Two or more races, 2.8% Hispanic of any race; Average household size: 2.91; Median age: 37.5; Age under 18: 30.0%; Age 65 and over: 13.9%; Males per 100 females: 119.1; Marriage status: 23.7% never married, 57.8% now married, 0.4% separated, 5.5% widowed, 13.0% divorced; Foreign born: 4.3%; Speak English only: 87.7%; With disability: 11.9%; Veterans: 7.0%; Ancestry: 21.6% German, 15.9% English, 10.9% Irish, 9.4% Polish, 9.0% Dutch
Employment: 19.2% management, business, and financial, 0.5% computer, engineering, and science, 18.2% education, legal, community service, arts, and media, 5.4% healthcare practitioners, 10.3% service, 14.9% sales and office, 17.9% natural resources, construction, and maintenance, 13.6% production, transportation, and material moving
Income: Per capita: $22,586; Median household: $63,125; Average household: $64,777; Households with income of $100,000 or more: 14.8%; Poverty rate: 5.9%
Educational Attainment: High school diploma or higher: 90.9%; Bachelor's degree or higher: 27.9%; Graduate/professional degree or higher: 13.6%
Housing: Homeownership rate: 93.3%; Median home value: $98,400; Median year structure built: 1955; Homeowner vacancy rate: 0.0%; Median selected monthly owner costs: $1,149 with a mortgage, $447 without a mortgage; Median gross rent: n/a per month; Rental vacancy rate: 0.0%
Health Insurance: 86.4% have insurance; 67.4% have private insurance; 26.1% have public insurance; 13.6% do not have insurance; 19.4% of children under 18 do not have insurance
Transportation: Commute: 79.6% car, 0.0% public transportation, 7.0% walk, 10.3% work from home; Mean travel time to work: 32.4 minutes

LITCHFIELD (town). Covers a land area of 29.992 square miles and a water area of 0.061 square miles. Located at 42.97° N. Lat; 75.16° W. Long. Elevation is 1,506 feet.
Population: 1,491; Growth (since 2000): 2.6%; Density: 49.7 persons per square mile; Race: 96.5% White, 0.0% Black/African American, 1.4% Asian, 0.0% American Indian/Alaska Native, 0.0% Native Hawaiian/Other Pacific Islander, 1.7% Two or more races, 1.1% Hispanic of any race; Average household size: 2.55; Median age: 46.6; Age under 18: 21.8%; Age 65 and over: 18.8%; Males per 100 females: 105.0; Marriage status: 28.8% never married, 54.2% now married, 2.0% separated, 4.5% widowed, 12.6% divorced; Foreign born: 3.0%; Speak English only: 93.0%; With disability: 9.9%; Veterans: 9.1%; Ancestry: 25.1% Irish, 18.2% German, 15.0% Italian, 13.3% English, 11.1% Polish
Employment: 12.8% management, business, and financial, 5.9% computer, engineering, and science, 9.3% education, legal, community service, arts, and media, 14.5% healthcare practitioners, 16.5% service, 16.5% sales and office, 13.9% natural resources, construction, and maintenance, 10.6% production, transportation, and material moving
Income: Per capita: $25,377; Median household: $57,644; Average household: $63,407; Households with income of $100,000 or more: 18.2%; Poverty rate: 9.2%
Educational Attainment: High school diploma or higher: 92.8%; Bachelor's degree or higher: 26.3%; Graduate/professional degree or higher: 8.5%

Housing: Homeownership rate: 86.8%; Median home value: $111,300; Median year structure built: 1972; Homeowner vacancy rate: 0.0%; Median selected monthly owner costs: $1,257 with a mortgage, $513 without a mortgage; Median gross rent: $636 per month; Rental vacancy rate: 0.0%
Health Insurance: 93.7% have insurance; 70.3% have private insurance; 41.0% have public insurance; 6.3% do not have insurance; 2.6% of children under 18 do not have insurance
Transportation: Commute: 91.6% car, 0.0% public transportation, 0.0% walk, 8.0% work from home; Mean travel time to work: 23.1 minutes

LITTLE FALLS (city). Covers a land area of 3.838 square miles and a water area of 0.151 square miles. Located at 43.04° N. Lat; 74.86° W. Long. Elevation is 420 feet.
Population: 4,790; Growth (since 2000): -7.7%; Density: 1,248.0 persons per square mile; Race: 96.9% White, 1.0% Black/African American, 1.0% Asian, 0.3% American Indian/Alaska Native, 0.0% Native Hawaiian/Other Pacific Islander, 0.6% Two or more races, 3.1% Hispanic of any race; Average household size: 2.48; Median age: 41.4; Age under 18: 23.3%; Age 65 and over: 17.6%; Males per 100 females: 88.3; Marriage status: 36.4% never married, 39.9% now married, 3.3% separated, 9.6% widowed, 14.1% divorced; Foreign born: 2.2%; Speak English only: 93.6%; With disability: 20.3%; Veterans: 8.5%; Ancestry: 22.5% Irish, 15.9% German, 12.8% Italian, 8.9% Polish, 8.5% English
Employment: 6.3% management, business, and financial, 2.8% computer, engineering, and science, 13.0% education, legal, community service, arts, and media, 6.5% healthcare practitioners, 23.3% service, 23.5% sales and office, 10.9% natural resources, construction, and maintenance, 13.8% production, transportation, and material moving
Income: Per capita: $23,081; Median household: $39,534; Average household: $56,650; Households with income of $100,000 or more: 11.1%; Poverty rate: 29.1%
Educational Attainment: High school diploma or higher: 88.9%; Bachelor's degree or higher: 24.8%; Graduate/professional degree or higher: 9.9%
School District(s)
Little Falls City SD (PK-12)
    Enrollment: 1,114 . . . . (315) 823-1470
Housing: Homeownership rate: 56.4%; Median home value: $75,100; Median year structure built: Before 1940; Homeowner vacancy rate: 9.1%; Median selected monthly owner costs: $960 with a mortgage, $466 without a mortgage; Median gross rent: $592 per month; Rental vacancy rate: 13.6%
Health Insurance: 94.7% have insurance; 53.8% have private insurance; 55.6% have public insurance; 5.3% do not have insurance; 2.8% of children under 18 do not have insurance
Hospitals: Little Falls Hospital (25 beds)
Safety: Violent crime rate: 34.0 per 10,000 population; Property crime rate: 261.2 per 10,000 population
Transportation: Commute: 83.6% car, 4.6% public transportation, 5.8% walk, 4.1% work from home; Mean travel time to work: 20.8 minutes
Additional Information Contacts
City of Little Falls. . . . . (315) 823-2400
http://www.cityoflittlefalls.net

LITTLE FALLS (town). Covers a land area of 22.340 square miles and a water area of 0.163 square miles. Located at 43.02° N. Lat; 74.89° W. Long. Elevation is 420 feet.
History: Home of Gen. Nicholas Herkimer, hero of Battle of Oriskany. Settled c.1725; incorporated as city 1895.
Population: 1,718; Growth (since 2000): 11.3%; Density: 76.9 persons per square mile; Race: 99.6% White, 0.0% Black/African American, 0.0% Asian, 0.0% American Indian/Alaska Native, 0.0% Native Hawaiian/Other Pacific Islander, 0.4% Two or more races, 0.0% Hispanic of any race; Average household size: 2.76; Median age: 43.1; Age under 18: 23.3%; Age 65 and over: 14.8%; Males per 100 females: 109.1; Marriage status: 28.8% never married, 56.7% now married, 2.4% separated, 5.5% widowed, 9.0% divorced; Foreign born: 2.2%; Speak English only: 91.5%; With disability: 9.0%; Veterans: 7.7%; Ancestry: 20.9% Irish, 19.3% German, 14.8% Italian, 11.4% American, 9.9% Polish
Employment: 15.6% management, business, and financial, 3.8% computer, engineering, and science, 5.8% education, legal, community service, arts, and media, 6.6% healthcare practitioners, 15.1% service, 19.1% sales and office, 12.7% natural resources, construction, and maintenance, 21.3% production, transportation, and material moving

Income: Per capita: $28,791; Median household: $64,830; Average household: $76,873; Households with income of $100,000 or more: 23.9%; Poverty rate: 7.2%

Educational Attainment: High school diploma or higher: 88.6%; Bachelor's degree or higher: 16.7%; Graduate/professional degree or higher: 8.6%

School District(s)

Little Falls City SD (PK-12)

    Enrollment: 1,114 .... (315) 823-1470

Housing: Homeownership rate: 86.5%; Median home value: $112,300; Median year structure built: 1965; Homeowner vacancy rate: 3.2%; Median selected monthly owner costs: $1,245 with a mortgage, $411 without a mortgage; Median gross rent: $1,097 per month; Rental vacancy rate: 11.6%

Health Insurance: 89.4% have insurance; 73.5% have private insurance; 27.3% have public insurance; 10.6% do not have insurance; 17.2% of children under 18 do not have insurance

Hospitals: Little Falls Hospital (25 beds)

Transportation: Commute: 95.6% car, 0.0% public transportation, 1.6% walk, 2.8% work from home; Mean travel time to work: 22.9 minutes

---

MANHEIM (town). Covers a land area of 29.136 square miles and a water area of 0.557 square miles. Located at 43.06° N. Lat; 74.80° W. Long.

Population: 3,248; Growth (since 2000): 2.4%; Density: 111.5 persons per square mile; Race: 98.4% White, 0.3% Black/African American, 0.0% Asian, 0.5% American Indian/Alaska Native, 0.0% Native Hawaiian/Other Pacific Islander, 0.6% Two or more races, 1.0% Hispanic of any race; Average household size: 2.53; Median age: 37.4; Age under 18: 27.5%; Age 65 and over: 17.4%; Males per 100 females: 96.5; Marriage status: 28.6% never married, 52.8% now married, 2.5% separated, 8.5% widowed, 10.0% divorced; Foreign born: 1.0%; Speak English only: 95.8%; With disability: 11.1%; Veterans: 11.8%; Ancestry: 20.2% German, 18.9% Italian, 11.7% Irish, 11.4% Polish, 10.7% English

Employment: 8.5% management, business, and financial, 1.4% computer, engineering, and science, 17.2% education, legal, community service, arts, and media, 7.1% healthcare practitioners, 14.5% service, 22.0% sales and office, 9.5% natural resources, construction, and maintenance, 20.0% production, transportation, and material moving

Income: Per capita: $21,261; Median household: $43,958; Average household: $53,721; Households with income of $100,000 or more: 14.5%; Poverty rate: 17.1%

Educational Attainment: High school diploma or higher: 85.6%; Bachelor's degree or higher: 17.7%; Graduate/professional degree or higher: 11.6%

Housing: Homeownership rate: 74.2%; Median home value: $80,800; Median year structure built: Before 1940; Homeowner vacancy rate: 1.5%; Median selected monthly owner costs: $1,047 with a mortgage, $418 without a mortgage; Median gross rent: $579 per month; Rental vacancy rate: 8.6%

Health Insurance: 93.3% have insurance; 59.0% have private insurance; 46.7% have public insurance; 6.7% do not have insurance; 10.1% of children under 18 do not have insurance

Transportation: Commute: 89.9% car, 0.0% public transportation, 4.0% walk, 4.0% work from home; Mean travel time to work: 23.6 minutes

---

MIDDLEVILLE (village). Covers a land area of 0.765 square miles and a water area of 0.050 square miles. Located at 43.14° N. Lat; 74.97° W. Long. Elevation is 597 feet.

Population: 555; Growth (since 2000): 0.9%; Density: 725.5 persons per square mile; Race: 96.9% White, 0.0% Black/African American, 0.0% Asian, 0.0% American Indian/Alaska Native, 0.0% Native Hawaiian/Other Pacific Islander, 3.1% Two or more races, 0.0% Hispanic of any race; Average household size: 2.52; Median age: 38.3; Age under 18: 31.0%; Age 65 and over: 17.5%; Males per 100 females: 91.8; Marriage status: 31.0% never married, 52.7% now married, 1.4% separated, 6.1% widowed, 10.3% divorced; Foreign born: 0.5%; Speak English only: 100.0%; With disability: 13.0%; Veterans: 8.8%; Ancestry: 29.7% German, 12.6% American, 11.2% Irish, 10.6% Italian, 9.9% English

Employment: 9.9% management, business, and financial, 1.2% computer, engineering, and science, 10.7% education, legal, community service, arts, and media, 10.3% healthcare practitioners, 9.1% service, 31.3% sales and office, 19.3% natural resources, construction, and maintenance, 8.2% production, transportation, and material moving

Income: Per capita: $25,055; Median household: $57,500; Average household: $63,113; Households with income of $100,000 or more: 21.4%; Poverty rate: 6.3%

Educational Attainment: High school diploma or higher: 87.9%; Bachelor's degree or higher: 18.6%; Graduate/professional degree or higher: 6.0%

Housing: Homeownership rate: 86.8%; Median home value: $89,900; Median year structure built: Before 1940; Homeowner vacancy rate: 3.5%; Median selected monthly owner costs: $1,406 with a mortgage, $425 without a mortgage; Median gross rent: $571 per month; Rental vacancy rate: 0.0%

Health Insurance: 98.7% have insurance; 75.4% have private insurance; 37.2% have public insurance; 1.3% do not have insurance; 0.0% of children under 18 do not have insurance

Transportation: Commute: 93.3% car, 0.0% public transportation, 5.8% walk, 0.8% work from home; Mean travel time to work: 34.0 minutes

---

MOHAWK (village). Covers a land area of 0.876 square miles and a water area of 0.027 square miles. Located at 43.01° N. Lat; 75.01° W. Long. Elevation is 413 feet.

History: Settled 1826, incorporated 1844.

Population: 2,551; Growth (since 2000): -4.1%; Density: 2,912.5 persons per square mile; Race: 98.8% White, 0.3% Black/African American, 0.0% Asian, 0.0% American Indian/Alaska Native, 0.0% Native Hawaiian/Other Pacific Islander, 0.9% Two or more races, 4.2% Hispanic of any race; Average household size: 2.34; Median age: 38.8; Age under 18: 18.5%; Age 65 and over: 17.6%; Males per 100 females: 91.0; Marriage status: 41.4% never married, 37.2% now married, 2.6% separated, 4.1% widowed, 17.3% divorced; Foreign born: 2.4%; Speak English only: 99.1%; With disability: 22.9%; Veterans: 8.0%; Ancestry: 31.6% German, 28.2% Irish, 18.3% Italian, 13.1% English, 9.5% Polish

Employment: 4.5% management, business, and financial, 1.1% computer, engineering, and science, 9.8% education, legal, community service, arts, and media, 9.7% healthcare practitioners, 30.2% service, 28.1% sales and office, 8.3% natural resources, construction, and maintenance, 8.2% production, transportation, and material moving

Income: Per capita: $20,681; Median household: $44,167; Average household: $47,543; Households with income of $100,000 or more: 6.0%; Poverty rate: 19.5%

Educational Attainment: High school diploma or higher: 92.0%; Bachelor's degree or higher: 19.5%; Graduate/professional degree or higher: 9.6%

Housing: Homeownership rate: 54.4%; Median home value: $79,900; Median year structure built: Before 1940; Homeowner vacancy rate: 0.0%; Median selected monthly owner costs: $965 with a mortgage, $366 without a mortgage; Median gross rent: $547 per month; Rental vacancy rate: 0.0%

Health Insurance: 92.1% have insurance; 53.8% have private insurance; 52.4% have public insurance; 7.9% do not have insurance; 6.0% of children under 18 do not have insurance

Transportation: Commute: 92.3% car, 4.7% public transportation, 0.0% walk, 2.9% work from home; Mean travel time to work: 16.3 minutes

---

NEWPORT (town). Covers a land area of 32.009 square miles and a water area of 0.443 square miles. Located at 43.18° N. Lat; 75.04° W. Long. Elevation is 663 feet.

Population: 2,221; Growth (since 2000): 1.3%; Density: 69.4 persons per square mile; Race: 95.4% White, 2.0% Black/African American, 0.0% Asian, 0.0% American Indian/Alaska Native, 0.0% Native Hawaiian/Other Pacific Islander, 2.4% Two or more races, 1.7% Hispanic of any race; Average household size: 2.61; Median age: 41.9; Age under 18: 26.2%; Age 65 and over: 15.3%; Males per 100 females: 94.6; Marriage status: 28.7% never married, 52.7% now married, 2.5% separated, 4.8% widowed, 13.7% divorced; Foreign born: 1.0%; Speak English only: 96.0%; With disability: 13.1%; Veterans: 12.1%; Ancestry: 19.1% German, 16.9% Irish, 12.4% Italian, 11.8% American, 10.7% Polish

Employment: 11.6% management, business, and financial, 3.7% computer, engineering, and science, 8.1% education, legal, community service, arts, and media, 9.7% healthcare practitioners, 16.6% service, 23.3% sales and office, 15.8% natural resources, construction, and maintenance, 11.2% production, transportation, and material moving

Income: Per capita: $25,276; Median household: $51,701; Average household: $64,731; Households with income of $100,000 or more: 24.4%; Poverty rate: 8.4%

Educational Attainment: High school diploma or higher: 89.0%; Bachelor's degree or higher: 15.6%; Graduate/professional degree or higher: 7.2%

School District(s)

West Canada Valley Central SD (PK-12)

 Enrollment: 707 . . . . (315) 845-6800

Housing: Homeownership rate: 83.4%; Median home value: $110,000; Median year structure built: 1971; Homeowner vacancy rate: 1.0%; Median selected monthly owner costs: $1,226 with a mortgage, $425 without a mortgage; Median gross rent: $472 per month; Rental vacancy rate: 6.7%

Health Insurance: 95.0% have insurance; 70.6% have private insurance; 38.2% have public insurance; 5.0% do not have insurance; 6.6% of children under 18 do not have insurance

Transportation: Commute: 90.0% car, 1.0% public transportation, 1.5% walk, 6.8% work from home; Mean travel time to work: 28.8 minutes

NEWPORT (village).

Covers a land area of 0.526 square miles and a water area of 0.064 square miles. Located at 43.19° N. Lat; 75.02° W. Long. Elevation is 663 feet.

Population: 598; Growth (since 2000): -6.6%; Density: 1,137.2 persons per square mile; Race: 91.0% White, 5.2% Black/African American, 0.0% Asian, 0.0% American Indian/Alaska Native, 0.0% Native Hawaiian/Other Pacific Islander, 3.5% Two or more races, 0.3% Hispanic of any race; Average household size: 2.30; Median age: 41.9; Age under 18: 23.9%; Age 65 and over: 18.6%; Males per 100 females: 91.6; Marriage status: 27.0% never married, 43.2% now married, 3.0% separated, 7.4% widowed, 22.3% divorced; Foreign born: 0.3%; Speak English only: 99.1%; With disability: 15.0%; Veterans: 14.4%; Ancestry: 22.6% German, 22.1% American, 20.1% Irish, 13.0% Italian, 11.0% English

Employment: 16.4% management, business, and financial, 5.7% computer, engineering, and science, 13.5% education, legal, community service, arts, and media, 4.5% healthcare practitioners, 8.2% service, 19.3% sales and office, 23.8% natural resources, construction, and maintenance, 8.6% production, transportation, and material moving

Income: Per capita: $24,375; Median household: $40,750; Average household: $53,787; Households with income of $100,000 or more: 13.4%; Poverty rate: 9.5%

Educational Attainment: High school diploma or higher: 90.0%; Bachelor's degree or higher: 21.6%; Graduate/professional degree or higher: 10.8%

School District(s)

West Canada Valley Central SD (PK-12)

 Enrollment: 707 . . . . (315) 845-6800

Housing: Homeownership rate: 60.0%; Median home value: $105,800; Median year structure built: Before 1940; Homeowner vacancy rate: 0.0%; Median selected monthly owner costs: $1,112 with a mortgage, $610 without a mortgage; Median gross rent: $439 per month; Rental vacancy rate: 5.5%

Health Insurance: 96.1% have insurance; 70.4% have private insurance; 45.1% have public insurance; 3.9% do not have insurance; 1.3% of children under 18 do not have insurance

Transportation: Commute: 86.2% car, 0.0% public transportation, 5.9% walk, 6.7% work from home; Mean travel time to work: 32.9 minutes

NORWAY (town).

Covers a land area of 35.560 square miles and a water area of 0.273 square miles. Located at 43.23° N. Lat; 74.95° W. Long. Elevation is 1,332 feet.

Population: 885; Growth (since 2000): 24.5%; Density: 24.9 persons per square mile; Race: 99.8% White, 0.2% Black/African American, 0.0% Asian, 0.0% American Indian/Alaska Native, 0.0% Native Hawaiian/Other Pacific Islander, 0.0% Two or more races, 0.1% Hispanic of any race; Average household size: 2.62; Median age: 46.0; Age under 18: 18.3%; Age 65 and over: 10.7%; Males per 100 females: 101.6; Marriage status: 28.3% never married, 60.2% now married, 1.9% separated, 2.9% widowed, 8.6% divorced; Foreign born: 0.7%; Speak English only: 99.0%; With disability: 12.4%; Veterans: 9.4%; Ancestry: 18.5% German, 17.7% English, 16.3% Irish, 9.4% Polish, 7.9% French

Employment: 12.0% management, business, and financial, 0.4% computer, engineering, and science, 9.1% education, legal, community service, arts, and media, 7.1% healthcare practitioners, 15.8% service, 22.7% sales and office, 14.2% natural resources, construction, and maintenance, 18.7% production, transportation, and material moving

Income: Per capita: $27,830; Median household: $58,088; Average household: $71,383; Households with income of $100,000 or more: 26.0%; Poverty rate: 10.7%

Educational Attainment: High school diploma or higher: 86.9%; Bachelor's degree or higher: 13.9%; Graduate/professional degree or higher: 5.2%

Housing: Homeownership rate: 84.3%; Median home value: $103,000; Median year structure built: 1983; Homeowner vacancy rate: 0.0%; Median selected monthly owner costs: $1,171 with a mortgage, $343 without a mortgage; Median gross rent: $664 per month; Rental vacancy rate: 13.1%

Health Insurance: 93.2% have insurance; 72.2% have private insurance; 31.2% have public insurance; 6.8% do not have insurance; 6.4% of children under 18 do not have insurance

Transportation: Commute: 94.0% car, 0.9% public transportation, 2.9% walk, 0.4% work from home; Mean travel time to work: 34.1 minutes

OHIO (town).

Covers a land area of 301.344 square miles and a water area of 6.227 square miles. Located at 43.46° N. Lat; 74.89° W. Long. Elevation is 1,371 feet.

Population: 1,011; Growth (since 2000): 9.7%; Density: 3.4 persons per square mile; Race: 98.0% White, 0.6% Black/African American, 0.4% Asian, 0.3% American Indian/Alaska Native, 0.0% Native Hawaiian/Other Pacific Islander, 0.7% Two or more races, 0.7% Hispanic of any race; Average household size: 2.33; Median age: 49.9; Age under 18: 19.3%; Age 65 and over: 19.8%; Males per 100 females: 104.1; Marriage status: 23.0% never married, 60.0% now married, 3.5% separated, 6.6% widowed, 10.5% divorced; Foreign born: 0.8%; Speak English only: 99.2%; With disability: 18.0%; Veterans: 16.9%; Ancestry: 24.7% German, 22.1% Irish, 15.1% Polish, 13.8% English, 7.2% American

Employment: 5.7% management, business, and financial, 1.9% computer, engineering, and science, 19.0% education, legal, community service, arts, and media, 1.9% healthcare practitioners, 13.3% service, 27.6% sales and office, 12.7% natural resources, construction, and maintenance, 17.9% production, transportation, and material moving

Income: Per capita: $22,879; Median household: $39,474; Average household: $53,098; Households with income of $100,000 or more: 11.8%; Poverty rate: 19.1%

Educational Attainment: High school diploma or higher: 95.3%; Bachelor's degree or higher: 16.0%; Graduate/professional degree or higher: 5.5%

Housing: Homeownership rate: 88.9%; Median home value: $94,400; Median year structure built: 1972; Homeowner vacancy rate: 0.0%; Median selected monthly owner costs: $942 with a mortgage, $361 without a mortgage; Median gross rent: $733 per month; Rental vacancy rate: 0.0%

Health Insurance: 92.6% have insurance; 49.3% have private insurance; 56.5% have public insurance; 7.4% do not have insurance; 5.4% of children under 18 do not have insurance

Transportation: Commute: 88.6% car, 0.0% public transportation, 4.0% walk, 7.4% work from home; Mean travel time to work: 36.3 minutes

OLD FORGE (CDP).

Covers a land area of 1.786 square miles and a water area of 0.178 square miles. Located at 43.71° N. Lat; 74.97° W. Long. Elevation is 1,736 feet.

Population: 598; Growth (since 2000): n/a; Density: 334.8 persons per square mile; Race: 91.6% White, 6.2% Black/African American, 0.0% Asian, 0.0% American Indian/Alaska Native, 0.0% Native Hawaiian/Other Pacific Islander, 0.0% Two or more races, 6.0% Hispanic of any race; Average household size: 1.76; Median age: 59.5; Age under 18: 5.9%; Age 65 and over: 34.9%; Males per 100 females: 95.3; Marriage status: 30.1% never married, 42.5% now married, 2.4% separated, 17.1% widowed, 10.3% divorced; Foreign born: 6.2%; Speak English only: 93.8%; With disability: 16.6%; Veterans: 17.6%; Ancestry: 21.4% German, 20.9% Irish, 16.6% English, 12.4% Dutch, 11.5% Welsh

Employment: 13.2% management, business, and financial, 0.0% computer, engineering, and science, 5.6% education, legal, community service, arts, and media, 0.0% healthcare practitioners, 23.1% service, 29.1% sales and office, 23.9% natural resources, construction, and maintenance, 5.1% production, transportation, and material moving

Income: Per capita: $31,462; Median household: $46,538; Average household: $60,267; Households with income of $100,000 or more: 12.5%; Poverty rate: 12.7%

Educational Attainment: High school diploma or higher: 88.3%; Bachelor's degree or higher: 14.1%; Graduate/professional degree or higher: 5.4%

School District(s)

Town of Webb Union Free SD (KG-12)

 Enrollment: 251 . . . . (315) 369-3222

Housing: Homeownership rate: 71.7%; Median home value: $200,000; Median year structure built: 1951; Homeowner vacancy rate: 0.0%; Median selected monthly owner costs: $827 with a mortgage, $634 without a mortgage; Median gross rent: $553 per month; Rental vacancy rate: 13.1%
Health Insurance: 86.0% have insurance; 48.0% have private insurance; 59.5% have public insurance; 14.0% do not have insurance; 0.0% of children under 18 do not have insurance
Transportation: Commute: 67.3% car, 0.0% public transportation, 0.0% walk, 32.7% work from home; Mean travel time to work: 14.3 minutes

POLAND (village).
Covers a land area of 0.543 square miles and a water area of 0.006 square miles. Located at 43.23° N. Lat; 75.06° W. Long. Elevation is 709 feet.
Population: 376; Growth (since 2000): -16.6%; Density: 692.5 persons per square mile; Race: 91.8% White, 0.8% Black/African American, 0.0% Asian, 0.5% American Indian/Alaska Native, 0.0% Native Hawaiian/Other Pacific Islander, 6.4% Two or more races, 0.5% Hispanic of any race; Average household size: 2.61; Median age: 36.4; Age under 18: 29.0%; Age 65 and over: 13.0%; Males per 100 females: 89.6; Marriage status: 26.4% never married, 52.4% now married, 1.5% separated, 8.1% widowed, 13.2% divorced; Foreign born: 1.9%; Speak English only: 98.8%; With disability: 13.6%; Veterans: 10.5%; Ancestry: 27.9% Irish, 20.7% German, 14.4% Polish, 11.2% American, 9.3% English
Employment: 21.7% management, business, and financial, 5.8% computer, engineering, and science, 5.3% education, legal, community service, arts, and media, 3.2% healthcare practitioners, 18.5% service, 26.5% sales and office, 8.5% natural resources, construction, and maintenance, 10.6% production, transportation, and material moving
Income: Per capita: $29,339; Median household: $53,646; Average household: $75,709; Households with income of $100,000 or more: 21.6%; Poverty rate: 19.9%
Educational Attainment: High school diploma or higher: 95.2%; Bachelor's degree or higher: 32.0%; Graduate/professional degree or higher: 8.8%

School District(s)
Poland Central SD (PK-12)
   Enrollment: 610 . . . . (315) 826-0203
Housing: Homeownership rate: 72.7%; Median home value: $99,200; Median year structure built: Before 1940; Homeowner vacancy rate: 0.0%; Median selected monthly owner costs: $1,321 with a mortgage, $371 without a mortgage; Median gross rent: $742 per month; Rental vacancy rate: 9.5%
Health Insurance: 86.7% have insurance; 62.0% have private insurance; 34.3% have public insurance; 13.3% do not have insurance; 27.4% of children under 18 do not have insurance
Transportation: Commute: 77.0% car, 1.1% public transportation, 9.1% walk, 9.6% work from home; Mean travel time to work: 19.7 minutes

RUSSIA (town).
Covers a land area of 56.962 square miles and a water area of 3.456 square miles. Located at 43.30° N. Lat; 75.07° W. Long. Elevation is 1,129 feet.
Population: 2,544; Growth (since 2000): 2.3%; Density: 44.7 persons per square mile; Race: 93.8% White, 0.5% Black/African American, 0.1% Asian, 2.1% American Indian/Alaska Native, 0.0% Native Hawaiian/Other Pacific Islander, 3.3% Two or more races, 0.7% Hispanic of any race; Average household size: 2.46; Median age: 40.9; Age under 18: 23.9%; Age 65 and over: 16.4%; Males per 100 females: 103.4; Marriage status: 25.2% never married, 56.6% now married, 1.4% separated, 7.6% widowed, 10.6% divorced; Foreign born: 2.8%; Speak English only: 91.1%; With disability: 15.0%; Veterans: 8.4%; Ancestry: 18.0% German, 14.6% Irish, 14.3% English, 9.5% Italian, 8.1% Polish
Employment: 13.3% management, business, and financial, 3.1% computer, engineering, and science, 14.7% education, legal, community service, arts, and media, 6.8% healthcare practitioners, 13.7% service, 24.0% sales and office, 11.8% natural resources, construction, and maintenance, 12.4% production, transportation, and material moving
Income: Per capita: $29,211; Median household: $52,759; Average household: $71,242; Households with income of $100,000 or more: 25.4%; Poverty rate: 12.4%
Educational Attainment: High school diploma or higher: 95.4%; Bachelor's degree or higher: 34.4%; Graduate/professional degree or higher: 14.5%
Housing: Homeownership rate: 84.8%; Median home value: $153,300; Median year structure built: 1965; Homeowner vacancy rate: 0.0%; Median

selected monthly owner costs: $1,401 with a mortgage, $513 without a mortgage; Median gross rent: $648 per month; Rental vacancy rate: 0.0%
Health Insurance: 89.4% have insurance; 65.1% have private insurance; 37.5% have public insurance; 10.6% do not have insurance; 16.5% of children under 18 do not have insurance
Transportation: Commute: 87.2% car, 1.1% public transportation, 3.1% walk, 7.9% work from home; Mean travel time to work: 32.0 minutes

SALISBURY (town).
Covers a land area of 107.366 square miles and a water area of 0.835 square miles. Located at 43.22° N. Lat; 74.80° W. Long. Elevation is 1,220 feet.
Population: 2,220; Growth (since 2000): 13.7%; Density: 20.7 persons per square mile; Race: 98.1% White, 0.1% Black/African American, 0.5% Asian, 0.2% American Indian/Alaska Native, 0.0% Native Hawaiian/Other Pacific Islander, 0.0% Two or more races, 2.0% Hispanic of any race; Average household size: 2.68; Median age: 38.8; Age under 18: 25.5%; Age 65 and over: 13.4%; Males per 100 females: 102.1; Marriage status: 35.9% never married, 44.6% now married, 1.0% separated, 7.2% widowed, 12.3% divorced; Foreign born: 2.1%; Speak English only: 91.3%; With disability: 19.0%; Veterans: 6.8%; Ancestry: 24.7% German, 17.2% Irish, 10.7% English, 10.5% Dutch, 8.1% American
Employment: 12.6% management, business, and financial, 1.6% computer, engineering, and science, 5.4% education, legal, community service, arts, and media, 6.9% healthcare practitioners, 19.6% service, 13.2% sales and office, 18.2% natural resources, construction, and maintenance, 22.5% production, transportation, and material moving
Income: Per capita: $20,277; Median household: $45,057; Average household: $54,243; Households with income of $100,000 or more: 9.9%; Poverty rate: 7.3%
Educational Attainment: High school diploma or higher: 75.7%; Bachelor's degree or higher: 7.1%; Graduate/professional degree or higher: 2.2%
Housing: Homeownership rate: 85.3%; Median home value: $86,800; Median year structure built: 1979; Homeowner vacancy rate: 0.0%; Median selected monthly owner costs: $991 with a mortgage, $356 without a mortgage; Median gross rent: $743 per month; Rental vacancy rate: 7.7%
Health Insurance: 90.6% have insurance; 61.1% have private insurance; 44.0% have public insurance; 9.4% do not have insurance; 4.1% of children under 18 do not have insurance
Transportation: Commute: 89.2% car, 0.0% public transportation, 5.5% walk, 4.6% work from home; Mean travel time to work: 30.0 minutes

SALISBURY CENTER (unincorporated postal area)
ZCTA: 13454
Covers a land area of 43.050 square miles and a water area of 0.283 square miles. Located at 43.22° N. Lat; 74.76° W. Long. Elevation is 1,073 feet.
Population: 644; Growth (since 2000): -9.6%; Density: 15.0 persons per square mile; Race: 98.0% White, 0.5% Black/African American, 1.6% Asian, 0.0% American Indian/Alaska Native, 0.0% Native Hawaiian/Other Pacific Islander, 0.0% Two or more races, 0.0% Hispanic of any race; Average household size: 2.11; Median age: 37.8; Age under 18: 20.0%; Age 65 and over: 19.1%; Males per 100 females: 99.0; Marriage status: 36.3% never married, 43.0% now married, 0.5% separated, 9.9% widowed, 10.8% divorced; Foreign born: 2.6%; Speak English only: 96.3%; With disability: 26.6%; Veterans: 6.6%; Ancestry: 24.4% German, 18.6% Irish, 16.3% American, 14.9% English, 5.7% French
Employment: 4.1% management, business, and financial, 0.0% computer, engineering, and science, 6.1% education, legal, community service, arts, and media, 3.7% healthcare practitioners, 33.7% service, 15.4% sales and office, 14.2% natural resources, construction, and maintenance, 22.8% production, transportation, and material moving
Income: Per capita: $19,668; Median household: $37,500; Average household: $43,587; Households with income of $100,000 or more: 3.8%; Poverty rate: 5.1%
Educational Attainment: High school diploma or higher: 77.1%; Bachelor's degree or higher: 5.4%; Graduate/professional degree or higher: 1.8%
Housing: Homeownership rate: 81.5%; Median home value: $89,200; Median year structure built: 1976; Homeowner vacancy rate: 0.0%; Median selected monthly owner costs: $948 with a mortgage, $343 without a mortgage; Median gross rent: $747 per month; Rental vacancy rate: 15.9%

Health Insurance: 93.5% have insurance; 72.2% have private insurance; 39.4% have public insurance; 6.5% do not have insurance; 5.7% of children under 18 do not have insurance

Transportation: Commute: 87.5% car, 0.0% public transportation, 6.5% walk, 4.7% work from home; Mean travel time to work: 26.6 minutes

SCHUYLER (town).
Covers a land area of 39.874 square miles and a water area of 0.358 square miles. Located at 43.11° N. Lat; 75.10° W. Long.

Population: 3,381; Growth (since 2000): -0.1%; Density: 84.8 persons per square mile; Race: 99.7% White, 0.0% Black/African American, 0.1% Asian, 0.0% American Indian/Alaska Native, 0.0% Native Hawaiian/Other Pacific Islander, 0.1% Two or more races, 0.9% Hispanic of any race; Average household size: 2.41; Median age: 47.2; Age under 18: 17.1%; Age 65 and over: 22.7%; Males per 100 females: 94.6; Marriage status: 26.0% never married, 56.6% now married, 1.4% separated, 5.8% widowed, 11.6% divorced; Foreign born: 4.2%; Speak English only: 95.3%; With disability: 12.0%; Veterans: 9.0%; Ancestry: 29.7% Italian, 20.0% Irish, 16.8% German, 10.9% Polish, 10.8% English

Employment: 8.3% management, business, and financial, 2.1% computer, engineering, and science, 10.6% education, legal, community service, arts, and media, 7.1% healthcare practitioners, 27.8% service, 25.3% sales and office, 6.2% natural resources, construction, and maintenance, 12.6% production, transportation, and material moving

Income: Per capita: $25,936; Median household: $51,025; Average household: $61,856; Households with income of $100,000 or more: 9.0%; Poverty rate: 7.0%

Educational Attainment: High school diploma or higher: 89.4%; Bachelor's degree or higher: 18.1%; Graduate/professional degree or higher: 9.3%

Housing: Homeownership rate: 83.2%; Median home value: $89,800; Median year structure built: 1981; Homeowner vacancy rate: 2.3%; Median selected monthly owner costs: $1,024 with a mortgage, $509 without a mortgage; Median gross rent: $821 per month; Rental vacancy rate: 0.0%

Health Insurance: 96.0% have insurance; 78.0% have private insurance; 36.4% have public insurance; 4.0% do not have insurance; 0.0% of children under 18 do not have insurance

Transportation: Commute: 97.1% car, 0.0% public transportation, 0.0% walk, 0.9% work from home; Mean travel time to work: 21.5 minutes

Additional Information Contacts

Town of Schuyler. . . . . (315) 733-7458
    http://townofschuyler.com

STARK (town).
Covers a land area of 31.833 square miles and a water area of 0.003 square miles. Located at 42.93° N. Lat; 74.82° W. Long.

Population: 833; Growth (since 2000): 8.6%; Density: 26.2 persons per square mile; Race: 99.3% White, 0.0% Black/African American, 0.1% Asian, 0.0% American Indian/Alaska Native, 0.0% Native Hawaiian/Other Pacific Islander, 0.6% Two or more races, 0.1% Hispanic of any race; Average household size: 2.56; Median age: 46.3; Age under 18: 25.1%; Age 65 and over: 16.6%; Males per 100 females: 112.6; Marriage status: 21.8% never married, 55.0% now married, 1.5% separated, 5.7% widowed, 17.6% divorced; Foreign born: 0.7%; Speak English only: 94.3%; With disability: 12.7%; Veterans: 7.4%; Ancestry: 27.6% German, 16.9% English, 12.6% Dutch, 12.5% Irish, 11.3% Polish

Employment: 11.3% management, business, and financial, 2.4% computer, engineering, and science, 13.4% education, legal, community service, arts, and media, 5.8% healthcare practitioners, 14.2% service, 13.4% sales and office, 20.7% natural resources, construction, and maintenance, 18.9% production, transportation, and material moving

Income: Per capita: $24,942; Median household: $54,028; Average household: $62,775; Households with income of $100,000 or more: 15.7%; Poverty rate: 5.7%

Educational Attainment: High school diploma or higher: 88.1%; Bachelor's degree or higher: 23.4%; Graduate/professional degree or higher: 7.5%

Housing: Homeownership rate: 86.2%; Median home value: $95,900; Median year structure built: 1943; Homeowner vacancy rate: 2.4%; Median selected monthly owner costs: $1,076 with a mortgage, $470 without a mortgage; Median gross rent: $532 per month; Rental vacancy rate: 13.5%

Health Insurance: 86.4% have insurance; 62.2% have private insurance; 31.5% have public insurance; 13.6% do not have insurance; 11.4% of children under 18 do not have insurance

Transportation: Commute: 83.4% car, 0.0% public transportation, 5.0% walk, 10.0% work from home; Mean travel time to work: 31.5 minutes

VAN HORNESVILLE (unincorporated postal area)
ZCTA: 13475

Covers a land area of 0.015 square miles and a water area of 0 square miles. Located at 42.89° N. Lat; 74.83° W. Long. Elevation is 1,152 feet.

Population: 23; Growth (since 2000): 228.6%; Density: 1,522.2 persons per square mile; Race: 100.0% White, 0.0% Black/African American, 0.0% Asian, 0.0% American Indian/Alaska Native, 0.0% Native Hawaiian/Other Pacific Islander, 0.0% Two or more races, 0.0% Hispanic of any race; Average household size: 1.77; Median age: 46.2; Age under 18: 34.8%; Age 65 and over: 0.0%; Males per 100 females: 100.0; Marriage status: 16.7% never married, 27.8% now married, 0.0% separated, 0.0% widowed, 55.6% divorced; Foreign born: 8.7%; Speak English only: 100.0%; With disability: 0.0%; Veterans: 0.0%; Ancestry: 34.8% Polish, 30.4% German, 30.4% Irish, 13.0% English, 13.0% Norwegian

Employment: 0.0% management, business, and financial, 37.5% computer, engineering, and science, 0.0% education, legal, community service, arts, and media, 37.5% healthcare practitioners, 0.0% service, 25.0% sales and office, 0.0% natural resources, construction, and maintenance, 0.0% production, transportation, and material moving

Income: Per capita: $28,670; Median household: n/a; Average household: $53,323; Households with income of $100,000 or more: 23.1%; Poverty rate: n/a

Educational Attainment: High school diploma or higher: 100.0%; Bachelor's degree or higher: 20.0%; Graduate/professional degree or higher: n/a

School District(s)

Van Hornesville-Owen D Young Central SD (KG-12)
    Enrollment: 190 . . . . (315) 858-0729

Housing: Homeownership rate: 23.1%; Median home value: n/a; Median year structure built: Before 1940; Homeowner vacancy rate: 0.0%; Median selected monthly owner costs: $0 with a mortgage, $0 without a mortgage; Median gross rent: n/a per month; Rental vacancy rate: 41.2%

Health Insurance: 56.5% have insurance; 56.5% have private insurance; 0.0% have public insurance; 43.5% do not have insurance; 37.5% of children under 18 do not have insurance

Transportation: Commute: 100.0% car, 0.0% public transportation, 0.0% walk, 0.0% work from home; Mean travel time to work: 38.8 minutes

WARREN (town).
Covers a land area of 37.791 square miles and a water area of 0.319 square miles. Located at 42.90° N. Lat; 74.94° W. Long. Elevation is 1,371 feet.

Population: 1,154; Growth (since 2000): 1.6%; Density: 30.5 persons per square mile; Race: 96.1% White, 1.4% Black/African American, 1.5% Asian, 0.2% American Indian/Alaska Native, 0.0% Native Hawaiian/Other Pacific Islander, 0.5% Two or more races, 2.3% Hispanic of any race; Average household size: 2.87; Median age: 38.0; Age under 18: 28.5%; Age 65 and over: 13.3%; Males per 100 females: 102.3; Marriage status: 27.0% never married, 57.5% now married, 3.3% separated, 6.1% widowed, 9.3% divorced; Foreign born: 9.7%; Speak English only: 90.5%; With disability: 10.8%; Veterans: 5.8%; Ancestry: 21.8% German, 15.4% English, 13.3% Irish, 8.4% Polish, 8.3% Italian

Employment: 18.5% management, business, and financial, 0.0% computer, engineering, and science, 10.0% education, legal, community service, arts, and media, 7.7% healthcare practitioners, 22.2% service, 12.2% sales and office, 17.3% natural resources, construction, and maintenance, 12.0% production, transportation, and material moving

Income: Per capita: $20,566; Median household: $55,000; Average household: $60,127; Households with income of $100,000 or more: 14.4%; Poverty rate: 17.9%

Educational Attainment: High school diploma or higher: 90.7%; Bachelor's degree or higher: 20.2%; Graduate/professional degree or higher: 8.1%

Housing: Homeownership rate: 81.2%; Median home value: $107,200; Median year structure built: 1971; Homeowner vacancy rate: 0.0%; Median selected monthly owner costs: $1,138 with a mortgage, $458 without a mortgage; Median gross rent: $787 per month; Rental vacancy rate: 6.5%

Health Insurance: 87.9% have insurance; 61.4% have private insurance; 36.1% have public insurance; 12.1% do not have insurance; 17.5% of children under 18 do not have insurance

Transportation: Commute: 83.2% car, 0.0% public transportation, 9.2% walk, 7.6% work from home; Mean travel time to work: 23.9 minutes

WEBB (town). Covers a land area of 452.284 square miles and a water area of 32.007 square miles. Located at 43.82° N. Lat; 75.04° W. Long.
Population: 1,300; Growth (since 2000): -32.0%; Density: 2.9 persons per square mile; Race: 96.2% White, 2.8% Black/African American, 0.0% Asian, 0.0% American Indian/Alaska Native, 0.0% Native Hawaiian/Other Pacific Islander, 0.0% Two or more races, 9.8% Hispanic of any race; Average household size: 1.89; Median age: 59.7; Age under 18: 4.2%; Age 65 and over: 38.3%; Males per 100 females: 101.2; Marriage status: 22.0% never married, 53.5% now married, 1.5% separated, 13.5% widowed, 11.1% divorced; Foreign born: 3.8%; Speak English only: 93.2%; With disability: 15.2%; Veterans: 13.0%; Ancestry: 22.2% American, 21.8% Irish, 20.7% German, 18.7% English, 8.5% French
Employment: 17.1% management, business, and financial, 0.7% computer, engineering, and science, 6.4% education, legal, community service, arts, and media, 1.6% healthcare practitioners, 19.7% service, 30.2% sales and office, 19.7% natural resources, construction, and maintenance, 4.6% production, transportation, and material moving
Income: Per capita: $35,429; Median household: $54,306; Average household: $68,383; Households with income of $100,000 or more: 17.5%; Poverty rate: 7.2%
Educational Attainment: High school diploma or higher: 93.0%; Bachelor's degree or higher: 25.1%; Graduate/professional degree or higher: 9.0%
Housing: Homeownership rate: 85.1%; Median home value: $267,300; Median year structure built: 1966; Homeowner vacancy rate: 9.1%; Median selected monthly owner costs: $1,536 with a mortgage, $650 without a mortgage; Median gross rent: $556 per month; Rental vacancy rate: 26.3%
Health Insurance: 90.0% have insurance; 64.5% have private insurance; 50.1% have public insurance; 10.0% do not have insurance; 0.0% of children under 18 do not have insurance
Safety: Violent crime rate: 0.0 per 10,000 population; Property crime rate: 27.6 per 10,000 population
Transportation: Commute: 74.7% car, 0.0% public transportation, 9.0% walk, 14.5% work from home; Mean travel time to work: 28.2 minutes

WEST WINFIELD (village). Covers a land area of 0.911 square miles and a water area of 0 square miles. Located at 42.88° N. Lat; 75.19° W. Long. Elevation is 1,191 feet.
Population: 750; Growth (since 2000): -13.0%; Density: 823.1 persons per square mile; Race: 94.1% White, 0.5% Black/African American, 0.3% Asian, 0.4% American Indian/Alaska Native, 0.3% Native Hawaiian/Other Pacific Islander, 4.4% Two or more races, 0.9% Hispanic of any race; Average household size: 2.29; Median age: 47.4; Age under 18: 18.8%; Age 65 and over: 22.8%; Males per 100 females: 84.0; Marriage status: 21.0% never married, 61.1% now married, 2.6% separated, 9.1% widowed, 8.8% divorced; Foreign born: 0.5%; Speak English only: 99.4%; With disability: 14.5%; Veterans: 10.8%; Ancestry: 25.2% Irish, 22.9% English, 13.2% German, 10.9% American, 8.8% Polish
Employment: 7.8% management, business, and financial, 5.2% computer, engineering, and science, 22.5% education, legal, community service, arts, and media, 6.4% healthcare practitioners, 21.4% service, 19.7% sales and office, 9.0% natural resources, construction, and maintenance, 8.1% production, transportation, and material moving
Income: Per capita: $28,768; Median household: $55,357; Average household: $64,750; Households with income of $100,000 or more: 18.3%; Poverty rate: 13.1%
Educational Attainment: High school diploma or higher: 91.4%; Bachelor's degree or higher: 30.0%; Graduate/professional degree or higher: 16.0%

School District(s)
Mount Markham Central SD (PK-12)
    Enrollment: 1,126 . . . . (315) 822-2824
Housing: Homeownership rate: 64.6%; Median home value: $107,400; Median year structure built: 1944; Homeowner vacancy rate: 3.6%; Median selected monthly owner costs: $1,173 with a mortgage, $434 without a mortgage; Median gross rent: $627 per month; Rental vacancy rate: 4.9%
Health Insurance: 94.7% have insurance; 69.7% have private insurance; 42.7% have public insurance; 5.3% do not have insurance; 5.9% of children under 18 do not have insurance
Newspapers: West Winfield Star (weekly circulation 1,400)
Transportation: Commute: 88.1% car, 0.0% public transportation, 4.9% walk, 5.5% work from home; Mean travel time to work: 22.4 minutes

WINFIELD (town). Covers a land area of 23.639 square miles and a water area of 0.012 square miles. Located at 42.90° N. Lat; 75.17° W. Long.
Population: 2,103; Growth (since 2000): -4.5%; Density: 89.0 persons per square mile; Race: 95.0% White, 0.8% Black/African American, 0.4% Asian, 0.1% American Indian/Alaska Native, 0.1% Native Hawaiian/Other Pacific Islander, 3.7% Two or more races, 1.7% Hispanic of any race; Average household size: 2.68; Median age: 42.8; Age under 18: 22.2%; Age 65 and over: 17.5%; Males per 100 females: 96.2; Marriage status: 25.6% never married, 59.2% now married, 2.4% separated, 5.7% widowed, 9.4% divorced; Foreign born: 2.9%; Speak English only: 96.3%; With disability: 13.9%; Veterans: 10.5%; Ancestry: 22.0% Irish, 19.4% English, 14.7% German, 9.6% Welsh, 8.6% American
Employment: 10.9% management, business, and financial, 4.4% computer, engineering, and science, 11.7% education, legal, community service, arts, and media, 4.9% healthcare practitioners, 23.0% service, 17.3% sales and office, 14.8% natural resources, construction, and maintenance, 13.0% production, transportation, and material moving
Income: Per capita: $26,171; Median household: $62,069; Average household: $69,044; Households with income of $100,000 or more: 17.5%; Poverty rate: 12.3%
Educational Attainment: High school diploma or higher: 88.8%; Bachelor's degree or higher: 21.5%; Graduate/professional degree or higher: 10.3%
Housing: Homeownership rate: 76.6%; Median home value: $111,600; Median year structure built: 1964; Homeowner vacancy rate: 1.3%; Median selected monthly owner costs: $1,137 with a mortgage, $450 without a mortgage; Median gross rent: $646 per month; Rental vacancy rate: 3.2%
Health Insurance: 95.9% have insurance; 73.4% have private insurance; 40.4% have public insurance; 4.1% do not have insurance; 1.8% of children under 18 do not have insurance
Transportation: Commute: 85.7% car, 1.1% public transportation, 5.4% walk, 7.3% work from home; Mean travel time to work: 25.7 minutes

Jefferson County

Located in northern New York; bounded on the west by Lake Ontario, and on the northwest by the Saint Lawrence River; drained by the Black and Indian Rivers. Covers a land area of 1,268.590 square miles, a water area of 588.632 square miles, and is located in the Eastern Time Zone at 44.00° N. Lat., 76.05° W. Long. The county was founded in 1805. County seat is Watertown.

Jefferson County is part of the Watertown-Fort Drum, NY Metropolitan Statistical Area. The entire metro area includes: Jefferson County, NY

Weather Station: Watertown | | | | | | | | | | | Elevation: 497 feet
	Jan	Feb	Mar	Apr	May	Jun	Jul	Aug	Sep	Oct	Nov	Dec
High	29	31	40	54	66	75	80	79	71	58	46	35
Low	10	12	22	35	47	56	61	60	52	40	31	18
Precip	3.3	2.7	2.7	3.2	3.6	3.3	3.4	4.0	4.3	4.2	4.6	3.7
Snow	31.0	25.4	13.0	3.4	tr	0.0	0.0	0.0	0.0	0.6	7.3	31.3

High and Low temperatures in degrees Fahrenheit; Precipitation and Snow in inches

Weather Station: Watertown Arpt | | | | | | | | | | | Elevation: 317 feet
	Jan	Feb	Mar	Apr	May	Jun	Jul	Aug	Sep	Oct	Nov	Dec
High	29	31	40	54	66	74	79	78	70	58	47	35
Low	10	11	20	33	44	53	58	56	48	38	30	17
Precip	2.6	2.2	2.3	3.0	3.0	2.8	2.7	3.1	3.7	3.7	3.8	3.1
Snow	na	na	na	na	na	na	na	na	na	na	na	na

High and Low temperatures in degrees Fahrenheit; Precipitation and Snow in inches

Population: 116,567; Growth (since 2000): 4.3%; Density: 91.9 persons per square mile; Race: 86.1% White, 5.8% Black/African American, 1.5% Asian, 0.6% American Indian/Alaska Native, 0.3% Native Hawaiian/Other Pacific Islander, 4.1% two or more races, 7.3% Hispanic of any race; Average household size: 2.54; Median age: 31.9; Age under 18: 24.5%; Age 65 and over: 12.2%; Males per 100 females: 103.8; Marriage status: 30.4% never married, 55.4% now married, 2.7% separated, 4.9% widowed, 9.3% divorced; Foreign born: 3.7%; Speak English only: 92.9%; With disability: 13.6%; Veterans: 13.7%; Ancestry: 18.3% Irish, 16.0% German, 9.9% English, 9.7% Italian, 9.1% French
Religion: Six largest groups: 18.2% Catholicism, 4.1% Methodist/Pietist, 2.1% Presbyterian-Reformed, 1.7% Baptist, 1.3% Muslim Estimate, 1.3% Holiness

Economy: Unemployment rate: 4.2%; Leading industries: 19.5 % retail trade; 13.3 % accommodation and food services; 11.3 % health care and social assistance; Farms: 876 totaling 290,811 acres; Company size: 2 employ 1,000 or more persons, 1 employs 500 to 999 persons, 34 employ 100 to 499 persons, 2,406 employ less than 100 persons; Business ownership: 2,027 women-owned, 62 Black-owned, 45 Hispanic-owned, 122 Asian-owned, n/a American Indian/Alaska Native-owned

Employment: 11.1% management, business, and financial, 3.2% computer, engineering, and science, 11.4% education, legal, community service, arts, and media, 6.6% healthcare practitioners, 22.1% service, 23.6% sales and office, 12.3% natural resources, construction, and maintenance, 9.8% production, transportation, and material moving

Income: Per capita: $24,717; Median household: $50,322; Average household: $63,176; Households with income of $100,000 or more: 17.4%; Poverty rate: 14.8%

Educational Attainment: High school diploma or higher: 90.3%; Bachelor's degree or higher: 21.4%; Graduate/professional degree or higher: 9.1%

Housing: Homeownership rate: 55.6%; Median home value: $149,300; Median year structure built: 1969; Homeowner vacancy rate: 2.6%; Median selected monthly owner costs: $1,247 with a mortgage, $476 without a mortgage; Median gross rent: $966 per month; Rental vacancy rate: 8.2%

Vital Statistics: Birth rate: 163.7 per 10,000 population; Death rate: 82.0 per 10,000 population; Age-adjusted cancer mortality rate: 178.2 deaths per 100,000 population

Health Insurance: 93.6% have insurance; 69.1% have private insurance; 38.5% have public insurance; 6.4% do not have insurance; 3.8% of children under 18 do not have insurance

Health Care: Physicians: 18.6 per 10,000 population; Dentists: 9.6 per 10,000 population; Hospital beds: 24.3 per 10,000 population; Hospital admissions: 816.4 per 10,000 population

Air Quality Index (AQI): Percent of Days: 94.8% good, 4.6% moderate, 0.6% unhealthy for sensitive individuals, 0.0% unhealthy, 0.0% very unhealthy; Annual median: 34; Annual maximum: 101

Transportation: Commute: 85.7% car, 0.3% public transportation, 6.5% walk, 5.0% work from home; Mean travel time to work: 17.4 minutes

2016 Presidential Election: 56.9% Trump, 36.1% Clinton, 4.4% Johnson, 1.6% Stein

National and State Parks: Brownville State Game Farm; Burnham Point State Park; Canoe Point and Picnic Point State Park; Cedar Point State Park; Grass Point State Park; Keewaydin Point State Park; Kring Point State Park; Long Point State Park; Mary Island State Park; Perch River State Game Management Area; Sackets Harbor Battlefield State Park; Southwich Beach State Park; Wellesley Island State Park; Westcott Beach State Park

Additional Information Contacts
Jefferson Government. . . . . (315) 785-3200
   http://www.co.jefferson.ny.us

Jefferson County Communities

ADAMS (town). Covers a land area of 42.270 square miles and a water area of 0.153 square miles. Located at 43.84° N. Lat; 76.05° W. Long. Elevation is 614 feet.

History: Incorporated 1851.

Population: 5,177; Growth (since 2000): 8.3%; Density: 122.5 persons per square mile; Race: 98.3% White, 0.2% Black/African American, 0.2% Asian, 0.1% American Indian/Alaska Native, 0.0% Native Hawaiian/Other Pacific Islander, 0.8% Two or more races, 2.1% Hispanic of any race; Average household size: 2.60; Median age: 35.8; Age under 18: 27.1%; Age 65 and over: 12.9%; Males per 100 females: 93.9; Marriage status: 26.9% never married, 58.2% now married, 4.6% separated, 5.5% widowed, 9.3% divorced; Foreign born: 1.3%; Speak English only: 98.6%; With disability: 14.4%; Veterans: 15.3%; Ancestry: 21.8% German, 20.3% Irish, 11.3% English, 9.4% Italian, 6.5% French

Employment: 11.6% management, business, and financial, 1.8% computer, engineering, and science, 16.8% education, legal, community service, arts, and media, 6.7% healthcare practitioners, 16.0% service, 25.8% sales and office, 17.5% natural resources, construction, and maintenance, 3.7% production, transportation, and material moving

Income: Per capita: $24,873; Median household: $54,271; Average household: $64,022; Households with income of $100,000 or more: 21.8%; Poverty rate: 15.3%

Educational Attainment: High school diploma or higher: 89.6%; Bachelor's degree or higher: 23.0%; Graduate/professional degree or higher: 12.1%

School District(s)
South Jefferson Central SD (PK-12)
   Enrollment: 1,936 . . . . (315) 583-6104

Housing: Homeownership rate: 67.2%; Median home value: $143,700; Median year structure built: 1967; Homeowner vacancy rate: 1.1%; Median selected monthly owner costs: $1,219 with a mortgage, $442 without a mortgage; Median gross rent: $832 per month; Rental vacancy rate: 4.7%

Health Insurance: 92.8% have insurance; 65.6% have private insurance; 41.0% have public insurance; 7.2% do not have insurance; 1.3% of children under 18 do not have insurance

Newspapers: Jefferson County Journal (weekly circulation 2,800)

Transportation: Commute: 94.5% car, 0.0% public transportation, 1.5% walk, 3.6% work from home; Mean travel time to work: 20.0 minutes

Additional Information Contacts
Town of Adams . . . . (315) 232-2467
   http://www.townofadams.com

ADAMS (village). Covers a land area of 1.447 square miles and a water area of 0 square miles. Located at 43.81° N. Lat; 76.02° W. Long. Elevation is 614 feet.

Population: 1,671; Growth (since 2000): 2.9%; Density: 1,154.8 persons per square mile; Race: 95.8% White, 0.0% Black/African American, 0.6% Asian, 0.4% American Indian/Alaska Native, 0.0% Native Hawaiian/Other Pacific Islander, 2.2% Two or more races, 5.5% Hispanic of any race; Average household size: 2.60; Median age: 32.2; Age under 18: 34.4%; Age 65 and over: 11.4%; Males per 100 females: 88.8; Marriage status: 29.0% never married, 51.7% now married, 5.9% separated, 6.9% widowed, 12.4% divorced; Foreign born: 3.2%; Speak English only: 98.0%; With disability: 15.2%; Veterans: 14.8%; Ancestry: 16.6% Irish, 13.6% German, 13.0% English, 10.1% Italian, 8.3% French

Employment: 9.6% management, business, and financial, 3.9% computer, engineering, and science, 16.7% education, legal, community service, arts, and media, 4.8% healthcare practitioners, 24.7% service, 19.7% sales and office, 10.5% natural resources, construction, and maintenance, 9.9% production, transportation, and material moving

Income: Per capita: $26,235; Median household: $54,531; Average household: $66,620; Households with income of $100,000 or more: 24.4%; Poverty rate: 16.7%

Educational Attainment: High school diploma or higher: 93.1%; Bachelor's degree or higher: 26.9%; Graduate/professional degree or higher: 13.0%

School District(s)
South Jefferson Central SD (PK-12)
   Enrollment: 1,936 . . . . (315) 583-6104

Housing: Homeownership rate: 61.6%; Median home value: $148,200; Median year structure built: Before 1940; Homeowner vacancy rate: 3.7%; Median selected monthly owner costs: $1,234 with a mortgage, $597 without a mortgage; Median gross rent: $746 per month; Rental vacancy rate: 11.0%

Health Insurance: 94.1% have insurance; 70.5% have private insurance; 38.1% have public insurance; 5.9% do not have insurance; 3.2% of children under 18 do not have insurance

Safety: Violent crime rate: 5.7 per 10,000 population; Property crime rate: 17.0 per 10,000 population

Newspapers: Jefferson County Journal (weekly circulation 2,800)

Transportation: Commute: 89.8% car, 0.0% public transportation, 4.9% walk, 4.0% work from home; Mean travel time to work: 25.5 minutes

ADAMS CENTER (CDP). Covers a land area of 4.855 square miles and a water area of 0.135 square miles. Located at 43.87° N. Lat; 75.99° W. Long. Elevation is 640 feet.

Population: 1,587; Growth (since 2000): 5.8%; Density: 326.9 persons per square mile; Race: 100.0% White, 0.0% Black/African American, 0.0% Asian, 0.0% American Indian/Alaska Native, 0.0% Native Hawaiian/Other Pacific Islander, 0.0% Two or more races, 0.8% Hispanic of any race; Average household size: 2.37; Median age: 44.3; Age under 18: 17.3%; Age 65 and over: 18.5%; Males per 100 females: 91.7; Marriage status: 26.6% never married, 62.7% now married, 6.5% separated, 2.9% widowed, 7.8% divorced; Foreign born: 0.0%; Speak English only: 100.0%; With disability: 21.2%; Veterans: 17.2%; Ancestry: 28.7% German, 24.8% Irish, 10.6% Italian, 8.3% English, 7.6% Canadian

Employment: 8.5% management, business, and financial, 0.0% computer, engineering, and science, 25.5% education, legal, community service, arts, and media, 0.0% healthcare practitioners, 11.0% service, 39.5% sales and office, 15.2% natural resources, construction, and maintenance, 0.3% production, transportation, and material moving
Income: Per capita: $25,555; Median household: $49,477; Average household: $60,618; Households with income of $100,000 or more: 18.5%; Poverty rate: 10.5%
Educational Attainment: High school diploma or higher: 86.3%; Bachelor's degree or higher: 22.6%; Graduate/professional degree or higher: 11.2%

School District(s)
South Jefferson Central SD (PK-12)
    Enrollment: 1,936 . . . . (315) 583-6104
Housing: Homeownership rate: 70.1%; Median home value: $115,200; Median year structure built: 1973; Homeowner vacancy rate: 0.0%; Median selected monthly owner costs: $1,140 with a mortgage, $355 without a mortgage; Median gross rent: $869 per month; Rental vacancy rate: 0.0%
Health Insurance: 95.0% have insurance; 64.1% have private insurance; 51.5% have public insurance; 5.0% do not have insurance; 0.0% of children under 18 do not have insurance
Transportation: Commute: 100.0% car, 0.0% public transportation, 0.0% walk, 0.0% work from home; Mean travel time to work: 13.2 minutes

ALEXANDRIA (town). Covers a land area of 72.657 square miles and a water area of 11.900 square miles. Located at 44.32° N. Lat; 75.88° W. Long.
History: Incorporated 1878.
Population: 4,084; Growth (since 2000): -0.3%; Density: 56.2 persons per square mile; Race: 96.9% White, 1.7% Black/African American, 0.3% Asian, 0.0% American Indian/Alaska Native, 0.0% Native Hawaiian/Other Pacific Islander, 0.9% Two or more races, 1.4% Hispanic of any race; Average household size: 2.32; Median age: 45.4; Age under 18: 18.2%; Age 65 and over: 18.4%; Males per 100 females: 100.3; Marriage status: 28.8% never married, 52.7% now married, 3.7% separated, 7.0% widowed, 11.4% divorced; Foreign born: 1.4%; Speak English only: 98.5%; With disability: 14.0%; Veterans: 8.3%; Ancestry: 26.0% Irish, 19.9% German, 11.1% French, 11.0% English, 7.4% Italian
Employment: 7.0% management, business, and financial, 1.2% computer, engineering, and science, 15.3% education, legal, community service, arts, and media, 2.7% healthcare practitioners, 27.5% service, 22.6% sales and office, 15.1% natural resources, construction, and maintenance, 8.5% production, transportation, and material moving
Income: Per capita: $28,900; Median household: $44,572; Average household: $67,234; Households with income of $100,000 or more: 20.3%; Poverty rate: 12.7%
Educational Attainment: High school diploma or higher: 89.2%; Bachelor's degree or higher: 21.4%; Graduate/professional degree or higher: 10.8%
Housing: Homeownership rate: 77.8%; Median home value: $123,700; Median year structure built: 1972; Homeowner vacancy rate: 6.0%; Median selected monthly owner costs: $1,173 with a mortgage, $475 without a mortgage; Median gross rent: $772 per month; Rental vacancy rate: 2.5%
Health Insurance: 92.0% have insurance; 64.0% have private insurance; 44.4% have public insurance; 8.0% do not have insurance; 2.1% of children under 18 do not have insurance
Transportation: Commute: 89.6% car, 0.5% public transportation, 3.7% walk, 4.7% work from home; Mean travel time to work: 17.5 minutes
Additional Information Contacts
Town of Alexandria . . . . (315) 482-9519
    http://www.townofalexandria.org

ALEXANDRIA BAY (village). Covers a land area of 0.766 square miles and a water area of 0.759 square miles. Located at 44.34° N. Lat; 75.92° W. Long. Elevation is 269 feet.
Population: 906; Growth (since 2000): -16.7%; Density: 1,182.6 persons per square mile; Race: 91.9% White, 5.3% Black/African American, 1.3% Asian, 0.0% American Indian/Alaska Native, 0.0% Native Hawaiian/Other Pacific Islander, 1.4% Two or more races, 1.0% Hispanic of any race; Average household size: 1.83; Median age: 49.8; Age under 18: 15.0%; Age 65 and over: 20.9%; Males per 100 females: 94.6; Marriage status: 28.8% never married, 43.3% now married, 2.7% separated, 8.2% widowed, 19.7% divorced; Foreign born: 3.4%; Speak English only: 97.4%; With disability: 17.5%; Veterans: 12.7%; Ancestry: 33.4% Irish, 14.6% German, 14.1% Italian, 14.0% English, 8.6% French

Employment: 7.7% management, business, and financial, 1.5% computer, engineering, and science, 21.8% education, legal, community service, arts, and media, 4.2% healthcare practitioners, 22.5% service, 23.6% sales and office, 12.6% natural resources, construction, and maintenance, 6.2% production, transportation, and material moving
Income: Per capita: $29,666; Median household: $43,182; Average household: $55,515; Households with income of $100,000 or more: 17.2%; Poverty rate: 11.8%
Educational Attainment: High school diploma or higher: 93.7%; Bachelor's degree or higher: 31.6%; Graduate/professional degree or higher: 17.3%

School District(s)
Alexandria Central SD (PK-12)
    Enrollment: 568 . . . . (315) 482-9971
Housing: Homeownership rate: 52.3%; Median home value: $114,500; Median year structure built: Before 1940; Homeowner vacancy rate: 8.7%; Median selected monthly owner costs: $1,221 with a mortgage, $466 without a mortgage; Median gross rent: $693 per month; Rental vacancy rate: 4.0%
Health Insurance: 94.1% have insurance; 63.0% have private insurance; 47.4% have public insurance; 5.9% do not have insurance; 2.9% of children under 18 do not have insurance
Hospitals: River Hospital (52 beds)
Safety: Violent crime rate: 9.4 per 10,000 population; Property crime rate: 47.1 per 10,000 population
Newspapers: Thousand Islands Sun (weekly circulation 6,700)
Transportation: Commute: 77.9% car, 0.0% public transportation, 15.6% walk, 2.6% work from home; Mean travel time to work: 14.7 minutes

ANTWERP (town). Covers a land area of 106.042 square miles and a water area of 2.378 square miles. Located at 44.22° N. Lat; 75.60° W. Long. Elevation is 512 feet.
Population: 1,644; Growth (since 2000): -8.3%; Density: 15.5 persons per square mile; Race: 97.1% White, 0.0% Black/African American, 0.0% Asian, 0.2% American Indian/Alaska Native, 0.0% Native Hawaiian/Other Pacific Islander, 2.7% Two or more races, 2.6% Hispanic of any race; Average household size: 2.65; Median age: 36.3; Age under 18: 27.3%; Age 65 and over: 12.2%; Males per 100 females: 101.7; Marriage status: 28.2% never married, 56.1% now married, 2.3% separated, 4.7% widowed, 11.1% divorced; Foreign born: 1.4%; Speak English only: 95.9%; With disability: 16.8%; Veterans: 12.7%; Ancestry: 17.6% Irish, 14.2% German, 11.6% French, 10.9% American, 9.3% English
Employment: 9.5% management, business, and financial, 0.4% computer, engineering, and science, 11.7% education, legal, community service, arts, and media, 7.5% healthcare practitioners, 16.0% service, 20.4% sales and office, 18.1% natural resources, construction, and maintenance, 16.4% production, transportation, and material moving
Income: Per capita: $23,485; Median household: $50,000; Average household: $61,528; Households with income of $100,000 or more: 16.4%; Poverty rate: 11.1%
Educational Attainment: High school diploma or higher: 84.6%; Bachelor's degree or higher: 9.1%; Graduate/professional degree or higher: 4.2%

School District(s)
Indian River Central SD (PK-12)
    Enrollment: 3,820 . . . . (315) 642-3441
Housing: Homeownership rate: 81.1%; Median home value: $119,100; Median year structure built: 1951; Homeowner vacancy rate: 1.1%; Median selected monthly owner costs: $1,205 with a mortgage, $460 without a mortgage; Median gross rent: $761 per month; Rental vacancy rate: 0.0%
Health Insurance: 91.3% have insurance; 61.9% have private insurance; 44.4% have public insurance; 8.7% do not have insurance; 4.6% of children under 18 do not have insurance
Transportation: Commute: 89.8% car, 0.1% public transportation, 1.1% walk, 6.4% work from home; Mean travel time to work: 30.6 minutes

ANTWERP (village). Covers a land area of 1.035 square miles and a water area of 0.033 square miles. Located at 44.20° N. Lat; 75.61° W. Long. Elevation is 512 feet.
Population: 537; Growth (since 2000): -25.0%; Density: 519.0 persons per square mile; Race: 98.7% White, 0.0% Black/African American, 0.0% Asian, 0.6% American Indian/Alaska Native, 0.0% Native Hawaiian/Other Pacific Islander, 0.7% Two or more races, 6.1% Hispanic of any race; Average household size: 2.58; Median age: 38.1; Age under 18: 27.2%; Age 65 and over: 14.7%; Males per 100 females: 100.6; Marriage status:

28.7% never married, 57.1% now married, 2.2% separated, 2.9% widowed, 11.3% divorced; Foreign born: 2.0%; Speak English only: 97.4%; With disability: 18.1%; Veterans: 19.3%; Ancestry: 17.3% English, 16.8% Irish, 10.8% Italian, 9.9% French, 8.4% German
Employment: 8.3% management, business, and financial, 1.6% computer, engineering, and science, 13.5% education, legal, community service, arts, and media, 3.1% healthcare practitioners, 16.6% service, 29.5% sales and office, 16.6% natural resources, construction, and maintenance, 10.9% production, transportation, and material moving
Income: Per capita: $22,358; Median household: $44,643; Average household: $56,643; Households with income of $100,000 or more: 8.7%; Poverty rate: 10.9%
Educational Attainment: High school diploma or higher: 90.1%; Bachelor's degree or higher: 11.0%; Graduate/professional degree or higher: 4.5%

School District(s)
Indian River Central SD (PK-12)
    Enrollment: 3,820 . . . . (315) 642-3441
Housing: Homeownership rate: 78.8%; Median home value: $104,200; Median year structure built: Before 1940; Homeowner vacancy rate: 3.3%; Median selected monthly owner costs: $1,317 with a mortgage, $555 without a mortgage; Median gross rent: $775 per month; Rental vacancy rate: 0.0%
Health Insurance: 90.4% have insurance; 64.9% have private insurance; 43.5% have public insurance; 9.6% do not have insurance; 10.3% of children under 18 do not have insurance
Transportation: Commute: 89.5% car, 0.5% public transportation, 2.4% walk, 7.1% work from home; Mean travel time to work: 27.4 minutes

BELLEVILLE (CDP). Covers a land area of 0.264 square miles and a water area of 0 square miles. Located at 43.78° N. Lat; 76.12° W. Long. Elevation is 459 feet.
Population: 160; Growth (since 2000): n/a; Density: 605.0 persons per square mile; Race: 100.0% White, 0.0% Black/African American, 0.0% Asian, 0.0% American Indian/Alaska Native, 0.0% Native Hawaiian/Other Pacific Islander, 0.0% Two or more races, 0.0% Hispanic of any race; Average household size: 2.62; Median age: 44.2; Age under 18: 38.7%; Age 65 and over: 8.1%; Males per 100 females: 93.2; Marriage status: 15.2% never married, 71.7% now married, 0.0% separated, 13.1% widowed, 0.0% divorced; Foreign born: 0.0%; Speak English only: 100.0%; With disability: 8.1%; Veterans: 0.0%; Ancestry: 10.6% European, 8.1% English, 8.1% Irish, 3.1% Dutch, 3.1% Scottish
Employment: 21.7% management, business, and financial, 0.0% computer, engineering, and science, 11.6% education, legal, community service, arts, and media, 0.0% healthcare practitioners, 8.7% service, 0.0% sales and office, 58.0% natural resources, construction, and maintenance, 0.0% production, transportation, and material moving
Income: Per capita: $26,032; Median household: $61,016; Average household: $69,436; Households with income of $100,000 or more: 24.6%; Poverty rate: n/a
Educational Attainment: High school diploma or higher: 100.0%; Bachelor's degree or higher: 17.7%; Graduate/professional degree or higher: 6.3%

School District(s)
Belleville Henderson Central SD (PK-12)
    Enrollment: 501 . . . . (315) 846-5826
Housing: Homeownership rate: 75.4%; Median home value: n/a; Median year structure built: 1978; Homeowner vacancy rate: 0.0%; Median selected monthly owner costs: $1,323 with a mortgage, n/a without a mortgage; Median gross rent: n/a per month; Rental vacancy rate: 0.0%
Health Insurance: 80.6% have insurance; 77.5% have private insurance; 11.3% have public insurance; 19.4% do not have insurance; 0.0% of children under 18 do not have insurance
Transportation: Commute: 68.7% car, 0.0% public transportation, 31.3% walk, 0.0% work from home; Mean travel time to work: 30.5 minutes

BLACK RIVER (village). Covers a land area of 1.791 square miles and a water area of 0.053 square miles. Located at 44.01° N. Lat; 75.80° W. Long. Elevation is 571 feet.
Population: 1,301; Growth (since 2000): 1.2%; Density: 726.3 persons per square mile; Race: 86.8% White, 1.8% Black/African American, 3.2% Asian, 0.0% American Indian/Alaska Native, 0.0% Native Hawaiian/Other Pacific Islander, 6.1% Two or more races, 1.8% Hispanic of any race; Average household size: 2.58; Median age: 34.4; Age under 18: 28.3%; Age 65 and over: 13.6%; Males per 100 females: 94.5; Marriage status:

17.3% never married, 70.4% now married, 4.3% separated, 4.8% widowed, 7.5% divorced; Foreign born: 6.8%; Speak English only: 90.7%; With disability: 20.0%; Veterans: 20.2%; Ancestry: 24.1% Irish, 14.5% German, 10.9% Italian, 10.8% English, 6.6% French
Employment: 12.2% management, business, and financial, 3.8% computer, engineering, and science, 13.4% education, legal, community service, arts, and media, 8.9% healthcare practitioners, 18.9% service, 25.1% sales and office, 5.0% natural resources, construction, and maintenance, 12.7% production, transportation, and material moving
Income: Per capita: $28,726; Median household: $60,500; Average household: $72,655; Households with income of $100,000 or more: 18.7%; Poverty rate: 6.3%
Educational Attainment: High school diploma or higher: 94.6%; Bachelor's degree or higher: 29.1%; Graduate/professional degree or higher: 10.0%

School District(s)
Carthage Central SD (KG-12)
    Enrollment: 3,239 . . . . (315) 493-5120
Housing: Homeownership rate: 56.7%; Median home value: $176,700; Median year structure built: 1955; Homeowner vacancy rate: 6.1%; Median selected monthly owner costs: $1,443 with a mortgage, $539 without a mortgage; Median gross rent: $793 per month; Rental vacancy rate: 4.0%
Health Insurance: 97.4% have insurance; 78.4% have private insurance; 38.2% have public insurance; 2.6% do not have insurance; 1.4% of children under 18 do not have insurance
Safety: Violent crime rate: 0.0 per 10,000 population; Property crime rate: 47.1 per 10,000 population
Transportation: Commute: 94.8% car, 0.0% public transportation, 0.6% walk, 1.5% work from home; Mean travel time to work: 16.5 minutes

BROWNVILLE (town). Covers a land area of 59.132 square miles and a water area of 7.320 square miles. Located at 44.03° N. Lat; 76.08° W. Long. Elevation is 348 feet.
Population: 6,329; Growth (since 2000): 8.3%; Density: 107.0 persons per square mile; Race: 97.0% White, 0.5% Black/African American, 1.4% Asian, 0.3% American Indian/Alaska Native, 0.0% Native Hawaiian/Other Pacific Islander, 0.8% Two or more races, 0.7% Hispanic of any race; Average household size: 2.57; Median age: 42.9; Age under 18: 21.8%; Age 65 and over: 15.1%; Males per 100 females: 97.3; Marriage status: 22.2% never married, 67.2% now married, 2.9% separated, 3.1% widowed, 7.5% divorced; Foreign born: 1.7%; Speak English only: 97.7%; With disability: 17.1%; Veterans: 12.3%; Ancestry: 20.1% Irish, 16.8% German, 14.3% French, 12.1% English, 9.5% Italian
Employment: 13.0% management, business, and financial, 1.0% computer, engineering, and science, 10.8% education, legal, community service, arts, and media, 6.2% healthcare practitioners, 24.6% service, 24.4% sales and office, 11.6% natural resources, construction, and maintenance, 8.4% production, transportation, and material moving
Income: Per capita: $26,322; Median household: $55,778; Average household: $67,153; Households with income of $100,000 or more: 24.5%; Poverty rate: 8.4%
Educational Attainment: High school diploma or higher: 91.4%; Bachelor's degree or higher: 20.5%; Graduate/professional degree or higher: 10.0%

School District(s)
General Brown Central SD (PK-12)
    Enrollment: 1,522 . . . . (315) 779-2300
Housing: Homeownership rate: 82.3%; Median home value: $152,400; Median year structure built: 1974; Homeowner vacancy rate: 0.4%; Median selected monthly owner costs: $1,234 with a mortgage, $470 without a mortgage; Median gross rent: $621 per month; Rental vacancy rate: 2.2%
Health Insurance: 94.5% have insurance; 76.1% have private insurance; 38.3% have public insurance; 5.5% do not have insurance; 4.1% of children under 18 do not have insurance
Transportation: Commute: 95.8% car, 0.1% public transportation, 1.4% walk, 2.2% work from home; Mean travel time to work: 19.4 minutes

BROWNVILLE (village). Covers a land area of 0.673 square miles and a water area of 0.004 square miles. Located at 44.01° N. Lat; 75.98° W. Long. Elevation is 348 feet.
Population: 1,037; Growth (since 2000): 1.5%; Density: 1,540.9 persons per square mile; Race: 98.0% White, 2.0% Black/African American, 0.0% Asian, 0.0% American Indian/Alaska Native, 0.0% Native Hawaiian/Other Pacific Islander, 0.0% Two or more races, 0.3% Hispanic of any race; Average household size: 2.53; Median age: 42.5; Age under 18: 25.9%;

Age 65 and over: 23.0%; Males per 100 females: 89.3; Marriage status: 24.5% never married, 63.2% now married, 2.9% separated, 5.7% widowed, 6.6% divorced; Foreign born: 0.0%; Speak English only: 99.3%; With disability: 22.4%; Veterans: 17.6%; Ancestry: 21.9% Irish, 21.1% German, 17.5% French, 10.0% French Canadian, 8.8% English

Employment: 12.7% management, business, and financial, 0.5% computer, engineering, and science, 13.2% education, legal, community service, arts, and media, 4.0% healthcare practitioners, 25.0% service, 28.1% sales and office, 12.7% natural resources, construction, and maintenance, 3.8% production, transportation, and material moving

Income: Per capita: $24,393; Median household: $48,750; Average household: $62,244; Households with income of $100,000 or more: 20.4%; Poverty rate: 4.6%

Educational Attainment: High school diploma or higher: 91.1%; Bachelor's degree or higher: 26.1%; Graduate/professional degree or higher: 11.9%

School District(s)
General Brown Central SD (PK-12)
    Enrollment: 1,522 . . . . (315) 779-2300

Housing: Homeownership rate: 65.6%; Median home value: $160,200; Median year structure built: Before 1940; Homeowner vacancy rate: 0.0%; Median selected monthly owner costs: $1,256 with a mortgage, $529 without a mortgage; Median gross rent: $763 per month; Rental vacancy rate: 0.0%

Health Insurance: 95.4% have insurance; 84.7% have private insurance; 33.3% have public insurance; 4.6% do not have insurance; 1.4% of children under 18 do not have insurance

Safety: Violent crime rate: 0.0 per 10,000 population; Property crime rate: 26.8 per 10,000 population

Transportation: Commute: 85.7% car, 0.5% public transportation, 4.1% walk, 7.0% work from home; Mean travel time to work: 14.8 minutes

---

CALCIUM (CDP). Covers a land area of 5.544 square miles and a water area of 0.002 square miles. Located at 44.05° N. Lat; 75.85° W. Long. Elevation is 469 feet.

Population: 4,119; Growth (since 2000): 23.1%; Density: 743.0 persons per square mile; Race: 55.4% White, 23.9% Black/African American, 8.8% Asian, 0.1% American Indian/Alaska Native, 0.0% Native Hawaiian/Other Pacific Islander, 7.3% Two or more races, 20.6% Hispanic of any race; Average household size: 2.48; Median age: 26.1; Age under 18: 25.3%; Age 65 and over: 2.5%; Males per 100 females: 102.5; Marriage status: 22.2% never married, 69.8% now married, 3.6% separated, 0.6% widowed, 7.3% divorced; Foreign born: 7.8%; Speak English only: 81.5%; With disability: 3.3%; Veterans: 16.4%; Ancestry: 10.0% French, 9.1% Italian, 8.3% German, 5.3% Irish, 4.8% English

Employment: 12.0% management, business, and financial, 6.2% computer, engineering, and science, 19.5% education, legal, community service, arts, and media, 1.1% healthcare practitioners, 20.6% service, 24.8% sales and office, 7.1% natural resources, construction, and maintenance, 8.7% production, transportation, and material moving

Income: Per capita: $22,651; Median household: $52,025; Average household: $54,518; Households with income of $100,000 or more: 6.5%; Poverty rate: 8.1%

Educational Attainment: High school diploma or higher: 90.6%; Bachelor's degree or higher: 33.5%; Graduate/professional degree or higher: 5.9%

School District(s)
Indian River Central SD (PK-12)
    Enrollment: 3,820 . . . . (315) 642-3441

Housing: Homeownership rate: 17.5%; Median home value: $156,900; Median year structure built: 1997; Homeowner vacancy rate: 0.0%; Median selected monthly owner costs: $1,420 with a mortgage, $284 without a mortgage; Median gross rent: $1,205 per month; Rental vacancy rate: 8.6%

Health Insurance: 90.6% have insurance; 72.0% have private insurance; 28.4% have public insurance; 9.4% do not have insurance; 1.9% of children under 18 do not have insurance

Transportation: Commute: 92.5% car, 0.0% public transportation, 0.0% walk, 5.5% work from home; Mean travel time to work: 13.9 minutes

---

CAPE VINCENT (town). Covers a land area of 56.353 square miles and a water area of 33.499 square miles. Located at 44.11° N. Lat; 76.29° W. Long. Elevation is 262 feet.

Population: 2,837; Growth (since 2000): -15.2%; Density: 50.3 persons per square mile; Race: 74.4% White, 14.2% Black/African American, 0.7%

Asian, 0.1% American Indian/Alaska Native, 0.0% Native Hawaiian/Other Pacific Islander, 5.0% Two or more races, 10.4% Hispanic of any race; Average household size: 2.25; Median age: 44.3; Age under 18: 13.9%; Age 65 and over: 18.0%; Males per 100 females: 177.1; Marriage status: 37.0% never married, 47.4% now married, 3.2% separated, 5.5% widowed, 10.2% divorced; Foreign born: 4.4%; Speak English only: 89.5%; With disability: 12.9%; Veterans: 9.1%; Ancestry: 17.8% Irish, 16.2% German, 9.1% English, 8.9% French, 7.4% Italian

Employment: 11.1% management, business, and financial, 3.3% computer, engineering, and science, 13.0% education, legal, community service, arts, and media, 6.0% healthcare practitioners, 18.3% service, 20.3% sales and office, 16.0% natural resources, construction, and maintenance, 11.9% production, transportation, and material moving

Income: Per capita: $21,449; Median household: $54,612; Average household: $66,720; Households with income of $100,000 or more: 20.6%; Poverty rate: 10.1%

Educational Attainment: High school diploma or higher: 81.5%; Bachelor's degree or higher: 17.4%; Graduate/professional degree or higher: 7.4%

School District(s)
Thousand Islands Central SD (KG-12)
    Enrollment: 947 . . . . (315) 686-5594

Housing: Homeownership rate: 81.9%; Median home value: $146,100; Median year structure built: 1976; Homeowner vacancy rate: 4.0%; Median selected monthly owner costs: $1,218 with a mortgage, $422 without a mortgage; Median gross rent: $633 per month; Rental vacancy rate: 7.0%

Health Insurance: 90.1% have insurance; 71.0% have private insurance; 42.6% have public insurance; 9.9% do not have insurance; 8.4% of children under 18 do not have insurance

Transportation: Commute: 86.1% car, 0.0% public transportation, 4.9% walk, 7.5% work from home; Mean travel time to work: 28.1 minutes

---

CAPE VINCENT (village). Covers a land area of 0.724 square miles and a water area of 0.025 square miles. Located at 44.12° N. Lat; 76.33° W. Long. Elevation is 262 feet.

Population: 743; Growth (since 2000): -2.2%; Density: 1,026.9 persons per square mile; Race: 94.9% White, 1.2% Black/African American, 0.7% Asian, 0.0% American Indian/Alaska Native, 0.0% Native Hawaiian/Other Pacific Islander, 3.2% Two or more races, 3.6% Hispanic of any race; Average household size: 2.41; Median age: 42.4; Age under 18: 28.7%; Age 65 and over: 19.5%; Males per 100 females: 92.6; Marriage status: 20.2% never married, 59.1% now married, 1.7% separated, 11.7% widowed, 9.0% divorced; Foreign born: 4.4%; Speak English only: 97.9%; With disability: 11.8%; Veterans: 18.7%; Ancestry: 27.1% German, 17.9% Irish, 14.8% French, 10.0% English, 9.3% Scottish

Employment: 8.1% management, business, and financial, 5.9% computer, engineering, and science, 13.7% education, legal, community service, arts, and media, 12.4% healthcare practitioners, 17.9% service, 14.7% sales and office, 14.3% natural resources, construction, and maintenance, 13.0% production, transportation, and material moving

Income: Per capita: $25,948; Median household: $49,375; Average household: $62,599; Households with income of $100,000 or more: 18.5%; Poverty rate: 5.5%

Educational Attainment: High school diploma or higher: 95.2%; Bachelor's degree or higher: 32.2%; Graduate/professional degree or higher: 11.4%

School District(s)
Thousand Islands Central SD (KG-12)
    Enrollment: 947 . . . . (315) 686-5594

Housing: Homeownership rate: 67.2%; Median home value: $137,500; Median year structure built: Before 1940; Homeowner vacancy rate: 5.3%; Median selected monthly owner costs: $1,214 with a mortgage, $512 without a mortgage; Median gross rent: $625 per month; Rental vacancy rate: 5.1%

Health Insurance: 87.3% have insurance; 69.3% have private insurance; 39.0% have public insurance; 12.7% do not have insurance; 11.0% of children under 18 do not have insurance

Safety: Violent crime rate: 0.0 per 10,000 population; Property crime rate: 55.9 per 10,000 population

Transportation: Commute: 84.7% car, 0.0% public transportation, 6.2% walk, 9.1% work from home; Mean travel time to work: 31.1 minutes

CARTHAGE (village). Covers a land area of 2.508 square miles and a water area of 0.170 square miles. Located at 43.99° N. Lat; 75.60° W. Long. Elevation is 768 feet.

History: Settled before 1801, incorporated 1841.

Population: 3,536; Growth (since 2000): -5.0%; Density: 1,410.1 persons per square mile; Race: 94.7% White, 0.9% Black/African American, 0.0% Asian, 0.0% American Indian/Alaska Native, 0.0% Native Hawaiian/Other Pacific Islander, 4.4% Two or more races, 1.7% Hispanic of any race; Average household size: 2.76; Median age: 29.3; Age under 18: 31.5%; Age 65 and over: 13.2%; Males per 100 females: 89.3; Marriage status: 32.5% never married, 47.8% now married, 4.9% separated, 5.3% widowed, 14.4% divorced; Foreign born: 1.0%; Speak English only: 97.8%; With disability: 21.6%; Veterans: 12.4%; Ancestry: 23.6% Irish, 16.8% Italian, 16.4% German, 10.4% French, 9.5% English

Employment: 13.5% management, business, and financial, 0.0% computer, engineering, and science, 6.5% education, legal, community service, arts, and media, 7.9% healthcare practitioners, 29.5% service, 17.0% sales and office, 21.8% natural resources, construction, and maintenance, 3.8% production, transportation, and material moving

Income: Per capita: $17,797; Median household: $43,074; Average household: $49,167; Households with income of $100,000 or more: 12.3%; Poverty rate: 31.5%

Educational Attainment: High school diploma or higher: 90.3%; Bachelor's degree or higher: 11.1%; Graduate/professional degree or higher: 6.0%

School District(s)
Carthage Central SD (KG-12)
    Enrollment: 3,239 . . . . (315) 493-5120

Housing: Homeownership rate: 41.1%; Median home value: $126,700; Median year structure built: Before 1940; Homeowner vacancy rate: 0.0%; Median selected monthly owner costs: $1,454 with a mortgage, $580 without a mortgage; Median gross rent: $914 per month; Rental vacancy rate: 6.8%

Health Insurance: 94.5% have insurance; 53.9% have private insurance; 50.0% have public insurance; 5.5% do not have insurance; 0.0% of children under 18 do not have insurance

Hospitals: Carthage Area Hospital (78 beds)

Safety: Violent crime rate: 20.4 per 10,000 population; Property crime rate: 166.4 per 10,000 population

Newspapers: Republican Tribune (weekly circulation 2,800)

Transportation: Commute: 89.6% car, 0.0% public transportation, 1.5% walk, 3.1% work from home; Mean travel time to work: 20.7 minutes

CHAMPION (town). Covers a land area of 44.184 square miles and a water area of 0.889 square miles. Located at 43.97° N. Lat; 75.71° W. Long. Elevation is 997 feet.

Population: 4,513; Growth (since 2000): 3.5%; Density: 102.1 persons per square mile; Race: 87.8% White, 3.7% Black/African American, 1.4% Asian, 0.0% American Indian/Alaska Native, 0.4% Native Hawaiian/Other Pacific Islander, 2.0% Two or more races, 8.7% Hispanic of any race; Average household size: 2.35; Median age: 41.2; Age under 18: 20.4%; Age 65 and over: 18.0%; Males per 100 females: 100.2; Marriage status: 23.7% never married, 58.1% now married, 0.9% separated, 6.8% widowed, 11.4% divorced; Foreign born: 3.2%; Speak English only: 92.5%; With disability: 20.7%; Veterans: 20.4%; Ancestry: 17.0% German, 14.8% Irish, 12.5% French, 10.2% English, 8.8% American

Employment: 11.9% management, business, and financial, 2.3% computer, engineering, and science, 15.4% education, legal, community service, arts, and media, 6.4% healthcare practitioners, 14.6% service, 23.0% sales and office, 12.0% natural resources, construction, and maintenance, 14.4% production, transportation, and material moving

Income: Per capita: $26,339; Median household: $52,931; Average household: $60,593; Households with income of $100,000 or more: 16.7%; Poverty rate: 11.2%

Educational Attainment: High school diploma or higher: 88.8%; Bachelor's degree or higher: 21.4%; Graduate/professional degree or higher: 6.6%

Housing: Homeownership rate: 62.0%; Median home value: $129,600; Median year structure built: 1973; Homeowner vacancy rate: 3.0%; Median selected monthly owner costs: $1,088 with a mortgage, $447 without a mortgage; Median gross rent: $871 per month; Rental vacancy rate: 12.0%

Health Insurance: 94.2% have insurance; 71.7% have private insurance; 40.3% have public insurance; 5.8% do not have insurance; 5.7% of children under 18 do not have insurance

Transportation: Commute: 92.5% car, 0.0% public transportation, 0.0% walk, 5.2% work from home; Mean travel time to work: 22.7 minutes

Additional Information Contacts
Town of Champion . . . . (315) 493-3240
    http://www.racog.org/Champion/Championhomepage.php

CHAUMONT (village). Covers a land area of 0.971 square miles and a water area of 0.093 square miles. Located at 44.07° N. Lat; 76.13° W. Long. Elevation is 289 feet.

Population: 887; Growth (since 2000): 49.8%; Density: 913.6 persons per square mile; Race: 93.8% White, 0.8% Black/African American, 0.0% Asian, 0.3% American Indian/Alaska Native, 0.0% Native Hawaiian/Other Pacific Islander, 5.1% Two or more races, 0.7% Hispanic of any race; Average household size: 2.95; Median age: 33.9; Age under 18: 28.5%; Age 65 and over: 16.6%; Males per 100 females: 90.8; Marriage status: 26.9% never married, 55.0% now married, 1.3% separated, 6.0% widowed, 12.1% divorced; Foreign born: 2.8%; Speak English only: 99.0%; With disability: 16.0%; Veterans: 10.0%; Ancestry: 22.4% Irish, 20.3% German, 11.7% Italian, 8.3% French, 5.4% English

Employment: 12.4% management, business, and financial, 5.6% computer, engineering, and science, 10.6% education, legal, community service, arts, and media, 4.8% healthcare practitioners, 30.2% service, 17.7% sales and office, 5.8% natural resources, construction, and maintenance, 13.0% production, transportation, and material moving

Income: Per capita: $24,322; Median household: $56,250; Average household: $72,651; Households with income of $100,000 or more: 27.4%; Poverty rate: 6.1%

Educational Attainment: High school diploma or higher: 92.1%; Bachelor's degree or higher: 20.0%; Graduate/professional degree or higher: 7.9%

School District(s)
Lyme Central SD (PK-12)
    Enrollment: 344 . . . . (315) 649-2417

Housing: Homeownership rate: 70.9%; Median home value: $139,300; Median year structure built: Before 1940; Homeowner vacancy rate: 3.2%; Median selected monthly owner costs: $1,333 with a mortgage, $494 without a mortgage; Median gross rent: $775 per month; Rental vacancy rate: 6.5%

Health Insurance: 95.1% have insurance; 71.5% have private insurance; 39.4% have public insurance; 4.9% do not have insurance; 8.7% of children under 18 do not have insurance

Transportation: Commute: 81.8% car, 0.5% public transportation, 13.7% walk, 4.0% work from home; Mean travel time to work: 20.6 minutes

CLAYTON (town). Covers a land area of 82.360 square miles and a water area of 21.671 square miles. Located at 44.20° N. Lat; 76.08° W. Long. Elevation is 276 feet.

History: North American freshwater craft at Antique Boat Museum, similar to one at Mystic, Connecticut; Thousand Islands Museum; Clayton Historic District. Incorporated 1872.

Population: 5,058; Growth (since 2000): 5.0%; Density: 61.4 persons per square mile; Race: 98.3% White, 0.8% Black/African American, 0.0% Asian, 0.0% American Indian/Alaska Native, 0.0% Native Hawaiian/Other Pacific Islander, 0.8% Two or more races, 1.2% Hispanic of any race; Average household size: 2.52; Median age: 39.8; Age under 18: 22.2%; Age 65 and over: 20.0%; Males per 100 females: 92.7; Marriage status: 24.4% never married, 61.8% now married, 1.8% separated, 6.0% widowed, 7.9% divorced; Foreign born: 1.3%; Speak English only: 98.4%; With disability: 8.5%; Veterans: 10.6%; Ancestry: 24.3% Irish, 21.0% German, 18.1% English, 14.0% French, 6.6% American

Employment: 10.5% management, business, and financial, 6.6% computer, engineering, and science, 10.1% education, legal, community service, arts, and media, 5.7% healthcare practitioners, 22.0% service, 22.3% sales and office, 13.0% natural resources, construction, and maintenance, 9.8% production, transportation, and material moving

Income: Per capita: $29,355; Median household: $68,220; Average household: $73,333; Households with income of $100,000 or more: 26.8%; Poverty rate: 7.0%

Educational Attainment: High school diploma or higher: 94.8%; Bachelor's degree or higher: 27.3%; Graduate/professional degree or higher: 13.6%

School District(s)
Thousand Islands Central SD (KG-12)
    Enrollment: 947 . . . . (315) 686-5594

Housing: Homeownership rate: 75.8%; Median home value: $168,900; Median year structure built: 1965; Homeowner vacancy rate: 2.9%; Median selected monthly owner costs: $1,415 with a mortgage, $518 without a mortgage; Median gross rent: $881 per month; Rental vacancy rate: 15.1%
Health Insurance: 94.4% have insurance; 72.0% have private insurance; 39.9% have public insurance; 5.6% do not have insurance; 0.5% of children under 18 do not have insurance
Transportation: Commute: 86.3% car, 0.0% public transportation, 5.2% walk, 5.9% work from home; Mean travel time to work: 22.3 minutes
Additional Information Contacts
Town of Clayton . . . . (315) 686-3512
   http://townofclayton.com

CLAYTON (village). Covers a land area of 1.613 square miles and a water area of 0.973 square miles. Located at 44.24° N. Lat; 76.08° W. Long. Elevation is 276 feet.
Population: 1,994; Growth (since 2000): 9.5%; Density: 1,236.2 persons per square mile; Race: 96.9% White, 2.1% Black/African American, 0.1% Asian, 0.0% American Indian/Alaska Native, 0.0% Native Hawaiian/Other Pacific Islander, 0.9% Two or more races, 0.3% Hispanic of any race; Average household size: 2.25; Median age: 38.9; Age under 18: 19.6%; Age 65 and over: 21.2%; Males per 100 females: 84.5; Marriage status: 33.0% never married, 46.6% now married, 2.7% separated, 7.9% widowed, 12.5% divorced; Foreign born: 0.9%; Speak English only: 99.9%; With disability: 9.9%; Veterans: 10.2%; Ancestry: 30.0% Irish, 22.9% German, 16.4% English, 14.2% French, 5.6% French Canadian
Employment: 8.6% management, business, and financial, 2.3% computer, engineering, and science, 8.8% education, legal, community service, arts, and media, 4.1% healthcare practitioners, 32.7% service, 19.5% sales and office, 15.2% natural resources, construction, and maintenance, 8.9% production, transportation, and material moving
Income: Per capita: $27,951; Median household: $50,431; Average household: $62,431; Households with income of $100,000 or more: 24.1%; Poverty rate: 11.1%
Educational Attainment: High school diploma or higher: 96.2%; Bachelor's degree or higher: 25.2%; Graduate/professional degree or higher: 10.0%
School District(s)
Thousand Islands Central SD (KG-12)
   Enrollment: 947 . . . . (315) 686-5594
Housing: Homeownership rate: 52.8%; Median home value: $153,300; Median year structure built: Before 1940; Homeowner vacancy rate: 0.0%; Median selected monthly owner costs: $1,277 with a mortgage, $657 without a mortgage; Median gross rent: $910 per month; Rental vacancy rate: 17.0%
Health Insurance: 92.3% have insurance; 63.2% have private insurance; 48.1% have public insurance; 7.7% do not have insurance; 0.0% of children under 18 do not have insurance
Safety: Violent crime rate: 5.3 per 10,000 population; Property crime rate: 26.6 per 10,000 population
Transportation: Commute: 78.2% car, 0.0% public transportation, 11.7% walk, 6.4% work from home; Mean travel time to work: 20.8 minutes

DEFERIET (village). Covers a land area of 0.650 square miles and a water area of 0.082 square miles. Located at 44.04° N. Lat; 75.68° W. Long. Elevation is 659 feet.
Population: 277; Growth (since 2000): -10.4%; Density: 426.2 persons per square mile; Race: 93.1% White, 0.0% Black/African American, 0.0% Asian, 0.0% American Indian/Alaska Native, 0.0% Native Hawaiian/Other Pacific Islander, 6.9% Two or more races, 3.2% Hispanic of any race; Average household size: 2.56; Median age: 27.9; Age under 18: 33.6%; Age 65 and over: 14.4%; Males per 100 females: 82.6; Marriage status: 38.2% never married, 38.7% now married, 2.0% separated, 7.4% widowed, 15.7% divorced; Foreign born: 2.2%; Speak English only: 89.8%; With disability: 12.3%; Veterans: 18.3%; Ancestry: 23.1% Irish, 20.6% French, 20.6% German, 13.0% Italian, 6.1% French Canadian
Employment: 8.5% management, business, and financial, 3.2% computer, engineering, and science, 4.3% education, legal, community service, arts, and media, 6.4% healthcare practitioners, 19.1% service, 31.9% sales and office, 17.0% natural resources, construction, and maintenance, 9.6% production, transportation, and material moving
Income: Per capita: $22,139; Median household: $50,000; Average household: $58,212; Households with income of $100,000 or more: 13.0%; Poverty rate: 21.4%

Educational Attainment: High school diploma or higher: 90.7%; Bachelor's degree or higher: 17.9%; Graduate/professional degree or higher: 4.3%
Housing: Homeownership rate: 64.8%; Median home value: $95,700; Median year structure built: Before 1940; Homeowner vacancy rate: 3.7%; Median selected monthly owner costs: $1,115 with a mortgage, $529 without a mortgage; Median gross rent: $967 per month; Rental vacancy rate: 0.0%
Health Insurance: 87.7% have insurance; 62.7% have private insurance; 41.4% have public insurance; 12.3% do not have insurance; 7.2% of children under 18 do not have insurance
Transportation: Commute: 96.1% car, 0.0% public transportation, 1.9% walk, 1.9% work from home; Mean travel time to work: 17.6 minutes

DEPAUVILLE (CDP). Covers a land area of 9.822 square miles and a water area of 0 square miles. Located at 44.14° N. Lat; 76.05° W. Long. Elevation is 305 feet.
Population: 278; Growth (since 2000): -45.7%; Density: 28.3 persons per square mile; Race: 100.0% White, 0.0% Black/African American, 0.0% Asian, 0.0% American Indian/Alaska Native, 0.0% Native Hawaiian/Other Pacific Islander, 0.0% Two or more races, 0.0% Hispanic of any race; Average household size: 3.16; Median age: 44.2; Age under 18: 29.1%; Age 65 and over: 8.3%; Males per 100 females: 103.2; Marriage status: 15.9% never married, 66.8% now married, 0.0% separated, 0.0% widowed, 17.3% divorced; Foreign born: 0.0%; Speak English only: 100.0%; With disability: 6.8%; Veterans: 20.8%; Ancestry: 24.5% German, 15.8% Polish, 13.7% Irish, 6.8% British, 6.5% Canadian
Employment: 6.6% management, business, and financial, 13.1% computer, engineering, and science, 5.8% education, legal, community service, arts, and media, 10.2% healthcare practitioners, 21.9% service, 24.1% sales and office, 12.4% natural resources, construction, and maintenance, 5.8% production, transportation, and material moving
Income: Per capita: $28,997; Median household: $69,375; Average household: $86,792; Households with income of $100,000 or more: 29.6%; Poverty rate: 32.4%
Educational Attainment: High school diploma or higher: 100.0%; Bachelor's degree or higher: 9.4%; Graduate/professional degree or higher: 9.4%
Housing: Homeownership rate: 93.2%; Median home value: $247,100; Median year structure built: 1972; Homeowner vacancy rate: 0.0%; Median selected monthly owner costs: $1,880 with a mortgage, n/a without a mortgage; Median gross rent: n/a per month; Rental vacancy rate: 0.0%
Health Insurance: 100.0% have insurance; 67.6% have private insurance; 49.3% have public insurance; 0.0% do not have insurance; 0.0% of children under 18 do not have insurance
Transportation: Commute: 75.9% car, 0.0% public transportation, 0.0% walk, 24.1% work from home; Mean travel time to work: 19.4 minutes

DEXTER (village). Covers a land area of 0.692 square miles and a water area of 0.063 square miles. Located at 44.01° N. Lat; 76.04° W. Long. Elevation is 282 feet.
History: Incorporated 1855.
Population: 1,213; Growth (since 2000): 8.3%; Density: 1,754.0 persons per square mile; Race: 96.4% White, 0.9% Black/African American, 0.0% Asian, 0.0% American Indian/Alaska Native, 0.0% Native Hawaiian/Other Pacific Islander, 2.7% Two or more races, 1.5% Hispanic of any race; Average household size: 2.44; Median age: 34.4; Age under 18: 25.4%; Age 65 and over: 13.4%; Males per 100 females: 91.6; Marriage status: 31.4% never married, 53.6% now married, 3.8% separated, 4.3% widowed, 10.7% divorced; Foreign born: 1.2%; Speak English only: 99.0%; With disability: 21.5%; Veterans: 10.5%; Ancestry: 28.3% Irish, 16.5% French, 13.1% German, 12.4% English, 5.9% Scottish
Employment: 15.6% management, business, and financial, 0.6% computer, engineering, and science, 13.6% education, legal, community service, arts, and media, 7.8% healthcare practitioners, 21.6% service, 24.0% sales and office, 7.8% natural resources, construction, and maintenance, 8.8% production, transportation, and material moving
Income: Per capita: $21,704; Median household: $35,000; Average household: $52,993; Households with income of $100,000 or more: 17.8%; Poverty rate: 22.9%
Educational Attainment: High school diploma or higher: 84.8%; Bachelor's degree or higher: 14.5%; Graduate/professional degree or higher: 7.0%

School District(s)

General Brown Central SD (PK-12)

Enrollment: 1,522 . . . . (315) 779-2300

Housing: Homeownership rate: 55.5%; Median home value: $119,100; Median year structure built: 1941; Homeowner vacancy rate: 0.0%; Median selected monthly owner costs: $1,137 with a mortgage, $466 without a mortgage; Median gross rent: $500 per month; Rental vacancy rate: 4.4%

Health Insurance: 97.9% have insurance; 65.6% have private insurance; 49.3% have public insurance; 2.1% do not have insurance; 3.4% of children under 18 do not have insurance

Transportation: Commute: 97.4% car, 0.0% public transportation, 1.8% walk, 0.8% work from home; Mean travel time to work: 19.9 minutes

---

ELLISBURG (town). Covers a land area of 85.146 square miles and a water area of 1.419 square miles. Located at 43.75° N. Lat; 76.11° W. Long. Elevation is 328 feet.

Population: 3,500; Growth (since 2000): -1.2%; Density: 41.1 persons per square mile; Race: 96.9% White, 1.7% Black/African American, 0.1% Asian, 0.5% American Indian/Alaska Native, 0.1% Native Hawaiian/Other Pacific Islander, 0.8% Two or more races, 1.5% Hispanic of any race; Average household size: 2.64; Median age: 40.5; Age under 18: 25.8%; Age 65 and over: 19.7%; Males per 100 females: 101.4; Marriage status: 19.9% never married, 66.7% now married, 0.9% separated, 3.9% widowed, 9.5% divorced; Foreign born: 1.3%; Speak English only: 92.9%; With disability: 11.2%; Veterans: 10.4%; Ancestry: 18.6% Irish, 18.0% German, 17.1% English, 5.8% American, 4.0% Italian

Employment: 15.7% management, business, and financial, 2.2% computer, engineering, and science, 10.5% education, legal, community service, arts, and media, 2.4% healthcare practitioners, 16.7% service, 24.1% sales and office, 19.4% natural resources, construction, and maintenance, 9.1% production, transportation, and material moving

Income: Per capita: $31,121; Median household: $58,679; Average household: $82,495; Households with income of $100,000 or more: 20.1%; Poverty rate: 10.6%

Educational Attainment: High school diploma or higher: 89.7%; Bachelor's degree or higher: 17.0%; Graduate/professional degree or higher: 5.5%

Housing: Homeownership rate: 80.9%; Median home value: $136,400; Median year structure built: 1968; Homeowner vacancy rate: 1.5%; Median selected monthly owner costs: $1,138 with a mortgage, $479 without a mortgage; Median gross rent: $866 per month; Rental vacancy rate: 4.9%

Health Insurance: 86.8% have insurance; 63.8% have private insurance; 34.4% have public insurance; 13.2% do not have insurance; 15.7% of children under 18 do not have insurance

Transportation: Commute: 86.6% car, 0.0% public transportation, 4.3% walk, 8.6% work from home; Mean travel time to work: 26.2 minutes

---

ELLISBURG (village). Covers a land area of 1.015 square miles and a water area of 0 square miles. Located at 43.73° N. Lat; 76.13° W. Long. Elevation is 328 feet.

Population: 282; Growth (since 2000): 4.8%; Density: 278.0 persons per square mile; Race: 97.2% White, 0.4% Black/African American, 1.1% Asian, 0.0% American Indian/Alaska Native, 0.7% Native Hawaiian/Other Pacific Islander, 0.7% Two or more races, 4.3% Hispanic of any race; Average household size: 2.85; Median age: 30.8; Age under 18: 30.5%; Age 65 and over: 11.3%; Males per 100 females: 108.5; Marriage status: 19.6% never married, 61.8% now married, 3.0% separated, 3.0% widowed, 15.6% divorced; Foreign born: 2.1%; Speak English only: 96.8%; With disability: 17.4%; Veterans: 13.8%; Ancestry: 16.0% German, 14.2% Irish, 13.1% English, 11.7% American, 8.2% Polish

Employment: 8.8% management, business, and financial, 7.2% computer, engineering, and science, 4.8% education, legal, community service, arts, and media, 1.6% healthcare practitioners, 16.0% service, 31.2% sales and office, 23.2% natural resources, construction, and maintenance, 7.2% production, transportation, and material moving

Income: Per capita: $20,812; Median household: $47,292; Average household: $57,841; Households with income of $100,000 or more: 14.1%; Poverty rate: 19.1%

Educational Attainment: High school diploma or higher: 93.9%; Bachelor's degree or higher: 14.5%; Graduate/professional degree or higher: 4.5%

Housing: Homeownership rate: 59.6%; Median home value: $134,200; Median year structure built: Before 1940; Homeowner vacancy rate: 0.0%; Median selected monthly owner costs: $1,054 with a mortgage, $400

without a mortgage; Median gross rent: $796 per month; Rental vacancy rate: 0.0%

Health Insurance: 94.0% have insurance; 61.0% have private insurance; 43.3% have public insurance; 6.0% do not have insurance; 0.0% of children under 18 do not have insurance

Transportation: Commute: 97.4% car, 0.0% public transportation, 0.9% walk, 0.0% work from home; Mean travel time to work: 27.3 minutes

---

EVANS MILLS (village). Covers a land area of 0.829 square miles and a water area of 0 square miles. Located at 44.09° N. Lat; 75.81° W. Long. Elevation is 423 feet.

Population: 463; Growth (since 2000): -23.5%; Density: 558.5 persons per square mile; Race: 94.8% White, 1.9% Black/African American, 0.4% Asian, 0.2% American Indian/Alaska Native, 0.0% Native Hawaiian/Other Pacific Islander, 2.6% Two or more races, 7.1% Hispanic of any race; Average household size: 2.14; Median age: 37.3; Age under 18: 14.9%; Age 65 and over: 14.9%; Males per 100 females: 103.6; Marriage status: 28.3% never married, 57.6% now married, 3.4% separated, 5.9% widowed, 8.3% divorced; Foreign born: 3.5%; Speak English only: 94.3%; With disability: 19.8%; Veterans: 23.1%; Ancestry: 19.9% Irish, 18.8% German, 9.3% French, 7.8% English, 7.6% Italian

Employment: 12.5% management, business, and financial, 2.3% computer, engineering, and science, 8.3% education, legal, community service, arts, and media, 7.4% healthcare practitioners, 20.8% service, 19.4% sales and office, 16.7% natural resources, construction, and maintenance, 12.5% production, transportation, and material moving

Income: Per capita: $28,385; Median household: $47,321; Average household: $63,096; Households with income of $100,000 or more: 20.1%; Poverty rate: 9.1%

Educational Attainment: High school diploma or higher: 88.8%; Bachelor's degree or higher: 23.1%; Graduate/professional degree or higher: 9.4%

School District(s)

Indian River Central SD (PK-12)

Enrollment: 3,820 . . . . (315) 642-3441

Housing: Homeownership rate: 52.2%; Median home value: $161,600; Median year structure built: 1951; Homeowner vacancy rate: 3.5%; Median selected monthly owner costs: $1,647 with a mortgage, $443 without a mortgage; Median gross rent: $822 per month; Rental vacancy rate: 7.1%

Health Insurance: 92.5% have insurance; 71.0% have private insurance; 40.3% have public insurance; 7.5% do not have insurance; 17.1% of children under 18 do not have insurance

Transportation: Commute: 93.3% car, 0.4% public transportation, 3.1% walk, 1.2% work from home; Mean travel time to work: 20.1 minutes

---

FELTS MILLS (CDP). Covers a land area of 0.329 square miles and a water area of 0 square miles. Located at 44.02° N. Lat; 75.76° W. Long. Elevation is 584 feet.

Population: 364; Growth (since 2000): n/a; Density: 1,107.2 persons per square mile; Race: 100.0% White, 0.0% Black/African American, 0.0% Asian, 0.0% American Indian/Alaska Native, 0.0% Native Hawaiian/Other Pacific Islander, 0.0% Two or more races, 8.5% Hispanic of any race; Average household size: 2.25; Median age: 33.4; Age under 18: 26.1%; Age 65 and over: 1.6%; Males per 100 females: 95.8; Marriage status: 24.2% never married, 59.1% now married, 23.8% separated, 11.5% widowed, 5.2% divorced; Foreign born: 0.0%; Speak English only: 90.4%; With disability: 23.6%; Veterans: 11.3%; Ancestry: 22.0% Irish, 17.3% English, 16.2% Polish, 14.8% French, 12.9% German

Employment: 9.5% management, business, and financial, 0.0% computer, engineering, and science, 0.0% education, legal, community service, arts, and media, 0.0% healthcare practitioners, 40.8% service, 14.8% sales and office, 6.5% natural resources, construction, and maintenance, 28.4% production, transportation, and material moving

Income: Per capita: $20,214; Median household: $39,886; Average household: $44,063; Households with income of $100,000 or more: n/a; Poverty rate: 3.3%

Educational Attainment: High school diploma or higher: 100.0%; Bachelor's degree or higher: 14.1%; Graduate/professional degree or higher: 6.1%

Housing: Homeownership rate: 84.6%; Median home value: n/a; Median year structure built: 1956; Homeowner vacancy rate: 0.0%; Median selected monthly owner costs: n/a with a mortgage, $349 without a mortgage; Median gross rent: $1,240 per month; Rental vacancy rate: 40.5%

Health Insurance: 94.2% have insurance; 74.1% have private insurance; 21.9% have public insurance; 5.8% do not have insurance; 0.0% of children under 18 do not have insurance
Transportation: Commute: 95.8% car, 0.0% public transportation, 4.2% walk, 0.0% work from home; Mean travel time to work: 12.3 minutes

FISHERS LANDING (CDP).
Covers a land area of 0.222 square miles and a water area of 0.002 square miles. Located at 44.28° N. Lat; 76.00° W. Long. Elevation is 262 feet.
Population: 59; Growth (since 2000): n/a; Density: 265.3 persons per square mile; Race: 100.0% White, 0.0% Black/African American, 0.0% Asian, 0.0% American Indian/Alaska Native, 0.0% Native Hawaiian/Other Pacific Islander, 0.0% Two or more races, 0.0% Hispanic of any race; Average household size: 1.74; Median age: 79.1; Age under 18: 0.0%; Age 65 and over: 66.1%; Males per 100 females: 102.3; Marriage status: 0.0% never married, 79.7% now married, 0.0% separated, 20.3% widowed, 0.0% divorced; Foreign born: 6.8%; Speak English only: 100.0%; With disability: 15.3%; Veterans: 40.7%; Ancestry: 28.8% Irish, 23.7% English, 22.0% German, 16.9% French, 8.5% Italian
Employment: 33.3% management, business, and financial, 0.0% computer, engineering, and science, 33.3% education, legal, community service, arts, and media, 0.0% healthcare practitioners, 33.3% service, 0.0% sales and office, 0.0% natural resources, construction, and maintenance, 0.0% production, transportation, and material moving
Income: Per capita: $32,400; Median household: n/a; Average household: $53,126; Households with income of $100,000 or more: 14.7%; Poverty rate: n/a
Educational Attainment: High school diploma or higher: 93.2%; Bachelor's degree or higher: 8.5%; Graduate/professional degree or higher: n/a
Housing: Homeownership rate: 100.0%; Median home value: $183,300; Median year structure built: 1985; Homeowner vacancy rate: 0.0%; Median selected monthly owner costs: n/a with a mortgage, $491 without a mortgage; Median gross rent: n/a per month; Rental vacancy rate: 100.0%
Health Insurance: 100.0% have insurance; 93.2% have private insurance; 66.1% have public insurance; 0.0% do not have insurance; 0.0% of children under 18 do not have insurance
Transportation: Commute: 100.0% car, 0.0% public transportation, 0.0% walk, 0.0% work from home; Mean travel time to work: 0.0 minutes

FORT DRUM (CDP).
Covers a land area of 14.329 square miles and a water area of 0.093 square miles. Located at 44.04° N. Lat; 75.79° W. Long.
Population: 13,819; Growth (since 2000): 14.0%; Density: 964.4 persons per square mile; Race: 66.4% White, 15.6% Black/African American, 1.8% Asian, 2.2% American Indian/Alaska Native, 2.0% Native Hawaiian/Other Pacific Islander, 7.7% Two or more races, 22.6% Hispanic of any race; Average household size: 3.02; Median age: 21.9; Age under 18: 29.7%; Age 65 and over: 0.1%; Males per 100 females: 135.5; Marriage status: 41.1% never married, 56.5% now married, 1.0% separated, 0.5% widowed, 1.9% divorced; Foreign born: 6.9%; Speak English only: 84.1%; With disability: 5.2%; Veterans: 16.5%; Ancestry: 18.7% German, 12.1% Irish, 6.6% Italian, 3.7% Polish, 3.6% English
Employment: 11.5% management, business, and financial, 5.8% computer, engineering, and science, 7.4% education, legal, community service, arts, and media, 5.7% healthcare practitioners, 26.2% service, 27.7% sales and office, 11.1% natural resources, construction, and maintenance, 4.6% production, transportation, and material moving
Income: Per capita: $18,442; Median household: $42,623; Average household: $51,499; Households with income of $100,000 or more: 8.5%; Poverty rate: 13.9%
Educational Attainment: High school diploma or higher: 95.4%; Bachelor's degree or higher: 25.0%; Graduate/professional degree or higher: 9.6%
Housing: Homeownership rate: 1.1%; Median home value: $157,700; Median year structure built: 1998; Homeowner vacancy rate: 0.0%; Median selected monthly owner costs: n/a with a mortgage, n/a without a mortgage; Median gross rent: $1,423 per month; Rental vacancy rate: 4.0%
Health Insurance: 97.4% have insurance; 93.0% have private insurance; 8.1% have public insurance; 2.6% do not have insurance; 0.7% of children under 18 do not have insurance
Transportation: Commute: 58.8% car, 0.0% public transportation, 25.3% walk, 12.2% work from home; Mean travel time to work: 8.6 minutes
Airports: Wheeler-Sack AAF (general aviation)

GLEN PARK (village).
Covers a land area of 0.708 square miles and a water area of 0.024 square miles. Located at 44.00° N. Lat; 75.96° W. Long. Elevation is 341 feet.
Population: 607; Growth (since 2000): 24.6%; Density: 857.2 persons per square mile; Race: 96.0% White, 0.3% Black/African American, 0.0% Asian, 0.0% American Indian/Alaska Native, 0.0% Native Hawaiian/Other Pacific Islander, 3.5% Two or more races, 0.7% Hispanic of any race; Average household size: 2.88; Median age: 35.3; Age under 18: 28.7%; Age 65 and over: 10.9%; Males per 100 females: 107.4; Marriage status: 29.4% never married, 55.7% now married, 2.7% separated, 6.5% widowed, 8.5% divorced; Foreign born: 1.0%; Speak English only: 98.7%; With disability: 15.6%; Veterans: 14.3%; Ancestry: 27.3% Irish, 18.1% German, 16.6% Italian, 12.5% English, 8.9% French
Employment: 12.7% management, business, and financial, 3.1% computer, engineering, and science, 12.4% education, legal, community service, arts, and media, 6.2% healthcare practitioners, 15.1% service, 30.2% sales and office, 10.0% natural resources, construction, and maintenance, 10.3% production, transportation, and material moving
Income: Per capita: $24,364; Median household: $52,917; Average household: $67,679; Households with income of $100,000 or more: 23.2%; Poverty rate: 12.5%
Educational Attainment: High school diploma or higher: 86.9%; Bachelor's degree or higher: 19.2%; Graduate/professional degree or higher: 6.2%
Housing: Homeownership rate: 77.7%; Median home value: $122,600; Median year structure built: Before 1940; Homeowner vacancy rate: 4.4%; Median selected monthly owner costs: $1,074 with a mortgage, $422 without a mortgage; Median gross rent: $925 per month; Rental vacancy rate: 0.0%
Health Insurance: 96.8% have insurance; 66.7% have private insurance; 41.9% have public insurance; 3.2% do not have insurance; 0.0% of children under 18 do not have insurance
Safety: Violent crime rate: 0.0 per 10,000 population; Property crime rate: 61.2 per 10,000 population
Transportation: Commute: 97.6% car, 0.0% public transportation, 0.7% walk, 0.7% work from home; Mean travel time to work: 18.7 minutes

GREAT BEND (CDP).
Covers a land area of 5.788 square miles and a water area of 0.056 square miles. Located at 44.02° N. Lat; 75.70° W. Long. Elevation is 663 feet.
Population: 1,023; Growth (since 2000): 27.7%; Density: 176.7 persons per square mile; Race: 91.4% White, 0.7% Black/African American, 1.2% Asian, 0.0% American Indian/Alaska Native, 1.8% Native Hawaiian/Other Pacific Islander, 3.8% Two or more races, 8.1% Hispanic of any race; Average household size: 2.72; Median age: 45.5; Age under 18: 16.9%; Age 65 and over: 26.3%; Males per 100 females: 112.3; Marriage status: 32.6% never married, 60.4% now married, 0.9% separated, 0.9% widowed, 6.1% divorced; Foreign born: 4.1%; Speak English only: 95.4%; With disability: 21.9%; Veterans: 27.8%; Ancestry: 26.5% French, 5.1% German, 5.1% Polish, 4.2% American, 3.9% English
Employment: 4.3% management, business, and financial, 0.0% computer, engineering, and science, 19.1% education, legal, community service, arts, and media, 5.7% healthcare practitioners, 15.9% service, 23.7% sales and office, 9.6% natural resources, construction, and maintenance, 21.6% production, transportation, and material moving
Income: Per capita: $24,943; Median household: $75,132; Average household: $64,165; Households with income of $100,000 or more: 22.3%; Poverty rate: 4.6%
Educational Attainment: High school diploma or higher: 93.3%; Bachelor's degree or higher: 16.2%; Graduate/professional degree or higher: 3.1%
Housing: Homeownership rate: 86.4%; Median home value: $116,400; Median year structure built: 1971; Homeowner vacancy rate: 6.6%; Median selected monthly owner costs: $1,011 with a mortgage, $376 without a mortgage; Median gross rent: $1,242 per month; Rental vacancy rate: 0.0%
Health Insurance: 93.2% have insurance; 56.6% have private insurance; 52.9% have public insurance; 6.8% do not have insurance; 16.5% of children under 18 do not have insurance
Transportation: Commute: 90.0% car, 0.0% public transportation, 0.0% walk, 6.6% work from home; Mean travel time to work: 18.6 minutes

HENDERSON (CDP). Covers a land area of 0.506 square miles and a water area of 0 square miles. Located at 43.85° N. Lat; 76.19° W. Long. Elevation is 348 feet.

Population: 163; Growth (since 2000): n/a; Density: 322.2 persons per square mile; Race: 95.7% White, 4.3% Black/African American, 0.0% Asian, 0.0% American Indian/Alaska Native, 0.0% Native Hawaiian/Other Pacific Islander, 0.0% Two or more races, 0.0% Hispanic of any race; Average household size: 2.06; Median age: 54.2; Age under 18: 10.4%; Age 65 and over: 34.4%; Males per 100 females: 88.2; Marriage status: 31.4% never married, 45.1% now married, 4.6% separated, 11.1% widowed, 12.4% divorced; Foreign born: 0.0%; Speak English only: 98.1%; With disability: 21.5%; Veterans: 13.5%; Ancestry: 26.4% Irish, 12.9% German, 8.6% English, 6.7% American, 5.5% French Canadian

Employment: 5.4% management, business, and financial, 0.0% computer, engineering, and science, 5.4% education, legal, community service, arts, and media, 2.7% healthcare practitioners, 13.5% service, 23.0% sales and office, 21.6% natural resources, construction, and maintenance, 28.4% production, transportation, and material moving

Income: Per capita: $22,629; Median household: $32,361; Average household: $48,842; Households with income of $100,000 or more: 13.9%; Poverty rate: 12.3%

Educational Attainment: High school diploma or higher: 89.9%; Bachelor's degree or higher: 9.3%; Graduate/professional degree or higher: 1.6%

Housing: Homeownership rate: 68.4%; Median home value: $105,000; Median year structure built: Before 1940; Homeowner vacancy rate: 14.3%; Median selected monthly owner costs: $1,075 with a mortgage, $431 without a mortgage; Median gross rent: $373 per month; Rental vacancy rate: 0.0%

Health Insurance: 96.8% have insurance; 69.0% have private insurance; 59.5% have public insurance; 3.2% do not have insurance; 0.0% of children under 18 do not have insurance

Transportation: Commute: 96.2% car, 0.0% public transportation, 3.8% walk, 0.0% work from home; Mean travel time to work: 26.2 minutes

HENDERSON (town). Covers a land area of 41.180 square miles and a water area of 11.756 square miles. Located at 43.86° N. Lat; 76.18° W. Long. Elevation is 348 feet.

Population: 1,509; Growth (since 2000): 9.6%; Density: 36.6 persons per square mile; Race: 97.4% White, 0.5% Black/African American, 0.0% Asian, 0.0% American Indian/Alaska Native, 0.0% Native Hawaiian/Other Pacific Islander, 1.6% Two or more races, 0.5% Hispanic of any race; Average household size: 2.26; Median age: 54.7; Age under 18: 13.9%; Age 65 and over: 34.4%; Males per 100 females: 102.4; Marriage status: 18.8% never married, 67.0% now married, 2.0% separated, 6.1% widowed, 8.1% divorced; Foreign born: 0.5%; Speak English only: 98.7%; With disability: 14.2%; Veterans: 11.5%; Ancestry: 19.8% English, 15.3% German, 12.5% Italian, 10.4% Irish, 8.7% American

Employment: 13.9% management, business, and financial, 1.4% computer, engineering, and science, 8.5% education, legal, community service, arts, and media, 3.5% healthcare practitioners, 12.6% service, 33.0% sales and office, 20.2% natural resources, construction, and maintenance, 7.0% production, transportation, and material moving

Income: Per capita: $37,008; Median household: $64,250; Average household: $83,534; Households with income of $100,000 or more: 33.0%; Poverty rate: 5.2%

Educational Attainment: High school diploma or higher: 90.8%; Bachelor's degree or higher: 24.2%; Graduate/professional degree or higher: 7.7%

Housing: Homeownership rate: 83.4%; Median home value: $175,800; Median year structure built: 1969; Homeowner vacancy rate: 5.6%; Median selected monthly owner costs: $1,349 with a mortgage, $526 without a mortgage; Median gross rent: $595 per month; Rental vacancy rate: 14.0%

Health Insurance: 98.1% have insurance; 77.8% have private insurance; 50.1% have public insurance; 1.9% do not have insurance; 0.0% of children under 18 do not have insurance

Transportation: Commute: 93.3% car, 0.0% public transportation, 2.4% walk, 3.5% work from home; Mean travel time to work: 24.2 minutes

HENDERSON HARBOR (unincorporated postal area)
ZCTA: 13651
Covers a land area of 2.449 square miles and a water area of 0.202 square miles. Located at 43.87° N. Lat; 76.18° W. Long. Elevation is 246 feet.

Population: 156; Growth (since 2000): n/a; Density: 63.7 persons per square mile; Race: 100.0% White, 0.0% Black/African American, 0.0% Asian, 0.0% American Indian/Alaska Native, 0.0% Native Hawaiian/Other Pacific Islander, 0.0% Two or more races, 0.0% Hispanic of any race; Average household size: 1.93; Median age: 67.2; Age under 18: 9.0%; Age 65 and over: 57.1%; Males per 100 females: 101.6; Marriage status: 4.8% never married, 80.0% now married, 0.0% separated, 2.1% widowed, 13.1% divorced; Foreign born: 0.0%; Speak English only: 100.0%; With disability: 3.9%; Veterans: 18.1%; Ancestry: 28.8% English, 16.7% French, 16.0% Irish, 15.4% Italian, 10.3% German

Employment: 35.8% management, business, and financial, 7.5% computer, engineering, and science, 17.0% education, legal, community service, arts, and media, 11.3% healthcare practitioners, 11.3% service, 17.0% sales and office, 0.0% natural resources, construction, and maintenance, 0.0% production, transportation, and material moving

Income: Per capita: $67,780; Median household: $105,417; Average household: $129,527; Households with income of $100,000 or more: 50.7%; Poverty rate: 1.9%

Educational Attainment: High school diploma or higher: 100.0%; Bachelor's degree or higher: 50.7%; Graduate/professional degree or higher: 27.5%

Housing: Homeownership rate: 75.3%; Median home value: $361,100; Median year structure built: 1964; Homeowner vacancy rate: 9.0%; Median selected monthly owner costs: $2,250 with a mortgage, $936 without a mortgage; Median gross rent: n/a per month; Rental vacancy rate: 0.0%

Health Insurance: 100.0% have insurance; 94.7% have private insurance; 63.8% have public insurance; 0.0% do not have insurance; 0.0% of children under 18 do not have insurance

Transportation: Commute: 84.2% car, 0.0% public transportation, 15.8% walk, 0.0% work from home; Mean travel time to work: 22.7 minutes

HERRINGS (village). Covers a land area of 0.281 square miles and a water area of 0.049 square miles. Located at 44.02° N. Lat; 75.66° W. Long. Elevation is 689 feet.

Population: 68; Growth (since 2000): -47.3%; Density: 241.7 persons per square mile; Race: 88.2% White, 1.5% Black/African American, 2.9% Asian, 0.0% American Indian/Alaska Native, 0.0% Native Hawaiian/Other Pacific Islander, 2.9% Two or more races, 4.4% Hispanic of any race; Average household size: 2.72; Median age: 56.7; Age under 18: 8.8%; Age 65 and over: 23.5%; Males per 100 females: 95.7; Marriage status: 23.4% never married, 60.9% now married, 0.0% separated, 6.3% widowed, 9.4% divorced; Foreign born: 8.8%; Speak English only: 88.2%; With disability: 21.2%; Veterans: 30.0%; Ancestry: 38.2% Irish, 13.2% German, 11.8% Ukrainian, 8.8% American, 5.9% English

Employment: 9.4% management, business, and financial, 0.0% computer, engineering, and science, 6.3% education, legal, community service, arts, and media, 3.1% healthcare practitioners, 28.1% service, 12.5% sales and office, 3.1% natural resources, construction, and maintenance, 37.5% production, transportation, and material moving

Income: Per capita: $24,922; Median household: $61,750; Average household: $70,196; Households with income of $100,000 or more: 28.0%; Poverty rate: 4.4%

Educational Attainment: High school diploma or higher: 83.1%; Bachelor's degree or higher: 8.5%; Graduate/professional degree or higher: 8.5%

Housing: Homeownership rate: 92.0%; Median home value: $91,700; Median year structure built: Before 1940; Homeowner vacancy rate: 0.0%; Median selected monthly owner costs: $867 with a mortgage, $483 without a mortgage; Median gross rent: n/a per month; Rental vacancy rate: 0.0%

Health Insurance: 97.0% have insurance; 75.8% have private insurance; 42.4% have public insurance; 3.0% do not have insurance; 0.0% of children under 18 do not have insurance

Transportation: Commute: 96.9% car, 0.0% public transportation, 0.0% walk, 0.0% work from home; Mean travel time to work: 26.4 minutes

HOUNSFIELD (town). Covers a land area of 48.915 square miles and a water area of 71.488 square miles. Located at 43.91° N. Lat; 76.31° W. Long.

Population: 3,476; Growth (since 2000): 4.6%; Density: 71.1 persons per square mile; Race: 95.1% White, 0.8% Black/African American, 1.6% Asian, 0.0% American Indian/Alaska Native, 0.0% Native Hawaiian/Other Pacific Islander, 2.0% Two or more races, 2.7% Hispanic of any race;

Average household size: 2.46; Median age: 33.5; Age under 18: 29.4%; Age 65 and over: 13.2%; Males per 100 females: 96.5; Marriage status: 30.4% never married, 55.2% now married, 2.1% separated, 4.5% widowed, 9.9% divorced; Foreign born: 6.2%; Speak English only: 87.9%; With disability: 13.6%; Veterans: 13.9%; Ancestry: 22.0% German, 17.1% Irish, 15.1% English, 7.9% French, 7.6% Italian

Employment: 9.0% management, business, and financial, 5.9% computer, engineering, and science, 11.0% education, legal, community service, arts, and media, 13.1% healthcare practitioners, 10.2% service, 23.6% sales and office, 15.0% natural resources, construction, and maintenance, 12.1% production, transportation, and material moving

Income: Per capita: $28,131; Median household: $52,971; Average household: $68,442; Households with income of $100,000 or more: 22.9%; Poverty rate: 18.0%

Educational Attainment: High school diploma or higher: 92.3%; Bachelor's degree or higher: 34.9%; Graduate/professional degree or higher: 15.7%

Housing: Homeownership rate: 52.1%; Median home value: $238,300; Median year structure built: 1982; Homeowner vacancy rate: 0.0%; Median selected monthly owner costs: $1,763 with a mortgage, $574 without a mortgage; Median gross rent: $1,022 per month; Rental vacancy rate: 6.5%

Health Insurance: 95.3% have insurance; 66.8% have private insurance; 42.7% have public insurance; 4.7% do not have insurance; 2.6% of children under 18 do not have insurance

Transportation: Commute: 92.1% car, 0.4% public transportation, 3.1% walk, 3.8% work from home; Mean travel time to work: 24.8 minutes

LA FARGEVILLE (CDP). Covers a land area of 3.318 square miles and a water area of 0.055 square miles. Located at 44.20° N. Lat; 75.96° W. Long. Elevation is 377 feet.

Population: 668; Growth (since 2000): 13.6%; Density: 201.3 persons per square mile; Race: 99.0% White, 0.0% Black/African American, 0.0% Asian, 0.0% American Indian/Alaska Native, 0.0% Native Hawaiian/Other Pacific Islander, 1.0% Two or more races, 2.8% Hispanic of any race; Average household size: 3.48; Median age: 40.7; Age under 18: 28.0%; Age 65 and over: 7.3%; Males per 100 females: 91.8; Marriage status: 32.9% never married, 53.3% now married, 4.0% separated, 7.1% widowed, 6.7% divorced; Foreign born: 3.9%; Speak English only: 97.6%; With disability: 7.8%; Veterans: 11.4%; Ancestry: 21.9% German, 14.5% Irish, 9.9% Italian, 9.4% English, 9.3% Scottish

Employment: 7.4% management, business, and financial, 6.6% computer, engineering, and science, 19.2% education, legal, community service, arts, and media, 5.9% healthcare practitioners, 3.3% service, 17.3% sales and office, 17.7% natural resources, construction, and maintenance, 22.5% production, transportation, and material moving

Income: Per capita: $25,623; Median household: $75,000; Average household: $87,441; Households with income of $100,000 or more: 22.9%; Poverty rate: 0.4%

Educational Attainment: High school diploma or higher: 90.0%; Bachelor's degree or higher: 28.9%; Graduate/professional degree or higher: 11.3%

School District(s)

La Fargeville Central SD (PK-12)

   Enrollment: 540 . . . . (315) 658-2241

Housing: Homeownership rate: 92.7%; Median home value: $124,300; Median year structure built: Before 1940; Homeowner vacancy rate: 0.0%; Median selected monthly owner costs: $1,297 with a mortgage, $383 without a mortgage; Median gross rent: $600 per month; Rental vacancy rate: 0.0%

Health Insurance: 89.1% have insurance; 64.7% have private insurance; 34.9% have public insurance; 10.9% do not have insurance; 16.3% of children under 18 do not have insurance

Transportation: Commute: 91.1% car, 0.0% public transportation, 0.0% walk, 8.9% work from home; Mean travel time to work: 21.0 minutes

LE RAY (town). Covers a land area of 73.643 square miles and a water area of 0.361 square miles. Located at 44.08° N. Lat; 75.80° W. Long.

Population: 22,473; Growth (since 2000): 13.3%; Density: 305.2 persons per square mile; Race: 68.3% White, 14.7% Black/African American, 2.9% Asian, 1.5% American Indian/Alaska Native, 1.2% Native Hawaiian/Other Pacific Islander, 7.3% Two or more races, 19.4% Hispanic of any race; Average household size: 2.80; Median age: 23.3; Age under 18: 27.6%; Age 65 and over: 2.1%; Males per 100 females: 123.5; Marriage status: 35.1% never married, 59.6% now married, 1.7% separated, 1.5%

widowed, 3.8% divorced; Foreign born: 6.5%; Speak English only: 85.4%; With disability: 6.5%; Veterans: 18.4%; Ancestry: 15.5% German, 11.9% Irish, 7.4% Italian, 5.1% English, 5.1% French

Employment: 11.7% management, business, and financial, 5.2% computer, engineering, and science, 10.4% education, legal, community service, arts, and media, 4.8% healthcare practitioners, 21.7% service, 26.9% sales and office, 11.7% natural resources, construction, and maintenance, 7.6% production, transportation, and material moving

Income: Per capita: $21,133; Median household: $48,759; Average household: $57,568; Households with income of $100,000 or more: 11.0%; Poverty rate: 10.8%

Educational Attainment: High school diploma or higher: 93.5%; Bachelor's degree or higher: 25.4%; Graduate/professional degree or higher: 8.4%

Housing: Homeownership rate: 17.4%; Median home value: $182,800; Median year structure built: 1994; Homeowner vacancy rate: 3.0%; Median selected monthly owner costs: $1,692 with a mortgage, $413 without a mortgage; Median gross rent: $1,308 per month; Rental vacancy rate: 6.5%

Health Insurance: 95.1% have insurance; 85.4% have private insurance; 16.6% have public insurance; 4.9% do not have insurance; 1.7% of children under 18 do not have insurance

Transportation: Commute: 70.4% car, 0.0% public transportation, 17.4% walk, 9.3% work from home; Mean travel time to work: 10.6 minutes

Additional Information Contacts

Town of Le Ray . . . . (315) 629-4052

   http://townofleray.org

LORRAINE (CDP). Covers a land area of 0.483 square miles and a water area of 0 square miles. Located at 43.77° N. Lat; 75.95° W. Long. Elevation is 1,001 feet.

Population: 77; Growth (since 2000): n/a; Density: 159.5 persons per square mile; Race: 100.0% White, 0.0% Black/African American, 0.0% Asian, 0.0% American Indian/Alaska Native, 0.0% Native Hawaiian/Other Pacific Islander, 0.0% Two or more races, 0.0% Hispanic of any race; Average household size: 2.48; Median age: 57.6; Age under 18: 7.8%; Age 65 and over: 29.9%; Males per 100 females: 102.3; Marriage status: 23.3% never married, 57.5% now married, 0.0% separated, 4.1% widowed, 15.1% divorced; Foreign born: 0.0%; Speak English only: 100.0%; With disability: 27.3%; Veterans: 22.5%; Ancestry: 15.6% French, 11.7% German, 9.1% Italian, 6.5% French Canadian, 3.9% American

Employment: 0.0% management, business, and financial, 0.0% computer, engineering, and science, 0.0% education, legal, community service, arts, and media, 13.3% healthcare practitioners, 50.0% service, 0.0% sales and office, 13.3% natural resources, construction, and maintenance, 23.3% production, transportation, and material moving

Income: Per capita: $19,373; Median household: $35,417; Average household: $50,219; Households with income of $100,000 or more: 9.7%; Poverty rate: 11.7%

Educational Attainment: High school diploma or higher: 80.0%; Bachelor's degree or higher: 4.6%; Graduate/professional degree or higher: 1.5%

Housing: Homeownership rate: 90.3%; Median home value: $91,700; Median year structure built: Before 1940; Homeowner vacancy rate: 0.0%; Median selected monthly owner costs: $925 with a mortgage, $470 without a mortgage; Median gross rent: n/a per month; Rental vacancy rate: 75.0%

Health Insurance: 97.4% have insurance; 55.8% have private insurance; 70.1% have public insurance; 2.6% do not have insurance; 0.0% of children under 18 do not have insurance

Transportation: Commute: 100.0% car, 0.0% public transportation, 0.0% walk, 0.0% work from home; Mean travel time to work: 24.0 minutes

LORRAINE (town). Covers a land area of 38.979 square miles and a water area of 0.018 square miles. Located at 43.75° N. Lat; 75.98° W. Long. Elevation is 1,001 feet.

Population: 846; Growth (since 2000): -9.0%; Density: 21.7 persons per square mile; Race: 97.4% White, 0.7% Black/African American, 0.5% Asian, 0.2% American Indian/Alaska Native, 0.0% Native Hawaiian/Other Pacific Islander, 0.9% Two or more races, 0.6% Hispanic of any race; Average household size: 2.67; Median age: 45.0; Age under 18: 20.6%; Age 65 and over: 12.6%; Males per 100 females: 103.7; Marriage status: 23.6% never married, 60.6% now married, 2.3% separated, 4.5% widowed, 11.3% divorced; Foreign born: 0.9%; Speak English only: 98.7%; With disability: 15.8%; Veterans: 10.6%; Ancestry: 15.2% English, 13.9% German, 13.5% Irish, 12.9% American, 12.8% French

Employment: 8.1% management, business, and financial, 1.9% computer, engineering, and science, 7.8% education, legal, community service, arts, and media, 6.1% healthcare practitioners, 23.1% service, 20.3% sales and office, 10.8% natural resources, construction, and maintenance, 21.9% production, transportation, and material moving
Income: Per capita: $21,978; Median household: $43,068; Average household: $58,206; Households with income of $100,000 or more: 19.2%; Poverty rate: 17.4%
Educational Attainment: High school diploma or higher: 83.9%; Bachelor's degree or higher: 13.8%; Graduate/professional degree or higher: 2.0%
Housing: Homeownership rate: 84.9%; Median home value: $108,800; Median year structure built: 1987; Homeowner vacancy rate: 1.1%; Median selected monthly owner costs: $1,188 with a mortgage, $453 without a mortgage; Median gross rent: $784 per month; Rental vacancy rate: 25.0%
Health Insurance: 88.9% have insurance; 55.2% have private insurance; 42.8% have public insurance; 11.1% do not have insurance; 4.9% of children under 18 do not have insurance
Transportation: Commute: 94.0% car, 0.0% public transportation, 1.7% walk, 3.7% work from home; Mean travel time to work: 24.9 minutes

---

LYME (town). Covers a land area of 55.813 square miles and a water area of 51.178 square miles. Located at 44.02° N. Lat; 76.23° W. Long.
Population: 2,451; Growth (since 2000): 21.6%; Density: 43.9 persons per square mile; Race: 97.1% White, 0.3% Black/African American, 0.2% Asian, 0.1% American Indian/Alaska Native, 0.0% Native Hawaiian/Other Pacific Islander, 2.3% Two or more races, 2.1% Hispanic of any race; Average household size: 2.57; Median age: 43.7; Age under 18: 22.3%; Age 65 and over: 19.4%; Males per 100 females: 101.9; Marriage status: 23.8% never married, 61.5% now married, 0.4% separated, 5.7% widowed, 9.0% divorced; Foreign born: 2.2%; Speak English only: 97.9%; With disability: 17.3%; Veterans: 8.8%; Ancestry: 23.1% Irish, 21.1% German, 9.6% English, 9.6% Italian, 7.8% French
Employment: 13.7% management, business, and financial, 1.9% computer, engineering, and science, 10.8% education, legal, community service, arts, and media, 3.8% healthcare practitioners, 31.4% service, 17.6% sales and office, 9.7% natural resources, construction, and maintenance, 11.0% production, transportation, and material moving
Income: Per capita: $28,016; Median household: $49,000; Average household: $71,856; Households with income of $100,000 or more: 24.5%; Poverty rate: 12.1%
Educational Attainment: High school diploma or higher: 89.4%; Bachelor's degree or higher: 22.3%; Graduate/professional degree or higher: 9.1%
Housing: Homeownership rate: 79.9%; Median home value: $161,000; Median year structure built: 1971; Homeowner vacancy rate: 3.6%; Median selected monthly owner costs: $1,421 with a mortgage, $515 without a mortgage; Median gross rent: $1,059 per month; Rental vacancy rate: 3.0%
Health Insurance: 95.7% have insurance; 64.7% have private insurance; 45.4% have public insurance; 4.3% do not have insurance; 4.1% of children under 18 do not have insurance
Transportation: Commute: 88.7% car, 0.2% public transportation, 4.9% walk, 5.7% work from home; Mean travel time to work: 22.3 minutes

---

MANNSVILLE (village). Covers a land area of 0.897 square miles and a water area of 0.033 square miles. Located at 43.72° N. Lat; 76.07° W. Long. Elevation is 620 feet.
Population: 404; Growth (since 2000): 1.0%; Density: 450.3 persons per square mile; Race: 88.4% White, 11.1% Black/African American, 0.0% Asian, 0.0% American Indian/Alaska Native, 0.0% Native Hawaiian/Other Pacific Islander, 0.5% Two or more races, 0.0% Hispanic of any race; Average household size: 2.95; Median age: 39.0; Age under 18: 24.8%; Age 65 and over: 14.9%; Males per 100 females: 91.4; Marriage status: 30.2% never married, 55.4% now married, 0.3% separated, 5.2% widowed, 9.2% divorced; Foreign born: 0.7%; Speak English only: 99.5%; With disability: 12.2%; Veterans: 20.5%; Ancestry: 22.3% German, 19.6% Irish, 13.4% English, 6.2% French Canadian, 5.0% French
Employment: 9.6% management, business, and financial, 2.1% computer, engineering, and science, 17.1% education, legal, community service, arts, and media, 8.2% healthcare practitioners, 17.1% service, 15.1% sales and office, 14.4% natural resources, construction, and maintenance, 16.4% production, transportation, and material moving

Income: Per capita: $25,728; Median household: $67,813; Average household: $73,433; Households with income of $100,000 or more: 23.4%; Poverty rate: 5.7%
Educational Attainment: High school diploma or higher: 88.1%; Bachelor's degree or higher: 17.0%; Graduate/professional degree or higher: 8.8%

School District(s)
South Jefferson Central SD (PK-12)
    Enrollment: 1,936 . . . . (315) 583-6104
Housing: Homeownership rate: 81.0%; Median home value: $134,400; Median year structure built: Before 1940; Homeowner vacancy rate: 0.0%; Median selected monthly owner costs: $1,222 with a mortgage, $442 without a mortgage; Median gross rent: $775 per month; Rental vacancy rate: 33.3%
Health Insurance: 83.6% have insurance; 67.2% have private insurance; 30.1% have public insurance; 16.4% do not have insurance; 1.9% of children under 18 do not have insurance
Transportation: Commute: 93.9% car, 0.0% public transportation, 1.4% walk, 1.4% work from home; Mean travel time to work: 28.1 minutes

---

NATURAL BRIDGE (CDP). Covers a land area of 1.389 square miles and a water area of 0 square miles. Located at 44.07° N. Lat; 75.50° W. Long. Elevation is 817 feet.
Population: 329; Growth (since 2000): -16.1%; Density: 236.8 persons per square mile; Race: 100.0% White, 0.0% Black/African American, 0.0% Asian, 0.0% American Indian/Alaska Native, 0.0% Native Hawaiian/Other Pacific Islander, 0.0% Two or more races, 0.0% Hispanic of any race; Average household size: 2.37; Median age: 49.6; Age under 18: 8.5%; Age 65 and over: 7.0%; Males per 100 females: 95.2; Marriage status: 24.3% never married, 58.8% now married, 0.0% separated, 7.6% widowed, 9.3% divorced; Foreign born: 0.0%; Speak English only: 100.0%; With disability: 38.6%; Veterans: 17.3%; Ancestry: 42.2% French, 41.6% English, 21.0% Italian, 17.9% Dutch, 11.9% German
Employment: 8.2% management, business, and financial, 0.0% computer, engineering, and science, 0.0% education, legal, community service, arts, and media, 10.1% healthcare practitioners, 22.2% service, 8.2% sales and office, 43.0% natural resources, construction, and maintenance, 8.2% production, transportation, and material moving
Income: Per capita: $30,458; Median household: n/a; Average household: $63,497; Households with income of $100,000 or more: 36.7%; Poverty rate: 3.3%
Educational Attainment: High school diploma or higher: 100.0%; Bachelor's degree or higher: n/a; Graduate/professional degree or higher: n/a
Housing: Homeownership rate: 90.6%; Median home value: n/a; Median year structure built: 1947; Homeowner vacancy rate: 0.0%; Median selected monthly owner costs: $916 with a mortgage, $491 without a mortgage; Median gross rent: n/a per month; Rental vacancy rate: 0.0%
Health Insurance: 76.0% have insurance; 59.0% have private insurance; 30.7% have public insurance; 24.0% do not have insurance; 0.0% of children under 18 do not have insurance
Transportation: Commute: 100.0% car, 0.0% public transportation, 0.0% walk, 0.0% work from home; Mean travel time to work: 19.5 minutes

---

ORLEANS (town). Covers a land area of 71.423 square miles and a water area of 6.620 square miles. Located at 44.22° N. Lat; 75.95° W. Long.
Population: 2,828; Growth (since 2000): 14.7%; Density: 39.6 persons per square mile; Race: 98.6% White, 0.4% Black/African American, 0.0% Asian, 0.3% American Indian/Alaska Native, 0.0% Native Hawaiian/Other Pacific Islander, 0.8% Two or more races, 2.5% Hispanic of any race; Average household size: 2.99; Median age: 41.8; Age under 18: 25.4%; Age 65 and over: 18.1%; Males per 100 females: 101.5; Marriage status: 29.2% never married, 57.4% now married, 3.0% separated, 6.8% widowed, 6.5% divorced; Foreign born: 1.6%; Speak English only: 89.8%; With disability: 11.6%; Veterans: 14.4%; Ancestry: 26.6% German, 19.1% Irish, 12.0% English, 10.2% French, 8.0% Italian
Employment: 8.9% management, business, and financial, 2.6% computer, engineering, and science, 10.9% education, legal, community service, arts, and media, 4.5% healthcare practitioners, 23.1% service, 16.8% sales and office, 17.1% natural resources, construction, and maintenance, 16.0% production, transportation, and material moving
Income: Per capita: $26,826; Median household: $61,438; Average household: $78,790; Households with income of $100,000 or more: 26.2%; Poverty rate: 7.5%

Educational Attainment: High school diploma or higher: 91.6%; Bachelor's degree or higher: 21.6%; Graduate/professional degree or higher: 8.6%

Housing: Homeownership rate: 89.3%; Median home value: $145,300; Median year structure built: 1972; Homeowner vacancy rate: 0.5%; Median selected monthly owner costs: $1,188 with a mortgage, $448 without a mortgage; Median gross rent: $942 per month; Rental vacancy rate: 11.4%

Health Insurance: 84.9% have insurance; 65.0% have private insurance; 35.3% have public insurance; 15.1% do not have insurance; 26.5% of children under 18 do not have insurance

Transportation: Commute: 86.8% car, 0.0% public transportation, 2.2% walk, 3.7% work from home; Mean travel time to work: 21.5 minutes

OXBOW (CDP). Covers a land area of 0.202 square miles and a water area of 0 square miles. Located at 44.29° N. Lat; 75.62° W. Long. Elevation is 354 feet.

Population: 112; Growth (since 2000): n/a; Density: 553.5 persons per square mile; Race: 100.0% White, 0.0% Black/African American, 0.0% Asian, 0.0% American Indian/Alaska Native, 0.0% Native Hawaiian/Other Pacific Islander, 0.0% Two or more races, 0.0% Hispanic of any race; Average household size: 3.20; Median age: 32.9; Age under 18: 33.9%; Age 65 and over: 13.4%; Males per 100 females: 92.9; Marriage status: 16.9% never married, 72.3% now married, 0.0% separated, 3.6% widowed, 7.2% divorced; Foreign born: 0.0%; Speak English only: 100.0%; With disability: 39.3%; Veterans: 8.1%; Ancestry: 25.9% French, 25.0% Irish, 8.0% American, 3.6% French Canadian, 2.7% Italian

Employment: 0.0% management, business, and financial, 0.0% computer, engineering, and science, 0.0% education, legal, community service, arts, and media, 5.0% healthcare practitioners, 37.5% service, 10.0% sales and office, 0.0% natural resources, construction, and maintenance, 47.5% production, transportation, and material moving

Income: Per capita: $18,478; Median household: $48,906; Average household: $59,577; Households with income of $100,000 or more: 14.3%; Poverty rate: n/a

Educational Attainment: High school diploma or higher: 63.5%; Bachelor's degree or higher: 2.7%; Graduate/professional degree or higher: n/a

Housing: Homeownership rate: 100.0%; Median home value: $72,500; Median year structure built: Before 1940; Homeowner vacancy rate: 0.0%; Median selected monthly owner costs: $1,225 with a mortgage, $372 without a mortgage; Median gross rent: n/a per month; Rental vacancy rate: 0.0%

Health Insurance: 95.5% have insurance; 59.8% have private insurance; 70.5% have public insurance; 4.5% do not have insurance; 0.0% of children under 18 do not have insurance

Transportation: Commute: 100.0% car, 0.0% public transportation, 0.0% walk, 0.0% work from home; Mean travel time to work: 37.5 minutes

PAMELIA (town). Covers a land area of 33.840 square miles and a water area of 1.369 square miles. Located at 44.06° N. Lat; 75.91° W. Long.

Population: 3,078; Growth (since 2000): 6.2%; Density: 91.0 persons per square mile; Race: 84.7% White, 5.3% Black/African American, 1.0% Asian, 0.3% American Indian/Alaska Native, 0.0% Native Hawaiian/Other Pacific Islander, 8.4% Two or more races, 4.3% Hispanic of any race; Average household size: 2.74; Median age: 36.4; Age under 18: 26.2%; Age 65 and over: 15.4%; Males per 100 females: 108.3; Marriage status: 24.3% never married, 62.5% now married, 1.7% separated, 3.4% widowed, 9.8% divorced; Foreign born: 2.6%; Speak English only: 93.4%; With disability: 11.8%; Veterans: 19.9%; Ancestry: 24.9% Irish, 16.6% German, 11.1% English, 8.2% Italian, 8.2% French

Employment: 18.1% management, business, and financial, 4.2% computer, engineering, and science, 8.3% education, legal, community service, arts, and media, 5.9% healthcare practitioners, 19.9% service, 16.5% sales and office, 18.0% natural resources, construction, and maintenance, 9.0% production, transportation, and material moving

Income: Per capita: $28,111; Median household: $70,518; Average household: $77,378; Households with income of $100,000 or more: 20.3%; Poverty rate: 9.2%

Educational Attainment: High school diploma or higher: 91.4%; Bachelor's degree or higher: 17.8%; Graduate/professional degree or higher: 7.0%

Housing: Homeownership rate: 69.4%; Median home value: $169,400; Median year structure built: 1975; Homeowner vacancy rate: 0.0%; Median

selected monthly owner costs: $1,338 with a mortgage, $423 without a mortgage; Median gross rent: $825 per month; Rental vacancy rate: 0.0%

Health Insurance: 85.4% have insurance; 73.7% have private insurance; 30.8% have public insurance; 14.6% do not have insurance; 22.1% of children under 18 do not have insurance

Transportation: Commute: 94.4% car, 0.0% public transportation, 5.1% walk, 0.5% work from home; Mean travel time to work: 13.8 minutes

PAMELIA CENTER (CDP). Covers a land area of 1.041 square miles and a water area of 0 square miles. Located at 44.04° N. Lat; 75.90° W. Long. Elevation is 469 feet.

Population: 367; Growth (since 2000): n/a; Density: 352.5 persons per square mile; Race: 93.5% White, 6.5% Black/African American, 0.0% Asian, 0.0% American Indian/Alaska Native, 0.0% Native Hawaiian/Other Pacific Islander, 0.0% Two or more races, 2.5% Hispanic of any race; Average household size: 2.10; Median age: 51.0; Age under 18: 8.2%; Age 65 and over: 28.1%; Males per 100 females: 107.9; Marriage status: 19.9% never married, 64.4% now married, 0.0% separated, 8.6% widowed, 7.1% divorced; Foreign born: 4.4%; Speak English only: 97.5%; With disability: 16.3%; Veterans: 38.7%; Ancestry: 32.4% English, 27.5% Italian, 26.4% German, 22.1% Irish, 6.0% Scottish

Employment: 21.9% management, business, and financial, 0.0% computer, engineering, and science, 5.1% education, legal, community service, arts, and media, 17.5% healthcare practitioners, 29.2% service, 0.0% sales and office, 26.3% natural resources, construction, and maintenance, 0.0% production, transportation, and material moving

Income: Per capita: $41,017; Median household: $85,250; Average household: $87,607; Households with income of $100,000 or more: 17.1%; Poverty rate: 2.5%

Educational Attainment: High school diploma or higher: 100.0%; Bachelor's degree or higher: 30.9%; Graduate/professional degree or higher: 21.9%

Housing: Homeownership rate: 77.7%; Median home value: $216,700; Median year structure built: 1985; Homeowner vacancy rate: 0.0%; Median selected monthly owner costs: $1,423 with a mortgage, n/a without a mortgage; Median gross rent: $1,297 per month; Rental vacancy rate: 0.0%

Health Insurance: 98.3% have insurance; 98.3% have private insurance; 40.8% have public insurance; 1.7% do not have insurance; 0.0% of children under 18 do not have insurance

Transportation: Commute: 100.0% car, 0.0% public transportation, 0.0% walk, 0.0% work from home; Mean travel time to work: 13.1 minutes

PHILADELPHIA (town). Covers a land area of 37.593 square miles and a water area of 0.021 square miles. Located at 44.15° N. Lat; 75.71° W. Long. Elevation is 486 feet.

Population: 1,860; Growth (since 2000): -13.1%; Density: 49.5 persons per square mile; Race: 89.5% White, 3.1% Black/African American, 0.9% Asian, 0.7% American Indian/Alaska Native, 0.0% Native Hawaiian/Other Pacific Islander, 5.4% Two or more races, 5.0% Hispanic of any race; Average household size: 2.44; Median age: 33.4; Age under 18: 24.5%; Age 65 and over: 13.7%; Males per 100 females: 89.4; Marriage status: 23.6% never married, 59.1% now married, 2.2% separated, 7.1% widowed, 10.2% divorced; Foreign born: 2.4%; Speak English only: 93.2%; With disability: 14.6%; Veterans: 15.5%; Ancestry: 17.6% German, 12.6% Irish, 10.2% English, 8.6% French, 6.7% American

Employment: 10.0% management, business, and financial, 1.7% computer, engineering, and science, 13.6% education, legal, community service, arts, and media, 3.8% healthcare practitioners, 19.7% service, 27.5% sales and office, 13.6% natural resources, construction, and maintenance, 9.8% production, transportation, and material moving

Income: Per capita: $23,803; Median household: $46,131; Average household: $57,048; Households with income of $100,000 or more: 14.6%; Poverty rate: 15.2%

Educational Attainment: High school diploma or higher: 91.1%; Bachelor's degree or higher: 21.1%; Graduate/professional degree or higher: 6.0%

School District(s)

Indian River Central SD (PK-12)
    Enrollment: 3,820 . . . . (315) 642-3441

Housing: Homeownership rate: 53.9%; Median home value: $135,000; Median year structure built: 1974; Homeowner vacancy rate: 0.0%; Median selected monthly owner costs: $1,087 with a mortgage, $479 without a mortgage; Median gross rent: $747 per month; Rental vacancy rate: 2.4%

Health Insurance: 92.5% have insurance; 72.7% have private insurance; 39.2% have public insurance; 7.5% do not have insurance; 5.9% of children under 18 do not have insurance
Transportation: Commute: 90.4% car, 0.4% public transportation, 2.6% walk, 5.1% work from home; Mean travel time to work: 20.2 minutes

---

PHILADELPHIA (village). Covers a land area of 0.904 square miles and a water area of 0 square miles. Located at 44.15° N. Lat; 75.71° W. Long. Elevation is 486 feet.
Population: 1,143; Growth (since 2000): -24.8%; Density: 1,264.1 persons per square mile; Race: 86.2% White, 3.5% Black/African American, 0.8% Asian, 0.8% American Indian/Alaska Native, 0.0% Native Hawaiian/Other Pacific Islander, 8.5% Two or more races, 7.3% Hispanic of any race; Average household size: 2.42; Median age: 30.3; Age under 18: 27.6%; Age 65 and over: 14.1%; Males per 100 females: 87.7; Marriage status: 25.5% never married, 60.9% now married, 2.9% separated, 6.0% widowed, 7.7% divorced; Foreign born: 1.9%; Speak English only: 92.2%; With disability: 14.2%; Veterans: 15.8%; Ancestry: 19.9% German, 13.6% Irish, 8.8% English, 7.3% American, 6.2% French
Employment: 8.6% management, business, and financial, 3.1% computer, engineering, and science, 13.5% education, legal, community service, arts, and media, 5.1% healthcare practitioners, 19.9% service, 28.7% sales and office, 9.7% natural resources, construction, and maintenance, 11.5% production, transportation, and material moving
Income: Per capita: $21,198; Median household: $37,679; Average household: $50,042; Households with income of $100,000 or more: 12.3%; Poverty rate: 18.2%
Educational Attainment: High school diploma or higher: 87.8%; Bachelor's degree or higher: 20.5%; Graduate/professional degree or higher: 7.0%

School District(s)
Indian River Central SD (PK-12)
    Enrollment: 3,820 . . . . (315) 642-3441
Housing: Homeownership rate: 40.4%; Median home value: $131,400; Median year structure built: 1972; Homeowner vacancy rate: 0.0%; Median selected monthly owner costs: $1,036 with a mortgage, $423 without a mortgage; Median gross rent: $691 per month; Rental vacancy rate: 3.0%
Health Insurance: 92.4% have insurance; 74.9% have private insurance; 38.1% have public insurance; 7.6% do not have insurance; 7.7% of children under 18 do not have insurance
Transportation: Commute: 92.3% car, 0.0% public transportation, 4.6% walk, 2.5% work from home; Mean travel time to work: 18.9 minutes

---

PIERREPONT MANOR (CDP). Covers a land area of 0.684 square miles and a water area of 0.004 square miles. Located at 43.74° N. Lat; 76.06° W. Long. Elevation is 623 feet.
Population: 177; Growth (since 2000): n/a; Density: 258.6 persons per square mile; Race: 90.4% White, 0.0% Black/African American, 0.0% Asian, 9.6% American Indian/Alaska Native, 0.0% Native Hawaiian/Other Pacific Islander, 0.0% Two or more races, 0.0% Hispanic of any race; Average household size: 5.06; Median age: n/a; Age under 18: 57.6%; Age 65 and over: 6.2%; Males per 100 females: 90.0; Marriage status: 0.0% never married, 100.0% now married, 9.3% separated, 0.0% widowed, 0.0% divorced; Foreign born: 9.6%; Speak English only: 45.2%; With disability: 5.6%; Veterans: 0.0%; Ancestry: 80.2% German, 6.8% American
Employment: 0.0% management, business, and financial, 0.0% computer, engineering, and science, 0.0% education, legal, community service, arts, and media, 0.0% healthcare practitioners, 0.0% service, 0.0% sales and office, 88.6% natural resources, construction, and maintenance, 11.4% production, transportation, and material moving
Income: Per capita: $8,592; Median household: $48,177; Average household: $44,183; Households with income of $100,000 or more: n/a; Poverty rate: n/a
Educational Attainment: High school diploma or higher: 24.3%; Bachelor's degree or higher: 5.7%; Graduate/professional degree or higher: n/a
Housing: Homeownership rate: 20.0%; Median home value: n/a; Median year structure built: Before 1940; Homeowner vacancy rate: 0.0%; Median selected monthly owner costs: n/a with a mortgage, n/a without a mortgage; Median gross rent: n/a per month; Rental vacancy rate: 0.0%
Health Insurance: 10.2% have insurance; 4.0% have private insurance; 6.2% have public insurance; 89.8% do not have insurance; 100.0% of children under 18 do not have insurance

Transportation: Commute: 100.0% car, 0.0% public transportation, 0.0% walk, 0.0% work from home; Mean travel time to work: 16.1 minutes

---

PLESSIS (CDP). Covers a land area of 0.346 square miles and a water area of 0 square miles. Located at 44.27° N. Lat; 75.86° W. Long. Elevation is 404 feet.
Population: 165; Growth (since 2000): n/a; Density: 477.2 persons per square mile; Race: 86.7% White, 13.3% Black/African American, 0.0% Asian, 0.0% American Indian/Alaska Native, 0.0% Native Hawaiian/Other Pacific Islander, 0.0% Two or more races, 0.0% Hispanic of any race; Average household size: 3.06; Median age: 21.9; Age under 18: 21.2%; Age 65 and over: 15.2%; Males per 100 females: 113.0; Marriage status: 49.0% never married, 27.3% now married, 0.0% separated, 0.0% widowed, 23.8% divorced; Foreign born: 0.0%; Speak English only: 100.0%; With disability: 3.0%; Veterans: 3.8%; Ancestry: 38.8% German, 38.8% Irish, 4.2% French, 3.0% English
Employment: 0.0% management, business, and financial, 0.0% computer, engineering, and science, 0.0% education, legal, community service, arts, and media, 8.5% healthcare practitioners, 29.3% service, 52.4% sales and office, 9.8% natural resources, construction, and maintenance, 0.0% production, transportation, and material moving
Income: Per capita: $26,347; Median household: $64,808; Average household: $78,935; Households with income of $100,000 or more: 13.0%; Poverty rate: n/a
Educational Attainment: High school diploma or higher: 100.0%; Bachelor's degree or higher: 8.6%; Graduate/professional degree or higher: n/a
Housing: Homeownership rate: 100.0%; Median home value: $142,100; Median year structure built: Before 1940; Homeowner vacancy rate: 0.0%; Median selected monthly owner costs: $1,464 with a mortgage, n/a without a mortgage; Median gross rent: n/a per month; Rental vacancy rate: 0.0%
Health Insurance: 95.2% have insurance; 50.9% have private insurance; 51.5% have public insurance; 4.8% do not have insurance; 0.0% of children under 18 do not have insurance
Transportation: Commute: 100.0% car, 0.0% public transportation, 0.0% walk, 0.0% work from home; Mean travel time to work: 20.7 minutes

---

REDWOOD (CDP). Covers a land area of 2.021 square miles and a water area of 0.534 square miles. Located at 44.30° N. Lat; 75.81° W. Long. Elevation is 367 feet.
Population: 677; Growth (since 2000): 15.9%; Density: 335.0 persons per square mile; Race: 96.3% White, 0.0% Black/African American, 0.0% Asian, 0.0% American Indian/Alaska Native, 0.0% Native Hawaiian/Other Pacific Islander, 2.2% Two or more races, 5.0% Hispanic of any race; Average household size: 3.08; Median age: 33.5; Age under 18: 19.8%; Age 65 and over: 6.2%; Males per 100 females: 100.3; Marriage status: 37.1% never married, 48.8% now married, 9.0% separated, 11.6% widowed, 2.6% divorced; Foreign born: 0.0%; Speak English only: 100.0%; With disability: 9.9%; Veterans: 0.0%; Ancestry: 40.0% Irish, 25.8% German, 7.4% French, 6.2% American, 5.3% English
Employment: 5.4% management, business, and financial, 0.0% computer, engineering, and science, 8.7% education, legal, community service, arts, and media, 0.0% healthcare practitioners, 44.5% service, 12.5% sales and office, 9.0% natural resources, construction, and maintenance, 20.0% production, transportation, and material moving
Income: Per capita: $12,087; Median household: $29,462; Average household: $35,180; Households with income of $100,000 or more: n/a; Poverty rate: 14.6%
Educational Attainment: High school diploma or higher: 82.1%; Bachelor's degree or higher: 5.2%; Graduate/professional degree or higher: 1.4%
Housing: Homeownership rate: 66.8%; Median home value: $68,200; Median year structure built: Before 1940; Homeowner vacancy rate: 13.5%; Median selected monthly owner costs: $894 with a mortgage, n/a without a mortgage; Median gross rent: $1,058 per month; Rental vacancy rate: 0.0%
Health Insurance: 92.0% have insurance; 59.8% have private insurance; 46.4% have public insurance; 8.0% do not have insurance; 0.0% of children under 18 do not have insurance
Transportation: Commute: 88.4% car, 3.0% public transportation, 0.0% walk, 8.5% work from home; Mean travel time to work: 19.6 minutes

RODMAN (CDP). Covers a land area of 0.116 square miles and a water area of 0 square miles. Located at 43.85° N. Lat; 75.94° W. Long. Elevation is 725 feet.

Population: 138; Growth (since 2000): n/a; Density: 1,190.5 persons per square mile; Race: 97.1% White, 0.0% Black/African American, 2.9% Asian, 0.0% American Indian/Alaska Native, 0.0% Native Hawaiian/Other Pacific Islander, 0.0% Two or more races, 0.0% Hispanic of any race; Average household size: 3.07; Median age: 41.4; Age under 18: 32.6%; Age 65 and over: 26.8%; Males per 100 females: 112.5; Marriage status: 8.3% never married, 85.4% now married, 4.2% separated, 0.0% widowed, 6.3% divorced; Foreign born: 4.3%; Speak English only: 94.5%; With disability: 0.0%; Veterans: 6.5%; Ancestry: 49.3% English, 19.6% German, 13.8% Irish, 13.0% American, 10.1% French

Employment: 5.9% management, business, and financial, 0.0% computer, engineering, and science, 19.6% education, legal, community service, arts, and media, 5.9% healthcare practitioners, 41.2% service, 19.6% sales and office, 0.0% natural resources, construction, and maintenance, 7.8% production, transportation, and material moving

Income: Per capita: $22,484; Median household: $57,917; Average household: $65,700; Households with income of $100,000 or more: 13.3%; Poverty rate: n/a

Educational Attainment: High school diploma or higher: 97.8%; Bachelor's degree or higher: 36.6%; Graduate/professional degree or higher: 20.4%

Housing: Homeownership rate: 93.3%; Median home value: $155,300; Median year structure built: Before 1940; Homeowner vacancy rate: 19.2%; Median selected monthly owner costs: $1,125 with a mortgage, $447 without a mortgage; Median gross rent: n/a per month; Rental vacancy rate: 0.0%

Health Insurance: 100.0% have insurance; 58.0% have private insurance; 49.3% have public insurance; 0.0% do not have insurance; 0.0% of children under 18 do not have insurance

Transportation: Commute: 100.0% car, 0.0% public transportation, 0.0% walk, 0.0% work from home; Mean travel time to work: 35.7 minutes

RODMAN (town). Covers a land area of 42.227 square miles and a water area of 0.053 square miles. Located at 43.84° N. Lat; 75.90° W. Long. Elevation is 725 feet.

Population: 1,220; Growth (since 2000): 6.4%; Density: 28.9 persons per square mile; Race: 98.4% White, 0.0% Black/African American, 0.3% Asian, 0.0% American Indian/Alaska Native, 0.0% Native Hawaiian/Other Pacific Islander, 1.2% Two or more races, 1.5% Hispanic of any race; Average household size: 2.93; Median age: 36.9; Age under 18: 27.0%; Age 65 and over: 13.4%; Males per 100 females: 104.5; Marriage status: 25.8% never married, 60.4% now married, 2.5% separated, 3.4% widowed, 10.5% divorced; Foreign born: 2.0%; Speak English only: 96.8%; With disability: 7.9%; Veterans: 10.5%; Ancestry: 21.1% Irish, 17.4% English, 12.6% German, 7.7% American, 6.6% French

Employment: 10.1% management, business, and financial, 2.2% computer, engineering, and science, 8.9% education, legal, community service, arts, and media, 5.4% healthcare practitioners, 21.9% service, 20.4% sales and office, 19.9% natural resources, construction, and maintenance, 11.1% production, transportation, and material moving

Income: Per capita: $26,876; Median household: $66,833; Average household: $76,480; Households with income of $100,000 or more: 30.0%; Poverty rate: 4.9%

Educational Attainment: High school diploma or higher: 88.7%; Bachelor's degree or higher: 19.4%; Graduate/professional degree or higher: 11.4%

Housing: Homeownership rate: 86.8%; Median home value: $161,000; Median year structure built: 1971; Homeowner vacancy rate: 2.7%; Median selected monthly owner costs: $1,188 with a mortgage, $507 without a mortgage; Median gross rent: $1,125 per month; Rental vacancy rate: 0.0%

Health Insurance: 94.4% have insurance; 73.7% have private insurance; 28.9% have public insurance; 5.6% do not have insurance; 1.8% of children under 18 do not have insurance

Transportation: Commute: 94.4% car, 0.0% public transportation, 3.0% walk, 2.7% work from home; Mean travel time to work: 21.1 minutes

RUTLAND (town). Covers a land area of 45.103 square miles and a water area of 0.275 square miles. Located at 43.94° N. Lat; 75.79° W. Long.

Population: 3,065; Growth (since 2000): 3.6%; Density: 68.0 persons per square mile; Race: 94.1% White, 1.3% Black/African American, 1.0%

Asian, 0.0% American Indian/Alaska Native, 0.0% Native Hawaiian/Other Pacific Islander, 2.9% Two or more races, 2.9% Hispanic of any race; Average household size: 2.67; Median age: 34.2; Age under 18: 29.6%; Age 65 and over: 11.9%; Males per 100 females: 98.8; Marriage status: 20.0% never married, 63.7% now married, 7.1% separated, 5.8% widowed, 10.5% divorced; Foreign born: 1.8%; Speak English only: 96.3%; With disability: 15.4%; Veterans: 18.9%; Ancestry: 20.7% Irish, 13.9% German, 12.9% English, 10.4% Italian, 8.0% French

Employment: 9.2% management, business, and financial, 4.2% computer, engineering, and science, 8.5% education, legal, community service, arts, and media, 12.0% healthcare practitioners, 19.1% service, 21.7% sales and office, 11.7% natural resources, construction, and maintenance, 13.5% production, transportation, and material moving

Income: Per capita: $24,180; Median household: $52,426; Average household: $63,946; Households with income of $100,000 or more: 14.7%; Poverty rate: 14.9%

Educational Attainment: High school diploma or higher: 92.2%; Bachelor's degree or higher: 22.4%; Graduate/professional degree or higher: 9.3%

Housing: Homeownership rate: 69.7%; Median home value: $153,000; Median year structure built: 1972; Homeowner vacancy rate: 3.2%; Median selected monthly owner costs: $1,380 with a mortgage, $503 without a mortgage; Median gross rent: $937 per month; Rental vacancy rate: 8.4%

Health Insurance: 96.0% have insurance; 66.4% have private insurance; 44.7% have public insurance; 4.0% do not have insurance; 1.5% of children under 18 do not have insurance

Transportation: Commute: 94.5% car, 0.0% public transportation, 1.4% walk, 3.3% work from home; Mean travel time to work: 17.3 minutes

SACKETS HARBOR (village). Covers a land area of 2.205 square miles and a water area of 0.006 square miles. Located at 43.94° N. Lat; 76.11° W. Long. Elevation is 282 feet.

History: In 1809 infantry was stationed here to enforce the Embargo Act and control smuggling. Following the outbreak of the War of 1812, it became the center of U.S. naval and military activity for Upper St. Lawrence Valley and Lake Ontario. Further expansion occurred during the 1830s and 1840s due to the Patriots War in Canada. Its growth led to the development of Pine Camp (Fort Drum) near Watertown. Zebulon Pike is buried here. Settled c.1801, Incorporated 1814.

Population: 1,534; Growth (since 2000): 10.7%; Density: 695.8 persons per square mile; Race: 92.8% White, 0.9% Black/African American, 0.8% Asian, 0.0% American Indian/Alaska Native, 0.0% Native Hawaiian/Other Pacific Islander, 4.6% Two or more races, 6.1% Hispanic of any race; Average household size: 2.23; Median age: 29.8; Age under 18: 28.2%; Age 65 and over: 12.6%; Males per 100 females: 98.4; Marriage status: 30.4% never married, 52.8% now married, 2.9% separated, 3.5% widowed, 13.3% divorced; Foreign born: 5.1%; Speak English only: 95.9%; With disability: 11.1%; Veterans: 18.4%; Ancestry: 19.1% Irish, 16.4% German, 14.7% English, 9.3% Italian, 8.7% French

Employment: 10.1% management, business, and financial, 5.6% computer, engineering, and science, 17.4% education, legal, community service, arts, and media, 18.7% healthcare practitioners, 10.1% service, 22.8% sales and office, 6.7% natural resources, construction, and maintenance, 8.4% production, transportation, and material moving

Income: Per capita: $32,129; Median household: $61,167; Average household: $71,114; Households with income of $100,000 or more: 22.9%; Poverty rate: 6.9%

Educational Attainment: High school diploma or higher: 95.4%; Bachelor's degree or higher: 50.8%; Graduate/professional degree or higher: 20.8%

School District(s)

Sackets Harbor Central SD (KG-12)
    Enrollment: 448 . . . . (315) 646-3575

Housing: Homeownership rate: 35.1%; Median home value: $251,000; Median year structure built: 1970; Homeowner vacancy rate: 0.0%; Median selected monthly owner costs: $1,659 with a mortgage, $621 without a mortgage; Median gross rent: $1,131 per month; Rental vacancy rate: 9.5%

Health Insurance: 94.2% have insurance; 80.8% have private insurance; 27.5% have public insurance; 5.8% do not have insurance; 6.2% of children under 18 do not have insurance

Safety: Violent crime rate: 0.0 per 10,000 population; Property crime rate: 0.0 per 10,000 population

Transportation: Commute: 92.1% car, 0.7% public transportation, 3.6% walk, 2.4% work from home; Mean travel time to work: 24.7 minutes

THERESA (town). Covers a land area of 64.943 square miles and a water area of 4.789 square miles. Located at 44.26° N. Lat; 75.77° W. Long. Elevation is 407 feet.
Population: 2,897; Growth (since 2000): 20.0%; Density: 44.6 persons per square mile; Race: 94.1% White, 0.5% Black/African American, 0.4% Asian, 0.4% American Indian/Alaska Native, 0.0% Native Hawaiian/Other Pacific Islander, 4.3% Two or more races, 4.0% Hispanic of any race; Average household size: 2.77; Median age: 37.3; Age under 18: 26.6%; Age 65 and over: 11.8%; Males per 100 females: 105.9; Marriage status: 28.5% never married, 54.5% now married, 2.1% separated, 8.1% widowed, 8.9% divorced; Foreign born: 2.1%; Speak English only: 96.6%; With disability: 14.9%; Veterans: 18.6%; Ancestry: 20.2% Irish, 15.5% German, 11.8% French, 9.7% English, 5.8% Italian
Employment: 13.2% management, business, and financial, 5.0% computer, engineering, and science, 9.7% education, legal, community service, arts, and media, 5.3% healthcare practitioners, 20.1% service, 18.9% sales and office, 14.3% natural resources, construction, and maintenance, 13.5% production, transportation, and material moving
Income: Per capita: $26,487; Median household: $62,708; Average household: $72,470; Households with income of $100,000 or more: 21.7%; Poverty rate: 12.9%
Educational Attainment: High school diploma or higher: 89.2%; Bachelor's degree or higher: 14.3%; Graduate/professional degree or higher: 6.3%

School District(s)
Indian River Central SD (PK-12)
    Enrollment: 3,820 . . . . (315) 642-3441
Housing: Homeownership rate: 70.4%; Median home value: $132,600; Median year structure built: 1974; Homeowner vacancy rate: 1.9%; Median selected monthly owner costs: $1,311 with a mortgage, $460 without a mortgage; Median gross rent: $951 per month; Rental vacancy rate: 9.6%
Health Insurance: 94.0% have insurance; 66.0% have private insurance; 45.4% have public insurance; 6.0% do not have insurance; 4.8% of children under 18 do not have insurance
Transportation: Commute: 94.9% car, 0.6% public transportation, 0.7% walk, 2.2% work from home; Mean travel time to work: 25.9 minutes

THERESA (village). Covers a land area of 1.252 square miles and a water area of 0.061 square miles. Located at 44.22° N. Lat; 75.80° W. Long. Elevation is 407 feet.
Population: 728; Growth (since 2000): -10.3%; Density: 581.5 persons per square mile; Race: 92.4% White, 0.8% Black/African American, 1.6% Asian, 1.2% American Indian/Alaska Native, 0.0% Native Hawaiian/Other Pacific Islander, 3.8% Two or more races, 6.7% Hispanic of any race; Average household size: 2.56; Median age: 37.4; Age under 18: 28.2%; Age 65 and over: 11.4%; Males per 100 females: 103.5; Marriage status: 30.5% never married, 48.8% now married, 4.7% separated, 10.4% widowed, 10.4% divorced; Foreign born: 6.5%; Speak English only: 90.9%; With disability: 17.2%; Veterans: 18.0%; Ancestry: 21.6% Irish, 17.3% German, 13.7% French, 6.5% American, 5.9% English
Employment: 8.3% management, business, and financial, 5.8% computer, engineering, and science, 11.2% education, legal, community service, arts, and media, 5.0% healthcare practitioners, 23.7% service, 27.7% sales and office, 11.2% natural resources, construction, and maintenance, 7.2% production, transportation, and material moving
Income: Per capita: $24,963; Median household: $52,143; Average household: $63,018; Households with income of $100,000 or more: 14.8%; Poverty rate: 8.7%
Educational Attainment: High school diploma or higher: 88.0%; Bachelor's degree or higher: 15.9%; Graduate/professional degree or higher: 8.5%

School District(s)
Indian River Central SD (PK-12)
    Enrollment: 3,820 . . . . (315) 642-3441
Housing: Homeownership rate: 66.9%; Median home value: $116,200; Median year structure built: Before 1940; Homeowner vacancy rate: 3.8%; Median selected monthly owner costs: $1,261 with a mortgage, $535 without a mortgage; Median gross rent: $817 per month; Rental vacancy rate: 17.5%
Health Insurance: 91.3% have insurance; 74.1% have private insurance; 41.4% have public insurance; 8.7% do not have insurance; 10.7% of children under 18 do not have insurance
Transportation: Commute: 92.9% car, 2.5% public transportation, 1.8% walk, 2.1% work from home; Mean travel time to work: 25.4 minutes

THOUSAND ISLAND PARK (CDP). Covers a land area of 0.293 square miles and a water area of 0 square miles. Located at 44.29° N. Lat; 76.03° W. Long. Elevation is 276 feet.
Population: 55; Growth (since 2000): n/a; Density: 187.7 persons per square mile; Race: 100.0% White, 0.0% Black/African American, 0.0% Asian, 0.0% American Indian/Alaska Native, 0.0% Native Hawaiian/Other Pacific Islander, 0.0% Two or more races, 0.0% Hispanic of any race; Average household size: 1.77; Median age: 73.3; Age under 18: 0.0%; Age 65 and over: 92.7%; Males per 100 females: 106.7; Marriage status: 0.0% never married, 83.6% now married, 0.0% separated, 16.4% widowed, 0.0% divorced; Foreign born: 0.0%; Speak English only: 100.0%; With disability: 18.2%; Veterans: 40.0%; Ancestry: 25.5% Lebanese, 25.5% English, 25.5% German, 25.5% Irish, 16.4% American
Employment: 17.9% management, business, and financial, 0.0% computer, engineering, and science, 17.9% education, legal, community service, arts, and media, 0.0% healthcare practitioners, 64.3% service, 0.0% sales and office, 0.0% natural resources, construction, and maintenance, 0.0% production, transportation, and material moving
Income: Per capita: $28,647; Median household: $57,946; Average household: $48,448; Households with income of $100,000 or more: n/a; Poverty rate: n/a
Educational Attainment: High school diploma or higher: 100.0%; Bachelor's degree or higher: 34.5%; Graduate/professional degree or higher: n/a
Housing: Homeownership rate: 100.0%; Median home value: $332,600; Median year structure built: Before 1940; Homeowner vacancy rate: 11.4%; Median selected monthly owner costs: $1,090 with a mortgage, n/a without a mortgage; Median gross rent: n/a per month; Rental vacancy rate: 0.0%
Health Insurance: 100.0% have insurance; 83.6% have private insurance; 100.0% have public insurance; 0.0% do not have insurance; 0.0% of children under 18 do not have insurance
Transportation: Commute: 67.9% car, 0.0% public transportation, 32.1% walk, 0.0% work from home; Mean travel time to work: 0.0 minutes

THREE MILE BAY (CDP). Covers a land area of 0.257 square miles and a water area of 0 square miles. Located at 44.08° N. Lat; 76.20° W. Long. Elevation is 259 feet.
Population: 213; Growth (since 2000): n/a; Density: 827.2 persons per square mile; Race: 100.0% White, 0.0% Black/African American, 0.0% Asian, 0.0% American Indian/Alaska Native, 0.0% Native Hawaiian/Other Pacific Islander, 0.0% Two or more races, 0.0% Hispanic of any race; Average household size: 2.32; Median age: 32.7; Age under 18: 28.6%; Age 65 and over: 13.1%; Males per 100 females: 95.7; Marriage status: 14.5% never married, 50.7% now married, 0.0% separated, 16.4% widowed, 18.4% divorced; Foreign born: 0.0%; Speak English only: 100.0%; With disability: 13.1%; Veterans: 13.1%; Ancestry: 44.6% Irish, 23.5% Dutch, 19.7% English, 16.4% Scottish, 8.9% French
Employment: 15.9% management, business, and financial, 0.0% computer, engineering, and science, 0.0% education, legal, community service, arts, and media, 8.8% healthcare practitioners, 48.7% service, 0.0% sales and office, 12.4% natural resources, construction, and maintenance, 14.2% production, transportation, and material moving
Income: Per capita: $19,432; Median household: n/a; Average household: $42,917; Households with income of $100,000 or more: 5.4%; Poverty rate: 5.2%
Educational Attainment: High school diploma or higher: 90.8%; Bachelor's degree or higher: 6.6%; Graduate/professional degree or higher: 3.3%
Housing: Homeownership rate: 88.0%; Median home value: n/a; Median year structure built: Before 1940; Homeowner vacancy rate: 0.0%; Median selected monthly owner costs: $925 with a mortgage, $371 without a mortgage; Median gross rent: n/a per month; Rental vacancy rate: 0.0%
Health Insurance: 100.0% have insurance; 45.1% have private insurance; 54.9% have public insurance; 0.0% do not have insurance; 0.0% of children under 18 do not have insurance
Transportation: Commute: 87.6% car, 0.0% public transportation, 0.0% walk, 12.4% work from home; Mean travel time to work: 22.5 minutes

WATERTOWN (city). County seat. Covers a land area of 9.020 square miles and a water area of 0.345 square miles. Located at 43.97° N. Lat; 75.91° W. Long. Elevation is 466 feet.
History: In 1800, five New Englanders hacked their way up from the Mohawk Valley, stopped at the rocky Black River Falls, and named the site Watertown. They built sawmills and gristmills along the river, and burned

piles of lumber for potash. The five and ten cent store originated in Watertown during county fair week in 1878. Frank W. Woolworth (1852-1910), a clerk in Moore & Smith's general store, piled leftover odds and ends on a table and put up a sign: "Any Article 5 cents." The entire stock was sold out in a few hours. Inspired by this success, Woolworth opened his first store in Utica the following year.

Population: 26,437; Growth (since 2000): -1.0%; Density: 2,931.0 persons per square mile; Race: 83.3% White, 7.4% Black/African American, 1.5% Asian, 1.0% American Indian/Alaska Native, 0.1% Native Hawaiian/Other Pacific Islander, 5.7% Two or more races, 7.2% Hispanic of any race; Average household size: 2.31; Median age: 31.1; Age under 18: 23.1%; Age 65 and over: 12.2%; Males per 100 females: 91.7; Marriage status: 34.7% never married, 46.0% now married, 3.8% separated, 6.2% widowed, 13.0% divorced; Foreign born: 4.1%; Speak English only: 93.8%; With disability: 16.2%; Veterans: 13.3%; Ancestry: 20.7% Irish, 14.8% Italian, 12.3% German, 9.8% French, 8.3% English

Employment: 9.9% management, business, and financial, 3.0% computer, engineering, and science, 12.5% education, legal, community service, arts, and media, 8.1% healthcare practitioners, 25.7% service, 25.4% sales and office, 6.5% natural resources, construction, and maintenance, 8.9% production, transportation, and material moving

Income: Per capita: $22,398; Median household: $40,767; Average household: $50,773; Households with income of $100,000 or more: 10.2%; Poverty rate: 24.7%

Educational Attainment: High school diploma or higher: 89.1%; Bachelor's degree or higher: 20.1%; Graduate/professional degree or higher: 8.9%

School District(s)
Jefferson-Lewis-Hamilton-Herkimer-Oneida Boces
    Enrollment: n/a . . . . (315) 779-7010
Watertown City SD (KG-12)
    Enrollment: 4,085 . . . . (315) 785-3700

Two-year College(s)
Jefferson Community College (Public)
    Enrollment: 3,460 . . . . (315) 786-2200
    Tuition: In-state $5,257; Out-of-state $8,017

Vocational/Technical School(s)
Jefferson Lewis BOCES-Practical Nursing Program (Public)
    Enrollment: 77 . . . . (315) 779-7200
    Tuition: In-state $11,792; Out-of-state $11,792

Housing: Homeownership rate: 40.3%; Median home value: $131,200; Median year structure built: Before 1940; Homeowner vacancy rate: 4.2%; Median selected monthly owner costs: $1,095 with a mortgage, $457 without a mortgage; Median gross rent: $826 per month; Rental vacancy rate: 10.9%

Health Insurance: 94.5% have insurance; 59.5% have private insurance; 48.6% have public insurance; 5.5% do not have insurance; 1.4% of children under 18 do not have insurance

Hospitals: Samaritan Medical Center (287 beds)

Safety: Violent crime rate: 54.0 per 10,000 population; Property crime rate: 409.4 per 10,000 population

Newspapers: Watertown Daily Times (daily circulation 29,500)

Transportation: Commute: 88.6% car, 1.3% public transportation, 4.5% walk, 2.1% work from home; Mean travel time to work: 14.8 minutes

Airports: Watertown International (primary service/non-hub)

Additional Information Contacts
City of Watertown . . . . (315) 785-7780
    http://www.citywatertown.org

WATERTOWN (town).
Covers a land area of 35.926 square miles and a water area of 0.101 square miles. Located at 43.93° N. Lat; 75.92° W. Long. Elevation is 466 feet.

History: Public Square Historic District in the city. Settled c.1800, Incorporated as a city 1869.

Population: 4,746; Growth (since 2000): 5.9%; Density: 132.1 persons per square mile; Race: 81.6% White, 5.2% Black/African American, 7.6% Asian, 0.4% American Indian/Alaska Native, 0.0% Native Hawaiian/Other Pacific Islander, 2.0% Two or more races, 7.0% Hispanic of any race; Average household size: 2.65; Median age: 38.8; Age under 18: 22.4%; Age 65 and over: 9.7%; Males per 100 females: 128.4; Marriage status: 35.0% never married, 50.6% now married, 1.8% separated, 5.5% widowed, 8.9% divorced; Foreign born: 7.7%; Speak English only: 87.9%; With disability: 9.6%; Veterans: 7.6%; Ancestry: 15.6% Irish, 13.9% German, 12.7% Italian, 8.1% English, 7.5% American

Employment: 6.4% management, business, and financial, 4.5% computer, engineering, and science, 10.0% education, legal, community service, arts, and media, 12.0% healthcare practitioners, 21.1% service, 23.4% sales and office, 10.5% natural resources, construction, and maintenance, 12.1% production, transportation, and material moving

Income: Per capita: $32,822; Median household: $77,264; Average household: $98,984; Households with income of $100,000 or more: 35.7%; Poverty rate: 6.2%

Educational Attainment: High school diploma or higher: 88.5%; Bachelor's degree or higher: 27.1%; Graduate/professional degree or higher: 14.0%

School District(s)
Jefferson-Lewis-Hamilton-Herkimer-Oneida Boces
    Enrollment: n/a . . . . (315) 779-7010
Watertown City SD (KG-12)
    Enrollment: 4,085 . . . . (315) 785-3700

Two-year College(s)
Jefferson Community College (Public)
    Enrollment: 3,460 . . . . (315) 786-2200
    Tuition: In-state $5,257; Out-of-state $8,017

Vocational/Technical School(s)
Jefferson Lewis BOCES-Practical Nursing Program (Public)
    Enrollment: 77 . . . . (315) 779-7200
    Tuition: In-state $11,792; Out-of-state $11,792

Housing: Homeownership rate: 77.7%; Median home value: $187,500; Median year structure built: 1977; Homeowner vacancy rate: 3.7%; Median selected monthly owner costs: $1,460 with a mortgage, $494 without a mortgage; Median gross rent: $1,084 per month; Rental vacancy rate: 7.7%

Health Insurance: 97.0% have insurance; 83.8% have private insurance; 23.6% have public insurance; 3.0% do not have insurance; 1.9% of children under 18 do not have insurance

Hospitals: Samaritan Medical Center (287 beds)

Newspapers: Watertown Daily Times (daily circulation 29,500)

Transportation: Commute: 91.7% car, 0.0% public transportation, 1.0% walk, 5.2% work from home; Mean travel time to work: 18.7 minutes

Airports: Watertown International (primary service/non-hub)

Additional Information Contacts
Town of Watertown . . . . (315) 782-8248
    http://www.townofwatertownny.org

WELLESLEY ISLAND (unincorporated postal area)
ZCTA: 13640

Covers a land area of 12.360 square miles and a water area of 0.256 square miles. Located at 44.30° N. Lat; 76.03° W. Long..

Population: 394; Growth (since 2000): 20.9%; Density: 31.9 persons per square mile; Race: 100.0% White, 0.0% Black/African American, 0.0% Asian, 0.0% American Indian/Alaska Native, 0.0% Native Hawaiian/Other Pacific Islander, 0.0% Two or more races, 0.0% Hispanic of any race; Average household size: 2.01; Median age: 64.1; Age under 18: 5.8%; Age 65 and over: 45.2%; Males per 100 females: 103.8; Marriage status: 11.1% never married, 77.4% now married, 1.1% separated, 8.4% widowed, 3.2% divorced; Foreign born: 4.1%; Speak English only: 97.7%; With disability: 3.6%; Veterans: 7.8%; Ancestry: 20.6% Italian, 15.2% Irish, 14.7% German, 14.0% English, 11.2% Norwegian

Employment: 24.2% management, business, and financial, 5.6% computer, engineering, and science, 35.5% education, legal, community service, arts, and media, 12.9% healthcare practitioners, 8.9% service, 7.3% sales and office, 0.0% natural resources, construction, and maintenance, 5.6% production, transportation, and material moving

Income: Per capita: $44,356; Median household: $46,667; Average household: $89,706; Households with income of $100,000 or more: 29.7%; Poverty rate: 4.8%

Educational Attainment: High school diploma or higher: 94.0%; Bachelor's degree or higher: 55.7%; Graduate/professional degree or higher: 26.2%

Housing: Homeownership rate: 96.4%; Median home value: $299,000; Median year structure built: 1983; Homeowner vacancy rate: 10.4%; Median selected monthly owner costs: $1,484 with a mortgage, $736 without a mortgage; Median gross rent: n/a per month; Rental vacancy rate: 0.0%

Health Insurance: 87.8% have insurance; 69.5% have private insurance; 49.2% have public insurance; 12.2% do not have insurance; 0.0% of children under 18 do not have insurance

Transportation: Commute: 71.8% car, 0.0% public transportation, 0.0% walk, 16.9% work from home; Mean travel time to work: 30.2 minutes

WEST CARTHAGE (village). Covers a land area of 1.297 square miles and a water area of 0.097 square miles. Located at 43.97° N. Lat; 75.62° W. Long. Elevation is 778 feet.

History: Incorporated 1888.

Population: 1,809; Growth (since 2000): -13.9%; Density: 1,395.3 persons per square mile; Race: 78.6% White, 6.6% Black/African American, 1.6% Asian, 0.0% American Indian/Alaska Native, 0.0% Native Hawaiian/Other Pacific Islander, 2.5% Two or more races, 15.9% Hispanic of any race; Average household size: 2.12; Median age: 31.6; Age under 18: 21.1%; Age 65 and over: 14.2%; Males per 100 females: 90.2; Marriage status: 22.4% never married, 56.5% now married, 1.8% separated, 8.3% widowed, 12.9% divorced; Foreign born: 2.0%; Speak English only: 87.4%; With disability: 24.3%; Veterans: 20.6%; Ancestry: 20.7% German, 20.2% Irish, 10.2% English, 8.5% French, 5.5% Polish

Employment: 4.5% management, business, and financial, 3.5% computer, engineering, and science, 10.9% education, legal, community service, arts, and media, 7.9% healthcare practitioners, 16.7% service, 31.5% sales and office, 11.3% natural resources, construction, and maintenance, 13.6% production, transportation, and material moving

Income: Per capita: $22,883; Median household: $41,898; Average household: $47,915; Households with income of $100,000 or more: 9.9%; Poverty rate: 14.0%

Educational Attainment: High school diploma or higher: 87.1%; Bachelor's degree or higher: 25.1%; Graduate/professional degree or higher: 9.8%

Housing: Homeownership rate: 31.7%; Median home value: $124,200; Median year structure built: Before 1940; Homeowner vacancy rate: 5.3%; Median selected monthly owner costs: $1,102 with a mortgage, $523 without a mortgage; Median gross rent: $796 per month; Rental vacancy rate: 12.2%

Health Insurance: 96.2% have insurance; 73.7% have private insurance; 45.6% have public insurance; 3.8% do not have insurance; 3.4% of children under 18 do not have insurance

Safety: Violent crime rate: 5.0 per 10,000 population; Property crime rate: 100.2 per 10,000 population

Transportation: Commute: 95.0% car, 0.0% public transportation, 0.0% walk, 0.6% work from home; Mean travel time to work: 21.1 minutes

Additional Information Contacts

Village of West Carthage . . . . (315) 493-2552
    http://villageofwestcarthage.org

WILNA (town). Covers a land area of 78.623 square miles and a water area of 0.878 square miles. Located at 44.06° N. Lat; 75.59° W. Long.

Population: 6,307; Growth (since 2000): 1.2%; Density: 80.2 persons per square mile; Race: 92.7% White, 2.0% Black/African American, 0.3% Asian, 0.0% American Indian/Alaska Native, 0.0% Native Hawaiian/Other Pacific Islander, 4.5% Two or more races, 2.1% Hispanic of any race; Average household size: 2.78; Median age: 29.1; Age under 18: 29.1%; Age 65 and over: 11.8%; Males per 100 females: 98.8; Marriage status: 37.6% never married, 46.3% now married, 3.8% separated, 6.0% widowed, 10.2% divorced; Foreign born: 2.2%; Speak English only: 97.1%; With disability: 17.2%; Veterans: 13.0%; Ancestry: 19.3% Irish, 15.0% French, 14.2% German, 12.5% Italian, 9.6% English

Employment: 14.6% management, business, and financial, 2.2% computer, engineering, and science, 5.1% education, legal, community service, arts, and media, 4.9% healthcare practitioners, 26.6% service, 20.7% sales and office, 16.3% natural resources, construction, and maintenance, 9.6% production, transportation, and material moving

Income: Per capita: $20,925; Median household: $46,519; Average household: $57,190; Households with income of $100,000 or more: 16.3%; Poverty rate: 21.4%

Educational Attainment: High school diploma or higher: 91.2%; Bachelor's degree or higher: 12.4%; Graduate/professional degree or higher: 4.9%

Housing: Homeownership rate: 52.5%; Median home value: $133,600; Median year structure built: 1952; Homeowner vacancy rate: 0.2%; Median selected monthly owner costs: $1,230 with a mortgage, $601 without a mortgage; Median gross rent: $857 per month; Rental vacancy rate: 4.9%

Health Insurance: 94.5% have insurance; 61.1% have private insurance; 43.1% have public insurance; 5.5% do not have insurance; 0.4% of children under 18 do not have insurance

Transportation: Commute: 84.2% car, 0.0% public transportation, 5.6% walk, 5.9% work from home; Mean travel time to work: 19.0 minutes

WORTH (town). Covers a land area of 43.218 square miles and a water area of 0.086 square miles. Located at 43.74° N. Lat; 75.84° W. Long. Elevation is 1,237 feet.

Population: 232; Growth (since 2000): -0.9%; Density: 5.4 persons per square mile; Race: 100.0% White, 0.0% Black/African American, 0.0% Asian, 0.0% American Indian/Alaska Native, 0.0% Native Hawaiian/Other Pacific Islander, 0.0% Two or more races, 0.0% Hispanic of any race; Average household size: 2.64; Median age: 39.3; Age under 18: 25.4%; Age 65 and over: 19.0%; Males per 100 females: 99.1; Marriage status: 11.9% never married, 64.8% now married, 3.4% separated, 10.2% widowed, 13.1% divorced; Foreign born: 0.0%; Speak English only: 96.6%; With disability: 11.6%; Veterans: 8.7%; Ancestry: 27.2% English, 25.9% Irish, 13.8% Italian, 9.5% American, 6.9% French

Employment: 16.0% management, business, and financial, 4.0% computer, engineering, and science, 19.0% education, legal, community service, arts, and media, 5.0% healthcare practitioners, 5.0% service, 22.0% sales and office, 19.0% natural resources, construction, and maintenance, 10.0% production, transportation, and material moving

Income: Per capita: $26,181; Median household: $61,250; Average household: $67,892; Households with income of $100,000 or more: 21.6%; Poverty rate: 27.6%

Educational Attainment: High school diploma or higher: 88.0%; Bachelor's degree or higher: 11.4%; Graduate/professional degree or higher: 5.4%

Housing: Homeownership rate: 90.9%; Median home value: $105,600; Median year structure built: 1977; Homeowner vacancy rate: 7.9%; Median selected monthly owner costs: $1,297 with a mortgage, $375 without a mortgage; Median gross rent: n/a per month; Rental vacancy rate: 0.0%

Health Insurance: 95.3% have insurance; 68.1% have private insurance; 44.8% have public insurance; 4.7% do not have insurance; 8.5% of children under 18 do not have insurance

Transportation: Commute: 95.8% car, 0.0% public transportation, 3.2% walk, 1.1% work from home; Mean travel time to work: 43.0 minutes

Kings County

See New York City

Lewis County

Located in north central New York; includes the foothills of the Adirondacks in the east; drained by the Black River. Covers a land area of 1,274.679 square miles, a water area of 15.282 square miles, and is located in the Eastern Time Zone at 43.79° N. Lat., 75.44° W. Long. The county was founded in 1805. County seat is Lowville.

Weather Station: Lowville										Elevation: 859 feet		
	Jan	Feb	Mar	Apr	May	Jun	Jul	Aug	Sep	Oct	Nov	Dec
High	26	29	37	52	65	74	78	77	69	56	44	32
Low	7	9	19	32	43	52	56	55	47	36	28	15
Precip	3.2	2.5	2.7	3.2	3.3	3.4	3.6	3.7	4.0	4.1	3.9	3.6
Snow	33.0	25.7	14.9	4.7	0.1	0.0	0.0	0.0	tr	0.8	9.3	32.9

High and Low temperatures in degrees Fahrenheit; Precipitation and Snow in inches

Population: 26,845; Growth (since 2000): -0.4%; Density: 21.1 persons per square mile; Race: 96.6% White, 0.7% Black/African American, 0.4% Asian, 0.2% American Indian/Alaska Native, 0.1% Native Hawaiian/Other Pacific Islander, 1.2% two or more races, 1.7% Hispanic of any race; Average household size: 2.59; Median age: 41.8; Age under 18: 23.3%; Age 65 and over: 16.7%; Males per 100 females: 101.1; Marriage status: 27.2% never married, 56.9% now married, 1.5% separated, 6.3% widowed, 9.6% divorced; Foreign born: 1.5%; Speak English only: 97.6%; With disability: 13.9%; Veterans: 9.3%; Ancestry: 27.9% German, 15.6% Irish, 11.3% French, 9.7% English, 5.8% Polish

Religion: Six largest groups: 23.8% Catholicism, 7.5% European Free-Church, 4.6% Methodist/Pietist, 1.8% Presbyterian-Reformed, 1.4% Non-denominational Protestant, 1.2% Baptist

Economy: Unemployment rate: 3.9%; Leading industries: 15.2 % retail trade; 14.3 % other services (except public administration); 12.6 % accommodation and food services; Farms: 634 totaling 181,741 acres; Company size: 0 employ 1,000 or more persons, 1 employs 500 to 999 persons, 6 employ 100 to 499 persons, 525 employ less than 100 persons;

Business ownership: 454 women-owned, n/a Black-owned, n/a Hispanic-owned, n/a Asian-owned, n/a American Indian/Alaska Native-owned

Employment: 11.0% management, business, and financial, 2.6% computer, engineering, and science, 10.2% education, legal, community service, arts, and media, 7.1% healthcare practitioners, 16.9% service, 18.0% sales and office, 18.4% natural resources, construction, and maintenance, 15.8% production, transportation, and material moving

Income: Per capita: $25,779; Median household: $51,475; Average household: $65,970; Households with income of $100,000 or more: 19.2%; Poverty rate: 14.2%

Educational Attainment: High school diploma or higher: 89.9%; Bachelor's degree or higher: 16.3%; Graduate/professional degree or higher: 7.2%

Housing: Homeownership rate: 78.0%; Median home value: $121,700; Median year structure built: 1969; Homeowner vacancy rate: 2.1%; Median selected monthly owner costs: $1,158 with a mortgage, $452 without a mortgage; Median gross rent: $742 per month; Rental vacancy rate: 8.8%

Vital Statistics: Birth rate: 114.9 per 10,000 population; Death rate: 102.1 per 10,000 population; Age-adjusted cancer mortality rate: 174.2 deaths per 100,000 population

Health Insurance: 92.2% have insurance; 69.4% have private insurance; 37.3% have public insurance; 7.8% do not have insurance; 6.7% of children under 18 do not have insurance

Health Care: Physicians: 9.0 per 10,000 population; Dentists: 1.9 per 10,000 population; Hospital beds: 69.4 per 10,000 population; Hospital admissions: 508.1 per 10,000 population

Transportation: Commute: 88.5% car, 0.3% public transportation, 5.4% walk, 4.7% work from home; Mean travel time to work: 24.5 minutes

2016 Presidential Election: 65.3% Trump, 27.8% Clinton, 4.4% Johnson, 1.2% Stein

National and State Parks: Sand Flats State Park; Whetstone Gulf State Park

Additional Information Contacts

Lewis Government . . . . (315) 376-5355
  http://www.lewiscountyny.org

Lewis County Communities

BEAVER FALLS (unincorporated postal area)
ZCTA: 13305

Covers a land area of 0.959 square miles and a water area of 0 square miles. Located at 43.89° N. Lat; 75.42° W. Long. Elevation is 807 feet.

Population: 417; Growth (since 2000): n/a; Density: 434.7 persons per square mile; Race: 100.0% White, 0.0% Black/African American, 0.0% Asian, 0.0% American Indian/Alaska Native, 0.0% Native Hawaiian/Other Pacific Islander, 0.0% Two or more races, 0.0% Hispanic of any race; Average household size: 3.26; Median age: 31.1; Age under 18: 32.4%; Age 65 and over: 11.3%; Males per 100 females: 99.3; Marriage status: 25.2% never married, 44.0% now married, 0.0% separated, 15.6% widowed, 15.2% divorced; Foreign born: 0.0%; Speak English only: 100.0%; With disability: 22.5%; Veterans: 18.8%; Ancestry: 36.0% French, 27.1% German, 24.5% Irish, 13.9% English, 12.2% Italian

Employment: 0.0% management, business, and financial, 0.0% computer, engineering, and science, 12.9% education, legal, community service, arts, and media, 11.3% healthcare practitioners, 26.8% service, 21.1% sales and office, 16.0% natural resources, construction, and maintenance, 11.9% production, transportation, and material moving

Income: Per capita: $22,802; Median household: $47,200; Average household: $71,233; Households with income of $100,000 or more: 17.2%; Poverty rate: n/a

Educational Attainment: High school diploma or higher: 88.2%; Bachelor's degree or higher: 28.3%; Graduate/professional degree or higher: n/a

School District(s)

Beaver River Central SD (PK-12)
  Enrollment: 885 . . . . (315) 346-1211

Housing: Homeownership rate: 76.6%; Median home value: $143,800; Median year structure built: 1964; Homeowner vacancy rate: 0.0%; Median selected monthly owner costs: $1,438 with a mortgage, $0 without a mortgage; Median gross rent: n/a per month; Rental vacancy rate: 0.0%

Health Insurance: 92.1% have insurance; 66.7% have private insurance; 30.0% have public insurance; 7.9% do not have insurance; 24.4% of children under 18 do not have insurance

Transportation: Commute: 100.0% car, 0.0% public transportation, 0.0% walk, 0.0% work from home; Mean travel time to work: 33.1 minutes

BRANTINGHAM (unincorporated postal area)
ZCTA: 13312

Covers a land area of 63.744 square miles and a water area of 1.013 square miles. Located at 43.70° N. Lat; 75.19° W. Long. Elevation is 1,253 feet.

Population: 424; Growth (since 2000): -38.5%; Density: 6.7 persons per square mile; Race: 99.1% White, 0.0% Black/African American, 0.0% Asian, 0.0% American Indian/Alaska Native, 0.0% Native Hawaiian/Other Pacific Islander, 0.9% Two or more races, 1.2% Hispanic of any race; Average household size: 2.27; Median age: 55.5; Age under 18: 17.9%; Age 65 and over: 29.7%; Males per 100 females: 106.9; Marriage status: 19.3% never married, 67.9% now married, 1.4% separated, 3.3% widowed, 9.5% divorced; Foreign born: 1.2%; Speak English only: 100.0%; With disability: 7.5%; Veterans: 9.8%; Ancestry: 34.2% German, 22.4% Irish, 14.4% Italian, 10.6% English, 10.6% French

Employment: 6.9% management, business, and financial, 0.0% computer, engineering, and science, 6.3% education, legal, community service, arts, and media, 4.6% healthcare practitioners, 31.0% service, 18.4% sales and office, 22.4% natural resources, construction, and maintenance, 10.3% production, transportation, and material moving

Income: Per capita: $32,007; Median household: $49,583; Average household: $72,141; Households with income of $100,000 or more: 23.0%; Poverty rate: 4.0%

Educational Attainment: High school diploma or higher: 95.7%; Bachelor's degree or higher: 30.2%; Graduate/professional degree or higher: 19.4%

Housing: Homeownership rate: 86.1%; Median home value: $240,400; Median year structure built: 1956; Homeowner vacancy rate: 0.0%; Median selected monthly owner costs: $1,433 with a mortgage, $634 without a mortgage; Median gross rent: $1,014 per month; Rental vacancy rate: 35.2%

Health Insurance: 98.3% have insurance; 75.9% have private insurance; 44.6% have public insurance; 1.7% do not have insurance; 0.0% of children under 18 do not have insurance

Transportation: Commute: 82.8% car, 0.0% public transportation, 10.3% walk, 1.7% work from home; Mean travel time to work: 25.0 minutes

CASTORLAND (village). Covers a land area of 0.321 square miles and a water area of 0 square miles. Located at 43.89° N. Lat; 75.52° W. Long. Elevation is 741 feet.

Population: 324; Growth (since 2000): 5.9%; Density: 1,009.2 persons per square mile; Race: 90.7% White, 0.0% Black/African American, 0.0% Asian, 0.0% American Indian/Alaska Native, 0.0% Native Hawaiian/Other Pacific Islander, 4.3% Two or more races, 10.5% Hispanic of any race; Average household size: 3.00; Median age: 28.5; Age under 18: 33.0%; Age 65 and over: 18.8%; Males per 100 females: 83.8; Marriage status: 30.1% never married, 55.1% now married, 5.5% separated, 6.4% widowed, 8.5% divorced; Foreign born: 4.0%; Speak English only: 88.9%; With disability: 14.7%; Veterans: 8.5%; Ancestry: 29.3% German, 9.6% English, 8.0% Irish, 6.8% Swiss, 3.4% Italian

Employment: 8.6% management, business, and financial, 4.3% computer, engineering, and science, 8.6% education, legal, community service, arts, and media, 2.2% healthcare practitioners, 15.1% service, 34.4% sales and office, 8.6% natural resources, construction, and maintenance, 18.3% production, transportation, and material moving

Income: Per capita: $21,573; Median household: $45,000; Average household: $62,271; Households with income of $100,000 or more: 12.1%; Poverty rate: 18.2%

Educational Attainment: High school diploma or higher: 84.1%; Bachelor's degree or higher: 11.3%; Graduate/professional degree or higher: 1.0%

Housing: Homeownership rate: 48.1%; Median home value: $106,300; Median year structure built: Before 1940; Homeowner vacancy rate: 0.0%; Median selected monthly owner costs: $1,163 with a mortgage, $561 without a mortgage; Median gross rent: $628 per month; Rental vacancy rate: 13.0%

Health Insurance: 94.4% have insurance; 54.9% have private insurance; 62.1% have public insurance; 5.6% do not have insurance; 5.3% of children under 18 do not have insurance
Transportation: Commute: 97.8% car, 0.0% public transportation, 0.0% walk, 2.2% work from home; Mean travel time to work: 18.0 minutes

CONSTABLEVILLE (village). Covers a land area of 1.118 square miles and a water area of 0 square miles. Located at 43.56° N. Lat; 75.43° W. Long. Elevation is 1,263 feet.
Population: 267; Growth (since 2000): -12.5%; Density: 238.7 persons per square mile; Race: 95.1% White, 0.0% Black/African American, 0.0% Asian, 0.0% American Indian/Alaska Native, 0.0% Native Hawaiian/Other Pacific Islander, 4.9% Two or more races, 1.1% Hispanic of any race; Average household size: 2.43; Median age: 41.9; Age under 18: 24.0%; Age 65 and over: 10.5%; Males per 100 females: 98.4; Marriage status: 34.3% never married, 52.4% now married, 1.9% separated, 5.2% widowed, 8.1% divorced; Foreign born: 0.0%; Speak English only: 99.2%; With disability: 11.2%; Veterans: 6.9%; Ancestry: 17.6% German, 15.7% Polish, 15.0% American, 12.7% Irish, 10.1% French
Employment: 19.5% management, business, and financial, 0.8% computer, engineering, and science, 9.3% education, legal, community service, arts, and media, 5.1% healthcare practitioners, 14.4% service, 21.2% sales and office, 20.3% natural resources, construction, and maintenance, 9.3% production, transportation, and material moving
Income: Per capita: $20,662; Median household: $48,125; Average household: $49,252; Households with income of $100,000 or more: 3.6%; Poverty rate: 17.2%
Educational Attainment: High school diploma or higher: 90.0%; Bachelor's degree or higher: 12.6%; Graduate/professional degree or higher: 5.3%

School District(s)
South Lewis Central SD (PK-12)
    Enrollment: 1,064 . . . . (315) 348-2500
Housing: Homeownership rate: 89.1%; Median home value: $79,200; Median year structure built: Before 1940; Homeowner vacancy rate: 5.8%; Median selected monthly owner costs: $1,144 with a mortgage, $537 without a mortgage; Median gross rent: $706 per month; Rental vacancy rate: 0.0%
Health Insurance: 91.4% have insurance; 64.4% have private insurance; 37.1% have public insurance; 8.6% do not have insurance; 12.5% of children under 18 do not have insurance
Transportation: Commute: 88.0% car, 0.0% public transportation, 3.4% walk, 5.1% work from home; Mean travel time to work: 29.1 minutes

COPENHAGEN (village). Covers a land area of 1.176 square miles and a water area of 0 square miles. Located at 43.89° N. Lat; 75.67° W. Long. Elevation is 1,165 feet.
Population: 803; Growth (since 2000): -7.2%; Density: 683.1 persons per square mile; Race: 95.8% White, 1.9% Black/African American, 0.4% Asian, 0.0% American Indian/Alaska Native, 0.0% Native Hawaiian/Other Pacific Islander, 2.0% Two or more races, 3.1% Hispanic of any race; Average household size: 2.28; Median age: 30.9; Age under 18: 16.2%; Age 65 and over: 14.6%; Males per 100 females: 103.8; Marriage status: 29.4% never married, 55.6% now married, 3.9% separated, 6.1% widowed, 9.0% divorced; Foreign born: 1.5%; Speak English only: 98.9%; With disability: 18.3%; Veterans: 13.4%; Ancestry: 25.0% German, 16.2% Irish, 15.6% French, 13.6% English, 6.8% Polish
Employment: 12.0% management, business, and financial, 4.3% computer, engineering, and science, 8.8% education, legal, community service, arts, and media, 5.1% healthcare practitioners, 24.8% service, 23.2% sales and office, 12.8% natural resources, construction, and maintenance, 9.1% production, transportation, and material moving
Income: Per capita: $26,883; Median household: $47,500; Average household: $60,648; Households with income of $100,000 or more: 18.8%; Poverty rate: 8.2%
Educational Attainment: High school diploma or higher: 91.0%; Bachelor's degree or higher: 11.4%; Graduate/professional degree or higher: 4.2%

School District(s)
Copenhagen Central SD (PK-12)
    Enrollment: 479 . . . . (315) 688-4411
Housing: Homeownership rate: 43.2%; Median home value: $137,900; Median year structure built: 1972; Homeowner vacancy rate: 11.1%; Median selected monthly owner costs: $1,325 with a mortgage, $487

without a mortgage; Median gross rent: $880 per month; Rental vacancy rate: 9.9%
Health Insurance: 94.2% have insurance; 77.6% have private insurance; 31.5% have public insurance; 5.8% do not have insurance; 10.8% of children under 18 do not have insurance
Transportation: Commute: 90.0% car, 0.0% public transportation, 6.1% walk, 3.8% work from home; Mean travel time to work: 22.2 minutes

CROGHAN (town). Covers a land area of 179.182 square miles and a water area of 2.849 square miles. Located at 43.97° N. Lat; 75.36° W. Long. Elevation is 827 feet.
History: American Maple Museum.
Population: 3,080; Growth (since 2000): -2.6%; Density: 17.2 persons per square mile; Race: 98.0% White, 0.6% Black/African American, 0.0% Asian, 0.0% American Indian/Alaska Native, 0.0% Native Hawaiian/Other Pacific Islander, 0.6% Two or more races, 1.0% Hispanic of any race; Average household size: 2.59; Median age: 42.8; Age under 18: 22.9%; Age 65 and over: 19.4%; Males per 100 females: 105.4; Marriage status: 25.7% never married, 61.5% now married, 1.0% separated, 6.3% widowed, 6.4% divorced; Foreign born: 1.0%; Speak English only: 99.9%; With disability: 17.3%; Veterans: 8.8%; Ancestry: 36.9% German, 13.5% French, 8.8% Irish, 8.8% English, 7.4% Italian
Employment: 9.3% management, business, and financial, 0.8% computer, engineering, and science, 12.6% education, legal, community service, arts, and media, 6.8% healthcare practitioners, 14.4% service, 14.9% sales and office, 15.2% natural resources, construction, and maintenance, 25.9% production, transportation, and material moving
Income: Per capita: $24,878; Median household: $42,500; Average household: $63,367; Households with income of $100,000 or more: 17.5%; Poverty rate: 9.0%
Educational Attainment: High school diploma or higher: 84.0%; Bachelor's degree or higher: 13.6%; Graduate/professional degree or higher: 5.9%
Housing: Homeownership rate: 79.7%; Median home value: $126,300; Median year structure built: 1969; Homeowner vacancy rate: 0.0%; Median selected monthly owner costs: $1,142 with a mortgage, $428 without a mortgage; Median gross rent: $621 per month; Rental vacancy rate: 7.3%
Health Insurance: 89.0% have insurance; 67.6% have private insurance; 37.0% have public insurance; 11.0% do not have insurance; 14.1% of children under 18 do not have insurance
Transportation: Commute: 90.7% car, 0.6% public transportation, 3.8% walk, 4.9% work from home; Mean travel time to work: 24.5 minutes

CROGHAN (village). Covers a land area of 0.434 square miles and a water area of 0 square miles. Located at 43.89° N. Lat; 75.39° W. Long. Elevation is 827 feet.
Population: 631; Growth (since 2000): -5.1%; Density: 1,454.4 persons per square mile; Race: 94.3% White, 0.0% Black/African American, 1.7% Asian, 0.3% American Indian/Alaska Native, 0.0% Native Hawaiian/Other Pacific Islander, 1.3% Two or more races, 2.7% Hispanic of any race; Average household size: 2.31; Median age: 42.9; Age under 18: 23.5%; Age 65 and over: 26.3%; Males per 100 females: 89.0; Marriage status: 21.9% never married, 58.8% now married, 0.6% separated, 12.4% widowed, 7.0% divorced; Foreign born: 5.1%; Speak English only: 97.1%; With disability: 21.2%; Veterans: 6.8%; Ancestry: 42.8% German, 16.2% French, 8.7% Irish, 4.8% American, 3.2% Swiss
Employment: 6.9% management, business, and financial, 0.0% computer, engineering, and science, 16.9% education, legal, community service, arts, and media, 4.8% healthcare practitioners, 24.7% service, 20.3% sales and office, 8.7% natural resources, construction, and maintenance, 17.7% production, transportation, and material moving
Income: Per capita: $22,215; Median household: $35,208; Average household: $52,309; Households with income of $100,000 or more: 15.0%; Poverty rate: 8.9%
Educational Attainment: High school diploma or higher: 83.6%; Bachelor's degree or higher: 14.4%; Graduate/professional degree or higher: 7.7%
Housing: Homeownership rate: 62.3%; Median home value: $112,800; Median year structure built: 1942; Homeowner vacancy rate: 0.0%; Median selected monthly owner costs: $1,270 with a mortgage, $447 without a mortgage; Median gross rent: $531 per month; Rental vacancy rate: 18.9%
Health Insurance: 96.4% have insurance; 66.4% have private insurance; 47.7% have public insurance; 3.6% do not have insurance; 2.5% of children under 18 do not have insurance

Transportation: Commute: 90.2% car, 0.0% public transportation, 5.8% walk, 4.0% work from home; Mean travel time to work: 22.7 minutes

DENMARK (town). Covers a land area of 50.602 square miles and a water area of 0.446 square miles. Located at 43.90° N. Lat; 75.63° W. Long. Elevation is 971 feet.
Population: 2,841; Growth (since 2000): 3.4%; Density: 56.1 persons per square mile; Race: 96.6% White, 0.5% Black/African American, 0.1% Asian, 0.0% American Indian/Alaska Native, 0.0% Native Hawaiian/Other Pacific Islander, 2.0% Two or more races, 3.8% Hispanic of any race; Average household size: 2.56; Median age: 37.2; Age under 18: 21.2%; Age 65 and over: 12.9%; Males per 100 females: 101.8; Marriage status: 29.6% never married, 59.4% now married, 3.3% separated, 4.5% widowed, 6.4% divorced; Foreign born: 1.1%; Speak English only: 97.0%; With disability: 14.1%; Veterans: 8.7%; Ancestry: 29.3% German, 17.5% Irish, 9.4% English, 7.5% French, 5.4% Polish
Employment: 14.1% management, business, and financial, 2.1% computer, engineering, and science, 9.1% education, legal, community service, arts, and media, 7.1% healthcare practitioners, 16.4% service, 21.3% sales and office, 17.1% natural resources, construction, and maintenance, 12.6% production, transportation, and material moving
Income: Per capita: $28,257; Median household: $56,806; Average household: $71,022; Households with income of $100,000 or more: 19.2%; Poverty rate: 9.0%
Educational Attainment: High school diploma or higher: 91.7%; Bachelor's degree or higher: 12.7%; Graduate/professional degree or higher: 4.6%
Housing: Homeownership rate: 69.5%; Median home value: $146,400; Median year structure built: 1975; Homeowner vacancy rate: 4.9%; Median selected monthly owner costs: $1,420 with a mortgage, $534 without a mortgage; Median gross rent: $851 per month; Rental vacancy rate: 11.2%
Health Insurance: 94.4% have insurance; 74.1% have private insurance; 32.5% have public insurance; 5.6% do not have insurance; 4.4% of children under 18 do not have insurance
Transportation: Commute: 91.0% car, 0.0% public transportation, 4.5% walk, 3.9% work from home; Mean travel time to work: 21.5 minutes

DIANA (town). Covers a land area of 137.094 square miles and a water area of 3.738 square miles. Located at 44.11° N. Lat; 75.37° W. Long.
Population: 1,650; Growth (since 2000): -0.7%; Density: 12.0 persons per square mile; Race: 97.9% White, 0.9% Black/African American, 0.0% Asian, 0.5% American Indian/Alaska Native, 0.0% Native Hawaiian/Other Pacific Islander, 0.7% Two or more races, 0.0% Hispanic of any race; Average household size: 2.52; Median age: 42.6; Age under 18: 21.0%; Age 65 and over: 17.0%; Males per 100 females: 95.8; Marriage status: 26.0% never married, 53.2% now married, 1.3% separated, 7.0% widowed, 13.8% divorced; Foreign born: 0.5%; Speak English only: 99.8%; With disability: 17.9%; Veterans: 12.4%; Ancestry: 18.1% German, 14.5% English, 10.8% French, 9.6% Italian, 9.3% Irish
Employment: 9.1% management, business, and financial, 4.1% computer, engineering, and science, 2.8% education, legal, community service, arts, and media, 4.2% healthcare practitioners, 21.8% service, 24.9% sales and office, 20.7% natural resources, construction, and maintenance, 12.4% production, transportation, and material moving
Income: Per capita: $21,238; Median household: $42,548; Average household: $51,995; Households with income of $100,000 or more: 12.2%; Poverty rate: 20.8%
Educational Attainment: High school diploma or higher: 85.1%; Bachelor's degree or higher: 13.4%; Graduate/professional degree or higher: 3.8%
Housing: Homeownership rate: 73.4%; Median home value: $107,800; Median year structure built: 1966; Homeowner vacancy rate: 4.8%; Median selected monthly owner costs: $1,129 with a mortgage, $414 without a mortgage; Median gross rent: $733 per month; Rental vacancy rate: 0.0%
Health Insurance: 91.6% have insurance; 66.2% have private insurance; 42.4% have public insurance; 8.4% do not have insurance; 3.9% of children under 18 do not have insurance
Transportation: Commute: 97.1% car, 0.0% public transportation, 1.7% walk, 0.0% work from home; Mean travel time to work: 27.5 minutes

GLENFIELD (unincorporated postal area)
ZCTA: 13343
Covers a land area of 56.180 square miles and a water area of 0.954 square miles. Located at 43.75° N. Lat; 75.31° W. Long. Elevation is 768 feet.

Population: 1,794; Growth (since 2000): 2.4%; Density: 31.9 persons per square mile; Race: 99.9% White, 0.1% Black/African American, 0.0% Asian, 0.0% American Indian/Alaska Native, 0.0% Native Hawaiian/Other Pacific Islander, 0.0% Two or more races, 0.5% Hispanic of any race; Average household size: 2.48; Median age: 46.5; Age under 18: 20.8%; Age 65 and over: 18.5%; Males per 100 females: 105.2; Marriage status: 19.8% never married, 62.6% now married, 1.5% separated, 5.6% widowed, 12.0% divorced; Foreign born: 0.0%; Speak English only: 98.8%; With disability: 12.4%; Veterans: 10.2%; Ancestry: 24.5% German, 18.7% Irish, 15.1% French, 7.9% English, 7.0% Hungarian
Employment: 14.9% management, business, and financial, 3.8% computer, engineering, and science, 7.8% education, legal, community service, arts, and media, 5.9% healthcare practitioners, 15.0% service, 23.0% sales and office, 13.5% natural resources, construction, and maintenance, 16.1% production, transportation, and material moving
Income: Per capita: $28,043; Median household: $59,306; Average household: $69,222; Households with income of $100,000 or more: 18.4%; Poverty rate: 10.8%
Educational Attainment: High school diploma or higher: 92.8%; Bachelor's degree or higher: 16.8%; Graduate/professional degree or higher: 6.4%

School District(s)
South Lewis Central SD (PK-12)
    Enrollment: 1,064 . . . . (315) 348-2500
Housing: Homeownership rate: 85.8%; Median home value: $104,000; Median year structure built: 1972; Homeowner vacancy rate: 0.5%; Median selected monthly owner costs: $1,060 with a mortgage, $446 without a mortgage; Median gross rent: $626 per month; Rental vacancy rate: 8.9%
Health Insurance: 89.6% have insurance; 66.4% have private insurance; 39.6% have public insurance; 10.4% do not have insurance; 14.4% of children under 18 do not have insurance
Transportation: Commute: 87.8% car, 0.0% public transportation, 4.0% walk, 6.3% work from home; Mean travel time to work: 25.7 minutes

GREIG (town). Covers a land area of 93.011 square miles and a water area of 1.354 square miles. Located at 43.70° N. Lat; 75.19° W. Long. Elevation is 807 feet.
Population: 1,294; Growth (since 2000): -5.2%; Density: 13.9 persons per square mile; Race: 96.9% White, 0.9% Black/African American, 0.0% Asian, 0.0% American Indian/Alaska Native, 0.0% Native Hawaiian/Other Pacific Islander, 1.8% Two or more races, 0.4% Hispanic of any race; Average household size: 2.32; Median age: 51.2; Age under 18: 17.9%; Age 65 and over: 22.2%; Males per 100 females: 106.4; Marriage status: 18.9% never married, 62.5% now married, 1.1% separated, 6.2% widowed, 12.5% divorced; Foreign born: 0.4%; Speak English only: 99.4%; With disability: 14.1%; Veterans: 8.3%; Ancestry: 25.3% German, 21.2% Irish, 18.6% French, 12.3% English, 7.3% Hungarian
Employment: 13.1% management, business, and financial, 2.4% computer, engineering, and science, 6.1% education, legal, community service, arts, and media, 5.9% healthcare practitioners, 19.7% service, 17.1% sales and office, 22.4% natural resources, construction, and maintenance, 13.4% production, transportation, and material moving
Income: Per capita: $31,449; Median household: $62,153; Average household: $72,998; Households with income of $100,000 or more: 22.1%; Poverty rate: 6.5%
Educational Attainment: High school diploma or higher: 93.6%; Bachelor's degree or higher: 21.1%; Graduate/professional degree or higher: 10.3%
Housing: Homeownership rate: 87.4%; Median home value: $137,100; Median year structure built: 1966; Homeowner vacancy rate: 1.8%; Median selected monthly owner costs: $1,176 with a mortgage, $482 without a mortgage; Median gross rent: $786 per month; Rental vacancy rate: 21.8%
Health Insurance: 92.2% have insurance; 68.3% have private insurance; 39.2% have public insurance; 7.8% do not have insurance; 11.6% of children under 18 do not have insurance
Transportation: Commute: 88.3% car, 0.0% public transportation, 5.0% walk, 3.4% work from home; Mean travel time to work: 27.1 minutes

HARRISBURG (town). Covers a land area of 39.882 square miles and a water area of 0.028 square miles. Located at 43.84° N. Lat; 75.67° W. Long. Elevation is 1,362 feet.
Population: 484; Growth (since 2000): 14.4%; Density: 12.1 persons per square mile; Race: 94.4% White, 0.0% Black/African American, 1.2%

Asian, 0.0% American Indian/Alaska Native, 0.0% Native Hawaiian/Other Pacific Islander, 4.3% Two or more races, 0.0% Hispanic of any race; Average household size: 2.97; Median age: 36.3; Age under 18: 30.2%; Age 65 and over: 12.0%; Males per 100 females: 117.4; Marriage status: 26.5% never married, 63.5% now married, 4.1% separated, 3.9% widowed, 6.1% divorced; Foreign born: 1.2%; Speak English only: 98.6%; With disability: 12.0%; Veterans: 8.6%; Ancestry: 25.8% Irish, 24.8% German, 9.7% Scottish, 7.6% French Canadian, 5.8% French

Employment: 12.5% management, business, and financial, 0.0% computer, engineering, and science, 8.8% education, legal, community service, arts, and media, 6.3% healthcare practitioners, 18.3% service, 15.4% sales and office, 27.1% natural resources, construction, and maintenance, 11.7% production, transportation, and material moving
Income: Per capita: $23,387; Median household: $57,292; Average household: $68,220; Households with income of $100,000 or more: 20.3%; Poverty rate: 18.0%
Educational Attainment: High school diploma or higher: 81.7%; Bachelor's degree or higher: 13.0%; Graduate/professional degree or higher: 4.0%
Housing: Homeownership rate: 94.5%; Median home value: $130,000; Median year structure built: 1975; Homeowner vacancy rate: 1.9%; Median selected monthly owner costs: $1,125 with a mortgage, $509 without a mortgage; Median gross rent: n/a per month; Rental vacancy rate: 47.1%
Health Insurance: 88.8% have insurance; 58.7% have private insurance; 39.7% have public insurance; 11.2% do not have insurance; 13.5% of children under 18 do not have insurance
Transportation: Commute: 87.1% car, 2.1% public transportation, 3.9% walk, 3.0% work from home; Mean travel time to work: 25.1 minutes

HARRISVILLE (village). Covers a land area of 0.737 square miles and a water area of 0.046 square miles. Located at 44.15° N. Lat; 75.32° W. Long. Elevation is 807 feet.

Population: 610; Growth (since 2000): -6.6%; Density: 827.2 persons per square mile; Race: 99.5% White, 0.0% Black/African American, 0.0% Asian, 0.5% American Indian/Alaska Native, 0.0% Native Hawaiian/Other Pacific Islander, 0.0% Two or more races, 0.0% Hispanic of any race; Average household size: 2.51; Median age: 40.8; Age under 18: 21.1%; Age 65 and over: 14.1%; Males per 100 females: 84.7; Marriage status: 22.5% never married, 47.0% now married, 3.4% separated, 10.5% widowed, 20.0% divorced; Foreign born: 0.0%; Speak English only: 99.5%; With disability: 20.7%; Veterans: 16.8%; Ancestry: 23.3% English, 13.9% Italian, 13.3% French, 13.1% Irish, 12.8% German
Employment: 17.4% management, business, and financial, 1.7% computer, engineering, and science, 4.1% education, legal, community service, arts, and media, 0.8% healthcare practitioners, 34.9% service, 20.3% sales and office, 11.2% natural resources, construction, and maintenance, 9.5% production, transportation, and material moving
Income: Per capita: $21,624; Median household: $41,979; Average household: $52,283; Households with income of $100,000 or more: 8.3%; Poverty rate: 22.5%
Educational Attainment: High school diploma or higher: 90.6%; Bachelor's degree or higher: 20.6%; Graduate/professional degree or higher: 4.2%

School District(s)
Harrisville Central SD (PK-12)
   Enrollment: 422 . . . . (315) 543-2707
Housing: Homeownership rate: 69.5%; Median home value: $74,600; Median year structure built: Before 1940; Homeowner vacancy rate: 6.6%; Median selected monthly owner costs: $1,075 with a mortgage, $571 without a mortgage; Median gross rent: $761 per month; Rental vacancy rate: 0.0%
Health Insurance: 91.0% have insurance; 60.3% have private insurance; 47.4% have public insurance; 9.0% do not have insurance; 0.0% of children under 18 do not have insurance
Transportation: Commute: 92.8% car, 0.0% public transportation, 4.2% walk, 0.0% work from home; Mean travel time to work: 27.6 minutes

LEWIS (town). Covers a land area of 64.607 square miles and a water area of 0.542 square miles. Located at 43.49° N. Lat; 75.56° W. Long.
Population: 782; Growth (since 2000): -8.8%; Density: 12.1 persons per square mile; Race: 95.0% White, 0.0% Black/African American, 3.6% Asian, 0.0% American Indian/Alaska Native, 0.0% Native Hawaiian/Other Pacific Islander, 1.4% Two or more races, 0.0% Hispanic of any race; Average household size: 2.44; Median age: 43.3; Age under 18: 19.8%; Age 65 and over: 9.7%; Males per 100 females: 109.3; Marriage status:

33.2% never married, 54.5% now married, 1.7% separated, 4.3% widowed, 8.0% divorced; Foreign born: 2.8%; Speak English only: 97.0%; With disability: 12.7%; Veterans: 8.5%; Ancestry: 45.7% German, 20.5% Irish, 11.0% Polish, 10.4% French, 9.5% American
Employment: 8.9% management, business, and financial, 2.5% computer, engineering, and science, 6.4% education, legal, community service, arts, and media, 9.5% healthcare practitioners, 19.3% service, 12.6% sales and office, 26.3% natural resources, construction, and maintenance, 14.5% production, transportation, and material moving
Income: Per capita: $22,942; Median household: $42,500; Average household: $55,137; Households with income of $100,000 or more: 17.5%; Poverty rate: 17.3%
Educational Attainment: High school diploma or higher: 92.2%; Bachelor's degree or higher: 12.5%; Graduate/professional degree or higher: 5.9%
Housing: Homeownership rate: 84.4%; Median home value: $94,100; Median year structure built: 1975; Homeowner vacancy rate: 4.3%; Median selected monthly owner costs: $909 with a mortgage, $450 without a mortgage; Median gross rent: $625 per month; Rental vacancy rate: 12.3%
Health Insurance: 89.0% have insurance; 58.6% have private insurance; 40.8% have public insurance; 11.0% do not have insurance; 0.0% of children under 18 do not have insurance
Transportation: Commute: 87.8% car, 0.9% public transportation, 1.2% walk, 10.1% work from home; Mean travel time to work: 39.2 minutes

LEYDEN (town). Covers a land area of 33.330 square miles and a water area of 0.222 square miles. Located at 43.53° N. Lat; 75.38° W. Long.
History: Originally known as Kelsey's Mills, it was renamed in 1839 in anticipation of becoming a thriving port upon completion of the Black River Canal.
Population: 1,808; Growth (since 2000): 0.9%; Density: 54.2 persons per square mile; Race: 99.3% White, 0.3% Black/African American, 0.0% Asian, 0.0% American Indian/Alaska Native, 0.0% Native Hawaiian/Other Pacific Islander, 0.3% Two or more races, 0.9% Hispanic of any race; Average household size: 2.57; Median age: 39.2; Age under 18: 28.0%; Age 65 and over: 16.6%; Males per 100 females: 97.7; Marriage status: 25.8% never married, 54.5% now married, 3.2% separated, 7.2% widowed, 12.4% divorced; Foreign born: 0.6%; Speak English only: 98.6%; With disability: 14.0%; Veterans: 9.6%; Ancestry: 31.4% German, 18.9% Irish, 12.4% Polish, 10.7% English, 8.7% French
Employment: 9.7% management, business, and financial, 0.5% computer, engineering, and science, 7.0% education, legal, community service, arts, and media, 7.0% healthcare practitioners, 14.4% service, 19.9% sales and office, 23.2% natural resources, construction, and maintenance, 18.2% production, transportation, and material moving
Income: Per capita: $23,209; Median household: $46,875; Average household: $58,977; Households with income of $100,000 or more: 15.1%; Poverty rate: 13.5%
Educational Attainment: High school diploma or higher: 92.2%; Bachelor's degree or higher: 10.1%; Graduate/professional degree or higher: 3.1%
Housing: Homeownership rate: 77.8%; Median home value: $85,700; Median year structure built: 1971; Homeowner vacancy rate: 0.0%; Median selected monthly owner costs: $1,108 with a mortgage, $418 without a mortgage; Median gross rent: $745 per month; Rental vacancy rate: 17.1%
Health Insurance: 92.8% have insurance; 66.6% have private insurance; 40.9% have public insurance; 7.2% do not have insurance; 2.2% of children under 18 do not have insurance
Transportation: Commute: 89.3% car, 0.0% public transportation, 3.3% walk, 5.3% work from home; Mean travel time to work: 24.1 minutes

LOWVILLE (town). Covers a land area of 37.834 square miles and a water area of 0.291 square miles. Located at 43.81° N. Lat; 75.52° W. Long. Elevation is 883 feet.
History: Lowville was the home of Dr. Franklin B. Hough (1822-1885), called the "father of American forestry" for his conservation activities. Settled 1798, incorporated in 1854.
Population: 4,888; Growth (since 2000): 7.5%; Density: 129.2 persons per square mile; Race: 94.8% White, 2.0% Black/African American, 1.1% Asian, 0.3% American Indian/Alaska Native, 0.5% Native Hawaiian/Other Pacific Islander, 1.1% Two or more races, 0.4% Hispanic of any race; Average household size: 2.63; Median age: 41.8; Age under 18: 23.6%; Age 65 and over: 19.1%; Males per 100 females: 91.1; Marriage status: 31.3% never married, 48.1% now married, 0.5% separated, 9.2%

widowed, 11.4% divorced; Foreign born: 2.1%; Speak English only: 97.1%; With disability: 13.2%; Veterans: 8.3%; Ancestry: 22.9% German, 17.9% Irish, 13.3% English, 9.0% French, 7.4% Scandinavian

Employment: 8.7% management, business, and financial, 6.0% computer, engineering, and science, 19.2% education, legal, community service, arts, and media, 10.9% healthcare practitioners, 16.2% service, 15.7% sales and office, 13.8% natural resources, construction, and maintenance, 9.3% production, transportation, and material moving

Income: Per capita: $27,164; Median household: $57,417; Average household: $72,017; Households with income of $100,000 or more: 28.9%; Poverty rate: 22.0%

Educational Attainment: High school diploma or higher: 91.8%; Bachelor's degree or higher: 26.2%; Graduate/professional degree or higher: 13.6%

School District(s)
Lowville Academy & Central SD (PK-12)
  Enrollment: 1,356 . . . . (315) 376-9000

Housing: Homeownership rate: 67.9%; Median home value: $144,600; Median year structure built: Before 1940; Homeowner vacancy rate: 0.0%; Median selected monthly owner costs: $1,215 with a mortgage, $473 without a mortgage; Median gross rent: $647 per month; Rental vacancy rate: 10.1%

Health Insurance: 98.4% have insurance; 80.2% have private insurance; 30.8% have public insurance; 1.6% do not have insurance; 1.4% of children under 18 do not have insurance

Hospitals: Lewis County General Hospital (160 beds)

Newspapers: Journal & Republican (weekly circulation 5,000)

Transportation: Commute: 86.1% car, 0.0% public transportation, 11.4% walk, 2.4% work from home; Mean travel time to work: 19.5 minutes

LOWVILLE (village). County seat. Covers a land area of 1.911 square miles and a water area of 0 square miles. Located at 43.79° N. Lat; 75.49° W. Long. Elevation is 883 feet.

Population: 3,180; Growth (since 2000): -8.5%; Density: 1,664.0 persons per square mile; Race: 93.9% White, 1.4% Black/African American, 1.7% Asian, 0.4% American Indian/Alaska Native, 0.7% Native Hawaiian/Other Pacific Islander, 1.6% Two or more races, 0.4% Hispanic of any race; Average household size: 2.36; Median age: 42.6; Age under 18: 21.4%; Age 65 and over: 18.6%; Males per 100 females: 90.2; Marriage status: 32.4% never married, 46.7% now married, 0.7% separated, 8.2% widowed, 12.7% divorced; Foreign born: 3.0%; Speak English only: 96.5%; With disability: 14.5%; Veterans: 9.4%; Ancestry: 21.5% German, 19.5% Irish, 7.2% Italian, 7.0% English, 6.7% French

Employment: 9.4% management, business, and financial, 8.8% computer, engineering, and science, 22.2% education, legal, community service, arts, and media, 10.5% healthcare practitioners, 9.5% service, 19.2% sales and office, 10.7% natural resources, construction, and maintenance, 9.7% production, transportation, and material moving

Income: Per capita: $30,075; Median household: $51,938; Average household: $70,505; Households with income of $100,000 or more: 28.0%; Poverty rate: 15.8%

Educational Attainment: High school diploma or higher: 91.5%; Bachelor's degree or higher: 30.6%; Graduate/professional degree or higher: 15.2%

School District(s)
Lowville Academy & Central SD (PK-12)
  Enrollment: 1,356 . . . . (315) 376-9000

Housing: Homeownership rate: 60.6%; Median home value: $142,800; Median year structure built: Before 1940; Homeowner vacancy rate: 0.0%; Median selected monthly owner costs: $1,184 with a mortgage, $503 without a mortgage; Median gross rent: $639 per month; Rental vacancy rate: 10.7%

Health Insurance: 97.8% have insurance; 75.3% have private insurance; 35.0% have public insurance; 2.2% do not have insurance; 2.4% of children under 18 do not have insurance

Hospitals: Lewis County General Hospital (160 beds)

Safety: Violent crime rate: 11.8 per 10,000 population; Property crime rate: 108.9 per 10,000 population

Newspapers: Journal & Republican (weekly circulation 5,000)

Transportation: Commute: 86.5% car, 0.0% public transportation, 10.1% walk, 3.4% work from home; Mean travel time to work: 19.9 minutes

LYONS FALLS (village). Covers a land area of 0.971 square miles and a water area of 0.093 square miles. Located at 43.62° N. Lat; 75.36° W. Long. Elevation is 830 feet.

History: Black River Canal, begun in 1838, completed in 1858, ceased operation in 1922. Never successfully competed with railroad. Completely abandoned in 1926 when its final function as a feeder of water to the New York State Barge Canal was assumed by Delta Lake (northeast of Rome) and Hinckley Reservoir, north of Utica.

Population: 613; Growth (since 2000): 3.7%; Density: 631.3 persons per square mile; Race: 98.2% White, 0.5% Black/African American, 0.0% Asian, 0.0% American Indian/Alaska Native, 0.0% Native Hawaiian/Other Pacific Islander, 1.3% Two or more races, 4.6% Hispanic of any race; Average household size: 2.37; Median age: 48.3; Age under 18: 24.5%; Age 65 and over: 25.3%; Males per 100 females: 102.9; Marriage status: 19.3% never married, 60.5% now married, 1.0% separated, 9.0% widowed, 11.3% divorced; Foreign born: 0.0%; Speak English only: 99.0%; With disability: 12.6%; Veterans: 15.8%; Ancestry: 23.5% German, 20.1% Irish, 12.4% French, 10.4% English, 7.2% Polish

Employment: 8.4% management, business, and financial, 5.5% computer, engineering, and science, 15.1% education, legal, community service, arts, and media, 1.3% healthcare practitioners, 20.2% service, 18.9% sales and office, 6.7% natural resources, construction, and maintenance, 23.9% production, transportation, and material moving

Income: Per capita: $23,566; Median household: $45,650; Average household: $54,415; Households with income of $100,000 or more: 13.1%; Poverty rate: 11.0%

Educational Attainment: High school diploma or higher: 85.5%; Bachelor's degree or higher: 13.8%; Graduate/professional degree or higher: 6.8%

Housing: Homeownership rate: 78.4%; Median home value: $94,300; Median year structure built: Before 1940; Homeowner vacancy rate: 0.0%; Median selected monthly owner costs: $1,027 with a mortgage, $488 without a mortgage; Median gross rent: $613 per month; Rental vacancy rate: 8.2%

Health Insurance: 92.5% have insurance; 67.5% have private insurance; 43.7% have public insurance; 7.5% do not have insurance; 14.3% of children under 18 do not have insurance

Transportation: Commute: 89.9% car, 0.0% public transportation, 3.9% walk, 4.4% work from home; Mean travel time to work: 24.7 minutes

LYONSDALE (town). Covers a land area of 68.743 square miles and a water area of 1.362 square miles. Located at 43.59° N. Lat; 75.24° W. Long. Elevation is 1,066 feet.

Population: 1,139; Growth (since 2000): -10.5%; Density: 16.6 persons per square mile; Race: 97.3% White, 0.5% Black/African American, 0.0% Asian, 1.5% American Indian/Alaska Native, 0.0% Native Hawaiian/Other Pacific Islander, 0.7% Two or more races, 0.4% Hispanic of any race; Average household size: 2.61; Median age: 43.5; Age under 18: 22.8%; Age 65 and over: 19.1%; Males per 100 females: 99.5; Marriage status: 25.8% never married, 54.9% now married, 2.9% separated, 6.4% widowed, 12.9% divorced; Foreign born: 0.8%; Speak English only: 98.5%; With disability: 22.2%; Veterans: 11.0%; Ancestry: 17.6% German, 17.5% Irish, 9.9% American, 9.7% English, 8.9% Italian

Employment: 7.8% management, business, and financial, 0.9% computer, engineering, and science, 8.0% education, legal, community service, arts, and media, 4.0% healthcare practitioners, 20.1% service, 16.3% sales and office, 24.6% natural resources, construction, and maintenance, 18.2% production, transportation, and material moving

Income: Per capita: $18,397; Median household: $41,250; Average household: $47,762; Households with income of $100,000 or more: 9.4%; Poverty rate: 26.7%

Educational Attainment: High school diploma or higher: 85.7%; Bachelor's degree or higher: 8.7%; Graduate/professional degree or higher: 4.3%

Housing: Homeownership rate: 76.2%; Median home value: $84,500; Median year structure built: 1976; Homeowner vacancy rate: 2.3%; Median selected monthly owner costs: $982 with a mortgage, $386 without a mortgage; Median gross rent: $699 per month; Rental vacancy rate: 0.0%

Health Insurance: 93.8% have insurance; 57.3% have private insurance; 56.2% have public insurance; 6.2% do not have insurance; 1.5% of children under 18 do not have insurance

Transportation: Commute: 87.6% car, 0.0% public transportation, 2.7% walk, 8.2% work from home; Mean travel time to work: 29.6 minutes

MARTINSBURG (town). Covers a land area of 75.684 square miles and a water area of 0.351 square miles. Located at 43.73° N. Lat; 75.54° W. Long. Elevation is 1,263 feet.

Population: 1,479; Growth (since 2000): 18.4%; Density: 19.5 persons per square mile; Race: 93.2% White, 0.3% Black/African American, 0.2% Asian, 0.3% American Indian/Alaska Native, 0.0% Native Hawaiian/Other Pacific Islander, 0.0% Two or more races, 8.4% Hispanic of any race; Average household size: 2.63; Median age: 37.4; Age under 18: 23.9%; Age 65 and over: 12.5%; Males per 100 females: 114.8; Marriage status: 34.2% never married, 48.4% now married, 1.3% separated, 7.3% widowed, 10.1% divorced; Foreign born: 6.6%; Speak English only: 89.3%; With disability: 11.2%; Veterans: 6.7%; Ancestry: 26.8% German, 17.1% Irish, 9.7% French, 8.5% Polish, 7.0% English

Employment: 15.1% management, business, and financial, 2.1% computer, engineering, and science, 5.8% education, legal, community service, arts, and media, 5.4% healthcare practitioners, 12.6% service, 21.1% sales and office, 23.1% natural resources, construction, and maintenance, 14.7% production, transportation, and material moving

Income: Per capita: $25,254; Median household: $51,894; Average household: $64,858; Households with income of $100,000 or more: 16.9%; Poverty rate: 16.4%

Educational Attainment: High school diploma or higher: 89.1%; Bachelor's degree or higher: 18.3%; Graduate/professional degree or higher: 6.1%

Housing: Homeownership rate: 79.4%; Median home value: $99,700; Median year structure built: 1960; Homeowner vacancy rate: 0.7%; Median selected monthly owner costs: $1,103 with a mortgage, $436 without a mortgage; Median gross rent: $647 per month; Rental vacancy rate: 10.5%

Health Insurance: 84.3% have insurance; 59.4% have private insurance; 37.1% have public insurance; 15.7% do not have insurance; 12.3% of children under 18 do not have insurance

Transportation: Commute: 71.2% car, 0.0% public transportation, 16.6% walk, 10.6% work from home; Mean travel time to work: 21.0 minutes

MONTAGUE (town). Covers a land area of 65.174 square miles and a water area of 0.163 square miles. Located at 43.72° N. Lat; 75.72° W. Long.

Population: 40; Growth (since 2000): -63.0%; Density: 0.6 persons per square mile; Race: 100.0% White, 0.0% Black/African American, 0.0% Asian, 0.0% American Indian/Alaska Native, 0.0% Native Hawaiian/Other Pacific Islander, 0.0% Two or more races, 2.5% Hispanic of any race; Average household size: 2.11; Median age: 55.6; Age under 18: 2.5%; Age 65 and over: 30.0%; Males per 100 females: 85.7; Marriage status: 22.5% never married, 62.5% now married, 0.0% separated, 0.0% widowed, 15.0% divorced; Foreign born: 0.0%; Speak English only: 100.0%; With disability: 17.5%; Veterans: 7.7%; Ancestry: 37.5% Irish, 30.0% Polish, 20.0% French, 12.5% Italian, 7.5% German

Employment: 36.8% management, business, and financial, 0.0% computer, engineering, and science, 5.3% education, legal, community service, arts, and media, 5.3% healthcare practitioners, 26.3% service, 0.0% sales and office, 10.5% natural resources, construction, and maintenance, 15.8% production, transportation, and material moving

Income: Per capita: $39,150; Median household: $41,875; Average household: $93,295; Households with income of $100,000 or more: 36.8%; Poverty rate: 2.5%

Educational Attainment: High school diploma or higher: 100.0%; Bachelor's degree or higher: 18.2%; Graduate/professional degree or higher: n/a

Housing: Homeownership rate: 100.0%; Median home value: $97,500; Median year structure built: 1985; Homeowner vacancy rate: 9.5%; Median selected monthly owner costs: n/a with a mortgage, $425 without a mortgage; Median gross rent: n/a per month; Rental vacancy rate: 0.0%

Health Insurance: 95.0% have insurance; 57.5% have private insurance; 52.5% have public insurance; 5.0% do not have insurance; 0.0% of children under 18 do not have insurance

Transportation: Commute: 89.5% car, 0.0% public transportation, 0.0% walk, 0.0% work from home; Mean travel time to work: 25.3 minutes

NEW BREMEN (town). Covers a land area of 55.589 square miles and a water area of 0.200 square miles. Located at 43.85° N. Lat; 75.37° W. Long. Elevation is 771 feet.

Population: 2,685; Growth (since 2000): -1.4%; Density: 48.3 persons per square mile; Race: 97.1% White, 0.5% Black/African American, 0.9% Asian, 0.1% American Indian/Alaska Native, 0.0% Native Hawaiian/Other Pacific Islander, 1.0% Two or more races, 1.2% Hispanic of any race;

Average household size: 2.93; Median age: 33.9; Age under 18: 29.5%; Age 65 and over: 13.9%; Males per 100 females: 98.7; Marriage status: 25.8% never married, 61.2% now married, 0.8% separated, 5.5% widowed, 7.5% divorced; Foreign born: 1.3%; Speak English only: 97.9%; With disability: 10.9%; Veterans: 8.9%; Ancestry: 35.5% German, 21.5% French, 11.0% Irish, 6.1% English, 5.8% American

Employment: 10.9% management, business, and financial, 2.3% computer, engineering, and science, 9.7% education, legal, community service, arts, and media, 5.7% healthcare practitioners, 17.3% service, 18.4% sales and office, 19.1% natural resources, construction, and maintenance, 16.6% production, transportation, and material moving

Income: Per capita: $23,515; Median household: $52,727; Average household: $68,101; Households with income of $100,000 or more: 20.8%; Poverty rate: 13.6%

Educational Attainment: High school diploma or higher: 90.5%; Bachelor's degree or higher: 16.7%; Graduate/professional degree or higher: 7.7%

Housing: Homeownership rate: 80.2%; Median home value: $128,200; Median year structure built: 1974; Homeowner vacancy rate: 2.0%; Median selected monthly owner costs: $1,178 with a mortgage, $459 without a mortgage; Median gross rent: $850 per month; Rental vacancy rate: 2.7%

Health Insurance: 89.4% have insurance; 66.3% have private insurance; 35.6% have public insurance; 10.6% do not have insurance; 12.1% of children under 18 do not have insurance

Transportation: Commute: 94.6% car, 0.5% public transportation, 1.9% walk, 3.0% work from home; Mean travel time to work: 27.3 minutes

OSCEOLA (town). Covers a land area of 87.007 square miles and a water area of 0.089 square miles. Located at 43.57° N. Lat; 75.69° W. Long. Elevation is 1,030 feet.

Population: 235; Growth (since 2000): -11.3%; Density: 2.7 persons per square mile; Race: 95.3% White, 0.0% Black/African American, 0.0% Asian, 0.0% American Indian/Alaska Native, 0.0% Native Hawaiian/Other Pacific Islander, 1.7% Two or more races, 4.7% Hispanic of any race; Average household size: 2.33; Median age: 50.8; Age under 18: 14.9%; Age 65 and over: 20.4%; Males per 100 females: 106.3; Marriage status: 24.8% never married, 56.8% now married, 1.0% separated, 5.8% widowed, 12.6% divorced; Foreign born: 3.8%; Speak English only: 100.0%; With disability: 9.4%; Veterans: 13.5%; Ancestry: 28.1% American, 22.1% Irish, 20.9% German, 8.9% French, 7.2% Italian

Employment: 10.0% management, business, and financial, 0.0% computer, engineering, and science, 10.0% education, legal, community service, arts, and media, 12.7% healthcare practitioners, 8.2% service, 25.5% sales and office, 9.1% natural resources, construction, and maintenance, 24.5% production, transportation, and material moving

Income: Per capita: $25,701; Median household: $45,938; Average household: $60,316; Households with income of $100,000 or more: 21.8%; Poverty rate: 18.3%

Educational Attainment: High school diploma or higher: 95.1%; Bachelor's degree or higher: 11.5%; Graduate/professional degree or higher: 9.3%

Housing: Homeownership rate: 87.1%; Median home value: $95,800; Median year structure built: 1980; Homeowner vacancy rate: 13.4%; Median selected monthly owner costs: $1,188 with a mortgage, $427 without a mortgage; Median gross rent: $792 per month; Rental vacancy rate: 0.0%

Health Insurance: 94.9% have insurance; 76.2% have private insurance; 42.1% have public insurance; 5.1% do not have insurance; 0.0% of children under 18 do not have insurance

Transportation: Commute: 84.1% car, 6.5% public transportation, 0.0% walk, 5.6% work from home; Mean travel time to work: 38.8 minutes

PINCKNEY (town). Covers a land area of 40.973 square miles and a water area of 0.142 square miles. Located at 43.83° N. Lat; 75.79° W. Long.

Population: 337; Growth (since 2000): 5.6%; Density: 8.2 persons per square mile; Race: 88.1% White, 0.0% Black/African American, 0.0% Asian, 1.2% American Indian/Alaska Native, 0.0% Native Hawaiian/Other Pacific Islander, 10.7% Two or more races, 0.0% Hispanic of any race; Average household size: 2.26; Median age: 36.9; Age under 18: 29.4%; Age 65 and over: 10.4%; Males per 100 females: 135.0; Marriage status: 40.9% never married, 45.6% now married, 1.9% separated, 2.7% widowed, 10.8% divorced; Foreign born: 0.0%; Speak English only: 87.2%; With disability: 9.8%; Veterans: 7.6%; Ancestry: 35.3% Polish, 35.0% German, 9.5% French, 5.3% Irish, 4.2% American

Employment: 7.2% management, business, and financial, 0.0% computer, engineering, and science, 4.8% education, legal, community service, arts, and media, 1.8% healthcare practitioners, 10.8% service, 10.2% sales and office, 23.4% natural resources, construction, and maintenance, 41.9% production, transportation, and material moving
Income: Per capita: $19,020; Median household: $37,031; Average household: $42,664; Households with income of $100,000 or more: 6.7%; Poverty rate: 26.3%
Educational Attainment: High school diploma or higher: 92.4%; Bachelor's degree or higher: 4.4%; Graduate/professional degree or higher: 2.2%
Housing: Homeownership rate: 63.1%; Median home value: $112,500; Median year structure built: 1989; Homeowner vacancy rate: 0.0%; Median selected monthly owner costs: $1,008 with a mortgage, $463 without a mortgage; Median gross rent: $1,116 per month; Rental vacancy rate: 1.8%
Health Insurance: 93.5% have insurance; 79.8% have private insurance; 54.0% have public insurance; 6.5% do not have insurance; 3.0% of children under 18 do not have insurance
Transportation: Commute: 94.5% car, 0.0% public transportation, 1.2% walk, 4.3% work from home; Mean travel time to work: 22.0 minutes

PORT LEYDEN (village). Covers a land area of 0.615 square miles and a water area of 0.042 square miles. Located at 43.59° N. Lat; 75.34° W. Long. Elevation is 892 feet.
Population: 688; Growth (since 2000): 3.5%; Density: 1,118.7 persons per square mile; Race: 98.8% White, 1.2% Black/African American, 0.0% Asian, 0.0% American Indian/Alaska Native, 0.0% Native Hawaiian/Other Pacific Islander, 0.0% Two or more races, 0.1% Hispanic of any race; Average household size: 2.63; Median age: 36.5; Age under 18: 29.7%; Age 65 and over: 16.1%; Males per 100 females: 92.0; Marriage status: 29.7% never married, 53.9% now married, 8.2% separated, 6.4% widowed, 10.0% divorced; Foreign born: 1.0%; Speak English only: 99.5%; With disability: 22.7%; Veterans: 9.1%; Ancestry: 25.1% German, 21.5% Irish, 16.6% Italian, 12.5% French, 6.0% English
Employment: 11.4% management, business, and financial, 0.8% computer, engineering, and science, 14.6% education, legal, community service, arts, and media, 5.7% healthcare practitioners, 14.6% service, 28.9% sales and office, 14.2% natural resources, construction, and maintenance, 9.8% production, transportation, and material moving
Income: Per capita: $18,317; Median household: $36,420; Average household: $47,842; Households with income of $100,000 or more: 13.6%; Poverty rate: 23.4%
Educational Attainment: High school diploma or higher: 92.4%; Bachelor's degree or higher: 9.7%; Graduate/professional degree or higher: 2.5%

School District(s)
South Lewis Central SD (PK-12)
   Enrollment: 1,064 . . . . (315) 348-2500
Housing: Homeownership rate: 65.8%; Median home value: $87,400; Median year structure built: Before 1940; Homeowner vacancy rate: 1.7%; Median selected monthly owner costs: $971 with a mortgage, $515 without a mortgage; Median gross rent: $727 per month; Rental vacancy rate: 12.3%
Health Insurance: 92.2% have insurance; 54.9% have private insurance; 50.3% have public insurance; 7.8% do not have insurance; 0.0% of children under 18 do not have insurance
Transportation: Commute: 95.7% car, 0.0% public transportation, 0.9% walk, 0.0% work from home; Mean travel time to work: 19.9 minutes

TURIN (town). Covers a land area of 31.176 square miles and a water area of 0.203 square miles. Located at 43.66° N. Lat; 75.43° W. Long. Elevation is 1,263 feet.
Population: 620; Growth (since 2000): -21.8%; Density: 19.9 persons per square mile; Race: 96.9% White, 0.0% Black/African American, 0.0% Asian, 0.0% American Indian/Alaska Native, 0.0% Native Hawaiian/Other Pacific Islander, 1.6% Two or more races, 4.5% Hispanic of any race; Average household size: 2.34; Median age: 46.2; Age under 18: 21.3%; Age 65 and over: 17.3%; Males per 100 females: 113.2; Marriage status: 23.3% never married, 63.9% now married, 0.6% separated, 3.6% widowed, 9.3% divorced; Foreign born: 2.7%; Speak English only: 96.2%; With disability: 7.9%; Veterans: 7.8%; Ancestry: 19.2% German, 11.8% Irish, 10.0% Italian, 9.5% Polish, 9.4% French
Employment: 14.4% management, business, and financial, 3.4% computer, engineering, and science, 9.5% education, legal, community

service, arts, and media, 2.9% healthcare practitioners, 19.0% service, 13.5% sales and office, 17.8% natural resources, construction, and maintenance, 19.5% production, transportation, and material moving
Income: Per capita: $31,725; Median household: $57,159; Average household: $73,724; Households with income of $100,000 or more: 20.7%; Poverty rate: 4.2%
Educational Attainment: High school diploma or higher: 94.9%; Bachelor's degree or higher: 14.8%; Graduate/professional degree or higher: 5.3%

School District(s)
South Lewis Central SD (PK-12)
   Enrollment: 1,064 . . . . (315) 348-2500
Housing: Homeownership rate: 90.4%; Median home value: $109,900; Median year structure built: 1962; Homeowner vacancy rate: 6.0%; Median selected monthly owner costs: $995 with a mortgage, $443 without a mortgage; Median gross rent: $970 per month; Rental vacancy rate: 0.0%
Health Insurance: 89.0% have insurance; 63.5% have private insurance; 37.9% have public insurance; 11.0% do not have insurance; 7.6% of children under 18 do not have insurance
Transportation: Commute: 89.4% car, 0.0% public transportation, 4.4% walk, 4.1% work from home; Mean travel time to work: 25.8 minutes

TURIN (village). Covers a land area of 1.026 square miles and a water area of 0 square miles. Located at 43.63° N. Lat; 75.41° W. Long. Elevation is 1,263 feet.
Population: 200; Growth (since 2000): -24.0%; Density: 194.9 persons per square mile; Race: 95.0% White, 0.0% Black/African American, 0.0% Asian, 0.0% American Indian/Alaska Native, 0.0% Native Hawaiian/Other Pacific Islander, 5.0% Two or more races, 9.5% Hispanic of any race; Average household size: 2.82; Median age: 32.7; Age under 18: 29.5%; Age 65 and over: 18.5%; Males per 100 females: 110.9; Marriage status: 26.2% never married, 58.6% now married, 2.1% separated, 0.7% widowed, 14.5% divorced; Foreign born: 0.0%; Speak English only: 100.0%; With disability: 7.5%; Veterans: 12.8%; Ancestry: 19.5% German, 11.0% Italian, 10.5% Irish, 8.0% French, 7.5% English
Employment: 7.2% management, business, and financial, 5.4% computer, engineering, and science, 10.8% education, legal, community service, arts, and media, 0.9% healthcare practitioners, 31.5% service, 12.6% sales and office, 7.2% natural resources, construction, and maintenance, 24.3% production, transportation, and material moving
Income: Per capita: $23,959; Median household: $58,750; Average household: $66,499; Households with income of $100,000 or more: 26.8%; Poverty rate: 7.7%
Educational Attainment: High school diploma or higher: 99.2%; Bachelor's degree or higher: 15.3%; Graduate/professional degree or higher: 5.1%

School District(s)
South Lewis Central SD (PK-12)
   Enrollment: 1,064 . . . . (315) 348-2500
Housing: Homeownership rate: 83.1%; Median home value: $81,500; Median year structure built: Before 1940; Homeowner vacancy rate: 0.0%; Median selected monthly owner costs: $782 with a mortgage, $500 without a mortgage; Median gross rent: n/a per month; Rental vacancy rate: 0.0%
Health Insurance: 96.5% have insurance; 54.5% have private insurance; 53.5% have public insurance; 3.5% do not have insurance; 0.0% of children under 18 do not have insurance
Transportation: Commute: 90.0% car, 0.0% public transportation, 0.0% walk, 10.0% work from home; Mean travel time to work: 27.0 minutes

WATSON (town). Covers a land area of 112.737 square miles and a water area of 2.960 square miles. Located at 43.83° N. Lat; 75.24° W. Long. Elevation is 748 feet.
Population: 1,864; Growth (since 2000): -6.2%; Density: 16.5 persons per square mile; Race: 99.0% White, 0.0% Black/African American, 0.0% Asian, 0.3% American Indian/Alaska Native, 0.0% Native Hawaiian/Other Pacific Islander, 0.7% Two or more races, 2.0% Hispanic of any race; Average household size: 2.61; Median age: 44.6; Age under 18: 20.4%; Age 65 and over: 17.8%; Males per 100 females: 103.6; Marriage status: 22.9% never married, 64.6% now married, 0.8% separated, 5.1% widowed, 7.4% divorced; Foreign born: 0.6%; Speak English only: 97.9%; With disability: 12.6%; Veterans: 13.4%; Ancestry: 24.7% German, 17.5% Irish, 11.4% American, 10.6% French, 6.9% English
Employment: 12.1% management, business, and financial, 2.5% computer, engineering, and science, 6.5% education, legal, community service, arts, and media, 9.3% healthcare practitioners, 15.3% service,

21.9% sales and office, 18.3% natural resources, construction, and maintenance, 14.1% production, transportation, and material moving

Income: Per capita: $28,996; Median household: $59,962; Average household: $73,640; Households with income of $100,000 or more: 19.1%; Poverty rate: 6.8%

Educational Attainment: High school diploma or higher: 91.9%; Bachelor's degree or higher: 15.7%; Graduate/professional degree or higher: 7.6%

Housing: Homeownership rate: 90.0%; Median home value: $128,900; Median year structure built: 1978; Homeowner vacancy rate: 2.7%; Median selected monthly owner costs: $1,153 with a mortgage, $418 without a mortgage; Median gross rent: $729 per month; Rental vacancy rate: 0.0%

Health Insurance: 90.4% have insurance; 71.9% have private insurance; 35.6% have public insurance; 9.6% do not have insurance; 7.1% of children under 18 do not have insurance

Transportation: Commute: 86.2% car, 0.0% public transportation, 2.3% walk, 10.3% work from home; Mean travel time to work: 23.7 minutes

WEST LEYDEN (unincorporated postal area)
ZCTA: 13489

Covers a land area of 42.699 square miles and a water area of 0.503 square miles. Located at 43.46° N. Lat; 75.55° W. Long. Elevation is 1,489 feet.

Population: 615; Growth (since 2000): -19.4%; Density: 14.4 persons per square mile; Race: 94.3% White, 1.1% Black/African American, 4.6% Asian, 0.0% American Indian/Alaska Native, 0.0% Native Hawaiian/Other Pacific Islander, 0.0% Two or more races, 0.0% Hispanic of any race; Average household size: 2.50; Median age: 44.4; Age under 18: 22.1%; Age 65 and over: 13.2%; Males per 100 females: 106.3; Marriage status: 32.3% never married, 56.0% now married, 0.4% separated, 5.3% widowed, 6.3% divorced; Foreign born: 4.4%; Speak English only: 91.4%; With disability: 12.9%; Veterans: 9.0%; Ancestry: 41.0% German, 19.0% Irish, 11.7% American, 10.4% French, 8.6% Polish

Employment: 13.6% management, business, and financial, 3.7% computer, engineering, and science, 7.8% education, legal, community service, arts, and media, 6.6% healthcare practitioners, 22.6% service, 11.9% sales and office, 14.8% natural resources, construction, and maintenance, 18.9% production, transportation, and material moving

Income: Per capita: $24,823; Median household: $51,250; Average household: $60,631; Households with income of $100,000 or more: 19.1%; Poverty rate: 11.5%

Educational Attainment: High school diploma or higher: 93.2%; Bachelor's degree or higher: 14.0%; Graduate/professional degree or higher: 5.8%

School District(s)
Adirondack Central SD (PK-12)
    Enrollment: 1,296 . . . . (315) 942-9200

Housing: Homeownership rate: 85.0%; Median home value: $103,900; Median year structure built: 1973; Homeowner vacancy rate: 5.4%; Median selected monthly owner costs: $920 with a mortgage, $435 without a mortgage; Median gross rent: $761 per month; Rental vacancy rate: 0.0%

Health Insurance: 87.8% have insurance; 60.5% have private insurance; 41.3% have public insurance; 12.2% do not have insurance; 0.0% of children under 18 do not have insurance

Transportation: Commute: 82.2% car, 1.3% public transportation, 1.7% walk, 14.8% work from home; Mean travel time to work: 35.9 minutes

WEST TURIN (town). Covers a land area of 102.054 square miles and a water area of 0.343 square miles. Located at 43.59° N. Lat; 75.51° W. Long.

Population: 1,619; Growth (since 2000): -3.3%; Density: 15.9 persons per square mile; Race: 97.6% White, 0.6% Black/African American, 0.0% Asian, 0.0% American Indian/Alaska Native, 0.0% Native Hawaiian/Other Pacific Islander, 1.4% Two or more races, 2.3% Hispanic of any race; Average household size: 2.46; Median age: 48.6; Age under 18: 21.4%; Age 65 and over: 16.4%; Males per 100 females: 102.4; Marriage status: 21.8% never married, 63.3% now married, 2.4% separated, 4.5% widowed, 10.4% divorced; Foreign born: 0.4%; Speak English only: 99.0%; With disability: 12.4%; Veterans: 8.6%; Ancestry: 26.1% German, 15.8% Irish, 10.8% English, 8.7% French, 7.7% Polish

Employment: 13.1% management, business, and financial, 2.0% computer, engineering, and science, 9.8% education, legal, community service, arts, and media, 3.9% healthcare practitioners, 23.5% service,

15.8% sales and office, 14.6% natural resources, construction, and maintenance, 17.3% production, transportation, and material moving

Income: Per capita: $28,549; Median household: $50,764; Average household: $70,176; Households with income of $100,000 or more: 13.5%; Poverty rate: 7.9%

Educational Attainment: High school diploma or higher: 89.5%; Bachelor's degree or higher: 13.6%; Graduate/professional degree or higher: 5.4%

Housing: Homeownership rate: 86.3%; Median home value: $103,300; Median year structure built: 1951; Homeowner vacancy rate: 1.0%; Median selected monthly owner costs: $1,191 with a mortgage, $507 without a mortgage; Median gross rent: $696 per month; Rental vacancy rate: 5.3%

Health Insurance: 92.5% have insurance; 68.0% have private insurance; 37.7% have public insurance; 7.5% do not have insurance; 8.3% of children under 18 do not have insurance

Transportation: Commute: 88.3% car, 0.7% public transportation, 4.0% walk, 3.7% work from home; Mean travel time to work: 28.9 minutes

Livingston County

Located in west central New York, in the Finger Lakes area; drained by the Genesee River; includes Conesus and Hemlock Lakes. Covers a land area of 631.762 square miles, a water area of 8.496 square miles, and is located in the Eastern Time Zone at 42.73° N. Lat., 77.77° W. Long. The county was founded in 1821. County seat is Geneseo.

Livingston County is part of the Rochester, NY Metropolitan Statistical Area. The entire metro area includes: Livingston County, NY; Monroe County, NY; Ontario County, NY; Orleans County, NY; Wayne County, NY; Yates County, NY

Weather Station: Avon   Elevation: 544 feet

	Jan	Feb	Mar	Apr	May	Jun	Jul	Aug	Sep	Oct	Nov	Dec
High	32	35	43	56	68	77	81	80	73	61	49	37
Low	17	17	24	35	45	55	59	58	50	40	32	23
Precip	1.8	1.6	2.4	2.7	2.8	3.3	3.3	3.4	3.4	2.7	2.7	2.1
Snow	13.3	10.5	10.7	2.1	0.2	0.0	0.0	0.0	0.0	tr	3.7	11.4

High and Low temperatures in degrees Fahrenheit; Precipitation and Snow in inches

Weather Station: Dansville   Elevation: 660 feet

	Jan	Feb	Mar	Apr	May	Jun	Jul	Aug	Sep	Oct	Nov	Dec
High	33	36	44	58	69	78	82	81	74	62	49	38
Low	16	17	24	35	45	54	59	57	50	39	32	22
Precip	1.5	1.2	1.9	2.5	2.9	3.4	3.6	3.4	3.4	2.7	2.5	1.9
Snow	8.4	6.2	5.6	1.0	0.1	0.0	0.0	0.0	0.0	tr	1.9	6.2

High and Low temperatures in degrees Fahrenheit; Precipitation and Snow in inches

Weather Station: Hemlock   Elevation: 901 feet

	Jan	Feb	Mar	Apr	May	Jun	Jul	Aug	Sep	Oct	Nov	Dec
High	32	34	43	56	68	76	80	79	71	59	48	37
Low	16	16	23	35	45	55	59	58	52	41	32	22
Precip	1.9	1.5	2.6	3.0	3.2	3.7	3.7	3.5	3.6	3.2	3.0	2.2
Snow	na	na	na	0.0	0.0	0.0	0.0	0.0	0.0	0.0	na	na

High and Low temperatures in degrees Fahrenheit; Precipitation and Snow in inches

Population: 64,373; Growth (since 2000): 0.1%; Density: 101.9 persons per square mile; Race: 93.3% White, 2.6% Black/African American, 1.4% Asian, 0.2% American Indian/Alaska Native, 0.0% Native Hawaiian/Other Pacific Islander, 1.8% two or more races, 3.4% Hispanic of any race; Average household size: 2.38; Median age: 40.4; Age under 18: 18.4%; Age 65 and over: 16.1%; Males per 100 females: 100.7; Marriage status: 34.8% never married, 48.8% now married, 1.9% separated, 6.0% widowed, 10.5% divorced; Foreign born: 3.6%; Speak English only: 93.5%; With disability: 13.2%; Veterans: 8.2%; Ancestry: 26.3% German, 21.2% Irish, 14.2% Italian, 13.5% English, 5.6% American

Religion: Six largest groups: 22.8% Catholicism, 4.9% Methodist/Pietist, 4.6% Non-denominational Protestant, 3.1% Presbyterian-Reformed, 1.1% Holiness, 0.8% Lutheran

Economy: Unemployment rate: 3.5%; Leading industries: 16.8 % retail trade; 12.6 % accommodation and food services; 12.2 % other services (except public administration); Farms: 661 totaling 194,945 acres; Company size: 0 employ 1,000 or more persons, 1 employs 500 to 999 persons, 16 employ 100 to 499 persons, 1,217 employ less than 100 persons; Business ownership: 1,436 women-owned, n/a Black-owned, n/a Hispanic-owned, 78 Asian-owned, n/a American Indian/Alaska Native-owned

Employment: 12.4% management, business, and financial, 4.1% computer, engineering, and science, 12.5% education, legal, community service, arts, and media, 5.3% healthcare practitioners, 19.0% service, 20.9% sales and office, 11.6% natural resources, construction, and maintenance, 14.1% production, transportation, and material moving
Income: Per capita: $25,882; Median household: $53,654; Average household: $66,113; Households with income of $100,000 or more: 20.7%; Poverty rate: 14.6%
Educational Attainment: High school diploma or higher: 89.1%; Bachelor's degree or higher: 23.7%; Graduate/professional degree or higher: 10.5%
Housing: Homeownership rate: 73.2%; Median home value: $125,000; Median year structure built: 1964; Homeowner vacancy rate: 1.0%; Median selected monthly owner costs: $1,287 with a mortgage, $542 without a mortgage; Median gross rent: $755 per month; Rental vacancy rate: 3.3%
Vital Statistics: Birth rate: 78.8 per 10,000 population; Death rate: 83.7 per 10,000 population; Age-adjusted cancer mortality rate: 180.4 deaths per 100,000 population
Health Insurance: 95.8% have insurance; 77.3% have private insurance; 34.7% have public insurance; 4.2% do not have insurance; 1.5% of children under 18 do not have insurance
Health Care: Physicians: 8.1 per 10,000 population; Dentists: 5.2 per 10,000 population; Hospital beds: 6.2 per 10,000 population; Hospital admissions: 368.2 per 10,000 population
Transportation: Commute: 88.4% car, 0.5% public transportation, 6.2% walk, 3.4% work from home; Mean travel time to work: 25.5 minutes
2016 Presidential Election: 57.6% Trump, 35.6% Clinton, 4.2% Johnson, 1.5% Stein
National and State Parks: Boyd-Parker State Park; Rattlesnake Hill State Wildlife Management Area
Additional Information Contacts
Livingston Government . . . . (585) 243-7010
   http://www.co.livingston.state.ny.us

Livingston County Communities

AVON (town). Covers a land area of 41.203 square miles and a water area of 0.055 square miles. Located at 42.90° N. Lat; 77.73° W. Long. Elevation is 650 feet.
History: Incorporated 1867.
Population: 6,979; Growth (since 2000): 8.3%; Density: 169.4 persons per square mile; Race: 95.8% White, 0.2% Black/African American, 1.8% Asian, 0.0% American Indian/Alaska Native, 0.0% Native Hawaiian/Other Pacific Islander, 1.9% Two or more races, 1.2% Hispanic of any race; Average household size: 2.35; Median age: 41.9; Age under 18: 21.3%; Age 65 and over: 17.0%; Males per 100 females: 96.9; Marriage status: 28.9% never married, 51.5% now married, 1.8% separated, 6.4% widowed, 13.2% divorced; Foreign born: 3.4%; Speak English only: 97.0%; With disability: 13.5%; Veterans: 9.0%; Ancestry: 26.4% Irish, 25.9% German, 16.7% English, 12.5% Italian, 6.3% American
Employment: 15.7% management, business, and financial, 6.1% computer, engineering, and science, 12.2% education, legal, community service, arts, and media, 4.5% healthcare practitioners, 14.9% service, 21.3% sales and office, 10.7% natural resources, construction, and maintenance, 14.6% production, transportation, and material moving
Income: Per capita: $29,012; Median household: $55,050; Average household: $68,109; Households with income of $100,000 or more: 22.7%; Poverty rate: 7.9%
Educational Attainment: High school diploma or higher: 94.4%; Bachelor's degree or higher: 30.6%; Graduate/professional degree or higher: 13.9%
School District(s)
Avon Central SD (KG-12)
   Enrollment: 1,010 . . . . (585) 226-2455
Housing: Homeownership rate: 71.2%; Median home value: $142,300; Median year structure built: 1967; Homeowner vacancy rate: 0.0%; Median selected monthly owner costs: $1,387 with a mortgage, $598 without a mortgage; Median gross rent: $810 per month; Rental vacancy rate: 3.5%
Health Insurance: 95.1% have insurance; 78.2% have private insurance; 32.6% have public insurance; 4.9% do not have insurance; 0.0% of children under 18 do not have insurance
Transportation: Commute: 92.5% car, 0.0% public transportation, 2.8% walk, 2.3% work from home; Mean travel time to work: 26.2 minutes

Additional Information Contacts
Town of Avon . . . . (585) 226-2425
   http://www.avon-ny.org/index_town.html

AVON (village). Covers a land area of 3.099 square miles and a water area of 0 square miles. Located at 42.91° N. Lat; 77.75° W. Long. Elevation is 650 feet.
Population: 3,293; Growth (since 2000): 10.6%; Density: 1,062.8 persons per square mile; Race: 94.4% White, 0.5% Black/African American, 0.6% Asian, 0.0% American Indian/Alaska Native, 0.0% Native Hawaiian/Other Pacific Islander, 4.0% Two or more races, 2.1% Hispanic of any race; Average household size: 2.47; Median age: 38.4; Age under 18: 20.9%; Age 65 and over: 17.6%; Males per 100 females: 90.7; Marriage status: 33.0% never married, 52.8% now married, 2.5% separated, 5.9% widowed, 8.4% divorced; Foreign born: 3.4%; Speak English only: 95.6%; With disability: 13.0%; Veterans: 7.1%; Ancestry: 30.2% Irish, 25.5% German, 18.6% Italian, 11.6% English, 8.0% Polish
Employment: 16.4% management, business, and financial, 6.6% computer, engineering, and science, 18.1% education, legal, community service, arts, and media, 3.3% healthcare practitioners, 13.0% service, 15.8% sales and office, 10.1% natural resources, construction, and maintenance, 16.6% production, transportation, and material moving
Income: Per capita: $29,963; Median household: $65,598; Average household: $74,748; Households with income of $100,000 or more: 29.0%; Poverty rate: 11.9%
Educational Attainment: High school diploma or higher: 96.3%; Bachelor's degree or higher: 35.5%; Graduate/professional degree or higher: 17.0%
School District(s)
Avon Central SD (KG-12)
   Enrollment: 1,010 . . . . (585) 226-2455
Housing: Homeownership rate: 64.5%; Median home value: $154,300; Median year structure built: 1959; Homeowner vacancy rate: 0.0%; Median selected monthly owner costs: $1,428 with a mortgage, $657 without a mortgage; Median gross rent: $684 per month; Rental vacancy rate: 6.3%
Health Insurance: 96.4% have insurance; 81.8% have private insurance; 31.7% have public insurance; 3.6% do not have insurance; 0.0% of children under 18 do not have insurance
Safety: Violent crime rate: 0.0 per 10,000 population; Property crime rate: 39.7 per 10,000 population
Transportation: Commute: 89.1% car, 0.0% public transportation, 5.1% walk, 2.4% work from home; Mean travel time to work: 22.0 minutes

BYERSVILLE (CDP). Covers a land area of 0.510 square miles and a water area of 0 square miles. Located at 42.58° N. Lat; 77.79° W. Long. Elevation is 1,358 feet.
Population: 32; Growth (since 2000): n/a; Density: 62.7 persons per square mile; Race: 93.8% White, 0.0% Black/African American, 0.0% Asian, 0.0% American Indian/Alaska Native, 0.0% Native Hawaiian/Other Pacific Islander, 6.3% Two or more races, 0.0% Hispanic of any race; Average household size: 1.78; Median age: 49.5; Age under 18: 6.2%; Age 65 and over: 12.5%; Males per 100 females: 88.0; Marriage status: 33.3% never married, 43.3% now married, 0.0% separated, 0.0% widowed, 23.3% divorced; Foreign born: 0.0%; Speak English only: 100.0%; With disability: 0.0%; Veterans: 26.7%; Ancestry: 59.4% German, 37.5% Italian, 12.5% European, 12.5% Scottish, 9.4% Irish
Employment: 19.0% management, business, and financial, 0.0% computer, engineering, and science, 0.0% education, legal, community service, arts, and media, 28.6% healthcare practitioners, 38.1% service, 0.0% sales and office, 0.0% natural resources, construction, and maintenance, 14.3% production, transportation, and material moving
Income: Per capita: $32,494; Median household: $68,750; Average household: $59,911; Households with income of $100,000 or more: 22.2%; Poverty rate: 12.5%
Educational Attainment: High school diploma or higher: 87.5%; Bachelor's degree or higher: 16.7%; Graduate/professional degree or higher: 16.7%
Housing: Homeownership rate: 100.0%; Median home value: $93,300; Median year structure built: Before 1940; Homeowner vacancy rate: 0.0%; Median selected monthly owner costs: $875 with a mortgage, n/a without a mortgage; Median gross rent: n/a per month; Rental vacancy rate: 0.0%
Health Insurance: 87.5% have insurance; 71.9% have private insurance; 46.9% have public insurance; 12.5% do not have insurance; 0.0% of children under 18 do not have insurance

Transportation: Commute: 81.0% car, 0.0% public transportation, 0.0% walk, 19.0% work from home; Mean travel time to work: 0.0 minutes

CALEDONIA (town).
Covers a land area of 43.875 square miles and a water area of 0.251 square miles. Located at 42.95° N. Lat; 77.82° W. Long. Elevation is 659 feet.
History: Incorporated 1887.
Population: 4,178; Growth (since 2000): -8.5%; Density: 95.2 persons per square mile; Race: 92.6% White, 2.3% Black/African American, 2.2% Asian, 0.0% American Indian/Alaska Native, 0.0% Native Hawaiian/Other Pacific Islander, 1.4% Two or more races, 2.6% Hispanic of any race; Average household size: 2.48; Median age: 44.4; Age under 18: 17.3%; Age 65 and over: 16.8%; Males per 100 females: 98.5; Marriage status: 27.3% never married, 53.2% now married, 1.6% separated, 8.2% widowed, 11.3% divorced; Foreign born: 5.6%; Speak English only: 95.1%; With disability: 12.2%; Veterans: 9.3%; Ancestry: 25.9% Irish, 23.8% German, 18.6% English, 16.2% Italian, 5.1% American
Employment: 11.6% management, business, and financial, 3.4% computer, engineering, and science, 9.5% education, legal, community service, arts, and media, 6.7% healthcare practitioners, 17.1% service, 21.0% sales and office, 14.2% natural resources, construction, and maintenance, 16.3% production, transportation, and material moving
Income: Per capita: $27,589; Median household: $53,891; Average household: $67,553; Households with income of $100,000 or more: 22.4%; Poverty rate: 5.1%
Educational Attainment: High school diploma or higher: 91.2%; Bachelor's degree or higher: 22.2%; Graduate/professional degree or higher: 8.7%

School District(s)
Caledonia-Mumford Central SD (PK-12)
    Enrollment: 813 . . . . (585) 538-3400
Housing: Homeownership rate: 80.0%; Median home value: $128,300; Median year structure built: 1965; Homeowner vacancy rate: 0.0%; Median selected monthly owner costs: $1,244 with a mortgage, $585 without a mortgage; Median gross rent: $741 per month; Rental vacancy rate: 0.0%
Health Insurance: 95.7% have insurance; 78.4% have private insurance; 32.8% have public insurance; 4.3% do not have insurance; 0.7% of children under 18 do not have insurance
Transportation: Commute: 93.3% car, 0.4% public transportation, 2.9% walk, 2.9% work from home; Mean travel time to work: 24.1 minutes
Additional Information Contacts
Town of Caledonia . . . . (585) 538-4927
    http://www.townofcaledoniany.com

CALEDONIA (village).
Covers a land area of 2.097 square miles and a water area of 0 square miles. Located at 42.98° N. Lat; 77.86° W. Long. Elevation is 659 feet.
Population: 2,037; Growth (since 2000): -12.5%; Density: 971.3 persons per square mile; Race: 95.7% White, 2.5% Black/African American, 0.4% Asian, 0.0% American Indian/Alaska Native, 0.0% Native Hawaiian/Other Pacific Islander, 0.5% Two or more races, 0.9% Hispanic of any race; Average household size: 2.21; Median age: 45.8; Age under 18: 15.9%; Age 65 and over: 18.8%; Males per 100 females: 94.6; Marriage status: 31.6% never married, 45.2% now married, 2.2% separated, 11.2% widowed, 12.0% divorced; Foreign born: 1.8%; Speak English only: 97.5%; With disability: 11.2%; Veterans: 11.4%; Ancestry: 24.9% German, 24.1% Italian, 23.0% Irish, 15.1% English, 5.2% American
Employment: 9.1% management, business, and financial, 3.3% computer, engineering, and science, 10.5% education, legal, community service, arts, and media, 4.4% healthcare practitioners, 19.2% service, 24.6% sales and office, 13.1% natural resources, construction, and maintenance, 15.9% production, transportation, and material moving
Income: Per capita: $27,440; Median household: $50,163; Average household: $60,049; Households with income of $100,000 or more: 15.5%; Poverty rate: 7.7%
Educational Attainment: High school diploma or higher: 93.1%; Bachelor's degree or higher: 20.8%; Graduate/professional degree or higher: 6.4%

School District(s)
Caledonia-Mumford Central SD (PK-12)
    Enrollment: 813 . . . . (585) 538-3400
Housing: Homeownership rate: 68.7%; Median home value: $119,200; Median year structure built: 1954; Homeowner vacancy rate: 0.0%; Median selected monthly owner costs: $1,208 with a mortgage, $529 without a mortgage; Median gross rent: $716 per month; Rental vacancy rate: 0.0%

Health Insurance: 96.0% have insurance; 77.2% have private insurance; 36.0% have public insurance; 4.0% do not have insurance; 0.0% of children under 18 do not have insurance
Safety: Violent crime rate: 9.5 per 10,000 population; Property crime rate: 4.7 per 10,000 population
Transportation: Commute: 93.7% car, 0.0% public transportation, 3.3% walk, 2.0% work from home; Mean travel time to work: 21.8 minutes

CONESUS (town).
Covers a land area of 32.891 square miles and a water area of 2.980 square miles. Located at 42.70° N. Lat; 77.64° W. Long. Elevation is 1,197 feet.
Population: 2,499; Growth (since 2000): 6.2%; Density: 76.0 persons per square mile; Race: 96.4% White, 1.7% Black/African American, 0.0% Asian, 0.9% American Indian/Alaska Native, 0.0% Native Hawaiian/Other Pacific Islander, 1.0% Two or more races, 1.7% Hispanic of any race; Average household size: 2.35; Median age: 48.4; Age under 18: 15.4%; Age 65 and over: 16.0%; Males per 100 females: 102.4; Marriage status: 26.6% never married, 59.2% now married, 1.2% separated, 5.2% widowed, 9.0% divorced; Foreign born: 3.9%; Speak English only: 96.7%; With disability: 12.2%; Veterans: 8.2%; Ancestry: 33.8% German, 27.7% Irish, 15.2% Italian, 11.7% English, 7.6% American
Employment: 7.7% management, business, and financial, 7.2% computer, engineering, and science, 11.3% education, legal, community service, arts, and media, 11.6% healthcare practitioners, 17.0% service, 20.7% sales and office, 12.5% natural resources, construction, and maintenance, 12.0% production, transportation, and material moving
Income: Per capita: $34,248; Median household: $68,295; Average household: $80,516; Households with income of $100,000 or more: 28.0%; Poverty rate: 11.0%
Educational Attainment: High school diploma or higher: 91.2%; Bachelor's degree or higher: 26.9%; Graduate/professional degree or higher: 10.1%
Housing: Homeownership rate: 91.6%; Median home value: $136,600; Median year structure built: 1978; Homeowner vacancy rate: 2.0%; Median selected monthly owner costs: $1,363 with a mortgage, $565 without a mortgage; Median gross rent: $861 per month; Rental vacancy rate: 16.0%
Health Insurance: 96.8% have insurance; 83.5% have private insurance; 27.1% have public insurance; 3.2% do not have insurance; 0.0% of children under 18 do not have insurance
Transportation: Commute: 96.2% car, 0.0% public transportation, 0.0% walk, 1.8% work from home; Mean travel time to work: 31.7 minutes

CONESUS HAMLET (CDP).
Covers a land area of 1.059 square miles and a water area of 0 square miles. Located at 42.73° N. Lat; 77.67° W. Long. Elevation is 1,207 feet.
Population: 450; Growth (since 2000): n/a; Density: 425.0 persons per square mile; Race: 100.0% White, 0.0% Black/African American, 0.0% Asian, 0.0% American Indian/Alaska Native, 0.0% Native Hawaiian/Other Pacific Islander, 0.0% Two or more races, 2.4% Hispanic of any race; Average household size: 2.78; Median age: 28.1; Age under 18: 26.4%; Age 65 and over: 4.9%; Males per 100 females: 91.3; Marriage status: 39.6% never married, 50.8% now married, 1.5% separated, 1.5% widowed, 8.2% divorced; Foreign born: 0.0%; Speak English only: 100.0%; With disability: 4.2%; Veterans: 8.5%; Ancestry: 58.2% German, 56.0% Irish, 12.2% English, 7.3% Italian, 4.4% Dutch
Employment: 0.0% management, business, and financial, 14.3% computer, engineering, and science, 5.9% education, legal, community service, arts, and media, 13.9% healthcare practitioners, 26.1% service, 26.9% sales and office, 13.0% natural resources, construction, and maintenance, 0.0% production, transportation, and material moving
Income: Per capita: $21,910; Median household: $57,232; Average household: $60,001; Households with income of $100,000 or more: 17.9%; Poverty rate: 5.1%
Educational Attainment: High school diploma or higher: 100.0%; Bachelor's degree or higher: 26.7%; Graduate/professional degree or higher: 7.6%
Housing: Homeownership rate: 72.2%; Median home value: $113,600; Median year structure built: 1941; Homeowner vacancy rate: 0.0%; Median selected monthly owner costs: $1,053 with a mortgage, $442 without a mortgage; Median gross rent: n/a per month; Rental vacancy rate: 27.4%
Health Insurance: 98.7% have insurance; 94.9% have private insurance; 13.3% have public insurance; 1.3% do not have insurance; 0.0% of children under 18 do not have insurance
Transportation: Commute: 100.0% car, 0.0% public transportation, 0.0% walk, 0.0% work from home; Mean travel time to work: 28.6 minutes

CONESUS LAKE (CDP). Covers a land area of 4.361 square miles and a water area of 5.050 square miles. Located at 42.80° N. Lat; 77.70° W. Long. Elevation is 846 feet.
Population: 2,409; Growth (since 2000): n/a; Density: 552.3 persons per square mile; Race: 95.5% White, 0.0% Black/African American, 1.4% Asian, 0.5% American Indian/Alaska Native, 0.5% Native Hawaiian/Other Pacific Islander, 2.1% Two or more races, 2.0% Hispanic of any race; Average household size: 1.90; Median age: 57.2; Age under 18: 9.4%; Age 65 and over: 29.2%; Males per 100 females: 105.2; Marriage status: 26.9% never married, 55.9% now married, 0.3% separated, 5.5% widowed, 11.6% divorced; Foreign born: 3.9%; Speak English only: 95.3%; With disability: 9.0%; Veterans: 7.4%; Ancestry: 29.0% German, 27.1% Irish, 22.5% Italian, 16.9% English, 7.3% American
Employment: 15.7% management, business, and financial, 4.2% computer, engineering, and science, 17.4% education, legal, community service, arts, and media, 8.5% healthcare practitioners, 15.4% service, 21.4% sales and office, 10.7% natural resources, construction, and maintenance, 6.7% production, transportation, and material moving
Income: Per capita: $46,958; Median household: $77,604; Average household: $89,424; Households with income of $100,000 or more: 30.3%; Poverty rate: 5.1%
Educational Attainment: High school diploma or higher: 98.4%; Bachelor's degree or higher: 39.2%; Graduate/professional degree or higher: 16.5%
Housing: Homeownership rate: 81.2%; Median home value: $217,300; Median year structure built: 1951; Homeowner vacancy rate: 0.0%; Median selected monthly owner costs: $1,694 with a mortgage, $698 without a mortgage; Median gross rent: $760 per month; Rental vacancy rate: 0.0%
Health Insurance: 98.7% have insurance; 87.3% have private insurance; 32.8% have public insurance; 1.3% do not have insurance; 0.0% of children under 18 do not have insurance
Transportation: Commute: 94.4% car, 0.0% public transportation, 0.0% walk, 5.2% work from home; Mean travel time to work: 32.3 minutes

CUMMINSVILLE (CDP). Covers a land area of 0.131 square miles and a water area of 0 square miles. Located at 42.57° N. Lat; 77.72° W. Long. Elevation is 640 feet.
Population: 170; Growth (since 2000): n/a; Density: 1,297.8 persons per square mile; Race: 100.0% White, 0.0% Black/African American, 0.0% Asian, 0.0% American Indian/Alaska Native, 0.0% Native Hawaiian/Other Pacific Islander, 0.0% Two or more races, 0.0% Hispanic of any race; Average household size: 1.45; Median age: 56.4; Age under 18: 0.0%; Age 65 and over: 14.7%; Males per 100 females: 77.7; Marriage status: 2.9% never married, 40.0% now married, 5.3% separated, 15.9% widowed, 41.2% divorced; Foreign born: 0.0%; Speak English only: 100.0%; With disability: 42.4%; Veterans: 11.8%; Ancestry: 31.2% Italian, 20.0% German, 16.5% American, 10.0% English
Employment: 0.0% management, business, and financial, 0.0% computer, engineering, and science, 0.0% education, legal, community service, arts, and media, 0.0% healthcare practitioners, 0.0% service, 48.7% sales and office, 28.2% natural resources, construction, and maintenance, 23.1% production, transportation, and material moving
Income: Per capita: $21,395; Median household: $19,531; Average household: $31,051; Households with income of $100,000 or more: 9.4%; Poverty rate: 42.4%
Educational Attainment: High school diploma or higher: 84.2%; Bachelor's degree or higher: n/a; Graduate/professional degree or higher: n/a
Housing: Homeownership rate: 70.1%; Median home value: $39,400; Median year structure built: 1969; Homeowner vacancy rate: 0.0%; Median selected monthly owner costs: n/a with a mortgage, $548 without a mortgage; Median gross rent: n/a per month; Rental vacancy rate: 0.0%
Health Insurance: 94.7% have insurance; 57.1% have private insurance; 57.1% have public insurance; 5.3% do not have insurance; 0.0% of children under 18 do not have insurance
Transportation: Commute: 100.0% car, 0.0% public transportation, 0.0% walk, 0.0% work from home; Mean travel time to work: 0.0 minutes

CUYLERVILLE (CDP). Covers a land area of 0.421 square miles and a water area of 0 square miles. Located at 42.78° N. Lat; 77.87° W. Long. Elevation is 571 feet.
Population: 215; Growth (since 2000): n/a; Density: 510.2 persons per square mile; Race: 100.0% White, 0.0% Black/African American, 0.0% Asian, 0.0% American Indian/Alaska Native, 0.0% Native Hawaiian/Other Pacific Islander, 0.0% Two or more races, 7.0% Hispanic of any race;

Average household size: 1.72; Median age: 56.2; Age under 18: 12.6%; Age 65 and over: 19.5%; Males per 100 females: 104.8; Marriage status: 23.4% never married, 65.4% now married, 2.7% separated, 8.5% widowed, 2.7% divorced; Foreign born: 0.0%; Speak English only: 100.0%; With disability: 10.2%; Veterans: 3.2%; Ancestry: 43.3% Italian, 34.0% German, 14.9% Irish, 9.3% Pennsylvania German, 8.4% English
Employment: 17.5% management, business, and financial, 0.0% computer, engineering, and science, 28.3% education, legal, community service, arts, and media, 5.0% healthcare practitioners, 10.8% service, 38.3% sales and office, 0.0% natural resources, construction, and maintenance, 0.0% production, transportation, and material moving
Income: Per capita: $28,361; Median household: $51,042; Average household: $49,586; Households with income of $100,000 or more: 12.8%; Poverty rate: 20.0%
Educational Attainment: High school diploma or higher: 94.0%; Bachelor's degree or higher: 45.1%; Graduate/professional degree or higher: 12.6%
Housing: Homeownership rate: 64.8%; Median home value: $104,200; Median year structure built: 1970; Homeowner vacancy rate: 0.0%; Median selected monthly owner costs: $997 with a mortgage, $420 without a mortgage; Median gross rent: $755 per month; Rental vacancy rate: 26.7%
Health Insurance: 98.1% have insurance; 92.6% have private insurance; 16.7% have public insurance; 1.9% do not have insurance; 0.0% of children under 18 do not have insurance
Transportation: Commute: 82.3% car, 0.0% public transportation, 0.0% walk, 17.7% work from home; Mean travel time to work: 19.2 minutes

DALTON (CDP). Covers a land area of 0.755 square miles and a water area of 0 square miles. Located at 42.54° N. Lat; 77.95° W. Long. Elevation is 1,342 feet.
Population: 397; Growth (since 2000): n/a; Density: 525.9 persons per square mile; Race: 100.0% White, 0.0% Black/African American, 0.0% Asian, 0.0% American Indian/Alaska Native, 0.0% Native Hawaiian/Other Pacific Islander, 0.0% Two or more races, 0.0% Hispanic of any race; Average household size: 2.76; Median age: 41.7; Age under 18: 24.2%; Age 65 and over: 17.9%; Males per 100 females: 102.2; Marriage status: 22.2% never married, 74.0% now married, 1.0% separated, 0.0% widowed, 3.8% divorced; Foreign born: 0.0%; Speak English only: 100.0%; With disability: 9.8%; Veterans: 6.0%; Ancestry: 32.5% Irish, 27.5% German, 25.9% English, 14.4% American, 9.8% Italian
Employment: 9.5% management, business, and financial, 0.0% computer, engineering, and science, 19.0% education, legal, community service, arts, and media, 4.8% healthcare practitioners, 11.6% service, 12.9% sales and office, 23.8% natural resources, construction, and maintenance, 18.4% production, transportation, and material moving
Income: Per capita: $30,344; Median household: $94,000; Average household: $86,550; Households with income of $100,000 or more: 37.5%; Poverty rate: 8.4%
Educational Attainment: High school diploma or higher: 98.6%; Bachelor's degree or higher: 18.1%; Graduate/professional degree or higher: 10.0%
Housing: Homeownership rate: 97.2%; Median home value: $89,400; Median year structure built: 1952; Homeowner vacancy rate: 0.0%; Median selected monthly owner costs: $774 with a mortgage, $565 without a mortgage; Median gross rent: n/a per month; Rental vacancy rate: 0.0%
Health Insurance: 97.0% have insurance; 81.4% have private insurance; 38.0% have public insurance; 3.0% do not have insurance; 0.0% of children under 18 do not have insurance
Transportation: Commute: 98.0% car, 2.0% public transportation, 0.0% walk, 0.0% work from home; Mean travel time to work: 38.4 minutes

DANSVILLE (village). Covers a land area of 2.608 square miles and a water area of 0 square miles. Located at 42.56° N. Lat; 77.70° W. Long. Elevation is 705 feet.
History: Clara Barton founded (1881) first local chapter of the American Red Cross here. Settled 1795, incorporated 1845.
Population: 4,499; Growth (since 2000): -6.9%; Density: 1,725.3 persons per square mile; Race: 95.1% White, 1.0% Black/African American, 0.0% Asian, 0.0% American Indian/Alaska Native, 0.0% Native Hawaiian/Other Pacific Islander, 2.4% Two or more races, 1.2% Hispanic of any race; Average household size: 2.20; Median age: 42.6; Age under 18: 22.5%; Age 65 and over: 15.3%; Males per 100 females: 89.2; Marriage status: 35.8% never married, 44.3% now married, 4.0% separated, 7.9% widowed, 12.0% divorced; Foreign born: 1.1%; Speak English only: 98.6%;

With disability: 16.2%; Veterans: 9.7%; Ancestry: 27.2% German, 24.3% Irish, 9.5% Polish, 8.9% English, 7.7% Italian
Employment: 7.0% management, business, and financial, 0.0% computer, engineering, and science, 16.6% education, legal, community service, arts, and media, 4.4% healthcare practitioners, 22.4% service, 17.8% sales and office, 11.6% natural resources, construction, and maintenance, 20.1% production, transportation, and material moving
Income: Per capita: $25,690; Median household: $37,553; Average household: $56,034; Households with income of $100,000 or more: 14.4%; Poverty rate: 25.5%
Educational Attainment: High school diploma or higher: 81.2%; Bachelor's degree or higher: 17.2%; Graduate/professional degree or higher: 11.2%

School District(s)
Dansville Central SD (PK-12)
    Enrollment: 1,493 . . . . (585) 335-4000
Housing: Homeownership rate: 59.0%; Median home value: $86,800; Median year structure built: Before 1940; Homeowner vacancy rate: 0.0%; Median selected monthly owner costs: $1,088 with a mortgage, $423 without a mortgage; Median gross rent: $672 per month; Rental vacancy rate: 0.0%
Health Insurance: 96.8% have insurance; 69.1% have private insurance; 47.0% have public insurance; 3.2% do not have insurance; 0.0% of children under 18 do not have insurance
Hospitals: Nicholas H Noyes Memorial Hospital (72 beds)
Safety: Violent crime rate: 8.9 per 10,000 population; Property crime rate: 236.5 per 10,000 population
Newspapers: Genesee County Express (weekly circulation 2,800)
Transportation: Commute: 83.5% car, 0.4% public transportation, 12.6% walk, 3.2% work from home; Mean travel time to work: 24.8 minutes
Additional Information Contacts
Village of Dansville . . . . (585) 335-5330
    http://dansvilleny.us

EAST AVON (CDP). Covers a land area of 1.310 square miles and a water area of 0 square miles. Located at 42.91° N. Lat; 77.71° W. Long. Elevation is 820 feet.
Population: 786; Growth (since 2000): n/a; Density: 600.1 persons per square mile; Race: 100.0% White, 0.0% Black/African American, 0.0% Asian, 0.0% American Indian/Alaska Native, 0.0% Native Hawaiian/Other Pacific Islander, 0.0% Two or more races, 0.0% Hispanic of any race; Average household size: 2.02; Median age: 35.7; Age under 18: 25.6%; Age 65 and over: 21.6%; Males per 100 females: 102.0; Marriage status: 23.7% never married, 38.6% now married, 4.0% separated, 5.8% widowed, 32.0% divorced; Foreign born: 0.0%; Speak English only: 100.0%; With disability: 29.5%; Veterans: 20.5%; Ancestry: 37.2% German, 18.1% Dutch, 17.6% English, 8.5% Polish, 8.4% Irish
Employment: 0.0% management, business, and financial, 6.8% computer, engineering, and science, 5.1% education, legal, community service, arts, and media, 10.1% healthcare practitioners, 36.1% service, 28.4% sales and office, 7.4% natural resources, construction, and maintenance, 6.1% production, transportation, and material moving
Income: Per capita: $21,254; Median household: $34,078; Average household: $43,051; Households with income of $100,000 or more: 3.9%; Poverty rate: 14.2%
Educational Attainment: High school diploma or higher: 87.0%; Bachelor's degree or higher: 27.7%; Graduate/professional degree or higher: 10.8%
Housing: Homeownership rate: 46.0%; Median home value: $147,300; Median year structure built: 1981; Homeowner vacancy rate: 0.0%; Median selected monthly owner costs: $1,633 with a mortgage, $605 without a mortgage; Median gross rent: $853 per month; Rental vacancy rate: 0.0%
Health Insurance: 95.7% have insurance; 62.1% have private insurance; 56.7% have public insurance; 4.3% do not have insurance; 0.0% of children under 18 do not have insurance
Transportation: Commute: 89.5% car, 0.0% public transportation, 0.0% walk, 0.0% work from home; Mean travel time to work: 22.4 minutes

FOWLERVILLE (CDP). Covers a land area of 0.901 square miles and a water area of 0 square miles. Located at 42.89° N. Lat; 77.85° W. Long. Elevation is 636 feet.
Population: 292; Growth (since 2000): n/a; Density: 324.0 persons per square mile; Race: 100.0% White, 0.0% Black/African American, 0.0% Asian, 0.0% American Indian/Alaska Native, 0.0% Native Hawaiian/Other Pacific Islander, 0.0% Two or more races, 0.0% Hispanic of any race;

Average household size: 2.43; Median age: 24.7; Age under 18: 23.6%; Age 65 and over: 15.4%; Males per 100 females: 110.2; Marriage status: 46.6% never married, 40.1% now married, 0.0% separated, 13.4% widowed, 0.0% divorced; Foreign born: 0.0%; Speak English only: 100.0%; With disability: 28.8%; Veterans: 8.5%; Ancestry: 45.2% Irish, 25.7% Italian, 25.3% French, 18.8% German, 18.2% Dutch
Employment: 17.7% management, business, and financial, 0.0% computer, engineering, and science, 0.0% education, legal, community service, arts, and media, 0.0% healthcare practitioners, 38.9% service, 23.9% sales and office, 19.5% natural resources, construction, and maintenance, 0.0% production, transportation, and material moving
Income: Per capita: $15,553; Median household: $16,368; Average household: $37,214; Households with income of $100,000 or more: 15.8%; Poverty rate: 55.5%
Educational Attainment: High school diploma or higher: 83.9%; Bachelor's degree or higher: 14.5%; Graduate/professional degree or higher: 8.1%
Housing: Homeownership rate: 43.3%; Median home value: $99,000; Median year structure built: Before 1940; Homeowner vacancy rate: 0.0%; Median selected monthly owner costs: $950 with a mortgage, n/a without a mortgage; Median gross rent: n/a per month; Rental vacancy rate: 0.0%
Health Insurance: 100.0% have insurance; 59.9% have private insurance; 70.9% have public insurance; 0.0% do not have insurance; 0.0% of children under 18 do not have insurance
Transportation: Commute: 100.0% car, 0.0% public transportation, 0.0% walk, 0.0% work from home; Mean travel time to work: 18.9 minutes

GENESEO (town). Covers a land area of 43.944 square miles and a water area of 1.198 square miles. Located at 42.81° N. Lat; 77.78° W. Long. Elevation is 771 feet.
History: Geneseo is best known for its association with the Wadsworth family. They became the squires of the middle Genesee in 1790. Members of the family served as legislators at the state and national levels.
Population: 10,715; Growth (since 2000): 11.0%; Density: 243.8 persons per square mile; Race: 91.5% White, 2.0% Black/African American, 3.5% Asian, 0.1% American Indian/Alaska Native, 0.0% Native Hawaiian/Other Pacific Islander, 2.7% Two or more races, 3.6% Hispanic of any race; Average household size: 2.33; Median age: 21.8; Age under 18: 10.8%; Age 65 and over: 12.4%; Males per 100 females: 84.0; Marriage status: 63.5% never married, 26.9% now married, 1.1% separated, 5.0% widowed, 4.6% divorced; Foreign born: 7.3%; Speak English only: 88.6%; With disability: 10.4%; Veterans: 5.5%; Ancestry: 22.8% German, 21.5% Irish, 19.0% Italian, 11.8% English, 5.0% Polish
Employment: 10.3% management, business, and financial, 2.9% computer, engineering, and science, 18.1% education, legal, community service, arts, and media, 5.1% healthcare practitioners, 26.6% service, 22.1% sales and office, 8.1% natural resources, construction, and maintenance, 6.8% production, transportation, and material moving
Income: Per capita: $21,914; Median household: $44,263; Average household: $64,799; Households with income of $100,000 or more: 21.3%; Poverty rate: 29.6%
Educational Attainment: High school diploma or higher: 90.1%; Bachelor's degree or higher: 39.0%; Graduate/professional degree or higher: 20.5%

School District(s)
Geneseo Central SD (KG-12)
    Enrollment: 890 . . . . (585) 243-3450
Four-year College(s)
SUNY College at Geneseo (Public)
    Enrollment: 5,652 . . . . (585) 245-5000
    Tuition: In-state $8,408; Out-of-state $18,026
Housing: Homeownership rate: 49.0%; Median home value: $170,600; Median year structure built: 1972; Homeowner vacancy rate: 0.0%; Median selected monthly owner costs: $1,623 with a mortgage, $674 without a mortgage; Median gross rent: $834 per month; Rental vacancy rate: 5.6%
Health Insurance: 98.1% have insurance; 85.7% have private insurance; 24.3% have public insurance; 1.9% do not have insurance; 1.7% of children under 18 do not have insurance
Newspapers: Livingston County News (weekly circulation 6,000)
Transportation: Commute: 68.8% car, 0.8% public transportation, 23.9% walk, 5.7% work from home; Mean travel time to work: 21.0 minutes
Additional Information Contacts
Town of Geneseo . . . . (585) 991-5000
    http://www.geneseony.org

GENESEO (village). County seat. Covers a land area of 2.839 square miles and a water area of 0 square miles. Located at 42.80° N. Lat; 77.81° W. Long. Elevation is 771 feet.

History: Major salt mine cave-in and diversion of surface drainage into subterranean channels occurred in 1995. Estates of the Wadsworth family, northeast and south of village. English-style Genesee Valley Hunt each fall. Seat of State University of N.Y. College at Geneseo. Settled c.1790, Incorporated 1832.

Population: 8,151; Growth (since 2000): 7.5%; Density: 2,871.2 persons per square mile; Race: 89.0% White, 2.6% Black/African American, 4.3% Asian, 0.1% American Indian/Alaska Native, 0.0% Native Hawaiian/Other Pacific Islander, 3.5% Two or more races, 4.4% Hispanic of any race; Average household size: 2.58; Median age: 20.8; Age under 18: 10.4%; Age 65 and over: 6.0%; Males per 100 females: 81.5; Marriage status: 79.1% never married, 15.7% now married, 1.3% separated, 2.4% widowed, 2.8% divorced; Foreign born: 8.6%; Speak English only: 85.5%; With disability: 8.5%; Veterans: 2.2%; Ancestry: 21.9% German, 19.4% Irish, 18.4% Italian, 9.7% English, 4.6% Polish

Employment: 7.8% management, business, and financial, 3.5% computer, engineering, and science, 19.8% education, legal, community service, arts, and media, 3.5% healthcare practitioners, 31.2% service, 25.2% sales and office, 4.1% natural resources, construction, and maintenance, 5.1% production, transportation, and material moving

Income: Per capita: $15,562; Median household: $35,038; Average household: $53,230; Households with income of $100,000 or more: 17.0%; Poverty rate: 41.4%

Educational Attainment: High school diploma or higher: 86.1%; Bachelor's degree or higher: 43.5%; Graduate/professional degree or higher: 24.5%

School District(s)
Geneseo Central SD (KG-12)
    Enrollment: 890 . . . . (585) 243-3450
Four-year College(s)
SUNY College at Geneseo (Public)
    Enrollment: 5,652 . . . . (585) 245-5000
    Tuition: In-state $8,408; Out-of-state $18,026

Housing: Homeownership rate: 39.2%; Median home value: $162,600; Median year structure built: 1968; Homeowner vacancy rate: 0.0%; Median selected monthly owner costs: $1,466 with a mortgage, $711 without a mortgage; Median gross rent: $769 per month; Rental vacancy rate: 4.8%

Health Insurance: 97.5% have insurance; 84.2% have private insurance; 21.2% have public insurance; 2.6% do not have insurance; 2.0% of children under 18 do not have insurance

Safety: Violent crime rate: 2.4 per 10,000 population; Property crime rate: 199.3 per 10,000 population

Newspapers: Livingston County News (weekly circulation 6,000)

Transportation: Commute: 57.8% car, 1.1% public transportation, 33.7% walk, 6.2% work from home; Mean travel time to work: 16.2 minutes

Additional Information Contacts
Village of Geneseo . . . . (585) 243-1177
    http://www.geneseony.org

GREIGSVILLE (CDP). Covers a land area of 0.710 square miles and a water area of 0 square miles. Located at 42.83° N. Lat; 77.90° W. Long. Elevation is 751 feet.

Population: 326; Growth (since 2000): n/a; Density: 458.9 persons per square mile; Race: 100.0% White, 0.0% Black/African American, 0.0% Asian, 0.0% American Indian/Alaska Native, 0.0% Native Hawaiian/Other Pacific Islander, 0.0% Two or more races, 0.0% Hispanic of any race; Average household size: 3.20; Median age: 25.0; Age under 18: 44.8%; Age 65 and over: 2.5%; Males per 100 females: 104.9; Marriage status: 41.0% never married, 55.1% now married, 0.0% separated, 0.0% widowed, 3.8% divorced; Foreign born: 0.0%; Speak English only: 100.0%; With disability: 3.1%; Veterans: 21.1%; Ancestry: 43.6% Italian, 34.4% German, 10.4% Dutch, 8.0% Irish, 7.7% American

Employment: 0.0% management, business, and financial, 14.5% computer, engineering, and science, 7.8% education, legal, community service, arts, and media, 0.0% healthcare practitioners, 31.6% service, 4.7% sales and office, 19.2% natural resources, construction, and maintenance, 22.3% production, transportation, and material moving

Income: Per capita: $28,921; Median household: $105,735; Average household: $92,469; Households with income of $100,000 or more: 54.9%; Poverty rate: n/a

Educational Attainment: High school diploma or higher: 94.5%; Bachelor's degree or higher: 16.5%; Graduate/professional degree or higher: 16.5%

Housing: Homeownership rate: 74.5%; Median home value: $86,500; Median year structure built: Before 1940; Homeowner vacancy rate: 0.0%; Median selected monthly owner costs: $1,250 with a mortgage, n/a without a mortgage; Median gross rent: n/a per month; Rental vacancy rate: 0.0%

Health Insurance: 97.2% have insurance; 94.5% have private insurance; 13.2% have public insurance; 2.8% do not have insurance; 0.0% of children under 18 do not have insurance

Transportation: Commute: 95.3% car, 0.0% public transportation, 0.0% walk, 4.7% work from home; Mean travel time to work: 25.5 minutes

GROVELAND (town). Covers a land area of 39.129 square miles and a water area of 0.725 square miles. Located at 42.71° N. Lat; 77.77° W. Long. Elevation is 614 feet.

Population: 3,344; Growth (since 2000): -13.2%; Density: 85.5 persons per square mile; Race: 68.5% White, 25.7% Black/African American, 0.3% Asian, 0.6% American Indian/Alaska Native, 0.0% Native Hawaiian/Other Pacific Islander, 3.0% Two or more races, 13.9% Hispanic of any race; Average household size: 2.61; Median age: 36.6; Age under 18: 9.5%; Age 65 and over: 6.0%; Males per 100 females: 334.9; Marriage status: 44.6% never married, 40.1% now married, 4.1% separated, 1.7% widowed, 13.6% divorced; Foreign born: 4.2%; Speak English only: 83.7%; With disability: 9.7%; Veterans: 9.8%; Ancestry: 14.4% German, 11.5% Irish, 9.6% Italian, 8.5% English, 4.6% African

Employment: 10.1% management, business, and financial, 2.5% computer, engineering, and science, 9.1% education, legal, community service, arts, and media, 7.9% healthcare practitioners, 13.5% service, 18.4% sales and office, 22.4% natural resources, construction, and maintenance, 16.1% production, transportation, and material moving

Income: Per capita: $12,436; Median household: $62,273; Average household: $77,876; Households with income of $100,000 or more: 27.7%; Poverty rate: 8.5%

Educational Attainment: High school diploma or higher: 80.3%; Bachelor's degree or higher: 9.5%; Graduate/professional degree or higher: 2.9%

Housing: Homeownership rate: 77.3%; Median home value: $145,900; Median year structure built: 1956; Homeowner vacancy rate: 2.3%; Median selected monthly owner costs: $1,278 with a mortgage, $592 without a mortgage; Median gross rent: $745 per month; Rental vacancy rate: 5.1%

Health Insurance: 92.9% have insurance; 68.1% have private insurance; 39.1% have public insurance; 7.1% do not have insurance; 3.5% of children under 18 do not have insurance

Transportation: Commute: 92.4% car, 0.0% public transportation, 4.0% walk, 3.6% work from home; Mean travel time to work: 26.3 minutes

GROVELAND STATION (CDP). Covers a land area of 0.586 square miles and a water area of 0 square miles. Located at 42.66° N. Lat; 77.77° W. Long. Elevation is 614 feet.

Population: 289; Growth (since 2000): n/a; Density: 492.9 persons per square mile; Race: 100.0% White, 0.0% Black/African American, 0.0% Asian, 0.0% American Indian/Alaska Native, 0.0% Native Hawaiian/Other Pacific Islander, 0.0% Two or more races, 0.0% Hispanic of any race; Average household size: 3.14; Median age: 33.2; Age under 18: 29.8%; Age 65 and over: 8.3%; Males per 100 females: 109.7; Marriage status: 26.9% never married, 54.8% now married, 0.9% separated, 5.0% widowed, 13.2% divorced; Foreign born: 0.0%; Speak English only: 100.0%; With disability: 11.8%; Veterans: 5.9%; Ancestry: 27.3% German, 23.2% English, 20.8% Irish, 14.9% Italian, 8.3% European

Employment: 10.0% management, business, and financial, 1.5% computer, engineering, and science, 7.7% education, legal, community service, arts, and media, 3.8% healthcare practitioners, 20.8% service, 20.8% sales and office, 16.2% natural resources, construction, and maintenance, 19.2% production, transportation, and material moving

Income: Per capita: $21,020; Median household: $52,500; Average household: $65,414; Households with income of $100,000 or more: 24.0%; Poverty rate: 15.0%

Educational Attainment: High school diploma or higher: 88.2%; Bachelor's degree or higher: 19.7%; Graduate/professional degree or higher: 3.4%

Housing: Homeownership rate: 88.0%; Median home value: $85,400; Median year structure built: Before 1940; Homeowner vacancy rate: 10.0%; Median selected monthly owner costs: $1,048 with a mortgage,

$559 without a mortgage; Median gross rent: $721 per month; Rental vacancy rate: 0.0%
Health Insurance: 96.5% have insurance; 61.9% have private insurance; 46.0% have public insurance; 3.5% do not have insurance; 0.0% of children under 18 do not have insurance
Transportation: Commute: 98.5% car, 0.0% public transportation, 0.0% walk, 1.5% work from home; Mean travel time to work: 27.7 minutes

HEMLOCK (CDP). Covers a land area of 1.863 square miles and a water area of 0 square miles. Located at 42.79° N. Lat; 77.61° W. Long. Elevation is 909 feet.
Population: 512; Growth (since 2000): n/a; Density: 274.9 persons per square mile; Race: 100.0% White, 0.0% Black/African American, 0.0% Asian, 0.0% American Indian/Alaska Native, 0.0% Native Hawaiian/Other Pacific Islander, 0.0% Two or more races, 0.0% Hispanic of any race; Average household size: 2.24; Median age: 36.9; Age under 18: 20.7%; Age 65 and over: 12.9%; Males per 100 females: 106.3; Marriage status: 6.9% never married, 63.5% now married, 0.0% separated, 17.0% widowed, 12.6% divorced; Foreign born: 0.0%; Speak English only: 96.7%; With disability: 4.3%; Veterans: 4.4%; Ancestry: 39.5% German, 9.6% English, 3.5% Austrian, 3.5% Dutch, 3.3% Irish
Employment: 0.0% management, business, and financial, 0.0% computer, engineering, and science, 0.0% education, legal, community service, arts, and media, 0.0% healthcare practitioners, 19.5% service, 12.8% sales and office, 21.5% natural resources, construction, and maintenance, 46.3% production, transportation, and material moving
Income: Per capita: $24,260; Median household: $62,014; Average household: $52,297; Households with income of $100,000 or more: n/a; Poverty rate: 10.0%
Educational Attainment: High school diploma or higher: 92.8%; Bachelor's degree or higher: 4.4%; Graduate/professional degree or higher: n/a
Housing: Homeownership rate: 84.7%; Median home value: $105,600; Median year structure built: Before 1940; Homeowner vacancy rate: 0.0%; Median selected monthly owner costs: $1,316 with a mortgage, n/a without a mortgage; Median gross rent: n/a per month; Rental vacancy rate: 0.0%
Health Insurance: 100.0% have insurance; 84.4% have private insurance; 25.2% have public insurance; 0.0% do not have insurance; 0.0% of children under 18 do not have insurance
Transportation: Commute: 98.7% car, 1.3% public transportation, 0.0% walk, 0.0% work from home; Mean travel time to work: 25.0 minutes

HUNT (CDP). Covers a land area of 0.119 square miles and a water area of 0 square miles. Located at 42.55° N. Lat; 77.99° W. Long. Elevation is 1,342 feet.
Population: 114; Growth (since 2000): n/a; Density: 957.2 persons per square mile; Race: 100.0% White, 0.0% Black/African American, 0.0% Asian, 0.0% American Indian/Alaska Native, 0.0% Native Hawaiian/Other Pacific Islander, 0.0% Two or more races, 2.6% Hispanic of any race; Average household size: 2.28; Median age: 41.8; Age under 18: 36.0%; Age 65 and over: 15.8%; Males per 100 females: 85.7; Marriage status: 17.3% never married, 66.7% now married, 3.7% separated, 16.0% widowed, 0.0% divorced; Foreign born: 10.5%; Speak English only: 82.4%; With disability: 19.3%; Veterans: 15.1%; Ancestry: 36.8% German, 28.9% Irish, 17.5% English, 10.5% Albanian, 3.5% Swedish
Employment: 20.0% management, business, and financial, 0.0% computer, engineering, and science, 0.0% education, legal, community service, arts, and media, 3.3% healthcare practitioners, 23.3% service, 0.0% sales and office, 33.3% natural resources, construction, and maintenance, 20.0% production, transportation, and material moving
Income: Per capita: $21,075; Median household: $44,167; Average household: $52,034; Households with income of $100,000 or more: 22.0%; Poverty rate: 11.4%
Educational Attainment: High school diploma or higher: 65.8%; Bachelor's degree or higher: 2.7%; Graduate/professional degree or higher: n/a
Housing: Homeownership rate: 100.0%; Median home value: $58,600; Median year structure built: 1949; Homeowner vacancy rate: 0.0%; Median selected monthly owner costs: $894 with a mortgage, n/a without a mortgage; Median gross rent: n/a per month; Rental vacancy rate: 0.0%
Health Insurance: 98.2% have insurance; 93.9% have private insurance; 25.4% have public insurance; 1.8% do not have insurance; 0.0% of children under 18 do not have insurance
Transportation: Commute: 54.2% car, 0.0% public transportation, 0.0% walk, 45.8% work from home; Mean travel time to work: 0.0 minutes

KYSORVILLE (CDP). Covers a land area of 0.827 square miles and a water area of 0 square miles. Located at 42.65° N. Lat; 77.79° W. Long. Elevation is 623 feet.
Population: 172; Growth (since 2000): n/a; Density: 208.1 persons per square mile; Race: 100.0% White, 0.0% Black/African American, 0.0% Asian, 0.0% American Indian/Alaska Native, 0.0% Native Hawaiian/Other Pacific Islander, 0.0% Two or more races, 3.5% Hispanic of any race; Average household size: 2.92; Median age: 34.5; Age under 18: 32.6%; Age 65 and over: 9.9%; Males per 100 females: 96.4; Marriage status: 16.4% never married, 81.0% now married, 6.0% separated, 0.0% widowed, 2.6% divorced; Foreign born: 0.0%; Speak English only: 100.0%; With disability: 17.4%; Veterans: 17.2%; Ancestry: 16.3% English, 15.7% German, 9.3% Irish, 7.0% American, 6.4% Lithuanian
Employment: 4.3% management, business, and financial, 0.0% computer, engineering, and science, 0.0% education, legal, community service, arts, and media, 4.3% healthcare practitioners, 47.8% service, 8.7% sales and office, 26.1% natural resources, construction, and maintenance, 8.7% production, transportation, and material moving
Income: Per capita: $21,967; Median household: $60,795; Average household: $63,456; Households with income of $100,000 or more: 10.2%; Poverty rate: 49.1%
Educational Attainment: High school diploma or higher: 57.5%; Bachelor's degree or higher: 5.7%; Graduate/professional degree or higher: 2.8%
Housing: Homeownership rate: 94.9%; Median home value: $44,000; Median year structure built: 1983; Homeowner vacancy rate: 0.0%; Median selected monthly owner costs: $860 with a mortgage, $323 without a mortgage; Median gross rent: n/a per month; Rental vacancy rate: 81.3%
Health Insurance: 100.0% have insurance; 79.1% have private insurance; 65.7% have public insurance; 0.0% do not have insurance; 0.0% of children under 18 do not have insurance
Transportation: Commute: 100.0% car, 0.0% public transportation, 0.0% walk, 0.0% work from home; Mean travel time to work: 30.7 minutes

LAKEVILLE (CDP). Covers a land area of 0.667 square miles and a water area of 0 square miles. Located at 42.84° N. Lat; 77.70° W. Long. Elevation is 823 feet.
Population: 994; Growth (since 2000): n/a; Density: 1,489.4 persons per square mile; Race: 85.2% White, 6.8% Black/African American, 7.9% Asian, 0.0% American Indian/Alaska Native, 0.0% Native Hawaiian/Other Pacific Islander, 0.0% Two or more races, 0.0% Hispanic of any race; Average household size: 2.97; Median age: 47.2; Age under 18: 28.7%; Age 65 and over: 14.6%; Males per 100 females: 84.8; Marriage status: 23.9% never married, 68.6% now married, 0.0% separated, 1.6% widowed, 6.0% divorced; Foreign born: 5.4%; Speak English only: 91.3%; With disability: 19.5%; Veterans: 7.6%; Ancestry: 24.5% Dutch, 20.9% Irish, 18.4% English, 14.0% German, 5.4% Lithuanian
Employment: 12.5% management, business, and financial, 3.9% computer, engineering, and science, 5.5% education, legal, community service, arts, and media, 0.0% healthcare practitioners, 58.8% service, 4.5% sales and office, 0.0% natural resources, construction, and maintenance, 14.8% production, transportation, and material moving
Income: Per capita: $14,554; Median household: $38,526; Average household: $43,281; Households with income of $100,000 or more: 13.0%; Poverty rate: 46.8%
Educational Attainment: High school diploma or higher: 80.2%; Bachelor's degree or higher: 11.8%; Graduate/professional degree or higher: 2.5%
Housing: Homeownership rate: 66.9%; Median home value: $152,800; Median year structure built: Before 1940; Homeowner vacancy rate: 0.0%; Median selected monthly owner costs: $1,422 with a mortgage, $554 without a mortgage; Median gross rent: $843 per month; Rental vacancy rate: 0.0%
Health Insurance: 83.1% have insurance; 40.0% have private insurance; 60.5% have public insurance; 16.9% do not have insurance; 0.0% of children under 18 do not have insurance
Transportation: Commute: 93.2% car, 0.0% public transportation, 5.8% walk, 0.0% work from home; Mean travel time to work: 18.1 minutes

LEICESTER (town). Covers a land area of 33.929 square miles and a water area of 0.004 square miles. Located at 42.76° N. Lat; 77.90° W. Long. Elevation is 650 feet.
Population: 2,138; Growth (since 2000): -6.5%; Density: 63.0 persons per square mile; Race: 93.5% White, 0.7% Black/African American, 0.4% Asian, 0.7% American Indian/Alaska Native, 0.0% Native Hawaiian/Other

Pacific Islander, 1.1% Two or more races, 4.4% Hispanic of any race; Average household size: 2.23; Median age: 45.3; Age under 18: 17.4%; Age 65 and over: 17.4%; Males per 100 females: 98.9; Marriage status: 27.8% never married, 53.3% now married, 1.0% separated, 5.0% widowed, 13.9% divorced; Foreign born: 4.3%; Speak English only: 95.2%; With disability: 10.9%; Veterans: 7.6%; Ancestry: 28.4% Italian, 27.2% German, 15.3% Irish, 11.1% Polish, 10.6% English

Employment: 14.8% management, business, and financial, 1.3% computer, engineering, and science, 12.9% education, legal, community service, arts, and media, 2.8% healthcare practitioners, 16.7% service, 21.0% sales and office, 19.1% natural resources, construction, and maintenance, 11.4% production, transportation, and material moving
Income: Per capita: $26,847; Median household: $54,038; Average household: $59,143; Households with income of $100,000 or more: 15.6%; Poverty rate: 11.2%
Educational Attainment: High school diploma or higher: 88.5%; Bachelor's degree or higher: 20.6%; Graduate/professional degree or higher: 6.5%
Housing: Homeownership rate: 74.5%; Median home value: $108,400; Median year structure built: 1974; Homeowner vacancy rate: 2.4%; Median selected monthly owner costs: $1,193 with a mortgage, $496 without a mortgage; Median gross rent: $782 per month; Rental vacancy rate: 9.3%
Health Insurance: 96.8% have insurance; 81.3% have private insurance; 35.1% have public insurance; 3.2% do not have insurance; 3.0% of children under 18 do not have insurance
Transportation: Commute: 87.5% car, 0.0% public transportation, 3.6% walk, 8.4% work from home; Mean travel time to work: 20.6 minutes

LEICESTER (village). Covers a land area of 0.367 square miles and a water area of 0 square miles. Located at 42.77° N. Lat; 77.90° W. Long. Elevation is 650 feet.
Population: 463; Growth (since 2000): -1.3%; Density: 1,260.8 persons per square mile; Race: 99.1% White, 0.0% Black/African American, 0.0% Asian, 0.0% American Indian/Alaska Native, 0.0% Native Hawaiian/Other Pacific Islander, 0.9% Two or more races, 0.2% Hispanic of any race; Average household size: 2.34; Median age: 44.9; Age under 18: 18.1%; Age 65 and over: 20.1%; Males per 100 females: 89.5; Marriage status: 27.2% never married, 52.1% now married, 2.0% separated, 6.8% widowed, 13.9% divorced; Foreign born: 0.2%; Speak English only: 99.1%; With disability: 12.3%; Veterans: 10.0%; Ancestry: 35.0% German, 24.0% Italian, 21.8% English, 21.8% Irish, 6.7% Polish
Employment: 11.1% management, business, and financial, 1.9% computer, engineering, and science, 11.1% education, legal, community service, arts, and media, 6.5% healthcare practitioners, 21.0% service, 23.3% sales and office, 14.1% natural resources, construction, and maintenance, 11.1% production, transportation, and material moving
Income: Per capita: $28,398; Median household: $63,636; Average household: $64,753; Households with income of $100,000 or more: 18.2%; Poverty rate: 3.7%
Educational Attainment: High school diploma or higher: 92.8%; Bachelor's degree or higher: 21.2%; Graduate/professional degree or higher: 9.6%
Housing: Homeownership rate: 74.2%; Median home value: $110,600; Median year structure built: 1955; Homeowner vacancy rate: 2.6%; Median selected monthly owner costs: $1,185 with a mortgage, $496 without a mortgage; Median gross rent: $838 per month; Rental vacancy rate: 7.3%
Health Insurance: 98.7% have insurance; 87.5% have private insurance; 32.6% have public insurance; 1.3% do not have insurance; 0.0% of children under 18 do not have insurance
Transportation: Commute: 100.0% car, 0.0% public transportation, 0.0% walk, 0.0% work from home; Mean travel time to work: 21.2 minutes

LIMA (town). Covers a land area of 31.891 square miles and a water area of 0.053 square miles. Located at 42.90° N. Lat; 77.61° W. Long. Elevation is 827 feet.
Population: 4,167; Growth (since 2000): -8.2%; Density: 130.7 persons per square mile; Race: 93.1% White, 0.4% Black/African American, 2.5% Asian, 0.0% American Indian/Alaska Native, 0.1% Native Hawaiian/Other Pacific Islander, 1.8% Two or more races, 4.0% Hispanic of any race; Average household size: 2.45; Median age: 41.4; Age under 18: 19.9%; Age 65 and over: 15.9%; Males per 100 females: 97.6; Marriage status: 29.6% never married, 56.1% now married, 1.1% separated, 4.5% widowed, 9.8% divorced; Foreign born: 6.6%; Speak English only: 93.5%; With disability: 11.6%; Veterans: 9.1%; Ancestry: 29.6% German, 23.4% Irish, 22.6% English, 11.4% Italian, 5.7% American

Employment: 15.5% management, business, and financial, 8.1% computer, engineering, and science, 11.5% education, legal, community service, arts, and media, 5.3% healthcare practitioners, 16.6% service, 18.6% sales and office, 6.8% natural resources, construction, and maintenance, 17.6% production, transportation, and material moving
Income: Per capita: $27,826; Median household: $58,606; Average household: $71,489; Households with income of $100,000 or more: 22.9%; Poverty rate: 9.4%
Educational Attainment: High school diploma or higher: 92.2%; Bachelor's degree or higher: 30.2%; Graduate/professional degree or higher: 10.7%

School District(s)
Honeoye Falls-Lima Central SD (KG-12)
    Enrollment: 2,212 . . . . (585) 624-7010
Two-year College(s)
Elim Bible Institute and College (Private, Not-for-profit, Evangelical Christian)
    Enrollment: 97 . . . . (585) 582-1230
    Tuition: In-state $7,942; Out-of-state $7,942
Housing: Homeownership rate: 74.9%; Median home value: $145,600; Median year structure built: 1974; Homeowner vacancy rate: 1.8%; Median selected monthly owner costs: $1,448 with a mortgage, $534 without a mortgage; Median gross rent: $720 per month; Rental vacancy rate: 5.7%
Health Insurance: 96.6% have insurance; 82.3% have private insurance; 29.9% have public insurance; 3.4% do not have insurance; 3.0% of children under 18 do not have insurance
Transportation: Commute: 89.1% car, 0.4% public transportation, 6.1% walk, 2.8% work from home; Mean travel time to work: 25.1 minutes
Additional Information Contacts
Town of Lima. . . . . (585) 582-1130
    http://www.lima-ny.org

LIMA (village). Covers a land area of 1.346 square miles and a water area of 0 square miles. Located at 42.91° N. Lat; 77.61° W. Long. Elevation is 827 feet.
Population: 2,445; Growth (since 2000): -0.6%; Density: 1,816.8 persons per square mile; Race: 89.6% White, 0.7% Black/African American, 2.9% Asian, 0.0% American Indian/Alaska Native, 0.1% Native Hawaiian/Other Pacific Islander, 3.1% Two or more races, 6.7% Hispanic of any race; Average household size: 2.43; Median age: 35.1; Age under 18: 22.9%; Age 65 and over: 13.9%; Males per 100 females: 93.1; Marriage status: 34.3% never married, 52.7% now married, 1.5% separated, 2.8% widowed, 10.2% divorced; Foreign born: 6.0%; Speak English only: 92.5%; With disability: 10.1%; Veterans: 7.3%; Ancestry: 32.6% German, 27.2% Irish, 15.1% English, 12.9% Italian, 3.7% American
Employment: 16.0% management, business, and financial, 7.3% computer, engineering, and science, 12.1% education, legal, community service, arts, and media, 3.3% healthcare practitioners, 18.5% service, 17.3% sales and office, 7.6% natural resources, construction, and maintenance, 18.0% production, transportation, and material moving
Income: Per capita: $25,568; Median household: $56,319; Average household: $68,387; Households with income of $100,000 or more: 21.8%; Poverty rate: 14.5%
Educational Attainment: High school diploma or higher: 91.0%; Bachelor's degree or higher: 27.9%; Graduate/professional degree or higher: 11.0%
School District(s)
Honeoye Falls-Lima Central SD (KG-12)
    Enrollment: 2,212 . . . . (585) 624-7010
Two-year College(s)
Elim Bible Institute and College (Private, Not-for-profit, Evangelical Christian)
    Enrollment: 97 . . . . (585) 582-1230
    Tuition: In-state $7,942; Out-of-state $7,942
Housing: Homeownership rate: 67.0%; Median home value: $134,100; Median year structure built: 1972; Homeowner vacancy rate: 0.0%; Median selected monthly owner costs: $1,321 with a mortgage, $553 without a mortgage; Median gross rent: $709 per month; Rental vacancy rate: 7.5%
Health Insurance: 96.6% have insurance; 80.0% have private insurance; 29.7% have public insurance; 3.4% do not have insurance; 1.5% of children under 18 do not have insurance
Transportation: Commute: 88.8% car, 0.1% public transportation, 6.1% walk, 2.5% work from home; Mean travel time to work: 25.8 minutes

LINWOOD (CDP). Covers a land area of 0.929 square miles and a water area of 0 square miles. Located at 42.90° N. Lat; 77.95° W. Long. Elevation is 938 feet.

Population: 70; Growth (since 2000): n/a; Density: 75.4 persons per square mile; Race: 91.4% White, 8.6% Black/African American, 0.0% Asian, 0.0% American Indian/Alaska Native, 0.0% Native Hawaiian/Other Pacific Islander, 0.0% Two or more races, 0.0% Hispanic of any race; Average household size: 2.12; Median age: 56.6; Age under 18: 0.0%; Age 65 and over: 44.3%; Males per 100 females: 100.0; Marriage status: 8.6% never married, 34.3% now married, 0.0% separated, 0.0% widowed, 57.1% divorced; Foreign born: 0.0%; Speak English only: 100.0%; With disability: 14.3%; Veterans: 11.4%; Ancestry: 57.1% English, 42.9% Irish, 21.4% German, 10.0% French

Employment: 44.4% management, business, and financial, 0.0% computer, engineering, and science, 0.0% education, legal, community service, arts, and media, 0.0% healthcare practitioners, 55.6% service, 0.0% sales and office, 0.0% natural resources, construction, and maintenance, 0.0% production, transportation, and material moving

Income: Per capita: $33,173; Median household: n/a; Average household: $70,821; Households with income of $100,000 or more: 24.2%; Poverty rate: 42.9%

Educational Attainment: High school diploma or higher: 100.0%; Bachelor's degree or higher: 21.4%; Graduate/professional degree or higher: 12.9%

Housing: Homeownership rate: 69.7%; Median home value: n/a; Median year structure built: 1975; Homeowner vacancy rate: 0.0%; Median selected monthly owner costs: n/a with a mortgage, n/a without a mortgage; Median gross rent: n/a per month; Rental vacancy rate: 0.0%

Health Insurance: 100.0% have insurance; 42.9% have private insurance; 87.1% have public insurance; 0.0% do not have insurance; 0.0% of children under 18 do not have insurance

Transportation: Commute: 100.0% car, 0.0% public transportation, 0.0% walk, 0.0% work from home; Mean travel time to work: 0.0 minutes

LIVONIA (town). Covers a land area of 38.262 square miles and a water area of 2.812 square miles. Located at 42.81° N. Lat; 77.65° W. Long. Elevation is 1,033 feet.

Population: 7,635; Growth (since 2000): 4.8%; Density: 199.5 persons per square mile; Race: 95.5% White, 1.3% Black/African American, 1.5% Asian, 0.2% American Indian/Alaska Native, 0.2% Native Hawaiian/Other Pacific Islander, 1.4% Two or more races, 0.7% Hispanic of any race; Average household size: 2.48; Median age: 43.4; Age under 18: 23.5%; Age 65 and over: 17.4%; Males per 100 females: 95.4; Marriage status: 25.9% never married, 58.3% now married, 0.8% separated, 5.4% widowed, 10.3% divorced; Foreign born: 2.0%; Speak English only: 96.4%; With disability: 12.2%; Veterans: 8.0%; Ancestry: 32.9% German, 22.8% Irish, 13.8% Italian, 11.8% English, 9.4% Dutch

Employment: 18.4% management, business, and financial, 7.1% computer, engineering, and science, 14.3% education, legal, community service, arts, and media, 5.9% healthcare practitioners, 19.3% service, 14.4% sales and office, 9.7% natural resources, construction, and maintenance, 11.0% production, transportation, and material moving

Income: Per capita: $29,974; Median household: $64,838; Average household: $74,399; Households with income of $100,000 or more: 25.2%; Poverty rate: 9.8%

Educational Attainment: High school diploma or higher: 94.4%; Bachelor's degree or higher: 29.6%; Graduate/professional degree or higher: 12.7%

School District(s)
Livonia Central SD (PK-12)
    Enrollment: 1,577 . . . . (585) 346-4000

Housing: Homeownership rate: 82.5%; Median home value: $152,300; Median year structure built: 1950; Homeowner vacancy rate: 0.9%; Median selected monthly owner costs: $1,457 with a mortgage, $618 without a mortgage; Median gross rent: $818 per month; Rental vacancy rate: 2.0%

Health Insurance: 95.3% have insurance; 76.4% have private insurance; 33.9% have public insurance; 4.7% do not have insurance; 0.0% of children under 18 do not have insurance

Transportation: Commute: 96.8% car, 0.3% public transportation, 0.7% walk, 1.4% work from home; Mean travel time to work: 26.1 minutes

Additional Information Contacts
Town of Livonia . . . . (585) 346-3710
    http://www.livoniany.org

LIVONIA (village). Covers a land area of 1.007 square miles and a water area of 0 square miles. Located at 42.82° N. Lat; 77.67° W. Long. Elevation is 1,033 feet.

Population: 1,105; Growth (since 2000): -19.5%; Density: 1,097.3 persons per square mile; Race: 96.7% White, 0.3% Black/African American, 0.0% Asian, 0.4% American Indian/Alaska Native, 0.0% Native Hawaiian/Other Pacific Islander, 2.6% Two or more races, 2.4% Hispanic of any race; Average household size: 2.23; Median age: 43.5; Age under 18: 23.4%; Age 65 and over: 15.3%; Males per 100 females: 92.0; Marriage status: 30.5% never married, 46.9% now married, 0.7% separated, 8.8% widowed, 13.7% divorced; Foreign born: 1.2%; Speak English only: 94.5%; With disability: 14.5%; Veterans: 8.3%; Ancestry: 32.1% German, 22.0% Irish, 16.0% English, 14.1% Italian, 6.5% Dutch

Employment: 18.1% management, business, and financial, 5.8% computer, engineering, and science, 9.9% education, legal, community service, arts, and media, 7.5% healthcare practitioners, 20.6% service, 19.8% sales and office, 11.7% natural resources, construction, and maintenance, 6.5% production, transportation, and material moving

Income: Per capita: $29,147; Median household: $57,813; Average household: $64,397; Households with income of $100,000 or more: 19.1%; Poverty rate: 13.0%

Educational Attainment: High school diploma or higher: 96.9%; Bachelor's degree or higher: 32.0%; Graduate/professional degree or higher: 14.0%

School District(s)
Livonia Central SD (PK-12)
    Enrollment: 1,577 . . . . (585) 346-4000

Housing: Homeownership rate: 70.5%; Median home value: $137,800; Median year structure built: Before 1940; Homeowner vacancy rate: 2.8%; Median selected monthly owner costs: $1,421 with a mortgage, $644 without a mortgage; Median gross rent: $688 per month; Rental vacancy rate: 6.6%

Health Insurance: 97.0% have insurance; 78.1% have private insurance; 32.9% have public insurance; 3.0% do not have insurance; 0.0% of children under 18 do not have insurance

Transportation: Commute: 91.3% car, 0.0% public transportation, 1.6% walk, 2.6% work from home; Mean travel time to work: 24.6 minutes

LIVONIA CENTER (CDP). Covers a land area of 0.817 square miles and a water area of 0 square miles. Located at 42.82° N. Lat; 77.64° W. Long. Elevation is 1,086 feet.

Population: 294; Growth (since 2000): n/a; Density: 360.0 persons per square mile; Race: 98.3% White, 1.7% Black/African American, 0.0% Asian, 0.0% American Indian/Alaska Native, 0.0% Native Hawaiian/Other Pacific Islander, 0.0% Two or more races, 0.0% Hispanic of any race; Average household size: 2.19; Median age: 52.6; Age under 18: 11.2%; Age 65 and over: 18.7%; Males per 100 females: 94.9; Marriage status: 20.4% never married, 79.6% now married, 9.9% separated, 0.0% widowed, 0.0% divorced; Foreign born: 0.7%; Speak English only: 100.0%; With disability: 21.4%; Veterans: 6.1%; Ancestry: 45.9% Irish, 37.8% Dutch, 13.9% English, 5.4% French, 5.1% American

Employment: 0.0% management, business, and financial, 24.7% computer, engineering, and science, 37.3% education, legal, community service, arts, and media, 0.0% healthcare practitioners, 1.2% service, 27.1% sales and office, 0.0% natural resources, construction, and maintenance, 9.6% production, transportation, and material moving

Income: Per capita: $38,199; Median household: $97,993; Average household: $81,024; Households with income of $100,000 or more: 26.4%; Poverty rate: 1.7%

Educational Attainment: High school diploma or higher: 97.1%; Bachelor's degree or higher: 46.1%; Graduate/professional degree or higher: 13.9%

Housing: Homeownership rate: 100.0%; Median home value: $165,300; Median year structure built: 2000; Homeowner vacancy rate: 0.0%; Median selected monthly owner costs: $1,669 with a mortgage, n/a without a mortgage; Median gross rent: n/a per month; Rental vacancy rate: 0.0%

Health Insurance: 100.0% have insurance; 84.0% have private insurance; 26.5% have public insurance; 0.0% do not have insurance; 0.0% of children under 18 do not have insurance

Transportation: Commute: 98.8% car, 0.0% public transportation, 0.0% walk, 1.2% work from home; Mean travel time to work: 23.1 minutes

MOUNT MORRIS (town). Covers a land area of 50.205 square miles and a water area of 0.106 square miles. Located at 42.66° N. Lat; 77.90° W. Long. Elevation is 630 feet.

Population: 4,340; Growth (since 2000): -5.0%; Density: 86.4 persons per square mile; Race: 93.7% White, 4.5% Black/African American, 0.0% Asian, 0.0% American Indian/Alaska Native, 0.0% Native Hawaiian/Other Pacific Islander, 0.4% Two or more races, 16.2% Hispanic of any race; Average household size: 2.37; Median age: 43.7; Age under 18: 20.2%; Age 65 and over: 22.1%; Males per 100 females: 95.7; Marriage status: 30.4% never married, 47.3% now married, 2.9% separated, 7.9% widowed, 14.5% divorced; Foreign born: 1.7%; Speak English only: 80.0%; With disability: 17.7%; Veterans: 7.9%; Ancestry: 23.7% German, 17.2% Irish, 16.5% Italian, 8.6% English, 6.3% American

Employment: 7.5% management, business, and financial, 1.1% computer, engineering, and science, 9.1% education, legal, community service, arts, and media, 2.3% healthcare practitioners, 29.0% service, 25.5% sales and office, 6.4% natural resources, construction, and maintenance, 19.2% production, transportation, and material moving

Income: Per capita: $21,081; Median household: $46,524; Average household: $51,856; Households with income of $100,000 or more: 12.9%; Poverty rate: 22.0%

Educational Attainment: High school diploma or higher: 82.1%; Bachelor's degree or higher: 13.0%; Graduate/professional degree or higher: 6.1%

School District(s)
Mount Morris Central SD (KG-12)
    Enrollment: 603 . . . . (585) 658-2568

Housing: Homeownership rate: 68.3%; Median home value: $83,500; Median year structure built: Before 1940; Homeowner vacancy rate: 1.2%; Median selected monthly owner costs: $1,190 with a mortgage, $550 without a mortgage; Median gross rent: $690 per month; Rental vacancy rate: 0.0%

Health Insurance: 87.5% have insurance; 56.2% have private insurance; 48.4% have public insurance; 12.5% do not have insurance; 9.1% of children under 18 do not have insurance

Transportation: Commute: 87.9% car, 1.5% public transportation, 2.7% walk, 0.7% work from home; Mean travel time to work: 17.2 minutes

Additional Information Contacts
Town of Mount Morris . . . . (585) 658-2730
    http://www.mountmorrisny.com/government/town.asp

MOUNT MORRIS (village). Covers a land area of 2.048 square miles and a water area of 0 square miles. Located at 42.72° N. Lat; 77.88° W. Long. Elevation is 630 feet.

Population: 2,511; Growth (since 2000): -23.1%; Density: 1,226.3 persons per square mile; Race: 89.8% White, 7.6% Black/African American, 0.0% Asian, 0.0% American Indian/Alaska Native, 0.0% Native Hawaiian/Other Pacific Islander, 0.1% Two or more races, 18.6% Hispanic of any race; Average household size: 2.16; Median age: 41.2; Age under 18: 21.6%; Age 65 and over: 16.0%; Males per 100 females: 98.7; Marriage status: 32.5% never married, 46.5% now married, 4.5% separated, 5.5% widowed, 15.5% divorced; Foreign born: 2.7%; Speak English only: 88.9%; With disability: 17.2%; Veterans: 8.5%; Ancestry: 23.9% Italian, 18.8% German, 14.9% Irish, 10.2% English, 4.1% French

Employment: 8.5% management, business, and financial, 1.7% computer, engineering, and science, 9.3% education, legal, community service, arts, and media, 1.8% healthcare practitioners, 32.0% service, 27.3% sales and office, 4.4% natural resources, construction, and maintenance, 14.8% production, transportation, and material moving

Income: Per capita: $21,469; Median household: $38,098; Average household: $46,096; Households with income of $100,000 or more: 10.8%; Poverty rate: 30.5%

Educational Attainment: High school diploma or higher: 90.1%; Bachelor's degree or higher: 16.0%; Graduate/professional degree or higher: 7.4%

School District(s)
Mount Morris Central SD (KG-12)
    Enrollment: 603 . . . . (585) 658-2568

Housing: Homeownership rate: 56.4%; Median home value: $67,500; Median year structure built: Before 1940; Homeowner vacancy rate: 2.0%; Median selected monthly owner costs: $1,123 with a mortgage, $515 without a mortgage; Median gross rent: $651 per month; Rental vacancy rate: 0.0%

Health Insurance: 92.6% have insurance; 59.5% have private insurance; 49.7% have public insurance; 7.4% do not have insurance; 0.0% of children under 18 do not have insurance

Safety: Violent crime rate: 21.1 per 10,000 population; Property crime rate: 235.1 per 10,000 population

Transportation: Commute: 93.5% car, 2.1% public transportation, 4.4% walk, 0.0% work from home; Mean travel time to work: 18.0 minutes

Additional Information Contacts
Village of Mount Morris . . . . (585) 658-4160
    http://www.mountmorrisny.com/government/village.asp

NORTH DANSVILLE (town). Covers a land area of 9.859 square miles and a water area of 0 square miles. Located at 42.56° N. Lat; 77.69° W. Long. Elevation is 705 feet.

Population: 5,375; Growth (since 2000): -6.3%; Density: 545.2 persons per square mile; Race: 95.9% White, 0.9% Black/African American, 0.0% Asian, 0.0% American Indian/Alaska Native, 0.0% Native Hawaiian/Other Pacific Islander, 2.0% Two or more races, 1.0% Hispanic of any race; Average household size: 2.15; Median age: 45.0; Age under 18: 20.4%; Age 65 and over: 16.5%; Males per 100 females: 89.5; Marriage status: 33.9% never married, 45.3% now married, 4.1% separated, 8.4% widowed, 12.3% divorced; Foreign born: 0.9%; Speak English only: 98.5%; With disability: 16.2%; Veterans: 9.5%; Ancestry: 26.9% German, 22.2% Irish, 9.9% English, 9.5% Italian, 8.9% Polish

Employment: 8.1% management, business, and financial, 0.7% computer, engineering, and science, 17.0% education, legal, community service, arts, and media, 4.5% healthcare practitioners, 19.5% service, 20.7% sales and office, 11.1% natural resources, construction, and maintenance, 18.3% production, transportation, and material moving

Income: Per capita: $27,154; Median household: $36,810; Average household: $58,417; Households with income of $100,000 or more: 13.6%; Poverty rate: 25.3%

Educational Attainment: High school diploma or higher: 82.3%; Bachelor's degree or higher: 16.6%; Graduate/professional degree or higher: 10.9%

Housing: Homeownership rate: 61.5%; Median home value: $85,200; Median year structure built: 1947; Homeowner vacancy rate: 0.0%; Median selected monthly owner costs: $1,088 with a mortgage, $409 without a mortgage; Median gross rent: $675 per month; Rental vacancy rate: 0.0%

Health Insurance: 95.6% have insurance; 68.6% have private insurance; 46.7% have public insurance; 4.4% do not have insurance; 0.0% of children under 18 do not have insurance

Transportation: Commute: 84.9% car, 0.4% public transportation, 10.7% walk, 3.8% work from home; Mean travel time to work: 24.2 minutes

NUNDA (town). Covers a land area of 37.094 square miles and a water area of 0.027 square miles. Located at 42.57° N. Lat; 77.88° W. Long. Elevation is 942 feet.

History: Incorporated 1839.

Population: 2,965; Growth (since 2000): -1.7%; Density: 79.9 persons per square mile; Race: 98.2% White, 0.7% Black/African American, 0.5% Asian, 0.0% American Indian/Alaska Native, 0.0% Native Hawaiian/Other Pacific Islander, 0.5% Two or more races, 0.4% Hispanic of any race; Average household size: 2.34; Median age: 46.9; Age under 18: 20.9%; Age 65 and over: 20.9%; Males per 100 females: 96.4; Marriage status: 23.6% never married, 57.0% now married, 0.9% separated, 7.4% widowed, 12.0% divorced; Foreign born: 0.9%; Speak English only: 99.1%; With disability: 14.4%; Veterans: 10.1%; Ancestry: 23.1% German, 21.0% Irish, 17.1% English, 9.3% Italian, 8.0% American

Employment: 7.3% management, business, and financial, 3.6% computer, engineering, and science, 12.8% education, legal, community service, arts, and media, 5.6% healthcare practitioners, 13.0% service, 28.0% sales and office, 14.9% natural resources, construction, and maintenance, 14.9% production, transportation, and material moving

Income: Per capita: $25,041; Median household: $53,042; Average household: $59,064; Households with income of $100,000 or more: 19.0%; Poverty rate: 16.7%

Educational Attainment: High school diploma or higher: 89.8%; Bachelor's degree or higher: 17.8%; Graduate/professional degree or higher: 8.2%

School District(s)
Dalton-Nunda Central SD (Keshequa) (PK-12)
    Enrollment: 714 . . . . (585) 468-2900

Housing: Homeownership rate: 76.0%; Median home value: $89,900; Median year structure built: 1952; Homeowner vacancy rate: 0.0%; Median

selected monthly owner costs: $1,085 with a mortgage, $475 without a mortgage; Median gross rent: $568 per month; Rental vacancy rate: 0.0%
Health Insurance: 98.5% have insurance; 75.6% have private insurance; 45.2% have public insurance; 1.5% do not have insurance; 0.0% of children under 18 do not have insurance
Safety: Violent crime rate: 3.4 per 10,000 population; Property crime rate: 40.7 per 10,000 population
Transportation: Commute: 92.3% car, 0.9% public transportation, 2.9% walk, 1.4% work from home; Mean travel time to work: 37.5 minutes

NUNDA (village).
Covers a land area of 0.993 square miles and a water area of 0 square miles. Located at 42.58° N. Lat; 77.94° W. Long. Elevation is 942 feet.
Population: 1,442; Growth (since 2000): 8.4%; Density: 1,451.5 persons per square mile; Race: 96.4% White, 1.5% Black/African American, 1.0% Asian, 0.0% American Indian/Alaska Native, 0.0% Native Hawaiian/Other Pacific Islander, 1.0% Two or more races, 0.8% Hispanic of any race; Average household size: 2.26; Median age: 44.3; Age under 18: 24.0%; Age 65 and over: 25.0%; Males per 100 females: 85.3; Marriage status: 26.8% never married, 49.6% now married, 1.2% separated, 8.9% widowed, 14.7% divorced; Foreign born: 1.9%; Speak English only: 98.7%; With disability: 21.2%; Veterans: 11.1%; Ancestry: 23.0% German, 18.2% Irish, 12.3% English, 9.4% American, 8.0% Italian
Employment: 5.0% management, business, and financial, 2.4% computer, engineering, and science, 18.8% education, legal, community service, arts, and media, 9.6% healthcare practitioners, 19.2% service, 26.0% sales and office, 12.0% natural resources, construction, and maintenance, 7.0% production, transportation, and material moving
Income: Per capita: $20,524; Median household: $35,833; Average household: $47,414; Households with income of $100,000 or more: 7.8%; Poverty rate: 28.8%
Educational Attainment: High school diploma or higher: 87.2%; Bachelor's degree or higher: 15.1%; Graduate/professional degree or higher: 8.5%

School District(s)
Dalton-Nunda Central SD (Keshequa) (PK-12)
    Enrollment: 714 . . . . (585) 468-2900
Housing: Homeownership rate: 57.7%; Median home value: $84,400; Median year structure built: Before 1940; Homeowner vacancy rate: 0.0%; Median selected monthly owner costs: $1,113 with a mortgage, $471 without a mortgage; Median gross rent: $559 per month; Rental vacancy rate: 0.0%
Health Insurance: 99.1% have insurance; 66.5% have private insurance; 59.1% have public insurance; 0.9% do not have insurance; 0.0% of children under 18 do not have insurance
Transportation: Commute: 90.1% car, 2.5% public transportation, 6.0% walk, 0.7% work from home; Mean travel time to work: 35.3 minutes

OSSIAN (town).
Covers a land area of 39.635 square miles and a water area of 0.028 square miles. Located at 42.51° N. Lat; 77.77° W. Long. Elevation is 1,342 feet.
Population: 786; Growth (since 2000): 4.7%; Density: 19.8 persons per square mile; Race: 98.1% White, 0.4% Black/African American, 0.0% Asian, 0.0% American Indian/Alaska Native, 0.0% Native Hawaiian/Other Pacific Islander, 1.5% Two or more races, 1.0% Hispanic of any race; Average household size: 2.46; Median age: 44.8; Age under 18: 26.1%; Age 65 and over: 18.3%; Males per 100 females: 112.1; Marriage status: 15.4% never married, 67.0% now married, 2.9% separated, 7.9% widowed, 9.7% divorced; Foreign born: 0.0%; Speak English only: 99.3%; With disability: 15.1%; Veterans: 10.8%; Ancestry: 29.8% German, 16.5% English, 15.4% Dutch, 11.1% American, 8.7% Italian
Employment: 14.9% management, business, and financial, 4.5% computer, engineering, and science, 9.0% education, legal, community service, arts, and media, 3.0% healthcare practitioners, 19.7% service, 14.6% sales and office, 22.1% natural resources, construction, and maintenance, 12.2% production, transportation, and material moving
Income: Per capita: $26,900; Median household: $65,938; Average household: $66,261; Households with income of $100,000 or more: 19.7%; Poverty rate: 5.4%
Educational Attainment: High school diploma or higher: 92.0%; Bachelor's degree or higher: 24.4%; Graduate/professional degree or higher: 9.6%
Housing: Homeownership rate: 92.5%; Median home value: $110,100; Median year structure built: 1975; Homeowner vacancy rate: 1.9%; Median

selected monthly owner costs: $1,222 with a mortgage, $531 without a mortgage; Median gross rent: $563 per month; Rental vacancy rate: 0.0%
Health Insurance: 97.2% have insurance; 81.3% have private insurance; 36.8% have public insurance; 2.8% do not have insurance; 0.5% of children under 18 do not have insurance
Transportation: Commute: 95.4% car, 2.8% public transportation, 0.0% walk, 0.0% work from home; Mean travel time to work: 26.0 minutes

PIFFARD (CDP).
Covers a land area of 0.934 square miles and a water area of 0 square miles. Located at 42.83° N. Lat; 77.86° W. Long. Elevation is 568 feet.
Population: 254; Growth (since 2000): n/a; Density: 272.0 persons per square mile; Race: 100.0% White, 0.0% Black/African American, 0.0% Asian, 0.0% American Indian/Alaska Native, 0.0% Native Hawaiian/Other Pacific Islander, 0.0% Two or more races, 3.9% Hispanic of any race; Average household size: 3.06; Median age: 32.4; Age under 18: 28.7%; Age 65 and over: 10.2%; Males per 100 females: 113.6; Marriage status: 21.0% never married, 44.8% now married, 0.0% separated, 0.0% widowed, 34.3% divorced; Foreign born: 0.0%; Speak English only: 96.1%; With disability: 42.9%; Veterans: 10.5%; Ancestry: 15.4% Irish, 15.0% Italian, 13.4% English, 12.2% German, 12.2% Scottish
Employment: 26.1% management, business, and financial, 0.0% computer, engineering, and science, 17.4% education, legal, community service, arts, and media, 7.8% healthcare practitioners, 0.0% service, 23.5% sales and office, 9.6% natural resources, construction, and maintenance, 15.7% production, transportation, and material moving
Income: Per capita: $20,956; Median household: $71,435; Average household: $63,025; Households with income of $100,000 or more: n/a; Poverty rate: 3.1%
Educational Attainment: High school diploma or higher: 89.4%; Bachelor's degree or higher: 11.8%; Graduate/professional degree or higher: 4.7%
Housing: Homeownership rate: 67.5%; Median home value: $102,300; Median year structure built: Before 1940; Homeowner vacancy rate: 0.0%; Median selected monthly owner costs: $982 with a mortgage, n/a without a mortgage; Median gross rent: n/a per month; Rental vacancy rate: 0.0%
Health Insurance: 100.0% have insurance; 61.0% have private insurance; 67.3% have public insurance; 0.0% do not have insurance; 0.0% of children under 18 do not have insurance
Transportation: Commute: 73.9% car, 0.0% public transportation, 26.1% walk, 0.0% work from home; Mean travel time to work: 15.2 minutes

PORTAGE (town).
Covers a land area of 26.399 square miles and a water area of 0.236 square miles. Located at 42.56° N. Lat; 77.99° W. Long. Elevation is 1,342 feet.
Population: 825; Growth (since 2000): -4.0%; Density: 31.3 persons per square mile; Race: 99.9% White, 0.1% Black/African American, 0.0% Asian, 0.0% American Indian/Alaska Native, 0.0% Native Hawaiian/Other Pacific Islander, 0.0% Two or more races, 0.5% Hispanic of any race; Average household size: 2.29; Median age: 44.9; Age under 18: 21.5%; Age 65 and over: 18.8%; Males per 100 females: 92.2; Marriage status: 23.9% never married, 57.1% now married, 2.5% separated, 7.2% widowed, 11.8% divorced; Foreign born: 2.3%; Speak English only: 96.7%; With disability: 14.3%; Veterans: 9.1%; Ancestry: 36.0% German, 23.6% English, 15.3% Irish, 8.2% American, 7.4% Italian
Employment: 9.4% management, business, and financial, 0.0% computer, engineering, and science, 6.5% education, legal, community service, arts, and media, 4.0% healthcare practitioners, 12.9% service, 27.8% sales and office, 19.9% natural resources, construction, and maintenance, 19.4% production, transportation, and material moving
Income: Per capita: $24,528; Median household: $47,237; Average household: $56,586; Households with income of $100,000 or more: 15.0%; Poverty rate: 14.2%
Educational Attainment: High school diploma or higher: 87.3%; Bachelor's degree or higher: 8.1%; Graduate/professional degree or higher: 2.4%
Housing: Homeownership rate: 84.7%; Median home value: $77,400; Median year structure built: 1956; Homeowner vacancy rate: 1.9%; Median selected monthly owner costs: $891 with a mortgage, $435 without a mortgage; Median gross rent: $596 per month; Rental vacancy rate: 0.0%
Health Insurance: 95.8% have insurance; 69.3% have private insurance; 43.2% have public insurance; 4.2% do not have insurance; 0.0% of children under 18 do not have insurance
Transportation: Commute: 88.1% car, 0.8% public transportation, 2.8% walk, 7.1% work from home; Mean travel time to work: 30.0 minutes

RETSOF (CDP). Covers a land area of 0.451 square miles and a water area of 0 square miles. Located at 42.83° N. Lat; 77.88° W. Long. Elevation is 728 feet.
Population: 174; Growth (since 2000): n/a; Density: 386.2 persons per square mile; Race: 86.8% White, 0.0% Black/African American, 0.0% Asian, 0.0% American Indian/Alaska Native, 0.0% Native Hawaiian/Other Pacific Islander, 13.2% Two or more races, 0.0% Hispanic of any race; Average household size: 2.83; Median age: 40.2; Age under 18: 24.1%; Age 65 and over: 16.1%; Males per 100 females: 86.8; Marriage status: 21.6% never married, 55.4% now married, 0.0% separated, 16.5% widowed, 6.5% divorced; Foreign born: 0.0%; Speak English only: 100.0%; With disability: 14.4%; Veterans: 0.0%; Ancestry: 20.1% American, 18.4% Italian, 13.8% Swedish, 10.9% British, 5.7% German
Employment: 0.0% management, business, and financial, 12.5% computer, engineering, and science, 12.5% education, legal, community service, arts, and media, 11.5% healthcare practitioners, 26.0% service, 20.8% sales and office, 0.0% natural resources, construction, and maintenance, 16.7% production, transportation, and material moving
Income: Per capita: $26,050; Median household: $54,306; Average household: $70,881; Households with income of $100,000 or more: 18.6%; Poverty rate: 2.9%
Educational Attainment: High school diploma or higher: 96.6%; Bachelor's degree or higher: 17.2%; Graduate/professional degree or higher: n/a

School District(s)
York Central SD (KG-12)
    Enrollment: 741 . . . . (585) 243-1730
Housing: Homeownership rate: 100.0%; Median home value: $87,700; Median year structure built: 1946; Homeowner vacancy rate: 0.0%; Median selected monthly owner costs: $905 with a mortgage, $527 without a mortgage; Median gross rent: n/a per month; Rental vacancy rate: 0.0%
Health Insurance: 96.0% have insurance; 89.7% have private insurance; 19.5% have public insurance; 4.0% do not have insurance; 15.2% of children under 18 do not have insurance
Transportation: Commute: 83.3% car, 2.1% public transportation, 14.6% walk, 0.0% work from home; Mean travel time to work: 22.2 minutes

SCOTTSBURG (CDP). Covers a land area of 0.164 square miles and a water area of 0 square miles. Located at 42.66° N. Lat; 77.71° W. Long. Elevation is 925 feet.
Population: 112; Growth (since 2000): n/a; Density: 680.9 persons per square mile; Race: 100.0% White, 0.0% Black/African American, 0.0% Asian, 0.0% American Indian/Alaska Native, 0.0% Native Hawaiian/Other Pacific Islander, 0.0% Two or more races, 0.0% Hispanic of any race; Average household size: 3.20; Median age: 50.3; Age under 18: 8.0%; Age 65 and over: 12.5%; Males per 100 females: 112.7; Marriage status: 28.2% never married, 59.2% now married, 0.0% separated, 5.8% widowed, 6.8% divorced; Foreign born: 0.0%; Speak English only: 100.0%; With disability: 12.5%; Veterans: 6.8%; Ancestry: 27.7% German, 24.1% European, 14.3% American, 10.7% Irish, 3.6% Dutch
Employment: 0.0% management, business, and financial, 0.0% computer, engineering, and science, 9.7% education, legal, community service, arts, and media, 0.0% healthcare practitioners, 23.6% service, 36.1% sales and office, 12.5% natural resources, construction, and maintenance, 18.1% production, transportation, and material moving
Income: Per capita: $24,682; Median household: $87,917; Average household: $77,549; Households with income of $100,000 or more: 8.6%; Poverty rate: 3.6%
Educational Attainment: High school diploma or higher: 100.0%; Bachelor's degree or higher: 14.3%; Graduate/professional degree or higher: 7.7%
Housing: Homeownership rate: 100.0%; Median home value: $89,400; Median year structure built: Before 1940; Homeowner vacancy rate: 0.0%; Median selected monthly owner costs: $1,000 with a mortgage, n/a without a mortgage; Median gross rent: n/a per month; Rental vacancy rate: 0.0%
Health Insurance: 75.9% have insurance; 68.8% have private insurance; 31.3% have public insurance; 24.1% do not have insurance; 0.0% of children under 18 do not have insurance
Transportation: Commute: 100.0% car, 0.0% public transportation, 0.0% walk, 0.0% work from home; Mean travel time to work: 31.5 minutes

SOUTH LIMA (CDP). Covers a land area of 0.883 square miles and a water area of 0 square miles. Located at 42.86° N. Lat; 77.68° W. Long. Elevation is 889 feet.
Population: 149; Growth (since 2000): n/a; Density: 168.8 persons per square mile; Race: 100.0% White, 0.0% Black/African American, 0.0% Asian, 0.0% American Indian/Alaska Native, 0.0% Native Hawaiian/Other Pacific Islander, 0.0% Two or more races, 0.0% Hispanic of any race; Average household size: 1.75; Median age: 61.1; Age under 18: 11.4%; Age 65 and over: 27.5%; Males per 100 females: 105.1; Marriage status: 15.2% never married, 56.8% now married, 0.0% separated, 28.0% widowed, 0.0% divorced; Foreign born: 5.4%; Speak English only: 100.0%; With disability: 31.5%; Veterans: 14.4%; Ancestry: 36.9% Irish, 25.5% English, 25.5% Italian, 8.1% German, 6.0% American
Employment: 22.7% management, business, and financial, 0.0% computer, engineering, and science, 0.0% education, legal, community service, arts, and media, 18.2% healthcare practitioners, 0.0% service, 18.2% sales and office, 0.0% natural resources, construction, and maintenance, 40.9% production, transportation, and material moving
Income: Per capita: $26,571; Median household: $35,375; Average household: $46,526; Households with income of $100,000 or more: 9.4%; Poverty rate: 12.1%
Educational Attainment: High school diploma or higher: 85.6%; Bachelor's degree or higher: 12.1%; Graduate/professional degree or higher: n/a
Housing: Homeownership rate: 65.9%; Median home value: $121,600; Median year structure built: Before 1940; Homeowner vacancy rate: 0.0%; Median selected monthly owner costs: n/a with a mortgage, $808 without a mortgage; Median gross rent: n/a per month; Rental vacancy rate: 0.0%
Health Insurance: 93.3% have insurance; 73.8% have private insurance; 59.1% have public insurance; 6.7% do not have insurance; 0.0% of children under 18 do not have insurance
Transportation: Commute: 100.0% car, 0.0% public transportation, 0.0% walk, 0.0% work from home; Mean travel time to work: 0.0 minutes

SPARTA (town). Covers a land area of 27.791 square miles and a water area of 0 square miles. Located at 42.63° N. Lat; 77.70° W. Long.
Population: 1,481; Growth (since 2000): -9.0%; Density: 53.3 persons per square mile; Race: 97.2% White, 1.1% Black/African American, 0.0% Asian, 0.2% American Indian/Alaska Native, 0.0% Native Hawaiian/Other Pacific Islander, 1.5% Two or more races, 0.0% Hispanic of any race; Average household size: 2.48; Median age: 49.4; Age under 18: 17.9%; Age 65 and over: 22.9%; Males per 100 females: 101.2; Marriage status: 20.5% never married, 62.9% now married, 0.6% separated, 8.0% widowed, 8.7% divorced; Foreign born: 2.8%; Speak English only: 94.8%; With disability: 15.9%; Veterans: 5.3%; Ancestry: 33.0% German, 18.7% Irish, 11.6% English, 8.1% Italian, 8.0% American
Employment: 5.9% management, business, and financial, 3.6% computer, engineering, and science, 8.6% education, legal, community service, arts, and media, 6.1% healthcare practitioners, 20.3% service, 23.9% sales and office, 16.2% natural resources, construction, and maintenance, 15.4% production, transportation, and material moving
Income: Per capita: $31,603; Median household: $67,250; Average household: $78,410; Households with income of $100,000 or more: 23.5%; Poverty rate: 7.4%
Educational Attainment: High school diploma or higher: 88.1%; Bachelor's degree or higher: 16.2%; Graduate/professional degree or higher: 7.4%
Housing: Homeownership rate: 95.0%; Median home value: $112,600; Median year structure built: 1972; Homeowner vacancy rate: 1.7%; Median selected monthly owner costs: $1,182 with a mortgage, $491 without a mortgage; Median gross rent: $775 per month; Rental vacancy rate: 0.0%
Health Insurance: 94.4% have insurance; 77.6% have private insurance; 36.9% have public insurance; 5.6% do not have insurance; 4.3% of children under 18 do not have insurance
Transportation: Commute: 91.1% car, 0.6% public transportation, 2.8% walk, 5.0% work from home; Mean travel time to work: 31.8 minutes

SPRINGWATER (town). Covers a land area of 53.105 square miles and a water area of 0.013 square miles. Located at 42.62° N. Lat; 77.57° W. Long. Elevation is 971 feet.
Population: 2,252; Growth (since 2000): -3.0%; Density: 42.4 persons per square mile; Race: 95.5% White, 1.8% Black/African American, 0.0% Asian, 0.7% American Indian/Alaska Native, 0.0% Native Hawaiian/Other Pacific Islander, 2.0% Two or more races, 0.1% Hispanic of any race; Average household size: 2.38; Median age: 45.3; Age under 18: 21.0%;

Age 65 and over: 17.2%; Males per 100 females: 105.3; Marriage status: 17.9% never married, 66.2% now married, 3.2% separated, 5.0% widowed, 10.9% divorced; Foreign born: 0.7%; Speak English only: 98.6%; With disability: 17.0%; Veterans: 7.9%; Ancestry: 33.0% German, 14.0% Irish, 12.2% English, 9.2% Italian, 7.2% American
Employment: 17.7% management, business, and financial, 3.6% computer, engineering, and science, 11.3% education, legal, community service, arts, and media, 7.2% healthcare practitioners, 8.7% service, 22.7% sales and office, 11.0% natural resources, construction, and maintenance, 17.7% production, transportation, and material moving
Income: Per capita: $27,319; Median household: $53,023; Average household: $64,607; Households with income of $100,000 or more: 19.2%; Poverty rate: 12.0%
Educational Attainment: High school diploma or higher: 85.3%; Bachelor's degree or higher: 21.3%; Graduate/professional degree or higher: 7.8%
Housing: Homeownership rate: 88.6%; Median home value: $111,500; Median year structure built: 1967; Homeowner vacancy rate: 5.8%; Median selected monthly owner costs: $1,152 with a mortgage, $518 without a mortgage; Median gross rent: $824 per month; Rental vacancy rate: 0.0%
Health Insurance: 96.9% have insurance; 78.2% have private insurance; 35.5% have public insurance; 3.1% do not have insurance; 0.0% of children under 18 do not have insurance
Transportation: Commute: 94.0% car, 0.4% public transportation, 0.5% walk, 3.7% work from home; Mean travel time to work: 35.3 minutes

SPRINGWATER HAMLET (CDP). Covers a land area of 1.331 square miles and a water area of 0 square miles. Located at 42.63° N. Lat; 77.60° W. Long.
Population: 527; Growth (since 2000): n/a; Density: 396.0 persons per square mile; Race: 99.6% White, 0.4% Black/African American, 0.0% Asian, 0.0% American Indian/Alaska Native, 0.0% Native Hawaiian/Other Pacific Islander, 0.0% Two or more races, 0.0% Hispanic of any race; Average household size: 2.73; Median age: 40.1; Age under 18: 27.1%; Age 65 and over: 10.4%; Males per 100 females: 107.2; Marriage status: 27.0% never married, 48.2% now married, 7.0% separated, 4.6% widowed, 20.2% divorced; Foreign born: 0.0%; Speak English only: 99.0%; With disability: 27.1%; Veterans: 6.8%; Ancestry: 23.3% German, 14.4% American, 9.1% English, 6.8% Irish, 2.8% Dutch
Employment: 19.2% management, business, and financial, 3.0% computer, engineering, and science, 2.5% education, legal, community service, arts, and media, 2.5% healthcare practitioners, 8.1% service, 26.8% sales and office, 7.6% natural resources, construction, and maintenance, 30.3% production, transportation, and material moving
Income: Per capita: $17,432; Median household: $38,864; Average household: $46,492; Households with income of $100,000 or more: 5.3%; Poverty rate: 24.9%
Educational Attainment: High school diploma or higher: 72.1%; Bachelor's degree or higher: 7.8%; Graduate/professional degree or higher: 3.2%
Housing: Homeownership rate: 74.7%; Median home value: $77,600; Median year structure built: Before 1940; Homeowner vacancy rate: 9.6%; Median selected monthly owner costs: $1,161 with a mortgage, $550 without a mortgage; Median gross rent: $950 per month; Rental vacancy rate: 0.0%
Health Insurance: 98.5% have insurance; 64.9% have private insurance; 48.6% have public insurance; 1.5% do not have insurance; 0.0% of children under 18 do not have insurance
Transportation: Commute: 94.9% car, 2.0% public transportation, 0.0% walk, 3.0% work from home; Mean travel time to work: 32.9 minutes

WADSWORTH (CDP). Covers a land area of 0.512 square miles and a water area of 0 square miles. Located at 42.82° N. Lat; 77.89° W. Long. Elevation is 741 feet.
Population: 338; Growth (since 2000): n/a; Density: 660.6 persons per square mile; Race: 100.0% White, 0.0% Black/African American, 0.0% Asian, 0.0% American Indian/Alaska Native, 0.0% Native Hawaiian/Other Pacific Islander, 0.0% Two or more races, 0.0% Hispanic of any race; Average household size: 2.60; Median age: 31.6; Age under 18: 35.8%; Age 65 and over: 13.3%; Males per 100 females: 106.5; Marriage status: 25.6% never married, 44.0% now married, 0.0% separated, 18.0% widowed, 12.4% divorced; Foreign born: 0.0%; Speak English only: 100.0%; With disability: 0.0%; Veterans: 0.0%; Ancestry: 70.4% Irish, 40.2% Italian, 22.8% German, 6.8% English, 3.3% Polish

Employment: 8.6% management, business, and financial, 5.5% computer, engineering, and science, 6.3% education, legal, community service, arts, and media, 0.0% healthcare practitioners, 21.1% service, 27.3% sales and office, 31.3% natural resources, construction, and maintenance, 0.0% production, transportation, and material moving
Income: Per capita: $24,311; Median household: $47,750; Average household: $61,235; Households with income of $100,000 or more: 26.2%; Poverty rate: n/a
Educational Attainment: High school diploma or higher: 68.8%; Bachelor's degree or higher: 25.8%; Graduate/professional degree or higher: n/a
Housing: Homeownership rate: 76.9%; Median home value: $77,600; Median year structure built: 1954; Homeowner vacancy rate: 0.0%; Median selected monthly owner costs: n/a with a mortgage, $470 without a mortgage; Median gross rent: n/a per month; Rental vacancy rate: 0.0%
Health Insurance: 96.7% have insurance; 78.4% have private insurance; 24.9% have public insurance; 3.3% do not have insurance; 0.0% of children under 18 do not have insurance
Transportation: Commute: 89.8% car, 0.0% public transportation, 10.2% walk, 0.0% work from home; Mean travel time to work: 13.3 minutes

WEBSTERS CROSSING (CDP). Covers a land area of 0.110 square miles and a water area of 0 square miles. Located at 42.67° N. Lat; 77.64° W. Long. Elevation is 1,339 feet.
Population: 20; Growth (since 2000): n/a; Density: 181.4 persons per square mile; Race: 100.0% White, 0.0% Black/African American, 0.0% Asian, 0.0% American Indian/Alaska Native, 0.0% Native Hawaiian/Other Pacific Islander, 0.0% Two or more races, 0.0% Hispanic of any race; Average household size: 2.00; Median age: 66.0; Age under 18: 0.0%; Age 65 and over: 50.0%; Males per 100 females: 97.1; Marriage status: 0.0% never married, 100.0% now married, 0.0% separated, 0.0% widowed, 0.0% divorced; Foreign born: 0.0%; Speak English only: 100.0%; With disability: 25.0%; Veterans: 25.0%; Ancestry: 25.0% Irish, 25.0% Italian
Employment: 0.0% management, business, and financial, 0.0% computer, engineering, and science, 0.0% education, legal, community service, arts, and media, 0.0% healthcare practitioners, 0.0% service, 100.0% sales and office, 0.0% natural resources, construction, and maintenance, 0.0% production, transportation, and material moving
Income: Per capita: $20,450; Median household: n/a; Average household: n/a; Households with income of $100,000 or more: n/a; Poverty rate: n/a
Educational Attainment: High school diploma or higher: 75.0%; Bachelor's degree or higher: n/a; Graduate/professional degree or higher: n/a
Housing: Homeownership rate: 100.0%; Median home value: n/a; Median year structure built: Before 1940; Homeowner vacancy rate: 63.0%; Median selected monthly owner costs: n/a with a mortgage, n/a without a mortgage; Median gross rent: n/a per month; Rental vacancy rate: 0.0%
Health Insurance: 100.0% have insurance; 100.0% have private insurance; 50.0% have public insurance; 0.0% do not have insurance; 0.0% of children under 18 do not have insurance
Transportation: Commute: 100.0% car, 0.0% public transportation, 0.0% walk, 0.0% work from home; Mean travel time to work: 0.0 minutes

WEST SPARTA (town). Covers a land area of 33.450 square miles and a water area of 0 square miles. Located at 42.61° N. Lat; 77.79° W. Long. Elevation is 617 feet.
Population: 1,373; Growth (since 2000): 10.4%; Density: 41.0 persons per square mile; Race: 94.4% White, 0.1% Black/African American, 2.5% Asian, 0.3% American Indian/Alaska Native, 0.0% Native Hawaiian/Other Pacific Islander, 2.0% Two or more races, 1.1% Hispanic of any race; Average household size: 2.58; Median age: 41.9; Age under 18: 20.1%; Age 65 and over: 14.6%; Males per 100 females: 101.8; Marriage status: 30.6% never married, 58.0% now married, 4.0% separated, 3.2% widowed, 8.3% divorced; Foreign born: 3.4%; Speak English only: 96.7%; With disability: 14.9%; Veterans: 12.4%; Ancestry: 20.6% German, 12.5% Irish, 9.5% Italian, 8.0% English, 7.3% American
Employment: 9.4% management, business, and financial, 1.9% computer, engineering, and science, 7.5% education, legal, community service, arts, and media, 4.9% healthcare practitioners, 17.8% service, 21.0% sales and office, 19.6% natural resources, construction, and maintenance, 17.8% production, transportation, and material moving
Income: Per capita: $24,303; Median household: $52,500; Average household: $62,273; Households with income of $100,000 or more: 16.7%; Poverty rate: 19.6%

Educational Attainment: High school diploma or higher: 83.3%; Bachelor's degree or higher: 14.2%; Graduate/professional degree or higher: 5.5%

Housing: Homeownership rate: 86.0%; Median home value: $91,800; Median year structure built: 1973; Homeowner vacancy rate: 1.9%; Median selected monthly owner costs: $1,135 with a mortgage, $458 without a mortgage; Median gross rent: $689 per month; Rental vacancy rate: 14.9%

Health Insurance: 95.2% have insurance; 74.6% have private insurance; 38.4% have public insurance; 4.8% do not have insurance; 3.5% of children under 18 do not have insurance

Transportation: Commute: 89.4% car, 0.3% public transportation, 0.4% walk, 8.0% work from home; Mean travel time to work: 31.1 minutes

---

WOODSVILLE (CDP). Covers a land area of 0.317 square miles and a water area of 0 square miles. Located at 42.58° N. Lat; 77.73° W. Long. Elevation is 646 feet.

Population: 124; Growth (since 2000): n/a; Density: 390.9 persons per square mile; Race: 100.0% White, 0.0% Black/African American, 0.0% Asian, 0.0% American Indian/Alaska Native, 0.0% Native Hawaiian/Other Pacific Islander, 0.0% Two or more races, 0.0% Hispanic of any race; Average household size: 2.64; Median age: 42.1; Age under 18: 16.9%; Age 65 and over: 12.1%; Males per 100 females: 116.2; Marriage status: 38.5% never married, 56.0% now married, 2.8% separated, 0.0% widowed, 5.5% divorced; Foreign born: 0.0%; Speak English only: 100.0%; With disability: 12.1%; Veterans: 3.9%; Ancestry: 26.6% German, 21.0% Irish, 17.7% American, 5.6% Italian, 4.8% English

Employment: 4.6% management, business, and financial, 6.2% computer, engineering, and science, 0.0% education, legal, community service, arts, and media, 6.2% healthcare practitioners, 24.6% service, 13.8% sales and office, 23.1% natural resources, construction, and maintenance, 21.5% production, transportation, and material moving

Income: Per capita: $22,473; Median household: $44,896; Average household: $57,628; Households with income of $100,000 or more: 14.9%; Poverty rate: 5.6%

Educational Attainment: High school diploma or higher: 88.5%; Bachelor's degree or higher: 8.0%; Graduate/professional degree or higher: 8.0%

Housing: Homeownership rate: 76.6%; Median home value: $61,300; Median year structure built: 1958; Homeowner vacancy rate: 20.0%; Median selected monthly owner costs: $592 with a mortgage, $450 without a mortgage; Median gross rent: n/a per month; Rental vacancy rate: 0.0%

Health Insurance: 82.3% have insurance; 71.8% have private insurance; 22.6% have public insurance; 17.7% do not have insurance; 0.0% of children under 18 do not have insurance

Transportation: Commute: 100.0% car, 0.0% public transportation, 0.0% walk, 0.0% work from home; Mean travel time to work: 23.9 minutes

---

YORK (town). Covers a land area of 49.100 square miles and a water area of 0.007 square miles. Located at 42.87° N. Lat; 77.89° W. Long. Elevation is 784 feet.

Population: 3,321; Growth (since 2000): 3.2%; Density: 67.6 persons per square mile; Race: 96.7% White, 0.2% Black/African American, 0.5% Asian, 0.0% American Indian/Alaska Native, 0.0% Native Hawaiian/Other Pacific Islander, 2.6% Two or more races, 0.4% Hispanic of any race; Average household size: 2.44; Median age: 42.4; Age under 18: 23.7%; Age 65 and over: 15.6%; Males per 100 females: 107.9; Marriage status: 24.9% never married, 55.6% now married, 0.7% separated, 6.8% widowed, 12.8% divorced; Foreign born: 0.6%; Speak English only: 97.8%; With disability: 13.3%; Veterans: 7.9%; Ancestry: 25.8% German, 22.8% Irish, 19.5% Italian, 16.2% English, 6.2% American

Employment: 14.0% management, business, and financial, 3.1% computer, engineering, and science, 7.0% education, legal, community service, arts, and media, 4.3% healthcare practitioners, 19.5% service, 21.5% sales and office, 14.6% natural resources, construction, and maintenance, 16.1% production, transportation, and material moving

Income: Per capita: $26,933; Median household: $55,101; Average household: $65,387; Households with income of $100,000 or more: 22.7%; Poverty rate: 8.4%

Educational Attainment: High school diploma or higher: 92.2%; Bachelor's degree or higher: 21.6%; Graduate/professional degree or higher: 9.7%

Housing: Homeownership rate: 78.0%; Median home value: $115,700; Median year structure built: 1941; Homeowner vacancy rate: 0.0%; Median selected monthly owner costs: $1,182 with a mortgage, $525 without a mortgage; Median gross rent: $762 per month; Rental vacancy rate: 0.0%

Health Insurance: 97.0% have insurance; 81.7% have private insurance; 34.2% have public insurance; 3.0% do not have insurance; 0.8% of children under 18 do not have insurance

Transportation: Commute: 90.0% car, 0.1% public transportation, 5.0% walk, 4.4% work from home; Mean travel time to work: 24.3 minutes

---

YORK HAMLET (CDP). Covers a land area of 2.754 square miles and a water area of 0 square miles. Located at 42.87° N. Lat; 77.89° W. Long. Elevation is 784 feet.

Population: 469; Growth (since 2000): n/a; Density: 170.3 persons per square mile; Race: 95.9% White, 0.0% Black/African American, 0.0% Asian, 0.0% American Indian/Alaska Native, 0.0% Native Hawaiian/Other Pacific Islander, 4.1% Two or more races, 0.0% Hispanic of any race; Average household size: 1.77; Median age: 56.9; Age under 18: 5.1%; Age 65 and over: 12.8%; Males per 100 females: 103.7; Marriage status: 20.7% never married, 62.6% now married, 0.0% separated, 5.9% widowed, 10.8% divorced; Foreign born: 0.0%; Speak English only: 94.0%; With disability: 5.1%; Veterans: 7.6%; Ancestry: 38.8% English, 23.2% German, 12.6% Italian, 11.9% American, 7.2% Irish

Employment: 20.0% management, business, and financial, 1.8% computer, engineering, and science, 9.6% education, legal, community service, arts, and media, 8.7% healthcare practitioners, 27.5% service, 12.2% sales and office, 13.1% natural resources, construction, and maintenance, 7.2% production, transportation, and material moving

Income: Per capita: $38,124; Median household: $60,625; Average household: $66,302; Households with income of $100,000 or more: 19.3%; Poverty rate: 5.1%

Educational Attainment: High school diploma or higher: 100.0%; Bachelor's degree or higher: 24.1%; Graduate/professional degree or higher: 9.9%

Housing: Homeownership rate: 82.3%; Median home value: $138,900; Median year structure built: Before 1940; Homeowner vacancy rate: 0.0%; Median selected monthly owner costs: $1,130 with a mortgage, $496 without a mortgage; Median gross rent: n/a per month; Rental vacancy rate: 0.0%

Health Insurance: 92.3% have insurance; 78.5% have private insurance; 24.5% have public insurance; 7.7% do not have insurance; 0.0% of children under 18 do not have insurance

Transportation: Commute: 89.6% car, 0.0% public transportation, 3.6% walk, 6.9% work from home; Mean travel time to work: 27.5 minutes

Madison County

Located in central New York; drained by the Chenango and Unadilla Rivers; includes Cazenovia Lake, part of Oneida Lake, and other lakes. Covers a land area of 654.842 square miles, a water area of 6.441 square miles, and is located in the Eastern Time Zone at 42.91° N. Lat., 75.66° W. Long. The county was founded in 1806. County seat is Wampsville.

Madison County is part of the Syracuse, NY Metropolitan Statistical Area. The entire metro area includes: Madison County, NY; Onondaga County, NY; Oswego County, NY

Weather Station: Morrisville 5 SW									Elevation: 1,299 feet		
	Jan	Feb	Mar	Apr	May	Jun	Jul	Aug	Sep	Oct	Nov	Dec
High	29	32	40	54	66	74	78	76	69	57	45	34
Low	11	13	20	33	43	52	56	55	49	37	29	19
Precip	3.2	3.0	3.4	3.7	4.1	4.5	4.0	3.6	4.3	4.1	3.9	3.9
Snow	30.5	25.7	21.1	5.6	0.2	0.0	0.0	0.0	tr	1.5	12.0	27.5

High and Low temperatures in degrees Fahrenheit; Precipitation and Snow in inches

Population: 71,760; Growth (since 2000): 3.3%; Density: 109.6 persons per square mile; Race: 94.8% White, 2.0% Black/African American, 0.8% Asian, 0.6% American Indian/Alaska Native, 0.1% Native Hawaiian/Other Pacific Islander, 1.4% two or more races, 2.1% Hispanic of any race; Average household size: 2.53; Median age: 41.3; Age under 18: 20.0%; Age 65 and over: 16.3%; Males per 100 females: 96.5; Marriage status: 34.4% never married, 48.7% now married, 2.2% separated, 5.8% widowed, 11.1% divorced; Foreign born: 2.4%; Speak English only: 95.7%; With disability: 12.1%; Veterans: 8.8%; Ancestry: 28.1% American, 15.7% Irish, 15.6% German, 12.0% English, 8.4% Italian

Religion: Six largest groups: 14.7% Catholicism, 5.8% Methodist/Pietist, 2.1% Baptist, 1.9% Presbyterian-Reformed, 1.3% Non-denominational Protestant, 1.3% Episcopalianism/Anglicanism

Economy: Unemployment rate: 3.8%; Leading industries: 14.7 % retail trade; 12.9 % construction; 12.2 % health care and social assistance;

Farms: 838 totaling 187,496 acres; Company size: 1 employs 1,000 or more persons, 3 employ 500 to 999 persons, 16 employ 100 to 499 persons, 1,391 employs less than 100 persons; Business ownership: 1,995 women-owned, 38 Black-owned, 68 Hispanic-owned, 37 Asian-owned, n/a American Indian/Alaska Native-owned

Employment: 13.7% management, business, and financial, 5.0% computer, engineering, and science, 12.0% education, legal, community service, arts, and media, 5.8% healthcare practitioners, 18.5% service, 22.3% sales and office, 10.4% natural resources, construction, and maintenance, 12.2% production, transportation, and material moving

Income: Per capita: $28,010; Median household: $58,365; Average household: $72,824; Households with income of $100,000 or more: 23.6%; Poverty rate: 11.1%

Educational Attainment: High school diploma or higher: 91.1%; Bachelor's degree or higher: 27.0%; Graduate/professional degree or higher: 11.5%

Housing: Homeownership rate: 76.0%; Median home value: $132,800; Median year structure built: 1961; Homeowner vacancy rate: 2.5%; Median selected monthly owner costs: $1,290 with a mortgage, $517 without a mortgage; Median gross rent: $755 per month; Rental vacancy rate: 4.8%

Vital Statistics: Birth rate: 89.2 per 10,000 population; Death rate: 84.1 per 10,000 population; Age-adjusted cancer mortality rate: 160.5 deaths per 100,000 population

Health Insurance: 95.1% have insurance; 73.8% have private insurance; 35.3% have public insurance; 4.9% do not have insurance; 3.0% of children under 18 do not have insurance

Health Care: Physicians: 15.7 per 10,000 population; Dentists: 3.4 per 10,000 population; Hospital beds: 35.9 per 10,000 population; Hospital admissions: 633.6 per 10,000 population

Transportation: Commute: 88.0% car, 0.6% public transportation, 5.4% walk, 4.7% work from home; Mean travel time to work: 23.3 minutes

2016 Presidential Election: 53.0% Trump, 38.8% Clinton, 5.3% Johnson, 1.7% Stein

National and State Parks: Chittenango Falls State Park

Additional Information Contacts
Madison Government .... (315) 366-2261
  http://www.madisoncounty.ny.gov

Madison County Communities

BOUCKVILLE (unincorporated postal area)
ZCTA: 13310

Covers a land area of 7.576 square miles and a water area of 0.092 square miles. Located at 42.89° N. Lat; 75.57° W. Long. Elevation is 1,142 feet.

Population: 459; Growth (since 2000): -6.5%; Density: 60.6 persons per square mile; Race: 100.0% White, 0.0% Black/African American, 0.0% Asian, 0.0% American Indian/Alaska Native, 0.0% Native Hawaiian/Other Pacific Islander, 0.0% Two or more races, 0.0% Hispanic of any race; Average household size: 2.33; Median age: 45.1; Age under 18: 14.2%; Age 65 and over: 13.5%; Males per 100 females: 85.7; Marriage status: 14.5% never married, 57.5% now married, 0.0% separated, 0.0% widowed, 28.0% divorced; Foreign born: 2.6%; Speak English only: 94.8%; With disability: 15.3%; Veterans: 16.5%; Ancestry: 32.7% American, 19.0% Irish, 14.2% German, 9.2% English, 8.1% Polish

Employment: 10.9% management, business, and financial, 20.5% computer, engineering, and science, 5.0% education, legal, community service, arts, and media, 4.5% healthcare practitioners, 12.3% service, 31.4% sales and office, 0.0% natural resources, construction, and maintenance, 15.5% production, transportation, and material moving

Income: Per capita: $19,218; Median household: $45,804; Average household: $43,531; Households with income of $100,000 or more: 6.6%; Poverty rate: 11.6%

Educational Attainment: High school diploma or higher: 83.2%; Bachelor's degree or higher: 14.2%; Graduate/professional degree or higher: 2.9%

Housing: Homeownership rate: 94.9%; Median home value: $105,300; Median year structure built: 1959; Homeowner vacancy rate: 0.0%; Median selected monthly owner costs: $1,508 with a mortgage, $408 without a mortgage; Median gross rent: n/a per month; Rental vacancy rate: 0.0%

Health Insurance: 100.0% have insurance; 58.6% have private insurance; 60.8% have public insurance; 0.0% do not have insurance; 0.0% of children under 18 do not have insurance

Transportation: Commute: 94.1% car, 0.0% public transportation, 0.0% walk, 0.0% work from home; Mean travel time to work: 19.3 minutes

BROOKFIELD (town). Covers a land area of 77.822 square miles and a water area of 0.196 square miles. Located at 42.81° N. Lat; 75.34° W. Long. Elevation is 1,381 feet.

Population: 2,387; Growth (since 2000): -0.7%; Density: 30.7 persons per square mile; Race: 99.4% White, 0.0% Black/African American, 0.0% Asian, 0.0% American Indian/Alaska Native, 0.0% Native Hawaiian/Other Pacific Islander, 0.4% Two or more races, 0.0% Hispanic of any race; Average household size: 2.53; Median age: 42.6; Age under 18: 24.3%; Age 65 and over: 19.2%; Males per 100 females: 97.0; Marriage status: 25.7% never married, 56.4% now married, 2.3% separated, 5.5% widowed, 12.4% divorced; Foreign born: 0.1%; Speak English only: 96.3%; With disability: 11.9%; Veterans: 11.8%; Ancestry: 20.0% German, 19.3% American, 13.3% Irish, 12.9% English, 5.5% Italian

Employment: 13.1% management, business, and financial, 2.5% computer, engineering, and science, 4.6% education, legal, community service, arts, and media, 5.6% healthcare practitioners, 18.6% service, 24.7% sales and office, 18.2% natural resources, construction, and maintenance, 12.6% production, transportation, and material moving

Income: Per capita: $24,912; Median household: $43,750; Average household: $60,874; Households with income of $100,000 or more: 15.6%; Poverty rate: 13.6%

Educational Attainment: High school diploma or higher: 90.2%; Bachelor's degree or higher: 16.0%; Graduate/professional degree or higher: 5.1%

School District(s)
Brookfield Central SD (PK-12)
  Enrollment: 245 .... (315) 899-3323

Housing: Homeownership rate: 83.2%; Median home value: $81,100; Median year structure built: 1971; Homeowner vacancy rate: 5.8%; Median selected monthly owner costs: $1,044 with a mortgage, $399 without a mortgage; Median gross rent: $805 per month; Rental vacancy rate: 0.0%

Health Insurance: 91.9% have insurance; 69.6% have private insurance; 39.4% have public insurance; 8.1% do not have insurance; 11.4% of children under 18 do not have insurance

Transportation: Commute: 96.9% car, 0.0% public transportation, 0.8% walk, 2.3% work from home; Mean travel time to work: 26.5 minutes

CANASTOTA (village). Covers a land area of 3.351 square miles and a water area of 0.004 square miles. Located at 43.08° N. Lat; 75.76° W. Long. Elevation is 430 feet.

History: International Boxing Hall of Fame is here. Incorporated 1835.

Population: 4,644; Growth (since 2000): 4.9%; Density: 1,385.9 persons per square mile; Race: 97.2% White, 0.0% Black/African American, 0.0% Asian, 0.0% American Indian/Alaska Native, 0.0% Native Hawaiian/Other Pacific Islander, 2.8% Two or more races, 0.0% Hispanic of any race; Average household size: 2.61; Median age: 34.6; Age under 18: 24.4%; Age 65 and over: 11.4%; Males per 100 females: 92.0; Marriage status: 35.6% never married, 47.0% now married, 4.5% separated, 5.3% widowed, 12.1% divorced; Foreign born: 0.0%; Speak English only: 98.7%; With disability: 10.9%; Veterans: 5.6%; Ancestry: 34.6% American, 15.6% Italian, 14.6% Irish, 14.0% German, 7.1% English

Employment: 15.4% management, business, and financial, 5.6% computer, engineering, and science, 6.6% education, legal, community service, arts, and media, 3.0% healthcare practitioners, 14.9% service, 31.8% sales and office, 9.0% natural resources, construction, and maintenance, 13.7% production, transportation, and material moving

Income: Per capita: $26,831; Median household: $57,069; Average household: $67,763; Households with income of $100,000 or more: 19.7%; Poverty rate: 8.7%

Educational Attainment: High school diploma or higher: 97.1%; Bachelor's degree or higher: 22.1%; Graduate/professional degree or higher: 9.1%

School District(s)
Canastota Central SD (PK-12)
  Enrollment: 1,402 .... (315) 697-2025

Housing: Homeownership rate: 56.9%; Median home value: $113,300; Median year structure built: 1948; Homeowner vacancy rate: 0.0%; Median selected monthly owner costs: $1,268 with a mortgage, $516 without a mortgage; Median gross rent: $676 per month; Rental vacancy rate: 7.4%

Health Insurance: 97.8% have insurance; 81.7% have private insurance; 27.2% have public insurance; 2.2% do not have insurance; 0.0% of children under 18 do not have insurance

Safety: Violent crime rate: 4.4 per 10,000 population; Property crime rate: 139.6 per 10,000 population
Newspapers: Cazenovia Republican (weekly circulation 2,800); Madison County Eagle (weekly circulation 8,700)
Transportation: Commute: 98.4% car, 0.0% public transportation, 0.0% walk, 0.8% work from home; Mean travel time to work: 23.9 minutes
Additional Information Contacts
Village of Canastota . . . . (315) 697-7559
    http://www.canastota.com

CAZENOVIA (town). Covers a land area of 49.870 square miles and a water area of 1.844 square miles. Located at 42.92° N. Lat; 75.86° W. Long. Elevation is 1,224 feet.

History: Seat of Cazenovia College. Settled 1793, incorporated 1810.
Population: 7,042; Growth (since 2000): 8.7%; Density: 141.2 persons per square mile; Race: 95.3% White, 2.9% Black/African American, 1.1% Asian, 0.2% American Indian/Alaska Native, 0.0% Native Hawaiian/Other Pacific Islander, 0.3% Two or more races, 2.7% Hispanic of any race; Average household size: 2.50; Median age: 44.8; Age under 18: 18.9%; Age 65 and over: 18.6%; Males per 100 females: 85.9; Marriage status: 34.9% never married, 51.8% now married, 3.5% separated, 4.6% widowed, 8.7% divorced; Foreign born: 3.2%; Speak English only: 96.2%; With disability: 11.3%; Veterans: 7.0%; Ancestry: 21.4% German, 20.9% American, 19.9% Irish, 16.2% English, 8.8% Italian
Employment: 18.1% management, business, and financial, 6.5% computer, engineering, and science, 17.2% education, legal, community service, arts, and media, 5.8% healthcare practitioners, 17.4% service, 19.6% sales and office, 6.9% natural resources, construction, and maintenance, 8.5% production, transportation, and material moving
Income: Per capita: $39,497; Median household: $74,464; Average household: $107,292; Households with income of $100,000 or more: 36.7%; Poverty rate: 6.1%
Educational Attainment: High school diploma or higher: 96.1%; Bachelor's degree or higher: 48.7%; Graduate/professional degree or higher: 21.0%

School District(s)
Cazenovia Central SD (KG-12)
    Enrollment: 1,455 . . . . (315) 655-1317
Four-year College(s)
Cazenovia College (Private, Not-for-profit)
    Enrollment: 893 . . . . (800) 654-3210
    Tuition: In-state $33,656; Out-of-state $33,656
Housing: Homeownership rate: 76.8%; Median home value: $261,200; Median year structure built: 1963; Homeowner vacancy rate: 2.9%; Median selected monthly owner costs: $1,904 with a mortgage, $830 without a mortgage; Median gross rent: $851 per month; Rental vacancy rate: 9.6%
Health Insurance: 97.2% have insurance; 82.5% have private insurance; 28.4% have public insurance; 2.8% do not have insurance; 0.6% of children under 18 do not have insurance
Transportation: Commute: 80.3% car, 0.6% public transportation, 9.3% walk, 8.3% work from home; Mean travel time to work: 26.6 minutes
Additional Information Contacts
Town of Cazenovia . . . . (315) 655-9213
    http://townofcazenovia.org/content

CAZENOVIA (village). Covers a land area of 1.873 square miles and a water area of 0 square miles. Located at 42.93° N. Lat; 75.85° W. Long. Elevation is 1,224 feet.

Population: 2,851; Growth (since 2000): 9.1%; Density: 1,521.9 persons per square mile; Race: 90.5% White, 7.1% Black/African American, 0.6% Asian, 0.4% American Indian/Alaska Native, 0.0% Native Hawaiian/Other Pacific Islander, 0.8% Two or more races, 4.8% Hispanic of any race; Average household size: 2.06; Median age: 37.8; Age under 18: 11.2%; Age 65 and over: 20.1%; Males per 100 females: 67.4; Marriage status: 48.5% never married, 33.3% now married, 2.7% separated, 6.5% widowed, 11.7% divorced; Foreign born: 2.9%; Speak English only: 95.0%; With disability: 12.3%; Veterans: 4.9%; Ancestry: 22.1% German, 19.2% Irish, 18.4% American, 15.2% English, 9.6% Italian
Employment: 10.9% management, business, and financial, 3.3% computer, engineering, and science, 22.9% education, legal, community service, arts, and media, 2.8% healthcare practitioners, 22.1% service, 26.0% sales and office, 6.3% natural resources, construction, and maintenance, 5.8% production, transportation, and material moving

Income: Per capita: $26,476; Median household: $52,917; Average household: $71,751; Households with income of $100,000 or more: 25.9%; Poverty rate: 11.4%
Educational Attainment: High school diploma or higher: 92.9%; Bachelor's degree or higher: 46.2%; Graduate/professional degree or higher: 21.0%

School District(s)
Cazenovia Central SD (KG-12)
    Enrollment: 1,455 . . . . (315) 655-1317
Four-year College(s)
Cazenovia College (Private, Not-for-profit)
    Enrollment: 893 . . . . (800) 654-3210
    Tuition: In-state $33,656; Out-of-state $33,656
Housing: Homeownership rate: 62.6%; Median home value: $196,600; Median year structure built: 1952; Homeowner vacancy rate: 0.0%; Median selected monthly owner costs: $1,601 with a mortgage, $809 without a mortgage; Median gross rent: $841 per month; Rental vacancy rate: 9.3%
Health Insurance: 97.5% have insurance; 79.8% have private insurance; 34.9% have public insurance; 2.5% do not have insurance; 1.7% of children under 18 do not have insurance
Safety: Violent crime rate: 17.6 per 10,000 population; Property crime rate: 129.9 per 10,000 population
Transportation: Commute: 64.6% car, 1.4% public transportation, 23.9% walk, 9.2% work from home; Mean travel time to work: 23.2 minutes

CHITTENANGO (village). Covers a land area of 2.441 square miles and a water area of 0 square miles. Located at 43.05° N. Lat; 75.87° W. Long. Elevation is 453 feet.

Population: 4,957; Growth (since 2000): 2.1%; Density: 2,030.6 persons per square mile; Race: 98.0% White, 1.0% Black/African American, 0.2% Asian, 0.0% American Indian/Alaska Native, 0.0% Native Hawaiian/Other Pacific Islander, 0.8% Two or more races, 1.3% Hispanic of any race; Average household size: 2.74; Median age: 37.6; Age under 18: 26.1%; Age 65 and over: 13.3%; Males per 100 females: 89.0; Marriage status: 28.5% never married, 54.2% now married, 2.2% separated, 4.1% widowed, 13.3% divorced; Foreign born: 1.6%; Speak English only: 98.6%; With disability: 10.9%; Veterans: 9.9%; Ancestry: 33.4% American, 16.5% German, 15.8% Irish, 11.2% Italian, 9.8% English
Employment: 14.8% management, business, and financial, 7.3% computer, engineering, and science, 10.7% education, legal, community service, arts, and media, 6.6% healthcare practitioners, 14.4% service, 27.3% sales and office, 7.9% natural resources, construction, and maintenance, 11.0% production, transportation, and material moving
Income: Per capita: $31,572; Median household: $74,293; Average household: $85,269; Households with income of $100,000 or more: 32.8%; Poverty rate: 4.9%
Educational Attainment: High school diploma or higher: 92.4%; Bachelor's degree or higher: 29.4%; Graduate/professional degree or higher: 11.0%

School District(s)
Chittenango Central SD (KG-12)
    Enrollment: 1,915 . . . . (315) 687-2840
Housing: Homeownership rate: 78.3%; Median home value: $127,100; Median year structure built: 1967; Homeowner vacancy rate: 8.2%; Median selected monthly owner costs: $1,268 with a mortgage, $555 without a mortgage; Median gross rent: $687 per month; Rental vacancy rate: 6.3%
Health Insurance: 95.4% have insurance; 78.2% have private insurance; 27.6% have public insurance; 4.6% do not have insurance; 0.0% of children under 18 do not have insurance
Safety: Violent crime rate: 10.2 per 10,000 population; Property crime rate: 51.1 per 10,000 population
Transportation: Commute: 95.6% car, 0.0% public transportation, 1.7% walk, 1.9% work from home; Mean travel time to work: 25.1 minutes
Additional Information Contacts
Village of Chittenango . . . . (315) 687-3936
    http://chittenango.org

DERUYTER (town). Covers a land area of 30.440 square miles and a water area of 0.833 square miles. Located at 42.77° N. Lat; 75.85° W. Long. Elevation is 1,286 feet.

Population: 1,495; Growth (since 2000): -2.4%; Density: 49.1 persons per square mile; Race: 91.0% White, 7.3% Black/African American, 0.9% Asian, 0.3% American Indian/Alaska Native, 0.0% Native Hawaiian/Other Pacific Islander, 0.5% Two or more races, 0.4% Hispanic of any race; Average household size: 2.79; Median age: 44.7; Age under 18: 30.9%;

Age 65 and over: 20.4%; Males per 100 females: 94.0; Marriage status: 22.0% never married, 62.1% now married, 2.6% separated, 5.8% widowed, 10.1% divorced; Foreign born: 1.3%; Speak English only: 93.4%; With disability: 9.9%; Veterans: 9.1%; Ancestry: 30.0% American, 13.9% English, 9.2% German, 8.1% Irish, 3.8% French
Employment: 15.8% management, business, and financial, 6.8% computer, engineering, and science, 8.0% education, legal, community service, arts, and media, 5.5% healthcare practitioners, 10.9% service, 25.8% sales and office, 13.9% natural resources, construction, and maintenance, 13.3% production, transportation, and material moving
Income: Per capita: $23,064; Median household: $56,563; Average household: $63,018; Households with income of $100,000 or more: 16.8%; Poverty rate: 14.7%
Educational Attainment: High school diploma or higher: 89.3%; Bachelor's degree or higher: 18.4%; Graduate/professional degree or higher: 9.1%

School District(s)
Deruyter Central SD (PK-12)
    Enrollment: 394 . . . . (315) 852-3400
Housing: Homeownership rate: 83.7%; Median home value: $105,800; Median year structure built: 1959; Homeowner vacancy rate: 0.0%; Median selected monthly owner costs: $1,071 with a mortgage, $498 without a mortgage; Median gross rent: $581 per month; Rental vacancy rate: 6.5%
Health Insurance: 90.6% have insurance; 57.0% have private insurance; 50.8% have public insurance; 9.4% do not have insurance; 9.1% of children under 18 do not have insurance
Transportation: Commute: 85.6% car, 0.0% public transportation, 7.0% walk, 5.3% work from home; Mean travel time to work: 32.8 minutes

DERUYTER (village). Covers a land area of 0.344 square miles and a water area of 0 square miles. Located at 42.76° N. Lat; 75.89° W. Long. Elevation is 1,286 feet.
Population: 482; Growth (since 2000): -9.2%; Density: 1,401.3 persons per square mile; Race: 97.1% White, 0.0% Black/African American, 2.9% Asian, 0.0% American Indian/Alaska Native, 0.0% Native Hawaiian/Other Pacific Islander, 0.0% Two or more races, 0.0% Hispanic of any race; Average household size: 2.47; Median age: 44.3; Age under 18: 32.8%; Age 65 and over: 19.9%; Males per 100 females: 79.4; Marriage status: 20.0% never married, 48.9% now married, 6.1% separated, 10.8% widowed, 20.3% divorced; Foreign born: 2.1%; Speak English only: 98.7%; With disability: 12.4%; Veterans: 9.6%; Ancestry: 47.9% American, 11.4% English, 7.5% Irish, 7.3% German, 5.0% Italian
Employment: 11.8% management, business, and financial, 1.8% computer, engineering, and science, 14.1% education, legal, community service, arts, and media, 4.7% healthcare practitioners, 18.2% service, 24.1% sales and office, 7.6% natural resources, construction, and maintenance, 17.6% production, transportation, and material moving
Income: Per capita: $22,260; Median household: $35,114; Average household: $52,717; Households with income of $100,000 or more: 11.4%; Poverty rate: 21.8%
Educational Attainment: High school diploma or higher: 92.1%; Bachelor's degree or higher: 22.0%; Graduate/professional degree or higher: 14.8%

School District(s)
Deruyter Central SD (PK-12)
    Enrollment: 394 . . . . (315) 852-3400
Housing: Homeownership rate: 63.6%; Median home value: $82,100; Median year structure built: Before 1940; Homeowner vacancy rate: 0.0%; Median selected monthly owner costs: $1,014 with a mortgage, $406 without a mortgage; Median gross rent: $558 per month; Rental vacancy rate: 7.8%
Health Insurance: 96.9% have insurance; 56.4% have private insurance; 60.4% have public insurance; 3.1% do not have insurance; 0.0% of children under 18 do not have insurance
Transportation: Commute: 83.5% car, 0.0% public transportation, 14.6% walk, 1.8% work from home; Mean travel time to work: 34.1 minutes

EARLVILLE (village). Covers a land area of 1.079 square miles and a water area of 0 square miles. Located at 42.74° N. Lat; 75.54° W. Long. Elevation is 1,099 feet.
Population: 1,206; Growth (since 2000): 52.5%; Density: 1,117.3 persons per square mile; Race: 94.6% White, 2.2% Black/African American, 0.0% Asian, 0.7% American Indian/Alaska Native, 0.0% Native Hawaiian/Other Pacific Islander, 0.9% Two or more races, 0.8% Hispanic of any race; Average household size: 2.88; Median age: 34.7; Age under 18: 31.7%;

Age 65 and over: 14.2%; Males per 100 females: 98.6; Marriage status: 29.3% never married, 52.9% now married, 2.5% separated, 10.4% widowed, 7.4% divorced; Foreign born: 0.5%; Speak English only: 97.9%; With disability: 10.1%; Veterans: 10.6%; Ancestry: 36.7% American, 14.5% Irish, 13.1% German, 12.6% English, 8.5% Italian
Employment: 13.5% management, business, and financial, 0.4% computer, engineering, and science, 14.3% education, legal, community service, arts, and media, 6.0% healthcare practitioners, 17.3% service, 27.5% sales and office, 10.0% natural resources, construction, and maintenance, 11.0% production, transportation, and material moving
Income: Per capita: $20,087; Median household: $44,563; Average household: $54,107; Households with income of $100,000 or more: 16.0%; Poverty rate: 12.6%
Educational Attainment: High school diploma or higher: 90.8%; Bachelor's degree or higher: 22.2%; Graduate/professional degree or higher: 9.5%
Housing: Homeownership rate: 68.5%; Median home value: $85,500; Median year structure built: Before 1940; Homeowner vacancy rate: 5.3%; Median selected monthly owner costs: $1,054 with a mortgage, $533 without a mortgage; Median gross rent: $838 per month; Rental vacancy rate: 0.0%
Health Insurance: 98.1% have insurance; 73.2% have private insurance; 41.9% have public insurance; 1.9% do not have insurance; 1.7% of children under 18 do not have insurance
Transportation: Commute: 95.0% car, 0.0% public transportation, 2.8% walk, 1.0% work from home; Mean travel time to work: 20.8 minutes

EATON (town). Covers a land area of 44.622 square miles and a water area of 0.949 square miles. Located at 42.89° N. Lat; 75.63° W. Long. Elevation is 1,204 feet.
Population: 4,792; Growth (since 2000): -0.7%; Density: 107.4 persons per square mile; Race: 86.0% White, 9.3% Black/African American, 1.9% Asian, 0.5% American Indian/Alaska Native, 0.0% Native Hawaiian/Other Pacific Islander, 1.6% Two or more races, 4.2% Hispanic of any race; Average household size: 2.53; Median age: 23.7; Age under 18: 14.9%; Age 65 and over: 12.0%; Males per 100 females: 102.5; Marriage status: 55.1% never married, 31.7% now married, 0.3% separated, 5.8% widowed, 7.4% divorced; Foreign born: 3.9%; Speak English only: 92.9%; With disability: 9.5%; Veterans: 3.7%; Ancestry: 39.9% American, 11.4% Irish, 9.4% German, 8.4% English, 5.2% Italian
Employment: 10.2% management, business, and financial, 6.0% computer, engineering, and science, 13.8% education, legal, community service, arts, and media, 7.9% healthcare practitioners, 21.2% service, 16.8% sales and office, 11.9% natural resources, construction, and maintenance, 12.2% production, transportation, and material moving
Income: Per capita: $18,240; Median household: $53,948; Average household: $65,320; Households with income of $100,000 or more: 16.0%; Poverty rate: 9.0%
Educational Attainment: High school diploma or higher: 84.0%; Bachelor's degree or higher: 21.2%; Graduate/professional degree or higher: 10.2%
Housing: Homeownership rate: 88.8%; Median home value: $122,500; Median year structure built: 1958; Homeowner vacancy rate: 0.8%; Median selected monthly owner costs: $1,097 with a mortgage, $477 without a mortgage; Median gross rent: $679 per month; Rental vacancy rate: 19.3%
Health Insurance: 92.2% have insurance; 72.4% have private insurance; 28.7% have public insurance; 7.8% do not have insurance; 6.4% of children under 18 do not have insurance
Transportation: Commute: 71.7% car, 1.0% public transportation, 18.2% walk, 7.4% work from home; Mean travel time to work: 18.6 minutes
Additional Information Contacts
Town of Eaton . . . . (315) 684-9111
    http://www.townofeaton.com

ERIEVILLE (unincorporated postal area)
ZCTA: 13061
    Covers a land area of 25.988 square miles and a water area of 0.976 square miles. Located at 42.87° N. Lat; 75.76° W. Long. Elevation is 1,545 feet.
Population: 1,039; Growth (since 2000): 11.7%; Density: 40.0 persons per square mile; Race: 97.6% White, 0.0% Black/African American, 0.0% Asian, 1.3% American Indian/Alaska Native, 0.0% Native Hawaiian/Other Pacific Islander, 0.0% Two or more races, 1.2% Hispanic of any race; Average household size: 2.39; Median age: 49.8; Age under 18: 14.7%; Age 65 and over: 21.4%; Males per 100 females:

116.7; Marriage status: 25.6% never married, 56.1% now married, 1.7% separated, 5.7% widowed, 12.6% divorced; Foreign born: 0.8%; Speak English only: 97.3%; With disability: 15.7%; Veterans: 10.0%; Ancestry: 20.1% English, 19.1% American, 18.7% German, 18.1% Irish, 6.9% Polish

Employment: 17.8% management, business, and financial, 4.7% computer, engineering, and science, 8.5% education, legal, community service, arts, and media, 8.3% healthcare practitioners, 14.0% service, 21.4% sales and office, 14.8% natural resources, construction, and maintenance, 10.2% production, transportation, and material moving

Income: Per capita: $31,991; Median household: $68,889; Average household: $74,572; Households with income of $100,000 or more: 23.1%; Poverty rate: 7.4%

Educational Attainment: High school diploma or higher: 96.6%; Bachelor's degree or higher: 32.9%; Graduate/professional degree or higher: 10.6%

Housing: Homeownership rate: 79.0%; Median home value: $184,600; Median year structure built: 1965; Homeowner vacancy rate: 0.0%; Median selected monthly owner costs: $1,259 with a mortgage, $521 without a mortgage; Median gross rent: $890 per month; Rental vacancy rate: 7.1%

Health Insurance: 94.4% have insurance; 70.5% have private insurance; 39.7% have public insurance; 5.6% do not have insurance; 5.4% of children under 18 do not have insurance

Transportation: Commute: 90.8% car, 0.0% public transportation, 0.0% walk, 8.2% work from home; Mean travel time to work: 30.5 minutes

---

FENNER (town). Covers a land area of 31.074 square miles and a water area of 0.048 square miles. Located at 42.97° N. Lat; 75.77° W. Long. Elevation is 1,552 feet.

Population: 1,620; Growth (since 2000): -3.6%; Density: 52.1 persons per square mile; Race: 98.5% White, 0.4% Black/African American, 0.0% Asian, 0.8% American Indian/Alaska Native, 0.0% Native Hawaiian/Other Pacific Islander, 0.2% Two or more races, 2.3% Hispanic of any race; Average household size: 2.52; Median age: 46.3; Age under 18: 19.6%; Age 65 and over: 17.7%; Males per 100 females: 107.2; Marriage status: 26.2% never married, 59.8% now married, 0.9% separated, 5.4% widowed, 8.6% divorced; Foreign born: 2.5%; Speak English only: 96.8%; With disability: 13.0%; Veterans: 9.9%; Ancestry: 30.4% American, 16.4% German, 15.2% English, 13.6% Irish, 6.5% French

Employment: 14.5% management, business, and financial, 7.9% computer, engineering, and science, 8.1% education, legal, community service, arts, and media, 6.8% healthcare practitioners, 16.4% service, 19.2% sales and office, 14.4% natural resources, construction, and maintenance, 12.7% production, transportation, and material moving

Income: Per capita: $34,189; Median household: $66,250; Average household: $84,198; Households with income of $100,000 or more: 27.2%; Poverty rate: 5.0%

Educational Attainment: High school diploma or higher: 95.8%; Bachelor's degree or higher: 26.4%; Graduate/professional degree or higher: 12.7%

Housing: Homeownership rate: 85.8%; Median home value: $128,200; Median year structure built: 1974; Homeowner vacancy rate: 1.4%; Median selected monthly owner costs: $1,199 with a mortgage, $421 without a mortgage; Median gross rent: $828 per month; Rental vacancy rate: 0.0%

Health Insurance: 95.6% have insurance; 72.6% have private insurance; 37.4% have public insurance; 4.4% do not have insurance; 0.0% of children under 18 do not have insurance

Transportation: Commute: 90.1% car, 0.7% public transportation, 3.8% walk, 5.4% work from home; Mean travel time to work: 25.7 minutes

---

GEORGETOWN (town). Covers a land area of 40.078 square miles and a water area of 0.099 square miles. Located at 42.79° N. Lat; 75.74° W. Long. Elevation is 1,411 feet.

Population: 531; Growth (since 2000): -43.9%; Density: 13.2 persons per square mile; Race: 98.9% White, 0.0% Black/African American, 0.0% Asian, 0.0% American Indian/Alaska Native, 0.0% Native Hawaiian/Other Pacific Islander, 1.1% Two or more races, 0.0% Hispanic of any race; Average household size: 2.58; Median age: 52.8; Age under 18: 6.4%; Age 65 and over: 21.7%; Males per 100 females: 142.3; Marriage status: 39.3% never married, 46.1% now married, 0.4% separated, 4.1% widowed, 10.5% divorced; Foreign born: 0.0%; Speak English only: 98.9%; With disability: 18.3%; Veterans: 4.8%; Ancestry: 32.0% American, 17.5% English, 10.0% German, 5.6% Dutch, 5.6% French

Employment: 12.8% management, business, and financial, 0.7% computer, engineering, and science, 8.9% education, legal, community service, arts, and media, 5.3% healthcare practitioners, 27.4% service, 17.8% sales and office, 18.1% natural resources, construction, and maintenance, 8.9% production, transportation, and material moving

Income: Per capita: $21,266; Median household: $44,500; Average household: $50,753; Households with income of $100,000 or more: 8.8%; Poverty rate: 16.0%

Educational Attainment: High school diploma or higher: 85.1%; Bachelor's degree or higher: 9.0%; Graduate/professional degree or higher: 2.6%

School District(s)

Georgetown-South Otselic Central SD (PK-12)

　Enrollment: 356 . . . . (315) 653-7218

Housing: Homeownership rate: 91.7%; Median home value: $79,400; Median year structure built: 1980; Homeowner vacancy rate: 9.6%; Median selected monthly owner costs: $1,049 with a mortgage, $450 without a mortgage; Median gross rent: $950 per month; Rental vacancy rate: 29.2%

Health Insurance: 89.5% have insurance; 56.7% have private insurance; 47.1% have public insurance; 10.5% do not have insurance; 0.0% of children under 18 do not have insurance

Transportation: Commute: 83.5% car, 0.0% public transportation, 9.9% walk, 5.9% work from home; Mean travel time to work: 27.5 minutes

---

HAMILTON (town). Covers a land area of 41.339 square miles and a water area of 0.116 square miles. Located at 42.79° N. Lat; 75.49° W. Long. Elevation is 1,122 feet.

History: Seat of Colgate University. Settled 1795, incorporated 1816.

Population: 6,539; Growth (since 2000): 14.1%; Density: 158.2 persons per square mile; Race: 85.5% White, 5.6% Black/African American, 4.4% Asian, 0.2% American Indian/Alaska Native, 0.0% Native Hawaiian/Other Pacific Islander, 3.7% Two or more races, 5.6% Hispanic of any race; Average household size: 2.39; Median age: 22.7; Age under 18: 14.1%; Age 65 and over: 12.3%; Males per 100 females: 90.0; Marriage status: 57.2% never married, 31.6% now married, 0.8% separated, 5.8% widowed, 5.4% divorced; Foreign born: 6.3%; Speak English only: 89.0%; With disability: 9.4%; Veterans: 3.8%; Ancestry: 21.3% American, 15.3% Irish, 13.9% German, 9.1% English, 8.5% Italian

Employment: 9.7% management, business, and financial, 4.5% computer, engineering, and science, 31.3% education, legal, community service, arts, and media, 3.3% healthcare practitioners, 17.4% service, 17.3% sales and office, 9.6% natural resources, construction, and maintenance, 6.8% production, transportation, and material moving

Income: Per capita: $23,544; Median household: $70,000; Average household: $78,652; Households with income of $100,000 or more: 28.9%; Poverty rate: 11.4%

Educational Attainment: High school diploma or higher: 93.1%; Bachelor's degree or higher: 50.9%; Graduate/professional degree or higher: 31.8%

School District(s)

Hamilton Central SD (PK-12)

　Enrollment: 575 . . . . (315) 824-6310

Four-year College(s)

Colgate University (Private, Not-for-profit)

　Enrollment: 2,894 . . . . (315) 228-1000

　Tuition: In-state $53,980; Out-of-state $53,980

Housing: Homeownership rate: 68.8%; Median home value: $170,000; Median year structure built: Before 1940; Homeowner vacancy rate: 1.3%; Median selected monthly owner costs: $1,310 with a mortgage, $655 without a mortgage; Median gross rent: $895 per month; Rental vacancy rate: 3.8%

Health Insurance: 97.7% have insurance; 88.0% have private insurance; 22.4% have public insurance; 2.3% do not have insurance; 1.5% of children under 18 do not have insurance

Hospitals: Community Memorial Hospital (88 beds)

Newspapers: Mid-York Weekly (weekly circulation 8,000)

Transportation: Commute: 64.5% car, 2.2% public transportation, 21.1% walk, 8.6% work from home; Mean travel time to work: 15.3 minutes

Airports: Hamilton Municipal (general aviation)

Additional Information Contacts

Town of Hamilton . . . . (315) 824-3380

　http://www.townofhamiltonny.org

HAMILTON (village).

Covers a land area of 2.486 square miles and a water area of 0.192 square miles. Located at 42.83° N. Lat; 75.55° W. Long. Elevation is 1,122 feet.

Population: 4,015; Growth (since 2000): 14.4%; Density: 1,614.8 persons per square mile; Race: 78.0% White, 8.4% Black/African American, 7.1% Asian, 0.2% American Indian/Alaska Native, 0.0% Native Hawaiian/Other Pacific Islander, 6.0% Two or more races, 5.8% Hispanic of any race; Average household size: 2.19; Median age: 21.3; Age under 18: 8.1%; Age 65 and over: 10.7%; Males per 100 females: 83.7; Marriage status: 75.7% never married, 15.9% now married, 0.8% separated, 4.9% widowed, 3.6% divorced; Foreign born: 9.8%; Speak English only: 84.9%; With disability: 6.8%; Veterans: 1.4%; Ancestry: 17.9% Irish, 17.8% American, 13.0% German, 9.9% English, 8.9% Italian

Employment: 9.4% management, business, and financial, 5.1% computer, engineering, and science, 38.3% education, legal, community service, arts, and media, 2.8% healthcare practitioners, 19.3% service, 14.8% sales and office, 5.7% natural resources, construction, and maintenance, 4.6% production, transportation, and material moving

Income: Per capita: $20,006; Median household: $65,150; Average household: $85,191; Households with income of $100,000 or more: 33.1%; Poverty rate: 17.7%

Educational Attainment: High school diploma or higher: 94.7%; Bachelor's degree or higher: 62.7%; Graduate/professional degree or higher: 43.3%

School District(s)

Hamilton Central SD (PK-12)

    Enrollment: 575 . . . . (315) 824-6310

Four-year College(s)

Colgate University (Private, Not-for-profit)

    Enrollment: 2,894 . . . . (315) 228-1000

    Tuition: In-state $53,980; Out-of-state $53,980

Housing: Homeownership rate: 56.2%; Median home value: $226,600; Median year structure built: Before 1940; Homeowner vacancy rate: 2.0%; Median selected monthly owner costs: $1,792 with a mortgage, $808 without a mortgage; Median gross rent: $823 per month; Rental vacancy rate: 5.5%

Health Insurance: 97.2% have insurance; 89.4% have private insurance; 18.5% have public insurance; 2.9% do not have insurance; 1.8% of children under 18 do not have insurance

Hospitals: Community Memorial Hospital (88 beds)

Safety: Violent crime rate: 0.0 per 10,000 population; Property crime rate: 14.6 per 10,000 population

Newspapers: Mid-York Weekly (weekly circulation 8,000)

Transportation: Commute: 46.5% car, 4.0% public transportation, 33.8% walk, 10.5% work from home; Mean travel time to work: 11.9 minutes

Airports: Hamilton Municipal (general aviation)

Additional Information Contacts

Village of Hamilton . . . . (315) 824-0002

    http://www.hamiltonny.com

HUBBARDSVILLE (unincorporated postal area)

ZCTA: 13355

Covers a land area of 29.107 square miles and a water area of 0.014 square miles. Located at 42.81° N. Lat; 75.43° W. Long. Elevation is 1,214 feet.

Population: 769; Growth (since 2000): 11.1%; Density: 26.4 persons per square mile; Race: 100.0% White, 0.0% Black/African American, 0.0% Asian, 0.0% American Indian/Alaska Native, 0.0% Native Hawaiian/Other Pacific Islander, 0.0% Two or more races, 0.0% Hispanic of any race; Average household size: 2.50; Median age: 37.1; Age under 18: 15.1%; Age 65 and over: 13.8%; Males per 100 females: 107.1; Marriage status: 33.1% never married, 56.2% now married, 2.7% separated, 5.4% widowed, 5.4% divorced; Foreign born: 0.4%; Speak English only: 98.7%; With disability: 19.0%; Veterans: 9.0%; Ancestry: 24.6% American, 22.1% Irish, 13.7% German, 10.5% Polish, 9.9% English

Employment: 5.7% management, business, and financial, 1.2% computer, engineering, and science, 5.5% education, legal, community service, arts, and media, 4.5% healthcare practitioners, 11.7% service, 24.4% sales and office, 36.1% natural resources, construction, and maintenance, 10.9% production, transportation, and material moving

Income: Per capita: $26,429; Median household: $58,611; Average household: $63,039; Households with income of $100,000 or more: 19.0%; Poverty rate: 5.6%

Educational Attainment: High school diploma or higher: 88.1%; Bachelor's degree or higher: 19.8%; Graduate/professional degree or higher: 4.8%

Housing: Homeownership rate: 67.0%; Median home value: $114,500; Median year structure built: Before 1940; Homeowner vacancy rate: 0.0%; Median selected monthly owner costs: $1,090 with a mortgage, $682 without a mortgage; Median gross rent: $797 per month; Rental vacancy rate: 0.0%

Health Insurance: 97.9% have insurance; 88.3% have private insurance; 22.4% have public insurance; 2.1% do not have insurance; 0.0% of children under 18 do not have insurance

Transportation: Commute: 86.2% car, 0.0% public transportation, 13.8% walk, 0.0% work from home; Mean travel time to work: 23.1 minutes

KIRKVILLE (unincorporated postal area)

ZCTA: 13082

Covers a land area of 23.571 square miles and a water area of 0.413 square miles. Located at 43.10° N. Lat; 75.96° W. Long..

Population: 4,685; Growth (since 2000): -6.5%; Density: 198.8 persons per square mile; Race: 98.4% White, 0.1% Black/African American, 0.0% Asian, 0.9% American Indian/Alaska Native, 0.0% Native Hawaiian/Other Pacific Islander, 0.6% Two or more races, 0.3% Hispanic of any race; Average household size: 2.65; Median age: 45.5; Age under 18: 18.5%; Age 65 and over: 21.6%; Males per 100 females: 93.8; Marriage status: 24.2% never married, 53.3% now married, 1.1% separated, 6.8% widowed, 15.8% divorced; Foreign born: 1.7%; Speak English only: 98.8%; With disability: 11.4%; Veterans: 11.5%; Ancestry: 26.5% Irish, 24.4% German, 18.5% English, 13.2% Italian, 9.0% Polish

Employment: 10.3% management, business, and financial, 5.9% computer, engineering, and science, 9.2% education, legal, community service, arts, and media, 4.6% healthcare practitioners, 16.2% service, 27.5% sales and office, 11.7% natural resources, construction, and maintenance, 14.6% production, transportation, and material moving

Income: Per capita: $30,870; Median household: $72,131; Average household: $76,808; Households with income of $100,000 or more: 27.4%; Poverty rate: 8.6%

Educational Attainment: High school diploma or higher: 90.5%; Bachelor's degree or higher: 25.4%; Graduate/professional degree or higher: 9.2%

Housing: Homeownership rate: 83.8%; Median home value: $137,600; Median year structure built: 1975; Homeowner vacancy rate: 6.1%; Median selected monthly owner costs: $1,377 with a mortgage, $558 without a mortgage; Median gross rent: $745 per month; Rental vacancy rate: 0.0%

Health Insurance: 95.6% have insurance; 74.5% have private insurance; 37.8% have public insurance; 4.4% do not have insurance; 0.0% of children under 18 do not have insurance

Transportation: Commute: 97.1% car, 0.0% public transportation, 0.8% walk, 2.2% work from home; Mean travel time to work: 21.4 minutes

LEBANON (town).

Covers a land area of 43.344 square miles and a water area of 0.336 square miles. Located at 42.78° N. Lat; 75.63° W. Long. Elevation is 1,345 feet.

Population: 1,539; Growth (since 2000): 15.8%; Density: 35.5 persons per square mile; Race: 95.6% White, 0.4% Black/African American, 0.2% Asian, 0.5% American Indian/Alaska Native, 0.0% Native Hawaiian/Other Pacific Islander, 3.2% Two or more races, 0.5% Hispanic of any race; Average household size: 2.98; Median age: 41.1; Age under 18: 28.1%; Age 65 and over: 13.8%; Males per 100 females: 105.9; Marriage status: 27.8% never married, 56.3% now married, 4.6% separated, 6.5% widowed, 9.4% divorced; Foreign born: 0.7%; Speak English only: 92.4%; With disability: 13.5%; Veterans: 12.5%; Ancestry: 34.6% American, 17.3% German, 11.0% English, 5.3% Irish, 3.8% Polish

Employment: 21.1% management, business, and financial, 1.2% computer, engineering, and science, 9.8% education, legal, community service, arts, and media, 6.3% healthcare practitioners, 22.8% service, 16.6% sales and office, 13.9% natural resources, construction, and maintenance, 8.2% production, transportation, and material moving

Income: Per capita: $26,284; Median household: $61,797; Average household: $75,830; Households with income of $100,000 or more: 24.2%; Poverty rate: 6.1%

Educational Attainment: High school diploma or higher: 88.7%; Bachelor's degree or higher: 22.7%; Graduate/professional degree or higher: 12.4%

Housing: Homeownership rate: 85.3%; Median home value: $121,300; Median year structure built: 1970; Homeowner vacancy rate: 0.0%; Median selected monthly owner costs: $1,323 with a mortgage, $473 without a mortgage; Median gross rent: $800 per month; Rental vacancy rate: 0.0%
Health Insurance: 86.2% have insurance; 58.2% have private insurance; 41.8% have public insurance; 13.8% do not have insurance; 16.9% of children under 18 do not have insurance
Transportation: Commute: 79.2% car, 0.3% public transportation, 7.4% walk, 12.5% work from home; Mean travel time to work: 23.5 minutes

LENOX (town).
Covers a land area of 36.243 square miles and a water area of 0.023 square miles. Located at 43.11° N. Lat; 75.76° W. Long. Elevation is 528 feet.
Population: 8,918; Growth (since 2000): 2.9%; Density: 246.1 persons per square mile; Race: 96.4% White, 0.2% Black/African American, 0.1% Asian, 0.1% American Indian/Alaska Native, 0.0% Native Hawaiian/Other Pacific Islander, 3.1% Two or more races, 0.1% Hispanic of any race; Average household size: 2.50; Median age: 42.1; Age under 18: 21.2%; Age 65 and over: 16.6%; Males per 100 females: 94.5; Marriage status: 33.1% never married, 47.7% now married, 3.3% separated, 7.1% widowed, 12.0% divorced; Foreign born: 0.5%; Speak English only: 97.9%; With disability: 14.9%; Veterans: 9.9%; Ancestry: 30.3% American, 15.2% German, 15.2% Irish, 12.5% Italian, 9.6% English
Employment: 13.6% management, business, and financial, 5.6% computer, engineering, and science, 6.3% education, legal, community service, arts, and media, 5.9% healthcare practitioners, 18.8% service, 26.8% sales and office, 10.0% natural resources, construction, and maintenance, 12.9% production, transportation, and material moving
Income: Per capita: $26,045; Median household: $52,313; Average household: $62,943; Households with income of $100,000 or more: 17.6%; Poverty rate: 11.0%
Educational Attainment: High school diploma or higher: 92.2%; Bachelor's degree or higher: 20.2%; Graduate/professional degree or higher: 7.0%
Housing: Homeownership rate: 68.2%; Median home value: $117,100; Median year structure built: 1959; Homeowner vacancy rate: 0.6%; Median selected monthly owner costs: $1,267 with a mortgage, $501 without a mortgage; Median gross rent: $804 per month; Rental vacancy rate: 5.1%
Health Insurance: 96.2% have insurance; 73.1% have private insurance; 36.4% have public insurance; 3.8% do not have insurance; 0.2% of children under 18 do not have insurance
Transportation: Commute: 96.8% car, 0.0% public transportation, 0.9% walk, 1.9% work from home; Mean travel time to work: 23.5 minutes
Additional Information Contacts
Town of Lenox . . . . (315) 697-7547
  http://www.lenoxny.com

LEONARDSVILLE (unincorporated postal area)
ZCTA: 13364
  Covers a land area of 2.956 square miles and a water area of 0 square miles. Located at 42.80° N. Lat; 75.26° W. Long. Elevation is 1,168 feet.
Population: 101; Growth (since 2000): n/a; Density: 34.2 persons per square mile; Race: 100.0% White, 0.0% Black/African American, 0.0% Asian, 0.0% American Indian/Alaska Native, 0.0% Native Hawaiian/Other Pacific Islander, 0.0% Two or more races, 0.0% Hispanic of any race; Average household size: 1.60; Median age: 50.3; Age under 18: 15.8%; Age 65 and over: 19.8%; Males per 100 females: 84.1; Marriage status: 22.2% never married, 47.8% now married, 0.0% separated, 0.0% widowed, 30.0% divorced; Foreign born: 0.0%; Speak English only: 100.0%; With disability: 8.9%; Veterans: 12.9%; Ancestry: 32.7% Irish, 24.8% American, 15.8% Dutch, 13.9% German, 5.9% Czech
Employment: 30.4% management, business, and financial, 0.0% computer, engineering, and science, 0.0% education, legal, community service, arts, and media, 5.8% healthcare practitioners, 0.0% service, 21.7% sales and office, 42.0% natural resources, construction, and maintenance, 0.0% production, transportation, and material moving
Income: Per capita: $24,733; Median household: $31,650; Average household: $38,067; Households with income of $100,000 or more: n/a; Poverty rate: 5.9%
Educational Attainment: High school diploma or higher: 100.0%; Bachelor's degree or higher: 20.0%; Graduate/professional degree or higher: n/a
Housing: Homeownership rate: 82.5%; Median home value: $61,100; Median year structure built: Before 1940; Homeowner vacancy rate:

35.6%; Median selected monthly owner costs: $1,028 with a mortgage, $544 without a mortgage; Median gross rent: n/a per month; Rental vacancy rate: 0.0%
Health Insurance: 96.0% have insurance; 90.1% have private insurance; 24.8% have public insurance; 4.0% do not have insurance; 0.0% of children under 18 do not have insurance
Transportation: Commute: 100.0% car, 0.0% public transportation, 0.0% walk, 0.0% work from home; Mean travel time to work: 41.9 minutes

LINCOLN (town).
Covers a land area of 24.999 square miles and a water area of 0.059 square miles. Located at 43.03° N. Lat; 75.73° W. Long. Elevation is 689 feet.
Population: 1,881; Growth (since 2000): 3.5%; Density: 75.2 persons per square mile; Race: 96.1% White, 0.3% Black/African American, 0.8% Asian, 0.2% American Indian/Alaska Native, 0.0% Native Hawaiian/Other Pacific Islander, 2.5% Two or more races, 0.7% Hispanic of any race; Average household size: 2.67; Median age: 43.6; Age under 18: 23.9%; Age 65 and over: 16.8%; Males per 100 females: 113.6; Marriage status: 24.3% never married, 61.6% now married, 1.5% separated, 6.5% widowed, 7.6% divorced; Foreign born: 1.2%; Speak English only: 97.9%; With disability: 12.9%; Veterans: 9.6%; Ancestry: 28.5% American, 16.8% Irish, 13.3% German, 11.9% English, 10.9% Italian
Employment: 19.0% management, business, and financial, 5.0% computer, engineering, and science, 9.0% education, legal, community service, arts, and media, 4.5% healthcare practitioners, 14.9% service, 22.7% sales and office, 12.5% natural resources, construction, and maintenance, 12.5% production, transportation, and material moving
Income: Per capita: $29,937; Median household: $64,300; Average household: $77,691; Households with income of $100,000 or more: 27.8%; Poverty rate: 7.6%
Educational Attainment: High school diploma or higher: 89.9%; Bachelor's degree or higher: 24.7%; Graduate/professional degree or higher: 9.8%
Housing: Homeownership rate: 88.9%; Median home value: $135,000; Median year structure built: 1975; Homeowner vacancy rate: 1.4%; Median selected monthly owner costs: $1,323 with a mortgage, $516 without a mortgage; Median gross rent: $821 per month; Rental vacancy rate: 0.0%
Health Insurance: 93.0% have insurance; 70.9% have private insurance; 36.5% have public insurance; 7.0% do not have insurance; 4.8% of children under 18 do not have insurance
Transportation: Commute: 93.5% car, 0.0% public transportation, 1.4% walk, 4.5% work from home; Mean travel time to work: 25.4 minutes

MADISON (town).
Covers a land area of 40.813 square miles and a water area of 0.576 square miles. Located at 42.89° N. Lat; 75.50° W. Long. Elevation is 1,204 feet.
Population: 2,946; Growth (since 2000): 5.2%; Density: 72.2 persons per square mile; Race: 98.9% White, 0.1% Black/African American, 0.1% Asian, 0.7% American Indian/Alaska Native, 0.0% Native Hawaiian/Other Pacific Islander, 0.1% Two or more races, 0.6% Hispanic of any race; Average household size: 2.27; Median age: 53.9; Age under 18: 13.2%; Age 65 and over: 26.2%; Males per 100 females: 99.9; Marriage status: 20.9% never married, 57.8% now married, 1.4% separated, 8.7% widowed, 12.5% divorced; Foreign born: 2.1%; Speak English only: 95.9%; With disability: 14.4%; Veterans: 11.0%; Ancestry: 43.2% American, 17.5% English, 11.8% Irish, 8.8% German, 5.2% Italian
Employment: 13.1% management, business, and financial, 1.9% computer, engineering, and science, 11.7% education, legal, community service, arts, and media, 8.6% healthcare practitioners, 17.2% service, 16.1% sales and office, 13.5% natural resources, construction, and maintenance, 17.8% production, transportation, and material moving
Income: Per capita: $28,715; Median household: $51,486; Average household: $62,725; Households with income of $100,000 or more: 15.9%; Poverty rate: 16.0%
Educational Attainment: High school diploma or higher: 90.7%; Bachelor's degree or higher: 29.1%; Graduate/professional degree or higher: 11.3%

School District(s)
Madison Central SD (PK-12)
  Enrollment: 478 . . . . (315) 893-1878
Housing: Homeownership rate: 86.3%; Median home value: $113,500; Median year structure built: 1963; Homeowner vacancy rate: 0.0%; Median selected monthly owner costs: $1,509 with a mortgage, $468 without a mortgage; Median gross rent: $491 per month; Rental vacancy rate: 1.2%

Health Insurance: 95.0% have insurance; 79.7% have private insurance; 45.0% have public insurance; 5.0% do not have insurance; 0.0% of children under 18 do not have insurance
Transportation: Commute: 96.7% car, 0.0% public transportation, 2.6% walk, 0.6% work from home; Mean travel time to work: 22.2 minutes

---

MADISON (village). Covers a land area of 0.502 square miles and a water area of 0 square miles. Located at 42.90° N. Lat; 75.51° W. Long. Elevation is 1,204 feet.
Population: 407; Growth (since 2000): 29.2%; Density: 810.7 persons per square mile; Race: 99.0% White, 0.0% Black/African American, 0.0% Asian, 0.0% American Indian/Alaska Native, 0.0% Native Hawaiian/Other Pacific Islander, 1.0% Two or more races, 4.4% Hispanic of any race; Average household size: 3.04; Median age: 32.5; Age under 18: 28.3%; Age 65 and over: 14.5%; Males per 100 females: 89.4; Marriage status: 30.1% never married, 58.8% now married, 5.6% separated, 3.9% widowed, 7.2% divorced; Foreign born: 0.5%; Speak English only: 98.9%; With disability: 12.0%; Veterans: 3.4%; Ancestry: 50.6% American, 13.0% Irish, 11.8% German, 9.1% English, 4.9% Welsh
Employment: 16.8% management, business, and financial, 3.9% computer, engineering, and science, 7.8% education, legal, community service, arts, and media, 12.3% healthcare practitioners, 16.2% service, 17.9% sales and office, 12.8% natural resources, construction, and maintenance, 12.3% production, transportation, and material moving
Income: Per capita: $21,297; Median household: $55,278; Average household: $62,295; Households with income of $100,000 or more: 10.5%; Poverty rate: 7.6%
Educational Attainment: High school diploma or higher: 84.2%; Bachelor's degree or higher: 15.8%; Graduate/professional degree or higher: 6.4%

School District(s)
Madison Central SD (PK-12)
    Enrollment: 478 . . . . (315) 893-1878
Housing: Homeownership rate: 68.7%; Median home value: $108,300; Median year structure built: Before 1940; Homeowner vacancy rate: 0.0%; Median selected monthly owner costs: $1,190 with a mortgage, $500 without a mortgage; Median gross rent: $817 per month; Rental vacancy rate: 6.7%
Health Insurance: 94.8% have insurance; 55.8% have private insurance; 55.5% have public insurance; 5.2% do not have insurance; 0.0% of children under 18 do not have insurance
Transportation: Commute: 83.1% car, 0.0% public transportation, 12.4% walk, 4.5% work from home; Mean travel time to work: 17.9 minutes

---

MORRISVILLE (village). Covers a land area of 1.153 square miles and a water area of 0 square miles. Located at 42.90° N. Lat; 75.64° W. Long. Elevation is 1,348 feet.
Population: 2,014; Growth (since 2000): -6.2%; Density: 1,747.5 persons per square mile; Race: 76.1% White, 17.2% Black/African American, 2.9% Asian, 0.0% American Indian/Alaska Native, 0.0% Native Hawaiian/Other Pacific Islander, 2.9% Two or more races, 8.3% Hispanic of any race; Average household size: 2.65; Median age: 20.8; Age under 18: 9.6%; Age 65 and over: 10.7%; Males per 100 females: 106.1; Marriage status: 77.7% never married, 15.4% now married, 0.5% separated, 3.4% widowed, 3.4% divorced; Foreign born: 5.1%; Speak English only: 88.5%; With disability: 4.3%; Veterans: 3.4%; Ancestry: 37.1% American, 12.0% Irish, 11.3% German, 6.5% English, 6.0% Italian
Employment: 5.9% management, business, and financial, 1.6% computer, engineering, and science, 21.8% education, legal, community service, arts, and media, 2.6% healthcare practitioners, 35.3% service, 16.2% sales and office, 11.4% natural resources, construction, and maintenance, 5.2% production, transportation, and material moving
Income: Per capita: $10,030; Median household: $51,985; Average household: $59,108; Households with income of $100,000 or more: 11.9%; Poverty rate: 16.5%
Educational Attainment: High school diploma or higher: 91.3%; Bachelor's degree or higher: 21.3%; Graduate/professional degree or higher: 12.3%

School District(s)
Morrisville-Eaton Central SD (PK-12)
    Enrollment: 694 . . . . (315) 684-9300
Four-year College(s)
Morrisville State College (Public)
    Enrollment: 3,063 . . . . (315) 684-6000
    Tuition: In-state $8,249; Out-of-state $17,899

Housing: Homeownership rate: 72.8%; Median home value: $121,900; Median year structure built: 1942; Homeowner vacancy rate: 4.5%; Median selected monthly owner costs: $1,240 with a mortgage, $708 without a mortgage; Median gross rent: $754 per month; Rental vacancy rate: 37.0%
Health Insurance: 93.9% have insurance; 83.4% have private insurance; 20.5% have public insurance; 6.1% do not have insurance; 5.3% of children under 18 do not have insurance
Transportation: Commute: 54.1% car, 1.2% public transportation, 36.9% walk, 6.1% work from home; Mean travel time to work: 13.1 minutes

---

MUNNSVILLE (village). Covers a land area of 0.849 square miles and a water area of 0 square miles. Located at 42.98° N. Lat; 75.59° W. Long. Elevation is 659 feet.
Population: 506; Growth (since 2000): 15.8%; Density: 595.7 persons per square mile; Race: 93.3% White, 0.0% Black/African American, 0.4% Asian, 0.4% American Indian/Alaska Native, 0.0% Native Hawaiian/Other Pacific Islander, 4.9% Two or more races, 1.0% Hispanic of any race; Average household size: 3.01; Median age: 28.0; Age under 18: 29.6%; Age 65 and over: 6.7%; Males per 100 females: 95.1; Marriage status: 37.6% never married, 48.9% now married, 4.2% separated, 4.5% widowed, 9.0% divorced; Foreign born: 0.4%; Speak English only: 98.2%; With disability: 9.3%; Veterans: 9.6%; Ancestry: 49.0% American, 10.3% German, 9.1% English, 7.5% Irish, 4.7% Italian
Employment: 8.9% management, business, and financial, 3.4% computer, engineering, and science, 11.0% education, legal, community service, arts, and media, 5.1% healthcare practitioners, 22.8% service, 21.1% sales and office, 9.3% natural resources, construction, and maintenance, 18.6% production, transportation, and material moving
Income: Per capita: $19,954; Median household: $48,571; Average household: $56,276; Households with income of $100,000 or more: 13.1%; Poverty rate: 16.0%
Educational Attainment: High school diploma or higher: 91.0%; Bachelor's degree or higher: 18.7%; Graduate/professional degree or higher: 6.1%

School District(s)
Stockbridge Valley Central SD (PK-12)
    Enrollment: 436 . . . . (315) 495-4400
Housing: Homeownership rate: 63.7%; Median home value: $89,300; Median year structure built: Before 1940; Homeowner vacancy rate: 0.0%; Median selected monthly owner costs: $1,082 with a mortgage, $475 without a mortgage; Median gross rent: $686 per month; Rental vacancy rate: 1.6%
Health Insurance: 93.5% have insurance; 63.4% have private insurance; 40.1% have public insurance; 6.5% do not have insurance; 2.5% of children under 18 do not have insurance
Transportation: Commute: 91.8% car, 0.0% public transportation, 4.3% walk, 3.9% work from home; Mean travel time to work: 19.4 minutes

---

NELSON (town). Covers a land area of 43.060 square miles and a water area of 0.996 square miles. Located at 42.89° N. Lat; 75.75° W. Long. Elevation is 1,437 feet.
Population: 1,924; Growth (since 2000): -2.0%; Density: 44.7 persons per square mile; Race: 97.5% White, 0.0% Black/African American, 0.9% Asian, 0.8% American Indian/Alaska Native, 0.0% Native Hawaiian/Other Pacific Islander, 0.2% Two or more races, 1.2% Hispanic of any race; Average household size: 2.49; Median age: 45.0; Age under 18: 22.3%; Age 65 and over: 20.2%; Males per 100 females: 104.3; Marriage status: 23.5% never married, 60.2% now married, 1.6% separated, 5.1% widowed, 11.1% divorced; Foreign born: 3.5%; Speak English only: 96.4%; With disability: 11.3%; Veterans: 9.8%; Ancestry: 23.9% American, 19.4% Irish, 18.3% German, 13.6% English, 7.3% Italian
Employment: 17.3% management, business, and financial, 7.5% computer, engineering, and science, 10.6% education, legal, community service, arts, and media, 11.1% healthcare practitioners, 14.6% service, 16.4% sales and office, 13.0% natural resources, construction, and maintenance, 9.5% production, transportation, and material moving
Income: Per capita: $31,058; Median household: $67,000; Average household: $75,236; Households with income of $100,000 or more: 27.4%; Poverty rate: 6.8%
Educational Attainment: High school diploma or higher: 95.1%; Bachelor's degree or higher: 35.3%; Graduate/professional degree or higher: 13.6%
Housing: Homeownership rate: 83.5%; Median home value: $178,400; Median year structure built: 1972; Homeowner vacancy rate: 0.0%; Median

selected monthly owner costs: $1,477 with a mortgage, $582 without a mortgage; Median gross rent: $897 per month; Rental vacancy rate: 0.0%
Health Insurance: 96.1% have insurance; 79.1% have private insurance; 33.9% have public insurance; 3.9% do not have insurance; 2.0% of children under 18 do not have insurance
Transportation: Commute: 90.2% car, 0.0% public transportation, 3.3% walk, 6.0% work from home; Mean travel time to work: 30.6 minutes

NEW WOODSTOCK (unincorporated postal area)
ZCTA: 13122

Covers a land area of 18.700 square miles and a water area of 0.015 square miles. Located at 42.84° N. Lat; 75.86° W. Long. Elevation is 1,306 feet.
Population: 1,377; Growth (since 2000): 13.9%; Density: 73.6 persons per square mile; Race: 99.7% White, 0.3% Black/African American, 0.0% Asian, 0.0% American Indian/Alaska Native, 0.0% Native Hawaiian/Other Pacific Islander, 0.0% Two or more races, 0.0% Hispanic of any race; Average household size: 3.05; Median age: 37.1; Age under 18: 32.5%; Age 65 and over: 9.3%; Males per 100 females: 93.1; Marriage status: 26.2% never married, 62.1% now married, 4.0% separated, 3.0% widowed, 8.6% divorced; Foreign born: 1.7%; Speak English only: 94.2%; With disability: 11.6%; Veterans: 13.1%; Ancestry: 22.7% American, 18.8% German, 13.6% Irish, 7.9% English, 6.8% Italian
Employment: 13.6% management, business, and financial, 9.4% computer, engineering, and science, 6.2% education, legal, community service, arts, and media, 8.6% healthcare practitioners, 16.2% service, 25.0% sales and office, 12.5% natural resources, construction, and maintenance, 8.6% production, transportation, and material moving
Income: Per capita: $25,746; Median household: $78,235; Average household: $77,428; Households with income of $100,000 or more: 23.2%; Poverty rate: 5.9%
Educational Attainment: High school diploma or higher: 92.7%; Bachelor's degree or higher: 18.5%; Graduate/professional degree or higher: 6.4%
Housing: Homeownership rate: 74.6%; Median home value: $237,500; Median year structure built: 1970; Homeowner vacancy rate: 0.0%; Median selected monthly owner costs: $1,900 with a mortgage, $715 without a mortgage; Median gross rent: $542 per month; Rental vacancy rate: 0.0%
Health Insurance: 91.8% have insurance; 70.7% have private insurance; 24.4% have public insurance; 8.2% do not have insurance; 8.1% of children under 18 do not have insurance
Transportation: Commute: 81.7% car, 0.0% public transportation, 1.4% walk, 13.7% work from home; Mean travel time to work: 36.1 minutes

NORTH BROOKFIELD (unincorporated postal area)
ZCTA: 13418

Covers a land area of 5.216 square miles and a water area of <.001 square miles. Located at 42.85° N. Lat; 75.38° W. Long. Elevation is 1,299 feet.
Population: 301; Growth (since 2000): -7.4%; Density: 57.7 persons per square mile; Race: 98.3% White, 0.0% Black/African American, 0.0% Asian, 0.0% American Indian/Alaska Native, 0.0% Native Hawaiian/Other Pacific Islander, 0.0% Two or more races, 0.0% Hispanic of any race; Average household size: 3.01; Median age: 41.4; Age under 18: 32.2%; Age 65 and over: 11.0%; Males per 100 females: 109.0; Marriage status: 42.9% never married, 42.5% now married, 0.0% separated, 6.1% widowed, 8.5% divorced; Foreign born: 0.0%; Speak English only: 100.0%; With disability: 6.6%; Veterans: 13.7%; Ancestry: 42.5% American, 15.3% German, 11.6% English, 8.0% European, 5.0% Italian
Employment: 17.4% management, business, and financial, 3.6% computer, engineering, and science, 0.0% education, legal, community service, arts, and media, 8.7% healthcare practitioners, 13.8% service, 15.9% sales and office, 14.5% natural resources, construction, and maintenance, 26.1% production, transportation, and material moving
Income: Per capita: $24,257; Median household: $58,750; Average household: $70,714; Households with income of $100,000 or more: 20.0%; Poverty rate: 12.6%
Educational Attainment: High school diploma or higher: 91.6%; Bachelor's degree or higher: 12.1%; Graduate/professional degree or higher: 3.2%
Housing: Homeownership rate: 80.0%; Median home value: $77,500; Median year structure built: 1971; Homeowner vacancy rate: 0.0%;

Median selected monthly owner costs: $960 with a mortgage, $491 without a mortgage; Median gross rent: n/a per month; Rental vacancy rate: 0.0%
Health Insurance: 99.0% have insurance; 58.1% have private insurance; 49.8% have public insurance; 1.0% do not have insurance; 0.0% of children under 18 do not have insurance
Transportation: Commute: 100.0% car, 0.0% public transportation, 0.0% walk, 0.0% work from home; Mean travel time to work: 20.8 minutes

ONEIDA (city). Covers a land area of 22.047 square miles and a water area of 0.082 square miles. Located at 43.07° N. Lat; 75.67° W. Long. Elevation is 430 feet.
History: The establishment and early growth of Oneida resulted from a shrewd bargain made by Sands Higinbotham, owner of the city site, with the railroad. The railroad received free right of way across his land, plus ample ground for a station, on the condition that it stop every passenger train at the depot for ten minutes for refreshments. Higinbotham then built the Railroad House to serve meals to passengers.
Population: 11,120; Growth (since 2000): 1.2%; Density: 504.4 persons per square mile; Race: 94.9% White, 1.7% Black/African American, 0.4% Asian, 2.3% American Indian/Alaska Native, 0.4% Native Hawaiian/Other Pacific Islander, 0.3% Two or more races, 3.3% Hispanic of any race; Average household size: 2.37; Median age: 41.8; Age under 18: 21.5%; Age 65 and over: 14.6%; Males per 100 females: 93.7; Marriage status: 34.3% never married, 45.3% now married, 2.9% separated, 5.2% widowed, 15.2% divorced; Foreign born: 3.6%; Speak English only: 95.2%; With disability: 13.1%; Veterans: 10.7%; Ancestry: 28.6% American, 16.8% Irish, 14.5% German, 11.2% English, 8.9% Italian
Employment: 9.7% management, business, and financial, 1.8% computer, engineering, and science, 13.4% education, legal, community service, arts, and media, 5.3% healthcare practitioners, 27.2% service, 22.9% sales and office, 7.4% natural resources, construction, and maintenance, 12.3% production, transportation, and material moving
Income: Per capita: $25,362; Median household: $44,388; Average household: $58,701; Households with income of $100,000 or more: 18.1%; Poverty rate: 19.0%
Educational Attainment: High school diploma or higher: 89.4%; Bachelor's degree or higher: 20.6%; Graduate/professional degree or higher: 6.6%

School District(s)
Oneida City SD (PK-12)
    Enrollment: 2,139 . . . . (315) 363-2550
Housing: Homeownership rate: 56.7%; Median home value: $110,000; Median year structure built: Before 1940; Homeowner vacancy rate: 2.7%; Median selected monthly owner costs: $1,188 with a mortgage, $488 without a mortgage; Median gross rent: $689 per month; Rental vacancy rate: 4.3%
Health Insurance: 95.8% have insurance; 63.9% have private insurance; 46.2% have public insurance; 4.2% do not have insurance; 2.7% of children under 18 do not have insurance
Hospitals: Oneida Healthcare Center (101 beds)
Safety: Violent crime rate: 22.7 per 10,000 population; Property crime rate: 344.6 per 10,000 population
Newspapers: Indian Country Today (weekly circulation 125,000); Oneida Daily Dispatch (daily circulation 6,600); Rome Observer (weekly circulation 11,000)
Transportation: Commute: 91.1% car, 1.5% public transportation, 2.2% walk, 1.6% work from home; Mean travel time to work: 19.8 minutes
Additional Information Contacts
City of Oneida . . . . (315) 363-7378
    http://www.oneidacity.com

PETERBORO (unincorporated postal area)
ZCTA: 13134

Covers a land area of 0.083 square miles and a water area of 0 square miles. Located at 42.97° N. Lat; 75.68° W. Long. Elevation is 1,296 feet.
Population: 181; Growth (since 2000): n/a; Density: 2,192.7 persons per square mile; Race: 92.3% White, 0.0% Black/African American, 0.0% Asian, 0.0% American Indian/Alaska Native, 0.0% Native Hawaiian/Other Pacific Islander, 7.7% Two or more races, 0.0% Hispanic of any race; Average household size: 3.23; Median age: 33.8; Age under 18: 19.9%; Age 65 and over: 5.0%; Males per 100 females: 70.0; Marriage status: 40.7% never married, 46.9% now married, 0.0% separated, 6.2% widowed, 6.2% divorced; Foreign born: 0.0%; Speak

English only: 98.7%; With disability: 7.7%; Veterans: 7.6%; Ancestry: 53.0% American, 11.6% German, 4.4% French, 4.4% Scotch-Irish, 1.7% English
Employment: 4.4% management, business, and financial, 3.3% computer, engineering, and science, 0.0% education, legal, community service, arts, and media, 0.0% healthcare practitioners, 21.1% service, 7.8% sales and office, 5.6% natural resources, construction, and maintenance, 57.8% production, transportation, and material moving
Income: Per capita: $22,621; Median household: $73,929; Average household: $71,564; Households with income of $100,000 or more: 44.6%; Poverty rate: 13.3%
Educational Attainment: High school diploma or higher: 61.5%; Bachelor's degree or higher: 15.6%; Graduate/professional degree or higher: 2.5%
Housing: Homeownership rate: 73.2%; Median home value: $83,800; Median year structure built: Before 1940; Homeowner vacancy rate: 0.0%; Median selected monthly owner costs: $1,832 with a mortgage, $0 without a mortgage; Median gross rent: $642 per month; Rental vacancy rate: 0.0%
Health Insurance: 100.0% have insurance; 60.8% have private insurance; 40.3% have public insurance; 0.0% do not have insurance; 0.0% of children under 18 do not have insurance
Transportation: Commute: 91.9% car, 0.0% public transportation, 0.0% walk, 4.1% work from home; Mean travel time to work: 32.1 minutes

SMITHFIELD (town).
Covers a land area of 24.274 square miles and a water area of 0.086 square miles. Located at 42.96° N. Lat; 75.66° W. Long.
Population: 1,513; Growth (since 2000): 25.6%; Density: 62.3 persons per square mile; Race: 91.7% White, 2.8% Black/African American, 0.0% Asian, 0.0% American Indian/Alaska Native, 0.0% Native Hawaiian/Other Pacific Islander, 5.6% Two or more races, 1.5% Hispanic of any race; Average household size: 3.13; Median age: 40.5; Age under 18: 21.2%; Age 65 and over: 13.0%; Males per 100 females: 101.6; Marriage status: 27.6% never married, 57.9% now married, 1.8% separated, 3.4% widowed, 11.1% divorced; Foreign born: 1.2%; Speak English only: 93.4%; With disability: 10.5%; Veterans: 4.8%; Ancestry: 36.0% American, 16.4% German, 8.9% English, 7.5% Irish, 3.9% Polish
Employment: 15.4% management, business, and financial, 2.2% computer, engineering, and science, 5.8% education, legal, community service, arts, and media, 4.9% healthcare practitioners, 15.1% service, 19.6% sales and office, 16.4% natural resources, construction, and maintenance, 20.6% production, transportation, and material moving
Income: Per capita: $26,702; Median household: $65,625; Average household: $77,927; Households with income of $100,000 or more: 26.5%; Poverty rate: 6.4%
Educational Attainment: High school diploma or higher: 86.2%; Bachelor's degree or higher: 13.1%; Graduate/professional degree or higher: 5.9%
Housing: Homeownership rate: 91.3%; Median home value: $110,800; Median year structure built: 1975; Homeowner vacancy rate: 0.0%; Median selected monthly owner costs: $1,464 with a mortgage, $466 without a mortgage; Median gross rent: $817 per month; Rental vacancy rate: 0.0%
Health Insurance: 88.5% have insurance; 66.6% have private insurance; 32.2% have public insurance; 11.5% do not have insurance; 16.0% of children under 18 do not have insurance
Transportation: Commute: 85.5% car, 0.8% public transportation, 2.8% walk, 8.9% work from home; Mean travel time to work: 25.6 minutes

STOCKBRIDGE (town).
Covers a land area of 31.655 square miles and a water area of 0 square miles. Located at 42.99° N. Lat; 75.59° W. Long. Elevation is 669 feet.
Population: 2,230; Growth (since 2000): 7.2%; Density: 70.4 persons per square mile; Race: 94.5% White, 0.0% Black/African American, 0.1% Asian, 0.9% American Indian/Alaska Native, 0.0% Native Hawaiian/Other Pacific Islander, 3.7% Two or more races, 2.6% Hispanic of any race; Average household size: 2.72; Median age: 40.1; Age under 18: 21.4%; Age 65 and over: 15.1%; Males per 100 females: 102.8; Marriage status: 30.7% never married, 54.9% now married, 2.8% separated, 4.2% widowed, 10.2% divorced; Foreign born: 0.1%; Speak English only: 98.2%; With disability: 10.8%; Veterans: 9.4%; Ancestry: 36.5% American, 13.9% German, 10.8% Irish, 8.4% Italian, 8.3% English
Employment: 8.5% management, business, and financial, 4.7% computer, engineering, and science, 5.9% education, legal, community service, arts, and media, 5.6% healthcare practitioners, 16.7% service, 19.9% sales and

office, 16.3% natural resources, construction, and maintenance, 22.5% production, transportation, and material moving
Income: Per capita: $23,686; Median household: $52,778; Average household: $61,151; Households with income of $100,000 or more: 17.8%; Poverty rate: 10.2%
Educational Attainment: High school diploma or higher: 91.9%; Bachelor's degree or higher: 12.7%; Graduate/professional degree or higher: 4.6%
Housing: Homeownership rate: 79.9%; Median home value: $91,800; Median year structure built: 1970; Homeowner vacancy rate: 0.0%; Median selected monthly owner costs: $1,153 with a mortgage, $463 without a mortgage; Median gross rent: $800 per month; Rental vacancy rate: 0.6%
Health Insurance: 96.4% have insurance; 71.5% have private insurance; 33.2% have public insurance; 3.6% do not have insurance; 0.8% of children under 18 do not have insurance
Transportation: Commute: 96.3% car, 0.0% public transportation, 2.2% walk, 0.8% work from home; Mean travel time to work: 22.5 minutes

SULLIVAN (town).
Covers a land area of 73.163 square miles and a water area of 0.199 square miles. Located at 43.09° N. Lat; 75.88° W. Long. Elevation is 456 feet.
Population: 15,283; Growth (since 2000): 1.9%; Density: 208.9 persons per square mile; Race: 98.2% White, 0.5% Black/African American, 0.2% Asian, 0.2% American Indian/Alaska Native, 0.0% Native Hawaiian/Other Pacific Islander, 0.4% Two or more races, 1.3% Hispanic of any race; Average household size: 2.65; Median age: 44.9; Age under 18: 20.9%; Age 65 and over: 16.7%; Males per 100 females: 96.8; Marriage status: 27.8% never married, 53.1% now married, 2.0% separated, 5.9% widowed, 13.2% divorced; Foreign born: 1.5%; Speak English only: 98.0%; With disability: 11.6%; Veterans: 10.5%; Ancestry: 24.6% American, 19.3% Irish, 18.0% German, 13.5% English, 9.4% Italian
Employment: 15.3% management, business, and financial, 6.7% computer, engineering, and science, 9.1% education, legal, community service, arts, and media, 5.5% healthcare practitioners, 15.0% service, 26.5% sales and office, 9.2% natural resources, construction, and maintenance, 12.7% production, transportation, and material moving
Income: Per capita: $31,489; Median household: $69,503; Average household: $79,677; Households with income of $100,000 or more: 29.3%; Poverty rate: 8.8%
Educational Attainment: High school diploma or higher: 90.9%; Bachelor's degree or higher: 27.0%; Graduate/professional degree or higher: 11.0%
Housing: Homeownership rate: 84.1%; Median home value: $143,000; Median year structure built: 1970; Homeowner vacancy rate: 5.2%; Median selected monthly owner costs: $1,292 with a mortgage, $542 without a mortgage; Median gross rent: $757 per month; Rental vacancy rate: 2.8%
Health Insurance: 95.1% have insurance; 75.7% have private insurance; 33.0% have public insurance; 4.9% do not have insurance; 1.0% of children under 18 do not have insurance
Transportation: Commute: 93.1% car, 0.0% public transportation, 1.7% walk, 4.7% work from home; Mean travel time to work: 25.3 minutes
Additional Information Contacts
Town of Sullivan . . . . (315) 687-7221
  http://townofsullivan.org/content

WAMPSVILLE (village).
County seat. Covers a land area of 1.009 square miles and a water area of 0.007 square miles. Located at 43.08° N. Lat; 75.71° W. Long. Elevation is 482 feet.
Population: 541; Growth (since 2000): -3.6%; Density: 536.3 persons per square mile; Race: 99.3% White, 0.0% Black/African American, 0.0% Asian, 0.7% American Indian/Alaska Native, 0.0% Native Hawaiian/Other Pacific Islander, 0.0% Two or more races, 0.0% Hispanic of any race; Average household size: 2.52; Median age: 41.8; Age under 18: 17.0%; Age 65 and over: 17.6%; Males per 100 females: 93.9; Marriage status: 39.3% never married, 42.4% now married, 2.1% separated, 9.1% widowed, 9.3% divorced; Foreign born: 0.4%; Speak English only: 100.0%; With disability: 10.9%; Veterans: 11.4%; Ancestry: 53.8% American, 13.7% English, 10.4% German, 9.4% Irish, 5.0% Italian
Employment: 14.3% management, business, and financial, 5.8% computer, engineering, and science, 8.5% education, legal, community service, arts, and media, 3.5% healthcare practitioners, 28.6% service, 20.5% sales and office, 11.6% natural resources, construction, and maintenance, 7.3% production, transportation, and material moving

Income: Per capita: $25,003; Median household: $42,344; Average household: $59,726; Households with income of $100,000 or more: 19.6%; Poverty rate: 20.5%

Educational Attainment: High school diploma or higher: 92.6%; Bachelor's degree or higher: 20.6%; Graduate/professional degree or higher: 9.2%

School District(s)

Oneida City SD (PK-12)

   Enrollment: 2,139 . . . . (315) 363-2550

Housing: Homeownership rate: 88.4%; Median home value: $137,500; Median year structure built: 1956; Homeowner vacancy rate: 7.3%; Median selected monthly owner costs: $1,065 with a mortgage, $539 without a mortgage; Median gross rent: $775 per month; Rental vacancy rate: 0.0%

Health Insurance: 96.9% have insurance; 71.3% have private insurance; 37.5% have public insurance; 3.1% do not have insurance; 3.8% of children under 18 do not have insurance

Transportation: Commute: 93.6% car, 0.0% public transportation, 4.8% walk, 1.6% work from home; Mean travel time to work: 19.3 minutes

WEST EATON (unincorporated postal area)

ZCTA: 13484

Covers a land area of 2.550 square miles and a water area of 0 square miles. Located at 42.87° N. Lat; 75.66° W. Long. Elevation is 1,358 feet.

Population: 187; Growth (since 2000): n/a; Density: 73.3 persons per square mile; Race: 100.0% White, 0.0% Black/African American, 0.0% Asian, 0.0% American Indian/Alaska Native, 0.0% Native Hawaiian/Other Pacific Islander, 0.0% Two or more races, 0.0% Hispanic of any race; Average household size: 3.22; Median age: 42.1; Age under 18: 46.5%; Age 65 and over: 0.0%; Males per 100 females: 102.3; Marriage status: 29.6% never married, 61.3% now married, 0.0% separated, 0.0% widowed, 9.2% divorced; Foreign born: 0.0%; Speak English only: 100.0%; With disability: 0.0%; Veterans: 0.0%; Ancestry: 93.0% American

Employment: 0.0% management, business, and financial, 45.0% computer, engineering, and science, 0.0% education, legal, community service, arts, and media, 13.0% healthcare practitioners, 42.0% service, 0.0% sales and office, 0.0% natural resources, construction, and maintenance, 0.0% production, transportation, and material moving

Income: Per capita: $26,406; Median household: n/a; Average household: n/a; Households with income of $100,000 or more: n/a; Poverty rate: n/a

Educational Attainment: High school diploma or higher: 100.0%; Bachelor's degree or higher: 13.0%; Graduate/professional degree or higher: n/a

Housing: Homeownership rate: 100.0%; Median home value: n/a; Median year structure built: Before 1940; Homeowner vacancy rate: 0.0%; Median selected monthly owner costs: $0 with a mortgage, $0 without a mortgage; Median gross rent: n/a per month; Rental vacancy rate: 0.0%

Health Insurance: 100.0% have insurance; 100.0% have private insurance; 0.0% have public insurance; 0.0% do not have insurance; 0.0% of children under 18 do not have insurance

Transportation: Commute: 58.0% car, 0.0% public transportation, 0.0% walk, 42.0% work from home; Mean travel time to work: 0.0 minutes

WEST EDMESTON (unincorporated postal area)

ZCTA: 13485

Covers a land area of 44.170 square miles and a water area of 0.160 square miles. Located at 42.79° N. Lat; 75.32° W. Long..

Population: 1,014; Growth (since 2000): 7.3%; Density: 23.0 persons per square mile; Race: 98.2% White, 0.5% Black/African American, 0.0% Asian, 0.0% American Indian/Alaska Native, 0.0% Native Hawaiian/Other Pacific Islander, 1.3% Two or more races, 0.4% Hispanic of any race; Average household size: 2.30; Median age: 48.2; Age under 18: 18.1%; Age 65 and over: 23.1%; Males per 100 females: 101.4; Marriage status: 21.2% never married, 62.7% now married, 3.5% separated, 5.5% widowed, 10.5% divorced; Foreign born: 1.3%; Speak English only: 97.6%; With disability: 17.9%; Veterans: 12.0%; Ancestry: 18.6% German, 14.4% English, 13.2% American, 9.0% Italian, 7.5% Irish

Employment: 13.4% management, business, and financial, 3.4% computer, engineering, and science, 10.0% education, legal, community service, arts, and media, 5.0% healthcare practitioners, 17.5% service, 25.1% sales and office, 11.2% natural resources, construction, and maintenance, 14.4% production, transportation, and material moving

Income: Per capita: $23,199; Median household: $39,792; Average household: $52,882; Households with income of $100,000 or more: 12.0%; Poverty rate: 15.6%

Educational Attainment: High school diploma or higher: 86.5%; Bachelor's degree or higher: 11.2%; Graduate/professional degree or higher: 5.1%

Housing: Homeownership rate: 87.1%; Median home value: $89,000; Median year structure built: 1979; Homeowner vacancy rate: 0.8%; Median selected monthly owner costs: $1,096 with a mortgage, $371 without a mortgage; Median gross rent: $740 per month; Rental vacancy rate: 0.0%

Health Insurance: 89.0% have insurance; 67.0% have private insurance; 37.9% have public insurance; 11.0% do not have insurance; 14.7% of children under 18 do not have insurance

Transportation: Commute: 91.0% car, 0.0% public transportation, 2.1% walk, 6.2% work from home; Mean travel time to work: 28.2 minutes

Manhattan Borough

See New York City

Monroe County

Located in western New York; bounded on the north by Lake Ontario; drained by the Genesee River. Covers a land area of 657.205 square miles, a water area of 709.524 square miles, and is located in the Eastern Time Zone at 43.46° N. Lat., 77.66° W. Long. The county was founded in 1821. County seat is Rochester.

Monroe County is part of the Rochester, NY Metropolitan Statistical Area. The entire metro area includes: Livingston County, NY; Monroe County, NY; Ontario County, NY; Orleans County, NY; Wayne County, NY; Yates County, NY

Weather Station: Rochester Intl Arpt   Elevation: 600 feet

	Jan	Feb	Mar	Apr	May	Jun	Jul	Aug	Sep	Oct	Nov	Dec
High	32	34	43	56	68	77	81	79	72	60	48	37
Low	18	19	26	37	47	56	61	60	52	42	33	23
Precip	2.4	1.9	2.6	2.8	2.8	3.4	3.2	3.5	3.4	2.7	2.9	2.6
Snow	27.0	21.3	17.0	3.9	0.4	tr	tr	0.0	tr	0.1	7.6	22.1

High and Low temperatures in degrees Fahrenheit; Precipitation and Snow in inches

Population: 748,680; Growth (since 2000): 1.8%; Density: 1,139.2 persons per square mile; Race: 75.9% White, 15.3% Black/African American, 3.7% Asian, 0.4% American Indian/Alaska Native, 0.0% Native Hawaiian/Other Pacific Islander, 2.9% two or more races, 8.3% Hispanic of any race; Average household size: 2.40; Median age: 38.6; Age under 18: 21.3%; Age 65 and over: 15.9%; Males per 100 females: 93.2; Marriage status: 37.5% never married, 46.2% now married, 2.2% separated, 6.0% widowed, 10.3% divorced; Foreign born: 8.5%; Speak English only: 86.6%; With disability: 13.3%; Veterans: 6.3%; Ancestry: 18.5% German, 17.6% Italian, 14.6% Irish, 10.0% English, 5.0% Polish

Religion: Six largest groups: 25.7% Catholicism, 4.8% Non-denominational Protestant, 2.8% Baptist, 2.3% Methodist/Pietist, 2.1% Lutheran, 2.0% Presbyterian-Reformed

Economy: Unemployment rate: 3.8%; Leading industries: 13.3 % retail trade; 11.4 % professional, scientific, and technical services; 10.9 % health care and social assistance; Farms: 475 totaling 98,676 acres; Company size: 25 employ 1,000 or more persons, 37 employ 500 to 999 persons, 452 employ 100 to 499 persons, 17,230 employ less than 100 persons; Business ownership: 20,290 women-owned, 5,333 Black-owned, 2,216 Hispanic-owned, 2,420 Asian-owned, 354 American Indian/Alaska Native-owned

Employment: 14.8% management, business, and financial, 7.3% computer, engineering, and science, 13.3% education, legal, community service, arts, and media, 7.4% healthcare practitioners, 17.6% service, 23.7% sales and office, 5.7% natural resources, construction, and maintenance, 10.2% production, transportation, and material moving

Income: Per capita: $31,291; Median household: $55,272; Average household: $75,077; Households with income of $100,000 or more: 24.2%; Poverty rate: 14.8%

Educational Attainment: High school diploma or higher: 90.3%; Bachelor's degree or higher: 37.1%; Graduate/professional degree or higher: 16.4%

Housing: Homeownership rate: 63.8%; Median home value: $142,300; Median year structure built: 1963; Homeowner vacancy rate: 1.0%; Median selected monthly owner costs: $1,380 with a mortgage, $596 without a mortgage; Median gross rent: $872 per month; Rental vacancy rate: 6.6%
Vital Statistics: Birth rate: 107.9 per 10,000 population; Death rate: 89.0 per 10,000 population; Age-adjusted cancer mortality rate: 160.5 deaths per 100,000 population
Health Insurance: 95.5% have insurance; 72.6% have private insurance; 36.9% have public insurance; 4.5% do not have insurance; 2.2% of children under 18 do not have insurance
Health Care: Physicians: 50.8 per 10,000 population; Dentists: 8.1 per 10,000 population; Hospital beds: 30.5 per 10,000 population; Hospital admissions: 1,351.8 per 10,000 population
Air Quality Index (AQI): Percent of Days: 85.8% good, 13.4% moderate, 0.8% unhealthy for sensitive individuals, 0.0% unhealthy, 0.0% very unhealthy; Annual median: 37; Annual maximum: 112
Transportation: Commute: 88.5% car, 3.1% public transportation, 3.2% walk, 3.8% work from home; Mean travel time to work: 20.1 minutes
2016 Presidential Election: 39.3% Trump, 54.2% Clinton, 3.8% Johnson, 1.5% Stein
National and State Parks: Hamlin Beach State Park
Additional Information Contacts
Monroe Government . . . . (585) 428-5301
  http://www.monroecounty.gov

Monroe County Communities

BRIGHTON (CDP). Covers a land area of 15.416 square miles and a water area of 0.168 square miles. Located at 43.12° N. Lat; 77.58° W. Long. Elevation is 446 feet.
Population: 36,753; Growth (since 2000): 3.3%; Density: 2,384.1 persons per square mile; Race: 79.3% White, 6.4% Black/African American, 10.8% Asian, 0.3% American Indian/Alaska Native, 0.0% Native Hawaiian/Other Pacific Islander, 2.5% Two or more races, 4.1% Hispanic of any race; Average household size: 2.18; Median age: 39.7; Age under 18: 17.6%; Age 65 and over: 19.8%; Males per 100 females: 89.3; Marriage status: 35.9% never married, 47.6% now married, 1.3% separated, 7.3% widowed, 9.2% divorced; Foreign born: 17.0%; Speak English only: 81.3%; With disability: 11.1%; Veterans: 5.8%; Ancestry: 17.8% German, 14.1% Irish, 12.4% Italian, 11.0% English, 5.3% Polish
Employment: 17.2% management, business, and financial, 12.4% computer, engineering, and science, 23.5% education, legal, community service, arts, and media, 10.6% healthcare practitioners, 11.2% service, 17.0% sales and office, 2.7% natural resources, construction, and maintenance, 5.4% production, transportation, and material moving
Income: Per capita: $43,174; Median household: $70,567; Average household: $97,641; Households with income of $100,000 or more: 33.9%; Poverty rate: 10.8%
Educational Attainment: High school diploma or higher: 95.9%; Bachelor's degree or higher: 65.3%; Graduate/professional degree or higher: 37.0%
Housing: Homeownership rate: 57.1%; Median home value: $171,800; Median year structure built: 1961; Homeowner vacancy rate: 0.8%; Median selected monthly owner costs: $1,680 with a mortgage, $751 without a mortgage; Median gross rent: $982 per month; Rental vacancy rate: 6.0%
Health Insurance: 96.2% have insurance; 83.4% have private insurance; 26.5% have public insurance; 3.8% do not have insurance; 2.9% of children under 18 do not have insurance
Safety: Violent crime rate: 7.7 per 10,000 population; Property crime rate: 213.4 per 10,000 population
Transportation: Commute: 87.3% car, 3.3% public transportation, 2.6% walk, 4.9% work from home; Mean travel time to work: 16.6 minutes
Additional Information Contacts
Town of Brighton . . . . (585) 784-5250
  http://www.townofbrighton.org

BROCKPORT (village). Covers a land area of 2.161 square miles and a water area of 0.047 square miles. Located at 43.21° N. Lat; 77.94° W. Long. Elevation is 518 feet.
History: Seat of State University of N.Y. College at Brockport. Incorporated 1829.
Population: 8,415; Growth (since 2000): 3.9%; Density: 3,893.2 persons per square mile; Race: 88.9% White, 4.1% Black/African American, 3.3% Asian, 0.1% American Indian/Alaska Native, 0.0% Native Hawaiian/Other Pacific Islander, 3.2% Two or more races, 5.0% Hispanic of any race;

Average household size: 2.36; Median age: 22.0; Age under 18: 12.5%; Age 65 and over: 11.6%; Males per 100 females: 88.3; Marriage status: 67.1% never married, 20.9% now married, 1.6% separated, 4.8% widowed, 7.3% divorced; Foreign born: 4.2%; Speak English only: 91.2%; With disability: 13.7%; Veterans: 4.5%; Ancestry: 19.5% German, 19.0% Irish, 17.8% Italian, 10.8% English, 6.8% Polish
Employment: 9.3% management, business, and financial, 4.2% computer, engineering, and science, 15.6% education, legal, community service, arts, and media, 2.7% healthcare practitioners, 23.8% service, 32.2% sales and office, 5.0% natural resources, construction, and maintenance, 7.2% production, transportation, and material moving
Income: Per capita: $17,340; Median household: $41,359; Average household: $51,692; Households with income of $100,000 or more: 13.1%; Poverty rate: 28.0%
Educational Attainment: High school diploma or higher: 90.6%; Bachelor's degree or higher: 37.5%; Graduate/professional degree or higher: 17.4%
School District(s)
Brockport Central SD (PK-12)
  Enrollment: 3,464 . . . . (585) 637-1810
Four-year College(s)
SUNY College at Brockport (Public)
  Enrollment: 8,313 . . . . (585) 395-2361
  Tuition: In-state $8,154; Out-of-state $17,804
Housing: Homeownership rate: 40.1%; Median home value: $115,400; Median year structure built: 1956; Homeowner vacancy rate: 0.0%; Median selected monthly owner costs: $1,251 with a mortgage, $618 without a mortgage; Median gross rent: $788 per month; Rental vacancy rate: 6.0%
Health Insurance: 94.3% have insurance; 77.0% have private insurance; 29.9% have public insurance; 5.7% do not have insurance; 3.0% of children under 18 do not have insurance
Safety: Violent crime rate: 24.1 per 10,000 population; Property crime rate: 103.5 per 10,000 population
Transportation: Commute: 64.9% car, 3.3% public transportation, 26.6% walk, 2.9% work from home; Mean travel time to work: 19.0 minutes
Additional Information Contacts
Village of Brockport . . . . (585) 637-5300
  http://brockportny.org

CHILI (town). Covers a land area of 39.499 square miles and a water area of 0.369 square miles. Located at 43.09° N. Lat; 77.75° W. Long.
History: The Town of Chili was established in 1822, once the hunting ground of the Seneca Indians. The first white settler was Captain Joseph Morgan who purchased land from Peter Sheffer of neighboring Wheatland. North Chili was a stop on the Underground Railroad.
Population: 28,742; Growth (since 2000): 4.0%; Density: 727.7 persons per square mile; Race: 84.9% White, 10.2% Black/African American, 1.5% Asian, 0.2% American Indian/Alaska Native, 0.0% Native Hawaiian/Other Pacific Islander, 2.6% Two or more races, 3.6% Hispanic of any race; Average household size: 2.57; Median age: 40.1; Age under 18: 20.8%; Age 65 and over: 15.0%; Males per 100 females: 93.5; Marriage status: 32.1% never married, 53.7% now married, 1.4% separated, 4.4% widowed, 9.8% divorced; Foreign born: 7.4%; Speak English only: 91.3%; With disability: 10.5%; Veterans: 6.1%; Ancestry: 25.8% German, 22.5% Italian, 17.9% Irish, 11.7% English, 7.1% Polish
Employment: 18.1% management, business, and financial, 9.1% computer, engineering, and science, 10.8% education, legal, community service, arts, and media, 7.9% healthcare practitioners, 13.3% service, 23.6% sales and office, 6.5% natural resources, construction, and maintenance, 10.8% production, transportation, and material moving
Income: Per capita: $32,803; Median household: $67,957; Average household: $83,434; Households with income of $100,000 or more: 29.3%; Poverty rate: 6.7%
Educational Attainment: High school diploma or higher: 94.8%; Bachelor's degree or higher: 37.4%; Graduate/professional degree or higher: 15.8%
Housing: Homeownership rate: 77.5%; Median home value: $142,000; Median year structure built: 1976; Homeowner vacancy rate: 0.5%; Median selected monthly owner costs: $1,408 with a mortgage, $558 without a mortgage; Median gross rent: $1,041 per month; Rental vacancy rate: 3.0%
Health Insurance: 96.0% have insurance; 82.0% have private insurance; 28.5% have public insurance; 4.0% do not have insurance; 2.5% of children under 18 do not have insurance

Transportation: Commute: 93.7% car, 0.1% public transportation, 1.6% walk, 3.9% work from home; Mean travel time to work: 19.5 minutes
Additional Information Contacts
Town of Chili . . . . (585) 889-3550
http://www.townofchili.org

CHURCHVILLE (village). Covers a land area of 1.153 square miles and a water area of 0.018 square miles. Located at 43.10° N. Lat; 77.88° W. Long. Elevation is 584 feet.
History: Frances E. Willard born here.
Population: 2,168; Growth (since 2000): 14.9%; Density: 1,879.8 persons per square mile; Race: 97.9% White, 0.2% Black/African American, 0.0% Asian, 0.0% American Indian/Alaska Native, 0.0% Native Hawaiian/Other Pacific Islander, 1.9% Two or more races, 4.0% Hispanic of any race; Average household size: 2.42; Median age: 43.3; Age under 18: 22.3%; Age 65 and over: 17.3%; Males per 100 females: 85.5; Marriage status: 26.3% never married, 54.8% now married, 2.8% separated, 6.5% widowed, 12.5% divorced; Foreign born: 0.8%; Speak English only: 96.8%; With disability: 13.5%; Veterans: 8.5%; Ancestry: 32.6% German, 24.6% Irish, 18.5% English, 16.9% Italian, 8.1% Scottish
Employment: 15.3% management, business, and financial, 5.7% computer, engineering, and science, 11.8% education, legal, community service, arts, and media, 4.1% healthcare practitioners, 22.1% service, 23.4% sales and office, 7.2% natural resources, construction, and maintenance, 10.4% production, transportation, and material moving
Income: Per capita: $28,947; Median household: $60,500; Average household: $69,707; Households with income of $100,000 or more: 20.0%; Poverty rate: 7.2%
Educational Attainment: High school diploma or higher: 96.7%; Bachelor's degree or higher: 37.7%; Graduate/professional degree or higher: 14.6%
School District(s)
Churchville-Chili Central SD (KG-12)
    Enrollment: 3,891 . . . . (585) 293-1800
Housing: Homeownership rate: 74.8%; Median home value: $132,000; Median year structure built: 1975; Homeowner vacancy rate: 0.4%; Median selected monthly owner costs: $1,294 with a mortgage, $530 without a mortgage; Median gross rent: $1,030 per month; Rental vacancy rate: 6.1%
Health Insurance: 97.5% have insurance; 83.5% have private insurance; 29.5% have public insurance; 2.5% do not have insurance; 0.0% of children under 18 do not have insurance
Transportation: Commute: 97.7% car, 0.0% public transportation, 1.0% walk, 1.3% work from home; Mean travel time to work: 22.9 minutes
Additional Information Contacts
Village of Churchville . . . . (585) 293-3720
http://www.churchville.net

CLARKSON (CDP). Covers a land area of 9.111 square miles and a water area of 0 square miles. Located at 43.24° N. Lat; 77.92° W. Long. Elevation is 427 feet.
Population: 4,355; Growth (since 2000): n/a; Density: 478.0 persons per square mile; Race: 96.5% White, 0.0% Black/African American, 0.4% Asian, 0.0% American Indian/Alaska Native, 0.0% Native Hawaiian/Other Pacific Islander, 2.3% Two or more races, 5.8% Hispanic of any race; Average household size: 2.53; Median age: 42.3; Age under 18: 29.0%; Age 65 and over: 13.8%; Males per 100 females: 93.2; Marriage status: 26.3% never married, 54.6% now married, 1.4% separated, 8.6% widowed, 10.5% divorced; Foreign born: 2.0%; Speak English only: 92.4%; With disability: 13.9%; Veterans: 8.9%; Ancestry: 27.4% German, 24.7% English, 21.8% Irish, 21.0% Italian, 11.4% Polish
Employment: 17.2% management, business, and financial, 6.3% computer, engineering, and science, 14.3% education, legal, community service, arts, and media, 9.0% healthcare practitioners, 16.8% service, 22.1% sales and office, 10.1% natural resources, construction, and maintenance, 4.2% production, transportation, and material moving
Income: Per capita: $27,518; Median household: $65,802; Average household: $68,960; Households with income of $100,000 or more: 24.7%; Poverty rate: 8.8%
Educational Attainment: High school diploma or higher: 95.3%; Bachelor's degree or higher: 42.2%; Graduate/professional degree or higher: 15.9%
Housing: Homeownership rate: 76.5%; Median home value: $144,200; Median year structure built: 1979; Homeowner vacancy rate: 0.0%; Median

selected monthly owner costs: $1,339 with a mortgage, $536 without a mortgage; Median gross rent: $775 per month; Rental vacancy rate: 0.0%
Health Insurance: 99.2% have insurance; 76.4% have private insurance; 34.9% have public insurance; 0.8% do not have insurance; 0.0% of children under 18 do not have insurance
Transportation: Commute: 96.5% car, 0.0% public transportation, 0.0% walk, 1.8% work from home; Mean travel time to work: 25.5 minutes

CLARKSON (town). Covers a land area of 33.183 square miles and a water area of 0.005 square miles. Located at 43.25° N. Lat; 77.93° W. Long. Elevation is 427 feet.
Population: 7,019; Growth (since 2000): 15.6%; Density: 211.5 persons per square mile; Race: 93.1% White, 0.3% Black/African American, 0.3% Asian, 0.0% American Indian/Alaska Native, 0.0% Native Hawaiian/Other Pacific Islander, 1.3% Two or more races, 9.3% Hispanic of any race; Average household size: 2.69; Median age: 44.2; Age under 18: 21.1%; Age 65 and over: 15.1%; Males per 100 females: 97.2; Marriage status: 29.6% never married, 53.5% now married, 0.8% separated, 8.5% widowed, 8.4% divorced; Foreign born: 6.5%; Speak English only: 90.2%; With disability: 12.1%; Veterans: 6.7%; Ancestry: 31.9% German, 22.8% English, 18.8% Italian, 15.9% Irish, 8.0% Polish
Employment: 14.5% management, business, and financial, 5.4% computer, engineering, and science, 10.5% education, legal, community service, arts, and media, 7.8% healthcare practitioners, 18.2% service, 19.1% sales and office, 16.5% natural resources, construction, and maintenance, 8.0% production, transportation, and material moving
Income: Per capita: $27,761; Median household: $71,576; Average household: $74,157; Households with income of $100,000 or more: 29.2%; Poverty rate: 6.3%
Educational Attainment: High school diploma or higher: 89.3%; Bachelor's degree or higher: 32.4%; Graduate/professional degree or higher: 14.4%
Housing: Homeownership rate: 79.6%; Median home value: $145,500; Median year structure built: 1979; Homeowner vacancy rate: 0.0%; Median selected monthly owner costs: $1,319 with a mortgage, $596 without a mortgage; Median gross rent: $783 per month; Rental vacancy rate: 0.0%
Health Insurance: 93.1% have insurance; 74.0% have private insurance; 30.6% have public insurance; 6.9% do not have insurance; 0.0% of children under 18 do not have insurance
Transportation: Commute: 88.5% car, 8.6% public transportation, 0.4% walk, 1.6% work from home; Mean travel time to work: 23.1 minutes
Additional Information Contacts
Town of Clarkson . . . . (585) 637-1130
http://www.clarksonny.org

EAST ROCHESTER (town/village). Covers a land area of 1.325 square miles and a water area of 0.004 square miles. Located at 43.11° N. Lat; 77.49° W. Long. Elevation is 420 feet.
History: East Rochester was originally known as the Village of Despatch when it was incorporated in 1897. It was designed as a planned community around the New York Central Railroad mainline that ran through the center of the village.
Population: 6,646; Growth (since 2000): -0.1%; Density: 5,017.2 persons per square mile; Race: 85.9% White, 7.8% Black/African American, 0.4% Asian, 0.3% American Indian/Alaska Native, 0.0% Native Hawaiian/Other Pacific Islander, 4.6% Two or more races, 5.1% Hispanic of any race; Average household size: 2.36; Median age: 35.9; Age under 18: 22.7%; Age 65 and over: 13.5%; Males per 100 females: 96.6; Marriage status: 38.2% never married, 39.9% now married, 2.5% separated, 5.6% widowed, 16.3% divorced; Foreign born: 3.9%; Speak English only: 92.1%; With disability: 11.9%; Veterans: 7.9%; Ancestry: 24.0% Italian, 20.0% German, 15.2% Irish, 9.2% English, 6.7% American
Employment: 8.9% management, business, and financial, 5.8% computer, engineering, and science, 11.8% education, legal, community service, arts, and media, 5.9% healthcare practitioners, 25.0% service, 24.5% sales and office, 7.2% natural resources, construction, and maintenance, 11.0% production, transportation, and material moving
Income: Per capita: $25,608; Median household: $49,275; Average household: $59,313; Households with income of $100,000 or more: 16.3%; Poverty rate: 15.0%
Educational Attainment: High school diploma or higher: 93.5%; Bachelor's degree or higher: 31.8%; Graduate/professional degree or higher: 13.5%

School District(s)
East Rochester Union Free SD (PK-12)
  Enrollment: 1,038 . . . . (585) 248-6302
Housing: Homeownership rate: 60.7%; Median home value: $97,300; Median year structure built: 1948; Homeowner vacancy rate: 5.0%; Median selected monthly owner costs: $1,250 with a mortgage, $519 without a mortgage; Median gross rent: $822 per month; Rental vacancy rate: 0.0%
Health Insurance: 92.2% have insurance; 68.0% have private insurance; 35.7% have public insurance; 7.8% do not have insurance; 2.1% of children under 18 do not have insurance
Safety: Violent crime rate: 6.0 per 10,000 population; Property crime rate: 133.1 per 10,000 population
Transportation: Commute: 90.7% car, 0.1% public transportation, 2.8% walk, 3.1% work from home; Mean travel time to work: 16.9 minutes
Additional Information Contacts
Village and Town of East Rochester . . . . (585) 586-3553
  http://eastrochester.org

FAIRPORT (village). Covers a land area of 1.589 square miles and a water area of 0.034 square miles. Located at 43.10° N. Lat; 77.44° W. Long. Elevation is 492 feet.
History: Incorporated 1867.
Population: 5,378; Growth (since 2000): -6.3%; Density: 3,384.9 persons per square mile; Race: 94.7% White, 0.1% Black/African American, 3.4% Asian, 0.0% American Indian/Alaska Native, 0.0% Native Hawaiian/Other Pacific Islander, 1.8% Two or more races, 5.8% Hispanic of any race; Average household size: 2.22; Median age: 46.1; Age under 18: 16.2%; Age 65 and over: 20.0%; Males per 100 females: 93.0; Marriage status: 27.3% never married, 54.9% now married, 2.8% separated, 4.4% widowed, 13.4% divorced; Foreign born: 7.0%; Speak English only: 95.7%; With disability: 9.9%; Veterans: 6.1%; Ancestry: 21.4% Irish, 20.6% German, 16.0% Italian, 15.8% English, 8.2% Polish
Employment: 14.3% management, business, and financial, 8.4% computer, engineering, and science, 16.6% education, legal, community service, arts, and media, 5.7% healthcare practitioners, 17.1% service, 28.9% sales and office, 3.1% natural resources, construction, and maintenance, 5.9% production, transportation, and material moving
Income: Per capita: $40,847; Median household: $72,647; Average household: $89,140; Households with income of $100,000 or more: 31.7%; Poverty rate: 3.1%
Educational Attainment: High school diploma or higher: 95.4%; Bachelor's degree or higher: 48.6%; Graduate/professional degree or higher: 24.8%
School District(s)
Fairport Central SD (KG-12)
  Enrollment: 6,061 . . . . (585) 421-2004
Monroe 1 Boces
  Enrollment: n/a . . . . (585) 383-2200
Housing: Homeownership rate: 73.3%; Median home value: $173,500; Median year structure built: 1950; Homeowner vacancy rate: 0.0%; Median selected monthly owner costs: $1,428 with a mortgage, $766 without a mortgage; Median gross rent: $909 per month; Rental vacancy rate: 6.0%
Health Insurance: 97.5% have insurance; 89.9% have private insurance; 26.0% have public insurance; 2.5% do not have insurance; 0.0% of children under 18 do not have insurance
Safety: Violent crime rate: 5.5 per 10,000 population; Property crime rate: 81.3 per 10,000 population
Transportation: Commute: 87.5% car, 0.5% public transportation, 3.1% walk, 8.1% work from home; Mean travel time to work: 18.7 minutes
Additional Information Contacts
Village of Fairport . . . . (585) 223-0313
  http://www.fairport.ny.us

GATES (CDP). Covers a land area of 1.979 square miles and a water area of 0.012 square miles. Located at 43.15° N. Lat; 77.70° W. Long.
Population: 5,153; Growth (since 2000): n/a; Density: 2,603.8 persons per square mile; Race: 86.4% White, 10.0% Black/African American, 1.5% Asian, 0.0% American Indian/Alaska Native, 0.0% Native Hawaiian/Other Pacific Islander, 2.1% Two or more races, 4.5% Hispanic of any race; Average household size: 2.55; Median age: 42.5; Age under 18: 19.7%; Age 65 and over: 22.7%; Males per 100 females: 90.9; Marriage status: 31.5% never married, 50.9% now married, 1.0% separated, 7.8% widowed, 9.7% divorced; Foreign born: 13.9%; Speak English only: 84.2%; With disability: 12.9%; Veterans: 8.2%; Ancestry: 30.7% Italian, 18.8% German, 9.8% English, 9.2% Irish, 5.1% French

Employment: 9.9% management, business, and financial, 5.5% computer, engineering, and science, 11.1% education, legal, community service, arts, and media, 4.5% healthcare practitioners, 17.6% service, 29.9% sales and office, 13.9% natural resources, construction, and maintenance, 7.6% production, transportation, and material moving
Income: Per capita: $28,217; Median household: $61,237; Average household: $69,361; Households with income of $100,000 or more: 19.1%; Poverty rate: 4.7%
Educational Attainment: High school diploma or higher: 85.8%; Bachelor's degree or higher: 20.6%; Graduate/professional degree or higher: 5.6%
Housing: Homeownership rate: 91.9%; Median home value: $117,800; Median year structure built: 1962; Homeowner vacancy rate: 0.0%; Median selected monthly owner costs: $1,143 with a mortgage, $547 without a mortgage; Median gross rent: $1,143 per month; Rental vacancy rate: 0.0%
Health Insurance: 97.9% have insurance; 86.4% have private insurance; 32.1% have public insurance; 2.1% do not have insurance; 0.0% of children under 18 do not have insurance
Transportation: Commute: 96.8% car, 0.5% public transportation, 0.5% walk, 2.3% work from home; Mean travel time to work: 16.7 minutes

GATES (town). Covers a land area of 15.200 square miles and a water area of 0.082 square miles. Located at 43.15° N. Lat; 77.71° W. Long.
Population: 28,653; Growth (since 2000): -2.1%; Density: 1,885.1 persons per square mile; Race: 79.5% White, 11.8% Black/African American, 3.8% Asian, 0.7% American Indian/Alaska Native, 0.1% Native Hawaiian/Other Pacific Islander, 2.9% Two or more races, 6.9% Hispanic of any race; Average household size: 2.39; Median age: 43.2; Age under 18: 19.5%; Age 65 and over: 20.4%; Males per 100 females: 91.1; Marriage status: 30.8% never married, 51.1% now married, 2.2% separated, 7.6% widowed, 10.5% divorced; Foreign born: 11.8%; Speak English only: 84.1%; With disability: 14.7%; Veterans: 7.8%; Ancestry: 25.2% Italian, 19.3% German, 12.7% Irish, 8.6% English, 4.8% Polish
Employment: 10.8% management, business, and financial, 4.9% computer, engineering, and science, 11.9% education, legal, community service, arts, and media, 6.5% healthcare practitioners, 17.9% service, 25.1% sales and office, 8.5% natural resources, construction, and maintenance, 14.4% production, transportation, and material moving
Income: Per capita: $27,836; Median household: $54,736; Average household: $64,771; Households with income of $100,000 or more: 18.3%; Poverty rate: 7.0%
Educational Attainment: High school diploma or higher: 87.3%; Bachelor's degree or higher: 23.1%; Graduate/professional degree or higher: 8.1%
Housing: Homeownership rate: 73.0%; Median home value: $117,100; Median year structure built: 1969; Homeowner vacancy rate: 1.2%; Median selected monthly owner costs: $1,245 with a mortgage, $537 without a mortgage; Median gross rent: $861 per month; Rental vacancy rate: 5.2%
Health Insurance: 96.3% have insurance; 77.0% have private insurance; 35.8% have public insurance; 3.7% do not have insurance; 1.9% of children under 18 do not have insurance
Safety: Violent crime rate: 20.9 per 10,000 population; Property crime rate: 292.8 per 10,000 population
Transportation: Commute: 94.2% car, 1.5% public transportation, 0.7% walk, 2.7% work from home; Mean travel time to work: 18.5 minutes
Additional Information Contacts
Town of Gates . . . . (585) 247-6100
  http://www.townofgates.org

GREECE (CDP). Covers a land area of 4.375 square miles and a water area of 0 square miles. Located at 43.21° N. Lat; 77.70° W. Long. Elevation is 430 feet.
Population: 15,185; Growth (since 2000): 3.9%; Density: 3,471.1 persons per square mile; Race: 87.3% White, 4.8% Black/African American, 2.6% Asian, 0.1% American Indian/Alaska Native, 0.0% Native Hawaiian/Other Pacific Islander, 4.4% Two or more races, 7.1% Hispanic of any race; Average household size: 2.38; Median age: 43.2; Age under 18: 18.8%; Age 65 and over: 20.7%; Males per 100 females: 88.8; Marriage status: 30.3% never married, 46.8% now married, 2.6% separated, 9.4% widowed, 13.5% divorced; Foreign born: 10.5%; Speak English only: 86.8%; With disability: 13.5%; Veterans: 8.0%; Ancestry: 29.4% Italian, 19.2% German, 14.3% Irish, 7.7% English, 4.9% Polish
Employment: 10.2% management, business, and financial, 5.0% computer, engineering, and science, 10.7% education, legal, community

service, arts, and media, 6.0% healthcare practitioners, 20.2% service, 28.0% sales and office, 6.8% natural resources, construction, and maintenance, 13.1% production, transportation, and material moving
Income: Per capita: $27,548; Median household: $53,684; Average household: $63,394; Households with income of $100,000 or more: 18.6%; Poverty rate: 7.1%
Educational Attainment: High school diploma or higher: 90.3%; Bachelor's degree or higher: 23.8%; Graduate/professional degree or higher: 8.6%
Housing: Homeownership rate: 73.3%; Median home value: $117,600; Median year structure built: 1964; Homeowner vacancy rate: 0.8%; Median selected monthly owner costs: $1,233 with a mortgage, $585 without a mortgage; Median gross rent: $856 per month; Rental vacancy rate: 6.9%
Health Insurance: 95.5% have insurance; 74.2% have private insurance; 40.3% have public insurance; 4.5% do not have insurance; 1.6% of children under 18 do not have insurance
Transportation: Commute: 94.1% car, 1.1% public transportation, 2.0% walk, 2.5% work from home; Mean travel time to work: 19.3 minutes

GREECE (town). Covers a land area of 47.518 square miles and a water area of 3.875 square miles. Located at 43.25° N. Lat; 77.70° W. Long. Elevation is 430 feet.
Population: 96,842; Growth (since 2000): 2.9%; Density: 2,038.0 persons per square mile; Race: 86.7% White, 6.5% Black/African American, 2.6% Asian, 0.2% American Indian/Alaska Native, 0.0% Native Hawaiian/Other Pacific Islander, 2.4% Two or more races, 5.3% Hispanic of any race; Average household size: 2.37; Median age: 43.8; Age under 18: 19.8%; Age 65 and over: 19.5%; Males per 100 females: 90.4; Marriage status: 29.5% never married, 51.0% now married, 1.6% separated, 7.9% widowed, 11.6% divorced; Foreign born: 6.9%; Speak English only: 90.0%; With disability: 13.3%; Veterans: 7.4%; Ancestry: 26.0% Italian, 21.7% German, 17.5% Irish, 10.5% English, 4.9% Polish
Employment: 14.2% management, business, and financial, 6.1% computer, engineering, and science, 10.0% education, legal, community service, arts, and media, 6.7% healthcare practitioners, 18.5% service, 25.1% sales and office, 6.8% natural resources, construction, and maintenance, 12.5% production, transportation, and material moving
Income: Per capita: $30,496; Median household: $57,202; Average household: $70,569; Households with income of $100,000 or more: 21.8%; Poverty rate: 8.4%
Educational Attainment: High school diploma or higher: 92.2%; Bachelor's degree or higher: 28.4%; Graduate/professional degree or higher: 10.2%
Housing: Homeownership rate: 72.2%; Median home value: $130,500; Median year structure built: 1971; Homeowner vacancy rate: 0.8%; Median selected monthly owner costs: $1,324 with a mortgage, $593 without a mortgage; Median gross rent: $909 per month; Rental vacancy rate: 7.3%
Health Insurance: 95.7% have insurance; 75.0% have private insurance; 37.2% have public insurance; 4.3% do not have insurance; 2.0% of children under 18 do not have insurance
Safety: Violent crime rate: 18.1 per 10,000 population; Property crime rate: 201.1 per 10,000 population
Transportation: Commute: 94.8% car, 0.7% public transportation, 1.2% walk, 2.6% work from home; Mean travel time to work: 20.0 minutes
Additional Information Contacts
Town of Greece. . . . . (585) 225-2000
    http://greeceny.gov

HAMLIN (CDP). Covers a land area of 7.710 square miles and a water area of 0 square miles. Located at 43.30° N. Lat; 77.92° W. Long. Elevation is 312 feet.
Population: 5,725; Growth (since 2000): n/a; Density: 742.5 persons per square mile; Race: 93.3% White, 4.9% Black/African American, 0.5% Asian, 0.0% American Indian/Alaska Native, 0.0% Native Hawaiian/Other Pacific Islander, 1.2% Two or more races, 2.1% Hispanic of any race; Average household size: 2.74; Median age: 36.1; Age under 18: 24.6%; Age 65 and over: 11.2%; Males per 100 females: 97.5; Marriage status: 33.4% never married, 50.5% now married, 1.5% separated, 3.4% widowed, 12.6% divorced; Foreign born: 2.8%; Speak English only: 95.8%; With disability: 13.8%; Veterans: 12.3%; Ancestry: 36.8% German, 20.0% Irish, 17.1% Italian, 14.3% English, 8.5% Polish
Employment: 8.5% management, business, and financial, 3.4% computer, engineering, and science, 8.9% education, legal, community service, arts, and media, 5.9% healthcare practitioners, 23.3% service, 28.0% sales and

office, 8.3% natural resources, construction, and maintenance, 13.7% production, transportation, and material moving
Income: Per capita: $24,280; Median household: $50,319; Average household: $64,912; Households with income of $100,000 or more: 20.4%; Poverty rate: 11.5%
Educational Attainment: High school diploma or higher: 91.8%; Bachelor's degree or higher: 20.9%; Graduate/professional degree or higher: 6.3%
Housing: Homeownership rate: 89.2%; Median home value: $99,700; Median year structure built: 1980; Homeowner vacancy rate: 1.8%; Median selected monthly owner costs: $1,171 with a mortgage, $543 without a mortgage; Median gross rent: $697 per month; Rental vacancy rate: 0.0%
Health Insurance: 96.3% have insurance; 73.0% have private insurance; 36.0% have public insurance; 3.7% do not have insurance; 0.6% of children under 18 do not have insurance
Transportation: Commute: 94.4% car, 0.0% public transportation, 0.6% walk, 3.6% work from home; Mean travel time to work: 29.7 minutes

HAMLIN (town). Covers a land area of 43.468 square miles and a water area of 1.122 square miles. Located at 43.32° N. Lat; 77.92° W. Long. Elevation is 312 feet.
Population: 9,093; Growth (since 2000): -2.8%; Density: 209.2 persons per square mile; Race: 95.0% White, 3.1% Black/African American, 0.4% Asian, 0.0% American Indian/Alaska Native, 0.0% Native Hawaiian/Other Pacific Islander, 1.4% Two or more races, 1.4% Hispanic of any race; Average household size: 2.71; Median age: 40.4; Age under 18: 22.6%; Age 65 and over: 13.4%; Males per 100 females: 98.7; Marriage status: 30.5% never married, 55.9% now married, 1.8% separated, 3.4% widowed, 10.2% divorced; Foreign born: 2.1%; Speak English only: 96.8%; With disability: 12.0%; Veterans: 11.0%; Ancestry: 35.7% German, 20.6% Irish, 14.7% Italian, 12.6% English, 8.3% Polish
Employment: 11.0% management, business, and financial, 4.3% computer, engineering, and science, 9.3% education, legal, community service, arts, and media, 5.0% healthcare practitioners, 19.4% service, 29.5% sales and office, 7.2% natural resources, construction, and maintenance, 14.3% production, transportation, and material moving
Income: Per capita: $27,105; Median household: $58,868; Average household: $71,693; Households with income of $100,000 or more: 25.4%; Poverty rate: 8.1%
Educational Attainment: High school diploma or higher: 92.5%; Bachelor's degree or higher: 24.5%; Graduate/professional degree or higher: 7.6%
Housing: Homeownership rate: 86.7%; Median home value: $113,000; Median year structure built: 1973; Homeowner vacancy rate: 1.1%; Median selected monthly owner costs: $1,253 with a mortgage, $548 without a mortgage; Median gross rent: $716 per month; Rental vacancy rate: 0.0%
Health Insurance: 96.3% have insurance; 76.9% have private insurance; 33.9% have public insurance; 3.7% do not have insurance; 0.9% of children under 18 do not have insurance
Transportation: Commute: 94.6% car, 0.0% public transportation, 0.8% walk, 3.8% work from home; Mean travel time to work: 29.1 minutes
Additional Information Contacts
Town of Hamlin . . . . (585) 964-2421
    http://www.hamlinny.org

HENRIETTA (town). Covers a land area of 35.351 square miles and a water area of 0.296 square miles. Located at 43.05° N. Lat; 77.64° W. Long. Elevation is 600 feet.
Population: 43,609; Growth (since 2000): 11.7%; Density: 1,233.6 persons per square mile; Race: 77.3% White, 9.1% Black/African American, 8.9% Asian, 0.4% American Indian/Alaska Native, 0.1% Native Hawaiian/Other Pacific Islander, 2.7% Two or more races, 4.0% Hispanic of any race; Average household size: 2.56; Median age: 33.6; Age under 18: 18.9%; Age 65 and over: 13.8%; Males per 100 females: 110.7; Marriage status: 41.0% never married, 45.3% now married, 1.5% separated, 4.1% widowed, 9.6% divorced; Foreign born: 13.7%; Speak English only: 83.2%; With disability: 13.0%; Veterans: 6.1%; Ancestry: 18.5% German, 13.4% Italian, 12.5% Irish, 8.4% English, 7.3% American
Employment: 14.0% management, business, and financial, 10.9% computer, engineering, and science, 11.0% education, legal, community service, arts, and media, 7.1% healthcare practitioners, 17.1% service, 23.8% sales and office, 6.0% natural resources, construction, and maintenance, 10.2% production, transportation, and material moving

Income: Per capita: $29,181; Median household: $62,883; Average household: $77,095; Households with income of $100,000 or more: 27.4%; Poverty rate: 13.0%

Educational Attainment: High school diploma or higher: 90.0%; Bachelor's degree or higher: 37.0%; Graduate/professional degree or higher: 15.5%

School District(s)
Rush-Henrietta Central SD (PK-12)
   Enrollment: 5,433 . . . . (585) 359-5012

Housing: Homeownership rate: 69.4%; Median home value: $141,300; Median year structure built: 1974; Homeowner vacancy rate: 1.0%; Median selected monthly owner costs: $1,320 with a mortgage, $558 without a mortgage; Median gross rent: $979 per month; Rental vacancy rate: 4.2%

Health Insurance: 96.8% have insurance; 80.4% have private insurance; 29.6% have public insurance; 3.2% do not have insurance; 1.3% of children under 18 do not have insurance

Transportation: Commute: 88.1% car, 3.0% public transportation, 4.9% walk, 3.2% work from home; Mean travel time to work: 18.5 minutes

Additional Information Contacts
Town of Henrietta . . . . (585) 334-7700
   http://www.henrietta.org

HILTON (village).
Covers a land area of 1.780 square miles and a water area of 0 square miles. Located at 43.29° N. Lat; 77.79° W. Long. Elevation is 279 feet.

Population: 5,896; Growth (since 2000): 0.7%; Density: 3,312.7 persons per square mile; Race: 95.3% White, 2.6% Black/African American, 0.3% Asian, 0.0% American Indian/Alaska Native, 0.0% Native Hawaiian/Other Pacific Islander, 1.5% Two or more races, 7.1% Hispanic of any race; Average household size: 2.74; Median age: 36.7; Age under 18: 27.6%; Age 65 and over: 10.5%; Males per 100 females: 91.2; Marriage status: 30.0% never married, 55.3% now married, 1.1% separated, 5.0% widowed, 9.6% divorced; Foreign born: 2.0%; Speak English only: 96.3%; With disability: 10.2%; Veterans: 9.2%; Ancestry: 28.3% Italian, 25.9% German, 18.2% Irish, 12.2% English, 6.8% American

Employment: 13.1% management, business, and financial, 6.2% computer, engineering, and science, 16.0% education, legal, community service, arts, and media, 9.8% healthcare practitioners, 13.8% service, 19.8% sales and office, 8.6% natural resources, construction, and maintenance, 12.7% production, transportation, and material moving

Income: Per capita: $28,237; Median household: $62,895; Average household: $75,453; Households with income of $100,000 or more: 26.7%; Poverty rate: 8.7%

Educational Attainment: High school diploma or higher: 95.3%; Bachelor's degree or higher: 28.1%; Graduate/professional degree or higher: 16.7%

School District(s)
Hilton Central SD (PK-12)
   Enrollment: 4,458 . . . . (585) 392-1000

Housing: Homeownership rate: 67.4%; Median home value: $132,600; Median year structure built: 1979; Homeowner vacancy rate: 0.0%; Median selected monthly owner costs: $1,277 with a mortgage, $554 without a mortgage; Median gross rent: $970 per month; Rental vacancy rate: 5.0%

Health Insurance: 100.0% have insurance; 85.0% have private insurance; 31.1% have public insurance; 0.0% do not have insurance; 0.0% of children under 18 do not have insurance

Transportation: Commute: 90.6% car, 0.0% public transportation, 3.0% walk, 4.0% work from home; Mean travel time to work: 26.2 minutes

Additional Information Contacts
Village of Hilton . . . . (585) 392-4144
   http://www.hiltonny.org

HONEOYE FALLS (village).
Covers a land area of 2.543 square miles and a water area of 0.052 square miles. Located at 42.95° N. Lat; 77.59° W. Long. Elevation is 656 feet.

History: Incorporated 1838.

Population: 2,752; Growth (since 2000): 6.1%; Density: 1,082.1 persons per square mile; Race: 97.1% White, 0.5% Black/African American, 0.6% Asian, 0.0% American Indian/Alaska Native, 0.0% Native Hawaiian/Other Pacific Islander, 1.8% Two or more races, 0.4% Hispanic of any race; Average household size: 2.31; Median age: 42.6; Age under 18: 23.1%; Age 65 and over: 18.5%; Males per 100 females: 88.6; Marriage status: 33.7% never married, 51.0% now married, 3.3% separated, 5.3% widowed, 10.1% divorced; Foreign born: 2.0%; Speak English only: 97.1%;

With disability: 12.9%; Veterans: 6.3%; Ancestry: 23.0% German, 19.1% Irish, 18.6% English, 12.7% Italian, 12.4% American

Employment: 11.1% management, business, and financial, 12.7% computer, engineering, and science, 17.2% education, legal, community service, arts, and media, 8.3% healthcare practitioners, 12.5% service, 19.1% sales and office, 10.4% natural resources, construction, and maintenance, 8.9% production, transportation, and material moving

Income: Per capita: $36,229; Median household: $67,750; Average household: $83,455; Households with income of $100,000 or more: 29.0%; Poverty rate: 11.9%

Educational Attainment: High school diploma or higher: 95.3%; Bachelor's degree or higher: 46.3%; Graduate/professional degree or higher: 22.4%

School District(s)
Honeoye Falls-Lima Central SD (KG-12)
   Enrollment: 2,212 . . . . (585) 624-7010

Housing: Homeownership rate: 62.2%; Median home value: $163,000; Median year structure built: 1959; Homeowner vacancy rate: 0.0%; Median selected monthly owner costs: $1,552 with a mortgage, $715 without a mortgage; Median gross rent: $826 per month; Rental vacancy rate: 4.9%

Health Insurance: 96.7% have insurance; 78.3% have private insurance; 32.5% have public insurance; 3.3% do not have insurance; 0.0% of children under 18 do not have insurance

Transportation: Commute: 87.0% car, 0.0% public transportation, 5.2% walk, 6.0% work from home; Mean travel time to work: 26.9 minutes

---

IRONDEQUOIT (CDP).
Covers a land area of 15.001 square miles and a water area of 1.833 square miles. Located at 43.21° N. Lat; 77.57° W. Long. Elevation is 381 feet.

History: Named for the Iroquoian translation of "bay". Settled 1791, organized 1839.

Population: 50,890; Growth (since 2000): -2.8%; Density: 3,392.4 persons per square mile; Race: 84.8% White, 9.1% Black/African American, 1.3% Asian, 0.1% American Indian/Alaska Native, 0.0% Native Hawaiian/Other Pacific Islander, 2.5% Two or more races, 8.7% Hispanic of any race; Average household size: 2.28; Median age: 44.2; Age under 18: 19.8%; Age 65 and over: 20.3%; Males per 100 females: 86.6; Marriage status: 30.6% never married, 50.4% now married, 1.9% separated, 7.0% widowed, 12.0% divorced; Foreign born: 7.6%; Speak English only: 87.1%; With disability: 13.7%; Veterans: 7.9%; Ancestry: 20.9% Italian, 20.8% German, 15.1% Irish, 9.9% English, 6.0% Polish

Employment: 16.1% management, business, and financial, 7.5% computer, engineering, and science, 12.8% education, legal, community service, arts, and media, 6.8% healthcare practitioners, 17.8% service, 23.5% sales and office, 5.8% natural resources, construction, and maintenance, 9.7% production, transportation, and material moving

Income: Per capita: $31,341; Median household: $56,986; Average household: $70,493; Households with income of $100,000 or more: 21.2%; Poverty rate: 8.6%

Educational Attainment: High school diploma or higher: 92.3%; Bachelor's degree or higher: 34.9%; Graduate/professional degree or higher: 13.6%

Housing: Homeownership rate: 77.9%; Median home value: $118,600; Median year structure built: 1955; Homeowner vacancy rate: 1.8%; Median selected monthly owner costs: $1,266 with a mortgage, $587 without a mortgage; Median gross rent: $878 per month; Rental vacancy rate: 6.2%

Health Insurance: 96.4% have insurance; 76.4% have private insurance; 36.4% have public insurance; 3.6% do not have insurance; 2.6% of children under 18 do not have insurance

Safety: Violent crime rate: 21.6 per 10,000 population; Property crime rate: 221.9 per 10,000 population

Transportation: Commute: 92.0% car, 1.8% public transportation, 1.2% walk, 3.6% work from home; Mean travel time to work: 20.1 minutes

Additional Information Contacts
Town of Irondequoit . . . . (585) 467-8840
   http://www.irondequoit.org

MENDON (town).
Covers a land area of 39.472 square miles and a water area of 0.515 square miles. Located at 42.98° N. Lat; 77.56° W. Long. Elevation is 561 feet.

Population: 9,250; Growth (since 2000): 10.5%; Density: 234.3 persons per square mile; Race: 95.9% White, 0.6% Black/African American, 2.1% Asian, 0.1% American Indian/Alaska Native, 0.0% Native Hawaiian/Other Pacific Islander, 1.3% Two or more races, 1.2% Hispanic of any race; Average household size: 2.64; Median age: 45.8; Age under 18: 24.3%;

Age 65 and over: 14.9%; Males per 100 females: 97.0; Marriage status: 25.5% never married, 64.1% now married, 1.7% separated, 4.8% widowed, 5.6% divorced; Foreign born: 3.7%; Speak English only: 96.7%; With disability: 8.3%; Veterans: 5.4%; Ancestry: 22.3% German, 19.6% Irish, 19.2% English, 14.1% Italian, 7.5% American

Employment: 20.5% management, business, and financial, 12.5% computer, engineering, and science, 16.1% education, legal, community service, arts, and media, 7.5% healthcare practitioners, 12.1% service, 16.7% sales and office, 4.9% natural resources, construction, and maintenance, 9.8% production, transportation, and material moving

Income: Per capita: $53,046; Median household: $97,902; Average household: $139,556; Households with income of $100,000 or more: 49.3%; Poverty rate: 7.9%

Educational Attainment: High school diploma or higher: 97.5%; Bachelor's degree or higher: 58.9%; Graduate/professional degree or higher: 29.4%

Housing: Homeownership rate: 82.4%; Median home value: $250,300; Median year structure built: 1974; Homeowner vacancy rate: 0.0%; Median selected monthly owner costs: $2,033 with a mortgage, $871 without a mortgage; Median gross rent: $869 per month; Rental vacancy rate: 3.6%

Health Insurance: 98.1% have insurance; 89.1% have private insurance; 21.4% have public insurance; 1.9% do not have insurance; 0.0% of children under 18 do not have insurance

Transportation: Commute: 88.9% car, 0.0% public transportation, 1.5% walk, 9.1% work from home; Mean travel time to work: 25.2 minutes

Additional Information Contacts

Town of Mendon . . . . (585) 624-6060
http://www.townofmendon.org

MUMFORD (unincorporated postal area)
ZCTA: 14511

Covers a land area of 2.309 square miles and a water area of 0.042 square miles. Located at 43.00° N. Lat; 77.89° W. Long. Elevation is 617 feet.

Population: 601; Growth (since 2000): n/a; Density: 260.3 persons per square mile; Race: 94.8% White, 1.5% Black/African American, 0.0% Asian, 0.0% American Indian/Alaska Native, 0.0% Native Hawaiian/Other Pacific Islander, 3.7% Two or more races, 0.0% Hispanic of any race; Average household size: 2.72; Median age: 31.7; Age under 18: 30.3%; Age 65 and over: 6.5%; Males per 100 females: 87.5%; Marriage status: 31.7% never married, 51.1% now married, 3.1% separated, 8.4% widowed, 8.8% divorced; Foreign born: 0.0%; Speak English only: 100.0%; With disability: 12.6%; Veterans: 2.1%; Ancestry: 63.2% German, 43.1% Irish, 11.0% American, 10.0% Italian, 9.8% English

Employment: 25.0% management, business, and financial, 0.0% computer, engineering, and science, 9.6% education, legal, community service, arts, and media, 5.4% healthcare practitioners, 13.5% service, 36.2% sales and office, 10.4% natural resources, construction, and maintenance, 0.0% production, transportation, and material moving

Income: Per capita: $21,305; Median household: $53,044; Average household: $56,210; Households with income of $100,000 or more: 16.3%; Poverty rate: 11.3%

Educational Attainment: High school diploma or higher: 100.0%; Bachelor's degree or higher: 52.9%; Graduate/professional degree or higher: 15.7%

Housing: Homeownership rate: 67.9%; Median home value: $120,800; Median year structure built: Before 1940; Homeowner vacancy rate: 0.0%; Median selected monthly owner costs: $1,380 with a mortgage, $0 without a mortgage; Median gross rent: n/a per month; Rental vacancy rate: 0.0%

Health Insurance: 95.5% have insurance; 83.9% have private insurance; 20.8% have public insurance; 4.5% do not have insurance; 7.7% of children under 18 do not have insurance

Transportation: Commute: 100.0% car, 0.0% public transportation, 0.0% walk, 0.0% work from home; Mean travel time to work: 22.2 minutes

NORTH CHILI (unincorporated postal area)
ZCTA: 14514

Covers a land area of 3.746 square miles and a water area of 0.012 square miles. Located at 43.11° N. Lat; 77.81° W. Long. Elevation is 584 feet.

Population: 6,812; Growth (since 2000): 44.3%; Density: 1,818.3 persons per square mile; Race: 89.7% White, 3.2% Black/African

American, 2.0% Asian, 0.0% American Indian/Alaska Native, 0.0% Native Hawaiian/Other Pacific Islander, 5.1% Two or more races, 3.7% Hispanic of any race; Average household size: 2.54; Median age: 42.1; Age under 18: 23.0%; Age 65 and over: 16.2%; Males per 100 females: 89.8; Marriage status: 30.5% never married, 55.0% now married, 1.4% separated, 5.7% widowed, 8.7% divorced; Foreign born: 8.2%; Speak English only: 90.0%; With disability: 11.5%; Veterans: 5.2%; Ancestry: 29.5% German, 22.0% Italian, 18.3% Irish, 13.9% English, 7.0% Polish

Employment: 20.4% management, business, and financial, 10.2% computer, engineering, and science, 13.2% education, legal, community service, arts, and media, 7.4% healthcare practitioners, 15.3% service, 19.3% sales and office, 5.3% natural resources, construction, and maintenance, 8.9% production, transportation, and material moving

Income: Per capita: $31,256; Median household: $62,381; Average household: $79,793; Households with income of $100,000 or more: 29.5%; Poverty rate: 9.0%

Educational Attainment: High school diploma or higher: 94.3%; Bachelor's degree or higher: 39.5%; Graduate/professional degree or higher: 17.8%

Housing: Homeownership rate: 68.7%; Median home value: $154,800; Median year structure built: 1986; Homeowner vacancy rate: 0.0%; Median selected monthly owner costs: $1,492 with a mortgage, $493 without a mortgage; Median gross rent: $990 per month; Rental vacancy rate: 8.7%

Health Insurance: 94.7% have insurance; 79.4% have private insurance; 29.0% have public insurance; 5.3% do not have insurance; 2.9% of children under 18 do not have insurance

Transportation: Commute: 95.9% car, 0.0% public transportation, 1.5% walk, 1.1% work from home; Mean travel time to work: 21.1 minutes

NORTH GATES (CDP). Covers a land area of 2.662 square miles and a water area of 0.026 square miles. Located at 43.17° N. Lat; 77.71° W. Long. Elevation is 525 feet.

Population: 9,644; Growth (since 2000): n/a; Density: 3,622.4 persons per square mile; Race: 73.7% White, 13.0% Black/African American, 6.1% Asian, 1.8% American Indian/Alaska Native, 0.2% Native Hawaiian/Other Pacific Islander, 3.3% Two or more races, 8.4% Hispanic of any race; Average household size: 2.21; Median age: 42.2; Age under 18: 18.6%; Age 65 and over: 19.9%; Males per 100 females: 90.9; Marriage status: 31.9% never married, 49.2% now married, 4.0% separated, 7.9% widowed, 11.0% divorced; Foreign born: 13.3%; Speak English only: 80.6%; With disability: 17.5%; Veterans: 6.4%; Ancestry: 23.0% Italian, 14.6% German, 12.3% Irish, 9.1% English, 4.0% Polish

Employment: 9.8% management, business, and financial, 6.3% computer, engineering, and science, 11.1% education, legal, community service, arts, and media, 4.7% healthcare practitioners, 19.3% service, 27.1% sales and office, 9.0% natural resources, construction, and maintenance, 12.8% production, transportation, and material moving

Income: Per capita: $26,138; Median household: $43,407; Average household: $56,886; Households with income of $100,000 or more: 15.0%; Poverty rate: 8.9%

Educational Attainment: High school diploma or higher: 82.7%; Bachelor's degree or higher: 19.7%; Graduate/professional degree or higher: 7.4%

Housing: Homeownership rate: 56.1%; Median home value: $115,200; Median year structure built: 1970; Homeowner vacancy rate: 4.1%; Median selected monthly owner costs: $1,203 with a mortgage, $559 without a mortgage; Median gross rent: $761 per month; Rental vacancy rate: 2.8%

Health Insurance: 96.3% have insurance; 70.0% have private insurance; 38.5% have public insurance; 3.7% do not have insurance; 1.9% of children under 18 do not have insurance

Transportation: Commute: 91.6% car, 4.1% public transportation, 0.7% walk, 2.7% work from home; Mean travel time to work: 21.3 minutes

OGDEN (town). Covers a land area of 36.476 square miles and a water area of 0.257 square miles. Located at 43.17° N. Lat; 77.81° W. Long.

Population: 20,194; Growth (since 2000): 9.2%; Density: 553.6 persons per square mile; Race: 95.7% White, 1.8% Black/African American, 0.7% Asian, 0.1% American Indian/Alaska Native, 0.0% Native Hawaiian/Other Pacific Islander, 1.4% Two or more races, 7.1% Hispanic of any race; Average household size: 2.69; Median age: 39.9; Age under 18: 21.2%; Age 65 and over: 13.2%; Males per 100 females: 94.0; Marriage status: 29.7% never married, 54.8% now married, 1.8% separated, 5.4% widowed, 10.1% divorced; Foreign born: 4.4%; Speak English only: 90.5%;

With disability: 10.4%; Veterans: 6.3%; Ancestry: 28.3% German, 24.6% Italian, 17.8% Irish, 14.5% English, 6.0% Polish
Employment: 18.3% management, business, and financial, 8.0% computer, engineering, and science, 13.2% education, legal, community service, arts, and media, 7.2% healthcare practitioners, 12.6% service, 24.1% sales and office, 6.4% natural resources, construction, and maintenance, 10.1% production, transportation, and material moving
Income: Per capita: $33,062; Median household: $74,159; Average household: $88,582; Households with income of $100,000 or more: 35.0%; Poverty rate: 7.4%
Educational Attainment: High school diploma or higher: 95.5%; Bachelor's degree or higher: 36.4%; Graduate/professional degree or higher: 14.8%
Housing: Homeownership rate: 75.2%; Median home value: $157,200; Median year structure built: 1977; Homeowner vacancy rate: 0.2%; Median selected monthly owner costs: $1,489 with a mortgage, $659 without a mortgage; Median gross rent: $964 per month; Rental vacancy rate: 0.0%
Health Insurance: 96.8% have insurance; 83.3% have private insurance; 26.3% have public insurance; 3.2% do not have insurance; 2.1% of children under 18 do not have insurance
Safety: Violent crime rate: 6.4 per 10,000 population; Property crime rate: 103.3 per 10,000 population
Transportation: Commute: 93.3% car, 0.1% public transportation, 1.9% walk, 4.3% work from home; Mean travel time to work: 20.0 minutes
Additional Information Contacts
Town of Ogden . . . . (585) 617-6100
  http://www.ogdenny.com

PARMA (town). Covers a land area of 42.023 square miles and a water area of 0.960 square miles. Located at 43.27° N. Lat; 77.80° W. Long.
Population: 15,800; Growth (since 2000): 6.6%; Density: 376.0 persons per square mile; Race: 97.0% White, 1.2% Black/African American, 0.6% Asian, 0.2% American Indian/Alaska Native, 0.0% Native Hawaiian/Other Pacific Islander, 0.8% Two or more races, 4.1% Hispanic of any race; Average household size: 2.71; Median age: 41.4; Age under 18: 23.8%; Age 65 and over: 14.1%; Males per 100 females: 98.7; Marriage status: 27.4% never married, 58.7% now married, 0.8% separated, 5.2% widowed, 8.7% divorced; Foreign born: 4.8%; Speak English only: 93.2%; With disability: 10.1%; Veterans: 8.7%; Ancestry: 27.7% German, 25.8% Italian, 20.0% Irish, 11.6% English, 5.0% Polish
Employment: 15.3% management, business, and financial, 5.9% computer, engineering, and science, 11.2% education, legal, community service, arts, and media, 9.0% healthcare practitioners, 13.1% service, 23.8% sales and office, 10.3% natural resources, construction, and maintenance, 11.4% production, transportation, and material moving
Income: Per capita: $30,262; Median household: $69,386; Average household: $80,356; Households with income of $100,000 or more: 30.5%; Poverty rate: 6.9%
Educational Attainment: High school diploma or higher: 95.6%; Bachelor's degree or higher: 29.8%; Graduate/professional degree or higher: 14.0%
Housing: Homeownership rate: 82.5%; Median home value: $147,100; Median year structure built: 1971; Homeowner vacancy rate: 0.0%; Median selected monthly owner costs: $1,370 with a mortgage, $553 without a mortgage; Median gross rent: $958 per month; Rental vacancy rate: 7.3%
Health Insurance: 97.7% have insurance; 84.6% have private insurance; 30.2% have public insurance; 2.3% do not have insurance; 0.9% of children under 18 do not have insurance
Transportation: Commute: 93.6% car, 0.0% public transportation, 1.7% walk, 3.8% work from home; Mean travel time to work: 25.5 minutes
Additional Information Contacts
Town of Parma . . . . (585) 392-9461
  http://www.parmany.org

PENFIELD (town). Covers a land area of 37.211 square miles and a water area of 0.634 square miles. Located at 43.15° N. Lat; 77.44° W. Long. Elevation is 423 feet.
Population: 37,245; Growth (since 2000): 7.5%; Density: 1,000.9 persons per square mile; Race: 91.1% White, 2.7% Black/African American, 3.1% Asian, 0.1% American Indian/Alaska Native, 0.0% Native Hawaiian/Other Pacific Islander, 2.5% Two or more races, 4.4% Hispanic of any race; Average household size: 2.43; Median age: 46.0; Age under 18: 23.0%; Age 65 and over: 20.8%; Males per 100 females: 93.0; Marriage status: 22.7% never married, 60.5% now married, 1.4% separated, 7.3% widowed, 9.5% divorced; Foreign born: 7.6%; Speak English only: 91.3%;

With disability: 9.9%; Veterans: 7.4%; Ancestry: 22.6% Italian, 20.5% German, 18.2% Irish, 14.3% English, 6.5% Polish
Employment: 21.1% management, business, and financial, 8.9% computer, engineering, and science, 14.4% education, legal, community service, arts, and media, 9.7% healthcare practitioners, 11.4% service, 24.5% sales and office, 4.0% natural resources, construction, and maintenance, 6.0% production, transportation, and material moving
Income: Per capita: $41,096; Median household: $80,879; Average household: $99,734; Households with income of $100,000 or more: 40.3%; Poverty rate: 4.3%
Educational Attainment: High school diploma or higher: 94.0%; Bachelor's degree or higher: 53.0%; Graduate/professional degree or higher: 24.8%
School District(s)
Penfield Central SD (KG-12)
  Enrollment: 4,581 . . . . (585) 249-5700
Housing: Homeownership rate: 82.7%; Median home value: $193,800; Median year structure built: 1976; Homeowner vacancy rate: 0.5%; Median selected monthly owner costs: $1,740 with a mortgage, $724 without a mortgage; Median gross rent: $891 per month; Rental vacancy rate: 10.9%
Health Insurance: 97.7% have insurance; 83.5% have private insurance; 30.6% have public insurance; 2.3% do not have insurance; 1.7% of children under 18 do not have insurance
Transportation: Commute: 91.7% car, 0.8% public transportation, 0.7% walk, 6.1% work from home; Mean travel time to work: 20.0 minutes
Additional Information Contacts
Town of Penfield . . . . (585) 340-8629
  http://www.penfield.org

PERINTON (town). Covers a land area of 34.186 square miles and a water area of 0.360 square miles. Located at 43.08° N. Lat; 77.43° W. Long.
Population: 46,660; Growth (since 2000): 1.2%; Density: 1,364.9 persons per square mile; Race: 92.3% White, 1.7% Black/African American, 3.9% Asian, 0.1% American Indian/Alaska Native, 0.0% Native Hawaiian/Other Pacific Islander, 1.6% Two or more races, 3.4% Hispanic of any race; Average household size: 2.44; Median age: 45.9; Age under 18: 21.6%; Age 65 and over: 20.0%; Males per 100 females: 92.6; Marriage status: 24.2% never married, 59.9% now married, 1.2% separated, 5.4% widowed, 10.4% divorced; Foreign born: 7.6%; Speak English only: 92.5%; With disability: 9.2%; Veterans: 7.3%; Ancestry: 23.3% German, 20.2% Italian, 19.8% Irish, 14.8% English, 6.4% Polish
Employment: 20.4% management, business, and financial, 9.9% computer, engineering, and science, 16.3% education, legal, community service, arts, and media, 7.3% healthcare practitioners, 13.4% service, 23.5% sales and office, 4.6% natural resources, construction, and maintenance, 4.6% production, transportation, and material moving
Income: Per capita: $42,555; Median household: $83,036; Average household: $102,790; Households with income of $100,000 or more: 40.1%; Poverty rate: 5.2%
Educational Attainment: High school diploma or higher: 96.5%; Bachelor's degree or higher: 57.1%; Graduate/professional degree or higher: 26.5%
Housing: Homeownership rate: 79.5%; Median home value: $196,600; Median year structure built: 1975; Homeowner vacancy rate: 0.3%; Median selected monthly owner costs: $1,641 with a mortgage, $679 without a mortgage; Median gross rent: $963 per month; Rental vacancy rate: 8.6%
Health Insurance: 97.3% have insurance; 86.0% have private insurance; 27.5% have public insurance; 2.7% do not have insurance; 1.6% of children under 18 do not have insurance
Transportation: Commute: 90.8% car, 0.7% public transportation, 1.4% walk, 6.2% work from home; Mean travel time to work: 20.9 minutes
Additional Information Contacts
Town of Perinton . . . . (585) 223-0770
  http://www.perinton.org

PITTSFORD (town). Covers a land area of 23.181 square miles and a water area of 0.209 square miles. Located at 43.07° N. Lat; 77.53° W. Long. Elevation is 492 feet.
History: Incorporated 1827.
Population: 29,507; Growth (since 2000): 8.4%; Density: 1,272.9 persons per square mile; Race: 87.7% White, 1.2% Black/African American, 8.7% Asian, 0.0% American Indian/Alaska Native, 0.0% Native Hawaiian/Other Pacific Islander, 1.7% Two or more races, 2.4% Hispanic of any race; Average household size: 2.56; Median age: 43.4; Age under 18: 22.7%;

Age 65 and over: 19.2%; Males per 100 females: 86.7; Marriage status: 28.8% never married, 59.0% now married, 0.7% separated, 6.1% widowed, 6.1% divorced; Foreign born: 10.4%; Speak English only: 88.4%; With disability: 8.0%; Veterans: 5.9%; Ancestry: 18.7% Irish, 17.4% German, 16.5% Italian, 14.8% English, 6.1% Polish

Employment: 22.8% management, business, and financial, 7.5% computer, engineering, and science, 21.3% education, legal, community service, arts, and media, 10.6% healthcare practitioners, 10.4% service, 21.4% sales and office, 2.0% natural resources, construction, and maintenance, 4.0% production, transportation, and material moving

Income: Per capita: $58,334; Median household: $110,544; Average household: $162,778; Households with income of $100,000 or more: 54.6%; Poverty rate: 3.3%

Educational Attainment: High school diploma or higher: 98.2%; Bachelor's degree or higher: 73.5%; Graduate/professional degree or higher: 40.1%

School District(s)
Pittsford Central SD (KG-12)
   Enrollment: 5,693 . . . . (585) 267-1004
Housing: Homeownership rate: 86.6%; Median home value: $270,400; Median year structure built: 1972; Homeowner vacancy rate: 1.3%; Median selected monthly owner costs: $2,264 with a mortgage, $950 without a mortgage; Median gross rent: $1,167 per month; Rental vacancy rate: 7.3%

Health Insurance: 98.8% have insurance; 92.8% have private insurance; 22.0% have public insurance; 1.2% do not have insurance; 0.9% of children under 18 do not have insurance

Transportation: Commute: 85.1% car, 0.2% public transportation, 4.5% walk, 8.7% work from home; Mean travel time to work: 18.3 minutes

Additional Information Contacts
Town of Pittsford . . . . (585) 248-6210
   http://townofpittsford.org

PITTSFORD (village). Covers a land area of 0.673 square miles and a water area of 0.019 square miles. Located at 43.09° N. Lat; 77.52° W. Long. Elevation is 492 feet.

Population: 1,699; Growth (since 2000): 19.8%; Density: 2,524.9 persons per square mile; Race: 91.6% White, 0.6% Black/African American, 2.5% Asian, 0.0% American Indian/Alaska Native, 0.0% Native Hawaiian/Other Pacific Islander, 4.5% Two or more races, 2.5% Hispanic of any race; Average household size: 2.24; Median age: 45.5; Age under 18: 22.1%; Age 65 and over: 15.6%; Males per 100 females: 86.1; Marriage status: 26.3% never married, 54.9% now married, 1.8% separated, 4.0% widowed, 14.7% divorced; Foreign born: 7.9%; Speak English only: 87.5%; With disability: 6.5%; Veterans: 6.2%; Ancestry: 23.2% Irish, 16.8% German, 15.1% English, 13.5% Italian, 8.0% American

Employment: 30.5% management, business, and financial, 5.8% computer, engineering, and science, 22.2% education, legal, community service, arts, and media, 9.6% healthcare practitioners, 8.3% service, 19.8% sales and office, 1.2% natural resources, construction, and maintenance, 2.7% production, transportation, and material moving

Income: Per capita: $60,512; Median household: $96,875; Average household: $139,518; Households with income of $100,000 or more: 48.7%; Poverty rate: 3.1%

Educational Attainment: High school diploma or higher: 98.9%; Bachelor's degree or higher: 71.2%; Graduate/professional degree or higher: 38.2%

School District(s)
Pittsford Central SD (KG-12)
   Enrollment: 5,693 . . . . (585) 267-1004
Housing: Homeownership rate: 74.5%; Median home value: $236,700; Median year structure built: Before 1940; Homeowner vacancy rate: 0.0%; Median selected monthly owner costs: $1,968 with a mortgage, $900 without a mortgage; Median gross rent: $1,184 per month; Rental vacancy rate: 0.0%

Health Insurance: 97.2% have insurance; 89.0% have private insurance; 22.0% have public insurance; 2.8% do not have insurance; 4.6% of children under 18 do not have insurance

Transportation: Commute: 85.3% car, 0.6% public transportation, 4.3% walk, 8.9% work from home; Mean travel time to work: 17.1 minutes

---

RIGA (town). Covers a land area of 34.962 square miles and a water area of 0.266 square miles. Located at 43.08° N. Lat; 77.87° W. Long. Elevation is 636 feet.

Population: 5,623; Growth (since 2000): 3.4%; Density: 160.8 persons per square mile; Race: 97.5% White, 1.0% Black/African American, 0.2% Asian, 0.0% American Indian/Alaska Native, 0.0% Native Hawaiian/Other Pacific Islander, 1.3% Two or more races, 2.7% Hispanic of any race; Average household size: 2.52; Median age: 47.8; Age under 18: 18.4%; Age 65 and over: 17.8%; Males per 100 females: 98.6; Marriage status: 24.6% never married, 60.7% now married, 3.1% separated, 6.0% widowed, 8.7% divorced; Foreign born: 1.9%; Speak English only: 96.3%; With disability: 12.2%; Veterans: 10.1%; Ancestry: 32.4% German, 20.2% Irish, 18.5% English, 16.4% Italian, 7.6% Polish

Employment: 13.5% management, business, and financial, 5.6% computer, engineering, and science, 12.0% education, legal, community service, arts, and media, 5.6% healthcare practitioners, 19.3% service, 23.2% sales and office, 8.7% natural resources, construction, and maintenance, 12.0% production, transportation, and material moving

Income: Per capita: $32,240; Median household: $68,430; Average household: $79,682; Households with income of $100,000 or more: 25.4%; Poverty rate: 7.2%

Educational Attainment: High school diploma or higher: 93.7%; Bachelor's degree or higher: 35.4%; Graduate/professional degree or higher: 13.9%

Housing: Homeownership rate: 88.5%; Median home value: $153,000; Median year structure built: 1973; Homeowner vacancy rate: 0.2%; Median selected monthly owner costs: $1,336 with a mortgage, $528 without a mortgage; Median gross rent: $1,013 per month; Rental vacancy rate: 5.4%

Health Insurance: 98.1% have insurance; 83.5% have private insurance; 34.0% have public insurance; 1.9% do not have insurance; 1.3% of children under 18 do not have insurance

Transportation: Commute: 97.4% car, 0.0% public transportation, 0.9% walk, 1.7% work from home; Mean travel time to work: 22.1 minutes

Additional Information Contacts
Town of Riga . . . . (585) 293-3880
   http://www.townofriga.org

ROCHESTER (city). County seat. Covers a land area of 35.781 square miles and a water area of 1.374 square miles. Located at 43.17° N. Lat; 77.62° W. Long. Elevation is 505 feet.

History: The first settler on the site of Rochester was Ebenezer "Indian" Allen, who was granted a 100-acre tract at the falls of the Genesee River on the condition that he erect a mill for use by the Native Americans. Allen built his mill in 1789. After changing hands several times, the area was finally purchased in 1803 by Colonel William Fitzhugh, Major Charles Carroll, and Colonel Nathaniel Rochester, all from Maryland. The village was incorporated as Rochesterville in 1817. The construction of the Erie Canal through Rochester assured the town supremacy over its neighbors. Rochester was the home of George Eastman, who invented and manufactured films for cameras. In 1888 the first Kodak camera was put on the market. The Eastman School of Music was later named for him. In 1840, the University of Rochester was founded by a convention of Baptists.

Population: 209,463; Growth (since 2000): -4.7%; Density: 5,854.1 persons per square mile; Race: 46.6% White, 40.7% Black/African American, 3.3% Asian, 1.0% American Indian/Alaska Native, 0.0% Native Hawaiian/Other Pacific Islander, 4.5% Two or more races, 17.8% Hispanic of any race; Average household size: 2.32; Median age: 31.7; Age under 18: 23.3%; Age 65 and over: 10.3%; Males per 100 females: 93.4; Marriage status: 56.2% never married, 27.5% now married, 3.9% separated, 5.2% widowed, 11.1% divorced; Foreign born: 8.7%; Speak English only: 80.4%; With disability: 17.9%; Veterans: 4.2%; Ancestry: 9.0% German, 8.7% Irish, 8.1% Italian, 5.1% English, 2.6% Polish

Employment: 9.5% management, business, and financial, 4.6% computer, engineering, and science, 12.8% education, legal, community service, arts, and media, 6.6% healthcare practitioners, 24.9% service, 24.2% sales and office, 4.7% natural resources, construction, and maintenance, 12.7% production, transportation, and material moving

Income: Per capita: $21,055; Median household: $32,347; Average household: $47,352; Households with income of $100,000 or more: 10.0%; Poverty rate: 33.1%

Educational Attainment: High school diploma or higher: 80.8%; Bachelor's degree or higher: 24.0%; Graduate/professional degree or higher: 9.9%

School District(s)

Brighton Central SD (KG-12)
Enrollment: 3,628 . . . . (585) 242-5200
Churchville-Chili Central SD (KG-12)
Enrollment: 3,891 . . . . (585) 293-1800
Discovery Charter School (KG-06)
Enrollment: 284. . . . . (585) 342-4032
East Irondequoit Central SD (PK-12)
Enrollment: 3,185 . . . . (585) 339-1210
Eugenio Maria De Hostos Charter School (KG-08)
Enrollment: 619 . . . . (585) 544-6170
Exploration Elementary CS - Science and Tech
Enrollment: n/a . . . . (585) 694-5234
Gates-Chili Central SD (PK-12)
Enrollment: 4,229 . . . . (585) 247-5050
Genesee Community Charter School (KG-06)
Enrollment: 217 . . . . (585) 697-1960
Greece Central SD (PK-12)
Enrollment: 11,083 . . . . (585) 966-2321
Penfield Central SD (KG-12)
Enrollment: 4,581 . . . . (585) 249-5700
Pittsford Central SD (KG-12)
Enrollment: 5,693 . . . . (585) 267-1004
Puc Achieve Charter School (05-07)
Enrollment: 286 . . . . (585) 471-6219
Renaissance Academy Charter School of the Arts (KG-04)
Enrollment: 327 . . . . (585) 225-4200
Rochester Academy Charter School (07-12)
Enrollment: 361 . . . . (585) 467-9201
Rochester City SD (PK-12)
Enrollment: 29,436 . . . . (585) 262-8378
Rochester Prep Charter School 3 (KG-KG)
Enrollment: 90 . . . . (585) 694-4072
Rush-Henrietta Central SD (PK-12)
Enrollment: 5,433 . . . . (585) 359-5012
True North Rochester Prep Charter School-West Camp (KG-08)
Enrollment: 761 . . . . (585) 368-5090
True North Rochester Preparatory Charter School (KG-10)
Enrollment: 1,003 . . . . (585) 436-8629
University Preparatory Charter School for Young Me (07-12)
Enrollment: 385. . . . . (585) 672-1280
Urban Choice Charter School (KG-08)
Enrollment: 397 . . . . (585) 288-5702
Vertus Charter School (09-11)
Enrollment: 251 . . . . (585) 747-8911
West Irondequoit Central SD (KG-12)
Enrollment: 3,597 . . . . (585) 336-2983
Young Women's College Prep Charter School of Rochester (07-11)
Enrollment: 345. . . . . (585) 254-0320

Four-year College(s)

Bryant & Stratton College-Greece (Private, For-profit)
Enrollment: 217 . . . . (585) 720-0660
Tuition: In-state $17,213; Out-of-state $17,213
Colgate Rochester Crozer Divinity School (Private, Not-for-profit)
Enrollment: 50. . . . . (585) 271-1320
Nazareth College (Private, Not-for-profit)
Enrollment: 2,900 . . . . (585) 389-2525
Tuition: In-state $33,549; Out-of-state $33,549
Northeastern Seminary (Private, Not-for-profit, Interdenominational)
Enrollment: 124. . . . . (585) 594-6000
Roberts Wesleyan College (Private, Not-for-profit, Free Methodist)
Enrollment: 1,740 . . . . (585) 594-6000
Tuition: In-state $30,686; Out-of-state $30,686
Rochester Institute of Technology (Private, Not-for-profit)
Enrollment: 16,584 . . . . (585) 475-2411
Tuition: In-state $40,068; Out-of-state $40,068
Saint John Fisher College (Private, Not-for-profit, Roman Catholic)
Enrollment: 3,776 . . . . (585) 385-8000
Tuition: In-state $33,120; Out-of-state $33,120
St Bernard's School of Theology and Ministry (Private, Not-for-profit, Roman Catholic)
Enrollment: 77. . . . . (585) 271-3657
Talmudical Institute of Upstate New York (Private, Not-for-profit)
Enrollment: 16. . . . . (716) 473-2810
Tuition: In-state $5,800; Out-of-state $5,800

University of Rochester (Private, Not-for-profit)
Enrollment: 11,648 . . . . (585) 275-3221
Tuition: In-state $52,020; Out-of-state $52,020

Two-year College(s)

Bryant & Stratton College-Henrietta (Private, For-profit)
Enrollment: 184 . . . . (585) 292-5627
Tuition: In-state $16,855; Out-of-state $16,855
Monroe Community College (Public)
Enrollment: 12,907 . . . . (585) 292-2000
Tuition: In-state $5,139; Out-of-state $9,419

Vocational/Technical School(s)

Continental School of Beauty Culture-Rochester (Private, For-profit)
Enrollment: 322. . . . . (585) 272-8060
Tuition: $12,690
Empire Beauty School-Rochester (Private, For-profit)
Enrollment: 76. . . . . (800) 920-4593
Tuition: $12,750
Isabella Graham Hart School of Practical Nursing (Private, Not-for-profit)
Enrollment: 70. . . . . (585) 922-1400
Tuition: $13,174
Monroe 2 Orleans BOCES-Center for Workforce Development (Public)
Enrollment: 74. . . . . (585) 349-9100
Tuition: $7,700
Onondaga School of Therapeutic Massage-Rochester (Private, For-profit)
Enrollment: 61. . . . . (585) 241-0070
Tuition: $15,575
Sharp Edgez Barber Institute (Private, For-profit)
Enrollment: 105 . . . . (585) 482-2808
Tuition: $8,000
Shear Ego International School of Hair Design (Private, For-profit)
Enrollment: 107 . . . . (585) 342-0070
Tuition: $13,740

Housing: Homeownership rate: 36.5%; Median home value: $79,400; Median year structure built: Before 1940; Homeowner vacancy rate: 1.3%; Median selected monthly owner costs: $1,032 with a mortgage; $467 without a mortgage; Median gross rent: $807 per month; Rental vacancy rate: 7.6%

Health Insurance: 92.6% have insurance; 51.2% have private insurance; 52.0% have public insurance; 7.4% do not have insurance; 3.0% of children under 18 do not have insurance

Hospitals: Highland Hospital (272 beds); Monroe Community Hospital (566 beds); Rochester General Hospital (528 beds); Strong Memorial Hospital (750 beds); Unity Hospital of Rochester (681 beds)

Safety: Violent crime rate: 89.7 per 10,000 population; Property crime rate: 380.4 per 10,000 population

Newspapers: City Newspaper (weekly circulation 40,000); Democrat & Chronicle (daily circulation 156,000)

Transportation: Commute: 79.3% car, 9.2% public transportation, 6.7% walk, 2.7% work from home; Mean travel time to work: 20.1 minutes; Amtrak: Train service available.

Airports: Greater Rochester International (primary service/small hub)

Additional Information Contacts
City of Rochester. . . . . (585) 428-5990
http://www.cityofrochester.gov

RUSH (town). Covers a land area of 30.332 square miles and a water area of 0.373 square miles. Located at 42.97° N. Lat; 77.67° W. Long. Elevation is 551 feet.

Population: 3,499; Growth (since 2000): -2.9%; Density: 115.4 persons per square mile; Race: 96.4% White, 2.6% Black/African American, 0.2% Asian, 0.0% American Indian/Alaska Native, 0.0% Native Hawaiian/Other Pacific Islander, 0.5% Two or more races, 3.5% Hispanic of any race; Average household size: 2.54; Median age: 49.3; Age under 18: 20.5%; Age 65 and over: 19.1%; Males per 100 females: 103.0; Marriage status: 23.2% never married, 61.1% now married, 1.6% separated, 4.4% widowed, 11.3% divorced; Foreign born: 3.0%; Speak English only: 96.9%; With disability: 10.8%; Veterans: 6.5%; Ancestry: 29.3% German, 23.7% Italian, 21.5% Irish, 13.0% English, 6.4% Polish

Employment: 11.9% management, business, and financial, 10.0% computer, engineering, and science, 11.5% education, legal, community service, arts, and media, 7.3% healthcare practitioners, 10.7% service, 27.6% sales and office, 11.8% natural resources, construction, and maintenance, 9.1% production, transportation, and material moving

Income: Per capita: $37,008; Median household: $85,046; Average household: $95,316; Households with income of $100,000 or more: 38.0%; Poverty rate: 4.9%
Educational Attainment: High school diploma or higher: 96.6%; Bachelor's degree or higher: 46.6%; Graduate/professional degree or higher: 21.0%

School District(s)
Rush-Henrietta Central SD (PK-12)
    Enrollment: 5,433 . . . . (585) 359-5012
Housing: Homeownership rate: 90.3%; Median home value: $190,300; Median year structure built: 1966; Homeowner vacancy rate: 1.6%; Median selected monthly owner costs: $1,756 with a mortgage, $595 without a mortgage; Median gross rent: $796 per month; Rental vacancy rate: 0.0%
Health Insurance: 98.3% have insurance; 82.4% have private insurance; 31.5% have public insurance; 1.7% do not have insurance; 0.0% of children under 18 do not have insurance
Transportation: Commute: 94.4% car, 0.0% public transportation, 0.0% walk, 3.9% work from home; Mean travel time to work: 23.0 minutes
Additional Information Contacts
Town of Rush . . . . (585) 533-1312
    http://townofrush.com

SCOTTSVILLE (village). Covers a land area of 1.082 square miles and a water area of 0.005 square miles. Located at 43.02° N. Lat; 77.75° W. Long. Elevation is 607 feet.
Population: 2,024; Growth (since 2000): -4.9%; Density: 1,870.2 persons per square mile; Race: 87.0% White, 9.7% Black/African American, 0.8% Asian, 0.0% American Indian/Alaska Native, 0.0% Native Hawaiian/Other Pacific Islander, 2.5% Two or more races, 6.7% Hispanic of any race; Average household size: 2.52; Median age: 40.9; Age under 18: 23.9%; Age 65 and over: 17.8%; Males per 100 females: 97.9; Marriage status: 28.0% never married, 53.4% now married, 2.1% separated, 6.5% widowed, 12.1% divorced; Foreign born: 2.6%; Speak English only: 93.6%; With disability: 14.6%; Veterans: 8.5%; Ancestry: 20.8% German, 18.7% Irish, 14.0% Italian, 13.6% English, 4.9% Polish
Employment: 10.2% management, business, and financial, 6.1% computer, engineering, and science, 18.8% education, legal, community service, arts, and media, 8.6% healthcare practitioners, 12.2% service, 22.5% sales and office, 10.4% natural resources, construction, and maintenance, 11.1% production, transportation, and material moving
Income: Per capita: $28,203; Median household: $59,911; Average household: $69,658; Households with income of $100,000 or more: 22.6%; Poverty rate: 17.1%
Educational Attainment: High school diploma or higher: 93.5%; Bachelor's degree or higher: 39.4%; Graduate/professional degree or higher: 18.1%

School District(s)
Wheatland-Chili Central SD (KG-12)
    Enrollment: 686 . . . . (585) 889-6246
Housing: Homeownership rate: 79.0%; Median home value: $127,000; Median year structure built: 1958; Homeowner vacancy rate: 0.0%; Median selected monthly owner costs: $1,210 with a mortgage, $617 without a mortgage; Median gross rent: $969 per month; Rental vacancy rate: 0.0%
Health Insurance: 93.9% have insurance; 73.7% have private insurance; 38.6% have public insurance; 6.1% do not have insurance; 0.8% of children under 18 do not have insurance
Transportation: Commute: 93.7% car, 0.0% public transportation, 3.3% walk, 2.5% work from home; Mean travel time to work: 24.4 minutes

SPENCERPORT (village). Covers a land area of 1.337 square miles and a water area of 0.032 square miles. Located at 43.19° N. Lat; 77.81° W. Long. Elevation is 554 feet.
History: Site of John T. Trowbridge's boyhood home. Incorporated 1867.
Population: 3,621; Growth (since 2000): 1.7%; Density: 2,707.6 persons per square mile; Race: 94.2% White, 2.9% Black/African American, 0.2% Asian, 0.0% American Indian/Alaska Native, 0.0% Native Hawaiian/Other Pacific Islander, 2.2% Two or more races, 0.5% Hispanic of any race; Average household size: 2.56; Median age: 41.3; Age under 18: 25.3%; Age 65 and over: 13.8%; Males per 100 females: 91.0; Marriage status: 30.4% never married, 52.2% now married, 4.3% separated, 5.4% widowed, 12.0% divorced; Foreign born: 2.4%; Speak English only: 98.4%; With disability: 10.8%; Veterans: 4.4%; Ancestry: 36.8% German, 26.1% Italian, 22.8% Irish, 10.5% English, 8.3% American
Employment: 19.6% management, business, and financial, 3.7% computer, engineering, and science, 15.3% education, legal, community

service, arts, and media, 5.3% healthcare practitioners, 15.9% service, 22.2% sales and office, 6.3% natural resources, construction, and maintenance, 11.7% production, transportation, and material moving
Income: Per capita: $32,509; Median household: $73,894; Average household: $82,515; Households with income of $100,000 or more: 35.2%; Poverty rate: 7.2%
Educational Attainment: High school diploma or higher: 98.1%; Bachelor's degree or higher: 39.7%; Graduate/professional degree or higher: 20.1%

School District(s)
Monroe 2-Orleans Boces
    Enrollment: n/a . . . . (585) 352-2410
Spencerport Central SD (KG-12)
    Enrollment: 3,620 . . . . (585) 349-5102
Housing: Homeownership rate: 68.1%; Median home value: $148,100; Median year structure built: 1958; Homeowner vacancy rate: 0.0%; Median selected monthly owner costs: $1,493 with a mortgage, $631 without a mortgage; Median gross rent: $938 per month; Rental vacancy rate: 0.0%
Health Insurance: 96.1% have insurance; 86.4% have private insurance; 23.5% have public insurance; 3.9% do not have insurance; 2.6% of children under 18 do not have insurance
Newspapers: Westside News Inc. (weekly circulation 33,000)
Transportation: Commute: 94.3% car, 0.1% public transportation, 1.8% walk, 3.9% work from home; Mean travel time to work: 18.6 minutes

SWEDEN (town). Covers a land area of 33.679 square miles and a water area of 0.152 square miles. Located at 43.18° N. Lat; 77.93° W. Long.
Population: 14,216; Growth (since 2000): 3.6%; Density: 422.1 persons per square mile; Race: 91.1% White, 2.9% Black/African American, 2.5% Asian, 0.0% American Indian/Alaska Native, 0.0% Native Hawaiian/Other Pacific Islander, 2.8% Two or more races, 4.8% Hispanic of any race; Average household size: 2.43; Median age: 24.8; Age under 18: 15.9%; Age 65 and over: 12.1%; Males per 100 females: 92.6; Marriage status: 53.9% never married, 34.3% now married, 2.1% separated, 3.9% widowed, 7.9% divorced; Foreign born: 3.7%; Speak English only: 91.7%; With disability: 11.4%; Veterans: 5.5%; Ancestry: 22.1% German, 21.1% Italian, 18.7% Irish, 13.0% English, 7.5% Polish
Employment: 10.7% management, business, and financial, 4.4% computer, engineering, and science, 15.2% education, legal, community service, arts, and media, 4.7% healthcare practitioners, 21.6% service, 29.5% sales and office, 5.6% natural resources, construction, and maintenance, 8.4% production, transportation, and material moving
Income: Per capita: $24,183; Median household: $50,317; Average household: $67,112; Households with income of $100,000 or more: 19.9%; Poverty rate: 18.5%
Educational Attainment: High school diploma or higher: 93.3%; Bachelor's degree or higher: 34.8%; Graduate/professional degree or higher: 16.6%
Housing: Homeownership rate: 55.9%; Median home value: $134,800; Median year structure built: 1969; Homeowner vacancy rate: 1.1%; Median selected monthly owner costs: $1,422 with a mortgage, $613 without a mortgage; Median gross rent: $804 per month; Rental vacancy rate: 6.2%
Health Insurance: 95.8% have insurance; 80.5% have private insurance; 29.6% have public insurance; 4.2% do not have insurance; 3.0% of children under 18 do not have insurance
Transportation: Commute: 77.8% car, 1.8% public transportation, 15.4% walk, 3.5% work from home; Mean travel time to work: 20.6 minutes
Additional Information Contacts
Town of Sweden . . . . (585) 637-2144
    http://www.townofsweden.org

WEBSTER (town). Covers a land area of 33.531 square miles and a water area of 1.707 square miles. Located at 43.23° N. Lat; 77.45° W. Long. Elevation is 446 feet.
History: Incorporated 1905.
Population: 44,224; Growth (since 2000): 16.6%; Density: 1,318.9 persons per square mile; Race: 91.0% White, 2.2% Black/African American, 3.8% Asian, 0.0% American Indian/Alaska Native, 0.0% Native Hawaiian/Other Pacific Islander, 2.7% Two or more races, 2.3% Hispanic of any race; Average household size: 2.47; Median age: 43.7; Age under 18: 21.4%; Age 65 and over: 18.6%; Males per 100 females: 93.7; Marriage status: 25.5% never married, 59.0% now married, 1.4% separated, 6.8% widowed, 8.7% divorced; Foreign born: 9.8%; Speak

English only: 88.7%; With disability: 10.5%; Veterans: 6.9%; Ancestry: 25.7% Italian, 23.4% German, 16.9% Irish, 11.9% English, 7.1% Polish
Employment: 18.4% management, business, and financial, 10.3% computer, engineering, and science, 11.9% education, legal, community service, arts, and media, 7.8% healthcare practitioners, 12.2% service, 23.1% sales and office, 6.9% natural resources, construction, and maintenance, 9.5% production, transportation, and material moving
Income: Per capita: $36,005; Median household: $75,552; Average household: $87,522; Households with income of $100,000 or more: 33.0%; Poverty rate: 4.9%
Educational Attainment: High school diploma or higher: 95.4%; Bachelor's degree or higher: 44.9%; Graduate/professional degree or higher: 20.0%

School District(s)
Webster Central SD (PK-12)
    Enrollment: 8,494 . . . . (585) 216-0001
Housing: Homeownership rate: 76.2%; Median home value: $180,200; Median year structure built: 1980; Homeowner vacancy rate: 1.1%; Median selected monthly owner costs: $1,618 with a mortgage, $672 without a mortgage; Median gross rent: $1,015 per month; Rental vacancy rate: 1.2%
Health Insurance: 96.8% have insurance; 83.6% have private insurance; 28.9% have public insurance; 3.2% do not have insurance; 2.3% of children under 18 do not have insurance
Safety: Violent crime rate: 7.1 per 10,000 population; Property crime rate: 91.1 per 10,000 population
Newspapers: Wayne County Mail (weekly circulation 2,400); Webster Herald (weekly circulation 4,200)
Transportation: Commute: 93.6% car, 0.2% public transportation, 1.3% walk, 4.1% work from home; Mean travel time to work: 20.3 minutes
Additional Information Contacts
Town of Webster . . . . (585) 872-1000
    http://www.ci.webster.ny.us

WEBSTER (village). Covers a land area of 2.202 square miles and a water area of <.001 square miles. Located at 43.22° N. Lat; 77.42° W. Long. Elevation is 446 feet.
Population: 5,558; Growth (since 2000): 6.6%; Density: 2,523.8 persons per square mile; Race: 75.4% White, 4.4% Black/African American, 12.1% Asian, 0.0% American Indian/Alaska Native, 0.0% Native Hawaiian/Other Pacific Islander, 7.1% Two or more races, 4.1% Hispanic of any race; Average household size: 2.20; Median age: 37.9; Age under 18: 20.2%; Age 65 and over: 14.9%; Males per 100 females: 89.4; Marriage status: 36.3% never married, 41.0% now married, 2.3% separated, 8.8% widowed, 13.9% divorced; Foreign born: 21.6%; Speak English only: 74.6%; With disability: 13.2%; Veterans: 6.3%; Ancestry: 20.5% German, 11.8% Italian, 11.4% English, 10.3% Irish, 5.3% Afghan
Employment: 11.8% management, business, and financial, 13.4% computer, engineering, and science, 12.5% education, legal, community service, arts, and media, 7.1% healthcare practitioners, 16.7% service, 20.7% sales and office, 6.4% natural resources, construction, and maintenance, 11.4% production, transportation, and material moving
Income: Per capita: $26,051; Median household: $43,750; Average household: $54,590; Households with income of $100,000 or more: 13.4%; Poverty rate: 18.6%
Educational Attainment: High school diploma or higher: 91.1%; Bachelor's degree or higher: 35.8%; Graduate/professional degree or higher: 17.3%

School District(s)
Webster Central SD (PK-12)
    Enrollment: 8,494 . . . . (585) 216-0001
Housing: Homeownership rate: 40.7%; Median home value: $149,700; Median year structure built: 1966; Homeowner vacancy rate: 4.2%; Median selected monthly owner costs: $1,287 with a mortgage, $554 without a mortgage; Median gross rent: $941 per month; Rental vacancy rate: 0.0%
Health Insurance: 92.4% have insurance; 63.6% have private insurance; 42.2% have public insurance; 7.6% do not have insurance; 0.9% of children under 18 do not have insurance
Newspapers: Wayne County Mail (weekly circulation 2,400); Webster Herald (weekly circulation 4,200)
Transportation: Commute: 90.7% car, 0.0% public transportation, 5.0% walk, 3.8% work from home; Mean travel time to work: 18.2 minutes
Additional Information Contacts
Village of Webster . . . . (585) 265-3770
    http://www.villageofwebster.com

WEST HENRIETTA (unincorporated postal area)
ZCTA: 14586
    Covers a land area of 11.146 square miles and a water area of 0.193 square miles. Located at 43.04° N. Lat; 77.69° W. Long. Elevation is 604 feet.
Population: 11,691; Growth (since 2000): 88.7%; Density: 1,048.9 persons per square mile; Race: 74.2% White, 7.5% Black/African American, 10.9% Asian, 0.6% American Indian/Alaska Native, 0.0% Native Hawaiian/Other Pacific Islander, 5.3% Two or more races, 3.9% Hispanic of any race; Average household size: 2.73; Median age: 34.8; Age under 18: 25.6%; Age 65 and over: 10.6%; Males per 100 females: 104.3; Marriage status: 32.9% never married, 53.8% now married, 1.6% separated, 4.1% widowed, 9.2% divorced; Foreign born: 14.5%; Speak English only: 82.6%; With disability: 9.8%; Veterans: 4.5%; Ancestry: 16.8% German, 13.5% Irish, 11.2% Italian, 8.2% English, 6.4% American
Employment: 18.8% management, business, and financial, 11.9% computer, engineering, and science, 12.8% education, legal, community service, arts, and media, 8.0% healthcare practitioners, 13.0% service, 20.3% sales and office, 4.2% natural resources, construction, and maintenance, 11.0% production, transportation, and material moving
Income: Per capita: $31,576; Median household: $82,076; Average household: $85,144; Households with income of $100,000 or more: 36.3%; Poverty rate: 8.1%
Educational Attainment: High school diploma or higher: 93.2%; Bachelor's degree or higher: 44.6%; Graduate/professional degree or higher: 20.0%

School District(s)
Rush-Henrietta Central SD (PK-12)
    Enrollment: 5,433 . . . . (585) 359-5012
Housing: Homeownership rate: 71.1%; Median home value: $179,000; Median year structure built: 1993; Homeowner vacancy rate: 0.4%; Median selected monthly owner costs: $1,569 with a mortgage, $590 without a mortgage; Median gross rent: $1,108 per month; Rental vacancy rate: 0.0%
Health Insurance: 95.9% have insurance; 79.7% have private insurance; 26.1% have public insurance; 4.1% do not have insurance; 2.6% of children under 18 do not have insurance
Transportation: Commute: 91.3% car, 0.3% public transportation, 2.9% walk, 4.5% work from home; Mean travel time to work: 20.0 minutes

WHEATLAND (town). Covers a land area of 30.411 square miles and a water area of 0.261 square miles. Located at 43.01° N. Lat; 77.82° W. Long. Elevation is 604 feet.
Population: 4,752; Growth (since 2000): -7.7%; Density: 156.3 persons per square mile; Race: 91.0% White, 7.1% Black/African American, 0.3% Asian, 0.0% American Indian/Alaska Native, 0.0% Native Hawaiian/Other Pacific Islander, 1.5% Two or more races, 3.6% Hispanic of any race; Average household size: 2.49; Median age: 33.7; Age under 18: 22.2%; Age 65 and over: 13.4%; Males per 100 females: 100.4; Marriage status: 31.2% never married, 51.4% now married, 2.5% separated, 5.7% widowed, 11.7% divorced; Foreign born: 1.7%; Speak English only: 96.9%; With disability: 12.8%; Veterans: 6.5%; Ancestry: 30.4% German, 23.5% Irish, 20.6% Italian, 11.2% English, 5.5% Polish
Employment: 16.3% management, business, and financial, 5.9% computer, engineering, and science, 11.1% education, legal, community service, arts, and media, 7.3% healthcare practitioners, 14.6% service, 25.4% sales and office, 9.5% natural resources, construction, and maintenance, 10.1% production, transportation, and material moving
Income: Per capita: $28,712; Median household: $59,744; Average household: $70,043; Households with income of $100,000 or more: 19.6%; Poverty rate: 13.5%
Educational Attainment: High school diploma or higher: 95.4%; Bachelor's degree or higher: 35.0%; Graduate/professional degree or higher: 14.1%
Housing: Homeownership rate: 67.9%; Median home value: $133,600; Median year structure built: 1971; Homeowner vacancy rate: 0.0%; Median selected monthly owner costs: $1,294 with a mortgage, $576 without a mortgage; Median gross rent: $1,045 per month; Rental vacancy rate: 0.0%
Health Insurance: 94.5% have insurance; 77.8% have private insurance; 33.2% have public insurance; 5.5% do not have insurance; 1.7% of children under 18 do not have insurance
Transportation: Commute: 95.8% car, 0.0% public transportation, 1.5% walk, 2.4% work from home; Mean travel time to work: 22.5 minutes

Additional Information Contacts
Town of Wheatland . . . . (585) 889-1553
http://www.townofwheatland.org

Montgomery County

Located in east central New York, in the Mohawk River Valley; crossed by the Barge Canal; drained by Schoharie Creek. Covers a land area of 403.043 square miles, a water area of 7.312 square miles, and is located in the Eastern Time Zone at 42.90° N. Lat., 74.44° W. Long. The county was founded in 1772. County seat is Fonda.

Montgomery County is part of the Amsterdam, NY Micropolitan Statistical Area. The entire metro area includes: Montgomery County, NY

Population: 49,500; Growth (since 2000): -0.4%; Density: 122.8 persons per square mile; Race: 88.2% White, 1.8% Black/African American, 0.8% Asian, 0.1% American Indian/Alaska Native, 0.0% Native Hawaiian/Other Pacific Islander, 3.6% two or more races, 13.2% Hispanic of any race; Average household size: 2.46; Median age: 41.1; Age under 18: 22.9%; Age 65 and over: 17.9%; Males per 100 females: 94.9; Marriage status: 32.4% never married, 47.9% now married, 2.9% separated, 8.3% widowed, 11.5% divorced; Foreign born: 3.4%; Speak English only: 85.7%; With disability: 15.9%; Veterans: 7.9%; Ancestry: 19.4% German, 15.4% Italian, 15.1% Irish, 11.0% Polish, 7.5% English
Religion: Six largest groups: 27.8% Catholicism, 4.4% Lutheran, 3.6% Presbyterian-Reformed, 2.6% Methodist/Pietist, 2.1% Non-denominational Protestant, 1.0% Baptist
Economy: Unemployment rate: 4.2%; Leading industries: 17.3 % health care and social assistance; 17.0 % retail trade; 11.1 % construction; Farms: 659 totaling 131,386 acres; Company size: 1 employs 1,000 or more persons, 2 employ 500 to 999 persons, 21 employs 100 to 499 persons, 1,057 employ less than 100 persons; Business ownership: 858 women-owned, 33 Black-owned, 109 Hispanic-owned, 85 Asian-owned, n/a American Indian/Alaska Native-owned
Employment: 11.5% management, business, and financial, 2.7% computer, engineering, and science, 9.9% education, legal, community service, arts, and media, 5.8% healthcare practitioners, 18.8% service, 23.9% sales and office, 9.6% natural resources, construction, and maintenance, 17.7% production, transportation, and material moving
Income: Per capita: $25,307; Median household: $47,449; Average household: $62,118; Households with income of $100,000 or more: 16.8%; Poverty rate: 19.6%
Educational Attainment: High school diploma or higher: 85.2%; Bachelor's degree or higher: 17.0%; Graduate/professional degree or higher: 6.9%
Housing: Homeownership rate: 68.9%; Median home value: $99,900; Median year structure built: 1944; Homeowner vacancy rate: 1.7%; Median selected monthly owner costs: $1,232 with a mortgage, $534 without a mortgage; Median gross rent: $732 per month; Rental vacancy rate: 5.6%
Vital Statistics: Birth rate: 127.7 per 10,000 population; Death rate: 111.9 per 10,000 population; Age-adjusted cancer mortality rate: 181.7 deaths per 100,000 population
Health Insurance: 91.8% have insurance; 61.1% have private insurance; 45.7% have public insurance; 8.2% do not have insurance; 9.6% of children under 18 do not have insurance
Health Care: Physicians: 13.6 per 10,000 population; Dentists: 6.5 per 10,000 population; Hospital beds: 58.9 per 10,000 population; Hospital admissions: 1,393.7 per 10,000 population
Transportation: Commute: 89.1% car, 1.3% public transportation, 3.6% walk, 3.7% work from home; Mean travel time to work: 24.5 minutes
2016 Presidential Election: 59.3% Trump, 34.6% Clinton, 3.6% Johnson, 1.4% Stein
National and State Parks: Schoharie Crossing State Historic Site
Additional Information Contacts
Montgomery Government . . . . (518) 853-8111
http://www.co.montgomery.ny.us

Montgomery County Communities

AMES (village). Covers a land area of 0.131 square miles and a water area of 0 square miles. Located at 42.84° N. Lat; 74.60° W. Long. Elevation is 705 feet.
Population: 161; Growth (since 2000): -6.9%; Density: 1,232.0 persons per square mile; Race: 98.8% White, 1.2% Black/African American, 0.0% Asian, 0.0% American Indian/Alaska Native, 0.0% Native Hawaiian/Other Pacific Islander, 0.0% Two or more races, 0.6% Hispanic of any race; Average household size: 2.48; Median age: 48.8; Age under 18: 13.0%; Age 65 and over: 21.7%; Males per 100 females: 107.1; Marriage status: 23.1% never married, 64.6% now married, 1.4% separated, 2.0% widowed, 10.2% divorced; Foreign born: 1.9%; Speak English only: 98.7%; With disability: 14.3%; Veterans: 13.6%; Ancestry: 20.5% English, 19.3% German, 14.3% Irish, 11.2% French, 9.3% Polish
Employment: 17.3% management, business, and financial, 0.0% computer, engineering, and science, 14.8% education, legal, community service, arts, and media, 4.9% healthcare practitioners, 11.1% service, 29.6% sales and office, 9.9% natural resources, construction, and maintenance, 12.3% production, transportation, and material moving
Income: Per capita: $33,702; Median household: $59,375; Average household: $89,345; Households with income of $100,000 or more: 35.3%; Poverty rate: 7.5%
Educational Attainment: High school diploma or higher: 83.3%; Bachelor's degree or higher: 20.0%; Graduate/professional degree or higher: 10.0%
Housing: Homeownership rate: 89.2%; Median home value: $103,100; Median year structure built: Before 1940; Homeowner vacancy rate: 0.0%; Median selected monthly owner costs: $975 with a mortgage, $450 without a mortgage; Median gross rent: $1,104 per month; Rental vacancy rate: 0.0%
Health Insurance: 96.3% have insurance; 73.9% have private insurance; 37.9% have public insurance; 3.7% do not have insurance; 0.0% of children under 18 do not have insurance
Transportation: Commute: 93.8% car, 0.0% public transportation, 0.0% walk, 1.2% work from home; Mean travel time to work: 32.8 minutes

AMSTERDAM (city). Covers a land area of 5.862 square miles and a water area of 0.391 square miles. Located at 42.94° N. Lat; 74.19° W. Long. Elevation is 361 feet.
History: Amsterdam was first settled by Albert Veeder, who came from Schenectady in 1783. The village of Amsterdam was so named in 1804. It began to grow in size and industrial importance after the Erie Canal was opened in 1825 and the Utica & Schenectady Railroad was constructed through it in 1836. The local carpet industry traces its beginnings to 1838, when William E. Greene established a carpet mill. The knitting industry was started by Greene in 1856.
Population: 17,974; Growth (since 2000): -2.1%; Density: 3,066.1 persons per square mile; Race: 75.2% White, 3.8% Black/African American, 0.6% Asian, 0.1% American Indian/Alaska Native, 0.0% Native Hawaiian/Other Pacific Islander, 6.7% Two or more races, 29.7% Hispanic of any race; Average household size: 2.46; Median age: 36.7; Age under 18: 23.6%; Age 65 and over: 16.9%; Males per 100 females: 90.0; Marriage status: 41.0% never married, 38.9% now married, 3.3% separated, 8.1% widowed, 12.0% divorced; Foreign born: 5.8%; Speak English only: 72.8%; With disability: 19.9%; Veterans: 7.0%; Ancestry: 17.5% Italian, 13.3% Irish, 11.9% German, 11.5% Polish, 4.8% English
Employment: 11.0% management, business, and financial, 2.5% computer, engineering, and science, 9.0% education, legal, community service, arts, and media, 4.1% healthcare practitioners, 21.9% service, 25.6% sales and office, 6.8% natural resources, construction, and maintenance, 19.0% production, transportation, and material moving
Income: Per capita: $21,931; Median household: $40,136; Average household: $53,271; Households with income of $100,000 or more: 13.1%; Poverty rate: 25.6%
Educational Attainment: High school diploma or higher: 82.5%; Bachelor's degree or higher: 14.6%; Graduate/professional degree or higher: 5.5%

School District(s)
Amsterdam City SD (PK-12)
    Enrollment: 3,906 . . . . (518) 843-3180
Broadalbin-Perth Central SD (PK-12)
    Enrollment: 1,826 . . . . (518) 954-2500
Housing: Homeownership rate: 53.2%; Median home value: $85,800; Median year structure built: Before 1940; Homeowner vacancy rate: 3.1%; Median selected monthly owner costs: $1,213 with a mortgage, $570 without a mortgage; Median gross rent: $757 per month; Rental vacancy rate: 4.1%
Health Insurance: 94.0% have insurance; 52.6% have private insurance; 54.4% have public insurance; 6.0% do not have insurance; 1.3% of children under 18 do not have insurance
Hospitals: Saint Mary's Hospital at Amsterdam (143 beds)

Safety: Violent crime rate: 17.5 per 10,000 population; Property crime rate: 191.7 per 10,000 population
Newspapers: Courier-Standard-Enterprise (weekly circulation 4,000); The Recorder (daily circulation 9,200)
Transportation: Commute: 86.0% car, 1.5% public transportation, 6.0% walk, 2.3% work from home; Mean travel time to work: 21.8 minutes; Amtrak: Train service available.
Additional Information Contacts
City of Amsterdam . . . . (518) 841-4300
  http://www.amsterdamny.gov

AMSTERDAM (town). Covers a land area of 29.701 square miles and a water area of 0.733 square miles. Located at 42.96° N. Lat; 74.17° W. Long. Elevation is 361 feet.
History: Historically famous for carpet manufacturing. The area was settled in 1783 and was named Amsterdam for its many early settlers from the Netherlands. Nearby stands Fort Johnson, home of the British colonial leader Sir William Johnson. Incorporated 1885.
Population: 6,001; Growth (since 2000): 3.1%; Density: 202.0 persons per square mile; Race: 98.1% White, 0.7% Black/African American, 0.0% Asian, 0.3% American Indian/Alaska Native, 0.0% Native Hawaiian/Other Pacific Islander, 0.5% Two or more races, 4.1% Hispanic of any race; Average household size: 2.19; Median age: 51.9; Age under 18: 15.7%; Age 65 and over: 26.0%; Males per 100 females: 92.0; Marriage status: 26.3% never married, 52.8% now married, 2.0% separated, 10.3% widowed, 10.6% divorced; Foreign born: 1.8%; Speak English only: 94.9%; With disability: 13.7%; Veterans: 8.3%; Ancestry: 22.9% Polish, 20.9% Italian, 19.2% German, 12.8% Irish, 9.1% English
Employment: 12.9% management, business, and financial, 2.6% computer, engineering, and science, 17.3% education, legal, community service, arts, and media, 7.6% healthcare practitioners, 12.9% service, 24.4% sales and office, 8.1% natural resources, construction, and maintenance, 14.2% production, transportation, and material moving
Income: Per capita: $36,001; Median household: $65,339; Average household: $79,909; Households with income of $100,000 or more: 25.8%; Poverty rate: 10.8%
Educational Attainment: High school diploma or higher: 89.6%; Bachelor's degree or higher: 25.0%; Graduate/professional degree or higher: 10.5%
School District(s)
Amsterdam City SD (PK-12)
  Enrollment: 3,906 . . . . (518) 843-3180
Broadalbin-Perth Central SD (PK-12)
  Enrollment: 1,826 . . . . (518) 954-2500
Housing: Homeownership rate: 83.4%; Median home value: $142,000; Median year structure built: 1954; Homeowner vacancy rate: 0.4%; Median selected monthly owner costs: $1,225 with a mortgage, $638 without a mortgage; Median gross rent: $747 per month; Rental vacancy rate: 13.1%
Health Insurance: 97.3% have insurance; 81.6% have private insurance; 39.4% have public insurance; 2.7% do not have insurance; 2.5% of children under 18 do not have insurance
Hospitals: Saint Mary's Hospital at Amsterdam (143 beds)
Newspapers: Courier-Standard-Enterprise (weekly circulation 4,000); The Recorder (daily circulation 9,200)
Transportation: Commute: 92.5% car, 2.5% public transportation, 0.4% walk, 2.6% work from home; Mean travel time to work: 25.0 minutes; Amtrak: Train service available.
Additional Information Contacts
Town of Amsterdam . . . . (518) 842-7961
  http://www.townofamsterdam.org

CANAJOHARIE (town). Covers a land area of 42.632 square miles and a water area of 0.501 square miles. Located at 42.87° N. Lat; 74.61° W. Long. Elevation is 308 feet.
History: Here are Van Alstyne House (1749), with historical collections, and a library and art gallery. Settled c.1730 by Dutch and Germans; incorporated 1829.
Population: 3,637; Growth (since 2000): -4.2%; Density: 85.3 persons per square mile; Race: 94.2% White, 1.7% Black/African American, 0.4% Asian, 0.1% American Indian/Alaska Native, 0.0% Native Hawaiian/Other Pacific Islander, 3.3% Two or more races, 3.1% Hispanic of any race; Average household size: 2.53; Median age: 37.2; Age under 18: 25.5%; Age 65 and over: 14.9%; Males per 100 females: 95.1; Marriage status: 35.6% never married, 45.5% now married, 1.2% separated, 6.7% widowed, 12.2% divorced; Foreign born: 2.3%; Speak English only: 94.7%;

With disability: 13.2%; Veterans: 8.3%; Ancestry: 30.7% German, 14.5% Irish, 11.3% Italian, 8.7% French, 7.3% Dutch
Employment: 18.6% management, business, and financial, 3.0% computer, engineering, and science, 9.4% education, legal, community service, arts, and media, 4.3% healthcare practitioners, 11.1% service, 27.8% sales and office, 7.0% natural resources, construction, and maintenance, 18.7% production, transportation, and material moving
Income: Per capita: $23,753; Median household: $50,031; Average household: $61,191; Households with income of $100,000 or more: 16.8%; Poverty rate: 21.1%
Educational Attainment: High school diploma or higher: 85.3%; Bachelor's degree or higher: 17.0%; Graduate/professional degree or higher: 7.8%
School District(s)
Canajoharie Central SD (PK-12)
  Enrollment: 968 . . . . (518) 673-6302
Housing: Homeownership rate: 66.0%; Median home value: $99,300; Median year structure built: Before 1940; Homeowner vacancy rate: 0.0%; Median selected monthly owner costs: $1,350 with a mortgage, $524 without a mortgage; Median gross rent: $723 per month; Rental vacancy rate: 7.8%
Health Insurance: 93.2% have insurance; 61.4% have private insurance; 43.9% have public insurance; 6.8% do not have insurance; 4.9% of children under 18 do not have insurance
Transportation: Commute: 92.2% car, 1.7% public transportation, 1.1% walk, 4.4% work from home; Mean travel time to work: 25.8 minutes

CANAJOHARIE (village). Covers a land area of 1.330 square miles and a water area of 0.068 square miles. Located at 42.90° N. Lat; 74.57° W. Long. Elevation is 308 feet.
Population: 2,015; Growth (since 2000): -10.7%; Density: 1,515.0 persons per square mile; Race: 91.1% White, 2.9% Black/African American, 0.7% Asian, 0.2% American Indian/Alaska Native, 0.0% Native Hawaiian/Other Pacific Islander, 5.0% Two or more races, 3.5% Hispanic of any race; Average household size: 2.36; Median age: 37.9; Age under 18: 23.4%; Age 65 and over: 18.9%; Males per 100 females: 90.7; Marriage status: 35.8% never married, 42.4% now married, 1.1% separated, 9.5% widowed, 12.4% divorced; Foreign born: 3.5%; Speak English only: 94.6%; With disability: 16.7%; Veterans: 7.6%; Ancestry: 29.3% German, 14.5% Irish, 9.9% Italian, 8.6% French, 7.6% English
Employment: 15.8% management, business, and financial, 3.7% computer, engineering, and science, 6.6% education, legal, community service, arts, and media, 4.6% healthcare practitioners, 15.7% service, 22.3% sales and office, 8.7% natural resources, construction, and maintenance, 22.5% production, transportation, and material moving
Income: Per capita: $21,801; Median household: $37,500; Average household: $51,919; Households with income of $100,000 or more: 12.4%; Poverty rate: 28.5%
Educational Attainment: High school diploma or higher: 82.6%; Bachelor's degree or higher: 15.6%; Graduate/professional degree or higher: 7.3%
School District(s)
Canajoharie Central SD (PK-12)
  Enrollment: 968 . . . . (518) 673-6302
Housing: Homeownership rate: 53.3%; Median home value: $93,700; Median year structure built: Before 1940; Homeowner vacancy rate: 0.0%; Median selected monthly owner costs: $1,303 with a mortgage, $564 without a mortgage; Median gross rent: $677 per month; Rental vacancy rate: 3.5%
Health Insurance: 92.2% have insurance; 53.7% have private insurance; 53.0% have public insurance; 7.8% do not have insurance; 3.4% of children under 18 do not have insurance
Safety: Violent crime rate: 0.0 per 10,000 population; Property crime rate: 75.0 per 10,000 population
Transportation: Commute: 92.4% car, 1.2% public transportation, 2.2% walk, 3.6% work from home; Mean travel time to work: 22.6 minutes

CHARLESTON (town). Covers a land area of 41.890 square miles and a water area of 0.973 square miles. Located at 42.82° N. Lat; 74.36° W. Long. Elevation is 1,138 feet.
Population: 1,374; Growth (since 2000): 6.3%; Density: 32.8 persons per square mile; Race: 98.8% White, 0.9% Black/African American, 0.0% Asian, 0.1% American Indian/Alaska Native, 0.0% Native Hawaiian/Other Pacific Islander, 0.0% Two or more races, 2.7% Hispanic of any race; Average household size: 2.60; Median age: 38.0; Age under 18: 23.8%;

Age 65 and over: 10.8%; Males per 100 females: 102.8; Marriage status: 30.7% never married, 57.6% now married, 4.4% separated, 2.2% widowed, 9.5% divorced; Foreign born: 1.9%; Speak English only: 98.2%; With disability: 10.1%; Veterans: 8.8%; Ancestry: 20.4% Irish, 14.4% Italian, 14.2% German, 11.0% Dutch, 10.3% Polish
Employment: 16.9% management, business, and financial, 2.5% computer, engineering, and science, 8.6% education, legal, community service, arts, and media, 7.2% healthcare practitioners, 14.0% service, 17.8% sales and office, 11.4% natural resources, construction, and maintenance, 21.5% production, transportation, and material moving
Income: Per capita: $33,936; Median household: $62,375; Average household: $88,973; Households with income of $100,000 or more: 27.4%; Poverty rate: 8.7%
Educational Attainment: High school diploma or higher: 93.0%; Bachelor's degree or higher: 20.5%; Graduate/professional degree or higher: 6.0%
Housing: Homeownership rate: 80.8%; Median home value: $148,900; Median year structure built: 1983; Homeowner vacancy rate: 3.6%; Median selected monthly owner costs: $1,414 with a mortgage, $620 without a mortgage; Median gross rent: $856 per month; Rental vacancy rate: 0.0%
Health Insurance: 93.8% have insurance; 73.7% have private insurance; 30.7% have public insurance; 6.2% do not have insurance; 6.4% of children under 18 do not have insurance
Transportation: Commute: 95.6% car, 0.5% public transportation, 0.0% walk, 3.2% work from home; Mean travel time to work: 40.8 minutes

---

FLORIDA (town). Covers a land area of 50.132 square miles and a water area of 1.274 square miles. Located at 42.89° N. Lat; 74.20° W. Long.
Population: 2,718; Growth (since 2000): -0.5%; Density: 54.2 persons per square mile; Race: 96.3% White, 0.0% Black/African American, 1.8% Asian, 0.0% American Indian/Alaska Native, 0.0% Native Hawaiian/Other Pacific Islander, 1.9% Two or more races, 3.2% Hispanic of any race; Average household size: 2.29; Median age: 49.2; Age under 18: 16.2%; Age 65 and over: 20.1%; Males per 100 females: 101.6; Marriage status: 24.8% never married, 58.6% now married, 3.7% separated, 4.9% widowed, 11.7% divorced; Foreign born: 2.0%; Speak English only: 95.0%; With disability: 15.7%; Veterans: 8.3%; Ancestry: 27.9% German, 24.9% Irish, 18.0% Polish, 16.5% Italian, 9.2% English
Employment: 9.5% management, business, and financial, 5.6% computer, engineering, and science, 10.8% education, legal, community service, arts, and media, 10.5% healthcare practitioners, 13.6% service, 18.6% sales and office, 14.5% natural resources, construction, and maintenance, 16.8% production, transportation, and material moving
Income: Per capita: $32,867; Median household: $49,293; Average household: $74,541; Households with income of $100,000 or more: 25.8%; Poverty rate: 13.9%
Educational Attainment: High school diploma or higher: 93.9%; Bachelor's degree or higher: 19.3%; Graduate/professional degree or higher: 10.1%
Housing: Homeownership rate: 81.8%; Median home value: $135,200; Median year structure built: 1971; Homeowner vacancy rate: 3.0%; Median selected monthly owner costs: $1,436 with a mortgage, $525 without a mortgage; Median gross rent: $778 per month; Rental vacancy rate: 0.0%
Health Insurance: 93.2% have insurance; 68.4% have private insurance; 46.6% have public insurance; 6.8% do not have insurance; 0.0% of children under 18 do not have insurance
Transportation: Commute: 92.5% car, 1.6% public transportation, 1.6% walk, 2.2% work from home; Mean travel time to work: 26.1 minutes

---

FONDA (village). County seat. Covers a land area of 0.539 square miles and a water area of 0.069 square miles. Located at 42.95° N. Lat; 74.37° W. Long. Elevation is 295 feet.
History: Formally a freight transfer point on the N.Y. Central railroad. Incorporated 1850.
Population: 772; Growth (since 2000): -4.7%; Density: 1,433.3 persons per square mile; Race: 91.5% White, 0.8% Black/African American, 0.0% Asian, 0.0% American Indian/Alaska Native, 0.0% Native Hawaiian/Other Pacific Islander, 3.2% Two or more races, 16.7% Hispanic of any race; Average household size: 2.78; Median age: 36.6; Age under 18: 29.4%; Age 65 and over: 9.8%; Males per 100 females: 96.3; Marriage status: 41.6% never married, 46.8% now married, 4.6% separated, 4.9% widowed, 6.7% divorced; Foreign born: 0.9%; Speak English only: 97.1%; With disability: 15.3%; Veterans: 7.9%; Ancestry: 24.5% Italian, 20.7% Irish, 15.9% German, 10.0% French, 9.1% Dutch

Employment: 10.6% management, business, and financial, 0.8% computer, engineering, and science, 4.4% education, legal, community service, arts, and media, 6.9% healthcare practitioners, 17.8% service, 22.8% sales and office, 13.9% natural resources, construction, and maintenance, 22.8% production, transportation, and material moving
Income: Per capita: $24,230; Median household: $62,000; Average household: $67,322; Households with income of $100,000 or more: 23.9%; Poverty rate: 8.4%
Educational Attainment: High school diploma or higher: 91.3%; Bachelor's degree or higher: 17.1%; Graduate/professional degree or higher: 6.8%

Fonda-Fultonville Central SD (PK-12)
    Enrollment: 1,401 . . . . (518) 853-4415
Housing: Homeownership rate: 65.6%; Median home value: $78,500; Median year structure built: Before 1940; Homeowner vacancy rate: 0.0%; Median selected monthly owner costs: $1,207 with a mortgage, $475 without a mortgage; Median gross rent: $603 per month; Rental vacancy rate: 0.0%
Health Insurance: 97.5% have insurance; 74.5% have private insurance; 31.1% have public insurance; 2.5% do not have insurance; 1.2% of children under 18 do not have insurance
Transportation: Commute: 84.8% car, 0.8% public transportation, 6.5% walk, 7.9% work from home; Mean travel time to work: 22.5 minutes

---

FORT HUNTER (unincorporated postal area)
ZCTA: 12069
    Covers a land area of 0.573 square miles and a water area of 0.118 square miles. Located at 42.95° N. Lat; 74.28° W. Long. Elevation is 292 feet.
Population: 167; Growth (since 2000): n/a; Density: 291.3 persons per square mile; Race: 100.0% White, 0.0% Black/African American, 0.0% Asian, 0.0% American Indian/Alaska Native, 0.0% Native Hawaiian/Other Pacific Islander, 0.0% Two or more races, 0.0% Hispanic of any race; Average household size: 2.29; Median age: 36.1; Age under 18: 29.3%; Age 65 and over: 20.4%; Males per 100 females: 111.6; Marriage status: 37.3% never married, 43.2% now married, 0.0% separated, 6.8% widowed, 12.7% divorced; Foreign born: 0.0%; Speak English only: 100.0%; With disability: 21.0%; Veterans: 0.0%; Ancestry: 72.5% Polish, 41.9% Irish, 37.1% German, 11.4% Dutch, 6.0% Swiss
Employment: 37.0% management, business, and financial, 0.0% computer, engineering, and science, 0.0% education, legal, community service, arts, and media, 0.0% healthcare practitioners, 0.0% service, 0.0% sales and office, 0.0% natural resources, construction, and maintenance, 63.0% production, transportation, and material moving
Income: Per capita: $16,428; Median household: $38,984; Average household: $35,927; Households with income of $100,000 or more: n/a; Poverty rate: 21.6%
Educational Attainment: High school diploma or higher: 95.3%; Bachelor's degree or higher: 7.1%; Graduate/professional degree or higher: 7.1%
Housing: Homeownership rate: 69.9%; Median home value: $86,300; Median year structure built: Before 1940; Homeowner vacancy rate: 22.7%; Median selected monthly owner costs: $0 with a mortgage, $439 without a mortgage; Median gross rent: n/a per month; Rental vacancy rate: 0.0%
Health Insurance: 89.2% have insurance; 26.3% have private insurance; 83.2% have public insurance; 10.8% do not have insurance; 0.0% of children under 18 do not have insurance
Transportation: Commute: 100.0% car, 0.0% public transportation, 0.0% walk, 0.0% work from home; Mean travel time to work: 0.0 minutes

---

FORT JOHNSON (village). Covers a land area of 0.737 square miles and a water area of 0.109 square miles. Located at 42.96° N. Lat; 74.24° W. Long. Elevation is 308 feet.
History: Fort Johnson (1749), once home of Sir William Johnson, is now a museum.
Population: 637; Growth (since 2000): 29.7%; Density: 864.7 persons per square mile; Race: 91.8% White, 5.7% Black/African American, 0.0% Asian, 0.0% American Indian/Alaska Native, 0.0% Native Hawaiian/Other Pacific Islander, 2.5% Two or more races, 11.1% Hispanic of any race; Average household size: 2.78; Median age: 43.9; Age under 18: 19.5%; Age 65 and over: 17.3%; Males per 100 females: 86.3; Marriage status: 32.1% never married, 48.7% now married, 7.6% separated, 5.3% widowed, 13.9% divorced; Foreign born: 1.7%; Speak English only: 96.3%;

With disability: 21.2%; Veterans: 12.3%; Ancestry: 18.5% Italian, 16.5% Irish, 15.1% Polish, 11.0% German, 9.1% English
Employment: 12.7% management, business, and financial, 4.8% computer, engineering, and science, 12.0% education, legal, community service, arts, and media, 5.5% healthcare practitioners, 8.6% service, 38.1% sales and office, 4.1% natural resources, construction, and maintenance, 14.1% production, transportation, and material moving
Income: Per capita: $26,866; Median household: $56,250; Average household: $71,494; Households with income of $100,000 or more: 23.6%; Poverty rate: 20.6%
Educational Attainment: High school diploma or higher: 93.0%; Bachelor's degree or higher: 22.0%; Graduate/professional degree or higher: 7.5%
Housing: Homeownership rate: 82.1%; Median home value: $90,600; Median year structure built: Before 1940; Homeowner vacancy rate: 4.1%; Median selected monthly owner costs: $1,282 with a mortgage, $570 without a mortgage; Median gross rent: $968 per month; Rental vacancy rate: 24.1%
Health Insurance: 97.6% have insurance; 81.0% have private insurance; 39.2% have public insurance; 2.4% do not have insurance; 0.0% of children under 18 do not have insurance
Transportation: Commute: 87.6% car, 0.7% public transportation, 3.5% walk, 0.7% work from home; Mean travel time to work: 27.0 minutes

FORT PLAIN (village). Covers a land area of 1.346 square miles and a water area of 0.057 square miles. Located at 42.93° N. Lat; 74.63° W. Long. Elevation is 305 feet.
History: Settled 1723, incorporated 1832.
Population: 1,698; Growth (since 2000): -25.8%; Density: 1,261.5 persons per square mile; Race: 92.2% White, 0.0% Black/African American, 3.8% Asian, 0.0% American Indian/Alaska Native, 0.0% Native Hawaiian/Other Pacific Islander, 2.8% Two or more races, 2.6% Hispanic of any race; Average household size: 2.24; Median age: 47.6; Age under 18: 18.3%; Age 65 and over: 27.4%; Males per 100 females: 89.7; Marriage status: 30.3% never married, 45.9% now married, 5.5% separated, 10.1% widowed, 13.7% divorced; Foreign born: 3.4%; Speak English only: 92.6%; With disability: 26.9%; Veterans: 8.3%; Ancestry: 28.2% German, 16.8% Irish, 15.2% English, 12.4% Italian, 8.8% American
Employment: 9.0% management, business, and financial, 3.7% computer, engineering, and science, 8.6% education, legal, community service, arts, and media, 4.1% healthcare practitioners, 19.4% service, 29.4% sales and office, 6.6% natural resources, construction, and maintenance, 19.3% production, transportation, and material moving
Income: Per capita: $20,953; Median household: $33,026; Average household: $46,546; Households with income of $100,000 or more: 8.4%; Poverty rate: 22.5%
Educational Attainment: High school diploma or higher: 85.2%; Bachelor's degree or higher: 12.9%; Graduate/professional degree or higher: 4.4%

School District(s)
Fort Plain Central SD (PK-12)
    Enrollment: 849 . . . . (518) 993-4000
Housing: Homeownership rate: 58.5%; Median home value: $68,700; Median year structure built: Before 1940; Homeowner vacancy rate: 5.6%; Median selected monthly owner costs: $1,038 with a mortgage, $530 without a mortgage; Median gross rent: $693 per month; Rental vacancy rate: 15.2%
Health Insurance: 97.1% have insurance; 57.4% have private insurance; 60.8% have public insurance; 2.9% do not have insurance; 0.0% of children under 18 do not have insurance
Safety: Violent crime rate: 22.6 per 10,000 population; Property crime rate: 289.3 per 10,000 population
Transportation: Commute: 89.0% car, 0.8% public transportation, 1.7% walk, 6.6% work from home; Mean travel time to work: 25.4 minutes

FULTONVILLE (village). Covers a land area of 0.477 square miles and a water area of 0.043 square miles. Located at 42.95° N. Lat; 74.37° W. Long. Elevation is 289 feet.
Population: 633; Growth (since 2000): -10.8%; Density: 1,326.5 persons per square mile; Race: 95.6% White, 0.0% Black/African American, 0.6% Asian, 0.0% American Indian/Alaska Native, 0.0% Native Hawaiian/Other Pacific Islander, 3.8% Two or more races, 1.6% Hispanic of any race; Average household size: 2.63; Median age: 32.2; Age under 18: 31.3%; Age 65 and over: 11.1%; Males per 100 females: 92.6; Marriage status: 40.0% never married, 41.6% now married, 4.4% separated, 7.1%

widowed, 11.3% divorced; Foreign born: 0.9%; Speak English only: 97.5%; With disability: 13.0%; Veterans: 7.1%; Ancestry: 25.8% German, 15.6% English, 15.6% Italian, 11.4% Irish, 5.2% Polish
Employment: 8.0% management, business, and financial, 1.6% computer, engineering, and science, 14.1% education, legal, community service, arts, and media, 3.8% healthcare practitioners, 27.2% service, 28.8% sales and office, 6.7% natural resources, construction, and maintenance, 9.9% production, transportation, and material moving
Income: Per capita: $20,820; Median household: $42,656; Average household: $55,210; Households with income of $100,000 or more: 11.7%; Poverty rate: 11.1%
Educational Attainment: High school diploma or higher: 84.7%; Bachelor's degree or higher: 15.3%; Graduate/professional degree or higher: 5.8%
Housing: Homeownership rate: 74.3%; Median home value: $85,000; Median year structure built: Before 1940; Homeowner vacancy rate: 0.0%; Median selected monthly owner costs: $978 with a mortgage, $458 without a mortgage; Median gross rent: $788 per month; Rental vacancy rate: 15.1%
Health Insurance: 94.0% have insurance; 69.2% have private insurance; 37.1% have public insurance; 6.0% do not have insurance; 4.5% of children under 18 do not have insurance
Transportation: Commute: 88.8% car, 0.0% public transportation, 7.5% walk, 3.7% work from home; Mean travel time to work: 20.9 minutes

GLEN (town). Covers a land area of 38.620 square miles and a water area of 0.706 square miles. Located at 42.90° N. Lat; 74.35° W. Long. Elevation is 686 feet.
Population: 2,234; Growth (since 2000): 0.5%; Density: 57.8 persons per square mile; Race: 94.3% White, 2.6% Black/African American, 0.4% Asian, 0.3% American Indian/Alaska Native, 0.0% Native Hawaiian/Other Pacific Islander, 2.0% Two or more races, 4.6% Hispanic of any race; Average household size: 2.75; Median age: 35.0; Age under 18: 26.2%; Age 65 and over: 12.0%; Males per 100 females: 110.7; Marriage status: 35.1% never married, 50.5% now married, 1.8% separated, 4.5% widowed, 9.9% divorced; Foreign born: 1.7%; Speak English only: 89.0%; With disability: 7.5%; Veterans: 5.4%; Ancestry: 21.6% German, 17.0% Irish, 12.3% English, 10.3% Italian, 8.1% Polish
Employment: 9.1% management, business, and financial, 3.4% computer, engineering, and science, 11.1% education, legal, community service, arts, and media, 3.0% healthcare practitioners, 21.4% service, 24.6% sales and office, 12.4% natural resources, construction, and maintenance, 15.0% production, transportation, and material moving
Income: Per capita: $21,816; Median household: $56,288; Average household: $62,444; Households with income of $100,000 or more: 14.3%; Poverty rate: 21.5%
Educational Attainment: High school diploma or higher: 84.4%; Bachelor's degree or higher: 18.2%; Graduate/professional degree or higher: 7.0%
Housing: Homeownership rate: 86.1%; Median home value: $103,900; Median year structure built: 1967; Homeowner vacancy rate: 0.0%; Median selected monthly owner costs: $1,322 with a mortgage, $503 without a mortgage; Median gross rent: $757 per month; Rental vacancy rate: 9.5%
Health Insurance: 85.8% have insurance; 71.6% have private insurance; 25.7% have public insurance; 14.2% do not have insurance; 30.3% of children under 18 do not have insurance
Transportation: Commute: 91.6% car, 0.0% public transportation, 3.7% walk, 4.7% work from home; Mean travel time to work: 25.6 minutes

HAGAMAN (village). Covers a land area of 1.498 square miles and a water area of 0.046 square miles. Located at 42.97° N. Lat; 74.16° W. Long. Elevation is 718 feet.
Population: 1,397; Growth (since 2000): 2.9%; Density: 932.9 persons per square mile; Race: 97.9% White, 0.0% Black/African American, 0.1% Asian, 0.0% American Indian/Alaska Native, 0.0% Native Hawaiian/Other Pacific Islander, 0.9% Two or more races, 3.9% Hispanic of any race; Average household size: 2.32; Median age: 47.6; Age under 18: 18.9%; Age 65 and over: 24.6%; Males per 100 females: 100.6; Marriage status: 24.5% never married, 52.4% now married, 1.3% separated, 7.9% widowed, 15.1% divorced; Foreign born: 0.6%; Speak English only: 93.6%; With disability: 14.5%; Veterans: 7.1%; Ancestry: 33.0% Polish, 31.4% German, 18.4% Irish, 17.5% Italian, 12.7% French
Employment: 15.8% management, business, and financial, 2.7% computer, engineering, and science, 11.4% education, legal, community service, arts, and media, 4.6% healthcare practitioners, 20.0% service,

16.0% sales and office, 10.1% natural resources, construction, and maintenance, 19.6% production, transportation, and material moving
Income: Per capita: $27,037; Median household: $57,585; Average household: $62,854; Households with income of $100,000 or more: 18.5%; Poverty rate: 11.4%
Educational Attainment: High school diploma or higher: 96.5%; Bachelor's degree or higher: 21.8%; Graduate/professional degree or higher: 9.7%
Housing: Homeownership rate: 85.2%; Median home value: $141,700; Median year structure built: 1945; Homeowner vacancy rate: 0.0%; Median selected monthly owner costs: $1,196 with a mortgage, $590 without a mortgage; Median gross rent: $825 per month; Rental vacancy rate: 12.0%
Health Insurance: 91.6% have insurance; 74.7% have private insurance; 38.3% have public insurance; 8.4% do not have insurance; 8.4% of children under 18 do not have insurance
Transportation: Commute: 97.0% car, 1.1% public transportation, 0.0% walk, 0.0% work from home; Mean travel time to work: 23.5 minutes

MINDEN (town). Covers a land area of 50.988 square miles and a water area of 0.449 square miles. Located at 42.93° N. Lat; 74.70° W. Long.
Population: 4,175; Growth (since 2000): -0.6%; Density: 81.9 persons per square mile; Race: 95.7% White, 0.0% Black/African American, 1.5% Asian, 0.0% American Indian/Alaska Native, 0.0% Native Hawaiian/Other Pacific Islander, 2.3% Two or more races, 1.5% Hispanic of any race; Average household size: 2.62; Median age: 41.4; Age under 18: 26.9%; Age 65 and over: 17.2%; Males per 100 females: 98.6; Marriage status: 23.6% never married, 56.7% now married, 4.2% separated, 8.1% widowed, 11.6% divorced; Foreign born: 2.0%; Speak English only: 84.2%; With disability: 16.2%; Veterans: 7.0%; Ancestry: 23.3% German, 15.1% Irish, 9.0% American, 8.9% English, 8.4% Italian
Employment: 6.0% management, business, and financial, 2.1% computer, engineering, and science, 7.6% education, legal, community service, arts, and media, 3.7% healthcare practitioners, 20.9% service, 22.7% sales and office, 12.0% natural resources, construction, and maintenance, 24.9% production, transportation, and material moving
Income: Per capita: $19,851; Median household: $41,278; Average household: $51,482; Households with income of $100,000 or more: 9.2%; Poverty rate: 21.1%
Educational Attainment: High school diploma or higher: 78.6%; Bachelor's degree or higher: 12.4%; Graduate/professional degree or higher: 4.9%
Housing: Homeownership rate: 76.2%; Median home value: $77,100; Median year structure built: 1942; Homeowner vacancy rate: 2.2%; Median selected monthly owner costs: $1,144 with a mortgage, $507 without a mortgage; Median gross rent: $656 per month; Rental vacancy rate: 18.4%
Health Insurance: 82.5% have insurance; 51.7% have private insurance; 46.7% have public insurance; 17.5% do not have insurance; 34.6% of children under 18 do not have insurance
Transportation: Commute: 88.0% car, 0.3% public transportation, 1.1% walk, 6.7% work from home; Mean travel time to work: 28.4 minutes
Additional Information Contacts
Town of Minden. . . . . (518) 993-3443
    http://townofminden.org

MOHAWK (town). Covers a land area of 34.681 square miles and a water area of 0.712 square miles. Located at 42.96° N. Lat; 74.40° W. Long.
Population: 3,761; Growth (since 2000): -3.6%; Density: 108.4 persons per square mile; Race: 93.6% White, 0.2% Black/African American, 1.8% Asian, 0.0% American Indian/Alaska Native, 0.0% Native Hawaiian/Other Pacific Islander, 3.3% Two or more races, 7.7% Hispanic of any race; Average household size: 2.35; Median age: 45.4; Age under 18: 21.1%; Age 65 and over: 17.6%; Males per 100 females: 97.9; Marriage status: 28.3% never married, 50.9% now married, 2.1% separated, 10.0% widowed, 10.8% divorced; Foreign born: 2.0%; Speak English only: 98.5%; With disability: 13.0%; Veterans: 7.0%; Ancestry: 24.4% German, 22.3% Irish, 18.7% Italian, 12.5% English, 10.6% Dutch
Employment: 12.5% management, business, and financial, 2.7% computer, engineering, and science, 3.3% education, legal, community service, arts, and media, 11.3% healthcare practitioners, 20.9% service, 21.5% sales and office, 10.3% natural resources, construction, and maintenance, 17.6% production, transportation, and material moving

Income: Per capita: $31,741; Median household: $62,617; Average household: $74,322; Households with income of $100,000 or more: 18.2%; Poverty rate: 5.4%
Educational Attainment: High school diploma or higher: 87.9%; Bachelor's degree or higher: 19.3%; Graduate/professional degree or higher: 7.8%
Housing: Homeownership rate: 84.2%; Median home value: $128,200; Median year structure built: 1965; Homeowner vacancy rate: 0.0%; Median selected monthly owner costs: $1,260 with a mortgage, $437 without a mortgage; Median gross rent: $693 per month; Rental vacancy rate: 0.0%
Health Insurance: 93.8% have insurance; 73.8% have private insurance; 36.2% have public insurance; 6.2% do not have insurance; 1.5% of children under 18 do not have insurance
Transportation: Commute: 93.4% car, 0.2% public transportation, 1.2% walk, 4.7% work from home; Mean travel time to work: 22.5 minutes

NELLISTON (village). Covers a land area of 1.105 square miles and a water area of 0.090 square miles. Located at 42.93° N. Lat; 74.61° W. Long. Elevation is 367 feet.
Population: 529; Growth (since 2000): -15.0%; Density: 478.8 persons per square mile; Race: 91.5% White, 0.0% Black/African American, 7.9% Asian, 0.0% American Indian/Alaska Native, 0.0% Native Hawaiian/Other Pacific Islander, 0.6% Two or more races, 3.4% Hispanic of any race; Average household size: 2.56; Median age: 45.8; Age under 18: 18.9%; Age 65 and over: 22.7%; Males per 100 females: 104.8; Marriage status: 28.3% never married, 48.7% now married, 2.0% separated, 12.5% widowed, 10.5% divorced; Foreign born: 5.3%; Speak English only: 88.3%; With disability: 21.9%; Veterans: 7.5%; Ancestry: 25.5% German, 15.5% Irish, 14.2% Dutch, 12.3% English, 10.8% Italian
Employment: 4.8% management, business, and financial, 0.0% computer, engineering, and science, 5.3% education, legal, community service, arts, and media, 2.7% healthcare practitioners, 17.1% service, 29.4% sales and office, 4.8% natural resources, construction, and maintenance, 35.8% production, transportation, and material moving
Income: Per capita: $20,828; Median household: $50,417; Average household: $52,379; Households with income of $100,000 or more: 8.7%; Poverty rate: 24.7%
Educational Attainment: High school diploma or higher: 79.5%; Bachelor's degree or higher: 11.4%; Graduate/professional degree or higher: 3.6%
Housing: Homeownership rate: 70.0%; Median home value: $86,300; Median year structure built: Before 1940; Homeowner vacancy rate: 0.0%; Median selected monthly owner costs: $1,100 with a mortgage, $503 without a mortgage; Median gross rent: $750 per month; Rental vacancy rate: 0.0%
Health Insurance: 93.0% have insurance; 59.4% have private insurance; 50.3% have public insurance; 7.0% do not have insurance; 0.0% of children under 18 do not have insurance
Transportation: Commute: 80.7% car, 0.0% public transportation, 11.2% walk, 7.0% work from home; Mean travel time to work: 30.1 minutes

PALATINE (town). Covers a land area of 41.072 square miles and a water area of 0.629 square miles. Located at 42.95° N. Lat; 74.54° W. Long. Elevation is 830 feet.
Population: 3,232; Growth (since 2000): 5.3%; Density: 78.7 persons per square mile; Race: 92.7% White, 0.2% Black/African American, 1.3% Asian, 0.0% American Indian/Alaska Native, 0.0% Native Hawaiian/Other Pacific Islander, 2.1% Two or more races, 4.7% Hispanic of any race; Average household size: 2.60; Median age: 42.7; Age under 18: 24.4%; Age 65 and over: 19.6%; Males per 100 females: 101.2; Marriage status: 20.2% never married, 57.6% now married, 2.6% separated, 10.3% widowed, 11.9% divorced; Foreign born: 3.1%; Speak English only: 91.6%; With disability: 13.5%; Veterans: 10.1%; Ancestry: 29.3% German, 17.5% Dutch, 12.1% Irish, 10.2% Italian, 8.3% English
Employment: 11.9% management, business, and financial, 1.8% computer, engineering, and science, 11.2% education, legal, community service, arts, and media, 5.2% healthcare practitioners, 20.5% service, 21.3% sales and office, 14.3% natural resources, construction, and maintenance, 13.8% production, transportation, and material moving
Income: Per capita: $24,040; Median household: $51,296; Average household: $61,311; Households with income of $100,000 or more: 16.8%; Poverty rate: 19.3%
Educational Attainment: High school diploma or higher: 85.2%; Bachelor's degree or higher: 16.4%; Graduate/professional degree or higher: 7.5%

Housing: Homeownership rate: 69.5%; Median home value: $93,700; Median year structure built: 1975; Homeowner vacancy rate: 0.7%; Median selected monthly owner costs: $1,188 with a mortgage, $535 without a mortgage; Median gross rent: $558 per month; Rental vacancy rate: 0.0%
Health Insurance: 85.5% have insurance; 58.1% have private insurance; 40.6% have public insurance; 14.5% do not have insurance; 22.1% of children under 18 do not have insurance
Transportation: Commute: 83.7% car, 1.1% public transportation, 6.3% walk, 8.5% work from home; Mean travel time to work: 21.8 minutes

PALATINE BRIDGE (village). Covers a land area of 0.883 square miles and a water area of 0.066 square miles. Located at 42.91° N. Lat; 74.58° W. Long. Elevation is 344 feet.

Population: 644; Growth (since 2000): -8.8%; Density: 729.4 persons per square mile; Race: 95.5% White, 0.8% Black/African American, 0.0% Asian, 0.0% American Indian/Alaska Native, 0.0% Native Hawaiian/Other Pacific Islander, 2.2% Two or more races, 1.6% Hispanic of any race; Average household size: 2.02; Median age: 56.7; Age under 18: 12.0%; Age 65 and over: 37.7%; Males per 100 females: 89.0; Marriage status: 19.2% never married, 43.4% now married, 2.7% separated, 22.7% widowed, 14.6% divorced; Foreign born: 0.0%; Speak English only: 96.5%; With disability: 29.1%; Veterans: 11.3%; Ancestry: 29.3% German, 12.9% Irish, 12.7% Italian, 12.6% English, 8.1% Dutch
Employment: 8.6% management, business, and financial, 3.0% computer, engineering, and science, 21.6% education, legal, community service, arts, and media, 5.6% healthcare practitioners, 19.0% service, 22.4% sales and office, 6.0% natural resources, construction, and maintenance, 13.8% production, transportation, and material moving
Income: Per capita: $27,306; Median household: $30,875; Average household: $55,513; Households with income of $100,000 or more: 14.2%; Poverty rate: 15.4%
Educational Attainment: High school diploma or higher: 89.0%; Bachelor's degree or higher: 20.0%; Graduate/professional degree or higher: 7.7%
Housing: Homeownership rate: 55.0%; Median home value: $90,800; Median year structure built: 1967; Homeowner vacancy rate: 3.7%; Median selected monthly owner costs: $1,182 with a mortgage, $534 without a mortgage; Median gross rent: $421 per month; Rental vacancy rate: 0.0%
Health Insurance: 95.0% have insurance; 59.5% have private insurance; 56.2% have public insurance; 5.0% do not have insurance; 0.0% of children under 18 do not have insurance
Transportation: Commute: 85.3% car, 5.8% public transportation, 1.2% walk, 7.0% work from home; Mean travel time to work: 25.9 minutes

ROOT (town). Covers a land area of 50.624 square miles and a water area of 0.426 square miles. Located at 42.84° N. Lat; 74.49° W. Long.

Population: 1,852; Growth (since 2000): 5.7%; Density: 36.6 persons per square mile; Race: 97.5% White, 0.4% Black/African American, 0.6% Asian, 0.0% American Indian/Alaska Native, 0.0% Native Hawaiian/Other Pacific Islander, 1.3% Two or more races, 1.7% Hispanic of any race; Average household size: 2.68; Median age: 38.4; Age under 18: 26.5%; Age 65 and over: 13.9%; Males per 100 females: 100.4; Marriage status: 24.5% never married, 55.3% now married, 3.3% separated, 9.9% widowed, 10.3% divorced; Foreign born: 1.3%; Speak English only: 94.6%; With disability: 13.6%; Veterans: 11.8%; Ancestry: 22.1% German, 12.8% Irish, 11.6% Italian, 10.4% English, 9.4% Dutch
Employment: 10.9% management, business, and financial, 3.1% computer, engineering, and science, 10.7% education, legal, community service, arts, and media, 3.7% healthcare practitioners, 15.7% service, 24.4% sales and office, 16.0% natural resources, construction, and maintenance, 15.5% production, transportation, and material moving
Income: Per capita: $22,310; Median household: $42,300; Average household: $59,018; Households with income of $100,000 or more: 20.8%; Poverty rate: 18.3%
Educational Attainment: High school diploma or higher: 82.5%; Bachelor's degree or higher: 16.5%; Graduate/professional degree or higher: 5.1%
Housing: Homeownership rate: 85.0%; Median home value: $106,700; Median year structure built: 1973; Homeowner vacancy rate: 1.8%; Median selected monthly owner costs: $1,194 with a mortgage, $480 without a mortgage; Median gross rent: $935 per month; Rental vacancy rate: 6.9%
Health Insurance: 89.3% have insurance; 62.1% have private insurance; 39.5% have public insurance; 10.7% do not have insurance; 12.3% of children under 18 do not have insurance

Transportation: Commute: 93.2% car, 0.3% public transportation, 0.5% walk, 5.3% work from home; Mean travel time to work: 30.7 minutes

SAINT JOHNSVILLE (town). Covers a land area of 16.841 square miles and a water area of 0.518 square miles. Located at 43.00° N. Lat; 74.68° W. Long. Elevation is 328 feet.

Population: 2,542; Growth (since 2000): -0.9%; Density: 150.9 persons per square mile; Race: 96.8% White, 0.7% Black/African American, 0.8% Asian, 0.0% American Indian/Alaska Native, 0.0% Native Hawaiian/Other Pacific Islander, 0.6% Two or more races, 2.4% Hispanic of any race; Average household size: 2.55; Median age: 36.5; Age under 18: 26.0%; Age 65 and over: 18.5%; Males per 100 females: 89.8; Marriage status: 31.2% never married, 45.6% now married, 4.0% separated, 10.7% widowed, 12.5% divorced; Foreign born: 2.6%; Speak English only: 90.5%; With disability: 14.6%; Veterans: 10.9%; Ancestry: 19.1% German, 14.7% Irish, 13.7% Italian, 9.2% American, 7.6% Dutch
Employment: 7.7% management, business, and financial, 1.4% computer, engineering, and science, 9.8% education, legal, community service, arts, and media, 8.4% healthcare practitioners, 24.9% service, 23.6% sales and office, 11.1% natural resources, construction, and maintenance, 13.0% production, transportation, and material moving
Income: Per capita: $19,702; Median household: $36,200; Average household: $51,375; Households with income of $100,000 or more: 11.4%; Poverty rate: 26.3%
Educational Attainment: High school diploma or higher: 85.8%; Bachelor's degree or higher: 12.1%; Graduate/professional degree or higher: 4.8%

School District(s)
Oppenheim-Ephratah-Saint Johnsville CSD (PK-12)
    Enrollment: 785. . . . . (518) 568-2011
Housing: Homeownership rate: 64.3%; Median home value: $80,600; Median year structure built: Before 1940; Homeowner vacancy rate: 2.7%; Median selected monthly owner costs: $976 with a mortgage, $496 without a mortgage; Median gross rent: $644 per month; Rental vacancy rate: 2.9%
Health Insurance: 86.8% have insurance; 49.6% have private insurance; 49.6% have public insurance; 13.2% do not have insurance; 21.1% of children under 18 do not have insurance
Transportation: Commute: 83.5% car, 1.5% public transportation, 11.9% walk, 1.6% work from home; Mean travel time to work: 21.6 minutes

SAINT JOHNSVILLE (village). Covers a land area of 0.878 square miles and a water area of 0.001 square miles. Located at 43.00° N. Lat; 74.68° W. Long. Elevation is 328 feet.

Population: 1,858; Growth (since 2000): 10.3%; Density: 2,117.3 persons per square mile; Race: 96.0% White, 1.0% Black/African American, 1.1% Asian, 0.0% American Indian/Alaska Native, 0.0% Native Hawaiian/Other Pacific Islander, 0.4% Two or more races, 3.3% Hispanic of any race; Average household size: 2.52; Median age: 35.9; Age under 18: 25.6%; Age 65 and over: 18.4%; Males per 100 females: 85.8; Marriage status: 33.0% never married, 44.2% now married, 4.6% separated, 10.8% widowed, 12.0% divorced; Foreign born: 3.0%; Speak English only: 94.8%; With disability: 17.1%; Veterans: 11.1%; Ancestry: 20.2% German, 17.2% Irish, 10.9% American, 10.2% Italian, 7.9% Dutch
Employment: 4.8% management, business, and financial, 1.0% computer, engineering, and science, 11.9% education, legal, community service, arts, and media, 10.0% healthcare practitioners, 20.1% service, 25.3% sales and office, 10.3% natural resources, construction, and maintenance, 16.7% production, transportation, and material moving
Income: Per capita: $19,577; Median household: $35,425; Average household: $50,884; Households with income of $100,000 or more: 10.2%; Poverty rate: 23.3%
Educational Attainment: High school diploma or higher: 87.3%; Bachelor's degree or higher: 13.5%; Graduate/professional degree or higher: 5.7%

School District(s)
Oppenheim-Ephratah-Saint Johnsville CSD (PK-12)
    Enrollment: 785. . . . . (518) 568-2011
Housing: Homeownership rate: 54.6%; Median home value: $72,100; Median year structure built: Before 1940; Homeowner vacancy rate: 0.0%; Median selected monthly owner costs: $1,011 with a mortgage, $537 without a mortgage; Median gross rent: $651 per month; Rental vacancy rate: 3.1%

Health Insurance: 93.0% have insurance; 50.5% have private insurance; 55.2% have public insurance; 7.0% do not have insurance; 3.8% of children under 18 do not have insurance
Safety: Violent crime rate: 24.0 per 10,000 population; Property crime rate: 119.8 per 10,000 population
Transportation: Commute: 80.6% car, 2.0% public transportation, 13.2% walk, 2.1% work from home; Mean travel time to work: 22.3 minutes

SPRAKERS (unincorporated postal area)
ZCTA: 12166
Covers a land area of 43.815 square miles and a water area of 0.303 square miles. Located at 42.83° N. Lat; 74.45° W. Long. Elevation is 302 feet.
Population: 1,353; Growth (since 2000): -9.9%; Density: 30.9 persons per square mile; Race: 96.3% White, 1.1% Black/African American, 0.6% Asian, 0.1% American Indian/Alaska Native, 0.0% Native Hawaiian/Other Pacific Islander, 1.6% Two or more races, 0.7% Hispanic of any race; Average household size: 2.48; Median age: 42.2; Age under 18: 23.1%; Age 65 and over: 17.6%; Males per 100 females: 107.1; Marriage status: 26.3% never married, 55.1% now married, 4.8% separated, 9.7% widowed, 8.9% divorced; Foreign born: 1.6%; Speak English only: 95.9%; With disability: 10.1%; Veterans: 12.0%; Ancestry: 20.3% German, 14.5% Irish, 10.3% English, 10.0% Polish, 9.8% Italian
Employment: 12.6% management, business, and financial, 4.0% computer, engineering, and science, 9.9% education, legal, community service, arts, and media, 4.6% healthcare practitioners, 16.7% service, 22.5% sales and office, 16.4% natural resources, construction, and maintenance, 13.2% production, transportation, and material moving
Income: Per capita: $25,355; Median household: $44,659; Average household: $62,374; Households with income of $100,000 or more: 21.5%; Poverty rate: 11.6%
Educational Attainment: High school diploma or higher: 85.8%; Bachelor's degree or higher: 17.5%; Graduate/professional degree or higher: 6.6%
Housing: Homeownership rate: 87.0%; Median home value: $118,200; Median year structure built: 1972; Homeowner vacancy rate: 2.2%; Median selected monthly owner costs: $1,346 with a mortgage, $491 without a mortgage; Median gross rent: n/a per month; Rental vacancy rate: 0.0%
Health Insurance: 90.9% have insurance; 71.0% have private insurance; 37.1% have public insurance; 9.1% do not have insurance; 11.0% of children under 18 do not have insurance
Transportation: Commute: 93.6% car, 1.0% public transportation, 0.7% walk, 3.9% work from home; Mean travel time to work: 37.2 minutes

TRIBES HILL (CDP). Covers a land area of 2.276 square miles and a water area of 0.135 square miles. Located at 42.95° N. Lat; 74.30° W. Long. Elevation is 420 feet.
Population: 1,016; Growth (since 2000): -0.8%; Density: 446.4 persons per square mile; Race: 92.5% White, 0.0% Black/African American, 3.5% Asian, 0.0% American Indian/Alaska Native, 0.0% Native Hawaiian/Other Pacific Islander, 3.9% Two or more races, 9.3% Hispanic of any race; Average household size: 2.14; Median age: 46.2; Age under 18: 22.9%; Age 65 and over: 26.0%; Males per 100 females: 93.6; Marriage status: 16.5% never married, 56.2% now married, 1.1% separated, 16.9% widowed, 10.4% divorced; Foreign born: 6.5%; Speak English only: 100.0%; With disability: 9.8%; Veterans: 6.6%; Ancestry: 22.2% Irish, 21.8% Italian, 16.8% German, 14.2% English, 13.0% French
Employment: 14.8% management, business, and financial, 8.6% computer, engineering, and science, 1.8% education, legal, community service, arts, and media, 6.8% healthcare practitioners, 14.5% service, 23.9% sales and office, 10.5% natural resources, construction, and maintenance, 19.1% production, transportation, and material moving
Income: Per capita: $37,041; Median household: $50,139; Average household: $77,800; Households with income of $100,000 or more: 19.4%; Poverty rate: 0.7%
Educational Attainment: High school diploma or higher: 89.7%; Bachelor's degree or higher: 14.7%; Graduate/professional degree or higher: 4.7%
Housing: Homeownership rate: 86.5%; Median home value: $114,500; Median year structure built: 1961; Homeowner vacancy rate: 0.0%; Median selected monthly owner costs: $1,125 with a mortgage, $361 without a mortgage; Median gross rent: $646 per month; Rental vacancy rate: 0.0%

Health Insurance: 97.1% have insurance; 87.4% have private insurance; 45.6% have public insurance; 2.9% do not have insurance; 0.0% of children under 18 do not have insurance
Transportation: Commute: 93.6% car, 0.0% public transportation, 0.0% walk, 6.4% work from home; Mean travel time to work: 22.0 minutes

Nassau County

Located in southeastern New York, on western Long Island; bounded on the west by Queens borough of New York city, on the south by the Atlantic Ocean, and on the north by Long Island Sound. Covers a land area of 284.716 square miles, a water area of 168.518 square miles, and is located in the Eastern Time Zone at 40.73° N. Lat., 73.59° W. Long. The county was founded in 1899. County seat is Mineola.

Nassau County is part of the New York-Newark-Jersey City, NY-NJ-PA Metropolitan Statistical Area. The entire metro area includes: Dutchess County-Putnam County, NY Metropolitan Division (Dutchess County, NY; Putnam County, NY); Nassau County-Suffolk County, NY Metropolitan Division (Nassau County, NY; Suffolk County, NY); Newark, NJ-PA Metropolitan Division (Essex County, NJ; Hunterdon County, NJ; Morris County, NJ; Somerset County, NJ; Sussex County, NJ; Union County, NJ; Pike County, PA); New York-Jersey City-White Plains, NY-NJ Metropolitan Division (Bergen County, NJ; Hudson County, NJ; Middlesex County, NJ; Monmouth County, NJ; Ocean County, NJ; Passaic County, NJ; Bronx County, NY; Kings County, NY; New York County, NY; Orange County, NY; Queens County, NY; Richmond County, NY; Rockland County, NY; Westchester County, NY)

Weather Station: Mineola   Elevation: 96 feet

	Jan	Feb	Mar	Apr	May	Jun	Jul	Aug	Sep	Oct	Nov	Dec
High	39	42	49	59	69	79	84	82	75	64	55	44
Low	26	27	33	42	50	60	66	65	58	47	40	31
Precip	3.5	2.7	4.3	4.4	4.0	3.9	4.4	3.7	3.8	4.0	3.8	3.7
Snow	4.9	6.4	3.6	0.6	0.0	0.0	0.0	0.0	0.0	0.0	0.1	4.2

High and Low temperatures in degrees Fahrenheit; Precipitation and Snow in inches

Weather Station: Wantagh Cedar Creek   Elevation: 9 feet

	Jan	Feb	Mar	Apr	May	Jun	Jul	Aug	Sep	Oct	Nov	Dec
High	38	40	47	56	66	76	81	81	74	64	54	43
Low	26	27	33	42	51	61	67	66	59	49	40	31
Precip	3.3	2.6	4.0	4.2	3.6	3.6	3.6	3.3	3.5	3.7	3.5	3.6
Snow	na	na	na	0.0	0.0	0.0	0.0	0.0	0.0	0.0	0.0	na

High and Low temperatures in degrees Fahrenheit; Precipitation and Snow in inches

Population: 1,363,069; Growth (since 2000): 2.1%; Density: 4,787.5 persons per square mile; Race: 68.9% White, 11.5% Black/African American, 9.1% Asian, 0.2% American Indian/Alaska Native, 0.0% Native Hawaiian/Other Pacific Islander, 3.4% two or more races, 16.4% Hispanic of any race; Average household size: 3.02; Median age: 41.5; Age under 18: 21.9%; Age 65 and over: 16.8%; Males per 100 females: 93.7; Marriage status: 32.0% never married, 55.0% now married, 1.5% separated, 6.4% widowed, 6.5% divorced; Foreign born: 22.0%; Speak English only: 72.0%; With disability: 8.5%; Veterans: 4.5%; Ancestry: 19.6% Italian, 14.2% Irish, 8.9% German, 4.6% Polish, 4.4% American
Religion: Six largest groups: 50.6% Catholicism, 6.0% Judaism, 1.4% Lutheran, 1.3% Eastern Liturgical (Orthodox), 1.3% Orthodox, 1.2% Methodist/Pietist
Economy: Unemployment rate: 3.3%; Leading industries: 14.7 % professional, scientific, and technical services; 12.6 % retail trade; 12.1 % health care and social assistance; Farms: 55 totaling 2,682 acres; Company size: 31 employs 1,000 or more persons, 29 employ 500 to 999 persons, 725 employ 100 to 499 persons, 47,475 employ less than 100 persons; Business ownership: 48,489 women-owned, 12,370 Black-owned, 16,700 Hispanic-owned, 15,866 Asian-owned, 606 American Indian/Alaska Native-owned
Employment: 17.7% management, business, and financial, 4.4% computer, engineering, and science, 14.6% education, legal, community service, arts, and media, 8.0% healthcare practitioners, 16.3% service, 25.3% sales and office, 6.6% natural resources, construction, and maintenance, 7.2% production, transportation, and material moving
Income: Per capita: $46,839; Median household: $105,744; Average household: $140,019; Households with income of $100,000 or more: 52.8%; Poverty rate: 5.9%

Educational Attainment: High school diploma or higher: 91.0%; Bachelor's degree or higher: 44.4%; Graduate/professional degree or higher: 20.0%

Housing: Homeownership rate: 80.6%; Median home value: $460,700; Median year structure built: 1955; Homeowner vacancy rate: 1.2%; Median selected monthly owner costs: $3,119 with a mortgage, $1,326 without a mortgage; Median gross rent: $1,663 per month; Rental vacancy rate: 4.5%

Vital Statistics: Birth rate: 103.5 per 10,000 population; Death rate: 81.9 per 10,000 population; Age-adjusted cancer mortality rate: 129.0 deaths per 100,000 population

Health Insurance: 94.2% have insurance; 80.3% have private insurance; 26.8% have public insurance; 5.8% do not have insurance; 2.7% of children under 18 do not have insurance

Health Care: Physicians: 68.9 per 10,000 population; Dentists: 12.1 per 10,000 population; Hospital beds: 31.6 per 10,000 population; Hospital admissions: 1,869.0 per 10,000 population

Air Quality Index (AQI): Percent of Days: 94.2% good, 5.8% moderate, 0.0% unhealthy for sensitive individuals, 0.0% unhealthy, 0.0% very unhealthy; Annual median: 21; Annual maximum: 64

Transportation: Commute: 75.8% car, 16.7% public transportation, 2.6% walk, 3.8% work from home; Mean travel time to work: 35.8 minutes

2016 Presidential Election: 45.1% Trump, 51.3% Clinton, 1.8% Johnson, 1.0% Stein

National and State Parks: Bethpage State Park; Hempstead Lake State Park; Jones Beach State Park; Oyster Bay National Wildlife Refuge; Planting Fields Arboretum State Historic Park; Sagamore Hill National Historic Site; Valley Stream State Park

Additional Information Contacts

Nassau Government . . . . (516) 571-2664
   http://www.nassaucountyny.gov

Nassau County Communities

ALBERTSON (CDP). Covers a land area of 0.680 square miles and a water area of 0 square miles. Located at 40.77° N. Lat; 73.65° W. Long. Elevation is 138 feet.

History: Albertson is a hamlet and census-designated place (CDP) in Nassau County, New York. The first European settler was John Seren in 1644, then Townsend Albertson started a farm and gristmill and the community became known as Albertson.

Population: 5,294; Growth (since 2000): 1.8%; Density: 7,790.3 persons per square mile; Race: 71.5% White, 1.4% Black/African American, 23.7% Asian, 1.5% American Indian/Alaska Native, 0.0% Native Hawaiian/Other Pacific Islander, 1.3% Two or more races, 9.2% Hispanic of any race; Average household size: 2.97; Median age: 45.9; Age under 18: 19.4%; Age 65 and over: 20.6%; Males per 100 females: 94.6; Marriage status: 28.0% never married, 57.3% now married, 0.5% separated, 8.6% widowed, 6.1% divorced; Foreign born: 26.5%; Speak English only: 64.4%; With disability: 9.9%; Veterans: 4.6%; Ancestry: 16.2% Italian, 15.6% Irish, 7.5% German, 5.7% Polish, 5.5% English

Employment: 23.3% management, business, and financial, 5.8% computer, engineering, and science, 17.0% education, legal, community service, arts, and media, 8.9% healthcare practitioners, 9.5% service, 22.9% sales and office, 5.7% natural resources, construction, and maintenance, 7.0% production, transportation, and material moving

Income: Per capita: $44,780; Median household: $113,889; Average household: $130,331; Households with income of $100,000 or more: 55.4%; Poverty rate: 2.5%

Educational Attainment: High school diploma or higher: 91.1%; Bachelor's degree or higher: 47.9%; Graduate/professional degree or higher: 25.9%

School District(s)

Herricks Union Free SD (KG-12)

   Enrollment: 3,926 . . . . (516) 305-8901

Mineola Union Free SD (PK-12)

   Enrollment: 2,872 . . . . (516) 237-2001

Housing: Homeownership rate: 96.0%; Median home value: $548,600; Median year structure built: 1954; Homeowner vacancy rate: 0.4%; Median selected monthly owner costs: $3,032 with a mortgage, $1,272 without a mortgage; Median gross rent: $2,617 per month; Rental vacancy rate: 0.0%

Health Insurance: 96.0% have insurance; 81.7% have private insurance; 30.8% have public insurance; 4.0% do not have insurance; 1.0% of children under 18 do not have insurance

Transportation: Commute: 84.4% car, 13.1% public transportation, 1.4% walk, 1.2% work from home; Mean travel time to work: 34.0 minutes

ATLANTIC BEACH (village). Covers a land area of 0.439 square miles and a water area of 0.601 square miles. Located at 40.59° N. Lat; 73.73° W. Long. Elevation is 7 feet.

Population: 1,473; Growth (since 2000): -25.8%; Density: 3,357.1 persons per square mile; Race: 94.3% White, 1.4% Black/African American, 2.2% Asian, 0.3% American Indian/Alaska Native, 0.0% Native Hawaiian/Other Pacific Islander, 1.8% Two or more races, 3.7% Hispanic of any race; Average household size: 2.35; Median age: 56.0; Age under 18: 17.2%; Age 65 and over: 25.9%; Males per 100 females: 91.0; Marriage status: 22.2% never married, 65.9% now married, 0.9% separated, 6.4% widowed, 5.5% divorced; Foreign born: 11.5%; Speak English only: 91.6%; With disability: 11.7%; Veterans: 5.4%; Ancestry: 17.7% Italian, 14.1% Irish, 11.9% American, 9.6% German, 7.9% Russian

Employment: 25.1% management, business, and financial, 1.7% computer, engineering, and science, 17.8% education, legal, community service, arts, and media, 9.5% healthcare practitioners, 14.2% service, 22.9% sales and office, 4.3% natural resources, construction, and maintenance, 4.4% production, transportation, and material moving

Income: Per capita: $88,834; Median household: $131,964; Average household: $206,758; Households with income of $100,000 or more: 61.1%; Poverty rate: 2.4%

Educational Attainment: High school diploma or higher: 97.3%; Bachelor's degree or higher: 54.4%; Graduate/professional degree or higher: 24.7%

Housing: Homeownership rate: 82.0%; Median home value: $763,600; Median year structure built: 1954; Homeowner vacancy rate: 4.5%; Median selected monthly owner costs: $3,773 with a mortgage, $1,501 without a mortgage; Median gross rent: $2,638 per month; Rental vacancy rate: 0.0%

Health Insurance: 97.7% have insurance; 84.8% have private insurance; 30.6% have public insurance; 2.3% do not have insurance; 0.0% of children under 18 do not have insurance

Transportation: Commute: 75.7% car, 13.8% public transportation, 2.1% walk, 8.4% work from home; Mean travel time to work: 42.6 minutes

BALDWIN (CDP). Covers a land area of 2.963 square miles and a water area of 0.025 square miles. Located at 40.66° N. Lat; 73.61° W. Long. Elevation is 23 feet.

History: Named for F.W. Baldwin, an early settler. Settled 1640s.

Population: 25,214; Growth (since 2000): 7.5%; Density: 8,509.2 persons per square mile; Race: 46.2% White, 35.5% Black/African American, 3.6% Asian, 0.0% American Indian/Alaska Native, 0.1% Native Hawaiian/Other Pacific Islander, 7.3% Two or more races, 25.0% Hispanic of any race; Average household size: 3.18; Median age: 40.2; Age under 18: 23.9%; Age 65 and over: 13.1%; Males per 100 females: 90.7; Marriage status: 34.0% never married, 52.1% now married, 2.1% separated, 5.3% widowed, 8.6% divorced; Foreign born: 25.1%; Speak English only: 71.0%; With disability: 7.2%; Veterans: 3.3%; Ancestry: 10.8% Irish, 10.2% Italian, 7.0% German, 7.0% Jamaican, 6.8% Haitian

Employment: 14.4% management, business, and financial, 4.2% computer, engineering, and science, 12.4% education, legal, community service, arts, and media, 10.6% healthcare practitioners, 18.2% service, 24.1% sales and office, 5.3% natural resources, construction, and maintenance, 10.8% production, transportation, and material moving

Income: Per capita: $36,033; Median household: $99,128; Average household: $111,592; Households with income of $100,000 or more: 49.1%; Poverty rate: 6.4%

Educational Attainment: High school diploma or higher: 91.0%; Bachelor's degree or higher: 35.6%; Graduate/professional degree or higher: 13.3%

School District(s)

Baldwin Union Free SD (KG-12)

   Enrollment: 4,708 . . . . (516) 434-6000

Housing: Homeownership rate: 82.4%; Median home value: $363,100; Median year structure built: 1946; Homeowner vacancy rate: 1.1%; Median selected monthly owner costs: $2,835 with a mortgage, $1,260 without a mortgage; Median gross rent: $1,665 per month; Rental vacancy rate: 3.3%

Health Insurance: 94.0% have insurance; 79.6% have private insurance; 23.6% have public insurance; 6.0% do not have insurance; 3.1% of children under 18 do not have insurance

Transportation: Commute: 77.0% car, 16.4% public transportation, 1.5% walk, 4.6% work from home; Mean travel time to work: 36.4 minutes

BALDWIN HARBOR (CDP). Covers a land area of 1.205 square miles and a water area of 0.522 square miles. Located at 40.63° N. Lat; 73.60° W. Long. Elevation is 13 feet.
Population: 7,335; Growth (since 2000): -10.0%; Density: 6,084.9 persons per square mile; Race: 59.0% White, 27.0% Black/African American, 4.3% Asian, 0.2% American Indian/Alaska Native, 0.0% Native Hawaiian/Other Pacific Islander, 4.2% Two or more races, 19.6% Hispanic of any race; Average household size: 3.00; Median age: 46.6; Age under 18: 18.7%; Age 65 and over: 15.4%; Males per 100 females: 93.1; Marriage status: 34.4% never married, 55.9% now married, 1.4% separated, 4.1% widowed, 5.7% divorced; Foreign born: 23.6%; Speak English only: 77.5%; With disability: 8.2%; Veterans: 4.3%; Ancestry: 13.5% Italian, 9.3% Irish, 8.6% German, 8.5% Haitian, 5.6% Jamaican
Employment: 20.5% management, business, and financial, 6.3% computer, engineering, and science, 16.3% education, legal, community service, arts, and media, 9.2% healthcare practitioners, 11.8% service, 23.2% sales and office, 7.0% natural resources, construction, and maintenance, 5.8% production, transportation, and material moving
Income: Per capita: $46,064; Median household: $118,654; Average household: $134,923; Households with income of $100,000 or more: 59.0%; Poverty rate: 6.0%
Educational Attainment: High school diploma or higher: 95.8%; Bachelor's degree or higher: 48.0%; Graduate/professional degree or higher: 22.3%
Housing: Homeownership rate: 92.2%; Median home value: $400,200; Median year structure built: 1957; Homeowner vacancy rate: 1.5%; Median selected monthly owner costs: $3,126 with a mortgage, $1,466 without a mortgage; Median gross rent: $3,009 per month; Rental vacancy rate: 0.0%
Health Insurance: 93.5% have insurance; 83.4% have private insurance; 22.7% have public insurance; 6.5% do not have insurance; 6.9% of children under 18 do not have insurance
Transportation: Commute: 74.6% car, 18.2% public transportation, 0.5% walk, 6.7% work from home; Mean travel time to work: 39.1 minutes

BARNUM ISLAND (CDP). Covers a land area of 0.879 square miles and a water area of 0.388 square miles. Located at 40.61° N. Lat; 73.65° W. Long. Elevation is 3 feet.
Population: 2,447; Growth (since 2000): -1.6%; Density: 2,782.7 persons per square mile; Race: 78.3% White, 4.1% Black/African American, 1.0% Asian, 2.2% American Indian/Alaska Native, 0.0% Native Hawaiian/Other Pacific Islander, 1.3% Two or more races, 21.3% Hispanic of any race; Average household size: 2.53; Median age: 47.3; Age under 18: 16.4%; Age 65 and over: 19.0%; Males per 100 females: 97.5; Marriage status: 32.0% never married, 56.4% now married, 3.4% separated, 5.2% widowed, 6.3% divorced; Foreign born: 10.1%; Speak English only: 76.2%; With disability: 17.6%; Veterans: 8.5%; Ancestry: 36.2% Italian, 14.1% Irish, 8.3% German, 3.8% American, 3.8% Russian
Employment: 8.7% management, business, and financial, 1.9% computer, engineering, and science, 22.3% education, legal, community service, arts, and media, 3.7% healthcare practitioners, 11.9% service, 26.5% sales and office, 10.1% natural resources, construction, and maintenance, 14.9% production, transportation, and material moving
Income: Per capita: $39,625; Median household: $94,063; Average household: $97,988; Households with income of $100,000 or more: 44.7%; Poverty rate: 9.6%
Educational Attainment: High school diploma or higher: 82.5%; Bachelor's degree or higher: 24.5%; Graduate/professional degree or higher: 10.9%
Housing: Homeownership rate: 72.6%; Median home value: $446,900; Median year structure built: 1965; Homeowner vacancy rate: 0.0%; Median selected monthly owner costs: $3,189 with a mortgage, $1,320 without a mortgage; Median gross rent: $1,375 per month; Rental vacancy rate: 0.0%
Health Insurance: 92.9% have insurance; 70.0% have private insurance; 40.4% have public insurance; 7.1% do not have insurance; 0.0% of children under 18 do not have insurance
Transportation: Commute: 69.0% car, 21.6% public transportation, 1.3% walk, 6.6% work from home; Mean travel time to work: 39.3 minutes

BAXTER ESTATES (village). Covers a land area of 0.182 square miles and a water area of 0 square miles. Located at 40.83° N. Lat; 73.69° W. Long. Elevation is 39 feet.
Population: 1,018; Growth (since 2000): 1.2%; Density: 5,578.6 persons per square mile; Race: 82.7% White, 0.0% Black/African American, 14.1% Asian, 0.0% American Indian/Alaska Native, 0.0% Native Hawaiian/Other Pacific Islander, 2.3% Two or more races, 15.0% Hispanic of any race; Average household size: 2.56; Median age: 42.5; Age under 18: 23.6%; Age 65 and over: 18.9%; Males per 100 females: 105.6; Marriage status: 27.8% never married, 58.4% now married, 0.4% separated, 7.1% widowed, 6.7% divorced; Foreign born: 34.1%; Speak English only: 66.5%; With disability: 4.8%; Veterans: 3.6%; Ancestry: 11.8% Italian, 11.4% Irish, 8.3% American, 7.2% German, 5.1% Russian
Employment: 28.1% management, business, and financial, 8.2% computer, engineering, and science, 20.1% education, legal, community service, arts, and media, 5.8% healthcare practitioners, 20.1% service, 14.1% sales and office, 1.5% natural resources, construction, and maintenance, 2.2% production, transportation, and material moving
Income: Per capita: $74,051; Median household: $124,063; Average household: $190,759; Households with income of $100,000 or more: 52.2%; Poverty rate: 10.4%
Educational Attainment: High school diploma or higher: 92.6%; Bachelor's degree or higher: 66.3%; Graduate/professional degree or higher: 34.5%
Housing: Homeownership rate: 68.0%; Median home value: $795,200; Median year structure built: 1941; Homeowner vacancy rate: 0.0%; Median selected monthly owner costs: $4,000+ with a mortgage, $1,501 without a mortgage; Median gross rent: $1,507 per month; Rental vacancy rate: 1.4%
Health Insurance: 90.2% have insurance; 81.0% have private insurance; 22.9% have public insurance; 9.8% do not have insurance; 0.0% of children under 18 do not have insurance
Transportation: Commute: 45.1% car, 34.6% public transportation, 7.5% walk, 7.0% work from home; Mean travel time to work: 44.3 minutes

BAY PARK (CDP). Covers a land area of 0.500 square miles and a water area of 0.102 square miles. Located at 40.63° N. Lat; 73.67° W. Long. Elevation is 10 feet.
Population: 1,650; Growth (since 2000): -28.3%; Density: 3,296.9 persons per square mile; Race: 86.1% White, 0.0% Black/African American, 13.9% Asian, 0.0% American Indian/Alaska Native, 0.0% Native Hawaiian/Other Pacific Islander, 0.0% Two or more races, 3.5% Hispanic of any race; Average household size: 2.56; Median age: 46.3; Age under 18: 14.9%; Age 65 and over: 20.0%; Males per 100 females: 91.8; Marriage status: 32.7% never married, 55.9% now married, 1.5% separated, 4.6% widowed, 6.8% divorced; Foreign born: 15.8%; Speak English only: 83.2%; With disability: 8.5%; Veterans: 7.9%; Ancestry: 38.7% Irish, 33.4% Italian, 16.1% German, 8.9% American, 8.2% English
Employment: 9.2% management, business, and financial, 0.0% computer, engineering, and science, 9.2% education, legal, community service, arts, and media, 3.1% healthcare practitioners, 38.0% service, 18.6% sales and office, 11.1% natural resources, construction, and maintenance, 10.7% production, transportation, and material moving
Income: Per capita: $30,930; Median household: $74,750; Average household: $79,785; Households with income of $100,000 or more: 29.3%; Poverty rate: 3.7%
Educational Attainment: High school diploma or higher: 96.3%; Bachelor's degree or higher: 17.3%; Graduate/professional degree or higher: 3.4%
Housing: Homeownership rate: 73.1%; Median home value: $325,900; Median year structure built: 1946; Homeowner vacancy rate: 9.9%; Median selected monthly owner costs: $2,605 with a mortgage, $1,037 without a mortgage; Median gross rent: $2,192 per month; Rental vacancy rate: 0.0%
Health Insurance: 97.2% have insurance; 64.8% have private insurance; 48.0% have public insurance; 2.8% do not have insurance; 0.0% of children under 18 do not have insurance
Transportation: Commute: 89.2% car, 8.0% public transportation, 1.1% walk, 1.7% work from home; Mean travel time to work: 30.2 minutes

BAYVILLE (village). Covers a land area of 1.450 square miles and a water area of 0.101 square miles. Located at 40.91° N. Lat; 73.56° W. Long. Elevation is 39 feet.
History: Incorporated 1919.

Population: 6,752; Growth (since 2000): -5.4%; Density: 4,656.7 persons per square mile; Race: 95.9% White, 0.1% Black/African American, 1.3% Asian, 0.3% American Indian/Alaska Native, 0.0% Native Hawaiian/Other Pacific Islander, 1.7% Two or more races, 5.7% Hispanic of any race; Average household size: 2.70; Median age: 47.6; Age under 18: 18.3%; Age 65 and over: 21.4%; Males per 100 females: 93.6; Marriage status: 29.3% never married, 59.2% now married, 1.8% separated, 5.5% widowed, 5.9% divorced; Foreign born: 9.7%; Speak English only: 86.4%; With disability: 11.9%; Veterans: 5.3%; Ancestry: 43.0% Italian, 26.7% Irish, 18.5% German, 8.8% Polish, 6.0% English

Employment: 18.8% management, business, and financial, 7.1% computer, engineering, and science, 19.0% education, legal, community service, arts, and media, 6.3% healthcare practitioners, 13.9% service, 20.6% sales and office, 9.3% natural resources, construction, and maintenance, 5.0% production, transportation, and material moving

Income: Per capita: $49,690; Median household: $102,722; Average household: $133,450; Households with income of $100,000 or more: 50.7%; Poverty rate: 4.2%

Educational Attainment: High school diploma or higher: 95.3%; Bachelor's degree or higher: 44.3%; Graduate/professional degree or higher: 21.8%

School District(s)

Locust Valley Central SD (KG-12)

   Enrollment: 2,085 . . . . (516) 277-5001

Housing: Homeownership rate: 80.0%; Median home value: $538,100; Median year structure built: 1961; Homeowner vacancy rate: 2.3%; Median selected monthly owner costs: $3,032 with a mortgage, $1,281 without a mortgage; Median gross rent: $1,506 per month; Rental vacancy rate: 0.0%

Health Insurance: 96.0% have insurance; 83.5% have private insurance; 29.1% have public insurance; 4.0% do not have insurance; 6.5% of children under 18 do not have insurance

Transportation: Commute: 81.6% car, 10.3% public transportation, 3.2% walk, 5.0% work from home; Mean travel time to work: 35.7 minutes

Additional Information Contacts

Village of Bayville . . . . (516) 628-1439

   http://bayvilleny.gov

BELLEROSE (village). Covers a land area of 0.125 square miles and a water area of 0 square miles. Located at 40.72° N. Lat; 73.72° W. Long. Elevation is 82 feet.

History: Settled 1908, incorporated 1924.

Population: 1,293; Growth (since 2000): 10.2%; Density: 10,323.9 persons per square mile; Race: 88.7% White, 1.5% Black/African American, 2.6% Asian, 0.0% American Indian/Alaska Native, 0.0% Native Hawaiian/Other Pacific Islander, 1.0% Two or more races, 14.6% Hispanic of any race; Average household size: 3.12; Median age: 42.7; Age under 18: 25.1%; Age 65 and over: 20.2%; Males per 100 females: 96.9; Marriage status: 29.7% never married, 60.2% now married, 1.0% separated, 4.5% widowed, 5.7% divorced; Foreign born: 7.1%; Speak English only: 86.6%; With disability: 9.0%; Veterans: 7.4%; Ancestry: 37.7% Irish, 29.5% Italian, 15.6% German, 8.5% Polish, 3.2% English

Employment: 24.1% management, business, and financial, 5.2% computer, engineering, and science, 24.8% education, legal, community service, arts, and media, 7.8% healthcare practitioners, 10.0% service, 21.4% sales and office, 2.9% natural resources, construction, and maintenance, 3.9% production, transportation, and material moving

Income: Per capita: $57,214; Median household: $178,125; Average household: $176,819; Households with income of $100,000 or more: 63.5%; Poverty rate: 7.0%

Educational Attainment: High school diploma or higher: 97.2%; Bachelor's degree or higher: 65.7%; Graduate/professional degree or higher: 35.3%

School District(s)

NYC Special Schools - District 75

   Enrollment: n/a . . . . (212) 802-1501

Housing: Homeownership rate: 95.4%; Median home value: $618,700; Median year structure built: Before 1940; Homeowner vacancy rate: 0.0%; Median selected monthly owner costs: $3,303 with a mortgage, $1,464 without a mortgage; Median gross rent: n/a per month; Rental vacancy rate: 26.9%

Health Insurance: 97.0% have insurance; 90.3% have private insurance; 20.1% have public insurance; 3.0% do not have insurance; 4.1% of children under 18 do not have insurance

Transportation: Commute: 67.9% car, 21.8% public transportation, 5.4% walk, 4.9% work from home; Mean travel time to work: 34.1 minutes

BELLEROSE TERRACE (CDP). Covers a land area of 0.125 square miles and a water area of 0 square miles. Located at 40.72° N. Lat; 73.73° W. Long. Elevation is 79 feet.

Population: 2,100; Growth (since 2000): -2.6%; Density: 16,850.8 persons per square mile; Race: 48.6% White, 0.0% Black/African American, 36.1% Asian, 0.7% American Indian/Alaska Native, 0.0% Native Hawaiian/Other Pacific Islander, 6.6% Two or more races, 23.9% Hispanic of any race; Average household size: 3.74; Median age: 38.6; Age under 18: 24.2%; Age 65 and over: 8.1%; Males per 100 females: 98.2; Marriage status: 28.8% never married, 59.7% now married, 0.4% separated, 5.2% widowed, 6.3% divorced; Foreign born: 43.0%; Speak English only: 49.3%; With disability: 3.6%; Veterans: 2.8%; Ancestry: 17.3% Irish, 8.9% Italian, 4.3% Polish, 3.2% American, 3.1% German

Employment: 17.4% management, business, and financial, 1.0% computer, engineering, and science, 12.1% education, legal, community service, arts, and media, 18.1% healthcare practitioners, 19.2% service, 19.3% sales and office, 5.4% natural resources, construction, and maintenance, 7.5% production, transportation, and material moving

Income: Per capita: $38,034; Median household: $106,550; Average household: $136,547; Households with income of $100,000 or more: 62.6%; Poverty rate: 0.4%

Educational Attainment: High school diploma or higher: 87.1%; Bachelor's degree or higher: 39.5%; Graduate/professional degree or higher: 14.4%

Housing: Homeownership rate: 87.7%; Median home value: $398,200; Median year structure built: Before 1940; Homeowner vacancy rate: 0.0%; Median selected monthly owner costs: $2,723 with a mortgage, $1,153 without a mortgage; Median gross rent: $1,240 per month; Rental vacancy rate: 0.0%

Health Insurance: 90.9% have insurance; 71.8% have private insurance; 25.4% have public insurance; 9.1% do not have insurance; 0.0% of children under 18 do not have insurance

Transportation: Commute: 72.6% car, 22.2% public transportation, 3.5% walk, 1.7% work from home; Mean travel time to work: 39.6 minutes

BELLMORE (CDP). Covers a land area of 2.359 square miles and a water area of 0.615 square miles. Located at 40.66° N. Lat; 73.53° W. Long. Elevation is 20 feet.

History: Bellmore was settled primarily by Englishmen who crossed Long Island Sound from Connecticut in the middle of the seventeenth century.

Population: 15,767; Growth (since 2000): -4.1%; Density: 6,685.1 persons per square mile; Race: 90.9% White, 1.7% Black/African American, 4.4% Asian, 0.0% American Indian/Alaska Native, 0.0% Native Hawaiian/Other Pacific Islander, 1.6% Two or more races, 7.2% Hispanic of any race; Average household size: 2.86; Median age: 44.2; Age under 18: 21.3%; Age 65 and over: 17.9%; Males per 100 females: 94.8; Marriage status: 25.3% never married, 62.9% now married, 1.2% separated, 7.0% widowed, 4.8% divorced; Foreign born: 11.5%; Speak English only: 86.2%; With disability: 9.3%; Veterans: 5.4%; Ancestry: 29.2% Italian, 15.9% Irish, 14.4% German, 6.5% Polish, 4.4% English

Employment: 18.9% management, business, and financial, 4.8% computer, engineering, and science, 22.4% education, legal, community service, arts, and media, 7.9% healthcare practitioners, 10.8% service, 23.6% sales and office, 4.6% natural resources, construction, and maintenance, 7.0% production, transportation, and material moving

Income: Per capita: $48,723; Median household: $125,736; Average household: $137,195; Households with income of $100,000 or more: 58.5%; Poverty rate: 2.5%

Educational Attainment: High school diploma or higher: 93.3%; Bachelor's degree or higher: 50.6%; Graduate/professional degree or higher: 21.0%

School District(s)

Bellmore Union Free SD (PK-06)

   Enrollment: 1,040 . . . . (516) 679-2909

Bellmore-Merrick Central High SD (07-12)

   Enrollment: 5,422 . . . . (516) 992-1001

North Bellmore Union Free SD (KG-06)

   Enrollment: 2,075 . . . . (516) 992-3000

Housing: Homeownership rate: 88.9%; Median home value: $457,900; Median year structure built: 1955; Homeowner vacancy rate: 1.0%; Median selected monthly owner costs: $3,142 with a mortgage, $1,329 without a

mortgage; Median gross rent: $1,845 per month; Rental vacancy rate: 3.6%

Health Insurance: 97.6% have insurance; 88.5% have private insurance; 23.5% have public insurance; 2.4% do not have insurance; 1.0% of children under 18 do not have insurance

Transportation: Commute: 77.0% car, 13.0% public transportation, 1.8% walk, 8.0% work from home; Mean travel time to work: 36.0 minutes

BETHPAGE (CDP). Covers a land area of 3.576 square miles and a water area of 0 square miles. Located at 40.75° N. Lat; 73.49° W. Long. Elevation is 105 feet.

History: Named for the biblical village of Bethpage, between Bethany and the Mount of Olives. A village restoration in Old Bethpage features 20 pre-Civil War buildings.

Population: 17,016; Growth (since 2000): 2.9%; Density: 4,758.6 persons per square mile; Race: 90.5% White, 0.8% Black/African American, 6.4% Asian, 0.1% American Indian/Alaska Native, 0.0% Native Hawaiian/Other Pacific Islander, 0.8% Two or more races, 7.4% Hispanic of any race; Average household size: 2.92; Median age: 45.7; Age under 18: 19.4%; Age 65 and over: 21.3%; Males per 100 females: 89.5; Marriage status: 26.0% never married, 59.5% now married, 0.6% separated, 8.5% widowed, 6.0% divorced; Foreign born: 13.1%; Speak English only: 82.6%; With disability: 10.8%; Veterans: 6.5%; Ancestry: 33.2% Italian, 22.0% Irish, 15.6% German, 6.6% Polish, 4.0% Greek

Employment: 19.1% management, business, and financial, 5.2% computer, engineering, and science, 14.3% education, legal, community service, arts, and media, 6.7% healthcare practitioners, 15.4% service, 27.4% sales and office, 6.4% natural resources, construction, and maintenance, 5.6% production, transportation, and material moving

Income: Per capita: $44,619; Median household: $114,364; Average household: $126,754; Households with income of $100,000 or more: 55.2%; Poverty rate: 2.0%

Educational Attainment: High school diploma or higher: 93.3%; Bachelor's degree or higher: 43.3%; Graduate/professional degree or higher: 15.9%

School District(s)

Bethpage Union Free SD (KG-12)
    Enrollment: 2,911 . . . . (516) 644-4001
Plainedge Union Free SD (KG-12)
    Enrollment: 2,992 . . . . (516) 992-7455

Four-year College(s)

Briarcliffe College (Private, For-profit)
    Enrollment: 108. . . . . (516) 918-3600

Housing: Homeownership rate: 91.0%; Median home value: $432,700; Median year structure built: 1957; Homeowner vacancy rate: 0.4%; Median selected monthly owner costs: $3,005 with a mortgage, $1,138 without a mortgage; Median gross rent: $1,816 per month; Rental vacancy rate: 14.8%

Health Insurance: 98.3% have insurance; 87.5% have private insurance; 27.6% have public insurance; 1.7% do not have insurance; 1.9% of children under 18 do not have insurance

Hospitals: Saint Joseph Hospital (223 beds)

Newspapers: Bethpage Tribune (weekly circulation 2,000)

Transportation: Commute: 83.5% car, 12.0% public transportation, 0.4% walk, 3.0% work from home; Mean travel time to work: 32.7 minutes

BROOKVILLE (village). Covers a land area of 3.937 square miles and a water area of 0.011 square miles. Located at 40.81° N. Lat; 73.57° W. Long. Elevation is 236 feet.

Population: 3,576; Growth (since 2000): 68.2%; Density: 908.3 persons per square mile; Race: 77.5% White, 6.3% Black/African American, 9.7% Asian, 0.0% American Indian/Alaska Native, 0.0% Native Hawaiian/Other Pacific Islander, 4.3% Two or more races, 9.3% Hispanic of any race; Average household size: 3.07; Median age: 22.9; Age under 18: 17.7%; Age 65 and over: 11.6%; Males per 100 females: 84.1; Marriage status: 49.5% never married, 46.4% now married, 0.5% separated, 2.8% widowed, 1.2% divorced; Foreign born: 14.6%; Speak English only: 78.1%; With disability: 6.0%; Veterans: 1.8%; Ancestry: 16.1% Italian, 9.7% Russian, 7.7% Irish, 7.2% Polish, 7.0% German

Employment: 26.7% management, business, and financial, 3.4% computer, engineering, and science, 13.9% education, legal, community service, arts, and media, 9.8% healthcare practitioners, 16.9% service, 26.8% sales and office, 1.4% natural resources, construction, and maintenance, 1.1% production, transportation, and material moving

Income: Per capita: $94,367; Median household: $250,000+; Average household: $425,300; Households with income of $100,000 or more: 77.0%; Poverty rate: 3.1%

Educational Attainment: High school diploma or higher: 98.6%; Bachelor's degree or higher: 76.1%; Graduate/professional degree or higher: 38.7%

Four-year College(s)

LIU Post (Private, Not-for-profit)
    Enrollment: 8,499 . . . . (516) 299-2900
    Tuition: In-state $36,978; Out-of-state $36,978

Housing: Homeownership rate: 93.6%; Median home value: $1,815,600; Median year structure built: 1965; Homeowner vacancy rate: 2.5%; Median selected monthly owner costs: $4,000+ with a mortgage, $1,501 without a mortgage; Median gross rent: $3,159 per month; Rental vacancy rate: 0.0%

Health Insurance: 96.7% have insurance; 88.6% have private insurance; 15.1% have public insurance; 3.3% do not have insurance; 0.0% of children under 18 do not have insurance

Transportation: Commute: 59.0% car, 11.2% public transportation, 16.4% walk, 12.4% work from home; Mean travel time to work: 31.7 minutes

CARLE PLACE (CDP). Covers a land area of 0.935 square miles and a water area of 0 square miles. Located at 40.75° N. Lat; 73.61° W. Long. Elevation is 108 feet.

History: The hamlet draws its name from the Carle House, a 32-room house built by Silas Carle in Westbury in the 1800s. An early name and current nickname is Frog Hollow; the local high school's sports teams are called the Frogs and the school colors are green and white.

Population: 4,918; Growth (since 2000): -6.3%; Density: 5,260.3 persons per square mile; Race: 76.2% White, 1.3% Black/African American, 11.8% Asian, 0.0% American Indian/Alaska Native, 0.0% Native Hawaiian/Other Pacific Islander, 5.7% Two or more races, 17.8% Hispanic of any race; Average household size: 2.75; Median age: 43.7; Age under 18: 17.6%; Age 65 and over: 21.1%; Males per 100 females: 96.5; Marriage status: 29.0% never married, 57.8% now married, 0.7% separated, 7.0% widowed, 6.2% divorced; Foreign born: 20.9%; Speak English only: 68.1%; With disability: 12.4%; Veterans: 5.4%; Ancestry: 18.7% Italian, 18.6% Irish, 14.7% German, 8.9% Polish, 6.8% Portuguese

Employment: 14.9% management, business, and financial, 5.8% computer, engineering, and science, 10.3% education, legal, community service, arts, and media, 10.2% healthcare practitioners, 19.6% service, 24.3% sales and office, 7.4% natural resources, construction, and maintenance, 7.5% production, transportation, and material moving

Income: Per capita: $44,068; Median household: $89,409; Average household: $119,297; Households with income of $100,000 or more: 44.3%; Poverty rate: 4.8%

Educational Attainment: High school diploma or higher: 86.9%; Bachelor's degree or higher: 37.9%; Graduate/professional degree or higher: 13.7%

School District(s)

Carle Place Union Free SD (KG-12)
    Enrollment: 1,358 . . . . (516) 622-6442

Housing: Homeownership rate: 73.8%; Median home value: $486,000; Median year structure built: 1954; Homeowner vacancy rate: 0.0%; Median selected monthly owner costs: $3,047 with a mortgage, $1,066 without a mortgage; Median gross rent: $1,725 per month; Rental vacancy rate: 15.4%

Health Insurance: 95.9% have insurance; 82.0% have private insurance; 31.3% have public insurance; 4.1% do not have insurance; 1.0% of children under 18 do not have insurance

Transportation: Commute: 82.5% car, 10.8% public transportation, 4.5% walk, 1.4% work from home; Mean travel time to work: 28.9 minutes

CEDARHURST (village). Covers a land area of 0.675 square miles and a water area of 0 square miles. Located at 40.63° N. Lat; 73.73° W. Long. Elevation is 30 feet.

History: Incorporated 1910.

Population: 6,685; Growth (since 2000): 8.5%; Density: 9,904.4 persons per square mile; Race: 80.5% White, 0.0% Black/African American, 0.7% Asian, 0.0% American Indian/Alaska Native, 0.0% Native Hawaiian/Other Pacific Islander, 0.3% Two or more races, 20.5% Hispanic of any race; Average household size: 3.46; Median age: 27.6; Age under 18: 29.7%; Age 65 and over: 14.3%; Males per 100 females: 93.8; Marriage status: 32.2% never married, 59.3% now married, 1.2% separated, 4.4% widowed, 4.1% divorced; Foreign born: 23.9%; Speak English only: 68.5%;

With disability: 5.3%; Veterans: 3.8%; Ancestry: 10.7% Eastern European, 6.5% German, 6.0% Italian, 5.7% European, 4.9% Russian
Employment: 19.1% management, business, and financial, 2.4% computer, engineering, and science, 10.9% education, legal, community service, arts, and media, 9.0% healthcare practitioners, 13.8% service, 22.9% sales and office, 14.3% natural resources, construction, and maintenance, 7.6% production, transportation, and material moving
Income: Per capita: $34,870; Median household: $93,558; Average household: $118,096; Households with income of $100,000 or more: 45.2%; Poverty rate: 5.0%
Educational Attainment: High school diploma or higher: 95.5%; Bachelor's degree or higher: 47.0%; Graduate/professional degree or higher: 25.2%

School District(s)
Lawrence Union Free SD (PK-12)
   Enrollment: 2,683 . . . . (516) 295-7030
Housing: Homeownership rate: 62.8%; Median home value: $524,000; Median year structure built: 1945; Homeowner vacancy rate: 0.0%; Median selected monthly owner costs: $3,170 with a mortgage, $1,099 without a mortgage; Median gross rent: $1,843 per month; Rental vacancy rate: 5.5%
Health Insurance: 95.7% have insurance; 83.8% have private insurance; 23.5% have public insurance; 4.3% do not have insurance; 0.8% of children under 18 do not have insurance
Transportation: Commute: 73.0% car, 7.9% public transportation, 12.1% walk, 3.6% work from home; Mean travel time to work: 34.4 minutes
Additional Information Contacts
Village of Cedarhurst. . . . . (516) 295-5770
   http://www.cedarhurst.gov

CENTRE ISLAND (village). Covers a land area of 1.090 square miles and a water area of 0.002 square miles. Located at 40.90° N. Lat; 73.52° W. Long. Elevation is 33 feet.
Population: 524; Growth (since 2000): 18.0%; Density: 480.7 persons per square mile; Race: 90.6% White, 0.4% Black/African American, 6.3% Asian, 0.0% American Indian/Alaska Native, 0.0% Native Hawaiian/Other Pacific Islander, 0.8% Two or more races, 3.6% Hispanic of any race; Average household size: 2.61; Median age: 51.0; Age under 18: 20.8%; Age 65 and over: 25.6%; Males per 100 females: 104.0; Marriage status: 26.2% never married, 62.4% now married, 0.5% separated, 6.6% widowed, 4.8% divorced; Foreign born: 13.2%; Speak English only: 82.3%; With disability: 5.7%; Veterans: 7.2%; Ancestry: 26.5% Italian, 17.6% German, 13.7% English, 13.2% Irish, 5.9% American
Employment: 33.6% management, business, and financial, 2.9% computer, engineering, and science, 23.1% education, legal, community service, arts, and media, 14.3% healthcare practitioners, 6.7% service, 15.5% sales and office, 2.9% natural resources, construction, and maintenance, 0.8% production, transportation, and material moving
Income: Per capita: $121,437; Median household: $140,625; Average household: $313,068; Households with income of $100,000 or more: 65.1%; Poverty rate: 5.7%
Educational Attainment: High school diploma or higher: 97.9%; Bachelor's degree or higher: 71.2%; Graduate/professional degree or higher: 39.1%
Housing: Homeownership rate: 94.0%; Median home value: $1,558,300; Median year structure built: 1954; Homeowner vacancy rate: 5.0%; Median selected monthly owner costs: $4,000+ with a mortgage, $1,501 without a mortgage; Median gross rent: n/a per month; Rental vacancy rate: 0.0%
Health Insurance: 100.0% have insurance; 94.1% have private insurance; 23.9% have public insurance; 0.0% do not have insurance; 0.0% of children under 18 do not have insurance
Safety: Violent crime rate: 0.0 per 10,000 population; Property crime rate: 24.5 per 10,000 population
Transportation: Commute: 61.3% car, 14.0% public transportation, 11.9% walk, 11.9% work from home; Mean travel time to work: 42.6 minutes

---

COVE NECK (village). Covers a land area of 1.284 square miles and a water area of 0.280 square miles. Located at 40.89° N. Lat; 73.50° W. Long. Elevation is 20 feet.
History: "Sagamore Hill," home of Theodore Roosevelt, is here.
Population: 262; Growth (since 2000): -12.7%; Density: 204.0 persons per square mile; Race: 96.9% White, 0.0% Black/African American, 3.1% Asian, 0.0% American Indian/Alaska Native, 0.0% Native Hawaiian/Other Pacific Islander, 0.0% Two or more races, 4.2% Hispanic of any race; Average household size: 2.54; Median age: 49.6; Age under 18: 24.8%;

Age 65 and over: 26.7%; Males per 100 females: 115.0; Marriage status: 16.8% never married, 72.3% now married, 0.0% separated, 6.9% widowed, 4.0% divorced; Foreign born: 10.7%; Speak English only: 94.9%; With disability: 3.8%; Veterans: 8.1%; Ancestry: 22.9% Irish, 16.4% German, 14.9% American, 10.3% Italian, 9.2% Polish
Employment: 43.3% management, business, and financial, 0.0% computer, engineering, and science, 19.2% education, legal, community service, arts, and media, 1.7% healthcare practitioners, 9.2% service, 21.7% sales and office, 0.8% natural resources, construction, and maintenance, 4.2% production, transportation, and material moving
Income: Per capita: $133,159; Median household: $157,813; Average household: $355,029; Households with income of $100,000 or more: 62.1%; Poverty rate: 4.2%
Educational Attainment: High school diploma or higher: 99.5%; Bachelor's degree or higher: 71.3%; Graduate/professional degree or higher: 35.6%
Housing: Homeownership rate: 84.5%; Median home value: 2 million+; Median year structure built: 1951; Homeowner vacancy rate: 0.0%; Median selected monthly owner costs: $4,000+ with a mortgage, $1,501 without a mortgage; Median gross rent: $3,500+ per month; Rental vacancy rate: 11.1%
Health Insurance: 99.2% have insurance; 90.5% have private insurance; 27.1% have public insurance; 0.8% do not have insurance; 0.0% of children under 18 do not have insurance
Transportation: Commute: 65.0% car, 15.8% public transportation, 5.0% walk, 12.5% work from home; Mean travel time to work: 31.5 minutes

---

EAST ATLANTIC BEACH (CDP). Covers a land area of 0.315 square miles and a water area of 0.368 square miles. Located at 40.59° N. Lat; 73.71° W. Long. Elevation is 69 feet.
Population: 1,943; Growth (since 2000): -13.9%; Density: 6,166.6 persons per square mile; Race: 97.3% White, 0.0% Black/African American, 0.9% Asian, 0.0% American Indian/Alaska Native, 0.0% Native Hawaiian/Other Pacific Islander, 1.1% Two or more races, 6.5% Hispanic of any race; Average household size: 2.54; Median age: 50.0; Age under 18: 11.1%; Age 65 and over: 23.3%; Males per 100 females: 101.1; Marriage status: 40.8% never married, 45.5% now married, 1.0% separated, 8.7% widowed, 5.0% divorced; Foreign born: 9.2%; Speak English only: 89.7%; With disability: 10.0%; Veterans: 6.0%; Ancestry: 28.3% Irish, 25.5% Italian, 8.1% Polish, 7.6% American, 7.3% German
Employment: 21.6% management, business, and financial, 0.0% computer, engineering, and science, 27.6% education, legal, community service, arts, and media, 3.1% healthcare practitioners, 8.6% service, 24.2% sales and office, 11.4% natural resources, construction, and maintenance, 3.4% production, transportation, and material moving
Income: Per capita: $80,957; Median household: $132,273; Average household: $200,382; Households with income of $100,000 or more: 60.8%; Poverty rate: 1.9%
Educational Attainment: High school diploma or higher: 97.5%; Bachelor's degree or higher: 56.4%; Graduate/professional degree or higher: 24.5%
Housing: Homeownership rate: 82.9%; Median home value: $615,700; Median year structure built: 1956; Homeowner vacancy rate: 3.7%; Median selected monthly owner costs: $3,481 with a mortgage, $1,354 without a mortgage; Median gross rent: $2,574 per month; Rental vacancy rate: 0.0%
Health Insurance: 96.4% have insurance; 79.8% have private insurance; 35.7% have public insurance; 3.6% do not have insurance; 0.0% of children under 18 do not have insurance
Transportation: Commute: 85.0% car, 8.1% public transportation, 4.0% walk, 2.9% work from home; Mean travel time to work: 36.7 minutes

---

EAST HILLS (village). Covers a land area of 2.273 square miles and a water area of 0 square miles. Located at 40.80° N. Lat; 73.63° W. Long. Elevation is 190 feet.
History: Incorporated 1931.
Population: 7,114; Growth (since 2000): 4.0%; Density: 3,130.3 persons per square mile; Race: 88.6% White, 0.6% Black/African American, 8.9% Asian, 0.2% American Indian/Alaska Native, 0.0% Native Hawaiian/Other Pacific Islander, 1.3% Two or more races, 4.7% Hispanic of any race; Average household size: 2.95; Median age: 43.9; Age under 18: 29.1%; Age 65 and over: 18.2%; Males per 100 females: 96.6; Marriage status: 16.1% never married, 76.4% now married, 0.2% separated, 4.9% widowed, 2.6% divorced; Foreign born: 12.9%; Speak English only: 81.9%;

With disability: 7.5%; Veterans: 4.3%; Ancestry: 14.9% Russian, 10.9% American, 9.5% Italian, 9.4% Polish, 4.9% Eastern European
Employment: 27.0% management, business, and financial, 5.3% computer, engineering, and science, 20.5% education, legal, community service, arts, and media, 15.5% healthcare practitioners, 3.5% service, 25.1% sales and office, 2.4% natural resources, construction, and maintenance, 0.6% production, transportation, and material moving
Income: Per capita: $89,604; Median household: $199,000; Average household: $263,894; Households with income of $100,000 or more: 77.8%; Poverty rate: 1.4%
Educational Attainment: High school diploma or higher: 98.1%; Bachelor's degree or higher: 80.9%; Graduate/professional degree or higher: 45.9%
Housing: Homeownership rate: 99.4%; Median home value: $970,100; Median year structure built: 1956; Homeowner vacancy rate: 0.0%; Median selected monthly owner costs: $4,000+ with a mortgage, $1,501 without a mortgage; Median gross rent: n/a per month; Rental vacancy rate: 0.0%
Health Insurance: 97.9% have insurance; 91.9% have private insurance; 18.4% have public insurance; 2.1% do not have insurance; 2.7% of children under 18 do not have insurance
Transportation: Commute: 73.3% car, 18.0% public transportation, 0.0% walk, 8.8% work from home; Mean travel time to work: 39.6 minutes
Additional Information Contacts
Village of East Hills . . . . (516) 621-5600
   http://www.villageofeasthills.org

EAST MASSAPEQUA (CDP). Covers a land area of 3.440 square miles and a water area of 0.113 square miles. Located at 40.68° N. Lat; 73.44° W. Long. Elevation is 16 feet.

History: East Massapequa is a hamlet within the Town of Oyster Bay in Nassau County, New York.
Population: 18,689; Growth (since 2000): -4.5%; Density: 5,433.2 persons per square mile; Race: 80.5% White, 13.5% Black/African American, 1.8% Asian, 0.1% American Indian/Alaska Native, 0.0% Native Hawaiian/Other Pacific Islander, 1.6% Two or more races, 13.2% Hispanic of any race; Average household size: 2.75; Median age: 44.1; Age under 18: 19.4%; Age 65 and over: 18.8%; Males per 100 females: 94.4; Marriage status: 30.0% never married, 53.6% now married, 1.6% separated, 8.0% widowed, 8.4% divorced; Foreign born: 12.6%; Speak English only: 86.3%; With disability: 11.6%; Veterans: 7.2%; Ancestry: 32.8% Italian, 22.2% Irish, 15.1% German, 5.3% English, 4.3% Haitian
Employment: 15.1% management, business, and financial, 4.6% computer, engineering, and science, 13.3% education, legal, community service, arts, and media, 6.8% healthcare practitioners, 19.4% service, 27.0% sales and office, 7.3% natural resources, construction, and maintenance, 6.6% production, transportation, and material moving
Income: Per capita: $43,656; Median household: $95,160; Average household: $118,132; Households with income of $100,000 or more: 48.2%; Poverty rate: 5.5%
Educational Attainment: High school diploma or higher: 94.2%; Bachelor's degree or higher: 37.9%; Graduate/professional degree or higher: 14.8%
Housing: Homeownership rate: 86.4%; Median home value: $424,400; Median year structure built: 1957; Homeowner vacancy rate: 5.2%; Median selected monthly owner costs: $2,984 with a mortgage, $1,321 without a mortgage; Median gross rent: $1,600 per month; Rental vacancy rate: 3.1%
Health Insurance: 96.2% have insurance; 82.1% have private insurance; 28.4% have public insurance; 3.8% do not have insurance; 1.5% of children under 18 do not have insurance
Transportation: Commute: 83.5% car, 12.5% public transportation, 0.5% walk, 2.8% work from home; Mean travel time to work: 35.4 minutes

EAST MEADOW (CDP). Covers a land area of 6.304 square miles and a water area of 0.024 square miles. Located at 40.72° N. Lat; 73.56° W. Long. Elevation is 72 feet.

History: Its name is derived from the meadow of Hempstead Plains east of the Meadow Brook (originally a brook, now replaced by a parkway of the same name).
Population: 37,195; Growth (since 2000): -0.7%; Density: 5,900.2 persons per square mile; Race: 74.0% White, 5.6% Black/African American, 11.0% Asian, 0.4% American Indian/Alaska Native, 0.0% Native Hawaiian/Other Pacific Islander, 2.8% Two or more races, 14.5% Hispanic of any race; Average household size: 2.91; Median age: 42.7; Age under 18: 18.0%; Age 65 and over: 18.8%; Males per 100 females: 98.2; Marriage status: 30.9% never married, 53.0% now married, 2.3% separated, 8.5% widowed, 7.6% divorced; Foreign born: 19.0%; Speak English only: 72.3%; With disability: 10.9%; Veterans: 5.4%; Ancestry: 21.7% Italian, 12.7% Irish, 8.4% German, 5.3% Polish, 4.0% American
Employment: 14.6% management, business, and financial, 3.8% computer, engineering, and science, 14.5% education, legal, community service, arts, and media, 8.6% healthcare practitioners, 16.2% service, 28.4% sales and office, 7.5% natural resources, construction, and maintenance, 6.5% production, transportation, and material moving
Income: Per capita: $39,549; Median household: $94,513; Average household: $116,731; Households with income of $100,000 or more: 48.1%; Poverty rate: 4.6%
Educational Attainment: High school diploma or higher: 91.1%; Bachelor's degree or higher: 38.1%; Graduate/professional degree or higher: 17.6%
School District(s)
East Meadow Union Free SD (KG-12)
   Enrollment: 7,160 . . . . (516) 478-5776
Housing: Homeownership rate: 87.9%; Median home value: $414,200; Median year structure built: 1956; Homeowner vacancy rate: 0.6%; Median selected monthly owner costs: $2,827 with a mortgage, $1,141 without a mortgage; Median gross rent: $1,921 per month; Rental vacancy rate: 3.0%
Health Insurance: 93.9% have insurance; 80.1% have private insurance; 29.9% have public insurance; 6.1% do not have insurance; 2.8% of children under 18 do not have insurance
Hospitals: Nassau University Medical Center (1,500 beds)
Transportation: Commute: 87.3% car, 8.1% public transportation, 0.8% walk, 3.3% work from home; Mean travel time to work: 31.2 minutes

EAST NORWICH (CDP). Covers a land area of 1.047 square miles and a water area of 0 square miles. Located at 40.85° N. Lat; 73.53° W. Long. Elevation is 207 feet.

Population: 2,888; Growth (since 2000): 8.0%; Density: 2,757.8 persons per square mile; Race: 94.6% White, 0.1% Black/African American, 2.1% Asian, 0.0% American Indian/Alaska Native, 0.0% Native Hawaiian/Other Pacific Islander, 2.8% Two or more races, 6.2% Hispanic of any race; Average household size: 2.98; Median age: 44.8; Age under 18: 23.6%; Age 65 and over: 17.3%; Males per 100 females: 91.6; Marriage status: 28.2% never married, 57.8% now married, 0.0% separated, 6.3% widowed, 7.8% divorced; Foreign born: 7.2%; Speak English only: 86.3%; With disability: 7.2%; Veterans: 5.4%; Ancestry: 40.8% Italian, 24.2% Irish, 13.9% German, 10.2% Polish, 5.6% English
Employment: 27.9% management, business, and financial, 4.7% computer, engineering, and science, 18.9% education, legal, community service, arts, and media, 7.7% healthcare practitioners, 9.7% service, 24.5% sales and office, 1.5% natural resources, construction, and maintenance, 5.1% production, transportation, and material moving
Income: Per capita: $65,020; Median household: $150,208; Average household: $193,247; Households with income of $100,000 or more: 68.1%; Poverty rate: 3.5%
Educational Attainment: High school diploma or higher: 96.4%; Bachelor's degree or higher: 60.1%; Graduate/professional degree or higher: 28.7%
School District(s)
Oyster Bay-East Norwich Central SD (PK-12)
   Enrollment: 1,621 . . . . (516) 624-6505
Housing: Homeownership rate: 95.4%; Median home value: $640,000; Median year structure built: 1956; Homeowner vacancy rate: 0.0%; Median selected monthly owner costs: $3,283 with a mortgage, $1,061 without a mortgage; Median gross rent: $2,368 per month; Rental vacancy rate: 24.1%
Health Insurance: 99.2% have insurance; 91.6% have private insurance; 23.6% have public insurance; 0.8% do not have insurance; 0.0% of children under 18 do not have insurance
Transportation: Commute: 79.5% car, 14.1% public transportation, 1.0% walk, 2.9% work from home; Mean travel time to work: 40.8 minutes

EAST ROCKAWAY (village). Covers a land area of 1.017 square miles and a water area of 0.014 square miles. Located at 40.64° N. Lat; 73.67° W. Long. Elevation is 10 feet.

History: Named for the Algonquian translation of "sand place". Settled c.1688. Incorporated 1900.
Population: 9,839; Growth (since 2000): -5.5%; Density: 9,678.9 persons per square mile; Race: 92.3% White, 0.9% Black/African American, 2.4%

Asian, 0.4% American Indian/Alaska Native, 0.0% Native Hawaiian/Other Pacific Islander, 1.9% Two or more races, 16.7% Hispanic of any race; Average household size: 2.66; Median age: 44.1; Age under 18: 21.5%; Age 65 and over: 15.0%; Males per 100 females: 89.3; Marriage status: 33.3% never married, 52.2% now married, 1.2% separated, 8.4% widowed, 6.2% divorced; Foreign born: 8.9%; Speak English only: 81.7%; With disability: 10.8%; Veterans: 5.6%; Ancestry: 28.7% Italian, 27.3% Irish, 7.9% German, 4.9% Russian, 4.3% Polish

Employment: 19.2% management, business, and financial, 4.7% computer, engineering, and science, 18.1% education, legal, community service, arts, and media, 5.4% healthcare practitioners, 17.4% service, 23.4% sales and office, 6.6% natural resources, construction, and maintenance, 5.3% production, transportation, and material moving

Income: Per capita: $47,888; Median household: $95,954; Average household: $126,434; Households with income of $100,000 or more: 46.3%; Poverty rate: 3.7%

Educational Attainment: High school diploma or higher: 95.9%; Bachelor's degree or higher: 45.7%; Graduate/professional degree or higher: 23.0%

School District(s)

East Rockaway Union Free SD (KG-12)
  Enrollment: 1,149 . . . . (516) 887-8300
Lynbrook Union Free SD (KG-12)
  Enrollment: 2,830 . . . . (516) 887-0253

Housing: Homeownership rate: 76.3%; Median home value: $444,700; Median year structure built: 1950; Homeowner vacancy rate: 0.0%; Median selected monthly owner costs: $3,273 with a mortgage, $1,205 without a mortgage; Median gross rent: $1,946 per month; Rental vacancy rate: 5.2%

Health Insurance: 95.9% have insurance; 81.0% have private insurance; 26.1% have public insurance; 4.1% do not have insurance; 1.7% of children under 18 do not have insurance

Transportation: Commute: 78.3% car, 17.5% public transportation, 2.4% walk, 1.2% work from home; Mean travel time to work: 35.9 minutes

Additional Information Contacts
Village of East Rockaway . . . . (516) 887-6300
  http://www.villageofeastrockaway.org

EAST WILLISTON (village). Covers a land area of 0.569 square miles and a water area of 0 square miles. Located at 40.76° N. Lat; 73.63° W. Long. Elevation is 118 feet.

History: Incorporated 1926.

Population: 2,582; Growth (since 2000): 3.2%; Density: 4,540.4 persons per square mile; Race: 83.2% White, 0.9% Black/African American, 10.8% Asian, 0.0% American Indian/Alaska Native, 0.0% Native Hawaiian/Other Pacific Islander, 3.5% Two or more races, 6.5% Hispanic of any race; Average household size: 3.21; Median age: 41.5; Age under 18: 26.9%; Age 65 and over: 16.9%; Males per 100 females: 97.8; Marriage status: 29.1% never married, 59.7% now married, 0.5% separated, 5.9% widowed, 5.3% divorced; Foreign born: 11.4%; Speak English only: 84.4%; With disability: 4.4%; Veterans: 2.9%; Ancestry: 28.7% Italian, 27.3% Irish, 15.1% German, 3.8% Polish, 3.4% American

Employment: 27.1% management, business, and financial, 4.5% computer, engineering, and science, 18.6% education, legal, community service, arts, and media, 14.8% healthcare practitioners, 6.4% service, 24.0% sales and office, 2.7% natural resources, construction, and maintenance, 2.0% production, transportation, and material moving

Income: Per capita: $73,275; Median household: $156,397; Average household: $233,941; Households with income of $100,000 or more: 75.2%; Poverty rate: 4.0%

Educational Attainment: High school diploma or higher: 98.4%; Bachelor's degree or higher: 69.5%; Graduate/professional degree or higher: 38.5%

School District(s)

East Williston Union Free SD (KG-12)
  Enrollment: 1,697 . . . . (516) 333-3758

Housing: Homeownership rate: 96.5%; Median home value: $815,900; Median year structure built: 1946; Homeowner vacancy rate: 0.0%; Median selected monthly owner costs: $4,000+ with a mortgage, $1,501 without a mortgage; Median gross rent: $3,500+ per month; Rental vacancy rate: 0.0%

Health Insurance: 98.0% have insurance; 90.5% have private insurance; 20.1% have public insurance; 2.0% do not have insurance; 0.6% of children under 18 do not have insurance

Transportation: Commute: 70.8% car, 25.1% public transportation, 1.1% walk, 2.7% work from home; Mean travel time to work: 35.6 minutes

Additional Information Contacts
Village of East Williston . . . . (516) 746-0782
  http://eastwilliston.org

ELMONT (CDP). Covers a land area of 3.369 square miles and a water area of 0.012 square miles. Located at 40.70° N. Lat; 73.71° W. Long. Elevation is 39 feet.

History: Elmont is famous as the home of Belmont Park horsracing tract, which hosts the Belmont Stakes, the third leg of the prestigious Triple Crown of thoroughbred racing.

Population: 36,636; Growth (since 2000): 12.2%; Density: 10,875.4 persons per square mile; Race: 21.1% White, 47.4% Black/African American, 13.9% Asian, 0.2% American Indian/Alaska Native, 0.0% Native Hawaiian/Other Pacific Islander, 5.6% Two or more races, 21.4% Hispanic of any race; Average household size: 3.73; Median age: 39.1; Age under 18: 19.9%; Age 65 and over: 13.2%; Males per 100 females: 92.9; Marriage status: 39.0% never married, 47.0% now married, 2.7% separated, 6.1% widowed, 7.9% divorced; Foreign born: 45.1%; Speak English only: 52.3%; With disability: 7.5%; Veterans: 2.4%; Ancestry: 15.6% Haitian, 9.9% Jamaican, 7.1% Italian, 3.0% German, 2.5% Irish

Employment: 10.3% management, business, and financial, 3.1% computer, engineering, and science, 9.1% education, legal, community service, arts, and media, 9.1% healthcare practitioners, 24.5% service, 25.4% sales and office, 8.3% natural resources, construction, and maintenance, 10.1% production, transportation, and material moving

Income: Per capita: $31,076; Median household: $94,353; Average household: $109,837; Households with income of $100,000 or more: 47.8%; Poverty rate: 7.7%

Educational Attainment: High school diploma or higher: 87.5%; Bachelor's degree or higher: 28.0%; Graduate/professional degree or higher: 9.7%

School District(s)

Elmont Union Free SD (PK-06)
  Enrollment: 3,783 . . . . (516) 326-5500
Sewanhaka Central High SD (07-12)
  Enrollment: 8,280 . . . . (516) 488-9800

Housing: Homeownership rate: 79.1%; Median home value: $374,900; Median year structure built: 1953; Homeowner vacancy rate: 3.0%; Median selected monthly owner costs: $2,879 with a mortgage, $1,101 without a mortgage; Median gross rent: $1,680 per month; Rental vacancy rate: 2.4%

Health Insurance: 92.5% have insurance; 71.6% have private insurance; 30.3% have public insurance; 7.5% do not have insurance; 3.4% of children under 18 do not have insurance

Newspapers: Elmont Herald (weekly circulation 3,000)

Transportation: Commute: 72.9% car, 22.1% public transportation, 2.5% walk, 1.7% work from home; Mean travel time to work: 40.2 minutes

FARMINGDALE (village). Covers a land area of 1.121 square miles and a water area of 0 square miles. Located at 40.73° N. Lat; 73.45° W. Long. Elevation is 72 feet.

History: Seat of State University of N.Y. at Farmingdale Settled 1695, incorporated 1904.

Population: 8,719; Growth (since 2000): 3.8%; Density: 7,780.0 persons per square mile; Race: 81.9% White, 4.1% Black/African American, 8.4% Asian, 0.2% American Indian/Alaska Native, 0.0% Native Hawaiian/Other Pacific Islander, 1.3% Two or more races, 11.7% Hispanic of any race; Average household size: 2.35; Median age: 47.1; Age under 18: 16.9%; Age 65 and over: 18.5%; Males per 100 females: 91.9; Marriage status: 28.9% never married, 52.2% now married, 1.1% separated, 8.5% widowed, 10.5% divorced; Foreign born: 15.1%; Speak English only: 84.1%; With disability: 10.4%; Veterans: 6.9%; Ancestry: 29.7% Italian, 19.3% Irish, 15.1% German, 5.8% English, 5.2% American

Employment: 17.2% management, business, and financial, 7.2% computer, engineering, and science, 14.8% education, legal, community service, arts, and media, 4.1% healthcare practitioners, 14.5% service, 27.2% sales and office, 7.0% natural resources, construction, and maintenance, 8.0% production, transportation, and material moving

Income: Per capita: $48,303; Median household: $84,654; Average household: $113,244; Households with income of $100,000 or more: 42.4%; Poverty rate: 7.0%

Educational Attainment: High school diploma or higher: 93.4%; Bachelor's degree or higher: 39.6%; Graduate/professional degree or higher: 14.8%

School District(s)
Farmingdale Union Free SD (KG-12)
  Enrollment: 5,825 . . . . (516) 434-5100
Four-year College(s)
Farmingdale State College (Public)
  Enrollment: 9,574 . . . . (631) 420-2000
  Tuition: In-state $8,076; Out-of-state $17,726
Housing: Homeownership rate: 66.9%; Median home value: $382,400; Median year structure built: 1960; Homeowner vacancy rate: 0.9%; Median selected monthly owner costs: $2,648 with a mortgage, $1,057 without a mortgage; Median gross rent: $1,627 per month; Rental vacancy rate: 10.4%
Health Insurance: 96.4% have insurance; 82.8% have private insurance; 26.7% have public insurance; 3.6% do not have insurance; 1.7% of children under 18 do not have insurance
Newspapers: South Bay's Neighbor (weekly circulation 255,000)
Transportation: Commute: 79.9% car, 14.7% public transportation, 1.4% walk, 2.0% work from home; Mean travel time to work: 34.9 minutes
Additional Information Contacts
Village of Farmingdale . . . . (516) 249-0093
  http://www.farmingdalevillage.com

FLORAL PARK (village). Covers a land area of 1.417 square miles and a water area of 0.013 square miles. Located at 40.72° N. Lat; 73.70° W. Long. Elevation is 89 feet.
History: Named to promote the beauty of the town. Incorporated 1908.
Population: 16,269; Growth (since 2000): 1.9%; Density: 11,478.5 persons per square mile; Race: 85.2% White, 1.0% Black/African American, 7.6% Asian, 0.0% American Indian/Alaska Native, 0.0% Native Hawaiian/Other Pacific Islander, 2.6% Two or more races, 10.5% Hispanic of any race; Average household size: 2.85; Median age: 42.1; Age under 18: 21.4%; Age 65 and over: 17.0%; Males per 100 females: 95.1; Marriage status: 28.5% never married, 59.8% now married, 1.3% separated, 5.5% widowed, 6.3% divorced; Foreign born: 13.2%; Speak English only: 84.7%; With disability: 7.9%; Veterans: 5.0%; Ancestry: 30.6% Irish, 25.4% Italian, 16.5% German, 5.2% English, 4.9% Polish
Employment: 19.5% management, business, and financial, 5.6% computer, engineering, and science, 20.0% education, legal, community service, arts, and media, 7.4% healthcare practitioners, 12.7% service, 24.1% sales and office, 5.7% natural resources, construction, and maintenance, 5.0% production, transportation, and material moving
Income: Per capita: $46,831; Median household: $107,917; Average household: $130,866; Households with income of $100,000 or more: 54.7%; Poverty rate: 2.1%
Educational Attainment: High school diploma or higher: 93.9%; Bachelor's degree or higher: 50.4%; Graduate/professional degree or higher: 21.9%

School District(s)
Floral Park-Bellerose Union Free SD (PK-06)
  Enrollment: 1,468 . . . . (516) 434-2725
NYC Special Schools - District 75
  Enrollment: n/a . . . . (212) 802-1501
Sewanhaka Central High SD (07-12)
  Enrollment: 8,280 . . . . (516) 488-9800
Housing: Homeownership rate: 78.1%; Median home value: $546,600; Median year structure built: Before 1940; Homeowner vacancy rate: 0.3%; Median selected monthly owner costs: $3,174 with a mortgage, $1,387 without a mortgage; Median gross rent: $1,514 per month; Rental vacancy rate: 2.0%
Health Insurance: 97.0% have insurance; 89.5% have private insurance; 21.5% have public insurance; 3.0% do not have insurance; 0.6% of children under 18 do not have insurance
Safety: Violent crime rate: 5.6 per 10,000 population; Property crime rate: 26.3 per 10,000 population
Newspapers: Nassau Border Papers (weekly circulation 29,000)
Transportation: Commute: 74.7% car, 18.8% public transportation, 2.9% walk, 2.7% work from home; Mean travel time to work: 35.0 minutes
Additional Information Contacts
Village of Floral Park. . . . . (516) 326-6300
  http://www.fpvillage.org

FLOWER HILL (village). Covers a land area of 1.618 square miles and a water area of 0 square miles. Located at 40.81° N. Lat; 73.68° W. Long. Elevation is 164 feet.
History: Incorporated 1931.
Population: 4,785; Growth (since 2000): 6.1%; Density: 2,956.9 persons per square mile; Race: 77.8% White, 0.8% Black/African American, 18.2% Asian, 0.0% American Indian/Alaska Native, 0.0% Native Hawaiian/Other Pacific Islander, 2.6% Two or more races, 5.7% Hispanic of any race; Average household size: 3.07; Median age: 44.0; Age under 18: 26.0%; Age 65 and over: 16.8%; Males per 100 females: 95.7; Marriage status: 23.1% never married, 64.4% now married, 1.2% separated, 5.4% widowed, 7.1% divorced; Foreign born: 22.8%; Speak English only: 72.1%; With disability: 6.2%; Veterans: 3.5%; Ancestry: 14.6% Italian, 12.8% Irish, 8.1% Russian, 7.2% Greek, 5.7% American
Employment: 30.0% management, business, and financial, 8.1% computer, engineering, and science, 20.6% education, legal, community service, arts, and media, 7.5% healthcare practitioners, 6.0% service, 24.7% sales and office, 1.2% natural resources, construction, and maintenance, 1.9% production, transportation, and material moving
Income: Per capita: $95,137; Median household: $178,750; Average household: $292,151; Households with income of $100,000 or more: 74.5%; Poverty rate: 1.9%
Educational Attainment: High school diploma or higher: 93.7%; Bachelor's degree or higher: 76.3%; Graduate/professional degree or higher: 35.9%
Housing: Homeownership rate: 91.4%; Median home value: $1,237,700; Median year structure built: 1955; Homeowner vacancy rate: 1.5%; Median selected monthly owner costs: $4,000+ with a mortgage, $1,501 without a mortgage; Median gross rent: $1,644 per month; Rental vacancy rate: 0.0%
Health Insurance: 97.1% have insurance; 90.2% have private insurance; 19.2% have public insurance; 2.9% do not have insurance; 4.5% of children under 18 do not have insurance
Transportation: Commute: 55.1% car, 31.1% public transportation, 2.0% walk, 11.8% work from home; Mean travel time to work: 42.3 minutes
Additional Information Contacts
Village of Flower Hill . . . . (516) 627-5000
  http://www.villageflowerhill.org

FRANKLIN SQUARE (CDP). Covers a land area of 2.878 square miles and a water area of 0 square miles. Located at 40.70° N. Lat; 73.68° W. Long. Elevation is 66 feet.
History: In late 1643, Robert Fordham and John Carman purchased 100 square miles of land from the Massapequak, Mericoke, Matinecock, and Rockaway tribes. This land now occupies the towns of Hempstead and North Hempstead. It's speculated that the name "Franklin Square" honors Benjamin Franklin.
Population: 32,482; Growth (since 2000): 10.7%; Density: 11,287.6 persons per square mile; Race: 69.2% White, 2.8% Black/African American, 13.1% Asian, 0.0% American Indian/Alaska Native, 0.0% Native Hawaiian/Other Pacific Islander, 3.4% Two or more races, 20.4% Hispanic of any race; Average household size: 3.36; Median age: 39.5; Age under 18: 21.6%; Age 65 and over: 16.9%; Males per 100 females: 91.1; Marriage status: 33.4% never married, 53.9% now married, 0.6% separated, 6.6% widowed, 6.1% divorced; Foreign born: 25.2%; Speak English only: 60.5%; With disability: 7.2%; Veterans: 4.4%; Ancestry: 33.3% Italian, 12.6% Irish, 8.0% German, 4.1% Polish, 2.7% Greek
Employment: 12.5% management, business, and financial, 4.5% computer, engineering, and science, 11.7% education, legal, community service, arts, and media, 8.6% healthcare practitioners, 17.6% service, 27.7% sales and office, 8.9% natural resources, construction, and maintenance, 8.5% production, transportation, and material moving
Income: Per capita: $34,193; Median household: $99,919; Average household: $111,068; Households with income of $100,000 or more: 50.0%; Poverty rate: 5.7%
Educational Attainment: High school diploma or higher: 89.3%; Bachelor's degree or higher: 32.1%; Graduate/professional degree or higher: 10.8%

School District(s)
Franklin Square Union Free SD (PK-06)
  Enrollment: 2,022 . . . . (516) 505-6975
Sewanhaka Central High SD (07-12)
  Enrollment: 8,280 . . . . (516) 488-9800
Valley Stream 13 Union Free SD (KG-06)
  Enrollment: 2,068 . . . . (516) 568-6100

Valley Stream Central High SD (07-12)

Enrollment: 4,571 . . . . (516) 872-5601

Housing: Homeownership rate: 83.1%; Median home value: $447,600; Median year structure built: 1953; Homeowner vacancy rate: 1.2%; Homeowner selected monthly owner costs: $3,018 with a mortgage, $1,234 without a mortgage; Median gross rent: $1,473 per month; Rental vacancy rate: 0.5%

Health Insurance: 94.4% have insurance; 77.3% have private insurance; 28.5% have public insurance; 5.6% do not have insurance; 1.9% of children under 18 do not have insurance

Transportation: Commute: 82.5% car, 11.9% public transportation, 2.1% walk, 3.1% work from home; Mean travel time to work: 35.0 minutes

---

FREEPORT (village). Covers a land area of 4.628 square miles and a water area of 0.241 square miles. Located at 40.65° N. Lat; 73.58° W. Long. Elevation is 20 feet.

History: Named for its port, used in colonial days by cargo ships to avoid British taxes. Settled as a village c.1650. Incorporated 1892.

Population: 43,380; Growth (since 2000): -0.9%; Density: 9,372.9 persons per square mile; Race: 40.5% White, 31.2% Black/African American, 1.0% Asian, 1.3% American Indian/Alaska Native, 0.0% Native Hawaiian/Other Pacific Islander, 16.1% Two or more races, 42.9% Hispanic of any race; Average household size: 3.14; Median age: 37.7; Age under 18: 21.7%; Age 65 and over: 15.0%; Males per 100 females: 94.9; Marriage status: 43.5% never married, 41.8% now married, 3.3% separated, 6.5% widowed, 8.2% divorced; Foreign born: 29.0%; Speak English only: 57.6%; With disability: 7.9%; Veterans: 3.3%; Ancestry: 7.5% Irish, 6.6% Italian, 4.8% German, 4.0% Jamaican, 2.9% American

Employment: 10.8% management, business, and financial, 2.9% computer, engineering, and science, 12.4% education, legal, community service, arts, and media, 6.0% healthcare practitioners, 24.0% service, 23.7% sales and office, 8.5% natural resources, construction, and maintenance, 11.7% production, transportation, and material moving

Income: Per capita: $29,899; Median household: $71,184; Average household: $90,199; Households with income of $100,000 or more: 35.1%; Poverty rate: 12.6%

Educational Attainment: High school diploma or higher: 80.8%; Bachelor's degree or higher: 27.8%; Graduate/professional degree or higher: 11.2%

School District(s)
Freeport Union Free SD (KG-12)

Enrollment: 6,952 . . . . (516) 867-5205

Housing: Homeownership rate: 67.6%; Median home value: $317,400; Median year structure built: 1953; Homeowner vacancy rate: 1.6%; Median selected monthly owner costs: $2,757 with a mortgage, $1,166 without a mortgage; Median gross rent: $1,385 per month; Rental vacancy rate: 0.7%

Health Insurance: 87.9% have insurance; 66.2% have private insurance; 32.8% have public insurance; 12.1% do not have insurance; 7.9% of children under 18 do not have insurance

Safety: Violent crime rate: 21.7 per 10,000 population; Property crime rate: 93.9 per 10,000 population

Transportation: Commute: 77.1% car, 13.2% public transportation, 5.8% walk, 3.4% work from home; Mean travel time to work: 32.2 minutes

Additional Information Contacts

Village of Freeport . . . . (516) 377-2200

http://www.freeportny.com

GARDEN CITY (village). Covers a land area of 5.330 square miles and a water area of 0.025 square miles. Located at 40.73° N. Lat; 73.65° W. Long. Elevation is 89 feet.

History: Named to promote the city as a beautiful place. Was founded in 1869 and planned by the merchant Alexander Stewart. In 1927, Charles Lindbergh began his historic transatlantic flight from nearby Roosevelt Field. Adelphi University is here. Incorporated 1919.

Population: 22,699; Growth (since 2000): 4.7%; Density: 4,258.7 persons per square mile; Race: 92.9% White, 1.8% Black/African American, 2.1% Asian, 0.0% American Indian/Alaska Native, 0.0% Native Hawaiian/Other Pacific Islander, 1.9% Two or more races, 4.5% Hispanic of any race; Average household size: 2.95; Median age: 42.7; Age under 18: 25.2%; Age 65 and over: 17.3%; Males per 100 females: 90.1; Marriage status: 29.9% never married, 60.3% now married, 0.4% separated, 6.1% widowed, 3.7% divorced; Foreign born: 7.1%; Speak English only: 89.9%; With disability: 6.9%; Veterans: 5.9%; Ancestry: 32.0% Irish, 31.8% Italian, 15.3% German, 5.5% English, 4.5% Polish

Employment: 29.8% management, business, and financial, 3.4% computer, engineering, and science, 18.8% education, legal, community service, arts, and media, 6.8% healthcare practitioners, 10.0% service, 26.3% sales and office, 1.5% natural resources, construction, and maintenance, 3.4% production, transportation, and material moving

Income: Per capita: $68,789; Median household: $161,163; Average household: $208,773; Households with income of $100,000 or more: 69.0%; Poverty rate: 2.8%

Educational Attainment: High school diploma or higher: 98.0%; Bachelor's degree or higher: 72.0%; Graduate/professional degree or higher: 33.8%

School District(s)
Garden City Union Free SD (KG-12)

Enrollment: 3,850 . . . . (516) 478-1010

Nassau Boces

Enrollment: n/a . . . . (516) 396-2200

Four-year College(s)
Adelphi University (Private, Not-for-profit)

Enrollment: 7,978 . . . . (516) 877-3000

Tuition: In-state $37,170; Out-of-state $37,170

Two-year College(s)
Nassau Community College (Public)

Enrollment: 19,059 . . . . (516) 572-7501

Tuition: In-state $5,632; Out-of-state $10,734

Housing: Homeownership rate: 94.2%; Median home value: $811,800; Median year structure built: 1948; Homeowner vacancy rate: 0.8%; Median selected monthly owner costs: $4,000+ with a mortgage, $1,501 without a mortgage; Median gross rent: $2,677 per month; Rental vacancy rate: 0.0%

Health Insurance: 98.1% have insurance; 92.2% have private insurance; 21.4% have public insurance; 1.9% do not have insurance; 0.4% of children under 18 do not have insurance

Safety: Violent crime rate: 0.9 per 10,000 population; Property crime rate: 94.8 per 10,000 population

Newspapers: Oyster Bay Guardian (weekly circulation 6,000); Richner Communications (weekly circulation 77,400)

Transportation: Commute: 65.7% car, 24.4% public transportation, 3.4% walk, 5.7% work from home; Mean travel time to work: 37.5 minutes

Additional Information Contacts

Village of Garden City . . . . (516) 465-4000

http://www.gardencityny.net

GARDEN CITY PARK (CDP). Covers a land area of 0.984 square miles and a water area of 0.007 square miles. Located at 40.74° N. Lat; 73.66° W. Long. Elevation is 105 feet.

History: Garden City Park is a hamlet and census-designated place (CDP) located in the Town of North Hempstead in Nassau County on Long Island.

Population: 8,332; Growth (since 2000): 10.3%; Density: 8,463.6 persons per square mile; Race: 40.4% White, 2.1% Black/African American, 44.5% Asian, 0.0% American Indian/Alaska Native, 0.0% Native Hawaiian/Other Pacific Islander, 2.6% Two or more races, 13.5% Hispanic of any race; Average household size: 3.32; Median age: 42.7; Age under 18: 20.4%; Age 65 and over: 19.7%; Males per 100 females: 93.8; Marriage status: 25.0% never married, 63.6% now married, 1.9% separated, 7.8% widowed, 3.7% divorced; Foreign born: 45.8%; Speak English only: 41.7%; With disability: 8.6%; Veterans: 4.3%; Ancestry: 13.9% Italian, 6.6% Irish, 5.0% German, 3.9% Polish, 2.7% Greek

Employment: 13.9% management, business, and financial, 6.6% computer, engineering, and science, 10.9% education, legal, community service, arts, and media, 14.1% healthcare practitioners, 14.8% service, 26.9% sales and office, 3.7% natural resources, construction, and maintenance, 9.1% production, transportation, and material moving

Income: Per capita: $39,702; Median household: $108,654; Average household: $127,372; Households with income of $100,000 or more: 54.0%; Poverty rate: 5.5%

Educational Attainment: High school diploma or higher: 91.3%; Bachelor's degree or higher: 41.0%; Graduate/professional degree or higher: 15.5%

School District(s)
Mineola Union Free SD (PK-12)

Enrollment: 2,872 . . . . (516) 237-2001

New Hyde Park-Garden City Park Union Free SD (KG-06)

Enrollment: 1,716 . . . . (516) 434-2305

Housing: Homeownership rate: 86.4%; Median home value: $590,100; Median year structure built: 1954; Homeowner vacancy rate: 0.0%; Median

selected monthly owner costs: $3,438 with a mortgage, $1,279 without a mortgage; Median gross rent: $1,713 per month; Rental vacancy rate: 0.0%

Health Insurance: 94.8% have insurance; 73.9% have private insurance; 33.8% have public insurance; 5.2% do not have insurance; 0.0% of children under 18 do not have insurance

Transportation: Commute: 74.6% car, 18.7% public transportation, 1.8% walk, 3.3% work from home; Mean travel time to work: 40.0 minutes

GARDEN CITY SOUTH (CDP).

Covers a land area of 0.404 square miles and a water area of 0 square miles. Located at 40.71° N. Lat; 73.66° W. Long. Elevation is 72 feet.

Population: 4,096; Growth (since 2000): 3.1%; Density: 10,132.4 persons per square mile; Race: 86.5% White, 0.3% Black/African American, 8.5% Asian, 0.0% American Indian/Alaska Native, 0.0% Native Hawaiian/Other Pacific Islander, 0.5% Two or more races, 9.0% Hispanic of any race; Average household size: 3.10; Median age: 41.0; Age under 18: 20.4%; Age 65 and over: 17.2%; Males per 100 females: 91.1; Marriage status: 27.3% never married, 56.8% now married, 0.2% separated, 7.6% widowed, 8.4% divorced; Foreign born: 14.7%; Speak English only: 78.2%; With disability: 9.7%; Veterans: 8.0%; Ancestry: 27.9% Italian, 24.7% Irish, 18.3% German, 4.8% Polish, 2.6% Greek

Employment: 15.3% management, business, and financial, 5.5% computer, engineering, and science, 20.0% education, legal, community service, arts, and media, 5.1% healthcare practitioners, 11.3% service, 29.0% sales and office, 5.6% natural resources, construction, and maintenance, 8.3% production, transportation, and material moving

Income: Per capita: $47,281; Median household: $114,088; Average household: $141,872; Households with income of $100,000 or more: 55.7%; Poverty rate: 4.0%

Educational Attainment: High school diploma or higher: 92.7%; Bachelor's degree or higher: 44.6%; Graduate/professional degree or higher: 22.9%

Housing: Homeownership rate: 91.0%; Median home value: $510,900; Median year structure built: 1951; Homeowner vacancy rate: 3.3%; Median selected monthly owner costs: $3,070 with a mortgage, $1,266 without a mortgage; Median gross rent: $1,442 per month; Rental vacancy rate: 0.0%

Health Insurance: 93.8% have insurance; 81.6% have private insurance; 23.5% have public insurance; 6.3% do not have insurance; 2.5% of children under 18 do not have insurance

Transportation: Commute: 82.8% car, 14.7% public transportation, 0.0% walk, 2.6% work from home; Mean travel time to work: 36.1 minutes

GLEN COVE (city).

Covers a land area of 6.655 square miles and a water area of 12.589 square miles. Located at 40.88° N. Lat; 73.64° W. Long. Elevation is 23 feet.

History: Settled 1668, attracted affluent class after Civil War. In 1920s it became core of the Gold Coast as mansions were built, including waterfront community on East Island at north end (once known as Morgans Island when owned by J.P. Morgan). In 19th century it attracted industry, including one of the world's largest starch factories. Incorporated as a city 1918.

Population: 27,376; Growth (since 2000): 2.8%; Density: 4,113.6 persons per square mile; Race: 62.5% White, 8.2% Black/African American, 3.9% Asian, 0.8% American Indian/Alaska Native, 0.0% Native Hawaiian/Other Pacific Islander, 3.8% Two or more races, 26.9% Hispanic of any race; Average household size: 2.77; Median age: 38.1; Age under 18: 21.1%; Age 65 and over: 18.2%; Males per 100 females: 94.9; Marriage status: 37.7% never married, 47.1% now married, 1.3% separated, 6.3% widowed, 8.9% divorced; Foreign born: 29.7%; Speak English only: 58.4%; With disability: 8.6%; Veterans: 4.7%; Ancestry: 20.3% Italian, 10.9% Irish, 7.0% German, 5.3% Polish, 3.5% English

Employment: 15.7% management, business, and financial, 2.8% computer, engineering, and science, 11.8% education, legal, community service, arts, and media, 5.4% healthcare practitioners, 27.4% service, 20.0% sales and office, 8.4% natural resources, construction, and maintenance, 8.5% production, transportation, and material moving

Income: Per capita: $39,760; Median household: $74,767; Average household: $109,733; Households with income of $100,000 or more: 36.1%; Poverty rate: 12.4%

Educational Attainment: High school diploma or higher: 81.6%; Bachelor's degree or higher: 37.8%; Graduate/professional degree or higher: 16.8%

School District(s)
Glen Cove City SD (PK-12)
    Enrollment: 3,310 . . . . (516) 801-7010
Four-year College(s)
Webb Institute (Private, Not-for-profit)
    Enrollment: 98. . . . . (516) 671-2213
    Tuition: In-state $48,775; Out-of-state $48,775

Housing: Homeownership rate: 51.1%; Median home value: $480,300; Median year structure built: 1957; Homeowner vacancy rate: 1.2%; Median selected monthly owner costs: $2,845 with a mortgage, $1,316 without a mortgage; Median gross rent: $1,742 per month; Rental vacancy rate: 6.1%

Health Insurance: 90.1% have insurance; 69.8% have private insurance; 32.5% have public insurance; 9.9% do not have insurance; 5.7% of children under 18 do not have insurance

Hospitals: Glen Cove Hospital (265 beds)

Safety: Violent crime rate: 2.9 per 10,000 population; Property crime rate: 55.1 per 10,000 population

Newspapers: Gold Coast Gazette (weekly circulation 4,000); Record-Pilot (weekly circulation 6,000)

Transportation: Commute: 81.8% car, 7.1% public transportation, 6.1% walk, 3.4% work from home; Mean travel time to work: 28.8 minutes

Additional Information Contacts
City of Glen Cove . . . . (516) 676-2000
    http://www.glencove-li.com

GLEN HEAD (CDP).

Covers a land area of 1.639 square miles and a water area of 0 square miles. Located at 40.84° N. Lat; 73.62° W. Long. Elevation is 112 feet.

History: Glen Head is consistently listed as one of the wealthiest zip codes on Long Island by a varierty of sources.

Population: 4,963; Growth (since 2000): 7.3%; Density: 3,028.6 persons per square mile; Race: 89.1% White, 2.3% Black/African American, 1.3% Asian, 0.0% American Indian/Alaska Native, 0.0% Native Hawaiian/Other Pacific Islander, 0.6% Two or more races, 12.1% Hispanic of any race; Average household size: 2.88; Median age: 43.2; Age under 18: 22.3%; Age 65 and over: 15.1%; Males per 100 females: 92.1; Marriage status: 27.0% never married, 63.2% now married, 1.5% separated, 3.6% widowed, 6.2% divorced; Foreign born: 18.6%; Speak English only: 73.4%; With disability: 5.7%; Veterans: 5.6%; Ancestry: 32.0% Italian, 19.5% Irish, 14.7% German, 5.9% Polish, 5.8% Russian

Employment: 26.6% management, business, and financial, 5.1% computer, engineering, and science, 11.7% education, legal, community service, arts, and media, 9.9% healthcare practitioners, 12.6% service, 22.3% sales and office, 6.4% natural resources, construction, and maintenance, 5.4% production, transportation, and material moving

Income: Per capita: $55,511; Median household: $107,125; Average household: $157,901; Households with income of $100,000 or more: 60.0%; Poverty rate: 2.1%

Educational Attainment: High school diploma or higher: 93.6%; Bachelor's degree or higher: 58.4%; Graduate/professional degree or higher: 31.0%

School District(s)
North Shore Central SD (KG-12)
    Enrollment: 2,688 . . . . (516) 277-7801

Housing: Homeownership rate: 84.7%; Median home value: $619,100; Median year structure built: 1955; Homeowner vacancy rate: 0.0%; Median selected monthly owner costs: $3,316 with a mortgage, $1,286 without a mortgage; Median gross rent: $2,012 per month; Rental vacancy rate: 0.0%

Health Insurance: 90.6% have insurance; 82.6% have private insurance; 19.2% have public insurance; 9.4% do not have insurance; 1.0% of children under 18 do not have insurance

Transportation: Commute: 81.6% car, 10.7% public transportation, 0.6% walk, 6.6% work from home; Mean travel time to work: 35.8 minutes

GLENWOOD LANDING (CDP).

Covers a land area of 0.972 square miles and a water area of 0 square miles. Located at 40.83° N. Lat; 73.64° W. Long. Elevation is 98 feet.

Population: 3,958; Growth (since 2000): 11.8%; Density: 4,073.8 persons per square mile; Race: 88.6% White, 3.2% Black/African American, 3.7% Asian, 0.0% American Indian/Alaska Native, 0.0% Native Hawaiian/Other Pacific Islander, 2.6% Two or more races, 5.7% Hispanic of any race; Average household size: 2.76; Median age: 43.6; Age under 18: 23.5%; Age 65 and over: 11.3%; Males per 100 females: 89.1; Marriage status:

29.2% never married, 55.9% now married, 2.3% separated, 4.9% widowed, 9.9% divorced; Foreign born: 8.4%; Speak English only: 89.4%; With disability: 5.1%; Veterans: 5.7%; Ancestry: 30.5% Italian, 27.8% Irish, 13.6% German, 7.7% Polish, 5.6% Eastern European

Employment: 22.7% management, business, and financial, 4.3% computer, engineering, and science, 19.5% education, legal, community service, arts, and media, 9.2% healthcare practitioners, 13.2% service, 21.8% sales and office, 4.6% natural resources, construction, and maintenance, 4.8% production, transportation, and material moving

Income: Per capita: $54,934; Median household: $123,454; Average household: $148,540; Households with income of $100,000 or more: 59.4%; Poverty rate: 2.3%

Educational Attainment: High school diploma or higher: 99.5%; Bachelor's degree or higher: 66.3%; Graduate/professional degree or higher: 34.9%

Housing: Homeownership rate: 89.1%; Median home value: $609,100; Median year structure built: 1954; Homeowner vacancy rate: 0.0%; Median selected monthly owner costs: $3,320 with a mortgage, $1,449 without a mortgage; Median gross rent: $1,645 per month; Rental vacancy rate: 0.0%

Health Insurance: 98.3% have insurance; 91.0% have private insurance; 18.7% have public insurance; 1.7% do not have insurance; 0.9% of children under 18 do not have insurance

Transportation: Commute: 82.7% car, 14.1% public transportation, 0.6% walk, 2.6% work from home; Mean travel time to work: 36.9 minutes

GREAT NECK (village).

Covers a land area of 1.329 square miles and a water area of 0.027 square miles. Located at 40.80° N. Lat; 73.73° W. Long. Elevation is 112 feet.

History: Great Neck, originally called "Madnan's Neck", was settled in the late 17th century, not long after settlers landed on Plymouth Rock. The area had previously been inhabited by the Mattinecock Native Americans.

Population: 10,272; Growth (since 2000): 7.7%; Density: 7,729.3 persons per square mile; Race: 87.9% White, 1.3% Black/African American, 8.8% Asian, 0.0% American Indian/Alaska Native, 0.0% Native Hawaiian/Other Pacific Islander, 0.9% Two or more races, 6.6% Hispanic of any race; Average household size: 3.22; Median age: 36.2; Age under 18: 29.9%; Age 65 and over: 18.8%; Males per 100 females: 96.5; Marriage status: 27.9% never married, 62.4% now married, 0.5% separated, 5.1% widowed, 4.7% divorced; Foreign born: 35.1%; Speak English only: 48.7%; With disability: 7.6%; Veterans: 3.0%; Ancestry: 25.7% Iranian, 8.7% American, 5.9% Israeli, 5.5% Russian, 4.7% Polish

Employment: 18.7% management, business, and financial, 5.6% computer, engineering, and science, 13.6% education, legal, community service, arts, and media, 13.9% healthcare practitioners, 9.9% service, 29.7% sales and office, 2.7% natural resources, construction, and maintenance, 5.8% production, transportation, and material moving

Income: Per capita: $41,070; Median household: $91,484; Average household: $130,107; Households with income of $100,000 or more: 46.1%; Poverty rate: 6.2%

Educational Attainment: High school diploma or higher: 90.9%; Bachelor's degree or higher: 53.1%; Graduate/professional degree or higher: 24.6%

School District(s)

Great Neck Union Free SD (PK-12)

    Enrollment: 6,664 . . . . (516) 441-4001

Housing: Homeownership rate: 76.3%; Median home value: $795,100; Median year structure built: 1951; Homeowner vacancy rate: 0.0%; Median selected monthly owner costs: $3,952 with a mortgage, $1,501 without a mortgage; Median gross rent: $1,768 per month; Rental vacancy rate: 12.9%

Health Insurance: 96.4% have insurance; 80.0% have private insurance; 31.0% have public insurance; 3.6% do not have insurance; 0.3% of children under 18 do not have insurance

Newspapers: Great Neck Record (weekly circulation 7,000)

Transportation: Commute: 65.5% car, 21.9% public transportation, 3.5% walk, 7.4% work from home; Mean travel time to work: 34.3 minutes

Additional Information Contacts

Village of Great Neck . . . . (516) 482-0019
    http://www.greatneckvillage.org

GREAT NECK ESTATES (village).

Covers a land area of 0.757 square miles and a water area of 0.044 square miles. Located at 40.79° N. Lat; 73.74° W. Long. Elevation is 82 feet.

History: Incorporated 1911.

Population: 2,840; Growth (since 2000): 3.0%; Density: 3,752.8 persons per square mile; Race: 91.1% White, 0.0% Black/African American, 6.8% Asian, 0.0% American Indian/Alaska Native, 0.0% Native Hawaiian/Other Pacific Islander, 2.1% Two or more races, 2.7% Hispanic of any race; Average household size: 3.01; Median age: 43.2; Age under 18: 28.8%; Age 65 and over: 19.8%; Males per 100 females: 90.4; Marriage status: 23.5% never married, 67.1% now married, 1.0% separated, 4.2% widowed, 5.2% divorced; Foreign born: 26.1%; Speak English only: 70.5%; With disability: 5.4%; Veterans: 2.1%; Ancestry: 14.2% Iranian, 11.5% Russian, 9.5% American, 8.0% Polish, 8.0% Eastern European

Employment: 22.2% management, business, and financial, 7.0% computer, engineering, and science, 22.5% education, legal, community service, arts, and media, 17.3% healthcare practitioners, 5.4% service, 23.7% sales and office, 1.8% natural resources, construction, and maintenance, 0.0% production, transportation, and material moving

Income: Per capita: $79,366; Median household: $158,182; Average household: $237,515; Households with income of $100,000 or more: 67.9%; Poverty rate: 6.7%

Educational Attainment: High school diploma or higher: 94.8%; Bachelor's degree or higher: 73.6%; Graduate/professional degree or higher: 44.7%

Housing: Homeownership rate: 91.6%; Median home value: $1,247,100; Median year structure built: Before 1940; Homeowner vacancy rate: 0.6%; Median selected monthly owner costs: $4,000+ with a mortgage, $1,501 without a mortgage; Median gross rent: $3,500+ per month; Rental vacancy rate: 0.0%

Health Insurance: 94.0% have insurance; 86.0% have private insurance; 18.7% have public insurance; 6.0% do not have insurance; 3.3% of children under 18 do not have insurance

Transportation: Commute: 57.5% car, 25.5% public transportation, 1.8% walk, 14.0% work from home; Mean travel time to work: 33.6 minutes

GREAT NECK GARDENS (CDP).

Covers a land area of 0.171 square miles and a water area of 0 square miles. Located at 40.80° N. Lat; 73.72° W. Long. Elevation is 98 feet.

Population: 1,240; Growth (since 2000): 13.9%; Density: 7,266.2 persons per square mile; Race: 64.4% White, 0.0% Black/African American, 33.2% Asian, 0.0% American Indian/Alaska Native, 0.0% Native Hawaiian/Other Pacific Islander, 2.3% Two or more races, 0.0% Hispanic of any race; Average household size: 3.91; Median age: 37.6; Age under 18: 38.3%; Age 65 and over: 15.4%; Males per 100 females: 99.7; Marriage status: 19.3% never married, 75.5% now married, 0.0% separated, 2.1% widowed, 3.1% divorced; Foreign born: 30.2%; Speak English only: 69.4%; With disability: 7.3%; Veterans: 6.7%; Ancestry: 14.9% Russian, 12.9% Polish, 12.3% Latvian, 6.8% Italian, 6.0% American

Employment: 35.6% management, business, and financial, 10.5% computer, engineering, and science, 5.1% education, legal, community service, arts, and media, 10.1% healthcare practitioners, 15.9% service, 22.8% sales and office, 0.0% natural resources, construction, and maintenance, 0.0% production, transportation, and material moving

Income: Per capita: $55,364; Median household: $195,865; Average household: $212,807; Households with income of $100,000 or more: 72.2%; Poverty rate: 5.4%

Educational Attainment: High school diploma or higher: 100.0%; Bachelor's degree or higher: 85.8%; Graduate/professional degree or higher: 22.8%

Housing: Homeownership rate: 92.4%; Median home value: $892,700; Median year structure built: 1948; Homeowner vacancy rate: 0.0%; Median selected monthly owner costs: $4,000+ with a mortgage, $1,501 without a mortgage; Median gross rent: n/a per month; Rental vacancy rate: 0.0%

Health Insurance: 89.4% have insurance; 81.9% have private insurance; 21.5% have public insurance; 10.6% do not have insurance; 11.8% of children under 18 do not have insurance

Transportation: Commute: 57.5% car, 31.1% public transportation, 2.7% walk, 3.4% work from home; Mean travel time to work: 41.9 minutes

GREAT NECK PLAZA (village).

Covers a land area of 0.312 square miles and a water area of 0 square miles. Located at 40.79° N. Lat; 73.73° W. Long. Elevation is 98 feet.

Population: 6,964; Growth (since 2000): 8.3%; Density: 22,308.3 persons per square mile; Race: 74.9% White, 2.7% Black/African American, 15.4% Asian, 1.4% American Indian/Alaska Native, 0.0% Native Hawaiian/Other Pacific Islander, 2.5% Two or more races, 10.3% Hispanic of any race; Average household size: 1.77; Median age: 52.5; Age under 18: 14.0%; Age 65 and over: 31.9%; Males per 100 females: 75.4; Marriage status:

23.4% never married, 46.8% now married, 1.2% separated, 14.8% widowed, 14.9% divorced; Foreign born: 28.1%; Speak English only: 66.1%; With disability: 14.3%; Veterans: 3.8%; Ancestry: 10.3% American, 9.8% Russian, 7.1% Polish, 5.6% Eastern European, 5.1% Italian

Employment: 23.0% management, business, and financial, 8.2% computer, engineering, and science, 19.4% education, legal, community service, arts, and media, 11.5% healthcare practitioners, 11.6% service, 21.2% sales and office, 2.4% natural resources, construction, and maintenance, 2.6% production, transportation, and material moving

Income: Per capita: $53,888; Median household: $74,303; Average household: $96,647; Households with income of $100,000 or more: 35.5%; Poverty rate: 6.7%

Educational Attainment: High school diploma or higher: 93.5%; Bachelor's degree or higher: 59.1%; Graduate/professional degree or higher: 27.2%

Housing: Homeownership rate: 54.6%; Median home value: $338,900; Median year structure built: 1957; Homeowner vacancy rate: 3.0%; Median selected monthly owner costs: $1,695 with a mortgage, $625 without a mortgage; Median gross rent: $1,839 per month; Rental vacancy rate: 0.0%

Health Insurance: 93.7% have insurance; 72.1% have private insurance; 40.2% have public insurance; 6.3% do not have insurance; 0.0% of children under 18 do not have insurance

Transportation: Commute: 44.2% car, 36.8% public transportation, 8.8% walk, 7.0% work from home; Mean travel time to work: 36.2 minutes

Additional Information Contacts

Village of Great Neck Plaza . . . . (516) 482-4500
  http://www.greatneckplaza.net

GREENVALE (CDP). Covers a land area of 0.252 square miles and a water area of 0 square miles. Located at 40.81° N. Lat; 73.63° W. Long. Elevation is 171 feet.

History: C.W. Post campus of Long Island University.

Population: 1,640; Growth (since 2000): -26.5%; Density: 6,504.0 persons per square mile; Race: 57.6% White, 0.0% Black/African American, 34.8% Asian, 0.0% American Indian/Alaska Native, 0.0% Native Hawaiian/Other Pacific Islander, 0.5% Two or more races, 8.8% Hispanic of any race; Average household size: 3.58; Median age: 33.6; Age under 18: 22.6%; Age 65 and over: 16.0%; Males per 100 females: 100.0; Marriage status: 42.0% never married, 50.5% now married, 0.6% separated, 2.3% widowed, 5.3% divorced; Foreign born: 36.3%; Speak English only: 60.8%; With disability: 6.0%; Veterans: 4.4%; Ancestry: 18.1% Irish, 16.4% Italian, 6.3% German, 3.0% Croatian, 2.6% American

Employment: 25.3% management, business, and financial, 2.5% computer, engineering, and science, 18.2% education, legal, community service, arts, and media, 9.0% healthcare practitioners, 14.2% service, 22.4% sales and office, 5.2% natural resources, construction, and maintenance, 3.3% production, transportation, and material moving

Income: Per capita: $55,177; Median household: $122,045; Average household: $190,371; Households with income of $100,000 or more: 72.8%; Poverty rate: 4.3%

Educational Attainment: High school diploma or higher: 95.9%; Bachelor's degree or higher: 58.3%; Graduate/professional degree or higher: 32.1%

School District(s)

Roslyn Union Free SD (PK-12)
  Enrollment: 3,112 . . . . (516) 801-5001

Housing: Homeownership rate: 63.3%; Median home value: $603,700; Median year structure built: 1956; Homeowner vacancy rate: 0.0%; Median selected monthly owner costs: $4,000+ with a mortgage, $1,397 without a mortgage; Median gross rent: $1,967 per month; Rental vacancy rate: 0.0%

Health Insurance: 94.5% have insurance; 86.5% have private insurance; 17.0% have public insurance; 5.5% do not have insurance; 0.0% of children under 18 do not have insurance

Transportation: Commute: 87.6% car, 12.4% public transportation, 0.0% walk, 0.0% work from home; Mean travel time to work: 33.4 minutes

HARBOR HILLS (CDP). Covers a land area of 0.118 square miles and a water area of 0.059 square miles. Located at 40.79° N. Lat; 73.75° W. Long. Elevation is 69 feet.

Population: 648; Growth (since 2000): 15.1%; Density: 5,473.8 persons per square mile; Race: 82.7% White, 0.0% Black/African American, 15.9% Asian, 0.0% American Indian/Alaska Native, 0.0% Native Hawaiian/Other Pacific Islander, 1.4% Two or more races, 3.4% Hispanic of any race;

Average household size: 3.41; Median age: 45.0; Age under 18: 29.9%; Age 65 and over: 17.6%; Males per 100 females: 89.1; Marriage status: 16.0% never married, 72.5% now married, 0.0% separated, 10.4% widowed, 1.1% divorced; Foreign born: 36.7%; Speak English only: 50.8%; With disability: 2.3%; Veterans: 4.8%; Ancestry: 50.3% Iranian, 6.3% German, 5.1% English, 4.6% Polish, 3.4% American

Employment: 34.8% management, business, and financial, 4.4% computer, engineering, and science, 22.0% education, legal, community service, arts, and media, 10.8% healthcare practitioners, 0.0% service, 23.0% sales and office, 5.1% natural resources, construction, and maintenance, 0.0% production, transportation, and material moving

Income: Per capita: $62,605; Median household: $166,296; Average household: $210,982; Households with income of $100,000 or more: 84.8%; Poverty rate: n/a

Educational Attainment: High school diploma or higher: 86.9%; Bachelor's degree or higher: 71.4%; Graduate/professional degree or higher: 45.1%

Housing: Homeownership rate: 100.0%; Median home value: $1,445,200; Median year structure built: 1949; Homeowner vacancy rate: 0.0%; Median selected monthly owner costs: $4,000+ with a mortgage, $1,501 without a mortgage; Median gross rent: n/a per month; Rental vacancy rate: 0.0%

Health Insurance: 86.7% have insurance; 83.3% have private insurance; 11.1% have public insurance; 13.3% do not have insurance; 10.8% of children under 18 do not have insurance

Transportation: Commute: 64.6% car, 25.6% public transportation, 0.0% walk, 9.8% work from home; Mean travel time to work: 42.4 minutes

HARBOR ISLE (CDP). Covers a land area of 0.173 square miles and a water area of 0.055 square miles. Located at 40.60° N. Lat; 73.66° W. Long. Elevation is 10 feet.

Population: 1,253; Growth (since 2000): -6.1%; Density: 7,239.8 persons per square mile; Race: 95.7% White, 1.0% Black/African American, 0.0% Asian, 0.0% American Indian/Alaska Native, 0.0% Native Hawaiian/Other Pacific Islander, 0.0% Two or more races, 17.6% Hispanic of any race; Average household size: 3.11; Median age: 45.4; Age under 18: 22.5%; Age 65 and over: 26.7%; Males per 100 females: 96.5; Marriage status: 20.7% never married, 67.0% now married, 0.0% separated, 6.5% widowed, 5.8% divorced; Foreign born: 8.9%; Speak English only: 88.8%; With disability: 12.7%; Veterans: 13.0%; Ancestry: 24.3% Irish, 20.1% German, 19.0% Italian, 7.5% American, 5.1% Polish

Employment: 17.7% management, business, and financial, 2.5% computer, engineering, and science, 11.7% education, legal, community service, arts, and media, 8.0% healthcare practitioners, 12.9% service, 34.5% sales and office, 4.3% natural resources, construction, and maintenance, 8.4% production, transportation, and material moving

Income: Per capita: $49,702; Median household: $103,125; Average household: $150,560; Households with income of $100,000 or more: 50.6%; Poverty rate: 1.8%

Educational Attainment: High school diploma or higher: 97.6%; Bachelor's degree or higher: 41.0%; Graduate/professional degree or higher: 15.2%

Housing: Homeownership rate: 100.0%; Median home value: $455,100; Median year structure built: 1956; Homeowner vacancy rate: 0.0%; Median selected monthly owner costs: $3,518 with a mortgage, $1,228 without a mortgage; Median gross rent: n/a per month; Rental vacancy rate: 0.0%

Health Insurance: 97.8% have insurance; 87.8% have private insurance; 36.6% have public insurance; 2.2% do not have insurance; 0.0% of children under 18 do not have insurance

Transportation: Commute: 70.9% car, 26.2% public transportation, 1.2% walk, 1.6% work from home; Mean travel time to work: 48.2 minutes

HEMPSTEAD (town). Covers a land area of 118.587 square miles and a water area of 73.000 square miles. Located at 40.63° N. Lat; 73.61° W. Long. Elevation is 56 feet.

History: In 1644, the first settlers of Hempstead found a well-watered grassy plain on which their cattle grew fat. The virgin soil was excellent for timothy, rye, wheat, and maize. The score or more families who made up the settlement prospered. Not before 1801, however, did the village begin to grow appreciably.

Population: 772,296; Growth (since 2000): 2.2%; Density: 6,512.5 persons per square mile; Race: 63.9% White, 17.0% Black/African American, 6.0% Asian, 0.3% American Indian/Alaska Native, 0.0% Native Hawaiian/Other Pacific Islander, 4.4% Two or more races, 20.1% Hispanic of any race; Average household size: 3.14; Median age: 40.1; Age under 18: 22.2%; Age 65 and over: 15.6%; Males per 100 females: 93.3;

Marriage status: 34.3% never married, 52.8% now married, 1.7% separated, 6.2% widowed, 6.7% divorced; Foreign born: 22.2%; Speak English only: 72.1%; With disability: 8.4%; Veterans: 4.4%; Ancestry: 18.3% Italian, 13.5% Irish, 8.3% German, 4.0% American, 4.0% Polish
Employment: 15.8% management, business, and financial, 3.8% computer, engineering, and science, 14.5% education, legal, community service, arts, and media, 7.4% healthcare practitioners, 18.1% service, 25.2% sales and office, 7.2% natural resources, construction, and maintenance, 8.0% production, transportation, and material moving
Income: Per capita: $41,052; Median household: $102,002; Average household: $126,525; Households with income of $100,000 or more: 50.8%; Poverty rate: 6.6%
Educational Attainment: High school diploma or higher: 89.6%; Bachelor's degree or higher: 39.4%; Graduate/professional degree or higher: 17.3%

School District(s)
Academy Charter School (KG-08)
    Enrollment: 945 . . . . (516) 408-2200
Evergreen Charter School (KG-05)
    Enrollment: 376 . . . . (516) 292-2060
Hempstead Union Free SD (PK-12)
    Enrollment: 8,392 . . . . (516) 434-4010
Uniondale Union Free SD (KG-12)
    Enrollment: 7,152 . . . . (516) 560-8824
Four-year College(s)
Hofstra University (Private, Not-for-profit)
    Enrollment: 11,131 . . . . (516) 463-6600
    Tuition: In-state $43,960; Out-of-state $43,960
Vocational/Technical School(s)
Access Careers (Private, For-profit)
    Enrollment: 47 . . . . (516) 433-0034
    Tuition: $1,300
Franklin Career Institute (Private, Not-for-profit)
    Enrollment: 271 . . . . (718) 535-3333
    Tuition: $18,856
Long Island Barber Institute (Private, For-profit)
    Enrollment: 44 . . . . (516) 486-5424
    Tuition: $7,500
Long Island Beauty School-Hempstead (Private, For-profit)
    Enrollment: 93 . . . . (516) 483-6259
    Tuition: $13,200
Housing: Homeownership rate: 80.8%; Median home value: $421,300; Median year structure built: 1953; Homeowner vacancy rate: 1.1%; Median selected monthly owner costs: $3,017 with a mortgage, $1,285 without a mortgage; Median gross rent: $1,554 per month; Rental vacancy rate: 3.9%
Health Insurance: 93.5% have insurance; 78.2% have private insurance; 27.6% have public insurance; 6.5% do not have insurance; 2.9% of children under 18 do not have insurance
Newspapers: Beacon Newspapers (weekly circulation 24,000)
Transportation: Commute: 76.0% car, 17.1% public transportation, 2.6% walk, 3.5% work from home; Mean travel time to work: 35.8 minutes
Additional Information Contacts
Town of Hempstead . . . . (516) 489-5000
    http://www.townofhempstead.org

HEMPSTEAD (village).
Covers a land area of 3.682 square miles and a water area of 0.005 square miles. Located at 40.70° N. Lat; 73.62° W. Long. Elevation is 56 feet.
History: The town grew significantly in the 1970s with the construction of nearby freeways, large retail outlets and the expansion of regional suburban industries. Settled in 1644 by English colonists who named it for their old home in England, Hemel-Hempstead. Seat of Hofstra University. Has many colonial houses and monuments. Founded as a village. Incorporated 1853.
Population: 55,698; Growth (since 2000): -1.5%; Density: 15,127.0 persons per square mile; Race: 13.8% White, 46.3% Black/African American, 1.7% Asian, 0.8% American Indian/Alaska Native, 0.0% Native Hawaiian/Other Pacific Islander, 5.0% Two or more races, 46.6% Hispanic of any race; Average household size: 3.50; Median age: 33.9; Age under 18: 27.0%; Age 65 and over: 10.3%; Males per 100 females: 97.1; Marriage status: 49.4% never married, 37.7% now married, 3.3% separated, 4.9% widowed, 8.0% divorced; Foreign born: 41.0%; Speak English only: 50.1%; With disability: 6.1%; Veterans: 3.0%; Ancestry: 8.4%

Jamaican, 3.6% Haitian, 1.7% Trinidadian and Tobagonian, 1.7% Italian, 1.4% Guyanese
Employment: 7.4% management, business, and financial, 2.1% computer, engineering, and science, 6.7% education, legal, community service, arts, and media, 3.8% healthcare practitioners, 35.2% service, 21.7% sales and office, 10.4% natural resources, construction, and maintenance, 12.7% production, transportation, and material moving
Income: Per capita: $22,825; Median household: $58,476; Average household: $75,726; Households with income of $100,000 or more: 27.5%; Poverty rate: 20.2%
Educational Attainment: High school diploma or higher: 69.5%; Bachelor's degree or higher: 18.9%; Graduate/professional degree or higher: 7.5%

School District(s)
Academy Charter School (KG-08)
    Enrollment: 945 . . . . (516) 408-2200
Evergreen Charter School (KG-05)
    Enrollment: 376 . . . . (516) 292-2060
Hempstead Union Free SD (PK-12)
    Enrollment: 8,392 . . . . (516) 434-4010
Uniondale Union Free SD (KG-12)
    Enrollment: 7,152 . . . . (516) 560-8824
Four-year College(s)
Hofstra University (Private, Not-for-profit)
    Enrollment: 11,131 . . . . (516) 463-6600
    Tuition: In-state $43,960; Out-of-state $43,960
Vocational/Technical School(s)
Access Careers (Private, For-profit)
    Enrollment: 47 . . . . (516) 433-0034
    Tuition: $1,300
Franklin Career Institute (Private, Not-for-profit)
    Enrollment: 271 . . . . (718) 535-3333
    Tuition: $18,856
Long Island Barber Institute (Private, For-profit)
    Enrollment: 44 . . . . (516) 486-5424
    Tuition: $7,500
Long Island Beauty School-Hempstead (Private, For-profit)
    Enrollment: 93 . . . . (516) 483-6259
    Tuition: $13,200
Housing: Homeownership rate: 43.4%; Median home value: $308,800; Median year structure built: 1956; Homeowner vacancy rate: 2.0%; Median selected monthly owner costs: $2,936 with a mortgage, $1,250 without a mortgage; Median gross rent: $1,350 per month; Rental vacancy rate: 8.6%
Health Insurance: 81.3% have insurance; 48.5% have private insurance; 41.9% have public insurance; 18.7% do not have insurance; 4.5% of children under 18 do not have insurance
Safety: Violent crime rate: 59.5 per 10,000 population; Property crime rate: 106.3 per 10,000 population
Newspapers: Beacon Newspapers (weekly circulation 24,000)
Transportation: Commute: 68.5% car, 23.3% public transportation, 4.0% walk, 2.1% work from home; Mean travel time to work: 32.1 minutes
Additional Information Contacts
Village of Hempstead . . . . (516) 489-3400
    http://www.villageofhempstead.org

HERRICKS (CDP).
Covers a land area of 0.573 square miles and a water area of 0 square miles. Located at 40.76° N. Lat; 73.66° W. Long. Elevation is 112 feet.
History: Named for Capt. James M. Herrick, it is an unincorporated entity, governed under the jurisdiction of the Town of North Hempstead. Mail delivery is provided by the New Hyde Park Post Office utilizing the 11040 Zip Code.
Population: 4,127; Growth (since 2000): 1.3%; Density: 7,197.5 persons per square mile; Race: 48.5% White, 0.3% Black/African American, 43.8% Asian, 0.4% American Indian/Alaska Native, 0.8% Native Hawaiian/Other Pacific Islander, 5.0% Two or more races, 7.5% Hispanic of any race; Average household size: 3.27; Median age: 41.6; Age under 18: 20.7%; Age 65 and over: 18.0%; Males per 100 females: 93.1; Marriage status: 30.7% never married, 58.2% now married, 0.3% separated, 6.0% widowed, 5.1% divorced; Foreign born: 36.4%; Speak English only: 52.2%; With disability: 8.7%; Veterans: 4.2%; Ancestry: 16.7% Italian, 9.6% Irish, 5.1% German, 4.4% Polish, 3.2% American
Employment: 22.4% management, business, and financial, 13.6% computer, engineering, and science, 10.2% education, legal, community

service, arts, and media, 15.3% healthcare practitioners, 12.1% service, 17.5% sales and office, 6.1% natural resources, construction, and maintenance, 2.8% production, transportation, and material moving
Income: Per capita: $48,798; Median household: $134,688; Average household: $157,473; Households with income of $100,000 or more: 63.7%; Poverty rate: 5.8%
Educational Attainment: High school diploma or higher: 95.1%; Bachelor's degree or higher: 54.6%; Graduate/professional degree or higher: 20.8%
Housing: Homeownership rate: 95.2%; Median home value: $620,600; Median year structure built: 1952; Homeowner vacancy rate: 2.0%; Median selected monthly owner costs: $3,250 with a mortgage, $1,501 without a mortgage; Median gross rent: $3,250 per month; Rental vacancy rate: 0.0%
Health Insurance: 94.3% have insurance; 80.9% have private insurance; 26.7% have public insurance; 5.7% do not have insurance; 1.8% of children under 18 do not have insurance
Transportation: Commute: 72.9% car, 22.3% public transportation, 1.8% walk, 3.0% work from home; Mean travel time to work: 41.6 minutes

HEWLETT (CDP). Covers a land area of 0.881 square miles and a water area of 0.018 square miles. Located at 40.64° N. Lat; 73.69° W. Long. Elevation is 23 feet.
History: Hewlett is a hamlet and census-designated place (CDP) in Nassau County, New York on the South Shore of Long Island, and usually included as one of the Five Towns in the southwestern corner of Nassau County.
Population: 6,268; Growth (since 2000): -11.2%; Density: 7,113.5 persons per square mile; Race: 82.6% White, 1.1% Black/African American, 9.9% Asian, 0.0% American Indian/Alaska Native, 0.0% Native Hawaiian/Other Pacific Islander, 0.3% Two or more races, 12.7% Hispanic of any race; Average household size: 2.68; Median age: 45.8; Age under 18: 20.0%; Age 65 and over: 22.1%; Males per 100 females: 92.5; Marriage status: 24.1% never married, 60.9% now married, 1.3% separated, 5.1% widowed, 9.8% divorced; Foreign born: 23.4%; Speak English only: 67.0%; With disability: 7.6%; Veterans: 5.7%; Ancestry: 17.9% Italian, 11.4% Russian, 10.9% Irish, 10.2% American, 8.6% Polish
Employment: 16.0% management, business, and financial, 2.4% computer, engineering, and science, 25.9% education, legal, community service, arts, and media, 11.9% healthcare practitioners, 12.6% service, 23.3% sales and office, 1.6% natural resources, construction, and maintenance, 6.4% production, transportation, and material moving
Income: Per capita: $46,033; Median household: $104,516; Average household: $122,442; Households with income of $100,000 or more: 51.0%; Poverty rate: 7.1%
Educational Attainment: High school diploma or higher: 94.7%; Bachelor's degree or higher: 50.7%; Graduate/professional degree or higher: 24.1%

School District(s)
Hewlett-Woodmere Union Free SD (PK-12)
    Enrollment: 3,098 . . . . (516) 792-4800
Housing: Homeownership rate: 79.7%; Median home value: $439,600; Median year structure built: 1956; Homeowner vacancy rate: 2.0%; Median selected monthly owner costs: $3,463 with a mortgage, $1,334 without a mortgage; Median gross rent: $1,401 per month; Rental vacancy rate: 0.0%
Health Insurance: 96.7% have insurance; 83.5% have private insurance; 30.1% have public insurance; 3.3% do not have insurance; 0.0% of children under 18 do not have insurance
Transportation: Commute: 77.7% car, 18.6% public transportation, 0.5% walk, 3.3% work from home; Mean travel time to work: 34.0 minutes

HEWLETT BAY PARK (village). Covers a land area of 0.337 square miles and a water area of 0.022 square miles. Located at 40.64° N. Lat; 73.70° W. Long. Elevation is 7 feet.
Population: 357; Growth (since 2000): -26.2%; Density: 1,059.8 persons per square mile; Race: 94.7% White, 1.4% Black/African American, 3.1% Asian, 0.0% American Indian/Alaska Native, 0.0% Native Hawaiian/Other Pacific Islander, 0.3% Two or more races, 5.0% Hispanic of any race; Average household size: 2.81; Median age: 50.6; Age under 18: 21.6%; Age 65 and over: 21.8%; Males per 100 females: 106.1; Marriage status: 20.1% never married, 71.4% now married, 0.3% separated, 5.3% widowed, 3.3% divorced; Foreign born: 21.0%; Speak English only: 69.5%; With disability: 2.8%; Veterans: 1.4%; Ancestry: 22.4% Russian, 8.1% Polish, 7.6% American, 5.6% Moroccan, 5.3% European

Employment: 33.3% management, business, and financial, 0.5% computer, engineering, and science, 15.3% education, legal, community service, arts, and media, 19.6% healthcare practitioners, 3.2% service, 23.3% sales and office, 2.6% natural resources, construction, and maintenance, 2.1% production, transportation, and material moving
Income: Per capita: $157,245; Median household: $233,750; Average household: $440,172; Households with income of $100,000 or more: 85.1%; Poverty rate: 0.8%
Educational Attainment: High school diploma or higher: 94.6%; Bachelor's degree or higher: 72.1%; Graduate/professional degree or higher: 39.5%
Housing: Homeownership rate: 98.4%; Median home value: $1,740,400; Median year structure built: 1954; Homeowner vacancy rate: 3.1%; Median selected monthly owner costs: $4,000+ with a mortgage, $1,501 without a mortgage; Median gross rent: n/a per month; Rental vacancy rate: 0.0%
Health Insurance: 98.6% have insurance; 93.3% have private insurance; 22.1% have public insurance; 1.4% do not have insurance; 3.7% of children under 18 do not have insurance
Transportation: Commute: 65.6% car, 14.8% public transportation, 1.6% walk, 18.0% work from home; Mean travel time to work: 39.8 minutes

HEWLETT HARBOR (village). Covers a land area of 0.726 square miles and a water area of 0.104 square miles. Located at 40.63° N. Lat; 73.68° W. Long. Elevation is 7 feet.
Population: 1,175; Growth (since 2000): -7.6%; Density: 1,617.9 persons per square mile; Race: 88.1% White, 2.1% Black/African American, 8.3% Asian, 0.0% American Indian/Alaska Native, 0.0% Native Hawaiian/Other Pacific Islander, 0.2% Two or more races, 1.4% Hispanic of any race; Average household size: 3.07; Median age: 46.3; Age under 18: 25.0%; Age 65 and over: 17.1%; Males per 100 females: 97.0; Marriage status: 27.4% never married, 62.7% now married, 0.6% separated, 5.7% widowed, 4.2% divorced; Foreign born: 14.7%; Speak English only: 80.4%; With disability: 7.6%; Veterans: 4.5%; Ancestry: 25.9% Russian, 14.7% American, 7.6% Eastern European, 5.7% Polish, 5.4% Italian
Employment: 24.6% management, business, and financial, 3.5% computer, engineering, and science, 18.2% education, legal, community service, arts, and media, 14.9% healthcare practitioners, 3.3% service, 31.8% sales and office, 0.0% natural resources, construction, and maintenance, 3.7% production, transportation, and material moving
Income: Per capita: $100,289; Median household: $218,750; Average household: $304,778; Households with income of $100,000 or more: 77.5%; Poverty rate: 3.1%
Educational Attainment: High school diploma or higher: 99.6%; Bachelor's degree or higher: 77.4%; Graduate/professional degree or higher: 41.4%
Housing: Homeownership rate: 99.2%; Median home value: $1,061,300; Median year structure built: 1957; Homeowner vacancy rate: 2.5%; Median selected monthly owner costs: $4,000+ with a mortgage, $1,501 without a mortgage; Median gross rent: n/a per month; Rental vacancy rate: 0.0%
Health Insurance: 99.1% have insurance; 91.2% have private insurance; 19.4% have public insurance; 0.9% do not have insurance; 0.0% of children under 18 do not have insurance
Transportation: Commute: 74.3% car, 14.1% public transportation, 1.2% walk, 10.4% work from home; Mean travel time to work: 42.8 minutes

HEWLETT NECK (village). Covers a land area of 0.193 square miles and a water area of 0.021 square miles. Located at 40.62° N. Lat; 73.70° W. Long. Elevation is 7 feet.
Population: 398; Growth (since 2000): -21.0%; Density: 2,066.5 persons per square mile; Race: 95.2% White, 2.8% Black/African American, 2.0% Asian, 0.0% American Indian/Alaska Native, 0.0% Native Hawaiian/Other Pacific Islander, 0.0% Two or more races, 2.5% Hispanic of any race; Average household size: 3.24; Median age: 42.6; Age under 18: 29.4%; Age 65 and over: 17.6%; Males per 100 females: 96.0; Marriage status: 25.3% never married, 68.0% now married, 0.3% separated, 4.7% widowed, 1.9% divorced; Foreign born: 14.8%; Speak English only: 69.9%; With disability: 7.5%; Veterans: 4.3%; Ancestry: 17.3% Russian, 8.3% Ukrainian, 7.0% Israeli, 7.0% Polish, 5.3% American
Employment: 32.7% management, business, and financial, 3.6% computer, engineering, and science, 23.6% education, legal, community service, arts, and media, 18.8% healthcare practitioners, 3.0% service, 16.4% sales and office, 0.6% natural resources, construction, and maintenance, 1.2% production, transportation, and material moving

Income: Per capita: $99,779; Median household: $212,750; Average household: $320,146; Households with income of $100,000 or more: 88.6%; Poverty rate: 0.5%
Educational Attainment: High school diploma or higher: 98.8%; Bachelor's degree or higher: 78.3%; Graduate/professional degree or higher: 45.7%
Housing: Homeownership rate: 99.2%; Median home value: $1,062,500; Median year structure built: 1943; Homeowner vacancy rate: 0.8%; Median selected monthly owner costs: $4,000+ with a mortgage, $1,501 without a mortgage; Median gross rent: n/a per month; Rental vacancy rate: 0.0%
Health Insurance: 98.5% have insurance; 90.7% have private insurance; 19.3% have public insurance; 1.5% do not have insurance; 1.5% of children under 18 do not have insurance
Transportation: Commute: 74.5% car, 15.8% public transportation, 0.6% walk, 9.1% work from home; Mean travel time to work: 42.9 minutes

HICKSVILLE (CDP).
Covers a land area of 6.791 square miles and a water area of 0.015 square miles. Located at 40.76° N. Lat; 73.52° W. Long. Elevation is 148 feet.
History: Named for Charles Hicks, a Quaker reformer. Founded 1648.
Population: 42,368; Growth (since 2000): 2.7%; Density: 6,238.9 persons per square mile; Race: 65.5% White, 4.3% Black/African American, 23.2% Asian, 0.2% American Indian/Alaska Native, 0.0% Native Hawaiian/Other Pacific Islander, 3.3% Two or more races, 15.6% Hispanic of any race; Average household size: 3.19; Median age: 43.9; Age under 18: 18.1%; Age 65 and over: 17.2%; Males per 100 females: 96.2; Marriage status: 31.5% never married, 56.7% now married, 1.3% separated, 6.6% widowed, 5.3% divorced; Foreign born: 30.5%; Speak English only: 62.8%; With disability: 9.0%; Veterans: 5.4%; Ancestry: 17.9% Italian, 16.6% Irish, 10.5% German, 3.9% Polish, 3.5% English
Employment: 14.1% management, business, and financial, 4.3% computer, engineering, and science, 12.0% education, legal, community service, arts, and media, 7.4% healthcare practitioners, 17.2% service, 28.6% sales and office, 7.6% natural resources, construction, and maintenance, 8.8% production, transportation, and material moving
Income: Per capita: $39,289; Median household: $104,188; Average household: $121,098; Households with income of $100,000 or more: 51.7%; Poverty rate: 4.6%
Educational Attainment: High school diploma or higher: 90.9%; Bachelor's degree or higher: 35.0%; Graduate/professional degree or higher: 12.5%

School District(s)
Hicksville Union Free SD (KG-12)
    Enrollment: 5,270 . . . . (516) 733-2105
Vocational/Technical School(s)
Brittany Beauty Academy (Private, For-profit)
    Enrollment: n/a . . . . (516) 822-5546
    Tuition: $14,000
Veeb Nassau County School of Practical Nursing (Public)
    Enrollment: 195 . . . . (516) 572-1704
    Tuition: In-state $16,725; Out-of-state $16,725
Housing: Homeownership rate: 86.7%; Median home value: $421,900; Median year structure built: 1954; Homeowner vacancy rate: 0.5%; Median selected monthly owner costs: $2,754 with a mortgage, $1,043 without a mortgage; Median gross rent: $1,820 per month; Rental vacancy rate: 12.3%
Health Insurance: 94.4% have insurance; 79.6% have private insurance; 27.3% have public insurance; 5.6% do not have insurance; 2.6% of children under 18 do not have insurance
Newspapers: Litmore Publishing (weekly circulation 58,000)
Transportation: Commute: 79.7% car, 12.3% public transportation, 2.6% walk, 3.2% work from home; Mean travel time to work: 33.8 minutes

INWOOD (CDP).
Covers a land area of 1.581 square miles and a water area of 0.483 square miles. Located at 40.62° N. Lat; 73.75° W. Long. Elevation is 7 feet.
History: Inwood is included among the Five Towns, an informal grouping of villages and hamlets in Nassau County on the South Shore of western Long Island adjoining the border with Queens County in New York City.
Population: 10,304; Growth (since 2000): 10.5%; Density: 6,515.4 persons per square mile; Race: 37.6% White, 23.8% Black/African American, 3.2% Asian, 0.7% American Indian/Alaska Native, 0.0% Native Hawaiian/Other Pacific Islander, 4.0% Two or more races, 45.1% Hispanic of any race; Average household size: 3.30; Median age: 34.9; Age under 18: 25.7%; Age 65 and over: 12.7%; Males per 100 females: 94.2;

Marriage status: 43.2% never married, 44.4% now married, 2.6% separated, 5.3% widowed, 7.2% divorced; Foreign born: 32.6%; Speak English only: 53.1%; With disability: 8.3%; Veterans: 2.6%; Ancestry: 15.3% Italian, 6.5% Irish, 4.0% American, 3.1% German, 1.8% Jamaican
Employment: 6.3% management, business, and financial, 1.1% computer, engineering, and science, 7.0% education, legal, community service, arts, and media, 3.1% healthcare practitioners, 32.8% service, 23.6% sales and office, 14.5% natural resources, construction, and maintenance, 11.6% production, transportation, and material moving
Income: Per capita: $23,142; Median household: $54,575; Average household: $72,033; Households with income of $100,000 or more: 22.0%; Poverty rate: 16.7%
Educational Attainment: High school diploma or higher: 74.8%; Bachelor's degree or higher: 15.8%; Graduate/professional degree or higher: 5.8%

School District(s)
Lawrence Union Free SD (PK-12)
    Enrollment: 2,683 . . . . (516) 295-7030
Housing: Homeownership rate: 46.6%; Median home value: $375,100; Median year structure built: 1947; Homeowner vacancy rate: 1.1%; Median selected monthly owner costs: $2,590 with a mortgage, $1,145 without a mortgage; Median gross rent: $1,362 per month; Rental vacancy rate: 1.0%
Health Insurance: 87.2% have insurance; 55.0% have private insurance; 43.3% have public insurance; 12.8% do not have insurance; 2.2% of children under 18 do not have insurance
Transportation: Commute: 68.1% car, 20.6% public transportation, 8.1% walk, 2.2% work from home; Mean travel time to work: 30.2 minutes

ISLAND PARK (village).
Covers a land area of 0.445 square miles and a water area of 0 square miles. Located at 40.61° N. Lat; 73.66° W. Long. Elevation is 7 feet.
History: Incorporated 1926.
Population: 4,765; Growth (since 2000): 0.7%; Density: 10,707.5 persons per square mile; Race: 81.7% White, 0.7% Black/African American, 2.1% Asian, 0.4% American Indian/Alaska Native, 0.0% Native Hawaiian/Other Pacific Islander, 3.2% Two or more races, 31.0% Hispanic of any race; Average household size: 2.90; Median age: 40.9; Age under 18: 17.9%; Age 65 and over: 17.7%; Males per 100 females: 95.6; Marriage status: 37.9% never married, 42.5% now married, 0.9% separated, 8.8% widowed, 10.8% divorced; Foreign born: 17.6%; Speak English only: 72.6%; With disability: 10.4%; Veterans: 6.7%; Ancestry: 27.6% Italian, 11.6% Irish, 11.6% German, 5.8% American, 4.6% Greek
Employment: 11.9% management, business, and financial, 5.7% computer, engineering, and science, 14.7% education, legal, community service, arts, and media, 2.4% healthcare practitioners, 21.1% service, 24.0% sales and office, 8.5% natural resources, construction, and maintenance, 11.6% production, transportation, and material moving
Income: Per capita: $36,789; Median household: $89,158; Average household: $104,893; Households with income of $100,000 or more: 45.1%; Poverty rate: 8.9%
Educational Attainment: High school diploma or higher: 91.3%; Bachelor's degree or higher: 26.8%; Graduate/professional degree or higher: 12.8%

School District(s)
Island Park Union Free SD (PK-08)
    Enrollment: 776 . . . . (516) 434-2600
Housing: Homeownership rate: 66.7%; Median home value: $370,900; Median year structure built: 1955; Homeowner vacancy rate: 0.9%; Median selected monthly owner costs: $2,950 with a mortgage, $1,112 without a mortgage; Median gross rent: $1,611 per month; Rental vacancy rate: 0.0%
Health Insurance: 91.7% have insurance; 71.6% have private insurance; 34.8% have public insurance; 8.3% do not have insurance; 1.1% of children under 18 do not have insurance
Newspapers: South Shore Tribune (weekly circulation 64,000)
Transportation: Commute: 78.7% car, 16.6% public transportation, 1.9% walk, 2.5% work from home; Mean travel time to work: 29.0 minutes
Additional Information Contacts
Village of Island Park . . . . (516) 431-0600
    http://www.villageofislandpark.com

JERICHO (CDP). Covers a land area of 3.943 square miles and a water area of 0.016 square miles. Located at 40.79° N. Lat; 73.54° W. Long. Elevation is 194 feet.

History: The English families who settled in Jericho were, or soon became, Quakers, members of the Society of Friends. Many fled from persecution in England and in the New England Colonies. They sought a peaceful existence as farmers. The name of the area was changed in 1692 from Lusum to Jericho after the town in the Middle East near the Jordan River mentioned in the Bible as part of the Promised Land.

Population: 14,014; Growth (since 2000): 7.4%; Density: 3,554.1 persons per square mile; Race: 61.7% White, 2.3% Black/African American, 31.9% Asian, 0.0% American Indian/Alaska Native, 0.0% Native Hawaiian/Other Pacific Islander, 2.6% Two or more races, 3.1% Hispanic of any race; Average household size: 2.95; Median age: 43.8; Age under 18: 23.1%; Age 65 and over: 14.1%; Males per 100 females: 93.8; Marriage status: 25.9% never married, 65.0% now married, 1.4% separated, 3.5% widowed, 5.6% divorced; Foreign born: 26.7%; Speak English only: 64.7%; With disability: 6.9%; Veterans: 2.8%; Ancestry: 10.1% Italian, 7.6% Russian, 6.8% Polish, 6.2% Eastern European, 5.3% American

Employment: 28.8% management, business, and financial, 8.1% computer, engineering, and science, 14.1% education, legal, community service, arts, and media, 12.3% healthcare practitioners, 6.5% service, 24.6% sales and office, 1.8% natural resources, construction, and maintenance, 3.7% production, transportation, and material moving

Income: Per capita: $71,613; Median household: $156,029; Average household: $211,804; Households with income of $100,000 or more: 71.7%; Poverty rate: 5.4%

Educational Attainment: High school diploma or higher: 96.8%; Bachelor's degree or higher: 70.0%; Graduate/professional degree or higher: 35.0%

School District(s)

Jericho Union Free SD (KG-12)
    Enrollment: 3,047 . . . . (516) 203-3600

Housing: Homeownership rate: 84.7%; Median home value: $732,100; Median year structure built: 1963; Homeowner vacancy rate: 0.4%; Median selected monthly owner costs: $4,000+ with a mortgage, $1,501 without a mortgage; Median gross rent: $1,935 per month; Rental vacancy rate: 0.0%

Health Insurance: 97.6% have insurance; 86.7% have private insurance; 21.5% have public insurance; 2.4% do not have insurance; 1.6% of children under 18 do not have insurance

Transportation: Commute: 69.6% car, 22.7% public transportation, 1.6% walk, 5.4% work from home; Mean travel time to work: 37.1 minutes

KENSINGTON (village). Covers a land area of 0.254 square miles and a water area of 0 square miles. Located at 40.79° N. Lat; 73.72° W. Long. Elevation is 128 feet.

Population: 1,131; Growth (since 2000): -6.5%; Density: 4,449.1 persons per square mile; Race: 82.9% White, 0.3% Black/African American, 16.1% Asian, 0.0% American Indian/Alaska Native, 0.0% Native Hawaiian/Other Pacific Islander, 0.3% Two or more races, 1.1% Hispanic of any race; Average household size: 2.67; Median age: 53.7; Age under 18: 21.9%; Age 65 and over: 33.0%; Males per 100 females: 91.3; Marriage status: 15.7% never married, 71.1% now married, 0.8% separated, 10.0% widowed, 3.1% divorced; Foreign born: 28.9%; Speak English only: 64.6%; With disability: 8.7%; Veterans: 5.0%; Ancestry: 14.3% Russian, 11.8% Polish, 9.2% Iranian, 8.0% Eastern European, 4.6% European

Employment: 30.2% management, business, and financial, 7.4% computer, engineering, and science, 21.2% education, legal, community service, arts, and media, 12.2% healthcare practitioners, 2.2% service, 23.8% sales and office, 0.0% natural resources, construction, and maintenance, 3.0% production, transportation, and material moving

Income: Per capita: $96,401; Median household: $164,821; Average household: $257,421; Households with income of $100,000 or more: 65.7%; Poverty rate: 5.0%

Educational Attainment: High school diploma or higher: 98.3%; Bachelor's degree or higher: 79.8%; Graduate/professional degree or higher: 48.8%

Housing: Homeownership rate: 93.9%; Median home value: $1,237,700; Median year structure built: Before 1940; Homeowner vacancy rate: 0.0%; Median selected monthly owner costs: $4,000+ with a mortgage, $1,501 without a mortgage; Median gross rent: $3,500+ per month; Rental vacancy rate: 13.3%

Health Insurance: 99.4% have insurance; 86.0% have private insurance; 33.6% have public insurance; 0.6% do not have insurance; 0.0% of children under 18 do not have insurance

Safety: Violent crime rate: 0.0 per 10,000 population; Property crime rate: 0.0 per 10,000 population

Transportation: Commute: 50.4% car, 29.3% public transportation, 6.2% walk, 14.0% work from home; Mean travel time to work: 36.2 minutes

KINGS POINT (village). Covers a land area of 3.355 square miles and a water area of 0.643 square miles. Located at 40.82° N. Lat; 73.74° W. Long. Elevation is 26 feet.

History: Seat of U.S. Merchant Marine Academy (established 1942). Incorporated 1924.

Population: 5,181; Growth (since 2000): 2.1%; Density: 1,544.1 persons per square mile; Race: 92.8% White, 1.3% Black/African American, 2.4% Asian, 0.0% American Indian/Alaska Native, 0.0% Native Hawaiian/Other Pacific Islander, 2.9% Two or more races, 1.9% Hispanic of any race; Average household size: 3.47; Median age: 34.1; Age under 18: 25.1%; Age 65 and over: 17.8%; Males per 100 females: 123.9; Marriage status: 36.4% never married, 59.3% now married, 0.4% separated, 2.4% widowed, 2.0% divorced; Foreign born: 29.7%; Speak English only: 61.4%; With disability: 7.4%; Veterans: 3.4%; Ancestry: 34.6% Iranian, 12.5% American, 7.2% German, 6.4% Irish, 5.6% Italian

Employment: 22.3% management, business, and financial, 4.3% computer, engineering, and science, 11.1% education, legal, community service, arts, and media, 9.5% healthcare practitioners, 7.9% service, 34.4% sales and office, 3.7% natural resources, construction, and maintenance, 7.1% production, transportation, and material moving

Income: Per capita: $72,044; Median household: $122,083; Average household: $277,635; Households with income of $100,000 or more: 60.1%; Poverty rate: 3.6%

Educational Attainment: High school diploma or higher: 89.9%; Bachelor's degree or higher: 55.8%; Graduate/professional degree or higher: 25.0%

Four-year College(s)

United States Merchant Marine Academy (Public)
    Enrollment: 975 . . . . (516) 726-5800
    Tuition: In-state $1,020; Out-of-state $1,020

Housing: Homeownership rate: 97.6%; Median home value: 2 million+; Median year structure built: 1959; Homeowner vacancy rate: 3.2%; Median selected monthly owner costs: $4,000+ with a mortgage, $1,501 without a mortgage; Median gross rent: n/a per month; Rental vacancy rate: 41.5%

Health Insurance: 96.8% have insurance; 87.3% have private insurance; 23.6% have public insurance; 3.2% do not have insurance; 1.8% of children under 18 do not have insurance

Safety: Violent crime rate: 3.8 per 10,000 population; Property crime rate: 19.1 per 10,000 population

Transportation: Commute: 65.4% car, 16.8% public transportation, 4.3% walk, 12.9% work from home; Mean travel time to work: 34.9 minutes

Additional Information Contacts

Village of Kings Point . . . . (516) 504-1000
    http://www.villageofkingspoint.org

LAKE SUCCESS (village). Covers a land area of 1.845 square miles and a water area of 0.050 square miles. Located at 40.76° N. Lat; 73.71° W. Long. Elevation is 203 feet.

History: Lake Success was the temporary home of the UN from 1946 to 1950. Settled c.1730, incorporated 1926.

Population: 3,112; Growth (since 2000): 11.3%; Density: 1,686.5 persons per square mile; Race: 49.8% White, 7.5% Black/African American, 39.7% Asian, 0.6% American Indian/Alaska Native, 0.0% Native Hawaiian/Other Pacific Islander, 1.5% Two or more races, 2.2% Hispanic of any race; Average household size: 3.48; Median age: 50.6; Age under 18: 20.6%; Age 65 and over: 31.0%; Males per 100 females: 78.8; Marriage status: 20.4% never married, 64.9% now married, 0.7% separated, 11.7% widowed, 3.0% divorced; Foreign born: 34.3%; Speak English only: 53.4%; With disability: 7.0%; Veterans: 4.7%; Ancestry: 6.1% German, 5.2% Armenian, 5.0% Italian, 3.9% American, 3.8% Russian

Employment: 23.9% management, business, and financial, 6.9% computer, engineering, and science, 14.8% education, legal, community service, arts, and media, 14.5% healthcare practitioners, 6.4% service, 30.2% sales and office, 0.0% natural resources, construction, and maintenance, 3.3% production, transportation, and material moving

Income: Per capita: $64,172; Median household: $167,083; Average household: $252,898; Households with income of $100,000 or more: 77.2%; Poverty rate: 5.0%

Educational Attainment: High school diploma or higher: 90.3%; Bachelor's degree or higher: 57.0%; Graduate/professional degree or higher: 27.2%

Housing: Homeownership rate: 96.8%; Median home value: $1,156,900; Median year structure built: 1955; Homeowner vacancy rate: 0.0%; Median selected monthly owner costs: $4,000+ with a mortgage, $1,501 without a mortgage; Median gross rent: $3,500+ per month; Rental vacancy rate: 0.0%

Health Insurance: 97.3% have insurance; 88.7% have private insurance; 21.4% have public insurance; 2.7% do not have insurance; 0.7% of children under 18 do not have insurance

Safety: Violent crime rate: 3.2 per 10,000 population; Property crime rate: 60.8 per 10,000 population

Transportation: Commute: 71.0% car, 18.1% public transportation, 1.7% walk, 8.8% work from home; Mean travel time to work: 36.7 minutes

LAKEVIEW (CDP).

Covers a land area of 1.000 square miles and a water area of 0.195 square miles. Located at 40.68° N. Lat; 73.65° W. Long. Elevation is 39 feet.

Population: 6,756; Growth (since 2000): 20.5%; Density: 6,756.5 persons per square mile; Race: 13.2% White, 74.6% Black/African American, 0.9% Asian, 0.2% American Indian/Alaska Native, 0.0% Native Hawaiian/Other Pacific Islander, 6.6% Two or more races, 18.4% Hispanic of any race; Average household size: 4.33; Median age: 34.4; Age under 18: 25.5%; Age 65 and over: 11.8%; Males per 100 females: 87.0; Marriage status: 43.1% never married, 42.1% now married, 4.0% separated, 8.0% widowed, 6.9% divorced; Foreign born: 25.1%; Speak English only: 73.0%; With disability: 8.4%; Veterans: 3.3%; Ancestry: 5.7% Haitian, 5.7% Jamaican, 4.5% Trinidadian and Tobagonian, 3.2% German, 2.1% West Indian

Employment: 8.4% management, business, and financial, 3.0% computer, engineering, and science, 11.3% education, legal, community service, arts, and media, 8.2% healthcare practitioners, 28.6% service, 24.6% sales and office, 10.2% natural resources, construction, and maintenance, 5.6% production, transportation, and material moving

Income: Per capita: $30,912; Median household: $115,750; Average household: $126,352; Households with income of $100,000 or more: 54.9%; Poverty rate: 4.5%

Educational Attainment: High school diploma or higher: 87.2%; Bachelor's degree or higher: 27.7%; Graduate/professional degree or higher: 14.0%

Housing: Homeownership rate: 93.1%; Median home value: $360,600; Median year structure built: 1959; Homeowner vacancy rate: 0.0%; Median selected monthly owner costs: $2,861 with a mortgage, $1,433 without a mortgage; Median gross rent: $2,621 per month; Rental vacancy rate: 17.2%

Health Insurance: 92.5% have insurance; 76.2% have private insurance; 26.2% have public insurance; 7.5% do not have insurance; 2.9% of children under 18 do not have insurance

Transportation: Commute: 72.8% car, 24.4% public transportation, 0.8% walk, 2.1% work from home; Mean travel time to work: 36.2 minutes

LATTINGTOWN (village).

Covers a land area of 3.755 square miles and a water area of 0.077 square miles. Located at 40.89° N. Lat; 73.60° W. Long. Elevation is 66 feet.

Population: 1,830; Growth (since 2000): -1.6%; Density: 487.3 persons per square mile; Race: 94.2% White, 1.1% Black/African American, 2.7% Asian, 0.0% American Indian/Alaska Native, 0.0% Native Hawaiian/Other Pacific Islander, 0.2% Two or more races, 5.6% Hispanic of any race; Average household size: 2.90; Median age: 50.2; Age under 18: 23.8%; Age 65 and over: 25.8%; Males per 100 females: 96.3; Marriage status: 22.0% never married, 63.4% now married, 1.0% separated, 5.9% widowed, 8.7% divorced; Foreign born: 13.3%; Speak English only: 82.2%; With disability: 7.3%; Veterans: 4.8%; Ancestry: 24.3% Italian, 13.8% German, 13.8% Irish, 9.3% Polish, 8.6% English

Employment: 29.4% management, business, and financial, 1.8% computer, engineering, and science, 16.3% education, legal, community service, arts, and media, 3.6% healthcare practitioners, 19.7% service, 22.2% sales and office, 3.5% natural resources, construction, and maintenance, 3.4% production, transportation, and material moving

Income: Per capita: $91,057; Median household: $123,393; Average household: $260,398; Households with income of $100,000 or more: 63.5%; Poverty rate: 4.2%

Educational Attainment: High school diploma or higher: 91.7%; Bachelor's degree or higher: 62.6%; Graduate/professional degree or higher: 29.9%

Housing: Homeownership rate: 83.6%; Median home value: $1,112,000; Median year structure built: 1955; Homeowner vacancy rate: 1.7%; Median selected monthly owner costs: $4,000+ with a mortgage, $1,501 without a mortgage; Median gross rent: $2,458 per month; Rental vacancy rate: 0.0%

Health Insurance: 97.3% have insurance; 86.5% have private insurance; 29.0% have public insurance; 2.7% do not have insurance; 1.8% of children under 18 do not have insurance

Transportation: Commute: 68.7% car, 11.4% public transportation, 6.1% walk, 11.9% work from home; Mean travel time to work: 34.5 minutes

LAUREL HOLLOW (village).

Covers a land area of 2.958 square miles and a water area of 0.204 square miles. Located at 40.86° N. Lat; 73.48° W. Long. Elevation is 108 feet.

History: Until 1935, called Laurelton.

Population: 1,982; Growth (since 2000): 2.7%; Density: 670.0 persons per square mile; Race: 89.6% White, 1.3% Black/African American, 6.6% Asian, 0.0% American Indian/Alaska Native, 0.0% Native Hawaiian/Other Pacific Islander, 1.6% Two or more races, 6.6% Hispanic of any race; Average household size: 3.28; Median age: 41.7; Age under 18: 32.6%; Age 65 and over: 15.2%; Males per 100 females: 93.8; Marriage status: 21.2% never married, 68.4% now married, 0.3% separated, 7.3% widowed, 3.1% divorced; Foreign born: 12.3%; Speak English only: 83.3%; With disability: 1.8%; Veterans: 4.0%; Ancestry: 19.9% Italian, 18.8% Irish, 15.1% German, 9.7% Polish, 8.0% English

Employment: 30.2% management, business, and financial, 5.6% computer, engineering, and science, 15.0% education, legal, community service, arts, and media, 11.8% healthcare practitioners, 7.9% service, 25.1% sales and office, 1.9% natural resources, construction, and maintenance, 2.5% production, transportation, and material moving

Income: Per capita: $99,272; Median household: $250,000+; Average household: $327,275; Households with income of $100,000 or more: 75.2%; Poverty rate: 6.3%

Educational Attainment: High school diploma or higher: 98.2%; Bachelor's degree or higher: 77.4%; Graduate/professional degree or higher: 45.8%

Housing: Homeownership rate: 95.7%; Median home value: $1,553,600; Median year structure built: 1968; Homeowner vacancy rate: 2.1%; Median selected monthly owner costs: $4,000+ with a mortgage, $1,501 without a mortgage; Median gross rent: $2,792 per month; Rental vacancy rate: 0.0%

Health Insurance: 98.6% have insurance; 92.7% have private insurance; 18.3% have public insurance; 1.4% do not have insurance; 2.0% of children under 18 do not have insurance

Transportation: Commute: 62.8% car, 21.2% public transportation, 4.9% walk, 9.8% work from home; Mean travel time to work: 44.1 minutes

LAWRENCE (village).

Covers a land area of 3.719 square miles and a water area of 0.912 square miles. Located at 40.60° N. Lat; 73.71° W. Long. Elevation is 23 feet.

History: Incorporated 1897.

Population: 6,553; Growth (since 2000): 0.5%; Density: 1,762.3 persons per square mile; Race: 96.9% White, 0.3% Black/African American, 1.8% Asian, 0.0% American Indian/Alaska Native, 0.0% Native Hawaiian/Other Pacific Islander, 0.0% Two or more races, 1.2% Hispanic of any race; Average household size: 3.07; Median age: 41.7; Age under 18: 30.7%; Age 65 and over: 22.0%; Males per 100 females: 92.2; Marriage status: 27.8% never married, 62.0% now married, 0.6% separated, 7.8% widowed, 2.3% divorced; Foreign born: 9.8%; Speak English only: 84.4%; With disability: 5.3%; Veterans: 2.2%; Ancestry: 25.6% Polish, 13.5% Russian, 11.4% American, 6.8% European, 6.6% Israeli

Employment: 18.2% management, business, and financial, 3.1% computer, engineering, and science, 27.2% education, legal, community service, arts, and media, 13.1% healthcare practitioners, 3.4% service, 32.4% sales and office, 0.5% natural resources, construction, and maintenance, 2.1% production, transportation, and material moving

Income: Per capita: $83,447; Median household: $129,609; Average household: $255,262; Households with income of $100,000 or more: 57.7%; Poverty rate: 4.8%

Educational Attainment: High school diploma or higher: 98.5%; Bachelor's degree or higher: 75.3%; Graduate/professional degree or higher: 44.8%

School District(s)
Lawrence Union Free SD (PK-12)
Enrollment: 2,683 . . . . (516) 295-7030

Four-year College(s)
Sh'or Yoshuv Rabbinical College (Private, Not-for-profit, Jewish)
Enrollment: 144 . . . . (516) 239-9002
Tuition: In-state $9,460; Out-of-state $9,460

Housing: Homeownership rate: 87.7%; Median home value: $889,100; Median year structure built: 1959; Homeowner vacancy rate: 3.7%; Median selected monthly owner costs: $4,000+ with a mortgage, $1,501 without a mortgage; Median gross rent: $1,668 per month; Rental vacancy rate: 0.0%

Health Insurance: 98.8% have insurance; 91.7% have private insurance; 25.8% have public insurance; 1.2% do not have insurance; 0.0% of children under 18 do not have insurance

Transportation: Commute: 68.1% car, 17.4% public transportation, 3.1% walk, 10.2% work from home; Mean travel time to work: 37.3 minutes

Additional Information Contacts
Village of Lawrence . . . . (516) 239-4600
http://www.villageoflawrence.org

LEVITTOWN (CDP).
Covers a land area of 6.811 square miles and a water area of 0.025 square miles. Located at 40.72° N. Lat; 73.51° W. Long. Elevation is 85 feet.

History: Named for William Levitt, developer of model suburban communities. It was originally developed by Levitt and Sons, Inc. a as mass-produced area of private, low-cost housing, and became the propotype for many postwar housing developments throughout the country. Founded 1947.

Population: 51,839; Growth (since 2000): -2.3%; Density: 7,611.0 persons per square mile; Race: 84.1% White, 1.4% Black/African American, 7.3% Asian, 0.0% American Indian/Alaska Native, 0.0% Native Hawaiian/Other Pacific Islander, 2.2% Two or more races, 14.6% Hispanic of any race; Average household size: 3.16; Median age: 42.0; Age under 18: 20.1%; Age 65 and over: 16.3%; Males per 100 females: 94.7; Marriage status: 30.5% never married, 56.0% now married, 1.7% separated, 6.8% widowed, 6.6% divorced; Foreign born: 14.1%; Speak English only: 82.0%; With disability: 10.1%; Veterans: 5.2%; Ancestry: 26.5% Italian, 21.2% Irish, 12.9% German, 4.3% Polish, 4.2% English

Employment: 15.0% management, business, and financial, 3.9% computer, engineering, and science, 13.5% education, legal, community service, arts, and media, 5.8% healthcare practitioners, 16.8% service, 28.5% sales and office, 7.0% natural resources, construction, and maintenance, 9.5% production, transportation, and material moving

Income: Per capita: $38,792; Median household: $108,179; Average household: $118,657; Households with income of $100,000 or more: 53.8%; Poverty rate: 4.6%

Educational Attainment: High school diploma or higher: 91.7%; Bachelor's degree or higher: 32.1%; Graduate/professional degree or higher: 12.7%

School District(s)
Island Trees Union Free SD (KG-12)
Enrollment: 2,279 . . . . (516) 520-2100
Levittown Union Free SD (KG-12)
Enrollment: 7,166 . . . . (516) 434-7020

Two-year College(s)
Hunter Business School (Private, For-profit)
Enrollment: 1,008 . . . . (516) 796-1000

Vocational/Technical School(s)
Brittany Beauty Academy (Private, For-profit)
Enrollment: 164 . . . . (516) 731-8300
Tuition: $14,000
Long Island Nail & Skin Care Institute (Private, For-profit)
Enrollment: 135 . . . . (516) 520-4800
Tuition: $9,395

Housing: Homeownership rate: 92.3%; Median home value: $367,700; Median year structure built: 1952; Homeowner vacancy rate: 0.6%; Median selected monthly owner costs: $2,829 with a mortgage, $1,153 without a mortgage; Median gross rent: $1,944 per month; Rental vacancy rate: 4.2%

Health Insurance: 96.3% have insurance; 84.7% have private insurance; 25.3% have public insurance; 3.7% do not have insurance; 2.4% of children under 18 do not have insurance

Transportation: Commute: 83.5% car, 11.4% public transportation, 1.6% walk, 1.9% work from home; Mean travel time to work: 32.8 minutes

LIDO BEACH (CDP).
Covers a land area of 1.739 square miles and a water area of 2.487 square miles. Located at 40.59° N. Lat; 73.60° W. Long. Elevation is 7 feet.

Population: 3,073; Growth (since 2000): 8.8%; Density: 1,767.2 persons per square mile; Race: 98.5% White, 0.2% Black/African American, 0.9% Asian, 0.0% American Indian/Alaska Native, 0.0% Native Hawaiian/Other Pacific Islander, 0.4% Two or more races, 5.8% Hispanic of any race; Average household size: 2.56; Median age: 52.7; Age under 18: 21.7%; Age 65 and over: 27.5%; Males per 100 females: 95.0; Marriage status: 19.8% never married, 69.4% now married, 0.7% separated, 5.8% widowed, 5.0% divorced; Foreign born: 10.0%; Speak English only: 89.3%; With disability: 15.2%; Veterans: 8.4%; Ancestry: 19.5% Irish, 19.1% Russian, 17.3% Italian, 9.5% Polish, 8.9% German

Employment: 21.3% management, business, and financial, 1.7% computer, engineering, and science, 18.6% education, legal, community service, arts, and media, 14.4% healthcare practitioners, 10.4% service, 30.6% sales and office, 0.6% natural resources, construction, and maintenance, 2.3% production, transportation, and material moving

Income: Per capita: $89,325; Median household: $161,111; Average household: $229,067; Households with income of $100,000 or more: 61.8%; Poverty rate: 2.1%

Educational Attainment: High school diploma or higher: 94.7%; Bachelor's degree or higher: 69.7%; Graduate/professional degree or higher: 40.4%

School District(s)
Long Beach City SD (PK-12)
Enrollment: 3,930 . . . . (516) 897-2104

Housing: Homeownership rate: 90.3%; Median home value: $666,900; Median year structure built: 1960; Homeowner vacancy rate: 5.5%; Median selected monthly owner costs: $3,882 with a mortgage, $1,501 without a mortgage; Median gross rent: $2,862 per month; Rental vacancy rate: 0.0%

Health Insurance: 99.4% have insurance; 89.2% have private insurance; 31.7% have public insurance; 0.6% do not have insurance; 0.0% of children under 18 do not have insurance

Transportation: Commute: 56.9% car, 21.4% public transportation, 1.8% walk, 19.9% work from home; Mean travel time to work: 41.4 minutes

LOCUST VALLEY (CDP).
Covers a land area of 0.914 square miles and a water area of 0.023 square miles. Located at 40.88° N. Lat; 73.59° W. Long. Elevation is 128 feet.

Population: 3,174; Growth (since 2000): -9.9%; Density: 3,474.1 persons per square mile; Race: 80.1% White, 3.0% Black/African American, 1.3% Asian, 0.3% American Indian/Alaska Native, 0.0% Native Hawaiian/Other Pacific Islander, 1.1% Two or more races, 11.7% Hispanic of any race; Average household size: 2.62; Median age: 40.0; Age under 18: 22.6%; Age 65 and over: 17.4%; Males per 100 females: 92.6; Marriage status: 33.2% never married, 52.9% now married, 2.7% separated, 5.5% widowed, 8.4% divorced; Foreign born: 18.3%; Speak English only: 77.5%; With disability: 8.9%; Veterans: 6.6%; Ancestry: 25.9% Irish, 23.2% Italian, 9.7% German, 6.1% Polish, 5.8% American

Employment: 25.1% management, business, and financial, 2.7% computer, engineering, and science, 14.7% education, legal, community service, arts, and media, 3.3% healthcare practitioners, 19.2% service, 17.7% sales and office, 6.7% natural resources, construction, and maintenance, 10.6% production, transportation, and material moving

Income: Per capita: $58,408; Median household: $98,125; Average household: $152,092; Households with income of $100,000 or more: 48.5%; Poverty rate: 7.5%

Educational Attainment: High school diploma or higher: 88.3%; Bachelor's degree or higher: 41.4%; Graduate/professional degree or higher: 14.5%

School District(s)
Locust Valley Central SD (KG-12)
Enrollment: 2,085 . . . . (516) 277-5001

Housing: Homeownership rate: 67.9%; Median home value: $574,200; Median year structure built: Before 1940; Homeowner vacancy rate: 2.3%; Median selected monthly owner costs: $3,095 with a mortgage, $1,050

without a mortgage; Median gross rent: $1,819 per month; Rental vacancy rate: 6.5%

Health Insurance: 87.9% have insurance; 77.0% have private insurance; 24.8% have public insurance; 12.1% do not have insurance; 8.1% of children under 18 do not have insurance

Newspapers: The Leader (weekly circulation 3,900)

Transportation: Commute: 78.6% car, 12.9% public transportation, 0.6% walk, 5.9% work from home; Mean travel time to work: 31.1 minutes

LONG BEACH (city). Covers a land area of 2.215 square miles and a water area of 1.680 square miles. Located at 40.59° N. Lat; 73.67° W. Long. Elevation is 7 feet.

History: Named for its beach on the Atlantic shore of Long Island. Incorporated 1922.

Population: 33,657; Growth (since 2000): -5.1%; Density: 15,197.3 persons per square mile; Race: 80.9% White, 6.3% Black/African American, 3.1% Asian, 0.1% American Indian/Alaska Native, 0.0% Native Hawaiian/Other Pacific Islander, 3.0% Two or more races, 14.5% Hispanic of any race; Average household size: 2.26; Median age: 44.3; Age under 18: 15.4%; Age 65 and over: 17.9%; Males per 100 females: 93.3; Marriage status: 37.7% never married, 43.5% now married, 2.4% separated, 6.5% widowed, 12.3% divorced; Foreign born: 14.6%; Speak English only: 82.0%; With disability: 10.9%; Veterans: 5.0%; Ancestry: 20.5% Irish, 17.5% Italian, 10.1% German, 7.3% American, 5.9% Russian

Employment: 20.3% management, business, and financial, 3.6% computer, engineering, and science, 17.3% education, legal, community service, arts, and media, 5.2% healthcare practitioners, 15.9% service, 26.7% sales and office, 6.2% natural resources, construction, and maintenance, 4.8% production, transportation, and material moving

Income: Per capita: $49,055; Median household: $85,619; Average household: $110,820; Households with income of $100,000 or more: 44.5%; Poverty rate: 7.7%

Educational Attainment: High school diploma or higher: 93.8%; Bachelor's degree or higher: 48.5%; Graduate/professional degree or higher: 23.2%

School District(s)
Long Beach City SD (PK-12)
    Enrollment: 3,930 . . . . (516) 897-2104

Four-year College(s)
Rabbinical College of Long Island (Private, Not-for-profit)
    Enrollment: 143 . . . . (516) 431-7414
    Tuition: In-state $8,800; Out-of-state $8,800

Housing: Homeownership rate: 57.7%; Median home value: $463,200; Median year structure built: 1957; Homeowner vacancy rate: 4.3%; Median selected monthly owner costs: $2,995 with a mortgage, $1,274 without a mortgage; Median gross rent: $1,806 per month; Rental vacancy rate: 3.5%

Health Insurance: 92.7% have insurance; 76.8% have private insurance; 29.4% have public insurance; 7.3% do not have insurance; 0.4% of children under 18 do not have insurance

Hospitals: Long Beach Medical Center (203 beds)

Safety: Violent crime rate: 6.2 per 10,000 population; Property crime rate: 58.9 per 10,000 population

Transportation: Commute: 71.3% car, 19.1% public transportation, 4.4% walk, 3.2% work from home; Mean travel time to work: 41.2 minutes

Additional Information Contacts
City of Long Beach . . . . (516) 431-1000
    http://www.longbeachny.org

LYNBROOK (village). Covers a land area of 2.014 square miles and a water area of 0 square miles. Located at 40.66° N. Lat; 73.67° W. Long. Elevation is 20 feet.

History: Old Church dates from 1800. The area was settled in 1785 and was called Bloomfield. The name Lynbrook(formed by reversing the syllables in Brooklyn) was adopted in 1895. Incorporated 1911.

Population: 19,706; Growth (since 2000): -1.0%; Density: 9,785.5 persons per square mile; Race: 82.9% White, 5.4% Black/African American, 3.3% Asian, 0.0% American Indian/Alaska Native, 0.0% Native Hawaiian/Other Pacific Islander, 3.6% Two or more races, 19.5% Hispanic of any race; Average household size: 2.77; Median age: 41.9; Age under 18: 21.5%; Age 65 and over: 16.3%; Males per 100 females: 90.2; Marriage status: 30.4% never married, 54.9% now married, 1.2% separated, 7.6% widowed, 7.1% divorced; Foreign born: 13.9%; Speak English only: 79.0%; With disability: 11.8%; Veterans: 5.8%; Ancestry: 30.7% Italian, 18.5% Irish, 11.2% German, 4.9% American, 3.5% Polish

Employment: 21.5% management, business, and financial, 3.4% computer, engineering, and science, 16.6% education, legal, community service, arts, and media, 6.7% healthcare practitioners, 13.0% service, 23.5% sales and office, 6.2% natural resources, construction, and maintenance, 9.1% production, transportation, and material moving

Income: Per capita: $43,445; Median household: $89,020; Average household: $117,359; Households with income of $100,000 or more: 46.6%; Poverty rate: 4.2%

Educational Attainment: High school diploma or higher: 94.2%; Bachelor's degree or higher: 41.3%; Graduate/professional degree or higher: 17.5%

School District(s)
Lynbrook Union Free SD (KG-12)
    Enrollment: 2,830 . . . . (516) 887-0253
Malverne Union Free SD (KG-12)
    Enrollment: 1,735 . . . . (516) 887-6405

Housing: Homeownership rate: 71.9%; Median home value: $426,800; Median year structure built: 1944; Homeowner vacancy rate: 1.6%; Median selected monthly owner costs: $3,173 with a mortgage, $1,295 without a mortgage; Median gross rent: $1,743 per month; Rental vacancy rate: 2.0%

Health Insurance: 96.3% have insurance; 85.7% have private insurance; 23.7% have public insurance; 3.7% do not have insurance; 2.3% of children under 18 do not have insurance

Safety: Violent crime rate: 9.2 per 10,000 population; Property crime rate: 52.1 per 10,000 population

Transportation: Commute: 73.4% car, 20.0% public transportation, 3.0% walk, 2.1% work from home; Mean travel time to work: 36.9 minutes

Additional Information Contacts
Village of Lynbrook . . . . (516) 599-8300
    http://www.lynbrookvillage.net

MALVERNE (village). Covers a land area of 1.058 square miles and a water area of 0 square miles. Located at 40.67° N. Lat; 73.67° W. Long. Elevation is 39 feet.

History: Settled in the early 1800s, incorporated 1921.

Population: 8,583; Growth (since 2000): -3.9%; Density: 8,114.0 persons per square mile; Race: 84.4% White, 6.3% Black/African American, 4.7% Asian, 0.3% American Indian/Alaska Native, 0.0% Native Hawaiian/Other Pacific Islander, 2.8% Two or more races, 6.6% Hispanic of any race; Average household size: 2.70; Median age: 48.4; Age under 18: 19.1%; Age 65 and over: 21.7%; Males per 100 females: 92.8; Marriage status: 26.2% never married, 59.5% now married, 0.7% separated, 7.3% widowed, 7.0% divorced; Foreign born: 10.8%; Speak English only: 89.3%; With disability: 10.1%; Veterans: 6.8%; Ancestry: 26.5% Italian, 23.5% Irish, 12.3% German, 7.6% American, 4.8% Polish

Employment: 22.9% management, business, and financial, 5.3% computer, engineering, and science, 15.1% education, legal, community service, arts, and media, 12.3% healthcare practitioners, 9.1% service, 25.4% sales and office, 7.2% natural resources, construction, and maintenance, 2.7% production, transportation, and material moving

Income: Per capita: $48,255; Median household: $106,250; Average household: $127,618; Households with income of $100,000 or more: 54.6%; Poverty rate: 2.8%

Educational Attainment: High school diploma or higher: 94.9%; Bachelor's degree or higher: 51.1%; Graduate/professional degree or higher: 24.1%

School District(s)
Malverne Union Free SD (KG-12)
    Enrollment: 1,735 . . . . (516) 887-6405

Housing: Homeownership rate: 95.8%; Median home value: $441,900; Median year structure built: 1944; Homeowner vacancy rate: 0.0%; Median selected monthly owner costs: $3,098 with a mortgage, $1,341 without a mortgage; Median gross rent: $1,328 per month; Rental vacancy rate: 0.0%

Health Insurance: 97.2% have insurance; 89.0% have private insurance; 27.2% have public insurance; 2.8% do not have insurance; 0.4% of children under 18 do not have insurance

Safety: Violent crime rate: 0.0 per 10,000 population; Property crime rate: 25.7 per 10,000 population

Transportation: Commute: 74.2% car, 18.3% public transportation, 1.9% walk, 4.6% work from home; Mean travel time to work: 37.5 minutes

Additional Information Contacts
Village of Malverne . . . . (516) 599-1200
    http://www.malvernevillage.org/index.html

MALVERNE PARK OAKS (CDP). Covers a land area of 0.130 square miles and a water area of 0 square miles. Located at 40.68° N. Lat; 73.66° W. Long. Elevation is 10 feet.
Population: 477; Growth (since 2000): 1.5%; Density: 3,663.1 persons per square mile; Race: 62.1% White, 8.8% Black/African American, 13.4% Asian, 0.0% American Indian/Alaska Native, 0.0% Native Hawaiian/Other Pacific Islander, 0.0% Two or more races, 15.7% Hispanic of any race; Average household size: 2.94; Median age: 50.1; Age under 18: 25.4%; Age 65 and over: 17.0%; Males per 100 females: 89.1; Marriage status: 22.3% never married, 73.9% now married, 0.0% separated, 3.8% widowed, 0.0% divorced; Foreign born: 28.1%; Speak English only: 74.0%; With disability: 2.7%; Veterans: 2.5%; Ancestry: 26.6% Italian, 19.5% Irish, 10.3% German, 8.8% French, 7.8% European
Employment: 35.8% management, business, and financial, 0.0% computer, engineering, and science, 19.0% education, legal, community service, arts, and media, 3.9% healthcare practitioners, 10.8% service, 30.6% sales and office, 0.0% natural resources, construction, and maintenance, 0.0% production, transportation, and material moving
Income: Per capita: $48,715; Median household: $110,278; Average household: $143,589; Households with income of $100,000 or more: 61.0%; Poverty rate: n/a
Educational Attainment: High school diploma or higher: 100.0%; Bachelor's degree or higher: 54.0%; Graduate/professional degree or higher: 34.5%
Housing: Homeownership rate: 100.0%; Median home value: $484,400; Median year structure built: 1951; Homeowner vacancy rate: 0.0%; Median selected monthly owner costs: $2,809 with a mortgage, n/a without a mortgage; Median gross rent: n/a per month; Rental vacancy rate: 0.0%
Health Insurance: 100.0% have insurance; 93.3% have private insurance; 21.0% have public insurance; 0.0% do not have insurance; 0.0% of children under 18 do not have insurance
Transportation: Commute: 64.7% car, 16.4% public transportation, 0.0% walk, 19.0% work from home; Mean travel time to work: 41.8 minutes

MANHASSET (CDP). Covers a land area of 2.382 square miles and a water area of 0.034 square miles. Located at 40.78° N. Lat; 73.69° W. Long. Elevation is 98 feet.
History: Manhasset is a Native American term that translates to "the island neighborhood." In 2005, a Wall Street Journal article ranked Manhasset as the best town for raising a family in the New York metropolitan area.
Population: 7,922; Growth (since 2000): -5.3%; Density: 3,326.1 persons per square mile; Race: 73.1% White, 8.5% Black/African American, 12.4% Asian, 0.4% American Indian/Alaska Native, 0.0% Native Hawaiian/Other Pacific Islander, 1.5% Two or more races, 10.9% Hispanic of any race; Average household size: 2.87; Median age: 45.0; Age under 18: 25.0%; Age 65 and over: 18.4%; Males per 100 females: 89.0; Marriage status: 30.4% never married, 56.9% now married, 0.7% separated, 5.9% widowed, 6.8% divorced; Foreign born: 20.4%; Speak English only: 71.3%; With disability: 4.9%; Veterans: 4.9%; Ancestry: 20.2% Italian, 15.7% Irish, 7.5% German, 6.6% American, 5.1% Greek
Employment: 26.3% management, business, and financial, 3.1% computer, engineering, and science, 13.1% education, legal, community service, arts, and media, 9.2% healthcare practitioners, 10.3% service, 26.9% sales and office, 4.1% natural resources, construction, and maintenance, 6.9% production, transportation, and material moving
Income: Per capita: $68,125; Median household: $130,433; Average household: $201,530; Households with income of $100,000 or more: 58.0%; Poverty rate: 4.2%
Educational Attainment: High school diploma or higher: 93.5%; Bachelor's degree or higher: 60.0%; Graduate/professional degree or higher: 28.7%

School District(s)
Manhasset Union Free SD (KG-12)
    Enrollment: 3,329 . . . . (516) 267-7700
Four-year College(s)
Elmezzi Graduate School of Molecular Medicine (Private, Not-for-profit)
    Enrollment: 11 . . . . (516) 562-3405
Housing: Homeownership rate: 78.9%; Median home value: $1,019,300; Median year structure built: Before 1940; Homeowner vacancy rate: 1.9%; Median selected monthly owner costs: $3,987 with a mortgage, $1,501 without a mortgage; Median gross rent: $1,402 per month; Rental vacancy rate: 7.2%

Health Insurance: 96.6% have insurance; 89.2% have private insurance; 20.9% have public insurance; 3.4% do not have insurance; 2.2% of children under 18 do not have insurance
Hospitals: North Shore University Hospital (900 beds)
Transportation: Commute: 57.4% car, 25.9% public transportation, 5.4% walk, 7.9% work from home; Mean travel time to work: 35.2 minutes

MANHASSET HILLS (CDP). Covers a land area of 0.591 square miles and a water area of 0 square miles. Located at 40.76° N. Lat; 73.68° W. Long. Elevation is 125 feet.
History: Manhasset is a Native American term that translates to "the island neighborhood. The Valley School, serving Manhasset's African American community, was closed in the 1960s by a desegregation lawsuit.
Population: 3,579; Growth (since 2000): -2.2%; Density: 6,053.6 persons per square mile; Race: 49.1% White, 0.0% Black/African American, 42.9% Asian, 0.0% American Indian/Alaska Native, 0.0% Native Hawaiian/Other Pacific Islander, 1.5% Two or more races, 11.0% Hispanic of any race; Average household size: 3.14; Median age: 47.1; Age under 18: 21.4%; Age 65 and over: 21.7%; Males per 100 females: 91.4; Marriage status: 22.6% never married, 67.5% now married, 0.1% separated, 7.1% widowed, 2.9% divorced; Foreign born: 37.0%; Speak English only: 47.2%; With disability: 7.2%; Veterans: 2.9%; Ancestry: 17.5% Italian, 5.1% Greek, 4.7% German, 2.9% Polish, 2.2% American
Employment: 24.2% management, business, and financial, 5.1% computer, engineering, and science, 13.4% education, legal, community service, arts, and media, 24.3% healthcare practitioners, 6.1% service, 19.8% sales and office, 6.1% natural resources, construction, and maintenance, 1.0% production, transportation, and material moving
Income: Per capita: $63,154; Median household: $155,234; Average household: $194,622; Households with income of $100,000 or more: 70.2%; Poverty rate: 0.5%
Educational Attainment: High school diploma or higher: 91.7%; Bachelor's degree or higher: 64.5%; Graduate/professional degree or higher: 38.2%
Housing: Homeownership rate: 98.2%; Median home value: $835,000; Median year structure built: 1962; Homeowner vacancy rate: 0.0%; Median selected monthly owner costs: $4,000+ with a mortgage, $1,501 without a mortgage; Median gross rent: n/a per month; Rental vacancy rate: 0.0%
Health Insurance: 96.5% have insurance; 90.5% have private insurance; 21.7% have public insurance; 3.5% do not have insurance; 4.6% of children under 18 do not have insurance
Transportation: Commute: 81.0% car, 13.6% public transportation, 0.4% walk, 5.0% work from home; Mean travel time to work: 38.6 minutes

MANORHAVEN (village). Covers a land area of 0.465 square miles and a water area of 0.166 square miles. Located at 40.84° N. Lat; 73.71° W. Long. Elevation is 13 feet.
History: Incorporated 1930.
Population: 6,627; Growth (since 2000): 8.0%; Density: 14,256.5 persons per square mile; Race: 72.2% White, 0.1% Black/African American, 20.1% Asian, 0.6% American Indian/Alaska Native, 0.1% Native Hawaiian/Other Pacific Islander, 2.5% Two or more races, 22.4% Hispanic of any race; Average household size: 2.76; Median age: 37.0; Age under 18: 28.5%; Age 65 and over: 10.9%; Males per 100 females: 96.9; Marriage status: 32.3% never married, 51.6% now married, 1.0% separated, 4.6% widowed, 11.5% divorced; Foreign born: 33.2%; Speak English only: 55.4%; With disability: 5.4%; Veterans: 3.5%; Ancestry: 16.0% Italian, 9.2% Irish, 8.4% American, 5.5% German, 4.3% Russian
Employment: 24.6% management, business, and financial, 6.8% computer, engineering, and science, 15.5% education, legal, community service, arts, and media, 4.9% healthcare practitioners, 10.5% service, 19.1% sales and office, 9.4% natural resources, construction, and maintenance, 9.2% production, transportation, and material moving
Income: Per capita: $46,468; Median household: $86,237; Average household: $127,164; Households with income of $100,000 or more: 42.7%; Poverty rate: 14.8%
Educational Attainment: High school diploma or higher: 92.9%; Bachelor's degree or higher: 51.4%; Graduate/professional degree or higher: 23.9%
Housing: Homeownership rate: 34.3%; Median home value: $557,000; Median year structure built: 1966; Homeowner vacancy rate: 7.8%; Median selected monthly owner costs: $2,741 with a mortgage, $1,226 without a mortgage; Median gross rent: $2,265 per month; Rental vacancy rate: 5.4%

Health Insurance: 86.6% have insurance; 73.1% have private insurance; 23.7% have public insurance; 13.4% do not have insurance; 13.7% of children under 18 do not have insurance

Transportation: Commute: 71.2% car, 20.5% public transportation, 3.4% walk, 2.7% work from home; Mean travel time to work: 45.4 minutes

Additional Information Contacts

Village of Manorhaven. . . . . (516) 883-7000
    http://www.manorhaven.org

MASSAPEQUA (CDP).

MASSAPEQUA (CDP). Covers a land area of 3.558 square miles and a water area of 0.436 square miles. Located at 40.67° N. Lat; 73.47° W. Long. Elevation is 23 feet.

History: Named for the Masapequa Indians. It is chiefly residential. Pop. figure also includes Arlyn Oaks, Crown Village, and Nassau Shores.

Population: 22,102; Growth (since 2000): -2.4%; Density: 6,212.4 persons per square mile; Race: 95.2% White, 0.4% Black/African American, 2.4% Asian, 0.3% American Indian/Alaska Native, 0.0% Native Hawaiian/Other Pacific Islander, 0.5% Two or more races, 5.4% Hispanic of any race; Average household size: 3.11; Median age: 43.8; Age under 18: 21.1%; Age 65 and over: 16.7%; Males per 100 females: 95.3; Marriage status: 30.6% never married, 58.2% now married, 1.9% separated, 5.7% widowed, 5.5% divorced; Foreign born: 5.5%; Speak English only: 93.0%; With disability: 8.2%; Veterans: 5.7%; Ancestry: 40.6% Italian, 27.8% Irish, 17.3% German, 5.1% Polish, 4.5% English

Employment: 19.0% management, business, and financial, 4.2% computer, engineering, and science, 14.4% education, legal, community service, arts, and media, 6.1% healthcare practitioners, 14.7% service, 27.7% sales and office, 8.9% natural resources, construction, and maintenance, 4.9% production, transportation, and material moving

Income: Per capita: $49,281; Median household: $123,384; Average household: $149,323; Households with income of $100,000 or more: 59.3%; Poverty rate: 2.4%

Educational Attainment: High school diploma or higher: 96.6%; Bachelor's degree or higher: 45.7%; Graduate/professional degree or higher: 16.8%

School District(s)

Massapequa Union Free SD (KG-12)
    Enrollment: 7,083 . . . . (516) 308-5000
Plainedge Union Free SD (KG-12)
    Enrollment: 2,992 . . . . (516) 992-7455

Housing: Homeownership rate: 94.1%; Median home value: $497,300; Median year structure built: 1955; Homeowner vacancy rate: 1.6%; Median selected monthly owner costs: $3,253 with a mortgage, $1,377 without a mortgage; Median gross rent: $2,065 per month; Rental vacancy rate: 11.0%

Health Insurance: 98.0% have insurance; 87.1% have private insurance; 24.9% have public insurance; 2.0% do not have insurance; 0.9% of children under 18 do not have insurance

Transportation: Commute: 80.5% car, 15.2% public transportation, 0.6% walk, 3.2% work from home; Mean travel time to work: 36.3 minutes

MASSAPEQUA PARK (village).

MASSAPEQUA PARK (village). Covers a land area of 2.210 square miles and a water area of 0.043 square miles. Located at 40.68° N. Lat; 73.45° W. Long. Elevation is 23 feet.

History: Named for the Masapequa Indians. Incorporated 1931.

Population: 17,223; Growth (since 2000): -1.6%; Density: 7,793.8 persons per square mile; Race: 96.6% White, 0.4% Black/African American, 1.7% Asian, 0.0% American Indian/Alaska Native, 0.0% Native Hawaiian/Other Pacific Islander, 0.4% Two or more races, 7.1% Hispanic of any race; Average household size: 3.07; Median age: 43.3; Age under 18: 23.5%; Age 65 and over: 17.1%; Males per 100 females: 94.1; Marriage status: 25.9% never married, 60.5% now married, 0.8% separated, 8.0% widowed, 5.6% divorced; Foreign born: 5.4%; Speak English only: 92.8%; With disability: 10.2%; Veterans: 6.3%; Ancestry: 44.2% Italian, 31.0% Irish, 17.8% German, 5.9% Polish, 4.5% English

Employment: 19.3% management, business, and financial, 4.4% computer, engineering, and science, 16.3% education, legal, community service, arts, and media, 7.8% healthcare practitioners, 14.2% service, 27.4% sales and office, 6.7% natural resources, construction, and maintenance, 3.9% production, transportation, and material moving

Income: Per capita: $45,418; Median household: $123,102; Average household: $136,173; Households with income of $100,000 or more: 61.2%; Poverty rate: 1.5%

Educational Attainment: High school diploma or higher: 96.2%; Bachelor's degree or higher: 42.9%; Graduate/professional degree or higher: 18.1%

School District(s)

Massapequa Union Free SD (KG-12)
    Enrollment: 7,083 . . . . (516) 308-5000

Housing: Homeownership rate: 97.4%; Median home value: $448,500; Median year structure built: 1956; Homeowner vacancy rate: 0.0%; Median selected monthly owner costs: $2,948 with a mortgage, $1,153 without a mortgage; Median gross rent: $2,245 per month; Rental vacancy rate: 0.0%

Health Insurance: 97.4% have insurance; 89.8% have private insurance; 23.5% have public insurance; 2.6% do not have insurance; 0.5% of children under 18 do not have insurance

Newspapers: Massapequa Post (weekly circulation 4,500)

Transportation: Commute: 80.1% car, 14.3% public transportation, 1.2% walk, 3.5% work from home; Mean travel time to work: 37.2 minutes

Additional Information Contacts

Village of Massapequa Park . . . . (516) 798-0244
    http://www.masspk.com

MATINECOCK (village).

MATINECOCK (village). Covers a land area of 2.658 square miles and a water area of 0.005 square miles. Located at 40.86° N. Lat; 73.58° W. Long. Elevation is 95 feet.

Population: 855; Growth (since 2000): 2.3%; Density: 321.7 persons per square mile; Race: 97.7% White, 0.0% Black/African American, 1.2% Asian, 0.0% American Indian/Alaska Native, 0.0% Native Hawaiian/Other Pacific Islander, 0.8% Two or more races, 4.6% Hispanic of any race; Average household size: 3.09; Median age: 45.0; Age under 18: 27.8%; Age 65 and over: 19.8%; Males per 100 females: 101.0; Marriage status: 26.5% never married, 61.9% now married, 0.0% separated, 5.5% widowed, 6.1% divorced; Foreign born: 4.1%; Speak English only: 87.1%; With disability: 4.9%; Veterans: 5.8%; Ancestry: 19.4% Irish, 13.0% Italian, 12.6% English, 11.0% German, 6.9% Scottish

Employment: 37.2% management, business, and financial, 3.5% computer, engineering, and science, 13.5% education, legal, community service, arts, and media, 9.9% healthcare practitioners, 5.4% service, 25.3% sales and office, 4.5% natural resources, construction, and maintenance, 0.6% production, transportation, and material moving

Income: Per capita: $114,487; Median household: $174,107; Average household: $355,522; Households with income of $100,000 or more: 70.3%; Poverty rate: 4.1%

Educational Attainment: High school diploma or higher: 97.8%; Bachelor's degree or higher: 80.3%; Graduate/professional degree or higher: 32.4%

Housing: Homeownership rate: 81.9%; Median home value: 2 million+; Median year structure built: 1952; Homeowner vacancy rate: 0.0%; Median selected monthly owner costs: $4,000+ with a mortgage, $1,501 without a mortgage; Median gross rent: $1,875 per month; Rental vacancy rate: 0.0%

Health Insurance: 99.3% have insurance; 92.4% have private insurance; 20.2% have public insurance; 0.7% do not have insurance; 0.0% of children under 18 do not have insurance

Transportation: Commute: 52.3% car, 21.2% public transportation, 6.2% walk, 19.6% work from home; Mean travel time to work: 41.8 minutes

Additional Information Contacts

Village of Matinecock . . . . (516) 671-7790
    http://www.matinecockvillage.org

MERRICK (CDP).

MERRICK (CDP). Covers a land area of 4.019 square miles and a water area of 1.133 square miles. Located at 40.65° N. Lat; 73.55° W. Long. Elevation is 16 feet.

History: The name Merrick is taken from "Meroke", the name (meaning peaceful) of the Algonquin tribe formerly indigenous to the area. It is served by the Merrick station on the Long Island Rail Road.

Population: 20,679; Growth (since 2000): -9.2%; Density: 5,144.8 persons per square mile; Race: 92.3% White, 2.7% Black/African American, 2.6% Asian, 0.0% American Indian/Alaska Native, 0.0% Native Hawaiian/Other Pacific Islander, 0.7% Two or more races, 6.4% Hispanic of any race; Average household size: 2.93; Median age: 44.3; Age under 18: 22.7%; Age 65 and over: 16.2%; Males per 100 females: 93.3; Marriage status: 26.5% never married, 62.9% now married, 1.1% separated, 5.7% widowed, 4.9% divorced; Foreign born: 12.3%; Speak English only: 85.6%; With disability: 7.6%; Veterans: 3.7%; Ancestry: 22.5% Italian, 14.4% Irish, 10.5% German, 9.7% Russian, 6.9% American

Employment: 23.7% management, business, and financial, 3.5% computer, engineering, and science, 21.9% education, legal, community service, arts, and media, 7.4% healthcare practitioners, 10.6% service, 23.9% sales and office, 5.3% natural resources, construction, and maintenance, 3.6% production, transportation, and material moving
Income: Per capita: $59,965; Median household: $147,572; Average household: $173,814; Households with income of $100,000 or more: 69.9%; Poverty rate: 3.2%
Educational Attainment: High school diploma or higher: 96.2%; Bachelor's degree or higher: 60.7%; Graduate/professional degree or higher: 31.1%

School District(s)
Bellmore-Merrick Central High SD (07-12)
    Enrollment: 5,422 . . . . (516) 992-1001
Merrick Union Free SD (KG-06)
    Enrollment: 1,473 . . . . (516) 992-7240
North Merrick Union Free SD (KG-06)
    Enrollment: 1,218 . . . . (516) 292-3694
Housing: Homeownership rate: 94.1%; Median home value: $543,400; Median year structure built: 1955; Homeowner vacancy rate: 0.3%; Median selected monthly owner costs: $3,381 with a mortgage, $1,501 without a mortgage; Median gross rent: $2,087 per month; Rental vacancy rate: 7.5%
Health Insurance: 97.5% have insurance; 89.1% have private insurance; 21.5% have public insurance; 2.5% do not have insurance; 0.7% of children under 18 do not have insurance
Newspapers: L & M Publications (weekly circulation 14,000)
Transportation: Commute: 69.7% car, 23.0% public transportation, 1.1% walk, 4.4% work from home; Mean travel time to work: 39.4 minutes

MILL NECK (village). Covers a land area of 2.609 square miles and a water area of 0.320 square miles. Located at 40.88° N. Lat; 73.56° W. Long. Elevation is 135 feet.
Population: 1,011; Growth (since 2000): 22.5%; Density: 387.5 persons per square mile; Race: 89.2% White, 0.0% Black/African American, 8.2% Asian, 0.0% American Indian/Alaska Native, 0.0% Native Hawaiian/Other Pacific Islander, 1.3% Two or more races, 4.2% Hispanic of any race; Average household size: 2.89; Median age: 50.0; Age under 18: 18.7%; Age 65 and over: 20.5%; Males per 100 females: 89.9; Marriage status: 24.1% never married, 66.4% now married, 0.8% separated, 5.0% widowed, 4.5% divorced; Foreign born: 13.1%; Speak English only: 82.5%; With disability: 4.8%; Veterans: 3.5%; Ancestry: 21.8% Italian, 17.9% Irish, 11.3% German, 11.0% English, 6.7% Polish
Employment: 30.4% management, business, and financial, 4.9% computer, engineering, and science, 12.5% education, legal, community service, arts, and media, 6.6% healthcare practitioners, 13.1% service, 26.9% sales and office, 2.1% natural resources, construction, and maintenance, 3.5% production, transportation, and material moving
Income: Per capita: $109,295; Median household: $190,938; Average household: $323,828; Households with income of $100,000 or more: 68.5%; Poverty rate: 5.8%
Educational Attainment: High school diploma or higher: 98.2%; Bachelor's degree or higher: 73.3%; Graduate/professional degree or higher: 32.0%
Housing: Homeownership rate: 89.7%; Median home value: $1,195,700; Median year structure built: 1957; Homeowner vacancy rate: 2.2%; Median selected monthly owner costs: $4,000+ with a mortgage, $1,501 without a mortgage; Median gross rent: $2,583 per month; Rental vacancy rate: 12.2%
Health Insurance: 97.3% have insurance; 88.0% have private insurance; 23.3% have public insurance; 2.7% do not have insurance; 0.0% of children under 18 do not have insurance
Transportation: Commute: 74.9% car, 10.5% public transportation, 2.9% walk, 10.3% work from home; Mean travel time to work: 38.0 minutes

MINEOLA (village). County seat. Covers a land area of 1.880 square miles and a water area of 0 square miles. Located at 40.75° N. Lat; 73.64° W. Long. Elevation is 108 feet.
History: Named for the Algonquian translation of "pleasant village". Incorporated 1906.
Population: 19,223; Growth (since 2000): -0.1%; Density: 10,227.6 persons per square mile; Race: 73.7% White, 2.5% Black/African American, 11.2% Asian, 0.0% American Indian/Alaska Native, 0.0% Native Hawaiian/Other Pacific Islander, 2.0% Two or more races, 19.4% Hispanic of any race; Average household size: 2.59; Median age: 41.9; Age under 18: 18.8%; Age 65 and over: 17.7%; Males per 100 females: 96.2; Marriage status: 30.6% never married, 55.0% now married, 1.8% separated, 5.7% widowed, 8.6% divorced; Foreign born: 29.3%; Speak English only: 61.3%; With disability: 6.4%; Veterans: 3.2%; Ancestry: 21.4% Italian, 19.2% Irish, 12.5% German, 8.5% Portuguese, 4.1% American
Employment: 17.2% management, business, and financial, 4.5% computer, engineering, and science, 12.6% education, legal, community service, arts, and media, 10.7% healthcare practitioners, 16.6% service, 21.8% sales and office, 8.1% natural resources, construction, and maintenance, 8.5% production, transportation, and material moving
Income: Per capita: $43,715; Median household: $90,027; Average household: $110,926; Households with income of $100,000 or more: 42.4%; Poverty rate: 5.3%
Educational Attainment: High school diploma or higher: 90.6%; Bachelor's degree or higher: 41.6%; Graduate/professional degree or higher: 18.4%

School District(s)
Mineola Union Free SD (PK-12)
    Enrollment: 2,872 . . . . (516) 237-2001
Four-year College(s)
New York College of Traditional Chinese Medicine (Private, Not-for-profit)
    Enrollment: 196 . . . . (516) 739-1545
Housing: Homeownership rate: 66.1%; Median home value: $456,200; Median year structure built: 1953; Homeowner vacancy rate: 0.5%; Median selected monthly owner costs: $2,737 with a mortgage, $1,141 without a mortgage; Median gross rent: $1,500 per month; Rental vacancy rate: 1.4%
Health Insurance: 95.2% have insurance; 81.7% have private insurance; 23.5% have public insurance; 4.8% do not have insurance; 2.3% of children under 18 do not have insurance
Hospitals: Winthrop - University Hospital (591 beds)
Newspapers: Anton Newspapers (weekly circulation 52,000)
Transportation: Commute: 77.2% car, 13.8% public transportation, 6.2% walk, 1.4% work from home; Mean travel time to work: 31.4 minutes
Additional Information Contacts
Village of Mineola . . . . (516) 746-0750
    http://www.mineola-ny.gov

MUNSEY PARK (village). Covers a land area of 0.518 square miles and a water area of 0 square miles. Located at 40.80° N. Lat; 73.68° W. Long. Elevation is 161 feet.
Population: 2,739; Growth (since 2000): 4.1%; Density: 5,284.6 persons per square mile; Race: 88.3% White, 0.0% Black/African American, 9.5% Asian, 0.0% American Indian/Alaska Native, 0.0% Native Hawaiian/Other Pacific Islander, 2.2% Two or more races, 2.5% Hispanic of any race; Average household size: 3.49; Median age: 41.8; Age under 18: 31.4%; Age 65 and over: 15.4%; Males per 100 females: 102.0; Marriage status: 22.5% never married, 71.4% now married, 0.0% separated, 3.3% widowed, 2.8% divorced; Foreign born: 14.8%; Speak English only: 86.0%; With disability: 4.3%; Veterans: 2.7%; Ancestry: 23.5% Irish, 21.0% Italian, 15.2% German, 8.2% Greek, 4.9% English
Employment: 36.3% management, business, and financial, 6.6% computer, engineering, and science, 17.6% education, legal, community service, arts, and media, 10.4% healthcare practitioners, 3.8% service, 20.2% sales and office, 2.4% natural resources, construction, and maintenance, 2.7% production, transportation, and material moving
Income: Per capita: $100,537; Median household: $250,000+; Average household: $350,541; Households with income of $100,000 or more: 86.4%; Poverty rate: 2.1%
Educational Attainment: High school diploma or higher: 98.7%; Bachelor's degree or higher: 84.2%; Graduate/professional degree or higher: 43.0%
Housing: Homeownership rate: 94.5%; Median home value: $1,505,700; Median year structure built: 1943; Homeowner vacancy rate: 1.3%; Median selected monthly owner costs: $4,000+ with a mortgage, $1,501 without a mortgage; Median gross rent: $1,717 per month; Rental vacancy rate: 0.0%
Health Insurance: 98.5% have insurance; 90.0% have private insurance; 15.8% have public insurance; 1.5% do not have insurance; 3.3% of children under 18 do not have insurance
Transportation: Commute: 40.5% car, 51.2% public transportation, 0.8% walk, 7.6% work from home; Mean travel time to work: 46.5 minutes

MUTTONTOWN (village). Covers a land area of 6.063 square miles and a water area of 0 square miles. Located at 40.83° N. Lat; 73.54° W. Long. Elevation is 292 feet.

History: During colonial times the area was used to raise sheep for wool and meat, thus giving the town its name "mutton". The village was incorporated in 1931.

Population: 3,661; Growth (since 2000): 7.3%; Density: 603.9 persons per square mile; Race: 71.9% White, 3.7% Black/African American, 23.0% Asian, 0.0% American Indian/Alaska Native, 0.0% Native Hawaiian/Other Pacific Islander, 0.9% Two or more races, 2.9% Hispanic of any race; Average household size: 3.08; Median age: 49.0; Age under 18: 23.3%; Age 65 and over: 18.3%; Males per 100 females: 99.8; Marriage status: 24.5% never married, 67.0% now married, 0.5% separated, 5.5% widowed, 3.0% divorced; Foreign born: 21.2%; Speak English only: 71.3%; With disability: 5.3%; Veterans: 2.1%; Ancestry: 11.2% Italian, 11.0% American, 8.7% Russian, 6.7% Irish, 6.3% Eastern European

Employment: 27.7% management, business, and financial, 4.1% computer, engineering, and science, 17.6% education, legal, community service, arts, and media, 14.9% healthcare practitioners, 4.9% service, 26.9% sales and office, 3.3% natural resources, construction, and maintenance, 0.5% production, transportation, and material moving

Income: Per capita: $125,610; Median household: $221,250; Average household: $387,953; Households with income of $100,000 or more: 81.8%; Poverty rate: 4.7%

Educational Attainment: High school diploma or higher: 98.2%; Bachelor's degree or higher: 73.4%; Graduate/professional degree or higher: 40.5%

Housing: Homeownership rate: 97.4%; Median home value: $1,632,500; Median year structure built: 1974; Homeowner vacancy rate: 2.7%; Median selected monthly owner costs: $4,000+ with a mortgage, $1,501 without a mortgage; Median gross rent: n/a per month; Rental vacancy rate: 35.4%

Health Insurance: 96.5% have insurance; 87.8% have private insurance; 18.4% have public insurance; 3.5% do not have insurance; 1.7% of children under 18 do not have insurance

Transportation: Commute: 70.2% car, 21.5% public transportation, 1.7% walk, 6.0% work from home; Mean travel time to work: 43.3 minutes

NEW CASSEL (CDP). Covers a land area of 1.479 square miles and a water area of 0 square miles. Located at 40.76° N. Lat; 73.56° W. Long. Elevation is 121 feet.

Population: 14,321; Growth (since 2000): 7.7%; Density: 9,682.0 persons per square mile; Race: 19.9% White, 39.7% Black/African American, 1.4% Asian, 0.1% American Indian/Alaska Native, 0.1% Native Hawaiian/Other Pacific Islander, 4.1% Two or more races, 51.9% Hispanic of any race; Average household size: 4.47; Median age: 32.1; Age under 18: 27.1%; Age 65 and over: 10.1%; Males per 100 females: 103.5; Marriage status: 45.3% never married, 46.1% now married, 3.0% separated, 5.2% widowed, 3.4% divorced; Foreign born: 45.6%; Speak English only: 36.5%; With disability: 6.9%; Veterans: 1.7%; Ancestry: 11.0% Haitian, 3.2% Italian, 2.9% Jamaican, 2.9% American, 1.1% Russian

Employment: 8.6% management, business, and financial, 3.4% computer, engineering, and science, 5.6% education, legal, community service, arts, and media, 4.0% healthcare practitioners, 25.3% service, 25.6% sales and office, 10.0% natural resources, construction, and maintenance, 17.5% production, transportation, and material moving

Income: Per capita: $24,387; Median household: $88,289; Average household: $100,488; Households with income of $100,000 or more: 39.6%; Poverty rate: 11.8%

Educational Attainment: High school diploma or higher: 74.7%; Bachelor's degree or higher: 22.3%; Graduate/professional degree or higher: 8.0%

Housing: Homeownership rate: 65.3%; Median home value: $334,300; Median year structure built: 1959; Homeowner vacancy rate: 0.0%; Median selected monthly owner costs: $2,832 with a mortgage, $1,121 without a mortgage; Median gross rent: $1,362 per month; Rental vacancy rate: 2.8%

Health Insurance: 81.5% have insurance; 63.1% have private insurance; 28.1% have public insurance; 18.5% do not have insurance; 14.6% of children under 18 do not have insurance

Transportation: Commute: 85.7% car, 8.2% public transportation, 2.7% walk, 1.7% work from home; Mean travel time to work: 27.8 minutes

NEW HYDE PARK (village). Covers a land area of 0.860 square miles and a water area of 0 square miles. Located at 40.73° N. Lat; 73.69° W. Long. Elevation is 105 feet.

History: Incorporated 1927.

Population: 9,906; Growth (since 2000): 4.0%; Density: 11,523.8 persons per square mile; Race: 53.5% White, 0.8% Black/African American, 32.5% Asian, 0.3% American Indian/Alaska Native, 0.5% Native Hawaiian/Other Pacific Islander, 2.9% Two or more races, 20.1% Hispanic of any race; Average household size: 3.43; Median age: 40.4; Age under 18: 21.8%; Age 65 and over: 13.8%; Males per 100 females: 94.0; Marriage status: 29.5% never married, 59.6% now married, 1.9% separated, 6.8% widowed, 4.0% divorced; Foreign born: 36.7%; Speak English only: 53.7%; With disability: 7.8%; Veterans: 1.9%; Ancestry: 16.7% Italian, 11.2% Irish, 9.9% German, 5.5% Polish, 3.2% American

Employment: 14.3% management, business, and financial, 6.1% computer, engineering, and science, 11.1% education, legal, community service, arts, and media, 13.0% healthcare practitioners, 16.6% service, 23.2% sales and office, 7.5% natural resources, construction, and maintenance, 8.3% production, transportation, and material moving

Income: Per capita: $38,907; Median household: $117,015; Average household: $130,282; Households with income of $100,000 or more: 58.3%; Poverty rate: 4.8%

Educational Attainment: High school diploma or higher: 90.7%; Bachelor's degree or higher: 44.7%; Graduate/professional degree or higher: 17.6%

School District(s)
Great Neck Union Free SD (PK-12)
  Enrollment: 6,664 . . . . (516) 441-4001
Herricks Union Free SD (KG-12)
  Enrollment: 3,926 . . . . (516) 305-8901
New Hyde Park-Garden City Park Union Free SD (KG-06)
  Enrollment: 1,716 . . . . (516) 434-2305
Sewanhaka Central High SD (07-12)
  Enrollment: 8,280 . . . . (516) 488-9800

Housing: Homeownership rate: 79.5%; Median home value: $499,000; Median year structure built: 1952; Homeowner vacancy rate: 0.0%; Median selected monthly owner costs: $2,979 with a mortgage, $1,222 without a mortgage; Median gross rent: $1,577 per month; Rental vacancy rate: 1.5%

Health Insurance: 91.2% have insurance; 73.6% have private insurance; 26.5% have public insurance; 8.8% do not have insurance; 3.2% of children under 18 do not have insurance

Hospitals: Long Island Jewish Medical Center (452 beds)

Transportation: Commute: 74.6% car, 20.1% public transportation, 2.6% walk, 1.8% work from home; Mean travel time to work: 34.1 minutes

Additional Information Contacts
Village of New Hyde Park . . . . (516) 354-0022
  http://www.vnhp.org

NORTH BELLMORE (CDP). Covers a land area of 2.620 square miles and a water area of 0 square miles. Located at 40.69° N. Lat; 73.54° W. Long. Elevation is 46 feet.

History: Bellmore, Long Island, serves as a suburb of New York City, a 45-minute train ride. John F. Kennedy Int'l Airport is located within 15 miles (24 km) of Bellmore.

Population: 19,994; Growth (since 2000): -0.4%; Density: 7,630.6 persons per square mile; Race: 89.7% White, 1.3% Black/African American, 6.1% Asian, 0.0% American Indian/Alaska Native, 0.0% Native Hawaiian/Other Pacific Islander, 1.9% Two or more races, 7.1% Hispanic of any race; Average household size: 3.06; Median age: 41.7; Age under 18: 20.4%; Age 65 and over: 15.0%; Males per 100 females: 93.8; Marriage status: 29.3% never married, 58.3% now married, 0.6% separated, 6.8% widowed, 5.5% divorced; Foreign born: 9.1%; Speak English only: 86.7%; With disability: 9.0%; Veterans: 4.9%; Ancestry: 26.1% Italian, 17.2% Irish, 13.5% German, 6.0% Polish, 5.8% American

Employment: 17.2% management, business, and financial, 6.9% computer, engineering, and science, 16.0% education, legal, community service, arts, and media, 9.0% healthcare practitioners, 10.2% service, 27.0% sales and office, 7.7% natural resources, construction, and maintenance, 5.9% production, transportation, and material moving

Income: Per capita: $47,019; Median household: $127,998; Average household: $140,352; Households with income of $100,000 or more: 62.8%; Poverty rate: 2.6%

Educational Attainment: High school diploma or higher: 95.1%; Bachelor's degree or higher: 47.6%; Graduate/professional degree or higher: 22.9%

School District(s)

North Bellmore Union Free SD (KG-06)

Enrollment: 2,075 . . . . (516) 992-3000

Housing: Homeownership rate: 89.7%; Median home value: $448,700; Median year structure built: 1956; Homeowner vacancy rate: 0.0%; Median selected monthly owner costs: $2,965 with a mortgage, $1,322 without a mortgage; Median gross rent: $1,468 per month; Rental vacancy rate: 5.2%

Health Insurance: 97.3% have insurance; 88.6% have private insurance; 23.8% have public insurance; 2.7% do not have insurance; 1.9% of children under 18 do not have insurance

Transportation: Commute: 82.0% car, 14.6% public transportation, 0.4% walk, 2.3% work from home; Mean travel time to work: 37.4 minutes

NORTH HEMPSTEAD (town). Covers a land area of 53.512 square miles and a water area of 15.598 square miles. Located at 40.80° N. Lat; 73.68° W. Long. Elevation is 102 feet.

History: First settled around 1643 as part of the town of Hempstead. Following the Revolutionary War, the Town of North Hempstead was split off in 1784.

Population: 231,085; Growth (since 2000): 3.8%; Density: 4,318.4 persons per square mile; Race: 66.9% White, 6.0% Black/African American, 18.2% Asian, 0.2% American Indian/Alaska Native, 0.1% Native Hawaiian/Other Pacific Islander, 2.2% Two or more races, 13.8% Hispanic of any race; Average household size: 2.95; Median age: 42.6; Age under 18: 22.8%; Age 65 and over: 19.3%; Males per 100 females: 94.5; Marriage status: 28.2% never married, 59.3% now married, 1.1% separated, 6.5% widowed, 6.0% divorced; Foreign born: 29.3%; Speak English only: 61.9%; With disability: 7.7%; Veterans: 3.8%; Ancestry: 13.8% Italian, 10.0% Irish, 6.6% German, 5.8% American, 4.8% Polish

Employment: 20.7% management, business, and financial, 5.5% computer, engineering, and science, 14.4% education, legal, community service, arts, and media, 10.8% healthcare practitioners, 12.3% service, 24.6% sales and office, 5.2% natural resources, construction, and maintenance, 6.5% production, transportation, and material moving

Income: Per capita: $56,755; Median household: $111,570; Average household: $165,932; Households with income of $100,000 or more: 55.3%; Poverty rate: 4.9%

Educational Attainment: High school diploma or higher: 91.2%; Bachelor's degree or higher: 54.3%; Graduate/professional degree or higher: 26.3%

Housing: Homeownership rate: 78.3%; Median home value: $662,600; Median year structure built: 1954; Homeowner vacancy rate: 1.0%; Median selected monthly owner costs: $3,548 with a mortgage, $1,501 without a mortgage; Median gross rent: $1,766 per month; Rental vacancy rate: 4.5%

Health Insurance: 93.9% have insurance; 81.6% have private insurance; 25.8% have public insurance; 6.1% do not have insurance; 3.6% of children under 18 do not have insurance

Transportation: Commute: 71.0% car, 19.7% public transportation, 3.1% walk, 4.9% work from home; Mean travel time to work: 36.1 minutes

Additional Information Contacts

Town of North Hempstead . . . . (516) 869-7646
http://www.northhempsteadny.gov

NORTH HILLS (village). Covers a land area of 2.759 square miles and a water area of 0 square miles. Located at 40.78° N. Lat; 73.68° W. Long. Elevation is 213 feet.

Population: 5,524; Growth (since 2000): 28.4%; Density: 2,002.1 persons per square mile; Race: 71.7% White, 2.7% Black/African American, 24.5% Asian, 0.0% American Indian/Alaska Native, 0.0% Native Hawaiian/Other Pacific Islander, 1.1% Two or more races, 0.1% Hispanic of any race; Average household size: 2.06; Median age: 62.6; Age under 18: 12.2%; Age 65 and over: 46.0%; Males per 100 females: 87.6; Marriage status: 13.0% never married, 69.2% now married, 0.0% separated, 11.5% widowed, 6.3% divorced; Foreign born: 27.0%; Speak English only: 74.6%; With disability: 12.3%; Veterans: 7.4%; Ancestry: 15.1% American, 11.7% Italian, 8.0% Russian, 6.7% Polish, 3.4% German

Employment: 25.6% management, business, and financial, 4.2% computer, engineering, and science, 11.5% education, legal, community service, arts, and media, 24.2% healthcare practitioners, 4.3% service,

29.3% sales and office, 0.1% natural resources, construction, and maintenance, 0.9% production, transportation, and material moving

Income: Per capita: $87,282; Median household: $121,184; Average household: $178,709; Households with income of $100,000 or more: 55.2%; Poverty rate: 1.0%

Educational Attainment: High school diploma or higher: 98.1%; Bachelor's degree or higher: 62.1%; Graduate/professional degree or higher: 36.2%

Housing: Homeownership rate: 87.3%; Median home value: $979,500; Median year structure built: 1986; Homeowner vacancy rate: 0.0%; Median selected monthly owner costs: $4,000+ with a mortgage, $1,501 without a mortgage; Median gross rent: $1,614 per month; Rental vacancy rate: 0.0%

Health Insurance: 98.3% have insurance; 80.6% have private insurance; 45.4% have public insurance; 1.7% do not have insurance; 0.0% of children under 18 do not have insurance

Transportation: Commute: 83.8% car, 9.1% public transportation, 0.5% walk, 6.6% work from home; Mean travel time to work: 30.6 minutes

Additional Information Contacts

Village of North Hills . . . . (516) 627-4832
http://www.villagenorthhills.com

NORTH LYNBROOK (CDP). Covers a land area of 0.087 square miles and a water area of 0 square miles. Located at 40.67° N. Lat; 73.67° W. Long. Elevation is 10 feet.

Population: 468; Growth (since 2000): -36.9%; Density: 5,408.8 persons per square mile; Race: 79.5% White, 0.0% Black/African American, 20.5% Asian, 0.0% American Indian/Alaska Native, 0.0% Native Hawaiian/Other Pacific Islander, 0.0% Two or more races, 20.7% Hispanic of any race; Average household size: 3.16; Median age: 48.8; Age under 18: 13.2%; Age 65 and over: 27.8%; Males per 100 females: 91.5; Marriage status: 27.8% never married, 58.1% now married, 0.0% separated, 8.4% widowed, 5.7% divorced; Foreign born: 27.6%; Speak English only: 69.2%; With disability: 6.8%; Veterans: 3.9%; Ancestry: 23.9% Italian, 8.8% German, 8.5% Irish, 6.6% Croatian, 4.3% French

Employment: 23.4% management, business, and financial, 0.0% computer, engineering, and science, 6.9% education, legal, community service, arts, and media, 6.1% healthcare practitioners, 12.6% service, 32.5% sales and office, 16.0% natural resources, construction, and maintenance, 2.6% production, transportation, and material moving

Income: Per capita: $44,126; Median household: $115,000; Average household: $135,181; Households with income of $100,000 or more: 69.6%; Poverty rate: n/a

Educational Attainment: High school diploma or higher: 92.3%; Bachelor's degree or higher: 33.1%; Graduate/professional degree or higher: 22.6%

Housing: Homeownership rate: 100.0%; Median home value: $436,400; Median year structure built: Before 1940; Homeowner vacancy rate: 0.0%; Median selected monthly owner costs: $3,771 with a mortgage, $1,243 without a mortgage; Median gross rent: n/a per month; Rental vacancy rate: 0.0%

Health Insurance: 95.7% have insurance; 81.6% have private insurance; 34.4% have public insurance; 4.3% do not have insurance; 0.0% of children under 18 do not have insurance

Transportation: Commute: 84.3% car, 4.0% public transportation, 8.5% walk, 3.1% work from home; Mean travel time to work: 34.6 minutes

NORTH MASSAPEQUA (CDP). Covers a land area of 2.995 square miles and a water area of 0.005 square miles. Located at 40.70° N. Lat; 73.47° W. Long. Elevation is 49 feet.

History: North Massapequa is a hamlet and census-designated place (CDP) located within the Town of Oyster Bay in Nassau County, New York.

Population: 18,591; Growth (since 2000): -2.9%; Density: 6,206.7 persons per square mile; Race: 94.8% White, 1.2% Black/African American, 1.7% Asian, 0.2% American Indian/Alaska Native, 0.0% Native Hawaiian/Other Pacific Islander, 1.2% Two or more races, 4.8% Hispanic of any race; Average household size: 3.01; Median age: 43.1; Age under 18: 21.5%; Age 65 and over: 15.7%; Males per 100 females: 93.1; Marriage status: 28.2% never married, 58.0% now married, 1.1% separated, 6.7% widowed, 7.0% divorced; Foreign born: 6.2%; Speak English only: 90.7%; With disability: 9.5%; Veterans: 6.1%; Ancestry: 42.0% Italian, 23.0% Irish, 15.3% German, 5.2% Polish, 3.4% American

Employment: 16.8% management, business, and financial, 5.1% computer, engineering, and science, 16.5% education, legal, community service, arts, and media, 7.0% healthcare practitioners, 15.9% service,

25.8% sales and office, 6.5% natural resources, construction, and maintenance, 6.5% production, transportation, and material moving
Income: Per capita: $45,169; Median household: $115,500; Average household: $132,608; Households with income of $100,000 or more: 58.1%; Poverty rate: 5.1%
Educational Attainment: High school diploma or higher: 96.0%; Bachelor's degree or higher: 37.6%; Graduate/professional degree or higher: 16.1%

School District(s)
Farmingdale Union Free SD (KG-12)
    Enrollment: 5,825 . . . . (516) 434-5100
Plainedge Union Free SD (KG-12)
    Enrollment: 2,992 . . . . (516) 992-7455
Housing: Homeownership rate: 95.0%; Median home value: $432,000; Median year structure built: 1956; Homeowner vacancy rate: 1.6%; Median selected monthly owner costs: $3,076 with a mortgage, $1,251 without a mortgage; Median gross rent: $1,799 per month; Rental vacancy rate: 0.0%
Health Insurance: 97.7% have insurance; 86.6% have private insurance; 23.7% have public insurance; 2.3% do not have insurance; 0.5% of children under 18 do not have insurance
Transportation: Commute: 84.9% car, 12.1% public transportation, 0.6% walk, 2.4% work from home; Mean travel time to work: 35.6 minutes

NORTH MERRICK (CDP).
Covers a land area of 1.719 square miles and a water area of 0.007 square miles. Located at 40.69° N. Lat; 73.56° W. Long. Elevation is 46 feet.
History: North Merrick is located on the south shore of Long Island.
Population: 12,436; Growth (since 2000): 5.0%; Density: 7,235.0 persons per square mile; Race: 89.9% White, 2.0% Black/African American, 5.4% Asian, 0.0% American Indian/Alaska Native, 0.0% Native Hawaiian/Other Pacific Islander, 1.2% Two or more races, 7.8% Hispanic of any race; Average household size: 3.20; Median age: 40.9; Age under 18: 24.5%; Age 65 and over: 15.2%; Males per 100 females: 95.6; Marriage status: 29.3% never married, 61.1% now married, 0.8% separated, 4.5% widowed, 5.1% divorced; Foreign born: 9.0%; Speak English only: 87.1%; With disability: 6.6%; Veterans: 6.2%; Ancestry: 30.0% Italian, 27.0% Irish, 14.3% German, 4.2% English, 4.1% Polish
Employment: 20.3% management, business, and financial, 3.8% computer, engineering, and science, 18.6% education, legal, community service, arts, and media, 5.5% healthcare practitioners, 11.8% service, 27.0% sales and office, 7.0% natural resources, construction, and maintenance, 6.1% production, transportation, and material moving
Income: Per capita: $46,794; Median household: $124,907; Average household: $147,236; Households with income of $100,000 or more: 60.8%; Poverty rate: 3.2%
Educational Attainment: High school diploma or higher: 94.4%; Bachelor's degree or higher: 48.5%; Graduate/professional degree or higher: 21.5%

School District(s)
North Bellmore Union Free SD (KG-06)
    Enrollment: 2,075 . . . . (516) 992-3000
North Merrick Union Free SD (KG-06)
    Enrollment: 1,218 . . . . (516) 292-3694
Housing: Homeownership rate: 94.5%; Median home value: $467,500; Median year structure built: 1955; Homeowner vacancy rate: 0.9%; Median selected monthly owner costs: $3,237 with a mortgage, $1,343 without a mortgage; Median gross rent: $2,306 per month; Rental vacancy rate: 11.3%
Health Insurance: 96.8% have insurance; 89.0% have private insurance; 21.1% have public insurance; 3.2% do not have insurance; 3.3% of children under 18 do not have insurance
Transportation: Commute: 79.3% car, 15.7% public transportation, 1.1% walk, 3.2% work from home; Mean travel time to work: 35.6 minutes

NORTH NEW HYDE PARK (CDP).
Covers a land area of 1.973 square miles and a water area of 0.022 square miles. Located at 40.75° N. Lat; 73.69° W. Long. Elevation is 115 feet.
History: North New Hyde Park is a census-designated place (CDP) in Nassau County, New York.
Population: 15,585; Growth (since 2000): 7.2%; Density: 7,900.5 persons per square mile; Race: 57.0% White, 1.6% Black/African American, 35.6% Asian, 0.2% American Indian/Alaska Native, 0.0% Native Hawaiian/Other Pacific Islander, 1.6% Two or more races, 7.7% Hispanic of any race; Average household size: 3.30; Median age: 43.9; Age under 18: 20.3%;

Age 65 and over: 18.7%; Males per 100 females: 93.2; Marriage status: 30.8% never married, 59.4% now married, 0.5% separated, 6.8% widowed, 3.0% divorced; Foreign born: 32.5%; Speak English only: 55.8%; With disability: 8.2%; Veterans: 4.3%; Ancestry: 21.0% Italian, 14.5% Irish, 7.6% German, 4.0% Polish, 2.0% American
Employment: 17.6% management, business, and financial, 6.5% computer, engineering, and science, 10.9% education, legal, community service, arts, and media, 13.2% healthcare practitioners, 9.6% service, 28.7% sales and office, 5.8% natural resources, construction, and maintenance, 7.7% production, transportation, and material moving
Income: Per capita: $46,909; Median household: $119,396; Average household: $151,011; Households with income of $100,000 or more: 62.9%; Poverty rate: 2.5%
Educational Attainment: High school diploma or higher: 90.2%; Bachelor's degree or higher: 49.0%; Graduate/professional degree or higher: 22.6%
Housing: Homeownership rate: 93.2%; Median home value: $563,700; Median year structure built: 1948; Homeowner vacancy rate: 0.6%; Median selected monthly owner costs: $3,213 with a mortgage, $1,258 without a mortgage; Median gross rent: $1,933 per month; Rental vacancy rate: 3.0%
Health Insurance: 95.0% have insurance; 84.2% have private insurance; 24.9% have public insurance; 5.0% do not have insurance; 0.6% of children under 18 do not have insurance
Transportation: Commute: 77.6% car, 17.5% public transportation, 1.5% walk, 2.2% work from home; Mean travel time to work: 37.4 minutes

NORTH VALLEY STREAM (CDP).
Covers a land area of 1.864 square miles and a water area of 0.033 square miles. Located at 40.68° N. Lat; 73.71° W. Long. Elevation is 39 feet.
History: North Valley Stream is a census-designated place (CDP) in the village of Valley Stream in Nassau County, New York.
Population: 19,153; Growth (since 2000): 21.3%; Density: 10,272.9 persons per square mile; Race: 24.0% White, 48.1% Black/African American, 13.1% Asian, 0.2% American Indian/Alaska Native, 0.1% Native Hawaiian/Other Pacific Islander, 4.2% Two or more races, 16.6% Hispanic of any race; Average household size: 3.48; Median age: 40.1; Age under 18: 19.8%; Age 65 and over: 15.5%; Males per 100 females: 87.6; Marriage status: 37.9% never married, 48.3% now married, 2.7% separated, 5.4% widowed, 8.4% divorced; Foreign born: 37.0%; Speak English only: 68.4%; With disability: 9.9%; Veterans: 4.5%; Ancestry: 8.3% Italian, 7.3% Jamaican, 4.7% Haitian, 4.2% American, 2.8% Guyanese
Employment: 15.5% management, business, and financial, 3.6% computer, engineering, and science, 13.0% education, legal, community service, arts, and media, 11.1% healthcare practitioners, 17.1% service, 25.4% sales and office, 6.3% natural resources, construction, and maintenance, 8.0% production, transportation, and material moving
Income: Per capita: $35,236; Median household: $104,541; Average household: $117,192; Households with income of $100,000 or more: 53.3%; Poverty rate: 3.8%
Educational Attainment: High school diploma or higher: 91.3%; Bachelor's degree or higher: 34.7%; Graduate/professional degree or higher: 13.5%
Housing: Homeownership rate: 88.7%; Median home value: $365,800; Median year structure built: 1952; Homeowner vacancy rate: 1.2%; Median selected monthly owner costs: $2,791 with a mortgage, $1,138 without a mortgage; Median gross rent: $1,738 per month; Rental vacancy rate: 0.0%
Health Insurance: 92.9% have insurance; 77.0% have private insurance; 26.3% have public insurance; 7.1% do not have insurance; 1.8% of children under 18 do not have insurance
Transportation: Commute: 77.9% car, 17.7% public transportation, 1.6% walk, 1.7% work from home; Mean travel time to work: 42.3 minutes

NORTH WANTAGH (CDP).
Covers a land area of 1.902 square miles and a water area of 0.009 square miles. Located at 40.69° N. Lat; 73.52° W. Long. Elevation is 36 feet.
Population: 12,019; Growth (since 2000): -1.1%; Density: 6,318.5 persons per square mile; Race: 94.8% White, 0.5% Black/African American, 1.9% Asian, 0.1% American Indian/Alaska Native, 0.0% Native Hawaiian/Other Pacific Islander, 1.7% Two or more races, 11.0% Hispanic of any race; Average household size: 2.93; Median age: 45.5; Age under 18: 20.2%; Age 65 and over: 20.1%; Males per 100 females: 91.5; Marriage status: 23.4% never married, 59.4% now married, 0.7% separated, 9.2% widowed, 7.9% divorced; Foreign born: 6.0%; Speak English only: 89.2%;

With disability: 9.7%; Veterans: 6.1%; Ancestry: 33.1% Italian, 20.9% Irish, 12.3% German, 4.9% American, 4.3% Polish

Employment: 19.7% management, business, and financial, 4.0% computer, engineering, and science, 18.1% education, legal, community service, arts, and media, 6.2% healthcare practitioners, 14.8% service, 24.6% sales and office, 5.5% natural resources, construction, and maintenance, 6.9% production, transportation, and material moving

Income: Per capita: $48,070; Median household: $123,951; Average household: $137,196; Households with income of $100,000 or more: 58.2%; Poverty rate: 2.2%

Educational Attainment: High school diploma or higher: 94.3%; Bachelor's degree or higher: 41.5%; Graduate/professional degree or higher: 17.9%

Housing: Homeownership rate: 93.9%; Median home value: $413,900; Median year structure built: 1955; Homeowner vacancy rate: 0.0%; Median selected monthly owner costs: $3,023 with a mortgage, $1,311 without a mortgage; Median gross rent: $1,109 per month; Rental vacancy rate: 3.5%

Health Insurance: 98.3% have insurance; 89.8% have private insurance; 26.2% have public insurance; 1.7% do not have insurance; 0.0% of children under 18 do not have insurance

Transportation: Commute: 83.4% car, 11.9% public transportation, 0.4% walk, 3.6% work from home; Mean travel time to work: 35.6 minutes

OCEANSIDE (CDP).

Covers a land area of 4.944 square miles and a water area of 0.473 square miles. Located at 40.63° N. Lat; 73.64° W. Long. Elevation is 13 feet.

History: Originally known as South Bay, the English government first call it Christian Hook in 1674 due to predominant religious affiliation of its colonists. Land development proceeded rapidly, and oyster sales dominated the economy.

Population: 30,710; Growth (since 2000): -6.2%; Density: 6,212.0 persons per square mile; Race: 92.6% White, 1.0% Black/African American, 2.3% Asian, 0.5% American Indian/Alaska Native, 0.0% Native Hawaiian/Other Pacific Islander, 1.0% Two or more races, 10.6% Hispanic of any race; Average household size: 2.85; Median age: 44.3; Age under 18: 20.2%; Age 65 and over: 17.1%; Males per 100 females: 92.8; Marriage status: 29.3% never married, 59.6% now married, 1.2% separated, 6.6% widowed, 4.6% divorced; Foreign born: 11.3%; Speak English only: 85.1%; With disability: 8.5%; Veterans: 4.8%; Ancestry: 30.6% Italian, 16.8% Irish, 9.3% German, 7.2% Polish, 6.0% Russian

Employment: 20.0% management, business, and financial, 3.7% computer, engineering, and science, 19.2% education, legal, community service, arts, and media, 4.0% healthcare practitioners, 14.5% service, 28.4% sales and office, 5.6% natural resources, construction, and maintenance, 4.6% production, transportation, and material moving

Income: Per capita: $45,731; Median household: $109,484; Average household: $127,670; Households with income of $100,000 or more: 53.9%; Poverty rate: 5.5%

Educational Attainment: High school diploma or higher: 95.0%; Bachelor's degree or higher: 44.6%; Graduate/professional degree or higher: 19.5%

School District(s)

Oceanside Union Free SD (KG-12)

    Enrollment: 5,552 . . . . (516) 678-1215

Housing: Homeownership rate: 88.0%; Median home value: $443,900; Median year structure built: 1955; Homeowner vacancy rate: 0.9%; Median selected monthly owner costs: $3,086 with a mortgage, $1,277 without a mortgage; Median gross rent: $1,355 per month; Rental vacancy rate: 2.1%

Health Insurance: 96.6% have insurance; 85.0% have private insurance; 24.0% have public insurance; 3.4% do not have insurance; 2.3% of children under 18 do not have insurance

Hospitals: South Nassau Communities Hospital (435 beds)

Transportation: Commute: 76.9% car, 15.8% public transportation, 1.6% walk, 5.1% work from home; Mean travel time to work: 36.9 minutes

OLD BETHPAGE (CDP).

Covers a land area of 4.182 square miles and a water area of 0.003 square miles. Located at 40.75° N. Lat; 73.46° W. Long. Elevation is 174 feet.

History: In 1695, Thomas Powell bought about 10,000 acres (40 sq. km.) from local Indian tribes, including the Marsapeque, Matinecoc, and Sacatogue, for 140 English pounds. Powell called his land Bethphage, because it was situated between two other places on Long Island, Jericho

and Jerusalem, just as the biblical town of Bethphage (meaning "house of figs") was situated between Jericho and Jerusalem in Israel.

Population: 5,624; Growth (since 2000): 4.1%; Density: 1,344.7 persons per square mile; Race: 93.0% White, 0.1% Black/African American, 5.8% Asian, 0.0% American Indian/Alaska Native, 0.0% Native Hawaiian/Other Pacific Islander, 1.0% Two or more races, 2.1% Hispanic of any race; Average household size: 2.95; Median age: 45.3; Age under 18: 22.2%; Age 65 and over: 17.5%; Males per 100 females: 93.2; Marriage status: 26.6% never married, 63.3% now married, 0.6% separated, 6.3% widowed, 3.8% divorced; Foreign born: 10.0%; Speak English only: 90.9%; With disability: 10.9%; Veterans: 4.5%; Ancestry: 31.0% Italian, 19.9% Irish, 10.2% Russian, 8.8% German, 5.7% Polish

Employment: 23.9% management, business, and financial, 6.2% computer, engineering, and science, 20.0% education, legal, community service, arts, and media, 7.7% healthcare practitioners, 9.4% service, 23.9% sales and office, 3.5% natural resources, construction, and maintenance, 5.5% production, transportation, and material moving

Income: Per capita: $55,348; Median household: $114,375; Average household: $160,928; Households with income of $100,000 or more: 56.6%; Poverty rate: 3.4%

Educational Attainment: High school diploma or higher: 95.4%; Bachelor's degree or higher: 56.8%; Graduate/professional degree or higher: 28.4%

School District(s)

Plainview-Old Bethpage Central SD (KG-12)

    Enrollment: 4,917 . . . . (516) 434-3001

Housing: Homeownership rate: 91.9%; Median home value: $570,000; Median year structure built: 1960; Homeowner vacancy rate: 1.2%; Median selected monthly owner costs: $3,802 with a mortgage, $1,501 without a mortgage; Median gross rent: n/a per month; Rental vacancy rate: 0.0%

Health Insurance: 96.1% have insurance; 84.4% have private insurance; 24.9% have public insurance; 3.9% do not have insurance; 4.8% of children under 18 do not have insurance

Transportation: Commute: 80.9% car, 11.2% public transportation, 1.1% walk, 5.5% work from home; Mean travel time to work: 31.4 minutes

OLD BROOKVILLE (village).

Covers a land area of 3.999 square miles and a water area of 0.001 square miles. Located at 40.84° N. Lat; 73.61° W. Long. Elevation is 92 feet.

Population: 2,022; Growth (since 2000): -6.7%; Density: 505.7 persons per square mile; Race: 79.9% White, 1.0% Black/African American, 13.0% Asian, 0.0% American Indian/Alaska Native, 0.0% Native Hawaiian/Other Pacific Islander, 3.6% Two or more races, 3.8% Hispanic of any race; Average household size: 3.18; Median age: 41.7; Age under 18: 26.9%; Age 65 and over: 16.6%; Males per 100 females: 102.5; Marriage status: 30.1% never married, 61.7% now married, 0.8% separated, 5.2% widowed, 3.0% divorced; Foreign born: 16.9%; Speak English only: 74.3%; With disability: 4.6%; Veterans: 4.4%; Ancestry: 32.0% Italian, 13.7% Irish, 8.7% German, 3.8% Russian, 3.7% American

Employment: 33.7% management, business, and financial, 0.0% computer, engineering, and science, 12.1% education, legal, community service, arts, and media, 16.3% healthcare practitioners, 7.9% service, 26.2% sales and office, 2.8% natural resources, construction, and maintenance, 1.0% production, transportation, and material moving

Income: Per capita: $107,304; Median household: $203,438; Average household: $342,472; Households with income of $100,000 or more: 73.8%; Poverty rate: 4.2%

Educational Attainment: High school diploma or higher: 96.0%; Bachelor's degree or higher: 72.9%; Graduate/professional degree or higher: 34.5%

Housing: Homeownership rate: 89.3%; Median home value: $1,972,700; Median year structure built: 1965; Homeowner vacancy rate: 0.7%; Median selected monthly owner costs: $4,000+ with a mortgage, $1,501 without a mortgage; Median gross rent: $2,781 per month; Rental vacancy rate: 0.0%

Health Insurance: 96.5% have insurance; 90.1% have private insurance; 18.6% have public insurance; 3.5% do not have insurance; 2.1% of children under 18 do not have insurance

Safety: Violent crime rate: 4.5 per 10,000 population; Property crime rate: 153.2 per 10,000 population

Transportation: Commute: 80.9% car, 9.6% public transportation, 0.0% walk, 9.5% work from home; Mean travel time to work: 35.4 minutes

OLD WESTBURY (village). Covers a land area of 8.573 square miles and a water area of 0 square miles. Located at 40.79° N. Lat; 73.60° W. Long. Elevation is 161 feet.

History: Westbury was named by Henry Willis, one of the first English settlers after a town in his home county of Wiltshire, England. Westbury had been a Quaker community of isolated farms until the railroad came in 1836.

Population: 4,711; Growth (since 2000): 11.4%; Density: 549.5 persons per square mile; Race: 67.2% White, 9.1% Black/African American, 17.8% Asian, 0.2% American Indian/Alaska Native, 0.0% Native Hawaiian/Other Pacific Islander, 3.9% Two or more races, 7.2% Hispanic of any race; Average household size: 3.19; Median age: 24.0; Age under 18: 17.6%; Age 65 and over: 12.8%; Males per 100 females: 94.5; Marriage status: 47.6% never married, 48.2% now married, 0.3% separated, 2.4% widowed, 1.8% divorced; Foreign born: 21.4%; Speak English only: 67.8%; With disability: 4.5%; Veterans: 1.4%; Ancestry: 8.7% Italian, 5.9% Irish, 5.8% Polish, 5.6% American, 5.5% German

Employment: 17.9% management, business, and financial, 3.6% computer, engineering, and science, 12.2% education, legal, community service, arts, and media, 17.5% healthcare practitioners, 16.4% service, 27.6% sales and office, 1.7% natural resources, construction, and maintenance, 3.0% production, transportation, and material moving

Income: Per capita: $75,045; Median household: $163,958; Average household: $325,450; Households with income of $100,000 or more: 75.3%; Poverty rate: 2.3%

Educational Attainment: High school diploma or higher: 98.2%; Bachelor's degree or higher: 76.6%; Graduate/professional degree or higher: 43.4%

School District(s)
East Williston Union Free SD (KG-12)
    Enrollment: 1,697 . . . . (516) 333-3758
Westbury Union Free SD (PK-12)
    Enrollment: 5,496 . . . . (516) 876-5016

Four-year College(s)
New York Institute of Technology (Private, Not-for-profit)
    Enrollment: 7,403 . . . . (516) 686-7516
    Tuition: In-state $35,870; Out-of-state $35,870
SUNY College at Old Westbury (Public)
    Enrollment: 4,910 . . . . (516) 876-3000
    Tuition: In-state $7,883; Out-of-state $17,533

Housing: Homeownership rate: 94.2%; Median home value: $1,729,800; Median year structure built: 1972; Homeowner vacancy rate: 1.7%; Median selected monthly owner costs: $4,000+ with a mortgage, $1,501 without a mortgage; Median gross rent: $1,175 per month; Rental vacancy rate: 0.0%

Health Insurance: 96.3% have insurance; 87.1% have private insurance; 17.2% have public insurance; 3.7% do not have insurance; 1.8% of children under 18 do not have insurance

Safety: Violent crime rate: 0.0 per 10,000 population; Property crime rate: 48.5 per 10,000 population

Transportation: Commute: 58.3% car, 11.8% public transportation, 14.2% walk, 13.7% work from home; Mean travel time to work: 29.8 minutes

Additional Information Contacts
Village of Old Westbury . . . . (516) 626-0800
    http://www.villageofoldwestbury.org

OYSTER BAY (CDP). Covers a land area of 1.233 square miles and a water area of 0.370 square miles. Located at 40.87° N. Lat; 73.53° W. Long. Elevation is 49 feet.

Population: 6,104; Growth (since 2000): -10.6%; Density: 4,948.7 persons per square mile; Race: 87.3% White, 2.8% Black/African American, 3.9% Asian, 0.0% American Indian/Alaska Native, 0.0% Native Hawaiian/Other Pacific Islander, 1.2% Two or more races, 9.6% Hispanic of any race; Average household size: 2.29; Median age: 46.3; Age under 18: 22.0%; Age 65 and over: 22.5%; Males per 100 females: 93.4; Marriage status: 26.1% never married, 53.0% now married, 2.0% separated, 12.8% widowed, 8.1% divorced; Foreign born: 12.7%; Speak English only: 83.3%; With disability: 13.2%; Veterans: 6.1%; Ancestry: 28.2% Italian, 26.0% Irish, 6.4% German, 4.7% English, 4.6% Polish

Employment: 25.0% management, business, and financial, 3.3% computer, engineering, and science, 15.6% education, legal, community service, arts, and media, 8.1% healthcare practitioners, 17.9% service, 19.3% sales and office, 5.0% natural resources, construction, and maintenance, 5.7% production, transportation, and material moving

Income: Per capita: $62,166; Median household: $92,952; Average household: $139,491; Households with income of $100,000 or more: 40.1%; Poverty rate: 2.9%

Educational Attainment: High school diploma or higher: 90.6%; Bachelor's degree or higher: 45.6%; Graduate/professional degree or higher: 19.3%

School District(s)
Oyster Bay-East Norwich Central SD (PK-12)
    Enrollment: 1,621 . . . . (516) 624-6505

Housing: Homeownership rate: 65.8%; Median home value: $562,600; Median year structure built: 1954; Homeowner vacancy rate: 0.0%; Median selected monthly owner costs: $3,413 with a mortgage, $1,027 without a mortgage; Median gross rent: $1,841 per month; Rental vacancy rate: 4.2%

Health Insurance: 96.2% have insurance; 83.7% have private insurance; 33.0% have public insurance; 3.8% do not have insurance; 1.8% of children under 18 do not have insurance

Transportation: Commute: 85.0% car, 7.9% public transportation, 4.3% walk, 2.1% work from home; Mean travel time to work: 28.1 minutes

OYSTER BAY (town). Covers a land area of 103.747 square miles and a water area of 65.652 square miles. Located at 40.80° N. Lat; 73.51° W. Long. Elevation is 49 feet.

History: Nearby is Theodore Roosevelt's estate, Sagamore Hill, which was made a national shrine in 1953 and a National Historic Site in 1963. Also of interest in Oyster Bay are several 18th-century houses, the Theodore Roosevelt Memorial Bird Sanctuary, a 12-acre wildlife sanctuary owned by the National Audubon Society, which adjoins Roosevelt's grave and the Oyster Bay National Wildlife Refuge. Settled 1653.

Population: 298,655; Growth (since 2000): 1.6%; Density: 2,878.7 persons per square mile; Race: 82.5% White, 2.7% Black/African American, 11.1% Asian, 0.1% American Indian/Alaska Native, 0.0% Native Hawaiian/Other Pacific Islander, 1.6% Two or more races, 8.2% Hispanic of any race; Average household size: 2.95; Median age: 44.2; Age under 18: 21.1%; Age 65 and over: 17.7%; Males per 100 females: 94.0; Marriage status: 28.0% never married, 59.4% now married, 1.2% separated, 6.8% widowed, 5.8% divorced; Foreign born: 15.8%; Speak English only: 79.7%; With disability: 8.8%; Veterans: 5.3%; Ancestry: 27.6% Italian, 18.7% Irish, 12.3% German, 5.8% Polish, 4.3% Russian

Employment: 20.3% management, business, and financial, 5.3% computer, engineering, and science, 15.0% education, legal, community service, arts, and media, 8.0% healthcare practitioners, 13.5% service, 26.5% sales and office, 5.8% natural resources, construction, and maintenance, 5.6% production, transportation, and material moving

Income: Per capita: $54,532; Median household: $120,826; Average household: $159,880; Households with income of $100,000 or more: 58.5%; Poverty rate: 3.9%

Educational Attainment: High school diploma or higher: 94.7%; Bachelor's degree or higher: 49.1%; Graduate/professional degree or higher: 21.8%

School District(s)
Oyster Bay-East Norwich Central SD (PK-12)
    Enrollment: 1,621 . . . . (516) 624-6505

Housing: Homeownership rate: 88.1%; Median home value: $485,900; Median year structure built: 1957; Homeowner vacancy rate: 1.1%; Median selected monthly owner costs: $3,202 with a mortgage, $1,311 without a mortgage; Median gross rent: $1,856 per month; Rental vacancy rate: 6.9%

Health Insurance: 96.8% have insurance; 86.0% have private insurance; 24.5% have public insurance; 3.2% do not have insurance; 1.6% of children under 18 do not have insurance

Transportation: Commute: 78.8% car, 14.2% public transportation, 1.7% walk, 4.1% work from home; Mean travel time to work: 35.3 minutes

Additional Information Contacts
Town of Oyster Bay . . . . (516) 624-6332
    http://www.oysterbaytown.com

OYSTER BAY COVE (village). Covers a land area of 4.187 square miles and a water area of 0.069 square miles. Located at 40.86° N. Lat; 73.51° W. Long. Elevation is 72 feet.

Population: 2,140; Growth (since 2000): -5.4%; Race: 85.2% White, 2.7% Black/African American, 9.6% Asian, 0.0% American Indian/Alaska Native, 0.0% Native Hawaiian/Other Pacific Islander, 0.8% Two or more races, 6.5% Hispanic of any race; Average household size: 3.07; Median age: 49.4; Age under 18: 18.8%;

Age 65 and over: 20.0%; Males per 100 females: 94.6; Marriage status: 23.8% never married, 68.8% now married, 0.9% separated, 3.4% widowed, 4.0% divorced; Foreign born: 15.2%; Speak English only: 79.3%; With disability: 6.3%; Veterans: 5.4%; Ancestry: 15.9% Italian, 14.8% Irish, 8.8% Russian, 7.9% German, 6.3% Polish

Employment: 29.0% management, business, and financial, 2.8% computer, engineering, and science, 13.4% education, legal, community service, arts, and media, 12.5% healthcare practitioners, 8.3% service, 28.5% sales and office, 3.0% natural resources, construction, and maintenance, 2.6% production, transportation, and material moving

Income: Per capita: $109,310; Median household: $226,667; Average household: $327,766; Households with income of $100,000 or more: 82.1%; Poverty rate: 0.4%

Educational Attainment: High school diploma or higher: 98.5%; Bachelor's degree or higher: 72.4%; Graduate/professional degree or higher: 37.4%

Housing: Homeownership rate: 93.7%; Median home value: $1,547,000; Median year structure built: 1974; Homeowner vacancy rate: 1.5%; Median selected monthly owner costs: $4,000+ with a mortgage, $1,501 without a mortgage; Median gross rent: $1,500 per month; Rental vacancy rate: 0.0%

Health Insurance: 97.9% have insurance; 92.7% have private insurance; 20.3% have public insurance; 2.1% do not have insurance; 0.9% of children under 18 do not have insurance

Safety: Violent crime rate: 0.0 per 10,000 population; Property crime rate: 32.3 per 10,000 population

Transportation: Commute: 78.3% car, 11.3% public transportation, 0.6% walk, 9.3% work from home; Mean travel time to work: 34.2 minutes

PLAINEDGE (CDP). Covers a land area of 1.404 square miles and a water area of 0 square miles. Located at 40.72° N. Lat; 73.48° W. Long. Elevation is 66 feet.

Population: 9,227; Growth (since 2000): 0.3%; Density: 6,571.5 persons per square mile; Race: 90.5% White, 0.0% Black/African American, 6.9% Asian, 0.0% American Indian/Alaska Native, 0.0% Native Hawaiian/Other Pacific Islander, 1.4% Two or more races, 8.9% Hispanic of any race; Average household size: 3.19; Median age: 41.0; Age under 18: 21.5%; Age 65 and over: 14.8%; Males per 100 females: 94.2; Marriage status: 29.5% never married, 58.2% now married, 1.6% separated, 6.0% widowed, 6.3% divorced; Foreign born: 9.9%; Speak English only: 89.3%; With disability: 8.6%; Veterans: 5.3%; Ancestry: 38.0% Italian, 26.8% Irish, 16.0% German, 6.8% Polish, 3.9% English

Employment: 16.3% management, business, and financial, 5.6% computer, engineering, and science, 15.4% education, legal, community service, arts, and media, 8.6% healthcare practitioners, 11.5% service, 27.4% sales and office, 8.2% natural resources, construction, and maintenance, 7.1% production, transportation, and material moving

Income: Per capita: $42,245; Median household: $118,917; Average household: $131,264; Households with income of $100,000 or more: 60.0%; Poverty rate: 2.5%

Educational Attainment: High school diploma or higher: 94.9%; Bachelor's degree or higher: 38.7%; Graduate/professional degree or higher: 15.2%

Housing: Homeownership rate: 89.0%; Median home value: $404,000; Median year structure built: 1956; Homeowner vacancy rate: 0.0%; Median selected monthly owner costs: $2,820 with a mortgage, $1,245 without a mortgage; Median gross rent: $1,945 per month; Rental vacancy rate: 13.9%

Health Insurance: 98.5% have insurance; 92.2% have private insurance; 19.3% have public insurance; 1.5% do not have insurance; 0.0% of children under 18 do not have insurance

Transportation: Commute: 86.7% car, 9.5% public transportation, 0.2% walk, 1.2% work from home; Mean travel time to work: 29.5 minutes

PLAINVIEW (CDP). Covers a land area of 5.733 square miles and a water area of 0.011 square miles. Located at 40.78° N. Lat; 73.47° W. Long. Elevation is 148 feet.

History: Plainview was settled in 1648, when Welsh settler Robert Williams bought land that included a small pond named the Moscopas, meaning "hole of dirt and water." Neighboring land was purchased by Thomas Powell in 1695 as part of the Bethpage Purchase, and the area was called "Mannatto Hill." Manitou was the Native American word for "god" or "spirit."

Population: 26,141; Growth (since 2000): 2.0%; Density: 4,559.9 persons per square mile; Race: 82.1% White, 0.8% Black/African American, 14.8%

Asian, 0.3% American Indian/Alaska Native, 0.0% Native Hawaiian/Other Pacific Islander, 1.2% Two or more races, 5.1% Hispanic of any race; Average household size: 2.89; Median age: 45.1; Age under 18: 22.6%; Age 65 and over: 19.9%; Males per 100 females: 93.3; Marriage status: 21.3% never married, 67.1% now married, 1.0% separated, 7.8% widowed, 3.8% divorced; Foreign born: 17.1%; Speak English only: 80.7%; With disability: 8.8%; Veterans: 4.5%; Ancestry: 15.9% Italian, 9.0% Russian, 8.2% Irish, 8.1% Polish, 7.4% German

Employment: 23.7% management, business, and financial, 6.3% computer, engineering, and science, 18.4% education, legal, community service, arts, and media, 8.4% healthcare practitioners, 9.7% service, 25.1% sales and office, 3.7% natural resources, construction, and maintenance, 4.7% production, transportation, and material moving

Income: Per capita: $56,873; Median household: $132,635; Average household: $163,355; Households with income of $100,000 or more: 62.1%; Poverty rate: 3.8%

Educational Attainment: High school diploma or higher: 95.7%; Bachelor's degree or higher: 63.2%; Graduate/professional degree or higher: 30.8%

School District(s)

Bethpage Union Free SD (KG-12)
Enrollment: 2,911 . . . . (516) 644-4001
Plainview-Old Bethpage Central SD (KG-12)
Enrollment: 4,917 . . . . (516) 434-3001
Syosset Central SD (KG-12)
Enrollment: 6,418 . . . . (516) 364-5605

Housing: Homeownership rate: 91.3%; Median home value: $536,600; Median year structure built: 1957; Homeowner vacancy rate: 0.4%; Median selected monthly owner costs: $3,330 with a mortgage, $1,461 without a mortgage; Median gross rent: $1,678 per month; Rental vacancy rate: 9.9%

Health Insurance: 97.6% have insurance; 87.5% have private insurance; 26.0% have public insurance; 2.4% do not have insurance; 1.1% of children under 18 do not have insurance

Hospitals: Plainview Hospital (239 beds)

Transportation: Commute: 74.3% car, 19.7% public transportation, 0.7% walk, 4.1% work from home; Mean travel time to work: 38.5 minutes

PLANDOME (village). Covers a land area of 0.495 square miles and a water area of 0.009 square miles. Located at 40.81° N. Lat; 73.70° W. Long. Elevation is 72 feet.

Population: 1,285; Growth (since 2000): 1.0%; Density: 2,597.3 persons per square mile; Race: 93.1% White, 0.0% Black/African American, 5.1% Asian, 0.0% American Indian/Alaska Native, 0.0% Native Hawaiian/Other Pacific Islander, 1.8% Two or more races, 3.4% Hispanic of any race; Average household size: 3.24; Median age: 45.0; Age under 18: 30.4%; Age 65 and over: 16.1%; Males per 100 females: 94.1; Marriage status: 25.1% never married, 69.6% now married, 0.5% separated, 3.6% widowed, 1.7% divorced; Foreign born: 8.6%; Speak English only: 86.8%; With disability: 4.6%; Veterans: 5.6%; Ancestry: 28.3% Irish, 25.6% Italian, 9.8% German, 7.0% American, 6.3% English

Employment: 36.2% management, business, and financial, 1.1% computer, engineering, and science, 16.8% education, legal, community service, arts, and media, 7.0% healthcare practitioners, 3.8% service, 32.6% sales and office, 2.0% natural resources, construction, and maintenance, 0.5% production, transportation, and material moving

Income: Per capita: $104,645; Median household: $233,523; Average household: $334,698; Households with income of $100,000 or more: 80.6%; Poverty rate: 2.0%

Educational Attainment: High school diploma or higher: 98.8%; Bachelor's degree or higher: 81.5%; Graduate/professional degree or higher: 41.4%

Housing: Homeownership rate: 94.2%; Median home value: $1,819,000; Median year structure built: Before 1940; Homeowner vacancy rate: 2.0%; Median selected monthly owner costs: $4,000+ with a mortgage, $1,501 without a mortgage; Median gross rent: n/a per month; Rental vacancy rate: 0.0%

Health Insurance: 99.6% have insurance; 96.0% have private insurance; 18.8% have public insurance; 0.4% do not have insurance; 0.0% of children under 18 do not have insurance

Transportation: Commute: 52.8% car, 40.3% public transportation, 0.5% walk, 5.6% work from home; Mean travel time to work: 41.3 minutes

PLANDOME HEIGHTS (village).

PLANDOME HEIGHTS (village). Covers a land area of 0.181 square miles and a water area of 0.007 square miles. Located at 40.80° N. Lat; 73.71° W. Long. Elevation is 89 feet.

Population: 935; Growth (since 2000): -3.7%; Density: 5,169.3 persons per square mile; Race: 83.6% White, 0.0% Black/African American, 15.1% Asian, 0.0% American Indian/Alaska Native, 0.0% Native Hawaiian/Other Pacific Islander, 0.1% Two or more races, 6.0% Hispanic of any race; Average household size: 2.98; Median age: 45.7; Age under 18: 28.4%; Age 65 and over: 15.7%; Males per 100 females: 92.5; Marriage status: 24.8% never married, 64.3% now married, 0.4% separated, 8.3% widowed, 2.7% divorced; Foreign born: 13.9%; Speak English only: 79.0%; With disability: 4.3%; Veterans: 2.1%; Ancestry: 22.1% Italian, 19.4% Irish, 9.5% German, 9.4% American, 6.1% English

Employment: 35.2% management, business, and financial, 6.6% computer, engineering, and science, 22.5% education, legal, community service, arts, and media, 9.8% healthcare practitioners, 3.7% service, 20.0% sales and office, 0.5% natural resources, construction, and maintenance, 1.7% production, transportation, and material moving

Income: Per capita: $89,082; Median household: $209,583; Average household: $254,305; Households with income of $100,000 or more: 74.5%; Poverty rate: 2.0%

Educational Attainment: High school diploma or higher: 99.4%; Bachelor's degree or higher: 84.5%; Graduate/professional degree or higher: 48.9%

Housing: Homeownership rate: 95.9%; Median home value: $1,111,300; Median year structure built: 1944; Homeowner vacancy rate: 0.0%; Median selected monthly owner costs: $4,000+ with a mortgage, $1,501 without a mortgage; Median gross rent: $3,250 per month; Rental vacancy rate: 0.0%

Health Insurance: 97.6% have insurance; 91.1% have private insurance; 17.5% have public insurance; 2.4% do not have insurance; 1.5% of children under 18 do not have insurance

Transportation: Commute: 53.3% car, 42.0% public transportation, 1.2% walk, 3.4% work from home; Mean travel time to work: 43.0 minutes

PLANDOME MANOR (village).

PLANDOME MANOR (village). Covers a land area of 0.484 square miles and a water area of 0.022 square miles. Located at 40.81° N. Lat; 73.70° W. Long. Elevation is 30 feet.

Population: 832; Growth (since 2000): -0.7%; Density: 1,717.6 persons per square mile; Race: 81.0% White, 0.0% Black/African American, 16.1% Asian, 0.0% American Indian/Alaska Native, 0.0% Native Hawaiian/Other Pacific Islander, 0.8% Two or more races, 4.1% Hispanic of any race; Average household size: 2.93; Median age: 45.3; Age under 18: 28.6%; Age 65 and over: 17.1%; Males per 100 females: 92.1; Marriage status: 18.8% never married, 71.4% now married, 0.3% separated, 6.6% widowed, 3.2% divorced; Foreign born: 13.9%; Speak English only: 81.6%; With disability: 5.9%; Veterans: 4.9%; Ancestry: 24.5% Italian, 23.2% Irish, 12.4% American, 9.7% German, 8.4% Polish

Employment: 27.4% management, business, and financial, 2.1% computer, engineering, and science, 27.9% education, legal, community service, arts, and media, 15.9% healthcare practitioners, 4.1% service, 16.9% sales and office, 5.1% natural resources, construction, and maintenance, 0.5% production, transportation, and material moving

Income: Per capita: $106,160; Median household: $195,000; Average household: $311,714; Households with income of $100,000 or more: 73.6%; Poverty rate: 1.9%

Educational Attainment: High school diploma or higher: 98.1%; Bachelor's degree or higher: 78.8%; Graduate/professional degree or higher: 42.3%

Housing: Homeownership rate: 94.4%; Median home value: $1,557,700; Median year structure built: 1958; Homeowner vacancy rate: 0.0%; Median selected monthly owner costs: $4,000+ with a mortgage, $1,501 without a mortgage; Median gross rent: $3,500+ per month; Rental vacancy rate: 0.0%

Health Insurance: 99.3% have insurance; 96.9% have private insurance; 17.7% have public insurance; 0.7% do not have insurance; 0.0% of children under 18 do not have insurance

Transportation: Commute: 66.8% car, 27.0% public transportation, 0.0% walk, 5.7% work from home; Mean travel time to work: 42.6 minutes

POINT LOOKOUT (CDP).

POINT LOOKOUT (CDP). Covers a land area of 0.226 square miles and a water area of 0 square miles. Located at 40.59° N. Lat; 73.58° W. Long. Elevation is 7 feet.

Population: 1,093; Growth (since 2000): -25.7%; Density: 4,835.9 persons per square mile; Race: 100.0% White, 0.0% Black/African American, 0.0% Asian, 0.0% American Indian/Alaska Native, 0.0% Native Hawaiian/Other Pacific Islander, 0.0% Two or more races, 3.8% Hispanic of any race; Average household size: 2.48; Median age: 45.9; Age under 18: 21.2%; Age 65 and over: 19.8%; Males per 100 females: 93.2; Marriage status: 28.1% never married, 63.2% now married, 4.2% separated, 4.6% widowed, 4.1% divorced; Foreign born: 0.8%; Speak English only: 100.0%; With disability: 8.6%; Veterans: 5.1%; Ancestry: 59.3% Irish, 25.1% German, 18.8% Italian, 9.9% Polish, 5.3% American

Employment: 31.6% management, business, and financial, 1.6% computer, engineering, and science, 15.1% education, legal, community service, arts, and media, 23.4% healthcare practitioners, 8.3% service, 11.8% sales and office, 8.2% natural resources, construction, and maintenance, 0.0% production, transportation, and material moving

Income: Per capita: $78,181; Median household: $146,389; Average household: $194,473; Households with income of $100,000 or more: 63.6%; Poverty rate: n/a

Educational Attainment: High school diploma or higher: 98.9%; Bachelor's degree or higher: 49.0%; Graduate/professional degree or higher: 22.0%

Housing: Homeownership rate: 75.7%; Median home value: $826,300; Median year structure built: Before 1940; Homeowner vacancy rate: 0.0%; Median selected monthly owner costs: $3,303 with a mortgage, $1,270 without a mortgage; Median gross rent: $2,292 per month; Rental vacancy rate: 0.0%

Health Insurance: 89.4% have insurance; 82.3% have private insurance; 25.1% have public insurance; 10.6% do not have insurance; 0.0% of children under 18 do not have insurance

Transportation: Commute: 73.0% car, 22.2% public transportation, 1.6% walk, 1.6% work from home; Mean travel time to work: 36.2 minutes

PORT WASHINGTON (CDP).

PORT WASHINGTON (CDP). Covers a land area of 4.185 square miles and a water area of 1.429 square miles. Located at 40.83° N. Lat; 73.68° W. Long. Elevation is 102 feet.

History: Named for George Washington, first President of the U.S. Initially important for extensive sand pits; center for seaplanes 1900-1920; early College of Long Island, 1920-1930s.

Population: 16,034; Growth (since 2000): 5.4%; Density: 3,831.4 persons per square mile; Race: 83.9% White, 2.1% Black/African American, 8.2% Asian, 0.0% American Indian/Alaska Native, 0.0% Native Hawaiian/Other Pacific Islander, 0.9% Two or more races, 15.9% Hispanic of any race; Average household size: 2.75; Median age: 43.0; Age under 18: 24.8%; Age 65 and over: 22.5%; Males per 100 females: 92.0; Marriage status: 21.7% never married, 63.4% now married, 1.3% separated, 7.6% widowed, 7.3% divorced; Foreign born: 19.8%; Speak English only: 75.7%; With disability: 8.6%; Veterans: 4.5%; Ancestry: 17.5% Italian, 12.7% Irish, 8.8% German, 6.2% American, 5.8% Polish

Employment: 24.5% management, business, and financial, 5.6% computer, engineering, and science, 20.3% education, legal, community service, arts, and media, 6.1% healthcare practitioners, 12.0% service, 21.1% sales and office, 6.4% natural resources, construction, and maintenance, 4.1% production, transportation, and material moving

Income: Per capita: $64,903; Median household: $120,233; Average household: $178,194; Households with income of $100,000 or more: 56.8%; Poverty rate: 2.3%

Educational Attainment: High school diploma or higher: 93.0%; Bachelor's degree or higher: 63.0%; Graduate/professional degree or higher: 29.0%

School District(s)

Port Washington Union Free SD (PK-12)
    Enrollment: 5,535 . . . . (516) 767-5005

Housing: Homeownership rate: 70.5%; Median home value: $771,400; Median year structure built: 1950; Homeowner vacancy rate: 1.0%; Median selected monthly owner costs: $3,996 with a mortgage, $1,501 without a mortgage; Median gross rent: $1,808 per month; Rental vacancy rate: 6.9%

Health Insurance: 94.4% have insurance; 82.4% have private insurance; 28.2% have public insurance; 5.6% do not have insurance; 2.8% of children under 18 do not have insurance

Safety: Violent crime rate: 2.6 per 10,000 population; Property crime rate: 51.1 per 10,000 population

Newspapers: Port Washington News (weekly circulation 8,000)

Transportation: Commute: 55.8% car, 28.6% public transportation, 6.5% walk, 6.8% work from home; Mean travel time to work: 38.7 minutes

PORT WASHINGTON NORTH (village).
Covers a land area of 0.478 square miles and a water area of 0.018 square miles. Located at 40.84° N. Lat; 73.70° W. Long. Elevation is 30 feet.

Population: 3,233; Growth (since 2000): 19.7%; Density: 6,769.8 persons per square mile; Race: 85.6% White, 5.0% Black/African American, 5.9% Asian, 0.0% American Indian/Alaska Native, 0.0% Native Hawaiian/Other Pacific Islander, 0.9% Two or more races, 15.3% Hispanic of any race; Average household size: 2.69; Median age: 43.5; Age under 18: 22.5%; Age 65 and over: 22.5%; Males per 100 females: 91.0; Marriage status: 29.7% never married, 57.4% now married, 0.4% separated, 6.6% widowed, 6.2% divorced; Foreign born: 20.8%; Speak English only: 77.6%; With disability: 8.0%; Veterans: 3.6%; Ancestry: 15.5% Italian, 12.0% Irish, 10.8% Polish, 9.7% American, 7.6% German

Employment: 15.1% management, business, and financial, 4.3% computer, engineering, and science, 25.9% education, legal, community service, arts, and media, 5.2% healthcare practitioners, 10.2% service, 32.8% sales and office, 2.3% natural resources, construction, and maintenance, 4.3% production, transportation, and material moving

Income: Per capita: $55,648; Median household: $96,750; Average household: $147,288; Households with income of $100,000 or more: 49.1%; Poverty rate: 4.8%

Educational Attainment: High school diploma or higher: 90.3%; Bachelor's degree or higher: 58.7%; Graduate/professional degree or higher: 25.7%

Housing: Homeownership rate: 62.4%; Median home value: $766,300; Median year structure built: 1968; Homeowner vacancy rate: 0.0%; Median selected monthly owner costs: $3,753 with a mortgage, $1,501 without a mortgage; Median gross rent: $1,908 per month; Rental vacancy rate: 0.0%

Health Insurance: 94.8% have insurance; 84.3% have private insurance; 26.9% have public insurance; 5.2% do not have insurance; 2.4% of children under 18 do not have insurance

Transportation: Commute: 69.0% car, 23.9% public transportation, 0.7% walk, 6.4% work from home; Mean travel time to work: 37.6 minutes

ROCKVILLE CENTRE (village).
Covers a land area of 3.247 square miles and a water area of 0.085 square miles. Located at 40.66° N. Lat; 73.64° W. Long. Elevation is 26 feet.

History: Named for Reverend Mordecai "Rock" Smith. Seat of Molloy Catholic College for Women. Incorporated 1893.

Population: 24,485; Growth (since 2000): -0.3%; Density: 7,540.3 persons per square mile; Race: 84.3% White, 5.3% Black/African American, 2.4% Asian, 0.0% American Indian/Alaska Native, 0.0% Native Hawaiian/Other Pacific Islander, 3.9% Two or more races, 12.5% Hispanic of any race; Average household size: 2.60; Median age: 42.1; Age under 18: 24.2%; Age 65 and over: 18.0%; Males per 100 females: 88.2; Marriage status: 30.8% never married, 56.1% now married, 1.5% separated, 6.4% widowed, 6.7% divorced; Foreign born: 10.2%; Speak English only: 85.6%; With disability: 9.3%; Veterans: 4.8%; Ancestry: 30.2% Irish, 23.4% Italian, 11.3% German, 5.1% Polish, 4.4% English

Employment: 25.2% management, business, and financial, 3.2% computer, engineering, and science, 22.0% education, legal, community service, arts, and media, 6.6% healthcare practitioners, 14.2% service, 20.8% sales and office, 4.5% natural resources, construction, and maintenance, 3.6% production, transportation, and material moving

Income: Per capita: $58,026; Median household: $105,444; Average household: $150,535; Households with income of $100,000 or more: 52.8%; Poverty rate: 5.5%

Educational Attainment: High school diploma or higher: 96.4%; Bachelor's degree or higher: 59.2%; Graduate/professional degree or higher: 29.0%

School District(s)
Rockville Centre Union Free SD (KG-12)
    Enrollment: 3,533 . . . . (516) 255-8920
Four-year College(s)
Molloy College (Private, Not-for-profit, Roman Catholic)
    Enrollment: 4,980 . . . . (516) 323-3000
    Tuition: In-state $30,310; Out-of-state $30,310

Housing: Homeownership rate: 67.8%; Median home value: $615,100; Median year structure built: 1946; Homeowner vacancy rate: 1.1%; Median selected monthly owner costs: $3,551 with a mortgage, $1,501 without a mortgage; Median gross rent: $1,554 per month; Rental vacancy rate: 0.7%

Health Insurance: 98.0% have insurance; 86.0% have private insurance; 25.5% have public insurance; 2.0% do not have insurance; 0.0% of children under 18 do not have insurance

Hospitals: Mercy Medical Center (375 beds)

Safety: Violent crime rate: 9.7 per 10,000 population; Property crime rate: 75.4 per 10,000 population

Transportation: Commute: 62.7% car, 26.0% public transportation, 4.1% walk, 5.3% work from home; Mean travel time to work: 39.2 minutes

Additional Information Contacts
Village of Rockville Centre . . . . (516) 678-9300
    http://www.rvcny.us

ROOSEVELT (CDP).
Covers a land area of 1.770 square miles and a water area of 0.010 square miles. Located at 40.68° N. Lat; 73.58° W. Long. Elevation is 39 feet.

History: Named for Franklin Delano Roosevelt, 32nd President of the U.S. Troubled school district was taken over by the State Department of Education in mid-1990s for restructuring and improvement.

Population: 16,091; Growth (since 2000): 1.5%; Density: 9,089.0 persons per square mile; Race: 16.0% White, 56.0% Black/African American, 0.1% Asian, 1.4% American Indian/Alaska Native, 0.0% Native Hawaiian/Other Pacific Islander, 13.7% Two or more races, 42.1% Hispanic of any race; Average household size: 3.75; Median age: 35.0; Age under 18: 21.5%; Age 65 and over: 11.8%; Males per 100 females: 93.0; Marriage status: 49.4% never married, 38.8% now married, 2.6% separated, 5.1% widowed, 6.7% divorced; Foreign born: 36.8%; Speak English only: 57.0%; With disability: 6.8%; Veterans: 2.3%; Ancestry: 4.7% Jamaican, 4.2% Haitian, 1.2% Guyanese, 1.0% Nigerian, 0.9% West Indian

Employment: 6.3% management, business, and financial, 1.4% computer, engineering, and science, 7.8% education, legal, community service, arts, and media, 4.8% healthcare practitioners, 29.8% service, 23.9% sales and office, 8.6% natural resources, construction, and maintenance, 17.5% production, transportation, and material moving

Income: Per capita: $24,997; Median household: $78,071; Average household: $87,703; Households with income of $100,000 or more: 39.3%; Poverty rate: 11.1%

Educational Attainment: High school diploma or higher: 72.2%; Bachelor's degree or higher: 16.4%; Graduate/professional degree or higher: 5.6%

School District(s)
Roosevelt Children's Academy Charter School (KG-08)
    Enrollment: 641 . . . . (516) 867-6202
Roosevelt Union Free SD (PK-12)
    Enrollment: 3,434 . . . . (516) 345-7001

Housing: Homeownership rate: 72.3%; Median home value: $278,500; Median year structure built: 1951; Homeowner vacancy rate: 3.0%; Median selected monthly owner costs: $2,572 with a mortgage, $1,126 without a mortgage; Median gross rent: $1,766 per month; Rental vacancy rate: 6.4%

Health Insurance: 84.2% have insurance; 60.7% have private insurance; 31.4% have public insurance; 15.8% do not have insurance; 7.0% of children under 18 do not have insurance

Transportation: Commute: 78.5% car, 15.2% public transportation, 2.4% walk, 2.5% work from home; Mean travel time to work: 32.5 minutes

ROSLYN (village).
Covers a land area of 0.645 square miles and a water area of 0.012 square miles. Located at 40.80° N. Lat; 73.65° W. Long. Elevation is 39 feet.

History: Cedarmere, home of William Cullen Bryant, is here. Incorporated 1932.

Population: 2,849; Growth (since 2000): 10.9%; Density: 4,416.5 persons per square mile; Race: 82.5% White, 0.6% Black/African American, 12.5% Asian, 0.0% American Indian/Alaska Native, 0.0% Native Hawaiian/Other Pacific Islander, 2.4% Two or more races, 6.0% Hispanic of any race; Average household size: 2.09; Median age: 49.7; Age under 18: 16.7%; Age 65 and over: 27.7%; Males per 100 females: 82.7; Marriage status: 25.9% never married, 45.5% now married, 0.5% separated, 14.4% widowed, 14.2% divorced; Foreign born: 20.9%; Speak English only: 76.2%; With disability: 10.2%; Veterans: 4.0%; Ancestry: 14.5% American, 10.0% Italian, 9.0% Iranian, 7.3% Russian, 6.2% Irish

Employment: 25.3% management, business, and financial, 6.4% computer, engineering, and science, 16.9% education, legal, community service, arts, and media, 13.6% healthcare practitioners, 10.8% service, 23.7% sales and office, 2.0% natural resources, construction, and maintenance, 1.3% production, transportation, and material moving

Income: Per capita: $73,940; Median household: $102,857; Average household: $164,122; Households with income of $100,000 or more: 51.4%; Poverty rate: 6.7%
Educational Attainment: High school diploma or higher: 95.9%; Bachelor's degree or higher: 67.5%; Graduate/professional degree or higher: 32.0%
Housing: Homeownership rate: 65.8%; Median home value: $468,400; Median year structure built: 1961; Homeowner vacancy rate: 2.3%; Median selected monthly owner costs: $3,361 with a mortgage, $1,338 without a mortgage; Median gross rent: $2,271 per month; Rental vacancy rate: 3.2%
Health Insurance: 91.6% have insurance; 82.1% have private insurance; 26.0% have public insurance; 8.4% do not have insurance; 5.8% of children under 18 do not have insurance
Hospitals: Saint Francis Hospital - Roslyn (279 beds)
Transportation: Commute: 77.2% car, 11.0% public transportation, 5.0% walk, 6.8% work from home; Mean travel time to work: 34.5 minutes

ROSLYN ESTATES (village). Covers a land area of 0.438 square miles and a water area of 0 square miles. Located at 40.79° N. Lat; 73.66° W. Long. Elevation is 233 feet.
Population: 1,127; Growth (since 2000): -6.9%; Density: 2,575.4 persons per square mile; Race: 93.4% White, 0.3% Black/African American, 5.9% Asian, 0.0% American Indian/Alaska Native, 0.0% Native Hawaiian/Other Pacific Islander, 0.4% Two or more races, 0.4% Hispanic of any race; Average household size: 2.92; Median age: 45.5; Age under 18: 29.0%; Age 65 and over: 20.5%; Males per 100 females: 96.7; Marriage status: 15.8% never married, 74.4% now married, 0.8% separated, 4.9% widowed, 4.8% divorced; Foreign born: 15.3%; Speak English only: 81.0%; With disability: 5.6%; Veterans: 3.3%; Ancestry: 19.8% American, 7.9% Russian, 7.7% Eastern European, 6.2% European, 6.1% Polish
Employment: 30.8% management, business, and financial, 1.8% computer, engineering, and science, 16.7% education, legal, community service, arts, and media, 20.3% healthcare practitioners, 2.4% service, 25.6% sales and office, 0.8% natural resources, construction, and maintenance, 1.6% production, transportation, and material moving
Income: Per capita: $114,189; Median household: $210,000; Average household: $337,432; Households with income of $100,000 or more: 72.8%; Poverty rate: 4.2%
Educational Attainment: High school diploma or higher: 99.2%; Bachelor's degree or higher: 80.0%; Graduate/professional degree or higher: 46.7%
Housing: Homeownership rate: 95.3%; Median home value: $1,077,500; Median year structure built: 1955; Homeowner vacancy rate: 0.0%; Median selected monthly owner costs: $4,000+ with a mortgage, $1,501 without a mortgage; Median gross rent: n/a per month; Rental vacancy rate: 14.3%
Health Insurance: 97.5% have insurance; 89.6% have private insurance; 20.9% have public insurance; 2.5% do not have insurance; 2.3% of children under 18 do not have insurance
Transportation: Commute: 75.5% car, 18.4% public transportation, 0.8% walk, 5.3% work from home; Mean travel time to work: 35.7 minutes

ROSLYN HARBOR (village). Covers a land area of 1.186 square miles and a water area of 0.002 square miles. Located at 40.81° N. Lat; 73.64° W. Long. Elevation is 108 feet.
Population: 922; Growth (since 2000): -9.9%; Density: 777.6 persons per square mile; Race: 84.2% White, 1.1% Black/African American, 13.1% Asian, 0.0% American Indian/Alaska Native, 0.0% Native Hawaiian/Other Pacific Islander, 1.6% Two or more races, 3.8% Hispanic of any race; Average household size: 2.88; Median age: 49.8; Age under 18: 21.3%; Age 65 and over: 23.8%; Males per 100 females: 90.4; Marriage status: 24.8% never married, 62.6% now married, 0.0% separated, 7.0% widowed, 5.6% divorced; Foreign born: 21.7%; Speak English only: 67.8%; With disability: 7.2%; Veterans: 3.4%; Ancestry: 14.8% American, 9.3% Italian, 9.1% Iranian, 7.8% Polish, 6.9% Russian
Employment: 22.9% management, business, and financial, 6.5% computer, engineering, and science, 18.4% education, legal, community service, arts, and media, 12.3% healthcare practitioners, 2.2% service, 34.1% sales and office, 2.2% natural resources, construction, and maintenance, 1.3% production, transportation, and material moving
Income: Per capita: $89,383; Median household: $200,000; Average household: $257,578; Households with income of $100,000 or more: 73.8%; Poverty rate: 3.0%

Educational Attainment: High school diploma or higher: 98.9%; Bachelor's degree or higher: 75.3%; Graduate/professional degree or higher: 43.1%
Housing: Homeownership rate: 91.9%; Median home value: $1,137,300; Median year structure built: 1960; Homeowner vacancy rate: 1.0%; Median selected monthly owner costs: $4,000+ with a mortgage, $1,501 without a mortgage; Median gross rent: $2,286 per month; Rental vacancy rate: 0.0%
Health Insurance: 97.2% have insurance; 86.6% have private insurance; 24.4% have public insurance; 2.8% do not have insurance; 3.3% of children under 18 do not have insurance
Transportation: Commute: 72.9% car, 18.1% public transportation, 0.0% walk, 8.9% work from home; Mean travel time to work: 35.7 minutes

ROSLYN HEIGHTS (CDP). Covers a land area of 1.476 square miles and a water area of 0 square miles. Located at 40.78° N. Lat; 73.64° W. Long. Elevation is 177 feet.
History: Ebenezer Close, stated that the rules [of the Post Office in setting up new names] specified a short, pleasant-sounding name which had not been chosen for any Post Office in the United States. Of the names proposed, only ten fitted the rules. Of these ten, the name Roslyn, said to have been proposed by Mr. Cairns because our valley reminded him of Roslin, Scotland, received the most votes and was subsequently approved by all.
Population: 6,802; Growth (since 2000): 8.1%; Density: 4,609.0 persons per square mile; Race: 66.1% White, 6.7% Black/African American, 21.9% Asian, 0.2% American Indian/Alaska Native, 0.0% Native Hawaiian/Other Pacific Islander, 1.9% Two or more races, 13.5% Hispanic of any race; Average household size: 3.24; Median age: 39.0; Age under 18: 24.5%; Age 65 and over: 14.9%; Males per 100 females: 94.4; Marriage status: 32.6% never married, 57.2% now married, 2.4% separated, 5.2% widowed, 5.1% divorced; Foreign born: 30.0%; Speak English only: 60.8%; With disability: 8.3%; Veterans: 3.2%; Ancestry: 11.4% Italian, 10.1% American, 5.3% Russian, 4.0% Polish, 3.8% German
Employment: 23.8% management, business, and financial, 3.6% computer, engineering, and science, 16.3% education, legal, community service, arts, and media, 14.1% healthcare practitioners, 14.5% service, 18.4% sales and office, 2.6% natural resources, construction, and maintenance, 6.6% production, transportation, and material moving
Income: Per capita: $53,711; Median household: $113,913; Average household: $169,639; Households with income of $100,000 or more: 55.9%; Poverty rate: 5.8%
Educational Attainment: High school diploma or higher: 93.7%; Bachelor's degree or higher: 63.6%; Graduate/professional degree or higher: 30.2%

School District(s)
East Williston Union Free SD (KG-12)
    Enrollment: 1,697 . . . . (516) 333-3758
Roslyn Union Free SD (PK-12)
    Enrollment: 3,112 . . . . (516) 801-5001
Housing: Homeownership rate: 79.4%; Median home value: $771,100; Median year structure built: 1959; Homeowner vacancy rate: 2.6%; Median selected monthly owner costs: $3,947 with a mortgage, $1,501 without a mortgage; Median gross rent: n/a per month; Rental vacancy rate: 9.3%
Health Insurance: 91.6% have insurance; 79.9% have private insurance; 23.0% have public insurance; 8.4% do not have insurance; 2.0% of children under 18 do not have insurance
Transportation: Commute: 69.5% car, 21.7% public transportation, 1.6% walk, 6.6% work from home; Mean travel time to work: 42.4 minutes

RUSSELL GARDENS (village). Covers a land area of 0.174 square miles and a water area of 0 square miles. Located at 40.78° N. Lat; 73.73° W. Long. Elevation is 131 feet.
Population: 878; Growth (since 2000): -18.2%; Density: 5,056.8 persons per square mile; Race: 69.8% White, 0.0% Black/African American, 28.8% Asian, 0.0% American Indian/Alaska Native, 0.0% Native Hawaiian/Other Pacific Islander, 1.3% Two or more races, 4.7% Hispanic of any race; Average household size: 2.72; Median age: 48.3; Age under 18: 20.8%; Age 65 and over: 21.3%; Males per 100 females: 94.0; Marriage status: 24.0% never married, 68.2% now married, 0.4% separated, 3.7% widowed, 4.2% divorced; Foreign born: 28.2%; Speak English only: 64.3%; With disability: 10.5%; Veterans: 4.2%; Ancestry: 10.7% Russian, 9.6% American, 9.0% Polish, 4.4% Italian, 4.3% Eastern European
Employment: 37.1% management, business, and financial, 5.1% computer, engineering, and science, 22.9% education, legal, community

service, arts, and media, 13.1% healthcare practitioners, 4.0% service, 16.4% sales and office, 1.1% natural resources, construction, and maintenance, 0.4% production, transportation, and material moving
Income: Per capita: $87,487; Median household: $177,813; Average household: $240,708; Households with income of $100,000 or more: 63.3%; Poverty rate: 1.9%
Educational Attainment: High school diploma or higher: 93.5%; Bachelor's degree or higher: 78.1%; Graduate/professional degree or higher: 44.7%
Housing: Homeownership rate: 76.6%; Median home value: $1,087,100; Median year structure built: 1946; Homeowner vacancy rate: 2.4%; Median selected monthly owner costs: $4,000+ with a mortgage, $1,501 without a mortgage; Median gross rent: $1,727 per month; Rental vacancy rate: 8.6%
Health Insurance: 97.6% have insurance; 86.4% have private insurance; 22.9% have public insurance; 2.4% do not have insurance; 1.1% of children under 18 do not have insurance
Transportation: Commute: 53.1% car, 40.3% public transportation, 0.9% walk, 5.3% work from home; Mean travel time to work: 42.8 minutes

SADDLE ROCK (village). Covers a land area of 0.246 square miles and a water area of 0.022 square miles. Located at 40.79° N. Lat; 73.75° W. Long. Elevation is 82 feet.
Population: 728; Growth (since 2000): -8.0%; Density: 2,957.8 persons per square mile; Race: 90.1% White, 2.7% Black/African American, 5.6% Asian, 0.0% American Indian/Alaska Native, 0.0% Native Hawaiian/Other Pacific Islander, 1.5% Two or more races, 1.1% Hispanic of any race; Average household size: 3.26; Median age: 46.5; Age under 18: 23.4%; Age 65 and over: 26.4%; Males per 100 females: 103.9; Marriage status: 19.8% never married, 68.1% now married, 0.0% separated, 5.0% widowed, 7.1% divorced; Foreign born: 39.6%; Speak English only: 46.7%; With disability: 8.9%; Veterans: 3.8%; Ancestry: 22.5% Iranian, 8.8% Polish, 5.9% Russian, 4.8% American, 3.4% Israeli
Employment: 25.6% management, business, and financial, 2.2% computer, engineering, and science, 17.7% education, legal, community service, arts, and media, 11.7% healthcare practitioners, 10.8% service, 29.1% sales and office, 0.6% natural resources, construction, and maintenance, 2.2% production, transportation, and material moving
Income: Per capita: $70,577; Median household: $162,083; Average household: $220,209; Households with income of $100,000 or more: 66.0%; Poverty rate: 3.3%
Educational Attainment: High school diploma or higher: 94.5%; Bachelor's degree or higher: 63.5%; Graduate/professional degree or higher: 32.6%
Housing: Homeownership rate: 95.1%; Median home value: $1,375,000; Median year structure built: 1957; Homeowner vacancy rate: 0.0%; Median selected monthly owner costs: $4,000+ with a mortgage, $1,501 without a mortgage; Median gross rent: n/a per month; Rental vacancy rate: 0.0%
Health Insurance: 98.2% have insurance; 84.5% have private insurance; 28.4% have public insurance; 1.8% do not have insurance; 1.2% of children under 18 do not have insurance
Transportation: Commute: 67.8% car, 24.5% public transportation, 0.0% walk, 7.7% work from home; Mean travel time to work: 39.6 minutes
Additional Information Contacts
Village of Saddle Rock . . . . (516) 482-9400
  http://www.saddlerock.org

SADDLE ROCK ESTATES (CDP). Covers a land area of 0.078 square miles and a water area of 0 square miles. Located at 40.79° N. Lat; 73.74° W. Long. Elevation is 26 feet.
Population: 253; Growth (since 2000): -40.3%; Density: 3,263.4 persons per square mile; Race: 84.6% White, 0.0% Black/African American, 15.4% Asian, 0.0% American Indian/Alaska Native, 0.0% Native Hawaiian/Other Pacific Islander, 0.0% Two or more races, 0.0% Hispanic of any race; Average household size: 2.81; Median age: 51.7; Age under 18: 18.2%; Age 65 and over: 13.4%; Males per 100 females: 99.1; Marriage status: 27.2% never married, 63.1% now married, 0.0% separated, 4.6% widowed, 5.1% divorced; Foreign born: 28.1%; Speak English only: 60.6%; With disability: 17.0%; Veterans: 3.9%; Ancestry: 10.7% American, 7.5% Finnish, 6.3% Iranian, 6.3% Polish, 3.6% Eastern European
Employment: 37.9% management, business, and financial, 17.7% computer, engineering, and science, 6.5% education, legal, community service, arts, and media, 0.0% healthcare practitioners, 0.0% service, 37.9% sales and office, 0.0% natural resources, construction, and maintenance, 0.0% production, transportation, and material moving

Income: Per capita: $53,369; Median household: $157,188; Average household: $146,353; Households with income of $100,000 or more: 67.8%; Poverty rate: n/a
Educational Attainment: High school diploma or higher: 94.3%; Bachelor's degree or higher: 75.3%; Graduate/professional degree or higher: 46.4%
Housing: Homeownership rate: 100.0%; Median home value: $1,218,800; Median year structure built: Before 1940; Homeowner vacancy rate: 0.0%; Median selected monthly owner costs: $4,000+ with a mortgage, $1,501 without a mortgage; Median gross rent: n/a per month; Rental vacancy rate: 0.0%
Health Insurance: 96.4% have insurance; 81.0% have private insurance; 34.0% have public insurance; 3.6% do not have insurance; 0.0% of children under 18 do not have insurance
Transportation: Commute: 37.1% car, 54.8% public transportation, 0.0% walk, 8.1% work from home; Mean travel time to work: 48.6 minutes

SALISBURY (CDP). Covers a land area of 1.737 square miles and a water area of 0.024 square miles. Located at 40.75° N. Lat; 73.56° W. Long. Elevation is 108 feet.
Population: 12,474; Growth (since 2000): 1.1%; Density: 7,181.8 persons per square mile; Race: 76.4% White, 0.8% Black/African American, 15.3% Asian, 0.2% American Indian/Alaska Native, 0.0% Native Hawaiian/Other Pacific Islander, 3.1% Two or more races, 13.6% Hispanic of any race; Average household size: 3.21; Median age: 42.9; Age under 18: 21.4%; Age 65 and over: 17.5%; Males per 100 females: 92.3; Marriage status: 28.3% never married, 60.5% now married, 0.6% separated, 6.4% widowed, 4.8% divorced; Foreign born: 25.6%; Speak English only: 66.8%; With disability: 10.3%; Veterans: 4.0%; Ancestry: 23.7% Italian, 12.4% Irish, 7.4% German, 4.0% Polish, 3.7% Afghan
Employment: 18.2% management, business, and financial, 6.7% computer, engineering, and science, 12.5% education, legal, community service, arts, and media, 9.2% healthcare practitioners, 13.5% service, 25.3% sales and office, 6.6% natural resources, construction, and maintenance, 8.0% production, transportation, and material moving
Income: Per capita: $42,365; Median household: $111,250; Average household: $131,432; Households with income of $100,000 or more: 56.0%; Poverty rate: 3.5%
Educational Attainment: High school diploma or higher: 92.0%; Bachelor's degree or higher: 44.6%; Graduate/professional degree or higher: 16.3%
Housing: Homeownership rate: 91.9%; Median home value: $439,200; Median year structure built: 1955; Homeowner vacancy rate: 0.3%; Median selected monthly owner costs: $2,981 with a mortgage, $1,233 without a mortgage; Median gross rent: $1,262 per month; Rental vacancy rate: 0.0%
Health Insurance: 96.1% have insurance; 85.0% have private insurance; 24.6% have public insurance; 3.9% do not have insurance; 1.5% of children under 18 do not have insurance
Transportation: Commute: 84.0% car, 10.9% public transportation, 0.8% walk, 3.7% work from home; Mean travel time to work: 34.9 minutes

SANDS POINT (village). Covers a land area of 4.230 square miles and a water area of 1.379 square miles. Located at 40.85° N. Lat; 73.70° W. Long. Elevation is 43 feet.
History: Sands Point promontory (lighthouse) is at tip of Manhasset Neck, Northwest of village.
Population: 2,856; Growth (since 2000): 2.5%; Density: 675.1 persons per square mile; Race: 87.3% White, 1.1% Black/African American, 9.5% Asian, 0.0% American Indian/Alaska Native, 0.0% Native Hawaiian/Other Pacific Islander, 1.4% Two or more races, 3.4% Hispanic of any race; Average household size: 2.94; Median age: 47.7; Age under 18: 26.5%; Age 65 and over: 18.1%; Males per 100 females: 95.7; Marriage status: 20.0% never married, 69.8% now married, 0.0% separated, 3.6% widowed, 6.7% divorced; Foreign born: 15.8%; Speak English only: 84.9%; With disability: 6.5%; Veterans: 2.2%; Ancestry: 12.9% Russian, 11.6% American, 9.5% Italian, 9.1% Polish, 8.5% Irish
Employment: 35.8% management, business, and financial, 6.1% computer, engineering, and science, 18.7% education, legal, community service, arts, and media, 5.0% healthcare practitioners, 6.3% service, 24.5% sales and office, 2.8% natural resources, construction, and maintenance, 0.7% production, transportation, and material moving
Income: Per capita: $136,542; Median household: $231,607; Average household: $405,772; Households with income of $100,000 or more: 84.2%; Poverty rate: 1.8%

Educational Attainment: High school diploma or higher: 96.2%; Bachelor's degree or higher: 82.2%; Graduate/professional degree or higher: 42.6%

Housing: Homeownership rate: 92.9%; Median home value: 2 million+; Median year structure built: 1959; Homeowner vacancy rate: 0.0%; Median selected monthly owner costs: $4,000+ with a mortgage, $1,501 without a mortgage; Median gross rent: $3,224 per month; Rental vacancy rate: 0.0%

Health Insurance: 99.8% have insurance; 92.4% have private insurance; 20.2% have public insurance; 0.2% do not have insurance; 0.0% of children under 18 do not have insurance

Safety: Violent crime rate: 0.0 per 10,000 population; Property crime rate: 34.4 per 10,000 population

Transportation: Commute: 52.8% car, 31.2% public transportation, 3.5% walk, 11.1% work from home; Mean travel time to work: 47.0 minutes

Additional Information Contacts
Village of Sands Point . . . . (516) 883-3044
http://www.sandspoint.org

SEA CLIFF (village). Covers a land area of 1.115 square miles and a water area of 0.847 square miles. Located at 40.85° N. Lat; 73.65° W. Long. Elevation is 184 feet.

History: Incorporated 1883.

Population: 5,085; Growth (since 2000): 0.4%; Density: 4,561.2 persons per square mile; Race: 91.2% White, 3.3% Black/African American, 1.0% Asian, 0.0% American Indian/Alaska Native, 0.0% Native Hawaiian/Other Pacific Islander, 2.2% Two or more races, 7.1% Hispanic of any race; Average household size: 2.64; Median age: 47.4; Age under 18: 21.9%; Age 65 and over: 16.4%; Males per 100 females: 94.0; Marriage status: 28.3% never married, 57.7% now married, 1.3% separated, 6.1% widowed, 7.9% divorced; Foreign born: 11.5%; Speak English only: 81.7%; With disability: 9.1%; Veterans: 3.9%; Ancestry: 26.0% Irish, 21.6% Italian, 16.2% German, 8.3% English, 7.1% Russian

Employment: 19.6% management, business, and financial, 5.4% computer, engineering, and science, 29.0% education, legal, community service, arts, and media, 6.0% healthcare practitioners, 10.4% service, 22.1% sales and office, 4.3% natural resources, construction, and maintenance, 3.3% production, transportation, and material moving

Income: Per capita: $56,688; Median household: $115,691; Average household: $150,244; Households with income of $100,000 or more: 59.4%; Poverty rate: 6.9%

Educational Attainment: High school diploma or higher: 97.9%; Bachelor's degree or higher: 65.4%; Graduate/professional degree or higher: 34.4%

School District(s)
North Shore Central SD (KG-12)
    Enrollment: 2,688 . . . . (516) 277-7801

Housing: Homeownership rate: 70.5%; Median home value: $658,000; Median year structure built: Before 1940; Homeowner vacancy rate: 1.7%; Median selected monthly owner costs: $3,400 with a mortgage, $1,429 without a mortgage; Median gross rent: $1,954 per month; Rental vacancy rate: 3.8%

Health Insurance: 96.6% have insurance; 90.2% have private insurance; 20.2% have public insurance; 3.4% do not have insurance; 0.0% of children under 18 do not have insurance

Transportation: Commute: 73.7% car, 14.4% public transportation, 4.6% walk, 7.0% work from home; Mean travel time to work: 33.7 minutes

Additional Information Contacts
Village of Sea Cliff . . . . (516) 671-0080
http://www.seacliff-ny.gov

SEAFORD (CDP). Covers a land area of 2.611 square miles and a water area of 0.054 square miles. Located at 40.67° N. Lat; 73.49° W. Long. Elevation is 10 feet.

History: The county Museum of Natural History is here. Settled 1643.

Population: 15,405; Growth (since 2000): -2.4%; Density: 5,901.0 persons per square mile; Race: 96.6% White, 0.0% Black/African American, 1.8% Asian, 0.1% American Indian/Alaska Native, 0.0% Native Hawaiian/Other Pacific Islander, 1.2% Two or more races, 6.4% Hispanic of any race; Average household size: 3.02; Median age: 42.1; Age under 18: 22.1%; Age 65 and over: 16.3%; Males per 100 females: 94.9; Marriage status: 29.9% never married, 59.6% now married, 1.2% separated, 4.5% widowed, 6.0% divorced; Foreign born: 7.8%; Speak English only: 91.1%; With disability: 8.6%; Veterans: 6.0%; Ancestry: 36.3% Italian, 30.4% Irish, 18.7% German, 4.1% Polish, 4.0% English

Employment: 17.3% management, business, and financial, 4.6% computer, engineering, and science, 15.7% education, legal, community service, arts, and media, 6.7% healthcare practitioners, 13.9% service, 24.9% sales and office, 11.0% natural resources, construction, and maintenance, 5.9% production, transportation, and material moving

Income: Per capita: $47,804; Median household: $123,177; Average household: $141,664; Households with income of $100,000 or more: 62.7%; Poverty rate: 3.3%

Educational Attainment: High school diploma or higher: 96.7%; Bachelor's degree or higher: 43.8%; Graduate/professional degree or higher: 17.7%

School District(s)
Levittown Union Free SD (KG-12)
    Enrollment: 7,166 . . . . (516) 434-7020
Seaford Union Free SD (KG-12)
    Enrollment: 2,265 . . . . (516) 592-4002

Housing: Homeownership rate: 89.8%; Median home value: $449,800; Median year structure built: 1957; Homeowner vacancy rate: 0.0%; Median selected monthly owner costs: $3,173 with a mortgage, $1,289 without a mortgage; Median gross rent: $1,950 per month; Rental vacancy rate: 0.0%

Health Insurance: 98.2% have insurance; 91.9% have private insurance; 21.9% have public insurance; 1.8% do not have insurance; 0.0% of children under 18 do not have insurance

Transportation: Commute: 78.7% car, 14.8% public transportation, 1.1% walk, 5.1% work from home; Mean travel time to work: 36.5 minutes

SEARINGTOWN (CDP). Covers a land area of 0.929 square miles and a water area of 0 square miles. Located at 40.77° N. Lat; 73.66° W. Long. Elevation is 125 feet.

History: The hamlet derives its name from the Searing family, once numerous in the area and among the first parishioners at the Methodist church that was erected in 1788.

Population: 4,572; Growth (since 2000): -9.2%; Density: 4,923.5 persons per square mile; Race: 50.9% White, 1.2% Black/African American, 43.1% Asian, 0.5% American Indian/Alaska Native, 0.0% Native Hawaiian/Other Pacific Islander, 2.3% Two or more races, 1.5% Hispanic of any race; Average household size: 3.18; Median age: 48.4; Age under 18: 19.6%; Age 65 and over: 23.1%; Males per 100 females: 95.4; Marriage status: 24.4% never married, 65.4% now married, 0.2% separated, 6.1% widowed, 4.1% divorced; Foreign born: 34.3%; Speak English only: 53.2%; With disability: 9.4%; Veterans: 4.6%; Ancestry: 10.8% Italian, 5.4% American, 5.1% Greek, 5.0% Polish, 4.4% Iranian

Employment: 26.5% management, business, and financial, 4.2% computer, engineering, and science, 11.8% education, legal, community service, arts, and media, 14.0% healthcare practitioners, 7.6% service, 30.3% sales and office, 4.1% natural resources, construction, and maintenance, 1.4% production, transportation, and material moving

Income: Per capita: $61,356; Median household: $154,570; Average household: $192,583; Households with income of $100,000 or more: 64.0%; Poverty rate: 3.2%

Educational Attainment: High school diploma or higher: 92.8%; Bachelor's degree or higher: 62.9%; Graduate/professional degree or higher: 34.1%

Housing: Homeownership rate: 98.1%; Median home value: $829,500; Median year structure built: 1961; Homeowner vacancy rate: 3.4%; Median selected monthly owner costs: $4,000+ with a mortgage, $1,501 without a mortgage; Median gross rent: n/a per month; Rental vacancy rate: 0.0%

Health Insurance: 97.0% have insurance; 85.8% have private insurance; 27.4% have public insurance; 3.0% do not have insurance; 1.3% of children under 18 do not have insurance

Transportation: Commute: 76.7% car, 15.2% public transportation, 1.6% walk, 4.5% work from home; Mean travel time to work: 39.0 minutes

SOUTH FARMINGDALE (CDP). Covers a land area of 2.218 square miles and a water area of 0.004 square miles. Located at 40.72° N. Lat; 73.45° W. Long. Elevation is 59 feet.

History: South Farmingdale is a hamlet and census-designated place (CDP) in the Town of Oyster Bay in Nassau County, New York.

Population: 15,294; Growth (since 2000): 1.5%; Density: 6,896.6 persons per square mile; Race: 89.0% White, 3.2% Black/African American, 5.3% Asian, 0.0% American Indian/Alaska Native, 0.0% Native Hawaiian/Other Pacific Islander, 1.0% Two or more races, 12.7% Hispanic of any race; Average household size: 3.13; Median age: 42.5; Age under 18: 22.2%; Age 65 and over: 15.3%; Males per 100 females: 95.7; Marriage status:

26.8% never married, 61.5% now married, 1.9% separated, 6.5% widowed, 5.2% divorced; Foreign born: 10.3%; Speak English only: 85.0%; With disability: 7.5%; Veterans: 5.4%; Ancestry: 41.0% Italian, 21.9% Irish, 16.7% German, 6.8% Polish, 3.1% English

Employment: 15.7% management, business, and financial, 4.7% computer, engineering, and science, 11.6% education, legal, community service, arts, and media, 5.3% healthcare practitioners, 18.1% service, 30.4% sales and office, 6.4% natural resources, construction, and maintenance, 7.9% production, transportation, and material moving

Income: Per capita: $40,187; Median household: $113,224; Average household: $122,583; Households with income of $100,000 or more: 56.2%; Poverty rate: 3.6%

Educational Attainment: High school diploma or higher: 94.8%; Bachelor's degree or higher: 34.5%; Graduate/professional degree or higher: 14.2%

Housing: Homeownership rate: 92.9%; Median home value: $388,700; Median year structure built: 1956; Homeowner vacancy rate: 0.5%; Median selected monthly owner costs: $2,790 with a mortgage, $1,163 without a mortgage; Median gross rent: $2,125 per month; Rental vacancy rate: 12.5%

Health Insurance: 97.3% have insurance; 84.5% have private insurance; 24.0% have public insurance; 2.7% do not have insurance; 0.2% of children under 18 do not have insurance

Transportation: Commute: 81.9% car, 11.6% public transportation, 1.4% walk, 4.7% work from home; Mean travel time to work: 32.6 minutes

SOUTH FLORAL PARK (village).
Covers a land area of 0.096 square miles and a water area of 0 square miles. Located at 40.71° N. Lat; 73.70° W. Long. Elevation is 72 feet.

History: Until 1931 called Jamaica Square.

Population: 2,006; Growth (since 2000): 27.1%; Density: 20,900.8 persons per square mile; Race: 14.4% White, 60.7% Black/African American, 10.5% Asian, 0.3% American Indian/Alaska Native, 0.0% Native Hawaiian/Other Pacific Islander, 5.3% Two or more races, 19.7% Hispanic of any race; Average household size: 3.60; Median age: 35.8; Age under 18: 23.5%; Age 65 and over: 10.0%; Males per 100 females: 87.1; Marriage status: 37.4% never married, 47.4% now married, 1.1% separated, 2.9% widowed, 12.3% divorced; Foreign born: 37.5%; Speak English only: 67.4%; With disability: 7.8%; Veterans: 2.2%; Ancestry: 10.6% Haitian, 5.5% Trinidadian and Tobagonian, 5.3% Jamaican, 2.8% Guyanese, 2.8% American

Employment: 18.2% management, business, and financial, 2.4% computer, engineering, and science, 13.6% education, legal, community service, arts, and media, 9.0% healthcare practitioners, 19.8% service, 21.7% sales and office, 6.9% natural resources, construction, and maintenance, 8.4% production, transportation, and material moving

Income: Per capita: $32,613; Median household: $95,781; Average household: $111,157; Households with income of $100,000 or more: 47.7%; Poverty rate: 1.7%

Educational Attainment: High school diploma or higher: 92.9%; Bachelor's degree or higher: 26.5%; Graduate/professional degree or higher: 9.8%

Housing: Homeownership rate: 82.8%; Median home value: $395,400; Median year structure built: 1956; Homeowner vacancy rate: 2.1%; Median selected monthly owner costs: $3,087 with a mortgage, $1,112 without a mortgage; Median gross rent: $1,458 per month; Rental vacancy rate: 9.4%

Health Insurance: 94.9% have insurance; 78.1% have private insurance; 26.9% have public insurance; 5.1% do not have insurance; 1.9% of children under 18 do not have insurance

Transportation: Commute: 75.4% car, 17.8% public transportation, 1.1% walk, 3.6% work from home; Mean travel time to work: 39.8 minutes

SOUTH HEMPSTEAD (CDP).
Covers a land area of 0.578 square miles and a water area of 0 square miles. Located at 40.68° N. Lat; 73.62° W. Long. Elevation is 43 feet.

Population: 3,044; Growth (since 2000): -4.5%; Density: 5,263.2 persons per square mile; Race: 82.6% White, 8.4% Black/African American, 1.6% Asian, 0.0% American Indian/Alaska Native, 0.0% Native Hawaiian/Other Pacific Islander, 1.2% Two or more races, 11.2% Hispanic of any race; Average household size: 2.99; Median age: 41.1; Age under 18: 25.0%; Age 65 and over: 14.7%; Males per 100 females: 93.3; Marriage status: 29.2% never married, 57.1% now married, 2.9% separated, 5.0% widowed, 8.7% divorced; Foreign born: 10.4%; Speak English only: 88.5%;

With disability: 6.6%; Veterans: 6.5%; Ancestry: 31.3% Irish, 23.3% Italian, 13.7% German, 6.5% Russian, 6.0% English

Employment: 21.9% management, business, and financial, 6.5% computer, engineering, and science, 16.6% education, legal, community service, arts, and media, 4.4% healthcare practitioners, 15.4% service, 22.0% sales and office, 10.3% natural resources, construction, and maintenance, 3.0% production, transportation, and material moving

Income: Per capita: $45,765; Median household: $113,750; Average household: $133,936; Households with income of $100,000 or more: 55.9%; Poverty rate: 3.6%

Educational Attainment: High school diploma or higher: 96.7%; Bachelor's degree or higher: 49.7%; Graduate/professional degree or higher: 22.8%

School District(s)
Rockville Centre Union Free SD (KG-12)
    Enrollment: 3,533 . . . . (516) 255-8920

Housing: Homeownership rate: 88.0%; Median home value: $398,000; Median year structure built: 1950; Homeowner vacancy rate: 2.7%; Median selected monthly owner costs: $2,871 with a mortgage, $1,367 without a mortgage; Median gross rent: $1,850 per month; Rental vacancy rate: 0.0%

Health Insurance: 94.6% have insurance; 79.4% have private insurance; 28.1% have public insurance; 5.4% do not have insurance; 2.5% of children under 18 do not have insurance

Transportation: Commute: 84.5% car, 11.1% public transportation, 1.2% walk, 2.7% work from home; Mean travel time to work: 33.4 minutes

SOUTH VALLEY STREAM (CDP).
Covers a land area of 0.873 square miles and a water area of 0 square miles. Located at 40.66° N. Lat; 73.72° W. Long. Elevation is 10 feet.

History: South Valley Stream is a hamlet in Nassau County, New York, located in the southern part of the Town of Hempstead.

Population: 6,924; Growth (since 2000): 22.8%; Density: 7,932.8 persons per square mile; Race: 41.9% White, 31.5% Black/African American, 16.1% Asian, 0.0% American Indian/Alaska Native, 0.1% Native Hawaiian/Other Pacific Islander, 2.7% Two or more races, 14.1% Hispanic of any race; Average household size: 3.39; Median age: 35.7; Age under 18: 24.1%; Age 65 and over: 13.9%; Males per 100 females: 92.1; Marriage status: 31.5% never married, 57.0% now married, 0.6% separated, 3.9% widowed, 7.6% divorced; Foreign born: 34.1%; Speak English only: 64.8%; With disability: 6.7%; Veterans: 3.5%; Ancestry: 6.5% Russian, 5.7% Italian, 5.6% American, 5.4% Haitian, 3.2% French

Employment: 19.6% management, business, and financial, 4.6% computer, engineering, and science, 13.4% education, legal, community service, arts, and media, 11.1% healthcare practitioners, 14.8% service, 23.6% sales and office, 7.5% natural resources, construction, and maintenance, 5.5% production, transportation, and material moving

Income: Per capita: $44,872; Median household: $132,619; Average household: $146,578; Households with income of $100,000 or more: 58.3%; Poverty rate: 3.0%

Educational Attainment: High school diploma or higher: 93.3%; Bachelor's degree or higher: 57.1%; Graduate/professional degree or higher: 26.4%

Housing: Homeownership rate: 85.4%; Median home value: $443,500; Median year structure built: 1954; Homeowner vacancy rate: 0.0%; Median selected monthly owner costs: $3,215 with a mortgage, $1,501 without a mortgage; Median gross rent: $1,261 per month; Rental vacancy rate: 4.2%

Health Insurance: 94.8% have insurance; 81.0% have private insurance; 23.7% have public insurance; 5.2% do not have insurance; 3.0% of children under 18 do not have insurance

Transportation: Commute: 64.2% car, 24.2% public transportation, 5.9% walk, 5.0% work from home; Mean travel time to work: 42.3 minutes

STEWART MANOR (village).
Covers a land area of 0.210 square miles and a water area of 0 square miles. Located at 40.72° N. Lat; 73.69° W. Long. Elevation is 85 feet.

History: Laid out 1926, incorporated 1927.

Population: 2,125; Growth (since 2000): 9.8%; Density: 10,133.9 persons per square mile; Race: 86.2% White, 2.2% Black/African American, 2.9% Asian, 0.0% American Indian/Alaska Native, 0.0% Native Hawaiian/Other Pacific Islander, 1.4% Two or more races, 12.5% Hispanic of any race; Average household size: 2.91; Median age: 44.2; Age under 18: 21.5%; Age 65 and over: 18.7%; Males per 100 females: 88.3; Marriage status: 27.5% never married, 58.9% now married, 0.4% separated, 7.9%

widowed, 5.8% divorced; Foreign born: 12.4%; Speak English only: 81.8%; With disability: 7.2%; Veterans: 5.2%; Ancestry: 34.5% Irish, 27.3% Italian, 16.3% German, 6.1% English, 4.5% Polish

Employment: 25.0% management, business, and financial, 5.6% computer, engineering, and science, 17.7% education, legal, community service, arts, and media, 7.2% healthcare practitioners, 12.9% service, 23.2% sales and office, 4.6% natural resources, construction, and maintenance, 3.9% production, transportation, and material moving

Income: Per capita: $56,185; Median household: $125,278; Average household: $159,073; Households with income of $100,000 or more: 67.8%; Poverty rate: 1.5%

Educational Attainment: High school diploma or higher: 97.0%; Bachelor's degree or higher: 56.7%; Graduate/professional degree or higher: 26.6%

School District(s)

Elmont Union Free SD (PK-06)
    Enrollment: 3,783 . . . . (516) 326-5500

Housing: Homeownership rate: 93.4%; Median home value: $570,200; Median year structure built: Before 1940; Homeowner vacancy rate: 1.9%; Median selected monthly owner costs: $3,159 with a mortgage, $1,283 without a mortgage; Median gross rent: $1,648 per month; Rental vacancy rate: 0.0%

Health Insurance: 93.8% have insurance; 88.0% have private insurance; 21.9% have public insurance; 6.2% do not have insurance; 2.8% of children under 18 do not have insurance

Transportation: Commute: 70.5% car, 23.1% public transportation, 2.0% walk, 4.1% work from home; Mean travel time to work: 38.6 minutes

SYOSSET (CDP).

Covers a land area of 4.974 square miles and a water area of 0 square miles. Located at 40.82° N. Lat; 73.50° W. Long. Elevation is 210 feet.

History: Syosset was established in 1846. Booming businesses in the area during this era included horse and livestock sales, cider milling, a pickle factory, and entrepreneur enterprises such as DV Horton's "Medicinal Root Beer".

Population: 19,669; Growth (since 2000): 6.1%; Density: 3,954.7 persons per square mile; Race: 68.3% White, 0.7% Black/African American, 27.8% Asian, 0.2% American Indian/Alaska Native, 0.0% Native Hawaiian/Other Pacific Islander, 1.6% Two or more races, 4.8% Hispanic of any race; Average household size: 3.08; Median age: 43.1; Age under 18: 25.2%; Age 65 and over: 15.9%; Males per 100 females: 98.3; Marriage status: 26.1% never married, 64.7% now married, 0.8% separated, 4.7% widowed, 4.4% divorced; Foreign born: 24.0%; Speak English only: 66.1%; With disability: 6.7%; Veterans: 3.8%; Ancestry: 18.7% Italian, 10.4% Irish, 9.3% German, 5.8% Polish, 5.3% Russian

Employment: 25.5% management, business, and financial, 9.5% computer, engineering, and science, 13.7% education, legal, community service, arts, and media, 10.4% healthcare practitioners, 6.4% service, 27.4% sales and office, 3.5% natural resources, construction, and maintenance, 3.6% production, transportation, and material moving

Income: Per capita: $64,061; Median household: $155,661; Average household: $195,781; Households with income of $100,000 or more: 69.4%; Poverty rate: 3.2%

Educational Attainment: High school diploma or higher: 95.7%; Bachelor's degree or higher: 64.1%; Graduate/professional degree or higher: 30.9%

School District(s)

Cold Spring Harbor Central SD (KG-12)
    Enrollment: 1,760 . . . . (631) 367-5931
NYC Special Schools - District 75
    Enrollment: n/a . . . . (212) 802-1501
Syosset Central SD (KG-12)
    Enrollment: 6,418 . . . . (516) 364-5605

Four-year College(s)

New York College of Health Professions (Private, Not-for-profit)
    Enrollment: 485 . . . . (516) 364-0808
    Tuition: In-state $14,226; Out-of-state $14,226

Housing: Homeownership rate: 91.5%; Median home value: $627,000; Median year structure built: 1957; Homeowner vacancy rate: 0.5%; Median selected monthly owner costs: $3,677 with a mortgage, $1,501 without a mortgage; Median gross rent: $2,762 per month; Rental vacancy rate: 0.0%

Health Insurance: 97.0% have insurance; 88.6% have private insurance; 21.0% have public insurance; 3.0% do not have insurance; 2.5% of children under 18 do not have insurance

Newspapers: Long Island Press (weekly circulation 65,000)

Transportation: Commute: 72.8% car, 18.5% public transportation, 1.5% walk, 6.3% work from home; Mean travel time to work: 38.5 minutes

THOMASTON (village).

Covers a land area of 0.408 square miles and a water area of 0 square miles. Located at 40.79° N. Lat; 73.72° W. Long. Elevation is 200 feet.

Population: 2,735; Growth (since 2000): 4.9%; Density: 6,710.9 persons per square mile; Race: 63.5% White, 1.7% Black/African American, 33.3% Asian, 0.2% American Indian/Alaska Native, 0.0% Native Hawaiian/Other Pacific Islander, 0.7% Two or more races, 3.1% Hispanic of any race; Average household size: 2.67; Median age: 45.3; Age under 18: 25.9%; Age 65 and over: 21.8%; Males per 100 females: 89.9; Marriage status: 21.1% never married, 62.8% now married, 1.6% separated, 6.5% widowed, 9.6% divorced; Foreign born: 31.7%; Speak English only: 55.1%; With disability: 6.7%; Veterans: 2.5%; Ancestry: 9.4% Russian, 5.8% Eastern European, 5.5% Polish, 4.4% American, 3.6% Italian

Employment: 28.2% management, business, and financial, 9.9% computer, engineering, and science, 20.6% education, legal, community service, arts, and media, 7.7% healthcare practitioners, 7.8% service, 20.2% sales and office, 1.5% natural resources, construction, and maintenance, 4.3% production, transportation, and material moving

Income: Per capita: $64,325; Median household: $117,279; Average household: $173,330; Households with income of $100,000 or more: 58.9%; Poverty rate: 10.1%

Educational Attainment: High school diploma or higher: 94.9%; Bachelor's degree or higher: 69.5%; Graduate/professional degree or higher: 42.9%

Housing: Homeownership rate: 79.9%; Median home value: $809,700; Median year structure built: 1951; Homeowner vacancy rate: 0.0%; Median selected monthly owner costs: $3,482 with a mortgage, $1,501 without a mortgage; Median gross rent: $1,988 per month; Rental vacancy rate: 7.2%

Health Insurance: 95.1% have insurance; 79.4% have private insurance; 28.7% have public insurance; 4.9% do not have insurance; 3.8% of children under 18 do not have insurance

Transportation: Commute: 52.0% car, 35.8% public transportation, 2.4% walk, 9.8% work from home; Mean travel time to work: 41.0 minutes

UNIONDALE (CDP).

Covers a land area of 2.707 square miles and a water area of 0 square miles. Located at 40.70° N. Lat; 73.59° W. Long. Elevation is 52 feet.

History: Named for the American union of states. Downtown suburban growth since the 1970s.

Population: 31,597; Growth (since 2000): 37.3%; Density: 11,674.3 persons per square mile; Race: 34.1% White, 38.2% Black/African American, 3.2% Asian, 0.7% American Indian/Alaska Native, 0.0% Native Hawaiian/Other Pacific Islander, 11.6% Two or more races, 35.4% Hispanic of any race; Average household size: 3.47; Median age: 32.9; Age under 18: 19.8%; Age 65 and over: 14.4%; Males per 100 females: 93.6; Marriage status: 47.4% never married, 39.7% now married, 2.2% separated, 5.8% widowed, 7.0% divorced; Foreign born: 34.5%; Speak English only: 56.5%; With disability: 7.5%; Veterans: 3.6%; Ancestry: 6.2% Jamaican, 5.6% Italian, 5.6% Haitian, 4.0% Irish, 2.9% American

Employment: 9.5% management, business, and financial, 2.2% computer, engineering, and science, 11.2% education, legal, community service, arts, and media, 7.4% healthcare practitioners, 25.9% service, 23.8% sales and office, 8.3% natural resources, construction, and maintenance, 11.7% production, transportation, and material moving

Income: Per capita: $26,436; Median household: $76,157; Average household: $98,706; Households with income of $100,000 or more: 37.2%; Poverty rate: 12.0%

Educational Attainment: High school diploma or higher: 79.8%; Bachelor's degree or higher: 26.4%; Graduate/professional degree or higher: 10.5%

School District(s)

Uniondale Union Free SD (KG-12)
    Enrollment: 7,152 . . . . (516) 560-8824

Housing: Homeownership rate: 70.1%; Median home value: $337,900; Median year structure built: 1955; Homeowner vacancy rate: 2.1%; Median selected monthly owner costs: $2,536 with a mortgage, $1,212 without a mortgage; Median gross rent: $1,649 per month; Rental vacancy rate: 6.0%

Health Insurance: 86.7% have insurance; 68.1% have private insurance; 28.7% have public insurance; 13.3% do not have insurance; 9.1% of children under 18 do not have insurance
Transportation: Commute: 78.7% car, 10.9% public transportation, 6.5% walk, 2.8% work from home; Mean travel time to work: 30.0 minutes

UNIVERSITY GARDENS (CDP). Covers a land area of 0.533 square miles and a water area of 0 square miles. Located at 40.78° N. Lat; 73.73° W. Long. Elevation is 144 feet.

History: Occupying the northern portion of Lake Success, this area was the temporary headquarters of the United Nations while its headquarters building in New York City was built. It borders the New York City borough of Queens.

Population: 4,208; Growth (since 2000): 1.7%; Density: 7,892.0 persons per square mile; Race: 53.0% White, 5.7% Black/African American, 36.7% Asian, 0.0% American Indian/Alaska Native, 0.0% Native Hawaiian/Other Pacific Islander, 0.6% Two or more races, 4.8% Hispanic of any race; Average household size: 2.49; Median age: 45.5; Age under 18: 21.9%; Age 65 and over: 18.1%; Males per 100 females: 92.6; Marriage status: 27.2% never married, 58.0% now married, 2.1% separated, 5.4% widowed, 9.4% divorced; Foreign born: 34.1%; Speak English only: 59.2%; With disability: 5.8%; Veterans: 2.9%; Ancestry: 9.6% Russian, 7.9% Polish, 6.9% American, 6.7% German, 5.2% Italian
Employment: 25.8% management, business, and financial, 7.9% computer, engineering, and science, 11.4% education, legal, community service, arts, and media, 7.8% healthcare practitioners, 9.4% service, 30.3% sales and office, 2.7% natural resources, construction, and maintenance, 4.6% production, transportation, and material moving
Income: Per capita: $59,382; Median household: $97,180; Average household: $148,931; Households with income of $100,000 or more: 48.0%; Poverty rate: 5.6%
Educational Attainment: High school diploma or higher: 93.8%; Bachelor's degree or higher: 63.5%; Graduate/professional degree or higher: 30.8%
Housing: Homeownership rate: 79.7%; Median home value: $641,000; Median year structure built: 1947; Homeowner vacancy rate: 0.0%; Median selected monthly owner costs: $2,885 with a mortgage, $1,364 without a mortgage; Median gross rent: $1,478 per month; Rental vacancy rate: 0.0%
Health Insurance: 98.4% have insurance; 89.2% have private insurance; 23.0% have public insurance; 1.6% do not have insurance; 0.9% of children under 18 do not have insurance
Transportation: Commute: 60.4% car, 34.8% public transportation, 1.8% walk, 2.5% work from home; Mean travel time to work: 43.8 minutes

UPPER BROOKVILLE (village). Covers a land area of 4.319 square miles and a water area of 0 square miles. Located at 40.85° N. Lat; 73.56° W. Long. Elevation is 157 feet.

Population: 1,535; Growth (since 2000): -14.8%; Density: 355.4 persons per square mile; Race: 76.6% White, 0.7% Black/African American, 19.0% Asian, 0.0% American Indian/Alaska Native, 0.0% Native Hawaiian/Other Pacific Islander, 3.3% Two or more races, 6.1% Hispanic of any race; Average household size: 3.12; Median age: 48.9; Age under 18: 17.1%; Age 65 and over: 21.4%; Males per 100 females: 94.3; Marriage status: 24.3% never married, 66.6% now married, 0.3% separated, 6.2% widowed, 2.9% divorced; Foreign born: 26.6%; Speak English only: 63.1%; With disability: 6.4%; Veterans: 4.4%; Ancestry: 14.4% Italian, 9.9% Irish, 8.2% German, 8.1% Greek, 5.8% Polish
Employment: 26.3% management, business, and financial, 3.1% computer, engineering, and science, 12.7% education, legal, community service, arts, and media, 11.9% healthcare practitioners, 6.9% service, 34.4% sales and office, 2.9% natural resources, construction, and maintenance, 1.9% production, transportation, and material moving
Income: Per capita: $110,051; Median household: $221,406; Average household: $333,414; Households with income of $100,000 or more: 73.6%; Poverty rate: 3.6%
Educational Attainment: High school diploma or higher: 97.2%; Bachelor's degree or higher: 61.1%; Graduate/professional degree or higher: 30.9%
Housing: Homeownership rate: 92.7%; Median home value: $1,816,200; Median year structure built: 1971; Homeowner vacancy rate: 4.9%; Median selected monthly owner costs: $4,000+ with a mortgage, $1,501 without a mortgage; Median gross rent: $1,850 per month; Rental vacancy rate: 0.0%

Health Insurance: 99.4% have insurance; 89.1% have private insurance; 26.1% have public insurance; 0.6% do not have insurance; 1.5% of children under 18 do not have insurance
Transportation: Commute: 81.3% car, 9.9% public transportation, 0.5% walk, 6.4% work from home; Mean travel time to work: 35.3 minutes

VALLEY STREAM (village). Covers a land area of 3.482 square miles and a water area of 0.017 square miles. Located at 40.66° N. Lat; 73.70° W. Long. Elevation is 16 feet.

History: Valley Stream was originally referred to as "the land between Near Rockaway and Jamaica." The northeast section received the name Tigertown, and in the mid 1880s, Rum Junction. The northern section of the Village was known as Cookie Hill, because of its racy reputation.
Population: 37,843; Growth (since 2000): 4.1%; Density: 10,867.8 persons per square mile; Race: 44.5% White, 25.1% Black/African American, 15.0% Asian, 0.0% American Indian/Alaska Native, 0.0% Native Hawaiian/Other Pacific Islander, 4.7% Two or more races, 25.2% Hispanic of any race; Average household size: 3.16; Median age: 40.8; Age under 18: 22.0%; Age 65 and over: 13.9%; Males per 100 females: 92.6; Marriage status: 32.9% never married, 53.4% now married, 1.7% separated, 5.4% widowed, 8.3% divorced; Foreign born: 34.9%; Speak English only: 61.7%; With disability: 9.3%; Veterans: 4.7%; Ancestry: 12.4% Italian, 7.1% Irish, 5.6% German, 4.1% American, 3.1% Haitian
Employment: 12.4% management, business, and financial, 3.8% computer, engineering, and science, 11.4% education, legal, community service, arts, and media, 9.7% healthcare practitioners, 19.0% service, 27.4% sales and office, 7.9% natural resources, construction, and maintenance, 8.4% production, transportation, and material moving
Income: Per capita: $37,726; Median household: $99,439; Average household: $115,558; Households with income of $100,000 or more: 49.8%; Poverty rate: 4.4%
Educational Attainment: High school diploma or higher: 90.8%; Bachelor's degree or higher: 37.4%; Graduate/professional degree or higher: 15.3%

School District(s)

Elmont Union Free SD (PK-06)
    Enrollment: 3,783 . . . . (516) 326-5500
Hewlett-Woodmere Union Free SD (PK-12)
    Enrollment: 3,098 . . . . (516) 792-4800
Valley Stream 13 Union Free SD (KG-06)
    Enrollment: 2,068 . . . . (516) 568-6100
Valley Stream 24 Union Free SD (KG-06)
    Enrollment: 1,124 . . . . (516) 434-2830
Valley Stream 30 Union Free SD (KG-06)
    Enrollment: 1,514 . . . . (516) 434-3600
Valley Stream Central High SD (07-12)
    Enrollment: 4,571 . . . . (516) 872-5601
Housing: Homeownership rate: 81.8%; Median home value: $385,400; Median year structure built: 1949; Homeowner vacancy rate: 0.8%; Median selected monthly owner costs: $2,951 with a mortgage, $1,180 without a mortgage; Median gross rent: $1,642 per month; Rental vacancy rate: 3.2%
Health Insurance: 92.6% have insurance; 75.7% have private insurance; 27.4% have public insurance; 7.4% do not have insurance; 4.9% of children under 18 do not have insurance
Hospitals: Franklin Hospital (305 beds)
Transportation: Commute: 70.0% car, 24.9% public transportation, 1.9% walk, 2.2% work from home; Mean travel time to work: 42.9 minutes
Additional Information Contacts
Village of Valley Stream . . . . (516) 825-4200
   http://www.vsvny.org

WANTAGH (CDP). Covers a land area of 3.830 square miles and a water area of 0.297 square miles. Located at 40.67° N. Lat; 73.51° W. Long. Elevation is 26 feet.

History: Wantagh was inhabited by the Merokee (or Merikoke) tribe of the Metoac Indians prior to European settlement in the mid-17th century. The Merokee were part of the greater Montauk tribe that loosely ruled Long Island's Native Americans. Wantagh was the chief of the Merokee tribe in 1647, and then the grand chief of the Montauk tribe from 1651-1658.
Population: 18,525; Growth (since 2000): -2.4%; Density: 4,836.4 persons per square mile; Race: 96.4% White, 0.3% Black/African American, 1.6% Asian, 0.0% American Indian/Alaska Native, 0.0% Native Hawaiian/Other Pacific Islander, 1.3% Two or more races, 6.5% Hispanic of any race; Average household size: 3.15; Median age: 42.5; Age under 18: 22.7%;

Age 65 and over: 16.1%; Males per 100 females: 93.5; Marriage status: 28.1% never married, 60.8% now married, 0.7% separated, 5.6% widowed, 5.5% divorced; Foreign born: 5.7%; Speak English only: 92.9%; With disability: 7.8%; Veterans: 5.1%; Ancestry: 30.7% Italian, 27.8% Irish, 17.9% German, 5.9% Polish, 4.9% American

Employment: 21.1% management, business, and financial, 6.2% computer, engineering, and science, 17.0% education, legal, community service, arts, and media, 5.9% healthcare practitioners, 12.6% service, 25.6% sales and office, 6.0% natural resources, construction, and maintenance, 5.6% production, transportation, and material moving

Income: Per capita: $51,667; Median household: $136,214; Average household: $160,581; Households with income of $100,000 or more: 66.6%; Poverty rate: 1.9%

Educational Attainment: High school diploma or higher: 96.8%; Bachelor's degree or higher: 44.9%; Graduate/professional degree or higher: 19.4%

School District(s)

Levittown Union Free SD (KG-12)
  Enrollment: 7,166 . . . . (516) 434-7020
Wantagh Union Free SD (KG-12)
  Enrollment: 3,004 . . . . (516) 679-6300

Housing: Homeownership rate: 94.3%; Median home value: $479,400; Median year structure built: 1955; Homeowner vacancy rate: 0.7%; Median selected monthly owner costs: $3,305 with a mortgage, $1,337 without a mortgage; Median gross rent: $1,756 per month; Rental vacancy rate: 0.0%

Health Insurance: 98.2% have insurance; 91.0% have private insurance; 20.3% have public insurance; 1.8% do not have insurance; 0.6% of children under 18 do not have insurance

Transportation: Commute: 78.4% car, 17.6% public transportation, 0.7% walk, 2.9% work from home; Mean travel time to work: 35.5 minutes

WEST HEMPSTEAD (CDP). Covers a land area of 2.656 square miles and a water area of 0.071 square miles. Located at 40.70° N. Lat; 73.65° W. Long. Elevation is 69 feet.

History: West Hempstead was home to the first international automobile race in the United States, running through farms and village streets, known as the Vanderbilt Cup.

Population: 19,841; Growth (since 2000): 6.0%; Density: 7,471.6 persons per square mile; Race: 67.3% White, 10.3% Black/African American, 8.4% Asian, 0.0% American Indian/Alaska Native, 0.0% Native Hawaiian/Other Pacific Islander, 4.6% Two or more races, 20.3% Hispanic of any race; Average household size: 3.36; Median age: 40.3; Age under 18: 23.4%; Age 65 and over: 14.8%; Males per 100 females: 96.4; Marriage status: 36.1% never married, 51.7% now married, 1.7% separated, 6.4% widowed, 5.8% divorced; Foreign born: 22.2%; Speak English only: 70.5%; With disability: 7.8%; Veterans: 5.0%; Ancestry: 19.4% Italian, 12.1% Irish, 9.3% German, 6.1% American, 3.0% Polish

Employment: 16.7% management, business, and financial, 4.6% computer, engineering, and science, 12.3% education, legal, community service, arts, and media, 7.4% healthcare practitioners, 17.3% service, 27.4% sales and office, 8.2% natural resources, construction, and maintenance, 6.1% production, transportation, and material moving

Income: Per capita: $40,662; Median household: $107,986; Average household: $132,957; Households with income of $100,000 or more: 53.8%; Poverty rate: 5.7%

Educational Attainment: High school diploma or higher: 90.5%; Bachelor's degree or higher: 38.4%; Graduate/professional degree or higher: 17.2%

School District(s)

West Hempstead Union Free SD (KG-12)
  Enrollment: 2,003 . . . . (516) 390-3107

Housing: Homeownership rate: 86.4%; Median home value: $428,000; Median year structure built: 1952; Homeowner vacancy rate: 0.5%; Median selected monthly owner costs: $2,879 with a mortgage, $1,241 without a mortgage; Median gross rent: $1,814 per month; Rental vacancy rate: 6.6%

Health Insurance: 94.6% have insurance; 80.9% have private insurance; 26.1% have public insurance; 5.4% do not have insurance; 2.1% of children under 18 do not have insurance

Transportation: Commute: 80.0% car, 13.2% public transportation, 1.7% walk, 3.7% work from home; Mean travel time to work: 34.6 minutes

WESTBURY (village). Covers a land area of 2.374 square miles and a water area of 0 square miles. Located at 40.76° N. Lat; 73.59° W. Long. Elevation is 105 feet.

History: Named for Westbury, England. Old Westbury Gardens and manor of former Phipps estate rivals formal gardens of Europe. Seat of N.Y. Institute of Technology's central campus; State University of N.Y. College at Old Westbury. Incorporated 1924.

Population: 15,396; Growth (since 2000): 7.9%; Density: 6,485.5 persons per square mile; Race: 47.4% White, 25.2% Black/African American, 9.2% Asian, 0.0% American Indian/Alaska Native, 0.1% Native Hawaiian/Other Pacific Islander, 4.7% Two or more races, 27.5% Hispanic of any race; Average household size: 3.15; Median age: 38.5; Age under 18: 20.2%; Age 65 and over: 15.4%; Males per 100 females: 96.2; Marriage status: 35.1% never married, 52.1% now married, 1.4% separated, 6.3% widowed, 6.5% divorced; Foreign born: 34.7%; Speak English only: 56.3%; With disability: 8.4%; Veterans: 3.6%; Ancestry: 13.8% Italian, 6.6% Irish, 4.6% German, 4.5% Haitian, 4.5% Jamaican

Employment: 13.9% management, business, and financial, 4.5% computer, engineering, and science, 12.0% education, legal, community service, arts, and media, 7.1% healthcare practitioners, 18.6% service, 25.0% sales and office, 7.4% natural resources, construction, and maintenance, 11.7% production, transportation, and material moving

Income: Per capita: $40,772; Median household: $96,563; Average household: $124,408; Households with income of $100,000 or more: 48.9%; Poverty rate: 6.2%

Educational Attainment: High school diploma or higher: 84.4%; Bachelor's degree or higher: 37.6%; Graduate/professional degree or higher: 17.7%

School District(s)

East Meadow Union Free SD (KG-12)
  Enrollment: 7,160 . . . . (516) 478-5776
Westbury Union Free SD (PK-12)
  Enrollment: 5,496 . . . . (516) 876-5016

Housing: Homeownership rate: 75.0%; Median home value: $437,900; Median year structure built: 1955; Homeowner vacancy rate: 1.3%; Median selected monthly owner costs: $2,986 with a mortgage, $1,348 without a mortgage; Median gross rent: $1,805 per month; Rental vacancy rate: 7.4%

Health Insurance: 88.1% have insurance; 76.7% have private insurance; 24.2% have public insurance; 11.9% do not have insurance; 7.2% of children under 18 do not have insurance

Transportation: Commute: 79.5% car, 12.8% public transportation, 1.7% walk, 4.2% work from home; Mean travel time to work: 33.3 minutes

Additional Information Contacts

Village of Westbury . . . . (516) 334-1700
  http://www.villageofwestbury.org

WILLISTON PARK (village). Covers a land area of 0.626 square miles and a water area of 0 square miles. Located at 40.76° N. Lat; 73.65° W. Long. Elevation is 125 feet.

History: Incorporated 1926.

Population: 7,334; Growth (since 2000): 1.0%; Density: 11,723.9 persons per square mile; Race: 78.4% White, 1.6% Black/African American, 13.4% Asian, 1.2% American Indian/Alaska Native, 0.0% Native Hawaiian/Other Pacific Islander, 1.5% Two or more races, 8.6% Hispanic of any race; Average household size: 2.83; Median age: 42.5; Age under 18: 22.3%; Age 65 and over: 17.3%; Males per 100 females: 92.4; Marriage status: 29.8% never married, 57.4% now married, 1.0% separated, 6.3% widowed, 6.6% divorced; Foreign born: 19.2%; Speak English only: 74.2%; With disability: 8.3%; Veterans: 6.4%; Ancestry: 31.2% Irish, 25.3% Italian, 14.5% German, 4.5% Polish, 3.5% Portuguese

Employment: 17.4% management, business, and financial, 4.9% computer, engineering, and science, 16.0% education, legal, community service, arts, and media, 8.2% healthcare practitioners, 11.5% service, 26.9% sales and office, 9.0% natural resources, construction, and maintenance, 6.0% production, transportation, and material moving

Income: Per capita: $47,440; Median household: $104,198; Average household: $132,264; Households with income of $100,000 or more: 53.7%; Poverty rate: 2.6%

Educational Attainment: High school diploma or higher: 92.8%; Bachelor's degree or higher: 48.1%; Graduate/professional degree or higher: 23.4%

School District(s)

Herricks Union Free SD (KG-12)
  Enrollment: 3,926 . . . . (516) 305-8901

Housing: Homeownership rate: 79.0%; Median home value: $498,700; Median year structure built: Before 1940; Homeowner vacancy rate: 0.4%; Median selected monthly owner costs: $2,790 with a mortgage, $1,237 without a mortgage; Median gross rent: $1,723 per month; Rental vacancy rate: 5.4%

Health Insurance: 97.1% have insurance; 90.2% have private insurance; 21.3% have public insurance; 2.9% do not have insurance; 2.2% of children under 18 do not have insurance

Transportation: Commute: 79.6% car, 16.4% public transportation, 2.0% walk, 1.2% work from home; Mean travel time to work: 33.7 minutes

Additional Information Contacts

Village of Williston Park . . . . (516) 746-2193
   http://www.villageofwillistonpark.org

WOODBURY (CDP). Covers a land area of 5.009 square miles and a water area of 0.016 square miles. Located at 40.82° N. Lat; 73.47° W. Long. Elevation is 164 feet.

History: Woodbury was originally a part of New Amsterdam. It was a Dutch colony until taken over by the British in the mid 1600s. According to records, one of the early names of this community was East Woods. Poet Walt Whitman and industrialist Andrew Mellon each once resided in Woodbury Hills.

Population: 8,684; Growth (since 2000): -3.6%; Density: 1,733.8 persons per square mile; Race: 85.4% White, 2.3% Black/African American, 11.1% Asian, 0.0% American Indian/Alaska Native, 0.0% Native Hawaiian/Other Pacific Islander, 0.8% Two or more races, 2.1% Hispanic of any race; Average household size: 2.60; Median age: 49.9; Age under 18: 19.7%; Age 65 and over: 27.6%; Males per 100 females: 87.4; Marriage status: 16.8% never married, 62.1% now married, 0.1% separated, 14.7% widowed, 6.4% divorced; Foreign born: 15.9%; Speak English only: 82.0%; With disability: 9.3%; Veterans: 4.3%; Ancestry: 14.3% Italian, 10.5% Russian, 8.9% Polish, 6.8% American, 6.1% German

Employment: 30.2% management, business, and financial, 5.5% computer, engineering, and science, 14.8% education, legal, community service, arts, and media, 17.0% healthcare practitioners, 5.3% service, 24.2% sales and office, 1.5% natural resources, construction, and maintenance, 1.6% production, transportation, and material moving

Income: Per capita: $84,161; Median household: $166,568; Average household: $239,946; Households with income of $100,000 or more: 66.2%; Poverty rate: 3.5%

Educational Attainment: High school diploma or higher: 94.2%; Bachelor's degree or higher: 65.2%; Graduate/professional degree or higher: 33.8%

School District(s)

Syosset Central SD (KG-12)
   Enrollment: 6,418 . . . . (516) 364-5605

Housing: Homeownership rate: 87.0%; Median home value: $831,100; Median year structure built: 1978; Homeowner vacancy rate: 1.7%; Median selected monthly owner costs: $4,000+ with a mortgage, $1,501 without a mortgage; Median gross rent: $2,367 per month; Rental vacancy rate: 0.0%

Health Insurance: 99.7% have insurance; 93.8% have private insurance; 22.8% have public insurance; 0.3% do not have insurance; 0.0% of children under 18 do not have insurance

Transportation: Commute: 76.0% car, 19.1% public transportation, 0.2% walk, 3.8% work from home; Mean travel time to work: 41.7 minutes

WOODMERE (CDP). Covers a land area of 2.551 square miles and a water area of 0.267 square miles. Located at 40.64° N. Lat; 73.72° W. Long. Elevation is 23 feet.

History: Woodmere is one of the Long Island communities known as the "Five Towns", which is usually said to comprise the villages of Lawrence and Cedarhurst, the hamlets of Woodmere and Inwood, and "The Hewletts." It gets its name from Samuel Wood, who opened a hotel there that flopped.

Population: 17,376; Growth (since 2000): 5.6%; Density: 6,812.7 persons per square mile; Race: 89.0% White, 4.6% Black/African American, 2.4% Asian, 0.0% American Indian/Alaska Native, 0.0% Native Hawaiian/Other Pacific Islander, 1.5% Two or more races, 7.6% Hispanic of any race; Average household size: 3.35; Median age: 34.7; Age under 18: 33.4%; Age 65 and over: 14.7%; Males per 100 females: 96.0; Marriage status: 25.2% never married, 64.6% now married, 0.7% separated, 6.4% widowed, 3.8% divorced; Foreign born: 12.6%; Speak English only: 74.8%; With disability: 7.9%; Veterans: 2.7%; Ancestry: 16.1% Polish, 11.6% American, 11.3% Russian, 6.5% Eastern European, 6.0% German

Employment: 22.3% management, business, and financial, 5.3% computer, engineering, and science, 23.9% education, legal, community service, arts, and media, 11.6% healthcare practitioners, 8.2% service, 20.0% sales and office, 4.2% natural resources, construction, and maintenance, 4.4% production, transportation, and material moving

Income: Per capita: $50,921; Median household: $132,553; Average household: $171,065; Households with income of $100,000 or more: 62.7%; Poverty rate: 4.3%

Educational Attainment: High school diploma or higher: 94.9%; Bachelor's degree or higher: 63.8%; Graduate/professional degree or higher: 37.4%

Housing: Homeownership rate: 88.9%; Median home value: $623,000; Median year structure built: 1957; Homeowner vacancy rate: 1.3%; Median selected monthly owner costs: $3,473 with a mortgage, $1,501 without a mortgage; Median gross rent: $1,791 per month; Rental vacancy rate: 9.7%

Health Insurance: 98.0% have insurance; 85.6% have private insurance; 22.7% have public insurance; 2.0% do not have insurance; 0.9% of children under 18 do not have insurance

Transportation: Commute: 69.5% car, 20.3% public transportation, 2.7% walk, 6.0% work from home; Mean travel time to work: 40.9 minutes

WOODSBURGH (village). Covers a land area of 0.340 square miles and a water area of 0.044 square miles. Located at 40.62° N. Lat; 73.71° W. Long. Elevation is 7 feet.

Population: 793; Growth (since 2000): -4.6%; Density: 2,329.3 persons per square mile; Race: 98.1% White, 0.5% Black/African American, 0.6% Asian, 0.0% American Indian/Alaska Native, 0.0% Native Hawaiian/Other Pacific Islander, 0.8% Two or more races, 1.5% Hispanic of any race; Average household size: 2.90; Median age: 45.1; Age under 18: 26.5%; Age 65 and over: 22.6%; Males per 100 females: 95.0; Marriage status: 19.3% never married, 74.4% now married, 2.1% separated, 3.4% widowed, 2.9% divorced; Foreign born: 8.7%; Speak English only: 75.8%; With disability: 8.1%; Veterans: 3.1%; Ancestry: 23.1% Polish, 14.0% Russian, 13.5% American, 8.8% Hungarian, 7.4% German

Employment: 13.8% management, business, and financial, 1.3% computer, engineering, and science, 25.9% education, legal, community service, arts, and media, 24.6% healthcare practitioners, 3.1% service, 27.7% sales and office, 0.5% natural resources, construction, and maintenance, 3.1% production, transportation, and material moving

Income: Per capita: $84,951; Median household: $185,625; Average household: $243,081; Households with income of $100,000 or more: 74.5%; Poverty rate: 4.4%

Educational Attainment: High school diploma or higher: 98.4%; Bachelor's degree or higher: 75.2%; Graduate/professional degree or higher: 45.8%

Housing: Homeownership rate: 94.9%; Median home value: $932,700; Median year structure built: 1948; Homeowner vacancy rate: 0.0%; Median selected monthly owner costs: $4,000+ with a mortgage, $1,501 without a mortgage; Median gross rent: $2,286 per month; Rental vacancy rate: 0.0%

Health Insurance: 100.0% have insurance; 88.9% have private insurance; 23.1% have public insurance; 0.0% do not have insurance; 0.0% of children under 18 do not have insurance

Transportation: Commute: 79.2% car, 13.0% public transportation, 1.0% walk, 6.5% work from home; Mean travel time to work: 33.6 minutes

New York City

Covers a land area of 302.643 square miles and a water area of 165.841 square miles. Located at 40.66° N. Lat; 73.93° W. Long. Elevation is 33 feet.

History: Adrien Block erected four trading houses in New York in 1613, prompting permanent settlement. In 1633, the first church was built, and that was soon followed by the establishment of Fort Amsterdam. After the battle of Long Island in 1776, when Sir William Howe's British forces defeated the forces of General George Washington, the city passed into English hands and remained in their control until 1783. Congress met in New York from 1785-1790, and it was here that George Washington was inaugurated as president.

Population: 8,560,072; Growth (since 2000): 6.9%; Density: 28,284.4 persons per square mile; Race: 42.8% White, 24.3% Black/African American, 14.0% Asian, 0.4% American Indian/Alaska Native, 0.1% Native Hawaiian/Other Pacific Islander, 3.3% Two or more races, 29.1% Hispanic of any race; Average household size: 2.67; Median age: 36.2; Age under

18: 21.0%; Age 65 and over: 13.6%; Males per 100 females: 90.4; Marriage status: 43.9% never married, 42.7% now married, 3.1% separated, 5.6% widowed, 7.8% divorced; Foreign born: 37.2%; Speak English only: 51.1%; With disability: 10.8%; Veterans: 2.4%; Ancestry: 6.4% Italian, 4.7% American, 4.4% Irish, 3.0% German, 2.7% Jamaican

Employment: 15.9% management, business, and financial, 4.4% computer, engineering, and science, 15.2% education, legal, community service, arts, and media, 5.2% healthcare practitioners, 22.8% service, 22.0% sales and office, 6.1% natural resources, construction, and maintenance, 8.4% production, transportation, and material moving

Income: Per capita: $35,761; Median household: $57,782; Average household: $93,196; Households with income of $100,000 or more: 29.3%; Poverty rate: 19.6%

Educational Attainment: High school diploma or higher: 81.1%; Bachelor's degree or higher: 36.7%; Graduate/professional degree or higher: 15.2%

Housing: Homeownership rate: 32.6%; Median home value: $538,700; Median year structure built: 1949; Homeowner vacancy rate: 1.8%; Median selected monthly owner costs: $2,588 with a mortgage, $836 without a mortgage; Median gross rent: $1,340 per month; Rental vacancy rate: 3.4%

Health Insurance: 90.2% have insurance; 56.6% have private insurance; 42.0% have public insurance; 9.8% do not have insurance; 3.0% of children under 18 do not have insurance

Safety: Violent crime rate: 53.9 per 10,000 population; Property crime rate: 144.9 per 10,000 population

Transportation: Commute: 26.6% car, 56.5% public transportation, 10.0% walk, 4.1% work from home; Mean travel time to work: 40.8 minutes; Amtrak: Train and bus service available.

Additional Information Contacts

Bronx Chamber of Commerce . . . . (718) 828-3900
   http://www.bronxchamber.org
Brooklyn Chamber of Commerce . . . . (718) 875-1000
   http://www.ibrooklyn.com
City of New York . . . . (212) 669-2400
   http://nyc.gov
Greater Harlem Chamber of Commerce . . . . (212) 862-7200
   http://greaterharlemchamber.com
Greater New York Chamber of Commerce . . . . (212) 686-7220
   http://www.ny-chamber.com
Greenwich Village-Chelsea Chamber of Commerce . . . . . . (646) 470-1773
   http://www.villagechelsea.com
Manhattan Chamber of Commerce . . . . (212) 479-7772
   http://www.manhattancc.org
New York Women's Chamber of Commerce . . . . (212) 491-9640
   http://www.nywcc.org
Queens Chamber of Commerce . . . . (718) 898-8500
   http://www.queenschamber.org
Rockaway Chamber of Commerce . . . . (718) 979-7030
   http://www.rockawaychamberofcommerce.com
Staten Island Chamber of Commerce . . . . (718) 727-1900
   http://www.sichamber.org

Five Boroughs of New York City

BRONX (borough). Aka Bronx County. Located in southeastern New York State; the northernmost borough of New York city, situated between Manhattan and the Westchester County line; bounded on the west by the Hudson River, on the southwest by Spuyten Duyvil Creek and the Harlem River, on the south by the East River, and on the east by Long Island Sound. Covers a land area of 42.096 square miles, a water area of 15.382 square miles, and is located in the Eastern Time Zone at 40.85° N. Lat., 73.85° W. Long. The county was founded in 1914.

Bronx County is part of the New York-Newark-Jersey City, NY-NJ-PA Metropolitan Statistical Area. The entire metro area includes: Dutchess County-Putnam County, NY Metropolitan Division (Dutchess County, NY; Putnam County, NY); Nassau County-Suffolk County, NY Metropolitan Division (Nassau County, NY; Suffolk County, NY); Newark, NJ-PA Metropolitan Division (Essex County, NJ; Hunterdon County, NJ; Morris County, NJ; Somerset County, NJ; Sussex County, NJ; Union County, NJ; Pike County, PA); New York-Jersey City-White Plains, NY-NJ Metropolitan Division (Bergen County, NJ; Hudson County, NJ; Middlesex County, NJ; Monmouth County, NJ; Ocean County, NJ; Passaic County, NJ; Bronx County, NY; Kings County, NY; New York County, NY; Orange County,

NY; Queens County, NY; Richmond County, NY; Rockland County, NY; Westchester County, NY)

Population: 1,455,846; Growth (since 2000): 9.2%; Density: 34,583.7 persons per square mile; Race: 21.0% White, 33.6% Black/African American, 3.7% Asian, 0.7% American Indian/Alaska Native, 0.1% Native Hawaiian/Other Pacific Islander, 3.5% two or more races, 55.7% Hispanic of any race; Average household size: 2.85; Median age: 33.6; Age under 18: 25.2%; Age 65 and over: 11.8%; Males per 100 females: 88.3; Marriage status: 48.8% never married, 36.5% now married, 5.2% separated, 5.6% widowed, 9.2% divorced; Foreign born: 35.3%; Speak English only: 40.7%; With disability: 14.6%; Veterans: 2.5%; Ancestry: 4.7% Jamaican, 3.0% Italian, 2.8% American, 2.6% African, 1.9% Irish

Religion: Six largest groups: 25.5% Catholicism, 2.8% Muslim Estimate, 1.8% Non-denominational Protestant, 1.7% Baptist, 1.2% Pentecostal, 1.0% Judaism

Economy: Unemployment rate: 5.4%; Leading industries: 23.0 % retail trade; 13.4 % health care and social assistance; 12.4 % real estate and rental and leasing; Farms: 1 totaling n/a acres; Company size: 22 employ 1,000 or more persons, 31 employs 500 to 999 persons, 279 employ 100 to 499 persons, 17,693 employ less than 100 persons; Business ownership: 68,705 women-owned, 42,720 Black-owned, 67,559 Hispanic-owned, 9,668 Asian-owned, 2,331 American Indian/Alaska Native-owned

Employment: 8.6% management, business, and financial, 2.0% computer, engineering, and science, 10.1% education, legal, community service, arts, and media, 4.3% healthcare practitioners, 33.4% service, 23.5% sales and office, 7.1% natural resources, construction, and maintenance, 11.1% production, transportation, and material moving

Income: Per capita: $19,721; Median household: $36,593; Average household: $53,730; Households with income of $100,000 or more: 13.9%; Poverty rate: 29.7%

Educational Attainment: High school diploma or higher: 71.5%; Bachelor's degree or higher: 19.4%; Graduate/professional degree or higher: 6.9%

Housing: Homeownership rate: 19.7%; Median home value: $371,800; Median year structure built: 1950; Homeowner vacancy rate: 2.0%; Median selected monthly owner costs: $2,370 with a mortgage, $734 without a mortgage; Median gross rent: $1,133 per month; Rental vacancy rate: 2.2%

Vital Statistics: Birth rate: 143.4 per 10,000 population; Death rate: 72.1 per 10,000 population; Age-adjusted cancer mortality rate: 138.8 deaths per 100,000 population

Health Insurance: 88.9% have insurance; 44.1% have private insurance; 54.6% have public insurance; 11.1% do not have insurance; 3.2% of children under 18 do not have insurance

Health Care: Physicians: 30.3 per 10,000 population; Dentists: 5.0 per 10,000 population; Hospital beds: 34.5 per 10,000 population; Hospital admissions: 1,288.1 per 10,000 population

Air Quality Index (AQI): Percent of Days: 79.7% good, 19.7% moderate, 0.5% unhealthy for sensitive individuals, 0.0% unhealthy, 0.0% very unhealthy; Annual median: 39; Annual maximum: 136

Transportation: Commute: 27.4% car, 60.2% public transportation, 7.6% walk, 3.1% work from home; Mean travel time to work: 44.2 minutes

2016 Presidential Election: 9.5% Trump, 88.5% Clinton, 0.6% Johnson, 1.1% Stein

National and State Parks: Roberto Clemente State Park

School District(s)

Academic Leadership Charter School (PK-07)
   Enrollment: 520 . . . . (718) 585-4215
Amber Charter School II (KG-01)
   Enrollment: 131 . . . . (646) 802-1140
American Dream Charter School (06-08)
   Enrollment: 245 . . . . (718) 585-3071
Atmosphere Academy Public Charter School (06-07)
   Enrollment: 239 . . . . (718) 696-0493
BGLIG-Shirley Rodriquez-Remeneski CS (KG-08)
   Enrollment: 433 . . . . (718) 993-1740
Boys Preparatory Charter School of New York (KG-03)
   Enrollment: 254 . . . . (212) 346-6000
Brilla College Preparatory Charter School (KG-04)
   Enrollment: 437 . . . . (347) 273-8439
Brilla College Preparatory Charter School Veritas
   Enrollment: n/a . . . . (347) 273-8439

Bronx Academy of Promise Charter School (KG-08)
  Enrollment: 609 . . . . (718) 293-6950
Bronx Charter School For Better Learning II (KG-01)
  Enrollment: 150 . . . . (718) 655-6660
Bronx Charter School For Excellence 2 (KG-01)
  Enrollment: 110 . . . . (718) 828-7301
Bronx Charter School For Excellence 3
  Enrollment: n/a . . . . (718) 828-7301
Bronx Charter School for Better Learning (PK-05)
  Enrollment: 522 . . . . (718) 655-6660
Bronx Charter School for Children (KG-05)
  Enrollment: 432 . . . . (718) 402-3300
Bronx Charter School for Excellence (KG-08)
  Enrollment: 801 . . . . (718) 828-7301
Bronx Charter School for the Arts (KG-05)
  Enrollment: 320 . . . . (718) 893-1042
Bronx Community Charter School (KG-06)
  Enrollment: 464 . . . . (718) 944-1400
Bronx Lighthouse Charter School (KG-12)
  Enrollment: 670 . . . . (646) 915-0025
Bronx Preparatory Charter School (06-12)
  Enrollment: 714 . . . . (718) 294-0841
Charter High School for Law and Social Justice (09-10)
  Enrollment: 248 . . . . (347) 696-0042
Children's Aid College Preparatory Charter School (KG-05)
  Enrollment: 413 . . . . (347) 871-9002
Dr Richard Izquierdo Health and Science Charter Sc (06-11)
  Enrollment: 742 . . . . (718) 378-0490
Equality Charter School (06-10)
  Enrollment: 528 . . . . (718) 320-3032
Family Life Academy Charter School (KG-08)
  Enrollment: 470 . . . . (718) 410-8100
Family Life Academy Charter School II (KG-05)
  Enrollment: 291 . . . . (718) 665-2805
Family Life Academy Charter School III (KG-03)
  Enrollment: 197 . . . . (718) 410-8100
Girls Preparatory Charter School of the Bronx (KG-07)
  Enrollment: 735 . . . . (718) 292-2113
Grand Concourse Academy Charter School (KG-06)
  Enrollment: 545 . . . . (718) 684-6505
Harriet Tubman Charter School (KG-08)
  Enrollment: 689 . . . . (718) 537-9912
Heketi Community Charter School (KG-05)
  Enrollment: 283 . . . . (718) 260-6004
Hyde Leadership Charter School (KG-12)
  Enrollment: 956 . . . . (718) 991-5500
Icahn Charter School 1 (KG-08)
  Enrollment: 323 . . . . (718) 716-8105
Icahn Charter School 2 (KG-08)
  Enrollment: 323 . . . . (718) 828-6107
Icahn Charter School 3 (KG-08)
  Enrollment: 318 . . . . (718) 828-0034
Icahn Charter School 5 (KG-06)
  Enrollment: 287 . . . . (718) 828-0034
Icahn Charter School 6 (KG-06)
  Enrollment: 292 . . . . (718) 294-1706
Icahn Charter School 7 (KG-05)
  Enrollment: 196 . . . . (718) 328-5480
International Leadership Charter School (09-12)
  Enrollment: 367 . . . . (718) 562-2300
Kipp Academy Charter School (KG-12)
  Enrollment: 1,106 . . . . (718) 665-3555
Legacy College Preparatory Charter School
  Enrollment: n/a . . . . (347) 746-1558
Metropolitan Lighthouse Charter School (KG-07)
  Enrollment: 474 . . . . (718) 893-0640
Mott Hall Charter School (06-08)
  Enrollment: 292 . . . . (718) 991-9139
Mott Haven Academy Charter School (PK-05)
  Enrollment: 304 . . . . (718) 292-7015
NYC Charter HS-Architecture Engineering Constructi (09-12)
  Enrollment: 426 . . . . (646) 400-5566
NYC Special Schools - District 75
  Enrollment: n/a . . . . (212) 802-1501
New Visions Aim Charter High School II (09-12)
  Enrollment: 198 . . . . (718) 861-7515

New Visions Charter High School For Humanities II (09-12)
  Enrollment: 463 . . . . (718) 665-5380
New Visions Charter High School for Advanced Math (09-12)
  Enrollment: 485 . . . . (718) 817-7683
New Visions Charter High School for the Humanities (09-12)
  Enrollment: 538 . . . . (718) 817-7686
New Visions Charter High School-Adv Math/Science II (09-12)
  Enrollment: 556 . . . . (718) 665-3671
New York Center for Autism Charter School Bronx
  Enrollment: n/a . . . . (212) 860-2580
New York City Geographic District # 7 (PK-12)
  Enrollment: 19,934 . . . . (718) 742-6500
New York City Geographic District # 8 (PK-12)
  Enrollment: 29,202 . . . . (718) 828-6653
New York City Geographic District # 9 (PK-12)
  Enrollment: 36,668 . . . . (718) 579-7143
New York City Geographic District #10 (PK-12)
  Enrollment: 56,751 . . . . (718) 741-5852
New York City Geographic District #11 (PK-12)
  Enrollment: 39,945 . . . . (718) 519-2620
New York City Geographic District #12 (PK-12)
  Enrollment: 24,305 . . . . (718) 328-2310
New York City Montessori Charter School (PK-05)
  Enrollment: 271 . . . . (347) 226-9094
Rosalyn Yalow Charter School (KG-02)
  Enrollment: 247 . . . . (347) 735-5480
South Bronx Charter School-Inter Cultures and Arts (KG-05)
  Enrollment: 422 . . . . (718) 292-5737
South Bronx Classical Charter School (KG-08)
  Enrollment: 488 . . . . (718) 860-4340
South Bronx Classical Charter School II (KG-04)
  Enrollment: 283 . . . . (718) 292-9526
South Bronx Classical Charter School III (KG-02)
  Enrollment: 162 . . . . (718) 860-4340
South Bronx Classical Charter School IV
  Enrollment: n/a . . . . (929) 285-3025
South Bronx Community Charter High School (09-09)
  Enrollment: 107 . . . . (646) 470-5594
South Bronx Early College Academy Charter School (06-07)
  Enrollment: 226 . . . . (929) 291-7700
Storefront Academy Charter School (KG-02)
  Enrollment: 134 . . . . (646) 476-1400
Success Academy Charter School-Bronx 1 (KG-06)
  Enrollment: 677 . . . . (347) 286-7950
Success Academy Charter School-Bronx 2 (KG-06)
  Enrollment: 725 . . . . (347) 286-7965
Success Academy Charter School-Bronx 3 (KG-04)
  Enrollment: 429 . . . . (646) 790-2145
Success Academy Charter School-Bronx 4 (KG-03)
  Enrollment: 398 . . . . (646) 558-0043
University Prep Charter High School (09-12)
  Enrollment: 404 . . . . (718) 585-0560

Four-year College(s)
CUNY Lehman College (Public)
  Enrollment: 14,130 . . . . (718) 960-8000
  Tuition: In-state $7,010; Out-of-state $14,400
College of Mount Saint Vincent (Private, Not-for-profit, Roman Catholic)
  Enrollment: 1,910 . . . . (718) 405-3200
  Tuition: In-state $37,100; Out-of-state $37,100
Fordham University (Private, Not-for-profit, Roman Catholic)
  Enrollment: 16,037 . . . . (718) 817-1000
  Tuition: In-state $50,986; Out-of-state $50,986
Monroe College (Private, For-profit)
  Enrollment: 6,310 . . . . (718) 933-6700
  Tuition: In-state $14,976; Out-of-state $14,976
Two-year College(s)
CUNY Bronx Community College (Public)
  Enrollment: 10,935 . . . . (718) 289-5100
  Tuition: In-state $5,206; Out-of-state $8,086
CUNY Hostos Community College (Public)
  Enrollment: 7,211 . . . . (718) 518-4444
  Tuition: In-state $5,208; Out-of-state $8,088
School of Professional Horticulture New York Botanical Garden (Private, Not-for-profit)

Enrollment: 19. . . . . (718) 817-8797
Tuition: In-state $7,500; Out-of-state $7,500

Vocational/Technical School(s)

American Beauty School (Private, For-profit)
Enrollment: 167. . . . . (718) 931-7400
Tuition: $8,190

Brittany Beauty Academy (Private, For-profit)
Enrollment: 108. . . . . (718) 220-0400
Tuition: $14,000

Hospitals: Bronx Childrens Psychiatric Center (78 beds); Bronx Psychiatric Center (360 beds); Bronx-Lebanon Hospital Center (847 beds); Calvary Hospital (225 beds); Hebrew Hospital Home (480 beds); Jacobi Medical Center (527 beds); Lincoln Medical and Mental Health Center (595 beds); Montefiore Medical Center (1062 beds); North Central Bronx Hospital (202 beds); Our Lady of Mercy Medical Center (345 beds); St. Barnabas Hospital (461 beds); Union Community Health Center (201 beds); Veterans Affairs Medical Center (459 beds); Weiler Hospital; Westchester Square Medical Center (205 beds)

Newspapers: Bronx Times Reporter (weekly circulation 57000); Co-Op City Times (weekly circulation 50000); Hagedorn Communications (weekly circulation 39300); Metro North Media (weekly circulation 53000); Norwood News (weekly circulation 15000); Riverdale Press (weekly circulation 14000)

Additional Information Contacts

Bronx County Government . . . . (718) 590-3557
http://bronxboropres.nyc.gov
Bronx Chamber of Commerce. (718) 828-3900
http://www.bronxchamber.org

BROOKLYN (borough). Aka Kings County. Located in southeastern New York State. One of the five counties/boroughs of New York City. Covers a land area of 70.816 square miles, a water area of 26.102 square miles, and is located in the Eastern Time Zone at 40.64° N. Lat., 73.95° W. Long. The county was founded in 1683.

Kings County is part of the New York-Newark-Jersey City, NY-NJ-PA Metropolitan Statistical Area. The entire metro area includes: Dutchess County-Putnam County, NY Metropolitan Division (Dutchess County, NY; Putnam County, NY); Nassau County-Suffolk County, NY Metropolitan Division (Nassau County, NY; Suffolk County, NY); Newark, NJ-PA Metropolitan Division (Essex County, NJ; Hunterdon County, NJ; Morris County, NJ; Somerset County, NJ; Sussex County, NJ; Union County, NJ; Pike County, PA); New York-Jersey City-White Plains, NY-NJ Metropolitan Division (Bergen County, NJ; Hudson County, NJ; Middlesex County, NJ; Monmouth County, NJ; Ocean County, NJ; Passaic County, NJ; Bronx County, NY; Kings County, NY; New York County, NY; Orange County, NY; Queens County, NY; Richmond County, NY; Rockland County, NY; Westchester County, NY)

Weather Station: New York Ave V Brooklyn   Elevation: 20 feet

	Jan	Feb	Mar	Apr	May	Jun	Jul	Aug	Sep	Oct	Nov	Dec
High	39	42	50	60	70	79	84	83	76	65	55	44
Low	27	29	35	45	54	64	70	69	62	50	42	32
Precip	3.5	2.7	4.2	4.4	4.2	3.9	4.8	3.7	3.7	3.7	3.8	3.3
Snow	6.6	7.3	3.9	0.7	0.0	0.0	0.0	0.0	0.0	tr	0.3	3.5

High and Low temperatures in degrees Fahrenheit; Precipitation and Snow in inches

Population: 2,635,121; Growth (since 2000): 6.9%; Density: 37,210.9 persons per square mile; Race: 43.2% White, 33.0% Black/African American, 11.9% Asian, 0.3% American Indian/Alaska Native, 0.0% Native Hawaiian/Other Pacific Islander, 2.7% two or more races, 19.3% Hispanic of any race; Average household size: 2.75; Median age: 34.8; Age under 18: 23.1%; Age 65 and over: 12.8%; Males per 100 females: 89.3; Marriage status: 44.1% never married, 43.3% now married, 3.1% separated, 5.4% widowed, 7.1% divorced; Foreign born: 36.9%; Speak English only: 54.1%; With disability: 10.3%; Veterans: 2.0%; Ancestry: 6.0% American, 5.1% Italian, 3.4% Irish, 3.3% Jamaican, 3.0% Haitian

Religion: Six largest groups: 24.9% Catholicism, 11.5% Judaism, 3.8% Muslim Estimate, 3.2% Baptist, 2.4% Non-denominational Protestant, 1.1% Pentecostal

Economy: Unemployment rate: 4.1%; Leading industries: 18.6 % retail trade; 11.5 % health care and social assistance; 10.5 % other services (except public administration); Farms: 10 totaling n/a acres; Company size: 42 employ 1,000 or more persons, 71 employs 500 to 999 persons, 620 employ 100 to 499 persons, 56,888 employ less than 100 persons; Business ownership: 118,489 women-owned, 63,209 Black-owned, 36,081

Hispanic-owned, 47,982 Asian-owned, 1,920 American Indian/Alaska Native-owned

Employment: 14.2% management, business, and financial, 4.5% computer, engineering, and science, 17.2% education, legal, community service, arts, and media, 4.9% healthcare practitioners, 23.1% service, 21.5% sales and office, 6.2% natural resources, construction, and maintenance, 8.5% production, transportation, and material moving

Income: Per capita: $29,928; Median household: $52,782; Average household: $80,782; Households with income of $100,000 or more: 26.2%; Poverty rate: 21.9%

Educational Attainment: High school diploma or higher: 80.7%; Bachelor's degree or higher: 35.2%; Graduate/professional degree or higher: 13.9%

Housing: Homeownership rate: 30.0%; Median home value: $623,900; Median year structure built: Before 1940; Homeowner vacancy rate: 1.8%; Median selected monthly owner costs: $2,723 with a mortgage, $843 without a mortgage; Median gross rent: $1,314 per month; Rental vacancy rate: 3.4%

Vital Statistics: Birth rate: 153.9 per 10,000 population; Death rate: 65.7 per 10,000 population; Age-adjusted cancer mortality rate: 139.7 deaths per 100,000 population

Health Insurance: 90.5% have insurance; 53.4% have private insurance; 44.5% have public insurance; 9.5% do not have insurance; 2.8% of children under 18 do not have insurance

Health Care: Physicians: 32.6 per 10,000 population; Dentists: 6.3 per 10,000 population; Hospital beds: 20.1 per 10,000 population; Hospital admissions: 775.9 per 10,000 population

Air Quality Index (AQI): Percent of Days: 90.1% good, 9.9% moderate, 0.0% unhealthy for sensitive individuals, 0.0% unhealthy, 0.0% very unhealthy; Annual median: 28; Annual maximum: 72

Transportation: Commute: 22.6% car, 61.8% public transportation, 8.6% walk, 4.3% work from home; Mean travel time to work: 42.4 minutes

2016 Presidential Election: 17.5% Trump, 79.5% Clinton, 0.9% Johnson, 1.5% Stein

National and State Parks: Empire - Fulton Ferry State Park; Gateway National Recreation Area

School District(s)

Achievement First Apollo Charter School (KG-06)
Enrollment: 758. . . . . (347) 471-2620
Achievement First Aspire Charter School (KG-04)
Enrollment: 439. . . . . (347) 838-0205
Achievement First Brownsville Charter School (KG-08)
Enrollment: 932. . . . . (347) 471-2600
Achievement First Bushwick Charter School (KG-12)
Enrollment: 1,067 . . . . (347) 471-2560
Achievement First Crown Heights Charter School (KG-12)
Enrollment: 1,025 . . . . (347) 471-2580
Achievement First East New York Charter School (KG-11)
Enrollment: 839. . . . . (718) 485-4924
Achievement First Endeavor Charter School (KG-12)
Enrollment: 1,053 . . . . (718) 622-4786
Achievement First Linden Charter School (KG-03)
Enrollment: 335. . . . . (347) 471-2700
Achievement First North Brooklyn Preparatory Charter School (KG-03)
Enrollment: 304. . . . . (347) 471-2690
Achievement First Voyager Charter School (05-05)
Enrollment: 67. . . . . (347) 471-2640
Bedford Stuyvesant Collegiate Charter School (05-12)
Enrollment: 345. . . . . (718) 669-7460
Bedford Stuyvesant New Beginnings Charter School (KG-08)
Enrollment: 661. . . . . (718) 453-1001
Beginning With Children Charter School II (KG-05)
Enrollment: 298. . . . . (718) 302-7700
Brooklyn Ascend Charter School (KG-09)
Enrollment: 1,266 . . . . (718) 907-9150
Brooklyn Charter School (The) (KG-05)
Enrollment: 234. . . . . (718) 302-2085
Brooklyn Dreams Charter School (KG-08)
Enrollment: 622. . . . . (718) 859-8400
Brooklyn East Collegiate Charter School (05-10)
Enrollment: 337. . . . . (718) 250-5760
Brooklyn Emerging Leaders Academy Charter School
Enrollment: n/a . . . . (347) 491-8320
Brooklyn Excelsior Charter School (KG-08)
Enrollment: 636. . . . . (718) 246-5681

Brooklyn Laboratory Charter School (06-08)
    Enrollment: 448 . . . . (347) 429-8439
Brooklyn Prospect Charter School (KG-12)
    Enrollment: 998 . . . . (716) 643-1086
Brooklyn Prospect Charter School-CSD 13 (06-06)
    Enrollment: 95 . . . . (347) 889-7041
Brooklyn Scholars Charter School (KG-08)
    Enrollment: 702 . . . . (718) 348-9360
Brooklyn Urban Garden Charter School (06-08)
    Enrollment: 284 . . . . (718) 280-9556
Brownsville Ascend Charter School (KG-07)
    Enrollment: 1,017 . . . . (347) 294-2600
Brownsville Collegiate Charter School (05-12)
    Enrollment: 330 . . . . (718) 636-0370
Bushwick Ascend Charter School (KG-06)
    Enrollment: 790 . . . . (718) 240-9162
Canarsie Ascend Charter School (KG-04)
    Enrollment: 566 . . . . (718) 907-0153
Central Brooklyn Ascend Charter School (KG-03)
    Enrollment: 346 . . . . (917) 246-4800
Citizens of the World Charter School 2 (KG-04)
    Enrollment: 331 . . . . (718) 221-5095
Citizens of the World Charter School New York 1 (KG-04)
    Enrollment: 319 . . . . (718) 384-1386
Collegiate Academy-Math-Personal AWA (06-06)
    Enrollment: 58 . . . . (917) 588-0276
Community Partnership Charter School (KG-08)
    Enrollment: 398 . . . . (718) 399-3824
Community Roots Charter School (KG-08)
    Enrollment: 474 . . . . (718) 858-1629
Compass Charter School (KG-03)
    Enrollment: 215 . . . . (718) 310-3588
Coney Island Preparatory Public Charter School (KG-11)
    Enrollment: 932 . . . . (718) 513-6951
Cultural Arts Academy Charter School At Spring Cre (KG-05)
    Enrollment: 277 . . . . (718) 683-3300
Excellence Boys Charter School of Bedford Stuyvesa (KG-12)
    Enrollment: 779 . . . . (718) 638-1830
Excellence Girls Charter School (KG-07)
    Enrollment: 1,336 . . . . (718) 638-1875
Explore Charter School (KG-08)
    Enrollment: 511 . . . . (718) 703-4484
Explore Empower Charter School (KG-08)
    Enrollment: 514 . . . . (718) 771-2090
Explore Exceed Charter School (KG-07)
    Enrollment: 492 . . . . (718) 989-6702
Explore Excel Charter School (KG-07)
    Enrollment: 526 . . . . (718) 303-3245
Hebrew Language Academy (KG-06)
    Enrollment: 612 . . . . (718) 377-7200
Hebrew Language Academy Charter School 2
    Enrollment: n/a . . . . (718) 682-5610
Hellenic Classical Charter School (PK-08)
    Enrollment: 478 . . . . (718) 499-0957
Hyde Leadership Charter School-Brooklyn (KG-05)
    Enrollment: 405 . . . . (718) 495-5620
Imagine Me Leadership Charter School (KG-05)
    Enrollment: 224 . . . . (347) 985-2140
International Charter School of New York (KG-02)
    Enrollment: 211 . . . . (718) 305-4199
Invictus Preparatory Charter School (05-08)
    Enrollment: 266 . . . . (718) 235-1682
Kings Collegiate Charter School (05-12)
    Enrollment: 433 . . . . (718) 342-6047
Kipp Amp Charter School (KG-12)
    Enrollment: 870 . . . . (718) 943-3710
La Cima Charter School (KG-05)
    Enrollment: 380 . . . . (718) 443-2136
Launch Expeditionary Learning Charter School (06-08)
    Enrollment: 321 . . . . (718) 604-6910
Leadership Preparatory Bedford Stuyvesant Charter (KG-09)
    Enrollment: 1,090 . . . . (718) 636-0360
Leadership Preparatory Brownsville Charter School (KG-07)
    Enrollment: 791 . . . . (718) 669-7461
Leadership Preparatory Canarsie Charter School (KG-08)
    Enrollment: 674 . . . . (347) 390-0560

Leadership Preparatory Ocean Hill Charter School (KG-07)
    Enrollment: 1,039 . . . . (718) 250-5767
Math Engineering And Science Academy Charter High School (09-12)
    Enrollment: 472 . . . . (718) 282-7426
NYC Special Schools - District 75
    Enrollment: n/a . . . . (212) 802-1501
New American Academy Charter School (KG-04)
    Enrollment: 324 . . . . (718) 968-6520
New Dawn Charter High School (09-12)
    Enrollment: 321 . . . . (347) 505-9102
New Hope Academy Charter School (KG-05)
    Enrollment: 401 . . . . (718) 337-8303
New Visions Aim Charter High School I (09-12)
    Enrollment: 218 . . . . (718) 269-7090
New Visions Charter High School For The Humanities III (09-12)
    Enrollment: 386 . . . . (718) 368-4145
New Visions Charter High School-Adv Math/Science III (09-12)
    Enrollment: 451 . . . . (646) 808-6590
New York City Geographic District #13 (PK-12)
    Enrollment: 21,183 . . . . (718) 636-3284
New York City Geographic District #14 (PK-12)
    Enrollment: 18,699 . . . . (718) 302-7600
New York City Geographic District #15 (PK-12)
    Enrollment: 31,978 . . . . (718) 935-4317
New York City Geographic District #16 (PK-12)
    Enrollment: 7,327 . . . . (718) 574-2828
New York City Geographic District #17 (PK-12)
    Enrollment: 22,488 . . . . (718) 221-4372
New York City Geographic District #18 (PK-12)
    Enrollment: 15,979 . . . . (718) 566-6008
New York City Geographic District #19 (PK-12)
    Enrollment: 23,240 . . . . (718) 240-2741
New York City Geographic District #20 (PK-12)
    Enrollment: 51,935 . . . . (718) 759-4912
New York City Geographic District #21 (PK-12)
    Enrollment: 35,393 . . . . (718) 648-0209
New York City Geographic District #22 (PK-12)
    Enrollment: 35,457 . . . . (718) 968-6248
New York City Geographic District #23 (PK-12)
    Enrollment: 9,777 . . . . (718) 240-3677
New York City Geographic District #32 (PK-12)
    Enrollment: 12,301 . . . . (718) 574-1100
Northside Charter High School (09-12)
    Enrollment: 401 . . . . (347) 390-1273
Ocean Hill Collegiate Charter School (05-10)
    Enrollment: 324 . . . . (718) 250-5765
Pave Academy Charter School (PK-08)
    Enrollment: 481 . . . . (718) 858-7813
Success Academy Charter School-Bedfor Stuyvesant 2 (KG-05)
    Enrollment: 366 . . . . (718) 704-1439
Success Academy Charter School-Bedford Stuyvesant 1 (KG-05)
    Enrollment: 565 . . . . (718) 635-3294
Success Academy Charter School-Bensonhurst (KG-03)
    Enrollment: 363 . . . . (347) 514-7082
Success Academy Charter School-Bergen Beach (KG-03)
    Enrollment: 387 . . . . (347) 817-2017
Success Academy Charter School-Cobble Hill (KG-05)
    Enrollment: 454 . . . . (718) 704-1460
Success Academy Charter School-Crown Heights (KG-04)
    Enrollment: 417 . . . . (646) 790-2129
Success Academy Charter School-Fort Greene (KG-04)
    Enrollment: 375 . . . . (646) 790-2137
Success Academy Charter School-NYC 10 (KG-01)
    Enrollment: 141 . . . . (646) 790-2173
Success Academy Charter School-NYC 8 (KG-01)
    Enrollment: 157 . . . . (646) 790-2150
Success Academy Charter School-NYC 9 (KG-01)
    Enrollment: 109 . . . . (646) 790-2125
Success Academy Charter School-Prospect Heights (KG-04)
    Enrollment: 390 . . . . (646) 790-2121
Success Academy Charter School-Williamsburg (KG-05)
    Enrollment: 523 . . . . (718) 704-1419
Summit Academy Charter School (06-12)
    Enrollment: 329 . . . . (718) 875-1403
Teaching Firms of America Professional Prep Charter (KG-05)
    Enrollment: 427 . . . . (718) 285-3787

UFT Charter School (02-12)
Enrollment: 300 . . . . (718) 927-5540
Unity Preparatory Charter School of Brooklyn (06-09)
Enrollment: 387 . . . . (718) 455-5046
Urban Dove Team Charter School (09-12)
Enrollment: 260 . . . . (718) 783-8232
Williamsburg Charter High School (09-12)
Enrollment: 956 . . . . (718) 782-9830
Williamsburg Collegiate Charter School (05-12)
Enrollment: 329 . . . . (718) 302-4018

Four-year College(s)

Bet Medrash Gadol Ateret Torah (Private, Not-for-profit)
Enrollment: 93 . . . . (718) 375-7100
Tuition: In-state $9,700; Out-of-state $9,700
Beth Hamedrash Shaarei Yosher Institute (Private, Not-for-profit)
Enrollment: 54 . . . . (718) 854-2290
Tuition: In-state $9,150; Out-of-state $9,150
Beth Hatalmud Rabbinical College (Private, Not-for-profit)
Enrollment: 11 . . . . (718) 259-2525
Tuition: In-state $8,500; Out-of-state $8,500
Brooklyn Law School (Private, Not-for-profit)
Enrollment: 1,151 . . . . (718) 625-2200
CUNY Brooklyn College (Public)
Enrollment: 17,803 . . . . (718) 951-5000
Tuition: In-state $7,040; Out-of-state $14,430
CUNY Medgar Evers College (Public)
Enrollment: 6,652 . . . . (718) 270-4900
Tuition: In-state $6,952; Out-of-state $14,342
CUNY New York City College of Technology (Public)
Enrollment: 17,279 . . . . (718) 260-5500
Tuition: In-state $6,920; Out-of-state $14,310
Central Yeshiva Beth Joseph (Private, Not-for-profit)
Enrollment: 40 . . . . (718) 951-6858
Tuition: In-state $11,000; Out-of-state $11,000
Central Yeshiva Tomchei Tmimim Lubavitz (Private, Not-for-profit)
Enrollment: 544 . . . . (718) 774-3430
Tuition: In-state $7,700; Out-of-state $7,700
LIU Brooklyn (Private, Not-for-profit)
Enrollment: 6,982 . . . . (718) 488-1011
Tuition: In-state $36,978; Out-of-state $36,978
Machzikei Hadath Rabbinical College (Private, Not-for-profit)
Enrollment: 146 . . . . (718) 854-8791
Tuition: In-state $11,300; Out-of-state $11,300
Mesivta Torah Vodaath Rabbinical Seminary (Private, Not-for-profit, Jewish)
Enrollment: 366 . . . . (718) 621-3651
Tuition: In-state $11,510; Out-of-state $11,510
Mesivta of Eastern Parkway-Yeshiva Zichron Meilech (Private, Not-for-profit)
Enrollment: 32 . . . . (718) 438-1002
Tuition: In-state $8,600; Out-of-state $8,600
Mirrer Yeshiva Cent Institute (Private, Not-for-profit, Jewish)
Enrollment: 183 . . . . (718) 645-0536
Tuition: In-state $7,260; Out-of-state $7,260
Pratt Institute-Main (Private, Not-for-profit)
Enrollment: 5,035 . . . . (718) 636-3600
Tuition: In-state $50,038; Out-of-state $50,038
Rabbinical Academy Mesivta Rabbi Chaim Berlin (Private, Not-for-profit)
Enrollment: 290 . . . . (718) 377-0777
Tuition: In-state $12,450; Out-of-state $12,450
Rabbinical College Bobover Yeshiva Bnei Zion (Private, Not-for-profit, Jewish)
Enrollment: 342 . . . . (718) 438-2018
Tuition: In-state $7,750; Out-of-state $7,750
Rabbinical College Ohr Yisroel (Private, Not-for-profit, Jewish)
Enrollment: 116 . . . . (718) 633-4715
Tuition: In-state $9,000; Out-of-state $9,000
Rabbinical College of Ohr Shimon Yisroel (Private, Not-for-profit, Jewish)
Enrollment: 227 . . . . (718) 855-4092
Tuition: In-state $13,600; Out-of-state $13,600
SUNY Downstate Medical Center (Public)
Enrollment: 1,792 . . . . (718) 270-2187
Saint Francis College (Private, Not-for-profit)
Enrollment: 2,362 . . . . (718) 522-2300
Tuition: In-state $26,188; Out-of-state $26,188

St. Joseph's College-New York (Private, Not-for-profit)
Enrollment: 1,176 . . . . (718) 940-5300
Tuition: In-state $26,550; Out-of-state $26,550
Talmudical Seminary Oholei Torah (Private, Not-for-profit)
Enrollment: 300 . . . . (718) 774-5050
Tuition: In-state $9,300; Out-of-state $9,300
Talmudical Seminary of Bobov (Private, Not-for-profit, Jewish)
Enrollment: 406 . . . . (718) 854-8700
Tuition: In-state $7,600; Out-of-state $7,600
Torah Temimah Talmudical Seminary (Private, Not-for-profit)
Enrollment: 66 . . . . (718) 853-8500
Tuition: In-state $10,750; Out-of-state $10,750
United Talmudical Seminary (Private, Not-for-profit, Jewish)
Enrollment: 2,722 . . . . (718) 963-9770
Tuition: In-state $13,800; Out-of-state $13,800
Yeshiva Derech Chaim (Private, Not-for-profit)
Enrollment: 138 . . . . (718) 438-5476
Tuition: In-state $11,800; Out-of-state $11,800
Yeshiva Gedola Ohr Yisrael (Private, Not-for-profit)
Enrollment: 39 . . . . (718) 382-8702
Tuition: In-state $7,300; Out-of-state $7,300
Yeshiva Gedolah Imrei Yosef D'spinka (Private, Not-for-profit, Jewish)
Enrollment: 105 . . . . (718) 851-8721
Tuition: In-state $8,000; Out-of-state $8,000
Yeshiva Karlin Stolin (Private, Not-for-profit)
Enrollment: 151 . . . . (718) 232-7800
Tuition: In-state $12,000; Out-of-state $12,000
Yeshiva Kollel Tifereth Elizer (Private, Not-for-profit)
Enrollment: 78 . . . . (929) 222-8090
Tuition: In-state $12,200; Out-of-state $12,200
Yeshiva Sholom Shachna (Private, Not-for-profit)
Enrollment: 105 . . . . (718) 253-1664
Tuition: In-state $10,700; Out-of-state $10,700
Yeshiva and Kollel Harbotzas Torah (Private, Not-for-profit)
Enrollment: n/a . . . . (718) 692-0208
Yeshiva of Machzikai Hadas (Private, Not-for-profit)
Enrollment: 413 . . . . (718) 853-2442
Tuition: In-state $9,200; Out-of-state $9,200
Yeshivas Novominsk (Private, Not-for-profit)
Enrollment: 154 . . . . (718) 438-2727
Tuition: In-state $10,000; Out-of-state $10,000
Yeshivat Mikdash Melech (Private, Not-for-profit)
Enrollment: n/a . . . . (718) 339-1090
Tuition: In-state $8,100; Out-of-state $8,100

Two-year College(s)

ASA College (Private, For-profit)
Enrollment: 4,686 . . . . (718) 522-9073
Tuition: In-state $12,728; Out-of-state $12,728
Associated Beth Rivkah Schools (Private, Not-for-profit)
Enrollment: 144 . . . . (718) 735-0400
Tuition: In-state $7,500; Out-of-state $7,500
CUNY Kingsborough Community College (Public)
Enrollment: 15,034 . . . . (718) 368-5000
Tuition: In-state $5,252; Out-of-state $8,132
Elyon College (Private, Not-for-profit)
Enrollment: 29 . . . . (718) 259-5600
Tuition: In-state $13,220; Out-of-state $13,220
Merkaz Bnos-Business School (Private, Not-for-profit, Jewish)
Enrollment: 73 . . . . (718) 234-4000
New York Methodist Hospital Center for Allied Health Education (Private, Not-for-profit)
Enrollment: 393 . . . . (718) 645-3500
Tuition: In-state $21,591; Out-of-state $21,591

Vocational/Technical School(s)

AMG School of Licensed Practical Nursing (Private, For-profit)
Enrollment: 163 . . . . (718) 596-5300
Tuition: $30,000
Allen School-Brooklyn (Private, For-profit)
Enrollment: 67 . . . . (718) 243-1700
Tuition: $16,280
Brittany Beauty Academy (Private, For-profit)
Enrollment: 81 . . . . (718) 745-1000
Tuition: $14,000

Charles Stuart School of Diamond Setting (Private, For-profit)
    Enrollment: 54. . . . . (718) 339-2640
    Tuition: $13,950
EDP School (Private, Not-for-profit)
    Enrollment: 159. . . . . (718) 332-6469
    Tuition: $4,200
Empire Beauty School-Brooklyn (Private, For-profit)
    Enrollment: 126. . . . . (800) 920-4593
    Tuition: $12,750
Manhattan School of Computer Technology (Private, Not-for-profit)
    Enrollment: 619. . . . . (212) 349-9768
    Tuition: $3,600
Seminar L'moros Bais Yaakov (Private, Not-for-profit)
    Enrollment: 405. . . . . (718) 851-2900
    Tuition: In-state $9,290; Out-of-state $9,290
Hospitals: Beth Israel Medical Center-Kings Highway Division (212 beds); Brookdale University Hospital and Medical Center (529 beds); Brooklyn Hospital Center (416 beds); Caledonian Hospital; Coney Island Hospital (387 beds); Interfaith Medical Center (277 beds); Kings County Hospital Center (627 beds); Kingsboro Psychiatric Center (305 beds); Kingsbrook Jewish Medical Center (864 beds); Long Island College Hospital (506 beds); Lutheran Medical Center (476 beds); Maimonides Medical Center (705 beds); NY Community Hospital of Brooklyn (134 beds); New York Methodist Hospital (576 beds); SUNY Downstate Medical Center (376 beds); St. Mary's Hospital (285 beds); VA New York Harbor Healthcare System (942 beds); Victory Memorial Hospital (346 beds); Woodhull Medical & Mental Health Center; Wyckoff Heights Medical Center (305 beds)
Newspapers: Brooklyn Daily Eagle (daily circulation 10100); Brooklyn Spectator (weekly circulation 9000); Brooklyn View (weekly circulation 135000); Canarsie Courier (weekly circulation 5000); Courier-Life Inc. (weekly circulation 390000); EWA Publications (weekly circulation 588000); Greenpoint Gazette (weekly circulation 5500); Home Reporter (weekly circulation 11000); Spring Creek Sun (weekly circulation 10500); The Brooklyn Paper (weekly circulation 259000)
Additional Information Contacts
Brooklyn Chamber of Commerce . . . . (718) 875-1000
    http://www.ibrooklyn.com
Kings County Government . . . . (718) 802-3700
    http://www.brooklyn-usa.org

MANHATTAN (borough). Aka New York County. Located in

southeastern New York State. One of the five counties/boroughs New York City. Covers a land area of 22.829 square miles, a water area of 10.762 square miles, and is located in the Eastern Time Zone at 40.78° N. Lat., 73.97° W. Long. The county was founded in 1683.

New York County is part of the New York-Newark-Jersey City, NY-NJ-PA Metropolitan Statistical Area. The entire metro area includes: Dutchess County-Putnam County, NY Metropolitan Division (Dutchess County, NY; Putnam County, NY); Nassau County-Suffolk County, NY Metropolitan Division (Nassau County, NY; Suffolk County, NY); Newark, NJ-PA Metropolitan Division (Essex County, NJ; Hunterdon County, NJ; Morris County, NJ; Somerset County, NJ; Sussex County, NJ; Union County, NJ; Pike County, PA); New York-Jersey City-White Plains, NY-NJ Metropolitan Division (Bergen County, NJ; Hudson County, NJ; Middlesex County, NJ; Monmouth County, NJ; Ocean County, NJ; Passaic County, NJ; Bronx County, NY; Kings County, NY; New York County, NY; Orange County, NY; Queens County, NY; Richmond County, NY; Rockland County, NY; Westchester County, NY)

Weather Station: New York Central Park Observ   Elevation: 131 feet

	Jan	Feb	Mar	Apr	May	Jun	Jul	Aug	Sep	Oct	Nov	Dec
High	39	42	50	62	72	80	85	84	76	65	55	44
Low	27	29	35	45	54	63	69	68	61	50	41	32
Precip	3.6	2.9	4.1	4.4	4.2	4.5	4.7	4.2	4.2	4.4	4.0	3.9
Snow	7.0	7.6	3.8	0.6	tr	0.0	tr	0.0	0.0	tr	0.3	4.3

High and Low temperatures in degrees Fahrenheit; Precipitation and Snow in inches

Population: 1,653,877; Growth (since 2000): 7.6%; Density: 72,447.3 persons per square mile; Race: 56.4% White, 14.9% Black/African American, 12.0% Asian, 0.4% American Indian/Alaska Native, 0.1% Native Hawaiian/Other Pacific Islander, 4.4% two or more races, 26.1% Hispanic of any race; Average household size: 2.10; Median age: 37.1; Age under 18: 14.5%; Age 65 and over: 15.3%; Males per 100 females: 88.5; Marriage status: 50.0% never married, 36.8% now married, 2.6%

separated, 4.8% widowed, 8.4% divorced; Foreign born: 28.9%; Speak English only: 60.0%; With disability: 10.2%; Veterans: 2.3%; Ancestry: 6.7% Irish, 6.1% German, 6.1% Italian, 5.2% American, 4.2% English
Religion: Six largest groups: 20.4% Catholicism, 6.2% Judaism, 2.7% Muslim Estimate, 2.7% Non-denominational Protestant, 2.4% Baptist, 1.7% Presbyterian-Reformed
Economy: Unemployment rate: 3.6%; Leading industries: 17.0 % professional, scientific, and technical services; 10.8 % retail trade; 10.6 % other services (except public administration); Farms: 6 totaling n/a acres; Company size: 204 employ 1,000 or more persons, 322 employ 500 to 999 persons, 2,948 employ 100 to 499 persons, 101,217 employ less than 100 persons; Business ownership: 114,896 women-owned, 24,859 Black-owned, 38,504 Hispanic-owned, 40,216 Asian-owned, 1,910 American Indian/Alaska Native-owned
Employment: 27.1% management, business, and financial, 6.5% computer, engineering, and science, 21.1% education, legal, community service, arts, and media, 5.3% healthcare practitioners, 13.9% service, 20.0% sales and office, 2.2% natural resources, construction, and maintenance, 3.8% production, transportation, and material moving
Income: Per capita: $69,529; Median household: $79,781; Average household: $146,019; Households with income of $100,000 or more: 42.4%; Poverty rate: 17.3%
Educational Attainment: High school diploma or higher: 86.8%; Bachelor's degree or higher: 60.7%; Graduate/professional degree or higher: 29.1%
Housing: Homeownership rate: 24.1%; Median home value: $915,300; Median year structure built: 1950; Homeowner vacancy rate: 2.3%; Median selected monthly owner costs: $3,112 with a mortgage, $946 without a mortgage; Median gross rent: $1,615 per month; Rental vacancy rate: 4.6%
Vital Statistics: Birth rate: 106.5 per 10,000 population; Death rate: 68.4 per 10,000 population; Age-adjusted cancer mortality rate: 120.7 deaths per 100,000 population
Health Insurance: 93.3% have insurance; 68.3% have private insurance; 33.3% have public insurance; 6.7% do not have insurance; 2.1% of children under 18 do not have insurance
Health Care: Physicians: 125.8 per 10,000 population; Dentists: 17.6 per 10,000 population; Hospital beds: 63.4 per 10,000 population; Hospital admissions: 2,712.4 per 10,000 population
Air Quality Index (AQI): Percent of Days: 72.6% good, 26.8% moderate, 0.5% unhealthy for sensitive individuals, 0.0% unhealthy, 0.0% very unhealthy; Annual median: 40; Annual maximum: 122
Transportation: Commute: 7.8% car, 59.4% public transportation, 20.4% walk, 6.7% work from home; Mean travel time to work: 31.8 minutes
2016 Presidential Election: 9.7% Trump, 86.6% Clinton, 1.4% Johnson, 1.4% Stein
National and State Parks: African Burial Ground National Monument; Castle Clinton National Monument; Federal Hall National Memorial; General Grant National Memorial; Governors Island National Monument; Hamilton Grange National Monument; Riverbank State Park; Theodore Roosevelt Birthplace National Historic Site
Airports: Downtown Manhattan/Wall St (general aviation); East 34th Street (general aviation); West 30th St. (general aviation)

School District(s)
Amber Charter School (KG-05)
    Enrollment: 497. . . . . (212) 534-9667
Broome Street Academy Charter High School (09-12)
    Enrollment: 318. . . . . (212) 453-0295
Capital Preparatory Harlem Charter School (06-07)
    Enrollment: 166. . . . . (212) 328-9370
Democracy Prep Endurance Charter School (06-10)
    Enrollment: 555. . . . . (212) 316-7602
Democracy Prep Harlem Charter School (KG-11)
    Enrollment: 896. . . . . (212) 281-1248
Democracy Preparatory Charter School (06-12)
    Enrollment: 705. . . . . (212) 281-3061
Dream Charter School (PK-08)
    Enrollment: 497. . . . . (212) 722-0232
East Harlem Scholars Academy Charter School (PK-05)
    Enrollment: 409. . . . . (212) 348-2518
East Harlem Scholars Academy Charter School II (PK-04)
    Enrollment: 264. . . . . (212) 348-2518
Future Leaders Institute Charter School (KG-08)
    Enrollment: 377. . . . . (212) 678-2868

Girls Preparatory Charter School of New York (KG-08)
   Enrollment: 631 . . . . (212) 388-0241
Global Community Charter School (KG-05)
   Enrollment: 441 . . . . (646) 360-2363
Great Oaks Charter School (06-08)
   Enrollment: 209 . . . . (212) 233-5152
Harbor Science and Arts Charter School (KG-08)
   Enrollment: 260 . . . . (917) 261-2700
Harlem Children's Zone Promise Academy Charter Sch (KG-12)
   Enrollment: 1,138 . . . . (646) 556-6275
Harlem Children's Zone Promise Academy II Charter (KG-11)
   Enrollment: 994 . . . . (212) 360-3255
Harlem Day Charter School (KG-08)
   Enrollment: 838 . . . . (212) 876-9953
Harlem Hebrew Language Academy Charter School (KG-04)
   Enrollment: 332 . . . . (212) 866-4608
Harlem Link Charter School (PK-05)
   Enrollment: 387 . . . . (212) 289-3249
Harlem Village Academy Charter School Ehvacs (KG-12)
   Enrollment: 980 . . . . (646) 812-9298
Harlem Village Academy Leadership Charter School (KG-12)
   Enrollment: 955 . . . . (646) 812-9400
Icahn Charter School 4 (KG-08)
   Enrollment: 316 . . . . (718) 828-0034
Inwood Academy for Leadership Charter School (05-12)
   Enrollment: 811 . . . . (212) 304-0103
John V Lindsay Wildcat Academy Charter School (09-12)
   Enrollment: 494 . . . . (212) 209-6036
Kipp Infinity Charter School (KG-12)
   Enrollment: 1,128 . . . . (212) 991-2600
Kipp NYC Washington Heights Academy Charter School (KG-09)
   Enrollment: 908 . . . . (212) 991-2620
Kipp Success Through Teamwork Achieve & Respon Col (KG-12)
   Enrollment: 815 . . . . (212) 991-2650
Manhattan Charter School (KG-05)
   Enrollment: 271 . . . . (212) 533-2743
Manhattan Charter School II (KG-05)
   Enrollment: 230 . . . . (212) 964-3792
NYC Special Schools - District 75
   Enrollment: n/a . . . . (212) 802-1501
Neighborhood Charter School of Harlem (KG-05)
   Enrollment: 375 . . . . (646) 701-7117
New Heights Academy Charter School (05-12)
   Enrollment: 749 . . . . (212) 283-5400
New York Center for Autism Charter School (KG-02)
   Enrollment: 32 . . . . (212) 860-2580
New York City Charter School of the Arts (06-06)
   Enrollment: 99 . . . . (347) 574-3446
New York City Geographic District # 1 (PK-12)
   Enrollment: 11,394 . . . . (212) 353-2948
New York City Geographic District # 2 (PK-12)
   Enrollment: 62,602 . . . . (212) 356-3739
New York City Geographic District # 3 (PK-12)
   Enrollment: 21,819 . . . . (212) 678-5857
New York City Geographic District # 4 (PK-12)
   Enrollment: 13,314 . . . . (212) 348-2873
New York City Geographic District # 5 (PK-12)
   Enrollment: 12,240 . . . . (212) 769-7500
New York City Geographic District # 6 (PK-12)
   Enrollment: 22,778 . . . . (212) 521-3757
New York French-American Charter School (KG-05)
   Enrollment: 254 . . . . (212) 666-4134
Opportunity Charter School (06-12)
   Enrollment: 425 . . . . (212) 866-6137
Rensaissance Charter High School for Innovation (09-12)
   Enrollment: 462 . . . . (212) 722-5871
School In The Square Public Charter School (06-06)
   Enrollment: 105 . . . . (718) 916-7683
Sisulu-Walker Charter School of Harlem (KG-05)
   Enrollment: 225 . . . . (212) 663-8216
St Hope Leadership Academy Charter School (05-08)
   Enrollment: 304 . . . . (212) 283-1204
Success Academy Charter School-Harlem 1 (PK-10)
   Enrollment: 1,156 . . . . (646) 277-7170
Success Academy Charter School-Harlem 2 (KG-07)
   Enrollment: 789 . . . . (646) 442-6600

Success Academy Charter School-Harlem 3 (KG-07)
   Enrollment: 822 . . . . (646) 747-6700
Success Academy Charter School-Harlem 4 (KG-07)
   Enrollment: 633 . . . . (646) 442-6500
Success Academy Charter School-Harlem 5 (KG-06)
   Enrollment: 678 . . . . (646) 380-2580
Success Academy Charter School-Harlem 6
   Enrollment: n/a . . . . (646) 569-5900
Success Academy Charter School-Hell's Kitchen (KG-04)
   Enrollment: 428 . . . . (646) 790-2153
Success Academy Charter School-Hudson Yards
   Enrollment: n/a . . . . (212) 845-9683
Success Academy Charter School-Union Square (KG-04)
   Enrollment: 454 . . . . (646) 790-2161
Success Academy Charter School-Upper West Side (KG-05)
   Enrollment: 652 . . . . (646) 274-1580
Success Academy Charter School-Washington Heights (KG-03)
   Enrollment: 379 . . . . (646) 558-0027
The Equity Project Charter School (05-08)
   Enrollment: 597 . . . . (646) 254-6451
Voice Charter School of New York (KG-08)
   Enrollment: 665 . . . . (718) 361-1694
Whin Music Community Charter School
   Enrollment: n/a . . . . (844) 489-0817

Four-year College(s)

American Musical and Dramatic Academy (Private, Not-for-profit)
   Enrollment: 1,515 . . . . (212) 787-5300
   Tuition: In-state $37,370; Out-of-state $37,370
Bank Street College of Education (Private, Not-for-profit)
   Enrollment: 704 . . . . (212) 875-4400
Barnard College (Private, Not-for-profit)
   Enrollment: 2,544 . . . . (212) 854-2003
   Tuition: In-state $52,662; Out-of-state $52,662
Berkeley College-New York (Private, For-profit)
   Enrollment: 3,635 . . . . (212) 986-4343
   Tuition: In-state $25,300; Out-of-state $25,300
Boricua College (Private, Not-for-profit)
   Enrollment: 883 . . . . (212) 694-1000
   Tuition: In-state $11,025; Out-of-state $11,025
CUNY Bernard M Baruch College (Public)
   Enrollment: 18,289 . . . . (646) 312-1000
   Tuition: In-state $7,062; Out-of-state $14,452
CUNY City College (Public)
   Enrollment: 16,001 . . . . (212) 650-7000
   Tuition: In-state $6,940; Out-of-state $14,330
CUNY Graduate School and University Center (Public)
   Enrollment: 7,674 . . . . (212) 817-7000
CUNY Hunter College (Public)
   Enrollment: 23,005 . . . . (212) 772-4000
   Tuition: In-state $6,982; Out-of-state $14,372
CUNY John Jay College of Criminal Justice (Public)
   Enrollment: 14,834 . . . . (212) 237-8000
   Tuition: In-state $7,070; Out-of-state $14,460
Christie's Education (Private, For-profit)
   Enrollment: 83 . . . . (212) 355-1501
Columbia University in the City of New York (Private, Not-for-profit)
   Enrollment: 30,454 . . . . (212) 854-1754
   Tuition: In-state $57,208; Out-of-state $57,208
Cooper Union for the Advancement of Science and Art (Private, Not-for-profit)
   Enrollment: 946 . . . . (212) 353-4100
   Tuition: In-state $45,100; Out-of-state $45,100
DeVry College of New York (Private, For-profit)
   Enrollment: 1,528 . . . . (212) 312-4300
   Tuition: In-state $18,020; Out-of-state $18,020
Fashion Institute of Technology (Public)
   Enrollment: 8,846 . . . . (212) 217-7999
   Tuition: In-state $5,483; Out-of-state $14,863
Hebrew Union College-Jewish Institute of Religion (Private, Not-for-profit, Jewish)
   Enrollment: 317 . . . . (212) 674-5300
Helene Fuld College of Nursing (Private, Not-for-profit)
   Enrollment: 480 . . . . (212) 616-7200
Icahn School of Medicine at Mount Sinai (Private, Not-for-profit)
   Enrollment: 1,208 . . . . (212) 241-6500

Jewish Theological Seminary of America (Private, Not-for-profit, Jewish)
Enrollment: 368. . . . . (212) 678-8000
Tuition: In-state $54,684; Out-of-state $54,684
LIM College (Private, For-profit)
Enrollment: 1,713. . . . . (212) 752-1530
Tuition: In-state $26,395; Out-of-state $26,395
Manhattan School of Music (Private, Not-for-profit)
Enrollment: 1,007. . . . . (212) 749-2802
Tuition: In-state $44,600; Out-of-state $44,600
Marymount Manhattan College (Private, Not-for-profit)
Enrollment: 2,150. . . . . (212) 517-0400
Tuition: In-state $31,950; Out-of-state $31,950
Mesivtha Tifereth Jerusalem of America (Private, Not-for-profit, Jewish)
Enrollment: 69. . . . . (212) 964-2830
Tuition: In-state $11,250; Out-of-state $11,250
Metropolitan College of New York (Private, Not-for-profit)
Enrollment: 1,113. . . . . (800) 338-4465
Tuition: In-state $19,180; Out-of-state $19,180
New York Academy of Art (Private, Not-for-profit)
Enrollment: 119. . . . . (212) 966-0300
New York College of Podiatric Medicine (Private, Not-for-profit)
Enrollment: 396. . . . . (212) 410-8000
New York Law School (Private, Not-for-profit)
Enrollment: 995. . . . . (212) 431-2100
New York School of Interior Design (Private, Not-for-profit)
Enrollment: 541. . . . . (212) 472-1500
Tuition: In-state $23,590; Out-of-state $23,590
New York Theological Seminary (Private, Not-for-profit, Interdenominational)
Enrollment: 359. . . . . (212) 870-1211
New York University (Private, Not-for-profit)
Enrollment: 51,123. . . . . (212) 998-1212
Tuition: In-state $50,464; Out-of-state $50,464
Pace University-New York (Private, Not-for-profit)
Enrollment: 12,986. . . . . (212) 346-1200
Tuition: In-state $43,986; Out-of-state $43,986
Pacific College of Oriental Medicine-New York (Private, For-profit)
Enrollment: 578. . . . . (212) 982-3456
Tuition: In-state $11,592; Out-of-state $11,592
Phillips School of Nursing at Mount Sinai Beth Israel (Private, Not-for-profit)
Enrollment: 178. . . . . (212) 614-6114
Tuition: In-state $34,700; Out-of-state $34,700
Relay Graduate School of Education (Private, Not-for-profit)
Enrollment: 3,186. . . . . (212) 228-1888
Rockefeller University (Private, Not-for-profit)
Enrollment: 232. . . . . (212) 327-8000
SUNY College of Optometry (Public)
Enrollment: 413. . . . . (212) 938-4000
School of Visual Arts (Private, For-profit)
Enrollment: 4,393. . . . . (212) 592-2000
Tuition: In-state $38,000; Out-of-state $38,000
Sotheby's Institute of Art-NY (Private, For-profit)
Enrollment: 268. . . . . (212) 517-3929
Teachers College at Columbia University (Private, Not-for-profit)
Enrollment: 4,701. . . . . (212) 678-3000
The General Theological Seminary (Private, Not-for-profit, Protestant Episcopal)
Enrollment: 45. . . . . (212) 243-5150
The Juilliard School (Private, Not-for-profit)
Enrollment: 927. . . . . (212) 799-5000
Tuition: In-state $43,170; Out-of-state $43,170
The King's College (Private, Not-for-profit, Interdenominational)
Enrollment: 555. . . . . (212) 659-7200
Tuition: In-state $35,400; Out-of-state $35,400
The New School (Private, Not-for-profit)
Enrollment: 10,389. . . . . (212) 229-5600
Tuition: In-state $47,276; Out-of-state $47,276
Touro College (Private, Not-for-profit)
Enrollment: 11,908. . . . . (646) 565-6000
Tuition: In-state $18,200; Out-of-state $18,200
Tri-State College of Acupuncture (Private, For-profit)
Enrollment: 123. . . . . (212) 242-2255
Union Theological Seminary in the City of New York (Private, Not-for-profit)
Enrollment: 217. . . . . (212) 662-7100

Weill Cornell Medical College (Private, Not-for-profit)
Enrollment: 1,107. . . . . (212) 746-1050
Yeshiva University (Private, Not-for-profit)
Enrollment: 6,330. . . . . (212) 960-5400
Tuition: In-state $42,000; Out-of-state $42,000

Two-year College(s)
American Academy McAllister Institute of Funeral Service (Private, Not-for-profit)
Enrollment: 480. . . . . (212) 757-1190
Tuition: In-state $17,085; Out-of-state $17,085
American Academy of Dramatic Arts-New York (Private, Not-for-profit)
Enrollment: 269. . . . . (212) 686-9244
Tuition: In-state $34,170; Out-of-state $34,170
CUNY Borough of Manhattan Community College (Public)
Enrollment: 26,932. . . . . (212) 220-8000
Tuition: In-state $5,170; Out-of-state $8,050
Circle in the Square Theatre School (Private, Not-for-profit)
Enrollment: 60. . . . . (212) 307-0388
Tuition: In-state $17,540; Out-of-state $17,540
Joffrey Ballet School (Private, For-profit)
Enrollment: 167. . . . . (888) 438-3808
Tuition: In-state $15,649; Out-of-state $15,649
Mandl School-The College of Allied Health (Private, For-profit)
Enrollment: 598. . . . . (212) 247-3434
Tuition: In-state $14,070; Out-of-state $14,070
Memorial Hospital School of Radiation Therapy Technology (Private, Not-for-profit)
Enrollment: 14. . . . . (212) 639-6835
Mildred Elley-New York Campus (Private, For-profit)
Enrollment: 1,077. . . . . (212) 380-9004
Tuition: In-state $13,365; Out-of-state $13,365
Neighborhood Playhouse School of the Theater (Private, Not-for-profit)
Enrollment: 98. . . . . (212) 688-3770
Tuition: In-state $16,200; Out-of-state $16,200
New York Career Institute (Private, For-profit)
Enrollment: n/a. . . . . (212) 962-0002
New York Conservatory for Dramatic Arts (Private, For-profit)
Enrollment: 237. . . . . (212) 645-0030
Tuition: In-state $33,242; Out-of-state $33,242
Stella and Charles Guttman Community College (Public)
Enrollment: 1,066. . . . . (646) 313-8000
Tuition: In-state $5,194; Out-of-state $8,074
Swedish Institute a College of Health Sciences (Private, For-profit)
Enrollment: 733. . . . . (212) 924-5900
Tuition: In-state $21,200; Out-of-state $21,200
The Ailey School (Private, Not-for-profit)
Enrollment: 113. . . . . (212) 405-9008
Tuition: In-state $12,265; Out-of-state $12,265
The Art Institute of New York City (Private, For-profit)
Enrollment: n/a. . . . . (212) 226-5500
Tuition: In-state $19,750; Out-of-state $19,750
The Collective School Of Music (Private, For-profit)
Enrollment: 32. . . . . (212) 741-0091
Tuition: In-state $30,250; Out-of-state $30,250
Wood Tobe-Coburn School (Private, For-profit)
Enrollment: n/a. . . . . (212) 686-9040
Tuition: In-state $16,920; Out-of-state $16,920

Vocational/Technical School(s)
Ace Institute of Technology (Private, For-profit)
Enrollment: 215. . . . . (212) 695-9700
Tuition: $10,450
American Academy of Personal Training (Private, For-profit)
Enrollment: 64. . . . . (212) 242-2278
Tuition: $5,725
Arrojo Cosmetology School (Private, For-profit)
Enrollment: 66. . . . . (646) 979-2265
Tuition: $17,000
Atelier Esthetique Institute of Esthetics (Private, For-profit)
Enrollment: 115. . . . . (212) 725-6130
Tuition: $8,100
Aveda Institute-New York (Private, For-profit)
Enrollment: 203. . . . . (212) 807-1492
Tuition: $17,395

Brittany Beauty Academy (Private, For-profit)
Enrollment: 103. . . . . (212) 868-7171
Tuition: $14,000
Carsten Institute of Cosmetology (Private, For-profit)
Enrollment: 94. . . . . (212) 675-4884
Tuition: $14,616
Christine Valmy International School for Esthetics Skin Care & Makeup
(Private, For-profit)
Enrollment: 387. . . . . (212) 779-7800
Tuition: $8,000
Culinary Tech Center (Private, For-profit)
Enrollment: 110. . . . . (646) 559-8551
Tuition: $12,195
Digital Film Academy (Private, For-profit)
Enrollment: 114. . . . . (212) 333-4013
Tuition: $17,630
Empire Beauty School-Manhattan (Private, For-profit)
Enrollment: 481. . . . . (800) 920-4593
Tuition: $12,750
Focus Personal Training Institute (Private, For-profit)
Enrollment: 70. . . . . (212) 319-3816
Tuition: $15,680
Gemological Institute of America-New York (Private, Not-for-profit)
Enrollment: 164. . . . . (212) 944-5900
Tuition: $21,000
Institute of Audio Research (Private, For-profit)
Enrollment: n/a . . . . (212) 777-8550
Tuition: $16,530
Institute of Culinary Education (Private, For-profit)
Enrollment: 558. . . . . (212) 847-0700
Tuition: $37,249
Lia Schorr Institute of Cosmetic Skin Care Training (Private, For-profit)
Enrollment: 11. . . . . (212) 486-9541
Tuition: $7,500
Manhattan Institute (Private, For-profit)
Enrollment: 634. . . . . (212) 564-1234
Tuition: $11,224
New Age Training (Private, For-profit)
Enrollment: 145. . . . . (212) 947-7940
Tuition: $12,300
SAE Institute of Technology-New York (Private, For-profit)
Enrollment: 259. . . . . (212) 944-9121
Tuition: $22,400
Studio Jewelers (Private, For-profit)
Enrollment: 34. . . . . (212) 686-1944
Tuition: $12,000
The International Culinary Center (Private, For-profit)
Enrollment: 462. . . . . (212) 219-8890
Tuition: $39,050

Hospitals: Bellevue Hospital Center (809 beds); Beth Israel Medical
Center (1368 beds); Cabrini Medical Center (493 beds); Cornerstone of
Medical Arts Center Hospital (100 beds); Department of Veteran Affairs NY
Harbor Health System (350 beds); Gracie Square Hospital (157 beds);
Harlem Hospital Center (272 beds); Hospital for Special Surgery (160
beds); Lenox Hill Hospital (652 beds); Manhattan Eye, Ear & Throat
Hospital (150 beds); Manhattan Psychiatric Center; Memorial
Sloan-Kettering Cancer Center (437 beds); Metropolitan Hospital Center
(341 beds); Mount Sinai Medical Center (1171 beds); NYU Hospital for
Joint Diseases (216 beds); NYU Langone Medical Center (724 beds); New
York - Presbyterian Hospital (2344 beds); New York Downtown Hospital
(155 beds); New York Eye and Ear Infirmary (103 beds); New York State
Psychiatric Institute (70 beds); North General Hospital (152 beds);
Rockefeller University Hospital (20 beds); SVCMC-Saint Vincent's Centers
NY & West Branches (756 beds); St. Luke's Roosevelt Hospital Center
(1046 beds); St. Vincent's Hospital & Medical Center of NY (727 beds); St.
Vincent's Midtown Hospital (150 beds)
Newspapers: AM New York (daily circulation 267000); Daily News (daily
circulation 603000); Downtown Express (weekly circulation 50000);
Manhattan Media (weekly circulation 57000); Metro New York (daily
circulation 327000); NY Town & Village (weekly circulation 8500); New
York Post (daily circulation 704000); New York Times (daily circulation
1040000); Resident Publications (weekly circulation 160000); The New
York Observer (weekly circulation 50000); The Villager (weekly circulation
26000); Village Voice (weekly circulation 253000); Wall Street Journal
(daily circulation 2100000)

Additional Information Contacts
City of New York . . . . (212) 669-2400
  http://nyc.gov
Greater Harlem Chamber of Commerce . . . . (212) 862-7200
  http://greaterharlemchamber.com
Greater New York Chamber of Commerce . . . . (212) 686-7220
  http://www.ny-chamber.com
Greenwich Village-Chelsea Chamber of Commerce . . . . . . (646) 470-1773
  http://www.villagechelsea.com
Manhattan Chamber of Commerce . . . . (212) 479-7772
  http://www.manhattancc.org
New York Women's Chamber of Commerce . . . . (212) 491-9640
  http://www.nywcc.org

QUEENS (borough). Aka Queens County. Located in southeastern
New York State, on Long Island; one of the five counties/boroughs New
York City; bounded on the west and north by the East River. Covers a land
area of 108.532 square miles, a water area of 69.675 square miles, and is
located in the Eastern Time Zone at 40.66° N. Lat., 73.84° W. Long. The
county was founded in 1683. County seat is Jamaica.

Queens County is part of the New York-Newark-Jersey City, NY-NJ-PA
Metropolitan Statistical Area. The entire metro area includes: Dutchess
County-Putnam County, NY Metropolitan Division (Dutchess County, NY;
Putnam County, NY); Nassau County-Suffolk County, NY Metropolitan
Division (Nassau County, NY; Suffolk County, NY); Newark, NJ-PA
Metropolitan Division (Essex County, NJ; Hunterdon County, NJ; Morris
County, NJ; Somerset County, NJ; Sussex County, NJ; Union County, NJ;
Pike County, PA); New York-Jersey City-White Plains, NY-NJ Metropolitan
Division (Bergen County, NJ; Hudson County, NJ; Middlesex County, NJ;
Monmouth County, NJ; Ocean County, NJ; Passaic County, NJ; Bronx
County, NY; Kings County, NY; New York County, NY; Orange County,
NY; Queens County, NY; Richmond County, NY; Rockland County, NY;
Westchester County, NY)

Weather Station: New York J F Kennedy Int'l Arpt								Elevation: 16 feet			
	Jan	Feb	Mar	Apr	May	Jun	Jul	Aug	Sep	Oct	Nov	Dec
High	39	42	49	59	68	78	83	82	75	64	54	44
Low	26	28	34	44	53	63	69	68	61	50	41	32
Precip	3.2	2.4	3.8	4.0	4.0	3.9	4.1	3.6	3.4	3.6	3.4	3.3
Snow	6.4	7.4	3.6	0.8	tr	0.0	tr	0.0	0.0	tr	0.3	4.2

High and Low temperatures in degrees Fahrenheit; Precipitation and Snow in inches

Weather Station: New York Laguardia Arpt								Elevation: 11 feet			
	Jan	Feb	Mar	Apr	May	Jun	Jul	Aug	Sep	Oct	Nov	Dec
High	39	42	49	61	71	80	85	84	76	65	54	44
Low	27	29	35	45	55	64	70	70	63	52	42	33
Precip	3.2	2.6	3.9	4.1	3.8	4.0	4.6	4.1	3.7	3.7	3.5	3.5
Snow	7.5	8.2	4.5	0.6	tr	0.0	tr	tr	0.0	tr	0.3	4.8

High and Low temperatures in degrees Fahrenheit; Precipitation and Snow in inches

Population: 2,339,280; Growth (since 2000): 4.9%; Density: 21,553.8
persons per square mile; Race: 39.7% White, 18.2% Black/African
American, 25.3% Asian, 0.4% American Indian/Alaska Native, 0.1% Native
Hawaiian/Other Pacific Islander, 3.4% two or more races, 28.0% Hispanic
of any race; Average household size: 2.97; Median age: 38.3; Age under
18: 20.2%; Age 65 and over: 14.3%; Males per 100 females: 93.8;
Marriage status: 38.5% never married, 47.9% now married, 2.6%
separated, 6.1% widowed, 7.5% divorced; Foreign born: 47.5%; Speak
English only: 44.0%; With disability: 9.6%; Veterans: 2.4%; Ancestry: 5.5%
Italian, 3.8% American, 3.7% Irish, 2.8% Jamaican, 2.8% Guyanese
Religion: Six largest groups: 30.4% Catholicism, 3.9% Judaism, 3.7%
Muslim Estimate, 1.7% Methodist/Pietist, 1.6% Eastern Liturgical
(Orthodox), 1.6% Orthodox
Economy: Unemployment rate: 3.5%; Leading industries: 16.1 % retail
trade; 12.2 % other services (except public administration); 11.6 %
construction; Farms: 6 totaling 442 acres; Company size: 43 employ 1,000
or more persons, 59 employ 500 to 999 persons, 612 employ 100 to 499
persons, 48,883 employ less than 100 persons; Business ownership:
97,982 women-owned, 30,783 Black-owned, 52,719 Hispanic-owned,
91,714 Asian-owned, 1,930 American Indian/Alaska Native-owned
Employment: 12.9% management, business, and financial, 4.0%
computer, engineering, and science, 11.1% education, legal, community
service, arts, and media, 5.3% healthcare practitioners, 24.6% service,
23.3% sales and office, 8.2% natural resources, construction, and
maintenance, 10.7% production, transportation, and material moving

Income: Per capita: $28,814; Median household: $62,008; Average household: $81,335; Households with income of $100,000 or more: 28.6%; Poverty rate: 13.7%

Educational Attainment: High school diploma or higher: 81.1%; Bachelor's degree or higher: 30.8%; Graduate/professional degree or higher: 11.3%

Housing: Homeownership rate: 44.5%; Median home value: $481,300; Median year structure built: 1951; Homeowner vacancy rate: 1.4%; Median selected monthly owner costs: $2,482 with a mortgage, $824 without a mortgage; Median gross rent: $1,456 per month; Rental vacancy rate: 2.7%

Vital Statistics: Birth rate: 125.9 per 10,000 population; Death rate: 66.3 per 10,000 population; Age-adjusted cancer mortality rate: 123.5 deaths per 100,000 population

Health Insurance: 87.8% have insurance; 56.8% have private insurance; 39.2% have public insurance; 12.2% do not have insurance; 3.7% of children under 18 do not have insurance

Health Care: Physicians: 26.3 per 10,000 population; Dentists: 7.2 per 10,000 population; Hospital beds: 12.9 per 10,000 population; Hospital admissions: 474.1 per 10,000 population

Air Quality Index (AQI): Percent of Days: 78.9% good, 19.5% moderate, 1.4% unhealthy for sensitive individuals, 0.3% unhealthy, 0.0% very unhealthy; Annual median: 39; Annual maximum: 151

Transportation: Commute: 38.5% car, 51.7% public transportation, 5.8% walk, 2.6% work from home; Mean travel time to work: 43.5 minutes

2016 Presidential Election: 21.8% Trump, 75.4% Clinton, 1.0% Johnson, 1.3% Stein

National and State Parks: Gateway National Recreation Area; Bayswater Point State Park; Gantry Plaza State Park

Airports: John F Kennedy International (primary service/large hub); La Guardia (primary service/large hub)

School District(s)

Academy of the City Charter School (KG-05)
Enrollment: 412 . . . . (718) 487-9857
Central Queens Academy Charter School (05-08)
Enrollment: 393 . . . . (718) 271-6200
Challenge Preparatory Charter School (KG-06)
Enrollment: 684 . . . . (718) 327-1352
Forte Preparatory Academy Charter School
Enrollment: n/a . . . . (347) 709-1197
Growing Up Green Charter School (KG-07)
Enrollment: 811 . . . . (347) 642-4306
Growing Up Green Charter School II (PK-02)
Enrollment: 184 . . . . (347) 642-4306
Merrick Academy-Queens Public Charter School (KG-05)
Enrollment: 554 . . . . (718) 479-3753
Middle Village Preparatory Charter School (06-08)
Enrollment: 378 . . . . (718) 869-2933
NYC Special Schools - District 75
Enrollment: n/a . . . . (212) 802-1501
New Visions Charter High School For The Humanities IV
Enrollment: n/a . . . . (212) 645-5110
New Visions Charter High School-Adv Math/Science IV (09-12)
Enrollment: 255 . . . . (718) 525-2041
New York City Geographic District #24 (PK-12)
Enrollment: 60,158 . . . . (718) 592-3357
New York City Geographic District #25 (PK-12)
Enrollment: 37,312 . . . . (718) 281-7605
New York City Geographic District #26 (PK-12)
Enrollment: 31,968 . . . . (718) 631-6943
New York City Geographic District #27 (PK-12)
Enrollment: 45,544 . . . . (718) 642-5770
New York City Geographic District #28 (PK-12)
Enrollment: 41,721 . . . . (718) 557-2618
New York City Geographic District #29 (PK-12)
Enrollment: 27,871 . . . . (718) 217-7740
New York City Geographic District #30 (PK-12)
Enrollment: 40,364 . . . . (718) 391-8323
Our World Neighborhood Charter School (KG-08)
Enrollment: 727 . . . . (718) 392-3405
Peninsula Preparatory Academy Charter School (KG-05)
Enrollment: 320 . . . . (347) 403-9231
Renaissance Charter School (The) (PK-12)
Enrollment: 549 . . . . (718) 803-0060

Riverton Street Charter School (KG-08)
Enrollment: 893 . . . . (718) 481-8200
Rochdale Early Advantage Charter School (PK-05)
Enrollment: 275 . . . . (718) 978-0075
Success Academy Charter School-NYC 13 (KG-01)
Enrollment: 159 . . . . (718) 704-1441
Success Academy Charter School-NYC 4 (KG-01)
Enrollment: 155 . . . . (718) 704-1421
Success Academy Charter School-Rosedale (KG-03)
Enrollment: 383 . . . . (347) 514-7060
Success Academy Charter School-Springfield Gardens (KG-03)
Enrollment: 333 . . . . (347) 602-4335

Four-year College(s)

Beis Medrash Heichal Dovid (Private, Not-for-profit, Jewish)
Enrollment: 125 . . . . (718) 868-2300
Tuition: In-state $9,375; Out-of-state $9,375
CUNY Queens College (Public)
Enrollment: 19,866 . . . . (718) 997-5000
Tuition: In-state $7,138; Out-of-state $14,528
CUNY School of Law (Public)
Enrollment: 488 . . . . (718) 340-4200
CUNY York College (Public)
Enrollment: 8,533 . . . . (718) 262-2000
Tuition: In-state $6,958; Out-of-state $14,348
Manhattan College (Private, Not-for-profit, Roman Catholic)
Enrollment: 4,242 . . . . (718) 862-8000
Tuition: In-state $41,412; Out-of-state $41,412
Plaza College (Private, For-profit)
Enrollment: 909 . . . . (718) 779-1430
Tuition: In-state $12,450; Out-of-state $12,450
Rabbinical Seminary of America (Private, Not-for-profit, Jewish)
Enrollment: 454 . . . . (718) 268-4700
Tuition: In-state $9,800; Out-of-state $9,800
SUNY Maritime College (Public)
Enrollment: 1,794 . . . . (718) 409-7200
Tuition: In-state $8,074; Out-of-state $17,724
St John's University-New York (Private, Not-for-profit, Roman Catholic)
Enrollment: 21,340 . . . . (718) 990-6161
Tuition: In-state $40,520; Out-of-state $40,520
Vaughn College of Aeronautics and Technology (Private, Not-for-profit)
Enrollment: 1,502 . . . . (718) 429-6600
Tuition: In-state $24,550; Out-of-state $24,550
Yeshiva Shaar Hatorah (Private, Not-for-profit, Jewish)
Enrollment: 111 . . . . (718) 846-1940
Tuition: In-state $15,235; Out-of-state $15,235
Yeshiva Zichron Aryeh (Private, Not-for-profit)
Enrollment: 24 . . . . (732) 370-3360
Tuition: In-state $8,750; Out-of-state $8,750
Yeshiva of Far Rockaway Derech Ayson Rabbinical Seminary (Private, Not-for-profit)
Enrollment: 33 . . . . (718) 327-7600
Tuition: In-state $11,750; Out-of-state $11,750
Yeshiva of the Telshe Alumni (Private, Not-for-profit)
Enrollment: 116 . . . . (718) 601-3523
Tuition: In-state $9,500; Out-of-state $9,500

Two-year College(s)

CUNY LaGuardia Community College (Public)
Enrollment: 19,373 . . . . (718) 482-7200
Tuition: In-state $5,218; Out-of-state $8,098
CUNY Queensborough Community College (Public)
Enrollment: 15,400 . . . . (718) 631-6262
Tuition: In-state $5,210; Out-of-state $8,090
Long Island Business Institute (Private, For-profit)
Enrollment: 717 . . . . (718) 939-5100
Tuition: In-state $14,475; Out-of-state $14,475
Miami Ad School-New York (Private, For-profit)
Enrollment: 110 . . . . (305) 538-3193
Tuition: In-state $19,400; Out-of-state $19,400
Neighborhood Playhouse School of the Theater (Private, Not-for-profit)
Enrollment: 98 . . . . (212) 688-3770
Tuition: In-state $16,200; Out-of-state $16,200
New York Automotive and Diesel Institute (Private, For-profit)
Enrollment: 169 . . . . (718) 658-0006
New York Medical Career Training Center (Private, For-profit)
Enrollment: 310 . . . . (718) 460-1717

St Paul's School of Nursing-Queens (Private, For-profit)
Enrollment: 582. . . . . (718) 357-0500
Tuition: In-state $36,771; Out-of-state $36,771
Vocational/Technical School(s)
Allen School-Jamaica (Private, For-profit)
Enrollment: 54. . . . . (718) 291-2200
Tuition: $16,280
Alliance Computing Solutions (Private, For-profit)
Enrollment: 23. . . . . (718) 661-9771
Tuition: $9,100
Apex Technical School (Private, For-profit)
Enrollment: 1,094 . . . . (212) 645-3300
Tuition: $18,295
Berk Trade and Business School (Private, For-profit)
Enrollment: 220. . . . . (718) 729-0909
Tuition: $11,225
Empire Beauty School-Queens (Private, For-profit)
Enrollment: 160. . . . . (800) 920-4593
Tuition: $12,750
Ferrara's Beauty School (Private, For-profit)
Enrollment: 73. . . . . (718) 544-8100
Tuition: $12,995
Grace International Beauty School (Private, For-profit)
Enrollment: 65. . . . . (718) 886-6660
Tuition: $7,800
Lincoln Technical Institute-Whitestone (Private, For-profit)
Enrollment: 587. . . . . (718) 640-9800
Tuition: $32,230
Metropolitan Learning Institute (Private, Not-for-profit)
Enrollment: 563. . . . . (718) 897-0482
Tuition: $16,500
Midway Paris Beauty School (Private, For-profit)
Enrollment: 125. . . . . (718) 418-2790
Tuition: $12,700
New York School for Medical and Dental Assistants (Private, For-profit)
Enrollment: 373. . . . . (718) 793-2330
Tuition: $14,065
Hospitals: Coler-Goldwater Specialty Hospital and Nursing Facility (2014 beds); Creedmoor Psychiatric Center (452 beds); Elmhurst Hospital Center (525 beds); Flushing Hospital Medical Center (293 beds); Forest Hills Hospital (222 beds); Forest Hills Hospital (312 beds); Hillside Hospital (223 beds); Holliswood Hospital (110 beds); Jamaica Hospital Medical Center (387 beds); New York Hospital Queens (439 beds); Peninsula Hospital Center (272 beds); Queens Childrens Psychiatric Center (86 beds); Queens Hospital Center (408 beds); St. John's Episcopal Hospital, South Shore (332 beds); St. Mary's Hospital for Children (95 beds)
Newspapers: Forum South (weekly circulation 60000); Queens Chronicle (weekly circulation 160000); Queens Gazette (weekly circulation 90000); Queens Ledger (weekly circulation 150000); Queens Times (weekly circulation 75000); Queens Tribune (weekly circulation 171000); Schneps Publications (weekly circulation 80000); The Wave (weekly circulation 13000); Times Newsweekly (weekly circulation 27000); Times/Ledger Newspapers (weekly circulation 45000); Woodside Herald (weekly circulation 16000)
Additional Information Contacts
Queens County Government. . . . . (718) 286-3000
http://www.queensbp.org
Queens Chamber of Commerce . . . . (718) 898-8500
http://www.queenschamber.org
Rockaway Chamber of Commerce . . . . (718) 979-7030
http://www.rockawaychamberofcommerce.com

Neighborhoods in Queens

ARVERNE (unincorporated postal area)
ZCTA: 11692
Covers a land area of 0.999 square miles and a water area of 0.070 square miles. Located at 40.59° N. Lat; 73.79° W. Long. Elevation is 7 feet.
Population: 20,242; Growth (since 2000): 27.4%; Density: 20,269.9 persons per square mile; Race: 24.4% White, 59.3% Black/African American, 5.9% Asian, 0.6% American Indian/Alaska Native, 0.0% Native Hawaiian/Other Pacific Islander, 2.4% Two or more races, 26.2% Hispanic of any race; Average household size: 3.02; Median age: 33.9; Age under 18: 28.6%; Age 65 and over: 10.9%; Males per 100 females:

84.0; Marriage status: 47.7% never married, 38.2% now married, 5.7% separated, 5.3% widowed, 8.8% divorced; Foreign born: 31.2%; Speak English only: 69.7%; With disability: 17.0%; Veterans: 2.6%; Ancestry: 7.9% Jamaican, 4.1% Guyanese, 3.1% Nigerian, 3.0% American, 2.1% Irish
Employment: 10.9% management, business, and financial, 2.7% computer, engineering, and science, 11.9% education, legal, community service, arts, and media, 6.9% healthcare practitioners, 28.7% service, 21.1% sales and office, 7.6% natural resources, construction, and maintenance, 10.3% production, transportation, and material moving
Income: Per capita: $21,492; Median household: $45,816; Average household: $62,707; Households with income of $100,000 or more: 18.5%; Poverty rate: 25.1%
Educational Attainment: High school diploma or higher: 75.5%; Bachelor's degree or higher: 22.4%; Graduate/professional degree or higher: 7.0%
Housing: Homeownership rate: 36.5%; Median home value: $362,300; Median year structure built: 1967; Homeowner vacancy rate: 0.7%; Median selected monthly owner costs: $2,542 with a mortgage, $583 without a mortgage; Median gross rent: $951 per month; Rental vacancy rate: 5.1%
Health Insurance: 91.9% have insurance; 50.3% have private insurance; 48.5% have public insurance; 8.1% do not have insurance; 2.4% of children under 18 do not have insurance
Transportation: Commute: 44.7% car, 48.5% public transportation, 2.7% walk, 2.1% work from home; Mean travel time to work: 57.0 minutes

ASTORIA (unincorporated postal area)
ZCTA: 11102
Covers a land area of 0.808 square miles and a water area of 0.003 square miles. Located at 40.77° N. Lat; 73.93° W. Long. Elevation is 23 feet.
Population: 33,727; Growth (since 2000): -7.1%; Density: 41,752.3 persons per square mile; Race: 56.9% White, 10.5% Black/African American, 16.3% Asian, 0.1% American Indian/Alaska Native, 0.1% Native Hawaiian/Other Pacific Islander, 2.6% Two or more races, 30.3% Hispanic of any race; Average household size: 2.45; Median age: 33.3; Age under 18: 15.4%; Age 65 and over: 11.0%; Males per 100 females: 99.7; Marriage status: 49.1% never married, 40.3% now married, 2.5% separated, 4.3% widowed, 6.3% divorced; Foreign born: 41.1%; Speak English only: 45.0%; With disability: 9.1%; Veterans: 1.7%; Ancestry: 7.0% Italian, 5.8% Irish, 4.8% American, 4.6% Greek, 3.9% German
Employment: 18.6% management, business, and financial, 5.7% computer, engineering, and science, 17.2% education, legal, community service, arts, and media, 2.9% healthcare practitioners, 24.0% service, 20.4% sales and office, 4.5% natural resources, construction, and maintenance, 6.7% production, transportation, and material moving
Income: Per capita: $35,275; Median household: $60,436; Average household: $82,508; Households with income of $100,000 or more: 29.3%; Poverty rate: 18.1%
Educational Attainment: High school diploma or higher: 83.2%; Bachelor's degree or higher: 46.5%; Graduate/professional degree or higher: 14.4%
Housing: Homeownership rate: 13.2%; Median home value: $560,200; Median year structure built: 1952; Homeowner vacancy rate: 1.3%; Median selected monthly owner costs: $2,621 with a mortgage, $918 without a mortgage; Median gross rent: $1,618 per month; Rental vacancy rate: 2.8%
Health Insurance: 87.6% have insurance; 57.3% have private insurance; 37.8% have public insurance; 12.4% do not have insurance; 1.0% of children under 18 do not have insurance
Transportation: Commute: 15.7% car, 71.5% public transportation, 6.1% walk, 4.1% work from home; Mean travel time to work: 39.3 minutes
ZCTA: 11103
Covers a land area of 0.711 square miles and a water area of 0 square miles. Located at 40.76° N. Lat; 73.91° W. Long. Elevation is 23 feet.
Population: 38,036; Growth (since 2000): -14.2%; Density: 53,490.8 persons per square mile; Race: 70.1% White, 2.7% Black/African American, 15.3% Asian, 0.2% American Indian/Alaska Native, 0.1% Native Hawaiian/Other Pacific Islander, 3.5% Two or more races, 23.5% Hispanic of any race; Average household size: 2.35; Median age: 33.8; Age under 18: 12.9%; Age 65 and over: 11.5%; Males per 100 females: 99.8; Marriage status: 48.8% never married, 39.4% now married, 2.1%

separated, 4.0% widowed, 7.8% divorced; Foreign born: 42.4%; Speak English only: 44.8%; With disability: 8.2%; Veterans: 1.9%; Ancestry: 11.6% Italian, 6.9% Irish, 6.3% German, 6.0% American, 5.5% Greek

Employment: 19.0% management, business, and financial, 7.2% computer, engineering, and science, 17.8% education, legal, community service, arts, and media, 4.0% healthcare practitioners, 19.6% service, 20.1% sales and office, 5.4% natural resources, construction, and maintenance, 6.9% production, transportation, and material moving

Income: Per capita: $36,827; Median household: $65,229; Average household: $81,512; Households with income of $100,000 or more: 29.3%; Poverty rate: 13.4%

Educational Attainment: High school diploma or higher: 86.7%; Bachelor's degree or higher: 48.9%; Graduate/professional degree or higher: 17.8%

Housing: Homeownership rate: 15.9%; Median home value: $762,700; Median year structure built: 1942; Homeowner vacancy rate: 1.0%; Median selected monthly owner costs: $2,922 with a mortgage, $997 without a mortgage; Median gross rent: $1,625 per month; Rental vacancy rate: 1.7%

Health Insurance: 87.1% have insurance; 61.6% have private insurance; 32.4% have public insurance; 12.9% do not have insurance; 3.5% of children under 18 do not have insurance

Transportation: Commute: 16.1% car, 72.3% public transportation, 6.6% walk, 2.6% work from home; Mean travel time to work: 38.5 minutes

ZCTA: 11105

Covers a land area of 1.632 square miles and a water area of 0 square miles. Located at 40.78° N. Lat; 73.91° W. Long. Elevation is 23 feet.

Population: 37,288; Growth (since 2000): -11.5%; Density: 22,848.7 persons per square mile; Race: 74.3% White, 2.5% Black/African American, 13.7% Asian, 0.3% American Indian/Alaska Native, 0.0% Native Hawaiian/Other Pacific Islander, 2.6% Two or more races, 21.4% Hispanic of any race; Average household size: 2.45; Median age: 35.1; Age under 18: 14.1%; Age 65 and over: 12.4%; Males per 100 females: 95.1; Marriage status: 45.0% never married, 43.1% now married, 1.8% separated, 5.3% widowed, 6.6% divorced; Foreign born: 37.6%; Speak English only: 45.0%; With disability: 8.6%; Veterans: 1.8%; Ancestry: 12.0% Italian, 12.0% Greek, 7.0% Irish, 5.8% German, 4.6% American

Employment: 18.8% management, business, and financial, 6.2% computer, engineering, and science, 20.1% education, legal, community service, arts, and media, 4.0% healthcare practitioners, 15.8% service, 22.2% sales and office, 5.5% natural resources, construction, and maintenance, 7.5% production, transportation, and material moving

Income: Per capita: $38,318; Median household: $68,050; Average household: $88,855; Households with income of $100,000 or more: 34.1%; Poverty rate: 9.8%

Educational Attainment: High school diploma or higher: 86.7%; Bachelor's degree or higher: 49.0%; Graduate/professional degree or higher: 17.0%

Housing: Homeownership rate: 26.6%; Median home value: $762,300; Median year structure built: 1941; Homeowner vacancy rate: 0.6%; Median selected monthly owner costs: $3,025 with a mortgage, $964 without a mortgage; Median gross rent: $1,644 per month; Rental vacancy rate: 3.1%

Health Insurance: 90.9% have insurance; 69.3% have private insurance; 30.2% have public insurance; 9.1% do not have insurance; 2.0% of children under 18 do not have insurance

Transportation: Commute: 23.0% car, 64.5% public transportation, 6.5% walk, 4.8% work from home; Mean travel time to work: 40.1 minutes

ZCTA: 11106

Covers a land area of 0.857 square miles and a water area of 0.014 square miles. Located at 40.76° N. Lat; 73.93° W. Long. Elevation is 23 feet.

Population: 40,111; Growth (since 2000): -7.0%; Density: 46,800.7 persons per square mile; Race: 53.8% White, 7.0% Black/African American, 21.3% Asian, 0.2% American Indian/Alaska Native, 0.0% Native Hawaiian/Other Pacific Islander, 4.7% Two or more races, 29.3% Hispanic of any race; Average household size: 2.33; Median age: 35.6; Age under 18: 14.7%; Age 65 and over: 13.0%; Males per 100 females: 94.7; Marriage status: 46.3% never married, 40.0% now married, 2.8% separated, 5.6% widowed, 8.1% divorced; Foreign born: 40.4%; Speak English only: 43.0%; With disability: 10.8%; Veterans: 2.0%; Ancestry: 8.0% Italian, 6.1% Irish, 5.4% American, 3.3% German, 3.2% Greek

Employment: 17.1% management, business, and financial, 6.2% computer, engineering, and science, 19.6% education, legal, community service, arts, and media, 4.1% healthcare practitioners, 20.1% service, 19.5% sales and office, 5.5% natural resources, construction, and maintenance, 7.9% production, transportation, and material moving

Income: Per capita: $35,257; Median household: $60,725; Average household: $78,578; Households with income of $100,000 or more: 27.7%; Poverty rate: 16.4%

Educational Attainment: High school diploma or higher: 85.2%; Bachelor's degree or higher: 47.7%; Graduate/professional degree or higher: 16.1%

Housing: Homeownership rate: 17.9%; Median home value: $502,800; Median year structure built: 1949; Homeowner vacancy rate: 0.3%; Median selected monthly owner costs: $2,442 with a mortgage, $802 without a mortgage; Median gross rent: $1,557 per month; Rental vacancy rate: 1.7%

Health Insurance: 89.4% have insurance; 62.4% have private insurance; 36.0% have public insurance; 10.6% do not have insurance; 1.4% of children under 18 do not have insurance

Transportation: Commute: 13.8% car, 71.4% public transportation, 8.1% walk, 3.9% work from home; Mean travel time to work: 38.4 minutes

BAYSIDE (unincorporated postal area)
ZCTA: 11360

Covers a land area of 1.425 square miles and a water area of 0 square miles. Located at 40.78° N. Lat; 73.78° W. Long. Elevation is 79 feet.

Population: 19,501; Growth (since 2000): 0.8%; Density: 13,683.6 persons per square mile; Race: 65.3% White, 0.9% Black/African American, 29.7% Asian, 0.3% American Indian/Alaska Native, 0.0% Native Hawaiian/Other Pacific Islander, 1.5% Two or more races, 9.0% Hispanic of any race; Average household size: 2.32; Median age: 48.4; Age under 18: 16.6%; Age 65 and over: 25.8%; Males per 100 females: 83.3; Marriage status: 24.3% never married, 56.8% now married, 1.2% separated, 10.4% widowed, 8.4% divorced; Foreign born: 35.6%; Speak English only: 49.3%; With disability: 12.4%; Veterans: 5.4%; Ancestry: 12.7% Italian, 6.2% Polish, 5.9% Russian, 5.5% Greek, 5.1% Irish

Employment: 20.7% management, business, and financial, 5.9% computer, engineering, and science, 16.1% education, legal, community service, arts, and media, 7.8% healthcare practitioners, 14.1% service, 24.5% sales and office, 7.0% natural resources, construction, and maintenance, 4.0% production, transportation, and material moving

Income: Per capita: $45,446; Median household: $84,476; Average household: $102,457; Households with income of $100,000 or more: 40.6%; Poverty rate: 7.9%

Educational Attainment: High school diploma or higher: 93.0%; Bachelor's degree or higher: 51.3%; Graduate/professional degree or higher: 22.4%

Housing: Homeownership rate: 70.7%; Median home value: $526,000; Median year structure built: 1967; Homeowner vacancy rate: 1.1%; Median selected monthly owner costs: $2,408 with a mortgage, $1,010 without a mortgage; Median gross rent: $2,007 per month; Rental vacancy rate: 4.5%

Health Insurance: 95.4% have insurance; 78.1% have private insurance; 34.8% have public insurance; 4.6% do not have insurance; 1.4% of children under 18 do not have insurance

Transportation: Commute: 64.3% car, 28.0% public transportation, 1.7% walk, 5.4% work from home; Mean travel time to work: 43.0 minutes

ZCTA: 11361

Covers a land area of 1.758 square miles and a water area of 0.019 square miles. Located at 40.76° N. Lat; 73.77° W. Long. Elevation is 79 feet.

Population: 29,072; Growth (since 2000): -0.5%; Density: 16,534.2 persons per square mile; Race: 50.1% White, 3.3% Black/African American, 39.0% Asian, 0.0% American Indian/Alaska Native, 0.0% Native Hawaiian/Other Pacific Islander, 2.2% Two or more races, 14.6% Hispanic of any race; Average household size: 2.75; Median age: 41.3; Age under 18: 18.4%; Age 65 and over: 17.4%; Males per 100 females: 91.7; Marriage status: 32.7% never married, 53.4% now married, 2.3% separated, 6.7% widowed, 7.2% divorced; Foreign born: 40.1%; Speak English only: 44.7%; With disability: 8.6%; Veterans: 3.4%; Ancestry: 12.7% Italian, 9.7% Irish, 5.3% Greek, 4.6% American, 4.1% German

Employment: 18.9% management, business, and financial, 5.7% computer, engineering, and science, 14.2% education, legal, community

service, arts, and media, 6.3% healthcare practitioners, 16.6% service, 25.7% sales and office, 6.2% natural resources, construction, and maintenance, 6.5% production, transportation, and material moving
Income: Per capita: $37,166; Median household: $82,020; Average household: $99,655; Households with income of $100,000 or more: 39.8%; Poverty rate: 9.0%
Educational Attainment: High school diploma or higher: 88.9%; Bachelor's degree or higher: 42.2%; Graduate/professional degree or higher: 17.4%
Housing: Homeownership rate: 57.9%; Median home value: $638,900; Median year structure built: 1954; Homeowner vacancy rate: 0.5%; Median selected monthly owner costs: $2,650 with a mortgage, $922 without a mortgage; Median gross rent: $1,722 per month; Rental vacancy rate: 2.3%
Health Insurance: 91.3% have insurance; 71.2% have private insurance; 31.3% have public insurance; 8.7% do not have insurance; 3.4% of children under 18 do not have insurance
Transportation: Commute: 61.2% car, 31.7% public transportation, 3.9% walk, 2.4% work from home; Mean travel time to work: 40.4 minutes

BREEZY POINT (unincorporated postal area)
ZCTA: 11697

Covers a land area of 2.220 square miles and a water area of <.001 square miles. Located at 40.56° N. Lat; 73.92° W. Long. Elevation is 7 feet.
Population: 3,702; Growth (since 2000): -12.4%; Density: 1,667.7 persons per square mile; Race: 96.2% White, 0.3% Black/African American, 0.2% Asian, 0.0% American Indian/Alaska Native, 0.0% Native Hawaiian/Other Pacific Islander, 0.0% Two or more races, 4.9% Hispanic of any race; Average household size: 2.64; Median age: 49.1; Age under 18: 22.0%; Age 65 and over: 24.1%; Males per 100 females: 86.0; Marriage status: 28.7% never married, 60.6% now married, 1.4% separated, 6.0% widowed, 4.7% divorced; Foreign born: 3.6%; Speak English only: 97.6%; With disability: 14.2%; Veterans: 10.9%; Ancestry: 59.8% Irish, 18.1% German, 17.0% Italian, 6.2% American, 4.1% English
Employment: 19.0% management, business, and financial, 2.6% computer, engineering, and science, 15.1% education, legal, community service, arts, and media, 8.3% healthcare practitioners, 18.3% service, 19.4% sales and office, 9.6% natural resources, construction, and maintenance, 7.7% production, transportation, and material moving
Income: Per capita: $48,159; Median household: $99,792; Average household: $124,884; Households with income of $100,000 or more: 49.9%; Poverty rate: 4.6%
Educational Attainment: High school diploma or higher: 97.1%; Bachelor's degree or higher: 48.1%; Graduate/professional degree or higher: 21.8%
Housing: Homeownership rate: 96.8%; Median home value: $556,400; Median year structure built: 1975; Homeowner vacancy rate: 0.0%; Median selected monthly owner costs: $2,105 with a mortgage, $614 without a mortgage; Median gross rent: n/a per month; Rental vacancy rate: 0.0%
Health Insurance: 98.3% have insurance; 91.1% have private insurance; 28.5% have public insurance; 1.7% do not have insurance; 3.4% of children under 18 do not have insurance
Transportation: Commute: 78.6% car, 12.2% public transportation, 3.9% walk, 4.9% work from home; Mean travel time to work: 44.8 minutes

CAMBRIA HEIGHTS (unincorporated postal area)
ZCTA: 11411

Covers a land area of 1.169 square miles and a water area of 0 square miles. Located at 40.69° N. Lat; 73.74° W. Long. Elevation is 49 feet.
Population: 19,990; Growth (since 2000): -6.1%; Density: 17,101.6 persons per square mile; Race: 2.1% White, 93.1% Black/African American, 0.3% Asian, 0.1% American Indian/Alaska Native, 0.0% Native Hawaiian/Other Pacific Islander, 1.8% Two or more races, 5.7% Hispanic of any race; Average household size: 3.30; Median age: 44.3; Age under 18: 18.4%; Age 65 and over: 19.6%; Males per 100 females: 81.1; Marriage status: 39.2% never married, 42.7% now married, 3.8% separated, 7.8% widowed, 10.3% divorced; Foreign born: 37.5%; Speak English only: 81.3%; With disability: 9.3%; Veterans: 4.4%; Ancestry: 19.7% Jamaican, 13.9% Haitian, 8.8% American, 4.3% West Indian, 3.3% Guyanese

Employment: 10.2% management, business, and financial, 2.9% computer, engineering, and science, 11.4% education, legal, community service, arts, and media, 10.1% healthcare practitioners, 25.8% service, 24.0% sales and office, 4.9% natural resources, construction, and maintenance, 10.7% production, transportation, and material moving
Income: Per capita: $33,473; Median household: $87,231; Average household: $101,581; Households with income of $100,000 or more: 42.1%; Poverty rate: 4.5%
Educational Attainment: High school diploma or higher: 91.4%; Bachelor's degree or higher: 32.5%; Graduate/professional degree or higher: 12.4%
Housing: Homeownership rate: 85.4%; Median home value: $417,400; Median year structure built: 1947; Homeowner vacancy rate: 0.9%; Median selected monthly owner costs: $2,403 with a mortgage, $773 without a mortgage; Median gross rent: $1,556 per month; Rental vacancy rate: 2.3%
Health Insurance: 92.4% have insurance; 70.5% have private insurance; 34.4% have public insurance; 7.6% do not have insurance; 4.4% of children under 18 do not have insurance
Transportation: Commute: 60.5% car, 36.4% public transportation, 0.6% walk, 1.8% work from home; Mean travel time to work: 47.1 minutes

COLLEGE POINT (unincorporated postal area)
ZCTA: 11356

Covers a land area of 1.571 square miles and a water area of 0 square miles. Located at 40.78° N. Lat; 73.84° W. Long. Elevation is 69 feet.
Population: 24,069; Growth (since 2000): 17.7%; Density: 15,317.1 persons per square mile; Race: 34.8% White, 2.4% Black/African American, 31.3% Asian, 0.1% American Indian/Alaska Native, 0.2% Native Hawaiian/Other Pacific Islander, 3.6% Two or more races, 39.8% Hispanic of any race; Average household size: 3.19; Median age: 38.0; Age under 18: 21.8%; Age 65 and over: 12.9%; Males per 100 females: 95.1; Marriage status: 31.3% never married, 55.3% now married, 2.2% separated, 6.5% widowed, 6.9% divorced; Foreign born: 49.0%; Speak English only: 28.1%; With disability: 6.2%; Veterans: 2.4%; Ancestry: 7.1% American, 6.6% Italian, 3.5% Irish, 3.0% German, 1.9% Greek
Employment: 13.0% management, business, and financial, 1.8% computer, engineering, and science, 7.4% education, legal, community service, arts, and media, 3.0% healthcare practitioners, 23.7% service, 27.6% sales and office, 12.3% natural resources, construction, and maintenance, 11.3% production, transportation, and material moving
Income: Per capita: $25,148; Median household: $59,712; Average household: $76,125; Households with income of $100,000 or more: 24.6%; Poverty rate: 13.1%
Educational Attainment: High school diploma or higher: 78.1%; Bachelor's degree or higher: 20.5%; Graduate/professional degree or higher: 6.1%
Housing: Homeownership rate: 48.1%; Median home value: $598,600; Median year structure built: 1951; Homeowner vacancy rate: 3.3%; Median selected monthly owner costs: $2,662 with a mortgage, $851 without a mortgage; Median gross rent: $1,603 per month; Rental vacancy rate: 3.9%
Health Insurance: 85.0% have insurance; 56.2% have private insurance; 35.1% have public insurance; 15.0% do not have insurance; 4.5% of children under 18 do not have insurance
Transportation: Commute: 58.4% car, 31.2% public transportation, 6.6% walk, 3.1% work from home; Mean travel time to work: 40.1 minutes

CORONA (unincorporated postal area)
ZCTA: 11368

Covers a land area of 2.632 square miles and a water area of 0.036 square miles. Located at 40.75° N. Lat; 73.85° W. Long. Elevation is 43 feet.
Population: 114,647; Growth (since 2000): 16.0%; Density: 43,559.8 persons per square mile; Race: 39.6% White, 12.1% Black/African American, 12.2% Asian, 0.6% American Indian/Alaska Native, 0.0% Native Hawaiian/Other Pacific Islander, 2.5% Two or more races, 73.2% Hispanic of any race; Average household size: 4.03; Median age: 32.0; Age under 18: 26.8%; Age 65 and over: 8.8%; Males per 100 females: 113.4; Marriage status: 45.9% never married, 42.4% now married, 3.4% separated, 4.6% widowed, 7.1% divorced; Foreign born: 59.6%; Speak English only: 13.7%; With disability: 10.5%; Veterans: 0.7%; Ancestry:

2.8% American, 1.0% Italian, 1.0% African, 0.9% Jamaican, 0.6% Other Subsaharan African

Employment: 4.6% management, business, and financial, 1.0% computer, engineering, and science, 4.8% education, legal, community service, arts, and media, 2.0% healthcare practitioners, 37.7% service, 18.3% sales and office, 16.8% natural resources, construction, and maintenance, 14.8% production, transportation, and material moving

Income: Per capita: $16,826; Median household: $47,862; Average household: $61,032; Households with income of $100,000 or more: 16.1%; Poverty rate: 20.7%

Educational Attainment: High school diploma or higher: 61.7%; Bachelor's degree or higher: 12.9%; Graduate/professional degree or higher: 3.4%

Housing: Homeownership rate: 22.1%; Median home value: $517,600; Median year structure built: 1960; Homeowner vacancy rate: 2.9%; Median selected monthly owner costs: $2,799 with a mortgage, $837 without a mortgage; Median gross rent: $1,526 per month; Rental vacancy rate: 1.2%

Health Insurance: 73.7% have insurance; 36.4% have private insurance; 48.5% have public insurance; 26.3% do not have insurance; 3.9% of children under 18 do not have insurance

Transportation: Commute: 21.3% car, 65.2% public transportation, 10.2% walk, 1.3% work from home; Mean travel time to work: 43.9 minutes

EAST ELMHURST (unincorporated postal area)
ZCTA: 11369

Covers a land area of 1.068 square miles and a water area of 0 square miles. Located at 40.76° N. Lat; 73.87° W. Long. Elevation is 75 feet.

Population: 37,325; Growth (since 2000): 3.4%; Density: 34,961.4 persons per square mile; Race: 27.1% White, 15.8% Black/African American, 13.4% Asian, 0.2% American Indian/Alaska Native, 0.0% Native Hawaiian/Other Pacific Islander, 3.3% Two or more races, 64.1% Hispanic of any race; Average household size: 3.39; Median age: 36.9; Age under 18: 21.7%; Age 65 and over: 13.9%; Males per 100 females: 99.8; Marriage status: 41.8% never married, 45.5% now married, 2.7% separated, 5.6% widowed, 7.0% divorced; Foreign born: 55.3%; Speak English only: 24.7%; With disability: 8.3%; Veterans: 1.9%; Ancestry: 5.9% American, 1.3% Italian, 1.0% Jamaican, 0.9% West Indian, 0.8% Irish

Employment: 7.8% management, business, and financial, 2.7% computer, engineering, and science, 8.0% education, legal, community service, arts, and media, 3.7% healthcare practitioners, 29.8% service, 22.0% sales and office, 12.6% natural resources, construction, and maintenance, 13.4% production, transportation, and material moving

Income: Per capita: $21,685; Median household: $53,426; Average household: $68,949; Households with income of $100,000 or more: 22.0%; Poverty rate: 15.7%

Educational Attainment: High school diploma or higher: 76.0%; Bachelor's degree or higher: 17.8%; Graduate/professional degree or higher: 6.2%

Housing: Homeownership rate: 51.7%; Median home value: $533,500; Median year structure built: 1946; Homeowner vacancy rate: 3.3%; Median selected monthly owner costs: $2,743 with a mortgage, $847 without a mortgage; Median gross rent: $1,456 per month; Rental vacancy rate: 1.3%

Health Insurance: 82.4% have insurance; 46.9% have private insurance; 44.1% have public insurance; 17.6% do not have insurance; 5.3% of children under 18 do not have insurance

Transportation: Commute: 32.7% car, 56.1% public transportation, 6.0% walk, 2.2% work from home; Mean travel time to work: 44.1 minutes

ZCTA: 11370

Covers a land area of 1.423 square miles and a water area of 0 square miles. Located at 40.77° N. Lat; 73.89° W. Long. Elevation is 75 feet.

Population: 33,789; Growth (since 2000): -21.7%; Density: 23,752.5 persons per square mile; Race: 42.0% White, 14.2% Black/African American, 22.2% Asian, 1.2% American Indian/Alaska Native, 0.0% Native Hawaiian/Other Pacific Islander, 1.8% Two or more races, 38.3% Hispanic of any race; Average household size: 3.14; Median age: 37.3; Age under 18: 16.4%; Age 65 and over: 11.7%; Males per 100 females: 162.0; Marriage status: 48.0% never married, 42.5% now married, 1.3% separated, 4.7% widowed, 4.7% divorced; Foreign born: 45.9%; Speak English only: 33.2%; With disability: 8.8%; Veterans: 1.3%; Ancestry: 6.6% American, 5.3% Italian, 4.6% Greek, 2.0% Irish, 1.1% Egyptian

Employment: 12.9% management, business, and financial, 3.2% computer, engineering, and science, 9.2% education, legal, community service, arts, and media, 4.2% healthcare practitioners, 26.3% service, 23.1% sales and office, 8.0% natural resources, construction, and maintenance, 13.0% production, transportation, and material moving

Income: Per capita: $22,720; Median household: $59,901; Average household: $84,987; Households with income of $100,000 or more: 28.8%; Poverty rate: 12.3%

Educational Attainment: High school diploma or higher: 73.4%; Bachelor's degree or higher: 21.8%; Graduate/professional degree or higher: 7.7%

Housing: Homeownership rate: 48.4%; Median home value: $627,100; Median year structure built: 1954; Homeowner vacancy rate: 2.1%; Median selected monthly owner costs: $2,830 with a mortgage, $900 without a mortgage; Median gross rent: $1,581 per month; Rental vacancy rate: 5.0%

Health Insurance: 90.9% have insurance; 57.0% have private insurance; 42.4% have public insurance; 9.1% do not have insurance; 1.1% of children under 18 do not have insurance

Transportation: Commute: 38.9% car, 53.0% public transportation, 3.7% walk, 2.5% work from home; Mean travel time to work: 39.0 minutes

ELMHURST (unincorporated postal area)
ZCTA: 11373

Covers a land area of 1.527 square miles and a water area of 0 square miles. Located at 40.74° N. Lat; 73.88° W. Long. Elevation is 26 feet.

Population: 96,353; Growth (since 2000): -8.9%; Density: 63,082.0 persons per square mile; Race: 24.2% White, 2.4% Black/African American, 50.7% Asian, 0.6% American Indian/Alaska Native, 0.0% Native Hawaiian/Other Pacific Islander, 2.5% Two or more races, 38.7% Hispanic of any race; Average household size: 3.18; Median age: 38.6; Age under 18: 19.1%; Age 65 and over: 13.3%; Males per 100 females: 103.1; Marriage status: 36.6% never married, 51.0% now married, 2.2% separated, 5.8% widowed, 6.6% divorced; Foreign born: 67.5%; Speak English only: 14.0%; With disability: 9.4%; Veterans: 1.0%; Ancestry: 2.6% American, 1.0% Irish, 0.8% Italian, 0.7% German, 0.5% Polish

Employment: 9.5% management, business, and financial, 3.5% computer, engineering, and science, 6.3% education, legal, community service, arts, and media, 4.8% healthcare practitioners, 34.3% service, 20.6% sales and office, 7.7% natural resources, construction, and maintenance, 13.3% production, transportation, and material moving

Income: Per capita: $22,249; Median household: $49,098; Average household: $65,321; Households with income of $100,000 or more: 19.8%; Poverty rate: 18.1%

Educational Attainment: High school diploma or higher: 73.6%; Bachelor's degree or higher: 26.2%; Graduate/professional degree or higher: 7.6%

Housing: Homeownership rate: 30.5%; Median home value: $530,900; Median year structure built: 1954; Homeowner vacancy rate: 0.3%; Median selected monthly owner costs: $2,478 with a mortgage, $813 without a mortgage; Median gross rent: $1,426 per month; Rental vacancy rate: 1.2%

Health Insurance: 81.6% have insurance; 42.9% have private insurance; 48.0% have public insurance; 18.4% do not have insurance; 3.1% of children under 18 do not have insurance

Transportation: Commute: 18.4% car, 70.2% public transportation, 7.7% walk, 1.6% work from home; Mean travel time to work: 42.5 minutes

FAR ROCKAWAY (unincorporated postal area)
ZCTA: 11691

Covers a land area of 2.834 square miles and a water area of 0.033 square miles. Located at 40.60° N. Lat; 73.76° W. Long. Elevation is 16 feet.

Population: 65,356; Growth (since 2000): 16.3%; Density: 23,063.2 persons per square mile; Race: 40.6% White, 46.3% Black/African American, 2.9% Asian, 0.1% American Indian/Alaska Native, 0.1% Native Hawaiian/Other Pacific Islander, 1.6% Two or more races, 27.7% Hispanic of any race; Average household size: 3.11; Median age: 31.9; Age under 18: 30.4%; Age 65 and over: 12.9%; Males per 100 females: 88.3; Marriage status: 43.1% never married, 40.7% now married, 5.0% separated, 6.9% widowed, 9.3% divorced; Foreign born: 30.3%; Speak English only: 64.6%; With disability: 16.8%; Veterans: 2.9%; Ancestry:

6.1% Jamaican, 5.9% American, 2.3% Guyanese, 2.1% Haitian, 1.9% Trinidadian and Tobagonian

Employment: 10.7% management, business, and financial, 1.9% computer, engineering, and science, 13.2% education, legal, community service, arts, and media, 6.3% healthcare practitioners, 31.5% service, 18.9% sales and office, 7.2% natural resources, construction, and maintenance, 10.4% production, transportation, and material moving

Income: Per capita: $19,799; Median household: $42,434; Average household: $58,683; Households with income of $100,000 or more: 17.5%; Poverty rate: 23.2%

Educational Attainment: High school diploma or higher: 72.8%; Bachelor's degree or higher: 23.2%; Graduate/professional degree or higher: 9.1%

Housing: Homeownership rate: 24.7%; Median home value: $440,700; Median year structure built: 1964; Homeowner vacancy rate: 2.5%; Median selected monthly owner costs: $2,818 with a mortgage, $888 without a mortgage; Median gross rent: $1,118 per month; Rental vacancy rate: 1.5%

Health Insurance: 91.3% have insurance; 49.4% have private insurance; 49.5% have public insurance; 8.7% do not have insurance; 2.5% of children under 18 do not have insurance

Transportation: Commute: 47.0% car, 39.7% public transportation, 7.6% walk, 2.9% work from home; Mean travel time to work: 49.6 minutes

ZCTA: 11693

Covers a land area of 0.997 square miles and a water area of 0 square miles. Located at 40.59° N. Lat; 73.81° W. Long. Elevation is 16 feet.

Population: 12,709; Growth (since 2000): 13.9%; Density: 12,745.4 persons per square mile; Race: 63.2% White, 20.1% Black/African American, 4.7% Asian, 0.0% American Indian/Alaska Native, 0.0% Native Hawaiian/Other Pacific Islander, 5.2% Two or more races, 27.9% Hispanic of any race; Average household size: 2.61; Median age: 38.5; Age under 18: 24.5%; Age 65 and over: 12.7%; Males per 100 females: 86.9; Marriage status: 43.6% never married, 37.3% now married, 3.7% separated, 7.7% widowed, 11.4% divorced; Foreign born: 22.3%; Speak English only: 64.5%; With disability: 16.6%; Veterans: 3.9%; Ancestry: 21.2% Irish, 10.4% Italian, 6.1% German, 6.1% Polish, 5.2% American

Employment: 10.0% management, business, and financial, 3.9% computer, engineering, and science, 11.6% education, legal, community service, arts, and media, 6.4% healthcare practitioners, 27.9% service, 19.1% sales and office, 13.8% natural resources, construction, and maintenance, 7.3% production, transportation, and material moving

Income: Per capita: $28,735; Median household: $57,443; Average household: $71,165; Households with income of $100,000 or more: 27.5%; Poverty rate: 14.4%

Educational Attainment: High school diploma or higher: 82.0%; Bachelor's degree or higher: 25.4%; Graduate/professional degree or higher: 10.3%

Housing: Homeownership rate: 49.2%; Median home value: $310,600; Median year structure built: 1962; Homeowner vacancy rate: 3.1%; Median selected monthly owner costs: $2,157 with a mortgage, $698 without a mortgage; Median gross rent: $1,011 per month; Rental vacancy rate: 5.4%

Health Insurance: 95.1% have insurance; 60.3% have private insurance; 42.3% have public insurance; 4.9% do not have insurance; 1.1% of children under 18 do not have insurance

Transportation: Commute: 50.3% car, 46.6% public transportation, 0.9% walk, 1.8% work from home; Mean travel time to work: 58.4 minutes

FLUSHING (unincorporated postal area)
ZCTA: 11354

Covers a land area of 2.167 square miles and a water area of 0.032 square miles. Located at 40.77° N. Lat; 73.83° W. Long. Elevation is 85 feet.

Population: 57,566; Growth (since 2000): 6.0%; Density: 26,564.1 persons per square mile; Race: 20.7% White, 3.6% Black/African American, 62.4% Asian, 0.2% American Indian/Alaska Native, 0.0% Native Hawaiian/Other Pacific Islander, 2.7% Two or more races, 16.0% Hispanic of any race; Average household size: 2.75; Median age: 44.2; Age under 18: 15.4%; Age 65 and over: 18.4%; Males per 100 females: 87.8; Marriage status: 30.7% never married, 53.1% now married, 2.8% separated, 8.6% widowed, 7.6% divorced; Foreign born: 65.6%; Speak English only: 21.2%; With disability: 8.3%; Veterans: 1.7%; Ancestry: 4.2% Italian, 4.2% American, 1.9% Irish, 1.3% Russian, 1.3% Greek

Employment: 11.5% management, business, and financial, 3.1% computer, engineering, and science, 6.6% education, legal, community service, arts, and media, 5.7% healthcare practitioners, 31.9% service, 26.2% sales and office, 6.2% natural resources, construction, and maintenance, 8.7% production, transportation, and material moving

Income: Per capita: $24,252; Median household: $44,512; Average household: $63,624; Households with income of $100,000 or more: 17.9%; Poverty rate: 21.0%

Educational Attainment: High school diploma or higher: 74.1%; Bachelor's degree or higher: 20.5%; Graduate/professional degree or higher: 7.0%

Housing: Homeownership rate: 39.5%; Median home value: $473,300; Median year structure built: 1958; Homeowner vacancy rate: 2.1%; Median selected monthly owner costs: $2,351 with a mortgage, $720 without a mortgage; Median gross rent: $1,412 per month; Rental vacancy rate: 4.2%

Health Insurance: 78.1% have insurance; 46.0% have private insurance; 37.5% have public insurance; 21.9% do not have insurance; 13.6% of children under 18 do not have insurance

Transportation: Commute: 40.9% car, 40.6% public transportation, 15.5% walk, 1.7% work from home; Mean travel time to work: 40.8 minutes

ZCTA: 11355

Covers a land area of 1.735 square miles and a water area of 0 square miles. Located at 40.75° N. Lat; 73.82° W. Long. Elevation is 85 feet.

Population: 82,890; Growth (since 2000): -0.5%; Density: 47,774.3 persons per square mile; Race: 12.8% White, 3.3% Black/African American, 72.7% Asian, 0.6% American Indian/Alaska Native, 0.1% Native Hawaiian/Other Pacific Islander, 2.4% Two or more races, 14.0% Hispanic of any race; Average household size: 2.99; Median age: 42.3; Age under 18: 16.7%; Age 65 and over: 16.7%; Males per 100 females: 93.2; Marriage status: 30.2% never married, 57.1% now married, 2.3% separated, 6.9% widowed, 5.7% divorced; Foreign born: 71.4%; Speak English only: 14.4%; With disability: 7.7%; Veterans: 1.3%; Ancestry: 1.9% American, 1.7% Italian, 0.8% Irish, 0.7% Russian, 0.6% Greek

Employment: 9.0% management, business, and financial, 4.1% computer, engineering, and science, 6.6% education, legal, community service, arts, and media, 4.1% healthcare practitioners, 32.4% service, 23.3% sales and office, 7.4% natural resources, construction, and maintenance, 13.1% production, transportation, and material moving

Income: Per capita: $20,034; Median household: $38,370; Average household: $55,963; Households with income of $100,000 or more: 16.0%; Poverty rate: 23.0%

Educational Attainment: High school diploma or higher: 70.3%; Bachelor's degree or higher: 19.8%; Graduate/professional degree or higher: 7.5%

Housing: Homeownership rate: 31.0%; Median home value: $533,000; Median year structure built: 1957; Homeowner vacancy rate: 2.5%; Median selected monthly owner costs: $2,391 with a mortgage, $797 without a mortgage; Median gross rent: $1,345 per month; Rental vacancy rate: 3.3%

Health Insurance: 77.6% have insurance; 38.4% have private insurance; 44.2% have public insurance; 22.4% do not have insurance; 8.6% of children under 18 do not have insurance

Transportation: Commute: 39.7% car, 43.3% public transportation, 14.6% walk, 1.5% work from home; Mean travel time to work: 39.9 minutes

ZCTA: 11358

Covers a land area of 1.949 square miles and a water area of 0 square miles. Located at 40.76° N. Lat; 73.80° W. Long. Elevation is 85 feet.

Population: 36,959; Growth (since 2000): -4.4%; Density: 18,959.1 persons per square mile; Race: 43.5% White, 1.2% Black/African American, 44.9% Asian, 0.2% American Indian/Alaska Native, 0.0% Native Hawaiian/Other Pacific Islander, 2.4% Two or more races, 16.5% Hispanic of any race; Average household size: 2.88; Median age: 43.5; Age under 18: 16.8%; Age 65 and over: 18.4%; Males per 100 females: 94.3; Marriage status: 31.0% never married, 56.7% now married, 1.7% separated, 6.3% widowed, 6.0% divorced; Foreign born: 48.5%; Speak English only: 33.8%; With disability: 6.5%; Veterans: 2.9%; Ancestry: 11.1% Italian, 6.6% Greek, 6.4% Irish, 4.1% American, 3.5% German

Employment: 15.6% management, business, and financial, 5.0% computer, engineering, and science, 12.7% education, legal, community service, arts, and media, 4.9% healthcare practitioners, 21.1% service, 25.0% sales and office, 7.2% natural resources, construction, and maintenance, 8.5% production, transportation, and material moving

Income: Per capita: $32,137; Median household: $65,932; Average household: $88,217; Households with income of $100,000 or more: 33.9%; Poverty rate: 9.9%
Educational Attainment: High school diploma or higher: 84.0%; Bachelor's degree or higher: 31.7%; Graduate/professional degree or higher: 12.5%
Housing: Homeownership rate: 56.0%; Median home value: $700,100; Median year structure built: 1945; Homeowner vacancy rate: 1.1%; Median selected monthly owner costs: $2,745 with a mortgage, $963 without a mortgage; Median gross rent: $1,583 per month; Rental vacancy rate: 4.6%
Health Insurance: 86.1% have insurance; 62.6% have private insurance; 32.1% have public insurance; 13.9% do not have insurance; 7.4% of children under 18 do not have insurance
Transportation: Commute: 53.1% car, 39.2% public transportation, 3.6% walk, 2.6% work from home; Mean travel time to work: 41.9 minutes

ZCTA: 11367

Covers a land area of 2.379 square miles and a water area of 0.186 square miles. Located at 40.73° N. Lat; 73.83° W. Long. Elevation is 85 feet.
Population: 43,496; Growth (since 2000): 13.8%; Density: 18,281.7 persons per square mile; Race: 56.1% White, 8.1% Black/African American, 26.5% Asian, 0.3% American Indian/Alaska Native, 0.0% Native Hawaiian/Other Pacific Islander, 4.3% Two or more races, 17.5% Hispanic of any race; Average household size: 2.90; Median age: 35.0; Age under 18: 24.4%; Age 65 and over: 14.9%; Males per 100 females: 91.0; Marriage status: 33.6% never married, 52.9% now married, 1.3% separated, 5.9% widowed, 7.5% divorced; Foreign born: 40.2%; Speak English only: 41.6%; With disability: 9.9%; Veterans: 3.1%; Ancestry: 7.0% Russian, 4.9% American, 4.4% Polish, 2.9% Italian, 2.2% German
Employment: 14.5% management, business, and financial, 4.6% computer, engineering, and science, 14.5% education, legal, community service, arts, and media, 8.5% healthcare practitioners, 19.3% service, 23.3% sales and office, 6.3% natural resources, construction, and maintenance, 9.0% production, transportation, and material moving
Income: Per capita: $27,413; Median household: $58,924; Average household: $78,082; Households with income of $100,000 or more: 27.6%; Poverty rate: 13.5%
Educational Attainment: High school diploma or higher: 84.4%; Bachelor's degree or higher: 38.2%; Graduate/professional degree or higher: 16.3%
Housing: Homeownership rate: 47.0%; Median home value: $394,300; Median year structure built: 1954; Homeowner vacancy rate: 1.4%; Median selected monthly owner costs: $1,970 with a mortgage, $717 without a mortgage; Median gross rent: $1,345 per month; Rental vacancy rate: 3.3%
Health Insurance: 93.0% have insurance; 64.2% have private insurance; 38.0% have public insurance; 7.0% do not have insurance; 2.6% of children under 18 do not have insurance
Transportation: Commute: 48.7% car, 40.6% public transportation, 7.3% walk, 2.2% work from home; Mean travel time to work: 42.0 minutes

FOREST HILLS (unincorporated postal area)
ZCTA: 11375

Covers a land area of 1.980 square miles and a water area of 0 square miles. Located at 40.72° N. Lat; 73.85° W. Long. Elevation is 59 feet.
Population: 72,937; Growth (since 2000): 3.9%; Density: 36,829.8 persons per square mile; Race: 61.9% White, 2.6% Black/African American, 28.4% Asian, 0.3% American Indian/Alaska Native, 0.1% Native Hawaiian/Other Pacific Islander, 4.1% Two or more races, 15.1% Hispanic of any race; Average household size: 2.23; Median age: 41.9; Age under 18: 19.0%; Age 65 and over: 19.1%; Males per 100 females: 85.7; Marriage status: 30.0% never married, 54.7% now married, 1.7% separated, 7.3% widowed, 8.0% divorced; Foreign born: 45.5%; Speak English only: 42.4%; With disability: 10.2%; Veterans: 2.4%; Ancestry: 9.6% Russian, 5.7% Italian, 5.0% American, 4.8% Polish, 4.7% Irish
Employment: 23.3% management, business, and financial, 8.2% computer, engineering, and science, 19.4% education, legal, community service, arts, and media, 8.3% healthcare practitioners, 11.0% service, 21.3% sales and office, 3.4% natural resources, construction, and maintenance, 5.1% production, transportation, and material moving

Income: Per capita: $46,430; Median household: $76,467; Average household: $101,342; Households with income of $100,000 or more: 37.7%; Poverty rate: 9.5%
Educational Attainment: High school diploma or higher: 93.1%; Bachelor's degree or higher: 59.5%; Graduate/professional degree or higher: 28.0%
Housing: Homeownership rate: 50.1%; Median home value: $382,700; Median year structure built: 1951; Homeowner vacancy rate: 1.8%; Median selected monthly owner costs: $1,802 with a mortgage, $598 without a mortgage; Median gross rent: $1,676 per month; Rental vacancy rate: 2.7%
Health Insurance: 95.0% have insurance; 75.5% have private insurance; 29.9% have public insurance; 5.0% do not have insurance; 2.9% of children under 18 do not have insurance
Transportation: Commute: 27.6% car, 62.0% public transportation, 5.4% walk, 4.2% work from home; Mean travel time to work: 43.0 minutes

FRESH MEADOWS (unincorporated postal area)
ZCTA: 11365

Covers a land area of 2.497 square miles and a water area of 0.018 square miles. Located at 40.74° N. Lat; 73.79° W. Long. Elevation is 36 feet.
Population: 45,565; Growth (since 2000): 9.6%; Density: 18,250.4 persons per square mile; Race: 35.3% White, 7.6% Black/African American, 44.6% Asian, 0.4% American Indian/Alaska Native, 0.0% Native Hawaiian/Other Pacific Islander, 3.5% Two or more races, 18.7% Hispanic of any race; Average household size: 2.91; Median age: 41.3; Age under 18: 20.0%; Age 65 and over: 15.1%; Males per 100 females: 89.2; Marriage status: 30.6% never married, 55.1% now married, 1.1% separated, 8.0% widowed, 6.4% divorced; Foreign born: 44.9%; Speak English only: 38.8%; With disability: 8.3%; Veterans: 3.7%; Ancestry: 5.1% Italian, 4.5% Irish, 2.9% Russian, 2.7% Polish, 2.6% German
Employment: 13.1% management, business, and financial, 5.1% computer, engineering, and science, 11.2% education, legal, community service, arts, and media, 6.7% healthcare practitioners, 20.4% service, 29.2% sales and office, 6.3% natural resources, construction, and maintenance, 7.9% production, transportation, and material moving
Income: Per capita: $29,830; Median household: $63,455; Average household: $82,750; Households with income of $100,000 or more: 30.0%; Poverty rate: 13.2%
Educational Attainment: High school diploma or higher: 86.1%; Bachelor's degree or higher: 35.5%; Graduate/professional degree or higher: 14.4%
Housing: Homeownership rate: 48.6%; Median home value: $638,700; Median year structure built: 1954; Homeowner vacancy rate: 0.5%; Median selected monthly owner costs: $2,786 with a mortgage, $915 without a mortgage; Median gross rent: $1,459 per month; Rental vacancy rate: 2.2%
Health Insurance: 90.9% have insurance; 63.1% have private insurance; 36.9% have public insurance; 9.1% do not have insurance; 2.5% of children under 18 do not have insurance
Transportation: Commute: 56.7% car, 37.3% public transportation, 3.1% walk, 2.1% work from home; Mean travel time to work: 45.4 minutes

ZCTA: 11366

Covers a land area of 1.095 square miles and a water area of 0 square miles. Located at 40.73° N. Lat; 73.79° W. Long. Elevation is 36 feet.
Population: 14,308; Growth (since 2000): 7.0%; Density: 13,071.3 persons per square mile; Race: 41.2% White, 5.6% Black/African American, 47.1% Asian, 0.0% American Indian/Alaska Native, 0.0% Native Hawaiian/Other Pacific Islander, 3.1% Two or more races, 8.0% Hispanic of any race; Average household size: 3.17; Median age: 40.5; Age under 18: 19.9%; Age 65 and over: 17.3%; Males per 100 females: 93.1; Marriage status: 34.1% never married, 55.1% now married, 2.1% separated, 5.6% widowed, 5.2% divorced; Foreign born: 51.4%; Speak English only: 33.3%; With disability: 7.9%; Veterans: 2.8%; Ancestry: 10.3% Russian, 3.5% American, 2.9% Italian, 2.8% Irish, 2.6% Polish
Employment: 15.2% management, business, and financial, 6.7% computer, engineering, and science, 11.5% education, legal, community service, arts, and media, 10.3% healthcare practitioners, 20.8% service, 24.5% sales and office, 5.3% natural resources, construction, and maintenance, 5.8% production, transportation, and material moving

Income: Per capita: $31,649; Median household: $67,115; Average household: $94,635; Households with income of $100,000 or more: 36.3%; Poverty rate: 13.3%

Educational Attainment: High school diploma or higher: 87.9%; Bachelor's degree or higher: 43.2%; Graduate/professional degree or higher: 16.3%

Housing: Homeownership rate: 70.1%; Median home value: $690,500; Median year structure built: 1951; Homeowner vacancy rate: 3.2%; Median selected monthly owner costs: $2,878 with a mortgage, $1,020 without a mortgage; Median gross rent: $1,624 per month; Rental vacancy rate: 1.3%

Health Insurance: 95.2% have insurance; 65.8% have private insurance; 41.0% have public insurance; 4.8% do not have insurance; 3.2% of children under 18 do not have insurance

Transportation: Commute: 51.9% car, 39.2% public transportation, 4.3% walk, 3.9% work from home; Mean travel time to work: 42.3 minutes

GLEN OAKS (unincorporated postal area)
ZCTA: 11004

Covers a land area of 0.950 square miles and a water area of 0 square miles. Located at 40.75° N. Lat; 73.71° W. Long. Elevation is 118 feet.

Population: 15,151; Growth (since 2000): 3.2%; Density: 15,946.5 persons per square mile; Race: 43.0% White, 7.4% Black/African American, 38.7% Asian, 0.7% American Indian/Alaska Native, 0.3% Native Hawaiian/Other Pacific Islander, 4.6% Two or more races, 14.2% Hispanic of any race; Average household size: 2.83; Median age: 44.5; Age under 18: 16.9%; Age 65 and over: 19.2%; Males per 100 females: 87.4; Marriage status: 30.9% never married, 52.4% now married, 0.8% separated, 7.9% widowed, 8.8% divorced; Foreign born: 37.6%; Speak English only: 56.8%; With disability: 11.2%; Veterans: 3.0%; Ancestry: 10.5% Irish, 10.0% Italian, 6.4% German, 4.9% American, 2.6% Polish

Employment: 15.4% management, business, and financial, 6.8% computer, engineering, and science, 10.0% education, legal, community service, arts, and media, 13.5% healthcare practitioners, 10.6% service, 27.8% sales and office, 6.3% natural resources, construction, and maintenance, 9.6% production, transportation, and material moving

Income: Per capita: $38,119; Median household: $93,315; Average household: $107,832; Households with income of $100,000 or more: 45.2%; Poverty rate: 6.2%

Educational Attainment: High school diploma or higher: 91.6%; Bachelor's degree or higher: 40.1%; Graduate/professional degree or higher: 16.5%

Housing: Homeownership rate: 73.0%; Median home value: $508,900; Median year structure built: 1954; Homeowner vacancy rate: 1.8%; Median selected monthly owner costs: $2,435 with a mortgage, $921 without a mortgage; Median gross rent: $1,431 per month; Rental vacancy rate: 0.0%

Health Insurance: 96.0% have insurance; 80.6% have private insurance; 26.2% have public insurance; 4.0% do not have insurance; 2.5% of children under 18 do not have insurance

Transportation: Commute: 72.8% car, 22.1% public transportation, 3.0% walk, 1.6% work from home; Mean travel time to work: 38.6 minutes

HOLLIS (unincorporated postal area)
ZCTA: 11423

Covers a land area of 1.411 square miles and a water area of 0 square miles. Located at 40.72° N. Lat; 73.77° W. Long. Elevation is 59 feet.

Population: 32,407; Growth (since 2000): 3.7%; Density: 22,968.9 persons per square mile; Race: 13.3% White, 37.5% Black/African American, 29.6% Asian, 1.1% American Indian/Alaska Native, 0.0% Native Hawaiian/Other Pacific Islander, 3.6% Two or more races, 14.0% Hispanic of any race; Average household size: 3.25; Median age: 39.9; Age under 18: 19.3%; Age 65 and over: 14.3%; Males per 100 females: 89.5; Marriage status: 39.2% never married, 47.0% now married, 2.3% separated, 5.4% widowed, 8.4% divorced; Foreign born: 53.0%; Speak English only: 60.0%; With disability: 10.8%; Veterans: 3.0%; Ancestry: 16.2% Guyanese, 6.8% Haitian, 6.5% Jamaican, 5.9% American, 2.0% Trinidadian and Tobagonian

Employment: 10.6% management, business, and financial, 3.6% computer, engineering, and science, 7.8% education, legal, community service, arts, and media, 7.3% healthcare practitioners, 26.5% service, 24.7% sales and office, 8.5% natural resources, construction, and maintenance, 10.9% production, transportation, and material moving

Income: Per capita: $27,902; Median household: $66,455; Average household: $84,986; Households with income of $100,000 or more: 29.2%; Poverty rate: 8.6%

Educational Attainment: High school diploma or higher: 83.0%; Bachelor's degree or higher: 28.4%; Graduate/professional degree or higher: 8.7%

Housing: Homeownership rate: 57.0%; Median home value: $458,100; Median year structure built: 1949; Homeowner vacancy rate: 0.0%; Median selected monthly owner costs: $2,433 with a mortgage, $903 without a mortgage; Median gross rent: $1,338 per month; Rental vacancy rate: 3.6%

Health Insurance: 90.5% have insurance; 58.2% have private insurance; 40.5% have public insurance; 9.5% do not have insurance; 1.9% of children under 18 do not have insurance

Transportation: Commute: 45.1% car, 46.8% public transportation, 2.9% walk, 3.6% work from home; Mean travel time to work: 46.7 minutes

HOWARD BEACH (unincorporated postal area)
ZCTA: 11414

Covers a land area of 2.300 square miles and a water area of 0.087 square miles. Located at 40.66° N. Lat; 73.84° W. Long. Elevation is 3 feet.

Population: 29,203; Growth (since 2000): 3.8%; Density: 12,698.8 persons per square mile; Race: 77.9% White, 2.8% Black/African American, 4.0% Asian, 0.0% American Indian/Alaska Native, 0.0% Native Hawaiian/Other Pacific Islander, 4.8% Two or more races, 23.5% Hispanic of any race; Average household size: 2.78; Median age: 45.2; Age under 18: 19.5%; Age 65 and over: 21.7%; Males per 100 females: 88.8; Marriage status: 30.8% never married, 52.4% now married, 2.3% separated, 8.2% widowed, 8.5% divorced; Foreign born: 20.5%; Speak English only: 63.9%; With disability: 14.4%; Veterans: 5.7%; Ancestry: 31.7% Italian, 11.4% Irish, 6.7% German, 6.1% Polish, 2.3% American

Employment: 14.9% management, business, and financial, 3.4% computer, engineering, and science, 13.0% education, legal, community service, arts, and media, 4.7% healthcare practitioners, 15.2% service, 28.1% sales and office, 8.1% natural resources, construction, and maintenance, 12.7% production, transportation, and material moving

Income: Per capita: $36,334; Median household: $72,632; Average household: $96,563; Households with income of $100,000 or more: 34.0%; Poverty rate: 11.8%

Educational Attainment: High school diploma or higher: 85.2%; Bachelor's degree or higher: 26.6%; Graduate/professional degree or higher: 9.7%

Housing: Homeownership rate: 69.6%; Median home value: $496,600; Median year structure built: 1962; Homeowner vacancy rate: 1.9%; Median selected monthly owner costs: $2,035 with a mortgage, $872 without a mortgage; Median gross rent: $1,509 per month; Rental vacancy rate: 0.0%

Health Insurance: 94.5% have insurance; 72.0% have private insurance; 37.4% have public insurance; 5.5% do not have insurance; 2.7% of children under 18 do not have insurance

Transportation: Commute: 68.1% car, 27.6% public transportation, 3.1% walk, 0.4% work from home; Mean travel time to work: 40.9 minutes

JACKSON HEIGHTS (unincorporated postal area)
ZCTA: 11372

Covers a land area of 0.737 square miles and a water area of 0 square miles. Located at 40.75° N. Lat; 73.88° W. Long. Elevation is 79 feet.

Population: 64,298; Growth (since 2000): -9.8%; Density: 87,189.3 persons per square mile; Race: 58.9% White, 2.7% Black/African American, 20.5% Asian, 0.2% American Indian/Alaska Native, 0.3% Native Hawaiian/Other Pacific Islander, 3.3% Two or more races, 59.3% Hispanic of any race; Average household size: 2.66; Median age: 39.7; Age under 18: 18.3%; Age 65 and over: 14.8%; Males per 100 females: 102.2; Marriage status: 43.2% never married, 41.0% now married, 3.3% separated, 5.4% widowed, 10.3% divorced; Foreign born: 59.6%; Speak English only: 20.2%; With disability: 8.6%; Veterans: 1.7%; Ancestry: 2.8% Irish, 2.7% Italian, 2.6% German, 2.0% American, 1.6% Russian

Employment: 12.7% management, business, and financial, 3.9% computer, engineering, and science, 10.5% education, legal, community service, arts, and media, 2.2% healthcare practitioners, 30.8% service, 20.6% sales and office, 6.6% natural resources, construction, and maintenance, 12.6% production, transportation, and material moving

Income: Per capita: $27,761; Median household: $53,963; Average household: $69,795; Households with income of $100,000 or more: 19.4%; Poverty rate: 14.0%

Educational Attainment: High school diploma or higher: 76.5%; Bachelor's degree or higher: 28.5%; Graduate/professional degree or higher: 10.2%

Housing: Homeownership rate: 30.6%; Median home value: $298,700; Median year structure built: 1946; Homeowner vacancy rate: 1.5%; Median selected monthly owner costs: $1,599 with a mortgage, $582 without a mortgage; Median gross rent: $1,390 per month; Rental vacancy rate: 2.3%

Health Insurance: 83.0% have insurance; 48.8% have private insurance; 42.9% have public insurance; 17.0% do not have insurance; 3.7% of children under 18 do not have insurance

Transportation: Commute: 21.0% car, 67.5% public transportation, 8.3% walk, 1.7% work from home; Mean travel time to work: 41.1 minutes

JAMAICA (unincorporated postal area)

ZCTA: 11430

Covers a land area of 7.118 square miles and a water area of 0.256 square miles. Located at 40.65° N. Lat; 73.79° W. Long. Elevation is 43 feet.

Population: 183; Growth (since 2000): -20.1%; Density: 25.7 persons per square mile; Race: 6.6% White, 78.1% Black/African American, 0.0% Asian, 0.0% American Indian/Alaska Native, 0.0% Native Hawaiian/Other Pacific Islander, 0.0% Two or more races, 32.2% Hispanic of any race; Average household size: 0.00; Median age: 45.5; Age under 18: 2.7%; Age 65 and over: 6.6%; Males per 100 females: 58.6; Marriage status: 76.4% never married, 14.0% now married, 2.8% separated, 2.8% widowed, 6.7% divorced; Foreign born: 6.6%; Speak English only: 69.7%; With disability: 33.3%; Veterans: 10.7%; Ancestry: 3.8% Guyanese

Employment: 0.0% management, business, and financial, 0.0% computer, engineering, and science, 0.0% education, legal, community service, arts, and media, 0.0% healthcare practitioners, 52.1% service, 29.6% sales and office, 8.5% natural resources, construction, and maintenance, 9.9% production, transportation, and material moving

Income: Per capita: $7,330; Median household: n/a; Average household: n/a; Households with income of $100,000 or more: n/a; Poverty rate: 78.1%

Educational Attainment: High school diploma or higher: 63.2%; Bachelor's degree or higher: 3.2%; Graduate/professional degree or higher: n/a

Housing: Homeownership rate: n/a; Median home value: n/a; Median year structure built: n/a; Homeowner vacancy rate: 0.0%; Median selected monthly owner costs: $0 with a mortgage, $0 without a mortgage; Median gross rent: n/a per month; Rental vacancy rate: 0.0%

Health Insurance: 83.6% have insurance; 0.0% have private insurance; 83.6% have public insurance; 16.4% do not have insurance; 0.0% of children under 18 do not have insurance

Transportation: Commute: 0.0% car, 82.8% public transportation, 17.2% walk, 0.0% work from home; Mean travel time to work: 70.3 minutes

ZCTA: 11432

Covers a land area of 2.149 square miles and a water area of 0 square miles. Located at 40.72° N. Lat; 73.79° W. Long. Elevation is 43 feet.

Population: 65,098; Growth (since 2000): 14.1%; Density: 30,290.4 persons per square mile; Race: 22.1% White, 15.6% Black/African American, 40.9% Asian, 0.5% American Indian/Alaska Native, 0.2% Native Hawaiian/Other Pacific Islander, 4.4% Two or more races, 25.7% Hispanic of any race; Average household size: 3.29; Median age: 35.1; Age under 18: 21.9%; Age 65 and over: 13.4%; Males per 100 females: 97.3; Marriage status: 39.7% never married, 48.1% now married, 2.0% separated, 5.4% widowed, 6.8% divorced; Foreign born: 57.1%; Speak English only: 31.6%; With disability: 8.6%; Veterans: 1.5%; Ancestry: 3.5% Guyanese, 2.4% Haitian, 2.3% Italian, 1.9% Irish, 1.8% American

Employment: 11.4% management, business, and financial, 3.7% computer, engineering, and science, 10.4% education, legal, community service, arts, and media, 6.1% healthcare practitioners, 24.5% service, 24.7% sales and office, 6.8% natural resources, construction, and maintenance, 12.4% production, transportation, and material moving

Income: Per capita: $23,174; Median household: $52,975; Average household: $75,650; Households with income of $100,000 or more: 23.7%; Poverty rate: 17.7%

Educational Attainment: High school diploma or higher: 78.2%; Bachelor's degree or higher: 35.0%; Graduate/professional degree or higher: 12.8%

Housing: Homeownership rate: 35.6%; Median home value: $563,400; Median year structure built: 1952; Homeowner vacancy rate: 0.9%; Median selected monthly owner costs: $2,619 with a mortgage, $926 without a mortgage; Median gross rent: $1,399 per month; Rental vacancy rate: 4.0%

Health Insurance: 88.4% have insurance; 47.4% have private insurance; 47.7% have public insurance; 11.6% do not have insurance; 4.0% of children under 18 do not have insurance

Transportation: Commute: 32.9% car, 54.3% public transportation, 8.6% walk, 2.8% work from home; Mean travel time to work: 45.6 minutes

ZCTA: 11433

Covers a land area of 1.552 square miles and a water area of 0 square miles. Located at 40.70° N. Lat; 73.79° W. Long. Elevation is 43 feet.

Population: 36,019; Growth (since 2000): 26.7%; Density: 23,208.7 persons per square mile; Race: 3.2% White, 67.6% Black/African American, 7.2% Asian, 0.3% American Indian/Alaska Native, 0.0% Native Hawaiian/Other Pacific Islander, 3.0% Two or more races, 19.4% Hispanic of any race; Average household size: 3.44; Median age: 34.4; Age under 18: 24.5%; Age 65 and over: 12.3%; Males per 100 females: 82.9; Marriage status: 51.8% never married, 35.7% now married, 4.0% separated, 5.3% widowed, 7.2% divorced; Foreign born: 39.2%; Speak English only: 73.6%; With disability: 10.6%; Veterans: 3.2%; Ancestry: 10.6% Jamaican, 7.8% Guyanese, 4.0% Trinidadian and Tobagonian, 2.8% American, 2.6% West Indian

Employment: 7.4% management, business, and financial, 1.5% computer, engineering, and science, 8.5% education, legal, community service, arts, and media, 3.3% healthcare practitioners, 34.8% service, 24.8% sales and office, 7.3% natural resources, construction, and maintenance, 12.4% production, transportation, and material moving

Income: Per capita: $20,816; Median household: $48,795; Average household: $66,108; Households with income of $100,000 or more: 20.7%; Poverty rate: 16.8%

Educational Attainment: High school diploma or higher: 77.4%; Bachelor's degree or higher: 17.8%; Graduate/professional degree or higher: 5.7%

Housing: Homeownership rate: 43.3%; Median home value: $388,200; Median year structure built: 1954; Homeowner vacancy rate: 4.3%; Median selected monthly owner costs: $2,494 with a mortgage, $655 without a mortgage; Median gross rent: $1,165 per month; Rental vacancy rate: 2.7%

Health Insurance: 85.9% have insurance; 44.3% have private insurance; 46.6% have public insurance; 14.1% do not have insurance; 6.1% of children under 18 do not have insurance

Transportation: Commute: 40.3% car, 52.9% public transportation, 4.8% walk, 1.4% work from home; Mean travel time to work: 48.1 minutes

ZCTA: 11434

Covers a land area of 3.239 square miles and a water area of 0.066 square miles. Located at 40.68° N. Lat; 73.78° W. Long. Elevation is 43 feet.

Population: 66,725; Growth (since 2000): 12.8%; Density: 20,601.8 persons per square mile; Race: 2.8% White, 87.7% Black/African American, 2.1% Asian, 0.1% American Indian/Alaska Native, 0.0% Native Hawaiian/Other Pacific Islander, 1.9% Two or more races, 8.1% Hispanic of any race; Average household size: 3.08; Median age: 37.5; Age under 18: 22.7%; Age 65 and over: 14.5%; Males per 100 females: 77.6; Marriage status: 47.7% never married, 35.4% now married, 4.3% separated, 6.4% widowed, 10.5% divorced; Foreign born: 32.1%; Speak English only: 88.9%; With disability: 11.7%; Veterans: 4.5%; Ancestry: 14.1% Jamaican, 4.4% Guyanese, 4.2% West Indian, 3.5% Haitian, 2.9% Trinidadian and Tobagonian

Employment: 9.7% management, business, and financial, 2.3% computer, engineering, and science, 10.3% education, legal, community service, arts, and media, 5.8% healthcare practitioners, 28.3% service, 25.7% sales and office, 6.4% natural resources, construction, and maintenance, 11.6% production, transportation, and material moving

Income: Per capita: $25,446; Median household: $60,702; Average household: $73,933; Households with income of $100,000 or more: 26.4%; Poverty rate: 10.4%

Educational Attainment: High school diploma or higher: 86.6%; Bachelor's degree or higher: 21.5%; Graduate/professional degree or higher: 6.3%
Housing: Homeownership rate: 49.2%; Median home value: $386,000; Median year structure built: 1961; Homeowner vacancy rate: 2.4%; Median selected monthly owner costs: $2,437 with a mortgage, $715 without a mortgage; Median gross rent: $1,130 per month; Rental vacancy rate: 1.1%
Health Insurance: 92.9% have insurance; 64.4% have private insurance; 37.7% have public insurance; 7.1% do not have insurance; 2.0% of children under 18 do not have insurance
Transportation: Commute: 46.9% car, 46.8% public transportation, 2.9% walk, 2.3% work from home; Mean travel time to work: 49.3 minutes

ZCTA: 11435
Covers a land area of 1.515 square miles and a water area of 0 square miles. Located at 40.70° N. Lat; 73.81° W. Long. Elevation is 43 feet.
Population: 59,214; Growth (since 2000): 9.9%; Density: 39,095.9 persons per square mile; Race: 19.3% White, 23.7% Black/African American, 23.8% Asian, 0.2% American Indian/Alaska Native, 0.0% Native Hawaiian/Other Pacific Islander, 4.7% Two or more races, 30.6% Hispanic of any race; Average household size: 3.09; Median age: 35.4; Age under 18: 21.0%; Age 65 and over: 12.1%; Males per 100 females: 96.4; Marriage status: 40.4% never married, 48.2% now married, 2.1% separated, 5.9% widowed, 5.5% divorced; Foreign born: 54.3%; Speak English only: 45.3%; With disability: 9.4%; Veterans: 1.7%; Ancestry: 10.1% Guyanese, 3.6% Jamaican, 3.1% Trinidadian and Tobagonian, 1.6% American, 1.4% Russian
Employment: 11.4% management, business, and financial, 4.5% computer, engineering, and science, 8.5% education, legal, community service, arts, and media, 5.5% healthcare practitioners, 23.9% service, 24.7% sales and office, 10.3% natural resources, construction, and maintenance, 11.3% production, transportation, and material moving
Income: Per capita: $25,498; Median household: $59,535; Average household: $74,494; Households with income of $100,000 or more: 24.7%; Poverty rate: 16.4%
Educational Attainment: High school diploma or higher: 76.7%; Bachelor's degree or higher: 27.3%; Graduate/professional degree or higher: 9.2%
Housing: Homeownership rate: 35.7%; Median home value: $363,900; Median year structure built: 1953; Homeowner vacancy rate: 1.6%; Median selected monthly owner costs: $2,283 with a mortgage, $737 without a mortgage; Median gross rent: $1,421 per month; Rental vacancy rate: 1.9%
Health Insurance: 85.7% have insurance; 45.2% have private insurance; 45.4% have public insurance; 14.3% do not have insurance; 5.0% of children under 18 do not have insurance
Transportation: Commute: 32.9% car, 58.7% public transportation, 5.0% walk, 1.9% work from home; Mean travel time to work: 47.4 minutes

ZCTA: 11436
Covers a land area of 0.788 square miles and a water area of 0 square miles. Located at 40.68° N. Lat; 73.80° W. Long. Elevation is 43 feet.
Population: 20,905; Growth (since 2000): 15.2%; Density: 26,534.8 persons per square mile; Race: 7.4% White, 62.0% Black/African American, 10.4% Asian, 0.7% American Indian/Alaska Native, 0.0% Native Hawaiian/Other Pacific Islander, 4.5% Two or more races, 15.7% Hispanic of any race; Average household size: 3.67; Median age: 35.9; Age under 18: 22.7%; Age 65 and over: 10.5%; Males per 100 females: 87.6; Marriage status: 42.6% never married, 42.4% now married, 3.4% separated, 7.3% widowed, 7.7% divorced; Foreign born: 40.5%; Speak English only: 78.7%; With disability: 12.0%; Veterans: 3.2%; Ancestry: 13.8% Guyanese, 6.9% Jamaican, 6.0% Trinidadian and Tobagonian, 3.9% West Indian, 2.7% Haitian
Employment: 8.7% management, business, and financial, 1.8% computer, engineering, and science, 7.6% education, legal, community service, arts, and media, 5.2% healthcare practitioners, 25.6% service, 26.5% sales and office, 12.7% natural resources, construction, and maintenance, 11.9% production, transportation, and material moving
Income: Per capita: $25,222; Median household: $69,259; Average household: $84,711; Households with income of $100,000 or more: 31.3%; Poverty rate: 11.7%
Educational Attainment: High school diploma or higher: 80.4%; Bachelor's degree or higher: 17.5%; Graduate/professional degree or higher: 5.9%

Housing: Homeownership rate: 71.6%; Median home value: $382,600; Median year structure built: 1950; Homeowner vacancy rate: 1.0%; Median selected monthly owner costs: $2,434 with a mortgage, $767 without a mortgage; Median gross rent: $1,492 per month; Rental vacancy rate: 4.5%
Health Insurance: 90.0% have insurance; 55.5% have private insurance; 42.1% have public insurance; 10.0% do not have insurance; 3.3% of children under 18 do not have insurance
Transportation: Commute: 49.4% car, 43.0% public transportation, 3.6% walk, 2.1% work from home; Mean travel time to work: 48.5 minutes

KEW GARDENS (unincorporated postal area)
ZCTA: 11415
Covers a land area of 0.568 square miles and a water area of 0 square miles. Located at 40.71° N. Lat; 73.83° W. Long. Elevation is 92 feet.
Population: 19,900; Growth (since 2000): -5.0%; Density: 35,026.0 persons per square mile; Race: 59.9% White, 5.6% Black/African American, 19.6% Asian, 0.3% American Indian/Alaska Native, 0.0% Native Hawaiian/Other Pacific Islander, 3.9% Two or more races, 24.0% Hispanic of any race; Average household size: 2.34; Median age: 38.6; Age under 18: 20.5%; Age 65 and over: 16.1%; Males per 100 females: 91.8; Marriage status: 37.7% never married, 47.5% now married, 1.5% separated, 5.9% widowed, 8.9% divorced; Foreign born: 41.9%; Speak English only: 42.3%; With disability: 9.1%; Veterans: 2.8%; Ancestry: 5.9% Russian, 4.9% American, 4.2% Polish, 3.5% Italian, 3.3% German
Employment: 18.9% management, business, and financial, 5.7% computer, engineering, and science, 17.6% education, legal, community service, arts, and media, 5.4% healthcare practitioners, 14.8% service, 22.4% sales and office, 5.2% natural resources, construction, and maintenance, 10.1% production, transportation, and material moving
Income: Per capita: $37,544; Median household: $65,981; Average household: $85,176; Households with income of $100,000 or more: 26.4%; Poverty rate: 12.0%
Educational Attainment: High school diploma or higher: 91.3%; Bachelor's degree or higher: 46.1%; Graduate/professional degree or higher: 19.9%
Housing: Homeownership rate: 35.5%; Median home value: $335,700; Median year structure built: 1948; Homeowner vacancy rate: 3.7%; Median selected monthly owner costs: $1,948 with a mortgage, $678 without a mortgage; Median gross rent: $1,461 per month; Rental vacancy rate: 3.7%
Health Insurance: 93.4% have insurance; 67.6% have private insurance; 32.7% have public insurance; 6.6% do not have insurance; 3.3% of children under 18 do not have insurance
Transportation: Commute: 31.5% car, 55.1% public transportation, 4.9% walk, 5.2% work from home; Mean travel time to work: 42.8 minutes

LITTLE NECK (unincorporated postal area)
ZCTA: 11362
Covers a land area of 2.517 square miles and a water area of 0.042 square miles. Located at 40.76° N. Lat; 73.74° W. Long. Elevation is 98 feet.
Population: 18,443; Growth (since 2000): 5.4%; Density: 7,327.8 persons per square mile; Race: 49.2% White, 1.0% Black/African American, 43.9% Asian, 0.0% American Indian/Alaska Native, 0.0% Native Hawaiian/Other Pacific Islander, 2.5% Two or more races, 8.9% Hispanic of any race; Average household size: 2.54; Median age: 48.9; Age under 18: 16.6%; Age 65 and over: 25.0%; Males per 100 females: 90.2; Marriage status: 27.0% never married, 56.9% now married, 1.7% separated, 9.0% widowed, 7.1% divorced; Foreign born: 40.7%; Speak English only: 46.8%; With disability: 10.9%; Veterans: 3.1%; Ancestry: 12.6% Italian, 5.9% Irish, 5.7% German, 4.9% Greek, 4.0% Polish
Employment: 18.1% management, business, and financial, 6.0% computer, engineering, and science, 15.5% education, legal, community service, arts, and media, 10.2% healthcare practitioners, 15.3% service, 25.0% sales and office, 4.3% natural resources, construction, and maintenance, 5.5% production, transportation, and material moving
Income: Per capita: $38,986; Median household: $80,828; Average household: $97,327; Households with income of $100,000 or more: 38.5%; Poverty rate: 7.4%
Educational Attainment: High school diploma or higher: 90.5%; Bachelor's degree or higher: 45.1%; Graduate/professional degree or higher: 20.8%

Housing: Homeownership rate: 80.1%; Median home value: $521,800; Median year structure built: 1957; Homeowner vacancy rate: 0.0%; Median selected monthly owner costs: $1,912 with a mortgage, $953 without a mortgage; Median gross rent: $1,682 per month; Rental vacancy rate: 1.6%
Health Insurance: 94.3% have insurance; 72.0% have private insurance; 36.3% have public insurance; 5.7% do not have insurance; 1.0% of children under 18 do not have insurance
Transportation: Commute: 64.4% car, 25.7% public transportation, 2.4% walk, 5.9% work from home; Mean travel time to work: 42.4 minutes

ZCTA: 11363

Covers a land area of 0.869 square miles and a water area of 0 square miles. Located at 40.77° N. Lat; 73.75° W. Long. Elevation is 98 feet.
Population: 7,423; Growth (since 2000): 7.3%; Density: 8,546.2 persons per square mile; Race: 59.7% White, 1.3% Black/African American, 30.2% Asian, 0.0% American Indian/Alaska Native, 0.0% Native Hawaiian/Other Pacific Islander, 4.5% Two or more races, 16.5% Hispanic of any race; Average household size: 2.83; Median age: 45.3; Age under 18: 20.1%; Age 65 and over: 20.6%; Males per 100 females: 90.6; Marriage status: 25.9% never married, 60.6% now married, 0.9% separated, 6.9% widowed, 6.6% divorced; Foreign born: 33.3%; Speak English only: 50.2%; With disability: 9.3%; Veterans: 3.9%; Ancestry: 19.9% Italian, 11.3% Irish, 6.3% American, 6.1% German, 4.6% Greek
Employment: 26.6% management, business, and financial, 4.9% computer, engineering, and science, 17.4% education, legal, community service, arts, and media, 5.6% healthcare practitioners, 11.0% service, 23.3% sales and office, 6.4% natural resources, construction, and maintenance, 4.8% production, transportation, and material moving
Income: Per capita: $46,719; Median household: $97,784; Average household: $128,817; Households with income of $100,000 or more: 48.5%; Poverty rate: 8.6%
Educational Attainment: High school diploma or higher: 96.2%; Bachelor's degree or higher: 51.0%; Graduate/professional degree or higher: 23.2%
Housing: Homeownership rate: 74.6%; Median home value: $817,100; Median year structure built: 1948; Homeowner vacancy rate: 0.4%; Median selected monthly owner costs: $3,553 with a mortgage, $1,152 without a mortgage; Median gross rent: $1,951 per month; Rental vacancy rate: 2.3%
Health Insurance: 94.4% have insurance; 80.9% have private insurance; 28.3% have public insurance; 5.6% do not have insurance; 1.3% of children under 18 do not have insurance
Transportation: Commute: 55.3% car, 36.6% public transportation, 3.1% walk, 3.5% work from home; Mean travel time to work: 42.5 minutes

LONG ISLAND CITY (unincorporated postal area)

ZCTA: 11101

Covers a land area of 2.615 square miles and a water area of 0.116 square miles. Located at 40.75° N. Lat; 73.94° W. Long. Elevation is 13 feet.
Population: 28,852; Growth (since 2000): 12.7%; Density: 11,031.6 persons per square mile; Race: 46.5% White, 16.7% Black/African American, 20.7% Asian, 0.5% American Indian/Alaska Native, 0.1% Native Hawaiian/Other Pacific Islander, 4.7% Two or more races, 27.5% Hispanic of any race; Average household size: 2.26; Median age: 34.8; Age under 18: 17.1%; Age 65 and over: 9.3%; Males per 100 females: 100.0; Marriage status: 47.7% never married, 40.5% now married, 3.3% separated, 3.8% widowed, 8.0% divorced; Foreign born: 36.2%; Speak English only: 53.7%; With disability: 8.0%; Veterans: 2.2%; Ancestry: 7.7% American, 5.4% Italian, 4.5% Irish, 3.6% German, 2.0% English
Employment: 22.7% management, business, and financial, 5.1% computer, engineering, and science, 16.4% education, legal, community service, arts, and media, 4.0% healthcare practitioners, 18.2% service, 21.3% sales and office, 4.6% natural resources, construction, and maintenance, 7.7% production, transportation, and material moving
Income: Per capita: $43,063; Median household: $57,866; Average household: $95,879; Households with income of $100,000 or more: 33.8%; Poverty rate: 18.6%
Educational Attainment: High school diploma or higher: 85.7%; Bachelor's degree or higher: 45.4%; Graduate/professional degree or higher: 18.6%
Housing: Homeownership rate: 17.0%; Median home value: $846,100; Median year structure built: 1946; Homeowner vacancy rate: 1.1%;

Median selected monthly owner costs: $3,416 with a mortgage, $779 without a mortgage; Median gross rent: $1,442 per month; Rental vacancy rate: 3.6%
Health Insurance: 91.2% have insurance; 59.8% have private insurance; 38.2% have public insurance; 8.8% do not have insurance; 2.8% of children under 18 do not have insurance
Transportation: Commute: 12.7% car, 76.2% public transportation, 5.5% walk, 3.5% work from home; Mean travel time to work: 35.8 minutes

ZCTA: 11109

Covers a land area of 0.040 square miles and a water area of 0.010 square miles. Located at 40.75° N. Lat; 73.96° W. Long. Elevation is 13 feet.
Population: 5,298; Growth (since 2000): n/a; Density: 132,037.4 persons per square mile; Race: 65.3% White, 4.0% Black/African American, 25.1% Asian, 0.0% American Indian/Alaska Native, 0.0% Native Hawaiian/Other Pacific Islander, 4.8% Two or more races, 6.6% Hispanic of any race; Average household size: 1.83; Median age: 31.5; Age under 18: 11.6%; Age 65 and over: 1.1%; Males per 100 females: 122.4; Marriage status: 41.5% never married, 51.7% now married, 1.8% separated, 2.3% widowed, 4.6% divorced; Foreign born: 36.6%; Speak English only: 58.2%; With disability: 2.4%; Veterans: 1.0%; Ancestry: 10.9% American, 9.8% Irish, 9.6% German, 7.0% Italian, 3.6% Polish
Employment: 36.7% management, business, and financial, 12.3% computer, engineering, and science, 21.7% education, legal, community service, arts, and media, 8.7% healthcare practitioners, 3.4% service, 16.4% sales and office, 0.8% natural resources, construction, and maintenance, 0.0% production, transportation, and material moving
Income: Per capita: $91,942; Median household: $137,452; Average household: $167,536; Households with income of $100,000 or more: 69.2%; Poverty rate: 7.1%
Educational Attainment: High school diploma or higher: 99.7%; Bachelor's degree or higher: 85.3%; Graduate/professional degree or higher: 43.5%
Housing: Homeownership rate: 6.8%; Median home value: $553,600; Median year structure built: 2009; Homeowner vacancy rate: 0.0%; Median selected monthly owner costs: $2,250 with a mortgage, $0 without a mortgage; Median gross rent: $3,059 per month; Rental vacancy rate: 3.9%
Health Insurance: 90.6% have insurance; 89.9% have private insurance; 4.0% have public insurance; 9.4% do not have insurance; 12.3% of children under 18 do not have insurance
Transportation: Commute: 12.0% car, 81.9% public transportation, 1.1% walk, 3.2% work from home; Mean travel time to work: 32.8 minutes

MASPETH (unincorporated postal area)

ZCTA: 11378

Covers a land area of 2.554 square miles and a water area of 0.056 square miles. Located at 40.72° N. Lat; 73.91° W. Long. Elevation is 30 feet.
Population: 35,844; Growth (since 2000): 5.3%; Density: 14,035.0 persons per square mile; Race: 74.0% White, 1.4% Black/African American, 11.1% Asian, 0.3% American Indian/Alaska Native, 0.1% Native Hawaiian/Other Pacific Islander, 2.6% Two or more races, 31.3% Hispanic of any race; Average household size: 2.82; Median age: 38.4; Age under 18: 21.7%; Age 65 and over: 13.2%; Males per 100 females: 95.9; Marriage status: 35.3% never married, 50.5% now married, 2.1% separated, 6.3% widowed, 7.9% divorced; Foreign born: 39.4%; Speak English only: 45.0%; With disability: 7.7%; Veterans: 2.8%; Ancestry: 17.5% Polish, 12.5% Irish, 12.3% Italian, 4.7% German, 3.9% American
Employment: 13.4% management, business, and financial, 3.5% computer, engineering, and science, 9.4% education, legal, community service, arts, and media, 4.2% healthcare practitioners, 21.6% service, 23.5% sales and office, 14.3% natural resources, construction, and maintenance, 10.1% production, transportation, and material moving
Income: Per capita: $32,263; Median household: $68,460; Average household: $86,987; Households with income of $100,000 or more: 30.6%; Poverty rate: 9.4%
Educational Attainment: High school diploma or higher: 85.9%; Bachelor's degree or higher: 27.4%; Graduate/professional degree or higher: 8.8%
Housing: Homeownership rate: 52.5%; Median home value: $574,900; Median year structure built: 1943; Homeowner vacancy rate: 0.5%; Median selected monthly owner costs: $2,544 with a mortgage, $823

without a mortgage; Median gross rent: $1,501 per month; Rental vacancy rate: 2.9%

Health Insurance: 88.7% have insurance; 63.9% have private insurance; 32.2% have public insurance; 11.3% do not have insurance; 3.2% of children under 18 do not have insurance

Transportation: Commute: 44.4% car, 46.6% public transportation, 5.0% walk, 2.8% work from home; Mean travel time to work: 41.6 minutes

MIDDLE VILLAGE (unincorporated postal area)
ZCTA: 11379

Covers a land area of 2.075 square miles and a water area of 0 square miles. Located at 40.72° N. Lat; 73.88° W. Long. Elevation is 98 feet.
Population: 37,524; Growth (since 2000): 29.5%; Density: 18,088.1 persons per square mile; Race: 79.5% White, 1.4% Black/African American, 10.6% Asian, 0.2% American Indian/Alaska Native, 0.0% Native Hawaiian/Other Pacific Islander, 2.4% Two or more races, 20.2% Hispanic of any race; Average household size: 2.75; Median age: 43.2; Age under 18: 18.8%; Age 65 and over: 18.5%; Males per 100 females: 90.4; Marriage status: 30.6% never married, 54.1% now married, 1.5% separated, 7.7% widowed, 7.7% divorced; Foreign born: 34.2%; Speak English only: 52.3%; With disability: 9.0%; Veterans: 3.4%; Ancestry: 24.0% Italian, 9.4% Irish, 8.3% German, 7.2% Polish, 4.2% American
Employment: 17.1% management, business, and financial, 4.2% computer, engineering, and science, 13.9% education, legal, community service, arts, and media, 6.4% healthcare practitioners, 17.2% service, 25.1% sales and office, 7.8% natural resources, construction, and maintenance, 8.4% production, transportation, and material moving
Income: Per capita: $36,301; Median household: $79,573; Average household: $95,587; Households with income of $100,000 or more: 38.6%; Poverty rate: 8.1%
Educational Attainment: High school diploma or higher: 87.1%; Bachelor's degree or higher: 33.3%; Graduate/professional degree or higher: 12.4%
Housing: Homeownership rate: 61.5%; Median home value: $615,200; Median year structure built: 1950; Homeowner vacancy rate: 0.2%; Median selected monthly owner costs: $2,652 with a mortgage, $810 without a mortgage; Median gross rent: $1,449 per month; Rental vacancy rate: 3.3%
Health Insurance: 93.0% have insurance; 73.4% have private insurance; 30.3% have public insurance; 7.0% do not have insurance; 1.8% of children under 18 do not have insurance
Transportation: Commute: 50.0% car, 41.0% public transportation, 5.7% walk, 2.4% work from home; Mean travel time to work: 41.7 minutes

OAKLAND GARDENS (unincorporated postal area)
ZCTA: 11364

Covers a land area of 2.466 square miles and a water area of 0 square miles. Located at 40.75° N. Lat; 73.76° W. Long. Elevation is 79 feet.
Population: 35,885; Growth (since 2000): 3.9%; Density: 14,551.9 persons per square mile; Race: 41.0% White, 2.6% Black/African American, 50.4% Asian, 0.3% American Indian/Alaska Native, 0.0% Native Hawaiian/Other Pacific Islander, 1.9% Two or more races, 9.8% Hispanic of any race; Average household size: 2.67; Median age: 44.7; Age under 18: 19.4%; Age 65 and over: 18.4%; Males per 100 females: 89.6; Marriage status: 29.2% never married, 56.3% now married, 1.9% separated, 6.0% widowed, 8.6% divorced; Foreign born: 45.3%; Speak English only: 40.0%; With disability: 8.1%; Veterans: 2.9%; Ancestry: 8.0% Italian, 5.7% Irish, 4.4% American, 3.5% Greek, 2.7% Polish
Employment: 17.7% management, business, and financial, 5.9% computer, engineering, and science, 12.0% education, legal, community service, arts, and media, 8.7% healthcare practitioners, 16.1% service, 25.2% sales and office, 6.3% natural resources, construction, and maintenance, 8.1% production, transportation, and material moving
Income: Per capita: $36,515; Median household: $71,030; Average household: $94,268; Households with income of $100,000 or more: 36.2%; Poverty rate: 8.9%
Educational Attainment: High school diploma or higher: 88.9%; Bachelor's degree or higher: 43.0%; Graduate/professional degree or higher: 17.9%
Housing: Homeownership rate: 73.8%; Median home value: $530,100; Median year structure built: 1954; Homeowner vacancy rate: 1.4%; Median selected monthly owner costs: $2,342 with a mortgage, $803

without a mortgage; Median gross rent: $1,685 per month; Rental vacancy rate: 1.8%

Health Insurance: 91.6% have insurance; 69.6% have private insurance; 32.5% have public insurance; 8.4% do not have insurance; 5.3% of children under 18 do not have insurance

Transportation: Commute: 60.2% car, 34.5% public transportation, 1.6% walk, 3.3% work from home; Mean travel time to work: 45.4 minutes

OZONE PARK (unincorporated postal area)
ZCTA: 11416

Covers a land area of 0.666 square miles and a water area of 0 square miles. Located at 40.68° N. Lat; 73.85° W. Long. Elevation is 33 feet.
Population: 27,567; Growth (since 2000): 16.5%; Density: 41,412.5 persons per square mile; Race: 28.0% White, 5.8% Black/African American, 33.5% Asian, 0.0% American Indian/Alaska Native, 0.1% Native Hawaiian/Other Pacific Islander, 6.4% Two or more races, 44.3% Hispanic of any race; Average household size: 3.81; Median age: 35.3; Age under 18: 23.5%; Age 65 and over: 9.8%; Males per 100 females: 99.0; Marriage status: 38.4% never married, 49.4% now married, 2.1% separated, 5.2% widowed, 6.9% divorced; Foreign born: 51.0%; Speak English only: 39.7%; With disability: 9.6%; Veterans: 2.2%; Ancestry: 6.3% Guyanese, 4.8% Italian, 2.2% Polish, 1.9% Trinidadian and Tobagonian, 1.7% Irish
Employment: 10.3% management, business, and financial, 3.1% computer, engineering, and science, 7.9% education, legal, community service, arts, and media, 4.3% healthcare practitioners, 27.6% service, 21.9% sales and office, 11.3% natural resources, construction, and maintenance, 13.7% production, transportation, and material moving
Income: Per capita: $21,709; Median household: $61,285; Average household: $76,532; Households with income of $100,000 or more: 26.1%; Poverty rate: 16.2%
Educational Attainment: High school diploma or higher: 76.6%; Bachelor's degree or higher: 20.4%; Graduate/professional degree or higher: 5.0%
Housing: Homeownership rate: 42.6%; Median home value: $502,100; Median year structure built: Before 1940; Homeowner vacancy rate: 0.9%; Median selected monthly owner costs: $2,646 with a mortgage, $800 without a mortgage; Median gross rent: $1,411 per month; Rental vacancy rate: 2.0%
Health Insurance: 88.2% have insurance; 46.5% have private insurance; 46.7% have public insurance; 11.8% do not have insurance; 3.3% of children under 18 do not have insurance
Transportation: Commute: 35.0% car, 54.8% public transportation, 5.4% walk, 3.4% work from home; Mean travel time to work: 47.7 minutes

ZCTA: 11417

Covers a land area of 1.119 square miles and a water area of 0 square miles. Located at 40.68° N. Lat; 73.84° W. Long. Elevation is 33 feet.
Population: 32,425; Growth (since 2000): 13.3%; Density: 28,975.9 persons per square mile; Race: 37.3% White, 6.9% Black/African American, 30.2% Asian, 0.2% American Indian/Alaska Native, 0.0% Native Hawaiian/Other Pacific Islander, 5.4% Two or more races, 37.5% Hispanic of any race; Average household size: 3.59; Median age: 37.9; Age under 18: 21.9%; Age 65 and over: 12.0%; Males per 100 females: 93.6; Marriage status: 36.2% never married, 51.7% now married, 1.9% separated, 5.6% widowed, 6.5% divorced; Foreign born: 45.0%; Speak English only: 46.6%; With disability: 10.1%; Veterans: 2.6%; Ancestry: 10.5% Italian, 6.6% Guyanese, 4.1% Irish, 2.6% Polish, 2.2% Trinidadian and Tobagonian
Employment: 11.3% management, business, and financial, 2.8% computer, engineering, and science, 9.5% education, legal, community service, arts, and media, 4.3% healthcare practitioners, 23.8% service, 26.3% sales and office, 10.2% natural resources, construction, and maintenance, 11.8% production, transportation, and material moving
Income: Per capita: $25,481; Median household: $69,989; Average household: $86,034; Households with income of $100,000 or more: 32.9%; Poverty rate: 15.6%
Educational Attainment: High school diploma or higher: 78.0%; Bachelor's degree or higher: 23.3%; Graduate/professional degree or higher: 7.3%
Housing: Homeownership rate: 60.2%; Median home value: $460,300; Median year structure built: 1940; Homeowner vacancy rate: 2.2%; Median selected monthly owner costs: $2,564 with a mortgage, $797

without a mortgage; Median gross rent: $1,457 per month; Rental vacancy rate: 2.1%

Health Insurance: 89.9% have insurance; 58.1% have private insurance; 39.6% have public insurance; 10.1% do not have insurance; 1.6% of children under 18 do not have insurance

Transportation: Commute: 43.5% car, 48.3% public transportation, 5.0% walk, 2.3% work from home; Mean travel time to work: 45.4 minutes

QUEENS (borough).
Covers a land area of 108.532 square miles and a water area of 69.675 square miles. Located at 40.66° N. Lat; 73.84° W. Long. Elevation is 43 feet.

Population: 2,339,280; Growth (since 2000): 4.9%; Density: 21,553.8 persons per square mile; Race: 39.7% White, 18.2% Black/African American, 25.3% Asian, 0.4% American Indian/Alaska Native, 0.1% Native Hawaiian/Other Pacific Islander, 3.4% Two or more races, 28.0% Hispanic of any race; Average household size: 2.97; Median age: 38.3; Age under 18: 20.2%; Age 65 and over: 14.3%; Males per 100 females: 93.8; Marriage status: 38.5% never married, 47.9% now married, 2.6% separated, 6.1% widowed, 7.5% divorced; Foreign born: 47.5%; Speak English only: 44.0%; With disability: 9.6%; Veterans: 2.4%; Ancestry: 5.5% Italian, 3.8% American, 3.7% Irish, 2.8% Jamaican, 2.8% Guyanese

Employment: 12.9% management, business, and financial, 4.0% computer, engineering, and science, 11.1% education, legal, community service, arts, and media, 5.3% healthcare practitioners, 24.6% service, 23.3% sales and office, 8.2% natural resources, construction, and maintenance, 10.7% production, transportation, and material moving

Income: Per capita: $28,814; Median household: $62,008; Average household: $81,335; Households with income of $100,000 or more: 28.6%; Poverty rate: 13.7%

Educational Attainment: High school diploma or higher: 81.1%; Bachelor's degree or higher: 30.8%; Graduate/professional degree or higher: 11.3%

Housing: Homeownership rate: 44.5%; Median home value: $481,300; Median year structure built: 1951; Homeowner vacancy rate: 1.4%; Median selected monthly owner costs: $2,482 with a mortgage, $824 without a mortgage; Median gross rent: $1,456 per month; Rental vacancy rate: 2.7%

Health Insurance: 87.8% have insurance; 56.8% have private insurance; 39.2% have public insurance; 12.2% do not have insurance; 3.7% of children under 18 do not have insurance

Newspapers: Forum South (weekly circulation 60,000); Queens Chronicle (weekly circulation 160,000); Queens Gazette (weekly circulation 90,000); Queens Ledger (weekly circulation 150,000); Queens Times (weekly circulation 75,000); Queens Tribune (weekly circulation 171,000); Schneps Publications (weekly circulation 80,000); The Wave (weekly circulation 13,000); Times Newsweekly (weekly circulation 27,000); Times/Ledger Newspapers (weekly circulation 45,000); Woodside Herald (weekly circulation 16,000)

Transportation: Commute: 38.5% car, 51.7% public transportation, 5.8% walk, 2.6% work from home; Mean travel time to work: 43.5 minutes

Additional Information Contacts
Borough of Queens . . . . (718) 286-3000
http://www.queensbp.org

QUEENS VILLAGE (unincorporated postal area)
ZCTA: 11427

Covers a land area of 1.576 square miles and a water area of 0 square miles. Located at 40.73° N. Lat; 73.75° W. Long. Elevation is 89 feet.

Population: 23,809; Growth (since 2000): 3.5%; Density: 15,104.4 persons per square mile; Race: 26.5% White, 22.0% Black/African American, 33.8% Asian, 0.5% American Indian/Alaska Native, 0.0% Native Hawaiian/Other Pacific Islander, 6.2% Two or more races, 16.8% Hispanic of any race; Average household size: 3.07; Median age: 42.1; Age under 18: 18.8%; Age 65 and over: 15.7%; Males per 100 females: 93.8; Marriage status: 33.5% never married, 54.1% now married, 1.6% separated, 6.1% widowed, 6.3% divorced; Foreign born: 47.3%; Speak English only: 49.0%; With disability: 8.8%; Veterans: 2.9%; Ancestry: 9.8% Guyanese, 4.7% American, 4.4% Haitian, 2.5% Irish, 2.2% Italian

Employment: 15.2% management, business, and financial, 3.5% computer, engineering, and science, 10.0% education, legal, community service, arts, and media, 10.4% healthcare practitioners, 19.4% service, 23.1% sales and office, 6.8% natural resources, construction, and maintenance, 11.6% production, transportation, and material moving

Income: Per capita: $32,110; Median household: $72,874; Average household: $96,719; Households with income of $100,000 or more: 35.2%; Poverty rate: 9.7%

Educational Attainment: High school diploma or higher: 86.1%; Bachelor's degree or higher: 32.0%; Graduate/professional degree or higher: 12.2%

Housing: Homeownership rate: 61.9%; Median home value: $475,900; Median year structure built: 1950; Homeowner vacancy rate: 1.8%; Median selected monthly owner costs: $2,540 with a mortgage, $848 without a mortgage; Median gross rent: $1,330 per month; Rental vacancy rate: 2.7%

Health Insurance: 91.7% have insurance; 66.4% have private insurance; 32.8% have public insurance; 8.3% do not have insurance; 3.8% of children under 18 do not have insurance

Transportation: Commute: 55.7% car, 39.3% public transportation, 1.8% walk, 2.6% work from home; Mean travel time to work: 45.2 minutes

ZCTA: 11428

Covers a land area of 0.833 square miles and a water area of 0 square miles. Located at 40.72° N. Lat; 73.74° W. Long. Elevation is 89 feet.

Population: 19,859; Growth (since 2000): -5.5%; Density: 23,851.2 persons per square mile; Race: 22.8% White, 19.0% Black/African American, 25.7% Asian, 0.1% American Indian/Alaska Native, 0.6% Native Hawaiian/Other Pacific Islander, 11.9% Two or more races, 24.8% Hispanic of any race; Average household size: 3.54; Median age: 40.0; Age under 18: 20.5%; Age 65 and over: 13.9%; Males per 100 females: 94.0; Marriage status: 33.7% never married, 56.1% now married, 2.1% separated, 5.0% widowed, 5.2% divorced; Foreign born: 50.2%; Speak English only: 55.2%; With disability: 7.5%; Veterans: 2.0%; Ancestry: 17.7% Guyanese, 4.9% Haitian, 3.7% American, 3.3% Italian, 2.2% Jamaican

Employment: 9.9% management, business, and financial, 2.6% computer, engineering, and science, 8.0% education, legal, community service, arts, and media, 6.3% healthcare practitioners, 22.0% service, 27.1% sales and office, 10.9% natural resources, construction, and maintenance, 13.2% production, transportation, and material moving

Income: Per capita: $25,256; Median household: $71,663; Average household: $82,700; Households with income of $100,000 or more: 32.0%; Poverty rate: 7.9%

Educational Attainment: High school diploma or higher: 83.5%; Bachelor's degree or higher: 18.4%; Graduate/professional degree or higher: 6.2%

Housing: Homeownership rate: 67.7%; Median home value: $451,600; Median year structure built: Before 1940; Homeowner vacancy rate: 0.9%; Median selected monthly owner costs: $2,501 with a mortgage, $789 without a mortgage; Median gross rent: $1,435 per month; Rental vacancy rate: 6.5%

Health Insurance: 91.6% have insurance; 67.3% have private insurance; 31.3% have public insurance; 8.4% do not have insurance; 5.4% of children under 18 do not have insurance

Transportation: Commute: 57.4% car, 38.0% public transportation, 1.5% walk, 1.6% work from home; Mean travel time to work: 45.2 minutes

ZCTA: 11429

Covers a land area of 1.301 square miles and a water area of 0 square miles. Located at 40.71° N. Lat; 73.74° W. Long. Elevation is 89 feet.

Population: 27,667; Growth (since 2000): 0.1%; Density: 21,264.7 persons per square mile; Race: 3.6% White, 78.2% Black/African American, 2.6% Asian, 0.8% American Indian/Alaska Native, 0.2% Native Hawaiian/Other Pacific Islander, 2.4% Two or more races, 12.5% Hispanic of any race; Average household size: 3.73; Median age: 39.5; Age under 18: 19.2%; Age 65 and over: 14.3%; Males per 100 females: 85.2; Marriage status: 49.2% never married, 38.6% now married, 2.6% separated, 5.1% widowed, 7.0% divorced; Foreign born: 43.0%; Speak English only: 65.9%; With disability: 9.4%; Veterans: 2.9%; Ancestry: 20.6% Haitian, 12.1% Jamaican, 5.4% Guyanese, 2.3% Trinidadian and Tobagonian, 2.1% West Indian

Employment: 9.1% management, business, and financial, 1.9% computer, engineering, and science, 12.5% education, legal, community service, arts, and media, 7.7% healthcare practitioners, 25.9% service, 27.0% sales and office, 6.6% natural resources, construction, and maintenance, 9.2% production, transportation, and material moving

Income: Per capita: $27,442; Median household: $80,464; Average household: $91,927; Households with income of $100,000 or more: 37.0%; Poverty rate: 10.0%

Educational Attainment: High school diploma or higher: 86.0%; Bachelor's degree or higher: 24.0%; Graduate/professional degree or higher: 8.2%

Housing: Homeownership rate: 70.5%; Median home value: $412,300; Median year structure built: 1946; Homeowner vacancy rate: 1.5%; Median selected monthly owner costs: $2,427 with a mortgage, $811 without a mortgage; Median gross rent: $1,411 per month; Rental vacancy rate: 1.6%

Health Insurance: 91.4% have insurance; 60.4% have private insurance; 38.0% have public insurance; 8.6% do not have insurance; 4.0% of children under 18 do not have insurance

Transportation: Commute: 52.9% car, 41.6% public transportation, 1.8% walk, 1.9% work from home; Mean travel time to work: 49.0 minutes

REGO PARK (unincorporated postal area)
ZCTA: 11374

Covers a land area of 0.934 square miles and a water area of 0 square miles. Located at 40.73° N. Lat; 73.86° W. Long. Elevation is 92 feet.

Population: 43,540; Growth (since 2000): -1.5%; Density: 46,599.7 persons per square mile; Race: 55.0% White, 4.0% Black/African American, 30.2% Asian, 0.2% American Indian/Alaska Native, 0.0% Native Hawaiian/Other Pacific Islander, 4.1% Two or more races, 17.3% Hispanic of any race; Average household size: 2.26; Median age: 44.0; Age under 18: 15.3%; Age 65 and over: 20.6%; Males per 100 females: 88.5; Marriage status: 32.7% never married, 51.2% now married, 2.8% separated, 7.9% widowed, 8.2% divorced; Foreign born: 59.1%; Speak English only: 29.7%; With disability: 12.7%; Veterans: 2.0%; Ancestry: 12.2% Russian, 3.9% Italian, 3.6% Polish, 3.3% Irish, 2.6% German

Employment: 18.6% management, business, and financial, 8.4% computer, engineering, and science, 12.3% education, legal, community service, arts, and media, 6.8% healthcare practitioners, 20.1% service, 21.5% sales and office, 3.6% natural resources, construction, and maintenance, 8.8% production, transportation, and material moving

Income: Per capita: $35,632; Median household: $56,863; Average household: $77,779; Households with income of $100,000 or more: 27.8%; Poverty rate: 13.4%

Educational Attainment: High school diploma or higher: 90.2%; Bachelor's degree or higher: 49.3%; Graduate/professional degree or higher: 19.9%

Housing: Homeownership rate: 36.8%; Median home value: $336,700; Median year structure built: 1953; Homeowner vacancy rate: 2.1%; Median selected monthly owner costs: $1,766 with a mortgage, $702 without a mortgage; Median gross rent: $1,453 per month; Rental vacancy rate: 2.7%

Health Insurance: 91.8% have insurance; 63.6% have private insurance; 38.0% have public insurance; 8.2% do not have insurance; 3.5% of children under 18 do not have insurance

Transportation: Commute: 26.5% car, 59.1% public transportation, 9.3% walk, 4.1% work from home; Mean travel time to work: 42.4 minutes

RICHMOND HILL (unincorporated postal area)
ZCTA: 11418

Covers a land area of 1.633 square miles and a water area of 0 square miles. Located at 40.70° N. Lat; 73.84° W. Long. Elevation is 59 feet.

Population: 39,267; Growth (since 2000): 7.4%; Density: 24,045.2 persons per square mile; Race: 39.7% White, 7.5% Black/African American, 26.1% Asian, 0.8% American Indian/Alaska Native, 0.0% Native Hawaiian/Other Pacific Islander, 5.2% Two or more races, 45.0% Hispanic of any race; Average household size: 3.56; Median age: 34.3; Age under 18: 24.3%; Age 65 and over: 9.5%; Males per 100 females: 100.5; Marriage status: 40.1% never married, 49.2% now married, 2.8% separated, 4.5% widowed, 6.3% divorced; Foreign born: 49.8%; Speak English only: 38.9%; With disability: 7.8%; Veterans: 1.5%; Ancestry: 6.0% Guyanese, 3.4% Italian, 3.1% Irish, 2.3% German, 1.7% Trinidadian and Tobagonian

Employment: 12.6% management, business, and financial, 3.1% computer, engineering, and science, 7.6% education, legal, community service, arts, and media, 4.5% healthcare practitioners, 25.7% service, 22.3% sales and office, 11.1% natural resources, construction, and maintenance, 13.1% production, transportation, and material moving

Income: Per capita: $24,653; Median household: $67,003; Average household: $82,300; Households with income of $100,000 or more: 29.6%; Poverty rate: 15.2%

Educational Attainment: High school diploma or higher: 77.4%; Bachelor's degree or higher: 27.8%; Graduate/professional degree or higher: 10.1%

Housing: Homeownership rate: 42.6%; Median home value: $477,500; Median year structure built: Before 1940; Homeowner vacancy rate: 0.8%; Median selected monthly owner costs: $2,610 with a mortgage, $795 without a mortgage; Median gross rent: $1,422 per month; Rental vacancy rate: 3.6%

Health Insurance: 85.1% have insurance; 49.3% have private insurance; 40.3% have public insurance; 14.9% do not have insurance; 3.2% of children under 18 do not have insurance

Transportation: Commute: 35.6% car, 53.0% public transportation, 6.1% walk, 3.6% work from home; Mean travel time to work: 43.9 minutes

RIDGEWOOD (unincorporated postal area)
ZCTA: 11385

Covers a land area of 3.613 square miles and a water area of 0.032 square miles. Located at 40.70° N. Lat; 73.89° W. Long. Elevation is 75 feet.

Population: 106,598; Growth (since 2000): 9.3%; Density: 29,506.0 persons per square mile; Race: 82.0% White, 2.0% Black/African American, 7.1% Asian, 0.2% American Indian/Alaska Native, 0.0% Native Hawaiian/Other Pacific Islander, 1.9% Two or more races, 44.2% Hispanic of any race; Average household size: 3.04; Median age: 35.4; Age under 18: 22.0%; Age 65 and over: 10.1%; Males per 100 females: 96.9; Marriage status: 41.2% never married, 46.3% now married, 2.9% separated, 5.2% widowed, 7.2% divorced; Foreign born: 41.2%; Speak English only: 42.7%; With disability: 6.3%; Veterans: 1.9%; Ancestry: 10.2% Polish, 8.4% Italian, 6.9% American, 4.5% German, 4.3% Irish

Employment: 10.3% management, business, and financial, 2.9% computer, engineering, and science, 10.6% education, legal, community service, arts, and media, 3.1% healthcare practitioners, 27.5% service, 22.4% sales and office, 11.4% natural resources, construction, and maintenance, 12.0% production, transportation, and material moving

Income: Per capita: $27,568; Median household: $64,481; Average household: $78,239; Households with income of $100,000 or more: 27.7%; Poverty rate: 12.5%

Educational Attainment: High school diploma or higher: 82.2%; Bachelor's degree or higher: 25.2%; Graduate/professional degree or higher: 8.5%

Housing: Homeownership rate: 32.1%; Median home value: $543,800; Median year structure built: Before 1940; Homeowner vacancy rate: 0.1%; Median selected monthly owner costs: $2,760 with a mortgage, $783 without a mortgage; Median gross rent: $1,399 per month; Rental vacancy rate: 3.6%

Health Insurance: 86.0% have insurance; 54.8% have private insurance; 36.6% have public insurance; 14.0% do not have insurance; 3.6% of children under 18 do not have insurance

Transportation: Commute: 29.4% car, 60.0% public transportation, 6.6% walk, 2.5% work from home; Mean travel time to work: 40.2 minutes

ROCKAWAY PARK (unincorporated postal area)
ZCTA: 11694

Covers a land area of 1.366 square miles and a water area of <.001 square miles. Located at 40.58° N. Lat; 73.84° W. Long. Elevation is 7 feet.

Population: 21,003; Growth (since 2000): 8.9%; Density: 15,379.6 persons per square mile; Race: 83.3% White, 7.0% Black/African American, 2.9% Asian, 0.6% American Indian/Alaska Native, 0.0% Native Hawaiian/Other Pacific Islander, 1.1% Two or more races, 13.8% Hispanic of any race; Average household size: 2.35; Median age: 49.0; Age under 18: 19.4%; Age 65 and over: 21.4%; Males per 100 females: 95.4; Marriage status: 34.7% never married, 49.6% now married, 4.0% separated, 7.9% widowed, 7.8% divorced; Foreign born: 14.4%; Speak English only: 79.9%; With disability: 19.5%; Veterans: 6.3%; Ancestry: 28.6% Irish, 15.8% Italian, 10.4% German, 7.3% American, 5.7% Polish

Employment: 16.3% management, business, and financial, 1.9% computer, engineering, and science, 21.3% education, legal, community service, arts, and media, 9.2% healthcare practitioners, 15.5% service, 21.3% sales and office, 9.0% natural resources, construction, and maintenance, 5.6% production, transportation, and material moving

Income: Per capita: $43,411; Median household: $77,547; Average household: $104,387; Households with income of $100,000 or more: 36.4%; Poverty rate: 8.1%
Educational Attainment: High school diploma or higher: 88.7%; Bachelor's degree or higher: 40.6%; Graduate/professional degree or higher: 17.3%
Housing: Homeownership rate: 50.8%; Median home value: $632,500; Median year structure built: 1953; Homeowner vacancy rate: 1.1%; Median selected monthly owner costs: $3,010 with a mortgage, $940 without a mortgage; Median gross rent: $1,297 per month; Rental vacancy rate: 5.2%
Health Insurance: 94.7% have insurance; 71.5% have private insurance; 37.1% have public insurance; 5.3% do not have insurance; 2.3% of children under 18 do not have insurance
Transportation: Commute: 63.7% car, 26.1% public transportation, 4.5% walk, 3.7% work from home; Mean travel time to work: 47.3 minutes

ROSEDALE (unincorporated postal area)
ZCTA: 11422

Covers a land area of 1.969 square miles and a water area of 0.079 square miles. Located at 40.66° N. Lat; 73.74° W. Long. Elevation is 16 feet.
Population: 33,479; Growth (since 2000): 10.0%; Density: 17,007.3 persons per square mile; Race: 6.5% White, 85.5% Black/African American, 2.1% Asian, 0.3% American Indian/Alaska Native, 0.0% Native Hawaiian/Other Pacific Islander, 2.3% Two or more races, 8.8% Hispanic of any race; Average household size: 3.45; Median age: 37.4; Age under 18: 20.9%; Age 65 and over: 12.0%; Males per 100 females: 83.2; Marriage status: 42.3% never married, 41.1% now married, 4.3% separated, 5.0% widowed, 11.6% divorced; Foreign born: 41.9%; Speak English only: 75.1%; With disability: 8.5%; Veterans: 2.9%; Ancestry: 17.6% Jamaican, 11.9% Haitian, 7.1% American, 5.3% West Indian, 4.6% Guyanese
Employment: 10.4% management, business, and financial, 1.6% computer, engineering, and science, 11.0% education, legal, community service, arts, and media, 8.8% healthcare practitioners, 25.3% service, 26.2% sales and office, 7.8% natural resources, construction, and maintenance, 8.8% production, transportation, and material moving
Income: Per capita: $30,216; Median household: $86,996; Average household: $96,500; Households with income of $100,000 or more: 40.5%; Poverty rate: 6.9%
Educational Attainment: High school diploma or higher: 88.9%; Bachelor's degree or higher: 27.5%; Graduate/professional degree or higher: 10.0%
Housing: Homeownership rate: 64.3%; Median home value: $418,400; Median year structure built: 1956; Homeowner vacancy rate: 1.2%; Median selected monthly owner costs: $2,535 with a mortgage, $778 without a mortgage; Median gross rent: $1,629 per month; Rental vacancy rate: 3.4%
Health Insurance: 93.2% have insurance; 71.8% have private insurance; 29.4% have public insurance; 6.8% do not have insurance; 2.4% of children under 18 do not have insurance
Transportation: Commute: 60.8% car, 34.6% public transportation, 1.3% walk, 2.2% work from home; Mean travel time to work: 50.2 minutes

SAINT ALBANS (unincorporated postal area)
ZCTA: 11412

Covers a land area of 1.646 square miles and a water area of 0 square miles. Located at 40.70° N. Lat; 73.76° W. Long. Elevation is 49 feet.
Population: 38,833; Growth (since 2000): 3.7%; Density: 23,585.7 persons per square mile; Race: 2.2% White, 87.6% Black/African American, 3.2% Asian, 0.4% American Indian/Alaska Native, 0.1% Native Hawaiian/Other Pacific Islander, 3.4% Two or more races, 6.5% Hispanic of any race; Average household size: 3.54; Median age: 39.5; Age under 18: 21.9%; Age 65 and over: 14.3%; Males per 100 females: 80.8; Marriage status: 44.7% never married, 38.9% now married, 4.2% separated, 6.6% widowed, 9.9% divorced; Foreign born: 35.6%; Speak English only: 85.6%; With disability: 10.0%; Veterans: 3.7%; Ancestry: 22.1% Jamaican, 8.7% American, 7.5% Haitian, 6.3% Guyanese, 3.5% Trinidadian and Tobagonian
Employment: 9.7% management, business, and financial, 1.8% computer, engineering, and science, 10.8% education, legal, community service, arts, and media, 6.7% healthcare practitioners, 29.8% service,

24.2% sales and office, 6.7% natural resources, construction, and maintenance, 10.4% production, transportation, and material moving
Income: Per capita: $27,935; Median household: $75,307; Average household: $89,346; Households with income of $100,000 or more: 35.7%; Poverty rate: 9.2%
Educational Attainment: High school diploma or higher: 87.6%; Bachelor's degree or higher: 23.0%; Graduate/professional degree or higher: 8.9%
Housing: Homeownership rate: 74.0%; Median home value: $412,200; Median year structure built: 1945; Homeowner vacancy rate: 0.9%; Median selected monthly owner costs: $2,533 with a mortgage, $810 without a mortgage; Median gross rent: $1,395 per month; Rental vacancy rate: 5.6%
Health Insurance: 91.6% have insurance; 66.0% have private insurance; 33.4% have public insurance; 8.4% do not have insurance; 3.1% of children under 18 do not have insurance
Transportation: Commute: 50.4% car, 43.5% public transportation, 2.3% walk, 2.6% work from home; Mean travel time to work: 49.8 minutes

SOUTH OZONE PARK (unincorporated postal area)
ZCTA: 11420

Covers a land area of 2.078 square miles and a water area of 0 square miles. Located at 40.67° N. Lat; 73.82° W. Long. Elevation is 26 feet.
Population: 49,396; Growth (since 2000): 8.6%; Density: 23,770.9 persons per square mile; Race: 15.9% White, 24.2% Black/African American, 29.1% Asian, 1.1% American Indian/Alaska Native, 0.1% Native Hawaiian/Other Pacific Islander, 6.8% Two or more races, 23.0% Hispanic of any race; Average household size: 3.73; Median age: 38.1; Age under 18: 21.0%; Age 65 and over: 11.7%; Males per 100 females: 93.7; Marriage status: 37.1% never married, 49.1% now married, 2.5% separated, 6.5% widowed, 7.4% divorced; Foreign born: 51.0%; Speak English only: 69.9%; With disability: 12.7%; Veterans: 2.1%; Ancestry: 16.3% Guyanese, 6.1% West Indian, 5.7% Trinidadian and Tobagonian, 3.1% Italian, 2.6% Jamaican
Employment: 8.9% management, business, and financial, 3.5% computer, engineering, and science, 7.6% education, legal, community service, arts, and media, 4.4% healthcare practitioners, 24.3% service, 28.5% sales and office, 11.1% natural resources, construction, and maintenance, 11.7% production, transportation, and material moving
Income: Per capita: $24,460; Median household: $66,220; Average household: $85,258; Households with income of $100,000 or more: 30.8%; Poverty rate: 11.2%
Educational Attainment: High school diploma or higher: 73.7%; Bachelor's degree or higher: 18.1%; Graduate/professional degree or higher: 4.6%
Housing: Homeownership rate: 67.4%; Median home value: $453,000; Median year structure built: 1946; Homeowner vacancy rate: 1.3%; Median selected monthly owner costs: $2,472 with a mortgage, $826 without a mortgage; Median gross rent: $1,457 per month; Rental vacancy rate: 2.5%
Health Insurance: 89.5% have insurance; 55.7% have private insurance; 41.0% have public insurance; 10.5% do not have insurance; 4.9% of children under 18 do not have insurance
Transportation: Commute: 51.3% car, 41.9% public transportation, 2.2% walk, 2.6% work from home; Mean travel time to work: 48.2 minutes

SOUTH RICHMOND HILL (unincorporated postal area)
ZCTA: 11419

Covers a land area of 1.129 square miles and a water area of 0 square miles. Located at 40.69° N. Lat; 73.82° W. Long..
Population: 52,392; Growth (since 2000): 7.2%; Density: 46,393.0 persons per square mile; Race: 10.5% White, 17.2% Black/African American, 29.7% Asian, 1.0% American Indian/Alaska Native, 0.0% Native Hawaiian/Other Pacific Islander, 6.1% Two or more races, 20.5% Hispanic of any race; Average household size: 4.11; Median age: 36.1; Age under 18: 20.4%; Age 65 and over: 10.3%; Males per 100 females: 99.6; Marriage status: 38.7% never married, 51.5% now married, 2.1% separated, 4.6% widowed, 5.3% divorced; Foreign born: 62.0%; Speak English only: 61.2%; With disability: 8.8%; Veterans: 1.2%; Ancestry: 17.3% Guyanese, 5.0% Trinidadian and Tobagonian, 2.0% West Indian, 1.5% Italian, 1.3% American
Employment: 7.8% management, business, and financial, 2.8% computer, engineering, and science, 7.2% education, legal, community

service, arts, and media, 3.7% healthcare practitioners, 24.4% service, 26.7% sales and office, 12.9% natural resources, construction, and maintenance, 14.5% production, transportation, and material moving
Income: Per capita: $22,049; Median household: $65,711; Average household: $82,122; Households with income of $100,000 or more: 27.9%; Poverty rate: 14.7%
Educational Attainment: High school diploma or higher: 71.6%; Bachelor's degree or higher: 19.6%; Graduate/professional degree or higher: 4.9%
Housing: Homeownership rate: 58.9%; Median home value: $460,300; Median year structure built: Before 1940; Homeowner vacancy rate: 1.5%; Median selected monthly owner costs: $2,569 with a mortgage, $835 without a mortgage; Median gross rent: $1,471 per month; Rental vacancy rate: 2.1%
Health Insurance: 86.9% have insurance; 43.7% have private insurance; 48.0% have public insurance; 13.1% do not have insurance; 3.1% of children under 18 do not have insurance
Transportation: Commute: 39.5% car, 51.9% public transportation, 6.0% walk, 1.1% work from home; Mean travel time to work: 47.0 minutes

SPRINGFIELD GARDENS (unincorporated postal area)
ZCTA: 11413

Covers a land area of 3.100 square miles and a water area of 0.033 square miles. Located at 40.67° N. Lat; 73.75° W. Long. Elevation is 30 feet.
Population: 42,895; Growth (since 2000): 7.7%; Density: 13,838.2 persons per square mile; Race: 2.2% White, 91.7% Black/African American, 1.3% Asian, 0.2% American Indian/Alaska Native, 0.2% Native Hawaiian/Other Pacific Islander, 1.6% Two or more races, 5.6% Hispanic of any race; Average household size: 3.52; Median age: 39.3; Age under 18: 21.7%; Age 65 and over: 15.5%; Males per 100 females: 83.2; Marriage status: 43.3% never married, 41.0% now married, 3.8% separated, 6.2% widowed, 9.4% divorced; Foreign born: 37.6%; Speak English only: 86.4%; With disability: 9.5%; Veterans: 4.1%; Ancestry: 24.3% Jamaican, 7.5% Haitian, 3.8% West Indian, 3.7% American, 3.3% Guyanese
Employment: 11.4% management, business, and financial, 2.4% computer, engineering, and science, 10.6% education, legal, community service, arts, and media, 7.1% healthcare practitioners, 27.9% service, 23.9% sales and office, 7.6% natural resources, construction, and maintenance, 9.2% production, transportation, and material moving
Income: Per capita: $30,087; Median household: $83,459; Average household: $97,251; Households with income of $100,000 or more: 40.0%; Poverty rate: 7.7%
Educational Attainment: High school diploma or higher: 88.2%; Bachelor's degree or higher: 26.0%; Graduate/professional degree or higher: 9.5%
Housing: Homeownership rate: 71.8%; Median home value: $430,700; Median year structure built: 1952; Homeowner vacancy rate: 1.2%; Median selected monthly owner costs: $2,532 with a mortgage, $844 without a mortgage; Median gross rent: $1,564 per month; Rental vacancy rate: 1.7%
Health Insurance: 92.8% have insurance; 68.2% have private insurance; 35.4% have public insurance; 7.2% do not have insurance; 3.3% of children under 18 do not have insurance
Transportation: Commute: 54.6% car, 39.6% public transportation, 2.3% walk, 2.5% work from home; Mean travel time to work: 51.5 minutes

SUNNYSIDE (unincorporated postal area)
ZCTA: 11104

Covers a land area of 0.390 square miles and a water area of 0 square miles. Located at 40.74° N. Lat; 73.92° W. Long. Elevation is 16 feet.
Population: 25,725; Growth (since 2000): -12.8%; Density: 65,961.7 persons per square mile; Race: 68.9% White, 1.5% Black/African American, 21.0% Asian, 0.1% American Indian/Alaska Native, 0.0% Native Hawaiian/Other Pacific Islander, 2.6% Two or more races, 30.8% Hispanic of any race; Average household size: 2.25; Median age: 38.6; Age under 18: 14.8%; Age 65 and over: 12.8%; Males per 100 females: 94.7; Marriage status: 43.7% never married, 44.8% now married, 2.2% separated, 4.1% widowed, 7.4% divorced; Foreign born: 48.0%; Speak English only: 36.6%; With disability: 7.2%; Veterans: 2.0%; Ancestry: 8.2% Irish, 5.4% Italian, 4.5% German, 3.9% Romanian, 3.8% American

Employment: 18.2% management, business, and financial, 4.8% computer, engineering, and science, 18.6% education, legal, community service, arts, and media, 4.5% healthcare practitioners, 21.2% service, 18.9% sales and office, 5.3% natural resources, construction, and maintenance, 8.7% production, transportation, and material moving
Income: Per capita: $37,114; Median household: $63,122; Average household: $80,386; Households with income of $100,000 or more: 26.2%; Poverty rate: 13.2%
Educational Attainment: High school diploma or higher: 86.5%; Bachelor's degree or higher: 45.9%; Graduate/professional degree or higher: 15.8%
Housing: Homeownership rate: 19.3%; Median home value: $414,200; Median year structure built: Before 1940; Homeowner vacancy rate: 0.5%; Median selected monthly owner costs: $1,974 with a mortgage, $745 without a mortgage; Median gross rent: $1,506 per month; Rental vacancy rate: 2.8%
Health Insurance: 85.3% have insurance; 58.1% have private insurance; 33.2% have public insurance; 14.7% do not have insurance; 3.1% of children under 18 do not have insurance
Transportation: Commute: 15.2% car, 71.2% public transportation, 4.9% walk, 5.3% work from home; Mean travel time to work: 38.3 minutes

WHITESTONE (unincorporated postal area)
ZCTA: 11357

Covers a land area of 2.802 square miles and a water area of 0 square miles. Located at 40.79° N. Lat; 73.81° W. Long. Elevation is 49 feet.
Population: 41,393; Growth (since 2000): 4.8%; Density: 14,773.5 persons per square mile; Race: 69.8% White, 0.5% Black/African American, 22.6% Asian, 0.2% American Indian/Alaska Native, 0.0% Native Hawaiian/Other Pacific Islander, 2.9% Two or more races, 14.5% Hispanic of any race; Average household size: 2.79; Median age: 44.8; Age under 18: 20.0%; Age 65 and over: 21.1%; Males per 100 females: 90.3; Marriage status: 27.5% never married, 58.2% now married, 1.5% separated, 7.4% widowed, 6.9% divorced; Foreign born: 33.7%; Speak English only: 49.5%; With disability: 11.3%; Veterans: 3.9%; Ancestry: 25.8% Italian, 8.4% Greek, 7.5% Irish, 4.9% German, 4.7% American
Employment: 17.6% management, business, and financial, 4.8% computer, engineering, and science, 14.1% education, legal, community service, arts, and media, 4.9% healthcare practitioners, 14.6% service, 29.2% sales and office, 8.4% natural resources, construction, and maintenance, 6.3% production, transportation, and material moving
Income: Per capita: $37,105; Median household: $81,053; Average household: $100,134; Households with income of $100,000 or more: 38.1%; Poverty rate: 5.4%
Educational Attainment: High school diploma or higher: 86.1%; Bachelor's degree or higher: 37.2%; Graduate/professional degree or higher: 13.9%
Housing: Homeownership rate: 76.2%; Median home value: $641,500; Median year structure built: 1956; Homeowner vacancy rate: 1.7%; Median selected monthly owner costs: $2,738 with a mortgage, $949 without a mortgage; Median gross rent: $1,742 per month; Rental vacancy rate: 6.9%
Health Insurance: 92.6% have insurance; 75.5% have private insurance; 30.2% have public insurance; 7.4% do not have insurance; 4.3% of children under 18 do not have insurance
Transportation: Commute: 70.0% car, 26.0% public transportation, 1.4% walk, 2.1% work from home; Mean travel time to work: 41.4 minutes

WOODHAVEN (unincorporated postal area)
ZCTA: 11421

Covers a land area of 1.288 square miles and a water area of 0 square miles. Located at 40.69° N. Lat; 73.86° W. Long. Elevation is 43 feet.
Population: 43,567; Growth (since 2000): 15.7%; Density: 33,823.5 persons per square mile; Race: 49.6% White, 4.2% Black/African American, 20.5% Asian, 0.6% American Indian/Alaska Native, 0.0% Native Hawaiian/Other Pacific Islander, 5.1% Two or more races, 58.0% Hispanic of any race; Average household size: 3.64; Median age: 37.5; Age under 18: 21.6%; Age 65 and over: 11.4%; Males per 100 females: 97.5; Marriage status: 38.7% never married, 48.9% now married, 2.5% separated, 4.7% widowed, 7.7% divorced; Foreign born: 48.1%; Speak English only: 32.4%; With disability: 8.0%; Veterans: 2.6%; Ancestry: 4.2% Italian, 3.2% Irish, 2.7% Polish, 2.6% German, 2.2% Guyanese

Employment: 9.1% management, business, and financial, 2.6% computer, engineering, and science, 8.6% education, legal, community service, arts, and media, 3.8% healthcare practitioners, 30.0% service, 24.3% sales and office, 9.0% natural resources, construction, and maintenance, 12.7% production, transportation, and material moving
Income: Per capita: $25,205; Median household: $69,053; Average household: $84,642; Households with income of $100,000 or more: 31.1%; Poverty rate: 11.8%
Educational Attainment: High school diploma or higher: 75.7%; Bachelor's degree or higher: 21.5%; Graduate/professional degree or higher: 5.9%
Housing: Homeownership rate: 57.2%; Median home value: $450,000; Median year structure built: Before 1940; Homeowner vacancy rate: 2.7%; Median selected monthly owner costs: $2,451 with a mortgage, $746 without a mortgage; Median gross rent: $1,542 per month; Rental vacancy rate: 3.8%
Health Insurance: 86.2% have insurance; 52.9% have private insurance; 39.3% have public insurance; 13.8% do not have insurance; 4.5% of children under 18 do not have insurance
Transportation: Commute: 33.3% car, 60.1% public transportation, 4.2% walk, 1.6% work from home; Mean travel time to work: 46.5 minutes

WOODSIDE (unincorporated postal area)
ZCTA: 11377

Covers a land area of 2.547 square miles and a water area of 0 square miles. Located at 40.74° N. Lat; 73.91° W. Long. Elevation is 59 feet.
Population: 89,688; Growth (since 2000): 1.5%; Density: 35,218.6 persons per square mile; Race: 48.5% White, 2.4% Black/African American, 37.9% Asian, 0.3% American Indian/Alaska Native, 0.0% Native Hawaiian/Other Pacific Islander, 3.3% Two or more races, 38.7% Hispanic of any race; Average household size: 2.84; Median age: 38.9; Age under 18: 17.4%; Age 65 and over: 13.8%; Males per 100 females: 101.4; Marriage status: 44.0% never married, 44.0% now married, 1.9% separated, 5.4% widowed, 6.5% divorced; Foreign born: 59.1%; Speak English only: 22.8%; With disability: 6.6%; Veterans: 2.1%; Ancestry: 4.2% Irish, 2.6% Italian, 1.9% American, 1.7% German, 1.3% Greek
Employment: 12.6% management, business, and financial, 4.7% computer, engineering, and science, 8.8% education, legal, community service, arts, and media, 3.0% healthcare practitioners, 25.3% service, 20.5% sales and office, 8.0% natural resources, construction, and maintenance, 17.2% production, transportation, and material moving
Income: Per capita: $25,978; Median household: $54,989; Average household: $69,474; Households with income of $100,000 or more: 19.6%; Poverty rate: 13.5%
Educational Attainment: High school diploma or higher: 76.8%; Bachelor's degree or higher: 28.9%; Graduate/professional degree or higher: 8.8%
Housing: Homeownership rate: 29.9%; Median home value: $482,600; Median year structure built: 1951; Homeowner vacancy rate: 1.2%; Median selected monthly owner costs: $2,086 with a mortgage, $744 without a mortgage; Median gross rent: $1,457 per month; Rental vacancy rate: 2.5%
Health Insurance: 83.4% have insurance; 45.2% have private insurance; 43.7% have public insurance; 16.6% do not have insurance; 3.3% of children under 18 do not have insurance
Transportation: Commute: 24.1% car, 67.2% public transportation, 5.2% walk, 2.0% work from home; Mean travel time to work: 37.6 minutes

End of Neighborhoods in Queens

STATEN ISLAND (borough). Aka Richmond County. Located in
southeastern New York State. One of the five counties/boroughs of New York City. Covers a land area of 58.370 square miles, a water area of 43.921 square miles, and is located in the Eastern Time Zone at 40.56° N. Lat., 74.14° W. Long. The county was founded in 1683. County seat is Saint George.

Richmond County is part of the New York-Newark-Jersey City, NY-NJ-PA Metropolitan Statistical Area. The entire metro area includes: Dutchess County-Putnam County, NY Metropolitan Division (Dutchess County, NY; Putnam County, NY); Nassau County-Suffolk County, NY Metropolitan Division (Nassau County, NY; Suffolk County, NY); Newark, NJ-PA Metropolitan Division (Essex County, NJ; Hunterdon County, NJ; Morris

County, NJ; Somerset County, NJ; Sussex County, NJ; Union County, NJ; Pike County, PA); New York-Jersey City-White Plains, NY-NJ Metropolitan Division (Bergen County, NJ; Hudson County, NJ; Middlesex County, NJ; Monmouth County, NJ; Ocean County, NJ; Passaic County, NJ; Bronx County, NY; Kings County, NY; New York County, NY; Orange County, NY; Queens County, NY; Richmond County, NY; Rockland County, NY; Westchester County, NY)

Population: 475,948; Growth (since 2000): 7.3%; Density: 8,153.9 persons per square mile; Race: 74.8% White, 10.3% Black/African American, 8.5% Asian, 0.3% American Indian/Alaska Native, 0.0% Native Hawaiian/Other Pacific Islander, 2.3% two or more races, 18.2% Hispanic of any race; Average household size: 2.82; Median age: 39.9; Age under 18: 22.1%; Age 65 and over: 15.1%; Males per 100 females: 94.1; Marriage status: 33.3% never married, 53.3% now married, 1.8% separated, 6.5% widowed, 6.9% divorced; Foreign born: 22.2%; Speak English only: 68.7%; With disability: 10.0%; Veterans: 4.6%; Ancestry: 30.2% Italian, 11.8% Irish, 6.1% American, 4.2% German, 3.6% Polish
Religion: Six largest groups: 54.2% Catholicism, 1.7% Muslim Estimate, 1.6% Eastern Liturgical (Orthodox), 1.6% Orthodox, 1.5% Judaism, 1.3% Non-denominational Protestant
Economy: Unemployment rate: 4.0%; Leading industries: 15.1 % retail trade; 14.1 % health care and social assistance; 13.5 % construction; Farms: 8 totaling n/a acres; Company size: 5 employ 1,000 or more persons, 7 employ 500 to 999 persons, 108 employ 100 to 499 persons, 9,120 employ less than 100 persons; Business ownership: 13,921 women-owned, 3,953 Black-owned, 4,241 Hispanic-owned, 4,242 Asian-owned, 179 American Indian/Alaska Native-owned
Employment: 14.4% management, business, and financial, 4.1% computer, engineering, and science, 14.3% education, legal, community service, arts, and media, 7.9% healthcare practitioners, 19.3% service, 23.2% sales and office, 8.7% natural resources, construction, and maintenance, 8.1% production, transportation, and material moving
Income: Per capita: $33,922; Median household: $76,244; Average household: $95,885; Households with income of $100,000 or more: 38.3%; Poverty rate: 12.9%
Educational Attainment: High school diploma or higher: 88.7%; Bachelor's degree or higher: 32.1%; Graduate/professional degree or higher: 13.0%
Housing: Homeownership rate: 69.5%; Median home value: $460,200; Median year structure built: 1972; Homeowner vacancy rate: 2.0%; Median selected monthly owner costs: $2,433 with a mortgage, $856 without a mortgage; Median gross rent: $1,229 per month; Rental vacancy rate: 6.5%
Vital Statistics: Birth rate: 111.2 per 10,000 population; Death rate: 82.9 per 10,000 population; Age-adjusted cancer mortality rate: 154.8 deaths per 100,000 population
Health Insurance: 94.1% have insurance; 70.8% have private insurance; 33.0% have public insurance; 5.9% do not have insurance; 2.5% of children under 18 do not have insurance
Health Care: Physicians: 39.8 per 10,000 population; Dentists: 6.7 per 10,000 population; Hospital beds: 28.2 per 10,000 population; Hospital admissions: 1,166.1 per 10,000 population
Air Quality Index (AQI): Percent of Days: 82.2% good, 15.9% moderate, 1.9% unhealthy for sensitive individuals, 0.0% unhealthy, 0.0% very unhealthy; Annual median: 37; Annual maximum: 136
Transportation: Commute: 64.0% car, 29.9% public transportation, 2.5% walk, 2.5% work from home; Mean travel time to work: 44.0 minutes
2016 Presidential Election: 56.1% Trump, 41.0% Clinton, 1.3% Johnson, 1.0% Stein
National and State Parks: Clay Pit Ponds State Park Preserve; Gateway National Recreation Area

School District(s)
Hawthorne-Cedar Knolls Union Free SD (KG-12)
  Enrollment: 240 . . . . (914) 749-2903
John W Lavelle Preparatory Charter School (06-12)
  Enrollment: 636 . . . . (347) 855-2238
NYC Special Schools - District 75
  Enrollment: n/a . . . . (212) 802-1501
New Ventures Charter School (09-12)
  Enrollment: 82 . . . . (347) 855-2238
New World Preparatory Charter School (06-08)
  Enrollment: 386 . . . . (718) 705-8900
New York City Geographic District #31 (PK-12)
  Enrollment: 62,815 . . . . (718) 420-5667

Four-year College(s)

College of Staten Island CUNY (Public)
  Enrollment: 13,594 . . . . (718) 982-2000
  Tuition: In-state $7,090; Out-of-state $14,480
Wagner College (Private, Not-for-profit, Lutheran Church in America)
  Enrollment: 2,271 . . . . (718) 390-3100
  Tuition: In-state $45,380; Out-of-state $45,380

Two-year College(s)

St Paul's School of Nursing-Staten Island (Private, For-profit)
  Enrollment: 532 . . . . (718) 517-7700
  Tuition: In-state $17,004; Out-of-state $17,004

Vocational/Technical School(s)

Academy of Cosmetology and Esthetics NYC (Private, For-profit)
  Enrollment: 87 . . . . (718) 979-9001
  Tuition: $14,500
Career School of NY (Private, Not-for-profit)
  Enrollment: 41 . . . . (718) 420-6440
  Tuition: $12,345

Hospitals: Richmond University Medical Center; South Beach Psychiatric Center (322 beds); St. Vincent's Staten Island/Bayley Seton Campuses (198 beds); Staten Island University Hospital (813 beds)

Newspapers: Staten Island Advance (daily circulation 58000)

Additional Information Contacts

Richmond County Government . . . . (718) 816-8200
  http://statenislandusa.com
Staten Island Chamber of Commerce . . . . (718) 727-1900
  http://www.sichamber.com

New York County

See New York City

Niagara County

Located in western New York; bounded on the west by the Niagara River and Lake Erie, and on the north by Lake Ontario; drained by Tonawanda Creek; includes Niagara Falls. Covers a land area of 522.359 square miles, a water area of 617.310 square miles, and is located in the Eastern Time Zone at 43.46° N. Lat., 78.79° W. Long. The county was founded in 1808. County seat is Lockport.

Niagara County is part of the Buffalo-Cheektowaga-Niagara Falls, NY Metropolitan Statistical Area. The entire metro area includes: Erie County, NY; Niagara County, NY

Population: 212,675; Growth (since 2000): -3.3%; Density: 407.1 persons per square mile; Race: 87.8% White, 7.2% Black/African American, 1.0% Asian, 1.1% American Indian/Alaska Native, 0.0% Native Hawaiian/Other Pacific Islander, 2.3% two or more races, 2.7% Hispanic of any race; Average household size: 2.37; Median age: 43.0; Age under 18: 20.3%; Age 65 and over: 17.7%; Males per 100 females: 94.2; Marriage status: 32.3% never married, 49.2% now married, 1.9% separated, 7.2% widowed, 11.2% divorced; Foreign born: 4.0%; Speak English only: 95.9%; With disability: 13.5%; Veterans: 8.7%; Ancestry: 23.9% German, 17.2% Italian, 15.0% Irish, 12.7% American, 11.0% Polish

Religion: Six largest groups: 24.0% Catholicism, 5.9% Lutheran, 4.1% Methodist/Pietist, 2.0% Presbyterian-Reformed, 1.9% Non-denominational Protestant, 1.3% Baptist

Economy: Unemployment rate: 4.1%; Leading industries: 16.3 % retail trade; 11.5 % accommodation and food services; 11.0 % other services (except public administration); Farms: 760 totaling 142,818 acres; Company size: 4 employ 1,000 or more persons, 3 employ 500 to 999 persons, 76 employ 100 to 499 persons, 4,501 employs less than 100 persons; Business ownership: 4,337 women-owned, 304 Black-owned, 171 Hispanic-owned, 187 Asian-owned, 123 American Indian/Alaska Native-owned

Employment: 12.2% management, business, and financial, 4.1% computer, engineering, and science, 10.4% education, legal, community service, arts, and media, 6.1% healthcare practitioners, 18.2% service, 26.2% sales and office, 9.0% natural resources, construction, and maintenance, 13.9% production, transportation, and material moving

Income: Per capita: $28,395; Median household: $51,656; Average household: $66,819; Households with income of $100,000 or more: 20.6%; Poverty rate: 13.4%

Educational Attainment: High school diploma or higher: 91.0%; Bachelor's degree or higher: 23.5%; Graduate/professional degree or higher: 9.8%

Housing: Homeownership rate: 71.5%; Median home value: $114,800; Median year structure built: 1954; Homeowner vacancy rate: 5.5%; Median selected monthly owner costs: $1,209 with a mortgage, $525 without a mortgage; Median gross rent: $669 per month; Rental vacancy rate: 15.5%

Vital Statistics: Birth rate: 99.5 per 10,000 population; Death rate: 109.8 per 10,000 population; Age-adjusted cancer mortality rate: 178.4 deaths per 100,000 population

Health Insurance: 95.1% have insurance; 72.3% have private insurance; 39.3% have public insurance; 4.9% do not have insurance; 2.4% of children under 18 do not have insurance

Health Care: Physicians: 11.5 per 10,000 population; Dentists: 5.2 per 10,000 population; Hospital beds: 25.6 per 10,000 population; Hospital admissions: 899.4 per 10,000 population

Air Quality Index (AQI): Percent of Days: 92.0% good, 7.6% moderate, 0.4% unhealthy for sensitive individuals, 0.0% unhealthy, 0.0% very unhealthy; Annual median: 35; Annual maximum: 105

Transportation: Commute: 93.3% car, 0.9% public transportation, 1.9% walk, 2.6% work from home; Mean travel time to work: 22.0 minutes

2016 Presidential Election: 56.2% Trump, 38.5% Clinton, 3.1% Johnson, 1.4% Stein

National and State Parks: Brydges State Park; Devils Hole State Park; Fort Niagara State Park; Fourmile Creek State Park; Joseph Davis State Park; Lower Niagara River State Park; New York State Reservation; Whirlpool State Park

Additional Information Contacts

Niagara Government . . . . (716) 439-7025
  http://www.niagaracounty.com

Niagara County Communities

APPLETON (unincorporated postal area)

ZCTA: 14008

Covers a land area of 24.452 square miles and a water area of 0.858 square miles. Located at 43.31° N. Lat; 78.62° W. Long. Elevation is 338 feet.

Population: 1,286; Growth (since 2000): -13.6%; Density: 52.6 persons per square mile; Race: 97.1% White, 0.3% Black/African American, 0.2% Asian, 2.3% American Indian/Alaska Native, 0.0% Native Hawaiian/Other Pacific Islander, 0.2% Two or more races, 0.2% Hispanic of any race; Average household size: 2.43; Median age: 48.7; Age under 18: 17.3%; Age 65 and over: 22.8%; Males per 100 females: 102.1; Marriage status: 20.9% never married, 57.4% now married, 1.1% separated, 8.2% widowed, 13.6% divorced; Foreign born: 0.9%; Speak English only: 99.5%; With disability: 13.1%; Veterans: 9.2%; Ancestry: 30.0% American, 18.8% German, 11.4% English, 10.3% Italian, 7.2% Irish

Employment: 9.1% management, business, and financial, 8.1% computer, engineering, and science, 6.6% education, legal, community service, arts, and media, 4.3% healthcare practitioners, 9.3% service, 35.2% sales and office, 11.7% natural resources, construction, and maintenance, 15.7% production, transportation, and material moving

Income: Per capita: $27,013; Median household: $56,691; Average household: $64,618; Households with income of $100,000 or more: 18.8%; Poverty rate: 14.2%

Educational Attainment: High school diploma or higher: 91.3%; Bachelor's degree or higher: 9.4%; Graduate/professional degree or higher: 1.7%

Housing: Homeownership rate: 78.5%; Median home value: $119,300; Median year structure built: Before 1940; Homeowner vacancy rate: 8.0%; Median selected monthly owner costs: $1,095 with a mortgage, $418 without a mortgage; Median gross rent: $833 per month; Rental vacancy rate: 28.2%

Health Insurance: 96.4% have insurance; 71.7% have private insurance; 42.1% have public insurance; 3.6% do not have insurance; 0.0% of children under 18 do not have insurance

Transportation: Commute: 86.1% car, 0.0% public transportation, 5.4% walk, 6.8% work from home; Mean travel time to work: 29.9 minutes

BARKER (village). Covers a land area of 0.420 square miles and a water area of 0 square miles. Located at 43.33° N. Lat; 78.55° W. Long. Elevation is 328 feet.
Population: 754; Growth (since 2000): 30.7%; Density: 1,796.0 persons per square mile; Race: 100.0% White, 0.0% Black/African American, 0.0% Asian, 0.0% American Indian/Alaska Native, 0.0% Native Hawaiian/Other Pacific Islander, 0.0% Two or more races, 26.4% Hispanic of any race; Average household size: 3.18; Median age: 30.4; Age under 18: 35.5%; Age 65 and over: 8.9%; Males per 100 females: 88.3; Marriage status: 30.5% never married, 54.7% now married, 0.8% separated, 4.5% widowed, 10.4% divorced; Foreign born: 4.4%; Speak English only: 85.5%; With disability: 6.8%; Veterans: 10.9%; Ancestry: 16.7% American, 14.3% German, 10.9% Irish, 10.6% English, 6.2% Italian
Employment: 17.8% management, business, and financial, 2.8% computer, engineering, and science, 5.9% education, legal, community service, arts, and media, 3.4% healthcare practitioners, 15.0% service, 18.8% sales and office, 16.9% natural resources, construction, and maintenance, 19.4% production, transportation, and material moving
Income: Per capita: $17,162; Median household: $42,083; Average household: $53,982; Households with income of $100,000 or more: 12.3%; Poverty rate: 15.1%
Educational Attainment: High school diploma or higher: 89.9%; Bachelor's degree or higher: 11.7%; Graduate/professional degree or higher: 4.7%

School District(s)
Barker Central SD (PK-12)
    Enrollment: 797 . . . . (716) 795-3832
Housing: Homeownership rate: 60.3%; Median home value: $98,800; Median year structure built: Before 1940; Homeowner vacancy rate: 0.0%; Median selected monthly owner costs: $1,033 with a mortgage, $540 without a mortgage; Median gross rent: $671 per month; Rental vacancy rate: 21.7%
Health Insurance: 79.6% have insurance; 41.0% have private insurance; 46.3% have public insurance; 20.4% do not have insurance; 12.7% of children under 18 do not have insurance
Transportation: Commute: 86.8% car, 0.0% public transportation, 4.8% walk, 8.4% work from home; Mean travel time to work: 21.8 minutes

BURT (unincorporated postal area)
ZCTA: 14028
    Covers a land area of 13.537 square miles and a water area of 0.512 square miles. Located at 43.32° N. Lat; 78.72° W. Long. Elevation is 315 feet.
Population: 1,548; Growth (since 2000): -10.9%; Density: 114.4 persons per square mile; Race: 96.4% White, 0.2% Black/African American, 0.1% Asian, 2.1% American Indian/Alaska Native, 0.0% Native Hawaiian/Other Pacific Islander, 1.2% Two or more races, 0.1% Hispanic of any race; Average household size: 2.38; Median age: 44.8; Age under 18: 16.7%; Age 65 and over: 14.9%; Males per 100 females: 104.7; Marriage status: 33.1% never married, 57.4% now married, 2.6% separated, 5.6% widowed, 3.8% divorced; Foreign born: 0.6%; Speak English only: 99.2%; With disability: 9.9%; Veterans: 10.0%; Ancestry: 33.0% German, 15.2% Irish, 14.3% English, 13.3% Italian, 9.0% Polish
Employment: 19.4% management, business, and financial, 4.8% computer, engineering, and science, 0.2% education, legal, community service, arts, and media, 6.2% healthcare practitioners, 17.1% service, 30.3% sales and office, 10.9% natural resources, construction, and maintenance, 9.3% production, transportation, and material moving
Income: Per capita: $35,390; Median household: $75,242; Average household: $82,462; Households with income of $100,000 or more: 36.7%; Poverty rate: 6.5%
Educational Attainment: High school diploma or higher: 94.5%; Bachelor's degree or higher: 27.0%; Graduate/professional degree or higher: 7.5%

School District(s)
Newfane Central SD (PK-12)
    Enrollment: 1,597 . . . . (716) 778-6888
Housing: Homeownership rate: 89.6%; Median home value: $116,400; Median year structure built: 1953; Homeowner vacancy rate: 14.1%; Median selected monthly owner costs: $1,108 with a mortgage, $758 without a mortgage; Median gross rent: $853 per month; Rental vacancy rate: 38.0%
Health Insurance: 92.5% have insurance; 74.4% have private insurance; 27.3% have public insurance; 7.5% do not have insurance; 0.0% of children under 18 do not have insurance

Transportation: Commute: 95.0% car, 0.0% public transportation, 0.0% walk, 5.0% work from home; Mean travel time to work: 27.9 minutes

CAMBRIA (town). Covers a land area of 39.710 square miles and a water area of 0 square miles. Located at 43.18° N. Lat; 78.82° W. Long. Elevation is 476 feet.
Population: 5,800; Growth (since 2000): 7.5%; Density: 146.1 persons per square mile; Race: 97.1% White, 1.9% Black/African American, 0.8% Asian, 0.0% American Indian/Alaska Native, 0.0% Native Hawaiian/Other Pacific Islander, 0.2% Two or more races, 0.0% Hispanic of any race; Average household size: 2.63; Median age: 46.1; Age under 18: 20.3%; Age 65 and over: 16.5%; Males per 100 females: 101.3; Marriage status: 29.7% never married, 55.2% now married, 0.3% separated, 7.8% widowed, 7.4% divorced; Foreign born: 2.6%; Speak English only: 99.0%; With disability: 10.0%; Veterans: 8.1%; Ancestry: 32.9% German, 20.0% American, 16.6% Irish, 15.5% Italian, 10.4% Polish
Employment: 10.3% management, business, and financial, 6.4% computer, engineering, and science, 4.9% education, legal, community service, arts, and media, 11.5% healthcare practitioners, 18.5% service, 23.4% sales and office, 14.5% natural resources, construction, and maintenance, 10.5% production, transportation, and material moving
Income: Per capita: $31,663; Median household: $71,136; Average household: $81,574; Households with income of $100,000 or more: 31.4%; Poverty rate: 5.8%
Educational Attainment: High school diploma or higher: 97.2%; Bachelor's degree or higher: 24.6%; Graduate/professional degree or higher: 8.7%
Housing: Homeownership rate: 89.5%; Median home value: $159,500; Median year structure built: 1964; Homeowner vacancy rate: 2.3%; Median selected monthly owner costs: $1,617 with a mortgage, $599 without a mortgage; Median gross rent: $757 per month; Rental vacancy rate: 0.0%
Health Insurance: 95.7% have insurance; 85.2% have private insurance; 26.9% have public insurance; 4.3% do not have insurance; 5.2% of children under 18 do not have insurance
Transportation: Commute: 96.4% car, 0.1% public transportation, 1.0% walk, 2.5% work from home; Mean travel time to work: 26.9 minutes
Additional Information Contacts
Town of Cambria . . . . (716) 433-7664
    http://www.townofcambria.com

GASPORT (CDP). Covers a land area of 2.869 square miles and a water area of 0.051 square miles. Located at 43.20° N. Lat; 78.58° W. Long. Elevation is 515 feet.
Population: 1,420; Growth (since 2000): 13.8%; Density: 494.9 persons per square mile; Race: 95.8% White, 1.1% Black/African American, 0.0% Asian, 0.8% American Indian/Alaska Native, 0.0% Native Hawaiian/Other Pacific Islander, 2.3% Two or more races, 0.0% Hispanic of any race; Average household size: 2.59; Median age: 35.7; Age under 18: 24.2%; Age 65 and over: 15.8%; Males per 100 females: 89.7; Marriage status: 35.1% never married, 41.9% now married, 2.8% separated, 5.2% widowed, 17.8% divorced; Foreign born: 1.1%; Speak English only: 97.4%; With disability: 6.2%; Veterans: 8.4%; Ancestry: 38.9% American, 22.3% German, 11.5% English, 7.0% Irish, 5.8% Polish
Employment: 8.8% management, business, and financial, 0.0% computer, engineering, and science, 1.6% education, legal, community service, arts, and media, 11.3% healthcare practitioners, 7.5% service, 11.2% sales and office, 18.6% natural resources, construction, and maintenance, 41.1% production, transportation, and material moving
Income: Per capita: $21,077; Median household: $47,778; Average household: $54,043; Households with income of $100,000 or more: 10.1%; Poverty rate: 9.9%
Educational Attainment: High school diploma or higher: 95.5%; Bachelor's degree or higher: 10.6%; Graduate/professional degree or higher: 3.4%

School District(s)
Royalton-Hartland Central SD (PK-12)
    Enrollment: 1,327 . . . . (716) 735-2000
Housing: Homeownership rate: 60.7%; Median home value: $83,300; Median year structure built: Before 1940; Homeowner vacancy rate: 0.0%; Median selected monthly owner costs: $1,071 with a mortgage, $548 without a mortgage; Median gross rent: $641 per month; Rental vacancy rate: 21.3%
Health Insurance: 100.0% have insurance; 85.1% have private insurance; 27.8% have public insurance; 0.0% do not have insurance; 0.0% of children under 18 do not have insurance

Transportation: Commute: 91.2% car, 6.2% public transportation, 0.0% walk, 2.5% work from home; Mean travel time to work: 26.4 minutes

HARTLAND (town).
Covers a land area of 52.378 square miles and a water area of 0.037 square miles. Located at 43.26° N. Lat; 78.55° W. Long. Elevation is 404 feet.

Population: 4,038; Growth (since 2000): -3.0%; Density: 77.1 persons per square mile; Race: 96.7% White, 0.1% Black/African American, 0.5% Asian, 1.3% American Indian/Alaska Native, 0.0% Native Hawaiian/Other Pacific Islander, 0.9% Two or more races, 1.0% Hispanic of any race; Average household size: 2.45; Median age: 47.9; Age under 18: 20.9%; Age 65 and over: 17.5%; Males per 100 females: 103.7; Marriage status: 19.6% never married, 67.0% now married, 1.4% separated, 7.0% widowed, 6.4% divorced; Foreign born: 1.4%; Speak English only: 98.7%; With disability: 11.6%; Veterans: 9.9%; Ancestry: 35.1% German, 19.8% Irish, 17.1% English, 12.3% Italian, 12.1% Polish

Employment: 14.8% management, business, and financial, 5.3% computer, engineering, and science, 8.5% education, legal, community service, arts, and media, 5.4% healthcare practitioners, 13.5% service, 26.7% sales and office, 10.4% natural resources, construction, and maintenance, 15.5% production, transportation, and material moving

Income: Per capita: $26,070; Median household: $56,801; Average household: $62,976; Households with income of $100,000 or more: 14.9%; Poverty rate: 10.1%

Educational Attainment: High school diploma or higher: 90.6%; Bachelor's degree or higher: 14.3%; Graduate/professional degree or higher: 6.4%

Housing: Homeownership rate: 83.5%; Median home value: $105,900; Median year structure built: 1954; Homeowner vacancy rate: 0.0%; Median selected monthly owner costs: $1,293 with a mortgage, $481 without a mortgage; Median gross rent: $594 per month; Rental vacancy rate: 20.5%

Health Insurance: 98.0% have insurance; 78.6% have private insurance; 40.9% have public insurance; 2.0% do not have insurance; 0.0% of children under 18 do not have insurance

Transportation: Commute: 92.0% car, 0.0% public transportation, 2.7% walk, 4.8% work from home; Mean travel time to work: 27.6 minutes

Additional Information Contacts

Town of Hartland . . . . (716) 735-7179
   http://townofhartland.org/content

LEWISTON (town).
Covers a land area of 37.121 square miles and a water area of 4.010 square miles. Located at 43.18° N. Lat; 78.95° W. Long. Elevation is 381 feet.

History: As with Lewis county, named after Governor Morgan Lewis. Settled c.1796, incorporated 1822.

Population: 15,991; Growth (since 2000): -1.6%; Density: 430.8 persons per square mile; Race: 94.5% White, 1.1% Black/African American, 1.2% Asian, 0.4% American Indian/Alaska Native, 0.0% Native Hawaiian/Other Pacific Islander, 1.6% Two or more races, 2.9% Hispanic of any race; Average household size: 2.26; Median age: 46.3; Age under 18: 15.0%; Age 65 and over: 22.8%; Males per 100 females: 88.7; Marriage status: 34.1% never married, 48.2% now married, 1.2% separated, 9.8% widowed, 7.9% divorced; Foreign born: 7.0%; Speak English only: 94.3%; With disability: 11.3%; Veterans: 8.8%; Ancestry: 25.7% Italian, 18.2% German, 15.9% Irish, 12.7% American, 10.7% Polish

Employment: 14.2% management, business, and financial, 3.3% computer, engineering, and science, 12.4% education, legal, community service, arts, and media, 7.9% healthcare practitioners, 18.5% service, 26.2% sales and office, 7.0% natural resources, construction, and maintenance, 10.4% production, transportation, and material moving

Income: Per capita: $33,577; Median household: $65,539; Average household: $81,269; Households with income of $100,000 or more: 26.6%; Poverty rate: 5.7%

Educational Attainment: High school diploma or higher: 95.4%; Bachelor's degree or higher: 36.7%; Graduate/professional degree or higher: 16.6%

School District(s)
Niagara-Wheatfield Central SD (PK-12)
   Enrollment: 3,668 . . . . (716) 215-3003

Housing: Homeownership rate: 81.2%; Median home value: $168,000; Median year structure built: 1959; Homeowner vacancy rate: 4.5%; Median selected monthly owner costs: $1,379 with a mortgage, $572 without a mortgage; Median gross rent: $765 per month; Rental vacancy rate: 4.6%

Health Insurance: 96.1% have insurance; 83.6% have private insurance; 30.3% have public insurance; 3.9% do not have insurance; 0.0% of children under 18 do not have insurance

Hospitals: Mount Saint Mary's Hospital & Health Center (179 beds)

Transportation: Commute: 91.5% car, 0.4% public transportation, 2.5% walk, 3.8% work from home; Mean travel time to work: 21.3 minutes

Additional Information Contacts

Town of Lewiston . . . . (716) 754-8213
   http://www.townoflewiston.us

LEWISTON (village).
Covers a land area of 1.097 square miles and a water area of 0.139 square miles. Located at 43.17° N. Lat; 79.04° W. Long. Elevation is 381 feet.

Population: 2,594; Growth (since 2000): -6.7%; Density: 2,365.4 persons per square mile; Race: 96.6% White, 0.0% Black/African American, 1.7% Asian, 0.8% American Indian/Alaska Native, 0.0% Native Hawaiian/Other Pacific Islander, 0.9% Two or more races, 0.5% Hispanic of any race; Average household size: 1.85; Median age: 53.2; Age under 18: 14.2%; Age 65 and over: 29.6%; Males per 100 females: 80.5; Marriage status: 25.8% never married, 50.3% now married, 1.8% separated, 13.0% widowed, 10.9% divorced; Foreign born: 7.2%; Speak English only: 97.8%; With disability: 9.0%; Veterans: 8.8%; Ancestry: 23.3% Italian, 17.9% American, 16.7% Irish, 15.2% English, 12.1% German

Employment: 17.5% management, business, and financial, 2.7% computer, engineering, and science, 9.3% education, legal, community service, arts, and media, 8.0% healthcare practitioners, 15.8% service, 37.2% sales and office, 3.2% natural resources, construction, and maintenance, 6.3% production, transportation, and material moving

Income: Per capita: $32,012; Median household: $48,056; Average household: $59,767; Households with income of $100,000 or more: 16.8%; Poverty rate: 9.2%

Educational Attainment: High school diploma or higher: 96.1%; Bachelor's degree or higher: 46.7%; Graduate/professional degree or higher: 15.4%

School District(s)
Niagara-Wheatfield Central SD (PK-12)
   Enrollment: 3,668 . . . . (716) 215-3003

Housing: Homeownership rate: 72.4%; Median home value: $153,000; Median year structure built: 1955; Homeowner vacancy rate: 9.4%; Median selected monthly owner costs: $1,252 with a mortgage, $548 without a mortgage; Median gross rent: $790 per month; Rental vacancy rate: 9.6%

Health Insurance: 97.2% have insurance; 81.5% have private insurance; 37.6% have public insurance; 2.8% do not have insurance; 0.0% of children under 18 do not have insurance

Hospitals: Mount Saint Mary's Hospital & Health Center (179 beds)

Transportation: Commute: 90.3% car, 0.0% public transportation, 0.0% walk, 6.8% work from home; Mean travel time to work: 20.4 minutes

LOCKPORT (city).
County seat. Covers a land area of 8.400 square miles and a water area of 0.046 square miles. Located at 43.17° N. Lat; 78.70° W. Long. Elevation is 614 feet.

Population: 20,676; Growth (since 2000): -7.2%; Density: 2,461.5 persons per square mile; Race: 87.6% White, 6.6% Black/African American, 1.5% Asian, 0.1% American Indian/Alaska Native, 0.0% Native Hawaiian/Other Pacific Islander, 3.7% Two or more races, 4.2% Hispanic of any race; Average household size: 2.27; Median age: 38.8; Age under 18: 22.4%; Age 65 and over: 15.0%; Males per 100 females: 91.3; Marriage status: 34.9% never married, 43.2% now married, 1.8% separated, 7.4% widowed, 14.4% divorced; Foreign born: 4.1%; Speak English only: 95.7%; With disability: 12.8%; Veterans: 8.0%; Ancestry: 24.9% German, 18.0% American, 15.9% Irish, 12.6% Italian, 10.5% English

Employment: 10.9% management, business, and financial, 3.7% computer, engineering, and science, 10.9% education, legal, community service, arts, and media, 4.9% healthcare practitioners, 16.3% service, 26.2% sales and office, 9.1% natural resources, construction, and maintenance, 18.0% production, transportation, and material moving

Income: Per capita: $25,808; Median household: $41,477; Average household: $57,862; Households with income of $100,000 or more: 14.0%; Poverty rate: 15.4%

Educational Attainment: High school diploma or higher: 87.5%; Bachelor's degree or higher: 21.0%; Graduate/professional degree or higher: 8.2%

School District(s)
Lockport City SD (KG-12)
   Enrollment: 4,746 . . . . (716) 478-4838

Starpoint Central SD (KG-12)
    Enrollment: 2,730 . . . . (716) 210-2352
Housing: Homeownership rate: 57.0%; Median home value: $88,500;
Median year structure built: Before 1940; Homeowner vacancy rate: 7.7%;
Median selected monthly owner costs: $1,086 with a mortgage, $503
without a mortgage; Median gross rent: $693 per month; Rental vacancy
rate: 19.1%
Health Insurance: 93.0% have insurance; 66.0% have private insurance;
42.4% have public insurance; 7.0% do not have insurance; 4.8% of
children under 18 do not have insurance
Hospitals: Eastern Niagara Hospital (134 beds)
Newspapers: Journal-Register (weekly circulation 1,900); Lockport
Union-Sun & Journal (daily circulation 2,700); Union-Sun & Journal (daily
circulation 11,500)
Transportation: Commute: 93.3% car, 0.2% public transportation, 2.1%
walk, 2.3% work from home; Mean travel time to work: 22.5 minutes
Additional Information Contacts
City of Lockport . . . . (716) 439-6676
    http://www.elockport.com

LOCKPORT (town). Covers a land area of 44.843 square miles and a
water area of 0.052 square miles. Located at 43.15° N. Lat; 78.69° W.
Long. Elevation is 614 feet.
History: Built around a series of locks on the old Erie Canal. Settled 1821,
incorporated 1865.
Population: 20,222; Growth (since 2000): 2.9%; Density: 450.9 persons
per square mile; Race: 91.6% White, 4.0% Black/African American, 1.2%
Asian, 0.3% American Indian/Alaska Native, 0.0% Native Hawaiian/Other
Pacific Islander, 1.7% Two or more races, 3.7% Hispanic of any race;
Average household size: 2.45; Median age: 43.0; Age under 18: 19.6%;
Age 65 and over: 18.0%; Males per 100 females: 98.9; Marriage status:
28.4% never married, 53.3% now married, 1.4% separated, 5.4%
widowed, 12.9% divorced; Foreign born: 2.7%; Speak English only: 95.2%;
With disability: 11.9%; Veterans: 7.3%; Ancestry: 26.0% German, 16.0%
American, 15.9% Irish, 15.6% Italian, 10.7% Polish
Employment: 14.4% management, business, and financial, 4.8%
computer, engineering, and science, 10.7% education, legal, community
service, arts, and media, 5.9% healthcare practitioners, 15.7% service,
26.0% sales and office, 10.0% natural resources, construction, and
maintenance, 12.6% production, transportation, and material moving
Income: Per capita: $30,548; Median household: $62,524; Average
household: $74,714; Households with income of $100,000 or more: 26.0%;
Poverty rate: 10.2%
Educational Attainment: High school diploma or higher: 92.3%;
Bachelor's degree or higher: 26.5%; Graduate/professional degree or
higher: 10.6%
School District(s)
Lockport City SD (KG-12)
    Enrollment: 4,746 . . . . (716) 478-4838
Starpoint Central SD (KG-12)
    Enrollment: 2,730 . . . . (716) 210-2352
Housing: Homeownership rate: 81.4%; Median home value: $133,200;
Median year structure built: 1981; Homeowner vacancy rate: 4.4%; Median
selected monthly owner costs: $1,470 with a mortgage, $627 without a
mortgage; Median gross rent: $554 per month; Rental vacancy rate: 21.1%
Health Insurance: 96.1% have insurance; 77.3% have private insurance;
36.3% have public insurance; 3.9% do not have insurance; 2.2% of
children under 18 do not have insurance
Hospitals: Eastern Niagara Hospital (134 beds)
Newspapers: Journal-Register (weekly circulation 1,900); Lockport
Union-Sun & Journal (daily circulation 2,700); Union-Sun & Journal (daily
circulation 11,500)
Transportation: Commute: 94.4% car, 0.6% public transportation, 2.0%
walk, 1.8% work from home; Mean travel time to work: 24.2 minutes
Additional Information Contacts
Town of Lockport . . . . (716) 439-9524
    http://www.elockport.com

MIDDLEPORT (village). Covers a land area of 0.872 square miles
and a water area of 0 square miles. Located at 43.21° N. Lat; 78.48° W.
Long. Elevation is 515 feet.
History: Grew after completion of Erie Canal (1825). Settled 1812,
incorporated 1859.
Population: 1,807; Growth (since 2000): -5.7%; Density: 2,072.4 persons
per square mile; Race: 96.3% White, 0.3% Black/African American, 0.3%

Asian, 0.4% American Indian/Alaska Native, 0.0% Native Hawaiian/Other
Pacific Islander, 1.1% Two or more races, 0.7% Hispanic of any race;
Average household size: 2.52; Median age: 38.1; Age under 18: 25.7%;
Age 65 and over: 13.6%; Males per 100 females: 91.1; Marriage status:
28.4% never married, 49.1% now married, 4.5% separated, 8.3%
widowed, 14.2% divorced; Foreign born: 1.0%; Speak English only: 98.2%;
With disability: 14.1%; Veterans: 9.0%; Ancestry: 29.2% American, 27.8%
German, 15.8% Irish, 11.8% English, 9.1% Polish
Employment: 7.2% management, business, and financial, 3.0% computer,
engineering, and science, 12.4% education, legal, community service, arts,
and media, 4.9% healthcare practitioners, 19.4% service, 22.2% sales and
office, 7.5% natural resources, construction, and maintenance, 23.4%
production, transportation, and material moving
Income: Per capita: $24,678; Median household: $46,944; Average
household: $61,386; Households with income of $100,000 or more: 13.6%;
Poverty rate: 11.4%
Educational Attainment: High school diploma or higher: 92.2%;
Bachelor's degree or higher: 14.3%; Graduate/professional degree or
higher: 5.8%
School District(s)
Royalton-Hartland Central SD (PK-12)
    Enrollment: 1,327 . . . . (716) 735-2000
Housing: Homeownership rate: 64.1%; Median home value: $89,000;
Median year structure built: Before 1940; Homeowner vacancy rate:
11.7%; Median selected monthly owner costs: $1,102 with a mortgage,
$536 without a mortgage; Median gross rent: $629 per month; Rental
vacancy rate: 6.2%
Health Insurance: 96.6% have insurance; 75.5% have private insurance;
35.1% have public insurance; 3.4% do not have insurance; 0.6% of
children under 18 do not have insurance
Safety: Violent crime rate: 17.0 per 10,000 population; Property crime rate:
169.9 per 10,000 population
Transportation: Commute: 96.4% car, 0.0% public transportation, 2.4%
walk, 1.2% work from home; Mean travel time to work: 24.6 minutes

NEWFANE (CDP). Covers a land area of 5.303 square miles and a
water area of 0 square miles. Located at 43.29° N. Lat; 78.69° W. Long.
Elevation is 344 feet.
Population: 4,024; Growth (since 2000): 28.6%; Density: 758.8 persons
per square mile; Race: 99.1% White, 0.5% Black/African American, 0.0%
Asian, 0.1% American Indian/Alaska Native, 0.0% Native Hawaiian/Other
Pacific Islander, 0.0% Two or more races, 0.3% Hispanic of any race;
Average household size: 2.39; Median age: 44.5; Age under 18: 21.0%;
Age 65 and over: 24.2%; Males per 100 females: 89.6; Marriage status:
22.0% never married, 52.9% now married, 0.5% separated, 11.9%
widowed, 13.1% divorced; Foreign born: 2.4%; Speak English only: 99.6%;
With disability: 9.5%; Veterans: 9.4%; Ancestry: 29.0% German, 25.0%
American, 13.8% Irish, 7.7% English, 7.0% Italian
Employment: 17.7% management, business, and financial, 4.9%
computer, engineering, and science, 7.4% education, legal, community
service, arts, and media, 9.6% healthcare practitioners, 22.6% service,
13.0% sales and office, 6.8% natural resources, construction, and
maintenance, 18.1% production, transportation, and material moving
Income: Per capita: $25,230; Median household: $47,373; Average
household: $60,657; Households with income of $100,000 or more: 17.1%;
Poverty rate: 10.7%
Educational Attainment: High school diploma or higher: 87.8%;
Bachelor's degree or higher: 18.5%; Graduate/professional degree or
higher: 6.0%
School District(s)
Newfane Central SD (PK-12)
    Enrollment: 1,597 . . . . (716) 778-6888
Housing: Homeownership rate: 83.8%; Median home value: $89,900;
Median year structure built: 1958; Homeowner vacancy rate: 2.8%; Median
selected monthly owner costs: $1,104 with a mortgage, $471 without a
mortgage; Median gross rent: $646 per month; Rental vacancy rate: 13.9%
Health Insurance: 88.5% have insurance; 70.5% have private insurance;
36.5% have public insurance; 11.5% do not have insurance; 6.5% of
children under 18 do not have insurance
Transportation: Commute: 98.8% car, 0.0% public transportation, 0.0%
walk, 1.2% work from home; Mean travel time to work: 22.4 minutes

NEWFANE (town).

Covers a land area of 51.823 square miles and a water area of 1.657 square miles. Located at 43.29° N. Lat; 78.69° W. Long. Elevation is 344 feet.

History: The Town of Newfane, in Niagara County, New York, was established in 1824 by James VanHorn and others. It is comprised of parts of the Towns of Hartland, Somerset, and Wilson.

Population: 9,432; Growth (since 2000): -2.3%; Density: 182.0 persons per square mile; Race: 97.7% White, 0.3% Black/African American, 0.0% Asian, 0.5% American Indian/Alaska Native, 0.0% Native Hawaiian/Other Pacific Islander, 1.4% Two or more races, 0.3% Hispanic of any race; Average household size: 2.41; Median age: 44.9; Age under 18: 18.3%; Age 65 and over: 18.6%; Males per 100 females: 96.4; Marriage status: 26.2% never married, 54.0% now married, 1.2% separated, 8.0% widowed, 11.9% divorced; Foreign born: 1.7%; Speak English only: 99.5%; With disability: 10.1%; Veterans: 8.8%; Ancestry: 30.9% German, 21.8% American, 15.6% Irish, 11.2% English, 8.8% Italian

Employment: 12.4% management, business, and financial, 5.3% computer, engineering, and science, 4.9% education, legal, community service, arts, and media, 8.3% healthcare practitioners, 18.3% service, 22.4% sales and office, 11.1% natural resources, construction, and maintenance, 17.3% production, transportation, and material moving

Income: Per capita: $28,016; Median household: $54,234; Average household: $66,751; Households with income of $100,000 or more: 20.0%; Poverty rate: 9.5%

Educational Attainment: High school diploma or higher: 90.5%; Bachelor's degree or higher: 17.9%; Graduate/professional degree or higher: 5.8%

School District(s)

Newfane Central SD (PK-12)
    Enrollment: 1,597 . . . . (716) 778-6888

Housing: Homeownership rate: 86.1%; Median home value: $108,600; Median year structure built: 1958; Homeowner vacancy rate: 4.3%; Median selected monthly owner costs: $1,149 with a mortgage, $498 without a mortgage; Median gross rent: $764 per month; Rental vacancy rate: 20.5%

Health Insurance: 91.8% have insurance; 73.5% have private insurance; 31.8% have public insurance; 8.2% do not have insurance; 4.7% of children under 18 do not have insurance

Transportation: Commute: 96.8% car, 0.1% public transportation, 0.7% walk, 2.5% work from home; Mean travel time to work: 24.8 minutes

Additional Information Contacts

Town of Newfane . . . . (716) 778-8531
    http://www.townofnewfane.com

NIAGARA (town).

Covers a land area of 9.484 square miles and a water area of 0 square miles. Located at 43.12° N. Lat; 78.98° W. Long.

History: Niagara was founded in 1812 as the "Town of Schlosser" after the local Fort Schlosser and British Army Captain Joseph Schlosser. In 1836 western parts of the town became the Town of Wheatfield, New York.

Population: 8,148; Growth (since 2000): -9.2%; Density: 859.2 persons per square mile; Race: 92.3% White, 4.2% Black/African American, 0.0% Asian, 3.2% American Indian/Alaska Native, 0.0% Native Hawaiian/Other Pacific Islander, 0.3% Two or more races, 2.8% Hispanic of any race; Average household size: 2.37; Median age: 44.3; Age under 18: 18.0%; Age 65 and over: 19.6%; Males per 100 females: 92.1; Marriage status: 34.4% never married, 44.5% now married, 3.2% separated, 8.6% widowed, 12.4% divorced; Foreign born: 4.7%; Speak English only: 95.6%; With disability: 13.1%; Veterans: 7.8%; Ancestry: 18.0% German, 17.5% Italian, 16.7% American, 12.1% Polish, 10.0% Irish

Employment: 7.0% management, business, and financial, 3.9% computer, engineering, and science, 8.0% education, legal, community service, arts, and media, 3.6% healthcare practitioners, 23.9% service, 30.1% sales and office, 12.9% natural resources, construction, and maintenance, 10.7% production, transportation, and material moving

Income: Per capita: $25,163; Median household: $43,465; Average household: $57,086; Households with income of $100,000 or more: 12.5%; Poverty rate: 13.1%

Educational Attainment: High school diploma or higher: 86.3%; Bachelor's degree or higher: 15.4%; Graduate/professional degree or higher: 5.6%

Housing: Homeownership rate: 71.8%; Median home value: $83,600; Median year structure built: 1963; Homeowner vacancy rate: 5.2%; Median selected monthly owner costs: $963 with a mortgage, $468 without a mortgage; Median gross rent: $752 per month; Rental vacancy rate: 6.0%

Health Insurance: 92.8% have insurance; 67.2% have private insurance; 42.3% have public insurance; 7.2% do not have insurance; 3.2% of children under 18 do not have insurance

Safety: Violent crime rate: 11.2 per 10,000 population; Property crime rate: 445.8 per 10,000 population

Transportation: Commute: 94.3% car, 1.5% public transportation, 0.6% walk, 3.2% work from home; Mean travel time to work: 17.2 minutes

Additional Information Contacts

Town of Niagara . . . . (716) 297-2150
    http://www.townofniagara.com

NIAGARA FALLS (city).

Covers a land area of 14.086 square miles and a water area of 2.742 square miles. Located at 43.09° N. Lat; 79.01° W. Long. Elevation is 614 feet.

History: Named for the Iroquois Indian translation of "at the neck". The first published view of Niagara Falls, reproduced in a volume in 1697, was a sketch made by Father Louis Hennepin, who visited the falls in 1678. In 1745 and 1750 the French built two forts near the falls to supplement Fort Niagara at the mouth of the river and to guard the upper end of the portage. Before the approach of the British in 1759, Chabert Joncaire, French master of the portage, burned the forts and retreated across the river. Under British occupation, Fort Schlosser was erected. Augustus Porter purchased the land immediately surrounding the falls in 1805 or 1806, and became master of the portage. Visioning a manufacturing center that would rival the English city, Porter named the settlement Manchester. The settlement and fort were burned in the War of 1812. The Niagara water power turned the first generator in 1881, and the falls continued to be a source of power for the surrounding area. The falls have been a tourist attraction since at least the early 19th century.

Population: 48,976; Growth (since 2000): -11.9%; Density: 3,476.9 persons per square mile; Race: 69.5% White, 22.6% Black/African American, 1.0% Asian, 1.5% American Indian/Alaska Native, 0.1% Native Hawaiian/Other Pacific Islander, 4.6% Two or more races, 3.6% Hispanic of any race; Average household size: 2.28; Median age: 38.6; Age under 18: 22.3%; Age 65 and over: 15.4%; Males per 100 females: 91.2; Marriage status: 41.4% never married, 39.2% now married, 3.0% separated, 7.3% widowed, 12.1% divorced; Foreign born: 4.8%; Speak English only: 95.0%; With disability: 16.2%; Veterans: 8.5%; Ancestry: 18.0% Italian, 12.9% American, 12.8% German, 12.2% Irish, 7.4% Polish

Employment: 8.9% management, business, and financial, 2.8% computer, engineering, and science, 10.8% education, legal, community service, arts, and media, 4.6% healthcare practitioners, 25.1% service, 27.9% sales and office, 7.0% natural resources, construction, and maintenance, 13.0% production, transportation, and material moving

Income: Per capita: $21,368; Median household: $33,965; Average household: $47,744; Households with income of $100,000 or more: 10.5%; Poverty rate: 27.5%

Educational Attainment: High school diploma or higher: 87.8%; Bachelor's degree or higher: 17.5%; Graduate/professional degree or higher: 7.1%

School District(s)

Niagara Charter School (KG-06)
    Enrollment: 345 . . . . (716) 297-4520
Niagara Falls City SD (PK-12)
    Enrollment: 7,200 . . . . (716) 286-4205
Niagara-Wheatfield Central SD (PK-12)
    Enrollment: 3,668 . . . . (716) 215-3003

Vocational/Technical School(s)

Cheryl Fells School of Business (Private, For-profit)
    Enrollment: 30 . . . . (716) 297-2750
    Tuition: $12,600

Housing: Homeownership rate: 57.2%; Median home value: $69,900; Median year structure built: 1942; Homeowner vacancy rate: 12.4%; Median selected monthly owner costs: $928 with a mortgage, $436 without a mortgage; Median gross rent: $645 per month; Rental vacancy rate: 17.8%

Health Insurance: 94.5% have insurance; 57.0% have private insurance; 52.4% have public insurance; 5.5% do not have insurance; 1.8% of children under 18 do not have insurance

Hospitals: Niagara Falls Memorial Medical Center

Safety: Violent crime rate: 112.4 per 10,000 population; Property crime rate: 482.8 per 10,000 population

Newspapers: Niagara Gazette (daily circulation 18,900)

Transportation: Commute: 89.9% car, 2.6% public transportation, 3.6% walk, 1.5% work from home; Mean travel time to work: 18.3 minutes; Amtrak: Train service available.
Airports: Niagara Falls International (primary service/non-hub)
Additional Information Contacts
City of Niagara Falls . . . . (716) 286-4393
   http://www.niagarafallsusa.org

NIAGARA UNIVERSITY (unincorporated postal area)
ZCTA: 14109
   Covers a land area of 0.474 square miles and a water area of 0 square miles. Located at 43.14° N. Lat; 79.03° W. Long..
   Population: 1,155; Growth (since 2000): n/a; Density: 2,438.9 persons per square mile; Race: 85.9% White, 4.8% Black/African American, 0.3% Asian, 0.0% American Indian/Alaska Native, 0.0% Native Hawaiian/Other Pacific Islander, 3.5% Two or more races, 7.8% Hispanic of any race; Average household size: 0.00; Median age: 19.4; Age under 18: 2.2%; Age 65 and over: 0.0%; Males per 100 females: 76.2; Marriage status: 100.0% never married, 0.0% now married, 0.0% separated, 0.0% widowed, 0.0% divorced; Foreign born: 3.5%; Speak English only: 93.6%; With disability: 3.9%; Veterans: 1.2%; Ancestry: 33.4% German, 27.8% Italian, 24.3% Irish, 11.5% Polish, 7.8% English
   Employment: 0.0% management, business, and financial, 0.0% computer, engineering, and science, 11.7% education, legal, community service, arts, and media, 2.2% healthcare practitioners, 45.2% service, 38.4% sales and office, 0.0% natural resources, construction, and maintenance, 2.5% production, transportation, and material moving
   Income: Per capita: $4,397; Median household: n/a; Average household: n/a; Households with income of $100,000 or more: n/a; Poverty rate: n/a
   Educational Attainment: High school diploma or higher: 100.0%; Bachelor's degree or higher: 27.3%; Graduate/professional degree or higher: n/a

Four-year College(s)
Niagara University (Private, Not-for-profit, Roman Catholic)
   Enrollment: 3,949 . . . . (716) 285-1212
   Tuition: In-state $31,950; Out-of-state $31,950
Two-year College(s)
Niagara University (Private, Not-for-profit, Roman Catholic)
   Enrollment: 3,949 . . . . (716) 285-1212
   Tuition: In-state $31,950; Out-of-state $31,950
Vocational/Technical School(s)
Niagara University (Private, Not-for-profit, Roman Catholic)
   Enrollment: 3,949 . . . . (716) 285-1212
   2016-17 Tuition: In-state $31,950; Out-of-state $31,950
   Housing: Homeownership rate: n/a; Median home value: n/a; Median year structure built: n/a; Homeowner vacancy rate: 0.0%; Median selected monthly owner costs: $0 with a mortgage, $0 without a mortgage; Median gross rent: n/a per month; Rental vacancy rate: 0.0%
   Health Insurance: 98.1% have insurance; 94.9% have private insurance; 3.2% have public insurance; 1.9% do not have insurance; 0.0% of children under 18 do not have insurance
   Transportation: Commute: 59.5% car, 0.0% public transportation, 36.5% walk, 1.9% work from home; Mean travel time to work: 12.7 minutes

NORTH TONAWANDA (city). Covers a land area of 10.100 square miles and a water area of 0.802 square miles. Located at 43.05° N. Lat; 78.87° W. Long. Elevation is 574 feet.
History: Named for its location north of Tonawanda. Settled c.1802. Incorporated as a city 1897.
Population: 30,752; Growth (since 2000): -7.5%; Density: 3,044.7 persons per square mile; Race: 95.2% White, 1.5% Black/African American, 0.4% Asian, 0.4% American Indian/Alaska Native, 0.0% Native Hawaiian/Other Pacific Islander, 1.9% Two or more races, 2.1% Hispanic of any race; Average household size: 2.24; Median age: 44.3; Age under 18: 18.6%; Age 65 and over: 18.5%; Males per 100 females: 95.3; Marriage status: 31.8% never married, 48.2% now married, 2.1% separated, 8.0% widowed, 12.1% divorced; Foreign born: 3.0%; Speak English only: 96.1%; With disability: 17.1%; Veterans: 9.2%; Ancestry: 30.5% German, 19.5% Italian, 18.7% Polish, 18.5% Irish, 10.2% English
Employment: 11.3% management, business, and financial, 4.5% computer, engineering, and science, 10.5% education, legal, community service, arts, and media, 6.0% healthcare practitioners, 16.9% service,

28.0% sales and office, 7.9% natural resources, construction, and maintenance, 14.9% production, transportation, and material moving
Income: Per capita: $29,344; Median household: $53,002; Average household: $64,678; Households with income of $100,000 or more: 19.1%; Poverty rate: 8.8%
Educational Attainment: High school diploma or higher: 92.7%; Bachelor's degree or higher: 24.5%; Graduate/professional degree or higher: 9.9%

School District(s)
Niagara-Wheatfield Central SD (PK-12)
   Enrollment: 3,668 . . . . (716) 215-3003
North Tonawanda City SD (KG-12)
   Enrollment: 3,593 . . . . (716) 807-3500
Vocational/Technical School(s)
Leon Studio One School of Hair Design & Career Training Center (Private, For-profit)
   Enrollment: n/a . . . . (716) 260-1652
   Housing: Homeownership rate: 68.9%; Median home value: $112,600; Median year structure built: 1954; Homeowner vacancy rate: 0.5%; Median selected monthly owner costs: $1,171 with a mortgage, $543 without a mortgage; Median gross rent: $666 per month; Rental vacancy rate: 9.5%
   Health Insurance: 95.8% have insurance; 76.0% have private insurance; 37.9% have public insurance; 4.2% do not have insurance; 1.5% of children under 18 do not have insurance
   Safety: Violent crime rate: 12.2 per 10,000 population; Property crime rate: 166.5 per 10,000 population
   Newspapers: Tonawanda News (daily circulation 8,000)
   Transportation: Commute: 94.7% car, 0.5% public transportation, 0.9% walk, 2.4% work from home; Mean travel time to work: 20.9 minutes
   Additional Information Contacts
City of North Tonawanda. . . . . (716) 695-8555
   http://www.northtonawanda.org

OLCOTT (CDP). Covers a land area of 4.547 square miles and a water area of 0.744 square miles. Located at 43.33° N. Lat; 78.70° W. Long. Elevation is 272 feet.
Population: 1,014; Growth (since 2000): -12.3%; Density: 223.0 persons per square mile; Race: 95.2% White, 0.2% Black/African American, 0.1% Asian, 2.8% American Indian/Alaska Native, 0.0% Native Hawaiian/Other Pacific Islander, 1.8% Two or more races, 0.0% Hispanic of any race; Average household size: 2.13; Median age: 45.8; Age under 18: 15.3%; Age 65 and over: 14.4%; Males per 100 females: 100.2; Marriage status: 35.5% never married, 42.7% now married, 3.1% separated, 7.7% widowed, 14.1% divorced; Foreign born: 0.8%; Speak English only: 99.7%; With disability: 8.6%; Veterans: 4.9%; Ancestry: 29.0% American, 21.2% German, 18.1% Irish, 12.4% English, 8.3% Dutch
Employment: 10.2% management, business, and financial, 2.7% computer, engineering, and science, 0.0% education, legal, community service, arts, and media, 12.9% healthcare practitioners, 26.2% service, 25.2% sales and office, 21.8% natural resources, construction, and maintenance, 1.0% production, transportation, and material moving
Income: Per capita: $27,180; Median household: $45,625; Average household: $56,996; Households with income of $100,000 or more: 14.3%; Poverty rate: 22.4%
Educational Attainment: High school diploma or higher: 97.1%; Bachelor's degree or higher: 18.1%; Graduate/professional degree or higher: 2.7%
Housing: Homeownership rate: 75.7%; Median home value: $99,000; Median year structure built: 1950; Homeowner vacancy rate: 5.3%; Median selected monthly owner costs: $1,099 with a mortgage, $445 without a mortgage; Median gross rent: $827 per month; Rental vacancy rate: 48.7%
Health Insurance: 97.9% have insurance; 60.5% have private insurance; 43.2% have public insurance; 2.1% do not have insurance; 0.0% of children under 18 do not have insurance
Transportation: Commute: 95.1% car, 0.0% public transportation, 1.9% walk, 3.0% work from home; Mean travel time to work: 30.2 minutes

PENDLETON (town). Covers a land area of 27.086 square miles and a water area of 0.270 square miles. Located at 43.10° N. Lat; 78.76° W. Long. Elevation is 581 feet.
Population: 6,583; Growth (since 2000): 8.8%; Density: 243.0 persons per square mile; Race: 98.7% White, 0.0% Black/African American, 0.3% Asian, 0.0% American Indian/Alaska Native, 0.0% Native Hawaiian/Other Pacific Islander, 0.9% Two or more races, 0.3% Hispanic of any race; Average household size: 2.84; Median age: 44.2; Age under 18: 20.2%;

Age 65 and over: 15.8%; Males per 100 females: 98.7; Marriage status: 28.0% never married, 60.6% now married, 0.4% separated, 5.3% widowed, 6.1% divorced; Foreign born: 1.8%; Speak English only: 99.0%; With disability: 10.4%; Veterans: 7.6%; Ancestry: 34.0% German, 20.6% Irish, 20.2% Italian, 18.2% Polish, 13.2% English

Employment: 12.7% management, business, and financial, 5.2% computer, engineering, and science, 13.3% education, legal, community service, arts, and media, 5.1% healthcare practitioners, 12.0% service, 28.6% sales and office, 10.7% natural resources, construction, and maintenance, 12.3% production, transportation, and material moving

Income: Per capita: $36,984; Median household: $90,570; Average household: $103,730; Households with income of $100,000 or more: 46.2%; Poverty rate: 4.6%

Educational Attainment: High school diploma or higher: 96.1%; Bachelor's degree or higher: 34.3%; Graduate/professional degree or higher: 12.9%

Housing: Homeownership rate: 94.0%; Median home value: $184,400; Median year structure built: 1972; Homeowner vacancy rate: 2.6%; Median selected monthly owner costs: $1,589 with a mortgage, $666 without a mortgage; Median gross rent: $1,087 per month; Rental vacancy rate: 18.8%

Health Insurance: 98.8% have insurance; 88.2% have private insurance; 23.3% have public insurance; 1.2% do not have insurance; 1.0% of children under 18 do not have insurance

Transportation: Commute: 96.8% car, 0.0% public transportation, 0.8% walk, 1.8% work from home; Mean travel time to work: 23.2 minutes

Additional Information Contacts
Town of Pendleton . . . . (716) 625-8833
    http://pendletonny.us

PORTER (town). Covers a land area of 33.055 square miles and a water area of 4.659 square miles. Located at 43.26° N. Lat; 78.97° W. Long.

Population: 6,616; Growth (since 2000): -4.4%; Density: 200.2 persons per square mile; Race: 96.9% White, 0.7% Black/African American, 0.2% Asian, 0.8% American Indian/Alaska Native, 0.0% Native Hawaiian/Other Pacific Islander, 0.7% Two or more races, 1.8% Hispanic of any race; Average household size: 2.49; Median age: 48.3; Age under 18: 20.7%; Age 65 and over: 19.0%; Males per 100 females: 100.3; Marriage status: 27.4% never married, 55.8% now married, 1.7% separated, 6.4% widowed, 10.4% divorced; Foreign born: 5.4%; Speak English only: 97.0%; With disability: 11.0%; Veterans: 10.3%; Ancestry: 23.5% German, 18.2% Italian, 17.2% American, 15.6% Irish, 11.1% Polish

Employment: 15.3% management, business, and financial, 3.9% computer, engineering, and science, 9.3% education, legal, community service, arts, and media, 9.0% healthcare practitioners, 13.6% service, 29.7% sales and office, 9.3% natural resources, construction, and maintenance, 9.9% production, transportation, and material moving

Income: Per capita: $34,523; Median household: $71,217; Average household: $84,422; Households with income of $100,000 or more: 31.9%; Poverty rate: 4.8%

Educational Attainment: High school diploma or higher: 93.2%; Bachelor's degree or higher: 31.8%; Graduate/professional degree or higher: 14.0%

Housing: Homeownership rate: 83.8%; Median home value: $151,700; Median year structure built: 1958; Homeowner vacancy rate: 5.7%; Median selected monthly owner costs: $1,348 with a mortgage, $529 without a mortgage; Median gross rent: $818 per month; Rental vacancy rate: 9.9%

Health Insurance: 94.5% have insurance; 79.5% have private insurance; 32.5% have public insurance; 5.5% do not have insurance; 4.0% of children under 18 do not have insurance

Transportation: Commute: 92.9% car, 0.0% public transportation, 2.4% walk, 3.9% work from home; Mean travel time to work: 25.8 minutes

Additional Information Contacts
Town of Porter . . . . (716) 745-3730
    http://www.townofporter.net

RANSOMVILLE (CDP). Covers a land area of 6.243 square miles and a water area of 0 square miles. Located at 43.24° N. Lat; 78.91° W. Long. Elevation is 325 feet.

Population: 1,626; Growth (since 2000): 9.3%; Density: 260.5 persons per square mile; Race: 94.5% White, 1.3% Black/African American, 0.0% Asian, 0.9% American Indian/Alaska Native, 0.0% Native Hawaiian/Other Pacific Islander, 2.1% Two or more races, 1.2% Hispanic of any race; Average household size: 2.80; Median age: 44.6; Age under 18: 25.8%;

Age 65 and over: 14.8%; Males per 100 females: 103.3; Marriage status: 26.5% never married, 56.4% now married, 0.7% separated, 5.1% widowed, 12.0% divorced; Foreign born: 3.3%; Speak English only: 100.0%; With disability: 8.3%; Veterans: 8.4%; Ancestry: 31.3% German, 25.7% American, 14.0% Irish, 10.7% Polish, 10.6% English

Employment: 14.7% management, business, and financial, 2.5% computer, engineering, and science, 8.1% education, legal, community service, arts, and media, 6.7% healthcare practitioners, 17.0% service, 27.3% sales and office, 11.9% natural resources, construction, and maintenance, 11.8% production, transportation, and material moving

Income: Per capita: $32,326; Median household: $80,761; Average household: $89,055; Households with income of $100,000 or more: 40.1%; Poverty rate: 1.4%

Educational Attainment: High school diploma or higher: 94.3%; Bachelor's degree or higher: 20.1%; Graduate/professional degree or higher: 6.8%

School District(s)
Wilson Central SD (PK-12)
    Enrollment: 1,183 . . . . (716) 751-9341

Housing: Homeownership rate: 82.2%; Median home value: $135,800; Median year structure built: 1947; Homeowner vacancy rate: 0.0%; Median selected monthly owner costs: $1,143 with a mortgage, $565 without a mortgage; Median gross rent: $1,125 per month; Rental vacancy rate: 0.0%

Health Insurance: 99.3% have insurance; 92.3% have private insurance; 22.0% have public insurance; 0.7% do not have insurance; 0.0% of children under 18 do not have insurance

Transportation: Commute: 93.5% car, 0.0% public transportation, 3.9% walk, 2.6% work from home; Mean travel time to work: 27.8 minutes

RAPIDS (CDP). Covers a land area of 3.644 square miles and a water area of 0 square miles. Located at 43.10° N. Long; 78.64° W. Long. Elevation is 591 feet.

Population: 1,336; Growth (since 2000): -1.5%; Density: 366.6 persons per square mile; Race: 98.2% White, 0.0% Black/African American, 0.0% Asian, 0.0% American Indian/Alaska Native, 0.0% Native Hawaiian/Other Pacific Islander, 0.5% Two or more races, 2.2% Hispanic of any race; Average household size: 2.73; Median age: 36.3; Age under 18: 26.0%; Age 65 and over: 11.8%; Males per 100 females: 99.3; Marriage status: 22.5% never married, 64.6% now married, 2.4% separated, 5.7% widowed, 7.2% divorced; Foreign born: 0.6%; Speak English only: 100.0%; With disability: 7.4%; Veterans: 3.7%; Ancestry: 32.1% American, 28.3% German, 16.8% Italian, 13.2% Irish, 8.7% Polish

Employment: 19.6% management, business, and financial, 1.7% computer, engineering, and science, 3.5% education, legal, community service, arts, and media, 15.1% healthcare practitioners, 28.8% service, 13.8% sales and office, 2.5% natural resources, construction, and maintenance, 15.0% production, transportation, and material moving

Income: Per capita: $33,928; Median household: $67,431; Average household: $90,039; Households with income of $100,000 or more: 46.6%; Poverty rate: 1.9%

Educational Attainment: High school diploma or higher: 92.0%; Bachelor's degree or higher: 38.1%; Graduate/professional degree or higher: 6.4%

Housing: Homeownership rate: 91.2%; Median home value: $173,700; Median year structure built: 1987; Homeowner vacancy rate: 19.4%; Median selected monthly owner costs: $1,732 with a mortgage, $611 without a mortgage; Median gross rent: n/a per month; Rental vacancy rate: 0.0%

Health Insurance: 100.0% have insurance; 93.6% have private insurance; 18.4% have public insurance; 0.0% do not have insurance; 0.0% of children under 18 do not have insurance

Transportation: Commute: 100.0% car, 0.0% public transportation, 0.0% walk, 0.0% work from home; Mean travel time to work: 24.4 minutes

ROYALTON (town). Covers a land area of 69.966 square miles and a water area of 0.311 square miles. Located at 43.15° N. Lat; 78.55° W. Long.

Population: 7,564; Growth (since 2000): -1.9%; Density: 108.1 persons per square mile; Race: 95.0% White, 1.1% Black/African American, 0.6% Asian, 0.3% American Indian/Alaska Native, 0.4% Native Hawaiian/Other Pacific Islander, 1.4% Two or more races, 2.8% Hispanic of any race; Average household size: 2.70; Median age: 41.1; Age under 18: 22.6%; Age 65 and over: 15.9%; Males per 100 females: 96.6; Marriage status: 28.8% never married, 56.7% now married, 1.5% separated, 4.9%

widowed, 9.6% divorced; Foreign born: 1.7%; Speak English only: 97.7%; With disability: 10.9%; Veterans: 9.2%; Ancestry: 34.0% German, 21.3% American, 12.6% Irish, 10.4% English, 9.9% Italian

Employment: 10.6% management, business, and financial, 1.9% computer, engineering, and science, 12.8% education, legal, community service, arts, and media, 6.2% healthcare practitioners, 19.3% service, 15.5% sales and office, 10.8% natural resources, construction, and maintenance, 22.9% production, transportation, and material moving

Income: Per capita: $26,991; Median household: $54,819; Average household: $71,839; Households with income of $100,000 or more: 23.5%; Poverty rate: 8.6%

Educational Attainment: High school diploma or higher: 92.4%; Bachelor's degree or higher: 17.6%; Graduate/professional degree or higher: 9.2%

Housing: Homeownership rate: 76.8%; Median home value: $113,600; Median year structure built: 1942; Homeowner vacancy rate: 2.7%; Median selected monthly owner costs: $1,174 with a mortgage, $562 without a mortgage; Median gross rent: $763 per month; Rental vacancy rate: 16.2%

Health Insurance: 98.6% have insurance; 78.0% have private insurance; 37.0% have public insurance; 1.4% do not have insurance; 0.2% of children under 18 do not have insurance

Transportation: Commute: 92.9% car, 1.2% public transportation, 1.2% walk, 3.2% work from home; Mean travel time to work: 25.2 minutes

Additional Information Contacts

Town of Royalton . . . . (716) 772-2431
    http://townofroyalton.org/content

SANBORN (CDP). Covers a land area of 2.633 square miles and a water area of 0 square miles. Located at 43.15° N. Lat; 78.88° W. Long. Elevation is 633 feet.

Population: 1,210; Growth (since 2000): n/a; Density: 459.5 persons per square mile; Race: 89.1% White, 7.2% Black/African American, 3.3% Asian, 0.4% American Indian/Alaska Native, 0.0% Native Hawaiian/Other Pacific Islander, 0.0% Two or more races, 0.0% Hispanic of any race; Average household size: 2.09; Median age: 50.2; Age under 18: 17.4%; Age 65 and over: 16.3%; Males per 100 females: 92.6; Marriage status: 30.6% never married, 39.7% now married, 0.0% separated, 10.3% widowed, 19.4% divorced; Foreign born: 5.0%; Speak English only: 95.9%; With disability: 16.1%; Veterans: 9.7%; Ancestry: 23.7% German, 17.7% English, 15.4% American, 15.2% Polish, 14.5% Irish

Employment: 9.0% management, business, and financial, 0.5% computer, engineering, and science, 4.9% education, legal, community service, arts, and media, 9.2% healthcare practitioners, 31.6% service, 26.8% sales and office, 6.3% natural resources, construction, and maintenance, 11.7% production, transportation, and material moving

Income: Per capita: $29,078; Median household: $57,232; Average household: $59,109; Households with income of $100,000 or more: 15.9%; Poverty rate: 4.9%

Educational Attainment: High school diploma or higher: 93.5%; Bachelor's degree or higher: 19.5%; Graduate/professional degree or higher: 7.2%

School District(s)

Niagara-Wheatfield Central SD (PK-12)
    Enrollment: 3,668 . . . . (716) 215-3003

Two-year College(s)

Niagara County Community College (Public)
    Enrollment: 5,439 . . . . (716) 614-6222
    Tuition: In-state $4,698; Out-of-state $11,034

Vocational/Technical School(s)

Orleans Niagara BOCES-Practical Nursing Program (Public)
    Enrollment: 62 . . . . (716) 731-6800
    Tuition: $13,049

Housing: Homeownership rate: 71.8%; Median home value: $127,700; Median year structure built: 1956; Homeowner vacancy rate: 3.3%; Median selected monthly owner costs: $1,103 with a mortgage, $554 without a mortgage; Median gross rent: $782 per month; Rental vacancy rate: 9.4%

Health Insurance: 95.2% have insurance; 85.0% have private insurance; 28.2% have public insurance; 4.8% do not have insurance; 0.0% of children under 18 do not have insurance

Transportation: Commute: 91.8% car, 0.3% public transportation, 0.2% walk, 7.7% work from home; Mean travel time to work: 19.5 minutes

---

SOMERSET (town). Covers a land area of 37.108 square miles and a water area of 0.063 square miles. Located at 43.34° N. Lat; 78.55° W. Long. Elevation is 305 feet.

Population: 2,706; Growth (since 2000): -5.5%; Density: 72.9 persons per square mile; Race: 98.3% White, 0.1% Black/African American, 0.1% Asian, 1.1% American Indian/Alaska Native, 0.0% Native Hawaiian/Other Pacific Islander, 0.3% Two or more races, 8.4% Hispanic of any race; Average household size: 2.71; Median age: 41.0; Age under 18: 25.3%; Age 65 and over: 16.4%; Males per 100 females: 101.1; Marriage status: 25.1% never married, 57.2% now married, 0.4% separated, 5.5% widowed, 12.2% divorced; Foreign born: 2.1%; Speak English only: 94.7%; With disability: 11.5%; Veterans: 11.6%; Ancestry: 26.1% American, 18.1% German, 10.1% Irish, 9.5% English, 8.4% Italian

Employment: 15.5% management, business, and financial, 4.9% computer, engineering, and science, 7.7% education, legal, community service, arts, and media, 3.0% healthcare practitioners, 13.7% service, 19.0% sales and office, 14.1% natural resources, construction, and maintenance, 22.1% production, transportation, and material moving

Income: Per capita: $26,290; Median household: $55,880; Average household: $70,086; Households with income of $100,000 or more: 20.2%; Poverty rate: 9.3%

Educational Attainment: High school diploma or higher: 90.8%; Bachelor's degree or higher: 15.6%; Graduate/professional degree or higher: 4.3%

Housing: Homeownership rate: 75.4%; Median home value: $113,200; Median year structure built: Before 1940; Homeowner vacancy rate: 5.0%; Median selected monthly owner costs: $1,109 with a mortgage, $547 without a mortgage; Median gross rent: $704 per month; Rental vacancy rate: 13.2%

Health Insurance: 90.7% have insurance; 67.7% have private insurance; 37.1% have public insurance; 9.3% do not have insurance; 6.5% of children under 18 do not have insurance

Transportation: Commute: 88.0% car, 0.0% public transportation, 2.1% walk, 7.5% work from home; Mean travel time to work: 28.8 minutes

---

SOUTH LOCKPORT (CDP). Covers a land area of 5.714 square miles and a water area of 0.014 square miles. Located at 43.14° N. Lat; 78.68° W. Long. Elevation is 633 feet.

Population: 7,654; Growth (since 2000): -10.5%; Density: 1,339.5 persons per square mile; Race: 88.7% White, 6.1% Black/African American, 1.2% Asian, 0.4% American Indian/Alaska Native, 0.0% Native Hawaiian/Other Pacific Islander, 2.2% Two or more races, 4.9% Hispanic of any race; Average household size: 2.33; Median age: 42.9; Age under 18: 21.9%; Age 65 and over: 19.3%; Males per 100 females: 90.7; Marriage status: 31.5% never married, 45.4% now married, 2.4% separated, 7.4% widowed, 15.7% divorced; Foreign born: 2.8%; Speak English only: 96.0%; With disability: 16.9%; Veterans: 8.9%; Ancestry: 28.0% German, 16.6% Italian, 16.0% Irish, 12.8% Polish, 12.3% American

Employment: 13.6% management, business, and financial, 1.8% computer, engineering, and science, 9.1% education, legal, community service, arts, and media, 5.6% healthcare practitioners, 18.2% service, 28.8% sales and office, 11.7% natural resources, construction, and maintenance, 11.1% production, transportation, and material moving

Income: Per capita: $25,299; Median household: $44,774; Average household: $57,971; Households with income of $100,000 or more: 16.5%; Poverty rate: 16.4%

Educational Attainment: High school diploma or higher: 88.3%; Bachelor's degree or higher: 16.7%; Graduate/professional degree or higher: 7.1%

Housing: Homeownership rate: 70.4%; Median home value: $92,200; Median year structure built: 1986; Homeowner vacancy rate: 6.6%; Median selected monthly owner costs: $1,375 with a mortgage, $681 without a mortgage; Median gross rent: $583 per month; Rental vacancy rate: 23.0%

Health Insurance: 93.8% have insurance; 65.2% have private insurance; 45.5% have public insurance; 6.2% do not have insurance; 3.1% of children under 18 do not have insurance

Transportation: Commute: 92.7% car, 1.7% public transportation, 2.8% walk, 1.1% work from home; Mean travel time to work: 24.3 minutes

---

TUSCARORA NATION RESERVATION (reservation). Covers a land area of 9.083 square miles and a water area of 0 square miles. Located at 43.16° N. Lat; 78.95° W. Long.

Population: 1,048; Growth (since 2000): -7.9%; Density: 115.4 persons per square mile; Race: 12.6% White, 0.0% Black/African American, 11.7% Asian, 68.4% American Indian/Alaska Native, 0.3% Native Hawaiian/Other

16182022242628303234363840424446485052545658606264666870

7375777981838587899193959799101103105107108109110111112113114115116117118119120121122123124125126127128129130131132133134135136137138139140141142143144145146147148149150151152153154155156157158159160161162163164165166167168169170171172173174175176177178179180181182183184185186187188189190191192193194195196197198199200201202203204205206207208209210211212213214215216217218219220

YOUNGSTOWN (village). Covers a land area of 1.097 square miles and a water area of 0.266 square miles. Located at 43.25° N. Lat; 79.04° W. Long. Elevation is 295 feet.

History: Just North is Fort Niagara, which has been restored.

Population: 1,894; Growth (since 2000): -3.2%; Density: 1,726.6 persons per square mile; Race: 97.8% White, 0.5% Black/African American, 0.5% Asian, 0.6% American Indian/Alaska Native, 0.0% Native Hawaiian/Other Pacific Islander, 0.5% Two or more races, 2.3% Hispanic of any race; Average household size: 2.45; Median age: 47.6; Age under 18: 20.6%; Age 65 and over: 24.0%; Males per 100 females: 96.2; Marriage status: 26.4% never married, 57.7% now married, 3.0% separated, 5.3% widowed, 10.6% divorced; Foreign born: 4.2%; Speak English only: 95.6%; With disability: 13.1%; Veterans: 8.6%; Ancestry: 20.5% German, 18.6% Italian, 17.8% Irish, 14.6% American, 12.1% English

Employment: 9.6% management, business, and financial, 3.1% computer, engineering, and science, 10.6% education, legal, community service, arts, and media, 8.4% healthcare practitioners, 19.0% service, 31.8% sales and office, 6.5% natural resources, construction, and maintenance, 10.9% production, transportation, and material moving

Income: Per capita: $34,878; Median household: $60,781; Average household: $84,674; Households with income of $100,000 or more: 22.0%; Poverty rate: 4.2%

Educational Attainment: High school diploma or higher: 96.7%; Bachelor's degree or higher: 32.1%; Graduate/professional degree or higher: 15.0%

School District(s)

Lewiston-Porter Central SD (PK-12)
    Enrollment: 2,030 . . . . (716) 286-7266

Housing: Homeownership rate: 77.7%; Median home value: $152,900; Median year structure built: 1956; Homeowner vacancy rate: 6.8%; Median selected monthly owner costs: $1,294 with a mortgage, $508 without a mortgage; Median gross rent: $698 per month; Rental vacancy rate: 10.9%

Health Insurance: 97.2% have insurance; 78.6% have private insurance; 40.7% have public insurance; 2.8% do not have insurance; 0.0% of children under 18 do not have insurance

Safety: Violent crime rate: 5.3 per 10,000 population; Property crime rate: 5.3 per 10,000 population

Transportation: Commute: 93.7% car, 0.0% public transportation, 2.2% walk, 2.6% work from home; Mean travel time to work: 24.2 minutes

Oneida County

Located in central New York; bounded partly on the west by Oneida Lake, rising to the Adirondacks in the east and northeast; drained by the Mohawk and Black Rivers; includes several lakes. Covers a land area of 1,212.429 square miles, a water area of 45.227 square miles, and is located in the Eastern Time Zone at 43.24° N. Lat., 75.43° W. Long. The county was founded in 1798. County seat is Utica.

Oneida County is part of the Utica-Rome, NY Metropolitan Statistical Area. The entire metro area includes: Herkimer County, NY; Oneida County, NY

Weather Station: Boonville 2 SSW										Elevation: 1,580 feet	
	Jan	Feb	Mar	Apr	May	Jun	Jul	Aug	Sep	Oct	Nov	Dec
High	25	28	36	51	63	71	75	74	66	54	41	30
Low	8	10	19	32	43	52	57	55	48	37	27	15
Precip	5.0	4.0	4.5	4.5	4.5	4.7	4.4	4.7	5.5	5.6	5.4	5.5
Snow	52.9	39.8	31.4	8.6	0.2	tr	0.0	0.0	tr	2.2	17.8	44.7

High and Low temperatures in degrees Fahrenheit; Precipitation and Snow in inches

Weather Station: Utica Oneida County Arpt										Elevation: 711 feet	
	Jan	Feb	Mar	Apr	May	Jun	Jul	Aug	Sep	Oct	Nov	Dec
High	29	32	41	55	68	76	80	79	71	58	46	34
Low	14	16	24	36	46	55	60	58	51	40	31	20
Precip	2.9	2.4	3.2	3.5	3.9	4.3	3.9	3.9	4.1	3.7	3.9	3.4
Snow	na	na	na	na	na	na	na	na	na	na	na	na

High and Low temperatures in degrees Fahrenheit; Precipitation and Snow in inches

Population: 232,324; Growth (since 2000): -1.3%; Density: 191.6 persons per square mile; Race: 85.6% White, 6.3% Black/African American, 4.0% Asian, 0.2% American Indian/Alaska Native, 0.0% Native Hawaiian/Other Pacific Islander, 2.4% two or more races, 5.4% Hispanic of any race; Average household size: 2.43; Median age: 41.0; Age under 18: 21.3%; Age 65 and over: 17.7%; Males per 100 females: 99.3; Marriage status: 34.6% never married, 46.7% now married, 2.2% separated, 7.5% widowed, 11.2% divorced; Foreign born: 7.5%; Speak English only: 88.1%;

With disability: 14.9%; Veterans: 9.0%; Ancestry: 17.2% American, 16.5% Italian, 14.5% Irish, 13.5% German, 8.7% Polish

Religion: Six largest groups: 36.9% Catholicism, 3.6% Methodist/Pietist, 1.9% Non-denominational Protestant, 1.6% Presbyterian-Reformed, 1.4% Baptist, 1.3% Lutheran

Economy: Unemployment rate: 3.9%; Leading industries: 16.9 % retail trade; 12.0 % health care and social assistance; 12.0 % accommodation and food services; Farms: 1,066 totaling 205,106 acres; Company size: 8 employ 1,000 or more persons, 11 employs 500 to 999 persons, 100 employ 100 to 499 persons, 4,783 employs less than 100 persons; Business ownership: 4,803 women-owned, 528 Black-owned, 484 Hispanic-owned, 583 Asian-owned, 90 American Indian/Alaska Native-owned

Employment: 12.1% management, business, and financial, 4.2% computer, engineering, and science, 11.7% education, legal, community service, arts, and media, 7.2% healthcare practitioners, 20.4% service, 23.4% sales and office, 8.3% natural resources, construction, and maintenance, 12.6% production, transportation, and material moving

Income: Per capita: $27,283; Median household: $51,316; Average household: $67,291; Households with income of $100,000 or more: 19.3%; Poverty rate: 16.6%

Educational Attainment: High school diploma or higher: 88.1%; Bachelor's degree or higher: 23.9%; Graduate/professional degree or higher: 9.7%

Housing: Homeownership rate: 66.6%; Median home value: $120,000; Median year structure built: 1955; Homeowner vacancy rate: 1.8%; Median selected monthly owner costs: $1,217 with a mortgage, $515 without a mortgage; Median gross rent: $735 per month; Rental vacancy rate: 6.1%

Vital Statistics: Birth rate: 106.5 per 10,000 population; Death rate: 106.9 per 10,000 population; Age-adjusted cancer mortality rate: 181.0 deaths per 100,000 population

Health Insurance: 95.0% have insurance; 66.5% have private insurance; 44.1% have public insurance; 5.0% do not have insurance; 2.8% of children under 18 do not have insurance

Health Care: Physicians: 23.0 per 10,000 population; Dentists: 5.6 per 10,000 population; Hospital beds: 64.9 per 10,000 population; Hospital admissions: 1,251.1 per 10,000 population

Air Quality Index (AQI): Percent of Days: 95.8% good, 4.2% moderate, 0.0% unhealthy for sensitive individuals, 0.0% unhealthy, 0.0% very unhealthy; Annual median: 20; Annual maximum: 62

Transportation: Commute: 90.1% car, 1.0% public transportation, 3.7% walk, 4.4% work from home; Mean travel time to work: 19.6 minutes

2016 Presidential Election: 56.5% Trump, 37.1% Clinton, 4.1% Johnson, 1.4% Stein

National and State Parks: Boonville Gorge State Park; Fort Stanwix National Monument; Verona Beach State Park

Additional Information Contacts

Oneida Government . . . . (315) 798-5794
    http://www.ocgov.net

Oneida County Communities

ALDER CREEK (unincorporated postal area)

ZCTA: 13301

Covers a land area of 2.443 square miles and a water area of 0.163 square miles. Located at 43.42° N. Lat; 75.22° W. Long. Elevation is 1,194 feet.

Population: 91; Growth (since 2000): -58.4%; Density: 37.2 persons per square mile; Race: 100.0% White, 0.0% Black/African American, 0.0% Asian, 0.0% American Indian/Alaska Native, 0.0% Native Hawaiian/Other Pacific Islander, 0.0% Two or more races, 0.0% Hispanic of any race; Average household size: 2.17; Median age: 57.8; Age under 18: 16.5%; Age 65 and over: 19.8%; Males per 100 females: 139.0; Marriage status: 10.5% never married, 65.8% now married, 0.0% separated, 23.7% widowed, 0.0% divorced; Foreign born: 0.0%; Speak English only: 100.0%; With disability: 19.8%; Veterans: 11.8%; Ancestry: 25.3% German, 19.8% English, 9.9% Irish, 9.9% Scottish

Employment: 0.0% management, business, and financial, 0.0% computer, engineering, and science, 0.0% education, legal, community service, arts, and media, 22.0% healthcare practitioners, 19.5% service, 39.0% sales and office, 19.5% natural resources, construction, and maintenance, 0.0% production, transportation, and material moving

Income: Per capita: $33,909; Median household: $76,250; Average household: $73,129; Households with income of $100,000 or more: 21.4%; Poverty rate: n/a

Educational Attainment: High school diploma or higher: 100.0%; Bachelor's degree or higher: 22.4%; Graduate/professional degree or higher: 11.8%

Housing: Homeownership rate: 100.0%; Median home value: $275,000; Median year structure built: 1970; Homeowner vacancy rate: 23.6%; Median selected monthly owner costs: $0 with a mortgage, $387 without a mortgage; Median gross rent: n/a per month; Rental vacancy rate: 0.0%

Health Insurance: 100.0% have insurance; 90.1% have private insurance; 38.5% have public insurance; 0.0% do not have insurance; 0.0% of children under 18 do not have insurance

Transportation: Commute: 100.0% car, 0.0% public transportation, 0.0% walk, 0.0% work from home; Mean travel time to work: 0.0 minutes

ANNSVILLE (town). Covers a land area of 60.167 square miles and a water area of 0.308 square miles. Located at 43.35° N. Lat; 75.61° W. Long.

Population: 2,979; Growth (since 2000): 0.8%; Density: 49.5 persons per square mile; Race: 95.5% White, 1.4% Black/African American, 0.5% Asian, 0.0% American Indian/Alaska Native, 0.0% Native Hawaiian/Other Pacific Islander, 2.1% Two or more races, 2.7% Hispanic of any race; Average household size: 2.69; Median age: 39.7; Age under 18: 24.2%; Age 65 and over: 13.0%; Males per 100 females: 102.4; Marriage status: 30.7% never married, 54.0% now married, 2.1% separated, 4.0% widowed, 11.2% divorced; Foreign born: 0.9%; Speak English only: 96.3%; With disability: 16.1%; Veterans: 11.5%; Ancestry: 28.6% American, 16.8% Irish, 16.0% German, 9.3% English, 9.1% Italian

Employment: 11.4% management, business, and financial, 1.6% computer, engineering, and science, 6.8% education, legal, community service, arts, and media, 3.7% healthcare practitioners, 19.3% service, 27.9% sales and office, 10.2% natural resources, construction, and maintenance, 19.1% production, transportation, and material moving

Income: Per capita: $22,415; Median household: $49,199; Average household: $57,622; Households with income of $100,000 or more: 15.8%; Poverty rate: 16.3%

Educational Attainment: High school diploma or higher: 87.4%; Bachelor's degree or higher: 10.4%; Graduate/professional degree or higher: 5.2%

Housing: Homeownership rate: 81.7%; Median home value: $99,400; Median year structure built: 1983; Homeowner vacancy rate: 1.5%; Median selected monthly owner costs: $1,139 with a mortgage, $458 without a mortgage; Median gross rent: $812 per month; Rental vacancy rate: 0.0%

Health Insurance: 95.2% have insurance; 64.7% have private insurance; 46.3% have public insurance; 4.8% do not have insurance; 1.5% of children under 18 do not have insurance

Transportation: Commute: 90.8% car, 0.0% public transportation, 2.3% walk, 6.1% work from home; Mean travel time to work: 26.9 minutes

AUGUSTA (town). Covers a land area of 27.728 square miles and a water area of 0 square miles. Located at 42.98° N. Lat; 75.50° W. Long. Elevation is 955 feet.

Population: 2,526; Growth (since 2000): 28.5%; Density: 91.1 persons per square mile; Race: 94.8% White, 2.3% Black/African American, 0.0% Asian, 0.0% American Indian/Alaska Native, 0.0% Native Hawaiian/Other Pacific Islander, 0.5% Two or more races, 2.7% Hispanic of any race; Average household size: 2.75; Median age: 37.7; Age under 18: 27.2%; Age 65 and over: 14.4%; Males per 100 females: 100.0; Marriage status: 28.7% never married, 50.2% now married, 1.4% separated, 4.5% widowed, 16.6% divorced; Foreign born: 2.6%; Speak English only: 88.0%; With disability: 11.2%; Veterans: 7.0%; Ancestry: 23.7% American, 16.1% German, 15.2% Irish, 12.0% English, 9.5% Italian

Employment: 11.9% management, business, and financial, 4.3% computer, engineering, and science, 10.3% education, legal, community service, arts, and media, 6.8% healthcare practitioners, 21.2% service, 18.9% sales and office, 17.5% natural resources, construction, and maintenance, 9.1% production, transportation, and material moving

Income: Per capita: $22,162; Median household: $51,793; Average household: $59,097; Households with income of $100,000 or more: 13.8%; Poverty rate: 19.4%

Educational Attainment: High school diploma or higher: 91.3%; Bachelor's degree or higher: 19.1%; Graduate/professional degree or higher: 4.9%

Housing: Homeownership rate: 81.2%; Median home value: $104,200; Median year structure built: Before 1940; Homeowner vacancy rate: 0.0%; Median selected monthly owner costs: $1,094 with a mortgage, $521

without a mortgage; Median gross rent: $765 per month; Rental vacancy rate: 3.9%

Health Insurance: 91.0% have insurance; 66.6% have private insurance; 37.9% have public insurance; 9.0% do not have insurance; 6.9% of children under 18 do not have insurance

Transportation: Commute: 85.9% car, 0.0% public transportation, 8.4% walk, 5.4% work from home; Mean travel time to work: 26.1 minutes

AVA (town). Covers a land area of 37.667 square miles and a water area of 0.038 square miles. Located at 43.41° N. Lat; 75.44° W. Long. Elevation is 1,371 feet.

Population: 588; Growth (since 2000): -18.9%; Density: 15.6 persons per square mile; Race: 92.5% White, 0.7% Black/African American, 3.6% Asian, 0.0% American Indian/Alaska Native, 1.0% Native Hawaiian/Other Pacific Islander, 2.0% Two or more races, 0.3% Hispanic of any race; Average household size: 2.31; Median age: 49.1; Age under 18: 17.0%; Age 65 and over: 16.5%; Males per 100 females: 104.2; Marriage status: 30.6% never married, 57.4% now married, 0.4% separated, 3.0% widowed, 8.9% divorced; Foreign born: 5.3%; Speak English only: 92.9%; With disability: 9.2%; Veterans: 13.7%; Ancestry: 33.3% American, 15.3% German, 13.6% Irish, 13.1% Polish, 11.4% English

Employment: 10.9% management, business, and financial, 0.0% computer, engineering, and science, 8.5% education, legal, community service, arts, and media, 1.0% healthcare practitioners, 21.5% service, 17.7% sales and office, 20.5% natural resources, construction, and maintenance, 19.8% production, transportation, and material moving

Income: Per capita: $23,815; Median household: $50,625; Average household: $54,169; Households with income of $100,000 or more: 11.8%; Poverty rate: 8.8%

Educational Attainment: High school diploma or higher: 88.2%; Bachelor's degree or higher: 14.1%; Graduate/professional degree or higher: 5.8%

Housing: Homeownership rate: 90.6%; Median home value: $99,500; Median year structure built: 1971; Homeowner vacancy rate: 2.9%; Median selected monthly owner costs: $1,110 with a mortgage, $399 without a mortgage; Median gross rent: $633 per month; Rental vacancy rate: 0.0%

Health Insurance: 96.4% have insurance; 70.7% have private insurance; 40.5% have public insurance; 3.6% do not have insurance; 0.0% of children under 18 do not have insurance

Transportation: Commute: 90.8% car, 0.0% public transportation, 1.4% walk, 7.8% work from home; Mean travel time to work: 30.2 minutes

BARNEVELD (village). Covers a land area of 0.192 square miles and a water area of 0 square miles. Located at 43.27° N. Lat; 75.19° W. Long. Elevation is 801 feet.

History: Nearby, in Steuben Memorial Park, is the reconstructed log cabin and the grave of Baron von Steuben.

Population: 261; Growth (since 2000): -21.4%; Density: 1,358.2 persons per square mile; Race: 100.0% White, 0.0% Black/African American, 0.0% Asian, 0.0% American Indian/Alaska Native, 0.0% Native Hawaiian/Other Pacific Islander, 0.0% Two or more races, 1.5% Hispanic of any race; Average household size: 1.98; Median age: 53.9; Age under 18: 18.4%; Age 65 and over: 28.7%; Males per 100 females: 104.3; Marriage status: 25.6% never married, 55.2% now married, 0.4% separated, 11.7% widowed, 7.6% divorced; Foreign born: 0.8%; Speak English only: 98.4%; With disability: 7.3%; Veterans: 14.1%; Ancestry: 27.2% American, 21.5% Irish, 16.1% German, 13.0% English, 9.6% Polish

Employment: 11.4% management, business, and financial, 3.6% computer, engineering, and science, 7.9% education, legal, community service, arts, and media, 10.7% healthcare practitioners, 25.7% service, 32.1% sales and office, 7.1% natural resources, construction, and maintenance, 1.4% production, transportation, and material moving

Income: Per capita: $34,075; Median household: $50,000; Average household: $72,389; Households with income of $100,000 or more: 13.6%; Poverty rate: 6.1%

Educational Attainment: High school diploma or higher: 96.4%; Bachelor's degree or higher: 36.0%; Graduate/professional degree or higher: 15.2%

Housing: Homeownership rate: 64.4%; Median home value: $132,500; Median year structure built: Before 1940; Homeowner vacancy rate: 4.5%; Median selected monthly owner costs: $1,200 with a mortgage, $658 without a mortgage; Median gross rent: $639 per month; Rental vacancy rate: 9.6%

Health Insurance: 93.9% have insurance; 64.4% have private insurance; 50.2% have public insurance; 6.1% do not have insurance; 16.0% of children under 18 do not have insurance
Transportation: Commute: 89.4% car, 0.0% public transportation, 0.0% walk, 10.6% work from home; Mean travel time to work: 22.8 minutes

BLOSSVALE (unincorporated postal area)
ZCTA: 13308
Covers a land area of 38.655 square miles and a water area of 0.663 square miles. Located at 43.25° N. Lat; 75.66° W. Long. Elevation is 420 feet.
Population: 2,816; Growth (since 2000): -42.1%; Density: 72.8 persons per square mile; Race: 98.8% White, 0.2% Black/African American, 0.0% Asian, 0.5% American Indian/Alaska Native, 0.0% Native Hawaiian/Other Pacific Islander, 0.5% Two or more races, 0.4% Hispanic of any race; Average household size: 2.32; Median age: 48.4; Age under 18: 16.2%; Age 65 and over: 22.1%; Males per 100 females: 99.1; Marriage status: 24.4% never married, 59.6% now married, 3.4% separated, 5.6% widowed, 10.3% divorced; Foreign born: 1.2%; Speak English only: 97.3%; With disability: 23.1%; Veterans: 14.7%; Ancestry: 18.3% German, 17.4% American, 17.4% Irish, 13.1% English, 9.6% Italian
Employment: 8.6% management, business, and financial, 3.6% computer, engineering, and science, 2.4% education, legal, community service, arts, and media, 1.1% healthcare practitioners, 18.0% service, 29.4% sales and office, 19.5% natural resources, construction, and maintenance, 17.3% production, transportation, and material moving
Income: Per capita: $26,393; Median household: $49,000; Average household: $59,918; Households with income of $100,000 or more: 15.3%; Poverty rate: 15.8%
Educational Attainment: High school diploma or higher: 83.3%; Bachelor's degree or higher: 11.4%; Graduate/professional degree or higher: 2.6%

School District(s)
Camden Central SD (PK-12)
   Enrollment: 2,225 . . . . (315) 245-4075
Housing: Homeownership rate: 87.1%; Median home value: $99,700; Median year structure built: 1975; Homeowner vacancy rate: 0.9%; Median selected monthly owner costs: $1,124 with a mortgage, $467 without a mortgage; Median gross rent: $800 per month; Rental vacancy rate: 0.0%
Health Insurance: 95.5% have insurance; 66.8% have private insurance; 51.4% have public insurance; 4.5% do not have insurance; 3.3% of children under 18 do not have insurance
Transportation: Commute: 97.2% car, 0.0% public transportation, 1.4% walk, 1.4% work from home; Mean travel time to work: 29.6 minutes

BOONVILLE (town). Covers a land area of 71.878 square miles and a water area of 0.698 square miles. Located at 43.46° N. Lat; 75.29° W. Long. Elevation is 1,148 feet.
History: Author and critic Walter D. Edmonds born here and lived in nearby Talcottville. Settled c.1791, incorporated 1855.
Population: 4,547; Growth (since 2000): -0.5%; Density: 63.3 persons per square mile; Race: 97.3% White, 0.2% Black/African American, 0.4% Asian, 0.2% American Indian/Alaska Native, 0.0% Native Hawaiian/Other Pacific Islander, 1.7% Two or more races, 1.9% Hispanic of any race; Average household size: 2.50; Median age: 45.4; Age under 18: 21.4%; Age 65 and over: 18.2%; Males per 100 females: 96.3; Marriage status: 31.9% never married, 47.5% now married, 1.6% separated, 9.8% widowed, 10.8% divorced; Foreign born: 1.1%; Speak English only: 96.9%; With disability: 15.0%; Veterans: 11.2%; Ancestry: 19.2% American, 16.9% German, 14.1% Irish, 10.3% Polish, 8.4% English
Employment: 10.3% management, business, and financial, 3.1% computer, engineering, and science, 9.9% education, legal, community service, arts, and media, 8.9% healthcare practitioners, 16.1% service, 22.7% sales and office, 12.9% natural resources, construction, and maintenance, 16.2% production, transportation, and material moving
Income: Per capita: $27,134; Median household: $58,346; Average household: $67,705; Households with income of $100,000 or more: 23.8%; Poverty rate: 15.6%
Educational Attainment: High school diploma or higher: 92.7%; Bachelor's degree or higher: 18.0%; Graduate/professional degree or higher: 8.7%

School District(s)
Adirondack Central SD (PK-12)
   Enrollment: 1,296 . . . . (315) 942-9200
Housing: Homeownership rate: 77.5%; Median home value: $110,300; Median year structure built: 1967; Homeowner vacancy rate: 0.9%; Median selected monthly owner costs: $1,012 with a mortgage, $420 without a mortgage; Median gross rent: $554 per month; Rental vacancy rate: 7.1%
Health Insurance: 94.9% have insurance; 71.3% have private insurance; 40.8% have public insurance; 5.1% do not have insurance; 6.9% of children under 18 do not have insurance
Newspapers: Boonville Herald (weekly circulation 4,400)
Transportation: Commute: 84.1% car, 0.0% public transportation, 7.9% walk, 7.4% work from home; Mean travel time to work: 23.8 minutes
Additional Information Contacts
Town of Boonville . . . . (315) 943-2064
   http://townofboonville.org/content

BOONVILLE (village). Covers a land area of 1.729 square miles and a water area of 0.004 square miles. Located at 43.48° N. Lat; 75.33° W. Long. Elevation is 1,148 feet.
Population: 2,113; Growth (since 2000): -1.2%; Density: 1,221.8 persons per square mile; Race: 98.2% White, 0.3% Black/African American, 0.0% Asian, 0.0% American Indian/Alaska Native, 0.0% Native Hawaiian/Other Pacific Islander, 1.6% Two or more races, 0.4% Hispanic of any race; Average household size: 2.41; Median age: 43.2; Age under 18: 22.9%; Age 65 and over: 21.6%; Males per 100 females: 91.0; Marriage status: 39.0% never married, 33.2% now married, 1.0% separated, 11.1% widowed, 16.7% divorced; Foreign born: 0.0%; Speak English only: 98.8%; With disability: 17.8%; Veterans: 10.7%; Ancestry: 20.3% German, 17.1% American, 16.4% Irish, 11.2% Polish, 6.8% French
Employment: 7.8% management, business, and financial, 1.6% computer, engineering, and science, 7.3% education, legal, community service, arts, and media, 9.1% healthcare practitioners, 17.8% service, 28.5% sales and office, 13.0% natural resources, construction, and maintenance, 15.0% production, transportation, and material moving
Income: Per capita: $21,173; Median household: $34,963; Average household: $50,364; Households with income of $100,000 or more: 14.9%; Poverty rate: 21.9%
Educational Attainment: High school diploma or higher: 90.1%; Bachelor's degree or higher: 12.4%; Graduate/professional degree or higher: 6.2%

School District(s)
Adirondack Central SD (PK-12)
   Enrollment: 1,296 . . . . (315) 942-9200
Housing: Homeownership rate: 61.3%; Median home value: $83,200; Median year structure built: Before 1940; Homeowner vacancy rate: 0.0%; Median selected monthly owner costs: $960 with a mortgage, $421 without a mortgage; Median gross rent: $540 per month; Rental vacancy rate: 8.6%
Health Insurance: 95.8% have insurance; 63.0% have private insurance; 48.3% have public insurance; 4.2% do not have insurance; 2.2% of children under 18 do not have insurance
Newspapers: Boonville Herald (weekly circulation 4,400)
Transportation: Commute: 86.2% car, 0.0% public transportation, 8.0% walk, 5.2% work from home; Mean travel time to work: 20.2 minutes
Additional Information Contacts
Village of Boonville . . . . (315) 943-2052
   http://village.boonville.ny.us/content

BRIDGEWATER (town). Covers a land area of 23.845 square miles and a water area of 0.012 square miles. Located at 42.90° N. Lat; 75.27° W. Long. Elevation is 1,211 feet.
Population: 1,411; Growth (since 2000): -15.6%; Density: 59.2 persons per square mile; Race: 98.3% White, 0.0% Black/African American, 0.0% Asian, 0.1% American Indian/Alaska Native, 0.0% Native Hawaiian/Other Pacific Islander, 1.4% Two or more races, 2.9% Hispanic of any race; Average household size: 2.60; Median age: 38.4; Age under 18: 23.0%; Age 65 and over: 11.3%; Males per 100 females: 104.6; Marriage status: 31.8% never married, 55.4% now married, 1.4% separated, 3.9% widowed, 8.9% divorced; Foreign born: 1.8%; Speak English only: 94.0%; With disability: 12.8%; Veterans: 7.7%; Ancestry: 22.3% American, 16.7% German, 15.2% Irish, 11.0% English, 8.9% Polish
Employment: 10.4% management, business, and financial, 3.7% computer, engineering, and science, 7.9% education, legal, community service, arts, and media, 5.1% healthcare practitioners, 19.6% service,

24.3% sales and office, 13.2% natural resources, construction, and maintenance, 15.7% production, transportation, and material moving
Income: Per capita: $22,882; Median household: $46,304; Average household: $58,218; Households with income of $100,000 or more: 16.0%; Poverty rate: 16.5%
Educational Attainment: High school diploma or higher: 89.7%; Bachelor's degree or higher: 13.6%; Graduate/professional degree or higher: 4.1%
Housing: Homeownership rate: 83.0%; Median home value: $81,800; Median year structure built: 1978; Homeowner vacancy rate: 3.2%; Median selected monthly owner costs: $1,029 with a mortgage, $456 without a mortgage; Median gross rent: $763 per month; Rental vacancy rate: 3.2%
Health Insurance: 92.2% have insurance; 64.1% have private insurance; 41.0% have public insurance; 7.8% do not have insurance; 4.1% of children under 18 do not have insurance
Transportation: Commute: 93.3% car, 0.0% public transportation, 2.8% walk, 3.4% work from home; Mean travel time to work: 23.8 minutes

BRIDGEWATER (village). Covers a land area of 0.607 square miles and a water area of 0 square miles. Located at 42.88° N. Lat; 75.25° W. Long. Elevation is 1,211 feet.
Population: 563; Growth (since 2000): -2.8%; Density: 928.2 persons per square mile; Race: 97.9% White, 0.0% Black/African American, 0.0% Asian, 0.0% American Indian/Alaska Native, 0.0% Native Hawaiian/Other Pacific Islander, 1.8% Two or more races, 5.9% Hispanic of any race; Average household size: 2.84; Median age: 30.0; Age under 18: 33.9%; Age 65 and over: 8.9%; Males per 100 females: 99.2; Marriage status: 35.4% never married, 48.9% now married, 0.2% separated, 4.2% widowed, 11.5% divorced; Foreign born: 3.0%; Speak English only: 90.6%; With disability: 9.8%; Veterans: 5.4%; Ancestry: 28.2% American, 17.9% Irish, 14.6% German, 11.5% English, 9.1% Dutch
Employment: 11.0% management, business, and financial, 1.6% computer, engineering, and science, 6.3% education, legal, community service, arts, and media, 3.5% healthcare practitioners, 27.1% service, 19.6% sales and office, 9.8% natural resources, construction, and maintenance, 21.2% production, transportation, and material moving
Income: Per capita: $17,847; Median household: $41,750; Average household: $49,663; Households with income of $100,000 or more: 6.5%; Poverty rate: 19.3%
Educational Attainment: High school diploma or higher: 83.7%; Bachelor's degree or higher: 10.5%; Graduate/professional degree or higher: 1.5%
Housing: Homeownership rate: 71.2%; Median home value: $67,500; Median year structure built: 1965; Homeowner vacancy rate: 3.4%; Median selected monthly owner costs: $950 with a mortgage, $488 without a mortgage; Median gross rent: $694 per month; Rental vacancy rate: 5.0%
Health Insurance: 90.1% have insurance; 54.9% have private insurance; 48.3% have public insurance; 9.9% do not have insurance; 6.0% of children under 18 do not have insurance
Transportation: Commute: 91.7% car, 0.0% public transportation, 7.9% walk, 0.4% work from home; Mean travel time to work: 22.4 minutes

CAMDEN (town). Covers a land area of 54.013 square miles and a water area of 0.141 square miles. Located at 43.35° N. Lat; 75.77° W. Long. Elevation is 502 feet.
History: Incorporated 1834.
Population: 4,915; Growth (since 2000): -2.2%; Density: 91.0 persons per square mile; Race: 96.6% White, 1.1% Black/African American, 0.4% Asian, 0.1% American Indian/Alaska Native, 0.0% Native Hawaiian/Other Pacific Islander, 1.8% Two or more races, 0.9% Hispanic of any race; Average household size: 2.49; Median age: 42.4; Age under 18: 24.1%; Age 65 and over: 18.3%; Males per 100 females: 97.8; Marriage status: 24.6% never married, 57.0% now married, 1.6% separated, 7.6% widowed, 10.8% divorced; Foreign born: 0.8%; Speak English only: 98.3%; With disability: 17.0%; Veterans: 11.3%; Ancestry: 30.9% American, 16.2% Irish, 11.5% German, 11.4% Italian
Employment: 9.7% management, business, and financial, 2.2% computer, engineering, and science, 14.3% education, legal, community service, arts, and media, 2.7% healthcare practitioners, 17.9% service, 23.5% sales and office, 9.4% natural resources, construction, and maintenance, 20.3% production, transportation, and material moving
Income: Per capita: $25,448; Median household: $49,142; Average household: $62,217; Households with income of $100,000 or more: 20.3%; Poverty rate: 12.8%

Educational Attainment: High school diploma or higher: 89.9%; Bachelor's degree or higher: 17.4%; Graduate/professional degree or higher: 6.4%
School District(s)
Camden Central SD (PK-12)
    Enrollment: 2,225 . . . . (315) 245-4075
Housing: Homeownership rate: 66.4%; Median home value: $109,400; Median year structure built: 1960; Homeowner vacancy rate: 2.2%; Median selected monthly owner costs: $1,096 with a mortgage, $428 without a mortgage; Median gross rent: $629 per month; Rental vacancy rate: 10.2%
Health Insurance: 93.1% have insurance; 69.1% have private insurance; 41.7% have public insurance; 6.9% do not have insurance; 0.6% of children under 18 do not have insurance
Newspapers: Queen Central News (weekly circulation 7,600)
Transportation: Commute: 91.7% car, 0.0% public transportation, 5.4% walk, 2.6% work from home; Mean travel time to work: 24.7 minutes

CAMDEN (village). Covers a land area of 2.436 square miles and a water area of 0 square miles. Located at 43.34° N. Lat; 75.75° W. Long. Elevation is 502 feet.
Population: 2,455; Growth (since 2000): 5.4%; Density: 1,007.7 persons per square mile; Race: 94.2% White, 1.3% Black/African American, 0.7% Asian, 0.1% American Indian/Alaska Native, 0.0% Native Hawaiian/Other Pacific Islander, 3.7% Two or more races, 1.3% Hispanic of any race; Average household size: 2.36; Median age: 39.4; Age under 18: 25.2%; Age 65 and over: 17.7%; Males per 100 females: 93.8; Marriage status: 29.8% never married, 43.0% now married, 1.7% separated, 11.1% widowed, 16.1% divorced; Foreign born: 1.3%; Speak English only: 98.2%; With disability: 18.2%; Veterans: 8.5%; Ancestry: 34.5% American, 15.8% Irish, 13.9% German, 10.8% English, 6.1% Italian
Employment: 9.7% management, business, and financial, 4.3% computer, engineering, and science, 15.3% education, legal, community service, arts, and media, 3.1% healthcare practitioners, 24.1% service, 22.9% sales and office, 7.2% natural resources, construction, and maintenance, 13.5% production, transportation, and material moving
Income: Per capita: $22,486; Median household: $39,688; Average household: $51,905; Households with income of $100,000 or more: 14.5%; Poverty rate: 17.1%
Educational Attainment: High school diploma or higher: 88.5%; Bachelor's degree or higher: 18.5%; Graduate/professional degree or higher: 6.9%
School District(s)
Camden Central SD (PK-12)
    Enrollment: 2,225 . . . . (315) 245-4075
Housing: Homeownership rate: 48.6%; Median home value: $97,300; Median year structure built: Before 1940; Homeowner vacancy rate: 0.0%; Median selected monthly owner costs: $1,090 with a mortgage, $527 without a mortgage; Median gross rent: $627 per month; Rental vacancy rate: 12.5%
Health Insurance: 92.0% have insurance; 62.0% have private insurance; 47.7% have public insurance; 8.0% do not have insurance; 0.0% of children under 18 do not have insurance
Safety: Violent crime rate: 4.6 per 10,000 population; Property crime rate: 110.0 per 10,000 population
Newspapers: Queen Central News (weekly circulation 7,600)
Transportation: Commute: 82.8% car, 0.0% public transportation, 12.7% walk, 3.8% work from home; Mean travel time to work: 23.6 minutes

CASSVILLE (unincorporated postal area)
ZCTA: 13318
    Covers a land area of 25.383 square miles and a water area of 0.012 square miles. Located at 42.92° N. Lat; 75.26° W. Long. Elevation is 1,240 feet.
Population: 1,279; Growth (since 2000): -10.5%; Density: 50.4 persons per square mile; Race: 99.1% White, 0.0% Black/African American, 0.0% Asian, 0.2% American Indian/Alaska Native, 0.0% Native Hawaiian/Other Pacific Islander, 0.8% Two or more races, 0.2% Hispanic of any race; Average household size: 2.77; Median age: 43.8; Age under 18: 20.8%; Age 65 and over: 14.9%; Males per 100 females: 104.8; Marriage status: 35.0% never married, 55.2% now married, 0.4% separated, 3.6% widowed, 6.2% divorced; Foreign born: 1.3%; Speak English only: 97.4%; With disability: 10.7%; Veterans: 6.2%; Ancestry: 12.6% Irish, 12.4% Polish, 11.8% Italian, 11.5% German, 10.7% American

Employment: 11.6% management, business, and financial, 2.7% computer, engineering, and science, 9.5% education, legal, community service, arts, and media, 4.6% healthcare practitioners, 17.8% service, 28.1% sales and office, 16.9% natural resources, construction, and maintenance, 8.7% production, transportation, and material moving
Income: Per capita: $26,649; Median household: $64,274; Average household: $72,289; Households with income of $100,000 or more: 29.3%; Poverty rate: 6.2%
Educational Attainment: High school diploma or higher: 94.1%; Bachelor's degree or higher: 15.6%; Graduate/professional degree or higher: 5.6%
Housing: Homeownership rate: 92.2%; Median home value: $133,100; Median year structure built: 1985; Homeowner vacancy rate: 2.3%; Median selected monthly owner costs: $1,250 with a mortgage, $497 without a mortgage; Median gross rent: $850 per month; Rental vacancy rate: 0.0%
Health Insurance: 96.0% have insurance; 78.7% have private insurance; 30.9% have public insurance; 4.0% do not have insurance; 0.7% of children under 18 do not have insurance
Transportation: Commute: 95.0% car, 0.0% public transportation, 0.0% walk, 4.5% work from home; Mean travel time to work: 22.4 minutes

CHADWICKS (CDP). Covers a land area of 1.327 square miles and a water area of 0 square miles. Located at 43.03° N. Lat; 75.27° W. Long. Elevation is 709 feet.
Population: 1,200; Growth (since 2000): n/a; Density: 904.2 persons per square mile; Race: 100.0% White, 0.0% Black/African American, 0.0% Asian, 0.0% American Indian/Alaska Native, 0.0% Native Hawaiian/Other Pacific Islander, 0.0% Two or more races, 2.9% Hispanic of any race; Average household size: 2.37; Median age: 44.9; Age under 18: 14.4%; Age 65 and over: 26.5%; Males per 100 females: 92.8; Marriage status: 30.0% never married, 49.5% now married, 2.4% separated, 5.5% widowed, 15.0% divorced; Foreign born: 2.7%; Speak English only: 90.0%; With disability: 17.7%; Veterans: 17.8%; Ancestry: 32.9% German, 23.6% Irish, 20.2% Italian, 11.9% Welsh, 11.5% English
Employment: 14.8% management, business, and financial, 6.2% computer, engineering, and science, 2.0% education, legal, community service, arts, and media, 18.3% healthcare practitioners, 31.8% service, 15.3% sales and office, 0.0% natural resources, construction, and maintenance, 11.5% production, transportation, and material moving
Income: Per capita: $24,966; Median household: $36,335; Average household: $56,988; Households with income of $100,000 or more: 12.0%; Poverty rate: 7.9%
Educational Attainment: High school diploma or higher: 93.8%; Bachelor's degree or higher: 23.7%; Graduate/professional degree or higher: 9.4%
Housing: Homeownership rate: 58.4%; Median home value: $110,800; Median year structure built: 1962; Homeowner vacancy rate: 0.0%; Median selected monthly owner costs: $1,500 with a mortgage, $443 without a mortgage; Median gross rent: $786 per month; Rental vacancy rate: 21.6%
Health Insurance: 94.7% have insurance; 62.7% have private insurance; 56.3% have public insurance; 5.3% do not have insurance; 0.0% of children under 18 do not have insurance
Transportation: Commute: 100.0% car, 0.0% public transportation, 0.0% walk, 0.0% work from home; Mean travel time to work: 17.2 minutes

CLARK MILLS (CDP). Covers a land area of 1.492 square miles and a water area of 0.019 square miles. Located at 43.09° N. Lat; 75.38° W. Long. Elevation is 515 feet.
Population: 1,769; Growth (since 2000): 24.2%; Density: 1,185.4 persons per square mile; Race: 95.7% White, 0.0% Black/African American, 3.6% Asian, 0.0% American Indian/Alaska Native, 0.0% Native Hawaiian/Other Pacific Islander, 0.7% Two or more races, 2.3% Hispanic of any race; Average household size: 1.92; Median age: 45.3; Age under 18: 17.8%; Age 65 and over: 18.8%; Males per 100 females: 95.0; Marriage status: 27.2% never married, 48.7% now married, 1.4% separated, 7.8% widowed, 16.2% divorced; Foreign born: 5.8%; Speak English only: 93.3%; With disability: 12.8%; Veterans: 11.7%; Ancestry: 29.8% American, 17.2% German, 13.4% Polish, 12.1% Italian, 9.6% English
Employment: 12.9% management, business, and financial, 1.9% computer, engineering, and science, 9.0% education, legal, community service, arts, and media, 14.8% healthcare practitioners, 15.4% service, 22.9% sales and office, 7.8% natural resources, construction, and maintenance, 15.4% production, transportation, and material moving

Income: Per capita: $30,165; Median household: $53,096; Average household: $58,049; Households with income of $100,000 or more: 8.6%; Poverty rate: 19.5%
Educational Attainment: High school diploma or higher: 94.4%; Bachelor's degree or higher: 28.7%; Graduate/professional degree or higher: 9.3%
Housing: Homeownership rate: 49.4%; Median home value: $86,500; Median year structure built: 1967; Homeowner vacancy rate: 0.0%; Median selected monthly owner costs: $1,133 with a mortgage, $525 without a mortgage; Median gross rent: $872 per month; Rental vacancy rate: 4.7%
Health Insurance: 98.8% have insurance; 65.7% have private insurance; 53.0% have public insurance; 1.2% do not have insurance; 0.0% of children under 18 do not have insurance
Transportation: Commute: 96.9% car, 0.0% public transportation, 2.0% walk, 1.1% work from home; Mean travel time to work: 19.7 minutes

CLAYVILLE (village). Covers a land area of 0.439 square miles and a water area of 0.004 square miles. Located at 42.98° N. Lat; 75.25° W. Long. Elevation is 961 feet.
Population: 283; Growth (since 2000): -36.4%; Density: 644.5 persons per square mile; Race: 99.6% White, 0.4% Black/African American, 0.0% Asian, 0.0% American Indian/Alaska Native, 0.0% Native Hawaiian/Other Pacific Islander, 0.0% Two or more races, 3.2% Hispanic of any race; Average household size: 2.36; Median age: 40.1; Age under 18: 22.3%; Age 65 and over: 9.5%; Males per 100 females: 113.4; Marriage status: 29.2% never married, 54.4% now married, 0.4% separated, 5.3% widowed, 11.1% divorced; Foreign born: 0.7%; Speak English only: 100.0%; With disability: 10.2%; Veterans: 9.5%; Ancestry: 34.6% American, 17.0% German, 15.9% Italian, 14.8% English, 12.0% Irish
Employment: 13.7% management, business, and financial, 2.7% computer, engineering, and science, 14.4% education, legal, community service, arts, and media, 2.7% healthcare practitioners, 19.9% service, 10.3% sales and office, 15.1% natural resources, construction, and maintenance, 21.2% production, transportation, and material moving
Income: Per capita: $24,552; Median household: $44,545; Average household: $59,162; Households with income of $100,000 or more: 12.5%; Poverty rate: 13.4%
Educational Attainment: High school diploma or higher: 87.6%; Bachelor's degree or higher: 19.9%; Graduate/professional degree or higher: 14.0%
Housing: Homeownership rate: 68.3%; Median home value: $95,000; Median year structure built: Before 1940; Homeowner vacancy rate: 3.5%; Median selected monthly owner costs: $1,125 with a mortgage, $456 without a mortgage; Median gross rent: $732 per month; Rental vacancy rate: 4.4%
Health Insurance: 90.1% have insurance; 72.8% have private insurance; 31.8% have public insurance; 9.9% do not have insurance; 12.3% of children under 18 do not have insurance
Transportation: Commute: 95.9% car, 0.0% public transportation, 0.0% walk, 4.1% work from home; Mean travel time to work: 20.1 minutes

CLINTON (village). Covers a land area of 0.626 square miles and a water area of 0 square miles. Located at 43.05° N. Lat; 75.38° W. Long. Elevation is 604 feet.
History: Seat of Hamilton College. Elihu Root was born here. Clinton Village Historic District. Incorporated 1843.
Population: 1,816; Growth (since 2000): -7.0%; Density: 2,901.6 persons per square mile; Race: 92.7% White, 1.3% Black/African American, 2.7% Asian, 0.0% American Indian/Alaska Native, 0.0% Native Hawaiian/Other Pacific Islander, 1.5% Two or more races, 4.2% Hispanic of any race; Average household size: 2.36; Median age: 40.1; Age under 18: 20.6%; Age 65 and over: 16.2%; Males per 100 females: 90.2; Marriage status: 29.2% never married, 52.5% now married, 2.1% separated, 6.2% widowed, 12.1% divorced; Foreign born: 5.6%; Speak English only: 92.6%; With disability: 9.7%; Veterans: 8.1%; Ancestry: 21.1% Irish, 18.7% German, 16.3% Italian, 10.7% English, 10.1% American
Employment: 16.9% management, business, and financial, 6.3% computer, engineering, and science, 23.0% education, legal, community service, arts, and media, 11.2% healthcare practitioners, 12.3% service, 17.2% sales and office, 3.3% natural resources, construction, and maintenance, 9.6% production, transportation, and material moving
Income: Per capita: $43,560; Median household: $63,906; Average household: $91,574; Households with income of $100,000 or more: 32.4%; Poverty rate: 9.7%

Educational Attainment: High school diploma or higher: 97.8%; Bachelor's degree or higher: 61.5%; Graduate/professional degree or higher: 34.1%

School District(s)
Clinton Central SD (KG-12)
  Enrollment: 1,271 . . . . (315) 557-2253
Four-year College(s)
Hamilton College (Private, Not-for-profit)
  Enrollment: 1,901 . . . . (315) 859-4011
  Tuition: In-state $52,770; Out-of-state $52,770
Housing: Homeownership rate: 65.9%; Median home value: $195,900; Median year structure built: Before 1940; Homeowner vacancy rate: 0.0%; Median selected monthly owner costs: $1,675 with a mortgage, $636 without a mortgage; Median gross rent: $894 per month; Rental vacancy rate: 0.0%
Health Insurance: 95.2% have insurance; 84.5% have private insurance; 24.2% have public insurance; 4.8% do not have insurance; 0.0% of children under 18 do not have insurance
Newspapers: Clinton Courier (weekly circulation 1,800)
Transportation: Commute: 84.4% car, 1.1% public transportation, 8.8% walk, 5.2% work from home; Mean travel time to work: 15.1 minutes

DEANSBORO (unincorporated postal area)
ZCTA: 13328
  Covers a land area of 15.864 square miles and a water area of 0 square miles. Located at 42.99° N. Lat; 75.43° W. Long. Elevation is 817 feet.
Population: 1,500; Growth (since 2000): 18.5%; Density: 94.6 persons per square mile; Race: 99.1% White, 0.3% Black/African American, 0.5% Asian, 0.0% American Indian/Alaska Native, 0.0% Native Hawaiian/Other Pacific Islander, 0.0% Two or more races, 0.4% Hispanic of any race; Average household size: 2.70; Median age: 36.5; Age under 18: 28.1%; Age 65 and over: 10.8%; Males per 100 females: 107.0; Marriage status: 20.3% never married, 66.8% now married, 2.9% separated, 3.1% widowed, 9.9% divorced; Foreign born: 0.5%; Speak English only: 95.5%; With disability: 8.3%; Veterans: 6.0%; Ancestry: 31.5% American, 21.0% German, 14.9% Irish, 11.9% English, 7.6% Polish
Employment: 12.0% management, business, and financial, 3.3% computer, engineering, and science, 21.1% education, legal, community service, arts, and media, 6.2% healthcare practitioners, 21.4% service, 12.2% sales and office, 10.3% natural resources, construction, and maintenance, 13.5% production, transportation, and material moving
Income: Per capita: $27,349; Median household: $61,932; Average household: $73,323; Households with income of $100,000 or more: 25.6%; Poverty rate: 10.9%
Educational Attainment: High school diploma or higher: 95.3%; Bachelor's degree or higher: 36.4%; Graduate/professional degree or higher: 12.7%
Housing: Homeownership rate: 84.3%; Median home value: $127,700; Median year structure built: 1959; Homeowner vacancy rate: 0.0%; Median selected monthly owner costs: $1,309 with a mortgage, $449 without a mortgage; Median gross rent: $544 per month; Rental vacancy rate: 0.0%
Health Insurance: 96.3% have insurance; 75.5% have private insurance; 27.5% have public insurance; 3.7% do not have insurance; 5.4% of children under 18 do not have insurance
Transportation: Commute: 94.1% car, 0.0% public transportation, 0.6% walk, 4.6% work from home; Mean travel time to work: 23.8 minutes

DEERFIELD (town). Covers a land area of 32.941 square miles and a water area of 0.107 square miles. Located at 43.19° N. Lat; 75.15° W. Long. Elevation is 443 feet.
Population: 4,129; Growth (since 2000): 5.7%; Density: 125.3 persons per square mile; Race: 95.3% White, 1.5% Black/African American, 1.6% Asian, 0.0% American Indian/Alaska Native, 0.0% Native Hawaiian/Other Pacific Islander, 1.6% Two or more races, 0.7% Hispanic of any race; Average household size: 2.64; Median age: 43.3; Age under 18: 20.9%; Age 65 and over: 15.2%; Males per 100 females: 98.7; Marriage status: 25.5% never married, 62.4% now married, 0.0% separated, 6.2% widowed, 6.0% divorced; Foreign born: 6.0%; Speak English only: 93.1%; With disability: 10.3%; Veterans: 8.4%; Ancestry: 26.0% Italian, 18.9% Polish, 17.7% German, 16.3% Irish, 8.4% American
Employment: 18.0% management, business, and financial, 5.3% computer, engineering, and science, 13.5% education, legal, community service, arts, and media, 9.6% healthcare practitioners, 14.5% service,

25.3% sales and office, 6.2% natural resources, construction, and maintenance, 7.6% production, transportation, and material moving
Income: Per capita: $33,345; Median household: $78,403; Average household: $85,776; Households with income of $100,000 or more: 36.2%; Poverty rate: 5.6%
Educational Attainment: High school diploma or higher: 94.5%; Bachelor's degree or higher: 33.4%; Graduate/professional degree or higher: 14.8%
Housing: Homeownership rate: 91.9%; Median home value: $144,300; Median year structure built: 1961; Homeowner vacancy rate: 0.9%; Median selected monthly owner costs: $1,372 with a mortgage, $531 without a mortgage; Median gross rent: $843 per month; Rental vacancy rate: 8.0%
Health Insurance: 94.8% have insurance; 84.0% have private insurance; 24.4% have public insurance; 5.2% do not have insurance; 3.6% of children under 18 do not have insurance
Transportation: Commute: 95.8% car, 0.0% public transportation, 0.8% walk, 3.3% work from home; Mean travel time to work: 19.5 minutes
Additional Information Contacts
Town of Deerfield . . . . (315) 724-0413
  http://townofdeerfield.org/content

DURHAMVILLE (CDP). Covers a land area of 1.372 square miles and a water area of 0 square miles. Located at 43.12° N. Lat; 75.67° W. Long. Elevation is 433 feet.
Population: 769; Growth (since 2000): n/a; Density: 560.5 persons per square mile; Race: 100.0% White, 0.0% Black/African American, 0.0% Asian, 0.0% American Indian/Alaska Native, 0.0% Native Hawaiian/Other Pacific Islander, 0.0% Two or more races, 0.0% Hispanic of any race; Average household size: 3.90; Median age: 15.8; Age under 18: 50.7%; Age 65 and over: 10.1%; Males per 100 females: 115.5; Marriage status: 36.5% never married, 40.6% now married, 13.0% separated, 18.1% widowed, 4.8% divorced; Foreign born: 0.0%; Speak English only: 100.0%; With disability: 34.9%; Veterans: 4.5%; Ancestry: 74.0% American, 12.7% German, 12.5% Scottish, 4.7% English, 4.0% Welsh
Employment: 0.0% management, business, and financial, 0.0% computer, engineering, and science, 0.0% education, legal, community service, arts, and media, 26.8% healthcare practitioners, 24.4% service, 19.0% sales and office, 0.0% natural resources, construction, and maintenance, 29.8% production, transportation, and material moving
Income: Per capita: $14,899; Median household: $48,583; Average household: $53,019; Households with income of $100,000 or more: 22.8%; Poverty rate: 64.4%
Educational Attainment: High school diploma or higher: 100.0%; Bachelor's degree or higher: 6.4%; Graduate/professional degree or higher: n/a

School District(s)
Oneida City SD (PK-12)
  Enrollment: 2,139 . . . . (315) 363-2550
Housing: Homeownership rate: 49.2%; Median home value: n/a; Median year structure built: 1956; Homeowner vacancy rate: 0.0%; Median selected monthly owner costs: $1,821 with a mortgage, n/a without a mortgage; Median gross rent: $1,311 per month; Rental vacancy rate: 0.0%
Health Insurance: 100.0% have insurance; 37.5% have private insurance; 71.7% have public insurance; 0.0% do not have insurance; 0.0% of children under 18 do not have insurance
Transportation: Commute: 100.0% car, 0.0% public transportation, 0.0% walk, 0.0% work from home; Mean travel time to work: 12.7 minutes

FLORENCE (town). Covers a land area of 54.922 square miles and a water area of 0.094 square miles. Located at 43.42° N. Lat; 75.74° W. Long. Elevation is 978 feet.
Population: 956; Growth (since 2000): -12.0%; Density: 17.4 persons per square mile; Race: 99.5% White, 0.0% Black/African American, 0.5% Asian, 0.0% American Indian/Alaska Native, 0.0% Native Hawaiian/Other Pacific Islander, 0.0% Two or more races, 0.0% Hispanic of any race; Average household size: 2.48; Median age: 42.5; Age under 18: 20.8%; Age 65 and over: 14.9%; Males per 100 females: 102.2; Marriage status: 31.2% never married, 53.7% now married, 1.7% separated, 4.2% widowed, 10.9% divorced; Foreign born: 0.5%; Speak English only: 98.4%; With disability: 15.6%; Veterans: 14.0%; Ancestry: 26.6% American, 19.6% Irish, 16.1% German, 10.7% English, 9.9% French
Employment: 4.3% management, business, and financial, 2.6% computer, engineering, and science, 7.6% education, legal, community service, arts, and media, 8.7% healthcare practitioners, 20.1% service, 18.0% sales and

office, 9.0% natural resources, construction, and maintenance, 29.8% production, transportation, and material moving
Income: Per capita: $20,359; Median household: $43,355; Average household: $50,189; Households with income of $100,000 or more: 12.2%; Poverty rate: 9.3%
Educational Attainment: High school diploma or higher: 82.8%; Bachelor's degree or higher: 7.9%; Graduate/professional degree or higher: 2.7%
Housing: Homeownership rate: 72.7%; Median home value: $89,000; Median year structure built: 1984; Homeowner vacancy rate: 0.0%; Median selected monthly owner costs: $995 with a mortgage, $448 without a mortgage; Median gross rent: $789 per month; Rental vacancy rate: 6.3%
Health Insurance: 93.9% have insurance; 62.7% have private insurance; 44.1% have public insurance; 6.1% do not have insurance; 2.8% of children under 18 do not have insurance
Transportation: Commute: 96.6% car, 0.0% public transportation, 0.0% walk, 1.9% work from home; Mean travel time to work: 31.4 minutes

FLOYD (town).
Covers a land area of 34.616 square miles and a water area of 0.175 square miles. Located at 43.24° N. Lat; 75.32° W. Long. Elevation is 561 feet.
Population: 3,800; Growth (since 2000): -1.8%; Density: 109.8 persons per square mile; Race: 97.7% White, 2.0% Black/African American, 0.0% Asian, 0.0% American Indian/Alaska Native, 0.0% Native Hawaiian/Other Pacific Islander, 0.3% Two or more races, 1.5% Hispanic of any race; Average household size: 2.57; Median age: 46.8; Age under 18: 21.5%; Age 65 and over: 17.5%; Males per 100 females: 102.6; Marriage status: 22.5% never married, 56.9% now married, 1.1% separated, 6.8% widowed, 13.9% divorced; Foreign born: 1.9%; Speak English only: 97.6%; With disability: 17.3%; Veterans: 10.3%; Ancestry: 25.0% American, 19.4% German, 16.3% Italian, 10.7% Irish, 7.7% English
Employment: 10.4% management, business, and financial, 2.9% computer, engineering, and science, 12.8% education, legal, community service, arts, and media, 9.6% healthcare practitioners, 18.0% service, 20.2% sales and office, 15.4% natural resources, construction, and maintenance, 10.7% production, transportation, and material moving
Income: Per capita: $34,710; Median household: $75,644; Average household: $86,789; Households with income of $100,000 or more: 31.7%; Poverty rate: 7.3%
Educational Attainment: High school diploma or higher: 96.2%; Bachelor's degree or higher: 21.7%; Graduate/professional degree or higher: 4.3%
Housing: Homeownership rate: 88.7%; Median home value: $121,500; Median year structure built: 1975; Homeowner vacancy rate: 2.3%; Median selected monthly owner costs: $1,415 with a mortgage, $554 without a mortgage; Median gross rent: $606 per month; Rental vacancy rate: 11.2%
Health Insurance: 93.0% have insurance; 68.9% have private insurance; 42.3% have public insurance; 7.0% do not have insurance; 7.2% of children under 18 do not have insurance
Transportation: Commute: 96.1% car, 0.0% public transportation, 0.9% walk, 1.6% work from home; Mean travel time to work: 19.3 minutes
Additional Information Contacts
Town of Floyd . . . . (315) 865-4256
  http://town.floyd.ny.us

FORESTPORT (town).
Covers a land area of 76.915 square miles and a water area of 1.985 square miles. Located at 43.50° N. Lat; 75.15° W. Long. Elevation is 1,122 feet.
Population: 1,486; Growth (since 2000): -12.2%; Density: 19.3 persons per square mile; Race: 97.2% White, 0.7% Black/African American, 0.1% Asian, 0.0% American Indian/Alaska Native, 0.0% Native Hawaiian/Other Pacific Islander, 1.7% Two or more races, 0.0% Hispanic of any race; Average household size: 2.06; Median age: 55.5; Age under 18: 10.5%; Age 65 and over: 28.9%; Males per 100 females: 105.8; Marriage status: 21.7% never married, 56.1% now married, 0.7% separated, 6.7% widowed, 15.5% divorced; Foreign born: 2.0%; Speak English only: 97.9%; With disability: 14.1%; Veterans: 13.8%; Ancestry: 22.7% German, 20.5% American, 17.4% Irish, 12.2% English, 11.4% Italian
Employment: 16.2% management, business, and financial, 2.0% computer, engineering, and science, 13.5% education, legal, community service, arts, and media, 5.8% healthcare practitioners, 14.1% service, 23.5% sales and office, 17.8% natural resources, construction, and maintenance, 7.1% production, transportation, and material moving

Income: Per capita: $30,605; Median household: $51,250; Average household: $61,832; Households with income of $100,000 or more: 17.4%; Poverty rate: 12.0%
Educational Attainment: High school diploma or higher: 91.5%; Bachelor's degree or higher: 23.3%; Graduate/professional degree or higher: 10.0%

School District(s)
Adirondack Central SD (PK-12)
  Enrollment: 1,296 . . . . (315) 942-9200
Housing: Homeownership rate: 89.3%; Median home value: $124,300; Median year structure built: 1966; Homeowner vacancy rate: 1.4%; Median selected monthly owner costs: $1,036 with a mortgage, $407 without a mortgage; Median gross rent: $540 per month; Rental vacancy rate: 0.0%
Health Insurance: 92.8% have insurance; 68.6% have private insurance; 49.6% have public insurance; 7.2% do not have insurance; 3.3% of children under 18 do not have insurance
Transportation: Commute: 88.5% car, 0.0% public transportation, 4.5% walk, 7.0% work from home; Mean travel time to work: 32.6 minutes

FRANKLIN SPRINGS (unincorporated postal area)
ZCTA: 13341
  Covers a land area of 0.184 square miles and a water area of 0 square miles. Located at 43.04° N. Lat; 75.40° W. Long. Elevation is 630 feet.
Population: 132; Growth (since 2000): 144.4%; Density: 716.8 persons per square mile; Race: 97.0% White, 0.0% Black/African American, 3.0% Asian, 0.0% American Indian/Alaska Native, 0.0% Native Hawaiian/Other Pacific Islander, 0.0% Two or more races, 0.0% Hispanic of any race; Average household size: 2.49; Median age: 42.8; Age under 18: 14.4%; Age 65 and over: 22.7%; Males per 100 females: 82.1; Marriage status: 16.2% never married, 83.8% now married, 0.0% separated, 0.0% widowed, 0.0% divorced; Foreign born: 3.0%; Speak English only: 90.8%; With disability: 0.0%; Veterans: 14.2%; Ancestry: 29.5% Italian, 20.5% Irish, 18.2% Turkish, 12.1% Hungarian, 11.4% American
Employment: 15.0% management, business, and financial, 5.0% computer, engineering, and science, 18.0% education, legal, community service, arts, and media, 21.0% healthcare practitioners, 20.0% service, 13.0% sales and office, 0.0% natural resources, construction, and maintenance, 8.0% production, transportation, and material moving
Income: Per capita: $45,345; Median household: $112,891; Average household: $109,696; Households with income of $100,000 or more: 77.4%; Poverty rate: n/a
Educational Attainment: High school diploma or higher: 100.0%; Bachelor's degree or higher: 55.6%; Graduate/professional degree or higher: 25.0%
Housing: Homeownership rate: 100.0%; Median home value: $127,300; Median year structure built: 1955; Homeowner vacancy rate: 0.0%; Median selected monthly owner costs: $1,453 with a mortgage, $0 without a mortgage; Median gross rent: n/a per month; Rental vacancy rate: 0.0%
Health Insurance: 100.0% have insurance; 96.2% have private insurance; 15.9% have public insurance; 0.0% do not have insurance; 0.0% of children under 18 do not have insurance
Transportation: Commute: 88.0% car, 4.0% public transportation, 5.0% walk, 3.0% work from home; Mean travel time to work: 21.4 minutes

HINCKLEY (unincorporated postal area)
ZCTA: 13352
  Covers a land area of 0.168 square miles and a water area of 0.017 square miles. Located at 43.31° N. Lat; 75.12° W. Long. Elevation is 1,197 feet.
Population: 38; Growth (since 2000): n/a; Density: 226.5 persons per square mile; Race: 100.0% White, 0.0% Black/African American, 0.0% Asian, 0.0% American Indian/Alaska Native, 0.0% Native Hawaiian/Other Pacific Islander, 0.0% Two or more races, 0.0% Hispanic of any race; Average household size: 0.00; Median age: n/a; Age under 18: 0.0%; Age 65 and over: 0.0%; Males per 100 females: 71.1; Marriage status: 0.0% never married, 0.0% now married, 0.0% separated, 0.0% widowed, 100.0% divorced; Foreign born: 0.0%; Speak English only: 28.9%; With disability: 71.1%; Veterans: 0.0%; Ancestry: 71.1% Italian, 28.9% English, 28.9% Irish
Employment: 0.0% management, business, and financial, 100.0% computer, engineering, and science, 0.0% education, legal, community service, arts, and media, 0.0% healthcare practitioners, 0.0% service,

0.0% sales and office, 0.0% natural resources, construction, and maintenance, 0.0% production, transportation, and material moving
Income: Per capita: n/a; Median household: n/a; Average household: n/a; Households with income of $100,000 or more: n/a; Poverty rate: 71.1%
Educational Attainment: High school diploma or higher: 100.0%; Bachelor's degree or higher: n/a; Graduate/professional degree or higher: n/a
Housing: Homeownership rate: 100.0%; Median home value: n/a; Median year structure built: Before 1940; Homeowner vacancy rate: 0.0%; Median selected monthly owner costs: $0 with a mortgage, $0 without a mortgage; Median gross rent: n/a per month; Rental vacancy rate: 0.0%
Health Insurance: 100.0% have insurance; 28.9% have private insurance; 71.1% have public insurance; 0.0% do not have insurance; 0.0% of children under 18 do not have insurance
Transportation: Commute: 100.0% car, 0.0% public transportation, 0.0% walk, 0.0% work from home; Mean travel time to work: 0.0 minutes

HOLLAND PATENT (village). Covers a land area of 0.506 square miles and a water area of 0.002 square miles. Located at 43.24° N. Lat; 75.26° W. Long. Elevation is 640 feet.

Population: 352; Growth (since 2000): -23.6%; Density: 696.3 persons per square mile; Race: 100.0% White, 0.0% Black/African American, 0.0% Asian, 0.0% American Indian/Alaska Native, 0.0% Native Hawaiian/Other Pacific Islander, 0.0% Two or more races, 0.0% Hispanic of any race; Average household size: 2.12; Median age: 49.0; Age under 18: 17.6%; Age 65 and over: 20.2%; Males per 100 females: 96.6; Marriage status: 29.2% never married, 46.3% now married, 0.6% separated, 6.3% widowed, 18.1% divorced; Foreign born: 1.1%; Speak English only: 98.0%; With disability: 4.0%; Veterans: 11.9%; Ancestry: 25.3% American, 18.8% English, 16.2% Irish, 9.9% German, 9.4% Italian
Employment: 7.6% management, business, and financial, 2.7% computer, engineering, and science, 17.8% education, legal, community service, arts, and media, 11.9% healthcare practitioners, 20.0% service, 17.8% sales and office, 8.1% natural resources, construction, and maintenance, 14.1% production, transportation, and material moving
Income: Per capita: $34,351; Median household: $67,500; Average household: $72,781; Households with income of $100,000 or more: 22.3%; Poverty rate: 10.5%
Educational Attainment: High school diploma or higher: 97.2%; Bachelor's degree or higher: 27.8%; Graduate/professional degree or higher: 14.7%

School District(s)
Holland Patent Central SD (PK-12)
    Enrollment: 1,441 . . . . (315) 865-7221
Housing: Homeownership rate: 75.3%; Median home value: $139,600; Median year structure built: Before 1940; Homeowner vacancy rate: 0.0%; Median selected monthly owner costs: $1,231 with a mortgage, $561 without a mortgage; Median gross rent: $714 per month; Rental vacancy rate: 28.1%
Health Insurance: 96.8% have insurance; 75.5% have private insurance; 38.9% have public insurance; 3.2% do not have insurance; 0.0% of children under 18 do not have insurance
Transportation: Commute: 88.9% car, 0.0% public transportation, 4.7% walk, 2.6% work from home; Mean travel time to work: 18.4 minutes
Additional Information Contacts
Village of Holland Patent . . . . (315) 865-4853
    http://village.holland-patent.ny.us/content

KIRKLAND (town). Covers a land area of 33.783 square miles and a water area of 0.051 square miles. Located at 43.04° N. Lat; 75.38° W. Long. Elevation is 528 feet.

Population: 10,171; Growth (since 2000): 0.3%; Density: 301.1 persons per square mile; Race: 91.2% White, 2.5% Black/African American, 3.3% Asian, 0.0% American Indian/Alaska Native, 0.0% Native Hawaiian/Other Pacific Islander, 1.5% Two or more races, 4.1% Hispanic of any race; Average household size: 2.22; Median age: 37.8; Age under 18: 14.5%; Age 65 and over: 18.9%; Males per 100 females: 90.5; Marriage status: 41.7% never married, 39.4% now married, 1.4% separated, 8.5% widowed, 10.4% divorced; Foreign born: 7.6%; Speak English only: 89.6%; With disability: 10.8%; Veterans: 7.5%; Ancestry: 19.4% German, 17.3% American, 16.2% Irish, 15.1% English, 12.1% Italian
Employment: 15.4% management, business, and financial, 5.4% computer, engineering, and science, 19.1% education, legal, community

service, arts, and media, 9.2% healthcare practitioners, 15.7% service, 22.7% sales and office, 3.7% natural resources, construction, and maintenance, 8.8% production, transportation, and material moving
Income: Per capita: $33,440; Median household: $63,542; Average household: $87,441; Households with income of $100,000 or more: 27.6%; Poverty rate: 9.5%
Educational Attainment: High school diploma or higher: 95.3%; Bachelor's degree or higher: 43.5%; Graduate/professional degree or higher: 20.9%
Housing: Homeownership rate: 63.8%; Median home value: $177,400; Median year structure built: 1956; Homeowner vacancy rate: 1.4%; Median selected monthly owner costs: $1,556 with a mortgage, $590 without a mortgage; Median gross rent: $882 per month; Rental vacancy rate: 2.9%
Health Insurance: 96.8% have insurance; 81.2% have private insurance; 30.4% have public insurance; 3.2% do not have insurance; 2.0% of children under 18 do not have insurance
Safety: Violent crime rate: 0.0 per 10,000 population; Property crime rate: 24.4 per 10,000 population
Transportation: Commute: 79.6% car, 0.8% public transportation, 12.9% walk, 6.5% work from home; Mean travel time to work: 16.3 minutes
Additional Information Contacts
Town of Kirkland . . . . (315) 853-5401
    http://townofkirkland.org/content

KNOXBORO (unincorporated postal area)
ZCTA: 13362
    Covers a land area of 0.276 square miles and a water area of 0 square miles. Located at 42.98° N. Lat; 75.52° W. Long. Elevation is 1,096 feet.
Population: 191; Growth (since 2000): n/a; Density: 692.0 persons per square mile; Race: 100.0% White, 0.0% Black/African American, 0.0% Asian, 0.0% American Indian/Alaska Native, 0.0% Native Hawaiian/Other Pacific Islander, 0.0% Two or more races, 0.0% Hispanic of any race; Average household size: 2.55; Median age: 38.8; Age under 18: 18.3%; Age 65 and over: 15.7%; Males per 100 females: 93.5; Marriage status: 45.6% never married, 26.7% now married, 0.0% separated, 0.0% widowed, 27.8% divorced; Foreign born: 0.0%; Speak English only: 100.0%; With disability: 13.0%; Veterans: 22.7%; Ancestry: 42.9% American, 21.5% German, 19.9% Italian, 15.2% Irish, 7.3% Welsh
Employment: 6.5% management, business, and financial, 0.0% computer, engineering, and science, 21.7% education, legal, community service, arts, and media, 6.5% healthcare practitioners, 18.5% service, 46.7% sales and office, 0.0% natural resources, construction, and maintenance, 0.0% production, transportation, and material moving
Income: Per capita: $31,334; Median household: n/a; Average household: $75,461; Households with income of $100,000 or more: 24.0%; Poverty rate: 8.9%
Educational Attainment: High school diploma or higher: 95.7%; Bachelor's degree or higher: 31.7%; Graduate/professional degree or higher: 23.0%
Housing: Homeownership rate: 78.7%; Median home value: n/a; Median year structure built: Before 1940; Homeowner vacancy rate: 0.0%; Median selected monthly owner costs: $1,132 with a mortgage, $0 without a mortgage; Median gross rent: n/a per month; Rental vacancy rate: 0.0%
Health Insurance: 100.0% have insurance; 90.8% have private insurance; 25.4% have public insurance; 0.0% do not have insurance; 0.0% of children under 18 do not have insurance
Transportation: Commute: 84.7% car, 0.0% public transportation, 0.0% walk, 15.3% work from home; Mean travel time to work: 33.9 minutes

LEE (town). Covers a land area of 45.106 square miles and a water area of 0.447 square miles. Located at 43.33° N. Lat; 75.52° W. Long. Elevation is 505 feet.

Population: 6,476; Growth (since 2000): -5.8%; Density: 143.6 persons per square mile; Race: 97.9% White, 0.9% Black/African American, 0.5% Asian, 0.0% American Indian/Alaska Native, 0.0% Native Hawaiian/Other Pacific Islander, 0.6% Two or more races, 0.7% Hispanic of any race; Average household size: 2.47; Median age: 46.7; Age under 18: 20.8%; Age 65 and over: 21.4%; Males per 100 females: 97.7; Marriage status: 23.8% never married, 58.3% now married, 1.9% separated, 8.8% widowed, 9.1% divorced; Foreign born: 1.2%; Speak English only: 98.1%; With disability: 13.1%; Veterans: 11.2%; Ancestry: 21.2% American, 17.2% Italian, 16.5% German, 13.9% Irish, 12.7% Polish

Employment: 12.4% management, business, and financial, 2.5% computer, engineering, and science, 10.9% education, legal, community service, arts, and media, 6.7% healthcare practitioners, 24.6% service, 18.4% sales and office, 11.7% natural resources, construction, and maintenance, 12.7% production, transportation, and material moving
Income: Per capita: $33,143; Median household: $66,796; Average household: $80,681; Households with income of $100,000 or more: 25.1%; Poverty rate: 5.8%
Educational Attainment: High school diploma or higher: 91.4%; Bachelor's degree or higher: 22.8%; Graduate/professional degree or higher: 7.9%
Housing: Homeownership rate: 85.9%; Median home value: $129,800; Median year structure built: 1968; Homeowner vacancy rate: 2.9%; Median selected monthly owner costs: $1,198 with a mortgage, $468 without a mortgage; Median gross rent: $1,006 per month; Rental vacancy rate: 0.0%
Health Insurance: 94.9% have insurance; 79.1% have private insurance; 37.2% have public insurance; 5.1% do not have insurance; 5.9% of children under 18 do not have insurance
Transportation: Commute: 94.5% car, 0.5% public transportation, 0.8% walk, 3.5% work from home; Mean travel time to work: 22.1 minutes
Additional Information Contacts
Town of Lee . . . . (315) 336-3438
  http://townofleeny.org/content

LEE CENTER (unincorporated postal area)
ZCTA: 13363

Covers a land area of 21.188 square miles and a water area of 0.045 square miles. Located at 43.32° N. Lat; 75.51° W. Long. Elevation is 617 feet.
Population: 2,115; Growth (since 2000): -11.8%; Density: 99.8 persons per square mile; Race: 99.2% White, 0.8% Black/African American, 0.0% Asian, 0.0% American Indian/Alaska Native, 0.0% Native Hawaiian/Other Pacific Islander, 0.0% Two or more races, 2.1% Hispanic of any race; Average household size: 2.39; Median age: 48.4; Age under 18: 16.5%; Age 65 and over: 19.6%; Males per 100 females: 98.7; Marriage status: 21.4% never married, 54.5% now married, 2.3% separated, 9.5% widowed, 14.5% divorced; Foreign born: 0.4%; Speak English only: 97.2%; With disability: 16.3%; Veterans: 11.9%; Ancestry: 20.5% American, 19.1% German, 16.0% Italian, 13.0% Polish, 10.6% English
Employment: 8.3% management, business, and financial, 1.4% computer, engineering, and science, 8.9% education, legal, community service, arts, and media, 4.0% healthcare practitioners, 23.4% service, 21.2% sales and office, 16.2% natural resources, construction, and maintenance, 16.6% production, transportation, and material moving
Income: Per capita: $30,392; Median household: $59,840; Average household: $70,995; Households with income of $100,000 or more: 20.8%; Poverty rate: 7.4%
Educational Attainment: High school diploma or higher: 92.5%; Bachelor's degree or higher: 19.0%; Graduate/professional degree or higher: 4.2%
Housing: Homeownership rate: 86.1%; Median home value: $115,500; Median year structure built: 1972; Homeowner vacancy rate: 8.1%; Median selected monthly owner costs: $1,123 with a mortgage, $464 without a mortgage; Median gross rent: $1,250 per month; Rental vacancy rate: 0.0%
Health Insurance: 98.0% have insurance; 81.3% have private insurance; 38.6% have public insurance; 2.0% do not have insurance; 0.0% of children under 18 do not have insurance
Transportation: Commute: 96.9% car, 0.0% public transportation, 0.0% walk, 3.1% work from home; Mean travel time to work: 25.3 minutes

MARCY (town). Covers a land area of 32.890 square miles and a water area of 0.428 square miles. Located at 43.17° N. Lat; 75.27° W. Long. Elevation is 604 feet.
Population: 9,406; Growth (since 2000): -0.7%; Density: 286.0 persons per square mile; Race: 82.6% White, 11.5% Black/African American, 0.5% Asian, 0.1% American Indian/Alaska Native, 0.0% Native Hawaiian/Other Pacific Islander, 2.6% Two or more races, 8.6% Hispanic of any race; Average household size: 2.68; Median age: 40.0; Age under 18: 15.4%; Age 65 and over: 11.7%; Males per 100 females: 208.9; Marriage status: 45.5% never married, 41.8% now married, 1.9% separated, 4.3% widowed, 8.4% divorced; Foreign born: 5.6%; Speak English only: 86.3%;

With disability: 11.3%; Veterans: 6.8%; Ancestry: 23.9% American, 15.1% Irish, 15.1% Italian, 13.8% German, 10.8% Polish
Employment: 8.6% management, business, and financial, 2.5% computer, engineering, and science, 20.0% education, legal, community service, arts, and media, 10.1% healthcare practitioners, 14.3% service, 26.9% sales and office, 9.9% natural resources, construction, and maintenance, 7.6% production, transportation, and material moving
Income: Per capita: $28,223; Median household: $79,601; Average household: $102,058; Households with income of $100,000 or more: 29.9%; Poverty rate: 6.3%
Educational Attainment: High school diploma or higher: 81.2%; Bachelor's degree or higher: 28.0%; Graduate/professional degree or higher: 10.0%

School District(s)
Whitesboro Central SD (KG-12)
  Enrollment: 3,262 . . . . (315) 266-3303
Housing: Homeownership rate: 84.4%; Median home value: $172,100; Median year structure built: 1969; Homeowner vacancy rate: 1.6%; Median selected monthly owner costs: $1,640 with a mortgage, $563 without a mortgage; Median gross rent: $859 per month; Rental vacancy rate: 0.0%
Health Insurance: 96.8% have insurance; 78.0% have private insurance; 33.7% have public insurance; 3.2% do not have insurance; 2.1% of children under 18 do not have insurance
Transportation: Commute: 89.0% car, 0.9% public transportation, 1.2% walk, 8.8% work from home; Mean travel time to work: 16.6 minutes
Additional Information Contacts
Town of Marcy . . . . (315) 768-4800
  http://townofmarcy.org/content

MARSHALL (town). Covers a land area of 32.802 square miles and a water area of 0 square miles. Located at 42.97° N. Lat; 75.39° W. Long. Elevation is 1,365 feet.
Population: 2,065; Growth (since 2000): -2.9%; Density: 63.0 persons per square mile; Race: 97.5% White, 0.6% Black/African American, 0.9% Asian, 0.0% American Indian/Alaska Native, 0.0% Native Hawaiian/Other Pacific Islander, 0.8% Two or more races, 2.6% Hispanic of any race; Average household size: 2.44; Median age: 39.3; Age under 18: 23.0%; Age 65 and over: 15.9%; Males per 100 females: 105.5; Marriage status: 24.2% never married, 61.9% now married, 3.0% separated, 5.2% widowed, 8.7% divorced; Foreign born: 1.5%; Speak English only: 95.7%; With disability: 10.6%; Veterans: 8.2%; Ancestry: 27.7% American, 18.8% Irish, 17.7% German, 12.2% English, 5.9% Polish
Employment: 13.6% management, business, and financial, 2.5% computer, engineering, and science, 15.4% education, legal, community service, arts, and media, 6.3% healthcare practitioners, 22.8% service, 12.6% sales and office, 7.6% natural resources, construction, and maintenance, 19.3% production, transportation, and material moving
Income: Per capita: $27,902; Median household: $55,385; Average household: $67,970; Households with income of $100,000 or more: 23.7%; Poverty rate: 9.8%
Educational Attainment: High school diploma or higher: 93.1%; Bachelor's degree or higher: 28.9%; Graduate/professional degree or higher: 10.7%
Housing: Homeownership rate: 84.8%; Median home value: $110,300; Median year structure built: 1962; Homeowner vacancy rate: 0.0%; Median selected monthly owner costs: $1,211 with a mortgage, $429 without a mortgage; Median gross rent: $659 per month; Rental vacancy rate: 0.0%
Health Insurance: 97.1% have insurance; 72.3% have private insurance; 34.2% have public insurance; 2.9% do not have insurance; 1.3% of children under 18 do not have insurance
Transportation: Commute: 92.3% car, 0.3% public transportation, 3.5% walk, 3.5% work from home; Mean travel time to work: 21.9 minutes

NEW HARTFORD (town). Covers a land area of 25.357 square miles and a water area of 0.118 square miles. Located at 43.06° N. Lat; 75.28° W. Long. Elevation is 541 feet.
History: Settled c.1787, incorporated 1870.
Population: 21,992; Growth (since 2000): 3.9%; Density: 867.3 persons per square mile; Race: 92.7% White, 2.4% Black/African American, 3.0% Asian, 0.3% American Indian/Alaska Native, 0.1% Native Hawaiian/Other Pacific Islander, 1.5% Two or more races, 1.8% Hispanic of any race; Average household size: 2.28; Median age: 47.5; Age under 18: 18.0%; Age 65 and over: 25.6%; Males per 100 females: 86.6; Marriage status: 28.8% never married, 50.3% now married, 1.1% separated, 10.6% widowed, 10.3% divorced; Foreign born: 6.6%; Speak English only: 92.2%;

With disability: 11.7%; Veterans: 9.6%; Ancestry: 24.3% Italian, 18.8% Irish, 17.1% German, 16.4% American, 11.3% Polish
Employment: 13.9% management, business, and financial, 6.7% computer, engineering, and science, 15.0% education, legal, community service, arts, and media, 11.2% healthcare practitioners, 15.6% service, 24.2% sales and office, 5.1% natural resources, construction, and maintenance, 8.3% production, transportation, and material moving
Income: Per capita: $37,958; Median household: $62,763; Average household: $88,684; Households with income of $100,000 or more: 28.8%; Poverty rate: 6.5%
Educational Attainment: High school diploma or higher: 95.6%; Bachelor's degree or higher: 40.4%; Graduate/professional degree or higher: 20.2%

School District(s)
New Hartford Central SD (KG-12)
    Enrollment: 2,572 . . . . (315) 624-1218
Oneida-Herkimer-Madison Boces
    Enrollment: n/a . . . . (315) 793-8560
Housing: Homeownership rate: 74.7%; Median home value: $155,600; Median year structure built: 1963; Homeowner vacancy rate: 2.6%; Median selected monthly owner costs: $1,438 with a mortgage, $584 without a mortgage; Median gross rent: $868 per month; Rental vacancy rate: 12.5%
Health Insurance: 97.7% have insurance; 83.6% have private insurance; 34.4% have public insurance; 2.3% do not have insurance; 1.1% of children under 18 do not have insurance
Safety: Violent crime rate: 7.9 per 10,000 population; Property crime rate: 292.9 per 10,000 population
Transportation: Commute: 94.7% car, 0.2% public transportation, 1.3% walk, 3.9% work from home; Mean travel time to work: 16.8 minutes
Additional Information Contacts
Town of New Hartford . . . . (315) 733-7500
    http://www.newhartfordtown.com

NEW HARTFORD (village). Covers a land area of 0.617 square miles and a water area of 0 square miles. Located at 43.07° N. Lat; 75.29° W. Long. Elevation is 541 feet.
Population: 1,898; Growth (since 2000): 0.6%; Density: 3,077.4 persons per square mile; Race: 97.4% White, 1.0% Black/African American, 0.9% Asian, 0.4% American Indian/Alaska Native, 0.0% Native Hawaiian/Other Pacific Islander, 0.3% Two or more races, 3.4% Hispanic of any race; Average household size: 2.28; Median age: 44.6; Age under 18: 23.0%; Age 65 and over: 19.9%; Males per 100 females: 82.5; Marriage status: 29.0% never married, 51.7% now married, 3.2% separated, 9.7% widowed, 9.6% divorced; Foreign born: 3.0%; Speak English only: 97.7%; With disability: 13.9%; Veterans: 6.9%; Ancestry: 27.2% Italian, 24.8% Irish, 20.4% German, 14.9% English, 10.5% American
Employment: 20.7% management, business, and financial, 5.4% computer, engineering, and science, 22.3% education, legal, community service, arts, and media, 3.9% healthcare practitioners, 10.8% service, 26.4% sales and office, 5.3% natural resources, construction, and maintenance, 5.4% production, transportation, and material moving
Income: Per capita: $37,312; Median household: $67,132; Average household: $83,867; Households with income of $100,000 or more: 34.6%; Poverty rate: 11.7%
Educational Attainment: High school diploma or higher: 99.2%; Bachelor's degree or higher: 47.1%; Graduate/professional degree or higher: 22.4%

School District(s)
New Hartford Central SD (KG-12)
    Enrollment: 2,572 . . . . (315) 624-1218
Oneida-Herkimer-Madison Boces
    Enrollment: n/a . . . . (315) 793-8560
Housing: Homeownership rate: 64.7%; Median home value: $152,700; Median year structure built: 1940; Homeowner vacancy rate: 1.1%; Median selected monthly owner costs: $1,439 with a mortgage, $558 without a mortgage; Median gross rent: $1,096 per month; Rental vacancy rate: 1.8%
Health Insurance: 97.5% have insurance; 87.1% have private insurance; 29.3% have public insurance; 2.5% do not have insurance; 2.6% of children under 18 do not have insurance
Transportation: Commute: 86.9% car, 0.1% public transportation, 8.8% walk, 3.7% work from home; Mean travel time to work: 15.2 minutes

NEW YORK MILLS (village). Covers a land area of 1.180 square miles and a water area of 0 square miles. Located at 43.10° N. Lat; 75.29° W. Long. Elevation is 466 feet.
History: Incorporated 1922.
Population: 3,581; Growth (since 2000): 12.2%; Density: 3,034.8 persons per square mile; Race: 93.5% White, 1.0% Black/African American, 3.1% Asian, 0.0% American Indian/Alaska Native, 0.0% Native Hawaiian/Other Pacific Islander, 2.5% Two or more races, 0.0% Hispanic of any race; Average household size: 2.13; Median age: 41.2; Age under 18: 22.5%; Age 65 and over: 19.2%; Males per 100 females: 92.1; Marriage status: 35.8% never married, 34.5% now married, 1.7% separated, 9.4% widowed, 20.4% divorced; Foreign born: 4.0%; Speak English only: 93.0%; With disability: 13.5%; Veterans: 12.4%; Ancestry: 21.1% Polish, 20.6% Italian, 19.2% Irish, 17.2% American, 9.9% German
Employment: 11.5% management, business, and financial, 7.2% computer, engineering, and science, 9.0% education, legal, community service, arts, and media, 6.8% healthcare practitioners, 17.6% service, 21.6% sales and office, 8.8% natural resources, construction, and maintenance, 17.6% production, transportation, and material moving
Income: Per capita: $24,882; Median household: $37,736; Average household: $51,147; Households with income of $100,000 or more: 10.8%; Poverty rate: 15.1%
Educational Attainment: High school diploma or higher: 95.8%; Bachelor's degree or higher: 20.3%; Graduate/professional degree or higher: 4.6%

School District(s)
New York Mills Union Free SD (KG-12)
    Enrollment: 571 . . . . (315) 768-8127
Housing: Homeownership rate: 42.7%; Median home value: $125,300; Median year structure built: 1951; Homeowner vacancy rate: 0.0%; Median selected monthly owner costs: $1,085 with a mortgage, $403 without a mortgage; Median gross rent: $801 per month; Rental vacancy rate: 4.8%
Health Insurance: 98.1% have insurance; 64.4% have private insurance; 53.1% have public insurance; 1.9% do not have insurance; 0.0% of children under 18 do not have insurance
Safety: Violent crime rate: 6.1 per 10,000 population; Property crime rate: 112.9 per 10,000 population
Transportation: Commute: 93.7% car, 0.8% public transportation, 3.6% walk, 1.8% work from home; Mean travel time to work: 14.5 minutes

NORTH BAY (unincorporated postal area)
ZCTA: 13123
    Covers a land area of 2.366 square miles and a water area of 0 square miles. Located at 43.23° N. Lat; 75.77° W. Long. Elevation is 476 feet.
    Population: 491; Growth (since 2000): n/a; Density: 207.5 persons per square mile; Race: 100.0% White, 0.0% Black/African American, 0.0% Asian, 0.0% American Indian/Alaska Native, 0.0% Native Hawaiian/Other Pacific Islander, 0.0% Two or more races, 0.0% Hispanic of any race; Average household size: 4.86; Median age: 27.0; Age under 18: 39.7%; Age 65 and over: 3.5%; Males per 100 females: 101.3; Marriage status: 40.9% never married, 39.2% now married, 17.9% separated, 5.7% widowed, 14.2% divorced; Foreign born: 0.0%; Speak English only: 100.0%; With disability: 7.5%; Veterans: 5.7%; Ancestry: 74.1% American, 17.9% English, 8.6% Norwegian, 7.9% Polish, 7.3% German
    Employment: 0.0% management, business, and financial, 0.0% computer, engineering, and science, 0.0% education, legal, community service, arts, and media, 0.0% healthcare practitioners, 32.9% service, 9.7% sales and office, 0.0% natural resources, construction, and maintenance, 57.4% production, transportation, and material moving
    Income: Per capita: $13,433; Median household: $55,825; Average household: $63,150; Households with income of $100,000 or more: 14.9%; Poverty rate: n/a
    Educational Attainment: High school diploma or higher: 86.6%; Bachelor's degree or higher: n/a; Graduate/professional degree or higher: n/a

School District(s)
Camden Central SD (PK-12)
    Enrollment: 2,225 . . . . (315) 245-4075
Housing: Homeownership rate: 100.0%; Median home value: $66,500; Median year structure built: 1943; Homeowner vacancy rate: 0.0%; Median selected monthly owner costs: $0 with a mortgage, $0 without a mortgage; Median gross rent: n/a per month; Rental vacancy rate: 100.0%

Health Insurance: 100.0% have insurance; 27.9% have private insurance; 78.8% have public insurance; 0.0% do not have insurance; 0.0% of children under 18 do not have insurance
Transportation: Commute: 100.0% car, 0.0% public transportation, 0.0% walk, 0.0% work from home; Mean travel time to work: 0.0 minutes

ONEIDA CASTLE (village).
Covers a land area of 0.514 square miles and a water area of 0 square miles. Located at 43.08° N. Lat; 75.63° W. Long. Elevation is 449 feet.
History: Center of Oneida Territory, site of chief settlement of Oneida people.
Population: 628; Growth (since 2000): 0.2%; Density: 1,221.9 persons per square mile; Race: 97.1% White, 0.0% Black/African American, 1.6% Asian, 0.6% American Indian/Alaska Native, 0.0% Native Hawaiian/Other Pacific Islander, 0.6% Two or more races, 0.8% Hispanic of any race; Average household size: 2.31; Median age: 45.8; Age under 18: 20.4%; Age 65 and over: 24.0%; Males per 100 females: 88.3; Marriage status: 25.9% never married, 50.9% now married, 1.8% separated, 6.3% widowed, 16.9% divorced; Foreign born: 3.2%; Speak English only: 96.6%; With disability: 12.6%; Veterans: 16.0%; Ancestry: 26.3% American, 16.2% German, 15.8% Italian, 14.6% English, 13.4% Irish
Employment: 4.9% management, business, and financial, 4.6% computer, engineering, and science, 9.2% education, legal, community service, arts, and media, 11.1% healthcare practitioners, 20.3% service, 23.6% sales and office, 9.2% natural resources, construction, and maintenance, 17.0% production, transportation, and material moving
Income: Per capita: $26,665; Median household: $47,273; Average household: $59,583; Households with income of $100,000 or more: 16.2%; Poverty rate: 9.7%
Educational Attainment: High school diploma or higher: 94.5%; Bachelor's degree or higher: 18.1%; Graduate/professional degree or higher: 4.0%
Housing: Homeownership rate: 72.1%; Median home value: $118,000; Median year structure built: Before 1940; Homeowner vacancy rate: 0.0%; Median selected monthly owner costs: $1,219 with a mortgage, $415 without a mortgage; Median gross rent: $817 per month; Rental vacancy rate: 0.0%
Health Insurance: 97.0% have insurance; 79.0% have private insurance; 35.7% have public insurance; 3.0% do not have insurance; 2.2% of children under 18 do not have insurance
Transportation: Commute: 95.7% car, 0.0% public transportation, 1.0% walk, 3.3% work from home; Mean travel time to work: 21.2 minutes

ORISKANY (village).
Covers a land area of 0.792 square miles and a water area of 0 square miles. Located at 43.16° N. Lat; 75.33° W. Long. Elevation is 430 feet.
History: Obelisk at Oriskany Battlefield (Northwest) marks site of an engagement (Aug. 6, 1777) of the Saratoga campaign, one of the bloodiest battles of the American Revolution. Incorporated 1914.
Population: 1,214; Growth (since 2000): -16.8%; Density: 1,533.6 persons per square mile; Race: 97.4% White, 1.5% Black/African American, 0.0% Asian, 0.0% American Indian/Alaska Native, 0.0% Native Hawaiian/Other Pacific Islander, 1.1% Two or more races, 0.6% Hispanic of any race; Average household size: 1.97; Median age: 49.3; Age under 18: 18.9%; Age 65 and over: 29.7%; Males per 100 females: 85.4; Marriage status: 28.8% never married, 42.9% now married, 1.7% separated, 12.1% widowed, 16.3% divorced; Foreign born: 2.3%; Speak English only: 99.1%; With disability: 20.8%; Veterans: 15.1%; Ancestry: 19.8% Italian, 19.2% American, 17.3% Irish, 16.2% English, 14.9% German
Employment: 7.5% management, business, and financial, 3.7% computer, engineering, and science, 16.4% education, legal, community service, arts, and media, 4.0% healthcare practitioners, 23.7% service, 31.4% sales and office, 1.7% natural resources, construction, and maintenance, 11.6% production, transportation, and material moving
Income: Per capita: $24,722; Median household: $41,458; Average household: $50,013; Households with income of $100,000 or more: 11.1%; Poverty rate: 11.2%
Educational Attainment: High school diploma or higher: 94.0%; Bachelor's degree or higher: 24.0%; Graduate/professional degree or higher: 7.7%
School District(s)
Oriskany Central SD (PK-12)
    Enrollment: 603 . . . . (315) 768-2058
Housing: Homeownership rate: 60.7%; Median home value: $116,100; Median year structure built: Before 1940; Homeowner vacancy rate: 5.4%;

Median selected monthly owner costs: $1,167 with a mortgage, $493 without a mortgage; Median gross rent: $989 per month; Rental vacancy rate: 2.2%
Health Insurance: 97.4% have insurance; 70.2% have private insurance; 48.1% have public insurance; 2.6% do not have insurance; 0.0% of children under 18 do not have insurance
Safety: Violent crime rate: 7.4 per 10,000 population; Property crime rate: 81.2 per 10,000 population
Transportation: Commute: 88.2% car, 0.6% public transportation, 5.1% walk, 5.3% work from home; Mean travel time to work: 14.2 minutes

ORISKANY FALLS (village).
Covers a land area of 0.506 square miles and a water area of 0 square miles. Located at 42.94° N. Lat; 75.46° W. Long. Elevation is 974 feet.
Population: 826; Growth (since 2000): 18.3%; Density: 1,631.7 persons per square mile; Race: 98.5% White, 0.5% Black/African American, 0.0% Asian, 0.0% American Indian/Alaska Native, 0.0% Native Hawaiian/Other Pacific Islander, 1.0% Two or more races, 0.0% Hispanic of any race; Average household size: 2.67; Median age: 33.9; Age under 18: 29.9%; Age 65 and over: 16.6%; Males per 100 females: 99.5; Marriage status: 25.3% never married, 51.8% now married, 2.8% separated, 7.9% widowed, 15.0% divorced; Foreign born: 0.5%; Speak English only: 97.6%; With disability: 13.4%; Veterans: 8.3%; Ancestry: 43.3% American, 18.3% Irish, 14.9% German, 11.0% English, 5.1% Polish
Employment: 7.5% management, business, and financial, 3.1% computer, engineering, and science, 6.5% education, legal, community service, arts, and media, 6.8% healthcare practitioners, 29.2% service, 23.9% sales and office, 13.7% natural resources, construction, and maintenance, 9.3% production, transportation, and material moving
Income: Per capita: $20,882; Median household: $53,095; Average household: $53,464; Households with income of $100,000 or more: 11.6%; Poverty rate: 15.6%
Educational Attainment: High school diploma or higher: 85.8%; Bachelor's degree or higher: 14.2%; Graduate/professional degree or higher: 3.2%
Housing: Homeownership rate: 61.4%; Median home value: $80,400; Median year structure built: Before 1940; Homeowner vacancy rate: 0.0%; Median selected monthly owner costs: $979 with a mortgage, $550 without a mortgage; Median gross rent: $756 per month; Rental vacancy rate: 5.6%
Health Insurance: 96.5% have insurance; 63.3% have private insurance; 46.0% have public insurance; 3.5% do not have insurance; 0.0% of children under 18 do not have insurance
Transportation: Commute: 93.5% car, 0.0% public transportation, 4.5% walk, 0.6% work from home; Mean travel time to work: 23.5 minutes

PARIS (town).
Covers a land area of 31.476 square miles and a water area of 0.015 square miles. Located at 42.97° N. Lat; 75.27° W. Long. Elevation is 1,489 feet.
Population: 4,331; Growth (since 2000): -6.0%; Density: 137.6 persons per square mile; Race: 94.0% White, 2.1% Black/African American, 1.7% Asian, 0.3% American Indian/Alaska Native, 0.0% Native Hawaiian/Other Pacific Islander, 2.0% Two or more races, 2.3% Hispanic of any race; Average household size: 2.48; Median age: 44.9; Age under 18: 19.4%; Age 65 and over: 16.6%; Males per 100 females: 97.7; Marriage status: 31.2% never married, 57.5% now married, 1.3% separated, 5.4% widowed, 6.0% divorced; Foreign born: 4.1%; Speak English only: 96.5%; With disability: 11.2%; Veterans: 9.9%; Ancestry: 16.7% American, 15.7% German, 13.2% Polish, 11.9% Italian, 11.4% Irish
Employment: 18.0% management, business, and financial, 5.0% computer, engineering, and science, 10.1% education, legal, community service, arts, and media, 8.6% healthcare practitioners, 17.1% service, 21.4% sales and office, 13.2% natural resources, construction, and maintenance, 6.5% production, transportation, and material moving
Income: Per capita: $32,803; Median household: $66,366; Average household: $80,743; Households with income of $100,000 or more: 26.9%; Poverty rate: 6.6%
Educational Attainment: High school diploma or higher: 94.8%; Bachelor's degree or higher: 29.1%; Graduate/professional degree or higher: 11.8%
Housing: Homeownership rate: 83.5%; Median home value: $154,500; Median year structure built: 1962; Homeowner vacancy rate: 1.8%; Median selected monthly owner costs: $1,371 with a mortgage, $647 without a mortgage; Median gross rent: $732 per month; Rental vacancy rate: 6.7%

Health Insurance: 94.9% have insurance; 80.0% have private insurance; 30.4% have public insurance; 5.1% do not have insurance; 0.9% of children under 18 do not have insurance

Transportation: Commute: 97.1% car, 0.0% public transportation, 0.0% walk, 2.0% work from home; Mean travel time to work: 21.4 minutes

Additional Information Contacts

Town of Paris . . . . (315) 839-5400
  http://town.paris.ny.us/content

PROSPECT (village).
Covers a land area of 0.208 square miles and a water area of 0 square miles. Located at 43.30° N. Lat; 75.15° W. Long. Elevation is 1,184 feet.

Population: 314; Growth (since 2000): -4.8%; Density: 1,510.5 persons per square mile; Race: 95.9% White, 0.0% Black/African American, 0.6% Asian, 0.0% American Indian/Alaska Native, 0.0% Native Hawaiian/Other Pacific Islander, 3.5% Two or more races, 0.6% Hispanic of any race; Average household size: 2.60; Median age: 42.8; Age under 18: 25.5%; Age 65 and over: 26.8%; Males per 100 females: 99.3; Marriage status: 23.4% never married, 46.4% now married, 0.4% separated, 13.4% widowed, 16.7% divorced; Foreign born: 0.6%; Speak English only: 99.3%; With disability: 9.0%; Veterans: 11.2%; Ancestry: 31.2% American, 19.7% German, 13.7% Irish, 11.5% English, 10.5% Italian

Employment: 14.6% management, business, and financial, 2.4% computer, engineering, and science, 7.3% education, legal, community service, arts, and media, 6.5% healthcare practitioners, 17.9% service, 27.6% sales and office, 6.5% natural resources, construction, and maintenance, 17.1% production, transportation, and material moving

Income: Per capita: $25,427; Median household: $51,875; Average household: $65,835; Households with income of $100,000 or more: 16.6%; Poverty rate: 7.0%

Educational Attainment: High school diploma or higher: 92.0%; Bachelor's degree or higher: 23.1%; Graduate/professional degree or higher: 6.2%

Housing: Homeownership rate: 95.0%; Median home value: $95,200; Median year structure built: Before 1940; Homeowner vacancy rate: 8.7%; Median selected monthly owner costs: $1,050 with a mortgage, $527 without a mortgage; Median gross rent: n/a per month; Rental vacancy rate: 45.5%

Health Insurance: 93.6% have insurance; 76.6% have private insurance; 39.1% have public insurance; 6.4% do not have insurance; 5.0% of children under 18 do not have insurance

Transportation: Commute: 96.8% car, 0.0% public transportation, 3.2% walk, 0.0% work from home; Mean travel time to work: 22.6 minutes

REMSEN (town).
Covers a land area of 35.465 square miles and a water area of 1.490 square miles. Located at 43.37° N. Lat; 75.15° W. Long. Elevation is 1,184 feet.

History: Reconstructed log cabin of Baron von Steuben, drillmaster to Continental Army, state historic site, 2 miles West.

Population: 1,612; Growth (since 2000): -17.7%; Density: 45.5 persons per square mile; Race: 99.3% White, 0.3% Black/African American, 0.2% Asian, 0.0% American Indian/Alaska Native, 0.0% Native Hawaiian/Other Pacific Islander, 0.1% Two or more races, 3.8% Hispanic of any race; Average household size: 2.24; Median age: 48.6; Age under 18: 15.9%; Age 65 and over: 17.1%; Males per 100 females: 99.7; Marriage status: 20.1% never married, 56.7% now married, 0.9% separated, 10.5% widowed, 12.7% divorced; Foreign born: 0.2%; Speak English only: 96.1%; With disability: 16.3%; Veterans: 9.1%; Ancestry: 19.2% German, 18.5% American, 15.6% Irish, 8.2% Italian, 8.9% Polish

Employment: 7.0% management, business, and financial, 2.2% computer, engineering, and science, 9.6% education, legal, community service, arts, and media, 4.5% healthcare practitioners, 14.9% service, 37.0% sales and office, 10.5% natural resources, construction, and maintenance, 14.4% production, transportation, and material moving

Income: Per capita: $30,102; Median household: $55,114; Average household: $66,270; Households with income of $100,000 or more: 18.9%; Poverty rate: 13.8%

Educational Attainment: High school diploma or higher: 94.4%; Bachelor's degree or higher: 17.9%; Graduate/professional degree or higher: 5.6%

School District(s)

Remsen Central SD (PK-12)
  Enrollment: 439 . . . . (315) 831-3797

Housing: Homeownership rate: 86.4%; Median home value: $115,000; Median year structure built: 1972; Homeowner vacancy rate: 4.3%; Median

selected monthly owner costs: $1,243 with a mortgage, $471 without a mortgage; Median gross rent: $769 per month; Rental vacancy rate: 14.9%

Health Insurance: 94.9% have insurance; 73.5% have private insurance; 39.4% have public insurance; 5.1% do not have insurance; 0.0% of children under 18 do not have insurance

Transportation: Commute: 94.0% car, 0.0% public transportation, 1.3% walk, 4.7% work from home; Mean travel time to work: 31.7 minutes

REMSEN (village).
Covers a land area of 0.372 square miles and a water area of 0 square miles. Located at 43.33° N. Lat; 75.19° W. Long. Elevation is 1,184 feet.

Population: 432; Growth (since 2000): -18.6%; Density: 1,160.3 persons per square mile; Race: 100.0% White, 0.0% Black/African American, 0.0% Asian, 0.0% American Indian/Alaska Native, 0.0% Native Hawaiian/Other Pacific Islander, 0.0% Two or more races, 10.6% Hispanic of any race; Average household size: 2.47; Median age: 41.9; Age under 18: 19.0%; Age 65 and over: 17.4%; Males per 100 females: 85.4; Marriage status: 33.5% never married, 42.5% now married, 2.8% separated, 11.7% widowed, 12.3% divorced; Foreign born: 0.0%; Speak English only: 90.2%; With disability: 20.6%; Veterans: 10.3%; Ancestry: 27.1% American, 17.6% Irish, 15.0% Italian, 11.6% German, 6.9% Welsh

Employment: 0.0% management, business, and financial, 0.0% computer, engineering, and science, 8.4% education, legal, community service, arts, and media, 7.8% healthcare practitioners, 11.7% service, 50.3% sales and office, 8.9% natural resources, construction, and maintenance, 12.8% production, transportation, and material moving

Income: Per capita: $20,506; Median household: $44,250; Average household: $48,665; Households with income of $100,000 or more: 6.3%; Poverty rate: 29.6%

Educational Attainment: High school diploma or higher: 91.8%; Bachelor's degree or higher: 8.8%; Graduate/professional degree or higher: 0.6%

School District(s)

Remsen Central SD (PK-12)
  Enrollment: 439 . . . . (315) 831-3797

Housing: Homeownership rate: 61.7%; Median home value: $91,400; Median year structure built: Before 1940; Homeowner vacancy rate: 10.7%; Median selected monthly owner costs: $1,120 with a mortgage, $463 without a mortgage; Median gross rent: $658 per month; Rental vacancy rate: 9.5%

Health Insurance: 90.7% have insurance; 48.4% have private insurance; 53.0% have public insurance; 9.3% do not have insurance; 0.0% of children under 18 do not have insurance

Transportation: Commute: 88.8% car, 0.0% public transportation, 5.0% walk, 6.1% work from home; Mean travel time to work: 28.2 minutes

ROME (city).
Covers a land area of 74.791 square miles and a water area of 0.811 square miles. Located at 43.23° N. Lat; 75.49° W. Long. Elevation is 456 feet.

History: Laid out c.1786 on the site of Fort Stanwix. The city was a busy portage point, and had great strategic importance during the French and Indian War and in the American Revolution. The Six Nation Treaty of 1768 was concluded here. Site of the Battle of Oriskany, one of the Revolution's bloodiest battles. Construction on the Erie Canal began (1817) in Rome. Incorporated as a city 1870.

Population: 32,589; Growth (since 2000): -6.8%; Density: 435.7 persons per square mile; Race: 88.3% White, 6.6% Black/African American, 1.3% Asian, 0.1% American Indian/Alaska Native, 0.0% Native Hawaiian/Other Pacific Islander, 2.5% Two or more races, 6.3% Hispanic of any race; Average household size: 2.36; Median age: 39.5; Age under 18: 20.8%; Age 65 and over: 17.3%; Males per 100 females: 105.6; Marriage status: 37.0% never married, 42.3% now married, 3.4% separated, 7.6% widowed, 13.1% divorced; Foreign born: 2.9%; Speak English only: 92.5%; With disability: 16.3%; Veterans: 11.0%; Ancestry: 22.6% American, 20.5% Italian, 14.0% Irish, 12.1% German, 7.0% English

Employment: 12.1% management, business, and financial, 5.4% computer, engineering, and science, 11.0% education, legal, community service, arts, and media, 7.7% healthcare practitioners, 21.7% service, 24.9% sales and office, 4.8% natural resources, construction, and maintenance, 12.5% production, transportation, and material moving

Income: Per capita: $24,970; Median household: $45,570; Average household: $59,662; Households with income of $100,000 or more: 15.1%; Poverty rate: 19.4%

Educational Attainment: High school diploma or higher: 87.1%; Bachelor's degree or higher: 20.5%; Graduate/professional degree or higher: 8.1%

School District(s)
New York State School for the Deaf (PK-12)
   Enrollment: 48 . . . . (315) 337-8400
Rome City SD (PK-12)
   Enrollment: 5,617 . . . . (315) 338-6521
Housing: Homeownership rate: 55.1%; Median home value: $94,900; Median year structure built: 1951; Homeowner vacancy rate: 1.6%; Median selected monthly owner costs: $1,144 with a mortgage, $549 without a mortgage; Median gross rent: $748 per month; Rental vacancy rate: 3.0%
Health Insurance: 95.4% have insurance; 65.3% have private insurance; 46.7% have public insurance; 4.6% do not have insurance; 0.5% of children under 18 do not have insurance
Hospitals: Rome Memorial Hospital (129 beds)
Safety: Violent crime rate: 22.1 per 10,000 population; Property crime rate: 174.8 per 10,000 population
Newspapers: Daily Sentinel (daily circulation 13,700)
Transportation: Commute: 90.3% car, 0.3% public transportation, 3.1% walk, 4.5% work from home; Mean travel time to work: 17.5 minutes; Amtrak: Train service available.
Airports: Griffiss International (general aviation)
Additional Information Contacts
City of Rome . . . . (315) 339-7658
   http://www.romenewyork.com

SANGERFIELD (town). Covers a land area of 30.802 square miles and a water area of 0.179 square miles. Located at 42.89° N. Lat; 75.38° W. Long. Elevation is 1,247 feet.
Population: 2,517; Growth (since 2000): -3.6%; Density: 81.7 persons per square mile; Race: 99.3% White, 0.4% Black/African American, 0.0% Asian, 0.0% American Indian/Alaska Native, 0.0% Native Hawaiian/Other Pacific Islander, 0.4% Two or more races, 0.6% Hispanic of any race; Average household size: 2.30; Median age: 47.9; Age under 18: 18.4%; Age 65 and over: 20.4%; Males per 100 females: 96.2; Marriage status: 26.5% never married, 51.9% now married, 1.9% separated, 8.6% widowed, 13.0% divorced; Foreign born: 0.2%; Speak English only: 99.3%; With disability: 13.5%; Veterans: 8.7%; Ancestry: 34.6% American, 15.4% Irish, 14.5% English, 13.8% German, 7.8% Italian
Employment: 13.7% management, business, and financial, 5.2% computer, engineering, and science, 10.3% education, legal, community service, arts, and media, 9.6% healthcare practitioners, 14.3% service, 18.6% sales and office, 13.1% natural resources, construction, and maintenance, 15.2% production, transportation, and material moving
Income: Per capita: $26,699; Median household: $52,539; Average household: $61,983; Households with income of $100,000 or more: 18.6%; Poverty rate: 11.6%
Educational Attainment: High school diploma or higher: 91.0%; Bachelor's degree or higher: 25.6%; Graduate/professional degree or higher: 9.6%
Housing: Homeownership rate: 64.5%; Median home value: $110,900; Median year structure built: Before 1940; Homeowner vacancy rate: 3.0%; Median selected monthly owner costs: $1,180 with a mortgage, $486 without a mortgage; Median gross rent: $638 per month; Rental vacancy rate: 2.9%
Health Insurance: 94.8% have insurance; 75.5% have private insurance; 34.1% have public insurance; 5.2% do not have insurance; 3.2% of children under 18 do not have insurance
Transportation: Commute: 89.3% car, 0.0% public transportation, 4.3% walk, 5.2% work from home; Mean travel time to work: 23.1 minutes

SAUQUOIT (unincorporated postal area)
ZCTA: 13456
   Covers a land area of 28.072 square miles and a water area of 0 square miles. Located at 43.00° N. Lat; 75.26° W. Long. Elevation is 866 feet.
Population: 4,107; Growth (since 2000): -4.0%; Density: 146.3 persons per square mile; Race: 93.8% White, 2.0% Black/African American, 1.8% Asian, 0.3% American Indian/Alaska Native, 0.0% Native Hawaiian/Other Pacific Islander, 2.1% Two or more races, 2.2% Hispanic of any race; Average household size: 2.56; Median age: 44.5; Age under 18: 20.2%; Age 65 and over: 16.8%; Males per 100 females: 94.2; Marriage status: 30.9% never married, 55.1% now married, 1.7% separated, 7.1% widowed, 7.0% divorced; Foreign born: 4.4%; Speak

English only: 95.7%; With disability: 10.6%; Veterans: 10.3%; Ancestry: 17.8% Irish, 17.4% Italian, 16.3% German, 16.1% Polish, 11.4% English
Employment: 18.9% management, business, and financial, 5.6% computer, engineering, and science, 10.7% education, legal, community service, arts, and media, 11.7% healthcare practitioners, 16.5% service, 20.0% sales and office, 9.2% natural resources, construction, and maintenance, 7.5% production, transportation, and material moving
Income: Per capita: $33,869; Median household: $66,049; Average household: $85,456; Households with income of $100,000 or more: 27.6%; Poverty rate: 6.8%
Educational Attainment: High school diploma or higher: 95.2%; Bachelor's degree or higher: 31.3%; Graduate/professional degree or higher: 14.0%
School District(s)
Sauquoit Valley Central SD (KG-12)
   Enrollment: 1,043 . . . . (315) 839-6311
Housing: Homeownership rate: 85.8%; Median home value: $150,200; Median year structure built: 1971; Homeowner vacancy rate: 0.7%; Median selected monthly owner costs: $1,390 with a mortgage, $638 without a mortgage; Median gross rent: $904 per month; Rental vacancy rate: 7.7%
Health Insurance: 95.8% have insurance; 80.1% have private insurance; 31.7% have public insurance; 4.2% do not have insurance; 0.0% of children under 18 do not have insurance
Transportation: Commute: 96.6% car, 0.1% public transportation, 0.0% walk, 2.2% work from home; Mean travel time to work: 20.9 minutes

SHERRILL (city). Covers a land area of 2.311 square miles and a water area of 0 square miles. Located at 43.07° N. Lat; 75.60° W. Long. Elevation is 495 feet.
History: Incorporated 1916.
Population: 3,054; Growth (since 2000): -3.0%; Density: 1,321.2 persons per square mile; Race: 97.9% White, 1.8% Black/African American, 0.0% Asian, 0.0% American Indian/Alaska Native, 0.0% Native Hawaiian/Other Pacific Islander, 0.1% Two or more races, 3.4% Hispanic of any race; Average household size: 2.38; Median age: 46.9; Age under 18: 21.3%; Age 65 and over: 23.4%; Males per 100 females: 93.5; Marriage status: 25.1% never married, 55.3% now married, 2.5% separated, 8.3% widowed, 11.2% divorced; Foreign born: 1.2%; Speak English only: 97.3%; With disability: 12.7%; Veterans: 8.8%; Ancestry: 23.1% German, 19.1% Irish, 15.8% Italian, 9.4% English, 8.3% Polish
Employment: 13.5% management, business, and financial, 2.0% computer, engineering, and science, 12.4% education, legal, community service, arts, and media, 13.1% healthcare practitioners, 18.7% service, 17.1% sales and office, 11.1% natural resources, construction, and maintenance, 12.2% production, transportation, and material moving
Income: Per capita: $31,695; Median household: $58,795; Average household: $73,341; Households with income of $100,000 or more: 22.8%; Poverty rate: 8.2%
Educational Attainment: High school diploma or higher: 94.3%; Bachelor's degree or higher: 28.9%; Graduate/professional degree or higher: 12.4%
School District(s)
Sherrill City SD (PK-12)
   Enrollment: 1,983 . . . . (315) 829-7425
Housing: Homeownership rate: 78.2%; Median home value: $147,500; Median year structure built: 1951; Homeowner vacancy rate: 0.0%; Median selected monthly owner costs: $1,276 with a mortgage, $462 without a mortgage; Median gross rent: $669 per month; Rental vacancy rate: 0.0%
Health Insurance: 96.8% have insurance; 81.0% have private insurance; 34.9% have public insurance; 3.2% do not have insurance; 4.4% of children under 18 do not have insurance
Safety: Violent crime rate: 0.0 per 10,000 population; Property crime rate: 69.0 per 10,000 population
Transportation: Commute: 94.2% car, 0.0% public transportation, 1.3% walk, 4.5% work from home; Mean travel time to work: 25.6 minutes
Additional Information Contacts
City of Sherrill . . . . (315) 363-2440
   http://www.sherrillny.org

STEUBEN (town). Covers a land area of 42.653 square miles and a water area of 0.048 square miles. Located at 43.35° N. Lat; 75.26° W. Long. Elevation is 928 feet.
Population: 1,237; Growth (since 2000): 5.5%; Density: 29.0 persons per square mile; Race: 99.2% White, 0.0% Black/African American, 0.4%

Asian, 0.0% American Indian/Alaska Native, 0.0% Native Hawaiian/Other Pacific Islander, 0.4% Two or more races, 0.0% Hispanic of any race; Average household size: 2.54; Median age: 45.8; Age under 18: 20.6%; Age 65 and over: 18.3%; Males per 100 females: 107.9; Marriage status: 25.6% never married, 60.4% now married, 0.7% separated, 2.2% widowed, 11.8% divorced; Foreign born: 1.2%; Speak English only: 97.7%; With disability: 8.8%; Veterans: 12.0%; Ancestry: 23.3% American, 18.7% German, 12.9% Irish, 12.1% English, 10.9% Polish
Employment: 15.6% management, business, and financial, 3.5% computer, engineering, and science, 8.7% education, legal, community service, arts, and media, 6.0% healthcare practitioners, 19.1% service, 16.2% sales and office, 9.2% natural resources, construction, and maintenance, 21.7% production, transportation, and material moving
Income: Per capita: $26,935; Median household: $59,375; Average household: $67,000; Households with income of $100,000 or more: 19.7%; Poverty rate: 9.3%
Educational Attainment: High school diploma or higher: 91.7%; Bachelor's degree or higher: 17.3%; Graduate/professional degree or higher: 4.6%
Housing: Homeownership rate: 87.1%; Median home value: $128,900; Median year structure built: 1980; Homeowner vacancy rate: 2.1%; Median selected monthly owner costs: $1,405 with a mortgage, $575 without a mortgage; Median gross rent: $700 per month; Rental vacancy rate: 0.0%
Health Insurance: 94.3% have insurance; 75.5% have private insurance; 31.7% have public insurance; 5.7% do not have insurance; 0.8% of children under 18 do not have insurance
Transportation: Commute: 94.9% car, 0.0% public transportation, 0.3% walk, 4.8% work from home; Mean travel time to work: 29.6 minutes

STITTVILLE (unincorporated postal area)

ZCTA: 13469

Covers a land area of 4.017 square miles and a water area of 0.073 square miles. Located at 43.21° N. Lat; 75.30° W. Long. Elevation is 538 feet.
Population: 995; Growth (since 2000): 23.3%; Density: 247.7 persons per square mile; Race: 99.1% White, 0.9% Black/African American, 0.0% Asian, 0.0% American Indian/Alaska Native, 0.0% Native Hawaiian/Other Pacific Islander, 0.0% Two or more races, 0.0% Hispanic of any race; Average household size: 2.68; Median age: 45.6; Age under 18: 23.8%; Age 65 and over: 17.3%; Males per 100 females: 101.2; Marriage status: 25.0% never married, 57.6% now married, 0.0% separated, 8.2% widowed, 9.1% divorced; Foreign born: 0.0%; Speak English only: 95.9%; With disability: 13.7%; Veterans: 5.8%; Ancestry: 34.1% American, 17.9% German, 8.1% Irish, 6.5% Italian, 5.9% Welsh
Employment: 0.0% management, business, and financial, 3.0% computer, engineering, and science, 20.4% education, legal, community service, arts, and media, 9.2% healthcare practitioners, 16.3% service, 23.4% sales and office, 22.2% natural resources, construction, and maintenance, 5.5% production, transportation, and material moving
Income: Per capita: $28,055; Median household: $80,357; Average household: $73,876; Households with income of $100,000 or more: 21.2%; Poverty rate: n/a
Educational Attainment: High school diploma or higher: 90.1%; Bachelor's degree or higher: 18.5%; Graduate/professional degree or higher: 7.6%
Housing: Homeownership rate: 89.8%; Median home value: $138,300; Median year structure built: 1955; Homeowner vacancy rate: 0.0%; Median selected monthly owner costs: $1,284 with a mortgage, $582 without a mortgage; Median gross rent: n/a per month; Rental vacancy rate: 0.0%
Health Insurance: 98.7% have insurance; 66.5% have private insurance; 42.7% have public insurance; 1.3% do not have insurance; 5.5% of children under 18 do not have insurance
Transportation: Commute: 97.5% car, 0.0% public transportation, 0.0% walk, 2.5% work from home; Mean travel time to work: 19.3 minutes

SYLVAN BEACH (village).

Covers a land area of 0.687 square miles and a water area of 0.021 square miles. Located at 43.21° N. Lat; 75.72° W. Long. Elevation is 374 feet.
Population: 682; Growth (since 2000): -36.3%; Density: 993.4 persons per square mile; Race: 93.8% White, 2.1% Black/African American, 0.0% Asian, 0.0% American Indian/Alaska Native, 0.0% Native Hawaiian/Other Pacific Islander, 4.1% Two or more races, 0.0% Hispanic of any race; Average household size: 1.89; Median age: 58.8; Age under 18: 7.8%; Age 65 and over: 43.5%; Males per 100 females: 98.0; Marriage status:

6.1% never married, 58.3% now married, 1.4% separated, 17.4% widowed, 18.2% divorced; Foreign born: 2.1%; Speak English only: 100.0%; With disability: 28.6%; Veterans: 18.6%; Ancestry: 31.8% American, 17.6% Italian, 16.9% Irish, 15.0% German, 12.3% English
Employment: 24.4% management, business, and financial, 0.0% computer, engineering, and science, 7.4% education, legal, community service, arts, and media, 6.3% healthcare practitioners, 4.0% service, 22.7% sales and office, 8.5% natural resources, construction, and maintenance, 26.7% production, transportation, and material moving
Income: Per capita: $26,111; Median household: $42,321; Average household: $49,327; Households with income of $100,000 or more: 11.1%; Poverty rate: 8.8%
Educational Attainment: High school diploma or higher: 86.3%; Bachelor's degree or higher: 17.7%; Graduate/professional degree or higher: 5.6%
Housing: Homeownership rate: 76.9%; Median home value: $97,900; Median year structure built: 1952; Homeowner vacancy rate: 9.5%; Median selected monthly owner costs: $1,135 with a mortgage, $460 without a mortgage; Median gross rent: $950 per month; Rental vacancy rate: 11.7%
Health Insurance: 96.9% have insurance; 65.4% have private insurance; 64.1% have public insurance; 3.1% do not have insurance; 0.0% of children under 18 do not have insurance
Transportation: Commute: 87.5% car, 0.0% public transportation, 0.0% walk, 12.5% work from home; Mean travel time to work: 25.7 minutes

TABERG (unincorporated postal area)

ZCTA: 13471

Covers a land area of 93.842 square miles and a water area of 0.368 square miles. Located at 43.36° N. Lat; 75.58° W. Long. Elevation is 518 feet.
Population: 3,341; Growth (since 2000): -3.6%; Density: 35.6 persons per square mile; Race: 94.6% White, 1.3% Black/African American, 0.4% Asian, 0.0% American Indian/Alaska Native, 0.0% Native Hawaiian/Other Pacific Islander, 3.2% Two or more races, 2.4% Hispanic of any race; Average household size: 2.63; Median age: 40.3; Age under 18: 24.1%; Age 65 and over: 14.8%; Males per 100 females: 101.7; Marriage status: 30.9% never married, 53.6% now married, 1.9% separated, 4.9% widowed, 10.6% divorced; Foreign born: 0.8%; Speak English only: 96.3%; With disability: 15.9%; Veterans: 11.6%; Ancestry: 28.6% American, 17.9% Irish, 16.7% German, 10.2% English, 7.9% Polish
Employment: 10.3% management, business, and financial, 1.4% computer, engineering, and science, 7.6% education, legal, community service, arts, and media, 5.0% healthcare practitioners, 24.4% service, 23.9% sales and office, 10.9% natural resources, construction, and maintenance, 16.4% production, transportation, and material moving
Income: Per capita: $21,858; Median household: $48,782; Average household: $55,386; Households with income of $100,000 or more: 14.2%; Poverty rate: 18.6%
Educational Attainment: High school diploma or higher: 86.7%; Bachelor's degree or higher: 10.9%; Graduate/professional degree or higher: 5.6%

School District(s)

Camden Central SD (PK-12)

    Enrollment: 2,225 . . . . (315) 245-4075
Housing: Homeownership rate: 81.9%; Median home value: $100,800; Median year structure built: 1984; Homeowner vacancy rate: 1.3%; Median selected monthly owner costs: $1,034 with a mortgage, $449 without a mortgage; Median gross rent: $807 per month; Rental vacancy rate: 0.0%
Health Insurance: 94.5% have insurance; 64.6% have private insurance; 46.5% have public insurance; 5.5% do not have insurance; 1.4% of children under 18 do not have insurance
Transportation: Commute: 92.0% car, 0.0% public transportation, 2.1% walk, 5.3% work from home; Mean travel time to work: 28.3 minutes

TRENTON (town).

Covers a land area of 43.376 square miles and a water area of 0.341 square miles. Located at 43.26° N. Lat; 75.21° W. Long.
Population: 4,574; Growth (since 2000): -2.1%; Density: 105.4 persons per square mile; Race: 97.7% White, 0.0% Black/African American, 0.2% Asian, 0.0% American Indian/Alaska Native, 0.0% Native Hawaiian/Other Pacific Islander, 2.1% Two or more races, 0.5% Hispanic of any race; Average household size: 2.60; Median age: 43.3; Age under 18: 24.5%; Age 65 and over: 16.4%; Males per 100 females: 100.3; Marriage status:

25.3% never married, 56.6% now married, 0.6% separated, 6.0% widowed, 12.1% divorced; Foreign born: 0.8%; Speak English only: 97.3%; With disability: 12.0%; Veterans: 11.0%; Ancestry: 22.1% American, 18.9% Irish, 16.3% German, 12.4% English, 11.9% Polish
Employment: 11.4% management, business, and financial, 3.5% computer, engineering, and science, 14.5% education, legal, community service, arts, and media, 5.4% healthcare practitioners, 13.6% service, 30.0% sales and office, 7.5% natural resources, construction, and maintenance, 14.2% production, transportation, and material moving
Income: Per capita: $31,394; Median household: $69,054; Average household: $82,106; Households with income of $100,000 or more: 29.9%; Poverty rate: 7.0%
Educational Attainment: High school diploma or higher: 93.0%; Bachelor's degree or higher: 31.4%; Graduate/professional degree or higher: 15.8%
Housing: Homeownership rate: 88.0%; Median home value: $151,700; Median year structure built: 1957; Homeowner vacancy rate: 2.5%; Median selected monthly owner costs: $1,477 with a mortgage, $568 without a mortgage; Median gross rent: $688 per month; Rental vacancy rate: 11.1%
Health Insurance: 89.8% have insurance; 73.3% have private insurance; 30.1% have public insurance; 10.2% do not have insurance; 24.0% of children under 18 do not have insurance
Transportation: Commute: 94.1% car, 0.2% public transportation, 1.0% walk, 4.0% work from home; Mean travel time to work: 27.1 minutes
Additional Information Contacts
Town of Trenton . . . . (315) 896-2664
  http://town.trenton.ny.us/content

UTICA (city). County seat. Covers a land area of 16.759 square miles and a water area of 0.256 square miles. Located at 43.10° N. Lat; 75.23° W. Long. Elevation is 456 feet.
History: The area around Utica was called "Yah-nun-da-da-sis," meaning "around the hill," by the Oneida people, in reference to the way their trails circled the nearby hills. The site was included in Cosby's Manor, a grant of 22,000 acres made by George II to William Cosby, governor of the Province of New York, and others in 1734. In 1758 the British erected Fort Schuyler. It was abandoned in the early 1760's. In 1798 the settlement was incorporated as a village, and the present name was determined by a chance selection from a hatful of paper slips. The Erie Canal brought new prosperity and the city was chartered in 1832. The textile industry, the backbone of Utica's economic structure, began with the opening of the woolen and cotton mills in the mid-1840's.
Population: 61,114; Growth (since 2000): 0.8%; Density: 3,646.7 persons per square mile; Race: 63.4% White, 15.8% Black/African American, 11.9% Asian, 0.3% American Indian/Alaska Native, 0.0% Native Hawaiian/Other Pacific Islander, 4.6% Two or more races, 12.3% Hispanic of any race; Average household size: 2.48; Median age: 34.0; Age under 18: 24.9%; Age 65 and over: 15.3%; Males per 100 females: 92.6; Marriage status: 43.8% never married, 37.0% now married, 2.6% separated, 7.8% widowed, 11.4% divorced; Foreign born: 19.4%; Speak English only: 70.8%; With disability: 18.4%; Veterans: 6.1%; Ancestry: 16.9% Italian, 9.8% Irish, 7.3% German, 6.4% American, 5.6% Yugoslavian
Employment: 9.2% management, business, and financial, 3.2% computer, engineering, and science, 11.0% education, legal, community service, arts, and media, 5.6% healthcare practitioners, 26.7% service, 23.9% sales and office, 6.4% natural resources, construction, and maintenance, 14.1% production, transportation, and material moving
Income: Per capita: $20,153; Median household: $33,873; Average household: $49,957; Households with income of $100,000 or more: 10.5%; Poverty rate: 30.4%
Educational Attainment: High school diploma or higher: 78.6%; Bachelor's degree or higher: 17.6%; Graduate/professional degree or higher: 6.2%
School District(s)
Utica Academy of Science Charter School (06-12)
  Enrollment: 409 . . . . (315) 266-1072
Utica City SD (PK-12)
  Enrollment: 10,311 . . . . (315) 792-2222
Whitesboro Central SD (KG-12)
  Enrollment: 3,262 . . . . (315) 266-3303
Four-year College(s)
SUNY Polytechnic Institute (Public)
  Enrollment: 2,912 . . . . (315) 792-7100
  Tuition: In-state $7,998; Out-of-state $17,648

Utica College (Private, Not-for-profit)
  Enrollment: 5,258 . . . . (315) 792-3111
  Tuition: In-state $20,676; Out-of-state $20,676
Two-year College(s)
Mohawk Valley Community College (Public)
  Enrollment: 6,506 . . . . (315) 792-5400
  Tuition: In-state $5,058; Out-of-state $9,308
Saint Elizabeth College of Nursing (Private, Not-for-profit, Roman Catholic)
  Enrollment: 202 . . . . (315) 801-8144
  Tuition: In-state $16,300; Out-of-state $21,264
Housing: Homeownership rate: 47.9%; Median home value: $89,400; Median year structure built: Before 1940; Homeowner vacancy rate: 2.4%; Median selected monthly owner costs: $1,074 with a mortgage, $479 without a mortgage; Median gross rent: $689 per month; Rental vacancy rate: 7.3%
Health Insurance: 93.4% have insurance; 46.2% have private insurance; 59.2% have public insurance; 6.6% do not have insurance; 2.9% of children under 18 do not have insurance
Hospitals: Faxton - Saint Luke's Healthcare; Saint Elizabeth Medical Center (201 beds)
Safety: Violent crime rate: 55.8 per 10,000 population; Property crime rate: 328.8 per 10,000 population
Newspapers: Observer-Dispatch (daily circulation 41,000)
Transportation: Commute: 85.8% car, 3.5% public transportation, 6.5% walk, 3.6% work from home; Mean travel time to work: 17.4 minutes; Amtrak: Train service available.
Additional Information Contacts
City of Utica . . . . (315) 792-0113
  http://www.cityofutica.com

VERNON (town). Covers a land area of 37.827 square miles and a water area of 0.011 square miles. Located at 43.07° N. Lat; 75.53° W. Long. Elevation is 633 feet.
Population: 5,416; Growth (since 2000): 1.5%; Density: 143.2 persons per square mile; Race: 96.5% White, 1.0% Black/African American, 0.6% Asian, 0.3% American Indian/Alaska Native, 0.0% Native Hawaiian/Other Pacific Islander, 1.6% Two or more races, 3.2% Hispanic of any race; Average household size: 2.50; Median age: 41.9; Age under 18: 19.0%; Age 65 and over: 15.6%; Males per 100 females: 98.0; Marriage status: 29.3% never married, 55.7% now married, 2.8% separated, 4.5% widowed, 10.4% divorced; Foreign born: 2.7%; Speak English only: 96.1%; With disability: 14.2%; Veterans: 8.7%; Ancestry: 33.2% American, 14.7% German, 13.4% Irish, 10.2% English, 9.1% Italian
Employment: 11.6% management, business, and financial, 4.5% computer, engineering, and science, 10.3% education, legal, community service, arts, and media, 9.8% healthcare practitioners, 17.0% service, 18.1% sales and office, 12.0% natural resources, construction, and maintenance, 16.8% production, transportation, and material moving
Income: Per capita: $30,791; Median household: $59,132; Average household: $75,316; Households with income of $100,000 or more: 26.9%; Poverty rate: 7.9%
Educational Attainment: High school diploma or higher: 91.9%; Bachelor's degree or higher: 18.5%; Graduate/professional degree or higher: 5.2%
School District(s)
Sherrill City SD (PK-12)
  Enrollment: 1,983 . . . . (315) 829-7425
Housing: Homeownership rate: 74.3%; Median home value: $122,500; Median year structure built: 1965; Homeowner vacancy rate: 2.7%; Median selected monthly owner costs: $1,331 with a mortgage, $423 without a mortgage; Median gross rent: $669 per month; Rental vacancy rate: 6.9%
Health Insurance: 94.9% have insurance; 74.7% have private insurance; 37.0% have public insurance; 5.1% do not have insurance; 2.1% of children under 18 do not have insurance
Transportation: Commute: 94.2% car, 0.6% public transportation, 1.7% walk, 1.4% work from home; Mean travel time to work: 22.0 minutes
Additional Information Contacts
Town of Vernon . . . . (315) 829-2422
  http://www.townofvernon.com

VERNON (village). Covers a land area of 0.946 square miles and a water area of 0.003 square miles. Located at 43.08° N. Lat; 75.54° W. Long. Elevation is 633 feet.
Population: 1,167; Growth (since 2000): 1.0%; Density: 1,233.7 persons per square mile; Race: 94.4% White, 0.0% Black/African American, 1.9%

Asian, 0.9% American Indian/Alaska Native, 0.0% Native Hawaiian/Other Pacific Islander, 2.7% Two or more races, 1.7% Hispanic of any race; Average household size: 2.24; Median age: 43.4; Age under 18: 15.3%; Age 65 and over: 18.7%; Males per 100 females: 99.7; Marriage status: 28.6% never married, 52.5% now married, 6.7% separated, 6.0% widowed, 12.9% divorced; Foreign born: 2.8%; Speak English only: 96.2%; With disability: 15.7%; Veterans: 10.1%; Ancestry: 36.8% American, 16.8% German, 12.5% Irish, 12.3% English, 10.3% Italian

Employment: 14.2% management, business, and financial, 1.1% computer, engineering, and science, 19.1% education, legal, community service, arts, and media, 2.6% healthcare practitioners, 18.9% service, 22.2% sales and office, 10.4% natural resources, construction, and maintenance, 11.4% production, transportation, and material moving

Income: Per capita: $28,691; Median household: $54,145; Average household: $62,651; Households with income of $100,000 or more: 20.6%; Poverty rate: 12.2%

Educational Attainment: High school diploma or higher: 92.8%; Bachelor's degree or higher: 20.5%; Graduate/professional degree or higher: 6.8%

School District(s)
Sherrill City SD (PK-12)
    Enrollment: 1,983 . . . . (315) 829-7425
Housing: Homeownership rate: 47.8%; Median home value: $116,100; Median year structure built: Before 1940; Homeowner vacancy rate: 1.2%; Median selected monthly owner costs: $1,332 with a mortgage, $516 without a mortgage; Median gross rent: $677 per month; Rental vacancy rate: 0.0%

Health Insurance: 96.9% have insurance; 72.8% have private insurance; 40.1% have public insurance; 3.1% do not have insurance; 0.0% of children under 18 do not have insurance

Safety: Violent crime rate: 8.6 per 10,000 population; Property crime rate: 180.6 per 10,000 population

Transportation: Commute: 89.9% car, 0.0% public transportation, 7.0% walk, 2.2% work from home; Mean travel time to work: 20.4 minutes

VERNON CENTER (unincorporated postal area)
ZCTA: 13477

Covers a land area of 20.250 square miles and a water area of 0 square miles. Located at 43.03° N. Lat; 75.51° W. Long. Elevation is 801 feet.

Population: 1,532; Growth (since 2000): 9.6%; Density: 75.7 persons per square mile; Race: 98.8% White, 1.2% Black/African American, 0.0% Asian, 0.0% American Indian/Alaska Native, 0.0% Native Hawaiian/Other Pacific Islander, 0.0% Two or more races, 0.0% Hispanic of any race; Average household size: 2.62; Median age: 32.6; Age under 18: 22.8%; Age 65 and over: 10.1%; Males per 100 females: 98.9; Marriage status: 33.1% never married, 58.5% now married, 2.9% separated, 1.6% widowed, 6.8% divorced; Foreign born: 0.9%; Speak English only: 98.9%; With disability: 9.7%; Veterans: 3.0%; Ancestry: 51.4% American, 16.5% German, 11.4% Polish, 8.6% Irish, 8.1% English

Employment: 9.3% management, business, and financial, 8.9% computer, engineering, and science, 7.8% education, legal, community service, arts, and media, 16.1% healthcare practitioners, 13.4% service, 10.6% sales and office, 17.9% natural resources, construction, and maintenance, 16.0% production, transportation, and material moving

Income: Per capita: $30,890; Median household: $47,862; Average household: $80,014; Households with income of $100,000 or more: 28.8%; Poverty rate: 8.8%

Educational Attainment: High school diploma or higher: 96.3%; Bachelor's degree or higher: 17.0%; Graduate/professional degree or higher: 2.2%

Housing: Homeownership rate: 79.0%; Median home value: $142,800; Median year structure built: 1977; Homeowner vacancy rate: 0.0%; Median selected monthly owner costs: $1,286 with a mortgage, $444 without a mortgage; Median gross rent: $598 per month; Rental vacancy rate: 0.0%

Health Insurance: 90.1% have insurance; 67.1% have private insurance; 34.4% have public insurance; 9.9% do not have insurance; 0.0% of children under 18 do not have insurance

Transportation: Commute: 98.2% car, 0.0% public transportation, 0.0% walk, 1.8% work from home; Mean travel time to work: 21.1 minutes

VERONA (CDP). Covers a land area of 1.878 square miles and a water area of 0 square miles. Located at 43.14° N. Lat; 75.57° W. Long. Elevation is 495 feet.

Population: 872; Growth (since 2000): n/a; Density: 464.3 persons per square mile; Race: 100.0% White, 0.0% Black/African American, 0.0% Asian, 0.0% American Indian/Alaska Native, 0.0% Native Hawaiian/Other Pacific Islander, 0.0% Two or more races, 0.0% Hispanic of any race; Average household size: 2.81; Median age: 37.3; Age under 18: 29.9%; Age 65 and over: 20.6%; Males per 100 females: 95.0; Marriage status: 17.1% never married, 59.4% now married, 0.0% separated, 13.7% widowed, 9.7% divorced; Foreign born: 0.0%; Speak English only: 100.0%; With disability: 7.1%; Veterans: 8.3%; Ancestry: 26.7% American, 18.1% English, 14.3% Italian, 10.6% Irish, 8.9% German

Employment: 12.8% management, business, and financial, 6.0% computer, engineering, and science, 0.0% education, legal, community service, arts, and media, 0.0% healthcare practitioners, 34.0% service, 14.3% sales and office, 15.5% natural resources, construction, and maintenance, 17.4% production, transportation, and material moving

Income: Per capita: $16,677; Median household: $44,423; Average household: $46,454; Households with income of $100,000 or more: n/a; Poverty rate: 15.7%

Educational Attainment: High school diploma or higher: 77.1%; Bachelor's degree or higher: 5.6%; Graduate/professional degree or higher: n/a

School District(s)
Madison-Oneida Boces
    Enrollment: n/a . . . . (315) 361-5510
Sherrill City SD (PK-12)
    Enrollment: 1,983 . . . . (315) 829-7425
Vocational/Technical School(s)
Madison Oneida BOCES-Practical Nursing Program (Public)
    Enrollment: 42 . . . . (315) 361-5800
    Tuition: $11,310
Housing: Homeownership rate: 86.1%; Median home value: $95,400; Median year structure built: 1963; Homeowner vacancy rate: 0.0%; Median selected monthly owner costs: $888 with a mortgage, $468 without a mortgage; Median gross rent: n/a per month; Rental vacancy rate: 0.0%

Health Insurance: 100.0% have insurance; 61.5% have private insurance; 59.2% have public insurance; 0.0% do not have insurance; 0.0% of children under 18 do not have insurance

Transportation: Commute: 96.2% car, 3.8% public transportation, 0.0% walk, 0.0% work from home; Mean travel time to work: 16.7 minutes

VERONA (town). Covers a land area of 69.230 square miles and a water area of 0.365 square miles. Located at 43.16° N. Lat; 75.63° W. Long. Elevation is 495 feet.

History: Site of Oneida Nation's Turning Stone Casino (68,000 square foot ; opened in 1990), first legal gambling casino in N.Y. state in over a century. Costing $10 million, it is one of the largest table game operations in the U.S. Owned and operated by the Oneida, one of 70 tribes across the U.S. who are allowed to offer gambling under the Indian Gaming Act of 1988, which was designed to generate wealth on impoverished reservations.

Population: 6,272; Growth (since 2000): -2.4%; Density: 90.6 persons per square mile; Race: 96.3% White, 1.8% Black/African American, 0.0% Asian, 0.0% American Indian/Alaska Native, 0.0% Native Hawaiian/Other Pacific Islander, 1.5% Two or more races, 0.3% Hispanic of any race; Average household size: 2.70; Median age: 42.6; Age under 18: 23.1%; Age 65 and over: 16.7%; Males per 100 females: 102.4; Marriage status: 28.8% never married, 53.3% now married, 3.1% separated, 6.1% widowed, 11.8% divorced; Foreign born: 0.3%; Speak English only: 98.4%; With disability: 17.6%; Veterans: 9.7%; Ancestry: 28.0% American, 17.6% Irish, 14.3% German, 14.3% Italian, 8.7% English

Employment: 12.2% management, business, and financial, 1.1% computer, engineering, and science, 4.6% education, legal, community service, arts, and media, 6.7% healthcare practitioners, 24.9% service, 15.1% sales and office, 13.9% natural resources, construction, and maintenance, 21.5% production, transportation, and material moving

Income: Per capita: $27,342; Median household: $58,000; Average household: $72,051; Households with income of $100,000 or more: 19.6%; Poverty rate: 18.0%

Educational Attainment: High school diploma or higher: 90.2%; Bachelor's degree or higher: 14.9%; Graduate/professional degree or higher: 5.6%

School District(s)

Madison-Oneida Boces

    Enrollment: n/a .... (315) 361-5510

Sherrill City SD (PK-12)

    Enrollment: 1,983 .... (315) 829-7425

Vocational/Technical School(s)

Madison Oneida BOCES-Practical Nursing Program (Public)

    Enrollment: 42 .... (315) 361-5800

    Tuition: $11,310

Housing: Homeownership rate: 80.6%; Median home value: $113,300; Median year structure built: 1965; Homeowner vacancy rate: 0.0%; Median selected monthly owner costs: $1,166 with a mortgage, $463 without a mortgage; Median gross rent: $738 per month; Rental vacancy rate: 10.5%

Health Insurance: 97.3% have insurance; 68.0% have private insurance; 46.6% have public insurance; 2.7% do not have insurance; 4.9% of children under 18 do not have insurance

Transportation: Commute: 90.0% car, 0.4% public transportation, 3.9% walk, 5.3% work from home; Mean travel time to work: 18.9 minutes

Additional Information Contacts

Town of Verona .... (315) 363-6799

    http://townverona.org/content

VERONA BEACH (unincorporated postal area)

ZCTA: 13162

Covers a land area of 1.758 square miles and a water area of 0.022 square miles. Located at 43.19° N. Lat; 75.71° W. Long. Elevation is 374 feet.

Population: 306; Growth (since 2000): n/a; Density: 174.1 persons per square mile; Race: 100.0% White, 0.0% Black/African American, 0.0% Asian, 0.0% American Indian/Alaska Native, 0.0% Native Hawaiian/Other Pacific Islander, 0.0% Two or more races, 0.0% Hispanic of any race; Average household size: 2.19; Median age: 42.6; Age under 18: 24.5%; Age 65 and over: 24.2%; Males per 100 females: 98.5; Marriage status: 29.8% never married, 20.5% now married, 0.0% separated, 11.2% widowed, 38.4% divorced; Foreign born: 0.0%; Speak English only: 100.0%; With disability: 0.0%; Veterans: 7.4%; Ancestry: 47.7% American, 19.3% Scotch-Irish, 13.1% Polish, 9.2% English, 5.6% Italian

Employment: 13.1% management, business, and financial, 0.0% computer, engineering, and science, 0.0% education, legal, community service, arts, and media, 0.0% healthcare practitioners, 0.0% service, 29.9% sales and office, 44.9% natural resources, construction, and maintenance, 12.1% production, transportation, and material moving

Income: Per capita: $85,031; Median household: n/a; Average household: $184,687; Households with income of $100,000 or more: 30.7%; Poverty rate: n/a

Educational Attainment: High school diploma or higher: 100.0%; Bachelor's degree or higher: 22.1%; Graduate/professional degree or higher: 14.9%

Housing: Homeownership rate: 85.7%; Median home value: $125,000; Median year structure built: 1970; Homeowner vacancy rate: 0.0%; Median selected monthly owner costs: $1,120 with a mortgage, $747 without a mortgage; Median gross rent: n/a per month; Rental vacancy rate: 0.0%

Health Insurance: 95.8% have insurance; 63.7% have private insurance; 56.2% have public insurance; 4.2% do not have insurance; 10.4% of children under 18 do not have insurance

Transportation: Commute: 100.0% car, 0.0% public transportation, 0.0% walk, 0.0% work from home; Mean travel time to work: 0.0 minutes

VIENNA (town). Covers a land area of 61.448 square miles and a water area of 33.628 square miles. Located at 43.23° N. Lat; 75.77° W. Long. Elevation is 463 feet.

Population: 5,445; Growth (since 2000): -6.4%; Density: 88.6 persons per square mile; Race: 99.0% White, 0.3% Black/African American, 0.0% Asian, 0.0% American Indian/Alaska Native, 0.0% Native Hawaiian/Other Pacific Islander, 0.8% Two or more races, 0.0% Hispanic of any race; Average household size: 2.55; Median age: 45.4; Age under 18: 24.1%; Age 65 and over: 18.7%; Males per 100 females: 102.0; Marriage status: 23.1% never married, 60.6% now married, 3.8% separated, 6.1% widowed, 10.1% divorced; Foreign born: 1.8%; Speak English only: 98.9%; With disability: 15.6%; Veterans: 12.3%; Ancestry: 29.3% American, 16.5% German, 13.8% Irish, 10.3% Italian, 10.2% English

Employment: 7.9% management, business, and financial, 3.4% computer, engineering, and science, 3.9% education, legal, community service, arts,

and media, 3.6% healthcare practitioners, 21.6% service, 20.9% sales and office, 18.8% natural resources, construction, and maintenance, 19.8% production, transportation, and material moving

Income: Per capita: $23,111; Median household: $50,924; Average household: $57,794; Households with income of $100,000 or more: 12.4%; Poverty rate: 19.3%

Educational Attainment: High school diploma or higher: 87.1%; Bachelor's degree or higher: 11.1%; Graduate/professional degree or higher: 4.2%

Housing: Homeownership rate: 81.6%; Median home value: $99,800; Median year structure built: 1968; Homeowner vacancy rate: 1.6%; Median selected monthly owner costs: $1,233 with a mortgage, $500 without a mortgage; Median gross rent: $1,046 per month; Rental vacancy rate: 11.5%

Health Insurance: 97.2% have insurance; 63.1% have private insurance; 52.2% have public insurance; 2.8% do not have insurance; 1.1% of children under 18 do not have insurance

Transportation: Commute: 94.4% car, 0.0% public transportation, 0.8% walk, 4.9% work from home; Mean travel time to work: 30.7 minutes

Additional Information Contacts

Town of Vienna .... (315) 245-2191

    http://townofvienna.ny.gov

WASHINGTON MILLS (CDP). Covers a land area of 0.670 square miles and a water area of 0 square miles. Located at 43.05° N. Lat; 75.28° W. Long. Elevation is 620 feet.

Population: 1,543; Growth (since 2000): n/a; Density: 2,303.7 persons per square mile; Race: 92.1% White, 1.4% Black/African American, 0.0% Asian, 0.0% American Indian/Alaska Native, 0.0% Native Hawaiian/Other Pacific Islander, 6.5% Two or more races, 6.7% Hispanic of any race; Average household size: 2.18; Median age: 36.1; Age under 18: 9.7%; Age 65 and over: 19.1%; Males per 100 females: 92.7; Marriage status: 44.7% never married, 42.8% now married, 3.9% separated, 4.0% widowed, 8.6% divorced; Foreign born: 9.3%; Speak English only: 94.9%; With disability: 6.2%; Veterans: 3.0%; Ancestry: 33.4% American, 21.5% Irish, 20.2% Italian, 9.2% German, 4.3% English

Employment: 6.5% management, business, and financial, 6.6% computer, engineering, and science, 6.8% education, legal, community service, arts, and media, 10.6% healthcare practitioners, 38.9% service, 23.3% sales and office, 1.9% natural resources, construction, and maintenance, 5.5% production, transportation, and material moving

Income: Per capita: $28,871; Median household: $55,881; Average household: $60,775; Households with income of $100,000 or more: 19.2%; Poverty rate: 11.1%

Educational Attainment: High school diploma or higher: 95.0%; Bachelor's degree or higher: 26.4%; Graduate/professional degree or higher: 12.1%

Housing: Homeownership rate: 52.9%; Median home value: $167,500; Median year structure built: 1968; Homeowner vacancy rate: 0.0%; Median selected monthly owner costs: $1,162 with a mortgage, $543 without a mortgage; Median gross rent: $946 per month; Rental vacancy rate: 15.1%

Health Insurance: 95.7% have insurance; 72.7% have private insurance; 36.0% have public insurance; 4.3% do not have insurance; 0.0% of children under 18 do not have insurance

Transportation: Commute: 100.0% car, 0.0% public transportation, 0.0% walk, 0.0% work from home; Mean travel time to work: 14.9 minutes

WATERVILLE (village). Covers a land area of 1.416 square miles and a water area of 0 square miles. Located at 42.93° N. Lat; 75.38° W. Long. Elevation is 1,201 feet.

History: George Eastman born here. Incorporated 1871.

Population: 1,610; Growth (since 2000): -6.4%; Density: 1,137.1 persons per square mile; Race: 98.3% White, 0.6% Black/African American, 0.0% Asian, 0.0% American Indian/Alaska Native, 0.0% Native Hawaiian/Other Pacific Islander, 1.0% Two or more races, 0.7% Hispanic of any race; Average household size: 2.24; Median age: 46.0; Age under 18: 16.5%; Age 65 and over: 24.0%; Males per 100 females: 91.2; Marriage status: 29.7% never married, 48.0% now married, 2.9% separated, 10.2% widowed, 12.2% divorced; Foreign born: 0.4%; Speak English only: 99.5%; With disability: 17.4%; Veterans: 8.0%; Ancestry: 29.4% American, 17.6% Irish, 17.1% German, 13.7% English, 8.6% Italian

Employment: 13.6% management, business, and financial, 5.0% computer, engineering, and science, 11.0% education, legal, community service, arts, and media, 8.5% healthcare practitioners, 18.4% service,

20.6% sales and office, 9.2% natural resources, construction, and maintenance, 13.6% production, transportation, and material moving

Income: Per capita: $26,642; Median household: $48,365; Average household: $60,898; Households with income of $100,000 or more: 21.0%; Poverty rate: 11.5%

Educational Attainment: High school diploma or higher: 94.2%; Bachelor's degree or higher: 28.8%; Graduate/professional degree or higher: 10.4%

School District(s)

Waterville Central SD (KG-12)

   Enrollment: 796 . . . . (315) 841-3910

Housing: Homeownership rate: 55.8%; Median home value: $110,400; Median year structure built: Before 1940; Homeowner vacancy rate: 5.3%; Median selected monthly owner costs: $1,252 with a mortgage, $541 without a mortgage; Median gross rent: $639 per month; Rental vacancy rate: 0.0%

Health Insurance: 96.0% have insurance; 76.7% have private insurance; 39.0% have public insurance; 4.0% do not have insurance; 3.8% of children under 18 do not have insurance

Newspapers: Waterville Times (weekly circulation 2,600)

Transportation: Commute: 89.5% car, 0.4% public transportation, 8.4% walk, 1.6% work from home; Mean travel time to work: 23.0 minutes

WESTDALE (unincorporated postal area)

ZCTA: 13483

Covers a land area of 6.920 square miles and a water area of 0.082 square miles. Located at 43.40° N. Lat; 75.83° W. Long. Elevation is 551 feet.

Population: 306; Growth (since 2000): 91.3%; Density: 44.2 persons per square mile; Race: 100.0% White, 0.0% Black/African American, 0.0% Asian, 0.0% American Indian/Alaska Native, 0.0% Native Hawaiian/Other Pacific Islander, 0.0% Two or more races, 0.0% Hispanic of any race; Average household size: 2.97; Median age: 35.9; Age under 18: 21.9%; Age 65 and over: 11.8%; Males per 100 females: 82.9; Marriage status: 38.6% never married, 47.9% now married, 3.5% separated, 4.2% widowed, 9.3% divorced; Foreign born: 0.0%; Speak English only: 100.0%; With disability: 10.1%; Veterans: 6.7%; Ancestry: 43.1% American, 14.1% Italian, 9.8% English, 7.2% Irish, 6.9% Ukrainian

Employment: 7.4% management, business, and financial, 0.0% computer, engineering, and science, 4.3% education, legal, community service, arts, and media, 3.7% healthcare practitioners, 20.2% service, 22.1% sales and office, 25.8% natural resources, construction, and maintenance, 16.6% production, transportation, and material moving

Income: Per capita: $21,271; Median household: n/a; Average household: $58,924; Households with income of $100,000 or more: 7.7%; Poverty rate: 3.3%

Educational Attainment: High school diploma or higher: 71.2%; Bachelor's degree or higher: n/a; Graduate/professional degree or higher: n/a

Housing: Homeownership rate: 69.9%; Median home value: $158,300; Median year structure built: 1976; Homeowner vacancy rate: 0.0%; Median selected monthly owner costs: $1,135 with a mortgage, $369 without a mortgage; Median gross rent: $875 per month; Rental vacancy rate: 0.0%

Health Insurance: 95.4% have insurance; 54.6% have private insurance; 44.1% have public insurance; 4.6% do not have insurance; 0.0% of children under 18 do not have insurance

Transportation: Commute: 100.0% car, 0.0% public transportation, 0.0% walk, 0.0% work from home; Mean travel time to work: 30.5 minutes

WESTERN (town). Covers a land area of 51.206 square miles and a water area of 3.465 square miles. Located at 43.35° N. Lat; 75.41° W. Long.

Population: 2,092; Growth (since 2000): 3.1%; Density: 40.9 persons per square mile; Race: 99.4% White, 0.0% Black/African American, 0.5% Asian, 0.0% American Indian/Alaska Native, 0.0% Native Hawaiian/Other Pacific Islander, 0.1% Two or more races, 0.0% Hispanic of any race; Average household size: 2.51; Median age: 45.1; Age under 18: 20.6%; Age 65 and over: 18.9%; Males per 100 females: 104.9; Marriage status: 25.1% never married, 57.7% now married, 0.0% separated, 6.8% widowed, 10.3% divorced; Foreign born: 1.2%; Speak English only: 96.6%; With disability: 13.3%; Veterans: 8.3%; Ancestry: 26.3% American, 21.0% German, 14.9% Irish, 12.0% Polish, 11.3% Italian

Employment: 13.1% management, business, and financial, 6.4% computer, engineering, and science, 2.6% education, legal, community service, arts, and media, 11.1% healthcare practitioners, 17.0% service, 27.7% sales and office, 15.4% natural resources, construction, and maintenance, 6.7% production, transportation, and material moving

Income: Per capita: $31,318; Median household: $63,019; Average household: $77,292; Households with income of $100,000 or more: 23.1%; Poverty rate: 8.2%

Educational Attainment: High school diploma or higher: 92.8%; Bachelor's degree or higher: 23.1%; Graduate/professional degree or higher: 9.0%

Housing: Homeownership rate: 77.5%; Median home value: $135,500; Median year structure built: 1964; Homeowner vacancy rate: 1.6%; Median selected monthly owner costs: $1,313 with a mortgage, $493 without a mortgage; Median gross rent: $850 per month; Rental vacancy rate: 0.0%

Health Insurance: 96.8% have insurance; 76.1% have private insurance; 38.4% have public insurance; 3.2% do not have insurance; 2.1% of children under 18 do not have insurance

Transportation: Commute: 93.0% car, 0.0% public transportation, 4.1% walk, 1.6% work from home; Mean travel time to work: 23.6 minutes

WESTERNVILLE (unincorporated postal area)

ZCTA: 13486

Covers a land area of 29.450 square miles and a water area of 3.465 square miles. Located at 43.35° N. Lat; 75.34° W. Long. Elevation is 561 feet.

Population: 837; Growth (since 2000): 0.6%; Density: 28.4 persons per square mile; Race: 100.0% White, 0.0% Black/African American, 0.0% Asian, 0.0% American Indian/Alaska Native, 0.0% Native Hawaiian/Other Pacific Islander, 0.0% Two or more races, 0.0% Hispanic of any race; Average household size: 2.29; Median age: 44.2; Age under 18: 19.7%; Age 65 and over: 19.4%; Males per 100 females: 99.3; Marriage status: 34.5% never married, 51.3% now married, 0.0% separated, 7.1% widowed, 7.1% divorced; Foreign born: 0.4%; Speak English only: 95.0%; With disability: 14.9%; Veterans: 8.2%; Ancestry: 24.5% American, 19.5% German, 15.2% Polish, 13.1% Irish, 9.7% English

Employment: 12.6% management, business, and financial, 7.7% computer, engineering, and science, 0.7% education, legal, community service, arts, and media, 9.7% healthcare practitioners, 15.3% service, 32.7% sales and office, 6.4% natural resources, construction, and maintenance, 14.9% production, transportation, and material moving

Income: Per capita: $30,023; Median household: $56,875; Average household: $67,700; Households with income of $100,000 or more: 16.6%; Poverty rate: 11.3%

Educational Attainment: High school diploma or higher: 92.8%; Bachelor's degree or higher: 19.0%; Graduate/professional degree or higher: 8.6%

Housing: Homeownership rate: 77.8%; Median home value: $101,600; Median year structure built: 1960; Homeowner vacancy rate: 2.4%; Median selected monthly owner costs: $1,408 with a mortgage, $430 without a mortgage; Median gross rent: $782 per month; Rental vacancy rate: 0.0%

Health Insurance: 91.6% have insurance; 70.1% have private insurance; 43.0% have public insurance; 8.4% do not have insurance; 5.7% of children under 18 do not have insurance

Transportation: Commute: 96.2% car, 0.0% public transportation, 3.8% walk, 0.0% work from home; Mean travel time to work: 22.5 minutes

WESTMORELAND (CDP). Covers a land area of 0.687 square miles and a water area of 0 square miles. Located at 43.12° N. Lat; 75.40° W. Long. Elevation is 522 feet.

Population: 776; Growth (since 2000): n/a; Density: 1,129.9 persons per square mile; Race: 73.5% White, 0.0% Black/African American, 10.1% Asian, 0.0% American Indian/Alaska Native, 0.0% Native Hawaiian/Other Pacific Islander, 16.5% Two or more races, 0.0% Hispanic of any race; Average household size: 2.69; Median age: 36.7; Age under 18: 33.9%; Age 65 and over: 9.9%; Males per 100 females: 95.9; Marriage status: 34.1% never married, 45.0% now married, 0.0% separated, 2.3% widowed, 18.5% divorced; Foreign born: 10.1%; Speak English only: 84.2%; With disability: 0.0%; Veterans: 9.9%; Ancestry: 24.9% American, 22.0% Greek, 16.5% Italian, 15.7% German, 14.9% English

Employment: 15.5% management, business, and financial, 4.0% computer, engineering, and science, 4.0% education, legal, community service, arts, and media, 0.0% healthcare practitioners, 39.2% service,

16.5% sales and office, 10.4% natural resources, construction, and maintenance, 10.4% production, transportation, and material moving
Income: Per capita: $25,418; Median household: $82,594; Average household: $68,307; Households with income of $100,000 or more: 23.2%; Poverty rate: n/a
Educational Attainment: High school diploma or higher: 100.0%; Bachelor's degree or higher: 21.2%; Graduate/professional degree or higher: 10.2%

School District(s)
Westmoreland Central SD (KG-12)
    Enrollment: 934 . . . . (315) 557-2614
Housing: Homeownership rate: 59.2%; Median home value: $168,800; Median year structure built: 1980; Homeowner vacancy rate: 0.0%; Median selected monthly owner costs: $2,188 with a mortgage, $659 without a mortgage; Median gross rent: n/a per month; Rental vacancy rate: 0.0%
Health Insurance: 94.1% have insurance; 82.0% have private insurance; 33.0% have public insurance; 5.9% do not have insurance; 0.0% of children under 18 do not have insurance
Transportation: Commute: 81.3% car, 0.0% public transportation, 0.0% walk, 18.7% work from home; Mean travel time to work: 23.5 minutes

WESTMORELAND (town). Covers a land area of 43.136 square miles and a water area of 0.015 square miles. Located at 43.12° N. Lat; 75.45° W. Long. Elevation is 522 feet.
Population: 6,115; Growth (since 2000): -1.5%; Density: 141.8 persons per square mile; Race: 91.6% White, 0.6% Black/African American, 1.9% Asian, 0.0% American Indian/Alaska Native, 0.2% Native Hawaiian/Other Pacific Islander, 5.8% Two or more races, 0.9% Hispanic of any race; Average household size: 2.46; Median age: 44.6; Age under 18: 22.9%; Age 65 and over: 17.1%; Males per 100 females: 100.4; Marriage status: 25.1% never married, 56.5% now married, 4.3% separated, 9.6% widowed, 8.8% divorced; Foreign born: 3.3%; Speak English only: 95.6%; With disability: 10.5%; Veterans: 7.5%; Ancestry: 18.5% German, 16.2% American, 15.7% Irish, 15.2% Italian, 14.6% Polish
Employment: 16.8% management, business, and financial, 5.9% computer, engineering, and science, 7.3% education, legal, community service, arts, and media, 3.0% healthcare practitioners, 20.0% service, 19.9% sales and office, 14.3% natural resources, construction, and maintenance, 12.8% production, transportation, and material moving
Income: Per capita: $29,893; Median household: $64,961; Average household: $74,008; Households with income of $100,000 or more: 24.9%; Poverty rate: 8.7%
Educational Attainment: High school diploma or higher: 91.4%; Bachelor's degree or higher: 22.9%; Graduate/professional degree or higher: 10.0%

School District(s)
Westmoreland Central SD (KG-12)
    Enrollment: 934 . . . . (315) 557-2614
Housing: Homeownership rate: 83.0%; Median home value: $151,100; Median year structure built: 1976; Homeowner vacancy rate: 0.0%; Median selected monthly owner costs: $1,413 with a mortgage, $586 without a mortgage; Median gross rent: $1,027 per month; Rental vacancy rate: 0.0%
Health Insurance: 93.5% have insurance; 77.2% have private insurance; 33.7% have public insurance; 6.5% do not have insurance; 2.9% of children under 18 do not have insurance
Transportation: Commute: 89.4% car, 0.0% public transportation, 0.7% walk, 10.0% work from home; Mean travel time to work: 27.7 minutes
Additional Information Contacts
Town of Westmoreland . . . . (315) 853-8001
    http://town.westmoreland.ny.us/content

WHITESBORO (village). Covers a land area of 1.050 square miles and a water area of 0 square miles. Located at 43.12° N. Lat; 75.30° W. Long. Elevation is 423 feet.
History: Settled 1784, incorporated 1813.
Population: 3,690; Growth (since 2000): -6.4%; Density: 3,515.6 persons per square mile; Race: 99.5% White, 0.0% Black/African American, 0.0% Asian, 0.5% American Indian/Alaska Native, 0.0% Native Hawaiian/Other Pacific Islander, 0.0% Two or more races, 0.7% Hispanic of any race; Average household size: 2.08; Median age: 42.7; Age under 18: 19.9%; Age 65 and over: 14.6%; Males per 100 females: 86.7; Marriage status: 37.1% never married, 33.4% now married, 5.6% separated, 5.7% widowed, 23.8% divorced; Foreign born: 0.8%; Speak English only: 98.6%;

With disability: 18.0%; Veterans: 8.1%; Ancestry: 24.9% American, 21.4% Irish, 16.2% Polish, 13.6% German, 13.0% Italian
Employment: 4.7% management, business, and financial, 4.1% computer, engineering, and science, 4.3% education, legal, community service, arts, and media, 3.6% healthcare practitioners, 31.8% service, 30.3% sales and office, 13.1% natural resources, construction, and maintenance, 8.1% production, transportation, and material moving
Income: Per capita: $26,171; Median household: $39,500; Average household: $52,670; Households with income of $100,000 or more: 4.8%; Poverty rate: 17.0%
Educational Attainment: High school diploma or higher: 91.5%; Bachelor's degree or higher: 15.7%; Graduate/professional degree or higher: 3.4%

School District(s)
Whitesboro Central SD (KG-12)
    Enrollment: 3,262 . . . . (315) 266-3303
Housing: Homeownership rate: 53.8%; Median home value: $94,100; Median year structure built: 1948; Homeowner vacancy rate: 1.4%; Median selected monthly owner costs: $1,087 with a mortgage, $508 without a mortgage; Median gross rent: $648 per month; Rental vacancy rate: 0.0%
Health Insurance: 96.4% have insurance; 66.2% have private insurance; 42.4% have public insurance; 3.6% do not have insurance; 0.0% of children under 18 do not have insurance
Safety: Violent crime rate: 0.0 per 10,000 population; Property crime rate: 98.6 per 10,000 population
Transportation: Commute: 90.2% car, 0.0% public transportation, 1.5% walk, 7.2% work from home; Mean travel time to work: 13.9 minutes
Additional Information Contacts
Village of Whitesboro . . . . (315) 736-1613
    http://village.whitesboro.ny.us/content

WHITESTOWN (town). Covers a land area of 27.318 square miles and a water area of 0.002 square miles. Located at 43.14° N. Lat; 75.34° W. Long.
Population: 18,509; Growth (since 2000): -0.7%; Density: 677.5 persons per square mile; Race: 97.1% White, 1.2% Black/African American, 0.9% Asian, 0.2% American Indian/Alaska Native, 0.0% Native Hawaiian/Other Pacific Islander, 0.7% Two or more races, 1.6% Hispanic of any race; Average household size: 2.23; Median age: 43.8; Age under 18: 19.5%; Age 65 and over: 18.9%; Males per 100 females: 96.0; Marriage status: 32.4% never married, 47.2% now married, 1.8% separated, 7.1% widowed, 13.4% divorced; Foreign born: 2.5%; Speak English only: 95.6%; With disability: 13.8%; Veterans: 11.2%; Ancestry: 21.0% Irish, 20.3% Italian, 18.5% Polish, 15.7% German, 15.7% American
Employment: 15.8% management, business, and financial, 5.2% computer, engineering, and science, 11.3% education, legal, community service, arts, and media, 5.6% healthcare practitioners, 18.7% service, 26.3% sales and office, 7.5% natural resources, construction, and maintenance, 9.6% production, transportation, and material moving
Income: Per capita: $31,591; Median household: $54,600; Average household: $70,410; Households with income of $100,000 or more: 18.9%; Poverty rate: 9.5%
Educational Attainment: High school diploma or higher: 93.1%; Bachelor's degree or higher: 27.9%; Graduate/professional degree or higher: 10.2%
Housing: Homeownership rate: 70.2%; Median home value: $127,800; Median year structure built: 1956; Homeowner vacancy rate: 0.6%; Median selected monthly owner costs: $1,208 with a mortgage, $523 without a mortgage; Median gross rent: $754 per month; Rental vacancy rate: 3.0%
Health Insurance: 97.1% have insurance; 76.7% have private insurance; 37.2% have public insurance; 2.9% do not have insurance; 0.0% of children under 18 do not have insurance
Safety: Violent crime rate: 1.1 per 10,000 population; Property crime rate: 32.6 per 10,000 population
Transportation: Commute: 92.2% car, 0.4% public transportation, 1.8% walk, 5.2% work from home; Mean travel time to work: 16.2 minutes
Additional Information Contacts
Town of Whitestown . . . . (315) 736-4224
    http://town.whitestown.ny.us/content

WOODGATE (unincorporated postal area)
ZCTA: 13494
    Covers a land area of 17.509 square miles and a water area of 0.408 square miles. Located at 43.53° N. Lat; 75.14° W. Long. Elevation is 1,480 feet.

Population: 232; Growth (since 2000): n/a; Density: 13.3 persons per square mile; Race: 99.1% White, 0.0% Black/African American, 0.9% Asian, 0.0% American Indian/Alaska Native, 0.0% Native Hawaiian/Other Pacific Islander, 0.0% Two or more races, 0.0% Hispanic of any race; Average household size: 2.23; Median age: 55.4; Age under 18: 3.0%; Age 65 and over: 29.3%; Males per 100 females: 107.9; Marriage status: 26.9% never married, 51.1% now married, 0.4% separated, 7.9% widowed, 14.1% divorced; Foreign born: 0.9%; Speak English only: 99.1%; With disability: 17.7%; Veterans: 15.1%; Ancestry: 22.4% American, 16.4% English, 14.2% Irish, 9.5% German, 9.5% Italian

Employment: 27.2% management, business, and financial, 0.0% computer, engineering, and science, 18.4% education, legal, community service, arts, and media, 12.3% healthcare practitioners, 3.5% service, 21.1% sales and office, 17.5% natural resources, construction, and maintenance, 0.0% production, transportation, and material moving

Income: Per capita: $37,136; Median household: $63,333; Average household: $80,463; Households with income of $100,000 or more: 30.8%; Poverty rate: 3.0%

Educational Attainment: High school diploma or higher: 88.2%; Bachelor's degree or higher: 24.6%; Graduate/professional degree or higher: 9.1%

Housing: Homeownership rate: 95.2%; Median home value: $158,500; Median year structure built: 1960; Homeowner vacancy rate: 0.0%; Median selected monthly owner costs: $1,107 with a mortgage, $403 without a mortgage; Median gross rent: n/a per month; Rental vacancy rate: 0.0%

Health Insurance: 94.0% have insurance; 78.4% have private insurance; 38.4% have public insurance; 6.0% do not have insurance; 0.0% of children under 18 do not have insurance

Transportation: Commute: 68.2% car, 0.0% public transportation, 6.5% walk, 25.2% work from home; Mean travel time to work: 29.3 minutes

YORKVILLE (village).

Covers a land area of 0.671 square miles and a water area of 0 square miles. Located at 43.11° N. Lat; 75.27° W. Long. Elevation is 433 feet.

History: Henry Inman, one of the most prominent and versatile of the first generation of American-trained artists, was born here in 1801.

Population: 2,629; Growth (since 2000): -1.7%; Density: 3,916.0 persons per square mile; Race: 98.1% White, 0.4% Black/African American, 1.1% Asian, 0.0% American Indian/Alaska Native, 0.0% Native Hawaiian/Other Pacific Islander, 0.5% Two or more races, 5.1% Hispanic of any race; Average household size: 2.49; Median age: 32.6; Age under 18: 23.2%; Age 65 and over: 14.9%; Males per 100 females: 95.4; Marriage status: 45.6% never married, 38.5% now married, 0.9% separated, 4.8% widowed, 11.1% divorced; Foreign born: 4.8%; Speak English only: 88.6%; With disability: 11.5%; Veterans: 8.4%; Ancestry: 22.2% Polish, 17.2% Irish, 16.5% German, 15.6% Italian, 12.4% American

Employment: 15.1% management, business, and financial, 2.1% computer, engineering, and science, 12.3% education, legal, community service, arts, and media, 4.8% healthcare practitioners, 17.5% service, 29.9% sales and office, 7.5% natural resources, construction, and maintenance, 10.7% production, transportation, and material moving

Income: Per capita: $26,444; Median household: $54,816; Average household: $64,034; Households with income of $100,000 or more: 9.4%; Poverty rate: 12.5%

Educational Attainment: High school diploma or higher: 93.9%; Bachelor's degree or higher: 24.6%; Graduate/professional degree or higher: 8.6%

Housing: Homeownership rate: 64.6%; Median home value: $92,500; Median year structure built: 1942; Homeowner vacancy rate: 0.0%; Median selected monthly owner costs: $1,055 with a mortgage, $534 without a mortgage; Median gross rent: $764 per month; Rental vacancy rate: 10.3%

Health Insurance: 93.3% have insurance; 70.6% have private insurance; 38.5% have public insurance; 6.7% do not have insurance; 0.0% of children under 18 do not have insurance

Safety: Violent crime rate: 19.2 per 10,000 population; Property crime rate: 92.1 per 10,000 population

Transportation: Commute: 92.1% car, 2.2% public transportation, 0.0% walk, 5.1% work from home; Mean travel time to work: 18.5 minutes

Onondaga County

Located in central New York, in the Finger Lakes area; drained by the Seneca and Oswego Rivers; includes Oneida and Skaneateles Lakes.

Covers a land area of 778.390 square miles, a water area of 27.228 square miles, and is located in the Eastern Time Zone at 43.01° N. Lat., 76.20° W. Long. The county was founded in 1794. County seat is Syracuse.

Onondaga County is part of the Syracuse, NY Metropolitan Statistical Area. The entire metro area includes: Madison County, NY; Onondaga County, NY; Oswego County, NY

Weather Station: Syracuse Hancock Int'l Arpt   Elevation: 410 feet

	Jan	Feb	Mar	Apr	May	Jun	Jul	Aug	Sep	Oct	Nov	Dec
High	32	34	43	57	69	77	82	80	72	60	48	37
Low	16	17	25	36	46	56	61	60	52	41	33	22
Precip	2.5	2.0	3.0	3.3	3.2	3.2	3.7	3.4	3.6	3.4	3.5	3.1
Snow	34.9	26.2	18.7	3.8	0.1	tr	tr	tr	tr	0.4	9.7	30.7

High and Low temperatures in degrees Fahrenheit; Precipitation and Snow in inches

Population: 467,669; Growth (since 2000): 2.0%; Density: 600.8 persons per square mile; Race: 79.9% White, 11.2% Black/African American, 3.9% Asian, 0.5% American Indian/Alaska Native, 0.0% Native Hawaiian/Other Pacific Islander, 3.4% two or more races, 4.7% Hispanic of any race; Average household size: 2.41; Median age: 38.8; Age under 18: 21.7%; Age 65 and over: 15.7%; Males per 100 females: 92.9; Marriage status: 36.6% never married, 46.8% now married, 2.0% separated, 6.0% widowed, 10.6% divorced; Foreign born: 7.6%; Speak English only: 89.5%; With disability: 12.5%; Veterans: 7.2%; Ancestry: 21.6% Irish, 17.0% Italian, 16.6% German, 10.7% English, 6.2% Polish

Religion: Six largest groups: 35.0% Catholicism, 4.4% Methodist/Pietist, 2.4% Baptist, 2.1% Non-denominational Protestant, 1.7% Lutheran, 1.5% Pentecostal

Economy: Unemployment rate: 3.5%; Leading industries: 14.2 % retail trade; 10.9 % health care and social assistance; 10.6 % other services (except public administration); Farms: 681 totaling 150,269 acres; Company size: 8 employ 1,000 or more persons, 36 employ 500 to 999 persons, 294 employ 100 to 499 persons, 11,371 employs less than 100 persons; Business ownership: 11,094 women-owned, 2,442 Black-owned, 834 Hispanic-owned, 1,222 Asian-owned, 223 American Indian/Alaska Native-owned

Employment: 14.4% management, business, and financial, 5.3% computer, engineering, and science, 13.8% education, legal, community service, arts, and media, 7.8% healthcare practitioners, 17.4% service, 25.3% sales and office, 6.7% natural resources, construction, and maintenance, 9.4% production, transportation, and material moving

Income: Per capita: $31,436; Median household: $57,271; Average household: $76,584; Households with income of $100,000 or more: 25.0%; Poverty rate: 14.9%

Educational Attainment: High school diploma or higher: 90.8%; Bachelor's degree or higher: 35.0%; Graduate/professional degree or higher: 15.4%

Housing: Homeownership rate: 64.9%; Median home value: $139,400; Median year structure built: 1961; Homeowner vacancy rate: 1.7%; Median selected monthly owner costs: $1,353 with a mortgage, $553 without a mortgage; Median gross rent: $823 per month; Rental vacancy rate: 6.6%

Vital Statistics: Birth rate: 110.8 per 10,000 population; Death rate: 90.0 per 10,000 population; Age-adjusted cancer mortality rate: 153.8 deaths per 100,000 population

Health Insurance: 94.8% have insurance; 73.4% have private insurance; 36.4% have public insurance; 5.2% do not have insurance; 3.0% of children under 18 do not have insurance

Health Care: Physicians: 52.1 per 10,000 population; Dentists: 7.5 per 10,000 population; Hospital beds: 39.4 per 10,000 population; Hospital admissions: 1,724.5 per 10,000 population

Air Quality Index (AQI): Percent of Days: 93.2% good, 6.8% moderate, 0.0% unhealthy for sensitive individuals, 0.0% unhealthy, 0.0% very unhealthy; Annual median: 35; Annual maximum: 93

Transportation: Commute: 87.5% car, 3.1% public transportation, 4.3% walk, 4.0% work from home; Mean travel time to work: 20.1 minutes

2016 Presidential Election: 40.1% Trump, 53.9% Clinton, 4.1% Johnson, 1.5% Stein

National and State Parks: Cicero Swamp State Wildlife Management Area; Clark Reservation State Park; Erie Canal State Park; Green Lakes State Park; Three Rivers State Wildlife Management Area

Additional Information Contacts

Onondaga Government . . . . (315) 435-2229
    http://www.ongov.net

Onondaga County Communities

APULIA STATION (unincorporated postal area)
ZCTA: 13020

Covers a land area of 0.468 square miles and a water area of 0 square miles. Located at 42.82° N. Lat; 76.07° W. Long. Elevation is 1,243 feet.

Population: 132; Growth (since 2000): n/a; Density: 282.3 persons per square mile; Race: 100.0% White, 0.0% Black/African American, 0.0% Asian, 0.0% American Indian/Alaska Native, 0.0% Native Hawaiian/Other Pacific Islander, 0.0% Two or more races, 0.0% Hispanic of any race; Average household size: 1.78; Median age: 46.1; Age under 18: 13.6%; Age 65 and over: 3.8%; Males per 100 females: 120.6; Marriage status: 22.8% never married, 42.1% now married, 0.0% separated, 0.0% widowed, 35.1% divorced; Foreign born: 0.0%; Speak English only: 98.5%; With disability: 1.5%; Veterans: 8.8%; Ancestry: 67.4% Irish, 30.3% Polish, 28.8% German, 26.5% Italian, 8.3% English

Employment: 6.2% management, business, and financial, 1.2% computer, engineering, and science, 0.0% education, legal, community service, arts, and media, 0.0% healthcare practitioners, 60.5% service, 8.6% sales and office, 9.9% natural resources, construction, and maintenance, 13.6% production, transportation, and material moving

Income: Per capita: $33,898; Median household: $56,750; Average household: $60,092; Households with income of $100,000 or more: 1.4%; Poverty rate: 5.3%

Educational Attainment: High school diploma or higher: 100.0%; Bachelor's degree or higher: 38.1%; Graduate/professional degree or higher: n/a

Housing: Homeownership rate: 100.0%; Median home value: $112,900; Median year structure built: 2001; Homeowner vacancy rate: 0.0%; Median selected monthly owner costs: $754 with a mortgage, $0 without a mortgage; Median gross rent: n/a per month; Rental vacancy rate: 0.0%

Health Insurance: 100.0% have insurance; 87.9% have private insurance; 15.9% have public insurance; 0.0% do not have insurance; 0.0% of children under 18 do not have insurance

Transportation: Commute: 100.0% car, 0.0% public transportation, 0.0% walk, 0.0% work from home; Mean travel time to work: 25.4 minutes

BALDWINSVILLE (village).
Covers a land area of 3.092 square miles and a water area of 0.180 square miles. Located at 43.16° N. Lat; 76.33° W. Long. Elevation is 381 feet.

History: Settled 1796, incorporated 1847.

Population: 7,532; Growth (since 2000): 6.8%; Density: 2,435.6 persons per square mile; Race: 96.4% White, 0.7% Black/African American, 0.5% Asian, 0.3% American Indian/Alaska Native, 0.0% Native Hawaiian/Other Pacific Islander, 1.9% Two or more races, 2.2% Hispanic of any race; Average household size: 2.26; Median age: 47.6; Age under 18: 19.1%; Age 65 and over: 23.8%; Males per 100 females: 89.8; Marriage status: 25.6% never married, 49.6% now married, 0.8% separated, 10.5% widowed, 14.4% divorced; Foreign born: 1.8%; Speak English only: 96.7%; With disability: 12.9%; Veterans: 8.9%; Ancestry: 28.2% German, 25.9% Irish, 17.1% English, 17.0% Italian, 7.6% French

Employment: 7.9% management, business, and financial, 7.9% computer, engineering, and science, 11.5% education, legal, community service, arts, and media, 7.8% healthcare practitioners, 15.9% service, 26.5% sales and office, 12.4% natural resources, construction, and maintenance, 10.1% production, transportation, and material moving

Income: Per capita: $29,542; Median household: $53,100; Average household: $66,223; Households with income of $100,000 or more: 20.1%; Poverty rate: 6.8%

Educational Attainment: High school diploma or higher: 94.1%; Bachelor's degree or higher: 29.0%; Graduate/professional degree or higher: 9.7%

School District(s)
Baldwinsville Central SD (KG-12)
    Enrollment: 5,604 . . . . (315) 638-6043

Housing: Homeownership rate: 61.4%; Median home value: $118,700; Median year structure built: 1960; Homeowner vacancy rate: 2.1%; Median selected monthly owner costs: $1,220 with a mortgage, $493 without a mortgage; Median gross rent: $777 per month; Rental vacancy rate: 1.4%

Health Insurance: 95.7% have insurance; 74.5% have private insurance; 37.9% have public insurance; 4.3% do not have insurance; 1.4% of children under 18 do not have insurance

Safety: Violent crime rate: 7.8 per 10,000 population; Property crime rate: 87.5 per 10,000 population

Transportation: Commute: 93.7% car, 0.1% public transportation, 2.2% walk, 4.0% work from home; Mean travel time to work: 22.1 minutes

Additional Information Contacts
Village of Baldwinsville . . . . (315) 635-3521
  http://www.baldwinsville.org

BREWERTON (CDP).
Covers a land area of 3.166 square miles and a water area of 0.172 square miles. Located at 43.23° N. Lat; 76.14° W. Long. Elevation is 384 feet.

History: Here are remains of Fort Brewerton (1759), now in state reservation.

Population: 4,011; Growth (since 2000): 16.2%; Density: 1,266.7 persons per square mile; Race: 94.8% White, 0.0% Black/African American, 2.6% Asian, 0.0% American Indian/Alaska Native, 0.0% Native Hawaiian/Other Pacific Islander, 1.8% Two or more races, 2.4% Hispanic of any race; Average household size: 2.51; Median age: 36.3; Age under 18: 25.3%; Age 65 and over: 11.7%; Males per 100 females: 96.6; Marriage status: 30.4% never married, 51.4% now married, 3.5% separated, 5.4% widowed, 12.8% divorced; Foreign born: 3.5%; Speak English only: 90.3%; With disability: 9.3%; Veterans: 6.2%; Ancestry: 20.9% German, 19.3% Italian, 17.6% English, 13.4% Irish, 11.5% Polish

Employment: 13.5% management, business, and financial, 6.3% computer, engineering, and science, 7.7% education, legal, community service, arts, and media, 4.0% healthcare practitioners, 19.9% service, 33.3% sales and office, 3.1% natural resources, construction, and maintenance, 12.2% production, transportation, and material moving

Income: Per capita: $30,910; Median household: $56,842; Average household: $75,781; Households with income of $100,000 or more: 27.7%; Poverty rate: 16.0%

Educational Attainment: High school diploma or higher: 91.4%; Bachelor's degree or higher: 20.6%; Graduate/professional degree or higher: 10.0%

School District(s)
Central Square Central SD (PK-12)
    Enrollment: 3,941 . . . . (315) 668-4220

Housing: Homeownership rate: 60.3%; Median home value: $143,900; Median year structure built: 1979; Homeowner vacancy rate: 0.0%; Median selected monthly owner costs: $1,494 with a mortgage, $604 without a mortgage; Median gross rent: $957 per month; Rental vacancy rate: 5.5%

Health Insurance: 94.0% have insurance; 67.2% have private insurance; 41.9% have public insurance; 6.0% do not have insurance; 0.9% of children under 18 do not have insurance

Transportation: Commute: 85.4% car, 3.2% public transportation, 4.7% walk, 6.1% work from home; Mean travel time to work: 23.2 minutes

BRIDGEPORT (CDP).
Covers a land area of 1.724 square miles and a water area of 0.015 square miles. Located at 43.15° N. Lat; 75.99° W. Long.

Population: 1,426; Growth (since 2000): -14.4%; Density: 827.3 persons per square mile; Race: 99.8% White, 0.2% Black/African American, 0.0% Asian, 0.0% American Indian/Alaska Native, 0.0% Native Hawaiian/Other Pacific Islander, 0.0% Two or more races, 7.8% Hispanic of any race; Average household size: 2.43; Median age: 48.2; Age under 18: 18.4%; Age 65 and over: 16.0%; Males per 100 females: 93.8; Marriage status: 26.9% never married, 44.7% now married, 0.4% separated, 8.0% widowed, 20.3% divorced; Foreign born: 1.1%; Speak English only: 98.9%; With disability: 21.5%; Veterans: 11.1%; Ancestry: 22.5% American, 20.4% German, 19.1% English, 13.0% Scottish, 8.4% Polish

Employment: 13.4% management, business, and financial, 1.3% computer, engineering, and science, 2.9% education, legal, community service, arts, and media, 1.8% healthcare practitioners, 26.0% service, 33.9% sales and office, 15.0% natural resources, construction, and maintenance, 5.8% production, transportation, and material moving

Income: Per capita: $25,250; Median household: $53,750; Average household: $59,339; Households with income of $100,000 or more: 19.1%; Poverty rate: 18.8%

Educational Attainment: High school diploma or higher: 88.0%; Bachelor's degree or higher: 3.9%; Graduate/professional degree or higher: 1.2%

School District(s)
Chittenango Central SD (KG-12)
    Enrollment: 1,915 . . . . (315) 687-2840

Housing: Homeownership rate: 74.7%; Median home value: $87,100; Median year structure built: 1962; Homeowner vacancy rate: 0.0%; Median selected monthly owner costs: $943 with a mortgage, $365 without a mortgage; Median gross rent: n/a per month; Rental vacancy rate: 0.0%
Health Insurance: 95.3% have insurance; 67.0% have private insurance; 39.5% have public insurance; 4.7% do not have insurance; 0.0% of children under 18 do not have insurance
Transportation: Commute: 89.5% car, 0.0% public transportation, 10.3% walk, 0.2% work from home; Mean travel time to work: 22.3 minutes

CAMILLUS (town). Covers a land area of 34.424 square miles and a water area of 0.017 square miles. Located at 43.07° N. Lat; 76.31° W. Long. Elevation is 433 feet.

History: Once a major cutlery manufacturing center. Incorporated 1852.
Population: 24,408; Growth (since 2000): 5.4%; Density: 709.0 persons per square mile; Race: 93.6% White, 1.3% Black/African American, 2.8% Asian, 0.3% American Indian/Alaska Native, 0.1% Native Hawaiian/Other Pacific Islander, 1.7% Two or more races, 2.7% Hispanic of any race; Average household size: 2.43; Median age: 42.7; Age under 18: 21.1%; Age 65 and over: 19.0%; Males per 100 females: 91.6; Marriage status: 28.8% never married, 54.7% now married, 1.8% separated, 6.2% widowed, 10.4% divorced; Foreign born: 6.1%; Speak English only: 91.6%; With disability: 9.8%; Veterans: 8.1%; Ancestry: 24.8% Irish, 21.6% Italian, 16.7% German, 14.3% English, 11.1% Polish
Employment: 15.2% management, business, and financial, 4.9% computer, engineering, and science, 14.9% education, legal, community service, arts, and media, 9.6% healthcare practitioners, 15.9% service, 25.4% sales and office, 6.3% natural resources, construction, and maintenance, 7.8% production, transportation, and material moving
Income: Per capita: $33,851; Median household: $68,087; Average household: $80,906; Households with income of $100,000 or more: 27.8%; Poverty rate: 5.8%
Educational Attainment: High school diploma or higher: 95.8%; Bachelor's degree or higher: 38.2%; Graduate/professional degree or higher: 16.8%
School District(s)
West Genesee Central SD (KG-12)
    Enrollment: 4,628 . . . . (315) 487-4562
Housing: Homeownership rate: 80.0%; Median home value: $142,900; Median year structure built: 1965; Homeowner vacancy rate: 1.0%; Median selected monthly owner costs: $1,360 with a mortgage, $568 without a mortgage; Median gross rent: $948 per month; Rental vacancy rate: 7.5%
Health Insurance: 94.8% have insurance; 82.4% have private insurance; 29.3% have public insurance; 5.2% do not have insurance; 5.4% of children under 18 do not have insurance
Safety: Violent crime rate: 6.5 per 10,000 population; Property crime rate: 120.3 per 10,000 population
Transportation: Commute: 94.3% car, 0.4% public transportation, 1.4% walk, 3.5% work from home; Mean travel time to work: 20.8 minutes
Additional Information Contacts
Town of Camillus. . . . . (315) 488-1335
    http://www.townofcamillus.com

CAMILLUS (village). Covers a land area of 0.390 square miles and a water area of 0 square miles. Located at 43.04° N. Lat; 76.31° W. Long. Elevation is 433 feet.

Population: 1,180; Growth (since 2000): -5.5%; Density: 3,023.3 persons per square mile; Race: 90.5% White, 5.5% Black/African American, 0.4% Asian, 0.0% American Indian/Alaska Native, 0.0% Native Hawaiian/Other Pacific Islander, 3.4% Two or more races, 2.2% Hispanic of any race; Average household size: 2.13; Median age: 40.4; Age under 18: 20.3%; Age 65 and over: 18.0%; Males per 100 females: 93.2; Marriage status: 39.7% never married, 40.5% now married, 4.0% separated, 8.7% widowed, 11.0% divorced; Foreign born: 4.8%; Speak English only: 95.8%; With disability: 14.4%; Veterans: 7.6%; Ancestry: 27.4% Irish, 20.7% English, 18.5% German, 14.2% Italian, 8.0% Polish
Employment: 16.8% management, business, and financial, 3.3% computer, engineering, and science, 10.8% education, legal, community service, arts, and media, 5.2% healthcare practitioners, 16.2% service, 29.7% sales and office, 10.2% natural resources, construction, and maintenance, 7.8% production, transportation, and material moving
Income: Per capita: $27,189; Median household: $48,867; Average household: $57,598; Households with income of $100,000 or more: 18.8%; Poverty rate: 11.0%

Educational Attainment: High school diploma or higher: 94.9%; Bachelor's degree or higher: 27.3%; Graduate/professional degree or higher: 10.1%
School District(s)
West Genesee Central SD (KG-12)
    Enrollment: 4,628 . . . . (315) 487-4562
Housing: Homeownership rate: 54.5%; Median home value: $108,600; Median year structure built: 1954; Homeowner vacancy rate: 1.6%; Median selected monthly owner costs: $1,231 with a mortgage, $489 without a mortgage; Median gross rent: $706 per month; Rental vacancy rate: 6.0%
Health Insurance: 93.1% have insurance; 68.9% have private insurance; 41.5% have public insurance; 6.9% do not have insurance; 2.5% of children under 18 do not have insurance
Transportation: Commute: 93.3% car, 1.8% public transportation, 0.5% walk, 3.8% work from home; Mean travel time to work: 21.0 minutes

CICERO (town). Covers a land area of 48.274 square miles and a water area of 0.191 square miles. Located at 43.17° N. Lat; 76.06° W. Long. Elevation is 394 feet.

Population: 31,326; Growth (since 2000): 12.0%; Density: 648.9 persons per square mile; Race: 94.7% White, 1.7% Black/African American, 1.3% Asian, 0.4% American Indian/Alaska Native, 0.0% Native Hawaiian/Other Pacific Islander, 1.6% Two or more races, 1.9% Hispanic of any race; Average household size: 2.56; Median age: 41.0; Age under 18: 22.9%; Age 65 and over: 14.1%; Males per 100 females: 96.1; Marriage status: 27.0% never married, 56.9% now married, 1.7% separated, 5.9% widowed, 10.3% divorced; Foreign born: 3.2%; Speak English only: 95.2%; With disability: 10.8%; Veterans: 6.3%; Ancestry: 24.9% Irish, 21.7% Italian, 19.5% German, 12.1% English, 8.0% Polish
Employment: 15.0% management, business, and financial, 6.0% computer, engineering, and science, 10.6% education, legal, community service, arts, and media, 8.0% healthcare practitioners, 15.6% service, 27.2% sales and office, 6.9% natural resources, construction, and maintenance, 10.7% production, transportation, and material moving
Income: Per capita: $34,949; Median household: $76,740; Average household: $88,139; Households with income of $100,000 or more: 34.6%; Poverty rate: 6.9%
Educational Attainment: High school diploma or higher: 94.9%; Bachelor's degree or higher: 31.9%; Graduate/professional degree or higher: 12.8%
School District(s)
North Syracuse Central SD (PK-12)
    Enrollment: 8,989 . . . . (315) 218-2151
Housing: Homeownership rate: 80.7%; Median home value: $151,000; Median year structure built: 1978; Homeowner vacancy rate: 1.3%; Median selected monthly owner costs: $1,463 with a mortgage, $586 without a mortgage; Median gross rent: $831 per month; Rental vacancy rate: 4.4%
Health Insurance: 95.6% have insurance; 80.2% have private insurance; 28.2% have public insurance; 4.4% do not have insurance; 2.9% of children under 18 do not have insurance
Safety: Violent crime rate: 4.1 per 10,000 population; Property crime rate: 93.7 per 10,000 population
Transportation: Commute: 93.5% car, 0.6% public transportation, 1.2% walk, 3.5% work from home; Mean travel time to work: 19.2 minutes
Additional Information Contacts
Town of Cicero . . . . (315) 699-8109
    http://ciceronewyork.net

CLAY (town). Covers a land area of 47.958 square miles and a water area of 0.901 square miles. Located at 43.18° N. Lat; 76.19° W. Long. Elevation is 394 feet.

Population: 59,626; Growth (since 2000): 1.4%; Density: 1,243.3 persons per square mile; Race: 89.5% White, 5.4% Black/African American, 1.9% Asian, 0.2% American Indian/Alaska Native, 0.0% Native Hawaiian/Other Pacific Islander, 2.8% Two or more races, 3.1% Hispanic of any race; Average household size: 2.50; Median age: 39.5; Age under 18: 22.1%; Age 65 and over: 14.5%; Males per 100 females: 93.9; Marriage status: 30.9% never married, 53.0% now married, 2.0% separated, 5.0% widowed, 11.1% divorced; Foreign born: 5.1%; Speak English only: 93.8%; With disability: 10.2%; Veterans: 8.2%; Ancestry: 25.2% Irish, 21.3% Italian, 20.2% German, 10.5% English, 7.2% Polish
Employment: 15.6% management, business, and financial, 6.1% computer, engineering, and science, 10.8% education, legal, community service, arts, and media, 8.8% healthcare practitioners, 14.7% service,

27.4% sales and office, 7.1% natural resources, construction, and maintenance, 9.6% production, transportation, and material moving
Income: Per capita: $33,102; Median household: $69,227; Average household: $81,627; Households with income of $100,000 or more: 28.4%; Poverty rate: 9.3%
Educational Attainment: High school diploma or higher: 94.5%; Bachelor's degree or higher: 35.1%; Graduate/professional degree or higher: 13.3%
Housing: Homeownership rate: 73.7%; Median home value: $142,300; Median year structure built: 1976; Homeowner vacancy rate: 1.4%; Median selected monthly owner costs: $1,405 with a mortgage, $548 without a mortgage; Median gross rent: $898 per month; Rental vacancy rate: 5.9%
Health Insurance: 96.3% have insurance; 81.4% have private insurance; 29.8% have public insurance; 3.7% do not have insurance; 1.5% of children under 18 do not have insurance
Transportation: Commute: 93.5% car, 0.8% public transportation, 1.2% walk, 3.9% work from home; Mean travel time to work: 20.0 minutes
Additional Information Contacts
Town of Clay . . . . (315) 652-3800
  http://www.townofclay.org

DE WITT (town). Covers a land area of 33.774 square miles and a water area of 0.092 square miles. Located at 43.05° N. Lat; 76.07° W. Long.
Population: 25,617; Growth (since 2000): 6.4%; Density: 758.5 persons per square mile; Race: 82.0% White, 7.0% Black/African American, 6.5% Asian, 0.3% American Indian/Alaska Native, 0.0% Native Hawaiian/Other Pacific Islander, 3.0% Two or more races, 2.8% Hispanic of any race; Average household size: 2.39; Median age: 42.3; Age under 18: 20.2%; Age 65 and over: 17.1%; Males per 100 females: 94.5; Marriage status: 35.1% never married, 49.4% now married, 1.4% separated, 5.3% widowed, 10.3% divorced; Foreign born: 11.9%; Speak English only: 85.3%; With disability: 13.2%; Veterans: 6.9%; Ancestry: 18.7% Irish, 16.2% Italian, 15.1% German, 11.6% English, 6.1% Polish
Employment: 15.9% management, business, and financial, 6.1% computer, engineering, and science, 15.9% education, legal, community service, arts, and media, 8.0% healthcare practitioners, 16.3% service, 24.8% sales and office, 5.2% natural resources, construction, and maintenance, 7.9% production, transportation, and material moving
Income: Per capita: $36,393; Median household: $65,665; Average household: $91,213; Households with income of $100,000 or more: 29.7%; Poverty rate: 9.8%
Educational Attainment: High school diploma or higher: 92.1%; Bachelor's degree or higher: 44.8%; Graduate/professional degree or higher: 22.9%
School District(s)
Jamesville-Dewitt Central SD (KG-12)
  Enrollment: 2,917 . . . . (315) 445-8304
Housing: Homeownership rate: 71.1%; Median home value: $153,700; Median year structure built: 1960; Homeowner vacancy rate: 0.8%; Median selected monthly owner costs: $1,484 with a mortgage, $575 without a mortgage; Median gross rent: $830 per month; Rental vacancy rate: 4.0%
Health Insurance: 95.8% have insurance; 79.3% have private insurance; 32.9% have public insurance; 4.2% do not have insurance; 2.4% of children under 18 do not have insurance
Safety: Violent crime rate: 18.9 per 10,000 population; Property crime rate: 281.4 per 10,000 population
Transportation: Commute: 88.4% car, 1.8% public transportation, 3.4% walk, 4.3% work from home; Mean travel time to work: 16.0 minutes
Additional Information Contacts
Town of De Witt . . . . (315) 446-3910
  http://www.townofdewitt.com

DELPHI FALLS (unincorporated postal area)
ZCTA: 13051
  Covers a land area of 0.236 square miles and a water area of 0 square miles. Located at 42.88° N. Lat; 75.91° W. Long. Elevation is 948 feet.
Population: 234; Growth (since 2000): n/a; Density: 992.7 persons per square mile; Race: 100.0% White, 0.0% Black/African American, 0.0% Asian, 0.0% American Indian/Alaska Native, 0.0% Native Hawaiian/Other Pacific Islander, 0.0% Two or more races, 0.0% Hispanic of any race; Average household size: 2.29; Median age: 40.8; Age under 18: 35.5%; Age 65 and over: 3.0%; Males per 100 females: 112.7; Marriage status: 8.6% never married, 91.4% now married, 0.0% separated, 0.0% widowed, 0.0% divorced; Foreign born: 0.0%; Speak

English only: 100.0%; With disability: 0.0%; Veterans: 0.0%; Ancestry: 53.0% English, 53.0% German, 23.9% Irish, 5.6% Eastern European, 3.4% Polish
Employment: 0.0% management, business, and financial, 0.0% computer, engineering, and science, 0.0% education, legal, community service, arts, and media, 0.0% healthcare practitioners, 0.0% service, 45.6% sales and office, 0.0% natural resources, construction, and maintenance, 54.4% production, transportation, and material moving
Income: Per capita: $20,409; Median household: n/a; Average household: $46,447; Households with income of $100,000 or more: n/a; Poverty rate: 53.0%
Educational Attainment: High school diploma or higher: 100.0%; Bachelor's degree or higher: 8.6%; Graduate/professional degree or higher: 8.6%
Housing: Homeownership rate: 40.2%; Median home value: n/a; Median year structure built: Before 1940; Homeowner vacancy rate: 0.0%; Median selected monthly owner costs: $0 with a mortgage, $0 without a mortgage; Median gross rent: $737 per month; Rental vacancy rate: 0.0%
Health Insurance: 76.9% have insurance; 41.5% have private insurance; 38.5% have public insurance; 23.1% do not have insurance; 0.0% of children under 18 do not have insurance
Transportation: Commute: 100.0% car, 0.0% public transportation, 0.0% walk, 0.0% work from home; Mean travel time to work: 0.0 minutes

EAST SYRACUSE (village). Covers a land area of 1.622 square miles and a water area of 0 square miles. Located at 43.06° N. Lat; 76.07° W. Long. Elevation is 433 feet.
Population: 3,017; Growth (since 2000): -5.1%; Density: 1,859.9 persons per square mile; Race: 95.5% White, 1.5% Black/African American, 0.3% Asian, 0.0% American Indian/Alaska Native, 0.0% Native Hawaiian/Other Pacific Islander, 1.3% Two or more races, 1.7% Hispanic of any race; Average household size: 2.24; Median age: 36.3; Age under 18: 21.9%; Age 65 and over: 11.2%; Males per 100 females: 99.7; Marriage status: 42.9% never married, 40.4% now married, 2.3% separated, 3.9% widowed, 12.7% divorced; Foreign born: 7.8%; Speak English only: 91.9%; With disability: 14.8%; Veterans: 6.7%; Ancestry: 24.1% Irish, 19.4% Italian, 16.1% German, 10.8% Polish, 8.3% English
Employment: 16.3% management, business, and financial, 4.1% computer, engineering, and science, 6.9% education, legal, community service, arts, and media, 4.3% healthcare practitioners, 22.5% service, 31.0% sales and office, 6.2% natural resources, construction, and maintenance, 8.7% production, transportation, and material moving
Income: Per capita: $24,688; Median household: $37,225; Average household: $53,935; Households with income of $100,000 or more: 14.3%; Poverty rate: 20.7%
Educational Attainment: High school diploma or higher: 88.4%; Bachelor's degree or higher: 19.7%; Graduate/professional degree or higher: 3.9%
School District(s)
East Syracuse-Minoa Central SD (PK-12)
  Enrollment: 3,431 . . . . (315) 434-3012
Housing: Homeownership rate: 47.7%; Median home value: $99,800; Median year structure built: Before 1940; Homeowner vacancy rate: 7.7%; Median selected monthly owner costs: $1,159 with a mortgage, $427 without a mortgage; Median gross rent: $727 per month; Rental vacancy rate: 5.9%
Health Insurance: 94.5% have insurance; 72.0% have private insurance; 38.0% have public insurance; 5.5% do not have insurance; 0.0% of children under 18 do not have insurance
Transportation: Commute: 85.5% car, 3.3% public transportation, 2.8% walk, 7.7% work from home; Mean travel time to work: 14.5 minutes

ELBRIDGE (town). Covers a land area of 37.539 square miles and a water area of 0.756 square miles. Located at 43.05° N. Lat; 76.44° W. Long. Elevation is 545 feet.
Population: 5,831; Growth (since 2000): -4.3%; Density: 155.3 persons per square mile; Race: 96.9% White, 0.3% Black/African American, 0.0% Asian, 0.3% American Indian/Alaska Native, 0.0% Native Hawaiian/Other Pacific Islander, 1.6% Two or more races, 2.4% Hispanic of any race; Average household size: 2.53; Median age: 46.5; Age under 18: 19.6%; Age 65 and over: 17.3%; Males per 100 females: 100.9; Marriage status: 28.6% never married, 51.4% now married, 3.9% separated, 5.8% widowed, 14.3% divorced; Foreign born: 2.6%; Speak English only: 96.4%;

With disability: 11.9%; Veterans: 9.3%; Ancestry: 29.5% Irish, 18.1% German, 15.5% English, 11.2% Italian, 9.3% Polish
Employment: 8.9% management, business, and financial, 2.7% computer, engineering, and science, 14.3% education, legal, community service, arts, and media, 4.5% healthcare practitioners, 15.5% service, 25.7% sales and office, 14.9% natural resources, construction, and maintenance, 13.4% production, transportation, and material moving
Income: Per capita: $29,587; Median household: $58,934; Average household: $73,833; Households with income of $100,000 or more: 24.0%; Poverty rate: 10.4%
Educational Attainment: High school diploma or higher: 87.7%; Bachelor's degree or higher: 23.9%; Graduate/professional degree or higher: 10.5%

School District(s)
Jordan-Elbridge Central SD (PK-12)
    Enrollment: 1,314 . . . . (315) 689-8500
Housing: Homeownership rate: 85.1%; Median home value: $121,600; Median year structure built: 1963; Homeowner vacancy rate: 2.9%; Median selected monthly owner costs: $1,217 with a mortgage, $477 without a mortgage; Median gross rent: $649 per month; Rental vacancy rate: 8.3%
Health Insurance: 92.2% have insurance; 74.5% have private insurance; 31.1% have public insurance; 7.8% do not have insurance; 1.8% of children under 18 do not have insurance
Transportation: Commute: 96.0% car, 0.4% public transportation, 1.0% walk, 2.1% work from home; Mean travel time to work: 22.2 minutes
Additional Information Contacts
Town of Elbridge . . . . (315) 689-9031
    http://www.townofelbridge.com

ELBRIDGE (village). Covers a land area of 1.126 square miles and a water area of 0 square miles. Located at 43.04° N. Lat; 76.44° W. Long. Elevation is 545 feet.
Population: 1,017; Growth (since 2000): -7.8%; Density: 903.4 persons per square mile; Race: 95.4% White, 0.0% Black/African American, 0.0% Asian, 1.6% American Indian/Alaska Native, 0.0% Native Hawaiian/Other Pacific Islander, 0.9% Two or more races, 4.8% Hispanic of any race; Average household size: 2.59; Median age: 47.5; Age under 18: 16.7%; Age 65 and over: 21.7%; Males per 100 females: 94.8; Marriage status: 29.3% never married, 52.0% now married, 0.7% separated, 5.6% widowed, 13.2% divorced; Foreign born: 3.9%; Speak English only: 92.5%; With disability: 14.1%; Veterans: 13.8%; Ancestry: 24.9% Irish, 17.0% English, 16.3% German, 13.5% Italian, 6.5% Polish
Employment: 10.4% management, business, and financial, 5.4% computer, engineering, and science, 13.1% education, legal, community service, arts, and media, 5.9% healthcare practitioners, 12.7% service, 25.9% sales and office, 15.8% natural resources, construction, and maintenance, 10.8% production, transportation, and material moving
Income: Per capita: $32,030; Median household: $68,393; Average household: $80,614; Households with income of $100,000 or more: 32.3%; Poverty rate: 5.7%
Educational Attainment: High school diploma or higher: 94.9%; Bachelor's degree or higher: 22.4%; Graduate/professional degree or higher: 6.9%

School District(s)
Jordan-Elbridge Central SD (PK-12)
    Enrollment: 1,314 . . . . (315) 689-8500
Housing: Homeownership rate: 74.3%; Median home value: $144,900; Median year structure built: 1962; Homeowner vacancy rate: 0.0%; Median selected monthly owner costs: $1,321 with a mortgage, $498 without a mortgage; Median gross rent: $838 per month; Rental vacancy rate: 9.0%
Health Insurance: 92.5% have insurance; 80.4% have private insurance; 33.6% have public insurance; 7.5% do not have insurance; 5.8% of children under 18 do not have insurance
Transportation: Commute: 90.6% car, 0.0% public transportation, 2.4% walk, 7.0% work from home; Mean travel time to work: 22.3 minutes

FABIUS (town). Covers a land area of 46.497 square miles and a water area of 0.275 square miles. Located at 42.82° N. Lat; 75.99° W. Long. Elevation is 1,266 feet.
Population: 2,306; Growth (since 2000): 16.8%; Density: 49.6 persons per square mile; Race: 90.9% White, 0.5% Black/African American, 0.7% Asian, 0.4% American Indian/Alaska Native, 0.0% Native Hawaiian/Other Pacific Islander, 0.6% Two or more races, 11.1% Hispanic of any race; Average household size: 2.87; Median age: 38.4; Age under 18: 22.6%; Age 65 and over: 11.4%; Males per 100 females: 104.2; Marriage status:

30.4% never married, 56.9% now married, 0.5% separated, 3.1% widowed, 9.6% divorced; Foreign born: 9.4%; Speak English only: 87.9%; With disability: 9.0%; Veterans: 6.5%; Ancestry: 23.2% German, 22.1% Irish, 17.1% English, 10.5% Italian, 5.8% Polish
Employment: 15.9% management, business, and financial, 2.7% computer, engineering, and science, 6.8% education, legal, community service, arts, and media, 5.8% healthcare practitioners, 16.9% service, 15.7% sales and office, 30.1% natural resources, construction, and maintenance, 6.2% production, transportation, and material moving
Income: Per capita: $32,417; Median household: $72,879; Average household: $90,817; Households with income of $100,000 or more: 31.6%; Poverty rate: 5.6%
Educational Attainment: High school diploma or higher: 93.2%; Bachelor's degree or higher: 27.5%; Graduate/professional degree or higher: 7.4%

School District(s)
Fabius-Pompey Central SD (KG-12)
    Enrollment: 663 . . . . (315) 683-5301
Housing: Homeownership rate: 88.4%; Median home value: $140,000; Median year structure built: 1960; Homeowner vacancy rate: 0.4%; Median selected monthly owner costs: $1,419 with a mortgage, $532 without a mortgage; Median gross rent: $755 per month; Rental vacancy rate: 5.1%
Health Insurance: 88.6% have insurance; 75.2% have private insurance; 23.9% have public insurance; 11.4% do not have insurance; 10.4% of children under 18 do not have insurance
Transportation: Commute: 75.3% car, 0.3% public transportation, 15.9% walk, 6.8% work from home; Mean travel time to work: 23.3 minutes

FABIUS (village). Covers a land area of 0.398 square miles and a water area of 0 square miles. Located at 42.83° N. Lat; 75.98° W. Long. Elevation is 1,266 feet.
Population: 315; Growth (since 2000): -11.3%; Density: 791.7 persons per square mile; Race: 99.0% White, 0.0% Black/African American, 0.0% Asian, 0.0% American Indian/Alaska Native, 0.0% Native Hawaiian/Other Pacific Islander, 0.6% Two or more races, 0.6% Hispanic of any race; Average household size: 2.46; Median age: 44.5; Age under 18: 25.7%; Age 65 and over: 15.9%; Males per 100 females: 89.2; Marriage status: 31.1% never married, 56.7% now married, 0.4% separated, 3.5% widowed, 8.7% divorced; Foreign born: 0.0%; Speak English only: 97.7%; With disability: 8.3%; Veterans: 7.3%; Ancestry: 34.3% Irish, 20.0% German, 19.4% English, 12.1% Italian, 5.4% American
Employment: 17.7% management, business, and financial, 3.7% computer, engineering, and science, 7.9% education, legal, community service, arts, and media, 6.1% healthcare practitioners, 16.5% service, 23.8% sales and office, 13.4% natural resources, construction, and maintenance, 11.0% production, transportation, and material moving
Income: Per capita: $32,343; Median household: $71,000; Average household: $81,059; Households with income of $100,000 or more: 25.7%; Poverty rate: 7.9%
Educational Attainment: High school diploma or higher: 96.7%; Bachelor's degree or higher: 31.3%; Graduate/professional degree or higher: 15.2%

School District(s)
Fabius-Pompey Central SD (KG-12)
    Enrollment: 663 . . . . (315) 683-5301
Housing: Homeownership rate: 78.1%; Median home value: $114,400; Median year structure built: Before 1940; Homeowner vacancy rate: 2.9%; Median selected monthly owner costs: $1,446 with a mortgage, $528 without a mortgage; Median gross rent: $625 per month; Rental vacancy rate: 15.2%
Health Insurance: 92.7% have insurance; 81.6% have private insurance; 27.6% have public insurance; 7.3% do not have insurance; 0.0% of children under 18 do not have insurance
Transportation: Commute: 91.5% car, 0.6% public transportation, 1.2% walk, 5.5% work from home; Mean travel time to work: 28.9 minutes

FAIRMOUNT (CDP). Covers a land area of 3.334 square miles and a water area of 0 square miles. Located at 43.04° N. Lat; 76.25° W. Long. Elevation is 492 feet.
Population: 9,986; Growth (since 2000): -7.5%; Density: 2,995.4 persons per square mile; Race: 94.1% White, 1.1% Black/African American, 2.4% Asian, 0.3% American Indian/Alaska Native, 0.0% Native Hawaiian/Other Pacific Islander, 1.7% Two or more races, 3.6% Hispanic of any race; Average household size: 2.37; Median age: 42.3; Age under 18: 19.8%; Age 65 and over: 19.6%; Males per 100 females: 88.5; Marriage status:

31.8% never married, 51.1% now married, 2.2% separated, 7.5% widowed, 9.6% divorced; Foreign born: 5.3%; Speak English only: 91.8%; With disability: 10.7%; Veterans: 8.1%; Ancestry: 26.2% Irish, 24.0% Italian, 16.1% German, 10.4% English, 10.1% Polish
Employment: 12.8% management, business, and financial, 2.9% computer, engineering, and science, 14.2% education, legal, community service, arts, and media, 10.3% healthcare practitioners, 18.4% service, 25.4% sales and office, 7.5% natural resources, construction, and maintenance, 8.5% production, transportation, and material moving
Income: Per capita: $30,230; Median household: $60,313; Average household: $69,814; Households with income of $100,000 or more: 20.2%; Poverty rate: 4.1%
Educational Attainment: High school diploma or higher: 95.7%; Bachelor's degree or higher: 32.5%; Graduate/professional degree or higher: 14.0%
Housing: Homeownership rate: 79.9%; Median home value: $124,100; Median year structure built: 1958; Homeowner vacancy rate: 1.7%; Median selected monthly owner costs: $1,211 with a mortgage, $533 without a mortgage; Median gross rent: $1,046 per month; Rental vacancy rate: 4.3%
Health Insurance: 94.5% have insurance; 79.2% have private insurance; 32.6% have public insurance; 5.5% do not have insurance; 6.5% of children under 18 do not have insurance
Transportation: Commute: 93.7% car, 0.5% public transportation, 2.7% walk, 3.1% work from home; Mean travel time to work: 20.6 minutes

FAYETTEVILLE (village).
Covers a land area of 1.746 square miles and a water area of 0 square miles. Located at 43.03° N. Lat; 76.00° W. Long. Elevation is 535 feet.
History: Incorporated 1844.
Population: 4,183; Growth (since 2000): -0.2%; Density: 2,395.3 persons per square mile; Race: 97.1% White, 0.9% Black/African American, 1.4% Asian, 0.0% American Indian/Alaska Native, 0.0% Native Hawaiian/Other Pacific Islander, 0.6% Two or more races, 1.4% Hispanic of any race; Average household size: 2.32; Median age: 45.7; Age under 18: 22.4%; Age 65 and over: 23.1%; Males per 100 females: 91.2; Marriage status: 23.3% never married, 60.8% now married, 0.5% separated, 5.5% widowed, 10.5% divorced; Foreign born: 3.8%; Speak English only: 96.3%; With disability: 10.8%; Veterans: 7.6%; Ancestry: 30.0% Irish, 20.0% German, 12.6% Italian, 12.1% English, 9.3% French
Employment: 15.7% management, business, and financial, 5.3% computer, engineering, and science, 18.2% education, legal, community service, arts, and media, 9.9% healthcare practitioners, 10.0% service, 29.9% sales and office, 5.9% natural resources, construction, and maintenance, 5.0% production, transportation, and material moving
Income: Per capita: $51,334; Median household: $76,402; Average household: $118,605; Households with income of $100,000 or more: 38.7%; Poverty rate: 4.3%
Educational Attainment: High school diploma or higher: 96.9%; Bachelor's degree or higher: 55.6%; Graduate/professional degree or higher: 31.8%

School District(s)
Fayetteville-Manlius Central SD (KG-12)
    Enrollment: 4,255 . . . . (315) 692-1200
Housing: Homeownership rate: 74.1%; Median home value: $177,700; Median year structure built: 1956; Homeowner vacancy rate: 0.0%; Median selected monthly owner costs: $1,683 with a mortgage, $820 without a mortgage; Median gross rent: $1,038 per month; Rental vacancy rate: 0.0%
Health Insurance: 96.9% have insurance; 75.4% have private insurance; 39.4% have public insurance; 3.1% do not have insurance; 1.9% of children under 18 do not have insurance
Transportation: Commute: 92.6% car, 0.0% public transportation, 1.5% walk, 5.4% work from home; Mean travel time to work: 20.7 minutes
Additional Information Contacts
Village of Fayetteville . . . . (315) 637-9864
   http://www.fayettevilleny.gov

GALEVILLE (CDP).
Covers a land area of 1.152 square miles and a water area of 0.006 square miles. Located at 43.09° N. Lat; 76.18° W. Long. Elevation is 423 feet.
Population: 4,599; Growth (since 2000): 2.7%; Density: 3,992.2 persons per square mile; Race: 83.2% White, 9.1% Black/African American, 6.7% Asian, 0.0% American Indian/Alaska Native, 0.0% Native Hawaiian/Other Pacific Islander, 1.0% Two or more races, 0.0% Hispanic of any race;

Average household size: 2.25; Median age: 44.2; Age under 18: 20.0%; Age 65 and over: 22.0%; Males per 100 females: 82.4; Marriage status: 31.1% never married, 49.2% now married, 2.4% separated, 10.4% widowed, 9.3% divorced; Foreign born: 10.2%; Speak English only: 88.3%; With disability: 15.2%; Veterans: 8.7%; Ancestry: 24.3% Italian, 22.9% German, 21.7% Irish, 9.8% English, 7.8% Polish
Employment: 6.9% management, business, and financial, 4.1% computer, engineering, and science, 7.1% education, legal, community service, arts, and media, 5.6% healthcare practitioners, 25.1% service, 34.9% sales and office, 4.5% natural resources, construction, and maintenance, 11.7% production, transportation, and material moving
Income: Per capita: $24,917; Median household: $46,394; Average household: $54,848; Households with income of $100,000 or more: 14.4%; Poverty rate: 14.5%
Educational Attainment: High school diploma or higher: 84.8%; Bachelor's degree or higher: 14.5%; Graduate/professional degree or higher: 4.7%
Housing: Homeownership rate: 71.9%; Median home value: $100,300; Median year structure built: 1957; Homeowner vacancy rate: 2.2%; Median selected monthly owner costs: $1,033 with a mortgage, $417 without a mortgage; Median gross rent: $786 per month; Rental vacancy rate: 12.1%
Health Insurance: 98.3% have insurance; 72.4% have private insurance; 46.5% have public insurance; 1.7% do not have insurance; 0.0% of children under 18 do not have insurance
Transportation: Commute: 94.5% car, 2.9% public transportation, 1.3% walk, 1.3% work from home; Mean travel time to work: 15.9 minutes

GEDDES (town).
Covers a land area of 9.156 square miles and a water area of 3.104 square miles. Located at 43.08° N. Lat; 76.22° W. Long.
Population: 16,786; Growth (since 2000): -5.4%; Density: 1,833.3 persons per square mile; Race: 90.3% White, 2.8% Black/African American, 0.6% Asian, 0.3% American Indian/Alaska Native, 0.1% Native Hawaiian/Other Pacific Islander, 5.0% Two or more races, 4.8% Hispanic of any race; Average household size: 2.37; Median age: 43.5; Age under 18: 20.2%; Age 65 and over: 20.5%; Males per 100 females: 87.4; Marriage status: 32.9% never married, 48.4% now married, 1.7% separated, 7.4% widowed, 11.3% divorced; Foreign born: 5.4%; Speak English only: 91.6%; With disability: 11.8%; Veterans: 8.5%; Ancestry: 27.6% Italian, 27.2% Irish, 15.0% German, 10.1% Polish, 8.7% English
Employment: 14.8% management, business, and financial, 3.1% computer, engineering, and science, 11.4% education, legal, community service, arts, and media, 6.7% healthcare practitioners, 21.7% service, 25.3% sales and office, 7.9% natural resources, construction, and maintenance, 9.0% production, transportation, and material moving
Income: Per capita: $29,173; Median household: $55,870; Average household: $68,046; Households with income of $100,000 or more: 20.7%; Poverty rate: 10.1%
Educational Attainment: High school diploma or higher: 92.5%; Bachelor's degree or higher: 30.4%; Graduate/professional degree or higher: 12.9%
Housing: Homeownership rate: 75.3%; Median home value: $128,300; Median year structure built: 1954; Homeowner vacancy rate: 2.5%; Median selected monthly owner costs: $1,201 with a mortgage, $522 without a mortgage; Median gross rent: $735 per month; Rental vacancy rate: 6.2%
Health Insurance: 95.2% have insurance; 78.7% have private insurance; 36.9% have public insurance; 4.8% do not have insurance; 3.3% of children under 18 do not have insurance
Safety: Violent crime rate: 6.8 per 10,000 population; Property crime rate: 209.9 per 10,000 population
Transportation: Commute: 92.1% car, 1.5% public transportation, 3.1% walk, 2.8% work from home; Mean travel time to work: 19.5 minutes
Additional Information Contacts
Town of Geddes . . . . (315) 468-3600
   http://www.townofgeddes.com

JAMESVILLE (unincorporated postal area)
ZCTA: 13078
    Covers a land area of 38.921 square miles and a water area of 0.463 square miles. Located at 42.96° N. Lat; 76.06° W. Long. Elevation is 607 feet.
Population: 10,439; Growth (since 2000): 21.0%; Density: 268.2 persons per square mile; Race: 79.1% White, 5.3% Black/African American, 10.4% Asian, 0.8% American Indian/Alaska Native, 0.0% Native Hawaiian/Other Pacific Islander, 4.3% Two or more races, 2.0% Hispanic of any race; Average household size: 2.52; Median age: 46.4;

Age under 18: 20.5%; Age 65 and over: 21.1%; Males per 100 females: 101.8; Marriage status: 28.0% never married, 56.1% now married, 1.2% separated, 8.1% widowed, 7.8% divorced; Foreign born: 11.6%; Speak English only: 86.5%; With disability: 11.0%; Veterans: 8.4%; Ancestry: 17.1% Irish, 16.0% Italian, 14.9% German, 12.9% English, 4.9% Polish
Employment: 19.7% management, business, and financial, 8.4% computer, engineering, and science, 14.4% education, legal, community service, arts, and media, 11.3% healthcare practitioners, 14.5% service, 20.2% sales and office, 6.8% natural resources, construction, and maintenance, 4.6% production, transportation, and material moving
Income: Per capita: $46,598; Median household: $87,596; Average household: $127,089; Households with income of $100,000 or more: 44.3%; Poverty rate: 6.3%
Educational Attainment: High school diploma or higher: 92.2%; Bachelor's degree or higher: 48.7%; Graduate/professional degree or higher: 25.2%

School District(s)
Jamesville-Dewitt Central SD (KG-12)
    Enrollment: 2,917 . . . . (315) 445-8304
Housing: Homeownership rate: 78.0%; Median home value: $198,300; Median year structure built: 1972; Homeowner vacancy rate: 0.0%; Median selected monthly owner costs: $1,698 with a mortgage, $748 without a mortgage; Median gross rent: $1,034 per month; Rental vacancy rate: 3.5%
Health Insurance: 94.1% have insurance; 80.2% have private insurance; 30.1% have public insurance; 5.9% do not have insurance; 5.1% of children under 18 do not have insurance
Transportation: Commute: 91.4% car, 0.9% public transportation, 0.4% walk, 6.6% work from home; Mean travel time to work: 21.0 minutes

JORDAN (village).
Covers a land area of 1.146 square miles and a water area of 0 square miles. Located at 43.07° N. Lat; 76.47° W. Long. Elevation is 413 feet.
History: Incorporated 1835.
Population: 1,427; Growth (since 2000): 8.6%; Density: 1,245.6 persons per square mile; Race: 97.6% White, 0.0% Black/African American, 0.0% Asian, 0.2% American Indian/Alaska Native, 0.0% Native Hawaiian/Other Pacific Islander, 2.0% Two or more races, 0.1% Hispanic of any race; Average household size: 2.46; Median age: 40.6; Age under 18: 21.4%; Age 65 and over: 14.7%; Males per 100 females: 102.1; Marriage status: 39.4% never married, 38.4% now married, 1.2% separated, 5.2% widowed, 16.9% divorced; Foreign born: 1.1%; Speak English only: 98.2%; With disability: 11.4%; Veterans: 11.0%; Ancestry: 34.4% Irish, 23.1% German, 15.5% English, 13.8% Polish, 7.7% French Canadian
Employment: 14.1% management, business, and financial, 2.7% computer, engineering, and science, 11.2% education, legal, community service, arts, and media, 5.6% healthcare practitioners, 11.7% service, 27.2% sales and office, 16.3% natural resources, construction, and maintenance, 11.2% production, transportation, and material moving
Income: Per capita: $27,510; Median household: $49,185; Average household: $66,836; Households with income of $100,000 or more: 20.6%; Poverty rate: 10.0%
Educational Attainment: High school diploma or higher: 92.7%; Bachelor's degree or higher: 27.2%; Graduate/professional degree or higher: 7.4%

School District(s)
Jordan-Elbridge Central SD (PK-12)
    Enrollment: 1,314 . . . . (315) 689-8500
Housing: Homeownership rate: 63.8%; Median home value: $98,300; Median year structure built: Before 1940; Homeowner vacancy rate: 4.2%; Median selected monthly owner costs: $1,191 with a mortgage, $495 without a mortgage; Median gross rent: $567 per month; Rental vacancy rate: 9.1%
Health Insurance: 94.2% have insurance; 68.5% have private insurance; 37.6% have public insurance; 5.8% do not have insurance; 3.7% of children under 18 do not have insurance
Safety: Violent crime rate: 0.0 per 10,000 population; Property crime rate: 7.6 per 10,000 population
Transportation: Commute: 94.7% car, 0.0% public transportation, 2.2% walk, 1.0% work from home; Mean travel time to work: 21.1 minutes

LAFAYETTE (town).
Covers a land area of 39.233 square miles and a water area of 0.413 square miles. Located at 42.91° N. Lat; 76.10° W. Long. Elevation is 1,132 feet.
Population: 4,913; Growth (since 2000): 1.7%; Density: 125.2 persons per square mile; Race: 86.4% White, 2.8% Black/African American, 5.9% Asian, 1.9% American Indian/Alaska Native, 0.0% Native Hawaiian/Other Pacific Islander, 2.9% Two or more races, 0.2% Hispanic of any race; Average household size: 2.43; Median age: 46.1; Age under 18: 20.7%; Age 65 and over: 16.9%; Males per 100 females: 99.4; Marriage status: 30.8% never married, 49.9% now married, 1.0% separated, 7.6% widowed, 11.7% divorced; Foreign born: 6.1%; Speak English only: 96.0%; With disability: 7.1%; Veterans: 7.0%; Ancestry: 23.7% Irish, 22.3% German, 17.4% Italian, 17.4% English, 4.3% French
Employment: 17.2% management, business, and financial, 6.6% computer, engineering, and science, 6.9% education, legal, community service, arts, and media, 5.2% healthcare practitioners, 22.1% service, 24.4% sales and office, 10.0% natural resources, construction, and maintenance, 7.6% production, transportation, and material moving
Income: Per capita: $33,651; Median household: $66,323; Average household: $80,547; Households with income of $100,000 or more: 32.1%; Poverty rate: 13.2%
Educational Attainment: High school diploma or higher: 94.5%; Bachelor's degree or higher: 36.0%; Graduate/professional degree or higher: 18.3%

School District(s)
Lafayette Central SD (PK-12)
    Enrollment: 923 . . . . (315) 677-9728
Housing: Homeownership rate: 77.0%; Median home value: $163,100; Median year structure built: 1970; Homeowner vacancy rate: 0.0%; Median selected monthly owner costs: $1,537 with a mortgage, $560 without a mortgage; Median gross rent: $945 per month; Rental vacancy rate: 11.2%
Health Insurance: 88.0% have insurance; 69.5% have private insurance; 30.6% have public insurance; 12.0% do not have insurance; 10.7% of children under 18 do not have insurance
Transportation: Commute: 96.5% car, 0.0% public transportation, 1.1% walk, 1.5% work from home; Mean travel time to work: 27.6 minutes
Additional Information Contacts
Town of La Fayette . . . . (315) 677-3674
    http://www.townoflafayette.com

LAKELAND (CDP).
Covers a land area of 1.483 square miles and a water area of 0 square miles. Located at 43.09° N. Lat; 76.24° W. Long. Elevation is 479 feet.
Population: 2,512; Growth (since 2000): -11.9%; Density: 1,693.4 persons per square mile; Race: 95.6% White, 3.4% Black/African American, 0.2% Asian, 0.0% American Indian/Alaska Native, 0.0% Native Hawaiian/Other Pacific Islander, 0.8% Two or more races, 0.8% Hispanic of any race; Average household size: 2.45; Median age: 50.4; Age under 18: 15.0%; Age 65 and over: 22.9%; Males per 100 females: 92.1; Marriage status: 24.9% never married, 60.2% now married, 1.0% separated, 4.4% widowed, 10.6% divorced; Foreign born: 10.1%; Speak English only: 89.1%; With disability: 11.4%; Veterans: 8.9%; Ancestry: 29.1% Italian, 16.6% Irish, 16.0% German, 15.7% Polish, 7.6% English
Employment: 13.2% management, business, and financial, 4.7% computer, engineering, and science, 8.9% education, legal, community service, arts, and media, 7.4% healthcare practitioners, 19.6% service, 26.1% sales and office, 7.8% natural resources, construction, and maintenance, 12.2% production, transportation, and material moving
Income: Per capita: $29,269; Median household: $59,000; Average household: $69,185; Households with income of $100,000 or more: 20.9%; Poverty rate: 3.1%
Educational Attainment: High school diploma or higher: 93.8%; Bachelor's degree or higher: 24.3%; Graduate/professional degree or higher: 9.2%
Housing: Homeownership rate: 81.9%; Median home value: $134,400; Median year structure built: 1970; Homeowner vacancy rate: 2.9%; Median selected monthly owner costs: $1,118 with a mortgage, $477 without a mortgage; Median gross rent: $1,019 per month; Rental vacancy rate: 12.3%
Health Insurance: 95.6% have insurance; 84.4% have private insurance; 34.8% have public insurance; 4.4% do not have insurance; 15.8% of children under 18 do not have insurance
Transportation: Commute: 98.1% car, 0.0% public transportation, 0.0% walk, 1.3% work from home; Mean travel time to work: 20.6 minutes

LIVERPOOL (village). Covers a land area of 0.757 square miles and a water area of 0 square miles. Located at 43.11° N. Lat; 76.21° W. Long. Elevation is 420 feet.
History: Incorporated 1830.
Population: 2,199; Growth (since 2000): -12.2%; Density: 2,904.5 persons per square mile; Race: 96.4% White, 1.5% Black/African American, 0.3% Asian, 0.0% American Indian/Alaska Native, 0.0% Native Hawaiian/Other Pacific Islander, 1.9% Two or more races, 1.7% Hispanic of any race; Average household size: 1.90; Median age: 48.3; Age under 18: 14.5%; Age 65 and over: 21.7%; Males per 100 females: 88.5; Marriage status: 38.6% never married, 42.7% now married, 2.1% separated, 8.2% widowed, 10.5% divorced; Foreign born: 3.3%; Speak English only: 99.0%; With disability: 8.4%; Veterans: 9.0%; Ancestry: 25.2% Italian, 24.1% Irish, 22.6% German, 16.0% English, 8.6% Polish
Employment: 13.7% management, business, and financial, 10.4% computer, engineering, and science, 16.8% education, legal, community service, arts, and media, 7.7% healthcare practitioners, 12.5% service, 23.6% sales and office, 7.8% natural resources, construction, and maintenance, 7.6% production, transportation, and material moving
Income: Per capita: $35,529; Median household: $55,761; Average household: $67,300; Households with income of $100,000 or more: 19.9%; Poverty rate: 7.2%
Educational Attainment: High school diploma or higher: 95.9%; Bachelor's degree or higher: 43.2%; Graduate/professional degree or higher: 19.7%
School District(s)
Liverpool Central SD (KG-12)
    Enrollment: 7,279 . . . . (315) 622-7125
Four-year College(s)
Bryant & Stratton College-Syracuse North (Private, For-profit)
    Enrollment: 258 . . . . (315) 652-6500
    Tuition: In-state $16,701; Out-of-state $16,701
Vocational/Technical School(s)
National Tractor Trailer School Inc-Liverpool (Private, For-profit)
    Enrollment: 61 . . . . (315) 451-2430
    Tuition: $10,248
Onondaga Cortland Madison BOCES (Public)
    Enrollment: 465 . . . . (315) 453-4455
    Tuition: $12,550
Housing: Homeownership rate: 66.3%; Median home value: $132,500; Median year structure built: 1948; Homeowner vacancy rate: 0.0%; Median selected monthly owner costs: $1,347 with a mortgage, $632 without a mortgage; Median gross rent: $891 per month; Rental vacancy rate: 4.9%
Health Insurance: 95.7% have insurance; 82.2% have private insurance; 29.9% have public insurance; 4.3% do not have insurance; 0.0% of children under 18 do not have insurance
Safety: Violent crime rate: 0.0 per 10,000 population; Property crime rate: 138.0 per 10,000 population
Transportation: Commute: 83.6% car, 2.9% public transportation, 3.6% walk, 9.4% work from home; Mean travel time to work: 18.1 minutes
Additional Information Contacts
Village of Liverpool . . . . (315) 457-3441
    http://www.villageofliverpool.org

LYNCOURT (CDP). Covers a land area of 1.243 square miles and a water area of 0 square miles. Located at 43.08° N. Lat; 76.13° W. Long. Elevation is 446 feet.
Population: 3,896; Growth (since 2000): -8.7%; Density: 3,134.2 persons per square mile; Race: 86.6% White, 2.2% Black/African American, 2.7% Asian, 0.0% American Indian/Alaska Native, 0.0% Native Hawaiian/Other Pacific Islander, 7.8% Two or more races, 4.3% Hispanic of any race; Average household size: 2.27; Median age: 41.3; Age under 18: 20.9%; Age 65 and over: 17.8%; Males per 100 females: 90.6; Marriage status: 39.4% never married, 38.8% now married, 1.2% separated, 8.6% widowed, 13.2% divorced; Foreign born: 4.3%; Speak English only: 94.0%; With disability: 14.2%; Veterans: 6.6%; Ancestry: 28.2% Italian, 24.4% Irish, 18.2% German, 8.7% Polish, 6.6% English
Employment: 15.9% management, business, and financial, 7.2% computer, engineering, and science, 6.0% education, legal, community service, arts, and media, 4.2% healthcare practitioners, 23.7% service, 26.6% sales and office, 6.1% natural resources, construction, and maintenance, 10.4% production, transportation, and material moving
Income: Per capita: $24,060; Median household: $50,044; Average household: $53,401; Households with income of $100,000 or more: 13.1%; Poverty rate: 15.2%

Educational Attainment: High school diploma or higher: 90.8%; Bachelor's degree or higher: 16.6%; Graduate/professional degree or higher: 3.8%
Housing: Homeownership rate: 73.0%; Median home value: $92,600; Median year structure built: 1956; Homeowner vacancy rate: 0.0%; Median selected monthly owner costs: $1,088 with a mortgage, $416 without a mortgage; Median gross rent: $815 per month; Rental vacancy rate: 5.3%
Health Insurance: 91.6% have insurance; 71.8% have private insurance; 40.1% have public insurance; 8.4% do not have insurance; 10.8% of children under 18 do not have insurance
Transportation: Commute: 96.0% car, 0.2% public transportation, 1.6% walk, 1.2% work from home; Mean travel time to work: 14.6 minutes

LYSANDER (town). Covers a land area of 61.715 square miles and a water area of 2.894 square miles. Located at 43.18° N. Lat; 76.37° W. Long. Elevation is 413 feet.
Population: 22,658; Growth (since 2000): 17.5%; Density: 367.1 persons per square mile; Race: 94.9% White, 1.8% Black/African American, 1.3% Asian, 0.3% American Indian/Alaska Native, 0.0% Native Hawaiian/Other Pacific Islander, 1.6% Two or more races, 2.9% Hispanic of any race; Average household size: 2.50; Median age: 44.5; Age under 18: 22.8%; Age 65 and over: 16.6%; Males per 100 females: 95.4; Marriage status: 23.2% never married, 61.2% now married, 0.7% separated, 5.3% widowed, 10.4% divorced; Foreign born: 2.9%; Speak English only: 96.0%; With disability: 8.8%; Veterans: 9.3%; Ancestry: 22.2% Irish, 20.9% German, 17.6% Italian, 16.4% English, 6.3% French
Employment: 15.9% management, business, and financial, 5.8% computer, engineering, and science, 15.4% education, legal, community service, arts, and media, 10.2% healthcare practitioners, 11.3% service, 23.9% sales and office, 6.3% natural resources, construction, and maintenance, 11.3% production, transportation, and material moving
Income: Per capita: $38,121; Median household: $79,625; Average household: $94,198; Households with income of $100,000 or more: 38.5%; Poverty rate: 6.8%
Educational Attainment: High school diploma or higher: 95.7%; Bachelor's degree or higher: 42.4%; Graduate/professional degree or higher: 17.4%
Housing: Homeownership rate: 80.2%; Median home value: $176,500; Median year structure built: 1980; Homeowner vacancy rate: 1.2%; Median selected monthly owner costs: $1,527 with a mortgage, $592 without a mortgage; Median gross rent: $824 per month; Rental vacancy rate: 6.4%
Health Insurance: 97.4% have insurance; 82.7% have private insurance; 29.3% have public insurance; 2.6% do not have insurance; 1.0% of children under 18 do not have insurance
Transportation: Commute: 92.8% car, 0.2% public transportation, 1.3% walk, 5.4% work from home; Mean travel time to work: 23.5 minutes
Additional Information Contacts
Town of Lysander . . . . (315) 638-0224
    http://www.townoflysander.org

MANLIUS (town). Covers a land area of 49.218 square miles and a water area of 0.735 square miles. Located at 43.05° N. Lat; 75.98° W. Long. Elevation is 591 feet.
History: Settled 1789 incorporated 1842,
Population: 32,282; Growth (since 2000): 1.3%; Density: 655.9 persons per square mile; Race: 89.9% White, 3.1% Black/African American, 3.5% Asian, 0.3% American Indian/Alaska Native, 0.0% Native Hawaiian/Other Pacific Islander, 2.6% Two or more races, 1.4% Hispanic of any race; Average household size: 2.46; Median age: 44.7; Age under 18: 24.1%; Age 65 and over: 20.0%; Males per 100 females: 91.2; Marriage status: 22.9% never married, 58.6% now married, 1.3% separated, 7.5% widowed, 11.0% divorced; Foreign born: 6.2%; Speak English only: 92.4%; With disability: 10.6%; Veterans: 8.1%; Ancestry: 26.4% Irish, 18.5% German, 15.8% Italian, 13.7% English, 5.6% Polish
Employment: 18.9% management, business, and financial, 5.6% computer, engineering, and science, 19.2% education, legal, community service, arts, and media, 9.9% healthcare practitioners, 11.5% service, 23.7% sales and office, 5.7% natural resources, construction, and maintenance, 5.5% production, transportation, and material moving
Income: Per capita: $44,864; Median household: $79,158; Average household: $109,217; Households with income of $100,000 or more: 38.5%; Poverty rate: 4.3%
Educational Attainment: High school diploma or higher: 96.7%; Bachelor's degree or higher: 52.2%; Graduate/professional degree or higher: 26.9%

School District(s)
Fayetteville-Manlius Central SD (KG-12)
Enrollment: 4,255 . . . . (315) 692-1200
Housing: Homeownership rate: 77.1%; Median home value: $184,200; Median year structure built: 1971; Homeowner vacancy rate: 0.1%; Median selected monthly owner costs: $1,742 with a mortgage, $731 without a mortgage; Median gross rent: $938 per month; Rental vacancy rate: 3.5%
Health Insurance: 96.9% have insurance; 80.8% have private insurance; 32.7% have public insurance; 3.1% do not have insurance; 3.2% of children under 18 do not have insurance
Safety: Violent crime rate: 6.9 per 10,000 population; Property crime rate: 138.9 per 10,000 population
Transportation: Commute: 91.1% car, 0.6% public transportation, 1.3% walk, 6.5% work from home; Mean travel time to work: 22.0 minutes
Additional Information Contacts
Town of Manlius . . . . (315) 637-3521
http://www.townofmanlius.org

MANLIUS (village). Covers a land area of 1.785 square miles and a water area of 0.002 square miles. Located at 43.00° N. Lat; 75.98° W. Long. Elevation is 591 feet.
Population: 4,566; Growth (since 2000): -5.3%; Density: 2,557.6 persons per square mile; Race: 88.3% White, 3.0% Black/African American, 5.2% Asian, 0.4% American Indian/Alaska Native, 0.0% Native Hawaiian/Other Pacific Islander, 3.1% Two or more races, 1.9% Hispanic of any race; Average household size: 2.38; Median age: 41.1; Age under 18: 24.3%; Age 65 and over: 18.3%; Males per 100 females: 87.4; Marriage status: 24.0% never married, 55.4% now married, 1.5% separated, 7.1% widowed, 13.5% divorced; Foreign born: 5.4%; Speak English only: 91.2%; With disability: 12.7%; Veterans: 6.9%; Ancestry: 25.1% Irish, 17.3% German, 13.4% English, 10.9% Italian, 5.7% Polish
Employment: 15.9% management, business, and financial, 4.0% computer, engineering, and science, 23.0% education, legal, community service, arts, and media, 7.1% healthcare practitioners, 12.7% service, 23.3% sales and office, 5.9% natural resources, construction, and maintenance, 8.1% production, transportation, and material moving
Income: Per capita: $36,497; Median household: $62,399; Average household: $85,116; Households with income of $100,000 or more: 32.3%; Poverty rate: 6.1%
Educational Attainment: High school diploma or higher: 96.6%; Bachelor's degree or higher: 56.0%; Graduate/professional degree or higher: 24.1%

School District(s)
Fayetteville-Manlius Central SD (KG-12)
Enrollment: 4,255 . . . . (315) 692-1200
Housing: Homeownership rate: 61.9%; Median home value: $198,400; Median year structure built: 1971; Homeowner vacancy rate: 0.0%; Median selected monthly owner costs: $1,832 with a mortgage, $774 without a mortgage; Median gross rent: $789 per month; Rental vacancy rate: 8.2%
Health Insurance: 97.3% have insurance; 78.6% have private insurance; 35.9% have public insurance; 2.7% do not have insurance; 2.2% of children under 18 do not have insurance
Transportation: Commute: 88.5% car, 2.1% public transportation, 2.3% walk, 6.9% work from home; Mean travel time to work: 25.3 minutes
Additional Information Contacts
Village of Manlius . . . . (315) 637-3521
http://www.townofmanlius.org

MARCELLUS (town). Covers a land area of 32.445 square miles and a water area of 0.140 square miles. Located at 42.94° N. Lat; 76.32° W. Long. Elevation is 682 feet.
History: Incorporated 1846.
Population: 6,179; Growth (since 2000): -2.2%; Density: 190.4 persons per square mile; Race: 97.1% White, 0.6% Black/African American, 1.3% Asian, 0.1% American Indian/Alaska Native, 0.0% Native Hawaiian/Other Pacific Islander, 0.9% Two or more races, 1.5% Hispanic of any race; Average household size: 2.50; Median age: 46.7; Age under 18: 22.4%; Age 65 and over: 17.8%; Males per 100 females: 97.7; Marriage status: 27.5% never married, 56.6% now married, 1.1% separated, 7.0% widowed, 9.0% divorced; Foreign born: 2.6%; Speak English only: 96.8%; With disability: 10.3%; Veterans: 8.1%; Ancestry: 32.3% Irish, 25.3% English, 22.5% German, 11.5% Italian, 6.3% Polish
Employment: 20.6% management, business, and financial, 5.2% computer, engineering, and science, 10.5% education, legal, community service, arts, and media, 6.6% healthcare practitioners, 15.1% service,

25.1% sales and office, 8.1% natural resources, construction, and maintenance, 8.7% production, transportation, and material moving
Income: Per capita: $38,145; Median household: $74,167; Average household: $93,127; Households with income of $100,000 or more: 34.5%; Poverty rate: 4.0%
Educational Attainment: High school diploma or higher: 98.0%; Bachelor's degree or higher: 40.2%; Graduate/professional degree or higher: 14.2%

School District(s)
Marcellus Central SD (KG-12)
Enrollment: 1,648 . . . . (315) 673-6000
Housing: Homeownership rate: 83.9%; Median home value: $175,600; Median year structure built: 1965; Homeowner vacancy rate: 0.8%; Median selected monthly owner costs: $1,669 with a mortgage, $629 without a mortgage; Median gross rent: $822 per month; Rental vacancy rate: 5.5%
Health Insurance: 94.5% have insurance; 84.0% have private insurance; 27.6% have public insurance; 5.5% do not have insurance; 7.9% of children under 18 do not have insurance
Transportation: Commute: 88.0% car, 0.3% public transportation, 2.4% walk, 8.5% work from home; Mean travel time to work: 23.4 minutes

MARCELLUS (village). Covers a land area of 0.622 square miles and a water area of 0 square miles. Located at 42.98° N. Lat; 76.34° W. Long. Elevation is 682 feet.
Population: 1,719; Growth (since 2000): -5.9%; Density: 2,764.4 persons per square mile; Race: 95.5% White, 0.7% Black/African American, 3.4% Asian, 0.3% American Indian/Alaska Native, 0.0% Native Hawaiian/Other Pacific Islander, 0.1% Two or more races, 0.6% Hispanic of any race; Average household size: 2.27; Median age: 43.9; Age under 18: 20.0%; Age 65 and over: 19.7%; Males per 100 females: 86.5; Marriage status: 35.1% never married, 47.6% now married, 2.4% separated, 8.4% widowed, 9.0% divorced; Foreign born: 3.9%; Speak English only: 95.5%; With disability: 11.5%; Veterans: 9.4%; Ancestry: 34.3% Irish, 25.5% German, 19.6% English, 10.6% Italian, 8.0% Polish
Employment: 18.9% management, business, and financial, 2.6% computer, engineering, and science, 14.3% education, legal, community service, arts, and media, 4.9% healthcare practitioners, 19.5% service, 26.4% sales and office, 4.0% natural resources, construction, and maintenance, 9.4% production, transportation, and material moving
Income: Per capita: $43,320; Median household: $56,250; Average household: $93,435; Households with income of $100,000 or more: 28.9%; Poverty rate: 3.5%
Educational Attainment: High school diploma or higher: 98.1%; Bachelor's degree or higher: 43.9%; Graduate/professional degree or higher: 15.6%

School District(s)
Marcellus Central SD (KG-12)
Enrollment: 1,648 . . . . (315) 673-6000
Housing: Homeownership rate: 56.5%; Median home value: $156,900; Median year structure built: 1957; Homeowner vacancy rate: 0.0%; Median selected monthly owner costs: $1,494 with a mortgage, $587 without a mortgage; Median gross rent: $818 per month; Rental vacancy rate: 6.5%
Health Insurance: 93.9% have insurance; 83.0% have private insurance; 29.4% have public insurance; 6.1% do not have insurance; 1.1% of children under 18 do not have insurance
Safety: Violent crime rate: 0.0 per 10,000 population; Property crime rate: 39.7 per 10,000 population
Transportation: Commute: 89.2% car, 0.4% public transportation, 6.0% walk, 4.3% work from home; Mean travel time to work: 21.4 minutes
Additional Information Contacts
Village of Marcellus . . . . (315) 673-3112
http://villageofmarcellus.com

MARIETTA (unincorporated postal area)
ZCTA: 13110
Covers a land area of 24.574 square miles and a water area of 0.010 square miles. Located at 42.90° N. Lat; 76.28° W. Long. Elevation is 797 feet.
Population: 2,298; Growth (since 2000): -7.0%; Density: 93.5 persons per square mile; Race: 97.6% White, 0.0% Black/African American, 0.4% Asian, 0.2% American Indian/Alaska Native, 0.0% Native Hawaiian/Other Pacific Islander, 1.8% Two or more races, 3.4% Hispanic of any race; Average household size: 2.42; Median age: 49.5; Age under 18: 21.7%; Age 65 and over: 19.1%; Males per 100 females: 106.9; Marriage status: 22.0% never married, 58.1% now married, 1.8%

separated, 8.9% widowed, 11.1% divorced; Foreign born: 2.4%; Speak English only: 95.9%; With disability: 11.8%; Veterans: 8.8%; Ancestry: 29.1% Irish, 21.2% German, 19.9% English, 9.2% Italian, 7.1% American

Employment: 15.3% management, business, and financial, 8.2% computer, engineering, and science, 13.4% education, legal, community service, arts, and media, 11.0% healthcare practitioners, 12.1% service, 20.7% sales and office, 11.7% natural resources, construction, and maintenance, 7.5% production, transportation, and material moving

Income: Per capita: $38,560; Median household: $77,431; Average household: $91,422; Households with income of $100,000 or more: 36.0%; Poverty rate: 6.0%

Educational Attainment: High school diploma or higher: 94.2%; Bachelor's degree or higher: 34.2%; Graduate/professional degree or higher: 13.4%

Housing: Homeownership rate: 89.9%; Median home value: $171,200; Median year structure built: 1973; Homeowner vacancy rate: 2.8%; Median selected monthly owner costs: $1,347 with a mortgage, $647 without a mortgage; Median gross rent: $720 per month; Rental vacancy rate: 0.0%

Health Insurance: 98.1% have insurance; 80.9% have private insurance; 32.9% have public insurance; 1.9% do not have insurance; 0.0% of children under 18 do not have insurance

Transportation: Commute: 87.0% car, 0.0% public transportation, 1.4% walk, 11.2% work from home; Mean travel time to work: 27.8 minutes

MATTYDALE (CDP). Covers a land area of 1.920 square miles and a water area of 0 square miles. Located at 43.10° N. Lat; 76.14° W. Long. Elevation is 404 feet.

Population: 6,611; Growth (since 2000): 3.8%; Density: 3,442.4 persons per square mile; Race: 85.9% White, 7.1% Black/African American, 1.2% Asian, 1.1% American Indian/Alaska Native, 0.0% Native Hawaiian/Other Pacific Islander, 4.4% Two or more races, 7.4% Hispanic of any race; Average household size: 2.56; Median age: 35.7; Age under 18: 25.9%; Age 65 and over: 12.8%; Males per 100 females: 91.5; Marriage status: 40.3% never married, 36.3% now married, 3.0% separated, 5.1% widowed, 18.3% divorced; Foreign born: 3.6%; Speak English only: 93.6%; With disability: 15.1%; Veterans: 7.8%; Ancestry: 23.6% Irish, 18.4% German, 14.9% Italian, 9.2% English, 7.6% Polish

Employment: 11.2% management, business, and financial, 2.0% computer, engineering, and science, 5.3% education, legal, community service, arts, and media, 2.7% healthcare practitioners, 21.4% service, 30.3% sales and office, 8.6% natural resources, construction, and maintenance, 18.4% production, transportation, and material moving

Income: Per capita: $24,008; Median household: $45,902; Average household: $59,634; Households with income of $100,000 or more: 9.5%; Poverty rate: 20.8%

Educational Attainment: High school diploma or higher: 88.0%; Bachelor's degree or higher: 14.5%; Graduate/professional degree or higher: 3.9%

Vocational/Technical School(s)
Continental School of Beauty Culture-Mattydale (Private, For-profit)
  Enrollment: 249 . . . . (585) 272-8060
  Tuition: $12,690

Housing: Homeownership rate: 65.7%; Median home value: $85,400; Median year structure built: 1953; Homeowner vacancy rate: 2.5%; Median selected monthly owner costs: $986 with a mortgage, $375 without a mortgage; Median gross rent: $875 per month; Rental vacancy rate: 7.6%

Health Insurance: 92.6% have insurance; 65.3% have private insurance; 44.6% have public insurance; 7.4% do not have insurance; 2.5% of children under 18 do not have insurance

Transportation: Commute: 87.3% car, 1.8% public transportation, 7.0% walk, 0.8% work from home; Mean travel time to work: 17.2 minutes

MEMPHIS (unincorporated postal area)
ZCTA: 13112

Covers a land area of 20.254 square miles and a water area of 1.328 square miles. Located at 43.11° N. Lat; 76.42° W. Long. Elevation is 433 feet.

Population: 1,850; Growth (since 2000): -3.7%; Density: 91.3 persons per square mile; Race: 99.7% White, 0.3% Black/African American, 0.0% Asian, 0.0% American Indian/Alaska Native, 0.0% Native Hawaiian/Other Pacific Islander, 0.0% Two or more races, 0.0% Hispanic of any race; Average household size: 2.65; Median age: 47.1; Age under 18: 21.7%; Age 65 and over: 20.1%; Males per 100 females:

106.2; Marriage status: 18.2% never married, 65.0% now married, 1.1% separated, 4.4% widowed, 12.3% divorced; Foreign born: 0.5%; Speak English only: 99.5%; With disability: 18.3%; Veterans: 6.5%; Ancestry: 22.8% German, 19.1% Irish, 17.4% Italian, 15.0% English, 7.5% American

Employment: 5.6% management, business, and financial, 0.6% computer, engineering, and science, 19.7% education, legal, community service, arts, and media, 4.9% healthcare practitioners, 14.1% service, 23.9% sales and office, 17.1% natural resources, construction, and maintenance, 14.1% production, transportation, and material moving

Income: Per capita: $26,919; Median household: $58,500; Average household: $70,998; Households with income of $100,000 or more: 19.1%; Poverty rate: 18.2%

Educational Attainment: High school diploma or higher: 94.2%; Bachelor's degree or higher: 23.8%; Graduate/professional degree or higher: 15.3%

Housing: Homeownership rate: 95.7%; Median home value: $137,100; Median year structure built: 1964; Homeowner vacancy rate: 0.0%; Median selected monthly owner costs: $1,305 with a mortgage, $443 without a mortgage; Median gross rent: n/a per month; Rental vacancy rate: 0.0%

Health Insurance: 97.7% have insurance; 75.7% have private insurance; 44.9% have public insurance; 2.3% do not have insurance; 2.6% of children under 18 do not have insurance

Transportation: Commute: 98.7% car, 0.0% public transportation, 0.0% walk, 0.0% work from home; Mean travel time to work: 26.9 minutes

MINOA (village). Covers a land area of 1.273 square miles and a water area of 0 square miles. Located at 43.07° N. Lat; 76.01° W. Long. Elevation is 413 feet.

Population: 3,519; Growth (since 2000): 5.1%; Density: 2,763.9 persons per square mile; Race: 92.4% White, 3.3% Black/African American, 0.0% Asian, 0.0% American Indian/Alaska Native, 0.0% Native Hawaiian/Other Pacific Islander, 4.3% Two or more races, 1.9% Hispanic of any race; Average household size: 2.53; Median age: 38.4; Age under 18: 26.0%; Age 65 and over: 18.1%; Males per 100 females: 88.0; Marriage status: 22.2% never married, 55.2% now married, 1.2% separated, 10.6% widowed, 12.0% divorced; Foreign born: 2.1%; Speak English only: 97.4%; With disability: 11.4%; Veterans: 6.9%; Ancestry: 27.3% Irish, 17.3% Italian, 14.7% English, 12.6% German, 5.1% Polish

Employment: 10.8% management, business, and financial, 8.9% computer, engineering, and science, 17.4% education, legal, community service, arts, and media, 6.5% healthcare practitioners, 17.4% service, 30.8% sales and office, 5.2% natural resources, construction, and maintenance, 3.0% production, transportation, and material moving

Income: Per capita: $28,298; Median household: $58,253; Average household: $70,040; Households with income of $100,000 or more: 20.2%; Poverty rate: 2.6%

Educational Attainment: High school diploma or higher: 98.8%; Bachelor's degree or higher: 33.1%; Graduate/professional degree or higher: 16.4%

School District(s)
East Syracuse-Minoa Central SD (PK-12)
  Enrollment: 3,431 . . . . (315) 434-3012

Housing: Homeownership rate: 76.3%; Median home value: $136,900; Median year structure built: 1972; Homeowner vacancy rate: 0.0%; Median selected monthly owner costs: $1,334 with a mortgage, $616 without a mortgage; Median gross rent: $786 per month; Rental vacancy rate: 0.0%

Health Insurance: 100.0% have insurance; 88.4% have private insurance; 26.2% have public insurance; 0.0% do not have insurance; 0.0% of children under 18 do not have insurance

Transportation: Commute: 94.6% car, 1.2% public transportation, 0.0% walk, 4.1% work from home; Mean travel time to work: 20.1 minutes

NEDROW (CDP). Covers a land area of 0.959 square miles and a water area of 0 square miles. Located at 42.98° N. Lat; 76.14° W. Long. Elevation is 472 feet.

Population: 2,332; Growth (since 2000): 3.0%; Density: 2,430.7 persons per square mile; Race: 63.3% White, 20.5% Black/African American, 0.9% Asian, 10.0% American Indian/Alaska Native, 0.0% Native Hawaiian/Other Pacific Islander, 5.4% Two or more races, 3.0% Hispanic of any race; Average household size: 2.49; Median age: 38.9; Age under 18: 22.1%; Age 65 and over: 13.1%; Males per 100 females: 91.6; Marriage status: 45.6% never married, 37.8% now married, 2.1% separated, 8.3% widowed, 8.4% divorced; Foreign born: 6.5%; Speak English only: 90.5%;

With disability: 17.6%; Veterans: 6.7%; Ancestry: 19.8% Irish, 13.9% German, 10.7% Italian, 7.9% English, 5.5% Scottish
Employment: 9.1% management, business, and financial, 5.0% computer, engineering, and science, 9.8% education, legal, community service, arts, and media, 6.7% healthcare practitioners, 23.9% service, 28.0% sales and office, 8.9% natural resources, construction, and maintenance, 8.6% production, transportation, and material moving
Income: Per capita: $29,133; Median household: $48,770; Average household: $71,049; Households with income of $100,000 or more: 16.8%; Poverty rate: 16.2%
Educational Attainment: High school diploma or higher: 87.5%; Bachelor's degree or higher: 18.1%; Graduate/professional degree or higher: 9.5%

School District(s)
Lafayette Central SD (PK-12)
    Enrollment: 923 . . . . (315) 677-9728
Onondaga Central SD (PK-12)
    Enrollment: 902 . . . . (315) 552-5000
Housing: Homeownership rate: 90.1%; Median home value: $84,600; Median year structure built: 1953; Homeowner vacancy rate: 1.9%; Median selected monthly owner costs: $994 with a mortgage, $462 without a mortgage; Median gross rent: $648 per month; Rental vacancy rate: 0.0%
Health Insurance: 95.7% have insurance; 64.6% have private insurance; 41.2% have public insurance; 4.3% do not have insurance; 0.0% of children under 18 do not have insurance
Transportation: Commute: 90.0% car, 2.2% public transportation, 5.8% walk, 2.1% work from home; Mean travel time to work: 18.1 minutes

NORTH SYRACUSE (village). Covers a land area of 1.958 square miles and a water area of 0 square miles. Located at 43.13° N. Lat; 76.13° W. Long. Elevation is 420 feet.
History: Incorporated 1925.
Population: 6,719; Growth (since 2000): -2.1%; Density: 3,432.0 persons per square mile; Race: 89.9% White, 3.7% Black/African American, 0.0% Asian, 0.7% American Indian/Alaska Native, 0.0% Native Hawaiian/Other Pacific Islander, 5.4% Two or more races, 2.4% Hispanic of any race; Average household size: 2.26; Median age: 42.0; Age under 18: 20.3%; Age 65 and over: 18.2%; Males per 100 females: 93.3; Marriage status: 31.7% never married, 43.2% now married, 5.1% separated, 8.3% widowed, 16.9% divorced; Foreign born: 1.9%; Speak English only: 97.1%; With disability: 17.5%; Veterans: 7.6%; Ancestry: 25.0% Irish, 22.2% German, 13.9% Italian, 13.2% English, 11.0% French
Employment: 12.0% management, business, and financial, 4.2% computer, engineering, and science, 9.4% education, legal, community service, arts, and media, 5.1% healthcare practitioners, 17.5% service, 32.8% sales and office, 8.5% natural resources, construction, and maintenance, 10.5% production, transportation, and material moving
Income: Per capita: $26,885; Median household: $43,844; Average household: $58,927; Households with income of $100,000 or more: 13.7%; Poverty rate: 12.4%
Educational Attainment: High school diploma or higher: 91.5%; Bachelor's degree or higher: 24.7%; Graduate/professional degree or higher: 7.0%

School District(s)
North Syracuse Central SD (PK-12)
    Enrollment: 8,989 . . . . (315) 218-2151
Housing: Homeownership rate: 61.8%; Median home value: $102,900; Median year structure built: 1958; Homeowner vacancy rate: 1.9%; Median selected monthly owner costs: $1,074 with a mortgage, $516 without a mortgage; Median gross rent: $826 per month; Rental vacancy rate: 5.6%
Health Insurance: 95.7% have insurance; 73.6% have private insurance; 39.9% have public insurance; 4.3% do not have insurance; 3.7% of children under 18 do not have insurance
Safety: Violent crime rate: 13.2 per 10,000 population; Property crime rate: 145.7 per 10,000 population
Transportation: Commute: 89.7% car, 0.7% public transportation, 4.1% walk, 3.0% work from home; Mean travel time to work: 18.0 minutes
Additional Information Contacts
Village of North Syracuse . . . . (315) 458-0900
    http://northsyracuseny.org

ONONDAGA (town). Covers a land area of 57.741 square miles and a water area of 0.096 square miles. Located at 42.98° N. Lat; 76.22° W. Long.
History: The town is named after the native Onondaga tribe, part of the Iroquois Confederacy. As early as 1600, Onondaga served as the capital of the Iroquois League and the primary settlement of the Onondaga people.
Population: 23,020; Growth (since 2000): 9.3%; Density: 398.7 persons per square mile; Race: 88.5% White, 4.2% Black/African American, 2.8% Asian, 1.2% American Indian/Alaska Native, 0.0% Native Hawaiian/Other Pacific Islander, 3.0% Two or more races, 3.0% Hispanic of any race; Average household size: 2.53; Median age: 42.9; Age under 18: 21.1%; Age 65 and over: 15.9%; Males per 100 females: 92.8; Marriage status: 31.7% never married, 54.7% now married, 2.1% separated, 6.4% widowed, 7.2% divorced; Foreign born: 5.8%; Speak English only: 91.8%; With disability: 9.4%; Veterans: 7.2%; Ancestry: 28.8% Irish, 18.6% Italian, 18.3% German, 12.8% English, 5.9% Polish
Employment: 18.4% management, business, and financial, 6.0% computer, engineering, and science, 15.1% education, legal, community service, arts, and media, 9.0% healthcare practitioners, 13.9% service, 25.4% sales and office, 6.5% natural resources, construction, and maintenance, 5.6% production, transportation, and material moving
Income: Per capita: $37,931; Median household: $80,495; Average household: $98,934; Households with income of $100,000 or more: 38.3%; Poverty rate: 5.6%
Educational Attainment: High school diploma or higher: 93.4%; Bachelor's degree or higher: 42.6%; Graduate/professional degree or higher: 18.6%
Housing: Homeownership rate: 80.4%; Median home value: $172,700; Median year structure built: 1972; Homeowner vacancy rate: 1.4%; Median selected monthly owner costs: $1,536 with a mortgage, $631 without a mortgage; Median gross rent: $949 per month; Rental vacancy rate: 5.5%
Health Insurance: 97.1% have insurance; 85.0% have private insurance; 25.0% have public insurance; 2.9% do not have insurance; 2.3% of children under 18 do not have insurance
Transportation: Commute: 92.9% car, 0.9% public transportation, 2.1% walk, 3.8% work from home; Mean travel time to work: 21.3 minutes
Additional Information Contacts
Town of Onondaga . . . . (315) 469-1583
    http://www.townofonondagany.com

ONONDAGA NATION RESERVATION (reservation). Covers a land area of 9.247 square miles and a water area of 0.046 square miles. Located at 42.93° N. Lat; 76.15° W. Long.
Population: 141; Growth (since 2000): -90.4%; Density: 15.2 persons per square mile; Race: 28.4% White, 0.0% Black/African American, 71.6% Asian, 0.0% American Indian/Alaska Native, 0.0% Native Hawaiian/Other Pacific Islander, 0.0% Two or more races, 28.4% Hispanic of any race; Average household size: 2.56; Median age: 76.4; Age under 18: 0.0%; Age 65 and over: 67.4%; Males per 100 females: 87.2; Marriage status: 0.0% never married, 100.0% now married, 0.0% separated, 0.0% widowed, 0.0% divorced; Foreign born: 61.0%; Speak English only: 0.0%; With disability: 39.0%; Veterans: 0.0%; Ancestry: n/a
Employment: 0.0% management, business, and financial, 100.0% computer, engineering, and science, 0.0% education, legal, community service, arts, and media, 0.0% healthcare practitioners, 0.0% service, 0.0% sales and office, 0.0% natural resources, construction, and maintenance, 0.0% production, transportation, and material moving
Income: Per capita: $38,301; Median household: n/a; Average household: n/a; Households with income of $100,000 or more: 100.0%; Poverty rate: n/a
Educational Attainment: High school diploma or higher: 39.0%; Bachelor's degree or higher: 39.0%; Graduate/professional degree or higher: n/a
Housing: Homeownership rate: 100.0%; Median home value: n/a; Median year structure built: n/a; Homeowner vacancy rate: 0.0%; Median selected monthly owner costs: n/a with a mortgage, n/a without a mortgage; Median gross rent: n/a per month; Rental vacancy rate: 0.0%
Health Insurance: 100.0% have insurance; 71.6% have private insurance; 67.4% have public insurance; 0.0% do not have insurance; 0.0% of children under 18 do not have insurance
Transportation: Commute: 0.0% car, 100.0% public transportation, 0.0% walk, 0.0% work from home; Mean travel time to work: 0.0 minutes

OTISCO (town). Covers a land area of 29.532 square miles and a water area of 1.629 square miles. Located at 42.86° N. Lat; 76.23° W. Long. Elevation is 1,480 feet.

Population: 2,558; Growth (since 2000): -0.1%; Density: 86.6 persons per square mile; Race: 97.7% White, 0.0% Black/African American, 0.0% Asian, 0.2% American Indian/Alaska Native, 0.0% Native Hawaiian/Other Pacific Islander, 2.2% Two or more races, 1.3% Hispanic of any race; Average household size: 2.58; Median age: 46.4; Age under 18: 21.7%; Age 65 and over: 15.6%; Males per 100 females: 105.7; Marriage status: 24.8% never married, 60.1% now married, 3.0% separated, 4.6% widowed, 10.5% divorced; Foreign born: 0.4%; Speak English only: 99.4%; With disability: 13.6%; Veterans: 8.4%; Ancestry: 29.4% German, 22.5% Irish, 19.7% English, 8.4% Italian, 7.0% Polish

Employment: 17.3% management, business, and financial, 4.3% computer, engineering, and science, 15.4% education, legal, community service, arts, and media, 5.2% healthcare practitioners, 16.3% service, 17.1% sales and office, 15.2% natural resources, construction, and maintenance, 9.2% production, transportation, and material moving

Income: Per capita: $32,418; Median household: $71,632; Average household: $82,229; Households with income of $100,000 or more: 30.6%; Poverty rate: 12.4%

Educational Attainment: High school diploma or higher: 94.3%; Bachelor's degree or higher: 30.3%; Graduate/professional degree or higher: 14.0%

Housing: Homeownership rate: 82.3%; Median home value: $172,300; Median year structure built: 1977; Homeowner vacancy rate: 0.0%; Median selected monthly owner costs: $1,299 with a mortgage, $580 without a mortgage; Median gross rent: $783 per month; Rental vacancy rate: 0.0%

Health Insurance: 92.2% have insurance; 71.4% have private insurance; 33.5% have public insurance; 7.8% do not have insurance; 3.4% of children under 18 do not have insurance

Transportation: Commute: 88.4% car, 0.5% public transportation, 0.3% walk, 9.6% work from home; Mean travel time to work: 24.6 minutes

POMPEY (town). Covers a land area of 66.378 square miles and a water area of 0.097 square miles. Located at 42.92° N. Lat; 75.99° W. Long. Elevation is 1,673 feet.

Population: 7,320; Growth (since 2000): 18.9%; Density: 110.3 persons per square mile; Race: 91.5% White, 0.8% Black/African American, 4.8% Asian, 0.5% American Indian/Alaska Native, 0.0% Native Hawaiian/Other Pacific Islander, 2.5% Two or more races, 2.8% Hispanic of any race; Average household size: 2.89; Median age: 44.7; Age under 18: 25.6%; Age 65 and over: 15.1%; Males per 100 females: 101.9; Marriage status: 24.0% never married, 64.2% now married, 0.8% separated, 3.9% widowed, 7.9% divorced; Foreign born: 4.3%; Speak English only: 90.6%; With disability: 8.2%; Veterans: 6.3%; Ancestry: 20.4% Irish, 19.6% German, 14.5% English, 10.1% Italian, 5.9% American

Employment: 22.4% management, business, and financial, 8.7% computer, engineering, and science, 11.2% education, legal, community service, arts, and media, 10.2% healthcare practitioners, 8.6% service, 20.6% sales and office, 10.7% natural resources, construction, and maintenance, 7.6% production, transportation, and material moving

Income: Per capita: $52,589; Median household: $111,049; Average household: $150,235; Households with income of $100,000 or more: 55.2%; Poverty rate: 3.5%

Educational Attainment: High school diploma or higher: 96.8%; Bachelor's degree or higher: 48.3%; Graduate/professional degree or higher: 21.7%

Housing: Homeownership rate: 92.0%; Median home value: $236,400; Median year structure built: 1975; Homeowner vacancy rate: 2.9%; Median selected monthly owner costs: $1,985 with a mortgage, $713 without a mortgage; Median gross rent: $741 per month; Rental vacancy rate: 19.4%

Health Insurance: 94.9% have insurance; 79.2% have private insurance; 26.9% have public insurance; 5.1% do not have insurance; 0.0% of children under 18 do not have insurance

Transportation: Commute: 95.2% car, 0.0% public transportation, 0.4% walk, 4.4% work from home; Mean travel time to work: 25.3 minutes

Additional Information Contacts

Town of Pompey . . . . (315) 682-9877
   http://www.townofpompey.com

SALINA (town). Covers a land area of 13.750 square miles and a water area of 1.311 square miles. Located at 43.10° N. Lat; 76.17° W. Long.

Population: 33,307; Growth (since 2000): 0.1%; Density: 2,422.3 persons per square mile; Race: 88.6% White, 4.9% Black/African American, 2.4%

Asian, 0.2% American Indian/Alaska Native, 0.0% Native Hawaiian/Other Pacific Islander, 3.5% Two or more races, 3.3% Hispanic of any race; Average household size: 2.25; Median age: 42.4; Age under 18: 20.0%; Age 65 and over: 19.9%; Males per 100 females: 90.4; Marriage status: 33.0% never married, 46.9% now married, 2.3% separated, 6.9% widowed, 13.2% divorced; Foreign born: 5.3%; Speak English only: 92.3%; With disability: 13.1%; Veterans: 8.6%; Ancestry: 25.3% Italian, 22.8% Irish, 20.3% German, 11.5% English, 7.9% Polish

Employment: 14.9% management, business, and financial, 5.2% computer, engineering, and science, 12.0% education, legal, community service, arts, and media, 6.2% healthcare practitioners, 17.1% service, 28.2% sales and office, 5.7% natural resources, construction, and maintenance, 10.8% production, transportation, and material moving

Income: Per capita: $30,097; Median household: $53,708; Average household: $66,440; Households with income of $100,000 or more: 17.9%; Poverty rate: 10.7%

Educational Attainment: High school diploma or higher: 91.4%; Bachelor's degree or higher: 28.1%; Graduate/professional degree or higher: 11.0%

Housing: Homeownership rate: 67.1%; Median home value: $110,900; Median year structure built: 1960; Homeowner vacancy rate: 2.1%; Median selected monthly owner costs: $1,164 with a mortgage, $481 without a mortgage; Median gross rent: $871 per month; Rental vacancy rate: 5.8%

Health Insurance: 95.8% have insurance; 76.9% have private insurance; 38.2% have public insurance; 4.2% do not have insurance; 2.4% of children under 18 do not have insurance

Transportation: Commute: 92.5% car, 1.5% public transportation, 2.2% walk, 2.6% work from home; Mean travel time to work: 18.1 minutes

Additional Information Contacts

Town of Salina . . . . (315) 457-2710
   http://www.salina.ny.us

SENECA KNOLLS (CDP). Covers a land area of 1.248 square miles and a water area of 0 square miles. Located at 43.12° N. Lat; 76.29° W. Long. Elevation is 407 feet.

Population: 2,136; Growth (since 2000): -0.1%; Density: 1,710.9 persons per square mile; Race: 98.3% White, 0.0% Black/African American, 0.0% Asian, 0.0% American Indian/Alaska Native, 0.0% Native Hawaiian/Other Pacific Islander, 1.7% Two or more races, 4.8% Hispanic of any race; Average household size: 2.20; Median age: 50.5; Age under 18: 16.3%; Age 65 and over: 21.5%; Males per 100 females: 94.5; Marriage status: 28.6% never married, 50.9% now married, 0.0% separated, 5.7% widowed, 14.8% divorced; Foreign born: 7.8%; Speak English only: 98.5%; With disability: 11.8%; Veterans: 11.0%; Ancestry: 36.2% Irish, 24.9% German, 22.7% English, 11.8% Italian, 9.8% French

Employment: 12.7% management, business, and financial, 5.7% computer, engineering, and science, 2.6% education, legal, community service, arts, and media, 10.5% healthcare practitioners, 14.7% service, 34.6% sales and office, 14.9% natural resources, construction, and maintenance, 4.5% production, transportation, and material moving

Income: Per capita: $26,986; Median household: $52,614; Average household: $57,815; Households with income of $100,000 or more: 14.6%; Poverty rate: 9.4%

Educational Attainment: High school diploma or higher: 96.0%; Bachelor's degree or higher: 11.2%; Graduate/professional degree or higher: 9.1%

Housing: Homeownership rate: 87.1%; Median home value: $94,800; Median year structure built: 1961; Homeowner vacancy rate: 0.0%; Median selected monthly owner costs: $1,007 with a mortgage, $509 without a mortgage; Median gross rent: $935 per month; Rental vacancy rate: 0.0%

Health Insurance: 98.6% have insurance; 78.1% have private insurance; 42.6% have public insurance; 1.4% do not have insurance; 0.0% of children under 18 do not have insurance

Transportation: Commute: 87.4% car, 1.9% public transportation, 7.2% walk, 3.5% work from home; Mean travel time to work: 20.7 minutes

SKANEATELES (town). Covers a land area of 42.606 square miles and a water area of 6.220 square miles. Located at 42.89° N. Lat; 76.41° W. Long. Elevation is 873 feet.

History: Village in a Historic District. Settled before 1800, incorporated 1833.

Population: 7,244; Growth (since 2000): -1.1%; Density: 170.0 persons per square mile; Race: 98.1% White, 0.0% Black/African American, 0.6% Asian, 0.4% American Indian/Alaska Native, 0.2% Native Hawaiian/Other Pacific Islander, 0.7% Two or more races, 0.4% Hispanic of any race;

Average household size: 2.26; Median age: 52.3; Age under 18: 19.8%; Age 65 and over: 25.2%; Males per 100 females: 94.2; Marriage status: 18.8% never married, 63.6% now married, 0.8% separated, 8.5% widowed, 9.0% divorced; Foreign born: 3.2%; Speak English only: 96.0%; With disability: 9.3%; Veterans: 7.2%; Ancestry: 28.3% Irish, 25.7% German, 21.9% English, 16.0% Italian, 8.3% Polish

Employment: 22.6% management, business, and financial, 4.0% computer, engineering, and science, 18.8% education, legal, community service, arts, and media, 9.5% healthcare practitioners, 12.3% service, 19.8% sales and office, 6.1% natural resources, construction, and maintenance, 6.9% production, transportation, and material moving

Income: Per capita: $61,452; Median household: $84,150; Average household: $138,522; Households with income of $100,000 or more: 42.7%; Poverty rate: 3.3%

Educational Attainment: High school diploma or higher: 98.7%; Bachelor's degree or higher: 54.4%; Graduate/professional degree or higher: 27.8%

School District(s)
Skaneateles Central SD (KG-12)
    Enrollment: 1,373 . . . . (315) 291-2221

Housing: Homeownership rate: 80.7%; Median home value: $290,100; Median year structure built: 1958; Homeowner vacancy rate: 1.3%; Median selected monthly owner costs: $1,952 with a mortgage, $780 without a mortgage; Median gross rent: $848 per month; Rental vacancy rate: 8.2%

Health Insurance: 95.8% have insurance; 87.5% have private insurance; 30.1% have public insurance; 4.2% do not have insurance; 2.7% of children under 18 do not have insurance

Transportation: Commute: 88.9% car, 0.4% public transportation, 4.0% walk, 6.1% work from home; Mean travel time to work: 22.8 minutes

Airports: Skaneateles Aero Drome (general aviation)

Additional Information Contacts
Town of Skaneateles . . . . (315) 685-3473
    http://www.townofskaneateles.com

SKANEATELES (village). Covers a land area of 1.414 square miles and a water area of 0.307 square miles. Located at 42.95° N. Lat; 76.43° W. Long. Elevation is 873 feet.

Population: 2,471; Growth (since 2000): -5.5%; Density: 1,748.0 persons per square mile; Race: 98.0% White, 0.0% Black/African American, 1.3% Asian, 0.0% American Indian/Alaska Native, 0.0% Native Hawaiian/Other Pacific Islander, 0.6% Two or more races, 0.3% Hispanic of any race; Average household size: 2.10; Median age: 51.7; Age under 18: 21.7%; Age 65 and over: 28.0%; Males per 100 females: 81.9; Marriage status: 15.6% never married, 62.1% now married, 0.8% separated, 9.7% widowed, 12.6% divorced; Foreign born: 4.6%; Speak English only: 96.0%; With disability: 8.7%; Veterans: 10.2%; Ancestry: 31.5% Irish, 23.8% English, 22.3% German, 11.3% Italian, 6.6% Polish

Employment: 27.2% management, business, and financial, 3.2% computer, engineering, and science, 22.3% education, legal, community service, arts, and media, 13.1% healthcare practitioners, 7.2% service, 17.2% sales and office, 4.0% natural resources, construction, and maintenance, 5.8% production, transportation, and material moving

Income: Per capita: $75,941; Median household: $82,500; Average household: $159,115; Households with income of $100,000 or more: 44.7%; Poverty rate: 4.2%

Educational Attainment: High school diploma or higher: 99.2%; Bachelor's degree or higher: 65.6%; Graduate/professional degree or higher: 32.8%

School District(s)
Skaneateles Central SD (KG-12)
    Enrollment: 1,373 . . . . (315) 291-2221

Housing: Homeownership rate: 69.8%; Median home value: $322,600; Median year structure built: Before 1940; Homeowner vacancy rate: 3.9%; Median selected monthly owner costs: $2,085 with a mortgage, $775 without a mortgage; Median gross rent: $845 per month; Rental vacancy rate: 8.6%

Health Insurance: 98.4% have insurance; 92.4% have private insurance; 31.1% have public insurance; 1.6% do not have insurance; 0.0% of children under 18 do not have insurance

Safety: Violent crime rate: 4.0 per 10,000 population; Property crime rate: 72.2 per 10,000 population

Transportation: Commute: 82.4% car, 1.2% public transportation, 6.1% walk, 9.0% work from home; Mean travel time to work: 25.3 minutes

Airports: Skaneateles Aero Drome (general aviation)

SKANEATELES FALLS (unincorporated postal area)
ZCTA: 13153
Covers a land area of 0.894 square miles and a water area of 0 square miles. Located at 43.00° N. Lat; 76.45° W. Long. Elevation is 705 feet.

Population: 343; Growth (since 2000): n/a; Density: 383.5 persons per square mile; Race: 100.0% White, 0.0% Black/African American, 0.0% Asian, 0.0% American Indian/Alaska Native, 0.0% Native Hawaiian/Other Pacific Islander, 0.0% Two or more races, 0.0% Hispanic of any race; Average household size: 2.21; Median age: 53.0; Age under 18: 7.6%; Age 65 and over: 17.5%; Males per 100 females: 111.1; Marriage status: 24.0% never married, 55.7% now married, 0.0% separated, 2.8% widowed, 17.5% divorced; Foreign born: 0.0%; Speak English only: 100.0%; With disability: 4.7%; Veterans: 6.3%; Ancestry: 42.6% German, 31.8% Irish, 20.7% English, 7.0% Italian, 4.7% French

Employment: 0.0% management, business, and financial, 0.0% computer, engineering, and science, 6.1% education, legal, community service, arts, and media, 10.6% healthcare practitioners, 25.3% service, 22.0% sales and office, 3.3% natural resources, construction, and maintenance, 32.7% production, transportation, and material moving

Income: Per capita: $25,218; Median household: $43,750; Average household: $52,967; Households with income of $100,000 or more: 3.2%; Poverty rate: 5.8%

Educational Attainment: High school diploma or higher: 96.2%; Bachelor's degree or higher: 12.6%; Graduate/professional degree or higher: 4.7%

Housing: Homeownership rate: 64.5%; Median home value: $155,000; Median year structure built: 1946; Homeowner vacancy rate: 0.0%; Median selected monthly owner costs: $1,654 with a mortgage, $438 without a mortgage; Median gross rent: $775 per month; Rental vacancy rate: 0.0%

Health Insurance: 100.0% have insurance; 89.2% have private insurance; 36.4% have public insurance; 0.0% do not have insurance; 0.0% of children under 18 do not have insurance

Transportation: Commute: 100.0% car, 0.0% public transportation, 0.0% walk, 0.0% work from home; Mean travel time to work: 17.9 minutes

SOLVAY (village). Covers a land area of 1.654 square miles and a water area of 0 square miles. Located at 43.06° N. Lat; 76.21° W. Long. Elevation is 499 feet.

History: In the 20th century, after earlier exploited salt springs had lost their deposits, brine wells provided basis for manufacturing of chlorines, caustic soda, and bicarbonate of soda. Former heavy-manufacturing and chemical-manufacturing have disappeared, mainly due to stricter environmental-quality standards. Incorporated 1894.

Population: 6,438; Growth (since 2000): -5.9%; Density: 3,893.5 persons per square mile; Race: 82.3% White, 2.5% Black/African American, 1.6% Asian, 0.7% American Indian/Alaska Native, 0.0% Native Hawaiian/Other Pacific Islander, 11.2% Two or more races, 10.1% Hispanic of any race; Average household size: 2.19; Median age: 39.4; Age under 18: 20.8%; Age 65 and over: 16.8%; Males per 100 females: 92.0; Marriage status: 39.3% never married, 40.4% now married, 3.4% separated, 7.0% widowed, 13.4% divorced; Foreign born: 5.5%; Speak English only: 88.9%; With disability: 14.3%; Veterans: 8.8%; Ancestry: 30.7% Italian, 26.4% Irish, 13.2% German, 7.4% Polish, 7.2% English

Employment: 11.4% management, business, and financial, 1.4% computer, engineering, and science, 8.0% education, legal, community service, arts, and media, 7.2% healthcare practitioners, 25.4% service, 26.4% sales and office, 8.9% natural resources, construction, and maintenance, 11.3% production, transportation, and material moving

Income: Per capita: $24,708; Median household: $45,746; Average household: $53,025; Households with income of $100,000 or more: 9.9%; Poverty rate: 16.0%

Educational Attainment: High school diploma or higher: 89.3%; Bachelor's degree or higher: 23.3%; Graduate/professional degree or higher: 7.5%

School District(s)
Solvay Union Free SD (PK-12)
    Enrollment: 1,510 . . . . (315) 468-1111

Housing: Homeownership rate: 54.6%; Median home value: $107,700; Median year structure built: 1949; Homeowner vacancy rate: 2.9%; Median selected monthly owner costs: $1,085 with a mortgage, $472 without a mortgage; Median gross rent: $684 per month; Rental vacancy rate: 4.3%

Health Insurance: 92.6% have insurance; 70.7% have private insurance; 39.7% have public insurance; 7.4% do not have insurance; 3.2% of children under 18 do not have insurance
Safety: Violent crime rate: 25.3 per 10,000 population; Property crime rate: 224.4 per 10,000 population
Transportation: Commute: 90.3% car, 2.5% public transportation, 4.0% walk, 3.2% work from home; Mean travel time to work: 19.3 minutes
Additional Information Contacts
Village of Solvay . . . . (315) 468-1670
    http://villageofsolvay.com

SPAFFORD (town). Covers a land area of 32.698 square miles and a water area of 6.518 square miles. Located at 42.83° N. Lat; 76.29° W. Long. Elevation is 1,686 feet.
Population: 1,658; Growth (since 2000): -0.2%; Density: 50.7 persons per square mile; Race: 99.3% White, 0.0% Black/African American, 0.0% Asian, 0.0% American Indian/Alaska Native, 0.0% Native Hawaiian/Other Pacific Islander, 0.5% Two or more races, 1.5% Hispanic of any race; Average household size: 2.39; Median age: 51.8; Age under 18: 19.5%; Age 65 and over: 21.5%; Males per 100 females: 98.6; Marriage status: 19.5% never married, 67.1% now married, 0.8% separated, 4.7% widowed, 8.7% divorced; Foreign born: 1.0%; Speak English only: 96.1%; With disability: 11.2%; Veterans: 7.6%; Ancestry: 27.1% German, 21.1% Irish, 16.9% English, 15.2% Italian, 6.2% American
Employment: 11.1% management, business, and financial, 8.0% computer, engineering, and science, 13.4% education, legal, community service, arts, and media, 13.6% healthcare practitioners, 11.4% service, 21.6% sales and office, 13.2% natural resources, construction, and maintenance, 7.7% production, transportation, and material moving
Income: Per capita: $45,025; Median household: $83,194; Average household: $105,983; Households with income of $100,000 or more: 40.7%; Poverty rate: 6.3%
Educational Attainment: High school diploma or higher: 96.8%; Bachelor's degree or higher: 47.0%; Graduate/professional degree or higher: 23.2%
Housing: Homeownership rate: 90.3%; Median home value: $223,100; Median year structure built: 1974; Homeowner vacancy rate: 2.9%; Median selected monthly owner costs: $1,621 with a mortgage, $657 without a mortgage; Median gross rent: $775 per month; Rental vacancy rate: 0.0%
Health Insurance: 97.4% have insurance; 90.6% have private insurance; 25.4% have public insurance; 2.6% do not have insurance; 0.9% of children under 18 do not have insurance
Transportation: Commute: 92.6% car, 0.0% public transportation, 1.6% walk, 5.0% work from home; Mean travel time to work: 30.2 minutes

SYRACUSE (city). County seat. Covers a land area of 25.043 square miles and a water area of 0.565 square miles. Located at 43.04° N. Lat; 76.14° W. Long. Elevation is 397 feet.
History: The beginnings and early growth of Syracuse are identified with salt. What the French soldiers and Jesuits saw in 1654 was a swamp. The salt springs were discovered by Father Simon LeMoyne. The first settler was Ephraim Webster, who arrived in 1786 and opened a trading station. Syracuse was incorporated as a village in 1825. The name was suggested by John Wilkinson, the first postmaster, who had read a poem describing the ancient Greek city in Sicily, which had also grown around a marsh and salt springs. In 1848, the villages of Syracuse and Salina, together with Lodi, were joined and incorporated as the city of Syracuse in 1881.
Population: 144,405; Growth (since 2000): -2.0%; Density: 5,766.2 persons per square mile; Race: 55.2% White, 29.0% Black/African American, 7.0% Asian, 0.9% American Indian/Alaska Native, 0.0% Native Hawaiian/Other Pacific Islander, 5.5% Two or more races, 9.1% Hispanic of any race; Average household size: 2.34; Median age: 30.6; Age under 18: 21.9%; Age 65 and over: 12.0%; Males per 100 females: 91.0; Marriage status: 54.0% never married, 30.2% now married, 2.9% separated, 5.8% widowed, 10.0% divorced; Foreign born: 12.5%; Speak English only: 81.7%; With disability: 16.2%; Veterans: 5.4%; Ancestry: 14.1% Irish, 11.7% Italian, 10.6% German, 5.2% English, 4.0% Polish
Employment: 9.4% management, business, and financial, 4.3% computer, engineering, and science, 15.5% education, legal, community service, arts, and media, 5.9% healthcare practitioners, 24.0% service, 25.2% sales and office, 5.1% natural resources, construction, and maintenance, 10.6% production, transportation, and material moving
Income: Per capita: $21,187; Median household: $34,716; Average household: $50,825; Households with income of $100,000 or more: 12.0%; Poverty rate: 32.6%

Educational Attainment: High school diploma or higher: 81.5%; Bachelor's degree or higher: 27.4%; Graduate/professional degree or higher: 12.4%
School District(s)
Lyncourt Union Free SD (PK-08)
    Enrollment: 412 . . . . (315) 455-7571
North Syracuse Central SD (PK-12)
    Enrollment: 8,989 . . . . (315) 218-2151
Onondaga-Cortland-Madison Boces
    Enrollment: n/a . . . . (315) 433-2602
Solvay Union Free SD (PK-12)
    Enrollment: 1,510 . . . . (315) 468-1111
Southside Academy Charter School (KG-08)
    Enrollment: 687 . . . . (315) 476-3019
Syracuse Academy of Science Charter School (KG-12)
    Enrollment: 926 . . . . (315) 428-8997
Syracuse City SD (PK-12)
    Enrollment: 21,015 . . . . (315) 435-4161
West Genesee Central SD (KG-12)
    Enrollment: 4,628 . . . . (315) 487-4562
Westhill Central SD (KG-12)
    Enrollment: 1,781 . . . . (315) 426-3218
Four-year College(s)
Le Moyne College (Private, Not-for-profit, Roman Catholic)
    Enrollment: 3,431 . . . . (315) 445-4100
    Tuition: In-state $33,905; Out-of-state $33,905
SUNY College of Environmental Science and Forestry (Public)
    Enrollment: 2,213 . . . . (315) 470-6500
    Tuition: In-state $8,543; Out-of-state $18,193
Syracuse University (Private, Not-for-profit)
    Enrollment: 22,484 . . . . (315) 443-1870
    Tuition: In-state $46,755; Out-of-state $46,755
Upstate Medical University (Public)
    Enrollment: 1,484 . . . . (315) 464-5540
Two-year College(s)
Bryant & Stratton College-Syracuse (Private, For-profit)
    Enrollment: 439 . . . . (315) 472-6603
    Tuition: In-state $17,550; Out-of-state $17,550
Onondaga Community College (Public)
    Enrollment: 10,659 . . . . (315) 498-2622
    Tuition: In-state $5,154; Out-of-state $9,724
Pomeroy College of Nursing at Crouse Hospital (Private, Not-for-profit)
    Enrollment: 265 . . . . (315) 470-7481
    Tuition: In-state $12,145; Out-of-state $12,145
St Joseph's College of Nursing at St Joseph's Hospital Health Center (Private, Not-for-profit, Roman Catholic)
    Enrollment: 298 . . . . (315) 448-5040
    Tuition: In-state $19,700; Out-of-state $19,700
Vocational/Technical School(s)
Onondaga School of Therapeutic Massage-Syracuse (Private, For-profit)
    Enrollment: 34 . . . . (315) 424-1159
    Tuition: $15,575
Housing: Homeownership rate: 38.3%; Median home value: $91,100; Median year structure built: 1945; Homeowner vacancy rate: 3.1%; Median selected monthly owner costs: $1,068 with a mortgage, $476 without a mortgage; Median gross rent: $769 per month; Rental vacancy rate: 7.5%
Health Insurance: 92.8% have insurance; 57.8% have private insurance; 47.9% have public insurance; 7.2% do not have insurance; 3.6% of children under 18 do not have insurance
Hospitals: Crouse Hospital (566 beds); Saint Joseph's Hospital Health Center (431 beds); Syracuse VA Medical Center (164 beds); University Hospital SUNY Health Science Center (356 beds)
Safety: Violent crime rate: 70.5 per 10,000 population; Property crime rate: 336.7 per 10,000 population
Newspapers: Eagle Newspapers (weekly circulation 51,000); Post-Standard (daily circulation 114,000); Syracuse New Times (weekly circulation 40,000)
Transportation: Commute: 73.7% car, 9.6% public transportation, 11.3% walk, 3.3% work from home; Mean travel time to work: 18.4 minutes; Amtrak: Train service available.
Airports: Syracuse Hancock International (primary service/small hub)
Additional Information Contacts
City of Syracuse . . . . (315) 448-8005
    http://www.syrgov.net/home.aspx

TULLY (town). Covers a land area of 25.754 square miles and a water area of 0.525 square miles. Located at 42.81° N. Lat; 76.14° W. Long. Elevation is 1,250 feet.

History: One of many former Finger Lake valleys, with rich agricultural soils.

Population: 2,718; Growth (since 2000): 0.3%; Density: 105.5 persons per square mile; Race: 95.5% White, 0.9% Black/African American, 1.1% Asian, 1.3% American Indian/Alaska Native, 0.0% Native Hawaiian/Other Pacific Islander, 0.7% Two or more races, 2.2% Hispanic of any race; Average household size: 2.60; Median age: 45.9; Age under 18: 23.5%; Age 65 and over: 17.6%; Males per 100 females: 95.6; Marriage status: 33.1% never married, 52.2% now married, 0.7% separated, 4.2% widowed, 10.4% divorced; Foreign born: 3.1%; Speak English only: 96.0%; With disability: 12.2%; Veterans: 11.1%; Ancestry: 29.7% Irish, 24.4% German, 16.2% English, 10.9% Italian, 5.7% French

Employment: 12.5% management, business, and financial, 5.4% computer, engineering, and science, 17.8% education, legal, community service, arts, and media, 8.2% healthcare practitioners, 17.4% service, 18.2% sales and office, 9.0% natural resources, construction, and maintenance, 11.6% production, transportation, and material moving

Income: Per capita: $37,452; Median household: $64,000; Average household: $95,835; Households with income of $100,000 or more: 36.3%; Poverty rate: 6.9%

Educational Attainment: High school diploma or higher: 93.3%; Bachelor's degree or higher: 44.9%; Graduate/professional degree or higher: 21.2%

School District(s)

Tully Central SD (KG-12)
    Enrollment: 819. . . . . (315) 696-6204

Housing: Homeownership rate: 73.4%; Median home value: $200,400; Median year structure built: 1976; Homeowner vacancy rate: 0.0%; Median selected monthly owner costs: $1,831 with a mortgage, $706 without a mortgage; Median gross rent: $844 per month; Rental vacancy rate: 6.7%

Health Insurance: 94.0% have insurance; 73.4% have private insurance; 35.4% have public insurance; 6.0% do not have insurance; 0.0% of children under 18 do not have insurance

Transportation: Commute: 86.5% car, 0.0% public transportation, 1.0% walk, 12.1% work from home; Mean travel time to work: 24.1 minutes

TULLY (village). Covers a land area of 0.717 square miles and a water area of 0 square miles. Located at 42.80° N. Lat; 76.11° W. Long. Elevation is 1,250 feet.

Population: 1,066; Growth (since 2000): 15.4%; Density: 1,485.8 persons per square mile; Race: 93.4% White, 1.8% Black/African American, 0.1% Asian, 3.3% American Indian/Alaska Native, 0.0% Native Hawaiian/Other Pacific Islander, 0.0% Two or more races, 4.7% Hispanic of any race; Average household size: 2.45; Median age: 36.7; Age under 18: 22.8%; Age 65 and over: 18.5%; Males per 100 females: 87.3; Marriage status: 42.3% never married, 33.7% now married, 0.4% separated, 7.0% widowed, 17.1% divorced; Foreign born: 2.3%; Speak English only: 96.2%; With disability: 17.5%; Veterans: 10.7%; Ancestry: 27.4% German, 21.9% English, 14.6% Irish, 13.9% Italian, 4.3% Dutch

Employment: 7.2% management, business, and financial, 6.6% computer, engineering, and science, 11.8% education, legal, community service, arts, and media, 9.1% healthcare practitioners, 21.7% service, 13.6% sales and office, 14.6% natural resources, construction, and maintenance, 15.3% production, transportation, and material moving

Income: Per capita: $27,031; Median household: $45,679; Average household: $63,754; Households with income of $100,000 or more: 19.6%; Poverty rate: 13.4%

Educational Attainment: High school diploma or higher: 89.0%; Bachelor's degree or higher: 28.7%; Graduate/professional degree or higher: 13.9%

School District(s)

Tully Central SD (KG-12)
    Enrollment: 819. . . . . (315) 696-6204

Housing: Homeownership rate: 47.1%; Median home value: $133,300; Median year structure built: Before 1940; Homeowner vacancy rate: 0.0%; Median selected monthly owner costs: $1,223 with a mortgage, $575 without a mortgage; Median gross rent: $843 per month; Rental vacancy rate: 0.0%

Health Insurance: 92.7% have insurance; 62.9% have private insurance; 45.1% have public insurance; 7.3% do not have insurance; 0.0% of children under 18 do not have insurance

Transportation: Commute: 85.1% car, 0.0% public transportation, 0.6% walk, 13.7% work from home; Mean travel time to work: 24.2 minutes

VAN BUREN (town). Covers a land area of 35.408 square miles and a water area of 0.704 square miles. Located at 43.12° N. Lat; 76.35° W. Long. Elevation is 499 feet.

Population: 13,366; Growth (since 2000): 5.5%; Density: 377.5 persons per square mile; Race: 95.2% White, 0.4% Black/African American, 1.1% Asian, 0.4% American Indian/Alaska Native, 0.0% Native Hawaiian/Other Pacific Islander, 2.4% Two or more races, 1.7% Hispanic of any race; Average household size: 2.24; Median age: 44.4; Age under 18: 19.0%; Age 65 and over: 20.7%; Males per 100 females: 94.9; Marriage status: 27.0% never married, 49.9% now married, 0.8% separated, 8.7% widowed, 14.5% divorced; Foreign born: 4.4%; Speak English only: 97.0%; With disability: 13.1%; Veterans: 10.2%; Ancestry: 29.0% Irish, 21.6% German, 15.4% English, 15.3% Italian, 7.9% French

Employment: 13.8% management, business, and financial, 6.3% computer, engineering, and science, 8.9% education, legal, community service, arts, and media, 10.0% healthcare practitioners, 15.4% service, 24.2% sales and office, 11.1% natural resources, construction, and maintenance, 10.3% production, transportation, and material moving

Income: Per capita: $29,498; Median household: $53,390; Average household: $65,321; Households with income of $100,000 or more: 20.2%; Poverty rate: 7.3%

Educational Attainment: High school diploma or higher: 94.2%; Bachelor's degree or higher: 25.8%; Graduate/professional degree or higher: 9.9%

Housing: Homeownership rate: 69.8%; Median home value: $118,700; Median year structure built: 1969; Homeowner vacancy rate: 2.1%; Median selected monthly owner costs: $1,191 with a mortgage, $490 without a mortgage; Median gross rent: $834 per month; Rental vacancy rate: 1.2%

Health Insurance: 94.6% have insurance; 76.2% have private insurance; 36.3% have public insurance; 5.4% do not have insurance; 1.3% of children under 18 do not have insurance

Transportation: Commute: 94.3% car, 0.6% public transportation, 1.7% walk, 3.4% work from home; Mean travel time to work: 23.5 minutes

Additional Information Contacts

Town of Van Buren . . . . (315) 635-3010
    http://www.townofvanburen.com

VILLAGE GREEN (CDP). Covers a land area of 1.154 square miles and a water area of 0.008 square miles. Located at 43.13° N. Lat; 76.31° W. Long. Elevation is 440 feet.

Population: 3,689; Growth (since 2000): -6.5%; Density: 3,196.9 persons per square mile; Race: 95.5% White, 0.0% Black/African American, 0.7% Asian, 0.6% American Indian/Alaska Native, 0.0% Native Hawaiian/Other Pacific Islander, 2.8% Two or more races, 0.0% Hispanic of any race; Average household size: 1.96; Median age: 38.1; Age under 18: 15.5%; Age 65 and over: 17.6%; Males per 100 females: 91.4; Marriage status: 30.6% never married, 44.4% now married, 1.7% separated, 8.1% widowed, 16.9% divorced; Foreign born: 4.8%; Speak English only: 97.0%; With disability: 11.3%; Veterans: 12.6%; Ancestry: 29.0% Irish, 22.6% German, 16.9% Italian, 13.7% English, 11.5% Polish

Employment: 14.8% management, business, and financial, 5.5% computer, engineering, and science, 7.6% education, legal, community service, arts, and media, 10.8% healthcare practitioners, 16.1% service, 28.9% sales and office, 3.2% natural resources, construction, and maintenance, 13.1% production, transportation, and material moving

Income: Per capita: $31,800; Median household: $51,063; Average household: $61,993; Households with income of $100,000 or more: 16.2%; Poverty rate: 5.3%

Educational Attainment: High school diploma or higher: 93.5%; Bachelor's degree or higher: 29.0%; Graduate/professional degree or higher: 9.4%

Housing: Homeownership rate: 59.6%; Median home value: $100,700; Median year structure built: 1975; Homeowner vacancy rate: 1.1%; Median selected monthly owner costs: $1,017 with a mortgage, $443 without a mortgage; Median gross rent: $880 per month; Rental vacancy rate: 0.0%

Health Insurance: 90.9% have insurance; 73.9% have private insurance; 34.2% have public insurance; 9.1% do not have insurance; 2.0% of children under 18 do not have insurance

Transportation: Commute: 98.1% car, 0.8% public transportation, 0.0% walk, 1.1% work from home; Mean travel time to work: 23.0 minutes

WARNERS (unincorporated postal area)

ZCTA: 13164

Covers a land area of 10.726 square miles and a water area of 0.009 square miles. Located at 43.10° N. Lat; 76.31° W. Long. Elevation is 430 feet.

Population: 2,449; Growth (since 2000): 39.2%; Density: 228.3 persons per square mile; Race: 94.4% White, 0.0% Black/African American, 3.6% Asian, 0.0% American Indian/Alaska Native, 0.0% Native Hawaiian/Other Pacific Islander, 1.8% Two or more races, 1.8% Hispanic of any race; Average household size: 3.03; Median age: 35.7; Age under 18: 31.4%; Age 65 and over: 11.1%; Males per 100 females: 105.6; Marriage status: 24.0% never married, 62.2% now married, 1.6% separated, 3.7% widowed, 10.1% divorced; Foreign born: 10.0%; Speak English only: 85.1%; With disability: 7.8%; Veterans: 8.4%; Ancestry: 21.4% Irish, 18.4% Polish, 17.6% English, 14.8% German, 14.5% Italian

Employment: 16.4% management, business, and financial, 9.4% computer, engineering, and science, 20.4% education, legal, community service, arts, and media, 13.1% healthcare practitioners, 11.4% service, 9.4% sales and office, 8.6% natural resources, construction, and maintenance, 11.2% production, transportation, and material moving

Income: Per capita: $28,243; Median household: $77,083; Average household: $83,587; Households with income of $100,000 or more: 35.8%; Poverty rate: 11.8%

Educational Attainment: High school diploma or higher: 91.1%; Bachelor's degree or higher: 34.3%; Graduate/professional degree or higher: 20.9%

Housing: Homeownership rate: 90.3%; Median home value: $167,500; Median year structure built: 1964; Homeowner vacancy rate: 0.0%; Median selected monthly owner costs: $1,619 with a mortgage, $471 without a mortgage; Median gross rent: $742 per month; Rental vacancy rate: 0.0%

Health Insurance: 93.8% have insurance; 77.1% have private insurance; 28.7% have public insurance; 6.2% do not have insurance; 2.5% of children under 18 do not have insurance

Transportation: Commute: 96.2% car, 0.0% public transportation, 0.6% walk, 3.1% work from home; Mean travel time to work: 23.4 minutes

WESTVALE (CDP).

Covers a land area of 1.364 square miles and a water area of 0 square miles. Located at 43.04° N. Lat; 76.22° W. Long. Elevation is 505 feet.

Population: 5,139; Growth (since 2000): -0.5%; Density: 3,766.7 persons per square mile; Race: 94.6% White, 3.5% Black/African American, 0.0% Asian, 0.0% American Indian/Alaska Native, 0.0% Native Hawaiian/Other Pacific Islander, 1.1% Two or more races, 1.6% Hispanic of any race; Average household size: 2.54; Median age: 43.0; Age under 18: 22.5%; Age 65 and over: 19.2%; Males per 100 females: 85.8; Marriage status: 31.5% never married, 53.1% now married, 0.6% separated, 5.6% widowed, 9.8% divorced; Foreign born: 3.5%; Speak English only: 94.6%; With disability: 8.5%; Veterans: 7.6%; Ancestry: 35.2% Irish, 24.5% Italian, 20.3% German, 10.5% Polish, 10.2% English

Employment: 19.5% management, business, and financial, 4.1% computer, engineering, and science, 18.6% education, legal, community service, arts, and media, 5.1% healthcare practitioners, 18.1% service, 24.5% sales and office, 6.1% natural resources, construction, and maintenance, 4.0% production, transportation, and material moving

Income: Per capita: $35,337; Median household: $78,553; Average household: $87,934; Households with income of $100,000 or more: 33.6%; Poverty rate: 6.8%

Educational Attainment: High school diploma or higher: 98.0%; Bachelor's degree or higher: 44.7%; Graduate/professional degree or higher: 22.9%

Housing: Homeownership rate: 95.1%; Median home value: $145,700; Median year structure built: 1954; Homeowner vacancy rate: 3.2%; Median selected monthly owner costs: $1,392 with a mortgage, $601 without a mortgage; Median gross rent: n/a per month; Rental vacancy rate: 0.0%

Health Insurance: 98.6% have insurance; 85.8% have private insurance; 33.2% have public insurance; 1.4% do not have insurance; 0.0% of children under 18 do not have insurance

Transportation: Commute: 91.9% car, 1.6% public transportation, 2.7% walk, 2.7% work from home; Mean travel time to work: 20.2 minutes

Ontario County

Located in west central New York, in the Finger Lakes area; bounded partly on the east by Seneca Lake; drained by Honeoye, Mud, and Flint Creeks; includes Canandaigua, Honeoye, and Canadice Lakes. Covers a land area of 644.065 square miles, a water area of 18.461 square miles, and is located in the Eastern Time Zone at 42.86° N. Lat., 77.30° W. Long. The county was founded in 1789. County seat is Canandaigua.

Ontario County is part of the Rochester, NY Metropolitan Statistical Area. The entire metro area includes: Livingston County, NY; Monroe County, NY; Ontario County, NY; Orleans County, NY; Wayne County, NY; Yates County, NY

Weather Station: Canandaigua 3 S									Elevation: 720 feet			
	Jan	Feb	Mar	Apr	May	Jun	Jul	Aug	Sep	Oct	Nov	Dec
High	33	35	42	55	67	77	81	79	72	60	49	38
Low	18	19	25	36	46	57	62	60	54	42	34	24
Precip	1.8	1.6	2.6	3.2	3.0	3.6	3.6	3.2	3.5	2.9	2.9	2.2
Snow	na	na	na	0.0	0.0	0.0	0.0	0.0	0.0	tr	tr	na

High and Low temperatures in degrees Fahrenheit; Precipitation and Snow in inches

Weather Station: Geneva Research Farm									Elevation: 717 feet			
	Jan	Feb	Mar	Apr	May	Jun	Jul	Aug	Sep	Oct	Nov	Dec
High	31	33	41	55	67	76	80	79	71	59	47	36
Low	16	17	25	36	47	56	61	59	52	41	33	22
Precip	1.7	1.5	2.4	2.9	3.0	3.6	3.4	3.0	3.6	3.2	2.8	2.2
Snow	13.7	11.6	11.3	2.3	tr	0.0	0.0	0.0	0.0	0.1	4.1	11.3

High and Low temperatures in degrees Fahrenheit; Precipitation and Snow in inches

Population: 109,491; Growth (since 2000): 9.2%; Density: 170.0 persons per square mile; Race: 92.7% White, 2.5% Black/African American, 1.3% Asian, 0.4% American Indian/Alaska Native, 0.1% Native Hawaiian/Other Pacific Islander, 1.5% two or more races, 4.4% Hispanic of any race; Average household size: 2.39; Median age: 43.4; Age under 18: 20.8%; Age 65 and over: 18.2%; Males per 100 females: 95.6; Marriage status: 29.4% never married, 52.8% now married, 2.3% separated, 6.7% widowed, 11.1% divorced; Foreign born: 3.9%; Speak English only: 92.9%; With disability: 11.9%; Veterans: 8.7%; Ancestry: 21.8% German, 18.4% Irish, 16.4% English, 14.8% Italian, 7.2% American

Religion: Six largest groups: 23.6% Catholicism, 5.8% Methodist/Pietist, 3.4% Presbyterian-Reformed, 2.0% Holiness, 1.9% Baptist, 1.4% Lutheran

Economy: Unemployment rate: 3.2%; Leading industries: 18.3 % retail trade; 11.5 % construction; 11.3 % accommodation and food services; Farms: 853 totaling 192,616 acres; Company size: 3 employ 1,000 or more persons, 4 employ 500 to 999 persons, 62 employ 100 to 499 persons, 2,851 employs less than 100 persons; Business ownership: 3,189 women-owned, 128 Black-owned, 103 Hispanic-owned, 78 Asian-owned, 73 American Indian/Alaska Native-owned

Employment: 15.4% management, business, and financial, 5.5% computer, engineering, and science, 12.5% education, legal, community service, arts, and media, 7.1% healthcare practitioners, 16.4% service, 23.2% sales and office, 8.3% natural resources, construction, and maintenance, 11.6% production, transportation, and material moving

Income: Per capita: $33,685; Median household: $61,710; Average household: $82,045; Households with income of $100,000 or more: 26.9%; Poverty rate: 9.7%

Educational Attainment: High school diploma or higher: 93.2%; Bachelor's degree or higher: 33.7%; Graduate/professional degree or higher: 14.9%

Housing: Homeownership rate: 73.2%; Median home value: $156,500; Median year structure built: 1972; Homeowner vacancy rate: 1.0%; Median selected monthly owner costs: $1,368 with a mortgage, $588 without a mortgage; Median gross rent: $837 per month; Rental vacancy rate: 7.0%

Vital Statistics: Birth rate: 93.1 per 10,000 population; Death rate: 97.1 per 10,000 population; Age-adjusted cancer mortality rate: 150.8 deaths per 100,000 population

Health Insurance: 95.0% have insurance; 75.9% have private insurance; 35.4% have public insurance; 5.0% do not have insurance; 3.3% of children under 18 do not have insurance

Health Care: Physicians: 26.2 per 10,000 population; Dentists: 5.6 per 10,000 population; Hospital beds: 76.0 per 10,000 population; Hospital admissions: 1,142.7 per 10,000 population

Transportation: Commute: 90.8% car, 0.7% public transportation, 3.5% walk, 4.2% work from home; Mean travel time to work: 23.2 minutes

2016 Presidential Election: 49.8% Trump, 42.5% Clinton, 4.8% Johnson, 1.6% Stein
National and State Parks: Ganondagan State Historic Site
Additional Information Contacts
Ontario Government . . . . (585) 396-4447
   http://www.co.ontario.ny.us

Ontario County Communities

BLOOMFIELD (village). Covers a land area of 1.397 square miles and a water area of 0 square miles. Located at 42.90° N. Lat; 77.42° W. Long. Elevation is 876 feet.
Population: 1,428; Growth (since 2000): 12.7%; Density: 1,022.3 persons per square mile; Race: 95.9% White, 2.5% Black/African American, 0.0% Asian, 0.0% American Indian/Alaska Native, 0.0% Native Hawaiian/Other Pacific Islander, 1.6% Two or more races, 2.8% Hispanic of any race; Average household size: 2.43; Median age: 44.0; Age under 18: 22.9%; Age 65 and over: 14.2%; Males per 100 females: 89.0; Marriage status: 29.9% never married, 57.1% now married, 3.2% separated, 3.3% widowed, 9.7% divorced; Foreign born: 0.0%; Speak English only: 98.1%; With disability: 11.8%; Veterans: 7.1%; Ancestry: 24.2% German, 22.3% Irish, 20.8% English, 13.8% American, 5.5% Italian
Employment: 22.6% management, business, and financial, 4.4% computer, engineering, and science, 6.3% education, legal, community service, arts, and media, 2.9% healthcare practitioners, 16.0% service, 28.2% sales and office, 8.1% natural resources, construction, and maintenance, 11.5% production, transportation, and material moving
Income: Per capita: $30,458; Median household: $59,583; Average household: $74,714; Households with income of $100,000 or more: 22.1%; Poverty rate: 18.9%
Educational Attainment: High school diploma or higher: 93.9%; Bachelor's degree or higher: 32.2%; Graduate/professional degree or higher: 7.0%

School District(s)
East Bloomfield Central SD (PK-12)
   Enrollment: 933 . . . . (585) 657-6121
Housing: Homeownership rate: 70.3%; Median home value: $141,300; Median year structure built: 1945; Homeowner vacancy rate: 2.4%; Median selected monthly owner costs: $1,269 with a mortgage, $625 without a mortgage; Median gross rent: $752 per month; Rental vacancy rate: 5.0%
Health Insurance: 97.1% have insurance; 74.3% have private insurance; 34.5% have public insurance; 2.9% do not have insurance; 0.0% of children under 18 do not have insurance
Transportation: Commute: 93.5% car, 0.1% public transportation, 0.0% walk, 5.8% work from home; Mean travel time to work: 25.6 minutes
Additional Information Contacts
Village of Bloomfield . . . . (585) 657-7554
   http://www.bloomfieldny.org

BRISTOL (town). Covers a land area of 36.694 square miles and a water area of 0.015 square miles. Located at 42.81° N. Lat; 77.43° W. Long. Elevation is 1,165 feet.
Population: 2,172; Growth (since 2000): -10.3%; Density: 59.2 persons per square mile; Race: 97.3% White, 0.2% Black/African American, 0.2% Asian, 0.1% American Indian/Alaska Native, 0.0% Native Hawaiian/Other Pacific Islander, 1.6% Two or more races, 0.8% Hispanic of any race; Average household size: 2.41; Median age: 50.5; Age under 18: 17.4%; Age 65 and over: 16.5%; Males per 100 females: 102.4; Marriage status: 23.1% never married, 59.1% now married, 1.8% separated, 6.7% widowed, 11.1% divorced; Foreign born: 2.1%; Speak English only: 98.7%; With disability: 10.7%; Veterans: 8.9%; Ancestry: 26.7% German, 24.6% English, 17.8% Irish, 8.1% Italian, 5.6% American
Employment: 11.3% management, business, and financial, 5.8% computer, engineering, and science, 11.2% education, legal, community service, arts, and media, 6.2% healthcare practitioners, 16.7% service, 15.8% sales and office, 16.3% natural resources, construction, and maintenance, 16.7% production, transportation, and material moving
Income: Per capita: $36,836; Median household: $71,982; Average household: $87,819; Households with income of $100,000 or more: 35.4%; Poverty rate: 4.5%
Educational Attainment: High school diploma or higher: 95.8%; Bachelor's degree or higher: 27.3%; Graduate/professional degree or higher: 11.6%
Housing: Homeownership rate: 95.6%; Median home value: $163,400; Median year structure built: 1977; Homeowner vacancy rate: 0.0%; Median

selected monthly owner costs: $1,511 with a mortgage, $536 without a mortgage; Median gross rent: $913 per month; Rental vacancy rate: 11.1%
Health Insurance: 95.3% have insurance; 81.1% have private insurance; 25.8% have public insurance; 4.7% do not have insurance; 8.7% of children under 18 do not have insurance
Transportation: Commute: 93.4% car, 0.0% public transportation, 1.2% walk, 5.4% work from home; Mean travel time to work: 28.9 minutes
Additional Information Contacts
Town of Bristol. . . . . (585) 229-2400
   http://www.townofbristol.org

CANADICE (town). Covers a land area of 29.851 square miles and a water area of 2.585 square miles. Located at 42.72° N. Lat; 77.56° W. Long.
Population: 1,736; Growth (since 2000): -6.0%; Density: 58.2 persons per square mile; Race: 98.8% White, 0.0% Black/African American, 0.0% Asian, 0.0% American Indian/Alaska Native, 0.0% Native Hawaiian/Other Pacific Islander, 0.5% Two or more races, 2.1% Hispanic of any race; Average household size: 2.31; Median age: 52.6; Age under 18: 15.0%; Age 65 and over: 17.6%; Males per 100 females: 103.7; Marriage status: 22.9% never married, 56.6% now married, 1.4% separated, 2.2% widowed, 18.3% divorced; Foreign born: 0.6%; Speak English only: 98.9%; With disability: 10.3%; Veterans: 10.2%; Ancestry: 35.7% German, 20.5% Irish, 13.7% English, 12.2% Italian, 5.8% Polish
Employment: 11.8% management, business, and financial, 6.2% computer, engineering, and science, 7.8% education, legal, community service, arts, and media, 5.3% healthcare practitioners, 14.0% service, 20.9% sales and office, 11.9% natural resources, construction, and maintenance, 22.2% production, transportation, and material moving
Income: Per capita: $34,068; Median household: $59,141; Average household: $78,246; Households with income of $100,000 or more: 26.8%; Poverty rate: 11.2%
Educational Attainment: High school diploma or higher: 88.2%; Bachelor's degree or higher: 24.2%; Graduate/professional degree or higher: 10.8%
Housing: Homeownership rate: 90.7%; Median home value: $149,700; Median year structure built: 1973; Homeowner vacancy rate: 3.8%; Median selected monthly owner costs: $1,203 with a mortgage, $538 without a mortgage; Median gross rent: $758 per month; Rental vacancy rate: 10.0%
Health Insurance: 93.8% have insurance; 77.6% have private insurance; 35.7% have public insurance; 6.2% do not have insurance; 1.4% of children under 18 do not have insurance
Transportation: Commute: 95.2% car, 0.0% public transportation, 1.2% walk, 2.4% work from home; Mean travel time to work: 35.7 minutes

CANANDAIGUA (city). County seat. Covers a land area of 4.594 square miles and a water area of 0.253 square miles. Located at 42.89° N. Lat; 77.28° W. Long. Elevation is 787 feet.
History: Built on the site of a Seneca Iroquois village, Canandaigua was an important railroad junction and home port for several steamboats by the mid-19th century. After the Civil War, local industries included brick works, several mills, and the regionally prominent McKechnie Brewery. Canandaigua was the site of the Susan B. Anthony trial in 1873.
Population: 10,402; Growth (since 2000): -7.7%; Density: 2,264.1 persons per square mile; Race: 94.0% White, 1.4% Black/African American, 1.5% Asian, 0.5% American Indian/Alaska Native, 0.9% Native Hawaiian/Other Pacific Islander, 0.5% Two or more races, 2.0% Hispanic of any race; Average household size: 2.13; Median age: 42.6; Age under 18: 19.7%; Age 65 and over: 21.1%; Males per 100 females: 88.8; Marriage status: 33.1% never married, 45.2% now married, 2.9% separated, 7.7% widowed, 13.9% divorced; Foreign born: 4.2%; Speak English only: 93.8%; With disability: 12.2%; Veterans: 8.6%; Ancestry: 23.1% German, 19.4% Irish, 17.3% English, 15.9% Italian, 7.0% American
Employment: 14.2% management, business, and financial, 4.4% computer, engineering, and science, 16.2% education, legal, community service, arts, and media, 9.3% healthcare practitioners, 19.2% service, 23.3% sales and office, 6.3% natural resources, construction, and maintenance, 7.1% production, transportation, and material moving
Income: Per capita: $34,928; Median household: $46,423; Average household: $74,724; Households with income of $100,000 or more: 21.0%; Poverty rate: 14.7%
Educational Attainment: High school diploma or higher: 95.2%; Bachelor's degree or higher: 39.5%; Graduate/professional degree or higher: 19.3%

School District(s)
Canandaigua City SD (PK-12)
    Enrollment: 3,588 . . . . (585) 396-3700
Two-year College(s)
Finger Lakes Community College (Public)
    Enrollment: 6,356 . . . . (585) 394-3500
    Tuition: In-state $5,096; Out-of-state $9,618
Housing: Homeownership rate: 56.3%; Median home value: $161,300; Median year structure built: 1951; Homeowner vacancy rate: 0.6%; Median selected monthly owner costs: $1,400 with a mortgage, $570 without a mortgage; Median gross rent: $804 per month; Rental vacancy rate: 7.7%
Health Insurance: 95.1% have insurance; 74.7% have private insurance; 39.5% have public insurance; 4.9% do not have insurance; 3.5% of children under 18 do not have insurance
Hospitals: Canandaigua VA Medical Center (251 beds); F F Thompson Hospital (113 beds)
Safety: Violent crime rate: 31.9 per 10,000 population; Property crime rate: 199.3 per 10,000 population
Newspapers: Daily Messenger (daily circulation 11,700); Messenger Post Media (weekly circulation 86,000)
Transportation: Commute: 86.1% car, 2.5% public transportation, 6.0% walk, 2.3% work from home; Mean travel time to work: 21.5 minutes
Additional Information Contacts
City of Canandaigua . . . . (585) 396-5000
    http://canandaigua.govoffice.com

CANANDAIGUA (town). Covers a land area of 56.796 square miles and a water area of 5.735 square miles. Located at 42.86° N. Lat; 77.31° W. Long. Elevation is 787 feet.
History: It is named from native word "Kah-nan-dah-kwe" meaning "the chosen spot" or "the chosen place."
Population: 10,733; Growth (since 2000): 40.3%; Density: 189.0 persons per square mile; Race: 95.4% White, 1.4% Black/African American, 0.6% Asian, 0.0% American Indian/Alaska Native, 0.3% Native Hawaiian/Other Pacific Islander, 1.6% Two or more races, 1.6% Hispanic of any race; Average household size: 2.29; Median age: 47.3; Age under 18: 18.9%; Age 65 and over: 21.5%; Males per 100 females: 95.6; Marriage status: 26.8% never married, 50.2% now married, 2.9% separated, 9.2% widowed, 13.8% divorced; Foreign born: 3.8%; Speak English only: 95.4%; With disability: 12.9%; Veterans: 7.4%; Ancestry: 21.7% German, 18.6% Irish, 16.8% English, 14.3% Italian, 7.9% American
Employment: 17.1% management, business, and financial, 5.2% computer, engineering, and science, 13.3% education, legal, community service, arts, and media, 7.8% healthcare practitioners, 13.4% service, 28.3% sales and office, 6.3% natural resources, construction, and maintenance, 8.5% production, transportation, and material moving
Income: Per capita: $37,398; Median household: $68,004; Average household: $87,220; Households with income of $100,000 or more: 33.0%; Poverty rate: 8.5%
Educational Attainment: High school diploma or higher: 95.8%; Bachelor's degree or higher: 41.0%; Graduate/professional degree or higher: 20.8%
School District(s)
Canandaigua City SD (PK-12)
    Enrollment: 3,588 . . . . (585) 396-3700
Two-year College(s)
Finger Lakes Community College (Public)
    Enrollment: 6,356 . . . . (585) 394-3500
    Tuition: In-state $5,096; Out-of-state $9,618
Housing: Homeownership rate: 68.4%; Median home value: $225,900; Median year structure built: 1991; Homeowner vacancy rate: 0.0%; Median selected monthly owner costs: $1,667 with a mortgage, $736 without a mortgage; Median gross rent: $994 per month; Rental vacancy rate: 10.2%
Health Insurance: 96.3% have insurance; 81.7% have private insurance; 32.9% have public insurance; 3.7% do not have insurance; 3.8% of children under 18 do not have insurance
Hospitals: Canandaigua VA Medical Center (251 beds); F F Thompson Hospital (113 beds)
Newspapers: Daily Messenger (daily circulation 11,700); Messenger Post Media (weekly circulation 86,000)
Transportation: Commute: 95.4% car, 0.3% public transportation, 0.3% walk, 4.0% work from home; Mean travel time to work: 24.4 minutes
Additional Information Contacts
Town of Canandaigua . . . . (585) 394-1120
    http://www.townofcanandaigua.org

CLIFTON SPRINGS (village). Covers a land area of 1.519 square miles and a water area of 0 square miles. Located at 42.96° N. Lat; 77.14° W. Long. Elevation is 577 feet.
Population: 2,286; Growth (since 2000): 2.8%; Density: 1,504.9 persons per square mile; Race: 94.0% White, 4.3% Black/African American, 0.2% Asian, 0.0% American Indian/Alaska Native, 0.0% Native Hawaiian/Other Pacific Islander, 1.3% Two or more races, 3.9% Hispanic of any race; Average household size: 2.32; Median age: 44.3; Age under 18: 21.3%; Age 65 and over: 24.8%; Males per 100 females: 80.7; Marriage status: 27.0% never married, 45.4% now married, 2.4% separated, 13.3% widowed, 14.3% divorced; Foreign born: 1.0%; Speak English only: 93.8%; With disability: 19.3%; Veterans: 9.6%; Ancestry: 19.8% Irish, 18.6% German, 15.7% English, 11.5% Italian, 9.7% Dutch
Employment: 11.1% management, business, and financial, 3.7% computer, engineering, and science, 10.9% education, legal, community service, arts, and media, 8.3% healthcare practitioners, 13.1% service, 27.0% sales and office, 8.2% natural resources, construction, and maintenance, 17.6% production, transportation, and material moving
Income: Per capita: $26,179; Median household: $41,652; Average household: $63,254; Households with income of $100,000 or more: 19.3%; Poverty rate: 11.9%
Educational Attainment: High school diploma or higher: 89.3%; Bachelor's degree or higher: 19.1%; Graduate/professional degree or higher: 9.2%
School District(s)
Phelps-Clifton Springs Central SD (KG-12)
    Enrollment: 1,550 . . . . (315) 548-6420
Housing: Homeownership rate: 55.4%; Median home value: $107,100; Median year structure built: Before 1940; Homeowner vacancy rate: 0.0%; Median selected monthly owner costs: $1,114 with a mortgage, $531 without a mortgage; Median gross rent: $621 per month; Rental vacancy rate: 4.1%
Health Insurance: 96.5% have insurance; 68.9% have private insurance; 47.2% have public insurance; 3.5% do not have insurance; 0.0% of children under 18 do not have insurance
Hospitals: Clifton Springs Hospital & Clinic (262 beds)
Transportation: Commute: 90.0% car, 1.0% public transportation, 6.3% walk, 0.9% work from home; Mean travel time to work: 20.3 minutes

CRYSTAL BEACH (CDP). Covers a land area of 0.682 square miles and a water area of 0.203 square miles. Located at 42.81° N. Lat; 77.26° W. Long. Elevation is 699 feet.
Population: 767; Growth (since 2000): n/a; Density: 1,125.4 persons per square mile; Race: 96.2% White, 0.0% Black/African American, 3.8% Asian, 0.0% American Indian/Alaska Native, 0.0% Native Hawaiian/Other Pacific Islander, 0.0% Two or more races, 3.7% Hispanic of any race; Average household size: 1.91; Median age: 51.3; Age under 18: 15.5%; Age 65 and over: 31.7%; Males per 100 females: 100.0; Marriage status: 21.7% never married, 63.6% now married, 3.8% separated, 2.9% widowed, 11.9% divorced; Foreign born: 10.7%; Speak English only: 92.4%; With disability: 12.9%; Veterans: 15.0%; Ancestry: 24.1% German, 17.5% Irish, 13.0% American, 8.1% Italian, 7.7% English
Employment: 10.9% management, business, and financial, 0.0% computer, engineering, and science, 13.3% education, legal, community service, arts, and media, 0.0% healthcare practitioners, 19.2% service, 21.6% sales and office, 18.0% natural resources, construction, and maintenance, 16.9% production, transportation, and material moving
Income: Per capita: $28,172; Median household: $45,448; Average household: $55,539; Households with income of $100,000 or more: 12.7%; Poverty rate: 21.3%
Educational Attainment: High school diploma or higher: 86.0%; Bachelor's degree or higher: 25.8%; Graduate/professional degree or higher: 15.1%
Housing: Homeownership rate: 76.6%; Median home value: $137,200; Median year structure built: 1978; Homeowner vacancy rate: 0.0%; Median selected monthly owner costs: $1,023 with a mortgage, $446 without a mortgage; Median gross rent: $810 per month; Rental vacancy rate: 0.0%
Health Insurance: 89.7% have insurance; 63.0% have private insurance; 46.9% have public insurance; 10.3% do not have insurance; 0.0% of children under 18 do not have insurance
Transportation: Commute: 100.0% car, 0.0% public transportation, 0.0% walk, 0.0% work from home; Mean travel time to work: 29.0 minutes

EAST BLOOMFIELD (town). Covers a land area of 33.195 square miles and a water area of 0.139 square miles. Located at 42.90° N. Lat; 77.42° W. Long. Elevation is 1,070 feet.

Population: 3,602; Growth (since 2000): 7.2%; Density: 108.5 persons per square mile; Race: 98.4% White, 1.0% Black/African American, 0.0% Asian, 0.0% American Indian/Alaska Native, 0.0% Native Hawaiian/Other Pacific Islander, 0.6% Two or more races, 1.6% Hispanic of any race; Average household size: 2.61; Median age: 41.8; Age under 18: 24.2%; Age 65 and over: 13.7%; Males per 100 females: 99.1; Marriage status: 28.0% never married, 57.4% now married, 2.4% separated, 3.2% widowed, 11.4% divorced; Foreign born: 0.4%; Speak English only: 97.6%; With disability: 9.6%; Veterans: 9.6%; Ancestry: 26.2% German, 25.5% Irish, 21.2% English, 11.4% American, 7.0% Italian

Employment: 18.0% management, business, and financial, 5.6% computer, engineering, and science, 8.4% education, legal, community service, arts, and media, 6.2% healthcare practitioners, 17.4% service, 28.1% sales and office, 6.3% natural resources, construction, and maintenance, 10.0% production, transportation, and material moving

Income: Per capita: $31,804; Median household: $71,100; Average household: $82,833; Households with income of $100,000 or more: 23.0%; Poverty rate: 9.2%

Educational Attainment: High school diploma or higher: 94.0%; Bachelor's degree or higher: 29.3%; Graduate/professional degree or higher: 8.2%

Housing: Homeownership rate: 80.5%; Median home value: $163,800; Median year structure built: 1964; Homeowner vacancy rate: 0.9%; Median selected monthly owner costs: $1,491 with a mortgage, $587 without a mortgage; Median gross rent: $760 per month; Rental vacancy rate: 3.2%

Health Insurance: 92.2% have insurance; 70.1% have private insurance; 32.9% have public insurance; 7.8% do not have insurance; 5.0% of children under 18 do not have insurance

Transportation: Commute: 92.3% car, 0.1% public transportation, 3.4% walk, 4.0% work from home; Mean travel time to work: 23.1 minutes

FARMINGTON (town). Covers a land area of 39.430 square miles and a water area of 0 square miles. Located at 42.99° N. Lat; 77.31° W. Long. Elevation is 561 feet.

Population: 12,891; Growth (since 2000): 21.8%; Density: 326.9 persons per square mile; Race: 93.0% White, 3.6% Black/African American, 0.6% Asian, 0.7% American Indian/Alaska Native, 0.1% Native Hawaiian/Other Pacific Islander, 1.2% Two or more races, 4.4% Hispanic of any race; Average household size: 2.44; Median age: 37.8; Age under 18: 25.5%; Age 65 and over: 13.8%; Males per 100 females: 95.8; Marriage status: 27.0% never married, 55.2% now married, 3.2% separated, 5.7% widowed, 12.1% divorced; Foreign born: 3.1%; Speak English only: 95.2%; With disability: 9.3%; Veterans: 9.3%; Ancestry: 25.1% German, 21.6% Irish, 16.4% Italian, 13.8% English, 11.4% American

Employment: 14.8% management, business, and financial, 9.8% computer, engineering, and science, 12.2% education, legal, community service, arts, and media, 8.6% healthcare practitioners, 13.9% service, 25.2% sales and office, 6.4% natural resources, construction, and maintenance, 9.3% production, transportation, and material moving

Income: Per capita: $32,923; Median household: $71,478; Average household: $80,334; Households with income of $100,000 or more: 29.7%; Poverty rate: 7.7%

Educational Attainment: High school diploma or higher: 96.3%; Bachelor's degree or higher: 37.8%; Graduate/professional degree or higher: 14.6%

Housing: Homeownership rate: 72.4%; Median home value: $158,800; Median year structure built: 1982; Homeowner vacancy rate: 1.1%; Median selected monthly owner costs: $1,308 with a mortgage, $594 without a mortgage; Median gross rent: $1,081 per month; Rental vacancy rate: 0.0%

Health Insurance: 95.8% have insurance; 77.9% have private insurance; 30.9% have public insurance; 4.2% do not have insurance; 3.8% of children under 18 do not have insurance

Transportation: Commute: 93.2% car, 1.0% public transportation, 0.0% walk, 4.8% work from home; Mean travel time to work: 25.5 minutes

Additional Information Contacts

Town of Farmington . . . . (315) 986-8100
    http://www.townoffarmingtonny.com

GENEVA (city). Covers a land area of 4.210 square miles and a water area of 1.632 square miles. Located at 42.86° N. Lat; 76.98° W. Long. Elevation is 443 feet.

History: Named for Geneva, Switzerland, by Swiss settlers. The area of the city of Geneva includes the site of the Native American settlement of Kanadesaga. After the Revolution, other settlers began to arrive. Captain Charles Williamson, agent for the Pulteney Estate, recognized the superb advantages of the site and laid out Main Street on the terrace overlooking the lake.

Population: 13,048; Growth (since 2000): -4.2%; Density: 3,099.2 persons per square mile; Race: 75.9% White, 10.2% Black/African American, 3.8% Asian, 1.4% American Indian/Alaska Native, 0.0% Native Hawaiian/Other Pacific Islander, 3.0% Two or more races, 17.4% Hispanic of any race; Average household size: 2.25; Median age: 29.6; Age under 18: 18.3%; Age 65 and over: 15.0%; Males per 100 females: 87.8; Marriage status: 51.9% never married, 33.3% now married, 1.9% separated, 5.8% widowed, 9.0% divorced; Foreign born: 8.3%; Speak English only: 79.2%; With disability: 12.5%; Veterans: 5.8%; Ancestry: 17.7% Italian, 17.1% Irish, 13.3% German, 9.2% English, 3.8% American

Employment: 9.6% management, business, and financial, 3.4% computer, engineering, and science, 18.0% education, legal, community service, arts, and media, 4.2% healthcare practitioners, 24.2% service, 21.9% sales and office, 6.4% natural resources, construction, and maintenance, 12.2% production, transportation, and material moving

Income: Per capita: $21,470; Median household: $40,920; Average household: $55,878; Households with income of $100,000 or more: 13.7%; Poverty rate: 18.9%

Educational Attainment: High school diploma or higher: 84.9%; Bachelor's degree or higher: 26.3%; Graduate/professional degree or higher: 13.2%

School District(s)
Geneva City SD (PK-12)
    Enrollment: 2,253 . . . . (315) 781-0400
Four-year College(s)
Hobart William Smith Colleges (Private, Not-for-profit)
    Enrollment: 2,244 . . . . (315) 781-3000
    Tuition: In-state $53,525; Out-of-state $53,525
Two-year College(s)
Finger Lakes Health College of Nursing (Private, Not-for-profit)
    Enrollment: 126 . . . . (315) 787-4005
    Tuition: In-state $11,540; Out-of-state $11,540
Vocational/Technical School(s)
Marion S Whelan School of Nursing of Geneva General Hospital (Private, Not-for-profit)
    Enrollment: 31 . . . . (315) 787-4005
    Tuition: In-state $9,150; Out-of-state $9,150

Housing: Homeownership rate: 49.1%; Median home value: $93,700; Median year structure built: Before 1940; Homeowner vacancy rate: 0.0%; Median selected monthly owner costs: $1,080 with a mortgage, $534 without a mortgage; Median gross rent: $738 per month; Rental vacancy rate: 9.2%

Health Insurance: 92.6% have insurance; 63.7% have private insurance; 41.6% have public insurance; 7.4% do not have insurance; 2.2% of children under 18 do not have insurance

Hospitals: Geneva General Hospital (136 beds)

Safety: Violent crime rate: 21.6 per 10,000 population; Property crime rate: 223.1 per 10,000 population

Newspapers: Finger Lakes Times (daily circulation 15,600)

Transportation: Commute: 79.2% car, 1.3% public transportation, 14.4% walk, 3.3% work from home; Mean travel time to work: 18.9 minutes

Additional Information Contacts

City of Geneva . . . . (315) 828-6550
    http://www.geneva.ny.us

GENEVA (town). Covers a land area of 19.091 square miles and a water area of 0.007 square miles. Located at 42.83° N. Lat; 77.01° W. Long. Elevation is 443 feet.

History: Hobart College and William Smith College are in the city. Settled 1788; Incorporated as village in 1812, as city in 1897.

Population: 3,260; Growth (since 2000): -0.9%; Density: 170.8 persons per square mile; Race: 77.4% White, 2.5% Black/African American, 7.3% Asian, 0.0% American Indian/Alaska Native, 0.0% Native Hawaiian/Other Pacific Islander, 3.3% Two or more races, 15.0% Hispanic of any race; Average household size: 2.16; Median age: 47.5; Age under 18: 18.8%; Age 65 and over: 25.2%; Males per 100 females: 91.7; Marriage status:

25.4% never married, 56.8% now married, 4.0% separated, 11.6% widowed, 6.2% divorced; Foreign born: 7.8%; Speak English only: 77.0%; With disability: 12.0%; Veterans: 10.7%; Ancestry: 21.1% Italian, 15.7% English, 14.9% German, 13.7% Irish, 4.6% Polish

Employment: 16.8% management, business, and financial, 2.7% computer, engineering, and science, 15.1% education, legal, community service, arts, and media, 7.4% healthcare practitioners, 17.7% service, 18.0% sales and office, 6.3% natural resources, construction, and maintenance, 16.1% production, transportation, and material moving

Income: Per capita: $29,327; Median household: $50,847; Average household: $63,485; Households with income of $100,000 or more: 15.0%; Poverty rate: 19.8%

Educational Attainment: High school diploma or higher: 93.9%; Bachelor's degree or higher: 33.7%; Graduate/professional degree or higher: 12.8%

School District(s)
Geneva City SD (PK-12)
   Enrollment: 2,253 . . . . (315) 781-0400

Four-year College(s)
Hobart William Smith Colleges (Private, Not-for-profit)
   Enrollment: 2,244 . . . . (315) 781-3000
   Tuition: In-state $53,525; Out-of-state $53,525

Two-year College(s)
Finger Lakes Health College of Nursing (Private, Not-for-profit)
   Enrollment: 126 . . . . (315) 787-4005
   Tuition: In-state $11,540; Out-of-state $11,540

Vocational/Technical School(s)
Marion S Whelan School of Nursing of Geneva General Hospital (Private, Not-for-profit)
   Enrollment: 31 . . . . (315) 787-4005
   Tuition: In-state $9,150; Out-of-state $9,150

Housing: Homeownership rate: 63.0%; Median home value: $185,400; Median year structure built: 1970; Homeowner vacancy rate: 0.0%; Median selected monthly owner costs: $1,393 with a mortgage, $644 without a mortgage; Median gross rent: $813 per month; Rental vacancy rate: 0.0%

Health Insurance: 94.0% have insurance; 72.7% have private insurance; 49.8% have public insurance; 6.0% do not have insurance; 3.7% of children under 18 do not have insurance

Hospitals: Geneva General Hospital (136 beds)

Newspapers: Finger Lakes Times (daily circulation 15,600)

Transportation: Commute: 91.6% car, 0.0% public transportation, 4.6% walk, 2.6% work from home; Mean travel time to work: 16.5 minutes

GORHAM (CDP). Covers a land area of 1.897 square miles and a water area of 0 square miles. Located at 42.80° N. Lat; 77.13° W. Long. Elevation is 889 feet.

Population: 680; Growth (since 2000): n/a; Density: 358.4 persons per square mile; Race: 100.0% White, 0.0% Black/African American, 0.0% Asian, 0.0% American Indian/Alaska Native, 0.0% Native Hawaiian/Other Pacific Islander, 0.0% Two or more races, 0.0% Hispanic of any race; Average household size: 2.75; Median age: 42.1; Age under 18: 26.3%; Age 65 and over: 9.1%; Males per 100 females: 86.4; Marriage status: 19.7% never married, 70.0% now married, 0.0% separated, 2.1% widowed, 8.1% divorced; Foreign born: 0.0%; Speak English only: 100.0%; With disability: 7.8%; Veterans: 20.4%; Ancestry: 16.2% Irish, 14.4% English, 12.4% German, 9.3% Italian, 6.3% French

Employment: 12.6% management, business, and financial, 15.2% computer, engineering, and science, 19.7% education, legal, community service, arts, and media, 0.0% healthcare practitioners, 20.1% service, 11.3% sales and office, 5.8% natural resources, construction, and maintenance, 15.2% production, transportation, and material moving

Income: Per capita: $25,932; Median household: $64,375; Average household: $70,441; Households with income of $100,000 or more: 29.6%; Poverty rate: 17.5%

Educational Attainment: High school diploma or higher: 100.0%; Bachelor's degree or higher: 35.9%; Graduate/professional degree or higher: 13.8%

School District(s)
Gorham-Middlesex Central SD (Marcus Whitman) (PK-12)
   Enrollment: 1,229 . . . . (585) 554-4848

Housing: Homeownership rate: 80.2%; Median home value: $99,300; Median year structure built: Before 1940; Homeowner vacancy rate: 0.0%; Median selected monthly owner costs: $936 with a mortgage, $540 without a mortgage; Median gross rent: n/a per month; Rental vacancy rate: 0.0%

Health Insurance: 96.3% have insurance; 71.2% have private insurance; 39.3% have public insurance; 3.7% do not have insurance; 0.0% of children under 18 do not have insurance

Transportation: Commute: 96.8% car, 0.0% public transportation, 0.0% walk, 3.2% work from home; Mean travel time to work: 24.9 minutes

GORHAM (town). Covers a land area of 48.854 square miles and a water area of 4.315 square miles. Located at 42.80° N. Lat; 77.20° W. Long. Elevation is 889 feet.

Population: 4,262; Growth (since 2000): 12.9%; Density: 87.2 persons per square mile; Race: 98.6% White, 0.2% Black/African American, 0.7% Asian, 0.0% American Indian/Alaska Native, 0.0% Native Hawaiian/Other Pacific Islander, 0.5% Two or more races, 1.9% Hispanic of any race; Average household size: 2.27; Median age: 48.9; Age under 18: 16.9%; Age 65 and over: 22.1%; Males per 100 females: 96.9; Marriage status: 23.1% never married, 59.2% now married, 1.9% separated, 5.6% widowed, 12.1% divorced; Foreign born: 2.7%; Speak English only: 94.5%; With disability: 11.5%; Veterans: 9.9%; Ancestry: 20.6% German, 16.0% Irish, 14.9% English, 13.3% American, 9.5% Italian

Employment: 11.7% management, business, and financial, 5.7% computer, engineering, and science, 9.7% education, legal, community service, arts, and media, 4.7% healthcare practitioners, 16.2% service, 21.3% sales and office, 15.7% natural resources, construction, and maintenance, 15.0% production, transportation, and material moving

Income: Per capita: $32,645; Median household: $57,240; Average household: $74,765; Households with income of $100,000 or more: 22.2%; Poverty rate: 9.5%

Educational Attainment: High school diploma or higher: 92.3%; Bachelor's degree or higher: 29.2%; Graduate/professional degree or higher: 13.5%

School District(s)
Gorham-Middlesex Central SD (Marcus Whitman) (PK-12)
   Enrollment: 1,229 . . . . (585) 554-4848

Housing: Homeownership rate: 85.6%; Median home value: $174,800; Median year structure built: 1967; Homeowner vacancy rate: 0.0%; Median selected monthly owner costs: $1,233 with a mortgage, $514 without a mortgage; Median gross rent: $636 per month; Rental vacancy rate: 0.0%

Health Insurance: 93.3% have insurance; 73.8% have private insurance; 36.9% have public insurance; 6.7% do not have insurance; 8.0% of children under 18 do not have insurance

Transportation: Commute: 94.0% car, 0.0% public transportation, 1.7% walk, 4.1% work from home; Mean travel time to work: 25.7 minutes

Additional Information Contacts
Town of Gorham . . . . (585) 526-6317
   http://www.gorham-ny.com

HALL (CDP). Covers a land area of 1.023 square miles and a water area of 0 square miles. Located at 42.80° N. Lat; 77.07° W. Long. Elevation is 935 feet.

Population: 192; Growth (since 2000): n/a; Density: 187.7 persons per square mile; Race: 100.0% White, 0.0% Black/African American, 0.0% Asian, 0.0% American Indian/Alaska Native, 0.0% Native Hawaiian/Other Pacific Islander, 0.0% Two or more races, 0.0% Hispanic of any race; Average household size: 2.23; Median age: 49.3; Age under 18: 15.6%; Age 65 and over: 5.2%; Males per 100 females: 101.9; Marriage status: 13.6% never married, 77.2% now married, 0.0% separated, 3.1% widowed, 6.2% divorced; Foreign born: 0.0%; Speak English only: 100.0%; With disability: 7.8%; Veterans: 0.0%; Ancestry: 34.4% English, 28.1% Irish, 27.6% German, 19.8% Italian, 13.0% Danish

Employment: 26.9% management, business, and financial, 0.0% computer, engineering, and science, 6.7% education, legal, community service, arts, and media, 0.0% healthcare practitioners, 3.0% service, 41.8% sales and office, 14.2% natural resources, construction, and maintenance, 7.5% production, transportation, and material moving

Income: Per capita: $40,050; Median household: $86,250; Average household: $90,080; Households with income of $100,000 or more: 50.0%; Poverty rate: 2.8%

Educational Attainment: High school diploma or higher: 94.4%; Bachelor's degree or higher: 27.2%; Graduate/professional degree or higher: 13.0%

Housing: Homeownership rate: 100.0%; Median home value: $121,200; Median year structure built: Before 1940; Homeowner vacancy rate: 0.0%; Median selected monthly owner costs: $1,190 with a mortgage, $437 without a mortgage; Median gross rent: n/a per month; Rental vacancy rate: 100.0%

Health Insurance: 91.1% have insurance; 82.8% have private insurance; 13.5% have public insurance; 8.9% do not have insurance; 0.0% of children under 18 do not have insurance

Transportation: Commute: 100.0% car, 0.0% public transportation, 0.0% walk, 0.0% work from home; Mean travel time to work: 24.9 minutes

HONEOYE (CDP). Covers a land area of 0.921 square miles and a water area of 0 square miles. Located at 42.79° N. Lat; 77.51° W. Long. Elevation is 814 feet.

Population: 777; Growth (since 2000): n/a; Density: 843.7 persons per square mile; Race: 97.8% White, 0.0% Black/African American, 0.0% Asian, 2.2% American Indian/Alaska Native, 0.0% Native Hawaiian/Other Pacific Islander, 0.0% Two or more races, 26.5% Hispanic of any race; Average household size: 3.22; Median age: 32.6; Age under 18: 23.7%; Age 65 and over: 15.2%; Males per 100 females: 107.5; Marriage status: 32.9% never married, 50.6% now married, 1.5% separated, 9.4% widowed, 7.1% divorced; Foreign born: 5.9%; Speak English only: 93.2%; With disability: 8.8%; Veterans: 5.2%; Ancestry: 52.3% Italian, 40.3% German, 13.4% Irish, 12.9% English, 8.0% French

Employment: 15.6% management, business, and financial, 0.0% computer, engineering, and science, 3.9% education, legal, community service, arts, and media, 0.0% healthcare practitioners, 12.4% service, 38.3% sales and office, 11.0% natural resources, construction, and maintenance, 18.8% production, transportation, and material moving

Income: Per capita: $15,955; Median household: $37,850; Average household: $48,678; Households with income of $100,000 or more: 18.7%; Poverty rate: 2.7%

Educational Attainment: High school diploma or higher: 97.8%; Bachelor's degree or higher: 8.9%; Graduate/professional degree or higher: 3.9%

School District(s)
Honeoye Central SD (KG-12)
    Enrollment: 604 . . . . (585) 229-4125

Housing: Homeownership rate: 52.7%; Median home value: n/a; Median year structure built: Before 1940; Homeowner vacancy rate: 23.0%; Median selected monthly owner costs: n/a with a mortgage, n/a without a mortgage; Median gross rent: $918 per month; Rental vacancy rate: 0.0%

Health Insurance: 92.9% have insurance; 43.6% have private insurance; 54.3% have public insurance; 7.1% do not have insurance; 0.0% of children under 18 do not have insurance

Transportation: Commute: 70.0% car, 0.0% public transportation, 30.0% walk, 0.0% work from home; Mean travel time to work: 24.5 minutes

HOPEWELL (town). Covers a land area of 35.676 square miles and a water area of 0.020 square miles. Located at 42.89° N. Lat; 77.20° W. Long.

Population: 3,736; Growth (since 2000): 11.7%; Density: 104.7 persons per square mile; Race: 93.4% White, 3.4% Black/African American, 0.0% Asian, 0.6% American Indian/Alaska Native, 0.0% Native Hawaiian/Other Pacific Islander, 2.1% Two or more races, 5.1% Hispanic of any race; Average household size: 2.75; Median age: 40.7; Age under 18: 23.9%; Age 65 and over: 16.1%; Males per 100 females: 112.8; Marriage status: 33.3% never married, 49.9% now married, 3.7% separated, 6.8% widowed, 10.0% divorced; Foreign born: 1.8%; Speak English only: 96.3%; With disability: 15.6%; Veterans: 6.0%; Ancestry: 20.3% German, 18.8% English, 14.6% Irish, 9.6% American, 9.4% Italian

Employment: 11.6% management, business, and financial, 5.8% computer, engineering, and science, 8.7% education, legal, community service, arts, and media, 8.3% healthcare practitioners, 19.3% service, 17.8% sales and office, 17.1% natural resources, construction, and maintenance, 11.3% production, transportation, and material moving

Income: Per capita: $23,589; Median household: $64,808; Average household: $69,175; Households with income of $100,000 or more: 21.1%; Poverty rate: 11.8%

Educational Attainment: High school diploma or higher: 90.1%; Bachelor's degree or higher: 21.9%; Graduate/professional degree or higher: 5.7%

Housing: Homeownership rate: 89.6%; Median home value: $123,200; Median year structure built: 1979; Homeowner vacancy rate: 0.0%; Median selected monthly owner costs: $1,344 with a mortgage, $588 without a mortgage; Median gross rent: $938 per month; Rental vacancy rate: 0.0%

Health Insurance: 94.1% have insurance; 66.7% have private insurance; 43.9% have public insurance; 5.9% do not have insurance; 3.2% of children under 18 do not have insurance

Transportation: Commute: 91.5% car, 0.7% public transportation, 3.7% walk, 2.6% work from home; Mean travel time to work: 27.6 minutes

IONIA (unincorporated postal area)
ZCTA: 14475

Covers a land area of 1.526 square miles and a water area of 0 square miles. Located at 42.94° N. Lat; 77.50° W. Long. Elevation is 889 feet.

Population: 257; Growth (since 2000): 15.2%; Density: 168.4 persons per square mile; Race: 96.9% White, 0.0% Black/African American, 0.0% Asian, 0.0% American Indian/Alaska Native, 0.0% Native Hawaiian/Other Pacific Islander, 0.0% Two or more races, 12.8% Hispanic of any race; Average household size: 2.38; Median age: 46.7; Age under 18: 25.7%; Age 65 and over: 28.8%; Males per 100 females: 93.4; Marriage status: 15.3% never married, 68.9% now married, 0.0% separated, 2.6% widowed, 13.3% divorced; Foreign born: 12.5%; Speak English only: 78.6%; With disability: 5.4%; Veterans: 2.6%; Ancestry: 35.0% Irish, 25.7% German, 21.4% English, 8.9% Scottish, 8.6% Italian

Employment: 12.9% management, business, and financial, 7.8% computer, engineering, and science, 8.6% education, legal, community service, arts, and media, 12.1% healthcare practitioners, 0.0% service, 17.2% sales and office, 16.4% natural resources, construction, and maintenance, 25.0% production, transportation, and material moving

Income: Per capita: $30,212; Median household: $66,875; Average household: $71,247; Households with income of $100,000 or more: 21.3%; Poverty rate: 5.1%

Educational Attainment: High school diploma or higher: 93.7%; Bachelor's degree or higher: 58.1%; Graduate/professional degree or higher: 16.8%

Housing: Homeownership rate: 95.4%; Median home value: $275,000; Median year structure built: 1984; Homeowner vacancy rate: 0.0%; Median selected monthly owner costs: $1,750 with a mortgage, $1,069 without a mortgage; Median gross rent: n/a per month; Rental vacancy rate: 78.3%

Health Insurance: 100.0% have insurance; 96.1% have private insurance; 31.9% have public insurance; 0.0% do not have insurance; 0.0% of children under 18 do not have insurance

Transportation: Commute: 94.5% car, 5.5% public transportation, 0.0% walk, 0.0% work from home; Mean travel time to work: 27.8 minutes

MANCHESTER (town). Covers a land area of 37.818 square miles and a water area of 0.032 square miles. Located at 42.99° N. Lat; 77.19° W. Long. Elevation is 591 feet.

History: Incorporated 1892.

Population: 9,369; Growth (since 2000): 1.2%; Density: 247.7 persons per square mile; Race: 96.8% White, 1.4% Black/African American, 0.0% Asian, 0.0% American Indian/Alaska Native, 0.0% Native Hawaiian/Other Pacific Islander, 1.2% Two or more races, 2.0% Hispanic of any race; Average household size: 2.46; Median age: 45.7; Age under 18: 20.0%; Age 65 and over: 20.1%; Males per 100 females: 94.2; Marriage status: 27.3% never married, 46.6% now married, 2.8% separated, 10.0% widowed, 16.2% divorced; Foreign born: 2.0%; Speak English only: 96.5%; With disability: 17.9%; Veterans: 12.3%; Ancestry: 20.3% Irish, 20.1% German, 17.9% English, 14.6% Italian, 8.4% Dutch

Employment: 10.3% management, business, and financial, 3.9% computer, engineering, and science, 8.4% education, legal, community service, arts, and media, 6.9% healthcare practitioners, 18.8% service, 23.9% sales and office, 11.6% natural resources, construction, and maintenance, 16.2% production, transportation, and material moving

Income: Per capita: $26,646; Median household: $51,250; Average household: $65,230; Households with income of $100,000 or more: 18.9%; Poverty rate: 11.7%

Educational Attainment: High school diploma or higher: 89.7%; Bachelor's degree or higher: 16.1%; Graduate/professional degree or higher: 5.6%

Housing: Homeownership rate: 78.5%; Median home value: $97,600; Median year structure built: 1958; Homeowner vacancy rate: 2.6%; Median selected monthly owner costs: $1,111 with a mortgage, $564 without a mortgage; Median gross rent: $689 per month; Rental vacancy rate: 7.3%

Health Insurance: 95.7% have insurance; 71.8% have private insurance; 43.3% have public insurance; 4.3% do not have insurance; 1.3% of children under 18 do not have insurance

Transportation: Commute: 93.3% car, 0.3% public transportation, 2.1% walk, 3.1% work from home; Mean travel time to work: 21.8 minutes

Additional Information Contacts
Town of Manchester . . . . (315) 462-6224
  http://manchesterny.org

MANCHESTER (village). Covers a land area of 1.176 square miles and a water area of 0 square miles. Located at 42.97° N. Lat; 77.23° W. Long. Elevation is 591 feet.
Population: 1,824; Growth (since 2000): 23.7%; Density: 1,550.7 persons per square mile; Race: 98.8% White, 0.0% Black/African American, 0.0% Asian, 0.1% American Indian/Alaska Native, 0.0% Native Hawaiian/Other Pacific Islander, 1.1% Two or more races, 2.5% Hispanic of any race; Average household size: 2.39; Median age: 37.2; Age under 18: 22.4%; Age 65 and over: 16.7%; Males per 100 females: 91.4; Marriage status: 29.1% never married, 47.7% now married, 2.3% separated, 10.9% widowed, 12.3% divorced; Foreign born: 0.8%; Speak English only: 96.9%; With disability: 13.4%; Veterans: 10.6%; Ancestry: 24.0% Irish, 20.2% German, 19.5% Italian, 19.2% English, 9.0% Dutch
Employment: 8.5% management, business, and financial, 4.3% computer, engineering, and science, 6.2% education, legal, community service, arts, and media, 5.6% healthcare practitioners, 24.7% service, 23.0% sales and office, 9.7% natural resources, construction, and maintenance, 17.9% production, transportation, and material moving
Income: Per capita: $25,165; Median household: $54,464; Average household: $59,434; Households with income of $100,000 or more: 12.2%; Poverty rate: 8.1%
Educational Attainment: High school diploma or higher: 91.6%; Bachelor's degree or higher: 16.8%; Graduate/professional degree or higher: 5.1%
Housing: Homeownership rate: 72.5%; Median home value: $93,100; Median year structure built: 1956; Homeowner vacancy rate: 1.8%; Median selected monthly owner costs: $1,036 with a mortgage, $547 without a mortgage; Median gross rent: $851 per month; Rental vacancy rate: 1.4%
Health Insurance: 94.7% have insurance; 74.5% have private insurance; 35.4% have public insurance; 5.3% do not have insurance; 0.0% of children under 18 do not have insurance
Safety: Violent crime rate: 0.0 per 10,000 population; Property crime rate: 6.1 per 10,000 population
Transportation: Commute: 96.6% car, 0.4% public transportation, 2.0% walk, 0.6% work from home; Mean travel time to work: 22.8 minutes

NAPLES (town). Covers a land area of 39.685 square miles and a water area of <.001 square miles. Located at 42.62° N. Lat; 77.43° W. Long. Elevation is 804 feet.
History: Incorporated 1894.
Population: 2,447; Growth (since 2000): 0.2%; Density: 61.7 persons per square mile; Race: 97.3% White, 0.6% Black/African American, 0.8% Asian, 0.0% American Indian/Alaska Native, 0.0% Native Hawaiian/Other Pacific Islander, 1.0% Two or more races, 2.0% Hispanic of any race; Average household size: 2.38; Median age: 51.0; Age under 18: 17.0%; Age 65 and over: 22.3%; Males per 100 females: 93.5; Marriage status: 28.0% never married, 52.7% now married, 3.1% separated, 9.3% widowed, 10.0% divorced; Foreign born: 2.7%; Speak English only: 96.5%; With disability: 11.7%; Veterans: 12.2%; Ancestry: 26.9% German, 18.5% Irish, 16.6% English, 11.2% Italian, 7.6% Dutch
Employment: 13.6% management, business, and financial, 2.9% computer, engineering, and science, 9.9% education, legal, community service, arts, and media, 11.6% healthcare practitioners, 23.4% service, 18.4% sales and office, 14.4% natural resources, construction, and maintenance, 5.8% production, transportation, and material moving
Income: Per capita: $25,535; Median household: $49,643; Average household: $59,977; Households with income of $100,000 or more: 18.2%; Poverty rate: 13.8%
Educational Attainment: High school diploma or higher: 92.6%; Bachelor's degree or higher: 24.6%; Graduate/professional degree or higher: 11.6%
School District(s)
Naples Central SD (PK-12)
  Enrollment: 724 . . . . (585) 374-7901
Housing: Homeownership rate: 80.6%; Median home value: $139,500; Median year structure built: 1956; Homeowner vacancy rate: 2.3%; Median selected monthly owner costs: $1,248 with a mortgage, $564 without a mortgage; Median gross rent: $689 per month; Rental vacancy rate: 4.8%
Health Insurance: 95.4% have insurance; 67.2% have private insurance; 47.4% have public insurance; 4.6% do not have insurance; 0.0% of children under 18 do not have insurance

Transportation: Commute: 90.2% car, 0.0% public transportation, 5.5% walk, 4.3% work from home; Mean travel time to work: 28.5 minutes

NAPLES (village). Covers a land area of 0.985 square miles and a water area of 0 square miles. Located at 42.62° N. Lat; 77.40° W. Long. Elevation is 804 feet.
Population: 998; Growth (since 2000): -6.9%; Density: 1,013.7 persons per square mile; Race: 94.3% White, 1.0% Black/African American, 2.0% Asian, 0.0% American Indian/Alaska Native, 0.0% Native Hawaiian/Other Pacific Islander, 2.1% Two or more races, 4.9% Hispanic of any race; Average household size: 2.40; Median age: 48.6; Age under 18: 17.3%; Age 65 and over: 19.9%; Males per 100 females: 86.6; Marriage status: 32.7% never married, 49.1% now married, 3.5% separated, 5.9% widowed, 12.4% divorced; Foreign born: 3.1%; Speak English only: 97.9%; With disability: 10.1%; Veterans: 13.0%; Ancestry: 28.6% German, 21.2% Irish, 19.0% English, 17.0% Italian, 4.5% Dutch
Employment: 10.2% management, business, and financial, 1.6% computer, engineering, and science, 14.4% education, legal, community service, arts, and media, 5.8% healthcare practitioners, 24.7% service, 25.8% sales and office, 10.7% natural resources, construction, and maintenance, 6.7% production, transportation, and material moving
Income: Per capita: $22,026; Median household: $41,136; Average household: $52,342; Households with income of $100,000 or more: 12.7%; Poverty rate: 19.1%
Educational Attainment: High school diploma or higher: 92.4%; Bachelor's degree or higher: 17.7%; Graduate/professional degree or higher: 8.2%
School District(s)
Naples Central SD (PK-12)
  Enrollment: 724 . . . . (585) 374-7901
Housing: Homeownership rate: 60.0%; Median home value: $110,700; Median year structure built: Before 1940; Homeowner vacancy rate: 3.0%; Median selected monthly owner costs: $1,279 with a mortgage, $534 without a mortgage; Median gross rent: $650 per month; Rental vacancy rate: 5.7%
Health Insurance: 94.1% have insurance; 58.9% have private insurance; 51.8% have public insurance; 5.9% do not have insurance; 0.0% of children under 18 do not have insurance
Transportation: Commute: 85.8% car, 0.0% public transportation, 11.4% walk, 2.8% work from home; Mean travel time to work: 23.2 minutes

PHELPS (town). Covers a land area of 64.951 square miles and a water area of 0.293 square miles. Located at 42.96° N. Lat; 77.05° W. Long. Elevation is 522 feet.
Population: 6,945; Growth (since 2000): -1.0%; Density: 106.9 persons per square mile; Race: 96.7% White, 1.1% Black/African American, 0.7% Asian, 0.0% American Indian/Alaska Native, 0.0% Native Hawaiian/Other Pacific Islander, 1.2% Two or more races, 0.8% Hispanic of any race; Average household size: 2.56; Median age: 45.1; Age under 18: 21.9%; Age 65 and over: 15.3%; Males per 100 females: 98.1; Marriage status: 24.1% never married, 58.9% now married, 2.3% separated, 5.7% widowed, 11.3% divorced; Foreign born: 1.9%; Speak English only: 96.7%; With disability: 13.9%; Veterans: 11.9%; Ancestry: 21.5% German, 20.6% English, 15.7% Irish, 11.3% Dutch, 10.8% American
Employment: 15.3% management, business, and financial, 3.5% computer, engineering, and science, 11.2% education, legal, community service, arts, and media, 6.2% healthcare practitioners, 16.4% service, 16.1% sales and office, 10.0% natural resources, construction, and maintenance, 21.4% production, transportation, and material moving
Income: Per capita: $31,608; Median household: $64,599; Average household: $80,215; Households with income of $100,000 or more: 23.4%; Poverty rate: 7.8%
Educational Attainment: High school diploma or higher: 91.1%; Bachelor's degree or higher: 22.0%; Graduate/professional degree or higher: 9.7%
Housing: Homeownership rate: 78.5%; Median home value: $127,300; Median year structure built: 1959; Homeowner vacancy rate: 0.0%; Median selected monthly owner costs: $1,223 with a mortgage, $509 without a mortgage; Median gross rent: $767 per month; Rental vacancy rate: 0.0%
Health Insurance: 95.2% have insurance; 80.3% have private insurance; 28.8% have public insurance; 4.8% do not have insurance; 4.7% of children under 18 do not have insurance
Transportation: Commute: 94.5% car, 0.4% public transportation, 2.8% walk, 2.2% work from home; Mean travel time to work: 19.3 minutes

Town of Phelps . . . . (315) 548-5691
http://www.phelpsny.com/residents/town

PHELPS (village). Covers a land area of 1.172 square miles and a water area of 0 square miles. Located at 42.96° N. Lat; 77.06° W. Long. Elevation is 522 feet.

Population: 1,744; Growth (since 2000): -11.4%; Density: 1,487.6 persons per square mile; Race: 98.4% White, 0.3% Black/African American, 0.5% Asian, 0.0% American Indian/Alaska Native, 0.0% Native Hawaiian/Other Pacific Islander, 0.9% Two or more races, 0.0% Hispanic of any race; Average household size: 2.24; Median age: 43.4; Age under 18: 20.9%; Age 65 and over: 19.3%; Males per 100 females: 93.5; Marriage status: 27.6% never married, 51.7% now married, 3.4% separated, 9.0% widowed, 11.8% divorced; Foreign born: 0.7%; Speak English only: 97.5%; With disability: 14.6%; Veterans: 14.0%; Ancestry: 27.1% Irish, 24.4% English, 24.4% German, 15.9% Dutch, 9.2% American
Employment: 16.0% management, business, and financial, 7.3% computer, engineering, and science, 9.1% education, legal, community service, arts, and media, 6.8% healthcare practitioners, 12.8% service, 20.6% sales and office, 11.5% natural resources, construction, and maintenance, 16.0% production, transportation, and material moving
Income: Per capita: $31,285; Median household: $61,125; Average household: $68,850; Households with income of $100,000 or more: 17.0%; Poverty rate: 3.9%
Educational Attainment: High school diploma or higher: 92.4%; Bachelor's degree or higher: 21.6%; Graduate/professional degree or higher: 11.1%
Housing: Homeownership rate: 65.5%; Median home value: $112,600; Median year structure built: Before 1940; Homeowner vacancy rate: 0.0%; Median selected monthly owner costs: $1,220 with a mortgage, $523 without a mortgage; Median gross rent: $716 per month; Rental vacancy rate: 0.0%
Health Insurance: 99.2% have insurance; 81.6% have private insurance; 35.5% have public insurance; 0.8% do not have insurance; 0.0% of children under 18 do not have insurance
Transportation: Commute: 95.6% car, 1.5% public transportation, 1.7% walk, 1.3% work from home; Mean travel time to work: 19.7 minutes
Additional Information Contacts
Village of Phelps . . . . (315) 548-3861
http://www.phelpsny.com/village

PORT GIBSON (CDP). Covers a land area of 1.171 square miles and a water area of 0.032 square miles. Located at 43.03° N. Lat; 77.16° W. Long. Elevation is 476 feet.

Population: 327; Growth (since 2000): n/a; Density: 279.2 persons per square mile; Race: 86.9% White, 0.9% Black/African American, 0.0% Asian, 0.0% American Indian/Alaska Native, 0.0% Native Hawaiian/Other Pacific Islander, 12.2% Two or more races, 0.0% Hispanic of any race; Average household size: 2.35; Median age: 39.2; Age under 18: 22.9%; Age 65 and over: 18.0%; Males per 100 females: 106.8; Marriage status: 25.4% never married, 54.5% now married, 0.0% separated, 3.4% widowed, 16.7% divorced; Foreign born: 0.0%; Speak English only: 100.0%; With disability: 15.9%; Veterans: 18.7%; Ancestry: 57.5% German, 28.1% Irish, 15.6% English, 14.1% Dutch, 9.2% American
Employment: 5.3% management, business, and financial, 6.1% computer, engineering, and science, 4.5% education, legal, community service, arts, and media, 12.9% healthcare practitioners, 30.3% service, 22.7% sales and office, 0.0% natural resources, construction, and maintenance, 18.2% production, transportation, and material moving
Income: Per capita: $26,655; Median household: $45,568; Average household: $61,713; Households with income of $100,000 or more: 18.7%; Poverty rate: 32.4%
Educational Attainment: High school diploma or higher: 79.6%; Bachelor's degree or higher: 10.0%; Graduate/professional degree or higher: 7.1%
Housing: Homeownership rate: 87.1%; Median home value: $96,000; Median year structure built: 1955; Homeowner vacancy rate: 0.0%; Median selected monthly owner costs: $900 with a mortgage, $314 without a mortgage; Median gross rent: $667 per month; Rental vacancy rate: 0.0%
Health Insurance: 99.1% have insurance; 70.0% have private insurance; 43.7% have public insurance; 0.9% do not have insurance; 0.0% of children under 18 do not have insurance
Transportation: Commute: 90.9% car, 0.0% public transportation, 0.0% walk, 9.1% work from home; Mean travel time to work: 25.4 minutes

RICHMOND (town). Covers a land area of 42.432 square miles and a water area of 1.960 square miles. Located at 42.79° N. Lat; 77.52° W. Long. Elevation is 814 feet.

Population: 3,293; Growth (since 2000): -4.6%; Density: 77.6 persons per square mile; Race: 94.7% White, 0.0% Black/African American, 0.0% Asian, 1.8% American Indian/Alaska Native, 0.0% Native Hawaiian/Other Pacific Islander, 3.1% Two or more races, 8.7% Hispanic of any race; Average household size: 2.62; Median age: 50.6; Age under 18: 15.5%; Age 65 and over: 20.1%; Males per 100 females: 105.1; Marriage status: 24.9% never married, 64.1% now married, 1.2% separated, 4.1% widowed, 6.9% divorced; Foreign born: 2.0%; Speak English only: 95.9%; With disability: 11.8%; Veterans: 8.1%; Ancestry: 27.6% German, 25.6% Italian, 18.3% English, 11.7% American, 8.7% Irish
Employment: 14.9% management, business, and financial, 11.1% computer, engineering, and science, 11.2% education, legal, community service, arts, and media, 2.3% healthcare practitioners, 10.7% service, 24.0% sales and office, 7.2% natural resources, construction, and maintenance, 18.6% production, transportation, and material moving
Income: Per capita: $27,833; Median household: $67,188; Average household: $71,479; Households with income of $100,000 or more: 26.7%; Poverty rate: 2.2%
Educational Attainment: High school diploma or higher: 97.4%; Bachelor's degree or higher: 27.4%; Graduate/professional degree or higher: 12.5%
Housing: Homeownership rate: 85.9%; Median home value: $163,300; Median year structure built: 1960; Homeowner vacancy rate: 6.5%; Median selected monthly owner costs: $1,229 with a mortgage, $770 without a mortgage; Median gross rent: $849 per month; Rental vacancy rate: 18.1%
Health Insurance: 94.2% have insurance; 68.1% have private insurance; 41.9% have public insurance; 5.8% do not have insurance; 0.0% of children under 18 do not have insurance
Transportation: Commute: 89.8% car, 0.0% public transportation, 7.3% walk, 3.0% work from home; Mean travel time to work: 31.3 minutes

SENECA (town). Covers a land area of 50.450 square miles and a water area of 0 square miles. Located at 42.83° N. Lat; 77.07° W. Long.

Population: 2,703; Growth (since 2000): -1.0%; Density: 53.6 persons per square mile; Race: 97.5% White, 0.1% Black/African American, 1.2% Asian, 0.0% American Indian/Alaska Native, 0.0% Native Hawaiian/Other Pacific Islander, 1.1% Two or more races, 1.7% Hispanic of any race; Average household size: 2.56; Median age: 46.7; Age under 18: 20.0%; Age 65 and over: 16.1%; Males per 100 females: 110.1; Marriage status: 21.7% never married, 62.9% now married, 1.3% separated, 6.2% widowed, 9.1% divorced; Foreign born: 2.2%; Speak English only: 95.9%; With disability: 9.8%; Veterans: 5.9%; Ancestry: 23.3% German, 18.5% English, 17.1% Italian, 16.8% Irish, 5.7% Dutch
Employment: 17.6% management, business, and financial, 1.9% computer, engineering, and science, 7.7% education, legal, community service, arts, and media, 7.8% healthcare practitioners, 14.2% service, 27.5% sales and office, 13.5% natural resources, construction, and maintenance, 9.9% production, transportation, and material moving
Income: Per capita: $33,359; Median household: $72,802; Average household: $85,157; Households with income of $100,000 or more: 32.0%; Poverty rate: 6.2%
Educational Attainment: High school diploma or higher: 92.6%; Bachelor's degree or higher: 27.3%; Graduate/professional degree or higher: 11.2%
Housing: Homeownership rate: 84.2%; Median home value: $138,300; Median year structure built: 1944; Homeowner vacancy rate: 2.9%; Median selected monthly owner costs: $1,225 with a mortgage, $477 without a mortgage; Median gross rent: $831 per month; Rental vacancy rate: 7.3%
Health Insurance: 89.8% have insurance; 77.1% have private insurance; 28.4% have public insurance; 10.2% do not have insurance; 20.3% of children under 18 do not have insurance
Transportation: Commute: 94.1% car, 0.5% public transportation, 0.3% walk, 4.6% work from home; Mean travel time to work: 21.5 minutes

SHORTSVILLE (village). Covers a land area of 0.668 square miles and a water area of 0 square miles. Located at 42.96° N. Lat; 77.22° W. Long. Elevation is 620 feet.

Population: 1,261; Growth (since 2000): -4.5%; Density: 1,888.9 persons per square mile; Race: 98.4% White, 1.3% Black/African American, 0.0% Asian, 0.0% American Indian/Alaska Native, 0.0% Native Hawaiian/Other Pacific Islander, 0.3% Two or more races, 0.0% Hispanic of any race; Average household size: 2.34; Median age: 49.0; Age under 18: 14.9%;

Age 65 and over: 18.7%; Males per 100 females: 96.3; Marriage status: 25.6% never married, 55.0% now married, 3.2% separated, 6.8% widowed, 12.6% divorced; Foreign born: 0.8%; Speak English only: 98.9%; With disability: 16.5%; Veterans: 11.7%; Ancestry: 21.6% Irish, 19.8% English, 19.7% German, 10.9% Italian, 8.5% Dutch

Employment: 9.9% management, business, and financial, 5.0% computer, engineering, and science, 11.3% education, legal, community service, arts, and media, 8.5% healthcare practitioners, 19.7% service, 25.0% sales and office, 6.7% natural resources, construction, and maintenance, 14.0% production, transportation, and material moving

Income: Per capita: $33,045; Median household: $62,353; Average household: $76,610; Households with income of $100,000 or more: 26.7%; Poverty rate: 7.5%

Educational Attainment: High school diploma or higher: 93.5%; Bachelor's degree or higher: 20.4%; Graduate/professional degree or higher: 5.7%

School District(s)
Manchester-Shortsville Central SD (Red Jacket) (PK-12)
    Enrollment: 845 . . . . (585) 289-3964
Housing: Homeownership rate: 82.3%; Median home value: $100,100; Median year structure built: Before 1940; Homeowner vacancy rate: 0.0%; Median selected monthly owner costs: $1,117 with a mortgage, $506 without a mortgage; Median gross rent: $602 per month; Rental vacancy rate: 31.2%

Health Insurance: 97.4% have insurance; 80.9% have private insurance; 34.8% have public insurance; 2.6% do not have insurance; 0.0% of children under 18 do not have insurance

Safety: Violent crime rate: 0.0 per 10,000 population; Property crime rate: 0.0 per 10,000 population

Transportation: Commute: 96.2% car, 0.0% public transportation, 0.6% walk, 1.0% work from home; Mean travel time to work: 22.5 minutes

SOUTH BRISTOL (town).
Covers a land area of 38.973 square miles and a water area of 3.051 square miles. Located at 42.70° N. Lat; 77.41° W. Long. Elevation is 1,086 feet.

Population: 1,695; Growth (since 2000): 3.0%; Density: 43.5 persons per square mile; Race: 98.7% White, 0.0% Black/African American, 0.2% Asian, 0.3% American Indian/Alaska Native, 0.0% Native Hawaiian/Other Pacific Islander, 0.8% Two or more races, 0.6% Hispanic of any race; Average household size: 2.14; Median age: 54.8; Age under 18: 16.0%; Age 65 and over: 27.4%; Males per 100 females: 100.3; Marriage status: 19.5% never married, 64.6% now married, 0.0% separated, 5.6% widowed, 10.3% divorced; Foreign born: 2.7%; Speak English only: 99.1%; With disability: 10.8%; Veterans: 9.3%; Ancestry: 27.0% German, 23.1% English, 19.1% Irish, 13.2% Italian, 6.5% Polish

Employment: 19.2% management, business, and financial, 2.1% computer, engineering, and science, 11.6% education, legal, community service, arts, and media, 6.4% healthcare practitioners, 18.8% service, 23.2% sales and office, 7.2% natural resources, construction, and maintenance, 11.5% production, transportation, and material moving

Income: Per capita: $46,226; Median household: $72,386; Average household: $99,519; Households with income of $100,000 or more: 33.4%; Poverty rate: 9.4%

Educational Attainment: High school diploma or higher: 97.9%; Bachelor's degree or higher: 46.1%; Graduate/professional degree or higher: 19.0%

Housing: Homeownership rate: 88.8%; Median home value: $230,000; Median year structure built: 1980; Homeowner vacancy rate: 0.0%; Median selected monthly owner costs: $1,615 with a mortgage, $738 without a mortgage; Median gross rent: $648 per month; Rental vacancy rate: 34.8%

Health Insurance: 97.0% have insurance; 79.4% have private insurance; 38.2% have public insurance; 3.0% do not have insurance; 0.0% of children under 18 do not have insurance

Transportation: Commute: 88.1% car, 0.0% public transportation, 0.4% walk, 10.8% work from home; Mean travel time to work: 30.9 minutes

STANLEY (unincorporated postal area)
ZCTA: 14561

Covers a land area of 51.876 square miles and a water area of 0 square miles. Located at 42.82° N. Lat; 77.13° W. Long. Elevation is 889 feet.
Population: 2,929; Growth (since 2000): 1.9%; Density: 56.5 persons per square mile; Race: 99.1% White, 0.1% Black/African American, 0.3% Asian, 0.0% American Indian/Alaska Native, 0.0% Native Hawaiian/Other Pacific Islander, 0.4% Two or more races, 1.5% Hispanic of any race; Average household size: 2.58; Median age: 41.9;

Age under 18: 21.4%; Age 65 and over: 11.2%; Males per 100 females: 104.6; Marriage status: 25.3% never married, 59.1% now married, 1.7% separated, 6.0% widowed, 9.6% divorced; Foreign born: 1.2%; Speak English only: 93.8%; With disability: 8.4%; Veterans: 7.9%; Ancestry: 22.1% German, 18.8% Irish, 18.0% English, 11.9% Italian, 9.0% Dutch

Employment: 14.9% management, business, and financial, 4.1% computer, engineering, and science, 11.1% education, legal, community service, arts, and media, 6.9% healthcare practitioners, 14.5% service, 23.3% sales and office, 12.4% natural resources, construction, and maintenance, 12.8% production, transportation, and material moving

Income: Per capita: $31,438; Median household: $65,850; Average household: $81,131; Households with income of $100,000 or more: 26.5%; Poverty rate: 7.9%

Educational Attainment: High school diploma or higher: 95.2%; Bachelor's degree or higher: 29.1%; Graduate/professional degree or higher: 10.0%

Housing: Homeownership rate: 83.8%; Median home value: $135,000; Median year structure built: Before 1940; Homeowner vacancy rate: 2.7%; Median selected monthly owner costs: $1,175 with a mortgage, $455 without a mortgage; Median gross rent: $824 per month; Rental vacancy rate: 0.0%

Health Insurance: 90.7% have insurance; 73.5% have private insurance; 31.2% have public insurance; 9.3% do not have insurance; 15.2% of children under 18 do not have insurance

Transportation: Commute: 93.3% car, 0.0% public transportation, 1.3% walk, 4.6% work from home; Mean travel time to work: 21.4 minutes

VICTOR (town).
Covers a land area of 35.918 square miles and a water area of 0.013 square miles. Located at 42.99° N. Lat; 77.43° W. Long. Elevation is 577 feet.

History: Incorporated 1879.

Population: 14,681; Growth (since 2000): 47.1%; Density: 408.7 persons per square mile; Race: 95.2% White, 1.0% Black/African American, 1.7% Asian, 0.4% American Indian/Alaska Native, 0.0% Native Hawaiian/Other Pacific Islander, 1.5% Two or more races, 0.5% Hispanic of any race; Average household size: 2.57; Median age: 42.9; Age under 18: 25.4%; Age 65 and over: 17.0%; Males per 100 females: 95.5; Marriage status: 22.9% never married, 65.1% now married, 1.1% separated, 5.1% widowed, 6.8% divorced; Foreign born: 5.6%; Speak English only: 93.2%; With disability: 8.1%; Veterans: 6.5%; Ancestry: 21.8% German, 19.1% Irish, 17.1% Italian, 16.1% English, 5.0% Polish

Employment: 24.9% management, business, and financial, 6.8% computer, engineering, and science, 13.9% education, legal, community service, arts, and media, 8.3% healthcare practitioners, 11.8% service, 25.0% sales and office, 3.4% natural resources, construction, and maintenance, 5.8% production, transportation, and material moving

Income: Per capita: $52,703; Median household: $98,167; Average household: $134,715; Households with income of $100,000 or more: 48.7%; Poverty rate: 2.3%

Educational Attainment: High school diploma or higher: 96.7%; Bachelor's degree or higher: 55.0%; Graduate/professional degree or higher: 25.8%

School District(s)
Victor Central SD (PK-12)
    Enrollment: 4,427 . . . . (585) 924-3252
Housing: Homeownership rate: 81.7%; Median home value: $258,200; Median year structure built: 1992; Homeowner vacancy rate: 0.0%; Median selected monthly owner costs: $2,046 with a mortgage, $785 without a mortgage; Median gross rent: $1,260 per month; Rental vacancy rate: 6.4%

Health Insurance: 97.9% have insurance; 87.7% have private insurance; 24.0% have public insurance; 2.1% do not have insurance; 0.6% of children under 18 do not have insurance

Transportation: Commute: 91.0% car, 0.4% public transportation, 0.6% walk, 8.0% work from home; Mean travel time to work: 21.3 minutes

Additional Information Contacts
Town of Victor . . . . (585) 742-5080
    http://www.victorny.org

VICTOR (village).
Covers a land area of 1.373 square miles and a water area of 0 square miles. Located at 42.98° N. Lat; 77.41° W. Long. Elevation is 577 feet.

Population: 2,757; Growth (since 2000): 13.3%; Density: 2,008.4 persons per square mile; Race: 95.7% White, 0.2% Black/African American, 1.5% Asian, 0.0% American Indian/Alaska Native, 0.0% Native Hawaiian/Other

Pacific Islander, 1.3% Two or more races, 1.1% Hispanic of any race; Average household size: 2.71; Median age: 40.5; Age under 18: 27.5%; Age 65 and over: 13.9%; Males per 100 females: 96.4; Marriage status: 30.6% never married, 57.3% now married, 3.0% separated, 5.0% widowed, 7.1% divorced; Foreign born: 2.5%; Speak English only: 97.1%; With disability: 9.5%; Veterans: 7.2%; Ancestry: 29.9% German, 22.1% Irish, 19.4% Italian, 15.7% English, 7.8% Polish

Employment: 19.1% management, business, and financial, 7.0% computer, engineering, and science, 12.6% education, legal, community service, arts, and media, 10.1% healthcare practitioners, 16.3% service, 24.3% sales and office, 1.9% natural resources, construction, and maintenance, 8.7% production, transportation, and material moving

Income: Per capita: $34,802; Median household: $83,625; Average household: $93,836; Households with income of $100,000 or more: 37.5%; Poverty rate: 4.8%

Educational Attainment: High school diploma or higher: 95.4%; Bachelor's degree or higher: 48.5%; Graduate/professional degree or higher: 22.0%

School District(s)

Victor Central SD (PK-12)
    Enrollment: 4,427 . . . . (585) 924-3252

Housing: Homeownership rate: 78.0%; Median home value: $194,400; Median year structure built: 1972; Homeowner vacancy rate: 0.0%; Median selected monthly owner costs: $1,436 with a mortgage, $738 without a mortgage; Median gross rent: $805 per month; Rental vacancy rate: 2.2%

Health Insurance: 97.4% have insurance; 84.4% have private insurance; 25.1% have public insurance; 2.6% do not have insurance; 0.0% of children under 18 do not have insurance

Transportation: Commute: 93.1% car, 0.8% public transportation, 1.3% walk, 4.8% work from home; Mean travel time to work: 21.0 minutes

WEST BLOOMFIELD (town). Covers a land area of 25.461 square miles and a water area of 0.039 square miles. Located at 42.89° N. Lat; 77.50° W. Long. Elevation is 948 feet.

Population: 2,516; Growth (since 2000): -1.3%; Density: 98.8 persons per square mile; Race: 98.2% White, 0.0% Black/African American, 0.0% Asian, 0.2% American Indian/Alaska Native, 0.0% Native Hawaiian/Other Pacific Islander, 0.7% Two or more races, 2.1% Hispanic of any race; Average household size: 2.26; Median age: 50.0; Age under 18: 16.8%; Age 65 and over: 24.3%; Males per 100 females: 100.8; Marriage status: 23.6% never married, 59.6% now married, 2.5% separated, 6.3% widowed, 10.5% divorced; Foreign born: 2.7%; Speak English only: 94.2%; With disability: 14.1%; Veterans: 14.6%; Ancestry: 28.7% German, 24.7% English, 19.1% Irish, 8.5% Italian, 5.8% American

Employment: 15.7% management, business, and financial, 3.3% computer, engineering, and science, 9.0% education, legal, community service, arts, and media, 3.6% healthcare practitioners, 10.7% service, 21.7% sales and office, 18.7% natural resources, construction, and maintenance, 17.2% production, transportation, and material moving

Income: Per capita: $30,546; Median household: $53,545; Average household: $68,821; Households with income of $100,000 or more: 22.1%; Poverty rate: 7.0%

Educational Attainment: High school diploma or higher: 90.8%; Bachelor's degree or higher: 25.5%; Graduate/professional degree or higher: 10.3%

Housing: Homeownership rate: 89.7%; Median home value: $120,400; Median year structure built: 1976; Homeowner vacancy rate: 2.6%; Median selected monthly owner costs: $1,208 with a mortgage, $559 without a mortgage; Median gross rent: $836 per month; Rental vacancy rate: 28.6%

Health Insurance: 93.5% have insurance; 78.3% have private insurance; 38.6% have public insurance; 6.5% do not have insurance; 0.0% of children under 18 do not have insurance

Transportation: Commute: 96.0% car, 0.5% public transportation, 1.3% walk, 2.3% work from home; Mean travel time to work: 24.6 minutes

Orange County

Located in southeastern New York; bounded on the east by the Hudson River, and on the southwest by the Delaware River and the New Jersey and Pennsylvania borders; includes parts of the Hudson highlands, the Ramapos, and the Shawangunk Range. Covers a land area of 811.686 square miles, a water area of 26.959 square miles, and is located in the Eastern Time Zone at 41.40° N. Lat., 74.31° W. Long. The county was founded in 1683. County seat is Goshen.

Orange County is part of the New York-Newark-Jersey City, NY-NJ-PA Metropolitan Statistical Area. The entire metro area includes: Dutchess County-Putnam County, NY Metropolitan Division (Dutchess County, NY; Putnam County, NY); Nassau County-Suffolk County, NY Metropolitan Division (Nassau County, NY; Suffolk County, NY); Newark, NJ-PA Metropolitan Division (Essex County, NJ; Hunterdon County, NJ; Morris County, NJ; Somerset County, NJ; Sussex County, NJ; Union County, NJ; Pike County, PA); New York-Jersey City-White Plains, NY-NJ Metropolitan Division (Bergen County, NJ; Hudson County, NJ; Middlesex County, NJ; Monmouth County, NJ; Ocean County, NJ; Passaic County, NJ; Bronx County, NY; Kings County, NY; New York County, NY; Orange County, NY; Queens County, NY; Richmond County, NY; Rockland County, NY; Westchester County, NY)

Weather Station: Middletown 2 NW   Elevation: 700 feet

	Jan	Feb	Mar	Apr	May	Jun	Jul	Aug	Sep	Oct	Nov	Dec
High	35	39	48	61	72	79	83	82	75	63	51	40
Low	19	20	28	39	49	58	63	62	54	43	34	25
Precip	2.7	2.3	3.1	4.0	4.1	4.5	4.0	4.0	4.2	3.8	3.6	3.1
Snow	na	na	na	tr	0.0	0.0	0.0	0.0	0.0	0.0	0.2	na

High and Low temperatures in degrees Fahrenheit; Precipitation and Snow in inches

Weather Station: Port Jervis   Elevation: 470 feet

	Jan	Feb	Mar	Apr	May	Jun	Jul	Aug	Sep	Oct	Nov	Dec
High	35	39	48	62	73	80	84	82	74	62	51	39
Low	17	19	26	37	47	56	61	60	52	40	32	22
Precip	3.0	2.7	3.7	4.0	4.0	4.3	4.0	3.8	4.5	4.2	3.6	3.6
Snow	12.2	9.4	7.1	1.7	0.0	0.0	0.0	0.0	0.0	tr	2.0	9.3

High and Low temperatures in degrees Fahrenheit; Precipitation and Snow in inches

Weather Station: Walden 1 ESE   Elevation: 379 feet

	Jan	Feb	Mar	Apr	May	Jun	Jul	Aug	Sep	Oct	Nov	Dec
High	34	38	46	59	70	78	83	81	74	62	51	39
Low	14	17	25	36	46	55	60	58	50	38	30	21
Precip	2.9	2.5	3.6	3.9	4.1	4.5	4.0	3.8	4.1	4.0	3.6	3.4
Snow	12.6	9.0	8.2	1.3	0.0	0.0	0.0	0.0	0.0	tr	1.5	8.6

High and Low temperatures in degrees Fahrenheit; Precipitation and Snow in inches

Weather Station: West Point   Elevation: 319 feet

	Jan	Feb	Mar	Apr	May	Jun	Jul	Aug	Sep	Oct	Nov	Dec
High	36	39	48	61	72	80	85	83	75	63	52	40
Low	21	23	30	40	50	59	64	63	55	45	36	26
Precip	3.6	2.8	3.9	4.2	4.1	4.6	4.5	4.4	4.5	4.8	4.4	4.1
Snow	11.5	9.4	5.8	0.2	0.0	0.0	0.0	0.0	0.0	tr	0.8	5.7

High and Low temperatures in degrees Fahrenheit; Precipitation and Snow in inches

Population: 378,174; Growth (since 2000): 10.8%; Density: 465.9 persons per square mile; Race: 74.1% White, 10.6% Black/African American, 2.6% Asian, 0.3% American Indian/Alaska Native, 0.1% Native Hawaiian/Other Pacific Islander, 3.5% two or more races, 19.7% Hispanic of any race; Average household size: 2.90; Median age: 36.9; Age under 18: 25.8%; Age 65 and over: 13.0%; Males per 100 females: 99.9; Marriage status: 34.4% never married, 52.0% now married, 2.0% separated, 5.3% widowed, 8.3% divorced; Foreign born: 10.8%; Speak English only: 75.3%; With disability: 12.0%; Veterans: 7.2%; Ancestry: 15.7% Irish, 15.4% Italian, 14.5% American, 10.2% German, 4.5% English

Religion: Six largest groups: 35.2% Catholicism, 6.5% Judaism, 2.1% Methodist/Pietist, 1.9% Presbyterian-Reformed, 1.2% Lutheran, 1.1% Pentecostal

Economy: Unemployment rate: 3.6%; Leading industries: 16.8 % retail trade; 11.8 % construction; 10.4 % other services (except public administration); Farms: 658 totaling 88,030 acres; Company size: 2 employ 1,000 or more persons, 10 employ 500 to 999 persons, 172 employ 100 to 499 persons, 9,272 employ less than 100 persons; Business ownership: 9,576 women-owned, 1,742 Black-owned, 2,678 Hispanic-owned, 1,630 Asian-owned, 130 American Indian/Alaska Native-owned

Employment: 13.1% management, business, and financial, 4.1% computer, engineering, and science, 12.4% education, legal, community service, arts, and media, 5.9% healthcare practitioners, 19.0% service, 25.7% sales and office, 8.2% natural resources, construction, and maintenance, 11.4% production, transportation, and material moving

Income: Per capita: $32,616; Median household: $75,146; Average household: $94,253; Households with income of $100,000 or more: 37.1%; Poverty rate: 12.2%

Educational Attainment: High school diploma or higher: 89.8%; Bachelor's degree or higher: 29.5%; Graduate/professional degree or higher: 12.4%

Housing: Homeownership rate: 68.4%; Median home value: $260,300; Median year structure built: 1970; Homeowner vacancy rate: 3.0%; Median selected monthly owner costs: $2,270 with a mortgage, $885 without a mortgage; Median gross rent: $1,187 per month; Rental vacancy rate: 4.7%

Vital Statistics: Birth rate: 127.8 per 10,000 population; Death rate: 72.8 per 10,000 population; Age-adjusted cancer mortality rate: 153.7 deaths per 100,000 population

Health Insurance: 94.2% have insurance; 72.4% have private insurance; 33.6% have public insurance; 5.8% do not have insurance; 2.3% of children under 18 do not have insurance

Health Care: Physicians: 23.0 per 10,000 population; Dentists: 6.9 per 10,000 population; Hospital beds: 25.8 per 10,000 population; Hospital admissions: 1,021.3 per 10,000 population

Air Quality Index (AQI): Percent of Days: 91.5% good, 8.5% moderate, 0.0% unhealthy for sensitive individuals, 0.0% unhealthy, 0.0% very unhealthy; Annual median: 34; Annual maximum: 82

Transportation: Commute: 84.1% car, 5.4% public transportation, 3.6% walk, 5.1% work from home; Mean travel time to work: 33.4 minutes

2016 Presidential Election: 50.4% Trump, 44.9% Clinton, 2.5% Johnson, 1.4% Stein

National and State Parks: Cherry Island State Wildlife Management Area; Hudson Highlands State Park; Sloop Hill State Unique Area; Storm King State Park

Additional Information Contacts

Orange Government . . . . (845) 291-2690
http://www.co.orange.ny.us

Orange County Communities

ARDEN (unincorporated postal area)

ZCTA: 10910

Covers a land area of 2.080 square miles and a water area of 0.042 square miles. Located at 41.28° N. Lat; 74.14° W. Long. Elevation is 512 feet.

Population: 25; Growth (since 2000): n/a; Density: 12.0 persons per square mile; Race: 100.0% White, 0.0% Black/African American, 0.0% Asian, 0.0% American Indian/Alaska Native, 0.0% Native Hawaiian/Other Pacific Islander, 0.0% Two or more races, 0.0% Hispanic of any race; Average household size: 0.00; Median age: n/a; Age under 18: 0.0%; Age 65 and over: 0.0%; Males per 100 females: 133.3; Marriage status: 0.0% never married, 0.0% now married, 0.0% separated, 100.0% widowed, 0.0% divorced; Foreign born: 0.0%; Speak English only: 100.0%; With disability: 0.0%; Veterans: 0.0%; Ancestry: 100.0% English, 100.0% Italian

Employment: 0.0% management, business, and financial, 100.0% computer, engineering, and science, 0.0% education, legal, community service, arts, and media, 0.0% healthcare practitioners, 0.0% service, 0.0% sales and office, 0.0% natural resources, construction, and maintenance, 0.0% production, transportation, and material moving

Income: Per capita: n/a; Median household: n/a; Average household: n/a; Households with income of $100,000 or more: 100.0%; Poverty rate: n/a

Educational Attainment: High school diploma or higher: 100.0%; Bachelor's degree or higher: 100.0%; Graduate/professional degree or higher: n/a

Housing: Homeownership rate: n/a; Median home value: n/a; Median year structure built: n/a; Homeowner vacancy rate: 0.0%; Median selected monthly owner costs: $0 with a mortgage, $0 without a mortgage; Median gross rent: n/a per month; Rental vacancy rate: 0.0%

Health Insurance: 100.0% have insurance; 100.0% have private insurance; 0.0% have public insurance; 0.0% do not have insurance; 0.0% of children under 18 do not have insurance

Transportation: Commute: 100.0% car, 0.0% public transportation, 0.0% walk, 0.0% work from home; Mean travel time to work: 0.0 minutes

BALMVILLE (CDP). Covers a land area of 2.117 square miles and a water area of 0.004 square miles. Located at 41.53° N. Lat; 74.02° W. Long. Elevation is 217 feet.

Population: 2,955; Growth (since 2000): -11.5%; Density: 1,395.5 persons per square mile; Race: 72.3% White, 12.7% Black/African American, 0.0% Asian, 0.0% American Indian/Alaska Native, 0.0% Native Hawaiian/Other

Pacific Islander, 9.7% Two or more races, 26.4% Hispanic of any race; Average household size: 2.49; Median age: 47.7; Age under 18: 18.9%; Age 65 and over: 19.9%; Males per 100 females: 96.5; Marriage status: 27.3% never married, 53.6% now married, 2.8% separated, 8.2% widowed, 11.0% divorced; Foreign born: 14.4%; Speak English only: 71.6%; With disability: 15.3%; Veterans: 6.2%; Ancestry: 13.0% Italian, 12.6% German, 11.5% Irish, 9.9% American, 3.9% English

Employment: 13.3% management, business, and financial, 2.8% computer, engineering, and science, 16.6% education, legal, community service, arts, and media, 6.4% healthcare practitioners, 21.1% service, 23.3% sales and office, 5.4% natural resources, construction, and maintenance, 11.0% production, transportation, and material moving

Income: Per capita: $37,295; Median household: $78,374; Average household: $91,481; Households with income of $100,000 or more: 32.2%; Poverty rate: 10.7%

Educational Attainment: High school diploma or higher: 93.2%; Bachelor's degree or higher: 30.3%; Graduate/professional degree or higher: 13.9%

Housing: Homeownership rate: 79.0%; Median home value: $269,000; Median year structure built: 1958; Homeowner vacancy rate: 2.1%; Median selected monthly owner costs: $2,446 with a mortgage, $786 without a mortgage; Median gross rent: $1,229 per month; Rental vacancy rate: 0.0%

Health Insurance: 92.8% have insurance; 75.2% have private insurance; 34.4% have public insurance; 7.2% do not have insurance; 5.0% of children under 18 do not have insurance

Transportation: Commute: 82.3% car, 5.8% public transportation, 0.6% walk, 11.3% work from home; Mean travel time to work: 34.9 minutes

BEAVER DAM LAKE (CDP).

Land/water area and latitude/longitude are not available.

Population: 1,640; Growth (since 2000): n/a; Density: n/a persons per square mile; Race: 90.1% White, 8.7% Black/African American, 0.0% Asian, 0.0% American Indian/Alaska Native, 0.0% Native Hawaiian/Other Pacific Islander, 1.2% Two or more races, 4.3% Hispanic of any race; Average household size: 2.66; Median age: 49.2; Age under 18: 18.2%; Age 65 and over: 20.4%; Males per 100 females: 103.1; Marriage status: 29.9% never married, 60.5% now married, 2.2% separated, 3.7% widowed, 5.9% divorced; Foreign born: 5.4%; Speak English only: 78.3%; With disability: 13.7%; Veterans: 13.6%; Ancestry: 33.2% Italian, 31.8% Irish, 14.9% German, 8.7% English, 6.6% Welsh

Employment: 13.1% management, business, and financial, 3.4% computer, engineering, and science, 13.6% education, legal, community service, arts, and media, 5.7% healthcare practitioners, 18.8% service, 24.1% sales and office, 17.0% natural resources, construction, and maintenance, 4.4% production, transportation, and material moving

Income: Per capita: $43,214; Median household: $111,875; Average household: $113,880; Households with income of $100,000 or more: 54.8%; Poverty rate: 6.3%

Educational Attainment: High school diploma or higher: 98.1%; Bachelor's degree or higher: 37.1%; Graduate/professional degree or higher: 15.6%

Housing: Homeownership rate: 92.7%; Median home value: $270,400; Median year structure built: 1979; Homeowner vacancy rate: 0.0%; Median selected monthly owner costs: $2,360 with a mortgage, $1,101 without a mortgage; Median gross rent: $1,255 per month; Rental vacancy rate: 0.0%

Health Insurance: 98.5% have insurance; 89.0% have private insurance; 34.8% have public insurance; 1.5% do not have insurance; 0.0% of children under 18 do not have insurance

Transportation: Commute: 89.8% car, 9.3% public transportation, 0.0% walk, 0.9% work from home; Mean travel time to work: 42.3 minutes

BLOOMING GROVE (town). Covers a land area of 34.736 square miles and a water area of 0.616 square miles. Located at 41.40° N. Lat; 74.18° W. Long. Elevation is 358 feet.

Population: 17,725; Growth (since 2000): 2.2%; Density: 510.3 persons per square mile; Race: 83.8% White, 6.4% Black/African American, 1.1% Asian, 0.0% American Indian/Alaska Native, 0.0% Native Hawaiian/Other Pacific Islander, 1.1% Two or more races, 16.6% Hispanic of any race; Average household size: 2.90; Median age: 41.7; Age under 18: 22.2%; Age 65 and over: 13.1%; Males per 100 females: 97.1; Marriage status: 33.0% never married, 54.6% now married, 2.1% separated, 4.6% widowed, 7.8% divorced; Foreign born: 8.1%; Speak English only: 84.6%;

With disability: 11.5%; Veterans: 6.6%; Ancestry: 25.2% Irish, 21.9% Italian, 15.5% American, 12.3% German, 4.3% English
Employment: 11.3% management, business, and financial, 4.9% computer, engineering, and science, 9.5% education, legal, community service, arts, and media, 7.3% healthcare practitioners, 18.5% service, 28.0% sales and office, 8.5% natural resources, construction, and maintenance, 12.0% production, transportation, and material moving
Income: Per capita: $38,230; Median household: $98,400; Average household: $107,979; Households with income of $100,000 or more: 48.7%; Poverty rate: 5.2%
Educational Attainment: High school diploma or higher: 94.7%; Bachelor's degree or higher: 30.3%; Graduate/professional degree or higher: 11.2%
Housing: Homeownership rate: 82.3%; Median home value: $268,900; Median year structure built: 1970; Homeowner vacancy rate: 2.3%; Median selected monthly owner costs: $2,391 with a mortgage, $970 without a mortgage; Median gross rent: $1,028 per month; Rental vacancy rate: 0.0%
Health Insurance: 97.0% have insurance; 86.9% have private insurance; 23.5% have public insurance; 3.0% do not have insurance; 1.5% of children under 18 do not have insurance
Safety: Violent crime rate: 9.3 per 10,000 population; Property crime rate: 52.3 per 10,000 population
Transportation: Commute: 90.0% car, 5.6% public transportation, 0.7% walk, 2.9% work from home; Mean travel time to work: 39.2 minutes
Additional Information Contacts
Town of Blooming Grove. . . . . (845) 496-3895
http://www.townofbloominggroveny.com

BULLVILLE (unincorporated postal area)
ZCTA: 10915

Covers a land area of 0.144 square miles and a water area of 0 square miles. Located at 41.55° N. Lat; 74.36° W. Long. Elevation is 515 feet.
Population: 75; Growth (since 2000): n/a; Density: 519.5 persons per square mile; Race: 100.0% White, 0.0% Black/African American, 0.0% Asian, 0.0% American Indian/Alaska Native, 0.0% Native Hawaiian/Other Pacific Islander, 0.0% Two or more races, 0.0% Hispanic of any race; Average household size: 2.20; Median age: 55.2; Age under 18: 0.0%; Age 65 and over: 0.0%; Males per 100 females: 124.5; Marriage status: 60.0% never married, 0.0% now married, 0.0% separated, 0.0% widowed, 40.0% divorced; Foreign born: 0.0%; Speak English only: 100.0%; With disability: 12.0%; Veterans: 0.0%; Ancestry: 40.0% French Canadian, 40.0% Italian, 12.0% American
Employment: 0.0% management, business, and financial, 0.0% computer, engineering, and science, 0.0% education, legal, community service, arts, and media, 0.0% healthcare practitioners, 52.0% service, 0.0% sales and office, 0.0% natural resources, construction, and maintenance, 48.0% production, transportation, and material moving
Income: Per capita: $45,464; Median household: n/a; Average household: n/a; Households with income of $100,000 or more: n/a; Poverty rate: n/a
Educational Attainment: High school diploma or higher: 88.0%; Bachelor's degree or higher: n/a; Graduate/professional degree or higher: n/a
Housing: Homeownership rate: 100.0%; Median home value: n/a; Median year structure built: n/a; Homeowner vacancy rate: 0.0%; Median selected monthly owner costs: $0 with a mortgage, $0 without a mortgage; Median gross rent: n/a per month; Rental vacancy rate: 0.0%
Health Insurance: 100.0% have insurance; 88.0% have private insurance; 12.0% have public insurance; 0.0% do not have insurance; 0.0% of children under 18 do not have insurance
Transportation: Commute: 100.0% car, 0.0% public transportation, 0.0% walk, 0.0% work from home; Mean travel time to work: 0.0 minutes

CAMPBELL HALL (unincorporated postal area)
ZCTA: 10916

Covers a land area of 20.201 square miles and a water area of 0.091 square miles. Located at 41.44° N. Lat; 74.25° W. Long. Elevation is 400 feet.
Population: 4,228; Growth (since 2000): 3.9%; Density: 209.3 persons per square mile; Race: 93.1% White, 0.7% Black/African American, 3.8% Asian, 0.0% American Indian/Alaska Native, 0.0% Native Hawaiian/Other Pacific Islander, 0.0% Two or more races, 6.9% Hispanic of any race; Average household size: 3.25; Median age: 41.9; Age under 18: 24.2%; Age 65 and over: 16.0%; Males per 100 females:

97.8; Marriage status: 31.3% never married, 61.1% now married, 0.0% separated, 4.6% widowed, 3.0% divorced; Foreign born: 8.6%; Speak English only: 88.3%; With disability: 11.6%; Veterans: 8.7%; Ancestry: 26.9% Italian, 22.4% Irish, 14.5% German, 6.3% English, 5.3% American
Employment: 19.2% management, business, and financial, 5.1% computer, engineering, and science, 11.9% education, legal, community service, arts, and media, 6.8% healthcare practitioners, 15.7% service, 23.3% sales and office, 12.1% natural resources, construction, and maintenance, 5.9% production, transportation, and material moving
Income: Per capita: $38,073; Median household: $104,238; Average household: $122,647; Households with income of $100,000 or more: 52.9%; Poverty rate: 7.5%
Educational Attainment: High school diploma or higher: 93.6%; Bachelor's degree or higher: 33.5%; Graduate/professional degree or higher: 10.7%
Housing: Homeownership rate: 93.2%; Median home value: $334,900; Median year structure built: 1977; Homeowner vacancy rate: 4.0%; Median selected monthly owner costs: $2,524 with a mortgage, $1,027 without a mortgage; Median gross rent: $1,631 per month; Rental vacancy rate: 0.0%
Health Insurance: 95.4% have insurance; 80.6% have private insurance; 24.9% have public insurance; 4.6% do not have insurance; 0.0% of children under 18 do not have insurance
Transportation: Commute: 92.0% car, 3.8% public transportation, 0.0% walk, 4.2% work from home; Mean travel time to work: 36.1 minutes

CENTRAL VALLEY (unincorporated postal area)
ZCTA: 10917

Covers a land area of 3.716 square miles and a water area of 0.031 square miles. Located at 41.32° N. Lat; 74.12° W. Long. Elevation is 522 feet.
Population: 1,862; Growth (since 2000): 12.8%; Density: 501.1 persons per square mile; Race: 86.0% White, 0.0% Black/African American, 2.8% Asian, 0.0% American Indian/Alaska Native, 0.0% Native Hawaiian/Other Pacific Islander, 5.1% Two or more races, 24.5% Hispanic of any race; Average household size: 3.19; Median age: 40.4; Age under 18: 24.9%; Age 65 and over: 15.0%; Males per 100 females: 102.5; Marriage status: 26.4% never married, 60.6% now married, 0.0% separated, 6.6% widowed, 6.3% divorced; Foreign born: 15.8%; Speak English only: 73.6%; With disability: 11.9%; Veterans: 7.4%; Ancestry: 23.3% Italian, 20.4% Irish, 17.5% American, 13.6% German, 6.6% English
Employment: 22.4% management, business, and financial, 2.1% computer, engineering, and science, 11.1% education, legal, community service, arts, and media, 12.2% healthcare practitioners, 11.5% service, 22.7% sales and office, 16.2% natural resources, construction, and maintenance, 1.9% production, transportation, and material moving
Income: Per capita: $41,346; Median household: $99,950; Average household: $129,959; Households with income of $100,000 or more: 49.9%; Poverty rate: 8.7%
Educational Attainment: High school diploma or higher: 96.0%; Bachelor's degree or higher: 33.2%; Graduate/professional degree or higher: 15.4%

School District(s)
Monroe-Woodbury Central SD (KG-12)
    Enrollment: 7,005 . . . . (845) 460-6200
Housing: Homeownership rate: 78.4%; Median home value: $298,700; Median year structure built: 1968; Homeowner vacancy rate: 0.0%; Median selected monthly owner costs: $2,950 with a mortgage, $989 without a mortgage; Median gross rent: $1,586 per month; Rental vacancy rate: 0.0%
Health Insurance: 95.9% have insurance; 89.8% have private insurance; 23.5% have public insurance; 4.1% do not have insurance; 3.3% of children under 18 do not have insurance
Transportation: Commute: 87.2% car, 9.1% public transportation, 0.0% walk, 1.7% work from home; Mean travel time to work: 40.2 minutes

CHESTER (town). Covers a land area of 25.049 square miles and a water area of 0.151 square miles. Located at 41.33° N. Lat; 74.28° W. Long. Elevation is 479 feet.
History: Hambletonian, famous trotter, foaled and buried here. Incorporated 1892.
Population: 11,971; Growth (since 2000): -1.4%; Density: 477.9 persons per square mile; Race: 74.5% White, 9.5% Black/African American, 5.8%

Asian, 0.6% American Indian/Alaska Native, 0.0% Native Hawaiian/Other Pacific Islander, 2.9% Two or more races, 18.3% Hispanic of any race; Average household size: 3.14; Median age: 37.1; Age under 18: 22.7%; Age 65 and over: 11.4%; Males per 100 females: 94.7; Marriage status: 32.8% never married, 53.9% now married, 1.7% separated, 2.9% widowed, 10.4% divorced; Foreign born: 12.4%; Speak English only: 83.8%; With disability: 10.8%; Veterans: 7.0%; Ancestry: 20.7% Italian, 17.1% Irish, 15.8% American, 6.7% German, 5.1% English

Employment: 11.7% management, business, and financial, 6.0% computer, engineering, and science, 16.9% education, legal, community service, arts, and media, 8.8% healthcare practitioners, 16.1% service, 24.8% sales and office, 7.4% natural resources, construction, and maintenance, 8.2% production, transportation, and material moving

Income: Per capita: $34,694; Median household: $101,250; Average household: $110,177; Households with income of $100,000 or more: 50.7%; Poverty rate: 5.8%

Educational Attainment: High school diploma or higher: 94.1%; Bachelor's degree or higher: 36.7%; Graduate/professional degree or higher: 15.0%

School District(s)

Chester Union Free SD (KG-12)
    Enrollment: 1,103 . . . . (845) 469-5052

Housing: Homeownership rate: 83.2%; Median home value: $278,300; Median year structure built: 1981; Homeowner vacancy rate: 1.3%; Median selected monthly owner costs: $2,394 with a mortgage, $885 without a mortgage; Median gross rent: $1,435 per month; Rental vacancy rate: 0.0%

Health Insurance: 95.2% have insurance; 82.1% have private insurance; 23.9% have public insurance; 4.8% do not have insurance; 2.4% of children under 18 do not have insurance

Safety: Violent crime rate: 8.8 per 10,000 population; Property crime rate: 8.8 per 10,000 population

Newspapers: Straus Newspapers (weekly circulation 27,000)

Transportation: Commute: 82.4% car, 8.7% public transportation, 4.1% walk, 4.2% work from home; Mean travel time to work: 37.3 minutes

CHESTER (village). Covers a land area of 2.148 square miles and a water area of 0 square miles. Located at 41.36° N. Lat; 74.28° W. Long. Elevation is 479 feet.

Population: 3,965; Growth (since 2000): 15.1%; Density: 1,845.8 persons per square mile; Race: 65.6% White, 13.2% Black/African American, 9.6% Asian, 0.8% American Indian/Alaska Native, 0.0% Native Hawaiian/Other Pacific Islander, 3.5% Two or more races, 31.4% Hispanic of any race; Average household size: 2.75; Median age: 39.3; Age under 18: 16.8%; Age 65 and over: 11.8%; Males per 100 females: 94.6; Marriage status: 39.3% never married, 41.6% now married, 3.6% separated, 4.4% widowed, 14.7% divorced; Foreign born: 15.1%; Speak English only: 83.1%; With disability: 15.4%; Veterans: 7.2%; Ancestry: 19.9% Italian, 15.3% Irish, 10.7% American, 6.2% German, 6.0% Jamaican

Employment: 11.5% management, business, and financial, 3.7% computer, engineering, and science, 10.1% education, legal, community service, arts, and media, 9.9% healthcare practitioners, 16.2% service, 30.9% sales and office, 6.7% natural resources, construction, and maintenance, 11.1% production, transportation, and material moving

Income: Per capita: $28,940; Median household: $68,500; Average household: $78,073; Households with income of $100,000 or more: 31.2%; Poverty rate: 12.7%

Educational Attainment: High school diploma or higher: 90.5%; Bachelor's degree or higher: 28.0%; Graduate/professional degree or higher: 7.5%

School District(s)

Chester Union Free SD (KG-12)
    Enrollment: 1,103 . . . . (845) 469-5052

Housing: Homeownership rate: 65.6%; Median home value: $199,000; Median year structure built: 1981; Homeowner vacancy rate: 3.5%; Median selected monthly owner costs: $1,959 with a mortgage, $784 without a mortgage; Median gross rent: $1,329 per month; Rental vacancy rate: 0.0%

Health Insurance: 94.6% have insurance; 77.3% have private insurance; 27.1% have public insurance; 5.4% do not have insurance; 3.5% of children under 18 do not have insurance

Safety: Violent crime rate: 15.2 per 10,000 population; Property crime rate: 133.8 per 10,000 population

Newspapers: Straus Newspapers (weekly circulation 27,000)

Transportation: Commute: 82.0% car, 9.2% public transportation, 4.9% walk, 3.9% work from home; Mean travel time to work: 31.1 minutes

CIRCLEVILLE (unincorporated postal area)
ZCTA: 10919
    Covers a land area of 4.116 square miles and a water area of 0.019 square miles. Located at 41.53° N. Lat; 74.39° W. Long. Elevation is 617 feet.

Population: 1,393; Growth (since 2000): 147.9%; Density: 338.4 persons per square mile; Race: 97.7% White, 0.8% Black/African American, 0.6% Asian, 0.0% American Indian/Alaska Native, 0.0% Native Hawaiian/Other Pacific Islander, 0.0% Two or more races, 7.7% Hispanic of any race; Average household size: 3.04; Median age: 43.8; Age under 18: 18.4%; Age 65 and over: 14.0%; Males per 100 females: 103.1; Marriage status: 33.4% never married, 51.5% now married, 2.5% separated, 3.7% widowed, 11.4% divorced; Foreign born: 7.7%; Speak English only: 92.3%; With disability: 10.5%; Veterans: 10.0%; Ancestry: 30.7% American, 23.9% Irish, 21.8% German, 13.9% Italian, 5.6% Polish

Employment: 18.0% management, business, and financial, 1.5% computer, engineering, and science, 11.3% education, legal, community service, arts, and media, 12.9% healthcare practitioners, 10.3% service, 22.5% sales and office, 13.9% natural resources, construction, and maintenance, 9.5% production, transportation, and material moving

Income: Per capita: $32,837; Median household: $100,341; Average household: $96,569; Households with income of $100,000 or more: 51.1%; Poverty rate: 5.4%

Educational Attainment: High school diploma or higher: 85.6%; Bachelor's degree or higher: 29.4%; Graduate/professional degree or higher: 18.7%

School District(s)

Pine Bush Central SD (PK-12)
    Enrollment: 5,266 . . . . (845) 744-2031

Housing: Homeownership rate: 96.3%; Median home value: $244,600; Median year structure built: 1958; Homeowner vacancy rate: 0.0%; Median selected monthly owner costs: $2,294 with a mortgage, $827 without a mortgage; Median gross rent: n/a per month; Rental vacancy rate: 0.0%

Health Insurance: 88.2% have insurance; 78.3% have private insurance; 21.3% have public insurance; 11.8% do not have insurance; 4.2% of children under 18 do not have insurance

Transportation: Commute: 86.0% car, 0.9% public transportation, 0.0% walk, 6.9% work from home; Mean travel time to work: 46.4 minutes

CORNWALL (town). Covers a land area of 26.653 square miles and a water area of 1.479 square miles. Located at 41.41° N. Lat; 74.06° W. Long.

History: Seat of N.Y. Military Academy and private schools. Incorporated 1884.

Population: 12,491; Growth (since 2000): 1.5%; Density: 468.7 persons per square mile; Race: 92.1% White, 0.2% Black/African American, 2.8% Asian, 0.0% American Indian/Alaska Native, 0.3% Native Hawaiian/Other Pacific Islander, 2.6% Two or more races, 10.9% Hispanic of any race; Average household size: 2.68; Median age: 42.8; Age under 18: 24.9%; Age 65 and over: 16.3%; Males per 100 females: 95.2; Marriage status: 29.9% never married, 54.0% now married, 1.7% separated, 5.1% widowed, 10.9% divorced; Foreign born: 4.7%; Speak English only: 89.0%; With disability: 11.5%; Veterans: 10.6%; Ancestry: 23.9% Irish, 19.1% Italian, 16.3% German, 12.1% American, 7.1% English

Employment: 20.8% management, business, and financial, 3.1% computer, engineering, and science, 18.3% education, legal, community service, arts, and media, 5.5% healthcare practitioners, 13.4% service, 27.1% sales and office, 5.0% natural resources, construction, and maintenance, 6.7% production, transportation, and material moving

Income: Per capita: $44,917; Median household: $89,520; Average household: $119,553; Households with income of $100,000 or more: 44.6%; Poverty rate: 3.9%

Educational Attainment: High school diploma or higher: 94.3%; Bachelor's degree or higher: 47.6%; Graduate/professional degree or higher: 22.9%

School District(s)

Cornwall Central SD (KG-12)
    Enrollment: 3,238 . . . . (845) 534-8009

Housing: Homeownership rate: 68.6%; Median home value: $321,100; Median year structure built: 1959; Homeowner vacancy rate: 3.9%; Median

selected monthly owner costs: $2,767 with a mortgage, $1,059 without a mortgage; Median gross rent: $1,353 per month; Rental vacancy rate: 9.1%

Health Insurance: 96.8% have insurance; 85.0% have private insurance; 26.3% have public insurance; 3.2% do not have insurance; 1.7% of children under 18 do not have insurance

Safety: Violent crime rate: 2.1 per 10,000 population; Property crime rate: 22.0 per 10,000 population

Newspapers: Cornwall Local (weekly circulation 3,300)

Transportation: Commute: 85.9% car, 3.5% public transportation, 1.6% walk, 7.9% work from home; Mean travel time to work: 32.4 minutes

Additional Information Contacts

Town of Cornwall . . . . (845) 534-9100
    http://www.cornwallny.com

CORNWALL-ON-HUDSON (village). Covers a land area of 1.987 square miles and a water area of 0.105 square miles. Located at 41.43° N. Lat; 74.02° W. Long. Elevation is 161 feet.

Population: 2,936; Growth (since 2000): -4.0%; Density: 1,477.7 persons per square mile; Race: 95.6% White, 0.0% Black/African American, 1.5% Asian, 0.0% American Indian/Alaska Native, 1.1% Native Hawaiian/Other Pacific Islander, 1.0% Two or more races, 7.3% Hispanic of any race; Average household size: 2.70; Median age: 42.7; Age under 18: 25.1%; Age 65 and over: 16.3%; Males per 100 females: 97.0; Marriage status: 30.4% never married, 57.9% now married, 1.6% separated, 2.8% widowed, 8.8% divorced; Foreign born: 3.5%; Speak English only: 91.1%; With disability: 7.5%; Veterans: 13.1%; Ancestry: 26.9% Irish, 17.7% Italian, 13.8% German, 11.4% American, 6.6% English

Employment: 21.9% management, business, and financial, 2.2% computer, engineering, and science, 25.4% education, legal, community service, arts, and media, 3.2% healthcare practitioners, 11.0% service, 25.4% sales and office, 4.9% natural resources, construction, and maintenance, 6.0% production, transportation, and material moving

Income: Per capita: $46,740; Median household: $103,017; Average household: $128,450; Households with income of $100,000 or more: 51.6%; Poverty rate: 3.7%

Educational Attainment: High school diploma or higher: 94.2%; Bachelor's degree or higher: 47.5%; Graduate/professional degree or higher: 21.7%

School District(s)

Cornwall Central SD (KG-12)
    Enrollment: 3,238 . . . . (845) 534-8009

Housing: Homeownership rate: 69.9%; Median home value: $310,000; Median year structure built: Before 1940; Homeowner vacancy rate: 2.0%; Median selected monthly owner costs: $2,825 with a mortgage, $973 without a mortgage; Median gross rent: $1,324 per month; Rental vacancy rate: 2.4%

Health Insurance: 95.3% have insurance; 86.5% have private insurance; 23.9% have public insurance; 4.7% do not have insurance; 5.9% of children under 18 do not have insurance

Safety: Violent crime rate: 10.3 per 10,000 population; Property crime rate: 75.5 per 10,000 population

Transportation: Commute: 85.7% car, 2.6% public transportation, 3.2% walk, 6.1% work from home; Mean travel time to work: 33.3 minutes

CRAWFORD (town). Covers a land area of 40.031 square miles and a water area of 0.084 square miles. Located at 41.57° N. Lat; 74.32° W. Long.

Population: 9,234; Growth (since 2000): 17.3%; Density: 230.7 persons per square mile; Race: 90.1% White, 4.1% Black/African American, 1.0% Asian, 0.0% American Indian/Alaska Native, 0.0% Native Hawaiian/Other Pacific Islander, 1.3% Two or more races, 10.5% Hispanic of any race; Average household size: 2.83; Median age: 42.3; Age under 18: 23.4%; Age 65 and over: 13.7%; Males per 100 females: 99.3; Marriage status: 34.4% never married, 51.8% now married, 1.4% separated, 5.5% widowed, 8.3% divorced; Foreign born: 5.1%; Speak English only: 89.2%; With disability: 12.4%; Veterans: 8.0%; Ancestry: 21.4% Irish, 20.8% Italian, 17.6% German, 12.6% American, 6.4% English

Employment: 10.8% management, business, and financial, 4.6% computer, engineering, and science, 12.4% education, legal, community service, arts, and media, 6.3% healthcare practitioners, 22.6% service, 19.2% sales and office, 12.9% natural resources, construction, and maintenance, 11.1% production, transportation, and material moving

Income: Per capita: $34,489; Median household: $80,282; Average household: $94,461; Households with income of $100,000 or more: 40.7%; Poverty rate: 9.0%

Educational Attainment: High school diploma or higher: 90.1%; Bachelor's degree or higher: 26.4%; Graduate/professional degree or higher: 11.4%

Housing: Homeownership rate: 80.5%; Median home value: $273,500; Median year structure built: 1983; Homeowner vacancy rate: 2.3%; Median selected monthly owner costs: $2,285 with a mortgage, $855 without a mortgage; Median gross rent: $975 per month; Rental vacancy rate: 6.3%

Health Insurance: 97.4% have insurance; 83.0% have private insurance; 26.0% have public insurance; 2.6% do not have insurance; 1.1% of children under 18 do not have insurance

Safety: Violent crime rate: 9.8 per 10,000 population; Property crime rate: 106.7 per 10,000 population

Transportation: Commute: 92.6% car, 1.1% public transportation, 1.4% walk, 3.7% work from home; Mean travel time to work: 38.0 minutes

Additional Information Contacts

Town of Crawford . . . . (845) 744-2029
    http://townofcrawford.org

CUDDEBACKVILLE (unincorporated postal area)

ZCTA: 12729
    Covers a land area of 22.195 square miles and a water area of 0.346 square miles. Located at 41.48° N. Lat; 74.62° W. Long. Elevation is 535 feet.

Population: 2,348; Growth (since 2000): 80.3%; Density: 105.8 persons per square mile; Race: 89.7% White, 1.6% Black/African American, 1.3% Asian, 0.0% American Indian/Alaska Native, 0.0% Native Hawaiian/Other Pacific Islander, 6.9% Two or more races, 3.1% Hispanic of any race; Average household size: 2.79; Median age: 47.2; Age under 18: 24.2%; Age 65 and over: 17.1%; Males per 100 females: 108.2; Marriage status: 33.6% never married, 53.3% now married, 2.9% separated, 6.4% widowed, 6.7% divorced; Foreign born: 2.5%; Speak English only: 92.1%; With disability: 23.4%; Veterans: 8.7%; Ancestry: 42.5% American, 15.0% German, 14.3% Irish, 11.3% Italian, 6.3% English

Employment: 7.5% management, business, and financial, 3.8% computer, engineering, and science, 4.2% education, legal, community service, arts, and media, 7.3% healthcare practitioners, 19.4% service, 28.7% sales and office, 17.5% natural resources, construction, and maintenance, 11.6% production, transportation, and material moving

Income: Per capita: $26,860; Median household: $49,091; Average household: $72,619; Households with income of $100,000 or more: 21.7%; Poverty rate: 20.4%

Educational Attainment: High school diploma or higher: 81.1%; Bachelor's degree or higher: 13.2%; Graduate/professional degree or higher: 4.1%

School District(s)

Port Jervis City SD (KG-12)
    Enrollment: 2,626 . . . . (845) 858-3100

Housing: Homeownership rate: 68.1%; Median home value: $141,600; Median year structure built: 1974; Homeowner vacancy rate: 3.9%; Median selected monthly owner costs: $1,780 with a mortgage, $770 without a mortgage; Median gross rent: $1,083 per month; Rental vacancy rate: 0.0%

Health Insurance: 98.1% have insurance; 55.5% have private insurance; 53.2% have public insurance; 1.9% do not have insurance; 0.0% of children under 18 do not have insurance

Transportation: Commute: 92.2% car, 0.2% public transportation, 0.0% walk, 2.8% work from home; Mean travel time to work: 24.5 minutes

DEERPARK (town). Covers a land area of 66.502 square miles and a water area of 1.452 square miles. Located at 41.44° N. Lat; 74.66° W. Long.

History: Deer Park, a hamlet and census-designated place (CDP), is a residential hamlet located in the pine barrens in the northeast corner of the town of Babylon. It grew out of Jacob Conklin's 1610 settlement of the Half Way Hollow Hills, later Wheatley Heights. Charles Wilson started what is now Deer Park in 1853 about eleven years after the Long Island Rail Road arrived in 1842.

Population: 7,799; Growth (since 2000): -0.8%; Density: 117.3 persons per square mile; Race: 91.3% White, 1.8% Black/African American, 1.0% Asian, 0.3% American Indian/Alaska Native, 0.0% Native Hawaiian/Other Pacific Islander, 3.2% Two or more races, 5.9% Hispanic of any race;

Average household size: 2.53; Median age: 44.8; Age under 18: 20.4%; Age 65 and over: 19.1%; Males per 100 females: 100.1; Marriage status: 30.8% never married, 53.5% now married, 2.3% separated, 7.4% widowed, 8.3% divorced; Foreign born: 2.3%; Speak English only: 93.7%; With disability: 19.8%; Veterans: 10.5%; Ancestry: 25.6% American, 17.9% Irish, 16.6% German, 13.5% Italian, 5.8% English

Employment: 8.3% management, business, and financial, 1.9% computer, engineering, and science, 8.4% education, legal, community service, arts, and media, 3.9% healthcare practitioners, 25.1% service, 24.4% sales and office, 12.2% natural resources, construction, and maintenance, 15.8% production, transportation, and material moving

Income: Per capita: $26,404; Median household: $51,838; Average household: $65,228; Households with income of $100,000 or more: 20.5%; Poverty rate: 14.3%

Educational Attainment: High school diploma or higher: 86.9%; Bachelor's degree or higher: 13.2%; Graduate/professional degree or higher: 4.3%

Housing: Homeownership rate: 82.7%; Median home value: $171,600; Median year structure built: 1968; Homeowner vacancy rate: 5.1%; Median selected monthly owner costs: $1,710 with a mortgage, $740 without a mortgage; Median gross rent: $1,063 per month; Rental vacancy rate: 11.2%

Health Insurance: 95.8% have insurance; 69.3% have private insurance; 40.8% have public insurance; 4.2% do not have insurance; 0.4% of children under 18 do not have insurance

Safety: Violent crime rate: 9.1 per 10,000 population; Property crime rate: 98.5 per 10,000 population

Transportation: Commute: 95.7% car, 0.8% public transportation, 0.7% walk, 1.4% work from home; Mean travel time to work: 30.0 minutes

Additional Information Contacts
Town of Deerpark . . . . (845) 856-2210
    http://townofdeerpark.org

FIRTHCLIFFE (CDP). Covers a land area of 2.965 square miles and a water area of 0.035 square miles. Located at 41.44° N. Lat; 74.03° W. Long. Elevation is 299 feet.

Population: 5,481; Growth (since 2000): 10.3%; Density: 1,848.7 persons per square mile; Race: 93.2% White, 0.4% Black/African American, 1.2% Asian, 0.0% American Indian/Alaska Native, 0.0% Native Hawaiian/Other Pacific Islander, 3.6% Two or more races, 13.1% Hispanic of any race; Average household size: 2.54; Median age: 42.6; Age under 18: 25.0%; Age 65 and over: 18.0%; Males per 100 females: 87.4; Marriage status: 30.3% never married, 48.4% now married, 2.0% separated, 7.0% widowed, 14.3% divorced; Foreign born: 3.7%; Speak English only: 92.2%; With disability: 13.5%; Veterans: 11.5%; Ancestry: 23.6% Irish, 20.8% Italian, 20.2% German, 7.8% English, 7.2% American

Employment: 21.2% management, business, and financial, 3.0% computer, engineering, and science, 13.1% education, legal, community service, arts, and media, 5.8% healthcare practitioners, 12.6% service, 28.7% sales and office, 4.5% natural resources, construction, and maintenance, 11.2% production, transportation, and material moving

Income: Per capita: $38,467; Median household: $73,268; Average household: $96,035; Households with income of $100,000 or more: 32.1%; Poverty rate: 2.4%

Educational Attainment: High school diploma or higher: 94.2%; Bachelor's degree or higher: 45.0%; Graduate/professional degree or higher: 21.1%

Housing: Homeownership rate: 57.4%; Median home value: $283,600; Median year structure built: 1960; Homeowner vacancy rate: 4.6%; Median selected monthly owner costs: $2,748 with a mortgage, $901 without a mortgage; Median gross rent: $1,357 per month; Rental vacancy rate: 11.2%

Health Insurance: 96.6% have insurance; 84.6% have private insurance; 28.6% have public insurance; 3.4% do not have insurance; 0.7% of children under 18 do not have insurance

Transportation: Commute: 87.6% car, 2.2% public transportation, 0.7% walk, 8.9% work from home; Mean travel time to work: 30.1 minutes

FLORIDA (village). Covers a land area of 2.251 square miles and a water area of 0.004 square miles. Located at 41.33° N. Lat; 74.35° W. Long. Elevation is 446 feet.

History: William H. Seward was born here.

Population: 2,845; Growth (since 2000): 10.7%; Density: 1,263.6 persons per square mile; Race: 79.1% White, 7.1% Black/African American, 1.0% Asian, 1.8% American Indian/Alaska Native, 0.0% Native Hawaiian/Other

Pacific Islander, 6.4% Two or more races, 18.1% Hispanic of any race; Average household size: 2.72; Median age: 41.9; Age under 18: 25.0%; Age 65 and over: 14.8%; Males per 100 females: 91.0; Marriage status: 25.8% never married, 58.5% now married, 3.5% separated, 7.4% widowed, 8.3% divorced; Foreign born: 8.6%; Speak English only: 83.8%; With disability: 11.2%; Veterans: 7.5%; Ancestry: 20.8% Italian, 18.4% Irish, 16.8% Polish, 14.5% German, 5.5% English

Employment: 18.7% management, business, and financial, 4.9% computer, engineering, and science, 12.3% education, legal, community service, arts, and media, 3.2% healthcare practitioners, 16.1% service, 27.3% sales and office, 9.0% natural resources, construction, and maintenance, 8.6% production, transportation, and material moving

Income: Per capita: $36,587; Median household: $85,655; Average household: $98,205; Households with income of $100,000 or more: 41.3%; Poverty rate: 2.7%

Educational Attainment: High school diploma or higher: 94.0%; Bachelor's degree or higher: 26.0%; Graduate/professional degree or higher: 8.0%

School District(s)
Florida Union Free SD (PK-12)
    Enrollment: 828 . . . . (845) 651-3095
Housing: Homeownership rate: 76.4%; Median home value: $257,800; Median year structure built: 1972; Homeowner vacancy rate: 0.0%; Median selected monthly owner costs: $2,262 with a mortgage, $914 without a mortgage; Median gross rent: $1,299 per month; Rental vacancy rate: 0.0%

Health Insurance: 98.1% have insurance; 84.9% have private insurance; 27.2% have public insurance; 1.9% do not have insurance; 0.0% of children under 18 do not have insurance

Safety: Violent crime rate: 3.5 per 10,000 population; Property crime rate: 14.0 per 10,000 population

Transportation: Commute: 93.4% car, 1.9% public transportation, 1.7% walk, 3.1% work from home; Mean travel time to work: 36.6 minutes

FORT MONTGOMERY (CDP). Covers a land area of 1.484 square miles and a water area of 0.031 square miles. Located at 41.34° N. Lat; 73.99° W. Long. Elevation is 161 feet.

Population: 1,623; Growth (since 2000): 14.5%; Density: 1,093.9 persons per square mile; Race: 72.9% White, 6.0% Black/African American, 2.6% Asian, 0.9% American Indian/Alaska Native, 0.0% Native Hawaiian/Other Pacific Islander, 2.8% Two or more races, 18.2% Hispanic of any race; Average household size: 2.80; Median age: 36.5; Age under 18: 20.1%; Age 65 and over: 10.8%; Males per 100 females: 104.6; Marriage status: 35.1% never married, 54.1% now married, 0.7% separated, 2.9% widowed, 7.9% divorced; Foreign born: 9.5%; Speak English only: 79.1%; With disability: 10.6%; Veterans: 8.6%; Ancestry: 25.0% Irish, 22.7% Italian, 16.6% German, 11.8% American, 7.3% English

Employment: 17.7% management, business, and financial, 9.8% computer, engineering, and science, 15.0% education, legal, community service, arts, and media, 6.4% healthcare practitioners, 12.5% service, 17.7% sales and office, 14.2% natural resources, construction, and maintenance, 6.7% production, transportation, and material moving

Income: Per capita: $40,393; Median household: $97,917; Average household: $108,818; Households with income of $100,000 or more: 46.6%; Poverty rate: 2.0%

Educational Attainment: High school diploma or higher: 91.2%; Bachelor's degree or higher: 44.8%; Graduate/professional degree or higher: 23.9%

School District(s)
Highland Falls Central SD (PK-12)
    Enrollment: 1,045 . . . . (845) 446-9575
Housing: Homeownership rate: 67.2%; Median home value: $273,500; Median year structure built: 1954; Homeowner vacancy rate: 3.5%; Median selected monthly owner costs: $2,286 with a mortgage, $959 without a mortgage; Median gross rent: $1,507 per month; Rental vacancy rate: 6.4%

Health Insurance: 95.9% have insurance; 87.9% have private insurance; 18.1% have public insurance; 4.1% do not have insurance; 17.7% of children under 18 do not have insurance

Transportation: Commute: 87.9% car, 5.2% public transportation, 1.4% walk, 5.6% work from home; Mean travel time to work: 32.9 minutes

GARDNERTOWN (CDP). Covers a land area of 4.826 square miles and a water area of 0.017 square miles. Located at 41.54° N. Lat; 74.06° W. Long. Elevation is 410 feet.

Population: 4,858; Growth (since 2000): 7.2%; Density: 1,006.7 persons per square mile; Race: 77.9% White, 9.3% Black/African American, 0.9% Asian, 0.0% American Indian/Alaska Native, 0.0% Native Hawaiian/Other Pacific Islander, 3.7% Two or more races, 16.6% Hispanic of any race; Average household size: 2.95; Median age: 37.2; Age under 18: 22.7%; Age 65 and over: 13.1%; Males per 100 females: 96.9; Marriage status: 34.5% never married, 48.2% now married, 4.2% separated, 6.6% widowed, 10.7% divorced; Foreign born: 11.1%; Speak English only: 78.0%; With disability: 11.0%; Veterans: 5.8%; Ancestry: 29.5% Italian, 16.4% Irish, 9.4% English, 7.4% German, 5.6% American

Employment: 11.4% management, business, and financial, 4.0% computer, engineering, and science, 13.5% education, legal, community service, arts, and media, 1.6% healthcare practitioners, 18.5% service, 29.5% sales and office, 7.2% natural resources, construction, and maintenance, 14.2% production, transportation, and material moving

Income: Per capita: $30,334; Median household: $72,260; Average household: $86,267; Households with income of $100,000 or more: 30.1%; Poverty rate: 3.0%

Educational Attainment: High school diploma or higher: 89.4%; Bachelor's degree or higher: 22.7%; Graduate/professional degree or higher: 9.9%

Housing: Homeownership rate: 81.4%; Median home value: $217,500; Median year structure built: 1958; Homeowner vacancy rate: 1.5%; Median selected monthly owner costs: $2,058 with a mortgage, $741 without a mortgage; Median gross rent: $1,099 per month; Rental vacancy rate: 11.8%

Health Insurance: 94.9% have insurance; 74.5% have private insurance; 33.6% have public insurance; 5.1% do not have insurance; 1.6% of children under 18 do not have insurance

Transportation: Commute: 92.2% car, 3.2% public transportation, 0.0% walk, 3.8% work from home; Mean travel time to work: 25.9 minutes

GOSHEN (town). Covers a land area of 43.642 square miles and a water area of 0.290 square miles. Located at 41.38° N. Lat; 74.35° W. Long. Elevation is 436 feet.

History: Good Time and Historic (or Harriman) harness-racing tracks are here; and the Hambletonian race is held here. Settled during 18th century; incorporated 1809.

Population: 13,864; Growth (since 2000): 7.4%; Density: 317.7 persons per square mile; Race: 83.4% White, 6.1% Black/African American, 3.2% Asian, 0.1% American Indian/Alaska Native, 0.0% Native Hawaiian/Other Pacific Islander, 3.1% Two or more races, 14.6% Hispanic of any race; Average household size: 2.73; Median age: 43.3; Age under 18: 20.8%; Age 65 and over: 18.5%; Males per 100 females: 102.2; Marriage status: 32.4% never married, 51.4% now married, 1.7% separated, 8.0% widowed, 8.2% divorced; Foreign born: 8.3%; Speak English only: 84.1%; With disability: 13.7%; Veterans: 7.7%; Ancestry: 20.8% Irish, 20.5% Italian, 15.4% American, 10.9% German, 6.7% Polish

Employment: 17.7% management, business, and financial, 4.1% computer, engineering, and science, 17.6% education, legal, community service, arts, and media, 7.1% healthcare practitioners, 13.8% service, 24.4% sales and office, 8.4% natural resources, construction, and maintenance, 6.9% production, transportation, and material moving

Income: Per capita: $39,621; Median household: $92,233; Average household: $116,272; Households with income of $100,000 or more: 44.6%; Poverty rate: 6.3%

Educational Attainment: High school diploma or higher: 91.1%; Bachelor's degree or higher: 37.6%; Graduate/professional degree or higher: 15.2%

School District(s)

Goshen Central SD (KG-12)
 Enrollment: 2,921 . . . . (845) 615-6720
Orange-Ulster Boces
 Enrollment: n/a . . . . (845) 291-0110

Vocational/Technical School(s)

Orange Ulster BOCES-Practical Nursing Program (Public)
 Enrollment: 84 . . . . (845) 291-0300
 Tuition: $13,437

Housing: Homeownership rate: 69.3%; Median home value: $306,000; Median year structure built: 1972; Homeowner vacancy rate: 2.2%; Median selected monthly owner costs: $2,663 with a mortgage, $895 without a

mortgage; Median gross rent: $1,236 per month; Rental vacancy rate: 9.2%

Health Insurance: 95.2% have insurance; 82.6% have private insurance; 26.5% have public insurance; 4.8% do not have insurance; 1.3% of children under 18 do not have insurance

Safety: Violent crime rate: 4.6 per 10,000 population; Property crime rate: 102.8 per 10,000 population

Newspapers: Goshen Independent (weekly circulation 2,300)

Transportation: Commute: 84.7% car, 4.9% public transportation, 2.6% walk, 7.3% work from home; Mean travel time to work: 36.0 minutes

Additional Information Contacts

Town of Goshen . . . . (845) 294-6250
 http://www.townofgoshen.org

GOSHEN (village). County seat. Covers a land area of 3.330 square miles and a water area of 0 square miles. Located at 41.40° N. Lat; 74.33° W. Long. Elevation is 436 feet.

Population: 5,381; Growth (since 2000): -5.2%; Density: 1,616.0 persons per square mile; Race: 82.2% White, 2.6% Black/African American, 3.0% Asian, 0.0% American Indian/Alaska Native, 0.0% Native Hawaiian/Other Pacific Islander, 5.6% Two or more races, 19.1% Hispanic of any race; Average household size: 2.49; Median age: 40.1; Age under 18: 23.2%; Age 65 and over: 18.8%; Males per 100 females: 87.6; Marriage status: 35.6% never married, 44.1% now married, 1.6% separated, 10.0% widowed, 10.4% divorced; Foreign born: 9.6%; Speak English only: 82.2%; With disability: 13.5%; Veterans: 6.1%; Ancestry: 22.1% Irish, 16.1% American, 15.6% Italian, 10.8% German, 8.1% English

Employment: 20.3% management, business, and financial, 2.1% computer, engineering, and science, 18.8% education, legal, community service, arts, and media, 7.7% healthcare practitioners, 15.0% service, 22.1% sales and office, 6.2% natural resources, construction, and maintenance, 7.9% production, transportation, and material moving

Income: Per capita: $38,118; Median household: $72,434; Average household: $95,042; Households with income of $100,000 or more: 35.2%; Poverty rate: 10.4%

Educational Attainment: High school diploma or higher: 93.1%; Bachelor's degree or higher: 44.2%; Graduate/professional degree or higher: 18.7%

School District(s)

Goshen Central SD (KG-12)
 Enrollment: 2,921 . . . . (845) 615-6720
Orange-Ulster Boces
 Enrollment: n/a . . . . (845) 291-0110

Vocational/Technical School(s)

Orange Ulster BOCES-Practical Nursing Program (Public)
 Enrollment: 84 . . . . (845) 291-0300
 Tuition: $13,437

Housing: Homeownership rate: 53.1%; Median home value: $287,700; Median year structure built: 1971; Homeowner vacancy rate: 2.1%; Median selected monthly owner costs: $2,296 with a mortgage, $1,014 without a mortgage; Median gross rent: $1,277 per month; Rental vacancy rate: 10.2%

Health Insurance: 93.5% have insurance; 79.4% have private insurance; 26.9% have public insurance; 6.5% do not have insurance; 2.8% of children under 18 do not have insurance

Safety: Violent crime rate: 7.5 per 10,000 population; Property crime rate: 97.1 per 10,000 population

Newspapers: Goshen Independent (weekly circulation 2,300)

Transportation: Commute: 83.4% car, 7.3% public transportation, 1.7% walk, 6.3% work from home; Mean travel time to work: 34.7 minutes

Additional Information Contacts

Village of Goshen . . . . (845) 294-6750
 http://www.villageofgoshen-ny.gov

GREENVILLE (town). Covers a land area of 30.015 square miles and a water area of 0.484 square miles. Located at 41.37° N. Lat; 74.60° W. Long. Elevation is 1,037 feet.

Population: 4,697; Growth (since 2000): 23.6%; Density: 156.5 persons per square mile; Race: 86.9% White, 1.8% Black/African American, 4.0% Asian, 0.0% American Indian/Alaska Native, 0.0% Native Hawaiian/Other Pacific Islander, 4.5% Two or more races, 9.0% Hispanic of any race; Average household size: 3.07; Median age: 40.7; Age under 18: 21.6%; Age 65 and over: 12.8%; Males per 100 females: 103.1; Marriage status: 32.0% never married, 59.9% now married, 0.0% separated, 3.5% widowed, 4.6% divorced; Foreign born: 6.2%; Speak English only: 87.2%;

With disability: 9.9%; Veterans: 7.5%; Ancestry: 19.4% Irish, 17.8% Italian, 17.0% American, 16.3% German, 7.6% Polish

Employment: 13.8% management, business, and financial, 2.8% computer, engineering, and science, 8.1% education, legal, community service, arts, and media, 6.1% healthcare practitioners, 20.8% service, 25.3% sales and office, 11.9% natural resources, construction, and maintenance, 11.1% production, transportation, and material moving

Income: Per capita: $37,565; Median household: $93,387; Average household: $113,259; Households with income of $100,000 or more: 47.3%; Poverty rate: 4.1%

Educational Attainment: High school diploma or higher: 96.6%; Bachelor's degree or higher: 24.0%; Graduate/professional degree or higher: 8.8%

Housing: Homeownership rate: 91.1%; Median home value: $274,400; Median year structure built: 1985; Homeowner vacancy rate: 2.9%; Median selected monthly owner costs: $2,291 with a mortgage, $866 without a mortgage; Median gross rent: $1,188 per month; Rental vacancy rate: 0.0%

Health Insurance: 95.1% have insurance; 83.9% have private insurance; 25.2% have public insurance; 4.9% do not have insurance; 1.2% of children under 18 do not have insurance

Transportation: Commute: 91.4% car, 0.8% public transportation, 0.0% walk, 7.8% work from home; Mean travel time to work: 40.8 minutes

Additional Information Contacts

Town of Greenville . . . . (518) 966-5055
   http://www.townofgreenvilleny.com

GREENWOOD LAKE (village). Covers a land area of 2.048 square miles and a water area of 0.424 square miles. Located at 41.22° N. Lat; 74.29° W. Long. Elevation is 630 feet.

Population: 3,116; Growth (since 2000): -8.6%; Density: 1,521.4 persons per square mile; Race: 79.8% White, 1.1% Black/African American, 0.0% Asian, 2.8% American Indian/Alaska Native, 0.0% Native Hawaiian/Other Pacific Islander, 16.4% Two or more races, 23.6% Hispanic of any race; Average household size: 2.60; Median age: 48.8; Age under 18: 20.5%; Age 65 and over: 7.9%; Males per 100 females: 98.4; Marriage status: 24.1% never married, 51.0% now married, 0.0% separated, 3.8% widowed, 21.1% divorced; Foreign born: 4.8%; Speak English only: 82.0%; With disability: 12.5%; Veterans: 8.9%; Ancestry: 20.0% American, 19.8% German, 16.4% Italian, 13.9% Irish, 4.7% Norwegian

Employment: 9.4% management, business, and financial, 17.5% computer, engineering, and science, 7.7% education, legal, community service, arts, and media, 4.3% healthcare practitioners, 20.3% service, 17.9% sales and office, 5.5% natural resources, construction, and maintenance, 17.5% production, transportation, and material moving

Income: Per capita: $38,391; Median household: $91,318; Average household: $96,243; Households with income of $100,000 or more: 48.5%; Poverty rate: 4.4%

Educational Attainment: High school diploma or higher: 88.3%; Bachelor's degree or higher: 23.3%; Graduate/professional degree or higher: 9.7%

School District(s)

Greenwood Lake Union Free SD (KG-08)
   Enrollment: 527 . . . . (845) 782-8678

Housing: Homeownership rate: 79.4%; Median home value: $260,000; Median year structure built: 1952; Homeowner vacancy rate: 0.0%; Median selected monthly owner costs: $2,012 with a mortgage, $1,059 without a mortgage; Median gross rent: $1,148 per month; Rental vacancy rate: 0.0%

Health Insurance: 94.6% have insurance; 84.2% have private insurance; 16.6% have public insurance; 5.4% do not have insurance; 0.0% of children under 18 do not have insurance

Safety: Violent crime rate: 3.2 per 10,000 population; Property crime rate: 67.9 per 10,000 population

Newspapers: Greenwood Lake News (weekly circulation 5,000)

Transportation: Commute: 83.9% car, 6.7% public transportation, 0.7% walk, 8.6% work from home; Mean travel time to work: 49.7 minutes

HAMPTONBURGH (town). Covers a land area of 26.758 square miles and a water area of 0.211 square miles. Located at 41.45° N. Lat; 74.24° W. Long. Elevation is 446 feet.

Population: 5,506; Growth (since 2000): 17.5%; Density: 205.8 persons per square mile; Race: 86.9% White, 3.5% Black/African American, 5.3% Asian, 0.0% American Indian/Alaska Native, 0.0% Native Hawaiian/Other Pacific Islander, 0.3% Two or more races, 8.8% Hispanic of any race;

Average household size: 3.37; Median age: 41.8; Age under 18: 23.8%; Age 65 and over: 13.4%; Males per 100 females: 97.5; Marriage status: 32.1% never married, 59.7% now married, 0.0% separated, 4.2% widowed, 4.0% divorced; Foreign born: 10.8%; Speak English only: 86.6%; With disability: 10.6%; Veterans: 8.8%; Ancestry: 22.7% Italian, 18.5% Irish, 14.0% German, 8.8% American, 6.2% English

Employment: 19.0% management, business, and financial, 3.2% computer, engineering, and science, 13.5% education, legal, community service, arts, and media, 6.5% healthcare practitioners, 14.7% service, 26.5% sales and office, 11.0% natural resources, construction, and maintenance, 5.7% production, transportation, and material moving

Income: Per capita: $35,681; Median household: $105,370; Average household: $118,886; Households with income of $100,000 or more: 52.4%; Poverty rate: 7.6%

Educational Attainment: High school diploma or higher: 93.4%; Bachelor's degree or higher: 32.4%; Graduate/professional degree or higher: 10.9%

Housing: Homeownership rate: 93.7%; Median home value: $349,800; Median year structure built: 1977; Homeowner vacancy rate: 3.2%; Median selected monthly owner costs: $2,588 with a mortgage, $1,064 without a mortgage; Median gross rent: $1,571 per month; Rental vacancy rate: 0.0%

Health Insurance: 94.9% have insurance; 82.3% have private insurance; 23.8% have public insurance; 5.1% do not have insurance; 0.0% of children under 18 do not have insurance

Transportation: Commute: 87.6% car, 4.1% public transportation, 0.4% walk, 7.6% work from home; Mean travel time to work: 34.5 minutes

Additional Information Contacts

Town of Hamptonburgh . . . . (845) 427-2424
   http://townofhamptonburgh.org/content

HARRIMAN (village). Covers a land area of 1.004 square miles and a water area of 0.018 square miles. Located at 41.31° N. Lat; 74.14° W. Long. Elevation is 538 feet.

Population: 2,965; Growth (since 2000): 31.7%; Density: 2,952.5 persons per square mile; Race: 51.5% White, 22.2% Black/African American, 4.6% Asian, 0.0% American Indian/Alaska Native, 0.0% Native Hawaiian/Other Pacific Islander, 3.0% Two or more races, 30.1% Hispanic of any race; Average household size: 2.85; Median age: 34.8; Age under 18: 24.9%; Age 65 and over: 4.9%; Males per 100 females: 94.4; Marriage status: 37.9% never married, 50.2% now married, 2.3% separated, 2.3% widowed, 9.6% divorced; Foreign born: 23.5%; Speak English only: 67.2%; With disability: 10.5%; Veterans: 3.6%; Ancestry: 12.4% American, 11.4% Irish, 9.1% Italian, 8.8% Jamaican, 6.0% German

Employment: 8.4% management, business, and financial, 3.6% computer, engineering, and science, 11.5% education, legal, community service, arts, and media, 4.8% healthcare practitioners, 26.4% service, 29.1% sales and office, 7.3% natural resources, construction, and maintenance, 8.9% production, transportation, and material moving

Income: Per capita: $31,039; Median household: $69,707; Average household: $85,720; Households with income of $100,000 or more: 29.3%; Poverty rate: 9.3%

Educational Attainment: High school diploma or higher: 92.2%; Bachelor's degree or higher: 32.3%; Graduate/professional degree or higher: 9.7%

School District(s)

Monroe-Woodbury Central SD (KG-12)
   Enrollment: 7,005 . . . . (845) 460-6200

Housing: Homeownership rate: 44.8%; Median home value: $176,400; Median year structure built: 1981; Homeowner vacancy rate: 0.0%; Median selected monthly owner costs: $2,455 with a mortgage, $1,032 without a mortgage; Median gross rent: $1,456 per month; Rental vacancy rate: 3.0%

Health Insurance: 90.4% have insurance; 76.1% have private insurance; 20.7% have public insurance; 9.6% do not have insurance; 6.6% of children under 18 do not have insurance

Safety: Violent crime rate: 4.1 per 10,000 population; Property crime rate: 77.0 per 10,000 population

Transportation: Commute: 80.8% car, 12.9% public transportation, 4.2% walk, 1.8% work from home; Mean travel time to work: 38.7 minutes

HIGHLAND FALLS (village).
Covers a land area of 1.090 square miles and a water area of 0.009 square miles. Located at 41.36° N. Lat; 73.97° W. Long. Elevation is 141 feet.
Population: 3,841; Growth (since 2000): 4.4%; Density: 3,522.6 persons per square mile; Race: 69.5% White, 18.2% Black/African American, 4.8% Asian, 0.3% American Indian/Alaska Native, 0.0% Native Hawaiian/Other Pacific Islander, 4.2% Two or more races, 14.2% Hispanic of any race; Average household size: 2.14; Median age: 41.7; Age under 18: 17.1%; Age 65 and over: 16.3%; Males per 100 females: 97.1; Marriage status: 41.3% never married, 47.1% now married, 2.4% separated, 1.8% widowed, 9.9% divorced; Foreign born: 14.4%; Speak English only: 79.6%; With disability: 13.5%; Veterans: 10.5%; Ancestry: 20.7% Irish, 13.1% Italian, 12.5% American, 11.5% German, 5.2% English
Employment: 13.3% management, business, and financial, 4.7% computer, engineering, and science, 14.8% education, legal, community service, arts, and media, 6.1% healthcare practitioners, 18.6% service, 24.3% sales and office, 7.5% natural resources, construction, and maintenance, 10.6% production, transportation, and material moving
Income: Per capita: $41,882; Median household: $74,278; Average household: $87,322; Households with income of $100,000 or more: 31.8%; Poverty rate: 4.6%
Educational Attainment: High school diploma or higher: 95.4%; Bachelor's degree or higher: 39.4%; Graduate/professional degree or higher: 17.8%

School District(s)
Highland Falls Central SD (PK-12)
    Enrollment: 1,045 . . . . (845) 446-9575
Housing: Homeownership rate: 48.1%; Median home value: $215,100; Median year structure built: 1946; Homeowner vacancy rate: 1.7%; Median selected monthly owner costs: $2,122 with a mortgage, $1,098 without a mortgage; Median gross rent: $1,168 per month; Rental vacancy rate: 0.0%
Health Insurance: 95.8% have insurance; 83.0% have private insurance; 31.0% have public insurance; 4.2% do not have insurance; 0.0% of children under 18 do not have insurance
Safety: Violent crime rate: 7.9 per 10,000 population; Property crime rate: 120.9 per 10,000 population
Newspapers: News Of The Highlands (weekly circulation 2,700)
Transportation: Commute: 88.0% car, 2.7% public transportation, 5.6% walk, 3.7% work from home; Mean travel time to work: 20.7 minutes

HIGHLAND MILLS (unincorporated postal area)
ZCTA: 10930
    Covers a land area of 13.876 square miles and a water area of 0.171 square miles. Located at 41.36° N. Lat; 74.11° W. Long. Elevation is 509 feet.
Population: 8,837; Growth (since 2000): 19.4%; Density: 636.9 persons per square mile; Race: 82.1% White, 6.8% Black/African American, 4.8% Asian, 0.0% American Indian/Alaska Native, 0.0% Native Hawaiian/Other Pacific Islander, 1.6% Two or more races, 17.0% Hispanic of any race; Average household size: 3.20; Median age: 40.8; Age under 18: 26.9%; Age 65 and over: 12.2%; Males per 100 females: 98.1; Marriage status: 28.7% never married, 60.0% now married, 1.7% separated, 5.0% widowed, 6.3% divorced; Foreign born: 15.3%; Speak English only: 81.4%; With disability: 12.7%; Veterans: 7.2%; Ancestry: 19.1% Irish, 18.3% Italian, 13.0% American, 9.4% German, 5.7% Polish
Employment: 15.1% management, business, and financial, 6.5% computer, engineering, and science, 12.5% education, legal, community service, arts, and media, 10.3% healthcare practitioners, 14.4% service, 27.8% sales and office, 6.0% natural resources, construction, and maintenance, 7.4% production, transportation, and material moving
Income: Per capita: $44,260; Median household: $131,832; Average household: $139,023; Households with income of $100,000 or more: 68.9%; Poverty rate: 6.2%
Educational Attainment: High school diploma or higher: 95.7%; Bachelor's degree or higher: 48.9%; Graduate/professional degree or higher: 24.7%
Housing: Homeownership rate: 92.1%; Median home value: $301,900; Median year structure built: 1982; Homeowner vacancy rate: 1.5%; Median selected monthly owner costs: $2,680 with a mortgage, $1,113 without a mortgage; Median gross rent: $1,151 per month; Rental vacancy rate: 0.0%
Health Insurance: 95.6% have insurance; 87.3% have private insurance; 19.8% have public insurance; 4.4% do not have insurance; 0.0% of children under 18 do not have insurance

Transportation: Commute: 84.1% car, 6.7% public transportation, 0.6% walk, 7.5% work from home; Mean travel time to work: 39.2 minutes

HIGHLANDS (town).
Covers a land area of 30.410 square miles and a water area of 3.060 square miles. Located at 41.37° N. Lat; 74.01° W. Long.
Population: 12,152; Growth (since 2000): -2.7%; Density: 399.6 persons per square mile; Race: 75.7% White, 9.9% Black/African American, 4.3% Asian, 0.4% American Indian/Alaska Native, 0.0% Native Hawaiian/Other Pacific Islander, 5.1% Two or more races, 12.5% Hispanic of any race; Average household size: 2.67; Median age: 23.2; Age under 18: 19.9%; Age 65 and over: 7.0%; Males per 100 females: 163.2; Marriage status: 55.7% never married, 37.2% now married, 1.0% separated, 1.4% widowed, 5.6% divorced; Foreign born: 8.3%; Speak English only: 82.8%; With disability: 9.8%; Veterans: 21.4%; Ancestry: 18.8% Irish, 16.6% German, 14.0% Italian, 11.4% American, 7.9% English
Employment: 14.8% management, business, and financial, 6.4% computer, engineering, and science, 18.7% education, legal, community service, arts, and media, 6.1% healthcare practitioners, 16.5% service, 21.0% sales and office, 8.2% natural resources, construction, and maintenance, 8.4% production, transportation, and material moving
Income: Per capita: $29,846; Median household: $87,526; Average household: $98,650; Households with income of $100,000 or more: 38.8%; Poverty rate: 3.2%
Educational Attainment: High school diploma or higher: 95.7%; Bachelor's degree or higher: 49.0%; Graduate/professional degree or higher: 26.8%
Housing: Homeownership rate: 41.2%; Median home value: $230,100; Median year structure built: 1953; Homeowner vacancy rate: 2.1%; Median selected monthly owner costs: $2,161 with a mortgage, $1,017 without a mortgage; Median gross rent: $1,436 per month; Rental vacancy rate: 0.7%
Health Insurance: 97.0% have insurance; 87.9% have private insurance; 20.2% have public insurance; 3.0% do not have insurance; 2.7% of children under 18 do not have insurance
Safety: Violent crime rate: 2.4 per 10,000 population; Property crime rate: 9.7 per 10,000 population
Transportation: Commute: 55.8% car, 1.9% public transportation, 21.2% walk, 20.1% work from home; Mean travel time to work: 18.3 minutes
Additional Information Contacts
Town of Highlands. . . . . (845) 446-4280
    http://townofhighlands.com

HOWELLS (unincorporated postal area)
ZCTA: 10932
    Covers a land area of 0.149 square miles and a water area of <.001 square miles. Located at 41.48° N. Lat; 74.46° W. Long. Elevation is 679 feet.
Population: 72; Growth (since 2000): n/a; Density: 482.4 persons per square mile; Race: 75.0% White, 0.0% Black/African American, 0.0% Asian, 0.0% American Indian/Alaska Native, 0.0% Native Hawaiian/Other Pacific Islander, 0.0% Two or more races, 25.0% Hispanic of any race; Average household size: 2.06; Median age: 59.9; Age under 18: 0.0%; Age 65 and over: 47.2%; Males per 100 females: 71.4; Marriage status: 27.8% never married, 72.2% now married, 0.0% separated, 0.0% widowed, 0.0% divorced; Foreign born: 23.6%; Speak English only: 75.0%; With disability: 23.6%; Veterans: 23.6%; Ancestry: 75.0% Irish
Employment: 0.0% management, business, and financial, 0.0% computer, engineering, and science, 0.0% education, legal, community service, arts, and media, 0.0% healthcare practitioners, 0.0% service, 100.0% sales and office, 0.0% natural resources, construction, and maintenance, 0.0% production, transportation, and material moving
Income: Per capita: $16,067; Median household: n/a; Average household: n/a; Households with income of $100,000 or more: n/a; Poverty rate: 25.0%
Educational Attainment: High school diploma or higher: 100.0%; Bachelor's degree or higher: 51.4%; Graduate/professional degree or higher: 27.8%
Housing: Homeownership rate: 100.0%; Median home value: n/a; Median year structure built: n/a; Homeowner vacancy rate: 0.0%; Median selected monthly owner costs: $0 with a mortgage, $0 without a mortgage; Median gross rent: n/a per month; Rental vacancy rate: 0.0%

Health Insurance: 100.0% have insurance; 100.0% have private insurance; 47.2% have public insurance; 0.0% do not have insurance; 0.0% of children under 18 do not have insurance
Transportation: Commute: 100.0% car, 0.0% public transportation, 0.0% walk, 0.0% work from home; Mean travel time to work: 0.0 minutes

HUGUENOT (unincorporated postal area)
ZCTA: 12746

Covers a land area of 14.181 square miles and a water area of 0.323 square miles. Located at 41.44° N. Lat; 74.66° W. Long. Elevation is 469 feet.
Population: 1,216; Growth (since 2000): 6.3%; Density: 85.7 persons per square mile; Race: 100.0% White, 0.0% Black/African American, 0.0% Asian, 0.0% American Indian/Alaska Native, 0.0% Native Hawaiian/Other Pacific Islander, 0.0% Two or more races, 0.0% Hispanic of any race; Average household size: 3.10; Median age: 33.3; Age under 18: 21.2%; Age 65 and over: 12.1%; Males per 100 females: 97.7; Marriage status: 36.0% never married, 57.3% now married, 0.0% separated, 0.8% widowed, 5.9% divorced; Foreign born: 1.0%; Speak English only: 96.9%; With disability: 14.0%; Veterans: 7.9%; Ancestry: 32.9% Irish, 18.4% German, 12.0% American, 11.7% Italian, 9.5% European
Employment: 3.1% management, business, and financial, 1.5% computer, engineering, and science, 10.8% education, legal, community service, arts, and media, 6.4% healthcare practitioners, 25.1% service, 18.0% sales and office, 12.9% natural resources, construction, and maintenance, 22.2% production, transportation, and material moving
Income: Per capita: $31,616; Median household: $90,690; Average household: $94,680; Households with income of $100,000 or more: 29.2%; Poverty rate: 1.0%
Educational Attainment: High school diploma or higher: 94.4%; Bachelor's degree or higher: 17.7%; Graduate/professional degree or higher: 8.1%
Housing: Homeownership rate: 85.9%; Median home value: $199,300; Median year structure built: 1965; Homeowner vacancy rate: 0.0%; Median selected monthly owner costs: $1,750 with a mortgage, $693 without a mortgage; Median gross rent: $1,132 per month; Rental vacancy rate: 46.0%
Health Insurance: 96.0% have insurance; 78.7% have private insurance; 26.6% have public insurance; 4.0% do not have insurance; 2.6% of children under 18 do not have insurance
Transportation: Commute: 94.6% car, 1.9% public transportation, 2.1% walk, 1.4% work from home; Mean travel time to work: 31.4 minutes

JOHNSON (unincorporated postal area)
ZCTA: 10933

Covers a land area of 1.092 square miles and a water area of 0.005 square miles. Located at 41.37° N. Lat; 74.51° W. Long. Elevation is 509 feet.
Population: 738; Growth (since 2000): n/a; Density: 675.7 persons per square mile; Race: 87.7% White, 0.0% Black/African American, 3.0% Asian, 0.0% American Indian/Alaska Native, 0.0% Native Hawaiian/Other Pacific Islander, 0.0% Two or more races, 1.5% Hispanic of any race; Average household size: 3.43; Median age: 30.7; Age under 18: 26.4%; Age 65 and over: 1.8%; Males per 100 females: 98.7; Marriage status: 32.6% never married, 59.9% now married, 0.0% separated, 7.5% widowed, 0.0% divorced; Foreign born: 2.6%; Speak English only: 95.0%; With disability: 24.5%; Veterans: 7.6%; Ancestry: 30.8% Italian, 29.4% American, 16.3% German, 7.5% Hungarian, 5.6% English
Employment: 10.7% management, business, and financial, 11.8% computer, engineering, and science, 3.3% education, legal, community service, arts, and media, 4.1% healthcare practitioners, 34.6% service, 30.8% sales and office, 4.7% natural resources, construction, and maintenance, 0.0% production, transportation, and material moving
Income: Per capita: $23,675; Median household: $95,320; Average household: $78,700; Households with income of $100,000 or more: 32.6%; Poverty rate: 9.3%
Educational Attainment: High school diploma or higher: 94.5%; Bachelor's degree or higher: 18.5%; Graduate/professional degree or higher: 1.9%
Housing: Homeownership rate: 94.9%; Median home value: $226,600; Median year structure built: 1992; Homeowner vacancy rate: 0.0%; Median selected monthly owner costs: $2,652 with a mortgage, $808

without a mortgage; Median gross rent: n/a per month; Rental vacancy rate: 0.0%
Health Insurance: 94.2% have insurance; 86.0% have private insurance; 15.6% have public insurance; 5.8% do not have insurance; 0.0% of children under 18 do not have insurance
Transportation: Commute: 97.0% car, 0.0% public transportation, 0.0% walk, 3.0% work from home; Mean travel time to work: 22.4 minutes

KIRYAS JOEL (village). Covers a land area of 1.109 square miles and a water area of 0.006 square miles. Located at 41.34° N. Lat; 74.17° W. Long. Elevation is 686 feet.
History: Founded in 1974 by the Satmar sect of Hasidic Jews to accommodate, in part, their burgeoning population in the Williamsburg section of Brooklyn.
Population: 22,794; Growth (since 2000): 73.5%; Density: 20,561.2 persons per square mile; Race: 99.5% White, 0.0% Black/African American, 0.0% Asian, 0.2% American Indian/Alaska Native, 0.0% Native Hawaiian/Other Pacific Islander, 0.2% Two or more races, 2.1% Hispanic of any race; Average household size: 5.50; Median age: 13.8; Age under 18: 60.4%; Age 65 and over: 2.2%; Males per 100 females: 107.3; Marriage status: 25.6% never married, 72.2% now married, 0.2% separated, 1.2% widowed, 0.9% divorced; Foreign born: 6.8%; Speak English only: 4.5%; With disability: 2.9%; Veterans: 0.5%; Ancestry: 26.9% American, 17.5% Hungarian, 3.1% Romanian, 2.6% European, 1.8% German
Employment: 14.6% management, business, and financial, 2.1% computer, engineering, and science, 20.1% education, legal, community service, arts, and media, 0.6% healthcare practitioners, 11.9% service, 37.8% sales and office, 4.3% natural resources, construction, and maintenance, 8.7% production, transportation, and material moving
Income: Per capita: $8,425; Median household: $30,525; Average household: $46,506; Households with income of $100,000 or more: 11.1%; Poverty rate: 48.0%
Educational Attainment: High school diploma or higher: 63.8%; Bachelor's degree or higher: 6.6%; Graduate/professional degree or higher: 0.5%
Housing: Homeownership rate: 28.4%; Median home value: $406,100; Median year structure built: 1997; Homeowner vacancy rate: 2.9%; Median selected monthly owner costs: $1,818 with a mortgage, $971 without a mortgage; Median gross rent: $1,111 per month; Rental vacancy rate: 0.5%
Health Insurance: 98.8% have insurance; 25.2% have private insurance; 80.3% have public insurance; 1.2% do not have insurance; 0.9% of children under 18 do not have insurance
Transportation: Commute: 44.9% car, 19.2% public transportation, 27.3% walk, 6.2% work from home; Mean travel time to work: 24.0 minutes

MAYBROOK (village). Covers a land area of 1.354 square miles and a water area of 0.006 square miles. Located at 41.49° N. Lat; 74.21° W. Long. Elevation is 420 feet.
History: Incorporated 1925.
Population: 3,298; Growth (since 2000): 6.9%; Density: 2,435.3 persons per square mile; Race: 71.0% White, 19.4% Black/African American, 1.6% Asian, 0.2% American Indian/Alaska Native, 0.3% Native Hawaiian/Other Pacific Islander, 5.7% Two or more races, 19.6% Hispanic of any race; Average household size: 2.48; Median age: 38.4; Age under 18: 15.7%; Age 65 and over: 11.5%; Males per 100 females: 86.0; Marriage status: 39.1% never married, 42.6% now married, 2.4% separated, 5.3% widowed, 13.0% divorced; Foreign born: 11.5%; Speak English only: 76.3%; With disability: 11.2%; Veterans: 8.2%; Ancestry: 19.7% Italian, 14.8% Irish, 11.9% American, 11.7% German, 3.4% Polish
Employment: 8.0% management, business, and financial, 6.8% computer, engineering, and science, 3.1% education, legal, community service, arts, and media, 6.1% healthcare practitioners, 25.5% service, 30.0% sales and office, 6.1% natural resources, construction, and maintenance, 14.3% production, transportation, and material moving
Income: Per capita: $32,896; Median household: $61,071; Average household: $78,413; Households with income of $100,000 or more: 30.7%; Poverty rate: 10.6%
Educational Attainment: High school diploma or higher: 91.4%; Bachelor's degree or higher: 24.3%; Graduate/professional degree or higher: 8.7%

School District(s)
Valley Central SD (Montgomery) (KG-12)
    Enrollment: 4,362 . . . . (845) 457-2400

Housing: Homeownership rate: 67.4%; Median home value: $178,200; Median year structure built: 1973; Homeowner vacancy rate: 3.5%; Median selected monthly owner costs: $1,712 with a mortgage, $640 without a mortgage; Median gross rent: $1,057 per month; Rental vacancy rate: 5.7%

Health Insurance: 89.6% have insurance; 70.6% have private insurance; 28.9% have public insurance; 10.4% do not have insurance; 4.5% of children under 18 do not have insurance

Safety: Violent crime rate: 8.5 per 10,000 population; Property crime rate: 22.8 per 10,000 population

Transportation: Commute: 81.3% car, 12.4% public transportation, 1.8% walk, 4.1% work from home; Mean travel time to work: 35.0 minutes

Additional Information Contacts

Village of Maybrook. . . . . (845) 427-2717
http://www.villageofmaybrook.com

MECHANICSTOWN (CDP). Covers a land area of 3.345 square miles and a water area of 0.056 square miles. Located at 41.45° N. Lat; 74.39° W. Long. Elevation is 531 feet.

Population: 6,904; Growth (since 2000): 13.9%; Density: 2,064.2 persons per square mile; Race: 54.5% White, 25.7% Black/African American, 1.8% Asian, 0.0% American Indian/Alaska Native, 0.4% Native Hawaiian/Other Pacific Islander, 6.1% Two or more races, 29.0% Hispanic of any race; Average household size: 2.35; Median age: 44.3; Age under 18: 18.8%; Age 65 and over: 21.8%; Males per 100 females: 84.7; Marriage status: 29.0% never married, 52.3% now married, 3.7% separated, 8.8% widowed, 9.9% divorced; Foreign born: 16.8%; Speak English only: 70.4%; With disability: 17.8%; Veterans: 4.9%; Ancestry: 17.0% American, 12.6% Italian, 8.6% Irish, 8.3% German, 4.7% Polish

Employment: 11.1% management, business, and financial, 0.7% computer, engineering, and science, 13.0% education, legal, community service, arts, and media, 2.9% healthcare practitioners, 16.6% service, 31.1% sales and office, 6.8% natural resources, construction, and maintenance, 17.7% production, transportation, and material moving

Income: Per capita: $29,914; Median household: $47,250; Average household: $69,787; Households with income of $100,000 or more: 20.4%; Poverty rate: 19.4%

Educational Attainment: High school diploma or higher: 88.7%; Bachelor's degree or higher: 19.8%; Graduate/professional degree or higher: 6.7%

Housing: Homeownership rate: 43.3%; Median home value: $204,100; Median year structure built: 1980; Homeowner vacancy rate: 2.6%; Median selected monthly owner costs: $1,878 with a mortgage, $953 without a mortgage; Median gross rent: $1,168 per month; Rental vacancy rate: 4.8%

Health Insurance: 91.0% have insurance; 71.1% have private insurance; 35.7% have public insurance; 9.0% do not have insurance; 0.0% of children under 18 do not have insurance

Transportation: Commute: 84.0% car, 3.1% public transportation, 5.2% walk, 1.0% work from home; Mean travel time to work: 40.1 minutes

MIDDLETOWN (city). Covers a land area of 5.076 square miles and a water area of 0.026 square miles. Located at 41.44° N. Lat; 74.42° W. Long. Elevation is 558 feet.

History: Settled 1756, Incorporated as a city 1888.

Population: 27,729; Growth (since 2000): 9.2%; Density: 5,462.9 persons per square mile; Race: 48.7% White, 21.6% Black/African American, 3.7% Asian, 0.3% American Indian/Alaska Native, 0.0% Native Hawaiian/Other Pacific Islander, 5.0% Two or more races, 41.2% Hispanic of any race; Average household size: 2.65; Median age: 35.8; Age under 18: 23.7%; Age 65 and over: 13.3%; Males per 100 females: 95.6; Marriage status: 41.1% never married, 45.8% now married, 2.9% separated, 5.3% widowed, 7.8% divorced; Foreign born: 17.6%; Speak English only: 63.0%; With disability: 13.9%; Veterans: 5.3%; Ancestry: 17.2% American, 6.6% Italian, 5.9% Irish, 4.6% German, 2.6% Polish

Employment: 10.6% management, business, and financial, 2.3% computer, engineering, and science, 8.4% education, legal, community service, arts, and media, 5.2% healthcare practitioners, 25.8% service, 24.8% sales and office, 7.6% natural resources, construction, and maintenance, 15.3% production, transportation, and material moving

Income: Per capita: $26,527; Median household: $52,021; Average household: $68,656; Households with income of $100,000 or more: 23.8%; Poverty rate: 17.3%

Educational Attainment: High school diploma or higher: 83.2%; Bachelor's degree or higher: 18.9%; Graduate/professional degree or higher: 7.1%

School District(s)
Middletown City SD (KG-12)
    Enrollment: 7,404 . . . . (845) 326-1158
Minisink Valley Central SD (KG-12)
    Enrollment: 3,841 . . . . (845) 355-5100

Two-year College(s)
Orange County Community College (Public)
    Enrollment: 6,601 . . . . (845) 344-6222
    Tuition: In-state $5,398; Out-of-state $10,174

Vocational/Technical School(s)
Beauty School of Middletown (Private, For-profit)
    Enrollment: 56. . . . . (845) 343-2171
    Tuition: $13,100

Housing: Homeownership rate: 55.0%; Median home value: $185,300; Median year structure built: 1956; Homeowner vacancy rate: 3.1%; Median selected monthly owner costs: $1,870 with a mortgage, $744 without a mortgage; Median gross rent: $1,126 per month; Rental vacancy rate: 6.4%

Health Insurance: 89.7% have insurance; 65.6% have private insurance; 36.8% have public insurance; 10.3% do not have insurance; 3.5% of children under 18 do not have insurance

Hospitals: Orange Regional Medical Center (174 beds)

Safety: Violent crime rate: 37.3 per 10,000 population; Property crime rate: 238.3 per 10,000 population

Newspapers: The Gazette (weekly circulation 9,000); Times Herald Record (daily circulation 79,100)

Transportation: Commute: 86.6% car, 4.3% public transportation, 2.5% walk, 3.7% work from home; Mean travel time to work: 30.5 minutes

Additional Information Contacts

City of Middletown. . . . . (845) 346-4101
http://www.middletown-ny.com

MINISINK (town). Covers a land area of 23.029 square miles and a water area of 0.144 square miles. Located at 41.32° N. Lat; 74.54° W. Long.

Population: 4,513; Growth (since 2000): 25.9%; Density: 196.0 persons per square mile; Race: 87.9% White, 2.2% Black/African American, 0.7% Asian, 0.7% American Indian/Alaska Native, 0.0% Native Hawaiian/Other Pacific Islander, 1.0% Two or more races, 13.5% Hispanic of any race; Average household size: 3.03; Median age: 40.8; Age under 18: 25.0%; Age 65 and over: 11.5%; Males per 100 females: 99.6; Marriage status: 31.7% never married, 54.7% now married, 1.5% separated, 5.5% widowed, 8.1% divorced; Foreign born: 6.0%; Speak English only: 88.5%; With disability: 17.0%; Veterans: 9.1%; Ancestry: 20.5% American, 19.7% Italian, 13.2% Irish, 11.5% German, 7.4% English

Employment: 18.9% management, business, and financial, 3.0% computer, engineering, and science, 8.7% education, legal, community service, arts, and media, 4.7% healthcare practitioners, 22.9% service, 27.6% sales and office, 8.2% natural resources, construction, and maintenance, 6.0% production, transportation, and material moving

Income: Per capita: $32,491; Median household: $88,689; Average household: $95,600; Households with income of $100,000 or more: 40.0%; Poverty rate: 5.7%

Educational Attainment: High school diploma or higher: 93.4%; Bachelor's degree or higher: 30.5%; Graduate/professional degree or higher: 12.5%

Housing: Homeownership rate: 83.1%; Median home value: $286,100; Median year structure built: 1980; Homeowner vacancy rate: 3.6%; Median selected monthly owner costs: $2,443 with a mortgage, $895 without a mortgage; Median gross rent: $1,227 per month; Rental vacancy rate: 0.0%

Health Insurance: 89.7% have insurance; 76.9% have private insurance; 24.5% have public insurance; 10.3% do not have insurance; 6.6% of children under 18 do not have insurance

Transportation: Commute: 89.1% car, 1.3% public transportation, 0.0% walk, 8.8% work from home; Mean travel time to work: 33.2 minutes

Additional Information Contacts

Town of Minisink . . . . (845) 726-3700
http://www.townofminisink.com

MONROE (town). Covers a land area of 19.976 square miles and a water area of 1.280 square miles. Located at 41.30° N. Lat; 74.20° W. Long. Elevation is 643 feet.

History: Incorporated 1894.

Population: 42,913; Growth (since 2000): 36.6%; Density: 2,148.2 persons per square mile; Race: 86.6% White, 3.2% Black/African American, 2.8% Asian, 0.3% American Indian/Alaska Native, 0.0% Native Hawaiian/Other Pacific Islander, 1.8% Two or more races, 11.3% Hispanic of any race; Average household size: 4.10; Median age: 21.2; Age under 18: 44.9%; Age 65 and over: 5.8%; Males per 100 females: 103.2; Marriage status: 29.2% never married, 63.2% now married, 1.0% separated, 3.1% widowed, 4.4% divorced; Foreign born: 10.4%; Speak English only: 39.0%; With disability: 6.7%; Veterans: 3.9%; Ancestry: 18.9% American, 10.0% Hungarian, 9.2% Italian, 8.3% Irish, 4.5% German

Employment: 13.8% management, business, and financial, 5.0% computer, engineering, and science, 17.0% education, legal, community service, arts, and media, 4.5% healthcare practitioners, 16.0% service, 29.4% sales and office, 5.9% natural resources, construction, and maintenance, 8.3% production, transportation, and material moving

Income: Per capita: $21,622; Median household: $66,482; Average household: $87,250; Households with income of $100,000 or more: 34.2%; Poverty rate: 28.6%

Educational Attainment: High school diploma or higher: 82.5%; Bachelor's degree or higher: 29.3%; Graduate/professional degree or higher: 11.3%

School District(s)

Greenwood Lake Union Free SD (KG-08)
    Enrollment: 527 . . . . (845) 782-8678
Kiryas Joel Village Union Free SD (PK-KG)
    Enrollment: 119 . . . . (845) 782-2300
Monroe-Woodbury Central SD (KG-12)
    Enrollment: 7,005 . . . . (845) 460-6200

Four-year College(s)

Uta Mesivta of Kiryas Joel (Private, Not-for-profit, Jewish)
    Enrollment: 1,864 . . . . (845) 783-9901
    Tuition: In-state $11,500; Out-of-state $11,500
Yeshivas Maharit D'Satmar (Private, Not-for-profit)
    Enrollment: 99 . . . . (845) 782-1380
    Tuition: In-state $11,500; Out-of-state $11,500

Housing: Homeownership rate: 58.2%; Median home value: $330,600; Median year structure built: 1985; Homeowner vacancy rate: 2.8%; Median selected monthly owner costs: $2,458 with a mortgage, $1,121 without a mortgage; Median gross rent: $1,228 per month; Rental vacancy rate: 1.2%

Health Insurance: 96.4% have insurance; 50.2% have private insurance; 54.6% have public insurance; 3.6% do not have insurance; 1.3% of children under 18 do not have insurance

Transportation: Commute: 69.1% car, 13.9% public transportation, 10.4% walk, 4.2% work from home; Mean travel time to work: 32.9 minutes

Additional Information Contacts

Town of Monroe . . . . (845) 783-1900
    http://www.monroeny.org

MONROE (village). Covers a land area of 3.453 square miles and a water area of 0.064 square miles. Located at 41.32° N. Lat; 74.18° W. Long. Elevation is 643 feet.

Population: 8,579; Growth (since 2000): 10.3%; Density: 2,484.3 persons per square mile; Race: 68.3% White, 6.7% Black/African American, 4.9% Asian, 1.0% American Indian/Alaska Native, 0.0% Native Hawaiian/Other Pacific Islander, 3.3% Two or more races, 26.8% Hispanic of any race; Average household size: 3.20; Median age: 35.1; Age under 18: 27.9%; Age 65 and over: 10.3%; Males per 100 females: 102.1; Marriage status: 29.9% never married, 60.9% now married, 1.9% separated, 5.1% widowed, 4.1% divorced; Foreign born: 15.1%; Speak English only: 72.5%; With disability: 11.6%; Veterans: 6.5%; Ancestry: 22.5% Italian, 19.3% Irish, 9.5% American, 5.9% German, 4.9% Polish

Employment: 12.3% management, business, and financial, 6.2% computer, engineering, and science, 16.9% education, legal, community service, arts, and media, 8.1% healthcare practitioners, 16.7% service, 27.3% sales and office, 4.5% natural resources, construction, and maintenance, 7.9% production, transportation, and material moving

Income: Per capita: $37,752; Median household: $107,000; Average household: $117,324; Households with income of $100,000 or more: 52.1%; Poverty rate: 2.9%

Educational Attainment: High school diploma or higher: 90.0%; Bachelor's degree or higher: 41.1%; Graduate/professional degree or higher: 18.2%

School District(s)

Greenwood Lake Union Free SD (KG-08)
    Enrollment: 527 . . . . (845) 782-8678
Kiryas Joel Village Union Free SD (PK-KG)
    Enrollment: 119 . . . . (845) 782-2300
Monroe-Woodbury Central SD (KG-12)
    Enrollment: 7,005 . . . . (845) 460-6200

Four-year College(s)

Uta Mesivta of Kiryas Joel (Private, Not-for-profit, Jewish)
    Enrollment: 1,864 . . . . (845) 783-9901
    Tuition: In-state $11,500; Out-of-state $11,500
Yeshivas Maharit D'Satmar (Private, Not-for-profit)
    Enrollment: 99 . . . . (845) 782-1380
    Tuition: In-state $11,500; Out-of-state $11,500

Housing: Homeownership rate: 76.9%; Median home value: $313,800; Median year structure built: 1975; Homeowner vacancy rate: 1.2%; Median selected monthly owner costs: $2,633 with a mortgage, $1,279 without a mortgage; Median gross rent: $1,535 per month; Rental vacancy rate: 3.1%

Health Insurance: 91.9% have insurance; 75.9% have private insurance; 26.7% have public insurance; 8.1% do not have insurance; 2.7% of children under 18 do not have insurance

Safety: Violent crime rate: 10.4 per 10,000 population; Property crime rate: 154.0 per 10,000 population

Transportation: Commute: 79.9% car, 9.5% public transportation, 2.3% walk, 3.3% work from home; Mean travel time to work: 33.5 minutes

Additional Information Contacts

Village of Monroe . . . . (845) 782-8341
    http://www.villageofmonroe.org

MONTGOMERY (town). Covers a land area of 50.256 square miles and a water area of 0.933 square miles. Located at 41.54° N. Lat; 74.21° W. Long. Elevation is 358 feet.

Population: 23,664; Growth (since 2000): 13.3%; Density: 470.9 persons per square mile; Race: 83.5% White, 6.9% Black/African American, 1.6% Asian, 0.0% American Indian/Alaska Native, 0.3% Native Hawaiian/Other Pacific Islander, 2.5% Two or more races, 14.8% Hispanic of any race; Average household size: 2.82; Median age: 38.3; Age under 18: 22.8%; Age 65 and over: 14.5%; Males per 100 females: 94.9; Marriage status: 31.6% never married, 52.0% now married, 2.3% separated, 6.4% widowed, 9.9% divorced; Foreign born: 6.2%; Speak English only: 87.7%; With disability: 13.1%; Veterans: 7.0%; Ancestry: 19.4% Irish, 17.9% Italian, 14.1% German, 14.0% American, 6.5% English

Employment: 10.8% management, business, and financial, 5.2% computer, engineering, and science, 14.2% education, legal, community service, arts, and media, 4.4% healthcare practitioners, 17.0% service, 27.4% sales and office, 8.4% natural resources, construction, and maintenance, 12.6% production, transportation, and material moving

Income: Per capita: $32,414; Median household: $75,587; Average household: $89,612; Households with income of $100,000 or more: 37.3%; Poverty rate: 7.6%

Educational Attainment: High school diploma or higher: 91.1%; Bachelor's degree or higher: 26.4%; Graduate/professional degree or higher: 11.3%

School District(s)

Valley Central SD (Montgomery) (KG-12)
    Enrollment: 4,362 . . . . (845) 457-2400

Housing: Homeownership rate: 71.4%; Median home value: $230,500; Median year structure built: 1970; Homeowner vacancy rate: 1.9%; Median selected monthly owner costs: $2,128 with a mortgage, $809 without a mortgage; Median gross rent: $1,172 per month; Rental vacancy rate: 4.1%

Health Insurance: 94.7% have insurance; 78.0% have private insurance; 30.4% have public insurance; 5.3% do not have insurance; 2.7% of children under 18 do not have insurance

Transportation: Commute: 89.6% car, 4.7% public transportation, 1.6% walk, 3.3% work from home; Mean travel time to work: 31.8 minutes

Airports: Orange County (general aviation)

Additional Information Contacts

Town of Montgomery . . . . (845) 457-2660
    http://www.townofmontgomery.com

MONTGOMERY (village).

Covers a land area of 1.406 square miles and a water area of 0.042 square miles. Located at 41.52° N. Lat; 74.24° W. Long. Elevation is 358 feet.

Population: 4,526; Growth (since 2000): 24.5%; Density: 3,219.8 persons per square mile; Race: 85.3% White, 5.1% Black/African American, 1.3% Asian, 0.0% American Indian/Alaska Native, 1.3% Native Hawaiian/Other Pacific Islander, 4.1% Two or more races, 14.6% Hispanic of any race; Average household size: 2.83; Median age: 41.4; Age under 18: 23.3%; Age 65 and over: 15.3%; Males per 100 females: 91.9; Marriage status: 27.8% never married, 55.8% now married, 2.3% separated, 6.4% widowed, 10.0% divorced; Foreign born: 3.9%; Speak English only: 87.6%; With disability: 13.3%; Veterans: 7.2%; Ancestry: 18.2% Irish, 15.5% Italian, 15.0% German, 14.9% American, 7.4% English

Employment: 12.7% management, business, and financial, 4.1% computer, engineering, and science, 15.9% education, legal, community service, arts, and media, 3.6% healthcare practitioners, 13.3% service, 28.3% sales and office, 11.6% natural resources, construction, and maintenance, 10.5% production, transportation, and material moving

Income: Per capita: $33,068; Median household: $83,292; Average household: $90,747; Households with income of $100,000 or more: 41.2%; Poverty rate: 5.2%

Educational Attainment: High school diploma or higher: 88.9%; Bachelor's degree or higher: 27.7%; Graduate/professional degree or higher: 11.0%

School District(s)

Valley Central SD (Montgomery) (KG-12)

    Enrollment: 4,362 . . . . (845) 457-2400

Housing: Homeownership rate: 61.8%; Median home value: $234,600; Median year structure built: 1977; Homeowner vacancy rate: 2.2%; Median selected monthly owner costs: $2,132 with a mortgage, $937 without a mortgage; Median gross rent: $1,175 per month; Rental vacancy rate: 6.0%

Health Insurance: 96.4% have insurance; 86.0% have private insurance; 28.2% have public insurance; 3.6% do not have insurance; 2.7% of children under 18 do not have insurance

Safety: Violent crime rate: 0.0 per 10,000 population; Property crime rate: 40.3 per 10,000 population

Transportation: Commute: 94.3% car, 0.4% public transportation, 0.4% walk, 1.8% work from home; Mean travel time to work: 31.5 minutes

Airports: Orange County (general aviation)

MOUNT HOPE (town).

Covers a land area of 25.134 square miles and a water area of 0.362 square miles. Located at 41.46° N. Lat; 74.53° W. Long. Elevation is 823 feet.

Population: 6,993; Growth (since 2000): 5.3%; Density: 278.2 persons per square mile; Race: 72.0% White, 16.6% Black/African American, 1.8% Asian, 0.2% American Indian/Alaska Native, 0.0% Native Hawaiian/Other Pacific Islander, 4.6% Two or more races, 16.5% Hispanic of any race; Average household size: 2.90; Median age: 44.4; Age under 18: 16.9%; Age 65 and over: 12.1%; Males per 100 females: 165.2; Marriage status: 34.9% never married, 49.4% now married, 2.9% separated, 3.0% widowed, 12.7% divorced; Foreign born: 8.4%; Speak English only: 82.9%; With disability: 13.0%; Veterans: 7.1%; Ancestry: 17.3% Irish, 16.1% Italian, 15.5% American, 11.1% German, 6.0% English

Employment: 11.5% management, business, and financial, 2.8% computer, engineering, and science, 15.1% education, legal, community service, arts, and media, 4.2% healthcare practitioners, 22.2% service, 21.6% sales and office, 14.2% natural resources, construction, and maintenance, 8.6% production, transportation, and material moving

Income: Per capita: $29,926; Median household: $81,722; Average household: $101,253; Households with income of $100,000 or more: 39.3%; Poverty rate: 12.5%

Educational Attainment: High school diploma or higher: 90.5%; Bachelor's degree or higher: 21.1%; Graduate/professional degree or higher: 9.1%

Housing: Homeownership rate: 87.6%; Median home value: $240,000; Median year structure built: 1972; Homeowner vacancy rate: 4.2%; Median selected monthly owner costs: $2,059 with a mortgage, $861 without a mortgage; Median gross rent: $1,317 per month; Rental vacancy rate: 2.9%

Health Insurance: 94.6% have insurance; 76.8% have private insurance; 30.0% have public insurance; 5.4% do not have insurance; 3.4% of children under 18 do not have insurance

Safety: Violent crime rate: 0.0 per 10,000 population; Property crime rate: 7.2 per 10,000 population

Transportation: Commute: 91.0% car, 3.3% public transportation, 0.3% walk, 5.3% work from home; Mean travel time to work: 42.1 minutes

Additional Information Contacts

Town of Mount Hope . . . . (845) 386-1460

    http://townofmounthope.org/content

MOUNTAIN LODGE PARK (CDP).

Covers a land area of 1.185 square miles and a water area of <.001 square miles. Located at 41.39° N. Lat; 74.14° W. Long. Elevation is 784 feet.

Population: 1,516; Growth (since 2000): n/a; Density: 1,279.2 persons per square mile; Race: 93.1% White, 2.9% Black/African American, 0.0% Asian, 0.0% American Indian/Alaska Native, 0.0% Native Hawaiian/Other Pacific Islander, 0.0% Two or more races, 10.2% Hispanic of any race; Average household size: 2.61; Median age: 28.7; Age under 18: 22.4%; Age 65 and over: 3.8%; Males per 100 females: 100.3; Marriage status: 47.8% never married, 36.9% now married, 0.0% separated, 4.7% widowed, 10.6% divorced; Foreign born: 4.0%; Speak English only: 90.7%; With disability: 21.4%; Veterans: 1.5%; Ancestry: 34.4% Irish, 27.1% German, 20.9% Italian, 16.6% American, 5.6% Swiss

Employment: 5.7% management, business, and financial, 3.1% computer, engineering, and science, 10.5% education, legal, community service, arts, and media, 8.5% healthcare practitioners, 15.7% service, 31.4% sales and office, 6.2% natural resources, construction, and maintenance, 19.0% production, transportation, and material moving

Income: Per capita: $30,265; Median household: $69,917; Average household: $77,089; Households with income of $100,000 or more: 26.9%; Poverty rate: 10.3%

Educational Attainment: High school diploma or higher: 83.3%; Bachelor's degree or higher: 16.1%; Graduate/professional degree or higher: 6.5%

Housing: Homeownership rate: 88.0%; Median home value: $177,800; Median year structure built: 1949; Homeowner vacancy rate: 8.4%; Median selected monthly owner costs: $1,755 with a mortgage, $569 without a mortgage; Median gross rent: n/a per month; Rental vacancy rate: 0.0%

Health Insurance: 92.7% have insurance; 88.8% have private insurance; 20.5% have public insurance; 7.3% do not have insurance; 15.0% of children under 18 do not have insurance

Transportation: Commute: 91.1% car, 7.7% public transportation, 0.0% walk, 1.2% work from home; Mean travel time to work: 44.6 minutes

MOUNTAINVILLE (unincorporated postal area)

ZCTA: 10953

    Covers a land area of 1.102 square miles and a water area of 0.013 square miles. Located at 41.40° N. Lat; 74.08° W. Long. Elevation is 299 feet.

Population: 125; Growth (since 2000): n/a; Density: 113.4 persons per square mile; Race: 100.0% White, 0.0% Black/African American, 0.0% Asian, 0.0% American Indian/Alaska Native, 0.0% Native Hawaiian/Other Pacific Islander, 0.0% Two or more races, 0.0% Hispanic of any race; Average household size: 1.92; Median age: 45.5; Age under 18: 19.2%; Age 65 and over: 20.0%; Males per 100 females: 121.1; Marriage status: 8.9% never married, 66.3% now married, 0.0% separated, 0.0% widowed, 24.8% divorced; Foreign born: 0.0%; Speak English only: 80.0%; With disability: 7.2%; Veterans: 0.0%; Ancestry: 55.2% American, 20.0% Eastern European, 16.8% Irish, 16.8% Italian, 8.0% English

Employment: 31.8% management, business, and financial, 0.0% computer, engineering, and science, 13.6% education, legal, community service, arts, and media, 0.0% healthcare practitioners, 0.0% service, 54.5% sales and office, 0.0% natural resources, construction, and maintenance, 0.0% production, transportation, and material moving

Income: Per capita: $58,662; Median household: n/a; Average household: $108,171; Households with income of $100,000 or more: 47.7%; Poverty rate: n/a

Educational Attainment: High school diploma or higher: 100.0%; Bachelor's degree or higher: 33.7%; Graduate/professional degree or higher: 33.7%

Housing: Homeownership rate: 100.0%; Median home value: $467,100; Median year structure built: 1967; Homeowner vacancy rate: 0.0%; Median selected monthly owner costs: $1,985 with a mortgage, $0 without a mortgage; Median gross rent: n/a per month; Rental vacancy rate: 0.0%

Health Insurance: 100.0% have insurance; 100.0% have private insurance; 20.0% have public insurance; 0.0% do not have insurance; 0.0% of children under 18 do not have insurance

Transportation: Commute: 100.0% car, 0.0% public transportation, 0.0% walk, 0.0% work from home; Mean travel time to work: 0.0 minutes

NEW HAMPTON (unincorporated postal area)

ZCTA: 10958

Covers a land area of 22.866 square miles and a water area of 0.139 square miles. Located at 41.37° N. Lat; 74.43° W. Long. Elevation is 538 feet.

Population: 3,286; Growth (since 2000): 10.8%; Density: 143.7 persons per square mile; Race: 89.3% White, 7.2% Black/African American, 0.3% Asian, 0.0% American Indian/Alaska Native, 0.0% Native Hawaiian/Other Pacific Islander, 0.5% Two or more races, 15.1% Hispanic of any race; Average household size: 3.00; Median age: 41.3; Age under 18: 20.1%; Age 65 and over: 13.2%; Males per 100 females: 112.5; Marriage status: 33.4% never married, 52.9% now married, 0.9% separated, 6.8% widowed, 6.8% divorced; Foreign born: 7.0%; Speak English only: 86.3%; With disability: 14.7%; Veterans: 11.6%; Ancestry: 20.5% American, 17.0% Irish, 16.6% German, 16.2% Italian, 8.9% Polish

Employment: 17.1% management, business, and financial, 3.3% computer, engineering, and science, 13.8% education, legal, community service, arts, and media, 3.1% healthcare practitioners, 17.0% service, 17.8% sales and office, 15.9% natural resources, construction, and maintenance, 11.9% production, transportation, and material moving

Income: Per capita: $31,177; Median household: $102,396; Average household: $103,201; Households with income of $100,000 or more: 52.4%; Poverty rate: 2.8%

Educational Attainment: High school diploma or higher: 87.1%; Bachelor's degree or higher: 33.5%; Graduate/professional degree or higher: 13.6%

Housing: Homeownership rate: 85.6%; Median home value: $290,400; Median year structure built: 1966; Homeowner vacancy rate: 0.0%; Median selected monthly owner costs: $2,255 with a mortgage, $981 without a mortgage; Median gross rent: $1,107 per month; Rental vacancy rate: 9.8%

Health Insurance: 93.7% have insurance; 79.5% have private insurance; 25.7% have public insurance; 6.3% do not have insurance; 0.6% of children under 18 do not have insurance

Transportation: Commute: 92.7% car, 3.1% public transportation, 2.3% walk, 0.8% work from home; Mean travel time to work: 30.0 minutes

NEW WINDSOR (CDP).

Covers a land area of 3.762 square miles and a water area of 0.042 square miles. Located at 41.47° N. Lat; 74.03° W. Long. Elevation is 161 feet.

Population: 8,916; Growth (since 2000): -1.8%; Density: 2,370.3 persons per square mile; Race: 76.2% White, 10.2% Black/African American, 1.2% Asian, 0.6% American Indian/Alaska Native, 0.0% Native Hawaiian/Other Pacific Islander, 3.9% Two or more races, 27.8% Hispanic of any race; Average household size: 2.53; Median age: 42.3; Age under 18: 19.6%; Age 65 and over: 16.3%; Males per 100 females: 95.3; Marriage status: 35.8% never married, 50.3% now married, 2.0% separated, 4.5% widowed, 9.4% divorced; Foreign born: 10.2%; Speak English only: 74.4%; With disability: 10.5%; Veterans: 8.6%; Ancestry: 15.9% Italian, 14.2% Irish, 10.2% German, 7.4% American, 3.7% Polish

Employment: 12.6% management, business, and financial, 2.7% computer, engineering, and science, 12.1% education, legal, community service, arts, and media, 6.0% healthcare practitioners, 18.2% service, 26.3% sales and office, 7.1% natural resources, construction, and maintenance, 15.0% production, transportation, and material moving

Income: Per capita: $34,918; Median household: $70,074; Average household: $85,823; Households with income of $100,000 or more: 31.3%; Poverty rate: 5.0%

Educational Attainment: High school diploma or higher: 92.5%; Bachelor's degree or higher: 23.2%; Graduate/professional degree or higher: 8.9%

School District(s)

Cornwall Central SD (KG-12)
    Enrollment: 3,238 . . . . (845) 534-8009
Newburgh City SD (PK-12)
    Enrollment: 11,390 . . . . (845) 563-3510
Washingtonville Central SD (PK-12)
    Enrollment: 4,137 . . . . (845) 497-4000

Four-year College(s)

Yeshiva Ohr Naftoli (Private, Not-for-profit)
    Enrollment: 24 . . . . (845) 784-4020
    Tuition: In-state $9,050; Out-of-state $9,050

Housing: Homeownership rate: 70.5%; Median home value: $228,900; Median year structure built: 1967; Homeowner vacancy rate: 5.2%; Median selected monthly owner costs: $2,027 with a mortgage, $902 without a mortgage; Median gross rent: $1,231 per month; Rental vacancy rate: 0.0%

Health Insurance: 94.3% have insurance; 76.8% have private insurance; 31.9% have public insurance; 5.7% do not have insurance; 0.0% of children under 18 do not have insurance

Newspapers: The Sentinel (weekly circulation 6,000)

Transportation: Commute: 92.4% car, 2.6% public transportation, 0.4% walk, 2.4% work from home; Mean travel time to work: 32.0 minutes

NEW WINDSOR (town).

Covers a land area of 34.070 square miles and a water area of 2.994 square miles. Located at 41.47° N. Lat; 74.11° W. Long. Elevation is 161 feet.

History: Was home of George Clinton. De Witt Clinton was born here.

Population: 26,799; Growth (since 2000): 17.2%; Density: 786.6 persons per square mile; Race: 69.6% White, 12.8% Black/African American, 3.4% Asian, 0.2% American Indian/Alaska Native, 0.0% Native Hawaiian/Other Pacific Islander, 4.1% Two or more races, 23.4% Hispanic of any race; Average household size: 2.78; Median age: 38.6; Age under 18: 22.4%; Age 65 and over: 14.1%; Males per 100 females: 95.4; Marriage status: 36.2% never married, 49.5% now married, 1.8% separated, 5.4% widowed, 8.9% divorced; Foreign born: 11.7%; Speak English only: 74.6%; With disability: 12.0%; Veterans: 8.0%; Ancestry: 18.0% Italian, 17.0% Irish, 9.3% German, 8.6% American, 4.3% Polish

Employment: 16.1% management, business, and financial, 4.0% computer, engineering, and science, 12.1% education, legal, community service, arts, and media, 6.6% healthcare practitioners, 17.8% service, 25.3% sales and office, 6.5% natural resources, construction, and maintenance, 11.5% production, transportation, and material moving

Income: Per capita: $34,976; Median household: $77,210; Average household: $95,169; Households with income of $100,000 or more: 37.3%; Poverty rate: 4.6%

Educational Attainment: High school diploma or higher: 94.2%; Bachelor's degree or higher: 30.9%; Graduate/professional degree or higher: 12.9%

School District(s)

Cornwall Central SD (KG-12)
    Enrollment: 3,238 . . . . (845) 534-8009
Newburgh City SD (PK-12)
    Enrollment: 11,390 . . . . (845) 563-3510
Washingtonville Central SD (PK-12)
    Enrollment: 4,137 . . . . (845) 497-4000

Four-year College(s)

Yeshiva Ohr Naftoli (Private, Not-for-profit)
    Enrollment: 24 . . . . (845) 784-4020
    Tuition: In-state $9,050; Out-of-state $9,050

Housing: Homeownership rate: 73.5%; Median home value: $248,900; Median year structure built: 1977; Homeowner vacancy rate: 3.3%; Median selected monthly owner costs: $2,297 with a mortgage, $895 without a mortgage; Median gross rent: $1,223 per month; Rental vacancy rate: 1.8%

Health Insurance: 94.6% have insurance; 78.0% have private insurance; 28.9% have public insurance; 5.4% do not have insurance; 1.8% of children under 18 do not have insurance

Safety: Violent crime rate: 9.4 per 10,000 population; Property crime rate: 131.5 per 10,000 population

Newspapers: The Sentinel (weekly circulation 6,000)

Transportation: Commute: 89.0% car, 5.3% public transportation, 1.1% walk, 3.6% work from home; Mean travel time to work: 34.3 minutes

Additional Information Contacts

Town of New Windsor . . . . (845) 563-4611
    http://town.new-windsor.ny.us

NEWBURGH (city).

Covers a land area of 3.804 square miles and a water area of 0.980 square miles. Located at 41.50° N. Lat; 74.02° W. Long. Elevation is 131 feet.

History: Has many old houses, and the streets run sharply to the river. At Hasbrouck House (1750; now a Museum), Washington made his headquarters from April 1782 to Aug. 1783. It was in Newburgh that the

Continental Army was disbanded. Mt. St. Mary College is in the city. West Point is located a few miles to the south. Settled 1709 by Palatines; Incorporated 1800.

Population: 28,444; Growth (since 2000): 0.7%; Density: 7,476.8 persons per square mile; Race: 35.1% White, 27.0% Black/African American, 1.2% Asian, 0.6% American Indian/Alaska Native, 0.0% Native Hawaiian/Other Pacific Islander, 4.5% Two or more races, 50.7% Hispanic of any race; Average household size: 3.00; Median age: 27.9; Age under 18: 33.0%; Age 65 and over: 8.6%; Males per 100 females: 94.6; Marriage status: 50.1% never married, 36.9% now married, 5.0% separated, 5.1% widowed, 7.9% divorced; Foreign born: 24.1%; Speak English only: 54.3%; With disability: 12.5%; Veterans: 3.4%; Ancestry: 8.1% American, 5.6% Irish, 5.0% Italian, 2.9% German, 2.6% Jamaican

Employment: 8.5% management, business, and financial, 2.2% computer, engineering, and science, 7.2% education, legal, community service, arts, and media, 3.0% healthcare practitioners, 28.3% service, 21.4% sales and office, 9.4% natural resources, construction, and maintenance, 20.0% production, transportation, and material moving

Income: Per capita: $18,312; Median household: $36,922; Average household: $54,121; Households with income of $100,000 or more: 15.7%; Poverty rate: 31.2%

Educational Attainment: High school diploma or higher: 72.0%; Bachelor's degree or higher: 14.2%; Graduate/professional degree or higher: 6.3%

School District(s)
Marlboro Central SD (KG-12)
 Enrollment: 1,942 . . . . (845) 236-5802
Newburgh City SD (PK-12)
 Enrollment: 11,390 . . . . (845) 563-3510
Newburgh Preparatory Charter High School (09-12)
 Enrollment: 65 . . . . (845) 565-4040
Valley Central SD (Montgomery) (KG-12)
 Enrollment: 4,362 . . . . (845) 457-2400

Four-year College(s)
Mount Saint Mary College (Private, Not-for-profit, Roman Catholic)
 Enrollment: 2,365 . . . . (845) 561-0800
 Tuition: In-state $29,920; Out-of-state $29,920

Housing: Homeownership rate: 32.0%; Median home value: $170,900; Median year structure built: Before 1940; Homeowner vacancy rate: 7.7%; Median selected monthly owner costs: $1,909 with a mortgage, $788 without a mortgage; Median gross rent: $1,118 per month; Rental vacancy rate: 8.3%

Health Insurance: 85.5% have insurance; 40.4% have private insurance; 52.8% have public insurance; 14.5% do not have insurance; 3.5% of children under 18 do not have insurance

Hospitals: Saint Luke's Cornwall Hospital (259 beds)

Safety: Violent crime rate: 123.6 per 10,000 population; Property crime rate: 266.0 per 10,000 population

Newspapers: Times Community Newspapers (weekly circulation 8,000)

Transportation: Commute: 71.9% car, 7.9% public transportation, 9.5% walk, 2.5% work from home; Mean travel time to work: 26.0 minutes

Airports: Stewart International (primary service/non-hub)

Additional Information Contacts
City of Newburgh . . . . (845) 569-7311
 http://www.cityofnewburgh-ny.gov

NEWBURGH (town).
Covers a land area of 42.678 square miles and a water area of 4.265 square miles. Located at 41.56° N. Lat; 74.06° W. Long. Elevation is 131 feet.

Population: 30,697; Growth (since 2000): 11.4%; Density: 719.3 persons per square mile; Race: 74.5% White, 12.8% Black/African American, 2.0% Asian, 0.1% American Indian/Alaska Native, 0.0% Native Hawaiian/Other Pacific Islander, 4.4% Two or more races, 18.8% Hispanic of any race; Average household size: 2.79; Median age: 41.2; Age under 18: 21.6%; Age 65 and over: 15.0%; Males per 100 females: 95.7; Marriage status: 28.4% never married, 55.8% now married, 2.1% separated, 6.2% widowed, 9.7% divorced; Foreign born: 9.5%; Speak English only: 81.0%; With disability: 10.4%; Veterans: 7.9%; Ancestry: 23.0% Italian, 18.2% Irish, 9.6% German, 9.0% American, 5.9% English

Employment: 13.3% management, business, and financial, 4.1% computer, engineering, and science, 13.0% education, legal, community service, arts, and media, 6.3% healthcare practitioners, 17.5% service, 26.6% sales and office, 9.0% natural resources, construction, and maintenance, 10.2% production, transportation, and material moving

Income: Per capita: $37,686; Median household: $86,010; Average household: $103,151; Households with income of $100,000 or more: 41.3%; Poverty rate: 7.0%

Educational Attainment: High school diploma or higher: 93.2%; Bachelor's degree or higher: 30.4%; Graduate/professional degree or higher: 12.2%

School District(s)
Marlboro Central SD (KG-12)
 Enrollment: 1,942 . . . . (845) 236-5802
Newburgh City SD (PK-12)
 Enrollment: 11,390 . . . . (845) 563-3510
Newburgh Preparatory Charter High School (09-12)
 Enrollment: 65 . . . . (845) 565-4040
Valley Central SD (Montgomery) (KG-12)
 Enrollment: 4,362 . . . . (845) 457-2400

Four-year College(s)
Mount Saint Mary College (Private, Not-for-profit, Roman Catholic)
 Enrollment: 2,365 . . . . (845) 561-0800
 Tuition: In-state $29,920; Out-of-state $29,920

Housing: Homeownership rate: 81.2%; Median home value: $250,600; Median year structure built: 1969; Homeowner vacancy rate: 2.8%; Median selected monthly owner costs: $2,210 with a mortgage, $805 without a mortgage; Median gross rent: $1,438 per month; Rental vacancy rate: 5.3%

Health Insurance: 94.2% have insurance; 77.7% have private insurance; 30.5% have public insurance; 5.8% do not have insurance; 5.4% of children under 18 do not have insurance

Hospitals: Saint Luke's Cornwall Hospital (259 beds)

Safety: Violent crime rate: 7.8 per 10,000 population; Property crime rate: 343.1 per 10,000 population

Newspapers: Times Community Newspapers (weekly circulation 8,000)

Transportation: Commute: 89.8% car, 4.8% public transportation, 0.5% walk, 4.4% work from home; Mean travel time to work: 31.0 minutes

Airports: Stewart International (primary service/non-hub)

Additional Information Contacts
Town of Newburgh . . . . (845) 564-4554
 http://www.townofnewburgh.org

ORANGE LAKE (CDP).
Covers a land area of 6.044 square miles and a water area of 0.656 square miles. Located at 41.54° N. Lat; 74.09° W. Long. Elevation is 492 feet.

Population: 6,603; Growth (since 2000): 8.5%; Density: 1,092.4 persons per square mile; Race: 58.7% White, 22.8% Black/African American, 4.4% Asian, 0.3% American Indian/Alaska Native, 0.0% Native Hawaiian/Other Pacific Islander, 7.0% Two or more races, 24.0% Hispanic of any race; Average household size: 2.72; Median age: 40.8; Age under 18: 21.1%; Age 65 and over: 18.6%; Males per 100 females: 93.4; Marriage status: 24.2% never married, 57.3% now married, 1.7% separated, 9.0% widowed, 9.6% divorced; Foreign born: 11.4%; Speak English only: 79.8%; With disability: 10.8%; Veterans: 5.0%; Ancestry: 18.5% Irish, 14.9% Italian, 11.6% American, 6.5% German, 3.5% English

Employment: 18.5% management, business, and financial, 1.2% computer, engineering, and science, 11.8% education, legal, community service, arts, and media, 10.7% healthcare practitioners, 17.6% service, 27.2% sales and office, 7.9% natural resources, construction, and maintenance, 5.2% production, transportation, and material moving

Income: Per capita: $41,016; Median household: $93,477; Average household: $111,785; Households with income of $100,000 or more: 46.2%; Poverty rate: 13.0%

Educational Attainment: High school diploma or higher: 94.0%; Bachelor's degree or higher: 31.9%; Graduate/professional degree or higher: 8.9%

Housing: Homeownership rate: 78.3%; Median home value: $237,400; Median year structure built: 1970; Homeowner vacancy rate: 2.2%; Median selected monthly owner costs: $2,126 with a mortgage, $668 without a mortgage; Median gross rent: $1,739 per month; Rental vacancy rate: 0.0%

Health Insurance: 96.1% have insurance; 76.3% have private insurance; 36.6% have public insurance; 3.9% do not have insurance; 0.0% of children under 18 do not have insurance

Transportation: Commute: 90.1% car, 4.0% public transportation, 0.0% walk, 5.4% work from home; Mean travel time to work: 35.0 minutes

OTISVILLE (village). Covers a land area of 0.764 square miles and a water area of 0 square miles. Located at 41.47° N. Lat; 74.54° W. Long. Elevation is 853 feet.

Population: 1,074; Growth (since 2000): 8.6%; Density: 1,405.4 persons per square mile; Race: 86.8% White, 2.5% Black/African American, 7.4% Asian, 0.0% American Indian/Alaska Native, 0.0% Native Hawaiian/Other Pacific Islander, 1.9% Two or more races, 10.3% Hispanic of any race; Average household size: 2.89; Median age: 41.1; Age under 18: 25.2%; Age 65 and over: 11.5%; Males per 100 females: 106.6; Marriage status: 26.1% never married, 56.9% now married, 2.8% separated, 2.2% widowed, 14.7% divorced; Foreign born: 8.0%; Speak English only: 86.2%; With disability: 18.2%; Veterans: 6.1%; Ancestry: 27.6% Irish, 21.3% American, 13.6% Italian, 8.8% German, 7.8% English

Employment: 9.2% management, business, and financial, 4.0% computer, engineering, and science, 19.6% education, legal, community service, arts, and media, 2.6% healthcare practitioners, 22.8% service, 19.0% sales and office, 11.5% natural resources, construction, and maintenance, 11.3% production, transportation, and material moving

Income: Per capita: $32,600; Median household: $71,094; Average household: $90,094; Households with income of $100,000 or more: 33.7%; Poverty rate: 9.2%

Educational Attainment: High school diploma or higher: 91.9%; Bachelor's degree or higher: 30.8%; Graduate/professional degree or higher: 15.6%

School District(s)

Minisink Valley Central SD (KG-12)
  Enrollment: 3,841 . . . . (845) 355-5100

Housing: Homeownership rate: 82.2%; Median home value: $189,900; Median year structure built: Before 1940; Homeowner vacancy rate: 3.2%; Median selected monthly owner costs: $1,991 with a mortgage, $761 without a mortgage; Median gross rent: $939 per month; Rental vacancy rate: 0.0%

Health Insurance: 88.0% have insurance; 72.3% have private insurance; 29.0% have public insurance; 12.0% do not have insurance; 14.5% of children under 18 do not have insurance

Transportation: Commute: 86.4% car, 4.8% public transportation, 1.9% walk, 6.9% work from home; Mean travel time to work: 32.6 minutes

Additional Information Contacts

Village of Otisville . . . . (845) 386-5172
  http://villageofotisville.com

PINE BUSH (CDP). Covers a land area of 2.106 square miles and a water area of 0.003 square miles. Located at 41.61° N. Lat; 74.30° W. Long. Elevation is 387 feet.

Population: 1,454; Growth (since 2000): -5.5%; Density: 690.3 persons per square mile; Race: 90.5% White, 3.0% Black/African American, 0.0% Asian, 0.0% American Indian/Alaska Native, 0.0% Native Hawaiian/Other Pacific Islander, 5.1% Two or more races, 14.2% Hispanic of any race; Average household size: 1.97; Median age: 47.6; Age under 18: 22.0%; Age 65 and over: 27.5%; Males per 100 females: 81.8; Marriage status: 31.0% never married, 35.4% now married, 1.8% separated, 15.7% widowed, 17.9% divorced; Foreign born: 4.9%; Speak English only: 84.3%; With disability: 19.8%; Veterans: 8.6%; Ancestry: 21.7% Italian, 17.6% Irish, 16.4% German, 9.3% German, 6.4% English

Employment: 9.1% management, business, and financial, 1.4% computer, engineering, and science, 15.8% education, legal, community service, arts, and media, 13.3% healthcare practitioners, 28.1% service, 16.0% sales and office, 5.9% natural resources, construction, and maintenance, 10.5% production, transportation, and material moving

Income: Per capita: $25,715; Median household: $26,964; Average household: $48,582; Households with income of $100,000 or more: 15.3%; Poverty rate: 23.5%

Educational Attainment: High school diploma or higher: 85.6%; Bachelor's degree or higher: 24.7%; Graduate/professional degree or higher: 11.1%

School District(s)

Pine Bush Central SD (PK-12)
  Enrollment: 5,266 . . . . (845) 744-2031

Housing: Homeownership rate: 51.6%; Median home value: $205,200; Median year structure built: 1988; Homeowner vacancy rate: 3.6%; Median selected monthly owner costs: $1,558 with a mortgage, $830 without a mortgage; Median gross rent: $805 per month; Rental vacancy rate: 6.5%

Health Insurance: 99.4% have insurance; 63.7% have private insurance; 52.2% have public insurance; 0.6% do not have insurance; 0.0% of children under 18 do not have insurance

Transportation: Commute: 83.3% car, 0.0% public transportation, 7.4% walk, 9.3% work from home; Mean travel time to work: 25.0 minutes

PINE ISLAND (unincorporated postal area)
ZCTA: 10969

Covers a land area of 11.221 square miles and a water area of 0.008 square miles. Located at 41.29° N. Lat; 74.49° W. Long. Elevation is 410 feet.

Population: 1,341; Growth (since 2000): 23.7%; Density: 119.5 persons per square mile; Race: 87.9% White, 4.3% Black/African American, 3.2% Asian, 0.0% American Indian/Alaska Native, 0.0% Native Hawaiian/Other Pacific Islander, 4.5% Two or more races, 5.5% Hispanic of any race; Average household size: 2.68; Median age: 44.9; Age under 18: 20.3%; Age 65 and over: 15.0%; Males per 100 females: 106.4; Marriage status: 34.3% never married, 53.4% now married, 2.7% separated, 6.1% widowed, 6.2% divorced; Foreign born: 8.8%; Speak English only: 91.9%; With disability: 8.2%; Veterans: 5.1%; Ancestry: 23.1% German, 22.2% Polish, 16.4% Irish, 11.5% Italian, 8.7% Dutch

Employment: 13.9% management, business, and financial, 1.6% computer, engineering, and science, 11.9% education, legal, community service, arts, and media, 9.1% healthcare practitioners, 20.2% service, 20.4% sales and office, 4.7% natural resources, construction, and maintenance, 18.1% production, transportation, and material moving

Income: Per capita: $42,143; Median household: $83,333; Average household: $111,936; Households with income of $100,000 or more: 41.4%; Poverty rate: 1.6%

Educational Attainment: High school diploma or higher: 94.2%; Bachelor's degree or higher: 22.2%; Graduate/professional degree or higher: 8.0%

Housing: Homeownership rate: 83.6%; Median home value: $283,600; Median year structure built: 1965; Homeowner vacancy rate: 0.0%; Median selected monthly owner costs: $2,271 with a mortgage, $784 without a mortgage; Median gross rent: $1,151 per month; Rental vacancy rate: 0.0%

Health Insurance: 95.4% have insurance; 83.5% have private insurance; 19.2% have public insurance; 4.6% do not have insurance; 0.0% of children under 18 do not have insurance

Transportation: Commute: 87.3% car, 4.2% public transportation, 0.0% walk, 8.5% work from home; Mean travel time to work: 36.1 minutes

PORT JERVIS (city). Covers a land area of 2.529 square miles and a water area of 0.180 square miles. Located at 41.38° N. Lat; 74.69° W. Long. Elevation is 440 feet.

History: Grew after opening (1828) of Delaware and Hudson Canal. It is one of the largest equestrian centers in nation. Settled before 1700, Incorporated 1907.

Population: 8,670; Growth (since 2000): -2.1%; Density: 3,428.3 persons per square mile; Race: 75.0% White, 14.7% Black/African American, 1.2% Asian, 0.8% American Indian/Alaska Native, 0.0% Native Hawaiian/Other Pacific Islander, 5.1% Two or more races, 8.5% Hispanic of any race; Average household size: 2.51; Median age: 40.5; Age under 18: 27.3%; Age 65 and over: 16.3%; Males per 100 females: 92.9; Marriage status: 37.3% never married, 41.6% now married, 1.9% separated, 9.5% widowed, 11.5% divorced; Foreign born: 5.6%; Speak English only: 92.9%; With disability: 17.8%; Veterans: 8.0%; Ancestry: 17.6% American, 17.2% German, 15.2% Irish, 11.4% Italian, 7.6% Polish

Employment: 8.4% management, business, and financial, 2.9% computer, engineering, and science, 8.7% education, legal, community service, arts, and media, 5.0% healthcare practitioners, 28.0% service, 20.1% sales and office, 9.2% natural resources, construction, and maintenance, 17.8% production, transportation, and material moving

Income: Per capita: $27,567; Median household: $46,500; Average household: $67,640; Households with income of $100,000 or more: 22.5%; Poverty rate: 18.0%

Educational Attainment: High school diploma or higher: 84.4%; Bachelor's degree or higher: 18.7%; Graduate/professional degree or higher: 6.2%

School District(s)

Port Jervis City SD (KG-12)
  Enrollment: 2,626 . . . . (845) 858-3100

Housing: Homeownership rate: 53.4%; Median home value: $160,800; Median year structure built: Before 1940; Homeowner vacancy rate: 4.5%; Median selected monthly owner costs: $1,632 with a mortgage, $791 without a mortgage; Median gross rent: $960 per month; Rental vacancy rate: 3.5%

Health Insurance: 91.8% have insurance; 60.6% have private insurance; 42.9% have public insurance; 8.2% do not have insurance; 4.2% of children under 18 do not have insurance
Hospitals: Bon Secours Community Hospital (183 beds)
Safety: Violent crime rate: 30.5 per 10,000 population; Property crime rate: 260.3 per 10,000 population
Transportation: Commute: 80.1% car, 0.6% public transportation, 8.9% walk, 6.5% work from home; Mean travel time to work: 26.0 minutes
Additional Information Contacts
City of Port Jervis . . . . (845) 858-4000
http://portjervisny.org

ROCK TAVERN (unincorporated postal area)
ZCTA: 12575
Covers a land area of 9.893 square miles and a water area of 0.254 square miles. Located at 41.47° N. Lat; 74.18° W. Long. Elevation is 417 feet.
Population: 2,034; Growth (since 2000): -2.6%; Density: 205.6 persons per square mile; Race: 81.2% White, 11.8% Black/African American, 1.9% Asian, 0.0% American Indian/Alaska Native, 0.0% Native Hawaiian/Other Pacific Islander, 2.1% Two or more races, 17.0% Hispanic of any race; Average household size: 2.66; Median age: 43.2; Age under 18: 18.5%; Age 65 and over: 8.4%; Males per 100 females: 94.7; Marriage status: 26.6% never married, 60.4% now married, 0.0% separated, 1.9% widowed, 11.1% divorced; Foreign born: 10.7%; Speak English only: 86.8%; With disability: 7.8%; Veterans: 6.9%; Ancestry: 29.3% Irish, 19.2% Italian, 17.4% American, 10.8% Polish, 4.5% German
Employment: 32.1% management, business, and financial, 8.9% computer, engineering, and science, 7.4% education, legal, community service, arts, and media, 7.1% healthcare practitioners, 12.4% service, 18.6% sales and office, 4.7% natural resources, construction, and maintenance, 9.0% production, transportation, and material moving
Income: Per capita: $50,728; Median household: $101,912; Average household: $130,990; Households with income of $100,000 or more: 51.7%; Poverty rate: n/a
Educational Attainment: High school diploma or higher: 100.0%; Bachelor's degree or higher: 43.8%; Graduate/professional degree or higher: 14.6%
Housing: Homeownership rate: 94.8%; Median home value: $341,600; Median year structure built: 1992; Homeowner vacancy rate: 0.0%; Median selected monthly owner costs: $2,556 with a mortgage, $1,019 without a mortgage; Median gross rent: n/a per month; Rental vacancy rate: 0.0%
Health Insurance: 95.1% have insurance; 93.7% have private insurance; 11.0% have public insurance; 4.9% do not have insurance; 0.0% of children under 18 do not have insurance
Transportation: Commute: 79.3% car, 12.4% public transportation, 1.8% walk, 6.5% work from home; Mean travel time to work: 50.7 minutes

SALISBURY MILLS (CDP). Covers a land area of 0.499 square miles and a water area of 0.005 square miles. Located at 41.43° N. Lat; 74.11° W. Long. Elevation is 305 feet.
Population: 241; Growth (since 2000): n/a; Density: 483.2 persons per square mile; Race: 87.6% White, 0.0% Black/African American, 0.0% Asian, 0.0% American Indian/Alaska Native, 0.0% Native Hawaiian/Other Pacific Islander, 8.7% Two or more races, 0.0% Hispanic of any race; Average household size: 3.89; Median age: 53.5; Age under 18: 6.6%; Age 65 and over: 19.1%; Males per 100 females: 103.8; Marriage status: 46.8% never married, 36.9% now married, 0.0% separated, 4.3% widowed, 12.0% divorced; Foreign born: 0.0%; Speak English only: 100.0%; With disability: 18.3%; Veterans: 7.6%; Ancestry: 36.1% Irish, 31.5% Italian, 24.9% English, 17.4% Polish, 16.2% Scotch-Irish
Employment: 15.2% management, business, and financial, 10.9% computer, engineering, and science, 10.9% education, legal, community service, arts, and media, 0.0% healthcare practitioners, 8.7% service, 26.1% sales and office, 28.3% natural resources, construction, and maintenance, 0.0% production, transportation, and material moving
Income: Per capita: $46,923; Median household: $143,750; Average household: $177,568; Households with income of $100,000 or more: 75.8%; Poverty rate: 8.7%
Educational Attainment: High school diploma or higher: 93.4%; Bachelor's degree or higher: 25.3%; Graduate/professional degree or higher: 11.5%

Housing: Homeownership rate: 85.5%; Median home value: $338,200; Median year structure built: 1945; Homeowner vacancy rate: 0.0%; Median selected monthly owner costs: $2,325 with a mortgage, n/a without a mortgage; Median gross rent: n/a per month; Rental vacancy rate: 0.0%
Health Insurance: 100.0% have insurance; 68.5% have private insurance; 51.9% have public insurance; 0.0% do not have insurance; 0.0% of children under 18 do not have insurance
Transportation: Commute: 69.4% car, 18.8% public transportation, 0.0% walk, 11.8% work from home; Mean travel time to work: 0.0 minutes

SCOTCHTOWN (CDP). Covers a land area of 4.226 square miles and a water area of 0.012 square miles. Located at 41.47° N. Lat; 74.37° W. Long. Elevation is 722 feet.
Population: 8,897; Growth (since 2000): -0.6%; Density: 2,105.5 persons per square mile; Race: 52.6% White, 25.0% Black/African American, 6.0% Asian, 1.3% American Indian/Alaska Native, 0.0% Native Hawaiian/Other Pacific Islander, 6.5% Two or more races, 24.9% Hispanic of any race; Average household size: 2.66; Median age: 38.8; Age under 18: 21.3%; Age 65 and over: 13.4%; Males per 100 females: 94.5; Marriage status: 36.9% never married, 52.8% now married, 1.1% separated, 3.8% widowed, 6.5% divorced; Foreign born: 12.4%; Speak English only: 73.5%; With disability: 14.3%; Veterans: 5.9%; Ancestry: 15.5% American, 14.2% Italian, 10.3% Irish, 6.1% German, 4.0% Polish
Employment: 11.5% management, business, and financial, 3.9% computer, engineering, and science, 8.0% education, legal, community service, arts, and media, 8.6% healthcare practitioners, 21.2% service, 30.4% sales and office, 5.6% natural resources, construction, and maintenance, 10.9% production, transportation, and material moving
Income: Per capita: $30,821; Median household: $66,542; Average household: $80,412; Households with income of $100,000 or more: 29.0%; Poverty rate: 7.3%
Educational Attainment: High school diploma or higher: 91.1%; Bachelor's degree or higher: 23.0%; Graduate/professional degree or higher: 9.3%
Housing: Homeownership rate: 59.1%; Median home value: $250,400; Median year structure built: 1976; Homeowner vacancy rate: 3.6%; Median selected monthly owner costs: $2,316 with a mortgage, $761 without a mortgage; Median gross rent: $1,278 per month; Rental vacancy rate: 4.1%
Health Insurance: 94.5% have insurance; 77.2% have private insurance; 26.8% have public insurance; 5.5% do not have insurance; 3.8% of children under 18 do not have insurance
Transportation: Commute: 93.5% car, 2.8% public transportation, 0.3% walk, 1.5% work from home; Mean travel time to work: 31.7 minutes

SLATE HILL (unincorporated postal area)
ZCTA: 10973
Covers a land area of 8.395 square miles and a water area of 0.129 square miles. Located at 41.38° N. Lat; 74.48° W. Long. Elevation is 499 feet.
Population: 2,377; Growth (since 2000): 26.0%; Density: 283.1 persons per square mile; Race: 88.4% White, 5.3% Black/African American, 1.3% Asian, 0.4% American Indian/Alaska Native, 0.0% Native Hawaiian/Other Pacific Islander, 1.3% Two or more races, 4.9% Hispanic of any race; Average household size: 2.92; Median age: 40.3; Age under 18: 20.5%; Age 65 and over: 9.8%; Males per 100 females: 100.9; Marriage status: 40.5% never married, 48.7% now married, 0.6% separated, 4.3% widowed, 6.5% divorced; Foreign born: 6.6%; Speak English only: 89.0%; With disability: 12.5%; Veterans: 5.9%; Ancestry: 26.8% Italian, 26.2% American, 21.8% Irish, 15.0% German, 5.6% English
Employment: 9.0% management, business, and financial, 4.8% computer, engineering, and science, 15.4% education, legal, community service, arts, and media, 11.8% healthcare practitioners, 12.6% service, 19.5% sales and office, 11.7% natural resources, construction, and maintenance, 15.3% production, transportation, and material moving
Income: Per capita: $39,565; Median household: $85,398; Average household: $113,804; Households with income of $100,000 or more: 43.4%; Poverty rate: 2.7%
Educational Attainment: High school diploma or higher: 96.1%; Bachelor's degree or higher: 30.6%; Graduate/professional degree or higher: 12.9%
Housing: Homeownership rate: 74.0%; Median home value: $270,500; Median year structure built: 1972; Homeowner vacancy rate: 0.0%; Median selected monthly owner costs: $2,253 with a mortgage, $970

without a mortgage; Median gross rent: $1,419 per month; Rental vacancy rate: 10.8%

Health Insurance: 92.8% have insurance; 78.8% have private insurance; 23.1% have public insurance; 7.2% do not have insurance; 0.0% of children under 18 do not have insurance

Transportation: Commute: 94.9% car, 2.1% public transportation, 0.2% walk, 2.3% work from home; Mean travel time to work: 27.5 minutes

SOUTH BLOOMING GROVE (village). Covers a land area of 4.674 square miles and a water area of 0.033 square miles. Located at 41.37° N. Lat; 74.17° W. Long. Elevation is 535 feet.

Population: 3,184; Growth (since 2000): n/a; Density: 681.2 persons per square mile; Race: 75.1% White, 10.1% Black/African American, 3.1% Asian, 0.0% American Indian/Alaska Native, 0.0% Native Hawaiian/Other Pacific Islander, 2.8% Two or more races, 17.9% Hispanic of any race; Average household size: 2.80; Median age: 38.5; Age under 18: 21.3%; Age 65 and over: 16.8%; Males per 100 females: 97.8; Marriage status: 32.3% never married, 54.7% now married, 2.5% separated, 5.5% widowed, 7.5% divorced; Foreign born: 14.0%; Speak English only: 73.5%; With disability: 9.8%; Veterans: 8.0%; Ancestry: 17.9% Irish, 17.3% American, 16.2% Italian, 9.3% German, 3.2% Jamaican

Employment: 9.9% management, business, and financial, 3.2% computer, engineering, and science, 12.7% education, legal, community service, arts, and media, 6.7% healthcare practitioners, 20.6% service, 24.8% sales and office, 8.3% natural resources, construction, and maintenance, 13.8% production, transportation, and material moving

Income: Per capita: $39,505; Median household: $86,379; Average household: $107,267; Households with income of $100,000 or more: 42.1%; Poverty rate: 6.8%

Educational Attainment: High school diploma or higher: 94.9%; Bachelor's degree or higher: 26.8%; Graduate/professional degree or higher: 12.1%

Housing: Homeownership rate: 77.9%; Median home value: $267,200; Median year structure built: 1967; Homeowner vacancy rate: 3.2%; Median selected monthly owner costs: $2,334 with a mortgage, $1,036 without a mortgage; Median gross rent: $1,234 per month; Rental vacancy rate: 0.0%

Health Insurance: 96.9% have insurance; 81.2% have private insurance; 31.5% have public insurance; 3.1% do not have insurance; 1.7% of children under 18 do not have insurance

Transportation: Commute: 92.4% car, 3.7% public transportation, 0.3% walk, 1.2% work from home; Mean travel time to work: 38.1 minutes

SOUTHFIELDS (unincorporated postal area)
ZCTA: 10975

Covers a land area of 5.883 square miles and a water area of 0.121 square miles. Located at 41.27° N. Lat; 74.17° W. Long. Elevation is 505 feet.

Population: 313; Growth (since 2000): 2.0%; Density: 53.2 persons per square mile; Race: 87.9% White, 0.0% Black/African American, 0.0% Asian, 0.0% American Indian/Alaska Native, 0.0% Native Hawaiian/Other Pacific Islander, 8.6% Two or more races, 19.2% Hispanic of any race; Average household size: 2.17; Median age: 44.3; Age under 18: 20.4%; Age 65 and over: 26.8%; Males per 100 females: 124.8; Marriage status: 25.7% never married, 55.6% now married, 0.0% separated, 0.0% widowed, 18.7% divorced; Foreign born: 0.0%; Speak English only: 90.7%; With disability: 21.1%; Veterans: 10.8%; Ancestry: 33.5% Irish, 31.3% Italian, 26.5% American, 11.5% Czech, 8.9% English

Employment: 0.0% management, business, and financial, 19.8% computer, engineering, and science, 5.5% education, legal, community service, arts, and media, 29.1% healthcare practitioners, 4.9% service, 40.7% sales and office, 0.0% natural resources, construction, and maintenance, 0.0% production, transportation, and material moving

Income: Per capita: $75,907; Median household: n/a; Average household: $166,031; Households with income of $100,000 or more: 43.0%; Poverty rate: n/a

Educational Attainment: High school diploma or higher: 100.0%; Bachelor's degree or higher: 28.1%; Graduate/professional degree or higher: 4.8%

Housing: Homeownership rate: 73.6%; Median home value: $181,900; Median year structure built: 1971; Homeowner vacancy rate: 0.0%; Median selected monthly owner costs: $1,861 with a mortgage, $0 without a mortgage; Median gross rent: n/a per month; Rental vacancy rate: 0.0%

Health Insurance: 100.0% have insurance; 81.8% have private insurance; 26.8% have public insurance; 0.0% do not have insurance; 0.0% of children under 18 do not have insurance

Transportation: Commute: 94.0% car, 6.0% public transportation, 0.0% walk, 0.0% work from home; Mean travel time to work: 58.9 minutes

SPARROW BUSH (unincorporated postal area)
ZCTA: 12780

Covers a land area of 23.825 square miles and a water area of 0.716 square miles. Located at 41.44° N. Lat; 74.73° W. Long. Elevation is 502 feet.

Population: 2,036; Growth (since 2000): -3.8%; Density: 85.5 persons per square mile; Race: 94.3% White, 1.2% Black/African American, 0.0% Asian, 0.0% American Indian/Alaska Native, 0.0% Native Hawaiian/Other Pacific Islander, 1.7% Two or more races, 7.3% Hispanic of any race; Average household size: 2.40; Median age: 42.0; Age under 18: 23.0%; Age 65 and over: 15.3%; Males per 100 females: 105.9; Marriage status: 31.1% never married, 50.8% now married, 1.5% separated, 8.2% widowed, 9.8% divorced; Foreign born: 1.2%; Speak English only: 94.8%; With disability: 18.2%; Veterans: 9.6%; Ancestry: 21.2% American, 18.6% German, 18.0% Irish, 12.8% Italian, 9.6% Dutch

Employment: 10.8% management, business, and financial, 1.6% computer, engineering, and science, 8.9% education, legal, community service, arts, and media, 0.0% healthcare practitioners, 25.8% service, 27.4% sales and office, 9.0% natural resources, construction, and maintenance, 16.5% production, transportation, and material moving

Income: Per capita: $24,108; Median household: $44,412; Average household: $56,638; Households with income of $100,000 or more: 19.4%; Poverty rate: 17.0%

Educational Attainment: High school diploma or higher: 87.5%; Bachelor's degree or higher: 12.7%; Graduate/professional degree or higher: 6.3%

Housing: Homeownership rate: 93.8%; Median home value: $145,000; Median year structure built: 1973; Homeowner vacancy rate: 10.1%; Median selected monthly owner costs: $1,726 with a mortgage, $562 without a mortgage; Median gross rent: $1,129 per month; Rental vacancy rate: 28.4%

Health Insurance: 94.6% have insurance; 81.3% have private insurance; 27.8% have public insurance; 5.4% do not have insurance; 0.0% of children under 18 do not have insurance

Transportation: Commute: 97.4% car, 0.8% public transportation, 0.0% walk, 0.8% work from home; Mean travel time to work: 37.3 minutes

STERLING FOREST (unincorporated postal area)
ZCTA: 10979

Covers a land area of 0.146 square miles and a water area of 0 square miles. Located at 41.18° N. Lat; 74.31° W. Long. Elevation is 656 feet.

Population: 262; Growth (since 2000): n/a; Density: 1,797.9 persons per square mile; Race: 61.5% White, 0.0% Black/African American, 0.0% Asian, 0.0% American Indian/Alaska Native, 0.0% Native Hawaiian/Other Pacific Islander, 38.5% Two or more races, 0.0% Hispanic of any race; Average household size: 2.88; Median age: 45.7; Age under 18: 26.7%; Age 65 and over: 0.0%; Males per 100 females: 107.1; Marriage status: 19.8% never married, 64.6% now married, 0.0% separated, 15.6% widowed, 0.0% divorced; Foreign born: 0.0%; Speak English only: 100.0%; With disability: 49.6%; Veterans: 0.0%; Ancestry: 50.4% Irish, 38.5% German, 26.7% French, 26.0% Russian, 11.5% Italian

Employment: 0.0% management, business, and financial, 0.0% computer, engineering, and science, 0.0% education, legal, community service, arts, and media, 0.0% healthcare practitioners, 44.9% service, 0.0% sales and office, 0.0% natural resources, construction, and maintenance, 55.1% production, transportation, and material moving

Income: Per capita: $19,981; Median household: $71,292; Average household: $55,052; Households with income of $100,000 or more: n/a; Poverty rate: n/a

Educational Attainment: High school diploma or higher: 100.0%; Bachelor's degree or higher: n/a; Graduate/professional degree or higher: n/a

Housing: Homeownership rate: 100.0%; Median home value: $224,200; Median year structure built: 1963; Homeowner vacancy rate: 0.0%; Median selected monthly owner costs: $0 with a mortgage, $0 without a mortgage; Median gross rent: n/a per month; Rental vacancy rate: 0.0%

Health Insurance: 100.0% have insurance; 76.3% have private insurance; 23.7% have public insurance; 0.0% do not have insurance; 0.0% of children under 18 do not have insurance
Transportation: Commute: 100.0% car, 0.0% public transportation, 0.0% walk, 0.0% work from home; Mean travel time to work: 0.0 minutes

THOMPSON RIDGE (unincorporated postal area)
ZCTA: 10985

Covers a land area of 0.257 square miles and a water area of 0 square miles. Located at 41.58° N. Lat; 74.37° W. Long. Elevation is 456 feet.
Population: 176; Growth (since 2000): 208.8%; Density: 684.6 persons per square mile; Race: 100.0% White, 0.0% Black/African American, 0.0% Asian, 0.0% American Indian/Alaska Native, 0.0% Native Hawaiian/Other Pacific Islander, 0.0% Two or more races, 0.0% Hispanic of any race; Average household size: 3.52; Median age: 33.3; Age under 18: 0.0%; Age 65 and over: 5.7%; Males per 100 females: 81.3; Marriage status: 59.1% never married, 35.2% now married, 0.0% separated, 0.0% widowed, 5.7% divorced; Foreign born: 35.2%; Speak English only: 64.8%; With disability: 24.4%; Veterans: 0.0%; Ancestry: 35.2% Albanian, 20.5% British West Indian, 18.2% English, 5.7% German, 5.1% Irish
Employment: 25.7% management, business, and financial, 0.0% computer, engineering, and science, 25.0% education, legal, community service, arts, and media, 0.0% healthcare practitioners, 0.0% service, 0.0% sales and office, 27.8% natural resources, construction, and maintenance, 21.5% production, transportation, and material moving
Income: Per capita: $47,868; Median household: $173,710; Average household: $160,814; Households with income of $100,000 or more: 80.0%; Poverty rate: 5.7%
Educational Attainment: High school diploma or higher: 93.2%; Bachelor's degree or higher: 11.4%; Graduate/professional degree or higher: 5.7%
Housing: Homeownership rate: 100.0%; Median home value: $268,800; Median year structure built: 1985; Homeowner vacancy rate: 0.0%; Median selected monthly owner costs: $0 with a mortgage, $0 without a mortgage; Median gross rent: n/a per month; Rental vacancy rate: 0.0%
Health Insurance: 79.0% have insurance; 73.3% have private insurance; 18.2% have public insurance; 21.0% do not have insurance; 0.0% of children under 18 do not have insurance
Transportation: Commute: 100.0% car, 0.0% public transportation, 0.0% walk, 0.0% work from home; Mean travel time to work: 0.0 minutes

TUXEDO (town). Covers a land area of 47.047 square miles and a water area of 2.299 square miles. Located at 41.24° N. Lat; 74.17° W. Long.

History: Tuxedo Park colony here, a private residential development begun (1886) by Pierre Lorillard, became known for its sports and social functions. King's College relocated here from Briarcliff Manor.
Population: 3,552; Growth (since 2000): 6.5%; Density: 75.5 persons per square mile; Race: 87.4% White, 4.5% Black/African American, 3.9% Asian, 0.0% American Indian/Alaska Native, 0.0% Native Hawaiian/Other Pacific Islander, 2.2% Two or more races, 9.0% Hispanic of any race; Average household size: 2.42; Median age: 47.0; Age under 18: 20.3%; Age 65 and over: 22.2%; Males per 100 females: 99.8; Marriage status: 29.1% never married, 53.9% now married, 1.6% separated, 8.5% widowed, 8.5% divorced; Foreign born: 11.5%; Speak English only: 84.9%; With disability: 12.7%; Veterans: 7.6%; Ancestry: 19.8% Italian, 18.1% Irish, 14.2% American, 8.4% German, 8.0% English
Employment: 20.9% management, business, and financial, 9.5% computer, engineering, and science, 13.3% education, legal, community service, arts, and media, 6.7% healthcare practitioners, 8.0% service, 34.4% sales and office, 4.6% natural resources, construction, and maintenance, 2.7% production, transportation, and material moving
Income: Per capita: $60,361; Median household: $104,625; Average household: $144,592; Households with income of $100,000 or more: 52.0%; Poverty rate: 2.9%
Educational Attainment: High school diploma or higher: 96.5%; Bachelor's degree or higher: 52.9%; Graduate/professional degree or higher: 21.2%
Housing: Homeownership rate: 78.5%; Median home value: $437,800; Median year structure built: 1965; Homeowner vacancy rate: 2.4%; Median selected monthly owner costs: $2,812 with a mortgage, $1,379 without a mortgage; Median gross rent: $1,695 per month; Rental vacancy rate: 2.8%

Health Insurance: 96.1% have insurance; 83.4% have private insurance; 27.6% have public insurance; 3.9% do not have insurance; 0.0% of children under 18 do not have insurance
Safety: Violent crime rate: 0.0 per 10,000 population; Property crime rate: 10.2 per 10,000 population
Transportation: Commute: 83.4% car, 9.1% public transportation, 0.7% walk, 6.8% work from home; Mean travel time to work: 40.7 minutes
Additional Information Contacts
Town of Tuxedo. . . . . (845) 351-4411
 http://www.tuxedogov.org

TUXEDO PARK (village). Covers a land area of 2.655 square miles and a water area of 0.566 square miles. Located at 41.20° N. Lat; 74.21° W. Long. Elevation is 407 feet.
Population: 536; Growth (since 2000): -26.7%; Density: 201.9 persons per square mile; Race: 93.7% White, 0.9% Black/African American, 3.4% Asian, 0.0% American Indian/Alaska Native, 0.0% Native Hawaiian/Other Pacific Islander, 2.1% Two or more races, 1.3% Hispanic of any race; Average household size: 2.59; Median age: 50.5; Age under 18: 21.6%; Age 65 and over: 27.4%; Males per 100 females: 104.3; Marriage status: 19.6% never married, 65.6% now married, 3.6% separated, 5.6% widowed, 9.2% divorced; Foreign born: 10.4%; Speak English only: 93.9%; With disability: 8.6%; Veterans: 7.6%; Ancestry: 24.3% Irish, 14.2% Italian, 13.6% German, 9.0% English, 6.9% American
Employment: 27.6% management, business, and financial, 7.0% computer, engineering, and science, 25.5% education, legal, community service, arts, and media, 3.7% healthcare practitioners, 6.6% service, 23.9% sales and office, 4.5% natural resources, construction, and maintenance, 1.2% production, transportation, and material moving
Income: Per capita: $90,717; Median household: $137,083; Average household: $227,941; Households with income of $100,000 or more: 59.8%; Poverty rate: 4.5%
Educational Attainment: High school diploma or higher: 97.3%; Bachelor's degree or higher: 69.4%; Graduate/professional degree or higher: 32.8%

School District(s)
Tuxedo Union Free SD (KG-12)
 Enrollment: 259. . . . . (845) 351-4799
Housing: Homeownership rate: 84.5%; Median home value: $1,088,000; Median year structure built: Before 1940; Homeowner vacancy rate: 7.2%; Median selected monthly owner costs: $4,000+ with a mortgage, $1,501 without a mortgage; Median gross rent: $1,375 per month; Rental vacancy rate: 22.0%
Health Insurance: 97.2% have insurance; 78.0% have private insurance; 30.4% have public insurance; 2.8% do not have insurance; 0.0% of children under 18 do not have insurance
Transportation: Commute: 65.0% car, 15.0% public transportation, 5.0% walk, 14.1% work from home; Mean travel time to work: 41.6 minutes

UNIONVILLE (village). Covers a land area of 0.310 square miles and a water area of 0 square miles. Located at 41.30° N. Lat; 74.56° W. Long. Elevation is 535 feet.
Population: 592; Growth (since 2000): 10.4%; Density: 1,907.2 persons per square mile; Race: 81.3% White, 2.0% Black/African American, 0.0% Asian, 0.0% American Indian/Alaska Native, 0.0% Native Hawaiian/Other Pacific Islander, 4.9% Two or more races, 29.1% Hispanic of any race; Average household size: 2.64; Median age: 42.3; Age under 18: 22.0%; Age 65 and over: 19.4%; Males per 100 females: 90.1; Marriage status: 22.2% never married, 44.7% now married, 2.8% separated, 8.9% widowed, 24.2% divorced; Foreign born: 11.1%; Speak English only: 79.9%; With disability: 14.0%; Veterans: 6.5%; Ancestry: 30.1% American, 17.7% Irish, 15.7% Italian, 9.0% German, 5.4% English
Employment: 10.7% management, business, and financial, 4.5% computer, engineering, and science, 9.6% education, legal, community service, arts, and media, 8.9% healthcare practitioners, 31.3% service, 14.1% sales and office, 13.1% natural resources, construction, and maintenance, 7.9% production, transportation, and material moving
Income: Per capita: $30,759; Median household: $73,750; Average household: $77,770; Households with income of $100,000 or more: 22.1%; Poverty rate: 3.5%
Educational Attainment: High school diploma or higher: 88.8%; Bachelor's degree or higher: 28.7%; Graduate/professional degree or higher: 10.0%
Housing: Homeownership rate: 82.9%; Median home value: $206,100; Median year structure built: Before 1940; Homeowner vacancy rate: 8.6%;

Median selected monthly owner costs: $1,542 with a mortgage, n/a without a mortgage; Median gross rent: $1,125 per month; Rental vacancy rate: 0.0%
Health Insurance: 90.0% have insurance; 66.9% have private insurance; 35.0% have public insurance; 10.0% do not have insurance; 4.8% of children under 18 do not have insurance
Transportation: Commute: 81.3% car, 5.7% public transportation, 0.0% walk, 10.2% work from home; Mean travel time to work: 39.2 minutes

VAILS GATE (CDP). Covers a land area of 1.061 square miles and a water area of 0 square miles. Located at 41.46° N. Lat; 74.05° W. Long. Elevation is 282 feet.
Population: 3,309; Growth (since 2000): -0.3%; Density: 3,118.3 persons per square mile; Race: 59.5% White, 20.1% Black/African American, 7.3% Asian, 0.0% American Indian/Alaska Native, 0.0% Native Hawaiian/Other Pacific Islander, 1.8% Two or more races, 21.0% Hispanic of any race; Average household size: 2.32; Median age: 40.0; Age under 18: 15.7%; Age 65 and over: 18.9%; Males per 100 females: 87.0; Marriage status: 37.2% never married, 41.4% now married, 1.5% separated, 11.2% widowed, 10.1% divorced; Foreign born: 21.4%; Speak English only: 68.8%; With disability: 17.8%; Veterans: 7.2%; Ancestry: 17.4% American, 14.5% Italian, 9.7% Irish, 8.6% German, 6.5% Haitian
Employment: 11.3% management, business, and financial, 1.7% computer, engineering, and science, 4.0% education, legal, community service, arts, and media, 9.5% healthcare practitioners, 25.8% service, 32.6% sales and office, 5.7% natural resources, construction, and maintenance, 9.4% production, transportation, and material moving
Income: Per capita: $27,135; Median household: $40,615; Average household: $61,928; Households with income of $100,000 or more: 18.6%; Poverty rate: 12.2%
Educational Attainment: High school diploma or higher: 88.3%; Bachelor's degree or higher: 18.0%; Graduate/professional degree or higher: 9.1%
Housing: Homeownership rate: 48.6%; Median home value: $204,100; Median year structure built: 1972; Homeowner vacancy rate: 0.0%; Median selected monthly owner costs: $2,206 with a mortgage, $496 without a mortgage; Median gross rent: $1,162 per month; Rental vacancy rate: 5.9%
Health Insurance: 90.7% have insurance; 63.2% have private insurance; 38.0% have public insurance; 9.3% do not have insurance; 10.5% of children under 18 do not have insurance
Transportation: Commute: 92.3% car, 3.4% public transportation, 2.7% walk, 1.0% work from home; Mean travel time to work: 29.0 minutes

WALDEN (village). Covers a land area of 1.968 square miles and a water area of 0.082 square miles. Located at 41.56° N. Lat; 74.19° W. Long. Elevation is 374 feet.
History: Former factory town. Incorporated 1855.
Population: 6,781; Growth (since 2000): 10.0%; Density: 3,445.5 persons per square mile; Race: 80.8% White, 6.8% Black/African American, 1.0% Asian, 0.0% American Indian/Alaska Native, 0.0% Native Hawaiian/Other Pacific Islander, 2.1% Two or more races, 15.8% Hispanic of any race; Average household size: 3.00; Median age: 35.9; Age under 18: 26.2%; Age 65 and over: 10.0%; Males per 100 females: 93.2; Marriage status: 38.3% never married, 48.2% now married, 4.7% separated, 6.7% widowed, 6.8% divorced; Foreign born: 5.4%; Speak English only: 89.4%; With disability: 15.6%; Veterans: 8.1%; Ancestry: 20.7% Irish, 17.9% Italian, 14.4% American, 12.8% German, 6.7% English
Employment: 9.2% management, business, and financial, 4.2% computer, engineering, and science, 13.8% education, legal, community service, arts, and media, 3.0% healthcare practitioners, 16.7% service, 31.2% sales and office, 8.5% natural resources, construction, and maintenance, 13.4% production, transportation, and material moving
Income: Per capita: $27,416; Median household: $70,147; Average household: $79,400; Households with income of $100,000 or more: 27.7%; Poverty rate: 10.9%
Educational Attainment: High school diploma or higher: 87.7%; Bachelor's degree or higher: 20.3%; Graduate/professional degree or higher: 9.6%
School District(s)
Valley Central SD (Montgomery) (KG-12)
    Enrollment: 4,362 . . . . (845) 457-2400
Housing: Homeownership rate: 65.4%; Median home value: $196,200; Median year structure built: 1954; Homeowner vacancy rate: 1.5%; Median selected monthly owner costs: $2,080 with a mortgage, $679 without a

mortgage; Median gross rent: $1,149 per month; Rental vacancy rate: 4.3%
Health Insurance: 95.6% have insurance; 76.4% have private insurance; 31.7% have public insurance; 4.4% do not have insurance; 0.8% of children under 18 do not have insurance
Safety: Violent crime rate: 10.5 per 10,000 population; Property crime rate: 119.5 per 10,000 population
Transportation: Commute: 92.4% car, 4.1% public transportation, 1.3% walk, 1.9% work from home; Mean travel time to work: 30.5 minutes
Additional Information Contacts
Village of Walden . . . . (845) 778-2177
    http://www.villageofwalden.org

WALLKILL (town). Covers a land area of 62.107 square miles and a water area of 0.736 square miles. Located at 41.49° N. Lat; 74.40° W. Long.
History: The original land patent for the town was dated 1724, but the town wasn't established until 1772. Wallkill's claim to fame during the American Revolution was the production of gunpowder in factories in Phillipsburgh and Craigville.
Population: 28,540; Growth (since 2000): 15.7%; Density: 459.5 persons per square mile; Race: 60.9% White, 18.7% Black/African American, 3.3% Asian, 0.9% American Indian/Alaska Native, 0.1% Native Hawaiian/Other Pacific Islander, 5.3% Two or more races, 23.5% Hispanic of any race; Average household size: 2.70; Median age: 40.8; Age under 18: 21.1%; Age 65 and over: 15.1%; Males per 100 females: 92.5; Marriage status: 34.4% never married, 52.6% now married, 1.8% separated, 4.7% widowed, 8.3% divorced; Foreign born: 12.9%; Speak English only: 76.0%; With disability: 14.5%; Veterans: 6.0%; Ancestry: 18.7% American, 13.1% Italian, 11.0% Irish, 8.9% German, 4.1% Polish
Employment: 11.2% management, business, and financial, 3.0% computer, engineering, and science, 9.0% education, legal, community service, arts, and media, 6.9% healthcare practitioners, 18.6% service, 29.6% sales and office, 8.6% natural resources, construction, and maintenance, 13.1% production, transportation, and material moving
Income: Per capita: $31,711; Median household: $65,035; Average household: $83,723; Households with income of $100,000 or more: 30.2%; Poverty rate: 11.0%
Educational Attainment: High school diploma or higher: 90.1%; Bachelor's degree or higher: 24.1%; Graduate/professional degree or higher: 10.6%
School District(s)
Wallkill Central SD (KG-12)
    Enrollment: 2,982 . . . . (845) 895-7100
Housing: Homeownership rate: 63.0%; Median home value: $247,400; Median year structure built: 1977; Homeowner vacancy rate: 3.2%; Median selected monthly owner costs: $2,189 with a mortgage, $795 without a mortgage; Median gross rent: $1,227 per month; Rental vacancy rate: 5.4%
Health Insurance: 93.7% have insurance; 76.5% have private insurance; 28.5% have public insurance; 6.3% do not have insurance; 1.7% of children under 18 do not have insurance
Safety: Violent crime rate: 22.5 per 10,000 population; Property crime rate: 218.8 per 10,000 population
Transportation: Commute: 89.8% car, 3.0% public transportation, 1.5% walk, 2.5% work from home; Mean travel time to work: 35.1 minutes
Additional Information Contacts
Town of Wallkill . . . . (845) 692-7800
    http://www.townofwallkill.com

WALTON PARK (CDP). Covers a land area of 2.329 square miles and a water area of 0.348 square miles. Located at 41.31° N. Lat; 74.23° W. Long. Elevation is 843 feet.
Population: 2,386; Growth (since 2000): 2.4%; Density: 1,024.4 persons per square mile; Race: 83.4% White, 3.1% Black/African American, 3.5% Asian, 0.0% American Indian/Alaska Native, 0.0% Native Hawaiian/Other Pacific Islander, 6.7% Two or more races, 6.7% Hispanic of any race; Average household size: 3.45; Median age: 38.1; Age under 18: 25.7%; Age 65 and over: 12.5%; Males per 100 females: 98.7; Marriage status: 35.4% never married, 49.4% now married, 1.5% separated, 4.5% widowed, 10.7% divorced; Foreign born: 10.0%; Speak English only: 85.6%; With disability: 11.1%; Veterans: 7.3%; Ancestry: 22.0% Irish, 21.2% Italian, 12.8% American, 12.5% German, 6.4% English
Employment: 17.1% management, business, and financial, 3.6% computer, engineering, and science, 13.3% education, legal, community

service, arts, and media, 6.6% healthcare practitioners, 13.8% service, 32.2% sales and office, 8.3% natural resources, construction, and maintenance, 5.2% production, transportation, and material moving
Income: Per capita: $33,484; Median household: $108,011; Average household: $112,812; Households with income of $100,000 or more: 57.2%; Poverty rate: 3.3%
Educational Attainment: High school diploma or higher: 95.6%; Bachelor's degree or higher: 37.3%; Graduate/professional degree or higher: 15.6%
Housing: Homeownership rate: 98.7%; Median home value: $306,300; Median year structure built: 1963; Homeowner vacancy rate: 3.2%; Median selected monthly owner costs: $2,537 with a mortgage, $1,157 without a mortgage; Median gross rent: n/a per month; Rental vacancy rate: 0.0%
Health Insurance: 98.0% have insurance; 84.9% have private insurance; 22.9% have public insurance; 2.0% do not have insurance; 1.6% of children under 18 do not have insurance
Transportation: Commute: 91.0% car, 5.2% public transportation, 0.0% walk, 2.3% work from home; Mean travel time to work: 37.3 minutes

WARWICK (town).
Covers a land area of 101.340 square miles and a water area of 3.546 square miles. Located at 41.26° N. Lat; 74.36° W. Long. Elevation is 518 feet.
History: Warwick was settled in 1746 by English immigrants from Warwickshire. Warwick Village Historic District. Incorporated in 1867.
Population: 31,305; Growth (since 2000): 1.8%; Density: 308.9 persons per square mile; Race: 84.8% White, 5.8% Black/African American, 1.3% Asian, 0.7% American Indian/Alaska Native, 0.2% Native Hawaiian/Other Pacific Islander, 4.4% Two or more races, 11.0% Hispanic of any race; Average household size: 2.65; Median age: 45.9; Age under 18: 21.8%; Age 65 and over: 17.0%; Males per 100 females: 100.0; Marriage status: 26.2% never married, 56.6% now married, 1.9% separated, 6.7% widowed, 10.5% divorced; Foreign born: 6.3%; Speak English only: 89.2%; With disability: 12.7%; Veterans: 8.9%; Ancestry: 24.1% Irish, 18.5% Italian, 15.9% German, 13.5% American, 6.8% English
Employment: 15.5% management, business, and financial, 5.5% computer, engineering, and science, 12.7% education, legal, community service, arts, and media, 5.4% healthcare practitioners, 17.4% service, 24.8% sales and office, 7.5% natural resources, construction, and maintenance, 11.3% production, transportation, and material moving
Income: Per capita: $43,990; Median household: $89,788; Average household: $115,147; Households with income of $100,000 or more: 44.7%; Poverty rate: 4.6%
Educational Attainment: High school diploma or higher: 94.2%; Bachelor's degree or higher: 37.1%; Graduate/professional degree or higher: 15.6%

School District(s)
Warwick Valley Central SD (KG-12)
    Enrollment: 3,631 . . . . (845) 987-3000
Housing: Homeownership rate: 77.8%; Median home value: $303,100; Median year structure built: 1968; Homeowner vacancy rate: 2.6%; Median selected monthly owner costs: $2,400 with a mortgage, $1,022 without a mortgage; Median gross rent: $1,107 per month; Rental vacancy rate: 1.5%
Health Insurance: 96.9% have insurance; 83.8% have private insurance; 27.0% have public insurance; 3.1% do not have insurance; 2.0% of children under 18 do not have insurance
Hospitals: Saint Anthony Community Hospital (73 beds)
Safety: Violent crime rate: 7.1 per 10,000 population; Property crime rate: 56.6 per 10,000 population
Newspapers: Warwick Valley Dispatch (weekly circulation 3,000)
Transportation: Commute: 84.5% car, 5.8% public transportation, 1.5% walk, 7.4% work from home; Mean travel time to work: 40.1 minutes
Additional Information Contacts
Town of Warwick. . . . . (845) 986-1124
    http://www.townofwarwick.org/index.shtml

WARWICK (village).
Covers a land area of 2.417 square miles and a water area of 0.004 square miles. Located at 41.26° N. Lat; 74.35° W. Long. Elevation is 518 feet.
Population: 6,801; Growth (since 2000): 6.1%; Density: 2,814.2 persons per square mile; Race: 89.1% White, 4.6% Black/African American, 0.6% Asian, 1.4% American Indian/Alaska Native, 1.0% Native Hawaiian/Other Pacific Islander, 0.8% Two or more races, 6.2% Hispanic of any race; Average household size: 2.26; Median age: 49.0; Age under 18: 20.1%; Age 65 and over: 27.2%; Males per 100 females: 82.8; Marriage status:

23.2% never married, 53.0% now married, 3.0% separated, 9.4% widowed, 14.4% divorced; Foreign born: 4.4%; Speak English only: 90.2%; With disability: 17.3%; Veterans: 12.8%; Ancestry: 27.8% Irish, 21.8% Italian, 15.2% German, 13.5% American, 6.5% English
Employment: 15.8% management, business, and financial, 3.5% computer, engineering, and science, 13.2% education, legal, community service, arts, and media, 6.0% healthcare practitioners, 20.4% service, 23.5% sales and office, 5.6% natural resources, construction, and maintenance, 12.0% production, transportation, and material moving
Income: Per capita: $36,907; Median household: $70,518; Average household: $82,976; Households with income of $100,000 or more: 33.2%; Poverty rate: 4.0%
Educational Attainment: High school diploma or higher: 92.9%; Bachelor's degree or higher: 37.0%; Graduate/professional degree or higher: 16.8%

School District(s)
Warwick Valley Central SD (KG-12)
    Enrollment: 3,631 . . . . (845) 987-3000
Housing: Homeownership rate: 57.6%; Median home value: $310,700; Median year structure built: 1969; Homeowner vacancy rate: 0.0%; Median selected monthly owner costs: $2,349 with a mortgage, $976 without a mortgage; Median gross rent: $969 per month; Rental vacancy rate: 3.0%
Health Insurance: 97.0% have insurance; 80.3% have private insurance; 36.6% have public insurance; 3.0% do not have insurance; 2.9% of children under 18 do not have insurance
Hospitals: Saint Anthony Community Hospital (73 beds)
Newspapers: Warwick Valley Dispatch (weekly circulation 3,000)
Transportation: Commute: 80.9% car, 5.8% public transportation, 5.5% walk, 5.9% work from home; Mean travel time to work: 34.6 minutes
Additional Information Contacts
Village of Warwick. . . . . (845) 986-2031
    http://www.villageofwarwick.org

WASHINGTON HEIGHTS (CDP).
Covers a land area of 1.486 square miles and a water area of 0.005 square miles. Located at 41.47° N. Lat; 74.42° W. Long. Elevation is 666 feet.
Population: 2,447; Growth (since 2000): 85.7%; Density: 1,646.3 persons per square mile; Race: 34.7% White, 15.7% Black/African American, 6.7% Asian, 0.0% American Indian/Alaska Native, 0.0% Native Hawaiian/Other Pacific Islander, 6.1% Two or more races, 40.6% Hispanic of any race; Average household size: 3.65; Median age: 31.2; Age under 18: 22.7%; Age 65 and over: 8.4%; Males per 100 females: 93.0; Marriage status: 43.9% never married, 45.0% now married, 0.0% separated, 0.8% widowed, 10.3% divorced; Foreign born: 24.4%; Speak English only: 56.4%; With disability: 13.3%; Veterans: 6.6%; Ancestry: 10.3% Italian, 9.2% German, 8.4% American, 5.9% Polish, 5.1% Irish
Employment: 8.0% management, business, and financial, 2.8% computer, engineering, and science, 1.9% education, legal, community service, arts, and media, 8.2% healthcare practitioners, 20.9% service, 24.5% sales and office, 7.7% natural resources, construction, and maintenance, 26.0% production, transportation, and material moving
Income: Per capita: $31,128; Median household: $101,484; Average household: $104,035; Households with income of $100,000 or more: 51.4%; Poverty rate: 4.1%
Educational Attainment: High school diploma or higher: 96.6%; Bachelor's degree or higher: 27.5%; Graduate/professional degree or higher: 16.2%
Housing: Homeownership rate: 84.2%; Median home value: $248,200; Median year structure built: 1964; Homeowner vacancy rate: 10.3%; Median selected monthly owner costs: $2,332 with a mortgage, n/a without a mortgage; Median gross rent: $1,455 per month; Rental vacancy rate: 0.0%
Health Insurance: 96.6% have insurance; 82.0% have private insurance; 19.2% have public insurance; 3.4% do not have insurance; 0.0% of children under 18 do not have insurance
Transportation: Commute: 92.4% car, 2.7% public transportation, 1.0% walk, 0.0% work from home; Mean travel time to work: 49.6 minutes

WASHINGTONVILLE (village).
Covers a land area of 2.538 square miles and a water area of 0.014 square miles. Located at 41.43° N. Lat; 74.16° W. Long. Elevation is 305 feet.
Population: 5,774; Growth (since 2000): -1.3%; Density: 2,274.9 persons per square mile; Race: 74.6% White, 8.7% Black/African American, 1.6% Asian, 0.1% American Indian/Alaska Native, 0.0% Native Hawaiian/Other Pacific Islander, 1.9% Two or more races, 24.2% Hispanic of any race;

Average household size: 2.76; Median age: 41.5; Age under 18: 22.8%; Age 65 and over: 13.3%; Males per 100 females: 93.9; Marriage status: 32.1% never married, 51.2% now married, 2.1% separated, 6.1% widowed, 10.6% divorced; Foreign born: 8.3%; Speak English only: 80.3%; With disability: 12.6%; Veterans: 5.0%; Ancestry: 24.2% Italian, 23.2% Irish, 11.4% American, 10.5% German, 4.6% English

Employment: 10.0% management, business, and financial, 7.7% computer, engineering, and science, 11.2% education, legal, community service, arts, and media, 8.8% healthcare practitioners, 14.8% service, 30.6% sales and office, 7.3% natural resources, construction, and maintenance, 9.6% production, transportation, and material moving

Income: Per capita: $35,823; Median household: $85,263; Average household: $96,050; Households with income of $100,000 or more: 42.2%; Poverty rate: 3.9%

Educational Attainment: High school diploma or higher: 93.8%; Bachelor's degree or higher: 34.9%; Graduate/professional degree or higher: 13.2%

School District(s)

Washingtonville Central SD (PK-12)

    Enrollment: 4,137 . . . . (845) 497-4000

Housing: Homeownership rate: 77.4%; Median home value: $234,800; Median year structure built: 1982; Homeowner vacancy rate: 1.4%; Median selected monthly owner costs: $2,348 with a mortgage, $918 without a mortgage; Median gross rent: $910 per month; Rental vacancy rate: 0.0%

Health Insurance: 97.7% have insurance; 86.0% have private insurance; 21.9% have public insurance; 2.3% do not have insurance; 0.0% of children under 18 do not have insurance

Safety: Violent crime rate: 5.2 per 10,000 population; Property crime rate: 57.4 per 10,000 population

Newspapers: Orange County Post (weekly circulation 2,600)

Transportation: Commute: 87.5% car, 8.5% public transportation, 1.1% walk, 1.5% work from home; Mean travel time to work: 39.2 minutes

Additional Information Contacts

Village of Washingtonville . . . . (845) 496-3221

WAWAYANDA (town). Covers a land area of 34.720 square miles and a water area of 0.309 square miles. Located at 41.38° N. Lat; 74.47° W. Long.

Population: 7,288; Growth (since 2000): 16.2%; Density: 209.9 persons per square mile; Race: 83.8% White, 5.8% Black/African American, 2.3% Asian, 0.1% American Indian/Alaska Native, 0.0% Native Hawaiian/Other Pacific Islander, 2.3% Two or more races, 11.6% Hispanic of any race; Average household size: 2.96; Median age: 40.3; Age under 18: 23.4%; Age 65 and over: 11.4%; Males per 100 females: 98.2; Marriage status: 38.7% never married, 50.0% now married, 2.3% separated, 4.9% widowed, 6.5% divorced; Foreign born: 7.0%; Speak English only: 83.7%; With disability: 11.9%; Veterans: 6.9%; Ancestry: 24.3% American, 19.4% Italian, 17.5% Irish, 15.2% German, 9.0% Polish

Employment: 10.2% management, business, and financial, 4.0% computer, engineering, and science, 13.5% education, legal, community service, arts, and media, 8.9% healthcare practitioners, 20.9% service, 20.9% sales and office, 10.3% natural resources, construction, and maintenance, 11.3% production, transportation, and material moving

Income: Per capita: $35,805; Median household: $88,676; Average household: $104,061; Households with income of $100,000 or more: 47.5%; Poverty rate: 8.9%

Educational Attainment: High school diploma or higher: 94.6%; Bachelor's degree or higher: 36.0%; Graduate/professional degree or higher: 14.8%

Housing: Homeownership rate: 74.2%; Median home value: $276,700; Median year structure built: 1974; Homeowner vacancy rate: 1.8%; Median selected monthly owner costs: $2,197 with a mortgage, $972 without a mortgage; Median gross rent: $1,424 per month; Rental vacancy rate: 6.2%

Health Insurance: 94.2% have insurance; 77.4% have private insurance; 27.2% have public insurance; 5.8% do not have insurance; 0.2% of children under 18 do not have insurance

Transportation: Commute: 94.7% car, 1.5% public transportation, 0.7% walk, 1.9% work from home; Mean travel time to work: 29.2 minutes

Additional Information Contacts

Town of Wawayanda. . . . . (845) 355-5700

    http://www.townofwawayanda.com

WEST POINT (CDP). Covers a land area of 19.749 square miles and a water area of 0.901 square miles. Located at 41.36° N. Lat; 74.02° W. Long. Elevation is 157 feet.

History: The site of the United States Military Reservation has been known as West Point since Revolutionary times. In 1802, Congress authorized the establishment of the military academy here. It became a military school of the first order under Major Sylvanus Thayer, superintendent from 1817 to 1833. Many Civil War leaders on both sides were graduates of West Point.

Population: 6,536; Growth (since 2000): -8.4%; Density: 330.9 persons per square mile; Race: 79.5% White, 6.1% Black/African American, 4.4% Asian, 0.4% American Indian/Alaska Native, 0.0% Native Hawaiian/Other Pacific Islander, 6.3% Two or more races, 10.3% Hispanic of any race; Average household size: 3.84; Median age: 21.2; Age under 18: 21.5%; Age 65 and over: 0.5%; Males per 100 females: 261.1; Marriage status: 70.8% never married, 26.7% now married, 0.1% separated, 0.4% widowed, 2.2% divorced; Foreign born: 4.4%; Speak English only: 85.7%; With disability: 3.8%; Veterans: 50.1%; Ancestry: 19.2% German, 15.5% Irish, 12.4% Italian, 10.7% American, 9.9% English

Employment: 14.9% management, business, and financial, 6.0% computer, engineering, and science, 30.3% education, legal, community service, arts, and media, 6.2% healthcare practitioners, 17.0% service, 17.4% sales and office, 2.8% natural resources, construction, and maintenance, 5.3% production, transportation, and material moving

Income: Per capita: $19,854; Median household: $100,039; Average household: $117,849; Households with income of $100,000 or more: 50.0%; Poverty rate: 1.3%

Educational Attainment: High school diploma or higher: 100.0%; Bachelor's degree or higher: 70.0%; Graduate/professional degree or higher: 45.0%

Four-year College(s)

United States Military Academy (Public)

    Enrollment: 4,491 . . . . (845) 938-4011

Housing: Homeownership rate: 1.1%; Median home value: n/a; Median year structure built: 1973; Homeowner vacancy rate: 0.0%; Median selected monthly owner costs: n/a with a mortgage, n/a without a mortgage; Median gross rent: $3,113 per month; Rental vacancy rate: 0.0%

Health Insurance: 100.0% have insurance; 97.1% have private insurance; 4.9% have public insurance; 0.0% do not have insurance; 0.0% of children under 18 do not have insurance

Transportation: Commute: 25.7% car, 0.6% public transportation, 37.0% walk, 34.9% work from home; Mean travel time to work: 9.5 minutes

WESTTOWN (unincorporated postal area)

ZCTA: 10998

    Covers a land area of 18.653 square miles and a water area of 0.141 square miles. Located at 41.32° N. Lat; 74.54° W. Long. Elevation is 502 feet.

    Population: 3,063; Growth (since 2000): -16.0%; Density: 164.2 persons per square mile; Race: 88.8% White, 2.9% Black/African American, 0.3% Asian, 1.0% American Indian/Alaska Native, 0.0% Native Hawaiian/Other Pacific Islander, 0.6% Two or more races, 13.9% Hispanic of any race; Average household size: 3.03; Median age: 41.4; Age under 18: 25.2%; Age 65 and over: 11.9%; Males per 100 females: 100.0; Marriage status: 33.5% never married, 56.0% now married, 1.7% separated, 3.7% widowed, 6.8% divorced; Foreign born: 6.1%; Speak English only: 88.0%; With disability: 15.5%; Veterans: 9.9%; Ancestry: 17.7% Italian, 16.3% American, 14.7% Irish, 11.1% German, 8.2% English

    Employment: 21.9% management, business, and financial, 0.0% computer, engineering, and science, 9.6% education, legal, community service, arts, and media, 4.3% healthcare practitioners, 19.4% service, 30.4% sales and office, 7.0% natural resources, construction, and maintenance, 7.5% production, transportation, and material moving

    Income: Per capita: $33,654; Median household: $88,548; Average household: $99,114; Households with income of $100,000 or more: 41.9%; Poverty rate: 5.4%

    Educational Attainment: High school diploma or higher: 93.8%; Bachelor's degree or higher: 33.4%; Graduate/professional degree or higher: 16.0%

    Housing: Homeownership rate: 81.1%; Median home value: $306,800; Median year structure built: 1985; Homeowner vacancy rate: 3.3%; Median selected monthly owner costs: $2,561 with a mortgage, $1,132

without a mortgage; Median gross rent: $1,306 per month; Rental vacancy rate: 0.0%

Health Insurance: 89.0% have insurance; 76.5% have private insurance; 25.1% have public insurance; 11.0% do not have insurance; 8.9% of children under 18 do not have insurance

Transportation: Commute: 88.1% car, 0.9% public transportation, 0.0% walk, 10.4% work from home; Mean travel time to work: 33.1 minutes

WOODBURY (town).
Covers a land area of 36.124 square miles and a water area of 1.076 square miles. Located at 41.33° N. Lat; 74.10° W. Long. Elevation is 482 feet.

Population: 11,628; Growth (since 2000): 22.9%; Density: 321.9 persons per square mile; Race: 80.0% White, 6.8% Black/African American, 5.0% Asian, 0.0% American Indian/Alaska Native, 0.0% Native Hawaiian/Other Pacific Islander, 2.0% Two or more races, 19.1% Hispanic of any race; Average household size: 3.26; Median age: 39.2; Age under 18: 27.6%; Age 65 and over: 11.4%; Males per 100 females: 98.7; Marriage status: 29.1% never married, 59.5% now married, 1.4% separated, 5.1% widowed, 6.3% divorced; Foreign born: 16.7%; Speak English only: 75.9%; With disability: 11.8%; Veterans: 6.6%; Ancestry: 17.8% Irish, 17.3% Italian, 13.8% American, 9.4% German, 5.1% Polish

Employment: 15.3% management, business, and financial, 5.6% computer, engineering, and science, 13.1% education, legal, community service, arts, and media, 9.8% healthcare practitioners, 14.6% service, 27.4% sales and office, 7.1% natural resources, construction, and maintenance, 7.1% production, transportation, and material moving

Income: Per capita: $40,714; Median household: $123,484; Average household: $130,167; Households with income of $100,000 or more: 62.1%; Poverty rate: 8.2%

Educational Attainment: High school diploma or higher: 95.2%; Bachelor's degree or higher: 44.4%; Graduate/professional degree or higher: 22.4%

Housing: Homeownership rate: 84.7%; Median home value: $305,500; Median year structure built: 1981; Homeowner vacancy rate: 1.3%; Median selected monthly owner costs: $2,715 with a mortgage, $1,095 without a mortgage; Median gross rent: $1,547 per month; Rental vacancy rate: 0.0%

Health Insurance: 96.0% have insurance; 86.4% have private insurance; 21.0% have public insurance; 4.0% do not have insurance; 0.5% of children under 18 do not have insurance

Safety: Violent crime rate: 3.6 per 10,000 population; Property crime rate: 458.4 per 10,000 population

Transportation: Commute: 83.1% car, 8.6% public transportation, 0.8% walk, 6.3% work from home; Mean travel time to work: 40.2 minutes

Additional Information Contacts

Town of Woodbury . . . . (845) 928-6829
http://www.townofwoodbury.com/home.shtml

WOODBURY (village).
Covers a land area of 35.602 square miles and a water area of 1.061 square miles. Located at 41.33° N. Lat; 74.10° W. Long. Elevation is 482 feet.

Population: 10,791; Growth (since 2000): n/a; Density: 303.1 persons per square mile; Race: 83.0% White, 5.6% Black/African American, 4.4% Asian, 0.0% American Indian/Alaska Native, 0.0% Native Hawaiian/Other Pacific Islander, 1.8% Two or more races, 18.1% Hispanic of any race; Average household size: 3.23; Median age: 40.1; Age under 18: 27.3%; Age 65 and over: 12.2%; Males per 100 females: 98.2; Marriage status: 29.0% never married, 59.0% now married, 1.4% separated, 5.3% widowed, 6.7% divorced; Foreign born: 15.4%; Speak English only: 77.3%; With disability: 12.2%; Veterans: 6.9%; Ancestry: 18.8% Irish, 18.1% Italian, 14.3% American, 9.9% German, 5.2% Polish

Employment: 15.6% management, business, and financial, 5.7% computer, engineering, and science, 12.6% education, legal, community service, arts, and media, 10.3% healthcare practitioners, 13.8% service, 27.8% sales and office, 7.6% natural resources, construction, and maintenance, 6.6% production, transportation, and material moving

Income: Per capita: $41,725; Median household: $125,589; Average household: $132,562; Households with income of $100,000 or more: 63.8%; Poverty rate: 8.2%

Educational Attainment: High school diploma or higher: 95.2%; Bachelor's degree or higher: 45.3%; Graduate/professional degree or higher: 22.9%

Housing: Homeownership rate: 88.4%; Median home value: $305,300; Median year structure built: 1980; Homeowner vacancy rate: 1.3%; Median selected monthly owner costs: $2,706 with a mortgage, $1,091 without a

mortgage; Median gross rent: $1,453 per month; Rental vacancy rate: 0.0%

Health Insurance: 95.8% have insurance; 86.0% have private insurance; 21.8% have public insurance; 4.2% do not have insurance; 0.6% of children under 18 do not have insurance

Transportation: Commute: 83.2% car, 7.9% public transportation, 0.9% walk, 6.8% work from home; Mean travel time to work: 39.7 minutes

Orleans County

Located in western New York; bounded on the north by Lake Ontario; drained by Oak Orchard Creek. Covers a land area of 391.259 square miles, a water area of 426.163 square miles, and is located in the Eastern Time Zone at 43.50° N. Lat., 78.23° W. Long. The county was founded in 1824. County seat is Albion.

Orleans County is part of the Rochester, NY Metropolitan Statistical Area. The entire metro area includes: Livingston County, NY; Monroe County, NY; Ontario County, NY; Orleans County, NY; Wayne County, NY; Yates County, NY

Weather Station: Albion 2 NE   Elevation: 439 feet

	Jan	Feb	Mar	Apr	May	Jun	Jul	Aug	Sep	Oct	Nov	Dec
High	32	35	44	57	69	78	82	80	73	61	49	37
Low	18	19	26	37	47	57	62	61	54	43	34	24
Precip	2.7	2.0	2.8	3.0	3.0	3.1	3.0	3.0	3.6	3.1	3.2	3.0
Snow	19.5	13.6	11.1	2.1	0.3	0.0	0.0	0.0	0.0	0.2	4.5	15.1

High and Low temperatures in degrees Fahrenheit; Precipitation and Snow in inches

Population: 41,584; Growth (since 2000): -5.9%; Density: 106.3 persons per square mile; Race: 89.2% White, 6.0% Black/African American, 0.7% Asian, 0.4% American Indian/Alaska Native, 0.1% Native Hawaiian/Other Pacific Islander, 2.0% two or more races, 4.7% Hispanic of any race; Average household size: 2.38; Median age: 42.8; Age under 18: 20.1%; Age 65 and over: 16.5%; Males per 100 females: 98.1; Marriage status: 30.0% never married, 51.4% now married, 2.7% separated, 6.2% widowed, 12.4% divorced; Foreign born: 3.4%; Speak English only: 94.2%; With disability: 17.2%; Veterans: 9.0%; Ancestry: 26.3% German, 16.8% English, 16.5% Irish, 11.6% Italian, 8.4% Polish

Religion: Six largest groups: 15.9% Catholicism, 8.4% Baptist, 5.5% Methodist/Pietist, 2.3% Lutheran, 1.8% Non-denominational Protestant, 1.8% Presbyterian-Reformed

Economy: Unemployment rate: 3.7%; Leading industries: 15.1 % other services (except public administration); 13.4 % retail trade; 13.2 % construction; Farms: 487 totaling 135,090 acres; Company size: 0 employ 1,000 or more persons, 1 employs 500 to 999 persons, 11 employs 100 to 499 persons, 638 employ less than 100 persons; Business ownership: 667 women-owned, 50 Black-owned, 41 Hispanic-owned, n/a Asian-owned, n/a American Indian/Alaska Native-owned

Employment: 12.2% management, business, and financial, 3.1% computer, engineering, and science, 8.8% education, legal, community service, arts, and media, 4.6% healthcare practitioners, 18.2% service, 21.4% sales and office, 13.1% natural resources, construction, and maintenance, 18.6% production, transportation, and material moving

Income: Per capita: $23,929; Median household: $49,223; Average household: $60,952; Households with income of $100,000 or more: 15.7%; Poverty rate: 15.9%

Educational Attainment: High school diploma or higher: 86.9%; Bachelor's degree or higher: 15.9%; Graduate/professional degree or higher: 6.2%

Housing: Homeownership rate: 75.0%; Median home value: $93,600; Median year structure built: 1951; Homeowner vacancy rate: 1.6%; Median selected monthly owner costs: $1,178 with a mortgage, $548 without a mortgage; Median gross rent: $683 per month; Rental vacancy rate: 1.4%

Vital Statistics: Birth rate: 105.2 per 10,000 population; Death rate: 100.3 per 10,000 population; Age-adjusted cancer mortality rate: 209.4 deaths per 100,000 population

Health Insurance: 93.6% have insurance; 66.7% have private insurance; 43.6% have public insurance; 6.4% do not have insurance; 7.0% of children under 18 do not have insurance

Health Care: Physicians: 4.1 per 10,000 population; Dentists: 2.4 per 10,000 population; Hospital beds: 15.5 per 10,000 population; Hospital admissions: 182.4 per 10,000 population

Transportation: Commute: 91.1% car, 0.5% public transportation, 2.2% walk, 3.4% work from home; Mean travel time to work: 24.1 minutes

2016 Presidential Election: 66.8% Trump, 27.3% Clinton, 4.2% Johnson, 1.1% Stein
National and State Parks: Golden Hill State Park; Iroquois National Wildlife Refuge; Lakeside Beach State Park
Additional Information Contacts
Orleans Government . . . . (585) 589-5334
  http://www.orleansny.com

Orleans County Communities

ALBION (town). Covers a land area of 25.257 square miles and a water area of 0.093 square miles. Located at 43.23° N. Lat; 78.21° W. Long. Elevation is 538 feet.
History: Albion was the home of George M. Pullman (1831-1897), originator of the Pullman railroad cars. Pullman was a cabinetmaker here from 1848 to 1855. Disgusted with the dirt, discomfort, and inconvenience of early railroad passenger cars, he conceived the idea of a car with the luxuries of beds and upholstered seats. Incorporated in 1828.
Population: 8,345; Growth (since 2000): 3.8%; Density: 330.4 persons per square mile; Race: 75.1% White, 18.7% Black/African American, 0.0% Asian, 0.4% American Indian/Alaska Native, 0.0% Native Hawaiian/Other Pacific Islander, 2.5% Two or more races, 8.6% Hispanic of any race; Average household size: 2.32; Median age: 37.2; Age under 18: 15.8%; Age 65 and over: 13.3%; Males per 100 females: 99.0; Marriage status: 41.0% never married, 41.0% now married, 3.9% separated, 6.0% widowed, 11.9% divorced; Foreign born: 7.7%; Speak English only: 93.2%; With disability: 22.1%; Veterans: 6.1%; Ancestry: 17.2% Irish, 16.5% German, 15.9% Italian, 12.0% English, 4.4% Polish
Employment: 11.3% management, business, and financial, 1.6% computer, engineering, and science, 7.0% education, legal, community service, arts, and media, 3.9% healthcare practitioners, 28.0% service, 18.0% sales and office, 15.7% natural resources, construction, and maintenance, 14.5% production, transportation, and material moving
Income: Per capita: $18,194; Median household: $39,706; Average household: $59,355; Households with income of $100,000 or more: 13.7%; Poverty rate: 25.1%
Educational Attainment: High school diploma or higher: 78.7%; Bachelor's degree or higher: 11.5%; Graduate/professional degree or higher: 3.7%
School District(s)
Albion Central SD (PK-12)
  Enrollment: 1,933 . . . . (585) 589-2056
Housing: Homeownership rate: 56.9%; Median home value: $89,700; Median year structure built: Before 1940; Homeowner vacancy rate: 2.9%; Median selected monthly owner costs: $1,240 with a mortgage, $573 without a mortgage; Median gross rent: $673 per month; Rental vacancy rate: 0.0%
Health Insurance: 94.4% have insurance; 57.4% have private insurance; 50.3% have public insurance; 5.6% do not have insurance; 3.5% of children under 18 do not have insurance
Transportation: Commute: 91.1% car, 0.0% public transportation, 3.8% walk, 1.7% work from home; Mean travel time to work: 20.0 minutes
Additional Information Contacts
Town of Albion. . . . . (585) 589-7048
  http://www.townofalbion.com

ALBION (village). County seat. Covers a land area of 2.920 square miles and a water area of 0 square miles. Located at 43.25° N. Lat; 78.19° W. Long. Elevation is 538 feet.
Population: 5,614; Growth (since 2000): -24.5%; Density: 1,922.9 persons per square mile; Race: 80.3% White, 11.2% Black/African American, 0.0% Asian, 0.0% American Indian/Alaska Native, 0.0% Native Hawaiian/Other Pacific Islander, 3.5% Two or more races, 7.8% Hispanic of any race; Average household size: 2.26; Median age: 38.2; Age under 18: 20.3%; Age 65 and over: 16.2%; Males per 100 females: 90.7; Marriage status: 29.1% never married, 50.6% now married, 3.1% separated, 7.4% widowed, 13.0% divorced; Foreign born: 8.3%; Speak English only: 94.3%; With disability: 25.5%; Veterans: 7.2%; Ancestry: 19.3% German, 18.8% Irish, 14.9% English, 14.2% Italian, 3.8% Polish
Employment: 12.1% management, business, and financial, 1.9% computer, engineering, and science, 5.6% education, legal, community service, arts, and media, 2.9% healthcare practitioners, 30.1% service, 17.4% sales and office, 17.3% natural resources, construction, and maintenance, 12.8% production, transportation, and material moving

Income: Per capita: $23,705; Median household: $32,259; Average household: $56,436; Households with income of $100,000 or more: 15.2%; Poverty rate: 25.9%
Educational Attainment: High school diploma or higher: 77.5%; Bachelor's degree or higher: 9.8%; Graduate/professional degree or higher: 2.2%
School District(s)
Albion Central SD (PK-12)
  Enrollment: 1,933 . . . . (585) 589-2056
Housing: Homeownership rate: 56.1%; Median home value: $77,600; Median year structure built: Before 1940; Homeowner vacancy rate: 3.1%; Median selected monthly owner costs: $1,122 with a mortgage, $508 without a mortgage; Median gross rent: $646 per month; Rental vacancy rate: 0.0%
Health Insurance: 94.6% have insurance; 57.6% have private insurance; 51.1% have public insurance; 5.4% do not have insurance; 4.0% of children under 18 do not have insurance
Safety: Violent crime rate: 52.2 per 10,000 population; Property crime rate: 323.0 per 10,000 population
Transportation: Commute: 90.4% car, 0.1% public transportation, 4.1% walk, 1.6% work from home; Mean travel time to work: 18.4 minutes
Additional Information Contacts
Village of Albion . . . . (585) 589-9176
  http://vil.albion.ny.us/content

BARRE (town). Covers a land area of 55.040 square miles and a water area of 0.011 square miles. Located at 43.18° N. Lat; 78.21° W. Long.
Population: 1,866; Growth (since 2000): -12.1%; Density: 33.9 persons per square mile; Race: 95.7% White, 1.7% Black/African American, 0.2% Asian, 0.3% American Indian/Alaska Native, 0.0% Native Hawaiian/Other Pacific Islander, 0.8% Two or more races, 3.1% Hispanic of any race; Average household size: 2.58; Median age: 48.7; Age under 18: 17.5%; Age 65 and over: 16.2%; Males per 100 females: 105.6; Marriage status: 21.4% never married, 64.6% now married, 3.2% separated, 5.6% widowed, 8.4% divorced; Foreign born: 1.6%; Speak English only: 96.6%; With disability: 14.3%; Veterans: 10.2%; Ancestry: 24.2% English, 22.6% German, 15.7% Irish, 9.1% American, 8.9% Polish
Employment: 9.2% management, business, and financial, 4.5% computer, engineering, and science, 11.8% education, legal, community service, arts, and media, 5.9% healthcare practitioners, 14.8% service, 19.2% sales and office, 17.2% natural resources, construction, and maintenance, 17.5% production, transportation, and material moving
Income: Per capita: $27,428; Median household: $58,828; Average household: $70,272; Households with income of $100,000 or more: 18.5%; Poverty rate: 8.7%
Educational Attainment: High school diploma or higher: 88.8%; Bachelor's degree or higher: 16.4%; Graduate/professional degree or higher: 6.0%
Housing: Homeownership rate: 91.6%; Median home value: $90,500; Median year structure built: 1944; Homeowner vacancy rate: 0.0%; Median selected monthly owner costs: $1,188 with a mortgage, $508 without a mortgage; Median gross rent: $775 per month; Rental vacancy rate: 0.0%
Health Insurance: 93.8% have insurance; 72.6% have private insurance; 39.3% have public insurance; 6.2% do not have insurance; 5.4% of children under 18 do not have insurance
Transportation: Commute: 92.9% car, 0.0% public transportation, 1.8% walk, 2.7% work from home; Mean travel time to work: 25.1 minutes

CARLTON (town). Covers a land area of 43.607 square miles and a water area of 0.801 square miles. Located at 43.34° N. Lat; 78.21° W. Long. Elevation is 344 feet.
Population: 2,901; Growth (since 2000): -2.0%; Density: 66.5 persons per square mile; Race: 94.9% White, 2.7% Black/African American, 0.3% Asian, 0.4% American Indian/Alaska Native, 0.0% Native Hawaiian/Other Pacific Islander, 1.2% Two or more races, 1.7% Hispanic of any race; Average household size: 2.31; Median age: 49.5; Age under 18: 16.6%; Age 65 and over: 22.9%; Males per 100 females: 102.3; Marriage status: 26.4% never married, 57.0% now married, 3.1% separated, 5.3% widowed, 11.3% divorced; Foreign born: 4.2%; Speak English only: 95.7%; With disability: 15.6%; Veterans: 10.0%; Ancestry: 32.9% German, 16.2% English, 15.1% Irish, 12.4% Italian, 12.1% Polish
Employment: 9.5% management, business, and financial, 5.2% computer, engineering, and science, 8.9% education, legal, community service, arts, and media, 3.8% healthcare practitioners, 14.6% service, 23.9% sales and

office, 16.9% natural resources, construction, and maintenance, 17.1% production, transportation, and material moving
Income: Per capita: $28,479; Median household: $57,607; Average household: $65,448; Households with income of $100,000 or more: 20.0%; Poverty rate: 14.7%
Educational Attainment: High school diploma or higher: 91.9%; Bachelor's degree or higher: 18.0%; Graduate/professional degree or higher: 7.9%
Housing: Homeownership rate: 83.6%; Median home value: $106,800; Median year structure built: 1955; Homeowner vacancy rate: 0.0%; Median selected monthly owner costs: $1,326 with a mortgage, $567 without a mortgage; Median gross rent: $885 per month; Rental vacancy rate: 0.0%
Health Insurance: 95.2% have insurance; 64.9% have private insurance; 50.2% have public insurance; 4.8% do not have insurance; 4.3% of children under 18 do not have insurance
Transportation: Commute: 93.1% car, 0.0% public transportation, 1.6% walk, 3.7% work from home; Mean travel time to work: 28.4 minutes

CLARENDON (town). Covers a land area of 35.219 square miles and a water area of 0 square miles. Located at 43.17° N. Lat; 78.06° W. Long. Elevation is 607 feet.
Population: 3,562; Growth (since 2000): 5.0%; Density: 101.1 persons per square mile; Race: 95.4% White, 1.8% Black/African American, 0.0% Asian, 0.8% American Indian/Alaska Native, 0.0% Native Hawaiian/Other Pacific Islander, 1.9% Two or more races, 0.2% Hispanic of any race; Average household size: 2.37; Median age: 48.8; Age under 18: 14.8%; Age 65 and over: 18.1%; Males per 100 females: 95.4; Marriage status: 23.9% never married, 58.9% now married, 1.5% separated, 4.9% widowed, 12.3% divorced; Foreign born: 0.4%; Speak English only: 98.9%; With disability: 10.9%; Veterans: 9.4%; Ancestry: 31.4% German, 23.7% English, 21.3% Irish, 11.7% Italian, 5.6% Polish
Employment: 8.9% management, business, and financial, 5.3% computer, engineering, and science, 5.3% education, legal, community service, arts, and media, 3.5% healthcare practitioners, 18.7% service, 28.7% sales and office, 9.9% natural resources, construction, and maintenance, 19.8% production, transportation, and material moving
Income: Per capita: $26,356; Median household: $52,330; Average household: $61,909; Households with income of $100,000 or more: 17.6%; Poverty rate: 13.0%
Educational Attainment: High school diploma or higher: 90.1%; Bachelor's degree or higher: 15.3%; Graduate/professional degree or higher: 4.6%
Housing: Homeownership rate: 84.9%; Median home value: $101,600; Median year structure built: 1975; Homeowner vacancy rate: 4.2%; Median selected monthly owner costs: $1,230 with a mortgage, $714 without a mortgage; Median gross rent: $740 per month; Rental vacancy rate: 0.0%
Health Insurance: 98.1% have insurance; 78.7% have private insurance; 39.3% have public insurance; 1.9% do not have insurance; 0.0% of children under 18 do not have insurance
Transportation: Commute: 97.0% car, 0.9% public transportation, 0.0% walk, 0.4% work from home; Mean travel time to work: 27.5 minutes

GAINES (town). Covers a land area of 34.419 square miles and a water area of 0.040 square miles. Located at 43.28° N. Lat; 78.20° W. Long. Elevation is 423 feet.
Population: 3,258; Growth (since 2000): -12.9%; Density: 94.7 persons per square mile; Race: 94.0% White, 2.5% Black/African American, 1.2% Asian, 0.0% American Indian/Alaska Native, 0.0% Native Hawaiian/Other Pacific Islander, 2.1% Two or more races, 2.3% Hispanic of any race; Average household size: 2.36; Median age: 44.8; Age under 18: 16.8%; Age 65 and over: 19.5%; Males per 100 females: 94.9; Marriage status: 27.2% never married, 52.7% now married, 1.7% separated, 4.6% widowed, 15.5% divorced; Foreign born: 1.0%; Speak English only: 98.4%; With disability: 21.5%; Veterans: 12.2%; Ancestry: 23.8% Irish, 21.0% German, 19.2% English, 11.1% Polish, 6.2% Italian
Employment: 13.4% management, business, and financial, 3.2% computer, engineering, and science, 9.8% education, legal, community service, arts, and media, 7.2% healthcare practitioners, 15.0% service, 25.2% sales and office, 14.2% natural resources, construction, and maintenance, 12.0% production, transportation, and material moving
Income: Per capita: $26,874; Median household: $55,257; Average household: $65,091; Households with income of $100,000 or more: 20.9%; Poverty rate: 10.1%

Educational Attainment: High school diploma or higher: 84.0%; Bachelor's degree or higher: 19.1%; Graduate/professional degree or higher: 9.2%
Housing: Homeownership rate: 79.1%; Median home value: $86,200; Median year structure built: 1975; Homeowner vacancy rate: 0.0%; Median selected monthly owner costs: $1,094 with a mortgage, $467 without a mortgage; Median gross rent: $763 per month; Rental vacancy rate: 0.0%
Health Insurance: 97.2% have insurance; 74.8% have private insurance; 42.9% have public insurance; 2.8% do not have insurance; 3.1% of children under 18 do not have insurance
Transportation: Commute: 93.3% car, 0.2% public transportation, 2.4% walk, 0.7% work from home; Mean travel time to work: 17.4 minutes

HOLLEY (village). Covers a land area of 1.268 square miles and a water area of 0 square miles. Located at 43.22° N. Lat; 78.03° W. Long. Elevation is 541 feet.
History: Incorporated 1867.
Population: 1,824; Growth (since 2000): 1.2%; Density: 1,438.4 persons per square mile; Race: 92.8% White, 2.6% Black/African American, 0.7% Asian, 0.1% American Indian/Alaska Native, 0.2% Native Hawaiian/Other Pacific Islander, 3.4% Two or more races, 3.6% Hispanic of any race; Average household size: 2.34; Median age: 36.4; Age under 18: 25.7%; Age 65 and over: 9.3%; Males per 100 females: 94.7; Marriage status: 37.0% never married, 39.9% now married, 3.5% separated, 6.0% widowed, 17.2% divorced; Foreign born: 2.7%; Speak English only: 95.3%; With disability: 13.2%; Veterans: 8.7%; Ancestry: 26.3% German, 23.1% Italian, 19.2% Irish, 11.7% English, 5.9% Polish
Employment: 11.9% management, business, and financial, 0.7% computer, engineering, and science, 4.6% education, legal, community service, arts, and media, 4.9% healthcare practitioners, 19.3% service, 26.0% sales and office, 11.5% natural resources, construction, and maintenance, 21.1% production, transportation, and material moving
Income: Per capita: $19,817; Median household: $38,667; Average household: $45,113; Households with income of $100,000 or more: 8.2%; Poverty rate: 23.7%
Educational Attainment: High school diploma or higher: 86.3%; Bachelor's degree or higher: 13.2%; Graduate/professional degree or higher: 5.7%

School District(s)
Holley Central SD (PK-12)
    Enrollment: 1,045 . . . . (585) 638-6316
Housing: Homeownership rate: 59.1%; Median home value: $81,000; Median year structure built: Before 1940; Homeowner vacancy rate: 1.7%; Median selected monthly owner costs: $985 with a mortgage, $438 without a mortgage; Median gross rent: $624 per month; Rental vacancy rate: 8.9%
Health Insurance: 94.4% have insurance; 64.7% have private insurance; 45.6% have public insurance; 5.6% do not have insurance; 0.4% of children under 18 do not have insurance
Safety: Violent crime rate: 17.6 per 10,000 population; Property crime rate: 163.8 per 10,000 population
Transportation: Commute: 94.6% car, 0.6% public transportation, 2.1% walk, 1.6% work from home; Mean travel time to work: 24.1 minutes

KENDALL (town). Covers a land area of 32.857 square miles and a water area of 0.061 square miles. Located at 43.33° N. Lat; 78.05° W. Long. Elevation is 338 feet.
Population: 2,659; Growth (since 2000): -6.3%; Density: 80.9 persons per square mile; Race: 97.3% White, 0.6% Black/African American, 0.0% Asian, 0.6% American Indian/Alaska Native, 0.0% Native Hawaiian/Other Pacific Islander, 0.8% Two or more races, 3.4% Hispanic of any race; Average household size: 2.60; Median age: 41.7; Age under 18: 26.1%; Age 65 and over: 15.5%; Males per 100 females: 101.9; Marriage status: 23.8% never married, 63.7% now married, 3.1% separated, 5.8% widowed, 6.8% divorced; Foreign born: 1.3%; Speak English only: 99.0%; With disability: 16.4%; Veterans: 9.3%; Ancestry: 35.3% German, 18.7% Irish, 14.4% English, 9.5% Italian, 8.0% American
Employment: 11.9% management, business, and financial, 4.1% computer, engineering, and science, 9.7% education, legal, community service, arts, and media, 4.4% healthcare practitioners, 11.2% service, 22.8% sales and office, 15.4% natural resources, construction, and maintenance, 20.5% production, transportation, and material moving
Income: Per capita: $25,841; Median household: $54,656; Average household: $67,962; Households with income of $100,000 or more: 14.3%; Poverty rate: 10.8%

Educational Attainment: High school diploma or higher: 93.4%; Bachelor's degree or higher: 17.9%; Graduate/professional degree or higher: 8.6%

School District(s)
Kendall Central SD (PK-12)
   Enrollment: 704 . . . . (585) 659-2741
Housing: Homeownership rate: 83.7%; Median home value: $112,400; Median year structure built: 1960; Homeowner vacancy rate: 1.8%; Median selected monthly owner costs: $1,166 with a mortgage, $624 without a mortgage; Median gross rent: $1,003 per month; Rental vacancy rate: 0.0%
Health Insurance: 93.6% have insurance; 71.2% have private insurance; 41.3% have public insurance; 6.4% do not have insurance; 4.4% of children under 18 do not have insurance
Transportation: Commute: 90.9% car, 0.4% public transportation, 1.2% walk, 6.3% work from home; Mean travel time to work: 32.1 minutes

KNOWLESVILLE (unincorporated postal area)
ZCTA: 14479

Covers a land area of 1.480 square miles and a water area of 0 square miles. Located at 43.24° N. Lat; 78.31° W. Long. Elevation is 512 feet.
Population: 207; Growth (since 2000): n/a; Density: 139.9 persons per square mile; Race: 100.0% White, 0.0% Black/African American, 0.0% Asian, 0.0% American Indian/Alaska Native, 0.0% Native Hawaiian/Other Pacific Islander, 0.0% Two or more races, 0.0% Hispanic of any race; Average household size: 2.20; Median age: 48.8; Age under 18: 24.6%; Age 65 and over: 14.0%; Males per 100 females: 97.8; Marriage status: 16.0% never married, 55.8% now married, 0.0% separated, 4.3% widowed, 23.9% divorced; Foreign born: 0.0%; Speak English only: 93.0%; With disability: 23.7%; Veterans: 22.4%; Ancestry: 21.7% German, 12.6% English, 9.2% French Canadian, 7.7% American, 7.2% Dutch
Employment: 9.6% management, business, and financial, 0.0% computer, engineering, and science, 0.0% education, legal, community service, arts, and media, 0.0% healthcare practitioners, 9.6% service, 10.8% sales and office, 15.7% natural resources, construction, and maintenance, 54.2% production, transportation, and material moving
Income: Per capita: $24,146; Median household: $56,875; Average household: $53,732; Households with income of $100,000 or more: 10.6%; Poverty rate: 17.9%
Educational Attainment: High school diploma or higher: 57.3%; Bachelor's degree or higher: n/a; Graduate/professional degree or higher: n/a
Housing: Homeownership rate: 90.4%; Median home value: n/a; Median year structure built: Before 1940; Homeowner vacancy rate: 0.0%; Median selected monthly owner costs: $0 with a mortgage, $414 without a mortgage; Median gross rent: n/a per month; Rental vacancy rate: 0.0%
Health Insurance: 71.5% have insurance; 46.9% have private insurance; 37.7% have public insurance; 28.5% do not have insurance; 64.7% of children under 18 do not have insurance
Transportation: Commute: 100.0% car, 0.0% public transportation, 0.0% walk, 0.0% work from home; Mean travel time to work: 27.0 minutes

LYNDONVILLE (village). Covers a land area of 1.024 square miles and a water area of 0 square miles. Located at 43.32° N. Lat; 78.39° W. Long. Elevation is 322 feet.
History: Incorporated 1903.
Population: 747; Growth (since 2000): -13.3%; Density: 729.1 persons per square mile; Race: 94.6% White, 0.9% Black/African American, 0.9% Asian, 0.3% American Indian/Alaska Native, 0.0% Native Hawaiian/Other Pacific Islander, 3.2% Two or more races, 1.3% Hispanic of any race; Average household size: 2.44; Median age: 37.7; Age under 18: 26.8%; Age 65 and over: 12.4%; Males per 100 females: 98.6; Marriage status: 27.0% never married, 50.3% now married, 1.6% separated, 3.1% widowed, 19.5% divorced; Foreign born: 1.1%; Speak English only: 96.7%; With disability: 10.4%; Veterans: 9.5%; Ancestry: 28.4% English, 23.6% German, 14.1% Irish, 10.8% Italian, 5.1% Scottish
Employment: 15.8% management, business, and financial, 1.2% computer, engineering, and science, 8.1% education, legal, community service, arts, and media, 2.8% healthcare practitioners, 10.6% service, 19.3% sales and office, 16.1% natural resources, construction, and maintenance, 26.1% production, transportation, and material moving

Income: Per capita: $25,830; Median household: $51,875; Average household: $63,518; Households with income of $100,000 or more: 15.0%; Poverty rate: 11.1%
Educational Attainment: High school diploma or higher: 90.1%; Bachelor's degree or higher: 17.6%; Graduate/professional degree or higher: 6.5%

School District(s)
Lyndonville Central SD (PK-12)
   Enrollment: 652 . . . . (585) 765-3101
Housing: Homeownership rate: 75.5%; Median home value: $87,400; Median year structure built: Before 1940; Homeowner vacancy rate: 0.0%; Median selected monthly owner costs: $1,084 with a mortgage, $516 without a mortgage; Median gross rent: $653 per month; Rental vacancy rate: 5.7%
Health Insurance: 97.3% have insurance; 68.7% have private insurance; 41.9% have public insurance; 2.7% do not have insurance; 0.0% of children under 18 do not have insurance
Transportation: Commute: 93.5% car, 0.0% public transportation, 4.9% walk, 1.6% work from home; Mean travel time to work: 25.6 minutes

MEDINA (village). Covers a land area of 3.299 square miles and a water area of 0.078 square miles. Located at 43.22° N. Lat; 78.39° W. Long. Elevation is 531 feet.
History: Incorporated 1832.
Population: 5,814; Growth (since 2000): -9.4%; Density: 1,762.5 persons per square mile; Race: 86.3% White, 7.0% Black/African American, 1.7% Asian, 0.0% American Indian/Alaska Native, 0.0% Native Hawaiian/Other Pacific Islander, 2.7% Two or more races, 6.3% Hispanic of any race; Average household size: 2.11; Median age: 42.0; Age under 18: 22.0%; Age 65 and over: 19.7%; Males per 100 females: 87.8; Marriage status: 29.2% never married, 47.6% now married, 1.8% separated, 8.6% widowed, 14.5% divorced; Foreign born: 1.9%; Speak English only: 94.2%; With disability: 21.8%; Veterans: 10.5%; Ancestry: 26.3% German, 16.7% English, 13.3% Irish, 13.0% Polish, 6.9% Italian
Employment: 12.7% management, business, and financial, 2.3% computer, engineering, and science, 13.3% education, legal, community service, arts, and media, 3.7% healthcare practitioners, 20.7% service, 18.3% sales and office, 9.5% natural resources, construction, and maintenance, 19.4% production, transportation, and material moving
Income: Per capita: $22,528; Median household: $39,741; Average household: $48,369; Households with income of $100,000 or more: 9.7%; Poverty rate: 13.9%
Educational Attainment: High school diploma or higher: 90.5%; Bachelor's degree or higher: 18.6%; Graduate/professional degree or higher: 7.4%

School District(s)
Medina Central SD (PK-12)
   Enrollment: 1,606 . . . . (585) 798-2700
Orleans-Niagara Boces
   Enrollment: n/a . . . . (716) 731-6800
Housing: Homeownership rate: 62.2%; Median home value: $71,300; Median year structure built: Before 1940; Homeowner vacancy rate: 0.5%; Median selected monthly owner costs: $1,061 with a mortgage, $551 without a mortgage; Median gross rent: $651 per month; Rental vacancy rate: 2.0%
Health Insurance: 96.5% have insurance; 64.6% have private insurance; 50.8% have public insurance; 3.5% do not have insurance; 0.0% of children under 18 do not have insurance
Hospitals: Medina Memorial Hospital (101 beds)
Safety: Violent crime rate: 41.8 per 10,000 population; Property crime rate: 259.6 per 10,000 population
Transportation: Commute: 82.3% car, 2.3% public transportation, 4.2% walk, 3.6% work from home; Mean travel time to work: 19.6 minutes
Additional Information Contacts
Village of Medina . . . . (585) 798-1790
   http://villagemedina.org/content

MURRAY (town). Covers a land area of 31.059 square miles and a water area of 0.040 square miles. Located at 43.26° N. Lat; 78.06° W. Long. Elevation is 410 feet.
Population: 4,784; Growth (since 2000): -23.6%; Density: 154.0 persons per square mile; Race: 93.8% White, 1.5% Black/African American, 0.6% Asian, 0.0% American Indian/Alaska Native, 0.1% Native Hawaiian/Other Pacific Islander, 1.3% Two or more races, 7.6% Hispanic of any race; Average household size: 2.48; Median age: 38.9; Age under 18: 23.8%;

Age 65 and over: 13.9%; Males per 100 females: 97.0; Marriage status: 31.8% never married, 44.1% now married, 3.7% separated, 7.2% widowed, 16.9% divorced; Foreign born: 3.3%; Speak English only: 91.7%; With disability: 14.3%; Veterans: 6.8%; Ancestry: 22.9% German, 21.5% Italian, 19.3% Irish, 12.2% English, 6.1% Polish
Employment: 13.3% management, business, and financial, 2.9% computer, engineering, and science, 6.4% education, legal, community service, arts, and media, 8.1% healthcare practitioners, 17.3% service, 23.2% sales and office, 13.4% natural resources, construction, and maintenance, 15.5% production, transportation, and material moving
Income: Per capita: $25,587; Median household: $43,839; Average household: $64,750; Households with income of $100,000 or more: 17.6%; Poverty rate: 19.1%
Educational Attainment: High school diploma or higher: 87.9%; Bachelor's degree or higher: 15.8%; Graduate/professional degree or higher: 5.9%
Housing: Homeownership rate: 75.1%; Median home value: $95,000; Median year structure built: 1953; Homeowner vacancy rate: 2.3%; Median selected monthly owner costs: $1,130 with a mortgage, $542 without a mortgage; Median gross rent: $620 per month; Rental vacancy rate: 6.2%
Health Insurance: 93.5% have insurance; 65.7% have private insurance; 44.1% have public insurance; 6.5% do not have insurance; 0.2% of children under 18 do not have insurance
Transportation: Commute: 94.1% car, 0.2% public transportation, 0.8% walk, 3.9% work from home; Mean travel time to work: 25.3 minutes
Additional Information Contacts
Town of Murray . . . . (585) 638-6570
http://www.townofmurray.org

RIDGEWAY (town).
Covers a land area of 50.026 square miles and a water area of 0.216 square miles. Located at 43.26° N. Lat; 78.38° W. Long. Elevation is 417 feet.
Population: 6,520; Growth (since 2000): -5.3%; Density: 130.3 persons per square mile; Race: 92.3% White, 3.5% Black/African American, 1.0% Asian, 0.0% American Indian/Alaska Native, 0.0% Native Hawaiian/Other Pacific Islander, 3.1% Two or more races, 2.3% Hispanic of any race; Average household size: 2.43; Median age: 38.8; Age under 18: 25.7%; Age 65 and over: 15.2%; Males per 100 females: 97.2; Marriage status: 25.7% never married, 55.6% now married, 1.0% separated, 6.8% widowed, 11.9% divorced; Foreign born: 2.3%; Speak English only: 92.7%; With disability: 19.7%; Veterans: 12.1%; Ancestry: 33.0% German, 16.5% English, 12.6% Polish, 11.2% Irish, 9.9% Italian
Employment: 12.6% management, business, and financial, 2.7% computer, engineering, and science, 13.5% education, legal, community service, arts, and media, 3.2% healthcare practitioners, 18.4% service, 19.3% sales and office, 9.4% natural resources, construction, and maintenance, 20.9% production, transportation, and material moving
Income: Per capita: $23,018; Median household: $46,979; Average household: $56,339; Households with income of $100,000 or more: 15.5%; Poverty rate: 13.7%
Educational Attainment: High school diploma or higher: 88.5%; Bachelor's degree or higher: 17.3%; Graduate/professional degree or higher: 7.0%
Housing: Homeownership rate: 75.9%; Median home value: $89,600; Median year structure built: Before 1940; Homeowner vacancy rate: 0.4%; Median selected monthly owner costs: $1,080 with a mortgage, $513 without a mortgage; Median gross rent: $667 per month; Rental vacancy rate: 3.1%
Health Insurance: 91.5% have insurance; 61.8% have private insurance; 43.0% have public insurance; 8.5% do not have insurance; 15.4% of children under 18 do not have insurance
Transportation: Commute: 86.5% car, 1.5% public transportation, 2.9% walk, 4.8% work from home; Mean travel time to work: 22.1 minutes

SHELBY (town).
Covers a land area of 46.390 square miles and a water area of 0.339 square miles. Located at 43.17° N. Lat; 78.39° W. Long. Elevation is 600 feet.
Population: 5,154; Growth (since 2000): -4.9%; Density: 111.1 persons per square mile; Race: 84.3% White, 7.4% Black/African American, 2.8% Asian, 0.3% American Indian/Alaska Native, 0.4% Native Hawaiian/Other Pacific Islander, 1.7% Two or more races, 7.9% Hispanic of any race; Average household size: 2.13; Median age: 44.4; Age under 18: 20.8%; Age 65 and over: 21.0%; Males per 100 females: 93.1; Marriage status: 32.2% never married, 48.0% now married, 2.5% separated, 7.8% widowed, 12.0% divorced; Foreign born: 3.9%; Speak English only: 91.1%;

With disability: 18.0%; Veterans: 8.7%; Ancestry: 25.8% German, 19.6% English, 12.6% Irish, 10.9% Polish, 5.3% Italian
Employment: 17.2% management, business, and financial, 1.3% computer, engineering, and science, 7.3% education, legal, community service, arts, and media, 3.7% healthcare practitioners, 20.7% service, 16.7% sales and office, 12.0% natural resources, construction, and maintenance, 21.2% production, transportation, and material moving
Income: Per capita: $22,711; Median household: $45,653; Average household: $49,193; Households with income of $100,000 or more: 8.3%; Poverty rate: 17.4%
Educational Attainment: High school diploma or higher: 90.4%; Bachelor's degree or higher: 17.6%; Graduate/professional degree or higher: 7.3%
Housing: Homeownership rate: 67.1%; Median home value: $82,600; Median year structure built: 1952; Homeowner vacancy rate: 1.8%; Median selected monthly owner costs: $1,164 with a mortgage, $546 without a mortgage; Median gross rent: $694 per month; Rental vacancy rate: 0.0%
Health Insurance: 90.9% have insurance; 66.6% have private insurance; 44.1% have public insurance; 9.1% do not have insurance; 10.6% of children under 18 do not have insurance
Transportation: Commute: 86.5% car, 0.8% public transportation, 4.1% walk, 4.0% work from home; Mean travel time to work: 20.7 minutes
Additional Information Contacts
Town of Shelby . . . . (585) 798-3120
http://www.townofshelbyny.org

WATERPORT (unincorporated postal area)
ZCTA: 14571
Covers a land area of 18.355 square miles and a water area of 0.505 square miles. Located at 43.34° N. Lat; 78.25° W. Long. Elevation is 351 feet.
Population: 1,061; Growth (since 2000): -5.2%; Density: 57.8 persons per square mile; Race: 93.1% White, 3.7% Black/African American, 0.8% Asian, 1.0% American Indian/Alaska Native, 0.0% Native Hawaiian/Other Pacific Islander, 0.0% Two or more races, 1.9% Hispanic of any race; Average household size: 2.21; Median age: 51.0; Age under 18: 17.6%; Age 65 and over: 29.1%; Males per 100 females: 103.5; Marriage status: 22.2% never married, 60.5% now married, 1.6% separated, 4.8% widowed, 12.4% divorced; Foreign born: 6.2%; Speak English only: 83.2%; With disability: 10.8%; Veterans: 8.6%; Ancestry: 24.0% German, 14.9% Irish, 14.7% Swiss, 12.8% English, 11.6% Italian
Employment: 16.6% management, business, and financial, 2.5% computer, engineering, and science, 15.9% education, legal, community service, arts, and media, 2.7% healthcare practitioners, 13.4% service, 30.7% sales and office, 10.2% natural resources, construction, and maintenance, 8.0% production, transportation, and material moving
Income: Per capita: $29,715; Median household: $47,632; Average household: $65,990; Households with income of $100,000 or more: 23.0%; Poverty rate: 26.2%
Educational Attainment: High school diploma or higher: 85.0%; Bachelor's degree or higher: 14.5%; Graduate/professional degree or higher: 8.8%
Housing: Homeownership rate: 95.2%; Median home value: $99,400; Median year structure built: 1950; Homeowner vacancy rate: 0.0%; Median selected monthly owner costs: $1,147 with a mortgage, $644 without a mortgage; Median gross rent: n/a per month; Rental vacancy rate: 0.0%
Health Insurance: 80.0% have insurance; 54.2% have private insurance; 47.5% have public insurance; 20.0% do not have insurance; 59.4% of children under 18 do not have insurance
Transportation: Commute: 79.5% car, 0.0% public transportation, 4.8% walk, 13.6% work from home; Mean travel time to work: 28.1 minutes

YATES (town).
Covers a land area of 37.387 square miles and a water area of 0 square miles. Located at 43.34° N. Lat; 78.39° W. Long. Elevation is 325 feet.
Population: 2,535; Growth (since 2000): 1.0%; Density: 67.8 persons per square mile; Race: 95.1% White, 0.3% Black/African American, 0.3% Asian, 1.8% American Indian/Alaska Native, 0.0% Native Hawaiian/Other Pacific Islander, 2.2% Two or more races, 2.0% Hispanic of any race; Average household size: 2.50; Median age: 44.7; Age under 18: 22.2%; Age 65 and over: 13.2%; Males per 100 females: 103.9; Marriage status: 23.1% never married, 56.3% now married, 2.6% separated, 5.9% widowed, 14.7% divorced; Foreign born: 0.9%; Speak English only: 92.6%;

With disability: 11.2%; Veterans: 8.6%; Ancestry: 33.3% German, 20.5% English, 13.5% Irish, 7.1% Polish, 6.7% Italian
Employment: 12.3% management, business, and financial, 2.9% computer, engineering, and science, 9.5% education, legal, community service, arts, and media, 4.1% healthcare practitioners, 10.6% service, 20.2% sales and office, 12.8% natural resources, construction, and maintenance, 27.5% production, transportation, and material moving
Income: Per capita: $27,523; Median household: $59,137; Average household: $69,602; Households with income of $100,000 or more: 17.9%; Poverty rate: 13.9%
Educational Attainment: High school diploma or higher: 87.2%; Bachelor's degree or higher: 15.6%; Graduate/professional degree or higher: 5.6%
Housing: Homeownership rate: 84.6%; Median home value: $96,400; Median year structure built: 1952; Homeowner vacancy rate: 1.8%; Median selected monthly owner costs: $1,238 with a mortgage, $581 without a mortgage; Median gross rent: $725 per month; Rental vacancy rate: 3.0%
Health Insurance: 89.1% have insurance; 68.9% have private insurance; 32.1% have public insurance; 10.9% do not have insurance; 15.3% of children under 18 do not have insurance
Transportation: Commute: 89.8% car, 0.0% public transportation, 2.3% walk, 6.2% work from home; Mean travel time to work: 29.8 minutes

Oswego County

Located in north central New York; bounded on the northwest by Lake Ontario, and on the south by Oneida Lake and the Oneida River; drained by the Oswego and Salmon Rivers. Covers a land area of 951.650 square miles, a water area of 360.433 square miles, and is located in the Eastern Time Zone at 43.46° N. Lat., 76.21° W. Long. The county was founded in 1816. County seat is Oswego.

Oswego County is part of the Syracuse, NY Metropolitan Statistical Area. The entire metro area includes: Madison County, NY; Onondaga County, NY; Oswego County, NY

Weather Station: Oswego East										Elevation: 350 feet	
	Jan	Feb	Mar	Apr	May	Jun	Jul	Aug	Sep	Oct	Nov	Dec
High	31	33	41	54	65	75	80	79	71	59	47	36
Low	18	19	26	37	47	56	62	61	54	44	35	24
Precip	3.6	2.8	3.2	3.5	3.3	3.0	3.1	3.4	3.9	4.1	4.5	3.8
Snow	45.0	32.8	17.1	3.8	tr	0.0	0.0	0.0	tr	0.2	8.5	34.6

High and Low temperatures in degrees Fahrenheit; Precipitation and Snow in inches

Population: 119,833; Growth (since 2000): -2.1%; Density: 125.9 persons per square mile; Race: 95.7% White, 1.0% Black/African American, 0.7% Asian, 0.2% American Indian/Alaska Native, 0.0% Native Hawaiian/Other Pacific Islander, 1.8% two or more races, 2.5% Hispanic of any race; Average household size: 2.51; Median age: 39.8; Age under 18: 21.5%; Age 65 and over: 14.8%; Males per 100 females: 99.4; Marriage status: 32.1% never married, 50.7% now married, 3.0% separated, 5.8% widowed, 11.4% divorced; Foreign born: 1.8%; Speak English only: 95.9%; With disability: 15.2%; Veterans: 9.3%; Ancestry: 21.0% Irish, 18.9% German, 14.2% Italian, 12.6% English, 7.3% French
Religion: Six largest groups: 20.8% Catholicism, 6.3% Methodist/Pietist, 1.8% Holiness, 1.7% Non-denominational Protestant, 0.9% Baptist, 0.7% Presbyterian-Reformed
Economy: Unemployment rate: 4.2%; Leading industries: 16.7 % retail trade; 14.7 % construction; 13.5 % accommodation and food services; Farms: 657 totaling 94,209 acres; Company size: 2 employ 1,000 or more persons, 3 employ 500 to 999 persons, 26 employ 100 to 499 persons, 2,107 employ less than 100 persons; Business ownership: 2,150 women-owned, 43 Black-owned, 69 Hispanic-owned, 152 Asian-owned, n/a American Indian/Alaska Native-owned
Employment: 10.2% management, business, and financial, 3.8% computer, engineering, and science, 9.9% education, legal, community service, arts, and media, 5.2% healthcare practitioners, 20.4% service, 23.0% sales and office, 12.1% natural resources, construction, and maintenance, 15.3% production, transportation, and material moving
Income: Per capita: $25,791; Median household: $51,755; Average household: $65,557; Households with income of $100,000 or more: 18.9%; Poverty rate: 18.3%
Educational Attainment: High school diploma or higher: 86.9%; Bachelor's degree or higher: 18.3%; Graduate/professional degree or higher: 7.8%

Housing: Homeownership rate: 72.6%; Median home value: $97,800; Median year structure built: 1970; Homeowner vacancy rate: 2.3%; Median selected monthly owner costs: $1,205 with a mortgage, $490 without a mortgage; Median gross rent: $748 per month; Rental vacancy rate: 5.6%
Vital Statistics: Birth rate: 97.1 per 10,000 population; Death rate: 89.5 per 10,000 population; Age-adjusted cancer mortality rate: 177.0 deaths per 100,000 population
Health Insurance: 93.9% have insurance; 64.8% have private insurance; 42.8% have public insurance; 6.1% do not have insurance; 4.0% of children under 18 do not have insurance
Health Care: Physicians: 7.4 per 10,000 population; Dentists: 4.4 per 10,000 population; Hospital beds: 8.2 per 10,000 population; Hospital admissions: 349.3 per 10,000 population
Air Quality Index (AQI): Percent of Days: 96.1% good, 3.9% moderate, 0.0% unhealthy for sensitive individuals, 0.0% unhealthy, 0.0% very unhealthy; Annual median: 34; Annual maximum: 87
Transportation: Commute: 90.3% car, 0.9% public transportation, 4.1% walk, 3.4% work from home; Mean travel time to work: 24.8 minutes
2016 Presidential Election: 57.5% Trump, 35.5% Clinton, 4.4% Johnson, 1.5% Stein
National and State Parks: Battle Island State Park; Fort Brewerton State Park; Happy Valley State Wildlife Management Area; Littlejohn State Game Management Area; Selkirk Shores State Park; Threemile Bay State Game Management Area
Additional Information Contacts
Oswego Government . . . . (315) 349-8385
http://www.co.oswego.ny.us

Oswego County Communities

ALBION (town). Covers a land area of 47.286 square miles and a water area of 0.532 square miles. Located at 43.49° N. Lat; 76.03° W. Long.
Population: 2,276; Growth (since 2000): 9.3%; Density: 48.1 persons per square mile; Race: 97.5% White, 0.2% Black/African American, 0.5% Asian, 0.0% American Indian/Alaska Native, 0.0% Native Hawaiian/Other Pacific Islander, 1.6% Two or more races, 0.9% Hispanic of any race; Average household size: 2.71; Median age: 40.1; Age under 18: 25.0%; Age 65 and over: 12.4%; Males per 100 females: 106.1; Marriage status: 29.0% never married, 51.7% now married, 3.6% separated, 3.8% widowed, 15.5% divorced; Foreign born: 0.8%; Speak English only: 95.7%; With disability: 14.2%; Veterans: 9.7%; Ancestry: 18.5% Irish, 16.2% German, 13.7% English, 8.3% French, 7.6% American
Employment: 10.0% management, business, and financial, 2.6% computer, engineering, and science, 7.7% education, legal, community service, arts, and media, 5.7% healthcare practitioners, 20.4% service, 17.0% sales and office, 16.3% natural resources, construction, and maintenance, 20.4% production, transportation, and material moving
Income: Per capita: $20,328; Median household: $46,810; Average household: $53,387; Households with income of $100,000 or more: 9.5%; Poverty rate: 21.6%
Educational Attainment: High school diploma or higher: 77.7%; Bachelor's degree or higher: 9.1%; Graduate/professional degree or higher: 4.2%
Housing: Homeownership rate: 80.0%; Median home value: $76,300; Median year structure built: 1982; Homeowner vacancy rate: 0.0%; Median selected monthly owner costs: $1,077 with a mortgage, $405 without a mortgage; Median gross rent: $852 per month; Rental vacancy rate: 0.0%
Health Insurance: 86.1% have insurance; 50.9% have private insurance; 45.6% have public insurance; 13.9% do not have insurance; 12.2% of children under 18 do not have insurance
Transportation: Commute: 90.1% car, 2.9% public transportation, 1.2% walk, 5.3% work from home; Mean travel time to work: 28.4 minutes

ALTMAR (village). Covers a land area of 2.069 square miles and a water area of 0.010 square miles. Located at 43.51° N. Lat; 76.01° W. Long. Elevation is 574 feet.
Population: 381; Growth (since 2000): 8.5%; Density: 184.1 persons per square mile; Race: 96.6% White, 0.3% Black/African American, 2.1% Asian, 0.0% American Indian/Alaska Native, 0.0% Native Hawaiian/Other Pacific Islander, 0.8% Two or more races, 0.3% Hispanic of any race; Average household size: 2.63; Median age: 39.4; Age under 18: 29.4%; Age 65 and over: 10.5%; Males per 100 females: 116.5; Marriage status: 39.2% never married, 33.3% now married, 3.1% separated, 4.5% widowed, 22.9% divorced; Foreign born: 3.1%; Speak English only: 95.9%;

With disability: 16.8%; Veterans: 3.7%; Ancestry: 24.1% Irish, 19.7% German, 14.2% English, 13.4% French, 8.7% Polish
Employment: 2.3% management, business, and financial, 3.8% computer, engineering, and science, 2.3% education, legal, community service, arts, and media, 1.5% healthcare practitioners, 31.1% service, 26.5% sales and office, 12.9% natural resources, construction, and maintenance, 19.7% production, transportation, and material moving
Income: Per capita: $15,674; Median household: $30,417; Average household: $40,099; Households with income of $100,000 or more: 4.8%; Poverty rate: 35.4%
Educational Attainment: High school diploma or higher: 74.4%; Bachelor's degree or higher: 5.2%; Graduate/professional degree or higher: 3.6%

School District(s)
Altmar Parish-Williamstown Central SD (PK-12)
    Enrollment: 1,238 . . . . (315) 625-5251
Housing: Homeownership rate: 62.8%; Median home value: $52,700; Median year structure built: 1973; Homeowner vacancy rate: 0.0%; Median selected monthly owner costs: $1,099 with a mortgage, $529 without a mortgage; Median gross rent: $738 per month; Rental vacancy rate: 0.0%
Health Insurance: 86.4% have insurance; 33.3% have private insurance; 60.1% have public insurance; 13.6% do not have insurance; 10.9% of children under 18 do not have insurance
Transportation: Commute: 89.4% car, 3.0% public transportation, 3.0% walk, 1.5% work from home; Mean travel time to work: 22.1 minutes

AMBOY (town). Covers a land area of 37.049 square miles and a water area of 0.692 square miles. Located at 43.38° N. Lat; 75.92° W. Long.
Population: 1,058; Growth (since 2000): -19.4%; Density: 28.6 persons per square mile; Race: 98.0% White, 0.1% Black/African American, 0.2% Asian, 0.4% American Indian/Alaska Native, 0.0% Native Hawaiian/Other Pacific Islander, 0.3% Two or more races, 1.0% Hispanic of any race; Average household size: 2.52; Median age: 43.5; Age under 18: 20.3%; Age 65 and over: 17.7%; Males per 100 females: 108.1; Marriage status: 28.1% never married, 55.1% now married, 3.2% separated, 5.3% widowed, 11.5% divorced; Foreign born: 0.5%; Speak English only: 98.7%; With disability: 18.1%; Veterans: 10.7%; Ancestry: 22.4% German, 16.4% Irish, 11.1% English, 8.0% Polish, 7.8% American
Employment: 14.2% management, business, and financial, 0.0% computer, engineering, and science, 3.4% education, legal, community service, arts, and media, 4.3% healthcare practitioners, 14.0% service, 29.8% sales and office, 10.4% natural resources, construction, and maintenance, 23.9% production, transportation, and material moving
Income: Per capita: $22,693; Median household: $47,321; Average household: $56,849; Households with income of $100,000 or more: 13.5%; Poverty rate: 16.9%
Educational Attainment: High school diploma or higher: 81.9%; Bachelor's degree or higher: 7.4%; Graduate/professional degree or higher: 0.8%
Housing: Homeownership rate: 84.5%; Median home value: $84,400; Median year structure built: 1979; Homeowner vacancy rate: 5.6%; Median selected monthly owner costs: $1,154 with a mortgage, $408 without a mortgage; Median gross rent: $682 per month; Rental vacancy rate: 0.0%
Health Insurance: 89.3% have insurance; 60.3% have private insurance; 44.3% have public insurance; 10.7% do not have insurance; 5.5% of children under 18 do not have insurance
Transportation: Commute: 97.7% car, 0.0% public transportation, 0.7% walk, 0.7% work from home; Mean travel time to work: 41.2 minutes

BERNHARDS BAY (unincorporated postal area)
ZCTA: 13028
    Covers a land area of 18.688 square miles and a water area of 0.302 square miles. Located at 43.30° N. Lat; 75.93° W. Long. Elevation is 390 feet.
Population: 1,445; Growth (since 2000): 4.7%; Density: 77.3 persons per square mile; Race: 98.2% White, 0.0% Black/African American, 0.0% Asian, 0.0% American Indian/Alaska Native, 0.0% Native Hawaiian/Other Pacific Islander, 1.8% Two or more races, 0.0% Hispanic of any race; Average household size: 2.61; Median age: 41.9; Age under 18: 21.4%; Age 65 and over: 18.6%; Males per 100 females: 113.3; Marriage status: 36.9% never married, 54.5% now married, 0.0% separated, 0.0% widowed, 8.6% divorced; Foreign born: 0.0%; Speak English only: 99.4%; With disability: 8.1%; Veterans: 10.3%; Ancestry: 33.1% Irish, 30.0% German, 18.0% English, 13.7% American, 11.3% Italian

Employment: 14.8% management, business, and financial, 1.5% computer, engineering, and science, 4.2% education, legal, community service, arts, and media, 9.6% healthcare practitioners, 24.0% service, 17.3% sales and office, 15.2% natural resources, construction, and maintenance, 13.5% production, transportation, and material moving
Income: Per capita: $32,372; Median household: $57,500; Average household: $85,373; Households with income of $100,000 or more: 25.5%; Poverty rate: 2.4%
Educational Attainment: High school diploma or higher: 84.8%; Bachelor's degree or higher: 12.3%; Graduate/professional degree or higher: 7.9%
Housing: Homeownership rate: 72.6%; Median home value: $175,800; Median year structure built: 1964; Homeowner vacancy rate: 2.9%; Median selected monthly owner costs: $1,797 with a mortgage, $494 without a mortgage; Median gross rent: $928 per month; Rental vacancy rate: 0.0%
Health Insurance: 89.0% have insurance; 62.7% have private insurance; 38.9% have public insurance; 11.0% do not have insurance; 10.7% of children under 18 do not have insurance
Transportation: Commute: 94.8% car, 0.0% public transportation, 2.4% walk, 2.8% work from home; Mean travel time to work: 32.0 minutes

BOYLSTON (town). Covers a land area of 39.152 square miles and a water area of 0.021 square miles. Located at 43.66° N. Lat; 75.95° W. Long.
Population: 507; Growth (since 2000): 0.4%; Density: 12.9 persons per square mile; Race: 95.5% White, 0.0% Black/African American, 0.0% Asian, 1.2% American Indian/Alaska Native, 0.0% Native Hawaiian/Other Pacific Islander, 3.4% Two or more races, 3.4% Hispanic of any race; Average household size: 2.49; Median age: 45.9; Age under 18: 24.1%; Age 65 and over: 18.9%; Males per 100 females: 115.3; Marriage status: 21.2% never married, 63.6% now married, 0.7% separated, 5.8% widowed, 9.4% divorced; Foreign born: 0.8%; Speak English only: 97.1%; With disability: 15.0%; Veterans: 19.7%; Ancestry: 21.3% English, 17.6% Irish, 17.2% German, 10.5% French, 4.9% Dutch
Employment: 6.6% management, business, and financial, 3.8% computer, engineering, and science, 5.2% education, legal, community service, arts, and media, 5.7% healthcare practitioners, 20.3% service, 13.2% sales and office, 25.9% natural resources, construction, and maintenance, 19.3% production, transportation, and material moving
Income: Per capita: $24,601; Median household: $54,444; Average household: $60,844; Households with income of $100,000 or more: 13.2%; Poverty rate: 14.7%
Educational Attainment: High school diploma or higher: 89.9%; Bachelor's degree or higher: 19.5%; Graduate/professional degree or higher: 7.1%
Housing: Homeownership rate: 92.6%; Median home value: $120,600; Median year structure built: 1975; Homeowner vacancy rate: 0.0%; Median selected monthly owner costs: $1,250 with a mortgage, $439 without a mortgage; Median gross rent: $850 per month; Rental vacancy rate: 0.0%
Health Insurance: 90.5% have insurance; 64.7% have private insurance; 43.2% have public insurance; 9.5% do not have insurance; 1.6% of children under 18 do not have insurance
Transportation: Commute: 94.7% car, 0.0% public transportation, 0.0% walk, 4.3% work from home; Mean travel time to work: 38.7 minutes

CENTRAL SQUARE (village). Covers a land area of 1.906 square miles and a water area of 0 square miles. Located at 43.29° N. Lat; 76.14° W. Long. Elevation is 449 feet.
Population: 1,938; Growth (since 2000): 17.7%; Density: 1,016.7 persons per square mile; Race: 98.9% White, 0.1% Black/African American, 0.0% Asian, 0.0% American Indian/Alaska Native, 0.0% Native Hawaiian/Other Pacific Islander, 1.0% Two or more races, 0.0% Hispanic of any race; Average household size: 2.14; Median age: 45.1; Age under 18: 20.5%; Age 65 and over: 21.1%; Males per 100 females: 83.5; Marriage status: 26.2% never married, 54.4% now married, 3.1% separated, 8.7% widowed, 10.7% divorced; Foreign born: 1.0%; Speak English only: 98.6%; With disability: 20.0%; Veterans: 10.6%; Ancestry: 27.5% German, 17.8% Irish, 17.0% English, 11.7% Italian, 11.2% French
Employment: 13.3% management, business, and financial, 3.4% computer, engineering, and science, 11.8% education, legal, community service, arts, and media, 5.6% healthcare practitioners, 18.1% service, 28.1% sales and office, 10.3% natural resources, construction, and maintenance, 9.5% production, transportation, and material moving

Income: Per capita: $27,701; Median household: $41,583; Average household: $58,153; Households with income of $100,000 or more: 15.6%; Poverty rate: 17.0%

Educational Attainment: High school diploma or higher: 91.1%; Bachelor's degree or higher: 23.6%; Graduate/professional degree or higher: 7.2%

School District(s)

Central Square Central SD (PK-12)

    Enrollment: 3,941 . . . . (315) 668-4220

Housing: Homeownership rate: 58.0%; Median home value: $144,400; Median year structure built: 1974; Homeowner vacancy rate: 3.3%; Median selected monthly owner costs: $1,323 with a mortgage, $624 without a mortgage; Median gross rent: $722 per month; Rental vacancy rate: 5.5%

Health Insurance: 98.6% have insurance; 69.9% have private insurance; 47.4% have public insurance; 1.4% do not have insurance; 0.0% of children under 18 do not have insurance

Safety: Violent crime rate: 0.0 per 10,000 population; Property crime rate: 179.2 per 10,000 population

Transportation: Commute: 96.6% car, 0.0% public transportation, 1.1% walk, 2.3% work from home; Mean travel time to work: 28.9 minutes

---

CLEVELAND (village). Covers a land area of 1.131 square miles and a water area of 0.093 square miles. Located at 43.24° N. Lat; 75.88° W. Long. Elevation is 436 feet.

Population: 683; Growth (since 2000): -9.9%; Density: 603.7 persons per square mile; Race: 98.1% White, 0.0% Black/African American, 0.0% Asian, 0.0% American Indian/Alaska Native, 0.0% Native Hawaiian/Other Pacific Islander, 1.9% Two or more races, 0.0% Hispanic of any race; Average household size: 2.46; Median age: 45.3; Age under 18: 18.7%; Age 65 and over: 13.5%; Males per 100 females: 106.0; Marriage status: 36.5% never married, 42.1% now married, 3.2% separated, 8.3% widowed, 13.1% divorced; Foreign born: 1.3%; Speak English only: 99.2%; With disability: 16.4%; Veterans: 7.2%; Ancestry: 22.0% German, 19.8% Irish, 12.0% Italian, 10.4% English, 8.5% Polish

Employment: 13.1% management, business, and financial, 3.1% computer, engineering, and science, 4.0% education, legal, community service, arts, and media, 4.4% healthcare practitioners, 19.0% service, 23.7% sales and office, 10.3% natural resources, construction, and maintenance, 22.4% production, transportation, and material moving

Income: Per capita: $25,750; Median household: $45,000; Average household: $62,268; Households with income of $100,000 or more: 16.2%; Poverty rate: 11.1%

Educational Attainment: High school diploma or higher: 90.9%; Bachelor's degree or higher: 10.3%; Graduate/professional degree or higher: 4.1%

School District(s)

Central Square Central SD (PK-12)

    Enrollment: 3,941 . . . . (315) 668-4220

Housing: Homeownership rate: 82.0%; Median home value: $84,200; Median year structure built: 1952; Homeowner vacancy rate: 0.0%; Median selected monthly owner costs: $1,193 with a mortgage, $463 without a mortgage; Median gross rent: $693 per month; Rental vacancy rate: 0.0%

Health Insurance: 89.2% have insurance; 61.3% have private insurance; 35.6% have public insurance; 10.8% do not have insurance; 1.4% of children under 18 do not have insurance

Transportation: Commute: 95.0% car, 0.6% public transportation, 2.2% walk, 2.2% work from home; Mean travel time to work: 43.1 minutes

---

CONSTANTIA (CDP). Covers a land area of 3.009 square miles and a water area of 0.007 square miles. Located at 43.26° N. Lat; 76.01° W. Long. Elevation is 384 feet.

Population: 991; Growth (since 2000): -10.5%; Density: 329.3 persons per square mile; Race: 96.4% White, 0.0% Black/African American, 0.0% Asian, 0.0% American Indian/Alaska Native, 0.0% Native Hawaiian/Other Pacific Islander, 3.6% Two or more races, 0.0% Hispanic of any race; Average household size: 1.97; Median age: 52.9; Age under 18: 11.1%; Age 65 and over: 24.2%; Males per 100 females: 106.3; Marriage status: 28.2% never married, 51.4% now married, 7.8% separated, 4.1% widowed, 16.3% divorced; Foreign born: 3.1%; Speak English only: 100.0%; With disability: 18.1%; Veterans: 5.3%; Ancestry: 21.6% English, 17.3% German, 14.2% Irish, 10.0% Polish, 6.6% Italian

Employment: 9.1% management, business, and financial, 9.5% computer, engineering, and science, 3.1% education, legal, community service, arts, and media, 9.3% healthcare practitioners, 8.9% service, 21.5% sales and

office, 17.5% natural resources, construction, and maintenance, 21.3% production, transportation, and material moving

Income: Per capita: $32,987; Median household: $56,167; Average household: $63,140; Households with income of $100,000 or more: 14.7%; Poverty rate: 10.2%

Educational Attainment: High school diploma or higher: 81.4%; Bachelor's degree or higher: 14.1%; Graduate/professional degree or higher: 3.0%

School District(s)

Central Square Central SD (PK-12)

    Enrollment: 3,941 . . . . (315) 668-4220

Housing: Homeownership rate: 78.2%; Median home value: $77,600; Median year structure built: 1961; Homeowner vacancy rate: 0.0%; Median selected monthly owner costs: $1,129 with a mortgage, $525 without a mortgage; Median gross rent: $622 per month; Rental vacancy rate: 18.5%

Health Insurance: 90.3% have insurance; 70.8% have private insurance; 33.5% have public insurance; 9.7% do not have insurance; 18.2% of children under 18 do not have insurance

Transportation: Commute: 96.5% car, 0.0% public transportation, 1.6% walk, 1.8% work from home; Mean travel time to work: 30.2 minutes

---

CONSTANTIA (town). Covers a land area of 56.765 square miles and a water area of 42.915 square miles. Located at 43.26° N. Lat; 75.96° W. Long. Elevation is 384 feet.

Population: 4,902; Growth (since 2000): -4.6%; Density: 86.4 persons per square mile; Race: 98.5% White, 0.0% Black/African American, 0.0% Asian, 0.0% American Indian/Alaska Native, 0.0% Native Hawaiian/Other Pacific Islander, 1.5% Two or more races, 0.0% Hispanic of any race; Average household size: 2.44; Median age: 46.2; Age under 18: 20.2%; Age 65 and over: 18.3%; Males per 100 females: 109.3; Marriage status: 28.4% never married, 57.2% now married, 4.5% separated, 3.6% widowed, 10.8% divorced; Foreign born: 1.2%; Speak English only: 99.7%; With disability: 12.4%; Veterans: 8.5%; Ancestry: 22.5% Irish, 22.1% German, 16.0% English, 11.4% American, 8.2% Italian

Employment: 14.3% management, business, and financial, 4.3% computer, engineering, and science, 4.3% education, legal, community service, arts, and media, 6.3% healthcare practitioners, 17.7% service, 19.8% sales and office, 17.9% natural resources, construction, and maintenance, 15.4% production, transportation, and material moving

Income: Per capita: $29,742; Median household: $57,010; Average household: $71,582; Households with income of $100,000 or more: 19.3%; Poverty rate: 6.6%

Educational Attainment: High school diploma or higher: 85.0%; Bachelor's degree or higher: 12.3%; Graduate/professional degree or higher: 5.6%

School District(s)

Central Square Central SD (PK-12)

    Enrollment: 3,941 . . . . (315) 668-4220

Housing: Homeownership rate: 80.1%; Median home value: $119,600; Median year structure built: 1973; Homeowner vacancy rate: 1.8%; Median selected monthly owner costs: $1,374 with a mortgage, $499 without a mortgage; Median gross rent: $845 per month; Rental vacancy rate: 5.9%

Health Insurance: 91.6% have insurance; 66.9% have private insurance; 35.8% have public insurance; 8.4% do not have insurance; 5.4% of children under 18 do not have insurance

Transportation: Commute: 96.3% car, 0.1% public transportation, 1.8% walk, 1.9% work from home; Mean travel time to work: 33.9 minutes

Additional Information Contacts

Town of Constantia . . . . (315) 623-7771

    http://townconstantia.org

FULTON (city). Covers a land area of 3.755 square miles and a water area of 1.001 square miles. Located at 43.30° N. Lat; 76.40° W. Long. Elevation is 361 feet.

History: Incorporated as village in 1835, as city in 1902.

Population: 11,509; Growth (since 2000): -2.9%; Density: 3,065.3 persons per square mile; Race: 95.9% White, 0.3% Black/African American, 0.1% Asian, 0.4% American Indian/Alaska Native, 0.0% Native Hawaiian/Other Pacific Islander, 1.2% Two or more races, 4.5% Hispanic of any race; Average household size: 2.41; Median age: 37.9; Age under 18: 24.2%; Age 65 and over: 14.8%; Males per 100 females: 91.9; Marriage status: 28.6% never married, 47.7% now married, 4.4% separated, 9.1% widowed, 14.6% divorced; Foreign born: 2.0%; Speak English only: 95.7%; With disability: 17.6%; Veterans: 8.0%; Ancestry: 23.8% Irish, 19.6% German, 15.7% Italian, 12.5% English, 6.3% French

Employment: 7.6% management, business, and financial, 3.7% computer, engineering, and science, 8.5% education, legal, community service, arts, and media, 5.5% healthcare practitioners, 21.4% service, 24.9% sales and office, 9.4% natural resources, construction, and maintenance, 19.1% production, transportation, and material moving
Income: Per capita: $22,024; Median household: $40,927; Average household: $52,481; Households with income of $100,000 or more: 12.1%; Poverty rate: 26.4%
Educational Attainment: High school diploma or higher: 84.5%; Bachelor's degree or higher: 16.3%; Graduate/professional degree or higher: 6.1%

School District(s)
Fulton City SD (KG-12)
    Enrollment: 3,471 . . . . (315) 593-5510
Mexico Central SD (PK-12)
    Enrollment: 2,170 . . . . (315) 963-8400
Housing: Homeownership rate: 56.1%; Median home value: $78,200; Median year structure built: 1942; Homeowner vacancy rate: 0.9%; Median selected monthly owner costs: $1,057 with a mortgage, $489 without a mortgage; Median gross rent: $715 per month; Rental vacancy rate: 6.9%
Health Insurance: 93.7% have insurance; 56.3% have private insurance; 50.9% have public insurance; 6.3% do not have insurance; 5.1% of children under 18 do not have insurance
Safety: Violent crime rate: 15.9 per 10,000 population; Property crime rate: 290.6 per 10,000 population
Newspapers: Fulton Patriot Advertiser (weekly circulation 5,700); The Valley News (weekly circulation 8,100)
Transportation: Commute: 90.9% car, 0.4% public transportation, 5.4% walk, 2.4% work from home; Mean travel time to work: 21.0 minutes
Additional Information Contacts
City of Fulton . . . . (315) 592-5390
    http://www.cityoffulton.com

GRANBY (town). Covers a land area of 44.713 square miles and a water area of 1.730 square miles. Located at 43.29° N. Lat; 76.44° W. Long.
Population: 6,627; Growth (since 2000): -5.5%; Density: 148.2 persons per square mile; Race: 97.3% White, 0.8% Black/African American, 0.0% Asian, 0.2% American Indian/Alaska Native, 0.0% Native Hawaiian/Other Pacific Islander, 1.6% Two or more races, 3.8% Hispanic of any race; Average household size: 2.69; Median age: 39.7; Age under 18: 21.8%; Age 65 and over: 14.8%; Males per 100 females: 104.7; Marriage status: 30.6% never married, 58.3% now married, 1.8% separated, 5.1% widowed, 6.0% divorced; Foreign born: 1.5%; Speak English only: 95.8%; With disability: 16.2%; Veterans: 7.2%; Ancestry: 15.8% Italian, 14.7% Irish, 11.7% English, 10.5% German, 9.2% French
Employment: 11.9% management, business, and financial, 6.2% computer, engineering, and science, 7.3% education, legal, community service, arts, and media, 7.8% healthcare practitioners, 25.3% service, 18.7% sales and office, 8.0% natural resources, construction, and maintenance, 14.7% production, transportation, and material moving
Income: Per capita: $31,445; Median household: $53,316; Average household: $84,117; Households with income of $100,000 or more: 20.7%; Poverty rate: 22.1%
Educational Attainment: High school diploma or higher: 83.2%; Bachelor's degree or higher: 18.0%; Graduate/professional degree or higher: 9.6%
Housing: Homeownership rate: 78.8%; Median home value: $89,400; Median year structure built: 1970; Homeowner vacancy rate: 4.4%; Median selected monthly owner costs: $1,241 with a mortgage, $444 without a mortgage; Median gross rent: $788 per month; Rental vacancy rate: 0.0%
Health Insurance: 97.2% have insurance; 59.2% have private insurance; 50.9% have public insurance; 2.8% do not have insurance; 2.2% of children under 18 do not have insurance
Transportation: Commute: 88.0% car, 0.0% public transportation, 2.8% walk, 3.7% work from home; Mean travel time to work: 22.7 minutes
Additional Information Contacts
Town of Granby . . . . (315) 598-6500
    http://towngranby.org/content

HANNIBAL (town). Covers a land area of 44.655 square miles and a water area of 0.171 square miles. Located at 43.31° N. Lat; 76.55° W. Long. Elevation is 328 feet.
Population: 4,701; Growth (since 2000): -5.2%; Density: 105.3 persons per square mile; Race: 95.5% White, 0.8% Black/African American, 0.6%

Asian, 0.0% American Indian/Alaska Native, 0.0% Native Hawaiian/Other Pacific Islander, 3.0% Two or more races, 1.6% Hispanic of any race; Average household size: 2.78; Median age: 39.4; Age under 18: 23.3%; Age 65 and over: 13.6%; Males per 100 females: 102.5; Marriage status: 30.7% never married, 46.4% now married, 2.5% separated, 7.8% widowed, 15.1% divorced; Foreign born: 1.3%; Speak English only: 97.2%; With disability: 20.3%; Veterans: 9.2%; Ancestry: 19.1% Irish, 17.6% Italian, 16.0% German, 13.6% English, 7.0% American
Employment: 7.3% management, business, and financial, 1.6% computer, engineering, and science, 5.7% education, legal, community service, arts, and media, 6.1% healthcare practitioners, 21.6% service, 25.0% sales and office, 12.0% natural resources, construction, and maintenance, 20.6% production, transportation, and material moving
Income: Per capita: $20,001; Median household: $49,386; Average household: $55,061; Households with income of $100,000 or more: 9.9%; Poverty rate: 18.4%
Educational Attainment: High school diploma or higher: 84.7%; Bachelor's degree or higher: 8.2%; Graduate/professional degree or higher: 2.2%

School District(s)
Hannibal Central SD (PK-12)
    Enrollment: 1,414 . . . . (315) 564-8100
Housing: Homeownership rate: 80.7%; Median home value: $82,800; Median year structure built: 1980; Homeowner vacancy rate: 3.1%; Median selected monthly owner costs: $1,157 with a mortgage, $400 without a mortgage; Median gross rent: $759 per month; Rental vacancy rate: 9.0%
Health Insurance: 94.0% have insurance; 55.8% have private insurance; 59.6% have public insurance; 6.0% do not have insurance; 2.9% of children under 18 do not have insurance
Transportation: Commute: 91.3% car, 2.1% public transportation, 2.5% walk, 4.0% work from home; Mean travel time to work: 25.7 minutes
Additional Information Contacts
Town of Hannibal . . . . (315) 564-6037
    http://hannibalny.org

HANNIBAL (village). Covers a land area of 1.152 square miles and a water area of 0 square miles. Located at 43.32° N. Lat; 76.58° W. Long. Elevation is 328 feet.
Population: 548; Growth (since 2000): 1.1%; Density: 475.5 persons per square mile; Race: 99.3% White, 0.0% Black/African American, 0.0% Asian, 0.0% American Indian/Alaska Native, 0.0% Native Hawaiian/Other Pacific Islander, 0.4% Two or more races, 2.4% Hispanic of any race; Average household size: 2.77; Median age: 40.5; Age under 18: 23.4%; Age 65 and over: 19.2%; Males per 100 females: 89.4; Marriage status: 32.3% never married, 44.9% now married, 2.8% separated, 5.5% widowed, 17.3% divorced; Foreign born: 1.1%; Speak English only: 96.4%; With disability: 19.5%; Veterans: 8.8%; Ancestry: 33.9% Irish, 16.2% English, 16.1% German, 14.1% Italian, 12.6% American
Employment: 6.3% management, business, and financial, 3.2% computer, engineering, and science, 9.5% education, legal, community service, arts, and media, 1.4% healthcare practitioners, 19.0% service, 25.8% sales and office, 7.2% natural resources, construction, and maintenance, 27.6% production, transportation, and material moving
Income: Per capita: $22,410; Median household: $54,074; Average household: $60,871; Households with income of $100,000 or more: 14.6%; Poverty rate: 10.9%
Educational Attainment: High school diploma or higher: 93.8%; Bachelor's degree or higher: 13.7%; Graduate/professional degree or higher: 5.1%

School District(s)
Hannibal Central SD (PK-12)
    Enrollment: 1,414 . . . . (315) 564-8100
Housing: Homeownership rate: 70.2%; Median home value: $91,100; Median year structure built: 1944; Homeowner vacancy rate: 4.8%; Median selected monthly owner costs: $1,105 with a mortgage, $452 without a mortgage; Median gross rent: $781 per month; Rental vacancy rate: 0.0%
Health Insurance: 98.5% have insurance; 62.0% have private insurance; 59.9% have public insurance; 1.5% do not have insurance; 0.0% of children under 18 do not have insurance
Transportation: Commute: 86.8% car, 0.0% public transportation, 8.5% walk, 4.7% work from home; Mean travel time to work: 23.4 minutes

HASTINGS (town).
Covers a land area of 45.645 square miles and a water area of 0.352 square miles. Located at 43.32° N. Lat; 76.16° W. Long. Elevation is 476 feet.

History: Hastings was the first town settled in Oswego County when Oliver Stevens built a building near the abandoned Fort Brewerton in 1789, where he traded with Indians and operated a tavern for the boatmen who frequented the nearby river and lake

Population: 9,289; Growth (since 2000): 5.5%; Density: 203.5 persons per square mile; Race: 96.6% White, 0.8% Black/African American, 0.7% Asian, 0.5% American Indian/Alaska Native, 0.0% Native Hawaiian/Other Pacific Islander, 1.4% Two or more races, 0.5% Hispanic of any race; Average household size: 2.50; Median age: 44.2; Age under 18: 21.2%; Age 65 and over: 15.4%; Males per 100 females: 97.3; Marriage status: 26.1% never married, 58.3% now married, 2.5% separated, 4.8% widowed, 10.9% divorced; Foreign born: 1.0%; Speak English only: 98.6%; With disability: 15.4%; Veterans: 10.4%; Ancestry: 23.2% German, 14.9% Irish, 12.7% English, 12.4% Italian, 8.8% American

Employment: 12.0% management, business, and financial, 4.0% computer, engineering, and science, 7.2% education, legal, community service, arts, and media, 5.0% healthcare practitioners, 16.9% service, 24.1% sales and office, 12.7% natural resources, construction, and maintenance, 18.1% production, transportation, and material moving

Income: Per capita: $27,249; Median household: $53,825; Average household: $66,781; Households with income of $100,000 or more: 21.0%; Poverty rate: 13.3%

Educational Attainment: High school diploma or higher: 87.2%; Bachelor's degree or higher: 14.2%; Graduate/professional degree or higher: 6.0%

Housing: Homeownership rate: 81.5%; Median home value: $118,700; Median year structure built: 1982; Homeowner vacancy rate: 2.3%; Median selected monthly owner costs: $1,289 with a mortgage, $515 without a mortgage; Median gross rent: $759 per month; Rental vacancy rate: 5.8%

Health Insurance: 97.2% have insurance; 67.5% have private insurance; 43.5% have public insurance; 2.8% do not have insurance; 0.6% of children under 18 do not have insurance

Transportation: Commute: 93.2% car, 0.9% public transportation, 0.9% walk, 3.6% work from home; Mean travel time to work: 28.5 minutes

Additional Information Contacts

Town of Hastings. . . . . (315) 668-2456
    http://www.hastingsny.org

LACONA (village).
Covers a land area of 1.110 square miles and a water area of 0.003 square miles. Located at 43.64° N. Lat; 76.07° W. Long. Elevation is 558 feet.

Population: 691; Growth (since 2000): 17.1%; Density: 622.6 persons per square mile; Race: 97.7% White, 0.1% Black/African American, 0.3% Asian, 0.0% American Indian/Alaska Native, 0.0% Native Hawaiian/Other Pacific Islander, 1.7% Two or more races, 0.1% Hispanic of any race; Average household size: 2.67; Median age: 34.9; Age under 18: 24.6%; Age 65 and over: 11.4%; Males per 100 females: 110.1; Marriage status: 41.4% never married, 37.8% now married, 2.2% separated, 6.4% widowed, 14.4% divorced; Foreign born: 0.4%; Speak English only: 97.9%; With disability: 19.0%; Veterans: 10.7%; Ancestry: 24.7% German, 16.2% English, 12.3% Irish, 9.1% Italian, 9.0% Polish

Employment: 13.8% management, business, and financial, 3.6% computer, engineering, and science, 5.9% education, legal, community service, arts, and media, 1.3% healthcare practitioners, 23.0% service, 26.3% sales and office, 12.8% natural resources, construction, and maintenance, 13.2% production, transportation, and material moving

Income: Per capita: $24,193; Median household: $62,969; Average household: $64,297; Households with income of $100,000 or more: 22.4%; Poverty rate: 23.4%

Educational Attainment: High school diploma or higher: 91.1%; Bachelor's degree or higher: 16.4%; Graduate/professional degree or higher: 7.0%

Housing: Homeownership rate: 59.6%; Median home value: $103,800; Median year structure built: Before 1940; Homeowner vacancy rate: 0.0%; Median selected monthly owner costs: $1,075 with a mortgage, $394 without a mortgage; Median gross rent: $635 per month; Rental vacancy rate: 0.0%

Health Insurance: 97.1% have insurance; 60.5% have private insurance; 45.2% have public insurance; 2.9% do not have insurance; 2.4% of children under 18 do not have insurance

Transportation: Commute: 94.3% car, 2.4% public transportation, 0.0% walk, 3.4% work from home; Mean travel time to work: 30.9 minutes

MALLORY (unincorporated postal area)
ZCTA: 13103

Covers a land area of 0.342 square miles and a water area of 0.015 square miles. Located at 43.33° N. Lat; 76.11° W. Long. Elevation is 413 feet.

Population: 320; Growth (since 2000): n/a; Density: 935.7 persons per square mile; Race: 95.0% White, 4.1% Black/African American, 0.0% Asian, 0.0% American Indian/Alaska Native, 0.0% Native Hawaiian/Other Pacific Islander, 0.9% Two or more races, 0.0% Hispanic of any race; Average household size: 2.50; Median age: 40.6; Age under 18: 23.7%; Age 65 and over: 8.1%; Males per 100 females: 109.0; Marriage status: 25.5% never married, 36.3% now married, 4.5% separated, 0.0% widowed, 38.2% divorced; Foreign born: 0.0%; Speak English only: 100.0%; With disability: 17.8%; Veterans: 2.9%; Ancestry: 24.7% American, 19.1% German, 17.5% English, 12.5% Irish, 8.1% French

Employment: 28.5% management, business, and financial, 5.3% computer, engineering, and science, 0.0% education, legal, community service, arts, and media, 0.0% healthcare practitioners, 15.9% service, 15.9% sales and office, 29.1% natural resources, construction, and maintenance, 5.3% production, transportation, and material moving

Income: Per capita: $24,508; Median household: $67,632; Average household: $61,195; Households with income of $100,000 or more: 26.6%; Poverty rate: 36.3%

Educational Attainment: High school diploma or higher: 89.7%; Bachelor's degree or higher: 18.1%; Graduate/professional degree or higher: n/a

Housing: Homeownership rate: 73.4%; Median home value: $131,600; Median year structure built: 1979; Homeowner vacancy rate: 0.0%; Median selected monthly owner costs: $1,386 with a mortgage, $579 without a mortgage; Median gross rent: $684 per month; Rental vacancy rate: 0.0%

Health Insurance: 82.8% have insurance; 39.7% have private insurance; 55.0% have public insurance; 17.2% do not have insurance; 0.0% of children under 18 do not have insurance

Transportation: Commute: 72.2% car, 0.0% public transportation, 0.0% walk, 27.8% work from home; Mean travel time to work: 0.0 minutes

MEXICO (town).
Covers a land area of 46.272 square miles and a water area of 0.717 square miles. Located at 43.46° N. Lat; 76.20° W. Long. Elevation is 410 feet.

Population: 5,127; Growth (since 2000): -1.0%; Density: 110.8 persons per square mile; Race: 95.5% White, 0.6% Black/African American, 0.4% Asian, 0.0% American Indian/Alaska Native, 0.0% Native Hawaiian/Other Pacific Islander, 2.9% Two or more races, 0.8% Hispanic of any race; Average household size: 2.61; Median age: 40.4; Age under 18: 23.1%; Age 65 and over: 14.6%; Males per 100 females: 98.4; Marriage status: 27.2% never married, 56.3% now married, 2.3% separated, 5.0% widowed, 11.4% divorced; Foreign born: 1.4%; Speak English only: 98.0%; With disability: 16.3%; Veterans: 9.8%; Ancestry: 20.3% English, 20.1% Irish, 18.3% German, 11.4% Italian, 10.0% American

Employment: 12.0% management, business, and financial, 6.4% computer, engineering, and science, 12.7% education, legal, community service, arts, and media, 5.6% healthcare practitioners, 21.1% service, 16.6% sales and office, 9.1% natural resources, construction, and maintenance, 16.5% production, transportation, and material moving

Income: Per capita: $28,441; Median household: $61,062; Average household: $72,303; Households with income of $100,000 or more: 24.7%; Poverty rate: 13.5%

Educational Attainment: High school diploma or higher: 90.3%; Bachelor's degree or higher: 20.8%; Graduate/professional degree or higher: 9.1%

School District(s)

Mexico Central SD (PK-12)
    Enrollment: 2,170 . . . . (315) 963-8400
Oswego Boces
    Enrollment: n/a . . . . (315) 963-4222

Vocational/Technical School(s)

Center for Instruction Technology & Innovation (CiTi) (Public)
    Enrollment: 57 . . . . (315) 963-4256
    Tuition: $12,910

Housing: Homeownership rate: 78.6%; Median home value: $120,700; Median year structure built: 1980; Homeowner vacancy rate: 2.9%; Median selected monthly owner costs: $1,308 with a mortgage, $572 without a mortgage; Median gross rent: $668 per month; Rental vacancy rate: 4.6%

Health Insurance: 95.5% have insurance; 69.0% have private insurance; 39.9% have public insurance; 4.5% do not have insurance; 1.6% of children under 18 do not have insurance
Newspapers: Oswego Co. Weeklies (weekly circulation 33,000)
Transportation: Commute: 93.4% car, 0.5% public transportation, 2.5% walk, 3.5% work from home; Mean travel time to work: 26.1 minutes
Additional Information Contacts
Town of Mexico . . . . (315) 963-7633
  http://town.mexicony.net

MEXICO (village). Covers a land area of 2.145 square miles and a water area of 0 square miles. Located at 43.47° N. Lat; 76.23° W. Long. Elevation is 410 feet.

Population: 1,707; Growth (since 2000): 8.6%; Density: 795.9 persons per square mile; Race: 96.4% White, 0.3% Black/African American, 0.5% Asian, 0.1% American Indian/Alaska Native, 0.0% Native Hawaiian/Other Pacific Islander, 1.7% Two or more races, 1.4% Hispanic of any race; Average household size: 2.47; Median age: 35.6; Age under 18: 28.4%; Age 65 and over: 10.5%; Males per 100 females: 84.1; Marriage status: 27.5% never married, 51.8% now married, 2.4% separated, 3.7% widowed, 17.1% divorced; Foreign born: 1.5%; Speak English only: 97.2%; With disability: 11.7%; Veterans: 9.3%; Ancestry: 22.0% Irish, 21.7% English, 13.0% German, 12.8% Italian, 10.4% French
Employment: 17.2% management, business, and financial, 6.5% computer, engineering, and science, 14.8% education, legal, community service, arts, and media, 4.1% healthcare practitioners, 23.3% service, 12.3% sales and office, 7.0% natural resources, construction, and maintenance, 14.8% production, transportation, and material moving
Income: Per capita: $28,879; Median household: $56,806; Average household: $69,347; Households with income of $100,000 or more: 21.1%; Poverty rate: 18.3%
Educational Attainment: High school diploma or higher: 93.8%; Bachelor's degree or higher: 23.0%; Graduate/professional degree or higher: 11.4%

School District(s)
Mexico Central SD (PK-12)
  Enrollment: 2,170 . . . . (315) 963-8400
Oswego Boces
  Enrollment: n/a . . . . (315) 963-4222
Vocational/Technical School(s)
Center for Instruction Technology & Innovation (CiTi) (Public)
  Enrollment: 57 . . . . (315) 963-4256
  Tuition: $12,910
Housing: Homeownership rate: 56.8%; Median home value: $115,600; Median year structure built: 1952; Homeowner vacancy rate: 0.8%; Median selected monthly owner costs: $1,306 with a mortgage, $594 without a mortgage; Median gross rent: $668 per month; Rental vacancy rate: 6.3%
Health Insurance: 95.1% have insurance; 61.8% have private insurance; 41.9% have public insurance; 4.9% do not have insurance; 2.0% of children under 18 do not have insurance
Newspapers: Oswego Co. Weeklies (weekly circulation 33,000)
Transportation: Commute: 87.8% car, 0.0% public transportation, 5.4% walk, 6.8% work from home; Mean travel time to work: 22.6 minutes

MINETTO (CDP). Covers a land area of 3.323 square miles and a water area of 0.263 square miles. Located at 43.40° N. Lat; 76.48° W. Long. Elevation is 325 feet.

Population: 991; Growth (since 2000): -8.7%; Density: 298.2 persons per square mile; Race: 98.6% White, 0.1% Black/African American, 0.6% Asian, 0.4% American Indian/Alaska Native, 0.0% Native Hawaiian/Other Pacific Islander, 0.3% Two or more races, 1.3% Hispanic of any race; Average household size: 2.12; Median age: 46.8; Age under 18: 18.7%; Age 65 and over: 22.3%; Males per 100 females: 100.9; Marriage status: 26.7% never married, 52.3% now married, 2.8% separated, 8.9% widowed, 12.2% divorced; Foreign born: 1.8%; Speak English only: 97.3%; With disability: 11.1%; Veterans: 11.2%; Ancestry: 22.6% German, 22.0% Irish, 18.2% Italian, 13.8% English, 11.3% Polish
Employment: 19.2% management, business, and financial, 2.1% computer, engineering, and science, 23.5% education, legal, community service, arts, and media, 5.4% healthcare practitioners, 10.9% service, 15.0% sales and office, 5.6% natural resources, construction, and maintenance, 18.3% production, transportation, and material moving
Income: Per capita: $36,354; Median household: $69,688; Average household: $78,407; Households with income of $100,000 or more: 29.0%; Poverty rate: 11.1%

Educational Attainment: High school diploma or higher: 95.8%; Bachelor's degree or higher: 42.4%; Graduate/professional degree or higher: 20.8%

School District(s)
Oswego City SD (KG-12)
  Enrollment: 3,723 . . . . (315) 341-2001
Housing: Homeownership rate: 84.1%; Median home value: $115,000; Median year structure built: 1958; Homeowner vacancy rate: 3.3%; Median selected monthly owner costs: $1,269 with a mortgage, $477 without a mortgage; Median gross rent: $611 per month; Rental vacancy rate: 0.0%
Health Insurance: 95.7% have insurance; 72.8% have private insurance; 37.2% have public insurance; 4.3% do not have insurance; 0.0% of children under 18 do not have insurance
Transportation: Commute: 93.5% car, 0.2% public transportation, 1.6% walk, 4.7% work from home; Mean travel time to work: 21.8 minutes

MINETTO (town). Covers a land area of 5.762 square miles and a water area of 0.279 square miles. Located at 43.40° N. Lat; 76.48° W. Long. Elevation is 325 feet.

Population: 1,556; Growth (since 2000): -6.4%; Density: 270.0 persons per square mile; Race: 98.7% White, 0.1% Black/African American, 0.4% Asian, 0.3% American Indian/Alaska Native, 0.0% Native Hawaiian/Other Pacific Islander, 0.6% Two or more races, 1.2% Hispanic of any race; Average household size: 2.23; Median age: 44.8; Age under 18: 20.6%; Age 65 and over: 20.6%; Males per 100 females: 98.2; Marriage status: 27.4% never married, 55.4% now married, 2.8% separated, 6.8% widowed, 10.4% divorced; Foreign born: 1.7%; Speak English only: 97.5%; With disability: 9.3%; Veterans: 11.0%; Ancestry: 24.6% Irish, 19.3% German, 17.4% Italian, 11.8% English, 10.9% Polish
Employment: 16.0% management, business, and financial, 2.9% computer, engineering, and science, 19.8% education, legal, community service, arts, and media, 4.0% healthcare practitioners, 13.4% service, 15.1% sales and office, 11.4% natural resources, construction, and maintenance, 17.4% production, transportation, and material moving
Income: Per capita: $34,419; Median household: $68,333; Average household: $76,518; Households with income of $100,000 or more: 26.9%; Poverty rate: 8.7%
Educational Attainment: High school diploma or higher: 95.8%; Bachelor's degree or higher: 38.6%; Graduate/professional degree or higher: 19.9%

School District(s)
Oswego City SD (KG-12)
  Enrollment: 3,723 . . . . (315) 341-2001
Housing: Homeownership rate: 84.3%; Median home value: $118,500; Median year structure built: 1965; Homeowner vacancy rate: 2.2%; Median selected monthly owner costs: $1,263 with a mortgage, $483 without a mortgage; Median gross rent: $633 per month; Rental vacancy rate: 0.0%
Health Insurance: 94.7% have insurance; 71.1% have private insurance; 36.5% have public insurance; 5.3% do not have insurance; 0.6% of children under 18 do not have insurance
Transportation: Commute: 94.6% car, 0.1% public transportation, 1.1% walk, 4.2% work from home; Mean travel time to work: 21.9 minutes

NEW HAVEN (town). Covers a land area of 31.099 square miles and a water area of 2.315 square miles. Located at 43.47° N. Lat; 76.32° W. Long. Elevation is 423 feet.

Population: 2,859; Growth (since 2000): -2.4%; Density: 91.9 persons per square mile; Race: 97.4% White, 0.5% Black/African American, 1.0% Asian, 0.0% American Indian/Alaska Native, 0.0% Native Hawaiian/Other Pacific Islander, 1.1% Two or more races, 0.0% Hispanic of any race; Average household size: 2.70; Median age: 41.9; Age under 18: 22.5%; Age 65 and over: 10.9%; Males per 100 females: 102.1; Marriage status: 29.3% never married, 50.9% now married, 2.6% separated, 4.7% widowed, 15.2% divorced; Foreign born: 0.5%; Speak English only: 95.4%; With disability: 13.7%; Veterans: 7.6%; Ancestry: 18.7% Irish, 15.6% German, 13.8% English, 9.3% American, 8.4% Italian
Employment: 6.9% management, business, and financial, 1.7% computer, engineering, and science, 8.2% education, legal, community service, arts, and media, 3.1% healthcare practitioners, 21.9% service, 22.9% sales and office, 21.6% natural resources, construction, and maintenance, 13.7% production, transportation, and material moving
Income: Per capita: $25,473; Median household: $53,920; Average household: $66,971; Households with income of $100,000 or more: 17.9%; Poverty rate: 12.6%

Educational Attainment: High school diploma or higher: 89.5%; Bachelor's degree or higher: 12.6%; Graduate/professional degree or higher: 4.9%

School District(s)
Mexico Central SD (PK-12)
    Enrollment: 2,170 . . . . (315) 963-8400
Housing: Homeownership rate: 78.5%; Median home value: $84,500; Median year structure built: 1978; Homeowner vacancy rate: 1.9%; Median selected monthly owner costs: $1,199 with a mortgage, $465 without a mortgage; Median gross rent: $930 per month; Rental vacancy rate: 14.6%
Health Insurance: 92.0% have insurance; 67.1% have private insurance; 34.8% have public insurance; 8.0% do not have insurance; 4.1% of children under 18 do not have insurance
Transportation: Commute: 94.9% car, 0.0% public transportation, 3.5% walk, 1.1% work from home; Mean travel time to work: 26.0 minutes

ORWELL (town). Covers a land area of 39.582 square miles and a water area of 1.684 square miles. Located at 43.56° N. Lat; 75.95° W. Long. Elevation is 801 feet.
Population: 1,533; Growth (since 2000): 22.2%; Density: 38.7 persons per square mile; Race: 93.5% White, 2.2% Black/African American, 0.0% Asian, 0.2% American Indian/Alaska Native, 0.0% Native Hawaiian/Other Pacific Islander, 1.5% Two or more races, 5.9% Hispanic of any race; Average household size: 3.08; Median age: 32.8; Age under 18: 29.5%; Age 65 and over: 11.9%; Males per 100 females: 117.3; Marriage status: 31.0% never married, 49.3% now married, 2.8% separated, 6.5% widowed, 13.2% divorced; Foreign born: 3.5%; Speak English only: 85.9%; With disability: 15.9%; Veterans: 9.4%; Ancestry: 20.4% German, 17.4% English, 14.0% Irish, 9.8% Italian, 6.6% French Canadian
Employment: 5.3% management, business, and financial, 4.2% computer, engineering, and science, 6.0% education, legal, community service, arts, and media, 8.2% healthcare practitioners, 16.0% service, 21.6% sales and office, 18.2% natural resources, construction, and maintenance, 20.5% production, transportation, and material moving
Income: Per capita: $22,115; Median household: $54,063; Average household: $67,553; Households with income of $100,000 or more: 22.8%; Poverty rate: 25.0%
Educational Attainment: High school diploma or higher: 81.9%; Bachelor's degree or higher: 15.9%; Graduate/professional degree or higher: 4.3%
Housing: Homeownership rate: 89.2%; Median home value: $87,900; Median year structure built: 1974; Homeowner vacancy rate: 4.1%; Median selected monthly owner costs: $1,210 with a mortgage, $428 without a mortgage; Median gross rent: $806 per month; Rental vacancy rate: 0.0%
Health Insurance: 87.9% have insurance; 57.7% have private insurance; 41.2% have public insurance; 12.1% do not have insurance; 14.3% of children under 18 do not have insurance
Transportation: Commute: 90.2% car, 2.0% public transportation, 2.2% walk, 5.6% work from home; Mean travel time to work: 38.5 minutes

OSWEGO (city). County seat. Covers a land area of 7.614 square miles and a water area of 3.614 square miles. Located at 43.46° N. Lat; 76.50° W. Long. Elevation is 285 feet.
History: The name of Oswego is of Indian origin, meaning "pouring out of waters." The strategic importance of the place led to the erection of a fort in 1722. Soon after military occupation ceased, settlement began. Its commanding position at the terminus of the inland water route made Oswego a busy port.
Population: 17,723; Growth (since 2000): -1.3%; Density: 2,327.7 persons per square mile; Race: 92.5% White, 1.9% Black/African American, 1.4% Asian, 0.2% American Indian/Alaska Native, 0.1% Native Hawaiian/Other Pacific Islander, 2.3% Two or more races, 4.7% Hispanic of any race; Average household size: 2.25; Median age: 34.9; Age under 18: 19.8%; Age 65 and over: 14.0%; Males per 100 females: 93.4; Marriage status: 41.1% never married, 41.6% now married, 3.8% separated, 6.2% widowed, 11.1% divorced; Foreign born: 3.2%; Speak English only: 93.4%; With disability: 12.7%; Veterans: 7.1%; Ancestry: 24.9% Irish, 20.6% Italian, 16.4% German, 9.9% English, 7.7% French
Employment: 9.7% management, business, and financial, 4.2% computer, engineering, and science, 13.5% education, legal, community service, arts, and media, 5.4% healthcare practitioners, 23.0% service, 25.9% sales and office, 7.2% natural resources, construction, and maintenance, 11.1% production, transportation, and material moving

Income: Per capita: $24,754; Median household: $38,464; Average household: $56,313; Households with income of $100,000 or more: 15.0%; Poverty rate: 28.0%
Educational Attainment: High school diploma or higher: 88.3%; Bachelor's degree or higher: 28.3%; Graduate/professional degree or higher: 14.3%

School District(s)
Oswego City SD (KG-12)
    Enrollment: 3,723 . . . . (315) 341-2001
Four-year College(s)
SUNY College at Oswego (Public)
    Enrollment: 8,026 . . . . (315) 312-2500
    Tuition: In-state $8,191; Out-of-state $17,841
Housing: Homeownership rate: 52.7%; Median home value: $84,200; Median year structure built: Before 1940; Homeowner vacancy rate: 3.2%; Median selected monthly owner costs: $1,078 with a mortgage, $512 without a mortgage; Median gross rent: $736 per month; Rental vacancy rate: 5.2%
Health Insurance: 93.0% have insurance; 66.9% have private insurance; 40.6% have public insurance; 7.0% do not have insurance; 3.0% of children under 18 do not have insurance
Hospitals: Oswego Hospital (74 beds)
Safety: Violent crime rate: 20.6 per 10,000 population; Property crime rate: 218.7 per 10,000 population
Newspapers: Oswego Palladium-Times (daily circulation 7,300)
Transportation: Commute: 86.2% car, 2.0% public transportation, 8.8% walk, 1.2% work from home; Mean travel time to work: 17.8 minutes
Additional Information Contacts
City of Oswego . . . . (315) 342-8116
    http://www.oswegony.org

OSWEGO (town). Covers a land area of 27.333 square miles and a water area of 2.016 square miles. Located at 43.40° N. Lat; 76.56° W. Long. Elevation is 285 feet.
History: Trading post established here after the English founded Oswego (1722) became vital to the Albany fur trade. Its strategic location prompted the building of Fort Oswego (1727), Fort George (1755) and Fort Ontario (1755), which were much contested in the colonial wars. Importance as a lake port came with the completion of the Barge Canal (1917) and the St. Lawrence Seaway (1959). Seat of State University College of Arts and Science at Oswego. Founded 1722, Incorporated as a city 1848.
Population: 7,938; Growth (since 2000): 8.9%; Density: 290.4 persons per square mile; Race: 86.3% White, 6.3% Black/African American, 2.6% Asian, 0.2% American Indian/Alaska Native, 0.0% Native Hawaiian/Other Pacific Islander, 2.9% Two or more races, 5.1% Hispanic of any race; Average household size: 2.75; Median age: 20.7; Age under 18: 11.8%; Age 65 and over: 8.4%; Males per 100 females: 101.2; Marriage status: 62.7% never married, 30.2% now married, 0.6% separated, 2.6% widowed, 4.5% divorced; Foreign born: 4.3%; Speak English only: 90.8%; With disability: 10.2%; Veterans: 4.1%; Ancestry: 25.9% Irish, 21.1% Italian, 18.0% German, 11.7% English, 9.8% Polish
Employment: 9.5% management, business, and financial, 4.9% computer, engineering, and science, 10.8% education, legal, community service, arts, and media, 3.1% healthcare practitioners, 32.9% service, 23.5% sales and office, 6.7% natural resources, construction, and maintenance, 8.5% production, transportation, and material moving
Income: Per capita: $20,615; Median household: $77,263; Average household: $87,959; Households with income of $100,000 or more: 32.9%; Poverty rate: 13.8%
Educational Attainment: High school diploma or higher: 92.0%; Bachelor's degree or higher: 33.2%; Graduate/professional degree or higher: 14.9%

School District(s)
Oswego City SD (KG-12)
    Enrollment: 3,723 . . . . (315) 341-2001
Four-year College(s)
SUNY College at Oswego (Public)
    Enrollment: 8,026 . . . . (315) 312-2500
    Tuition: In-state $8,191; Out-of-state $17,841
Housing: Homeownership rate: 90.2%; Median home value: $141,700; Median year structure built: 1974; Homeowner vacancy rate: 0.0%; Median selected monthly owner costs: $1,427 with a mortgage, $571 without a mortgage; Median gross rent: $1,013 per month; Rental vacancy rate: 0.0%

Health Insurance: 97.3% have insurance; 81.0% have private insurance; 23.9% have public insurance; 2.7% do not have insurance; 1.5% of children under 18 do not have insurance
Hospitals: Oswego Hospital (74 beds)
Newspapers: Oswego Palladium-Times (daily circulation 7,300)
Transportation: Commute: 73.5% car, 1.3% public transportation, 19.6% walk, 4.1% work from home; Mean travel time to work: 19.6 minutes
Additional Information Contacts
Town of Oswego . . . . (315) 343-2586
  http://www.townofoswego.com

PALERMO (town). Covers a land area of 40.464 square miles and a water area of 0.279 square miles. Located at 43.37° N. Lat; 76.26° W. Long. Elevation is 469 feet.

Population: 3,611; Growth (since 2000): -2.0%; Density: 89.2 persons per square mile; Race: 96.8% White, 0.0% Black/African American, 1.2% Asian, 0.0% American Indian/Alaska Native, 0.0% Native Hawaiian/Other Pacific Islander, 1.9% Two or more races, 0.3% Hispanic of any race; Average household size: 2.63; Median age: 43.0; Age under 18: 20.5%; Age 65 and over: 14.9%; Males per 100 females: 101.5; Marriage status: 29.9% never married, 53.5% now married, 2.1% separated, 7.1% widowed, 9.5% divorced; Foreign born: 2.1%; Speak English only: 94.7%; With disability: 14.9%; Veterans: 11.0%; Ancestry: 22.6% Irish, 17.1% German, 13.8% English, 11.7% French, 10.4% Italian
Employment: 10.5% management, business, and financial, 2.5% computer, engineering, and science, 9.2% education, legal, community service, arts, and media, 8.0% healthcare practitioners, 18.3% service, 18.0% sales and office, 14.3% natural resources, construction, and maintenance, 19.3% production, transportation, and material moving
Income: Per capita: $23,851; Median household: $50,587; Average household: $61,590; Households with income of $100,000 or more: 15.8%; Poverty rate: 13.7%
Educational Attainment: High school diploma or higher: 87.8%; Bachelor's degree or higher: 11.6%; Graduate/professional degree or higher: 3.8%
Housing: Homeownership rate: 77.4%; Median home value: $94,300; Median year structure built: 1977; Homeowner vacancy rate: 0.0%; Median selected monthly owner costs: $1,242 with a mortgage, $470 without a mortgage; Median gross rent: $767 per month; Rental vacancy rate: 0.0%
Health Insurance: 92.8% have insurance; 61.8% have private insurance; 44.0% have public insurance; 7.2% do not have insurance; 2.4% of children under 18 do not have insurance
Transportation: Commute: 97.9% car, 0.7% public transportation, 1.4% walk, 0.0% work from home; Mean travel time to work: 28.9 minutes

PARISH (town). Covers a land area of 41.725 square miles and a water area of 0.225 square miles. Located at 43.40° N. Lat; 76.06° W. Long. Elevation is 495 feet.

Population: 2,509; Growth (since 2000): -6.9%; Density: 60.1 persons per square mile; Race: 98.2% White, 0.0% Black/African American, 0.6% Asian, 0.0% American Indian/Alaska Native, 0.0% Native Hawaiian/Other Pacific Islander, 1.1% Two or more races, 0.8% Hispanic of any race; Average household size: 2.69; Median age: 42.3; Age under 18: 23.0%; Age 65 and over: 13.9%; Males per 100 females: 98.0; Marriage status: 31.2% never married, 52.6% now married, 1.4% separated, 6.1% widowed, 10.0% divorced; Foreign born: 0.8%; Speak English only: 97.9%; With disability: 12.6%; Veterans: 10.1%; Ancestry: 22.3% German, 17.2% Irish, 9.6% Polish, 9.4% English, 9.0% French
Employment: 7.8% management, business, and financial, 3.6% computer, engineering, and science, 9.6% education, legal, community service, arts, and media, 7.0% healthcare practitioners, 15.9% service, 25.7% sales and office, 10.3% natural resources, construction, and maintenance, 20.1% production, transportation, and material moving
Income: Per capita: $30,353; Median household: $56,845; Average household: $80,109; Households with income of $100,000 or more: 22.3%; Poverty rate: 15.6%
Educational Attainment: High school diploma or higher: 87.1%; Bachelor's degree or higher: 15.2%; Graduate/professional degree or higher: 6.0%

School District(s)
Altmar Parish-Williamstown Central SD (PK-12)
  Enrollment: 1,238 . . . . (315) 625-5251
Housing: Homeownership rate: 84.9%; Median home value: $112,700; Median year structure built: 1974; Homeowner vacancy rate: 3.0%; Median

selected monthly owner costs: $1,218 with a mortgage, $497 without a mortgage; Median gross rent: $809 per month; Rental vacancy rate: 0.0%
Health Insurance: 94.3% have insurance; 70.6% have private insurance; 35.9% have public insurance; 5.7% do not have insurance; 0.3% of children under 18 do not have insurance
Transportation: Commute: 92.9% car, 0.0% public transportation, 4.5% walk, 2.1% work from home; Mean travel time to work: 32.3 minutes

PARISH (village). Covers a land area of 1.605 square miles and a water area of 0 square miles. Located at 43.41° N. Lat; 76.13° W. Long. Elevation is 495 feet.

Population: 516; Growth (since 2000): 0.8%; Density: 321.5 persons per square mile; Race: 97.5% White, 0.0% Black/African American, 0.0% Asian, 0.2% American Indian/Alaska Native, 0.0% Native Hawaiian/Other Pacific Islander, 2.3% Two or more races, 3.7% Hispanic of any race; Average household size: 2.79; Median age: 32.6; Age under 18: 25.0%; Age 65 and over: 13.4%; Males per 100 females: 99.1; Marriage status: 41.5% never married, 41.3% now married, 1.5% separated, 5.7% widowed, 11.4% divorced; Foreign born: 2.7%; Speak English only: 98.7%; With disability: 11.4%; Veterans: 9.0%; Ancestry: 23.3% German, 20.3% Irish, 14.5% English, 11.2% Polish, 8.3% American
Employment: 7.1% management, business, and financial, 2.2% computer, engineering, and science, 9.7% education, legal, community service, arts, and media, 3.4% healthcare practitioners, 17.5% service, 26.9% sales and office, 15.7% natural resources, construction, and maintenance, 17.5% production, transportation, and material moving
Income: Per capita: $25,597; Median household: $56,750; Average household: $70,124; Households with income of $100,000 or more: 17.8%; Poverty rate: 12.5%
Educational Attainment: High school diploma or higher: 94.8%; Bachelor's degree or higher: 23.0%; Graduate/professional degree or higher: 9.5%

School District(s)
Altmar Parish-Williamstown Central SD (PK-12)
  Enrollment: 1,238 . . . . (315) 625-5251
Housing: Homeownership rate: 69.7%; Median home value: $97,400; Median year structure built: Before 1940; Homeowner vacancy rate: 0.0%; Median selected monthly owner costs: $1,202 with a mortgage, $605 without a mortgage; Median gross rent: $760 per month; Rental vacancy rate: 0.0%
Health Insurance: 90.9% have insurance; 63.8% have private insurance; 38.8% have public insurance; 9.1% do not have insurance; 1.4% of children under 18 do not have insurance
Transportation: Commute: 87.1% car, 0.0% public transportation, 9.1% walk, 1.5% work from home; Mean travel time to work: 25.6 minutes

PENNELLVILLE (unincorporated postal area)
ZCTA: 13132
  Covers a land area of 23.726 square miles and a water area of 0.407 square miles. Located at 43.27° N. Lat; 76.25° W. Long. Elevation is 413 feet.

Population: 3,575; Growth (since 2000): -17.1%; Density: 150.7 persons per square mile; Race: 95.6% White, 0.2% Black/African American, 1.2% Asian, 0.0% American Indian/Alaska Native, 0.0% Native Hawaiian/Other Pacific Islander, 3.0% Two or more races, 0.3% Hispanic of any race; Average household size: 2.40; Median age: 47.9; Age under 18: 17.7%; Age 65 and over: 19.8%; Males per 100 females: 104.7; Marriage status: 25.1% never married, 53.9% now married, 4.9% separated, 7.6% widowed, 13.4% divorced; Foreign born: 1.2%; Speak English only: 98.7%; With disability: 16.3%; Veterans: 8.0%; Ancestry: 30.1% Irish, 29.3% German, 9.5% Italian, 9.1% English, 6.2% Polish
Employment: 11.8% management, business, and financial, 4.4% computer, engineering, and science, 7.2% education, legal, community service, arts, and media, 0.9% healthcare practitioners, 12.6% service, 37.2% sales and office, 21.9% natural resources, construction, and maintenance, 4.1% production, transportation, and material moving
Income: Per capita: $29,995; Median household: $60,185; Average household: $73,126; Households with income of $100,000 or more: 26.3%; Poverty rate: 11.5%
Educational Attainment: High school diploma or higher: 92.1%; Bachelor's degree or higher: 22.0%; Graduate/professional degree or higher: 9.3%
Housing: Homeownership rate: 86.8%; Median home value: $102,800; Median year structure built: 1981; Homeowner vacancy rate: 0.0%; Median selected monthly owner costs: $1,328 with a mortgage, $629

without a mortgage; Median gross rent: $905 per month; Rental vacancy rate: 0.0%

Health Insurance: 94.8% have insurance; 66.6% have private insurance; 43.5% have public insurance; 5.2% do not have insurance; 0.0% of children under 18 do not have insurance

Transportation: Commute: 92.5% car, 0.0% public transportation, 1.5% walk, 6.0% work from home; Mean travel time to work: 22.3 minutes

PHOENIX (village). Covers a land area of 1.171 square miles and a water area of 0.119 square miles. Located at 43.23° N. Lat; 76.30° W. Long. Elevation is 371 feet.

History: Incorporated 1849.

Population: 2,388; Growth (since 2000): 6.1%; Density: 2,040.1 persons per square mile; Race: 92.7% White, 0.2% Black/African American, 1.5% Asian, 0.3% American Indian/Alaska Native, 0.0% Native Hawaiian/Other Pacific Islander, 5.2% Two or more races, 2.4% Hispanic of any race; Average household size: 2.33; Median age: 34.6; Age under 18: 25.2%; Age 65 and over: 10.8%; Males per 100 females: 90.7; Marriage status: 35.5% never married, 44.6% now married, 4.4% separated, 6.4% widowed, 13.5% divorced; Foreign born: 2.6%; Speak English only: 95.3%; With disability: 13.2%; Veterans: 8.9%; Ancestry: 26.5% German, 19.7% Irish, 12.8% Italian, 10.3% English, 9.9% American

Employment: 8.4% management, business, and financial, 4.9% computer, engineering, and science, 8.6% education, legal, community service, arts, and media, 2.8% healthcare practitioners, 17.8% service, 31.7% sales and office, 11.3% natural resources, construction, and maintenance, 14.6% production, transportation, and material moving

Income: Per capita: $26,432; Median household: $41,217; Average household: $62,557; Households with income of $100,000 or more: 12.2%; Poverty rate: 21.7%

Educational Attainment: High school diploma or higher: 87.4%; Bachelor's degree or higher: 13.2%; Graduate/professional degree or higher: 4.8%

School District(s)
Phoenix Central SD (PK-12)
    Enrollment: 1,849 . . . . (315) 695-1555
Housing: Homeownership rate: 37.4%; Median home value: $87,300; Median year structure built: 1949; Homeowner vacancy rate: 0.0%; Median selected monthly owner costs: $1,165 with a mortgage, $548 without a mortgage; Median gross rent: $662 per month; Rental vacancy rate: 2.1%
Health Insurance: 93.4% have insurance; 54.0% have private insurance; 52.6% have public insurance; 6.6% do not have insurance; 0.0% of children under 18 do not have insurance
Safety: Violent crime rate: 8.8 per 10,000 population; Property crime rate: 97.1 per 10,000 population
Transportation: Commute: 96.0% car, 0.3% public transportation, 0.7% walk, 2.9% work from home; Mean travel time to work: 24.5 minutes

PULASKI (village). Covers a land area of 3.484 square miles and a water area of 0.106 square miles. Located at 43.57° N. Lat; 76.12° W. Long. Elevation is 371 feet.

History: Incorporated 1832.

Population: 2,132; Growth (since 2000): -11.1%; Density: 612.0 persons per square mile; Race: 97.3% White, 0.0% Black/African American, 0.8% Asian, 0.0% American Indian/Alaska Native, 0.0% Native Hawaiian/Other Pacific Islander, 1.9% Two or more races, 0.8% Hispanic of any race; Average household size: 2.30; Median age: 36.3; Age under 18: 25.2%; Age 65 and over: 17.5%; Males per 100 females: 93.9; Marriage status: 33.7% never married, 43.9% now married, 5.5% separated, 7.3% widowed, 15.0% divorced; Foreign born: 1.4%; Speak English only: 98.9%; With disability: 20.6%; Veterans: 11.1%; Ancestry: 26.1% German, 21.2% Irish, 15.6% English, 12.6% French, 7.5% American

Employment: 9.7% management, business, and financial, 3.1% computer, engineering, and science, 12.8% education, legal, community service, arts, and media, 4.5% healthcare practitioners, 20.6% service, 23.4% sales and office, 14.1% natural resources, construction, and maintenance, 11.9% production, transportation, and material moving

Income: Per capita: $22,357; Median household: $36,302; Average household: $50,189; Households with income of $100,000 or more: 12.5%; Poverty rate: 22.3%

Educational Attainment: High school diploma or higher: 90.0%; Bachelor's degree or higher: 16.0%; Graduate/professional degree or higher: 6.1%

School District(s)
Pulaski Central SD (PK-12)
    Enrollment: 1,114 . . . . (315) 298-5188
Housing: Homeownership rate: 45.2%; Median home value: $99,700; Median year structure built: 1950; Homeowner vacancy rate: 4.3%; Median selected monthly owner costs: $1,131 with a mortgage, $531 without a mortgage; Median gross rent: $692 per month; Rental vacancy rate: 2.3%
Health Insurance: 97.4% have insurance; 60.2% have private insurance; 51.8% have public insurance; 2.6% do not have insurance; 1.6% of children under 18 do not have insurance
Transportation: Commute: 88.3% car, 0.5% public transportation, 6.1% walk, 3.1% work from home; Mean travel time to work: 27.1 minutes

REDFIELD (town). Covers a land area of 89.817 square miles and a water area of 3.606 square miles. Located at 43.59° N. Lat; 75.83° W. Long. Elevation is 948 feet.

Population: 486; Growth (since 2000): -19.9%; Density: 5.4 persons per square mile; Race: 100.0% White, 0.0% Black/African American, 0.0% Asian, 0.0% American Indian/Alaska Native, 0.0% Native Hawaiian/Other Pacific Islander, 0.0% Two or more races, 0.0% Hispanic of any race; Average household size: 2.49; Median age: 44.6; Age under 18: 19.1%; Age 65 and over: 24.3%; Males per 100 females: 103.7; Marriage status: 19.7% never married, 58.7% now married, 2.0% separated, 8.9% widowed, 12.7% divorced; Foreign born: 1.2%; Speak English only: 97.8%; With disability: 18.1%; Veterans: 11.5%; Ancestry: 22.8% German, 14.8% American, 13.6% English, 13.6% Irish, 11.5% Italian

Employment: 18.0% management, business, and financial, 5.2% computer, engineering, and science, 12.4% education, legal, community service, arts, and media, 2.6% healthcare practitioners, 11.9% service, 18.6% sales and office, 16.0% natural resources, construction, and maintenance, 15.5% production, transportation, and material moving

Income: Per capita: $22,426; Median household: $50,688; Average household: $53,916; Households with income of $100,000 or more: 10.7%; Poverty rate: 14.8%

Educational Attainment: High school diploma or higher: 94.7%; Bachelor's degree or higher: 13.1%; Graduate/professional degree or higher: 8.1%

Housing: Homeownership rate: 90.3%; Median home value: $100,000; Median year structure built: 1982; Homeowner vacancy rate: 8.3%; Median selected monthly owner costs: $930 with a mortgage, $396 without a mortgage; Median gross rent: $475 per month; Rental vacancy rate: 29.6%
Health Insurance: 94.9% have insurance; 69.1% have private insurance; 45.5% have public insurance; 5.1% do not have insurance; 3.2% of children under 18 do not have insurance
Transportation: Commute: 93.1% car, 0.0% public transportation, 0.0% walk, 3.7% work from home; Mean travel time to work: 35.1 minutes

RICHLAND (town). Covers a land area of 57.248 square miles and a water area of 2.801 square miles. Located at 43.55° N. Lat; 76.15° W. Long. Elevation is 545 feet.

Population: 5,642; Growth (since 2000): -3.1%; Density: 98.6 persons per square mile; Race: 98.4% White, 0.5% Black/African American, 0.3% Asian, 0.0% American Indian/Alaska Native, 0.0% Native Hawaiian/Other Pacific Islander, 0.8% Two or more races, 0.9% Hispanic of any race; Average household size: 2.61; Median age: 36.8; Age under 18: 28.4%; Age 65 and over: 18.2%; Males per 100 females: 99.2; Marriage status: 25.5% never married, 53.8% now married, 3.7% separated, 7.6% widowed, 13.0% divorced; Foreign born: 1.6%; Speak English only: 91.3%; With disability: 17.4%; Veterans: 10.9%; Ancestry: 26.1% German, 17.0% Irish, 10.3% English, 9.7% French, 9.4% Italian

Employment: 9.8% management, business, and financial, 2.6% computer, engineering, and science, 13.2% education, legal, community service, arts, and media, 5.3% healthcare practitioners, 18.1% service, 23.7% sales and office, 15.2% natural resources, construction, and maintenance, 12.1% production, transportation, and material moving

Income: Per capita: $22,693; Median household: $44,527; Average household: $58,633; Households with income of $100,000 or more: 19.0%; Poverty rate: 22.3%

Educational Attainment: High school diploma or higher: 86.4%; Bachelor's degree or higher: 15.3%; Graduate/professional degree or higher: 7.0%

Housing: Homeownership rate: 68.0%; Median home value: $102,900; Median year structure built: 1964; Homeowner vacancy rate: 5.8%; Median selected monthly owner costs: $1,139 with a mortgage, $503 without a mortgage; Median gross rent: $724 per month; Rental vacancy rate: 3.7%

Health Insurance: 89.1% have insurance; 59.0% have private insurance; 44.6% have public insurance; 10.9% do not have insurance; 21.4% of children under 18 do not have insurance
Transportation: Commute: 88.2% car, 0.2% public transportation, 4.8% walk, 5.2% work from home; Mean travel time to work: 23.6 minutes

SAND RIDGE (CDP).
Covers a land area of 2.399 square miles and a water area of 0.036 square miles. Located at 43.26° N. Lat; 76.24° W. Long. Elevation is 433 feet.
Population: 698; Growth (since 2000): -23.0%; Density: 291.0 persons per square mile; Race: 100.0% White, 0.0% Black/African American, 0.0% Asian, 0.0% American Indian/Alaska Native, 0.0% Native Hawaiian/Other Pacific Islander, 0.0% Two or more races, 0.0% Hispanic of any race; Average household size: 2.31; Median age: 48.3; Age under 18: 14.3%; Age 65 and over: 21.3%; Males per 100 females: 105.6; Marriage status: 27.0% never married, 54.6% now married, 7.1% separated, 15.8% widowed, 2.6% divorced; Foreign born: 0.0%; Speak English only: 100.0%; With disability: 30.8%; Veterans: 12.5%; Ancestry: 29.9% German, 16.9% Irish, 10.6% French, 10.3% Italian, 7.3% American
Employment: 5.6% management, business, and financial, 6.0% computer, engineering, and science, 4.9% education, legal, community service, arts, and media, 0.0% healthcare practitioners, 24.9% service, 22.1% sales and office, 30.2% natural resources, construction, and maintenance, 6.3% production, transportation, and material moving
Income: Per capita: $21,141; Median household: $42,159; Average household: $47,135; Households with income of $100,000 or more: 4.6%; Poverty rate: 9.0%
Educational Attainment: High school diploma or higher: 79.1%; Bachelor's degree or higher: 2.7%; Graduate/professional degree or higher: 2.7%
Housing: Homeownership rate: 94.0%; Median home value: $72,700; Median year structure built: 1973; Homeowner vacancy rate: 0.0%; Median selected monthly owner costs: $1,293 with a mortgage, $547 without a mortgage; Median gross rent: n/a per month; Rental vacancy rate: 0.0%
Health Insurance: 82.7% have insurance; 41.3% have private insurance; 61.5% have public insurance; 17.3% do not have insurance; 0.0% of children under 18 do not have insurance
Transportation: Commute: 100.0% car, 0.0% public transportation, 0.0% walk, 0.0% work from home; Mean travel time to work: 20.5 minutes

SANDY CREEK (town).
Covers a land area of 42.284 square miles and a water area of 4.157 square miles. Located at 43.63° N. Lat; 76.12° W. Long. Elevation is 499 feet.
Population: 3,817; Growth (since 2000): -1.2%; Density: 90.3 persons per square mile; Race: 98.0% White, 0.2% Black/African American, 0.4% Asian, 0.0% American Indian/Alaska Native, 0.0% Native Hawaiian/Other Pacific Islander, 1.4% Two or more races, 0.4% Hispanic of any race; Average household size: 2.38; Median age: 45.0; Age under 18: 19.4%; Age 65 and over: 18.2%; Males per 100 females: 102.9; Marriage status: 24.7% never married, 57.0% now married, 2.9% separated, 5.9% widowed, 12.4% divorced; Foreign born: 1.2%; Speak English only: 99.2%; With disability: 18.3%; Veterans: 10.6%; Ancestry: 22.8% German, 20.0% English, 19.7% Irish, 7.1% French, 6.0% Polish
Employment: 15.5% management, business, and financial, 2.0% computer, engineering, and science, 9.8% education, legal, community service, arts, and media, 4.6% healthcare practitioners, 20.7% service, 20.4% sales and office, 14.3% natural resources, construction, and maintenance, 12.6% production, transportation, and material moving
Income: Per capita: $27,291; Median household: $58,750; Average household: $64,102; Households with income of $100,000 or more: 17.1%; Poverty rate: 13.2%
Educational Attainment: High school diploma or higher: 89.0%; Bachelor's degree or higher: 13.3%; Graduate/professional degree or higher: 5.7%

School District(s)
Sandy Creek Central SD (PK-12)
   Enrollment: 830 . . . . (315) 387-3445
Housing: Homeownership rate: 77.8%; Median home value: $105,600; Median year structure built: 1972; Homeowner vacancy rate: 0.6%; Median selected monthly owner costs: $1,124 with a mortgage, $436 without a mortgage; Median gross rent: $672 per month; Rental vacancy rate: 21.1%
Health Insurance: 95.1% have insurance; 67.8% have private insurance; 46.1% have public insurance; 4.9% do not have insurance; 0.5% of children under 18 do not have insurance

Transportation: Commute: 95.7% car, 0.6% public transportation, 0.8% walk, 2.9% work from home; Mean travel time to work: 30.3 minutes

SANDY CREEK (village).
Covers a land area of 1.351 square miles and a water area of 0 square miles. Located at 43.64° N. Lat; 76.09° W. Long. Elevation is 499 feet.
Population: 782; Growth (since 2000): -0.9%; Density: 578.7 persons per square mile; Race: 98.6% White, 0.8% Black/African American, 0.0% Asian, 0.0% American Indian/Alaska Native, 0.1% Native Hawaiian/Other Pacific Islander, 0.5% Two or more races, 0.5% Hispanic of any race; Average household size: 2.58; Median age: 32.8; Age under 18: 27.1%; Age 65 and over: 12.8%; Males per 100 females: 95.7; Marriage status: 21.4% never married, 59.5% now married, 4.6% separated, 5.3% widowed, 13.7% divorced; Foreign born: 1.9%; Speak English only: 99.0%; With disability: 14.6%; Veterans: 13.3%; Ancestry: 29.0% English, 19.1% German, 16.4% Irish, 9.3% Scottish, 7.3% Dutch
Employment: 12.1% management, business, and financial, 4.3% computer, engineering, and science, 7.0% education, legal, community service, arts, and media, 6.7% healthcare practitioners, 18.0% service, 18.8% sales and office, 16.1% natural resources, construction, and maintenance, 17.2% production, transportation, and material moving
Income: Per capita: $23,264; Median household: $51,985; Average household: $58,245; Households with income of $100,000 or more: 11.2%; Poverty rate: 13.4%
Educational Attainment: High school diploma or higher: 95.1%; Bachelor's degree or higher: 13.1%; Graduate/professional degree or higher: 5.5%

School District(s)
Sandy Creek Central SD (PK-12)
   Enrollment: 830 . . . . (315) 387-3445
Housing: Homeownership rate: 67.0%; Median home value: $93,100; Median year structure built: 1944; Homeowner vacancy rate: 3.3%; Median selected monthly owner costs: $939 with a mortgage, $472 without a mortgage; Median gross rent: $682 per month; Rental vacancy rate: 5.7%
Health Insurance: 94.2% have insurance; 69.8% have private insurance; 35.9% have public insurance; 5.8% do not have insurance; 0.0% of children under 18 do not have insurance
Transportation: Commute: 95.3% car, 0.8% public transportation, 1.1% walk, 2.7% work from home; Mean travel time to work: 25.3 minutes

SCHROEPPEL (town).
Covers a land area of 42.201 square miles and a water area of 0.996 square miles. Located at 43.26° N. Lat; 76.28° W. Long.
Population: 8,291; Growth (since 2000): -3.2%; Density: 196.5 persons per square mile; Race: 96.3% White, 0.1% Black/African American, 0.6% Asian, 0.1% American Indian/Alaska Native, 0.0% Native Hawaiian/Other Pacific Islander, 2.9% Two or more races, 1.3% Hispanic of any race; Average household size: 2.53; Median age: 41.8; Age under 18: 21.9%; Age 65 and over: 15.9%; Males per 100 females: 99.8; Marriage status: 29.2% never married, 52.5% now married, 3.7% separated, 6.8% widowed, 11.4% divorced; Foreign born: 1.1%; Speak English only: 98.5%; With disability: 17.3%; Veterans: 8.9%; Ancestry: 24.4% German, 21.6% Irish, 11.6% Italian, 9.5% English, 7.1% French
Employment: 9.8% management, business, and financial, 3.3% computer, engineering, and science, 11.0% education, legal, community service, arts, and media, 2.6% healthcare practitioners, 14.3% service, 30.2% sales and office, 16.4% natural resources, construction, and maintenance, 12.4% production, transportation, and material moving
Income: Per capita: $27,766; Median household: $57,946; Average household: $70,080; Households with income of $100,000 or more: 21.5%; Poverty rate: 16.3%
Educational Attainment: High school diploma or higher: 88.8%; Bachelor's degree or higher: 19.1%; Graduate/professional degree or higher: 8.0%
Housing: Homeownership rate: 71.7%; Median home value: $99,500; Median year structure built: 1974; Homeowner vacancy rate: 0.0%; Median selected monthly owner costs: $1,288 with a mortgage, $569 without a mortgage; Median gross rent: $719 per month; Rental vacancy rate: 1.5%
Health Insurance: 94.5% have insurance; 62.3% have private insurance; 45.4% have public insurance; 5.5% do not have insurance; 0.0% of children under 18 do not have insurance
Transportation: Commute: 89.5% car, 0.7% public transportation, 0.9% walk, 8.4% work from home; Mean travel time to work: 23.8 minutes

Additional Information Contacts
Town of Schroeppel . . . . (315) 695-2778
  http://townofschroeppel.com/content

SCRIBA (town). Covers a land area of 40.571 square miles and a water area of 3.342 square miles. Located at 43.46° N. Lat; 76.42° W. Long. Elevation is 367 feet.

Population: 6,667; Growth (since 2000): -9.1%; Density: 164.3 persons per square mile; Race: 97.8% White, 0.0% Black/African American, 1.1% Asian, 0.1% American Indian/Alaska Native, 0.0% Native Hawaiian/Other Pacific Islander, 1.0% Two or more races, 4.2% Hispanic of any race; Average household size: 2.32; Median age: 45.1; Age under 18: 19.5%; Age 65 and over: 15.5%; Males per 100 females: 98.0; Marriage status: 20.9% never married, 60.2% now married, 3.3% separated, 4.3% widowed, 14.6% divorced; Foreign born: 2.1%; Speak English only: 96.8%; With disability: 15.3%; Veterans: 14.0%; Ancestry: 19.4% Italian, 18.0% Irish, 15.3% English, 11.5% German, 9.3% French

Employment: 12.7% management, business, and financial, 3.4% computer, engineering, and science, 10.6% education, legal, community service, arts, and media, 7.5% healthcare practitioners, 18.6% service, 20.6% sales and office, 10.7% natural resources, construction, and maintenance, 15.9% production, transportation, and material moving

Income: Per capita: $32,446; Median household: $59,110; Average household: $75,119; Households with income of $100,000 or more: 26.5%; Poverty rate: 12.8%

Educational Attainment: High school diploma or higher: 83.5%; Bachelor's degree or higher: 20.6%; Graduate/professional degree or higher: 5.0%

Housing: Homeownership rate: 79.8%; Median home value: $112,700; Median year structure built: 1981; Homeowner vacancy rate: 2.1%; Median selected monthly owner costs: $1,364 with a mortgage, $501 without a mortgage; Median gross rent: $754 per month; Rental vacancy rate: 6.9%

Health Insurance: 95.3% have insurance; 74.8% have private insurance; 36.2% have public insurance; 4.7% do not have insurance; 0.1% of children under 18 do not have insurance

Transportation: Commute: 91.2% car, 2.2% public transportation, 1.1% walk, 2.2% work from home; Mean travel time to work: 21.9 minutes

Additional Information Contacts
Town of Scriba . . . . (315) 343-3375
  http://scribany.org

SUNY OSWEGO (CDP). Covers a land area of 0.324 square miles and a water area of 0.302 square miles. Located at 43.46° N. Lat; 76.54° W. Long.

Population: 3,733; Growth (since 2000): n/a; Density: 11,505.8 persons per square mile; Race: 74.1% White, 13.2% Black/African American, 4.7% Asian, 0.3% American Indian/Alaska Native, 0.0% Native Hawaiian/Other Pacific Islander, 5.1% Two or more races, 9.9% Hispanic of any race; Average household size: 0.00; Median age: 19.6; Age under 18: 1.2%; Age 65 and over: 0.0%; Males per 100 females: 95.7; Marriage status: 99.7% never married, 0.3% now married, 0.0% separated, 0.0% widowed, 0.0% divorced; Foreign born: 6.8%; Speak English only: 85.1%; With disability: 4.2%; Veterans: 0.0%; Ancestry: 29.3% Irish, 26.8% Italian, 21.5% German, 8.4% Polish, 7.4% English

Employment: 3.5% management, business, and financial, 3.7% computer, engineering, and science, 5.7% education, legal, community service, arts, and media, 0.0% healthcare practitioners, 42.4% service, 40.6% sales and office, 1.7% natural resources, construction, and maintenance, 2.3% production, transportation, and material moving

Income: Per capita: $7,007; Median household: n/a; Average household: n/a; Households with income of $100,000 or more: n/a; Poverty rate: n/a

Educational Attainment: High school diploma or higher: n/a; Bachelor's degree or higher: n/a; Graduate/professional degree or higher: n/a

Housing: Homeownership rate: n/a; Median home value: n/a; Median year structure built: n/a; Homeowner vacancy rate: n/a; Median selected monthly owner costs: n/a with a mortgage, n/a without a mortgage; Median gross rent: n/a per month; Rental vacancy rate: n/a

Health Insurance: 99.1% have insurance; 89.3% have private insurance; 11.5% have public insurance; 0.9% do not have insurance; 1.0% of children under 18 do not have insurance

Transportation: Commute: 27.2% car, 4.0% public transportation, 61.1% walk, 7.7% work from home; Mean travel time to work: 9.6 minutes

VOLNEY (town). Covers a land area of 48.240 square miles and a water area of 0.916 square miles. Located at 43.36° N. Lat; 76.37° W. Long. Elevation is 443 feet.

Population: 5,792; Growth (since 2000): -5.0%; Density: 120.1 persons per square mile; Race: 98.5% White, 0.1% Black/African American, 0.0% Asian, 0.0% American Indian/Alaska Native, 0.0% Native Hawaiian/Other Pacific Islander, 1.5% Two or more races, 1.6% Hispanic of any race; Average household size: 2.87; Median age: 41.8; Age under 18: 23.7%; Age 65 and over: 16.8%; Males per 100 females: 101.5; Marriage status: 24.0% never married, 61.4% now married, 3.8% separated, 6.1% widowed, 8.5% divorced; Foreign born: 1.5%; Speak English only: 97.9%; With disability: 14.7%; Veterans: 15.3%; Ancestry: 25.1% Irish, 19.8% German, 12.8% Italian, 10.4% French Canadian, 9.2% English

Employment: 7.0% management, business, and financial, 2.9% computer, engineering, and science, 11.4% education, legal, community service, arts, and media, 5.5% healthcare practitioners, 18.8% service, 20.7% sales and office, 17.2% natural resources, construction, and maintenance, 16.5% production, transportation, and material moving

Income: Per capita: $25,271; Median household: $59,097; Average household: $71,430; Households with income of $100,000 or more: 21.3%; Poverty rate: 15.3%

Educational Attainment: High school diploma or higher: 88.0%; Bachelor's degree or higher: 20.3%; Graduate/professional degree or higher: 8.5%

Housing: Homeownership rate: 80.4%; Median home value: $101,800; Median year structure built: 1981; Homeowner vacancy rate: 3.0%; Median selected monthly owner costs: $1,190 with a mortgage, $573 without a mortgage; Median gross rent: $919 per month; Rental vacancy rate: 10.8%

Health Insurance: 91.0% have insurance; 61.6% have private insurance; 42.3% have public insurance; 9.0% do not have insurance; 6.1% of children under 18 do not have insurance

Transportation: Commute: 94.1% car, 0.0% public transportation, 0.0% walk, 5.9% work from home; Mean travel time to work: 23.6 minutes

Additional Information Contacts
Town of Volney . . . . (315) 593-8288
  http://www.townofvolney.com

WEST MONROE (town). Covers a land area of 33.746 square miles and a water area of 4.841 square miles. Located at 43.31° N. Lat; 76.09° W. Long. Elevation is 397 feet.

Population: 4,179; Growth (since 2000): -5.6%; Density: 123.8 persons per square mile; Race: 97.3% White, 0.3% Black/African American, 0.0% Asian, 0.0% American Indian/Alaska Native, 0.0% Native Hawaiian/Other Pacific Islander, 1.4% Two or more races, 0.9% Hispanic of any race; Average household size: 2.41; Median age: 42.7; Age under 18: 22.8%; Age 65 and over: 13.1%; Males per 100 females: 106.4; Marriage status: 29.3% never married, 47.6% now married, 1.8% separated, 5.8% widowed, 17.3% divorced; Foreign born: 0.2%; Speak English only: 97.2%; With disability: 16.2%; Veterans: 11.4%; Ancestry: 22.8% Irish, 22.2% German, 12.7% English, 12.0% Italian, 8.1% American

Employment: 9.0% management, business, and financial, 4.5% computer, engineering, and science, 9.4% education, legal, community service, arts, and media, 2.9% healthcare practitioners, 18.7% service, 21.5% sales and office, 16.3% natural resources, construction, and maintenance, 17.6% production, transportation, and material moving

Income: Per capita: $28,528; Median household: $58,141; Average household: $67,631; Households with income of $100,000 or more: 23.4%; Poverty rate: 16.5%

Educational Attainment: High school diploma or higher: 89.7%; Bachelor's degree or higher: 11.7%; Graduate/professional degree or higher: 4.6%

Housing: Homeownership rate: 81.8%; Median home value: $127,200; Median year structure built: 1982; Homeowner vacancy rate: 1.5%; Median selected monthly owner costs: $1,383 with a mortgage, $538 without a mortgage; Median gross rent: $852 per month; Rental vacancy rate: 0.0%

Health Insurance: 95.1% have insurance; 61.2% have private insurance; 51.7% have public insurance; 4.9% do not have insurance; 0.9% of children under 18 do not have insurance

Transportation: Commute: 92.3% car, 0.7% public transportation, 1.0% walk, 6.0% work from home; Mean travel time to work: 32.0 minutes

Additional Information Contacts
Town of West Monroe . . . . (315) 668-8314
  http://www.townofwestmonroe-ny.us

WILLIAMSTOWN (town). Covers a land area of 38.672 square miles and a water area of 0.491 square miles. Located at 43.46° N. Lat; 75.89° W. Long. Elevation is 600 feet.

Population: 1,234; Growth (since 2000): -8.6%; Density: 31.9 persons per square mile; Race: 97.0% White, 0.0% Black/African American, 0.0% Asian, 0.0% American Indian/Alaska Native, 0.0% Native Hawaiian/Other Pacific Islander, 3.0% Two or more races, 0.3% Hispanic of any race; Average household size: 2.89; Median age: 35.9; Age under 18: 24.4%; Age 65 and over: 13.0%; Males per 100 females: 102.1; Marriage status: 34.4% never married, 51.3% now married, 1.2% separated, 5.0% widowed, 9.2% divorced; Foreign born: 0.6%; Speak English only: 95.2%; With disability: 15.6%; Veterans: 11.7%; Ancestry: 22.0% Irish, 13.3% English, 12.8% American, 12.6% German, 6.1% French

Employment: 5.7% management, business, and financial, 3.0% computer, engineering, and science, 6.6% education, legal, community service, arts, and media, 2.5% healthcare practitioners, 23.5% service, 20.6% sales and office, 15.4% natural resources, construction, and maintenance, 22.6% production, transportation, and material moving

Income: Per capita: $21,968; Median household: $54,489; Average household: $62,079; Households with income of $100,000 or more: 17.8%; Poverty rate: 7.8%

Educational Attainment: High school diploma or higher: 82.9%; Bachelor's degree or higher: 7.3%; Graduate/professional degree or higher: 0.9%

Housing: Homeownership rate: 86.2%; Median home value: $81,600; Median year structure built: 1979; Homeowner vacancy rate: 5.6%; Median selected monthly owner costs: $1,098 with a mortgage, $393 without a mortgage; Median gross rent: $689 per month; Rental vacancy rate: 20.3%

Health Insurance: 92.8% have insurance; 58.4% have private insurance; 47.6% have public insurance; 7.2% do not have insurance; 4.2% of children under 18 do not have insurance

Transportation: Commute: 95.3% car, 0.7% public transportation, 0.5% walk, 3.0% work from home; Mean travel time to work: 34.8 minutes

Otsego County

Located in central New York; bounded on the west by the Unadilla River; drained by the Susquehanna River; includes Canadarago Lake and other lakes. Covers a land area of 1,001.700 square miles, a water area of 14.052 square miles, and is located in the Eastern Time Zone at 42.63° N. Lat., 75.03° W. Long. The county was founded in 1791. County seat is Cooperstown.

Otsego County is part of the Oneonta, NY Micropolitan Statistical Area. The entire metro area includes: Otsego County, NY

Weather Station: Cherry Valley 2 NNE | | | | | | Elevation: 1,359 feet

	Jan	Feb	Mar	Apr	May	Jun	Jul	Aug	Sep	Oct	Nov	Dec
High	28	32	40	54	66	74	78	76	69	57	46	33
Low	12	14	22	34	44	53	58	57	49	38	30	18
Precip	3.3	2.8	3.9	4.1	4.4	4.5	4.5	4.2	4.0	3.9	3.8	3.3
Snow	32.8	21.1	22.1	5.9	0.4	0.0	0.0	0.0	tr	1.1	9.2	24.5

High and Low temperatures in degrees Fahrenheit; Precipitation and Snow in inches

Weather Station: Cooperstown | | | | | | Elevation: 1,200 feet

	Jan	Feb	Mar	Apr	May	Jun	Jul	Aug	Sep	Oct	Nov	Dec
High	31	34	42	56	68	76	80	78	71	59	47	35
Low	12	13	21	33	43	52	57	56	48	37	29	19
Precip	2.9	2.4	3.4	3.7	3.9	4.5	4.3	4.0	3.8	3.8	3.3	3.1
Snow	21.7	16.4	15.3	4.0	0.1	0.0	0.0	0.0	tr	0.5	6.1	18.0

High and Low temperatures in degrees Fahrenheit; Precipitation and Snow in inches

Weather Station: Maryland 6 SW | | | | | | Elevation: 3,911 feet

	Jan	Feb	Mar	Apr	May	Jun	Jul	Aug	Sep	Oct	Nov	Dec
High	31	33	42	56	67	75	79	78	70	59	47	35
Low	12	12	20	32	41	51	55	54	47	36	29	19
Precip	3.2	2.5	3.4	3.5	3.6	4.3	4.4	3.5	3.6	3.5	3.4	3.2
Snow	21.2	16.0	13.3	3.3	0.2	0.0	0.0	0.0	0.0	0.8	6.0	16.0

High and Low temperatures in degrees Fahrenheit; Precipitation and Snow in inches

Population: 60,750; Growth (since 2000): -1.5%; Density: 60.6 persons per square mile; Race: 93.5% White, 2.0% Black/African American, 1.4% Asian, 0.2% American Indian/Alaska Native, 0.0% Native Hawaiian/Other Pacific Islander, 1.9% two or more races, 3.5% Hispanic of any race; Average household size: 2.33; Median age: 42.0; Age under 18: 16.6%; Age 65 and over: 19.3%; Males per 100 females: 93.7; Marriage status: 35.3% never married, 48.6% now married, 2.0% separated, 6.3% widowed, 9.9% divorced; Foreign born: 3.6%; Speak English only: 94.0%; With disability: 12.9%; Veterans: 8.3%; Ancestry: 21.1% German, 19.1% Irish, 14.7% English, 12.7% Italian, 5.1% American

Religion: Six largest groups: 18.6% Catholicism, 8.5% Methodist/Pietist, 2.1% Episcopalianism/Anglicanism, 1.8% Presbyterian-Reformed, 1.7% Baptist, 1.6% Non-denominational Protestant

Economy: Unemployment rate: 3.5%; Leading industries: 19.3 % retail trade; 15.0 % accommodation and food services; 11.3 % health care and social assistance; Farms: 995 totaling 180,750 acres; Company size: 1 employs 1,000 or more persons, 3 employ 500 to 999 persons, 23 employ 100 to 499 persons, 1,382 employ less than 100 persons; Business ownership: 1,400 women-owned, 27 Black-owned, 143 Hispanic-owned, 53 Asian-owned, n/a American Indian/Alaska Native-owned

Employment: 13.1% management, business, and financial, 2.6% computer, engineering, and science, 13.2% education, legal, community service, arts, and media, 7.7% healthcare practitioners, 20.2% service, 22.6% sales and office, 9.5% natural resources, construction, and maintenance, 11.0% production, transportation, and material moving

Income: Per capita: $26,688; Median household: $51,254; Average household: $66,706; Households with income of $100,000 or more: 19.7%; Poverty rate: 16.1%

Educational Attainment: High school diploma or higher: 91.0%; Bachelor's degree or higher: 29.6%; Graduate/professional degree or higher: 14.3%

Housing: Homeownership rate: 74.3%; Median home value: $141,900; Median year structure built: 1955; Homeowner vacancy rate: 1.6%; Median selected monthly owner costs: $1,274 with a mortgage, $462 without a mortgage; Median gross rent: $808 per month; Rental vacancy rate: 8.7%

Vital Statistics: Birth rate: 84.4 per 10,000 population; Death rate: 103.7 per 10,000 population; Age-adjusted cancer mortality rate: 167.7 deaths per 100,000 population

Health Insurance: 93.6% have insurance; 71.7% have private insurance; 38.2% have public insurance; 6.4% do not have insurance; 4.9% of children under 18 do not have insurance

Health Care: Physicians: 60.5 per 10,000 population; Dentists: 5.5 per 10,000 population; Hospital beds: 56.8 per 10,000 population; Hospital admissions: 1,847.1 per 10,000 population

Transportation: Commute: 82.2% car, 2.2% public transportation, 8.7% walk, 5.1% work from home; Mean travel time to work: 22.4 minutes

2016 Presidential Election: 51.8% Trump, 40.7% Clinton, 4.2% Johnson, 2.0% Stein

National and State Parks: Gilbert Lake State Park

Additional Information Contacts

Otsego Government . . . . (607) 547-4276
   http://www.otsegocounty.com

Otsego County Communities

BURLINGTON (town). Covers a land area of 44.891 square miles and a water area of 0.122 square miles. Located at 42.72° N. Lat; 75.14° W. Long. Elevation is 1,535 feet.

Population: 1,145; Growth (since 2000): 5.5%; Density: 25.5 persons per square mile; Race: 99.0% White, 0.0% Black/African American, 0.3% Asian, 0.0% American Indian/Alaska Native, 0.0% Native Hawaiian/Other Pacific Islander, 0.7% Two or more races, 0.7% Hispanic of any race; Average household size: 2.75; Median age: 41.6; Age under 18: 23.0%; Age 65 and over: 15.8%; Males per 100 females: 108.4; Marriage status: 29.6% never married, 55.5% now married, 1.6% separated, 5.0% widowed, 9.9% divorced; Foreign born: 0.5%; Speak English only: 95.1%; With disability: 12.4%; Veterans: 5.1%; Ancestry: 31.0% German, 19.6% Irish, 9.3% American, 9.1% French, 8.6% English

Employment: 13.5% management, business, and financial, 2.5% computer, engineering, and science, 8.9% education, legal, community service, arts, and media, 4.2% healthcare practitioners, 19.7% service, 24.7% sales and office, 8.9% natural resources, construction, and maintenance, 17.7% production, transportation, and material moving

Income: Per capita: $23,223; Median household: $51,307; Average household: $62,681; Households with income of $100,000 or more: 17.5%; Poverty rate: 16.2%

Educational Attainment: High school diploma or higher: 93.4%; Bachelor's degree or higher: 17.7%; Graduate/professional degree or higher: 5.5%

Housing: Homeownership rate: 88.7%; Median home value: $113,500; Median year structure built: 1959; Homeowner vacancy rate: 2.6%; Median

selected monthly owner costs: $1,122 with a mortgage, $444 without a mortgage; Median gross rent: $1,000 per month; Rental vacancy rate: 0.0%

Health Insurance: 87.6% have insurance; 56.7% have private insurance; 44.7% have public insurance; 12.4% do not have insurance; 21.4% of children under 18 do not have insurance

Transportation: Commute: 93.8% car, 2.0% public transportation, 0.6% walk, 1.0% work from home; Mean travel time to work: 22.4 minutes

BURLINGTON FLATS (unincorporated postal area)
ZCTA: 13315

Covers a land area of 49.097 square miles and a water area of 0.170 square miles. Located at 42.74° N. Lat; 75.14° W. Long. Elevation is 1,289 feet.

Population: 1,444; Growth (since 2000): 3.4%; Density: 29.4 persons per square mile; Race: 99.2% White, 0.0% Black/African American, 0.2% Asian, 0.0% American Indian/Alaska Native, 0.0% Native Hawaiian/Other Pacific Islander, 0.6% Two or more races, 1.0% Hispanic of any race; Average household size: 2.76; Median age: 42.3; Age under 18: 22.4%; Age 65 and over: 14.1%; Males per 100 females: 109.0; Marriage status: 27.8% never married, 58.7% now married, 1.2% separated, 4.2% widowed, 9.3% divorced; Foreign born: 0.6%; Speak English only: 94.6%; With disability: 10.6%; Veterans: 7.0%; Ancestry: 28.1% German, 20.5% Irish, 8.9% English, 8.2% French, 7.3% American

Employment: 10.7% management, business, and financial, 3.2% computer, engineering, and science, 7.2% education, legal, community service, arts, and media, 4.2% healthcare practitioners, 20.7% service, 23.5% sales and office, 13.7% natural resources, construction, and maintenance, 16.9% production, transportation, and material moving

Income: Per capita: $23,625; Median household: $56,923; Average household: $64,482; Households with income of $100,000 or more: 19.6%; Poverty rate: 15.4%

Educational Attainment: High school diploma or higher: 93.5%; Bachelor's degree or higher: 16.0%; Graduate/professional degree or higher: 5.7%

Housing: Homeownership rate: 91.0%; Median home value: $119,100; Median year structure built: 1959; Homeowner vacancy rate: 2.1%; Median selected monthly owner costs: $1,092 with a mortgage, $440 without a mortgage; Median gross rent: $1,125 per month; Rental vacancy rate: 0.0%

Health Insurance: 89.1% have insurance; 60.5% have private insurance; 41.3% have public insurance; 10.9% do not have insurance; 17.6% of children under 18 do not have insurance

Transportation: Commute: 94.1% car, 1.9% public transportation, 0.0% walk, 0.9% work from home; Mean travel time to work: 25.5 minutes

BUTTERNUTS (town). Covers a land area of 53.829 square miles and a water area of 0.040 square miles. Located at 42.47° N. Lat; 75.32° W. Long.

Population: 1,864; Growth (since 2000): 4.0%; Density: 34.6 persons per square mile; Race: 98.1% White, 0.0% Black/African American, 0.4% Asian, 0.0% American Indian/Alaska Native, 0.0% Native Hawaiian/Other Pacific Islander, 1.4% Two or more races, 1.0% Hispanic of any race; Average household size: 2.42; Median age: 50.1; Age under 18: 16.2%; Age 65 and over: 23.3%; Males per 100 females: 97.6; Marriage status: 22.5% never married, 59.4% now married, 1.4% separated, 7.8% widowed, 10.3% divorced; Foreign born: 2.9%; Speak English only: 97.4%; With disability: 15.8%; Veterans: 9.6%; Ancestry: 22.4% German, 21.0% English, 17.4% Irish, 10.1% American, 6.7% Italian

Employment: 14.1% management, business, and financial, 1.9% computer, engineering, and science, 13.6% education, legal, community service, arts, and media, 5.0% healthcare practitioners, 11.4% service, 21.3% sales and office, 11.8% natural resources, construction, and maintenance, 21.0% production, transportation, and material moving

Income: Per capita: $25,461; Median household: $46,917; Average household: $60,665; Households with income of $100,000 or more: 15.9%; Poverty rate: 15.5%

Educational Attainment: High school diploma or higher: 89.4%; Bachelor's degree or higher: 26.1%; Graduate/professional degree or higher: 11.1%

Housing: Homeownership rate: 86.6%; Median home value: $135,000; Median year structure built: 1968; Homeowner vacancy rate: 1.6%; Median selected monthly owner costs: $1,192 with a mortgage, $410 without a mortgage; Median gross rent: $826 per month; Rental vacancy rate: 0.0%

Health Insurance: 94.8% have insurance; 69.9% have private insurance; 45.3% have public insurance; 5.2% do not have insurance; 1.5% of children under 18 do not have insurance

Transportation: Commute: 89.3% car, 0.3% public transportation, 4.7% walk, 5.6% work from home; Mean travel time to work: 25.7 minutes

CHERRY VALLEY (town). Covers a land area of 40.375 square miles and a water area of 0.007 square miles. Located at 42.81° N. Lat; 74.72° W. Long. Elevation is 1,345 feet.

History: Burned (Nov. 11, 1778) during American Revolution by Native American and Tory forces; over 40 people killed. Settled c.1740.

Population: 1,313; Growth (since 2000): 3.7%; Density: 32.5 persons per square mile; Race: 97.6% White, 0.2% Black/African American, 0.9% Asian, 0.0% American Indian/Alaska Native, 0.0% Native Hawaiian/Other Pacific Islander, 1.3% Two or more races, 1.1% Hispanic of any race; Average household size: 2.51; Median age: 43.0; Age under 18: 22.3%; Age 65 and over: 18.2%; Males per 100 females: 92.9; Marriage status: 23.1% never married, 62.8% now married, 0.7% separated, 2.5% widowed, 11.5% divorced; Foreign born: 2.7%; Speak English only: 93.6%; With disability: 13.2%; Veterans: 8.2%; Ancestry: 24.9% German, 16.8% English, 12.1% Irish, 12.0% Italian, 5.4% European

Employment: 15.6% management, business, and financial, 2.3% computer, engineering, and science, 13.3% education, legal, community service, arts, and media, 4.3% healthcare practitioners, 12.4% service, 30.0% sales and office, 11.3% natural resources, construction, and maintenance, 10.8% production, transportation, and material moving

Income: Per capita: $28,038; Median household: $59,048; Average household: $69,095; Households with income of $100,000 or more: 22.0%; Poverty rate: 12.3%

Educational Attainment: High school diploma or higher: 94.1%; Bachelor's degree or higher: 33.1%; Graduate/professional degree or higher: 16.2%

School District(s)
Cherry Valley-Springfield Central SD (PK-12)
    Enrollment: 507 . . . . (607) 264-9332

Housing: Homeownership rate: 77.8%; Median home value: $164,600; Median year structure built: Before 1940; Homeowner vacancy rate: 0.0%; Median selected monthly owner costs: $1,446 with a mortgage, $535 without a mortgage; Median gross rent: $799 per month; Rental vacancy rate: 0.0%

Health Insurance: 92.2% have insurance; 78.1% have private insurance; 35.0% have public insurance; 7.8% do not have insurance; 8.9% of children under 18 do not have insurance

Transportation: Commute: 83.3% car, 1.3% public transportation, 7.7% walk, 7.7% work from home; Mean travel time to work: 25.9 minutes

CHERRY VALLEY (village). Covers a land area of 0.510 square miles and a water area of <.001 square miles. Located at 42.80° N. Lat; 74.75° W. Long. Elevation is 1,345 feet.

Population: 544; Growth (since 2000): -8.1%; Density: 1,067.5 persons per square mile; Race: 94.3% White, 0.4% Black/African American, 2.2% Asian, 0.0% American Indian/Alaska Native, 0.0% Native Hawaiian/Other Pacific Islander, 3.1% Two or more races, 2.2% Hispanic of any race; Average household size: 2.43; Median age: 42.4; Age under 18: 22.1%; Age 65 and over: 24.1%; Males per 100 females: 81.2; Marriage status: 21.1% never married, 58.2% now married, 0.5% separated, 2.7% widowed, 18.0% divorced; Foreign born: 4.2%; Speak English only: 93.8%; With disability: 16.7%; Veterans: 14.4%; Ancestry: 18.2% German, 15.4% English, 11.9% Irish, 5.3% Dutch, 5.3% Welsh

Employment: 9.4% management, business, and financial, 2.3% computer, engineering, and science, 9.4% education, legal, community service, arts, and media, 3.4% healthcare practitioners, 13.5% service, 42.5% sales and office, 7.1% natural resources, construction, and maintenance, 12.4% production, transportation, and material moving

Income: Per capita: $24,899; Median household: $51,042; Average household: $58,652; Households with income of $100,000 or more: 15.3%; Poverty rate: 10.7%

Educational Attainment: High school diploma or higher: 96.3%; Bachelor's degree or higher: 37.9%; Graduate/professional degree or higher: 17.8%

School District(s)
Cherry Valley-Springfield Central SD (PK-12)
    Enrollment: 507 . . . . (607) 264-9332

Housing: Homeownership rate: 68.6%; Median home value: $129,700; Median year structure built: Before 1940; Homeowner vacancy rate: 0.0%;

Median selected monthly owner costs: $1,346 with a mortgage, $423 without a mortgage; Median gross rent: $767 per month; Rental vacancy rate: 0.0%
Health Insurance: 95.4% have insurance; 78.3% have private insurance; 43.4% have public insurance; 4.6% do not have insurance; 4.2% of children under 18 do not have insurance
Transportation: Commute: 72.9% car, 1.2% public transportation, 17.8% walk, 8.1% work from home; Mean travel time to work: 24.5 minutes

COOPERSTOWN (village). County seat. Covers a land area of 1.635 square miles and a water area of 0.210 square miles. Located at 42.70° N. Lat; 74.93° W. Long. Elevation is 1,227 feet.

History: Founded by William Cooper, who brought his family here in 1787. His son, James Fenimore Cooper, made his home here after returning from abroad in 1833, and the region is described in his Leatherstocking Tales. Fenimore House is the headquarters of N.Y. State Historical Association. Other attractions include Farmers' Museum and the famous National Baseball Hall of Fame and Museum, which commemorates the founding (1839) of baseball here by Abner Doubleday. Incorporated 1807.
Population: 1,941; Growth (since 2000): -4.5%; Density: 1,187.4 persons per square mile; Race: 88.2% White, 2.6% Black/African American, 7.6% Asian, 0.9% American Indian/Alaska Native, 0.0% Native Hawaiian/Other Pacific Islander, 0.6% Two or more races, 2.0% Hispanic of any race; Average household size: 1.99; Median age: 51.6; Age under 18: 12.6%; Age 65 and over: 20.7%; Males per 100 females: 81.4; Marriage status: 28.4% never married, 53.4% now married, 2.9% separated, 7.8% widowed, 10.5% divorced; Foreign born: 8.6%; Speak English only: 89.5%; With disability: 9.4%; Veterans: 7.6%; Ancestry: 22.0% Irish, 21.1% English, 18.2% German, 13.4% Italian, 6.3% Scottish
Employment: 13.5% management, business, and financial, 3.1% computer, engineering, and science, 18.0% education, legal, community service, arts, and media, 25.3% healthcare practitioners, 12.7% service, 20.3% sales and office, 4.1% natural resources, construction, and maintenance, 2.9% production, transportation, and material moving
Income: Per capita: $47,528; Median household: $63,750; Average household: $97,821; Households with income of $100,000 or more: 28.7%; Poverty rate: 7.5%
Educational Attainment: High school diploma or higher: 97.2%; Bachelor's degree or higher: 55.9%; Graduate/professional degree or higher: 36.1%

School District(s)
Cooperstown Central SD (KG-12)
    Enrollment: 903 . . . . (607) 547-5364
Housing: Homeownership rate: 60.9%; Median home value: $271,600; Median year structure built: Before 1940; Homeowner vacancy rate: 1.9%; Median selected monthly owner costs: $2,005 with a mortgage, $867 without a mortgage; Median gross rent: $834 per month; Rental vacancy rate: 15.0%
Health Insurance: 96.5% have insurance; 83.1% have private insurance; 30.7% have public insurance; 3.5% do not have insurance; 3.8% of children under 18 do not have insurance
Hospitals: Mary Imogene Bassett Hospital (180 beds)
Newspapers: Cooperstown Crier (weekly circulation 2,500); Freeman's Journal (weekly circulation 2,500); Hometown Oneonta (weekly circulation 9,700)
Transportation: Commute: 53.8% car, 1.2% public transportation, 36.1% walk, 6.8% work from home; Mean travel time to work: 12.8 minutes

DECATUR (town). Covers a land area of 20.562 square miles and a water area of 0.197 square miles. Located at 42.66° N. Lat; 74.71° W. Long. Elevation is 1,617 feet.

Population: 308; Growth (since 2000): -24.9%; Density: 15.0 persons per square mile; Race: 90.6% White, 0.6% Black/African American, 2.6% Asian, 0.0% American Indian/Alaska Native, 0.0% Native Hawaiian/Other Pacific Islander, 6.2% Two or more races, 2.3% Hispanic of any race; Average household size: 2.57; Median age: 43.5; Age under 18: 20.5%; Age 65 and over: 22.4%; Males per 100 females: 105.2; Marriage status: 24.0% never married, 58.0% now married, 0.8% separated, 10.8% widowed, 7.2% divorced; Foreign born: 3.2%; Speak English only: 94.2%; With disability: 10.1%; Veterans: 7.3%; Ancestry: 23.4% German, 17.9% English, 15.6% Irish, 8.8% American, 6.5% Slovene
Employment: 7.8% management, business, and financial, 3.4% computer, engineering, and science, 6.9% education, legal, community service, arts, and media, 9.5% healthcare practitioners, 25.0% service, 18.1% sales and

office, 16.4% natural resources, construction, and maintenance, 12.9% production, transportation, and material moving
Income: Per capita: $25,928; Median household: $47,500; Average household: $68,832; Households with income of $100,000 or more: 25.0%; Poverty rate: 19.5%
Educational Attainment: High school diploma or higher: 85.8%; Bachelor's degree or higher: 21.5%; Graduate/professional degree or higher: 11.0%
Housing: Homeownership rate: 85.8%; Median home value: $154,800; Median year structure built: 1957; Homeowner vacancy rate: 3.7%; Median selected monthly owner costs: $1,325 with a mortgage, $608 without a mortgage; Median gross rent: $550 per month; Rental vacancy rate: 19.0%
Health Insurance: 93.2% have insurance; 68.2% have private insurance; 40.6% have public insurance; 6.8% do not have insurance; 0.0% of children under 18 do not have insurance
Transportation: Commute: 92.2% car, 0.0% public transportation, 5.2% walk, 2.6% work from home; Mean travel time to work: 37.2 minutes

EAST SPRINGFIELD (unincorporated postal area)
ZCTA: 13333

Covers a land area of 1.701 square miles and a water area of 0.003 square miles. Located at 42.84° N. Lat; 74.82° W. Long. Elevation is 1,322 feet.
Population: 36; Growth (since 2000): -74.6%; Density: 21.2 persons per square mile; Race: 100.0% White, 0.0% Black/African American, 0.0% Asian, 0.0% American Indian/Alaska Native, 0.0% Native Hawaiian/Other Pacific Islander, 0.0% Two or more races, 0.0% Hispanic of any race; Average household size: 2.12; Median age: 70.3; Age under 18: 0.0%; Age 65 and over: 61.1%; Males per 100 females: 106.7; Marriage status: 30.6% never married, 63.9% now married, 0.0% separated, 5.6% widowed, 0.0% divorced; Foreign born: 0.0%; Speak English only: 100.0%; With disability: 8.3%; Veterans: 13.9%; Ancestry: 44.4% German, 27.8% American, 22.2% Scottish, 16.7% European, 16.7% French
Employment: 0.0% management, business, and financial, 0.0% computer, engineering, and science, 0.0% education, legal, community service, arts, and media, 50.0% healthcare practitioners, 0.0% service, 50.0% sales and office, 0.0% natural resources, construction, and maintenance, 0.0% production, transportation, and material moving
Income: Per capita: $17,647; Median household: $33,750; Average household: $36,994; Households with income of $100,000 or more: n/a; Poverty rate: 41.7%
Educational Attainment: High school diploma or higher: 100.0%; Bachelor's degree or higher: 32.1%; Graduate/professional degree or higher: 32.1%
Housing: Homeownership rate: 100.0%; Median home value: $141,300; Median year structure built: Before 1940; Homeowner vacancy rate: 0.0%; Median selected monthly owner costs: $0 with a mortgage, $0 without a mortgage; Median gross rent: n/a per month; Rental vacancy rate: 0.0%
Health Insurance: 100.0% have insurance; 91.7% have private insurance; 69.4% have public insurance; 0.0% do not have insurance; 0.0% of children under 18 do not have insurance
Transportation: Commute: 100.0% car, 0.0% public transportation, 0.0% walk, 0.0% work from home; Mean travel time to work: 0.0 minutes

EAST WORCESTER (unincorporated postal area)
ZCTA: 12064

Covers a land area of 11.429 square miles and a water area of 0.014 square miles. Located at 42.61° N. Lat; 74.66° W. Long. Elevation is 1,463 feet.
Population: 370; Growth (since 2000): -22.9%; Density: 32.4 persons per square mile; Race: 89.2% White, 9.5% Black/African American, 0.0% Asian, 0.0% American Indian/Alaska Native, 1.4% Native Hawaiian/Other Pacific Islander, 0.0% Two or more races, 0.0% Hispanic of any race; Average household size: 1.81; Median age: 59.4; Age under 18: 8.6%; Age 65 and over: 37.8%; Males per 100 females: 121.7; Marriage status: 8.0% never married, 59.5% now married, 11.2% separated, 7.4% widowed, 25.1% divorced; Foreign born: 1.1%; Speak English only: 98.9%; With disability: 23.0%; Veterans: 18.6%; Ancestry: 34.6% Irish, 27.8% German, 8.6% English, 6.8% Italian, 4.1% Eastern European
Employment: 9.5% management, business, and financial, 0.0% computer, engineering, and science, 7.4% education, legal, community service, arts, and media, 13.5% healthcare practitioners, 27.7% service,

12.2% sales and office, 16.2% natural resources, construction, and maintenance, 13.5% production, transportation, and material moving
Income: Per capita: $26,590; Median household: $44,545; Average household: $48,825; Households with income of $100,000 or more: 2.0%; Poverty rate: 16.2%
Educational Attainment: High school diploma or higher: 82.0%; Bachelor's degree or higher: 14.2%; Graduate/professional degree or higher: 5.0%
Housing: Homeownership rate: 80.4%; Median home value: $93,300; Median year structure built: Before 1940; Homeowner vacancy rate: 0.0%; Median selected monthly owner costs: $1,121 with a mortgage, $443 without a mortgage; Median gross rent: $708 per month; Rental vacancy rate: 28.6%
Health Insurance: 95.9% have insurance; 60.0% have private insurance; 63.0% have public insurance; 4.1% do not have insurance; 0.0% of children under 18 do not have insurance
Transportation: Commute: 97.3% car, 2.7% public transportation, 0.0% walk, 0.0% work from home; Mean travel time to work: 40.9 minutes

EDMESTON (CDP). Covers a land area of 4.345 square miles and a water area of 0 square miles. Located at 42.70° N. Lat; 75.25° W. Long. Elevation is 1,204 feet.
Population: 642; Growth (since 2000): n/a; Density: 147.8 persons per square mile; Race: 97.2% White, 0.5% Black/African American, 1.2% Asian, 0.0% American Indian/Alaska Native, 0.0% Native Hawaiian/Other Pacific Islander, 0.5% Two or more races, 0.9% Hispanic of any race; Average household size: 2.38; Median age: 40.6; Age under 18: 22.6%; Age 65 and over: 17.8%; Males per 100 females: 93.8; Marriage status: 30.2% never married, 56.8% now married, 0.6% separated, 2.5% widowed, 10.5% divorced; Foreign born: 3.0%; Speak English only: 100.0%; With disability: 11.1%; Veterans: 11.7%; Ancestry: 40.2% English, 16.0% German, 15.3% Irish, 6.9% Dutch, 6.1% French
Employment: 11.9% management, business, and financial, 2.3% computer, engineering, and science, 14.5% education, legal, community service, arts, and media, 16.6% healthcare practitioners, 16.9% service, 15.4% sales and office, 21.2% natural resources, construction, and maintenance, 1.2% production, transportation, and material moving
Income: Per capita: $31,152; Median household: $58,000; Average household: $73,620; Households with income of $100,000 or more: 20.0%; Poverty rate: 8.3%
Educational Attainment: High school diploma or higher: 94.8%; Bachelor's degree or higher: 22.7%; Graduate/professional degree or higher: 12.1%

School District(s)
Edmeston Central SD (PK-12)
    Enrollment: 426 . . . . (607) 965-8931
Housing: Homeownership rate: 77.8%; Median home value: $119,100; Median year structure built: 1947; Homeowner vacancy rate: 0.0%; Median selected monthly owner costs: $1,076 with a mortgage, $448 without a mortgage; Median gross rent: $664 per month; Rental vacancy rate: 14.3%
Health Insurance: 97.5% have insurance; 84.7% have private insurance; 31.2% have public insurance; 2.5% do not have insurance; 0.0% of children under 18 do not have insurance
Transportation: Commute: 85.5% car, 0.9% public transportation, 6.1% walk, 2.3% work from home; Mean travel time to work: 17.7 minutes

EDMESTON (town). Covers a land area of 44.297 square miles and a water area of 0.084 square miles. Located at 42.72° N. Lat; 75.26° W. Long. Elevation is 1,204 feet.
Population: 1,766; Growth (since 2000): -3.2%; Density: 39.9 persons per square mile; Race: 96.9% White, 1.9% Black/African American, 0.5% Asian, 0.0% American Indian/Alaska Native, 0.0% Native Hawaiian/Other Pacific Islander, 0.5% Two or more races, 1.4% Hispanic of any race; Average household size: 2.45; Median age: 45.7; Age under 18: 19.6%; Age 65 and over: 21.3%; Males per 100 females: 97.2; Marriage status: 31.0% never married, 51.9% now married, 0.9% separated, 3.4% widowed, 13.7% divorced; Foreign born: 2.5%; Speak English only: 97.1%; With disability: 14.1%; Veterans: 9.2%; Ancestry: 30.2% English, 17.0% German, 16.4% Irish, 7.9% American, 5.6% French
Employment: 15.5% management, business, and financial, 3.2% computer, engineering, and science, 10.4% education, legal, community service, arts, and media, 9.9% healthcare practitioners, 16.7% service, 17.0% sales and office, 19.5% natural resources, construction, and maintenance, 7.7% production, transportation, and material moving

Income: Per capita: $26,683; Median household: $56,071; Average household: $68,399; Households with income of $100,000 or more: 19.3%; Poverty rate: 10.9%
Educational Attainment: High school diploma or higher: 95.0%; Bachelor's degree or higher: 19.1%; Graduate/professional degree or higher: 7.3%

School District(s)
Edmeston Central SD (PK-12)
    Enrollment: 426 . . . . (607) 965-8931
Housing: Homeownership rate: 83.6%; Median home value: $129,700; Median year structure built: 1957; Homeowner vacancy rate: 0.0%; Median selected monthly owner costs: $1,180 with a mortgage, $444 without a mortgage; Median gross rent: $677 per month; Rental vacancy rate: 8.2%
Health Insurance: 93.1% have insurance; 74.1% have private insurance; 38.6% have public insurance; 6.9% do not have insurance; 6.8% of children under 18 do not have insurance
Transportation: Commute: 86.6% car, 1.8% public transportation, 3.9% walk, 3.3% work from home; Mean travel time to work: 21.9 minutes

EXETER (town). Covers a land area of 32.078 square miles and a water area of 0.615 square miles. Located at 42.80° N. Lat; 75.08° W. Long.
Population: 818; Growth (since 2000): -14.3%; Density: 25.5 persons per square mile; Race: 98.4% White, 0.0% Black/African American, 1.5% Asian, 0.1% American Indian/Alaska Native, 0.0% Native Hawaiian/Other Pacific Islander, 0.0% Two or more races, 0.0% Hispanic of any race; Average household size: 2.17; Median age: 49.5; Age under 18: 16.3%; Age 65 and over: 18.1%; Males per 100 females: 90.9; Marriage status: 22.4% never married, 58.6% now married, 1.1% separated, 5.0% widowed, 14.0% divorced; Foreign born: 3.5%; Speak English only: 99.6%; With disability: 12.2%; Veterans: 11.2%; Ancestry: 16.3% Irish, 13.6% German, 12.2% English, 7.1% Italian, 6.8% American
Employment: 12.0% management, business, and financial, 2.1% computer, engineering, and science, 4.9% education, legal, community service, arts, and media, 7.8% healthcare practitioners, 14.1% service, 29.7% sales and office, 15.6% natural resources, construction, and maintenance, 13.8% production, transportation, and material moving
Income: Per capita: $27,922; Median household: $52,837; Average household: $60,505; Households with income of $100,000 or more: 20.1%; Poverty rate: 19.0%
Educational Attainment: High school diploma or higher: 91.0%; Bachelor's degree or higher: 20.9%; Graduate/professional degree or higher: 6.7%
Housing: Homeownership rate: 89.4%; Median home value: $112,500; Median year structure built: 1968; Homeowner vacancy rate: 2.3%; Median selected monthly owner costs: $1,103 with a mortgage, $312 without a mortgage; Median gross rent: $913 per month; Rental vacancy rate: 0.0%
Health Insurance: 94.5% have insurance; 66.7% have private insurance; 43.0% have public insurance; 5.5% do not have insurance; 2.2% of children under 18 do not have insurance
Transportation: Commute: 93.7% car, 0.0% public transportation, 0.0% walk, 6.3% work from home; Mean travel time to work: 24.3 minutes

FLY CREEK (unincorporated postal area)
ZCTA: 13337
Covers a land area of 18.498 square miles and a water area of 0.116 square miles. Located at 42.76° N. Lat; 75.00° W. Long. Elevation is 1,302 feet.
Population: 708; Growth (since 2000): -18.4%; Density: 38.3 persons per square mile; Race: 93.9% White, 0.0% Black/African American, 4.2% Asian, 0.0% American Indian/Alaska Native, 0.0% Native Hawaiian/Other Pacific Islander, 1.8% Two or more races, 2.8% Hispanic of any race; Average household size: 2.16; Median age: 51.7; Age under 18: 15.4%; Age 65 and over: 24.2%; Males per 100 females: 101.5; Marriage status: 22.4% never married, 61.5% now married, 4.1% separated, 5.2% widowed, 10.9% divorced; Foreign born: 5.5%; Speak English only: 92.4%; With disability: 3.2%; Veterans: 5.7%; Ancestry: 24.6% German, 16.1% English, 13.8% Irish, 10.2% European, 6.9% Polish
Employment: 9.8% management, business, and financial, 0.0% computer, engineering, and science, 22.0% education, legal, community service, arts, and media, 19.0% healthcare practitioners, 24.9% service, 16.3% sales and office, 2.1% natural resources, construction, and maintenance, 5.9% production, transportation, and material moving

Income: Per capita: $45,913; Median household: $69,286; Average household: $97,351; Households with income of $100,000 or more: 19.8%; Poverty rate: 13.4%

Educational Attainment: High school diploma or higher: 100.0%; Bachelor's degree or higher: 55.4%; Graduate/professional degree or higher: 30.8%

Housing: Homeownership rate: 74.1%; Median home value: $362,500; Median year structure built: Before 1940; Homeowner vacancy rate: 0.0%; Median selected monthly owner costs: $2,313 with a mortgage, $619 without a mortgage; Median gross rent: $743 per month; Rental vacancy rate: 0.0%

Health Insurance: 98.0% have insurance; 73.0% have private insurance; 38.6% have public insurance; 2.0% do not have insurance; 0.0% of children under 18 do not have insurance

Transportation: Commute: 84.6% car, 0.0% public transportation, 4.2% walk, 11.3% work from home; Mean travel time to work: 15.4 minutes

GARRATTSVILLE (unincorporated postal area)
ZCTA: 13342

Covers a land area of 7.941 square miles and a water area of 0.056 square miles. Located at 42.65° N. Lat; 75.20° W. Long. Elevation is 1,302 feet.

Population: 271; Growth (since 2000): 16.8%; Density: 34.1 persons per square mile; Race: 100.0% White, 0.0% Black/African American, 0.0% Asian, 0.0% American Indian/Alaska Native, 0.0% Native Hawaiian/Other Pacific Islander, 0.0% Two or more races, 0.0% Hispanic of any race; Average household size: 2.51; Median age: 50.9; Age under 18: 15.1%; Age 65 and over: 18.1%; Males per 100 females: 79.3; Marriage status: 29.6% never married, 63.9% now married, 1.3% separated, 1.3% widowed, 5.2% divorced; Foreign born: 0.0%; Speak English only: 97.3%; With disability: 11.4%; Veterans: 7.8%; Ancestry: 24.4% Irish, 16.6% English, 15.5% German, 13.7% French, 9.2% Italian

Employment: 20.1% management, business, and financial, 3.4% computer, engineering, and science, 16.1% education, legal, community service, arts, and media, 0.0% healthcare practitioners, 10.9% service, 30.5% sales and office, 4.0% natural resources, construction, and maintenance, 14.9% production, transportation, and material moving

Income: Per capita: $32,439; Median household: $70,000; Average household: $80,889; Households with income of $100,000 or more: 26.0%; Poverty rate: n/a

Educational Attainment: High school diploma or higher: 95.1%; Bachelor's degree or higher: 22.4%; Graduate/professional degree or higher: 12.2%

Housing: Homeownership rate: 97.2%; Median home value: $165,200; Median year structure built: 1981; Homeowner vacancy rate: 14.6%; Median selected monthly owner costs: $1,302 with a mortgage, $467 without a mortgage; Median gross rent: n/a per month; Rental vacancy rate: 0.0%

Health Insurance: 97.0% have insurance; 83.4% have private insurance; 30.6% have public insurance; 3.0% do not have insurance; 0.0% of children under 18 do not have insurance

Transportation: Commute: 87.8% car, 0.0% public transportation, 4.9% walk, 7.3% work from home; Mean travel time to work: 21.5 minutes

GILBERTSVILLE (village).
Covers a land area of 1.003 square miles and a water area of 0 square miles. Located at 42.47° N. Lat; 75.32° W. Long. Elevation is 1,093 feet.

Population: 367; Growth (since 2000): -2.1%; Density: 366.0 persons per square mile; Race: 95.6% White, 0.0% Black/African American, 2.2% Asian, 0.0% American Indian/Alaska Native, 0.0% Native Hawaiian/Other Pacific Islander, 2.2% Two or more races, 0.3% Hispanic of any race; Average household size: 2.31; Median age: 54.2; Age under 18: 16.6%; Age 65 and over: 29.2%; Males per 100 females: 70.5; Marriage status: 19.6% never married, 58.1% now married, 4.0% separated, 9.9% widowed, 12.4% divorced; Foreign born: 8.4%; Speak English only: 97.2%; With disability: 20.2%; Veterans: 10.8%; Ancestry: 26.7% English, 21.0% German, 15.5% Irish, 9.5% Italian, 7.9% Polish

Employment: 14.8% management, business, and financial, 3.6% computer, engineering, and science, 17.8% education, legal, community service, arts, and media, 3.0% healthcare practitioners, 13.0% service, 24.9% sales and office, 4.1% natural resources, construction, and maintenance, 18.9% production, transportation, and material moving

Income: Per capita: $30,480; Median household: $55,750; Average household: $68,678; Households with income of $100,000 or more: 21.4%; Poverty rate: 11.7%

Educational Attainment: High school diploma or higher: 90.5%; Bachelor's degree or higher: 33.3%; Graduate/professional degree or higher: 14.3%

School District(s)
Gilbertsville-Mount Upton Central SD (PK-12)
  Enrollment: 379 . . . . (607) 783-2207

Housing: Homeownership rate: 71.1%; Median home value: $136,500; Median year structure built: Before 1940; Homeowner vacancy rate: 0.0%; Median selected monthly owner costs: $970 with a mortgage, $513 without a mortgage; Median gross rent: $555 per month; Rental vacancy rate: 0.0%

Health Insurance: 94.8% have insurance; 68.4% have private insurance; 50.4% have public insurance; 5.2% do not have insurance; 7.6% of children under 18 do not have insurance

Transportation: Commute: 84.0% car, 1.3% public transportation, 5.1% walk, 9.0% work from home; Mean travel time to work: 24.4 minutes

HARTWICK (CDP).
Covers a land area of 3.457 square miles and a water area of 0 square miles. Located at 42.66° N. Lat; 75.06° W. Long. Elevation is 1,329 feet.

Population: 601; Growth (since 2000): n/a; Density: 173.8 persons per square mile; Race: 98.5% White, 0.0% Black/African American, 0.0% Asian, 0.0% American Indian/Alaska Native, 0.0% Native Hawaiian/Other Pacific Islander, 1.5% Two or more races, 0.0% Hispanic of any race; Average household size: 2.55; Median age: 36.5; Age under 18: 23.1%; Age 65 and over: 7.5%; Males per 100 females: 96.6; Marriage status: 34.0% never married, 49.8% now married, 3.0% separated, 7.9% widowed, 8.3% divorced; Foreign born: 0.8%; Speak English only: 98.4%; With disability: 9.3%; Veterans: 7.6%; Ancestry: 41.6% German, 22.0% Irish, 11.0% English, 7.7% Scottish, 7.2% American

Employment: 16.1% management, business, and financial, 0.0% computer, engineering, and science, 9.9% education, legal, community service, arts, and media, 11.6% healthcare practitioners, 29.7% service, 15.0% sales and office, 5.1% natural resources, construction, and maintenance, 12.5% production, transportation, and material moving

Income: Per capita: $28,165; Median household: $50,000; Average household: $71,304; Households with income of $100,000 or more: 25.4%; Poverty rate: 11.1%

Educational Attainment: High school diploma or higher: 95.9%; Bachelor's degree or higher: 32.9%; Graduate/professional degree or higher: 11.8%

Housing: Homeownership rate: 71.6%; Median home value: $135,900; Median year structure built: 1940; Homeowner vacancy rate: 0.0%; Median selected monthly owner costs: $1,326 with a mortgage, $387 without a mortgage; Median gross rent: n/a per month; Rental vacancy rate: 19.3%

Health Insurance: 93.7% have insurance; 75.9% have private insurance; 30.9% have public insurance; 6.3% do not have insurance; 3.1% of children under 18 do not have insurance

Transportation: Commute: 87.8% car, 6.1% public transportation, 1.5% walk, 4.7% work from home; Mean travel time to work: 25.9 minutes

HARTWICK (town).
Covers a land area of 40.082 square miles and a water area of 0.342 square miles. Located at 42.64° N. Lat; 75.02° W. Long. Elevation is 1,329 feet.

Population: 2,047; Growth (since 2000): -7.1%; Density: 51.1 persons per square mile; Race: 96.0% White, 0.3% Black/African American, 1.1% Asian, 0.0% American Indian/Alaska Native, 0.0% Native Hawaiian/Other Pacific Islander, 1.8% Two or more races, 0.8% Hispanic of any race; Average household size: 2.52; Median age: 41.6; Age under 18: 21.5%; Age 65 and over: 15.5%; Males per 100 females: 100.4; Marriage status: 32.4% never married, 51.7% now married, 4.9% separated, 5.3% widowed, 10.6% divorced; Foreign born: 2.3%; Speak English only: 96.0%; With disability: 11.0%; Veterans: 10.0%; Ancestry: 28.3% German, 22.0% Irish, 16.5% English, 12.0% Italian, 6.9% French

Employment: 12.8% management, business, and financial, 2.3% computer, engineering, and science, 11.2% education, legal, community service, arts, and media, 9.7% healthcare practitioners, 24.8% service, 21.3% sales and office, 7.8% natural resources, construction, and maintenance, 10.0% production, transportation, and material moving

Income: Per capita: $28,078; Median household: $49,345; Average household: $69,693; Households with income of $100,000 or more: 23.0%; Poverty rate: 16.3%

Educational Attainment: High school diploma or higher: 93.7%; Bachelor's degree or higher: 29.6%; Graduate/professional degree or higher: 14.0%

Housing: Homeownership rate: 74.2%; Median home value: $171,100; Median year structure built: 1967; Homeowner vacancy rate: 2.4%; Median selected monthly owner costs: $1,314 with a mortgage, $449 without a mortgage; Median gross rent: $792 per month; Rental vacancy rate: 13.3%

Health Insurance: 95.7% have insurance; 71.8% have private insurance; 37.7% have public insurance; 4.3% do not have insurance; 2.8% of children under 18 do not have insurance

Transportation: Commute: 89.7% car, 3.4% public transportation, 1.5% walk, 4.5% work from home; Mean travel time to work: 22.7 minutes

Additional Information Contacts

Town of Hartwick. . . . . (607) 293-8123
http://townofhartwick.org

LAURENS (town). Covers a land area of 42.049 square miles and a water area of 0.119 square miles. Located at 42.54° N. Lat; 75.12° W. Long. Elevation is 1,112 feet.

Population: 2,637; Growth (since 2000): 9.8%; Density: 62.7 persons per square mile; Race: 98.7% White, 0.5% Black/African American, 0.4% Asian, 0.0% American Indian/Alaska Native, 0.0% Native Hawaiian/Other Pacific Islander, 0.3% Two or more races, 3.3% Hispanic of any race; Average household size: 2.39; Median age: 47.4; Age under 18: 18.3%; Age 65 and over: 21.6%; Males per 100 females: 91.2; Marriage status: 22.6% never married, 56.5% now married, 2.3% separated, 7.2% widowed, 13.7% divorced; Foreign born: 5.7%; Speak English only: 95.2%; With disability: 10.5%; Veterans: 10.2%; Ancestry: 27.7% Irish, 26.7% German, 16.9% English, 8.5% Italian, 5.1% Scottish

Employment: 10.8% management, business, and financial, 3.7% computer, engineering, and science, 10.4% education, legal, community service, arts, and media, 7.4% healthcare practitioners, 22.2% service, 28.6% sales and office, 10.4% natural resources, construction, and maintenance, 6.4% production, transportation, and material moving

Income: Per capita: $26,891; Median household: $55,523; Average household: $63,051; Households with income of $100,000 or more: 21.2%; Poverty rate: 15.6%

Educational Attainment: High school diploma or higher: 91.2%; Bachelor's degree or higher: 27.4%; Graduate/professional degree or higher: 11.8%

School District(s)

Laurens Central SD (KG-12)
    Enrollment: 334. . . . . (607) 432-2050

Housing: Homeownership rate: 82.9%; Median home value: $134,700; Median year structure built: 1971; Homeowner vacancy rate: 1.6%; Median selected monthly owner costs: $1,146 with a mortgage, $471 without a mortgage; Median gross rent: $690 per month; Rental vacancy rate: 2.1%

Health Insurance: 92.6% have insurance; 69.7% have private insurance; 41.2% have public insurance; 7.4% do not have insurance; 4.6% of children under 18 do not have insurance

Transportation: Commute: 94.5% car, 0.2% public transportation, 2.1% walk, 3.3% work from home; Mean travel time to work: 25.3 minutes

---

LAURENS (village). Covers a land area of 0.128 square miles and a water area of 0 square miles. Located at 42.53° N. Lat; 75.09° W. Long. Elevation is 1,112 feet.

Population: 234; Growth (since 2000): -15.5%; Density: 1,822.3 persons per square mile; Race: 98.7% White, 0.9% Black/African American, 0.0% Asian, 0.0% American Indian/Alaska Native, 0.0% Native Hawaiian/Other Pacific Islander, 0.0% Two or more races, 7.7% Hispanic of any race; Average household size: 2.52; Median age: 36.0; Age under 18: 26.5%; Age 65 and over: 14.5%; Males per 100 females: 67.5; Marriage status: 21.3% never married, 56.9% now married, 0.6% separated, 7.5% widowed, 14.4% divorced; Foreign born: 3.8%; Speak English only: 90.6%; With disability: 19.2%; Veterans: 9.9%; Ancestry: 24.8% Irish, 23.9% German, 12.8% Italian, 11.5% English, 9.8% Dutch

Employment: 17.7% management, business, and financial, 0.0% computer, engineering, and science, 4.4% education, legal, community service, arts, and media, 6.2% healthcare practitioners, 18.6% service, 33.6% sales and office, 7.1% natural resources, construction, and maintenance, 12.4% production, transportation, and material moving

Income: Per capita: $21,845; Median household: $47,188; Average household: $56,458; Households with income of $100,000 or more: 17.2%; Poverty rate: 14.1%

Educational Attainment: High school diploma or higher: 95.7%; Bachelor's degree or higher: 20.2%; Graduate/professional degree or higher: 3.7%

School District(s)

Laurens Central SD (KG-12)
    Enrollment: 334. . . . . (607) 432-2050

Housing: Homeownership rate: 68.8%; Median home value: $107,100; Median year structure built: Before 1940; Homeowner vacancy rate: 0.0%; Median selected monthly owner costs: $1,052 with a mortgage, $450 without a mortgage; Median gross rent: $660 per month; Rental vacancy rate: 0.0%

Health Insurance: 90.2% have insurance; 67.9% have private insurance; 38.5% have public insurance; 9.8% do not have insurance; 0.0% of children under 18 do not have insurance

Transportation: Commute: 85.0% car, 1.8% public transportation, 8.0% walk, 5.3% work from home; Mean travel time to work: 21.6 minutes

---

MARYLAND (town). Covers a land area of 52.406 square miles and a water area of 0.135 square miles. Located at 42.55° N. Lat; 74.87° W. Long. Elevation is 1,230 feet.

Population: 1,913; Growth (since 2000): -0.4%; Density: 36.5 persons per square mile; Race: 97.7% White, 0.1% Black/African American, 0.0% Asian, 0.0% American Indian/Alaska Native, 0.0% Native Hawaiian/Other Pacific Islander, 2.0% Two or more races, 1.1% Hispanic of any race; Average household size: 2.39; Median age: 48.4; Age under 18: 16.6%; Age 65 and over: 20.8%; Males per 100 females: 97.6; Marriage status: 24.9% never married, 59.1% now married, 2.8% separated, 8.2% widowed, 7.8% divorced; Foreign born: 1.2%; Speak English only: 99.4%; With disability: 19.6%; Veterans: 6.3%; Ancestry: 22.9% English, 19.6% German, 19.4% Irish, 9.4% Italian, 6.7% Polish

Employment: 10.7% management, business, and financial, 0.4% computer, engineering, and science, 9.2% education, legal, community service, arts, and media, 6.7% healthcare practitioners, 23.7% service, 23.5% sales and office, 9.7% natural resources, construction, and maintenance, 16.1% production, transportation, and material moving

Income: Per capita: $24,272; Median household: $48,700; Average household: $57,697; Households with income of $100,000 or more: 13.3%; Poverty rate: 17.8%

Educational Attainment: High school diploma or higher: 90.4%; Bachelor's degree or higher: 20.4%; Graduate/professional degree or higher: 8.4%

Housing: Homeownership rate: 75.5%; Median home value: $117,700; Median year structure built: 1963; Homeowner vacancy rate: 0.0%; Median selected monthly owner costs: $1,188 with a mortgage, $467 without a mortgage; Median gross rent: $683 per month; Rental vacancy rate: 0.0%

Health Insurance: 93.2% have insurance; 64.0% have private insurance; 48.2% have public insurance; 6.8% do not have insurance; 3.3% of children under 18 do not have insurance

Transportation: Commute: 94.3% car, 0.0% public transportation, 1.1% walk, 3.6% work from home; Mean travel time to work: 25.4 minutes

---

MIDDLEFIELD (town). Covers a land area of 63.334 square miles and a water area of 0.371 square miles. Located at 42.70° N. Lat; 74.86° W. Long. Elevation is 1,250 feet.

Population: 1,882; Growth (since 2000): -16.3%; Density: 29.7 persons per square mile; Race: 96.0% White, 1.6% Black/African American, 1.5% Asian, 0.3% American Indian/Alaska Native, 0.0% Native Hawaiian/Other Pacific Islander, 0.5% Two or more races, 2.1% Hispanic of any race; Average household size: 2.13; Median age: 53.9; Age under 18: 13.1%; Age 65 and over: 26.6%; Males per 100 females: 100.4; Marriage status: 28.3% never married, 55.6% now married, 2.0% separated, 7.5% widowed, 8.5% divorced; Foreign born: 2.8%; Speak English only: 95.2%; With disability: 10.4%; Veterans: 12.5%; Ancestry: 27.2% German, 16.7% English, 13.5% Irish, 11.3% Italian, 6.4% French

Employment: 15.9% management, business, and financial, 2.2% computer, engineering, and science, 10.5% education, legal, community service, arts, and media, 13.7% healthcare practitioners, 18.0% service, 18.2% sales and office, 15.6% natural resources, construction, and maintenance, 5.8% production, transportation, and material moving

Income: Per capita: $37,152; Median household: $63,810; Average household: $82,819; Households with income of $100,000 or more: 25.3%; Poverty rate: 6.7%

Educational Attainment: High school diploma or higher: 91.7%; Bachelor's degree or higher: 40.9%; Graduate/professional degree or higher: 29.0%

Housing: Homeownership rate: 81.7%; Median home value: $249,700; Median year structure built: 1971; Homeowner vacancy rate: 0.0%; Median

selected monthly owner costs: $1,602 with a mortgage, $516 without a mortgage; Median gross rent: $883 per month; Rental vacancy rate: 0.0%
Health Insurance: 91.7% have insurance; 78.6% have private insurance; 38.7% have public insurance; 8.3% do not have insurance; 14.6% of children under 18 do not have insurance
Transportation: Commute: 82.2% car, 0.6% public transportation, 8.4% walk, 7.4% work from home; Mean travel time to work: 19.9 minutes

MILFORD (town).
Covers a land area of 46.117 square miles and a water area of 1.030 square miles. Located at 42.55° N. Lat; 74.98° W. Long. Elevation is 1,207 feet.
Population: 2,937; Growth (since 2000): 0.0%; Density: 63.7 persons per square mile; Race: 97.5% White, 1.0% Black/African American, 0.4% Asian, 0.0% American Indian/Alaska Native, 0.0% Native Hawaiian/Other Pacific Islander, 0.8% Two or more races, 0.5% Hispanic of any race; Average household size: 2.30; Median age: 45.6; Age under 18: 17.2%; Age 65 and over: 23.3%; Males per 100 females: 99.9; Marriage status: 30.0% never married, 54.9% now married, 2.9% separated, 2.5% widowed, 12.6% divorced; Foreign born: 1.3%; Speak English only: 97.2%; With disability: 14.3%; Veterans: 11.6%; Ancestry: 25.6% German, 17.4% Irish, 15.7% English, 15.0% Italian, 7.9% American
Employment: 17.2% management, business, and financial, 1.9% computer, engineering, and science, 8.4% education, legal, community service, arts, and media, 6.0% healthcare practitioners, 19.7% service, 25.1% sales and office, 7.4% natural resources, construction, and maintenance, 14.4% production, transportation, and material moving
Income: Per capita: $29,027; Median household: $55,383; Average household: $67,230; Households with income of $100,000 or more: 17.9%; Poverty rate: 14.0%
Educational Attainment: High school diploma or higher: 90.5%; Bachelor's degree or higher: 24.3%; Graduate/professional degree or higher: 9.3%

School District(s)
Milford Central SD (PK-12)
    Enrollment: 399 . . . . (607) 286-3341
Housing: Homeownership rate: 71.8%; Median home value: $140,600; Median year structure built: 1958; Homeowner vacancy rate: 2.7%; Median selected monthly owner costs: $1,365 with a mortgage, $494 without a mortgage; Median gross rent: $928 per month; Rental vacancy rate: 0.0%
Health Insurance: 95.8% have insurance; 67.5% have private insurance; 47.5% have public insurance; 4.2% do not have insurance; 3.2% of children under 18 do not have insurance
Transportation: Commute: 90.9% car, 2.6% public transportation, 1.5% walk, 3.3% work from home; Mean travel time to work: 27.4 minutes

MILFORD (village).
Covers a land area of 0.424 square miles and a water area of 0 square miles. Located at 42.59° N. Lat; 74.95° W. Long. Elevation is 1,207 feet.
Population: 384; Growth (since 2000): -24.9%; Density: 905.1 persons per square mile; Race: 88.0% White, 6.0% Black/African American, 3.4% Asian, 0.0% American Indian/Alaska Native, 0.0% Native Hawaiian/Other Pacific Islander, 2.3% Two or more races, 2.6% Hispanic of any race; Average household size: 2.01; Median age: 49.3; Age under 18: 15.1%; Age 65 and over: 18.0%; Males per 100 females: 91.2; Marriage status: 25.7% never married, 55.6% now married, 1.2% separated, 5.6% widowed, 13.0% divorced; Foreign born: 3.9%; Speak English only: 93.3%; With disability: 13.5%; Veterans: 11.0%; Ancestry: 18.8% German, 11.5% Italian, 11.2% Irish, 10.9% English, 5.2% American
Employment: 12.4% management, business, and financial, 1.9% computer, engineering, and science, 10.0% education, legal, community service, arts, and media, 13.9% healthcare practitioners, 21.1% service, 18.2% sales and office, 10.0% natural resources, construction, and maintenance, 12.4% production, transportation, and material moving
Income: Per capita: $30,576; Median household: $43,125; Average household: $61,667; Households with income of $100,000 or more: 17.8%; Poverty rate: 10.4%
Educational Attainment: High school diploma or higher: 87.5%; Bachelor's degree or higher: 26.6%; Graduate/professional degree or higher: 15.6%

School District(s)
Milford Central SD (PK-12)
    Enrollment: 399 . . . . (607) 286-3341
Housing: Homeownership rate: 56.0%; Median home value: $104,200; Median year structure built: Before 1940; Homeowner vacancy rate: 3.5%; Median selected monthly owner costs: $1,265 with a mortgage, $458

without a mortgage; Median gross rent: $625 per month; Rental vacancy rate: 0.0%
Health Insurance: 97.4% have insurance; 72.4% have private insurance; 40.4% have public insurance; 2.6% do not have insurance; 5.2% of children under 18 do not have insurance
Transportation: Commute: 93.2% car, 1.0% public transportation, 1.9% walk, 3.9% work from home; Mean travel time to work: 23.3 minutes

MORRIS (town).
Covers a land area of 39.067 square miles and a water area of 0.126 square miles. Located at 42.54° N. Lat; 75.26° W. Long. Elevation is 1,145 feet.
Population: 1,824; Growth (since 2000): -2.3%; Density: 46.7 persons per square mile; Race: 96.3% White, 0.0% Black/African American, 0.7% Asian, 0.0% American Indian/Alaska Native, 0.0% Native Hawaiian/Other Pacific Islander, 2.6% Two or more races, 1.3% Hispanic of any race; Average household size: 2.68; Median age: 42.8; Age under 18: 19.5%; Age 65 and over: 19.2%; Males per 100 females: 97.9; Marriage status: 26.7% never married, 60.8% now married, 1.9% separated, 5.7% widowed, 6.9% divorced; Foreign born: 3.2%; Speak English only: 97.3%; With disability: 14.1%; Veterans: 11.2%; Ancestry: 21.3% German, 18.6% Irish, 12.5% English, 11.7% Italian, 8.6% American
Employment: 11.4% management, business, and financial, 7.7% computer, engineering, and science, 12.3% education, legal, community service, arts, and media, 7.2% healthcare practitioners, 16.8% service, 21.5% sales and office, 12.8% natural resources, construction, and maintenance, 10.4% production, transportation, and material moving
Income: Per capita: $26,670; Median household: $50,859; Average household: $69,596; Households with income of $100,000 or more: 20.0%; Poverty rate: 17.4%
Educational Attainment: High school diploma or higher: 92.2%; Bachelor's degree or higher: 26.0%; Graduate/professional degree or higher: 7.9%

School District(s)
Morris Central SD (PK-12)
    Enrollment: 373 . . . . (607) 263-6102
Housing: Homeownership rate: 76.9%; Median home value: $127,900; Median year structure built: Before 1940; Homeowner vacancy rate: 4.0%; Median selected monthly owner costs: $1,186 with a mortgage, $456 without a mortgage; Median gross rent: $679 per month; Rental vacancy rate: 3.1%
Health Insurance: 98.2% have insurance; 70.6% have private insurance; 47.9% have public insurance; 1.8% do not have insurance; 0.0% of children under 18 do not have insurance
Transportation: Commute: 79.3% car, 2.0% public transportation, 6.2% walk, 10.5% work from home; Mean travel time to work: 25.1 minutes

MORRIS (village).
Covers a land area of 0.746 square miles and a water area of 0.008 square miles. Located at 42.55° N. Lat; 75.25° W. Long. Elevation is 1,145 feet.
Population: 489; Growth (since 2000): -17.3%; Density: 655.8 persons per square mile; Race: 97.5% White, 0.0% Black/African American, 0.0% Asian, 0.0% American Indian/Alaska Native, 0.0% Native Hawaiian/Other Pacific Islander, 1.0% Two or more races, 3.7% Hispanic of any race; Average household size: 2.35; Median age: 37.8; Age under 18: 20.0%; Age 65 and over: 26.8%; Males per 100 females: 95.6; Marriage status: 32.4% never married, 52.3% now married, 3.9% separated, 8.1% widowed, 7.1% divorced; Foreign born: 3.7%; Speak English only: 96.1%; With disability: 10.6%; Veterans: 8.2%; Ancestry: 28.4% German, 21.9% Irish, 16.8% English, 13.5% American, 11.0% Italian
Employment: 19.2% management, business, and financial, 2.7% computer, engineering, and science, 13.8% education, legal, community service, arts, and media, 14.3% healthcare practitioners, 22.8% service, 18.3% sales and office, 1.3% natural resources, construction, and maintenance, 7.6% production, transportation, and material moving
Income: Per capita: $29,291; Median household: $43,906; Average household: $68,460; Households with income of $100,000 or more: 17.1%; Poverty rate: 19.9%
Educational Attainment: High school diploma or higher: 96.4%; Bachelor's degree or higher: 33.5%; Graduate/professional degree or higher: 10.1%

School District(s)
Morris Central SD (PK-12)
    Enrollment: 373 . . . . (607) 263-6102
Housing: Homeownership rate: 59.0%; Median home value: $110,800; Median year structure built: Before 1940; Homeowner vacancy rate: 5.5%;

Median selected monthly owner costs: $1,113 with a mortgage, $488 without a mortgage; Median gross rent: $643 per month; Rental vacancy rate: 5.6%
Health Insurance: 97.8% have insurance; 73.8% have private insurance; 52.1% have public insurance; 2.2% do not have insurance; 0.0% of children under 18 do not have insurance
Transportation: Commute: 85.3% car, 0.0% public transportation, 13.8% walk, 0.0% work from home; Mean travel time to work: 22.4 minutes

MOUNT VISION (unincorporated postal area)
ZCTA: 13810
Covers a land area of 40.028 square miles and a water area of 0.183 square miles. Located at 42.61° N. Lat; 75.11° W. Long. Elevation is 1,171 feet.
Population: 1,060; Growth (since 2000): -18.2%; Density: 26.5 persons per square mile; Race: 96.5% White, 0.7% Black/African American, 1.9% Asian, 0.0% American Indian/Alaska Native, 0.1% Native Hawaiian/Other Pacific Islander, 0.6% Two or more races, 1.1% Hispanic of any race; Average household size: 2.13; Median age: 50.6; Age under 18: 11.0%; Age 65 and over: 19.1%; Males per 100 females: 93.4; Marriage status: 28.2% never married, 49.2% now married, 0.3% separated, 7.1% widowed, 15.5% divorced; Foreign born: 6.1%; Speak English only: 98.4%; With disability: 6.3%; Veterans: 9.4%; Ancestry: 25.6% Irish, 20.2% German, 17.2% English, 12.9% Italian, 7.6% Dutch
Employment: 18.0% management, business, and financial, 1.8% computer, engineering, and science, 9.8% education, legal, community service, arts, and media, 6.6% healthcare practitioners, 18.0% service, 24.6% sales and office, 14.4% natural resources, construction, and maintenance, 6.8% production, transportation, and material moving
Income: Per capita: $29,910; Median household: $44,489; Average household: $63,020; Households with income of $100,000 or more: 14.6%; Poverty rate: 13.0%
Educational Attainment: High school diploma or higher: 94.8%; Bachelor's degree or higher: 25.8%; Graduate/professional degree or higher: 12.7%
Housing: Homeownership rate: 82.9%; Median home value: $123,800; Median year structure built: 1955; Homeowner vacancy rate: 3.5%; Median selected monthly owner costs: $1,147 with a mortgage, $504 without a mortgage; Median gross rent: $678 per month; Rental vacancy rate: 4.3%
Health Insurance: 94.4% have insurance; 74.7% have private insurance; 36.6% have public insurance; 5.6% do not have insurance; 0.0% of children under 18 do not have insurance
Transportation: Commute: 96.0% car, 0.0% public transportation, 2.0% walk, 2.0% work from home; Mean travel time to work: 33.9 minutes

NEW LISBON (town). Covers a land area of 44.355 square miles and a water area of 0.301 square miles. Located at 42.62° N. Lat; 75.13° W. Long. Elevation is 1,247 feet.
Population: 1,068; Growth (since 2000): -4.3%; Density: 24.1 persons per square mile; Race: 97.7% White, 0.0% Black/African American, 0.8% Asian, 0.0% American Indian/Alaska Native, 0.1% Native Hawaiian/Other Pacific Islander, 0.9% Two or more races, 1.7% Hispanic of any race; Average household size: 2.36; Median age: 47.6; Age under 18: 16.4%; Age 65 and over: 14.9%; Males per 100 females: 90.8; Marriage status: 26.7% never married, 57.8% now married, 1.0% separated, 5.7% widowed, 9.8% divorced; Foreign born: 2.7%; Speak English only: 95.6%; With disability: 12.0%; Veterans: 8.5%; Ancestry: 18.3% English, 17.2% Irish, 14.8% German, 11.6% Italian, 7.6% American
Employment: 14.4% management, business, and financial, 2.3% computer, engineering, and science, 9.4% education, legal, community service, arts, and media, 5.7% healthcare practitioners, 16.6% service, 23.8% sales and office, 12.2% natural resources, construction, and maintenance, 15.6% production, transportation, and material moving
Income: Per capita: $32,305; Median household: $58,625; Average household: $75,306; Households with income of $100,000 or more: 20.3%; Poverty rate: 7.3%
Educational Attainment: High school diploma or higher: 94.1%; Bachelor's degree or higher: 22.0%; Graduate/professional degree or higher: 10.2%
Housing: Homeownership rate: 87.2%; Median home value: $122,800; Median year structure built: 1976; Homeowner vacancy rate: 4.4%; Median selected monthly owner costs: $1,166 with a mortgage, $414 without a mortgage; Median gross rent: $850 per month; Rental vacancy rate: 0.0%

Health Insurance: 96.2% have insurance; 75.9% have private insurance; 33.9% have public insurance; 3.8% do not have insurance; 0.0% of children under 18 do not have insurance
Transportation: Commute: 93.4% car, 0.0% public transportation, 2.8% walk, 3.8% work from home; Mean travel time to work: 28.8 minutes

ONEONTA (city). Covers a land area of 4.361 square miles and a water area of 0.004 square miles. Located at 42.45° N. Lat; 75.07° W. Long. Elevation is 1,112 feet.
History: Oneonta grew after the coming of the railroad in 1865; however, no vestiges of importance as a railroad center exist today. Brotherhood of Railroad Brakemen founded here in 1883), which was renamed Brotherhood of Railroad Trainmen in 1889. Seat of the State University of N.Y. College at Oneonta and Hartwick College. National Soccer Hall of Fame. Settled c.1780, Incorporated as a city 1909.
Population: 13,932; Growth (since 2000): 4.8%; Density: 3,194.4 persons per square mile; Race: 87.2% White, 4.8% Black/African American, 2.8% Asian, 0.3% American Indian/Alaska Native, 0.0% Native Hawaiian/Other Pacific Islander, 3.2% Two or more races, 8.0% Hispanic of any race; Average household size: 2.21; Median age: 21.9; Age under 18: 11.1%; Age 65 and over: 11.6%; Males per 100 females: 83.9; Marriage status: 63.9% never married, 26.0% now married, 1.3% separated, 4.3% widowed, 5.9% divorced; Foreign born: 5.6%; Speak English only: 89.6%; With disability: 11.3%; Veterans: 5.3%; Ancestry: 22.5% Irish, 20.4% Italian, 17.6% German, 9.6% English, 5.4% Polish
Employment: 11.3% management, business, and financial, 2.5% computer, engineering, and science, 19.3% education, legal, community service, arts, and media, 6.0% healthcare practitioners, 27.2% service, 25.0% sales and office, 4.3% natural resources, construction, and maintenance, 4.5% production, transportation, and material moving
Income: Per capita: $19,408; Median household: $41,377; Average household: $58,892; Households with income of $100,000 or more: 16.3%; Poverty rate: 25.6%
Educational Attainment: High school diploma or higher: 92.6%; Bachelor's degree or higher: 42.6%; Graduate/professional degree or higher: 21.6%

School District(s)
Oneonta City SD (KG-12)
    Enrollment: 1,724 . . . . (607) 433-8200
Four-year College(s)
Hartwick College (Private, Not-for-profit)
    Enrollment: 1,201 . . . . (607) 431-4000
    Tuition: In-state $44,134; Out-of-state $44,134
SUNY Oneonta (Public)
    Enrollment: 6,358 . . . . (607) 436-3500
    Tuition: In-state $8,166; Out-of-state $17,816
Vocational/Technical School(s)
Otsego Area BOCES-Practical Nursing Program (Public)
    Enrollment: 37. . . . . (607) 431-2562
    Tuition: $10,200
Housing: Homeownership rate: 46.0%; Median home value: $147,000; Median year structure built: Before 1940; Homeowner vacancy rate: 1.4%; Median selected monthly owner costs: $1,366 with a mortgage, $466 without a mortgage; Median gross rent: $859 per month; Rental vacancy rate: 9.2%
Health Insurance: 93.8% have insurance; 75.0% have private insurance; 28.5% have public insurance; 6.2% do not have insurance; 3.9% of children under 18 do not have insurance
Hospitals: Aurelia Osborn Fox Memorial Hospital (128 beds)
Safety: Violent crime rate: 19.3 per 10,000 population; Property crime rate: 167.5 per 10,000 population
Newspapers: Daily Star (daily circulation 15,900)
Transportation: Commute: 63.2% car, 5.6% public transportation, 24.2% walk, 3.8% work from home; Mean travel time to work: 14.9 minutes
Airports: Oneonta Municipal (general aviation)
Additional Information Contacts
City of Oneonta . . . . (607) 432-6450
    http://www.oneonta.ny.us

ONEONTA (town). Covers a land area of 32.911 square miles and a water area of 0.252 square miles. Located at 42.43° N. Lat; 75.10° W. Long. Elevation is 1,112 feet.
Population: 5,088; Growth (since 2000): 1.9%; Density: 154.6 persons per square mile; Race: 88.2% White, 5.1% Black/African American, 1.3% Asian, 0.2% American Indian/Alaska Native, 0.0% Native Hawaiian/Other

Pacific Islander, 2.2% Two or more races, 6.2% Hispanic of any race; Average household size: 2.35; Median age: 43.8; Age under 18: 17.4%; Age 65 and over: 22.2%; Males per 100 females: 97.1; Marriage status: 30.4% never married, 48.6% now married, 1.5% separated, 7.9% widowed, 13.1% divorced; Foreign born: 4.3%; Speak English only: 92.1%; With disability: 14.9%; Veterans: 9.3%; Ancestry: 24.5% German, 12.9% Italian, 11.6% Irish, 9.8% English, 5.5% American
Employment: 12.6% management, business, and financial, 4.5% computer, engineering, and science, 18.2% education, legal, community service, arts, and media, 8.8% healthcare practitioners, 17.6% service, 22.0% sales and office, 9.5% natural resources, construction, and maintenance, 6.8% production, transportation, and material moving
Income: Per capita: $29,465; Median household: $55,972; Average household: $72,949; Households with income of $100,000 or more: 25.9%; Poverty rate: 22.2%
Educational Attainment: High school diploma or higher: 91.1%; Bachelor's degree or higher: 37.8%; Graduate/professional degree or higher: 19.3%

School District(s)
Oneonta City SD (KG-12)
    Enrollment: 1,724 . . . . (607) 433-8200
Four-year College(s)
Hartwick College (Private, Not-for-profit)
    Enrollment: 1,201 . . . . (607) 431-4000
    Tuition: In-state $44,134; Out-of-state $44,134
SUNY Oneonta (Public)
    Enrollment: 6,358 . . . . (607) 436-3500
    Tuition: In-state $8,166; Out-of-state $17,816
Vocational/Technical School(s)
Otsego Area BOCES-Practical Nursing Program (Public)
    Enrollment: 37 . . . . (607) 431-2562
    Tuition: $10,200
Housing: Homeownership rate: 86.6%; Median home value: $153,700; Median year structure built: 1967; Homeowner vacancy rate: 2.6%; Median selected monthly owner costs: $1,322 with a mortgage, $449 without a mortgage; Median gross rent: $876 per month; Rental vacancy rate: 12.7%
Health Insurance: 89.9% have insurance; 67.4% have private insurance; 38.9% have public insurance; 10.1% do not have insurance; 3.0% of children under 18 do not have insurance
Hospitals: Aurelia Osborn Fox Memorial Hospital (128 beds)
Newspapers: Daily Star (daily circulation 15,900)
Transportation: Commute: 85.6% car, 2.2% public transportation, 1.9% walk, 9.8% work from home; Mean travel time to work: 21.4 minutes
Airports: Oneonta Municipal (general aviation)
Additional Information Contacts
Town of Oneonta . . . . (607) 432-2900
    http://www.townofoneonta.org

OTEGO (town). Covers a land area of 45.633 square miles and a water area of 0.076 square miles. Located at 42.46° N. Lat; 75.19° W. Long. Elevation is 1,070 feet.
Population: 2,961; Growth (since 2000): -7.0%; Density: 64.9 persons per square mile; Race: 95.9% White, 0.3% Black/African American, 0.6% Asian, 0.1% American Indian/Alaska Native, 0.0% Native Hawaiian/Other Pacific Islander, 3.0% Two or more races, 0.1% Hispanic of any race; Average household size: 2.36; Median age: 49.6; Age under 18: 15.1%; Age 65 and over: 23.1%; Males per 100 females: 94.1; Marriage status: 27.8% never married, 52.9% now married, 0.1% separated, 9.8% widowed, 9.5% divorced; Foreign born: 3.6%; Speak English only: 97.8%; With disability: 11.3%; Veterans: 9.0%; Ancestry: 21.2% German, 18.9% Irish, 18.5% English, 13.8% Italian, 6.3% French
Employment: 14.9% management, business, and financial, 1.9% computer, engineering, and science, 14.0% education, legal, community service, arts, and media, 1.9% healthcare practitioners, 20.3% service, 21.6% sales and office, 6.4% natural resources, construction, and maintenance, 19.0% production, transportation, and material moving
Income: Per capita: $26,577; Median household: $50,000; Average household: $62,140; Households with income of $100,000 or more: 20.2%; Poverty rate: 9.6%
Educational Attainment: High school diploma or higher: 90.2%; Bachelor's degree or higher: 26.6%; Graduate/professional degree or higher: 13.0%

School District(s)
Otego-Unadilla Central SD (KG-12)
    Enrollment: 893 . . . . (607) 988-5038

Housing: Homeownership rate: 81.8%; Median home value: $132,400; Median year structure built: 1978; Homeowner vacancy rate: 1.0%; Median selected monthly owner costs: $1,287 with a mortgage, $571 without a mortgage; Median gross rent: $742 per month; Rental vacancy rate: 26.9%
Health Insurance: 95.3% have insurance; 72.8% have private insurance; 37.1% have public insurance; 4.7% do not have insurance; 0.0% of children under 18 do not have insurance
Transportation: Commute: 92.6% car, 0.0% public transportation, 2.7% walk, 1.3% work from home; Mean travel time to work: 23.2 minutes

OTEGO (village). Covers a land area of 1.159 square miles and a water area of 0 square miles. Located at 42.39° N. Lat; 75.18° W. Long. Elevation is 1,070 feet.
Population: 1,146; Growth (since 2000): 8.9%; Density: 988.4 persons per square mile; Race: 91.4% White, 0.2% Black/African American, 1.6% Asian, 0.0% American Indian/Alaska Native, 0.0% Native Hawaiian/Other Pacific Islander, 6.9% Two or more races, 0.2% Hispanic of any race; Average household size: 2.36; Median age: 42.6; Age under 18: 18.8%; Age 65 and over: 16.9%; Males per 100 females: 90.2; Marriage status: 30.4% never married, 57.0% now married, 0.3% separated, 4.8% widowed, 7.8% divorced; Foreign born: 5.8%; Speak English only: 98.4%; With disability: 13.1%; Veterans: 8.9%; Ancestry: 21.1% Irish, 18.7% German, 15.2% English, 10.2% French, 8.2% Dutch
Employment: 11.7% management, business, and financial, 2.4% computer, engineering, and science, 17.6% education, legal, community service, arts, and media, 4.9% healthcare practitioners, 24.4% service, 23.9% sales and office, 5.2% natural resources, construction, and maintenance, 10.0% production, transportation, and material moving
Income: Per capita: $27,896; Median household: $57,788; Average household: $65,606; Households with income of $100,000 or more: 20.0%; Poverty rate: 9.8%
Educational Attainment: High school diploma or higher: 96.5%; Bachelor's degree or higher: 37.2%; Graduate/professional degree or higher: 17.6%

School District(s)
Otego-Unadilla Central SD (KG-12)
    Enrollment: 893 . . . . (607) 988-5038
Housing: Homeownership rate: 72.4%; Median home value: $138,700; Median year structure built: 1954; Homeowner vacancy rate: 2.8%; Median selected monthly owner costs: $1,282 with a mortgage, $495 without a mortgage; Median gross rent: $715 per month; Rental vacancy rate: 20.0%
Health Insurance: 94.7% have insurance; 75.6% have private insurance; 33.9% have public insurance; 5.3% do not have insurance; 0.0% of children under 18 do not have insurance
Transportation: Commute: 84.6% car, 0.0% public transportation, 4.1% walk, 2.9% work from home; Mean travel time to work: 20.2 minutes

OTSEGO (town). Covers a land area of 53.890 square miles and a water area of 5.162 square miles. Located at 42.76° N. Lat; 74.96° W. Long.
Population: 3,794; Growth (since 2000): -2.8%; Density: 70.4 persons per square mile; Race: 91.5% White, 1.6% Black/African American, 3.9% Asian, 0.3% American Indian/Alaska Native, 0.0% Native Hawaiian/Other Pacific Islander, 2.6% Two or more races, 2.1% Hispanic of any race; Average household size: 2.09; Median age: 51.4; Age under 18: 14.0%; Age 65 and over: 24.6%; Males per 100 females: 85.6; Marriage status: 24.5% never married, 54.4% now married, 2.8% separated, 10.1% widowed, 11.0% divorced; Foreign born: 6.5%; Speak English only: 91.0%; With disability: 7.7%; Veterans: 7.8%; Ancestry: 19.8% English, 19.0% Irish, 16.6% German, 10.0% Italian, 5.1% Scottish
Employment: 16.3% management, business, and financial, 1.8% computer, engineering, and science, 18.7% education, legal, community service, arts, and media, 19.8% healthcare practitioners, 17.2% service, 16.9% sales and office, 5.2% natural resources, construction, and maintenance, 4.0% production, transportation, and material moving
Income: Per capita: $44,073; Median household: $69,583; Average household: $95,758; Households with income of $100,000 or more: 28.4%; Poverty rate: 9.1%
Educational Attainment: High school diploma or higher: 96.6%; Bachelor's degree or higher: 50.5%; Graduate/professional degree or higher: 28.1%
Housing: Homeownership rate: 71.9%; Median home value: $297,600; Median year structure built: Before 1940; Homeowner vacancy rate: 1.5%; Median selected monthly owner costs: $1,716 with a mortgage, $715

without a mortgage; Median gross rent: $789 per month; Rental vacancy rate: 12.0%

Health Insurance: 96.2% have insurance; 83.9% have private insurance; 29.6% have public insurance; 3.8% do not have insurance; 0.0% of children under 18 do not have insurance

Transportation: Commute: 69.5% car, 2.1% public transportation, 18.8% walk, 8.3% work from home; Mean travel time to work: 15.9 minutes

---

PITTSFIELD (town). Covers a land area of 37.986 square miles and a water area of 0.116 square miles. Located at 42.61° N. Lat; 75.27° W. Long. Elevation is 1,155 feet.

Population: 1,303; Growth (since 2000): 0.6%; Density: 34.3 persons per square mile; Race: 96.4% White, 0.5% Black/African American, 0.5% Asian, 0.2% American Indian/Alaska Native, 0.0% Native Hawaiian/Other Pacific Islander, 2.4% Two or more races, 1.9% Hispanic of any race; Average household size: 2.71; Median age: 44.3; Age under 18: 21.6%; Age 65 and over: 16.4%; Males per 100 females: 103.0; Marriage status: 26.8% never married, 59.7% now married, 3.3% separated, 7.1% widowed, 6.4% divorced; Foreign born: 2.9%; Speak English only: 94.4%; With disability: 14.2%; Veterans: 5.6%; Ancestry: 19.6% German, 16.6% Italian, 14.5% Irish, 12.5% English, 6.1% French

Employment: 16.6% management, business, and financial, 2.5% computer, engineering, and science, 5.0% education, legal, community service, arts, and media, 8.7% healthcare practitioners, 14.7% service, 24.7% sales and office, 9.2% natural resources, construction, and maintenance, 18.6% production, transportation, and material moving

Income: Per capita: $26,038; Median household: $47,500; Average household: $69,613; Households with income of $100,000 or more: 26.1%; Poverty rate: 13.4%

Educational Attainment: High school diploma or higher: 85.8%; Bachelor's degree or higher: 17.0%; Graduate/professional degree or higher: 4.2%

Housing: Homeownership rate: 90.8%; Median home value: $102,500; Median year structure built: 1974; Homeowner vacancy rate: 0.0%; Median selected monthly owner costs: $1,346 with a mortgage, $370 without a mortgage; Median gross rent: $817 per month; Rental vacancy rate: 8.3%

Health Insurance: 90.3% have insurance; 69.0% have private insurance; 33.1% have public insurance; 9.7% do not have insurance; 10.9% of children under 18 do not have insurance

Transportation: Commute: 85.2% car, 4.3% public transportation, 5.1% walk, 3.4% work from home; Mean travel time to work: 30.3 minutes

---

PLAINFIELD (town). Covers a land area of 29.500 square miles and a water area of 0 square miles. Located at 42.83° N. Lat; 75.19° W. Long.

Population: 903; Growth (since 2000): -8.4%; Density: 30.6 persons per square mile; Race: 96.6% White, 0.2% Black/African American, 1.7% Asian, 0.0% American Indian/Alaska Native, 0.0% Native Hawaiian/Other Pacific Islander, 1.6% Two or more races, 0.8% Hispanic of any race; Average household size: 2.43; Median age: 45.8; Age under 18: 20.9%; Age 65 and over: 22.6%; Males per 100 females: 102.4; Marriage status: 21.4% never married, 60.8% now married, 0.9% separated, 6.6% widowed, 11.1% divorced; Foreign born: 2.0%; Speak English only: 94.8%; With disability: 17.6%; Veterans: 8.4%; Ancestry: 17.8% German, 13.2% English, 9.7% American, 9.7% Irish, 8.0% Italian

Employment: 15.4% management, business, and financial, 5.7% computer, engineering, and science, 8.5% education, legal, community service, arts, and media, 3.3% healthcare practitioners, 8.7% service, 18.5% sales and office, 23.9% natural resources, construction, and maintenance, 15.9% production, transportation, and material moving

Income: Per capita: $26,684; Median household: $52,250; Average household: $64,264; Households with income of $100,000 or more: 19.6%; Poverty rate: 12.2%

Educational Attainment: High school diploma or higher: 88.1%; Bachelor's degree or higher: 15.9%; Graduate/professional degree or higher: 5.2%

Housing: Homeownership rate: 83.1%; Median home value: $90,500; Median year structure built: 1971; Homeowner vacancy rate: 0.0%; Median selected monthly owner costs: $1,144 with a mortgage, $378 without a mortgage; Median gross rent: $631 per month; Rental vacancy rate: 0.0%

Health Insurance: 93.5% have insurance; 67.2% have private insurance; 43.7% have public insurance; 6.5% do not have insurance; 16.9% of children under 18 do not have insurance

Transportation: Commute: 90.1% car, 0.5% public transportation, 2.3% walk, 6.3% work from home; Mean travel time to work: 30.0 minutes

---

PORTLANDVILLE (unincorporated postal area)
ZCTA: 13834

Covers a land area of 0.348 square miles and a water area of 0.041 square miles. Located at 42.53° N. Lat; 74.97° W. Long. Elevation is 1,152 feet.

Population: 238; Growth (since 2000): 40.0%; Density: 684.3 persons per square mile; Race: 97.1% White, 2.9% Black/African American, 0.0% Asian, 0.0% American Indian/Alaska Native, 0.0% Native Hawaiian/Other Pacific Islander, 0.0% Two or more races, 0.0% Hispanic of any race; Average household size: 3.72; Median age: 27.1; Age under 18: 31.5%; Age 65 and over: 6.7%; Males per 100 females: 114.5; Marriage status: 63.9% never married, 31.9% now married, 0.0% separated, 0.0% widowed, 4.2% divorced; Foreign born: 0.0%; Speak English only: 100.0%; With disability: 3.4%; Veterans: 9.8%; Ancestry: 42.4% Italian, 39.5% Swedish, 35.3% German, 28.6% European, 23.9% Greek

Employment: 39.2% management, business, and financial, 0.0% computer, engineering, and science, 7.2% education, legal, community service, arts, and media, 11.2% healthcare practitioners, 0.0% service, 21.6% sales and office, 20.8% natural resources, construction, and maintenance, 0.0% production, transportation, and material moving

Income: Per capita: $16,393; Median household: $71,037; Average household: $60,895; Households with income of $100,000 or more: n/a; Poverty rate: 2.9%

Educational Attainment: High school diploma or higher: 100.0%; Bachelor's degree or higher: 28.9%; Graduate/professional degree or higher: 6.6%

Housing: Homeownership rate: 25.0%; Median home value: n/a; Median year structure built: 1941; Homeowner vacancy rate: 0.0%; Median selected monthly owner costs: $0 with a mortgage, $0 without a mortgage; Median gross rent: $1,556 per month; Rental vacancy rate: 0.0%

Health Insurance: 100.0% have insurance; 97.1% have private insurance; 9.7% have public insurance; 0.0% do not have insurance; 0.0% of children under 18 do not have insurance

Transportation: Commute: 88.0% car, 5.6% public transportation, 6.4% walk, 0.0% work from home; Mean travel time to work: 17.9 minutes

---

RICHFIELD (town). Covers a land area of 30.858 square miles and a water area of 1.598 square miles. Located at 42.85° N. Lat; 75.05° W. Long. Elevation is 1,476 feet.

History: Health resort until mid-20th century; sulphur springs. Incorporated 1934.

Population: 2,147; Growth (since 2000): -11.4%; Density: 69.6 persons per square mile; Race: 95.6% White, 1.1% Black/African American, 1.4% Asian, 0.4% American Indian/Alaska Native, 0.0% Native Hawaiian/Other Pacific Islander, 1.4% Two or more races, 1.2% Hispanic of any race; Average household size: 2.22; Median age: 45.0; Age under 18: 16.3%; Age 65 and over: 18.2%; Males per 100 females: 95.6; Marriage status: 27.2% never married, 54.3% now married, 3.2% separated, 6.1% widowed, 12.4% divorced; Foreign born: 2.2%; Speak English only: 94.7%; With disability: 14.8%; Veterans: 9.8%; Ancestry: 26.4% Irish, 15.3% German, 12.7% Dutch, 11.4% English, 7.2% French

Employment: 10.1% management, business, and financial, 1.5% computer, engineering, and science, 7.9% education, legal, community service, arts, and media, 10.1% healthcare practitioners, 15.5% service, 25.8% sales and office, 15.4% natural resources, construction, and maintenance, 13.7% production, transportation, and material moving

Income: Per capita: $27,783; Median household: $49,429; Average household: $61,391; Households with income of $100,000 or more: 12.8%; Poverty rate: 10.9%

Educational Attainment: High school diploma or higher: 91.2%; Bachelor's degree or higher: 17.9%; Graduate/professional degree or higher: 8.8%

Housing: Homeownership rate: 69.1%; Median home value: $118,000; Median year structure built: Before 1940; Homeowner vacancy rate: 3.2%; Median selected monthly owner costs: $1,158 with a mortgage, $446 without a mortgage; Median gross rent: $685 per month; Rental vacancy rate: 3.0%

Health Insurance: 88.5% have insurance; 60.6% have private insurance; 45.3% have public insurance; 11.5% do not have insurance; 8.6% of children under 18 do not have insurance

Transportation: Commute: 87.8% car, 0.3% public transportation, 8.9% walk, 2.0% work from home; Mean travel time to work: 24.7 minutes

RICHFIELD SPRINGS (village). Covers a land area of 1.007 square miles and a water area of 0 square miles. Located at 42.85° N. Lat; 74.99° W. Long. Elevation is 1,312 feet.

Population: 1,102; Growth (since 2000): -12.2%; Density: 1,094.8 persons per square mile; Race: 95.2% White, 1.2% Black/African American, 1.8% Asian, 0.8% American Indian/Alaska Native, 0.0% Native Hawaiian/Other Pacific Islander, 0.8% Two or more races, 2.4% Hispanic of any race; Average household size: 2.05; Median age: 43.4; Age under 18: 15.3%; Age 65 and over: 13.8%; Males per 100 females: 89.5; Marriage status: 29.4% never married, 52.0% now married, 3.1% separated, 4.2% widowed, 14.4% divorced; Foreign born: 2.9%; Speak English only: 95.8%; With disability: 15.6%; Veterans: 8.1%; Ancestry: 23.8% Irish, 15.8% German, 11.3% English, 6.7% French, 6.3% Italian

Employment: 7.4% management, business, and financial, 2.0% computer, engineering, and science, 9.5% education, legal, community service, arts, and media, 3.1% healthcare practitioners, 19.9% service, 29.6% sales and office, 13.3% natural resources, construction, and maintenance, 15.3% production, transportation, and material moving

Income: Per capita: $22,343; Median household: $34,866; Average household: $45,913; Households with income of $100,000 or more: 5.7%; Poverty rate: 17.7%

Educational Attainment: High school diploma or higher: 87.3%; Bachelor's degree or higher: 16.6%; Graduate/professional degree or higher: 8.4%

School District(s)
Richfield Springs Central SD (PK-12)
    Enrollment: 454 . . . . (315) 858-0610
Housing: Homeownership rate: 54.3%; Median home value: $98,500; Median year structure built: Before 1940; Homeowner vacancy rate: 2.9%; Median selected monthly owner costs: $1,220 with a mortgage, $463 without a mortgage; Median gross rent: $663 per month; Rental vacancy rate: 3.6%

Health Insurance: 90.2% have insurance; 57.1% have private insurance; 47.9% have public insurance; 9.8% do not have insurance; 2.0% of children under 18 do not have insurance

Transportation: Commute: 83.8% car, 0.6% public transportation, 13.4% walk, 2.2% work from home; Mean travel time to work: 25.0 minutes

ROSEBOOM (town). Covers a land area of 33.407 square miles and a water area of 0.104 square miles. Located at 42.73° N. Lat; 74.71° W. Long. Elevation is 1,289 feet.

Population: 664; Growth (since 2000): -2.9%; Density: 19.9 persons per square mile; Race: 97.4% White, 0.8% Black/African American, 0.3% Asian, 0.0% American Indian/Alaska Native, 0.0% Native Hawaiian/Other Pacific Islander, 1.5% Two or more races, 0.0% Hispanic of any race; Average household size: 2.30; Median age: 47.6; Age under 18: 21.2%; Age 65 and over: 20.6%; Males per 100 females: 102.6; Marriage status: 28.7% never married, 55.6% now married, 1.1% separated, 7.9% widowed, 7.9% divorced; Foreign born: 0.8%; Speak English only: 95.1%; With disability: 11.4%; Veterans: 6.5%; Ancestry: 16.1% German, 13.3% English, 13.3% Irish, 9.9% Italian, 6.0% Dutch

Employment: 10.0% management, business, and financial, 2.0% computer, engineering, and science, 14.0% education, legal, community service, arts, and media, 5.4% healthcare practitioners, 18.9% service, 29.8% sales and office, 10.6% natural resources, construction, and maintenance, 9.2% production, transportation, and material moving

Income: Per capita: $25,382; Median household: $46,875; Average household: $57,498; Households with income of $100,000 or more: 12.1%; Poverty rate: 13.5%

Educational Attainment: High school diploma or higher: 89.5%; Bachelor's degree or higher: 23.3%; Graduate/professional degree or higher: 10.0%

Housing: Homeownership rate: 87.5%; Median home value: $119,700; Median year structure built: 1966; Homeowner vacancy rate: 0.0%; Median selected monthly owner costs: $1,192 with a mortgage, $427 without a mortgage; Median gross rent: $900 per month; Rental vacancy rate: 0.0%

Health Insurance: 96.8% have insurance; 69.1% have private insurance; 44.7% have public insurance; 3.2% do not have insurance; 0.7% of children under 18 do not have insurance

Transportation: Commute: 93.1% car, 1.2% public transportation, 0.9% walk, 4.5% work from home; Mean travel time to work: 25.3 minutes

SCHENEVUS (CDP). Covers a land area of 1.029 square miles and a water area of 0 square miles. Located at 42.55° N. Lat; 74.83° W. Long. Elevation is 1,302 feet.

Population: 501; Growth (since 2000): n/a; Density: 487.1 persons per square mile; Race: 100.0% White, 0.0% Black/African American, 0.0% Asian, 0.0% American Indian/Alaska Native, 0.0% Native Hawaiian/Other Pacific Islander, 0.0% Two or more races, 0.0% Hispanic of any race; Average household size: 2.39; Median age: 46.7; Age under 18: 8.0%; Age 65 and over: 19.6%; Males per 100 females: 88.7; Marriage status: 34.3% never married, 50.3% now married, 0.0% separated, 6.9% widowed, 8.5% divorced; Foreign born: 0.0%; Speak English only: 98.8%; With disability: 18.2%; Veterans: 1.3%; Ancestry: 32.9% English, 26.5% Irish, 13.2% German, 9.4% French, 5.2% Italian

Employment: 4.7% management, business, and financial, 1.3% computer, engineering, and science, 10.0% education, legal, community service, arts, and media, 7.3% healthcare practitioners, 33.3% service, 19.0% sales and office, 9.7% natural resources, construction, and maintenance, 14.7% production, transportation, and material moving

Income: Per capita: $20,282; Median household: $41,600; Average household: $46,760; Households with income of $100,000 or more: 7.6%; Poverty rate: 19.0%

Educational Attainment: High school diploma or higher: 93.9%; Bachelor's degree or higher: 19.4%; Graduate/professional degree or higher: 5.8%

School District(s)
Schenevus Central SD (PK-12)
    Enrollment: 390 . . . . (607) 638-5530
Housing: Homeownership rate: 64.8%; Median home value: $102,300; Median year structure built: Before 1940; Homeowner vacancy rate: 0.0%; Median selected monthly owner costs: $1,151 with a mortgage, $497 without a mortgage; Median gross rent: $600 per month; Rental vacancy rate: 0.0%

Health Insurance: 94.4% have insurance; 71.3% have private insurance; 39.3% have public insurance; 5.6% do not have insurance; 12.0% of children under 18 do not have insurance

Transportation: Commute: 89.7% car, 0.0% public transportation, 1.3% walk, 5.7% work from home; Mean travel time to work: 26.2 minutes

SPRINGFIELD (town). Covers a land area of 42.894 square miles and a water area of 2.614 square miles. Located at 42.83° N. Lat; 74.87° W. Long. Elevation is 1,355 feet.

Population: 1,342; Growth (since 2000): -0.6%; Density: 31.3 persons per square mile; Race: 100.0% White, 0.0% Black/African American, 0.0% Asian, 0.0% American Indian/Alaska Native, 0.0% Native Hawaiian/Other Pacific Islander, 0.0% Two or more races, 0.4% Hispanic of any race; Average household size: 2.48; Median age: 45.5; Age under 18: 21.5%; Age 65 and over: 22.0%; Males per 100 females: 105.8; Marriage status: 22.3% never married, 60.5% now married, 1.5% separated, 8.0% widowed, 9.3% divorced; Foreign born: 1.0%; Speak English only: 89.2%; With disability: 15.0%; Veterans: 8.0%; Ancestry: 21.2% English, 18.3% German, 11.3% Irish, 9.0% Dutch, 8.5% American

Employment: 15.9% management, business, and financial, 0.9% computer, engineering, and science, 7.3% education, legal, community service, arts, and media, 10.4% healthcare practitioners, 15.6% service, 16.6% sales and office, 22.1% natural resources, construction, and maintenance, 11.2% production, transportation, and material moving

Income: Per capita: $24,525; Median household: $46,818; Average household: $61,154; Households with income of $100,000 or more: 17.4%; Poverty rate: 10.2%

Educational Attainment: High school diploma or higher: 88.1%; Bachelor's degree or higher: 25.0%; Graduate/professional degree or higher: 14.7%

Housing: Homeownership rate: 77.9%; Median home value: $157,500; Median year structure built: 1950; Homeowner vacancy rate: 1.9%; Median selected monthly owner costs: $1,142 with a mortgage, $353 without a mortgage; Median gross rent: $618 per month; Rental vacancy rate: 0.0%

Health Insurance: 85.8% have insurance; 61.1% have private insurance; 42.0% have public insurance; 14.2% do not have insurance; 18.7% of children under 18 do not have insurance

Transportation: Commute: 78.1% car, 0.5% public transportation, 6.9% walk, 12.1% work from home; Mean travel time to work: 22.4 minutes

SPRINGFIELD CENTER (unincorporated postal area)
ZCTA: 13468

Covers a land area of 9.726 square miles and a water area of 0.108 square miles. Located at 42.85° N. Lat; 74.85° W. Long. Elevation is 1,260 feet.

Population: 419; Growth (since 2000): -8.7%; Density: 43.1 persons per square mile; Race: 100.0% White, 0.0% Black/African American, 0.0% Asian, 0.0% American Indian/Alaska Native, 0.0% Native Hawaiian/Other Pacific Islander, 0.0% Two or more races, 1.2% Hispanic of any race; Average household size: 2.69; Median age: 35.6; Age under 18: 27.7%; Age 65 and over: 14.3%; Males per 100 females: 93.6; Marriage status: 18.7% never married, 67.1% now married, 1.0% separated, 5.8% widowed, 8.4% divorced; Foreign born: 0.0%; Speak English only: 82.8%; With disability: 11.7%; Veterans: 6.3%; Ancestry: 28.2% English, 14.3% Irish, 10.5% Dutch, 9.8% Swiss, 7.9% German

Employment: 7.2% management, business, and financial, 1.4% computer, engineering, and science, 9.6% education, legal, community service, arts, and media, 17.7% healthcare practitioners, 21.1% service, 16.7% sales and office, 14.4% natural resources, construction, and maintenance, 12.0% production, transportation, and material moving

Income: Per capita: $26,402; Median household: $58,750; Average household: $70,625; Households with income of $100,000 or more: 20.5%; Poverty rate: 10.5%

Educational Attainment: High school diploma or higher: 85.9%; Bachelor's degree or higher: 34.1%; Graduate/professional degree or higher: 24.1%

Housing: Homeownership rate: 70.5%; Median home value: $171,700; Median year structure built: 1963; Homeowner vacancy rate: 0.0%; Median selected monthly owner costs: $1,833 with a mortgage, $425 without a mortgage; Median gross rent: $584 per month; Rental vacancy rate: 0.0%

Health Insurance: 82.1% have insurance; 63.5% have private insurance; 37.0% have public insurance; 17.9% do not have insurance; 21.6% of children under 18 do not have insurance

Transportation: Commute: 84.1% car, 1.5% public transportation, 8.0% walk, 6.5% work from home; Mean travel time to work: 27.1 minutes

UNADILLA (town). Covers a land area of 46.254 square miles and a water area of 0.419 square miles. Located at 42.37° N. Lat; 75.33° W. Long. Elevation is 1,010 feet.

History: During the early years of the Revolution, Native American villages in the vicinity of Unadilla were gathering places for Tories bent on destruction of frontier patriot settlements. In 1778, an American force destroyed the villages. The place began to grow with construction of the Catskill Turnpike soon after 1800. Settled in 1790, incorporated in 1827.

Population: 4,224; Growth (since 2000): -7.1%; Density: 91.3 persons per square mile; Race: 95.4% White, 0.4% Black/African American, 0.0% Asian, 0.3% American Indian/Alaska Native, 0.0% Native Hawaiian/Other Pacific Islander, 0.8% Two or more races, 3.6% Hispanic of any race; Average household size: 2.40; Median age: 46.1; Age under 18: 21.7%; Age 65 and over: 21.8%; Males per 100 females: 98.0; Marriage status: 21.0% never married, 59.5% now married, 3.6% separated, 8.1% widowed, 11.4% divorced; Foreign born: 2.2%; Speak English only: 97.7%; With disability: 15.9%; Veterans: 9.1%; Ancestry: 26.9% German, 19.5% English, 18.6% Irish, 8.6% Italian, 7.4% American

Employment: 12.7% management, business, and financial, 1.1% computer, engineering, and science, 8.8% education, legal, community service, arts, and media, 3.5% healthcare practitioners, 20.3% service, 18.2% sales and office, 9.3% natural resources, construction, and maintenance, 26.0% production, transportation, and material moving

Income: Per capita: $26,380; Median household: $50,801; Average household: $61,400; Households with income of $100,000 or more: 17.4%; Poverty rate: 15.8%

Educational Attainment: High school diploma or higher: 85.6%; Bachelor's degree or higher: 13.7%; Graduate/professional degree or higher: 6.0%

School District(s)
Otego-Unadilla Central SD (KG-12)
    Enrollment: 893. . . . . (607) 988-5038

Housing: Homeownership rate: 84.2%; Median home value: $93,900; Median year structure built: 1965; Homeowner vacancy rate: 0.3%; Median selected monthly owner costs: $1,122 with a mortgage, $409 without a mortgage; Median gross rent: $692 per month; Rental vacancy rate: 13.7%

Health Insurance: 96.9% have insurance; 75.6% have private insurance; 41.7% have public insurance; 3.1% do not have insurance; 2.6% of children under 18 do not have insurance

Transportation: Commute: 90.9% car, 0.2% public transportation, 0.8% walk, 6.0% work from home; Mean travel time to work: 26.7 minutes

UNADILLA (village). Covers a land area of 1.037 square miles and a water area of 0.049 square miles. Located at 42.33° N. Lat; 75.31° W. Long. Elevation is 1,010 feet.

Population: 1,031; Growth (since 2000): -8.5%; Density: 994.6 persons per square mile; Race: 97.7% White, 0.0% Black/African American, 0.0% Asian, 1.3% American Indian/Alaska Native, 0.0% Native Hawaiian/Other Pacific Islander, 1.1% Two or more races, 1.8% Hispanic of any race; Average household size: 2.35; Median age: 38.0; Age under 18: 28.4%; Age 65 and over: 17.0%; Males per 100 females: 90.9; Marriage status: 26.4% never married, 52.2% now married, 3.6% separated, 5.6% widowed, 15.8% divorced; Foreign born: 0.5%; Speak English only: 98.5%; With disability: 15.8%; Veterans: 7.7%; Ancestry: 38.7% German, 29.5% Irish, 19.9% English, 14.1% Italian, 5.9% French

Employment: 7.4% management, business, and financial, 3.6% computer, engineering, and science, 8.1% education, legal, community service, arts, and media, 3.8% healthcare practitioners, 12.1% service, 29.2% sales and office, 12.8% natural resources, construction, and maintenance, 22.9% production, transportation, and material moving

Income: Per capita: $26,648; Median household: $51,354; Average household: $61,344; Households with income of $100,000 or more: 18.9%; Poverty rate: 12.2%

Educational Attainment: High school diploma or higher: 85.4%; Bachelor's degree or higher: 17.1%; Graduate/professional degree or higher: 4.5%

School District(s)
Otego-Unadilla Central SD (KG-12)
    Enrollment: 893. . . . . (607) 988-5038

Housing: Homeownership rate: 70.4%; Median home value: $93,900; Median year structure built: Before 1940; Homeowner vacancy rate: 1.6%; Median selected monthly owner costs: $1,071 with a mortgage, $506 without a mortgage; Median gross rent: $656 per month; Rental vacancy rate: 11.0%

Health Insurance: 93.2% have insurance; 67.1% have private insurance; 42.4% have public insurance; 6.8% do not have insurance; 8.5% of children under 18 do not have insurance

Transportation: Commute: 94.3% car, 0.9% public transportation, 1.8% walk, 2.3% work from home; Mean travel time to work: 24.7 minutes

WELLS BRIDGE (unincorporated postal area)
ZCTA: 13859

Covers a land area of 0.480 square miles and a water area of 0.030 square miles. Located at 42.37° N. Lat; 75.25° W. Long. Elevation is 1,043 feet.

Population: 279; Growth (since 2000): 31.0%; Density: 581.5 persons per square mile; Race: 96.8% White, 0.0% Black/African American, 0.0% Asian, 0.0% American Indian/Alaska Native, 0.0% Native Hawaiian/Other Pacific Islander, 3.2% Two or more races, 0.0% Hispanic of any race; Average household size: 2.45; Median age: 34.8; Age under 18: 24.7%; Age 65 and over: 16.8%; Males per 100 females: 104.5; Marriage status: 24.3% never married, 71.9% now married, 0.0% separated, 0.0% widowed, 3.8% divorced; Foreign born: 0.0%; Speak English only: 100.0%; With disability: 11.5%; Veterans: 3.8%; Ancestry: 33.0% Norwegian, 26.5% German, 24.7% Australian, 22.9% English, 7.5% Irish

Employment: 8.2% management, business, and financial, 0.0% computer, engineering, and science, 0.0% education, legal, community service, arts, and media, 0.0% healthcare practitioners, 29.9% service, 20.9% sales and office, 0.0% natural resources, construction, and maintenance, 41.0% production, transportation, and material moving

Income: Per capita: $31,782; Median household: $66,250; Average household: $74,372; Households with income of $100,000 or more: 9.6%; Poverty rate: 3.2%

Educational Attainment: High school diploma or higher: 85.5%; Bachelor's degree or higher: n/a; Graduate/professional degree or higher: n/a

Housing: Homeownership rate: 83.3%; Median home value: $115,600; Median year structure built: 1962; Homeowner vacancy rate: 0.0%; Median selected monthly owner costs: $1,301 with a mortgage, $0

without a mortgage; Median gross rent: n/a per month; Rental vacancy rate: 0.0%
Health Insurance: 100.0% have insurance; 88.5% have private insurance; 20.1% have public insurance; 0.0% do not have insurance; 0.0% of children under 18 do not have insurance
Transportation: Commute: 100.0% car, 0.0% public transportation, 0.0% walk, 0.0% work from home; Mean travel time to work: 0.0 minutes

WEST END (CDP). Covers a land area of 3.652 square miles and a water area of 0.075 square miles. Located at 42.48° N. Lat; 75.09° W. Long. Elevation is 1,280 feet.
Population: 1,530; Growth (since 2000): -15.6%; Density: 418.9 persons per square mile; Race: 92.8% White, 3.2% Black/African American, 0.0% Asian, 0.0% American Indian/Alaska Native, 0.0% Native Hawaiian/Other Pacific Islander, 1.1% Two or more races, 6.5% Hispanic of any race; Average household size: 1.92; Median age: 55.6; Age under 18: 12.0%; Age 65 and over: 30.7%; Males per 100 females: 92.8; Marriage status: 28.4% never married, 49.9% now married, 4.1% separated, 11.5% widowed, 10.2% divorced; Foreign born: 6.5%; Speak English only: 93.2%; With disability: 24.9%; Veterans: 10.0%; Ancestry: 16.1% German, 12.4% Irish, 11.3% Italian, 9.0% American, 7.5% English
Employment: 5.7% management, business, and financial, 6.7% computer, engineering, and science, 23.5% education, legal, community service, arts, and media, 18.3% healthcare practitioners, 24.8% service, 17.1% sales and office, 2.2% natural resources, construction, and maintenance, 1.7% production, transportation, and material moving
Income: Per capita: $30,125; Median household: $40,313; Average household: $57,898; Households with income of $100,000 or more: 18.6%; Poverty rate: 24.1%
Educational Attainment: High school diploma or higher: 85.9%; Bachelor's degree or higher: 39.2%; Graduate/professional degree or higher: 21.8%
Housing: Homeownership rate: 84.3%; Median home value: $121,800; Median year structure built: 1961; Homeowner vacancy rate: 6.7%; Median selected monthly owner costs: $1,035 with a mortgage, $382 without a mortgage; Median gross rent: $878 per month; Rental vacancy rate: 13.5%
Health Insurance: 92.7% have insurance; 70.7% have private insurance; 45.0% have public insurance; 7.3% do not have insurance; 0.0% of children under 18 do not have insurance
Transportation: Commute: 96.5% car, 2.8% public transportation, 0.0% walk, 0.0% work from home; Mean travel time to work: 19.3 minutes

WEST ONEONTA (unincorporated postal area)
ZCTA: 13861
Covers a land area of 4.410 square miles and a water area of 0.017 square miles. Located at 42.51° N. Lat; 75.15° W. Long. Elevation is 1,138 feet.
Population: 328; Growth (since 2000): -49.7%; Density: 74.4 persons per square mile; Race: 79.9% White, 2.7% Black/African American, 0.0% Asian, 0.0% American Indian/Alaska Native, 0.0% Native Hawaiian/Other Pacific Islander, 17.4% Two or more races, 0.0% Hispanic of any race; Average household size: 2.83; Median age: 38.0; Age under 18: 26.5%; Age 65 and over: 23.8%; Males per 100 females: 100.0; Marriage status: 10.9% never married, 62.1% now married, 0.0% separated, 0.0% widowed, 27.0% divorced; Foreign born: 0.0%; Speak English only: 97.3%; With disability: 12.2%; Veterans: 18.3%; Ancestry: 28.4% German, 17.4% Irish, 10.4% American, 9.1% French, 7.9% Scottish
Employment: 4.7% management, business, and financial, 3.3% computer, engineering, and science, 8.7% education, legal, community service, arts, and media, 12.7% healthcare practitioners, 35.3% service, 16.0% sales and office, 13.3% natural resources, construction, and maintenance, 6.0% production, transportation, and material moving
Income: Per capita: $36,931; Median household: $110,375; Average household: $103,048; Households with income of $100,000 or more: 52.6%; Poverty rate: 13.1%
Educational Attainment: High school diploma or higher: 89.4%; Bachelor's degree or higher: 41.2%; Graduate/professional degree or higher: 19.0%
Housing: Homeownership rate: 87.9%; Median home value: $178,100; Median year structure built: 1975; Homeowner vacancy rate: 0.0%; Median selected monthly owner costs: $1,094 with a mortgage, $0 without a mortgage; Median gross rent: n/a per month; Rental vacancy rate: 0.0%

Health Insurance: 91.8% have insurance; 77.7% have private insurance; 34.1% have public insurance; 8.2% do not have insurance; 0.0% of children under 18 do not have insurance
Transportation: Commute: 96.9% car, 0.0% public transportation, 0.0% walk, 3.1% work from home; Mean travel time to work: 39.1 minutes

WESTFORD (town). Covers a land area of 33.853 square miles and a water area of 0.056 square miles. Located at 42.64° N. Lat; 74.82° W. Long. Elevation is 1,562 feet.
Population: 835; Growth (since 2000): 6.5%; Density: 24.7 persons per square mile; Race: 95.9% White, 1.1% Black/African American, 0.5% Asian, 0.0% American Indian/Alaska Native, 0.0% Native Hawaiian/Other Pacific Islander, 2.3% Two or more races, 1.1% Hispanic of any race; Average household size: 2.45; Median age: 44.2; Age under 18: 21.9%; Age 65 and over: 16.5%; Males per 100 females: 99.5; Marriage status: 25.0% never married, 59.3% now married, 2.0% separated, 2.0% widowed, 13.7% divorced; Foreign born: 1.8%; Speak English only: 98.0%; With disability: 14.3%; Veterans: 9.0%; Ancestry: 19.4% German, 19.3% Irish, 14.1% English, 10.8% Italian, 10.3% Dutch
Employment: 13.2% management, business, and financial, 8.0% computer, engineering, and science, 6.9% education, legal, community service, arts, and media, 3.8% healthcare practitioners, 19.9% service, 20.1% sales and office, 13.7% natural resources, construction, and maintenance, 14.4% production, transportation, and material moving
Income: Per capita: $26,208; Median household: $55,865; Average household: $66,637; Households with income of $100,000 or more: 19.1%; Poverty rate: 5.9%
Educational Attainment: High school diploma or higher: 92.1%; Bachelor's degree or higher: 26.9%; Graduate/professional degree or higher: 7.1%
Housing: Homeownership rate: 82.0%; Median home value: $139,000; Median year structure built: 1973; Homeowner vacancy rate: 2.5%; Median selected monthly owner costs: $1,319 with a mortgage, $461 without a mortgage; Median gross rent: $791 per month; Rental vacancy rate: 0.0%
Health Insurance: 98.3% have insurance; 77.6% have private insurance; 40.5% have public insurance; 1.7% do not have insurance; 0.5% of children under 18 do not have insurance
Transportation: Commute: 90.8% car, 0.0% public transportation, 1.7% walk, 7.0% work from home; Mean travel time to work: 29.0 minutes

WORCESTER (CDP). Covers a land area of 8.563 square miles and a water area of 0.046 square miles. Located at 42.61° N. Lat; 74.74° W. Long. Elevation is 1,335 feet.
Population: 953; Growth (since 2000): n/a; Density: 111.3 persons per square mile; Race: 94.8% White, 2.0% Black/African American, 0.0% Asian, 0.0% American Indian/Alaska Native, 0.0% Native Hawaiian/Other Pacific Islander, 2.1% Two or more races, 10.0% Hispanic of any race; Average household size: 2.36; Median age: 47.4; Age under 18: 22.7%; Age 65 and over: 31.7%; Males per 100 females: 90.9; Marriage status: 21.3% never married, 58.1% now married, 2.0% separated, 8.6% widowed, 12.0% divorced; Foreign born: 0.4%; Speak English only: 96.3%; With disability: 11.3%; Veterans: 11.5%; Ancestry: 26.7% Irish, 19.4% Italian, 16.5% German, 11.6% French, 6.4% English
Employment: 1.9% management, business, and financial, 2.8% computer, engineering, and science, 8.8% education, legal, community service, arts, and media, 11.0% healthcare practitioners, 22.9% service, 22.6% sales and office, 17.6% natural resources, construction, and maintenance, 12.5% production, transportation, and material moving
Income: Per capita: $23,481; Median household: $43,239; Average household: $55,969; Households with income of $100,000 or more: 16.2%; Poverty rate: 14.8%
Educational Attainment: High school diploma or higher: 82.2%; Bachelor's degree or higher: 26.4%; Graduate/professional degree or higher: 11.9%

School District(s)
Worcester Central SD (PK-12)
　　Enrollment: 371 . . . . (607) 397-8785
Housing: Homeownership rate: 79.0%; Median home value: $102,700; Median year structure built: Before 1940; Homeowner vacancy rate: 0.0%; Median selected monthly owner costs: $940 with a mortgage, $381 without a mortgage; Median gross rent: $947 per month; Rental vacancy rate: 27.8%
Health Insurance: 89.7% have insurance; 60.5% have private insurance; 57.3% have public insurance; 10.3% do not have insurance; 17.1% of children under 18 do not have insurance

Transportation: Commute: 93.6% car, 0.0% public transportation, 2.9% walk, 3.5% work from home; Mean travel time to work: 28.6 minutes

WORCESTER (town).
Covers a land area of 46.710 square miles and a water area of 0.163 square miles. Located at 42.58° N. Lat; 74.72° W. Long. Elevation is 1,335 feet.
Population: 2,035; Growth (since 2000): -7.8%; Density: 43.6 persons per square mile; Race: 94.7% White, 2.7% Black/African American, 0.0% Asian, 0.0% American Indian/Alaska Native, 0.0% Native Hawaiian/Other Pacific Islander, 1.9% Two or more races, 5.6% Hispanic of any race; Average household size: 2.22; Median age: 51.2; Age under 18: 19.2%; Age 65 and over: 29.9%; Males per 100 females: 97.9; Marriage status: 21.3% never married, 55.6% now married, 3.1% separated, 8.1% widowed, 14.9% divorced; Foreign born: 2.2%; Speak English only: 95.4%; With disability: 14.4%; Veterans: 13.2%; Ancestry: 25.5% Irish, 19.7% German, 15.4% Italian, 13.0% French, 6.2% English
Employment: 9.2% management, business, and financial, 1.9% computer, engineering, and science, 8.3% education, legal, community service, arts, and media, 11.7% healthcare practitioners, 19.0% service, 20.2% sales and office, 14.1% natural resources, construction, and maintenance, 15.5% production, transportation, and material moving
Income: Per capita: $25,722; Median household: $44,545; Average household: $57,150; Households with income of $100,000 or more: 16.3%; Poverty rate: 16.5%
Educational Attainment: High school diploma or higher: 83.9%; Bachelor's degree or higher: 21.9%; Graduate/professional degree or higher: 10.0%
School District(s)
Worcester Central SD (PK-12)
    Enrollment: 371 . . . . (607) 397-8785
Housing: Homeownership rate: 80.3%; Median home value: $106,300; Median year structure built: 1955; Homeowner vacancy rate: 2.7%; Median selected monthly owner costs: $1,093 with a mortgage, $457 without a mortgage; Median gross rent: $742 per month; Rental vacancy rate: 21.1%
Health Insurance: 93.5% have insurance; 63.2% have private insurance; 56.0% have public insurance; 6.5% do not have insurance; 9.4% of children under 18 do not have insurance
Transportation: Commute: 92.6% car, 2.0% public transportation, 3.1% walk, 2.3% work from home; Mean travel time to work: 37.6 minutes

Putnam County

Located in southeastern New York; bounded on the west by the Hudson River, and on the east by Connecticut; includes part of the Taconic Mountains. Covers a land area of 230.312 square miles, a water area of 15.939 square miles, and is located in the Eastern Time Zone at 41.43° N. Lat., 73.74° W. Long. The county was founded in 1812. County seat is Carmel.

Putnam County is part of the New York-Newark-Jersey City, NY-NJ-PA Metropolitan Statistical Area. The entire metro area includes: Dutchess County-Putnam County, NY Metropolitan Division (Dutchess County, NY; Putnam County, NY); Nassau County-Suffolk County, NY Metropolitan Division (Nassau County, NY; Suffolk County, NY); Newark, NJ-PA Metropolitan Division (Essex County, NJ; Hunterdon County, NJ; Morris County, NJ; Somerset County, NJ; Sussex County, NJ; Union County, NJ; Pike County, PA); New York-Jersey City-White Plains, NY-NJ Metropolitan Division (Bergen County, NJ; Hudson County, NJ; Middlesex County, NJ; Monmouth County, NJ; Ocean County, NJ; Passaic County, NJ; Bronx County, NY; Kings County, NY; New York County, NY; Orange County, NY; Queens County, NY; Richmond County, NY; Rockland County, NY; Westchester County, NY)

Population: 99,464; Growth (since 2000): 3.9%; Density: 431.9 persons per square mile; Race: 89.1% White, 2.4% Black/African American, 2.2% Asian, 0.3% American Indian/Alaska Native, 0.0% Native Hawaiian/Other Pacific Islander, 2.4% two or more races, 13.8% Hispanic of any race; Average household size: 2.82; Median age: 43.8; Age under 18: 20.9%; Age 65 and over: 15.6%; Males per 100 females: 99.7; Marriage status: 28.3% never married, 58.7% now married, 1.4% separated, 5.0% widowed, 7.9% divorced; Foreign born: 13.3%; Speak English only: 80.9%; With disability: 10.6%; Veterans: 5.3%; Ancestry: 27.9% Italian, 22.2% Irish, 12.4% German, 6.1% English, 4.7% American

Religion: Six largest groups: 41.5% Catholicism, 1.2% Methodist/Pietist, 1.2% Lutheran, 1.2% Judaism, 1.0% Episcopalianism/Anglicanism, 0.8% Presbyterian-Reformed
Economy: Unemployment rate: 3.4%; Leading industries: 19.9 % construction; 11.5 % retail trade; 10.6 % professional, scientific, and technical services; Farms: 72 totaling 5,908 acres; Company size: 0 employ 1,000 or more persons, 2 employ 500 to 999 persons, 19 employ 100 to 499 persons, 2,854 employ less than 100 persons; Business ownership: 3,373 women-owned, 266 Black-owned, 709 Hispanic-owned, 357 Asian-owned, 26 American Indian/Alaska Native-owned
Employment: 15.5% management, business, and financial, 5.0% computer, engineering, and science, 14.9% education, legal, community service, arts, and media, 6.1% healthcare practitioners, 16.7% service, 25.1% sales and office, 10.6% natural resources, construction, and maintenance, 6.0% production, transportation, and material moving
Income: Per capita: $44,063; Median household: $99,608; Average household: $124,736; Households with income of $100,000 or more: 49.8%; Poverty rate: 4.8%
Educational Attainment: High school diploma or higher: 92.8%; Bachelor's degree or higher: 38.5%; Graduate/professional degree or higher: 16.4%
Housing: Homeownership rate: 81.9%; Median home value: $357,700; Median year structure built: 1968; Homeowner vacancy rate: 0.8%; Median selected monthly owner costs: $2,708 with a mortgage, $1,107 without a mortgage; Median gross rent: $1,334 per month; Rental vacancy rate: 4.8%
Vital Statistics: Birth rate: 82.5 per 10,000 population; Death rate: 74.4 per 10,000 population; Age-adjusted cancer mortality rate: 132.5 deaths per 100,000 population
Health Insurance: 94.3% have insurance; 81.7% have private insurance; 25.4% have public insurance; 5.7% do not have insurance; 2.9% of children under 18 do not have insurance
Health Care: Physicians: 19.7 per 10,000 population; Dentists: 5.7 per 10,000 population; Hospital beds: 31.3 per 10,000 population; Hospital admissions: 1,077.9 per 10,000 population
Air Quality Index (AQI): Percent of Days: 94.2% good, 5.0% moderate, 0.8% unhealthy for sensitive individuals, 0.0% unhealthy, 0.0% very unhealthy; Annual median: 34; Annual maximum: 112
Transportation: Commute: 84.4% car, 8.5% public transportation, 1.2% walk, 5.3% work from home; Mean travel time to work: 39.2 minutes
2016 Presidential Election: 55.6% Trump, 39.9% Clinton, 2.4% Johnson, 1.2% Stein
National and State Parks: Clarence Fahnestock Memorial State Park
Additional Information Contacts
Putnam Government . . . . (845) 225-3641
    http://www.putnamcountyny.com

Putnam County Communities

BREWSTER (village).
Covers a land area of 0.467 square miles and a water area of 0.004 square miles. Located at 41.40° N. Lat; 73.61° W. Long. Elevation is 466 feet.
History: Jurist James Kent born nearby, 1763. Settled 1850, incorporated 1894.
Population: 2,360; Growth (since 2000): 9.2%; Density: 5,051.2 persons per square mile; Race: 62.5% White, 5.3% Black/African American, 1.4% Asian, 2.6% American Indian/Alaska Native, 0.0% Native Hawaiian/Other Pacific Islander, 4.7% Two or more races, 63.4% Hispanic of any race; Average household size: 2.74; Median age: 32.9; Age under 18: 19.5%; Age 65 and over: 8.5%; Males per 100 females: 161.2; Marriage status: 45.5% never married, 46.3% now married, 1.8% separated, 2.3% widowed, 5.9% divorced; Foreign born: 53.4%; Speak English only: 40.0%; With disability: 9.5%; Veterans: 4.0%; Ancestry: 7.6% Irish, 5.6% Italian, 5.2% American, 3.7% English, 3.6% German
Employment: 9.6% management, business, and financial, 1.6% computer, engineering, and science, 3.1% education, legal, community service, arts, and media, 0.6% healthcare practitioners, 33.4% service, 20.9% sales and office, 21.9% natural resources, construction, and maintenance, 8.8% production, transportation, and material moving
Income: Per capita: $26,123; Median household: $54,950; Average household: $70,072; Households with income of $100,000 or more: 23.4%; Poverty rate: 16.7%
Educational Attainment: High school diploma or higher: 61.8%; Bachelor's degree or higher: 16.6%; Graduate/professional degree or higher: 6.8%

Brewster Central SD (KG-12)
    Enrollment: 3,159 . . . . (845) 279-8000
Housing: Homeownership rate: 23.2%; Median home value: $265,600;
Median year structure built: 1954; Homeowner vacancy rate: 0.0%; Median
selected monthly owner costs: $2,356 with a mortgage, $960 without a
mortgage; Median gross rent: $1,173 per month; Rental vacancy rate:
2.1%
Health Insurance: 60.7% have insurance; 39.5% have private insurance;
28.5% have public insurance; 39.3% do not have insurance; 6.9% of
children under 18 do not have insurance
Safety: Violent crime rate: 4.3 per 10,000 population; Property crime rate:
68.6 per 10,000 population
Transportation: Commute: 78.6% car, 10.7% public transportation, 5.2%
walk, 2.2% work from home; Mean travel time to work: 30.3 minutes

BREWSTER HILL (CDP). Covers a land area of 0.870 square miles
and a water area of 0.110 square miles. Located at 41.42° N. Lat; 73.61°
W. Long. Elevation is 617 feet.
Population: 1,618; Growth (since 2000): -27.3%; Density: 1,859.3 persons
per square mile; Race: 84.5% White, 0.0% Black/African American, 6.1%
Asian, 0.0% American Indian/Alaska Native, 0.0% Native Hawaiian/Other
Pacific Islander, 7.0% Two or more races, 10.1% Hispanic of any race;
Average household size: 2.62; Median age: 47.7; Age under 18: 18.0%;
Age 65 and over: 20.0%; Males per 100 females: 98.0; Marriage status:
11.4% never married, 65.1% now married, 0.0% separated, 6.3%
widowed, 17.2% divorced; Foreign born: 7.2%; Speak English only: 83.7%;
With disability: 15.4%; Veterans: 12.9%; Ancestry: 35.5% Italian, 26.5%
Irish, 15.9% German, 11.2% English, 7.6% Polish
Employment: 9.6% management, business, and financial, 11.3%
computer, engineering, and science, 22.7% education, legal, community
service, arts, and media, 0.0% healthcare practitioners, 14.3% service,
30.4% sales and office, 8.3% natural resources, construction, and
maintenance, 3.3% production, transportation, and material moving
Income: Per capita: $37,681; Median household: $84,732; Average
household: $95,666; Households with income of $100,000 or more: 40.4%;
Poverty rate: n/a
Educational Attainment: High school diploma or higher: 89.7%;
Bachelor's degree or higher: 33.6%; Graduate/professional degree or
higher: 15.1%
Housing: Homeownership rate: 100.0%; Median home value: $333,000;
Median year structure built: 1958; Homeowner vacancy rate: 0.0%; Median
selected monthly owner costs: $2,520 with a mortgage, $813 without a
mortgage; Median gross rent: n/a per month; Rental vacancy rate: 100.0%
Health Insurance: 80.4% have insurance; 69.2% have private insurance;
29.7% have public insurance; 19.6% do not have insurance; 35.0% of
children under 18 do not have insurance
Transportation: Commute: 86.1% car, 9.6% public transportation, 0.0%
walk, 4.3% work from home; Mean travel time to work: 37.0 minutes

CARMEL (town). County seat. Covers a land area of 35.907 square
miles and a water area of 4.786 square miles. Located at 41.39° N. Lat;
73.72° W. Long. Elevation is 561 feet.
Population: 34,328; Growth (since 2000): 4.0%; Density: 956.0 persons
per square mile; Race: 90.8% White, 1.1% Black/African American, 2.9%
Asian, 0.0% American Indian/Alaska Native, 0.0% Native Hawaiian/Other
Pacific Islander, 2.1% Two or more races, 10.9% Hispanic of any race;
Average household size: 2.89; Median age: 43.9; Age under 18: 20.8%;
Age 65 and over: 15.9%; Males per 100 females: 98.4; Marriage status:
27.9% never married, 59.9% now married, 1.2% separated, 5.2%
widowed, 7.0% divorced; Foreign born: 13.9%; Speak English only: 81.3%;
With disability: 10.5%; Veterans: 4.9%; Ancestry: 31.1% Italian, 23.5%
Irish, 11.9% German, 4.9% American, 4.7% Polish
Employment: 14.6% management, business, and financial, 4.7%
computer, engineering, and science, 14.6% education, legal, community
service, arts, and media, 7.4% healthcare practitioners, 16.4% service,
24.2% sales and office, 12.7% natural resources, construction, and
maintenance, 5.4% production, transportation, and material moving
Income: Per capita: $44,260; Median household: $100,790; Average
household: $125,607; Households with income of $100,000 or more:
50.4%; Poverty rate: 3.3%
Educational Attainment: High school diploma or higher: 93.2%;
Bachelor's degree or higher: 37.1%; Graduate/professional degree or
higher: 15.5%

Carmel Central SD (KG-12)
    Enrollment: 4,210 . . . . (845) 878-2094
Housing: Homeownership rate: 81.3%; Median home value: $376,300;
Median year structure built: 1969; Homeowner vacancy rate: 0.3%; Median
selected monthly owner costs: $3,009 with a mortgage, $1,160 without a
mortgage; Median gross rent: $1,292 per month; Rental vacancy rate:
4.8%
Health Insurance: 94.9% have insurance; 83.3% have private insurance;
23.8% have public insurance; 5.1% do not have insurance; 2.4% of
children under 18 do not have insurance
Hospitals: Putnam Hospital Center (164 beds)
Safety: Violent crime rate: 2.6 per 10,000 population; Property crime rate:
36.5 per 10,000 population
Newspapers: Putnam County Courier (weekly circulation 4,800)
Transportation: Commute: 87.4% car, 6.6% public transportation, 1.1%
walk, 4.4% work from home; Mean travel time to work: 38.0 minutes
Additional Information Contacts
Town of Carmel . . . . (845) 628-1500
    http://www.ci.carmel.ny.us

CARMEL HAMLET (CDP). Covers a land area of 8.335 square
miles and a water area of 2.055 square miles. Located at 41.42° N. Lat;
73.69° W. Long.
Population: 6,392; Growth (since 2000): 13.1%; Density: 766.9 persons
per square mile; Race: 84.7% White, 2.4% Black/African American, 6.1%
Asian, 0.0% American Indian/Alaska Native, 0.0% Native Hawaiian/Other
Pacific Islander, 4.9% Two or more races, 14.3% Hispanic of any race;
Average household size: 2.68; Median age: 48.0; Age under 18: 19.4%;
Age 65 and over: 21.7%; Males per 100 females: 98.6; Marriage status:
27.4% never married, 54.7% now married, 1.1% separated, 11.1%
widowed, 6.8% divorced; Foreign born: 9.7%; Speak English only: 85.6%;
With disability: 14.6%; Veterans: 6.3%; Ancestry: 27.1% Italian, 21.9%
Irish, 12.5% German, 7.9% Polish, 6.0% English
Employment: 13.0% management, business, and financial, 3.5%
computer, engineering, and science, 15.1% education, legal, community
service, arts, and media, 7.7% healthcare practitioners, 7.8% service,
34.6% sales and office, 12.5% natural resources, construction, and
maintenance, 6.0% production, transportation, and material moving
Income: Per capita: $42,892; Median household: $93,287; Average
household: $115,326; Households with income of $100,000 or more:
44.5%; Poverty rate: 4.3%
Educational Attainment: High school diploma or higher: 90.9%;
Bachelor's degree or higher: 35.1%; Graduate/professional degree or
higher: 15.7%
Housing: Homeownership rate: 71.9%; Median home value: $324,400;
Median year structure built: 1971; Homeowner vacancy rate: 0.0%; Median
selected monthly owner costs: $3,248 with a mortgage, $1,085 without a
mortgage; Median gross rent: $1,257 per month; Rental vacancy rate:
6.5%
Health Insurance: 94.3% have insurance; 75.5% have private insurance;
33.5% have public insurance; 5.7% do not have insurance; 7.6% of
children under 18 do not have insurance
Transportation: Commute: 87.5% car, 7.0% public transportation, 0.4%
walk, 5.1% work from home; Mean travel time to work: 38.9 minutes

COLD SPRING (village). Covers a land area of 0.594 square miles
and a water area of 0.005 square miles. Located at 41.42° N. Lat; 73.95°
W. Long. Elevation is 115 feet.
History: Settled before the American Revolution; incorporated 1846.
Population: 1,834; Growth (since 2000): -7.5%; Density: 3,089.0 persons
per square mile; Race: 91.1% White, 0.7% Black/African American, 1.7%
Asian, 1.3% American Indian/Alaska Native, 0.0% Native Hawaiian/Other
Pacific Islander, 2.7% Two or more races, 4.3% Hispanic of any race;
Average household size: 2.18; Median age: 47.0; Age under 18: 17.6%;
Age 65 and over: 18.7%; Males per 100 females: 90.6; Marriage status:
29.1% never married, 55.1% now married, 3.6% separated, 4.9%
widowed, 10.9% divorced; Foreign born: 9.3%; Speak English only: 88.1%;
With disability: 13.4%; Veterans: 9.8%; Ancestry: 22.7% Italian, 20.8%
Irish, 13.2% German, 12.5% English, 5.3% Polish
Employment: 15.9% management, business, and financial, 5.8%
computer, engineering, and science, 27.1% education, legal, community
service, arts, and media, 4.4% healthcare practitioners, 17.8% service,
19.1% sales and office, 5.0% natural resources, construction, and
maintenance, 4.8% production, transportation, and material moving

Income: Per capita: $47,768; Median household: $93,839; Average household: $101,909; Households with income of $100,000 or more: 47.9%; Poverty rate: 5.5%

Educational Attainment: High school diploma or higher: 97.5%; Bachelor's degree or higher: 55.5%; Graduate/professional degree or higher: 24.7%

School District(s)

Haldane Central SD (KG-12)
    Enrollment: 833. . . . . (845) 265-9254
Housing: Homeownership rate: 63.3%; Median home value: $419,600; Median year structure built: Before 1940; Homeowner vacancy rate: 3.4%; Median selected monthly owner costs: $2,540 with a mortgage, $1,148 without a mortgage; Median gross rent: $1,372 per month; Rental vacancy rate: 4.3%

Health Insurance: 96.1% have insurance; 83.7% have private insurance; 24.2% have public insurance; 3.9% do not have insurance; 1.5% of children under 18 do not have insurance

Newspapers: Putnam County News & Recorder (weekly circulation 4,200)

Transportation: Commute: 52.3% car, 33.2% public transportation, 5.5% walk, 7.4% work from home; Mean travel time to work: 52.6 minutes

GARRISON (unincorporated postal area)
ZCTA: 10524

Covers a land area of 20.802 square miles and a water area of 0.324 square miles. Located at 41.38° N. Lat; 73.93° W. Long. Elevation is 49 feet.

Population: 4,303; Growth (since 2000): 1.7%; Density: 206.9 persons per square mile; Race: 86.8% White, 3.3% Black/African American, 3.0% Asian, 0.0% American Indian/Alaska Native, 0.0% Native Hawaiian/Other Pacific Islander, 5.2% Two or more races, 6.8% Hispanic of any race; Average household size: 2.74; Median age: 49.4; Age under 18: 17.0%; Age 65 and over: 21.7%; Males per 100 females: 95.4; Marriage status: 26.3% never married, 63.6% now married, 1.1% separated, 3.9% widowed, 6.2% divorced; Foreign born: 10.6%; Speak English only: 89.0%; With disability: 9.6%; Veterans: 7.1%; Ancestry: 26.2% Irish, 22.2% Italian, 10.8% German, 7.9% English, 5.8% American

Employment: 18.7% management, business, and financial, 3.5% computer, engineering, and science, 19.2% education, legal, community service, arts, and media, 6.5% healthcare practitioners, 12.2% service, 20.3% sales and office, 8.9% natural resources, construction, and maintenance, 10.7% production, transportation, and material moving

Income: Per capita: $59,305; Median household: $125,912; Average household: $171,332; Households with income of $100,000 or more: 63.5%; Poverty rate: 6.7%

Educational Attainment: High school diploma or higher: 95.9%; Bachelor's degree or higher: 52.1%; Graduate/professional degree or higher: 26.8%

School District(s)

Garrison Union Free SD (KG-08)
    Enrollment: 212 . . . . (845) 424-3689
Housing: Homeownership rate: 90.9%; Median home value: $459,300; Median year structure built: 1967; Homeowner vacancy rate: 0.5%; Median selected monthly owner costs: $2,769 with a mortgage, $1,300 without a mortgage; Median gross rent: $1,735 per month; Rental vacancy rate: 9.3%

Health Insurance: 97.5% have insurance; 83.8% have private insurance; 29.5% have public insurance; 2.5% do not have insurance; 0.0% of children under 18 do not have insurance

Transportation: Commute: 71.7% car, 15.5% public transportation, 0.6% walk, 11.5% work from home; Mean travel time to work: 39.4 minutes

KENT (town). Covers a land area of 40.504 square miles and a water area of 2.822 square miles. Located at 41.46° N. Lat; 73.73° W. Long.
History: Kent was part of the Philipse Patent of 1679, when it was populated by the Wappinger tribe. Daniel Nimham (1724-1778) was the last chief of the Wappingers and was the most prominent Native American of his time in the Hudson Valley.

Population: 13,406; Growth (since 2000): -4.3%; Density: 331.0 persons per square mile; Race: 85.1% White, 5.7% Black/African American, 1.1% Asian, 0.6% American Indian/Alaska Native, 0.0% Native Hawaiian/Other Pacific Islander, 2.2% Two or more races, 16.1% Hispanic of any race; Average household size: 2.81; Median age: 45.9; Age under 18: 20.0%; Age 65 and over: 17.2%; Males per 100 females: 98.9; Marriage status:

26.2% never married, 57.5% now married, 2.2% separated, 6.4% widowed, 9.9% divorced; Foreign born: 14.4%; Speak English only: 78.7%; With disability: 13.7%; Veterans: 6.7%; Ancestry: 25.1% Italian, 22.1% Irish, 11.4% German, 5.7% English, 5.4% Polish

Employment: 13.8% management, business, and financial, 3.5% computer, engineering, and science, 11.6% education, legal, community service, arts, and media, 6.2% healthcare practitioners, 19.5% service, 27.3% sales and office, 11.8% natural resources, construction, and maintenance, 6.3% production, transportation, and material moving

Income: Per capita: $44,046; Median household: $91,090; Average household: $124,065; Households with income of $100,000 or more: 46.3%; Poverty rate: 4.7%

Educational Attainment: High school diploma or higher: 93.5%; Bachelor's degree or higher: 32.2%; Graduate/professional degree or higher: 13.9%

Housing: Homeownership rate: 85.4%; Median home value: $285,900; Median year structure built: 1964; Homeowner vacancy rate: 1.9%; Median selected monthly owner costs: $2,432 with a mortgage, $1,006 without a mortgage; Median gross rent: $1,499 per month; Rental vacancy rate: 4.3%

Health Insurance: 94.7% have insurance; 79.8% have private insurance; 30.5% have public insurance; 5.3% do not have insurance; 2.7% of children under 18 do not have insurance

Safety: Violent crime rate: 0.8 per 10,000 population; Property crime rate: 46.8 per 10,000 population

Transportation: Commute: 89.1% car, 5.3% public transportation, 0.9% walk, 3.9% work from home; Mean travel time to work: 41.3 minutes

Additional Information Contacts

Town of Kent . . . . (845) 225-3943
    http://www.townofkentny.com

LAKE CARMEL (CDP). Covers a land area of 5.161 square miles and a water area of 0.333 square miles. Located at 41.46° N. Lat; 73.67° W. Long. Elevation is 801 feet.

Population: 8,201; Growth (since 2000): -5.3%; Density: 1,589.0 persons per square mile; Race: 81.2% White, 5.8% Black/African American, 1.6% Asian, 1.0% American Indian/Alaska Native, 0.0% Native Hawaiian/Other Pacific Islander, 1.9% Two or more races, 21.1% Hispanic of any race; Average household size: 2.79; Median age: 43.8; Age under 18: 21.4%; Age 65 and over: 15.3%; Males per 100 females: 99.9; Marriage status: 26.4% never married, 58.4% now married, 2.3% separated, 6.7% widowed, 8.5% divorced; Foreign born: 16.3%; Speak English only: 75.1%; With disability: 12.7%; Veterans: 6.2%; Ancestry: 28.3% Italian, 21.0% Irish, 11.0% German, 6.5% Polish, 4.4% American

Employment: 13.6% management, business, and financial, 4.1% computer, engineering, and science, 11.1% education, legal, community service, arts, and media, 4.3% healthcare practitioners, 19.1% service, 30.5% sales and office, 11.1% natural resources, construction, and maintenance, 6.2% production, transportation, and material moving

Income: Per capita: $36,880; Median household: $86,957; Average household: $100,508; Households with income of $100,000 or more: 42.0%; Poverty rate: 4.9%

Educational Attainment: High school diploma or higher: 93.2%; Bachelor's degree or higher: 29.4%; Graduate/professional degree or higher: 11.5%

Housing: Homeownership rate: 87.0%; Median home value: $269,500; Median year structure built: 1961; Homeowner vacancy rate: 1.1%; Median selected monthly owner costs: $2,307 with a mortgage, $910 without a mortgage; Median gross rent: $1,612 per month; Rental vacancy rate: 7.5%

Health Insurance: 93.5% have insurance; 79.1% have private insurance; 28.2% have public insurance; 6.5% do not have insurance; 4.1% of children under 18 do not have insurance

Transportation: Commute: 90.5% car, 6.3% public transportation, 0.0% walk, 3.2% work from home; Mean travel time to work: 42.9 minutes

LAKE PEEKSKILL (unincorporated postal area)
ZCTA: 10537

Covers a land area of 1.077 square miles and a water area of 0.095 square miles. Located at 41.34° N. Lat; 73.88° W. Long. Elevation is 315 feet.

Population: 1,661; Growth (since 2000): -18.3%; Density: 1,542.3 persons per square mile; Race: 86.7% White, 9.6% Black/African American, 0.0% Asian, 0.0% American Indian/Alaska Native, 0.0% Native Hawaiian/Other Pacific Islander, 3.7% Two or more races, 7.3%

Hispanic of any race; Average household size: 2.64; Median age: 47.6; Age under 18: 10.4%; Age 65 and over: 14.0%; Males per 100 females: 101.0; Marriage status: 34.7% never married, 47.9% now married, 3.3% separated, 3.4% widowed, 14.0% divorced; Foreign born: 17.8%; Speak English only: 80.6%; With disability: 7.1%; Veterans: 8.1%; Ancestry: 29.6% German, 25.4% Italian, 24.0% Irish, 8.6% Albanian, 7.3% American

Employment: 28.4% management, business, and financial, 2.8% computer, engineering, and science, 19.7% education, legal, community service, arts, and media, 3.7% healthcare practitioners, 12.4% service, 21.8% sales and office, 9.3% natural resources, construction, and maintenance, 1.9% production, transportation, and material moving

Income: Per capita: $42,354; Median household: $100,729; Average household: $107,088; Households with income of $100,000 or more: 50.6%; Poverty rate: 5.3%

Educational Attainment: High school diploma or higher: 94.7%; Bachelor's degree or higher: 52.2%; Graduate/professional degree or higher: 16.3%

Housing: Homeownership rate: 88.9%; Median home value: $258,000; Median year structure built: 1953; Homeowner vacancy rate: 13.5%; Median selected monthly owner costs: $2,116 with a mortgage, $783 without a mortgage; Median gross rent: $1,125 per month; Rental vacancy rate: 0.0%

Health Insurance: 97.2% have insurance; 70.7% have private insurance; 35.8% have public insurance; 2.8% do not have insurance; 0.0% of children under 18 do not have insurance

Transportation: Commute: 88.1% car, 7.4% public transportation, 0.0% walk, 1.9% work from home; Mean travel time to work: 42.2 minutes

MAHOPAC (CDP). Covers a land area of 5.279 square miles and a water area of 1.171 square miles. Located at 41.37° N. Lat; 73.74° W. Long. Elevation is 666 feet.

History: Mahopac was originally inhabited by the Wappinger Native Americans, an Algonquian tribe. The land was patented in 1697 by Adolphus Philipse, son of a wealthy Anglo-Dutch gentryman.

Population: 8,742; Growth (since 2000): 3.1%; Density: 1,655.8 persons per square mile; Race: 90.0% White, 0.0% Black/African American, 2.0% Asian, 0.0% American Indian/Alaska Native, 0.0% Native Hawaiian/Other Pacific Islander, 1.9% Two or more races, 13.1% Hispanic of any race; Average household size: 2.79; Median age: 42.2; Age under 18: 19.4%; Age 65 and over: 15.0%; Males per 100 females: 101.2; Marriage status: 31.8% never married, 57.8% now married, 1.5% separated, 3.3% widowed, 7.1% divorced; Foreign born: 22.7%; Speak English only: 71.8%; With disability: 9.3%; Veterans: 3.2%; Ancestry: 30.1% Italian, 16.4% Irish, 9.8% Albanian, 9.6% German, 6.2% American

Employment: 13.6% management, business, and financial, 6.4% computer, engineering, and science, 14.8% education, legal, community service, arts, and media, 6.5% healthcare practitioners, 19.8% service, 21.6% sales and office, 12.9% natural resources, construction, and maintenance, 4.4% production, transportation, and material moving

Income: Per capita: $42,988; Median household: $87,594; Average household: $115,793; Households with income of $100,000 or more: 45.7%; Poverty rate: 4.0%

Educational Attainment: High school diploma or higher: 91.9%; Bachelor's degree or higher: 39.2%; Graduate/professional degree or higher: 19.7%

School District(s)
Mahopac Central SD (KG-12)
Enrollment: 4,270 . . . . (845) 628-3415

Housing: Homeownership rate: 70.1%; Median home value: $368,800; Median year structure built: 1966; Homeowner vacancy rate: 0.0%; Median selected monthly owner costs: $2,776 with a mortgage, $1,159 without a mortgage; Median gross rent: $1,236 per month; Rental vacancy rate: 0.0%

Health Insurance: 92.8% have insurance; 80.7% have private insurance; 21.8% have public insurance; 7.2% do not have insurance; 0.8% of children under 18 do not have insurance

Newspapers: Putnam County Press (weekly circulation 12,000)

Transportation: Commute: 82.2% car, 7.8% public transportation, 3.8% walk, 4.9% work from home; Mean travel time to work: 35.8 minutes

NELSONVILLE (village). Covers a land area of 1.034 square miles and a water area of 0.001 square miles. Located at 41.43° N. Lat; 73.95° W. Long. Elevation is 187 feet.

Population: 719; Growth (since 2000): 27.3%; Density: 695.5 persons per square mile; Race: 93.2% White, 0.3% Black/African American, 1.9% Asian, 0.0% American Indian/Alaska Native, 0.0% Native Hawaiian/Other Pacific Islander, 0.8% Two or more races, 17.9% Hispanic of any race; Average household size: 3.21; Median age: 36.7; Age under 18: 34.2%; Age 65 and over: 8.6%; Males per 100 females: 97.5; Marriage status: 27.3% never married, 60.4% now married, 0.6% separated, 5.9% widowed, 6.3% divorced; Foreign born: 7.4%; Speak English only: 88.2%; With disability: 6.2%; Veterans: 3.9%; Ancestry: 28.0% Italian, 25.2% Irish, 14.7% German, 10.4% English, 6.0% Polish

Employment: 18.5% management, business, and financial, 9.3% computer, engineering, and science, 25.9% education, legal, community service, arts, and media, 3.2% healthcare practitioners, 16.6% service, 14.1% sales and office, 7.7% natural resources, construction, and maintenance, 4.8% production, transportation, and material moving

Income: Per capita: $41,099; Median household: $98,393; Average household: $139,381; Households with income of $100,000 or more: 48.0%; Poverty rate: 1.5%

Educational Attainment: High school diploma or higher: 94.9%; Bachelor's degree or higher: 54.0%; Graduate/professional degree or higher: 27.2%

Housing: Homeownership rate: 77.8%; Median home value: $417,100; Median year structure built: 1952; Homeowner vacancy rate: 0.0%; Median selected monthly owner costs: $2,691 with a mortgage, $1,090 without a mortgage; Median gross rent: $1,539 per month; Rental vacancy rate: 0.0%

Health Insurance: 95.8% have insurance; 88.8% have private insurance; 17.1% have public insurance; 4.2% do not have insurance; 0.0% of children under 18 do not have insurance

Transportation: Commute: 67.2% car, 21.9% public transportation, 0.6% walk, 8.0% work from home; Mean travel time to work: 46.3 minutes

PATTERSON (town). Covers a land area of 32.208 square miles and a water area of 0.696 square miles. Located at 41.48° N. Lat; 73.59° W. Long. Elevation is 443 feet.

History: Patterson is located in a valley which was formerly part of the Patterson Great Swamp. The village, originally named Franklin, was settled about 1770 by Scots discharged from the British army after service in the French and Indian War. The present name was adopted in 1808 when the legislature passed a law abolishing the numerous "Franklins" in the state. The town was then named after Matthew Patterson, an early settler.

Population: 11,974; Growth (since 2000): 5.9%; Density: 371.8 persons per square mile; Race: 86.4% White, 4.8% Black/African American, 3.6% Asian, 0.3% American Indian/Alaska Native, 0.2% Native Hawaiian/Other Pacific Islander, 1.8% Two or more races, 18.0% Hispanic of any race; Average household size: 2.90; Median age: 40.5; Age under 18: 20.2%; Age 65 and over: 13.7%; Males per 100 females: 102.4; Marriage status: 33.2% never married, 55.8% now married, 0.9% separated, 5.1% widowed, 6.0% divorced; Foreign born: 12.7%; Speak English only: 74.5%; With disability: 11.0%; Veterans: 4.3%; Ancestry: 22.4% Italian, 15.0% Irish, 10.1% German, 7.6% English, 4.4% American

Employment: 13.5% management, business, and financial, 4.7% computer, engineering, and science, 13.8% education, legal, community service, arts, and media, 5.1% healthcare practitioners, 17.5% service, 30.2% sales and office, 7.0% natural resources, construction, and maintenance, 8.1% production, transportation, and material moving

Income: Per capita: $33,852; Median household: $94,875; Average household: $108,335; Households with income of $100,000 or more: 45.9%; Poverty rate: 10.8%

Educational Attainment: High school diploma or higher: 91.8%; Bachelor's degree or higher: 33.8%; Graduate/professional degree or higher: 13.6%

School District(s)
Carmel Central SD (KG-12)
Enrollment: 4,210 . . . . (845) 878-2094

Housing: Homeownership rate: 81.6%; Median home value: $322,100; Median year structure built: 1972; Homeowner vacancy rate: 0.0%; Median selected monthly owner costs: $2,622 with a mortgage, $988 without a mortgage; Median gross rent: $1,197 per month; Rental vacancy rate: 6.3%

Health Insurance: 92.5% have insurance; 78.5% have private insurance; 26.8% have public insurance; 7.5% do not have insurance; 6.1% of children under 18 do not have insurance
Transportation: Commute: 85.4% car, 7.3% public transportation, 2.4% walk, 4.1% work from home; Mean travel time to work: 38.9 minutes
Additional Information Contacts
Town of Patterson . . . . (845) 878-6500
   http://www.pattersonny.org

PEACH LAKE (CDP). Covers a land area of 2.664 square miles and a water area of 0.380 square miles. Located at 41.37° N. Lat; 73.58° W. Long. Elevation is 561 feet.
Population: 1,659; Growth (since 2000): -0.7%; Density: 622.8 persons per square mile; Race: 98.7% White, 0.7% Black/African American, 0.4% Asian, 0.0% American Indian/Alaska Native, 0.0% Native Hawaiian/Other Pacific Islander, 0.2% Two or more races, 5.7% Hispanic of any race; Average household size: 2.88; Median age: 46.3; Age under 18: 22.8%; Age 65 and over: 16.9%; Males per 100 females: 95.8; Marriage status: 27.3% never married, 59.1% now married, 2.7% separated, 5.9% widowed, 7.7% divorced; Foreign born: 4.5%; Speak English only: 92.5%; With disability: 7.3%; Veterans: 6.4%; Ancestry: 29.8% Italian, 29.2% Irish, 14.6% German, 10.3% English, 7.6% Polish
Employment: 11.9% management, business, and financial, 6.2% computer, engineering, and science, 18.6% education, legal, community service, arts, and media, 9.2% healthcare practitioners, 17.8% service, 24.3% sales and office, 7.2% natural resources, construction, and maintenance, 4.7% production, transportation, and material moving
Income: Per capita: $47,032; Median household: $116,106; Average household: $131,365; Households with income of $100,000 or more: 56.6%; Poverty rate: 1.3%
Educational Attainment: High school diploma or higher: 95.8%; Bachelor's degree or higher: 55.3%; Graduate/professional degree or higher: 21.3%
Housing: Homeownership rate: 90.6%; Median home value: $408,700; Median year structure built: 1964; Homeowner vacancy rate: 3.5%; Median selected monthly owner costs: $2,514 with a mortgage, $875 without a mortgage; Median gross rent: $2,150 per month; Rental vacancy rate: 0.0%
Health Insurance: 97.8% have insurance; 90.8% have private insurance; 22.4% have public insurance; 2.2% do not have insurance; 1.9% of children under 18 do not have insurance
Transportation: Commute: 84.8% car, 4.1% public transportation, 0.0% walk, 8.6% work from home; Mean travel time to work: 34.8 minutes

PHILIPSTOWN (town). Covers a land area of 48.785 square miles and a water area of 2.785 square miles. Located at 41.41° N. Lat; 73.92° W. Long.
Population: 9,763; Growth (since 2000): 3.6%; Density: 200.1 persons per square mile; Race: 91.1% White, 2.0% Black/African American, 1.8% Asian, 0.2% American Indian/Alaska Native, 0.0% Native Hawaiian/Other Pacific Islander, 3.3% Two or more races, 7.0% Hispanic of any race; Average household size: 2.62; Median age: 47.5; Age under 18: 19.9%; Age 65 and over: 19.8%; Males per 100 females: 95.8; Marriage status: 26.6% never married, 61.3% now married, 1.6% separated, 4.9% widowed, 7.2% divorced; Foreign born: 7.8%; Speak English only: 90.7%; With disability: 10.8%; Veterans: 7.5%; Ancestry: 24.3% Italian, 23.7% Irish, 13.6% German, 11.4% English, 4.4% Polish
Employment: 19.1% management, business, and financial, 5.2% computer, engineering, and science, 20.0% education, legal, community service, arts, and media, 4.9% healthcare practitioners, 15.4% service, 22.2% sales and office, 6.5% natural resources, construction, and maintenance, 6.7% production, transportation, and material moving
Income: Per capita: $56,419; Median household: $108,103; Average household: $151,194; Households with income of $100,000 or more: 55.4%; Poverty rate: 5.0%
Educational Attainment: High school diploma or higher: 96.7%; Bachelor's degree or higher: 52.3%; Graduate/professional degree or higher: 24.7%
Housing: Homeownership rate: 81.1%; Median home value: $479,900; Median year structure built: 1967; Homeowner vacancy rate: 0.9%; Median selected monthly owner costs: $2,794 with a mortgage, $1,196 without a mortgage; Median gross rent: $1,475 per month; Rental vacancy rate: 3.8%

Health Insurance: 96.5% have insurance; 83.5% have private insurance; 27.7% have public insurance; 3.5% do not have insurance; 0.2% of children under 18 do not have insurance
Transportation: Commute: 66.5% car, 19.5% public transportation, 1.4% walk, 11.5% work from home; Mean travel time to work: 44.0 minutes
Additional Information Contacts
Town of Philipstown . . . . (845) 265-3329
   http://philipstown.com

PUTNAM LAKE (CDP). Covers a land area of 3.841 square miles and a water area of 0.419 square miles. Located at 41.47° N. Lat; 73.55° W. Long. Elevation is 512 feet.
Population: 3,506; Growth (since 2000): -9.1%; Density: 912.7 persons per square mile; Race: 86.9% White, 5.9% Black/African American, 1.3% Asian, 0.0% American Indian/Alaska Native, 0.0% Native Hawaiian/Other Pacific Islander, 4.2% Two or more races, 14.5% Hispanic of any race; Average household size: 2.60; Median age: 46.9; Age under 18: 19.3%; Age 65 and over: 13.1%; Males per 100 females: 102.4; Marriage status: 29.2% never married, 57.4% now married, 1.2% separated, 4.9% widowed, 8.5% divorced; Foreign born: 10.3%; Speak English only: 80.6%; With disability: 13.7%; Veterans: 5.6%; Ancestry: 31.5% Italian, 21.8% Irish, 10.0% German, 8.1% English, 4.5% American
Employment: 10.2% management, business, and financial, 4.7% computer, engineering, and science, 15.6% education, legal, community service, arts, and media, 4.5% healthcare practitioners, 20.8% service, 28.3% sales and office, 8.4% natural resources, construction, and maintenance, 7.6% production, transportation, and material moving
Income: Per capita: $40,468; Median household: $95,238; Average household: $104,342; Households with income of $100,000 or more: 47.3%; Poverty rate: 1.6%
Educational Attainment: High school diploma or higher: 92.3%; Bachelor's degree or higher: 31.6%; Graduate/professional degree or higher: 12.2%
Housing: Homeownership rate: 85.4%; Median home value: $228,100; Median year structure built: 1952; Homeowner vacancy rate: 0.0%; Median selected monthly owner costs: $1,984 with a mortgage, $728 without a mortgage; Median gross rent: $1,518 per month; Rental vacancy rate: 0.0%
Health Insurance: 97.4% have insurance; 85.1% have private insurance; 26.1% have public insurance; 2.6% do not have insurance; 0.0% of children under 18 do not have insurance
Transportation: Commute: 92.5% car, 4.5% public transportation, 0.5% walk, 2.3% work from home; Mean travel time to work: 37.2 minutes

PUTNAM VALLEY (town). Covers a land area of 41.175 square miles and a water area of 1.605 square miles. Located at 41.40° N. Lat; 73.84° W. Long. Elevation is 161 feet.
Population: 11,705; Growth (since 2000): 9.5%; Density: 284.3 persons per square mile; Race: 92.8% White, 1.1% Black/African American, 0.7% Asian, 0.4% American Indian/Alaska Native, 0.0% Native Hawaiian/Other Pacific Islander, 3.6% Two or more races, 10.6% Hispanic of any race; Average household size: 2.88; Median age: 44.1; Age under 18: 21.7%; Age 65 and over: 14.7%; Males per 100 females: 101.1; Marriage status: 23.4% never married, 63.5% now married, 2.0% separated, 4.2% widowed, 8.9% divorced; Foreign born: 10.6%; Speak English only: 83.7%; With disability: 9.6%; Veterans: 4.2%; Ancestry: 30.0% Italian, 24.4% Irish, 16.2% German, 7.8% English, 4.8% American
Employment: 20.6% management, business, and financial, 7.4% computer, engineering, and science, 14.1% education, legal, community service, arts, and media, 5.7% healthcare practitioners, 13.3% service, 24.1% sales and office, 10.8% natural resources, construction, and maintenance, 4.1% production, transportation, and material moving
Income: Per capita: $46,956; Median household: $115,133; Average household: $132,487; Households with income of $100,000 or more: 54.8%; Poverty rate: 3.9%
Educational Attainment: High school diploma or higher: 94.1%; Bachelor's degree or higher: 42.3%; Graduate/professional degree or higher: 16.0%
School District(s)
Putnam Valley Central SD (KG-12)
   Enrollment: 1,717 . . . . (845) 528-8143
Housing: Homeownership rate: 90.8%; Median home value: $378,100; Median year structure built: 1961; Homeowner vacancy rate: 2.3%; Median selected monthly owner costs: $2,817 with a mortgage, $1,118 without a

mortgage; Median gross rent: $1,553 per month; Rental vacancy rate: 0.0%

Health Insurance: 98.2% have insurance; 87.7% have private insurance; 23.1% have public insurance; 1.8% do not have insurance; 0.0% of children under 18 do not have insurance

Transportation: Commute: 85.7% car, 8.9% public transportation, 0.6% walk, 4.2% work from home; Mean travel time to work: 42.3 minutes

Additional Information Contacts

Town of Putnam Valley . . . . (845) 526-2121
http://www.putnamvalley.com

SOUTHEAST (town). Covers a land area of 31.734 square miles and a water area of 3.245 square miles. Located at 41.41° N. Lat; 73.60° W. Long.

History: The Tilly Foster Iron Mine (established 1790), located on a 128-acre farm owned by Tilly Foster, was the largest of a number of mines in the area. The town was named after this mine. For a time high-grade iron ore was shipped from here to Pennsylvania. Became open-pit mine in 1889, closed in 1897 after an avalanche.

Population: 18,288; Growth (since 2000): 5.6%; Density: 576.3 persons per square mile; Race: 87.2% White, 2.0% Black/African American, 2.1% Asian, 0.4% American Indian/Alaska Native, 0.0% Native Hawaiian/Other Pacific Islander, 2.1% Two or more races, 20.2% Hispanic of any race; Average household size: 2.73; Median age: 41.5; Age under 18: 22.1%; Age 65 and over: 13.4%; Males per 100 females: 102.5; Marriage status: 31.6% never married, 54.9% now married, 1.1% separated, 4.4% widowed, 9.2% divorced; Foreign born: 16.1%; Speak English only: 78.7%; With disability: 9.0%; Veterans: 5.2%; Ancestry: 28.0% Italian, 22.2% Irish, 12.4% German, 6.1% English, 4.5% American

Employment: 14.6% management, business, and financial, 5.2% computer, engineering, and science, 16.2% education, legal, community service, arts, and media, 5.3% healthcare practitioners, 17.8% service, 24.4% sales and office, 10.0% natural resources, construction, and maintenance, 6.6% production, transportation, and material moving

Income: Per capita: $41,944; Median household: $95,222; Average household: $113,542; Households with income of $100,000 or more: 47.0%; Poverty rate: 4.6%

Educational Attainment: High school diploma or higher: 89.0%; Bachelor's degree or higher: 39.2%; Graduate/professional degree or higher: 17.2%

Housing: Homeownership rate: 75.5%; Median home value: $344,700; Median year structure built: 1976; Homeowner vacancy rate: 0.4%; Median selected monthly owner costs: $2,444 with a mortgage, $1,051 without a mortgage; Median gross rent: $1,330 per month; Rental vacancy rate: 5.7%

Health Insurance: 90.3% have insurance; 77.6% have private insurance; 23.8% have public insurance; 9.7% do not have insurance; 5.0% of children under 18 do not have insurance

Transportation: Commute: 83.5% car, 8.8% public transportation, 1.0% walk, 5.9% work from home; Mean travel time to work: 36.1 minutes

Additional Information Contacts

Town of Southeast . . . . (845) 279-4313
http://www.townofsoutheast-ny.com/Home

Queens County and Borough

See New York City

Rensselaer County

Located in eastern New York; bounded on the west by the Hudson River, and on the east by Massachusetts and Vermont; includes part of the Taconic Mountains; drained by the Hoosic River. Covers a land area of 652.431 square miles, a water area of 12.962 square miles, and is located in the Eastern Time Zone at 42.71° N. Lat., 73.51° W. Long. The county was founded in 1791. County seat is Troy.

Rensselaer County is part of the Albany-Schenectady-Troy, NY Metropolitan Statistical Area. The entire metro area includes: Albany County, NY; Rensselaer County, NY; Saratoga County, NY; Schenectady County, NY; Schoharie County, NY

Weather Station: Grafton   Elevation: 1,560 feet

	Jan	Feb	Mar	Apr	May	Jun	Jul	Aug	Sep	Oct	Nov	Dec
High	28	32	41	54	66	74	78	76	68	57	45	33
Low	12	15	23	34	45	53	58	57	50	39	29	18
Precip	2.9	2.6	3.6	3.9	4.5	4.2	4.5	4.5	4.2	4.0	4.0	3.2
Snow	20.6	14.9	15.4	5.9	0.2	0.0	0.0	0.0	tr	1.3	7.2	17.8

High and Low temperatures in degrees Fahrenheit; Precipitation and Snow in inches

Weather Station: Troy Lock and Dam   Elevation: 23 feet

	Jan	Feb	Mar	Apr	May	Jun	Jul	Aug	Sep	Oct	Nov	Dec
High	32	35	44	59	70	79	84	82	74	62	49	37
Low	15	17	25	37	48	58	63	61	53	41	32	22
Precip	2.2	1.9	3.0	3.3	3.7	4.2	4.4	4.1	3.3	3.7	3.1	2.6
Snow	12.7	8.0	7.5	1.3	0.0	0.0	0.0	0.0	0.0	0.1	1.8	7.2

High and Low temperatures in degrees Fahrenheit; Precipitation and Snow in inches

Population: 159,800; Growth (since 2000): 4.8%; Density: 244.9 persons per square mile; Race: 86.5% White, 6.5% Black/African American, 2.5% Asian, 0.1% American Indian/Alaska Native, 0.0% Native Hawaiian/Other Pacific Islander, 3.5% two or more races, 4.6% Hispanic of any race; Average household size: 2.39; Median age: 39.9; Age under 18: 20.1%; Age 65 and over: 15.6%; Males per 100 females: 97.5; Marriage status: 36.3% never married, 48.0% now married, 2.3% separated, 6.3% widowed, 9.4% divorced; Foreign born: 4.9%; Speak English only: 92.6%; With disability: 13.6%; Veterans: 7.6%; Ancestry: 25.2% Irish, 17.6% German, 15.7% Italian, 9.9% English, 7.7% French

Religion: Six largest groups: 28.1% Catholicism, 3.4% Methodist/Pietist, 1.9% Presbyterian-Reformed, 1.5% Lutheran, 1.3% Baptist, 1.3% Non-denominational Protestant

Economy: Unemployment rate: 3.4%; Leading industries: 14.3 % construction; 14.1 % retail trade; 12.1 % health care and social assistance; Farms: 495 totaling 88,763 acres; Company size: 3 employ 1,000 or more persons, 2 employ 500 to 999 persons, 63 employ 100 to 499 persons, 2,929 employ less than 100 persons; Business ownership: 3,632 women-owned, 560 Black-owned, 256 Hispanic-owned, 197 Asian-owned, 99 American Indian/Alaska Native-owned

Employment: 15.4% management, business, and financial, 7.3% computer, engineering, and science, 11.3% education, legal, community service, arts, and media, 6.0% healthcare practitioners, 16.8% service, 24.4% sales and office, 8.3% natural resources, construction, and maintenance, 10.6% production, transportation, and material moving

Income: Per capita: $33,067; Median household: $63,166; Average household: $80,038; Households with income of $100,000 or more: 27.9%; Poverty rate: 12.6%

Educational Attainment: High school diploma or higher: 91.8%; Bachelor's degree or higher: 29.8%; Graduate/professional degree or higher: 12.8%

Housing: Homeownership rate: 63.4%; Median home value: $183,400; Median year structure built: 1958; Homeowner vacancy rate: 1.5%; Median selected monthly owner costs: $1,608 with a mortgage, $637 without a mortgage; Median gross rent: $908 per month; Rental vacancy rate: 3.5%

Vital Statistics: Birth rate: 100.2 per 10,000 population; Death rate: 98.1 per 10,000 population; Age-adjusted cancer mortality rate: 166.8 deaths per 100,000 population

Health Insurance: 95.2% have insurance; 75.8% have private insurance; 34.0% have public insurance; 4.8% do not have insurance; 2.0% of children under 18 do not have insurance

Health Care: Physicians: 18.6 per 10,000 population; Dentists: 4.4 per 10,000 population; Hospital beds: 24.1 per 10,000 population; Hospital admissions: 760.5 per 10,000 population

Transportation: Commute: 89.1% car, 3.0% public transportation, 3.7% walk, 3.4% work from home; Mean travel time to work: 24.4 minutes

2016 Presidential Election: 47.1% Trump, 45.7% Clinton, 4.1% Johnson, 1.9% Stein

National and State Parks: Crailo State Historic Site; State Forest Rensselaer Number 3

Additional Information Contacts

Rensselaer Government . . . . (518) 270-4080
http://www.rensco.com

Rensselaer County Communities

AVERILL PARK (CDP). Covers a land area of 2.933 square miles and a water area of 0.118 square miles. Located at 42.64° N. Lat; 73.55° W. Long. Elevation is 784 feet.
Population: 1,368; Growth (since 2000): -9.8%; Density: 466.5 persons per square mile; Race: 92.8% White, 0.0% Black/African American, 0.0% Asian, 7.2% American Indian/Alaska Native, 0.0% Native Hawaiian/Other Pacific Islander, 0.0% Two or more races, 7.2% Hispanic of any race; Average household size: 2.31; Median age: 45.5; Age under 18: 16.5%; Age 65 and over: 13.0%; Males per 100 females: 99.9; Marriage status: 22.4% never married, 54.6% now married, 4.7% separated, 7.0% widowed, 15.9% divorced; Foreign born: 8.6%; Speak English only: 83.4%; With disability: 8.6%; Veterans: 6.0%; Ancestry: 22.7% Irish, 20.5% German, 14.0% Polish, 13.9% Italian, 13.5% English
Employment: 15.9% management, business, and financial, 11.0% computer, engineering, and science, 7.9% education, legal, community service, arts, and media, 4.4% healthcare practitioners, 25.1% service, 20.1% sales and office, 7.5% natural resources, construction, and maintenance, 8.0% production, transportation, and material moving
Income: Per capita: $36,611; Median household: $76,912; Average household: $83,223; Households with income of $100,000 or more: 30.9%; Poverty rate: 1.0%
Educational Attainment: High school diploma or higher: 88.9%; Bachelor's degree or higher: 25.0%; Graduate/professional degree or higher: 7.7%

School District(s)
Averill Park Central SD (KG-12)
    Enrollment: 2,784 . . . . (518) 674-7055
Housing: Homeownership rate: 78.7%; Median home value: $212,900; Median year structure built: 1959; Homeowner vacancy rate: 0.0%; Median selected monthly owner costs: $1,653 with a mortgage, $587 without a mortgage; Median gross rent: $631 per month; Rental vacancy rate: 0.0%
Health Insurance: 92.8% have insurance; 88.8% have private insurance; 18.2% have public insurance; 7.2% do not have insurance; 0.0% of children under 18 do not have insurance
Newspapers: The Advertiser (weekly circulation 48,000)
Transportation: Commute: 84.4% car, 3.8% public transportation, 11.9% walk, 0.0% work from home; Mean travel time to work: 25.6 minutes

BERLIN (town). Covers a land area of 59.603 square miles and a water area of 0.319 square miles. Located at 42.66° N. Lat; 73.38° W. Long. Elevation is 840 feet.
Population: 1,565; Growth (since 2000): -17.7%; Density: 26.3 persons per square mile; Race: 99.2% White, 0.0% Black/African American, 0.5% Asian, 0.0% American Indian/Alaska Native, 0.0% Native Hawaiian/Other Pacific Islander, 0.3% Two or more races, 0.3% Hispanic of any race; Average household size: 2.14; Median age: 49.4; Age under 18: 15.1%; Age 65 and over: 23.2%; Males per 100 females: 96.9; Marriage status: 19.6% never married, 57.3% now married, 1.0% separated, 13.3% widowed, 9.7% divorced; Foreign born: 0.3%; Speak English only: 98.6%; With disability: 19.4%; Veterans: 12.7%; Ancestry: 31.4% German, 23.1% Irish, 16.5% English, 11.4% Italian, 9.8% French
Employment: 12.7% management, business, and financial, 7.1% computer, engineering, and science, 13.0% education, legal, community service, arts, and media, 6.8% healthcare practitioners, 13.8% service, 14.7% sales and office, 22.2% natural resources, construction, and maintenance, 9.7% production, transportation, and material moving
Income: Per capita: $29,955; Median household: $50,357; Average household: $63,088; Households with income of $100,000 or more: 21.0%; Poverty rate: 9.4%
Educational Attainment: High school diploma or higher: 90.6%; Bachelor's degree or higher: 27.3%; Graduate/professional degree or higher: 18.4%

School District(s)
Berlin Central SD (PK-12)
    Enrollment: 727. . . . . (518) 658-1500
Housing: Homeownership rate: 78.5%; Median home value: $143,500; Median year structure built: 1965; Homeowner vacancy rate: 1.9%; Median selected monthly owner costs: $1,198 with a mortgage, $548 without a mortgage; Median gross rent: $825 per month; Rental vacancy rate: 14.7%
Health Insurance: 94.9% have insurance; 80.3% have private insurance; 36.8% have public insurance; 5.1% do not have insurance; 11.0% of children under 18 do not have insurance

Transportation: Commute: 97.3% car, 0.3% public transportation, 0.9% walk, 1.5% work from home; Mean travel time to work: 36.8 minutes

BRUNSWICK (town). Covers a land area of 44.347 square miles and a water area of 0.280 square miles. Located at 42.75° N. Lat; 73.58° W. Long. Elevation is 518 feet.
Population: 12,499; Growth (since 2000): 7.2%; Density: 281.8 persons per square mile; Race: 94.8% White, 1.1% Black/African American, 2.0% Asian, 0.0% American Indian/Alaska Native, 0.0% Native Hawaiian/Other Pacific Islander, 1.2% Two or more races, 1.9% Hispanic of any race; Average household size: 2.36; Median age: 47.5; Age under 18: 15.5%; Age 65 and over: 19.0%; Males per 100 females: 97.5; Marriage status: 26.3% never married, 57.2% now married, 1.1% separated, 5.9% widowed, 10.7% divorced; Foreign born: 3.5%; Speak English only: 95.4%; With disability: 13.5%; Veterans: 8.2%; Ancestry: 35.0% Irish, 20.1% German, 18.8% Italian, 11.0% French, 10.5% English
Employment: 15.9% management, business, and financial, 8.0% computer, engineering, and science, 12.2% education, legal, community service, arts, and media, 7.9% healthcare practitioners, 12.4% service, 27.3% sales and office, 7.8% natural resources, construction, and maintenance, 8.6% production, transportation, and material moving
Income: Per capita: $46,122; Median household: $86,115; Average household: $107,183; Households with income of $100,000 or more: 40.3%; Poverty rate: 3.4%
Educational Attainment: High school diploma or higher: 96.3%; Bachelor's degree or higher: 39.2%; Graduate/professional degree or higher: 18.2%
Housing: Homeownership rate: 76.1%; Median home value: $215,100; Median year structure built: 1967; Homeowner vacancy rate: 2.6%; Median selected monthly owner costs: $1,720 with a mortgage, $678 without a mortgage; Median gross rent: $1,091 per month; Rental vacancy rate: 5.4%
Health Insurance: 96.1% have insurance; 86.1% have private insurance; 27.7% have public insurance; 3.9% do not have insurance; 2.4% of children under 18 do not have insurance
Transportation: Commute: 91.7% car, 0.6% public transportation, 1.8% walk, 5.1% work from home; Mean travel time to work: 24.0 minutes
Additional Information Contacts
Town of Brunswick . . . . (518) 279-3461
    http://www.townofbrunswick.org

BUSKIRK (unincorporated postal area)
ZCTA: 12028
    Covers a land area of 22.573 square miles and a water area of 0.274 square miles. Located at 42.93° N. Lat; 73.44° W. Long. Elevation is 364 feet.
    Population: 945; Growth (since 2000): -14.1%; Density: 41.9 persons per square mile; Race: 97.7% White, 0.0% Black/African American, 1.0% Asian, 0.0% American Indian/Alaska Native, 0.0% Native Hawaiian/Other Pacific Islander, 1.4% Two or more races, 3.7% Hispanic of any race; Average household size: 2.98; Median age: 40.6; Age under 18: 22.8%; Age 65 and over: 13.0%; Males per 100 females: 102.8; Marriage status: 22.9% never married, 61.8% now married, 0.0% separated, 7.2% widowed, 8.0% divorced; Foreign born: 5.3%; Speak English only: 93.0%; With disability: 14.7%; Veterans: 8.8%; Ancestry: 22.6% German, 15.0% French, 10.2% Irish, 10.1% English, 8.7% Polish
    Employment: 10.4% management, business, and financial, 4.1% computer, engineering, and science, 6.4% education, legal, community service, arts, and media, 7.2% healthcare practitioners, 25.1% service, 18.0% sales and office, 2.9% natural resources, construction, and maintenance, 25.9% production, transportation, and material moving
    Income: Per capita: $30,238; Median household: $69,338; Average household: $88,944; Households with income of $100,000 or more: 27.4%; Poverty rate: 1.9%
    Educational Attainment: High school diploma or higher: 93.2%; Bachelor's degree or higher: 22.0%; Graduate/professional degree or higher: 9.3%
    Housing: Homeownership rate: 85.5%; Median home value: $154,300; Median year structure built: 1982; Homeowner vacancy rate: 0.0%; Median selected monthly owner costs: $1,276 with a mortgage, $680 without a mortgage; Median gross rent: n/a per month; Rental vacancy rate: 0.0%
    Health Insurance: 96.2% have insurance; 75.8% have private insurance; 30.2% have public insurance; 3.8% do not have insurance; 0.0% of children under 18 do not have insurance

Transportation: Commute: 89.9% car, 2.1% public transportation, 0.0% walk, 8.0% work from home; Mean travel time to work: 31.5 minutes

CASTLETON-ON-HUDSON (village).
Covers a land area of 0.714 square miles and a water area of <.001 square miles. Located at 42.53° N. Lat; 73.75° W. Long. Elevation is 151 feet.

History: Settled by the Dutch c.1630; incorporated 1827.

Population: 1,350; Growth (since 2000): -16.6%; Density: 1,890.6 persons per square mile; Race: 93.9% White, 2.4% Black/African American, 0.0% Asian, 0.2% American Indian/Alaska Native, 0.0% Native Hawaiian/Other Pacific Islander, 2.4% Two or more races, 6.1% Hispanic of any race; Average household size: 2.39; Median age: 43.0; Age under 18: 23.2%; Age 65 and over: 17.7%; Males per 100 females: 88.4; Marriage status: 26.4% never married, 53.0% now married, 1.7% separated, 11.1% widowed, 9.5% divorced; Foreign born: 2.6%; Speak English only: 95.9%; With disability: 11.2%; Veterans: 6.9%; Ancestry: 23.5% Irish, 23.3% German, 20.7% Italian, 11.6% English, 7.6% Polish

Employment: 17.7% management, business, and financial, 7.1% computer, engineering, and science, 12.1% education, legal, community service, arts, and media, 4.9% healthcare practitioners, 15.6% service, 27.1% sales and office, 6.9% natural resources, construction, and maintenance, 8.7% production, transportation, and material moving

Income: Per capita: $32,835; Median household: $71,667; Average household: $80,890; Households with income of $100,000 or more: 29.4%; Poverty rate: 6.8%

Educational Attainment: High school diploma or higher: 93.7%; Bachelor's degree or higher: 38.8%; Graduate/professional degree or higher: 17.7%

School District(s)
East Greenbush Central SD (KG-12)
    Enrollment: 4,096 . . . . (518) 207-2531
Rensselaer-Columbia-Greene Boces
    Enrollment: n/a . . . . (518) 479-6882
Schodack Central SD (KG-12)
    Enrollment: 900 . . . . (518) 732-2297

Housing: Homeownership rate: 70.8%; Median home value: $165,500; Median year structure built: Before 1940; Homeowner vacancy rate: 2.6%; Median selected monthly owner costs: $1,713 with a mortgage, $681 without a mortgage; Median gross rent: $823 per month; Rental vacancy rate: 0.0%

Health Insurance: 97.6% have insurance; 85.5% have private insurance; 23.2% have public insurance; 2.4% do not have insurance; 0.0% of children under 18 do not have insurance

Transportation: Commute: 95.2% car, 1.4% public transportation, 1.2% walk, 2.3% work from home; Mean travel time to work: 26.5 minutes

CHERRY PLAIN (unincorporated postal area)
ZCTA: 12040

Covers a land area of 1.307 square miles and a water area of 0 square miles. Located at 42.64° N. Lat; 73.35° W. Long..

Population: 161; Growth (since 2000): n/a; Density: 123.2 persons per square mile; Race: 100.0% White, 0.0% Black/African American, 0.0% Asian, 0.0% American Indian/Alaska Native, 0.0% Native Hawaiian/Other Pacific Islander, 0.0% Two or more races, 3.1% Hispanic of any race; Average household size: 2.56; Median age: 50.6; Age under 18: 17.4%; Age 65 and over: 3.7%; Males per 100 females: 105.5; Marriage status: 6.0% never married, 81.2% now married, 0.0% separated, 0.0% widowed, 12.8% divorced; Foreign born: 0.0%; Speak English only: 100.0%; With disability: 26.1%; Veterans: 3.8%; Ancestry: 45.3% Italian, 40.4% Irish, 16.1% American, 14.3% German, 8.7% French

Employment: 5.8% management, business, and financial, 3.5% computer, engineering, and science, 14.0% education, legal, community service, arts, and media, 0.0% healthcare practitioners, 12.8% service, 5.8% sales and office, 41.9% natural resources, construction, and maintenance, 16.3% production, transportation, and material moving

Income: Per capita: $16,372; Median household: $40,809; Average household: $41,817; Households with income of $100,000 or more: 12.7%; Poverty rate: 16.1%

Educational Attainment: High school diploma or higher: 85.9%; Bachelor's degree or higher: 8.7%; Graduate/professional degree or higher: 3.3%

School District(s)
Berlin Central SD (PK-12)
    Enrollment: 727 . . . . (518) 658-1500

Housing: Homeownership rate: 100.0%; Median home value: n/a; Median year structure built: Before 1940; Homeowner vacancy rate: 0.0%; Median selected monthly owner costs: $1,294 with a mortgage, $850 without a mortgage; Median gross rent: n/a per month; Rental vacancy rate: 0.0%

Health Insurance: 67.7% have insurance; 46.6% have private insurance; 24.8% have public insurance; 32.3% do not have insurance; 100.0% of children under 18 do not have insurance

Transportation: Commute: 100.0% car, 0.0% public transportation, 0.0% walk, 0.0% work from home; Mean travel time to work: 20.1 minutes

CROPSEYVILLE (unincorporated postal area)
ZCTA: 12052

Covers a land area of 30.302 square miles and a water area of 1.047 square miles. Located at 42.75° N. Lat; 73.48° W. Long. Elevation is 558 feet.

Population: 1,713; Growth (since 2000): 71.3%; Density: 56.5 persons per square mile; Race: 96.3% White, 0.0% Black/African American, 1.1% Asian, 0.0% American Indian/Alaska Native, 0.0% Native Hawaiian/Other Pacific Islander, 2.6% Two or more races, 0.3% Hispanic of any race; Average household size: 2.39; Median age: 44.3; Age under 18: 20.1%; Age 65 and over: 14.2%; Males per 100 females: 105.8; Marriage status: 33.4% never married, 49.7% now married, 6.4% separated, 3.9% widowed, 13.0% divorced; Foreign born: 3.3%; Speak English only: 97.9%; With disability: 8.0%; Veterans: 6.8%; Ancestry: 37.7% Irish, 19.3% German, 15.0% English, 14.4% French, 9.9% Italian

Employment: 12.6% management, business, and financial, 12.6% computer, engineering, and science, 10.8% education, legal, community service, arts, and media, 6.7% healthcare practitioners, 16.4% service, 22.6% sales and office, 13.3% natural resources, construction, and maintenance, 5.1% production, transportation, and material moving

Income: Per capita: $33,465; Median household: $66,579; Average household: $79,759; Households with income of $100,000 or more: 28.7%; Poverty rate: 11.5%

Educational Attainment: High school diploma or higher: 94.8%; Bachelor's degree or higher: 28.3%; Graduate/professional degree or higher: 10.3%

Housing: Homeownership rate: 82.1%; Median home value: $169,000; Median year structure built: 1976; Homeowner vacancy rate: 0.0%; Median selected monthly owner costs: $1,435 with a mortgage, $537 without a mortgage; Median gross rent: $850 per month; Rental vacancy rate: 0.0%

Health Insurance: 91.0% have insurance; 69.4% have private insurance; 31.3% have public insurance; 9.0% do not have insurance; 0.8% of children under 18 do not have insurance

Transportation: Commute: 95.9% car, 0.0% public transportation, 0.0% walk, 3.9% work from home; Mean travel time to work: 39.1 minutes

EAGLE BRIDGE (unincorporated postal area)
ZCTA: 12057

Covers a land area of 35.163 square miles and a water area of 0.012 square miles. Located at 42.97° N. Lat; 73.35° W. Long. Elevation is 404 feet.

Population: 2,162; Growth (since 2000): 26.2%; Density: 61.5 persons per square mile; Race: 96.9% White, 0.0% Black/African American, 2.8% Asian, 0.3% American Indian/Alaska Native, 0.0% Native Hawaiian/Other Pacific Islander, 0.0% Two or more races, 0.0% Hispanic of any race; Average household size: 2.49; Median age: 48.7; Age under 18: 19.0%; Age 65 and over: 19.9%; Males per 100 females: 99.5; Marriage status: 26.5% never married, 57.3% now married, 2.0% separated, 3.7% widowed, 12.5% divorced; Foreign born: 1.3%; Speak English only: 99.7%; With disability: 11.8%; Veterans: 12.4%; Ancestry: 23.8% American, 18.9% Irish, 15.0% English, 14.9% German, 8.8% French

Employment: 11.5% management, business, and financial, 0.0% computer, engineering, and science, 6.1% education, legal, community service, arts, and media, 5.1% healthcare practitioners, 25.1% service, 16.4% sales and office, 11.9% natural resources, construction, and maintenance, 23.9% production, transportation, and material moving

Income: Per capita: $26,963; Median household: $60,625; Average household: $66,008; Households with income of $100,000 or more: 24.0%; Poverty rate: 2.5%

Educational Attainment: High school diploma or higher: 92.6%; Bachelor's degree or higher: 13.2%; Graduate/professional degree or higher: 4.2%

Housing: Homeownership rate: 87.1%; Median home value: $179,000; Median year structure built: 1973; Homeowner vacancy rate: 0.0%; Median selected monthly owner costs: $1,174 with a mortgage, $775 without a mortgage; Median gross rent: $710 per month; Rental vacancy rate: 0.0%

Health Insurance: 98.9% have insurance; 77.3% have private insurance; 39.2% have public insurance; 1.1% do not have insurance; 0.0% of children under 18 do not have insurance

Transportation: Commute: 86.3% car, 0.8% public transportation, 7.8% walk, 5.2% work from home; Mean travel time to work: 26.0 minutes

---

EAST GREENBUSH (CDP). Covers a land area of 2.664 square miles and a water area of 0.006 square miles. Located at 42.59° N. Lat; 73.70° W. Long. Elevation is 341 feet.

Population: 4,582; Growth (since 2000): 12.2%; Density: 1,719.9 persons per square mile; Race: 90.0% White, 2.2% Black/African American, 5.1% Asian, 0.0% American Indian/Alaska Native, 0.0% Native Hawaiian/Other Pacific Islander, 2.5% Two or more races, 0.7% Hispanic of any race; Average household size: 2.54; Median age: 46.1; Age under 18: 20.4%; Age 65 and over: 15.4%; Males per 100 females: 95.3; Marriage status: 27.4% never married, 58.9% now married, 1.0% separated, 6.3% widowed, 7.4% divorced; Foreign born: 7.2%; Speak English only: 92.0%; With disability: 12.1%; Veterans: 10.9%; Ancestry: 18.3% Irish, 17.5% German, 15.7% Italian, 9.9% English, 7.2% Polish

Employment: 23.1% management, business, and financial, 14.2% computer, engineering, and science, 18.8% education, legal, community service, arts, and media, 4.8% healthcare practitioners, 8.2% service, 21.1% sales and office, 5.2% natural resources, construction, and maintenance, 4.6% production, transportation, and material moving

Income: Per capita: $42,184; Median household: $85,588; Average household: $105,002; Households with income of $100,000 or more: 41.1%; Poverty rate: 4.2%

Educational Attainment: High school diploma or higher: 97.8%; Bachelor's degree or higher: 48.9%; Graduate/professional degree or higher: 28.1%

School District(s)
East Greenbush Central SD (KG-12)
    Enrollment: 4,096 . . . . (518) 207-2531

Housing: Homeownership rate: 67.5%; Median home value: $246,900; Median year structure built: 1977; Homeowner vacancy rate: 0.0%; Median selected monthly owner costs: $1,930 with a mortgage, $740 without a mortgage; Median gross rent: $1,147 per month; Rental vacancy rate: 0.0%

Health Insurance: 97.7% have insurance; 88.1% have private insurance; 22.7% have public insurance; 2.3% do not have insurance; 2.6% of children under 18 do not have insurance

Transportation: Commute: 93.7% car, 1.7% public transportation, 0.8% walk, 2.7% work from home; Mean travel time to work: 19.5 minutes

---

EAST GREENBUSH (town). Covers a land area of 24.020 square miles and a water area of 0.274 square miles. Located at 42.61° N. Lat; 73.70° W. Long. Elevation is 341 feet.

Population: 16,403; Growth (since 2000): 5.4%; Density: 682.9 persons per square mile; Race: 92.1% White, 2.0% Black/African American, 4.2% Asian, 0.0% American Indian/Alaska Native, 0.0% Native Hawaiian/Other Pacific Islander, 1.1% Two or more races, 2.0% Hispanic of any race; Average household size: 2.37; Median age: 45.1; Age under 18: 21.5%; Age 65 and over: 17.8%; Males per 100 females: 91.2; Marriage status: 26.2% never married, 57.4% now married, 2.1% separated, 6.5% widowed, 9.8% divorced; Foreign born: 6.0%; Speak English only: 92.5%; With disability: 11.7%; Veterans: 9.0%; Ancestry: 26.9% Irish, 20.0% German, 19.6% Italian, 10.5% English, 7.5% Polish

Employment: 18.5% management, business, and financial, 9.3% computer, engineering, and science, 13.9% education, legal, community service, arts, and media, 6.5% healthcare practitioners, 10.6% service, 28.1% sales and office, 6.4% natural resources, construction, and maintenance, 6.6% production, transportation, and material moving

Income: Per capita: $40,087; Median household: $77,342; Average household: $95,125; Households with income of $100,000 or more: 37.0%; Poverty rate: 5.3%

Educational Attainment: High school diploma or higher: 95.6%; Bachelor's degree or higher: 42.0%; Graduate/professional degree or higher: 20.8%

School District(s)
East Greenbush Central SD (KG-12)
    Enrollment: 4,096 . . . . (518) 207-2531

Housing: Homeownership rate: 77.9%; Median home value: $207,600; Median year structure built: 1975; Homeowner vacancy rate: 1.3%; Median selected monthly owner costs: $1,746 with a mortgage, $654 without a mortgage; Median gross rent: $1,094 per month; Rental vacancy rate: 0.0%

Health Insurance: 97.0% have insurance; 88.0% have private insurance; 25.3% have public insurance; 3.0% do not have insurance; 1.5% of children under 18 do not have insurance

Safety: Violent crime rate: 4.3 per 10,000 population; Property crime rate: 203.5 per 10,000 population

Transportation: Commute: 94.1% car, 1.5% public transportation, 0.8% walk, 3.1% work from home; Mean travel time to work: 19.1 minutes

Additional Information Contacts
Town of East Greenbush . . . . (518) 477-4775
    http://eastgreenbush.org

EAST NASSAU (village). Covers a land area of 4.863 square miles and a water area of 0.009 square miles. Located at 42.54° N. Lat; 73.50° W. Long. Elevation is 571 feet.

Population: 579; Growth (since 2000): 1.4%; Density: 119.1 persons per square mile; Race: 90.8% White, 1.0% Black/African American, 0.9% Asian, 0.9% American Indian/Alaska Native, 0.0% Native Hawaiian/Other Pacific Islander, 5.4% Two or more races, 6.6% Hispanic of any race; Average household size: 2.67; Median age: 40.0; Age under 18: 26.4%; Age 65 and over: 13.8%; Males per 100 females: 105.2; Marriage status: 27.0% never married, 56.2% now married, 5.2% separated, 5.2% widowed, 11.6% divorced; Foreign born: 3.3%; Speak English only: 96.7%; With disability: 7.3%; Veterans: 8.2%; Ancestry: 23.3% Irish, 22.5% German, 13.3% Italian, 7.9% English, 6.0% American

Employment: 14.0% management, business, and financial, 9.9% computer, engineering, and science, 8.9% education, legal, community service, arts, and media, 9.9% healthcare practitioners, 15.4% service, 14.7% sales and office, 17.1% natural resources, construction, and maintenance, 10.2% production, transportation, and material moving

Income: Per capita: $29,836; Median household: $66,875; Average household: $77,230; Households with income of $100,000 or more: 29.5%; Poverty rate: 5.4%

Educational Attainment: High school diploma or higher: 95.3%; Bachelor's degree or higher: 29.4%; Graduate/professional degree or higher: 12.0%

Housing: Homeownership rate: 84.3%; Median home value: $180,700; Median year structure built: 1944; Homeowner vacancy rate: 6.2%; Median selected monthly owner costs: $1,553 with a mortgage, $725 without a mortgage; Median gross rent: $858 per month; Rental vacancy rate: 15.0%

Health Insurance: 94.3% have insurance; 75.1% have private insurance; 32.6% have public insurance; 5.7% do not have insurance; 0.0% of children under 18 do not have insurance

Transportation: Commute: 91.1% car, 1.4% public transportation, 1.4% walk, 4.8% work from home; Mean travel time to work: 34.1 minutes

---

EAST SCHODACK (unincorporated postal area)
ZCTA: 12063

    Covers a land area of 1.425 square miles and a water area of 0.004 square miles. Located at 42.57° N. Lat; 73.64° W. Long. Elevation is 456 feet.

Population: 361; Growth (since 2000): 88.0%; Density: 253.3 persons per square mile; Race: 97.8% White, 0.0% Black/African American, 2.2% Asian, 0.0% American Indian/Alaska Native, 0.0% Native Hawaiian/Other Pacific Islander, 0.0% Two or more races, 0.0% Hispanic of any race; Average household size: 2.62; Median age: 34.3; Age under 18: 23.0%; Age 65 and over: 20.8%; Males per 100 females: 93.0; Marriage status: 19.4% never married, 72.3% now married, 5.8% separated, 0.0% widowed, 8.3% divorced; Foreign born: 2.2%; Speak English only: 97.4%; With disability: 22.2%; Veterans: 10.8%; Ancestry: 21.9% German, 18.6% Irish, 14.4% English, 11.1% Italian, 10.5% American

Employment: 20.6% management, business, and financial, 7.4% computer, engineering, and science, 0.0% education, legal, community service, arts, and media, 18.9% healthcare practitioners, 0.0% service,

45.1% sales and office, 8.0% natural resources, construction, and maintenance, 0.0% production, transportation, and material moving
Income: Per capita: $38,766; Median household: $81,607; Average household: $99,633; Households with income of $100,000 or more: 36.9%; Poverty rate: n/a
Educational Attainment: High school diploma or higher: 100.0%; Bachelor's degree or higher: 47.7%; Graduate/professional degree or higher: 24.0%
Housing: Homeownership rate: 75.4%; Median home value: $198,100; Median year structure built: 1957; Homeowner vacancy rate: 0.0%; Median selected monthly owner costs: $1,596 with a mortgage, $926 without a mortgage; Median gross rent: n/a per month; Rental vacancy rate: 0.0%
Health Insurance: 90.6% have insurance; 70.9% have private insurance; 40.4% have public insurance; 9.4% do not have insurance; 0.0% of children under 18 do not have insurance
Transportation: Commute: 100.0% car, 0.0% public transportation, 0.0% walk, 0.0% work from home; Mean travel time to work: 24.1 minutes

GRAFTON (town). Covers a land area of 44.721 square miles and a water area of 1.241 square miles. Located at 42.76° N. Lat; 73.46° W. Long. Elevation is 1,473 feet.
Population: 2,438; Growth (since 2000): 22.7%; Density: 54.5 persons per square mile; Race: 97.8% White, 0.0% Black/African American, 1.0% Asian, 0.0% American Indian/Alaska Native, 0.0% Native Hawaiian/Other Pacific Islander, 1.2% Two or more races, 3.0% Hispanic of any race; Average household size: 2.36; Median age: 45.1; Age under 18: 21.0%; Age 65 and over: 15.4%; Males per 100 females: 102.5; Marriage status: 32.1% never married, 52.9% now married, 4.1% separated, 4.4% widowed, 10.6% divorced; Foreign born: 1.9%; Speak English only: 97.4%; With disability: 8.6%; Veterans: 7.5%; Ancestry: 34.6% Irish, 20.7% German, 14.0% English, 13.1% French, 9.1% Dutch
Employment: 18.0% management, business, and financial, 8.5% computer, engineering, and science, 10.5% education, legal, community service, arts, and media, 6.3% healthcare practitioners, 15.9% service, 18.9% sales and office, 13.1% natural resources, construction, and maintenance, 8.7% production, transportation, and material moving
Income: Per capita: $34,172; Median household: $65,465; Average household: $79,611; Households with income of $100,000 or more: 30.5%; Poverty rate: 9.8%
Educational Attainment: High school diploma or higher: 94.6%; Bachelor's degree or higher: 30.0%; Graduate/professional degree or higher: 10.4%
Housing: Homeownership rate: 84.4%; Median home value: $172,800; Median year structure built: 1976; Homeowner vacancy rate: 0.0%; Median selected monthly owner costs: $1,499 with a mortgage, $542 without a mortgage; Median gross rent: $935 per month; Rental vacancy rate: 0.0%
Health Insurance: 94.3% have insurance; 74.7% have private insurance; 31.5% have public insurance; 5.7% do not have insurance; 0.0% of children under 18 do not have insurance
Transportation: Commute: 93.3% car, 0.0% public transportation, 0.9% walk, 5.2% work from home; Mean travel time to work: 38.9 minutes

HAMPTON MANOR (CDP). Covers a land area of 0.624 square miles and a water area of 0.023 square miles. Located at 42.62° N. Lat; 73.72° W. Long. Elevation is 207 feet.
Population: 2,172; Growth (since 2000): -14.0%; Density: 3,480.2 persons per square mile; Race: 92.2% White, 2.2% Black/African American, 2.0% Asian, 0.0% American Indian/Alaska Native, 0.0% Native Hawaiian/Other Pacific Islander, 1.5% Two or more races, 2.2% Hispanic of any race; Average household size: 2.12; Median age: 41.9; Age under 18: 23.5%; Age 65 and over: 18.0%; Males per 100 females: 90.9; Marriage status: 33.8% never married, 53.9% now married, 1.6% separated, 5.9% widowed, 6.5% divorced; Foreign born: 3.5%; Speak English only: 94.9%; With disability: 14.7%; Veterans: 5.4%; Ancestry: 39.2% Irish, 21.4% Italian, 19.3% German, 8.1% English, 7.9% French
Employment: 10.8% management, business, and financial, 2.4% computer, engineering, and science, 9.4% education, legal, community service, arts, and media, 4.3% healthcare practitioners, 16.8% service, 36.6% sales and office, 7.9% natural resources, construction, and maintenance, 11.7% production, transportation, and material moving
Income: Per capita: $28,771; Median household: $46,250; Average household: $59,841; Households with income of $100,000 or more: 17.2%; Poverty rate: 13.8%

Educational Attainment: High school diploma or higher: 91.9%; Bachelor's degree or higher: 20.4%; Graduate/professional degree or higher: 14.0%
Housing: Homeownership rate: 75.5%; Median home value: $155,500; Median year structure built: 1950; Homeowner vacancy rate: 0.0%; Median selected monthly owner costs: $1,479 with a mortgage, $521 without a mortgage; Median gross rent: $793 per month; Rental vacancy rate: 0.0%
Health Insurance: 97.8% have insurance; 79.9% have private insurance; 37.5% have public insurance; 2.2% do not have insurance; 0.0% of children under 18 do not have insurance
Transportation: Commute: 96.5% car, 2.2% public transportation, 0.0% walk, 0.0% work from home; Mean travel time to work: 16.3 minutes

HOOSICK (town). Covers a land area of 63.032 square miles and a water area of 0.113 square miles. Located at 42.88° N. Lat; 73.35° W. Long. Elevation is 482 feet.
History: Bennington Battlefield Park is Northeast. Hoosick Falls Historic District. Incorporated 1827.
Population: 6,833; Growth (since 2000): 1.1%; Density: 108.4 persons per square mile; Race: 98.4% White, 0.0% Black/African American, 0.1% Asian, 0.1% American Indian/Alaska Native, 0.0% Native Hawaiian/Other Pacific Islander, 1.2% Two or more races, 2.4% Hispanic of any race; Average household size: 2.46; Median age: 43.1; Age under 18: 22.9%; Age 65 and over: 17.2%; Males per 100 females: 90.7; Marriage status: 34.1% never married, 49.3% now married, 4.6% separated, 7.1% widowed, 9.6% divorced; Foreign born: 1.6%; Speak English only: 96.5%; With disability: 16.2%; Veterans: 10.5%; Ancestry: 26.3% Irish, 13.5% German, 10.4% French, 10.1% English, 8.6% Italian
Employment: 13.4% management, business, and financial, 2.8% computer, engineering, and science, 6.9% education, legal, community service, arts, and media, 9.0% healthcare practitioners, 18.8% service, 22.1% sales and office, 9.0% natural resources, construction, and maintenance, 18.1% production, transportation, and material moving
Income: Per capita: $26,226; Median household: $51,214; Average household: $64,317; Households with income of $100,000 or more: 19.7%; Poverty rate: 15.3%
Educational Attainment: High school diploma or higher: 94.2%; Bachelor's degree or higher: 20.8%; Graduate/professional degree or higher: 3.4%
Housing: Homeownership rate: 67.0%; Median home value: $150,500; Median year structure built: Before 1940; Homeowner vacancy rate: 3.0%; Median selected monthly owner costs: $1,435 with a mortgage, $650 without a mortgage; Median gross rent: $880 per month; Rental vacancy rate: 0.0%
Health Insurance: 94.8% have insurance; 68.5% have private insurance; 42.5% have public insurance; 5.2% do not have insurance; 1.5% of children under 18 do not have insurance
Transportation: Commute: 94.3% car, 0.6% public transportation, 1.6% walk, 3.5% work from home; Mean travel time to work: 27.6 minutes
Additional Information Contacts
Town of Hoosick . . . . (518) 686-4571
  http://townofhoosick.org

HOOSICK FALLS (village). Covers a land area of 1.598 square miles and a water area of 0 square miles. Located at 42.90° N. Lat; 73.35° W. Long. Elevation is 446 feet.
Population: 3,426; Growth (since 2000): -0.3%; Density: 2,143.9 persons per square mile; Race: 98.3% White, 0.0% Black/African American, 0.3% Asian, 0.1% American Indian/Alaska Native, 0.0% Native Hawaiian/Other Pacific Islander, 1.3% Two or more races, 1.5% Hispanic of any race; Average household size: 2.29; Median age: 45.0; Age under 18: 18.3%; Age 65 and over: 19.3%; Males per 100 females: 87.5; Marriage status: 36.2% never married, 46.3% now married, 6.3% separated, 7.3% widowed, 10.1% divorced; Foreign born: 1.9%; Speak English only: 96.5%; With disability: 20.2%; Veterans: 9.7%; Ancestry: 25.0% Irish, 12.4% German, 11.9% American, 10.9% Italian, 10.1% Polish
Employment: 9.3% management, business, and financial, 1.5% computer, engineering, and science, 8.0% education, legal, community service, arts, and media, 7.3% healthcare practitioners, 17.6% service, 27.4% sales and office, 6.9% natural resources, construction, and maintenance, 22.0% production, transportation, and material moving
Income: Per capita: $27,997; Median household: $49,447; Average household: $63,545; Households with income of $100,000 or more: 18.1%; Poverty rate: 13.1%

Educational Attainment: High school diploma or higher: 94.6%; Bachelor's degree or higher: 20.8%; Graduate/professional degree or higher: 4.9%

School District(s)
Hoosick Falls Central SD (PK-12)

    Enrollment: 1,128 . . . . (518) 686-7012

Housing: Homeownership rate: 59.4%; Median home value: $112,400; Median year structure built: Before 1940; Homeowner vacancy rate: 3.0%; Median selected monthly owner costs: $1,334 with a mortgage, $673 without a mortgage; Median gross rent: $842 per month; Rental vacancy rate: 0.0%

Health Insurance: 95.0% have insurance; 73.0% have private insurance; 41.1% have public insurance; 5.0% do not have insurance; 0.0% of children under 18 do not have insurance

Safety: Violent crime rate: 5.9 per 10,000 population; Property crime rate: 114.5 per 10,000 population

Transportation: Commute: 96.8% car, 0.0% public transportation, 2.2% walk, 0.9% work from home; Mean travel time to work: 30.5 minutes

JOHNSONVILLE (unincorporated postal area)
ZCTA: 12094

Covers a land area of 28.234 square miles and a water area of 0.582 square miles. Located at 42.90° N. Lat; 73.49° W. Long. Elevation is 377 feet.

Population: 2,532; Growth (since 2000): 17.1%; Density: 89.7 persons per square mile; Race: 100.0% White, 0.0% Black/African American, 0.0% Asian, 0.0% American Indian/Alaska Native, 0.0% Native Hawaiian/Other Pacific Islander, 0.0% Two or more races, 0.2% Hispanic of any race; Average household size: 2.77; Median age: 35.8; Age under 18: 33.5%; Age 65 and over: 12.4%; Males per 100 females: 100.4; Marriage status: 21.6% never married, 67.9% now married, 6.3% separated, 4.1% widowed, 6.5% divorced; Foreign born: 0.2%; Speak English only: 99.8%; With disability: 12.0%; Veterans: 10.2%; Ancestry: 34.2% German, 33.9% Irish, 11.8% French, 9.6% English, 7.1% French Canadian

Employment: 14.2% management, business, and financial, 5.3% computer, engineering, and science, 6.0% education, legal, community service, arts, and media, 18.5% healthcare practitioners, 9.7% service, 17.8% sales and office, 17.0% natural resources, construction, and maintenance, 11.5% production, transportation, and material moving

Income: Per capita: $30,922; Median household: $81,850; Average household: $85,325; Households with income of $100,000 or more: 30.1%; Poverty rate: 8.2%

Educational Attainment: High school diploma or higher: 92.9%; Bachelor's degree or higher: 24.2%; Graduate/professional degree or higher: 10.0%

Housing: Homeownership rate: 84.6%; Median home value: $182,400; Median year structure built: 1973; Homeowner vacancy rate: 6.3%; Median selected monthly owner costs: $1,476 with a mortgage, $620 without a mortgage; Median gross rent: $1,052 per month; Rental vacancy rate: 0.0%

Health Insurance: 96.0% have insurance; 83.6% have private insurance; 26.1% have public insurance; 4.0% do not have insurance; 0.0% of children under 18 do not have insurance

Transportation: Commute: 95.3% car, 0.0% public transportation, 0.9% walk, 1.7% work from home; Mean travel time to work: 39.2 minutes

MELROSE (unincorporated postal area)
ZCTA: 12121

Covers a land area of 20.614 square miles and a water area of 2.959 square miles. Located at 42.84° N. Lat; 73.61° W. Long. Elevation is 390 feet.

Population: 1,680; Growth (since 2000): -7.0%; Density: 81.5 persons per square mile; Race: 96.8% White, 1.4% Black/African American, 0.4% Asian, 0.0% American Indian/Alaska Native, 0.0% Native Hawaiian/Other Pacific Islander, 0.8% Two or more races, 0.6% Hispanic of any race; Average household size: 2.75; Median age: 46.6; Age under 18: 18.1%; Age 65 and over: 20.8%; Males per 100 females: 97.3; Marriage status: 20.0% never married, 66.6% now married, 1.9% separated, 5.8% widowed, 7.6% divorced; Foreign born: 2.4%; Speak English only: 97.3%; With disability: 9.4%; Veterans: 6.5%; Ancestry: 19.3% Irish, 14.1% German, 13.5% English, 9.7% French, 9.3% Italian

Employment: 20.4% management, business, and financial, 8.0% computer, engineering, and science, 5.5% education, legal, community service, arts, and media, 3.7% healthcare practitioners, 14.9% service,

---

34.5% sales and office, 4.2% natural resources, construction, and maintenance, 8.8% production, transportation, and material moving

Income: Per capita: $32,726; Median household: $79,817; Average household: $86,984; Households with income of $100,000 or more: 29.6%; Poverty rate: 3.5%

Educational Attainment: High school diploma or higher: 95.7%; Bachelor's degree or higher: 20.0%; Graduate/professional degree or higher: 8.2%

Housing: Homeownership rate: 95.2%; Median home value: $199,800; Median year structure built: 1970; Homeowner vacancy rate: 0.0%; Median selected monthly owner costs: $1,639 with a mortgage, $605 without a mortgage; Median gross rent: n/a per month; Rental vacancy rate: 0.0%

Health Insurance: 99.2% have insurance; 89.9% have private insurance; 31.3% have public insurance; 0.8% do not have insurance; 0.0% of children under 18 do not have insurance

Transportation: Commute: 96.6% car, 0.0% public transportation, 0.0% walk, 2.5% work from home; Mean travel time to work: 31.2 minutes

NASSAU (town). Covers a land area of 44.444 square miles and a water area of 0.792 square miles. Located at 42.55° N. Lat; 73.54° W. Long. Elevation is 404 feet.

Population: 4,804; Growth (since 2000): -0.3%; Density: 108.1 persons per square mile; Race: 96.9% White, 0.4% Black/African American, 0.3% Asian, 0.1% American Indian/Alaska Native, 0.0% Native Hawaiian/Other Pacific Islander, 1.4% Two or more races, 2.0% Hispanic of any race; Average household size: 2.53; Median age: 43.2; Age under 18: 23.5%; Age 65 and over: 16.3%; Males per 100 females: 102.0; Marriage status: 25.4% never married, 58.1% now married, 3.6% separated, 5.5% widowed, 10.9% divorced; Foreign born: 1.8%; Speak English only: 98.6%; With disability: 17.1%; Veterans: 7.1%; Ancestry: 27.4% Irish, 26.0% German, 16.8% Italian, 10.7% English, 6.8% Polish

Employment: 16.1% management, business, and financial, 5.7% computer, engineering, and science, 8.5% education, legal, community service, arts, and media, 5.7% healthcare practitioners, 17.0% service, 19.5% sales and office, 12.1% natural resources, construction, and maintenance, 15.6% production, transportation, and material moving

Income: Per capita: $34,005; Median household: $73,208; Average household: $85,223; Households with income of $100,000 or more: 36.1%; Poverty rate: 6.2%

Educational Attainment: High school diploma or higher: 93.0%; Bachelor's degree or higher: 24.2%; Graduate/professional degree or higher: 11.5%

School District(s)
East Greenbush Central SD (KG-12)

    Enrollment: 4,096 . . . . (518) 207-2531

Housing: Homeownership rate: 78.2%; Median home value: $183,900; Median year structure built: 1954; Homeowner vacancy rate: 1.3%; Median selected monthly owner costs: $1,648 with a mortgage, $705 without a mortgage; Median gross rent: $883 per month; Rental vacancy rate: 14.6%

Health Insurance: 97.7% have insurance; 84.6% have private insurance; 33.5% have public insurance; 2.3% do not have insurance; 0.4% of children under 18 do not have insurance

Transportation: Commute: 96.1% car, 1.0% public transportation, 0.5% walk, 1.7% work from home; Mean travel time to work: 28.6 minutes

Additional Information Contacts

Town of Nassau . . . . (518) 766-2343
    http://townofnassau.org/content

NASSAU (village). Covers a land area of 0.699 square miles and a water area of 0 square miles. Located at 42.51° N. Lat; 73.61° W. Long. Elevation is 404 feet.

Population: 1,010; Growth (since 2000): -13.0%; Density: 1,445.4 persons per square mile; Race: 95.7% White, 0.2% Black/African American, 0.0% Asian, 0.2% American Indian/Alaska Native, 0.0% Native Hawaiian/Other Pacific Islander, 3.7% Two or more races, 2.8% Hispanic of any race; Average household size: 2.34; Median age: 40.2; Age under 18: 22.0%; Age 65 and over: 15.7%; Males per 100 females: 94.0; Marriage status: 26.4% never married, 61.0% now married, 1.6% separated, 3.8% widowed, 8.8% divorced; Foreign born: 0.6%; Speak English only: 98.1%; With disability: 16.6%; Veterans: 7.0%; Ancestry: 38.3% Irish, 33.0% German, 14.7% Italian, 13.9% English, 6.1% American

Employment: 11.4% management, business, and financial, 4.1% computer, engineering, and science, 11.8% education, legal, community service, arts, and media, 5.3% healthcare practitioners, 17.5% service,

27.6% sales and office, 11.6% natural resources, construction, and maintenance, 10.7% production, transportation, and material moving
Income: Per capita: $32,071; Median household: $67,308; Average household: $75,260; Households with income of $100,000 or more: 25.1%; Poverty rate: 6.7%
Educational Attainment: High school diploma or higher: 93.1%; Bachelor's degree or higher: 25.1%; Graduate/professional degree or higher: 9.4%

School District(s)
East Greenbush Central SD (KG-12)
    Enrollment: 4,096 . . . . (518) 207-2531
Housing: Homeownership rate: 63.0%; Median home value: $165,600; Median year structure built: 1943; Homeowner vacancy rate: 2.9%; Median selected monthly owner costs: $1,603 with a mortgage, $703 without a mortgage; Median gross rent: $753 per month; Rental vacancy rate: 11.6%
Health Insurance: 97.8% have insurance; 83.9% have private insurance; 30.6% have public insurance; 2.2% do not have insurance; 2.2% of children under 18 do not have insurance
Safety: Violent crime rate: 26.9 per 10,000 population; Property crime rate: 26.9 per 10,000 population
Transportation: Commute: 92.0% car, 2.4% public transportation, 1.3% walk, 3.6% work from home; Mean travel time to work: 27.8 minutes

NORTH GREENBUSH (town). Covers a land area of 18.545 square miles and a water area of 0.363 square miles. Located at 42.67° N. Lat; 73.67° W. Long.
Population: 12,147; Growth (since 2000): 12.4%; Density: 655.0 persons per square mile; Race: 95.0% White, 2.2% Black/African American, 0.9% Asian, 0.0% American Indian/Alaska Native, 0.0% Native Hawaiian/Other Pacific Islander, 1.4% Two or more races, 3.9% Hispanic of any race; Average household size: 2.33; Median age: 47.0; Age under 18: 17.2%; Age 65 and over: 22.2%; Males per 100 females: 88.8; Marriage status: 28.0% never married, 53.5% now married, 1.5% separated, 9.8% widowed, 8.8% divorced; Foreign born: 6.0%; Speak English only: 91.3%; With disability: 12.8%; Veterans: 9.7%; Ancestry: 27.2% Irish, 23.1% German, 21.3% Italian, 10.1% English, 8.2% Polish
Employment: 20.3% management, business, and financial, 7.6% computer, engineering, and science, 13.0% education, legal, community service, arts, and media, 5.4% healthcare practitioners, 14.8% service, 24.5% sales and office, 6.6% natural resources, construction, and maintenance, 7.8% production, transportation, and material moving
Income: Per capita: $41,003; Median household: $76,113; Average household: $95,877; Households with income of $100,000 or more: 37.0%; Poverty rate: 3.3%
Educational Attainment: High school diploma or higher: 93.4%; Bachelor's degree or higher: 37.3%; Graduate/professional degree or higher: 16.4%
Housing: Homeownership rate: 72.3%; Median home value: $214,400; Median year structure built: 1965; Homeowner vacancy rate: 0.4%; Median selected monthly owner costs: $1,684 with a mortgage, $622 without a mortgage; Median gross rent: $1,137 per month; Rental vacancy rate: 1.8%
Health Insurance: 97.0% have insurance; 84.9% have private insurance; 29.0% have public insurance; 3.0% do not have insurance; 0.9% of children under 18 do not have insurance
Safety: Violent crime rate: 6.5 per 10,000 population; Property crime rate: 124.2 per 10,000 population
Transportation: Commute: 92.0% car, 0.6% public transportation, 0.9% walk, 6.1% work from home; Mean travel time to work: 21.6 minutes
Additional Information Contacts
Town of North Greenbush . . . . (518) 283-4306
    http://www.townofng.com

PETERSBURGH (town). Aka Petersburg. Covers a land area of 41.605 square miles and a water area of 0.003 square miles. Located at 42.78° N. Lat; 73.33° W. Long.
Population: 1,532; Growth (since 2000): -2.0%; Density: 36.8 persons per square mile; Race: 98.8% White, 0.0% Black/African American, 0.0% Asian, 0.0% American Indian/Alaska Native, 0.0% Native Hawaiian/Other Pacific Islander, 1.0% Two or more races, 1.7% Hispanic of any race; Average household size: 2.34; Median age: 49.6; Age under 18: 14.7%; Age 65 and over: 24.7%; Males per 100 females: 110.9; Marriage status: 21.5% never married, 51.9% now married, 1.1% separated, 8.1% widowed, 18.5% divorced; Foreign born: 4.9%; Speak English only: 96.8%;

With disability: 16.9%; Veterans: 11.4%; Ancestry: 25.0% Irish, 23.7% German, 17.6% English, 9.5% Italian, 8.7% French
Employment: 15.3% management, business, and financial, 2.4% computer, engineering, and science, 10.3% education, legal, community service, arts, and media, 6.1% healthcare practitioners, 16.1% service, 17.6% sales and office, 8.9% natural resources, construction, and maintenance, 23.4% production, transportation, and material moving
Income: Per capita: $31,318; Median household: $53,472; Average household: $70,871; Households with income of $100,000 or more: 23.6%; Poverty rate: 9.7%
Educational Attainment: High school diploma or higher: 86.2%; Bachelor's degree or higher: 22.9%; Graduate/professional degree or higher: 11.2%
Housing: Homeownership rate: 88.9%; Median home value: $141,900; Median year structure built: 1976; Homeowner vacancy rate: 0.5%; Median selected monthly owner costs: $1,373 with a mortgage, $511 without a mortgage; Median gross rent: $727 per month; Rental vacancy rate: 11.0%
Health Insurance: 93.2% have insurance; 72.0% have private insurance; 39.9% have public insurance; 6.8% do not have insurance; 0.0% of children under 18 do not have insurance
Transportation: Commute: 92.3% car, 0.4% public transportation, 2.9% walk, 4.4% work from home; Mean travel time to work: 34.2 minutes

PITTSTOWN (town). Covers a land area of 61.628 square miles and a water area of 3.216 square miles. Located at 42.87° N. Lat; 73.52° W. Long. Elevation is 568 feet.
Population: 5,717; Growth (since 2000): 1.3%; Density: 92.8 persons per square mile; Race: 99.4% White, 0.0% Black/African American, 0.0% Asian, 0.0% American Indian/Alaska Native, 0.0% Native Hawaiian/Other Pacific Islander, 0.6% Two or more races, 0.6% Hispanic of any race; Average household size: 2.72; Median age: 38.5; Age under 18: 23.7%; Age 65 and over: 13.8%; Males per 100 females: 99.5; Marriage status: 21.3% never married, 62.6% now married, 3.0% separated, 7.3% widowed, 8.8% divorced; Foreign born: 2.0%; Speak English only: 98.2%; With disability: 12.5%; Veterans: 8.4%; Ancestry: 32.2% German, 24.2% Irish, 13.9% English, 7.9% Italian, 5.5% French
Employment: 14.1% management, business, and financial, 6.9% computer, engineering, and science, 6.1% education, legal, community service, arts, and media, 10.6% healthcare practitioners, 16.5% service, 24.7% sales and office, 10.6% natural resources, construction, and maintenance, 10.5% production, transportation, and material moving
Income: Per capita: $34,018; Median household: $79,698; Average household: $89,848; Households with income of $100,000 or more: 32.7%; Poverty rate: 6.3%
Educational Attainment: High school diploma or higher: 93.3%; Bachelor's degree or higher: 22.7%; Graduate/professional degree or higher: 9.0%
Housing: Homeownership rate: 83.6%; Median home value: $187,100; Median year structure built: 1973; Homeowner vacancy rate: 3.0%; Median selected monthly owner costs: $1,639 with a mortgage, $632 without a mortgage; Median gross rent: $882 per month; Rental vacancy rate: 0.0%
Health Insurance: 95.3% have insurance; 86.3% have private insurance; 23.8% have public insurance; 4.7% do not have insurance; 0.1% of children under 18 do not have insurance
Transportation: Commute: 96.0% car, 0.0% public transportation, 0.0% walk, 2.4% work from home; Mean travel time to work: 36.5 minutes
Additional Information Contacts
Town of Pittstown . . . . (518) 753-4222
    http://pittstown.us

POESTENKILL (CDP). Covers a land area of 5.876 square miles and a water area of 0.066 square miles. Located at 42.70° N. Lat; 73.54° W. Long. Elevation is 479 feet.
Population: 916; Growth (since 2000): -10.5%; Density: 155.9 persons per square mile; Race: 99.1% White, 0.0% Black/African American, 0.0% Asian, 0.9% American Indian/Alaska Native, 0.0% Native Hawaiian/Other Pacific Islander, 0.0% Two or more races, 0.0% Hispanic of any race; Average household size: 2.24; Median age: 48.1; Age under 18: 20.0%; Age 65 and over: 27.7%; Males per 100 females: 90.8; Marriage status: 21.4% never married, 49.3% now married, 1.4% separated, 13.7% widowed, 15.6% divorced; Foreign born: 0.0%; Speak English only: 96.4%; With disability: 11.8%; Veterans: 5.9%; Ancestry: 34.8% Irish, 17.4% English, 16.9% French, 14.5% Italian, 11.2% German
Employment: 9.6% management, business, and financial, 5.3% computer, engineering, and science, 2.7% education, legal, community service, arts,

and media, 10.3% healthcare practitioners, 14.9% service, 36.2% sales and office, 15.1% natural resources, construction, and maintenance, 5.9% production, transportation, and material moving
Income: Per capita: $37,468; Median household: $87,188; Average household: $82,394; Households with income of $100,000 or more: 39.1%; Poverty rate: 4.8%
Educational Attainment: High school diploma or higher: 93.0%; Bachelor's degree or higher: 12.9%; Graduate/professional degree or higher: 8.5%

School District(s)
Averill Park Central SD (KG-12)
    Enrollment: 2,784 . . . . (518) 674-7055
Housing: Homeownership rate: 89.5%; Median home value: $204,200; Median year structure built: 1959; Homeowner vacancy rate: 0.0%; Median selected monthly owner costs: $1,691 with a mortgage, $632 without a mortgage; Median gross rent: $675 per month; Rental vacancy rate: 0.0%
Health Insurance: 98.0% have insurance; 86.1% have private insurance; 38.2% have public insurance; 2.0% do not have insurance; 0.0% of children under 18 do not have insurance
Transportation: Commute: 98.3% car, 0.0% public transportation, 0.0% walk, 1.7% work from home; Mean travel time to work: 30.5 minutes

POESTENKILL (town). Covers a land area of 32.355 square miles and a water area of 0.220 square miles. Located at 42.70° N. Lat; 73.52° W. Long. Elevation is 479 feet.
Population: 4,508; Growth (since 2000): 11.2%; Density: 139.3 persons per square mile; Race: 98.2% White, 0.6% Black/African American, 0.0% Asian, 0.2% American Indian/Alaska Native, 0.0% Native Hawaiian/Other Pacific Islander, 1.1% Two or more races, 1.3% Hispanic of any race; Average household size: 2.71; Median age: 43.5; Age under 18: 23.6%; Age 65 and over: 15.0%; Males per 100 females: 98.4; Marriage status: 25.1% never married, 59.1% now married, 1.0% separated, 6.1% widowed, 9.7% divorced; Foreign born: 1.0%; Speak English only: 97.3%; With disability: 7.8%; Veterans: 6.9%; Ancestry: 25.5% Irish, 18.8% German, 17.1% English, 16.7% Italian, 9.1% French
Employment: 14.7% management, business, and financial, 8.2% computer, engineering, and science, 7.8% education, legal, community service, arts, and media, 6.4% healthcare practitioners, 16.9% service, 28.4% sales and office, 8.1% natural resources, construction, and maintenance, 9.5% production, transportation, and material moving
Income: Per capita: $41,401; Median household: $95,876; Average household: $109,687; Households with income of $100,000 or more: 41.9%; Poverty rate: 4.1%
Educational Attainment: High school diploma or higher: 94.5%; Bachelor's degree or higher: 30.6%; Graduate/professional degree or higher: 14.2%

School District(s)
Averill Park Central SD (KG-12)
    Enrollment: 2,784 . . . . (518) 674-7055
Housing: Homeownership rate: 82.5%; Median home value: $212,300; Median year structure built: 1962; Homeowner vacancy rate: 1.8%; Median selected monthly owner costs: $1,817 with a mortgage, $609 without a mortgage; Median gross rent: $748 per month; Rental vacancy rate: 0.0%
Health Insurance: 98.6% have insurance; 91.1% have private insurance; 21.7% have public insurance; 1.4% do not have insurance; 0.6% of children under 18 do not have insurance
Transportation: Commute: 96.9% car, 0.0% public transportation, 0.7% walk, 1.3% work from home; Mean travel time to work: 26.9 minutes
Additional Information Contacts
Town of Poestenkill . . . . (518) 283-5100
    http://poestenkillny.com/content

RENSSELAER (city). Covers a land area of 3.171 square miles and a water area of 0.334 square miles. Located at 42.65° N. Lat; 73.73° W. Long. Elevation is 16 feet.
History: The city was formed by the union of several villages within the tract granted to Kiliaen Van Rensselaer by the chartered Dutch West Indies Company. At the 17th-century Fort Crailo, now a museum, the British surgeon Richard Shuckburg is said to have written "Yankee Doodle." Settled 1630 by Dutch, incorporated 1897.
Population: 9,375; Growth (since 2000): 20.8%; Density: 2,956.9 persons per square mile; Race: 77.1% White, 5.6% Black/African American, 7.9% Asian, 0.1% American Indian/Alaska Native, 0.0% Native Hawaiian/Other Pacific Islander, 6.7% Two or more races, 5.9% Hispanic of any race; Average household size: 2.25; Median age: 34.9; Age under 18: 20.5%;

Age 65 and over: 14.1%; Males per 100 females: 92.7; Marriage status: 38.8% never married, 42.5% now married, 4.0% separated, 8.7% widowed, 10.1% divorced; Foreign born: 7.2%; Speak English only: 93.5%; With disability: 15.1%; Veterans: 9.0%; Ancestry: 27.2% Irish, 17.8% German, 13.4% Italian, 5.7% French, 5.6% English
Employment: 14.5% management, business, and financial, 3.7% computer, engineering, and science, 9.9% education, legal, community service, arts, and media, 8.0% healthcare practitioners, 19.6% service, 20.0% sales and office, 13.3% natural resources, construction, and maintenance, 10.9% production, transportation, and material moving
Income: Per capita: $29,622; Median household: $49,773; Average household: $65,326; Households with income of $100,000 or more: 20.5%; Poverty rate: 15.3%
Educational Attainment: High school diploma or higher: 89.3%; Bachelor's degree or higher: 25.2%; Graduate/professional degree or higher: 11.5%

School District(s)
East Greenbush Central SD (KG-12)
    Enrollment: 4,096 . . . . (518) 207-2531
New York State Office of Children and Family Services (OCFS) (06-12)
    Enrollment: 311 . . . . (518) 473-7793
Rensselaer City SD (PK-12)
    Enrollment: 1,156 . . . . (518) 465-7509
Housing: Homeownership rate: 39.4%; Median home value: $126,800; Median year structure built: 1946; Homeowner vacancy rate: 0.7%; Median selected monthly owner costs: $1,265 with a mortgage, $574 without a mortgage; Median gross rent: $916 per month; Rental vacancy rate: 2.4%
Health Insurance: 93.6% have insurance; 63.9% have private insurance; 43.4% have public insurance; 6.4% do not have insurance; 2.4% of children under 18 do not have insurance
Safety: Violent crime rate: 13.9 per 10,000 population; Property crime rate: 125.4 per 10,000 population
Transportation: Commute: 89.0% car, 5.4% public transportation, 1.2% walk, 3.1% work from home; Mean travel time to work: 22.3 minutes; Amtrak: Train service available.
Additional Information Contacts
City of Rensselaer . . . . (518) 462-4266
    http://www.rensselaerny.gov/Home.aspx

SAND LAKE (town). Covers a land area of 35.049 square miles and a water area of 1.120 square miles. Located at 42.63° N. Lat; 73.54° W. Long. Elevation is 781 feet.
Population: 8,476; Growth (since 2000): 6.1%; Density: 241.8 persons per square mile; Race: 97.8% White, 0.5% Black/African American, 0.0% Asian, 1.2% American Indian/Alaska Native, 0.0% Native Hawaiian/Other Pacific Islander, 0.1% Two or more races, 2.2% Hispanic of any race; Average household size: 2.60; Median age: 45.0; Age under 18: 20.0%; Age 65 and over: 17.3%; Males per 100 females: 98.3; Marriage status: 25.1% never married, 61.2% now married, 1.2% separated, 5.6% widowed, 8.2% divorced; Foreign born: 4.1%; Speak English only: 94.1%; With disability: 9.2%; Veterans: 9.2%; Ancestry: 24.4% German, 20.5% Irish, 15.5% Italian, 11.0% English, 9.0% Polish
Employment: 14.2% management, business, and financial, 9.0% computer, engineering, and science, 10.6% education, legal, community service, arts, and media, 4.4% healthcare practitioners, 17.7% service, 22.2% sales and office, 11.0% natural resources, construction, and maintenance, 10.8% production, transportation, and material moving
Income: Per capita: $40,117; Median household: $87,259; Average household: $103,608; Households with income of $100,000 or more: 40.1%; Poverty rate: 4.6%
Educational Attainment: High school diploma or higher: 93.0%; Bachelor's degree or higher: 32.9%; Graduate/professional degree or higher: 15.5%
Housing: Homeownership rate: 90.3%; Median home value: $231,500; Median year structure built: 1968; Homeowner vacancy rate: 1.7%; Median selected monthly owner costs: $1,721 with a mortgage, $777 without a mortgage; Median gross rent: $774 per month; Rental vacancy rate: 7.0%
Health Insurance: 96.7% have insurance; 88.2% have private insurance; 25.4% have public insurance; 3.3% do not have insurance; 0.7% of children under 18 do not have insurance
Transportation: Commute: 92.9% car, 1.1% public transportation, 2.5% walk, 2.0% work from home; Mean travel time to work: 25.0 minutes
Additional Information Contacts
Town of Sand Lake . . . . (518) 674-2026
    http://townofsandlake.us/content

SCHAGHTICOKE (town).
Covers a land area of 49.747 square miles and a water area of 2.114 square miles. Located at 42.88° N. Lat; 73.61° W. Long. Elevation is 358 feet.

History: On the northern border of the county, north of Troy, the town contains a village, also called Schaghticoke, and part of the village of Valley Falls. It was named for the Native American tribe formed in the seventeenth century from remnant peoples of eastern New York and New England, which has one of the oldest reservations in the United States.

Population: 7,615; Growth (since 2000): 2.1%; Density: 153.1 persons per square mile; Race: 93.8% White, 2.8% Black/African American, 0.9% Asian, 0.1% American Indian/Alaska Native, 0.0% Native Hawaiian/Other Pacific Islander, 1.9% Two or more races, 1.4% Hispanic of any race; Average household size: 2.66; Median age: 42.7; Age under 18: 21.3%; Age 65 and over: 18.6%; Males per 100 females: 98.8; Marriage status: 28.2% never married, 55.8% now married, 1.8% separated, 7.9% widowed, 8.1% divorced; Foreign born: 2.7%; Speak English only: 95.9%; With disability: 12.7%; Veterans: 7.8%; Ancestry: 31.8% Irish, 16.1% Italian, 13.1% French, 12.4% English, 11.6% German

Employment: 17.6% management, business, and financial, 4.5% computer, engineering, and science, 7.1% education, legal, community service, arts, and media, 4.9% healthcare practitioners, 16.0% service, 25.2% sales and office, 12.2% natural resources, construction, and maintenance, 12.5% production, transportation, and material moving

Income: Per capita: $32,106; Median household: $69,923; Average household: $84,077; Households with income of $100,000 or more: 30.0%; Poverty rate: 11.7%

Educational Attainment: High school diploma or higher: 90.3%; Bachelor's degree or higher: 17.7%; Graduate/professional degree or higher: 4.5%

School District(s)
Hoosic Valley Central SD (KG-12)
    Enrollment: 951. . . . . (518) 753-4450

Housing: Homeownership rate: 85.7%; Median home value: $177,800; Median year structure built: 1964; Homeowner vacancy rate: 0.2%; Median selected monthly owner costs: $1,562 with a mortgage, $601 without a mortgage; Median gross rent: $729 per month; Rental vacancy rate: 0.0%

Health Insurance: 96.2% have insurance; 77.4% have private insurance; 35.0% have public insurance; 3.8% do not have insurance; 1.2% of children under 18 do not have insurance

Transportation: Commute: 97.0% car, 0.3% public transportation, 0.1% walk, 1.6% work from home; Mean travel time to work: 28.5 minutes

Additional Information Contacts
Town of Schaghticoke. . . . . (518) 753-6915
    http://townofschaghticoke.org/content

SCHAGHTICOKE (village).
Covers a land area of 0.758 square miles and a water area of 0.235 square miles. Located at 42.90° N. Lat; 73.59° W. Long. Elevation is 358 feet.

Population: 568; Growth (since 2000): -16.0%; Density: 749.2 persons per square mile; Race: 99.1% White, 0.0% Black/African American, 0.0% Asian, 0.9% American Indian/Alaska Native, 0.0% Native Hawaiian/Other Pacific Islander, 0.0% Two or more races, 0.0% Hispanic of any race; Average household size: 2.38; Median age: 39.8; Age under 18: 24.8%; Age 65 and over: 18.5%; Males per 100 females: 110.7; Marriage status: 26.1% never married, 52.6% now married, 2.0% separated, 6.7% widowed, 14.6% divorced; Foreign born: 0.0%; Speak English only: 97.4%; With disability: 23.1%; Veterans: 11.9%; Ancestry: 24.5% Irish, 20.6% German, 13.6% Italian, 11.1% French, 9.9% English

Employment: 4.2% management, business, and financial, 7.6% computer, engineering, and science, 5.1% education, legal, community service, arts, and media, 5.5% healthcare practitioners, 11.8% service, 26.2% sales and office, 26.2% natural resources, construction, and maintenance, 13.5% production, transportation, and material moving

Income: Per capita: $24,856; Median household: $47,656; Average household: $58,794; Households with income of $100,000 or more: 15.9%; Poverty rate: 23.1%

Educational Attainment: High school diploma or higher: 86.8%; Bachelor's degree or higher: 13.2%; Graduate/professional degree or higher: 4.9%

School District(s)
Hoosic Valley Central SD (KG-12)
    Enrollment: 951. . . . . (518) 753-4450

Housing: Homeownership rate: 65.7%; Median home value: $154,600; Median year structure built: Before 1940; Homeowner vacancy rate: 0.0%; Median selected monthly owner costs: $1,409 with a mortgage, $557 without a mortgage; Median gross rent: $608 per month; Rental vacancy rate: 0.0%

Health Insurance: 93.5% have insurance; 68.3% have private insurance; 47.7% have public insurance; 6.5% do not have insurance; 0.0% of children under 18 do not have insurance

Transportation: Commute: 94.9% car, 0.0% public transportation, 2.1% walk, 2.1% work from home; Mean travel time to work: 31.5 minutes

SCHODACK (town).
Covers a land area of 61.927 square miles and a water area of 1.676 square miles. Located at 42.53° N. Lat; 73.68° W. Long.

Population: 13,156; Growth (since 2000): 4.9%; Density: 212.4 persons per square mile; Race: 94.8% White, 1.7% Black/African American, 0.3% Asian, 0.0% American Indian/Alaska Native, 0.1% Native Hawaiian/Other Pacific Islander, 2.5% Two or more races, 1.8% Hispanic of any race; Average household size: 2.59; Median age: 44.1; Age under 18: 20.7%; Age 65 and over: 17.1%; Males per 100 females: 97.2; Marriage status: 27.7% never married, 59.6% now married, 3.1% separated, 5.6% widowed, 7.1% divorced; Foreign born: 1.9%; Speak English only: 97.0%; With disability: 11.6%; Veterans: 7.8%; Ancestry: 22.8% German, 21.2% Irish, 16.1% Italian, 16.1% English, 8.2% French

Employment: 19.0% management, business, and financial, 7.8% computer, engineering, and science, 7.9% education, legal, community service, arts, and media, 5.9% healthcare practitioners, 14.4% service, 27.1% sales and office, 7.2% natural resources, construction, and maintenance, 10.7% production, transportation, and material moving

Income: Per capita: $40,457; Median household: $79,740; Average household: $103,964; Households with income of $100,000 or more: 38.8%; Poverty rate: 3.6%

Educational Attainment: High school diploma or higher: 93.5%; Bachelor's degree or higher: 31.4%; Graduate/professional degree or higher: 13.4%

Housing: Homeownership rate: 80.2%; Median home value: $216,200; Median year structure built: 1967; Homeowner vacancy rate: 0.2%; Median selected monthly owner costs: $1,828 with a mortgage, $705 without a mortgage; Median gross rent: $887 per month; Rental vacancy rate: 0.0%

Health Insurance: 94.2% have insurance; 83.4% have private insurance; 27.0% have public insurance; 5.8% do not have insurance; 3.1% of children under 18 do not have insurance

Safety: Violent crime rate: 2.6 per 10,000 population; Property crime rate: 36.8 per 10,000 population

Transportation: Commute: 94.2% car, 1.0% public transportation, 0.1% walk, 4.5% work from home; Mean travel time to work: 23.5 minutes

Additional Information Contacts
Town of Schodack. . . . . (518) 477-7918
    http://www.schodack.org

SCHODACK LANDING (unincorporated postal area)
ZCTA: 12156
    Covers a land area of 14.344 square miles and a water area of 0.682 square miles. Located at 42.48° N. Lat; 73.75° W. Long. Elevation is 59 feet.

    Population: 1,068; Growth (since 2000): 15.7%; Density: 74.5 persons per square mile; Race: 100.0% White, 0.0% Black/African American, 0.0% Asian, 0.0% American Indian/Alaska Native, 0.0% Native Hawaiian/Other Pacific Islander, 0.0% Two or more races, 0.0% Hispanic of any race; Average household size: 2.77; Median age: 36.8; Age under 18: 34.2%; Age 65 and over: 6.9%; Males per 100 females: 103.4; Marriage status: 32.1% never married, 59.1% now married, 0.6% separated, 0.0% widowed, 8.9% divorced; Foreign born: 0.4%; Speak English only: 100.0%; With disability: 5.9%; Veterans: 3.3%; Ancestry: 28.1% English, 21.1% Syrian, 19.4% American, 17.0% German, 14.0% Irish

    Employment: 33.9% management, business, and financial, 4.0% computer, engineering, and science, 8.5% education, legal, community service, arts, and media, 12.9% healthcare practitioners, 2.0% service, 24.6% sales and office, 7.9% natural resources, construction, and maintenance, 6.1% production, transportation, and material moving

    Income: Per capita: $33,812; Median household: $68,393; Average household: $92,554; Households with income of $100,000 or more: 36.1%; Poverty rate: 5.9%

    Educational Attainment: High school diploma or higher: 87.3%; Bachelor's degree or higher: 27.7%; Graduate/professional degree or higher: 18.4%

Housing: Homeownership rate: 80.3%; Median home value: $307,300; Median year structure built: 1976; Homeowner vacancy rate: 0.0%; Median selected monthly owner costs: $1,823 with a mortgage, $760 without a mortgage; Median gross rent: $725 per month; Rental vacancy rate: 0.0%

Health Insurance: 92.7% have insurance; 91.5% have private insurance; 8.1% have public insurance; 7.3% do not have insurance; 0.0% of children under 18 do not have insurance

Transportation: Commute: 95.6% car, 0.0% public transportation, 0.0% walk, 2.6% work from home; Mean travel time to work: 23.2 minutes

STEPHENTOWN (town). Covers a land area of 57.880 square miles and a water area of 0.196 square miles. Located at 42.55° N. Lat; 73.41° W. Long. Elevation is 876 feet.

Population: 2,906; Growth (since 2000): 1.1%; Density: 50.2 persons per square mile; Race: 99.6% White, 0.0% Black/African American, 0.3% Asian, 0.0% American Indian/Alaska Native, 0.0% Native Hawaiian/Other Pacific Islander, 0.1% Two or more races, 0.4% Hispanic of any race; Average household size: 2.26; Median age: 46.5; Age under 18: 18.2%; Age 65 and over: 18.7%; Males per 100 females: 100.5; Marriage status: 30.2% never married, 57.7% now married, 1.1% separated, 3.0% widowed, 9.1% divorced; Foreign born: 0.9%; Speak English only: 98.1%; With disability: 13.9%; Veterans: 7.9%; Ancestry: 24.4% German, 24.4% Irish, 18.4% Italian, 17.1% English, 12.9% French

Employment: 14.5% management, business, and financial, 6.0% computer, engineering, and science, 8.3% education, legal, community service, arts, and media, 5.3% healthcare practitioners, 22.5% service, 16.3% sales and office, 11.9% natural resources, construction, and maintenance, 15.2% production, transportation, and material moving

Income: Per capita: $38,510; Median household: $68,906; Average household: $87,159; Households with income of $100,000 or more: 30.4%; Poverty rate: 9.3%

Educational Attainment: High school diploma or higher: 96.1%; Bachelor's degree or higher: 22.5%; Graduate/professional degree or higher: 13.3%

Housing: Homeownership rate: 84.0%; Median home value: $152,100; Median year structure built: 1982; Homeowner vacancy rate: 0.0%; Median selected monthly owner costs: $1,259 with a mortgage, $546 without a mortgage; Median gross rent: $754 per month; Rental vacancy rate: 3.6%

Health Insurance: 93.8% have insurance; 81.0% have private insurance; 28.3% have public insurance; 6.2% do not have insurance; 0.0% of children under 18 do not have insurance

Transportation: Commute: 90.7% car, 0.0% public transportation, 3.0% walk, 6.0% work from home; Mean travel time to work: 34.6 minutes

TROY (city). County seat. Covers a land area of 10.357 square miles and a water area of 0.700 square miles. Located at 42.74° N. Lat; 73.68° W. Long. Elevation is 33 feet.

History: The early name of Troy was Pa-an-pa-ack, "field of standing corn." The site was part of the patroonship granted to Kiliaen Van Rensselaer by the Dutch West India Company. For 120 years, it was occupied by Dutch farmers. Some argument took place about the name, but "Troy" was selected in 1789 at a public meeting.

Population: 49,826; Growth (since 2000): 1.3%; Density: 4,810.8 persons per square mile; Race: 69.8% White, 17.1% Black/African American, 4.1% Asian, 0.1% American Indian/Alaska Native, 0.0% Native Hawaiian/Other Pacific Islander, 7.3% Two or more races, 9.7% Hispanic of any race; Average household size: 2.25; Median age: 30.6; Age under 18: 20.0%; Age 65 and over: 10.9%; Males per 100 females: 102.1; Marriage status: 55.0% never married, 30.7% now married, 2.3% separated, 4.9% widowed, 9.5% divorced; Foreign born: 7.4%; Speak English only: 87.1%; With disability: 15.5%; Veterans: 5.3%; Ancestry: 21.7% Irish, 14.7% Italian, 9.9% German, 6.5% French, 6.0% English

Employment: 12.0% management, business, and financial, 7.8% computer, engineering, and science, 13.8% education, legal, community service, arts, and media, 4.5% healthcare practitioners, 20.6% service, 24.2% sales and office, 6.1% natural resources, construction, and maintenance, 11.0% production, transportation, and material moving

Income: Per capita: $22,955; Median household: $40,911; Average household: $55,043; Households with income of $100,000 or more: 14.6%; Poverty rate: 26.1%

Educational Attainment: High school diploma or higher: 87.2%; Bachelor's degree or higher: 25.7%; Graduate/professional degree or higher: 9.8%

Housing: Homeownership rate: 36.8%; Median home value: $144,400; Median year structure built: Before 1940; Homeowner vacancy rate: 2.4%; Median selected monthly owner costs: $1,458 with a mortgage, $598 without a mortgage; Median gross rent: $879 per month; Rental vacancy rate: 4.3%

Health Insurance: 93.9% have insurance; 62.1% have private insurance; 42.4% have public insurance; 6.1% do not have insurance; 2.8% of children under 18 do not have insurance

Hospitals: Saint Mary's Hospital - Troy (201 beds); Samaritan Hospital (238 beds)

Safety: Violent crime rate: 70.7 per 10,000 population; Property crime rate: 348.9 per 10,000 population

Newspapers: The Record (daily circulation 15,200)

Transportation: Commute: 77.8% car, 7.9% public transportation, 10.4% walk, 2.9% work from home; Mean travel time to work: 22.3 minutes

Additional Information Contacts
City of Troy . . . . (518) 279-7134
    http://www.troyny.gov

VALLEY FALLS (village). Covers a land area of 0.463 square miles and a water area of 0.025 square miles. Located at 42.90° N. Lat; 73.56° W. Long. Elevation is 335 feet.

Population: 500; Growth (since 2000): 1.8%; Density: 1,078.9 persons per square mile; Race: 97.4% White, 0.0% Black/African American, 0.8% Asian, 0.0% American Indian/Alaska Native, 0.0% Native Hawaiian/Other Pacific Islander, 1.4% Two or more races, 1.0% Hispanic of any race; Average household size: 2.76; Median age: 38.3; Age under 18: 23.4%; Age 65 and over: 14.4%; Males per 100 females: 86.4; Marriage status: 33.8% never married, 58.3% now married, 1.0% separated, 3.6% widowed, 4.3% divorced; Foreign born: 0.8%; Speak English only: 99.0%; With disability: 12.6%; Veterans: 9.4%; Ancestry: 33.2% Irish, 20.4% German, 16.4% English, 14.2% Italian, 10.0% Polish

Employment: 11.9% management, business, and financial, 5.1% computer, engineering, and science, 7.9% education, legal, community service, arts, and media, 7.5% healthcare practitioners, 24.1% service, 14.6% sales and office, 7.5% natural resources, construction, and maintenance, 21.3% production, transportation, and material moving

Income: Per capita: $38,520; Median household: $74,583; Average household: $101,492; Households with income of $100,000 or more: 41.4%; Poverty rate: 4.0%

Educational Attainment: High school diploma or higher: 98.2%; Bachelor's degree or higher: 32.0%; Graduate/professional degree or higher: 12.7%

Housing: Homeownership rate: 73.5%; Median home value: $145,800; Median year structure built: Before 1940; Homeowner vacancy rate: 5.0%; Median selected monthly owner costs: $1,527 with a mortgage, $650 without a mortgage; Median gross rent: $926 per month; Rental vacancy rate: 0.0%

Health Insurance: 98.6% have insurance; 89.8% have private insurance; 24.8% have public insurance; 1.4% do not have insurance; 1.6% of children under 18 do not have insurance
Transportation: Commute: 97.2% car, 0.0% public transportation, 0.4% walk, 2.0% work from home; Mean travel time to work: 30.4 minutes

WEST SAND LAKE (CDP). Covers a land area of 4.704 square miles and a water area of 0.088 square miles. Located at 42.64° N. Lat; 73.59° W. Long. Elevation is 525 feet.
Population: 2,907; Growth (since 2000): 19.2%; Density: 618.0 persons per square mile; Race: 97.3% White, 1.5% Black/African American, 0.0% Asian, 0.1% American Indian/Alaska Native, 0.0% Native Hawaiian/Other Pacific Islander, 0.0% Two or more races, 1.5% Hispanic of any race; Average household size: 2.96; Median age: 40.3; Age under 18: 25.7%; Age 65 and over: 9.9%; Males per 100 females: 94.7; Marriage status: 26.5% never married, 61.9% now married, 0.0% separated, 5.8% widowed, 5.8% divorced; Foreign born: 3.4%; Speak English only: 95.1%; With disability: 5.9%; Veterans: 8.0%; Ancestry: 23.3% German, 16.2% Irish, 11.2% Italian, 8.4% English, 8.1% French
Employment: 15.4% management, business, and financial, 7.8% computer, engineering, and science, 10.7% education, legal, community service, arts, and media, 3.0% healthcare practitioners, 12.0% service, 25.6% sales and office, 11.5% natural resources, construction, and maintenance, 14.0% production, transportation, and material moving
Income: Per capita: $37,426; Median household: $90,321; Average household: $110,303; Households with income of $100,000 or more: 42.2%; Poverty rate: 8.0%
Educational Attainment: High school diploma or higher: 91.3%; Bachelor's degree or higher: 40.9%; Graduate/professional degree or higher: 23.8%

School District(s)
Averill Park Central SD (KG-12)
    Enrollment: 2,784 . . . . (518) 674-7055
Housing: Homeownership rate: 92.6%; Median home value: $218,100; Median year structure built: 1964; Homeowner vacancy rate: 5.3%; Median selected monthly owner costs: $1,726 with a mortgage, $853 without a mortgage; Median gross rent: $774 per month; Rental vacancy rate: 24.7%
Health Insurance: 96.9% have insurance; 86.3% have private insurance; 20.2% have public insurance; 3.1% do not have insurance; 0.0% of children under 18 do not have insurance
Transportation: Commute: 95.2% car, 1.3% public transportation, 0.8% walk, 2.3% work from home; Mean travel time to work: 25.4 minutes

WYNANTSKILL (CDP). Covers a land area of 2.360 square miles and a water area of 0.003 square miles. Located at 42.69° N. Lat; 73.64° W. Long. Elevation is 335 feet.
Population: 3,077; Growth (since 2000): 2.0%; Density: 1,304.0 persons per square mile; Race: 95.5% White, 3.7% Black/African American, 0.0% Asian, 0.0% American Indian/Alaska Native, 0.0% Native Hawaiian/Other Pacific Islander, 0.8% Two or more races, 3.2% Hispanic of any race; Average household size: 2.35; Median age: 44.4; Age under 18: 16.7%; Age 65 and over: 14.4%; Males per 100 females: 90.2; Marriage status: 32.9% never married, 55.0% now married, 1.5% separated, 7.8% widowed, 4.4% divorced; Foreign born: 3.3%; Speak English only: 93.0%; With disability: 12.2%; Veterans: 5.7%; Ancestry: 33.0% Irish, 27.4% Italian, 22.1% German, 15.9% French, 8.9% Polish
Employment: 15.3% management, business, and financial, 7.1% computer, engineering, and science, 9.7% education, legal, community service, arts, and media, 4.5% healthcare practitioners, 19.0% service, 27.4% sales and office, 9.7% natural resources, construction, and maintenance, 7.3% production, transportation, and material moving
Income: Per capita: $35,131; Median household: $67,037; Average household: $81,361; Households with income of $100,000 or more: 31.3%; Poverty rate: 2.2%
Educational Attainment: High school diploma or higher: 93.9%; Bachelor's degree or higher: 25.8%; Graduate/professional degree or higher: 9.9%

School District(s)
Wynantskill Union Free SD (KG-08)
    Enrollment: 360 . . . . (518) 283-4679
Housing: Homeownership rate: 83.1%; Median home value: $191,800; Median year structure built: 1956; Homeowner vacancy rate: 0.0%; Median selected monthly owner costs: $1,566 with a mortgage, $557 without a mortgage; Median gross rent: $830 per month; Rental vacancy rate: 0.0%

Health Insurance: 97.9% have insurance; 85.5% have private insurance; 23.3% have public insurance; 2.1% do not have insurance; 0.0% of children under 18 do not have insurance
Transportation: Commute: 92.6% car, 1.0% public transportation, 2.7% walk, 3.7% work from home; Mean travel time to work: 23.1 minutes

Richmond County

See New York City

Rockland County

Located in southeastern New York; bounded on the east by the Hudson River, and on the southwest and south by New Jersey; includes part of the Ramapo Mountains; drained by the Hackensack and Ramapo Rivers. Covers a land area of 173.550 square miles, a water area of 25.792 square miles, and is located in the Eastern Time Zone at 41.15° N. Lat., 74.02° W. Long. The county was founded in 1798. County seat is New City.

Rockland County is part of the New York-Newark-Jersey City, NY-NJ-PA Metropolitan Statistical Area. The entire metro area includes: Dutchess County-Putnam County, NY Metropolitan Division (Dutchess County, NY; Putnam County, NY); Nassau County-Suffolk County, NY Metropolitan Division (Nassau County, NY; Suffolk County, NY); Newark, NJ-PA Metropolitan Division (Essex County, NJ; Hunterdon County, NJ; Morris County, NJ; Somerset County, NJ; Sussex County, NJ; Union County, NJ; Pike County, PA); New York-Jersey City-White Plains, NY-NJ Metropolitan Division (Bergen County, NJ; Hudson County, NJ; Middlesex County, NJ; Monmouth County, NJ; Ocean County, NJ; Passaic County, NJ; Bronx County, NY; Kings County, NY; New York County, NY; Orange County, NY; Queens County, NY; Richmond County, NY; Rockland County, NY; Westchester County, NY)

Population: 325,027; Growth (since 2000): 13.3%; Density: 1,872.8 persons per square mile; Race: 70.9% White, 12.5% Black/African American, 6.1% Asian, 0.2% American Indian/Alaska Native, 0.0% Native Hawaiian/Other Pacific Islander, 2.6% two or more races, 17.3% Hispanic of any race; Average household size: 3.18; Median age: 36.2; Age under 18: 27.7%; Age 65 and over: 15.1%; Males per 100 females: 96.3; Marriage status: 32.6% never married, 54.8% now married, 1.7% separated, 5.8% widowed, 6.9% divorced; Foreign born: 21.4%; Speak English only: 61.6%; With disability: 9.3%; Veterans: 3.9%; Ancestry: 13.5% Irish, 13.4% Italian, 8.0% American, 6.2% German, 4.7% Haitian
Religion: Six largest groups: 35.1% Catholicism, 22.0% Judaism, 2.8% Non-denominational Protestant, 1.5% Muslim Estimate, 1.3% Baptist, 0.9% Eastern Liturgical (Orthodox)
Economy: Unemployment rate: 3.5%; Leading industries: 13.3 % professional, scientific, and technical services; 13.2 % retail trade; 11.6 % health care and social assistance; Farms: 23 totaling 526 acres; Company size: 5 employ 1,000 or more persons, 14 employ 500 to 999 persons, 149 employ 100 to 499 persons, 9,855 employ less than 100 persons; Business ownership: 9,433 women-owned, 2,180 Black-owned, 3,221 Hispanic-owned, 2,376 Asian-owned, 119 American Indian/Alaska Native-owned
Employment: 15.8% management, business, and financial, 4.6% computer, engineering, and science, 15.9% education, legal, community service, arts, and media, 8.0% healthcare practitioners, 19.3% service, 23.0% sales and office, 6.7% natural resources, construction, and maintenance, 6.7% production, transportation, and material moving
Income: Per capita: $36,898; Median household: $88,571; Average household: $116,063; Households with income of $100,000 or more: 45.0%; Poverty rate: 14.2%
Educational Attainment: High school diploma or higher: 87.3%; Bachelor's degree or higher: 40.4%; Graduate/professional degree or higher: 18.5%
Housing: Homeownership rate: 68.9%; Median home value: $425,100; Median year structure built: 1969; Homeowner vacancy rate: 1.3%; Median selected monthly owner costs: $3,035 with a mortgage, $1,298 without a mortgage; Median gross rent: $1,420 per month; Rental vacancy rate: 4.2%
Vital Statistics: Birth rate: 160.0 per 10,000 population; Death rate: 73.8 per 10,000 population; Age-adjusted cancer mortality rate: 115.1 deaths per 100,000 population

Health Insurance: 92.7% have insurance; 65.5% have private insurance; 38.9% have public insurance; 7.3% do not have insurance; 3.8% of children under 18 do not have insurance
Health Care: Physicians: 34.9 per 10,000 population; Dentists: 9.9 per 10,000 population; Hospital beds: 39.4 per 10,000 population; Hospital admissions: 875.1 per 10,000 population
Air Quality Index (AQI): Percent of Days: 93.2% good, 6.6% moderate, 0.3% unhealthy for sensitive individuals, 0.0% unhealthy, 0.0% very unhealthy; Annual median: 35; Annual maximum: 105
Transportation: Commute: 81.3% car, 8.6% public transportation, 3.4% walk, 5.0% work from home; Mean travel time to work: 31.0 minutes
2016 Presidential Election: 45.1% Trump, 51.3% Clinton, 1.7% Johnson, 1.0% Stein
National and State Parks: Bear Mountain State Park; Blauvelt State Park; High Tor State Park; Hook Mountain State Park; Iona Island Component Hudson River National Estuarine Research Reserve; Palisades State Park; Piermont Marsh Component Hudson River National Estuarine Research Reserve; Rockland Lake State Park; Stony Point State Park; Tallman Mountain State Park
Additional Information Contacts
Rockland Government . . . . (845) 638-5070
    http://www.co.rockland.ny.us

Rockland County Communities

AIRMONT (village). Covers a land area of 4.643 square miles and a water area of 0.002 square miles. Located at 41.10° N. Lat; 74.10° W. Long. Elevation is 587 feet.
Population: 8,869; Growth (since 2000): 13.7%; Density: 1,910.2 persons per square mile; Race: 85.4% White, 2.6% Black/African American, 6.5% Asian, 0.1% American Indian/Alaska Native, 0.2% Native Hawaiian/Other Pacific Islander, 1.9% Two or more races, 9.1% Hispanic of any race; Average household size: 3.39; Median age: 36.5; Age under 18: 29.3%; Age 65 and over: 17.5%; Males per 100 females: 90.6; Marriage status: 27.0% never married, 62.4% now married, 1.5% separated, 6.1% widowed, 4.5% divorced; Foreign born: 15.5%; Speak English only: 64.3%; With disability: 8.5%; Veterans: 5.2%; Ancestry: 14.8% Italian, 12.3% American, 9.4% Irish, 4.2% Eastern European, 3.9% English
Employment: 22.1% management, business, and financial, 5.3% computer, engineering, and science, 16.0% education, legal, community service, arts, and media, 8.8% healthcare practitioners, 12.6% service, 26.1% sales and office, 6.4% natural resources, construction, and maintenance, 2.7% production, transportation, and material moving
Income: Per capita: $36,117; Median household: $94,606; Average household: $122,227; Households with income of $100,000 or more: 48.7%; Poverty rate: 8.0%
Educational Attainment: High school diploma or higher: 88.1%; Bachelor's degree or higher: 43.0%; Graduate/professional degree or higher: 19.7%
Housing: Homeownership rate: 74.1%; Median home value: $470,600; Median year structure built: 1971; Homeowner vacancy rate: 0.0%; Median selected monthly owner costs: $3,317 with a mortgage, $1,439 without a mortgage; Median gross rent: $1,396 per month; Rental vacancy rate: 2.8%
Health Insurance: 96.9% have insurance; 65.7% have private insurance; 43.7% have public insurance; 3.1% do not have insurance; 0.3% of children under 18 do not have insurance
Transportation: Commute: 82.4% car, 8.3% public transportation, 0.3% walk, 7.5% work from home; Mean travel time to work: 29.9 minutes
Additional Information Contacts
Village of Airmont . . . . (845) 357-8111
    http://www.airmont.org

BARDONIA (CDP). Covers a land area of 2.574 square miles and a water area of 0.355 square miles. Located at 41.11° N. Lat; 73.98° W. Long. Elevation is 295 feet.
History: Bardonia is named for the Bardon Brothers - John and the twins Phillip and Conrad - who came from Bavaria in the 1849 and opened several businesses.
Population: 3,695; Growth (since 2000): -15.4%; Density: 1,435.6 persons per square mile; Race: 85.3% White, 1.9% Black/African American, 10.2% Asian, 0.0% American Indian/Alaska Native, 0.0% Native Hawaiian/Other Pacific Islander, 2.6% Two or more races, 3.7% Hispanic of any race; Average household size: 2.75; Median age: 51.4; Age under 18: 17.7%; Age 65 and over: 30.1%; Males per 100 females: 93.0; Marriage status:

26.8% never married, 56.5% now married, 0.2% separated, 7.5% widowed, 9.2% divorced; Foreign born: 14.7%; Speak English only: 83.7%; With disability: 10.4%; Veterans: 3.4%; Ancestry: 36.0% Italian, 24.5% Irish, 6.1% German, 5.4% Polish, 4.7% Russian
Employment: 21.5% management, business, and financial, 4.0% computer, engineering, and science, 15.0% education, legal, community service, arts, and media, 15.7% healthcare practitioners, 13.9% service, 19.7% sales and office, 4.3% natural resources, construction, and maintenance, 5.9% production, transportation, and material moving
Income: Per capita: $59,454; Median household: $112,554; Average household: $160,240; Households with income of $100,000 or more: 56.8%; Poverty rate: 1.7%
Educational Attainment: High school diploma or higher: 94.0%; Bachelor's degree or higher: 55.5%; Graduate/professional degree or higher: 23.3%
School District(s)
Clarkstown Central SD (KG-12)
    Enrollment: 8,156 . . . . (845) 639-6418
Housing: Homeownership rate: 85.0%; Median home value: $542,800; Median year structure built: 1973; Homeowner vacancy rate: 0.0%; Median selected monthly owner costs: $3,371 with a mortgage, $1,426 without a mortgage; Median gross rent: n/a per month; Rental vacancy rate: 0.0%
Health Insurance: 99.0% have insurance; 88.9% have private insurance; 33.9% have public insurance; 1.0% do not have insurance; 0.0% of children under 18 do not have insurance
Transportation: Commute: 83.5% car, 5.7% public transportation, 0.0% walk, 8.6% work from home; Mean travel time to work: 34.0 minutes

BLAUVELT (CDP). Covers a land area of 4.502 square miles and a water area of 0.105 square miles. Located at 41.07° N. Lat; 73.95° W. Long. Elevation is 197 feet.
History: Blauvelt section of Palisades Interstate Park is here.
Population: 5,794; Growth (since 2000): 11.3%; Density: 1,287.0 persons per square mile; Race: 88.1% White, 2.1% Black/African American, 5.5% Asian, 0.0% American Indian/Alaska Native, 0.0% Native Hawaiian/Other Pacific Islander, 2.1% Two or more races, 10.7% Hispanic of any race; Average household size: 3.27; Median age: 37.7; Age under 18: 24.7%; Age 65 and over: 16.0%; Males per 100 females: 95.0; Marriage status: 34.4% never married, 57.1% now married, 1.7% separated, 5.4% widowed, 3.1% divorced; Foreign born: 13.0%; Speak English only: 84.3%; With disability: 9.2%; Veterans: 4.4%; Ancestry: 33.2% Irish, 20.1% Italian, 10.3% German, 6.6% American, 4.1% Polish
Employment: 17.3% management, business, and financial, 5.2% computer, engineering, and science, 23.1% education, legal, community service, arts, and media, 5.7% healthcare practitioners, 16.8% service, 22.1% sales and office, 6.6% natural resources, construction, and maintenance, 3.2% production, transportation, and material moving
Income: Per capita: $46,081; Median household: $126,410; Average household: $159,539; Households with income of $100,000 or more: 62.5%; Poverty rate: 3.6%
Educational Attainment: High school diploma or higher: 93.5%; Bachelor's degree or higher: 55.8%; Graduate/professional degree or higher: 23.8%
School District(s)
South Orangetown Central SD (KG-12)
    Enrollment: 3,114 . . . . (845) 680-1050
Housing: Homeownership rate: 96.4%; Median home value: $497,700; Median year structure built: 1963; Homeowner vacancy rate: 0.0%; Median selected monthly owner costs: $3,538 with a mortgage, $1,483 without a mortgage; Median gross rent: n/a per month; Rental vacancy rate: 0.0%
Health Insurance: 93.0% have insurance; 83.7% have private insurance; 22.0% have public insurance; 7.0% do not have insurance; 10.1% of children under 18 do not have insurance
Transportation: Commute: 87.1% car, 6.0% public transportation, 2.4% walk, 4.2% work from home; Mean travel time to work: 31.4 minutes

CHESTNUT RIDGE (village). Covers a land area of 4.968 square miles and a water area of 0.003 square miles. Located at 41.08° N. Lat; 74.05° W. Long. Elevation is 417 feet.
Population: 8,118; Growth (since 2000): 3.7%; Density: 1,634.1 persons per square mile; Race: 61.6% White, 23.9% Black/African American, 5.3% Asian, 0.0% American Indian/Alaska Native, 0.0% Native Hawaiian/Other Pacific Islander, 3.0% Two or more races, 11.2% Hispanic of any race; Average household size: 3.18; Median age: 37.6; Age under 18: 26.8%; Age 65 and over: 18.3%; Males per 100 females: 94.6; Marriage status:

28.0% never married, 60.1% now married, 1.0% separated, 4.8% widowed, 7.1% divorced; Foreign born: 18.4%; Speak English only: 73.8%; With disability: 9.9%; Veterans: 6.0%; Ancestry: 9.6% Italian, 8.0% American, 6.9% Irish, 6.0% German, 4.2% Polish

Employment: 15.3% management, business, and financial, 5.9% computer, engineering, and science, 17.1% education, legal, community service, arts, and media, 13.5% healthcare practitioners, 15.0% service, 21.6% sales and office, 4.2% natural resources, construction, and maintenance, 7.5% production, transportation, and material moving

Income: Per capita: $38,987; Median household: $94,464; Average household: $123,106; Households with income of $100,000 or more: 49.0%; Poverty rate: 8.4%

Educational Attainment: High school diploma or higher: 92.8%; Bachelor's degree or higher: 44.8%; Graduate/professional degree or higher: 20.3%

School District(s)

East Ramapo Central SD (Spring Valley) (KG-12)
 Enrollment: 9,010 . . . . (845) 577-6011

Housing: Homeownership rate: 85.2%; Median home value: $440,700; Median year structure built: 1965; Homeowner vacancy rate: 0.3%; Median selected monthly owner costs: $3,142 with a mortgage, $1,246 without a mortgage; Median gross rent: $1,436 per month; Rental vacancy rate: 4.6%

Health Insurance: 95.5% have insurance; 68.6% have private insurance; 39.1% have public insurance; 4.5% do not have insurance; 0.5% of children under 18 do not have insurance

Transportation: Commute: 81.5% car, 7.5% public transportation, 2.7% walk, 7.2% work from home; Mean travel time to work: 31.3 minutes

Additional Information Contacts

Village of Chestnut Ridge . . . . (845) 425-2805
 http://www.chestnutridgevillage.org

CLARKSTOWN (town).
Covers a land area of 38.475 square miles and a water area of 8.593 square miles. Located at 41.13° N. Lat; 73.97° W. Long.

History: The town of Clarkstown was created in 1791 in Orange County, before Rockland County was formed. In 2008 Clarkstown became one of 600 municipalities nationwide to sign the United States Mayor's Climate Protection Agreement to reduce carbon dioxide emissions to seven percent below the 1990 levels by 2012.

Population: 87,224; Growth (since 2000): 6.3%; Density: 2,267.0 persons per square mile; Race: 70.9% White, 11.2% Black/African American, 10.4% Asian, 0.2% American Indian/Alaska Native, 0.0% Native Hawaiian/Other Pacific Islander, 3.3% Two or more races, 14.0% Hispanic of any race; Average household size: 2.89; Median age: 44.3; Age under 18: 21.8%; Age 65 and over: 18.9%; Males per 100 females: 94.1; Marriage status: 28.9% never married, 57.3% now married, 1.4% separated, 6.8% widowed, 7.1% divorced; Foreign born: 21.3%; Speak English only: 71.1%; With disability: 9.8%; Veterans: 4.3%; Ancestry: 20.6% Italian, 17.1% Irish, 6.8% German, 5.2% American, 4.6% Haitian

Employment: 18.7% management, business, and financial, 5.9% computer, engineering, and science, 14.5% education, legal, community service, arts, and media, 10.3% healthcare practitioners, 16.0% service, 23.0% sales and office, 5.7% natural resources, construction, and maintenance, 5.9% production, transportation, and material moving

Income: Per capita: $47,603; Median household: $111,025; Average household: $135,868; Households with income of $100,000 or more: 55.9%; Poverty rate: 6.1%

Educational Attainment: High school diploma or higher: 91.4%; Bachelor's degree or higher: 49.8%; Graduate/professional degree or higher: 22.7%

Housing: Homeownership rate: 79.7%; Median home value: $445,100; Median year structure built: 1970; Homeowner vacancy rate: 0.8%; Median selected monthly owner costs: $3,092 with a mortgage, $1,357 without a mortgage; Median gross rent: $1,564 per month; Rental vacancy rate: 7.8%

Health Insurance: 95.3% have insurance; 80.1% have private insurance; 29.0% have public insurance; 4.7% do not have insurance; 2.6% of children under 18 do not have insurance

Safety: Violent crime rate: 10.9 per 10,000 population; Property crime rate: 137.5 per 10,000 population

Transportation: Commute: 85.3% car, 7.9% public transportation, 1.2% walk, 4.6% work from home; Mean travel time to work: 33.2 minutes

Additional Information Contacts

Town of Clarkstown . . . . (845) 639-2000
 http://www.town.clarkstown.ny.us

CONGERS (CDP).
Covers a land area of 3.068 square miles and a water area of 0.744 square miles. Located at 41.15° N. Lat; 73.94° W. Long. Elevation is 177 feet.

History: Congers, named after Abraham B. Conger, was settled in the late 17th century by Dutch, German and English settlers. It was originally known as Cedar Grove Corner and then Waldberg, which is German for "forest mountain."

Population: 8,389; Growth (since 2000): 1.0%; Density: 2,734.4 persons per square mile; Race: 82.4% White, 1.8% Black/African American, 9.8% Asian, 0.4% American Indian/Alaska Native, 0.0% Native Hawaiian/Other Pacific Islander, 3.2% Two or more races, 13.7% Hispanic of any race; Average household size: 3.02; Median age: 43.6; Age under 18: 21.3%; Age 65 and over: 17.8%; Males per 100 females: 93.6; Marriage status: 29.8% never married, 55.4% now married, 2.6% separated, 7.1% widowed, 7.7% divorced; Foreign born: 17.6%; Speak English only: 75.9%; With disability: 10.7%; Veterans: 4.5%; Ancestry: 32.6% Italian, 24.3% Irish, 9.7% German, 4.1% American, 3.8% English

Employment: 21.3% management, business, and financial, 4.4% computer, engineering, and science, 15.0% education, legal, community service, arts, and media, 8.6% healthcare practitioners, 15.1% service, 23.4% sales and office, 6.5% natural resources, construction, and maintenance, 5.6% production, transportation, and material moving

Income: Per capita: $45,241; Median household: $113,333; Average household: $135,394; Households with income of $100,000 or more: 57.8%; Poverty rate: 4.3%

Educational Attainment: High school diploma or higher: 90.7%; Bachelor's degree or higher: 44.6%; Graduate/professional degree or higher: 22.0%

School District(s)

Clarkstown Central SD (KG-12)
 Enrollment: 8,156 . . . . (845) 639-6418

Housing: Homeownership rate: 84.3%; Median home value: $453,900; Median year structure built: 1967; Homeowner vacancy rate: 1.1%; Median selected monthly owner costs: $3,284 with a mortgage, $1,404 without a mortgage; Median gross rent: $1,582 per month; Rental vacancy rate: 7.1%

Health Insurance: 95.1% have insurance; 81.9% have private insurance; 24.9% have public insurance; 4.9% do not have insurance; 3.7% of children under 18 do not have insurance

Transportation: Commute: 88.5% car, 6.9% public transportation, 0.3% walk, 4.3% work from home; Mean travel time to work: 32.3 minutes

GARNERVILLE (unincorporated postal area)
ZCTA: 10923

 Covers a land area of 1.967 square miles and a water area of 0.036 square miles. Located at 41.20° N. Lat; 74.00° W. Long. Elevation is 210 feet.

Population: 8,553; Growth (since 2000): -7.8%; Density: 4,348.9 persons per square mile; Race: 62.5% White, 10.3% Black/African American, 6.5% Asian, 0.0% American Indian/Alaska Native, 0.0% Native Hawaiian/Other Pacific Islander, 3.6% Two or more races, 38.2% Hispanic of any race; Average household size: 3.19; Median age: 37.8; Age under 18: 23.1%; Age 65 and over: 12.1%; Males per 100 females: 94.2; Marriage status: 34.4% never married, 53.6% now married, 1.8% separated, 3.7% widowed, 8.3% divorced; Foreign born: 25.4%; Speak English only: 60.1%; With disability: 9.0%; Veterans: 4.5%; Ancestry: 17.3% Italian, 14.3% Irish, 8.7% German, 3.9% Polish, 3.8% Haitian

Employment: 10.6% management, business, and financial, 3.5% computer, engineering, and science, 11.2% education, legal, community service, arts, and media, 8.1% healthcare practitioners, 25.6% service, 23.5% sales and office, 6.7% natural resources, construction, and maintenance, 10.9% production, transportation, and material moving

Income: Per capita: $31,866; Median household: $82,813; Average household: $99,827; Households with income of $100,000 or more: 40.0%; Poverty rate: 11.2%

Educational Attainment: High school diploma or higher: 85.7%; Bachelor's degree or higher: 28.4%; Graduate/professional degree or higher: 13.1%

School District(s)

Haverstraw-Stony Point CSD (North Rockland) (KG-12)
 Enrollment: 7,981 . . . . (845) 942-3002

Housing: Homeownership rate: 62.3%; Median home value: $332,300; Median year structure built: 1972; Homeowner vacancy rate: 0.0%; Median selected monthly owner costs: $2,954 with a mortgage, $1,026 without a mortgage; Median gross rent: $1,442 per month; Rental vacancy rate: 4.8%

Health Insurance: 89.3% have insurance; 63.8% have private insurance; 34.9% have public insurance; 10.7% do not have insurance; 1.4% of children under 18 do not have insurance

Transportation: Commute: 85.7% car, 6.5% public transportation, 0.9% walk, 3.5% work from home; Mean travel time to work: 31.6 minutes

GRAND VIEW-ON-HUDSON (village). Covers a land area of 0.176 square miles and a water area of <.001 square miles. Located at 41.07° N. Lat; 73.92° W. Long. Elevation is -3 feet.

Population: 348; Growth (since 2000): 22.5%; Density: 1,981.6 persons per square mile; Race: 97.7% White, 0.0% Black/African American, 1.1% Asian, 0.0% American Indian/Alaska Native, 0.0% Native Hawaiian/Other Pacific Islander, 1.1% Two or more races, 12.4% Hispanic of any race; Average household size: 2.38; Median age: 51.5; Age under 18: 20.7%; Age 65 and over: 25.9%; Males per 100 females: 80.4; Marriage status: 20.1% never married, 65.5% now married, 4.8% separated, 7.2% widowed, 7.2% divorced; Foreign born: 11.2%; Speak English only: 91.9%; With disability: 2.9%; Veterans: 7.6%; Ancestry: 11.5% Irish, 11.2% German, 9.8% Swedish, 9.2% Russian, 7.8% English

Employment: 33.9% management, business, and financial, 1.6% computer, engineering, and science, 31.3% education, legal, community service, arts, and media, 8.3% healthcare practitioners, 5.2% service, 14.1% sales and office, 2.6% natural resources, construction, and maintenance, 3.1% production, transportation, and material moving

Income: Per capita: $81,907; Median household: $123,750; Average household: $198,521; Households with income of $100,000 or more: 69.9%; Poverty rate: 1.7%

Educational Attainment: High school diploma or higher: 99.6%; Bachelor's degree or higher: 80.0%; Graduate/professional degree or higher: 42.3%

Housing: Homeownership rate: 81.5%; Median home value: $968,800; Median year structure built: Before 1940; Homeowner vacancy rate: 2.5%; Median selected monthly owner costs: $4,000+ with a mortgage, $1,501 without a mortgage; Median gross rent: $3,341 per month; Rental vacancy rate: 12.9%

Health Insurance: 99.4% have insurance; 90.5% have private insurance; 27.6% have public insurance; 0.6% do not have insurance; 0.0% of children under 18 do not have insurance

Transportation: Commute: 72.7% car, 13.9% public transportation, 0.0% walk, 12.3% work from home; Mean travel time to work: 46.1 minutes

HAVERSTRAW (town). Covers a land area of 22.155 square miles and a water area of 5.260 square miles. Located at 41.20° N. Lat; 74.04° W. Long. Elevation is 33 feet.

History: In Haverstraw, James Wood discovered the modern system of burning brick, and set up brickyards in the town. At its peak, the industry included 40 brickyards.

Population: 37,497; Growth (since 2000): 10.9%; Density: 1,692.5 persons per square mile; Race: 54.5% White, 15.7% Black/African American, 4.6% Asian, 0.0% American Indian/Alaska Native, 0.0% Native Hawaiian/Other Pacific Islander, 3.8% Two or more races, 45.1% Hispanic of any race; Average household size: 3.05; Median age: 36.8; Age under 18: 23.7%; Age 65 and over: 13.5%; Males per 100 females: 94.0; Marriage status: 36.2% never married, 48.4% now married, 2.6% separated, 5.3% widowed, 10.1% divorced; Foreign born: 29.9%; Speak English only: 52.2%; With disability: 11.5%; Veterans: 3.8%; Ancestry: 12.0% Irish, 12.0% Italian, 5.5% German, 4.7% Haitian, 3.3% American

Employment: 8.5% management, business, and financial, 3.5% computer, engineering, and science, 10.0% education, legal, community service, arts, and media, 7.3% healthcare practitioners, 26.9% service, 23.7% sales and office, 8.0% natural resources, construction, and maintenance, 12.1% production, transportation, and material moving

Income: Per capita: $31,234; Median household: $73,619; Average household: $92,842; Households with income of $100,000 or more: 37.6%; Poverty rate: 11.1%

Educational Attainment: High school diploma or higher: 82.5%; Bachelor's degree or higher: 28.4%; Graduate/professional degree or higher: 11.3%

School District(s)
Haverstraw-Stony Point CSD (North Rockland) (KG-12)
　Enrollment: 7,981 . . . . (845) 942-3002

Housing: Homeownership rate: 60.4%; Median home value: $295,800; Median year structure built: 1971; Homeowner vacancy rate: 1.7%; Median selected monthly owner costs: $2,695 with a mortgage, $1,205 without a mortgage; Median gross rent: $1,425 per month; Rental vacancy rate: 1.6%

Health Insurance: 89.9% have insurance; 61.5% have private insurance; 39.3% have public insurance; 10.1% do not have insurance; 2.6% of children under 18 do not have insurance

Safety: Violent crime rate: 11.2 per 10,000 population; Property crime rate: 79.4 per 10,000 population

Transportation: Commute: 82.7% car, 8.1% public transportation, 2.8% walk, 4.4% work from home; Mean travel time to work: 30.0 minutes

Additional Information Contacts
Town of Haverstraw . . . . (845) 942-3727
　http://townofhaverstraw.us

HAVERSTRAW (village). Covers a land area of 1.980 square miles and a water area of 3.057 square miles. Located at 41.18° N. Lat; 73.94° W. Long. Elevation is 33 feet.

Population: 12,181; Growth (since 2000): 20.4%; Density: 6,151.8 persons per square mile; Race: 45.3% White, 11.2% Black/African American, 1.7% Asian, 0.0% American Indian/Alaska Native, 0.0% Native Hawaiian/Other Pacific Islander, 2.1% Two or more races, 68.7% Hispanic of any race; Average household size: 3.21; Median age: 33.5; Age under 18: 26.8%; Age 65 and over: 12.8%; Males per 100 females: 94.4; Marriage status: 37.7% never married, 46.2% now married, 4.1% separated, 6.4% widowed, 9.7% divorced; Foreign born: 38.3%; Speak English only: 35.0%; With disability: 14.8%; Veterans: 3.8%; Ancestry: 8.1% Irish, 4.8% Italian, 2.6% German, 2.0% American, 2.0% Polish

Employment: 5.5% management, business, and financial, 2.0% computer, engineering, and science, 7.7% education, legal, community service, arts, and media, 5.7% healthcare practitioners, 32.7% service, 21.6% sales and office, 8.1% natural resources, construction, and maintenance, 16.7% production, transportation, and material moving

Income: Per capita: $24,435; Median household: $56,862; Average household: $75,876; Households with income of $100,000 or more: 29.1%; Poverty rate: 16.3

Educational Attainment: High school diploma or higher: 72.5%; Bachelor's degree or higher: 21.8%; Graduate/professional degree or higher: 7.7%

School District(s)
Haverstraw-Stony Point CSD (North Rockland) (KG-12)
　Enrollment: 7,981 . . . . (845) 942-3002

Housing: Homeownership rate: 40.2%; Median home value: $248,100; Median year structure built: 1956; Homeowner vacancy rate: 2.1%; Median selected monthly owner costs: $2,684 with a mortgage, $1,071 without a mortgage; Median gross rent: $1,331 per month; Rental vacancy rate: 0.7%

Health Insurance: 87.8% have insurance; 46.5% have private insurance; 49.2% have public insurance; 12.2% do not have insurance; 1.8% of children under 18 do not have insurance

Transportation: Commute: 76.6% car, 13.6% public transportation, 4.4% walk, 2.7% work from home; Mean travel time to work: 28.7 minutes

Additional Information Contacts
Village of Haverstraw . . . . (845) 429-0300
　http://www.voh-ny.com/index.htm

HILLBURN (village). Covers a land area of 2.251 square miles and a water area of 0.018 square miles. Located at 41.13° N. Lat; 74.17° W. Long. Elevation is 308 feet.

History: Incorporated 1893.

Population: 1,019; Growth (since 2000): 15.7%; Density: 452.7 persons per square mile; Race: 37.1% White, 23.0% Black/African American, 3.2% Asian, 5.2% American Indian/Alaska Native, 0.0% Native Hawaiian/Other Pacific Islander, 11.8% Two or more races, 27.3% Hispanic of any race; Average household size: 3.32; Median age: 40.2; Age under 18: 25.7%; Age 65 and over: 11.2%; Males per 100 females: 108.6; Marriage status: 31.5% never married, 54.3% now married, 1.5% separated, 4.0% widowed, 10.2% divorced; Foreign born: 25.1%; Speak English only: 59.1%; With disability: 10.8%; Veterans: 5.7%; Ancestry: 13.0% Haitian, 10.5% Irish, 9.1% Italian, 8.2% American, 5.6% Russian

Employment: 10.0% management, business, and financial, 7.1% computer, engineering, and science, 10.2% education, legal, community service, arts, and media, 3.7% healthcare practitioners, 27.4% service, 16.3% sales and office, 11.8% natural resources, construction, and maintenance, 13.4% production, transportation, and material moving
Income: Per capita: $28,423; Median household: $68,542; Average household: $85,541; Households with income of $100,000 or more: 37.1%; Poverty rate: 10.4%
Educational Attainment: High school diploma or higher: 88.2%; Bachelor's degree or higher: 28.1%; Graduate/professional degree or higher: 10.4%
Housing: Homeownership rate: 70.4%; Median home value: $298,800; Median year structure built: Before 1940; Homeowner vacancy rate: 2.7%; Median selected monthly owner costs: $2,655 with a mortgage, $1,064 without a mortgage; Median gross rent: $1,703 per month; Rental vacancy rate: 6.0%
Health Insurance: 90.6% have insurance; 67.7% have private insurance; 31.0% have public insurance; 9.4% do not have insurance; 1.9% of children under 18 do not have insurance
Transportation: Commute: 84.0% car, 9.7% public transportation, 2.2% walk, 4.0% work from home; Mean travel time to work: 30.1 minutes
Additional Information Contacts
Village of Hillburn . . . . (845) 357-2036
    http://www.hillburn.org

HILLCREST (CDP).
Covers a land area of 1.297 square miles and a water area of 0 square miles. Located at 41.13° N. Lat; 74.04° W. Long. Elevation is 512 feet.
Population: 7,697; Growth (since 2000): 8.3%; Density: 5,932.6 persons per square mile; Race: 28.2% White, 48.1% Black/African American, 10.2% Asian, 0.2% American Indian/Alaska Native, 0.0% Native Hawaiian/Other Pacific Islander, 4.9% Two or more races, 25.9% Hispanic of any race; Average household size: 4.05; Median age: 38.3; Age under 18: 21.2%; Age 65 and over: 16.0%; Males per 100 females: 96.1; Marriage status: 39.0% never married, 46.2% now married, 1.3% separated, 6.7% widowed, 8.1% divorced; Foreign born: 45.7%; Speak English only: 49.5%; With disability: 10.0%; Veterans: 3.6%; Ancestry: 17.4% Haitian, 13.1% Jamaican, 5.7% American, 2.3% Italian, 2.1% African
Employment: 6.4% management, business, and financial, 1.0% computer, engineering, and science, 10.4% education, legal, community service, arts, and media, 9.3% healthcare practitioners, 31.5% service, 17.3% sales and office, 12.4% natural resources, construction, and maintenance, 11.6% production, transportation, and material moving
Income: Per capita: $31,108; Median household: $94,265; Average household: $119,812; Households with income of $100,000 or more: 49.0%; Poverty rate: 4.4%
Educational Attainment: High school diploma or higher: 81.7%; Bachelor's degree or higher: 28.8%; Graduate/professional degree or higher: 8.9%
Housing: Homeownership rate: 84.7%; Median home value: $355,900; Median year structure built: 1963; Homeowner vacancy rate: 1.2%; Median selected monthly owner costs: $2,786 with a mortgage, $1,280 without a mortgage; Median gross rent: $1,458 per month; Rental vacancy rate: 1.8%
Health Insurance: 88.1% have insurance; 65.6% have private insurance; 36.4% have public insurance; 11.9% do not have insurance; 7.9% of children under 18 do not have insurance
Transportation: Commute: 89.3% car, 5.7% public transportation, 0.7% walk, 1.0% work from home; Mean travel time to work: 26.9 minutes

KASER (village).
Covers a land area of 0.172 square miles and a water area of 0 square miles. Located at 41.12° N. Lat; 74.07° W. Long. Elevation is 538 feet.
Population: 5,138; Growth (since 2000): 54.9%; Density: 29,823.0 persons per square mile; Race: 99.6% White, 0.0% Black/African American, 0.3% Asian, 0.0% American Indian/Alaska Native, 0.0% Native Hawaiian/Other Pacific Islander, 0.1% Two or more races, 0.0% Hispanic of any race; Average household size: 5.48; Median age: 15.7; Age under 18: 56.7%; Age 65 and over: 2.7%; Males per 100 females: 105.5; Marriage status: 30.9% never married, 66.9% now married, 0.3% separated, 0.6% widowed, 1.5% divorced; Foreign born: 7.3%; Speak English only: 4.0%; With disability: 3.4%; Veterans: 0.3%; Ancestry: 30.6% American, 24.9% Hungarian, 13.2% European, 7.0% Israeli, 5.1% Romanian

Employment: 9.3% management, business, and financial, 6.6% computer, engineering, and science, 48.4% education, legal, community service, arts, and media, 0.0% healthcare practitioners, 4.6% service, 26.2% sales and office, 0.8% natural resources, construction, and maintenance, 4.2% production, transportation, and material moving
Income: Per capita: $5,463; Median household: $17,564; Average household: $29,520; Households with income of $100,000 or more: 3.5%; Poverty rate: 76.1%
Educational Attainment: High school diploma or higher: 68.9%; Bachelor's degree or higher: 4.4%; Graduate/professional degree or higher: 2.0%
Housing: Homeownership rate: 5.4%; Median home value: $812,500; Median year structure built: 1996; Homeowner vacancy rate: 19.0%; Median selected monthly owner costs: $4,000+ with a mortgage, n/a without a mortgage; Median gross rent: $911 per month; Rental vacancy rate: 0.0%
Health Insurance: 98.3% have insurance; 6.4% have private insurance; 94.1% have public insurance; 1.7% do not have insurance; 0.7% of children under 18 do not have insurance
Transportation: Commute: 34.0% car, 11.3% public transportation, 44.8% walk, 5.0% work from home; Mean travel time to work: 14.2 minutes

MONSEY (CDP).
Covers a land area of 2.273 square miles and a water area of 0.014 square miles. Located at 41.11° N. Lat; 74.08° W. Long. Elevation is 545 feet.
History: Rockland County was inhabited by the Munsee band of Lenape Native Americans, or Delaware Indians, of the Algonquian tribe. Monsey Glen, an Indian encampment, is located west of the intersection of NY 59 and NY 306, where rock shelters are still visible. The Monsey railroad station is named for Munsee, a Lenape chief, and was built in 1841.
Population: 22,043; Growth (since 2000): 52.0%; Density: 9,698.9 persons per square mile; Race: 95.8% White, 3.0% Black/African American, 0.1% Asian, 0.0% American Indian/Alaska Native, 0.0% Native Hawaiian/Other Pacific Islander, 0.2% Two or more races, 2.0% Hispanic of any race; Average household size: 5.41; Median age: 16.2; Age under 18: 54.5%; Age 65 and over: 5.8%; Males per 100 females: 106.0; Marriage status: 32.8% never married, 63.8% now married, 0.3% separated, 1.9% widowed, 1.5% divorced; Foreign born: 10.3%; Speak English only: 22.7%; With disability: 5.7%; Veterans: 0.7%; Ancestry: 20.7% American, 18.2% European, 15.0% Hungarian, 8.0% Polish, 4.1% Israeli
Employment: 16.1% management, business, and financial, 3.3% computer, engineering, and science, 34.3% education, legal, community service, arts, and media, 2.0% healthcare practitioners, 9.4% service, 27.1% sales and office, 2.6% natural resources, construction, and maintenance, 5.2% production, transportation, and material moving
Income: Per capita: $12,356; Median household: $37,925; Average household: $64,969; Households with income of $100,000 or more: 16.8%; Poverty rate: 44.1%
Educational Attainment: High school diploma or higher: 78.8%; Bachelor's degree or higher: 16.5%; Graduate/professional degree or higher: 7.2%

School District(s)
East Ramapo Central SD (Spring Valley) (KG-12)
    Enrollment: 9,010 . . . . (845) 577-6011
Four-year College(s)
Bais Binyomin Academy (Private, Not-for-profit)
    Enrollment: 25 . . . . (845) 207-0330
    Tuition: In-state $8,000; Out-of-state $8,000
Bais Medrash Elyon (Private, Not-for-profit)
    Enrollment: 68 . . . . (845) 371-2481
    Tuition: In-state $8,600; Out-of-state $8,600
Beth Medrash Meor Yitzchok (Private, Not-for-profit)
    Enrollment: 129 . . . . (845) 426-3488
    Tuition: In-state $9,100; Out-of-state $9,100
Mechon L'hoyroa (Private, Not-for-profit)
    Enrollment: 40 . . . . (845) 425-9565
    Tuition: In-state $8,400; Out-of-state $8,400
Rabbinical College Beth Shraga (Private, Not-for-profit)
    Enrollment: 39 . . . . (845) 356-1980
    Tuition: In-state $12,950; Out-of-state $12,950
Yeshiva D'monsey Rabbinical College (Private, Not-for-profit)
    Enrollment: 76 . . . . (845) 352-5852
    Tuition: In-state $6,800; Out-of-state $6,800

Yeshiva Gedolah Kesser Torah (Private, Not-for-profit)
  Enrollment: 71 . . . . (845) 406-4308
  Tuition: In-state $11,300; Out-of-state $11,300
Yeshiva Shaar Ephraim (Private, For-profit)
  Enrollment: 117 . . . . (845) 426-3116
  Tuition: In-state $13,675; Out-of-state $13,675
Yeshivath Viznitz (Private, Not-for-profit)
  Enrollment: 690 . . . . (845) 731-3700
  Tuition: In-state $10,000; Out-of-state $10,000
Housing: Homeownership rate: 39.5%; Median home value: $617,400; Median year structure built: 1990; Homeowner vacancy rate: 0.4%; Median selected monthly owner costs: $3,276 with a mortgage, $1,501 without a mortgage; Median gross rent: $1,434 per month; Rental vacancy rate: 2.8%
Health Insurance: 94.2% have insurance; 26.6% have private insurance; 72.9% have public insurance; 5.8% do not have insurance; 4.7% of children under 18 do not have insurance
Transportation: Commute: 65.6% car, 9.4% public transportation, 14.5% walk, 7.9% work from home; Mean travel time to work: 22.7 minutes

MONTEBELLO (village). Covers a land area of 4.346 square miles and a water area of 0.010 square miles. Located at 41.13° N. Lat; 74.11° W. Long. Elevation is 318 feet.
History: Montebello was incorporated in 1986.
Population: 4,658; Growth (since 2000): 26.3%; Density: 1,071.7 persons per square mile; Race: 83.0% White, 5.1% Black/African American, 8.6% Asian, 0.0% American Indian/Alaska Native, 0.0% Native Hawaiian/Other Pacific Islander, 1.1% Two or more races, 4.7% Hispanic of any race; Average household size: 2.98; Median age: 48.0; Age under 18: 23.4%; Age 65 and over: 18.9%; Males per 100 females: 93.1; Marriage status: 26.6% never married, 55.7% now married, 0.7% separated, 10.2% widowed, 7.5% divorced; Foreign born: 13.1%; Speak English only: 85.0%; With disability: 10.6%; Veterans: 3.3%; Ancestry: 27.0% Italian, 12.3% German, 10.8% Irish, 6.0% American, 5.9% Polish
Employment: 29.8% management, business, and financial, 3.7% computer, engineering, and science, 17.2% education, legal, community service, arts, and media, 18.5% healthcare practitioners, 7.4% service, 16.8% sales and office, 3.0% natural resources, construction, and maintenance, 3.7% production, transportation, and material moving
Income: Per capita: $69,203; Median household: $157,798; Average household: $204,380; Households with income of $100,000 or more: 65.9%; Poverty rate: 2.9%
Educational Attainment: High school diploma or higher: 95.8%; Bachelor's degree or higher: 65.6%; Graduate/professional degree or higher: 39.8%
Housing: Homeownership rate: 91.6%; Median home value: $624,000; Median year structure built: 1978; Homeowner vacancy rate: 0.0%; Median selected monthly owner costs: $4,000+ with a mortgage, $1,501 without a mortgage; Median gross rent: $1,715 per month; Rental vacancy rate: 0.0%
Health Insurance: 98.0% have insurance; 88.2% have private insurance; 22.4% have public insurance; 2.0% do not have insurance; 0.0% of children under 18 do not have insurance
Transportation: Commute: 84.4% car, 9.1% public transportation, 0.0% walk, 6.6% work from home; Mean travel time to work: 36.2 minutes
Additional Information Contacts
Village of Montebello . . . . (845) 368-2211
  http://www.villageofmontebello.com

MOUNT IVY (CDP). Covers a land area of 1.467 square miles and a water area of 0 square miles. Located at 41.19° N. Lat; 74.03° W. Long. Elevation is 463 feet.
Population: 6,808; Growth (since 2000): 4.2%; Density: 4,641.1 persons per square mile; Race: 57.6% White, 21.5% Black/African American, 4.1% Asian, 0.0% American Indian/Alaska Native, 0.0% Native Hawaiian/Other Pacific Islander, 7.9% Two or more races, 27.2% Hispanic of any race; Average household size: 2.45; Median age: 40.5; Age under 18: 22.5%; Age 65 and over: 12.9%; Males per 100 females: 90.2; Marriage status: 30.7% never married, 48.7% now married, 0.5% separated, 4.8% widowed, 15.8% divorced; Foreign born: 24.9%; Speak English only: 64.2%; With disability: 8.0%; Veterans: 2.3%; Ancestry: 15.0% Italian, 14.9% Irish, 7.7% German, 7.1% American, 5.3% Haitian
Employment: 11.6% management, business, and financial, 4.5% computer, engineering, and science, 12.1% education, legal, community service, arts, and media, 10.6% healthcare practitioners, 20.1% service,

25.8% sales and office, 7.7% natural resources, construction, and maintenance, 7.6% production, transportation, and material moving
Income: Per capita: $37,441; Median household: $73,768; Average household: $89,114; Households with income of $100,000 or more: 37.4%; Poverty rate: 8.0%
Educational Attainment: High school diploma or higher: 90.6%; Bachelor's degree or higher: 34.3%; Graduate/professional degree or higher: 13.7%
Housing: Homeownership rate: 66.1%; Median home value: $221,500; Median year structure built: 1977; Homeowner vacancy rate: 5.0%; Median selected monthly owner costs: $2,265 with a mortgage, $1,174 without a mortgage; Median gross rent: $1,613 per month; Rental vacancy rate: 6.2%
Health Insurance: 91.3% have insurance; 67.4% have private insurance; 36.5% have public insurance; 8.7% do not have insurance; 4.9% of children under 18 do not have insurance
Transportation: Commute: 87.9% car, 2.8% public transportation, 1.1% walk, 7.9% work from home; Mean travel time to work: 30.5 minutes

NANUET (CDP). Covers a land area of 5.433 square miles and a water area of 0.005 square miles. Located at 41.10° N. Lat; 74.02° W. Long. Elevation is 299 feet.
History: Named for a local Indian chief. International Shrine of St. Anthony is here.
Population: 18,312; Growth (since 2000): 9.6%; Density: 3,370.7 persons per square mile; Race: 62.0% White, 16.6% Black/African American, 13.0% Asian, 0.4% American Indian/Alaska Native, 0.0% Native Hawaiian/Other Pacific Islander, 3.7% Two or more races, 15.0% Hispanic of any race; Average household size: 2.76; Median age: 44.0; Age under 18: 21.2%; Age 65 and over: 18.3%; Males per 100 females: 89.4; Marriage status: 29.7% never married, 55.1% now married, 1.0% separated, 7.4% widowed, 7.8% divorced; Foreign born: 29.1%; Speak English only: 63.1%; With disability: 10.5%; Veterans: 3.8%; Ancestry: 18.7% Irish, 18.0% Italian, 8.5% Haitian, 6.9% German, 3.3% Polish
Employment: 15.6% management, business, and financial, 4.6% computer, engineering, and science, 13.9% education, legal, community service, arts, and media, 10.5% healthcare practitioners, 17.5% service, 24.1% sales and office, 6.5% natural resources, construction, and maintenance, 7.3% production, transportation, and material moving
Income: Per capita: $41,761; Median household: $97,250; Average household: $114,073; Households with income of $100,000 or more: 49.2%; Poverty rate: 8.1%
Educational Attainment: High school diploma or higher: 88.5%; Bachelor's degree or higher: 43.5%; Graduate/professional degree or higher: 16.7%
School District(s)
Nanuet Union Free SD (KG-12)
  Enrollment: 2,224 . . . . (845) 627-9888
Vocational/Technical School(s)
Capri Cosmetology Learning Centers (Private, For-profit)
  Enrollment: 245 . . . . (845) 623-6339
  Tuition: $14,100
Housing: Homeownership rate: 70.3%; Median home value: $381,600; Median year structure built: 1975; Homeowner vacancy rate: 0.2%; Median selected monthly owner costs: $2,985 with a mortgage, $1,209 without a mortgage; Median gross rent: $1,865 per month; Rental vacancy rate: 9.2%
Health Insurance: 96.6% have insurance; 75.1% have private insurance; 34.7% have public insurance; 3.4% do not have insurance; 0.0% of children under 18 do not have insurance
Newspapers: Rockland County Times (weekly circulation 12,000)
Transportation: Commute: 86.8% car, 7.5% public transportation, 0.9% walk, 3.8% work from home; Mean travel time to work: 32.9 minutes

NEW CITY (CDP). County seat. Covers a land area of 15.582 square miles and a water area of 0.793 square miles. Located at 41.15° N. Lat; 73.99° W. Long. Elevation is 157 feet.
History: New City is the county seat, and most populous community of Rockland County. Its downtown is one of the main business districts in the county.
Population: 34,338; Growth (since 2000): 0.9%; Density: 2,203.7 persons per square mile; Race: 74.6% White, 9.3% Black/African American, 10.1% Asian, 0.1% American Indian/Alaska Native, 0.0% Native Hawaiian/Other Pacific Islander, 3.1% Two or more races, 10.1% Hispanic of any race; Average household size: 3.02; Median age: 44.4; Age under 18: 22.6%;

Age 65 and over: 18.6%; Males per 100 females: 96.4; Marriage status: 27.7% never married, 61.3% now married, 1.0% separated, 5.4% widowed, 5.7% divorced; Foreign born: 18.4%; Speak English only: 75.2%; With disability: 8.7%; Veterans: 5.1%; Ancestry: 17.8% Italian, 15.2% Irish, 7.3% German, 6.5% Russian, 6.1% Polish

Employment: 20.7% management, business, and financial, 6.4% computer, engineering, and science, 14.9% education, legal, community service, arts, and media, 11.2% healthcare practitioners, 12.7% service, 23.8% sales and office, 4.7% natural resources, construction, and maintenance, 5.5% production, transportation, and material moving

Income: Per capita: $51,569; Median household: $124,765; Average household: $153,966; Households with income of $100,000 or more: 63.2%; Poverty rate: 4.2%

Educational Attainment: High school diploma or higher: 94.6%; Bachelor's degree or higher: 58.4%; Graduate/professional degree or higher: 28.3%

School District(s)

Clarkstown Central SD (KG-12)
    Enrollment: 8,156 . . . . (845) 639-6418
East Ramapo Central SD (Spring Valley) (KG-12)
    Enrollment: 9,010 . . . . (845) 577-6011

Housing: Homeownership rate: 89.4%; Median home value: $472,800; Median year structure built: 1969; Homeowner vacancy rate: 1.1%; Median selected monthly owner costs: $3,158 with a mortgage, $1,422 without a mortgage; Median gross rent: $1,366 per month; Rental vacancy rate: 10.2%

Health Insurance: 96.9% have insurance; 85.9% have private insurance; 25.4% have public insurance; 3.1% do not have insurance; 1.3% of children under 18 do not have insurance

Transportation: Commute: 85.0% car, 8.5% public transportation, 0.7% walk, 4.8% work from home; Mean travel time to work: 35.5 minutes

NEW HEMPSTEAD (village).

Covers a land area of 2.853 square miles and a water area of 0.010 square miles. Located at 41.15° N. Lat; 74.05° W. Long. Elevation is 581 feet.

History: New Hempstead, formally known as Kakiat, is a village in the Town of Ramapo. Joseph Berger of The New York Times said in a 1997 article that New Hempstead was one of several Town of Ramapo villages formed by non-Jewish people and more secular Jewish people "to preserve the sparse Better Homes and Gardens ambiance that attracted them to Rockland County.

Population: 5,359; Growth (since 2000): 12.4%; Density: 1,878.2 persons per square mile; Race: 62.2% White, 18.7% Black/African American, 4.0% Asian, 0.0% American Indian/Alaska Native, 0.0% Native Hawaiian/Other Pacific Islander, 1.0% Two or more races, 19.1% Hispanic of any race; Average household size: 4.51; Median age: 31.9; Age under 18: 30.5%; Age 65 and over: 10.0%; Males per 100 females: 99.6; Marriage status: 40.8% never married, 51.1% now married, 1.7% separated, 6.3% widowed, 1.8% divorced; Foreign born: 22.5%; Speak English only: 67.4%; With disability: 4.7%; Veterans: 2.8%; Ancestry: 14.9% American, 8.3% Polish, 8.3% Russian, 6.3% European, 4.1% Hungarian

Employment: 16.9% management, business, and financial, 2.1% computer, engineering, and science, 16.4% education, legal, community service, arts, and media, 6.5% healthcare practitioners, 17.8% service, 27.1% sales and office, 9.2% natural resources, construction, and maintenance, 4.1% production, transportation, and material moving

Income: Per capita: $31,333; Median household: $114,205; Average household: $133,939; Households with income of $100,000 or more: 60.5%; Poverty rate: 1.3%

Educational Attainment: High school diploma or higher: 91.5%; Bachelor's degree or higher: 37.9%; Graduate/professional degree or higher: 17.4%

Housing: Homeownership rate: 91.1%; Median home value: $485,200; Median year structure built: 1965; Homeowner vacancy rate: 0.0%; Median selected monthly owner costs: $3,123 with a mortgage, $1,501 without a mortgage; Median gross rent: $1,963 per month; Rental vacancy rate: 0.0%

Health Insurance: 84.2% have insurance; 62.0% have private insurance; 28.5% have public insurance; 15.8% do not have insurance; 5.9% of children under 18 do not have insurance

Transportation: Commute: 79.5% car, 10.8% public transportation, 0.0% walk, 7.3% work from home; Mean travel time to work: 37.1 minutes

NEW SQUARE (village).

Covers a land area of 0.356 square miles and a water area of 0 square miles. Located at 41.14° N. Lat; 74.03° W. Long. Elevation is 489 feet.

History: A community of Orthodox Hasidic Jews of the Skvirer sect lives here.

Population: 7,995; Growth (since 2000): 72.9%; Density: 22,438.6 persons per square mile; Race: 99.3% White, 0.2% Black/African American, 0.0% Asian, 0.2% American Indian/Alaska Native, 0.0% Native Hawaiian/Other Pacific Islander, 0.4% Two or more races, 1.0% Hispanic of any race; Average household size: 5.96; Median age: 13.9; Age under 18: 61.2%; Age 65 and over: 1.8%; Males per 100 females: 107.5; Marriage status: 29.7% never married, 69.2% now married, 0.0% separated, 1.0% widowed, 0.1% divorced; Foreign born: 3.7%; Speak English only: 5.8%; With disability: 2.7%; Veterans: 0.4%; Ancestry: 32.9% Hungarian, 18.9% American, 14.5% European, 6.9% Polish, 4.9% Russian

Employment: 12.4% management, business, and financial, 2.7% computer, engineering, and science, 34.7% education, legal, community service, arts, and media, 0.7% healthcare practitioners, 15.8% service, 24.7% sales and office, 5.0% natural resources, construction, and maintenance, 4.0% production, transportation, and material moving

Income: Per capita: $6,568; Median household: $23,924; Average household: $38,543; Households with income of $100,000 or more: 9.0%; Poverty rate: 64.4%

Educational Attainment: High school diploma or higher: 70.3%; Bachelor's degree or higher: 3.9%; Graduate/professional degree or higher: 0.9%

Housing: Homeownership rate: 13.5%; Median home value: $338,200; Median year structure built: 1996; Homeowner vacancy rate: 0.0%; Median selected monthly owner costs: $2,542 with a mortgage, n/a without a mortgage; Median gross rent: $1,376 per month; Rental vacancy rate: 0.0%

Health Insurance: 99.8% have insurance; 13.6% have private insurance; 89.5% have public insurance; 0.2% do not have insurance; 0.1% of children under 18 do not have insurance

Transportation: Commute: 36.4% car, 8.1% public transportation, 44.4% walk, 6.3% work from home; Mean travel time to work: 15.2 minutes

NYACK (village).

Covers a land area of 0.770 square miles and a water area of 0.838 square miles. Located at 41.09° N. Lat; 73.91° W. Long. Elevation is 72 feet.

History: Was a 19th-century health resort, port, and boat-building center. Birthplace of artist Edward Hopper. Settled 1684, incorporated 1833.

Population: 7,057; Growth (since 2000): 4.7%; Density: 9,168.8 persons per square mile; Race: 63.3% White, 24.6% Black/African American, 3.6% Asian, 0.0% American Indian/Alaska Native, 0.0% Native Hawaiian/Other Pacific Islander, 4.8% Two or more races, 19.3% Hispanic of any race; Average household size: 2.14; Median age: 42.3; Age under 18: 17.7%; Age 65 and over: 18.1%; Males per 100 females: 86.3; Marriage status: 38.6% never married, 45.8% now married, 3.6% separated, 5.1% widowed, 10.6% divorced; Foreign born: 22.0%; Speak English only: 73.6%; With disability: 15.2%; Veterans: 3.2%; Ancestry: 20.9% Irish, 9.7% Italian, 8.5% German, 7.2% Haitian, 3.0% English

Employment: 15.6% management, business, and financial, 5.6% computer, engineering, and science, 20.6% education, legal, community service, arts, and media, 9.0% healthcare practitioners, 24.1% service, 18.8% sales and office, 2.3% natural resources, construction, and maintenance, 4.1% production, transportation, and material moving

Income: Per capita: $41,654; Median household: $65,884; Average household: $87,917; Households with income of $100,000 or more: 25.9%; Poverty rate: 13.2%

Educational Attainment: High school diploma or higher: 88.3%; Bachelor's degree or higher: 50.4%; Graduate/professional degree or higher: 23.9%

School District(s)

Nyack Union Free SD (KG-12)
    Enrollment: 3,083 . . . . (845) 353-7015

Four-year College(s)

Nyack College (Private, Not-for-profit, Christ and Missionary Alliance Church)
    Enrollment: 2,455 . . . . (845) 675-4400
    Tuition: In-state $25,350; Out-of-state $25,350

Housing: Homeownership rate: 30.5%; Median home value: $463,600; Median year structure built: 1956; Homeowner vacancy rate: 7.0%; Median selected monthly owner costs: $2,810 with a mortgage, $1,374 without a

mortgage; Median gross rent: $1,514 per month; Rental vacancy rate: 7.8%
Health Insurance: 91.0% have insurance; 66.8% have private insurance; 34.9% have public insurance; 9.0% do not have insurance; 6.3% of children under 18 do not have insurance
Hospitals: Nyack Hospital (375 beds)
Transportation: Commute: 75.7% car, 11.3% public transportation, 8.7% walk, 3.5% work from home; Mean travel time to work: 29.4 minutes
Additional Information Contacts
Village of Nyack. . . . . (845) 358-0548
  http://nyack-ny.gov

ORANGEBURG (CDP). Covers a land area of 3.073 square miles and a water area of 0 square miles. Located at 41.05° N. Lat; 73.94° W. Long. Elevation is 118 feet.
Population: 4,217; Growth (since 2000): 24.5%; Density: 1,372.5 persons per square mile; Race: 81.5% White, 4.2% Black/African American, 10.5% Asian, 0.1% American Indian/Alaska Native, 0.0% Native Hawaiian/Other Pacific Islander, 1.3% Two or more races, 11.9% Hispanic of any race; Average household size: 2.40; Median age: 46.3; Age under 18: 14.3%; Age 65 and over: 25.3%; Males per 100 females: 73.8; Marriage status: 43.4% never married, 42.8% now married, 1.3% separated, 9.3% widowed, 4.5% divorced; Foreign born: 18.2%; Speak English only: 79.5%; With disability: 15.5%; Veterans: 4.9%; Ancestry: 33.2% Irish, 19.8% Italian, 9.8% German, 7.7% American, 4.9% Polish
Employment: 14.5% management, business, and financial, 2.9% computer, engineering, and science, 17.0% education, legal, community service, arts, and media, 8.3% healthcare practitioners, 19.9% service, 23.8% sales and office, 7.0% natural resources, construction, and maintenance, 6.7% production, transportation, and material moving
Income: Per capita: $37,324; Median household: $86,211; Average household: $103,690; Households with income of $100,000 or more: 43.7%; Poverty rate: 8.5%
Educational Attainment: High school diploma or higher: 90.0%; Bachelor's degree or higher: 51.1%; Graduate/professional degree or higher: 22.4%

School District(s)
South Orangetown Central SD (KG-12)
  Enrollment: 3,114 . . . . (845) 680-1050
Four-year College(s)
Dominican College of Blauvelt (Private, Not-for-profit)
  Enrollment: 1,954 . . . . (845) 359-7800
  Tuition: In-state $28,448; Out-of-state $28,448
LIU Hudson at Rockland (Private, Not-for-profit)
  Enrollment: n/a . . . . (845) 359-7200
Housing: Homeownership rate: 70.7%; Median home value: $449,400; Median year structure built: 1966; Homeowner vacancy rate: 2.7%; Median selected monthly owner costs: $3,110 with a mortgage, $1,213 without a mortgage; Median gross rent: $933 per month; Rental vacancy rate: 7.2%
Health Insurance: 96.8% have insurance; 81.0% have private insurance; 33.6% have public insurance; 3.2% do not have insurance; 0.0% of children under 18 do not have insurance
Transportation: Commute: 84.9% car, 4.4% public transportation, 5.5% walk, 4.9% work from home; Mean travel time to work: 28.8 minutes

ORANGETOWN (town). Covers a land area of 24.098 square miles and a water area of 7.268 square miles. Located at 41.05° N. Lat; 73.95° W. Long. Elevation is 200 feet.
History: Orangetown was first settled around 1680, the first town formed in Rockland County. Its Dutch settlers purchased land from the Tappan Indians in 1686.
Population: 50,365; Growth (since 2000): 5.6%; Density: 2,090.0 persons per square mile; Race: 81.2% White, 6.0% Black/African American, 7.3% Asian, 0.6% American Indian/Alaska Native, 0.0% Native Hawaiian/Other Pacific Islander, 2.3% Two or more races, 10.6% Hispanic of any race; Average household size: 2.65; Median age: 43.0; Age under 18: 20.1%; Age 65 and over: 18.8%; Males per 100 females: 92.3; Marriage status: 34.6% never married, 52.2% now married, 1.4% separated, 6.3% widowed, 6.9% divorced; Foreign born: 16.1%; Speak English only: 81.3%; With disability: 10.4%; Veterans: 4.6%; Ancestry: 30.4% Irish, 17.0% Italian, 10.0% German, 5.7% American, 4.3% English
Employment: 17.8% management, business, and financial, 5.4% computer, engineering, and science, 19.7% education, legal, community service, arts, and media, 7.5% healthcare practitioners, 17.6% service,

21.7% sales and office, 6.5% natural resources, construction, and maintenance, 3.8% production, transportation, and material moving
Income: Per capita: $49,876; Median household: $98,782; Average household: $136,220; Households with income of $100,000 or more: 49.5%; Poverty rate: 6.5%
Educational Attainment: High school diploma or higher: 91.3%; Bachelor's degree or higher: 51.2%; Graduate/professional degree or higher: 23.4%
Housing: Homeownership rate: 73.5%; Median home value: $472,800; Median year structure built: 1961; Homeowner vacancy rate: 1.8%; Median selected monthly owner costs: $3,218 with a mortgage, $1,269 without a mortgage; Median gross rent: $1,470 per month; Rental vacancy rate: 5.4%
Health Insurance: 95.0% have insurance; 81.4% have private insurance; 27.9% have public insurance; 5.0% do not have insurance; 6.1% of children under 18 do not have insurance
Safety: Violent crime rate: 12.2 per 10,000 population; Property crime rate: 80.2 per 10,000 population
Transportation: Commute: 81.9% car, 9.0% public transportation, 3.0% walk, 5.4% work from home; Mean travel time to work: 32.8 minutes
Additional Information Contacts
Town of Orangetown. . . . . (845) 359-5100
  http://www.orangetown.com

PALISADES (unincorporated postal area)
ZCTA: 10964
  Covers a land area of 2.466 square miles and a water area of 0 square miles. Located at 41.02° N. Lat; 73.91° W. Long. Elevation is 194 feet.
  Population: 1,372; Growth (since 2000): 7.0%; Density: 556.3 persons per square mile; Race: 83.5% White, 1.9% Black/African American, 12.0% Asian, 0.8% American Indian/Alaska Native, 0.0% Native Hawaiian/Other Pacific Islander, 1.8% Two or more races, 4.1% Hispanic of any race; Average household size: 2.60; Median age: 52.2; Age under 18: 13.8%; Age 65 and over: 30.2%; Males per 100 females: 95.2; Marriage status: 36.5% never married, 47.6% now married, 0.0% separated, 12.3% widowed, 3.6% divorced; Foreign born: 24.3%; Speak English only: 73.1%; With disability: 18.1%; Veterans: 4.3%; Ancestry: 26.8% Irish, 15.8% German, 11.7% Italian, 10.9% Polish, 6.6% Russian
  Employment: 35.3% management, business, and financial, 1.5% computer, engineering, and science, 22.7% education, legal, community service, arts, and media, 5.5% healthcare practitioners, 9.6% service, 17.9% sales and office, 4.6% natural resources, construction, and maintenance, 3.0% production, transportation, and material moving
  Income: Per capita: $70,664; Median household: $121,528; Average household: $190,383; Households with income of $100,000 or more: 52.2%; Poverty rate: 7.9%
  Educational Attainment: High school diploma or higher: 94.4%; Bachelor's degree or higher: 48.2%; Graduate/professional degree or higher: 26.2%
  Housing: Homeownership rate: 77.1%; Median home value: $602,000; Median year structure built: 1960; Homeowner vacancy rate: 0.0%; Median selected monthly owner costs: $4,000 with a mortgage, $1,501 without a mortgage; Median gross rent: $1,854 per month; Rental vacancy rate: 0.0%
  Health Insurance: 95.0% have insurance; 80.3% have private insurance; 33.5% have public insurance; 5.0% do not have insurance; 0.0% of children under 18 do not have insurance
  Transportation: Commute: 84.2% car, 1.4% public transportation, 2.3% walk, 12.1% work from home; Mean travel time to work: 33.9 minutes

PEARL RIVER (CDP). Covers a land area of 6.799 square miles and a water area of 0.400 square miles. Located at 41.06° N. Lat; 74.01° W. Long. Elevation is 243 feet.
History: In 1696, Pearl River was originally part of a larger portion of land known as the Kakiat Patent that was granted to Daniel Honan and Michael Hawdon. In 1713, the land was split into north and south plots. After the Revolutionary War, the land was further divided and sold. In the early 1870s, the town was divided into five different parts: Middletown, Sickletown, Pascack, Muddy Brook, and Naurashaun.
Population: 16,116; Growth (since 2000): 3.6%; Density: 2,370.4 persons per square mile; Race: 88.4% White, 2.3% Black/African American, 4.9% Asian, 1.4% American Indian/Alaska Native, 0.0% Native Hawaiian/Other Pacific Islander, 0.8% Two or more races, 7.3% Hispanic of any race; Average household size: 2.79; Median age: 42.2; Age under 18: 22.8%; Age 65 and over: 18.2%; Males per 100 females: 95.8; Marriage status:

28.8% never married, 58.4% now married, 0.8% separated, 6.5% widowed, 6.3% divorced; Foreign born: 13.3%; Speak English only: 86.9%; With disability: 8.2%; Veterans: 5.4%; Ancestry: 44.1% Irish, 19.4% Italian, 11.2% German, 5.7% American, 2.7% English

Employment: 16.6% management, business, and financial, 6.0% computer, engineering, and science, 19.6% education, legal, community service, arts, and media, 5.6% healthcare practitioners, 20.1% service, 20.2% sales and office, 10.0% natural resources, construction, and maintenance, 1.8% production, transportation, and material moving

Income: Per capita: $50,116; Median household: $105,897; Average household: $138,119; Households with income of $100,000 or more: 52.4%; Poverty rate: 5.7%

Educational Attainment: High school diploma or higher: 91.0%; Bachelor's degree or higher: 45.3%; Graduate/professional degree or higher: 20.2%

School District(s)
Pearl River Union Free SD (KG-12)
    Enrollment: 2,522 . . . . (845) 620-3922

Housing: Homeownership rate: 80.7%; Median home value: $453,700; Median year structure built: 1961; Homeowner vacancy rate: 1.3%; Median selected monthly owner costs: $3,145 with a mortgage, $1,058 without a mortgage; Median gross rent: $1,372 per month; Rental vacancy rate: 2.1%

Health Insurance: 95.4% have insurance; 86.2% have private insurance; 24.7% have public insurance; 4.6% do not have insurance; 7.0% of children under 18 do not have insurance

Transportation: Commute: 82.2% car, 10.2% public transportation, 1.1% walk, 5.5% work from home; Mean travel time to work: 35.2 minutes

PIERMONT (village). Covers a land area of 0.679 square miles and a water area of 0.473 square miles. Located at 41.04° N. Lat; 73.91° W. Long. Elevation is 92 feet.

History: Until the 1980s, manufacturing (paperboard, silk ribbons). Site of Camp Shanks, which was operational during World Wars I and II. Pier (1 mile long) from which village takes its name was used for embarkation of troops. Site where 1983 Woody Allen movie *The Purple Rose of Cairo* was filmed. Incorporated 1847.

Population: 2,574; Growth (since 2000): -1.3%; Density: 3,788.2 persons per square mile; Race: 82.8% White, 4.0% Black/African American, 7.3% Asian, 0.0% American Indian/Alaska Native, 0.0% Native Hawaiian/Other Pacific Islander, 4.4% Two or more races, 11.0% Hispanic of any race; Average household size: 2.14; Median age: 49.1; Age under 18: 15.7%; Age 65 and over: 23.0%; Males per 100 females: 89.9; Marriage status: 29.4% never married, 54.4% now married, 1.5% separated, 2.4% widowed, 13.8% divorced; Foreign born: 14.8%; Speak English only: 80.5%; With disability: 7.0%; Veterans: 6.5%; Ancestry: 19.7% Irish, 17.9% Italian, 12.5% English, 7.1% American, 5.1% German

Employment: 20.7% management, business, and financial, 7.7% computer, engineering, and science, 17.4% education, legal, community service, arts, and media, 9.7% healthcare practitioners, 14.9% service, 22.7% sales and office, 5.1% natural resources, construction, and maintenance, 1.7% production, transportation, and material moving

Income: Per capita: $79,432; Median household: $104,549; Average household: $169,325; Households with income of $100,000 or more: 53.1%; Poverty rate: 4.9%

Educational Attainment: High school diploma or higher: 95.0%; Bachelor's degree or higher: 68.4%; Graduate/professional degree or higher: 37.0%

School District(s)
South Orangetown Central SD (KG-12)
    Enrollment: 3,114 . . . . (845) 680-1050

Housing: Homeownership rate: 68.8%; Median home value: $575,400; Median year structure built: 1964; Homeowner vacancy rate: 3.1%; Median selected monthly owner costs: $3,154 with a mortgage, $1,492 without a mortgage; Median gross rent: $1,631 per month; Rental vacancy rate: 7.4%

Health Insurance: 96.5% have insurance; 83.4% have private insurance; 32.8% have public insurance; 3.5% do not have insurance; 0.0% of children under 18 do not have insurance

Safety: Violent crime rate: 0.0 per 10,000 population; Property crime rate: 46.6 per 10,000 population

Transportation: Commute: 82.8% car, 4.6% public transportation, 0.2% walk, 9.7% work from home; Mean travel time to work: 34.1 minutes

POMONA (village). Covers a land area of 2.397 square miles and a water area of 0 square miles. Located at 41.19° N. Lat; 74.05° W. Long. Elevation is 456 feet.

Population: 3,103; Growth (since 2000): 13.8%; Density: 1,294.4 persons per square mile; Race: 71.0% White, 15.6% Black/African American, 10.0% Asian, 0.0% American Indian/Alaska Native, 0.0% Native Hawaiian/Other Pacific Islander, 2.6% Two or more races, 8.8% Hispanic of any race; Average household size: 3.10; Median age: 40.0; Age under 18: 24.2%; Age 65 and over: 16.4%; Males per 100 females: 99.2; Marriage status: 31.1% never married, 57.0% now married, 0.8% separated, 6.7% widowed, 5.2% divorced; Foreign born: 21.0%; Speak English only: 73.4%; With disability: 7.3%; Veterans: 4.7%; Ancestry: 10.9% Polish, 9.8% Italian, 7.7% Russian, 7.6% German, 6.0% Eastern European

Employment: 16.8% management, business, and financial, 10.5% computer, engineering, and science, 16.5% education, legal, community service, arts, and media, 13.4% healthcare practitioners, 11.6% service, 25.0% sales and office, 3.7% natural resources, construction, and maintenance, 2.5% production, transportation, and material moving

Income: Per capita: $47,010; Median household: $118,246; Average household: $142,862; Households with income of $100,000 or more: 61.2%; Poverty rate: 9.2%

Educational Attainment: High school diploma or higher: 93.9%; Bachelor's degree or higher: 60.8%; Graduate/professional degree or higher: 29.3%

Housing: Homeownership rate: 91.1%; Median home value: $498,600; Median year structure built: 1976; Homeowner vacancy rate: 0.0%; Median selected monthly owner costs: $3,469 with a mortgage, $1,499 without a mortgage; Median gross rent: $2,262 per month; Rental vacancy rate: 0.0%

Health Insurance: 94.2% have insurance; 70.3% have private insurance; 34.8% have public insurance; 5.8% do not have insurance; 2.6% of children under 18 do not have insurance

Transportation: Commute: 80.7% car, 7.0% public transportation, 0.3% walk, 9.6% work from home; Mean travel time to work: 32.4 minutes

RAMAPO (town). Covers a land area of 61.198 square miles and a water area of 0.696 square miles. Located at 41.14° N. Lat; 74.10° W. Long. Elevation is 331 feet.

History: Ramapo was formerly known as New Hempstead then later Hampstead. The city name, recorded variously as Ramopuck, Ramapock, or Ramapough, is Native American for either "sweet water" or "sloping/slanting rocks."

Population: 134,440; Growth (since 2000): 23.4%; Density: 2,196.8 persons per square mile; Race: 70.5% White, 15.4% Black/African American, 3.7% Asian, 0.1% American Indian/Alaska Native, 0.0% Native Hawaiian/Other Pacific Islander, 1.7% Two or more races, 14.1% Hispanic of any race; Average household size: 3.79; Median age: 28.0; Age under 18: 36.2%; Age 65 and over: 11.5%; Males per 100 females: 100.0; Marriage status: 33.5% never married, 55.7% now married, 1.9% separated, 5.0% widowed, 5.8% divorced; Foreign born: 22.4%; Speak English only: 47.5%; With disability: 7.8%; Veterans: 3.0%; Ancestry: 12.5% American, 7.6% Hungarian, 7.1% European, 6.3% Haitian, 6.1% Italian

Employment: 14.8% management, business, and financial, 3.8% computer, engineering, and science, 17.5% education, legal, community service, arts, and media, 7.1% healthcare practitioners, 20.3% service, 23.2% sales and office, 6.9% natural resources, construction, and maintenance, 6.5% production, transportation, and material moving

Income: Per capita: $26,148; Median household: $69,245; Average household: $96,306; Households with income of $100,000 or more: 34.9%; Poverty rate: 24.0%

Educational Attainment: High school diploma or higher: 82.6%; Bachelor's degree or higher: 32.1%; Graduate/professional degree or higher: 15.2%

Housing: Homeownership rate: 57.9%; Median home value: $417,300; Median year structure built: 1970; Homeowner vacancy rate: 1.2%; Median selected monthly owner costs: $3,002 with a mortgage, $1,331 without a mortgage; Median gross rent: $1,354 per month; Rental vacancy rate: 2.5%

Health Insurance: 90.6% have insurance; 48.9% have private insurance; 50.8% have public insurance; 9.4% do not have insurance; 4.0% of children under 18 do not have insurance

Safety: Violent crime rate: 4.7 per 10,000 population; Property crime rate: 73.7 per 10,000 population

Transportation: Commute: 75.8% car, 9.9% public transportation, 6.1% walk, 5.6% work from home; Mean travel time to work: 28.5 minutes

Additional Information Contacts

Town of Ramapo . . . . (845) 357-5100
  http://www.ramapo.org

SLOATSBURG (village). Covers a land area of 2.467 square miles and a water area of 0.038 square miles. Located at 41.16° N. Lat; 74.19° W. Long. Elevation is 341 feet.

History: Settled before 1775, incorporated 1929.

Population: 3,142; Growth (since 2000): 0.8%; Density: 1,273.6 persons per square mile; Race: 90.1% White, 5.8% Black/African American, 1.3% Asian, 0.0% American Indian/Alaska Native, 0.0% Native Hawaiian/Other Pacific Islander, 0.9% Two or more races, 15.0% Hispanic of any race; Average household size: 2.82; Median age: 42.0; Age under 18: 22.4%; Age 65 and over: 14.7%; Males per 100 females: 104.2; Marriage status: 33.6% never married, 51.2% now married, 1.4% separated, 6.0% widowed, 9.2% divorced; Foreign born: 13.7%; Speak English only: 84.0%; With disability: 12.4%; Veterans: 6.4%; Ancestry: 30.8% Italian, 21.5% Irish, 13.5% German, 6.6% English, 6.0% American

Employment: 14.9% management, business, and financial, 3.6% computer, engineering, and science, 20.6% education, legal, community service, arts, and media, 4.7% healthcare practitioners, 17.9% service, 22.8% sales and office, 9.7% natural resources, construction, and maintenance, 5.9% production, transportation, and material moving

Income: Per capita: $36,623; Median household: $91,042; Average household: $101,922; Households with income of $100,000 or more: 46.1%; Poverty rate: 4.9%

Educational Attainment: High school diploma or higher: 94.3%; Bachelor's degree or higher: 38.1%; Graduate/professional degree or higher: 14.7%

School District(s)

Ramapo Central SD (Suffern) (KG-12)
  Enrollment: 4,337 . . . . (845) 357-7783

Housing: Homeownership rate: 79.2%; Median home value: $302,200; Median year structure built: 1957; Homeowner vacancy rate: 0.6%; Median selected monthly owner costs: $2,576 with a mortgage, $1,308 without a mortgage; Median gross rent: $1,470 per month; Rental vacancy rate: 0.0%

Health Insurance: 94.1% have insurance; 80.8% have private insurance; 25.2% have public insurance; 5.9% do not have insurance; 1.4% of children under 18 do not have insurance

Transportation: Commute: 87.9% car, 4.6% public transportation, 1.7% walk, 5.8% work from home; Mean travel time to work: 31.7 minutes

SOUTH NYACK (village). Covers a land area of 0.605 square miles and a water area of 1.079 square miles. Located at 41.08° N. Lat; 73.92° W. Long. Elevation is 72 feet.

History: Incorporated 1878.

Population: 3,546; Growth (since 2000): 2.1%; Density: 5,861.1 persons per square mile; Race: 71.0% White, 15.9% Black/African American, 5.1% Asian, 0.8% American Indian/Alaska Native, 0.3% Native Hawaiian/Other Pacific Islander, 5.3% Two or more races, 9.8% Hispanic of any race; Average household size: 2.27; Median age: 40.9; Age under 18: 14.6%; Age 65 and over: 16.9%; Males per 100 females: 87.1; Marriage status: 45.6% never married, 40.3% now married, 0.5% separated, 5.3% widowed, 8.7% divorced; Foreign born: 13.9%; Speak English only: 78.4%; With disability: 12.5%; Veterans: 3.8%; Ancestry: 15.6% Irish, 12.5% German, 12.0% Italian, 10.9% Haitian, 8.7% English

Employment: 19.3% management, business, and financial, 7.3% computer, engineering, and science, 24.5% education, legal, community service, arts, and media, 7.4% healthcare practitioners, 10.7% service, 21.7% sales and office, 4.2% natural resources, construction, and maintenance, 4.8% production, transportation, and material moving

Income: Per capita: $49,608; Median household: $99,643; Average household: $135,814; Households with income of $100,000 or more: 50.0%; Poverty rate: 5.3%

Educational Attainment: High school diploma or higher: 97.3%; Bachelor's degree or higher: 59.9%; Graduate/professional degree or higher: 28.8%

Housing: Homeownership rate: 61.0%; Median home value: $462,600; Median year structure built: Before 1940; Homeowner vacancy rate: 3.3%; Median selected monthly owner costs: $3,596 with a mortgage, $1,501 without a mortgage; Median gross rent: $1,688 per month; Rental vacancy rate: 6.8%

Health Insurance: 96.1% have insurance; 80.8% have private insurance; 28.4% have public insurance; 3.9% do not have insurance; 1.9% of children under 18 do not have insurance

Safety: Violent crime rate: 8.5 per 10,000 population; Property crime rate: 42.5 per 10,000 population

Transportation: Commute: 73.3% car, 14.3% public transportation, 4.7% walk, 7.5% work from home; Mean travel time to work: 31.7 minutes

SPARKILL (CDP). Covers a land area of 0.529 square miles and a water area of 0 square miles. Located at 41.03° N. Lat; 73.93° W. Long. Elevation is 52 feet.

Population: 1,893; Growth (since 2000): n/a; Density: 3,575.6 persons per square mile; Race: 63.8% White, 4.4% Black/African American, 12.6% Asian, 0.0% American Indian/Alaska Native, 0.0% Native Hawaiian/Other Pacific Islander, 7.9% Two or more races, 17.7% Hispanic of any race; Average household size: 3.09; Median age: 37.3; Age under 18: 24.3%; Age 65 and over: 9.2%; Males per 100 females: 96.9; Marriage status: 37.3% never married, 51.8% now married, 0.0% separated, 5.2% widowed, 5.6% divorced; Foreign born: 22.4%; Speak English only: 66.8%; With disability: 7.9%; Veterans: 0.0%; Ancestry: 16.6% Italian, 10.1% Irish, 7.1% German, 5.8% Polish, 5.5% Greek

Employment: 14.9% management, business, and financial, 6.0% computer, engineering, and science, 17.7% education, legal, community service, arts, and media, 9.6% healthcare practitioners, 14.4% service, 27.1% sales and office, 5.6% natural resources, construction, and maintenance, 4.6% production, transportation, and material moving

Income: Per capita: $45,378; Median household: $114,871; Average household: $137,478; Households with income of $100,000 or more: 60.4%; Poverty rate: 5.4%

Educational Attainment: High school diploma or higher: 95.0%; Bachelor's degree or higher: 56.6%; Graduate/professional degree or higher: 23.8%

Four-year College(s)

St. Thomas Aquinas College (Private, Not-for-profit)
  Enrollment: 1,915 . . . . (845) 398-4000
  Tuition: In-state $30,750; Out-of-state $30,750

Housing: Homeownership rate: 91.2%; Median home value: $446,800; Median year structure built: 1964; Homeowner vacancy rate: 0.0%; Median selected monthly owner costs: $3,110 with a mortgage, $1,257 without a mortgage; Median gross rent: n/a per month; Rental vacancy rate: 0.0%

Health Insurance: 98.3% have insurance; 89.0% have private insurance; 17.5% have public insurance; 1.7% do not have insurance; 0.0% of children under 18 do not have insurance

Transportation: Commute: 85.8% car, 12.2% public transportation, 0.0% walk, 1.9% work from home; Mean travel time to work: 36.5 minutes

SPRING VALLEY (village). Covers a land area of 2.016 square miles and a water area of 0.002 square miles. Located at 41.11° N. Lat; 74.05° W. Long. Elevation is 446 feet.

History: Named for a spring in the area. Incorporated 1902.

Population: 32,538; Growth (since 2000): 27.8%; Density: 16,142.0 persons per square mile; Race: 34.8% White, 37.6% Black/African American, 2.5% Asian, 0.0% American Indian/Alaska Native, 0.0% Native Hawaiian/Other Pacific Islander, 2.0% Two or more races, 29.9% Hispanic of any race; Average household size: 3.62; Median age: 29.6; Age under 18: 33.1%; Age 65 and over: 8.1%; Males per 100 females: 103.1; Marriage status: 40.0% never married, 48.2% now married, 4.2% separated, 4.6% widowed, 7.2% divorced; Foreign born: 42.3%; Speak English only: 32.9%; With disability: 7.3%; Veterans: 1.8%; Ancestry: 19.1% Haitian, 8.1% American, 3.7% Hungarian, 3.5% Jamaican, 3.1% Polish

Employment: 8.7% management, business, and financial, 2.0% computer, engineering, and science, 8.3% education, legal, community service, arts, and media, 4.1% healthcare practitioners, 35.0% service, 22.0% sales and office, 10.0% natural resources, construction, and maintenance, 9.9% production, transportation, and material moving

Income: Per capita: $20,518; Median household: $43,434; Average household: $67,677; Households with income of $100,000 or more: 17.0%; Poverty rate: 25.9%

Educational Attainment: High school diploma or higher: 68.3%; Bachelor's degree or higher: 15.4%; Graduate/professional degree or higher: 5.1%

School District(s)

East Ramapo Central SD (Spring Valley) (KG-12)
  Enrollment: 9,010 . . . . (845) 577-6011

Four-year College(s)

Be'er Yaakov Talmudic Seminary (Private, Not-for-profit)
Enrollment: 510 . . . . (845) 406-9699
Tuition: In-state $9,300; Out-of-state $9,300
Housing: Homeownership rate: 28.0%; Median home value: $278,600; Median year structure built: 1968; Homeowner vacancy rate: 3.0%; Median selected monthly owner costs: $2,200 with a mortgage, $880 without a mortgage; Median gross rent: $1,293 per month; Rental vacancy rate: 3.6%
Health Insurance: 80.0% have insurance; 34.3% have private insurance; 51.6% have public insurance; 20.0% do not have insurance; 6.6% of children under 18 do not have insurance
Safety: Violent crime rate: 40.6 per 10,000 population; Property crime rate: 118.9 per 10,000 population
Transportation: Commute: 72.9% car, 14.2% public transportation, 5.2% walk, 2.2% work from home; Mean travel time to work: 26.1 minutes
Additional Information Contacts
Village of Spring Valley . . . . (845) 352-1100
http://www.villagespringvalley.org

STONY POINT (CDP).

Covers a land area of 5.442 square miles and a water area of 1.293 square miles. Located at 41.23° N. Lat; 74.00° W. Long. Elevation is 118 feet.
Population: 12,920; Growth (since 2000): 10.0%; Density: 2,374.3 persons per square mile; Race: 77.3% White, 10.0% Black/African American, 1.8% Asian, 0.2% American Indian/Alaska Native, 0.0% Native Hawaiian/Other Pacific Islander, 3.2% Two or more races, 19.4% Hispanic of any race; Average household size: 2.99; Median age: 41.8; Age under 18: 21.4%; Age 65 and over: 17.3%; Males per 100 females: 96.5; Marriage status: 33.0% never married, 56.2% now married, 1.8% separated, 6.3% widowed, 4.5% divorced; Foreign born: 10.2%; Speak English only: 81.5%; With disability: 12.1%; Veterans: 6.0%; Ancestry: 27.1% Italian, 24.0% Irish, 12.6% German, 5.1% English, 2.8% American
Employment: 16.2% management, business, and financial, 3.5% computer, engineering, and science, 13.7% education, legal, community service, arts, and media, 6.1% healthcare practitioners, 18.0% service, 24.6% sales and office, 9.3% natural resources, construction, and maintenance, 8.6% production, transportation, and material moving
Income: Per capita: $38,628; Median household: $94,519; Average household: $112,723; Households with income of $100,000 or more: 48.0%; Poverty rate: 7.5%
Educational Attainment: High school diploma or higher: 94.0%; Bachelor's degree or higher: 32.4%; Graduate/professional degree or higher: 14.6%

School District(s)

Haverstraw-Stony Point CSD (North Rockland) (KG-12)
Enrollment: 7,981 . . . . (845) 942-3002
Housing: Homeownership rate: 83.2%; Median home value: $359,400; Median year structure built: 1968; Homeowner vacancy rate: 2.2%; Median selected monthly owner costs: $2,923 with a mortgage, $1,115 without a mortgage; Median gross rent: $1,557 per month; Rental vacancy rate: 13.7%
Health Insurance: 95.2% have insurance; 83.8% have private insurance; 26.7% have public insurance; 4.8% do not have insurance; 3.0% of children under 18 do not have insurance
Transportation: Commute: 91.4% car, 3.0% public transportation, 0.2% walk, 3.0% work from home; Mean travel time to work: 31.8 minutes

STONY POINT (town).

Covers a land area of 27.624 square miles and a water area of 3.975 square miles. Located at 41.25° N. Lat; 74.00° W. Long. Elevation is 118 feet.
History: Named for a local rocky bluff that projects into the Hudson River. Nearby is Stony Point Museum (1936) in battlefield reservation (part of Palisades Interstate Park), commemorating storming of Stony Point by "Mad" Anthony Wayne's Continental forces in July 1779.
Population: 15,501; Growth (since 2000): 8.8%; Density: 561.1 persons per square mile; Race: 79.5% White, 8.6% Black/African American, 1.9% Asian, 0.2% American Indian/Alaska Native, 0.0% Native Hawaiian/Other Pacific Islander, 3.1% Two or more races, 17.9% Hispanic of any race; Average household size: 2.96; Median age: 43.0; Age under 18: 21.2%; Age 65 and over: 16.8%; Males per 100 females: 97.1; Marriage status: 31.5% never married, 56.9% now married, 1.6% separated, 6.0% widowed, 5.6% divorced; Foreign born: 10.0%; Speak English only: 82.2%; With disability: 11.1%; Veterans: 6.0%; Ancestry: 26.6% Italian, 23.9% Irish, 13.3% German, 6.1% English, 3.5% American

Employment: 18.2% management, business, and financial, 3.3% computer, engineering, and science, 15.1% education, legal, community service, arts, and media, 5.4% healthcare practitioners, 16.9% service, 23.7% sales and office, 9.3% natural resources, construction, and maintenance, 7.9% production, transportation, and material moving
Income: Per capita: $41,431; Median household: $101,630; Average household: $119,660; Households with income of $100,000 or more: 51.0%; Poverty rate: 6.9%
Educational Attainment: High school diploma or higher: 93.5%; Bachelor's degree or higher: 35.7%; Graduate/professional degree or higher: 16.7%

School District(s)

Haverstraw-Stony Point CSD (North Rockland) (KG-12)
Enrollment: 7,981 . . . . (845) 942-3002
Housing: Homeownership rate: 84.4%; Median home value: $371,300; Median year structure built: 1970; Homeowner vacancy rate: 1.8%; Median selected monthly owner costs: $2,971 with a mortgage, $1,141 without a mortgage; Median gross rent: $1,499 per month; Rental vacancy rate: 12.3%
Health Insurance: 95.4% have insurance; 84.6% have private insurance; 25.7% have public insurance; 4.6% do not have insurance; 3.1% of children under 18 do not have insurance
Safety: Violent crime rate: 5.8 per 10,000 population; Property crime rate: 48.9 per 10,000 population
Transportation: Commute: 90.5% car, 4.0% public transportation, 0.3% walk, 3.3% work from home; Mean travel time to work: 32.0 minutes
Additional Information Contacts
Town of Stony Point . . . . (845) 786-2716
http://www.townofstonypoint.org

SUFFERN (village).

Covers a land area of 2.089 square miles and a water area of 0.028 square miles. Located at 41.11° N. Lat; 74.14° W. Long. Elevation is 312 feet.
History: Named for John Suffern, original member of the first state legislature. Incorporated 1896.
Population: 10,984; Growth (since 2000): -0.2%; Density: 5,258.9 persons per square mile; Race: 77.6% White, 3.6% Black/African American, 7.1% Asian, 0.0% American Indian/Alaska Native, 0.0% Native Hawaiian/Other Pacific Islander, 3.1% Two or more races, 19.6% Hispanic of any race; Average household size: 2.50; Median age: 42.7; Age under 18: 18.5%; Age 65 and over: 19.5%; Males per 100 females: 94.6; Marriage status: 31.5% never married, 51.9% now married, 2.3% separated, 6.3% widowed, 10.2% divorced; Foreign born: 20.7%; Speak English only: 73.1%; With disability: 12.7%; Veterans: 4.9%; Ancestry: 18.1% Italian, 15.2% Irish, 9.1% German, 8.1% Polish, 7.6% American
Employment: 15.6% management, business, and financial, 7.3% computer, engineering, and science, 17.0% education, legal, community service, arts, and media, 5.4% healthcare practitioners, 18.5% service, 23.8% sales and office, 6.4% natural resources, construction, and maintenance, 6.0% production, transportation, and material moving
Income: Per capita: $39,887; Median household: $87,554; Average household: $99,314; Households with income of $100,000 or more: 42.6%; Poverty rate: 7.1%
Educational Attainment: High school diploma or higher: 92.3%; Bachelor's degree or higher: 42.8%; Graduate/professional degree or higher: 22.0%

School District(s)

East Ramapo Central SD (Spring Valley) (KG-12)
Enrollment: 9,010 . . . . (845) 577-6011
Ramapo Central SD (Suffern) (KG-12)
Enrollment: 4,337 . . . . (845) 357-7783

Four-year College(s)

Yeshiva Shaarei Torah of Rockland (Private, Not-for-profit, Jewish)
Enrollment: 93 . . . . (845) 352-3431
Tuition: In-state $12,500; Out-of-state $12,500

Two-year College(s)

Rockland Community College (Public)
Enrollment: 6,950 . . . . (845) 574-4000
Tuition: In-state $5,037; Out-of-state $9,623
Housing: Homeownership rate: 72.0%; Median home value: $311,000; Median year structure built: 1970; Homeowner vacancy rate: 2.3%; Median selected monthly owner costs: $2,535 with a mortgage, $1,051 without a mortgage; Median gross rent: $1,355 per month; Rental vacancy rate: 1.7%

Health Insurance: 92.0% have insurance; 75.2% have private insurance; 30.9% have public insurance; 8.0% do not have insurance; 1.7% of children under 18 do not have insurance
Hospitals: Good Samaritan Hospital of Suffern (370 beds)
Safety: Violent crime rate: 10.9 per 10,000 population; Property crime rate: 55.5 per 10,000 population
Transportation: Commute: 81.7% car, 10.3% public transportation, 2.9% walk, 4.7% work from home; Mean travel time to work: 32.9 minutes
Additional Information Contacts
Village of Suffern . . . . (845) 357-2600
 http://www.suffernvillage.com

TAPPAN (CDP). Covers a land area of 2.771 square miles and a water area of 0.006 square miles. Located at 41.03° N. Lat; 73.95° W. Long. Elevation is 43 feet.
History: De Wint Mansion was Washington's headquarters in 1780 and 1783. John Andre, British spy in the American Revolution, was tried and hanged here.
Population: 7,049; Growth (since 2000): 4.3%; Density: 2,544.0 persons per square mile; Race: 79.9% White, 1.2% Black/African American, 16.4% Asian, 0.0% American Indian/Alaska Native, 0.0% Native Hawaiian/Other Pacific Islander, 0.8% Two or more races, 8.5% Hispanic of any race; Average household size: 2.97; Median age: 45.8; Age under 18: 20.9%; Age 65 and over: 22.4%; Males per 100 females: 95.4; Marriage status: 27.4% never married, 57.2% now married, 1.0% separated, 7.9% widowed, 7.5% divorced; Foreign born: 20.8%; Speak English only: 75.1%; With disability: 8.5%; Veterans: 5.1%; Ancestry: 24.1% Irish, 16.9% Italian, 8.6% German, 6.5% American, 4.4% English
Employment: 21.4% management, business, and financial, 2.8% computer, engineering, and science, 15.2% education, legal, community service, arts, and media, 10.4% healthcare practitioners, 13.4% service, 26.2% sales and office, 3.1% natural resources, construction, and maintenance, 7.5% production, transportation, and material moving
Income: Per capita: $53,896; Median household: $112,143; Average household: $158,822; Households with income of $100,000 or more: 54.5%; Poverty rate: 3.1%
Educational Attainment: High school diploma or higher: 91.5%; Bachelor's degree or higher: 51.8%; Graduate/professional degree or higher: 22.6%
School District(s)
South Orangetown Central SD (KG-12)
 Enrollment: 3,114 . . . . (845) 680-1050
Housing: Homeownership rate: 93.9%; Median home value: $478,600; Median year structure built: 1967; Homeowner vacancy rate: 0.0%; Median selected monthly owner costs: $2,965 with a mortgage, $1,362 without a mortgage; Median gross rent: $2,227 per month; Rental vacancy rate: 18.6%
Health Insurance: 97.6% have insurance; 84.9% have private insurance; 28.1% have public insurance; 2.4% do not have insurance; 3.1% of children under 18 do not have insurance
Transportation: Commute: 91.3% car, 5.0% public transportation, 0.5% walk, 2.9% work from home; Mean travel time to work: 31.7 minutes

THIELLS (CDP). Covers a land area of 1.827 square miles and a water area of 0.031 square miles. Located at 41.20° N. Lat; 74.01° W. Long. Elevation is 272 feet.
Population: 5,511; Growth (since 2000): 15.8%; Density: 3,016.7 persons per square mile; Race: 73.8% White, 10.6% Black/African American, 7.5% Asian, 0.0% American Indian/Alaska Native, 0.0% Native Hawaiian/Other Pacific Islander, 2.1% Two or more races, 23.1% Hispanic of any race; Average household size: 3.41; Median age: 43.9; Age under 18: 18.8%; Age 65 and over: 16.7%; Males per 100 females: 94.9; Marriage status: 35.0% never married, 53.7% now married, 2.2% separated, 4.2% widowed, 7.2% divorced; Foreign born: 15.0%; Speak English only: 71.0%; With disability: 9.7%; Veterans: 4.4%; Ancestry: 24.0% Italian, 20.0% Irish, 8.5% German, 4.2% Haitian, 3.4% English
Employment: 13.0% management, business, and financial, 4.0% computer, engineering, and science, 16.2% education, legal, community service, arts, and media, 7.3% healthcare practitioners, 21.1% service, 28.8% sales and office, 5.4% natural resources, construction, and maintenance, 4.3% production, transportation, and material moving
Income: Per capita: $38,307; Median household: $122,614; Average household: $126,216; Households with income of $100,000 or more: 61.6%; Poverty rate: 2.8%

Educational Attainment: High school diploma or higher: 94.4%; Bachelor's degree or higher: 42.1%; Graduate/professional degree or higher: 15.3%
School District(s)
Haverstraw-Stony Point CSD (North Rockland) (KG-12)
 Enrollment: 7,981 . . . . (845) 942-3002
Housing: Homeownership rate: 90.5%; Median home value: $373,000; Median year structure built: 1973; Homeowner vacancy rate: 0.0%; Median selected monthly owner costs: $3,042 with a mortgage, $1,338 without a mortgage; Median gross rent: $1,925 per month; Rental vacancy rate: 0.0%
Health Insurance: 94.6% have insurance; 81.7% have private insurance; 25.7% have public insurance; 5.4% do not have insurance; 1.5% of children under 18 do not have insurance
Transportation: Commute: 87.7% car, 6.7% public transportation, 1.5% walk, 2.7% work from home; Mean travel time to work: 32.1 minutes

TOMKINS COVE (unincorporated postal area)
ZCTA: 10986
 Covers a land area of 10.801 square miles and a water area of 0.173 square miles. Located at 41.29° N. Lat; 74.00° W. Long. Elevation is 144 feet.
Population: 1,831; Growth (since 2000): 5.3%; Density: 169.5 persons per square mile; Race: 90.2% White, 2.3% Black/African American, 1.3% Asian, 0.0% American Indian/Alaska Native, 0.0% Native Hawaiian/Other Pacific Islander, 4.2% Two or more races, 11.6% Hispanic of any race; Average household size: 3.09; Median age: 42.9; Age under 18: 23.8%; Age 65 and over: 9.1%; Males per 100 females: 100.6; Marriage status: 27.3% never married, 61.6% now married, 0.8% separated, 3.2% widowed, 8.0% divorced; Foreign born: 9.2%; Speak English only: 83.7%; With disability: 4.3%; Veterans: 6.8%; Ancestry: 26.1% Irish, 22.1% Italian, 18.0% German, 13.1% English, 8.8% Norwegian
Employment: 29.5% management, business, and financial, 1.5% computer, engineering, and science, 21.6% education, legal, community service, arts, and media, 2.4% healthcare practitioners, 13.1% service, 19.7% sales and office, 10.4% natural resources, construction, and maintenance, 1.8% production, transportation, and material moving
Income: Per capita: $56,319; Median household: $126,959; Average household: $172,136; Households with income of $100,000 or more: 66.0%; Poverty rate: 3.6%
Educational Attainment: High school diploma or higher: 94.9%; Bachelor's degree or higher: 53.4%; Graduate/professional degree or higher: 23.2%
Housing: Homeownership rate: 89.2%; Median home value: $469,500; Median year structure built: 1978; Homeowner vacancy rate: 0.0%; Median selected monthly owner costs: $3,250 with a mortgage, $1,501 without a mortgage; Median gross rent: $1,205 per month; Rental vacancy rate: 0.0%
Health Insurance: 99.5% have insurance; 93.3% have private insurance; 14.9% have public insurance; 0.5% do not have insurance; 1.7% of children under 18 do not have insurance
Transportation: Commute: 85.8% car, 7.6% public transportation, 1.1% walk, 5.4% work from home; Mean travel time to work: 35.0 minutes

UPPER NYACK (village). Covers a land area of 1.222 square miles and a water area of 3.143 square miles. Located at 41.12° N. Lat; 73.91° W. Long. Elevation is 187 feet.
Population: 2,204; Growth (since 2000): 18.3%; Density: 1,804.0 persons per square mile; Race: 86.8% White, 6.7% Black/African American, 2.9% Asian, 0.2% American Indian/Alaska Native, 0.0% Native Hawaiian/Other Pacific Islander, 2.6% Two or more races, 5.4% Hispanic of any race; Average household size: 2.55; Median age: 46.8; Age under 18: 24.7%; Age 65 and over: 20.4%; Males per 100 females: 100.1; Marriage status: 30.3% never married, 55.1% now married, 0.6% separated, 6.7% widowed, 7.9% divorced; Foreign born: 9.4%; Speak English only: 90.5%; With disability: 9.3%; Veterans: 4.5%; Ancestry: 20.0% Irish, 17.0% Italian, 11.7% German, 11.5% American, 6.0% English
Employment: 20.2% management, business, and financial, 9.6% computer, engineering, and science, 26.8% education, legal, community service, arts, and media, 5.5% healthcare practitioners, 11.1% service, 17.1% sales and office, 7.9% natural resources, construction, and maintenance, 1.9% production, transportation, and material moving

Income: Per capita: $68,405; Median household: $127,167; Average household: $186,291; Households with income of $100,000 or more: 63.4%; Poverty rate: 2.6%

Educational Attainment: High school diploma or higher: 97.7%; Bachelor's degree or higher: 64.2%; Graduate/professional degree or higher: 35.1%

School District(s)

Nyack Union Free SD (KG-12)
    Enrollment: 3,083 . . . . (845) 353-7015

Housing: Homeownership rate: 88.1%; Median home value: $531,400; Median year structure built: 1954; Homeowner vacancy rate: 0.0%; Median selected monthly owner costs: $3,259 with a mortgage, $1,501 without a mortgage; Median gross rent: $1,714 per month; Rental vacancy rate: 0.0%

Health Insurance: 96.1% have insurance; 88.6% have private insurance; 23.3% have public insurance; 3.9% do not have insurance; 0.0% of children under 18 do not have insurance

Transportation: Commute: 76.9% car, 8.8% public transportation, 0.9% walk, 13.2% work from home; Mean travel time to work: 33.4 minutes

VALLEY COTTAGE (CDP).

Covers a land area of 4.309 square miles and a water area of 0.023 square miles. Located at 41.12° N. Lat; 73.94° W. Long. Elevation is 177 feet.

History: Valley Cottage is a hamlet and census-designated place in the town of Clarkstown, Rockland County, New York.

Population: 10,230; Growth (since 2000): 10.4%; Density: 2,374.4 persons per square mile; Race: 70.4% White, 6.5% Black/African American, 14.4% Asian, 0.2% American Indian/Alaska Native, 0.0% Native Hawaiian/Other Pacific Islander, 5.1% Two or more races, 18.9% Hispanic of any race; Average household size: 2.84; Median age: 45.9; Age under 18: 21.7%; Age 65 and over: 19.6%; Males per 100 females: 92.1; Marriage status: 25.7% never married, 57.1% now married, 1.8% separated, 9.7% widowed, 7.5% divorced; Foreign born: 18.2%; Speak English only: 72.5%; With disability: 12.3%; Veterans: 4.7%; Ancestry: 27.9% Italian, 16.0% Irish, 5.6% American, 4.1% Polish, 4.0% English

Employment: 15.7% management, business, and financial, 6.5% computer, engineering, and science, 14.1% education, legal, community service, arts, and media, 10.2% healthcare practitioners, 22.2% service, 22.3% sales and office, 6.4% natural resources, construction, and maintenance, 2.7% production, transportation, and material moving

Income: Per capita: $41,779; Median household: $105,148; Average household: $117,141; Households with income of $100,000 or more: 52.9%; Poverty rate: 6.2%

Educational Attainment: High school diploma or higher: 90.7%; Bachelor's degree or higher: 45.3%; Graduate/professional degree or higher: 19.1%

School District(s)

Nyack Union Free SD (KG-12)
    Enrollment: 3,083 . . . . (845) 353-7015

Housing: Homeownership rate: 81.8%; Median home value: $385,800; Median year structure built: 1971; Homeowner vacancy rate: 1.5%; Median selected monthly owner costs: $2,740 with a mortgage, $1,170 without a mortgage; Median gross rent: $1,607 per month; Rental vacancy rate: 0.0%

Health Insurance: 92.8% have insurance; 78.8% have private insurance; 27.4% have public insurance; 7.2% do not have insurance; 8.0% of children under 18 do not have insurance

Transportation: Commute: 85.9% car, 7.8% public transportation, 1.9% walk, 4.3% work from home; Mean travel time to work: 32.7 minutes

VIOLA (CDP).

Covers a land area of 2.678 square miles and a water area of <.001 square miles. Located at 41.13° N. Lat; 74.08° W. Long. Elevation is 571 feet.

History: Viola was originally known as Mechanicsville. The well known Alms House (or "County Poor House") was established in 1837, at Viola, in the Town of Ramapo, for the poor and destitute (debtors). The inmates contributed to their upkeep by tending the farm.

Population: 6,331; Growth (since 2000): 6.7%; Density: 2,363.9 persons per square mile; Race: 89.7% White, 4.3% Black/African American, 1.8% Asian, 0.0% American Indian/Alaska Native, 0.0% Native Hawaiian/Other Pacific Islander, 0.7% Two or more races, 4.7% Hispanic of any race; Average household size: 3.61; Median age: 26.6; Age under 18: 34.8%; Age 65 and over: 17.2%; Males per 100 females: 96.0; Marriage status: 36.8% never married, 48.7% now married, 1.4% separated, 10.0% widowed, 4.5% divorced; Foreign born: 14.8%; Speak English only: 59.1%;

With disability: 11.2%; Veterans: 2.1%; Ancestry: 15.8% American, 9.7% Polish, 8.8% Hungarian, 8.5% European, 6.7% German

Employment: 22.4% management, business, and financial, 4.1% computer, engineering, and science, 25.4% education, legal, community service, arts, and media, 9.2% healthcare practitioners, 6.1% service, 26.6% sales and office, 2.0% natural resources, construction, and maintenance, 4.1% production, transportation, and material moving

Income: Per capita: $29,956; Median household: $56,596; Average household: $105,760; Households with income of $100,000 or more: 37.8%; Poverty rate: 15.6%

Educational Attainment: High school diploma or higher: 87.6%; Bachelor's degree or higher: 42.4%; Graduate/professional degree or higher: 24.8%

Housing: Homeownership rate: 52.6%; Median home value: $638,400; Median year structure built: 1979; Homeowner vacancy rate: 2.3%; Median selected monthly owner costs: $3,928 with a mortgage, $1,501 without a mortgage; Median gross rent: $1,366 per month; Rental vacancy rate: 0.0%

Health Insurance: 84.4% have insurance; 55.3% have private insurance; 43.1% have public insurance; 15.6% do not have insurance; 18.7% of children under 18 do not have insurance

Transportation: Commute: 70.6% car, 8.7% public transportation, 5.3% walk, 13.3% work from home; Mean travel time to work: 31.8 minutes

WESLEY HILLS (village).

Covers a land area of 3.353 square miles and a water area of 0.023 square miles. Located at 41.16° N. Lat; 74.08° W. Long. Elevation is 531 feet.

History: Wesley Hills, originally named Wesley Chapel, named after a chapel built in 1829 by a circuit-riding preacher named James Sherwood. The northeast corner of Grandview Avenue and Route 202 was the Kakiat Airstrip. Early air-mail delivery was flown from there.

Population: 5,890; Growth (since 2000): 21.5%; Density: 1,756.8 persons per square mile; Race: 94.2% White, 0.8% Black/African American, 3.4% Asian, 0.2% American Indian/Alaska Native, 0.0% Native Hawaiian/Other Pacific Islander, 0.6% Two or more races, 2.1% Hispanic of any race; Average household size: 3.63; Median age: 30.0; Age under 18: 35.4%; Age 65 and over: 15.9%; Males per 100 females: 101.0; Marriage status: 26.8% never married, 69.5% now married, 1.2% separated, 1.7% widowed, 2.1% divorced; Foreign born: 11.9%; Speak English only: 81.0%; With disability: 6.4%; Veterans: 2.4%; Ancestry: 14.5% American, 13.2% Polish, 11.8% European, 10.5% Russian, 6.6% Italian

Employment: 21.9% management, business, and financial, 5.0% computer, engineering, and science, 14.0% education, legal, community service, arts, and media, 16.4% healthcare practitioners, 8.1% service, 27.7% sales and office, 5.6% natural resources, construction, and maintenance, 1.3% production, transportation, and material moving

Income: Per capita: $38,555; Median household: $115,250; Average household: $139,259; Households with income of $100,000 or more: 57.0%; Poverty rate: 1.8%

Educational Attainment: High school diploma or higher: 94.0%; Bachelor's degree or higher: 61.0%; Graduate/professional degree or higher: 38.3%

Housing: Homeownership rate: 94.0%; Median home value: $567,600; Median year structure built: 1967; Homeowner vacancy rate: 0.0%; Median selected monthly owner costs: $3,457 with a mortgage, $1,501 without a mortgage; Median gross rent: $1,637 per month; Rental vacancy rate: 0.0%

Health Insurance: 99.0% have insurance; 88.6% have private insurance; 30.5% have public insurance; 1.0% do not have insurance; 1.0% of children under 18 do not have insurance

Transportation: Commute: 81.2% car, 4.7% public transportation, 1.6% walk, 12.5% work from home; Mean travel time to work: 35.1 minutes

Additional Information Contacts

Village of Wesley Hills . . . . (845) 354-0400
    http://www.wesleyhills.org

WEST HAVERSTRAW (village).

Covers a land area of 1.519 square miles and a water area of 0.024 square miles. Located at 41.21° N. Lat; 73.99° W. Long. Elevation is 108 feet.

History: Named, probably, for a variation of the Dutch translation of "oat-straw," or for a Dutch name. Incorporated 1883.

Population: 10,353; Growth (since 2000): 0.6%; Density: 6,813.7 persons per square mile; Race: 52.0% White, 17.6% Black/African American, 4.7% Asian, 0.0% American Indian/Alaska Native, 0.0% Native Hawaiian/Other Pacific Islander, 4.5% Two or more races, 50.0% Hispanic of any race;

Average household size: 3.35; Median age: 33.8; Age under 18: 25.6%; Age 65 and over: 10.2%; Males per 100 females: 94.8; Marriage status: 39.4% never married, 47.5% now married, 3.1% separated, 4.2% widowed, 8.8% divorced; Foreign born: 31.4%; Speak English only: 48.7%; With disability: 9.9%; Veterans: 4.3%; Ancestry: 11.9% Irish, 11.8% Italian, 7.7% Haitian, 5.8% German, 2.9% American

Employment: 5.8% management, business, and financial, 3.3% computer, engineering, and science, 6.5% education, legal, community service, arts, and media, 4.7% healthcare practitioners, 31.2% service, 21.5% sales and office, 10.5% natural resources, construction, and maintenance, 16.5% production, transportation, and material moving

Income: Per capita: $26,795; Median household: $67,988; Average household: $87,532; Households with income of $100,000 or more: 31.1%; Poverty rate: 11.6%

Educational Attainment: High school diploma or higher: 78.9%; Bachelor's degree or higher: 18.0%; Graduate/professional degree or higher: 7.9%

School District(s)
Haverstraw-Stony Point CSD (North Rockland) (KG-12)
   Enrollment: 7,981 . . . . (845) 942-3002

Housing: Homeownership rate: 59.4%; Median home value: $265,600; Median year structure built: 1965; Homeowner vacancy rate: 0.0%; Median selected monthly owner costs: $2,645 with a mortgage, $938 without a mortgage; Median gross rent: $1,460 per month; Rental vacancy rate: 0.0%

Health Insurance: 87.9% have insurance; 61.9% have private insurance; 37.2% have public insurance; 12.1% do not have insurance; 3.1% of children under 18 do not have insurance

Hospitals: Helen Hayes Hospital (155 beds)

Transportation: Commute: 82.8% car, 7.2% public transportation, 3.4% walk, 4.2% work from home; Mean travel time to work: 28.9 minutes

Additional Information Contacts
Village of West Haverstraw . . . . (845) 947-2800
   http://westhaverstraw.wordpress.com

WEST NYACK (CDP). Covers a land area of 2.940 square miles and a water area of 0.021 square miles. Located at 41.09° N. Lat; 73.97° W. Long. Elevation is 75 feet.

Population: 3,947; Growth (since 2000): 20.3%; Density: 1,342.6 persons per square mile; Race: 81.2% White, 1.4% Black/African American, 8.6% Asian, 0.0% American Indian/Alaska Native, 0.0% Native Hawaiian/Other Pacific Islander, 2.3% Two or more races, 13.4% Hispanic of any race; Average household size: 2.66; Median age: 47.9; Age under 18: 20.9%; Age 65 and over: 17.8%; Males per 100 females: 96.0; Marriage status: 24.7% never married, 59.3% now married, 2.1% separated, 8.2% widowed, 7.8% divorced; Foreign born: 12.1%; Speak English only: 77.3%; With disability: 6.4%; Veterans: 4.3%; Ancestry: 25.4% Italian, 25.2% Irish, 9.4% American, 9.3% German, 8.5% English

Employment: 18.1% management, business, and financial, 9.7% computer, engineering, and science, 15.3% education, legal, community service, arts, and media, 9.4% healthcare practitioners, 13.9% service, 24.0% sales and office, 2.3% natural resources, construction, and maintenance, 7.2% production, transportation, and material moving

Income: Per capita: $56,189; Median household: $140,185; Average household: $149,371; Households with income of $100,000 or more: 62.8%; Poverty rate: 6.2%

Educational Attainment: High school diploma or higher: 97.6%; Bachelor's degree or higher: 47.6%; Graduate/professional degree or higher: 26.2%

School District(s)
Clarkstown Central SD (KG-12)
   Enrollment: 8,156 . . . . (845) 639-6418
Rockland Boces
   Enrollment: n/a . . . . (845) 627-4701

Vocational/Technical School(s)
Rockland County BOCES-Practical Nursing Program (Public)
   Enrollment: 47 . . . . (845) 627-4770
   Tuition: $14,800

Housing: Homeownership rate: 94.4%; Median home value: $483,800; Median year structure built: 1965; Homeowner vacancy rate: 0.0%; Median selected monthly owner costs: $2,989 with a mortgage, $1,304 without a mortgage; Median gross rent: $874 per month; Rental vacancy rate: 0.0%

Health Insurance: 97.2% have insurance; 85.6% have private insurance; 25.8% have public insurance; 2.8% do not have insurance; 0.0% of children under 18 do not have insurance

Newspapers: Rockland Review (weekly circulation 20,000)

Transportation: Commute: 85.4% car, 8.1% public transportation, 0.0% walk, 5.5% work from home; Mean travel time to work: 30.4 minutes

Saint Lawrence County

Located in northern New York; bounded on the northwest by the Saint Lawrence River; drained by the Saint Regis, Indian, Grass, Oswegatchie, and Raquette Rivers; plains area, rising to the Adirondacks in the southeast; includes Black and Cranberry Lak Covers a land area of 2,680.377 square miles, a water area of 141.062 square miles, and is located in the Eastern Time Zone at 44.49° N. Lat., 75.07° W. Long. The county was founded in 1802. County seat is Canton.

Saint Lawrence County is part of the Ogdensburg-Massena, NY Micropolitan Statistical Area. The entire metro area includes: St. Lawrence County, NY

Weather Station: Canton 4 SE — Elevation: 399 feet

	Jan	Feb	Mar	Apr	May	Jun	Jul	Aug	Sep	Oct	Nov	Dec
High	26	29	39	53	66	74	79	77	69	57	45	32
Low	5	8	18	33	44	54	58	56	48	37	28	14
Precip	2.1	1.8	2.1	2.9	3.1	3.3	3.9	3.7	4.0	3.9	3.4	2.6
Snow	20.1	16.9	12.4	3.7	tr	0.0	0.0	0.0	tr	0.6	5.8	18.5

High and Low temperatures in degrees Fahrenheit; Precipitation and Snow in inches

Weather Station: Gouverneur 3 NW — Elevation: 419 feet

	Jan	Feb	Mar	Apr	May	Jun	Jul	Aug	Sep	Oct	Nov	Dec
High	27	31	40	55	67	76	80	79	71	58	45	33
Low	6	8	18	32	42	52	56	55	46	36	28	14
Precip	2.3	2.0	2.2	3.0	3.1	3.3	3.6	3.4	3.9	4.0	3.7	2.7
Snow	21.9	18.2	13.6	3.9	tr	tr	0.0	0.0	tr	1.0	6.8	19.2

High and Low temperatures in degrees Fahrenheit; Precipitation and Snow in inches

Weather Station: Lawrenceville 3 SW — Elevation: 500 feet

	Jan	Feb	Mar	Apr	May	Jun	Jul	Aug	Sep	Oct	Nov	Dec
High	27	30	40	55	68	76	80	79	71	58	45	32
Low	8	10	20	33	45	54	59	57	49	39	29	15
Precip	2.2	1.9	2.3	3.0	3.0	3.9	4.1	3.9	4.1	3.7	3.5	2.7
Snow	15.7	14.0	13.3	4.1	0.2	0.0	0.0	0.0	0.0	0.5	6.3	14.3

High and Low temperatures in degrees Fahrenheit; Precipitation and Snow in inches

Weather Station: Massena Arpt — Elevation: 213 feet

	Jan	Feb	Mar	Apr	May	Jun	Jul	Aug	Sep	Oct	Nov	Dec
High	24	28	39	54	67	76	81	78	70	57	44	31
Low	5	8	19	33	45	53	58	56	48	37	28	14
Precip	2.2	1.9	2.3	2.8	3.1	3.4	3.6	3.5	3.6	3.2	3.1	2.6
Snow	na	na	na	na	na	na	na	na	na	na	na	na

High and Low temperatures in degrees Fahrenheit; Precipitation and Snow in inches

Weather Station: Wanakena Ranger School — Elevation: 1,509 feet

	Jan	Feb	Mar	Apr	May	Jun	Jul	Aug	Sep	Oct	Nov	Dec
High	27	30	38	52	66	74	78	76	68	55	43	31
Low	4	5	14	30	41	50	54	53	45	35	25	12
Precip	2.8	2.3	2.7	3.0	3.8	4.0	4.7	4.2	4.6	4.1	3.9	3.1
Snow	29.6	25.3	17.3	6.0	0.3	0.0	0.0	0.0	tr	1.6	11.2	25.8

High and Low temperatures in degrees Fahrenheit; Precipitation and Snow in inches

Population: 110,817; Growth (since 2000): -1.0%; Density: 41.3 persons per square mile; Race: 93.0% White, 2.4% Black/African American, 1.1% Asian, 0.7% American Indian/Alaska Native, 0.1% Native Hawaiian/Other Pacific Islander, 1.8% two or more races, 2.3% Hispanic of any race; Average household size: 2.38; Median age: 38.0; Age under 18: 20.5%; Age 65 and over: 15.8%; Males per 100 females: 103.2; Marriage status: 36.2% never married, 46.8% now married, 2.2% separated, 6.6% widowed, 10.3% divorced; Foreign born: 4.1%; Speak English only: 92.1%; With disability: 15.8%; Veterans: 8.9%; Ancestry: 17.6% Irish, 13.1% French, 11.7% English, 9.9% German, 6.5% Italian

Religion: Six largest groups: 21.9% Catholicism, 3.8% Methodist/Pietist, 2.3% Presbyterian-Reformed, 1.7% European Free-Church, 1.2% Non-denominational Protestant, 1.1% Episcopalianism/Anglicanism

Economy: Unemployment rate: 4.5%; Leading industries: 20.0 % retail trade; 12.4 % health care and social assistance; 12.4 % accommodation and food services; Farms: 1,303 totaling 356,909 acres; Company size: 3 employ 1,000 or more persons, 2 employ 500 to 999 persons, 27 employ 100 to 499 persons, 1,889 employ less than 100 persons; Business ownership: 1,744 women-owned, n/a Black-owned, n/a Hispanic-owned, 75 Asian-owned, 81 American Indian/Alaska Native-owned

Employment: 11.1% management, business, and financial, 2.4% computer, engineering, and science, 14.3% education, legal, community service, arts, and media, 6.4% healthcare practitioners, 22.6% service, 21.4% sales and office, 11.4% natural resources, construction, and maintenance, 10.4% production, transportation, and material moving

Income: Per capita: $23,554; Median household: $48,330; Average household: $61,209; Households with income of $100,000 or more: 15.8%; Poverty rate: 19.4%

Educational Attainment: High school diploma or higher: 88.1%; Bachelor's degree or higher: 23.1%; Graduate/professional degree or higher: 11.6%

Housing: Homeownership rate: 72.5%; Median home value: $88,000; Median year structure built: 1960; Homeowner vacancy rate: 2.4%; Median selected monthly owner costs: $1,069 with a mortgage, $449 without a mortgage; Median gross rent: $723 per month; Rental vacancy rate: 4.1%

Vital Statistics: Birth rate: 102.8 per 10,000 population; Death rate: 97.2 per 10,000 population; Age-adjusted cancer mortality rate: 149.9 deaths per 100,000 population

Health Insurance: 92.3% have insurance; 67.2% have private insurance; 40.3% have public insurance; 7.7% do not have insurance; 8.7% of children under 18 do not have insurance

Health Care: Physicians: 15.5 per 10,000 population; Dentists: 3.8 per 10,000 population; Hospital beds: 38.6 per 10,000 population; Hospital admissions: 993.7 per 10,000 population

Transportation: Commute: 86.9% car, 0.5% public transportation, 6.1% walk, 5.1% work from home; Mean travel time to work: 20.9 minutes

2016 Presidential Election: 50.9% Trump, 42.1% Clinton, 3.7% Johnson, 2.1% Stein

National and State Parks: Adirondack State Park; Cedar Island State Park; Cold Spring Brook State Forest; Coles Creek State Park; Degrasse State Forest; Donnerville State Forest; Greenwood Creek State Forest; Higley Flow State Park; Jacques Cartier State Park; Orebed Creek State Forest; Saint Lawrence State Forest; Saint Lawrence State Park; Silver Hill State Forest; Stammer Creek State Forest; Taylor Creek State Forest; Trout Lake State Forest; Whippoorwill Corners State Forest; Wilson Hill State Fish and Game Managemen

Additional Information Contacts

Saint Lawrence Government . . . . (315) 379-2276
  http://www.co.st-lawrence.ny.us

Saint Lawrence County Communities

BRASHER (town). Covers a land area of 91.103 square miles and a water area of 0.967 square miles. Located at 44.89° N. Lat; 74.72° W. Long.

Population: 2,597; Growth (since 2000): 11.1%; Density: 28.5 persons per square mile; Race: 94.5% White, 0.7% Black/African American, 1.0% Asian, 1.3% American Indian/Alaska Native, 0.0% Native Hawaiian/Other Pacific Islander, 1.8% Two or more races, 2.0% Hispanic of any race; Average household size: 2.68; Median age: 36.5; Age under 18: 29.1%; Age 65 and over: 11.9%; Males per 100 females: 96.4; Marriage status: 29.9% never married, 52.9% now married, 1.7% separated, 5.5% widowed, 11.6% divorced; Foreign born: 1.3%; Speak English only: 95.8%; With disability: 17.3%; Veterans: 9.6%; Ancestry: 17.6% Irish, 13.8% French, 10.4% American, 10.1% English, 8.2% Italian

Employment: 7.9% management, business, and financial, 1.7% computer, engineering, and science, 16.1% education, legal, community service, arts, and media, 4.6% healthcare practitioners, 18.3% service, 19.2% sales and office, 23.2% natural resources, construction, and maintenance, 9.1% production, transportation, and material moving

Income: Per capita: $22,517; Median household: $54,102; Average household: $59,711; Households with income of $100,000 or more: 11.6%; Poverty rate: 11.6%

Educational Attainment: High school diploma or higher: 89.0%; Bachelor's degree or higher: 13.9%; Graduate/professional degree or higher: 6.2%

Housing: Homeownership rate: 76.7%; Median home value: $91,800; Median year structure built: 1971; Homeowner vacancy rate: 1.7%; Median selected monthly owner costs: $1,082 with a mortgage, $440 without a mortgage; Median gross rent: $732 per month; Rental vacancy rate: 0.0%

Health Insurance: 93.9% have insurance; 64.0% have private insurance; 45.6% have public insurance; 6.1% do not have insurance; 0.0% of children under 18 do not have insurance

Transportation: Commute: 94.4% car, 0.0% public transportation, 0.5% walk, 5.1% work from home; Mean travel time to work: 25.2 minutes

BRASHER FALLS (CDP). Covers a land area of 1.638 square miles and a water area of 0.101 square miles. Located at 44.81° N. Lat; 74.79° W. Long. Elevation is 289 feet.

Population: 692; Growth (since 2000): n/a; Density: 422.5 persons per square mile; Race: 98.8% White, 0.3% Black/African American, 0.9% Asian, 0.0% American Indian/Alaska Native, 0.0% Native Hawaiian/Other Pacific Islander, 0.0% Two or more races, 0.0% Hispanic of any race; Average household size: 2.40; Median age: 29.7; Age under 18: 27.0%; Age 65 and over: 19.7%; Males per 100 females: 89.5; Marriage status: 32.1% never married, 49.9% now married, 2.1% separated, 6.3% widowed, 11.7% divorced; Foreign born: 1.4%; Speak English only: 97.9% With disability: 21.2%; Veterans: 10.7%; Ancestry: 18.9% Irish, 9.1% English, 7.5% French, 6.5% Italian, 5.9% French Canadian

Employment: 6.4% management, business, and financial, 5.8% computer, engineering, and science, 27.3% education, legal, community service, arts, and media, 9.6% healthcare practitioners, 6.4% service, 6.1% sales and office, 32.3% natural resources, construction, and maintenance, 6.1% production, transportation, and material moving

Income: Per capita: $24,966; Median household: $63,333; Average household: $60,305; Households with income of $100,000 or more: 3.8%; Poverty rate: 26.2%

Educational Attainment: High school diploma or higher: 91.3%; Bachelor's degree or higher: 20.7%; Graduate/professional degree or higher: 6.8%

School District(s)

Brasher Falls Central SD (PK-12)
  Enrollment: 1,034 . . . . (315) 389-5131

Housing: Homeownership rate: 61.8%; Median home value: $114,600; Median year structure built: 1955; Homeowner vacancy rate: 0.0%; Median selected monthly owner costs: $1,250 with a mortgage, $543 without a mortgage; Median gross rent: $685 per month; Rental vacancy rate: 0.0%

Health Insurance: 92.8% have insurance; 61.0% have private insurance; 49.3% have public insurance; 7.2% do not have insurance; 0.0% of children under 18 do not have insurance

Transportation: Commute: 91.6% car, 0.0% public transportation, 0.0% walk, 8.4% work from home; Mean travel time to work: 28.8 minutes

BRIER HILL (unincorporated postal area)
ZCTA: 13614
  Covers a land area of 8.966 square miles and a water area of 0 square miles. Located at 44.53° N. Lat; 75.69° W. Long. Elevation is 341 feet.

Population: 208; Growth (since 2000): -28.0%; Density: 23.2 persons per square mile; Race: 91.3% White, 0.0% Black/African American, 0.0% Asian, 7.2% American Indian/Alaska Native, 0.0% Native Hawaiian/Other Pacific Islander, 1.4% Two or more races, 0.0% Hispanic of any race; Average household size: 2.29; Median age: 57.0; Age under 18: 8.2%; Age 65 and over: 37.5%; Males per 100 females: 85.9; Marriage status: 21.0% never married, 59.5% now married, 0.0% separated, 10.8% widowed, 8.7% divorced; Foreign born: 1.9%; Speak English only: 100.0%; With disability: 23.6%; Veterans: 5.2%; Ancestry: 35.1% Irish, 24.0% English, 16.3% German, 13.9% French, 9.1% Italian

Employment: 6.6% management, business, and financial, 0.0% computer, engineering, and science, 11.8% education, legal, community service, arts, and media, 28.9% healthcare practitioners, 14.5% service, 14.5% sales and office, 18.4% natural resources, construction, and maintenance, 5.3% production, transportation, and material moving

Income: Per capita: $20,845; Median household: $25,625; Average household: $45,442; Households with income of $100,000 or more: 16.5%; Poverty rate: 19.2%

Educational Attainment: High school diploma or higher: 73.3%; Bachelor's degree or higher: 5.3%; Graduate/professional degree or higher: n/a

Housing: Homeownership rate: 70.3%; Median home value: $60,000; Median year structure built: 1995; Homeowner vacancy rate: 0.0%; Median selected monthly owner costs: $758 with a mortgage, $385 without a mortgage; Median gross rent: n/a per month; Rental vacancy rate: 0.0%

Health Insurance: 96.2% have insurance; 36.5% have private insurance; 73.1% have public insurance; 3.8% do not have insurance; 0.0% of children under 18 do not have insurance

Transportation: Commute: 86.8% car, 0.0% public transportation, 0.0% walk, 13.2% work from home; Mean travel time to work: 27.0 minutes

CANTON (town). Covers a land area of 104.765 square miles and a water area of 1.098 square miles. Located at 44.57° N. Lat; 75.21° W. Long. Elevation is 377 feet.

History: Seat of Saint Lawrence University and the State University of N.Y. College of Technology. Frederic Remington born here. Irving Bacheller born in nearby Pierrepont. Settled 1799, incorporated 1845.

Population: 11,198; Growth (since 2000): 8.4%; Density: 106.9 persons per square mile; Race: 90.7% White, 3.9% Black/African American, 2.1% Asian, 0.4% American Indian/Alaska Native, 0.2% Native Hawaiian/Other Pacific Islander, 1.6% Two or more races, 2.7% Hispanic of any race; Average household size: 2.21; Median age: 27.8; Age under 18: 13.0%; Age 65 and over: 14.9%; Males per 100 females: 96.2; Marriage status: 54.0% never married, 32.1% now married, 1.2% separated, 7.3% widowed, 6.6% divorced; Foreign born: 6.3%; Speak English only: 91.2%; With disability: 10.8%; Veterans: 5.8%; Ancestry: 16.3% Irish, 9.6% English, 8.4% German, 7.0% Italian, 6.6% French

Employment: 9.9% management, business, and financial, 3.8% computer, engineering, and science, 25.9% education, legal, community service, arts, and media, 6.0% healthcare practitioners, 16.4% service, 23.2% sales and office, 7.2% natural resources, construction, and maintenance, 7.5% production, transportation, and material moving

Income: Per capita: $22,482; Median household: $56,523; Average household: $68,501; Households with income of $100,000 or more: 19.0%; Poverty rate: 16.9%

Educational Attainment: High school diploma or higher: 90.2%; Bachelor's degree or higher: 39.0%; Graduate/professional degree or higher: 21.9%

School District(s)
Canton Central SD (PK-12)
    Enrollment: 1,324 . . . . (315) 386-8561
Saint Lawrence-Lewis Boces
    Enrollment: n/a . . . . (315) 386-4504

Four-year College(s)
SUNY College of Technology at Canton (Public)
    Enrollment: 3,180 . . . . (315) 386-7011
    Tuition: In-state $8,130; Out-of-state $12,320
St Lawrence University (Private, Not-for-profit)
    Enrollment: 2,493 . . . . (315) 229-5011
    Tuition: In-state $52,990; Out-of-state $52,990

Housing: Homeownership rate: 70.1%; Median home value: $113,600; Median year structure built: 1956; Homeowner vacancy rate: 5.9%; Median selected monthly owner costs: $1,255 with a mortgage, $497 without a mortgage; Median gross rent: $915 per month; Rental vacancy rate: 2.5%

Health Insurance: 92.8% have insurance; 74.5% have private insurance; 30.6% have public insurance; 7.2% do not have insurance; 4.2% of children under 18 do not have insurance

Newspapers: St. Lawrence Plaindealer (weekly circulation 3,500)

Transportation: Commute: 72.2% car, 2.3% public transportation, 16.6% walk, 6.3% work from home; Mean travel time to work: 19.1 minutes

Additional Information Contacts
Town of Canton . . . . (315) 386-2871
    http://www.cantonnewyork.us

CANTON (village). County seat. Covers a land area of 3.576 square miles and a water area of 0.100 square miles. Located at 44.60° N. Lat; 75.17° W. Long. Elevation is 377 feet.

Population: 6,553; Growth (since 2000): 11.4%; Density: 1,832.3 persons per square mile; Race: 87.8% White, 6.5% Black/African American, 1.9% Asian, 0.6% American Indian/Alaska Native, 0.3% Native Hawaiian/Other Pacific Islander, 1.2% Two or more races, 3.5% Hispanic of any race; Average household size: 1.92; Median age: 21.9; Age under 18: 7.7%; Age 65 and over: 12.4%; Males per 100 females: 97.7; Marriage status: 68.2% never married, 22.2% now married, 0.3% separated, 4.0% widowed, 5.6% divorced; Foreign born: 7.3%; Speak English only: 89.9%; With disability: 6.8%; Veterans: 3.9%; Ancestry: 13.5% Irish, 9.0% English, 7.7% German, 7.3% Italian, 4.7% French

Employment: 9.7% management, business, and financial, 5.5% computer, engineering, and science, 36.9% education, legal, community service, arts, and media, 4.2% healthcare practitioners, 15.3% service, 20.0% sales and office, 2.3% natural resources, construction, and maintenance, 6.0% production, transportation, and material moving

Income: Per capita: $19,104; Median household: $54,115; Average household: $70,003; Households with income of $100,000 or more: 22.3%; Poverty rate: 19.6%

Educational Attainment: High school diploma or higher: 93.6%; Bachelor's degree or higher: 53.2%; Graduate/professional degree or higher: 30.1%

School District(s)
Canton Central SD (PK-12)
    Enrollment: 1,324 . . . . (315) 386-8561
Saint Lawrence-Lewis Boces
    Enrollment: n/a . . . . (315) 386-4504

Four-year College(s)
SUNY College of Technology at Canton (Public)
    Enrollment: 3,180 . . . . (315) 386-7011
    Tuition: In-state $8,130; Out-of-state $12,320
St Lawrence University (Private, Not-for-profit)
    Enrollment: 2,493 . . . . (315) 229-5011
    Tuition: In-state $52,990; Out-of-state $52,990

Housing: Homeownership rate: 51.4%; Median home value: $161,300; Median year structure built: 1942; Homeowner vacancy rate: 10.8%; Median selected monthly owner costs: $1,343 with a mortgage, $719 without a mortgage; Median gross rent: $904 per month; Rental vacancy rate: 3.2%

Health Insurance: 93.8% have insurance; 82.4% have private insurance; 21.2% have public insurance; 6.2% do not have insurance; 4.3% of children under 18 do not have insurance

Safety: Violent crime rate: 1.5 per 10,000 population; Property crime rate: 32.0 per 10,000 population

Newspapers: St. Lawrence Plaindealer (weekly circulation 3,500)

Transportation: Commute: 52.6% car, 4.1% public transportation, 32.9% walk, 6.2% work from home; Mean travel time to work: 16.9 minutes

Additional Information Contacts
Village of Canton . . . . (315) 386-2871
    http://www.cantonnewyork.us

CHASE MILLS (unincorporated postal area)
ZCTA: 13621

    Covers a land area of 27.207 square miles and a water area of 0.825 square miles. Located at 44.83° N. Lat; 75.08° W. Long. Elevation is 269 feet.

Population: 482; Growth (since 2000): -31.0%; Density: 17.7 persons per square mile; Race: 98.1% White, 0.2% Black/African American, 0.0% Asian, 0.0% American Indian/Alaska Native, 0.0% Native Hawaiian/Other Pacific Islander, 1.7% Two or more races, 1.7% Hispanic of any race; Average household size: 2.24; Median age: 41.2; Age under 18: 23.2%; Age 65 and over: 9.8%; Males per 100 females: 101.2; Marriage status: 36.7% never married, 41.3% now married, 1.6% separated, 9.1% widowed, 12.9% divorced; Foreign born: 3.1%; Speak English only: 96.7%; With disability: 14.9%; Veterans: 8.9%; Ancestry: 16.2% Scottish, 15.1% French, 13.1% Irish, 11.8% English, 10.8% French Canadian

Employment: 6.8% management, business, and financial, 0.0% computer, engineering, and science, 10.6% education, legal, community service, arts, and media, 5.6% healthcare practitioners, 32.3% service, 12.4% sales and office, 13.0% natural resources, construction, and maintenance, 19.3% production, transportation, and material moving

Income: Per capita: $22,616; Median household: $42,788; Average household: $50,748; Households with income of $100,000 or more: 17.7%; Poverty rate: 25.3%

Educational Attainment: High school diploma or higher: 81.2%; Bachelor's degree or higher: 21.9%; Graduate/professional degree or higher: 14.0%

Housing: Homeownership rate: 83.3%; Median home value: $79,400; Median year structure built: 1974; Homeowner vacancy rate: 5.3%; Median selected monthly owner costs: $856 with a mortgage, $300 without a mortgage; Median gross rent: $1,135 per month; Rental vacancy rate: 0.0%

Health Insurance: 97.7% have insurance; 57.1% have private insurance; 54.4% have public insurance; 2.3% do not have insurance; 0.0% of children under 18 do not have insurance

Transportation: Commute: 91.3% car, 0.0% public transportation, 0.0% walk, 8.7% work from home; Mean travel time to work: 28.1 minutes

CHILDWOLD (unincorporated postal area)
ZCTA: 12922

    Covers a land area of 43.968 square miles and a water area of 1.404 square miles. Located at 44.29° N. Lat; 74.70° W. Long. Elevation is 1,627 feet.

Population: 41; Growth (since 2000): -29.3%; Density: 0.9 persons per square mile; Race: 97.6% White, 2.4% Black/African American, 0.0% Asian, 0.0% American Indian/Alaska Native, 0.0% Native Hawaiian/Other Pacific Islander, 0.0% Two or more races, 0.0% Hispanic of any race; Average household size: 2.05; Median age: 56.9; Age under 18: 9.8%; Age 65 and over: 36.6%; Males per 100 females: 103.1; Marriage status: 28.2% never married, 41.0% now married, 0.0% separated, 7.7% widowed, 23.1% divorced; Foreign born: 0.0%; Speak English only: 97.4%; With disability: 29.3%; Veterans: 5.4%; Ancestry: 41.5% German, 31.7% Irish, 19.5% French, 19.5% Scottish, 12.2% English

Employment: 22.2% management, business, and financial, 0.0% computer, engineering, and science, 5.6% education, legal, community service, arts, and media, 0.0% healthcare practitioners, 27.8% service, 33.3% sales and office, 0.0% natural resources, construction, and maintenance, 11.1% production, transportation, and material moving

Income: Per capita: $26,520; Median household: n/a; Average household: $49,365; Households with income of $100,000 or more: 10.0%; Poverty rate: 12.2%

Educational Attainment: High school diploma or higher: 91.9%; Bachelor's degree or higher: 21.6%; Graduate/professional degree or higher: 5.4%

Housing: Homeownership rate: 90.0%; Median home value: n/a; Median year structure built: 1963; Homeowner vacancy rate: 0.0%; Median selected monthly owner costs: $0 with a mortgage, $530 without a mortgage; Median gross rent: n/a per month; Rental vacancy rate: 0.0%

Health Insurance: 85.4% have insurance; 70.7% have private insurance; 48.8% have public insurance; 14.6% do not have insurance; 0.0% of children under 18 do not have insurance

Transportation: Commute: 94.4% car, 0.0% public transportation, 0.0% walk, 0.0% work from home; Mean travel time to work: 39.7 minutes

CHIPPEWA BAY (unincorporated postal area)
ZCTA: 13623

Covers a land area of 0.396 square miles and a water area of 0 square miles. Located at 44.45° N. Lat; 75.75° W. Long. Elevation is 289 feet.
Population: 18; Growth (since 2000): n/a; Density: 45.4 persons per square mile; Race: 100.0% White, 0.0% Black/African American, 0.0% Asian, 0.0% American Indian/Alaska Native, 0.0% Native Hawaiian/Other Pacific Islander, 0.0% Two or more races, 0.0% Hispanic of any race; Average household size: 1.80; Median age: 58.3; Age under 18: 0.0%; Age 65 and over: 16.7%; Males per 100 females: 104.2; Marriage status: 44.4% never married, 0.0% now married, 0.0% separated, 16.7% widowed, 38.9% divorced; Foreign born: 0.0%; Speak English only: 100.0%; With disability: 44.4%; Veterans: 16.7%; Ancestry: 38.9% American, 38.9% European

Employment: 0.0% management, business, and financial, 0.0% computer, engineering, and science, 0.0% education, legal, community service, arts, and media, 50.0% healthcare practitioners, 0.0% service, 0.0% sales and office, 0.0% natural resources, construction, and maintenance, 50.0% production, transportation, and material moving

Income: Per capita: $30,028; Median household: $63,333; Average household: $53,090; Households with income of $100,000 or more: n/a; Poverty rate: 44.4%

Educational Attainment: High school diploma or higher: 42.9%; Bachelor's degree or higher: 21.4%; Graduate/professional degree or higher: n/a

Housing: Homeownership rate: 60.0%; Median home value: n/a; Median year structure built: 1953; Homeowner vacancy rate: 0.0%; Median selected monthly owner costs: $0 with a mortgage, $0 without a mortgage; Median gross rent: n/a per month; Rental vacancy rate: 0.0%

Health Insurance: 100.0% have insurance; 33.3% have private insurance; 83.3% have public insurance; 0.0% do not have insurance; 0.0% of children under 18 do not have insurance

Transportation: Commute: 100.0% car, 0.0% public transportation, 0.0% walk, 0.0% work from home; Mean travel time to work: 0.0 minutes

CLARE (town). Covers a land area of 96.556 square miles and a water area of 0.698 square miles. Located at 44.36° N. Lat; 75.01° W. Long. Elevation is 820 feet.
Population: 161; Growth (since 2000): 43.8%; Density: 1.7 persons per square mile; Race: 100.0% White, 0.0% Black/African American, 0.0% Asian, 0.0% American Indian/Alaska Native, 0.0% Native Hawaiian/Other Pacific Islander, 0.0% Two or more races, 0.0% Hispanic of any race;

Average household size: 3.43; Median age: 36.1; Age under 18: 31.7%; Age 65 and over: 9.3%; Males per 100 females: 98.1; Marriage status: 40.3% never married, 44.4% now married, 0.8% separated, 5.6% widowed, 9.7% divorced; Foreign born: 0.0%; Speak English only: 100.0%; With disability: 12.4%; Veterans: 8.2%; Ancestry: 20.5% Irish, 19.3% Italian, 16.8% American, 13.0% French, 12.4% English

Employment: 4.5% management, business, and financial, 0.0% computer, engineering, and science, 3.0% education, legal, community service, arts, and media, 10.6% healthcare practitioners, 22.7% service, 25.8% sales and office, 19.7% natural resources, construction, and maintenance, 13.6% production, transportation, and material moving

Income: Per capita: $18,064; Median household: $49,531; Average household: $56,036; Households with income of $100,000 or more: 4.2%; Poverty rate: 25.5%

Educational Attainment: High school diploma or higher: 82.5%; Bachelor's degree or higher: 8.2%; Graduate/professional degree or higher: 2.1%

Housing: Homeownership rate: 97.9%; Median home value: $63,600; Median year structure built: 1985; Homeowner vacancy rate: 0.0%; Median selected monthly owner costs: $1,075 with a mortgage, $375 without a mortgage; Median gross rent: n/a per month; Rental vacancy rate: 0.0%

Health Insurance: 75.2% have insurance; 47.2% have private insurance; 34.2% have public insurance; 24.8% do not have insurance; 41.2% of children under 18 do not have insurance

Transportation: Commute: 96.9% car, 0.0% public transportation, 0.0% walk, 0.0% work from home; Mean travel time to work: 30.0 minutes

CLIFTON (town). Covers a land area of 134.360 square miles and a water area of 15.985 square miles. Located at 44.20° N. Lat; 74.89° W. Long.
Population: 651; Growth (since 2000): -17.7%; Density: 4.8 persons per square mile; Race: 95.4% White, 0.0% Black/African American, 0.9% Asian, 0.3% American Indian/Alaska Native, 0.0% Native Hawaiian/Other Pacific Islander, 3.1% Two or more races, 0.6% Hispanic of any race; Average household size: 2.25; Median age: 53.8; Age under 18: 15.7%; Age 65 and over: 23.7%; Males per 100 females: 109.2; Marriage status: 21.8% never married, 58.4% now married, 2.4% separated, 11.8% widowed, 8.0% divorced; Foreign born: 0.9%; Speak English only: 95.1%; With disability: 25.3%; Veterans: 14.6%; Ancestry: 16.9% Irish, 16.7% English, 14.1% French, 7.7% French Canadian, 4.9% Italian

Employment: 11.7% management, business, and financial, 0.0% computer, engineering, and science, 8.4% education, legal, community service, arts, and media, 4.2% healthcare practitioners, 29.9% service, 22.0% sales and office, 8.9% natural resources, construction, and maintenance, 15.0% production, transportation, and material moving

Income: Per capita: $24,048; Median household: $37,917; Average household: $53,839; Households with income of $100,000 or more: 13.2%; Poverty rate: 25.3%

Educational Attainment: High school diploma or higher: 83.6%; Bachelor's degree or higher: 19.4%; Graduate/professional degree or higher: 6.7%

Housing: Homeownership rate: 81.0%; Median home value: $73,300; Median year structure built: 1957; Homeowner vacancy rate: 3.9%; Median selected monthly owner costs: $1,190 with a mortgage, $405 without a mortgage; Median gross rent: $664 per month; Rental vacancy rate: 0.0%

Health Insurance: 95.7% have insurance; 57.8% have private insurance; 57.0% have public insurance; 4.3% do not have insurance; 5.6% of children under 18 do not have insurance

Transportation: Commute: 84.8% car, 0.0% public transportation, 5.4% walk, 7.8% work from home; Mean travel time to work: 31.6 minutes

COLTON (CDP). Covers a land area of 1.688 square miles and a water area of 0.073 square miles. Located at 44.57° N. Lat; 74.95° W. Long. Elevation is 873 feet.
Population: 376; Growth (since 2000): n/a; Density: 222.7 persons per square mile; Race: 98.9% White, 0.0% Black/African American, 1.1% Asian, 0.0% American Indian/Alaska Native, 0.0% Native Hawaiian/Other Pacific Islander, 0.0% Two or more races, 2.1% Hispanic of any race; Average household size: 2.39; Median age: 48.4; Age under 18: 18.1%; Age 65 and over: 13.3%; Males per 100 females: 93.8; Marriage status: 14.1% never married, 64.5% now married, 0.0% separated, 10.2% widowed, 11.2% divorced; Foreign born: 2.9%; Speak English only: 96.8%; With disability: 23.9%; Veterans: 1.0%; Ancestry: 26.6% Irish, 17.6% French Canadian, 17.3% English, 14.9% French, 10.4% American

Employment: 11.7% management, business, and financial, 7.6% computer, engineering, and science, 29.8% education, legal, community service, arts, and media, 0.0% healthcare practitioners, 18.1% service, 25.7% sales and office, 3.5% natural resources, construction, and maintenance, 3.5% production, transportation, and material moving
Income: Per capita: $29,521; Median household: $56,875; Average household: $69,429; Households with income of $100,000 or more: 27.4%; Poverty rate: 9.0%
Educational Attainment: High school diploma or higher: 92.4%; Bachelor's degree or higher: 23.6%; Graduate/professional degree or higher: 15.6%

School District(s)
Colton-Pierrepont Central SD (PK-12)
    Enrollment: 331 . . . . (315) 262-2100
Housing: Homeownership rate: 84.1%; Median home value: $98,800; Median year structure built: Before 1940; Homeowner vacancy rate: 0.0%; Median selected monthly owner costs: $1,121 with a mortgage, $459 without a mortgage; Median gross rent: $617 per month; Rental vacancy rate: 0.0%
Health Insurance: 85.6% have insurance; 63.0% have private insurance; 34.8% have public insurance; 14.4% do not have insurance; 16.9% of children under 18 do not have insurance
Transportation: Commute: 90.5% car, 0.0% public transportation, 1.8% walk, 7.7% work from home; Mean travel time to work: 20.6 minutes

COLTON (town). Covers a land area of 241.702 square miles and a water area of 13.252 square miles. Located at 44.37° N. Lat; 74.81° W. Long. Elevation is 873 feet.
Population: 1,516; Growth (since 2000): 4.3%; Density: 6.3 persons per square mile; Race: 98.7% White, 0.3% Black/African American, 0.5% Asian, 0.0% American Indian/Alaska Native, 0.0% Native Hawaiian/Other Pacific Islander, 0.5% Two or more races, 0.6% Hispanic of any race; Average household size: 2.24; Median age: 52.9; Age under 18: 17.8%; Age 65 and over: 25.3%; Males per 100 females: 104.9; Marriage status: 18.6% never married, 58.5% now married, 1.8% separated, 12.1% widowed, 10.8% divorced; Foreign born: 2.8%; Speak English only: 96.3%; With disability: 22.8%; Veterans: 8.7%; Ancestry: 26.7% English, 24.6% Irish, 14.4% French, 11.2% German, 7.2% French Canadian
Employment: 13.9% management, business, and financial, 4.5% computer, engineering, and science, 23.5% education, legal, community service, arts, and media, 5.2% healthcare practitioners, 16.0% service, 22.5% sales and office, 6.7% natural resources, construction, and maintenance, 7.7% production, transportation, and material moving
Income: Per capita: $30,778; Median household: $56,800; Average household: $68,829; Households with income of $100,000 or more: 27.9%; Poverty rate: 11.1%
Educational Attainment: High school diploma or higher: 95.1%; Bachelor's degree or higher: 33.2%; Graduate/professional degree or higher: 20.8%

School District(s)
Colton-Pierrepont Central SD (PK-12)
    Enrollment: 331 . . . . (315) 262-2100
Housing: Homeownership rate: 88.2%; Median home value: $132,200; Median year structure built: 1970; Homeowner vacancy rate: 0.0%; Median selected monthly owner costs: $1,237 with a mortgage, $452 without a mortgage; Median gross rent: $613 per month; Rental vacancy rate: 0.0%
Health Insurance: 94.3% have insurance; 74.6% have private insurance; 43.5% have public insurance; 5.7% do not have insurance; 4.7% of children under 18 do not have insurance
Transportation: Commute: 93.4% car, 0.0% public transportation, 1.1% walk, 5.0% work from home; Mean travel time to work: 22.5 minutes

CRANBERRY LAKE (CDP). Covers a land area of 19.437 square miles and a water area of 0.276 square miles. Located at 44.18° N. Lat; 74.87° W. Long. Elevation is 1,489 feet.
Population: 157; Growth (since 2000): n/a; Density: 8.1 persons per square mile; Race: 100.0% White, 0.0% Black/African American, 0.0% Asian, 0.0% American Indian/Alaska Native, 0.0% Native Hawaiian/Other Pacific Islander, 0.0% Two or more races, 0.0% Hispanic of any race; Average household size: 2.04; Median age: 61.9; Age under 18: 9.6%; Age 65 and over: 42.0%; Males per 100 females: 115.1; Marriage status: 22.8% never married, 62.8% now married, 0.0% separated, 10.3% widowed, 4.1% divorced; Foreign born: 0.0%; Speak English only: 98.7%; With disability: 18.5%; Veterans: 19.0%; Ancestry: 33.1% English, 18.5% Irish, 12.1% French, 7.6% Swedish, 5.7% French Canadian

Employment: 39.0% management, business, and financial, 0.0% computer, engineering, and science, 9.8% education, legal, community service, arts, and media, 0.0% healthcare practitioners, 31.7% service, 9.8% sales and office, 9.8% natural resources, construction, and maintenance, 0.0% production, transportation, and material moving
Income: Per capita: $32,271; Median household: $51,719; Average household: $64,062; Households with income of $100,000 or more: 18.2%; Poverty rate: 17.2%
Educational Attainment: High school diploma or higher: 95.1%; Bachelor's degree or higher: 45.8%; Graduate/professional degree or higher: 17.6%
Housing: Homeownership rate: 90.9%; Median home value: $187,500; Median year structure built: 1960; Homeowner vacancy rate: 3.8%; Median selected monthly owner costs: $1,563 with a mortgage, n/a without a mortgage; Median gross rent: n/a per month; Rental vacancy rate: 0.0%
Health Insurance: 94.3% have insurance; 82.2% have private insurance; 50.3% have public insurance; 5.7% do not have insurance; 0.0% of children under 18 do not have insurance
Transportation: Commute: 80.5% car, 0.0% public transportation, 9.8% walk, 9.8% work from home; Mean travel time to work: 31.5 minutes

DE KALB (town). Covers a land area of 82.523 square miles and a water area of 0.684 square miles. Located at 44.48° N. Lat; 75.37° W. Long. Elevation is 331 feet.
Population: 2,270; Growth (since 2000): 2.6%; Density: 27.5 persons per square mile; Race: 97.9% White, 0.7% Black/African American, 0.2% Asian, 0.0% American Indian/Alaska Native, 0.0% Native Hawaiian/Other Pacific Islander, 1.1% Two or more races, 0.4% Hispanic of any race; Average household size: 2.86; Median age: 33.3; Age under 18: 30.7%; Age 65 and over: 13.9%; Males per 100 females: 103.9; Marriage status: 34.6% never married, 52.2% now married, 3.6% separated, 5.5% widowed, 7.7% divorced; Foreign born: 2.2%; Speak English only: 89.8%; With disability: 15.3%; Veterans: 10.1%; Ancestry: 17.0% Irish, 11.2% French, 10.2% German, 8.7% American, 7.8% English
Employment: 9.0% management, business, and financial, 0.7% computer, engineering, and science, 4.8% education, legal, community service, arts, and media, 6.3% healthcare practitioners, 22.6% service, 22.6% sales and office, 24.4% natural resources, construction, and maintenance, 9.6% production, transportation, and material moving
Income: Per capita: $20,429; Median household: $50,298; Average household: $59,120; Households with income of $100,000 or more: 10.5%; Poverty rate: 23.0%
Educational Attainment: High school diploma or higher: 77.8%; Bachelor's degree or higher: 15.1%; Graduate/professional degree or higher: 5.5%
Housing: Homeownership rate: 86.4%; Median home value: $92,100; Median year structure built: 1959; Homeowner vacancy rate: 0.0%; Median selected monthly owner costs: $922 with a mortgage, $422 without a mortgage; Median gross rent: $585 per month; Rental vacancy rate: 12.3%
Health Insurance: 80.0% have insurance; 53.6% have private insurance; 43.0% have public insurance; 20.0% do not have insurance; 27.6% of children under 18 do not have insurance
Transportation: Commute: 85.4% car, 0.0% public transportation, 2.4% walk, 7.7% work from home; Mean travel time to work: 26.4 minutes

DE PEYSTER (town). Covers a land area of 42.927 square miles and a water area of 2.169 square miles. Located at 44.54° N. Lat; 75.46° W. Long. Elevation is 374 feet.
Population: 1,216; Growth (since 2000): 29.9%; Density: 28.3 persons per square mile; Race: 98.6% White, 0.8% Black/African American, 0.0% Asian, 0.2% American Indian/Alaska Native, 0.2% Native Hawaiian/Other Pacific Islander, 0.1% Two or more races, 0.7% Hispanic of any race; Average household size: 3.85; Median age: 26.1; Age under 18: 38.5%; Age 65 and over: 11.1%; Males per 100 females: 102.0; Marriage status: 33.1% never married, 57.3% now married, 3.0% separated, 4.3% widowed, 5.3% divorced; Foreign born: 2.0%; Speak English only: 59.5%; With disability: 13.0%; Veterans: 5.2%; Ancestry: 13.0% Irish, 11.8% German, 11.6% Dutch, 11.4% Pennsylvania German, 9.5% French
Employment: 28.1% management, business, and financial, 0.5% computer, engineering, and science, 9.6% education, legal, community service, arts, and media, 6.0% healthcare practitioners, 11.9% service, 12.2% sales and office, 14.5% natural resources, construction, and maintenance, 17.1% production, transportation, and material moving

Income: Per capita: $14,324; Median household: $44,063; Average household: $55,303; Households with income of $100,000 or more: 20.2%; Poverty rate: 39.0%
Educational Attainment: High school diploma or higher: 67.7%; Bachelor's degree or higher: 12.6%; Graduate/professional degree or higher: 4.4%
Housing: Homeownership rate: 89.9%; Median home value: $78,700; Median year structure built: 1973; Homeowner vacancy rate: 0.0%; Median selected monthly owner costs: $914 with a mortgage, $335 without a mortgage; Median gross rent: $690 per month; Rental vacancy rate: 0.0%
Health Insurance: 56.0% have insurance; 34.1% have private insurance; 30.7% have public insurance; 44.0% do not have insurance; 55.4% of children under 18 do not have insurance
Transportation: Commute: 63.0% car, 0.0% public transportation, 4.5% walk, 25.7% work from home; Mean travel time to work: 25.0 minutes

DEKALB JUNCTION (CDP).

Covers a land area of 3.883 square miles and a water area of 0.062 square miles. Located at 44.51° N. Lat; 75.29° W. Long.
Population: 568; Growth (since 2000): n/a; Density: 146.3 persons per square mile; Race: 99.1% White, 0.9% Black/African American, 0.0% Asian, 0.0% American Indian/Alaska Native, 0.0% Native Hawaiian/Other Pacific Islander, 0.0% Two or more races, 0.9% Hispanic of any race; Average household size: 2.96; Median age: 33.4; Age under 18: 27.8%; Age 65 and over: 9.2%; Males per 100 females: 107.6; Marriage status: 37.6% never married, 54.4% now married, 9.6% separated, 1.4% widowed, 6.7% divorced; Foreign born: 2.6%; Speak English only: 92.9%; With disability: 18.5%; Veterans: 15.1%; Ancestry: 15.8% Irish, 12.7% Dutch, 12.3% French, 10.9% American, 9.2% English
Employment: 5.5% management, business, and financial, 0.0% computer, engineering, and science, 4.2% education, legal, community service, arts, and media, 4.2% healthcare practitioners, 32.4% service, 27.7% sales and office, 19.7% natural resources, construction, and maintenance, 6.3% production, transportation, and material moving
Income: Per capita: $22,686; Median household: $57,132; Average household: $70,331; Households with income of $100,000 or more: 18.5%; Poverty rate: 7.5%
Educational Attainment: High school diploma or higher: 77.7%; Bachelor's degree or higher: 20.9%; Graduate/professional degree or higher: 1.1%

School District(s)
Hermon-Dekalb Central SD (PK-12)
    Enrollment: 420 . . . . (315) 347-3442
Housing: Homeownership rate: 92.6%; Median home value: $67,200; Median year structure built: 1956; Homeowner vacancy rate: 0.0%; Median selected monthly owner costs: $1,096 with a mortgage, $281 without a mortgage; Median gross rent: n/a per month; Rental vacancy rate: 51.7%
Health Insurance: 87.1% have insurance; 71.7% have private insurance; 30.3% have public insurance; 12.9% do not have insurance; 9.5% of children under 18 do not have insurance
Transportation: Commute: 91.4% car, 0.0% public transportation, 0.0% walk, 0.0% work from home; Mean travel time to work: 18.7 minutes

EDWARDS (town).

Covers a land area of 50.471 square miles and a water area of 0.831 square miles. Located at 44.29° N. Lat; 75.28° W. Long. Elevation is 669 feet.
Population: 1,046; Growth (since 2000): -8.9%; Density: 20.7 persons per square mile; Race: 96.5% White, 0.0% Black/African American, 0.6% Asian, 0.0% American Indian/Alaska Native, 0.0% Native Hawaiian/Other Pacific Islander, 2.9% Two or more races, 0.7% Hispanic of any race; Average household size: 2.46; Median age: 44.1; Age under 18: 19.4%; Age 65 and over: 20.8%; Males per 100 females: 94.9; Marriage status: 31.7% never married, 50.9% now married, 1.9% separated, 9.8% widowed, 7.6% divorced; Foreign born: 5.0%; Speak English only: 93.2%; With disability: 19.3%; Veterans: 9.6%; Ancestry: 16.9% English, 13.6% French Canadian, 12.4% German, 10.8% Irish, 9.9% American
Employment: 6.6% management, business, and financial, 4.5% computer, engineering, and science, 7.3% education, legal, community service, arts, and media, 8.3% healthcare practitioners, 23.4% service, 18.2% sales and office, 12.5% natural resources, construction, and maintenance, 19.1% production, transportation, and material moving
Income: Per capita: $22,898; Median household: $50,250; Average household: $55,222; Households with income of $100,000 or more: 8.1%; Poverty rate: 11.3%

Educational Attainment: High school diploma or higher: 90.0%; Bachelor's degree or higher: 13.1%; Graduate/professional degree or higher: 3.9%
Housing: Homeownership rate: 72.9%; Median home value: $72,200; Median year structure built: 1964; Homeowner vacancy rate: 0.0%; Median selected monthly owner costs: $1,063 with a mortgage, $463 without a mortgage; Median gross rent: $714 per month; Rental vacancy rate: 0.0%
Health Insurance: 94.6% have insurance; 65.6% have private insurance; 51.2% have public insurance; 5.4% do not have insurance; 0.9% of children under 18 do not have insurance
Transportation: Commute: 84.1% car, 1.4% public transportation, 3.8% walk, 6.7% work from home; Mean travel time to work: 35.3 minutes

FINE (town).

Covers a land area of 166.799 square miles and a water area of 2.618 square miles. Located at 44.15° N. Lat; 75.09° W. Long. Elevation is 965 feet.
Population: 1,412; Growth (since 2000): -12.9%; Density: 8.5 persons per square mile; Race: 95.9% White, 0.6% Black/African American, 0.7% Asian, 0.9% American Indian/Alaska Native, 0.0% Native Hawaiian/Other Pacific Islander, 1.5% Two or more races, 1.6% Hispanic of any race; Average household size: 2.12; Median age: 53.5; Age under 18: 15.9%; Age 65 and over: 27.5%; Males per 100 females: 108.6; Marriage status: 19.0% never married, 60.2% now married, 4.0% separated, 8.2% widowed, 12.5% divorced; Foreign born: 1.4%; Speak English only: 94.3%; With disability: 23.4%; Veterans: 17.3%; Ancestry: 25.1% English, 20.5% French, 15.7% Irish, 11.4% German, 7.5% American
Employment: 15.9% management, business, and financial, 1.5% computer, engineering, and science, 9.6% education, legal, community service, arts, and media, 7.4% healthcare practitioners, 24.1% service, 20.2% sales and office, 11.9% natural resources, construction, and maintenance, 9.4% production, transportation, and material moving
Income: Per capita: $26,260; Median household: $45,795; Average household: $57,567; Households with income of $100,000 or more: 16.5%; Poverty rate: 16.6%
Educational Attainment: High school diploma or higher: 84.1%; Bachelor's degree or higher: 14.1%; Graduate/professional degree or higher: 6.8%
Housing: Homeownership rate: 78.7%; Median home value: $80,900; Median year structure built: 1953; Homeowner vacancy rate: 2.0%; Median selected monthly owner costs: $980 with a mortgage, $460 without a mortgage; Median gross rent: $609 per month; Rental vacancy rate: 2.7%
Health Insurance: 97.6% have insurance; 69.1% have private insurance; 53.3% have public insurance; 2.4% do not have insurance; 0.0% of children under 18 do not have insurance
Transportation: Commute: 83.0% car, 0.0% public transportation, 3.5% walk, 12.5% work from home; Mean travel time to work: 32.9 minutes

FOWLER (town).

Covers a land area of 59.325 square miles and a water area of 1.368 square miles. Located at 44.28° N. Lat; 75.40° W. Long. Elevation is 591 feet.
Population: 2,138; Growth (since 2000): -1.9%; Density: 36.0 persons per square mile; Race: 97.1% White, 0.6% Black/African American, 0.7% Asian, 0.2% American Indian/Alaska Native, 0.0% Native Hawaiian/Other Pacific Islander, 1.4% Two or more races, 0.6% Hispanic of any race; Average household size: 2.51; Median age: 42.6; Age under 18: 20.2%; Age 65 and over: 17.1%; Males per 100 females: 102.0; Marriage status: 22.3% never married, 64.2% now married, 1.9% separated, 6.3% widowed, 7.2% divorced; Foreign born: 1.6%; Speak English only: 94.9%; With disability: 14.3%; Veterans: 10.1%; Ancestry: 16.7% Irish, 13.7% French, 12.4% English, 8.4% American, 7.1% German
Employment: 10.4% management, business, and financial, 2.3% computer, engineering, and science, 5.8% education, legal, community service, arts, and media, 4.7% healthcare practitioners, 25.9% service, 20.2% sales and office, 18.5% natural resources, construction, and maintenance, 12.1% production, transportation, and material moving
Income: Per capita: $26,576; Median household: $46,094; Average household: $65,111; Households with income of $100,000 or more: 16.5%; Poverty rate: 16.0%
Educational Attainment: High school diploma or higher: 89.1%; Bachelor's degree or higher: 13.4%; Graduate/professional degree or higher: 4.8%
Housing: Homeownership rate: 83.8%; Median home value: $101,400; Median year structure built: 1977; Homeowner vacancy rate: 0.7%; Median selected monthly owner costs: $1,070 with a mortgage, $388 without a mortgage; Median gross rent: $930 per month; Rental vacancy rate: 9.2%

Health Insurance: 94.9% have insurance; 66.7% have private insurance; 46.6% have public insurance; 5.1% do not have insurance; 0.0% of children under 18 do not have insurance
Transportation: Commute: 97.3% car, 0.0% public transportation, 0.0% walk, 2.7% work from home; Mean travel time to work: 25.4 minutes

GOUVERNEUR (town). Covers a land area of 71.217 square miles and a water area of 1.074 square miles. Located at 44.36° N. Lat; 75.49° W. Long. Elevation is 440 feet.

History: Named for Gouverneur Morris, whose mansion still stands. Laid out 1787, Incorporated 1850.
Population: 7,023; Growth (since 2000): -5.3%; Density: 98.6 persons per square mile; Race: 89.2% White, 6.7% Black/African American, 0.0% Asian, 0.2% American Indian/Alaska Native, 0.0% Native Hawaiian/Other Pacific Islander, 1.3% Two or more races, 5.0% Hispanic of any race; Average household size: 2.47; Median age: 36.3; Age under 18: 21.6%; Age 65 and over: 11.1%; Males per 100 females: 127.8; Marriage status: 36.3% never married, 44.7% now married, 2.3% separated, 7.3% widowed, 11.7% divorced; Foreign born: 2.4%; Speak English only: 92.1%; With disability: 16.2%; Veterans: 9.7%; Ancestry: 15.3% Irish, 11.5% German, 10.5% English, 9.0% French, 6.5% Italian
Employment: 7.4% management, business, and financial, 0.5% computer, engineering, and science, 9.5% education, legal, community service, arts, and media, 9.6% healthcare practitioners, 14.8% service, 23.9% sales and office, 19.2% natural resources, construction, and maintenance, 15.1% production, transportation, and material moving
Income: Per capita: $17,023; Median household: $34,651; Average household: $47,676; Households with income of $100,000 or more: 7.2%; Poverty rate: 26.6%
Educational Attainment: High school diploma or higher: 83.9%; Bachelor's degree or higher: 10.4%; Graduate/professional degree or higher: 4.8%

School District(s)
Gouverneur Central SD (PK-12)
    Enrollment: 1,561 . . . . (315) 287-4870
Housing: Homeownership rate: 62.2%; Median home value: $91,100; Median year structure built: 1955; Homeowner vacancy rate: 4.2%; Median selected monthly owner costs: $1,063 with a mortgage, $438 without a mortgage; Median gross rent: $732 per month; Rental vacancy rate: 12.1%
Health Insurance: 89.8% have insurance; 49.2% have private insurance; 51.2% have public insurance; 10.2% do not have insurance; 11.2% of children under 18 do not have insurance
Hospitals: Gouverneur Hospital
Newspapers: Gouverneur Tribune-Press (weekly circulation 4,000)
Transportation: Commute: 92.9% car, 0.0% public transportation, 1.2% walk, 3.3% work from home; Mean travel time to work: 22.9 minutes
Additional Information Contacts
Town of Gouverneur . . . . (315) 287-2340
    http://www.gouverneurny.com

GOUVERNEUR (village). Covers a land area of 2.191 square miles and a water area of 0.087 square miles. Located at 44.34° N. Lat; 75.47° W. Long. Elevation is 440 feet.

Population: 3,795; Growth (since 2000): -11.0%; Density: 1,732.3 persons per square mile; Race: 96.4% White, 2.2% Black/African American, 0.0% Asian, 0.2% American Indian/Alaska Native, 0.0% Native Hawaiian/Other Pacific Islander, 0.7% Two or more races, 0.7% Hispanic of any race; Average household size: 2.43; Median age: 35.7; Age under 18: 23.1%; Age 65 and over: 15.2%; Males per 100 females: 93.8; Marriage status: 37.5% never married, 39.9% now married, 1.4% separated, 9.7% widowed, 12.8% divorced; Foreign born: 1.3%; Speak English only: 98.5%; With disability: 15.7%; Veterans: 12.6%; Ancestry: 15.0% Irish, 12.8% German, 12.4% French, 11.9% English, 6.0% French Canadian
Employment: 8.4% management, business, and financial, 1.0% computer, engineering, and science, 7.2% education, legal, community service, arts, and media, 8.8% healthcare practitioners, 13.4% service, 23.5% sales and office, 21.8% natural resources, construction, and maintenance, 15.8% production, transportation, and material moving
Income: Per capita: $18,366; Median household: $34,217; Average household: $45,315; Households with income of $100,000 or more: 9.0%; Poverty rate: 30.8%
Educational Attainment: High school diploma or higher: 88.6%; Bachelor's degree or higher: 9.2%; Graduate/professional degree or higher: 6.8%

School District(s)
Gouverneur Central SD (PK-12)
    Enrollment: 1,561 . . . . (315) 287-4870
Housing: Homeownership rate: 46.5%; Median home value: $93,500; Median year structure built: Before 1940; Homeowner vacancy rate: 8.6%; Median selected monthly owner costs: $959 with a mortgage, $474 without a mortgage; Median gross rent: $646 per month; Rental vacancy rate: 13.5%
Health Insurance: 90.3% have insurance; 44.7% have private insurance; 59.7% have public insurance; 9.7% do not have insurance; 1.6% of children under 18 do not have insurance
Hospitals: Gouverneur Hospital
Newspapers: Gouverneur Tribune-Press (weekly circulation 4,000)
Transportation: Commute: 95.0% car, 0.0% public transportation, 0.8% walk, 1.0% work from home; Mean travel time to work: 24.3 minutes

HAILESBORO (CDP). Covers a land area of 4.727 square miles and a water area of 0.080 square miles. Located at 44.31° N. Lat; 75.43° W. Long. Elevation is 492 feet.

Population: 731; Growth (since 2000): n/a; Density: 154.6 persons per square mile; Race: 97.9% White, 0.7% Black/African American, 0.0% Asian, 0.0% American Indian/Alaska Native, 0.0% Native Hawaiian/Other Pacific Islander, 1.4% Two or more races, 0.0% Hispanic of any race; Average household size: 2.59; Median age: 33.8; Age under 18: 23.5%; Age 65 and over: 16.7%; Males per 100 females: 89.1; Marriage status: 17.5% never married, 70.1% now married, 0.9% separated, 8.3% widowed, 4.2% divorced; Foreign born: 4.7%; Speak English only: 88.7%; With disability: 6.9%; Veterans: 6.3%; Ancestry: 23.7% Irish, 17.1% French, 10.5% American, 10.1% English, 9.8% Italian
Employment: 12.1% management, business, and financial, 2.5% computer, engineering, and science, 3.8% education, legal, community service, arts, and media, 1.7% healthcare practitioners, 23.8% service, 23.3% sales and office, 27.1% natural resources, construction, and maintenance, 5.8% production, transportation, and material moving
Income: Per capita: $23,863; Median household: $43,942; Average household: $60,714; Households with income of $100,000 or more: 11.4%; Poverty rate: 25.0%
Educational Attainment: High school diploma or higher: 86.1%; Bachelor's degree or higher: 14.1%; Graduate/professional degree or higher: 6.7%
Housing: Homeownership rate: 75.4%; Median home value: $144,600; Median year structure built: 1966; Homeowner vacancy rate: 0.0%; Median selected monthly owner costs: $1,037 with a mortgage, $415 without a mortgage; Median gross rent: $1,579 per month; Rental vacancy rate: 16.9%
Health Insurance: 95.3% have insurance; 64.0% have private insurance; 42.3% have public insurance; 4.7% do not have insurance; 0.0% of children under 18 do not have insurance
Transportation: Commute: 100.0% car, 0.0% public transportation, 0.0% walk, 0.0% work from home; Mean travel time to work: 29.9 minutes

HAMMOND (town). Covers a land area of 62.197 square miles and a water area of 15.709 square miles. Located at 44.44° N. Lat; 75.73° W. Long. Elevation is 358 feet.

Population: 1,316; Growth (since 2000): 9.0%; Density: 21.2 persons per square mile; Race: 97.4% White, 0.2% Black/African American, 0.5% Asian, 0.0% American Indian/Alaska Native, 0.0% Native Hawaiian/Other Pacific Islander, 1.8% Two or more races, 0.7% Hispanic of any race; Average household size: 2.51; Median age: 39.6; Age under 18: 23.6%; Age 65 and over: 18.5%; Males per 100 females: 97.2; Marriage status: 33.5% never married, 50.5% now married, 2.4% separated, 7.8% widowed, 8.2% divorced; Foreign born: 1.6%; Speak English only: 97.2%; With disability: 15.7%; Veterans: 10.2%; Ancestry: 19.9% Irish, 14.1% German, 12.5% French, 10.8% English, 10.3% Italian
Employment: 17.2% management, business, and financial, 1.2% computer, engineering, and science, 7.4% education, legal, community service, arts, and media, 6.8% healthcare practitioners, 19.3% service, 23.8% sales and office, 16.4% natural resources, construction, and maintenance, 7.9% production, transportation, and material moving
Income: Per capita: $24,222; Median household: $50,234; Average household: $59,545; Households with income of $100,000 or more: 13.7%; Poverty rate: 29.0%
Educational Attainment: High school diploma or higher: 83.0%; Bachelor's degree or higher: 22.5%; Graduate/professional degree or higher: 12.5%

School District(s)
Hammond Central SD (PK-12)
   Enrollment: 291 . . . . (315) 324-5931
Housing: Homeownership rate: 74.7%; Median home value: $80,300; Median year structure built: 1965; Homeowner vacancy rate: 4.1%; Median selected monthly owner costs: $1,023 with a mortgage, $446 without a mortgage; Median gross rent: $726 per month; Rental vacancy rate: 0.0%
Health Insurance: 90.5% have insurance; 54.3% have private insurance; 53.8% have public insurance; 9.5% do not have insurance; 10.3% of children under 18 do not have insurance
Transportation: Commute: 80.7% car, 0.4% public transportation, 4.7% walk, 12.2% work from home; Mean travel time to work: 28.8 minutes

HAMMOND (village). Covers a land area of 0.586 square miles and a water area of 0 square miles. Located at 44.45° N. Lat; 75.69° W. Long. Elevation is 358 feet.

Population: 312; Growth (since 2000): 3.3%; Density: 532.8 persons per square mile; Race: 96.2% White, 1.0% Black/African American, 0.6% Asian, 0.0% American Indian/Alaska Native, 0.0% Native Hawaiian/Other Pacific Islander, 2.2% Two or more races, 1.9% Hispanic of any race; Average household size: 2.50; Median age: 34.2; Age under 18: 24.4%; Age 65 and over: 14.7%; Males per 100 females: 78.3; Marriage status: 32.6% never married, 48.5% now married, 0.4% separated, 11.3% widowed, 7.5% divorced; Foreign born: 0.6%; Speak English only: 99.7%; With disability: 20.6%; Veterans: 7.0%; Ancestry: 23.7% German, 18.3% French, 16.0% Italian, 13.5% English, 9.9% Dutch
Employment: 3.9% management, business, and financial, 2.4% computer, engineering, and science, 11.0% education, legal, community service, arts, and media, 4.7% healthcare practitioners, 24.4% service, 33.1% sales and office, 11.0% natural resources, construction, and maintenance, 9.4% production, transportation, and material moving
Income: Per capita: $17,301; Median household: $32,292; Average household: $41,330; Households with income of $100,000 or more: 8.8%; Poverty rate: 31.7%
Educational Attainment: High school diploma or higher: 90.0%; Bachelor's degree or higher: 16.3%; Graduate/professional degree or higher: 11.0%

School District(s)
Hammond Central SD (PK-12)
   Enrollment: 291 . . . . (315) 324-5931
Housing: Homeownership rate: 60.8%; Median home value: $61,800; Median year structure built: Before 1940; Homeowner vacancy rate: 0.0%; Median selected monthly owner costs: $930 with a mortgage, $400 without a mortgage; Median gross rent: $635 per month; Rental vacancy rate: 0.0%
Health Insurance: 91.2% have insurance; 51.0% have private insurance; 50.7% have public insurance; 8.8% do not have insurance; 3.7% of children under 18 do not have insurance
Transportation: Commute: 81.8% car, 0.0% public transportation, 11.6% walk, 5.0% work from home; Mean travel time to work: 30.3 minutes

HANNAWA FALLS (CDP). Covers a land area of 5.110 square miles and a water area of 0.302 square miles. Located at 44.60° N. Lat; 74.97° W. Long. Elevation is 558 feet.

Population: 1,010; Growth (since 2000): n/a; Density: 197.6 persons per square mile; Race: 95.0% White, 0.8% Black/African American, 2.3% Asian, 0.0% American Indian/Alaska Native, 0.0% Native Hawaiian/Other Pacific Islander, 2.0% Two or more races, 2.0% Hispanic of any race; Average household size: 2.29; Median age: 46.3; Age under 18: 18.3%; Age 65 and over: 25.3%; Males per 100 females: 107.6; Marriage status: 26.6% never married, 61.3% now married, 0.0% separated, 7.3% widowed, 4.7% divorced; Foreign born: 4.8%; Speak English only: 99.4%; With disability: 11.3%; Veterans: 9.3%; Ancestry: 17.9% French, 16.9% Irish, 15.0% English, 10.6% German, 8.2% Italian
Employment: 7.2% management, business, and financial, 3.4% computer, engineering, and science, 27.5% education, legal, community service, arts, and media, 13.8% healthcare practitioners, 11.0% service, 21.0% sales and office, 4.4% natural resources, construction, and maintenance, 11.7% production, transportation, and material moving
Income: Per capita: $28,643; Median household: $54,917; Average household: $67,317; Households with income of $100,000 or more: 27.0%; Poverty rate: 17.0%
Educational Attainment: High school diploma or higher: 92.6%; Bachelor's degree or higher: 33.7%; Graduate/professional degree or higher: 20.5%

Housing: Homeownership rate: 79.1%; Median home value: $145,800; Median year structure built: 1982; Homeowner vacancy rate: 0.0%; Median selected monthly owner costs: $1,233 with a mortgage, $724 without a mortgage; Median gross rent: $859 per month; Rental vacancy rate: 32.8%
Health Insurance: 100.0% have insurance; 88.4% have private insurance; 37.0% have public insurance; 0.0% do not have insurance; 0.0% of children under 18 do not have insurance
Transportation: Commute: 95.1% car, 0.0% public transportation, 0.0% walk, 4.9% work from home; Mean travel time to work: 19.8 minutes

HERMON (town). Covers a land area of 53.146 square miles and a water area of 1.080 square miles. Located at 44.40° N. Lat; 75.29° W. Long. Elevation is 499 feet.

Population: 909; Growth (since 2000): -15.0%; Density: 17.1 persons per square mile; Race: 95.6% White, 1.0% Black/African American, 0.0% Asian, 0.0% American Indian/Alaska Native, 1.4% Native Hawaiian/Other Pacific Islander, 1.4% Two or more races, 1.8% Hispanic of any race; Average household size: 2.27; Median age: 48.1; Age under 18: 17.3%; Age 65 and over: 22.2%; Males per 100 females: 97.5; Marriage status: 25.3% never married, 52.6% now married, 3.7% separated, 10.1% widowed, 12.1% divorced; Foreign born: 2.6%; Speak English only: 95.7%; With disability: 17.6%; Veterans: 12.0%; Ancestry: 17.5% English, 15.0% Irish, 13.2% French, 7.2% German, 6.6% American
Employment: 11.3% management, business, and financial, 1.3% computer, engineering, and science, 10.1% education, legal, community service, arts, and media, 6.0% healthcare practitioners, 35.0% service, 16.9% sales and office, 11.3% natural resources, construction, and maintenance, 8.1% production, transportation, and material moving
Income: Per capita: $24,016; Median household: $44,489; Average household: $53,635; Households with income of $100,000 or more: 9.0%; Poverty rate: 14.8%
Educational Attainment: High school diploma or higher: 86.1%; Bachelor's degree or higher: 16.4%; Graduate/professional degree or higher: 6.4%
Housing: Homeownership rate: 78.9%; Median home value: $82,800; Median year structure built: 1950; Homeowner vacancy rate: 1.6%; Median selected monthly owner costs: $1,013 with a mortgage, $478 without a mortgage; Median gross rent: $607 per month; Rental vacancy rate: 9.7%
Health Insurance: 92.1% have insurance; 68.1% have private insurance; 45.1% have public insurance; 7.9% do not have insurance; 3.6% of children under 18 do not have insurance
Transportation: Commute: 97.9% car, 0.0% public transportation, 1.3% walk, 0.8% work from home; Mean travel time to work: 34.4 minutes

HERMON (village). Covers a land area of 0.380 square miles and a water area of 0 square miles. Located at 44.47° N. Lat; 75.23° W. Long. Elevation is 499 feet.

Population: 353; Growth (since 2000): -12.2%; Density: 929.2 persons per square mile; Race: 93.8% White, 2.5% Black/African American, 0.0% Asian, 0.0% American Indian/Alaska Native, 0.3% Native Hawaiian/Other Pacific Islander, 3.1% Two or more races, 3.4% Hispanic of any race; Average household size: 1.97; Median age: 38.9; Age under 18: 18.4%; Age 65 and over: 22.9%; Males per 100 females: 84.3; Marriage status: 36.9% never married, 35.5% now married, 4.8% separated, 10.3% widowed, 17.2% divorced; Foreign born: 2.5%; Speak English only: 98.8%; With disability: 22.4%; Veterans: 11.8%; Ancestry: 22.9% Irish, 15.9% English, 13.3% German, 11.0% Italian, 6.2% French
Employment: 8.6% management, business, and financial, 3.6% computer, engineering, and science, 7.1% education, legal, community service, arts, and media, 12.9% healthcare practitioners, 27.1% service, 18.6% sales and office, 4.3% natural resources, construction, and maintenance, 17.9% production, transportation, and material moving
Income: Per capita: $22,829; Median household: $36,328; Average household: $46,271; Households with income of $100,000 or more: 7.8%; Poverty rate: 24.5%
Educational Attainment: High school diploma or higher: 79.8%; Bachelor's degree or higher: 19.0%; Graduate/professional degree or higher: 6.6%
Housing: Homeownership rate: 65.0%; Median home value: $72,800; Median year structure built: Before 1940; Homeowner vacancy rate: 4.2%; Median selected monthly owner costs: $1,038 with a mortgage, $482 without a mortgage; Median gross rent: $575 per month; Rental vacancy rate: 12.7%

Health Insurance: 89.8% have insurance; 63.5% have private insurance; 49.3% have public insurance; 10.2% do not have insurance; 0.0% of children under 18 do not have insurance

Transportation: Commute: 93.8% car, 0.0% public transportation, 3.9% walk, 2.3% work from home; Mean travel time to work: 30.6 minutes

HEUVELTON (village). Covers a land area of 0.761 square miles and a water area of 0.107 square miles. Located at 44.62° N. Lat; 75.40° W. Long. Elevation is 315 feet.

Population: 680; Growth (since 2000): -15.4%; Density: 893.9 persons per square mile; Race: 96.9% White, 1.0% Black/African American, 0.0% Asian, 0.7% American Indian/Alaska Native, 0.0% Native Hawaiian/Other Pacific Islander, 0.9% Two or more races, 0.7% Hispanic of any race; Average household size: 2.40; Median age: 43.4; Age under 18: 22.9%; Age 65 and over: 12.9%; Males per 100 females: 84.0; Marriage status: 26.1% never married, 57.8% now married, 4.7% separated, 7.8% widowed, 8.3% divorced; Foreign born: 3.5%; Speak English only: 96.8%; With disability: 15.0%; Veterans: 6.1%; Ancestry: 18.7% English, 15.4% Irish, 12.1% French, 8.2% American, 8.2% French Canadian

Employment: 9.8% management, business, and financial, 2.9% computer, engineering, and science, 6.6% education, legal, community service, arts, and media, 10.7% healthcare practitioners, 30.6% service, 19.9% sales and office, 9.2% natural resources, construction, and maintenance, 10.1% production, transportation, and material moving

Income: Per capita: $27,656; Median household: $58,750; Average household: $64,666; Households with income of $100,000 or more: 23.7%; Poverty rate: 9.3%

Educational Attainment: High school diploma or higher: 92.0%; Bachelor's degree or higher: 19.8%; Graduate/professional degree or higher: 10.3%

School District(s)

Heuvelton Central SD (PK-12)

    Enrollment: 527 . . . . (315) 344-2414

Housing: Homeownership rate: 74.6%; Median home value: $83,400; Median year structure built: Before 1940; Homeowner vacancy rate: 1.4%; Median selected monthly owner costs: $1,088 with a mortgage, $481 without a mortgage; Median gross rent: $612 per month; Rental vacancy rate: 10.0%

Health Insurance: 95.0% have insurance; 75.0% have private insurance; 34.3% have public insurance; 5.0% do not have insurance; 0.0% of children under 18 do not have insurance

Transportation: Commute: 91.5% car, 0.0% public transportation, 4.6% walk, 3.3% work from home; Mean travel time to work: 26.5 minutes

HOPKINTON (town). Covers a land area of 185.340 square miles and a water area of 1.704 square miles. Located at 44.54° N. Lat; 74.66° W. Long. Elevation is 794 feet.

Population: 1,121; Growth (since 2000): 9.9%; Density: 6.0 persons per square mile; Race: 96.5% White, 0.0% Black/African American, 0.7% Asian, 1.2% American Indian/Alaska Native, 0.0% Native Hawaiian/Other Pacific Islander, 1.2% Two or more races, 1.9% Hispanic of any race; Average household size: 2.73; Median age: 41.1; Age under 18: 30.3%; Age 65 and over: 20.3%; Males per 100 females: 104.8; Marriage status: 24.7% never married, 61.9% now married, 2.0% separated, 4.9% widowed, 8.4% divorced; Foreign born: 1.6%; Speak English only: 98.2%; With disability: 15.0%; Veterans: 12.8%; Ancestry: 22.8% Irish, 21.4% German, 13.2% French, 8.4% English, 8.2% American

Employment: 13.9% management, business, and financial, 13.1% computer, engineering, and science, 10.6% education, legal, community service, arts, and media, 6.1% healthcare practitioners, 20.0% service, 11.9% sales and office, 15.6% natural resources, construction, and maintenance, 8.9% production, transportation, and material moving

Income: Per capita: $21,286; Median household: $42,917; Average household: $57,053; Households with income of $100,000 or more: 15.6%; Poverty rate: 10.2%

Educational Attainment: High school diploma or higher: 86.8%; Bachelor's degree or higher: 22.1%; Graduate/professional degree or higher: 9.4%

Housing: Homeownership rate: 90.8%; Median home value: $86,900; Median year structure built: 1966; Homeowner vacancy rate: 1.3%; Median selected monthly owner costs: $1,186 with a mortgage, $467 without a mortgage; Median gross rent: $705 per month; Rental vacancy rate: 0.0%

Health Insurance: 90.5% have insurance; 65.0% have private insurance; 39.2% have public insurance; 9.5% do not have insurance; 7.8% of children under 18 do not have insurance

Transportation: Commute: 93.7% car, 0.0% public transportation, 4.6% walk, 1.7% work from home; Mean travel time to work: 28.6 minutes

LAWRENCE (town). Covers a land area of 47.610 square miles and a water area of 0.058 square miles. Located at 44.75° N. Lat; 74.68° W. Long.

Population: 1,847; Growth (since 2000): 19.5%; Density: 38.8 persons per square mile; Race: 94.8% White, 0.2% Black/African American, 1.4% Asian, 0.6% American Indian/Alaska Native, 0.0% Native Hawaiian/Other Pacific Islander, 2.8% Two or more races, 2.3% Hispanic of any race; Average household size: 2.91; Median age: 36.2; Age under 18: 32.1%; Age 65 and over: 11.7%; Males per 100 females: 102.9; Marriage status: 30.5% never married, 54.2% now married, 1.1% separated, 3.9% widowed, 11.5% divorced; Foreign born: 2.5%; Speak English only: 84.5%; With disability: 17.1%; Veterans: 11.3%; Ancestry: 18.1% French, 14.0% German, 13.0% English, 9.6% Irish, 7.4% American

Employment: 9.5% management, business, and financial, 0.7% computer, engineering, and science, 6.6% education, legal, community service, arts, and media, 6.6% healthcare practitioners, 28.1% service, 20.5% sales and office, 11.0% natural resources, construction, and maintenance, 17.1% production, transportation, and material moving

Income: Per capita: $19,103; Median household: $43,030; Average household: $55,963; Households with income of $100,000 or more: 12.2%; Poverty rate: 28.4%

Educational Attainment: High school diploma or higher: 79.7%; Bachelor's degree or higher: 13.9%; Graduate/professional degree or higher: 5.7%

Housing: Homeownership rate: 81.7%; Median home value: $73,800; Median year structure built: 1972; Homeowner vacancy rate: 3.4%; Median selected monthly owner costs: $1,069 with a mortgage, $414 without a mortgage; Median gross rent: $575 per month; Rental vacancy rate: 0.0%

Health Insurance: 82.6% have insurance; 54.1% have private insurance; 38.7% have public insurance; 17.4% do not have insurance; 27.0% of children under 18 do not have insurance

Transportation: Commute: 87.7% car, 0.0% public transportation, 5.2% walk, 5.6% work from home; Mean travel time to work: 24.4 minutes

LISBON (town). Covers a land area of 108.280 square miles and a water area of 5.636 square miles. Located at 44.70° N. Lat; 75.31° W. Long. Elevation is 338 feet.

Population: 4,080; Growth (since 2000): 0.8%; Density: 37.7 persons per square mile; Race: 97.8% White, 0.7% Black/African American, 0.0% Asian, 0.2% American Indian/Alaska Native, 0.0% Native Hawaiian/Other Pacific Islander, 1.3% Two or more races, 0.2% Hispanic of any race; Average household size: 2.42; Median age: 43.5; Age under 18: 24.2%; Age 65 and over: 16.6%; Males per 100 females: 101.3; Marriage status: 24.0% never married, 55.9% now married, 0.3% separated, 5.9% widowed, 14.3% divorced; Foreign born: 3.4%; Speak English only: 93.9%; With disability: 15.4%; Veterans: 10.6%; Ancestry: 15.2% Irish, 11.4% French, 9.9% French Canadian, 6.7% Italian, 6.1% American

Employment: 9.0% management, business, and financial, 0.6% computer, engineering, and science, 11.3% education, legal, community service, arts, and media, 7.8% healthcare practitioners, 31.4% service, 16.5% sales and office, 12.6% natural resources, construction, and maintenance, 10.9% production, transportation, and material moving

Income: Per capita: $30,013; Median household: $61,131; Average household: $72,164; Households with income of $100,000 or more: 23.5%; Poverty rate: 9.3%

Educational Attainment: High school diploma or higher: 88.7%; Bachelor's degree or higher: 17.1%; Graduate/professional degree or higher: 8.1%

School District(s)

Lisbon Central SD (PK-12)

    Enrollment: 600 . . . . (315) 393-4951

Housing: Homeownership rate: 85.8%; Median home value: $89,700; Median year structure built: 1974; Homeowner vacancy rate: 0.0%; Median selected monthly owner costs: $1,086 with a mortgage, $398 without a mortgage; Median gross rent: n/a per month; Rental vacancy rate: 0.0%

Health Insurance: 93.1% have insurance; 74.0% have private insurance; 33.4% have public insurance; 6.9% do not have insurance; 9.4% of children under 18 do not have insurance

Transportation: Commute: 96.1% car, 0.0% public transportation, 1.6% walk, 2.2% work from home; Mean travel time to work: 20.8 minutes

Additional Information Contacts
Town of Lisbon . . . . (315) 393-5988
http://www.lisbonny.net

LOUISVILLE (town). Covers a land area of 48.525 square miles and a water area of 15.342 square miles. Located at 44.91° N. Lat; 75.01° W. Long. Elevation is 217 feet.

Population: 3,108; Growth (since 2000): -2.7%; Density: 64.0 persons per square mile; Race: 94.4% White, 0.0% Black/African American, 1.2% Asian, 1.0% American Indian/Alaska Native, 0.0% Native Hawaiian/Other Pacific Islander, 2.7% Two or more races, 2.8% Hispanic of any race; Average household size: 2.23; Median age: 50.7; Age under 18: 15.7%; Age 65 and over: 19.4%; Males per 100 females: 93.2; Marriage status: 21.3% never married, 60.1% now married, 3.9% separated, 7.3% widowed, 11.3% divorced; Foreign born: 3.5%; Speak English only: 96.3%; With disability: 19.3%; Veterans: 8.1%; Ancestry: 23.6% Irish, 17.6% French, 13.8% English, 9.6% German, 6.0% American

Employment: 18.8% management, business, and financial, 1.9% computer, engineering, and science, 13.2% education, legal, community service, arts, and media, 4.5% healthcare practitioners, 23.3% service, 21.2% sales and office, 13.4% natural resources, construction, and maintenance, 3.7% production, transportation, and material moving

Income: Per capita: $35,128; Median household: $65,204; Average household: $77,489; Households with income of $100,000 or more: 25.2%; Poverty rate: 6.4%

Educational Attainment: High school diploma or higher: 91.2%; Bachelor's degree or higher: 33.5%; Graduate/professional degree or higher: 15.1%

Housing: Homeownership rate: 80.3%; Median home value: $119,900; Median year structure built: 1973; Homeowner vacancy rate: 2.5%; Median selected monthly owner costs: $1,198 with a mortgage, $511 without a mortgage; Median gross rent: $769 per month; Rental vacancy rate: 0.0%

Health Insurance: 95.9% have insurance; 84.3% have private insurance; 32.5% have public insurance; 4.1% do not have insurance; 0.0% of children under 18 do not have insurance

Transportation: Commute: 92.3% car, 0.0% public transportation, 0.5% walk, 6.7% work from home; Mean travel time to work: 19.5 minutes

MACOMB (town). Covers a land area of 60.717 square miles and a water area of 2.428 square miles. Located at 44.44° N. Lat; 75.57° W. Long.

Population: 995; Growth (since 2000): 17.6%; Density: 16.4 persons per square mile; Race: 97.0% White, 0.6% Black/African American, 0.9% Asian, 0.3% American Indian/Alaska Native, 0.0% Native Hawaiian/Other Pacific Islander, 0.3% Two or more races, 1.2% Hispanic of any race; Average household size: 2.68; Median age: 40.0; Age under 18: 21.9%; Age 65 and over: 18.1%; Males per 100 females: 116.7; Marriage status: 31.5% never married, 52.0% now married, 1.6% separated, 6.2% widowed, 10.3% divorced; Foreign born: 3.7%; Speak English only: 93.7%; With disability: 15.5%; Veterans: 7.7%; Ancestry: 16.7% American, 14.4% English, 11.2% Irish, 7.6% Polish, 7.2% French

Employment: 8.1% management, business, and financial, 2.0% computer, engineering, and science, 7.6% education, legal, community service, arts, and media, 11.2% healthcare practitioners, 21.8% service, 21.6% sales and office, 16.2% natural resources, construction, and maintenance, 11.4% production, transportation, and material moving

Income: Per capita: $24,904; Median household: $51,705; Average household: $66,747; Households with income of $100,000 or more: 17.5%; Poverty rate: 26.5%

Educational Attainment: High school diploma or higher: 88.6%; Bachelor's degree or higher: 15.0%; Graduate/professional degree or higher: 7.1%

Housing: Homeownership rate: 85.4%; Median home value: $87,300; Median year structure built: 1965; Homeowner vacancy rate: 0.0%; Median selected monthly owner costs: $1,097 with a mortgage, $422 without a mortgage; Median gross rent: n/a per month; Rental vacancy rate: 18.2%

Health Insurance: 89.8% have insurance; 60.7% have private insurance; 46.2% have public insurance; 10.2% do not have insurance; 3.9% of children under 18 do not have insurance

Transportation: Commute: 90.7% car, 0.5% public transportation, 2.1% walk, 6.7% work from home; Mean travel time to work: 29.6 minutes

MADRID (CDP). Covers a land area of 3.727 square miles and a water area of 0.133 square miles. Located at 44.75° N. Lat; 75.13° W. Long. Elevation is 325 feet.

Population: 688; Growth (since 2000): n/a; Density: 184.6 persons per square mile; Race: 95.6% White, 1.0% Black/African American, 0.0% Asian, 1.5% American Indian/Alaska Native, 0.0% Native Hawaiian/Other Pacific Islander, 1.9% Two or more races, 2.5% Hispanic of any race; Average household size: 2.38; Median age: 49.3; Age under 18: 18.7%; Age 65 and over: 28.5%; Males per 100 females: 102.4; Marriage status: 29.8% never married, 50.8% now married, 4.7% separated, 11.7% widowed, 7.6% divorced; Foreign born: 2.5%; Speak English only: 96.3%; With disability: 27.0%; Veterans: 4.5%; Ancestry: 17.7% English, 15.0% French, 11.6% Irish, 8.9% German, 8.4% Scottish

Employment: 15.0% management, business, and financial, 4.3% computer, engineering, and science, 8.3% education, legal, community service, arts, and media, 4.0% healthcare practitioners, 24.1% service, 20.6% sales and office, 18.6% natural resources, construction, and maintenance, 5.1% production, transportation, and material moving

Income: Per capita: $20,813; Median household: $44,750; Average household: $51,345; Households with income of $100,000 or more: 12.2%; Poverty rate: 24.7%

Educational Attainment: High school diploma or higher: 79.3%; Bachelor's degree or higher: 22.2%; Graduate/professional degree or higher: 10.5%

School District(s)

Madrid-Waddington Central SD (PK-12)
    Enrollment: 697 . . . . (315) 322-5746

Housing: Homeownership rate: 63.9%; Median home value: $82,700; Median year structure built: Before 1940; Homeowner vacancy rate: 0.0%; Median selected monthly owner costs: $1,250 with a mortgage, $550 without a mortgage; Median gross rent: $657 per month; Rental vacancy rate: 0.0%

Health Insurance: 92.0% have insurance; 54.9% have private insurance; 56.3% have public insurance; 8.0% do not have insurance; 13.6% of children under 18 do not have insurance

Transportation: Commute: 82.1% car, 0.0% public transportation, 6.1% walk, 10.6% work from home; Mean travel time to work: 23.0 minutes

MADRID (town). Covers a land area of 52.984 square miles and a water area of 0.598 square miles. Located at 44.77° N. Lat; 75.13° W. Long. Elevation is 325 feet.

Population: 1,699; Growth (since 2000): -7.1%; Density: 32.1 persons per square mile; Race: 95.2% White, 0.5% Black/African American, 0.2% Asian, 0.6% American Indian/Alaska Native, 0.0% Native Hawaiian/Other Pacific Islander, 2.9% Two or more races, 3.2% Hispanic of any race; Average household size: 2.50; Median age: 41.0; Age under 18: 22.7%; Age 65 and over: 19.4%; Males per 100 females: 101.7; Marriage status: 27.1% never married, 56.2% now married, 3.1% separated, 8.1% widowed, 8.5% divorced; Foreign born: 3.2%; Speak English only: 95.1%; With disability: 19.2%; Veterans: 7.9%; Ancestry: 15.9% English, 15.5% Irish, 15.2% French, 10.2% Scottish, 9.1% German

Employment: 14.2% management, business, and financial, 1.9% computer, engineering, and science, 8.7% education, legal, community service, arts, and media, 5.9% healthcare practitioners, 23.8% service, 20.6% sales and office, 16.7% natural resources, construction, and maintenance, 8.3% production, transportation, and material moving

Income: Per capita: $23,305; Median household: $47,313; Average household: $58,650; Households with income of $100,000 or more: 16.7%; Poverty rate: 20.4%

Educational Attainment: High school diploma or higher: 85.4%; Bachelor's degree or higher: 23.5%; Graduate/professional degree or higher: 9.5%

School District(s)

Madrid-Waddington Central SD (PK-12)
    Enrollment: 697 . . . . (315) 322-5746

Housing: Homeownership rate: 76.8%; Median home value: $92,700; Median year structure built: 1957; Homeowner vacancy rate: 1.9%; Median selected monthly owner costs: $1,205 with a mortgage, $494 without a mortgage; Median gross rent: $686 per month; Rental vacancy rate: 0.0%

Health Insurance: 94.0% have insurance; 64.2% have private insurance; 49.3% have public insurance; 6.0% do not have insurance; 6.5% of children under 18 do not have insurance

Transportation: Commute: 89.8% car, 0.0% public transportation, 3.8% walk, 5.9% work from home; Mean travel time to work: 22.3 minutes

MASSENA (town). Covers a land area of 44.369 square miles and a water area of 11.774 square miles. Located at 44.96° N. Lat; 74.83° W. Long. Elevation is 230 feet.

History: Settled 1792, incorporated 1886.
Population: 12,471; Growth (since 2000): -5.0%; Density: 281.1 persons per square mile; Race: 93.6% White, 0.2% Black/African American, 1.3% Asian, 2.0% American Indian/Alaska Native, 0.0% Native Hawaiian/Other Pacific Islander, 2.7% Two or more races, 0.6% Hispanic of any race; Average household size: 2.19; Median age: 41.3; Age under 18: 22.2%; Age 65 and over: 18.5%; Males per 100 females: 91.9; Marriage status: 31.0% never married, 47.1% now married, 2.8% separated, 8.3% widowed, 13.6% divorced; Foreign born: 4.6%; Speak English only: 93.9%; With disability: 19.4%; Veterans: 9.8%; Ancestry: 23.2% Irish, 21.2% French, 11.0% French Canadian, 10.4% English, 8.2% German
Employment: 16.1% management, business, and financial, 2.3% computer, engineering, and science, 11.4% education, legal, community service, arts, and media, 4.4% healthcare practitioners, 21.7% service, 22.9% sales and office, 8.2% natural resources, construction, and maintenance, 13.0% production, transportation, and material moving
Income: Per capita: $23,292; Median household: $41,066; Average household: $50,910; Households with income of $100,000 or more: 11.9%; Poverty rate: 24.4%
Educational Attainment: High school diploma or higher: 89.3%; Bachelor's degree or higher: 23.6%; Graduate/professional degree or higher: 11.2%

School District(s)
Massena Central SD (PK-12)
    Enrollment: 2,704 . . . . (315) 764-3700
Housing: Homeownership rate: 66.2%; Median home value: $76,600; Median year structure built: 1954; Homeowner vacancy rate: 2.8%; Median selected monthly owner costs: $934 with a mortgage, $447 without a mortgage; Median gross rent: $711 per month; Rental vacancy rate: 2.9%
Health Insurance: 95.0% have insurance; 62.9% have private insurance; 49.4% have public insurance; 5.0% do not have insurance; 1.9% of children under 18 do not have insurance
Hospitals: Massena Memorial Hospital (50 beds)
Newspapers: Daily Courier-Observer (daily circulation 4,900)
Transportation: Commute: 91.6% car, 0.4% public transportation, 3.4% walk, 3.1% work from home; Mean travel time to work: 17.7 minutes
Airports: Massena International-Richards Field (commercial service–non-primary)
Additional Information Contacts
Town of Massena . . . . (315) 769-5228
    http://www.massena.ny.us

MASSENA (village). Covers a land area of 4.524 square miles and a water area of 0.200 square miles. Located at 44.93° N. Lat; 74.89° W. Long. Elevation is 230 feet.
Population: 10,839; Growth (since 2000): -3.3%; Density: 2,395.7 persons per square mile; Race: 94.3% White, 0.2% Black/African American, 1.4% Asian, 1.8% American Indian/Alaska Native, 0.0% Native Hawaiian/Other Pacific Islander, 2.1% Two or more races, 0.6% Hispanic of any race; Average household size: 2.21; Median age: 38.6; Age under 18: 22.5%; Age 65 and over: 16.9%; Males per 100 females: 90.6; Marriage status: 31.1% never married, 47.4% now married, 2.9% separated, 8.5% widowed, 13.0% divorced; Foreign born: 4.1%; Speak English only: 94.6%; With disability: 19.0%; Veterans: 9.4%; Ancestry: 25.2% Irish, 21.4% French, 11.0% English, 10.6% French Canadian, 8.3% Italian
Employment: 15.6% management, business, and financial, 2.9% computer, engineering, and science, 12.4% education, legal, community service, arts, and media, 4.9% healthcare practitioners, 19.5% service, 24.6% sales and office, 7.4% natural resources, construction, and maintenance, 12.7% production, transportation, and material moving
Income: Per capita: $23,293; Median household: $40,970; Average household: $51,422; Households with income of $100,000 or more: 12.3%; Poverty rate: 24.0%
Educational Attainment: High school diploma or higher: 89.1%; Bachelor's degree or higher: 23.8%; Graduate/professional degree or higher: 11.7%

School District(s)
Massena Central SD (PK-12)
    Enrollment: 2,704 . . . . (315) 764-3700
Housing: Homeownership rate: 65.4%; Median home value: $75,100; Median year structure built: 1953; Homeowner vacancy rate: 3.3%; Median

selected monthly owner costs: $933 with a mortgage, $470 without a mortgage; Median gross rent: $715 per month; Rental vacancy rate: 3.2%
Health Insurance: 95.3% have insurance; 63.5% have private insurance; 48.4% have public insurance; 4.7% do not have insurance; 1.4% of children under 18 do not have insurance
Hospitals: Massena Memorial Hospital (50 beds)
Newspapers: Daily Courier-Observer (daily circulation 4,900)
Transportation: Commute: 92.3% car, 0.2% public transportation, 3.5% walk, 2.2% work from home; Mean travel time to work: 16.8 minutes
Airports: Massena International-Richards Field (commercial service–non-primary)
Additional Information Contacts
Village of Massena . . . . (315) 769-8625
    http://www.massenaworks.com

MORRISTOWN (town). Covers a land area of 45.721 square miles and a water area of 13.724 square miles. Located at 44.53° N. Lat; 75.63° W. Long. Elevation is 289 feet.
Population: 1,704; Growth (since 2000): -16.9%; Density: 37.3 persons per square mile; Race: 94.4% White, 0.2% Black/African American, 0.5% Asian, 1.5% American Indian/Alaska Native, 0.0% Native Hawaiian/Other Pacific Islander, 3.5% Two or more races, 2.9% Hispanic of any race; Average household size: 2.25; Median age: 52.8; Age under 18: 16.0%; Age 65 and over: 25.5%; Males per 100 females: 96.4; Marriage status: 21.0% never married, 56.8% now married, 2.1% separated, 8.5% widowed, 13.7% divorced; Foreign born: 3.7%; Speak English only: 90.1%; With disability: 16.8%; Veterans: 11.0%; Ancestry: 18.1% German, 15.8% Irish, 13.7% English, 9.0% American, 8.6% French
Employment: 12.9% management, business, and financial, 0.3% computer, engineering, and science, 12.8% education, legal, community service, arts, and media, 8.1% healthcare practitioners, 14.3% service, 28.0% sales and office, 10.6% natural resources, construction, and maintenance, 13.1% production, transportation, and material moving
Income: Per capita: $35,438; Median household: $50,402; Average household: $80,382; Households with income of $100,000 or more: 21.4%; Poverty rate: 18.6%
Educational Attainment: High school diploma or higher: 85.3%; Bachelor's degree or higher: 18.8%; Graduate/professional degree or higher: 6.7%

School District(s)
Morristown Central SD (PK-12)
    Enrollment: 342 . . . . (315) 375-8814
Housing: Homeownership rate: 78.7%; Median home value: $101,800; Median year structure built: 1959; Homeowner vacancy rate: 6.7%; Median selected monthly owner costs: $1,229 with a mortgage, $453 without a mortgage; Median gross rent: $819 per month; Rental vacancy rate: 16.8%
Health Insurance: 93.5% have insurance; 59.0% have private insurance; 53.1% have public insurance; 6.5% do not have insurance; 1.1% of children under 18 do not have insurance
Transportation: Commute: 90.5% car, 0.8% public transportation, 4.1% walk, 4.4% work from home; Mean travel time to work: 25.1 minutes

MORRISTOWN (village). Covers a land area of 0.980 square miles and a water area of 0.042 square miles. Located at 44.58° N. Lat; 75.65° W. Long. Elevation is 289 feet.
Population: 328; Growth (since 2000): -28.1%; Density: 334.6 persons per square mile; Race: 97.6% White, 0.9% Black/African American, 0.6% Asian, 0.0% American Indian/Alaska Native, 0.0% Native Hawaiian/Other Pacific Islander, 0.9% Two or more races, 0.3% Hispanic of any race; Average household size: 2.27; Median age: 42.4; Age under 18: 14.0%; Age 65 and over: 21.6%; Males per 100 females: 85.4; Marriage status: 35.7% never married, 50.8% now married, 0.7% separated, 7.1% widowed, 6.4% divorced; Foreign born: 5.5%; Speak English only: 96.2%; With disability: 16.8%; Veterans: 8.9%; Ancestry: 31.1% Irish, 15.5% German, 12.2% French Canadian, 10.4% American, 9.1% English
Employment: 7.4% management, business, and financial, 1.1% computer, engineering, and science, 6.9% education, legal, community service, arts, and media, 8.6% healthcare practitioners, 15.4% service, 36.0% sales and office, 7.4% natural resources, construction, and maintenance, 17.1% production, transportation, and material moving
Income: Per capita: $29,764; Median household: $68,125; Average household: $69,053; Households with income of $100,000 or more: 20.2%; Poverty rate: 8.5%

Educational Attainment: High school diploma or higher: 89.2%; Bachelor's degree or higher: 20.9%; Graduate/professional degree or higher: 6.0%

School District(s)
Morristown Central SD (PK-12)
.....Enrollment: 342...................................... (315) 375-8814
Housing: Homeownership rate: 80.6%; Median home value: $82,500; Median year structure built: 1944; Homeowner vacancy rate: 14.0%; Median selected monthly owner costs: $1,179 with a mortgage, $340 without a mortgage; Median gross rent: $1,009 per month; Rental vacancy rate: 0.0%
Health Insurance: 94.5% have insurance; 75.6% have private insurance; 46.3% have public insurance; 5.5% do not have insurance; 5.5% of children under 18 do not have insurance
Transportation: Commute: 92.5% car, 2.9% public transportation, 0.6% walk, 2.9% work from home; Mean travel time to work: 28.3 minutes

NEWTON FALLS (unincorporated postal area)
ZCTA: 13666

Covers a land area of 39.110 square miles and a water area of 3.442 square miles. Located at 44.22° N. Lat; 74.93° W. Long. Elevation is 1,496 feet.
Population: 241; Growth (since 2000): n/a; Density: 6.2 persons per square mile; Race: 96.7% White, 0.0% Black/African American, 0.0% Asian, 0.0% American Indian/Alaska Native, 0.0% Native Hawaiian/Other Pacific Islander, 2.9% Two or more races, 1.2% Hispanic of any race; Average household size: 2.43; Median age: 45.2; Age under 18: 13.3%; Age 65 and over: 20.3%; Males per 100 females: 101.5; Marriage status: 22.7% never married, 53.7% now married, 1.9% separated, 13.9% widowed, 9.7% divorced; Foreign born: 0.0%; Speak English only: 89.3%; With disability: 29.5%; Veterans: 10.0%; Ancestry: 17.8% French, 12.4% English, 10.4% Irish, 8.7% French Canadian, 5.8% American
Employment: 9.7% management, business, and financial, 0.0% computer, engineering, and science, 9.7% education, legal, community service, arts, and media, 9.7% healthcare practitioners, 26.9% service, 37.6% sales and office, 4.3% natural resources, construction, and maintenance, 2.2% production, transportation, and material moving
Income: Per capita: $25,900; Median household: $23,917; Average household: $62,617; Households with income of $100,000 or more: 18.2%; Poverty rate: 33.2%
Educational Attainment: High school diploma or higher: 76.2%; Bachelor's degree or higher: 13.8%; Graduate/professional degree or higher: 2.1%
Housing: Homeownership rate: 81.8%; Median home value: n/a; Median year structure built: 1952; Homeowner vacancy rate: 8.0%; Median selected monthly owner costs: $1,114 with a mortgage, $325 without a mortgage; Median gross rent: n/a per month; Rental vacancy rate: 0.0%
Health Insurance: 97.1% have insurance; 38.6% have private insurance; 73.0% have public insurance; 2.9% do not have insurance; 0.0% of children under 18 do not have insurance
Transportation: Commute: 93.4% car, 0.0% public transportation, 0.0% walk, 2.2% work from home; Mean travel time to work: 24.4 minutes

NICHOLVILLE (unincorporated postal area)
ZCTA: 12965

Covers a land area of 9.535 square miles and a water area of 0.025 square miles. Located at 44.70° N. Lat; 74.69° W. Long. Elevation is 791 feet.
Population: 558; Growth (since 2000): 14.1%; Density: 58.5 persons per square mile; Race: 98.6% White, 0.0% Black/African American, 1.4% Asian, 0.0% American Indian/Alaska Native, 0.0% Native Hawaiian/Other Pacific Islander, 0.0% Two or more races, 0.5% Hispanic of any race; Average household size: 3.10; Median age: 38.5; Age under 18: 31.5%; Age 65 and over: 14.5%; Males per 100 females: 91.8; Marriage status: 28.0% never married, 63.3% now married, 0.0% separated, 3.3% widowed, 5.4% divorced; Foreign born: 1.4%; Speak English only: 98.4%; With disability: 10.8%; Veterans: 14.1%; Ancestry: 21.3% English, 10.8% French Canadian, 10.8% Italian, 10.0% Scottish, 8.6% French
Employment: 6.0% management, business, and financial, 9.8% computer, engineering, and science, 6.5% education, legal, community service, arts, and media, 7.6% healthcare practitioners, 23.4% service,

31.0% sales and office, 12.0% natural resources, construction, and maintenance, 3.8% production, transportation, and material moving
Income: Per capita: $19,171; Median household: $41,375; Average household: $57,822; Households with income of $100,000 or more: 14.4%; Poverty rate: 7.0%
Educational Attainment: High school diploma or higher: 90.9%; Bachelor's degree or higher: 19.8%; Graduate/professional degree or higher: 10.1%
Housing: Homeownership rate: 88.3%; Median home value: $80,300; Median year structure built: Before 1940; Homeowner vacancy rate: 0.0%; Median selected monthly owner costs: $1,113 with a mortgage, $472 without a mortgage; Median gross rent: n/a per month; Rental vacancy rate: 0.0%
Health Insurance: 94.4% have insurance; 72.8% have private insurance; 32.4% have public insurance; 5.6% do not have insurance; 0.0% of children under 18 do not have insurance
Transportation: Commute: 90.8% car, 0.0% public transportation, 3.8% walk, 3.3% work from home; Mean travel time to work: 27.9 minutes

NORFOLK (CDP).
Covers a land area of 2.702 square miles and a water area of 0.112 square miles. Located at 44.79° N. Lat; 74.99° W. Long. Elevation is 259 feet.
Population: 1,432; Growth (since 2000): 7.3%; Density: 530.0 persons per square mile; Race: 93.5% White, 1.9% Black/African American, 0.0% Asian, 2.5% American Indian/Alaska Native, 0.0% Native Hawaiian/Other Pacific Islander, 2.1% Two or more races, 1.5% Hispanic of any race; Average household size: 2.53; Median age: 25.1; Age under 18: 32.6%; Age 65 and over: 6.2%; Males per 100 females: 98.1; Marriage status: 44.8% never married, 40.6% now married, 0.6% separated, 9.7% widowed, 4.9% divorced; Foreign born: 1.4%; Speak English only: 88.7%; With disability: 8.1%; Veterans: 6.4%; Ancestry: 33.0% German, 21.9% Irish, 16.9% Swiss, 12.7% English, 11.1% French
Employment: 16.2% management, business, and financial, 2.4% computer, engineering, and science, 9.6% education, legal, community service, arts, and media, 2.4% healthcare practitioners, 32.3% service, 19.4% sales and office, 15.6% natural resources, construction, and maintenance, 2.1% production, transportation, and material moving
Income: Per capita: $18,082; Median household: $37,778; Average household: $45,263; Households with income of $100,000 or more: 7.6%; Poverty rate: 34.4%
Educational Attainment: High school diploma or higher: 90.7%; Bachelor's degree or higher: 22.1%; Graduate/professional degree or higher: 11.9%
Housing: Homeownership rate: 58.1%; Median home value: $96,500; Median year structure built: Before 1940; Homeowner vacancy rate: 0.0%; Median selected monthly owner costs: $1,045 with a mortgage, $473 without a mortgage; Median gross rent: $738 per month; Rental vacancy rate: 0.0%
Health Insurance: 80.2% have insurance; 65.7% have private insurance; 24.0% have public insurance; 19.8% do not have insurance; 32.6% of children under 18 do not have insurance
Transportation: Commute: 93.9% car, 2.5% public transportation, 1.8% walk, 0.0% work from home; Mean travel time to work: 26.8 minutes

NORFOLK (town).
Covers a land area of 56.740 square miles and a water area of 1.004 square miles. Located at 44.84° N. Lat; 74.93° W. Long. Elevation is 259 feet.
History: Settled in 1809. Amish people moved into the area in the mid-1970s and opened a cheese mill, cheese factories, sawmills, and gristmills; they are no longer here. William P. Rogers, who grew up here, was appointed U.S. Attorney General in 1958.
Population: 4,580; Growth (since 2000): 0.3%; Density: 80.7 persons per square mile; Race: 97.2% White, 0.6% Black/African American, 0.0% Asian, 1.4% American Indian/Alaska Native, 0.0% Native Hawaiian/Other Pacific Islander, 0.7% Two or more races, 0.5% Hispanic of any race; Average household size: 2.54; Median age: 34.9; Age under 18: 26.3%; Age 65 and over: 13.6%; Males per 100 females: 99.0; Marriage status: 27.9% never married, 58.5% now married, 0.8% separated, 6.3% widowed, 7.4% divorced; Foreign born: 1.7%; Speak English only: 95.0%; With disability: 12.0%; Veterans: 10.6%; Ancestry: 20.5% Irish, 17.7% French, 16.0% German, 13.2% English, 6.0% French Canadian
Employment: 9.0% management, business, and financial, 2.2% computer, engineering, and science, 9.0% education, legal, community service, arts, and media, 2.7% healthcare practitioners, 34.1% service, 23.3% sales and

office, 12.0% natural resources, construction, and maintenance, 7.6% production, transportation, and material moving

Income: Per capita: $23,601; Median household: $46,758; Average household: $58,954; Households with income of $100,000 or more: 12.2%; Poverty rate: 20.9%

Educational Attainment: High school diploma or higher: 91.0%; Bachelor's degree or higher: 15.5%; Graduate/professional degree or higher: 7.1%

Housing: Homeownership rate: 74.0%; Median home value: $78,600; Median year structure built: 1962; Homeowner vacancy rate: 2.0%; Median selected monthly owner costs: $1,025 with a mortgage, $427 without a mortgage; Median gross rent: $767 per month; Rental vacancy rate: 0.0%

Health Insurance: 89.1% have insurance; 65.9% have private insurance; 36.7% have public insurance; 10.9% do not have insurance; 14.1% of children under 18 do not have insurance

Safety: Violent crime rate: 0.0 per 10,000 population; Property crime rate: 2.2 per 10,000 population

Transportation: Commute: 95.7% car, 1.4% public transportation, 0.6% walk, 1.8% work from home; Mean travel time to work: 23.1 minutes

Additional Information Contacts

Town of Norfolk . . . . (315) 384-4821
http://www.norfolkny.us

NORTH LAWRENCE (unincorporated postal area)
ZCTA: 12967

Covers a land area of 37.607 square miles and a water area of 0.032 square miles. Located at 44.77° N. Lat; 74.66° W. Long. Elevation is 338 feet.

Population: 1,216; Growth (since 2000): 10.6%; Density: 32.3 persons per square mile; Race: 96.5% White, 0.2% Black/African American, 0.0% Asian, 0.5% American Indian/Alaska Native, 0.0% Native Hawaiian/Other Pacific Islander, 2.3% Two or more races, 4.5% Hispanic of any race; Average household size: 2.87; Median age: 36.2; Age under 18: 31.9%; Age 65 and over: 10.3%; Males per 100 females: 106.6; Marriage status: 29.4% never married, 55.0% now married, 1.4% separated, 5.1% widowed, 10.4% divorced; Foreign born: 2.1%; Speak English only: 78.7%; With disability: 18.3%; Veterans: 8.3%; Ancestry: 20.1% German, 17.1% French, 9.1% American, 9.1% English, 8.4% Irish

Employment: 13.4% management, business, and financial, 0.7% computer, engineering, and science, 3.3% education, legal, community service, arts, and media, 6.3% healthcare practitioners, 29.9% service, 17.4% sales and office, 8.7% natural resources, construction, and maintenance, 20.4% production, transportation, and material moving

Income: Per capita: $19,465; Median household: $43,950; Average household: $56,943; Households with income of $100,000 or more: 9.7%; Poverty rate: 34.4%

Educational Attainment: High school diploma or higher: 78.9%; Bachelor's degree or higher: 11.5%; Graduate/professional degree or higher: 4.1%

Housing: Homeownership rate: 83.5%; Median home value: $68,300; Median year structure built: 1974; Homeowner vacancy rate: 2.5%; Median selected monthly owner costs: $1,020 with a mortgage, $392 without a mortgage; Median gross rent: n/a per month; Rental vacancy rate: 0.0%

Health Insurance: 77.3% have insurance; 50.9% have private insurance; 36.8% have public insurance; 22.7% do not have insurance; 39.9% of children under 18 do not have insurance

Transportation: Commute: 86.9% car, 0.0% public transportation, 3.2% walk, 8.5% work from home; Mean travel time to work: 25.4 minutes

NORWOOD (village). Covers a land area of 2.095 square miles and a water area of 0.169 square miles. Located at 44.75° N. Lat; 75.00° W. Long. Elevation is 331 feet.

History: Originally an Adirondack-Saint Lawrence Valley railroad center and industrial village, but now purely a residential community. Incorporated 1871.

Population: 1,686; Growth (since 2000): 0.1%; Density: 804.8 persons per square mile; Race: 96.9% White, 0.4% Black/African American, 1.2% Asian, 0.8% American Indian/Alaska Native, 0.3% Native Hawaiian/Other Pacific Islander, 0.4% Two or more races, 0.9% Hispanic of any race; Average household size: 2.22; Median age: 42.8; Age under 18: 20.8%; Age 65 and over: 22.7%; Males per 100 females: 97.0; Marriage status: 28.0% never married, 52.0% now married, 2.2% separated, 7.5% widowed, 12.4% divorced; Foreign born: 2.0%; Speak English only: 97.9%;

With disability: 19.0%; Veterans: 11.9%; Ancestry: 19.8% Irish, 16.1% French, 15.5% English, 12.5% French Canadian, 9.0% Italian

Employment: 12.5% management, business, and financial, 1.6% computer, engineering, and science, 21.8% education, legal, community service, arts, and media, 8.8% healthcare practitioners, 22.9% service, 18.2% sales and office, 7.8% natural resources, construction, and maintenance, 6.3% production, transportation, and material moving

Income: Per capita: $23,470; Median household: $42,228; Average household: $51,639; Households with income of $100,000 or more: 8.8%; Poverty rate: 18.4%

Educational Attainment: High school diploma or higher: 92.7%; Bachelor's degree or higher: 26.3%; Graduate/professional degree or higher: 13.1%

School District(s)

Norwood-Norfolk Central SD (PK-12)
Enrollment: 1,043 . . . . (315) 353-6631

Housing: Homeownership rate: 66.6%; Median home value: $76,000; Median year structure built: Before 1940; Homeowner vacancy rate: 1.4%; Median selected monthly owner costs: $902 with a mortgage, $475 without a mortgage; Median gross rent: $639 per month; Rental vacancy rate: 6.4%

Health Insurance: 90.4% have insurance; 66.2% have private insurance; 41.6% have public insurance; 9.6% do not have insurance; 11.3% of children under 18 do not have insurance

Safety: Violent crime rate: 12.6 per 10,000 population; Property crime rate: 37.9 per 10,000 population

Transportation: Commute: 97.5% car, 0.0% public transportation, 1.2% walk, 1.3% work from home; Mean travel time to work: 18.8 minutes

OGDENSBURG (city). Covers a land area of 4.956 square miles and a water area of 3.181 square miles. Located at 44.71° N. Lat; 75.46° W. Long. Elevation is 295 feet.

History: Settled by French missionaries and trappers 1749; was strategically important in the War of 1812. Seat of Mater Dei, and Wadhams Hall Seminary and College and a Museum with works of Frederic Remington, who lived here. Rhoda Fox Graves was the first woman to serve the state's Assembly and Senate. Incorporated as a city 1868.

Population: 10,851; Growth (since 2000): -12.2%; Density: 2,189.6 persons per square mile; Race: 85.0% White, 7.4% Black/African American, 1.0% Asian, 0.6% American Indian/Alaska Native, 0.1% Native Hawaiian/Other Pacific Islander, 2.9% Two or more races, 5.3% Hispanic of any race; Average household size: 2.22; Median age: 39.8; Age under 18: 19.3%; Age 65 and over: 14.9%; Males per 100 females: 120.6; Marriage status: 35.4% never married, 46.0% now married, 4.3% separated, 6.5% widowed, 12.2% divorced; Foreign born: 4.9%; Speak English only: 90.1%; With disability: 19.2%; Veterans: 8.0%; Ancestry: 17.1% Irish, 14.0% French, 9.4% English, 9.0% German, 7.8% American

Employment: 8.9% management, business, and financial, 1.1% computer, engineering, and science, 12.6% education, legal, community service, arts, and media, 10.1% healthcare practitioners, 23.6% service, 23.6% sales and office, 5.9% natural resources, construction, and maintenance, 14.2% production, transportation, and material moving

Income: Per capita: $23,241; Median household: $38,901; Average household: $60,345; Households with income of $100,000 or more: 12.0%; Poverty rate: 20.8%

Educational Attainment: High school diploma or higher: 83.5%; Bachelor's degree or higher: 16.8%; Graduate/professional degree or higher: 6.8%

School District(s)

Ogdensburg City SD (PK-12)
Enrollment: 1,677 . . . . (315) 393-0900

Housing: Homeownership rate: 59.3%; Median home value: $68,100; Median year structure built: Before 1940; Homeowner vacancy rate: 1.5%; Median selected monthly owner costs: $990 with a mortgage, $477 without a mortgage; Median gross rent: $602 per month; Rental vacancy rate: 3.2%

Health Insurance: 93.2% have insurance; 64.5% have private insurance; 44.8% have public insurance; 6.8% do not have insurance; 4.2% of children under 18 do not have insurance

Hospitals: Claxton - Hepburn Medical Center (159 beds)

Safety: Violent crime rate: 27.1 per 10,000 population; Property crime rate: 356.6 per 10,000 population

Newspapers: Canton Rural News (weekly circulation 13,000); Ogdensburg Journal (daily circulation 5,800); The Advance News (weekly circulation 11,000)

Transportation: Commute: 91.8% car, 0.1% public transportation, 3.8% walk, 2.1% work from home; Mean travel time to work: 13.6 minutes

Airports: Ogdensburg International (commercial service–non-primary)

Additional Information Contacts

City of Ogdensburg . . . . (315) 393-3540
    http://www.ogdensburg.org

OSWEGATCHIE (town).
Covers a land area of 65.498 square miles and a water area of 5.705 square miles. Located at 44.63° N. Lat; 75.49° W. Long. Elevation is 1,355 feet.

Population: 4,375; Growth (since 2000): 0.1%; Density: 66.8 persons per square mile; Race: 98.7% White, 0.4% Black/African American, 0.2% Asian, 0.1% American Indian/Alaska Native, 0.2% Native Hawaiian/Other Pacific Islander, 0.3% Two or more races, 0.1% Hispanic of any race; Average household size: 2.60; Median age: 46.1; Age under 18: 25.3%; Age 65 and over: 20.4%; Males per 100 females: 91.7; Marriage status: 23.8% never married, 53.3% now married, 1.2% separated, 10.6% widowed, 12.3% divorced; Foreign born: 2.8%; Speak English only: 86.8%; With disability: 15.9%; Veterans: 11.5%; Ancestry: 13.6% Irish, 12.4% French, 11.6% German, 9.9% English, 8.2% Pennsylvania German

Employment: 15.3% management, business, and financial, 1.0% computer, engineering, and science, 6.6% education, legal, community service, arts, and media, 7.1% healthcare practitioners, 27.5% service, 25.7% sales and office, 9.3% natural resources, construction, and maintenance, 7.4% production, transportation, and material moving

Income: Per capita: $24,387; Median household: $56,919; Average household: $63,578; Households with income of $100,000 or more: 17.9%; Poverty rate: 24.8%

Educational Attainment: High school diploma or higher: 85.4%; Bachelor's degree or higher: 18.2%; Graduate/professional degree or higher: 8.9%

Housing: Homeownership rate: 89.8%; Median home value: $100,800; Median year structure built: 1969; Homeowner vacancy rate: 1.8%; Median selected monthly owner costs: $987 with a mortgage, $453 without a mortgage; Median gross rent: $626 per month; Rental vacancy rate: 4.7%

Health Insurance: 83.1% have insurance; 59.6% have private insurance; 38.9% have public insurance; 16.9% do not have insurance; 36.1% of children under 18 do not have insurance

Transportation: Commute: 91.2% car, 0.0% public transportation, 1.8% walk, 6.9% work from home; Mean travel time to work: 19.0 minutes

PARISHVILLE (CDP).
Covers a land area of 3.292 square miles and a water area of 0.067 square miles. Located at 44.63° N. Lat; 74.79° W. Long. Elevation is 892 feet.

Population: 787; Growth (since 2000): n/a; Density: 239.0 persons per square mile; Race: 97.5% White, 0.0% Black/African American, 0.0% Asian, 0.0% American Indian/Alaska Native, 0.0% Native Hawaiian/Other Pacific Islander, 1.8% Two or more races, 3.7% Hispanic of any race; Average household size: 2.37; Median age: 29.8; Age under 18: 25.8%; Age 65 and over: 11.2%; Males per 100 females: 93.7; Marriage status: 20.2% never married, 56.7% now married, 7.1% separated, 8.5% widowed, 14.6% divorced; Foreign born: 2.3%; Speak English only: 93.9%; With disability: 15.9%; Veterans: 16.6%; Ancestry: 26.7% English, 21.9% Irish, 15.8% Italian, 12.3% French Canadian, 11.9% French

Employment: 4.7% management, business, and financial, 8.0% computer, engineering, and science, 15.6% education, legal, community service, arts, and media, 6.8% healthcare practitioners, 11.2% service, 26.8% sales and office, 15.6% natural resources, construction, and maintenance, 11.2% production, transportation, and material moving

Income: Per capita: $23,010; Median household: $49,200; Average household: $55,612; Households with income of $100,000 or more: 13.2%; Poverty rate: 19.9%

Educational Attainment: High school diploma or higher: 93.4%; Bachelor's degree or higher: 25.7%; Graduate/professional degree or higher: 12.2%

School District(s)
Parishville-Hopkinton Central SD (PK-12)
    Enrollment: 461 . . . . (315) 265-4642

Housing: Homeownership rate: 67.2%; Median home value: $85,100; Median year structure built: Before 1940; Homeowner vacancy rate: 0.0%; Median selected monthly owner costs: $887 with a mortgage, $349 without

a mortgage; Median gross rent: $805 per month; Rental vacancy rate: 0.0%

Health Insurance: 96.6% have insurance; 63.5% have private insurance; 49.7% have public insurance; 3.4% do not have insurance; 0.0% of children under 18 do not have insurance

Transportation: Commute: 98.2% car, 0.0% public transportation, 0.0% walk, 1.8% work from home; Mean travel time to work: 36.0 minutes

PARISHVILLE (town).
Covers a land area of 98.159 square miles and a water area of 3.270 square miles. Located at 44.55° N. Lat; 74.78° W. Long. Elevation is 892 feet.

Population: 2,237; Growth (since 2000): 9.2%; Density: 22.8 persons per square mile; Race: 96.9% White, 0.0% Black/African American, 1.1% Asian, 0.5% American Indian/Alaska Native, 0.0% Native Hawaiian/Other Pacific Islander, 1.2% Two or more races, 1.3% Hispanic of any race; Average household size: 2.32; Median age: 40.2; Age under 18: 19.8%; Age 65 and over: 15.4%; Males per 100 females: 103.3; Marriage status: 28.8% never married, 54.6% now married, 3.7% separated, 4.6% widowed, 12.1% divorced; Foreign born: 1.7%; Speak English only: 94.7%; With disability: 13.5%; Veterans: 13.3%; Ancestry: 20.2% Irish, 16.5% English, 11.6% French, 10.7% French Canadian, 8.9% German

Employment: 9.9% management, business, and financial, 4.1% computer, engineering, and science, 12.9% education, legal, community service, arts, and media, 7.2% healthcare practitioners, 22.3% service, 18.0% sales and office, 14.3% natural resources, construction, and maintenance, 11.3% production, transportation, and material moving

Income: Per capita: $26,021; Median household: $51,000; Average household: $60,276; Households with income of $100,000 or more: 14.6%; Poverty rate: 15.6%

Educational Attainment: High school diploma or higher: 92.6%; Bachelor's degree or higher: 27.2%; Graduate/professional degree or higher: 12.8%

School District(s)
Parishville-Hopkinton Central SD (PK-12)
    Enrollment: 461 . . . . (315) 265-4642

Housing: Homeownership rate: 68.0%; Median home value: $89,700; Median year structure built: 1971; Homeowner vacancy rate: 0.0%; Median selected monthly owner costs: $1,064 with a mortgage, $419 without a mortgage; Median gross rent: $883 per month; Rental vacancy rate: 0.0%

Health Insurance: 91.1% have insurance; 67.6% have private insurance; 39.9% have public insurance; 8.9% do not have insurance; 5.0% of children under 18 do not have insurance

Transportation: Commute: 93.1% car, 0.0% public transportation, 0.0% walk, 6.9% work from home; Mean travel time to work: 26.0 minutes

PIERCEFIELD (town).
Covers a land area of 104.155 square miles and a water area of 6.910 square miles. Located at 44.22° N. Lat; 74.60° W. Long. Elevation is 1,572 feet.

Population: 226; Growth (since 2000): -25.9%; Density: 2.2 persons per square mile; Race: 95.1% White, 0.4% Black/African American, 0.0% Asian, 0.0% American Indian/Alaska Native, 0.0% Native Hawaiian/Other Pacific Islander, 2.2% Two or more races, 4.4% Hispanic of any race; Average household size: 2.19; Median age: 55.0; Age under 18: 15.0%; Age 65 and over: 31.9%; Males per 100 females: 93.8; Marriage status: 19.9% never married, 63.8% now married, 2.0% separated, 2.0% widowed, 14.3% divorced; Foreign born: 3.1%; Speak English only: 94.8%; With disability: 22.6%; Veterans: 11.5%; Ancestry: 21.7% German, 21.2% Irish, 16.4% English, 14.6% Italian, 11.9% French

Employment: 14.3% management, business, and financial, 1.9% computer, engineering, and science, 12.4% education, legal, community service, arts, and media, 4.8% healthcare practitioners, 28.6% service, 23.8% sales and office, 11.4% natural resources, construction, and maintenance, 2.9% production, transportation, and material moving

Income: Per capita: $25,620; Median household: $55,750; Average household: $56,661; Households with income of $100,000 or more: 8.7%; Poverty rate: 10.2%

Educational Attainment: High school diploma or higher: 92.6%; Bachelor's degree or higher: 30.2%; Graduate/professional degree or higher: 9.5%

Housing: Homeownership rate: 93.2%; Median home value: $110,000; Median year structure built: 1959; Homeowner vacancy rate: 0.0%; Median selected monthly owner costs: $1,268 with a mortgage, $494 without a mortgage; Median gross rent: n/a per month; Rental vacancy rate: 0.0%

Health Insurance: 92.0% have insurance; 73.0% have private insurance; 43.4% have public insurance; 8.0% do not have insurance; 0.0% of children under 18 do not have insurance
Transportation: Commute: 97.9% car, 0.0% public transportation, 0.0% walk, 1.0% work from home; Mean travel time to work: 24.2 minutes

PIERREPONT (town). Covers a land area of 60.252 square miles and a water area of 0.468 square miles. Located at 44.53° N. Lat; 75.01° W. Long. Elevation is 741 feet.
Population: 2,546; Growth (since 2000): -4.8%; Density: 42.3 persons per square mile; Race: 96.9% White, 0.4% Black/African American, 1.1% Asian, 0.1% American Indian/Alaska Native, 0.2% Native Hawaiian/Other Pacific Islander, 1.4% Two or more races, 1.1% Hispanic of any race; Average household size: 2.53; Median age: 44.6; Age under 18: 20.0%; Age 65 and over: 19.6%; Males per 100 females: 103.2; Marriage status: 25.1% never married, 63.4% now married, 1.8% separated, 4.3% widowed, 7.3% divorced; Foreign born: 2.3%; Speak English only: 99.0%; With disability: 12.2%; Veterans: 9.8%; Ancestry: 20.0% English, 18.5% Irish, 13.9% French, 9.3% German, 7.8% American
Employment: 6.8% management, business, and financial, 4.2% computer, engineering, and science, 17.8% education, legal, community service, arts, and media, 9.8% healthcare practitioners, 19.4% service, 21.2% sales and office, 12.9% natural resources, construction, and maintenance, 7.9% production, transportation, and material moving
Income: Per capita: $26,588; Median household: $57,298; Average household: $67,514; Households with income of $100,000 or more: 19.5%; Poverty rate: 12.0%
Educational Attainment: High school diploma or higher: 90.6%; Bachelor's degree or higher: 25.8%; Graduate/professional degree or higher: 12.5%
Housing: Homeownership rate: 86.8%; Median home value: $133,800; Median year structure built: 1978; Homeowner vacancy rate: 0.0%; Median selected monthly owner costs: $1,230 with a mortgage, $509 without a mortgage; Median gross rent: $905 per month; Rental vacancy rate: 25.3%
Health Insurance: 96.2% have insurance; 77.7% have private insurance; 38.9% have public insurance; 3.8% do not have insurance; 0.0% of children under 18 do not have insurance
Transportation: Commute: 93.5% car, 0.0% public transportation, 0.4% walk, 6.2% work from home; Mean travel time to work: 22.8 minutes

PITCAIRN (town). Covers a land area of 58.518 square miles and a water area of 0.937 square miles. Located at 44.22° N. Lat; 75.27° W. Long. Elevation is 781 feet.
Population: 825; Growth (since 2000): 5.4%; Density: 14.1 persons per square mile; Race: 98.7% White, 0.0% Black/African American, 0.5% Asian, 0.1% American Indian/Alaska Native, 0.0% Native Hawaiian/Other Pacific Islander, 0.7% Two or more races, 1.1% Hispanic of any race; Average household size: 2.68; Median age: 38.4; Age under 18: 28.6%; Age 65 and over: 15.9%; Males per 100 females: 105.8; Marriage status: 28.8% never married, 55.5% now married, 4.6% separated, 4.1% widowed, 11.7% divorced; Foreign born: 3.0%; Speak English only: 96.7%; With disability: 18.9%; Veterans: 11.7%; Ancestry: 13.7% American, 12.6% Irish, 11.4% English, 9.9% German, 9.2% French
Employment: 5.3% management, business, and financial, 0.7% computer, engineering, and science, 10.3% education, legal, community service, arts, and media, 4.3% healthcare practitioners, 24.6% service, 19.6% sales and office, 18.6% natural resources, construction, and maintenance, 16.6% production, transportation, and material moving
Income: Per capita: $21,077; Median household: $43,750; Average household: $57,428; Households with income of $100,000 or more: 18.8%; Poverty rate: 18.6%
Educational Attainment: High school diploma or higher: 82.6%; Bachelor's degree or higher: 8.6%; Graduate/professional degree or higher: 5.8%
Housing: Homeownership rate: 84.1%; Median home value: $83,700; Median year structure built: 1977; Homeowner vacancy rate: 2.6%; Median selected monthly owner costs: $1,175 with a mortgage, $365 without a mortgage; Median gross rent: $672 per month; Rental vacancy rate: 0.0%
Health Insurance: 92.0% have insurance; 64.1% have private insurance; 44.7% have public insurance; 8.0% do not have insurance; 0.0% of children under 18 do not have insurance
Transportation: Commute: 98.3% car, 0.0% public transportation, 0.0% walk, 1.7% work from home; Mean travel time to work: 33.1 minutes

POTSDAM (town). Covers a land area of 101.403 square miles and a water area of 2.049 square miles. Located at 44.68° N. Lat; 75.04° W. Long. Elevation is 433 feet.
History: In 1804, William Bullard and others came to Potsdam from Massachusetts, pooled their resources, and purchased a tract of land on which they established the "Union." Property was held in common, an accurate account of labor and materials contributed by each member was kept, and all proceeds were divided pro rata annually. The group prospered for a few years but dissolved in 1810, when the land was evenly divided among the members. In the 19th century, sandstone quarries near Potsdam employed hundreds of workers. Seat of State University of New York College at Potsdam and Clarkson University. Incorporated in 1831.
Population: 16,197; Growth (since 2000): 1.5%; Density: 159.7 persons per square mile; Race: 88.3% White, 4.2% Black/African American, 2.9% Asian, 0.6% American Indian/Alaska Native, 0.0% Native Hawaiian/Other Pacific Islander, 2.5% Two or more races, 4.0% Hispanic of any race; Average household size: 2.26; Median age: 24.3; Age under 18: 13.6%; Age 65 and over: 11.0%; Males per 100 females: 107.9; Marriage status: 58.0% never married, 30.9% now married, 1.3% separated, 3.6% widowed, 7.5% divorced; Foreign born: 7.4%; Speak English only: 89.5%; With disability: 11.3%; Veterans: 5.7%; Ancestry: 15.2% Irish, 11.4% English, 9.9% German, 9.3% French, 8.4% Italian
Employment: 10.3% management, business, and financial, 3.4% computer, engineering, and science, 24.6% education, legal, community service, arts, and media, 4.8% healthcare practitioners, 21.6% service, 21.5% sales and office, 7.2% natural resources, construction, and maintenance, 6.7% production, transportation, and material moving
Income: Per capita: $21,837; Median household: $51,743; Average household: $67,692; Households with income of $100,000 or more: 20.1%; Poverty rate: 19.3%
Educational Attainment: High school diploma or higher: 92.4%; Bachelor's degree or higher: 40.9%; Graduate/professional degree or higher: 25.7%

School District(s)
Potsdam Central SD (PK-12)
   Enrollment: 1,358 . . . . (315) 265-2000
Four-year College(s)
Clarkson University (Private, Not-for-profit)
   Enrollment: 4,233 . . . . (315) 268-6400
   Tuition: In-state $47,950; Out-of-state $47,950
SUNY College at Potsdam (Public)
   Enrollment: 3,587 . . . . (315) 267-2000
   Tuition: In-state $8,221; Out-of-state $17,871
Housing: Homeownership rate: 60.6%; Median home value: $103,700; Median year structure built: 1961; Homeowner vacancy rate: 2.2%; Median selected monthly owner costs: $1,234 with a mortgage, $480 without a mortgage; Median gross rent: $756 per month; Rental vacancy rate: 4.1%
Health Insurance: 95.9% have insurance; 79.5% have private insurance; 27.5% have public insurance; 4.1% do not have insurance; 4.7% of children under 18 do not have insurance
Hospitals: Canton - Potsdam Hospital (94 beds)
Newspapers: North Country This Week (weekly circulation 10,500)
Transportation: Commute: 72.7% car, 0.9% public transportation, 19.5% walk, 5.5% work from home; Mean travel time to work: 16.3 minutes
Airports: Potsdam Municipal/Damon Field (general aviation)
Additional Information Contacts
Town of Potsdam . . . . (315) 265-3430
   http://www.potsdamny.us

POTSDAM (village). Covers a land area of 4.447 square miles and a water area of 0.495 square miles. Located at 44.67° N. Lat; 74.99° W. Long. Elevation is 433 feet.
Population: 9,710; Growth (since 2000): 3.0%; Density: 2,183.5 persons per square mile; Race: 85.8% White, 6.5% Black/African American, 3.1% Asian, 0.7% American Indian/Alaska Native, 0.0% Native Hawaiian/Other Pacific Islander, 1.5% Two or more races, 6.0% Hispanic of any race; Average household size: 2.09; Median age: 21.0; Age under 18: 8.5%; Age 65 and over: 7.3%; Males per 100 females: 113.9; Marriage status: 75.1% never married, 16.4% now married, 1.0% separated, 3.2% widowed, 5.3% divorced; Foreign born: 9.8%; Speak English only: 87.1%; With disability: 8.9%; Veterans: 3.2%; Ancestry: 14.3% Irish, 9.7% English, 9.5% German, 8.5% Italian, 4.8% French
Employment: 9.0% management, business, and financial, 3.6% computer, engineering, and science, 29.8% education, legal, community service, arts, and media, 1.8% healthcare practitioners, 20.8% service, 24.6% sales and

office, 3.7% natural resources, construction, and maintenance, 6.7% production, transportation, and material moving

Income: Per capita: $15,359; Median household: $31,667; Average household: $58,506; Households with income of $100,000 or more: 15.7%; Poverty rate: 27.5%

Educational Attainment: High school diploma or higher: 91.4%; Bachelor's degree or higher: 53.7%; Graduate/professional degree or higher: 35.3%

School District(s)
Potsdam Central SD (PK-12)
    Enrollment: 1,358 . . . . (315) 265-2000
Four-year College(s)
Clarkson University (Private, Not-for-profit)
    Enrollment: 4,233 . . . . (315) 268-6400
    Tuition: In-state $47,950; Out-of-state $47,950
SUNY College at Potsdam (Public)
    Enrollment: 3,587 . . . . (315) 267-2000
    Tuition: In-state $8,221; Out-of-state $17,871

Housing: Homeownership rate: 39.5%; Median home value: $104,000; Median year structure built: 1958; Homeowner vacancy rate: 3.1%; Median selected monthly owner costs: $1,306 with a mortgage, $574 without a mortgage; Median gross rent: $740 per month; Rental vacancy rate: 3.8%

Health Insurance: 95.7% have insurance; 81.0% have private insurance; 21.7% have public insurance; 4.3% do not have insurance; 4.7% of children under 18 do not have insurance

Hospitals: Canton - Potsdam Hospital (94 beds)

Safety: Violent crime rate: 10.2 per 10,000 population; Property crime rate: 92.2 per 10,000 population

Newspapers: North Country This Week (weekly circulation 10,500)

Transportation: Commute: 52.2% car, 1.3% public transportation, 37.5% walk, 7.6% work from home; Mean travel time to work: 12.9 minutes

Airports: Potsdam Municipal/Damon Field (general aviation)

Additional Information Contacts
Village of Potsdam . . . . (315) 265-7480
    http://www.vi.potsdam.ny.us

PYRITES (unincorporated postal area)
ZCTA: 13677

Covers a land area of 0.196 square miles and a water area of 0.031 square miles. Located at 44.51° N. Lat; 75.18° W. Long. Elevation is 502 feet.

Population: 106; Growth (since 2000): n/a; Density: 539.5 persons per square mile; Race: 100.0% White, 0.0% Black/African American, 0.0% Asian, 0.0% American Indian/Alaska Native, 0.0% Native Hawaiian/Other Pacific Islander, 0.0% Two or more races, 0.0% Hispanic of any race; Average household size: 4.24; Median age: 52.9; Age under 18: 0.0%; Age 65 and over: 24.5%; Males per 100 females: 78.8; Marriage status: 56.6% never married, 28.3% now married, 0.0% separated, 15.1% widowed, 0.0% divorced; Foreign born: 0.0%; Speak English only: 100.0%; With disability: 34.0%; Veterans: 23.6%; Ancestry: 50.9% English, 29.2% French, 17.9% American

Employment: 44.1% management, business, and financial, 0.0% computer, engineering, and science, 0.0% education, legal, community service, arts, and media, 0.0% healthcare practitioners, 55.9% service, 0.0% sales and office, 0.0% natural resources, construction, and maintenance, 0.0% production, transportation, and material moving

Income: Per capita: $25,912; Median household: n/a; Average household: n/a; Households with income of $100,000 or more: 60.0%; Poverty rate: 10.4%

Educational Attainment: High school diploma or higher: 64.4%; Bachelor's degree or higher: n/a; Graduate/professional degree or higher: n/a

Housing: Homeownership rate: 60.0%; Median home value: n/a; Median year structure built: n/a; Homeowner vacancy rate: 0.0%; Median selected monthly owner costs: $0 with a mortgage, $0 without a mortgage; Median gross rent: n/a per month; Rental vacancy rate: 0.0%

Health Insurance: 100.0% have insurance; 89.6% have private insurance; 71.7% have public insurance; 0.0% do not have insurance; 0.0% of children under 18 do not have insurance

Transportation: Commute: 100.0% car, 0.0% public transportation, 0.0% walk, 0.0% work from home; Mean travel time to work: 0.0 minutes

RAYMONDVILLE (unincorporated postal area)
ZCTA: 13678

Covers a land area of 0.785 square miles and a water area of 0.039 square miles. Located at 44.81° N. Lat; 74.99° W. Long. Elevation is 253 feet.

Population: 254; Growth (since 2000): n/a; Density: 323.5 persons per square mile; Race: 100.0% White, 0.0% Black/African American, 0.0% Asian, 0.0% American Indian/Alaska Native, 0.0% Native Hawaiian/Other Pacific Islander, 0.0% Two or more races, 0.0% Hispanic of any race; Average household size: 2.65; Median age: 33.8; Age under 18: 18.5%; Age 65 and over: 22.8%; Males per 100 females: 93.6; Marriage status: 44.4% never married, 55.6% now married, 0.0% separated, 0.0% widowed, 0.0% divorced; Foreign born: 0.0%; Speak English only: 100.0%; With disability: 11.8%; Veterans: 10.6%; Ancestry: 28.0% English, 28.0% Scottish, 23.6% Irish, 17.7% French, 11.4% Norwegian

Employment: 0.0% management, business, and financial, 0.0% computer, engineering, and science, 0.0% education, legal, community service, arts, and media, 32.6% healthcare practitioners, 33.7% service, 6.7% sales and office, 0.0% natural resources, construction, and maintenance, 27.0% production, transportation, and material moving

Income: Per capita: $24,098; Median household: n/a; Average household: $63,423; Households with income of $100,000 or more: 8.3%; Poverty rate: 5.5%

Educational Attainment: High school diploma or higher: 85.9%; Bachelor's degree or higher: n/a; Graduate/professional degree or higher: n/a

Housing: Homeownership rate: 53.1%; Median home value: n/a; Median year structure built: 1955; Homeowner vacancy rate: 0.0%; Median selected monthly owner costs: $0 with a mortgage, $0 without a mortgage; Median gross rent: $640 per month; Rental vacancy rate: 0.0%

Health Insurance: 100.0% have insurance; 90.9% have private insurance; 29.1% have public insurance; 0.0% do not have insurance; 0.0% of children under 18 do not have insurance

Transportation: Commute: 100.0% car, 0.0% public transportation, 0.0% walk, 0.0% work from home; Mean travel time to work: 0.0 minutes

RENSSELAER FALLS (village). Covers a land area of 0.291
square miles and a water area of 0.027 square miles. Located at 44.59° N. Lat; 75.32° W. Long. Elevation is 328 feet.

Population: 374; Growth (since 2000): 11.0%; Density: 1,287.1 persons per square mile; Race: 97.3% White, 1.6% Black/African American, 0.0% Asian, 0.0% American Indian/Alaska Native, 0.0% Native Hawaiian/Other Pacific Islander, 0.3% Two or more races, 0.8% Hispanic of any race; Average household size: 2.51; Median age: 32.9; Age under 18: 31.0%; Age 65 and over: 9.9%; Males per 100 females: 91.9; Marriage status: 32.8% never married, 47.5% now married, 1.5% separated, 10.2% widowed, 9.4% divorced; Foreign born: 0.5%; Speak English only: 97.6%; With disability: 17.1%; Veterans: 3.5%; Ancestry: 21.1% French, 21.1% Irish, 11.5% English, 7.0% American, 7.0% French Canadian

Employment: 0.7% management, business, and financial, 4.0% computer, engineering, and science, 21.9% education, legal, community service, arts, and media, 8.6% healthcare practitioners, 33.1% service, 19.2% sales and office, 6.6% natural resources, construction, and maintenance, 6.0% production, transportation, and material moving

Income: Per capita: $24,708; Median household: $33,250; Average household: $63,153; Households with income of $100,000 or more: 16.8%; Poverty rate: 24.5%

Educational Attainment: High school diploma or higher: 88.1%; Bachelor's degree or higher: 24.2%; Graduate/professional degree or higher: 17.2%

Housing: Homeownership rate: 79.2%; Median home value: $67,000; Median year structure built: Before 1940; Homeowner vacancy rate: 0.0%; Median selected monthly owner costs: $888 with a mortgage, $348 without a mortgage; Median gross rent: $856 per month; Rental vacancy rate: 0.0%

Health Insurance: 86.1% have insurance; 50.8% have private insurance; 46.8% have public insurance; 13.9% do not have insurance; 7.6% of children under 18 do not have insurance

Transportation: Commute: 91.2% car, 1.4% public transportation, 2.0% walk, 5.4% work from home; Mean travel time to work: 26.8 minutes

RICHVILLE (village). Covers a land area of 0.738 square miles and a water area of 0 square miles. Located at 44.42° N. Lat; 75.39° W. Long. Elevation is 407 feet.

Population: 297; Growth (since 2000): 8.4%; Density: 402.3 persons per square mile; Race: 97.6% White, 0.7% Black/African American, 0.0% Asian, 0.0% American Indian/Alaska Native, 0.3% Native Hawaiian/Other Pacific Islander, 1.3% Two or more races, 0.7% Hispanic of any race; Average household size: 2.54; Median age: 36.8; Age under 18: 30.3%; Age 65 and over: 11.4%; Males per 100 females: 105.7; Marriage status: 31.3% never married, 49.1% now married, 0.9% separated, 8.9% widowed, 10.7% divorced; Foreign born: 1.3%; Speak English only: 98.9%; With disability: 11.5%; Veterans: 16.1%; Ancestry: 22.2% Irish, 19.9% English, 13.8% French, 10.1% American, 7.1% French Canadian
Employment: 11.0% management, business, and financial, 1.1% computer, engineering, and science, 3.3% education, legal, community service, arts, and media, 7.7% healthcare practitioners, 20.9% service, 31.9% sales and office, 15.4% natural resources, construction, and maintenance, 8.8% production, transportation, and material moving
Income: Per capita: $22,480; Median household: $40,938; Average household: $59,062; Households with income of $100,000 or more: 12.0%; Poverty rate: 15.2%
Educational Attainment: High school diploma or higher: 90.9%; Bachelor's degree or higher: 9.6%; Graduate/professional degree or higher: 3.7%
Housing: Homeownership rate: 92.3%; Median home value: $79,000; Median year structure built: Before 1940; Homeowner vacancy rate: 0.0%; Median selected monthly owner costs: $854 with a mortgage, $419 without a mortgage; Median gross rent: $644 per month; Rental vacancy rate: 0.0%
Health Insurance: 96.6% have insurance; 65.8% have private insurance; 46.8% have public insurance; 3.4% do not have insurance; 3.2% of children under 18 do not have insurance
Transportation: Commute: 89.8% car, 0.0% public transportation, 5.7% walk, 3.4% work from home; Mean travel time to work: 32.1 minutes

ROSSIE (town). Covers a land area of 37.880 square miles and a water area of 1.363 square miles. Located at 44.33° N. Lat; 75.62° W. Long. Elevation is 276 feet.

Population: 980; Growth (since 2000): 24.5%; Density: 25.9 persons per square mile; Race: 99.2% White, 0.1% Black/African American, 0.0% Asian, 0.0% American Indian/Alaska Native, 0.0% Native Hawaiian/Other Pacific Islander, 0.7% Two or more races, 1.8% Hispanic of any race; Average household size: 3.16; Median age: 32.1; Age under 18: 32.2%; Age 65 and over: 10.7%; Males per 100 females: 99.3; Marriage status: 35.9% never married, 47.8% now married, 0.4% separated, 6.1% widowed, 10.1% divorced; Foreign born: 3.3%; Speak English only: 85.2%; With disability: 14.3%; Veterans: 6.4%; Ancestry: 23.3% German, 16.5% Irish, 7.6% French, 7.0% American, 6.0% English
Employment: 11.3% management, business, and financial, 0.3% computer, engineering, and science, 8.8% education, legal, community service, arts, and media, 4.2% healthcare practitioners, 12.5% service, 16.4% sales and office, 27.2% natural resources, construction, and maintenance, 19.3% production, transportation, and material moving
Income: Per capita: $16,127; Median household: $45,156; Average household: $50,391; Households with income of $100,000 or more: 11.3%; Poverty rate: 29.7%
Educational Attainment: High school diploma or higher: 80.3%; Bachelor's degree or higher: 11.8%; Graduate/professional degree or higher: 7.7%
Housing: Homeownership rate: 82.9%; Median home value: $85,600; Median year structure built: 1977; Homeowner vacancy rate: 3.0%; Median selected monthly owner costs: $1,279 with a mortgage, $447 without a mortgage; Median gross rent: $739 per month; Rental vacancy rate: 0.0%
Health Insurance: 80.8% have insurance; 47.1% have private insurance; 46.4% have public insurance; 19.2% do not have insurance; 35.8% of children under 18 do not have insurance
Transportation: Commute: 88.2% car, 0.0% public transportation, 0.6% walk, 11.3% work from home; Mean travel time to work: 31.5 minutes

RUSSELL (town). Covers a land area of 96.675 square miles and a water area of 0.618 square miles. Located at 44.40° N. Lat; 75.14° W. Long. Elevation is 617 feet.
Population: 1,843; Growth (since 2000): 2.3%; Density: 19.1 persons per square mile; Race: 98.2% White, 0.0% Black/African American, 0.0% Asian, 0.3% American Indian/Alaska Native, 0.0% Native Hawaiian/Other

Pacific Islander, 1.5% Two or more races, 0.2% Hispanic of any race; Average household size: 2.51; Median age: 43.9; Age under 18: 23.3%; Age 65 and over: 14.9%; Males per 100 females: 103.7; Marriage status: 24.6% never married, 61.6% now married, 3.2% separated, 5.4% widowed, 8.3% divorced; Foreign born: 1.8%; Speak English only: 97.1%; With disability: 15.0%; Veterans: 10.3%; Ancestry: 17.0% French, 16.5% English, 15.1% Irish, 7.7% German, 6.3% Scottish
Employment: 4.7% management, business, and financial, 1.9% computer, engineering, and science, 7.7% education, legal, community service, arts, and media, 12.4% healthcare practitioners, 25.7% service, 24.3% sales and office, 9.4% natural resources, construction, and maintenance, 13.9% production, transportation, and material moving
Income: Per capita: $27,038; Median household: $48,047; Average household: $67,153; Households with income of $100,000 or more: 17.3%; Poverty rate: 10.6%
Educational Attainment: High school diploma or higher: 90.3%; Bachelor's degree or higher: 21.9%; Graduate/professional degree or higher: 8.8%

School District(s)
Edwards-Knox Central SD (PK-12)
   Enrollment: 569 . . . . (315) 562-8130
Housing: Homeownership rate: 86.3%; Median home value: $83,100; Median year structure built: 1983; Homeowner vacancy rate: 1.4%; Median selected monthly owner costs: $1,069 with a mortgage, $376 without a mortgage; Median gross rent: $673 per month; Rental vacancy rate: 9.0%
Health Insurance: 95.5% have insurance; 70.9% have private insurance; 40.5% have public insurance; 4.5% do not have insurance; 3.2% of children under 18 do not have insurance
Transportation: Commute: 94.0% car, 0.0% public transportation, 0.4% walk, 5.6% work from home; Mean travel time to work: 29.3 minutes

SOUTH COLTON (unincorporated postal area)
ZCTA: 13687
   Covers a land area of 134.416 square miles and a water area of 9.784 square miles. Located at 44.43° N. Lat; 74.84° W. Long. Elevation is 935 feet.
Population: 438; Growth (since 2000): 31.5%; Density: 3.3 persons per square mile; Race: 100.0% White, 0.0% Black/African American, 0.0% Asian, 0.0% American Indian/Alaska Native, 0.0% Native Hawaiian/Other Pacific Islander, 0.0% Two or more races, 0.0% Hispanic of any race; Average household size: 2.32; Median age: 49.0; Age under 18: 19.6%; Age 65 and over: 21.2%; Males per 100 females: 108.3; Marriage status: 27.5% never married, 45.8% now married, 2.0% separated, 10.9% widowed, 15.8% divorced; Foreign born: 1.4%; Speak English only: 99.3%; With disability: 25.6%; Veterans: 16.8%; Ancestry: 46.1% English, 16.7% Irish, 15.5% French, 4.3% Dutch, 4.1% Scotch-Irish
Employment: 12.1% management, business, and financial, 2.9% computer, engineering, and science, 22.5% education, legal, community service, arts, and media, 11.0% healthcare practitioners, 16.2% service, 17.9% sales and office, 11.0% natural resources, construction, and maintenance, 6.4% production, transportation, and material moving
Income: Per capita: $28,066; Median household: $47,292; Average household: $64,644; Households with income of $100,000 or more: 24.4%; Poverty rate: 12.3%
Educational Attainment: High school diploma or higher: 98.1%; Bachelor's degree or higher: 28.4%; Graduate/professional degree or higher: 17.0%
Housing: Homeownership rate: 87.3%; Median home value: $105,300; Median year structure built: 1973; Homeowner vacancy rate: 0.0%; Median selected monthly owner costs: $861 with a mortgage, $419 without a mortgage; Median gross rent: $600 per month; Rental vacancy rate: 0.0%
Health Insurance: 95.2% have insurance; 74.7% have private insurance; 43.4% have public insurance; 4.8% do not have insurance; 0.0% of children under 18 do not have insurance
Transportation: Commute: 93.5% car, 0.0% public transportation, 2.2% walk, 4.3% work from home; Mean travel time to work: 29.2 minutes

STAR LAKE (CDP). Covers a land area of 4.338 square miles and a water area of 0.426 square miles. Located at 44.17° N. Lat; 75.04° W. Long. Elevation is 1,486 feet.
Population: 699; Growth (since 2000): -18.7%; Density: 161.2 persons per square mile; Race: 95.7% White, 0.7% Black/African American, 1.1% Asian, 0.3% American Indian/Alaska Native, 0.0% Native Hawaiian/Other

Pacific Islander, 1.9% Two or more races, 1.4% Hispanic of any race; Average household size: 2.13; Median age: 52.2; Age under 18: 19.6%; Age 65 and over: 26.8%; Males per 100 females: 105.3; Marriage status: 19.6% never married, 57.2% now married, 6.2% separated, 11.8% widowed, 11.4% divorced; Foreign born: 1.9%; Speak English only: 96.7%; With disability: 26.9%; Veterans: 14.6%; Ancestry: 24.9% French, 18.0% English, 15.2% Irish, 7.9% German, 6.0% Italian
Employment: 9.7% management, business, and financial, 1.2% computer, engineering, and science, 10.4% education, legal, community service, arts, and media, 6.6% healthcare practitioners, 23.9% service, 17.4% sales and office, 15.4% natural resources, construction, and maintenance, 15.4% production, transportation, and material moving
Income: Per capita: $25,712; Median household: $41,932; Average household: $55,413; Households with income of $100,000 or more: 15.7%; Poverty rate: 17.7%
Educational Attainment: High school diploma or higher: 81.5%; Bachelor's degree or higher: 13.6%; Graduate/professional degree or higher: 7.5%

School District(s)
Clifton-Fine Central SD (PK-12)
    Enrollment: 302 . . . . (315) 848-3333
Housing: Homeownership rate: 69.5%; Median home value: $75,000; Median year structure built: 1954; Homeowner vacancy rate: 0.0%; Median selected monthly owner costs: $886 with a mortgage, $532 without a mortgage; Median gross rent: $500 per month; Rental vacancy rate: 3.9%
Health Insurance: 97.1% have insurance; 71.0% have private insurance; 46.9% have public insurance; 2.9% do not have insurance; 4.2% of children under 18 do not have insurance
Hospitals: Clifton Fine Hospital
Transportation: Commute: 87.4% car, 0.0% public transportation, 1.2% walk, 9.8% work from home; Mean travel time to work: 32.5 minutes

STOCKHOLM (town). Covers a land area of 93.897 square miles and a water area of 0.392 square miles. Located at 44.75° N. Lat; 74.86° W. Long.
Population: 3,647; Growth (since 2000): 1.5%; Density: 38.8 persons per square mile; Race: 99.5% White, 0.0% Black/African American, 0.0% Asian, 0.0% American Indian/Alaska Native, 0.0% Native Hawaiian/Other Pacific Islander, 0.5% Two or more races, 0.0% Hispanic of any race; Average household size: 2.36; Median age: 40.1; Age under 18: 25.9%; Age 65 and over: 16.8%; Males per 100 females: 104.9; Marriage status: 20.8% never married, 53.5% now married, 2.3% separated, 7.7% widowed, 18.1% divorced; Foreign born: 2.8%; Speak English only: 93.9%; With disability: 24.1%; Veterans: 12.1%; Ancestry: 19.9% Irish, 16.4% French, 12.7% English, 12.2% French Canadian, 11.5% Italian
Employment: 9.9% management, business, and financial, 4.5% computer, engineering, and science, 10.3% education, legal, community service, arts, and media, 6.0% healthcare practitioners, 29.1% service, 12.0% sales and office, 15.6% natural resources, construction, and maintenance, 12.6% production, transportation, and material moving
Income: Per capita: $21,345; Median household: $40,804; Average household: $49,474; Households with income of $100,000 or more: 10.7%; Poverty rate: 17.8%
Educational Attainment: High school diploma or higher: 95.1%; Bachelor's degree or higher: 18.3%; Graduate/professional degree or higher: 8.0%
Housing: Homeownership rate: 80.3%; Median home value: $77,500; Median year structure built: 1972; Homeowner vacancy rate: 4.2%; Median selected monthly owner costs: $1,022 with a mortgage, $427 without a mortgage; Median gross rent: $820 per month; Rental vacancy rate: 0.0%
Health Insurance: 95.2% have insurance; 63.4% have private insurance; 50.9% have public insurance; 4.8% do not have insurance; 0.0% of children under 18 do not have insurance
Transportation: Commute: 83.4% car, 0.0% public transportation, 3.4% walk, 12.8% work from home; Mean travel time to work: 22.9 minutes

WADDINGTON (town). Covers a land area of 51.606 square miles and a water area of 6.367 square miles. Located at 44.83° N. Lat; 75.19° W. Long. Elevation is 272 feet.
Population: 2,032; Growth (since 2000): -8.1%; Density: 39.4 persons per square mile; Race: 94.3% White, 0.0% Black/African American, 0.0% Asian, 2.2% American Indian/Alaska Native, 0.0% Native Hawaiian/Other Pacific Islander, 1.2% Two or more races, 1.2% Hispanic of any race; Average household size: 2.35; Median age: 42.7; Age under 18: 24.8%; Age 65 and over: 17.0%; Males per 100 females: 91.9; Marriage status:

31.8% never married, 47.4% now married, 2.7% separated, 7.8% widowed, 12.9% divorced; Foreign born: 2.3%; Speak English only: 99.7%; With disability: 17.0%; Veterans: 13.2%; Ancestry: 26.4% Irish, 19.4% French, 13.2% English, 9.8% German, 9.6% French Canadian
Employment: 10.8% management, business, and financial, 3.1% computer, engineering, and science, 8.4% education, legal, community service, arts, and media, 8.0% healthcare practitioners, 26.2% service, 12.6% sales and office, 18.7% natural resources, construction, and maintenance, 12.2% production, transportation, and material moving
Income: Per capita: $29,805; Median household: $60,500; Average household: $69,248; Households with income of $100,000 or more: 26.0%; Poverty rate: 13.3%
Educational Attainment: High school diploma or higher: 92.4%; Bachelor's degree or higher: 21.7%; Graduate/professional degree or higher: 8.5%
Housing: Homeownership rate: 72.7%; Median home value: $117,700; Median year structure built: 1973; Homeowner vacancy rate: 2.1%; Median selected monthly owner costs: $1,055 with a mortgage, $437 without a mortgage; Median gross rent: $841 per month; Rental vacancy rate: 0.0%
Health Insurance: 93.8% have insurance; 72.5% have private insurance; 38.1% have public insurance; 6.2% do not have insurance; 8.1% of children under 18 do not have insurance
Transportation: Commute: 97.3% car, 0.0% public transportation, 1.5% walk, 0.9% work from home; Mean travel time to work: 24.1 minutes

WADDINGTON (village). Covers a land area of 2.180 square miles and a water area of 0.187 square miles. Located at 44.86° N. Lat; 75.20° W. Long. Elevation is 272 feet.
Population: 891; Growth (since 2000): -3.5%; Density: 408.7 persons per square mile; Race: 92.7% White, 4.6% Black/African American, 0.0% Asian, 0.0% American Indian/Alaska Native, 0.0% Native Hawaiian/Other Pacific Islander, 2.7% Two or more races, 2.7% Hispanic of any race; Average household size: 2.10; Median age: 47.2; Age under 18: 21.4%; Age 65 and over: 22.0%; Males per 100 females: 82.0; Marriage status: 26.1% never married, 53.7% now married, 5.3% separated, 9.0% widowed, 11.2% divorced; Foreign born: 3.7%; Speak English only: 99.3%; With disability: 21.9%; Veterans: 10.5%; Ancestry: 30.8% Irish, 22.0% French, 16.3% English, 9.7% German, 6.8% Italian
Employment: 14.8% management, business, and financial, 5.4% computer, engineering, and science, 8.8% education, legal, community service, arts, and media, 2.4% healthcare practitioners, 33.2% service, 16.9% sales and office, 16.3% natural resources, construction, and maintenance, 2.1% production, transportation, and material moving
Income: Per capita: $30,437; Median household: $42,039; Average household: $62,711; Households with income of $100,000 or more: 21.3%; Poverty rate: 13.5%
Educational Attainment: High school diploma or higher: 92.4%; Bachelor's degree or higher: 26.2%; Graduate/professional degree or higher: 7.9%
Housing: Homeownership rate: 64.2%; Median home value: $128,900; Median year structure built: 1960; Homeowner vacancy rate: 0.0%; Median selected monthly owner costs: $1,111 with a mortgage, $513 without a mortgage; Median gross rent: $765 per month; Rental vacancy rate: 0.0%
Health Insurance: 97.5% have insurance; 76.0% have private insurance; 41.3% have public insurance; 2.5% do not have insurance; 0.0% of children under 18 do not have insurance
Transportation: Commute: 95.9% car, 0.0% public transportation, 0.9% walk, 2.2% work from home; Mean travel time to work: 23.1 minutes

WANAKENA (unincorporated postal area)
ZCTA: 13695
    Covers a land area of 17.001 square miles and a water area of 0.334 square miles. Located at 44.10° N. Lat; 74.92° W. Long. Elevation is 1,503 feet.
    Population: 154; Growth (since 2000): n/a; Density: 9.1 persons per square mile; Race: 85.7% White, 2.6% Black/African American, 0.0% Asian, 6.5% American Indian/Alaska Native, 0.0% Native Hawaiian/Other Pacific Islander, 2.6% Two or more races, 0.0% Hispanic of any race; Average household size: 1.90; Median age: 52.9; Age under 18: 5.2%; Age 65 and over: 37.7%; Males per 100 females: 179.2; Marriage status: 38.9% never married, 59.1% now married, 0.0% separated, 2.0% widowed, 0.0% divorced; Foreign born: 0.0%; Speak English only: 95.5%; With disability: 21.4%; Veterans: 15.1%; Ancestry: 33.8% English, 29.2% Irish, 14.9% Dutch, 11.0% Scottish, 8.4% French Canadian

Employment: 43.8% management, business, and financial, 0.0% computer, engineering, and science, 0.0% education, legal, community service, arts, and media, 7.5% healthcare practitioners, 23.8% service, 11.3% sales and office, 5.0% natural resources, construction, and maintenance, 8.8% production, transportation, and material moving
Income: Per capita: $31,116; Median household: $100,556; Average household: $84,421; Households with income of $100,000 or more: 53.8%; Poverty rate: n/a
Educational Attainment: High school diploma or higher: 100.0%; Bachelor's degree or higher: 40.7%; Graduate/professional degree or higher: 11.0%
Housing: Homeownership rate: 100.0%; Median home value: $241,200; Median year structure built: 1948; Homeowner vacancy rate: 0.0%; Median selected monthly owner costs: $1,698 with a mortgage, $694 without a mortgage; Median gross rent: n/a per month; Rental vacancy rate: 0.0%
Health Insurance: 100.0% have insurance; 94.2% have private insurance; 37.7% have public insurance; 0.0% do not have insurance; 0.0% of children under 18 do not have insurance
Transportation: Commute: 51.5% car, 0.0% public transportation, 5.9% walk, 42.6% work from home; Mean travel time to work: 15.5 minutes

WEST STOCKHOLM (unincorporated postal area)
ZCTA: 13696
Covers a land area of 1.862 square miles and a water area of 0 square miles. Located at 44.69° N. Lat; 74.89° W. Long. Elevation is 384 feet.
Population: 44; Growth (since 2000): n/a; Density: 23.6 persons per square mile; Race: 100.0% White, 0.0% Black/African American, 0.0% Asian, 0.0% American Indian/Alaska Native, 0.0% Native Hawaiian/Other Pacific Islander, 0.0% Two or more races, 0.0% Hispanic of any race; Average household size: 1.63; Median age: 60.4; Age under 18: 0.0%; Age 65 and over: 27.3%; Males per 100 females: 102.3; Marriage status: 27.3% never married, 72.7% now married, 0.0% separated, 0.0% widowed, 0.0% divorced; Foreign born: 0.0%; Speak English only: 100.0%; With disability: 0.0%; Veterans: 0.0%; Ancestry: 61.4% Irish, 27.3% English
Employment: 27.3% management, business, and financial, 0.0% computer, engineering, and science, 0.0% education, legal, community service, arts, and media, 0.0% healthcare practitioners, 0.0% service, 0.0% sales and office, 0.0% natural resources, construction, and maintenance, 72.7% production, transportation, and material moving
Income: Per capita: $56,650; Median household: n/a; Average household: n/a; Households with income of $100,000 or more: 55.6%; Poverty rate: n/a
Educational Attainment: High school diploma or higher: 100.0%; Bachelor's degree or higher: n/a; Graduate/professional degree or higher: n/a
Housing: Homeownership rate: 55.6%; Median home value: n/a; Median year structure built: Before 1940; Homeowner vacancy rate: 78.3%; Median selected monthly owner costs: $0 with a mortgage, $0 without a mortgage; Median gross rent: n/a per month; Rental vacancy rate: 0.0%
Health Insurance: 100.0% have insurance; 100.0% have private insurance; 27.3% have public insurance; 0.0% do not have insurance; 0.0% of children under 18 do not have insurance
Transportation: Commute: 58.6% car, 0.0% public transportation, 0.0% walk, 41.4% work from home; Mean travel time to work: 0.0 minutes

WINTHROP (CDP).
Covers a land area of 2.777 square miles and a water area of 0.023 square miles. Located at 44.80° N. Lat; 74.81° W. Long. Elevation is 325 feet.
Population: 338; Growth (since 2000): n/a; Density: 121.7 persons per square mile; Race: 97.6% White, 0.0% Black/African American, 0.0% Asian, 0.0% American Indian/Alaska Native, 0.0% Native Hawaiian/Other Pacific Islander, 2.4% Two or more races, 0.0% Hispanic of any race; Average household size: 2.21; Median age: 42.8; Age under 18: 15.7%; Age 65 and over: 8.3%; Males per 100 females: 96.9; Marriage status: 10.2% never married, 36.1% now married, 6.0% separated, 22.1% widowed, 31.6% divorced; Foreign born: 5.0%; Speak English only: 94.4%; With disability: 39.6%; Veterans: 9.5%; Ancestry: 39.6% Welsh, 12.4% Irish, 9.2% English, 8.0% French, 5.0% Scottish
Employment: 0.0% management, business, and financial, 0.0% computer, engineering, and science, 26.7% education, legal, community service, arts, and media, 31.0% healthcare practitioners, 12.9% service, 0.0% sales and

office, 14.7% natural resources, construction, and maintenance, 14.7% production, transportation, and material moving
Income: Per capita: $39,008; Median household: $51,210; Average household: $82,858; Households with income of $100,000 or more: 22.2%; Poverty rate: 10.1%
Educational Attainment: High school diploma or higher: 100.0%; Bachelor's degree or higher: 22.8%; Graduate/professional degree or higher: 15.4%
Housing: Homeownership rate: 75.2%; Median home value: $39,600; Median year structure built: Before 1940; Homeowner vacancy rate: 0.0%; Median selected monthly owner costs: $1,308 with a mortgage, n/a without a mortgage; Median gross rent: n/a per month; Rental vacancy rate: 0.0%
Health Insurance: 71.3% have insurance; 50.3% have private insurance; 29.3% have public insurance; 28.7% do not have insurance; 0.0% of children under 18 do not have insurance
Transportation: Commute: 100.0% car, 0.0% public transportation, 0.0% walk, 0.0% work from home; Mean travel time to work: 21.8 minutes

Saratoga County

Located in eastern New York, partly in the Adirondacks; bounded on the east by the Hudson River, and on the south by the Mohawk River; includes Saratoga Lake. Covers a land area of 809.984 square miles, a water area of 33.824 square miles, and is located in the Eastern Time Zone at 43.11° N. Lat., 73.86° W. Long. The county was founded in 1791. County seat is Ballston Spa.

Saratoga County is part of the Albany-Schenectady-Troy, NY Metropolitan Statistical Area. The entire metro area includes: Albany County, NY; Rensselaer County, NY; Saratoga County, NY; Schenectady County, NY; Schoharie County, NY

Weather Station: Conklingville Dam										Elevation: 808 feet		
	Jan	Feb	Mar	Apr	May	Jun	Jul	Aug	Sep	Oct	Nov	Dec
High	29	33	41	54	66	74	78	77	69	58	46	33
Low	9	12	21	33	45	54	58	57	49	38	30	17
Precip	3.4	2.8	4.0	3.7	4.1	4.1	4.2	4.0	3.8	3.7	3.8	3.8
Snow	19.9	13.8	13.8	2.6	tr	0.0	0.0	0.0	0.0	0.1	3.7	16.5

High and Low temperatures in degrees Fahrenheit; Precipitation and Snow in inches

Weather Station: Saratoga Springs 4 SW										Elevation: 310 feet		
	Jan	Feb	Mar	Apr	May	Jun	Jul	Aug	Sep	Oct	Nov	Dec
High	31	35	45	60	72	80	83	82	74	61	48	36
Low	12	15	24	35	46	55	60	58	50	39	30	19
Precip	3.2	2.5	3.5	3.7	4.1	4.3	4.3	4.1	3.7	3.8	3.8	3.6
Snow	19.1	12.6	11.6	2.3	tr	0.0	0.0	0.0	tr	0.1	3.1	14.2

High and Low temperatures in degrees Fahrenheit; Precipitation and Snow in inches

Population: 226,632; Growth (since 2000): 13.0%; Density: 279.8 persons per square mile; Race: 93.2% White, 1.7% Black/African American, 2.8% Asian, 0.2% American Indian/Alaska Native, 0.0% Native Hawaiian/Other Pacific Islander, 1.6% two or more races, 3.0% Hispanic of any race; Average household size: 2.39; Median age: 42.3; Age under 18: 20.9%; Age 65 and over: 16.5%; Males per 100 females: 96.9; Marriage status: 28.1% never married, 56.3% now married, 1.7% separated, 5.3% widowed, 10.3% divorced; Foreign born: 5.3%; Speak English only: 93.1%; With disability: 11.3%; Veterans: 9.0%; Ancestry: 23.5% Irish, 18.0% Italian, 16.5% German, 12.5% English, 8.0% French
Religion: Six largest groups: 23.9% Catholicism, 4.1% Methodist/Pietist, 3.1% Non-denominational Protestant, 1.9% Episcopalianism/Anglicanism, 1.2% Lutheran, 1.2% Presbyterian-Reformed
Economy: Unemployment rate: 3.1%; Leading industries: 14.2 % retail trade; 12.7 % construction; 11.9 % professional, scientific, and technical services; Farms: 583 totaling 78,849 acres; Company size: 5 employ 1,000 or more persons, 6 employ 500 to 999 persons, 73 employ 100 to 499 persons, 5,194 employ less than 100 persons; Business ownership: 5,863 women-owned, 190 Black-owned, 268 Hispanic-owned, 636 Asian-owned, 43 American Indian/Alaska Native-owned
Employment: 17.9% management, business, and financial, 8.7% computer, engineering, and science, 12.6% education, legal, community service, arts, and media, 6.5% healthcare practitioners, 14.3% service, 23.5% sales and office, 7.7% natural resources, construction, and maintenance, 8.7% production, transportation, and material moving
Income: Per capita: $39,653; Median household: $77,548; Average household: $96,086; Households with income of $100,000 or more: 36.9%; Poverty rate: 6.6%

Educational Attainment: High school diploma or higher: 93.9%; Bachelor's degree or higher: 40.4%; Graduate/professional degree or higher: 17.0%

Housing: Homeownership rate: 71.5%; Median home value: $243,600; Median year structure built: 1981; Homeowner vacancy rate: 0.9%; Median selected monthly owner costs: $1,727 with a mortgage, $605 without a mortgage; Median gross rent: $1,046 per month; Rental vacancy rate: 4.5%

Vital Statistics: Birth rate: 94.0 per 10,000 population; Death rate: 84.5 per 10,000 population; Age-adjusted cancer mortality rate: 160.0 deaths per 100,000 population

Health Insurance: 96.2% have insurance; 82.3% have private insurance; 29.0% have public insurance; 3.8% do not have insurance; 1.5% of children under 18 do not have insurance

Health Care: Physicians: 22.5 per 10,000 population; Dentists: 6.4 per 10,000 population; Hospital beds: 13.0 per 10,000 population; Hospital admissions: 518.5 per 10,000 population

Air Quality Index (AQI): Percent of Days: 96.3% good, 3.7% moderate, 0.0% unhealthy for sensitive individuals, 0.0% unhealthy, 0.0% very unhealthy; Annual median: 34; Annual maximum: 90

Transportation: Commute: 90.7% car, 0.8% public transportation, 1.9% walk, 5.9% work from home; Mean travel time to work: 25.3 minutes

2016 Presidential Election: 47.8% Trump, 44.6% Clinton, 4.5% Johnson, 1.6% Stein

National and State Parks: Moreau Lake State Park; New York State Game Management Area; Peebles Island State Park; Saratoga National Historical Park; Saratoga Spa State Park; Wilkinson National Recreation Trail

Additional Information Contacts
Saratoga Government . . . . (518) 885-2213
  http://www.saratogacountyny.gov

Saratoga County Communities

BALLSTON (town). Covers a land area of 29.576 square miles and a water area of 0.462 square miles. Located at 42.95° N. Lat; 73.89° W. Long.

History: Founded in 1785, the town was purchased by Eliphalet Ball from the Mcdonald brothers, and he paid the brothers one barrel of rum for the right to name the town after himself. Over time the name was shortened to Ballston.

Population: 10,576; Growth (since 2000): 21.2%; Density: 357.6 persons per square mile; Race: 95.3% White, 0.8% Black/African American, 2.5% Asian, 0.0% American Indian/Alaska Native, 0.2% Native Hawaiian/Other Pacific Islander, 1.0% Two or more races, 3.6% Hispanic of any race; Average household size: 2.60; Median age: 44.5; Age under 18: 23.2%; Age 65 and over: 18.4%; Males per 100 females: 91.5; Marriage status: 26.8% never married, 57.9% now married, 1.7% separated, 5.4% widowed, 10.0% divorced; Foreign born: 3.6%; Speak English only: 94.3%; With disability: 10.9%; Veterans: 6.8%; Ancestry: 23.1% Irish, 22.8% German, 18.4% Italian, 16.5% English, 7.7% French

Employment: 17.6% management, business, and financial, 7.7% computer, engineering, and science, 13.4% education, legal, community service, arts, and media, 5.7% healthcare practitioners, 13.4% service, 25.9% sales and office, 7.7% natural resources, construction, and maintenance, 8.5% production, transportation, and material moving

Income: Per capita: $39,667; Median household: $89,449; Average household: $104,022; Households with income of $100,000 or more: 43.2%; Poverty rate: 6.9%

Educational Attainment: High school diploma or higher: 95.5%; Bachelor's degree or higher: 46.2%; Graduate/professional degree or higher: 20.8%

Housing: Homeownership rate: 76.6%; Median home value: $278,800; Median year structure built: 1976; Homeowner vacancy rate: 1.7%; Median selected monthly owner costs: $1,803 with a mortgage, $620 without a mortgage; Median gross rent: $1,048 per month; Rental vacancy rate: 0.0%

Health Insurance: 98.0% have insurance; 81.5% have private insurance; 33.3% have public insurance; 2.0% do not have insurance; 0.0% of children under 18 do not have insurance

Transportation: Commute: 91.7% car, 1.6% public transportation, 1.0% walk, 5.1% work from home; Mean travel time to work: 25.6 minutes

Additional Information Contacts
Town of Ballston . . . . (518) 885-8502
  http://www.townofballstonny.org

BALLSTON LAKE (unincorporated postal area)
ZCTA: 12019

  Covers a land area of 29.500 square miles and a water area of 0.493 square miles. Located at 42.93° N. Lat; 73.88° W. Long. Elevation is 266 feet.

Population: 14,396; Growth (since 2000): 8.1%; Density: 488.0 persons per square mile; Race: 92.4% White, 1.2% Black/African American, 3.9% Asian, 0.0% American Indian/Alaska Native, 0.1% Native Hawaiian/Other Pacific Islander, 2.4% Two or more races, 1.2% Hispanic of any race; Average household size: 2.45; Median age: 45.7; Age under 18: 20.7%; Age 65 and over: 20.4%; Males per 100 females: 98.9; Marriage status: 23.2% never married, 62.9% now married, 0.9% separated, 6.2% widowed, 7.7% divorced; Foreign born: 6.2%; Speak English only: 93.7%; With disability: 7.9%; Veterans: 8.6%; Ancestry: 22.7% Irish, 18.6% Italian, 17.8% German, 14.6% English, 9.3% Polish

Employment: 18.4% management, business, and financial, 10.5% computer, engineering, and science, 12.8% education, legal, community service, arts, and media, 10.6% healthcare practitioners, 11.8% service, 23.9% sales and office, 6.6% natural resources, construction, and maintenance, 5.3% production, transportation, and material moving

Income: Per capita: $46,269; Median household: $98,600; Average household: $113,837; Households with income of $100,000 or more: 49.0%; Poverty rate: 3.2%

Educational Attainment: High school diploma or higher: 96.8%; Bachelor's degree or higher: 48.7%; Graduate/professional degree or higher: 25.2%

School District(s)
Burnt Hills-Ballston Lake Central SD (KG-12)
  Enrollment: 3,091 . . . . (518) 399-9141
Shenendehowa Central SD (KG-12)
  Enrollment: 9,856 . . . . (518) 881-0610

Housing: Homeownership rate: 79.9%; Median home value: $278,400; Median year structure built: 1975; Homeowner vacancy rate: 1.4%; Median selected monthly owner costs: $1,924 with a mortgage, $646 without a mortgage; Median gross rent: $1,018 per month; Rental vacancy rate: 0.0%

Health Insurance: 98.3% have insurance; 89.5% have private insurance; 28.4% have public insurance; 1.7% do not have insurance; 1.6% of children under 18 do not have insurance

Transportation: Commute: 92.7% car, 1.5% public transportation, 0.5% walk, 5.0% work from home; Mean travel time to work: 25.7 minutes

BALLSTON SPA (village). County seat. Covers a land area of 1.599 square miles and a water area of 0.009 square miles. Located at 43.01° N. Lat; 73.85° W. Long. Elevation is 315 feet.

History: Formerly a popular resort. Settled 1771, incorporated 1807.

Population: 5,278; Growth (since 2000): -5.0%; Density: 3,301.8 persons per square mile; Race: 93.0% White, 2.3% Black/African American, 1.6% Asian, 1.4% American Indian/Alaska Native, 0.0% Native Hawaiian/Other Pacific Islander, 1.5% Two or more races, 5.6% Hispanic of any race; Average household size: 2.21; Median age: 40.6; Age under 18: 20.4%; Age 65 and over: 20.3%; Males per 100 females: 94.2; Marriage status: 29.2% never married, 46.7% now married, 1.2% separated, 10.3% widowed, 13.8% divorced; Foreign born: 4.9%; Speak English only: 91.6%; With disability: 10.3%; Veterans: 9.0%; Ancestry: 17.7% Irish, 16.2% German, 15.6% Italian, 15.0% English, 9.5% French

Employment: 12.1% management, business, and financial, 11.4% computer, engineering, and science, 13.0% education, legal, community service, arts, and media, 4.7% healthcare practitioners, 22.6% service, 21.1% sales and office, 5.5% natural resources, construction, and maintenance, 9.4% production, transportation, and material moving

Income: Per capita: $30,420; Median household: $56,358; Average household: $68,311; Households with income of $100,000 or more: 23.6%; Poverty rate: 11.1%

Educational Attainment: High school diploma or higher: 93.5%; Bachelor's degree or higher: 36.1%; Graduate/professional degree or higher: 14.4%

School District(s)
Ballston Spa Central SD (KG-12)
  Enrollment: 4,160 . . . . (518) 884-7195
Vocational/Technical School(s)
John Paolo's Xtreme Beauty Institute-Goldwell Product Artistry (Private, For-profit)
  Enrollment: 23 . . . . (518) 583-3700
  Tuition: $13,500

Housing: Homeownership rate: 52.2%; Median home value: $217,900; Median year structure built: Before 1940; Homeowner vacancy rate: 0.0%; Median selected monthly owner costs: $1,667 with a mortgage, $513 without a mortgage; Median gross rent: $898 per month; Rental vacancy rate: 0.0%

Health Insurance: 95.2% have insurance; 69.8% have private insurance; 42.3% have public insurance; 4.8% do not have insurance; 1.7% of children under 18 do not have insurance

Safety: Violent crime rate: 1.9 per 10,000 population; Property crime rate: 90.5 per 10,000 population

Newspapers: Ballston Journal (weekly circulation 2,200)

Transportation: Commute: 84.4% car, 3.0% public transportation, 3.6% walk, 7.3% work from home; Mean travel time to work: 25.0 minutes

BURNT HILLS (unincorporated postal area)
ZCTA: 12027

Covers a land area of 7.172 square miles and a water area of 0.022 square miles. Located at 42.94° N. Lat; 73.91° W. Long. Elevation is 407 feet.

Population: 3,930; Growth (since 2000): 7.4%; Density: 548.0 persons per square mile; Race: 97.1% White, 0.6% Black/African American, 1.5% Asian, 0.0% American Indian/Alaska Native, 0.0% Native Hawaiian/Other Pacific Islander, 0.9% Two or more races, 1.8% Hispanic of any race; Average household size: 2.66; Median age: 45.0; Age under 18: 25.4%; Age 65 and over: 16.3%; Males per 100 females: 91.4; Marriage status: 24.3% never married, 62.3% now married, 2.1% separated, 3.6% widowed, 9.9% divorced; Foreign born: 2.4%; Speak English only: 96.8%; With disability: 10.1%; Veterans: 6.9%; Ancestry: 25.7% German, 25.6% Irish, 24.5% Italian, 16.2% English, 8.5% Polish

Employment: 20.1% management, business, and financial, 9.8% computer, engineering, and science, 13.9% education, legal, community service, arts, and media, 4.9% healthcare practitioners, 8.3% service, 28.1% sales and office, 7.7% natural resources, construction, and maintenance, 7.1% production, transportation, and material moving

Income: Per capita: $42,852; Median household: $92,159; Average household: $114,914; Households with income of $100,000 or more: 48.3%; Poverty rate: 0.6%

Educational Attainment: High school diploma or higher: 98.7%; Bachelor's degree or higher: 58.1%; Graduate/professional degree or higher: 21.7%

School District(s)
Burnt Hills-Ballston Lake Central SD (KG-12)

    Enrollment: 3,091 . . . . (518) 399-9141

Housing: Homeownership rate: 82.7%; Median home value: $259,000; Median year structure built: 1967; Homeowner vacancy rate: 0.7%; Median selected monthly owner costs: $1,650 with a mortgage, $609 without a mortgage; Median gross rent: $1,248 per month; Rental vacancy rate: 0.0%

Health Insurance: 98.1% have insurance; 89.0% have private insurance; 24.3% have public insurance; 1.9% do not have insurance; 0.0% of children under 18 do not have insurance

Transportation: Commute: 92.7% car, 0.4% public transportation, 0.0% walk, 6.2% work from home; Mean travel time to work: 27.6 minutes

CHARLTON (town). Covers a land area of 32.774 square miles and a water area of 0.188 square miles. Located at 42.96° N. Lat; 73.99° W. Long. Elevation is 495 feet.

Population: 4,185; Growth (since 2000): 5.8%; Density: 127.7 persons per square mile; Race: 98.9% White, 0.5% Black/African American, 0.0% Asian, 0.0% American Indian/Alaska Native, 0.0% Native Hawaiian/Other Pacific Islander, 0.5% Two or more races, 0.5% Hispanic of any race; Average household size: 2.49; Median age: 49.1; Age under 18: 19.9%; Age 65 and over: 20.8%; Males per 100 females: 96.5; Marriage status: 22.2% never married, 64.1% now married, 2.2% separated, 5.2% widowed, 8.5% divorced; Foreign born: 1.2%; Speak English only: 98.3%; With disability: 8.9%; Veterans: 9.5%; Ancestry: 25.4% German, 19.7% Irish, 18.9% English, 18.4% Polish, 16.0% Italian

Employment: 16.2% management, business, and financial, 8.2% computer, engineering, and science, 7.9% education, legal, community service, arts, and media, 8.8% healthcare practitioners, 15.8% service, 26.5% sales and office, 13.0% natural resources, construction, and maintenance, 3.6% production, transportation, and material moving

Income: Per capita: $39,070; Median household: $82,394; Average household: $97,702; Households with income of $100,000 or more: 35.9%; Poverty rate: 2.8%

Educational Attainment: High school diploma or higher: 95.2%; Bachelor's degree or higher: 35.8%; Graduate/professional degree or higher: 14.4%

Housing: Homeownership rate: 95.2%; Median home value: $252,800; Median year structure built: 1966; Homeowner vacancy rate: 0.4%; Median selected monthly owner costs: $1,781 with a mortgage, $723 without a mortgage; Median gross rent: n/a per month; Rental vacancy rate: 0.0%

Health Insurance: 99.3% have insurance; 91.5% have private insurance; 26.6% have public insurance; 0.7% do not have insurance; 0.0% of children under 18 do not have insurance

Transportation: Commute: 95.0% car, 0.1% public transportation, 0.0% walk, 4.4% work from home; Mean travel time to work: 27.5 minutes

Additional Information Contacts

Town of Charlton . . . . (518) 384-0152
  http://www.townofcharlton.org

CLIFTON PARK (town). Covers a land area of 48.202 square miles and a water area of 2.004 square miles. Located at 42.86° N. Lat; 73.82° W. Long. Elevation is 344 feet.

History: Clifton Park was first settled in the 17th century. It was named in 1707 by Nanning Harmansen, who wrote to Lord Cornbury requesting a Patent for Land he bought from the Native Americans known as Shenendehowa, and that the patent to be known by "Your name of Cliftons Park."

Population: 36,884; Growth (since 2000): 11.8%; Density: 765.2 persons per square mile; Race: 88.4% White, 3.0% Black/African American, 5.7% Asian, 0.1% American Indian/Alaska Native, 0.1% Native Hawaiian/Other Pacific Islander, 1.6% Two or more races, 3.3% Hispanic of any race; Average household size: 2.55; Median age: 42.8; Age under 18: 23.0%; Age 65 and over: 17.4%; Males per 100 females: 95.2; Marriage status: 24.3% never married, 62.0% now married, 1.5% separated, 4.8% widowed, 8.9% divorced; Foreign born: 8.3%; Speak English only: 88.9%; With disability: 7.5%; Veterans: 8.2%; Ancestry: 24.2% Irish, 19.5% Italian, 18.2% German, 11.5% English, 7.3% Polish

Employment: 22.4% management, business, and financial, 12.6% computer, engineering, and science, 14.2% education, legal, community service, arts, and media, 7.7% healthcare practitioners, 8.9% service, 22.5% sales and office, 6.3% natural resources, construction, and maintenance, 5.4% production, transportation, and material moving

Income: Per capita: $45,870; Median household: $101,738; Average household: $117,191; Households with income of $100,000 or more: 51.3%; Poverty rate: 3.6%

Educational Attainment: High school diploma or higher: 97.5%; Bachelor's degree or higher: 55.7%; Graduate/professional degree or higher: 26.0%

School District(s)
Shenendehowa Central SD (KG-12)

    Enrollment: 9,856 . . . . (518) 881-0610

Housing: Homeownership rate: 82.0%; Median home value: $280,700; Median year structure built: 1982; Homeowner vacancy rate: 0.3%; Median selected monthly owner costs: $1,911 with a mortgage, $674 without a mortgage; Median gross rent: $1,174 per month; Rental vacancy rate: 7.2%

Health Insurance: 98.1% have insurance; 89.1% have private insurance; 24.0% have public insurance; 1.9% do not have insurance; 0.5% of children under 18 do not have insurance

Transportation: Commute: 91.9% car, 1.0% public transportation, 0.5% walk, 5.7% work from home; Mean travel time to work: 25.4 minutes

Additional Information Contacts

Town of Clifton Park . . . . (518) 371-6651
  http://www.cliftonpark.org

CORINTH (town). Covers a land area of 56.763 square miles and a water area of 1.372 square miles. Located at 43.23° N. Lat; 73.92° W. Long. Elevation is 610 feet.

History: Incorporated 1886.

Population: 6,484; Growth (since 2000): 8.3%; Density: 114.2 persons per square mile; Race: 97.2% White, 0.8% Black/African American, 0.0% Asian, 0.0% American Indian/Alaska Native, 0.0% Native Hawaiian/Other Pacific Islander, 2.0% Two or more races, 3.3% Hispanic of any race; Average household size: 2.58; Median age: 41.4; Age under 18: 23.1%; Age 65 and over: 16.6%; Males per 100 females: 96.5; Marriage status: 25.3% never married, 59.0% now married, 2.7% separated, 5.9% widowed, 9.9% divorced; Foreign born: 2.3%; Speak English only: 95.8%;

With disability: 19.8%; Veterans: 12.3%; Ancestry: 13.8% Irish, 11.2% French, 10.8% German, 10.7% English, 9.4% Italian
Employment: 5.9% management, business, and financial, 4.9% computer, engineering, and science, 8.4% education, legal, community service, arts, and media, 4.3% healthcare practitioners, 24.9% service, 23.0% sales and office, 12.4% natural resources, construction, and maintenance, 16.2% production, transportation, and material moving
Income: Per capita: $25,327; Median household: $55,465; Average household: $65,398; Households with income of $100,000 or more: 22.4%; Poverty rate: 11.0%
Educational Attainment: High school diploma or higher: 86.8%; Bachelor's degree or higher: 18.4%; Graduate/professional degree or higher: 4.8%

School District(s)
Corinth Central SD (KG-12)
    Enrollment: 1,205 . . . . (518) 654-2601
Housing: Homeownership rate: 79.5%; Median home value: $148,900; Median year structure built: 1967; Homeowner vacancy rate: 0.0%; Median selected monthly owner costs: $1,286 with a mortgage, $484 without a mortgage; Median gross rent: $894 per month; Rental vacancy rate: 2.7%
Health Insurance: 95.2% have insurance; 69.9% have private insurance; 39.5% have public insurance; 4.8% do not have insurance; 0.6% of children under 18 do not have insurance
Transportation: Commute: 92.5% car, 0.4% public transportation, 2.4% walk, 4.6% work from home; Mean travel time to work: 27.1 minutes
Additional Information Contacts
Town of Corinth. . . . . (518) 654-9232
    http://townofcorinthny.com

CORINTH (village). Covers a land area of 1.067 square miles and a water area of 0.039 square miles. Located at 43.25° N. Lat; 73.83° W. Long. Elevation is 610 feet.
Population: 2,651; Growth (since 2000): 7.2%; Density: 2,485.4 persons per square mile; Race: 95.3% White, 0.4% Black/African American, 0.0% Asian, 0.0% American Indian/Alaska Native, 0.0% Native Hawaiian/Other Pacific Islander, 4.3% Two or more races, 2.0% Hispanic of any race; Average household size: 2.63; Median age: 37.4; Age under 18: 25.4%; Age 65 and over: 13.1%; Males per 100 females: 93.3; Marriage status: 27.7% never married, 55.0% now married, 3.8% separated, 6.2% widowed, 11.1% divorced; Foreign born: 1.8%; Speak English only: 95.3%; With disability: 22.6%; Veterans: 12.1%; Ancestry: 17.9% Irish, 13.9% English, 13.4% Italian, 12.3% German, 11.8% French
Employment: 6.9% management, business, and financial, 2.7% computer, engineering, and science, 8.5% education, legal, community service, arts, and media, 4.0% healthcare practitioners, 25.6% service, 23.3% sales and office, 12.2% natural resources, construction, and maintenance, 16.8% production, transportation, and material moving
Income: Per capita: $21,044; Median household: $45,250; Average household: $55,412; Households with income of $100,000 or more: 15.3%; Poverty rate: 17.8%
Educational Attainment: High school diploma or higher: 85.0%; Bachelor's degree or higher: 13.1%; Graduate/professional degree or higher: 3.7%

School District(s)
Corinth Central SD (KG-12)
    Enrollment: 1,205 . . . . (518) 654-2601
Housing: Homeownership rate: 61.9%; Median home value: $141,600; Median year structure built: Before 1940; Homeowner vacancy rate: 0.0%; Median selected monthly owner costs: $1,218 with a mortgage, $469 without a mortgage; Median gross rent: $899 per month; Rental vacancy rate: 3.5%
Health Insurance: 89.3% have insurance; 57.1% have private insurance; 45.4% have public insurance; 10.7% do not have insurance; 1.2% of children under 18 do not have insurance
Transportation: Commute: 87.6% car, 1.1% public transportation, 6.5% walk, 4.5% work from home; Mean travel time to work: 27.8 minutes

COUNTRY KNOLLS (CDP). Covers a land area of 1.582 square miles and a water area of <.001 square miles. Located at 42.91° N. Lat; 73.81° W. Long. Elevation is 282 feet.
Population: 2,063; Growth (since 2000): -4.3%; Density: 1,304.1 persons per square mile; Race: 86.9% White, 4.0% Black/African American, 8.8% Asian, 0.0% American Indian/Alaska Native, 0.0% Native Hawaiian/Other Pacific Islander, 0.3% Two or more races, 2.0% Hispanic of any race; Average household size: 2.77; Median age: 43.3; Age under 18: 26.0%;

Age 65 and over: 25.0%; Males per 100 females: 100.0; Marriage status: 16.2% never married, 74.7% now married, 1.1% separated, 5.2% widowed, 3.8% divorced; Foreign born: 9.1%; Speak English only: 91.7%; With disability: 6.3%; Veterans: 8.8%; Ancestry: 28.2% Irish, 15.0% English, 14.3% Italian, 10.8% German, 9.0% American
Employment: 25.2% management, business, and financial, 13.8% computer, engineering, and science, 15.4% education, legal, community service, arts, and media, 13.8% healthcare practitioners, 10.4% service, 12.8% sales and office, 2.3% natural resources, construction, and maintenance, 6.3% production, transportation, and material moving
Income: Per capita: $46,025; Median household: $114,306; Average household: $128,043; Households with income of $100,000 or more: 62.2%; Poverty rate: 2.9%
Educational Attainment: High school diploma or higher: 99.0%; Bachelor's degree or higher: 65.9%; Graduate/professional degree or higher: 35.3%
Housing: Homeownership rate: 98.4%; Median home value: $279,800; Median year structure built: 1971; Homeowner vacancy rate: 0.0%; Median selected monthly owner costs: $1,904 with a mortgage, $625 without a mortgage; Median gross rent: n/a per month; Rental vacancy rate: 0.0%
Health Insurance: 98.4% have insurance; 90.5% have private insurance; 28.2% have public insurance; 1.6% do not have insurance; 0.0% of children under 18 do not have insurance
Transportation: Commute: 94.2% car, 1.9% public transportation, 0.0% walk, 3.1% work from home; Mean travel time to work: 25.2 minutes

DAY (town). Covers a land area of 64.112 square miles and a water area of 5.420 square miles. Located at 43.32° N. Lat; 74.03° W. Long.
Population: 716; Growth (since 2000): -22.2%; Density: 11.2 persons per square mile; Race: 98.5% White, 0.0% Black/African American, 0.0% Asian, 0.0% American Indian/Alaska Native, 0.0% Native Hawaiian/Other Pacific Islander, 1.4% Two or more races, 0.4% Hispanic of any race; Average household size: 2.03; Median age: 57.1; Age under 18: 10.2%; Age 65 and over: 32.0%; Males per 100 females: 110.8; Marriage status: 15.3% never married, 61.9% now married, 2.1% separated, 6.9% widowed, 15.9% divorced; Foreign born: 2.0%; Speak English only: 98.6%; With disability: 26.4%; Veterans: 12.7%; Ancestry: 19.1% Irish, 14.2% English, 13.4% German, 9.8% Italian, 8.9% Polish
Employment: 11.8% management, business, and financial, 4.4% computer, engineering, and science, 8.5% education, legal, community service, arts, and media, 3.0% healthcare practitioners, 22.1% service, 21.0% sales and office, 19.9% natural resources, construction, and maintenance, 9.2% production, transportation, and material moving
Income: Per capita: $29,725; Median household: $50,789; Average household: $59,457; Households with income of $100,000 or more: 14.4%; Poverty rate: 16.8%
Educational Attainment: High school diploma or higher: 84.8%; Bachelor's degree or higher: 18.6%; Graduate/professional degree or higher: 7.4%
Housing: Homeownership rate: 87.8%; Median home value: $164,900; Median year structure built: 1973; Homeowner vacancy rate: 5.0%; Median selected monthly owner costs: $1,446 with a mortgage, $405 without a mortgage; Median gross rent: $786 per month; Rental vacancy rate: 15.7%
Health Insurance: 92.7% have insurance; 67.7% have private insurance; 53.6% have public insurance; 7.3% do not have insurance; 0.0% of children under 18 do not have insurance
Transportation: Commute: 91.9% car, 0.0% public transportation, 4.6% walk, 3.5% work from home; Mean travel time to work: 46.1 minutes

EDINBURG (town). Covers a land area of 60.169 square miles and a water area of 6.925 square miles. Located at 43.22° N. Lat; 74.07° W. Long. Elevation is 889 feet.
Population: 1,428; Growth (since 2000): 3.2%; Density: 23.7 persons per square mile; Race: 99.2% White, 0.3% Black/African American, 0.6% Asian, 0.0% American Indian/Alaska Native, 0.0% Native Hawaiian/Other Pacific Islander, 0.0% Two or more races, 0.4% Hispanic of any race; Average household size: 2.27; Median age: 52.0; Age under 18: 13.9%; Age 65 and over: 27.2%; Males per 100 females: 106.5; Marriage status: 23.5% never married, 58.9% now married, 1.7% separated, 6.8% widowed, 10.8% divorced; Foreign born: 0.7%; Speak English only: 98.6%; With disability: 14.9%; Veterans: 14.5%; Ancestry: 16.7% Irish, 15.0% German, 12.6% English, 9.7% Italian, 9.3% American
Employment: 8.6% management, business, and financial, 3.4% computer, engineering, and science, 6.7% education, legal, community service, arts, and media, 10.4% healthcare practitioners, 20.2% service, 18.9% sales

and office, 22.8% natural resources, construction, and maintenance, 8.9% production, transportation, and material moving
Income: Per capita: $31,966; Median household: $58,352; Average household: $72,048; Households with income of $100,000 or more: 22.1%; Poverty rate: 7.4%
Educational Attainment: High school diploma or higher: 89.2%; Bachelor's degree or higher: 17.1%; Graduate/professional degree or higher: 7.5%

School District(s)
Edinburg Common SD (PK-12)
    Enrollment: 81 . . . . (518) 863-8412
Housing: Homeownership rate: 91.3%; Median home value: $237,700; Median year structure built: 1974; Homeowner vacancy rate: 2.7%; Median selected monthly owner costs: $1,330 with a mortgage, $396 without a mortgage; Median gross rent: $732 per month; Rental vacancy rate: 0.0%
Health Insurance: 93.1% have insurance; 82.8% have private insurance; 35.3% have public insurance; 6.9% do not have insurance; 9.5% of children under 18 do not have insurance
Transportation: Commute: 97.3% car, 0.5% public transportation, 0.0% walk, 2.3% work from home; Mean travel time to work: 37.2 minutes
Additional Information Contacts
Town of Edinburg . . . . (518) 863-2034
    http://www.edinburgny.com

GALWAY (town).
Covers a land area of 43.824 square miles and a water area of 1.180 square miles. Located at 43.03° N. Lat; 74.03° W. Long. Elevation is 830 feet.
Population: 3,547; Growth (since 2000): -1.2%; Density: 80.9 persons per square mile; Race: 95.7% White, 0.6% Black/African American, 0.0% Asian, 1.8% American Indian/Alaska Native, 0.0% Native Hawaiian/Other Pacific Islander, 1.9% Two or more races, 2.1% Hispanic of any race; Average household size: 2.28; Median age: 48.3; Age under 18: 20.6%; Age 65 and over: 22.2%; Males per 100 females: 105.3; Marriage status: 20.9% never married, 65.8% now married, 1.5% separated, 4.9% widowed, 8.5% divorced; Foreign born: 2.7%; Speak English only: 91.1%; With disability: 10.8%; Veterans: 10.7%; Ancestry: 31.4% Irish, 22.3% Italian, 19.3% German, 14.3% English, 10.2% Polish
Employment: 18.7% management, business, and financial, 4.4% computer, engineering, and science, 12.2% education, legal, community service, arts, and media, 11.9% healthcare practitioners, 17.2% service, 16.7% sales and office, 11.5% natural resources, construction, and maintenance, 7.4% production, transportation, and material moving
Income: Per capita: $35,692; Median household: $68,688; Average household: $81,908; Households with income of $100,000 or more: 32.6%; Poverty rate: 9.5%
Educational Attainment: High school diploma or higher: 94.9%; Bachelor's degree or higher: 38.6%; Graduate/professional degree or higher: 17.3%

School District(s)
Galway Central SD (KG-12)
    Enrollment: 822 . . . . (518) 882-1033
Housing: Homeownership rate: 88.0%; Median home value: $247,100; Median year structure built: 1973; Homeowner vacancy rate: 0.1%; Median selected monthly owner costs: $1,447 with a mortgage, $511 without a mortgage; Median gross rent: $950 per month; Rental vacancy rate: 0.0%
Health Insurance: 98.9% have insurance; 84.6% have private insurance; 35.3% have public insurance; 1.1% do not have insurance; 0.5% of children under 18 do not have insurance
Transportation: Commute: 92.7% car, 0.1% public transportation, 1.0% walk, 6.2% work from home; Mean travel time to work: 27.6 minutes

GALWAY (village).
Covers a land area of 0.256 square miles and a water area of 0 square miles. Located at 43.02° N. Lat; 74.03° W. Long. Elevation is 830 feet.
Population: 228; Growth (since 2000): 6.5%; Density: 890.7 persons per square mile; Race: 99.1% White, 0.9% Black/African American, 0.0% Asian, 0.0% American Indian/Alaska Native, 0.0% Native Hawaiian/Other Pacific Islander, 0.0% Two or more races, 2.6% Hispanic of any race; Average household size: 2.65; Median age: 36.6; Age under 18: 27.6%; Age 65 and over: 18.9%; Males per 100 females: 92.3; Marriage status: 20.6% never married, 54.1% now married, 2.4% separated, 7.1% widowed, 18.2% divorced; Foreign born: 0.9%; Speak English only: 99.0%; With disability: 10.5%; Veterans: 0.0%; Ancestry: 28.5% Italian, 27.2% Irish, 25.9% German, 22.4% English, 7.9% French Canadian

Employment: 13.4% management, business, and financial, 6.7% computer, engineering, and science, 16.0% education, legal, community service, arts, and media, 0.8% healthcare practitioners, 27.7% service, 16.8% sales and office, 10.1% natural resources, construction, and maintenance, 8.4% production, transportation, and material moving
Income: Per capita: $23,039; Median household: $59,167; Average household: $64,758; Households with income of $100,000 or more: 22.1%; Poverty rate: 15.0%
Educational Attainment: High school diploma or higher: 100.0%; Bachelor's degree or higher: 35.5%; Graduate/professional degree or higher: 18.7%

School District(s)
Galway Central SD (KG-12)
    Enrollment: 822 . . . . (518) 882-1033
Housing: Homeownership rate: 73.3%; Median home value: $163,300; Median year structure built: Before 1940; Homeowner vacancy rate: 1.6%; Median selected monthly owner costs: $1,438 with a mortgage, $738 without a mortgage; Median gross rent: $700 per month; Rental vacancy rate: 0.0%
Health Insurance: 93.4% have insurance; 63.2% have private insurance; 43.0% have public insurance; 6.6% do not have insurance; 6.3% of children under 18 do not have insurance
Transportation: Commute: 82.4% car, 0.0% public transportation, 10.9% walk, 6.7% work from home; Mean travel time to work: 30.7 minutes

GANSEVOORT (unincorporated postal area)
ZCTA: 12831
    Covers a land area of 67.169 square miles and a water area of 0.992 square miles. Located at 43.20° N. Lat; 73.69° W. Long. Elevation is 239 feet.
Population: 17,585; Growth (since 2000): 23.8%; Density: 261.8 persons per square mile; Race: 96.1% White, 1.9% Black/African American, 0.3% Asian, 0.0% American Indian/Alaska Native, 0.0% Native Hawaiian/Other Pacific Islander, 0.9% Two or more races, 2.8% Hispanic of any race; Average household size: 2.68; Median age: 40.1; Age under 18: 25.5%; Age 65 and over: 10.5%; Males per 100 females: 102.5; Marriage status: 25.4% never married, 60.4% now married, 1.5% separated, 4.5% widowed, 9.7% divorced; Foreign born: 2.2%; Speak English only: 96.3%; With disability: 9.6%; Veterans: 6.9%; Ancestry: 28.4% Irish, 16.2% Italian, 14.6% German, 12.9% English, 9.6% French
Employment: 18.9% management, business, and financial, 8.0% computer, engineering, and science, 14.3% education, legal, community service, arts, and media, 6.0% healthcare practitioners, 13.2% service, 22.5% sales and office, 7.9% natural resources, construction, and maintenance, 9.3% production, transportation, and material moving
Income: Per capita: $35,736; Median household: $82,443; Average household: $96,014; Households with income of $100,000 or more: 38.7%; Poverty rate: 5.1%
Educational Attainment: High school diploma or higher: 94.7%; Bachelor's degree or higher: 36.2%; Graduate/professional degree or higher: 15.2%
Housing: Homeownership rate: 76.4%; Median home value: $235,600; Median year structure built: 1990; Homeowner vacancy rate: 0.0%; Median selected monthly owner costs: $1,705 with a mortgage, $570 without a mortgage; Median gross rent: $1,057 per month; Rental vacancy rate: 0.0%
Health Insurance: 97.1% have insurance; 82.4% have private insurance; 24.5% have public insurance; 2.9% do not have insurance; 0.3% of children under 18 do not have insurance
Transportation: Commute: 94.7% car, 0.3% public transportation, 0.7% walk, 3.6% work from home; Mean travel time to work: 28.3 minutes

GREENFIELD (town).
Covers a land area of 67.388 square miles and a water area of 0.299 square miles. Located at 43.14° N. Lat; 73.87° W. Long. Elevation is 591 feet.
Population: 7,789; Growth (since 2000): 5.8%; Density: 115.6 persons per square mile; Race: 96.3% White, 0.4% Black/African American, 0.5% Asian, 0.2% American Indian/Alaska Native, 0.0% Native Hawaiian/Other Pacific Islander, 1.8% Two or more races, 1.2% Hispanic of any race; Average household size: 2.41; Median age: 46.1; Age under 18: 21.9%; Age 65 and over: 18.8%; Males per 100 females: 98.0; Marriage status: 21.7% never married, 62.9% now married, 1.4% separated, 6.7% widowed, 8.7% divorced; Foreign born: 2.4%; Speak English only: 96.3%; With disability: 15.0%; Veterans: 9.8%; Ancestry: 23.8% Irish, 20.0% German, 18.7% English, 11.0% Italian, 9.2% French

Employment: 17.6% management, business, and financial, 6.3% computer, engineering, and science, 12.6% education, legal, community service, arts, and media, 5.8% healthcare practitioners, 15.1% service, 22.7% sales and office, 11.9% natural resources, construction, and maintenance, 8.0% production, transportation, and material moving
Income: Per capita: $36,875; Median household: $74,806; Average household: $88,947; Households with income of $100,000 or more: 35.3%; Poverty rate: 11.8%
Educational Attainment: High school diploma or higher: 91.0%; Bachelor's degree or higher: 36.4%; Graduate/professional degree or higher: 16.2%
Housing: Homeownership rate: 76.5%; Median home value: $238,200; Median year structure built: 1985; Homeowner vacancy rate: 1.1%; Median selected monthly owner costs: $1,752 with a mortgage, $554 without a mortgage; Median gross rent: $1,359 per month; Rental vacancy rate: 13.1%
Health Insurance: 94.6% have insurance; 78.8% have private insurance; 33.4% have public insurance; 5.4% do not have insurance; 1.3% of children under 18 do not have insurance
Transportation: Commute: 88.7% car, 0.3% public transportation, 0.5% walk, 7.9% work from home; Mean travel time to work: 25.7 minutes
Additional Information Contacts
Town of Greenfield . . . . (518) 893-7432
  http://www.townofgreenfield.com

GREENFIELD CENTER (unincorporated postal area)
ZCTA: 12833
  Covers a land area of 35.246 square miles and a water area of 0.152 square miles. Located at 43.15° N. Lat; 73.84° W. Long. Elevation is 686 feet.
Population: 4,388; Growth (since 2000): -2.3%; Density: 124.5 persons per square mile; Race: 95.0% White, 0.5% Black/African American, 0.8% Asian, 0.4% American Indian/Alaska Native, 0.0% Native Hawaiian/Other Pacific Islander, 3.3% Two or more races, 0.6% Hispanic of any race; Average household size: 2.55; Median age: 44.7; Age under 18: 22.5%; Age 65 and over: 12.3%; Males per 100 females: 100.0; Marriage status: 22.6% never married, 66.8% now married, 2.1% separated, 5.0% widowed, 5.6% divorced; Foreign born: 1.7%; Speak English only: 95.9%; With disability: 10.8%; Veterans: 7.4%; Ancestry: 23.7% German, 22.3% Irish, 18.8% English, 11.2% Italian, 10.6% French
Employment: 16.1% management, business, and financial, 7.6% computer, engineering, and science, 11.1% education, legal, community service, arts, and media, 4.9% healthcare practitioners, 17.3% service, 26.0% sales and office, 8.5% natural resources, construction, and maintenance, 8.5% production, transportation, and material moving
Income: Per capita: $35,867; Median household: $80,469; Average household: $91,135; Households with income of $100,000 or more: 38.3%; Poverty rate: 10.9%
Educational Attainment: High school diploma or higher: 88.7%; Bachelor's degree or higher: 34.7%; Graduate/professional degree or higher: 14.5%
School District(s)
Saratoga Springs City SD (KG-12)
  Enrollment: 6,412 . . . . (518) 583-4708
Housing: Homeownership rate: 85.6%; Median home value: $238,200; Median year structure built: 1983; Homeowner vacancy rate: 0.0%; Median selected monthly owner costs: $1,747 with a mortgage, $455 without a mortgage; Median gross rent: $895 per month; Rental vacancy rate: 9.2%
Health Insurance: 94.9% have insurance; 79.7% have private insurance; 27.1% have public insurance; 5.1% do not have insurance; 2.3% of children under 18 do not have insurance
Transportation: Commute: 89.2% car, 0.6% public transportation, 0.0% walk, 6.6% work from home; Mean travel time to work: 25.1 minutes

HADLEY (CDP). Covers a land area of 1.117 square miles and a water area of 0.199 square miles. Located at 43.30° N. Lat; 73.83° W. Long. Elevation is 630 feet.
Population: 838; Growth (since 2000): n/a; Density: 750.0 persons per square mile; Race: 97.6% White, 0.0% Black/African American, 0.0% Asian, 0.0% American Indian/Alaska Native, 0.0% Native Hawaiian/Other Pacific Islander, 2.4% Two or more races, 1.4% Hispanic of any race; Average household size: 2.28; Median age: 47.6; Age under 18: 21.4%; Age 65 and over: 21.5%; Males per 100 females: 94.4; Marriage status:

9.1% never married, 76.4% now married, 0.7% separated, 5.3% widowed, 9.2% divorced; Foreign born: 2.5%; Speak English only: 97.5%; With disability: 15.3%; Veterans: 21.7%; Ancestry: 20.5% French, 14.9% American, 14.9% Irish, 13.0% Italian, 11.9% German
Employment: 6.4% management, business, and financial, 1.4% computer, engineering, and science, 15.4% education, legal, community service, arts, and media, 1.7% healthcare practitioners, 30.4% service, 15.1% sales and office, 16.8% natural resources, construction, and maintenance, 12.8% production, transportation, and material moving
Income: Per capita: $28,246; Median household: $48,750; Average household: $64,757; Households with income of $100,000 or more: 13.9%; Poverty rate: 5.9%
Educational Attainment: High school diploma or higher: 92.3%; Bachelor's degree or higher: 18.3%; Graduate/professional degree or higher: 4.6%
Housing: Homeownership rate: 80.7%; Median home value: $154,400; Median year structure built: 1966; Homeowner vacancy rate: 3.6%; Median selected monthly owner costs: $1,327 with a mortgage, $379 without a mortgage; Median gross rent: $828 per month; Rental vacancy rate: 0.0%
Health Insurance: 96.5% have insurance; 73.5% have private insurance; 40.9% have public insurance; 3.5% do not have insurance; 0.0% of children under 18 do not have insurance
Transportation: Commute: 86.5% car, 0.0% public transportation, 0.0% walk, 13.5% work from home; Mean travel time to work: 43.0 minutes

HADLEY (town). Covers a land area of 39.705 square miles and a water area of 1.380 square miles. Located at 43.34° N. Lat; 73.91° W. Long. Elevation is 630 feet.
Population: 1,839; Growth (since 2000): -6.7%; Density: 46.3 persons per square mile; Race: 96.5% White, 0.0% Black/African American, 0.0% Asian, 0.0% American Indian/Alaska Native, 0.0% Native Hawaiian/Other Pacific Islander, 3.3% Two or more races, 0.9% Hispanic of any race; Average household size: 2.44; Median age: 47.9; Age under 18: 19.4%; Age 65 and over: 18.4%; Males per 100 females: 99.6; Marriage status: 16.7% never married, 71.3% now married, 0.3% separated, 4.8% widowed, 7.2% divorced; Foreign born: 2.6%; Speak English only: 98.9%; With disability: 14.5%; Veterans: 14.4%; Ancestry: 17.4% Irish, 17.2% French, 13.1% Italian, 12.6% American, 12.0% English
Employment: 6.2% management, business, and financial, 6.2% computer, engineering, and science, 12.1% education, legal, community service, arts, and media, 4.6% healthcare practitioners, 20.9% service, 18.9% sales and office, 16.3% natural resources, construction, and maintenance, 14.8% production, transportation, and material moving
Income: Per capita: $29,210; Median household: $58,750; Average household: $71,709; Households with income of $100,000 or more: 21.8%; Poverty rate: 5.3%
Educational Attainment: High school diploma or higher: 89.3%; Bachelor's degree or higher: 19.6%; Graduate/professional degree or higher: 4.5%
Housing: Homeownership rate: 85.2%; Median home value: $166,000; Median year structure built: 1973; Homeowner vacancy rate: 3.8%; Median selected monthly owner costs: $1,438 with a mortgage, $423 without a mortgage; Median gross rent: $825 per month; Rental vacancy rate: 0.0%
Health Insurance: 95.7% have insurance; 75.2% have private insurance; 34.5% have public insurance; 4.3% do not have insurance; 1.2% of children under 18 do not have insurance
Transportation: Commute: 88.6% car, 0.5% public transportation, 1.5% walk, 9.4% work from home; Mean travel time to work: 34.9 minutes
Additional Information Contacts
Town of Hadley . . . . (518) 696-3112
  http://www.townofhadley.org

HALFMOON (town). Covers a land area of 32.580 square miles and a water area of 1.050 square miles. Located at 42.86° N. Lat; 73.73° W. Long. Elevation is 276 feet.
Population: 23,660; Growth (since 2000): 28.1%; Density: 726.2 persons per square mile; Race: 88.9% White, 2.0% Black/African American, 6.3% Asian, 0.4% American Indian/Alaska Native, 0.1% Native Hawaiian/Other Pacific Islander, 1.9% Two or more races, 4.4% Hispanic of any race; Average household size: 2.29; Median age: 41.8; Age under 18: 19.8%; Age 65 and over: 16.0%; Males per 100 females: 95.6; Marriage status: 27.3% never married, 56.1% now married, 1.7% separated, 5.1% widowed, 11.6% divorced; Foreign born: 10.8%; Speak English only: 88.3%; With disability: 9.0%; Veterans: 8.0%; Ancestry: 20.1% Irish, 16.8% Italian, 16.5% German, 11.2% English, 8.9% French

Employment: 18.4% management, business, and financial, 11.2% computer, engineering, and science, 10.7% education, legal, community service, arts, and media, 6.4% healthcare practitioners, 14.9% service, 23.6% sales and office, 7.0% natural resources, construction, and maintenance, 7.7% production, transportation, and material moving
Income: Per capita: $42,095; Median household: $75,948; Average household: $96,314; Households with income of $100,000 or more: 36.5%; Poverty rate: 7.0%
Educational Attainment: High school diploma or higher: 93.5%; Bachelor's degree or higher: 44.4%; Graduate/professional degree or higher: 18.8%
Housing: Homeownership rate: 64.7%; Median home value: $246,400; Median year structure built: 1990; Homeowner vacancy rate: 1.2%; Median selected monthly owner costs: $1,738 with a mortgage, $614 without a mortgage; Median gross rent: $1,131 per month; Rental vacancy rate: 1.7%
Health Insurance: 95.0% have insurance; 82.6% have private insurance; 27.7% have public insurance; 5.0% do not have insurance; 0.5% of children under 18 do not have insurance
Transportation: Commute: 93.2% car, 0.3% public transportation, 1.5% walk, 4.0% work from home; Mean travel time to work: 23.9 minutes
Additional Information Contacts
Town of Halfmoon . . . . (518) 371-2592
    http://www.townofhalfmoon.org

MALTA (town). Covers a land area of 27.922 square miles and a water area of 3.532 square miles. Located at 42.98° N. Lat; 73.79° W. Long. Elevation is 341 feet.
Population: 15,373; Growth (since 2000): 18.2%; Density: 550.6 persons per square mile; Race: 94.6% White, 0.9% Black/African American, 2.9% Asian, 0.0% American Indian/Alaska Native, 0.0% Native Hawaiian/Other Pacific Islander, 1.5% Two or more races, 2.9% Hispanic of any race; Average household size: 2.30; Median age: 42.9; Age under 18: 20.1%; Age 65 and over: 16.2%; Males per 100 females: 98.6; Marriage status: 24.5% never married, 59.4% now married, 0.3% separated, 5.6% widowed, 10.5% divorced; Foreign born: 5.4%; Speak English only: 94.2%; With disability: 10.2%; Veterans: 10.3%; Ancestry: 25.3% Irish, 19.3% Italian, 18.8% German, 14.6% English, 7.3% Polish
Employment: 19.1% management, business, and financial, 11.7% computer, engineering, and science, 13.5% education, legal, community service, arts, and media, 5.0% healthcare practitioners, 11.6% service, 26.5% sales and office, 6.4% natural resources, construction, and maintenance, 6.1% production, transportation, and material moving
Income: Per capita: $44,645; Median household: $87,188; Average household: $103,286; Households with income of $100,000 or more: 41.6%; Poverty rate: 3.0%
Educational Attainment: High school diploma or higher: 97.1%; Bachelor's degree or higher: 44.6%; Graduate/professional degree or higher: 18.5%
Housing: Homeownership rate: 70.1%; Median home value: $249,200; Median year structure built: 1986; Homeowner vacancy rate: 0.8%; Median selected monthly owner costs: $1,908 with a mortgage, $668 without a mortgage; Median gross rent: $1,085 per month; Rental vacancy rate: 7.0%
Health Insurance: 98.3% have insurance; 89.5% have private insurance; 23.2% have public insurance; 1.7% do not have insurance; 0.8% of children under 18 do not have insurance
Transportation: Commute: 92.2% car, 1.3% public transportation, 0.5% walk, 5.6% work from home; Mean travel time to work: 24.8 minutes
Additional Information Contacts
Town of Malta . . . . (518) 899-2552
    http://www.malta-town.org

MECHANICVILLE (city). Covers a land area of 0.841 square miles and a water area of 0.079 square miles. Located at 42.90° N. Lat; 73.69° W. Long. Elevation is 89 feet.
History: Settled before 1700; incorporated as village in 1859, as city in 1915.
Population: 5,177; Growth (since 2000): 3.1%; Density: 6,158.4 persons per square mile; Race: 91.8% White, 3.5% Black/African American, 0.7% Asian, 0.0% American Indian/Alaska Native, 0.0% Native Hawaiian/Other Pacific Islander, 3.8% Two or more races, 3.5% Hispanic of any race; Average household size: 2.19; Median age: 35.8; Age under 18: 20.7%; Age 65 and over: 14.5%; Males per 100 females: 87.0; Marriage status: 38.9% never married, 37.1% now married, 4.6% separated, 7.3%

widowed, 16.7% divorced; Foreign born: 2.1%; Speak English only: 97.5%; With disability: 16.0%; Veterans: 12.4%; Ancestry: 32.1% Italian, 23.6% Irish, 12.7% German, 11.6% English, 8.6% French
Employment: 11.2% management, business, and financial, 5.0% computer, engineering, and science, 13.1% education, legal, community service, arts, and media, 2.5% healthcare practitioners, 17.6% service, 29.8% sales and office, 9.5% natural resources, construction, and maintenance, 11.3% production, transportation, and material moving
Income: Per capita: $25,805; Median household: $44,625; Average household: $56,524; Households with income of $100,000 or more: 19.4%; Poverty rate: 18.7%
Educational Attainment: High school diploma or higher: 89.7%; Bachelor's degree or higher: 20.6%; Graduate/professional degree or higher: 4.2%

School District(s)
Mechanicville City SD (KG-12)
    Enrollment: 1,356 . . . . (518) 664-5727
Housing: Homeownership rate: 36.5%; Median home value: $159,200; Median year structure built: Before 1940; Homeowner vacancy rate: 0.7%; Median selected monthly owner costs: $1,521 with a mortgage, $585 without a mortgage; Median gross rent: $814 per month; Rental vacancy rate: 5.6%
Health Insurance: 93.7% have insurance; 70.0% have private insurance; 38.0% have public insurance; 6.3% do not have insurance; 1.7% of children under 18 do not have insurance
Safety: Violent crime rate: 25.6 per 10,000 population; Property crime rate: 106.3 per 10,000 population
Newspapers: The Express (weekly circulation 2,800)
Transportation: Commute: 93.2% car, 0.3% public transportation, 3.5% walk, 3.0% work from home; Mean travel time to work: 26.3 minutes
Additional Information Contacts
City of Mechanicville . . . . (518) 664-9884
    http://www.mechanicville.com

MIDDLE GROVE (unincorporated postal area)
ZCTA: 12850
    Covers a land area of 46.763 square miles and a water area of 0.883 square miles. Located at 43.10° N. Lat; 73.98° W. Long. Elevation is 551 feet.
Population: 3,291; Growth (since 2000): 46.8%; Density: 70.4 persons per square mile; Race: 97.3% White, 0.2% Black/African American, 0.2% Asian, 0.0% American Indian/Alaska Native, 0.0% Native Hawaiian/Other Pacific Islander, 0.8% Two or more races, 1.2% Hispanic of any race; Average household size: 2.63; Median age: 39.5; Age under 18: 26.2%; Age 65 and over: 15.6%; Males per 100 females: 109.2; Marriage status: 21.2% never married, 64.4% now married, 0.7% separated, 2.6% widowed, 11.7% divorced; Foreign born: 1.6%; Speak English only: 99.6%; With disability: 8.9%; Veterans: 11.0%; Ancestry: 26.7% Irish, 21.7% Italian, 15.7% German, 15.3% English, 10.0% Polish
Employment: 13.5% management, business, and financial, 7.0% computer, engineering, and science, 13.7% education, legal, community service, arts, and media, 8.7% healthcare practitioners, 17.6% service, 15.3% sales and office, 17.7% natural resources, construction, and maintenance, 6.5% production, transportation, and material moving
Income: Per capita: $34,501; Median household: $76,316; Average household: $91,018; Households with income of $100,000 or more: 32.9%; Poverty rate: 14.7%
Educational Attainment: High school diploma or higher: 92.6%; Bachelor's degree or higher: 36.0%; Graduate/professional degree or higher: 15.1%
Housing: Homeownership rate: 81.6%; Median home value: $241,200; Median year structure built: 1981; Homeowner vacancy rate: 0.0%; Median selected monthly owner costs: $1,883 with a mortgage, $560 without a mortgage; Median gross rent: $1,153 per month; Rental vacancy rate: 0.0%
Health Insurance: 95.5% have insurance; 81.2% have private insurance; 28.3% have public insurance; 4.5% do not have insurance; 0.0% of children under 18 do not have insurance
Transportation: Commute: 87.9% car, 0.3% public transportation, 0.8% walk, 10.5% work from home; Mean travel time to work: 29.0 minutes

MILTON (CDP). Covers a land area of 1.487 square miles and a water area of 0.005 square miles. Located at 43.04° N. Lat; 73.85° W. Long. Elevation is 420 feet.

Population: 3,321; Growth (since 2000): 23.4%; Density: 2,234.0 persons per square mile; Race: 97.4% White, 0.0% Black/African American, 1.9% Asian, 0.0% American Indian/Alaska Native, 0.0% Native Hawaiian/Other Pacific Islander, 0.7% Two or more races, 1.7% Hispanic of any race; Average household size: 2.45; Median age: 41.6; Age under 18: 18.0%; Age 65 and over: 17.1%; Males per 100 females: 91.4; Marriage status: 30.0% never married, 55.3% now married, 1.3% separated, 4.3% widowed, 10.4% divorced; Foreign born: 3.9%; Speak English only: 96.8%; With disability: 11.8%; Veterans: 10.5%; Ancestry: 21.9% Italian, 20.1% Irish, 17.5% German, 12.5% Polish, 12.1% English

Employment: 14.6% management, business, and financial, 5.4% computer, engineering, and science, 16.3% education, legal, community service, arts, and media, 5.2% healthcare practitioners, 14.9% service, 24.4% sales and office, 8.8% natural resources, construction, and maintenance, 10.4% production, transportation, and material moving

Income: Per capita: $37,175; Median household: $82,950; Average household: $92,112; Households with income of $100,000 or more: 34.1%; Poverty rate: 1.1%

Educational Attainment: High school diploma or higher: 99.1%; Bachelor's degree or higher: 46.2%; Graduate/professional degree or higher: 19.7%

Housing: Homeownership rate: 81.1%; Median home value: $212,600; Median year structure built: 1991; Homeowner vacancy rate: 0.0%; Median selected monthly owner costs: $1,586 with a mortgage, $611 without a mortgage; Median gross rent: $1,502 per month; Rental vacancy rate: 0.0%

Health Insurance: 97.1% have insurance; 84.5% have private insurance; 26.3% have public insurance; 2.9% do not have insurance; 0.0% of children under 18 do not have insurance

Transportation: Commute: 97.6% car, 0.0% public transportation, 0.0% walk, 2.4% work from home; Mean travel time to work: 24.4 minutes

MILTON (town). Covers a land area of 35.690 square miles and a water area of 0.064 square miles. Located at 43.05° N. Lat; 73.90° W. Long. Elevation is 420 feet.

History: In 1959, the film, The Fugitive Kid, based on a play by Tennessee Williams, starring Marlon Brando and Anna Magnani, was filmed in Milton. The main street was reconstructed to resemble an old town in the deep south.

Population: 19,120; Growth (since 2000): 11.8%; Density: 535.7 persons per square mile; Race: 94.7% White, 1.2% Black/African American, 1.5% Asian, 0.8% American Indian/Alaska Native, 0.0% Native Hawaiian/Other Pacific Islander, 1.8% Two or more races, 2.1% Hispanic of any race; Average household size: 2.46; Median age: 39.6; Age under 18: 23.0%; Age 65 and over: 13.3%; Males per 100 females: 100.9; Marriage status: 30.8% never married, 53.4% now married, 2.2% separated, 4.3% widowed, 11.4% divorced; Foreign born: 3.1%; Speak English only: 95.0%; With disability: 12.7%; Veterans: 9.3%; Ancestry: 20.3% Irish, 19.3% Italian, 16.0% German, 11.9% English, 9.1% French

Employment: 13.8% management, business, and financial, 8.0% computer, engineering, and science, 12.2% education, legal, community service, arts, and media, 4.8% healthcare practitioners, 17.3% service, 23.1% sales and office, 8.0% natural resources, construction, and maintenance, 12.8% production, transportation, and material moving

Income: Per capita: $33,680; Median household: $66,875; Average household: $84,460; Households with income of $100,000 or more: 30.1%; Poverty rate: 9.1%

Educational Attainment: High school diploma or higher: 92.6%; Bachelor's degree or higher: 34.0%; Graduate/professional degree or higher: 12.3%

Housing: Homeownership rate: 72.5%; Median home value: $194,000; Median year structure built: 1982; Homeowner vacancy rate: 0.1%; Median selected monthly owner costs: $1,534 with a mortgage, $586 without a mortgage; Median gross rent: $1,032 per month; Rental vacancy rate: 1.9%

Health Insurance: 95.2% have insurance; 76.3% have private insurance; 33.3% have public insurance; 4.8% do not have insurance; 2.0% of children under 18 do not have insurance

Transportation: Commute: 92.0% car, 0.8% public transportation, 1.9% walk, 4.2% work from home; Mean travel time to work: 25.2 minutes

Additional Information Contacts

Town of Milton . . . . (518) 885-9220
http://www.townofmiltonny.org

MOREAU (town). Covers a land area of 41.924 square miles and a water area of 1.657 square miles. Located at 43.25° N. Lat; 73.67° W. Long. Elevation is 341 feet.

Population: 15,263; Growth (since 2000): 10.4%; Density: 364.1 persons per square mile; Race: 96.1% White, 1.7% Black/African American, 0.4% Asian, 0.1% American Indian/Alaska Native, 0.0% Native Hawaiian/Other Pacific Islander, 1.4% Two or more races, 1.8% Hispanic of any race; Average household size: 2.37; Median age: 44.1; Age under 18: 20.2%; Age 65 and over: 15.1%; Males per 100 females: 100.2; Marriage status: 28.1% never married, 53.2% now married, 2.4% separated, 6.4% widowed, 12.2% divorced; Foreign born: 1.5%; Speak English only: 97.6%; With disability: 12.9%; Veterans: 7.2%; Ancestry: 21.7% Irish, 13.7% French, 12.9% Italian, 12.6% English, 10.4% German

Employment: 12.2% management, business, and financial, 4.2% computer, engineering, and science, 8.9% education, legal, community service, arts, and media, 6.5% healthcare practitioners, 16.4% service, 27.3% sales and office, 8.7% natural resources, construction, and maintenance, 15.8% production, transportation, and material moving

Income: Per capita: $30,148; Median household: $61,392; Average household: $72,122; Households with income of $100,000 or more: 26.5%; Poverty rate: 7.3%

Educational Attainment: High school diploma or higher: 93.0%; Bachelor's degree or higher: 19.8%; Graduate/professional degree or higher: 6.4%

Housing: Homeownership rate: 70.5%; Median home value: $181,300; Median year structure built: 1974; Homeowner vacancy rate: 0.0%; Median selected monthly owner costs: $1,440 with a mortgage, $554 without a mortgage; Median gross rent: $914 per month; Rental vacancy rate: 1.4%

Health Insurance: 95.0% have insurance; 79.0% have private insurance; 30.9% have public insurance; 5.0% do not have insurance; 1.3% of children under 18 do not have insurance

Transportation: Commute: 95.3% car, 0.2% public transportation, 1.5% walk, 2.5% work from home; Mean travel time to work: 21.6 minutes

Additional Information Contacts

Town of Moreau . . . . (518) 792-1030
http://www.townofmoreau.org

NORTH BALLSTON SPA (CDP). Covers a land area of 0.824 square miles and a water area of 0.004 square miles. Located at 43.02° N. Lat; 73.85° W. Long.

Population: 1,481; Growth (since 2000): 19.7%; Density: 1,797.4 persons per square mile; Race: 85.3% White, 4.3% Black/African American, 0.0% Asian, 5.0% American Indian/Alaska Native, 0.0% Native Hawaiian/Other Pacific Islander, 5.2% Two or more races, 0.7% Hispanic of any race; Average household size: 2.31; Median age: 40.5; Age under 18: 18.1%; Age 65 and over: 11.1%; Males per 100 females: 96.8; Marriage status: 30.7% never married, 45.1% now married, 1.0% separated, 5.2% widowed, 19.0% divorced; Foreign born: 1.9%; Speak English only: 90.5%; With disability: 13.7%; Veterans: 11.9%; Ancestry: 21.8% Irish, 20.5% German, 18.5% Italian, 10.0% English, 7.1% French

Employment: 5.2% management, business, and financial, 6.7% computer, engineering, and science, 26.4% education, legal, community service, arts, and media, 1.3% healthcare practitioners, 12.6% service, 28.2% sales and office, 7.9% natural resources, construction, and maintenance, 11.8% production, transportation, and material moving

Income: Per capita: $33,614; Median household: $66,595; Average household: $76,698; Households with income of $100,000 or more: 33.6%; Poverty rate: 6.8%

Educational Attainment: High school diploma or higher: 84.5%; Bachelor's degree or higher: 26.7%; Graduate/professional degree or higher: 8.8%

Housing: Homeownership rate: 79.3%; Median home value: $182,900; Median year structure built: 1960; Homeowner vacancy rate: 0.0%; Median selected monthly owner costs: $1,203 with a mortgage, $509 without a mortgage; Median gross rent: n/a per month; Rental vacancy rate: 0.0%

Health Insurance: 93.9% have insurance; 79.4% have private insurance; 28.3% have public insurance; 6.1% do not have insurance; 0.0% of children under 18 do not have insurance

Transportation: Commute: 100.0% car, 0.0% public transportation, 0.0% walk, 0.0% work from home; Mean travel time to work: 22.9 minutes

NORTHUMBERLAND (town). Covers a land area of 32.299 square miles and a water area of 0.619 square miles. Located at 43.16° N. Lat; 73.63° W. Long. Elevation is 112 feet.

Population: 5,140; Growth (since 2000): 11.7%; Density: 159.1 persons per square mile; Race: 95.6% White, 1.3% Black/African American, 0.2% Asian, 0.5% American Indian/Alaska Native, 0.0% Native Hawaiian/Other Pacific Islander, 1.6% Two or more races, 3.9% Hispanic of any race; Average household size: 2.78; Median age: 41.4; Age under 18: 24.0%; Age 65 and over: 11.2%; Males per 100 females: 103.5; Marriage status: 23.6% never married, 65.1% now married, 1.7% separated, 5.2% widowed, 6.0% divorced; Foreign born: 1.1%; Speak English only: 96.5%; With disability: 12.9%; Veterans: 9.5%; Ancestry: 20.8% Irish, 15.5% English, 14.0% German, 11.1% Italian, 8.1% American

Employment: 14.1% management, business, and financial, 6.8% computer, engineering, and science, 11.1% education, legal, community service, arts, and media, 6.3% healthcare practitioners, 17.3% service, 25.0% sales and office, 11.2% natural resources, construction, and maintenance, 8.2% production, transportation, and material moving

Income: Per capita: $33,156; Median household: $81,900; Average household: $92,781; Households with income of $100,000 or more: 38.3%; Poverty rate: 7.6%

Educational Attainment: High school diploma or higher: 92.0%; Bachelor's degree or higher: 28.2%; Graduate/professional degree or higher: 10.1%

Housing: Homeownership rate: 90.3%; Median home value: $197,200; Median year structure built: 1987; Homeowner vacancy rate: 1.3%; Median selected monthly owner costs: $1,606 with a mortgage, $468 without a mortgage; Median gross rent: $1,102 per month; Rental vacancy rate: 0.0%

Health Insurance: 97.7% have insurance; 83.6% have private insurance; 26.8% have public insurance; 2.3% do not have insurance; 0.6% of children under 18 do not have insurance

Transportation: Commute: 93.7% car, 0.0% public transportation, 1.2% walk, 5.1% work from home; Mean travel time to work: 28.6 minutes

Additional Information Contacts

Town of Northumberland . . . . (518) 792-9179
    http://www.townofnorthumberland.org

PORTER CORNERS (unincorporated postal area)
ZCTA: 12859

Covers a land area of 22.017 square miles and a water area of 0.058 square miles. Located at 43.17° N. Lat; 73.92° W. Long. Elevation is 663 feet.

Population: 2,122; Growth (since 2000): 7.0%; Density: 96.4 persons per square mile; Race: 100.0% White, 0.0% Black/African American, 0.0% Asian, 0.0% American Indian/Alaska Native, 0.0% Native Hawaiian/Other Pacific Islander, 0.0% Two or more races, 0.6% Hispanic of any race; Average household size: 2.45; Median age: 38.4; Age under 18: 23.3%; Age 65 and over: 13.5%; Males per 100 females: 101.1; Marriage status: 27.6% never married, 56.5% now married, 0.4% separated, 4.9% widowed, 11.0% divorced; Foreign born: 0.7%; Speak English only: 98.1%; With disability: 17.1%; Veterans: 9.3%; Ancestry: 18.1% English, 16.2% Irish, 14.3% German, 9.0% French, 7.4% Dutch

Employment: 15.0% management, business, and financial, 2.9% computer, engineering, and science, 8.8% education, legal, community service, arts, and media, 4.6% healthcare practitioners, 10.0% service, 23.7% sales and office, 18.9% natural resources, construction, and maintenance, 16.0% production, transportation, and material moving

Income: Per capita: $32,629; Median household: $66,250; Average household: $80,620; Households with income of $100,000 or more: 32.6%; Poverty rate: 12.8%

Educational Attainment: High school diploma or higher: 86.4%; Bachelor's degree or higher: 18.4%; Graduate/professional degree or higher: 8.5%

Housing: Homeownership rate: 84.0%; Median home value: $175,200; Median year structure built: 1986; Homeowner vacancy rate: 0.0%; Median selected monthly owner costs: $1,541 with a mortgage, $583 without a mortgage; Median gross rent: $1,321 per month; Rental vacancy rate: 0.0%

Health Insurance: 94.6% have insurance; 75.0% have private insurance; 32.3% have public insurance; 5.4% do not have insurance; 0.0% of children under 18 do not have insurance

Transportation: Commute: 96.9% car, 0.0% public transportation, 0.0% walk, 2.2% work from home; Mean travel time to work: 29.8 minutes

PROVIDENCE (town). Covers a land area of 43.996 square miles and a water area of 1.098 square miles. Located at 43.12° N. Lat; 74.04° W. Long.

Population: 2,188; Growth (since 2000): 18.8%; Density: 49.7 persons per square mile; Race: 97.9% White, 0.3% Black/African American, 0.0% Asian, 0.0% American Indian/Alaska Native, 0.0% Native Hawaiian/Other Pacific Islander, 1.6% Two or more races, 2.1% Hispanic of any race; Average household size: 2.60; Median age: 44.0; Age under 18: 20.9%; Age 65 and over: 14.4%; Males per 100 females: 111.1; Marriage status: 28.8% never married, 56.6% now married, 0.6% separated, 4.7% widowed, 9.9% divorced; Foreign born: 2.1%; Speak English only: 98.9%; With disability: 12.1%; Veterans: 11.6%; Ancestry: 17.9% German, 17.3% Italian, 13.8% Irish, 12.5% Polish, 10.6% English

Employment: 13.5% management, business, and financial, 5.2% computer, engineering, and science, 7.8% education, legal, community service, arts, and media, 8.2% healthcare practitioners, 15.0% service, 16.4% sales and office, 21.1% natural resources, construction, and maintenance, 12.8% production, transportation, and material moving

Income: Per capita: $32,270; Median household: $66,458; Average household: $84,197; Households with income of $100,000 or more: 26.8%; Poverty rate: 7.1%

Educational Attainment: High school diploma or higher: 87.1%; Bachelor's degree or higher: 19.4%; Graduate/professional degree or higher: 5.7%

Housing: Homeownership rate: 86.3%; Median home value: $175,600; Median year structure built: 1986; Homeowner vacancy rate: 1.2%; Median selected monthly owner costs: $1,638 with a mortgage, $441 without a mortgage; Median gross rent: $976 per month; Rental vacancy rate: 0.0%

Health Insurance: 94.6% have insurance; 82.4% have private insurance; 26.5% have public insurance; 5.4% do not have insurance; 0.0% of children under 18 do not have insurance

Transportation: Commute: 96.1% car, 0.3% public transportation, 0.4% walk, 2.8% work from home; Mean travel time to work: 34.6 minutes

REXFORD (unincorporated postal area)
ZCTA: 12148

Covers a land area of 15.649 square miles and a water area of 1.280 square miles. Located at 42.83° N. Lat; 73.85° W. Long. Elevation is 249 feet.

Population: 4,716; Growth (since 2000): 61.0%; Density: 301.4 persons per square mile; Race: 93.3% White, 0.9% Black/African American, 5.4% Asian, 0.0% American Indian/Alaska Native, 0.0% Native Hawaiian/Other Pacific Islander, 0.3% Two or more races, 3.5% Hispanic of any race; Average household size: 2.52; Median age: 44.7; Age under 18: 24.6%; Age 65 and over: 16.6%; Males per 100 females: 93.2; Marriage status: 21.7% never married, 63.6% now married, 0.9% separated, 6.4% widowed, 8.2% divorced; Foreign born: 9.3%; Speak English only: 85.6%; With disability: 6.7%; Veterans: 8.6%; Ancestry: 21.6% Italian, 19.1% Irish, 16.4% German, 11.2% English, 8.2% Polish

Employment: 21.0% management, business, and financial, 13.8% computer, engineering, and science, 12.6% education, legal, community service, arts, and media, 8.8% healthcare practitioners, 10.3% service, 25.1% sales and office, 6.7% natural resources, construction, and maintenance, 1.7% production, transportation, and material moving

Income: Per capita: $47,534; Median household: $107,302; Average household: $119,716; Households with income of $100,000 or more: 56.5%; Poverty rate: 2.7%

Educational Attainment: High school diploma or higher: 97.4%; Bachelor's degree or higher: 54.0%; Graduate/professional degree or higher: 31.5%

School District(s)

Niskayuna Central SD (KG-12)
    Enrollment: 4,223 . . . . (518) 377-4666

Housing: Homeownership rate: 87.0%; Median home value: $317,000; Median year structure built: 1991; Homeowner vacancy rate: 0.0%; Median selected monthly owner costs: $2,202 with a mortgage, $760 without a mortgage; Median gross rent: $2,693 per month; Rental vacancy rate: 25.5%

Health Insurance: 99.6% have insurance; 89.9% have private insurance; 23.9% have public insurance; 0.4% do not have insurance; 0.0% of children under 18 do not have insurance

Transportation: Commute: 87.1% car, 0.0% public transportation, 0.4% walk, 11.4% work from home; Mean travel time to work: 23.7 minutes

ROCK CITY FALLS (unincorporated postal area)
ZCTA: 12863

Covers a land area of 3.594 square miles and a water area of 0 square miles. Located at 43.06° N. Lat; 73.93° W. Long. Elevation is 453 feet.

Population: 763; Growth (since 2000): 28.0%; Density: 212.3 persons per square mile; Race: 100.0% White, 0.0% Black/African American, 0.0% Asian, 0.0% American Indian/Alaska Native, 0.0% Native Hawaiian/Other Pacific Islander, 0.0% Two or more races, 2.2% Hispanic of any race; Average household size: 2.77; Median age: 39.3; Age under 18: 20.6%; Age 65 and over: 15.3%; Males per 100 females: 98.1; Marriage status: 22.4% never married, 69.1% now married, 2.8% separated, 1.3% widowed, 7.2% divorced; Foreign born: 0.0%; Speak English only: 98.9%; With disability: 15.9%; Veterans: 12.3%; Ancestry: 19.4% Italian, 14.3% English, 10.6% German, 9.4% Irish, 8.8% American

Employment: 9.0% management, business, and financial, 6.2% computer, engineering, and science, 16.8% education, legal, community service, arts, and media, 9.4% healthcare practitioners, 8.3% service, 21.4% sales and office, 12.2% natural resources, construction, and maintenance, 16.6% production, transportation, and material moving

Income: Per capita: $40,279; Median household: $116,125; Average household: $111,952; Households with income of $100,000 or more: 62.2%; Poverty rate: 3.7%

Educational Attainment: High school diploma or higher: 94.9%; Bachelor's degree or higher: 38.6%; Graduate/professional degree or higher: 18.1%

Housing: Homeownership rate: 84.7%; Median home value: $285,000; Median year structure built: 1991; Homeowner vacancy rate: 0.0%; Median selected monthly owner costs: $2,159 with a mortgage, $644 without a mortgage; Median gross rent: $888 per month; Rental vacancy rate: 0.0%

Health Insurance: 97.3% have insurance; 79.6% have private insurance; 31.2% have public insurance; 2.7% do not have insurance; 0.0% of children under 18 do not have insurance

Transportation: Commute: 88.5% car, 0.0% public transportation, 0.0% walk, 7.1% work from home; Mean travel time to work: 29.3 minutes

ROUND LAKE (village).
Covers a land area of 1.123 square miles and a water area of 0.107 square miles. Located at 42.94° N. Lat; 73.80° W. Long. Elevation is 164 feet.

Population: 631; Growth (since 2000): 4.5%; Density: 561.8 persons per square mile; Race: 97.5% White, 0.6% Black/African American, 0.5% Asian, 0.0% American Indian/Alaska Native, 0.0% Native Hawaiian/Other Pacific Islander, 1.4% Two or more races, 1.6% Hispanic of any race; Average household size: 2.15; Median age: 50.5; Age under 18: 13.3%; Age 65 and over: 17.0%; Males per 100 females: 89.4; Marriage status: 19.1% never married, 58.6% now married, 2.4% separated, 6.2% widowed, 16.2% divorced; Foreign born: 3.3%; Speak English only: 95.7%; With disability: 13.3%; Veterans: 10.4%; Ancestry: 22.8% Irish, 17.9% English, 16.0% German, 11.4% Italian, 7.8% French

Employment: 20.2% management, business, and financial, 16.6% computer, engineering, and science, 12.7% education, legal, community service, arts, and media, 4.1% healthcare practitioners, 8.8% service, 21.5% sales and office, 8.0% natural resources, construction, and maintenance, 8.0% production, transportation, and material moving

Income: Per capita: $43,827; Median household: $83,542; Average household: $94,220; Households with income of $100,000 or more: 35.8%; Poverty rate: 4.8%

Educational Attainment: High school diploma or higher: 95.9%; Bachelor's degree or higher: 52.8%; Graduate/professional degree or higher: 18.5%

Housing: Homeownership rate: 82.6%; Median home value: $205,700; Median year structure built: Before 1940; Homeowner vacancy rate: 0.0%; Median selected monthly owner costs: $1,693 with a mortgage, $686 without a mortgage; Median gross rent: $1,070 per month; Rental vacancy rate: 12.1%

Health Insurance: 94.8% have insurance; 82.6% have private insurance; 25.7% have public insurance; 5.2% do not have insurance; 0.0% of children under 18 do not have insurance

Transportation: Commute: 88.1% car, 0.0% public transportation, 3.4% walk, 8.5% work from home; Mean travel time to work: 24.2 minutes

Additional Information Contacts

Village of Round Lake . . . . (518) 899-2800
  http://www.roundlakevillage.org

SARATOGA (town).
Covers a land area of 40.562 square miles and a water area of 2.339 square miles. Located at 43.05° N. Lat; 73.65° W. Long.

History: Saratoga was named for a Mohawk Indian word that described the Indian hunting grounds located along both sides of the Hudson River. Thought to derive from either 'Se-rach-ta-gue' meaning 'the hillside country of the quiet river" or 'sharató:ken,' meaning "where you get a blister on your heels."

Population: 5,716; Growth (since 2000): 11.2%; Density: 140.9 persons per square mile; Race: 94.4% White, 3.2% Black/African American, 1.0% Asian, 0.2% American Indian/Alaska Native, 0.0% Native Hawaiian/Other Pacific Islander, 1.2% Two or more races, 5.0% Hispanic of any race; Average household size: 2.59; Median age: 39.9; Age under 18: 24.4%; Age 65 and over: 14.4%; Males per 100 females: 98.5; Marriage status: 31.8% never married, 53.1% now married, 2.8% separated, 4.4% widowed, 10.7% divorced; Foreign born: 3.9%; Speak English only: 94.4%; With disability: 12.3%; Veterans: 11.6%; Ancestry: 24.8% Irish, 16.5% German, 11.6% Italian, 11.3% French, 11.2% English

Employment: 18.7% management, business, and financial, 4.8% computer, engineering, and science, 10.2% education, legal, community service, arts, and media, 4.6% healthcare practitioners, 16.7% service, 24.6% sales and office, 11.1% natural resources, construction, and maintenance, 9.2% production, transportation, and material moving

Income: Per capita: $34,465; Median household: $70,018; Average household: $89,623; Households with income of $100,000 or more: 31.0%; Poverty rate: 6.7%

Educational Attainment: High school diploma or higher: 91.5%; Bachelor's degree or higher: 31.0%; Graduate/professional degree or higher: 10.7%

Housing: Homeownership rate: 78.9%; Median home value: $214,300; Median year structure built: 1970; Homeowner vacancy rate: 1.9%; Median selected monthly owner costs: $1,687 with a mortgage, $543 without a mortgage; Median gross rent: $922 per month; Rental vacancy rate: 0.0%

Health Insurance: 91.9% have insurance; 74.2% have private insurance; 31.6% have public insurance; 8.1% do not have insurance; 11.3% of children under 18 do not have insurance

Transportation: Commute: 91.8% car, 2.0% public transportation, 0.6% walk, 5.5% work from home; Mean travel time to work: 25.9 minutes

Additional Information Contacts

Town of Saratoga . . . . (518) 695-3644
  http://www.townofsaratoga.com

SARATOGA SPRINGS (city).
Covers a land area of 28.065 square miles and a water area of 0.807 square miles. Located at 43.07° N. Lat; 73.78° W. Long. Elevation is 299 feet.

History: The growth and development of Saratoga Springs has been closely associated with its mineral springs, the waters of which began to be used in 1774. Rumors of the healing powers of the water circulated. In 1789, Gideon Putnam arrived and in 1802 he erected the three-story Union Hall, a hotel for visitors. People were attracted to the spot, and Putnam was ready to sell them lots around his hotel.

Population: 27,682; Growth (since 2000): 5.7%; Density: 986.4 persons per square mile; Race: 92.4% White, 2.1% Black/African American, 3.5% Asian, 0.1% American Indian/Alaska Native, 0.0% Native Hawaiian/Other Pacific Islander, 1.5% Two or more races, 3.2% Hispanic of any race; Average household size: 2.03; Median age: 39.7; Age under 18: 15.4%; Age 65 and over: 18.9%; Males per 100 females: 93.4; Marriage status: 37.9% never married, 46.0% now married, 1.9% separated, 5.2% widowed, 10.8% divorced; Foreign born: 6.7%; Speak English only: 89.6%; With disability: 11.0%; Veterans: 9.5%; Ancestry: 26.7% Irish, 18.8% Italian, 17.6% German, 12.6% English, 6.4% Polish

Employment: 21.8% management, business, and financial, 9.7% computer, engineering, and science, 17.7% education, legal, community service, arts, and media, 8.0% healthcare practitioners, 14.1% service, 19.7% sales and office, 4.5% natural resources, construction, and maintenance, 4.5% production, transportation, and material moving

Income: Per capita: $49,481; Median household: $76,775; Average household: $110,927; Households with income of $100,000 or more: 36.7%; Poverty rate: 6.8%

Educational Attainment: High school diploma or higher: 94.8%; Bachelor's degree or higher: 55.2%; Graduate/professional degree or higher: 26.2%

School District(s)

Saratoga Springs City SD (KG-12)
  Enrollment: 6,412 . . . . (518) 583-4708

Four-year College(s)
SUNY Empire State College (Public)
    Enrollment: 10,977 . . . . (518) 587-2100
    Tuition: In-state $7,185; Out-of-state $16,835
Skidmore College (Private, Not-for-profit)
    Enrollment: 2,684 . . . . (518) 580-5000
    Tuition: In-state $52,596; Out-of-state $52,596
Housing: Homeownership rate: 54.8%; Median home value: $343,200; Median year structure built: 1974; Homeowner vacancy rate: 2.1%; Median selected monthly owner costs: $1,969 with a mortgage, $758 without a mortgage; Median gross rent: $1,089 per month; Rental vacancy rate: 7.4%
Health Insurance: 96.4% have insurance; 84.0% have private insurance; 27.7% have public insurance; 3.6% do not have insurance; 1.0% of children under 18 do not have insurance
Hospitals: Saratoga Hospital (243 beds)
Safety: Violent crime rate: 20.0 per 10,000 population; Property crime rate: 164.2 per 10,000 population
Newspapers: Community News (weekly circulation 28,000); The Saratogian (daily circulation 10,300)
Transportation: Commute: 78.0% car, 1.4% public transportation, 7.8% walk, 12.0% work from home; Mean travel time to work: 23.4 minutes; Amtrak: Train and bus service available.
Airports: Saratoga County (general aviation)
Additional Information Contacts
City of Saratoga Springs . . . . (518) 587-3550
    http://www.saratoga-springs.org

SCHUYLERVILLE (village). Covers a land area of 0.533 square miles and a water area of 0.054 square miles. Located at 43.10° N. Lat; 73.58° W. Long. Elevation is 128 feet.
Population: 1,567; Growth (since 2000): 30.9%; Density: 2,939.9 persons per square mile; Race: 92.9% White, 6.3% Black/African American, 0.0% Asian, 0.1% American Indian/Alaska Native, 0.0% Native Hawaiian/Other Pacific Islander, 0.8% Two or more races, 2.2% Hispanic of any race; Average household size: 2.50; Median age: 34.4; Age under 18: 27.2%; Age 65 and over: 11.1%; Males per 100 females: 89.3; Marriage status: 30.7% never married, 47.6% now married, 3.1% separated, 7.7% widowed, 14.1% divorced; Foreign born: 4.5%; Speak English only: 94.7%; With disability: 14.1%; Veterans: 9.8%; Ancestry: 19.6% Irish, 17.9% Italian, 14.9% German, 11.7% English, 10.8% French
Employment: 16.0% management, business, and financial, 3.5% computer, engineering, and science, 8.9% education, legal, community service, arts, and media, 4.2% healthcare practitioners, 19.4% service, 22.7% sales and office, 13.3% natural resources, construction, and maintenance, 12.0% production, transportation, and material moving
Income: Per capita: $26,164; Median household: $60,536; Average household: $65,945; Households with income of $100,000 or more: 16.7%; Poverty rate: 9.6%
Educational Attainment: High school diploma or higher: 89.4%; Bachelor's degree or higher: 23.0%; Graduate/professional degree or higher: 7.2%
School District(s)
Schuylerville Central SD (KG-12)
    Enrollment: 1,614 . . . . (518) 695-3255
Housing: Homeownership rate: 58.1%; Median home value: $155,400; Median year structure built: Before 1940; Homeowner vacancy rate: 0.0%; Median selected monthly owner costs: $1,505 with a mortgage, $667 without a mortgage; Median gross rent: $867 per month; Rental vacancy rate: 0.0%
Health Insurance: 97.0% have insurance; 72.8% have private insurance; 34.3% have public insurance; 3.0% do not have insurance; 3.0% of children under 18 do not have insurance
Transportation: Commute: 95.8% car, 0.8% public transportation, 1.6% walk, 1.8% work from home; Mean travel time to work: 25.5 minutes

SOUTH GLENS FALLS (village). Covers a land area of 1.358 square miles and a water area of 0.132 square miles. Located at 43.29° N. Lat; 73.63° W. Long. Elevation is 344 feet.
History: Incorporated 1895.
Population: 3,595; Growth (since 2000): 6.7%; Density: 2,646.5 persons per square mile; Race: 95.0% White, 2.7% Black/African American, 1.6% Asian, 0.4% American Indian/Alaska Native, 0.0% Native Hawaiian/Other Pacific Islander, 0.3% Two or more races, 4.1% Hispanic of any race; Average household size: 2.06; Median age: 39.9; Age under 18: 20.7%;

Age 65 and over: 16.6%; Males per 100 females: 90.2; Marriage status: 34.1% never married, 40.8% now married, 3.2% separated, 6.6% widowed, 18.5% divorced; Foreign born: 1.3%; Speak English only: 97.7%; With disability: 15.5%; Veterans: 9.4%; Ancestry: 16.5% Irish, 16.0% German, 15.9% Italian, 11.7% English, 9.9% French
Employment: 14.1% management, business, and financial, 2.2% computer, engineering, and science, 7.4% education, legal, community service, arts, and media, 4.5% healthcare practitioners, 18.7% service, 23.7% sales and office, 6.4% natural resources, construction, and maintenance, 23.1% production, transportation, and material moving
Income: Per capita: $24,441; Median household: $40,216; Average household: $50,735; Households with income of $100,000 or more: 10.6%; Poverty rate: 12.9%
Educational Attainment: High school diploma or higher: 91.1%; Bachelor's degree or higher: 16.8%; Graduate/professional degree or higher: 4.3%
School District(s)
South Glens Falls Central SD (PK-12)
    Enrollment: 3,157 . . . . (518) 793-9617
Housing: Homeownership rate: 45.9%; Median home value: $144,900; Median year structure built: 1952; Homeowner vacancy rate: 0.0%; Median selected monthly owner costs: $1,337 with a mortgage, $516 without a mortgage; Median gross rent: $845 per month; Rental vacancy rate: 2.8%
Health Insurance: 95.0% have insurance; 63.4% have private insurance; 46.7% have public insurance; 5.0% do not have insurance; 0.0% of children under 18 do not have insurance
Safety: Violent crime rate: 28.0 per 10,000 population; Property crime rate: 196.2 per 10,000 population
Transportation: Commute: 91.0% car, 0.0% public transportation, 4.7% walk, 3.3% work from home; Mean travel time to work: 21.9 minutes

STILLWATER (town). Covers a land area of 41.191 square miles and a water area of 2.383 square miles. Located at 42.97° N. Lat; 73.69° W. Long. Elevation is 92 feet.
History: The American Revolutionary battles (Sept. 19, 1777, and Oct. 7, 1777) fought near here are commemorated by Saratoga National Historical Park, 9 miles Southeast of Saratoga Springs.
Population: 8,586; Growth (since 2000): 14.1%; Density: 208.4 persons per square mile; Race: 96.4% White, 1.6% Black/African American, 1.1% Asian, 0.4% American Indian/Alaska Native, 0.0% Native Hawaiian/Other Pacific Islander, 0.3% Two or more races, 2.7% Hispanic of any race; Average household size: 2.57; Median age: 43.4; Age under 18: 22.0%; Age 65 and over: 16.8%; Males per 100 females: 100.8; Marriage status: 23.5% never married, 64.2% now married, 0.9% separated, 5.4% widowed, 6.9% divorced; Foreign born: 4.3%; Speak English only: 97.0%; With disability: 13.7%; Veterans: 9.1%; Ancestry: 26.7% Italian, 25.2% Irish, 12.6% French, 11.1% English, 8.9% Polish
Employment: 17.2% management, business, and financial, 3.9% computer, engineering, and science, 10.6% education, legal, community service, arts, and media, 7.1% healthcare practitioners, 12.2% service, 27.4% sales and office, 7.4% natural resources, construction, and maintenance, 14.2% production, transportation, and material moving
Income: Per capita: $38,943; Median household: $78,795; Average household: $99,283; Households with income of $100,000 or more: 38.9%; Poverty rate: 3.9%
Educational Attainment: High school diploma or higher: 91.3%; Bachelor's degree or higher: 25.8%; Graduate/professional degree or higher: 7.7%
School District(s)
Stillwater Central SD (PK-12)
    Enrollment: 1,112 . . . . (518) 373-6100
Housing: Homeownership rate: 85.2%; Median home value: $240,000; Median year structure built: 1984; Homeowner vacancy rate: 1.0%; Median selected monthly owner costs: $1,832 with a mortgage, $607 without a mortgage; Median gross rent: $1,089 per month; Rental vacancy rate: 0.0%
Health Insurance: 95.7% have insurance; 78.0% have private insurance; 30.7% have public insurance; 4.3% do not have insurance; 0.1% of children under 18 do not have insurance
Safety: Violent crime rate: 1.5 per 10,000 population; Property crime rate: 46.5 per 10,000 population
Transportation: Commute: 91.3% car, 1.2% public transportation, 0.3% walk, 6.8% work from home; Mean travel time to work: 28.9 minutes

Additional Information Contacts
Town of Stillwater . . . . (518) 664-6148
  http://www.stillwaterny.org

STILLWATER (village).

Covers a land area of 1.258 square miles and a water area of 0.204 square miles. Located at 42.94° N. Lat; 73.64° W. Long. Elevation is 92 feet.

Population: 1,894; Growth (since 2000): 15.2%; Density: 1,505.5 persons per square mile; Race: 95.6% White, 1.9% Black/African American, 0.6% Asian, 0.3% American Indian/Alaska Native, 0.0% Native Hawaiian/Other Pacific Islander, 1.5% Two or more races, 1.2% Hispanic of any race; Average household size: 2.68; Median age: 35.6; Age under 18: 26.5%; Age 65 and over: 12.0%; Males per 100 females: 93.8; Marriage status: 29.4% never married, 56.8% now married, 1.6% separated, 5.2% widowed, 8.6% divorced; Foreign born: 3.8%; Speak English only: 95.7%; With disability: 13.6%; Veterans: 8.6%; Ancestry: 35.7% Irish, 23.7% Italian, 13.3% English, 12.4% French, 11.9% German

Employment: 8.6% management, business, and financial, 2.8% computer, engineering, and science, 9.1% education, legal, community service, arts, and media, 6.1% healthcare practitioners, 16.0% service, 30.3% sales and office, 9.0% natural resources, construction, and maintenance, 18.3% production, transportation, and material moving

Income: Per capita: $29,621; Median household: $73,571; Average household: $78,769; Households with income of $100,000 or more: 29.6%; Poverty rate: 6.2%

Educational Attainment: High school diploma or higher: 92.8%; Bachelor's degree or higher: 19.5%; Graduate/professional degree or higher: 5.2%

School District(s)
Stillwater Central SD (PK-12)
  Enrollment: 1,112 . . . . (518) 373-6100

Housing: Homeownership rate: 71.8%; Median home value: $193,500; Median year structure built: 1967; Homeowner vacancy rate: 5.5%; Median selected monthly owner costs: $1,452 with a mortgage, $582 without a mortgage; Median gross rent: $956 per month; Rental vacancy rate: 0.0%

Health Insurance: 93.8% have insurance; 73.1% have private insurance; 31.3% have public insurance; 6.2% do not have insurance; 0.6% of children under 18 do not have insurance

Transportation: Commute: 95.0% car, 0.6% public transportation, 1.1% walk, 1.8% work from home; Mean travel time to work: 29.2 minutes

VICTORY (village).

Covers a land area of 0.525 square miles and a water area of 0 square miles. Located at 43.09° N. Lat; 73.59° W. Long. Elevation is 203 feet.

Population: 540; Growth (since 2000): -0.7%; Density: 1,027.6 persons per square mile; Race: 93.5% White, 3.1% Black/African American, 0.0% Asian, 1.5% American Indian/Alaska Native, 0.0% Native Hawaiian/Other Pacific Islander, 1.9% Two or more races, 3.0% Hispanic of any race; Average household size: 2.76; Median age: 33.0; Age under 18: 24.8%; Age 65 and over: 10.6%; Males per 100 females: 101.0; Marriage status: 38.1% never married, 47.5% now married, 3.5% separated, 2.8% widowed, 11.6% divorced; Foreign born: 0.9%; Speak English only: 95.5%; With disability: 16.5%; Veterans: 14.5%; Ancestry: 31.9% Irish, 22.2% French, 11.1% Italian, 10.9% American, 10.7% German

Employment: 8.6% management, business, and financial, 2.2% computer, engineering, and science, 10.4% education, legal, community service, arts, and media, 1.9% healthcare practitioners, 28.0% service, 22.8% sales and office, 11.6% natural resources, construction, and maintenance, 14.6% production, transportation, and material moving

Income: Per capita: $22,310; Median household: $51,154; Average household: $61,696; Households with income of $100,000 or more: 17.8%; Poverty rate: 20.2%

Educational Attainment: High school diploma or higher: 82.7%; Bachelor's degree or higher: 15.0%; Graduate/professional degree or higher: 6.7%

Housing: Homeownership rate: 72.4%; Median home value: $138,100; Median year structure built: Before 1940; Homeowner vacancy rate: 3.6%; Median selected monthly owner costs: $1,313 with a mortgage, $476 without a mortgage; Median gross rent: $983 per month; Rental vacancy rate: 0.0%

Health Insurance: 87.2% have insurance; 61.9% have private insurance; 35.6% have public insurance; 12.8% do not have insurance; 21.4% of children under 18 do not have insurance

Transportation: Commute: 94.0% car, 0.0% public transportation, 0.0% walk, 6.0% work from home; Mean travel time to work: 25.5 minutes

VICTORY MILLS (unincorporated postal area)

ZCTA: 12884

Covers a land area of 0.498 square miles and a water area of 0 square miles. Located at 43.09° N. Lat; 73.59° W. Long. Elevation is 203 feet.

Population: 460; Growth (since 2000): n/a; Density: 923.5 persons per square mile; Race: 95.7% White, 3.7% Black/African American, 0.0% Asian, 0.0% American Indian/Alaska Native, 0.0% Native Hawaiian/Other Pacific Islander, 0.7% Two or more races, 0.7% Hispanic of any race; Average household size: 2.77; Median age: 36.3; Age under 18: 24.3%; Age 65 and over: 9.3%; Males per 100 females: 98.4; Marriage status: 36.7% never married, 42.5% now married, 5.8% separated, 2.2% widowed, 18.5% divorced; Foreign born: 5.2%; Speak English only: 88.3%; With disability: 25.0%; Veterans: 10.6%; Ancestry: 26.5% Irish, 25.4% French, 14.8% Italian, 12.4% English, 11.3% German

Employment: 10.5% management, business, and financial, 2.2% computer, engineering, and science, 7.2% education, legal, community service, arts, and media, 1.7% healthcare practitioners, 34.3% service, 13.8% sales and office, 10.5% natural resources, construction, and maintenance, 19.9% production, transportation, and material moving

Income: Per capita: $20,115; Median household: $43,750; Average household: $56,848; Households with income of $100,000 or more: 12.0%; Poverty rate: 28.3%

Educational Attainment: High school diploma or higher: 76.9%; Bachelor's degree or higher: 9.9%; Graduate/professional degree or higher: 4.0%

Housing: Homeownership rate: 77.1%; Median home value: $127,800; Median year structure built: Before 1940; Homeowner vacancy rate: 0.0%; Median selected monthly owner costs: $1,207 with a mortgage, $478 without a mortgage; Median gross rent: $1,024 per month; Rental vacancy rate: 0.0%

Health Insurance: 82.2% have insurance; 45.0% have private insurance; 45.7% have public insurance; 17.8% do not have insurance; 22.7% of children under 18 do not have insurance

Transportation: Commute: 97.2% car, 0.0% public transportation, 0.0% walk, 2.8% work from home; Mean travel time to work: 22.9 minutes

WATERFORD (town).

Covers a land area of 6.567 square miles and a water area of 0.845 square miles. Located at 42.80° N. Lat; 73.69° W. Long. Elevation is 69 feet.

History: Incorporated 1794.

Population: 8,456; Growth (since 2000): -0.7%; Density: 1,287.7 persons per square mile; Race: 93.8% White, 0.7% Black/African American, 2.4% Asian, 0.4% American Indian/Alaska Native, 0.0% Native Hawaiian/Other Pacific Islander, 1.8% Two or more races, 3.2% Hispanic of any race; Average household size: 2.33; Median age: 38.4; Age under 18: 19.3%; Age 65 and over: 14.2%; Males per 100 females: 96.0; Marriage status: 38.0% never married, 48.5% now married, 1.6% separated, 5.8% widowed, 7.8% divorced; Foreign born: 5.4%; Speak English only: 94.9%; With disability: 14.5%; Veterans: 7.0%; Ancestry: 24.5% Irish, 16.8% Italian, 13.3% German, 10.6% French, 10.4% English

Employment: 14.2% management, business, and financial, 6.8% computer, engineering, and science, 7.8% education, legal, community service, arts, and media, 5.8% healthcare practitioners, 19.0% service, 27.1% sales and office, 6.6% natural resources, construction, and maintenance, 12.8% production, transportation, and material moving

Income: Per capita: $32,867; Median household: $63,402; Average household: $76,104; Households with income of $100,000 or more: 26.5%; Poverty rate: 7.4%

Educational Attainment: High school diploma or higher: 91.3%; Bachelor's degree or higher: 24.6%; Graduate/professional degree or higher: 7.6%

School District(s)
Waterford-Halfmoon Union Free SD (KG-12)
  Enrollment: 807 . . . . (518) 237-0800

Housing: Homeownership rate: 58.3%; Median home value: $208,400; Median year structure built: 1960; Homeowner vacancy rate: 0.0%; Median selected monthly owner costs: $1,566 with a mortgage, $503 without a mortgage; Median gross rent: $918 per month; Rental vacancy rate: 3.1%

Health Insurance: 94.1% have insurance; 79.2% have private insurance; 29.9% have public insurance; 5.9% do not have insurance; 11.2% of children under 18 do not have insurance

Safety: Violent crime rate: 5.9 per 10,000 population; Property crime rate: 48.2 per 10,000 population

Transportation: Commute: 90.1% car, 1.0% public transportation, 2.4% walk, 5.9% work from home; Mean travel time to work: 21.6 minutes
Additional Information Contacts
Town of Waterford . . . . (518) 235-8282
    http://www.town.waterford.ny.us

WATERFORD (village). Covers a land area of 0.283 square miles and a water area of 0.075 square miles. Located at 42.79° N. Lat; 73.68° W. Long. Elevation is 69 feet.
Population: 2,180; Growth (since 2000): -1.1%; Density: 7,707.5 persons per square mile; Race: 88.0% White, 1.5% Black/African American, 6.6% Asian, 0.0% American Indian/Alaska Native, 0.0% Native Hawaiian/Other Pacific Islander, 2.9% Two or more races, 7.6% Hispanic of any race; Average household size: 2.18; Median age: 38.7; Age under 18: 17.8%; Age 65 and over: 11.5%; Males per 100 females: 97.2; Marriage status: 39.3% never married, 44.0% now married, 3.3% separated, 3.5% widowed, 13.1% divorced; Foreign born: 4.9%; Speak English only: 93.7%; With disability: 16.9%; Veterans: 5.5%; Ancestry: 31.1% Irish, 20.5% Italian, 11.7% German, 9.6% French, 8.9% Polish
Employment: 18.6% management, business, and financial, 3.6% computer, engineering, and science, 10.2% education, legal, community service, arts, and media, 3.4% healthcare practitioners, 24.4% service, 21.6% sales and office, 8.9% natural resources, construction, and maintenance, 9.3% production, transportation, and material moving
Income: Per capita: $26,645; Median household: $50,000; Average household: $57,915; Households with income of $100,000 or more: 12.4%; Poverty rate: 12.9%
Educational Attainment: High school diploma or higher: 87.0%; Bachelor's degree or higher: 24.9%; Graduate/professional degree or higher: 6.4%

School District(s)
Waterford-Halfmoon Union Free SD (KG-12)
    Enrollment: 807 . . . . (518) 237-0800
Housing: Homeownership rate: 42.0%; Median home value: $158,500; Median year structure built: Before 1940; Homeowner vacancy rate: 0.0%; Median selected monthly owner costs: $1,414 with a mortgage, $490 without a mortgage; Median gross rent: $828 per month; Rental vacancy rate: 0.0%
Health Insurance: 92.4% have insurance; 68.6% have private insurance; 36.1% have public insurance; 7.6% do not have insurance; 6.0% of children under 18 do not have insurance
Transportation: Commute: 83.0% car, 4.0% public transportation, 8.2% walk, 2.9% work from home; Mean travel time to work: 24.8 minutes
Additional Information Contacts
Village of Waterford . . . . (518) 235-9898
    http://www.waterfordny.org

WILTON (town). Covers a land area of 35.834 square miles and a water area of 0.118 square miles. Located at 43.15° N. Lat; 73.73° W. Long. Elevation is 348 feet.
Population: 16,823; Growth (since 2000): 34.5%; Density: 469.5 persons per square mile; Race: 94.5% White, 1.6% Black/African American, 2.0% Asian, 0.0% American Indian/Alaska Native, 0.0% Native Hawaiian/Other Pacific Islander, 1.3% Two or more races, 2.8% Hispanic of any race; Average household size: 2.50; Median age: 41.9; Age under 18: 23.1%; Age 65 and over: 14.3%; Males per 100 females: 96.3; Marriage status: 24.2% never married, 59.2% now married, 1.0% separated, 4.3% widowed, 12.3% divorced; Foreign born: 4.2%; Speak English only: 95.7%; With disability: 10.6%; Veterans: 8.3%; Ancestry: 30.4% Irish, 20.1% Italian, 17.6% German, 10.0% English, 8.6% French
Employment: 23.0% management, business, and financial, 8.7% computer, engineering, and science, 14.9% education, legal, community service, arts, and media, 7.0% healthcare practitioners, 12.9% service, 20.4% sales and office, 5.2% natural resources, construction, and maintenance, 8.0% production, transportation, and material moving
Income: Per capita: $40,003; Median household: $84,692; Average household: $99,844; Households with income of $100,000 or more: 41.1%; Poverty rate: 4.7%
Educational Attainment: High school diploma or higher: 94.4%; Bachelor's degree or higher: 44.2%; Graduate/professional degree or higher: 19.4%

School District(s)
South Glens Falls Central SD (PK-12)
    Enrollment: 3,157 . . . . (518) 793-9617

Housing: Homeownership rate: 72.3%; Median home value: $271,500; Median year structure built: 1994; Homeowner vacancy rate: 0.6%; Median selected monthly owner costs: $1,791 with a mortgage, $619 without a mortgage; Median gross rent: $1,317 per month; Rental vacancy rate: 2.2%
Health Insurance: 96.8% have insurance; 82.7% have private insurance; 26.6% have public insurance; 3.2% do not have insurance; 0.7% of children under 18 do not have insurance
Transportation: Commute: 92.7% car, 0.4% public transportation, 0.7% walk, 5.5% work from home; Mean travel time to work: 27.9 minutes
Additional Information Contacts
Town of Wilton . . . . (518) 587-1939
    http://www.townofwilton.com

Schenectady County

Located in eastern New York; bounded on the north by Schoharie Creek; crossed by the Mohawk River. Covers a land area of 204.516 square miles, a water area of 4.870 square miles, and is located in the Eastern Time Zone at 42.82° N. Lat., 74.04° W. Long. The county was founded in 1809. County seat is Schenectady.

Schenectady County is part of the Albany-Schenectady-Troy, NY Metropolitan Statistical Area. The entire metro area includes: Albany County, NY; Rensselaer County, NY; Saratoga County, NY; Schenectady County, NY; Schoharie County, NY

Population: 155,239; Growth (since 2000): 5.9%; Density: 759.1 persons per square mile; Race: 77.8% White, 10.3% Black/African American, 4.7% Asian, 0.2% American Indian/Alaska Native, 0.0% Native Hawaiian/Other Pacific Islander, 3.5% two or more races, 6.7% Hispanic of any race; Average household size: 2.80; Median age: 39.8; Age under 18: 21.7%; Age 65 and over: 16.2%; Males per 100 females: 93.7; Marriage status: 36.7% never married, 45.4% now married, 2.1% separated, 6.9% widowed, 11.0% divorced; Foreign born: 10.6%; Speak English only: 89.8%; With disability: 13.6%; Veterans: 7.4%; Ancestry: 19.4% Italian, 16.9% Irish, 14.1% German, 8.2% English, 7.7% Polish
Religion: Six largest groups: 28.6% Catholicism, 3.9% Muslim Estimate, 3.7% Presbyterian-Reformed, 2.1% Lutheran, 2.1% Methodist/Pietist, 1.5% Judaism
Economy: Unemployment rate: 3.7%; Leading industries: 14.9 % retail trade; 14.1 % health care and social assistance; 12.1 % construction; Farms: 169 totaling 19,868 acres; Company size: 5 employ 1,000 or more persons, 5 employ 500 to 999 persons, 59 employ 100 to 499 persons, 2,991 employs less than 100 persons; Business ownership: 3,414 women-owned, 817 Black-owned, 348 Hispanic-owned, 465 Asian-owned, 64 American Indian/Alaska Native-owned
Employment: 13.8% management, business, and financial, 6.7% computer, engineering, and science, 11.6% education, legal, community service, arts, and media, 6.1% healthcare practitioners, 19.1% service, 25.9% sales and office, 6.7% natural resources, construction, and maintenance, 10.2% production, transportation, and material moving
Income: Per capita: $29,981; Median household: $61,315; Average household: $77,444; Households with income of $100,000 or more: 26.6%; Poverty rate: 12.4%
Educational Attainment: High school diploma or higher: 90.2%; Bachelor's degree or higher: 30.8%; Graduate/professional degree or higher: 13.5%
Housing: Homeownership rate: 67.8%; Median home value: $164,100; Median year structure built: 1951; Homeowner vacancy rate: 1.9%; Median selected monthly owner costs: $1,559 with a mortgage, $624 without a mortgage; Median gross rent: $894 per month; Rental vacancy rate: 7.3%
Vital Statistics: Birth rate: 114.6 per 10,000 population; Death rate: 94.0 per 10,000 population; Age-adjusted cancer mortality rate: 156.6 deaths per 100,000 population
Health Insurance: 94.5% have insurance; 70.5% have private insurance; 38.1% have public insurance; 5.5% do not have insurance; 2.7% of children under 18 do not have insurance
Health Care: Physicians: 27.3 per 10,000 population; Dentists: 8.1 per 10,000 population; Hospital beds: 50.1 per 10,000 population; Hospital admissions: 1,700.5 per 10,000 population
Transportation: Commute: 88.8% car, 3.9% public transportation, 2.9% walk, 3.1% work from home; Mean travel time to work: 22.9 minutes
2016 Presidential Election: 43.0% Trump, 50.2% Clinton, 3.9% Johnson, 1.7% Stein

Additional Information Contacts
Schenectady Government . . . . (518) 388-4282
   http://www.schenectadycounty.com

Schenectady County Communities

ALPLAUS (unincorporated postal area)
ZCTA: 12008
   Covers a land area of 0.831 square miles and a water area of 0.175 square miles. Located at 42.85° N. Lat; 73.91° W. Long. Elevation is 259 feet.
   Population: 513; Growth (since 2000): 19.0%; Density: 617.1 persons per square mile; Race: 86.7% White, 0.0% Black/African American, 12.9% Asian, 0.4% American Indian/Alaska Native, 0.0% Native Hawaiian/Other Pacific Islander, 0.0% Two or more races, 9.9% Hispanic of any race; Average household size: 3.13; Median age: 41.5; Age under 18: 24.8%; Age 65 and over: 18.3%; Males per 100 females: 103.7; Marriage status: 15.8% never married, 60.9% now married, 2.3% separated, 7.0% widowed, 16.3% divorced; Foreign born: 8.2%; Speak English only: 88.3%; With disability: 13.8%; Veterans: 11.1%; Ancestry: 32.4% Italian, 20.3% Irish, 11.9% German, 10.7% French, 7.4% English
   Employment: 7.9% management, business, and financial, 13.5% computer, engineering, and science, 24.9% education, legal, community service, arts, and media, 11.8% healthcare practitioners, 6.6% service, 26.6% sales and office, 7.0% natural resources, construction, and maintenance, 1.7% production, transportation, and material moving
   Income: Per capita: $39,391; Median household: $103,472; Average household: $113,869; Households with income of $100,000 or more: 52.2%; Poverty rate: 1.2%
   Educational Attainment: High school diploma or higher: 93.1%; Bachelor's degree or higher: 55.9%; Graduate/professional degree or higher: 30.8%
   Housing: Homeownership rate: 92.5%; Median home value: $234,700; Median year structure built: Before 1940; Homeowner vacancy rate: 0.0%; Median selected monthly owner costs: $1,955 with a mortgage, $506 without a mortgage; Median gross rent: n/a per month; Rental vacancy rate: 0.0%
   Health Insurance: 98.2% have insurance; 90.4% have private insurance; 24.8% have public insurance; 1.8% do not have insurance; 0.0% of children under 18 do not have insurance
   Transportation: Commute: 89.5% car, 0.0% public transportation, 0.0% walk, 10.5% work from home; Mean travel time to work: 24.6 minutes

DELANSON (village). Covers a land area of 0.644 square miles and a water area of 0.003 square miles. Located at 42.75° N. Lat; 74.18° W. Long. Elevation is 817 feet.
   Population: 352; Growth (since 2000): -8.6%; Density: 546.7 persons per square mile; Race: 98.9% White, 0.0% Black/African American, 1.1% Asian, 0.0% American Indian/Alaska Native, 0.0% Native Hawaiian/Other Pacific Islander, 0.0% Two or more races, 2.0% Hispanic of any race; Average household size: 3.06; Median age: 34.2; Age under 18: 28.1%; Age 65 and over: 10.2%; Males per 100 females: 96.4; Marriage status: 39.0% never married, 56.5% now married, 0.4% separated, 2.2% widowed, 2.2% divorced; Foreign born: 2.3%; Speak English only: 99.4%; With disability: 6.0%; Veterans: 5.9%; Ancestry: 22.4% American, 21.3% German, 21.0% Irish, 15.1% Italian, 9.4% English
   Employment: 27.2% management, business, and financial, 5.9% computer, engineering, and science, 12.4% education, legal, community service, arts, and media, 1.2% healthcare practitioners, 19.5% service, 18.9% sales and office, 8.9% natural resources, construction, and maintenance, 5.9% production, transportation, and material moving
   Income: Per capita: $30,696; Median household: $75,625; Average household: $86,369; Households with income of $100,000 or more: 35.7%; Poverty rate: 3.4%
   Educational Attainment: High school diploma or higher: 93.2%; Bachelor's degree or higher: 23.0%; Graduate/professional degree or higher: 8.5%

School District(s)
Duanesburg Central SD (KG-12)
   Enrollment: 740 . . . . (518) 895-2279
   Housing: Homeownership rate: 73.0%; Median home value: $180,600; Median year structure built: Before 1940; Homeowner vacancy rate: 4.4%; Median selected monthly owner costs: $1,609 with a mortgage, $650 without a mortgage; Median gross rent: $1,266 per month; Rental vacancy rate: 0.0%

Health Insurance: 97.2% have insurance; 84.4% have private insurance; 23.9% have public insurance; 2.8% do not have insurance; 0.0% of children under 18 do not have insurance
Transportation: Commute: 98.2% car, 0.0% public transportation, 0.0% walk, 1.8% work from home; Mean travel time to work: 29.3 minutes

DUANE LAKE (CDP). Covers a land area of 2.401 square miles and a water area of 0.194 square miles. Located at 42.75° N. Lat; 74.11° W. Long. Elevation is 922 feet.
   Population: 246; Growth (since 2000): -31.1%; Density: 102.4 persons per square mile; Race: 78.0% White, 4.1% Black/African American, 0.0% Asian, 0.0% American Indian/Alaska Native, 0.0% Native Hawaiian/Other Pacific Islander, 10.2% Two or more races, 17.9% Hispanic of any race; Average household size: 2.30; Median age: 45.9; Age under 18: 20.7%; Age 65 and over: 25.2%; Males per 100 females: 97.0; Marriage status: 8.2% never married, 84.1% now married, 0.0% separated, 0.0% widowed, 7.7% divorced; Foreign born: 0.0%; Speak English only: 100.0%; With disability: 0.0%; Veterans: 15.9%; Ancestry: 26.8% German, 17.1% Dutch, 13.4% Polish, 12.6% Irish, 6.5% American
   Employment: 22.8% management, business, and financial, 12.8% computer, engineering, and science, 17.4% education, legal, community service, arts, and media, 0.0% healthcare practitioners, 10.7% service, 27.5% sales and office, 8.7% natural resources, construction, and maintenance, 0.0% production, transportation, and material moving
   Income: Per capita: $48,839; Median household: $121,645; Average household: $116,269; Households with income of $100,000 or more: 75.7%; Poverty rate: n/a
   Educational Attainment: High school diploma or higher: 100.0%; Bachelor's degree or higher: 59.8%; Graduate/professional degree or higher: 35.8%
   Housing: Homeownership rate: 100.0%; Median home value: $255,200; Median year structure built: 1957; Homeowner vacancy rate: 0.0%; Median selected monthly owner costs: $2,074 with a mortgage, n/a without a mortgage; Median gross rent: n/a per month; Rental vacancy rate: 0.0%
   Health Insurance: 83.7% have insurance; 83.7% have private insurance; 31.3% have public insurance; 16.3% do not have insurance; 0.0% of children under 18 do not have insurance
   Transportation: Commute: 82.6% car, 0.0% public transportation, 10.1% walk, 7.4% work from home; Mean travel time to work: 24.1 minutes

DUANESBURG (CDP). Covers a land area of 2.449 square miles and a water area of 0.096 square miles. Located at 42.76° N. Lat; 74.13° W. Long. Elevation is 718 feet.
   Population: 328; Growth (since 2000): -3.2%; Density: 133.9 persons per square mile; Race: 100.0% White, 0.0% Black/African American, 0.0% Asian, 0.0% American Indian/Alaska Native, 0.0% Native Hawaiian/Other Pacific Islander, 0.0% Two or more races, 19.5% Hispanic of any race; Average household size: 4.90; Median age: 43.6; Age under 18: 11.9%; Age 65 and over: 10.4%; Males per 100 females: 89.8; Marriage status: 0.0% never married, 100.0% now married, 0.0% separated, 0.0% widowed, 0.0% divorced; Foreign born: 0.0%; Speak English only: 92.4%; With disability: 7.3%; Veterans: 41.2%; Ancestry: 36.3% Polish, 35.7% English, 24.4% French, 24.4% Italian, 19.5% American
   Employment: 10.1% management, business, and financial, 0.0% computer, engineering, and science, 0.0% education, legal, community service, arts, and media, 0.0% healthcare practitioners, 0.0% service, 48.6% sales and office, 31.2% natural resources, construction, and maintenance, 10.1% production, transportation, and material moving
   Income: Per capita: $34,864; Median household: $113,681; Average household: $114,245; Households with income of $100,000 or more: 62.7%; Poverty rate: n/a
   Educational Attainment: High school diploma or higher: 100.0%; Bachelor's degree or higher: 36.0%; Graduate/professional degree or higher: 8.3%
   Housing: Homeownership rate: 100.0%; Median home value: $158,900; Median year structure built: 1964; Homeowner vacancy rate: 0.0%; Median selected monthly owner costs: n/a with a mortgage, n/a without a mortgage; Median gross rent: n/a per month; Rental vacancy rate: 0.0%
   Health Insurance: 100.0% have insurance; 94.5% have private insurance; 5.5% have public insurance; 0.0% do not have insurance; 0.0% of children under 18 do not have insurance
   Transportation: Commute: 100.0% car, 0.0% public transportation, 0.0% walk, 0.0% work from home; Mean travel time to work: 0.0 minutes

DUANESBURG (town). Covers a land area of 70.782 square miles and a water area of 1.250 square miles. Located at 42.78° N. Lat; 74.17° W. Long. Elevation is 718 feet.

Population: 6,573; Growth (since 2000): 13.2%; Density: 92.9 persons per square mile; Race: 95.4% White, 0.5% Black/African American, 1.7% Asian, 0.0% American Indian/Alaska Native, 0.0% Native Hawaiian/Other Pacific Islander, 2.1% Two or more races, 4.9% Hispanic of any race; Average household size: 3.40; Median age: 38.9; Age under 18: 21.8%; Age 65 and over: 10.2%; Males per 100 females: 100.5; Marriage status: 37.5% never married, 53.5% now married, 1.3% separated, 2.8% widowed, 6.2% divorced; Foreign born: 2.2%; Speak English only: 98.2%; With disability: 8.6%; Veterans: 10.9%; Ancestry: 23.9% German, 21.8% Irish, 10.6% American, 10.1% English, 9.7% Italian

Employment: 9.9% management, business, and financial, 6.5% computer, engineering, and science, 8.4% education, legal, community service, arts, and media, 3.6% healthcare practitioners, 14.9% service, 31.7% sales and office, 15.7% natural resources, construction, and maintenance, 9.4% production, transportation, and material moving

Income: Per capita: $30,184; Median household: $84,127; Average household: $92,518; Households with income of $100,000 or more: 35.3%; Poverty rate: 7.6%

Educational Attainment: High school diploma or higher: 92.9%; Bachelor's degree or higher: 23.5%; Graduate/professional degree or higher: 11.1%

Housing: Homeownership rate: 86.1%; Median home value: $209,200; Median year structure built: 1971; Homeowner vacancy rate: 0.2%; Median selected monthly owner costs: $1,781 with a mortgage, $692 without a mortgage; Median gross rent: $1,234 per month; Rental vacancy rate: 0.0%

Health Insurance: 93.7% have insurance; 75.6% have private insurance; 28.4% have public insurance; 6.3% do not have insurance; 0.4% of children under 18 do not have insurance

Transportation: Commute: 92.7% car, 0.0% public transportation, 0.8% walk, 6.2% work from home; Mean travel time to work: 30.8 minutes

Additional Information Contacts

Town of Duanesburg . . . . (518) 895-8920
  http://www.duanesburg.net

EAST GLENVILLE (CDP). Covers a land area of 7.165 square miles and a water area of 0.287 square miles. Located at 42.86° N. Lat; 73.92° W. Long. Elevation is 361 feet.

Population: 6,339; Growth (since 2000): 4.5%; Density: 884.7 persons per square mile; Race: 93.8% White, 0.3% Black/African American, 3.5% Asian, 0.0% American Indian/Alaska Native, 0.0% Native Hawaiian/Other Pacific Islander, 1.6% Two or more races, 3.8% Hispanic of any race; Average household size: 2.67; Median age: 45.1; Age under 18: 22.0%; Age 65 and over: 22.5%; Males per 100 females: 92.5; Marriage status: 25.0% never married, 56.8% now married, 1.3% separated, 9.1% widowed, 9.2% divorced; Foreign born: 5.1%; Speak English only: 92.0%; With disability: 12.8%; Veterans: 10.8%; Ancestry: 22.1% Irish, 19.9% Italian, 14.9% German, 11.3% Polish, 9.8% English

Employment: 17.7% management, business, and financial, 8.8% computer, engineering, and science, 17.5% education, legal, community service, arts, and media, 9.5% healthcare practitioners, 13.6% service, 22.0% sales and office, 7.9% natural resources, construction, and maintenance, 3.0% production, transportation, and material moving

Income: Per capita: $34,909; Median household: $79,375; Average household: $87,705; Households with income of $100,000 or more: 33.1%; Poverty rate: 4.0%

Educational Attainment: High school diploma or higher: 95.9%; Bachelor's degree or higher: 38.5%; Graduate/professional degree or higher: 17.5%

Housing: Homeownership rate: 77.6%; Median home value: $207,000; Median year structure built: 1965; Homeowner vacancy rate: 1.1%; Median selected monthly owner costs: $1,702 with a mortgage, $643 without a mortgage; Median gross rent: $1,165 per month; Rental vacancy rate: 10.7%

Health Insurance: 96.2% have insurance; 85.8% have private insurance; 29.4% have public insurance; 3.8% do not have insurance; 5.6% of children under 18 do not have insurance

Transportation: Commute: 94.9% car, 1.3% public transportation, 0.3% walk, 3.5% work from home; Mean travel time to work: 24.7 minutes

GLENVILLE (town). Covers a land area of 49.186 square miles and a water area of 1.490 square miles. Located at 42.89° N. Lat; 73.99° W. Long. Elevation is 705 feet.

Population: 29,506; Growth (since 2000): 4.7%; Density: 599.9 persons per square mile; Race: 94.7% White, 1.6% Black/African American, 1.5% Asian, 0.0% American Indian/Alaska Native, 0.1% Native Hawaiian/Other Pacific Islander, 1.8% Two or more races, 3.0% Hispanic of any race; Average household size: 2.69; Median age: 42.8; Age under 18: 21.4%; Age 65 and over: 18.9%; Males per 100 females: 94.0; Marriage status: 29.9% never married, 51.4% now married, 1.5% separated, 7.4% widowed, 11.3% divorced; Foreign born: 3.3%; Speak English only: 95.4%; With disability: 11.9%; Veterans: 9.4%; Ancestry: 23.5% Irish, 20.9% Italian, 19.4% German, 12.9% English, 9.9% Polish

Employment: 16.1% management, business, and financial, 6.9% computer, engineering, and science, 13.3% education, legal, community service, arts, and media, 7.0% healthcare practitioners, 15.3% service, 28.6% sales and office, 5.9% natural resources, construction, and maintenance, 6.8% production, transportation, and material moving

Income: Per capita: $34,732; Median household: $75,018; Average household: $86,440; Households with income of $100,000 or more: 33.2%; Poverty rate: 5.8%

Educational Attainment: High school diploma or higher: 95.9%; Bachelor's degree or higher: 36.9%; Graduate/professional degree or higher: 16.5%

Housing: Homeownership rate: 77.2%; Median home value: $185,500; Median year structure built: 1957; Homeowner vacancy rate: 1.2%; Median selected monthly owner costs: $1,654 with a mortgage, $637 without a mortgage; Median gross rent: $995 per month; Rental vacancy rate: 7.4%

Health Insurance: 95.9% have insurance; 81.6% have private insurance; 29.5% have public insurance; 4.1% do not have insurance; 3.4% of children under 18 do not have insurance

Safety: Violent crime rate: 6.5 per 10,000 population; Property crime rate: 214.3 per 10,000 population

Transportation: Commute: 94.4% car, 1.3% public transportation, 1.7% walk, 2.3% work from home; Mean travel time to work: 23.5 minutes

Additional Information Contacts

Town of Glenville. . . . . (518) 688-1200
  http://www.townofglenville.org

MARIAVILLE LAKE (CDP). Covers a land area of 5.623 square miles and a water area of 0.380 square miles. Located at 42.82° N. Lat; 74.17° W. Long. Elevation is 1,289 feet.

Population: 475; Growth (since 2000): -33.1%; Density: 84.5 persons per square mile; Race: 93.7% White, 0.0% Black/African American, 2.1% Asian, 0.0% American Indian/Alaska Native, 0.0% Native Hawaiian/Other Pacific Islander, 4.2% Two or more races, 0.0% Hispanic of any race; Average household size: 3.03; Median age: 41.1; Age under 18: 15.6%; Age 65 and over: 12.4%; Males per 100 females: 109.9; Marriage status: 46.8% never married, 48.7% now married, 0.0% separated, 0.0% widowed, 4.5% divorced; Foreign born: 3.2%; Speak English only: 96.8%; With disability: 13.6%; Veterans: 5.8%; Ancestry: 42.9% Irish, 30.1% German, 11.2% French, 10.7% American, 6.9% Swedish

Employment: 3.9% management, business, and financial, 4.2% computer, engineering, and science, 9.4% education, legal, community service, arts, and media, 0.0% healthcare practitioners, 18.1% service, 37.7% sales and office, 12.9% natural resources, construction, and maintenance, 13.9% production, transportation, and material moving

Income: Per capita: $24,228; Median household: $54,926; Average household: $63,611; Households with income of $100,000 or more: 19.1%; Poverty rate: 11.6%

Educational Attainment: High school diploma or higher: 97.1%; Bachelor's degree or higher: 34.0%; Graduate/professional degree or higher: 18.6%

Housing: Homeownership rate: 100.0%; Median home value: $187,500; Median year structure built: 1970; Homeowner vacancy rate: 0.0%; Median selected monthly owner costs: $1,161 with a mortgage, $770 without a mortgage; Median gross rent: n/a per month; Rental vacancy rate: 0.0%

Health Insurance: 96.0% have insurance; 77.9% have private insurance; 31.8% have public insurance; 4.0% do not have insurance; 0.0% of children under 18 do not have insurance

Transportation: Commute: 94.5% car, 0.0% public transportation, 0.0% walk, 5.5% work from home; Mean travel time to work: 28.1 minutes

NISKAYUNA (town).
Covers a land area of 14.152 square miles and a water area of 0.890 square miles. Located at 42.80° N. Lat; 73.87° W. Long. Elevation is 292 feet.

Population: 22,243; Growth (since 2000): 9.6%; Density: 1,571.8 persons per square mile; Race: 82.6% White, 4.4% Black/African American, 9.6% Asian, 0.1% American Indian/Alaska Native, 0.0% Native Hawaiian/Other Pacific Islander, 2.4% Two or more races, 4.2% Hispanic of any race; Average household size: 2.97; Median age: 43.2; Age under 18: 25.7%; Age 65 and over: 18.9%; Males per 100 females: 93.0; Marriage status: 24.6% never married, 60.1% now married, 0.8% separated, 6.3% widowed, 9.0% divorced; Foreign born: 16.7%; Speak English only: 81.5%; With disability: 12.0%; Veterans: 6.2%; Ancestry: 18.5% Italian, 16.5% Irish, 15.8% German, 8.8% English, 7.4% Polish

Employment: 20.9% management, business, and financial, 15.3% computer, engineering, and science, 17.3% education, legal, community service, arts, and media, 7.3% healthcare practitioners, 7.4% service, 21.3% sales and office, 5.7% natural resources, construction, and maintenance, 4.7% production, transportation, and material moving

Income: Per capita: $45,049; Median household: $105,398; Average household: $129,699; Households with income of $100,000 or more: 53.9%; Poverty rate: 5.0%

Educational Attainment: High school diploma or higher: 96.6%; Bachelor's degree or higher: 58.6%; Graduate/professional degree or higher: 33.0%

Housing: Homeownership rate: 81.9%; Median home value: $261,700; Median year structure built: 1965; Homeowner vacancy rate: 0.3%; Median selected monthly owner costs: $2,053 with a mortgage, $829 without a mortgage; Median gross rent: $1,122 per month; Rental vacancy rate: 2.9%

Health Insurance: 96.4% have insurance; 83.4% have private insurance; 28.2% have public insurance; 3.6% do not have insurance; 1.6% of children under 18 do not have insurance

Safety: Violent crime rate: 6.7 per 10,000 population; Property crime rate: 182.3 per 10,000 population

Transportation: Commute: 92.0% car, 0.6% public transportation, 1.3% walk, 4.9% work from home; Mean travel time to work: 21.0 minutes

Additional Information Contacts

Town of Niskayuna . . . . (518) 386-4500
    http://www.niskayuna.org

PATTERSONVILLE (unincorporated postal area)
ZCTA: 12137

Covers a land area of 23.978 square miles and a water area of 0.396 square miles. Located at 42.86° N. Lat; 74.13° W. Long. Elevation is 269 feet.

Population: 1,998; Growth (since 2000): 29.4%; Density: 83.3 persons per square mile; Race: 95.5% White, 0.0% Black/African American, 2.4% Asian, 0.0% American Indian/Alaska Native, 0.0% Native Hawaiian/Other Pacific Islander, 2.1% Two or more races, 3.4% Hispanic of any race; Average household size: 2.91; Median age: 39.1; Age under 18: 15.4%; Age 65 and over: 12.0%; Males per 100 females: 98.7; Marriage status: 35.3% never married, 53.5% now married, 3.6% separated, 2.0% widowed, 9.2% divorced; Foreign born: 3.2%; Speak English only: 97.4%; With disability: 9.4%; Veterans: 8.5%; Ancestry: 25.9% Irish, 23.3% German, 20.1% Italian, 15.0% Polish, 14.1% French

Employment: 8.7% management, business, and financial, 2.5% computer, engineering, and science, 9.6% education, legal, community service, arts, and media, 3.4% healthcare practitioners, 17.2% service, 27.3% sales and office, 9.9% natural resources, construction, and maintenance, 21.4% production, transportation, and material moving

Income: Per capita: $27,285; Median household: $64,213; Average household: $71,825; Households with income of $100,000 or more: 18.2%; Poverty rate: 9.2%

Educational Attainment: High school diploma or higher: 89.6%; Bachelor's degree or higher: 20.3%; Graduate/professional degree or higher: 11.0%

Housing: Homeownership rate: 82.1%; Median home value: $184,300; Median year structure built: 1972; Homeowner vacancy rate: 0.0%; Median selected monthly owner costs: $1,471 with a mortgage, $605 without a mortgage; Median gross rent: $767 per month; Rental vacancy rate: 0.0%

Health Insurance: 94.3% have insurance; 70.0% have private insurance; 37.4% have public insurance; 5.7% do not have insurance; 1.7% of children under 18 do not have insurance

Transportation: Commute: 95.6% car, 0.0% public transportation, 1.9% walk, 1.5% work from home; Mean travel time to work: 34.3 minutes

PRINCETOWN (town).
Covers a land area of 23.924 square miles and a water area of 0.287 square miles. Located at 42.81° N. Lat; 74.08° W. Long. Elevation is 420 feet.

Population: 1,797; Growth (since 2000): -15.7%; Density: 75.1 persons per square mile; Race: 99.5% White, 0.5% Black/African American, 0.0% Asian, 0.0% American Indian/Alaska Native, 0.0% Native Hawaiian/Other Pacific Islander, 0.0% Two or more races, 1.5% Hispanic of any race; Average household size: 2.79; Median age: 49.4; Age under 18: 16.9%; Age 65 and over: 24.6%; Males per 100 females: 100.5; Marriage status: 24.8% never married, 60.3% now married, 0.6% separated, 4.9% widowed, 9.9% divorced; Foreign born: 3.6%; Speak English only: 93.6%; With disability: 10.0%; Veterans: 10.5%; Ancestry: 22.1% Italian, 20.9% Irish, 14.8% German, 13.8% English, 10.5% Polish

Employment: 14.2% management, business, and financial, 8.5% computer, engineering, and science, 15.3% education, legal, community service, arts, and media, 2.0% healthcare practitioners, 19.4% service, 19.7% sales and office, 9.6% natural resources, construction, and maintenance, 11.2% production, transportation, and material moving

Income: Per capita: $38,464; Median household: $84,750; Average household: $97,839; Households with income of $100,000 or more: 34.6%; Poverty rate: 4.0%

Educational Attainment: High school diploma or higher: 89.8%; Bachelor's degree or higher: 35.1%; Graduate/professional degree or higher: 12.5%

Housing: Homeownership rate: 90.6%; Median home value: $206,000; Median year structure built: 1974; Homeowner vacancy rate: 0.7%; Median selected monthly owner costs: $1,746 with a mortgage, $641 without a mortgage; Median gross rent: $866 per month; Rental vacancy rate: 16.7%

Health Insurance: 97.9% have insurance; 81.0% have private insurance; 36.2% have public insurance; 2.1% do not have insurance; 0.0% of children under 18 do not have insurance

Transportation: Commute: 91.7% car, 1.1% public transportation, 2.0% walk, 3.8% work from home; Mean travel time to work: 26.4 minutes

ROTTERDAM (CDP).
Covers a land area of 6.933 square miles and a water area of 0.006 square miles. Located at 42.78° N. Lat; 73.95° W. Long. Elevation is 338 feet.

Population: 20,470; Growth (since 2000): -0.3%; Density: 2,952.4 persons per square mile; Race: 91.0% White, 3.7% Black/African American, 1.1% Asian, 0.1% American Indian/Alaska Native, 0.0% Native Hawaiian/Other Pacific Islander, 3.4% Two or more races, 5.6% Hispanic of any race; Average household size: 2.79; Median age: 41.2; Age under 18: 21.8%; Age 65 and over: 19.1%; Males per 100 females: 90.9; Marriage status: 31.4% never married, 46.7% now married, 1.8% separated, 8.0% widowed, 14.0% divorced; Foreign born: 3.4%; Speak English only: 94.1%; With disability: 12.8%; Veterans: 9.8%; Ancestry: 32.9% Italian, 18.4% Irish, 14.9% German, 9.5% Polish, 8.7% English

Employment: 12.8% management, business, and financial, 5.0% computer, engineering, and science, 8.6% education, legal, community service, arts, and media, 4.4% healthcare practitioners, 23.1% service, 28.2% sales and office, 6.7% natural resources, construction, and maintenance, 11.1% production, transportation, and material moving

Income: Per capita: $27,069; Median household: $60,615; Average household: $68,645; Households with income of $100,000 or more: 21.6%; Poverty rate: 8.8%

Educational Attainment: High school diploma or higher: 92.7%; Bachelor's degree or higher: 20.8%; Graduate/professional degree or higher: 6.8%

Housing: Homeownership rate: 79.8%; Median home value: $158,600; Median year structure built: 1954; Homeowner vacancy rate: 3.7%; Median selected monthly owner costs: $1,396 with a mortgage, $522 without a mortgage; Median gross rent: $949 per month; Rental vacancy rate: 2.7%

Health Insurance: 96.2% have insurance; 75.8% have private insurance; 36.6% have public insurance; 3.8% do not have insurance; 1.9% of children under 18 do not have insurance

Transportation: Commute: 94.4% car, 0.8% public transportation, 0.9% walk, 2.6% work from home; Mean travel time to work: 22.3 minutes

ROTTERDAM (town).
Covers a land area of 35.692 square miles and a water area of 0.768 square miles. Located at 42.81° N. Lat; 74.01° W. Long. Elevation is 338 feet.

History: Settled c.1670, incorporated 1821.

Population: 29,415; Growth (since 2000): 3.9%; Density: 824.1 persons per square mile; Race: 92.9% White, 2.7% Black/African American, 1.4% Asian, 0.1% American Indian/Alaska Native, 0.0% Native Hawaiian/Other Pacific Islander, 2.4% Two or more races, 4.9% Hispanic of any race; Average household size: 2.83; Median age: 41.6; Age under 18: 21.8%; Age 65 and over: 18.4%; Males per 100 females: 92.2; Marriage status: 32.4% never married, 46.7% now married, 1.5% separated, 7.4% widowed, 13.5% divorced; Foreign born: 3.9%; Speak English only: 93.8%; With disability: 12.2%; Veterans: 9.2%; Ancestry: 32.7% Italian, 20.7% Irish, 15.4% German, 10.6% Polish, 8.6% English
Employment: 13.8% management, business, and financial, 4.9% computer, engineering, and science, 8.8% education, legal, community service, arts, and media, 5.2% healthcare practitioners, 23.1% service, 25.9% sales and office, 7.1% natural resources, construction, and maintenance, 11.3% production, transportation, and material moving
Income: Per capita: $29,130; Median household: $65,629; Average household: $74,964; Households with income of $100,000 or more: 26.1%; Poverty rate: 7.5%
Educational Attainment: High school diploma or higher: 92.7%; Bachelor's degree or higher: 23.9%; Graduate/professional degree or higher: 8.5%
Housing: Homeownership rate: 78.5%; Median home value: $166,700; Median year structure built: 1957; Homeowner vacancy rate: 3.0%; Median selected monthly owner costs: $1,487 with a mortgage, $564 without a mortgage; Median gross rent: $953 per month; Rental vacancy rate: 3.1%
Health Insurance: 96.6% have insurance; 78.4% have private insurance; 33.8% have public insurance; 3.4% do not have insurance; 1.6% of children under 18 do not have insurance
Safety: Violent crime rate: 12.5 per 10,000 population; Property crime rate: 278.2 per 10,000 population
Transportation: Commute: 93.8% car, 0.6% public transportation, 1.5% walk, 2.5% work from home; Mean travel time to work: 22.6 minutes
Additional Information Contacts
Town of Rotterdam . . . . (518) 355-7575
   http://rotterdamny.org

ROTTERDAM JUNCTION (unincorporated postal area)
ZCTA: 12150
   Covers a land area of 1.096 square miles and a water area of 0.094 square miles. Located at 42.88° N. Lat; 74.05° W. Long. Elevation is 249 feet.
Population: 903; Growth (since 2000): 8.0%; Density: 823.6 persons per square mile; Race: 100.0% White, 0.0% Black/African American, 0.0% Asian, 0.0% American Indian/Alaska Native, 0.0% Native Hawaiian/Other Pacific Islander, 0.0% Two or more races, 0.0% Hispanic of any race; Average household size: 3.16; Median age: 44.7; Age under 18: 15.7%; Age 65 and over: 25.5%; Males per 100 females: 91.2; Marriage status: 49.2% never married, 23.2% now married, 1.4% separated, 15.3% widowed, 12.2% divorced; Foreign born: 14.2%; Speak English only: 77.6%; With disability: 8.7%; Veterans: 8.1%; Ancestry: 55.4% Italian, 17.7% Irish, 12.5% Polish, 8.9% American, 7.5% German
Employment: 6.6% management, business, and financial, 2.7% computer, engineering, and science, 10.9% education, legal, community service, arts, and media, 7.9% healthcare practitioners, 36.6% service, 15.3% sales and office, 14.5% natural resources, construction, and maintenance, 5.4% production, transportation, and material moving
Income: Per capita: $27,849; Median household: $66,944; Average household: $73,179; Households with income of $100,000 or more: 30.0%; Poverty rate: 1.6%
Educational Attainment: High school diploma or higher: 77.9%; Bachelor's degree or higher: 19.8%; Graduate/professional degree or higher: 0.9%
Housing: Homeownership rate: 88.5%; Median home value: $155,400; Median year structure built: 1961; Homeowner vacancy rate: 0.0%; Median selected monthly owner costs: $1,395 with a mortgage, $619 without a mortgage; Median gross rent: n/a per month; Rental vacancy rate: 0.0%
Health Insurance: 91.8% have insurance; 77.9% have private insurance; 30.5% have public insurance; 8.2% do not have insurance; 0.0% of children under 18 do not have insurance
Transportation: Commute: 95.2% car, 0.0% public transportation, 0.0% walk, 4.8% work from home; Mean travel time to work: 25.1 minutes

SCHENECTADY (city). County seat. Covers a land area of 10.779 square miles and a water area of 0.185 square miles. Located at 42.80° N. Lat; 73.93° W. Long. Elevation is 243 feet.
History: The site of Schenectady was called "Schonowe" meaning "big flats" by the Mohawk people. In 1662, Arent Van Curler, with a small group of Dutchmen, emigrated from Albany to the "Groote Vlachte" ("big flats") and purchased land. The first major migration of English into Schenectady began about 1700. In 1848, a locomotive factory was organized that was Schenectady's largest industry for a half century. In 1886, Thomas A. Edison bought two abandoned factory buildings for the Edison Company. In 1892 it was consolidated with the Thompson-Huston Company of Lynn, Massachusetts, to form the General Electric Company. Schenectady became the city that "lights and hauls the world."
Population: 65,705; Growth (since 2000): 6.3%; Density: 6,095.4 persons per square mile; Race: 59.4% White, 20.9% Black/African American, 6.4% Asian, 0.5% American Indian/Alaska Native, 0.0% Native Hawaiian/Other Pacific Islander, 5.4% Two or more races, 10.3% Hispanic of any race; Average household size: 2.73; Median age: 36.4; Age under 18: 20.7%; Age 65 and over: 13.4%; Males per 100 females: 93.7; Marriage status: 45.7% never married, 36.2% now married, 3.3% separated, 7.2% widowed, 10.9% divorced; Foreign born: 15.9%; Speak English only: 87.4%; With disability: 16.1%; Veterans: 5.7%; Ancestry: 13.9% Italian, 11.7% Irish, 9.7% German, 5.5% Guyanese, 5.5% Polish
Employment: 10.7% management, business, and financial, 4.6% computer, engineering, and science, 10.5% education, legal, community service, arts, and media, 6.1% healthcare practitioners, 23.4% service, 25.5% sales and office, 5.9% natural resources, construction, and maintenance, 13.2% production, transportation, and material moving
Income: Per capita: $22,874; Median household: $43,174; Average household: $55,574; Households with income of $100,000 or more: 14.0%; Poverty rate: 21.0%
Educational Attainment: High school diploma or higher: 83.9%; Bachelor's degree or higher: 22.3%; Graduate/professional degree or higher: 8.0%

School District(s)
Guilderland Central SD (KG-12)
   Enrollment: 4,879 . . . . (518) 456-6200
Niskayuna Central SD (KG-12)
   Enrollment: 4,223 . . . . (518) 377-4666
Rotterdam-Mohonasen Central SD (KG-12)
   Enrollment: 2,789 . . . . (518) 356-8200
Schalmont Central SD (KG-12)
   Enrollment: 1,850 . . . . (518) 355-9200
Schenectady City SD (PK-12)
   Enrollment: 9,816 . . . . (518) 370-8100
Four-year College(s)
Union College (Private, Not-for-profit)
   Enrollment: 2,267 . . . . (518) 388-6000
   Tuition: In-state $53,490; Out-of-state $53,490
Two-year College(s)
Belanger School of Nursing (Private, Not-for-profit)
   Enrollment: 114 . . . . (518) 243-4471
   Tuition: In-state $11,014; Out-of-state $11,014
Schenectady County Community College (Public)
   Enrollment: 6,588 . . . . (518) 381-1200
   Tuition: In-state $4,593; Out-of-state $8,529
Vocational/Technical School(s)
Modern Welding School (Private, For-profit)
   Enrollment: 98 . . . . (518) 374-1216
   Tuition: $15,300
Paul Mitchell the School-Schenectady (Private, For-profit)
   Enrollment: 157 . . . . (518) 370-4590
   Tuition: $13,000
Housing: Homeownership rate: 51.9%; Median home value: $110,800; Median year structure built: Before 1940; Homeowner vacancy rate: 2.8%; Median selected monthly owner costs: $1,312 with a mortgage, $569 without a mortgage; Median gross rent: $854 per month; Rental vacancy rate: 8.7%
Health Insurance: 92.2% have insurance; 56.7% have private insurance; 48.3% have public insurance; 7.8% do not have insurance; 3.6% of children under 18 do not have insurance
Hospitals: Ellis Hospital (368 beds); Sunnyview Hospital & Rehabilitation Center (104 beds)
Safety: Violent crime rate: 89.2 per 10,000 population; Property crime rate: 317.9 per 10,000 population

Newspapers: Daily Gazette (daily circulation 52,000)
Transportation: Commute: 81.8% car, 8.5% public transportation, 5.1% walk, 2.7% work from home; Mean travel time to work: 22.2 minutes; Amtrak: Train service available.
Airports: Schenectady County (general aviation)
Additional Information Contacts
City of Schenectady . . . . (518) 382-5199
    http://www.cityofschenectady.com

SCOTIA (village). Covers a land area of 1.685 square miles and a water area of 0.104 square miles. Located at 42.83° N. Lat; 73.96° W. Long. Elevation is 243 feet.
History: Scotia Naval Supply Depot closed. Settled before 1660, incorporated 1904.
Population: 7,775; Growth (since 2000): -2.3%; Density: 4,613.1 persons per square mile; Race: 93.9% White, 3.5% Black/African American, 0.5% Asian, 0.1% American Indian/Alaska Native, 0.0% Native Hawaiian/Other Pacific Islander, 1.4% Two or more races, 2.3% Hispanic of any race; Average household size: 2.57; Median age: 38.5; Age under 18: 23.2%; Age 65 and over: 14.1%; Males per 100 females: 93.9; Marriage status: 31.1% never married, 48.8% now married, 2.3% separated, 5.6% widowed, 14.4% divorced; Foreign born: 1.4%; Speak English only: 98.2%; With disability: 9.9%; Veterans: 7.8%; Ancestry: 28.4% Irish, 18.7% Italian, 17.7% German, 12.4% English, 10.3% Polish
Employment: 13.6% management, business, and financial, 4.6% computer, engineering, and science, 9.8% education, legal, community service, arts, and media, 4.4% healthcare practitioners, 19.0% service, 35.9% sales and office, 5.1% natural resources, construction, and maintenance, 7.7% production, transportation, and material moving
Income: Per capita: $30,866; Median household: $61,000; Average household: $71,032; Households with income of $100,000 or more: 24.1%; Poverty rate: 7.4%
Educational Attainment: High school diploma or higher: 97.1%; Bachelor's degree or higher: 33.1%; Graduate/professional degree or higher: 13.9%

School District(s)
Burnt Hills-Ballston Lake Central SD (KG-12)
    Enrollment: 3,091 . . . . (518) 399-9141
Scotia-Glenville Central SD (KG-12)
    Enrollment: 2,485 . . . . (518) 382-1215
Housing: Homeownership rate: 72.9%; Median home value: $138,600; Median year structure built: Before 1940; Homeowner vacancy rate: 3.0%; Median selected monthly owner costs: $1,508 with a mortgage, $556 without a mortgage; Median gross rent: $793 per month; Rental vacancy rate: 3.9%
Health Insurance: 95.7% have insurance; 78.9% have private insurance; 28.7% have public insurance; 4.3% do not have insurance; 1.2% of children under 18 do not have insurance
Safety: Violent crime rate: 15.7 per 10,000 population; Property crime rate: 133.3 per 10,000 population
Transportation: Commute: 90.4% car, 2.4% public transportation, 4.6% walk, 1.6% work from home; Mean travel time to work: 20.5 minutes
Additional Information Contacts
Village of Scotia . . . . (518) 374-1071
    http://www.villageofscotia.org

Schoharie County

Located in east central New York, partly in the Catskills; crossed by The Helderbergs; drained by Schoharie and Catskill Creeks. Covers a land area of 621.819 square miles, a water area of 4.508 square miles, and is located in the Eastern Time Zone at 42.59° N. Lat., 74.44° W. Long. The county was founded in 1795. County seat is Schoharie.

Schoharie County is part of the Albany-Schenectady-Troy, NY Metropolitan Statistical Area. The entire metro area includes: Albany County, NY; Rensselaer County, NY; Saratoga County, NY; Schenectady County, NY; Schoharie County, NY

Weather Station: Lansing Manor   Elevation: 1,100 feet

	Jan	Feb	Mar	Apr	May	Jun	Jul	Aug	Sep	Oct	Nov	Dec
High	34	35	44	57	68	77	81	80	72	60	49	38
Low	13	13	22	33	43	53	57	56	49	37	30	19
Precip	2.5	2.0	3.0	3.4	3.7	4.2	4.7	3.5	3.6	4.3	2.9	2.4
Snow	17.0	9.8	10.9	2.2	tr	0.0	0.0	0.0	0.0	0.6	3.7	11.2

High and Low temperatures in degrees Fahrenheit; Precipitation and Snow in inches

Population: 31,611; Growth (since 2000): 0.1%; Density: 50.8 persons per square mile; Race: 96.0% White, 1.6% Black/African American, 0.9% Asian, 0.2% American Indian/Alaska Native, 0.0% Native Hawaiian/Other Pacific Islander, 1.1% two or more races, 3.0% Hispanic of any race; Average household size: 2.41; Median age: 44.1; Age under 18: 18.1%; Age 65 and over: 19.4%; Males per 100 females: 100.0; Marriage status: 32.0% never married, 48.6% now married, 2.3% separated, 7.3% widowed, 12.1% divorced; Foreign born: 2.9%; Speak English only: 96.0%; With disability: 16.0%; Veterans: 9.6%; Ancestry: 25.9% German, 21.7% Irish, 12.7% Italian, 9.4% English, 7.8% Dutch
Religion: Six largest groups: 20.7% Catholicism, 6.3% Methodist/Pietist, 4.6% Lutheran, 2.4% Presbyterian-Reformed, 1.6% Non-denominational Protestant, 1.2% Latter-day Saints
Economy: Unemployment rate: 3.8%; Leading industries: 16.6 % retail trade; 14.5 % construction; 11.2 % accommodation and food services; Farms: 532 totaling 98,369 acres; Company size: 0 employ 1,000 or more persons, 1 employs 500 to 999 persons, 5 employ 100 to 499 persons, 572 employ less than 100 persons; Business ownership: 590 women-owned, n/a Black-owned, n/a Hispanic-owned, n/a Asian-owned, n/a American Indian/Alaska Native-owned
Employment: 14.4% management, business, and financial, 4.0% computer, engineering, and science, 11.2% education, legal, community service, arts, and media, 4.3% healthcare practitioners, 18.3% service, 22.3% sales and office, 13.7% natural resources, construction, and maintenance, 11.8% production, transportation, and material moving
Income: Per capita: $26,953; Median household: $51,842; Average household: $65,357; Households with income of $100,000 or more: 18.8%; Poverty rate: 13.9%
Educational Attainment: High school diploma or higher: 88.7%; Bachelor's degree or higher: 21.6%; Graduate/professional degree or higher: 8.9%
Housing: Homeownership rate: 75.5%; Median home value: $143,300; Median year structure built: 1973; Homeowner vacancy rate: 2.0%; Median selected monthly owner costs: $1,327 with a mortgage, $539 without a mortgage; Median gross rent: $781 per month; Rental vacancy rate: 4.8%
Vital Statistics: Birth rate: 72.6 per 10,000 population; Death rate: 89.1 per 10,000 population; Age-adjusted cancer mortality rate: 153.4 deaths per 100,000 population
Health Insurance: 95.0% have insurance; 69.7% have private insurance; 42.7% have public insurance; 5.0% do not have insurance; 2.9% of children under 18 do not have insurance
Health Care: Physicians: 6.0 per 10,000 population; Dentists: 2.9 per 10,000 population; Hospital beds: 12.7 per 10,000 population; Hospital admissions: 231.8 per 10,000 population
Transportation: Commute: 87.5% car, 1.1% public transportation, 5.9% walk, 4.7% work from home; Mean travel time to work: 29.7 minutes
2016 Presidential Election: 62.9% Trump, 30.2% Clinton, 3.8% Johnson, 2.0% Stein
National and State Parks: Max V Shaul State Park; Mine Kill State Park
Additional Information Contacts
Schoharie Government . . . . (518) 295-8114
    http://www.schohariecounty-ny.gov

Schoharie County Communities

BLENHEIM (town). Covers a land area of 33.933 square miles and a water area of 0.461 square miles. Located at 42.49° N. Lat; 74.52° W. Long.
Population: 323; Growth (since 2000): -2.1%; Density: 9.5 persons per square mile; Race: 98.1% White, 1.5% Black/African American, 0.3% Asian, 0.0% American Indian/Alaska Native, 0.0% Native Hawaiian/Other Pacific Islander, 0.0% Two or more races, 2.8% Hispanic of any race; Average household size: 2.43; Median age: 47.2; Age under 18: 19.8%; Age 65 and over: 30.7%; Males per 100 females: 96.4; Marriage status: 23.7% never married, 58.1% now married, 4.8% separated, 5.6% widowed, 12.6% divorced; Foreign born: 4.3%; Speak English only: 95.2%; With disability: 21.4%; Veterans: 12.7%; Ancestry: 36.2% German, 22.9% Irish, 12.4% Dutch, 9.3% Polish, 8.7% Italian
Employment: 16.8% management, business, and financial, 3.2% computer, engineering, and science, 12.8% education, legal, community service, arts, and media, 6.4% healthcare practitioners, 23.2% service, 24.0% sales and office, 1.6% natural resources, construction, and maintenance, 12.0% production, transportation, and material moving

Income: Per capita: $25,137; Median household: $44,583; Average household: $57,887; Households with income of $100,000 or more: 14.3%; Poverty rate: 15.6%
Educational Attainment: High school diploma or higher: 91.0%; Bachelor's degree or higher: 27.0%; Graduate/professional degree or higher: 10.3%
Housing: Homeownership rate: 87.2%; Median home value: $130,000; Median year structure built: 1976; Homeowner vacancy rate: 3.3%; Median selected monthly owner costs: $1,155 with a mortgage, $479 without a mortgage; Median gross rent: $744 per month; Rental vacancy rate: 22.2%
Health Insurance: 97.5% have insurance; 69.0% have private insurance; 47.1% have public insurance; 2.5% do not have insurance; 0.0% of children under 18 do not have insurance
Transportation: Commute: 90.2% car, 0.0% public transportation, 1.6% walk, 6.5% work from home; Mean travel time to work: 28.8 minutes

BROOME (town). Covers a land area of 47.741 square miles and a water area of 0.250 square miles. Located at 42.50° N. Lat; 74.29° W. Long.
Population: 790; Growth (since 2000): -16.6%; Density: 16.5 persons per square mile; Race: 97.6% White, 0.3% Black/African American, 0.4% Asian, 0.0% American Indian/Alaska Native, 0.0% Native Hawaiian/Other Pacific Islander, 0.4% Two or more races, 6.5% Hispanic of any race; Average household size: 2.04; Median age: 53.2; Age under 18: 10.1%; Age 65 and over: 28.6%; Males per 100 females: 107.9; Marriage status: 24.8% never married, 57.1% now married, 4.2% separated, 6.7% widowed, 11.4% divorced; Foreign born: 6.6%; Speak English only: 94.4%; With disability: 13.3%; Veterans: 10.0%; Ancestry: 23.7% Irish, 19.4% German, 12.7% Italian, 8.6% English, 7.6% American
Employment: 7.6% management, business, and financial, 2.1% computer, engineering, and science, 9.7% education, legal, community service, arts, and media, 1.2% healthcare practitioners, 14.9% service, 24.0% sales and office, 20.7% natural resources, construction, and maintenance, 19.8% production, transportation, and material moving
Income: Per capita: $30,647; Median household: $48,077; Average household: $61,488; Households with income of $100,000 or more: 16.2%; Poverty rate: 9.0%
Educational Attainment: High school diploma or higher: 87.0%; Bachelor's degree or higher: 14.5%; Graduate/professional degree or higher: 6.9%
Housing: Homeownership rate: 93.0%; Median home value: $139,600; Median year structure built: 1977; Homeowner vacancy rate: 0.8%; Median selected monthly owner costs: $1,423 with a mortgage, $544 without a mortgage; Median gross rent: n/a per month; Rental vacancy rate: 0.0%
Health Insurance: 91.6% have insurance; 72.0% have private insurance; 39.5% have public insurance; 8.4% do not have insurance; 3.4% of children under 18 do not have insurance
Transportation: Commute: 85.3% car, 4.6% public transportation, 2.1% walk, 7.0% work from home; Mean travel time to work: 36.3 minutes

CARLISLE (town). Covers a land area of 34.124 square miles and a water area of 0.128 square miles. Located at 42.74° N. Lat; 74.44° W. Long. Elevation is 1,283 feet.
Population: 1,839; Growth (since 2000): 4.6%; Density: 53.9 persons per square mile; Race: 93.1% White, 1.2% Black/African American, 3.6% Asian, 0.2% American Indian/Alaska Native, 0.0% Native Hawaiian/Other Pacific Islander, 1.1% Two or more races, 3.3% Hispanic of any race; Average household size: 2.52; Median age: 42.0; Age under 18: 17.2%; Age 65 and over: 13.9%; Males per 100 females: 100.0; Marriage status: 31.4% never married, 53.6% now married, 1.5% separated, 4.1% widowed, 11.0% divorced; Foreign born: 2.4%; Speak English only: 96.1%; With disability: 8.4%; Veterans: 9.2%; Ancestry: 24.6% German, 20.5% Irish, 11.4% English, 9.0% Italian, 7.9% American
Employment: 21.4% management, business, and financial, 4.0% computer, engineering, and science, 9.8% education, legal, community service, arts, and media, 4.9% healthcare practitioners, 14.0% service, 15.6% sales and office, 19.2% natural resources, construction, and maintenance, 11.2% production, transportation, and material moving
Income: Per capita: $29,968; Median household: $57,407; Average household: $74,043; Households with income of $100,000 or more: 19.5%; Poverty rate: 11.7%
Educational Attainment: High school diploma or higher: 90.3%; Bachelor's degree or higher: 27.6%; Graduate/professional degree or higher: 8.0%

Housing: Homeownership rate: 80.1%; Median home value: $140,000; Median year structure built: 1973; Homeowner vacancy rate: 0.5%; Median selected monthly owner costs: $1,384 with a mortgage, $524 without a mortgage; Median gross rent: $808 per month; Rental vacancy rate: 0.0%
Health Insurance: 94.3% have insurance; 74.7% have private insurance; 30.1% have public insurance; 5.7% do not have insurance; 0.9% of children under 18 do not have insurance
Transportation: Commute: 91.1% car, 0.0% public transportation, 3.4% walk, 4.9% work from home; Mean travel time to work: 31.5 minutes

CENTRAL BRIDGE (CDP). Covers a land area of 1.843 square miles and a water area of 0.014 square miles. Located at 42.71° N. Lat; 74.35° W. Long. Elevation is 620 feet.
Population: 238; Growth (since 2000): n/a; Density: 129.1 persons per square mile; Race: 89.5% White, 0.0% Black/African American, 0.0% Asian, 0.0% American Indian/Alaska Native, 0.0% Native Hawaiian/Other Pacific Islander, 10.5% Two or more races, 0.0% Hispanic of any race; Average household size: 2.22; Median age: 37.9; Age under 18: 16.4%; Age 65 and over: 43.3%; Males per 100 females: 97.7; Marriage status: 18.0% never married, 82.0% now married, 8.5% separated, 0.0% widowed, 0.0% divorced; Foreign born: 0.0%; Speak English only: 100.0%; With disability: 11.3%; Veterans: 27.1%; Ancestry: 52.5% German, 17.2% Norwegian, 14.7% French, 14.3% Irish, 10.9% Italian
Employment: 19.8% management, business, and financial, 8.6% computer, engineering, and science, 22.2% education, legal, community service, arts, and media, 0.0% healthcare practitioners, 0.0% service, 29.6% sales and office, 0.0% natural resources, construction, and maintenance, 19.8% production, transportation, and material moving
Income: Per capita: $15,048; Median household: $31,536; Average household: $35,370; Households with income of $100,000 or more: n/a; Poverty rate: 28.6%
Educational Attainment: High school diploma or higher: 84.4%; Bachelor's degree or higher: 13.3%; Graduate/professional degree or higher: 4.0%
Housing: Homeownership rate: 58.9%; Median home value: $79,000; Median year structure built: 1953; Homeowner vacancy rate: 0.0%; Median selected monthly owner costs: n/a with a mortgage, n/a without a mortgage; Median gross rent: $632 per month; Rental vacancy rate: 0.0%
Health Insurance: 100.0% have insurance; 100.0% have private insurance; 50.8% have public insurance; 0.0% do not have insurance; 0.0% of children under 18 do not have insurance
Transportation: Commute: 89.2% car, 0.0% public transportation, 0.0% walk, 10.8% work from home; Mean travel time to work: 0.0 minutes

CHARLOTTEVILLE (unincorporated postal area)
ZCTA: 12036
Covers a land area of 7.406 square miles and a water area of 0.008 square miles. Located at 42.54° N. Lat; 74.67° W. Long. Elevation is 1,604 feet.
Population: 270; Growth (since 2000): 1.9%; Density: 36.5 persons per square mile; Race: 98.5% White, 0.0% Black/African American, 1.5% Asian, 0.0% American Indian/Alaska Native, 0.0% Native Hawaiian/Other Pacific Islander, 0.0% Two or more races, 10.0% Hispanic of any race; Average household size: 2.43; Median age: 41.1; Age under 18: 20.7%; Age 65 and over: 21.9%; Males per 100 females: 103.6; Marriage status: 44.3% never married, 32.9% now married, 0.0% separated, 11.9% widowed, 11.0% divorced; Foreign born: 8.5%; Speak English only: 87.7%; With disability: 18.1%; Veterans: 9.8%; Ancestry: 24.1% German, 18.5% American, 18.1% Irish, 11.5% Dutch, 6.3% Swiss
Employment: 7.8% management, business, and financial, 5.2% computer, engineering, and science, 3.5% education, legal, community service, arts, and media, 0.0% healthcare practitioners, 26.1% service, 19.1% sales and office, 11.3% natural resources, construction, and maintenance, 27.0% production, transportation, and material moving
Income: Per capita: $22,631; Median household: $41,696; Average household: $49,629; Households with income of $100,000 or more: 8.1%; Poverty rate: 26.7%
Educational Attainment: High school diploma or higher: 83.9%; Bachelor's degree or higher: 16.6%; Graduate/professional degree or higher: 8.3%
Housing: Homeownership rate: 91.9%; Median home value: $147,200; Median year structure built: 1964; Homeowner vacancy rate: 0.0%; Median selected monthly owner costs: $1,150 with a mortgage, $400

without a mortgage; Median gross rent: n/a per month; Rental vacancy rate: 0.0%
Health Insurance: 92.2% have insurance; 44.4% have private insurance; 59.3% have public insurance; 7.8% do not have insurance; 0.0% of children under 18 do not have insurance
Transportation: Commute: 82.0% car, 5.4% public transportation, 5.4% walk, 3.6% work from home; Mean travel time to work: 33.9 minutes

COBLESKILL (town).
Covers a land area of 30.599 square miles and a water area of 0.179 square miles. Located at 42.69° N. Lat; 74.44° W. Long. Elevation is 922 feet.
History: The Borst & Burnhans Plant began in Cobleskill in 1800 as a feed, flour, and grist mill, and became famous for its pancake flour in 1890. The Harder Refrigerator Plant, established in 1859, made threshing machines, silos, manure spreaders, and refrigerators. Seat of State University of N.Y. College. of Agriculture and Technology at Cobleskill. Cobleskill Historic District. Settled in 1752, incorporated in 1868.
Population: 6,484; Growth (since 2000): 1.2%; Density: 211.9 persons per square mile; Race: 91.6% White, 5.7% Black/African American, 0.2% Asian, 0.4% American Indian/Alaska Native, 0.2% Native Hawaiian/Other Pacific Islander, 1.7% Two or more races, 3.7% Hispanic of any race; Average household size: 2.27; Median age: 33.1; Age under 18: 15.4%; Age 65 and over: 17.4%; Males per 100 females: 94.9; Marriage status: 46.6% never married, 33.4% now married, 2.0% separated, 7.9% widowed, 12.2% divorced; Foreign born: 2.7%; Speak English only: 94.7%; With disability: 15.6%; Veterans: 6.7%; Ancestry: 22.5% Irish, 18.2% German, 14.6% Italian, 7.6% American, 6.6% English
Employment: 10.0% management, business, and financial, 3.5% computer, engineering, and science, 12.8% education, legal, community service, arts, and media, 4.7% healthcare practitioners, 29.4% service, 22.9% sales and office, 7.8% natural resources, construction, and maintenance, 8.9% production, transportation, and material moving
Income: Per capita: $23,440; Median household: $40,313; Average household: $62,288; Households with income of $100,000 or more: 19.8%; Poverty rate: 18.2%
Educational Attainment: High school diploma or higher: 89.9%; Bachelor's degree or higher: 23.6%; Graduate/professional degree or higher: 11.4%

School District(s)
Cobleskill-Richmondville Central SD (PK-12)
   Enrollment: 1,718 . . . . (518) 234-4032
Four-year College(s)
SUNY College of Agriculture and Technology at Cobleskill (Public)
   Enrollment: 2,291 . . . . (518) 255-5525
   Tuition: In-state $8,139; Out-of-state $17,789
Housing: Homeownership rate: 49.8%; Median home value: $151,800; Median year structure built: 1969; Homeowner vacancy rate: 0.0%; Median selected monthly owner costs: $1,480 with a mortgage, $560 without a mortgage; Median gross rent: $797 per month; Rental vacancy rate: 4.6%
Health Insurance: 95.7% have insurance; 68.9% have private insurance; 40.7% have public insurance; 4.3% do not have insurance; 3.7% of children under 18 do not have insurance
Hospitals: Cobleskill Regional Hospital (40 beds)
Newspapers: Cobleskill Times-Journal (weekly circulation 6,000)
Transportation: Commute: 72.8% car, 1.0% public transportation, 20.4% walk, 4.6% work from home; Mean travel time to work: 20.3 minutes
Additional Information Contacts
Town of Cobleskill . . . . (518) 234-1719
   http://www.townofcobleskill.com

COBLESKILL (village).
Covers a land area of 3.572 square miles and a water area of 0.004 square miles. Located at 42.68° N. Lat; 74.49° W. Long. Elevation is 922 feet.
Population: 4,697; Growth (since 2000): 3.6%; Density: 1,315.0 persons per square mile; Race: 88.6% White, 7.8% Black/African American, 0.3% Asian, 0.6% American Indian/Alaska Native, 0.2% Native Hawaiian/Other Pacific Islander, 2.2% Two or more races, 5.1% Hispanic of any race; Average household size: 2.23; Median age: 24.9; Age under 18: 13.7%; Age 65 and over: 14.9%; Males per 100 females: 93.0; Marriage status: 57.2% never married, 25.9% now married, 2.2% separated, 6.8% widowed, 10.1% divorced; Foreign born: 3.4%; Speak English only: 93.4%; With disability: 18.2%; Veterans: 5.8%; Ancestry: 22.7% Irish, 18.9% German, 13.0% Italian, 7.8% American, 5.9% English
Employment: 8.7% management, business, and financial, 3.5% computer, engineering, and science, 7.5% education, legal, community service, arts,

and media, 4.5% healthcare practitioners, 37.2% service, 23.7% sales and office, 7.1% natural resources, construction, and maintenance, 7.9% production, transportation, and material moving
Income: Per capita: $18,824; Median household: $34,495; Average household: $52,553; Households with income of $100,000 or more: 14.9%; Poverty rate: 24.9%
Educational Attainment: High school diploma or higher: 84.1%; Bachelor's degree or higher: 24.3%; Graduate/professional degree or higher: 9.6%

School District(s)
Cobleskill-Richmondville Central SD (PK-12)
   Enrollment: 1,718 . . . . (518) 234-4032
Four-year College(s)
SUNY College of Agriculture and Technology at Cobleskill (Public)
   Enrollment: 2,291 . . . . (518) 255-5525
   Tuition: In-state $8,139; Out-of-state $17,789
Housing: Homeownership rate: 33.4%; Median home value: $137,300; Median year structure built: 1965; Homeowner vacancy rate: 0.0%; Median selected monthly owner costs: $1,525 with a mortgage, $633 without a mortgage; Median gross rent: $777 per month; Rental vacancy rate: 5.2%
Health Insurance: 95.3% have insurance; 68.5% have private insurance; 38.5% have public insurance; 4.7% do not have insurance; 4.9% of children under 18 do not have insurance
Hospitals: Cobleskill Regional Hospital (40 beds)
Safety: Violent crime rate: 13.2 per 10,000 population; Property crime rate: 244.5 per 10,000 population
Newspapers: Cobleskill Times-Journal (weekly circulation 6,000)
Transportation: Commute: 65.9% car, 1.4% public transportation, 28.3% walk, 2.6% work from home; Mean travel time to work: 19.4 minutes
Additional Information Contacts
Village of Cobleskill . . . . (518) 234-3891
   http://www.schohariecounty-ny.gov/CountyWebSite/villcob

CONESVILLE (town).
Covers a land area of 39.466 square miles and a water area of 0.404 square miles. Located at 42.40° N. Lat; 74.34° W. Long. Elevation is 1,381 feet.
Population: 785; Growth (since 2000): 8.1%; Density: 19.9 persons per square mile; Race: 95.5% White, 0.0% Black/African American, 0.9% Asian, 0.0% American Indian/Alaska Native, 0.0% Native Hawaiian/Other Pacific Islander, 0.6% Two or more races, 10.3% Hispanic of any race; Average household size: 2.34; Median age: 52.6; Age under 18: 10.7%; Age 65 and over: 26.4%; Males per 100 females: 96.3; Marriage status: 23.9% never married, 55.3% now married, 2.8% separated, 3.6% widowed, 17.2% divorced; Foreign born: 9.0%; Speak English only: 88.4%; With disability: 16.3%; Veterans: 9.3%; Ancestry: 22.0% German, 21.5% Irish, 18.5% Italian, 12.6% English, 9.2% Dutch
Employment: 13.8% management, business, and financial, 2.1% computer, engineering, and science, 13.0% education, legal, community service, arts, and media, 2.4% healthcare practitioners, 23.9% service, 13.8% sales and office, 17.8% natural resources, construction, and maintenance, 13.3% production, transportation, and material moving
Income: Per capita: $28,722; Median household: $54,044; Average household: $61,983; Households with income of $100,000 or more: 16.4%; Poverty rate: 12.9%
Educational Attainment: High school diploma or higher: 88.1%; Bachelor's degree or higher: 19.8%; Graduate/professional degree or higher: 9.5%
Housing: Homeownership rate: 94.6%; Median home value: $119,000; Median year structure built: 1981; Homeowner vacancy rate: 1.9%; Median selected monthly owner costs: $1,056 with a mortgage, $505 without a mortgage; Median gross rent: n/a per month; Rental vacancy rate: 10.0%
Health Insurance: 90.4% have insurance; 67.1% have private insurance; 41.7% have public insurance; 9.6% do not have insurance; 4.1% of children under 18 do not have insurance
Transportation: Commute: 81.8% car, 2.3% public transportation, 1.5% walk, 13.8% work from home; Mean travel time to work: 42.2 minutes

ESPERANCE (town).
Covers a land area of 19.666 square miles and a water area of 0.371 square miles. Located at 42.75° N. Lat; 74.32° W. Long. Elevation is 581 feet.
Population: 1,858; Growth (since 2000): -9.1%; Density: 94.5 persons per square mile; Race: 98.1% White, 0.0% Black/African American, 0.5% Asian, 0.0% American Indian/Alaska Native, 0.0% Native Hawaiian/Other Pacific Islander, 1.4% Two or more races, 2.7% Hispanic of any race; Average household size: 2.47; Median age: 43.6; Age under 18: 21.7%;

Age 65 and over: 20.0%; Males per 100 females: 101.6; Marriage status: 27.8% never married, 53.0% now married, 2.7% separated, 8.1% widowed, 11.1% divorced; Foreign born: 1.6%; Speak English only: 99.1%; With disability: 16.5%; Veterans: 10.0%; Ancestry: 27.1% German, 16.5% Irish, 11.2% Dutch, 10.2% Italian, 7.7% English

Employment: 12.0% management, business, and financial, 4.6% computer, engineering, and science, 8.3% education, legal, community service, arts, and media, 5.1% healthcare practitioners, 16.8% service, 26.3% sales and office, 11.2% natural resources, construction, and maintenance, 15.7% production, transportation, and material moving

Income: Per capita: $29,225; Median household: $57,734; Average household: $69,744; Households with income of $100,000 or more: 18.6%; Poverty rate: 10.2%

Educational Attainment: High school diploma or higher: 91.6%; Bachelor's degree or higher: 17.0%; Graduate/professional degree or higher: 4.8%

Housing: Homeownership rate: 82.7%; Median home value: $113,000; Median year structure built: 1974; Homeowner vacancy rate: 5.9%; Median selected monthly owner costs: $1,391 with a mortgage, $473 without a mortgage; Median gross rent: $982 per month; Rental vacancy rate: 0.0%

Health Insurance: 94.2% have insurance; 77.7% have private insurance; 39.8% have public insurance; 5.8% do not have insurance; 1.6% of children under 18 do not have insurance

Transportation: Commute: 95.0% car, 0.0% public transportation, 1.7% walk, 1.7% work from home; Mean travel time to work: 29.8 minutes

Additional Information Contacts

Town of Esperance . . . . (518) 875-6109
  http://townofesperance.org

ESPERANCE (village). Covers a land area of 0.491 square miles and a water area of 0.030 square miles. Located at 42.76° N. Lat; 74.26° W. Long. Elevation is 581 feet.

Population: 394; Growth (since 2000): 3.7%; Density: 802.3 persons per square mile; Race: 97.7% White, 0.0% Black/African American, 2.3% Asian, 0.0% American Indian/Alaska Native, 0.0% Native Hawaiian/Other Pacific Islander, 0.0% Two or more races, 3.8% Hispanic of any race; Average household size: 2.79; Median age: 39.0; Age under 18: 27.4%; Age 65 and over: 15.5%; Males per 100 females: 106.6; Marriage status: 29.1% never married, 51.8% now married, 1.9% separated, 7.4% widowed, 11.7% divorced; Foreign born: 1.8%; Speak English only: 99.0%; With disability: 15.5%; Veterans: 10.4%; Ancestry: 29.7% German, 24.9% Irish, 12.9% Italian, 10.7% French, 9.6% Scottish

Employment: 9.6% management, business, and financial, 8.5% computer, engineering, and science, 10.2% education, legal, community service, arts, and media, 4.5% healthcare practitioners, 15.3% service, 26.6% sales and office, 12.4% natural resources, construction, and maintenance, 13.0% production, transportation, and material moving

Income: Per capita: $24,290; Median household: $60,511; Average household: $63,026; Households with income of $100,000 or more: 19.1%; Poverty rate: 5.9%

Educational Attainment: High school diploma or higher: 96.1%; Bachelor's degree or higher: 14.1%; Graduate/professional degree or higher: 7.5%

Housing: Homeownership rate: 85.1%; Median home value: $133,300; Median year structure built: 1950; Homeowner vacancy rate: 0.0%; Median selected monthly owner costs: $1,286 with a mortgage, $633 without a mortgage; Median gross rent: $1,250 per month; Rental vacancy rate: 0.0%

Health Insurance: 94.6% have insurance; 75.8% have private insurance; 32.5% have public insurance; 5.4% do not have insurance; 6.3% of children under 18 do not have insurance

Transportation: Commute: 90.0% car, 0.0% public transportation, 5.0% walk, 1.7% work from home; Mean travel time to work: 35.8 minutes

FULTON (town). Covers a land area of 64.978 square miles and a water area of 0.027 square miles. Located at 42.59° N. Lat; 74.45° W. Long.

Population: 1,313; Growth (since 2000): -12.2%; Density: 20.2 persons per square mile; Race: 97.7% White, 0.2% Black/African American, 0.0% Asian, 0.2% American Indian/Alaska Native, 0.0% Native Hawaiian/Other Pacific Islander, 1.9% Two or more races, 0.2% Hispanic of any race; Average household size: 2.39; Median age: 43.6; Age under 18: 21.3%; Age 65 and over: 18.3%; Males per 100 females: 127.8; Marriage status: 24.8% never married, 55.0% now married, 2.3% separated, 10.0% widowed, 10.2% divorced; Foreign born: 3.5%; Speak English only: 96.7%;

With disability: 20.0%; Veterans: 13.3%; Ancestry: 35.6% German, 20.1% Irish, 12.0% Dutch, 8.3% English, 8.0% Italian

Employment: 10.3% management, business, and financial, 2.1% computer, engineering, and science, 8.6% education, legal, community service, arts, and media, 10.1% healthcare practitioners, 15.0% service, 16.5% sales and office, 24.0% natural resources, construction, and maintenance, 13.3% production, transportation, and material moving

Income: Per capita: $27,909; Median household: $40,114; Average household: $65,654; Households with income of $100,000 or more: 18.9%; Poverty rate: 12.6%

Educational Attainment: High school diploma or higher: 82.3%; Bachelor's degree or higher: 17.7%; Graduate/professional degree or higher: 7.4%

Housing: Homeownership rate: 82.1%; Median home value: $121,800; Median year structure built: 1974; Homeowner vacancy rate: 2.6%; Median selected monthly owner costs: $1,140 with a mortgage, $485 without a mortgage; Median gross rent: $803 per month; Rental vacancy rate: 0.0%

Health Insurance: 95.0% have insurance; 64.8% have private insurance; 48.9% have public insurance; 5.0% do not have insurance; 0.0% of children under 18 do not have insurance

Transportation: Commute: 90.2% car, 1.1% public transportation, 2.2% walk, 4.7% work from home; Mean travel time to work: 29.6 minutes

FULTONHAM (unincorporated postal area)
ZCTA: 12071

Covers a land area of 9.231 square miles and a water area of 0 square miles. Located at 42.55° N. Lat; 74.42° W. Long. Elevation is 702 feet.

Population: 360; Growth (since 2000): 29.0%; Density: 39.0 persons per square mile; Race: 98.6% White, 0.8% Black/African American, 0.0% Asian, 0.6% American Indian/Alaska Native, 0.0% Native Hawaiian/Other Pacific Islander, 0.0% Two or more races, 0.0% Hispanic of any race; Average household size: 2.88; Median age: 38.8; Age under 18: 26.7%; Age 65 and over: 18.3%; Males per 100 females: 104.5; Marriage status: 30.7% never married, 47.1% now married, 1.1% separated, 18.9% widowed, 3.2% divorced; Foreign born: 11.7%; Speak English only: 92.9%; With disability: 25.0%; Veterans: 7.6%; Ancestry: 46.9% German, 14.2% Dutch, 10.6% Danish, 9.7% English, 8.3% Polish

Employment: 17.7% management, business, and financial, 0.0% computer, engineering, and science, 3.1% education, legal, community service, arts, and media, 10.0% healthcare practitioners, 5.4% service, 27.7% sales and office, 11.5% natural resources, construction, and maintenance, 24.6% production, transportation, and material moving

Income: Per capita: $25,105; Median household: $52,375; Average household: $69,890; Households with income of $100,000 or more: 23.2%; Poverty rate: 20.3%

Educational Attainment: High school diploma or higher: 83.8%; Bachelor's degree or higher: 13.6%; Graduate/professional degree or higher: n/a

Housing: Homeownership rate: 72.0%; Median home value: $153,100; Median year structure built: 1971; Homeowner vacancy rate: 0.0%; Median selected monthly owner costs: $1,203 with a mortgage, $632 without a mortgage; Median gross rent: n/a per month; Rental vacancy rate: 0.0%

Health Insurance: 96.1% have insurance; 66.1% have private insurance; 39.2% have public insurance; 3.9% do not have insurance; 0.0% of children under 18 do not have insurance

Transportation: Commute: 91.5% car, 0.0% public transportation, 0.0% walk, 8.5% work from home; Mean travel time to work: 24.4 minutes

GILBOA (town). Covers a land area of 57.800 square miles and a water area of 1.576 square miles. Located at 42.43° N. Lat; 74.45° W. Long. Elevation is 1,027 feet.

Population: 1,303; Growth (since 2000): 7.2%; Density: 22.5 persons per square mile; Race: 97.5% White, 0.1% Black/African American, 0.0% Asian, 0.0% American Indian/Alaska Native, 0.0% Native Hawaiian/Other Pacific Islander, 1.5% Two or more races, 3.6% Hispanic of any race; Average household size: 2.67; Median age: 47.6; Age under 18: 17.5%; Age 65 and over: 22.3%; Males per 100 females: 104.9; Marriage status: 26.6% never married, 58.0% now married, 2.8% separated, 5.7% widowed, 9.7% divorced; Foreign born: 3.7%; Speak English only: 95.2%; With disability: 16.2%; Veterans: 8.7%; Ancestry: 30.6% German, 26.3% Irish, 13.8% Italian, 9.8% Dutch, 9.7% English

Employment: 9.2% management, business, and financial, 1.2% computer, engineering, and science, 9.9% education, legal, community service, arts,

and media, 6.0% healthcare practitioners, 13.4% service, 25.7% sales and office, 16.3% natural resources, construction, and maintenance, 18.3% production, transportation, and material moving

Income: Per capita: $30,493; Median household: $64,265; Average household: $78,483; Households with income of $100,000 or more: 22.4%; Poverty rate: 8.2%

Educational Attainment: High school diploma or higher: 91.3%; Bachelor's degree or higher: 16.4%; Graduate/professional degree or higher: 6.5%

School District(s)
Gilboa-Conesville Central SD (PK-12)
    Enrollment: 304.............................. (607) 588-7541

Housing: Homeownership rate: 84.2%; Median home value: $140,100; Median year structure built: 1981; Homeowner vacancy rate: 0.0%; Median selected monthly owner costs: $1,209 with a mortgage, $368 without a mortgage; Median gross rent: $900 per month; Rental vacancy rate: 0.0%

Health Insurance: 88.0% have insurance; 64.2% have private insurance; 43.7% have public insurance; 12.0% do not have insurance; 20.8% of children under 18 do not have insurance

Transportation: Commute: 94.5% car, 0.0% public transportation, 2.5% walk, 3.0% work from home; Mean travel time to work: 26.2 minutes

HOWES CAVE (unincorporated postal area)
ZCTA: 12092

Covers a land area of 14.957 square miles and a water area of 0.172 square miles. Located at 42.70° N. Lat; 74.38° W. Long. Elevation is 781 feet.

Population: 730; Growth (since 2000): -15.2%; Density: 48.8 persons per square mile; Race: 96.6% White, 0.0% Black/African American, 0.0% Asian, 0.0% American Indian/Alaska Native, 0.0% Native Hawaiian/Other Pacific Islander, 3.4% Two or more races, 1.2% Hispanic of any race; Average household size: 2.13; Median age: 51.5; Age under 18: 16.4%; Age 65 and over: 27.8%; Males per 100 females: 97.0; Marriage status: 24.8% never married, 43.2% now married, 2.9% separated, 19.5% widowed, 12.5% divorced; Foreign born: 1.8%; Speak English only: 98.1%; With disability: 17.0%; Veterans: 3.4%; Ancestry: 29.9% German, 20.1% American, 16.4% Italian, 14.4% Irish, 11.1% Dutch

Employment: 21.4% management, business, and financial, 7.0% computer, engineering, and science, 11.1% education, legal, community service, arts, and media, 3.5% healthcare practitioners, 11.7% service, 8.5% sales and office, 15.5% natural resources, construction, and maintenance, 21.1% production, transportation, and material moving

Income: Per capita: $26,604; Median household: $32,692; Average household: $56,142; Households with income of $100,000 or more: 17.5%; Poverty rate: 7.7%

Educational Attainment: High school diploma or higher: 95.0%; Bachelor's degree or higher: 16.1%; Graduate/professional degree or higher: 5.0%

Housing: Homeownership rate: 65.8%; Median home value: $111,800; Median year structure built: 1973; Homeowner vacancy rate: 0.0%; Median selected monthly owner costs: $1,169 with a mortgage, $455 without a mortgage; Median gross rent: $738 per month; Rental vacancy rate: 0.0%

Health Insurance: 93.7% have insurance; 61.0% have private insurance; 58.9% have public insurance; 6.3% do not have insurance; 0.0% of children under 18 do not have insurance

Transportation: Commute: 76.0% car, 0.0% public transportation, 10.2% walk, 13.8% work from home; Mean travel time to work: 23.9 minutes

JEFFERSON (town). Covers a land area of 43.251 square miles and a water area of 0.163 square miles. Located at 42.49° N. Lat; 74.61° W. Long. Elevation is 1,867 feet.

Population: 1,443; Growth (since 2000): 12.3%; Density: 33.4 persons per square mile; Race: 99.2% White, 0.1% Black/African American, 0.3% Asian, 0.0% American Indian/Alaska Native, 0.0% Native Hawaiian/Other Pacific Islander, 0.3% Two or more races, 3.0% Hispanic of any race; Average household size: 2.38; Median age: 48.5; Age under 18: 20.1%; Age 65 and over: 20.2%; Males per 100 females: 105.8; Marriage status: 25.6% never married, 54.1% now married, 1.9% separated, 7.7% widowed, 12.6% divorced; Foreign born: 3.0%; Speak English only: 97.0%; With disability: 17.5%; Veterans: 8.5%; Ancestry: 28.8% German, 20.7% Irish, 18.6% Italian, 11.6% English, 6.4% Dutch

Employment: 13.9% management, business, and financial, 3.1% computer, engineering, and science, 14.9% education, legal, community service, arts, and media, 3.1% healthcare practitioners, 14.5% service, 22.2% sales and office, 13.6% natural resources, construction, and maintenance, 14.7% production, transportation, and material moving

Income: Per capita: $26,995; Median household: $51,534; Average household: $64,131; Households with income of $100,000 or more: 12.9%; Poverty rate: 10.1%

Educational Attainment: High school diploma or higher: 81.2%; Bachelor's degree or higher: 21.3%; Graduate/professional degree or higher: 9.1%

School District(s)
Jefferson Central SD (PK-12)
    Enrollment: 246.............................. (607) 652-7821

Housing: Homeownership rate: 84.3%; Median home value: $166,000; Median year structure built: 1977; Homeowner vacancy rate: 0.0%; Median selected monthly owner costs: $1,265 with a mortgage, $573 without a mortgage; Median gross rent: $537 per month; Rental vacancy rate: 0.0%

Health Insurance: 89.9% have insurance; 66.5% have private insurance; 45.6% have public insurance; 10.1% do not have insurance; 14.0% of children under 18 do not have insurance

Transportation: Commute: 89.4% car, 1.2% public transportation, 2.2% walk, 6.2% work from home; Mean travel time to work: 29.7 minutes

MIDDLEBURGH (town). Covers a land area of 49.111 square miles and a water area of 0.098 square miles. Located at 42.62° N. Lat; 74.31° W. Long. Elevation is 640 feet.

Population: 3,594; Growth (since 2000): 2.2%; Density: 73.2 persons per square mile; Race: 97.5% White, 1.1% Black/African American, 1.3% Asian, 0.0% American Indian/Alaska Native, 0.0% Native Hawaiian/Other Pacific Islander, 0.1% Two or more races, 3.6% Hispanic of any race; Average household size: 2.23; Median age: 49.1; Age under 18: 15.7%; Age 65 and over: 24.8%; Males per 100 females: 94.6; Marriage status: 33.0% never married, 44.6% now married, 1.8% separated, 9.4% widowed, 12.9% divorced; Foreign born: 1.3%; Speak English only: 96.1%; With disability: 25.9%; Veterans: 12.6%; Ancestry: 27.4% German, 21.0% Irish, 11.4% Dutch, 10.8% Italian, 10.7% English

Employment: 16.1% management, business, and financial, 6.4% computer, engineering, and science, 13.6% education, legal, community service, arts, and media, 3.9% healthcare practitioners, 14.2% service, 18.8% sales and office, 14.5% natural resources, construction, and maintenance, 12.6% production, transportation, and material moving

Income: Per capita: $28,216; Median household: $48,317; Average household: $61,930; Households with income of $100,000 or more: 18.2%; Poverty rate: 15.3%

Educational Attainment: High school diploma or higher: 86.8%; Bachelor's degree or higher: 20.6%; Graduate/professional degree or higher: 8.5%

School District(s)
Middleburgh Central SD (PK-12)
    Enrollment: 804.............................. (518) 827-3625

Housing: Homeownership rate: 80.7%; Median home value: $114,800; Median year structure built: 1951; Homeowner vacancy rate: 3.9%; Median selected monthly owner costs: $1,114 with a mortgage, $578 without a mortgage; Median gross rent: $798 per month; Rental vacancy rate: 13.0%

Health Insurance: 96.7% have insurance; 69.4% have private insurance; 49.8% have public insurance; 3.3% do not have insurance; 1.6% of children under 18 do not have insurance

Transportation: Commute: 94.3% car, 2.1% public transportation, 1.9% walk, 1.7% work from home; Mean travel time to work: 35.8 minutes

MIDDLEBURGH (village). Covers a land area of 1.247 square miles and a water area of 0 square miles. Located at 42.60° N. Lat; 74.33° W. Long. Elevation is 640 feet.

Population: 1,542; Growth (since 2000): 10.3%; Density: 1,236.2 persons per square mile; Race: 96.6% White, 0.2% Black/African American, 2.9% Asian, 0.0% American Indian/Alaska Native, 0.0% Native Hawaiian/Other Pacific Islander, 0.3% Two or more races, 7.3% Hispanic of any race; Average household size: 2.29; Median age: 43.5; Age under 18: 20.9%; Age 65 and over: 20.6%; Males per 100 females: 85.9; Marriage status: 36.3% never married, 43.2% now married, 1.3% separated, 5.8% widowed, 14.7% divorced; Foreign born: 2.9%; Speak English only: 91.6%; With disability: 20.4%; Veterans: 9.3%; Ancestry: 27.0% Irish, 23.9% German, 14.6% English, 8.8% Dutch, 8.6% Italian

Employment: 15.1% management, business, and financial, 1.3% computer, engineering, and science, 14.3% education, legal, community service, arts, and media, 6.0% healthcare practitioners, 19.4% service, 23.0% sales and office, 9.2% natural resources, construction, and maintenance, 11.8% production, transportation, and material moving
Income: Per capita: $25,198; Median household: $47,292; Average household: $56,592; Households with income of $100,000 or more: 12.1%; Poverty rate: 14.9%
Educational Attainment: High school diploma or higher: 90.3%; Bachelor's degree or higher: 21.5%; Graduate/professional degree or higher: 11.6%

School District(s)
Middleburgh Central SD (PK-12)
    Enrollment: 804 . . . . (518) 827-3625
Housing: Homeownership rate: 66.8%; Median home value: $128,300; Median year structure built: 1956; Homeowner vacancy rate: 1.3%; Median selected monthly owner costs: $1,259 with a mortgage, $750 without a mortgage; Median gross rent: $754 per month; Rental vacancy rate: 17.2%
Health Insurance: 94.4% have insurance; 76.8% have private insurance; 37.9% have public insurance; 5.6% do not have insurance; 2.8% of children under 18 do not have insurance
Transportation: Commute: 91.4% car, 0.8% public transportation, 4.0% walk, 3.7% work from home; Mean travel time to work: 26.8 minutes

NORTH BLENHEIM (unincorporated postal area)
ZCTA: 12131
    Covers a land area of 7.065 square miles and a water area of 0.405 square miles. Located at 42.46° N. Lat; 74.46° W. Long. Elevation is 791 feet.
Population: 111; Growth (since 2000): -48.8%; Density: 15.7 persons per square mile; Race: 100.0% White, 0.0% Black/African American, 0.0% Asian, 0.0% American Indian/Alaska Native, 0.0% Native Hawaiian/Other Pacific Islander, 0.0% Two or more races, 0.0% Hispanic of any race; Average household size: 2.85; Median age: 43.6; Age under 18: 18.0%; Age 65 and over: 28.8%; Males per 100 females: 117.0; Marriage status: 31.6% never married, 48.4% now married, 3.2% separated, 5.3% widowed, 14.7% divorced; Foreign born: 2.7%; Speak English only: 93.5%; With disability: 31.5%; Veterans: 8.8%; Ancestry: 50.5% German, 20.7% Irish, 14.4% Polish, 12.6% Italian, 11.7% American
Employment: 5.6% management, business, and financial, 11.1% computer, engineering, and science, 8.3% education, legal, community service, arts, and media, 8.3% healthcare practitioners, 30.6% service, 11.1% sales and office, 0.0% natural resources, construction, and maintenance, 25.0% production, transportation, and material moving
Income: Per capita: $25,884; Median household: $53,750; Average household: $65,456; Households with income of $100,000 or more: 15.4%; Poverty rate: 21.1%
Educational Attainment: High school diploma or higher: 85.0%; Bachelor's degree or higher: 15.0%; Graduate/professional degree or higher: 11.3%
Housing: Homeownership rate: 79.5%; Median home value: $144,300; Median year structure built: 1987; Homeowner vacancy rate: 11.4%; Median selected monthly owner costs: $1,719 with a mortgage, $467 without a mortgage; Median gross rent: n/a per month; Rental vacancy rate: 0.0%
Health Insurance: 98.2% have insurance; 66.7% have private insurance; 54.1% have public insurance; 1.8% do not have insurance; 0.0% of children under 18 do not have insurance
Transportation: Commute: 73.5% car, 0.0% public transportation, 5.9% walk, 14.7% work from home; Mean travel time to work: 22.2 minutes

RICHMONDVILLE (town). Covers a land area of 30.160 square miles and a water area of 0.065 square miles. Located at 42.64° N. Lat; 74.55° W. Long. Elevation is 1,096 feet.
Population: 2,488; Growth (since 2000): 3.2%; Density: 82.5 persons per square mile; Race: 96.9% White, 0.8% Black/African American, 1.0% Asian, 0.9% American Indian/Alaska Native, 0.0% Native Hawaiian/Other Pacific Islander, 0.4% Two or more races, 0.7% Hispanic of any race; Average household size: 2.46; Median age: 40.0; Age under 18: 19.9%; Age 65 and over: 15.7%; Males per 100 females: 94.5; Marriage status: 30.7% never married, 43.3% now married, 0.4% separated, 8.5% widowed, 17.4% divorced; Foreign born: 2.2%; Speak English only: 98.7%; With disability: 14.1%; Veterans: 11.0%; Ancestry: 30.4% Irish, 29.3% German, 12.0% Italian, 8.9% English, 6.7% Dutch

Employment: 13.9% management, business, and financial, 2.8% computer, engineering, and science, 10.3% education, legal, community service, arts, and media, 4.3% healthcare practitioners, 22.3% service, 27.4% sales and office, 9.7% natural resources, construction, and maintenance, 9.3% production, transportation, and material moving
Income: Per capita: $26,004; Median household: $48,750; Average household: $61,172; Households with income of $100,000 or more: 18.1%; Poverty rate: 15.7%
Educational Attainment: High school diploma or higher: 89.2%; Bachelor's degree or higher: 22.8%; Graduate/professional degree or higher: 11.2%

School District(s)
Cobleskill-Richmondville Central SD (PK-12)
    Enrollment: 1,718 . . . . (518) 234-4032
Housing: Homeownership rate: 66.4%; Median home value: $150,500; Median year structure built: 1974; Homeowner vacancy rate: 5.2%; Median selected monthly owner costs: $1,591 with a mortgage, $503 without a mortgage; Median gross rent: $756 per month; Rental vacancy rate: 6.4%
Health Insurance: 97.7% have insurance; 63.7% have private insurance; 46.9% have public insurance; 2.3% do not have insurance; 0.0% of children under 18 do not have insurance
Transportation: Commute: 90.5% car, 1.2% public transportation, 4.5% walk, 3.0% work from home; Mean travel time to work: 28.3 minutes

RICHMONDVILLE (village). Covers a land area of 1.846 square miles and a water area of 0 square miles. Located at 42.63° N. Lat; 74.56° W. Long. Elevation is 1,096 feet.
Population: 906; Growth (since 2000): 15.3%; Density: 490.7 persons per square mile; Race: 94.7% White, 0.1% Black/African American, 1.8% Asian, 2.4% American Indian/Alaska Native, 0.0% Native Hawaiian/Other Pacific Islander, 1.0% Two or more races, 0.6% Hispanic of any race; Average household size: 2.81; Median age: 35.0; Age under 18: 21.3%; Age 65 and over: 16.0%; Males per 100 females: 82.5; Marriage status: 41.9% never married, 41.3% now married, 0.4% separated, 6.5% widowed, 10.4% divorced; Foreign born: 2.6%; Speak English only: 98.3%; With disability: 15.3%; Veterans: 11.9%; Ancestry: 24.5% German, 23.8% Irish, 14.3% Italian, 8.3% American, 6.3% Dutch
Employment: 8.1% management, business, and financial, 0.0% computer, engineering, and science, 13.2% education, legal, community service, arts, and media, 5.6% healthcare practitioners, 18.8% service, 27.7% sales and office, 12.6% natural resources, construction, and maintenance, 14.0% production, transportation, and material moving
Income: Per capita: $25,446; Median household: $61,058; Average household: $66,440; Households with income of $100,000 or more: 20.7%; Poverty rate: 12.1%
Educational Attainment: High school diploma or higher: 83.5%; Bachelor's degree or higher: 16.2%; Graduate/professional degree or higher: 9.8%

School District(s)
Cobleskill-Richmondville Central SD (PK-12)
    Enrollment: 1,718 . . . . (518) 234-4032
Housing: Homeownership rate: 54.9%; Median home value: $134,700; Median year structure built: 1962; Homeowner vacancy rate: 10.7%; Median selected monthly owner costs: $1,435 with a mortgage, $614 without a mortgage; Median gross rent: $664 per month; Rental vacancy rate: 4.6%
Health Insurance: 96.7% have insurance; 65.9% have private insurance; 48.0% have public insurance; 3.3% do not have insurance; 0.0% of children under 18 do not have insurance
Transportation: Commute: 87.7% car, 3.5% public transportation, 5.4% walk, 3.3% work from home; Mean travel time to work: 32.1 minutes

SCHOHARIE (town). Covers a land area of 29.830 square miles and a water area of 0.129 square miles. Located at 42.68° N. Lat; 74.31° W. Long. Elevation is 600 feet.
History: Has 18th-century buildings including Old Stone Fort; 1772, now a museum. Incorporated 1867.
Population: 3,039; Growth (since 2000): -7.9%; Density: 101.9 persons per square mile; Race: 96.7% White, 1.3% Black/African American, 0.3% Asian, 0.0% American Indian/Alaska Native, 0.0% Native Hawaiian/Other Pacific Islander, 1.4% Two or more races, 1.3% Hispanic of any race; Average household size: 2.50; Median age: 47.9; Age under 18: 20.2%; Age 65 and over: 22.6%; Males per 100 females: 93.5; Marriage status: 24.9% never married, 59.5% now married, 3.0% separated, 5.8% widowed, 9.8% divorced; Foreign born: 3.8%; Speak English only: 97.0%;

With disability: 13.9%; Veterans: 9.1%; Ancestry: 32.0% German, 15.9% Irish, 12.9% Italian, 12.3% English, 7.2% French
Employment: 22.1% management, business, and financial, 6.6% computer, engineering, and science, 10.7% education, legal, community service, arts, and media, 3.8% healthcare practitioners, 6.1% service, 30.1% sales and office, 12.3% natural resources, construction, and maintenance, 8.2% production, transportation, and material moving
Income: Per capita: $28,182; Median household: $58,514; Average household: $69,297; Households with income of $100,000 or more: 21.7%; Poverty rate: 9.4%
Educational Attainment: High school diploma or higher: 88.0%; Bachelor's degree or higher: 22.3%; Graduate/professional degree or higher: 8.1%

School District(s)
Schoharie Central SD (PK-12)
    Enrollment: 940................................ (518) 295-6679
Housing: Homeownership rate: 78.3%; Median home value: $161,200; Median year structure built: 1975; Homeowner vacancy rate: 2.0%; Median selected monthly owner costs: $1,333 with a mortgage, $585 without a mortgage; Median gross rent: $713 per month; Rental vacancy rate: 5.1%
Health Insurance: 99.1% have insurance; 80.6% have private insurance; 40.0% have public insurance; 0.9% do not have insurance; 0.0% of children under 18 do not have insurance
Transportation: Commute: 94.4% car, 2.3% public transportation, 2.3% walk, 1.0% work from home; Mean travel time to work: 30.7 minutes

SCHOHARIE (village). County seat. Covers a land area of 1.658 square miles and a water area of <.001 square miles. Located at 42.67° N. Lat; 74.31° W. Long. Elevation is 600 feet.
Population: 778; Growth (since 2000): -24.5%; Density: 469.1 persons per square mile; Race: 91.5% White, 5.1% Black/African American, 0.9% Asian, 0.0% American Indian/Alaska Native, 0.0% Native Hawaiian/Other Pacific Islander, 1.3% Two or more races, 3.3% Hispanic of any race; Average household size: 2.14; Median age: 50.7; Age under 18: 13.9%; Age 65 and over: 29.2%; Males per 100 females: 91.7; Marriage status: 31.2% never married, 41.5% now married, 0.6% separated, 10.8% widowed, 16.4% divorced; Foreign born: 4.2%; Speak English only: 95.9%; With disability: 24.5%; Veterans: 7.9%; Ancestry: 19.5% German, 16.1% Irish, 12.5% Dutch, 11.4% European, 6.9% English
Employment: 17.5% management, business, and financial, 1.9% computer, engineering, and science, 10.7% education, legal, community service, arts, and media, 3.2% healthcare practitioners, 9.4% service, 26.9% sales and office, 9.1% natural resources, construction, and maintenance, 21.1% production, transportation, and material moving
Income: Per capita: $31,318; Median household: $52,321; Average household: $65,208; Households with income of $100,000 or more: 16.9%; Poverty rate: 14.9%
Educational Attainment: High school diploma or higher: 83.4%; Bachelor's degree or higher: 15.8%; Graduate/professional degree or higher: 9.2%

School District(s)
Schoharie Central SD (PK-12)
    Enrollment: 940................................ (518) 295-6679
Housing: Homeownership rate: 60.7%; Median home value: $154,000; Median year structure built: 1944; Homeowner vacancy rate: 8.2%; Median selected monthly owner costs: $1,583 with a mortgage, $658 without a mortgage; Median gross rent: $756 per month; Rental vacancy rate: 9.5%
Health Insurance: 98.6% have insurance; 71.5% have private insurance; 51.6% have public insurance; 1.4% do not have insurance; 0.0% of children under 18 do not have insurance
Safety: Violent crime rate: 0.0 per 10,000 population; Property crime rate: 0.0 per 10,000 population
Transportation: Commute: 89.2% car, 4.3% public transportation, 5.0% walk, 1.4% work from home; Mean travel time to work: 20.8 minutes

SEWARD (town). Covers a land area of 36.377 square miles and a water area of 0.079 square miles. Located at 42.71° N. Lat; 74.58° W. Long. Elevation is 1,184 feet.
Population: 1,664; Growth (since 2000): 1.6%; Density: 45.7 persons per square mile; Race: 97.8% White, 0.1% Black/African American, 1.3% Asian, 0.2% American Indian/Alaska Native, 0.0% Native Hawaiian/Other Pacific Islander, 0.6% Two or more races, 2.2% Hispanic of any race; Average household size: 2.56; Median age: 46.2; Age under 18: 20.9%; Age 65 and over: 16.3%; Males per 100 females: 100.8; Marriage status: 23.5% never married, 59.7% now married, 5.3% separated, 5.8%

widowed, 11.0% divorced; Foreign born: 1.8%; Speak English only: 97.9%; With disability: 13.4%; Veterans: 11.1%; Ancestry: 29.2% German, 19.5% Irish, 14.2% Italian, 8.2% French, 7.2% English
Employment: 14.3% management, business, and financial, 3.5% computer, engineering, and science, 13.0% education, legal, community service, arts, and media, 3.2% healthcare practitioners, 12.0% service, 19.9% sales and office, 20.2% natural resources, construction, and maintenance, 13.9% production, transportation, and material moving
Income: Per capita: $26,846; Median household: $55,508; Average household: $66,219; Households with income of $100,000 or more: 20.2%; Poverty rate: 15.6%
Educational Attainment: High school diploma or higher: 88.9%; Bachelor's degree or higher: 24.7%; Graduate/professional degree or higher: 6.7%
Housing: Homeownership rate: 89.1%; Median home value: $149,200; Median year structure built: 1971; Homeowner vacancy rate: 1.2%; Median selected monthly owner costs: $1,412 with a mortgage, $538 without a mortgage; Median gross rent: $1,118 per month; Rental vacancy rate: 8.1%
Health Insurance: 95.4% have insurance; 72.5% have private insurance; 40.7% have public insurance; 4.6% do not have insurance; 0.0% of children under 18 do not have insurance
Transportation: Commute: 86.8% car, 1.3% public transportation, 1.8% walk, 8.5% work from home; Mean travel time to work: 34.8 minutes

SHARON (town). Covers a land area of 39.062 square miles and a water area of 0.098 square miles. Located at 42.78° N. Lat; 74.61° W. Long. Elevation is 1,184 feet.
History: Former health resort, with sulphur springs.
Population: 1,918; Growth (since 2000): 4.1%; Density: 49.1 persons per square mile; Race: 95.9% White, 0.1% Black/African American, 2.9% Asian, 0.0% American Indian/Alaska Native, 0.0% Native Hawaiian/Other Pacific Islander, 1.0% Two or more races, 2.9% Hispanic of any race; Average household size: 2.45; Median age: 42.7; Age under 18: 18.2%; Age 65 and over: 18.4%; Males per 100 females: 105.6; Marriage status: 29.7% never married, 50.9% now married, 1.2% separated, 7.5% widowed, 11.9% divorced; Foreign born: 3.5%; Speak English only: 93.3%; With disability: 12.5%; Veterans: 10.2%; Ancestry: 21.7% Irish, 21.3% German, 15.5% Italian, 11.6% English, 6.4% Dutch
Employment: 18.5% management, business, and financial, 2.9% computer, engineering, and science, 9.2% education, legal, community service, arts, and media, 1.7% healthcare practitioners, 16.8% service, 18.4% sales and office, 17.5% natural resources, construction, and maintenance, 14.4% production, transportation, and material moving
Income: Per capita: $25,946; Median household: $50,526; Average household: $61,895; Households with income of $100,000 or more: 19.0%; Poverty rate: 13.4%
Educational Attainment: High school diploma or higher: 90.7%; Bachelor's degree or higher: 19.0%; Graduate/professional degree or higher: 6.9%
Housing: Homeownership rate: 69.3%; Median home value: $151,000; Median year structure built: 1956; Homeowner vacancy rate: 2.7%; Median selected monthly owner costs: $1,366 with a mortgage, $581 without a mortgage; Median gross rent: $836 per month; Rental vacancy rate: 0.0%
Health Insurance: 93.5% have insurance; 62.7% have private insurance; 46.2% have public insurance; 6.5% do not have insurance; 1.7% of children under 18 do not have insurance
Transportation: Commute: 85.2% car, 1.0% public transportation, 3.9% walk, 9.6% work from home; Mean travel time to work: 30.3 minutes

SHARON SPRINGS (village). Covers a land area of 1.827 square miles and a water area of 0 square miles. Located at 42.79° N. Lat; 74.61° W. Long. Elevation is 1,102 feet.
Population: 472; Growth (since 2000): -13.7%; Density: 258.4 persons per square mile; Race: 89.0% White, 0.0% Black/African American, 8.5% Asian, 0.0% American Indian/Alaska Native, 0.0% Native Hawaiian/Other Pacific Islander, 2.5% Two or more races, 0.0% Hispanic of any race; Average household size: 2.29; Median age: 46.6; Age under 18: 13.1%; Age 65 and over: 21.0%; Males per 100 females: 100.7; Marriage status: 32.1% never married, 36.5% now married, 0.5% separated, 11.9% widowed, 19.4% divorced; Foreign born: 7.2%; Speak English only: 90.7%; With disability: 18.6%; Veterans: 9.0%; Ancestry: 25.8% Irish, 19.1% Italian, 17.8% German, 16.9% English, 9.3% French
Employment: 15.7% management, business, and financial, 5.6% computer, engineering, and science, 15.2% education, legal, community

service, arts, and media, 5.1% healthcare practitioners, 16.7% service, 18.7% sales and office, 13.1% natural resources, construction, and maintenance, 10.1% production, transportation, and material moving
Income: Per capita: $26,449; Median household: $37,841; Average household: $59,469; Households with income of $100,000 or more: 14.6%; Poverty rate: 21.2%
Educational Attainment: High school diploma or higher: 85.3%; Bachelor's degree or higher: 22.2%; Graduate/professional degree or higher: 6.1%

School District(s)
Sharon Springs Central SD (KG-12)
    Enrollment: 268 . . . . (518) 284-2266
Housing: Homeownership rate: 52.8%; Median home value: $108,900; Median year structure built: 1946; Homeowner vacancy rate: 0.0%; Median selected monthly owner costs: $1,354 with a mortgage, $650 without a mortgage; Median gross rent: $761 per month; Rental vacancy rate: 0.0%
Health Insurance: 96.0% have insurance; 59.1% have private insurance; 53.8% have public insurance; 4.0% do not have insurance; 0.0% of children under 18 do not have insurance
Transportation: Commute: 91.9% car, 1.0% public transportation, 1.0% walk, 6.1% work from home; Mean travel time to work: 28.3 minutes

SLOANSVILLE (unincorporated postal area)
ZCTA: 12160
    Covers a land area of 17.720 square miles and a water area of 0.139 square miles. Located at 42.76° N. Lat; 74.38° W. Long. Elevation is 679 feet.
Population: 945; Growth (since 2000): -19.7%; Density: 53.3 persons per square mile; Race: 99.5% White, 0.0% Black/African American, 0.0% Asian, 0.3% American Indian/Alaska Native, 0.0% Native Hawaiian/Other Pacific Islander, 0.2% Two or more races, 5.0% Hispanic of any race; Average household size: 2.73; Median age: 45.9; Age under 18: 21.1%; Age 65 and over: 16.7%; Males per 100 females: 104.8; Marriage status: 20.5% never married, 66.7% now married, 2.2% separated, 5.8% widowed, 7.0% divorced; Foreign born: 1.7%; Speak English only: 97.2%; With disability: 13.1%; Veterans: 11.3%; Ancestry: 26.0% German, 25.6% Irish, 16.4% Dutch, 8.7% English, 8.4% American
Employment: 15.7% management, business, and financial, 4.9% computer, engineering, and science, 11.7% education, legal, community service, arts, and media, 1.4% healthcare practitioners, 16.0% service, 21.4% sales and office, 15.7% natural resources, construction, and maintenance, 13.3% production, transportation, and material moving
Income: Per capita: $31,467; Median household: $66,667; Average household: $83,895; Households with income of $100,000 or more: 23.1%; Poverty rate: 9.9%
Educational Attainment: High school diploma or higher: 93.0%; Bachelor's degree or higher: 21.5%; Graduate/professional degree or higher: 5.6%
Housing: Homeownership rate: 87.9%; Median home value: $145,000; Median year structure built: 1972; Homeowner vacancy rate: 0.0%; Median selected monthly owner costs: $1,569 with a mortgage, $521 without a mortgage; Median gross rent: $1,050 per month; Rental vacancy rate: 0.0%
Health Insurance: 91.9% have insurance; 69.1% have private insurance; 37.5% have public insurance; 8.1% do not have insurance; 0.0% of children under 18 do not have insurance
Transportation: Commute: 91.1% car, 0.0% public transportation, 0.0% walk, 7.3% work from home; Mean travel time to work: 32.1 minutes

SUMMIT (town). Covers a land area of 37.085 square miles and a water area of 0.399 square miles. Located at 42.57° N. Lat; 74.60° W. Long. Elevation is 2,116 feet.
Population: 1,066; Growth (since 2000): -5.1%; Density: 28.7 persons per square mile; Race: 96.6% White, 0.1% Black/African American, 0.4% Asian, 0.0% American Indian/Alaska Native, 0.0% Native Hawaiian/Other Pacific Islander, 2.9% Two or more races, 2.8% Hispanic of any race; Average household size: 2.47; Median age: 44.0; Age under 18: 21.8%; Age 65 and over: 20.4%; Males per 100 females: 115.4; Marriage status: 28.9% never married, 49.4% now married, 2.1% separated, 9.3% widowed, 12.4% divorced; Foreign born: 4.0%; Speak English only: 95.1%; With disability: 16.4%; Veterans: 10.6%; Ancestry: 30.8% German, 26.5% Irish, 12.4% American, 9.8% English, 8.0% Italian
Employment: 17.1% management, business, and financial, 3.1% computer, engineering, and science, 8.0% education, legal, community

service, arts, and media, 0.7% healthcare practitioners, 26.6% service, 26.2% sales and office, 7.1% natural resources, construction, and maintenance, 11.3% production, transportation, and material moving
Income: Per capita: $24,938; Median household: $51,726; Average household: $58,515; Households with income of $100,000 or more: 14.6%; Poverty rate: 19.3%
Educational Attainment: High school diploma or higher: 89.1%; Bachelor's degree or higher: 23.2%; Graduate/professional degree or higher: 8.4%
Housing: Homeownership rate: 93.3%; Median home value: $152,100; Median year structure built: 1974; Homeowner vacancy rate: 0.0%; Median selected monthly owner costs: $1,090 with a mortgage, $486 without a mortgage; Median gross rent: $929 per month; Rental vacancy rate: 9.4%
Health Insurance: 94.9% have insurance; 63.4% have private insurance; 47.6% have public insurance; 5.1% do not have insurance; 0.0% of children under 18 do not have insurance
Transportation: Commute: 94.0% car, 0.0% public transportation, 0.0% walk, 5.1% work from home; Mean travel time to work: 36.5 minutes

WARNERVILLE (unincorporated postal area)
ZCTA: 12187
    Covers a land area of 23.019 square miles and a water area of 0.023 square miles. Located at 42.62° N. Lat; 74.46° W. Long. Elevation is 925 feet.
Population: 449; Growth (since 2000): -34.4%; Density: 19.5 persons per square mile; Race: 100.0% White, 0.0% Black/African American, 0.0% Asian, 0.0% American Indian/Alaska Native, 0.0% Native Hawaiian/Other Pacific Islander, 0.0% Two or more races, 1.8% Hispanic of any race; Average household size: 2.26; Median age: 50.9; Age under 18: 18.9%; Age 65 and over: 21.6%; Males per 100 females: 108.1; Marriage status: 20.9% never married, 53.6% now married, 4.0% separated, 8.6% widowed, 16.9% divorced; Foreign born: 1.3%; Speak English only: 97.9%; With disability: 18.0%; Veterans: 11.5%; Ancestry: 23.2% German, 20.3% Irish, 15.1% Italian, 12.9% English, 8.7% European
Employment: 7.6% management, business, and financial, 3.3% computer, engineering, and science, 20.4% education, legal, community service, arts, and media, 1.9% healthcare practitioners, 28.0% service, 23.7% sales and office, 5.7% natural resources, construction, and maintenance, 9.5% production, transportation, and material moving
Income: Per capita: $28,798; Median household: $49,732; Average household: $61,743; Households with income of $100,000 or more: 16.1%; Poverty rate: 10.5%
Educational Attainment: High school diploma or higher: 97.0%; Bachelor's degree or higher: 31.2%; Graduate/professional degree or higher: 19.8%
Housing: Homeownership rate: 92.5%; Median home value: $189,300; Median year structure built: 1976; Homeowner vacancy rate: 0.0%; Median selected monthly owner costs: $1,590 with a mortgage, $733 without a mortgage; Median gross rent: $836 per month; Rental vacancy rate: 51.6%
Health Insurance: 95.5% have insurance; 63.0% have private insurance; 42.5% have public insurance; 4.5% do not have insurance; 0.0% of children under 18 do not have insurance
Transportation: Commute: 80.3% car, 0.0% public transportation, 14.6% walk, 5.1% work from home; Mean travel time to work: 24.6 minutes

WEST FULTON (unincorporated postal area)
ZCTA: 12194
    Covers a land area of 15.429 square miles and a water area of 0.009 square miles. Located at 42.53° N. Lat; 74.45° W. Long. Elevation is 1,158 feet.
Population: 158; Growth (since 2000): -26.5%; Density: 10.2 persons per square mile; Race: 97.5% White, 0.0% Black/African American, 0.0% Asian, 0.0% American Indian/Alaska Native, 0.0% Native Hawaiian/Other Pacific Islander, 2.5% Two or more races, 0.0% Hispanic of any race; Average household size: 2.47; Median age: 37.0; Age under 18: 29.7%; Age 65 and over: 20.3%; Males per 100 females: 99.0; Marriage status: 12.1% never married, 65.5% now married, 1.7% separated, 4.3% widowed, 18.1% divorced; Foreign born: 0.0%; Speak English only: 100.0%; With disability: 17.7%; Veterans: 13.5%; Ancestry: 23.4% German, 17.7% Irish, 15.2% French, 12.0% Dutch, 10.8% English

Employment: 12.5% management, business, and financial, 7.5% computer, engineering, and science, 12.5% education, legal, community service, arts, and media, 5.0% healthcare practitioners, 5.0% service, 15.0% sales and office, 35.0% natural resources, construction, and maintenance, 7.5% production, transportation, and material moving
Income: Per capita: $25,153; Median household: $45,500; Average household: $61,292; Households with income of $100,000 or more: 12.5%; Poverty rate: 3.2%
Educational Attainment: High school diploma or higher: 93.5%; Bachelor's degree or higher: 17.6%; Graduate/professional degree or higher: 6.5%
Housing: Homeownership rate: 100.0%; Median home value: $82,000; Median year structure built: 1969; Homeowner vacancy rate: 0.0%; Median selected monthly owner costs: $1,023 with a mortgage, $467 without a mortgage; Median gross rent: n/a per month; Rental vacancy rate: 0.0%
Health Insurance: 100.0% have insurance; 68.4% have private insurance; 54.4% have public insurance; 0.0% do not have insurance; 0.0% of children under 18 do not have insurance
Transportation: Commute: 82.5% car, 0.0% public transportation, 0.0% walk, 17.5% work from home; Mean travel time to work: 42.1 minutes

WRIGHT (town). Covers a land area of 28.636 square miles and a water area of 0.082 square miles. Located at 42.67° N. Lat; 74.21° W. Long.
Population: 1,704; Growth (since 2000): 10.1%; Density: 59.5 persons per square mile; Race: 98.7% White, 0.3% Black/African American, 0.6% Asian, 0.0% American Indian/Alaska Native, 0.0% Native Hawaiian/Other Pacific Islander, 0.5% Two or more races, 3.6% Hispanic of any race; Average household size: 2.70; Median age: 43.8; Age under 18: 22.7%; Age 65 and over: 12.7%; Males per 100 females: 105.5; Marriage status: 27.8% never married, 56.8% now married, 2.5% separated, 4.5% widowed, 10.9% divorced; Foreign born: 2.8%; Speak English only: 96.9%; With disability: 13.2%; Veterans: 9.8%; Ancestry: 23.9% German, 21.5% Irish, 11.2% Dutch, 10.4% English, 10.3% Italian
Employment: 11.4% management, business, and financial, 6.1% computer, engineering, and science, 8.1% education, legal, community service, arts, and media, 7.3% healthcare practitioners, 19.3% service, 21.8% sales and office, 17.1% natural resources, construction, and maintenance, 9.0% production, transportation, and material moving
Income: Per capita: $27,950; Median household: $60,192; Average household: $73,586; Households with income of $100,000 or more: 20.2%; Poverty rate: 15.4%
Educational Attainment: High school diploma or higher: 92.0%; Bachelor's degree or higher: 24.0%; Graduate/professional degree or higher: 13.8%
Housing: Homeownership rate: 87.5%; Median home value: $160,500; Median year structure built: 1977; Homeowner vacancy rate: 0.0%; Median selected monthly owner costs: $1,516 with a mortgage, $548 without a mortgage; Median gross rent: $775 per month; Rental vacancy rate: 0.0%
Health Insurance: 92.8% have insurance; 69.1% have private insurance; 39.0% have public insurance; 7.2% do not have insurance; 2.2% of children under 18 do not have insurance
Transportation: Commute: 90.7% car, 0.0% public transportation, 2.6% walk, 6.0% work from home; Mean travel time to work: 31.2 minutes

Schuyler County

Located in west central New York, in the Finger Lakes region; drained by Cayuta and Catherine Creeks; includes Lamoka and Cayuta Lakes and part of Seneca Lake. Covers a land area of 328.333 square miles, a water area of 13.995 square miles, and is located in the Eastern Time Zone at 42.42° N. Lat., 76.94° W. Long. The county was founded in 1854. County seat is Watkins Glen.
Population: 18,112; Growth (since 2000): -5.8%; Density: 55.2 persons per square mile; Race: 96.6% White, 1.4% Black/African American, 0.5% Asian, 0.1% American Indian/Alaska Native, 0.0% Native Hawaiian/Other Pacific Islander, 1.3% two or more races, 1.8% Hispanic of any race; Average household size: 2.39; Median age: 45.7; Age under 18: 19.9%; Age 65 and over: 19.4%; Males per 100 females: 98.9; Marriage status: 28.3% never married, 52.1% now married, 3.2% separated, 6.0% widowed, 13.6% divorced; Foreign born: 1.7%; Speak English only: 96.5%; With disability: 16.1%; Veterans: 10.4%; Ancestry: 18.2% Irish, 16.8% American, 15.5% English, 15.5% German, 10.4% Italian

Religion: Six largest groups: 12.9% Catholicism, 6.1% Methodist/Pietist, 3.2% Baptist, 2.7% Presbyterian-Reformed, 0.8% Episcopalianism/Anglicanism, 0.8% Non-denominational Protestant
Economy: Unemployment rate: 3.5%; Leading industries: 19.1 % accommodation and food services; 14.6 % retail trade; 11.7 % other services (except public administration); Farms: 393 totaling 69,222 acres; Company size: 0 employ 1,000 or more persons, 0 employ 500 to 999 persons, 8 employ 100 to 499 persons, 375 employ less than 100 persons; Business ownership: 440 women-owned, n/a Black-owned, n/a Hispanic-owned, n/a Asian-owned, n/a American Indian/Alaska Native-owned
Employment: 12.9% management, business, and financial, 4.2% computer, engineering, and science, 10.5% education, legal, community service, arts, and media, 7.4% healthcare practitioners, 19.0% service, 19.9% sales and office, 11.0% natural resources, construction, and maintenance, 15.0% production, transportation, and material moving
Income: Per capita: $25,285; Median household: $47,810; Average household: $60,353; Households with income of $100,000 or more: 16.5%; Poverty rate: 15.3%
Educational Attainment: High school diploma or higher: 89.7%; Bachelor's degree or higher: 22.1%; Graduate/professional degree or higher: 10.2%
Housing: Homeownership rate: 76.4%; Median home value: $114,700; Median year structure built: 1962; Homeowner vacancy rate: 0.4%; Median selected monthly owner costs: $1,133 with a mortgage, $471 without a mortgage; Median gross rent: $741 per month; Rental vacancy rate: 12.8%
Vital Statistics: Birth rate: 101.7 per 10,000 population; Death rate: 102.8 per 10,000 population; Age-adjusted cancer mortality rate: 210.5 deaths per 100,000 population
Health Insurance: 93.1% have insurance; 66.4% have private insurance; 42.2% have public insurance; 6.9% do not have insurance; 3.3% of children under 18 do not have insurance
Health Care: Physicians: 10.6 per 10,000 population; Dentists: 2.2 per 10,000 population; Hospital beds: 80.6 per 10,000 population; Hospital admissions: 442.8 per 10,000 population
Transportation: Commute: 90.5% car, 0.8% public transportation, 3.2% walk, 4.4% work from home; Mean travel time to work: 24.8 minutes
2016 Presidential Election: 57.6% Trump, 35.2% Clinton, 3.5% Johnson, 2.5% Stein
National and State Parks: Cliffside State Forest; Connecticut Hill State Game Management Area; Finger Lakes National Forest; Green Mountain National Forest-Hector Ranger District; Watkins Glen State Park
Additional Information Contacts
Schuyler Government . . . . (607) 535-8133
  http://www.schuylercounty.us

Schuyler County Communities

ALPINE (unincorporated postal area)
ZCTA: 14805
  Covers a land area of 27.655 square miles and a water area of 0.599 square miles. Located at 42.35° N. Lat; 76.72° W. Long. Elevation is 1,165 feet.
Population: 1,146; Growth (since 2000): -5.1%; Density: 41.4 persons per square mile; Race: 97.2% White, 1.9% Black/African American, 0.0% Asian, 0.5% American Indian/Alaska Native, 0.0% Native Hawaiian/Other Pacific Islander, 0.3% Two or more races, 2.1% Hispanic of any race; Average household size: 2.75; Median age: 42.2; Age under 18: 24.6%; Age 65 and over: 12.1%; Males per 100 females: 100.0; Marriage status: 35.8% never married, 52.8% now married, 0.8% separated, 4.2% widowed, 7.3% divorced; Foreign born: 1.7%; Speak English only: 97.9%; With disability: 11.5%; Veterans: 11.1%; Ancestry: 24.1% Irish, 15.0% American, 14.9% Italian, 11.4% English, 9.4% German
Employment: 9.5% management, business, and financial, 3.0% computer, engineering, and science, 13.0% education, legal, community service, arts, and media, 8.8% healthcare practitioners, 15.3% service, 20.6% sales and office, 13.9% natural resources, construction, and maintenance, 15.8% production, transportation, and material moving
Income: Per capita: $26,594; Median household: $56,563; Average household: $71,919; Households with income of $100,000 or more: 27.0%; Poverty rate: 15.5%
Educational Attainment: High school diploma or higher: 93.4%; Bachelor's degree or higher: 30.0%; Graduate/professional degree or higher: 9.1%

Housing: Homeownership rate: 80.1%; Median home value: $120,900; Median year structure built: 1964; Homeowner vacancy rate: 0.0%; Median selected monthly owner costs: $1,191 with a mortgage, $469 without a mortgage; Median gross rent: $859 per month; Rental vacancy rate: 0.0%

Health Insurance: 96.9% have insurance; 72.4% have private insurance; 36.4% have public insurance; 3.1% do not have insurance; 0.0% of children under 18 do not have insurance

Transportation: Commute: 89.2% car, 1.4% public transportation, 4.7% walk, 2.3% work from home; Mean travel time to work: 28.6 minutes

BEAVER DAMS (unincorporated postal area)

ZCTA: 14812

Covers a land area of 77.543 square miles and a water area of 0.085 square miles. Located at 42.30° N. Lat; 77.01° W. Long. Elevation is 1,263 feet.

Population: 3,071; Growth (since 2000): -21.9%; Density: 39.6 persons per square mile; Race: 97.2% White, 1.5% Black/African American, 0.4% Asian, 0.0% American Indian/Alaska Native, 0.0% Native Hawaiian/Other Pacific Islander, 0.3% Two or more races, 2.2% Hispanic of any race; Average household size: 2.55; Median age: 38.1; Age under 18: 24.0%; Age 65 and over: 12.4%; Males per 100 females: 111.6; Marriage status: 31.1% never married, 53.9% now married, 3.7% separated, 5.5% widowed, 9.4% divorced; Foreign born: 1.5%; Speak English only: 97.0%; With disability: 15.7%; Veterans: 7.9%; Ancestry: 24.5% American, 15.9% Irish, 13.7% German, 12.1% English, 8.2% Italian

Employment: 8.0% management, business, and financial, 6.2% computer, engineering, and science, 7.6% education, legal, community service, arts, and media, 4.8% healthcare practitioners, 20.0% service, 20.5% sales and office, 15.4% natural resources, construction, and maintenance, 17.5% production, transportation, and material moving

Income: Per capita: $23,339; Median household: $52,303; Average household: $60,663; Households with income of $100,000 or more: 14.7%; Poverty rate: 12.9%

Educational Attainment: High school diploma or higher: 89.3%; Bachelor's degree or higher: 15.0%; Graduate/professional degree or higher: 5.2%

Housing: Homeownership rate: 86.6%; Median home value: $86,500; Median year structure built: 1973; Homeowner vacancy rate: 0.9%; Median selected monthly owner costs: $1,051 with a mortgage, $445 without a mortgage; Median gross rent: $711 per month; Rental vacancy rate: 27.3%

Health Insurance: 96.3% have insurance; 69.9% have private insurance; 37.8% have public insurance; 3.7% do not have insurance; 1.8% of children under 18 do not have insurance

Transportation: Commute: 94.2% car, 0.0% public transportation, 2.3% walk, 2.3% work from home; Mean travel time to work: 25.4 minutes

BURDETT (village). Covers a land area of 0.962 square miles and a water area of 0 square miles. Located at 42.42° N. Lat; 76.84° W. Long. Elevation is 978 feet.

Population: 469; Growth (since 2000): 31.4%; Density: 487.3 persons per square mile; Race: 97.4% White, 0.0% Black/African American, 2.3% Asian, 0.2% American Indian/Alaska Native, 0.0% Native Hawaiian/Other Pacific Islander, 0.0% Two or more races, 0.0% Hispanic of any race; Average household size: 2.30; Median age: 48.3; Age under 18: 19.0%; Age 65 and over: 24.9%; Males per 100 females: 87.8; Marriage status: 29.2% never married, 54.8% now married, 2.2% separated, 4.7% widowed, 11.3% divorced; Foreign born: 1.1%; Speak English only: 98.0%; With disability: 12.4%; Veterans: 5.8%; Ancestry: 26.0% German, 19.6% Italian, 16.4% English, 15.6% American, 13.0% Irish

Employment: 15.2% management, business, and financial, 6.6% computer, engineering, and science, 13.6% education, legal, community service, arts, and media, 8.1% healthcare practitioners, 14.6% service, 12.1% sales and office, 11.1% natural resources, construction, and maintenance, 18.7% production, transportation, and material moving

Income: Per capita: $25,930; Median household: $53,182; Average household: $58,942; Households with income of $100,000 or more: 10.8%; Poverty rate: 12.1%

Educational Attainment: High school diploma or higher: 94.2%; Bachelor's degree or higher: 31.7%; Graduate/professional degree or higher: 11.2%

Housing: Homeownership rate: 84.8%; Median home value: $124,000; Median year structure built: Before 1940; Homeowner vacancy rate: 5.5%;

Median selected monthly owner costs: $1,438 with a mortgage, $529 without a mortgage; Median gross rent: $738 per month; Rental vacancy rate: 0.0%

Health Insurance: 95.1% have insurance; 73.6% have private insurance; 45.2% have public insurance; 4.9% do not have insurance; 3.2% of children under 18 do not have insurance

Transportation: Commute: 85.2% car, 1.0% public transportation, 3.1% walk, 10.7% work from home; Mean travel time to work: 24.3 minutes

CATHARINE (town). Covers a land area of 32.295 square miles and a water area of 0.605 square miles. Located at 42.34° N. Lat; 76.73° W. Long. Elevation is 1,178 feet.

Population: 1,704; Growth (since 2000): -11.7%; Density: 52.8 persons per square mile; Race: 97.9% White, 0.4% Black/African American, 0.0% Asian, 0.5% American Indian/Alaska Native, 0.0% Native Hawaiian/Other Pacific Islander, 1.2% Two or more races, 1.4% Hispanic of any race; Average household size: 2.53; Median age: 43.0; Age under 18: 23.8%; Age 65 and over: 17.5%; Males per 100 females: 96.2; Marriage status: 29.3% never married, 49.1% now married, 1.7% separated, 7.8% widowed, 13.8% divorced; Foreign born: 0.7%; Speak English only: 98.0%; With disability: 14.8%; Veterans: 9.5%; Ancestry: 19.0% Irish, 18.4% American, 14.0% English, 12.6% German, 10.1% Polish

Employment: 11.2% management, business, and financial, 2.6% computer, engineering, and science, 9.8% education, legal, community service, arts, and media, 3.5% healthcare practitioners, 21.9% service, 19.5% sales and office, 11.6% natural resources, construction, and maintenance, 19.8% production, transportation, and material moving

Income: Per capita: $23,470; Median household: $49,821; Average household: $58,923; Households with income of $100,000 or more: 14.3%; Poverty rate: 15.3%

Educational Attainment: High school diploma or higher: 92.2%; Bachelor's degree or higher: 22.3%; Graduate/professional degree or higher: 8.8%

Housing: Homeownership rate: 76.8%; Median home value: $109,400; Median year structure built: 1953; Homeowner vacancy rate: 0.6%; Median selected monthly owner costs: $1,136 with a mortgage, $510 without a mortgage; Median gross rent: $663 per month; Rental vacancy rate: 14.6%

Health Insurance: 91.9% have insurance; 68.2% have private insurance; 39.9% have public insurance; 8.1% do not have insurance; 4.2% of children under 18 do not have insurance

Transportation: Commute: 90.8% car, 1.6% public transportation, 3.4% walk, 2.5% work from home; Mean travel time to work: 27.8 minutes

CAYUTA (town). Covers a land area of 20.319 square miles and a water area of <.001 square miles. Located at 42.27° N. Lat; 76.68° W. Long. Elevation is 1,102 feet.

Population: 458; Growth (since 2000): -16.0%; Density: 22.5 persons per square mile; Race: 93.7% White, 4.8% Black/African American, 0.0% Asian, 0.2% American Indian/Alaska Native, 0.0% Native Hawaiian/Other Pacific Islander, 1.3% Two or more races, 2.2% Hispanic of any race; Average household size: 2.21; Median age: 43.8; Age under 18: 16.4%; Age 65 and over: 14.4%; Males per 100 females: 100.7; Marriage status: 27.1% never married, 53.1% now married, 0.0% separated, 6.7% widowed, 13.1% divorced; Foreign born: 2.4%; Speak English only: 98.8%; With disability: 18.3%; Veterans: 9.7%; Ancestry: 15.3% Irish, 12.7% American, 12.7% German, 10.5% Italian, 9.4% French

Employment: 7.9% management, business, and financial, 2.2% computer, engineering, and science, 9.2% education, legal, community service, arts, and media, 0.4% healthcare practitioners, 32.0% service, 15.8% sales and office, 11.0% natural resources, construction, and maintenance, 21.5% production, transportation, and material moving

Income: Per capita: $20,129; Median household: $40,313; Average household: $44,892; Households with income of $100,000 or more: 7.2%; Poverty rate: 19.9%

Educational Attainment: High school diploma or higher: 85.9%; Bachelor's degree or higher: 11.6%; Graduate/professional degree or higher: 5.2%

Housing: Homeownership rate: 74.9%; Median home value: $77,600; Median year structure built: 1979; Homeowner vacancy rate: 0.0%; Median selected monthly owner costs: $1,156 with a mortgage, $377 without a mortgage; Median gross rent: $860 per month; Rental vacancy rate: 11.5%

Health Insurance: 90.8% have insurance; 54.1% have private insurance; 48.5% have public insurance; 9.2% do not have insurance; 2.4% of children under 18 do not have insurance

Transportation: Commute: 97.3% car, 0.0% public transportation, 0.0% walk, 0.0% work from home; Mean travel time to work: 26.1 minutes

DIX (town). Covers a land area of 36.258 square miles and a water area of 0.454 square miles. Located at 42.33° N. Lat; 76.90° W. Long.
Population: 3,897; Growth (since 2000): -7.1%; Density: 107.5 persons per square mile; Race: 95.0% White, 2.9% Black/African American, 0.7% Asian, 0.0% American Indian/Alaska Native, 0.0% Native Hawaiian/Other Pacific Islander, 1.2% Two or more races, 2.0% Hispanic of any race; Average household size: 2.38; Median age: 43.8; Age under 18: 19.7%; Age 65 and over: 18.9%; Males per 100 females: 93.0; Marriage status: 28.0% never married, 53.6% now married, 5.9% separated, 6.1% widowed, 12.3% divorced; Foreign born: 1.6%; Speak English only: 98.0%; With disability: 17.4%; Veterans: 11.3%; Ancestry: 23.6% American, 18.0% Irish, 13.2% English, 12.1% German, 8.9% Italian
Employment: 6.3% management, business, and financial, 2.4% computer, engineering, and science, 8.5% education, legal, community service, arts, and media, 11.4% healthcare practitioners, 25.4% service, 20.2% sales and office, 10.7% natural resources, construction, and maintenance, 15.0% production, transportation, and material moving
Income: Per capita: $24,732; Median household: $42,616; Average household: $58,709; Households with income of $100,000 or more: 16.8%; Poverty rate: 13.7%
Educational Attainment: High school diploma or higher: 89.5%; Bachelor's degree or higher: 14.4%; Graduate/professional degree or higher: 5.7%
Housing: Homeownership rate: 70.8%; Median home value: $105,400; Median year structure built: 1949; Homeowner vacancy rate: 0.0%; Median selected monthly owner costs: $1,032 with a mortgage, $459 without a mortgage; Median gross rent: $627 per month; Rental vacancy rate: 13.7%
Health Insurance: 91.1% have insurance; 63.8% have private insurance; 39.5% have public insurance; 8.9% do not have insurance; 3.5% of children under 18 do not have insurance
Transportation: Commute: 86.6% car, 0.2% public transportation, 7.9% walk, 3.0% work from home; Mean travel time to work: 20.8 minutes

HECTOR (town). Covers a land area of 102.369 square miles and a water area of 10.214 square miles. Located at 42.46° N. Lat; 76.78° W. Long. Elevation is 853 feet.
History: The town is named after Hector Ely, who was the firstborn son of the town founders. The area was originally under the dominion of the Iroquois and became part of the Central New York Military Tract, used to pay soldiers of the American Revolution. The area's first permanent settler arrived in 1791.
Population: 4,935; Growth (since 2000): 1.7%; Density: 48.2 persons per square mile; Race: 97.8% White, 0.0% Black/African American, 0.7% Asian, 0.0% American Indian/Alaska Native, 0.0% Native Hawaiian/Other Pacific Islander, 1.5% Two or more races, 1.2% Hispanic of any race; Average household size: 2.23; Median age: 49.1; Age under 18: 14.1%; Age 65 and over: 21.4%; Males per 100 females: 102.2; Marriage status: 31.3% never married, 51.4% now married, 1.1% separated, 4.5% widowed, 12.9% divorced; Foreign born: 2.4%; Speak English only: 94.7%; With disability: 10.4%; Veterans: 8.4%; Ancestry: 21.4% Irish, 19.7% English, 18.7% German, 12.7% Italian, 10.4% American
Employment: 16.0% management, business, and financial, 5.2% computer, engineering, and science, 13.2% education, legal, community service, arts, and media, 8.4% healthcare practitioners, 13.4% service, 21.4% sales and office, 12.1% natural resources, construction, and maintenance, 10.3% production, transportation, and material moving
Income: Per capita: $28,590; Median household: $50,785; Average household: $62,320; Households with income of $100,000 or more: 16.9%; Poverty rate: 10.8%
Educational Attainment: High school diploma or higher: 94.0%; Bachelor's degree or higher: 34.9%; Graduate/professional degree or higher: 19.4%
Housing: Homeownership rate: 83.3%; Median home value: $144,100; Median year structure built: 1961; Homeowner vacancy rate: 0.5%; Median selected monthly owner costs: $1,195 with a mortgage, $500 without a mortgage; Median gross rent: $815 per month; Rental vacancy rate: 15.7%
Health Insurance: 94.6% have insurance; 73.3% have private insurance; 39.0% have public insurance; 5.4% do not have insurance; 0.4% of children under 18 do not have insurance
Transportation: Commute: 91.7% car, 1.2% public transportation, 1.2% walk, 6.0% work from home; Mean travel time to work: 25.4 minutes

Additional Information Contacts
Town of Hector . . . . (607) 546-5286
    http://home.htva.net/~townofhector

MONTOUR (town). Covers a land area of 18.579 square miles and a water area of 0.005 square miles. Located at 42.34° N. Lat; 76.83° W. Long. Elevation is 482 feet.
History: Chequaga (or Shequaga) Falls here attract tourists, especially when snowmelt in the spring enhances the awesome spectacle.
Population: 2,380; Growth (since 2000): -2.7%; Density: 128.1 persons per square mile; Race: 99.2% White, 0.0% Black/African American, 0.3% Asian, 0.3% American Indian/Alaska Native, 0.0% Native Hawaiian/Other Pacific Islander, 0.0% Two or more races, 0.5% Hispanic of any race; Average household size: 2.34; Median age: 46.2; Age under 18: 22.2%; Age 65 and over: 21.3%; Males per 100 females: 92.5; Marriage status: 25.8% never married, 44.4% now married, 3.6% separated, 7.5% widowed, 22.3% divorced; Foreign born: 1.5%; Speak English only: 98.2%; With disability: 22.7%; Veterans: 13.1%; Ancestry: 17.5% American, 15.1% English, 15.1% Irish, 11.1% German, 10.0% Italian
Employment: 15.4% management, business, and financial, 6.3% computer, engineering, and science, 7.9% education, legal, community service, arts, and media, 3.7% healthcare practitioners, 18.3% service, 20.2% sales and office, 9.8% natural resources, construction, and maintenance, 18.3% production, transportation, and material moving
Income: Per capita: $22,571; Median household: $44,116; Average household: $53,331; Households with income of $100,000 or more: 15.4%; Poverty rate: 20.7%
Educational Attainment: High school diploma or higher: 87.2%; Bachelor's degree or higher: 16.7%; Graduate/professional degree or higher: 4.6%
Housing: Homeownership rate: 60.3%; Median home value: $108,600; Median year structure built: 1956; Homeowner vacancy rate: 0.0%; Median selected monthly owner costs: $1,156 with a mortgage, $428 without a mortgage; Median gross rent: $668 per month; Rental vacancy rate: 10.8%
Health Insurance: 95.7% have insurance; 60.5% have private insurance; 49.9% have public insurance; 4.3% do not have insurance; 0.0% of children under 18 do not have insurance
Transportation: Commute: 92.6% car, 1.9% public transportation, 2.0% walk, 3.1% work from home; Mean travel time to work: 23.2 minutes

MONTOUR FALLS (village). Covers a land area of 3.008 square miles and a water area of 0.024 square miles. Located at 42.35° N. Lat; 76.85° W. Long. Elevation is 449 feet.
Population: 1,737; Growth (since 2000): -3.3%; Density: 577.4 persons per square mile; Race: 95.7% White, 2.8% Black/African American, 0.3% Asian, 0.3% American Indian/Alaska Native, 0.0% Native Hawaiian/Other Pacific Islander, 0.0% Two or more races, 1.0% Hispanic of any race; Average household size: 2.33; Median age: 47.6; Age under 18: 22.1%; Age 65 and over: 28.3%; Males per 100 females: 81.6; Marriage status: 25.0% never married, 38.1% now married, 3.9% separated, 12.7% widowed, 24.2% divorced; Foreign born: 2.9%; Speak English only: 97.4%; With disability: 23.0%; Veterans: 11.7%; Ancestry: 21.3% American, 15.7% Irish, 10.3% English, 9.9% German, 8.2% Italian
Employment: 11.7% management, business, and financial, 4.2% computer, engineering, and science, 7.5% education, legal, community service, arts, and media, 4.7% healthcare practitioners, 22.5% service, 17.3% sales and office, 12.0% natural resources, construction, and maintenance, 20.1% production, transportation, and material moving
Income: Per capita: $19,960; Median household: $39,922; Average household: $48,053; Households with income of $100,000 or more: 13.9%; Poverty rate: 25.1%
Educational Attainment: High school diploma or higher: 84.6%; Bachelor's degree or higher: 13.2%; Graduate/professional degree or higher: 4.9%

School District(s)
Odessa-Montour Central SD (PK-12)
    Enrollment: 776 . . . . (607) 594-3341
Housing: Homeownership rate: 52.2%; Median home value: $103,800; Median year structure built: 1950; Homeowner vacancy rate: 0.0%; Median selected monthly owner costs: $1,127 with a mortgage, $425 without a mortgage; Median gross rent: $632 per month; Rental vacancy rate: 13.0%
Health Insurance: 95.8% have insurance; 46.9% have private insurance; 60.9% have public insurance; 4.2% do not have insurance; 0.0% of children under 18 do not have insurance
Hospitals: Schuyler Hospital (169 beds)

Transportation: Commute: 97.2% car, 0.0% public transportation, 1.1% walk, 1.1% work from home; Mean travel time to work: 21.1 minutes

ODESSA (village). Covers a land area of 1.137 square miles and a water area of 0 square miles. Located at 42.33° N. Lat; 76.79° W. Long. Elevation is 1,043 feet.

Population: 566; Growth (since 2000): -8.3%; Density: 498.0 persons per square mile; Race: 97.3% White, 1.1% Black/African American, 0.0% Asian, 0.4% American Indian/Alaska Native, 0.0% Native Hawaiian/Other Pacific Islander, 1.2% Two or more races, 0.7% Hispanic of any race; Average household size: 2.30; Median age: 43.6; Age under 18: 20.0%; Age 65 and over: 17.8%; Males per 100 females: 94.4; Marriage status: 22.6% never married, 49.8% now married, 3.5% separated, 9.6% widowed, 18.0% divorced; Foreign born: 0.0%; Speak English only: 98.0%; With disability: 11.3%; Veterans: 8.6%; Ancestry: 19.1% English, 18.9% American, 17.0% Irish, 13.4% Polish, 10.1% German
Employment: 10.5% management, business, and financial, 1.0% computer, engineering, and science, 6.8% education, legal, community service, arts, and media, 6.1% healthcare practitioners, 25.8% service, 18.6% sales and office, 8.1% natural resources, construction, and maintenance, 23.1% production, transportation, and material moving
Income: Per capita: $25,114; Median household: $49,375; Average household: $59,246; Households with income of $100,000 or more: 15.0%; Poverty rate: 18.2%
Educational Attainment: High school diploma or higher: 94.7%; Bachelor's degree or higher: 22.8%; Graduate/professional degree or higher: 10.4%

School District(s)
Odessa-Montour Central SD (PK-12)
    Enrollment: 776 . . . . (607) 594-3341
Housing: Homeownership rate: 67.5%; Median home value: $110,600; Median year structure built: 1946; Homeowner vacancy rate: 1.8%; Median selected monthly owner costs: $1,158 with a mortgage, $540 without a mortgage; Median gross rent: $583 per month; Rental vacancy rate: 0.0%
Health Insurance: 87.5% have insurance; 62.5% have private insurance; 39.6% have public insurance; 12.5% do not have insurance; 14.3% of children under 18 do not have insurance
Transportation: Commute: 90.2% car, 1.4% public transportation, 7.8% walk, 0.7% work from home; Mean travel time to work: 27.3 minutes

ORANGE (town). Covers a land area of 54.069 square miles and a water area of 0.385 square miles. Located at 42.34° N. Lat; 77.04° W. Long.

Population: 1,350; Growth (since 2000): -22.9%; Density: 25.0 persons per square mile; Race: 93.1% White, 4.0% Black/African American, 1.0% Asian, 0.0% American Indian/Alaska Native, 0.0% Native Hawaiian/Other Pacific Islander, 1.9% Two or more races, 0.6% Hispanic of any race; Average household size: 2.47; Median age: 41.0; Age under 18: 19.9%; Age 65 and over: 15.3%; Males per 100 females: 126.0; Marriage status: 28.3% never married, 55.3% now married, 2.8% separated, 6.2% widowed, 10.2% divorced; Foreign born: 1.9%; Speak English only: 98.1%; With disability: 18.4%; Veterans: 8.4%; Ancestry: 19.9% German, 15.3% American, 14.9% Irish, 11.7% English, 10.4% Italian
Employment: 12.7% management, business, and financial, 7.4% computer, engineering, and science, 12.1% education, legal, community service, arts, and media, 6.8% healthcare practitioners, 20.0% service, 17.0% sales and office, 11.0% natural resources, construction, and maintenance, 12.9% production, transportation, and material moving
Income: Per capita: $26,833; Median household: $47,813; Average household: $69,308; Households with income of $100,000 or more: 19.0%; Poverty rate: 20.7%
Educational Attainment: High school diploma or higher: 88.2%; Bachelor's degree or higher: 18.2%; Graduate/professional degree or higher: 3.9%
Housing: Homeownership rate: 83.7%; Median home value: $86,600; Median year structure built: 1980; Homeowner vacancy rate: 2.0%; Median selected monthly owner costs: $1,105 with a mortgage, $474 without a mortgage; Median gross rent: $688 per month; Rental vacancy rate: 16.0%
Health Insurance: 95.8% have insurance; 68.7% have private insurance; 42.4% have public insurance; 4.2% do not have insurance; 3.5% of children under 18 do not have insurance
Transportation: Commute: 92.4% car, 0.0% public transportation, 3.2% walk, 1.8% work from home; Mean travel time to work: 31.4 minutes

READING (town). Covers a land area of 27.149 square miles and a water area of 0 square miles. Located at 42.42° N. Lat; 76.94° W. Long.

Population: 1,548; Growth (since 2000): -13.3%; Density: 57.0 persons per square mile; Race: 93.5% White, 1.9% Black/African American, 0.6% Asian, 0.3% American Indian/Alaska Native, 0.0% Native Hawaiian/Other Pacific Islander, 3.0% Two or more races, 7.4% Hispanic of any race; Average household size: 2.48; Median age: 46.4; Age under 18: 23.4%; Age 65 and over: 17.8%; Males per 100 females: 95.3; Marriage status: 20.1% never married, 58.3% now married, 2.9% separated, 6.8% widowed, 14.8% divorced; Foreign born: 2.2%; Speak English only: 93.3%; With disability: 16.1%; Veterans: 12.2%; Ancestry: 24.9% German, 21.2% Irish, 20.9% English, 12.4% Italian, 6.1% American
Employment: 19.6% management, business, and financial, 3.4% computer, engineering, and science, 10.4% education, legal, community service, arts, and media, 6.2% healthcare practitioners, 15.6% service, 16.8% sales and office, 12.1% natural resources, construction, and maintenance, 15.9% production, transportation, and material moving
Income: Per capita: $27,878; Median household: $60,395; Average household: $69,654; Households with income of $100,000 or more: 23.6%; Poverty rate: 13.6%
Educational Attainment: High school diploma or higher: 87.8%; Bachelor's degree or higher: 22.3%; Graduate/professional degree or higher: 12.0%
Housing: Homeownership rate: 84.2%; Median home value: $150,700; Median year structure built: 1966; Homeowner vacancy rate: 0.0%; Median selected monthly owner costs: $1,141 with a mortgage, $484 without a mortgage; Median gross rent: $850 per month; Rental vacancy rate: 15.5%
Health Insurance: 90.5% have insurance; 67.0% have private insurance; 37.7% have public insurance; 9.5% do not have insurance; 11.1% of children under 18 do not have insurance
Transportation: Commute: 89.2% car, 0.3% public transportation, 3.7% walk, 6.0% work from home; Mean travel time to work: 22.8 minutes

ROCK STREAM (unincorporated postal area)
ZCTA: 14878

Covers a land area of 16.039 square miles and a water area of 0 square miles. Located at 42.45° N. Lat; 76.94° W. Long..
Population: 504; Growth (since 2000): -32.5%; Density: 31.4 persons per square mile; Race: 97.8% White, 0.0% Black/African American, 1.2% Asian, 0.0% American Indian/Alaska Native, 0.0% Native Hawaiian/Other Pacific Islander, 1.0% Two or more races, 3.2% Hispanic of any race; Average household size: 2.08; Median age: 49.6; Age under 18: 16.5%; Age 65 and over: 21.0%; Males per 100 females: 100.8; Marriage status: 14.1% never married, 62.6% now married, 3.0% separated, 6.4% widowed, 16.9% divorced; Foreign born: 1.8%; Speak English only: 87.7%; With disability: 9.3%; Veterans: 21.4%; Ancestry: 23.6% Irish, 22.0% German, 21.0% English, 9.5% French, 8.3% American
Employment: 24.7% management, business, and financial, 3.2% computer, engineering, and science, 17.2% education, legal, community service, arts, and media, 4.5% healthcare practitioners, 17.9% service, 7.8% sales and office, 15.9% natural resources, construction, and maintenance, 8.8% production, transportation, and material moving
Income: Per capita: $43,828; Median household: $65,313; Average household: $91,181; Households with income of $100,000 or more: 32.7%; Poverty rate: 5.0%
Educational Attainment: High school diploma or higher: 94.9%; Bachelor's degree or higher: 24.3%; Graduate/professional degree or higher: 17.9%
Housing: Homeownership rate: 85.1%; Median home value: $137,000; Median year structure built: 1952; Homeowner vacancy rate: 0.0%; Median selected monthly owner costs: $1,108 with a mortgage, $565 without a mortgage; Median gross rent: $733 per month; Rental vacancy rate: 0.0%
Health Insurance: 84.1% have insurance; 68.1% have private insurance; 36.7% have public insurance; 15.9% do not have insurance; 7.9% of children under 18 do not have insurance
Transportation: Commute: 84.4% car, 0.0% public transportation, 8.4% walk, 5.5% work from home; Mean travel time to work: 22.2 minutes

TYRONE (town). Covers a land area of 37.296 square miles and a water area of 2.332 square miles. Located at 42.44° N. Lat; 77.04° W. Long. Elevation is 1,171 feet.

Population: 1,840; Growth (since 2000): 7.4%; Density: 49.3 persons per square mile; Race: 97.7% White, 1.1% Black/African American, 0.2%

Asian, 0.0% American Indian/Alaska Native, 0.0% Native Hawaiian/Other Pacific Islander, 0.8% Two or more races, 0.7% Hispanic of any race; Average household size: 2.83; Median age: 42.3; Age under 18: 26.9%; Age 65 and over: 19.6%; Males per 100 females: 95.7; Marriage status: 29.2% never married, 55.9% now married, 5.9% separated, 5.6% widowed, 9.2% divorced; Foreign born: 0.3%; Speak English only: 96.0%; With disability: 19.4%; Veterans: 11.5%; Ancestry: 28.2% American, 13.5% Irish, 11.5% German, 11.4% English, 7.8% Polish

Employment: 11.9% management, business, and financial, 2.9% computer, engineering, and science, 9.6% education, legal, community service, arts, and media, 7.0% healthcare practitioners, 19.4% service, 20.5% sales and office, 8.5% natural resources, construction, and maintenance, 20.4% production, transportation, and material moving

Income: Per capita: $20,753; Median household: $52,434; Average household: $58,800; Households with income of $100,000 or more: 13.0%; Poverty rate: 20.2%

Educational Attainment: High school diploma or higher: 82.9%; Bachelor's degree or higher: 14.4%; Graduate/professional degree or higher: 6.7%

Housing: Homeownership rate: 78.2%; Median home value: $111,700; Median year structure built: 1962; Homeowner vacancy rate: 0.0%; Median selected monthly owner costs: $994 with a mortgage, $449 without a mortgage; Median gross rent: $763 per month; Rental vacancy rate: 0.0%

Health Insurance: 92.1% have insurance; 59.6% have private insurance; 50.1% have public insurance; 7.9% do not have insurance; 4.0% of children under 18 do not have insurance

Transportation: Commute: 90.1% car, 0.0% public transportation, 0.8% walk, 7.4% work from home; Mean travel time to work: 28.7 minutes

WATKINS GLEN (village). County seat. Covers a land area of 1.559 square miles and a water area of 0.383 square miles. Located at 42.38° N. Lat; 76.87° W. Long. Elevation is 463 feet.

History: The resort hotel here is famed for its mineral spring water. An international Grand Prix sports-car race was held here annually until 1981. Incorporated 1842.

Population: 2,006; Growth (since 2000): -6.7%; Density: 1,286.7 persons per square mile; Race: 94.8% White, 1.7% Black/African American, 1.3% Asian, 0.0% American Indian/Alaska Native, 0.0% Native Hawaiian/Other Pacific Islander, 2.1% Two or more races, 5.4% Hispanic of any race; Average household size: 2.45; Median age: 39.1; Age under 18: 22.7%; Age 65 and over: 17.7%; Males per 100 females: 87.2; Marriage status: 35.1% never married, 44.0% now married, 4.0% separated, 5.6% widowed, 15.3% divorced; Foreign born: 1.5%; Speak English only: 98.6%; With disability: 19.7%; Veterans: 12.1%; Ancestry: 17.7% Irish, 16.1% American, 15.8% German, 15.8% Italian, 10.3% English

Employment: 9.5% management, business, and financial, 0.6% computer, engineering, and science, 11.6% education, legal, community service, arts, and media, 8.7% healthcare practitioners, 23.3% service, 23.4% sales and office, 8.6% natural resources, construction, and maintenance, 14.3% production, transportation, and material moving

Income: Per capita: $24,151; Median household: $45,938; Average household: $59,052; Households with income of $100,000 or more: 15.4%; Poverty rate: 19.3%

Educational Attainment: High school diploma or higher: 87.0%; Bachelor's degree or higher: 20.9%; Graduate/professional degree or higher: 8.3%

School District(s)

Watkins Glen Central SD (PK-12)

    Enrollment: 1,082 . . . . (607) 535-3220

Housing: Homeownership rate: 61.2%; Median home value: $122,400; Median year structure built: Before 1940; Homeowner vacancy rate: 0.0%; Median selected monthly owner costs: $1,081 with a mortgage, $503 without a mortgage; Median gross rent: $673 per month; Rental vacancy rate: 9.0%

Health Insurance: 93.9% have insurance; 62.8% have private insurance; 44.1% have public insurance; 6.1% do not have insurance; 0.8% of children under 18 do not have insurance

Safety: Violent crime rate: 5.3 per 10,000 population; Property crime rate: 100.2 per 10,000 population

Transportation: Commute: 77.0% car, 0.7% public transportation, 14.1% walk, 6.8% work from home; Mean travel time to work: 20.7 minutes

Seneca County

Located in west central New York, in the Finger Lakes region; bounded on the east by Cayuga Lake and the Seneca River, and partly on the west by Seneca Lake. Covers a land area of 323.705 square miles, a water area of 66.734 square miles, and is located in the Eastern Time Zone at 42.78° N. Lat., 76.83° W. Long. The county was founded in 1804. County seat is Waterloo.

Seneca County is part of the Seneca Falls, NY Micropolitan Statistical Area. The entire metro area includes: Seneca County, NY

Population: 34,843; Growth (since 2000): 4.5%; Density: 107.6 persons per square mile; Race: 91.6% White, 4.9% Black/African American, 0.7% Asian, 0.3% American Indian/Alaska Native, 0.0% Native Hawaiian/Other Pacific Islander, 1.8% two or more races, 3.3% Hispanic of any race; Average household size: 2.34; Median age: 42.2; Age under 18: 20.1%; Age 65 and over: 17.7%; Males per 100 females: 109.9; Marriage status: 31.5% never married, 49.3% now married, 2.0% separated, 6.6% widowed, 12.6% divorced; Foreign born: 2.2%; Speak English only: 93.4%; With disability: 16.6%; Veterans: 9.2%; Ancestry: 19.4% German, 17.0% Irish, 15.9% Italian, 13.3% English, 7.3% American

Religion: Six largest groups: 3.1% Methodist/Pietist, 2.7% Catholicism, 2.1% European Free-Church, 1.9% Presbyterian-Reformed, 1.7% Non-denominational Protestant, 1.4% Latter-day Saints

Economy: Unemployment rate: 3.1%; Leading industries: 23.6 % retail trade; 11.7 % other services (except public administration); 11.0 % accommodation and food services; Farms: 584 totaling 130,206 acres; Company size: 0 employ 1,000 or more persons, 1 employs 500 to 999 persons, 10 employ 100 to 499 persons, 706 employ less than 100 persons; Business ownership: 561 women-owned, n/a Black-owned, n/a Hispanic-owned, 46 Asian-owned, n/a American Indian/Alaska Native-owned

Employment: 13.2% management, business, and financial, 2.7% computer, engineering, and science, 11.7% education, legal, community service, arts, and media, 5.4% healthcare practitioners, 17.6% service, 23.9% sales and office, 11.1% natural resources, construction, and maintenance, 14.3% production, transportation, and material moving

Income: Per capita: $26,541; Median household: $51,601; Average household: $67,092; Households with income of $100,000 or more: 18.7%; Poverty rate: 11.8%

Educational Attainment: High school diploma or higher: 85.9%; Bachelor's degree or higher: 20.5%; Graduate/professional degree or higher: 8.6%

Housing: Homeownership rate: 73.2%; Median home value: $98,400; Median year structure built: 1958; Homeowner vacancy rate: 1.1%; Median selected monthly owner costs: $1,127 with a mortgage, $503 without a mortgage; Median gross rent: $750 per month; Rental vacancy rate: 5.9%

Vital Statistics: Birth rate: 103.2 per 10,000 population; Death rate: 92.5 per 10,000 population; Age-adjusted cancer mortality rate: 183.5 deaths per 100,000 population

Health Insurance: 90.3% have insurance; 69.8% have private insurance; 38.6% have public insurance; 9.7% do not have insurance; 12.1% of children under 18 do not have insurance

Health Care: Physicians: 3.5 per 10,000 population; Dentists: 2.6 per 10,000 population; Hospital beds: 0.0 per 10,000 population; Hospital admissions: 0.0 per 10,000 population

Air Quality Index (AQI): Percent of Days: 100.0% good, 0.0% moderate, 0.0% unhealthy for sensitive individuals, 0.0% unhealthy, 0.0% very unhealthy; Annual median: 0; Annual maximum: 20

Transportation: Commute: 89.9% car, 0.7% public transportation, 3.3% walk, 4.0% work from home; Mean travel time to work: 22.3 minutes

2016 Presidential Election: 51.8% Trump, 40.8% Clinton, 4.6% Johnson, 1.9% Stein

National and State Parks: Cayuga Lake State Park; Lodi Point State Marine Park; Montezuma National Wildlife Refuge; Sampson State Park; Seneca Lake State Park; Women's Rights National Historical Park

Additional Information Contacts

Seneca Government . . . . (315) 539-1771
   http://www.co.seneca.ny.us

Seneca County Communities

COVERT (town). Covers a land area of 31.385 square miles and a water area of 6.195 square miles. Located at 42.58° N. Lat; 76.70° W. Long. Elevation is 906 feet.
Population: 2,224; Growth (since 2000): -0.1%; Density: 70.9 persons per square mile; Race: 97.5% White, 0.0% Black/African American, 0.9% Asian, 0.6% American Indian/Alaska Native, 0.0% Native Hawaiian/Other Pacific Islander, 1.0% Two or more races, 1.1% Hispanic of any race; Average household size: 2.40; Median age: 46.2; Age under 18: 21.3%; Age 65 and over: 23.3%; Males per 100 females: 105.9; Marriage status: 27.7% never married, 55.5% now married, 0.7% separated, 5.2% widowed, 11.6% divorced; Foreign born: 3.5%; Speak English only: 95.3%; With disability: 15.2%; Veterans: 9.5%; Ancestry: 19.6% English, 16.7% Irish, 14.7% Italian, 13.4% German, 7.5% American
Employment: 18.7% management, business, and financial, 2.1% computer, engineering, and science, 12.7% education, legal, community service, arts, and media, 7.5% healthcare practitioners, 14.6% service, 24.8% sales and office, 10.3% natural resources, construction, and maintenance, 9.2% production, transportation, and material moving
Income: Per capita: $28,637; Median household: $58,393; Average household: $69,023; Households with income of $100,000 or more: 19.6%; Poverty rate: 8.3%
Educational Attainment: High school diploma or higher: 91.6%; Bachelor's degree or higher: 28.6%; Graduate/professional degree or higher: 13.6%
Housing: Homeownership rate: 82.6%; Median home value: $126,600; Median year structure built: 1954; Homeowner vacancy rate: 0.8%; Median selected monthly owner costs: $1,178 with a mortgage, $573 without a mortgage; Median gross rent: $875 per month; Rental vacancy rate: 18.0%
Health Insurance: 94.6% have insurance; 78.1% have private insurance; 36.1% have public insurance; 5.4% do not have insurance; 7.5% of children under 18 do not have insurance
Transportation: Commute: 87.4% car, 3.5% public transportation, 4.1% walk, 5.0% work from home; Mean travel time to work: 27.5 minutes

FAYETTE (town). Covers a land area of 54.819 square miles and a water area of 11.583 square miles. Located at 42.84° N. Lat; 76.86° W. Long. Elevation is 607 feet.
Population: 3,881; Growth (since 2000): 6.5%; Density: 70.8 persons per square mile; Race: 96.1% White, 0.0% Black/African American, 0.6% Asian, 0.0% American Indian/Alaska Native, 0.0% Native Hawaiian/Other Pacific Islander, 2.8% Two or more races, 1.9% Hispanic of any race; Average household size: 2.42; Median age: 49.5; Age under 18: 20.6%; Age 65 and over: 21.3%; Males per 100 females: 97.2; Marriage status: 19.9% never married, 63.0% now married, 1.9% separated, 6.0% widowed, 11.1% divorced; Foreign born: 2.5%; Speak English only: 96.2%; With disability: 16.2%; Veterans: 11.2%; Ancestry: 25.3% German, 18.1% Irish, 15.5% English, 15.4% Italian, 5.4% Swiss
Employment: 18.8% management, business, and financial, 2.1% computer, engineering, and science, 9.9% education, legal, community service, arts, and media, 4.6% healthcare practitioners, 14.4% service, 24.3% sales and office, 8.9% natural resources, construction, and maintenance, 17.0% production, transportation, and material moving
Income: Per capita: $31,472; Median household: $63,137; Average household: $76,283; Households with income of $100,000 or more: 22.9%; Poverty rate: 11.1%
Educational Attainment: High school diploma or higher: 88.6%; Bachelor's degree or higher: 22.8%; Graduate/professional degree or higher: 6.7%
Housing: Homeownership rate: 82.2%; Median home value: $109,200; Median year structure built: 1969; Homeowner vacancy rate: 2.9%; Median selected monthly owner costs: $1,293 with a mortgage, $529 without a mortgage; Median gross rent: $807 per month; Rental vacancy rate: 7.2%
Health Insurance: 86.0% have insurance; 69.7% have private insurance; 36.0% have public insurance; 14.0% do not have insurance; 20.8% of children under 18 do not have insurance
Transportation: Commute: 91.0% car, 0.3% public transportation, 2.8% walk, 3.6% work from home; Mean travel time to work: 19.2 minutes

INTERLAKEN (village). Covers a land area of 0.267 square miles and a water area of 0 square miles. Located at 42.62° N. Lat; 76.72° W. Long. Elevation is 906 feet.
Population: 626; Growth (since 2000): -7.1%; Density: 2,341.1 persons per square mile; Race: 96.0% White, 0.0% Black/African American, 1.0% Asian, 0.0% American Indian/Alaska Native, 0.0% Native Hawaiian/Other Pacific Islander, 3.0% Two or more races, 0.2% Hispanic of any race; Average household size: 2.49; Median age: 37.8; Age under 18: 19.0%; Age 65 and over: 11.5%; Males per 100 females: 99.3; Marriage status: 41.6% never married, 40.3% now married, 0.7% separated, 3.9% widowed, 14.2% divorced; Foreign born: 4.8%; Speak English only: 95.3%; With disability: 15.3%; Veterans: 5.1%; Ancestry: 25.6% English, 19.0% Irish, 14.4% German, 10.5% Italian, 8.8% American
Employment: 13.2% management, business, and financial, 0.6% computer, engineering, and science, 19.2% education, legal, community service, arts, and media, 3.7% healthcare practitioners, 19.2% service, 23.4% sales and office, 8.7% natural resources, construction, and maintenance, 12.1% production, transportation, and material moving
Income: Per capita: $25,203; Median household: $54,250; Average household: $63,465; Households with income of $100,000 or more: 14.7%; Poverty rate: 15.8%
Educational Attainment: High school diploma or higher: 87.2%; Bachelor's degree or higher: 33.9%; Graduate/professional degree or higher: 16.0%

School District(s)
South Seneca Central SD (KG-12)
    Enrollment: 745 . . . . (607) 869-9636
Housing: Homeownership rate: 78.1%; Median home value: $83,800; Median year structure built: Before 1940; Homeowner vacancy rate: 0.0%; Median selected monthly owner costs: $1,101 with a mortgage, $526 without a mortgage; Median gross rent: $664 per month; Rental vacancy rate: 10.9%
Health Insurance: 93.1% have insurance; 65.7% have private insurance; 38.7% have public insurance; 6.9% do not have insurance; 6.8% of children under 18 do not have insurance
Safety: Violent crime rate: 0.0 per 10,000 population; Property crime rate: 32.2 per 10,000 population
Transportation: Commute: 94.3% car, 1.7% public transportation, 2.8% walk, 1.1% work from home; Mean travel time to work: 26.5 minutes

JUNIUS (town). Covers a land area of 26.709 square miles and a water area of 0.145 square miles. Located at 42.97° N. Lat; 76.91° W. Long. Elevation is 443 feet.
Population: 1,485; Growth (since 2000): 9.0%; Density: 55.6 persons per square mile; Race: 98.9% White, 0.0% Black/African American, 0.2% Asian, 0.0% American Indian/Alaska Native, 0.0% Native Hawaiian/Other Pacific Islander, 0.9% Two or more races, 4.0% Hispanic of any race; Average household size: 2.77; Median age: 37.4; Age under 18: 28.1%; Age 65 and over: 17.8%; Males per 100 females: 103.5; Marriage status: 23.5% never married, 56.6% now married, 2.3% separated, 7.6% widowed, 12.3% divorced; Foreign born: 1.2%; Speak English only: 94.8%; With disability: 14.3%; Veterans: 12.5%; Ancestry: 21.7% German, 14.2% Italian, 13.0% American, 10.7% English, 9.2% French
Employment: 11.5% management, business, and financial, 4.6% computer, engineering, and science, 6.3% education, legal, community service, arts, and media, 1.9% healthcare practitioners, 15.9% service, 23.7% sales and office, 8.5% natural resources, construction, and maintenance, 27.8% production, transportation, and material moving
Income: Per capita: $23,452; Median household: $50,500; Average household: $64,643; Households with income of $100,000 or more: 16.8%; Poverty rate: 10.4%
Educational Attainment: High school diploma or higher: 80.6%; Bachelor's degree or higher: 10.9%; Graduate/professional degree or higher: 2.7%
Housing: Homeownership rate: 82.8%; Median home value: $94,400; Median year structure built: 1974; Homeowner vacancy rate: 2.8%; Median selected monthly owner costs: $1,045 with a mortgage, $468 without a mortgage; Median gross rent: $707 per month; Rental vacancy rate: 0.0%
Health Insurance: 86.8% have insurance; 64.0% have private insurance; 37.6% have public insurance; 13.2% do not have insurance; 13.8% of children under 18 do not have insurance
Transportation: Commute: 91.8% car, 0.0% public transportation, 5.1% walk, 2.7% work from home; Mean travel time to work: 20.3 minutes

LODI (town). Covers a land area of 34.190 square miles and a water area of 5.574 square miles. Located at 42.59° N. Lat; 76.83° W. Long. Elevation is 1,106 feet.
Population: 1,546; Growth (since 2000): 4.7%; Density: 45.2 persons per square mile; Race: 98.3% White, 0.3% Black/African American, 0.2% Asian, 0.1% American Indian/Alaska Native, 0.0% Native Hawaiian/Other Pacific Islander, 0.6% Two or more races, 0.9% Hispanic of any race; Average household size: 2.17; Median age: 47.8; Age under 18: 19.1%; Age 65 and over: 22.9%; Males per 100 females: 104.2; Marriage status: 24.4% never married, 57.6% now married, 1.8% separated, 7.7% widowed, 10.4% divorced; Foreign born: 1.0%; Speak English only: 92.4%; With disability: 16.2%; Veterans: 9.7%; Ancestry: 20.5% Irish, 19.6% English, 18.0% German, 15.3% American, 7.8% Dutch
Employment: 11.5% management, business, and financial, 3.7% computer, engineering, and science, 16.1% education, legal, community service, arts, and media, 2.3% healthcare practitioners, 21.8% service, 16.1% sales and office, 17.7% natural resources, construction, and maintenance, 10.8% production, transportation, and material moving
Income: Per capita: $26,805; Median household: $48,750; Average household: $57,961; Households with income of $100,000 or more: 13.5%; Poverty rate: 8.7%
Educational Attainment: High school diploma or higher: 86.3%; Bachelor's degree or higher: 19.6%; Graduate/professional degree or higher: 9.9%
Housing: Homeownership rate: 82.0%; Median home value: $118,800; Median year structure built: 1971; Homeowner vacancy rate: 0.0%; Median selected monthly owner costs: $1,134 with a mortgage, $544 without a mortgage; Median gross rent: $656 per month; Rental vacancy rate: 3.0%
Health Insurance: 89.2% have insurance; 69.5% have private insurance; 38.0% have public insurance; 10.8% do not have insurance; 15.9% of children under 18 do not have insurance
Transportation: Commute: 90.2% car, 0.3% public transportation, 2.2% walk, 3.6% work from home; Mean travel time to work: 30.2 minutes

LODI (village). Covers a land area of 0.551 square miles and a water area of 0.002 square miles. Located at 42.61° N. Lat; 76.82° W. Long. Elevation is 1,106 feet.
Population: 328; Growth (since 2000): -3.0%; Density: 595.1 persons per square mile; Race: 98.8% White, 0.0% Black/African American, 0.0% Asian, 0.3% American Indian/Alaska Native, 0.0% Native Hawaiian/Other Pacific Islander, 0.0% Two or more races, 1.5% Hispanic of any race; Average household size: 2.25; Median age: 42.5; Age under 18: 14.0%; Age 65 and over: 13.7%; Males per 100 females: 122.1; Marriage status: 23.9% never married, 57.1% now married, 5.2% separated, 3.1% widowed, 15.9% divorced; Foreign born: 1.5%; Speak English only: 99.7%; With disability: 12.5%; Veterans: 7.4%; Ancestry: 20.7% English, 16.2% Irish, 13.4% American, 12.5% German, 9.1% Italian
Employment: 4.5% management, business, and financial, 9.7% computer, engineering, and science, 16.1% education, legal, community service, arts, and media, 1.9% healthcare practitioners, 25.8% service, 12.9% sales and office, 11.6% natural resources, construction, and maintenance, 17.4% production, transportation, and material moving
Income: Per capita: $24,992; Median household: $42,353; Average household: $56,007; Households with income of $100,000 or more: 16.5%; Poverty rate: 14.0%
Educational Attainment: High school diploma or higher: 90.5%; Bachelor's degree or higher: 20.9%; Graduate/professional degree or higher: 13.8%
Housing: Homeownership rate: 71.2%; Median home value: $66,700; Median year structure built: Before 1940; Homeowner vacancy rate: 0.0%; Median selected monthly owner costs: $938 with a mortgage, $431 without a mortgage; Median gross rent: $736 per month; Rental vacancy rate: 8.7%
Health Insurance: 90.2% have insurance; 59.8% have private insurance; 45.1% have public insurance; 9.8% do not have insurance; 4.3% of children under 18 do not have insurance
Transportation: Commute: 88.0% car, 1.3% public transportation, 6.0% walk, 0.0% work from home; Mean travel time to work: 23.7 minutes

OVID (town). Covers a land area of 30.861 square miles and a water area of 7.893 square miles. Located at 42.65° N. Lat; 76.80° W. Long. Elevation is 968 feet.
Population: 2,313; Growth (since 2000): -16.1%; Density: 74.9 persons per square mile; Race: 94.7% White, 1.1% Black/African American, 1.1% Asian, 1.3% American Indian/Alaska Native, 0.0% Native Hawaiian/Other

Pacific Islander, 1.5% Two or more races, 1.3% Hispanic of any race; Average household size: 2.42; Median age: 38.0; Age under 18: 24.5%; Age 65 and over: 17.8%; Males per 100 females: 101.1; Marriage status: 26.0% never married, 55.4% now married, 3.3% separated, 7.3% widowed, 11.3% divorced; Foreign born: 1.1%; Speak English only: 91.7%; With disability: 18.2%; Veterans: 9.0%; Ancestry: 21.0% German, 16.4% English, 14.7% Irish, 12.1% American, 5.6% Italian
Employment: 14.7% management, business, and financial, 2.7% computer, engineering, and science, 13.2% education, legal, community service, arts, and media, 6.1% healthcare practitioners, 23.4% service, 19.5% sales and office, 11.6% natural resources, construction, and maintenance, 8.8% production, transportation, and material moving
Income: Per capita: $25,479; Median household: $43,920; Average household: $62,397; Households with income of $100,000 or more: 17.1%; Poverty rate: 13.6%
Educational Attainment: High school diploma or higher: 86.5%; Bachelor's degree or higher: 23.5%; Graduate/professional degree or higher: 10.6%
School District(s)
South Seneca Central SD (KG-12)
    Enrollment: 745 . . . . (607) 869-9636
Housing: Homeownership rate: 77.0%; Median home value: $99,100; Median year structure built: 1958; Homeowner vacancy rate: 1.9%; Median selected monthly owner costs: $1,097 with a mortgage, $477 without a mortgage; Median gross rent: $629 per month; Rental vacancy rate: 5.5%
Health Insurance: 85.1% have insurance; 62.0% have private insurance; 40.3% have public insurance; 14.9% do not have insurance; 18.6% of children under 18 do not have insurance
Transportation: Commute: 86.0% car, 0.7% public transportation, 6.3% walk, 5.8% work from home; Mean travel time to work: 28.1 minutes

OVID (village). Covers a land area of 0.398 square miles and a water area of 0 square miles. Located at 42.68° N. Lat; 76.82° W. Long. Elevation is 968 feet.
Population: 647; Growth (since 2000): 5.7%; Density: 1,627.4 persons per square mile; Race: 90.3% White, 1.4% Black/African American, 3.6% Asian, 1.9% American Indian/Alaska Native, 0.0% Native Hawaiian/Other Pacific Islander, 1.7% Two or more races, 3.4% Hispanic of any race; Average household size: 2.78; Median age: 28.8; Age under 18: 30.8%; Age 65 and over: 11.1%; Males per 100 females: 93.6; Marriage status: 30.4% never married, 47.8% now married, 2.1% separated, 9.5% widowed, 12.2% divorced; Foreign born: 2.9%; Speak English only: 96.9%; With disability: 12.5%; Veterans: 10.3%; Ancestry: 29.5% German, 23.0% Irish, 13.8% English, 5.1% French, 4.3% Scottish
Employment: 12.0% management, business, and financial, 2.7% computer, engineering, and science, 15.1% education, legal, community service, arts, and media, 0.7% healthcare practitioners, 29.6% service, 22.3% sales and office, 13.7% natural resources, construction, and maintenance, 3.8% production, transportation, and material moving
Income: Per capita: $27,097; Median household: $49,779; Average household: $76,707; Households with income of $100,000 or more: 17.6%; Poverty rate: 11.4%
Educational Attainment: High school diploma or higher: 90.5%; Bachelor's degree or higher: 21.7%; Graduate/professional degree or higher: 13.0%
School District(s)
South Seneca Central SD (KG-12)
    Enrollment: 745 . . . . (607) 869-9636
Housing: Homeownership rate: 73.0%; Median home value: $90,000; Median year structure built: Before 1940; Homeowner vacancy rate: 7.6%; Median selected monthly owner costs: $986 with a mortgage, $450 without a mortgage; Median gross rent: $649 per month; Rental vacancy rate: 15.9%
Health Insurance: 91.3% have insurance; 63.5% have private insurance; 40.8% have public insurance; 8.7% do not have insurance; 0.0% of children under 18 do not have insurance
Transportation: Commute: 87.3% car, 0.0% public transportation, 8.6% walk, 4.1% work from home; Mean travel time to work: 26.6 minutes

ROMULUS (CDP). Covers a land area of 0.609 square miles and a water area of 0 square miles. Located at 42.75° N. Lat; 76.84° W. Long. Elevation is 718 feet.
Population: 504; Growth (since 2000): n/a; Density: 828.1 persons per square mile; Race: 99.6% White, 0.0% Black/African American, 0.0% Asian, 0.0% American Indian/Alaska Native, 0.0% Native Hawaiian/Other

Pacific Islander, 0.4% Two or more races, 10.9% Hispanic of any race; Average household size: 2.83; Median age: 33.8; Age under 18: 28.4%; Age 65 and over: 16.3%; Males per 100 females: 96.6; Marriage status: 34.8% never married, 52.5% now married, 0.0% separated, 5.1% widowed, 7.6% divorced; Foreign born: 0.2%; Speak English only: 99.1%; With disability: 17.9%; Veterans: 8.9%; Ancestry: 21.6% English, 20.4% German, 17.7% Irish, 14.9% American, 11.1% Italian

Employment: 5.4% management, business, and financial, 0.0% computer, engineering, and science, 2.2% education, legal, community service, arts, and media, 16.6% healthcare practitioners, 15.2% service, 32.3% sales and office, 12.6% natural resources, construction, and maintenance, 15.7% production, transportation, and material moving

Income: Per capita: $18,895; Median household: $46,417; Average household: $53,215; Households with income of $100,000 or more: 1.7%; Poverty rate: 21.4%

Educational Attainment: High school diploma or higher: 87.8%; Bachelor's degree or higher: 5.5%; Graduate/professional degree or higher: 1.6%

School District(s)

Romulus Central SD (PK-12)

    Enrollment: 447 . . . . (607) 869-5391

Housing: Homeownership rate: 74.3%; Median home value: $70,500; Median year structure built: 1950; Homeowner vacancy rate: 0.0%; Median selected monthly owner costs: $850 with a mortgage, $434 without a mortgage; Median gross rent: $836 per month; Rental vacancy rate: 18.2%

Health Insurance: 89.7% have insurance; 59.9% have private insurance; 45.0% have public insurance; 10.3% do not have insurance; 13.3% of children under 18 do not have insurance

Transportation: Commute: 86.1% car, 0.9% public transportation, 10.8% walk, 1.3% work from home; Mean travel time to work: 21.9 minutes

ROMULUS (town).

Covers a land area of 37.792 square miles and a water area of 13.591 square miles. Located at 42.71° N. Lat; 76.83° W. Long. Elevation is 718 feet.

History: The town is named after the mythical founder of Rome, Romulus, a name assigned by a clerk with an interest in the classics. Before the American Revolution, this area was controlled by both the Cayuga tribe and the Seneca tribe. Jesuit missionaries visited the area in the 17th Century. A punitive action in 1779 destroyed native villages and drove many of the Native Americans away. Romulus contains the area of Kendaia (Apple Town), a former Iroquois (Cayuga) village destroyed by the residents in anticipation of the arrival of the Sullivan Expedition on September 5, 1779.

Population: 4,347; Growth (since 2000): 113.5%; Density: 115.0 persons per square mile; Race: 63.3% White, 30.9% Black/African American, 0.1% Asian, 1.2% American Indian/Alaska Native, 0.0% Native Hawaiian/Other Pacific Islander, 2.1% Two or more races, 11.1% Hispanic of any race; Average household size: 2.47; Median age: 36.2; Age under 18: 10.8%; Age 65 and over: 9.3%; Males per 100 females: 264.2; Marriage status: 51.7% never married, 34.5% now married, 3.3% separated, 3.4% widowed, 10.3% divorced; Foreign born: 3.1%; Speak English only: 87.1%; With disability: 15.9%; Veterans: 4.9%; Ancestry: 15.8% German, 11.0% Irish, 6.5% English, 6.5% Italian, 5.2% American

Employment: 11.8% management, business, and financial, 3.5% computer, engineering, and science, 9.5% education, legal, community service, arts, and media, 3.2% healthcare practitioners, 22.2% service, 27.1% sales and office, 11.7% natural resources, construction, and maintenance, 11.1% production, transportation, and material moving

Income: Per capita: $14,780; Median household: $57,550; Average household: $69,046; Households with income of $100,000 or more: 15.5%; Poverty rate: 8.1%

Educational Attainment: High school diploma or higher: 68.5%; Bachelor's degree or higher: 8.6%; Graduate/professional degree or higher: 3.9%

School District(s)

Romulus Central SD (PK-12)

    Enrollment: 447 . . . . (607) 869-5391

Housing: Homeownership rate: 64.8%; Median home value: $99,400; Median year structure built: 1953; Homeowner vacancy rate: 0.0%; Median selected monthly owner costs: $1,026 with a mortgage, $421 without a mortgage; Median gross rent: $849 per month; Rental vacancy rate: 1.8%

Health Insurance: 80.4% have insurance; 62.8% have private insurance; 35.1% have public insurance; 19.6% do not have insurance; 25.5% of children under 18 do not have insurance

Transportation: Commute: 82.4% car, 0.2% public transportation, 8.3% walk, 3.6% work from home; Mean travel time to work: 26.3 minutes

Additional Information Contacts

Town of Romulus . . . . (607) 869-9326
  http://www.romulustown.com

SENECA FALLS (town).

Covers a land area of 24.217 square miles and a water area of 3.242 square miles. Located at 42.91° N. Lat; 76.79° W. Long. Elevation is 449 feet.

History: Seneca Falls owes its early industrial development to the 50-foot waterfall which provided power, and its fame to great women who mothered the causes of woman's suffrage, anti-slavery, and temperance. Amelia Jenks Bloomer (1818-1894), wife of the local postmaster, did not invent the bloomers but she introduced them and advocated them as a uniform for women fighting for suffrage. Elizabeth Cady Stanton (1815-1902) moved to Seneca Falls in 1847, and the two called together the first convention of women fighting for suffrage. Susan B. Anthony (1820-1906) also joined the group and was president of the American Women's Suffrage Association until 1900.

Population: 8,838; Growth (since 2000): -5.4%; Density: 364.9 persons per square mile; Race: 93.6% White, 2.3% Black/African American, 1.9% Asian, 0.1% American Indian/Alaska Native, 0.0% Native Hawaiian/Other Pacific Islander, 2.0% Two or more races, 2.4% Hispanic of any race; Average household size: 2.23; Median age: 42.7; Age under 18: 18.6%; Age 65 and over: 17.9%; Males per 100 females: 97.5; Marriage status: 32.1% never married, 48.9% now married, 2.0% separated, 7.7% widowed, 11.4% divorced; Foreign born: 3.3%; Speak English only: 92.6%; With disability: 15.8%; Veterans: 8.7%; Ancestry: 23.2% Italian, 21.2% Irish, 16.3% German, 14.2% English, 6.3% American

Employment: 14.8% management, business, and financial, 3.5% computer, engineering, and science, 14.1% education, legal, community service, arts, and media, 5.2% healthcare practitioners, 18.3% service, 24.3% sales and office, 8.3% natural resources, construction, and maintenance, 11.6% production, transportation, and material moving

Income: Per capita: $30,273; Median household: $50,407; Average household: $69,559; Households with income of $100,000 or more: 22.0%; Poverty rate: 12.5%

Educational Attainment: High school diploma or higher: 91.7%; Bachelor's degree or higher: 28.9%; Graduate/professional degree or higher: 12.2%

School District(s)

Seneca Falls Central SD (KG-12)

    Enrollment: 1,325 . . . . (315) 568-5818

Four-year College(s)

New York Chiropractic College (Private, Not-for-profit)

    Enrollment: 926 . . . . (315) 568-3000

Housing: Homeownership rate: 66.5%; Median home value: $100,700; Median year structure built: 1952; Homeowner vacancy rate: 1.2%; Median selected monthly owner costs: $1,165 with a mortgage, $509 without a mortgage; Median gross rent: $750 per month; Rental vacancy rate: 8.0%

Health Insurance: 94.1% have insurance; 72.2% have private insurance; 39.9% have public insurance; 5.9% do not have insurance; 3.7% of children under 18 do not have insurance

Safety: Violent crime rate: 12.5 per 10,000 population; Property crime rate: 271.3 per 10,000 population

Transportation: Commute: 89.0% car, 0.5% public transportation, 3.5% walk, 4.4% work from home; Mean travel time to work: 21.3 minutes

Additional Information Contacts

Town of Seneca Falls . . . . (315) 568-8013
  http://www.senecafalls.com

SENECA FALLS (CDP).

Covers a land area of 4.414 square miles and a water area of 0.157 square miles. Located at 42.91° N. Lat; 76.80° W. Long. Elevation is 449 feet.

History: Elizabeth Cady Stanton lived here and helped organize first women's rights convention in U.S., held here in 1848. Women's Rights National Historic Park and Museum, located in the restored Elizabeth Cady Stanton House, and the National Women's Hall of Fame are here. Settled 1787, Incorporated 1831.

Population: 6,171; Growth (since 2000): -10.1%; Density: 1,398.2 persons per square mile; Race: 93.9% White, 2.2% Black/African American, 1.6% Asian, 0.1% American Indian/Alaska Native, 0.0% Native Hawaiian/Other Pacific Islander, 2.0% Two or more races, 1.9% Hispanic of any race; Average household size: 2.27; Median age: 43.6; Age under 18: 19.5%; Age 65 and over: 18.8%; Males per 100 females: 95.5; Marriage status:

30.0% never married, 48.3% now married, 1.9% separated, 9.2% widowed, 12.5% divorced; Foreign born: 3.2%; Speak English only: 93.7%; With disability: 16.3%; Veterans: 9.5%; Ancestry: 24.4% Italian, 23.1% Irish, 15.9% English, 14.2% German, 7.2% American

Employment: 15.5% management, business, and financial, 4.2% computer, engineering, and science, 11.3% education, legal, community service, arts, and media, 6.6% healthcare practitioners, 17.5% service, 26.7% sales and office, 7.1% natural resources, construction, and maintenance, 11.1% production, transportation, and material moving

Income: Per capita: $27,907; Median household: $48,347; Average household: $64,474; Households with income of $100,000 or more: 18.8%; Poverty rate: 13.7%

Educational Attainment: High school diploma or higher: 91.6%; Bachelor's degree or higher: 28.7%; Graduate/professional degree or higher: 10.2%

School District(s)
Seneca Falls Central SD (KG-12)
Enrollment: 1,325 . . . . (315) 568-5818

Four-year College(s)
New York Chiropractic College (Private, Not-for-profit)
Enrollment: 926 . . . . (315) 568-3000

Housing: Homeownership rate: 68.1%; Median home value: $91,200; Median year structure built: Before 1940; Homeowner vacancy rate: 1.7%; Median selected monthly owner costs: $1,076 with a mortgage, $473 without a mortgage; Median gross rent: $742 per month; Rental vacancy rate: 11.6%

Health Insurance: 93.8% have insurance; 70.7% have private insurance; 43.4% have public insurance; 6.2% do not have insurance; 4.2% of children under 18 do not have insurance

Transportation: Commute: 87.9% car, 0.4% public transportation, 4.1% walk, 5.0% work from home; Mean travel time to work: 19.5 minutes

Additional Information Contacts
Village of Seneca Falls . . . . (315) 568-8107
http://www.senecafalls.com/village-listings.php

TYRE (town). Covers a land area of 30.054 square miles and a water area of 3.060 square miles. Located at 42.99° N. Lat; 76.79° W. Long. Elevation is 410 feet.

Population: 935; Growth (since 2000): 4.0%; Density: 31.1 persons per square mile; Race: 99.6% White, 0.0% Black/African American, 0.0% Asian, 0.4% American Indian/Alaska Native, 0.0% Native Hawaiian/Other Pacific Islander, 0.0% Two or more races, 0.0% Hispanic of any race; Average household size: 2.55; Median age: 39.3; Age under 18: 27.2%; Age 65 and over: 12.4%; Males per 100 females: 101.9; Marriage status: 30.0% never married, 51.8% now married, 1.1% separated, 5.5% widowed, 12.6% divorced; Foreign born: 0.7%; Speak English only: 96.6%; With disability: 11.4%; Veterans: 10.4%; Ancestry: 20.9% Italian, 19.9% German, 17.9% Irish, 15.0% English, 8.2% American

Employment: 12.6% management, business, and financial, 2.1% computer, engineering, and science, 10.0% education, legal, community service, arts, and media, 4.2% healthcare practitioners, 10.5% service, 20.2% sales and office, 17.9% natural resources, construction, and maintenance, 22.6% production, transportation, and material moving

Income: Per capita: $26,479; Median household: $54,375; Average household: $68,693; Households with income of $100,000 or more: 23.6%; Poverty rate: 12.5%

Educational Attainment: High school diploma or higher: 86.0%; Bachelor's degree or higher: 21.2%; Graduate/professional degree or higher: 8.3%

Housing: Homeownership rate: 88.0%; Median home value: $94,300; Median year structure built: 1963; Homeowner vacancy rate: 0.0%; Median selected monthly owner costs: $1,164 with a mortgage, $457 without a mortgage; Median gross rent: $567 per month; Rental vacancy rate: 12.0%

Health Insurance: 86.6% have insurance; 65.6% have private insurance; 36.5% have public insurance; 13.4% do not have insurance; 18.5% of children under 18 do not have insurance

Transportation: Commute: 93.1% car, 0.5% public transportation, 1.9% walk, 4.0% work from home; Mean travel time to work: 22.3 minutes

VARICK (town). Covers a land area of 31.994 square miles and a water area of 13.676 square miles. Located at 42.78° N. Lat; 76.85° W. Long.

Population: 1,808; Growth (since 2000): 4.6%; Density: 56.5 persons per square mile; Race: 95.5% White, 1.4% Black/African American, 0.1% Asian, 0.0% American Indian/Alaska Native, 0.0% Native Hawaiian/Other Pacific Islander, 1.7% Two or more races, 4.2% Hispanic of any race;

Average household size: 2.62; Median age: 38.2; Age under 18: 29.0%; Age 65 and over: 21.5%; Males per 100 females: 105.4; Marriage status: 22.7% never married, 60.4% now married, 0.5% separated, 6.5% widowed, 10.4% divorced; Foreign born: 1.4%; Speak English only: 91.3%; With disability: 13.2%; Veterans: 11.0%; Ancestry: 26.3% German, 14.4% English, 13.8% Irish, 10.9% American, 10.7% Italian

Employment: 18.2% management, business, and financial, 2.6% computer, engineering, and science, 3.5% education, legal, community service, arts, and media, 9.2% healthcare practitioners, 12.5% service, 23.2% sales and office, 15.0% natural resources, construction, and maintenance, 15.9% production, transportation, and material moving

Income: Per capita: $29,358; Median household: $59,844; Average household: $81,737; Households with income of $100,000 or more: 26.0%; Poverty rate: 9.9%

Educational Attainment: High school diploma or higher: 84.4%; Bachelor's degree or higher: 26.2%; Graduate/professional degree or higher: 11.1%

Housing: Homeownership rate: 88.4%; Median home value: $144,000; Median year structure built: 1972; Homeowner vacancy rate: 2.0%; Median selected monthly owner costs: $1,240 with a mortgage, $583 without a mortgage; Median gross rent: $877 per month; Rental vacancy rate: 14.0%

Health Insurance: 79.2% have insurance; 59.5% have private insurance; 37.8% have public insurance; 20.8% do not have insurance; 37.1% of children under 18 do not have insurance

Transportation: Commute: 87.6% car, 0.0% public transportation, 3.6% walk, 8.5% work from home; Mean travel time to work: 24.5 minutes

WATERLOO (town). Covers a land area of 21.668 square miles and a water area of 0.147 square miles. Located at 42.92° N. Lat; 76.91° W. Long. Elevation is 453 feet.

History: Official birthplace of the Memorial Day celebaration, May 5, 1866 (celebrated on May 30). Incorporated 1824.

Population: 7,466; Growth (since 2000): -5.1%; Density: 344.6 persons per square mile; Race: 96.1% White, 1.5% Black/African American, 0.0% Asian, 0.1% American Indian/Alaska Native, 0.0% Native Hawaiian/Other Pacific Islander, 2.0% Two or more races, 2.1% Hispanic of any race; Average household size: 2.25; Median age: 44.3; Age under 18: 20.8%; Age 65 and over: 17.4%; Males per 100 females: 92.3; Marriage status: 31.5% never married, 42.8% now married, 1.7% separated, 7.6% widowed, 18.1% divorced; Foreign born: 1.1%; Speak English only: 96.8%; With disability: 19.9%; Veterans: 10.4%; Ancestry: 21.3% German, 19.8% Italian, 17.5% Irish, 10.7% English, 5.6% American

Employment: 6.9% management, business, and financial, 1.6% computer, engineering, and science, 11.5% education, legal, community service, arts, and media, 6.3% healthcare practitioners, 17.9% service, 25.6% sales and office, 13.4% natural resources, construction, and maintenance, 16.9% production, transportation, and material moving

Income: Per capita: $25,995; Median household: $49,337; Average household: $59,132; Households with income of $100,000 or more: 12.8%; Poverty rate: 14.2%

Educational Attainment: High school diploma or higher: 88.2%; Bachelor's degree or higher: 14.2%; Graduate/professional degree or higher: 6.4%

School District(s)
Waterloo Central SD (PK-12)
Enrollment: 1,645 . . . . (315) 539-1500

Housing: Homeownership rate: 66.7%; Median home value: $77,800; Median year structure built: 1957; Homeowner vacancy rate: 0.0%; Median selected monthly owner costs: $993 with a mortgage, $485 without a mortgage; Median gross rent: $728 per month; Rental vacancy rate: 1.5%

Health Insurance: 95.2% have insurance; 72.9% have private insurance; 40.4% have public insurance; 4.8% do not have insurance; 2.6% of children under 18 do not have insurance

Transportation: Commute: 93.7% car, 0.6% public transportation, 1.2% walk, 2.8% work from home; Mean travel time to work: 19.6 minutes

WATERLOO (village). County seat. Covers a land area of 2.157 square miles and a water area of 0.047 square miles. Located at 42.90° N. Lat; 76.86° W. Long. Elevation is 453 feet.

Population: 5,247; Growth (since 2000): 2.7%; Density: 2,432.5 persons per square mile; Race: 96.2% White, 0.1% Black/African American, 0.0% Asian, 0.0% American Indian/Alaska Native, 0.0% Native Hawaiian/Other Pacific Islander, 3.7% Two or more races, 1.0% Hispanic of any race; Average household size: 2.38; Median age: 40.8; Age under 18: 21.0%; Age 65 and over: 17.8%; Males per 100 females: 86.5; Marriage status:

33.3% never married, 43.2% now married, 1.7% separated, 7.9% widowed, 15.5% divorced; Foreign born: 0.7%; Speak English only: 98.4%; With disability: 17.0%; Veterans: 8.6%; Ancestry: 24.6% Irish, 22.3% Italian, 21.2% German, 12.7% English, 7.6% Dutch

Employment: 9.0% management, business, and financial, 2.5% computer, engineering, and science, 8.5% education, legal, community service, arts, and media, 6.1% healthcare practitioners, 19.6% service, 23.6% sales and office, 12.7% natural resources, construction, and maintenance, 18.0% production, transportation, and material moving

Income: Per capita: $27,193; Median household: $51,958; Average household: $65,653; Households with income of $100,000 or more: 19.9%; Poverty rate: 13.7%

Educational Attainment: High school diploma or higher: 90.5%; Bachelor's degree or higher: 17.9%; Graduate/professional degree or higher: 4.7%

School District(s)

Waterloo Central SD (PK-12)

Enrollment: 1,645 . . . . (315) 539-1500

Housing: Homeownership rate: 68.9%; Median home value: $83,200; Median year structure built: 1951; Homeowner vacancy rate: 0.0%; Median selected monthly owner costs: $1,049 with a mortgage, $585 without a mortgage; Median gross rent: $649 per month; Rental vacancy rate: 0.0%

Health Insurance: 96.6% have insurance; 76.8% have private insurance; 41.1% have public insurance; 3.4% do not have insurance; 0.7% of children under 18 do not have insurance

Safety: Violent crime rate: 10.0 per 10,000 population; Property crime rate: 152.1 per 10,000 population

Transportation: Commute: 92.1% car, 0.5% public transportation, 1.8% walk, 2.8% work from home; Mean travel time to work: 20.1 minutes

Additional Information Contacts

Village of Waterloo . . . . (315) 539-9131
  http://www.waterloony.com

WILLARD (unincorporated postal area)

ZCTA: 14588

Covers a land area of 0.241 square miles and a water area of 0 square miles. Located at 42.68° N. Lat; 76.87° W. Long. Elevation is 600 feet.

Population: 707; Growth (since 2000): n/a; Density: 2,936.1 persons per square mile; Race: 50.5% White, 42.0% Black/African American, 0.8% Asian, 1.3% American Indian/Alaska Native, 0.0% Native Hawaiian/Other Pacific Islander, 4.5% Two or more races, 13.0% Hispanic of any race; Average household size: 1.72; Median age: 36.4; Age under 18: 1.8%; Age 65 and over: 5.0%; Males per 100 females: 813.4; Marriage status: 61.7% never married, 23.2% now married, 1.6% separated, 1.3% widowed, 13.9% divorced; Foreign born: 1.6%; Speak English only: 90.5%; With disability: 41.8%; Veterans: 2.3%; Ancestry: 12.2% English, 11.5% Irish, 9.2% German, 6.1% Italian, 3.5% American

Employment: 0.0% management, business, and financial, 0.0% computer, engineering, and science, 0.0% education, legal, community service, arts, and media, 0.0% healthcare practitioners, 30.8% service, 41.5% sales and office, 20.0% natural resources, construction, and maintenance, 7.7% production, transportation, and material moving

Income: Per capita: $9,116; Median household: n/a; Average household: $62,625; Households with income of $100,000 or more: 21.9%; Poverty rate: n/a

Educational Attainment: High school diploma or higher: 64.4%; Bachelor's degree or higher: 1.5%; Graduate/professional degree or higher: 1.5%

Housing: Homeownership rate: 85.9%; Median home value: $98,800; Median year structure built: Before 1940; Homeowner vacancy rate: 0.0%; Median selected monthly owner costs: $766 with a mortgage, $0 without a mortgage; Median gross rent: n/a per month; Rental vacancy rate: 0.0%

Health Insurance: 100.0% have insurance; 87.3% have private insurance; 44.5% have public insurance; 0.0% do not have insurance; 0.0% of children under 18 do not have insurance

Transportation: Commute: 100.0% car, 0.0% public transportation, 0.0% walk, 0.0% work from home; Mean travel time to work: 0.0 minutes

---

Staten Island Borough

See New York City

Steuben County

Located in southern New York, partly in the Finger Lakes region; bounded on the south by Pennsylvania; drained by the Canisteo, Cohocton, Tioga, and Chemung Rivers; includes part of Keuka Lake. Covers a land area of 1,390.559 square miles, a water area of 13.524 square miles, and is located in the Eastern Time Zone at 42.27° N. Lat., 77.39° W. Long. The county was founded in 1796. County seat is Bath.

Steuben County is part of the Corning, NY Micropolitan Statistical Area. The entire metro area includes: Steuben County, NY

Weather Station: Bath — Elevation: 1,120 feet

	Jan	Feb	Mar	Apr	May	Jun	Jul	Aug	Sep	Oct	Nov	Dec
High	32	35	43	56	68	77	81	79	72	60	47	36
Low	13	14	21	32	41	50	55	54	46	35	29	19
Precip	1.7	1.5	2.1	2.8	2.9	3.8	3.2	2.8	3.4	2.5	2.7	2.1
Snow	11.1	9.1	10.3	1.5	tr	tr	0.0	0.0	0.0	tr	3.6	9.2

High and Low temperatures in degrees Fahrenheit; Precipitation and Snow in inches

Population: 97,539; Growth (since 2000): -1.2%; Density: 70.1 persons per square mile; Race: 94.9% White, 1.6% Black/African American, 1.5% Asian, 0.1% American Indian/Alaska Native, 0.0% Native Hawaiian/Other Pacific Islander, 1.5% two or more races, 1.6% Hispanic of any race; Average household size: 2.37; Median age: 42.4; Age under 18: 22.1%; Age 65 and over: 17.9%; Males per 100 females: 98.5; Marriage status: 27.5% never married, 53.5% now married, 2.8% separated, 6.7% widowed, 12.3% divorced; Foreign born: 2.8%; Speak English only: 94.9%; With disability: 15.8%; Veterans: 11.3%; Ancestry: 20.6% German, 17.4% Irish, 13.5% English, 10.9% American, 8.3% Italian

Religion: Six largest groups: 14.1% Catholicism, 6.4% Methodist/Pietist, 3.9% Holiness, 2.5% Non-denominational Protestant, 1.9% Presbyterian-Reformed, 1.8% Baptist

Economy: Unemployment rate: 4.0%; Leading industries: 18.3 % retail trade; 12.9 % health care and social assistance; 12.5 % other services (except public administration); Farms: 1,667 totaling 405,727 acres; Company size: 0 employ 1,000 or more persons, 5 employ 500 to 999 persons, 37 employ 100 to 499 persons, 1,764 employ less than 100 persons; Business ownership: 1,741 women-owned, n/a Black-owned, 34 Hispanic-owned, 166 Asian-owned, n/a American Indian/Alaska Native-owned

Employment: 12.2% management, business, and financial, 5.6% computer, engineering, and science, 11.0% education, legal, community service, arts, and media, 5.6% healthcare practitioners, 18.5% service, 20.2% sales and office, 11.0% natural resources, construction, and maintenance, 15.9% production, transportation, and material moving

Income: Per capita: $27,731; Median household: $50,157; Average household: $66,573; Households with income of $100,000 or more: 17.9%; Poverty rate: 14.5%

Educational Attainment: High school diploma or higher: 89.9%; Bachelor's degree or higher: 22.6%; Graduate/professional degree or higher: 11.0%

Housing: Homeownership rate: 71.8%; Median home value: $95,300; Median year structure built: 1960; Homeowner vacancy rate: 1.4%; Median selected monthly owner costs: $1,119 with a mortgage, $472 without a mortgage; Median gross rent: $691 per month; Rental vacancy rate: 4.8%

Vital Statistics: Birth rate: 107.3 per 10,000 population; Death rate: 104.2 per 10,000 population; Age-adjusted cancer mortality rate: 177.6 deaths per 100,000 population

Health Insurance: 92.8% have insurance; 67.2% have private insurance; 41.5% have public insurance; 7.2% do not have insurance; 7.3% of children under 18 do not have insurance

Health Care: Physicians: 15.4 per 10,000 population; Dentists: 3.7 per 10,000 population; Hospital beds: 63.5 per 10,000 population; Hospital admissions: 726.6 per 10,000 population

Air Quality Index (AQI): Percent of Days: 96.1% good, 3.9% moderate, 0.0% unhealthy for sensitive individuals, 0.0% unhealthy, 0.0% very unhealthy; Annual median: 34; Annual maximum: 91

Transportation: Commute: 90.3% car, 0.6% public transportation, 4.3% walk, 3.4% work from home; Mean travel time to work: 21.7 minutes

2016 Presidential Election: 63.9% Trump, 29.8% Clinton, 4.0% Johnson, 1.4% Stein

National and State Parks: Stony Brook State Park

Additional Information Contacts

Steuben Government . . . . (607) 776-9631
  http://www.steubencony.org

Steuben County Communities

ADDISON (town). Covers a land area of 25.545 square miles and a water area of 0.142 square miles. Located at 42.13° N. Lat; 77.23° W. Long. Elevation is 997 feet.

History: Incorporated 1873.

Population: 2,537; Growth (since 2000): -3.9%; Density: 99.3 persons per square mile; Race: 96.8% White, 0.5% Black/African American, 0.6% Asian, 0.2% American Indian/Alaska Native, 0.0% Native Hawaiian/Other Pacific Islander, 0.6% Two or more races, 1.4% Hispanic of any race; Average household size: 2.54; Median age: 38.5; Age under 18: 25.4%; Age 65 and over: 16.0%; Males per 100 females: 93.7; Marriage status: 26.3% never married, 58.5% now married, 6.2% separated, 5.3% widowed, 9.9% divorced; Foreign born: 2.1%; Speak English only: 97.7%; With disability: 16.3%; Veterans: 9.3%; Ancestry: 17.6% Irish, 16.1% German, 15.2% American, 13.4% English, 6.9% Italian

Employment: 9.8% management, business, and financial, 4.7% computer, engineering, and science, 9.7% education, legal, community service, arts, and media, 4.9% healthcare practitioners, 18.6% service, 26.8% sales and office, 7.9% natural resources, construction, and maintenance, 17.7% production, transportation, and material moving

Income: Per capita: $24,325; Median household: $52,685; Average household: $62,040; Households with income of $100,000 or more: 20.7%; Poverty rate: 14.9%

Educational Attainment: High school diploma or higher: 93.7%; Bachelor's degree or higher: 18.1%; Graduate/professional degree or higher: 7.8%

School District(s)
Addison Central SD (PK-12)
    Enrollment: 1,140 . . . . (607) 359-2244

Housing: Homeownership rate: 73.1%; Median home value: $84,800; Median year structure built: 1941; Homeowner vacancy rate: 1.7%; Median selected monthly owner costs: $1,011 with a mortgage, $493 without a mortgage; Median gross rent: $584 per month; Rental vacancy rate: 5.6%

Health Insurance: 91.3% have insurance; 63.1% have private insurance; 43.3% have public insurance; 8.7% do not have insurance; 6.0% of children under 18 do not have insurance

Safety: Violent crime rate: 19.9 per 10,000 population; Property crime rate: 51.6 per 10,000 population

Newspapers: Addison Post (weekly circulation 6,400)

Transportation: Commute: 93.6% car, 0.0% public transportation, 3.1% walk, 2.8% work from home; Mean travel time to work: 23.7 minutes

ADDISON (village). Covers a land area of 1.893 square miles and a water area of 0 square miles. Located at 42.11° N. Lat; 77.23° W. Long. Elevation is 997 feet.

Population: 1,826; Growth (since 2000): 1.6%; Density: 964.7 persons per square mile; Race: 96.1% White, 0.7% Black/African American, 0.4% Asian, 0.3% American Indian/Alaska Native, 0.0% Native Hawaiian/Other Pacific Islander, 0.8% Two or more races, 1.9% Hispanic of any race; Average household size: 2.66; Median age: 35.7; Age under 18: 27.7%; Age 65 and over: 11.7%; Males per 100 females: 91.4; Marriage status: 32.8% never married, 54.8% now married, 6.2% separated, 4.3% widowed, 8.1% divorced; Foreign born: 2.2%; Speak English only: 97.3%; With disability: 13.6%; Veterans: 11.6%; Ancestry: 15.8% Irish, 15.5% English, 15.5% German, 12.7% American, 9.0% Italian

Employment: 6.5% management, business, and financial, 6.3% computer, engineering, and science, 10.5% education, legal, community service, arts, and media, 6.2% healthcare practitioners, 19.5% service, 28.7% sales and office, 6.7% natural resources, construction, and maintenance, 15.7% production, transportation, and material moving

Income: Per capita: $23,676; Median household: $54,853; Average household: $63,250; Households with income of $100,000 or more: 19.2%; Poverty rate: 16.3%

Educational Attainment: High school diploma or higher: 93.4%; Bachelor's degree or higher: 16.9%; Graduate/professional degree or higher: 8.2%

School District(s)
Addison Central SD (PK-12)
    Enrollment: 1,140 . . . . (607) 359-2244

Housing: Homeownership rate: 70.0%; Median home value: $76,700; Median year structure built: Before 1940; Homeowner vacancy rate: 2.6%; Median selected monthly owner costs: $978 with a mortgage, $497 without

a mortgage; Median gross rent: $650 per month; Rental vacancy rate: 7.2%

Health Insurance: 91.3% have insurance; 64.9% have private insurance; 38.3% have public insurance; 8.7% do not have insurance; 7.7% of children under 18 do not have insurance

Newspapers: Addison Post (weekly circulation 6,400)

Transportation: Commute: 92.0% car, 0.0% public transportation, 3.6% walk, 3.7% work from home; Mean travel time to work: 23.9 minutes

ARKPORT (village). Covers a land area of 0.694 square miles and a water area of 0 square miles. Located at 42.39° N. Lat; 77.70° W. Long. Elevation is 1,184 feet.

Population: 755; Growth (since 2000): -9.3%; Density: 1,087.5 persons per square mile; Race: 98.4% White, 0.0% Black/African American, 0.4% Asian, 0.0% American Indian/Alaska Native, 0.0% Native Hawaiian/Other Pacific Islander, 0.0% Two or more races, 0.0% Hispanic of any race; Average household size: 2.29; Median age: 39.1; Age under 18: 24.4%; Age 65 and over: 16.3%; Males per 100 females: 83.1; Marriage status: 30.5% never married, 49.2% now married, 8.9% separated, 7.1% widowed, 13.2% divorced; Foreign born: 2.1%; Speak English only: 96.1%; With disability: 16.8%; Veterans: 10.9%; Ancestry: 23.4% Irish, 22.9% German, 16.2% English, 13.0% Italian, 9.3% American

Employment: 12.5% management, business, and financial, 1.4% computer, engineering, and science, 13.8% education, legal, community service, arts, and media, 8.7% healthcare practitioners, 16.8% service, 23.0% sales and office, 12.5% natural resources, construction, and maintenance, 11.4% production, transportation, and material moving

Income: Per capita: $27,663; Median household: $55,000; Average household: $63,187; Households with income of $100,000 or more: 17.0%; Poverty rate: 4.5%

Educational Attainment: High school diploma or higher: 90.8%; Bachelor's degree or higher: 24.4%; Graduate/professional degree or higher: 10.8%

School District(s)
Arkport Central SD (KG-12)
    Enrollment: 451 . . . . (607) 295-7471

Housing: Homeownership rate: 72.7%; Median home value: $88,800; Median year structure built: 1953; Homeowner vacancy rate: 2.8%; Median selected monthly owner costs: $1,036 with a mortgage, $433 without a mortgage; Median gross rent: $663 per month; Rental vacancy rate: 7.2%

Health Insurance: 94.3% have insurance; 79.3% have private insurance; 31.4% have public insurance; 5.7% do not have insurance; 7.9% of children under 18 do not have insurance

Transportation: Commute: 89.7% car, 0.0% public transportation, 4.9% walk, 1.4% work from home; Mean travel time to work: 21.2 minutes

ATLANTA (unincorporated postal area)
ZCTA: 14808

Covers a land area of 3.369 square miles and a water area of 0 square miles. Located at 42.56° N. Lat; 77.47° W. Long. Elevation is 1,309 feet.

Population: 488; Growth (since 2000): -18.0%; Density: 144.8 persons per square mile; Race: 97.5% White, 0.0% Black/African American, 0.0% Asian, 0.0% American Indian/Alaska Native, 0.0% Native Hawaiian/Other Pacific Islander, 1.6% Two or more races, 2.3% Hispanic of any race; Average household size: 2.37; Median age: 56.0; Age under 18: 18.2%; Age 65 and over: 29.3%; Males per 100 females: 119.7; Marriage status: 23.7% never married, 48.4% now married, 1.9% separated, 5.0% widowed, 22.8% divorced; Foreign born: 4.5%; Speak English only: 97.5%; With disability: 29.5%; Veterans: 14.0%; Ancestry: 18.2% German, 16.0% English, 15.0% Irish, 9.0% Italian, 6.4% French

Employment: 5.9% management, business, and financial, 1.8% computer, engineering, and science, 4.7% education, legal, community service, arts, and media, 0.0% healthcare practitioners, 12.9% service, 26.5% sales and office, 10.6% natural resources, construction, and maintenance, 37.6% production, transportation, and material moving

Income: Per capita: $28,739; Median household: $55,781; Average household: $69,353; Households with income of $100,000 or more: 12.0%; Poverty rate: 8.8%

Educational Attainment: High school diploma or higher: 84.0%; Bachelor's degree or higher: 9.9%; Graduate/professional degree or higher: 5.3%

Housing: Homeownership rate: 83.0%; Median home value: $71,300; Median year structure built: Before 1940; Homeowner vacancy rate: 7.8%; Median selected monthly owner costs: $900 with a mortgage,

$450 without a mortgage; Median gross rent: $729 per month; Rental vacancy rate: 26.1%

Health Insurance: 98.8% have insurance; 69.7% have private insurance; 51.4% have public insurance; 1.2% do not have insurance; 0.0% of children under 18 do not have insurance

Transportation: Commute: 90.6% car, 0.0% public transportation, 5.9% walk, 3.5% work from home; Mean travel time to work: 22.0 minutes

---

AVOCA (town). Covers a land area of 36.249 square miles and a water area of 0.041 square miles. Located at 42.42° N. Lat; 77.45° W. Long. Elevation is 1,194 feet.

History: Settled 1843, incorporated 1883.

Population: 2,013; Growth (since 2000): -13.0%; Density: 55.5 persons per square mile; Race: 97.8% White, 0.5% Black/African American, 0.0% Asian, 0.0% American Indian/Alaska Native, 0.3% Native Hawaiian/Other Pacific Islander, 0.3% Two or more races, 1.0% Hispanic of any race; Average household size: 2.28; Median age: 47.0; Age under 18: 18.0%; Age 65 and over: 20.0%; Males per 100 females: 104.7; Marriage status: 28.3% never married, 53.2% now married, 1.4% separated, 5.6% widowed, 13.0% divorced; Foreign born: 1.1%; Speak English only: 97.3%; With disability: 21.1%; Veterans: 12.4%; Ancestry: 21.4% German, 16.9% English, 14.6% Irish, 12.5% American, 7.7% Italian

Employment: 14.7% management, business, and financial, 3.6% computer, engineering, and science, 6.8% education, legal, community service, arts, and media, 4.5% healthcare practitioners, 15.3% service, 24.0% sales and office, 11.5% natural resources, construction, and maintenance, 19.5% production, transportation, and material moving

Income: Per capita: $24,123; Median household: $45,152; Average household: $55,699; Households with income of $100,000 or more: 13.0%; Poverty rate: 18.3%

Educational Attainment: High school diploma or higher: 91.4%; Bachelor's degree or higher: 17.1%; Graduate/professional degree or higher: 7.5%

School District(s)

Avoca Central SD (PK-12)

    Enrollment: 442 . . . . (607) 566-2221

Housing: Homeownership rate: 73.1%; Median home value: $84,500; Median year structure built: 1962; Homeowner vacancy rate: 1.6%; Median selected monthly owner costs: $1,144 with a mortgage, $396 without a mortgage; Median gross rent: $685 per month; Rental vacancy rate: 2.9%

Health Insurance: 95.0% have insurance; 61.6% have private insurance; 50.9% have public insurance; 5.0% do not have insurance; 0.8% of children under 18 do not have insurance

Transportation: Commute: 93.4% car, 0.7% public transportation, 1.2% walk, 2.9% work from home; Mean travel time to work: 26.4 minutes

---

AVOCA (village). Covers a land area of 1.326 square miles and a water area of 0.002 square miles. Located at 42.41° N. Lat; 77.42° W. Long. Elevation is 1,194 feet.

Population: 950; Growth (since 2000): -5.8%; Density: 716.4 persons per square mile; Race: 98.1% White, 0.4% Black/African American, 0.0% Asian, 0.0% American Indian/Alaska Native, 0.2% Native Hawaiian/Other Pacific Islander, 0.3% Two or more races, 1.1% Hispanic of any race; Average household size: 2.45; Median age: 39.6; Age under 18: 20.4%; Age 65 and over: 15.4%; Males per 100 females: 100.4; Marriage status: 29.0% never married, 50.3% now married, 1.8% separated, 5.4% widowed, 15.4% divorced; Foreign born: 0.2%; Speak English only: 99.3%; With disability: 17.5%; Veterans: 15.1%; Ancestry: 27.1% German, 20.6% English, 16.7% Irish, 8.7% Italian, 7.5% Scottish

Employment: 12.2% management, business, and financial, 5.9% computer, engineering, and science, 6.3% education, legal, community service, arts, and media, 6.6% healthcare practitioners, 17.6% service, 25.3% sales and office, 10.0% natural resources, construction, and maintenance, 16.1% production, transportation, and material moving

Income: Per capita: $24,013; Median household: $50,217; Average household: $59,223; Households with income of $100,000 or more: 12.3%; Poverty rate: 16.4%

Educational Attainment: High school diploma or higher: 97.3%; Bachelor's degree or higher: 20.3%; Graduate/professional degree or higher: 6.4%

School District(s)

Avoca Central SD (PK-12)

    Enrollment: 442 . . . . (607) 566-2221

Housing: Homeownership rate: 71.6%; Median home value: $77,100; Median year structure built: Before 1940; Homeowner vacancy rate: 3.5%;

Median selected monthly owner costs: $1,139 with a mortgage, $390 without a mortgage; Median gross rent: $627 per month; Rental vacancy rate: 6.1%

Health Insurance: 93.5% have insurance; 62.8% have private insurance; 45.8% have public insurance; 6.5% do not have insurance; 1.5% of children under 18 do not have insurance

Transportation: Commute: 93.1% car, 1.4% public transportation, 2.3% walk, 0.9% work from home; Mean travel time to work: 24.0 minutes

---

BATH (town). Covers a land area of 95.319 square miles and a water area of 0.559 square miles. Located at 42.32° N. Lat; 77.32° W. Long. Elevation is 1,109 feet.

History: Bath is the site of the first clearing in Steuben County, made in 1793 by Colonel Charles Williamson (1757-1808), agent for the Pulteney Estate. Williamson chose the site of Bath on the Cohocton River as the location of a future metropolis that was to be the trading, industrial, and distribution center for the entire region. He was too energetic to wait for the normal processes of settlement. His plan was to build the city first, which would then attract settlers. Williamson's overhasty promotions cost his principals more than a million dollars, and he was dismissed from his position in 1801. Incorporated in 1816.

Population: 12,123; Growth (since 2000): 0.2%; Density: 127.2 persons per square mile; Race: 94.2% White, 3.3% Black/African American, 0.9% Asian, 0.3% American Indian/Alaska Native, 0.0% Native Hawaiian/Other Pacific Islander, 1.1% Two or more races, 2.7% Hispanic of any race; Average household size: 2.23; Median age: 45.1; Age under 18: 20.1%; Age 65 and over: 19.3%; Males per 100 females: 103.4; Marriage status: 28.0% never married, 46.3% now married, 2.8% separated, 8.2% widowed, 17.5% divorced; Foreign born: 2.0%; Speak English only: 96.8%; With disability: 19.2%; Veterans: 15.1%; Ancestry: 19.4% German, 14.6% Irish, 13.7% American, 11.5% English, 7.1% Italian

Employment: 7.1% management, business, and financial, 3.5% computer, engineering, and science, 13.1% education, legal, community service, arts, and media, 6.6% healthcare practitioners, 21.8% service, 20.2% sales and office, 10.3% natural resources, construction, and maintenance, 17.4% production, transportation, and material moving

Income: Per capita: $24,566; Median household: $41,176; Average household: $56,746; Households with income of $100,000 or more: 11.2%; Poverty rate: 17.3%

Educational Attainment: High school diploma or higher: 87.0%; Bachelor's degree or higher: 16.2%; Graduate/professional degree or higher: 7.2%

School District(s)

Bath Central SD (PK-12)

    Enrollment: 1,607 . . . . (607) 776-3301

Housing: Homeownership rate: 63.2%; Median home value: $83,900; Median year structure built: 1962; Homeowner vacancy rate: 1.4%; Median selected monthly owner costs: $1,086 with a mortgage, $480 without a mortgage; Median gross rent: $615 per month; Rental vacancy rate: 2.3%

Health Insurance: 94.8% have insurance; 61.0% have private insurance; 51.2% have public insurance; 5.2% do not have insurance; 1.2% of children under 18 do not have insurance

Hospitals: Bath VA Medical Center (440 beds); Ira Davenport Memorial Hospital (66 beds)

Newspapers: Courier-Advocate (weekly circulation 11,000)

Transportation: Commute: 86.4% car, 1.9% public transportation, 5.8% walk, 3.4% work from home; Mean travel time to work: 19.3 minutes

Additional Information Contacts

Town of Bath . . . . (607) 776-7013

    http://www.townofbathny.org

BATH (village). County seat. Covers a land area of 3.175 square miles and a water area of <.001 square miles. Located at 42.34° N. Lat; 77.32° W. Long. Elevation is 1,109 feet.

Population: 5,611; Growth (since 2000): -0.5%; Density: 1,767.5 persons per square mile; Race: 93.2% White, 4.0% Black/African American, 1.3% Asian, 0.1% American Indian/Alaska Native, 0.0% Native Hawaiian/Other Pacific Islander, 1.3% Two or more races, 1.8% Hispanic of any race; Average household size: 2.05; Median age: 44.7; Age under 18: 19.9%; Age 65 and over: 21.1%; Males per 100 females: 93.1; Marriage status: 28.0% never married, 42.7% now married, 3.1% separated, 10.0% widowed, 19.2% divorced; Foreign born: 2.9%; Speak English only: 95.4%; With disability: 22.4%; Veterans: 15.6%; Ancestry: 23.3% German, 16.0% American, 13.4% English, 13.0% Irish, 9.4% Polish

Employment: 5.1% management, business, and financial, 4.1% computer, engineering, and science, 11.8% education, legal, community service, arts, and media, 7.0% healthcare practitioners, 23.1% service, 27.6% sales and office, 2.9% natural resources, construction, and maintenance, 18.5% production, transportation, and material moving
Income: Per capita: $25,070; Median household: $34,877; Average household: $51,878; Households with income of $100,000 or more: 6.6%; Poverty rate: 18.1%
Educational Attainment: High school diploma or higher: 90.7%; Bachelor's degree or higher: 15.0%; Graduate/professional degree or higher: 6.4%

School District(s)
Bath Central SD (PK-12)
    Enrollment: 1,607 . . . . (607) 776-3301
Housing: Homeownership rate: 51.3%; Median home value: $78,500; Median year structure built: 1949; Homeowner vacancy rate: 1.6%; Median selected monthly owner costs: $1,048 with a mortgage, $464 without a mortgage; Median gross rent: $597 per month; Rental vacancy rate: 3.3%
Health Insurance: 93.9% have insurance; 56.1% have private insurance; 55.6% have public insurance; 6.1% do not have insurance; 2.5% of children under 18 do not have insurance
Hospitals: Bath VA Medical Center (440 beds); Ira Davenport Memorial Hospital (66 beds)
Safety: Violent crime rate: 27.0 per 10,000 population; Property crime rate: 309.6 per 10,000 population
Newspapers: Courier-Advocate (weekly circulation 11,000)
Transportation: Commute: 79.7% car, 3.2% public transportation, 9.5% walk, 3.7% work from home; Mean travel time to work: 15.7 minutes
Additional Information Contacts
Village of Bath . . . . (607) 776-3811
    http://www.villageofbath.org

BRADFORD (town).
Covers a land area of 25.122 square miles and a water area of 0.114 square miles. Located at 42.33° N. Lat; 77.13° W. Long. Elevation is 1,119 feet.
Population: 806; Growth (since 2000): 5.6%; Density: 32.1 persons per square mile; Race: 97.8% White, 0.0% Black/African American, 0.0% Asian, 0.2% American Indian/Alaska Native, 0.0% Native Hawaiian/Other Pacific Islander, 2.0% Two or more races, 0.4% Hispanic of any race; Average household size: 2.50; Median age: 40.5; Age under 18: 22.6%; Age 65 and over: 17.1%; Males per 100 females: 104.1; Marriage status: 22.4% never married, 63.3% now married, 2.5% separated, 5.7% widowed, 8.6% divorced; Foreign born: 0.7%; Speak English only: 99.3%; With disability: 18.1%; Veterans: 14.1%; Ancestry: 20.0% American, 16.3% Polish, 13.6% German, 12.5% Irish, 11.4% English
Employment: 12.1% management, business, and financial, 5.5% computer, engineering, and science, 10.3% education, legal, community service, arts, and media, 8.4% healthcare practitioners, 15.3% service, 22.4% sales and office, 13.5% natural resources, construction, and maintenance, 12.4% production, transportation, and material moving
Income: Per capita: $22,346; Median household: $48,438; Average household: $55,595; Households with income of $100,000 or more: 10.8%; Poverty rate: 16.3%
Educational Attainment: High school diploma or higher: 78.7%; Bachelor's degree or higher: 12.7%; Graduate/professional degree or higher: 4.3%

School District(s)
Bradford Central SD (PK-12)
    Enrollment: 289 . . . . (607) 583-4616
Housing: Homeownership rate: 84.2%; Median home value: $81,900; Median year structure built: 1980; Homeowner vacancy rate: 0.0%; Median selected monthly owner costs: $1,082 with a mortgage, $438 without a mortgage; Median gross rent: $742 per month; Rental vacancy rate: 0.0%
Health Insurance: 92.7% have insurance; 65.8% have private insurance; 41.7% have public insurance; 7.3% do not have insurance; 0.0% of children under 18 do not have insurance
Transportation: Commute: 86.0% car, 0.0% public transportation, 2.8% walk, 11.2% work from home; Mean travel time to work: 25.3 minutes

CAMERON (town).
Covers a land area of 46.704 square miles and a water area of 0.058 square miles. Located at 42.23° N. Lat; 77.42° W. Long. Elevation is 1,070 feet.
Population: 911; Growth (since 2000): -11.9%; Density: 19.5 persons per square mile; Race: 98.8% White, 0.0% Black/African American, 0.0% Asian, 0.0% American Indian/Alaska Native, 0.1% Native Hawaiian/Other

Pacific Islander, 0.9% Two or more races, 0.2% Hispanic of any race; Average household size: 2.60; Median age: 38.8; Age under 18: 25.5%; Age 65 and over: 17.7%; Males per 100 females: 106.8; Marriage status: 20.5% never married, 56.1% now married, 2.0% separated, 8.9% widowed, 14.5% divorced; Foreign born: 2.1%; Speak English only: 92.2%; With disability: 19.8%; Veterans: 11.5%; Ancestry: 14.2% American, 13.0% German, 11.9% Irish, 10.6% English, 7.8% Swiss
Employment: 12.2% management, business, and financial, 4.5% computer, engineering, and science, 1.8% education, legal, community service, arts, and media, 4.2% healthcare practitioners, 14.0% service, 19.4% sales and office, 20.9% natural resources, construction, and maintenance, 23.0% production, transportation, and material moving
Income: Per capita: $23,222; Median household: $43,500; Average household: $59,543; Households with income of $100,000 or more: 12.3%; Poverty rate: 25.5%
Educational Attainment: High school diploma or higher: 84.2%; Bachelor's degree or higher: 7.1%; Graduate/professional degree or higher: 3.5%
Housing: Homeownership rate: 79.7%; Median home value: $82,100; Median year structure built: 1980; Homeowner vacancy rate: 6.7%; Median selected monthly owner costs: $1,225 with a mortgage, $394 without a mortgage; Median gross rent: $686 per month; Rental vacancy rate: 0.0%
Health Insurance: 84.6% have insurance; 59.7% have private insurance; 42.7% have public insurance; 15.4% do not have insurance; 17.4% of children under 18 do not have insurance
Transportation: Commute: 97.3% car, 0.0% public transportation, 0.9% walk, 1.2% work from home; Mean travel time to work: 30.5 minutes

CAMERON MILLS (unincorporated postal area)
ZCTA: 14820
    Covers a land area of 30.740 square miles and a water area of 0.026 square miles. Located at 42.19° N. Lat; 77.36° W. Long. Elevation is 1,033 feet.
Population: 829; Growth (since 2000): 3.1%; Density: 27.0 persons per square mile; Race: 99.3% White, 0.2% Black/African American, 0.0% Asian, 0.0% American Indian/Alaska Native, 0.0% Native Hawaiian/Other Pacific Islander, 0.2% Two or more races, 1.0% Hispanic of any race; Average household size: 2.65; Median age: 41.4; Age under 18: 23.9%; Age 65 and over: 12.7%; Males per 100 females: 100.0; Marriage status: 20.8% never married, 66.6% now married, 2.8% separated, 3.1% widowed, 9.5% divorced; Foreign born: 0.0%; Speak English only: 95.1%; With disability: 11.2%; Veterans: 14.4%; Ancestry: 18.0% German, 16.9% American, 14.7% English, 11.5% Irish, 7.8% Polish
Employment: 13.3% management, business, and financial, 2.3% computer, engineering, and science, 4.6% education, legal, community service, arts, and media, 8.7% healthcare practitioners, 9.6% service, 22.0% sales and office, 24.3% natural resources, construction, and maintenance, 15.1% production, transportation, and material moving
Income: Per capita: $21,810; Median household: $49,063; Average household: $57,412; Households with income of $100,000 or more: 12.7%; Poverty rate: 20.7%
Educational Attainment: High school diploma or higher: 81.4%; Bachelor's degree or higher: 4.7%; Graduate/professional degree or higher: 2.6%

School District(s)
Addison Central SD (PK-12)
    Enrollment: 1,140 . . . . (607) 359-2244
Housing: Homeownership rate: 81.2%; Median home value: $84,800; Median year structure built: 1982; Homeowner vacancy rate: 2.7%; Median selected monthly owner costs: $1,147 with a mortgage, $423 without a mortgage; Median gross rent: $658 per month; Rental vacancy rate: 0.0%
Health Insurance: 89.7% have insurance; 55.6% have private insurance; 49.1% have public insurance; 10.3% do not have insurance; 0.0% of children under 18 do not have insurance
Transportation: Commute: 84.3% car, 0.0% public transportation, 11.6% walk, 4.1% work from home; Mean travel time to work: 27.9 minutes

CAMPBELL (CDP).
Covers a land area of 1.761 square miles and a water area of 0 square miles. Located at 42.24° N. Lat; 77.19° W. Long. Elevation is 1,014 feet.
Population: 659; Growth (since 2000): n/a; Density: 374.1 persons per square mile; Race: 97.7% White, 2.3% Black/African American, 0.0%

Asian, 0.0% American Indian/Alaska Native, 0.0% Native Hawaiian/Other Pacific Islander, 0.0% Two or more races, 2.1% Hispanic of any race; Average household size: 2.35; Median age: 39.2; Age under 18: 23.1%; Age 65 and over: 6.2%; Males per 100 females: 90.6; Marriage status: 28.0% never married, 55.6% now married, 2.4% separated, 6.7% widowed, 9.7% divorced; Foreign born: 1.5%; Speak English only: 100.0%; With disability: 14.0%; Veterans: 17.0%; Ancestry: 34.3% American, 11.2% English, 10.9% Italian, 5.6% German, 4.1% Irish

Employment: 1.7% management, business, and financial, 8.8% computer, engineering, and science, 8.8% education, legal, community service, arts, and media, 4.4% healthcare practitioners, 33.4% service, 14.5% sales and office, 15.9% natural resources, construction, and maintenance, 12.5% production, transportation, and material moving

Income: Per capita: $19,902; Median household: $32,455; Average household: $46,651; Households with income of $100,000 or more: 13.5%; Poverty rate: 20.8%

Educational Attainment: High school diploma or higher: 88.4%; Bachelor's degree or higher: 19.8%; Graduate/professional degree or higher: 14.7%

School District(s)

Campbell-Savona Central SD (PK-12)

    Enrollment: 858 . . . . (607) 527-9800

Housing: Homeownership rate: 75.5%; Median home value: $82,600; Median year structure built: 1970; Homeowner vacancy rate: 0.0%; Median selected monthly owner costs: $1,099 with a mortgage, $450 without a mortgage; Median gross rent: $698 per month; Rental vacancy rate: 0.0%

Health Insurance: 89.4% have insurance; 78.6% have private insurance; 22.2% have public insurance; 10.6% do not have insurance; 0.0% of children under 18 do not have insurance

Transportation: Commute: 100.0% car, 0.0% public transportation, 0.0% walk, 0.0% work from home; Mean travel time to work: 26.9 minutes

CAMPBELL (town). Covers a land area of 40.685 square miles and a water area of 0.094 square miles. Located at 42.23° N. Lat; 77.17° W. Long. Elevation is 1,014 feet.

Population: 3,319; Growth (since 2000): -10.1%; Density: 81.6 persons per square mile; Race: 97.7% White, 0.5% Black/African American, 0.2% Asian, 0.5% American Indian/Alaska Native, 0.0% Native Hawaiian/Other Pacific Islander, 1.1% Two or more races, 2.5% Hispanic of any race; Average household size: 2.25; Median age: 49.0; Age under 18: 17.7%; Age 65 and over: 24.3%; Males per 100 females: 96.5; Marriage status: 19.5% never married, 62.0% now married, 2.5% separated, 6.9% widowed, 11.5% divorced; Foreign born: 0.9%; Speak English only: 96.9%; With disability: 17.9%; Veterans: 13.7%; Ancestry: 19.6% English, 17.7% American, 14.3% German, 10.8% Irish, 7.2% Italian

Employment: 13.5% management, business, and financial, 4.4% computer, engineering, and science, 8.2% education, legal, community service, arts, and media, 4.2% healthcare practitioners, 22.1% service, 10.0% sales and office, 13.7% natural resources, construction, and maintenance, 24.0% production, transportation, and material moving

Income: Per capita: $28,986; Median household: $46,853; Average household: $65,544; Households with income of $100,000 or more: 20.6%; Poverty rate: 10.6%

Educational Attainment: High school diploma or higher: 88.4%; Bachelor's degree or higher: 17.5%; Graduate/professional degree or higher: 7.1%

School District(s)

Campbell-Savona Central SD (PK-12)

    Enrollment: 858 . . . . (607) 527-9800

Housing: Homeownership rate: 87.3%; Median home value: $87,800; Median year structure built: 1974; Homeowner vacancy rate: 2.4%; Median selected monthly owner costs: $1,266 with a mortgage, $458 without a mortgage; Median gross rent: $717 per month; Rental vacancy rate: 0.0%

Health Insurance: 92.6% have insurance; 66.7% have private insurance; 42.0% have public insurance; 7.4% do not have insurance; 12.9% of children under 18 do not have insurance

Transportation: Commute: 91.3% car, 2.2% public transportation, 3.4% walk, 3.1% work from home; Mean travel time to work: 22.1 minutes

CANISTEO (town). Covers a land area of 54.351 square miles and a water area of 0.009 square miles. Located at 42.24° N. Lat; 77.54° W. Long. Elevation is 1,135 feet.

History: Settled before 1790, incorporated 1873.

Population: 3,298; Growth (since 2000): -8.0%; Density: 60.7 persons per square mile; Race: 98.4% White, 0.7% Black/African American, 0.4%

Asian, 0.0% American Indian/Alaska Native, 0.0% Native Hawaiian/Other Pacific Islander, 0.4% Two or more races, 0.7% Hispanic of any race; Average household size: 2.49; Median age: 44.2; Age under 18: 21.8%; Age 65 and over: 21.0%; Males per 100 females: 95.8; Marriage status: 28.3% never married, 55.1% now married, 3.4% separated, 7.2% widowed, 9.4% divorced; Foreign born: 1.2%; Speak English only: 99.3%; With disability: 18.0%; Veterans: 10.1%; Ancestry: 22.3% German, 21.0% Irish, 14.3% English, 8.8% American, 5.9% Italian

Employment: 10.0% management, business, and financial, 2.0% computer, engineering, and science, 10.4% education, legal, community service, arts, and media, 9.9% healthcare practitioners, 21.7% service, 20.5% sales and office, 14.4% natural resources, construction, and maintenance, 11.1% production, transportation, and material moving

Income: Per capita: $27,236; Median household: $51,907; Average household: $68,271; Households with income of $100,000 or more: 14.4%; Poverty rate: 15.5%

Educational Attainment: High school diploma or higher: 90.7%; Bachelor's degree or higher: 19.2%; Graduate/professional degree or higher: 8.5%

School District(s)

Canisteo-Greenwood CSD (PK-12)

    Enrollment: 992 . . . . (607) 698-4225

Housing: Homeownership rate: 79.2%; Median home value: $84,800; Median year structure built: 1943; Homeowner vacancy rate: 2.0%; Median selected monthly owner costs: $915 with a mortgage, $397 without a mortgage; Median gross rent: $586 per month; Rental vacancy rate: 0.0%

Health Insurance: 95.7% have insurance; 69.5% have private insurance; 45.1% have public insurance; 4.3% do not have insurance; 1.0% of children under 18 do not have insurance

Transportation: Commute: 92.0% car, 0.1% public transportation, 4.8% walk, 2.9% work from home; Mean travel time to work: 26.6 minutes

CANISTEO (village). Covers a land area of 0.934 square miles and a water area of 0 square miles. Located at 42.27° N. Lat; 77.61° W. Long. Elevation is 1,135 feet.

Population: 2,333; Growth (since 2000): -0.1%; Density: 2,498.7 persons per square mile; Race: 97.7% White, 1.0% Black/African American, 0.5% Asian, 0.0% American Indian/Alaska Native, 0.0% Native Hawaiian/Other Pacific Islander, 0.6% Two or more races, 0.3% Hispanic of any race; Average household size: 2.51; Median age: 42.8; Age under 18: 23.7%; Age 65 and over: 20.4%; Males per 100 females: 90.8; Marriage status: 29.9% never married, 54.4% now married, 1.8% separated, 7.0% widowed, 8.6% divorced; Foreign born: 1.2%; Speak English only: 99.0%; With disability: 18.2%; Veterans: 9.6%; Ancestry: 20.7% Irish, 19.5% German, 17.7% English, 7.3% Italian, 6.2% American

Employment: 11.6% management, business, and financial, 1.0% computer, engineering, and science, 11.1% education, legal, community service, arts, and media, 11.3% healthcare practitioners, 23.1% service, 20.3% sales and office, 11.0% natural resources, construction, and maintenance, 10.4% production, transportation, and material moving

Income: Per capita: $28,814; Median household: $53,208; Average household: $72,761; Households with income of $100,000 or more: 14.3%; Poverty rate: 13.9%

Educational Attainment: High school diploma or higher: 93.8%; Bachelor's degree or higher: 21.9%; Graduate/professional degree or higher: 10.1%

School District(s)

Canisteo-Greenwood CSD (PK-12)

    Enrollment: 992 . . . . (607) 698-4225

Housing: Homeownership rate: 75.3%; Median home value: $80,700; Median year structure built: Before 1940; Homeowner vacancy rate: 3.1%; Median selected monthly owner costs: $920 with a mortgage, $405 without a mortgage; Median gross rent: $591 per month; Rental vacancy rate: 0.0%

Health Insurance: 94.8% have insurance; 69.2% have private insurance; 45.0% have public insurance; 5.2% do not have insurance; 1.3% of children under 18 do not have insurance

Safety: Violent crime rate: 0.0 per 10,000 population; Property crime rate: 36.8 per 10,000 population

Transportation: Commute: 92.6% car, 0.1% public transportation, 5.3% walk, 1.6% work from home; Mean travel time to work: 23.0 minutes

CATON (town). Covers a land area of 37.565 square miles and a water area of 0.434 square miles. Located at 42.04° N. Lat; 77.02° W. Long. Elevation is 1,424 feet.

Population: 1,903; Growth (since 2000): -9.3%; Density: 50.7 persons per square mile; Race: 97.3% White, 0.3% Black/African American, 0.4% Asian, 0.0% American Indian/Alaska Native, 0.0% Native Hawaiian/Other Pacific Islander, 0.9% Two or more races, 1.6% Hispanic of any race; Average household size: 2.61; Median age: 45.3; Age under 18: 21.3%; Age 65 and over: 16.0%; Males per 100 females: 101.0; Marriage status: 23.0% never married, 65.7% now married, 2.4% separated, 3.2% widowed, 8.1% divorced; Foreign born: 1.2%; Speak English only: 98.2%; With disability: 12.2%; Veterans: 11.1%; Ancestry: 16.5% German, 16.1% Irish, 13.7% English, 12.8% American, 7.5% Italian

Employment: 16.0% management, business, and financial, 4.4% computer, engineering, and science, 10.9% education, legal, community service, arts, and media, 3.6% healthcare practitioners, 14.8% service, 21.8% sales and office, 12.0% natural resources, construction, and maintenance, 16.6% production, transportation, and material moving

Income: Per capita: $31,812; Median household: $73,646; Average household: $82,647; Households with income of $100,000 or more: 27.3%; Poverty rate: 7.6%

Educational Attainment: High school diploma or higher: 91.5%; Bachelor's degree or higher: 24.6%; Graduate/professional degree or higher: 10.7%

Housing: Homeownership rate: 92.2%; Median home value: $118,000; Median year structure built: 1974; Homeowner vacancy rate: 0.0%; Median selected monthly owner costs: $1,351 with a mortgage, $556 without a mortgage; Median gross rent: $870 per month; Rental vacancy rate: 0.0%

Health Insurance: 96.0% have insurance; 82.6% have private insurance; 29.5% have public insurance; 4.0% do not have insurance; 5.6% of children under 18 do not have insurance

Transportation: Commute: 97.5% car, 0.6% public transportation, 0.7% walk, 0.7% work from home; Mean travel time to work: 27.2 minutes

COHOCTON (town). Covers a land area of 56.083 square miles and a water area of 0.007 square miles. Located at 42.52° N. Lat; 77.48° W. Long. Elevation is 1,319 feet.

Population: 2,360; Growth (since 2000): -10.1%; Density: 42.1 persons per square mile; Race: 97.5% White, 0.3% Black/African American, 0.0% Asian, 0.1% American Indian/Alaska Native, 0.0% Native Hawaiian/Other Pacific Islander, 1.9% Two or more races, 2.5% Hispanic of any race; Average household size: 2.60; Median age: 43.0; Age under 18: 23.7%; Age 65 and over: 14.9%; Males per 100 females: 105.0; Marriage status: 26.4% never married, 56.0% now married, 2.0% separated, 5.9% widowed, 11.7% divorced; Foreign born: 0.9%; Speak English only: 98.8%; With disability: 17.7%; Veterans: 10.4%; Ancestry: 30.8% German, 15.9% English, 15.7% Irish, 7.0% Italian, 4.6% French

Employment: 7.9% management, business, and financial, 0.9% computer, engineering, and science, 7.5% education, legal, community service, arts, and media, 4.9% healthcare practitioners, 17.9% service, 20.2% sales and office, 13.2% natural resources, construction, and maintenance, 27.5% production, transportation, and material moving

Income: Per capita: $24,427; Median household: $49,034; Average household: $63,656; Households with income of $100,000 or more: 15.0%; Poverty rate: 13.2%

Educational Attainment: High school diploma or higher: 89.1%; Bachelor's degree or higher: 13.0%; Graduate/professional degree or higher: 6.0%

School District(s)
Wayland-Cohocton Central SD (PK-12)
    Enrollment: 1,335 . . . . (585) 728-2211

Housing: Homeownership rate: 86.4%; Median home value: $78,800; Median year structure built: 1944; Homeowner vacancy rate: 3.2%; Median selected monthly owner costs: $1,007 with a mortgage, $425 without a mortgage; Median gross rent: $667 per month; Rental vacancy rate: 12.9%

Health Insurance: 96.8% have insurance; 68.1% have private insurance; 43.5% have public insurance; 3.2% do not have insurance; 0.3% of children under 18 do not have insurance

Transportation: Commute: 89.2% car, 0.0% public transportation, 3.1% walk, 4.6% work from home; Mean travel time to work: 27.0 minutes

COHOCTON (village). Covers a land area of 1.501 square miles and a water area of 0 square miles. Located at 42.50° N. Lat; 77.50° W. Long. Elevation is 1,319 feet.

Population: 900; Growth (since 2000): 5.4%; Density: 599.4 persons per square mile; Race: 98.1% White, 0.3% Black/African American, 0.0% Asian, 0.3% American Indian/Alaska Native, 0.0% Native Hawaiian/Other Pacific Islander, 1.1% Two or more races, 0.1% Hispanic of any race; Average household size: 2.79; Median age: 34.4; Age under 18: 27.9%; Age 65 and over: 8.7%; Males per 100 females: 93.5; Marriage status: 29.9% never married, 58.2% now married, 2.3% separated, 5.2% widowed, 6.6% divorced; Foreign born: 0.0%; Speak English only: 99.5%; With disability: 20.1%; Veterans: 9.1%; Ancestry: 22.4% German, 17.3% English, 10.2% Irish, 8.2% French Canadian, 7.7% Italian

Employment: 5.8% management, business, and financial, 1.5% computer, engineering, and science, 14.3% education, legal, community service, arts, and media, 2.8% healthcare practitioners, 20.6% service, 20.6% sales and office, 14.1% natural resources, construction, and maintenance, 20.4% production, transportation, and material moving

Income: Per capita: $19,335; Median household: $44,545; Average household: $55,876; Households with income of $100,000 or more: 12.7%; Poverty rate: 21.9%

Educational Attainment: High school diploma or higher: 90.2%; Bachelor's degree or higher: 13.6%; Graduate/professional degree or higher: 6.9%

School District(s)
Wayland-Cohocton Central SD (PK-12)
    Enrollment: 1,335 . . . . (585) 728-2211

Housing: Homeownership rate: 73.4%; Median home value: $74,600; Median year structure built: Before 1940; Homeowner vacancy rate: 0.0%; Median selected monthly owner costs: $883 with a mortgage, $421 without a mortgage; Median gross rent: $632 per month; Rental vacancy rate: 6.7%

Health Insurance: 94.3% have insurance; 55.3% have private insurance; 48.7% have public insurance; 5.7% do not have insurance; 0.7% of children under 18 do not have insurance

Transportation: Commute: 90.4% car, 0.0% public transportation, 2.8% walk, 4.4% work from home; Mean travel time to work: 25.5 minutes

COOPERS PLAINS (CDP). Covers a land area of 0.824 square miles and a water area of 0 square miles. Located at 42.18° N. Lat; 77.14° W. Long. Elevation is 984 feet.

Population: 435; Growth (since 2000): n/a; Density: 527.6 persons per square mile; Race: 100.0% White, 0.0% Black/African American, 0.0% Asian, 0.0% American Indian/Alaska Native, 0.0% Native Hawaiian/Other Pacific Islander, 0.0% Two or more races, 0.0% Hispanic of any race; Average household size: 2.25; Median age: 54.7; Age under 18: 26.4%; Age 65 and over: 32.6%; Males per 100 females: 101.3; Marriage status: 22.2% never married, 55.0% now married, 0.0% separated, 19.4% widowed, 3.4% divorced; Foreign born: 0.0%; Speak English only: 100.0%; With disability: 28.7%; Veterans: 9.7%; Ancestry: 19.1% American, 9.2% Polish, 8.7% German, 6.9% Scottish, 6.4% English

Employment: 10.8% management, business, and financial, 16.2% computer, engineering, and science, 0.0% education, legal, community service, arts, and media, 0.0% healthcare practitioners, 7.4% service, 44.6% sales and office, 6.8% natural resources, construction, and maintenance, 14.2% production, transportation, and material moving

Income: Per capita: $23,520; Median household: $48,438; Average household: $52,534; Households with income of $100,000 or more: n/a; Poverty rate: 14.3%

Educational Attainment: High school diploma or higher: 100.0%; Bachelor's degree or higher: 20.3%; Graduate/professional degree or higher: n/a

Housing: Homeownership rate: 100.0%; Median home value: $89,200; Median year structure built: Before 1940; Homeowner vacancy rate: 0.0%; Median selected monthly owner costs: $1,038 with a mortgage, $273 without a mortgage; Median gross rent: n/a per month; Rental vacancy rate: 0.0%

Health Insurance: 100.0% have insurance; 71.5% have private insurance; 58.9% have public insurance; 0.0% do not have insurance; 0.0% of children under 18 do not have insurance

Transportation: Commute: 100.0% car, 0.0% public transportation, 0.0% walk, 0.0% work from home; Mean travel time to work: 18.2 minutes

CORNING (city). Covers a land area of 3.084 square miles and a water area of 0.177 square miles. Located at 42.15° N. Lat; 77.06° W. Long. Elevation is 932 feet.

History: The glass industry, for which the city is famous, began in 1868. Corning glass Museum and the Rockwell Museum, with the largest collection of Western art in the Eastern U.S. and the world's largest collection of Steuben glass, are located in the city. In 1972 the city was heavily damaged by flooding in the wake of Hurricane Agnes. Settled 1788; Incorporated as a city 1890.

Population: 10,870; Growth (since 2000): 0.3%; Density: 3,524.9 persons per square mile; Race: 91.7% White, 2.9% Black/African American, 2.4% Asian, 0.1% American Indian/Alaska Native, 0.0% Native Hawaiian/Other Pacific Islander, 2.5% Two or more races, 1.5% Hispanic of any race; Average household size: 2.07; Median age: 39.2; Age under 18: 20.5%; Age 65 and over: 15.0%; Males per 100 females: 93.1; Marriage status: 36.4% never married, 44.0% now married, 3.0% separated, 5.9% widowed, 13.8% divorced; Foreign born: 5.3%; Speak English only: 93.6%; With disability: 13.7%; Veterans: 9.1%; Ancestry: 17.7% Irish, 15.6% German, 12.6% English, 10.8% Italian, 9.9% American

Employment: 14.6% management, business, and financial, 7.4% computer, engineering, and science, 13.2% education, legal, community service, arts, and media, 4.7% healthcare practitioners, 21.1% service, 22.0% sales and office, 5.1% natural resources, construction, and maintenance, 11.8% production, transportation, and material moving

Income: Per capita: $31,174; Median household: $47,466; Average household: $65,144; Households with income of $100,000 or more: 18.3%; Poverty rate: 16.6%

Educational Attainment: High school diploma or higher: 93.5%; Bachelor's degree or higher: 32.9%; Graduate/professional degree or higher: 17.3%

School District(s)
Corning City SD (PK-12)
    Enrollment: 4,725 . . . . (607) 936-3704

Two-year College(s)
Corning Community College (Public)
    Enrollment: 3,834 . . . . (607) 962-9011
    Tuition: In-state $5,076; Out-of-state $9,594

Housing: Homeownership rate: 51.9%; Median home value: $105,200; Median year structure built: Before 1940; Homeowner vacancy rate: 1.0%; Median selected monthly owner costs: $1,136 with a mortgage, $516 without a mortgage; Median gross rent: $729 per month; Rental vacancy rate: 4.7%

Health Insurance: 93.9% have insurance; 69.2% have private insurance; 37.1% have public insurance; 6.1% do not have insurance; 1.5% of children under 18 do not have insurance

Hospitals: Corning Hospital (99 beds)

Safety: Violent crime rate: 37.2 per 10,000 population; Property crime rate: 246.5 per 10,000 population

Newspapers: The Leader (daily circulation 12,800)

Transportation: Commute: 86.7% car, 0.1% public transportation, 8.5% walk, 1.7% work from home; Mean travel time to work: 15.1 minutes

Additional Information Contacts
City of Corning. . . . . (607) 962-0340
    http://www.cityofcorning.com

CORNING (town). Covers a land area of 36.850 square miles and a water area of 0.503 square miles. Located at 42.15° N. Lat; 77.01° W. Long. Elevation is 932 feet.

Population: 6,285; Growth (since 2000): -2.2%; Density: 170.6 persons per square mile; Race: 93.2% White, 2.9% Black/African American, 2.0% Asian, 0.5% American Indian/Alaska Native, 0.0% Native Hawaiian/Other Pacific Islander, 1.2% Two or more races, 1.0% Hispanic of any race; Average household size: 2.50; Median age: 42.5; Age under 18: 23.4%; Age 65 and over: 15.7%; Males per 100 females: 99.4; Marriage status: 24.7% never married, 59.9% now married, 1.7% separated, 5.8% widowed, 9.7% divorced; Foreign born: 2.3%; Speak English only: 95.4%; With disability: 15.9%; Veterans: 12.7%; Ancestry: 20.9% German, 16.1% Irish, 11.5% English, 9.7% Italian, 9.0% American

Employment: 14.7% management, business, and financial, 9.7% computer, engineering, and science, 11.8% education, legal, community service, arts, and media, 6.2% healthcare practitioners, 18.9% service, 16.7% sales and office, 7.9% natural resources, construction, and maintenance, 14.0% production, transportation, and material moving

Income: Per capita: $35,286; Median household: $57,697; Average household: $88,742; Households with income of $100,000 or more: 25.9%; Poverty rate: 7.8%

Educational Attainment: High school diploma or higher: 88.8%; Bachelor's degree or higher: 29.8%; Graduate/professional degree or higher: 16.2%

School District(s)
Corning City SD (PK-12)
    Enrollment: 4,725 . . . . (607) 936-3704

Two-year College(s)
Corning Community College (Public)
    Enrollment: 3,834 . . . . (607) 962-9011
    Tuition: In-state $5,076; Out-of-state $9,594

Housing: Homeownership rate: 76.9%; Median home value: $109,100; Median year structure built: 1958; Homeowner vacancy rate: 0.4%; Median selected monthly owner costs: $1,181 with a mortgage, $479 without a mortgage; Median gross rent: $869 per month; Rental vacancy rate: 1.4%

Health Insurance: 91.9% have insurance; 71.7% have private insurance; 35.5% have public insurance; 8.1% do not have insurance; 11.5% of children under 18 do not have insurance

Hospitals: Corning Hospital (99 beds)

Newspapers: The Leader (daily circulation 12,800)

Transportation: Commute: 96.3% car, 0.0% public transportation, 1.8% walk, 1.7% work from home; Mean travel time to work: 17.6 minutes

Additional Information Contacts
Town of Corning . . . . (607) 936-6114
    http://www.townofcorningny.org

DANSVILLE (town). Covers a land area of 48.368 square miles and a water area of 0.068 square miles. Located at 42.46° N. Lat; 77.66° W. Long.

Population: 1,879; Growth (since 2000): -5.0%; Density: 38.8 persons per square mile; Race: 99.0% White, 0.4% Black/African American, 0.3% Asian, 0.0% American Indian/Alaska Native, 0.0% Native Hawaiian/Other Pacific Islander, 0.0% Two or more races, 0.9% Hispanic of any race; Average household size: 2.61; Median age: 43.2; Age under 18: 22.7%; Age 65 and over: 12.2%; Males per 100 females: 104.0; Marriage status: 30.3% never married, 52.1% now married, 2.6% separated, 4.0% widowed, 13.6% divorced; Foreign born: 0.6%; Speak English only: 99.2%; With disability: 14.5%; Veterans: 9.2%; Ancestry: 31.1% German, 18.7% Irish, 11.1% American, 10.0% English, 7.3% Italian

Employment: 12.8% management, business, and financial, 1.6% computer, engineering, and science, 5.4% education, legal, community service, arts, and media, 7.5% healthcare practitioners, 19.7% service, 17.6% sales and office, 13.8% natural resources, construction, and maintenance, 21.7% production, transportation, and material moving

Income: Per capita: $22,653; Median household: $46,875; Average household: $58,398; Households with income of $100,000 or more: 13.3%; Poverty rate: 17.9%

Educational Attainment: High school diploma or higher: 86.3%; Bachelor's degree or higher: 15.0%; Graduate/professional degree or higher: 7.6%

Housing: Homeownership rate: 81.8%; Median home value: $93,500; Median year structure built: 1978; Homeowner vacancy rate: 0.5%; Median selected monthly owner costs: $1,185 with a mortgage, $454 without a mortgage; Median gross rent: $846 per month; Rental vacancy rate: 7.1%

Health Insurance: 86.7% have insurance; 60.7% have private insurance; 40.7% have public insurance; 13.3% do not have insurance; 7.1% of children under 18 do not have insurance

Transportation: Commute: 94.8% car, 0.0% public transportation, 1.8% walk, 3.1% work from home; Mean travel time to work: 28.5 minutes

ERWIN (town). Covers a land area of 38.656 square miles and a water area of 0.501 square miles. Located at 42.13° N. Lat; 77.15° W. Long.

Population: 8,387; Growth (since 2000): 16.1%; Density: 217.0 persons per square mile; Race: 84.6% White, 4.0% Black/African American, 9.6% Asian, 0.0% American Indian/Alaska Native, 0.0% Native Hawaiian/Other Pacific Islander, 1.5% Two or more races, 2.4% Hispanic of any race; Average household size: 2.35; Median age: 39.8; Age under 18: 24.0%; Age 65 and over: 17.4%; Males per 100 females: 95.0; Marriage status: 23.8% never married, 59.1% now married, 1.8% separated, 6.5% widowed, 10.7% divorced; Foreign born: 10.9%; Speak English only: 87.1%; With disability: 9.3%; Veterans: 7.5%; Ancestry: 16.1% German, 15.3% Irish, 9.9% English, 9.3% Italian, 8.6% American

Employment: 17.7% management, business, and financial, 15.8% computer, engineering, and science, 14.9% education, legal, community service, arts, and media, 2.8% healthcare practitioners, 10.0% service, 23.6% sales and office, 5.4% natural resources, construction, and maintenance, 9.7% production, transportation, and material moving
Income: Per capita: $43,070; Median household: $67,227; Average household: $103,049; Households with income of $100,000 or more: 35.9%; Poverty rate: 8.5%
Educational Attainment: High school diploma or higher: 95.7%; Bachelor's degree or higher: 47.5%; Graduate/professional degree or higher: 26.1%
Housing: Homeownership rate: 66.0%; Median home value: $145,400; Median year structure built: 1972; Homeowner vacancy rate: 2.6%; Median selected monthly owner costs: $1,353 with a mortgage, $563 without a mortgage; Median gross rent: $961 per month; Rental vacancy rate: 4.5%
Health Insurance: 97.8% have insurance; 85.1% have private insurance; 26.7% have public insurance; 2.2% do not have insurance; 0.2% of children under 18 do not have insurance
Transportation: Commute: 91.3% car, 0.2% public transportation, 2.2% walk, 5.2% work from home; Mean travel time to work: 17.3 minutes
Additional Information Contacts
Town of Erwin . . . . (607) 936-3652
    http://www.erwinny.org

FREMONT (town). Covers a land area of 32.036 square miles and a water area of 0.154 square miles. Located at 42.39° N. Lat; 77.61° W. Long. Elevation is 1,529 feet.
Population: 1,000; Growth (since 2000): 3.7%; Density: 31.2 persons per square mile; Race: 98.8% White, 0.0% Black/African American, 0.0% Asian, 0.0% American Indian/Alaska Native, 0.0% Native Hawaiian/Other Pacific Islander, 1.2% Two or more races, 0.6% Hispanic of any race; Average household size: 2.33; Median age: 47.1; Age under 18: 16.3%; Age 65 and over: 21.8%; Males per 100 females: 104.0; Marriage status: 21.7% never married, 56.6% now married, 1.5% separated, 7.6% widowed, 14.1% divorced; Foreign born: 0.6%; Speak English only: 100.0%; With disability: 13.7%; Veterans: 9.4%; Ancestry: 25.0% Irish, 19.8% German, 15.5% English, 9.2% Italian, 7.4% American
Employment: 10.7% management, business, and financial, 2.2% computer, engineering, and science, 7.5% education, legal, community service, arts, and media, 15.6% healthcare practitioners, 8.8% service, 20.6% sales and office, 19.1% natural resources, construction, and maintenance, 15.4% production, transportation, and material moving
Income: Per capita: $26,429; Median household: $55,144; Average household: $61,486; Households with income of $100,000 or more: 17.0%; Poverty rate: 8.3%
Educational Attainment: High school diploma or higher: 93.1%; Bachelor's degree or higher: 12.7%; Graduate/professional degree or higher: 6.0%
Housing: Homeownership rate: 87.6%; Median home value: $93,500; Median year structure built: 1960; Homeowner vacancy rate: 0.0%; Median selected monthly owner costs: $1,266 with a mortgage, $448 without a mortgage; Median gross rent: $661 per month; Rental vacancy rate: 0.0%
Health Insurance: 94.3% have insurance; 73.4% have private insurance; 39.0% have public insurance; 5.7% do not have insurance; 7.4% of children under 18 do not have insurance
Transportation: Commute: 83.6% car, 0.0% public transportation, 2.8% walk, 10.9% work from home; Mean travel time to work: 21.6 minutes

GANG MILLS (CDP). Covers a land area of 4.378 square miles and a water area of 0.023 square miles. Located at 42.16° N. Lat; 77.13° W. Long. Elevation is 935 feet.
Population: 4,254; Growth (since 2000): 28.8%; Density: 971.7 persons per square mile; Race: 73.0% White, 7.7% Black/African American, 16.7% Asian, 0.0% American Indian/Alaska Native, 0.0% Native Hawaiian/Other Pacific Islander, 2.4% Two or more races, 3.9% Hispanic of any race; Average household size: 2.35; Median age: 37.8; Age under 18: 25.3%; Age 65 and over: 13.5%; Males per 100 females: 95.1; Marriage status: 23.2% never married, 59.9% now married, 0.4% separated, 6.3% widowed, 10.7% divorced; Foreign born: 17.1%; Speak English only: 77.4%; With disability: 9.1%; Veterans: 7.3%; Ancestry: 13.8% German, 10.0% Irish, 9.6% Italian, 7.1% English, 6.1% Polish
Employment: 14.6% management, business, and financial, 22.3% computer, engineering, and science, 14.2% education, legal, community service, arts, and media, 4.8% healthcare practitioners, 6.7% service,

22.8% sales and office, 5.7% natural resources, construction, and maintenance, 9.0% production, transportation, and material moving
Income: Per capita: $46,228; Median household: $92,981; Average household: $113,175; Households with income of $100,000 or more: 47.8%; Poverty rate: 8.6%
Educational Attainment: High school diploma or higher: 95.9%; Bachelor's degree or higher: 60.1%; Graduate/professional degree or higher: 34.4%
Housing: Homeownership rate: 56.6%; Median home value: $171,900; Median year structure built: 1981; Homeowner vacancy rate: 0.0%; Median selected monthly owner costs: $1,484 with a mortgage, $657 without a mortgage; Median gross rent: $1,109 per month; Rental vacancy rate: 5.6%
Health Insurance: 99.2% have insurance; 90.5% have private insurance; 22.2% have public insurance; 0.8% do not have insurance; 0.0% of children under 18 do not have insurance
Transportation: Commute: 94.9% car, 0.0% public transportation, 0.6% walk, 4.5% work from home; Mean travel time to work: 15.6 minutes

GREENWOOD (town). Covers a land area of 41.339 square miles and a water area of 0.007 square miles. Located at 42.15° N. Lat; 77.66° W. Long. Elevation is 1,562 feet.
Population: 683; Growth (since 2000): -19.6%; Density: 16.5 persons per square mile; Race: 99.3% White, 0.0% Black/African American, 0.0% Asian, 0.0% American Indian/Alaska Native, 0.0% Native Hawaiian/Other Pacific Islander, 0.7% Two or more races, 0.0% Hispanic of any race; Average household size: 2.36; Median age: 47.8; Age under 18: 21.7%; Age 65 and over: 25.5%; Males per 100 females: 103.8; Marriage status: 20.2% never married, 61.6% now married, 2.1% separated, 7.2% widowed, 10.9% divorced; Foreign born: 1.5%; Speak English only: 98.9%; With disability: 18.2%; Veterans: 12.0%; Ancestry: 20.9% German, 20.1% English, 18.2% Irish, 5.7% Dutch, 5.4% American
Employment: 16.1% management, business, and financial, 0.7% computer, engineering, and science, 14.7% education, legal, community service, arts, and media, 2.1% healthcare practitioners, 11.2% service, 18.9% sales and office, 20.7% natural resources, construction, and maintenance, 15.4% production, transportation, and material moving
Income: Per capita: $25,908; Median household: $54,375; Average household: $61,991; Households with income of $100,000 or more: 17.9%; Poverty rate: 11.2%
Educational Attainment: High school diploma or higher: 91.4%; Bachelor's degree or higher: 12.8%; Graduate/professional degree or higher: 4.9%

School District(s)
Canisteo-Greenwood CSD (PK-12)
    Enrollment: 992 . . . . (607) 698-4225
Housing: Homeownership rate: 85.5%; Median home value: $90,300; Median year structure built: Before 1940; Homeowner vacancy rate: 2.4%; Median selected monthly owner costs: $958 with a mortgage, $425 without a mortgage; Median gross rent: $650 per month; Rental vacancy rate: 14.3%
Health Insurance: 91.4% have insurance; 72.9% have private insurance; 41.9% have public insurance; 8.6% do not have insurance; 10.7% of children under 18 do not have insurance
Transportation: Commute: 88.2% car, 2.6% public transportation, 0.0% walk, 9.2% work from home; Mean travel time to work: 31.7 minutes

HAMMONDSPORT (village). Covers a land area of 0.345 square miles and a water area of 0.020 square miles. Located at 42.41° N. Lat; 77.22° W. Long. Elevation is 755 feet.
History: Birthplace of Glenn Curtiss, who made aviation experiments in the village. Museum. Incorporated 1871.
Population: 542; Growth (since 2000): -25.9%; Density: 1,570.5 persons per square mile; Race: 93.5% White, 0.9% Black/African American, 0.0% Asian, 0.0% American Indian/Alaska Native, 0.0% Native Hawaiian/Other Pacific Islander, 5.0% Two or more races, 2.8% Hispanic of any race; Average household size: 1.94; Median age: 53.9; Age under 18: 18.6%; Age 65 and over: 32.7%; Males per 100 females: 95.0; Marriage status: 11.4% never married, 65.3% now married, 3.5% separated, 8.6% widowed, 14.7% divorced; Foreign born: 2.4%; Speak English only: 95.6%; With disability: 14.7%; Veterans: 13.2%; Ancestry: 27.9% German, 19.9% English, 14.6% Irish, 11.4% Italian, 9.4% American
Employment: 15.3% management, business, and financial, 1.3% computer, engineering, and science, 22.6% education, legal, community service, arts, and media, 7.2% healthcare practitioners, 13.2% service,

26.8% sales and office, 2.1% natural resources, construction, and maintenance, 11.5% production, transportation, and material moving
Income: Per capita: $31,099; Median household: $39,500; Average household: $60,509; Households with income of $100,000 or more: 16.9%; Poverty rate: 12.5%
Educational Attainment: High school diploma or higher: 97.6%; Bachelor's degree or higher: 35.4%; Graduate/professional degree or higher: 11.8%

School District(s)
Hammondsport Central SD (PK-12)
  Enrollment: 487 . . . . (607) 569-5200
Housing: Homeownership rate: 62.6%; Median home value: $120,200; Median year structure built: Before 1940; Homeowner vacancy rate: 0.0%; Median selected monthly owner costs: $1,100 with a mortgage, $455 without a mortgage; Median gross rent: $716 per month; Rental vacancy rate: 10.3%
Health Insurance: 93.7% have insurance; 63.3% have private insurance; 54.4% have public insurance; 6.3% do not have insurance; 8.7% of children under 18 do not have insurance
Safety: Violent crime rate: 47.3 per 10,000 population; Property crime rate: 94.6 per 10,000 population
Transportation: Commute: 83.1% car, 2.5% public transportation, 8.9% walk, 3.8% work from home; Mean travel time to work: 18.5 minutes

HARTSVILLE (town). Covers a land area of 36.143 square miles and a water area of 0.056 square miles. Located at 42.22° N. Lat; 77.66° W. Long. Elevation is 1,480 feet.
Population: 699; Growth (since 2000): 19.5%; Density: 19.3 persons per square mile; Race: 97.4% White, 2.1% Black/African American, 0.0% Asian, 0.0% American Indian/Alaska Native, 0.0% Native Hawaiian/Other Pacific Islander, 0.4% Two or more races, 0.3% Hispanic of any race; Average household size: 2.40; Median age: 41.5; Age under 18: 25.8%; Age 65 and over: 18.9%; Males per 100 females: 116.7; Marriage status: 20.3% never married, 59.6% now married, 1.8% separated, 5.3% widowed, 14.8% divorced; Foreign born: 1.7%; Speak English only: 98.2%; With disability: 10.4%; Veterans: 8.3%; Ancestry: 22.9% Irish, 18.5% Italian, 12.0% German, 10.2% American, 9.3% English
Employment: 10.1% management, business, and financial, 1.8% computer, engineering, and science, 11.3% education, legal, community service, arts, and media, 4.3% healthcare practitioners, 16.2% service, 20.1% sales and office, 24.7% natural resources, construction, and maintenance, 11.6% production, transportation, and material moving
Income: Per capita: $29,243; Median household: $58,295; Average household: $71,033; Households with income of $100,000 or more: 18.6%; Poverty rate: 5.0%
Educational Attainment: High school diploma or higher: 96.5%; Bachelor's degree or higher: 21.0%; Graduate/professional degree or higher: 9.6%
Housing: Homeownership rate: 87.3%; Median home value: $112,000; Median year structure built: 1976; Homeowner vacancy rate: 0.0%; Median selected monthly owner costs: $1,191 with a mortgage, $382 without a mortgage; Median gross rent: $1,059 per month; Rental vacancy rate: 7.5%
Health Insurance: 94.3% have insurance; 86.3% have private insurance; 30.2% have public insurance; 5.7% do not have insurance; 0.0% of children under 18 do not have insurance
Transportation: Commute: 97.6% car, 0.0% public transportation, 0.0% walk, 2.4% work from home; Mean travel time to work: 26.3 minutes

HORNBY (town). Covers a land area of 40.850 square miles and a water area of 0.038 square miles. Located at 42.24° N. Lat; 77.03° W. Long. Elevation is 1,522 feet.
Population: 1,736; Growth (since 2000): -0.3%; Density: 42.5 persons per square mile; Race: 97.2% White, 1.3% Black/African American, 0.2% Asian, 0.0% American Indian/Alaska Native, 0.2% Native Hawaiian/Other Pacific Islander, 1.0% Two or more races, 1.0% Hispanic of any race; Average household size: 2.56; Median age: 42.3; Age under 18: 22.0%; Age 65 and over: 13.7%; Males per 100 females: 99.5; Marriage status: 24.2% never married, 60.1% now married, 1.8% separated, 3.4% widowed, 12.2% divorced; Foreign born: 1.2%; Speak English only: 98.5%; With disability: 13.5%; Veterans: 7.5%; Ancestry: 18.8% English, 16.4% American, 16.2% German, 16.0% Irish, 10.9% Italian
Employment: 12.1% management, business, and financial, 7.0% computer, engineering, and science, 7.1% education, legal, community service, arts, and media, 6.0% healthcare practitioners, 16.1% service,

23.1% sales and office, 18.5% natural resources, construction, and maintenance, 10.2% production, transportation, and material moving
Income: Per capita: $26,901; Median household: $55,893; Average household: $68,205; Households with income of $100,000 or more: 19.6%; Poverty rate: 5.9%
Educational Attainment: High school diploma or higher: 88.9%; Bachelor's degree or higher: 19.6%; Graduate/professional degree or higher: 8.9%
Housing: Homeownership rate: 89.2%; Median home value: $98,900; Median year structure built: 1970; Homeowner vacancy rate: 1.3%; Median selected monthly owner costs: $1,207 with a mortgage, $534 without a mortgage; Median gross rent: $760 per month; Rental vacancy rate: 0.0%
Health Insurance: 94.8% have insurance; 69.5% have private insurance; 39.5% have public insurance; 5.2% do not have insurance; 3.5% of children under 18 do not have insurance
Transportation: Commute: 94.6% car, 0.0% public transportation, 2.3% walk, 3.2% work from home; Mean travel time to work: 22.3 minutes

HORNELL (city). Covers a land area of 2.837 square miles and a water area of 0 square miles. Located at 42.33° N. Lat; 77.66° W. Long. Elevation is 1,161 feet.
History: Settled 1790, incorporated 1906.
Population: 8,332; Growth (since 2000): -7.6%; Density: 2,936.7 persons per square mile; Race: 94.1% White, 1.1% Black/African American, 0.8% Asian, 0.2% American Indian/Alaska Native, 0.0% Native Hawaiian/Other Pacific Islander, 3.2% Two or more races, 2.3% Hispanic of any race; Average household size: 2.39; Median age: 38.2; Age under 18: 23.8%; Age 65 and over: 16.0%; Males per 100 females: 93.6; Marriage status: 37.5% never married, 42.5% now married, 2.9% separated, 7.1% widowed, 12.9% divorced; Foreign born: 2.7%; Speak English only: 96.4%; With disability: 17.6%; Veterans: 11.9%; Ancestry: 22.7% Irish, 19.0% German, 14.0% Italian, 13.3% English, 6.9% American
Employment: 7.6% management, business, and financial, 3.8% computer, engineering, and science, 11.3% education, legal, community service, arts, and media, 5.0% healthcare practitioners, 26.0% service, 19.2% sales and office, 10.0% natural resources, construction, and maintenance, 17.1% production, transportation, and material moving
Income: Per capita: $20,531; Median household: $40,400; Average household: $49,815; Households with income of $100,000 or more: 9.1%; Poverty rate: 20.9%
Educational Attainment: High school diploma or higher: 89.7%; Bachelor's degree or higher: 19.0%; Graduate/professional degree or higher: 8.6%

School District(s)
Hornell City SD (KG-12)
  Enrollment: 1,711 . . . . (607) 324-1302
Housing: Homeownership rate: 56.8%; Median home value: $66,200; Median year structure built: Before 1940; Homeowner vacancy rate: 0.0%; Median selected monthly owner costs: $923 with a mortgage, $389 without a mortgage; Median gross rent: $616 per month; Rental vacancy rate: 11.3%
Health Insurance: 95.1% have insurance; 58.5% have private insurance; 52.0% have public insurance; 4.9% do not have insurance; 1.8% of children under 18 do not have insurance
Hospitals: Saint James Mercy Hospital (297 beds)
Safety: Violent crime rate: 4.9 per 10,000 population; Property crime rate: 121.8 per 10,000 population
Newspapers: Evening Tribune (daily circulation 4,200); Hornell Spectator (weekly circulation 14,500)
Transportation: Commute: 89.1% car, 0.6% public transportation, 8.3% walk, 0.9% work from home; Mean travel time to work: 17.3 minutes
Airports: Hornell Municipal (general aviation)
Additional Information Contacts
City of Hornell . . . . (607) 324-7421
  http://www.cityofhornell.com

HORNELLSVILLE (town). Covers a land area of 43.325 square miles and a water area of 0.216 square miles. Located at 42.33° N. Lat; 77.68° W. Long.
Population: 4,075; Growth (since 2000): 0.8%; Density: 94.1 persons per square mile; Race: 96.3% White, 0.1% Black/African American, 0.5% Asian, 0.1% American Indian/Alaska Native, 0.0% Native Hawaiian/Other Pacific Islander, 2.7% Two or more races, 3.4% Hispanic of any race; Average household size: 2.15; Median age: 48.6; Age under 18: 17.8%; Age 65 and over: 25.1%; Males per 100 females: 89.7; Marriage status:

26.1% never married, 47.9% now married, 2.6% separated, 15.1% widowed, 10.9% divorced; Foreign born: 2.3%; Speak English only: 96.5%; With disability: 19.7%; Veterans: 14.2%; Ancestry: 25.3% German, 24.2% Irish, 20.0% English, 12.3% Italian, 8.6% American

Employment: 15.1% management, business, and financial, 2.9% computer, engineering, and science, 14.0% education, legal, community service, arts, and media, 8.5% healthcare practitioners, 19.8% service, 18.3% sales and office, 9.6% natural resources, construction, and maintenance, 11.8% production, transportation, and material moving

Income: Per capita: $27,016; Median household: $46,506; Average household: $59,458; Households with income of $100,000 or more: 15.0%; Poverty rate: 14.5%

Educational Attainment: High school diploma or higher: 93.9%; Bachelor's degree or higher: 25.9%; Graduate/professional degree or higher: 14.2%

Housing: Homeownership rate: 74.5%; Median home value: $104,300; Median year structure built: 1968; Homeowner vacancy rate: 1.2%; Median selected monthly owner costs: $1,044 with a mortgage, $527 without a mortgage; Median gross rent: $627 per month; Rental vacancy rate: 1.4%

Health Insurance: 95.9% have insurance; 73.8% have private insurance; 44.3% have public insurance; 4.1% do not have insurance; 2.1% of children under 18 do not have insurance

Transportation: Commute: 92.2% car, 0.2% public transportation, 2.1% walk, 3.7% work from home; Mean travel time to work: 20.6 minutes

Additional Information Contacts

Town of Hornellsville . . . . (607) 295-9660
http://www.townofhornellsville.com

HOWARD (town). Covers a land area of 60.546 square miles and a water area of 0.220 square miles. Located at 42.34° N. Lat; 77.51° W. Long. Elevation is 1,650 feet.

Population: 1,581; Growth (since 2000): 10.6%; Density: 26.1 persons per square mile; Race: 98.5% White, 0.8% Black/African American, 0.3% Asian, 0.0% American Indian/Alaska Native, 0.0% Native Hawaiian/Other Pacific Islander, 0.5% Two or more races, 0.2% Hispanic of any race; Average household size: 2.70; Median age: 41.2; Age under 18: 25.7%; Age 65 and over: 14.8%; Males per 100 females: 106.6; Marriage status: 24.6% never married, 64.4% now married, 3.7% separated, 7.7% widowed, 3.2% divorced; Foreign born: 0.5%; Speak English only: 98.9%; With disability: 13.1%; Veterans: 10.0%; Ancestry: 29.0% German, 21.3% English, 20.4% Irish, 6.6% American, 6.2% Dutch

Employment: 8.5% management, business, and financial, 5.0% computer, engineering, and science, 11.5% education, legal, community service, arts, and media, 3.2% healthcare practitioners, 18.9% service, 19.6% sales and office, 13.1% natural resources, construction, and maintenance, 20.2% production, transportation, and material moving

Income: Per capita: $23,932; Median household: $58,419; Average household: $64,476; Households with income of $100,000 or more: 20.2%; Poverty rate: 13.3%

Educational Attainment: High school diploma or higher: 93.7%; Bachelor's degree or higher: 15.8%; Graduate/professional degree or higher: 6.2%

Housing: Homeownership rate: 80.3%; Median home value: $88,400; Median year structure built: 1972; Homeowner vacancy rate: 0.0%; Median selected monthly owner costs: $1,102 with a mortgage, $457 without a mortgage; Median gross rent: $747 per month; Rental vacancy rate: 0.0%

Health Insurance: 95.3% have insurance; 68.8% have private insurance; 41.0% have public insurance; 4.7% do not have insurance; 0.0% of children under 18 do not have insurance

Transportation: Commute: 89.0% car, 0.6% public transportation, 3.7% walk, 6.2% work from home; Mean travel time to work: 24.6 minutes

JASPER (town). Covers a land area of 52.644 square miles and a water area of 0.023 square miles. Located at 42.14° N. Lat; 77.53° W. Long. Elevation is 1,572 feet.

Population: 1,606; Growth (since 2000): 26.5%; Density: 30.5 persons per square mile; Race: 99.4% White, 0.1% Black/African American, 0.2% Asian, 0.0% American Indian/Alaska Native, 0.0% Native Hawaiian/Other Pacific Islander, 0.0% Two or more races, 0.2% Hispanic of any race; Average household size: 3.53; Median age: 24.4; Age under 18: 38.3%; Age 65 and over: 11.4%; Males per 100 females: 100.3; Marriage status: 25.5% never married, 61.0% now married, 2.3% separated, 6.9% widowed, 6.6% divorced; Foreign born: 1.8%; Speak English only: 62.5%; With disability: 14.0%; Veterans: 7.9%; Ancestry: 25.5% German, 11.8% Pennsylvania German, 10.1% Irish, 9.2% American, 8.6% Swiss

Employment: 16.7% management, business, and financial, 1.0% computer, engineering, and science, 6.1% education, legal, community service, arts, and media, 1.8% healthcare practitioners, 11.6% service, 21.0% sales and office, 20.0% natural resources, construction, and maintenance, 21.8% production, transportation, and material moving

Income: Per capita: $14,676; Median household: $38,333; Average household: $51,614; Households with income of $100,000 or more: 9.1%; Poverty rate: 24.0%

Educational Attainment: High school diploma or higher: 75.0%; Bachelor's degree or higher: 7.8%; Graduate/professional degree or higher: 3.8%

School District(s)

Jasper-Troupsburg Central SD (PK-12)
    Enrollment: 491 . . . . (607) 792-3675

Housing: Homeownership rate: 80.2%; Median home value: $93,800; Median year structure built: 1977; Homeowner vacancy rate: 0.0%; Median selected monthly owner costs: $1,179 with a mortgage, $349 without a mortgage; Median gross rent: $550 per month; Rental vacancy rate: 0.0%

Health Insurance: 57.7% have insurance; 35.1% have private insurance; 32.6% have public insurance; 42.3% do not have insurance; 58.8% of children under 18 do not have insurance

Transportation: Commute: 71.4% car, 2.6% public transportation, 14.3% walk, 7.2% work from home; Mean travel time to work: 29.1 minutes

KANONA (unincorporated postal area)
ZCTA: 14856

Covers a land area of 0.377 square miles and a water area of 0 square miles. Located at 42.38° N. Lat; 77.37° W. Long. Elevation is 1,145 feet.

Population: 219; Growth (since 2000): n/a; Density: 580.8 persons per square mile; Race: 100.0% White, 0.0% Black/African American, 0.0% Asian, 0.0% American Indian/Alaska Native, 0.0% Native Hawaiian/Other Pacific Islander, 0.0% Two or more races, 0.0% Hispanic of any race; Average household size: 2.43; Median age: 23.2; Age under 18: 47.5%; Age 65 and over: 0.0%; Males per 100 females: 117.1; Marriage status: 50.4% never married, 0.0% now married, 0.0% separated, 0.0% widowed, 49.6% divorced; Foreign born: 0.0%; Speak English only: 100.0%; With disability: 0.0%; Veterans: 0.0%; Ancestry: 26.0% German, 15.1% Russian, 13.2% Irish

Employment: 0.0% management, business, and financial, 0.0% computer, engineering, and science, 25.2% education, legal, community service, arts, and media, 0.0% healthcare practitioners, 24.3% service, 21.7% sales and office, 28.7% natural resources, construction, and maintenance, 0.0% production, transportation, and material moving

Income: Per capita: $10,516; Median household: n/a; Average household: $26,794; Households with income of $100,000 or more: n/a; Poverty rate: n/a

Educational Attainment: High school diploma or higher: 69.5%; Bachelor's degree or higher: n/a; Graduate/professional degree or higher: n/a

Housing: Homeownership rate: 32.2%; Median home value: n/a; Median year structure built: Before 1940; Homeowner vacancy rate: 0.0%; Median selected monthly owner costs: $0 with a mortgage, $0 without a mortgage; Median gross rent: n/a per month; Rental vacancy rate: 0.0%

Health Insurance: 84.9% have insurance; 26.0% have private insurance; 58.9% have public insurance; 15.1% do not have insurance; 0.0% of children under 18 do not have insurance

Transportation: Commute: 75.7% car, 0.0% public transportation, 24.3% walk, 0.0% work from home; Mean travel time to work: 0.0 minutes

LINDLEY (town). Covers a land area of 37.597 square miles and a water area of 0.271 square miles. Located at 42.04° N. Lat; 77.15° W. Long. Elevation is 1,010 feet.

Population: 2,001; Growth (since 2000): 4.6%; Density: 53.2 persons per square mile; Race: 97.0% White, 0.1% Black/African American, 0.0% Asian, 0.0% American Indian/Alaska Native, 0.0% Native Hawaiian/Other Pacific Islander, 2.9% Two or more races, 0.3% Hispanic of any race; Average household size: 2.57; Median age: 42.0; Age under 18: 25.2%; Age 65 and over: 17.1%; Males per 100 females: 102.6; Marriage status: 27.6% never married, 56.4% now married, 3.0% separated, 2.8% widowed, 13.3% divorced; Foreign born: 1.4%; Speak English only: 98.0%; With disability: 12.1%; Veterans: 12.6%; Ancestry: 23.2% German, 21.0% Irish, 18.4% American, 8.3% English, 5.2% Italian

Income: Per capita: $14,916; Median household: $40,625; Average household: $44,032; Households with income of $100,000 or more: 3.4%; Poverty rate: 8.1%

Educational Attainment: High school diploma or higher: 84.2%; Bachelor's degree or higher: 12.0%; Graduate/professional degree or higher: 5.5%

School District(s)
Prattsburgh Central SD (PK-12)
    Enrollment: 396. . . . . (607) 522-3795
Housing: Homeownership rate: 76.5%; Median home value: $65,800; Median year structure built: 1947; Homeowner vacancy rate: 6.4%; Median selected monthly owner costs: $657 with a mortgage, $404 without a mortgage; Median gross rent: $595 per month; Rental vacancy rate: 20.3%

Health Insurance: 91.4% have insurance; 43.1% have private insurance; 62.7% have public insurance; 8.6% do not have insurance; 3.7% of children under 18 do not have insurance

Transportation: Commute: 79.5% car, 0.0% public transportation, 11.2% walk, 1.9% work from home; Mean travel time to work: 21.2 minutes

PRATTSBURGH (town). Covers a land area of 51.666 square miles and a water area of 0.050 square miles. Located at 42.54° N. Lat; 77.33° W. Long. Elevation is 1,463 feet.

Population: 2,202; Growth (since 2000): 6.7%; Density: 42.6 persons per square mile; Race: 96.9% White, 0.4% Black/African American, 0.6% Asian, 0.0% American Indian/Alaska Native, 0.0% Native Hawaiian/Other Pacific Islander, 1.2% Two or more races, 3.8% Hispanic of any race; Average household size: 2.66; Median age: 43.0; Age under 18: 24.6%; Age 65 and over: 18.5%; Males per 100 females: 100.3; Marriage status: 24.0% never married, 63.1% now married, 2.3% separated, 3.4% widowed, 9.5% divorced; Foreign born: 1.5%; Speak English only: 95.3%; With disability: 12.0%; Veterans: 11.3%; Ancestry: 25.7% German, 20.6% Irish, 13.6% English, 8.7% American, 8.1% Polish

Employment: 9.6% management, business, and financial, 3.3% computer, engineering, and science, 7.7% education, legal, community service, arts, and media, 6.7% healthcare practitioners, 19.2% service, 16.7% sales and office, 21.0% natural resources, construction, and maintenance, 15.8% production, transportation, and material moving

Income: Per capita: $24,053; Median household: $50,031; Average household: $63,742; Households with income of $100,000 or more: 14.3%; Poverty rate: 8.0%

Educational Attainment: High school diploma or higher: 88.0%; Bachelor's degree or higher: 16.3%; Graduate/professional degree or higher: 5.7%

School District(s)
Prattsburgh Central SD (PK-12)
    Enrollment: 396. . . . . (607) 522-3795
Housing: Homeownership rate: 87.5%; Median home value: $92,100; Median year structure built: 1982; Homeowner vacancy rate: 1.9%; Median selected monthly owner costs: $1,100 with a mortgage, $452 without a mortgage; Median gross rent: $589 per month; Rental vacancy rate: 13.4%

Health Insurance: 91.6% have insurance; 60.4% have private insurance; 50.0% have public insurance; 8.4% do not have insurance; 9.4% of children under 18 do not have insurance

Transportation: Commute: 87.1% car, 0.0% public transportation, 4.5% walk, 4.8% work from home; Mean travel time to work: 28.3 minutes

PULTENEY (town). Covers a land area of 33.137 square miles and a water area of 3.317 square miles. Located at 42.53° N. Lat; 77.20° W. Long. Elevation is 1,053 feet.

Population: 1,387; Growth (since 2000): -1.3%; Density: 41.9 persons per square mile; Race: 99.6% White, 0.0% Black/African American, 0.0% Asian, 0.0% American Indian/Alaska Native, 0.0% Native Hawaiian/Other Pacific Islander, 0.4% Two or more races, 0.0% Hispanic of any race; Average household size: 2.21; Median age: 46.5; Age under 18: 22.9%; Age 65 and over: 24.2%; Males per 100 females: 96.8; Marriage status: 18.5% never married, 62.0% now married, 3.6% separated, 8.9% widowed, 10.6% divorced; Foreign born: 1.2%; Speak English only: 91.0%; With disability: 12.8%; Veterans: 9.7%; Ancestry: 23.4% German, 16.6% English, 15.1% Irish, 8.7% French, 6.9% Dutch

Employment: 20.5% management, business, and financial, 4.2% computer, engineering, and science, 9.2% education, legal, community service, arts, and media, 4.8% healthcare practitioners, 13.6% service, 22.1% sales and office, 11.5% natural resources, construction, and maintenance, 14.0% production, transportation, and material moving

Income: Per capita: $28,255; Median household: $50,764; Average household: $62,526; Households with income of $100,000 or more: 20.5%; Poverty rate: 12.1%

Educational Attainment: High school diploma or higher: 91.9%; Bachelor's degree or higher: 31.1%; Graduate/professional degree or higher: 19.9%

Housing: Homeownership rate: 90.8%; Median home value: $125,600; Median year structure built: 1972; Homeowner vacancy rate: 2.2%; Median selected monthly owner costs: $1,026 with a mortgage, $403 without a mortgage; Median gross rent: $661 per month; Rental vacancy rate: 0.0%

Health Insurance: 86.2% have insurance; 63.1% have private insurance; 41.8% have public insurance; 13.8% do not have insurance; 23.0% of children under 18 do not have insurance

Transportation: Commute: 86.5% car, 0.0% public transportation, 0.7% walk, 10.5% work from home; Mean travel time to work: 27.8 minutes

RATHBONE (town). Covers a land area of 36.017 square miles and a water area of 0.102 square miles. Located at 42.13° N. Lat; 77.34° W. Long. Elevation is 1,001 feet.

Population: 1,143; Growth (since 2000): 5.8%; Density: 31.7 persons per square mile; Race: 98.9% White, 0.8% Black/African American, 0.0% Asian, 0.0% American Indian/Alaska Native, 0.0% Native Hawaiian/Other Pacific Islander, 0.0% Two or more races, 0.7% Hispanic of any race; Average household size: 3.02; Median age: 35.0; Age under 18: 27.1%; Age 65 and over: 14.2%; Males per 100 females: 110.5; Marriage status: 26.3% never married, 65.1% now married, 1.9% separated, 3.2% widowed, 5.3% divorced; Foreign born: 1.4%; Speak English only: 81.0%; With disability: 12.1%; Veterans: 11.9%; Ancestry: 21.8% German, 20.7% American, 15.8% English, 9.5% Irish, 6.7% Polish

Employment: 9.6% management, business, and financial, 2.6% computer, engineering, and science, 8.5% education, legal, community service, arts, and media, 7.7% healthcare practitioners, 9.4% service, 22.2% sales and office, 20.9% natural resources, construction, and maintenance, 19.0% production, transportation, and material moving

Income: Per capita: $19,022; Median household: $44,545; Average household: $58,526; Households with income of $100,000 or more: 17.5%; Poverty rate: 24.9%

Educational Attainment: High school diploma or higher: 76.2%; Bachelor's degree or higher: 8.7%; Graduate/professional degree or higher: 5.0%

Housing: Homeownership rate: 82.3%; Median home value: $122,600; Median year structure built: 1983; Homeowner vacancy rate: 0.0%; Median selected monthly owner costs: $967 with a mortgage, $456 without a mortgage; Median gross rent: $595 per month; Rental vacancy rate: 13.0%

Health Insurance: 67.2% have insurance; 51.6% have private insurance; 27.6% have public insurance; 32.8% do not have insurance; 44.1% of children under 18 do not have insurance

Transportation: Commute: 91.0% car, 0.0% public transportation, 0.9% walk, 6.7% work from home; Mean travel time to work: 31.8 minutes

REXVILLE (unincorporated postal area)
ZCTA: 14877

Covers a land area of 42.288 square miles and a water area of 0.146 square miles. Located at 42.06° N. Lat; 77.68° W. Long. Elevation is 1,841 feet.

Population: 395; Growth (since 2000): -39.3%; Density: 9.3 persons per square mile; Race: 95.2% White, 0.0% Black/African American, 0.0% Asian, 0.0% American Indian/Alaska Native, 0.0% Native Hawaiian/Other Pacific Islander, 4.8% Two or more races, 0.0% Hispanic of any race; Average household size: 2.32; Median age: 50.8; Age under 18: 19.2%; Age 65 and over: 25.8%; Males per 100 females: 114.4; Marriage status: 21.6% never married, 49.7% now married, 2.8% separated, 6.5% widowed, 22.2% divorced; Foreign born: 2.8%; Speak English only: 96.2%; With disability: 18.2%; Veterans: 8.2%; Ancestry: 24.6% English, 23.5% Irish, 19.2% German, 7.8% American, 6.8% Dutch

Employment: 9.8% management, business, and financial, 4.9% computer, engineering, and science, 7.9% education, legal, community service, arts, and media, 2.4% healthcare practitioners, 20.1% service, 17.7% sales and office, 27.4% natural resources, construction, and maintenance, 9.8% production, transportation, and material moving

Income: Per capita: $29,131; Median household: $53,333; Average household: $67,612; Households with income of $100,000 or more: 25.4%; Poverty rate: 14.9%

Educational Attainment: High school diploma or higher: 91.7%; Bachelor's degree or higher: 17.3%; Graduate/professional degree or higher: 5.0%
Housing: Homeownership rate: 80.6%; Median home value: $103,000; Median year structure built: 1972; Homeowner vacancy rate: 4.2%; Median selected monthly owner costs: $1,269 with a mortgage, $488 without a mortgage; Median gross rent: $677 per month; Rental vacancy rate: 0.0%
Health Insurance: 90.1% have insurance; 64.1% have private insurance; 44.3% have public insurance; 9.9% do not have insurance; 14.5% of children under 18 do not have insurance
Transportation: Commute: 80.6% car, 0.0% public transportation, 2.5% walk, 16.3% work from home; Mean travel time to work: 38.1 minutes

RIVERSIDE (village). Covers a land area of 0.301 square miles and a water area of 0.006 square miles. Located at 42.16° N. Lat; 77.08° W. Long. Elevation is 938 feet.
Population: 657; Growth (since 2000): 10.6%; Density: 2,179.2 persons per square mile; Race: 94.2% White, 0.0% Black/African American, 5.8% Asian, 0.0% American Indian/Alaska Native, 0.0% Native Hawaiian/Other Pacific Islander, 0.0% Two or more races, 0.3% Hispanic of any race; Average household size: 2.48; Median age: 41.0; Age under 18: 26.0%; Age 65 and over: 24.4%; Males per 100 females: 96.4; Marriage status: 19.2% never married, 55.8% now married, 3.0% separated, 9.9% widowed, 15.1% divorced; Foreign born: 4.3%; Speak English only: 90.5%; With disability: 17.2%; Veterans: 14.0%; Ancestry: 30.4% German, 15.4% Irish, 13.7% American, 12.8% English, 6.5% Welsh
Employment: 3.9% management, business, and financial, 9.7% computer, engineering, and science, 17.4% education, legal, community service, arts, and media, 2.7% healthcare practitioners, 32.9% service, 11.6% sales and office, 1.2% natural resources, construction, and maintenance, 20.5% production, transportation, and material moving
Income: Per capita: $22,528; Median household: $43,594; Average household: $56,921; Households with income of $100,000 or more: 7.2%; Poverty rate: 19.9%
Educational Attainment: High school diploma or higher: 89.9%; Bachelor's degree or higher: 11.9%; Graduate/professional degree or higher: 3.8%
Housing: Homeownership rate: 84.9%; Median home value: $77,000; Median year structure built: 1947; Homeowner vacancy rate: 0.0%; Median selected monthly owner costs: $869 with a mortgage, $356 without a mortgage; Median gross rent: $979 per month; Rental vacancy rate: 0.0%
Health Insurance: 91.8% have insurance; 64.8% have private insurance; 53.6% have public insurance; 8.2% do not have insurance; 11.0% of children under 18 do not have insurance
Transportation: Commute: 87.0% car, 0.0% public transportation, 7.9% walk, 4.3% work from home; Mean travel time to work: 18.9 minutes

SAVONA (village). Covers a land area of 1.040 square miles and a water area of 0 square miles. Located at 42.28° N. Lat; 77.22° W. Long. Elevation is 1,053 feet.
Population: 866; Growth (since 2000): 5.4%; Density: 833.0 persons per square mile; Race: 90.4% White, 1.5% Black/African American, 3.7% Asian, 0.3% American Indian/Alaska Native, 0.0% Native Hawaiian/Other Pacific Islander, 2.0% Two or more races, 4.2% Hispanic of any race; Average household size: 2.62; Median age: 32.6; Age under 18: 27.5%; Age 65 and over: 9.2%; Males per 100 females: 93.2; Marriage status: 32.5% never married, 44.0% now married, 2.3% separated, 6.1% widowed, 17.5% divorced; Foreign born: 1.8%; Speak English only: 96.0%; With disability: 11.7%; Veterans: 12.6%; Ancestry: 26.1% German, 13.2% Irish, 10.5% English, 10.4% American, 7.9% Italian
Employment: 3.7% management, business, and financial, 1.3% computer, engineering, and science, 7.3% education, legal, community service, arts, and media, 3.9% healthcare practitioners, 25.1% service, 26.4% sales and office, 17.8% natural resources, construction, and maintenance, 14.4% production, transportation, and material moving
Income: Per capita: $19,649; Median household: $48,594; Average household: $51,850; Households with income of $100,000 or more: 10.3%; Poverty rate: 26.1%
Educational Attainment: High school diploma or higher: 92.0%; Bachelor's degree or higher: 9.5%; Graduate/professional degree or higher: 1.6%
School District(s)
Campbell-Savona Central SD (PK-12)
    Enrollment: 858 . . . . (607) 527-9800

Housing: Homeownership rate: 72.3%; Median home value: $82,000; Median year structure built: Before 1940; Homeowner vacancy rate: 0.0%; Median selected monthly owner costs: $1,082 with a mortgage, $378 without a mortgage; Median gross rent: $680 per month; Rental vacancy rate: 0.0%
Health Insurance: 94.6% have insurance; 57.0% have private insurance; 51.4% have public insurance; 5.4% do not have insurance; 0.8% of children under 18 do not have insurance
Transportation: Commute: 93.1% car, 0.8% public transportation, 4.0% walk, 2.1% work from home; Mean travel time to work: 24.2 minutes

SOUTH CORNING (village). Covers a land area of 0.617 square miles and a water area of 0 square miles. Located at 42.13° N. Lat; 77.04° W. Long. Elevation is 951 feet.
Population: 1,176; Growth (since 2000): 2.5%; Density: 1,907.0 persons per square mile; Race: 86.4% White, 11.1% Black/African American, 0.3% Asian, 0.0% American Indian/Alaska Native, 0.0% Native Hawaiian/Other Pacific Islander, 2.2% Two or more races, 0.9% Hispanic of any race; Average household size: 2.21; Median age: 43.0; Age under 18: 17.9%; Age 65 and over: 18.0%; Males per 100 females: 95.7; Marriage status: 25.2% never married, 52.7% now married, 4.0% separated, 9.1% widowed, 13.0% divorced; Foreign born: 0.9%; Speak English only: 98.4%; With disability: 18.0%; Veterans: 12.2%; Ancestry: 23.6% German, 17.3% Irish, 15.1% English, 11.4% Italian, 8.2% American
Employment: 13.1% management, business, and financial, 3.6% computer, engineering, and science, 8.2% education, legal, community service, arts, and media, 5.0% healthcare practitioners, 15.6% service, 23.3% sales and office, 9.3% natural resources, construction, and maintenance, 21.9% production, transportation, and material moving
Income: Per capita: $27,812; Median household: $55,921; Average household: $62,243; Households with income of $100,000 or more: 20.7%; Poverty rate: 7.6%
Educational Attainment: High school diploma or higher: 93.2%; Bachelor's degree or higher: 27.6%; Graduate/professional degree or higher: 11.1%
Housing: Homeownership rate: 66.5%; Median home value: $90,700; Median year structure built: 1953; Homeowner vacancy rate: 1.9%; Median selected monthly owner costs: $1,206 with a mortgage, $495 without a mortgage; Median gross rent: $1,003 per month; Rental vacancy rate: 4.3%
Health Insurance: 91.5% have insurance; 73.7% have private insurance; 34.6% have public insurance; 8.5% do not have insurance; 9.0% of children under 18 do not have insurance
Transportation: Commute: 95.4% car, 0.0% public transportation, 2.2% walk, 1.7% work from home; Mean travel time to work: 17.2 minutes

THURSTON (town). Covers a land area of 36.353 square miles and a water area of 0.165 square miles. Located at 42.23° N. Lat; 77.28° W. Long. Elevation is 1,263 feet.
Population: 1,284; Growth (since 2000): -1.9%; Density: 35.3 persons per square mile; Race: 99.3% White, 0.0% Black/African American, 0.0% Asian, 0.3% American Indian/Alaska Native, 0.0% Native Hawaiian/Other Pacific Islander, 0.4% Two or more races, 0.5% Hispanic of any race; Average household size: 2.59; Median age: 45.1; Age under 18: 21.2%; Age 65 and over: 15.6%; Males per 100 females: 102.4; Marriage status: 23.1% never married, 63.3% now married, 2.6% separated, 5.2% widowed, 8.4% divorced; Foreign born: 0.5%; Speak English only: 97.8%; With disability: 16.9%; Veterans: 13.0%; Ancestry: 22.6% American, 22.1% German, 16.7% English, 14.4% Irish, 4.6% Polish
Employment: 10.0% management, business, and financial, 5.0% computer, engineering, and science, 4.1% education, legal, community service, arts, and media, 6.8% healthcare practitioners, 17.2% service, 21.6% sales and office, 16.6% natural resources, construction, and maintenance, 18.6% production, transportation, and material moving
Income: Per capita: $23,178; Median household: $54,750; Average household: $59,785; Households with income of $100,000 or more: 15.8%; Poverty rate: 11.1%
Educational Attainment: High school diploma or higher: 83.0%; Bachelor's degree or higher: 11.2%; Graduate/professional degree or higher: 4.4%
Housing: Homeownership rate: 84.4%; Median home value: $84,600; Median year structure built: 1975; Homeowner vacancy rate: 0.0%; Median selected monthly owner costs: $1,059 with a mortgage, $541 without a mortgage; Median gross rent: $682 per month; Rental vacancy rate: 12.5%

Health Insurance: 95.7% have insurance; 71.3% have private insurance; 40.8% have public insurance; 4.3% do not have insurance; 2.4% of children under 18 do not have insurance
Transportation: Commute: 90.3% car, 0.0% public transportation, 8.6% walk, 1.1% work from home; Mean travel time to work: 24.2 minutes

TROUPSBURG (town). Covers a land area of 61.238 square miles and a water area of 0.028 square miles. Located at 42.07° N. Lat; 77.53° W. Long. Elevation is 1,663 feet.
Population: 1,200; Growth (since 2000): 6.6%; Density: 19.6 persons per square mile; Race: 99.3% White, 0.0% Black/African American, 0.4% Asian, 0.0% American Indian/Alaska Native, 0.0% Native Hawaiian/Other Pacific Islander, 0.3% Two or more races, 0.1% Hispanic of any race; Average household size: 3.05; Median age: 36.2; Age under 18: 28.8%; Age 65 and over: 13.8%; Males per 100 females: 103.6; Marriage status: 23.8% never married, 58.3% now married, 0.8% separated, 6.1% widowed, 11.8% divorced; Foreign born: 0.4%; Speak English only: 90.7%; With disability: 12.5%; Veterans: 6.1%; Ancestry: 21.9% German, 18.2% English, 12.0% American, 9.6% Irish, 6.2% Italian
Employment: 14.5% management, business, and financial, 1.9% computer, engineering, and science, 7.7% education, legal, community service, arts, and media, 2.1% healthcare practitioners, 9.8% service, 26.3% sales and office, 21.8% natural resources, construction, and maintenance, 16.0% production, transportation, and material moving
Income: Per capita: $18,707; Median household: $52,375; Average household: $56,682; Households with income of $100,000 or more: 5.6%; Poverty rate: 24.2%
Educational Attainment: High school diploma or higher: 87.3%; Bachelor's degree or higher: 14.1%; Graduate/professional degree or higher: 6.8%

School District(s)
Jasper-Troupsburg Central SD (PK-12)
    Enrollment: 491 . . . . (607) 792-3675
Housing: Homeownership rate: 88.3%; Median home value: $107,800; Median year structure built: 1975; Homeowner vacancy rate: 4.8%; Median selected monthly owner costs: $1,226 with a mortgage, $623 without a mortgage; Median gross rent: $795 per month; Rental vacancy rate: 0.0%
Health Insurance: 85.6% have insurance; 51.8% have private insurance; 45.2% have public insurance; 14.4% do not have insurance; 18.2% of children under 18 do not have insurance
Transportation: Commute: 82.4% car, 0.0% public transportation, 4.7% walk, 13.0% work from home; Mean travel time to work: 30.9 minutes

TUSCARORA (town). Covers a land area of 37.627 square miles and a water area of 0.085 square miles. Located at 42.05° N. Lat; 77.26° W. Long.
Population: 1,351; Growth (since 2000): -3.5%; Density: 35.9 persons per square mile; Race: 97.7% White, 0.0% Black/African American, 0.5% Asian, 0.0% American Indian/Alaska Native, 0.0% Native Hawaiian/Other Pacific Islander, 1.4% Two or more races, 0.0% Hispanic of any race; Average household size: 2.43; Median age: 41.3; Age under 18: 22.0%; Age 65 and over: 15.2%; Males per 100 females: 101.8; Marriage status: 24.1% never married, 60.0% now married, 5.7% separated, 5.7% widowed, 10.2% divorced; Foreign born: 1.6%; Speak English only: 96.1%; With disability: 14.7%; Veterans: 10.4%; Ancestry: 18.4% Irish, 17.2% American, 17.2% German, 8.7% English, 5.3% Italian
Employment: 8.0% management, business, and financial, 7.3% computer, engineering, and science, 5.8% education, legal, community service, arts, and media, 11.3% healthcare practitioners, 7.5% service, 17.5% sales and office, 20.4% natural resources, construction, and maintenance, 22.1% production, transportation, and material moving
Income: Per capita: $22,732; Median household: $44,856; Average household: $55,176; Households with income of $100,000 or more: 12.0%; Poverty rate: 17.1%
Educational Attainment: High school diploma or higher: 85.2%; Bachelor's degree or higher: 16.2%; Graduate/professional degree or higher: 5.0%
Housing: Homeownership rate: 79.2%; Median home value: $91,900; Median year structure built: 1977; Homeowner vacancy rate: 0.0%; Median selected monthly owner costs: $1,214 with a mortgage, $575 without a mortgage; Median gross rent: $823 per month; Rental vacancy rate: 4.1%
Health Insurance: 92.6% have insurance; 68.2% have private insurance; 38.6% have public insurance; 7.4% do not have insurance; 7.6% of children under 18 do not have insurance

Transportation: Commute: 95.8% car, 0.0% public transportation, 1.1% walk, 1.1% work from home; Mean travel time to work: 32.5 minutes

URBANA (town). Covers a land area of 40.946 square miles and a water area of 3.231 square miles. Located at 42.41° N. Lat; 77.23° W. Long. Elevation is 728 feet.
Population: 2,131; Growth (since 2000): -16.3%; Density: 52.0 persons per square mile; Race: 95.2% White, 3.1% Black/African American, 0.0% Asian, 0.0% American Indian/Alaska Native, 0.0% Native Hawaiian/Other Pacific Islander, 1.3% Two or more races, 1.5% Hispanic of any race; Average household size: 2.11; Median age: 55.5; Age under 18: 15.8%; Age 65 and over: 31.1%; Males per 100 females: 100.1; Marriage status: 17.1% never married, 57.3% now married, 3.4% separated, 10.5% widowed, 15.1% divorced; Foreign born: 1.8%; Speak English only: 98.5%; With disability: 18.5%; Veterans: 13.5%; Ancestry: 18.2% English, 17.6% German, 11.7% Irish, 9.0% American, 6.9% Italian
Employment: 15.0% management, business, and financial, 3.9% computer, engineering, and science, 15.9% education, legal, community service, arts, and media, 4.7% healthcare practitioners, 19.0% service, 19.1% sales and office, 6.8% natural resources, construction, and maintenance, 15.5% production, transportation, and material moving
Income: Per capita: $34,162; Median household: $52,045; Average household: $75,446; Households with income of $100,000 or more: 20.5%; Poverty rate: 13.7%
Educational Attainment: High school diploma or higher: 90.5%; Bachelor's degree or higher: 26.5%; Graduate/professional degree or higher: 13.3%
Housing: Homeownership rate: 74.5%; Median home value: $138,400; Median year structure built: 1949; Homeowner vacancy rate: 0.0%; Median selected monthly owner costs: $1,134 with a mortgage, $454 without a mortgage; Median gross rent: $726 per month; Rental vacancy rate: 10.2%
Health Insurance: 96.2% have insurance; 67.1% have private insurance; 48.5% have public insurance; 3.8% do not have insurance; 2.7% of children under 18 do not have insurance
Transportation: Commute: 89.8% car, 0.6% public transportation, 4.3% walk, 4.4% work from home; Mean travel time to work: 18.8 minutes

WAYLAND (town). Covers a land area of 38.738 square miles and a water area of 0.600 square miles. Located at 42.52° N. Lat; 77.60° W. Long. Elevation is 1,375 feet.
History: Incorporated 1877.
Population: 3,988; Growth (since 2000): -7.6%; Density: 102.9 persons per square mile; Race: 98.8% White, 0.2% Black/African American, 0.0% Asian, 0.1% American Indian/Alaska Native, 0.0% Native Hawaiian/Other Pacific Islander, 0.9% Two or more races, 0.6% Hispanic of any race; Average household size: 2.28; Median age: 48.9; Age under 18: 17.6%; Age 65 and over: 19.1%; Males per 100 females: 95.0; Marriage status: 27.7% never married, 52.5% now married, 4.7% separated, 5.6% widowed, 14.2% divorced; Foreign born: 0.4%; Speak English only: 98.7%; With disability: 20.2%; Veterans: 10.6%; Ancestry: 41.9% German, 23.6% Irish, 13.8% English, 5.9% American, 5.7% Dutch
Employment: 7.2% management, business, and financial, 3.2% computer, engineering, and science, 8.8% education, legal, community service, arts, and media, 6.7% healthcare practitioners, 21.2% service, 19.4% sales and office, 11.1% natural resources, construction, and maintenance, 22.5% production, transportation, and material moving
Income: Per capita: $25,717; Median household: $51,029; Average household: $58,441; Households with income of $100,000 or more: 16.0%; Poverty rate: 10.7%
Educational Attainment: High school diploma or higher: 88.8%; Bachelor's degree or higher: 12.6%; Graduate/professional degree or higher: 5.8%

School District(s)
Wayland-Cohocton Central SD (PK-12)
    Enrollment: 1,335 . . . . (585) 728-2211
Housing: Homeownership rate: 74.0%; Median home value: $93,800; Median year structure built: 1960; Homeowner vacancy rate: 3.2%; Median selected monthly owner costs: $983 with a mortgage, $530 without a mortgage; Median gross rent: $656 per month; Rental vacancy rate: 0.9%
Health Insurance: 96.2% have insurance; 71.8% have private insurance; 41.7% have public insurance; 3.8% do not have insurance; 0.0% of children under 18 do not have insurance
Transportation: Commute: 90.3% car, 2.2% public transportation, 3.1% walk, 2.2% work from home; Mean travel time to work: 28.3 minutes

Additional Information Contacts
Town of Wayland .... (585) 728-5660
   http://townofwayland.org/content

WAYLAND (village). Covers a land area of 1.130 square miles and a water area of 0.058 square miles. Located at 42.56° N. Lat; 77.60° W. Long. Elevation is 1,375 feet.

Population: 1,788; Growth (since 2000): -5.5%; Density: 1,582.9 persons per square mile; Race: 98.5% White, 0.3% Black/African American, 0.0% Asian, 0.2% American Indian/Alaska Native, 0.0% Native Hawaiian/Other Pacific Islander, 0.9% Two or more races, 0.6% Hispanic of any race; Average household size: 2.36; Median age: 42.6; Age under 18: 24.0%; Age 65 and over: 14.4%; Males per 100 females: 94.3; Marriage status: 26.9% never married, 52.3% now married, 2.6% separated, 5.3% widowed, 15.6% divorced; Foreign born: 0.8%; Speak English only: 98.7%; With disability: 21.3%; Veterans: 8.7%; Ancestry: 38.8% German, 18.7% Irish, 15.2% English, 9.2% American, 6.0% Dutch

Employment: 8.2% management, business, and financial, 4.5% computer, engineering, and science, 10.1% education, legal, community service, arts, and media, 8.4% healthcare practitioners, 19.5% service, 20.9% sales and office, 8.0% natural resources, construction, and maintenance, 20.5% production, transportation, and material moving

Income: Per capita: $24,546; Median household: $43,646; Average household: $58,134; Households with income of $100,000 or more: 11.8%; Poverty rate: 11.8%

Educational Attainment: High school diploma or higher: 89.9%; Bachelor's degree or higher: 15.2%; Graduate/professional degree or higher: 8.8%

School District(s)
Wayland-Cohocton Central SD (PK-12)
   Enrollment: 1,335 .... (585) 728-2211

Housing: Homeownership rate: 66.4%; Median home value: $91,500; Median year structure built: Before 1940; Homeowner vacancy rate: 3.8%; Median selected monthly owner costs: $1,015 with a mortgage, $520 without a mortgage; Median gross rent: $599 per month; Rental vacancy rate: 1.6%

Health Insurance: 96.5% have insurance; 64.3% have private insurance; 45.7% have public insurance; 3.5% do not have insurance; 0.0% of children under 18 do not have insurance

Transportation: Commute: 92.4% car, 0.6% public transportation, 2.2% walk, 2.4% work from home; Mean travel time to work: 23.5 minutes

WAYNE (town). Covers a land area of 20.582 square miles and a water area of 2.014 square miles. Located at 42.43° N. Lat; 77.14° W. Long. Elevation is 1,168 feet.

Population: 1,020; Growth (since 2000): -12.4%; Density: 49.6 persons per square mile; Race: 99.4% White, 0.5% Black/African American, 0.0% Asian, 0.1% American Indian/Alaska Native, 0.0% Native Hawaiian/Other Pacific Islander, 0.0% Two or more races, 0.0% Hispanic of any race; Average household size: 2.23; Median age: 53.7; Age under 18: 15.7%; Age 65 and over: 24.9%; Males per 100 females: 97.2; Marriage status: 21.0% never married, 62.6% now married, 1.4% separated, 4.8% widowed, 11.5% divorced; Foreign born: 0.5%; Speak English only: 98.3%; With disability: 19.6%; Veterans: 10.3%; Ancestry: 24.5% Irish, 17.3% German, 15.6% English, 14.0% American, 8.1% Polish

Employment: 16.6% management, business, and financial, 2.5% computer, engineering, and science, 13.0% education, legal, community service, arts, and media, 6.6% healthcare practitioners, 14.4% service, 27.3% sales and office, 8.7% natural resources, construction, and maintenance, 10.9% production, transportation, and material moving

Income: Per capita: $35,588; Median household: $55,500; Average household: $77,907; Households with income of $100,000 or more: 28.4%; Poverty rate: 10.3%

Educational Attainment: High school diploma or higher: 92.9%; Bachelor's degree or higher: 34.8%; Graduate/professional degree or higher: 14.9%

Housing: Homeownership rate: 93.9%; Median home value: $168,900; Median year structure built: 1966; Homeowner vacancy rate: 1.8%; Median selected monthly owner costs: $1,188 with a mortgage, $593 without a mortgage; Median gross rent: $1,113 per month; Rental vacancy rate: 24.3%

Health Insurance: 92.6% have insurance; 69.0% have private insurance; 46.5% have public insurance; 7.4% do not have insurance; 9.4% of children under 18 do not have insurance

Transportation: Commute: 94.8% car, 0.0% public transportation, 2.3% walk, 2.9% work from home; Mean travel time to work: 27.2 minutes

WEST UNION (town). Covers a land area of 40.903 square miles and a water area of 0.146 square miles. Located at 42.04° N. Lat; 77.69° W. Long. Elevation is 2,257 feet.

Population: 279; Growth (since 2000): -30.1%; Density: 6.8 persons per square mile; Race: 93.2% White, 0.0% Black/African American, 0.0% Asian, 0.0% American Indian/Alaska Native, 0.0% Native Hawaiian/Other Pacific Islander, 6.8% Two or more races, 0.0% Hispanic of any race; Average household size: 2.49; Median age: 47.4; Age under 18: 20.1%; Age 65 and over: 18.6%; Males per 100 females: 113.7; Marriage status: 25.2% never married, 60.0% now married, 3.9% separated, 3.5% widowed, 11.3% divorced; Foreign born: 1.4%; Speak English only: 96.5%; With disability: 16.1%; Veterans: 9.4%; Ancestry: 23.3% Irish, 20.8% German, 15.4% English, 10.0% American, 8.2% Italian

Employment: 14.2% management, business, and financial, 6.7% computer, engineering, and science, 2.5% education, legal, community service, arts, and media, 3.3% healthcare practitioners, 12.5% service, 18.3% sales and office, 30.0% natural resources, construction, and maintenance, 12.5% production, transportation, and material moving

Income: Per capita: $26,394; Median household: $43,125; Average household: $65,292; Households with income of $100,000 or more: 20.6%; Poverty rate: 9.7%

Educational Attainment: High school diploma or higher: 90.7%; Bachelor's degree or higher: 6.9%; Graduate/professional degree or higher: 3.4%

Housing: Homeownership rate: 74.1%; Median home value: $100,700; Median year structure built: 1974; Homeowner vacancy rate: 6.7%; Median selected monthly owner costs: $1,143 with a mortgage, $463 without a mortgage; Median gross rent: $669 per month; Rental vacancy rate: 0.0%

Health Insurance: 83.5% have insurance; 64.5% have private insurance; 38.4% have public insurance; 16.5% do not have insurance; 29.3% of children under 18 do not have insurance

Transportation: Commute: 82.4% car, 0.0% public transportation, 3.4% walk, 13.4% work from home; Mean travel time to work: 31.8 minutes

WHEELER (town). Covers a land area of 46.066 square miles and a water area of 0.061 square miles. Located at 42.44° N. Lat; 77.34° W. Long. Elevation is 1,257 feet.

Population: 1,151; Growth (since 2000): -8.9%; Density: 25.0 persons per square mile; Race: 94.3% White, 3.0% Black/African American, 0.2% Asian, 0.0% American Indian/Alaska Native, 0.0% Native Hawaiian/Other Pacific Islander, 2.5% Two or more races, 1.3% Hispanic of any race; Average household size: 2.44; Median age: 43.4; Age under 18: 21.2%; Age 65 and over: 19.6%; Males per 100 females: 106.9; Marriage status: 22.3% never married, 56.6% now married, 4.2% separated, 6.4% widowed, 14.7% divorced; Foreign born: 0.4%; Speak English only: 94.6%; With disability: 16.2%; Veterans: 12.1%; Ancestry: 28.2% German, 27.4% Irish, 13.0% English, 8.0% American, 5.6% Dutch

Employment: 14.8% management, business, and financial, 5.8% computer, engineering, and science, 7.6% education, legal, community service, arts, and media, 2.8% healthcare practitioners, 22.5% service, 15.7% sales and office, 17.1% natural resources, construction, and maintenance, 13.7% production, transportation, and material moving

Income: Per capita: $26,302; Median household: $48,750; Average household: $64,856; Households with income of $100,000 or more: 12.1%; Poverty rate: 13.9%

Educational Attainment: High school diploma or higher: 83.2%; Bachelor's degree or higher: 19.0%; Graduate/professional degree or higher: 7.8%

Housing: Homeownership rate: 85.6%; Median home value: $100,600; Median year structure built: 1975; Homeowner vacancy rate: 1.0%; Median selected monthly owner costs: $973 with a mortgage, $464 without a mortgage; Median gross rent: $833 per month; Rental vacancy rate: 0.0%

Health Insurance: 81.7% have insurance; 59.4% have private insurance; 38.2% have public insurance; 18.3% do not have insurance; 27.4% of children under 18 do not have insurance

Transportation: Commute: 91.8% car, 0.0% public transportation, 0.0% walk, 5.6% work from home; Mean travel time to work: 25.7 minutes

WOODHULL (town). Covers a land area of 55.390 square miles and a water area of 0.033 square miles. Located at 42.05° N. Lat; 77.39° W. Long. Elevation is 1,322 feet.

Population: 1,999; Growth (since 2000): 31.2%; Density: 36.1 persons per square mile; Race: 99.2% White, 0.0% Black/African American, 0.0% Asian, 0.0% American Indian/Alaska Native, 0.0% Native Hawaiian/Other Pacific Islander, 0.8% Two or more races, 0.0% Hispanic of any race; Average household size: 2.92; Median age: 33.7; Age under 18: 30.9%; Age 65 and over: 13.7%; Males per 100 females: 101.3; Marriage status: 29.9% never married, 51.4% now married, 1.5% separated, 4.8% widowed, 13.9% divorced; Foreign born: 0.3%; Speak English only: 88.5%; With disability: 12.9%; Veterans: 11.1%; Ancestry: 19.3% American, 15.0% English, 12.6% German, 11.6% Irish, 5.5% Pennsylvania German

Employment: 7.1% management, business, and financial, 1.1% computer, engineering, and science, 11.8% education, legal, community service, arts, and media, 3.9% healthcare practitioners, 19.6% service, 15.4% sales and office, 19.2% natural resources, construction, and maintenance, 21.9% production, transportation, and material moving

Income: Per capita: $18,946; Median household: $43,571; Average household: $55,283; Households with income of $100,000 or more: 14.1%; Poverty rate: 26.4%

Educational Attainment: High school diploma or higher: 86.8%; Bachelor's degree or higher: 10.9%; Graduate/professional degree or higher: 3.6%

Housing: Homeownership rate: 85.5%; Median home value: $81,600; Median year structure built: 1972; Homeowner vacancy rate: 0.7%; Median selected monthly owner costs: $971 with a mortgage, $361 without a mortgage; Median gross rent: $636 per month; Rental vacancy rate: 8.3%

Health Insurance: 81.3% have insurance; 59.3% have private insurance; 36.4% have public insurance; 18.7% do not have insurance; 29.3% of children under 18 do not have insurance

Transportation: Commute: 92.7% car, 1.6% public transportation, 2.5% walk, 3.3% work from home; Mean travel time to work: 33.2 minutes

Suffolk County

Located in southeastern New York; on Long Island, bounded on the south by the Atlantic Ocean, on the east by Block Island Sound, and on the north by Long Island Sound; includes many bays and inlets. Covers a land area of 912.051 square miles, a water area of 1,461.082 square miles, and is located in the Eastern Time Zone at 40.94° N. Lat., 72.69° W. Long. The county was founded in 1683. County seat is Riverhead.

Suffolk County is part of the New York-Newark-Jersey City, NY-NJ-PA Metropolitan Statistical Area. The entire metro area includes: Dutchess County-Putnam County, NY Metropolitan Division (Dutchess County, NY; Putnam County, NY); Nassau County-Suffolk County, NY Metropolitan Division (Nassau County, NY; Suffolk County, NY); Newark, NJ-PA Metropolitan Division (Essex County, NJ; Hunterdon County, NJ; Morris County, NJ; Somerset County, NJ; Sussex County, NJ; Union County, NJ; Pike County, PA); New York-Jersey City-White Plains, NY-NJ Metropolitan Division (Bergen County, NJ; Hudson County, NJ; Middlesex County, NJ; Monmouth County, NJ; Ocean County, NJ; Passaic County, NJ; Bronx County, NY; Kings County, NY; New York County, NY; Orange County, NY; Queens County, NY; Richmond County, NY; Rockland County, NY; Westchester County, NY)

Weather Station: Bridgehampton										Elevation: 60 feet		
	Jan	Feb	Mar	Apr	May	Jun	Jul	Aug	Sep	Oct	Nov	Dec
High	39	40	47	56	66	75	81	80	74	63	54	44
Low	23	25	30	39	48	57	63	63	55	44	37	28
Precip	4.0	3.5	4.9	4.7	3.7	4.2	3.4	4.0	4.4	4.2	4.4	4.3
Snow	7.7	7.9	5.3	0.9	0.0	0.0	0.0	0.0	0.0	tr	0.7	4.0

High and Low temperatures in degrees Fahrenheit; Precipitation and Snow in inches

Weather Station: Islip-Macarthur Arpt										Elevation: 83 feet		
	Jan	Feb	Mar	Apr	May	Jun	Jul	Aug	Sep	Oct	Nov	Dec
High	39	41	48	58	68	77	82	81	74	64	54	44
Low	24	25	31	41	50	60	66	65	58	46	37	28
Precip	3.8	3.0	4.4	4.3	3.8	4.1	3.3	4.3	3.8	4.0	3.6	4.2
Snow	na	na	na	na	na	na	na	na	na	na	na	na

High and Low temperatures in degrees Fahrenheit; Precipitation and Snow in inches

Weather Station: Riverhead Research Farm										Elevation: 100 feet		
	Jan	Feb	Mar	Apr	May	Jun	Jul	Aug	Sep	Oct	Nov	Dec
High	40	42	49	60	71	79	84	83	76	65	55	45
Low	25	26	32	41	50	60	65	65	58	48	40	30
Precip	3.7	3.1	4.5	4.5	3.9	4.1	3.2	3.9	3.8	4.2	4.3	4.0
Snow	8.5	7.6	5.1	0.7	0.0	0.0	0.0	0.0	0.0	0.0	0.5	4.7

High and Low temperatures in degrees Fahrenheit; Precipitation and Snow in inches

Weather Station: Setauket Strong										Elevation: 40 feet		
	Jan	Feb	Mar	Apr	May	Jun	Jul	Aug	Sep	Oct	Nov	Dec
High	40	42	50	61	71	79	83	82	76	65	55	45
Low	25	26	31	41	49	59	65	64	58	47	38	30
Precip	3.4	2.7	4.0	4.4	3.7	3.9	na	3.6	3.8	3.6	3.6	3.5
Snow	2.5	3.3	1.3	0.2	0.0	0.0	0.0	0.0	0.0	0.0	tr	na

High and Low temperatures in degrees Fahrenheit; Precipitation and Snow in inches

Population: 1,497,595; Growth (since 2000): 5.5%; Density: 1,642.0 persons per square mile; Race: 80.5% White, 7.8% Black/African American, 3.9% Asian, 0.2% American Indian/Alaska Native, 0.0% Native Hawaiian/Other Pacific Islander, 2.5% two or more races, 18.6% Hispanic of any race; Average household size: 3.00; Median age: 41.0; Age under 18: 22.0%; Age 65 and over: 15.6%; Males per 100 females: 96.8; Marriage status: 32.8% never married, 52.8% now married, 1.7% separated, 6.3% widowed, 8.1% divorced; Foreign born: 15.6%; Speak English only: 77.3%; With disability: 9.5%; Veterans: 5.7%; Ancestry: 24.8% Italian, 18.9% Irish, 14.3% German, 4.9% Polish, 4.5% English

Religion: Six largest groups: 58.9% Catholicism, 2.2% Lutheran, 1.7% Methodist/Pietist, 1.6% Non-denominational Protestant, 1.4% Judaism, 1.3% Muslim Estimate

Economy: Unemployment rate: 3.3%; Leading industries: 14.7 % construction; 13.4 % retail trade; 11.6 % professional, scientific, and technical services; Farms: 604 totaling 35,975 acres; Company size: 24 employ 1,000 or more persons, 45 employ 500 to 999 persons, 747 employ 100 to 499 persons, 48,333 employ less than 100 persons; Business ownership: 48,272 women-owned, 7,112 Black-owned, 15,418 Hispanic-owned, 7,686 Asian-owned, 715 American Indian/Alaska Native-owned

Employment: 14.7% management, business, and financial, 4.5% computer, engineering, and science, 12.9% education, legal, community service, arts, and media, 6.4% healthcare practitioners, 17.2% service, 25.7% sales and office, 9.4% natural resources, construction, and maintenance, 9.4% production, transportation, and material moving

Income: Per capita: $40,277; Median household: $92,838; Average household: $118,116; Households with income of $100,000 or more: 46.4%; Poverty rate: 7.2%

Educational Attainment: High school diploma or higher: 90.1%; Bachelor's degree or higher: 35.0%; Graduate/professional degree or higher: 15.8%

Housing: Homeownership rate: 80.3%; Median home value: $379,400; Median year structure built: 1968; Homeowner vacancy rate: 1.4%; Median selected monthly owner costs: $2,744 with a mortgage, $1,165 without a mortgage; Median gross rent: $1,646 per month; Rental vacancy rate: 5.3%

Vital Statistics: Birth rate: 103.9 per 10,000 population; Death rate: 85.6 per 10,000 population; Age-adjusted cancer mortality rate: 147.7 deaths per 100,000 population

Health Insurance: 93.5% have insurance; 77.9% have private insurance; 28.6% have public insurance; 6.5% do not have insurance; 2.7% of children under 18 do not have insurance

Health Care: Physicians: 34.0 per 10,000 population; Dentists: 8.3 per 10,000 population; Hospital beds: 29.2 per 10,000 population; Hospital admissions: 1,128.7 per 10,000 population

Air Quality Index (AQI): Percent of Days: 85.8% good, 11.8% moderate, 1.9% unhealthy for sensitive individuals, 0.5% unhealthy, 0.0% very unhealthy; Annual median: 39; Annual maximum: 159

Transportation: Commute: 87.4% car, 6.4% public transportation, 1.5% walk, 3.6% work from home; Mean travel time to work: 32.0 minutes

2016 Presidential Election: 51.5% Trump, 44.6% Clinton, 2.0% Johnson, 1.2% Stein

National and State Parks: Amagansett National Wildlife Refuge; Babylon Marsh State Tidal Wetlands; Belmont Lake State Park; Brookhaven State Park; Caleb Smith State Park; Camp Hero State Park; Captree State Park; Caumsett State Park; Connetquot River State Park; Conscience Point National Wildlife Refuge; Elizabeth Alexandra Morton National Wildlife Refuge; Fire Island National Seashore; Gilgo State Park; Heckscher State Park; Hither Hills State Park; Montauk Downs State Park; Montauk Point

State Park; Orient Beach State Park; Petteanger Island State Tidal Wetlands; Robert Moses State Park; Seatuck National Wildlife Refuge; Sunken Meadow State Park; Target Rock National Wildlife Refuge; Wertheim National Wildlife Refuge; Wildwood State Park

Additional Information Contacts
Suffolk Government . . . . (631) 852-2000
http://www.suffolkcountyny.gov

Suffolk County Communities

AMAGANSETT (CDP). Covers a land area of 6.527 square miles and a water area of 0.024 square miles. Located at 40.99° N. Lat; 72.13° W. Long. Elevation is 30 feet.
Population: 817; Growth (since 2000): -23.4%; Density: 125.2 persons per square mile; Race: 97.1% White, 1.2% Black/African American, 0.0% Asian, 0.0% American Indian/Alaska Native, 0.0% Native Hawaiian/Other Pacific Islander, 0.5% Two or more races, 8.0% Hispanic of any race; Average household size: 2.29; Median age: 56.9; Age under 18: 11.1%; Age 65 and over: 37.8%; Males per 100 females: 107.3; Marriage status: 27.7% never married, 56.0% now married, 1.0% separated, 9.6% widowed, 6.7% divorced; Foreign born: 12.2%; Speak English only: 89.5%; With disability: 12.4%; Veterans: 6.3%; Ancestry: 23.1% Irish, 22.9% German, 16.2% English, 15.7% Italian, 10.8% Russian
Employment: 18.6% management, business, and financial, 4.6% computer, engineering, and science, 17.9% education, legal, community service, arts, and media, 0.0% healthcare practitioners, 19.3% service, 20.5% sales and office, 17.6% natural resources, construction, and maintenance, 1.4% production, transportation, and material moving
Income: Per capita: $66,838; Median household: $85,417; Average household: $148,148; Households with income of $100,000 or more: 42.0%; Poverty rate: 5.8%
Educational Attainment: High school diploma or higher: 92.4%; Bachelor's degree or higher: 47.9%; Graduate/professional degree or higher: 22.4%

School District(s)
Amagansett Union Free SD (PK-10)
    Enrollment: 116 . . . . (631) 267-3572
Housing: Homeownership rate: 82.4%; Median home value: $1,673,900; Median year structure built: 1975; Homeowner vacancy rate: 0.0%; Median selected monthly owner costs: $2,425 with a mortgage, $908 without a mortgage; Median gross rent: $1,855 per month; Rental vacancy rate: 24.4%
Health Insurance: 89.2% have insurance; 81.0% have private insurance; 34.9% have public insurance; 10.8% do not have insurance; 0.0% of children under 18 do not have insurance
Transportation: Commute: 81.4% car, 3.8% public transportation, 0.0% walk, 14.8% work from home; Mean travel time to work: 28.8 minutes

AMITYVILLE (village). Covers a land area of 2.113 square miles and a water area of 0.363 square miles. Located at 40.67° N. Lat; 73.42° W. Long. Elevation is 20 feet.
History: Settled 1780, incorporated 1894.
Population: 9,513; Growth (since 2000): 0.8%; Density: 4,502.2 persons per square mile; Race: 72.9% White, 6.4% Black/African American, 1.7% Asian, 0.1% American Indian/Alaska Native, 0.0% Native Hawaiian/Other Pacific Islander, 1.5% Two or more races, 23.0% Hispanic of any race; Average household size: 2.72; Median age: 44.4; Age under 18: 20.5%; Age 65 and over: 19.0%; Males per 100 females: 91.5; Marriage status: 29.3% never married, 50.8% now married, 0.9% separated, 8.0% widowed, 12.0% divorced; Foreign born: 14.9%; Speak English only: 76.4%; With disability: 10.6%; Veterans: 7.2%; Ancestry: 25.3% Irish, 23.4% Italian, 13.6% German, 5.3% Polish, 5.2% English
Employment: 12.7% management, business, and financial, 8.3% computer, engineering, and science, 11.4% education, legal, community service, arts, and media, 8.1% healthcare practitioners, 16.1% service, 25.8% sales and office, 5.8% natural resources, construction, and maintenance, 11.8% production, transportation, and material moving
Income: Per capita: $40,029; Median household: $98,268; Average household: $109,619; Households with income of $100,000 or more: 48.8%; Poverty rate: 12.4%
Educational Attainment: High school diploma or higher: 93.3%; Bachelor's degree or higher: 37.0%; Graduate/professional degree or higher: 12.8%

School District(s)
Amityville Union Free SD (PK-12)
    Enrollment: 3,150 . . . . (631) 565-6019
Two-year College(s)
Island Drafting and Technical Institute (Private, For-profit)
    Enrollment: 90 . . . . (631) 691-8733
    Tuition: In-state $16,650; Out-of-state $16,650
Vocational/Technical School(s)
Branford Hall Career Institute-Amityville (Private, For-profit)
    Enrollment: 252 . . . . (631) 608-9113
    Tuition: $14,666
Housing: Homeownership rate: 70.4%; Median home value: $382,200; Median year structure built: 1957; Homeowner vacancy rate: 0.6%; Median selected monthly owner costs: $2,773 with a mortgage, $1,402 without a mortgage; Median gross rent: $1,553 per month; Rental vacancy rate: 9.0%
Health Insurance: 91.7% have insurance; 72.0% have private insurance; 35.4% have public insurance; 8.3% do not have insurance; 0.0% of children under 18 do not have insurance
Safety: Violent crime rate: 11.6 per 10,000 population; Property crime rate: 132.7 per 10,000 population
Newspapers: Amityville Record (weekly circulation 2,900)
Transportation: Commute: 75.2% car, 13.9% public transportation, 2.1% walk, 5.5% work from home; Mean travel time to work: 34.1 minutes
Additional Information Contacts
Village of Amityville . . . . (631) 264-6000
http://www.amityville.com

AQUEBOGUE (CDP). Covers a land area of 3.812 square miles and a water area of 0.099 square miles. Located at 40.94° N. Lat; 72.62° W. Long. Elevation is 36 feet.
Population: 1,635; Growth (since 2000): -27.5%; Density: 428.9 persons per square mile; Race: 93.8% White, 6.2% Black/African American, 0.0% Asian, 0.0% American Indian/Alaska Native, 0.0% Native Hawaiian/Other Pacific Islander, 0.0% Two or more races, 7.5% Hispanic of any race; Average household size: 2.14; Median age: 48.8; Age under 18: 11.6%; Age 65 and over: 16.1%; Males per 100 females: 92.4; Marriage status: 36.7% never married, 48.5% now married, 0.0% separated, 3.0% widowed, 11.8% divorced; Foreign born: 10.0%; Speak English only: 86.5%; With disability: 15.0%; Veterans: 11.1%; Ancestry: 30.9% Irish, 22.0% Italian, 16.8% German, 15.8% Polish, 13.1% English
Employment: 17.2% management, business, and financial, 8.4% computer, engineering, and science, 16.9% education, legal, community service, arts, and media, 12.2% healthcare practitioners, 13.5% service, 7.9% sales and office, 20.7% natural resources, construction, and maintenance, 3.2% production, transportation, and material moving
Income: Per capita: $54,221; Median household: $64,172; Average household: $116,486; Households with income of $100,000 or more: 35.8%; Poverty rate: 0.4%
Educational Attainment: High school diploma or higher: 96.6%; Bachelor's degree or higher: 35.0%; Graduate/professional degree or higher: 25.5%

School District(s)
Riverhead Central SD (KG-12)
    Enrollment: 5,517 . . . . (631) 369-6717
Housing: Homeownership rate: 80.0%; Median home value: $425,900; Median year structure built: 1976; Homeowner vacancy rate: 0.0%; Median selected monthly owner costs: $2,611 with a mortgage, $1,124 without a mortgage; Median gross rent: $2,007 per month; Rental vacancy rate: 0.0%
Health Insurance: 87.5% have insurance; 74.1% have private insurance; 21.9% have public insurance; 12.5% do not have insurance; 0.0% of children under 18 do not have insurance
Transportation: Commute: 90.9% car, 1.4% public transportation, 0.0% walk, 5.7% work from home; Mean travel time to work: 26.6 minutes

ASHAROKEN (village). Covers a land area of 1.471 square miles and a water area of 5.015 square miles. Located at 40.94° N. Lat; 73.39° W. Long. Elevation is 13 feet.
Population: 446; Growth (since 2000): -28.6%; Density: 303.3 persons per square mile; Race: 96.0% White, 0.0% Black/African American, 2.7% Asian, 0.7% American Indian/Alaska Native, 0.0% Native Hawaiian/Other Pacific Islander, 0.7% Two or more races, 1.1% Hispanic of any race; Average household size: 2.51; Median age: 55.7; Age under 18: 19.5%; Age 65 and over: 29.8%; Males per 100 females: 107.6; Marriage status:

19.5% never married, 69.6% now married, 2.1% separated, 5.6% widowed, 5.3% divorced; Foreign born: 6.3%; Speak English only: 91.8%; With disability: 9.0%; Veterans: 10.9%; Ancestry: 33.6% Irish, 24.7% Italian, 18.6% German, 7.0% English, 6.1% Polish

Employment: 28.2% management, business, and financial, 7.3% computer, engineering, and science, 13.6% education, legal, community service, arts, and media, 12.1% healthcare practitioners, 5.3% service, 26.7% sales and office, 3.9% natural resources, construction, and maintenance, 2.9% production, transportation, and material moving

Income: Per capita: $136,992; Median household: $241,250; Average household: $339,044; Households with income of $100,000 or more: 71.3%; Poverty rate: 3.1%

Educational Attainment: High school diploma or higher: 100.0%; Bachelor's degree or higher: 67.6%; Graduate/professional degree or higher: 29.8%

Housing: Homeownership rate: 89.9%; Median home value: $1,155,000; Median year structure built: 1958; Homeowner vacancy rate: 5.5%; Median selected monthly owner costs: $4,000+ with a mortgage, $1,501 without a mortgage; Median gross rent: $3,500+ per month; Rental vacancy rate: 40.0%

Health Insurance: 100.0% have insurance; 89.2% have private insurance; 33.0% have public insurance; 0.0% do not have insurance; 0.0% of children under 18 do not have insurance

Safety: Violent crime rate: 0.0 per 10,000 population; Property crime rate: 30.9 per 10,000 population

Transportation: Commute: 87.7% car, 4.9% public transportation, 0.0% walk, 6.4% work from home; Mean travel time to work: 45.1 minutes

BABYLON (town). Covers a land area of 52.319 square miles and a water area of 61.861 square miles. Located at 40.68° N. Lat; 73.32° W. Long. Elevation is 7 feet.

History: The 1st U.S. wireless station was built here by Marconi. Settled 1689, incorporated as a village 1893.

Population: 213,199; Growth (since 2000): 0.7%; Density: 4,075.0 persons per square mile; Race: 67.6% White, 16.5% Black/African American, 3.4% Asian, 0.2% American Indian/Alaska Native, 0.0% Native Hawaiian/Other Pacific Islander, 3.5% Two or more races, 22.1% Hispanic of any race; Average household size: 3.18; Median age: 39.7; Age under 18: 21.4%; Age 65 and over: 14.0%; Males per 100 females: 93.7; Marriage status: 35.5% never married, 49.5% now married, 2.0% separated, 6.5% widowed, 8.5% divorced; Foreign born: 19.8%; Speak English only: 73.2%; With disability: 10.5%; Veterans: 5.3%; Ancestry: 24.6% Italian, 16.7% Irish, 11.6% German, 5.0% Polish, 3.4% American

Employment: 12.1% management, business, and financial, 4.0% computer, engineering, and science, 10.8% education, legal, community service, arts, and media, 5.4% healthcare practitioners, 19.2% service, 27.0% sales and office, 9.8% natural resources, construction, and maintenance, 11.8% production, transportation, and material moving

Income: Per capita: $33,875; Median household: $86,339; Average household: $102,521; Households with income of $100,000 or more: 42.5%; Poverty rate: 7.4%

Educational Attainment: High school diploma or higher: 88.0%; Bachelor's degree or higher: 25.8%; Graduate/professional degree or higher: 9.7%

School District(s)
Babylon Union Free SD (KG-12)
    Enrollment: 1,606 . . . . (631) 893-7925

Housing: Homeownership rate: 76.2%; Median home value: $343,700; Median year structure built: 1960; Homeowner vacancy rate: 1.6%; Median selected monthly owner costs: $2,687 with a mortgage, $1,172 without a mortgage; Median gross rent: $1,603 per month; Rental vacancy rate: 5.1%

Health Insurance: 92.4% have insurance; 74.2% have private insurance; 30.3% have public insurance; 7.6% do not have insurance; 3.2% of children under 18 do not have insurance

Newspapers: Babylon Beacon (weekly circulation 3,400)

Transportation: Commute: 86.0% car, 8.3% public transportation, 1.8% walk, 2.4% work from home; Mean travel time to work: 30.9 minutes

Additional Information Contacts
Town of Babylon . . . . (631) 957-3000
    http://www.townofbabylon.com

BABYLON (village). Covers a land area of 2.445 square miles and a water area of 0.343 square miles. Located at 40.69° N. Lat; 73.33° W. Long. Elevation is 7 feet.

Population: 12,177; Growth (since 2000): -3.5%; Density: 4,980.5 persons per square mile; Race: 89.5% White, 1.3% Black/African American, 3.6% Asian, 0.2% American Indian/Alaska Native, 0.0% Native Hawaiian/Other Pacific Islander, 4.8% Two or more races, 8.1% Hispanic of any race; Average household size: 2.83; Median age: 43.1; Age under 18: 19.4%; Age 65 and over: 14.8%; Males per 100 females: 94.5; Marriage status: 31.5% never married, 56.0% now married, 1.1% separated, 5.6% widowed, 6.9% divorced; Foreign born: 9.6%; Speak English only: 90.7%; With disability: 8.8%; Veterans: 6.1%; Ancestry: 30.1% Irish, 29.7% Italian, 17.7% German, 7.5% English, 5.5% Polish

Employment: 18.6% management, business, and financial, 5.5% computer, engineering, and science, 22.5% education, legal, community service, arts, and media, 3.9% healthcare practitioners, 10.9% service, 24.1% sales and office, 8.2% natural resources, construction, and maintenance, 6.3% production, transportation, and material moving

Income: Per capita: $53,963; Median household: $123,110; Average household: $147,206; Households with income of $100,000 or more: 58.4%; Poverty rate: 4.5%

Educational Attainment: High school diploma or higher: 96.9%; Bachelor's degree or higher: 50.9%; Graduate/professional degree or higher: 23.1%

School District(s)
Babylon Union Free SD (KG-12)
    Enrollment: 1,606 . . . . (631) 893-7925

Housing: Homeownership rate: 76.2%; Median home value: $453,400; Median year structure built: 1954; Homeowner vacancy rate: 1.7%; Median selected monthly owner costs: $3,148 with a mortgage, $1,405 without a mortgage; Median gross rent: $1,805 per month; Rental vacancy rate: 1.4%

Health Insurance: 97.3% have insurance; 88.2% have private insurance; 20.8% have public insurance; 2.7% do not have insurance; 0.9% of children under 18 do not have insurance

Newspapers: Babylon Beacon (weekly circulation 3,400)

Transportation: Commute: 78.1% car, 14.2% public transportation, 1.5% walk, 5.7% work from home; Mean travel time to work: 34.5 minutes

Additional Information Contacts
Village of Babylon . . . . (631) 669-1212
    http://www.villageofbabylonny.gov

BAITING HOLLOW (CDP). Covers a land area of 3.213 square miles and a water area of 0 square miles. Located at 40.96° N. Lat; 72.74° W. Long. Elevation is 105 feet.

Population: 1,637; Growth (since 2000): 13.0%; Density: 509.5 persons per square mile; Race: 92.6% White, 1.2% Black/African American, 3.5% Asian, 0.0% American Indian/Alaska Native, 0.0% Native Hawaiian/Other Pacific Islander, 2.3% Two or more races, 8.4% Hispanic of any race; Average household size: 2.53; Median age: 52.6; Age under 18: 15.6%; Age 65 and over: 29.3%; Males per 100 females: 97.1; Marriage status: 18.4% never married, 64.1% now married, 0.5% separated, 8.8% widowed, 8.7% divorced; Foreign born: 11.4%; Speak English only: 83.1%; With disability: 12.0%; Veterans: 8.1%; Ancestry: 24.4% Irish, 24.4% Italian, 21.0% German, 7.8% Polish, 5.6% English

Employment: 8.5% management, business, and financial, 5.2% computer, engineering, and science, 14.5% education, legal, community service, arts, and media, 5.8% healthcare practitioners, 14.5% service, 37.4% sales and office, 5.8% natural resources, construction, and maintenance, 8.3% production, transportation, and material moving

Income: Per capita: $52,517; Median household: $98,750; Average household: $131,417; Households with income of $100,000 or more: 47.7%; Poverty rate: 4.5%

Educational Attainment: High school diploma or higher: 97.5%; Bachelor's degree or higher: 36.5%; Graduate/professional degree or higher: 22.0%

Housing: Homeownership rate: 90.2%; Median home value: $397,700; Median year structure built: 1987; Homeowner vacancy rate: 0.0%; Median selected monthly owner costs: $3,062 with a mortgage, $1,130 without a mortgage; Median gross rent: $2,152 per month; Rental vacancy rate: 0.0%

Health Insurance: 97.6% have insurance; 83.5% have private insurance; 37.4% have public insurance; 2.4% do not have insurance; 0.0% of children under 18 do not have insurance

Transportation: Commute: 85.1% car, 5.5% public transportation, 0.0% walk, 5.0% work from home; Mean travel time to work: 29.4 minutes

---

BAY SHORE (CDP). Covers a land area of 5.368 square miles and a water area of 0.159 square miles. Located at 40.73° N. Lat; 73.25° W. Long. Elevation is 16 feet.
History: Named for its location on Great South Bay. Founded 1708.
Population: 30,392; Growth (since 2000): 27.4%; Density: 5,662.1 persons per square mile; Race: 51.7% White, 24.0% Black/African American, 3.5% Asian, 0.7% American Indian/Alaska Native, 0.0% Native Hawaiian/Other Pacific Islander, 6.3% Two or more races, 38.3% Hispanic of any race; Average household size: 3.32; Median age: 34.7; Age under 18: 25.9%; Age 65 and over: 10.8%; Males per 100 females: 94.1; Marriage status: 38.1% never married, 47.1% now married, 3.1% separated, 5.0% widowed, 9.8% divorced; Foreign born: 22.4%; Speak English only: 65.5%; With disability: 11.0%; Veterans: 4.1%; Ancestry: 15.3% Italian, 14.6% Irish, 8.6% German, 3.2% Haitian, 2.9% English
Employment: 12.1% management, business, and financial, 1.6% computer, engineering, and science, 11.0% education, legal, community service, arts, and media, 5.0% healthcare practitioners, 23.9% service, 26.2% sales and office, 7.8% natural resources, construction, and maintenance, 12.3% production, transportation, and material moving
Income: Per capita: $31,036; Median household: $80,123; Average household: $98,001; Households with income of $100,000 or more: 38.5%; Poverty rate: 9.7%
Educational Attainment: High school diploma or higher: 85.0%; Bachelor's degree or higher: 30.6%; Graduate/professional degree or higher: 14.1%

School District(s)
Bay Shore Union Free SD (KG-12)
    Enrollment: 6,141 . . . . (631) 968-1115
Brentwood Union Free SD (PK-12)
    Enrollment: 20,013 . . . . (631) 434-2325
Fire Island Union Free SD (PK-06)
    Enrollment: 25 . . . . (631) 583-5626
Housing: Homeownership rate: 62.5%; Median home value: $323,000; Median year structure built: 1959; Homeowner vacancy rate: 0.5%; Median selected monthly owner costs: $2,674 with a mortgage, $1,143 without a mortgage; Median gross rent: $1,477 per month; Rental vacancy rate: 4.2%
Health Insurance: 91.4% have insurance; 71.9% have private insurance; 27.8% have public insurance; 8.6% do not have insurance; 2.1% of children under 18 do not have insurance
Hospitals: Southside Hospital (377 beds)
Transportation: Commute: 81.1% car, 11.2% public transportation, 2.6% walk, 3.6% work from home; Mean travel time to work: 33.8 minutes

---

BAYPORT (CDP). Covers a land area of 3.720 square miles and a water area of 0.076 square miles. Located at 40.75° N. Lat; 73.06° W. Long. Elevation is 16 feet.
History: Bayport is a hamlet and a census-designated place (CDP) in Suffolk County, Long Island, New York.
Population: 8,181; Growth (since 2000): -5.6%; Density: 2,199.3 persons per square mile; Race: 92.6% White, 1.6% Black/African American, 1.8% Asian, 0.6% American Indian/Alaska Native, 0.0% Native Hawaiian/Other Pacific Islander, 2.8% Two or more races, 6.8% Hispanic of any race; Average household size: 2.60; Median age: 47.0; Age under 18: 21.6%; Age 65 and over: 19.7%; Males per 100 females: 92.2; Marriage status: 24.8% never married, 55.2% now married, 1.6% separated, 9.2% widowed, 10.8% divorced; Foreign born: 5.2%; Speak English only: 93.3%; With disability: 10.3%; Veterans: 9.1%; Ancestry: 31.3% Italian, 28.5% Irish, 25.4% German, 8.3% English, 6.2% Polish
Employment: 15.6% management, business, and financial, 4.0% computer, engineering, and science, 17.6% education, legal, community service, arts, and media, 9.2% healthcare practitioners, 12.7% service, 24.2% sales and office, 7.4% natural resources, construction, and maintenance, 9.4% production, transportation, and material moving
Income: Per capita: $47,840; Median household: $93,125; Average household: $122,940; Households with income of $100,000 or more: 47.7%; Poverty rate: 4.8%
Educational Attainment: High school diploma or higher: 93.8%; Bachelor's degree or higher: 44.1%; Graduate/professional degree or higher: 22.4%

School District(s)
Bayport-Blue Point Union Free SD (KG-12)
    Enrollment: 2,230 . . . . (631) 472-7860
Housing: Homeownership rate: 73.4%; Median home value: $429,500; Median year structure built: 1968; Homeowner vacancy rate: 0.0%; Median selected monthly owner costs: $3,248 with a mortgage, $1,372 without a mortgage; Median gross rent: $1,651 per month; Rental vacancy rate: 3.3%
Health Insurance: 97.6% have insurance; 86.8% have private insurance; 28.1% have public insurance; 2.4% do not have insurance; 2.4% of children under 18 do not have insurance
Transportation: Commute: 87.8% car, 6.2% public transportation, 0.0% walk, 5.8% work from home; Mean travel time to work: 31.1 minutes

---

BAYWOOD (CDP). Covers a land area of 2.260 square miles and a water area of 0 square miles. Located at 40.75° N. Lat; 73.29° W. Long. Elevation is 59 feet.
Population: 7,360; Growth (since 2000): -2.8%; Density: 3,256.1 persons per square mile; Race: 61.1% White, 16.5% Black/African American, 2.1% Asian, 1.3% American Indian/Alaska Native, 0.0% Native Hawaiian/Other Pacific Islander, 4.5% Two or more races, 35.3% Hispanic of any race; Average household size: 3.25; Median age: 39.8; Age under 18: 22.9%; Age 65 and over: 10.0%; Males per 100 females: 100.5; Marriage status: 36.1% never married, 48.2% now married, 2.3% separated, 6.8% widowed, 8.9% divorced; Foreign born: 17.8%; Speak English only: 71.4%; With disability: 10.3%; Veterans: 6.8%; Ancestry: 16.1% Italian, 14.0% Irish, 7.6% German, 3.2% American, 2.5% English
Employment: 9.1% management, business, and financial, 2.9% computer, engineering, and science, 8.6% education, legal, community service, arts, and media, 4.8% healthcare practitioners, 19.8% service, 30.0% sales and office, 10.3% natural resources, construction, and maintenance, 14.6% production, transportation, and material moving
Income: Per capita: $28,856; Median household: $78,328; Average household: $88,758; Households with income of $100,000 or more: 37.8%; Poverty rate: 8.0%
Educational Attainment: High school diploma or higher: 88.4%; Bachelor's degree or higher: 20.0%; Graduate/professional degree or higher: 5.7%
Housing: Homeownership rate: 82.0%; Median home value: $281,600; Median year structure built: 1959; Homeowner vacancy rate: 0.6%; Median selected monthly owner costs: $2,293 with a mortgage, $991 without a mortgage; Median gross rent: $1,464 per month; Rental vacancy rate: 0.0%
Health Insurance: 89.0% have insurance; 70.6% have private insurance; 25.2% have public insurance; 11.0% do not have insurance; 3.6% of children under 18 do not have insurance
Transportation: Commute: 86.7% car, 7.9% public transportation, 0.5% walk, 3.7% work from home; Mean travel time to work: 31.0 minutes

---

BELLE TERRE (village). Covers a land area of 0.885 square miles and a water area of 0 square miles. Located at 40.96° N. Lat; 73.07° W. Long. Elevation is 161 feet.
Population: 679; Growth (since 2000): -18.4%; Density: 767.4 persons per square mile; Race: 94.1% White, 0.0% Black/African American, 4.7% Asian, 0.0% American Indian/Alaska Native, 0.0% Native Hawaiian/Other Pacific Islander, 1.2% Two or more races, 2.4% Hispanic of any race; Average household size: 2.64; Median age: 50.6; Age under 18: 22.1%; Age 65 and over: 23.6%; Males per 100 females: 101.0; Marriage status: 17.4% never married, 73.7% now married, 0.9% separated, 6.4% widowed, 2.4% divorced; Foreign born: 13.0%; Speak English only: 86.8%; With disability: 7.1%; Veterans: 8.5%; Ancestry: 23.3% Italian, 18.9% German, 18.7% Irish, 6.8% American, 6.6% Russian
Employment: 22.8% management, business, and financial, 9.8% computer, engineering, and science, 13.2% education, legal, community service, arts, and media, 20.3% healthcare practitioners, 5.8% service, 24.0% sales and office, 2.2% natural resources, construction, and maintenance, 1.8% production, transportation, and material moving
Income: Per capita: $129,224; Median household: $210,250; Average household: $350,982; Households with income of $100,000 or more: 76.6%; Poverty rate: 3.5%
Educational Attainment: High school diploma or higher: 98.6%; Bachelor's degree or higher: 71.4%; Graduate/professional degree or higher: 48.1%
Housing: Homeownership rate: 96.5%; Median home value: $841,800; Median year structure built: 1970; Homeowner vacancy rate: 0.0%; Median

selected monthly owner costs: $4,000+ with a mortgage, $1,501 without a mortgage; Median gross rent: n/a per month; Rental vacancy rate: 0.0%
Health Insurance: 99.4% have insurance; 85.6% have private insurance; 29.6% have public insurance; 0.6% do not have insurance; 0.0% of children under 18 do not have insurance
Transportation: Commute: 87.2% car, 3.5% public transportation, 0.0% walk, 7.7% work from home; Mean travel time to work: 32.9 minutes

BELLPORT (village).
Covers a land area of 1.445 square miles and a water area of 0.091 square miles. Located at 40.75° N. Lat; 72.94° W. Long. Elevation is 26 feet.
Population: 2,050; Growth (since 2000): -13.2%; Density: 1,418.7 persons per square mile; Race: 93.5% White, 1.0% Black/African American, 3.0% Asian, 1.1% American Indian/Alaska Native, 0.0% Native Hawaiian/Other Pacific Islander, 1.4% Two or more races, 2.5% Hispanic of any race; Average household size: 2.40; Median age: 54.1; Age under 18: 15.9%; Age 65 and over: 27.2%; Males per 100 females: 93.5; Marriage status: 20.1% never married, 65.4% now married, 1.3% separated, 7.6% widowed, 6.9% divorced; Foreign born: 9.5%; Speak English only: 89.4%; With disability: 7.9%; Veterans: 7.5%; Ancestry: 31.5% Irish, 27.2% German, 17.0% Italian, 10.0% English, 4.4% Hungarian
Employment: 18.5% management, business, and financial, 5.9% computer, engineering, and science, 25.2% education, legal, community service, arts, and media, 6.6% healthcare practitioners, 17.2% service, 19.1% sales and office, 3.9% natural resources, construction, and maintenance, 3.5% production, transportation, and material moving
Income: Per capita: $61,858; Median household: $103,438; Average household: $143,873; Households with income of $100,000 or more: 50.6%; Poverty rate: 4.3%
Educational Attainment: High school diploma or higher: 96.7%; Bachelor's degree or higher: 55.2%; Graduate/professional degree or higher: 32.5%

School District(s)
South Country Central SD (PK-12)
    Enrollment: 4,515 . . . . (631) 730-1510
Housing: Homeownership rate: 88.5%; Median home value: $459,600; Median year structure built: 1957; Homeowner vacancy rate: 3.8%; Median selected monthly owner costs: $2,890 with a mortgage, $1,364 without a mortgage; Median gross rent: $1,667 per month; Rental vacancy rate: 3.9%
Health Insurance: 98.0% have insurance; 86.1% have private insurance; 36.5% have public insurance; 2.0% do not have insurance; 0.0% of children under 18 do not have insurance
Transportation: Commute: 84.0% car, 4.6% public transportation, 3.6% walk, 2.9% work from home; Mean travel time to work: 29.1 minutes
Additional Information Contacts
Village of Bellport . . . . (631) 286-0327
    http://www.bellportvillage.com

BLUE POINT (CDP).
Covers a land area of 1.794 square miles and a water area of 0.006 square miles. Located at 40.75° N. Lat; 73.04° W. Long. Elevation is 10 feet.
History: Bluepoint oysters take their name from here.
Population: 4,742; Growth (since 2000): 7.6%; Density: 2,643.8 persons per square mile; Race: 98.8% White, 0.1% Black/African American, 0.6% Asian, 0.0% American Indian/Alaska Native, 0.0% Native Hawaiian/Other Pacific Islander, 0.4% Two or more races, 9.0% Hispanic of any race; Average household size: 2.92; Median age: 43.4; Age under 18: 23.2%; Age 65 and over: 15.1%; Males per 100 females: 96.7; Marriage status: 31.7% never married, 55.0% now married, 1.6% separated, 5.9% widowed, 7.4% divorced; Foreign born: 4.0%; Speak English only: 91.3%; With disability: 6.2%; Veterans: 5.6%; Ancestry: 41.4% Irish, 33.1% German, 27.5% Italian, 6.4% English, 3.3% Polish
Employment: 17.8% management, business, and financial, 5.2% computer, engineering, and science, 17.6% education, legal, community service, arts, and media, 9.1% healthcare practitioners, 13.4% service, 18.4% sales and office, 9.5% natural resources, construction, and maintenance, 9.0% production, transportation, and material moving
Income: Per capita: $44,522; Median household: $117,313; Average household: $126,692; Households with income of $100,000 or more: 54.9%; Poverty rate: 3.4%
Educational Attainment: High school diploma or higher: 95.2%; Bachelor's degree or higher: 44.1%; Graduate/professional degree or higher: 21.0%

School District(s)
Bayport-Blue Point Union Free SD (KG-12)
    Enrollment: 2,230 . . . . (631) 472-7860
Housing: Homeownership rate: 86.7%; Median home value: $401,800; Median year structure built: 1959; Homeowner vacancy rate: 2.1%; Median selected monthly owner costs: $3,039 with a mortgage, $1,278 without a mortgage; Median gross rent: $1,659 per month; Rental vacancy rate: 0.0%
Health Insurance: 95.3% have insurance; 88.4% have private insurance; 19.7% have public insurance; 4.7% do not have insurance; 6.1% of children under 18 do not have insurance
Transportation: Commute: 91.6% car, 4.6% public transportation, 0.4% walk, 2.3% work from home; Mean travel time to work: 31.2 minutes

BOHEMIA (CDP).
Covers a land area of 8.620 square miles and a water area of 0.037 square miles. Located at 40.78° N. Lat; 73.13° W. Long. Elevation is 66 feet.
History: Bohemia was founded in 1855 by Slavic immigrants who were the first Europeans to settle there in large numbers. They came from a mountainous village in the Central European Kingdom of Bohemia, for which the town was named.
Population: 9,282; Growth (since 2000): -6.0%; Density: 1,076.9 persons per square mile; Race: 97.0% White, 1.0% Black/African American, 1.2% Asian, 0.0% American Indian/Alaska Native, 0.0% Native Hawaiian/Other Pacific Islander, 0.6% Two or more races, 8.9% Hispanic of any race; Average household size: 2.72; Median age: 42.2; Age under 18: 21.1%; Age 65 and over: 14.5%; Males per 100 females: 97.0; Marriage status: 33.1% never married, 50.4% now married, 1.5% separated, 5.1% widowed, 11.4% divorced; Foreign born: 5.9%; Speak English only: 88.6%; With disability: 9.2%; Veterans: 7.0%; Ancestry: 34.6% Italian, 22.7% Irish, 17.0% German, 4.0% American, 3.7% Polish
Employment: 14.3% management, business, and financial, 3.9% computer, engineering, and science, 13.3% education, legal, community service, arts, and media, 5.8% healthcare practitioners, 17.1% service, 26.6% sales and office, 9.4% natural resources, construction, and maintenance, 9.6% production, transportation, and material moving
Income: Per capita: $39,488; Median household: $85,927; Average household: $105,312; Households with income of $100,000 or more: 43.1%; Poverty rate: 6.8%
Educational Attainment: High school diploma or higher: 92.7%; Bachelor's degree or higher: 28.5%; Graduate/professional degree or higher: 14.2%

School District(s)
Connetquot Central SD (PK-12)
    Enrollment: 5,982 . . . . (631) 244-2215
Vocational/Technical School(s)
Branford Hall Career Institute-Bohemia Campus (Private, For-profit)
    Enrollment: 265 . . . . (631) 589-1222
    Tuition: $14,666
Housing: Homeownership rate: 77.0%; Median home value: $384,900; Median year structure built: 1971; Homeowner vacancy rate: 0.0%; Median selected monthly owner costs: $2,954 with a mortgage, $1,192 without a mortgage; Median gross rent: $1,693 per month; Rental vacancy rate: 3.6%
Health Insurance: 96.7% have insurance; 85.9% have private insurance; 22.9% have public insurance; 3.3% do not have insurance; 1.3% of children under 18 do not have insurance
Transportation: Commute: 90.5% car, 6.9% public transportation, 1.3% walk, 0.4% work from home; Mean travel time to work: 32.4 minutes

BRENTWOOD (CDP).
Covers a land area of 10.981 square miles and a water area of 0 square miles. Located at 40.78° N. Lat; 73.25° W. Long. Elevation is 79 feet.
History: Josiah Warren led (1851) an experiment in communal living in Brentwood.
Population: 63,115; Growth (since 2000): 17.1%; Density: 5,747.9 persons per square mile; Race: 58.8% White, 14.6% Black/African American, 1.6% Asian, 0.5% American Indian/Alaska Native, 0.0% Native Hawaiian/Other Pacific Islander, 5.1% Two or more races, 66.7% Hispanic of any race; Average household size: 4.56; Median age: 32.6; Age under 18: 26.4%; Age 65 and over: 8.6%; Males per 100 females: 103.6; Marriage status: 45.2% never married, 42.0% now married, 2.8% separated, 4.5% widowed, 8.3% divorced; Foreign born: 42.0%; Speak English only: 29.2%; With disability: 8.2%; Veterans: 3.5%; Ancestry: 4.2% Italian, 3.5% Haitian, 2.9% Irish, 1.6% German, 1.3% American

Employment: 6.2% management, business, and financial, 2.1% computer, engineering, and science, 5.0% education, legal, community service, arts, and media, 3.4% healthcare practitioners, 26.6% service, 22.8% sales and office, 10.7% natural resources, construction, and maintenance, 23.2% production, transportation, and material moving
Income: Per capita: $22,661; Median household: $74,127; Average household: $93,756; Households with income of $100,000 or more: 34.5%; Poverty rate: 12.3%
Educational Attainment: High school diploma or higher: 69.5%; Bachelor's degree or higher: 13.0%; Graduate/professional degree or higher: 4.0%

School District(s)
Brentwood Union Free SD (PK-12)
   Enrollment: 20,013 . . . . (631) 434-2325
Four-year College(s)
LIU Brentwood (Private, Not-for-profit)
   Enrollment: 165 . . . . (631) 287-8500
Vocational/Technical School(s)
Eastern Suffolk BOCES (Public)
   Enrollment: 261 . . . . (631) 233-4450
   Tuition: $14,840
Housing: Homeownership rate: 72.8%; Median home value: $285,500; Median year structure built: 1963; Homeowner vacancy rate: 0.9%; Median selected monthly owner costs: $2,311 with a mortgage, $938 without a mortgage; Median gross rent: $1,348 per month; Rental vacancy rate: 4.5%
Health Insurance: 84.8% have insurance; 60.6% have private insurance; 32.6% have public insurance; 15.2% do not have insurance; 6.5% of children under 18 do not have insurance
Transportation: Commute: 91.9% car, 3.6% public transportation, 1.6% walk, 1.4% work from home; Mean travel time to work: 26.8 minutes

BRIDGEHAMPTON (CDP). Covers a land area of 13.010 square miles and a water area of 0.623 square miles. Located at 40.95° N. Lat; 72.31° W. Long. Elevation is 43 feet.
Population: 1,149; Growth (since 2000): -16.8%; Density: 88.3 persons per square mile; Race: 82.1% White, 15.7% Black/African American, 1.2% Asian, 0.0% American Indian/Alaska Native, 0.0% Native Hawaiian/Other Pacific Islander, 1.0% Two or more races, 20.5% Hispanic of any race; Average household size: 2.26; Median age: 50.5; Age under 18: 15.3%; Age 65 and over: 34.1%; Males per 100 females: 101.1; Marriage status: 28.2% never married, 54.5% now married, 2.7% separated, 7.3% widowed, 10.0% divorced; Foreign born: 17.4%; Speak English only: 80.2%; With disability: 6.5%; Veterans: 7.3%; Ancestry: 15.6% Irish, 11.4% German, 10.7% English, 7.9% Polish, 4.8% Italian
Employment: 20.6% management, business, and financial, 0.0% computer, engineering, and science, 11.3% education, legal, community service, arts, and media, 1.7% healthcare practitioners, 19.9% service, 25.8% sales and office, 11.5% natural resources, construction, and maintenance, 9.1% production, transportation, and material moving
Income: Per capita: $76,582; Median household: $88,194; Average household: $169,378; Households with income of $100,000 or more: 48.1%; Poverty rate: 4.2%
Educational Attainment: High school diploma or higher: 92.9%; Bachelor's degree or higher: 46.1%; Graduate/professional degree or higher: 14.8%

School District(s)
Bridgehampton Union Free SD (PK-12)
   Enrollment: 209 . . . . (631) 537-0271
Housing: Homeownership rate: 86.0%; Median home value: $1,278,800; Median year structure built: 1980; Homeowner vacancy rate: 2.6%; Median selected monthly owner costs: $2,495 with a mortgage, $1,090 without a mortgage; Median gross rent: $1,279 per month; Rental vacancy rate: 0.0%
Health Insurance: 88.9% have insurance; 80.4% have private insurance; 37.6% have public insurance; 11.1% do not have insurance; 0.0% of children under 18 do not have insurance
Newspapers: Dan's Papers (weekly circulation 69,000)
Transportation: Commute: 76.3% car, 7.9% public transportation, 5.7% walk, 9.6% work from home; Mean travel time to work: 24.2 minutes

BRIGHTWATERS (village). Covers a land area of 0.976 square miles and a water area of 0.023 square miles. Located at 40.72° N. Lat; 73.26° W. Long. Elevation is 23 feet.
History: Laid out 1907, incorporated 1916.

Population: 3,096; Growth (since 2000): -4.7%; Density: 3,171.2 persons per square mile; Race: 88.8% White, 2.1% Black/African American, 2.1% Asian, 0.0% American Indian/Alaska Native, 0.0% Native Hawaiian/Other Pacific Islander, 2.1% Two or more races, 9.0% Hispanic of any race; Average household size: 2.77; Median age: 46.8; Age under 18: 23.4%; Age 65 and over: 16.5%; Males per 100 females: 97.6; Marriage status: 22.8% never married, 64.4% now married, 1.1% separated, 6.3% widowed, 6.4% divorced; Foreign born: 5.9%; Speak English only: 89.3%; With disability: 10.2%; Veterans: 9.3%; Ancestry: 33.1% Irish, 27.7% Italian, 19.8% German, 7.1% English, 5.2% Polish
Employment: 19.7% management, business, and financial, 3.2% computer, engineering, and science, 18.4% education, legal, community service, arts, and media, 13.5% healthcare practitioners, 13.3% service, 20.9% sales and office, 7.4% natural resources, construction, and maintenance, 3.5% production, transportation, and material moving
Income: Per capita: $60,678; Median household: $123,152; Average household: $165,299; Households with income of $100,000 or more: 61.2%; Poverty rate: 1.0%
Educational Attainment: High school diploma or higher: 96.9%; Bachelor's degree or higher: 58.7%; Graduate/professional degree or higher: 29.2%
Housing: Homeownership rate: 94.6%; Median home value: $503,400; Median year structure built: 1946; Homeowner vacancy rate: 0.5%; Median selected monthly owner costs: $3,391 with a mortgage, $1,501 without a mortgage; Median gross rent: $1,097 per month; Rental vacancy rate: 0.0%
Health Insurance: 97.8% have insurance; 91.5% have private insurance; 22.1% have public insurance; 2.2% do not have insurance; 1.2% of children under 18 do not have insurance
Transportation: Commute: 85.6% car, 9.3% public transportation, 1.6% walk, 3.6% work from home; Mean travel time to work: 33.8 minutes

BROOKHAVEN (CDP). Covers a land area of 5.761 square miles and a water area of 0.146 square miles. Located at 40.78° N. Lat; 72.91° W. Long. Elevation is 10 feet.
Population: 3,523; Growth (since 2000): -1.3%; Density: 611.5 persons per square mile; Race: 87.3% White, 7.7% Black/African American, 0.1% Asian, 0.0% American Indian/Alaska Native, 0.0% Native Hawaiian/Other Pacific Islander, 3.9% Two or more races, 12.7% Hispanic of any race; Average household size: 2.68; Median age: 50.1; Age under 18: 20.1%; Age 65 and over: 21.8%; Males per 100 females: 93.2; Marriage status: 29.7% never married, 51.6% now married, 1.1% separated, 8.5% widowed, 10.2% divorced; Foreign born: 10.6%; Speak English only: 81.7%; With disability: 13.6%; Veterans: 7.5%; Ancestry: 27.2% Italian, 19.8% Irish, 14.6% German, 5.9% Polish, 3.8% Lebanese
Employment: 15.7% management, business, and financial, 4.4% computer, engineering, and science, 11.9% education, legal, community service, arts, and media, 11.3% healthcare practitioners, 17.1% service, 22.4% sales and office, 11.3% natural resources, construction, and maintenance, 5.8% production, transportation, and material moving
Income: Per capita: $38,767; Median household: $80,769; Average household: $117,686; Households with income of $100,000 or more: 43.4%; Poverty rate: 10.5%
Educational Attainment: High school diploma or higher: 83.3%; Bachelor's degree or higher: 34.9%; Graduate/professional degree or higher: 18.4%

School District(s)
South Country Central SD (PK-12)
   Enrollment: 4,515 . . . . (631) 730-1510
Housing: Homeownership rate: 80.4%; Median home value: $421,100; Median year structure built: 1972; Homeowner vacancy rate: 0.8%; Median selected monthly owner costs: $2,865 with a mortgage, $1,310 without a mortgage; Median gross rent: $1,353 per month; Rental vacancy rate: 0.0%
Health Insurance: 94.0% have insurance; 73.0% have private insurance; 36.7% have public insurance; 6.0% do not have insurance; 1.0% of children under 18 do not have insurance
Transportation: Commute: 86.8% car, 6.9% public transportation, 0.3% walk, 5.4% work from home; Mean travel time to work: 34.4 minutes

BROOKHAVEN (town).

Covers a land area of 259.439 square miles and a water area of 272.097 square miles. Located at 40.86° N. Lat; 72.96° W. Long. Elevation is 10 feet.

History: Brookhaven was the home of William Floyd (1743-1821), Revolutionary War soldier, statesman, and signer of the Declaration of Independence.

Population: 487,731; Growth (since 2000): 8.8%; Density: 1,879.9 persons per square mile; Race: 85.4% White, 5.7% Black/African American, 4.8% Asian, 0.2% American Indian/Alaska Native, 0.0% Native Hawaiian/Other Pacific Islander, 2.1% Two or more races, 15.4% Hispanic of any race; Average household size: 2.94; Median age: 39.5; Age under 18: 22.2%; Age 65 and over: 14.5%; Males per 100 females: 97.2; Marriage status: 33.7% never married, 52.0% now married, 1.7% separated, 5.9% widowed, 8.5% divorced; Foreign born: 12.5%; Speak English only: 80.8%; With disability: 9.7%; Veterans: 5.9%; Ancestry: 27.8% Italian, 20.2% Irish, 16.5% German, 5.2% American, 4.6% Polish

Employment: 14.1% management, business, and financial, 5.2% computer, engineering, and science, 12.5% education, legal, community service, arts, and media, 7.4% healthcare practitioners, 16.6% service, 25.6% sales and office, 9.7% natural resources, construction, and maintenance, 8.9% production, transportation, and material moving

Income: Per capita: $37,341; Median household: $89,594; Average household: $108,666; Households with income of $100,000 or more: 44.1%; Poverty rate: 7.5%

Educational Attainment: High school diploma or higher: 91.3%; Bachelor's degree or higher: 32.4%; Graduate/professional degree or higher: 15.2%

School District(s)

South Country Central SD (PK-12)

    Enrollment: 4,515 . . . . (631) 730-1510

Housing: Homeownership rate: 79.1%; Median home value: $332,200; Median year structure built: 1974; Homeowner vacancy rate: 1.4%; Median selected monthly owner costs: $2,606 with a mortgage, $1,098 without a mortgage; Median gross rent: $1,670 per month; Rental vacancy rate: 4.5%

Health Insurance: 94.4% have insurance; 78.4% have private insurance; 28.7% have public insurance; 5.6% do not have insurance; 1.8% of children under 18 do not have insurance

Transportation: Commute: 90.5% car, 4.1% public transportation, 1.3% walk, 3.2% work from home; Mean travel time to work: 33.2 minutes

Additional Information Contacts

Town of Brookhaven . . . . (631) 451-6300

    http://www.brookhaven.org

CALVERTON (CDP).

Covers a land area of 28.027 square miles and a water area of 0.501 square miles. Located at 40.92° N. Lat; 72.77° W. Long. Elevation is 30 feet.

History: Calverton was first called "Baiting Hollow Station" when the Long Island Railroad arrived in 1844. The station closed in 1958, but the sheltered shed for the station remained standing as of 2007. The area's native American name was Conungum or Kanungum, meaning "fixed line" or "boundary."

Population: 6,517; Growth (since 2000): 14.3%; Density: 232.5 persons per square mile; Race: 88.2% White, 3.6% Black/African American, 1.3% Asian, 0.0% American Indian/Alaska Native, 0.0% Native Hawaiian/Other Pacific Islander, 6.9% Two or more races, 15.7% Hispanic of any race; Average household size: 2.03; Median age: 54.0; Age under 18: 9.6%; Age 65 and over: 34.9%; Males per 100 females: 91.5; Marriage status: 22.5% never married, 50.4% now married, 2.1% separated, 14.2% widowed, 12.9% divorced; Foreign born: 8.0%; Speak English only: 87.9%; With disability: 14.1%; Veterans: 13.2%; Ancestry: 23.0% Irish, 19.6% Italian, 16.6% German, 10.3% Polish, 6.5% English

Employment: 17.8% management, business, and financial, 2.9% computer, engineering, and science, 7.2% education, legal, community service, arts, and media, 2.4% healthcare practitioners, 18.8% service, 30.7% sales and office, 9.2% natural resources, construction, and maintenance, 11.1% production, transportation, and material moving

Income: Per capita: $32,907; Median household: $50,763; Average household: $65,155; Households with income of $100,000 or more: 17.7%; Poverty rate: 10.8%

Educational Attainment: High school diploma or higher: 86.9%; Bachelor's degree or higher: 16.7%; Graduate/professional degree or higher: 5.2%

School District(s)

Riverhead Central SD (KG-12)

    Enrollment: 5,517 . . . . (631) 369-6717

Riverhead Charter School (KG-08)

    Enrollment: 409 . . . . (631) 369-5800

Housing: Homeownership rate: 84.8%; Median home value: $222,000; Median year structure built: 1985; Homeowner vacancy rate: 1.8%; Median selected monthly owner costs: $1,900 with a mortgage, $861 without a mortgage; Median gross rent: $1,856 per month; Rental vacancy rate: 0.0%

Health Insurance: 91.4% have insurance; 72.3% have private insurance; 49.5% have public insurance; 8.6% do not have insurance; 0.0% of children under 18 do not have insurance

Transportation: Commute: 93.5% car, 0.0% public transportation, 3.6% walk, 2.9% work from home; Mean travel time to work: 26.7 minutes

CENTER MORICHES (CDP).

Covers a land area of 5.217 square miles and a water area of 0.415 square miles. Located at 40.80° N. Lat; 72.80° W. Long. Elevation is 26 feet.

History: Center Moriches is a hamlet in Suffolk County, New York. It is the location of the historic Masury Estate Ballroom and Terry-Ketcham Inn, both listed on the National Register of Historic Places.

Population: 8,743; Growth (since 2000): 31.4%; Density: 1,675.9 persons per square mile; Race: 92.6% White, 2.1% Black/African American, 1.1% Asian, 0.0% American Indian/Alaska Native, 0.0% Native Hawaiian/Other Pacific Islander, 1.7% Two or more races, 10.5% Hispanic of any race; Average household size: 3.14; Median age: 39.1; Age under 18: 26.0%; Age 65 and over: 10.6%; Males per 100 females: 102.0; Marriage status: 28.8% never married, 60.8% now married, 0.7% separated, 3.9% widowed, 6.5% divorced; Foreign born: 5.8%; Speak English only: 88.9%; With disability: 7.6%; Veterans: 5.5%; Ancestry: 28.6% Irish, 25.3% Italian, 23.1% German, 7.7% Polish, 7.1% English

Employment: 11.4% management, business, and financial, 2.3% computer, engineering, and science, 16.7% education, legal, community service, arts, and media, 8.1% healthcare practitioners, 19.4% service, 23.7% sales and office, 13.4% natural resources, construction, and maintenance, 5.0% production, transportation, and material moving

Income: Per capita: $39,904; Median household: $98,931; Average household: $122,981; Households with income of $100,000 or more: 48.8%; Poverty rate: 3.8%

Educational Attainment: High school diploma or higher: 93.8%; Bachelor's degree or higher: 29.9%; Graduate/professional degree or higher: 18.2%

School District(s)

Center Moriches Union Free SD (KG-12)

    Enrollment: 1,586 . . . . (631) 878-0052

Housing: Homeownership rate: 83.3%; Median home value: $385,300; Median year structure built: 1974; Homeowner vacancy rate: 4.1%; Median selected monthly owner costs: $2,736 with a mortgage, $1,326 without a mortgage; Median gross rent: $1,559 per month; Rental vacancy rate: 0.0%

Health Insurance: 94.1% have insurance; 86.0% have private insurance; 20.4% have public insurance; 5.9% do not have insurance; 2.2% of children under 18 do not have insurance

Newspapers: The Press (weekly circulation 3,000)

Transportation: Commute: 93.5% car, 0.2% public transportation, 1.6% walk, 4.7% work from home; Mean travel time to work: 30.5 minutes

CENTEREACH (CDP).

Covers a land area of 8.714 square miles and a water area of 0 square miles. Located at 40.87° N. Lat; 73.08° W. Long. Elevation is 98 feet.

History: Centereach was first called West Middle Island, as was known as New Village until the early 20th century. In 1916, it was discovered that another town in Updstate New York had the same name, and it was changed to Centereach, due to its central location on Long Island.

Population: 31,953; Growth (since 2000): 17.1%; Density: 3,666.7 persons per square mile; Race: 88.6% White, 2.7% Black/African American, 5.2% Asian, 0.2% American Indian/Alaska Native, 0.2% Native Hawaiian/Other Pacific Islander, 1.8% Two or more races, 15.3% Hispanic of any race; Average household size: 3.28; Median age: 38.0; Age under 18: 22.2%; Age 65 and over: 14.1%; Males per 100 females: 99.7; Marriage status: 32.2% never married, 53.7% now married, 2.0% separated, 6.9% widowed, 7.3% divorced; Foreign born: 11.3%; Speak English only: 83.7%; With disability: 10.0%; Veterans: 5.7%; Ancestry: 32.6% Italian, 23.4% Irish, 18.5% German, 4.2% Polish, 3.7% American

Employment: 15.9% management, business, and financial, 4.6% computer, engineering, and science, 9.2% education, legal, community service, arts, and media, 7.0% healthcare practitioners, 18.5% service, 27.6% sales and office, 8.6% natural resources, construction, and maintenance, 8.6% production, transportation, and material moving

Income: Per capita: $35,887; Median household: $98,025; Average household: $113,562; Households with income of $100,000 or more: 49.4%; Poverty rate: 5.5%

Educational Attainment: High school diploma or higher: 91.8%; Bachelor's degree or higher: 29.1%; Graduate/professional degree or higher: 12.2%

School District(s)
Middle Country Central SD (PK-12)

　Enrollment: 9,933 . . . . (631) 285-8005

Housing: Homeownership rate: 84.9%; Median home value: $335,400; Median year structure built: 1968; Homeowner vacancy rate: 0.5%; Median selected monthly owner costs: $2,645 with a mortgage, $1,080 without a mortgage; Median gross rent: $1,891 per month; Rental vacancy rate: 4.8%

Health Insurance: 94.8% have insurance; 82.4% have private insurance; 24.4% have public insurance; 5.2% do not have insurance; 1.8% of children under 18 do not have insurance

Transportation: Commute: 94.0% car, 3.2% public transportation, 0.4% walk, 1.8% work from home; Mean travel time to work: 29.1 minutes

CENTERPORT (CDP). Covers a land area of 2.104 square miles and a water area of 0.190 square miles. Located at 40.90° N. Lat; 73.37° W. Long. Elevation is 49 feet.

History: Formerly known as Little Cow Harbor about 1700, Centreport in 1836, and then the present Centerport after 1895. The name refers to its geographic position midway between the east and west boundaries of the township of Huntington.

Population: 5,380; Growth (since 2000): -1.2%; Density: 2,556.6 persons per square mile; Race: 97.3% White, 0.8% Black/African American, 0.7% Asian, 0.0% American Indian/Alaska Native, 0.0% Native Hawaiian/Other Pacific Islander, 1.2% Two or more races, 3.4% Hispanic of any race; Average household size: 2.74; Median age: 45.7; Age under 18: 23.1%; Age 65 and over: 17.1%; Males per 100 females: 91.1; Marriage status: 22.7% never married, 60.9% now married, 1.1% separated, 6.6% widowed, 9.9% divorced; Foreign born: 4.5%; Speak English only: 95.6%; With disability: 6.2%; Veterans: 4.0%; Ancestry: 40.1% Irish, 33.0% Italian, 22.0% German, 7.9% English, 5.1% American

Employment: 28.5% management, business, and financial, 5.5% computer, engineering, and science, 21.7% education, legal, community service, arts, and media, 9.1% healthcare practitioners, 5.7% service, 20.7% sales and office, 4.5% natural resources, construction, and maintenance, 4.3% production, transportation, and material moving

Income: Per capita: $62,114; Median household: $120,391; Average household: $166,987; Households with income of $100,000 or more: 58.8%; Poverty rate: 2.8%

Educational Attainment: High school diploma or higher: 97.7%; Bachelor's degree or higher: 59.4%; Graduate/professional degree or higher: 29.6%

School District(s)
Harborfields Central SD (KG-12)

　Enrollment: 3,217 . . . . (631) 754-5320

Housing: Homeownership rate: 92.9%; Median home value: $595,600; Median year structure built: 1957; Homeowner vacancy rate: 0.0%; Median selected monthly owner costs: $3,392 with a mortgage, $1,405 without a mortgage; Median gross rent: $1,842 per month; Rental vacancy rate: 0.0%

Health Insurance: 97.7% have insurance; 89.3% have private insurance; 23.6% have public insurance; 2.3% do not have insurance; 0.0% of children under 18 do not have insurance

Transportation: Commute: 72.6% car, 16.2% public transportation, 0.7% walk, 9.1% work from home; Mean travel time to work: 37.1 minutes

CENTRAL ISLIP (CDP). Covers a land area of 7.111 square miles and a water area of 0 square miles. Located at 40.78° N. Lat; 73.19° W. Long. Elevation is 89 feet.

History: Central Islip was home to the Secatogue tribe of Algonquin native-American people before the arrival of European settlers.

Population: 33,253; Growth (since 2000): 4.1%; Density: 4,676.2 persons per square mile; Race: 48.3% White, 27.2% Black/African American, 2.7% Asian, 0.2% American Indian/Alaska Native, 0.0% Native Hawaiian/Other

Pacific Islander, 6.5% Two or more races, 45.6% Hispanic of any race; Average household size: 3.57; Median age: 34.2; Age under 18: 24.4%; Age 65 and over: 9.7%; Males per 100 females: 98.5; Marriage status: 46.1% never married, 39.3% now married, 2.1% separated, 5.5% widowed, 9.2% divorced; Foreign born: 34.2%; Speak English only: 48.6%; With disability: 9.5%; Veterans: 4.1%; Ancestry: 5.8% Italian, 5.4% Irish, 4.8% German, 4.1% African, 3.1% Haitian

Employment: 7.0% management, business, and financial, 1.9% computer, engineering, and science, 6.5% education, legal, community service, arts, and media, 5.4% healthcare practitioners, 23.3% service, 25.6% sales and office, 9.4% natural resources, construction, and maintenance, 20.8% production, transportation, and material moving

Income: Per capita: $24,830; Median household: $67,804; Average household: $81,255; Households with income of $100,000 or more: 29.1%; Poverty rate: 13.0%

Educational Attainment: High school diploma or higher: 74.3%; Bachelor's degree or higher: 15.8%; Graduate/professional degree or higher: 5.7%

School District(s)
Central Islip Union Free SD (PK-12)

　Enrollment: 7,609 . . . . (631) 348-5001

Housing: Homeownership rate: 66.2%; Median home value: $254,900; Median year structure built: 1973; Homeowner vacancy rate: 0.7%; Median selected monthly owner costs: $2,324 with a mortgage, $1,018 without a mortgage; Median gross rent: $1,553 per month; Rental vacancy rate: 3.4%

Health Insurance: 85.6% have insurance; 61.1% have private insurance; 33.1% have public insurance; 14.4% do not have insurance; 4.5% of children under 18 do not have insurance

Transportation: Commute: 90.7% car, 6.2% public transportation, 1.1% walk, 0.8% work from home; Mean travel time to work: 27.9 minutes

COLD SPRING HARBOR (CDP). Covers a land area of 3.665 square miles and a water area of 0.169 square miles. Located at 40.86° N. Lat; 73.45° W. Long. Elevation is 33 feet.

History: Was 19th-century whaling port.

Population: 5,088; Growth (since 2000): 2.3%; Density: 1,388.2 persons per square mile; Race: 90.2% White, 0.2% Black/African American, 4.3% Asian, 0.0% American Indian/Alaska Native, 0.0% Native Hawaiian/Other Pacific Islander, 2.0% Two or more races, 6.1% Hispanic of any race; Average household size: 2.96; Median age: 45.7; Age under 18: 24.4%; Age 65 and over: 15.1%; Males per 100 females: 96.3; Marriage status: 26.1% never married, 62.8% now married, 0.9% separated, 5.1% widowed, 6.0% divorced; Foreign born: 9.3%; Speak English only: 85.7%; With disability: 6.5%; Veterans: 5.7%; Ancestry: 27.4% Italian, 24.1% Irish, 17.6% German, 10.7% English, 5.8% American

Employment: 35.4% management, business, and financial, 4.8% computer, engineering, and science, 21.7% education, legal, community service, arts, and media, 5.1% healthcare practitioners, 5.8% service, 21.9% sales and office, 3.2% natural resources, construction, and maintenance, 2.1% production, transportation, and material moving

Income: Per capita: $81,109; Median household: $173,088; Average household: $240,848; Households with income of $100,000 or more: 73.3%; Poverty rate: 2.1%

Educational Attainment: High school diploma or higher: 97.8%; Bachelor's degree or higher: 69.8%; Graduate/professional degree or higher: 34.2%

School District(s)
Cold Spring Harbor Central SD (KG-12)

　Enrollment: 1,760 . . . . (631) 367-5931

Housing: Homeownership rate: 85.8%; Median home value: $763,900; Median year structure built: 1958; Homeowner vacancy rate: 0.0%; Median selected monthly owner costs: $4,000+ with a mortgage, $1,501 without a mortgage; Median gross rent: $2,889 per month; Rental vacancy rate: 11.7%

Health Insurance: 99.0% have insurance; 92.4% have private insurance; 18.1% have public insurance; 1.0% do not have insurance; 0.0% of children under 18 do not have insurance

Transportation: Commute: 69.3% car, 21.2% public transportation, 0.9% walk, 6.8% work from home; Mean travel time to work: 39.8 minutes

COMMACK (CDP). Covers a land area of 11.969 square miles and a water area of 0 square miles. Located at 40.84° N. Lat; 73.28° W. Long. Elevation is 131 feet.

History: Commack is home to the oldest Methodist Church building in New York state, built in 1789 as the Comac Church. It is listed on the National Register of Historic Places and is one of the oldest buildings in Commack.

Population: 37,117; Growth (since 2000): 2.1%; Density: 3,101.2 persons per square mile; Race: 90.6% White, 1.7% Black/African American, 4.6% Asian, 0.0% American Indian/Alaska Native, 0.0% Native Hawaiian/Other Pacific Islander, 2.2% Two or more races, 5.9% Hispanic of any race; Average household size: 3.03; Median age: 46.2; Age under 18: 21.2%; Age 65 and over: 18.7%; Males per 100 females: 94.1; Marriage status: 27.1% never married, 60.2% now married, 0.7% separated, 7.1% widowed, 5.6% divorced; Foreign born: 9.4%; Speak English only: 87.1%; With disability: 8.6%; Veterans: 6.4%; Ancestry: 34.6% Italian, 19.2% Irish, 13.0% German, 6.7% Polish, 4.7% Russian

Employment: 20.2% management, business, and financial, 5.2% computer, engineering, and science, 16.5% education, legal, community service, arts, and media, 8.0% healthcare practitioners, 12.5% service, 26.9% sales and office, 5.4% natural resources, construction, and maintenance, 5.3% production, transportation, and material moving

Income: Per capita: $48,513; Median household: $124,461; Average household: $143,371; Households with income of $100,000 or more: 60.8%; Poverty rate: 3.9%

Educational Attainment: High school diploma or higher: 96.7%; Bachelor's degree or higher: 48.9%; Graduate/professional degree or higher: 22.6%

School District(s)
Commack Union Free SD (KG-12)
    Enrollment: 6,307 . . . . (631) 912-2010

Housing: Homeownership rate: 92.0%; Median home value: $471,300; Median year structure built: 1964; Homeowner vacancy rate: 0.8%; Median selected monthly owner costs: $3,192 with a mortgage, $1,332 without a mortgage; Median gross rent: $1,683 per month; Rental vacancy rate: 5.5%

Health Insurance: 97.4% have insurance; 87.2% have private insurance; 23.9% have public insurance; 2.6% do not have insurance; 1.6% of children under 18 do not have insurance

Transportation: Commute: 87.4% car, 6.7% public transportation, 1.1% walk, 3.8% work from home; Mean travel time to work: 33.4 minutes

COPIAGUE (CDP). Covers a land area of 3.218 square miles and a water area of 0.028 square miles. Located at 40.67° N. Lat; 73.39° W. Long. Elevation is 23 feet.

History: Copiague is an unincorporated place within the Town of Babylon.

Population: 22,926; Growth (since 2000): 4.6%; Density: 7,123.5 persons per square mile; Race: 67.6% White, 8.4% Black/African American, 1.8% Asian, 0.6% American Indian/Alaska Native, 0.0% Native Hawaiian/Other Pacific Islander, 5.2% Two or more races, 37.0% Hispanic of any race; Average household size: 3.22; Median age: 41.1; Age under 18: 20.1%; Age 65 and over: 12.7%; Males per 100 females: 99.2; Marriage status: 38.8% never married, 46.2% now married, 2.2% separated, 5.9% widowed, 9.1% divorced; Foreign born: 28.9%; Speak English only: 60.5%; With disability: 10.4%; Veterans: 3.7%; Ancestry: 21.8% Italian, 17.2% Irish, 12.9% German, 4.6% Polish, 2.8% American

Employment: 12.3% management, business, and financial, 3.5% computer, engineering, and science, 6.5% education, legal, community service, arts, and media, 3.1% healthcare practitioners, 20.6% service, 24.8% sales and office, 11.1% natural resources, construction, and maintenance, 18.1% production, transportation, and material moving

Income: Per capita: $29,052; Median household: $72,517; Average household: $88,263; Households with income of $100,000 or more: 34.8%; Poverty rate: 6.7%

Educational Attainment: High school diploma or higher: 80.4%; Bachelor's degree or higher: 18.8%; Graduate/professional degree or higher: 6.4%

School District(s)
Copiague Union Free SD (KG-12)
    Enrollment: 5,137 . . . . (631) 842-4015
Vocational/Technical School(s)
Electrical Training Center (Private, For-profit)
    Enrollment: 114. . . . . (631) 226-8021
    Tuition: $11,000

Housing: Homeownership rate: 79.7%; Median home value: $298,600; Median year structure built: 1960; Homeowner vacancy rate: 1.1%; Median

selected monthly owner costs: $2,454 with a mortgage, $1,071 without a mortgage; Median gross rent: $1,650 per month; Rental vacancy rate: 5.4%

Health Insurance: 90.8% have insurance; 66.4% have private insurance; 34.3% have public insurance; 9.2% do not have insurance; 5.4% of children under 18 do not have insurance

Transportation: Commute: 84.6% car, 8.5% public transportation, 2.4% walk, 1.5% work from home; Mean travel time to work: 28.8 minutes

CORAM (CDP). Covers a land area of 13.824 square miles and a water area of 0 square miles. Located at 40.88° N. Lat; 73.01° W. Long. Elevation is 95 feet.

History: Coram is the oldest settlement in the central part of the town of Brookhaven. Its early name was "Wincoram." Its first white settler was likely William Satterly, who opened a tavern in 1677.

Population: 40,713; Growth (since 2000): 16.6%; Density: 2,945.0 persons per square mile; Race: 78.6% White, 10.4% Black/African American, 6.5% Asian, 0.3% American Indian/Alaska Native, 0.1% Native Hawaiian/Other Pacific Islander, 2.0% Two or more races, 18.9% Hispanic of any race; Average household size: 2.77; Median age: 40.3; Age under 18: 22.4%; Age 65 and over: 13.4%; Males per 100 females: 93.2; Marriage status: 33.4% never married, 50.6% now married, 1.6% separated, 6.0% widowed, 10.0% divorced; Foreign born: 17.0%; Speak English only: 78.1%; With disability: 8.8%; Veterans: 5.2%; Ancestry: 24.0% Italian, 15.3% Irish, 12.0% German, 8.4% American, 4.3% English

Employment: 12.6% management, business, and financial, 4.1% computer, engineering, and science, 13.6% education, legal, community service, arts, and media, 6.7% healthcare practitioners, 17.1% service, 27.0% sales and office, 9.5% natural resources, construction, and maintenance, 9.4% production, transportation, and material moving

Income: Per capita: $35,967; Median household: $82,151; Average household: $96,453; Households with income of $100,000 or more: 37.4%; Poverty rate: 4.6%

Educational Attainment: High school diploma or higher: 92.5%; Bachelor's degree or higher: 34.2%; Graduate/professional degree or higher: 14.3%

School District(s)
Longwood Central SD (KG-12)
    Enrollment: 9,164 . . . . (631) 345-2172

Housing: Homeownership rate: 69.0%; Median home value: $308,600; Median year structure built: 1979; Homeowner vacancy rate: 2.0%; Median selected monthly owner costs: $2,571 with a mortgage, $1,060 without a mortgage; Median gross rent: $1,839 per month; Rental vacancy rate: 5.5%

Health Insurance: 95.5% have insurance; 77.5% have private insurance; 28.6% have public insurance; 4.5% do not have insurance; 1.4% of children under 18 do not have insurance

Transportation: Commute: 90.5% car, 3.7% public transportation, 0.8% walk, 2.9% work from home; Mean travel time to work: 35.5 minutes

CUTCHOGUE (CDP). Covers a land area of 9.723 square miles and a water area of 0.427 square miles. Located at 41.02° N. Lat; 72.49° W. Long. Elevation is 30 feet.

Population: 3,213; Growth (since 2000): 12.8%; Density: 330.4 persons per square mile; Race: 96.9% White, 0.8% Black/African American, 1.6% Asian, 0.0% American Indian/Alaska Native, 0.0% Native Hawaiian/Other Pacific Islander, 0.0% Two or more races, 2.6% Hispanic of any race; Average household size: 2.55; Median age: 52.3; Age under 18: 18.1%; Age 65 and over: 28.6%; Males per 100 females: 102.0; Marriage status: 23.9% never married, 58.2% now married, 2.1% separated, 6.8% widowed, 11.0% divorced; Foreign born: 10.1%; Speak English only: 87.1%; With disability: 12.3%; Veterans: 10.3%; Ancestry: 19.5% Irish, 19.4% Italian, 18.2% English, 16.5% German, 8.9% Polish

Employment: 15.0% management, business, and financial, 3.1% computer, engineering, and science, 16.1% education, legal, community service, arts, and media, 8.4% healthcare practitioners, 11.1% service, 26.8% sales and office, 11.5% natural resources, construction, and maintenance, 8.1% production, transportation, and material moving

Income: Per capita: $48,116; Median household: $93,125; Average household: $119,900; Households with income of $100,000 or more: 45.7%; Poverty rate: 2.3%

Educational Attainment: High school diploma or higher: 95.9%; Bachelor's degree or higher: 45.2%; Graduate/professional degree or higher: 19.2%

School District(s)
Mattituck-Cutchogue Union Free SD (KG-12)
    Enrollment: 1,198 . . . . (631) 298-4242
Housing: Homeownership rate: 91.1%; Median home value: $514,400;
Median year structure built: 1974; Homeowner vacancy rate: 0.0%; Median
selected monthly owner costs: $2,721 with a mortgage, $1,224 without a
mortgage; Median gross rent: $1,658 per month; Rental vacancy rate:
0.0%
Health Insurance: 95.2% have insurance; 82.4% have private insurance;
40.9% have public insurance; 4.8% do not have insurance; 0.0% of
children under 18 do not have insurance
Transportation: Commute: 85.2% car, 3.9% public transportation, 1.6%
walk, 8.6% work from home; Mean travel time to work: 35.7 minutes

DEER PARK (CDP).
Covers a land area of 6.168 square miles and a
water area of 0.004 square miles. Located at 40.76° N. Lat; 73.32° W.
Long. Elevation is 85 feet.
History: Deer Park is a residential hamlet located in the pine barrens in
the northeast corner of the town of Babylon. It grew out of Jacob Conklin's
1610 settlement of the Half Way Hollow Hills, later Wheatley Heights.
Charles Wilson founded Deer Park in 1853 about eleven years after the
Long Island Rail Road arrived in 1842.
Population: 27,653; Growth (since 2000): -2.3%; Density: 4,483.6 persons
per square mile; Race: 70.5% White, 13.7% Black/African American, 8.2%
Asian, 0.0% American Indian/Alaska Native, 0.0% Native Hawaiian/Other
Pacific Islander, 2.9% Two or more races, 15.7% Hispanic of any race;
Average household size: 3.12; Median age: 40.4; Age under 18: 22.4%;
Age 65 and over: 14.7%; Males per 100 females: 93.8; Marriage status:
32.3% never married, 53.5% now married, 2.3% separated, 7.3%
widowed, 6.8% divorced; Foreign born: 18.9%; Speak English only: 73.2%;
With disability: 10.3%; Veterans: 5.9%; Ancestry: 32.0% Italian, 14.8%
Irish, 9.9% German, 3.4% American, 3.3% Polish
Employment: 13.7% management, business, and financial, 4.2%
computer, engineering, and science, 10.1% education, legal, community
service, arts, and media, 7.0% healthcare practitioners, 19.1% service,
25.4% sales and office, 11.3% natural resources, construction, and
maintenance, 9.1% production, transportation, and material moving
Income: Per capita: $34,247; Median household: $86,919; Average
household: $101,410; Households with income of $100,000 or more:
44.7%; Poverty rate: 8.2%
Educational Attainment: High school diploma or higher: 89.6%;
Bachelor's degree or higher: 27.5%; Graduate/professional degree or
higher: 10.1%
School District(s)
Deer Park Union Free SD (PK-12)
    Enrollment: 4,166 . . . . (631) 274-4010
Housing: Homeownership rate: 84.2%; Median home value: $353,700;
Median year structure built: 1963; Homeowner vacancy rate: 1.1%; Median
selected monthly owner costs: $2,709 with a mortgage, $1,102 without a
mortgage; Median gross rent: $1,576 per month; Rental vacancy rate:
4.2%
Health Insurance: 94.0% have insurance; 79.0% have private insurance;
27.6% have public insurance; 6.0% do not have insurance; 4.8% of
children under 18 do not have insurance
Transportation: Commute: 89.2% car, 6.0% public transportation, 2.5%
walk, 1.0% work from home; Mean travel time to work: 30.9 minutes

DERING HARBOR (village).
Covers a land area of 0.246 square
miles and a water area of 0.013 square miles. Located at 41.09° N. Lat;
72.34° W. Long. Elevation is 7 feet.
Population: 8; Growth (since 2000): -38.5%; Density: 32.6 persons per
square mile; Race: 100.0% White, 0.0% Black/African American, 0.0%
Asian, 0.0% American Indian/Alaska Native, 0.0% Native Hawaiian/Other
Pacific Islander, 0.0% Two or more races, 0.0% Hispanic of any race;
Average household size: 1.60; Median age: 68.3; Age under 18: 0.0%;
Age 65 and over: 62.5%; Males per 100 females: 120.0; Marriage status:
37.5% never married, 0.0% now married, 0.0% separated, 25.0%
widowed, 37.5% divorced; Foreign born: 0.0%; Speak English only:
100.0%; With disability: 25.0%; Veterans: 0.0%; Ancestry: 100.0% English
Employment: n/a management, business, and financial, n/a computer,
engineering, and science, n/a education, legal, community service, arts,
and media, n/a healthcare practitioners, n/a service, n/a sales and office,
n/a natural resources, construction, and maintenance, n/a production,
transportation, and material moving

Income: Per capita: $69,888; Median household: n/a; Average household:
n/a; Households with income of $100,000 or more: 60.0%; Poverty rate:
n/a
Educational Attainment: High school diploma or higher: 100.0%;
Bachelor's degree or higher: 100.0%; Graduate/professional degree or
higher: 60.0%
Housing: Homeownership rate: 60.0%; Median home value: n/a; Median
year structure built: 1974; Homeowner vacancy rate: 0.0%; Median
selected monthly owner costs: n/a with a mortgage, n/a without a
mortgage; Median gross rent: n/a per month; Rental vacancy rate: 0.0%
Health Insurance: 100.0% have insurance; 100.0% have private
insurance; 62.5% have public insurance; 0.0% do not have insurance;
0.0% of children under 18 do not have insurance
Transportation: Commute: n/a car, n/a public transportation, n/a walk, n/a
work from home; Mean travel time to work: 0.0 minutes

DIX HILLS (CDP).
Covers a land area of 15.946 square miles and a
water area of 0 square miles. Located at 40.80° N. Lat; 73.34° W. Long.
Elevation is 203 feet.
History: Settlers traded goods with the Secatogue tribe for land that
became Dix Hills in 1699, originally called Dick's Hills. Lore has it that it
was named for local native Dick Pechegan. Scholar William Wallace
Tooker notes that the addition of the English name "Dick" to the indigenous
name "Pechegan" was a common practice. The area was mostly used for
farming until after World War II.
Population: 27,647; Growth (since 2000): 6.2%; Density: 1,733.7 persons
per square mile; Race: 77.0% White, 4.5% Black/African American, 16.1%
Asian, 0.1% American Indian/Alaska Native, 0.1% Native Hawaiian/Other
Pacific Islander, 1.2% Two or more races, 6.0% Hispanic of any race;
Average household size: 3.30; Median age: 44.0; Age under 18: 23.9%;
Age 65 and over: 16.1%; Males per 100 females: 98.9; Marriage status:
25.5% never married, 66.3% now married, 0.9% separated, 4.2%
widowed, 4.0% divorced; Foreign born: 18.2%; Speak English only: 75.8%;
With disability: 6.7%; Veterans: 3.2%; Ancestry: 22.5% Italian, 12.3% Irish,
9.1% German, 6.7% Polish, 5.1% Russian
Employment: 23.3% management, business, and financial, 5.4%
computer, engineering, and science, 15.1% education, legal, community
service, arts, and media, 12.8% healthcare practitioners, 8.1% service,
26.2% sales and office, 3.5% natural resources, construction, and
maintenance, 5.7% production, transportation, and material moving
Income: Per capita: $61,176; Median household: $152,263; Average
household: $199,642; Households with income of $100,000 or more:
70.2%; Poverty rate: 4.0%
Educational Attainment: High school diploma or higher: 96.9%;
Bachelor's degree or higher: 61.8%; Graduate/professional degree or
higher: 31.1%
School District(s)
Commack Union Free SD (KG-12)
    Enrollment: 6,307 . . . . (631) 912-2010
Half Hollow Hills Central SD (KG-12)
    Enrollment: 8,354 . . . . (631) 592-3008
Western Suffolk Boces
    Enrollment: n/a . . . . (631) 549-4900
Four-year College(s)
Five Towns College (Private, For-profit)
    Enrollment: 670 . . . . (631) 424-7000
    Tuition: In-state $19,360; Out-of-state $19,360
Housing: Homeownership rate: 94.7%; Median home value: $694,600;
Median year structure built: 1968; Homeowner vacancy rate: 1.3%; Median
selected monthly owner costs: $4,000+ with a mortgage, $1,501 without a
mortgage; Median gross rent: $1,916 per month; Rental vacancy rate:
15.5%
Health Insurance: 96.5% have insurance; 86.6% have private insurance;
23.0% have public insurance; 3.5% do not have insurance; 1.4% of
children under 18 do not have insurance
Transportation: Commute: 84.4% car, 10.2% public transportation, 0.4%
walk, 4.7% work from home; Mean travel time to work: 36.7 minutes

EAST FARMINGDALE (CDP).
Covers a land area of 5.715 square
miles and a water area of 0.020 square miles. Located at 40.73° N. Lat;
73.42° W. Long. Elevation is 69 feet.
History: East Farmingdale's first European settler was Thomas Powell,
who arrived in 1687. On October 18, 1695, he purchased a 15-square-mile
tract of land from three Native American tribes, known as the Bethpage
Purchase.

Population: 6,222; Growth (since 2000): 15.2%; Density: 1,088.7 persons per square mile; Race: 59.2% White, 11.3% Black/African American, 9.1% Asian, 0.1% American Indian/Alaska Native, 0.0% Native Hawaiian/Other Pacific Islander, 7.5% Two or more races, 24.7% Hispanic of any race; Average household size: 3.11; Median age: 33.1; Age under 18: 22.1%; Age 65 and over: 12.5%; Males per 100 females: 100.9; Marriage status: 38.5% never married, 46.6% now married, 1.4% separated, 6.1% widowed, 8.8% divorced; Foreign born: 24.6%; Speak English only: 68.2%; With disability: 8.8%; Veterans: 3.8%; Ancestry: 23.8% Italian, 12.8% German, 12.5% Irish, 4.3% Polish, 2.5% Greek

Employment: 13.7% management, business, and financial, 4.3% computer, engineering, and science, 9.7% education, legal, community service, arts, and media, 4.9% healthcare practitioners, 18.1% service, 32.9% sales and office, 8.7% natural resources, construction, and maintenance, 7.7% production, transportation, and material moving

Income: Per capita: $35,975; Median household: $84,408; Average household: $115,398; Households with income of $100,000 or more: 44.6%; Poverty rate: 7.4%

Educational Attainment: High school diploma or higher: 90.2%; Bachelor's degree or higher: 29.8%; Graduate/professional degree or higher: 10.3%

Housing: Homeownership rate: 68.2%; Median home value: $400,700; Median year structure built: 1966; Homeowner vacancy rate: 2.0%; Median selected monthly owner costs: $2,862 with a mortgage, $1,000 without a mortgage; Median gross rent: $1,552 per month; Rental vacancy rate: 5.4%

Health Insurance: 92.0% have insurance; 76.1% have private insurance; 26.0% have public insurance; 8.0% do not have insurance; 2.2% of children under 18 do not have insurance

Transportation: Commute: 76.3% car, 12.3% public transportation, 4.1% walk, 5.1% work from home; Mean travel time to work: 29.4 minutes

EAST HAMPTON (town). Covers a land area of 74.328 square miles and a water area of 312.224 square miles. Located at 41.09° N. Lat; 72.11° W. Long. Elevation is 33 feet.

History: Birthplace of John Howard Payne, whose home is now a museum. The village has 3 historic districts containing other significant buildings. Settled 1648, incorporated 1920.

Population: 21,935; Growth (since 2000): 11.2%; Density: 295.1 persons per square mile; Race: 93.4% White, 2.5% Black/African American, 2.0% Asian, 0.2% American Indian/Alaska Native, 0.0% Native Hawaiian/Other Pacific Islander, 0.9% Two or more races, 20.9% Hispanic of any race; Average household size: 2.42; Median age: 51.0; Age under 18: 16.4%; Age 65 and over: 25.9%; Males per 100 females: 101.5; Marriage status: 26.5% never married, 60.0% now married, 0.5% separated, 6.3% widowed, 7.2% divorced; Foreign born: 21.0%; Speak English only: 73.6%; With disability: 10.6%; Veterans: 6.0%; Ancestry: 15.7% Irish, 13.9% Italian, 13.4% German, 9.7% English, 5.9% American

Employment: 14.3% management, business, and financial, 2.7% computer, engineering, and science, 15.3% education, legal, community service, arts, and media, 4.0% healthcare practitioners, 21.1% service, 20.8% sales and office, 16.9% natural resources, construction, and maintenance, 4.8% production, transportation, and material moving

Income: Per capita: $62,904; Median household: $92,516; Average household: $149,434; Households with income of $100,000 or more: 45.2%; Poverty rate: 9.3%

Educational Attainment: High school diploma or higher: 92.0%; Bachelor's degree or higher: 44.2%; Graduate/professional degree or higher: 19.2%

School District(s)
East Hampton Union Free SD (KG-12)
    Enrollment: 1,814 . . . . (631) 329-4104
Springs Union Free SD (PK-11)
    Enrollment: 764 . . . . (631) 324-0144

Housing: Homeownership rate: 84.3%; Median home value: $807,500; Median year structure built: 1978; Homeowner vacancy rate: 1.1%; Median selected monthly owner costs: $2,854 with a mortgage, $992 without a mortgage; Median gross rent: $1,777 per month; Rental vacancy rate: 14.5%

Health Insurance: 90.7% have insurance; 72.8% have private insurance; 37.3% have public insurance; 9.3% do not have insurance; 5.1% of children under 18 do not have insurance

Safety: Violent crime rate: 8.5 per 10,000 population; Property crime rate: 113.4 per 10,000 population

Newspapers: East Hampton Star (weekly circulation 15,000); The Independent (weekly circulation 25,000)

Transportation: Commute: 77.5% car, 8.5% public transportation, 3.5% walk, 9.1% work from home; Mean travel time to work: 26.5 minutes

Airports: East Hampton (general aviation)

Additional Information Contacts
Town of East Hampton . . . . (631) 324-4141
    http://www.town.east-hampton.ny.us

EAST HAMPTON (village). Covers a land area of 4.764 square miles and a water area of 0.138 square miles. Located at 40.95° N. Lat; 72.20° W. Long. Elevation is 33 feet.

Population: 1,130; Growth (since 2000): -15.3%; Density: 237.2 persons per square mile; Race: 92.5% White, 1.3% Black/African American, 2.1% Asian, 0.0% American Indian/Alaska Native, 0.0% Native Hawaiian/Other Pacific Islander, 3.5% Two or more races, 9.4% Hispanic of any race; Average household size: 2.05; Median age: 61.4; Age under 18: 9.4%; Age 65 and over: 41.8%; Males per 100 females: 90.7; Marriage status: 19.3% never married, 57.9% now married, 1.2% separated, 10.3% widowed, 12.5% divorced; Foreign born: 20.4%; Speak English only: 81.9%; With disability: 8.8%; Veterans: 7.4%; Ancestry: 17.1% English, 14.2% German, 11.9% Italian, 10.0% Irish, 8.5% French

Employment: 28.4% management, business, and financial, 3.2% computer, engineering, and science, 15.1% education, legal, community service, arts, and media, 4.5% healthcare practitioners, 15.8% service, 21.3% sales and office, 10.5% natural resources, construction, and maintenance, 1.1% production, transportation, and material moving

Income: Per capita: $113,552; Median household: $103,269; Average household: $228,114; Households with income of $100,000 or more: 51.2%; Poverty rate: 8.0%

Educational Attainment: High school diploma or higher: 94.1%; Bachelor's degree or higher: 61.6%; Graduate/professional degree or higher: 30.3%

School District(s)
East Hampton Union Free SD (KG-12)
    Enrollment: 1,814 . . . . (631) 329-4104
Springs Union Free SD (PK-11)
    Enrollment: 764 . . . . (631) 324-0144

Housing: Homeownership rate: 76.6%; Median home value: $1,665,800; Median year structure built: 1953; Homeowner vacancy rate: 7.0%; Median selected monthly owner costs: $4,000+ with a mortgage, $1,304 without a mortgage; Median gross rent: $2,260 per month; Rental vacancy rate: 6.2%

Health Insurance: 91.0% have insurance; 78.9% have private insurance; 44.0% have public insurance; 9.0% do not have insurance; 0.0% of children under 18 do not have insurance

Safety: Violent crime rate: 8.9 per 10,000 population; Property crime rate: 437.1 per 10,000 population

Newspapers: East Hampton Star (weekly circulation 15,000); The Independent (weekly circulation 25,000)

Transportation: Commute: 60.6% car, 12.8% public transportation, 12.8% walk, 8.5% work from home; Mean travel time to work: 20.5 minutes

Airports: East Hampton (general aviation)

EAST HAMPTON NORTH (CDP). Covers a land area of 5.639 square miles and a water area of 0 square miles. Located at 40.97° N. Lat; 72.19° W. Long.

Population: 4,615; Growth (since 2000): 28.7%; Density: 818.4 persons per square mile; Race: 96.7% White, 2.2% Black/African American, 0.3% Asian, 0.0% American Indian/Alaska Native, 0.0% Native Hawaiian/Other Pacific Islander, 0.3% Two or more races, 31.8% Hispanic of any race; Average household size: 2.54; Median age: 45.9; Age under 18: 19.3%; Age 65 and over: 19.3%; Males per 100 females: 99.3; Marriage status: 35.7% never married, 51.2% now married, 0.4% separated, 5.7% widowed, 7.4% divorced; Foreign born: 28.1%; Speak English only: 62.9%; With disability: 12.7%; Veterans: 3.1%; Ancestry: 17.1% Irish, 10.2% German, 9.8% Italian, 6.5% English, 5.1% French

Employment: 9.3% management, business, and financial, 2.3% computer, engineering, and science, 17.5% education, legal, community service, arts, and media, 1.6% healthcare practitioners, 19.9% service, 20.0% sales and office, 20.7% natural resources, construction, and maintenance, 8.6% production, transportation, and material moving

Income: Per capita: $47,920; Median household: $94,025; Average household: $117,780; Households with income of $100,000 or more: 46.0%; Poverty rate: 6.4%

Educational Attainment: High school diploma or higher: 88.4%; Bachelor's degree or higher: 32.1%; Graduate/professional degree or higher: 14.6%
Housing: Homeownership rate: 79.1%; Median home value: $680,700; Median year structure built: 1983; Homeowner vacancy rate: 0.0%; Median selected monthly owner costs: $2,682 with a mortgage, $841 without a mortgage; Median gross rent: $1,079 per month; Rental vacancy rate: 4.3%
Health Insurance: 90.9% have insurance; 62.0% have private insurance; 38.5% have public insurance; 9.1% do not have insurance; 0.0% of children under 18 do not have insurance
Transportation: Commute: 84.1% car, 6.8% public transportation, 2.0% walk, 6.5% work from home; Mean travel time to work: 27.1 minutes

EAST ISLIP (CDP). Covers a land area of 3.950 square miles and a water area of 0.109 square miles. Located at 40.73° N. Lat; 73.19° W. Long. Elevation is 16 feet.
History: Originally referred to as "East of Islip", the town was named in 1890 by William Nicoll, an English aristocrat who purchased the surrounding land in 1683 to build a family residence.
Population: 13,616; Growth (since 2000): -3.3%; Density: 3,447.3 persons per square mile; Race: 94.1% White, 1.2% Black/African American, 1.4% Asian, 0.0% American Indian/Alaska Native, 0.0% Native Hawaiian/Other Pacific Islander, 0.1% Two or more races, 7.6% Hispanic of any race; Average household size: 3.17; Median age: 41.0; Age under 18: 23.9%; Age 65 and over: 13.7%; Males per 100 females: 96.2; Marriage status: 31.5% never married, 54.2% now married, 1.4% separated, 8.0% widowed, 6.3% divorced; Foreign born: 4.6%; Speak English only: 92.7%; With disability: 6.1%; Veterans: 5.5%; Ancestry: 34.7% Italian, 33.1% Irish, 19.2% German, 5.6% Polish, 5.4% English
Employment: 16.7% management, business, and financial, 4.5% computer, engineering, and science, 17.4% education, legal, community service, arts, and media, 6.7% healthcare practitioners, 10.3% service, 23.4% sales and office, 14.0% natural resources, construction, and maintenance, 7.1% production, transportation, and material moving
Income: Per capita: $44,526; Median household: $120,528; Average household: $138,864; Households with income of $100,000 or more: 62.2%; Poverty rate: 7.4%
Educational Attainment: High school diploma or higher: 95.3%; Bachelor's degree or higher: 41.8%; Graduate/professional degree or higher: 20.6%
School District(s)
East Islip Union Free SD (KG-12)
    Enrollment: 3,822 . . . . (631) 224-2000
Housing: Homeownership rate: 90.1%; Median home value: $400,500; Median year structure built: 1959; Homeowner vacancy rate: 0.8%; Median selected monthly owner costs: $2,909 with a mortgage, $1,267 without a mortgage; Median gross rent: $1,772 per month; Rental vacancy rate: 13.6%
Health Insurance: 97.5% have insurance; 89.5% have private insurance; 19.4% have public insurance; 2.5% do not have insurance; 0.6% of children under 18 do not have insurance
Transportation: Commute: 88.4% car, 6.6% public transportation, 1.3% walk, 3.3% work from home; Mean travel time to work: 34.3 minutes

EAST MARION (CDP). Covers a land area of 2.238 square miles and a water area of 0.128 square miles. Located at 41.13° N. Lat; 72.35° W. Long. Elevation is 33 feet.
Population: 885; Growth (since 2000): 17.1%; Density: 395.4 persons per square mile; Race: 94.1% White, 0.7% Black/African American, 0.3% Asian, 0.0% American Indian/Alaska Native, 0.0% Native Hawaiian/Other Pacific Islander, 4.9% Two or more races, 5.0% Hispanic of any race; Average household size: 2.05; Median age: 61.0; Age under 18: 11.6%; Age 65 and over: 39.4%; Males per 100 females: 102.2; Marriage status: 24.1% never married, 53.4% now married, 0.0% separated, 13.0% widowed, 9.6% divorced; Foreign born: 12.5%; Speak English only: 83.5%; With disability: 15.9%; Veterans: 11.4%; Ancestry: 21.4% Irish, 18.6% German, 16.5% Italian, 15.5% English, 9.6% Greek
Employment: 17.3% management, business, and financial, 3.9% computer, engineering, and science, 16.8% education, legal, community service, arts, and media, 9.8% healthcare practitioners, 18.2% service, 22.1% sales and office, 10.3% natural resources, construction, and maintenance, 1.7% production, transportation, and material moving

Income: Per capita: $47,648; Median household: $72,566; Average household: $94,191; Households with income of $100,000 or more: 32.0%; Poverty rate: 3.5%
Educational Attainment: High school diploma or higher: 92.4%; Bachelor's degree or higher: 38.0%; Graduate/professional degree or higher: 19.4%
Housing: Homeownership rate: 81.7%; Median home value: $618,600; Median year structure built: 1979; Homeowner vacancy rate: 0.0%; Median selected monthly owner costs: $2,677 with a mortgage, $954 without a mortgage; Median gross rent: $1,654 per month; Rental vacancy rate: 16.0%
Health Insurance: 95.1% have insurance; 73.0% have private insurance; 48.9% have public insurance; 4.9% do not have insurance; 5.7% of children under 18 do not have insurance
Transportation: Commute: 83.9% car, 0.8% public transportation, 2.5% walk, 12.7% work from home; Mean travel time to work: 38.8 minutes

EAST MORICHES (CDP). Covers a land area of 5.477 square miles and a water area of 0.149 square miles. Located at 40.81° N. Lat; 72.76° W. Long. Elevation is 30 feet.
History: East Moriches is a hamlet (and census-designated place) in Suffolk County, New York. The name Moriches comes from Meritces, a Native American who owned land on Moriches Neck.
Population: 5,177; Growth (since 2000): 13.8%; Density: 945.3 persons per square mile; Race: 97.1% White, 1.8% Black/African American, 0.3% Asian, 0.0% American Indian/Alaska Native, 0.0% Native Hawaiian/Other Pacific Islander, 0.4% Two or more races, 3.8% Hispanic of any race; Average household size: 2.72; Median age: 44.4; Age under 18: 20.3%; Age 65 and over: 16.0%; Males per 100 females: 96.4; Marriage status: 27.8% never married, 60.0% now married, 1.0% separated, 5.5% widowed, 6.6% divorced; Foreign born: 3.0%; Speak English only: 95.4%; With disability: 9.7%; Veterans: 8.6%; Ancestry: 33.2% Italian, 28.5% Irish, 19.5% German, 9.0% English, 8.3% Polish
Employment: 19.2% management, business, and financial, 4.0% computer, engineering, and science, 12.0% education, legal, community service, arts, and media, 8.9% healthcare practitioners, 16.2% service, 21.5% sales and office, 13.0% natural resources, construction, and maintenance, 5.2% production, transportation, and material moving
Income: Per capita: $44,399; Median household: $102,020; Average household: $119,929; Households with income of $100,000 or more: 54.3%; Poverty rate: 4.8%
Educational Attainment: High school diploma or higher: 96.1%; Bachelor's degree or higher: 34.8%; Graduate/professional degree or higher: 20.2%
School District(s)
East Moriches Union Free SD (KG-08)
    Enrollment: 727 . . . . (631) 878-0162
Housing: Homeownership rate: 80.8%; Median home value: $412,900; Median year structure built: 1980; Homeowner vacancy rate: 2.7%; Median selected monthly owner costs: $2,977 with a mortgage, $1,356 without a mortgage; Median gross rent: $1,755 per month; Rental vacancy rate: 3.6%
Health Insurance: 94.7% have insurance; 83.4% have private insurance; 22.5% have public insurance; 5.3% do not have insurance; 0.0% of children under 18 do not have insurance
Transportation: Commute: 89.0% car, 3.0% public transportation, 0.0% walk, 8.0% work from home; Mean travel time to work: 32.2 minutes

EAST NORTHPORT (CDP). Covers a land area of 5.161 square miles and a water area of 0 square miles. Located at 40.88° N. Lat; 73.32° W. Long. Elevation is 223 feet.
History: On July 30, 1656, land was purchased from Chief Asharoken, head of the Matinecocks Native American tribe, part of which is known today as East Northport.
Population: 19,465; Growth (since 2000): -6.6%; Density: 3,771.6 persons per square mile; Race: 96.1% White, 0.9% Black/African American, 1.3% Asian, 0.0% American Indian/Alaska Native, 0.1% Native Hawaiian/Other Pacific Islander, 0.8% Two or more races, 7.5% Hispanic of any race; Average household size: 2.76; Median age: 44.8; Age under 18: 21.2%; Age 65 and over: 15.8%; Males per 100 females: 97.8; Marriage status: 29.3% never married, 56.0% now married, 0.8% separated, 6.3% widowed, 8.3% divorced; Foreign born: 6.8%; Speak English only: 91.6%; With disability: 8.5%; Veterans: 6.5%; Ancestry: 32.2% Italian, 26.2% Irish, 16.1% German, 6.4% English, 5.5% American

Employment: 18.4% management, business, and financial, 5.2% computer, engineering, and science, 17.7% education, legal, community service, arts, and media, 4.6% healthcare practitioners, 14.4% service, 26.0% sales and office, 8.9% natural resources, construction, and maintenance, 4.8% production, transportation, and material moving
Income: Per capita: $42,107; Median household: $100,846; Average household: $113,509; Households with income of $100,000 or more: 51.1%; Poverty rate: 4.1%
Educational Attainment: High school diploma or higher: 95.0%; Bachelor's degree or higher: 45.2%; Graduate/professional degree or higher: 20.5%

School District(s)
Northport-East Northport Union Free SD (KG-12)
  Enrollment: 5,547 . . . . (631) 262-6604
Housing: Homeownership rate: 82.7%; Median home value: $452,900; Median year structure built: 1958; Homeowner vacancy rate: 0.0%; Median selected monthly owner costs: $2,762 with a mortgage, $1,090 without a mortgage; Median gross rent: $1,850 per month; Rental vacancy rate: 0.0%
Health Insurance: 96.2% have insurance; 85.3% have private insurance; 26.7% have public insurance; 3.8% do not have insurance; 0.0% of children under 18 do not have insurance
Transportation: Commute: 85.3% car, 7.7% public transportation, 0.7% walk, 5.6% work from home; Mean travel time to work: 33.8 minutes

EAST PATCHOGUE (CDP). Covers a land area of 8.346 square miles and a water area of 0.131 square miles. Located at 40.77° N. Lat; 72.98° W. Long. Elevation is 23 feet.
History: Patchogue is a village on the south shore of Long Island in Suffolk County, New York.
Population: 22,796; Growth (since 2000): 9.5%; Density: 2,731.4 persons per square mile; Race: 90.4% White, 3.7% Black/African American, 2.5% Asian, 0.0% American Indian/Alaska Native, 0.0% Native Hawaiian/Other Pacific Islander, 1.7% Two or more races, 19.4% Hispanic of any race; Average household size: 2.66; Median age: 41.1; Age under 18: 20.8%; Age 65 and over: 16.9%; Males per 100 females: 95.3; Marriage status: 32.5% never married, 49.3% now married, 2.1% separated, 6.8% widowed, 11.4% divorced; Foreign born: 12.0%; Speak English only: 78.6%; With disability: 10.7%; Veterans: 6.0%; Ancestry: 33.5% Italian, 21.7% Irish, 17.9% German, 6.1% English, 3.2% Polish
Employment: 12.5% management, business, and financial, 5.0% computer, engineering, and science, 13.4% education, legal, community service, arts, and media, 6.4% healthcare practitioners, 15.5% service, 23.9% sales and office, 14.1% natural resources, construction, and maintenance, 9.3% production, transportation, and material moving
Income: Per capita: $35,378; Median household: $72,083; Average household: $91,318; Households with income of $100,000 or more: 35.9%; Poverty rate: 9.0%
Educational Attainment: High school diploma or higher: 87.0%; Bachelor's degree or higher: 26.2%; Graduate/professional degree or higher: 12.3%

School District(s)
South Country Central SD (PK-12)
  Enrollment: 4,515 . . . . (631) 730-1510
Housing: Homeownership rate: 64.8%; Median home value: $315,300; Median year structure built: 1971; Homeowner vacancy rate: 0.5%; Median selected monthly owner costs: $2,564 with a mortgage, $1,047 without a mortgage; Median gross rent: $1,373 per month; Rental vacancy rate: 1.7%
Health Insurance: 91.1% have insurance; 75.9% have private insurance; 30.2% have public insurance; 8.9% do not have insurance; 3.3% of children under 18 do not have insurance
Transportation: Commute: 90.6% car, 4.3% public transportation, 0.9% walk, 3.0% work from home; Mean travel time to work: 32.0 minutes

EAST QUOGUE (CDP). Covers a land area of 8.874 square miles and a water area of 2.685 square miles. Located at 40.85° N. Lat; 72.58° W. Long. Elevation is 13 feet.
History: East Quogue, originally settled in 1673 as Fourth Neck, is a hamlet and census-designated place (CDP) in Suffolk County, New York.
Population: 4,898; Growth (since 2000): 14.8%; Density: 552.0 persons per square mile; Race: 93.9% White, 0.1% Black/African American, 2.0% Asian, 0.3% American Indian/Alaska Native, 0.0% Native Hawaiian/Other Pacific Islander, 2.2% Two or more races, 5.9% Hispanic of any race; Average household size: 2.60; Median age: 46.0; Age under 18: 23.7%;

Age 65 and over: 18.0%; Males per 100 females: 96.4; Marriage status: 25.9% never married, 59.3% now married, 1.3% separated, 5.2% widowed, 9.6% divorced; Foreign born: 4.9%; Speak English only: 92.2%; With disability: 8.5%; Veterans: 6.3%; Ancestry: 31.3% Italian, 29.4% Irish, 17.8% German, 14.0% Polish, 6.9% English
Employment: 16.9% management, business, and financial, 2.1% computer, engineering, and science, 14.9% education, legal, community service, arts, and media, 7.3% healthcare practitioners, 13.4% service, 25.7% sales and office, 13.0% natural resources, construction, and maintenance, 6.7% production, transportation, and material moving
Income: Per capita: $42,577; Median household: $83,684; Average household: $108,062; Households with income of $100,000 or more: 42.8%; Poverty rate: 2.7%
Educational Attainment: High school diploma or higher: 95.7%; Bachelor's degree or higher: 39.7%; Graduate/professional degree or higher: 21.2%

School District(s)
East Quogue Union Free SD (KG-06)
  Enrollment: 406. . . . . (631) 653-5210
Housing: Homeownership rate: 84.7%; Median home value: $526,900; Median year structure built: 1973; Homeowner vacancy rate: 4.5%; Median selected monthly owner costs: $2,727 with a mortgage, $964 without a mortgage; Median gross rent: $1,860 per month; Rental vacancy rate: 0.0%
Health Insurance: 95.6% have insurance; 86.2% have private insurance; 27.8% have public insurance; 4.4% do not have insurance; 1.4% of children under 18 do not have insurance
Transportation: Commute: 92.2% car, 3.6% public transportation, 0.3% walk, 3.9% work from home; Mean travel time to work: 31.6 minutes

EAST SHOREHAM (CDP). Covers a land area of 5.367 square miles and a water area of 0 square miles. Located at 40.95° N. Lat; 72.88° W. Long. Elevation is 121 feet.
Population: 6,788; Growth (since 2000): 16.9%; Density: 1,264.7 persons per square mile; Race: 93.9% White, 1.0% Black/African American, 3.4% Asian, 0.0% American Indian/Alaska Native, 0.0% Native Hawaiian/Other Pacific Islander, 1.2% Two or more races, 11.8% Hispanic of any race; Average household size: 3.27; Median age: 40.3; Age under 18: 27.9%; Age 65 and over: 11.2%; Males per 100 females: 101.8; Marriage status: 24.5% never married, 66.0% now married, 1.4% separated, 3.9% widowed, 5.7% divorced; Foreign born: 8.1%; Speak English only: 90.0%; With disability: 6.6%; Veterans: 7.5%; Ancestry: 27.5% Italian, 23.4% Irish, 16.3% German, 9.3% Polish, 8.9% American
Employment: 13.8% management, business, and financial, 5.2% computer, engineering, and science, 20.4% education, legal, community service, arts, and media, 5.4% healthcare practitioners, 14.0% service, 25.6% sales and office, 8.0% natural resources, construction, and maintenance, 7.7% production, transportation, and material moving
Income: Per capita: $43,148; Median household: $125,603; Average household: $139,191; Households with income of $100,000 or more: 67.4%; Poverty rate: 3.3%
Educational Attainment: High school diploma or higher: 95.3%; Bachelor's degree or higher: 45.7%; Graduate/professional degree or higher: 26.4%
Housing: Homeownership rate: 92.7%; Median home value: $414,700; Median year structure built: 1974; Homeowner vacancy rate: 0.5%; Median selected monthly owner costs: $2,919 with a mortgage, $1,400 without a mortgage; Median gross rent: $2,515 per month; Rental vacancy rate: 0.0%
Health Insurance: 97.5% have insurance; 90.5% have private insurance; 17.6% have public insurance; 2.5% do not have insurance; 0.6% of children under 18 do not have insurance
Transportation: Commute: 95.1% car, 2.4% public transportation, 0.0% walk, 2.5% work from home; Mean travel time to work: 37.0 minutes

EASTPORT (CDP). Covers a land area of 5.258 square miles and a water area of 0.130 square miles. Located at 40.84° N. Lat; 72.73° W. Long. Elevation is 30 feet.
Population: 1,981; Growth (since 2000): 36.2%; Density: 376.7 persons per square mile; Race: 96.0% White, 0.9% Black/African American, 1.0% Asian, 0.0% American Indian/Alaska Native, 0.0% Native Hawaiian/Other Pacific Islander, 1.2% Two or more races, 9.2% Hispanic of any race; Average household size: 2.58; Median age: 49.5; Age under 18: 13.7%; Age 65 and over: 27.2%; Males per 100 females: 99.2; Marriage status: 34.6% never married, 56.6% now married, 0.7% separated, 2.9%

widowed, 5.9% divorced; Foreign born: 8.7%; Speak English only: 88.5%; With disability: 12.3%; Veterans: 8.5%; Ancestry: 26.9% German, 19.6% Irish, 15.0% Italian, 10.7% English, 6.8% American

Employment: 13.4% management, business, and financial, 3.1% computer, engineering, and science, 11.2% education, legal, community service, arts, and media, 11.8% healthcare practitioners, 19.4% service, 20.9% sales and office, 17.1% natural resources, construction, and maintenance, 3.0% production, transportation, and material moving

Income: Per capita: $48,825; Median household: $106,094; Average household: $130,193; Households with income of $100,000 or more: 53.9%; Poverty rate: 6.8%

Educational Attainment: High school diploma or higher: 96.3%; Bachelor's degree or higher: 46.1%; Graduate/professional degree or higher: 23.3%

School District(s)

Eastport-South Manor CSD (PK-12)

   Enrollment: 3,474 . . . . (631) 801-3011

Housing: Homeownership rate: 76.2%; Median home value: $498,000; Median year structure built: 1990; Homeowner vacancy rate: 0.0%; Median selected monthly owner costs: $2,946 with a mortgage, $1,230 without a mortgage; Median gross rent: $1,453 per month; Rental vacancy rate: 0.0%

Health Insurance: 96.2% have insurance; 82.9% have private insurance; 32.9% have public insurance; 3.8% do not have insurance; 0.0% of children under 18 do not have insurance

Transportation: Commute: 84.8% car, 0.3% public transportation, 3.8% walk, 11.2% work from home; Mean travel time to work: 27.8 minutes

EATONS NECK (CDP). Covers a land area of 1.005 square miles and a water area of 0 square miles. Located at 40.93° N. Lat; 73.39° W. Long. Elevation is 16 feet.

Population: 1,575; Growth (since 2000): 13.5%; Density: 1,567.8 persons per square mile; Race: 96.4% White, 0.0% Black/African American, 2.4% Asian, 0.0% American Indian/Alaska Native, 0.0% Native Hawaiian/Other Pacific Islander, 1.2% Two or more races, 2.0% Hispanic of any race; Average household size: 2.91; Median age: 49.8; Age under 18: 19.2%; Age 65 and over: 22.6%; Males per 100 females: 96.1; Marriage status: 26.4% never married, 66.4% now married, 0.4% separated, 3.8% widowed, 3.5% divorced; Foreign born: 5.0%; Speak English only: 90.3%; With disability: 8.6%; Veterans: 8.3%; Ancestry: 29.7% Irish, 24.8% German, 18.8% Italian, 11.9% American, 5.4% English

Employment: 20.3% management, business, and financial, 2.0% computer, engineering, and science, 23.6% education, legal, community service, arts, and media, 8.7% healthcare practitioners, 7.0% service, 26.5% sales and office, 8.8% natural resources, construction, and maintenance, 3.0% production, transportation, and material moving

Income: Per capita: $61,921; Median household: $128,750; Average household: $176,541; Households with income of $100,000 or more: 57.8%; Poverty rate: 5.0%

Educational Attainment: High school diploma or higher: 99.5%; Bachelor's degree or higher: 62.3%; Graduate/professional degree or higher: 31.4%

Housing: Homeownership rate: 97.6%; Median home value: $710,400; Median year structure built: 1962; Homeowner vacancy rate: 0.0%; Median selected monthly owner costs: $4,000+ with a mortgage, $1,461 without a mortgage; Median gross rent: n/a per month; Rental vacancy rate: 0.0%

Health Insurance: 98.2% have insurance; 88.5% have private insurance; 26.5% have public insurance; 1.8% do not have insurance; 0.0% of children under 18 do not have insurance

Transportation: Commute: 82.0% car, 6.6% public transportation, 1.5% walk, 9.0% work from home; Mean travel time to work: 47.3 minutes

ELWOOD (CDP). Covers a land area of 4.782 square miles and a water area of 0 square miles. Located at 40.85° N. Lat; 73.34° W. Long. Elevation is 184 feet.

Population: 11,592; Growth (since 2000): 6.2%; Density: 2,424.3 persons per square mile; Race: 78.2% White, 7.1% Black/African American, 9.8% Asian, 0.0% American Indian/Alaska Native, 0.0% Native Hawaiian/Other Pacific Islander, 1.7% Two or more races, 8.0% Hispanic of any race; Average household size: 3.15; Median age: 42.1; Age under 18: 24.7%; Age 65 and over: 15.0%; Males per 100 females: 94.0; Marriage status: 28.7% never married, 61.0% now married, 0.7% separated, 4.6% widowed, 5.7% divorced; Foreign born: 15.8%; Speak English only: 78.8%; With disability: 8.9%; Veterans: 4.6%; Ancestry: 28.7% Italian, 21.4% Irish, 13.5% German, 6.8% Polish, 6.1% English

Employment: 20.0% management, business, and financial, 6.7% computer, engineering, and science, 14.6% education, legal, community service, arts, and media, 7.5% healthcare practitioners, 12.7% service, 26.0% sales and office, 6.0% natural resources, construction, and maintenance, 6.6% production, transportation, and material moving

Income: Per capita: $45,899; Median household: $111,675; Average household: $141,605; Households with income of $100,000 or more: 55.8%; Poverty rate: 4.3%

Educational Attainment: High school diploma or higher: 94.1%; Bachelor's degree or higher: 46.7%; Graduate/professional degree or higher: 18.5%

School District(s)

Elwood Union Free SD (KG-12)

   Enrollment: 2,227 . . . . (631) 266-5400

Housing: Homeownership rate: 92.8%; Median home value: $494,100; Median year structure built: 1964; Homeowner vacancy rate: 0.6%; Median selected monthly owner costs: $3,331 with a mortgage, $1,451 without a mortgage; Median gross rent: $2,142 per month; Rental vacancy rate: 7.4%

Health Insurance: 97.2% have insurance; 83.3% have private insurance; 26.9% have public insurance; 2.8% do not have insurance; 2.5% of children under 18 do not have insurance

Transportation: Commute: 84.4% car, 9.1% public transportation, 1.0% walk, 3.8% work from home; Mean travel time to work: 33.3 minutes

FARMINGVILLE (CDP). Covers a land area of 4.124 square miles and a water area of 0 square miles. Located at 40.84° N. Lat; 73.04° W. Long. Elevation is 105 feet.

Population: 15,250; Growth (since 2000): -7.3%; Density: 3,697.9 persons per square mile; Race: 85.9% White, 2.1% Black/African American, 6.2% Asian, 0.0% American Indian/Alaska Native, 0.0% Native Hawaiian/Other Pacific Islander, 2.0% Two or more races, 14.0% Hispanic of any race; Average household size: 3.27; Median age: 38.9; Age under 18: 21.6%; Age 65 and over: 12.0%; Males per 100 females: 99.7; Marriage status: 31.8% never married, 56.4% now married, 1.8% separated, 5.3% widowed, 6.5% divorced; Foreign born: 12.4%; Speak English only: 78.6%; With disability: 9.5%; Veterans: 5.3%; Ancestry: 30.3% Italian, 18.9% Irish, 16.3% German, 5.1% Polish, 3.9% American

Employment: 11.3% management, business, and financial, 6.6% computer, engineering, and science, 7.3% education, legal, community service, arts, and media, 7.0% healthcare practitioners, 20.2% service, 26.1% sales and office, 10.5% natural resources, construction, and maintenance, 11.1% production, transportation, and material moving

Income: Per capita: $35,683; Median household: $94,852; Average household: $111,206; Households with income of $100,000 or more: 48.5%; Poverty rate: 4.1%

Educational Attainment: High school diploma or higher: 91.3%; Bachelor's degree or higher: 25.9%; Graduate/professional degree or higher: 8.8%

School District(s)

Sachem Central SD (KG-12)

   Enrollment: 13,427 . . . . (631) 471-1336

Housing: Homeownership rate: 86.7%; Median home value: $332,900; Median year structure built: 1971; Homeowner vacancy rate: 1.5%; Median selected monthly owner costs: $2,440 with a mortgage, $1,123 without a mortgage; Median gross rent: $1,750 per month; Rental vacancy rate: 0.0%

Health Insurance: 93.6% have insurance; 79.0% have private insurance; 25.4% have public insurance; 6.4% do not have insurance; 2.3% of children under 18 do not have insurance

Transportation: Commute: 92.9% car, 3.2% public transportation, 0.6% walk, 2.4% work from home; Mean travel time to work: 35.1 minutes

FIRE ISLAND (CDP). Covers a land area of 9.226 square miles and a water area of 29.044 square miles. Located at 40.64° N. Lat; 73.20° W. Long. Elevation is 3 feet.

Population: 246; Growth (since 2000): -20.6%; Density: 26.7 persons per square mile; Race: 94.3% White, 0.0% Black/African American, 2.8% Asian, 0.4% American Indian/Alaska Native, 0.0% Native Hawaiian/Other Pacific Islander, 0.0% Two or more races, 24.8% Hispanic of any race; Average household size: 3.23; Median age: 38.8; Age under 18: 24.0%; Age 65 and over: 15.0%; Males per 100 females: 121.2; Marriage status: 27.3% never married, 61.9% now married, 0.5% separated, 6.2% widowed, 4.6% divorced; Foreign born: 21.5%; Speak English only: 70.5%;

With disability: 13.1%; Veterans: 9.0%; Ancestry: 13.4% Italian, 11.8% Irish, 10.6% German, 8.9% American, 5.3% Polish
Employment: 12.5% management, business, and financial, 7.5% computer, engineering, and science, 13.3% education, legal, community service, arts, and media, 5.8% healthcare practitioners, 11.7% service, 23.3% sales and office, 11.7% natural resources, construction, and maintenance, 14.2% production, transportation, and material moving
Income: Per capita: $36,205; Median household: $98,125; Average household: $109,448; Households with income of $100,000 or more: 48.0%; Poverty rate: 10.6%
Educational Attainment: High school diploma or higher: 82.0%; Bachelor's degree or higher: 36.5%; Graduate/professional degree or higher: 18.0%
Housing: Homeownership rate: 81.3%; Median home value: $490,000; Median year structure built: 1966; Homeowner vacancy rate: 1.6%; Median selected monthly owner costs: $3,167 with a mortgage, $817 without a mortgage; Median gross rent: $1,625 per month; Rental vacancy rate: 0.0%
Health Insurance: 94.1% have insurance; 79.3% have private insurance; 26.6% have public insurance; 5.9% do not have insurance; 4.7% of children under 18 do not have insurance
Transportation: Commute: 75.4% car, 1.6% public transportation, 4.0% walk, 8.7% work from home; Mean travel time to work: 26.1 minutes

FISHERS ISLAND (CDP).
Covers a land area of 4.076 square miles and a water area of 0.147 square miles. Located at 41.27° N. Lat; 71.97° W. Long. Elevation is 16 feet.
Population: 230; Growth (since 2000): -20.4%; Density: 56.4 persons per square mile; Race: 97.0% White, 0.0% Black/African American, 0.0% Asian, 0.0% American Indian/Alaska Native, 0.0% Native Hawaiian/Other Pacific Islander, 1.7% Two or more races, 1.3% Hispanic of any race; Average household size: 2.90; Median age: 52.5; Age under 18: 20.4%; Age 65 and over: 23.0%; Males per 100 females: 100.0; Marriage status: 17.8% never married, 69.2% now married, 1.1% separated, 10.3% widowed, 2.7% divorced; Foreign born: 1.7%; Speak English only: 92.9%; With disability: 3.0%; Veterans: 13.7%; Ancestry: 17.8% Irish, 17.0% English, 10.0% Italian, 9.6% Polish, 7.0% French
Employment: 14.5% management, business, and financial, 0.0% computer, engineering, and science, 8.4% education, legal, community service, arts, and media, 1.5% healthcare practitioners, 9.9% service, 39.7% sales and office, 12.2% natural resources, construction, and maintenance, 13.7% production, transportation, and material moving
Income: Per capita: $53,707; Median household: $150,703; Average household: $154,456; Households with income of $100,000 or more: 68.9%; Poverty rate: 0.9%
Educational Attainment: High school diploma or higher: 96.6%; Bachelor's degree or higher: 52.5%; Graduate/professional degree or higher: 33.5%

School District(s)
Fishers Island Union Free School District (PK-12)
    Enrollment: 67 . . . . (631) 788-7444
Housing: Homeownership rate: 66.2%; Median home value: $1,179,700; Median year structure built: 1945; Homeowner vacancy rate: 0.0%; Median selected monthly owner costs: n/a with a mortgage, $1,501 without a mortgage; Median gross rent: $1,388 per month; Rental vacancy rate: 39.5%
Health Insurance: 87.8% have insurance; 83.0% have private insurance; 26.1% have public insurance; 12.2% do not have insurance; 0.0% of children under 18 do not have insurance
Transportation: Commute: 40.5% car, 19.8% public transportation, 38.2% walk, 1.5% work from home; Mean travel time to work: 13.4 minutes
Airports: Elizabeth Field (general aviation)

FLANDERS (CDP).
Covers a land area of 11.461 square miles and a water area of 0.174 square miles. Located at 40.89° N. Lat; 72.61° W. Long. Elevation is 7 feet.
Population: 5,144; Growth (since 2000): 41.1%; Density: 448.8 persons per square mile; Race: 89.2% White, 8.1% Black/African American, 1.8% Asian, 0.0% American Indian/Alaska Native, 0.0% Native Hawaiian/Other Pacific Islander, 0.8% Two or more races, 58.1% Hispanic of any race; Average household size: 3.66; Median age: 36.1; Age under 18: 34.5%; Age 65 and over: 7.7%; Males per 100 females: 114.6; Marriage status: 35.7% never married, 49.3% now married, 3.0% separated, 6.1% widowed, 8.9% divorced; Foreign born: 34.0%; Speak English only: 39.4%

With disability: 5.4%; Veterans: 2.1%; Ancestry: 7.9% French, 5.9% German, 4.8% Russian, 4.6% Polish, 4.3% Norwegian
Employment: 2.0% management, business, and financial, 0.0% computer, engineering, and science, 6.5% education, legal, community service, arts, and media, 9.0% healthcare practitioners, 23.7% service, 16.6% sales and office, 40.4% natural resources, construction, and maintenance, 1.9% production, transportation, and material moving
Income: Per capita: $27,981; Median household: $75,735; Average household: $93,561; Households with income of $100,000 or more: 39.6%; Poverty rate: 8.7%
Educational Attainment: High school diploma or higher: 84.8%; Bachelor's degree or higher: 18.1%; Graduate/professional degree or higher: 9.9%
Housing: Homeownership rate: 80.9%; Median home value: $291,400; Median year structure built: 1967; Homeowner vacancy rate: 0.0%; Median selected monthly owner costs: $2,145 with a mortgage, $662 without a mortgage; Median gross rent: $2,127 per month; Rental vacancy rate: 0.0%
Health Insurance: 71.3% have insurance; 37.3% have private insurance; 40.8% have public insurance; 28.7% do not have insurance; 9.8% of children under 18 do not have insurance
Transportation: Commute: 89.0% car, 6.8% public transportation, 1.1% walk, 3.1% work from home; Mean travel time to work: 22.8 minutes

FORT SALONGA (CDP).
Covers a land area of 9.829 square miles and a water area of 0.111 square miles. Located at 40.90° N. Lat; 73.30° W. Long. Elevation is 33 feet.
History: The name evolved from the Revolutionary War British Fort Salonga, or Fort Slongo, (named after one of the fort's architects) once located near the border of Huntington Township and The Town of Smithtown, overlooking the Long Island Sound.
Population: 10,155; Growth (since 2000): 5.4%; Density: 1,033.1 persons per square mile; Race: 96.5% White, 0.6% Black/African American, 1.2% Asian, 0.0% American Indian/Alaska Native, 0.0% Native Hawaiian/Other Pacific Islander, 1.0% Two or more races, 5.5% Hispanic of any race; Average household size: 2.89; Median age: 47.6; Age under 18: 22.8%; Age 65 and over: 20.0%; Males per 100 females: 100.5; Marriage status: 26.2% never married, 62.0% now married, 0.6% separated, 7.0% widowed, 4.7% divorced; Foreign born: 5.1%; Speak English only: 93.6%; With disability: 7.7%; Veterans: 6.5%; Ancestry: 33.0% Italian, 20.8% Irish, 20.7% German, 8.8% Polish, 7.1% English
Employment: 22.2% management, business, and financial, 6.0% computer, engineering, and science, 21.1% education, legal, community service, arts, and media, 7.4% healthcare practitioners, 10.6% service, 19.5% sales and office, 10.8% natural resources, construction, and maintenance, 2.4% production, transportation, and material moving
Income: Per capita: $60,471; Median household: $131,818; Average household: $175,105; Households with income of $100,000 or more: 66.3%; Poverty rate: 6.4%
Educational Attainment: High school diploma or higher: 98.2%; Bachelor's degree or higher: 52.7%; Graduate/professional degree or higher: 25.4%
Housing: Homeownership rate: 93.0%; Median home value: $678,300; Median year structure built: 1965; Homeowner vacancy rate: 2.2%; Median selected monthly owner costs: $3,671 with a mortgage, $1,501 without a mortgage; Median gross rent: $1,777 per month; Rental vacancy rate: 0.0%
Health Insurance: 96.4% have insurance; 85.4% have private insurance; 24.1% have public insurance; 3.6% do not have insurance; 1.2% of children under 18 do not have insurance
Transportation: Commute: 84.2% car, 8.5% public transportation, 0.0% walk, 6.1% work from home; Mean travel time to work: 39.7 minutes

GILGO (CDP).
Covers a land area of 4.996 square miles and a water area of 6.707 square miles. Located at 40.64° N. Lat; 73.38° W. Long.
Population: 146; Growth (since 2000): n/a; Density: 29.2 persons per square mile; Race: 100.0% White, 0.0% Black/African American, 0.0% Asian, 0.0% American Indian/Alaska Native, 0.0% Native Hawaiian/Other Pacific Islander, 0.0% Two or more races, 0.0% Hispanic of any race; Average household size: 2.61; Median age: 70.1; Age under 18: 6.8%; Age 65 and over: 51.4%; Males per 100 females: 118.3; Marriage status: 17.6% never married, 82.4% now married, 0.0% separated, 0.0% widowed, 0.0% divorced; Foreign born: 0.0%; Speak English only: 100.0%; With disability: 19.2%; Veterans: 20.6%; Ancestry: 61.6% German, 61.6% Italian, 32.2% English, 13.0% Welsh, 6.2% Scottish

Employment: 40.4% management, business, and financial, 0.0% computer, engineering, and science, 42.3% education, legal, community service, arts, and media, 17.3% healthcare practitioners, 0.0% service, 0.0% sales and office, 0.0% natural resources, construction, and maintenance, 0.0% production, transportation, and material moving
Income: Per capita: $40,413; Median household: n/a; Average household: $100,502; Households with income of $100,000 or more: 32.2%; Poverty rate: n/a
Educational Attainment: High school diploma or higher: 100.0%; Bachelor's degree or higher: 86.8%; Graduate/professional degree or higher: 55.1%
Housing: Homeownership rate: 100.0%; Median home value: $375,700; Median year structure built: Before 1940; Homeowner vacancy rate: 0.0%; Median selected monthly owner costs: n/a with a mortgage, $1,284 without a mortgage; Median gross rent: n/a per month; Rental vacancy rate: 0.0%
Health Insurance: 100.0% have insurance; 100.0% have private insurance; 51.4% have public insurance; 0.0% do not have insurance; 0.0% of children under 18 do not have insurance
Transportation: Commute: 82.7% car, 17.3% public transportation, 0.0% walk, 0.0% work from home; Mean travel time to work: 0.0 minutes

GORDON HEIGHTS (CDP). Covers a land area of 1.705 square miles and a water area of 0.014 square miles. Located at 40.86° N. Lat; 72.96° W. Long. Elevation is 154 feet.
Population: 3,573; Growth (since 2000): 15.5%; Density: 2,095.9 persons per square mile; Race: 49.2% White, 42.6% Black/African American, 0.7% Asian, 0.0% American Indian/Alaska Native, 1.3% Native Hawaiian/Other Pacific Islander, 2.9% Two or more races, 33.0% Hispanic of any race; Average household size: 3.34; Median age: 29.5; Age under 18: 31.2%; Age 65 and over: 6.2%; Males per 100 females: 100.2; Marriage status: 54.2% never married, 30.7% now married, 3.6% separated, 2.9% widowed, 12.3% divorced; Foreign born: 16.7%; Speak English only: 72.4%; With disability: 12.5%; Veterans: 3.3%; Ancestry: 6.8% Italian, 4.8% French, 3.7% German, 3.1% American, 3.1% Irish
Employment: 5.8% management, business, and financial, 6.0% computer, engineering, and science, 11.9% education, legal, community service, arts, and media, 9.8% healthcare practitioners, 24.8% service, 21.2% sales and office, 7.1% natural resources, construction, and maintenance, 13.5% production, transportation, and material moving
Income: Per capita: $24,637; Median household: $71,214; Average household: $79,559; Households with income of $100,000 or more: 31.9%; Poverty rate: 16.1%
Educational Attainment: High school diploma or higher: 86.4%; Bachelor's degree or higher: 21.4%; Graduate/professional degree or higher: 11.0%
Housing: Homeownership rate: 69.5%; Median home value: $255,400; Median year structure built: 1990; Homeowner vacancy rate: 4.1%; Median selected monthly owner costs: $2,297 with a mortgage, $1,138 without a mortgage; Median gross rent: $1,701 per month; Rental vacancy rate: 0.0%
Health Insurance: 92.2% have insurance; 58.0% have private insurance; 42.1% have public insurance; 7.8% do not have insurance; 0.0% of children under 18 do not have insurance
Transportation: Commute: 93.4% car, 4.3% public transportation, 0.0% walk, 1.5% work from home; Mean travel time to work: 29.1 minutes

GREAT RIVER (CDP). Covers a land area of 4.597 square miles and a water area of 0.595 square miles. Located at 40.72° N. Lat; 73.16° W. Long. Elevation is 13 feet.
Population: 1,441; Growth (since 2000): -6.8%; Density: 313.5 persons per square mile; Race: 98.4% White, 0.0% Black/African American, 1.0% Asian, 0.0% American Indian/Alaska Native, 0.0% Native Hawaiian/Other Pacific Islander, 0.6% Two or more races, 4.4% Hispanic of any race; Average household size: 3.15; Median age: 45.4; Age under 18: 25.6%; Age 65 and over: 13.5%; Males per 100 females: 105.4; Marriage status: 27.7% never married, 63.5% now married, 0.2% separated, 6.7% widowed, 2.2% divorced; Foreign born: 3.9%; Speak English only: 94.6%; With disability: 7.1%; Veterans: 5.9%; Ancestry: 37.3% Irish, 30.0% Italian, 23.0% German, 11.9% English, 7.0% French
Employment: 29.6% management, business, and financial, 2.8% computer, engineering, and science, 28.8% education, legal, community service, arts, and media, 6.2% healthcare practitioners, 5.2% service, 17.7% sales and office, 4.2% natural resources, construction, and maintenance, 5.5% production, transportation, and material moving

Income: Per capita: $50,050; Median household: $117,443; Average household: $153,758; Households with income of $100,000 or more: 60.9%; Poverty rate: 5.0%
Educational Attainment: High school diploma or higher: 98.4%; Bachelor's degree or higher: 57.2%; Graduate/professional degree or higher: 36.0%
Housing: Homeownership rate: 87.5%; Median home value: $614,900; Median year structure built: 1964; Homeowner vacancy rate: 4.8%; Median selected monthly owner costs: $3,940 with a mortgage, $1,501 without a mortgage; Median gross rent: $2,040 per month; Rental vacancy rate: 0.0%
Health Insurance: 97.8% have insurance; 90.8% have private insurance; 17.5% have public insurance; 2.2% do not have insurance; 0.0% of children under 18 do not have insurance
Transportation: Commute: 88.9% car, 5.8% public transportation, 1.0% walk, 4.3% work from home; Mean travel time to work: 29.4 minutes

GREENLAWN (CDP). Covers a land area of 3.722 square miles and a water area of 0.003 square miles. Located at 40.86° N. Lat; 73.36° W. Long. Elevation is 226 feet.
Population: 13,850; Growth (since 2000): 4.2%; Density: 3,721.5 persons per square mile; Race: 72.2% White, 16.5% Black/African American, 3.6% Asian, 0.2% American Indian/Alaska Native, 0.0% Native Hawaiian/Other Pacific Islander, 2.8% Two or more races, 10.3% Hispanic of any race; Average household size: 3.07; Median age: 43.3; Age under 18: 25.5%; Age 65 and over: 19.1%; Males per 100 females: 92.4; Marriage status: 28.8% never married, 52.4% now married, 1.1% separated, 9.5% widowed, 9.3% divorced; Foreign born: 15.4%; Speak English only: 80.4%; With disability: 8.0%; Veterans: 5.5%; Ancestry: 19.7% Italian, 16.0% Irish, 15.1% German, 5.6% English, 5.3% American
Employment: 16.0% management, business, and financial, 5.3% computer, engineering, and science, 13.1% education, legal, community service, arts, and media, 7.9% healthcare practitioners, 19.4% service, 23.6% sales and office, 5.4% natural resources, construction, and maintenance, 9.2% production, transportation, and material moving
Income: Per capita: $41,222; Median household: $88,996; Average household: $123,768; Households with income of $100,000 or more: 43.6%; Poverty rate: 6.7%
Educational Attainment: High school diploma or higher: 92.0%; Bachelor's degree or higher: 42.8%; Graduate/professional degree or higher: 18.9%

School District(s)
Harborfields Central SD (KG-12)
    Enrollment: 3,217 . . . . (631) 754-5320
Housing: Homeownership rate: 80.6%; Median home value: $460,500; Median year structure built: 1960; Homeowner vacancy rate: 3.1%; Median selected monthly owner costs: $3,046 with a mortgage, $1,285 without a mortgage; Median gross rent: $684 per month; Rental vacancy rate: 7.1%
Health Insurance: 94.0% have insurance; 81.8% have private insurance; 24.8% have public insurance; 6.0% do not have insurance; 5.2% of children under 18 do not have insurance
Transportation: Commute: 86.9% car, 9.0% public transportation, 0.2% walk, 3.5% work from home; Mean travel time to work: 31.9 minutes

GREENPORT (village). Covers a land area of 0.956 square miles and a water area of 0.249 square miles. Located at 41.10° N. Lat; 72.37° W. Long. Elevation is 10 feet.
History: By 1840 pursuit of offshore whaling, practiced by both Native Americans and European residents, had turned into a way of industry with ships leaving Cold Springs Harbor, Sag Harbor, and Greenport on 3-year whaling voyages. Greenport Village Historic District. Incorporated 1838.
Population: 2,057; Growth (since 2000): 0.4%; Density: 2,151.9 persons per square mile; Race: 80.4% White, 14.7% Black/African American, 0.7% Asian, 0.0% American Indian/Alaska Native, 0.0% Native Hawaiian/Other Pacific Islander, 2.2% Two or more races, 21.1% Hispanic of any race; Average household size: 2.32; Median age: 46.5; Age under 18: 19.3%; Age 65 and over: 18.9%; Males per 100 females: 100.8; Marriage status: 33.1% never married, 43.5% now married, 1.2% separated, 11.3% widowed, 12.1% divorced; Foreign born: 17.2%; Speak English only: 80.5%; With disability: 11.8%; Veterans: 5.5%; Ancestry: 17.8% Irish, 11.7% German, 10.4% English, 10.3% Italian, 6.5% Polish
Employment: 7.1% management, business, and financial, 5.3% computer, engineering, and science, 9.1% education, legal, community service, arts, and media, 5.3% healthcare practitioners, 27.1% service, 26.0% sales and

office, 11.5% natural resources, construction, and maintenance, 8.6% production, transportation, and material moving

Income: Per capita: $34,211; Median household: $56,799; Average household: $80,495; Households with income of $100,000 or more: 25.8%; Poverty rate: 13.8%

Educational Attainment: High school diploma or higher: 82.4%; Bachelor's degree or higher: 29.8%; Graduate/professional degree or higher: 11.7%

School District(s)

Greenport Union Free SD (PK-12)
   Enrollment: 692 . . . . (631) 477-1950

Housing: Homeownership rate: 53.9%; Median home value: $510,000; Median year structure built: Before 1940; Homeowner vacancy rate: 6.5%; Median selected monthly owner costs: $2,382 with a mortgage, $752 without a mortgage; Median gross rent: $1,483 per month; Rental vacancy rate: 15.9%

Health Insurance: 85.3% have insurance; 64.1% have private insurance; 36.9% have public insurance; 14.7% do not have insurance; 2.6% of children under 18 do not have insurance

Hospitals: Eastern Long Island Hospital (90 beds)

Transportation: Commute: 74.9% car, 6.7% public transportation, 12.1% walk, 3.3% work from home; Mean travel time to work: 23.8 minutes

GREENPORT WEST (CDP). Covers a land area of 3.209 square miles and a water area of 0.125 square miles. Located at 41.09° N. Lat; 72.39° W. Long. Elevation is 7 feet.

Population: 2,064; Growth (since 2000): 22.9%; Density: 643.1 persons per square mile; Race: 97.1% White, 1.7% Black/African American, 0.0% Asian, 0.0% American Indian/Alaska Native, 0.0% Native Hawaiian/Other Pacific Islander, 1.1% Two or more races, 18.5% Hispanic of any race; Average household size: 2.13; Median age: 60.0; Age under 18: 9.6%; Age 65 and over: 41.6%; Males per 100 females: 82.8; Marriage status: 25.3% never married, 57.0% now married, 1.0% separated, 12.6% widowed, 5.2% divorced; Foreign born: 14.1%; Speak English only: 79.0%; With disability: 15.6%; Veterans: 9.3%; Ancestry: 18.9% Italian, 13.8% German, 12.7% Irish, 11.0% Polish, 10.8% English

Employment: 20.7% management, business, and financial, 4.2% computer, engineering, and science, 17.9% education, legal, community service, arts, and media, 2.5% healthcare practitioners, 19.3% service, 18.9% sales and office, 6.8% natural resources, construction, and maintenance, 9.6% production, transportation, and material moving

Income: Per capita: $48,985; Median household: $63,355; Average household: $106,396; Households with income of $100,000 or more: 30.7%; Poverty rate: 12.2%

Educational Attainment: High school diploma or higher: 92.8%; Bachelor's degree or higher: 41.7%; Graduate/professional degree or higher: 23.1%

Housing: Homeownership rate: 76.6%; Median home value: $478,400; Median year structure built: 1985; Homeowner vacancy rate: 1.1%; Median selected monthly owner costs: $2,113 with a mortgage, $856 without a mortgage; Median gross rent: $1,135 per month; Rental vacancy rate: 12.3%

Health Insurance: 91.8% have insurance; 70.0% have private insurance; 57.9% have public insurance; 8.2% do not have insurance; 0.0% of children under 18 do not have insurance

Transportation: Commute: 71.8% car, 7.6% public transportation, 7.5% walk, 8.4% work from home; Mean travel time to work: 26.1 minutes

HALESITE (CDP). Covers a land area of 0.889 square miles and a water area of 0.092 square miles. Located at 40.89° N. Lat; 73.41° W. Long. Elevation is 26 feet.

Population: 2,770; Growth (since 2000): 7.3%; Density: 3,116.3 persons per square mile; Race: 96.6% White, 2.1% Black/African American, 1.3% Asian, 0.0% American Indian/Alaska Native, 0.0% Native Hawaiian/Other Pacific Islander, 0.0% Two or more races, 9.1% Hispanic of any race; Average household size: 2.59; Median age: 46.5; Age under 18: 23.1%; Age 65 and over: 17.9%; Males per 100 females: 101.0; Marriage status: 18.5% never married, 62.0% now married, 1.1% separated, 7.0% widowed, 12.5% divorced; Foreign born: 12.0%; Speak English only: 89.8%; With disability: 5.0%; Veterans: 6.3%; Ancestry: 26.6% Irish, 25.8% Italian, 13.8% German, 9.4% American, 7.8% English

Employment: 19.5% management, business, and financial, 5.1% computer, engineering, and science, 30.5% education, legal, community service, arts, and media, 5.4% healthcare practitioners, 6.9% service,

24.3% sales and office, 3.4% natural resources, construction, and maintenance, 4.9% production, transportation, and material moving

Income: Per capita: $61,348; Median household: $126,651; Average household: $156,968; Households with income of $100,000 or more: 70.3%; Poverty rate: 1.2%

Educational Attainment: High school diploma or higher: 98.4%; Bachelor's degree or higher: 58.6%; Graduate/professional degree or higher: 34.0%

Housing: Homeownership rate: 88.9%; Median home value: $570,900; Median year structure built: 1953; Homeowner vacancy rate: 0.0%; Median selected monthly owner costs: $3,267 with a mortgage, $1,331 without a mortgage; Median gross rent: $1,995 per month; Rental vacancy rate: 0.0%

Health Insurance: 99.1% have insurance; 89.4% have private insurance; 19.6% have public insurance; 0.9% do not have insurance; 0.0% of children under 18 do not have insurance

Transportation: Commute: 80.2% car, 10.9% public transportation, 2.0% walk, 6.9% work from home; Mean travel time to work: 32.2 minutes

HAMPTON BAYS (CDP). Covers a land area of 12.954 square miles and a water area of 5.174 square miles. Located at 40.87° N. Lat; 72.52° W. Long. Elevation is 33 feet.

History: Until 1922 called Good Ground.

Population: 13,457; Growth (since 2000): 10.0%; Density: 1,038.9 persons per square mile; Race: 91.7% White, 1.2% Black/African American, 0.3% Asian, 0.0% American Indian/Alaska Native, 0.0% Native Hawaiian/Other Pacific Islander, 2.6% Two or more races, 28.6% Hispanic of any race; Average household size: 2.53; Median age: 43.8; Age under 18: 18.6%; Age 65 and over: 18.4%; Males per 100 females: 106.0; Marriage status: 29.5% never married, 53.4% now married, 1.5% separated, 8.4% widowed, 8.7% divorced; Foreign born: 26.0%; Speak English only: 68.3%; With disability: 11.2%; Veterans: 6.4%; Ancestry: 20.7% Irish, 16.1% Italian, 13.2% German, 7.3% English, 6.7% Polish

Employment: 10.3% management, business, and financial, 2.2% computer, engineering, and science, 9.6% education, legal, community service, arts, and media, 5.9% healthcare practitioners, 25.4% service, 21.5% sales and office, 18.3% natural resources, construction, and maintenance, 6.7% production, transportation, and material moving

Income: Per capita: $41,535; Median household: $77,447; Average household: $101,687; Households with income of $100,000 or more: 35.8%; Poverty rate: 7.4%

Educational Attainment: High school diploma or higher: 90.7%; Bachelor's degree or higher: 33.1%; Graduate/professional degree or higher: 13.6%

School District(s)

Hampton Bays Union Free SD (PK-12)
   Enrollment: 2,096 . . . . (631) 723-2100

Housing: Homeownership rate: 70.8%; Median home value: $433,900; Median year structure built: 1973; Homeowner vacancy rate: 1.7%; Median selected monthly owner costs: $2,571 with a mortgage, $962 without a mortgage; Median gross rent: $1,705 per month; Rental vacancy rate: 0.0%

Health Insurance: 84.8% have insurance; 64.8% have private insurance; 34.8% have public insurance; 15.2% do not have insurance; 5.0% of children under 18 do not have insurance

Transportation: Commute: 88.0% car, 4.9% public transportation, 1.7% walk, 4.0% work from home; Mean travel time to work: 30.2 minutes

HAUPPAUGE (CDP). Covers a land area of 10.713 square miles and a water area of 0.148 square miles. Located at 40.82° N. Lat; 73.21° W. Long. Elevation is 62 feet.

History: Happague's name derives from the Native American Algonquian term for "overflowed land."

Population: 19,852; Growth (since 2000): -1.2%; Density: 1,853.1 persons per square mile; Race: 86.5% White, 4.2% Black/African American, 6.3% Asian, 0.1% American Indian/Alaska Native, 0.0% Native Hawaiian/Other Pacific Islander, 1.1% Two or more races, 6.6% Hispanic of any race; Average household size: 2.83; Median age: 45.0; Age under 18: 21.2%; Age 65 and over: 18.3%; Males per 100 females: 96.4; Marriage status: 26.7% never married, 60.2% now married, 1.4% separated, 6.9% widowed, 6.3% divorced; Foreign born: 12.7%; Speak English only: 82.7%; With disability: 9.3%; Veterans: 6.6%; Ancestry: 31.7% Italian, 18.4% Irish, 14.9% German, 5.0% Polish, 3.9% American

Employment: 18.6% management, business, and financial, 7.4% computer, engineering, and science, 13.2% education, legal, community

service, arts, and media, 6.3% healthcare practitioners, 13.8% service, 27.4% sales and office, 6.5% natural resources, construction, and maintenance, 6.8% production, transportation, and material moving
Income: Per capita: $45,228; Median household: $108,547; Average household: $124,898; Households with income of $100,000 or more: 55.0%; Poverty rate: 3.2%
Educational Attainment: High school diploma or higher: 96.6%; Bachelor's degree or higher: 45.9%; Graduate/professional degree or higher: 21.1%

School District(s)
Hauppauge Union Free SD (KG-12)
   Enrollment: 3,609 . . . . (631) 761-8208
Vocational/Technical School(s)
Long Island Beauty School-Hauppauge (Private, For-profit)
   Enrollment: 198 . . . . (631) 724-0440
   Tuition: $13,200
Housing: Homeownership rate: 83.9%; Median home value: $459,500; Median year structure built: 1968; Homeowner vacancy rate: 1.7%; Median selected monthly owner costs: $2,968 with a mortgage, $1,230 without a mortgage; Median gross rent: $1,972 per month; Rental vacancy rate: 8.8%
Health Insurance: 96.9% have insurance; 86.6% have private insurance; 24.7% have public insurance; 3.1% do not have insurance; 2.2% of children under 18 do not have insurance
Transportation: Commute: 89.2% car, 5.7% public transportation, 0.4% walk, 3.2% work from home; Mean travel time to work: 31.6 minutes

HEAD OF THE HARBOR (village). Covers a land area of 2.807 square miles and a water area of 0.228 square miles. Located at 40.90° N. Lat; 73.16° W. Long. Elevation is 121 feet.
Population: 1,308; Growth (since 2000): -9.6%; Density: 466.0 persons per square mile; Race: 90.7% White, 2.6% Black/African American, 4.4% Asian, 0.0% American Indian/Alaska Native, 0.0% Native Hawaiian/Other Pacific Islander, 1.4% Two or more races, 7.9% Hispanic of any race; Average household size: 2.77; Median age: 48.0; Age under 18: 17.2%; Age 65 and over: 20.9%; Males per 100 females: 102.2; Marriage status: 34.3% never married, 55.9% now married, 0.9% separated, 6.3% widowed, 3.5% divorced; Foreign born: 10.3%; Speak English only: 89.9%; With disability: 10.5%; Veterans: 5.6%; Ancestry: 20.3% Italian, 18.7% German, 18.0% Irish, 8.9% English, 5.0% Russian
Employment: 31.0% management, business, and financial, 7.3% computer, engineering, and science, 18.2% education, legal, community service, arts, and media, 12.5% healthcare practitioners, 8.3% service, 18.6% sales and office, 0.0% natural resources, construction, and maintenance, 4.1% production, transportation, and material moving
Income: Per capita: $98,078; Median household: $156,250; Average household: $264,318; Households with income of $100,000 or more: 70.4%; Poverty rate: 5.0%
Educational Attainment: High school diploma or higher: 97.7%; Bachelor's degree or higher: 65.5%; Graduate/professional degree or higher: 36.9%
Housing: Homeownership rate: 90.3%; Median home value: $887,600; Median year structure built: 1967; Homeowner vacancy rate: 3.8%; Median selected monthly owner costs: $4,000+ with a mortgage, $1,501 without a mortgage; Median gross rent: $2,025 per month; Rental vacancy rate: 0.0%
Health Insurance: 97.1% have insurance; 88.9% have private insurance; 22.2% have public insurance; 2.9% do not have insurance; 2.7% of children under 18 do not have insurance
Transportation: Commute: 86.4% car, 2.9% public transportation, 0.0% walk, 10.2% work from home; Mean travel time to work: 28.5 minutes

HOLBROOK (CDP). Covers a land area of 7.183 square miles and a water area of 0 square miles. Located at 40.79° N. Lat; 73.07° W. Long. Elevation is 118 feet.
History: Holbrook is located in the towns of Islip and Brookhaven, divided by the Main Line of the Long Island Rail Road.
Population: 26,117; Growth (since 2000): -5.1%; Density: 3,636.1 persons per square mile; Race: 92.4% White, 2.6% Black/African American, 2.1% Asian, 0.5% American Indian/Alaska Native, 0.2% Native Hawaiian/Other Pacific Islander, 1.8% Two or more races, 9.5% Hispanic of any race; Average household size: 2.95; Median age: 42.4; Age under 18: 21.2%; Age 65 and over: 15.1%; Males per 100 females: 93.2; Marriage status: 30.2% never married, 55.9% now married, 1.0% separated, 5.4% widowed, 8.6% divorced; Foreign born: 6.0%; Speak English only: 91.2%;

With disability: 10.3%; Veterans: 6.5%; Ancestry: 35.6% Italian, 23.8% Irish, 19.3% German, 5.6% Polish, 4.2% English
Employment: 13.9% management, business, and financial, 4.0% computer, engineering, and science, 13.2% education, legal, community service, arts, and media, 5.6% healthcare practitioners, 17.5% service, 30.2% sales and office, 8.6% natural resources, construction, and maintenance, 6.9% production, transportation, and material moving
Income: Per capita: $39,825; Median household: $98,242; Average household: $113,698; Households with income of $100,000 or more: 48.2%; Poverty rate: 3.1%
Educational Attainment: High school diploma or higher: 94.8%; Bachelor's degree or higher: 33.3%; Graduate/professional degree or higher: 14.2%

School District(s)
Sachem Central SD (KG-12)
   Enrollment: 13,427 . . . . (631) 471-1336
Housing: Homeownership rate: 80.8%; Median home value: $359,100; Median year structure built: 1975; Homeowner vacancy rate: 0.0%; Median selected monthly owner costs: $2,532 with a mortgage, $1,046 without a mortgage; Median gross rent: $1,890 per month; Rental vacancy rate: 6.9%
Health Insurance: 95.7% have insurance; 87.1% have private insurance; 24.0% have public insurance; 4.3% do not have insurance; 3.0% of children under 18 do not have insurance
Transportation: Commute: 90.5% car, 5.4% public transportation, 0.6% walk, 2.6% work from home; Mean travel time to work: 32.2 minutes

HOLTSVILLE (CDP). Covers a land area of 7.113 square miles and a water area of 0 square miles. Located at 40.81° N. Lat; 73.04° W. Long. Elevation is 105 feet.
History: Holtsville included only a few farmhouses until 1843, when the Long Island Rail Road opened its Waverly Station. As another post office named Waverly already existed in Upstate New York, the name of the hamlet was changed to Holtsville in 1860, in honor of U.S. Postmaster General Joseph Holt.
Population: 20,201; Growth (since 2000): 18.8%; Density: 2,840.0 persons per square mile; Race: 89.7% White, 3.5% Black/African American, 3.6% Asian, 0.0% American Indian/Alaska Native, 0.0% Native Hawaiian/Other Pacific Islander, 2.0% Two or more races, 14.7% Hispanic of any race; Average household size: 3.01; Median age: 41.4; Age under 18: 22.0%; Age 65 and over: 13.0%; Males per 100 females: 93.5; Marriage status: 30.2% never married, 57.0% now married, 1.3% separated, 4.5% widowed, 8.3% divorced; Foreign born: 10.9%; Speak English only: 82.7%; With disability: 9.2%; Veterans: 5.9%; Ancestry: 31.8% Italian, 23.3% Irish, 18.1% German, 6.4% English, 5.8% Polish
Employment: 15.9% management, business, and financial, 5.9% computer, engineering, and science, 10.9% education, legal, community service, arts, and media, 6.6% healthcare practitioners, 14.9% service, 25.6% sales and office, 10.4% natural resources, construction, and maintenance, 9.7% production, transportation, and material moving
Income: Per capita: $40,751; Median household: $98,955; Average household: $118,327; Households with income of $100,000 or more: 49.3%; Poverty rate: 5.2%
Educational Attainment: High school diploma or higher: 92.7%; Bachelor's degree or higher: 29.8%; Graduate/professional degree or higher: 12.1%

School District(s)
Sachem Central SD (KG-12)
   Enrollment: 13,427 . . . . (631) 471-1336
Housing: Homeownership rate: 79.3%; Median home value: $350,100; Median year structure built: 1976; Homeowner vacancy rate: 0.6%; Median selected monthly owner costs: $2,510 with a mortgage, $1,066 without a mortgage; Median gross rent: $1,636 per month; Rental vacancy rate: 5.1%
Health Insurance: 94.9% have insurance; 83.6% have private insurance; 22.2% have public insurance; 5.1% do not have insurance; 2.9% of children under 18 do not have insurance
Transportation: Commute: 91.8% car, 4.7% public transportation, 0.5% walk, 3.0% work from home; Mean travel time to work: 33.0 minutes

HUNTINGTON (CDP). Covers a land area of 7.594 square miles and a water area of 0.140 square miles. Located at 40.88° N. Lat; 73.41° W. Long. Elevation is 75 feet.
History: The central business district, called Huntington Village locally, is old and well developed, but it is not incorporated and does not have a

village form of government. Huntington is the birthplace of singer Mariah Carey and actor Ralph Macchio. It is also where world-renowned jazz musicians John Coltrane and his wife Alice Coltrane (harpist and pianist) lived in the later years of their life together; he died in Huntington in 1967.
Population: 17,371; Growth (since 2000): -5.6%; Density: 2,287.6 persons per square mile; Race: 92.6% White, 1.9% Black/African American, 3.1% Asian, 0.0% American Indian/Alaska Native, 0.0% Native Hawaiian/Other Pacific Islander, 1.0% Two or more races, 6.9% Hispanic of any race; Average household size: 2.46; Median age: 47.1; Age under 18: 19.0%; Age 65 and over: 19.4%; Males per 100 females: 96.5; Marriage status: 27.1% never married, 57.4% now married, 1.9% separated, 6.2% widowed, 9.4% divorced; Foreign born: 10.5%; Speak English only: 89.7%; With disability: 6.9%; Veterans: 6.0%; Ancestry: 27.7% Italian, 23.9% Irish, 16.3% German, 8.0% English, 6.3% American
Employment: 24.8% management, business, and financial, 8.6% computer, engineering, and science, 22.4% education, legal, community service, arts, and media, 6.0% healthcare practitioners, 9.0% service, 19.4% sales and office, 5.3% natural resources, construction, and maintenance, 4.6% production, transportation, and material moving
Income: Per capita: $62,445; Median household: $117,021; Average household: $152,620; Households with income of $100,000 or more: 55.2%; Poverty rate: 6.5%
Educational Attainment: High school diploma or higher: 97.0%; Bachelor's degree or higher: 62.4%; Graduate/professional degree or higher: 32.6%

School District(s)
Cold Spring Harbor Central SD (KG-12)
    Enrollment: 1,760 . . . . (631) 367-5931
Elwood Union Free SD (KG-12)
    Enrollment: 2,227 . . . . (631) 266-5400
Huntington Union Free SD (KG-12)
    Enrollment: 4,675 . . . . (631) 673-2038
South Huntington Union Free SD (KG-12)
    Enrollment: 6,091 . . . . (631) 812-3070
Housing: Homeownership rate: 82.1%; Median home value: $573,600; Median year structure built: 1955; Homeowner vacancy rate: 1.7%; Median selected monthly owner costs: $3,345 with a mortgage, $1,501 without a mortgage; Median gross rent: $1,893 per month; Rental vacancy rate: 6.9%
Health Insurance: 97.9% have insurance; 88.6% have private insurance; 23.9% have public insurance; 2.1% do not have insurance; 0.6% of children under 18 do not have insurance
Hospitals: Huntington Hospital (408 beds)
Newspapers: Long Islander Newspapers (weekly circulation 33,500)
Transportation: Commute: 75.5% car, 13.1% public transportation, 1.5% walk, 9.0% work from home; Mean travel time to work: 37.3 minutes

HUNTINGTON (town). Covers a land area of 94.123 square miles and a water area of 42.988 square miles. Located at 40.88° N. Lat; 73.38° W. Long. Elevation is 75 feet.
History: Named for Huntingdon, England, or to mean "hunting town" for its abundance of game. Seat of Immaculate Conception College, World Friends College. Settled 1653.
Population: 204,011; Growth (since 2000): 4.5%; Density: 2,167.5 persons per square mile; Race: 82.9% White, 4.8% Black/African American, 5.6% Asian, 0.1% American Indian/Alaska Native, 0.0% Native Hawaiian/Other Pacific Islander, 1.4% Two or more races, 12.2% Hispanic of any race; Average household size: 2.93; Median age: 44.3; Age under 18: 22.8%; Age 65 and over: 17.7%; Males per 100 females: 96.9; Marriage status: 28.0% never married, 58.4% now married, 1.3% separated, 6.5% widowed, 7.1% divorced; Foreign born: 13.9%; Speak English only: 80.7%; With disability: 7.7%; Veterans: 5.2%; Ancestry: 24.8% Italian, 18.2% Irish, 13.5% German, 5.4% Polish, 5.4% American
Employment: 20.0% management, business, and financial, 5.3% computer, engineering, and science, 17.0% education, legal, community service, arts, and media, 7.2% healthcare practitioners, 13.2% service, 25.0% sales and office, 6.4% natural resources, construction, and maintenance, 5.9% production, transportation, and material moving
Income: Per capita: $52,523; Median household: $112,790; Average household: $151,755; Households with income of $100,000 or more: 55.5%; Poverty rate: 6.4%
Educational Attainment: High school diploma or higher: 93.4%; Bachelor's degree or higher: 51.4%; Graduate/professional degree or higher: 24.4%

School District(s)
Cold Spring Harbor Central SD (KG-12)
    Enrollment: 1,760 . . . . (631) 367-5931
Elwood Union Free SD (KG-12)
    Enrollment: 2,227 . . . . (631) 266-5400
Huntington Union Free SD (KG-12)
    Enrollment: 4,675 . . . . (631) 673-2038
South Huntington Union Free SD (KG-12)
    Enrollment: 6,091 . . . . (631) 812-3070
Housing: Homeownership rate: 85.4%; Median home value: $520,600; Median year structure built: 1962; Homeowner vacancy rate: 1.7%; Median selected monthly owner costs: $3,208 with a mortgage, $1,384 without a mortgage; Median gross rent: $1,767 per month; Rental vacancy rate: 7.8%
Health Insurance: 95.0% have insurance; 82.5% have private insurance; 26.2% have public insurance; 5.0% do not have insurance; 3.1% of children under 18 do not have insurance
Hospitals: Huntington Hospital (408 beds)
Newspapers: Long Islander Newspapers (weekly circulation 33,500)
Transportation: Commute: 81.7% car, 10.3% public transportation, 1.3% walk, 5.5% work from home; Mean travel time to work: 34.6 minutes
Additional Information Contacts
Town of Huntington . . . . (631) 351-3206
   http://www.huntingtonny.gov

HUNTINGTON BAY (village). Covers a land area of 0.998 square miles and a water area of 0.897 square miles. Located at 40.90° N. Lat; 73.41° W. Long. Elevation is 16 feet.
History: Site of capture of Nathan Hale by British forces during American Revolution.
Population: 1,458; Growth (since 2000): -2.5%; Density: 1,460.6 persons per square mile; Race: 96.2% White, 0.0% Black/African American, 2.5% Asian, 0.6% American Indian/Alaska Native, 0.0% Native Hawaiian/Other Pacific Islander, 0.0% Two or more races, 0.5% Hispanic of any race; Average household size: 2.63; Median age: 52.9; Age under 18: 16.6%; Age 65 and over: 26.6%; Males per 100 females: 97.9; Marriage status: 25.7% never married, 60.9% now married, 1.3% separated, 7.8% widowed, 5.6% divorced; Foreign born: 9.1%; Speak English only: 89.5%; With disability: 5.7%; Veterans: 6.9%; Ancestry: 27.6% Italian, 23.9% Irish, 12.5% English, 11.7% German, 8.7% American
Employment: 37.0% management, business, and financial, 3.0% computer, engineering, and science, 17.0% education, legal, community service, arts, and media, 5.4% healthcare practitioners, 5.5% service, 28.0% sales and office, 1.7% natural resources, construction, and maintenance, 2.4% production, transportation, and material moving
Income: Per capita: $98,864; Median household: $183,500; Average household: $256,724; Households with income of $100,000 or more: 69.9%; Poverty rate: 7.3%
Educational Attainment: High school diploma or higher: 99.1%; Bachelor's degree or higher: 70.8%; Graduate/professional degree or higher: 30.3%
Housing: Homeownership rate: 93.9%; Median home value: $1,091,500; Median year structure built: 1953; Homeowner vacancy rate: 2.0%; Median selected monthly owner costs: $4,000+ with a mortgage, $1,501 without a mortgage; Median gross rent: n/a per month; Rental vacancy rate: 20.9%
Health Insurance: 99.2% have insurance; 90.4% have private insurance; 31.1% have public insurance; 0.8% do not have insurance; 0.0% of children under 18 do not have insurance
Safety: Violent crime rate: 0.0 per 10,000 population; Property crime rate: 41.8 per 10,000 population
Transportation: Commute: 68.9% car, 16.8% public transportation, 0.0% walk, 13.8% work from home; Mean travel time to work: 41.6 minutes

HUNTINGTON STATION (CDP). Covers a land area of 5.474 square miles and a water area of 0.004 square miles. Located at 40.84° N. Lat; 73.40° W. Long. Elevation is 217 feet.
History: Named for Huntingdon, England, or to mean "hunting town". Walt Whitman born here.
Population: 33,338; Growth (since 2000): 11.5%; Density: 6,090.1 persons per square mile; Race: 62.8% White, 9.4% Black/African American, 3.1% Asian, 0.2% American Indian/Alaska Native, 0.0% Native Hawaiian/Other Pacific Islander, 1.8% Two or more races, 37.8% Hispanic of any race; Average household size: 3.32; Median age: 36.9; Age under 18: 26.8%; Age 65 and over: 11.0%; Males per 100 females: 104.4; Marriage status: 36.2% never married, 50.7% now married, 2.2%

separated, 4.9% widowed, 8.1% divorced; Foreign born: 25.8%; Speak English only: 56.9%; With disability: 7.3%; Veterans: 3.7%; Ancestry: 15.0% Italian, 11.4% Irish, 10.2% German, 4.9% American, 4.2% Polish
Employment: 11.8% management, business, and financial, 3.8% computer, engineering, and science, 13.3% education, legal, community service, arts, and media, 4.9% healthcare practitioners, 24.6% service, 21.1% sales and office, 9.2% natural resources, construction, and maintenance, 11.4% production, transportation, and material moving
Income: Per capita: $32,140; Median household: $82,077; Average household: $101,856; Households with income of $100,000 or more: 40.5%; Poverty rate: 14.5%
Educational Attainment: High school diploma or higher: 79.6%; Bachelor's degree or higher: 34.3%; Graduate/professional degree or higher: 14.8%

School District(s)
Huntington Union Free SD (KG-12)
    Enrollment: 4,675 . . . . (631) 673-2038
South Huntington Union Free SD (KG-12)
    Enrollment: 6,091 . . . . (631) 812-3070
Housing: Homeownership rate: 73.1%; Median home value: $356,900; Median year structure built: 1958; Homeowner vacancy rate: 2.3%; Median selected monthly owner costs: $2,600 with a mortgage, $1,197 without a mortgage; Median gross rent: $1,703 per month; Rental vacancy rate: 8.8%
Health Insurance: 84.7% have insurance; 64.7% have private insurance; 28.8% have public insurance; 15.3% do not have insurance; 9.1% of children under 18 do not have insurance
Transportation: Commute: 81.1% car, 9.9% public transportation, 2.7% walk, 4.2% work from home; Mean travel time to work: 30.3 minutes

ISLANDIA (village). Covers a land area of 2.220 square miles and a water area of 0 square miles. Located at 40.81° N. Lat; 73.17° W. Long. Elevation is 66 feet.
Population: 3,352; Growth (since 2000): 9.6%; Density: 1,510.0 persons per square mile; Race: 63.3% White, 12.8% Black/African American, 11.4% Asian, 0.0% American Indian/Alaska Native, 0.0% Native Hawaiian/Other Pacific Islander, 0.9% Two or more races, 25.5% Hispanic of any race; Average household size: 3.32; Median age: 41.0; Age under 18: 18.7%; Age 65 and over: 13.2%; Males per 100 females: 88.1; Marriage status: 37.4% never married, 44.6% now married, 2.3% separated, 6.6% widowed, 11.4% divorced; Foreign born: 26.2%; Speak English only: 62.2%; With disability: 6.5%; Veterans: 5.2%; Ancestry: 15.1% Italian, 8.0% Irish, 5.2% German, 4.9% Trinidadian and Tobagonian, 3.6% American
Employment: 13.8% management, business, and financial, 4.3% computer, engineering, and science, 8.2% education, legal, community service, arts, and media, 4.0% healthcare practitioners, 22.1% service, 28.4% sales and office, 8.6% natural resources, construction, and maintenance, 10.6% production, transportation, and material moving
Income: Per capita: $32,653; Median household: $90,966; Average household: $102,609; Households with income of $100,000 or more: 44.6%; Poverty rate: 3.1%
Educational Attainment: High school diploma or higher: 87.9%; Bachelor's degree or higher: 22.6%; Graduate/professional degree or higher: 6.8%

School District(s)
Central Islip Union Free SD (PK-12)
    Enrollment: 7,609 . . . . (631) 348-5001

Vocational/Technical School(s)
New York Institute of Beauty (Private, For-profit)
    Enrollment: 165 . . . . (631) 582-4737
    Tuition: $9,795
Housing: Homeownership rate: 89.2%; Median home value: $305,300; Median year structure built: 1969; Homeowner vacancy rate: 4.2%; Median selected monthly owner costs: $2,509 with a mortgage, $1,135 without a mortgage; Median gross rent: $1,854 per month; Rental vacancy rate: 11.2%
Health Insurance: 91.5% have insurance; 72.5% have private insurance; 25.5% have public insurance; 8.5% do not have insurance; 0.0% of children under 18 do not have insurance
Transportation: Commute: 89.7% car, 4.5% public transportation, 0.2% walk, 3.2% work from home; Mean travel time to work: 33.0 minutes

ISLIP (CDP). Covers a land area of 4.800 square miles and a water area of 0.119 square miles. Located at 40.74° N. Lat; 73.22° W. Long. Elevation is 13 feet.
History: Islip is one of ten towns in Suffolk County located on the south shore of Long Island. Within the Town of Islip is a smaller, unincorporated hamlet and census-designated place also named Islip.
Population: 18,254; Growth (since 2000): -11.3%; Density: 3,802.9 persons per square mile; Race: 85.4% White, 4.6% Black/African American, 2.4% Asian, 0.0% American Indian/Alaska Native, 0.0% Native Hawaiian/Other Pacific Islander, 1.2% Two or more races, 17.1% Hispanic of any race; Average household size: 3.03; Median age: 42.0; Age under 18: 21.2%; Age 65 and over: 13.9%; Males per 100 females: 95.6; Marriage status: 33.7% never married, 52.8% now married, 1.5% separated, 5.9% widowed, 7.6% divorced; Foreign born: 12.4%; Speak English only: 83.4%; With disability: 9.8%; Veterans: 6.4%; Ancestry: 28.9% Irish, 26.9% Italian, 18.3% German, 4.0% English, 3.2% Polish
Employment: 15.9% management, business, and financial, 3.6% computer, engineering, and science, 13.6% education, legal, community service, arts, and media, 5.7% healthcare practitioners, 17.0% service, 27.2% sales and office, 9.2% natural resources, construction, and maintenance, 7.9% production, transportation, and material moving
Income: Per capita: $40,309; Median household: $98,525; Average household: $117,485; Households with income of $100,000 or more: 49.2%; Poverty rate: 7.0%
Educational Attainment: High school diploma or higher: 91.2%; Bachelor's degree or higher: 35.1%; Graduate/professional degree or higher: 14.3%

School District(s)
Islip Union Free SD (KG-12)
    Enrollment: 2,859 . . . . (631) 650-8210
Housing: Homeownership rate: 85.6%; Median home value: $368,300; Median year structure built: 1962; Homeowner vacancy rate: 1.4%; Median selected monthly owner costs: $2,804 with a mortgage, $1,235 without a mortgage; Median gross rent: $1,438 per month; Rental vacancy rate: 7.1%
Health Insurance: 95.0% have insurance; 80.7% have private insurance; 26.3% have public insurance; 5.0% do not have insurance; 2.6% of children under 18 do not have insurance
Transportation: Commute: 87.2% car, 7.9% public transportation, 0.5% walk, 3.7% work from home; Mean travel time to work: 32.8 minutes
Airports: Long Island MacArthur (primary service/small hub)

ISLIP (town). Covers a land area of 104.114 square miles and a water area of 58.891 square miles. Located at 40.71° N. Lat; 73.20° W. Long. Elevation is 13 feet.
History: Islip is one of ten towns in Suffolk County located on the south shore of Long Island.
Population: 335,302; Growth (since 2000): 3.9%; Density: 3,220.5 persons per square mile; Race: 72.5% White, 10.5% Black/African American, 2.6% Asian, 0.3% American Indian/Alaska Native, 0.1% Native Hawaiian/Other Pacific Islander, 3.9% Two or more races, 30.8% Hispanic of any race; Average household size: 3.35; Median age: 38.0; Age under 18: 23.6%; Age 65 and over: 12.6%; Males per 100 females: 97.2; Marriage status: 36.3% never married, 49.6% now married, 2.0% separated, 5.9% widowed, 8.2% divorced; Foreign born: 20.6%; Speak English only: 67.9%; With disability: 9.3%; Veterans: 5.3%; Ancestry: 20.7% Italian, 17.2% Irish, 12.1% German, 3.1% Polish, 3.1% English
Employment: 12.1% management, business, and financial, 3.3% computer, engineering, and science, 11.3% education, legal, community service, arts, and media, 5.0% healthcare practitioners, 19.9% service, 26.1% sales and office, 9.2% natural resources, construction, and maintenance, 13.2% production, transportation, and material moving
Income: Per capita: $34,222; Median household: $90,278; Average household: $109,660; Households with income of $100,000 or more: 44.7%; Poverty rate: 8.0%
Educational Attainment: High school diploma or higher: 85.2%; Bachelor's degree or higher: 28.3%; Graduate/professional degree or higher: 12.4%

School District(s)
Islip Union Free SD (KG-12)
    Enrollment: 2,859 . . . . (631) 650-8210
Housing: Homeownership rate: 78.0%; Median home value: $352,200; Median year structure built: 1965; Homeowner vacancy rate: 1.0%; Median selected monthly owner costs: $2,650 with a mortgage, $1,179 without a

mortgage; Median gross rent: $1,620 per month; Rental vacancy rate: 4.6%

Health Insurance: 91.8% have insurance; 75.1% private insurance; 27.6% have public insurance; 8.2% do not have insurance; 3.3% of children under 18 do not have insurance

Transportation: Commute: 88.8% car, 6.6% public transportation, 1.2% walk, 2.3% work from home; Mean travel time to work: 30.7 minutes

Airports: Long Island MacArthur (primary service/small hub)

Additional Information Contacts

Town of Islip . . . . (631) 224-5490
http://www.townofislip-ny.gov

ISLIP TERRACE (CDP). Covers a land area of 1.347 square miles and a water area of 0 square miles. Located at 40.75° N. Lat; 73.19° W. Long. Elevation is 23 feet.

Population: 5,611; Growth (since 2000): -0.5%; Density: 4,164.9 persons per square mile; Race: 92.0% White, 1.8% Black/African American, 3.5% Asian, 0.0% American Indian/Alaska Native, 0.0% Native Hawaiian/Other Pacific Islander, 1.4% Two or more races, 13.7% Hispanic of any race; Average household size: 3.42; Median age: 39.1; Age under 18: 24.7%; Age 65 and over: 11.1%; Males per 100 females: 99.7; Marriage status: 32.4% never married, 54.2% now married, 2.8% separated, 6.7% widowed, 6.7% divorced; Foreign born: 6.6%; Speak English only: 90.8%; With disability: 6.6%; Veterans: 4.8%; Ancestry: 34.1% Italian, 27.4% Irish, 18.4% German, 5.6% French, 3.4% English

Employment: 13.4% management, business, and financial, 3.9% computer, engineering, and science, 14.7% education, legal, community service, arts, and media, 3.8% healthcare practitioners, 15.3% service, 30.0% sales and office, 10.6% natural resources, construction, and maintenance, 8.4% production, transportation, and material moving

Income: Per capita: $38,156; Median household: $108,438; Average household: $125,847; Households with income of $100,000 or more: 53.8%; Poverty rate: 4.6%

Educational Attainment: High school diploma or higher: 92.4%; Bachelor's degree or higher: 25.8%; Graduate/professional degree or higher: 9.0%

School District(s)

East Islip Union Free SD (KG-12)
    Enrollment: 3,822 . . . . (631) 224-2000

Housing: Homeownership rate: 89.5%; Median home value: $351,300; Median year structure built: 1961; Homeowner vacancy rate: 0.0%; Median selected monthly owner costs: $2,650 with a mortgage, $1,147 without a mortgage; Median gross rent: $1,100 per month; Rental vacancy rate: 0.0%

Health Insurance: 95.2% have insurance; 85.2% have private insurance; 21.3% have public insurance; 4.8% do not have insurance; 0.0% of children under 18 do not have insurance

Transportation: Commute: 91.2% car, 4.7% public transportation, 1.1% walk, 2.4% work from home; Mean travel time to work: 30.0 minutes

JAMESPORT (CDP). Covers a land area of 4.496 square miles and a water area of 0.027 square miles. Located at 40.96° N. Lat; 72.58° W. Long. Elevation is 16 feet.

Population: 1,012; Growth (since 2000): -33.7%; Density: 225.1 persons per square mile; Race: 96.4% White, 2.3% Black/African American, 0.0% Asian, 0.0% American Indian/Alaska Native, 0.0% Native Hawaiian/Other Pacific Islander, 0.0% Two or more races, 1.3% Hispanic of any race; Average household size: 2.49; Median age: 49.7; Age under 18: 16.1%; Age 65 and over: 32.3%; Males per 100 females: 97.2; Marriage status: 35.3% never married, 52.1% now married, 0.0% separated, 6.7% widowed, 5.8% divorced; Foreign born: 2.3%; Speak English only: 67.6%; With disability: 8.5%; Veterans: 10.5%; Ancestry: 30.8% Albanian, 25.5% German, 25.0% Irish, 10.5% English, 7.1% Italian

Employment: 34.2% management, business, and financial, 12.5% computer, engineering, and science, 0.0% education, legal, community service, arts, and media, 15.1% healthcare practitioners, 7.5% service, 30.7% sales and office, 0.0% natural resources, construction, and maintenance, 0.0% production, transportation, and material moving

Income: Per capita: $51,114; Median household: $84,775; Average household: $126,808; Households with income of $100,000 or more: 36.1%; Poverty rate: 3.0%

Educational Attainment: High school diploma or higher: 96.3%; Bachelor's degree or higher: 40.1%; Graduate/professional degree or higher: 28.2%

Housing: Homeownership rate: 94.5%; Median home value: n/a; Median year structure built: 1967; Homeowner vacancy rate: 21.9%; Median selected monthly owner costs: n/a with a mortgage, $1,018 without a mortgage; Median gross rent: n/a per month; Rental vacancy rate: 0.0%

Health Insurance: 80.2% have insurance; 58.9% have private insurance; 51.0% have public insurance; 19.8% do not have insurance; 0.0% of children under 18 do not have insurance

Transportation: Commute: 87.1% car, 0.0% public transportation, 3.9% walk, 9.0% work from home; Mean travel time to work: 35.7 minutes

KINGS PARK (CDP). Covers a land area of 6.199 square miles and a water area of 0.391 square miles. Located at 40.89° N. Lat; 73.25° W. Long. Elevation is 174 feet.

History: Developed as utopian community in 1872; became farm for insane in 1885. State psychiatric center opened 1892.

Population: 16,733; Growth (since 2000): 3.6%; Density: 2,699.2 persons per square mile; Race: 91.4% White, 1.1% Black/African American, 4.6% Asian, 0.0% American Indian/Alaska Native, 0.0% Native Hawaiian/Other Pacific Islander, 0.6% Two or more races, 5.3% Hispanic of any race; Average household size: 2.66; Median age: 46.0; Age under 18: 19.9%; Age 65 and over: 21.3%; Males per 100 females: 93.7; Marriage status: 27.4% never married, 57.0% now married, 0.8% separated, 8.4% widowed, 7.2% divorced; Foreign born: 7.5%; Speak English only: 89.6%; With disability: 9.1%; Veterans: 6.3%; Ancestry: 30.6% Italian, 26.1% Irish, 21.0% German, 7.8% English, 5.8% Polish

Employment: 15.2% management, business, and financial, 4.4% computer, engineering, and science, 16.4% education, legal, community service, arts, and media, 8.5% healthcare practitioners, 12.9% service, 28.7% sales and office, 8.3% natural resources, construction, and maintenance, 5.6% production, transportation, and material moving

Income: Per capita: $47,738; Median household: $99,469; Average household: $126,101; Households with income of $100,000 or more: 49.8%; Poverty rate: 3.7%

Educational Attainment: High school diploma or higher: 94.8%; Bachelor's degree or higher: 43.5%; Graduate/professional degree or higher: 19.3%

School District(s)

Kings Park Central SD (KG-12)
    Enrollment: 3,335 . . . . (631) 269-3310

Housing: Homeownership rate: 79.9%; Median home value: $425,900; Median year structure built: 1967; Homeowner vacancy rate: 0.1%; Median selected monthly owner costs: $2,825 with a mortgage, $1,205 without a mortgage; Median gross rent: $1,445 per month; Rental vacancy rate: 3.8%

Health Insurance: 97.2% have insurance; 86.5% have private insurance; 26.8% have public insurance; 2.8% do not have insurance; 1.8% of children under 18 do not have insurance

Transportation: Commute: 85.8% car, 10.1% public transportation, 0.9% walk, 3.1% work from home; Mean travel time to work: 36.0 minutes

LAKE GROVE (village). Covers a land area of 2.947 square miles and a water area of 0.001 square miles. Located at 40.86° N. Lat; 73.12° W. Long. Elevation is 118 feet.

Population: 11,205; Growth (since 2000): 9.3%; Density: 3,802.4 persons per square mile; Race: 89.1% White, 1.6% Black/African American, 5.8% Asian, 0.0% American Indian/Alaska Native, 0.0% Native Hawaiian/Other Pacific Islander, 1.7% Two or more races, 7.5% Hispanic of any race; Average household size: 2.96; Median age: 40.9; Age under 18: 20.5%; Age 65 and over: 15.7%; Males per 100 females: 98.6; Marriage status: 31.5% never married, 54.6% now married, 1.5% separated, 6.8% widowed, 7.1% divorced; Foreign born: 12.5%; Speak English only: 84.8%; With disability: 8.0%; Veterans: 6.5%; Ancestry: 34.2% Italian, 25.5% Irish, 16.6% German, 5.0% English, 4.5% Polish

Employment: 14.5% management, business, and financial, 5.8% computer, engineering, and science, 14.1% education, legal, community service, arts, and media, 6.1% healthcare practitioners, 16.1% service, 29.6% sales and office, 7.5% natural resources, construction, and maintenance, 6.4% production, transportation, and material moving

Income: Per capita: $43,477; Median household: $101,816; Average household: $124,452; Households with income of $100,000 or more: 51.1%; Poverty rate: 5.1%

Educational Attainment: High school diploma or higher: 94.2%; Bachelor's degree or higher: 38.0%; Graduate/professional degree or higher: 17.6%

School District(s)

Middle Country Central SD (PK-12)

    Enrollment: 9,933 . . . . (631) 285-8005

Sachem Central SD (KG-12)

    Enrollment: 13,427 . . . . (631) 471-1336

Housing: Homeownership rate: 81.8%; Median home value: $388,400; Median year structure built: 1970; Homeowner vacancy rate: 1.1%; Median selected monthly owner costs: $2,725 with a mortgage, $1,069 without a mortgage; Median gross rent: $1,766 per month; Rental vacancy rate: 5.9%

Health Insurance: 94.9% have insurance; 83.3% have private insurance; 25.4% have public insurance; 5.1% do not have insurance; 0.4% of children under 18 do not have insurance

Transportation: Commute: 86.3% car, 8.8% public transportation, 1.1% walk, 2.8% work from home; Mean travel time to work: 35.7 minutes

Additional Information Contacts

Village of Lake Grove . . . . (631) 585-2000

    http://www.lakegroveny.gov

LAKE RONKONKOMA (CDP). Covers a land area of 4.940 square miles and a water area of 0.003 square miles. Located at 40.83° N. Lat; 73.11° W. Long. Elevation is 72 feet.

History: The actual Lake Ronkonkoma, adjacent to the hamlet, is the largest lake on Long Island. It is a "groundwater lake," not fed by streams, with no surface outlet.

Population: 20,393; Growth (since 2000): 3.5%; Density: 4,127.9 persons per square mile; Race: 86.2% White, 3.0% Black/African American, 6.0% Asian, 0.1% American Indian/Alaska Native, 0.0% Native Hawaiian/Other Pacific Islander, 2.0% Two or more races, 11.4% Hispanic of any race; Average household size: 2.94; Median age: 40.1; Age under 18: 22.3%; Age 65 and over: 15.0%; Males per 100 females: 94.6; Marriage status: 32.5% never married, 50.9% now married, 1.9% separated, 7.6% widowed, 9.1% divorced; Foreign born: 13.8%; Speak English only: 79.5%; With disability: 11.5%; Veterans: 7.5%; Ancestry: 32.5% Italian, 22.9% Irish, 13.8% German, 5.8% Polish, 4.0% English

Employment: 14.3% management, business, and financial, 5.4% computer, engineering, and science, 12.0% education, legal, community service, arts, and media, 5.9% healthcare practitioners, 17.3% service, 27.8% sales and office, 8.5% natural resources, construction, and maintenance, 8.8% production, transportation, and material moving

Income: Per capita: $35,756; Median household: $89,410; Average household: $101,556; Households with income of $100,000 or more: 43.5%; Poverty rate: 7.3%

Educational Attainment: High school diploma or higher: 91.3%; Bachelor's degree or higher: 28.4%; Graduate/professional degree or higher: 11.8%

School District(s)

Sachem Central SD (KG-12)

    Enrollment: 13,427 . . . . (631) 471-1336

Housing: Homeownership rate: 73.7%; Median home value: $344,300; Median year structure built: 1966; Homeowner vacancy rate: 0.0%; Median selected monthly owner costs: $2,583 with a mortgage, $902 without a mortgage; Median gross rent: $1,444 per month; Rental vacancy rate: 0.0%

Health Insurance: 96.8% have insurance; 81.8% have private insurance; 28.2% have public insurance; 3.2% do not have insurance; 0.2% of children under 18 do not have insurance

Transportation: Commute: 89.1% car, 6.3% public transportation, 0.9% walk, 2.4% work from home; Mean travel time to work: 31.9 minutes

---

LAUREL (CDP). Covers a land area of 3.000 square miles and a water area of 0.074 square miles. Located at 40.97° N. Lat; 72.56° W. Long. Elevation is 20 feet.

Population: 1,003; Growth (since 2000): -15.6%; Density: 334.3 persons per square mile; Race: 97.3% White, 1.4% Black/African American, 0.0% Asian, 0.0% American Indian/Alaska Native, 0.0% Native Hawaiian/Other Pacific Islander, 0.6% Two or more races, 18.1% Hispanic of any race; Average household size: 2.59; Median age: 44.7; Age under 18: 17.1%; Age 65 and over: 24.6%; Males per 100 females: 102.9; Marriage status: 30.3% never married, 62.1% now married, 10.9% separated, 2.6% widowed, 5.1% divorced; Foreign born: 5.9%; Speak English only: 98.4%; With disability: 12.5%; Veterans: 9.1%; Ancestry: 44.7% Irish, 24.9% Polish, 11.9% German, 10.5% Italian, 7.2% Czech

Employment: 17.4% management, business, and financial, 0.0% computer, engineering, and science, 18.1% education, legal, community

service, arts, and media, 14.2% healthcare practitioners, 16.5% service, 20.0% sales and office, 13.8% natural resources, construction, and maintenance, 0.0% production, transportation, and material moving

Income: Per capita: $58,489; Median household: $127,569; Average household: $143,931; Households with income of $100,000 or more: 53.8%; Poverty rate: 3.1%

Educational Attainment: High school diploma or higher: 96.5%; Bachelor's degree or higher: 47.6%; Graduate/professional degree or higher: 31.3%

Housing: Homeownership rate: 94.2%; Median home value: $535,800; Median year structure built: 1972; Homeowner vacancy rate: 0.0%; Median selected monthly owner costs: $2,690 with a mortgage, $1,165 without a mortgage; Median gross rent: n/a per month; Rental vacancy rate: 0.0%

Health Insurance: 95.9% have insurance; 71.6% have private insurance; 44.0% have public insurance; 4.1% do not have insurance; 0.0% of children under 18 do not have insurance

Transportation: Commute: 91.5% car, 6.0% public transportation, 1.1% walk, 1.4% work from home; Mean travel time to work: 21.2 minutes

---

LINDENHURST (village). Covers a land area of 3.760 square miles and a water area of 0.057 square miles. Located at 40.69° N. Lat; 73.37° W. Long. Elevation is 30 feet.

History: Named for Linden, Germany. Incorporated 1923.

Population: 27,257; Growth (since 2000): -2.0%; Density: 7,248.8 persons per square mile; Race: 89.6% White, 2.7% Black/African American, 1.5% Asian, 0.1% American Indian/Alaska Native, 0.0% Native Hawaiian/Other Pacific Islander, 2.3% Two or more races, 18.5% Hispanic of any race; Average household size: 3.08; Median age: 41.6; Age under 18: 18.8%; Age 65 and over: 14.1%; Males per 100 females: 94.6; Marriage status: 33.2% never married, 53.2% now married, 1.4% separated, 5.3% widowed, 8.3% divorced; Foreign born: 16.3%; Speak English only: 75.7%; With disability: 10.3%; Veterans: 5.7%; Ancestry: 31.2% Italian, 23.4% Irish, 16.4% German, 9.9% Polish, 3.1% American

Employment: 11.7% management, business, and financial, 3.3% computer, engineering, and science, 12.0% education, legal, community service, arts, and media, 4.4% healthcare practitioners, 18.9% service, 27.5% sales and office, 11.1% natural resources, construction, and maintenance, 11.1% production, transportation, and material moving

Income: Per capita: $34,633; Median household: $89,724; Average household: $100,890; Households with income of $100,000 or more: 42.1%; Poverty rate: 5.6%

Educational Attainment: High school diploma or higher: 89.2%; Bachelor's degree or higher: 23.9%; Graduate/professional degree or higher: 8.7%

School District(s)

Lindenhurst Union Free SD (KG-12)

    Enrollment: 6,004 . . . . (631) 867-3001

Housing: Homeownership rate: 78.3%; Median home value: $348,400; Median year structure built: 1957; Homeowner vacancy rate: 1.8%; Median selected monthly owner costs: $2,722 with a mortgage, $1,225 without a mortgage; Median gross rent: $1,480 per month; Rental vacancy rate: 7.3%

Health Insurance: 95.2% have insurance; 79.0% have private insurance; 27.5% have public insurance; 4.8% do not have insurance; 4.7% of children under 18 do not have insurance

Transportation: Commute: 87.9% car, 8.2% public transportation, 1.9% walk, 1.5% work from home; Mean travel time to work: 33.6 minutes

Additional Information Contacts

Village of Lindenhurst . . . . (631) 957-7500

    http://www.villageoflindenhurst.com

LLOYD HARBOR (village). Covers a land area of 9.363 square miles and a water area of 1.296 square miles. Located at 40.92° N. Lat; 73.44° W. Long. Elevation is 138 feet.

History: In 1654, the Matinecock Native Americans sold 3,000 acres (12 km_) of what is now called Lloyd Neck to English settlers from Oyster Bay. The Matinecock referred to the region as Caumsett (place by sharp rock). In 1676, James Lloyd acquired the neck, which was then taken over by his son Henry.

Population: 3,702; Growth (since 2000): 0.7%; Density: 395.4 persons per square mile; Race: 93.4% White, 0.3% Black/African American, 4.8% Asian, 0.0% American Indian/Alaska Native, 0.0% Native Hawaiian/Other Pacific Islander, 1.3% Two or more races, 2.9% Hispanic of any race; Average household size: 2.99; Median age: 46.5; Age under 18: 28.4%; Age 65 and over: 17.4%; Males per 100 females: 99.7; Marriage status:

24.0% never married, 67.8% now married, 0.2% separated, 4.3% widowed, 3.8% divorced; Foreign born: 8.8%; Speak English only: 90.8%; With disability: 6.2%; Veterans: 6.2%; Ancestry: 22.6% Irish, 21.9% Italian, 16.8% German, 7.7% English, 7.6% American

Employment: 24.1% management, business, and financial, 2.8% computer, engineering, and science, 23.5% education, legal, community service, arts, and media, 8.7% healthcare practitioners, 8.3% service, 26.5% sales and office, 4.1% natural resources, construction, and maintenance, 2.1% production, transportation, and material moving
Income: Per capita: $114,928; Median household: $211,087; Average household: $345,588; Households with income of $100,000 or more: 73.7%; Poverty rate: 4.2%
Educational Attainment: High school diploma or higher: 98.4%; Bachelor's degree or higher: 74.9%; Graduate/professional degree or higher: 40.9%
Housing: Homeownership rate: 94.0%; Median home value: $1,403,900; Median year structure built: 1963; Homeowner vacancy rate: 1.3%; Median selected monthly owner costs: $4,000+ with a mortgage, $1,501 without a mortgage; Median gross rent: $1,159 per month; Rental vacancy rate: 17.6%
Health Insurance: 98.6% have insurance; 92.0% have private insurance; 19.9% have public insurance; 1.4% do not have insurance; 2.3% of children under 18 do not have insurance
Safety: Violent crime rate: 5.4 per 10,000 population; Property crime rate: 24.4 per 10,000 population
Transportation: Commute: 68.9% car, 17.1% public transportation, 2.3% walk, 8.0% work from home; Mean travel time to work: 43.5 minutes

MANORVILLE (CDP). Covers a land area of 25.469 square miles and a water area of 0.042 square miles. Located at 40.86° N. Lat; 72.79° W. Long. Elevation is 52 feet.
Population: 14,522; Growth (since 2000): 30.5%; Density: 570.2 persons per square mile; Race: 91.8% White, 3.0% Black/African American, 1.2% Asian, 0.0% American Indian/Alaska Native, 0.0% Native Hawaiian/Other Pacific Islander, 2.1% Two or more races, 10.1% Hispanic of any race; Average household size: 3.01; Median age: 40.0; Age under 18: 26.2%; Age 65 and over: 13.7%; Males per 100 females: 98.0; Marriage status: 29.7% never married, 54.9% now married, 1.5% separated, 7.6% widowed, 7.8% divorced; Foreign born: 4.9%; Speak English only: 92.9%; With disability: 7.6%; Veterans: 7.5%; Ancestry: 39.6% Italian, 24.2% Irish, 20.9% German, 4.5% English, 4.1% Polish
Employment: 19.3% management, business, and financial, 6.3% computer, engineering, and science, 15.1% education, legal, community service, arts, and media, 11.0% healthcare practitioners, 12.0% service, 20.8% sales and office, 6.3% natural resources, construction, and maintenance, 9.1% production, transportation, and material moving
Income: Per capita: $40,638; Median household: $104,643; Average household: $120,090; Households with income of $100,000 or more: 52.5%; Poverty rate: 4.7%
Educational Attainment: High school diploma or higher: 94.5%; Bachelor's degree or higher: 36.3%; Graduate/professional degree or higher: 19.1%

School District(s)
Eastport-South Manor CSD (PK-12)
   Enrollment: 3,474 . . . . (631) 801-3011
Housing: Homeownership rate: 85.0%; Median home value: $409,400; Median year structure built: 1993; Homeowner vacancy rate: 0.0%; Median selected monthly owner costs: $3,306 with a mortgage, $921 without a mortgage; Median gross rent: $1,585 per month; Rental vacancy rate: 5.8%
Health Insurance: 96.9% have insurance; 84.6% have private insurance; 24.1% have public insurance; 3.1% do not have insurance; 2.5% of children under 18 do not have insurance
Transportation: Commute: 93.6% car, 1.4% public transportation, 0.4% walk, 4.2% work from home; Mean travel time to work: 32.7 minutes

MASTIC (CDP). Covers a land area of 3.897 square miles and a water area of 0.085 square miles. Located at 40.81° N. Lat; 72.85° W. Long. Elevation is 30 feet.
History: The hamlet was originally called Forge, and was chaned to Mastic in 1893. The Poospatuck Indian Reservation lies in the town's southern end.
Population: 15,574; Growth (since 2000): 0.9%; Density: 3,996.5 persons per square mile; Race: 82.5% White, 10.7% Black/African American, 1.5% Asian, 0.2% American Indian/Alaska Native, 0.0% Native Hawaiian/Other

Pacific Islander, 0.7% Two or more races, 25.0% Hispanic of any race; Average household size: 3.52; Median age: 35.3; Age under 18: 27.6%; Age 65 and over: 8.2%; Males per 100 females: 100.1; Marriage status: 35.7% never married, 50.7% now married, 1.4% separated, 4.1% widowed, 9.5% divorced; Foreign born: 17.7%; Speak English only: 72.5%; With disability: 9.0%; Veterans: 4.3%; Ancestry: 26.1% Italian, 20.5% Irish, 17.1% German, 4.6% Polish, 3.3% English
Employment: 8.4% management, business, and financial, 1.8% computer, engineering, and science, 6.3% education, legal, community service, arts, and media, 5.4% healthcare practitioners, 22.2% service, 27.7% sales and office, 11.8% natural resources, construction, and maintenance, 16.5% production, transportation, and material moving
Income: Per capita: $25,701; Median household: $76,729; Average household: $85,940; Households with income of $100,000 or more: 34.9%; Poverty rate: 11.9%
Educational Attainment: High school diploma or higher: 84.5%; Bachelor's degree or higher: 14.7%; Graduate/professional degree or higher: 3.6%
Housing: Homeownership rate: 77.9%; Median home value: $238,500; Median year structure built: 1975; Homeowner vacancy rate: 3.0%; Median selected monthly owner costs: $2,339 with a mortgage, $1,081 without a mortgage; Median gross rent: $1,681 per month; Rental vacancy rate: 4.0%
Health Insurance: 89.0% have insurance; 63.7% have private insurance; 33.2% have public insurance; 11.0% do not have insurance; 1.2% of children under 18 do not have insurance
Transportation: Commute: 91.7% car, 4.3% public transportation, 1.5% walk, 2.2% work from home; Mean travel time to work: 31.3 minutes

MASTIC BEACH (village). Covers a land area of 4.715 square miles and a water area of 0.265 square miles. Located at 40.77° N. Lat; 72.84° W. Long. Elevation is 7 feet.
History: Mastic Beach is on a peninsula extending into Moriches Bay. Created in 1928, there are marinas, private docks, and several historic sites. There is sailing, swimming, fishing, birding, hiking, camping and shopping.
Population: 14,850; Growth (since 2000): 28.6%; Density: 3,149.6 persons per square mile; Race: 80.2% White, 12.3% Black/African American, 0.6% Asian, 0.3% American Indian/Alaska Native, 0.0% Native Hawaiian/Other Pacific Islander, 4.8% Two or more races, 16.6% Hispanic of any race; Average household size: 2.97; Median age: 36.8; Age under 18: 23.9%; Age 65 and over: 9.9%; Males per 100 females: 98.6; Marriage status: 42.6% never married, 45.0% now married, 2.1% separated, 5.5% widowed, 6.8% divorced; Foreign born: 8.3%; Speak English only: 84.8%; With disability: 10.6%; Veterans: 5.8%; Ancestry: 26.4% Italian, 20.6% Irish, 18.8% German, 4.9% English, 3.9% Polish
Employment: 11.4% management, business, and financial, 5.5% computer, engineering, and science, 7.3% education, legal, community service, arts, and media, 9.1% healthcare practitioners, 15.9% service, 25.3% sales and office, 14.4% natural resources, construction, and maintenance, 11.2% production, transportation, and material moving
Income: Per capita: $27,466; Median household: $66,065; Average household: $79,445; Households with income of $100,000 or more: 28.4%; Poverty rate: 15.1%
Educational Attainment: High school diploma or higher: 89.1%; Bachelor's degree or higher: 16.2%; Graduate/professional degree or higher: 6.1%

School District(s)
William Floyd Union Free SD (KG-12)
   Enrollment: 8,837 . . . . (631) 874-1201
Housing: Homeownership rate: 72.7%; Median home value: $193,300; Median year structure built: 1967; Homeowner vacancy rate: 2.6%; Median selected monthly owner costs: $2,022 with a mortgage, $891 without a mortgage; Median gross rent: $1,787 per month; Rental vacancy rate: 1.3%
Health Insurance: 88.9% have insurance; 66.1% have private insurance; 35.1% have public insurance; 11.1% do not have insurance; 5.9% of children under 18 do not have insurance
Transportation: Commute: 91.5% car, 4.5% public transportation, 0.5% walk, 2.6% work from home; Mean travel time to work: 38.4 minutes

MATTITUCK (CDP). Covers a land area of 8.996 square miles and a water area of 0.364 square miles. Located at 41.00° N. Lat; 72.54° W. Long. Elevation is 16 feet.

History: Mattituck is believed to havebeen named for the Native American "Great Creek." Mattituck Creek has been dredged and is used extensively by pleasure craft on Long Island Sound.

Population: 4,818; Growth (since 2000): 14.8%; Density: 535.6 persons per square mile; Race: 96.0% White, 0.0% Black/African American, 0.4% Asian, 2.8% American Indian/Alaska Native, 0.0% Native Hawaiian/Other Pacific Islander, 0.8% Two or more races, 3.0% Hispanic of any race; Average household size: 2.47; Median age: 52.0; Age under 18: 16.1%; Age 65 and over: 22.5%; Males per 100 females: 98.2; Marriage status: 28.8% never married, 55.8% now married, 0.0% separated, 7.2% widowed, 8.2% divorced; Foreign born: 6.6%; Speak English only: 90.5%; With disability: 11.9%; Veterans: 8.6%; Ancestry: 26.2% Irish, 18.0% German, 17.0% Italian, 14.2% English, 13.1% Polish

Employment: 15.7% management, business, and financial, 2.5% computer, engineering, and science, 16.4% education, legal, community service, arts, and media, 1.9% healthcare practitioners, 18.6% service, 18.3% sales and office, 18.6% natural resources, construction, and maintenance, 8.1% production, transportation, and material moving

Income: Per capita: $47,469; Median household: $81,432; Average household: $114,301; Households with income of $100,000 or more: 42.8%; Poverty rate: 3.5%

Educational Attainment: High school diploma or higher: 94.4%; Bachelor's degree or higher: 39.3%; Graduate/professional degree or higher: 18.8%

School District(s)

Mattituck-Cutchogue Union Free SD (KG-12)
　　Enrollment: 1,198 . . . . (631) 298-4242

Housing: Homeownership rate: 85.7%; Median home value: $560,600; Median year structure built: 1961; Homeowner vacancy rate: 0.0%; Median selected monthly owner costs: $2,382 with a mortgage, $1,073 without a mortgage; Median gross rent: $1,332 per month; Rental vacancy rate: 15.7%

Health Insurance: 93.8% have insurance; 83.4% have private insurance; 31.8% have public insurance; 6.2% do not have insurance; 12.0% of children under 18 do not have insurance

Newspapers: Suffolk Times (weekly circulation 12,000); The News-Review (weekly circulation 5,000)

Transportation: Commute: 86.3% car, 2.2% public transportation, 0.5% walk, 8.6% work from home; Mean travel time to work: 27.5 minutes

Airports: Mattituck (general aviation)

MEDFORD (CDP). Covers a land area of 10.797 square miles and a water area of 0 square miles. Located at 40.82° N. Lat; 72.99° W. Long. Elevation is 89 feet.

Population: 24,129; Growth (since 2000): 9.8%; Density: 2,234.8 persons per square mile; Race: 87.0% White, 6.6% Black/African American, 3.2% Asian, 0.1% American Indian/Alaska Native, 0.0% Native Hawaiian/Other Pacific Islander, 2.0% Two or more races, 21.6% Hispanic of any race; Average household size: 3.00; Median age: 40.6; Age under 18: 21.6%; Age 65 and over: 15.0%; Males per 100 females: 96.5; Marriage status: 37.3% never married, 47.4% now married, 2.9% separated, 7.0% widowed, 8.3% divorced; Foreign born: 11.8%; Speak English only: 78.5%; With disability: 8.3%; Veterans: 6.3%; Ancestry: 25.4% Italian, 21.3% Irish, 19.0% German, 4.0% Polish, 3.9% American

Employment: 16.0% management, business, and financial, 5.8% computer, engineering, and science, 8.5% education, legal, community service, arts, and media, 5.9% healthcare practitioners, 17.1% service, 26.2% sales and office, 10.6% natural resources, construction, and maintenance, 10.0% production, transportation, and material moving

Income: Per capita: $35,051; Median household: $87,413; Average household: $101,798; Households with income of $100,000 or more: 44.7%; Poverty rate: 9.2%

Educational Attainment: High school diploma or higher: 91.5%; Bachelor's degree or higher: 27.9%; Graduate/professional degree or higher: 10.5%

School District(s)

Patchogue-Medford Union Free SD (KG-12)
　　Enrollment: 7,666 . . . . (631) 687-6380

Housing: Homeownership rate: 84.7%; Median home value: $298,900; Median year structure built: 1975; Homeowner vacancy rate: 0.7%; Median selected monthly owner costs: $2,511 with a mortgage, $1,006 without a

mortgage; Median gross rent: $1,779 per month; Rental vacancy rate: 1.5%

Health Insurance: 94.9% have insurance; 79.8% have private insurance; 28.7% have public insurance; 5.1% do not have insurance; 2.3% of children under 18 do not have insurance

Transportation: Commute: 91.2% car, 4.1% public transportation, 0.5% walk, 3.7% work from home; Mean travel time to work: 33.5 minutes

MELVILLE (CDP). Covers a land area of 12.086 square miles and a water area of <.001 square miles. Located at 40.78° N. Lat; 73.41° W. Long. Elevation is 135 feet.

History: Poet Walt Whitman was born in a shingle-sided farmhouse that still sits, though rather improbably, on a heavily commercial stretch of Route 110 in Melville, squeezed between a film developer and a furniture store.

Population: 18,418; Growth (since 2000): 26.7%; Density: 1,524.0 persons per square mile; Race: 84.0% White, 6.0% Black/African American, 7.3% Asian, 0.0% American Indian/Alaska Native, 0.2% Native Hawaiian/Other Pacific Islander, 1.2% Two or more races, 7.2% Hispanic of any race; Average household size: 2.68; Median age: 48.5; Age under 18: 20.2%; Age 65 and over: 26.6%; Males per 100 females: 89.9; Marriage status: 23.3% never married, 60.9% now married, 1.2% separated, 10.1% widowed, 5.7% divorced; Foreign born: 13.3%; Speak English only: 84.9%; With disability: 9.0%; Veterans: 6.1%; Ancestry: 21.3% Italian, 8.4% Irish, 8.1% German, 7.8% Russian, 6.4% American

Employment: 20.8% management, business, and financial, 4.5% computer, engineering, and science, 16.1% education, legal, community service, arts, and media, 7.9% healthcare practitioners, 9.4% service, 35.4% sales and office, 2.6% natural resources, construction, and maintenance, 3.3% production, transportation, and material moving

Income: Per capita: $64,157; Median household: $123,655; Average household: $171,141; Households with income of $100,000 or more: 55.2%; Poverty rate: 4.5%

Educational Attainment: High school diploma or higher: 95.7%; Bachelor's degree or higher: 56.4%; Graduate/professional degree or higher: 27.8%

School District(s)

Half Hollow Hills Central SD (KG-12)
　　Enrollment: 8,354 . . . . (631) 592-3008
South Huntington Union Free SD (KG-12)
　　Enrollment: 6,091 . . . . (631) 812-3070

Housing: Homeownership rate: 86.6%; Median home value: $635,000; Median year structure built: 1981; Homeowner vacancy rate: 3.5%; Median selected monthly owner costs: $3,443 with a mortgage, $1,289 without a mortgage; Median gross rent: $2,079 per month; Rental vacancy rate: 11.5%

Health Insurance: 98.9% have insurance; 86.4% have private insurance; 31.4% have public insurance; 1.1% do not have insurance; 0.0% of children under 18 do not have insurance

Newspapers: Newsday (daily circulation 368,000)

Transportation: Commute: 81.9% car, 9.5% public transportation, 0.8% walk, 7.4% work from home; Mean travel time to work: 33.3 minutes

MIDDLE ISLAND (CDP). Covers a land area of 8.239 square miles and a water area of 0.059 square miles. Located at 40.89° N. Lat; 72.95° W. Long. Elevation is 82 feet.

Population: 10,405; Growth (since 2000): 7.2%; Density: 1,262.9 persons per square mile; Race: 78.3% White, 15.1% Black/African American, 3.2% Asian, 0.0% American Indian/Alaska Native, 0.0% Native Hawaiian/Other Pacific Islander, 1.6% Two or more races, 9.5% Hispanic of any race; Average household size: 2.45; Median age: 44.6; Age under 18: 20.7%; Age 65 and over: 22.0%; Males per 100 females: 92.7; Marriage status: 31.2% never married, 49.4% now married, 1.2% separated, 8.8% widowed, 10.6% divorced; Foreign born: 9.2%; Speak English only: 89.7%; With disability: 13.1%; Veterans: 8.3%; Ancestry: 27.7% Italian, 16.7% Irish, 13.9% German, 8.0% American, 5.6% Polish

Employment: 14.8% management, business, and financial, 5.0% computer, engineering, and science, 15.6% education, legal, community service, arts, and media, 6.4% healthcare practitioners, 17.7% service, 22.3% sales and office, 9.4% natural resources, construction, and maintenance, 8.8% production, transportation, and material moving

Income: Per capita: $33,802; Median household: $69,450; Average household: $82,154; Households with income of $100,000 or more: 32.0%; Poverty rate: 10.5%

Educational Attainment: High school diploma or higher: 93.5%; Bachelor's degree or higher: 27.8%; Graduate/professional degree or higher: 13.1%

School District(s)
Longwood Central SD (KG-12)
   Enrollment: 9,164 . . . . (631) 345-2172

Housing: Homeownership rate: 76.5%; Median home value: $272,400; Median year structure built: 1980; Homeowner vacancy rate: 1.7%; Median selected monthly owner costs: $2,177 with a mortgage, $1,119 without a mortgage; Median gross rent: $1,672 per month; Rental vacancy rate: 10.6%

Health Insurance: 94.9% have insurance; 73.8% have private insurance; 38.7% have public insurance; 5.1% do not have insurance; 4.2% of children under 18 do not have insurance

Transportation: Commute: 93.8% car, 4.4% public transportation, 0.2% walk, 1.5% work from home; Mean travel time to work: 34.5 minutes

MILLER PLACE (CDP).
Covers a land area of 6.552 square miles and a water area of 0 square miles. Located at 40.94° N. Lat; 72.99° W. Long. Elevation is 131 feet.

History: Miller Place is named for the Miller family, settlers of the area in the 17th century. For most of its history, the community functioned as an agriculture-based society.

Population: 11,709; Growth (since 2000): 10.7%; Density: 1,787.2 persons per square mile; Race: 95.0% White, 0.2% Black/African American, 3.2% Asian, 0.0% American Indian/Alaska Native, 0.0% Native Hawaiian/Other Pacific Islander, 1.6% Two or more races, 7.9% Hispanic of any race; Average household size: 2.98; Median age: 41.3; Age under 18: 26.4%; Age 65 and over: 14.9%; Males per 100 females: 98.4; Marriage status: 27.6% never married, 58.4% now married, 1.0% separated, 4.3% widowed, 9.8% divorced; Foreign born: 5.7%; Speak English only: 90.0%; With disability: 9.4%; Veterans: 5.5%; Ancestry: 31.4% Italian, 21.0% Irish, 16.6% German, 9.8% American, 4.1% English

Employment: 16.1% management, business, and financial, 4.9% computer, engineering, and science, 13.6% education, legal, community service, arts, and media, 10.7% healthcare practitioners, 15.3% service, 23.6% sales and office, 10.7% natural resources, construction, and maintenance, 5.1% production, transportation, and material moving

Income: Per capita: $45,494; Median household: $119,963; Average household: $133,285; Households with income of $100,000 or more: 57.4%; Poverty rate: 3.9%

Educational Attainment: High school diploma or higher: 97.7%; Bachelor's degree or higher: 46.3%; Graduate/professional degree or higher: 23.3%

School District(s)
Miller Place Union Free SD (KG-12)
   Enrollment: 2,708 . . . . (631) 474-2700

Housing: Homeownership rate: 94.5%; Median home value: $423,800; Median year structure built: 1975; Homeowner vacancy rate: 1.2%; Median selected monthly owner costs: $3,214 with a mortgage, $1,366 without a mortgage; Median gross rent: $1,441 per month; Rental vacancy rate: 0.0%

Health Insurance: 98.9% have insurance; 88.6% have private insurance; 22.8% have public insurance; 1.1% do not have insurance; 0.5% of children under 18 do not have insurance

Transportation: Commute: 89.8% car, 5.3% public transportation, 0.3% walk, 4.6% work from home; Mean travel time to work: 39.5 minutes

MONTAUK (CDP).
Covers a land area of 17.479 square miles and a water area of 2.252 square miles. Located at 41.05° N. Lat; 71.95° W. Long. Elevation is 33 feet.

History: Name derived from Montauk word for hilly land. Founded on land bought from Montauks in 1686 by settlers from nearby East Hampton to raise cattle. Site of oldest cattle ranch in U.S.

Population: 3,662; Growth (since 2000): -4.9%; Density: 209.5 persons per square mile; Race: 96.4% White, 1.1% Black/African American, 0.8% Asian, 0.5% American Indian/Alaska Native, 0.0% Native Hawaiian/Other Pacific Islander, 0.6% Two or more races, 10.6% Hispanic of any race; Average household size: 2.33; Median age: 56.0; Age under 18: 10.4%; Age 65 and over: 32.9%; Males per 100 females: 99.8; Marriage status: 23.5% never married, 63.4% now married, 0.0% separated, 10.6% widowed, 2.6% divorced; Foreign born: 11.5%; Speak English only: 81.4%; With disability: 17.8%; Veterans: 9.0%; Ancestry: 22.7% Irish, 20.5% Italian, 16.0% German, 11.0% English, 4.8% American

Employment: 10.2% management, business, and financial, 1.9% computer, engineering, and science, 12.6% education, legal, community service, arts, and media, 6.5% healthcare practitioners, 30.9% service, 18.5% sales and office, 13.8% natural resources, construction, and maintenance, 5.6% production, transportation, and material moving

Income: Per capita: $45,852; Median household: $87,717; Average household: $105,529; Households with income of $100,000 or more: 37.7%; Poverty rate: 5.4%

Educational Attainment: High school diploma or higher: 94.2%; Bachelor's degree or higher: 37.8%; Graduate/professional degree or higher: 10.9%

School District(s)
Montauk Union Free SD (PK-08)
   Enrollment: 330 . . . . (631) 668-2474

Housing: Homeownership rate: 87.1%; Median home value: $871,300; Median year structure built: 1978; Homeowner vacancy rate: 0.6%; Median selected monthly owner costs: $2,655 with a mortgage, $988 without a mortgage; Median gross rent: $2,048 per month; Rental vacancy rate: 49.7%

Health Insurance: 92.5% have insurance; 74.6% have private insurance; 44.4% have public insurance; 7.5% do not have insurance; 6.0% of children under 18 do not have insurance

Transportation: Commute: 82.1% car, 2.0% public transportation, 3.0% walk, 10.4% work from home; Mean travel time to work: 22.5 minutes

Airports: Montauk (general aviation)

MORICHES (CDP).
Covers a land area of 2.050 square miles and a water area of 0.227 square miles. Located at 40.81° N. Lat; 72.83° W. Long. Elevation is 23 feet.

Population: 3,092; Growth (since 2000): 33.3%; Density: 1,508.6 persons per square mile; Race: 74.9% White, 9.6% Black/African American, 6.7% Asian, 0.5% American Indian/Alaska Native, 0.0% Native Hawaiian/Other Pacific Islander, 6.3% Two or more races, 4.1% Hispanic of any race; Average household size: 2.11; Median age: 44.5; Age under 18: 22.3%; Age 65 and over: 19.0%; Males per 100 females: 93.6; Marriage status: 29.1% never married, 55.5% now married, 8.7% separated, 6.4% widowed, 9.1% divorced; Foreign born: 11.0%; Speak English only: 82.9%; With disability: 7.7%; Veterans: 4.7%; Ancestry: 37.7% Italian, 23.2% Irish, 12.3% German, 4.0% Polish, 2.8% French

Employment: 16.1% management, business, and financial, 4.5% computer, engineering, and science, 4.1% education, legal, community service, arts, and media, 9.2% healthcare practitioners, 14.6% service, 36.4% sales and office, 7.4% natural resources, construction, and maintenance, 7.8% production, transportation, and material moving

Income: Per capita: $43,134; Median household: $60,290; Average household: $90,016; Households with income of $100,000 or more: 29.9%; Poverty rate: 4.7%

Educational Attainment: High school diploma or higher: 90.6%; Bachelor's degree or higher: 35.1%; Graduate/professional degree or higher: 20.6%

School District(s)
William Floyd Union Free SD (KG-12)
   Enrollment: 8,837 . . . . (631) 874-1201

Housing: Homeownership rate: 45.7%; Median home value: $340,700; Median year structure built: 1987; Homeowner vacancy rate: 0.0%; Median selected monthly owner costs: $3,074 with a mortgage, $1,308 without a mortgage; Median gross rent: $1,709 per month; Rental vacancy rate: 5.1%

Health Insurance: 92.5% have insurance; 83.2% have private insurance; 27.0% have public insurance; 7.5% do not have insurance; 13.5% of children under 18 do not have insurance

Transportation: Commute: 89.8% car, 4.1% public transportation, 1.0% walk, 5.1% work from home; Mean travel time to work: 35.1 minutes

MOUNT SINAI (CDP).
Covers a land area of 5.999 square miles and a water area of 0.419 square miles. Located at 40.94° N. Lat; 73.02° W. Long. Elevation is 33 feet.

Population: 11,976; Growth (since 2000): 37.1%; Density: 1,996.3 persons per square mile; Race: 91.0% White, 0.4% Black/African American, 3.8% Asian, 0.5% American Indian/Alaska Native, 0.0% Native Hawaiian/Other Pacific Islander, 3.4% Two or more races, 14.6% Hispanic of any race; Average household size: 2.95; Median age: 42.0; Age under 18: 24.2%; Age 65 and over: 19.4%; Males per 100 females: 95.3; Marriage status: 25.0% never married, 64.8% now married, 1.3% separated, 4.9% widowed, 5.3% divorced; Foreign born: 10.0%; Speak

English only: 83.0%; With disability: 9.0%; Veterans: 6.3%; Ancestry: 26.9% Italian, 20.0% Irish, 15.7% German, 9.7% American, 7.2% Polish
Employment: 19.9% management, business, and financial, 6.3% computer, engineering, and science, 12.9% education, legal, community service, arts, and media, 8.5% healthcare practitioners, 16.2% service, 24.2% sales and office, 7.9% natural resources, construction, and maintenance, 4.2% production, transportation, and material moving
Income: Per capita: $47,726; Median household: $114,310; Average household: $138,110; Households with income of $100,000 or more: 59.7%; Poverty rate: 7.4%
Educational Attainment: High school diploma or higher: 94.0%; Bachelor's degree or higher: 42.9%; Graduate/professional degree or higher: 18.4%

School District(s)
Mount Sinai Union Free SD (KG-12)
    Enrollment: 2,333 . . . . (631) 870-2550
Housing: Homeownership rate: 92.2%; Median home value: $446,500; Median year structure built: 1979; Homeowner vacancy rate: 0.0%; Median selected monthly owner costs: $3,183 with a mortgage, $1,347 without a mortgage; Median gross rent: $1,392 per month; Rental vacancy rate: 0.0%
Health Insurance: 96.8% have insurance; 82.5% have private insurance; 31.5% have public insurance; 3.2% do not have insurance; 0.1% of children under 18 do not have insurance
Transportation: Commute: 91.9% car, 1.9% public transportation, 0.4% walk, 5.4% work from home; Mean travel time to work: 32.1 minutes

NAPEAGUE (CDP).
Covers a land area of 3.678 square miles and a water area of 0.080 square miles. Located at 40.99° N. Lat; 72.07° W. Long. Elevation is 7 feet.
Population: 129; Growth (since 2000): -42.2%; Density: 35.1 persons per square mile; Race: 100.0% White, 0.0% Black/African American, 0.0% Asian, 0.0% American Indian/Alaska Native, 0.0% Native Hawaiian/Other Pacific Islander, 0.0% Two or more races, 0.0% Hispanic of any race; Average household size: 2.02; Median age: 54.7; Age under 18: 17.8%; Age 65 and over: 10.1%; Males per 100 females: 92.3; Marriage status: 10.4% never married, 81.1% now married, 0.0% separated, 4.7% widowed, 3.8% divorced; Foreign born: 0.0%; Speak English only: 100.0%; With disability: 3.9%; Veterans: 0.0%; Ancestry: 34.9% American, 10.1% Polish, 9.3% English, 9.3% Italian, 5.4% German
Employment: 27.9% management, business, and financial, 0.0% computer, engineering, and science, 12.8% education, legal, community service, arts, and media, 12.8% healthcare practitioners, 0.0% service, 43.0% sales and office, 3.5% natural resources, construction, and maintenance, 0.0% production, transportation, and material moving
Income: Per capita: $85,754; Median household: n/a; Average household: $174,109; Households with income of $100,000 or more: 54.7%; Poverty rate: 3.9%
Educational Attainment: High school diploma or higher: 100.0%; Bachelor's degree or higher: 61.3%; Graduate/professional degree or higher: 48.1%
Housing: Homeownership rate: 82.8%; Median home value: n/a; Median year structure built: 1984; Homeowner vacancy rate: 20.9%; Median selected monthly owner costs: n/a with a mortgage, $825 without a mortgage; Median gross rent: n/a per month; Rental vacancy rate: 0.0%
Health Insurance: 100.0% have insurance; 96.1% have private insurance; 10.1% have public insurance; 0.0% do not have insurance; 0.0% of children under 18 do not have insurance
Transportation: Commute: 54.7% car, 0.0% public transportation, 0.0% walk, 45.3% work from home; Mean travel time to work: 0.0 minutes

NESCONSET (CDP).
Covers a land area of 3.821 square miles and a water area of 0.003 square miles. Located at 40.85° N. Lat; 73.15° W. Long. Elevation is 118 feet.
History: Nesconset is a hamlet and census-designated place (CDP) in Suffolk County, Long Island, New York.
Population: 13,674; Growth (since 2000): 14.0%; Density: 3,578.6 persons per square mile; Race: 93.1% White, 0.4% Black/African American, 4.6% Asian, 0.0% American Indian/Alaska Native, 0.0% Native Hawaiian/Other Pacific Islander, 0.9% Two or more races, 4.2% Hispanic of any race; Average household size: 2.97; Median age: 43.5; Age under 18: 24.6%; Age 65 and over: 18.5%; Males per 100 females: 94.6; Marriage status: 23.8% never married, 62.3% now married, 0.7% separated, 6.0% widowed, 7.9% divorced; Foreign born: 9.1%; Speak

English only: 87.5%; With disability: 7.9%; Veterans: 3.3%; Ancestry: 37.6% Italian, 26.7% Irish, 19.0% German, 8.2% English, 5.8% Polish
Employment: 19.6% management, business, and financial, 5.5% computer, engineering, and science, 19.1% education, legal, community service, arts, and media, 5.7% healthcare practitioners, 14.0% service, 23.6% sales and office, 8.5% natural resources, construction, and maintenance, 4.1% production, transportation, and material moving
Income: Per capita: $46,045; Median household: $119,453; Average household: $136,040; Households with income of $100,000 or more: 60.0%; Poverty rate: 2.9%
Educational Attainment: High school diploma or higher: 94.8%; Bachelor's degree or higher: 48.8%; Graduate/professional degree or higher: 23.6%

School District(s)
Smithtown Central SD (KG-12)
    Enrollment: 9,344 . . . . (631) 382-2006
Housing: Homeownership rate: 87.7%; Median home value: $457,900; Median year structure built: 1973; Homeowner vacancy rate: 0.0%; Median selected monthly owner costs: $3,043 with a mortgage, $1,443 without a mortgage; Median gross rent: $1,900 per month; Rental vacancy rate: 19.7%
Health Insurance: 98.7% have insurance; 92.3% have private insurance; 22.5% have public insurance; 1.3% do not have insurance; 0.4% of children under 18 do not have insurance
Transportation: Commute: 89.9% car, 5.3% public transportation, 0.0% walk, 4.1% work from home; Mean travel time to work: 33.8 minutes

NEW SUFFOLK (CDP).
Covers a land area of 0.556 square miles and a water area of 0.054 square miles. Located at 41.00° N. Lat; 72.48° W. Long. Elevation is 26 feet.
Population: 243; Growth (since 2000): -27.9%; Density: 436.7 persons per square mile; Race: 95.9% White, 4.1% Black/African American, 0.0% Asian, 0.0% American Indian/Alaska Native, 0.0% Native Hawaiian/Other Pacific Islander, 0.0% Two or more races, 0.0% Hispanic of any race; Average household size: 1.91; Median age: 56.9; Age under 18: 8.6%; Age 65 and over: 32.9%; Males per 100 females: 84.7; Marriage status: 20.7% never married, 58.1% now married, 0.0% separated, 10.6% widowed, 10.6% divorced; Foreign born: 9.5%; Speak English only: 100.0%; With disability: 7.4%; Veterans: 13.1%; Ancestry: 31.7% German, 21.4% English, 15.2% Polish, 13.6% Irish, 10.7% Italian
Employment: 2.8% management, business, and financial, 0.0% computer, engineering, and science, 19.6% education, legal, community service, arts, and media, 4.7% healthcare practitioners, 20.6% service, 39.3% sales and office, 1.9% natural resources, construction, and maintenance, 11.2% production, transportation, and material moving
Income: Per capita: $53,516; Median household: $66,477; Average household: $100,045; Households with income of $100,000 or more: 43.3%; Poverty rate: 7.4%
Educational Attainment: High school diploma or higher: 97.1%; Bachelor's degree or higher: 54.9%; Graduate/professional degree or higher: 18.9%

School District(s)
New Suffolk Common SD (PK-06)
    Enrollment: 12 . . . . (631) 734-6940
Housing: Homeownership rate: 78.0%; Median home value: $702,200; Median year structure built: Before 1940; Homeowner vacancy rate: 5.7%; Median selected monthly owner costs: $2,550 with a mortgage, $764 without a mortgage; Median gross rent: $2,000 per month; Rental vacancy rate: 0.0%
Health Insurance: 97.1% have insurance; 88.9% have private insurance; 39.5% have public insurance; 2.9% do not have insurance; 0.0% of children under 18 do not have insurance
Transportation: Commute: 66.7% car, 0.0% public transportation, 25.7% walk, 7.6% work from home; Mean travel time to work: 21.6 minutes

NISSEQUOGUE (village).
Covers a land area of 3.782 square miles and a water area of 0.194 square miles. Located at 40.91° N. Lat; 73.19° W. Long. Elevation is 85 feet.
Population: 1,641; Growth (since 2000): 6.4%; Density: 433.9 persons per square mile; Race: 94.9% White, 1.8% Black/African American, 1.0% Asian, 1.5% American Indian/Alaska Native, 0.0% Native Hawaiian/Other Pacific Islander, 0.7% Two or more races, 4.5% Hispanic of any race; Average household size: 2.96; Median age: 51.0; Age under 18: 20.5%; Age 65 and over: 22.5%; Males per 100 females: 107.5; Marriage status: 24.7% never married, 66.9% now married, 0.5% separated, 4.0%

widowed, 4.3% divorced; Foreign born: 8.0%; Speak English only: 94.2%; With disability: 8.2%; Veterans: 6.0%; Ancestry: 30.5% Italian, 26.4% Irish, 18.1% German, 5.7% American, 4.7% Greek

Employment: 23.4% management, business, and financial, 5.0% computer, engineering, and science, 19.1% education, legal, community service, arts, and media, 13.1% healthcare practitioners, 7.4% service, 25.1% sales and office, 3.2% natural resources, construction, and maintenance, 3.7% production, transportation, and material moving

Income: Per capita: $98,728; Median household: $181,250; Average household: $291,288; Households with income of $100,000 or more: 80.9%; Poverty rate: 3.6%

Educational Attainment: High school diploma or higher: 97.3%; Bachelor's degree or higher: 61.7%; Graduate/professional degree or higher: 40.2%

Housing: Homeownership rate: 97.1%; Median home value: $1,032,300; Median year structure built: 1976; Homeowner vacancy rate: 3.0%; Median selected monthly owner costs: $4,000+ with a mortgage, $1,501 without a mortgage; Median gross rent: $2,333 per month; Rental vacancy rate: 61.0%

Health Insurance: 97.6% have insurance; 90.9% have private insurance; 24.5% have public insurance; 2.4% do not have insurance; 0.0% of children under 18 do not have insurance

Safety: Violent crime rate: 0.0 per 10,000 population; Property crime rate: 40.1 per 10,000 population

Transportation: Commute: 86.8% car, 3.5% public transportation, 1.6% walk, 8.1% work from home; Mean travel time to work: 27.2 minutes

NORTH AMITYVILLE (CDP). Covers a land area of 2.354 square miles and a water area of 0 square miles. Located at 40.70° N. Lat; 73.41° W. Long. Elevation is 33 feet.

History: North Amityville is a hamlet in Suffolk County, New York.

Population: 19,774; Growth (since 2000): 19.3%; Density: 8,399.6 persons per square mile; Race: 13.9% White, 55.6% Black/African American, 1.9% Asian, 0.0% American Indian/Alaska Native, 0.0% Native Hawaiian/Other Pacific Islander, 6.5% Two or more races, 34.8% Hispanic of any race; Average household size: 3.87; Median age: 34.0; Age under 18: 24.2%; Age 65 and over: 11.6%; Males per 100 females: 85.7; Marriage status: 49.3% never married, 36.5% now married, 3.2% separated, 6.5% widowed, 7.7% divorced; Foreign born: 31.7%; Speak English only: 61.2%; With disability: 10.2%; Veterans: 3.1%; Ancestry: 8.1% Haitian, 7.4% Jamaican, 7.0% American, 3.8% Italian, 2.4% German

Employment: 5.0% management, business, and financial, 2.0% computer, engineering, and science, 6.9% education, legal, community service, arts, and media, 7.1% healthcare practitioners, 32.3% service, 24.4% sales and office, 7.0% natural resources, construction, and maintenance, 15.4% production, transportation, and material moving

Income: Per capita: $23,554; Median household: $72,500; Average household: $82,884; Households with income of $100,000 or more: 34.3%; Poverty rate: 8.5%

Educational Attainment: High school diploma or higher: 79.2%; Bachelor's degree or higher: 17.6%; Graduate/professional degree or higher: 6.2%

Housing: Homeownership rate: 64.3%; Median home value: $278,700; Median year structure built: 1968; Homeowner vacancy rate: 0.5%; Median selected monthly owner costs: $2,544 with a mortgage, $1,118 without a mortgage; Median gross rent: $1,315 per month; Rental vacancy rate: 6.2%

Health Insurance: 85.9% have insurance; 61.2% have private insurance; 36.0% have public insurance; 14.1% do not have insurance; 2.6% of children under 18 do not have insurance

Transportation: Commute: 86.5% car, 5.7% public transportation, 2.9% walk, 1.2% work from home; Mean travel time to work: 25.8 minutes

NORTH BABYLON (CDP). Covers a land area of 3.370 square miles and a water area of 0.053 square miles. Located at 40.73° N. Lat; 73.33° W. Long. Elevation is 23 feet.

History: North Babylon is a hamlet and census-designated place (CDP) in Suffolk County, New York.

Population: 17,182; Growth (since 2000): -3.9%; Density: 5,098.8 persons per square mile; Race: 82.8% White, 8.4% Black/African American, 2.6% Asian, 0.1% American Indian/Alaska Native, 0.0% Native Hawaiian/Other Pacific Islander, 1.8% Two or more races, 16.5% Hispanic of any race; Average household size: 2.97; Median age: 42.8; Age under 18: 21.6%; Age 65 and over: 13.8%; Males per 100 females: 93.8; Marriage status: 30.8% never married, 53.2% now married, 1.8% separated, 6.3%

widowed, 9.7% divorced; Foreign born: 12.4%; Speak English only: 82.1%; With disability: 12.2%; Veterans: 6.5%; Ancestry: 31.1% Italian, 21.8% Irish, 13.1% German, 5.3% Polish, 3.6% American

Employment: 13.7% management, business, and financial, 5.8% computer, engineering, and science, 11.2% education, legal, community service, arts, and media, 6.6% healthcare practitioners, 15.0% service, 28.5% sales and office, 9.3% natural resources, construction, and maintenance, 9.9% production, transportation, and material moving

Income: Per capita: $38,715; Median household: $95,463; Average household: $110,313; Households with income of $100,000 or more: 47.6%; Poverty rate: 5.6%

Educational Attainment: High school diploma or higher: 93.5%; Bachelor's degree or higher: 28.6%; Graduate/professional degree or higher: 12.1%

School District(s)
North Babylon Union Free SD (KG-12)
    Enrollment: 4,719 . . . . (631) 620-7011

Housing: Homeownership rate: 83.1%; Median home value: $340,500; Median year structure built: 1958; Homeowner vacancy rate: 3.3%; Median selected monthly owner costs: $2,655 with a mortgage, $1,084 without a mortgage; Median gross rent: $1,864 per month; Rental vacancy rate: 4.7%

Health Insurance: 93.6% have insurance; 79.8% have private insurance; 27.7% have public insurance; 6.4% do not have insurance; 2.6% of children under 18 do not have insurance

Transportation: Commute: 89.8% car, 6.0% public transportation, 0.7% walk, 2.7% work from home; Mean travel time to work: 29.9 minutes

Airports: Republic (commercial service–non-primary)

NORTH BAY SHORE (CDP). Covers a land area of 3.252 square miles and a water area of 0 square miles. Located at 40.76° N. Lat; 73.26° W. Long. Elevation is 36 feet.

History: North Bay Shore is an unincorporated neighborhood on Long Island in the Town of Islip in Suffolk County.The area is a suburb of New York City.

Population: 21,886; Growth (since 2000): 46.0%; Density: 6,730.1 persons per square mile; Race: 29.2% White, 18.0% Black/African American, 2.4% Asian, 0.9% American Indian/Alaska Native, 0.0% Native Hawaiian/Other Pacific Islander, 12.2% Two or more races, 66.3% Hispanic of any race; Average household size: 4.95; Median age: 30.5; Age under 18: 28.3%; Age 65 and over: 6.2%; Males per 100 females: 103.7; Marriage status: 42.8% never married, 46.9% now married, 3.5% separated, 3.4% widowed, 6.9% divorced; Foreign born: 41.8%; Speak English only: 34.0%; With disability: 9.0%; Veterans: 2.9%; Ancestry: 3.0% American, 2.4% Irish, 2.4% Haitian, 2.3% German, 2.1% Italian

Employment: 6.8% management, business, and financial, 1.4% computer, engineering, and science, 4.2% education, legal, community service, arts, and media, 2.4% healthcare practitioners, 27.9% service, 24.2% sales and office, 10.2% natural resources, construction, and maintenance, 22.9% production, transportation, and material moving

Income: Per capita: $22,902; Median household: $83,325; Average household: $102,029; Households with income of $100,000 or more: 39.0%; Poverty rate: 9.7%

Educational Attainment: High school diploma or higher: 67.4%; Bachelor's degree or higher: 11.5%; Graduate/professional degree or higher: 3.7%

Housing: Homeownership rate: 75.3%; Median home value: $288,300; Median year structure built: 1967; Homeowner vacancy rate: 1.9%; Median selected monthly owner costs: $2,537 with a mortgage, $1,026 without a mortgage; Median gross rent: $1,703 per month; Rental vacancy rate: 5.6%

Health Insurance: 87.7% have insurance; 61.5% have private insurance; 32.5% have public insurance; 12.3% do not have insurance; 2.4% of children under 18 do not have insurance

Transportation: Commute: 88.4% car, 6.9% public transportation, 1.3% walk, 1.1% work from home; Mean travel time to work: 31.1 minutes

NORTH BELLPORT (CDP). Covers a land area of 4.936 square miles and a water area of 0 square miles. Located at 40.79° N. Lat; 72.95° W. Long. Elevation is 46 feet.

History: North Bellport is a hamlet and census-designated place (CDP) in Suffolk County, New York.

Population: 11,561; Growth (since 2000): 28.4%; Density: 2,342.0 persons per square mile; Race: 68.9% White, 23.0% Black/African American, 3.8% Asian, 0.0% American Indian/Alaska Native, 0.0% Native

Hawaiian/Other Pacific Islander, 2.8% Two or more races, 32.7% Hispanic of any race; Average household size: 3.31; Median age: 33.1; Age under 18: 27.7%; Age 65 and over: 7.8%; Males per 100 females: 98.5; Marriage status: 45.2% never married, 41.5% now married, 4.3% separated, 3.7% widowed, 9.6% divorced; Foreign born: 20.9%; Speak English only: 66.8%; With disability: 9.3%; Veterans: 4.7%; Ancestry: 20.6% Italian, 11.8% Irish, 7.4% German, 3.3% English, 2.5% Polish
Employment: 14.2% management, business, and financial, 3.8% computer, engineering, and science, 6.1% education, legal, community service, arts, and media, 4.8% healthcare practitioners, 19.6% service, 24.6% sales and office, 13.5% natural resources, construction, and maintenance, 13.5% production, transportation, and material moving
Income: Per capita: $25,600; Median household: $63,621; Average household: $79,251; Households with income of $100,000 or more: 27.2%; Poverty rate: 17.9%
Educational Attainment: High school diploma or higher: 81.6%; Bachelor's degree or higher: 18.3%; Graduate/professional degree or higher: 6.9%
Housing: Homeownership rate: 57.8%; Median home value: $260,900; Median year structure built: 1978; Homeowner vacancy rate: 1.1%; Median selected monthly owner costs: $2,320 with a mortgage, $983 without a mortgage; Median gross rent: $2,067 per month; Rental vacancy rate: 6.6%
Health Insurance: 90.4% have insurance; 63.6% have private insurance; 38.2% have public insurance; 9.6% do not have insurance; 0.6% of children under 18 do not have insurance
Transportation: Commute: 90.2% car, 5.3% public transportation, 0.9% walk, 1.7% work from home; Mean travel time to work: 31.4 minutes

NORTH GREAT RIVER (CDP). Covers a land area of 2.325 square miles and a water area of 0.023 square miles. Located at 40.76° N. Lat; 73.16° W. Long. Elevation is 30 feet.
Population: 3,720; Growth (since 2000): -5.3%; Density: 1,600.0 persons per square mile; Race: 91.5% White, 4.1% Black/African American, 2.8% Asian, 0.0% American Indian/Alaska Native, 0.0% Native Hawaiian/Other Pacific Islander, 1.6% Two or more races, 6.6% Hispanic of any race; Average household size: 2.90; Median age: 46.2; Age under 18: 19.7%; Age 65 and over: 21.0%; Males per 100 females: 97.9; Marriage status: 36.1% never married, 47.3% now married, 0.4% separated, 10.0% widowed, 6.6% divorced; Foreign born: 8.0%; Speak English only: 89.7%; With disability: 5.6%; Veterans: 6.4%; Ancestry: 32.5% Italian, 29.7% Irish, 25.3% German, 4.7% English, 3.5% Polish
Employment: 15.1% management, business, and financial, 7.2% computer, engineering, and science, 11.0% education, legal, community service, arts, and media, 5.5% healthcare practitioners, 17.8% service, 31.4% sales and office, 5.9% natural resources, construction, and maintenance, 6.1% production, transportation, and material moving
Income: Per capita: $37,270; Median household: $80,000; Average household: $104,540; Households with income of $100,000 or more: 40.0%; Poverty rate: 5.7%
Educational Attainment: High school diploma or higher: 91.2%; Bachelor's degree or higher: 27.3%; Graduate/professional degree or higher: 9.8%
Housing: Homeownership rate: 78.5%; Median home value: $353,900; Median year structure built: 1967; Homeowner vacancy rate: 2.6%; Median selected monthly owner costs: $2,843 with a mortgage, $1,313 without a mortgage; Median gross rent: $1,849 per month; Rental vacancy rate: 6.8%
Health Insurance: 97.9% have insurance; 87.7% have private insurance; 28.7% have public insurance; 2.1% do not have insurance; 0.1% of children under 18 do not have insurance
Transportation: Commute: 88.5% car, 6.0% public transportation, 1.0% walk, 3.6% work from home; Mean travel time to work: 26.1 minutes

NORTH HAVEN (village). Covers a land area of 2.713 square miles and a water area of 0 square miles. Located at 41.02° N. Lat; 72.31° W. Long. Elevation is 20 feet.
Population: 931; Growth (since 2000): 25.3%; Density: 343.2 persons per square mile; Race: 98.8% White, 0.0% Black/African American, 0.3% Asian, 0.0% American Indian/Alaska Native, 0.5% Native Hawaiian/Other Pacific Islander, 0.3% Two or more races, 1.1% Hispanic of any race; Average household size: 2.45; Median age: 51.0; Age under 18: 22.1%; Age 65 and over: 25.0%; Males per 100 females: 91.5; Marriage status: 18.7% never married, 68.3% now married, 1.1% separated, 5.3% widowed, 7.7% divorced; Foreign born: 6.2%; Speak English only: 97.6%;

With disability: 9.2%; Veterans: 8.3%; Ancestry: 29.3% Irish, 20.9% Italian, 16.0% English, 13.9% German, 5.0% Polish
Employment: 22.1% management, business, and financial, 6.4% computer, engineering, and science, 14.7% education, legal, community service, arts, and media, 4.1% healthcare practitioners, 12.2% service, 25.7% sales and office, 13.3% natural resources, construction, and maintenance, 1.4% production, transportation, and material moving
Income: Per capita: $95,959; Median household: $117,500; Average household: $235,028; Households with income of $100,000 or more: 61.9%; Poverty rate: 3.3%
Educational Attainment: High school diploma or higher: 97.7%; Bachelor's degree or higher: 60.5%; Graduate/professional degree or higher: 29.8%
Housing: Homeownership rate: 95.3%; Median home value: $1,108,100; Median year structure built: 1973; Homeowner vacancy rate: 3.7%; Median selected monthly owner costs: $3,571 with a mortgage, $1,186 without a mortgage; Median gross rent: $3,000 per month; Rental vacancy rate: 10.0%
Health Insurance: 95.9% have insurance; 86.3% have private insurance; 29.5% have public insurance; 4.1% do not have insurance; 2.4% of children under 18 do not have insurance
Transportation: Commute: 70.6% car, 9.9% public transportation, 3.0% walk, 14.5% work from home; Mean travel time to work: 27.2 minutes

NORTH LINDENHURST (CDP). Covers a land area of 1.920 square miles and a water area of 0 square miles. Located at 40.71° N. Lat; 73.39° W. Long. Elevation is 43 feet.
History: North Lindenhurst is a hamlet (and census-designated place) in Suffolk County, New York.
Population: 10,788; Growth (since 2000): -8.3%; Density: 5,619.9 persons per square mile; Race: 84.3% White, 6.7% Black/African American, 1.4% Asian, 0.0% American Indian/Alaska Native, 0.0% Native Hawaiian/Other Pacific Islander, 1.4% Two or more races, 22.1% Hispanic of any race; Average household size: 3.05; Median age: 37.8; Age under 18: 21.2%; Age 65 and over: 12.2%; Males per 100 females: 96.3; Marriage status: 32.1% never married, 52.1% now married, 2.8% separated, 6.7% widowed, 9.0% divorced; Foreign born: 27.7%; Speak English only: 64.1%; With disability: 8.9%; Veterans: 5.3%; Ancestry: 23.3% Italian, 18.3% Irish, 11.4% German, 7.8% Polish, 2.8% English
Employment: 7.6% management, business, and financial, 2.9% computer, engineering, and science, 9.5% education, legal, community service, arts, and media, 3.9% healthcare practitioners, 21.8% service, 34.7% sales and office, 11.0% natural resources, construction, and maintenance, 8.7% production, transportation, and material moving
Income: Per capita: $31,286; Median household: $70,694; Average household: $90,666; Households with income of $100,000 or more: 36.9%; Poverty rate: 5.9%
Educational Attainment: High school diploma or higher: 85.1%; Bachelor's degree or higher: 17.4%; Graduate/professional degree or higher: 6.4%
Housing: Homeownership rate: 68.8%; Median home value: $337,900; Median year structure built: 1958; Homeowner vacancy rate: 0.8%; Median selected monthly owner costs: $2,754 with a mortgage, $1,151 without a mortgage; Median gross rent: $1,554 per month; Rental vacancy rate: 4.1%
Health Insurance: 90.5% have insurance; 71.8% have private insurance; 30.1% have public insurance; 9.5% do not have insurance; 2.7% of children under 18 do not have insurance
Transportation: Commute: 89.9% car, 6.6% public transportation, 0.9% walk, 1.6% work from home; Mean travel time to work: 28.5 minutes

NORTH PATCHOGUE (CDP). Covers a land area of 1.978 square miles and a water area of 0.052 square miles. Located at 40.78° N. Lat; 73.02° W. Long. Elevation is 49 feet.
History: North Patchogue is a hamlet and census-designated place (CDP) in Suffolk County, New York.
Population: 6,869; Growth (since 2000): -12.2%; Density: 3,473.4 persons per square mile; Race: 94.7% White, 3.2% Black/African American, 1.3% Asian, 0.0% American Indian/Alaska Native, 0.0% Native Hawaiian/Other Pacific Islander, 0.8% Two or more races, 25.5% Hispanic of any race; Average household size: 2.89; Median age: 39.1; Age under 18: 22.7%; Age 65 and over: 13.6%; Males per 100 females: 98.2; Marriage status: 29.0% never married, 58.8% now married, 0.5% separated, 4.7% widowed, 7.5% divorced; Foreign born: 15.2%; Speak English only: 74.5%;

With disability: 9.6%; Veterans: 6.9%; Ancestry: 28.5% Italian, 23.5% Irish, 19.3% German, 4.6% English, 3.3% Polish
Employment: 12.8% management, business, and financial, 4.3% computer, engineering, and science, 11.3% education, legal, community service, arts, and media, 5.7% healthcare practitioners, 15.5% service, 25.3% sales and office, 16.9% natural resources, construction, and maintenance, 8.2% production, transportation, and material moving
Income: Per capita: $32,310; Median household: $83,750; Average household: $88,847; Households with income of $100,000 or more: 43.5%; Poverty rate: 9.2%
Educational Attainment: High school diploma or higher: 90.9%; Bachelor's degree or higher: 20.7%; Graduate/professional degree or higher: 5.8%
Housing: Homeownership rate: 87.5%; Median home value: $280,300; Median year structure built: 1961; Homeowner vacancy rate: 2.2%; Median selected monthly owner costs: $2,515 with a mortgage, $981 without a mortgage; Median gross rent: $1,389 per month; Rental vacancy rate: 0.0%
Health Insurance: 96.8% have insurance; 79.6% have private insurance; 27.9% have public insurance; 3.2% do not have insurance; 0.6% of children under 18 do not have insurance
Transportation: Commute: 93.9% car, 2.0% public transportation, 1.1% walk, 2.3% work from home; Mean travel time to work: 30.3 minutes

NORTH SEA (CDP).
Covers a land area of 11.052 square miles and a water area of 1.041 square miles. Located at 40.93° N. Lat; 72.41° W. Long. Elevation is 16 feet.
Population: 4,465; Growth (since 2000): -0.6%; Density: 404.0 persons per square mile; Race: 96.0% White, 0.5% Black/African American, 3.5% Asian, 0.0% American Indian/Alaska Native, 0.0% Native Hawaiian/Other Pacific Islander, 0.0% Two or more races, 9.9% Hispanic of any race; Average household size: 2.41; Median age: 48.1; Age under 18: 17.0%; Age 65 and over: 26.0%; Males per 100 females: 103.7; Marriage status: 26.1% never married, 58.3% now married, 1.1% separated, 7.2% widowed, 8.4% divorced; Foreign born: 18.0%; Speak English only: 80.2%; With disability: 9.1%; Veterans: 5.6%; Ancestry: 16.8% Irish, 13.8% German, 12.9% Italian, 11.0% English, 9.9% Polish
Employment: 18.1% management, business, and financial, 2.8% computer, engineering, and science, 11.4% education, legal, community service, arts, and media, 7.1% healthcare practitioners, 19.4% service, 25.1% sales and office, 12.5% natural resources, construction, and maintenance, 3.6% production, transportation, and material moving
Income: Per capita: $65,997; Median household: $82,976; Average household: $155,280; Households with income of $100,000 or more: 44.7%; Poverty rate: 7.7%
Educational Attainment: High school diploma or higher: 96.0%; Bachelor's degree or higher: 49.5%; Graduate/professional degree or higher: 16.1%
Housing: Homeownership rate: 79.9%; Median home value: $817,200; Median year structure built: 1979; Homeowner vacancy rate: 3.5%; Median selected monthly owner costs: $2,806 with a mortgage, $856 without a mortgage; Median gross rent: $1,934 per month; Rental vacancy rate: 0.0%
Health Insurance: 92.0% have insurance; 75.1% have private insurance; 34.2% have public insurance; 8.0% do not have insurance; 6.4% of children under 18 do not have insurance
Transportation: Commute: 81.9% car, 7.6% public transportation, 2.3% walk, 6.5% work from home; Mean travel time to work: 25.7 minutes

NORTHAMPTON (CDP).
Covers a land area of 11.551 square miles and a water area of 0.100 square miles. Located at 40.88° N. Lat; 72.68° W. Long. Elevation is 151 feet.
Population: 420; Growth (since 2000): -10.3%; Density: 36.4 persons per square mile; Race: 55.2% White, 33.8% Black/African American, 2.4% Asian, 0.0% American Indian/Alaska Native, 0.0% Native Hawaiian/Other Pacific Islander, 8.6% Two or more races, 38.3% Hispanic of any race; Average household size: 2.94; Median age: 34.9; Age under 18: 12.4%; Age 65 and over: 13.6%; Males per 100 females: 108.8; Marriage status: 51.4% never married, 45.4% now married, 2.7% separated, 0.0% widowed, 3.3% divorced; Foreign born: 6.0%; Speak English only: 81.0%; With disability: 23.1%; Veterans: 1.9%; Ancestry: 20.0% Italian, 8.3% Ukrainian, 6.4% English, 6.4% Finnish, 5.2% German
Employment: 6.3% management, business, and financial, 0.0% computer, engineering, and science, 7.0% education, legal, community service, arts, and media, 25.0% healthcare practitioners, 10.9% service, 35.6% sales

and office, 6.3% natural resources, construction, and maintenance, 8.8% production, transportation, and material moving
Income: Per capita: $35,765; Median household: $106,607; Average household: $101,410; Households with income of $100,000 or more: 53.2%; Poverty rate: 26.2%
Educational Attainment: High school diploma or higher: 87.1%; Bachelor's degree or higher: 29.1%; Graduate/professional degree or higher: 22.0%
Housing: Homeownership rate: 59.4%; Median home value: $317,300; Median year structure built: 1966; Homeowner vacancy rate: 0.0%; Median selected monthly owner costs: $1,864 with a mortgage, $863 without a mortgage; Median gross rent: n/a per month; Rental vacancy rate: 0.0%
Health Insurance: 95.2% have insurance; 89.3% have private insurance; 17.1% have public insurance; 4.8% do not have insurance; 0.0% of children under 18 do not have insurance
Transportation: Commute: 88.4% car, 0.0% public transportation, 11.6% walk, 0.0% work from home; Mean travel time to work: 27.9 minutes

NORTHPORT (village).
Covers a land area of 2.308 square miles and a water area of 0.222 square miles. Located at 40.90° N. Lat; 73.34° W. Long. Elevation is 59 feet.
History: Although it was known by the name of Northport since at least 1837, the village of Northport was formally incorporated in 1894, the first village to do so in Huntington Township. Over the years Northport has expanded from its original borders, annexing other established communities.
Population: 7,405; Growth (since 2000): -2.6%; Density: 3,208.0 persons per square mile; Race: 96.6% White, 1.4% Black/African American, 1.2% Asian, 0.0% American Indian/Alaska Native, 0.0% Native Hawaiian/Other Pacific Islander, 0.8% Two or more races, 4.1% Hispanic of any race; Average household size: 2.43; Median age: 48.3; Age under 18: 20.0%; Age 65 and over: 22.2%; Males per 100 females: 95.5; Marriage status: 23.5% never married, 58.7% now married, 2.4% separated, 6.0% widowed, 11.8% divorced; Foreign born: 6.8%; Speak English only: 92.5%; With disability: 8.0%; Veterans: 7.2%; Ancestry: 31.2% Italian, 20.2% Irish, 14.5% German, 12.9% English, 6.0% American
Employment: 21.1% management, business, and financial, 5.8% computer, engineering, and science, 17.3% education, legal, community service, arts, and media, 7.7% healthcare practitioners, 8.9% service, 27.5% sales and office, 6.5% natural resources, construction, and maintenance, 5.1% production, transportation, and material moving
Income: Per capita: $56,892; Median household: $108,850; Average household: $137,811; Households with income of $100,000 or more: 53.3%; Poverty rate: 4.5%
Educational Attainment: High school diploma or higher: 97.2%; Bachelor's degree or higher: 61.6%; Graduate/professional degree or higher: 28.1%

School District(s)
Kings Park Central SD (KG-12)
    Enrollment: 3,335 . . . . (631) 269-3310
Northport-East Northport Union Free SD (KG-12)
    Enrollment: 5,547 . . . . (631) 262-6604
Two-year College(s)
Western Suffolk BOCES (Public)
    Enrollment: 265 . . . . (631) 261-3600
Housing: Homeownership rate: 78.4%; Median home value: $562,600; Median year structure built: 1954; Homeowner vacancy rate: 2.4%; Median selected monthly owner costs: $2,958 with a mortgage, $1,270 without a mortgage; Median gross rent: $1,414 per month; Rental vacancy rate: 18.9%
Health Insurance: 98.0% have insurance; 85.4% have private insurance; 29.9% have public insurance; 2.0% do not have insurance; 3.3% of children under 18 do not have insurance
Hospitals: Northport VA Medical Center (524 beds)
Safety: Violent crime rate: 5.5 per 10,000 population; Property crime rate: 57.3 per 10,000 population
Transportation: Commute: 79.8% car, 10.8% public transportation, 1.7% walk, 2.9% work from home; Mean travel time to work: 35.4 minutes
Additional Information Contacts
Village of Northport . . . . (631) 261-7502
    http://www.northportny.gov

NORTHVILLE (CDP). Covers a land area of 7.404 square miles and a water area of 0.021 square miles. Located at 40.98° N. Lat; 72.63° W. Long. Elevation is 59 feet.

Population: 1,677; Growth (since 2000): 109.4%; Density: 226.5 persons per square mile; Race: 94.1% White, 1.4% Black/African American, 0.0% Asian, 0.0% American Indian/Alaska Native, 0.0% Native Hawaiian/Other Pacific Islander, 0.0% Two or more races, 11.2% Hispanic of any race; Average household size: 2.36; Median age: 56.9; Age under 18: 14.5%; Age 65 and over: 35.7%; Males per 100 females: 99.4; Marriage status: 12.5% never married, 73.1% now married, 4.0% separated, 13.7% widowed, 0.7% divorced; Foreign born: 11.7%; Speak English only: 81.4%; With disability: 9.5%; Veterans: 5.9%; Ancestry: 15.8% American, 15.0% Italian, 12.7% Irish, 9.6% European, 8.8% Polish
Employment: 46.2% management, business, and financial, 0.0% computer, engineering, and science, 2.9% education, legal, community service, arts, and media, 0.0% healthcare practitioners, 26.1% service, 20.6% sales and office, 3.2% natural resources, construction, and maintenance, 1.0% production, transportation, and material moving
Income: Per capita: $35,646; Median household: $76,250; Average household: $82,339; Households with income of $100,000 or more: 35.5%; Poverty rate: 0.7%
Educational Attainment: High school diploma or higher: 96.3%; Bachelor's degree or higher: 23.7%; Graduate/professional degree or higher: 10.6%
Housing: Homeownership rate: 93.0%; Median home value: $454,000; Median year structure built: 2001; Homeowner vacancy rate: 5.5%; Median selected monthly owner costs: $2,916 with a mortgage, $1,028 without a mortgage; Median gross rent: n/a per month; Rental vacancy rate: 0.0%
Health Insurance: 99.0% have insurance; 95.9% have private insurance; 36.9% have public insurance; 1.0% do not have insurance; 0.0% of children under 18 do not have insurance
Transportation: Commute: 90.6% car, 1.9% public transportation, 7.5% walk, 0.0% work from home; Mean travel time to work: 32.3 minutes

NORTHWEST HARBOR (CDP). Covers a land area of 14.473 square miles and a water area of 1.580 square miles. Located at 41.00° N. Lat; 72.22° W. Long. Elevation is 79 feet.

History: Northwest Harbor is named for the bay on the South Fork of Long Island connecting Sag Harbor, Shelter Island and East Hampton town to Gardiners Bay and the open waters of the Atlantic Ocean. The bay derives its name from being northwest of East Hampton village.
Population: 2,835; Growth (since 2000): -7.3%; Density: 195.9 persons per square mile; Race: 89.1% White, 2.2% Black/African American, 1.4% Asian, 0.0% American Indian/Alaska Native, 0.0% Native Hawaiian/Other Pacific Islander, 2.6% Two or more races, 19.9% Hispanic of any race; Average household size: 2.10; Median age: 55.6; Age under 18: 9.1%; Age 65 and over: 31.6%; Males per 100 females: 96.6; Marriage status: 19.7% never married, 62.4% now married, 1.6% separated, 7.0% widowed, 11.0% divorced; Foreign born: 18.6%; Speak English only: 78.0%; With disability: 10.6%; Veterans: 6.2%; Ancestry: 16.4% Italian, 13.4% Irish, 8.5% Russian, 8.2% Polish, 7.0% English
Employment: 18.8% management, business, and financial, 6.4% computer, engineering, and science, 17.8% education, legal, community service, arts, and media, 4.3% healthcare practitioners, 20.1% service, 17.9% sales and office, 8.4% natural resources, construction, and maintenance, 6.3% production, transportation, and material moving
Income: Per capita: $110,733; Median household: $157,708; Average household: $231,216; Households with income of $100,000 or more: 60.4%; Poverty rate: 7.7%
Educational Attainment: High school diploma or higher: 98.5%; Bachelor's degree or higher: 56.3%; Graduate/professional degree or higher: 29.0%
Housing: Homeownership rate: 94.0%; Median home value: $901,700; Median year structure built: 1979; Homeowner vacancy rate: 1.2%; Median selected monthly owner costs: $2,492 with a mortgage, $1,302 without a mortgage; Median gross rent: $1,003 per month; Rental vacancy rate: 0.0%
Health Insurance: 97.2% have insurance; 82.2% have private insurance; 40.6% have public insurance; 2.8% do not have insurance; 6.1% of children under 18 do not have insurance
Transportation: Commute: 62.0% car, 17.0% public transportation, 8.2% walk, 12.8% work from home; Mean travel time to work: 28.1 minutes

NOYACK (CDP). Covers a land area of 8.404 square miles and a water area of 0.322 square miles. Located at 40.98° N. Lat; 72.35° W. Long. Elevation is 26 feet.

Population: 3,808; Growth (since 2000): 41.2%; Density: 453.1 persons per square mile; Race: 89.3% White, 3.3% Black/African American, 5.7% Asian, 0.0% American Indian/Alaska Native, 0.0% Native Hawaiian/Other Pacific Islander, 0.4% Two or more races, 16.5% Hispanic of any race; Average household size: 2.76; Median age: 41.0; Age under 18: 22.8%; Age 65 and over: 16.6%; Males per 100 females: 93.1; Marriage status: 36.6% never married, 41.3% now married, 0.5% separated, 7.5% widowed, 14.6% divorced; Foreign born: 24.0%; Speak English only: 75.3%; With disability: 7.9%; Veterans: 4.4%; Ancestry: 19.5% Irish, 18.9% Italian, 18.3% German, 8.3% English, 4.9% American
Employment: 27.7% management, business, and financial, 3.5% computer, engineering, and science, 17.6% education, legal, community service, arts, and media, 1.2% healthcare practitioners, 15.6% service, 18.8% sales and office, 13.4% natural resources, construction, and maintenance, 2.2% production, transportation, and material moving
Income: Per capita: $48,480; Median household: $86,979; Average household: $130,283; Households with income of $100,000 or more: 46.1%; Poverty rate: 4.2%
Educational Attainment: High school diploma or higher: 95.7%; Bachelor's degree or higher: 57.7%; Graduate/professional degree or higher: 22.6%
Housing: Homeownership rate: 80.4%; Median home value: $714,900; Median year structure built: 1976; Homeowner vacancy rate: 1.8%; Median selected monthly owner costs: $3,116 with a mortgage, $871 without a mortgage; Median gross rent: $2,122 per month; Rental vacancy rate: 0.0%
Health Insurance: 83.7% have insurance; 69.9% have private insurance; 27.5% have public insurance; 16.3% do not have insurance; 1.5% of children under 18 do not have insurance
Transportation: Commute: 81.5% car, 2.7% public transportation, 0.0% walk, 14.1% work from home; Mean travel time to work: 19.5 minutes

OAK BEACH-CAPTREE (CDP). Covers a land area of 2.756 square miles and a water area of 0.920 square miles. Located at 40.65° N. Lat; 73.27° W. Long.

Population: 37; Growth (since 2000): n/a; Density: 13.4 persons per square mile; Race: 100.0% White, 0.0% Black/African American, 0.0% Asian, 0.0% American Indian/Alaska Native, 0.0% Native Hawaiian/Other Pacific Islander, 0.0% Two or more races, 0.0% Hispanic of any race; Average household size: 0.00; Median age: n/a; Age under 18: 0.0%; Age 65 and over: 27.0%; Males per 100 females: 100.0; Marriage status: 0.0% never married, 0.0% now married, 0.0% separated, 0.0% widowed, 100.0% divorced; Foreign born: 0.0%; Speak English only: 100.0%; With disability: 0.0%; Veterans: 0.0%; Ancestry: 73.0% German, 27.0% Irish
Employment: 0.0% management, business, and financial, 100.0% computer, engineering, and science, 0.0% education, legal, community service, arts, and media, 0.0% healthcare practitioners, 0.0% service, 0.0% sales and office, 0.0% natural resources, construction, and maintenance, 0.0% production, transportation, and material moving
Income: Per capita: n/a; Median household: n/a; Average household: n/a; Households with income of $100,000 or more: 27.0%; Poverty rate: n/a
Educational Attainment: High school diploma or higher: 100.0%; Bachelor's degree or higher: 100.0%; Graduate/professional degree or higher: 100.0%
Housing: Homeownership rate: 100.0%; Median home value: n/a; Median year structure built: 1976; Homeowner vacancy rate: 0.0%; Median selected monthly owner costs: n/a with a mortgage, n/a without a mortgage; Median gross rent: n/a per month; Rental vacancy rate: 0.0%
Health Insurance: 100.0% have insurance; 100.0% have private insurance; 27.0% have public insurance; 0.0% do not have insurance; 0.0% of children under 18 do not have insurance
Transportation: Commute: 100.0% car, 0.0% public transportation, 0.0% walk, 0.0% work from home; Mean travel time to work: 0.0 minutes

OAKDALE (CDP). Covers a land area of 3.417 square miles and a water area of 0.394 square miles. Located at 40.74° N. Lat; 73.13° W. Long. Elevation is 10 feet.

History: Seat of Dowling College.
Population: 7,274; Growth (since 2000): -9.9%; Density: 2,128.6 persons per square mile; Race: 95.9% White, 2.2% Black/African American, 0.6% Asian, 0.0% American Indian/Alaska Native, 0.0% Native Hawaiian/Other Pacific Islander, 0.8% Two or more races, 7.3% Hispanic of any race;

Average household size: 2.50; Median age: 46.5; Age under 18: 17.0%; Age 65 and over: 19.5%; Males per 100 females: 91.1; Marriage status: 28.0% never married, 55.5% now married, 1.4% separated, 7.4% widowed, 9.2% divorced; Foreign born: 6.4%; Speak English only: 91.4%; With disability: 13.0%; Veterans: 7.5%; Ancestry: 34.7% Italian, 23.5% Irish, 20.4% German, 6.5% English, 5.5% Polish

Employment: 17.6% management, business, and financial, 5.0% computer, engineering, and science, 18.7% education, legal, community service, arts, and media, 5.1% healthcare practitioners, 16.0% service, 22.8% sales and office, 7.9% natural resources, construction, and maintenance, 6.8% production, transportation, and material moving

Income: Per capita: $45,128; Median household: $89,375; Average household: $112,624; Households with income of $100,000 or more: 45.0%; Poverty rate: 3.4%

Educational Attainment: High school diploma or higher: 94.6%; Bachelor's degree or higher: 34.3%; Graduate/professional degree or higher: 18.8%

School District(s)
Connetquot Central SD (PK-12)
   Enrollment: 5,982 . . . . (631) 244-2215
Vocational/Technical School(s)
Eastern Suffolk BOCES (Public)
   Enrollment: n/a . . . . (631) 233-4450
   Tuition: $10,190

Housing: Homeownership rate: 85.6%; Median home value: $424,600; Median year structure built: 1969; Homeowner vacancy rate: 2.4%; Median selected monthly owner costs: $2,958 with a mortgage, $1,377 without a mortgage; Median gross rent: $1,488 per month; Rental vacancy rate: 0.0%

Health Insurance: 94.8% have insurance; 83.5% have private insurance; 27.6% have public insurance; 5.2% do not have insurance; 1.6% of children under 18 do not have insurance

Transportation: Commute: 87.2% car, 7.8% public transportation, 1.7% walk, 3.0% work from home; Mean travel time to work: 32.9 minutes

OCEAN BEACH (village).
Covers a land area of 0.141 square miles and a water area of 0 square miles. Located at 40.65° N. Lat; 73.16° W. Long. Elevation is 3 feet.

Population: 24; Growth (since 2000): -82.6%; Density: 169.8 persons per square mile; Race: 100.0% White, 0.0% Black/African American, 0.0% Asian, 0.0% American Indian/Alaska Native, 0.0% Native Hawaiian/Other Pacific Islander, 0.0% Two or more races, 0.0% Hispanic of any race; Average household size: 1.50; Median age: 55.8; Age under 18: 0.0%; Age 65 and over: 16.7%; Males per 100 females: 146.9; Marriage status: 62.5% never married, 16.7% now married, 0.0% separated, 8.3% widowed, 12.5% divorced; Foreign born: 4.2%; Speak English only: 100.0%; With disability: 33.3%; Veterans: 25.0%; Ancestry: 25.0% Scottish, 12.5% German, 8.3% English, 8.3% French, 8.3% Italian

Employment: 25.0% management, business, and financial, 0.0% computer, engineering, and science, 0.0% education, legal, community service, arts, and media, 6.3% healthcare practitioners, 6.3% service, 43.8% sales and office, 12.5% natural resources, construction, and maintenance, 6.3% production, transportation, and material moving

Income: Per capita: $47,313; Median household: n/a; Average household: $70,969; Households with income of $100,000 or more: 37.6%; Poverty rate: 25.0%

Educational Attainment: High school diploma or higher: 100.0%; Bachelor's degree or higher: 41.7%; Graduate/professional degree or higher: 29.2%

Housing: Homeownership rate: 100.0%; Median home value: n/a; Median year structure built: 1946; Homeowner vacancy rate: 0.0%; Median selected monthly owner costs: $2,750 with a mortgage, $1,050 without a mortgage; Median gross rent: n/a per month; Rental vacancy rate: 0.0%

Health Insurance: 95.8% have insurance; 70.8% have private insurance; 41.7% have public insurance; 4.2% do not have insurance; 0.0% of children under 18 do not have insurance

Safety: Violent crime rate: 0.0 per 10,000 population; Property crime rate: 975.6 per 10,000 population

Transportation: Commute: 31.3% car, 0.0% public transportation, 6.3% walk, 12.5% work from home; Mean travel time to work: 16.1 minutes

Additional Information Contacts
Village of Ocean Beach . . . . (631) 583-5940
   http://www.villageofoceanbeach.org

OLD FIELD (village).
Covers a land area of 2.070 square miles and a water area of 0.121 square miles. Located at 40.96° N. Lat; 73.15° W. Long. Elevation is 7 feet.

Population: 826; Growth (since 2000): -12.8%; Density: 399.1 persons per square mile; Race: 84.7% White, 1.2% Black/African American, 12.6% Asian, 0.0% American Indian/Alaska Native, 0.0% Native Hawaiian/Other Pacific Islander, 1.1% Two or more races, 2.9% Hispanic of any race; Average household size: 2.64; Median age: 49.2; Age under 18: 20.6%; Age 65 and over: 18.2%; Males per 100 females: 104.5; Marriage status: 20.9% never married, 68.6% now married, 0.9% separated, 6.1% widowed, 4.5% divorced; Foreign born: 19.0%; Speak English only: 82.5%; With disability: 6.1%; Veterans: 3.5%; Ancestry: 13.2% Italian, 11.4% Irish, 9.8% German, 8.2% American, 6.8% English

Employment: 26.0% management, business, and financial, 7.6% computer, engineering, and science, 18.3% education, legal, community service, arts, and media, 22.4% healthcare practitioners, 5.0% service, 17.1% sales and office, 1.7% natural resources, construction, and maintenance, 1.9% production, transportation, and material moving

Income: Per capita: $126,419; Median household: $203,500; Average household: $336,871; Households with income of $100,000 or more: 80.9%; Poverty rate: 5.8%

Educational Attainment: High school diploma or higher: 98.5%; Bachelor's degree or higher: 78.3%; Graduate/professional degree or higher: 58.0%

Housing: Homeownership rate: 92.5%; Median home value: $1,081,100; Median year structure built: 1968; Homeowner vacancy rate: 0.0%; Median selected monthly owner costs: $4,000+ with a mortgage, $1,501 without a mortgage; Median gross rent: $1,875 per month; Rental vacancy rate: 0.0%

Health Insurance: 99.3% have insurance; 90.7% have private insurance; 21.9% have public insurance; 0.7% do not have insurance; 1.1% of children under 18 do not have insurance

Transportation: Commute: 85.1% car, 7.0% public transportation, 0.7% walk, 6.0% work from home; Mean travel time to work: 30.5 minutes
Additional Information Contacts
Village of Old Field . . . . (631) 941-9412
   http://www.oldfieldny.org

ORIENT (CDP).
Covers a land area of 5.122 square miles and a water area of 1.032 square miles. Located at 41.14° N. Lat; 72.26° W. Long. Elevation is 13 feet.

Population: 718; Growth (since 2000): 1.3%; Density: 140.2 persons per square mile; Race: 97.8% White, 0.0% Black/African American, 0.0% Asian, 1.0% American Indian/Alaska Native, 0.0% Native Hawaiian/Other Pacific Islander, 1.3% Two or more races, 1.9% Hispanic of any race; Average household size: 2.12; Median age: 64.4; Age under 18: 9.7%; Age 65 and over: 48.5%; Males per 100 females: 89.5; Marriage status: 15.8% never married, 69.2% now married, 0.6% separated, 5.3% widowed, 9.7% divorced; Foreign born: 1.9%; Speak English only: 95.2%; With disability: 19.8%; Veterans: 18.8%; Ancestry: 25.2% English, 24.5% Irish, 22.0% German, 11.7% Italian, 10.4% Polish

Employment: 18.0% management, business, and financial, 0.0% computer, engineering, and science, 18.3% education, legal, community service, arts, and media, 11.2% healthcare practitioners, 18.0% service, 16.6% sales and office, 13.6% natural resources, construction, and maintenance, 4.4% production, transportation, and material moving

Income: Per capita: $48,720; Median household: $71,125; Average household: $103,034; Households with income of $100,000 or more: 27.2%; Poverty rate: 6.1%

Educational Attainment: High school diploma or higher: 95.2%; Bachelor's degree or higher: 31.6%; Graduate/professional degree or higher: 13.3%

School District(s)
Oysterponds Union Free SD (PK-06)
   Enrollment: 92 . . . . (631) 323-2410
Housing: Homeownership rate: 87.6%; Median home value: $736,700; Median year structure built: 1966; Homeowner vacancy rate: 2.3%; Median selected monthly owner costs: $2,542 with a mortgage, $1,057 without a mortgage; Median gross rent: $1,577 per month; Rental vacancy rate: 0.0%

Health Insurance: 96.2% have insurance; 76.0% have private insurance; 59.2% have public insurance; 3.8% do not have insurance; 0.0% of children under 18 do not have insurance

Transportation: Commute: 72.9% car, 8.6% public transportation, 2.7% walk, 13.1% work from home; Mean travel time to work: 40.2 minutes

PATCHOGUE (village). Covers a land area of 2.255 square miles and a water area of 0.262 square miles. Located at 40.76° N. Lat; 73.02° W. Long. Elevation is 20 feet.

History: Patchogue is a village on the south shore of Long Island in Suffolk County, New York.

Population: 12,425; Growth (since 2000): 4.2%; Density: 5,508.9 persons per square mile; Race: 84.5% White, 5.1% Black/African American, 2.2% Asian, 0.4% American Indian/Alaska Native, 0.0% Native Hawaiian/Other Pacific Islander, 2.1% Two or more races, 33.9% Hispanic of any race; Average household size: 2.44; Median age: 36.4; Age under 18: 22.6%; Age 65 and over: 11.7%; Males per 100 females: 100.2; Marriage status: 38.3% never married, 45.1% now married, 2.5% separated, 4.8% widowed, 11.8% divorced; Foreign born: 17.0%; Speak English only: 67.4%; With disability: 10.3%; Veterans: 3.5%; Ancestry: 21.5% Italian, 16.2% German, 16.2% Irish, 6.0% English, 3.4% American

Employment: 15.8% management, business, and financial, 3.7% computer, engineering, and science, 10.9% education, legal, community service, arts, and media, 5.0% healthcare practitioners, 18.2% service, 22.5% sales and office, 9.7% natural resources, construction, and maintenance, 14.3% production, transportation, and material moving

Income: Per capita: $35,936; Median household: $69,595; Average household: $85,509; Households with income of $100,000 or more: 30.8%; Poverty rate: 15.3%

Educational Attainment: High school diploma or higher: 85.8%; Bachelor's degree or higher: 29.1%; Graduate/professional degree or higher: 11.5%

School District(s)
Eastern Suffolk Boces
  Enrollment: n/a . . . . (631) 687-3006
Patchogue-Medford Union Free SD (KG-12)
  Enrollment: 7,666 . . . . (631) 687-6380

Four-year College(s)
St. Joseph's College-Long Island (Private, Not-for-profit)
  Enrollment: 3,966 . . . . (631) 687-5100
  Tuition: In-state $26,560; Out-of-state $26,560

Housing: Homeownership rate: 52.3%; Median home value: $300,100; Median year structure built: 1966; Homeowner vacancy rate: 1.0%; Median selected monthly owner costs: $2,298 with a mortgage, $1,010 without a mortgage; Median gross rent: $1,474 per month; Rental vacancy rate: 4.2%

Health Insurance: 87.3% have insurance; 69.7% have private insurance; 30.4% have public insurance; 12.7% do not have insurance; 3.1% of children under 18 do not have insurance

Hospitals: Brookhaven Memorial Hospital Medical Center (321 beds)

Newspapers: Long Island Advance (weekly circulation 11,000)

Transportation: Commute: 87.0% car, 3.7% public transportation, 4.9% walk, 2.3% work from home; Mean travel time to work: 29.9 minutes

Additional Information Contacts
Village of Patchogue . . . . (631) 475-4300
  http://www.patchoguevillage.org

PECONIC (CDP). Covers a land area of 3.380 square miles and a water area of 0.126 square miles. Located at 41.04° N. Lat; 72.46° W. Long. Elevation is 30 feet.

Population: 536; Growth (since 2000): -50.4%; Density: 158.6 persons per square mile; Race: 100.0% White, 0.0% Black/African American, 0.0% Asian, 0.0% American Indian/Alaska Native, 0.0% Native Hawaiian/Other Pacific Islander, 0.0% Two or more races, 19.8% Hispanic of any race; Average household size: 1.88; Median age: 60.3; Age under 18: 3.2%; Age 65 and over: 42.0%; Males per 100 females: 109.5; Marriage status: 13.3% never married, 64.7% now married, 0.0% separated, 12.1% widowed, 9.8% divorced; Foreign born: 25.6%; Speak English only: 74.4%; With disability: 16.0%; Veterans: 13.5%; Ancestry: 22.4% German, 14.4% Irish, 11.4% Italian, 10.8% Polish, 5.4% English

Employment: 22.4% management, business, and financial, 6.8% computer, engineering, and science, 3.8% education, legal, community service, arts, and media, 4.2% healthcare practitioners, 16.3% service, 23.2% sales and office, 18.6% natural resources, construction, and maintenance, 4.6% production, transportation, and material moving

Income: Per capita: $62,592; Median household: $64,583; Average household: $112,048; Households with income of $100,000 or more: 35.8%; Poverty rate: n/a

Educational Attainment: High school diploma or higher: 90.9%; Bachelor's degree or higher: 32.5%; Graduate/professional degree or higher: 24.6%

Housing: Homeownership rate: 93.0%; Median home value: $557,100; Median year structure built: 1982; Homeowner vacancy rate: 0.0%; Median selected monthly owner costs: $2,172 with a mortgage, $850 without a mortgage; Median gross rent: n/a per month; Rental vacancy rate: 0.0%

Health Insurance: 80.2% have insurance; 71.8% have private insurance; 46.8% have public insurance; 19.8% do not have insurance; 0.0% of children under 18 do not have insurance

Transportation: Commute: 79.5% car, 4.6% public transportation, 0.0% walk, 16.0% work from home; Mean travel time to work: 16.3 minutes

POOSPATUCK RESERVATION (reservation). Covers a land area of 0.113 square miles and a water area of 0.057 square miles. Located at 40.79° N. Lat; 72.83° W. Long.

Population: 748; Growth (since 2000): 176.0%; Density: 6,638.6 persons per square mile; Race: 15.6% White, 21.0% Black/African American, 0.0% Asian, 53.3% American Indian/Alaska Native, 0.0% Native Hawaiian/Other Pacific Islander, 10.0% Two or more races, 5.1% Hispanic of any race; Average household size: 3.22; Median age: 31.4; Age under 18: 18.0%; Age 65 and over: 8.6%; Males per 100 females: 88.4; Marriage status: 61.3% never married, 30.1% now married, 2.4% separated, 2.7% widowed, 6.0% divorced; Foreign born: 3.3%; Speak English only: 96.0%; With disability: 14.3%; Veterans: 3.6%; Ancestry: 5.2% Irish, 5.1% German, 4.4% Belizean, 3.9% French, 3.9% Italian

Employment: 10.3% management, business, and financial, 0.0% computer, engineering, and science, 9.5% education, legal, community service, arts, and media, 6.5% healthcare practitioners, 19.8% service, 24.4% sales and office, 13.4% natural resources, construction, and maintenance, 16.0% production, transportation, and material moving

Income: Per capita: $17,203; Median household: $33,750; Average household: $49,561; Households with income of $100,000 or more: 12.1%; Poverty rate: 24.1%

Educational Attainment: High school diploma or higher: 75.3%; Bachelor's degree or higher: 7.0%; Graduate/professional degree or higher: 2.3%

Housing: Homeownership rate: 78.9%; Median home value: $159,800; Median year structure built: 1981; Homeowner vacancy rate: 0.0%; Median selected monthly owner costs: $1,476 with a mortgage, $455 without a mortgage; Median gross rent: $1,556 per month; Rental vacancy rate: 0.0%

Health Insurance: 69.7% have insurance; 34.0% have private insurance; 42.8% have public insurance; 30.3% do not have insurance; 14.5% of children under 18 do not have insurance

Transportation: Commute: 78.6% car, 0.0% public transportation, 17.2% walk, 0.0% work from home; Mean travel time to work: 25.9 minutes

POQUOTT (village). Covers a land area of 0.439 square miles and a water area of 0.147 square miles. Located at 40.95° N. Lat; 73.09° W. Long. Elevation is 66 feet.

Population: 992; Growth (since 2000): 1.7%; Density: 2,258.4 persons per square mile; Race: 88.0% White, 1.1% Black/African American, 6.6% Asian, 0.0% American Indian/Alaska Native, 0.0% Native Hawaiian/Other Pacific Islander, 3.7% Two or more races, 6.7% Hispanic of any race; Average household size: 2.71; Median age: 46.7; Age under 18: 23.5%; Age 65 and over: 18.4%; Males per 100 females: 97.3; Marriage status: 25.8% never married, 60.7% now married, 0.4% separated, 4.0% widowed, 9.4% divorced; Foreign born: 14.1%; Speak English only: 88.4%; With disability: 6.0%; Veterans: 3.6%; Ancestry: 22.5% Italian, 18.4% German, 18.2% Irish, 9.9% American, 3.8% English

Employment: 18.8% management, business, and financial, 11.0% computer, engineering, and science, 22.7% education, legal, community service, arts, and media, 15.7% healthcare practitioners, 6.6% service, 16.5% sales and office, 6.0% natural resources, construction, and maintenance, 2.7% production, transportation, and material moving

Income: Per capita: $93,565; Median household: $167,500; Average household: $254,642; Households with income of $100,000 or more: 67.7%; Poverty rate: 3.0%

Educational Attainment: High school diploma or higher: 97.1%; Bachelor's degree or higher: 67.0%; Graduate/professional degree or higher: 41.7%

Housing: Homeownership rate: 91.3%; Median home value: $564,400; Median year structure built: 1958; Homeowner vacancy rate: 0.0%; Median selected monthly owner costs: $3,328 with a mortgage, $1,501 without a mortgage; Median gross rent: $2,154 per month; Rental vacancy rate: 0.0%

Health Insurance: 97.3% have insurance; 88.4% have private insurance; 21.6% have public insurance; 2.7% do not have insurance; 0.0% of children under 18 do not have insurance

Transportation: Commute: 86.0% car, 4.3% public transportation, 0.4% walk, 8.3% work from home; Mean travel time to work: 30.7 minutes

PORT JEFFERSON (village). Covers a land area of 3.057 square miles and a water area of 0.027 square miles. Located at 40.94° N. Lat; 73.05° W. Long. Elevation is 3 feet.

History: Port Jefferson at one time was a small ship building community, with the name Drowned Meadow. The community leaders, realizing this was a poor name for the ship building business, eventually changed its name to Port Jefferson in 1836 after President Thomas Jefferson. The town was once a major whaling port, especially in the 1880s. The Village of Port Jefferson was incorporated in 1964.

Population: 7,833; Growth (since 2000): -0.1%; Density: 2,562.5 persons per square mile; Race: 86.5% White, 2.2% Black/African American, 7.6% Asian, 0.0% American Indian/Alaska Native, 0.0% Native Hawaiian/Other Pacific Islander, 2.3% Two or more races, 10.0% Hispanic of any race; Average household size: 2.50; Median age: 45.0; Age under 18: 21.0%; Age 65 and over: 22.2%; Males per 100 females: 97.5; Marriage status: 28.0% never married, 57.2% now married, 0.8% separated, 5.7% widowed, 9.1% divorced; Foreign born: 16.8%; Speak English only: 82.6%; With disability: 7.6%; Veterans: 5.7%; Ancestry: 17.9% Italian, 16.3% Irish, 12.5% German, 10.2% American, 8.8% English

Employment: 17.9% management, business, and financial, 9.8% computer, engineering, and science, 19.8% education, legal, community service, arts, and media, 13.4% healthcare practitioners, 12.7% service, 19.3% sales and office, 4.8% natural resources, construction, and maintenance, 2.3% production, transportation, and material moving

Income: Per capita: $53,135; Median household: $99,258; Average household: $133,966; Households with income of $100,000 or more: 49.4%; Poverty rate: 6.6%

Educational Attainment: High school diploma or higher: 97.9%; Bachelor's degree or higher: 59.9%; Graduate/professional degree or higher: 41.0%

School District(s)
Port Jefferson Union Free SD (PK-12)
    Enrollment: 1,143 . . . . (631) 791-4221

Housing: Homeownership rate: 69.1%; Median home value: $514,200; Median year structure built: 1971; Homeowner vacancy rate: 2.1%; Median selected monthly owner costs: $3,095 with a mortgage, $1,210 without a mortgage; Median gross rent: $1,581 per month; Rental vacancy rate: 0.0%

Health Insurance: 96.8% have insurance; 85.6% have private insurance; 29.0% have public insurance; 3.2% do not have insurance; 0.5% of children under 18 do not have insurance

Hospitals: John T Mather Memorial Hospital of Port Jefferson (248 beds); Saint Charles Hospital (231 beds)

Transportation: Commute: 89.5% car, 5.8% public transportation, 0.7% walk, 4.0% work from home; Mean travel time to work: 30.2 minutes

Additional Information Contacts
Village of Port Jefferson . . . . (631) 473-4724
    http://www.portjeff.com

PORT JEFFERSON STATION (CDP). Covers a land area of 2.666 square miles and a water area of 0 square miles. Located at 40.93° N. Lat; 73.07° W. Long. Elevation is 177 feet.

History: Port Jefferson Station was first called by the Native American name *Comsewogue*.

Population: 7,306; Growth (since 2000): -2.9%; Density: 2,740.5 persons per square mile; Race: 82.5% White, 2.9% Black/African American, 8.1% Asian, 0.3% American Indian/Alaska Native, 0.0% Native Hawaiian/Other Pacific Islander, 2.6% Two or more races, 14.2% Hispanic of any race; Average household size: 2.72; Median age: 39.3; Age under 18: 18.4%; Age 65 and over: 17.2%; Males per 100 females: 95.8; Marriage status: 30.4% never married, 56.2% now married, 1.1% separated, 6.5% widowed, 6.9% divorced; Foreign born: 11.6%; Speak English only: 80.2%; With disability: 8.9%; Veterans: 6.1%; Ancestry: 24.9% Italian, 17.8% Irish, 12.7% German, 8.0% American, 6.3% Polish

Employment: 16.5% management, business, and financial, 10.9% computer, engineering, and science, 14.9% education, legal, community service, arts, and media, 5.9% healthcare practitioners, 10.4% service, 25.1% sales and office, 8.7% natural resources, construction, and maintenance, 7.6% production, transportation, and material moving

Income: Per capita: $40,200; Median household: $92,174; Average household: $108,594; Households with income of $100,000 or more: 43.8%; Poverty rate: 5.0%

Educational Attainment: High school diploma or higher: 93.1%; Bachelor's degree or higher: 37.2%; Graduate/professional degree or higher: 18.0%

School District(s)
Brookhaven-Comsewogue Union Free SD (KG-12)
    Enrollment: 3,815 . . . . (631) 474-8105

Housing: Homeownership rate: 72.9%; Median home value: $355,800; Median year structure built: 1968; Homeowner vacancy rate: 2.1%; Median selected monthly owner costs: $2,798 with a mortgage, $1,121 without a mortgage; Median gross rent: $1,674 per month; Rental vacancy rate: 2.8%

Health Insurance: 93.6% have insurance; 76.6% have private insurance; 30.4% have public insurance; 6.4% do not have insurance; 2.3% of children under 18 do not have insurance

Transportation: Commute: 91.1% car, 4.8% public transportation, 0.8% walk, 2.1% work from home; Mean travel time to work: 36.5 minutes

QUIOGUE (CDP).
Land/water area and latitude/longitude are not available.

Population: 728; Growth (since 2000): n/a; Density: n/a persons per square mile; Race: 87.9% White, 0.0% Black/African American, 1.1% Asian, 3.4% American Indian/Alaska Native, 0.0% Native Hawaiian/Other Pacific Islander, 7.6% Two or more races, 36.8% Hispanic of any race; Average household size: 2.53; Median age: 46.6; Age under 18: 11.8%; Age 65 and over: 10.3%; Males per 100 females: 88.7; Marriage status: 37.2% never married, 45.0% now married, 0.0% separated, 9.9% widowed, 7.8% divorced; Foreign born: 28.8%; Speak English only: 71.2%; With disability: 5.8%; Veterans: 4.4%; Ancestry: 12.0% Polish, 11.4% German, 9.8% Italian, 8.8% English, 8.4% Swedish

Employment: 7.8% management, business, and financial, 0.0% computer, engineering, and science, 13.8% education, legal, community service, arts, and media, 6.3% healthcare practitioners, 14.8% service, 24.4% sales and office, 26.9% natural resources, construction, and maintenance, 6.0% production, transportation, and material moving

Income: Per capita: $38,129; Median household: n/a; Average household: $91,078; Households with income of $100,000 or more: 43.1%; Poverty rate: 10.3%

Educational Attainment: High school diploma or higher: 93.3%; Bachelor's degree or higher: 32.4%; Graduate/professional degree or higher: 11.3%

Housing: Homeownership rate: 77.4%; Median home value: $498,900; Median year structure built: 1967; Homeowner vacancy rate: 0.0%; Median selected monthly owner costs: $2,333 with a mortgage, n/a without a mortgage; Median gross rent: $1,896 per month; Rental vacancy rate: 11.0%

Health Insurance: 87.0% have insurance; 74.3% have private insurance; 18.7% have public insurance; 13.0% do not have insurance; 0.0% of children under 18 do not have insurance

Transportation: Commute: 89.3% car, 2.0% public transportation, 0.0% walk, 8.7% work from home; Mean travel time to work: 31.0 minutes

QUOGUE (village). Covers a land area of 4.191 square miles and a water area of 0.773 square miles. Located at 40.82° N. Lat; 72.60° W. Long. Elevation is 16 feet.

History: Region originally occupied by Native American tribe of Shinnecocks because of rich hunting and fishing. Nearby Hampton Bays was called Good Ground until 1922. Settled in 1686, when known as Fourth Neck, then Atlanticville, until adoption of present name in 1891.

Population: 932; Growth (since 2000): -8.4%; Density: 222.4 persons per square mile; Race: 89.8% White, 4.5% Black/African American, 3.8% Asian, 0.0% American Indian/Alaska Native, 0.0% Native Hawaiian/Other Pacific Islander, 1.9% Two or more races, 3.5% Hispanic of any race; Average household size: 2.28; Median age: 55.7; Age under 18: 16.4%; Age 65 and over: 33.8%; Males per 100 females: 91.9; Marriage status: 13.3% never married, 64.6% now married, 1.4% separated, 8.3% widowed, 13.9% divorced; Foreign born: 3.9%; Speak English only: 93.2%; With disability: 10.8%; Veterans: 4.0%; Ancestry: 19.0% Italian, 18.8% Irish, 11.9% German, 9.2% European, 7.2% English

Employment: 29.1% management, business, and financial, 0.0% computer, engineering, and science, 17.0% education, legal, community service, arts, and media, 7.1% healthcare practitioners, 0.3% service,

38.0% sales and office, 3.3% natural resources, construction, and maintenance, 5.3% production, transportation, and material moving
Income: Per capita: $56,681; Median household: $93,625; Average household: $129,386; Households with income of $100,000 or more: 48.6%; Poverty rate: 6.7%
Educational Attainment: High school diploma or higher: 98.8%; Bachelor's degree or higher: 68.8%; Graduate/professional degree or higher: 34.2%

School District(s)
Quogue Union Free SD (PK-06)
    Enrollment: 103 . . . . (631) 653-4285
Housing: Homeownership rate: 82.5%; Median home value: $1,193,500; Median year structure built: 1981; Homeowner vacancy rate: 0.0%; Median selected monthly owner costs: $3,116 with a mortgage, $1,224 without a mortgage; Median gross rent: $1,588 per month; Rental vacancy rate: 0.0%
Health Insurance: 96.1% have insurance; 86.3% have private insurance; 33.5% have public insurance; 3.9% do not have insurance; 7.2% of children under 18 do not have insurance
Safety: Violent crime rate: 0.0 per 10,000 population; Property crime rate: 248.5 per 10,000 population
Transportation: Commute: 74.8% car, 6.0% public transportation, 0.0% walk, 18.4% work from home; Mean travel time to work: 36.4 minutes

REMSENBURG-SPEONK (CDP).
Covers a land area of 3.602 square miles and a water area of 0.081 square miles. Located at 40.82° N. Lat; 72.71° W. Long. Elevation is 30 feet.
Population: 2,179; Growth (since 2000): -18.5%; Density: 604.9 persons per square mile; Race: 89.9% White, 3.9% Black/African American, 4.9% Asian, 0.0% American Indian/Alaska Native, 0.0% Native Hawaiian/Other Pacific Islander, 1.4% Two or more races, 13.0% Hispanic of any race; Average household size: 2.55; Median age: 44.3; Age under 18: 20.7%; Age 65 and over: 19.3%; Males per 100 females: 94.4; Marriage status: 20.9% never married, 68.6% now married, 0.0% separated, 2.5% widowed, 8.0% divorced; Foreign born: 8.2%; Speak English only: 85.2%; With disability: 4.6%; Veterans: 4.3%; Ancestry: 21.5% Irish, 20.0% German, 19.8% Italian, 8.7% English, 3.9% Polish
Employment: 25.0% management, business, and financial, 2.7% computer, engineering, and science, 10.6% education, legal, community service, arts, and media, 7.3% healthcare practitioners, 14.5% service, 17.2% sales and office, 9.4% natural resources, construction, and maintenance, 13.3% production, transportation, and material moving
Income: Per capita: $47,439; Median household: $87,083; Average household: $117,023; Households with income of $100,000 or more: 46.8%; Poverty rate: 9.5%
Educational Attainment: High school diploma or higher: 98.1%; Bachelor's degree or higher: 39.7%; Graduate/professional degree or higher: 16.9%

School District(s)
Remsenburg-Speonk Union Free SD (KG-06)
    Enrollment: 142 . . . . (631) 325-0203
Housing: Homeownership rate: 83.8%; Median home value: $619,100; Median year structure built: 1982; Homeowner vacancy rate: 4.9%; Median selected monthly owner costs: $2,437 with a mortgage, $1,117 without a mortgage; Median gross rent: $1,372 per month; Rental vacancy rate: 6.8%
Health Insurance: 90.4% have insurance; 78.0% have private insurance; 29.8% have public insurance; 9.6% do not have insurance; 0.0% of children under 18 do not have insurance
Transportation: Commute: 94.4% car, 2.5% public transportation, 0.0% walk, 3.1% work from home; Mean travel time to work: 23.1 minutes

RIDGE (CDP).
Covers a land area of 13.211 square miles and a water area of 0.093 square miles. Located at 40.90° N. Lat; 72.89° W. Long. Elevation is 92 feet.
Population: 12,958; Growth (since 2000): -3.2%; Density: 980.9 persons per square mile; Race: 87.2% White, 6.4% Black/African American, 4.2% Asian, 0.4% American Indian/Alaska Native, 0.0% Native Hawaiian/Other Pacific Islander, 1.2% Two or more races, 5.6% Hispanic of any race; Average household size: 2.35; Median age: 50.4; Age under 18: 17.3%; Age 65 and over: 29.2%; Males per 100 females: 85.0; Marriage status: 24.0% never married, 53.4% now married, 1.3% separated, 11.4% widowed, 11.3% divorced; Foreign born: 7.7%; Speak English only: 91.0%; With disability: 17.3%; Veterans: 9.7%; Ancestry: 29.3% Italian, 20.8% Irish, 20.3% German, 8.0% American, 7.2% Polish

Employment: 14.3% management, business, and financial, 6.7% computer, engineering, and science, 10.8% education, legal, community service, arts, and media, 4.6% healthcare practitioners, 17.4% service, 25.8% sales and office, 7.9% natural resources, construction, and maintenance, 12.5% production, transportation, and material moving
Income: Per capita: $36,830; Median household: $63,375; Average household: $84,947; Households with income of $100,000 or more: 29.1%; Poverty rate: 7.7%
Educational Attainment: High school diploma or higher: 90.7%; Bachelor's degree or higher: 23.1%; Graduate/professional degree or higher: 13.6%

School District(s)
Longwood Central SD (KG-12)
    Enrollment: 9,164 . . . . (631) 345-2172
Housing: Homeownership rate: 85.1%; Median home value: $274,800; Median year structure built: 1978; Homeowner vacancy rate: 2.8%; Median selected monthly owner costs: $2,491 with a mortgage, $868 without a mortgage; Median gross rent: $1,361 per month; Rental vacancy rate: 9.9%
Health Insurance: 97.0% have insurance; 77.3% have private insurance; 43.1% have public insurance; 3.0% do not have insurance; 0.9% of children under 18 do not have insurance
Transportation: Commute: 92.2% car, 3.2% public transportation, 0.0% walk, 4.3% work from home; Mean travel time to work: 32.1 minutes

RIVERHEAD (CDP).
Covers a land area of 15.082 square miles and a water area of 0.305 square miles. Located at 40.95° N. Lat; 72.68° W. Long. Elevation is 13 feet.
Population: 14,124; Growth (since 2000): 34.3%; Density: 936.5 persons per square mile; Race: 72.9% White, 21.4% Black/African American, 1.1% Asian, 2.0% American Indian/Alaska Native, 0.0% Native Hawaiian/Other Pacific Islander, 0.8% Two or more races, 20.3% Hispanic of any race; Average household size: 2.51; Median age: 45.3; Age under 18: 17.7%; Age 65 and over: 21.4%; Males per 100 females: 103.5; Marriage status: 38.0% never married, 42.7% now married, 2.7% separated, 8.9% widowed, 10.4% divorced; Foreign born: 21.5%; Speak English only: 71.2%; With disability: 16.0%; Veterans: 7.2%; Ancestry: 12.8% Irish, 12.6% Polish, 12.2% German, 9.3% Italian, 3.5% English
Employment: 6.3% management, business, and financial, 4.0% computer, engineering, and science, 5.3% education, legal, community service, arts, and media, 2.7% healthcare practitioners, 22.4% service, 32.1% sales and office, 18.7% natural resources, construction, and maintenance, 8.6% production, transportation, and material moving
Income: Per capita: $29,824; Median household: $53,882; Average household: $73,217; Households with income of $100,000 or more: 21.6%; Poverty rate: 15.7%
Educational Attainment: High school diploma or higher: 79.5%; Bachelor's degree or higher: 17.6%; Graduate/professional degree or higher: 5.2%

School District(s)
Riverhead Central SD (KG-12)
    Enrollment: 5,517 . . . . (631) 369-6717
Four-year College(s)
LIU Riverhead (Private, Not-for-profit)
    Enrollment: 106 . . . . (631) 287-8010
Vocational/Technical School(s)
Eastern Suffolk BOCES (Public)
    Enrollment: 11 . . . . (631) 233-4450
    Tuition: $10,190
Housing: Homeownership rate: 60.6%; Median home value: $309,900; Median year structure built: 1977; Homeowner vacancy rate: 0.7%; Median selected monthly owner costs: $2,188 with a mortgage, $788 without a mortgage; Median gross rent: $1,360 per month; Rental vacancy rate: 4.0%
Health Insurance: 87.7% have insurance; 57.4% have private insurance; 44.6% have public insurance; 12.3% do not have insurance; 3.1% of children under 18 do not have insurance
Hospitals: Peconic Bay Medical Center (214 beds)
Newspapers: Suffolk Life Papers (weekly circulation 570,000)
Transportation: Commute: 89.2% car, 2.0% public transportation, 1.3% walk, 6.0% work from home; Mean travel time to work: 24.6 minutes

RIVERHEAD (town). County seat. Covers a land area of 67.426 square miles and a water area of 133.841 square miles. Located at 40.98° N. Lat; 72.71° W. Long. Elevation is 13 feet.

History: Named for its location at the head of the Peconic River. Museum of Suffolk County Historical Society is here.

Population: 33,839; Growth (since 2000): 22.3%; Density: 501.9 persons per square mile; Race: 85.6% White, 9.7% Black/African American, 1.0% Asian, 0.9% American Indian/Alaska Native, 0.0% Native Hawaiian/Other Pacific Islander, 1.5% Two or more races, 13.5% Hispanic of any race; Average household size: 2.47; Median age: 48.7; Age under 18: 16.5%; Age 65 and over: 23.9%; Males per 100 females: 99.0; Marriage status: 29.8% never married, 52.7% now married, 2.0% separated, 8.5% widowed, 9.0% divorced; Foreign born: 13.4%; Speak English only: 80.6%; With disability: 13.8%; Veterans: 9.1%; Ancestry: 18.5% Irish, 17.6% Italian, 13.8% German, 10.8% Polish, 5.5% American

Employment: 15.0% management, business, and financial, 5.6% computer, engineering, and science, 8.8% education, legal, community service, arts, and media, 5.1% healthcare practitioners, 18.3% service, 28.2% sales and office, 11.8% natural resources, construction, and maintenance, 7.2% production, transportation, and material moving

Income: Per capita: $37,970; Median household: $66,147; Average household: $92,089; Households with income of $100,000 or more: 31.1%; Poverty rate: 9.5%

Educational Attainment: High school diploma or higher: 88.0%; Bachelor's degree or higher: 27.0%; Graduate/professional degree or higher: 11.9%

School District(s)

Riverhead Central SD (KG-12)
    Enrollment: 5,517 . . . . (631) 369-6717

Four-year College(s)

LIU Riverhead (Private, Not-for-profit)
    Enrollment: 106 . . . . (631) 287-8010

Vocational/Technical School(s)

Eastern Suffolk BOCES (Public)
    Enrollment: 11 . . . . (631) 233-4450
    Tuition: $10,190

Housing: Homeownership rate: 79.0%; Median home value: $350,000; Median year structure built: 1982; Homeowner vacancy rate: 2.4%; Median selected monthly owner costs: $2,547 with a mortgage, $963 without a mortgage; Median gross rent: $1,372 per month; Rental vacancy rate: 4.2%

Health Insurance: 92.2% have insurance; 72.9% have private insurance; 38.2% have public insurance; 7.8% do not have insurance; 2.4% of children under 18 do not have insurance

Hospitals: Peconic Bay Medical Center (214 beds)

Newspapers: Suffolk Life Papers (weekly circulation 570,000)

Transportation: Commute: 89.6% car, 1.5% public transportation, 2.0% walk, 5.6% work from home; Mean travel time to work: 27.6 minutes

Additional Information Contacts

Town of Riverhead . . . . (631) 727-3200
    http://www.townofriverheadny.gov

RIVERSIDE (CDP). Covers a land area of 2.717 square miles and a water area of 0.113 square miles. Located at 40.91° N. Lat; 72.67° W. Long. Elevation is 180 feet.

Population: 4,068; Growth (since 2000): 41.5%; Density: 1,497.2 persons per square mile; Race: 52.1% White, 32.8% Black/African American, 0.3% Asian, 0.0% American Indian/Alaska Native, 0.0% Native Hawaiian/Other Pacific Islander, 11.7% Two or more races, 19.8% Hispanic of any race; Average household size: 1.89; Median age: 36.0; Age under 18: 4.3%; Age 65 and over: 9.8%; Males per 100 females: 178.0; Marriage status: 67.4% never married, 20.8% now married, 1.1% separated, 6.8% widowed, 5.1% divorced; Foreign born: 13.4%; Speak English only: 88.7%; With disability: 19.2%; Veterans: 7.6%; Ancestry: 4.2% Irish, 4.0% English, 3.7% German, 3.2% Italian, 1.5% American

Employment: 2.9% management, business, and financial, 9.5% computer, engineering, and science, 6.6% education, legal, community service, arts, and media, 0.0% healthcare practitioners, 2.6% service, 25.6% sales and office, 44.7% natural resources, construction, and maintenance, 8.1% production, transportation, and material moving

Income: Per capita: $18,819; Median household: $38,889; Average household: $54,728; Households with income of $100,000 or more: 17.2%; Poverty rate: 17.4%

Educational Attainment: High school diploma or higher: 70.2%; Bachelor's degree or higher: 6.3%; Graduate/professional degree or higher: 0.4%

Housing: Homeownership rate: 63.5%; Median home value: $78,900; Median year structure built: 1967; Homeowner vacancy rate: 4.7%; Median selected monthly owner costs: $1,485 with a mortgage, $719 without a mortgage; Median gross rent: $1,711 per month; Rental vacancy rate: 0.0%

Health Insurance: 69.4% have insurance; 48.0% have private insurance; 44.0% have public insurance; 30.6% do not have insurance; 0.0% of children under 18 do not have insurance

Transportation: Commute: 88.0% car, 0.0% public transportation, 10.5% walk, 0.0% work from home; Mean travel time to work: 18.9 minutes

ROCKY POINT (CDP). Covers a land area of 11.298 square miles and a water area of 0 square miles. Located at 40.94° N. Lat; 72.94° W. Long. Elevation is 194 feet.

Population: 13,094; Growth (since 2000): 28.6%; Density: 1,158.9 persons per square mile; Race: 95.2% White, 0.5% Black/African American, 0.4% Asian, 0.2% American Indian/Alaska Native, 0.0% Native Hawaiian/Other Pacific Islander, 1.0% Two or more races, 8.6% Hispanic of any race; Average household size: 2.89; Median age: 38.2; Age under 18: 25.4%; Age 65 and over: 10.6%; Males per 100 females: 98.7; Marriage status: 32.1% never married, 53.7% now married, 1.1% separated, 3.8% widowed, 10.4% divorced; Foreign born: 6.3%; Speak English only: 89.6%; With disability: 10.9%; Veterans: 5.2%; Ancestry: 30.8% Italian, 24.6% Irish, 22.3% German, 9.7% American, 5.0% English

Employment: 14.3% management, business, and financial, 2.1% computer, engineering, and science, 14.8% education, legal, community service, arts, and media, 9.7% healthcare practitioners, 16.1% service, 24.2% sales and office, 11.3% natural resources, construction, and maintenance, 7.6% production, transportation, and material moving

Income: Per capita: $39,533; Median household: $94,589; Average household: $111,483; Households with income of $100,000 or more: 46.1%; Poverty rate: 3.8%

Educational Attainment: High school diploma or higher: 94.1%; Bachelor's degree or higher: 35.6%; Graduate/professional degree or higher: 18.5%

School District(s)

Rocky Point Union Free SD (KG-12)
    Enrollment: 3,157 . . . . (631) 849-7561

Housing: Homeownership rate: 83.6%; Median home value: $293,800; Median year structure built: 1967; Homeowner vacancy rate: 3.2%; Median selected monthly owner costs: $2,483 with a mortgage, $1,140 without a mortgage; Median gross rent: $1,418 per month; Rental vacancy rate: 18.7%

Health Insurance: 93.9% have insurance; 78.6% have private insurance; 24.0% have public insurance; 6.1% do not have insurance; 1.5% of children under 18 do not have insurance

Newspapers: The North Shore Sun (weekly circulation 5,000)

Transportation: Commute: 94.4% car, 2.5% public transportation, 0.8% walk, 1.7% work from home; Mean travel time to work: 36.2 minutes

RONKONKOMA (CDP). Covers a land area of 7.833 square miles and a water area of 0.332 square miles. Located at 40.80° N. Lat; 73.13° W. Long. Elevation is 112 feet.

History: Since 1988, Ronkonkoma has been the end of electrification along the Long Island Rail Road's Main Line. The track between Hicksville and Ronkonkoma is referred to as the Ronkonkoma Branch.

Population: 18,628; Growth (since 2000): -7.0%; Density: 2,378.2 persons per square mile; Race: 87.6% White, 2.7% Black/African American, 5.4% Asian, 0.3% American Indian/Alaska Native, 0.5% Native Hawaiian/Other Pacific Islander, 2.1% Two or more races, 9.6% Hispanic of any race; Average household size: 3.05; Median age: 39.7; Age under 18: 21.3%; Age 65 and over: 13.9%; Males per 100 females: 98.3; Marriage status: 34.5% never married, 52.9% now married, 1.5% separated, 4.9% widowed, 7.7% divorced; Foreign born: 9.8%; Speak English only: 86.0%; With disability: 10.6%; Veterans: 5.8%; Ancestry: 32.4% Italian, 27.5% Irish, 19.1% German, 5.7% Polish, 3.8% English

Employment: 13.7% management, business, and financial, 5.7% computer, engineering, and science, 12.1% education, legal, community service, arts, and media, 5.6% healthcare practitioners, 16.0% service, 27.6% sales and office, 8.7% natural resources, construction, and maintenance, 10.6% production, transportation, and material moving

Income: Per capita: $36,736; Median household: $97,143; Average household: $107,501; Households with income of $100,000 or more: 48.1%; Poverty rate: 5.2%

Educational Attainment: High school diploma or higher: 94.3%; Bachelor's degree or higher: 31.5%; Graduate/professional degree or higher: 12.9%

School District(s)

Connetquot Central SD (PK-12)
    Enrollment: 5,982 . . . . (631) 244-2215
Housing: Homeownership rate: 80.2%; Median home value: $338,200; Median year structure built: 1970; Homeowner vacancy rate: 0.7%; Median selected monthly owner costs: $2,524 with a mortgage, $1,103 without a mortgage; Median gross rent: $1,574 per month; Rental vacancy rate: 3.2%

Health Insurance: 93.9% have insurance; 81.5% have private insurance; 24.7% have public insurance; 6.1% do not have insurance; 3.7% of children under 18 do not have insurance

Transportation: Commute: 90.8% car, 6.3% public transportation, 1.1% walk, 1.2% work from home; Mean travel time to work: 30.1 minutes

---

SAG HARBOR (village). Covers a land area of 1.804 square miles and a water area of 0.522 square miles. Located at 41.00° N. Lat; 72.29° W. Long. Elevation is 26 feet.

History: An important 19th-century whaling port. National Historic District. The *Long Island Herald* (1791) was L.I.'s first local paper. The Whalers' Church and Whalers' Museum, noted for their architecture, are among its historic buildings. Had first customhouse in N.Y., and first post office on L.I., established 1794. Settled 1720—1730, Incorporated 1846.

Population: 2,151; Growth (since 2000): -7.0%; Density: 1,192.3 persons per square mile; Race: 83.8% White, 10.2% Black/African American, 2.7% Asian, 0.0% American Indian/Alaska Native, 0.0% Native Hawaiian/Other Pacific Islander, 1.7% Two or more races, 15.8% Hispanic of any race; Average household size: 2.41; Median age: 48.3; Age under 18: 17.0%; Age 65 and over: 25.4%; Males per 100 females: 88.4; Marriage status: 28.5% never married, 52.0% now married, 1.3% separated, 9.0% widowed, 10.5% divorced; Foreign born: 19.7%; Speak English only: 80.3%; With disability: 9.4%; Veterans: 5.4%; Ancestry: 17.8% Irish, 13.5% Italian, 12.7% German, 11.3% English, 5.3% American

Employment: 11.2% management, business, and financial, 3.0% computer, engineering, and science, 21.7% education, legal, community service, arts, and media, 3.8% healthcare practitioners, 18.1% service, 23.2% sales and office, 12.2% natural resources, construction, and maintenance, 6.8% production, transportation, and material moving

Income: Per capita: $66,283; Median household: $90,536; Average household: $156,653; Households with income of $100,000 or more: 46.3%; Poverty rate: 11.4%

Educational Attainment: High school diploma or higher: 92.2%; Bachelor's degree or higher: 47.7%; Graduate/professional degree or higher: 21.6%

School District(s)

Sag Harbor Union Free SD (PK-12)
    Enrollment: 976 . . . . (631) 725-5300
Housing: Homeownership rate: 69.8%; Median home value: $993,500; Median year structure built: 1968; Homeowner vacancy rate: 0.8%; Median selected monthly owner costs: $3,614 with a mortgage, $1,057 without a mortgage; Median gross rent: $1,899 per month; Rental vacancy rate: 12.1%

Health Insurance: 89.9% have insurance; 69.3% have private insurance; 40.8% have public insurance; 10.1% do not have insurance; 3.1% of children under 18 do not have insurance

Safety: Violent crime rate: 0.0 per 10,000 population; Property crime rate: 0.0 per 10,000 population

Newspapers: Sag Harbor Express (weekly circulation 2,500)

Transportation: Commute: 75.0% car, 6.7% public transportation, 5.3% walk, 11.6% work from home; Mean travel time to work: 22.2 minutes

---

SAGAPONACK (village). Covers a land area of 4.414 square miles and a water area of 0.240 square miles. Located at 40.93° N. Lat; 72.27° W. Long. Elevation is 23 feet.

Population: 221; Growth (since 2000): -62.0%; Density: 50.1 persons per square mile; Race: 95.5% White, 4.5% Black/African American, 0.0% Asian, 0.0% American Indian/Alaska Native, 0.0% Native Hawaiian/Other Pacific Islander, 0.0% Two or more races, 0.9% Hispanic of any race; Average household size: 2.23; Median age: 56.6; Age under 18: 23.1%; Age 65 and over: 35.3%; Males per 100 females: 93.2; Marriage status:

10.2% never married, 73.3% now married, 0.0% separated, 10.2% widowed, 6.3% divorced; Foreign born: 10.4%; Speak English only: 90.3%; With disability: 5.4%; Veterans: 4.1%; Ancestry: 23.5% German, 17.2% English, 16.7% Italian, 15.8% Irish, 7.7% Russian

Employment: 19.8% management, business, and financial, 6.6% computer, engineering, and science, 25.3% education, legal, community service, arts, and media, 9.9% healthcare practitioners, 4.4% service, 22.0% sales and office, 4.4% natural resources, construction, and maintenance, 7.7% production, transportation, and material moving

Income: Per capita: $124,811; Median household: n/a; Average household: $254,797; Households with income of $100,000 or more: 67.6%; Poverty rate: n/a

Educational Attainment: High school diploma or higher: 100.0%; Bachelor's degree or higher: 78.2%; Graduate/professional degree or higher: 25.3%

School District(s)

Sagaponack Common SD (KG-04)
    Enrollment: 9 . . . . (631) 537-0651
Housing: Homeownership rate: 92.9%; Median home value: 2 million+; Median year structure built: 1980; Homeowner vacancy rate: 4.2%; Median selected monthly owner costs: $3,350 with a mortgage, $1,217 without a mortgage; Median gross rent: n/a per month; Rental vacancy rate: 0.0%

Health Insurance: 100.0% have insurance; 88.7% have private insurance; 39.8% have public insurance; 0.0% do not have insurance; 0.0% of children under 18 do not have insurance

Transportation: Commute: 45.1% car, 3.3% public transportation, 2.2% walk, 48.4% work from home; Mean travel time to work: 10.6 minutes

---

SAINT JAMES (CDP). Covers a land area of 4.559 square miles and a water area of <.001 square miles. Located at 40.88° N. Lat; 73.15° W. Long. Elevation is 151 feet.

History: In the early 20th century, St. James was a popular vacation spot for celebraties of stage and screen, including Lionel, Ethel, and John Barrymore, Buster Keaton, Myrna Loy, and Irving Berlin.

Population: 13,536; Growth (since 2000): 2.0%; Density: 2,968.8 persons per square mile; Race: 94.3% White, 0.2% Black/African American, 3.5% Asian, 0.0% American Indian/Alaska Native, 0.0% Native Hawaiian/Other Pacific Islander, 1.2% Two or more races, 5.9% Hispanic of any race; Average household size: 2.77; Median age: 46.2; Age under 18: 21.1%; Age 65 and over: 20.0%; Males per 100 females: 90.8; Marriage status: 29.4% never married, 53.7% now married, 1.1% separated, 9.6% widowed, 7.2% divorced; Foreign born: 6.3%; Speak English only: 90.1%; With disability: 11.1%; Veterans: 7.4%; Ancestry: 32.2% Italian, 26.7% Irish, 20.8% German, 5.1% English, 4.5% American

Employment: 19.0% management, business, and financial, 5.7% computer, engineering, and science, 18.2% education, legal, community service, arts, and media, 7.1% healthcare practitioners, 11.6% service, 24.1% sales and office, 8.5% natural resources, construction, and maintenance, 5.8% production, transportation, and material moving

Income: Per capita: $46,144; Median household: $102,868; Average household: $128,208; Households with income of $100,000 or more: 50.9%; Poverty rate: 3.9%

Educational Attainment: High school diploma or higher: 93.2%; Bachelor's degree or higher: 44.4%; Graduate/professional degree or higher: 22.8%

School District(s)

Smithtown Central SD (KG-12)
    Enrollment: 9,344 . . . . (631) 382-2006
Housing: Homeownership rate: 91.1%; Median home value: $445,000; Median year structure built: 1967; Homeowner vacancy rate: 1.8%; Median selected monthly owner costs: $3,250 with a mortgage, $1,143 without a mortgage; Median gross rent: $1,683 per month; Rental vacancy rate: 8.5%

Health Insurance: 96.8% have insurance; 87.0% have private insurance; 25.0% have public insurance; 3.2% do not have insurance; 4.3% of children under 18 do not have insurance

Transportation: Commute: 90.0% car, 5.7% public transportation, 0.5% walk, 3.0% work from home; Mean travel time to work: 33.8 minutes

---

SALTAIRE (village). Covers a land area of 0.233 square miles and a water area of 0.051 square miles. Located at 40.64° N. Lat; 73.19° W. Long. Elevation is 3 feet.

Population: 10; Growth (since 2000): -76.7%; Density: 43.0 persons per square mile; Race: 100.0% White, 0.0% Black/African American, 0.0% Asian, 0.0% American Indian/Alaska Native, 0.0% Native Hawaiian/Other

Pacific Islander, 0.0% Two or more races, 0.0% Hispanic of any race; Average household size: 1.67; Median age: 66.3; Age under 18: 20.0%; Age 65 and over: 70.0%; Males per 100 females: 105.6; Marriage status: 0.0% never married, 75.0% now married, 0.0% separated, 25.0% widowed, 0.0% divorced; Foreign born: 10.0%; Speak English only: 100.0%; With disability: 10.0%; Veterans: 25.0%; Ancestry: 40.0% English, 20.0% American, 20.0% Irish, 10.0% Albanian, 10.0% German

Employment: 25.0% management, business, and financial, 0.0% computer, engineering, and science, 50.0% education, legal, community service, arts, and media, 0.0% healthcare practitioners, 0.0% service, 25.0% sales and office, 0.0% natural resources, construction, and maintenance, 0.0% production, transportation, and material moving

Income: Per capita: $70,870; Median household: n/a; Average household: $127,817; Households with income of $100,000 or more: 50.0%; Poverty rate: n/a

Educational Attainment: High school diploma or higher: 100.0%; Bachelor's degree or higher: 75.0%; Graduate/professional degree or higher: 37.5%

Housing: Homeownership rate: 66.7%; Median home value: $1,875,000; Median year structure built: 1965; Homeowner vacancy rate: 0.0%; Median selected monthly owner costs: n/a with a mortgage, n/a without a mortgage; Median gross rent: n/a per month; Rental vacancy rate: 0.0%

Health Insurance: 90.0% have insurance; 90.0% have private insurance; 60.0% have public insurance; 10.0% do not have insurance; 0.0% of children under 18 do not have insurance

Transportation: Commute: 0.0% car, 50.0% public transportation, 0.0% walk, 50.0% work from home; Mean travel time to work: 0.0 minutes

Additional Information Contacts

Village of Saltaire . . . . (631) 583-5566
   http://www.saltaire.org

SAYVILLE (CDP). Covers a land area of 5.289 square miles and a water area of 0.065 square miles. Located at 40.75° N. Lat; 73.09° W. Long. Elevation is 20 feet.

History: The earliest known inhabitants of Sayville were the Secatogue tribe of the Algonquian tribe. It was founded by John Edwards, who built the first house in Sayville in 1761.

Population: 16,143; Growth (since 2000): -3.5%; Density: 3,052.1 persons per square mile; Race: 95.0% White, 1.0% Black/African American, 2.2% Asian, 0.0% American Indian/Alaska Native, 0.2% Native Hawaiian/Other Pacific Islander, 1.4% Two or more races, 5.6% Hispanic of any race; Average household size: 2.77; Median age: 45.3; Age under 18: 21.6%; Age 65 and over: 19.8%; Males per 100 females: 89.5; Marriage status: 26.6% never married, 56.2% now married, 1.5% separated, 9.8% widowed, 7.4% divorced; Foreign born: 5.1%; Speak English only: 93.4%; With disability: 8.5%; Veterans: 7.3%; Ancestry: 31.0% Italian, 30.7% Irish, 20.3% German, 6.2% English, 4.4% Polish

Employment: 18.1% management, business, and financial, 4.7% computer, engineering, and science, 20.1% education, legal, community service, arts, and media, 5.4% healthcare practitioners, 13.1% service, 26.4% sales and office, 6.8% natural resources, construction, and maintenance, 5.4% production, transportation, and material moving

Income: Per capita: $47,222; Median household: $105,987; Average household: $130,353; Households with income of $100,000 or more: 53.4%; Poverty rate: 5.0%

Educational Attainment: High school diploma or higher: 92.3%; Bachelor's degree or higher: 44.3%; Graduate/professional degree or higher: 21.8%

School District(s)

Sayville Union Free SD (KG-12)
   Enrollment: 2,954 . . . . (631) 244-6510

Housing: Homeownership rate: 78.3%; Median home value: $433,500; Median year structure built: 1964; Homeowner vacancy rate: 2.8%; Median selected monthly owner costs: $3,063 with a mortgage, $1,289 without a mortgage; Median gross rent: $1,762 per month; Rental vacancy rate: 1.9%

Health Insurance: 98.5% have insurance; 88.8% have private insurance; 24.8% have public insurance; 1.5% do not have insurance; 0.4% of children under 18 do not have insurance

Newspapers: Islip Bulletin (weekly circulation 3,000); Suffolk Co. News (weekly circulation 15,000)

Transportation: Commute: 88.4% car, 8.4% public transportation, 0.9% walk, 2.1% work from home; Mean travel time to work: 34.3 minutes

---

SELDEN (CDP). Covers a land area of 4.321 square miles and a water area of 0 square miles. Located at 40.87° N. Lat; 73.05° W. Long. Elevation is 89 feet.

History: The town's early resident was Captain Daniel Roe (1740-1820), who fought in the French and Indian War and served as a captain in the Revolutionary War, and for whom Captain Daniel Roe Highway is named.

Population: 19,928; Growth (since 2000): -8.8%; Density: 4,611.6 persons per square mile; Race: 85.5% White, 4.4% Black/African American, 6.9% Asian, 0.1% American Indian/Alaska Native, 0.0% Native Hawaiian/Other Pacific Islander, 1.0% Two or more races, 18.2% Hispanic of any race; Average household size: 3.24; Median age: 38.7; Age under 18: 21.1%; Age 65 and over: 12.9%; Males per 100 females: 98.4; Marriage status: 33.6% never married, 50.6% now married, 2.1% separated, 5.7% widowed, 10.1% divorced; Foreign born: 15.5%; Speak English only: 77.0%; With disability: 10.5%; Veterans: 5.8%; Ancestry: 28.4% Italian, 19.7% Irish, 15.2% German, 5.3% American, 3.4% English

Employment: 9.9% management, business, and financial, 4.8% computer, engineering, and science, 8.1% education, legal, community service, arts, and media, 6.2% healthcare practitioners, 19.7% service, 31.9% sales and office, 10.8% natural resources, construction, and maintenance, 8.7% production, transportation, and material moving

Income: Per capita: $30,646; Median household: $85,926; Average household: $93,563; Households with income of $100,000 or more: 41.0%; Poverty rate: 6.9%

Educational Attainment: High school diploma or higher: 91.2%; Bachelor's degree or higher: 23.5%; Graduate/professional degree or higher: 8.3%

School District(s)

Middle Country Central SD (PK-12)
   Enrollment: 9,933 . . . . (631) 285-8005

Two-year College(s)

Suffolk County Community College (Public)
   Enrollment: 26,756 . . . . (631) 451-4110
   Tuition: In-state $5,600; Out-of-state $10,470

Housing: Homeownership rate: 78.3%; Median home value: $299,400; Median year structure built: 1968; Homeowner vacancy rate: 0.6%; Median selected monthly owner costs: $2,459 with a mortgage, $1,062 without a mortgage; Median gross rent: $1,634 per month; Rental vacancy rate: 1.8%

Health Insurance: 93.2% have insurance; 71.6% have private insurance; 31.5% have public insurance; 6.8% do not have insurance; 0.3% of children under 18 do not have insurance

Transportation: Commute: 92.7% car, 4.1% public transportation, 0.2% walk, 2.6% work from home; Mean travel time to work: 33.6 minutes

---

SETAUKET-EAST SETAUKET (CDP). Covers a land area of 8.520 square miles and a water area of 0.805 square miles. Located at 40.93° N. Lat; 73.10° W. Long.

History: The region was first settled in the 1650s. During the American Revolutionary War, the Culper Spy Ring headed by Benjamin Tallmadge passed information about British troop movements gathered in New York City to George Washington. The 1777 Battle of Setauket was fought here.

Population: 13,654; Growth (since 2000): -14.3%; Density: 1,602.6 persons per square mile; Race: 85.9% White, 1.3% Black/African American, 8.8% Asian, 0.1% American Indian/Alaska Native, 0.0% Native Hawaiian/Other Pacific Islander, 2.9% Two or more races, 5.3% Hispanic of any race; Average household size: 2.75; Median age: 45.9; Age under 18: 22.8%; Age 65 and over: 17.1%; Males per 100 females: 94.7; Marriage status: 25.1% never married, 60.1% now married, 1.1% separated, 6.0% widowed, 8.8% divorced; Foreign born: 12.6%; Speak English only: 85.3%; With disability: 7.9%; Veterans: 4.8%; Ancestry: 25.5% Italian, 20.7% Irish, 17.5% German, 7.5% American, 6.9% English

Employment: 16.6% management, business, and financial, 7.7% computer, engineering, and science, 22.1% education, legal, community service, arts, and media, 11.7% healthcare practitioners, 10.2% service, 23.2% sales and office, 5.0% natural resources, construction, and maintenance, 3.5% production, transportation, and material moving

Income: Per capita: $61,452; Median household: $141,863; Average household: $168,017; Households with income of $100,000 or more: 64.4%; Poverty rate: 1.8%

Educational Attainment: High school diploma or higher: 97.1%; Bachelor's degree or higher: 63.6%; Graduate/professional degree or higher: 36.6%

Three Village Central SD (KG-12)
  Enrollment: 6,299 . . . . (631) 730-4010
Housing: Homeownership rate: 93.1%; Median home value: $464,800;
Median year structure built: 1968; Homeowner vacancy rate: 2.2%; Median
selected monthly owner costs: $3,052 with a mortgage, $1,463 without a
mortgage; Median gross rent: $1,885 per month; Rental vacancy rate:
20.7%
Health Insurance: 97.9% have insurance; 90.3% have private insurance;
21.1% have public insurance; 2.1% do not have insurance; 0.1% of
children under 18 do not have insurance
Newspapers: Times-Beacon Record Newspapers (weekly circulation
50,000)
Transportation: Commute: 86.9% car, 4.6% public transportation, 1.0%
walk, 6.8% work from home; Mean travel time to work: 32.3 minutes

SHELTER ISLAND (CDP). Covers a land area of 6.549 square

miles and a water area of 0.142 square miles. Located at 41.06° N. Lat;
72.32° W. Long. Elevation is 52 feet.
Population: 1,371; Growth (since 2000): 11.1%; Density: 209.3 persons
per square mile; Race: 96.4% White, 0.0% Black/African American, 0.0%
Asian, 0.0% American Indian/Alaska Native, 0.0% Native Hawaiian/Other
Pacific Islander, 0.0% Two or more races, 8.6% Hispanic of any race;
Average household size: 2.18; Median age: 50.1; Age under 18: 28.4%;
Age 65 and over: 26.0%; Males per 100 females: 103.5; Marriage status:
19.8% never married, 62.8% now married, 0.0% separated, 5.1%
widowed, 12.2% divorced; Foreign born: 5.5%; Speak English only: 92.7%;
With disability: 6.7%; Veterans: 20.4%; Ancestry: 45.8% Irish, 31.3%
English, 27.2% German, 15.5% Scottish, 5.0% Czech
Employment: 24.8% management, business, and financial, 0.0%
computer, engineering, and science, 2.4% education, legal, community
service, arts, and media, 10.5% healthcare practitioners, 33.6% service,
7.3% sales and office, 8.6% natural resources, construction, and
maintenance, 12.7% production, transportation, and material moving
Income: Per capita: $52,729; Median household: $110,148; Average
household: $115,639; Households with income of $100,000 or more:
50.6%; Poverty rate: 4.3%
Educational Attainment: High school diploma or higher: 98.4%;
Bachelor's degree or higher: 54.1%; Graduate/professional degree or
higher: 23.7%

School District(s)
Shelter Island Union Free SD (PK-12)
  Enrollment: 228 . . . . (631) 749-0302
Housing: Homeownership rate: 86.3%; Median home value: $690,600;
Median year structure built: 1972; Homeowner vacancy rate: 4.1%; Median
selected monthly owner costs: $2,652 with a mortgage, $632 without a
mortgage; Median gross rent: n/a per month; Rental vacancy rate: 0.0%
Health Insurance: 95.8% have insurance; 87.7% have private insurance;
29.8% have public insurance; 4.2% do not have insurance; 0.0% of
children under 18 do not have insurance
Newspapers: Shelter Island Reporter (weekly circulation 3,200)
Transportation: Commute: 97.6% car, 0.0% public transportation, 0.0%
walk, 2.4% work from home; Mean travel time to work: 26.2 minutes

SHELTER ISLAND (town). Covers a land area of 12.165 square

miles and a water area of 16.944 square miles. Located at 41.06° N. Lat;
72.32° W. Long. Elevation is 52 feet.
Population: 2,643; Growth (since 2000): 18.6%; Density: 217.3 persons
per square mile; Race: 97.5% White, 0.0% Black/African American, 0.6%
Asian, 0.0% American Indian/Alaska Native, 0.0% Native Hawaiian/Other
Pacific Islander, 0.0% Two or more races, 4.5% Hispanic of any race;
Average household size: 2.18; Median age: 50.9; Age under 18: 23.2%;
Age 65 and over: 33.1%; Males per 100 females: 97.2; Marriage status:
21.5% never married, 58.5% now married, 0.0% separated, 7.2%
widowed, 12.8% divorced; Foreign born: 5.1%; Speak English only: 93.3%;
With disability: 8.0%; Veterans: 18.8%; Ancestry: 31.9% Irish, 21.9%
English, 18.7% German, 14.5% Polish, 11.7% Italian
Employment: 24.0% management, business, and financial, 3.7%
computer, engineering, and science, 10.1% education, legal, community
service, arts, and media, 5.8% healthcare practitioners, 24.9% service,
13.7% sales and office, 4.8% natural resources, construction, and
maintenance, 13.0% production, transportation, and material moving
Income: Per capita: $56,503; Median household: $110,530; Average
household: $124,995; Households with income of $100,000 or more:
55.9%; Poverty rate: 2.3%

Educational Attainment: High school diploma or higher: 99.2%;
Bachelor's degree or higher: 59.9%; Graduate/professional degree or
higher: 27.3%

School District(s)
Shelter Island Union Free SD (PK-12)
  Enrollment: 228 . . . . (631) 749-0302
Housing: Homeownership rate: 89.3%; Median home value: $785,600;
Median year structure built: 1978; Homeowner vacancy rate: 2.1%; Median
selected monthly owner costs: $2,903 with a mortgage, $681 without a
mortgage; Median gross rent: $2,092 per month; Rental vacancy rate:
0.0%
Health Insurance: 96.3% have insurance; 87.2% have private insurance;
36.4% have public insurance; 3.7% do not have insurance; 6.1% of
children under 18 do not have insurance
Newspapers: Shelter Island Reporter (weekly circulation 3,200)
Transportation: Commute: 90.6% car, 1.3% public transportation, 0.3%
walk, 7.8% work from home; Mean travel time to work: 34.1 minutes

SHELTER ISLAND HEIGHTS (CDP). Covers a land area of

5.370 square miles and a water area of 0.279 square miles. Located at
41.07° N. Lat; 72.37° W. Long. Elevation is 56 feet.
Population: 1,264; Growth (since 2000): 28.8%; Density: 235.4 persons
per square mile; Race: 98.7% White, 0.0% Black/African American, 1.3%
Asian, 0.0% American Indian/Alaska Native, 0.0% Native Hawaiian/Other
Pacific Islander, 0.0% Two or more races, 0.0% Hispanic of any race;
Average household size: 2.20; Median age: 57.6; Age under 18: 17.7%;
Age 65 and over: 40.6%; Males per 100 females: 89.5; Marriage status:
23.1% never married, 54.6% now married, 0.0% separated, 9.0%
widowed, 13.3% divorced; Foreign born: 4.7%; Speak English only: 93.8%;
With disability: 9.3%; Veterans: 17.4%; Ancestry: 28.2% Polish, 19.5%
Italian, 16.9% Irish, 11.2% English, 9.7% German
Employment: 23.0% management, business, and financial, 8.3%
computer, engineering, and science, 19.7% education, legal, community
service, arts, and media, 0.0% healthcare practitioners, 13.9% service,
21.8% sales and office, 0.0% natural resources, construction, and
maintenance, 13.3% production, transportation, and material moving
Income: Per capita: $60,512; Median household: $120,787; Average
household: $135,603; Households with income of $100,000 or more:
61.9%; Poverty rate: n/a
Educational Attainment: High school diploma or higher: 100.0%;
Bachelor's degree or higher: 65.6%; Graduate/professional degree or
higher: 30.7%
Housing: Homeownership rate: 92.9%; Median home value: $912,100;
Median year structure built: 1981; Homeowner vacancy rate: 0.0%; Median
selected monthly owner costs: $3,272 with a mortgage, $1,244 without a
mortgage; Median gross rent: n/a per month; Rental vacancy rate: 0.0%
Health Insurance: 96.8% have insurance; 86.6% have private insurance;
43.4% have public insurance; 3.2% do not have insurance; 14.4% of
children under 18 do not have insurance
Transportation: Commute: 81.8% car, 3.0% public transportation, 0.8%
walk, 14.4% work from home; Mean travel time to work: 45.4 minutes

SHINNECOCK HILLS (CDP). Covers a land area of 2.839 square

miles and a water area of 0.201 square miles. Located at 40.89° N. Lat;
72.46° W. Long. Elevation is 79 feet.
Population: 2,428; Growth (since 2000): 38.8%; Density: 855.2 persons
per square mile; Race: 84.1% White, 0.3% Black/African American, 14.3%
Asian, 0.0% American Indian/Alaska Native, 0.0% Native Hawaiian/Other
Pacific Islander, 0.3% Two or more races, 12.6% Hispanic of any race;
Average household size: 2.27; Median age: 46.3; Age under 18: 13.1%;
Age 65 and over: 22.0%; Males per 100 females: 104.9; Marriage status:
34.4% never married, 43.1% now married, 0.9% separated, 6.5%
widowed, 16.0% divorced; Foreign born: 24.0%; Speak English only:
69.4%; With disability: 5.8%; Veterans: 4.2%; Ancestry: 15.5% Irish, 15.3%
German, 9.4% Italian, 7.0% Polish, 6.7% English
Employment: 19.1% management, business, and financial, 5.1%
computer, engineering, and science, 13.6% education, legal, community
service, arts, and media, 13.5% healthcare practitioners, 8.7% service,
20.9% sales and office, 10.4% natural resources, construction, and
maintenance, 8.7% production, transportation, and material moving
Income: Per capita: $62,981; Median household: $102,051; Average
household: $151,170; Households with income of $100,000 or more:
53.2%; Poverty rate: 9.9%

Educational Attainment: High school diploma or higher: 96.8%; Bachelor's degree or higher: 50.5%; Graduate/professional degree or higher: 24.4%

Housing: Homeownership rate: 74.2%; Median home value: $711,800; Median year structure built: 1975; Homeowner vacancy rate: 3.0%; Median selected monthly owner costs: $2,534 with a mortgage, $997 without a mortgage; Median gross rent: $1,929 per month; Rental vacancy rate: 0.0%

Health Insurance: 84.0% have insurance; 60.9% have private insurance; 38.3% have public insurance; 16.0% do not have insurance; 3.7% of children under 18 do not have insurance

Transportation: Commute: 64.0% car, 19.5% public transportation, 6.0% walk, 8.3% work from home; Mean travel time to work: 30.0 minutes

---

SHINNECOCK RESERVATION (reservation). Covers a land area of 1.349 square miles and a water area of 0 square miles. Located at 40.87° N. Lat; 72.43° W. Long.

Population: 59; Growth (since 2000): -88.3%; Density: 43.7 persons per square mile; Race: 0.0% White, 0.0% Black/African American, 18.6% Asian, 74.6% American Indian/Alaska Native, 0.0% Native Hawaiian/Other Pacific Islander, 6.8% Two or more races, 0.0% Hispanic of any race; Average household size: 2.68; Median age: 33.6; Age under 18: 28.8%; Age 65 and over: 10.2%; Males per 100 females: 88.1; Marriage status: 11.9% never married, 59.5% now married, 0.0% separated, 19.0% widowed, 9.5% divorced; Foreign born: 10.2%; Speak English only: 79.2%; With disability: 8.5%; Veterans: 7.1%; Ancestry: n/a.

Employment: 0.0% management, business, and financial, 0.0% computer, engineering, and science, 0.0% education, legal, community service, arts, and media, 0.0% healthcare practitioners, 25.9% service, 55.6% sales and office, 0.0% natural resources, construction, and maintenance, 18.5% production, transportation, and material moving

Income: Per capita: $24,890; Median household: n/a; Average household: $54,127; Households with income of $100,000 or more: 13.6%; Poverty rate: 15.3%

Educational Attainment: High school diploma or higher: 73.8%; Bachelor's degree or higher: 7.1%; Graduate/professional degree or higher: n/a

Housing: Homeownership rate: 81.8%; Median home value: n/a; Median year structure built: 1983; Homeowner vacancy rate: 0.0%; Median selected monthly owner costs: n/a with a mortgage, $414 without a mortgage; Median gross rent: n/a per month; Rental vacancy rate: 33.3%

Health Insurance: 44.1% have insurance; 30.5% have private insurance; 18.6% have public insurance; 55.9% do not have insurance; 100.0% of children under 18 do not have insurance

Transportation: Commute: 100.0% car, 0.0% public transportation, 0.0% walk, 0.0% work from home; Mean travel time to work: 0.0 minutes

---

SHIRLEY (CDP). Covers a land area of 11.455 square miles and a water area of 0.432 square miles. Located at 40.80° N. Lat; 72.87° W. Long. Elevation is 52 feet.

History: Shirley is notable as the western terminus of Atlantic Crossing 1, a major submarine telecommunications cable linking the United States with the UK, Germany, and the Netherlands. The town is named for Walter T. Shirley, who developed the area on Mastic Bay into an affordable enclave.

Population: 27,186; Growth (since 2000): 7.1%; Density: 2,373.2 persons per square mile; Race: 85.3% White, 8.4% Black/African American, 1.8% Asian, 0.5% American Indian/Alaska Native, 0.0% Native Hawaiian/Other Pacific Islander, 1.2% Two or more races, 21.2% Hispanic of any race; Average household size: 3.46; Median age: 35.3; Age under 18: 23.3%; Age 65 and over: 10.8%; Males per 100 females: 99.4; Marriage status: 36.7% never married, 50.7% now married, 2.7% separated, 4.2% widowed, 8.4% divorced; Foreign born: 13.8%; Speak English only: 76.1%; With disability: 10.4%; Veterans: 4.7%; Ancestry: 33.0% Italian, 15.6% Irish, 14.9% German, 4.1% Polish, 3.6% American

Employment: 12.9% management, business, and financial, 3.4% computer, engineering, and science, 9.8% education, legal, community service, arts, and media, 7.3% healthcare practitioners, 17.8% service, 24.9% sales and office, 11.4% natural resources, construction, and maintenance, 12.4% production, transportation, and material moving

Income: Per capita: $28,596; Median household: $84,312; Average household: $94,481; Households with income of $100,000 or more: 38.1%; Poverty rate: 11.1%

Educational Attainment: High school diploma or higher: 85.0%; Bachelor's degree or higher: 18.2%; Graduate/professional degree or higher: 7.9%

William Floyd Union Free SD (KG-12)
    Enrollment: 8,837 . . . . (631) 874-1201

Housing: Homeownership rate: 82.7%; Median home value: $253,200; Median year structure built: 1977; Homeowner vacancy rate: 2.7%; Median selected monthly owner costs: $2,341 with a mortgage, $1,002 without a mortgage; Median gross rent: $2,032 per month; Rental vacancy rate: 0.0%

Health Insurance: 92.3% have insurance; 68.9% have private insurance; 35.0% have public insurance; 7.7% do not have insurance; 1.4% of children under 18 do not have insurance

Newspapers: South Shore Press (weekly circulation 45,000)

Transportation: Commute: 92.5% car, 3.5% public transportation, 0.9% walk, 2.4% work from home; Mean travel time to work: 34.8 minutes

---

SHOREHAM (village). Covers a land area of 0.448 square miles and a water area of 0 square miles. Located at 40.96° N. Lat; 72.91° W. Long. Elevation is 66 feet.

Population: 449; Growth (since 2000): 7.7%; Density: 1,001.4 persons per square mile; Race: 97.6% White, 0.0% Black/African American, 0.7% Asian, 0.0% American Indian/Alaska Native, 0.0% Native Hawaiian/Other Pacific Islander, 1.3% Two or more races, 1.8% Hispanic of any race; Average household size: 2.72; Median age: 52.9; Age under 18: 18.9%; Age 65 and over: 30.5%; Males per 100 females: 101.1; Marriage status: 20.3% never married, 67.1% now married, 1.1% separated, 7.2% widowed, 5.3% divorced; Foreign born: 6.9%; Speak English only: 94.4%; With disability: 3.8%; Veterans: 4.4%; Ancestry: 27.8% Italian, 22.5% German, 18.3% Irish, 14.9% American, 10.5% English

Employment: 24.3% management, business, and financial, 10.9% computer, engineering, and science, 16.5% education, legal, community service, arts, and media, 14.8% healthcare practitioners, 5.7% service, 17.4% sales and office, 5.7% natural resources, construction, and maintenance, 4.8% production, transportation, and material moving

Income: Per capita: $61,848; Median household: $136,042; Average household: $171,370; Households with income of $100,000 or more: 70.3%; Poverty rate: 8.2%

Educational Attainment: High school diploma or higher: 98.3%; Bachelor's degree or higher: 66.9%; Graduate/professional degree or higher: 47.3%

Shoreham-Wading River Central SD (KG-12)
    Enrollment: 2,272 . . . . (631) 821-8105

Housing: Homeownership rate: 96.4%; Median home value: $497,100; Median year structure built: 1965; Homeowner vacancy rate: 3.0%; Median selected monthly owner costs: $3,400 with a mortgage, $1,501 without a mortgage; Median gross rent: n/a per month; Rental vacancy rate: 45.5%

Health Insurance: 97.6% have insurance; 91.3% have private insurance; 31.6% have public insurance; 2.4% do not have insurance; 0.0% of children under 18 do not have insurance

Transportation: Commute: 86.2% car, 4.9% public transportation, 0.9% walk, 8.0% work from home; Mean travel time to work: 32.0 minutes

---

SMITHTOWN (CDP). Covers a land area of 11.629 square miles and a water area of 0.485 square miles. Located at 40.86° N. Lat; 73.22° W. Long. Elevation is 59 feet.

History: Smithtown, originally known as "Smithfield," was first settled around 1665. Local legend has it that after rescuing a Native American Chief's kidnapped daughter, Richard Smith was told that the Chief would grant title to all of the land Smith could encircle in one day, on a bull. Smith chose to ride the bull on the longest day of the year (summer solstice)—to enable him to ride longer "in one day." The land he acquired in this way is said to approximate the current town's location. There is a large anatomically correct statue of Smith's bull, known as Whisper, at the fork of Jericho Turnpike and St. Johnland Road.

Population: 26,340; Growth (since 2000): -2.1%; Density: 2,265.1 persons per square mile; Race: 92.6% White, 1.2% Black/African American, 3.8% Asian, 0.0% American Indian/Alaska Native, 0.0% Native Hawaiian/Other Pacific Islander, 1.1% Two or more races, 4.8% Hispanic of any race; Average household size: 2.91; Median age: 46.1; Age under 18: 20.7%; Age 65 and over: 19.0%; Males per 100 females: 94.5; Marriage status: 28.5% never married, 57.6% now married, 1.2% separated, 7.5% widowed, 6.4% divorced; Foreign born: 6.5%; Speak English only: 89.5%;

With disability: 9.2%; Veterans: 5.6%; Ancestry: 36.3% Italian, 21.1% Irish, 18.8% German, 6.6% Polish, 4.8% American
Employment: 20.5% management, business, and financial, 5.5% computer, engineering, and science, 16.9% education, legal, community service, arts, and media, 6.8% healthcare practitioners, 12.5% service, 26.7% sales and office, 6.8% natural resources, construction, and maintenance, 4.2% production, transportation, and material moving
Income: Per capita: $49,983; Median household: $126,402; Average household: $145,128; Households with income of $100,000 or more: 62.3%; Poverty rate: 2.9%
Educational Attainment: High school diploma or higher: 94.4%; Bachelor's degree or higher: 48.3%; Graduate/professional degree or higher: 22.9%

School District(s)
Hauppauge Union Free SD (KG-12)
    Enrollment: 3,609 . . . . (631) 761-8208
Smithtown Central SD (KG-12)
    Enrollment: 9,344 . . . . (631) 382-2006
Housing: Homeownership rate: 88.0%; Median home value: $483,900; Median year structure built: 1967; Homeowner vacancy rate: 0.9%; Median selected monthly owner costs: $3,164 with a mortgage, $1,335 without a mortgage; Median gross rent: $1,455 per month; Rental vacancy rate: 0.8%
Health Insurance: 98.0% have insurance; 89.7% have private insurance; 22.4% have public insurance; 2.0% do not have insurance; 1.3% of children under 18 do not have insurance
Hospitals: Saint Catherine of Siena Hospital (311 beds)
Newspapers: ESP Publications (weekly circulation 31,000); Mid Island News (weekly circulation 2,200); Smithtown News Inc. (weekly circulation 37,000)
Transportation: Commute: 86.5% car, 6.1% public transportation, 0.6% walk, 5.7% work from home; Mean travel time to work: 34.3 minutes

SMITHTOWN (town). Covers a land area of 53.698 square miles and a water area of 57.752 square miles. Located at 40.92° N. Lat; 73.18° W. Long. Elevation is 59 feet.
History: Smithtown, originally known as "Smithfield," was first settled around 1665. Legend has it that Richard Smith rescued a Native American Chief's kidnapped daughter, and was granted title to all of the land Smith could encircle in one day, on a bull. In this way, he acquired the current town. A large statue of Smith's bull, known as Whisper, is at the fork of Jericho Turnpike and St. Johnland Road.
Population: 117,863; Growth (since 2000): 1.9%; Density: 2,194.9 persons per square mile; Race: 91.9% White, 1.1% Black/African American, 4.3% Asian, 0.0% American Indian/Alaska Native, 0.0% Native Hawaiian/Other Pacific Islander, 1.3% Two or more races, 5.2% Hispanic of any race; Average household size: 2.88; Median age: 45.5; Age under 18: 21.7%; Age 65 and over: 18.8%; Males per 100 females: 94.8; Marriage status: 26.9% never married, 59.6% now married, 0.9% separated, 7.1% widowed, 6.4% divorced; Foreign born: 8.1%; Speak English only: 88.6%; With disability: 8.9%; Veterans: 6.0%; Ancestry: 34.7% Italian, 23.2% Irish, 18.1% German, 6.2% Polish, 5.4% English
Employment: 19.6% management, business, and financial, 5.7% computer, engineering, and science, 16.8% education, legal, community service, arts, and media, 7.6% healthcare practitioners, 12.5% service, 25.9% sales and office, 6.7% natural resources, construction, and maintenance, 5.2% production, transportation, and material moving
Income: Per capita: $50,255; Median household: $118,836; Average household: $142,682; Households with income of $100,000 or more: 58.8%; Poverty rate: 3.2%
Educational Attainment: High school diploma or higher: 95.5%; Bachelor's degree or higher: 48.0%; Graduate/professional degree or higher: 22.9%

School District(s)
Hauppauge Union Free SD (KG-12)
    Enrollment: 3,609 . . . . (631) 761-8208
Smithtown Central SD (KG-12)
    Enrollment: 9,344 . . . . (631) 382-2006
Housing: Homeownership rate: 88.9%; Median home value: $466,700; Median year structure built: 1967; Homeowner vacancy rate: 0.8%; Median selected monthly owner costs: $3,142 with a mortgage, $1,299 without a mortgage; Median gross rent: $1,653 per month; Rental vacancy rate: 6.9%

Health Insurance: 97.7% have insurance; 88.7% have private insurance; 23.5% have public insurance; 2.3% do not have insurance; 1.4% of children under 18 do not have insurance
Hospitals: Saint Catherine of Siena Hospital (311 beds)
Newspapers: ESP Publications (weekly circulation 31,000); Mid Island News (weekly circulation 2,200); Smithtown News Inc. (weekly circulation 37,000)
Transportation: Commute: 87.8% car, 6.4% public transportation, 0.6% walk, 4.3% work from home; Mean travel time to work: 33.6 minutes
Additional Information Contacts
Town of Smithtown . . . . (631) 360-7620
    http://www.smithtowninfo.com

SOUND BEACH (CDP). Covers a land area of 1.637 square miles and a water area of 0 square miles. Located at 40.96° N. Lat; 72.97° W. Long. Elevation is 177 feet.
Population: 8,040; Growth (since 2000): -18.0%; Density: 4,912.5 persons per square mile; Race: 94.6% White, 0.4% Black/African American, 0.5% Asian, 3.0% American Indian/Alaska Native, 0.0% Native Hawaiian/Other Pacific Islander, 0.3% Two or more races, 6.1% Hispanic of any race; Average household size: 2.86; Median age: 44.6; Age under 18: 19.1%; Age 65 and over: 16.2%; Males per 100 females: 97.0; Marriage status: 30.7% never married, 54.6% now married, 0.9% separated, 6.8% widowed, 7.9% divorced; Foreign born: 6.8%; Speak English only: 89.6%; With disability: 13.8%; Veterans: 5.2%; Ancestry: 26.1% Italian, 24.1% Irish, 21.2% German, 12.8% American, 5.9% English
Employment: 8.3% management, business, and financial, 4.2% computer, engineering, and science, 13.2% education, legal, community service, arts, and media, 7.5% healthcare practitioners, 22.3% service, 28.0% sales and office, 10.3% natural resources, construction, and maintenance, 6.2% production, transportation, and material moving
Income: Per capita: $40,754; Median household: $82,550; Average household: $114,580; Households with income of $100,000 or more: 43.3%; Poverty rate: 5.8%
Educational Attainment: High school diploma or higher: 94.7%; Bachelor's degree or higher: 43.2%; Graduate/professional degree or higher: 16.6%
Housing: Homeownership rate: 93.1%; Median home value: $292,700; Median year structure built: 1962; Homeowner vacancy rate: 0.0%; Median selected monthly owner costs: $2,553 with a mortgage, $1,112 without a mortgage; Median gross rent: $1,438 per month; Rental vacancy rate: 14.3%
Health Insurance: 95.4% have insurance; 74.3% have private insurance; 36.3% have public insurance; 4.6% do not have insurance; 1.5% of children under 18 do not have insurance
Transportation: Commute: 88.9% car, 4.9% public transportation, 0.8% walk, 4.5% work from home; Mean travel time to work: 36.2 minutes

SOUTH HUNTINGTON (CDP). Covers a land area of 3.409 square miles and a water area of 0 square miles. Located at 40.82° N. Lat; 73.39° W. Long. Elevation is 207 feet.
History: South Huntington is the birthplace of Walt Whitman, and a shopping mall named after him is nearby.
Population: 9,733; Growth (since 2000): 2.8%; Density: 2,855.4 persons per square mile; Race: 85.0% White, 2.0% Black/African American, 6.9% Asian, 0.0% American Indian/Alaska Native, 0.0% Native Hawaiian/Other Pacific Islander, 0.8% Two or more races, 12.5% Hispanic of any race; Average household size: 2.86; Median age: 44.7; Age under 18: 18.4%; Age 65 and over: 18.3%; Males per 100 females: 96.7; Marriage status: 29.7% never married, 55.0% now married, 1.9% separated, 8.1% widowed, 7.2% divorced; Foreign born: 11.1%; Speak English only: 81.6%; With disability: 9.9%; Veterans: 4.3%; Ancestry: 28.0% Italian, 24.6% Irish, 18.6% German, 5.5% Polish, 5.3% American
Employment: 17.8% management, business, and financial, 6.2% computer, engineering, and science, 15.1% education, legal, community service, arts, and media, 6.1% healthcare practitioners, 12.7% service, 26.8% sales and office, 11.7% natural resources, construction, and maintenance, 3.5% production, transportation, and material moving
Income: Per capita: $43,226; Median household: $101,189; Average household: $121,179; Households with income of $100,000 or more: 50.9%; Poverty rate: 8.1%
Educational Attainment: High school diploma or higher: 94.6%; Bachelor's degree or higher: 42.8%; Graduate/professional degree or higher: 18.3%

Housing: Homeownership rate: 87.4%; Median home value: $421,100; Median year structure built: 1958; Homeowner vacancy rate: 2.8%; Median selected monthly owner costs: $2,884 with a mortgage, $1,214 without a mortgage; Median gross rent: $1,814 per month; Rental vacancy rate: 0.0%

Health Insurance: 97.3% have insurance; 82.5% have private insurance; 29.9% have public insurance; 2.7% do not have insurance; 1.5% of children under 18 do not have insurance

Transportation: Commute: 85.5% car, 7.5% public transportation, 0.7% walk, 4.3% work from home; Mean travel time to work: 32.6 minutes

SOUTH JAMESPORT (unincorporated postal area)
ZCTA: 11970

Covers a land area of 0.562 square miles and a water area of 0.027 square miles. Located at 40.94° N. Lat; 72.58° W. Long. Elevation is 3 feet.

Population: 104; Growth (since 2000): -67.4%; Density: 185.2 persons per square mile; Race: 100.0% White, 0.0% Black/African American, 0.0% Asian, 0.0% American Indian/Alaska Native, 0.0% Native Hawaiian/Other Pacific Islander, 0.0% Two or more races, 0.0% Hispanic of any race; Average household size: 1.17; Median age: 55.9; Age under 18: 0.0%; Age 65 and over: 28.8%; Males per 100 females: 83.2; Marriage status: 53.8% never married, 28.8% now married, 0.0% separated, 0.0% widowed, 17.3% divorced; Foreign born: 0.0%; Speak English only: 100.0%; With disability: 0.0%; Veterans: 14.4%; Ancestry: 53.8% Irish, 31.7% Italian, 17.3% Hungarian, 14.4% English, 14.4% Polish

Employment: 0.0% management, business, and financial, 0.0% computer, engineering, and science, 0.0% education, legal, community service, arts, and media, 0.0% healthcare practitioners, 0.0% service, 100.0% sales and office, 0.0% natural resources, construction, and maintenance, 0.0% production, transportation, and material moving

Income: Per capita: $33,124; Median household: n/a; Average household: $38,707; Households with income of $100,000 or more: 16.9%; Poverty rate: 17.3%

Educational Attainment: High school diploma or higher: 100.0%; Bachelor's degree or higher: 17.3%; Graduate/professional degree or higher: n/a

Housing: Homeownership rate: 79.8%; Median home value: n/a; Median year structure built: 1981; Homeowner vacancy rate: 36.0%; Median selected monthly owner costs: $0 with a mortgage, $0 without a mortgage; Median gross rent: n/a per month; Rental vacancy rate: 0.0%

Health Insurance: 46.2% have insurance; 28.8% have private insurance; 46.2% have public insurance; 53.8% do not have insurance; 0.0% of children under 18 do not have insurance

Transportation: Commute: 45.5% car, 0.0% public transportation, 54.5% walk, 0.0% work from home; Mean travel time to work: 0.0 minutes

SOUTHAMPTON (town). Covers a land area of 139.195 square miles and a water area of 154.510 square miles. Located at 40.88° N. Lat; 72.46° W. Long. Elevation is 26 feet.

History: Known for its many fine estates and celebrity residents. Parrish Memorial Art Museum is here, as is Southampton College of Long Island University. Settled 1640 as first English settlement in state, incorporated 1894.

Population: 58,024; Growth (since 2000): 6.1%; Density: 416.9 persons per square mile; Race: 87.4% White, 5.7% Black/African American, 2.5% Asian, 0.1% American Indian/Alaska Native, 0.0% Native Hawaiian/Other Pacific Islander, 2.4% Two or more races, 20.2% Hispanic of any race; Average household size: 2.55; Median age: 45.3; Age under 18: 19.0%; Age 65 and over: 20.0%; Males per 100 females: 104.6; Marriage status: 31.5% never married, 51.7% now married, 1.4% separated, 7.2% widowed, 9.7% divorced; Foreign born: 19.0%; Speak English only: 76.6%; With disability: 9.2%; Veterans: 5.9%; Ancestry: 17.8% Irish, 14.4% Italian, 13.4% German, 8.1% English, 6.8% Polish

Employment: 15.3% management, business, and financial, 2.6% computer, engineering, and science, 12.6% education, legal, community service, arts, and media, 6.3% healthcare practitioners, 18.3% service, 22.3% sales and office, 17.2% natural resources, construction, and maintenance, 5.4% production, transportation, and material moving

Income: Per capita: $49,374; Median household: $83,150; Average household: $128,721; Households with income of $100,000 or more: 43.7%; Poverty rate: 7.8%

Educational Attainment: High school diploma or higher: 91.7%; Bachelor's degree or higher: 39.7%; Graduate/professional degree or higher: 17.1%

School District(s)
Southampton Union Free SD (PK-12)
    Enrollment: 1,710 . . . . (631) 591-4510
Tuckahoe Common SD (PK-08)
    Enrollment: 361 . . . . (631) 283-3550

Housing: Homeownership rate: 78.1%; Median home value: $626,400; Median year structure built: 1974; Homeowner vacancy rate: 2.7%; Median selected monthly owner costs: $2,670 with a mortgage, $973 without a mortgage; Median gross rent: $1,779 per month; Rental vacancy rate: 2.2%

Health Insurance: 87.2% have insurance; 70.3% have private insurance; 33.0% have public insurance; 12.8% do not have insurance; 4.4% of children under 18 do not have insurance

Hospitals: Southampton Hospital (168 beds)

Safety: Violent crime rate: 12.2 per 10,000 population; Property crime rate: 119.8 per 10,000 population

Transportation: Commute: 82.8% car, 6.1% public transportation, 2.6% walk, 7.4% work from home; Mean travel time to work: 26.5 minutes

Airports: Southampton (general aviation)

Additional Information Contacts
Town of Southampton . . . . (631) 287-5740
    http://www.southamptontownny.gov

SOUTHAMPTON (village). Covers a land area of 6.422 square miles and a water area of 0.797 square miles. Located at 40.88° N. Lat; 72.40° W. Long. Elevation is 26 feet.

Population: 3,256; Growth (since 2000): -17.9%; Density: 507.0 persons per square mile; Race: 80.8% White, 13.5% Black/African American, 1.7% Asian, 0.5% American Indian/Alaska Native, 0.0% Native Hawaiian/Other Pacific Islander, 0.2% Two or more races, 4.5% Hispanic of any race; Average household size: 2.25; Median age: 56.9; Age under 18: 15.3%; Age 65 and over: 32.5%; Males per 100 females: 96.2; Marriage status: 27.8% never married, 47.8% now married, 0.8% separated, 9.7% widowed, 14.6% divorced; Foreign born: 11.3%; Speak English only: 89.5%; With disability: 11.9%; Veterans: 7.9%; Ancestry: 21.9% Irish, 16.0% German, 10.6% Italian, 10.2% English, 10.2% Polish

Employment: 21.2% management, business, and financial, 3.2% computer, engineering, and science, 16.9% education, legal, community service, arts, and media, 2.4% healthcare practitioners, 22.1% service, 24.7% sales and office, 9.5% natural resources, construction, and maintenance, 0.0% production, transportation, and material moving

Income: Per capita: $62,701; Median household: $78,864; Average household: $148,494; Households with income of $100,000 or more: 44.3%; Poverty rate: 11.6%

Educational Attainment: High school diploma or higher: 95.8%; Bachelor's degree or higher: 52.3%; Graduate/professional degree or higher: 21.0%

School District(s)
Southampton Union Free SD (PK-12)
    Enrollment: 1,710 . . . . (631) 591-4510
Tuckahoe Common SD (PK-08)
    Enrollment: 361 . . . . (631) 283-3550

Housing: Homeownership rate: 82.9%; Median home value: $1,195,700; Median year structure built: 1962; Homeowner vacancy rate: 3.5%; Median selected monthly owner costs: $3,542 with a mortgage, $1,005 without a mortgage; Median gross rent: $1,718 per month; Rental vacancy rate: 4.2%

Health Insurance: 96.8% have insurance; 88.6% have private insurance; 30.7% have public insurance; 3.2% do not have insurance; 0.0% of children under 18 do not have insurance

Hospitals: Southampton Hospital (168 beds)

Safety: Violent crime rate: 6.0 per 10,000 population; Property crime rate: 253.9 per 10,000 population

Transportation: Commute: 72.9% car, 8.7% public transportation, 3.4% walk, 14.4% work from home; Mean travel time to work: 20.3 minutes

Airports: Southampton (general aviation)

SOUTHOLD (CDP). Covers a land area of 10.465 square miles and a water area of 0.855 square miles. Located at 41.06° N. Lat; 72.43° W. Long. Elevation is 23 feet.

Population: 6,474; Growth (since 2000): 18.5%; Density: 618.7 persons per square mile; Race: 98.8% White, 0.1% Black/African American, 0.8%

Asian, 0.0% American Indian/Alaska Native, 0.0% Native Hawaiian/Other Pacific Islander, 0.2% Two or more races, 5.7% Hispanic of any race; Average household size: 2.45; Median age: 51.8; Age under 18: 17.8%; Age 65 and over: 29.1%; Males per 100 females: 95.1; Marriage status: 27.8% never married, 58.5% now married, 1.2% separated, 5.4% widowed, 8.3% divorced; Foreign born: 10.9%; Speak English only: 90.3%; With disability: 12.0%; Veterans: 8.4%; Ancestry: 27.8% Irish, 21.5% Italian, 20.4% Polish, 18.1% German, 9.2% English

Employment: 13.9% management, business, and financial, 1.2% computer, engineering, and science, 10.2% education, legal, community service, arts, and media, 6.2% healthcare practitioners, 17.9% service, 28.6% sales and office, 13.3% natural resources, construction, and maintenance, 8.7% production, transportation, and material moving

Income: Per capita: $50,656; Median household: $82,222; Average household: $117,297; Households with income of $100,000 or more: 41.4%; Poverty rate: 9.7%

Educational Attainment: High school diploma or higher: 96.2%; Bachelor's degree or higher: 38.9%; Graduate/professional degree or higher: 18.0%

School District(s)

Southold Union Free SD (PK-12)

    Enrollment: 786 . . . . (631) 765-5400

Housing: Homeownership rate: 86.0%; Median home value: $524,400; Median year structure built: 1975; Homeowner vacancy rate: 0.6%; Median selected monthly owner costs: $2,391 with a mortgage, $952 without a mortgage; Median gross rent: $1,434 per month; Rental vacancy rate: 15.7%

Health Insurance: 94.4% have insurance; 80.5% have private insurance; 40.1% have public insurance; 5.6% do not have insurance; 7.8% of children under 18 do not have insurance

Transportation: Commute: 79.5% car, 7.0% public transportation, 3.8% walk, 4.7% work from home; Mean travel time to work: 30.7 minutes

---

SOUTHOLD (town).

Covers a land area of 53.783 square miles and a water area of 349.917 square miles. Located at 41.14° N. Lat; 72.32° W. Long. Elevation is 23 feet.

History: The Algonquian-speaking Shinnecock tribes lived in eastern Long Island before European colonization. Southold was settled by English colonists in 1640, and in most histories is reported as the first English settlement on Long Island in the future New York State.

Population: 22,241; Growth (since 2000): 8.0%; Density: 413.5 persons per square mile; Race: 95.8% White, 1.8% Black/African American, 0.6% Asian, 0.6% American Indian/Alaska Native, 0.0% Native Hawaiian/Other Pacific Islander, 0.8% Two or more races, 7.9% Hispanic of any race; Average household size: 2.38; Median age: 53.0; Age under 18: 15.9%; Age 65 and over: 28.9%; Males per 100 females: 96.9; Marriage status: 26.7% never married, 57.0% now married, 1.3% separated, 7.7% widowed, 8.7% divorced; Foreign born: 10.5%; Speak English only: 87.9%; With disability: 12.7%; Veterans: 9.3%; Ancestry: 23.7% Irish, 17.4% Italian, 16.8% German, 13.9% Polish, 12.6% English

Employment: 14.9% management, business, and financial, 2.5% computer, engineering, and science, 13.8% education, legal, community service, arts, and media, 5.6% healthcare practitioners, 17.9% service, 24.0% sales and office, 13.7% natural resources, construction, and maintenance, 7.7% production, transportation, and material moving

Income: Per capita: $48,444; Median household: $79,438; Average household: $112,019; Households with income of $100,000 or more: 39.5%; Poverty rate: 6.8%

Educational Attainment: High school diploma or higher: 93.8%; Bachelor's degree or higher: 39.5%; Graduate/professional degree or higher: 19.1%

School District(s)

Southold Union Free SD (PK-12)

    Enrollment: 786 . . . . (631) 765-5400

Housing: Homeownership rate: 82.9%; Median home value: $544,400; Median year structure built: 1971; Homeowner vacancy rate: 0.9%; Median selected monthly owner costs: $2,459 with a mortgage, $1,005 without a mortgage; Median gross rent: $1,434 per month; Rental vacancy rate: 14.0%

Health Insurance: 93.1% have insurance; 78.1% have private insurance; 40.9% have public insurance; 6.9% do not have insurance; 5.5% of children under 18 do not have insurance

Safety: Violent crime rate: 8.5 per 10,000 population; Property crime rate: 107.1 per 10,000 population

Transportation: Commute: 80.9% car, 5.2% public transportation, 4.1% walk, 6.9% work from home; Mean travel time to work: 28.9 minutes

Additional Information Contacts

Town of Southold . . . . (631) 765-1800
    http://southoldtown.northfork.net

SPRINGS (CDP).

Covers a land area of 8.479 square miles and a water area of 0.757 square miles. Located at 41.02° N. Lat; 72.17° W. Long. Elevation is 10 feet.

Population: 7,205; Growth (since 2000): 45.6%; Density: 849.7 persons per square mile; Race: 93.7% White, 1.1% Black/African American, 4.6% Asian, 0.3% American Indian/Alaska Native, 0.0% Native Hawaiian/Other Pacific Islander, 0.3% Two or more races, 24.3% Hispanic of any race; Average household size: 2.66; Median age: 45.5; Age under 18: 22.2%; Age 65 and over: 21.3%; Males per 100 females: 108.5; Marriage status: 23.9% never married, 66.6% now married, 0.3% separated, 2.5% widowed, 7.0% divorced; Foreign born: 24.2%; Speak English only: 69.6%; With disability: 5.9%; Veterans: 6.0%; Ancestry: 15.2% German, 12.6% Italian, 11.4% Irish, 9.3% English, 9.0% American

Employment: 14.9% management, business, and financial, 1.6% computer, engineering, and science, 13.8% education, legal, community service, arts, and media, 4.5% healthcare practitioners, 19.3% service, 22.6% sales and office, 22.7% natural resources, construction, and maintenance, 0.7% production, transportation, and material moving

Income: Per capita: $55,412; Median household: $85,946; Average household: $142,135; Households with income of $100,000 or more: 41.2%; Poverty rate: 13.0%

Educational Attainment: High school diploma or higher: 90.3%; Bachelor's degree or higher: 46.5%; Graduate/professional degree or higher: 19.6%

Housing: Homeownership rate: 86.7%; Median home value: $674,000; Median year structure built: 1978; Homeowner vacancy rate: 0.0%; Median selected monthly owner costs: $3,013 with a mortgage, $1,012 without a mortgage; Median gross rent: $2,050 per month; Rental vacancy rate: 0.0%

Health Insurance: 87.6% have insurance; 73.3% have private insurance; 30.6% have public insurance; 12.4% do not have insurance; 8.4% of children under 18 do not have insurance

Transportation: Commute: 80.8% car, 9.7% public transportation, 1.4% walk, 6.5% work from home; Mean travel time to work: 29.7 minutes

---

STONY BROOK (CDP).

Covers a land area of 5.815 square miles and a water area of 0.139 square miles. Located at 40.91° N. Lat; 73.13° W. Long. Elevation is 89 feet.

History: Named for its location, and to promote the town. Restored 1941 to resemble 18th-century village. State University of New York at Stony Brook, one of the university's four graduate centers, and the State University of New York Health Science Center are here.

Population: 13,308; Growth (since 2000): -3.1%; Density: 2,288.7 persons per square mile; Race: 84.9% White, 1.0% Black/African American, 11.9% Asian, 0.0% American Indian/Alaska Native, 0.2% Native Hawaiian/Other Pacific Islander, 1.7% Two or more races, 3.5% Hispanic of any race; Average household size: 2.89; Median age: 45.8; Age under 18: 21.9%; Age 65 and over: 21.5%; Males per 100 females: 95.9; Marriage status: 24.4% never married, 61.5% now married, 1.2% separated, 6.6% widowed, 7.5% divorced; Foreign born: 14.2%; Speak English only: 82.2%; With disability: 8.5%; Veterans: 6.5%; Ancestry: 26.7% Italian, 20.5% Irish, 17.5% German, 6.1% English, 4.9% American

Employment: 16.9% management, business, and financial, 11.0% computer, engineering, and science, 22.1% education, legal, community service, arts, and media, 12.7% healthcare practitioners, 9.3% service, 21.5% sales and office, 3.3% natural resources, construction, and maintenance, 3.2% production, transportation, and material moving

Income: Per capita: $55,188; Median household: $131,308; Average household: $156,051; Households with income of $100,000 or more: 61.8%; Poverty rate: 7.4%

Educational Attainment: High school diploma or higher: 96.9%; Bachelor's degree or higher: 67.2%; Graduate/professional degree or higher: 39.7%

School District(s)

Three Village Central SD (KG-12)

    Enrollment: 6,299 . . . . (631) 730-4010

Four-year College(s)
Stony Brook University (Public)
Enrollment: 25,989 . . . . (631) 632-6000
Tuition: In-state $9,257; Out-of-state $26,767
Housing: Homeownership rate: 91.4%; Median home value: $447,600; Median year structure built: 1966; Homeowner vacancy rate: 0.3%; Median selected monthly owner costs: $3,242 with a mortgage, $1,437 without a mortgage; Median gross rent: $2,497 per month; Rental vacancy rate: 8.8%
Health Insurance: 98.5% have insurance; 89.7% have private insurance; 26.0% have public insurance; 1.5% do not have insurance; 0.4% of children under 18 do not have insurance
Hospitals: University Hospital - Stony Brook (540 beds)
Transportation: Commute: 86.0% car, 4.9% public transportation, 1.7% walk, 6.0% work from home; Mean travel time to work: 28.8 minutes
Airports: Health Sciences Center Unv Hospital (general aviation)

STONY BROOK UNIVERSITY (CDP).
Covers a land area of 1.697 square miles and a water area of 0 square miles. Located at 40.91° N. Lat; 73.12° W. Long.
History: Stony Brook is a hamlet and census-designated place (CDP) in the Town of Brookhaven in Suffolk County, New York, on the North Shore of Long Island. It is the home of Stony Brook University.
Population: 9,059; Growth (since 2000): n/a; Density: 5,336.9 persons per square mile; Race: 35.1% White, 10.2% Black/African American, 45.0% Asian, 0.1% American Indian/Alaska Native, 0.0% Native Hawaiian/Other Pacific Islander, 6.3% Two or more races, 9.4% Hispanic of any race; Average household size: 3.05; Median age: 20.4; Age under 18: 1.7%; Age 65 and over: 4.1%; Males per 100 females: 110.0; Marriage status: 93.5% never married, 3.9% now married, 0.0% separated, 2.3% widowed, 0.3% divorced; Foreign born: 32.4%; Speak English only: 41.6%; With disability: 4.0%; Veterans: 4.0%; Ancestry: 10.2% Italian, 9.1% Irish, 6.2% German, 3.2% Polish, 1.7% English
Employment: 8.0% management, business, and financial, 12.4% computer, engineering, and science, 20.5% education, legal, community service, arts, and media, 3.4% healthcare practitioners, 15.7% service, 36.2% sales and office, 2.0% natural resources, construction, and maintenance, 1.7% production, transportation, and material moving
Income: Per capita: $5,389; Median household: $155,179; Average household: $163,557; Households with income of $100,000 or more: 71.3%; Poverty rate: n/a
Educational Attainment: High school diploma or higher: 89.1%; Bachelor's degree or higher: 51.1%; Graduate/professional degree or higher: 14.6%
Housing: Homeownership rate: n/a; Median home value: $578,100; Median year structure built: 1963; Homeowner vacancy rate: n/a; Median selected monthly owner costs: $2,313 with a mortgage, n/a without a mortgage; Median gross rent: n/a per month; Rental vacancy rate: n/a
Health Insurance: 96.0% have insurance; 82.0% have private insurance; 16.0% have public insurance; 4.0% do not have insurance; 1.0% of children under 18 do not have insurance
Transportation: Commute: 22.2% car, 11.0% public transportation, 57.1% walk, 7.8% work from home; Mean travel time to work: 17.8 minutes

TERRYVILLE (CDP).
Covers a land area of 3.213 square miles and a water area of 0 square miles. Located at 40.91° N. Lat; 73.05° W. Long. Elevation is 151 feet.
Population: 12,379; Growth (since 2000): 16.9%; Density: 3,852.8 persons per square mile; Race: 87.8% White, 5.6% Black/African American, 2.1% Asian, 0.0% American Indian/Alaska Native, 0.0% Native Hawaiian/Other Pacific Islander, 3.1% Two or more races, 18.9% Hispanic of any race; Average household size: 3.31; Median age: 42.2; Age under 18: 23.5%; Age 65 and over: 17.2%; Males per 100 females: 93.5; Marriage status: 27.8% never married, 59.9% now married, 1.7% separated, 6.4% widowed, 5.9% divorced; Foreign born: 15.0%; Speak English only: 77.6%; With disability: 10.0%; Veterans: 5.3%; Ancestry: 25.1% Italian, 16.0% Irish, 13.3% American, 10.8% German, 6.0% Polish
Employment: 12.4% management, business, and financial, 3.3% computer, engineering, and science, 17.1% education, legal, community service, arts, and media, 4.7% healthcare practitioners, 19.4% service, 26.5% sales and office, 8.1% natural resources, construction, and maintenance, 8.5% production, transportation, and material moving
Income: Per capita: $34,918; Median household: $101,840; Average household: $111,018; Households with income of $100,000 or more: 51.1%; Poverty rate: 9.3%

Educational Attainment: High school diploma or higher: 88.6%; Bachelor's degree or higher: 33.8%; Graduate/professional degree or higher: 14.6%
Housing: Homeownership rate: 81.0%; Median home value: $352,000; Median year structure built: 1973; Homeowner vacancy rate: 0.0%; Median selected monthly owner costs: $2,837 with a mortgage, $1,164 without a mortgage; Median gross rent: $2,144 per month; Rental vacancy rate: 3.3%
Health Insurance: 97.2% have insurance; 81.6% have private insurance; 28.5% have public insurance; 2.8% do not have insurance; 2.1% of children under 18 do not have insurance
Transportation: Commute: 94.8% car, 2.2% public transportation, 0.3% walk, 2.0% work from home; Mean travel time to work: 34.9 minutes

TUCKAHOE (CDP).
Covers a land area of 4.140 square miles and a water area of 0.458 square miles. Located at 40.90° N. Lat; 72.44° W. Long. Elevation is 49 feet.
Population: 1,068; Growth (since 2000): -38.7%; Density: 257.9 persons per square mile; Race: 71.9% White, 20.3% Black/African American, 1.4% Asian, 0.0% American Indian/Alaska Native, 0.0% Native Hawaiian/Other Pacific Islander, 0.5% Two or more races, 22.2% Hispanic of any race; Average household size: 2.40; Median age: 50.9; Age under 18: 13.6%; Age 65 and over: 27.0%; Males per 100 females: 101.0; Marriage status: 27.9% never married, 69.2% now married, 0.0% separated, 0.0% widowed, 3.0% divorced; Foreign born: 20.5%; Speak English only: 76.9%; With disability: 9.9%; Veterans: 5.3%; Ancestry: 15.1% Irish, 13.5% German, 12.2% English, 7.1% Italian, 4.8% Austrian
Employment: 11.1% management, business, and financial, 0.4% computer, engineering, and science, 23.5% education, legal, community service, arts, and media, 7.8% healthcare practitioners, 23.9% service, 24.1% sales and office, 6.7% natural resources, construction, and maintenance, 2.5% production, transportation, and material moving
Income: Per capita: $45,385; Median household: $80,000; Average household: $108,739; Households with income of $100,000 or more: 47.6%; Poverty rate: 11.8%
Educational Attainment: High school diploma or higher: 81.0%; Bachelor's degree or higher: 29.9%; Graduate/professional degree or higher: 11.0%
Housing: Homeownership rate: 77.4%; Median home value: $770,800; Median year structure built: 1969; Homeowner vacancy rate: 0.0%; Median selected monthly owner costs: $2,798 with a mortgage, $1,233 without a mortgage; Median gross rent: $2,037 per month; Rental vacancy rate: 20.5%
Health Insurance: 81.9% have insurance; 70.8% have private insurance; 37.3% have public insurance; 18.1% do not have insurance; 20.4% of children under 18 do not have insurance
Transportation: Commute: 81.8% car, 6.1% public transportation, 3.1% walk, 8.6% work from home; Mean travel time to work: 21.4 minutes

UPTON (unincorporated postal area)
ZCTA: 11973
Covers a land area of 4.408 square miles and a water area of 0.004 square miles. Located at 40.87° N. Lat; 72.88° W. Long. Elevation is 89 feet.
Population: 42; Growth (since 2000): n/a; Density: 9.5 persons per square mile; Race: 38.1% White, 23.8% Black/African American, 38.1% Asian, 0.0% American Indian/Alaska Native, 0.0% Native Hawaiian/Other Pacific Islander, 0.0% Two or more races, 14.3% Hispanic of any race; Average household size: 0.00; Median age: 19.8; Age under 18: 14.3%; Age 65 and over: 0.0%; Males per 100 females: All males; Marriage status: 88.1% never married, 11.9% now married, 0.0% separated, 0.0% widowed, 0.0% divorced; Foreign born: 11.9%; Speak English only: 35.7%; With disability: 0.0%; Veterans: 0.0%; Ancestry: 11.9% Austrian, 11.9% Russian
Employment: 0.0% management, business, and financial, 50.0% computer, engineering, and science, 25.0% education, legal, community service, arts, and media, 0.0% healthcare practitioners, 0.0% service, 25.0% sales and office, 0.0% natural resources, construction, and maintenance, 0.0% production, transportation, and material moving
Income: Per capita: $5,386; Median household: n/a; Average household: n/a; Households with income of $100,000 or more: n/a; Poverty rate: n/a
Educational Attainment: High school diploma or higher: 100.0%; Bachelor's degree or higher: 100.0%; Graduate/professional degree or higher: 100.0%

Housing: Homeownership rate: n/a; Median home value: n/a; Median year structure built: 1975; Homeowner vacancy rate: 0.0%; Median selected monthly owner costs: $0 with a mortgage, $0 without a mortgage; Median gross rent: n/a per month; Rental vacancy rate: 100.0%

Health Insurance: 88.1% have insurance; 88.1% have private insurance; 0.0% have public insurance; 11.9% do not have insurance; 0.0% of children under 18 do not have insurance

Transportation: Commute: 0.0% car, 0.0% public transportation, 100.0% walk, 0.0% work from home; Mean travel time to work: 13.3 minutes

VILLAGE OF THE BRANCH (village). Covers a land area of 0.948 square miles and a water area of 0.030 square miles. Located at 40.85° N. Lat; 73.18° W. Long. Elevation is 62 feet.

Population: 1,927; Growth (since 2000): 1.7%; Density: 2,032.9 persons per square mile; Race: 94.8% White, 0.6% Black/African American, 2.5% Asian, 0.0% American Indian/Alaska Native, 0.0% Native Hawaiian/Other Pacific Islander, 1.3% Two or more races, 3.1% Hispanic of any race; Average household size: 3.08; Median age: 40.0; Age under 18: 29.2%; Age 65 and over: 14.1%; Males per 100 females: 89.4; Marriage status: 26.6% never married, 63.1% now married, 0.1% separated, 5.5% widowed, 4.8% divorced; Foreign born: 5.1%; Speak English only: 93.6%; With disability: 7.6%; Veterans: 3.4%; Ancestry: 35.3% Italian, 26.3% Irish, 20.1% German, 11.2% Polish, 4.2% Russian

Employment: 21.5% management, business, and financial, 3.8% computer, engineering, and science, 18.8% education, legal, community service, arts, and media, 9.5% healthcare practitioners, 9.4% service, 26.7% sales and office, 7.2% natural resources, construction, and maintenance, 3.1% production, transportation, and material moving

Income: Per capita: $52,629; Median household: $132,656; Average household: $162,238; Households with income of $100,000 or more: 66.4%; Poverty rate: 2.2%

Educational Attainment: High school diploma or higher: 98.4%; Bachelor's degree or higher: 63.1%; Graduate/professional degree or higher: 35.6%

Housing: Homeownership rate: 91.5%; Median home value: $516,100; Median year structure built: 1967; Homeowner vacancy rate: 0.0%; Median selected monthly owner costs: $3,303 with a mortgage, $1,438 without a mortgage; Median gross rent: $1,880 per month; Rental vacancy rate: 22.4%

Health Insurance: 96.9% have insurance; 90.4% have private insurance; 17.0% have public insurance; 3.1% do not have insurance; 4.4% of children under 18 do not have insurance

Transportation: Commute: 84.3% car, 10.1% public transportation, 0.4% walk, 4.3% work from home; Mean travel time to work: 36.5 minutes

WADING RIVER (CDP). Covers a land area of 9.803 square miles and a water area of 0.039 square miles. Located at 40.95° N. Lat; 72.82° W. Long. Elevation is 92 feet.

History: Wading River lies in both the Towns of Riverhead and Brookhaven. Its name comes from the original Algonquian name, Pauquaconsuk, meaning "the place where we wade for thick, round-shelled clams." "Wading River" was adopted by the first English colonists.

Population: 8,367; Growth (since 2000): 25.5%; Density: 853.5 persons per square mile; Race: 96.5% White, 0.7% Black/African American, 0.7% Asian, 0.1% American Indian/Alaska Native, 0.0% Native Hawaiian/Other Pacific Islander, 0.9% Two or more races, 6.0% Hispanic of any race; Average household size: 2.98; Median age: 40.9; Age under 18: 21.7%; Age 65 and over: 14.3%; Males per 100 females: 100.1; Marriage status: 26.5% never married, 66.1% now married, 1.2% separated, 2.8% widowed, 4.6% divorced; Foreign born: 7.5%; Speak English only: 90.2%; With disability: 9.7%; Veterans: 8.9%; Ancestry: 27.7% Italian, 20.6% Irish, 14.6% German, 13.8% American, 8.6% Polish

Employment: 19.2% management, business, and financial, 8.5% computer, engineering, and science, 13.3% education, legal, community service, arts, and media, 8.1% healthcare practitioners, 15.5% service, 23.4% sales and office, 4.5% natural resources, construction, and maintenance, 7.4% production, transportation, and material moving

Income: Per capita: $47,002; Median household: $116,709; Average household: $137,239; Households with income of $100,000 or more: 55.9%; Poverty rate: 4.8%

Educational Attainment: High school diploma or higher: 95.1%; Bachelor's degree or higher: 45.8%; Graduate/professional degree or higher: 21.7%

School District(s)
Little Flower Union Free SD (03-12)
    Enrollment: 18 . . . . (631) 929-4300
Shoreham-Wading River Central SD (KG-12)
    Enrollment: 2,272 . . . . (631) 821-8105

Housing: Homeownership rate: 94.5%; Median home value: $398,900; Median year structure built: 1977; Homeowner vacancy rate: 1.6%; Median selected monthly owner costs: $2,915 with a mortgage, $1,208 without a mortgage; Median gross rent: n/a per month; Rental vacancy rate: 18.3%

Health Insurance: 97.6% have insurance; 90.0% have private insurance; 20.0% have public insurance; 2.4% do not have insurance; 3.4% of children under 18 do not have insurance

Newspapers: The Community Journal (weekly circulation 7,000)

Transportation: Commute: 90.0% car, 0.8% public transportation, 1.6% walk, 6.5% work from home; Mean travel time to work: 30.5 minutes

WAINSCOTT (CDP). Covers a land area of 6.728 square miles and a water area of 0.496 square miles. Located at 40.96° N. Lat; 72.25° W. Long. Elevation is 23 feet.

Population: 498; Growth (since 2000): -20.7%; Density: 74.0 persons per square mile; Race: 94.2% White, 3.4% Black/African American, 0.0% Asian, 0.0% American Indian/Alaska Native, 0.0% Native Hawaiian/Other Pacific Islander, 1.4% Two or more races, 20.9% Hispanic of any race; Average household size: 2.24; Median age: 48.1; Age under 18: 12.4%; Age 65 and over: 28.9%; Males per 100 females: 115.9; Marriage status: 36.5% never married, 46.1% now married, 0.0% separated, 8.9% widowed, 8.5% divorced; Foreign born: 18.9%; Speak English only: 75.2%; With disability: 13.8%; Veterans: 8.5%; Ancestry: 23.5% English, 14.5% Italian, 13.5% German, 12.9% Irish, 8.0% Scottish

Employment: 23.9% management, business, and financial, 5.1% computer, engineering, and science, 13.7% education, legal, community service, arts, and media, 4.6% healthcare practitioners, 6.1% service, 30.5% sales and office, 8.6% natural resources, construction, and maintenance, 7.6% production, transportation, and material moving

Income: Per capita: $44,374; Median household: $72,237; Average household: $107,961; Households with income of $100,000 or more: 47.5%; Poverty rate: 26.7%

Educational Attainment: High school diploma or higher: 90.9%; Bachelor's degree or higher: 41.9%; Graduate/professional degree or higher: 21.2%

School District(s)
Wainscott Common SD (KG-03)
    Enrollment: 27 . . . . (631) 537-1080

Housing: Homeownership rate: 81.4%; Median home value: $1,316,700; Median year structure built: 1982; Homeowner vacancy rate: 6.0%; Median selected monthly owner costs: $4,000+ with a mortgage, $871 without a mortgage; Median gross rent: $1,775 per month; Rental vacancy rate: 0.0%

Health Insurance: 90.7% have insurance; 70.4% have private insurance; 48.1% have public insurance; 9.3% do not have insurance; 0.0% of children under 18 do not have insurance

Transportation: Commute: 82.2% car, 0.5% public transportation, 4.6% walk, 11.7% work from home; Mean travel time to work: 9.2 minutes

WATER MILL (CDP). Covers a land area of 10.541 square miles and a water area of 1.483 square miles. Located at 40.92° N. Lat; 72.35° W. Long. Elevation is 33 feet.

Population: 2,196; Growth (since 2000): 27.4%; Density: 208.3 persons per square mile; Race: 91.0% White, 0.2% Black/African American, 5.1% Asian, 0.5% American Indian/Alaska Native, 0.0% Native Hawaiian/Other Pacific Islander, 3.2% Two or more races, 12.2% Hispanic of any race; Average household size: 2.50; Median age: 53.6; Age under 18: 12.3%; Age 65 and over: 23.5%; Males per 100 females: 102.2; Marriage status: 21.5% never married, 64.0% now married, 4.9% separated, 8.6% widowed, 5.8% divorced; Foreign born: 24.4%; Speak English only: 78.2%; With disability: 6.7%; Veterans: 4.8%; Ancestry: 17.1% English, 15.5% Irish, 10.5% Italian, 8.7% German, 7.3% Swiss

Employment: 21.8% management, business, and financial, 5.8% computer, engineering, and science, 12.8% education, legal, community service, arts, and media, 6.3% healthcare practitioners, 9.6% service, 21.3% sales and office, 13.7% natural resources, construction, and maintenance, 8.7% production, transportation, and material moving

Income: Per capita: $90,193; Median household: $107,702; Average household: $222,059; Households with income of $100,000 or more: 54.4%; Poverty rate: 8.4%

Educational Attainment: High school diploma or higher: 97.0%; Bachelor's degree or higher: 56.7%; Graduate/professional degree or higher: 25.5%

Housing: Homeownership rate: 92.8%; Median home value: $1,675,700; Median year structure built: 1983; Homeowner vacancy rate: 2.3%; Median selected monthly owner costs: $3,769 with a mortgage, $1,178 without a mortgage; Median gross rent: $2,827 per month; Rental vacancy rate: 0.0%

Health Insurance: 86.8% have insurance; 79.4% have private insurance; 24.3% have public insurance; 13.2% do not have insurance; 0.0% of children under 18 do not have insurance

Transportation: Commute: 69.4% car, 10.0% public transportation, 8.4% walk, 9.8% work from home; Mean travel time to work: 23.8 minutes

WEST BABYLON (CDP).
Covers a land area of 7.767 square miles and a water area of 0.309 square miles. Located at 40.71° N. Lat; 73.36° W. Long. Elevation is 39 feet.

History: West Babylon's first one-room schoolhouse was erected in the early 1800s, on South Country Road (Montauk Highway), just east of Great East Neck Road. During the winter of 1836, poet Walt Whitman taught school in West Babylon.

Population: 43,168; Growth (since 2000): -0.7%; Density: 5,557.9 persons per square mile; Race: 76.8% White, 11.1% Black/African American, 3.5% Asian, 0.1% American Indian/Alaska Native, 0.1% Native Hawaiian/Other Pacific Islander, 2.3% Two or more races, 18.3% Hispanic of any race; Average household size: 3.15; Median age: 41.0; Age under 18: 20.6%; Age 65 and over: 16.0%; Males per 100 females: 91.8; Marriage status: 31.2% never married, 51.8% now married, 1.8% separated, 7.9% widowed, 9.1% divorced; Foreign born: 14.6%; Speak English only: 79.8%; With disability: 11.1%; Veterans: 6.0%; Ancestry: 31.4% Italian, 18.3% Irish, 13.5% German, 6.0% Polish, 3.3% English

Employment: 13.8% management, business, and financial, 3.7% computer, engineering, and science, 11.2% education, legal, community service, arts, and media, 4.8% healthcare practitioners, 15.2% service, 29.8% sales and office, 10.4% natural resources, construction, and maintenance, 11.0% production, transportation, and material moving

Income: Per capita: $35,234; Median household: $86,611; Average household: $105,362; Households with income of $100,000 or more: 43.2%; Poverty rate: 5.5%

Educational Attainment: High school diploma or higher: 89.7%; Bachelor's degree or higher: 24.5%; Graduate/professional degree or higher: 8.6%

School District(s)
West Babylon Union Free SD (KG-12)

    Enrollment: 3,944 . . . . (631) 376-7001

Housing: Homeownership rate: 75.9%; Median home value: $343,000; Median year structure built: 1962; Homeowner vacancy rate: 1.1%; Median selected monthly owner costs: $2,727 with a mortgage, $1,261 without a mortgage; Median gross rent: $1,694 per month; Rental vacancy rate: 3.9%

Health Insurance: 93.5% have insurance; 77.6% have private insurance; 29.4% have public insurance; 6.5% do not have insurance; 2.3% of children under 18 do not have insurance

Transportation: Commute: 87.5% car, 8.4% public transportation, 0.8% walk, 2.7% work from home; Mean travel time to work: 32.6 minutes

WEST BAY SHORE (CDP).
Covers a land area of 2.193 square miles and a water area of 0.094 square miles. Located at 40.71° N. Lat; 73.27° W. Long. Elevation is 13 feet.

Population: 4,745; Growth (since 2000): -0.6%; Density: 2,164.1 persons per square mile; Race: 87.8% White, 1.7% Black/African American, 4.0% Asian, 0.0% American Indian/Alaska Native, 0.0% Native Hawaiian/Other Pacific Islander, 4.3% Two or more races, 17.4% Hispanic of any race; Average household size: 2.86; Median age: 42.8; Age under 18: 22.5%; Age 65 and over: 22.3%; Males per 100 females: 96.7; Marriage status: 22.3% never married, 63.3% now married, 2.2% separated, 7.8% widowed, 6.6% divorced; Foreign born: 10.4%; Speak English only: 88.5%; With disability: 11.5%; Veterans: 5.9%; Ancestry: 25.2% Italian, 23.0% Irish, 19.8% German, 5.8% English, 5.1% Polish

Employment: 18.8% management, business, and financial, 4.9% computer, engineering, and science, 23.4% education, legal, community service, arts, and media, 4.1% healthcare practitioners, 11.7% service,

24.6% sales and office, 7.2% natural resources, construction, and maintenance, 5.3% production, transportation, and material moving

Income: Per capita: $50,216; Median household: $112,257; Average household: $139,501; Households with income of $100,000 or more: 58.7%; Poverty rate: 2.9%

Educational Attainment: High school diploma or higher: 95.6%; Bachelor's degree or higher: 48.0%; Graduate/professional degree or higher: 26.4%

Housing: Homeownership rate: 95.6%; Median home value: $412,600; Median year structure built: 1962; Homeowner vacancy rate: 1.4%; Median selected monthly owner costs: $3,046 with a mortgage, $1,501 without a mortgage; Median gross rent: $1,938 per month; Rental vacancy rate: 0.0%

Health Insurance: 97.4% have insurance; 86.1% have private insurance; 31.7% have public insurance; 2.6% do not have insurance; 2.5% of children under 18 do not have insurance

Transportation: Commute: 84.9% car, 10.6% public transportation, 1.5% walk, 1.7% work from home; Mean travel time to work: 35.2 minutes

WEST HAMPTON DUNES (village).
Covers a land area of 0.329 square miles and a water area of 0.085 square miles. Located at 40.78° N. Lat; 72.71° W. Long. Elevation is 7 feet.

Population: 62; Growth (since 2000): 463.6%; Density: 188.2 persons per square mile; Race: 85.5% White, 3.2% Black/African American, 0.0% Asian, 4.8% American Indian/Alaska Native, 0.0% Native Hawaiian/Other Pacific Islander, 0.0% Two or more races, 6.5% Hispanic of any race; Average household size: 2.21; Median age: 65.4; Age under 18: 11.3%; Age 65 and over: 56.5%; Males per 100 females: 139.1; Marriage status: 0.0% never married, 96.4% now married, 0.0% separated, 0.0% widowed, 3.6% divorced; Foreign born: 9.7%; Speak English only: 89.7%; With disability: 6.5%; Veterans: 25.5%; Ancestry: 41.9% Italian, 9.7% Russian, 8.1% Irish, 6.5% Austrian, 6.5% German

Employment: 26.1% management, business, and financial, 8.7% computer, engineering, and science, 21.7% education, legal, community service, arts, and media, 0.0% healthcare practitioners, 0.0% service, 34.8% sales and office, 0.0% natural resources, construction, and maintenance, 8.7% production, transportation, and material moving

Income: Per capita: $74,273; Median household: $118,333; Average household: $160,843; Households with income of $100,000 or more: 57.1%; Poverty rate: n/a

Educational Attainment: High school diploma or higher: 100.0%; Bachelor's degree or higher: 78.2%; Graduate/professional degree or higher: 40.0%

Housing: Homeownership rate: 89.3%; Median home value: n/a; Median year structure built: 1993; Homeowner vacancy rate: 0.0%; Median selected monthly owner costs: $4,000+ with a mortgage, $1,501 without a mortgage; Median gross rent: n/a per month; Rental vacancy rate: 0.0%

Health Insurance: 100.0% have insurance; 85.5% have private insurance; 59.7% have public insurance; 0.0% do not have insurance; 0.0% of children under 18 do not have insurance

Transportation: Commute: 52.2% car, 0.0% public transportation, 30.4% walk, 17.4% work from home; Mean travel time to work: 32.6 minutes

WEST HILLS (CDP).
Covers a land area of 4.926 square miles and a water area of 0 square miles. Located at 40.82° N. Lat; 73.43° W. Long. Elevation is 348 feet.

History: The community of West Hills is home to West Hills County Park, the location of Jayne's Hill which is the natural highest point on Long Island (400 feet). This area includes picturesque, well-groomed nature trails, including the historic Walt Whitman Trail.

Population: 5,349; Growth (since 2000): -4.6%; Density: 1,085.9 persons per square mile; Race: 89.3% White, 0.9% Black/African American, 5.1% Asian, 0.4% American Indian/Alaska Native, 0.0% Native Hawaiian/Other Pacific Islander, 2.2% Two or more races, 7.9% Hispanic of any race; Average household size: 2.82; Median age: 48.4; Age under 18: 19.9%; Age 65 and over: 19.0%; Males per 100 females: 97.4; Marriage status: 25.5% never married, 64.5% now married, 1.5% separated, 5.1% widowed, 5.0% divorced; Foreign born: 9.4%; Speak English only: 84.3%; With disability: 5.7%; Veterans: 5.0%; Ancestry: 28.5% Italian, 20.7% Irish, 19.6% German, 9.4% American, 6.9% Polish

Employment: 27.0% management, business, and financial, 3.9% computer, engineering, and science, 21.8% education, legal, community service, arts, and media, 6.0% healthcare practitioners, 7.4% service, 24.9% sales and office, 4.9% natural resources, construction, and maintenance, 4.0% production, transportation, and material moving

Income: Per capita: $61,288; Median household: $124,167; Average household: $168,802; Households with income of $100,000 or more: 60.2%; Poverty rate: 2.0%

Educational Attainment: High school diploma or higher: 96.2%; Bachelor's degree or higher: 57.2%; Graduate/professional degree or higher: 25.9%

Housing: Homeownership rate: 94.4%; Median home value: $595,200; Median year structure built: 1959; Homeowner vacancy rate: 1.1%; Median selected monthly owner costs: $3,238 with a mortgage, $1,449 without a mortgage; Median gross rent: $2,639 per month; Rental vacancy rate: 0.0%

Health Insurance: 98.5% have insurance; 88.0% have private insurance; 22.5% have public insurance; 1.5% do not have insurance; 0.7% of children under 18 do not have insurance

Transportation: Commute: 76.2% car, 14.9% public transportation, 2.0% walk, 6.5% work from home; Mean travel time to work: 37.2 minutes

WEST ISLIP (CDP). Covers a land area of 6.329 square miles and a water area of 0.437 square miles. Located at 40.71° N. Lat; 73.29° W. Long. Elevation is 20 feet.

History: The first people to settle in this area more than one thousand years ago were the Secatogue Indians. An Indian burial ground was discovered north of West Islip beach enabling historians to reconstruct a village of these Indians who lived along the edges of the Great South Bay, Sampawams Creek, Trues Creek and Willetts Creek.

Population: 27,117; Growth (since 2000): -6.2%; Density: 4,284.7 persons per square mile; Race: 95.3% White, 0.8% Black/African American, 1.1% Asian, 0.0% American Indian/Alaska Native, 0.0% Native Hawaiian/Other Pacific Islander, 1.5% Two or more races, 7.7% Hispanic of any race; Average household size: 3.12; Median age: 42.9; Age under 18: 21.6%; Age 65 and over: 15.0%; Males per 100 females: 96.2; Marriage status: 29.6% never married, 55.2% now married, 0.9% separated, 7.7% widowed, 7.5% divorced; Foreign born: 5.2%; Speak English only: 91.0%; With disability: 9.1%; Veterans: 5.8%; Ancestry: 37.9% Italian, 30.2% Irish, 18.7% German, 4.8% Polish, 4.6% English

Employment: 15.4% management, business, and financial, 3.1% computer, engineering, and science, 16.1% education, legal, community service, arts, and media, 6.1% healthcare practitioners, 15.1% service, 29.7% sales and office, 8.3% natural resources, construction, and maintenance, 6.2% production, transportation, and material moving

Income: Per capita: $42,428; Median household: $111,687; Average household: $129,041; Households with income of $100,000 or more: 56.5%; Poverty rate: 5.3%

Educational Attainment: High school diploma or higher: 94.7%; Bachelor's degree or higher: 37.9%; Graduate/professional degree or higher: 17.9%

School District(s)
West Islip Union Free SD (KG-12)
    Enrollment: 4,415 . . . . (631) 930-1560

Housing: Homeownership rate: 94.6%; Median home value: $407,300; Median year structure built: 1958; Homeowner vacancy rate: 0.1%; Median selected monthly owner costs: $2,978 with a mortgage, $1,373 without a mortgage; Median gross rent: $1,589 per month; Rental vacancy rate: 5.9%

Health Insurance: 96.1% have insurance; 85.1% have private insurance; 22.7% have public insurance; 3.9% do not have insurance; 2.4% of children under 18 do not have insurance

Hospitals: Good Samaritan Hospital Medical Center (437 beds)

Transportation: Commute: 87.7% car, 7.4% public transportation, 1.2% walk, 3.2% work from home; Mean travel time to work: 31.2 minutes

WEST SAYVILLE (CDP). Covers a land area of 2.100 square miles and a water area of 0.007 square miles. Located at 40.73° N. Lat; 73.11° W. Long. Elevation is 13 feet.

History: West Sayville is a hamlet in Suffolk County, New York. It was inhabited by the Secatogue Tribe of the Algonquin Nation. The name Secatogue means "black meadow lands."

Population: 4,824; Growth (since 2000): -3.6%; Density: 2,297.6 persons per square mile; Race: 96.2% White, 0.2% Black/African American, 1.0% Asian, 0.4% American Indian/Alaska Native, 0.0% Native Hawaiian/Other Pacific Islander, 1.4% Two or more races, 4.6% Hispanic of any race; Average household size: 2.88; Median age: 45.4; Age under 18: 21.5%; Age 65 and over: 16.1%; Males per 100 females: 92.4; Marriage status: 30.5% never married, 55.7% now married, 1.2% separated, 6.4% widowed, 7.4% divorced; Foreign born: 3.3%; Speak English only: 95.2%;

With disability: 11.9%; Veterans: 8.7%; Ancestry: 31.9% Italian, 29.4% Irish, 22.5% German, 4.8% English, 3.6% Polish

Employment: 18.0% management, business, and financial, 8.2% computer, engineering, and science, 17.1% education, legal, community service, arts, and media, 5.6% healthcare practitioners, 11.3% service, 24.9% sales and office, 7.8% natural resources, construction, and maintenance, 7.2% production, transportation, and material moving

Income: Per capita: $39,131; Median household: $95,938; Average household: $109,917; Households with income of $100,000 or more: 48.7%; Poverty rate: 4.5%

Educational Attainment: High school diploma or higher: 93.3%; Bachelor's degree or higher: 36.4%; Graduate/professional degree or higher: 14.4%

School District(s)
Sayville Union Free SD (KG-12)
    Enrollment: 2,954 . . . . (631) 244-6510

Housing: Homeownership rate: 84.5%; Median home value: $367,900; Median year structure built: 1956; Homeowner vacancy rate: 1.4%; Median selected monthly owner costs: $2,651 with a mortgage, $1,102 without a mortgage; Median gross rent: $1,621 per month; Rental vacancy rate: 0.0%

Health Insurance: 93.4% have insurance; 82.6% have private insurance; 24.5% have public insurance; 6.6% do not have insurance; 1.7% of children under 18 do not have insurance

Transportation: Commute: 88.0% car, 8.8% public transportation, 0.0% walk, 3.3% work from home; Mean travel time to work: 35.2 minutes

WESTHAMPTON (CDP). Covers a land area of 12.674 square miles and a water area of 2.191 square miles. Located at 40.85° N. Lat; 72.66° W. Long. Elevation is 36 feet.

History: Like most of Southern Long Island shore zone, suffering from significant beach erosion due to a succession of mid-1990s Atlantic hurricanes. Part of the original Quogue Purchase of 1666. Westhampton's first summerhouse built by Gen. John A. Dix in 1879; then a three-day journey by stage from Brooklyn until L.I. Railroad extended to Sag Harbor in 1870. By 1920s Westhampton and The Hamptons were the summering place for the rich and famous. Incorporated 1928.

Population: 2,672; Growth (since 2000): -6.9%; Density: 210.8 persons per square mile; Race: 92.6% White, 3.6% Black/African American, 1.8% Asian, 0.0% American Indian/Alaska Native, 0.0% Native Hawaiian/Other Pacific Islander, 0.6% Two or more races, 11.9% Hispanic of any race; Average household size: 2.49; Median age: 51.7; Age under 18: 21.7%; Age 65 and over: 26.5%; Males per 100 females: 97.2; Marriage status: 20.8% never married, 56.7% now married, 1.6% separated, 9.9% widowed, 12.6% divorced; Foreign born: 12.9%; Speak English only: 83.5%; With disability: 10.0%; Veterans: 9.6%; Ancestry: 22.4% Irish, 19.6% Italian, 13.2% German, 12.3% Polish, 6.9% English

Employment: 16.4% management, business, and financial, 2.3% computer, engineering, and science, 13.5% education, legal, community service, arts, and media, 4.2% healthcare practitioners, 12.1% service, 28.9% sales and office, 15.9% natural resources, construction, and maintenance, 6.7% production, transportation, and material moving

Income: Per capita: $53,604; Median household: $101,327; Average household: $140,114; Households with income of $100,000 or more: 52.7%; Poverty rate: 10.5%

Educational Attainment: High school diploma or higher: 93.8%; Bachelor's degree or higher: 44.6%; Graduate/professional degree or higher: 22.7%

Housing: Homeownership rate: 81.5%; Median home value: $721,600; Median year structure built: 1980; Homeowner vacancy rate: 5.8%; Median selected monthly owner costs: $2,537 with a mortgage, $1,095 without a mortgage; Median gross rent: $2,038 per month; Rental vacancy rate: 2.1%

Health Insurance: 92.5% have insurance; 77.7% have private insurance; 30.0% have public insurance; 7.5% do not have insurance; 4.9% of children under 18 do not have insurance

Transportation: Commute: 75.3% car, 8.1% public transportation, 1.9% walk, 12.6% work from home; Mean travel time to work: 25.3 minutes

WESTHAMPTON BEACH (village). Covers a land area of 2.931 square miles and a water area of 0.072 square miles. Located at 40.81° N. Lat; 72.65° W. Long. Elevation is 7 feet.

Population: 1,799; Growth (since 2000): -5.4%; Density: 613.8 persons per square mile; Race: 92.3% White, 1.6% Black/African American, 1.1% Asian, 0.4% American Indian/Alaska Native, 0.0% Native Hawaiian/Other

Pacific Islander, 4.6% Two or more races, 11.0% Hispanic of any race; Average household size: 2.44; Median age: 47.5; Age under 18: 23.2%; Age 65 and over: 26.5%; Males per 100 females: 109.6; Marriage status: 24.9% never married, 55.3% now married, 0.8% separated, 8.0% widowed, 11.8% divorced; Foreign born: 12.8%; Speak English only: 87.2%; With disability: 11.5%; Veterans: 6.9%; Ancestry: 21.7% Irish, 17.7% Italian, 16.7% German, 11.1% English, 6.2% Polish

Employment: 19.2% management, business, and financial, 3.9% computer, engineering, and science, 16.3% education, legal, community service, arts, and media, 6.6% healthcare practitioners, 10.8% service, 24.9% sales and office, 10.7% natural resources, construction, and maintenance, 7.6% production, transportation, and material moving

Income: Per capita: $66,394; Median household: $84,808; Average household: $160,600; Households with income of $100,000 or more: 44.9%; Poverty rate: 5.6%

Educational Attainment: High school diploma or higher: 98.0%; Bachelor's degree or higher: 51.6%; Graduate/professional degree or higher: 26.3%

School District(s)
Westhampton Beach Union Free SD (KG-12)
    Enrollment: 1,798 . . . . (631) 288-3800
Housing: Homeownership rate: 71.5%; Median home value: $660,400; Median year structure built: 1970; Homeowner vacancy rate: 4.8%; Median selected monthly owner costs: $2,857 with a mortgage, $1,074 without a mortgage; Median gross rent: $1,859 per month; Rental vacancy rate: 3.7%

Health Insurance: 93.4% have insurance; 75.7% have private insurance; 35.5% have public insurance; 6.6% do not have insurance; 5.2% of children under 18 do not have insurance

Safety: Violent crime rate: 0.0 per 10,000 population; Property crime rate: 214.2 per 10,000 population

Transportation: Commute: 74.8% car, 11.4% public transportation, 4.6% walk, 6.8% work from home; Mean travel time to work: 35.6 minutes

Airports: Francis S Gabreski (general aviation)

Additional Information Contacts
Village of Westhampton Beach . . . . (631) 288-1654
    http://www.whbvillage.com

WHEATLEY HEIGHTS (CDP). Covers a land area of 1.302 square miles and a water area of 0 square miles. Located at 40.76° N. Lat; 73.37° W. Long. Elevation is 102 feet.

Population: 5,038; Growth (since 2000): 0.5%; Density: 3,870.2 persons per square mile; Race: 30.0% White, 50.8% Black/African American, 10.4% Asian, 0.0% American Indian/Alaska Native, 0.0% Native Hawaiian/Other Pacific Islander, 3.1% Two or more races, 14.3% Hispanic of any race; Average household size: 3.75; Median age: 36.6; Age under 18: 24.3%; Age 65 and over: 10.3%; Males per 100 females: 91.6; Marriage status: 39.9% never married, 49.6% now married, 1.6% separated, 4.6% widowed, 5.9% divorced; Foreign born: 23.8%; Speak English only: 73.4%; With disability: 8.7%; Veterans: 4.1%; Ancestry: 8.6% Haitian, 6.5% Italian, 6.4% American, 6.0% Irish, 5.0% German

Employment: 13.1% management, business, and financial, 5.6% computer, engineering, and science, 15.0% education, legal, community service, arts, and media, 9.7% healthcare practitioners, 14.7% service, 30.2% sales and office, 4.5% natural resources, construction, and maintenance, 7.3% production, transportation, and material moving

Income: Per capita: $34,688; Median household: $111,641; Average household: $123,213; Households with income of $100,000 or more: 56.4%; Poverty rate: 2.6%

Educational Attainment: High school diploma or higher: 94.3%; Bachelor's degree or higher: 41.6%; Graduate/professional degree or higher: 18.5%

Housing: Homeownership rate: 85.2%; Median home value: $382,100; Median year structure built: 1966; Homeowner vacancy rate: 3.9%; Median selected monthly owner costs: $2,946 with a mortgage, $1,240 without a mortgage; Median gross rent: $1,366 per month; Rental vacancy rate: 7.1%

Health Insurance: 95.2% have insurance; 81.3% have private insurance; 22.1% have public insurance; 4.8% do not have insurance; 2.4% of children under 18 do not have insurance

Transportation: Commute: 83.1% car, 11.0% public transportation, 0.9% walk, 3.1% work from home; Mean travel time to work: 34.7 minutes

WYANDANCH (CDP). Covers a land area of 4.473 square miles and a water area of 0.003 square miles. Located at 40.75° N. Lat; 73.38° W. Long. Elevation is 56 feet.

History: Wyandanch is named after Chief Wyandanch, a leader of the Montaukett Native American tribe during the 17th century.

Population: 11,315; Growth (since 2000): 7.3%; Density: 2,529.4 persons per square mile; Race: 20.3% White, 59.5% Black/African American, 0.5% Asian, 1.5% American Indian/Alaska Native, 0.0% Native Hawaiian/Other Pacific Islander, 7.2% Two or more races, 34.1% Hispanic of any race; Average household size: 4.03; Median age: 32.1; Age under 18: 27.0%; Age 65 and over: 9.8%; Males per 100 females: 96.4; Marriage status: 53.7% never married, 34.2% now married, 3.7% separated, 4.5% widowed, 7.6% divorced; Foreign born: 25.2%; Speak English only: 63.0%; With disability: 11.2%; Veterans: 4.4%; Ancestry: 7.3% Haitian, 5.4% Jamaican, 4.1% American, 2.3% African, 1.5% Italian

Employment: 6.5% management, business, and financial, 2.8% computer, engineering, and science, 7.7% education, legal, community service, arts, and media, 4.8% healthcare practitioners, 28.7% service, 17.1% sales and office, 10.5% natural resources, construction, and maintenance, 22.0% production, transportation, and material moving

Income: Per capita: $20,230; Median household: $59,861; Average household: $72,895; Households with income of $100,000 or more: 26.3%; Poverty rate: 22.2%

Educational Attainment: High school diploma or higher: 77.9%; Bachelor's degree or higher: 13.5%; Graduate/professional degree or higher: 4.2%

School District(s)
Wyandanch Union Free SD (PK-12)
    Enrollment: 2,688 . . . . (631) 870-0401
Housing: Homeownership rate: 61.2%; Median home value: $244,000; Median year structure built: 1967; Homeowner vacancy rate: 6.6%; Median selected monthly owner costs: $2,265 with a mortgage, $1,004 without a mortgage; Median gross rent: $1,635 per month; Rental vacancy rate: 4.9%

Health Insurance: 86.9% have insurance; 51.8% have private insurance; 45.4% have public insurance; 13.1% do not have insurance; 4.2% of children under 18 do not have insurance

Transportation: Commute: 84.1% car, 8.5% public transportation, 3.1% walk, 3.2% work from home; Mean travel time to work: 25.8 minutes

YAPHANK (CDP). Covers a land area of 13.649 square miles and a water area of 0.123 square miles. Located at 40.83° N. Lat; 72.92° W. Long. Elevation is 39 feet.

History: US Camp Upton here was a US Army induction center in World Wars I and II.

Population: 6,308; Growth (since 2000): 25.5%; Density: 462.2 persons per square mile; Race: 83.4% White, 7.7% Black/African American, 2.7% Asian, 0.1% American Indian/Alaska Native, 0.0% Native Hawaiian/Other Pacific Islander, 3.5% Two or more races, 13.3% Hispanic of any race; Average household size: 2.77; Median age: 38.6; Age under 18: 18.7%; Age 65 and over: 11.0%; Males per 100 females: 119.4; Marriage status: 39.3% never married, 47.9% now married, 0.9% separated, 2.4% widowed, 10.4% divorced; Foreign born: 9.3%; Speak English only: 87.2%; With disability: 10.7%; Veterans: 6.3%; Ancestry: 25.9% Italian, 24.1% Irish, 21.3% German, 5.5% English, 5.0% Polish

Employment: 15.4% management, business, and financial, 2.3% computer, engineering, and science, 16.0% education, legal, community service, arts, and media, 5.6% healthcare practitioners, 16.7% service, 24.3% sales and office, 8.7% natural resources, construction, and maintenance, 11.0% production, transportation, and material moving

Income: Per capita: $38,075; Median household: $97,664; Average household: $109,326; Households with income of $100,000 or more: 48.2%; Poverty rate: 4.9%

Educational Attainment: High school diploma or higher: 90.7%; Bachelor's degree or higher: 27.5%; Graduate/professional degree or higher: 12.4%

School District(s)
Longwood Central SD (KG-12)
    Enrollment: 9,164 . . . . (631) 345-2172
Housing: Homeownership rate: 85.5%; Median home value: $310,800; Median year structure built: 1982; Homeowner vacancy rate: 0.0%; Median selected monthly owner costs: $2,452 with a mortgage, $953 without a mortgage; Median gross rent: $2,140 per month; Rental vacancy rate: 6.3%

Health Insurance: 95.7% have insurance; 82.3% have private insurance; 24.6% have public insurance; 4.3% do not have insurance; 0.0% of children under 18 do not have insurance

Transportation: Commute: 94.7% car, 2.0% public transportation, 0.6% walk, 2.3% work from home; Mean travel time to work: 34.2 minutes

Sullivan County

Located in southeastern New York; bounded on the west and southwest by the Delaware River and the Pennsylvania border; drained by the Neversink River; includes parts of the Catskills and the Shawangunk Range, and many lakes. Covers a land area of 968.132 square miles, a water area of 28.591 square miles, and is located in the Eastern Time Zone at 41.72° N. Lat., 74.76° W. Long. The county was founded in 1809. County seat is Monticello.

Weather Station: Liberty 1 NE									Elevation: 1,548 feet			
	Jan	Feb	Mar	Apr	May	Jun	Jul	Aug	Sep	Oct	Nov	Dec
High	30	34	42	55	66	74	79	78	70	59	47	34
Low	12	14	22	33	43	51	56	55	47	36	28	18
Precip	3.7	2.8	3.8	4.6	4.8	5.0	4.9	4.5	4.9	4.5	3.9	4.2
Snow	18.6	12.7	12.7	3.3	tr	0.0	0.0	0.0	0.0	0.3	4.0	15.1

High and Low temperatures in degrees Fahrenheit; Precipitation and Snow in inches

Population: 75,783; Growth (since 2000): 2.5%; Density: 78.3 persons per square mile; Race: 81.4% White, 8.6% Black/African American, 1.6% Asian, 0.3% American Indian/Alaska Native, 0.0% Native Hawaiian/Other Pacific Islander, 3.5% two or more races, 15.4% Hispanic of any race; Average household size: 2.59; Median age: 42.6; Age under 18: 21.4%; Age 65 and over: 17.5%; Males per 100 females: 104.4; Marriage status: 34.1% never married, 48.8% now married, 3.0% separated, 7.1% widowed, 9.9% divorced; Foreign born: 9.4%; Speak English only: 85.5%; With disability: 16.3%; Veterans: 8.1%; Ancestry: 19.0% German, 15.7% Irish, 12.9% Italian, 6.2% Polish, 6.0% English

Religion: Six largest groups: 19.8% Catholicism, 5.6% Judaism, 4.0% Methodist/Pietist, 3.9% Muslim Estimate, 1.7% Hindu, 1.5% Presbyterian-Reformed

Economy: Unemployment rate: 3.5%; Leading industries: 14.6 % retail trade; 12.7 % accommodation and food services; 11.5 % construction; Farms: 321 totaling 53,859 acres; Company size: 1 employs 1,000 or more persons, 2 employ 500 to 999 persons, 27 employ 100 to 499 persons, 1,869 employ less than 100 persons; Business ownership: 2,105 women-owned, 377 Black-owned, 447 Hispanic-owned, 219 Asian-owned, 26 American Indian/Alaska Native-owned

Employment: 10.2% management, business, and financial, 2.5% computer, engineering, and science, 12.4% education, legal, community service, arts, and media, 6.1% healthcare practitioners, 22.7% service, 23.8% sales and office, 11.4% natural resources, construction, and maintenance, 10.9% production, transportation, and material moving

Income: Per capita: $28,224; Median household: $53,877; Average household: $72,552; Households with income of $100,000 or more: 21.3%; Poverty rate: 15.9%

Educational Attainment: High school diploma or higher: 86.4%; Bachelor's degree or higher: 23.4%; Graduate/professional degree or higher: 9.9%

Housing: Homeownership rate: 66.9%; Median home value: $167,900; Median year structure built: 1971; Homeowner vacancy rate: 5.2%; Median selected monthly owner costs: $1,582 with a mortgage, $658 without a mortgage; Median gross rent: $860 per month; Rental vacancy rate: 11.2%

Vital Statistics: Birth rate: 103.1 per 10,000 population; Death rate: 97.8 per 10,000 population; Age-adjusted cancer mortality rate: 189.8 deaths per 100,000 population

Health Insurance: 92.3% have insurance; 64.6% have private insurance; 43.2% have public insurance; 7.7% do not have insurance; 1.9% of children under 18 do not have insurance

Health Care: Physicians: 11.0 per 10,000 population; Dentists: 4.0 per 10,000 population; Hospital beds: 25.2 per 10,000 population; Hospital admissions: 556.9 per 10,000 population

Transportation: Commute: 89.0% car, 2.2% public transportation, 2.8% walk, 4.7% work from home; Mean travel time to work: 30.6 minutes

2016 Presidential Election: 53.2% Trump, 42.0% Clinton, 2.5% Johnson, 1.7% Stein

Additional Information Contacts

Sullivan Government . . . . (845) 794-3000
http://co.sullivan.ny.us

Sullivan County Communities

BARRYVILLE (unincorporated postal area)
ZCTA: 12719

Covers a land area of 17.233 square miles and a water area of 0.443 square miles. Located at 41.50° N. Lat; 74.90° W. Long. Elevation is 594 feet.

Population: 1,289; Growth (since 2000): 27.4%; Density: 74.8 persons per square mile; Race: 95.5% White, 3.4% Black/African American, 0.6% Asian, 0.0% American Indian/Alaska Native, 0.0% Native Hawaiian/Other Pacific Islander, 0.0% Two or more races, 5.2% Hispanic of any race; Average household size: 2.33; Median age: 52.6; Age under 18: 14.0%; Age 65 and over: 25.6%; Males per 100 females: 109.5; Marriage status: 28.8% never married, 54.5% now married, 4.5% separated, 5.6% widowed, 11.1% divorced; Foreign born: 10.9%; Speak English only: 89.6%; With disability: 20.2%; Veterans: 10.2%; Ancestry: 23.7% German, 15.2% Irish, 10.9% Italian, 9.5% English, 8.0% Polish

Employment: 12.5% management, business, and financial, 8.8% computer, engineering, and science, 14.2% education, legal, community service, arts, and media, 9.6% healthcare practitioners, 17.6% service, 20.1% sales and office, 5.2% natural resources, construction, and maintenance, 12.1% production, transportation, and material moving

Income: Per capita: $39,021; Median household: $56,923; Average household: $92,102; Households with income of $100,000 or more: 28.7%; Poverty rate: 11.6%

Educational Attainment: High school diploma or higher: 82.1%; Bachelor's degree or higher: 32.1%; Graduate/professional degree or higher: 9.8%

Housing: Homeownership rate: 79.2%; Median home value: $205,000; Median year structure built: 1971; Homeowner vacancy rate: 2.0%; Median selected monthly owner costs: $1,690 with a mortgage, $586 without a mortgage; Median gross rent: $991 per month; Rental vacancy rate: 0.0%

Health Insurance: 88.5% have insurance; 66.0% have private insurance; 43.0% have public insurance; 11.5% do not have insurance; 10.8% of children under 18 do not have insurance

Transportation: Commute: 84.9% car, 0.0% public transportation, 0.0% walk, 12.4% work from home; Mean travel time to work: 44.6 minutes

BETHEL (town). Covers a land area of 85.265 square miles and a water area of 4.693 square miles. Located at 41.69° N. Lat; 74.85° W. Long. Elevation is 1,325 feet.

History: Site of the 3-day Woodstock rock festival, July 1969.

Population: 4,156; Growth (since 2000): -4.7%; Density: 48.7 persons per square mile; Race: 94.8% White, 2.2% Black/African American, 0.6% Asian, 1.1% American Indian/Alaska Native, 0.0% Native Hawaiian/Other Pacific Islander, 0.8% Two or more races, 8.7% Hispanic of any race; Average household size: 2.28; Median age: 48.0; Age under 18: 15.7%; Age 65 and over: 19.9%; Males per 100 females: 110.6; Marriage status: 36.3% never married, 44.1% now married, 1.4% separated, 7.5% widowed, 12.1% divorced; Foreign born: 6.3%; Speak English only: 91.8%; With disability: 12.1%; Veterans: 9.7%; Ancestry: 25.1% Irish, 23.5% Italian, 19.2% German, 8.5% American, 5.9% Polish

Employment: 11.1% management, business, and financial, 3.1% computer, engineering, and science, 8.7% education, legal, community service, arts, and media, 8.6% healthcare practitioners, 21.5% service, 19.8% sales and office, 17.1% natural resources, construction, and maintenance, 10.1% production, transportation, and material moving

Income: Per capita: $35,110; Median household: $63,922; Average household: $81,614; Households with income of $100,000 or more: 23.4%; Poverty rate: 12.9%

Educational Attainment: High school diploma or higher: 84.3%; Bachelor's degree or higher: 24.3%; Graduate/professional degree or higher: 6.1%

Housing: Homeownership rate: 68.5%; Median home value: $171,500; Median year structure built: 1961; Homeowner vacancy rate: 8.2%; Median selected monthly owner costs: $1,473 with a mortgage, $729 without a mortgage; Median gross rent: $790 per month; Rental vacancy rate: 2.5%

Health Insurance: 94.1% have insurance; 72.5% have private insurance; 39.7% have public insurance; 5.9% do not have insurance; 0.6% of children under 18 do not have insurance

Transportation: Commute: 95.5% car, 1.5% public transportation, 0.0% walk, 2.3% work from home; Mean travel time to work: 27.8 minutes

Additional Information Contacts
Town of Bethel . . . . (845) 583-4350
http://www.town.bethel.ny.us

BLOOMINGBURG (village).

Covers a land area of 0.309 square miles and a water area of 0 square miles. Located at 41.56° N. Lat; 74.44° W. Long. Elevation is 515 feet.

History: Also spelled Bloomingburgh.

Population: 389; Growth (since 2000): 10.2%; Density: 1,259.9 persons per square mile; Race: 92.0% White, 5.7% Black/African American, 0.0% Asian, 0.0% American Indian/Alaska Native, 0.0% Native Hawaiian/Other Pacific Islander, 0.8% Two or more races, 8.0% Hispanic of any race; Average household size: 2.70; Median age: 35.2; Age under 18: 21.3%; Age 65 and over: 18.3%; Males per 100 females: 92.7; Marriage status: 30.9% never married, 44.3% now married, 3.5% separated, 10.5% widowed, 14.3% divorced; Foreign born: 5.9%; Speak English only: 90.8%; With disability: 15.4%; Veterans: 3.6%; Ancestry: 26.0% Irish, 16.7% Italian, 11.1% German, 9.0% Polish, 8.0% English

Employment: 7.8% management, business, and financial, 3.3% computer, engineering, and science, 3.3% education, legal, community service, arts, and media, 15.0% healthcare practitioners, 19.6% service, 30.1% sales and office, 15.7% natural resources, construction, and maintenance, 5.2% production, transportation, and material moving

Income: Per capita: $19,186; Median household: $31,667; Average household: $47,618; Households with income of $100,000 or more: 16.7%; Poverty rate: 27.8%

Educational Attainment: High school diploma or higher: 90.0%; Bachelor's degree or higher: 4.2%; Graduate/professional degree or higher: n/a

Housing: Homeownership rate: 34.0%; Median home value: $221,300; Median year structure built: 1942; Homeowner vacancy rate: 9.2%; Median selected monthly owner costs: $1,875 with a mortgage, $817 without a mortgage; Median gross rent: $855 per month; Rental vacancy rate: 19.0%

Health Insurance: 94.1% have insurance; 54.5% have private insurance; 54.2% have public insurance; 5.9% do not have insurance; 0.0% of children under 18 do not have insurance

Transportation: Commute: 90.8% car, 5.2% public transportation, 0.7% walk, 2.0% work from home; Mean travel time to work: 31.7 minutes

BURLINGHAM (unincorporated postal area)

ZCTA: 12722

Covers a land area of 0.278 square miles and a water area of 0 square miles. Located at 41.59° N. Lat; 74.37° W. Long. Elevation is 400 feet.

Population: 126; Growth (since 2000): n/a; Density: 452.7 persons per square mile; Race: 100.0% White, 0.0% Black/African American, 0.0% Asian, 0.0% American Indian/Alaska Native, 0.0% Native Hawaiian/Other Pacific Islander, 0.0% Two or more races, 0.0% Hispanic of any race; Average household size: 1.62; Median age: 59.8; Age under 18: 0.0%; Age 65 and over: 45.2%; Males per 100 females: 100.0; Marriage status: 40.5% never married, 59.5% now married, 14.3% separated, 0.0% widowed, 0.0% divorced; Foreign born: 0.0%; Speak English only: 100.0%; With disability: 64.3%; Veterans: 0.0%; Ancestry: 23.8% Austrian, 23.8% French, 23.8% Irish, 21.4% Yugoslavian

Employment: 0.0% management, business, and financial, 0.0% computer, engineering, and science, 0.0% education, legal, community service, arts, and media, 0.0% healthcare practitioners, 37.5% service, 0.0% sales and office, 62.5% natural resources, construction, and maintenance, 0.0% production, transportation, and material moving

Income: Per capita: $52,400; Median household: $73,250; Average household: $84,762; Households with income of $100,000 or more: 23.1%; Poverty rate: n/a

Educational Attainment: High school diploma or higher: 71.4%; Bachelor's degree or higher: n/a; Graduate/professional degree or higher: n/a

Housing: Homeownership rate: 100.0%; Median home value: n/a; Median year structure built: 1949; Homeowner vacancy rate: 0.0%; Median selected monthly owner costs: $0 with a mortgage, $0 without a mortgage; Median gross rent: n/a per month; Rental vacancy rate: 0.0%

Health Insurance: 100.0% have insurance; 100.0% have private insurance; 69.0% have public insurance; 0.0% do not have insurance; 0.0% of children under 18 do not have insurance

Transportation: Commute: 37.5% car, 0.0% public transportation, 0.0% walk, 62.5% work from home; Mean travel time to work: 0.0 minutes

CALLICOON (CDP).

Covers a land area of 0.359 square miles and a water area of 0.086 square miles. Located at 41.77° N. Lat; 75.06° W. Long. Elevation is 840 feet.

Population: 225; Growth (since 2000): 4.2%; Density: 627.3 persons per square mile; Race: 72.9% White, 15.6% Black/African American, 0.0% Asian, 0.0% American Indian/Alaska Native, 0.0% Native Hawaiian/Other Pacific Islander, 5.3% Two or more races, 6.2% Hispanic of any race; Average household size: 1.72; Median age: 43.2; Age under 18: 12.9%; Age 65 and over: 17.8%; Males per 100 females: 85.6; Marriage status: 51.7% never married, 46.0% now married, 0.0% separated, 0.0% widowed, 2.4% divorced; Foreign born: 4.4%; Speak English only: 100.0%; With disability: 17.8%; Veterans: 20.4%; Ancestry: 32.4% German, 13.3% Italian, 11.1% West Indian, 8.0% Scottish, 7.1% Irish

Employment: 3.4% management, business, and financial, 0.0% computer, engineering, and science, 28.6% education, legal, community service, arts, and media, 0.0% healthcare practitioners, 6.8% service, 28.6% sales and office, 20.4% natural resources, construction, and maintenance, 12.2% production, transportation, and material moving

Income: Per capita: $31,584; Median household: $42,450; Average household: $51,048; Households with income of $100,000 or more: 3.8%; Poverty rate: 4.0%

Educational Attainment: High school diploma or higher: 100.0%; Bachelor's degree or higher: 22.8%; Graduate/professional degree or higher: 7.1%

Housing: Homeownership rate: 49.6%; Median home value: $215,600; Median year structure built: Before 1940; Homeowner vacancy rate: 0.0%; Median selected monthly owner costs: $1,484 with a mortgage, $597 without a mortgage; Median gross rent: $769 per month; Rental vacancy rate: 0.0%

Health Insurance: 81.3% have insurance; 67.6% have private insurance; 41.3% have public insurance; 18.7% do not have insurance; 0.0% of children under 18 do not have insurance

Hospitals: Catskill Regional Medical Center - G Hermann Site

Newspapers: Sullivan County Democrat (weekly circulation 8,300)

Transportation: Commute: 58.5% car, 0.0% public transportation, 10.2% walk, 31.3% work from home; Mean travel time to work: 28.0 minutes

CALLICOON (town).

Covers a land area of 48.591 square miles and a water area of 0.355 square miles. Located at 41.84° N. Lat; 74.92° W. Long. Elevation is 840 feet.

History: Seat of St. Joseph Seraphic Seminary.

Population: 2,964; Growth (since 2000): -2.9%; Density: 61.0 persons per square mile; Race: 94.2% White, 1.1% Black/African American, 1.8% Asian, 0.0% American Indian/Alaska Native, 0.0% Native Hawaiian/Other Pacific Islander, 2.8% Two or more races, 6.7% Hispanic of any race; Average household size: 2.52; Median age: 48.6; Age under 18: 21.8%; Age 65 and over: 24.1%; Males per 100 females: 99.3; Marriage status: 22.5% never married, 57.8% now married, 0.2% separated, 5.0% widowed, 14.7% divorced; Foreign born: 5.3%; Speak English only: 96.8%; With disability: 15.5%; Veterans: 8.8%; Ancestry: 31.7% German, 20.2% Irish, 15.4% American, 10.3% English, 5.3% Polish

Employment: 9.6% management, business, and financial, 3.4% computer, engineering, and science, 18.2% education, legal, community service, arts, and media, 3.4% healthcare practitioners, 17.5% service, 22.4% sales and office, 15.4% natural resources, construction, and maintenance, 10.1% production, transportation, and material moving

Income: Per capita: $28,873; Median household: $67,608; Average household: $69,610; Households with income of $100,000 or more: 25.2%; Poverty rate: 6.8%

Educational Attainment: High school diploma or higher: 95.5%; Bachelor's degree or higher: 27.5%; Graduate/professional degree or higher: 12.5%

Housing: Homeownership rate: 79.1%; Median home value: $170,600; Median year structure built: 1966; Homeowner vacancy rate: 3.0%; Median selected monthly owner costs: $1,331 with a mortgage, $685 without a mortgage; Median gross rent: $811 per month; Rental vacancy rate: 0.8%

Health Insurance: 94.0% have insurance; 80.8% have private insurance; 35.9% have public insurance; 6.0% do not have insurance; 0.0% of children under 18 do not have insurance

Hospitals: Catskill Regional Medical Center - G Hermann Site

Newspapers: Sullivan County Democrat (weekly circulation 8,300)

Transportation: Commute: 89.6% car, 1.0% public transportation, 1.4% walk, 8.0% work from home; Mean travel time to work: 31.0 minutes

CALLICOON CENTER (unincorporated postal area)
ZCTA: 12724

Covers a land area of 7.556 square miles and a water area of <.001 square miles. Located at 41.84° N. Lat; 74.96° W. Long. Elevation is 1,253 feet.

Population: 404; Growth (since 2000): 36.5%; Density: 53.5 persons per square mile; Race: 88.6% White, 0.0% Black/African American, 3.0% Asian, 0.0% American Indian/Alaska Native, 0.0% Native Hawaiian/Other Pacific Islander, 8.4% Two or more races, 0.0% Hispanic of any race; Average household size: 2.61; Median age: 45.1; Age under 18: 21.8%; Age 65 and over: 26.7%; Males per 100 females: 100.8; Marriage status: 37.4% never married, 51.1% now married, 0.0% separated, 6.1% widowed, 5.5% divorced; Foreign born: 0.0%; Speak English only: 100.0%; With disability: 10.1%; Veterans: 10.4%; Ancestry: 43.3% German, 40.8% Irish, 5.0% French, 1.7% American

Employment: 26.6% management, business, and financial, 0.0% computer, engineering, and science, 13.3% education, legal, community service, arts, and media, 0.0% healthcare practitioners, 5.1% service, 41.1% sales and office, 13.9% natural resources, construction, and maintenance, 0.0% production, transportation, and material moving

Income: Per capita: $34,812; Median household: $64,491; Average household: $74,739; Households with income of $100,000 or more: 27.7%; Poverty rate: 5.0%

Educational Attainment: High school diploma or higher: 100.0%; Bachelor's degree or higher: 16.7%; Graduate/professional degree or higher: 7.0%

Housing: Homeownership rate: 81.9%; Median home value: n/a; Median year structure built: 1952; Homeowner vacancy rate: 0.0%; Median selected monthly owner costs: $0 with a mortgage, $491 without a mortgage; Median gross rent: n/a per month; Rental vacancy rate: 0.0%

Health Insurance: 94.6% have insurance; 94.6% have private insurance; 29.7% have public insurance; 5.4% do not have insurance; 0.0% of children under 18 do not have insurance

Transportation: Commute: 89.9% car, 0.0% public transportation, 0.0% walk, 10.1% work from home; Mean travel time to work: 54.3 minutes

CLARYVILLE (unincorporated postal area)
ZCTA: 12725

Covers a land area of 67.785 square miles and a water area of 0.104 square miles. Located at 41.98° N. Lat; 74.57° W. Long. Elevation is 1,617 feet.

Population: 146; Growth (since 2000): -43.8%; Density: 2.2 persons per square mile; Race: 89.7% White, 0.0% Black/African American, 4.8% Asian, 0.0% American Indian/Alaska Native, 0.0% Native Hawaiian/Other Pacific Islander, 0.0% Two or more races, 6.8% Hispanic of any race; Average household size: 1.72; Median age: 60.5; Age under 18: 5.5%; Age 65 and over: 39.0%; Males per 100 females: 102.2; Marriage status: 23.9% never married, 65.2% now married, 0.0% separated, 7.2% widowed, 3.6% divorced; Foreign born: 11.6%; Speak English only: 87.8%; With disability: 17.1%; Veterans: 11.6%; Ancestry: 27.4% Irish, 21.9% German, 13.7% Polish, 12.3% Dutch, 12.3% English

Employment: 11.8% management, business, and financial, 2.9% computer, engineering, and science, 33.8% education, legal, community service, arts, and media, 13.2% healthcare practitioners, 13.2% service, 8.8% sales and office, 10.3% natural resources, construction, and maintenance, 5.9% production, transportation, and material moving

Income: Per capita: $42,618; Median household: $78,333; Average household: $81,958; Households with income of $100,000 or more: 29.0%; Poverty rate: 20.9%

Educational Attainment: High school diploma or higher: 98.4%; Bachelor's degree or higher: 53.9%; Graduate/professional degree or higher: 16.4%

Housing: Homeownership rate: 85.5%; Median home value: $237,500; Median year structure built: 1956; Homeowner vacancy rate: 8.5%; Median selected monthly owner costs: $1,625 with a mortgage, $583 without a mortgage; Median gross rent: n/a per month; Rental vacancy rate: 0.0%

Health Insurance: 92.5% have insurance; 72.6% have private insurance; 52.7% have public insurance; 7.5% do not have insurance; 0.0% of children under 18 do not have insurance

Transportation: Commute: 69.2% car, 4.6% public transportation, 0.0% walk, 23.1% work from home; Mean travel time to work: 28.8 minutes

COCHECTON (town). Covers a land area of 36.241 square miles and a water area of 0.790 square miles. Located at 41.68° N. Lat; 74.99° W. Long. Elevation is 732 feet.

Population: 1,521; Growth (since 2000): 14.5%; Density: 42.0 persons per square mile; Race: 92.8% White, 2.9% Black/African American, 0.4% Asian, 0.4% American Indian/Alaska Native, 0.0% Native Hawaiian/Other Pacific Islander, 1.1% Two or more races, 6.6% Hispanic of any race; Average household size: 2.44; Median age: 44.1; Age under 18: 20.0%; Age 65 and over: 20.4%; Males per 100 females: 100.6; Marriage status: 31.2% never married, 54.2% now married, 1.0% separated, 6.8% widowed, 7.7% divorced; Foreign born: 6.8%; Speak English only: 94.0%; With disability: 12.2%; Veterans: 10.8%; Ancestry: 29.4% German, 20.5% Irish, 11.2% Italian, 8.2% American, 6.6% English

Employment: 20.0% management, business, and financial, 1.6% computer, engineering, and science, 17.1% education, legal, community service, arts, and media, 3.9% healthcare practitioners, 10.1% service, 17.1% sales and office, 19.3% natural resources, construction, and maintenance, 10.9% production, transportation, and material moving

Income: Per capita: $33,328; Median household: $60,909; Average household: $79,735; Households with income of $100,000 or more: 28.2%; Poverty rate: 12.6%

Educational Attainment: High school diploma or higher: 97.6%; Bachelor's degree or higher: 28.1%; Graduate/professional degree or higher: 16.0%

Housing: Homeownership rate: 76.5%; Median home value: $173,400; Median year structure built: 1966; Homeowner vacancy rate: 5.0%; Median selected monthly owner costs: $1,519 with a mortgage, $576 without a mortgage; Median gross rent: $884 per month; Rental vacancy rate: 12.5%

Health Insurance: 93.0% have insurance; 76.0% have private insurance; 34.8% have public insurance; 7.0% do not have insurance; 0.0% of children under 18 do not have insurance

Transportation: Commute: 89.3% car, 0.6% public transportation, 0.4% walk, 9.1% work from home; Mean travel time to work: 34.0 minutes

DELAWARE (town). Covers a land area of 34.941 square miles and a water area of 0.703 square miles. Located at 41.75° N. Lat; 75.00° W. Long.

Population: 2,594; Growth (since 2000): -4.6%; Density: 74.2 persons per square mile; Race: 82.5% White, 5.4% Black/African American, 2.6% Asian, 0.2% American Indian/Alaska Native, 0.0% Native Hawaiian/Other Pacific Islander, 2.0% Two or more races, 11.0% Hispanic of any race; Average household size: 2.34; Median age: 46.1; Age under 18: 17.0%; Age 65 and over: 21.6%; Males per 100 females: 96.3; Marriage status: 38.7% never married, 48.3% now married, 2.7% separated, 6.5% widowed, 6.5% divorced; Foreign born: 9.5%; Speak English only: 84.4%; With disability: 10.9%; Veterans: 9.9%; Ancestry: 32.8% German, 20.0% Irish, 9.2% English, 7.6% Italian, 4.4% French

Employment: 7.3% management, business, and financial, 1.3% computer, engineering, and science, 20.2% education, legal, community service, arts, and media, 5.0% healthcare practitioners, 22.4% service, 16.5% sales and office, 18.6% natural resources, construction, and maintenance, 8.7% production, transportation, and material moving

Income: Per capita: $30,096; Median household: $60,227; Average household: $72,511; Households with income of $100,000 or more: 19.9%; Poverty rate: 11.8%

Educational Attainment: High school diploma or higher: 93.3%; Bachelor's degree or higher: 31.3%; Graduate/professional degree or higher: 14.2%

Housing: Homeownership rate: 75.0%; Median home value: $188,900; Median year structure built: 1958; Homeowner vacancy rate: 0.9%; Median selected monthly owner costs: $1,508 with a mortgage, $639 without a mortgage; Median gross rent: $855 per month; Rental vacancy rate: 0.0%

Health Insurance: 92.9% have insurance; 74.1% have private insurance; 38.2% have public insurance; 7.1% do not have insurance; 3.0% of children under 18 do not have insurance

Transportation: Commute: 80.8% car, 1.6% public transportation, 4.6% walk, 12.4% work from home; Mean travel time to work: 30.0 minutes

ELDRED (unincorporated postal area)
ZCTA: 12732

Covers a land area of 25.067 square miles and a water area of 0.760 square miles. Located at 41.55° N. Lat; 74.87° W. Long. Elevation is 971 feet.

Population: 700; Growth (since 2000): -22.2%; Density: 27.9 persons per square mile; Race: 96.7% White, 0.0% Black/African American,

2.6% Asian, 0.0% American Indian/Alaska Native, 0.0% Native Hawaiian/Other Pacific Islander, 0.0% Two or more races, 0.7% Hispanic of any race; Average household size: 2.01; Median age: 50.4; Age under 18: 19.1%; Age 65 and over: 19.9%; Males per 100 females: 91.2; Marriage status: 19.0% never married, 62.7% now married, 0.9% separated, 5.4% widowed, 13.0% divorced; Foreign born: 6.3%; Speak English only: 99.2%; With disability: 9.3%; Veterans: 7.1%; Ancestry: 42.9% German, 32.0% Irish, 12.7% French, 11.6% English, 10.9% Italian

Employment: 16.3% management, business, and financial, 1.4% computer, engineering, and science, 2.3% education, legal, community service, arts, and media, 4.6% healthcare practitioners, 8.9% service, 16.0% sales and office, 26.9% natural resources, construction, and maintenance, 23.5% production, transportation, and material moving
Income: Per capita: $39,208; Median household: $40,625; Average household: $75,995; Households with income of $100,000 or more: 12.9%; Poverty rate: 15.3%
Educational Attainment: High school diploma or higher: 98.0%; Bachelor's degree or higher: 22.9%; Graduate/professional degree or higher: 5.8%

School District(s)
Eldred Central SD (PK-12)
    Enrollment: 606 . . . . (845) 456-1100
Housing: Homeownership rate: 77.0%; Median home value: $174,300; Median year structure built: 1969; Homeowner vacancy rate: 0.0%; Median selected monthly owner costs: $1,125 with a mortgage, $668 without a mortgage; Median gross rent: $1,131 per month; Rental vacancy rate: 16.7%
Health Insurance: 83.3% have insurance; 67.0% have private insurance; 28.9% have public insurance; 16.7% do not have insurance; 3.6% of children under 18 do not have insurance
Transportation: Commute: 95.1% car, 0.0% public transportation, 2.0% walk, 1.2% work from home; Mean travel time to work: 45.6 minutes

FALLSBURG (town). Covers a land area of 77.622 square miles and a water area of 1.488 square miles. Located at 41.74° N. Lat; 74.60° W. Long. Elevation is 1,207 feet.
History: Fallsburg takes its name from a waterfall on the Neversink River and was established in 1826. The town is in the heart of a once popular predominately Jewish summer resort area known as the Catskills Borscht Belt.
Population: 12,929; Growth (since 2000): 5.7%; Density: 166.6 persons per square mile; Race: 72.2% White, 11.9% Black/African American, 2.2% Asian, 0.5% American Indian/Alaska Native, 0.0% Native Hawaiian/Other Pacific Islander, 4.1% Two or more races, 21.6% Hispanic of any race; Average household size: 2.61; Median age: 40.7; Age under 18: 21.5%; Age 65 and over: 16.6%; Males per 100 females: 124.0; Marriage status: 38.8% never married, 46.2% now married, 2.6% separated, 6.3% widowed, 8.7% divorced; Foreign born: 12.4%; Speak English only: 75.4%; With disability: 21.0%; Veterans: 7.2%; Ancestry: 12.6% German, 10.3% Irish, 9.6% Italian, 9.5% Polish, 4.3% Russian
Employment: 9.8% management, business, and financial, 3.5% computer, engineering, and science, 16.8% education, legal, community service, arts, and media, 5.3% healthcare practitioners, 23.2% service, 22.4% sales and office, 8.4% natural resources, construction, and maintenance, 10.6% production, transportation, and material moving
Income: Per capita: $20,424; Median household: $41,584; Average household: $57,624; Households with income of $100,000 or more: 15.5%; Poverty rate: 27.3%
Educational Attainment: High school diploma or higher: 80.3%; Bachelor's degree or higher: 20.1%; Graduate/professional degree or higher: 9.0%

School District(s)
Fallsburg Central SD (PK-12)
    Enrollment: 1,397 . . . . (845) 434-6800
Housing: Homeownership rate: 62.4%; Median home value: $156,100; Median year structure built: 1982; Homeowner vacancy rate: 7.3%; Median selected monthly owner costs: $1,386 with a mortgage, $607 without a mortgage; Median gross rent: $791 per month; Rental vacancy rate: 15.8%
Health Insurance: 92.1% have insurance; 51.5% have private insurance; 55.3% have public insurance; 7.9% do not have insurance; 2.9% of children under 18 do not have insurance
Safety: Violent crime rate: 10.8 per 10,000 population; Property crime rate: 88.9 per 10,000 population

Transportation: Commute: 83.5% car, 5.1% public transportation, 4.4% walk, 4.9% work from home; Mean travel time to work: 26.0 minutes
Additional Information Contacts
Town of Fallsburg . . . . (845) 434-8810
    http://www.townoffallsburg.com

FERNDALE (unincorporated postal area)
ZCTA: 12734
    Covers a land area of 13.772 square miles and a water area of 0.036 square miles. Located at 41.73° N. Lat; 74.75° W. Long. Elevation is 1,345 feet.
Population: 984; Growth (since 2000): 17.6%; Density: 71.4 persons per square mile; Race: 95.2% White, 0.0% Black/African American, 0.0% Asian, 0.0% American Indian/Alaska Native, 0.0% Native Hawaiian/Other Pacific Islander, 1.1% Two or more races, 32.1% Hispanic of any race; Average household size: 2.72; Median age: 34.6; Age under 18: 26.2%; Age 65 and over: 16.2%; Males per 100 females: 114.1; Marriage status: 17.6% never married, 66.3% now married, 5.6% separated, 8.9% widowed, 7.2% divorced; Foreign born: 6.0%; Speak English only: 82.7%; With disability: 14.4%; Veterans: 2.6%; Ancestry: 15.9% German, 13.8% Italian, 9.1% Irish, 8.0% English, 6.4% French
Employment: 5.0% management, business, and financial, 1.1% computer, engineering, and science, 24.7% education, legal, community service, arts, and media, 4.1% healthcare practitioners, 30.3% service, 17.0% sales and office, 8.5% natural resources, construction, and maintenance, 9.2% production, transportation, and material moving
Income: Per capita: $25,562; Median household: $73,300; Average household: $67,550; Households with income of $100,000 or more: 12.0%; Poverty rate: 4.3%
Educational Attainment: High school diploma or higher: 83.3%; Bachelor's degree or higher: 24.6%; Graduate/professional degree or higher: 10.8%
Housing: Homeownership rate: 71.8%; Median home value: $180,700; Median year structure built: 1967; Homeowner vacancy rate: 9.8%; Median selected monthly owner costs: $2,006 with a mortgage, $660 without a mortgage; Median gross rent: $810 per month; Rental vacancy rate: 0.0%
Health Insurance: 94.9% have insurance; 84.0% have private insurance; 24.0% have public insurance; 5.1% do not have insurance; 0.0% of children under 18 do not have insurance
Transportation: Commute: 100.0% car, 0.0% public transportation, 0.0% walk, 0.0% work from home; Mean travel time to work: 16.0 minutes

FORESTBURGH (town). Covers a land area of 54.781 square miles and a water area of 1.532 square miles. Located at 41.56° N. Lat; 74.71° W. Long.
Population: 1,103; Growth (since 2000): 32.4%; Density: 20.1 persons per square mile; Race: 96.3% White, 1.2% Black/African American, 2.0% Asian, 0.4% American Indian/Alaska Native, 0.0% Native Hawaiian/Other Pacific Islander, 0.2% Two or more races, 2.8% Hispanic of any race; Average household size: 2.43; Median age: 52.1; Age under 18: 15.3%; Age 65 and over: 22.3%; Males per 100 females: 99.3; Marriage status: 21.7% never married, 62.0% now married, 2.1% separated, 5.9% widowed, 10.5% divorced; Foreign born: 8.7%; Speak English only: 90.7%; With disability: 17.2%; Veterans: 10.6%; Ancestry: 27.0% German, 22.2% Irish, 15.1% Italian, 8.4% English, 4.4% French
Employment: 21.9% management, business, and financial, 3.6% computer, engineering, and science, 16.8% education, legal, community service, arts, and media, 5.3% healthcare practitioners, 15.2% service, 18.1% sales and office, 12.5% natural resources, construction, and maintenance, 6.7% production, transportation, and material moving
Income: Per capita: $49,143; Median household: $76,000; Average household: $112,157; Households with income of $100,000 or more: 36.6%; Poverty rate: 3.6%
Educational Attainment: High school diploma or higher: 91.6%; Bachelor's degree or higher: 34.1%; Graduate/professional degree or higher: 18.6%
Housing: Homeownership rate: 85.0%; Median home value: $196,800; Median year structure built: 1972; Homeowner vacancy rate: 2.4%; Median selected monthly owner costs: $2,027 with a mortgage, $744 without a mortgage; Median gross rent: $1,125 per month; Rental vacancy rate: 8.2%

Health Insurance: 96.3% have insurance; 80.0% have private insurance; 32.4% have public insurance; 3.7% do not have insurance; 0.0% of children under 18 do not have insurance
Transportation: Commute: 89.1% car, 1.0% public transportation, 1.4% walk, 5.4% work from home; Mean travel time to work: 36.8 minutes

FREMONT (town). Covers a land area of 50.186 square miles and a water area of 1.046 square miles. Located at 41.87° N. Lat; 75.03° W. Long.

Population: 1,234; Growth (since 2000): -11.3%; Density: 24.6 persons per square mile; Race: 91.5% White, 7.4% Black/African American, 0.4% Asian, 0.0% American Indian/Alaska Native, 0.0% Native Hawaiian/Other Pacific Islander, 0.4% Two or more races, 3.4% Hispanic of any race; Average household size: 2.37; Median age: 47.9; Age under 18: 18.4%; Age 65 and over: 23.6%; Males per 100 females: 106.4; Marriage status: 28.4% never married, 55.8% now married, 3.0% separated, 9.5% widowed, 6.3% divorced; Foreign born: 4.9%; Speak English only: 93.9%; With disability: 19.9%; Veterans: 12.9%; Ancestry: 34.9% German, 21.9% Irish, 15.6% American, 15.6% Italian, 7.7% English
Employment: 16.2% management, business, and financial, 4.5% computer, engineering, and science, 19.3% education, legal, community service, arts, and media, 2.8% healthcare practitioners, 25.2% service, 13.2% sales and office, 13.4% natural resources, construction, and maintenance, 5.5% production, transportation, and material moving
Income: Per capita: $29,561; Median household: $56,042; Average household: $69,317; Households with income of $100,000 or more: 26.3%; Poverty rate: 9.0%
Educational Attainment: High school diploma or higher: 85.9%; Bachelor's degree or higher: 34.4%; Graduate/professional degree or higher: 18.5%
Housing: Homeownership rate: 89.7%; Median home value: $190,800; Median year structure built: 1962; Homeowner vacancy rate: 2.1%; Median selected monthly owner costs: $1,386 with a mortgage, $543 without a mortgage; Median gross rent: $690 per month; Rental vacancy rate: 0.0%
Health Insurance: 97.2% have insurance; 87.2% have private insurance; 35.6% have public insurance; 2.8% do not have insurance; 0.0% of children under 18 do not have insurance
Transportation: Commute: 89.9% car, 0.8% public transportation, 1.1% walk, 8.2% work from home; Mean travel time to work: 34.8 minutes

FREMONT CENTER (unincorporated postal area)
ZCTA: 12736

Covers a land area of 6.086 square miles and a water area of <.001 square miles. Located at 41.85° N. Lat; 75.02° W. Long. Elevation is 1,240 feet.
Population: 56; Growth (since 2000): -63.2%; Density: 9.2 persons per square mile; Race: 100.0% White, 0.0% Black/African American, 0.0% Asian, 0.0% American Indian/Alaska Native, 0.0% Native Hawaiian/Other Pacific Islander, 0.0% Two or more races, 16.1% Hispanic of any race; Average household size: 1.93; Median age: 49.5; Age under 18: 5.4%; Age 65 and over: 21.4%; Males per 100 females: 114.5; Marriage status: 0.0% never married, 88.7% now married, 22.6% separated, 0.0% widowed, 11.3% divorced; Foreign born: 10.7%; Speak English only: 78.6%; With disability: 39.3%; Veterans: 7.5%; Ancestry: 58.9% German, 17.9% Irish, 7.1% Italian
Employment: 13.0% management, business, and financial, 0.0% computer, engineering, and science, 17.4% education, legal, community service, arts, and media, 17.4% healthcare practitioners, 0.0% service, 17.4% sales and office, 17.4% natural resources, construction, and maintenance, 17.4% production, transportation, and material moving
Income: Per capita: $21,916; Median household: n/a; Average household: $40,548; Households with income of $100,000 or more: 10.3%; Poverty rate: 32.1%
Educational Attainment: High school diploma or higher: 83.0%; Bachelor's degree or higher: 13.2%; Graduate/professional degree or higher: 5.7%
Housing: Homeownership rate: 100.0%; Median home value: n/a; Median year structure built: 1976; Homeowner vacancy rate: 0.0%; Median selected monthly owner costs: $0 with a mortgage, $813 without a mortgage; Median gross rent: n/a per month; Rental vacancy rate: 0.0%
Health Insurance: 89.3% have insurance; 62.5% have private insurance; 42.9% have public insurance; 10.7% do not have insurance; 0.0% of children under 18 do not have insurance

Transportation: Commute: 100.0% car, 0.0% public transportation, 0.0% walk, 0.0% work from home; Mean travel time to work: 25.0 minutes

GLEN SPEY (unincorporated postal area)
ZCTA: 12737

Covers a land area of 35.801 square miles and a water area of 2.321 square miles. Located at 41.50° N. Lat; 74.80° W. Long. Elevation is 1,283 feet.
Population: 1,826; Growth (since 2000): 21.7%; Density: 51.0 persons per square mile; Race: 90.1% White, 1.0% Black/African American, 5.4% Asian, 0.0% American Indian/Alaska Native, 0.0% Native Hawaiian/Other Pacific Islander, 1.4% Two or more races, 12.9% Hispanic of any race; Average household size: 2.75; Median age: 41.2; Age under 18: 26.8%; Age 65 and over: 17.3%; Males per 100 females: 101.7; Marriage status: 22.3% never married, 59.1% now married, 2.4% separated, 6.1% widowed, 12.5% divorced; Foreign born: 11.8%; Speak English only: 82.6%; With disability: 15.3%; Veterans: 9.4%; Ancestry: 19.9% German, 17.6% Irish, 12.4% Italian, 10.1% Polish, 5.9% Ukrainian
Employment: 15.4% management, business, and financial, 5.0% computer, engineering, and science, 13.2% education, legal, community service, arts, and media, 3.7% healthcare practitioners, 17.1% service, 12.7% sales and office, 20.2% natural resources, construction, and maintenance, 12.8% production, transportation, and material moving
Income: Per capita: $29,035; Median household: $75,488; Average household: $77,693; Households with income of $100,000 or more: 26.4%; Poverty rate: 11.0%
Educational Attainment: High school diploma or higher: 93.9%; Bachelor's degree or higher: 30.8%; Graduate/professional degree or higher: 16.6%

School District(s)
Eldred Central SD (PK-12)
    Enrollment: 606 . . . . (845) 456-1100
Housing: Homeownership rate: 85.5%; Median home value: $202,700; Median year structure built: 1974; Homeowner vacancy rate: 5.0%; Median selected monthly owner costs: $1,892 with a mortgage, $733 without a mortgage; Median gross rent: $855 per month; Rental vacancy rate: 15.5%
Health Insurance: 93.4% have insurance; 69.7% have private insurance; 37.8% have public insurance; 6.6% do not have insurance; 2.2% of children under 18 do not have insurance
Transportation: Commute: 91.7% car, 1.6% public transportation, 2.5% walk, 4.2% work from home; Mean travel time to work: 40.7 minutes

GLEN WILD (unincorporated postal area)
ZCTA: 12738

Covers a land area of 6.559 square miles and a water area of 0.047 square miles. Located at 41.68° N. Lat; 74.59° W. Long. Elevation is 1,322 feet.
Population: 431; Growth (since 2000): 34.7%; Density: 65.7 persons per square mile; Race: 100.0% White, 0.0% Black/African American, 0.0% Asian, 0.0% American Indian/Alaska Native, 0.0% Native Hawaiian/Other Pacific Islander, 0.0% Two or more races, 35.7% Hispanic of any race; Average household size: 2.71; Median age: 35.2; Age under 18: 22.3%; Age 65 and over: 11.6%; Males per 100 females: 93.9; Marriage status: 28.1% never married, 57.3% now married, 3.9% separated, 6.6% widowed, 8.1% divorced; Foreign born: 1.2%; Speak English only: 92.2%; With disability: 14.8%; Veterans: 13.1%; Ancestry: 24.1% Scottish, 23.0% Italian, 13.7% German, 11.6% Irish, 5.1% Dutch
Employment: 11.0% management, business, and financial, 0.0% computer, engineering, and science, 12.3% education, legal, community service, arts, and media, 17.6% healthcare practitioners, 11.0% service, 44.5% sales and office, 0.0% natural resources, construction, and maintenance, 3.5% production, transportation, and material moving
Income: Per capita: $22,910; Median household: $61,830; Average household: $67,357; Households with income of $100,000 or more: 20.8%; Poverty rate: 14.2%
Educational Attainment: High school diploma or higher: 83.6%; Bachelor's degree or higher: 46.6%; Graduate/professional degree or higher: 9.6%
Housing: Homeownership rate: 56.6%; Median home value: $190,900; Median year structure built: 1979; Homeowner vacancy rate: 0.0%; Median selected monthly owner costs: $1,353 with a mortgage, $0

without a mortgage; Median gross rent: $899 per month; Rental vacancy rate: 0.0%

Health Insurance: 100.0% have insurance; 79.1% have private insurance; 28.3% have public insurance; 0.0% do not have insurance; 0.0% of children under 18 do not have insurance

Transportation: Commute: 90.5% car, 0.0% public transportation, 0.0% walk, 9.5% work from home; Mean travel time to work: 32.5 minutes

GRAHAMSVILLE (unincorporated postal area)
ZCTA: 12740

Covers a land area of 74.355 square miles and a water area of 1.051 square miles. Located at 41.94° N. Lat; 74.43° W. Long. Elevation is 968 feet.

Population: 1,659; Growth (since 2000): -20.5%; Density: 22.3 persons per square mile; Race: 89.3% White, 1.9% Black/African American, 0.0% Asian, 0.0% American Indian/Alaska Native, 0.0% Native Hawaiian/Other Pacific Islander, 2.0% Two or more races, 12.4% Hispanic of any race; Average household size: 2.61; Median age: 45.5; Age under 18: 21.7%; Age 65 and over: 21.0%; Males per 100 females: 98.5; Marriage status: 26.5% never married, 60.0% now married, 2.1% separated, 6.5% widowed, 7.0% divorced; Foreign born: 4.6%; Speak English only: 93.4%; With disability: 13.0%; Veterans: 10.5%; Ancestry: 21.1% German, 15.4% English, 12.7% Italian, 9.5% Irish, 6.8% Polish

Employment: 15.3% management, business, and financial, 5.0% computer, engineering, and science, 7.9% education, legal, community service, arts, and media, 4.4% healthcare practitioners, 32.3% service, 18.4% sales and office, 12.1% natural resources, construction, and maintenance, 4.6% production, transportation, and material moving

Income: Per capita: $32,641; Median household: $70,608; Average household: $81,828; Households with income of $100,000 or more: 26.6%; Poverty rate: 13.0%

Educational Attainment: High school diploma or higher: 88.0%; Bachelor's degree or higher: 19.6%; Graduate/professional degree or higher: 10.6%

School District(s)
Tri-Valley Central SD (PK-12)
    Enrollment: 1,064 . . . . (845) 985-2296

Housing: Homeownership rate: 76.1%; Median home value: $228,800; Median year structure built: 1970; Homeowner vacancy rate: 1.2%; Median selected monthly owner costs: $1,519 with a mortgage, $550 without a mortgage; Median gross rent: $1,203 per month; Rental vacancy rate: 0.0%

Health Insurance: 96.6% have insurance; 82.1% have private insurance; 35.5% have public insurance; 3.4% do not have insurance; 0.0% of children under 18 do not have insurance

Transportation: Commute: 95.1% car, 0.7% public transportation, 1.1% walk, 1.0% work from home; Mean travel time to work: 34.7 minutes

HANKINS (unincorporated postal area)
ZCTA: 12741

Covers a land area of 8.248 square miles and a water area of 0.122 square miles. Located at 41.84° N. Lat; 75.08° W. Long. Elevation is 807 feet.

Population: 247; Growth (since 2000): -2.0%; Density: 29.9 persons per square mile; Race: 98.4% White, 1.6% Black/African American, 0.0% Asian, 0.0% American Indian/Alaska Native, 0.0% Native Hawaiian/Other Pacific Islander, 0.0% Two or more races, 2.8% Hispanic of any race; Average household size: 2.06; Median age: 47.0; Age under 18: 23.9%; Age 65 and over: 20.6%; Males per 100 females: 104.1; Marriage status: 34.8% never married, 54.3% now married, 1.9% separated, 7.1% widowed, 3.8% divorced; Foreign born: 3.6%; Speak English only: 97.1%; With disability: 21.9%; Veterans: 3.7%; Ancestry: 44.5% Irish, 42.5% German, 16.6% Italian, 11.3% Northern European, 8.5% English

Employment: 25.6% management, business, and financial, 4.7% computer, engineering, and science, 27.9% education, legal, community service, arts, and media, 0.0% healthcare practitioners, 19.8% service, 14.0% sales and office, 2.3% natural resources, construction, and maintenance, 5.8% production, transportation, and material moving

Income: Per capita: $30,730; Median household: $57,857; Average household: $63,678; Households with income of $100,000 or more: 32.5%; Poverty rate: 4.5%

Educational Attainment: High school diploma or higher: 87.0%; Bachelor's degree or higher: 46.7%; Graduate/professional degree or higher: 21.3%

Housing: Homeownership rate: 82.5%; Median home value: $219,400; Median year structure built: Before 1940; Homeowner vacancy rate: 0.0%; Median selected monthly owner costs: $850 with a mortgage, $500 without a mortgage; Median gross rent: $675 per month; Rental vacancy rate: 0.0%

Health Insurance: 100.0% have insurance; 91.9% have private insurance; 26.3% have public insurance; 0.0% do not have insurance; 0.0% of children under 18 do not have insurance

Transportation: Commute: 94.7% car, 0.0% public transportation, 0.0% walk, 5.3% work from home; Mean travel time to work: 55.7 minutes

HARRIS (unincorporated postal area)
ZCTA: 12742

Covers a land area of 2.150 square miles and a water area of 0.008 square miles. Located at 41.72° N. Lat; 74.72° W. Long. Elevation is 1,181 feet.

Population: 68; Growth (since 2000): -48.5%; Density: 31.6 persons per square mile; Race: 100.0% White, 0.0% Black/African American, 0.0% Asian, 0.0% American Indian/Alaska Native, 0.0% Native Hawaiian/Other Pacific Islander, 0.0% Two or more races, 0.0% Hispanic of any race; Average household size: 1.94; Median age: 62.7; Age under 18: 11.8%; Age 65 and over: 47.1%; Males per 100 females: 101.1; Marriage status: 16.7% never married, 63.3% now married, 0.0% separated, 0.0% widowed, 20.0% divorced; Foreign born: 19.1%; Speak English only: 100.0%; With disability: 19.1%; Veterans: 11.7%; Ancestry: 29.4% Irish, 19.1% Brazilian, 10.3% German, 10.3% Welsh, 8.8% Slavic

Employment: 0.0% management, business, and financial, 0.0% computer, engineering, and science, 22.7% education, legal, community service, arts, and media, 0.0% healthcare practitioners, 0.0% service, 54.5% sales and office, 22.7% natural resources, construction, and maintenance, 0.0% production, transportation, and material moving

Income: Per capita: $23,471; Median household: n/a; Average household: $47,280; Households with income of $100,000 or more: 14.3%; Poverty rate: n/a

Educational Attainment: High school diploma or higher: 100.0%; Bachelor's degree or higher: 26.7%; Graduate/professional degree or higher: 16.7%

Housing: Homeownership rate: 51.4%; Median home value: n/a; Median year structure built: 1945; Homeowner vacancy rate: 0.0%; Median selected monthly owner costs: $0 with a mortgage, $0 without a mortgage; Median gross rent: $608 per month; Rental vacancy rate: 0.0%

Health Insurance: 100.0% have insurance; 70.6% have private insurance; 76.5% have public insurance; 0.0% do not have insurance; 0.0% of children under 18 do not have insurance

Hospitals: Catskill Regional Medical Center (263 beds)

Transportation: Commute: 100.0% car, 0.0% public transportation, 0.0% walk, 0.0% work from home; Mean travel time to work: 0.0 minutes

HIGHLAND (town). Covers a land area of 50.056 square miles and a water area of 1.867 square miles. Located at 41.57° N. Lat; 74.89° W. Long.

Population: 2,328; Growth (since 2000): -3.2%; Density: 46.5 persons per square mile; Race: 96.3% White, 1.9% Black/African American, 1.3% Asian, 0.0% American Indian/Alaska Native, 0.0% Native Hawaiian/Other Pacific Islander, 0.0% Two or more races, 3.5% Hispanic of any race; Average household size: 2.20; Median age: 51.0; Age under 18: 17.8%; Age 65 and over: 22.2%; Males per 100 females: 102.4; Marriage status: 24.8% never married, 54.8% now married, 2.9% separated, 8.0% widowed, 12.4% divorced; Foreign born: 9.3%; Speak English only: 92.7%; With disability: 17.1%; Veterans: 7.3%; Ancestry: 30.8% German, 25.0% Irish, 12.2% Italian, 9.2% English, 6.1% Polish

Employment: 12.8% management, business, and financial, 5.6% computer, engineering, and science, 10.9% education, legal, community service, arts, and media, 7.1% healthcare practitioners, 14.0% service, 21.3% sales and office, 15.2% natural resources, construction, and maintenance, 13.0% production, transportation, and material moving

Income: Per capita: $35,208; Median household: $50,246; Average household: $77,399; Households with income of $100,000 or more: 20.1%; Poverty rate: 14.3%

Educational Attainment: High school diploma or higher: 89.3%; Bachelor's degree or higher: 25.4%; Graduate/professional degree or higher: 8.6%

Housing: Homeownership rate: 73.6%; Median home value: $194,100; Median year structure built: 1969; Homeowner vacancy rate: 1.1%; Median selected monthly owner costs: $1,496 with a mortgage, $639 without a mortgage; Median gross rent: $1,090 per month; Rental vacancy rate: 8.3%
Health Insurance: 87.8% have insurance; 63.1% have private insurance; 42.0% have public insurance; 12.2% do not have insurance; 5.7% of children under 18 do not have insurance
Transportation: Commute: 89.5% car, 0.8% public transportation, 0.8% walk, 6.8% work from home; Mean travel time to work: 43.2 minutes

HIGHLAND LAKE (unincorporated postal area)
ZCTA: 12743
Covers a land area of 8.192 square miles and a water area of 0.623 square miles. Located at 41.55° N. Lat; 74.83° W. Long. Elevation is 1,332 feet.
Population: 389; Growth (since 2000): 28.4%; Density: 47.5 persons per square mile; Race: 98.7% White, 0.0% Black/African American, 1.3% Asian, 0.0% American Indian/Alaska Native, 0.0% Native Hawaiian/Other Pacific Islander, 0.0% Two or more races, 2.6% Hispanic of any race; Average household size: 2.32; Median age: 50.9; Age under 18: 21.1%; Age 65 and over: 23.7%; Males per 100 females: 103.7; Marriage status: 23.0% never married, 36.4% now married, 1.8% separated, 17.6% widowed, 23.0% divorced; Foreign born: 9.8%; Speak English only: 91.8%; With disability: 25.2%; Veterans: 4.9%; Ancestry: 33.9% German, 23.9% Irish, 16.7% Italian, 13.4% Scottish, 11.8% English
Employment: 5.0% management, business, and financial, 6.0% computer, engineering, and science, 33.0% education, legal, community service, arts, and media, 8.0% healthcare practitioners, 5.0% service, 18.0% sales and office, 16.0% natural resources, construction, and maintenance, 9.0% production, transportation, and material moving
Income: Per capita: $30,809; Median household: $51,635; Average household: $74,195; Households with income of $100,000 or more: 23.7%; Poverty rate: 20.8%
Educational Attainment: High school diploma or higher: 93.2%; Bachelor's degree or higher: 22.9%; Graduate/professional degree or higher: 10.6%
Housing: Homeownership rate: 66.1%; Median home value: $206,900; Median year structure built: 1969; Homeowner vacancy rate: 0.0%; Median selected monthly owner costs: $1,883 with a mortgage, $625 without a mortgage; Median gross rent: $1,206 per month; Rental vacancy rate: 0.0%
Health Insurance: 92.5% have insurance; 53.2% have private insurance; 63.0% have public insurance; 7.5% do not have insurance; 0.0% of children under 18 do not have insurance
Transportation: Commute: 83.0% car, 7.0% public transportation, 0.0% walk, 10.0% work from home; Mean travel time to work: 45.5 minutes

HORTONVILLE (CDP). Covers a land area of 0.756 square miles and a water area of 0 square miles. Located at 41.77° N. Lat; 75.02° W. Long. Elevation is 804 feet.
Population: 130; Growth (since 2000): n/a; Density: 172.0 persons per square mile; Race: 96.9% White, 0.0% Black/African American, 0.0% Asian, 0.0% American Indian/Alaska Native, 0.0% Native Hawaiian/Other Pacific Islander, 3.1% Two or more races, 0.0% Hispanic of any race; Average household size: 1.71; Median age: 63.6; Age under 18: 0.0%; Age 65 and over: 48.5%; Males per 100 females: 96.4; Marriage status: 28.5% never married, 54.6% now married, 0.0% separated, 3.8% widowed, 13.1% divorced; Foreign born: 8.5%; Speak English only: 86.9%; With disability: 26.9%; Veterans: 10.8%; Ancestry: 46.9% German, 23.1% Irish, 16.9% English, 14.6% Scandinavian, 10.8% Norwegian
Employment: 0.0% management, business, and financial, 0.0% computer, engineering, and science, 0.0% education, legal, community service, arts, and media, 0.0% healthcare practitioners, 48.1% service, 19.2% sales and office, 32.7% natural resources, construction, and maintenance, 0.0% production, transportation, and material moving
Income: Per capita: $35,727; Median household: $58,000; Average household: $59,357; Households with income of $100,000 or more: 6.6%; Poverty rate: 3.8%
Educational Attainment: High school diploma or higher: 89.2%; Bachelor's degree or higher: 19.2%; Graduate/professional degree or higher: n/a
Housing: Homeownership rate: 61.8%; Median home value: $126,300; Median year structure built: 1949; Homeowner vacancy rate: 0.0%; Median

selected monthly owner costs: $1,175 with a mortgage, $520 without a mortgage; Median gross rent: $720 per month; Rental vacancy rate: 0.0%
Health Insurance: 95.4% have insurance; 74.6% have private insurance; 60.8% have public insurance; 4.6% do not have insurance; 0.0% of children under 18 do not have insurance
Transportation: Commute: 76.1% car, 0.0% public transportation, 23.9% walk, 0.0% work from home; Mean travel time to work: 39.3 minutes

HURLEYVILLE (unincorporated postal area)
ZCTA: 12747
Covers a land area of 13.954 square miles and a water area of 0.452 square miles. Located at 41.75° N. Lat; 74.69° W. Long. Elevation is 1,319 feet.
Population: 1,857; Growth (since 2000): -4.2%; Density: 133.1 persons per square mile; Race: 72.6% White, 14.4% Black/African American, 9.7% Asian, 0.0% American Indian/Alaska Native, 0.0% Native Hawaiian/Other Pacific Islander, 2.6% Two or more races, 11.7% Hispanic of any race; Average household size: 2.63; Median age: 47.6; Age under 18: 16.7%; Age 65 and over: 22.5%; Males per 100 females: 95.7; Marriage status: 24.8% never married, 63.0% now married, 7.2% separated, 8.5% widowed, 3.6% divorced; Foreign born: 15.5%; Speak English only: 84.6%; With disability: 16.3%; Veterans: 4.3%; Ancestry: 17.9% Irish, 17.8% German, 5.1% English, 3.6% Hungarian, 3.6% Italian
Employment: 11.4% management, business, and financial, 1.4% computer, engineering, and science, 20.8% education, legal, community service, arts, and media, 3.1% healthcare practitioners, 19.0% service, 23.9% sales and office, 12.0% natural resources, construction, and maintenance, 8.3% production, transportation, and material moving
Income: Per capita: $28,779; Median household: $64,708; Average household: $75,152; Households with income of $100,000 or more: 20.3%; Poverty rate: 24.7%
Educational Attainment: High school diploma or higher: 85.6%; Bachelor's degree or higher: 29.2%; Graduate/professional degree or higher: 12.5%
Housing: Homeownership rate: 72.3%; Median home value: $162,800; Median year structure built: 1960; Homeowner vacancy rate: 9.6%; Median selected monthly owner costs: $1,500 with a mortgage, $480 without a mortgage; Median gross rent: $898 per month; Rental vacancy rate: 0.0%
Health Insurance: 82.7% have insurance; 64.1% have private insurance; 33.0% have public insurance; 17.3% do not have insurance; 20.4% of children under 18 do not have insurance
Transportation: Commute: 84.3% car, 0.7% public transportation, 4.7% walk, 10.3% work from home; Mean travel time to work: 19.4 minutes

JEFFERSONVILLE (village). Covers a land area of 0.405 square miles and a water area of 0.033 square miles. Located at 41.78° N. Lat; 74.93° W. Long. Elevation is 1,050 feet.
Population: 306; Growth (since 2000): -27.1%; Density: 754.7 persons per square mile; Race: 85.9% White, 2.9% Black/African American, 9.2% Asian, 0.0% American Indian/Alaska Native, 0.0% Native Hawaiian/Other Pacific Islander, 1.3% Two or more races, 7.5% Hispanic of any race; Average household size: 2.41; Median age: 46.0; Age under 18: 15.4%; Age 65 and over: 22.9%; Males per 100 females: 106.3; Marriage status: 40.7% never married, 44.0% now married, 2.2% separated, 6.7% widowed, 8.6% divorced; Foreign born: 12.7%; Speak English only: 86.7%; With disability: 13.1%; Veterans: 5.0%; Ancestry: 27.5% German, 10.5% Irish, 10.1% Italian, 9.2% American, 7.2% English
Employment: 9.8% management, business, and financial, 3.5% computer, engineering, and science, 12.1% education, legal, community service, arts, and media, 1.7% healthcare practitioners, 39.3% service, 19.7% sales and office, 5.8% natural resources, construction, and maintenance, 8.1% production, transportation, and material moving
Income: Per capita: $26,210; Median household: $55,000; Average household: $59,691; Households with income of $100,000 or more: 9.5%; Poverty rate: 12.6%
Educational Attainment: High school diploma or higher: 92.9%; Bachelor's degree or higher: 31.7%; Graduate/professional degree or higher: 16.1%

School District(s)
Sullivan West Central SD (PK-12)
    Enrollment: 1,086 . . . . (845) 482-4610
Housing: Homeownership rate: 56.0%; Median home value: $141,900; Median year structure built: Before 1940; Homeowner vacancy rate: 1.5%;

Median selected monthly owner costs: $1,390 with a mortgage, $743 without a mortgage; Median gross rent: $793 per month; Rental vacancy rate: 3.8%
Health Insurance: 89.9% have insurance; 72.2% have private insurance; 32.4% have public insurance; 10.1% do not have insurance; 0.0% of children under 18 do not have insurance
Transportation: Commute: 70.1% car, 0.0% public transportation, 10.4% walk, 19.5% work from home; Mean travel time to work: 23.9 minutes

KAUNEONGA LAKE (unincorporated postal area)
ZCTA: 12749

Covers a land area of 2.942 square miles and a water area of 0.026 square miles. Located at 41.70° N. Lat; 74.84° W. Long. Elevation is 1,348 feet.
Population: 340; Growth (since 2000): 35.5%; Density: 115.6 persons per square mile; Race: 100.0% White, 0.0% Black/African American, 0.0% Asian, 0.0% American Indian/Alaska Native, 0.0% Native Hawaiian/Other Pacific Islander, 0.0% Two or more races, 0.0% Hispanic of any race; Average household size: 1.74; Median age: 55.5; Age under 18: 5.3%; Age 65 and over: 26.2%; Males per 100 females: 106.9; Marriage status: 32.0% never married, 32.9% now married, 0.0% separated, 16.5% widowed, 18.6% divorced; Foreign born: 6.8%; Speak English only: 100.0%; With disability: 5.0%; Veterans: 5.9%; Ancestry: 28.5% Irish, 22.1% German, 20.3% Italian, 13.5% Polish, 10.9% American
Employment: 30.0% management, business, and financial, 0.0% computer, engineering, and science, 0.0% education, legal, community service, arts, and media, 2.9% healthcare practitioners, 27.1% service, 23.7% sales and office, 16.4% natural resources, construction, and maintenance, 0.0% production, transportation, and material moving
Income: Per capita: $34,753; Median household: $52,829; Average household: $60,089; Households with income of $100,000 or more: 24.1%; Poverty rate: 17.9%
Educational Attainment: High school diploma or higher: 93.1%; Bachelor's degree or higher: 15.2%; Graduate/professional degree or higher: n/a
Housing: Homeownership rate: 33.3%; Median home value: n/a; Median year structure built: 1965; Homeowner vacancy rate: 9.7%; Median selected monthly owner costs: $0 with a mortgage, $0 without a mortgage; Median gross rent: $643 per month; Rental vacancy rate: 0.0%
Health Insurance: 100.0% have insurance; 94.4% have private insurance; 31.5% have public insurance; 0.0% do not have insurance; 0.0% of children under 18 do not have insurance
Transportation: Commute: 97.1% car, 0.0% public transportation, 0.0% walk, 2.9% work from home; Mean travel time to work: 19.0 minutes

KENOZA LAKE (unincorporated postal area)
ZCTA: 12750

Covers a land area of 4.255 square miles and a water area of 0.221 square miles. Located at 41.73° N. Lat; 74.97° W. Long. Elevation is 1,060 feet.
Population: 274; Growth (since 2000): n/a; Density: 64.4 persons per square mile; Race: 86.1% White, 12.0% Black/African American, 0.0% Asian, 1.8% American Indian/Alaska Native, 0.0% Native Hawaiian/Other Pacific Islander, 0.0% Two or more races, 0.0% Hispanic of any race; Average household size: 3.47; Median age: 39.1; Age under 18: 20.1%; Age 65 and over: 8.8%; Males per 100 females: 88.9; Marriage status: 37.1% never married, 60.3% now married, 8.3% separated, 2.6% widowed, 0.0% divorced; Foreign born: 2.2%; Speak English only: 95.5%; With disability: 12.0%; Veterans: 2.7%; Ancestry: 27.7% German, 11.3% Slovak, 9.9% American, 9.1% Scotch-Irish, 8.4% French
Employment: 0.0% management, business, and financial, 7.3% computer, engineering, and science, 4.3% education, legal, community service, arts, and media, 7.3% healthcare practitioners, 39.0% service, 11.6% sales and office, 18.9% natural resources, construction, and maintenance, 11.6% production, transportation, and material moving
Income: Per capita: $30,522; Median household: $78,125; Average household: $98,004; Households with income of $100,000 or more: 39.3%; Poverty rate: 12.0%
Educational Attainment: High school diploma or higher: 96.9%; Bachelor's degree or higher: 19.9%; Graduate/professional degree or higher: 13.6%

Housing: Homeownership rate: 74.7%; Median home value: $169,200; Median year structure built: 1971; Homeowner vacancy rate: 0.0%; Median selected monthly owner costs: $1,589 with a mortgage, $900 without a mortgage; Median gross rent: $1,250 per month; Rental vacancy rate: 0.0%
Health Insurance: 100.0% have insurance; 74.1% have private insurance; 32.5% have public insurance; 0.0% do not have insurance; 0.0% of children under 18 do not have insurance
Transportation: Commute: 92.7% car, 0.0% public transportation, 0.0% walk, 7.3% work from home; Mean travel time to work: 31.7 minutes

KIAMESHA LAKE (unincorporated postal area)
ZCTA: 12751

Covers a land area of 3.417 square miles and a water area of 0.465 square miles. Located at 41.70° N. Lat; 74.66° W. Long. Elevation is 1,417 feet.
Population: 1,206; Growth (since 2000): 211.6%; Density: 352.9 persons per square mile; Race: 72.5% White, 19.7% Black/African American, 1.5% Asian, 0.0% American Indian/Alaska Native, 0.0% Native Hawaiian/Other Pacific Islander, 4.1% Two or more races, 12.2% Hispanic of any race; Average household size: 3.91; Median age: 17.5; Age under 18: 50.0%; Age 65 and over: 2.7%; Males per 100 females: 98.5; Marriage status: 42.6% never married, 48.6% now married, 0.0% separated, 3.9% widowed, 4.9% divorced; Foreign born: 6.6%; Speak English only: 77.2%; With disability: 9.5%; Veterans: 1.2%; Ancestry: 11.6% Italian, 11.4% German, 8.5% Polish, 5.1% English, 4.6% American
Employment: 1.2% management, business, and financial, 2.3% computer, engineering, and science, 17.8% education, legal, community service, arts, and media, 6.8% healthcare practitioners, 41.6% service, 15.0% sales and office, 8.9% natural resources, construction, and maintenance, 6.5% production, transportation, and material moving
Income: Per capita: $14,174; Median household: $50,288; Average household: $55,651; Households with income of $100,000 or more: 9.4%; Poverty rate: 26.0%
Educational Attainment: High school diploma or higher: 88.2%; Bachelor's degree or higher: 20.0%; Graduate/professional degree or higher: 8.7%
Housing: Homeownership rate: 41.1%; Median home value: $158,800; Median year structure built: 1977; Homeowner vacancy rate: 0.0%; Median selected monthly owner costs: $1,120 with a mortgage, $611 without a mortgage; Median gross rent: $894 per month; Rental vacancy rate: 8.8%
Health Insurance: 95.4% have insurance; 44.9% have private insurance; 60.4% have public insurance; 4.6% do not have insurance; 0.0% of children under 18 do not have insurance
Transportation: Commute: 75.2% car, 3.9% public transportation, 11.1% walk, 7.0% work from home; Mean travel time to work: 17.6 minutes

LAKE HUNTINGTON (unincorporated postal area)
ZCTA: 12752

Covers a land area of 1.733 square miles and a water area of 0.141 square miles. Located at 41.68° N. Lat; 74.99° W. Long. Elevation is 1,217 feet.
Population: 262; Growth (since 2000): 80.7%; Density: 151.2 persons per square mile; Race: 97.7% White, 2.3% Black/African American, 0.0% Asian, 0.0% American Indian/Alaska Native, 0.0% Native Hawaiian/Other Pacific Islander, 0.0% Two or more races, 5.3% Hispanic of any race; Average household size: 2.18; Median age: 38.5; Age under 18: 17.6%; Age 65 and over: 11.8%; Males per 100 females: 112.3; Marriage status: 45.3% never married, 30.2% now married, 0.0% separated, 17.2% widowed, 7.3% divorced; Foreign born: 0.8%; Speak English only: 97.1%; With disability: 17.6%; Veterans: 7.9%; Ancestry: 45.0% German, 31.7% Irish, 14.5% Italian, 10.7% Dutch, 10.7% Polish
Employment: 20.8% management, business, and financial, 5.6% computer, engineering, and science, 7.2% education, legal, community service, arts, and media, 5.6% healthcare practitioners, 12.0% service, 16.0% sales and office, 16.0% natural resources, construction, and maintenance, 16.8% production, transportation, and material moving
Income: Per capita: $30,233; Median household: $40,000; Average household: $63,353; Households with income of $100,000 or more: 13.4%; Poverty rate: 3.1%

Educational Attainment: High school diploma or higher: 100.0%; Bachelor's degree or higher: 20.9%; Graduate/professional degree or higher: 12.8%

School District(s)

Sullivan West Central SD (PK-12)

    Enrollment: 1,086 . . . . (845) 482-4610

Housing: Homeownership rate: 62.5%; Median home value: $170,600; Median year structure built: 1944; Homeowner vacancy rate: 9.6%; Median selected monthly owner costs: $1,250 with a mortgage, $704 without a mortgage; Median gross rent: $815 per month; Rental vacancy rate: 20.9%

Health Insurance: 85.9% have insurance; 79.8% have private insurance; 22.9% have public insurance; 14.1% do not have insurance; 0.0% of children under 18 do not have insurance

Transportation: Commute: 88.5% car, 0.0% public transportation, 2.5% walk, 9.0% work from home; Mean travel time to work: 26.0 minutes

LIBERTY (town). Covers a land area of 79.579 square miles and a water area of 1.158 square miles. Located at 41.81° N. Lat; 74.78° W. Long. Elevation is 1,506 feet.

History: Settled 1793, incorporated 1870.

Population: 9,462; Growth (since 2000): -1.8%; Density: 118.9 persons per square mile; Race: 84.5% White, 6.3% Black/African American, 1.8% Asian, 0.2% American Indian/Alaska Native, 0.0% Native Hawaiian/Other Pacific Islander, 2.6% Two or more races, 22.4% Hispanic of any race; Average household size: 2.70; Median age: 41.5; Age under 18: 20.6%; Age 65 and over: 15.7%; Males per 100 females: 99.0; Marriage status: 37.1% never married, 44.2% now married, 4.1% separated, 7.8% widowed, 10.9% divorced; Foreign born: 9.6%; Speak English only: 86.1%; With disability: 18.9%; Veterans: 7.1%; Ancestry: 19.5% German, 16.0% Irish, 9.7% Italian, 5.4% Polish, 5.2% Dutch

Employment: 7.6% management, business, and financial, 1.4% computer, engineering, and science, 10.6% education, legal, community service, arts, and media, 6.4% healthcare practitioners, 24.7% service, 22.6% sales and office, 10.4% natural resources, construction, and maintenance, 16.4% production, transportation, and material moving

Income: Per capita: $24,901; Median household: $41,048; Average household: $63,082; Households with income of $100,000 or more: 16.8%; Poverty rate: 17.2%

Educational Attainment: High school diploma or higher: 82.2%; Bachelor's degree or higher: 16.6%; Graduate/professional degree or higher: 8.1%

School District(s)

Liberty Central SD (PK-12)

    Enrollment: 1,692 . . . . (845) 292-6990

Sullivan Boces

    Enrollment: n/a . . . . (845) 295-4016

Housing: Homeownership rate: 56.0%; Median home value: $130,700; Median year structure built: 1965; Homeowner vacancy rate: 2.9%; Median selected monthly owner costs: $1,563 with a mortgage, $690 without a mortgage; Median gross rent: $773 per month; Rental vacancy rate: 5.5%

Health Insurance: 91.2% have insurance; 53.8% have private insurance; 47.8% have public insurance; 8.8% do not have insurance; 0.6% of children under 18 do not have insurance

Transportation: Commute: 94.5% car, 0.1% public transportation, 1.6% walk, 2.1% work from home; Mean travel time to work: 23.4 minutes

Additional Information Contacts

Town of Liberty . . . . (845) 292-5110

    http://www.townofliberty.org

LIBERTY (village). Covers a land area of 2.602 square miles and a water area of 0.004 square miles. Located at 41.80° N. Lat; 74.74° W. Long. Elevation is 1,506 feet.

Population: 4,175; Growth (since 2000): 5.0%; Density: 1,604.3 persons per square mile; Race: 78.2% White, 7.5% Black/African American, 1.9% Asian, 0.0% American Indian/Alaska Native, 0.0% Native Hawaiian/Other Pacific Islander, 3.0% Two or more races, 28.4% Hispanic of any race; Average household size: 2.61; Median age: 39.7; Age under 18: 22.7%; Age 65 and over: 14.1%; Males per 100 females: 93.4; Marriage status: 38.9% never married, 38.2% now married, 5.3% separated, 8.6% widowed, 14.3% divorced; Foreign born: 11.8%; Speak English only: 85.0%; With disability: 25.2%; Veterans: 6.0%; Ancestry: 25.1% German, 15.0% Irish, 7.8% Dutch, 7.4% Italian, 6.2% Polish

Employment: 7.8% management, business, and financial, 2.1% computer, engineering, and science, 6.8% education, legal, community service, arts,

and media, 2.6% healthcare practitioners, 16.8% service, 30.2% sales and office, 4.6% natural resources, construction, and maintenance, 29.0% production, transportation, and material moving

Income: Per capita: $19,902; Median household: $29,688; Average household: $48,528; Households with income of $100,000 or more: 12.2%; Poverty rate: 26.4%

Educational Attainment: High school diploma or higher: 79.6%; Bachelor's degree or higher: 12.9%; Graduate/professional degree or higher: 4.8%

School District(s)

Liberty Central SD (PK-12)

    Enrollment: 1,692 . . . . (845) 292-6990

Sullivan Boces

    Enrollment: n/a . . . . (845) 295-4016

Housing: Homeownership rate: 37.8%; Median home value: $106,100; Median year structure built: 1955; Homeowner vacancy rate: 4.4%; Median selected monthly owner costs: $1,427 with a mortgage, $725 without a mortgage; Median gross rent: $742 per month; Rental vacancy rate: 8.2%

Health Insurance: 87.8% have insurance; 32.1% have private insurance; 63.5% have public insurance; 12.2% do not have insurance; 1.3% of children under 18 do not have insurance

Safety: Violent crime rate: 64.2 per 10,000 population; Property crime rate: 340.7 per 10,000 population

Transportation: Commute: 94.5% car, 0.0% public transportation, 0.0% walk, 1.8% work from home; Mean travel time to work: 25.7 minutes

Additional Information Contacts

Village of Liberty . . . . (845) 292-2250

    http://www.libertyvillageny.org

LIVINGSTON MANOR (CDP). Covers a land area of 3.081 square miles and a water area of 0.012 square miles. Located at 41.89° N. Lat; 74.82° W. Long. Elevation is 1,401 feet.

Population: 1,061; Growth (since 2000): -21.7%; Density: 344.4 persons per square mile; Race: 69.6% White, 0.0% Black/African American, 0.0% Asian, 0.0% American Indian/Alaska Native, 0.0% Native Hawaiian/Other Pacific Islander, 3.8% Two or more races, 21.7% Hispanic of any race; Average household size: 2.59; Median age: 42.5; Age under 18: 13.0%; Age 65 and over: 6.1%; Males per 100 females: 96.6; Marriage status: 29.6% never married, 50.8% now married, 19.8% separated, 6.1% widowed, 13.4% divorced; Foreign born: 13.1%; Speak English only: 78.3%; With disability: 14.0%; Veterans: 5.1%; Ancestry: 28.7% German, 8.0% English, 7.7% Dutch, 7.6% Polish, 6.7% Italian

Employment: 2.4% management, business, and financial, 0.0% computer, engineering, and science, 8.5% education, legal, community service, arts, and media, 0.0% healthcare practitioners, 37.7% service, 23.4% sales and office, 6.3% natural resources, construction, and maintenance, 21.7% production, transportation, and material moving

Income: Per capita: $22,176; Median household: $48,578; Average household: $52,891; Households with income of $100,000 or more: 10.2%; Poverty rate: 21.8%

Educational Attainment: High school diploma or higher: 74.5%; Bachelor's degree or higher: 13.8%; Graduate/professional degree or higher: n/a

School District(s)

Livingston Manor Central SD (PK-12)

    Enrollment: 488 . . . . (845) 439-4400

Housing: Homeownership rate: 59.8%; Median home value: $85,900; Median year structure built: 1955; Homeowner vacancy rate: 8.2%; Median selected monthly owner costs: $1,486 with a mortgage, $607 without a mortgage; Median gross rent: $1,080 per month; Rental vacancy rate: 21.1%

Health Insurance: 84.2% have insurance; 55.3% have private insurance; 36.0% have public insurance; 15.8% do not have insurance; 0.0% of children under 18 do not have insurance

Transportation: Commute: 90.7% car, 0.0% public transportation, 7.5% walk, 1.8% work from home; Mean travel time to work: 32.8 minutes

LOCH SHELDRAKE (CDP).
Land/water area and latitude/longitude are not available.

Population: 1,073; Growth (since 2000): n/a; Density: n/a persons per square mile; Race: 63.6% White, 12.4% Black/African American, 2.0% Asian, 0.0% American Indian/Alaska Native, 0.0% Native Hawaiian/Other Pacific Islander, 2.3% Two or more races, 25.4% Hispanic of any race; Average household size: 2.44; Median age: 32.3; Age under 18: 8.3%; Age 65 and over: 12.9%; Males per 100 females: 110.3; Marriage status:

47.7% never married, 45.9% now married, 4.9% separated, 2.4% widowed, 4.0% divorced; Foreign born: 12.1%; Speak English only: 60.3%; With disability: 18.8%; Veterans: 8.6%; Ancestry: 16.8% Polish, 13.3% Irish, 9.3% American, 8.3% Dutch, 5.5% German

Employment: 13.3% management, business, and financial, 15.3% computer, engineering, and science, 10.6% education, legal, community service, arts, and media, 10.9% healthcare practitioners, 29.1% service, 8.1% sales and office, 12.6% natural resources, construction, and maintenance, 0.0% production, transportation, and material moving

Income: Per capita: $23,674; Median household: n/a; Average household: $73,926; Households with income of $100,000 or more: 23.6%; Poverty rate: 22.8%

Educational Attainment: High school diploma or higher: 87.0%; Bachelor's degree or higher: 31.4%; Graduate/professional degree or higher: 15.7%

Two-year College(s)

Sullivan County Community College (Public)
 Enrollment: 1,565 . . . . (845) 434-5750
 Tuition: In-state $5,690; Out-of-state $10,504

Housing: Homeownership rate: 83.2%; Median home value: $117,100; Median year structure built: 1983; Homeowner vacancy rate: 0.0%; Median selected monthly owner costs: $1,481 with a mortgage, $420 without a mortgage; Median gross rent: n/a per month; Rental vacancy rate: 32.0%

Health Insurance: 86.6% have insurance; 68.0% have private insurance; 38.0% have public insurance; 13.4% do not have insurance; 10.9% of children under 18 do not have insurance

Transportation: Commute: 43.0% car, 30.4% public transportation, 8.6% walk, 14.3% work from home; Mean travel time to work: 74.9 minutes

LUMBERLAND (town).

Covers a land area of 46.539 square miles and a water area of 2.807 square miles. Located at 41.49° N. Lat; 74.81° W. Long.

Population: 2,389; Growth (since 2000): 23.2%; Density: 51.3 persons per square mile; Race: 91.3% White, 0.8% Black/African American, 4.3% Asian, 0.0% American Indian/Alaska Native, 0.0% Native Hawaiian/Other Pacific Islander, 1.0% Two or more races, 12.5% Hispanic of any race; Average household size: 2.74; Median age: 45.3; Age under 18: 23.6%; Age 65 and over: 18.5%; Males per 100 females: 100.5; Marriage status: 22.8% never married, 57.4% now married, 2.0% separated, 5.9% widowed, 13.9% divorced; Foreign born: 10.6%; Speak English only: 83.8%; With disability: 16.5%; Veterans: 9.5%; Ancestry: 24.8% German, 17.0% Irish, 11.6% Italian, 8.4% Polish, 6.8% English

Employment: 13.5% management, business, and financial, 4.4% computer, engineering, and science, 13.1% education, legal, community service, arts, and media, 4.1% healthcare practitioners, 19.0% service, 14.7% sales and office, 16.5% natural resources, construction, and maintenance, 14.8% production, transportation, and material moving

Income: Per capita: $30,491; Median household: $71,682; Average household: $81,241; Households with income of $100,000 or more: 25.7%; Poverty rate: 11.6%

Educational Attainment: High school diploma or higher: 92.8%; Bachelor's degree or higher: 30.9%; Graduate/professional degree or higher: 15.4%

Housing: Homeownership rate: 87.6%; Median home value: $198,600; Median year structure built: 1971; Homeowner vacancy rate: 4.2%; Median selected monthly owner costs: $1,821 with a mortgage, $738 without a mortgage; Median gross rent: $855 per month; Rental vacancy rate: 14.2%

Health Insurance: 93.5% have insurance; 72.4% have private insurance; 36.3% have public insurance; 6.5% do not have insurance; 2.0% of children under 18 do not have insurance

Transportation: Commute: 89.7% car, 1.2% public transportation, 1.9% walk, 7.2% work from home; Mean travel time to work: 41.0 minutes

MAMAKATING (town).

Covers a land area of 96.108 square miles and a water area of 2.561 square miles. Located at 41.59° N. Lat; 74.50° W. Long. Elevation is 577 feet.

Population: 11,649; Growth (since 2000): 5.9%; Density: 121.2 persons per square mile; Race: 88.1% White, 5.2% Black/African American, 1.1% Asian, 0.2% American Indian/Alaska Native, 0.0% Native Hawaiian/Other Pacific Islander, 2.0% Two or more races, 11.7% Hispanic of any race; Average household size: 2.87; Median age: 41.0; Age under 18: 22.5%; Age 65 and over: 12.8%; Males per 100 females: 102.2; Marriage status: 29.5% never married, 53.7% now married, 3.9% separated, 5.8% widowed, 10.9% divorced; Foreign born: 7.2%; Speak English only: 89.6%;

With disability: 14.2%; Veterans: 8.1%; Ancestry: 21.8% Italian, 21.4% German, 21.1% Irish, 8.1% English, 7.5% Polish

Employment: 9.6% management, business, and financial, 2.1% computer, engineering, and science, 8.7% education, legal, community service, arts, and media, 6.1% healthcare practitioners, 21.3% service, 31.3% sales and office, 10.0% natural resources, construction, and maintenance, 10.9% production, transportation, and material moving

Income: Per capita: $31,608; Median household: $64,770; Average household: $85,570; Households with income of $100,000 or more: 28.8%; Poverty rate: 8.3%

Educational Attainment: High school diploma or higher: 90.3%; Bachelor's degree or higher: 20.5%; Graduate/professional degree or higher: 8.1%

Housing: Homeownership rate: 78.1%; Median home value: $184,800; Median year structure built: 1969; Homeowner vacancy rate: 5.6%; Median selected monthly owner costs: $1,931 with a mortgage, $822 without a mortgage; Median gross rent: $1,108 per month; Rental vacancy rate: 18.6%

Health Insurance: 92.9% have insurance; 76.5% have private insurance; 31.4% have public insurance; 7.1% do not have insurance; 2.6% of children under 18 do not have insurance

Transportation: Commute: 92.6% car, 2.9% public transportation, 0.6% walk, 3.6% work from home; Mean travel time to work: 37.1 minutes

Additional Information Contacts
Town of Mamakating. . . . . (845) 888-3002
 http://www.mamakating.org

MONGAUP VALLEY (unincorporated postal area)

ZCTA: 12762

Covers a land area of 6.342 square miles and a water area of 0.490 square miles. Located at 41.66° N. Lat; 74.79° W. Long. Elevation is 1,112 feet.

Population: 596; Growth (since 2000): 74.3%; Density: 94.0 persons per square mile; Race: 97.5% White, 0.0% Black/African American, 0.0% Asian, 0.0% American Indian/Alaska Native, 0.0% Native Hawaiian/Other Pacific Islander, 0.0% Two or more races, 16.8% Hispanic of any race; Average household size: 2.66; Median age: 33.1; Age under 18: 33.4%; Age 65 and over: 21.5%; Males per 100 females: 101.6; Marriage status: 54.3% never married, 29.6% now married, 1.5% separated, 2.1% widowed, 14.0% divorced; Foreign born: 1.8%; Speak English only: 93.0%; With disability: 10.7%; Veterans: 1.8%; Ancestry: 31.0% American, 22.0% German, 15.9% Italian, 12.2% Irish, 4.7% Russian

Employment: 0.0% management, business, and financial, 0.0% computer, engineering, and science, 0.0% education, legal, community service, arts, and media, 20.5% healthcare practitioners, 29.7% service, 34.6% sales and office, 11.4% natural resources, construction, and maintenance, 3.8% production, transportation, and material moving

Income: Per capita: $19,570; Median household: $38,571; Average household: $50,328; Households with income of $100,000 or more: 7.6%; Poverty rate: 32.9%

Educational Attainment: High school diploma or higher: 75.0%; Bachelor's degree or higher: 25.3%; Graduate/professional degree or higher: 7.5%

Housing: Homeownership rate: 58.5%; Median home value: n/a; Median year structure built: 1978; Homeowner vacancy rate: 0.0%; Median selected monthly owner costs: $0 with a mortgage, $797 without a mortgage; Median gross rent: $850 per month; Rental vacancy rate: 0.0%

Health Insurance: 93.6% have insurance; 45.0% have private insurance; 62.9% have public insurance; 6.4% do not have insurance; 0.0% of children under 18 do not have insurance

Transportation: Commute: 100.0% car, 0.0% public transportation, 0.0% walk, 0.0% work from home; Mean travel time to work: 20.1 minutes

MONTICELLO (village).

County seat. Covers a land area of 3.985 square miles and a water area of 0.024 square miles. Located at 41.65° N. Lat; 74.69° W. Long. Elevation is 1,512 feet.

History: Incorporated 1830.

Population: 6,562; Growth (since 2000): 0.8%; Density: 1,646.8 persons per square mile; Race: 47.7% White, 31.2% Black/African American, 2.8% Asian, 0.0% American Indian/Alaska Native, 0.0% Native Hawaiian/Other Pacific Islander, 13.0% Two or more races, 32.2% Hispanic of any race; Average household size: 2.49; Median age: 34.8; Age under 18: 26.5%;

Age 65 and over: 16.0%; Males per 100 females: 97.1; Marriage status: 46.9% never married, 35.5% now married, 2.9% separated, 7.8% widowed, 9.8% divorced; Foreign born: 17.2%; Speak English only: 74.6%; With disability: 20.6%; Veterans: 5.8%; Ancestry: 8.2% German, 6.3% Italian, 5.2% Irish, 4.5% Jamaican, 3.9% American

Employment: 7.0% management, business, and financial, 0.8% computer, engineering, and science, 7.1% education, legal, community service, arts, and media, 6.9% healthcare practitioners, 33.4% service, 25.7% sales and office, 7.6% natural resources, construction, and maintenance, 11.6% production, transportation, and material moving

Income: Per capita: $16,923; Median household: $31,169; Average household: $41,296; Households with income of $100,000 or more: 6.8%; Poverty rate: 27.2%

Educational Attainment: High school diploma or higher: 81.9%; Bachelor's degree or higher: 19.0%; Graduate/professional degree or higher: 4.7%

School District(s)

Monticello Central SD (KG-12)

Enrollment: 3,020 . . . . (845) 794-7700

Housing: Homeownership rate: 26.7%; Median home value: $83,700; Median year structure built: 1955; Homeowner vacancy rate: 6.5%; Median selected monthly owner costs: $1,358 with a mortgage, $591 without a mortgage; Median gross rent: $876 per month; Rental vacancy rate: 8.8%

Health Insurance: 86.3% have insurance; 35.5% have private insurance; 62.5% have public insurance; 13.7% do not have insurance; 1.4% of children under 18 do not have insurance

Safety: Violent crime rate: 56.5 per 10,000 population; Property crime rate: 285.6 per 10,000 population

Transportation: Commute: 75.8% car, 4.5% public transportation, 11.5% walk, 3.0% work from home; Mean travel time to work: 24.6 minutes

Airports: Sullivan County International (general aviation)

Additional Information Contacts

Village of Monticello . . . . (845) 794-6130
   http://www.villageofmonticello.com

MOUNTAIN DALE (unincorporated postal area)

ZCTA: 12763

Covers a land area of 14.269 square miles and a water area of 0.177 square miles. Located at 41.68° N. Lat; 74.52° W. Long. Elevation is 1,010 feet.

Population: 664; Growth (since 2000): -13.3%; Density: 46.5 persons per square mile; Race: 92.3% White, 4.2% Black/African American, 0.0% Asian, 0.0% American Indian/Alaska Native, 0.0% Native Hawaiian/Other Pacific Islander, 1.4% Two or more races, 22.3% Hispanic of any race; Average household size: 2.91; Median age: 35.3; Age under 18: 26.8%; Age 65 and over: 18.1%; Males per 100 females: 112.2; Marriage status: 32.3% never married, 59.2% now married, 1.8% separated, 5.9% widowed, 2.6% divorced; Foreign born: 9.6%; Speak English only: 84.8%; With disability: 13.1%; Veterans: 7.2%; Ancestry: 20.5% Polish, 13.7% Italian, 11.7% German, 9.9% Hungarian, 8.4% Irish

Employment: 5.2% management, business, and financial, 0.0% computer, engineering, and science, 17.9% education, legal, community service, arts, and media, 2.5% healthcare practitioners, 22.5% service, 36.1% sales and office, 14.8% natural resources, construction, and maintenance, 0.9% production, transportation, and material moving

Income: Per capita: $24,320; Median household: $67,734; Average household: $69,422; Households with income of $100,000 or more: 15.5%; Poverty rate: 16.2%

Educational Attainment: High school diploma or higher: 95.0%; Bachelor's degree or higher: 12.1%; Graduate/professional degree or higher: 5.5%

Housing: Homeownership rate: 76.7%; Median home value: $162,900; Median year structure built: 1975; Homeowner vacancy rate: 4.0%; Median selected monthly owner costs: $1,532 with a mortgage, $675 without a mortgage; Median gross rent: $841 per month; Rental vacancy rate: 0.0%

Health Insurance: 97.3% have insurance; 64.9% have private insurance; 47.7% have public insurance; 2.7% do not have insurance; 0.0% of children under 18 do not have insurance

Transportation: Commute: 84.3% car, 0.0% public transportation, 3.7% walk, 12.0% work from home; Mean travel time to work: 24.5 minutes

NARROWSBURG (CDP). Covers a land area of 1.366 square miles and a water area of 0.134 square miles. Located at 41.60° N. Lat; 75.06° W. Long. Elevation is 676 feet.

Population: 339; Growth (since 2000): -18.1%; Density: 248.1 persons per square mile; Race: 88.5% White, 6.8% Black/African American, 2.4% Asian, 2.4% American Indian/Alaska Native, 0.0% Native Hawaiian/Other Pacific Islander, 0.0% Two or more races, 0.0% Hispanic of any race; Average household size: 2.02; Median age: 61.4; Age under 18: 6.5%; Age 65 and over: 45.1%; Males per 100 females: 109.2; Marriage status: 21.7% never married, 57.3% now married, 0.0% separated, 4.3% widowed, 16.7% divorced; Foreign born: 5.0%; Speak English only: 95.5%; With disability: 19.2%; Veterans: 9.8%; Ancestry: 23.0% German, 19.2% Irish, 10.0% Italian, 8.3% English, 6.2% Welsh

Employment: 20.2% management, business, and financial, 0.0% computer, engineering, and science, 8.5% education, legal, community service, arts, and media, 0.0% healthcare practitioners, 26.4% service, 29.5% sales and office, 9.3% natural resources, construction, and maintenance, 6.2% production, transportation, and material moving

Income: Per capita: $26,542; Median household: $43,594; Average household: $51,500; Households with income of $100,000 or more: 7.8%; Poverty rate: 8.8%

Educational Attainment: High school diploma or higher: 84.9%; Bachelor's degree or higher: 28.5%; Graduate/professional degree or higher: 8.1%

Housing: Homeownership rate: 72.6%; Median home value: $163,400; Median year structure built: 1944; Homeowner vacancy rate: 10.3%; Median selected monthly owner costs: $1,201 with a mortgage, $629 without a mortgage; Median gross rent: $683 per month; Rental vacancy rate: 0.0%

Health Insurance: 85.3% have insurance; 59.9% have private insurance; 58.1% have public insurance; 14.7% do not have insurance; 0.0% of children under 18 do not have insurance

Newspapers: The River Reporter (weekly circulation 4,500)

Transportation: Commute: 72.9% car, 8.5% public transportation, 8.5% walk, 10.1% work from home; Mean travel time to work: 23.6 minutes

NEVERSINK (town). Covers a land area of 82.773 square miles and a water area of 3.491 square miles. Located at 41.87° N. Lat; 74.59° W. Long. Elevation is 1,634 feet.

Population: 3,456; Growth (since 2000): -2.7%; Density: 41.8 persons per square mile; Race: 91.5% White, 2.3% Black/African American, 0.0% Asian, 0.0% American Indian/Alaska Native, 0.0% Native Hawaiian/Other Pacific Islander, 3.1% Two or more races, 6.1% Hispanic of any race; Average household size: 2.82; Median age: 40.3; Age under 18: 26.6%; Age 65 and over: 14.6%; Males per 100 females: 96.5; Marriage status: 23.4% never married, 66.8% now married, 1.3% separated, 5.3% widowed, 4.5% divorced; Foreign born: 5.6%; Speak English only: 95.7%; With disability: 9.2%; Veterans: 11.5%; Ancestry: 18.3% Irish, 16.6% German, 9.6% Italian, 8.7% English, 6.8% European

Employment: 11.5% management, business, and financial, 6.4% computer, engineering, and science, 9.6% education, legal, community service, arts, and media, 6.0% healthcare practitioners, 27.9% service, 20.8% sales and office, 14.0% natural resources, construction, and maintenance, 3.9% production, transportation, and material moving

Income: Per capita: $31,445; Median household: $73,176; Average household: $86,955; Households with income of $100,000 or more: 30.1%; Poverty rate: 7.6%

Educational Attainment: High school diploma or higher: 88.1%; Bachelor's degree or higher: 25.4%; Graduate/professional degree or higher: 12.6%

Housing: Homeownership rate: 77.1%; Median home value: $209,700; Median year structure built: 1977; Homeowner vacancy rate: 0.0%; Median selected monthly owner costs: $1,405 with a mortgage, $655 without a mortgage; Median gross rent: $927 per month; Rental vacancy rate: 0.0%

Health Insurance: 97.5% have insurance; 84.7% have private insurance; 27.5% have public insurance; 2.5% do not have insurance; 0.0% of children under 18 do not have insurance

Transportation: Commute: 97.8% car, 0.3% public transportation, 0.5% walk, 0.5% work from home; Mean travel time to work: 30.2 minutes

NORTH BRANCH (unincorporated postal area)

ZCTA: 12766

Covers a land area of 8.037 square miles and a water area of 0.005 square miles. Located at 41.82° N. Lat; 74.98° W. Long. Elevation is 1,037 feet.

Population: 350; Growth (since 2000): -23.2%; Density: 43.5 persons per square mile; Race: 100.0% White, 0.0% Black/African American, 0.0% Asian, 0.0% American Indian/Alaska Native, 0.0% Native Hawaiian/Other Pacific Islander, 0.0% Two or more races, 0.0% Hispanic of any race; Average household size: 2.46; Median age: 51.1; Age under 18: 28.6%; Age 65 and over: 40.9%; Males per 100 females: 98.6; Marriage status: 12.9% never married, 58.2% now married, 0.0% separated, 13.9% widowed, 15.0% divorced; Foreign born: 1.7%; Speak English only: 98.3%; With disability: 22.6%; Veterans: 18.0%; Ancestry: 50.9% German, 16.0% American, 10.9% English, 8.0% Irish, 2.6% Polish

Employment: 0.0% management, business, and financial, 0.0% computer, engineering, and science, 4.6% education, legal, community service, arts, and media, 6.5% healthcare practitioners, 16.7% service, 45.4% sales and office, 16.7% natural resources, construction, and maintenance, 10.2% production, transportation, and material moving

Income: Per capita: $30,327; Median household: $68,661; Average household: $68,494; Households with income of $100,000 or more: 23.2%; Poverty rate: 1.7%

Educational Attainment: High school diploma or higher: 84.4%; Bachelor's degree or higher: 30.4%; Graduate/professional degree or higher: 6.4%

Housing: Homeownership rate: 94.4%; Median home value: $164,500; Median year structure built: 1984; Homeowner vacancy rate: 5.0%; Median selected monthly owner costs: $1,449 with a mortgage, $669 without a mortgage; Median gross rent: n/a per month; Rental vacancy rate: 0.0%

Health Insurance: 100.0% have insurance; 87.4% have private insurance; 60.3% have public insurance; 0.0% do not have insurance; 0.0% of children under 18 do not have insurance

Transportation: Commute: 100.0% car, 0.0% public transportation, 0.0% walk, 0.0% work from home; Mean travel time to work: 19.0 minutes

OBERNBURG (unincorporated postal area)
ZCTA: 12767

Covers a land area of 2.957 square miles and a water area of 0.016 square miles. Located at 41.84° N. Lat; 74.99° W. Long. Elevation is 1,657 feet.

Population: 108; Growth (since 2000): n/a; Density: 36.5 persons per square mile; Race: 100.0% White, 0.0% Black/African American, 0.0% Asian, 0.0% American Indian/Alaska Native, 0.0% Native Hawaiian/Other Pacific Islander, 0.0% Two or more races, 13.9% Hispanic of any race; Average household size: 2.77; Median age: 34.8; Age under 18: 24.1%; Age 65 and over: 11.1%; Males per 100 females: 103.2; Marriage status: 41.5% never married, 44.7% now married, 4.3% separated, 10.6% widowed, 3.2% divorced; Foreign born: 0.0%; Speak English only: 96.2%; With disability: 10.2%; Veterans: 2.4%; Ancestry: 59.3% German, 24.1% Irish, 3.7% American, 2.8% Polish, 2.8% Portuguese

Employment: 5.7% management, business, and financial, 5.7% computer, engineering, and science, 20.8% education, legal, community service, arts, and media, 0.0% healthcare practitioners, 17.0% service, 13.2% sales and office, 37.7% natural resources, construction, and maintenance, 0.0% production, transportation, and material moving

Income: Per capita: $34,841; Median household: $108,250; Average household: $93,715; Households with income of $100,000 or more: 53.8%; Poverty rate: 5.6%

Educational Attainment: High school diploma or higher: 95.2%; Bachelor's degree or higher: 38.1%; Graduate/professional degree or higher: 20.6%

Housing: Homeownership rate: 100.0%; Median home value: $98,800; Median year structure built: 1952; Homeowner vacancy rate: 0.0%; Median selected monthly owner costs: $1,875 with a mortgage, $592 without a mortgage; Median gross rent: n/a per month; Rental vacancy rate: 0.0%

Health Insurance: 100.0% have insurance; 97.2% have private insurance; 24.1% have public insurance; 0.0% do not have insurance; 0.0% of children under 18 do not have insurance

Transportation: Commute: 100.0% car, 0.0% public transportation, 0.0% walk, 0.0% work from home; Mean travel time to work: 27.3 minutes

PARKSVILLE (unincorporated postal area)
ZCTA: 12768

Covers a land area of 34.840 square miles and a water area of 0.521 square miles. Located at 41.86° N. Lat; 74.73° W. Long. Elevation is 1,670 feet.

Population: 781; Growth (since 2000): -24.2%; Density: 22.4 persons per square mile; Race: 98.8% White, 0.0% Black/African American, 0.0% Asian, 1.2% American Indian/Alaska Native, 0.0% Native Hawaiian/Other Pacific Islander, 0.0% Two or more races, 31.5% Hispanic of any race; Average household size: 2.31; Median age: 49.2; Age under 18: 14.1%; Age 65 and over: 17.3%; Males per 100 females: 134.6; Marriage status: 37.1% never married, 45.8% now married, 0.0% separated, 7.9% widowed, 9.2% divorced; Foreign born: 3.2%; Speak English only: 93.4%; With disability: 20.4%; Veterans: 4.9%; Ancestry: 24.2% Irish, 21.4% Italian, 10.2% German, 7.3% American, 4.9% Scottish

Employment: 7.0% management, business, and financial, 0.9% computer, engineering, and science, 11.1% education, legal, community service, arts, and media, 6.8% healthcare practitioners, 46.7% service, 23.9% sales and office, 3.6% natural resources, construction, and maintenance, 0.0% production, transportation, and material moving

Income: Per capita: $34,064; Median household: $64,278; Average household: $68,761; Households with income of $100,000 or more: 23.7%; Poverty rate: 2.7%

Educational Attainment: High school diploma or higher: 93.2%; Bachelor's degree or higher: 16.0%; Graduate/professional degree or higher: 2.1%

Housing: Homeownership rate: 67.8%; Median home value: $130,500; Median year structure built: 1974; Homeowner vacancy rate: 3.4%; Median selected monthly owner costs: $1,275 with a mortgage, $450 without a mortgage; Median gross rent: $672 per month; Rental vacancy rate: 0.0%

Health Insurance: 96.4% have insurance; 84.4% have private insurance; 28.7% have public insurance; 3.6% do not have insurance; 0.0% of children under 18 do not have insurance

Transportation: Commute: 94.4% car, 0.0% public transportation, 0.0% walk, 3.8% work from home; Mean travel time to work: 29.2 minutes

PHILLIPSPORT (unincorporated postal area)
ZCTA: 12769

Covers a land area of 4.935 square miles and a water area of 0 square miles. Located at 41.66° N. Lat; 74.47° W. Long. Elevation is 499 feet.

Population: 195; Growth (since 2000): n/a; Density: 39.5 persons per square mile; Race: 100.0% White, 0.0% Black/African American, 0.0% Asian, 0.0% American Indian/Alaska Native, 0.0% Native Hawaiian/Other Pacific Islander, 0.0% Two or more races, 3.6% Hispanic of any race; Average household size: 1.68; Median age: 53.6; Age under 18: 12.3%; Age 65 and over: 6.2%; Males per 100 females: 107.4; Marriage status: 0.0% never married, 43.3% now married, 0.0% separated, 5.3% widowed, 51.5% divorced; Foreign born: 0.0%; Speak English only: 91.2%; With disability: 3.6%; Veterans: 4.7%; Ancestry: 34.9% Polish, 30.8% German, 30.3% Russian, 22.6% English, 18.5% Italian

Employment: 0.0% management, business, and financial, 0.0% computer, engineering, and science, 9.6% education, legal, community service, arts, and media, 42.3% healthcare practitioners, 0.0% service, 9.6% sales and office, 19.2% natural resources, construction, and maintenance, 19.2% production, transportation, and material moving

Income: Per capita: $41,865; Median household: $76,250; Average household: $71,039; Households with income of $100,000 or more: 25.0%; Poverty rate: n/a

Educational Attainment: High school diploma or higher: 100.0%; Bachelor's degree or higher: 33.3%; Graduate/professional degree or higher: 14.6%

Housing: Homeownership rate: 78.4%; Median home value: $131,500; Median year structure built: 1953; Homeowner vacancy rate: 0.0%; Median selected monthly owner costs: $1,182 with a mortgage, $0 without a mortgage; Median gross rent: n/a per month; Rental vacancy rate: 46.8%

Health Insurance: 86.2% have insurance; 75.9% have private insurance; 10.3% have public insurance; 13.8% do not have insurance; 0.0% of children under 18 do not have insurance

Transportation: Commute: 100.0% car, 0.0% public transportation, 0.0% walk, 0.0% work from home; Mean travel time to work: 38.8 minutes

POND EDDY (unincorporated postal area)
ZCTA: 12770

Covers a land area of 4.499 square miles and a water area of 0.274 square miles. Located at 41.45° N. Lat; 74.84° W. Long. Elevation is 554 feet.

Population: 295; Growth (since 2000): 8.5%; Density: 65.6 persons per square mile; Race: 91.9% White, 0.0% Black/African American, 0.0% Asian, 0.0% American Indian/Alaska Native, 0.0% Native Hawaiian/Other Pacific Islander, 0.0% Two or more races, 21.0% Hispanic of any race; Average household size: 2.71; Median age: 53.9; Age under 18: 8.5%; Age 65 and over: 16.3%; Males per 100 females: 88.5; Marriage status: 23.8% never married, 53.8% now married, 0.0% separated, 4.5% widowed, 17.8% divorced; Foreign born: 7.1%; Speak English only: 84.3%; With disability: 16.9%; Veterans: 7.4%; Ancestry: 39.3% German, 13.2% Irish, 11.2% Italian, 10.8% Portuguese, 8.1% American

Employment: 0.0% management, business, and financial, 0.0% computer, engineering, and science, 9.8% education, legal, community service, arts, and media, 0.0% healthcare practitioners, 44.7% service, 36.4% sales and office, 4.5% natural resources, construction, and maintenance, 4.5% production, transportation, and material moving

Income: Per capita: $27,351; Median household: $70,703; Average household: $69,909; Households with income of $100,000 or more: 11.9%; Poverty rate: 8.8%

Educational Attainment: High school diploma or higher: 97.8%; Bachelor's degree or higher: 15.5%; Graduate/professional degree or higher: 12.9%

Housing: Homeownership rate: 89.0%; Median home value: $183,900; Median year structure built: 1949; Homeowner vacancy rate: 4.0%; Median selected monthly owner costs: $1,558 with a mortgage, $938 without a mortgage; Median gross rent: n/a per month; Rental vacancy rate: 0.0%

Health Insurance: 97.3% have insurance; 84.7% have private insurance; 26.8% have public insurance; 2.7% do not have insurance; 0.0% of children under 18 do not have insurance

Transportation: Commute: 88.0% car, 0.0% public transportation, 0.0% walk, 12.0% work from home; Mean travel time to work: 31.3 minutes

ROCK HILL (CDP).
Covers a land area of 3.657 square miles and a water area of 0.946 square miles. Located at 41.61° N. Lat; 74.58° W. Long. Elevation is 1,378 feet.

Population: 1,494; Growth (since 2000): 41.5%; Density: 408.5 persons per square mile; Race: 85.3% White, 9.3% Black/African American, 2.0% Asian, 0.0% American Indian/Alaska Native, 0.0% Native Hawaiian/Other Pacific Islander, 3.3% Two or more races, 6.4% Hispanic of any race; Average household size: 2.69; Median age: 43.0; Age under 18: 19.5%; Age 65 and over: 21.4%; Males per 100 females: 97.7; Marriage status: 25.6% never married, 61.0% now married, 0.9% separated, 8.0% widowed, 5.4% divorced; Foreign born: 15.0%; Speak English only: 80.9%; With disability: 10.3%; Veterans: 7.2%; Ancestry: 16.7% Italian, 15.4% German, 9.8% American, 8.7% English, 6.6% Ukrainian

Employment: 12.7% management, business, and financial, 1.1% computer, engineering, and science, 19.4% education, legal, community service, arts, and media, 11.2% healthcare practitioners, 9.6% service, 26.9% sales and office, 12.0% natural resources, construction, and maintenance, 7.1% production, transportation, and material moving

Income: Per capita: $40,390; Median household: $100,625; Average household: $106,846; Households with income of $100,000 or more: 50.6%; Poverty rate: 3.2%

Educational Attainment: High school diploma or higher: 96.2%; Bachelor's degree or higher: 47.2%; Graduate/professional degree or higher: 21.0%

Housing: Homeownership rate: 87.4%; Median home value: $223,100; Median year structure built: 1976; Homeowner vacancy rate: 9.0%; Median selected monthly owner costs: $2,237 with a mortgage, $830 without a mortgage; Median gross rent: $1,200 per month; Rental vacancy rate: 42.6%

Health Insurance: 94.2% have insurance; 86.9% have private insurance; 25.2% have public insurance; 5.8% do not have insurance; 2.5% of children under 18 do not have insurance

Transportation: Commute: 95.1% car, 1.9% public transportation, 1.0% walk, 1.9% work from home; Mean travel time to work: 35.6 minutes

ROCKLAND (town).
Covers a land area of 94.156 square miles and a water area of 1.114 square miles. Located at 41.96° N. Lat; 74.79° W. Long. Elevation is 1,293 feet.

Population: 3,662; Growth (since 2000): -6.4%; Density: 38.9 persons per square mile; Race: 81.4% White, 5.9% Black/African American, 0.1% Asian, 0.0% American Indian/Alaska Native, 0.0% Native Hawaiian/Other Pacific Islander, 4.9% Two or more races, 6.4% Hispanic of any race; Average household size: 2.39; Median age: 44.6; Age under 18: 23.0%; Age 65 and over: 17.5%; Males per 100 females: 101.7; Marriage status: 28.9% never married, 49.8% now married, 8.3% separated, 12.0% widowed, 9.3% divorced; Foreign born: 5.2%; Speak English only: 92.1%; With disability: 12.5%; Veterans: 8.8%; Ancestry: 26.0% German, 15.3% Irish, 13.4% Italian, 8.7% English, 6.3% Polish

Employment: 8.6% management, business, and financial, 0.0% computer, engineering, and science, 17.9% education, legal, community service, arts, and media, 4.2% healthcare practitioners, 26.9% service, 20.6% sales and office, 9.5% natural resources, construction, and maintenance, 12.4% production, transportation, and material moving

Income: Per capita: $38,437; Median household: $49,226; Average household: $89,757; Households with income of $100,000 or more: 20.7%; Poverty rate: 20.4%

Educational Attainment: High school diploma or higher: 87.7%; Bachelor's degree or higher: 27.3%; Graduate/professional degree or higher: 12.4%

Housing: Homeownership rate: 69.7%; Median home value: $160,700; Median year structure built: 1969; Homeowner vacancy rate: 7.9%; Median selected monthly owner costs: $1,436 with a mortgage, $637 without a mortgage; Median gross rent: $1,048 per month; Rental vacancy rate: 14.4%

Health Insurance: 92.8% have insurance; 69.1% have private insurance; 38.6% have public insurance; 7.2% do not have insurance; 1.8% of children under 18 do not have insurance

Transportation: Commute: 90.1% car, 0.0% public transportation, 4.6% walk, 5.3% work from home; Mean travel time to work: 28.7 minutes

ROSCOE (CDP).
Covers a land area of 0.718 square miles and a water area of 0.002 square miles. Located at 41.93° N. Lat; 74.92° W. Long. Elevation is 1,296 feet.

Population: 607; Growth (since 2000): 1.7%; Density: 845.3 persons per square mile; Race: 100.0% White, 0.0% Black/African American, 0.0% Asian, 0.0% American Indian/Alaska Native, 0.0% Native Hawaiian/Other Pacific Islander, 0.0% Two or more races, 0.0% Hispanic of any race; Average household size: 2.21; Median age: 46.3; Age under 18: 29.2%; Age 65 and over: 21.6%; Males per 100 females: 88.5; Marriage status: 37.6% never married, 36.4% now married, 0.0% separated, 16.6% widowed, 9.3% divorced; Foreign born: 4.4%; Speak English only: 100.0%; With disability: 6.4%; Veterans: 8.8%; Ancestry: 30.5% Irish, 28.3% German, 24.4% Italian, 15.3% English, 11.4% French

Employment: 14.6% management, business, and financial, 0.0% computer, engineering, and science, 15.2% education, legal, community service, arts, and media, 9.6% healthcare practitioners, 18.5% service, 8.9% sales and office, 20.2% natural resources, construction, and maintenance, 12.9% production, transportation, and material moving

Income: Per capita: $48,580; Median household: $50,927; Average household: $109,534; Households with income of $100,000 or more: 25.9%; Poverty rate: 4.0%

Educational Attainment: High school diploma or higher: 96.3%; Bachelor's degree or higher: 44.2%; Graduate/professional degree or higher: 18.6%

School District(s)

Roscoe Central SD (PK-12)

    Enrollment: 256 . . . . (607) 498-4126

Housing: Homeownership rate: 76.4%; Median home value: $157,700; Median year structure built: Before 1940; Homeowner vacancy rate: 0.0%; Median selected monthly owner costs: $1,692 with a mortgage, $705 without a mortgage; Median gross rent: n/a per month; Rental vacancy rate: 0.0%

Health Insurance: 95.1% have insurance; 79.7% have private insurance; 34.4% have public insurance; 4.9% do not have insurance; 0.0% of children under 18 do not have insurance

Transportation: Commute: 86.8% car, 0.0% public transportation, 9.2% walk, 4.0% work from home; Mean travel time to work: 27.1 minutes

SMALLWOOD (CDP).
Covers a land area of 1.505 square miles and a water area of 0.118 square miles. Located at 41.66° N. Lat; 74.82° W. Long. Elevation is 1,201 feet.

Population: 689; Growth (since 2000): 21.7%; Density: 457.9 persons per square mile; Race: 96.4% White, 0.0% Black/African American, 3.6% Asian, 0.0% American Indian/Alaska Native, 0.0% Native Hawaiian/Other Pacific Islander, 0.0% Two or more races, 4.2% Hispanic of any race; Average household size: 2.70; Median age: 47.6; Age under 18: 16.3%; Age 65 and over: 7.7%; Males per 100 females: 99.3; Marriage status: 43.4% never married, 35.7% now married, 0.0% separated, 1.7% widowed, 19.2% divorced; Foreign born: 4.6%; Speak English only: 99.9%; With disability: 6.2%; Veterans: 8.3%; Ancestry: 35.3% Irish, 22.4% German, 20.0% Italian, 8.3% Norwegian, 7.8% Polish

Employment: 18.8% management, business, and financial, 0.0% computer, engineering, and science, 0.0% education, legal, community service, arts, and media, 8.3% healthcare practitioners, 2.7% service, 29.0% sales and office, 18.8% natural resources, construction, and maintenance, 22.5% production, transportation, and material moving

Income: Per capita: $45,904; Median household: $135,375; Average household: $115,916; Households with income of $100,000 or more: 50.6%; Poverty rate: 3.8%

Educational Attainment: High school diploma or higher: 84.3%; Bachelor's degree or higher: 36.4%; Graduate/professional degree or higher: 10.4%

Housing: Homeownership rate: 78.8%; Median home value: $204,300; Median year structure built: 1944; Homeowner vacancy rate: 14.5%; Median selected monthly owner costs: $1,146 with a mortgage, $1,026 without a mortgage; Median gross rent: n/a per month; Rental vacancy rate: 0.0%

Health Insurance: 95.5% have insurance; 84.2% have private insurance; 20.3% have public insurance; 4.5% do not have insurance; 3.6% of children under 18 do not have insurance

Transportation: Commute: 94.2% car, 0.0% public transportation, 0.0% walk, 2.9% work from home; Mean travel time to work: 29.4 minutes

SOUTH FALLSBURG (CDP).
Covers a land area of 5.947 square miles and a water area of 0.155 square miles. Located at 41.73° N. Lat; 74.64° W. Long. Elevation is 1,266 feet.

Population: 2,299; Growth (since 2000): 11.5%; Density: 386.6 persons per square mile; Race: 68.9% White, 9.4% Black/African American, 0.3% Asian, 0.0% American Indian/Alaska Native, 0.0% Native Hawaiian/Other Pacific Islander, 2.0% Two or more races, 27.4% Hispanic of any race; Average household size: 3.28; Median age: 30.6; Age under 18: 40.2%; Age 65 and over: 19.1%; Males per 100 females: 99.0; Marriage status: 35.1% never married, 32.1% now married, 0.0% separated, 15.6% widowed, 17.3% divorced; Foreign born: 10.8%; Speak English only: 73.0%; With disability: 18.7%; Veterans: 2.9%; Ancestry: 13.6% German, 12.7% Polish, 3.3% Italian, 2.5% Russian, 2.3% Dutch

Employment: 4.3% management, business, and financial, 0.0% computer, engineering, and science, 20.7% education, legal, community service, arts, and media, 1.0% healthcare practitioners, 31.2% service, 12.2% sales and office, 11.1% natural resources, construction, and maintenance, 19.5% production, transportation, and material moving

Income: Per capita: $11,769; Median household: $24,757; Average household: $36,539; Households with income of $100,000 or more: 6.8%; Poverty rate: 59.2%

Educational Attainment: High school diploma or higher: 60.1%; Bachelor's degree or higher: 9.2%; Graduate/professional degree or higher: 7.1%

Four-year College(s)
Yeshivath Zichron Moshe (Private, Not-for-profit)
  Enrollment: 199. . . . . (845) 434-5240
  Tuition: In-state $12,740; Out-of-state $12,740

Housing: Homeownership rate: 30.7%; Median home value: $169,800; Median year structure built: 1980; Homeowner vacancy rate: 22.1%; Median selected monthly owner costs: $2,009 with a mortgage, $786 without a mortgage; Median gross rent: $593 per month; Rental vacancy rate: 26.7%

Health Insurance: 93.7% have insurance; 24.3% have private insurance; 79.3% have public insurance; 6.3% do not have insurance; 0.0% of children under 18 do not have insurance

Transportation: Commute: 74.7% car, 7.0% public transportation, 11.6% walk, 0.0% work from home; Mean travel time to work: 15.1 minutes

SUMMITVILLE (unincorporated postal area)
ZCTA: 12781

Covers a land area of 4.267 square miles and a water area of 0 square miles. Located at 41.62° N. Lat; 74.47° W. Long. Elevation is 548 feet.

Population: 142; Growth (since 2000): n/a; Density: 33.3 persons per square mile; Race: 53.5% White, 35.2% Black/African American, 0.0% Asian, 0.0% American Indian/Alaska Native, 0.0% Native Hawaiian/Other Pacific Islander, 0.0% Two or more races, 59.2% Hispanic of any race; Average household size: 2.68; Median age: 44.4; Age under 18: 27.5%; Age 65 and over: 22.5%; Males per 100 females: 106.0; Marriage status: 10.7% never married, 89.3% now married, 0.0% separated, 0.0% widowed, 0.0% divorced; Foreign born: 0.0%; Speak English only: 79.6%; With disability: 10.6%; Veterans: 8.7%; Ancestry: 38.0% Irish, 7.7% Italian

Employment: 0.0% management, business, and financial, 0.0% computer, engineering, and science, 0.0% education, legal, community service, arts, and media, 0.0% healthcare practitioners, 34.1% service, 65.9% sales and office, 0.0% natural resources, construction, and maintenance, 0.0% production, transportation, and material moving

Income: Per capita: $21,670; Median household: n/a; Average household: $54,498; Households with income of $100,000 or more: 17.0%; Poverty rate: 7.7%

Educational Attainment: High school diploma or higher: 100.0%; Bachelor's degree or higher: n/a; Graduate/professional degree or higher: n/a

Housing: Homeownership rate: 100.0%; Median home value: n/a; Median year structure built: 1942; Homeowner vacancy rate: 46.5%; Median selected monthly owner costs: $0 with a mortgage, $0 without a mortgage; Median gross rent: n/a per month; Rental vacancy rate: 0.0%

Health Insurance: 92.3% have insurance; 92.3% have private insurance; 22.5% have public insurance; 7.7% do not have insurance; 0.0% of children under 18 do not have insurance

Transportation: Commute: 100.0% car, 0.0% public transportation, 0.0% walk, 0.0% work from home; Mean travel time to work: 0.0 minutes

SWAN LAKE (unincorporated postal area)
ZCTA: 12783

Covers a land area of 33.251 square miles and a water area of 1.096 square miles. Located at 41.74° N. Lat; 74.83° W. Long. Elevation is 1,345 feet.

Population: 1,820; Growth (since 2000): -16.1%; Density: 54.7 persons per square mile; Race: 87.6% White, 8.1% Black/African American, 1.4% Asian, 1.0% American Indian/Alaska Native, 0.0% Native Hawaiian/Other Pacific Islander, 1.4% Two or more races, 15.5% Hispanic of any race; Average household size: 3.13; Median age: 40.0; Age under 18: 20.1%; Age 65 and over: 15.3%; Males per 100 females: 137.3; Marriage status: 37.8% never married, 45.9% now married, 3.9% separated, 6.4% widowed, 9.9% divorced; Foreign born: 6.5%; Speak English only: 81.8%; With disability: 17.7%; Veterans: 7.2%; Ancestry: 28.7% Italian, 20.3% Irish, 13.4% German, 6.4% Polish, 6.1% Hungarian

Employment: 10.5% management, business, and financial, 2.3% computer, engineering, and science, 23.3% education, legal, community service, arts, and media, 5.1% healthcare practitioners, 25.0% service, 10.1% sales and office, 16.0% natural resources, construction, and maintenance, 7.7% production, transportation, and material moving

Income: Per capita: $23,503; Median household: $66,917; Average household: $74,440; Households with income of $100,000 or more: 22.1%; Poverty rate: 12.9%

Educational Attainment: High school diploma or higher: 79.6%; Bachelor's degree or higher: 18.5%; Graduate/professional degree or higher: 6.0%

Housing: Homeownership rate: 84.2%; Median home value: $157,100; Median year structure built: 1963; Homeowner vacancy rate: 0.0%; Median selected monthly owner costs: $1,832 with a mortgage, $655 without a mortgage; Median gross rent: $954 per month; Rental vacancy rate: 0.0%

Health Insurance: 91.1% have insurance; 53.2% have private insurance; 49.5% have public insurance; 8.9% do not have insurance; 0.0% of children under 18 do not have insurance

Transportation: Commute: 86.6% car, 4.1% public transportation, 5.4% walk, 3.9% work from home; Mean travel time to work: 19.0 minutes

THOMPSON (town). Covers a land area of 84.089 square miles and a water area of 3.408 square miles. Located at 41.65° N. Lat; 74.68° W. Long.

Population: 15,034; Growth (since 2000): 6.0%; Density: 178.8 persons per square mile; Race: 66.2% White, 19.7% Black/African American, 2.2% Asian, 0.0% American Indian/Alaska Native, 0.0% Native Hawaiian/Other Pacific Islander, 7.6% Two or more races, 23.6% Hispanic of any race; Average household size: 2.62; Median age: 39.4; Age under 18: 23.4%; Age 65 and over: 17.9%; Males per 100 females: 99.3; Marriage status: 41.3% never married, 41.5% now married, 2.5% separated, 8.2% widowed, 9.0% divorced; Foreign born: 12.9%; Speak English only: 79.1%; With disability: 17.0%; Veterans: 6.4%; Ancestry: 11.4% Italian, 9.5% German, 7.3% Irish, 4.5% English, 3.8% American

Employment: 8.6% management, business, and financial, 1.5% computer, engineering, and science, 9.9% education, legal, community service, arts, and media, 8.0% healthcare practitioners, 25.9% service, 27.0% sales and office, 9.1% natural resources, construction, and maintenance, 9.9% production, transportation, and material moving

Income: Per capita: $24,711; Median household: $42,175; Average household: $64,464; Households with income of $100,000 or more: 18.1%; Poverty rate: 19.6%

Educational Attainment: High school diploma or higher: 85.5%; Bachelor's degree or higher: 23.8%; Graduate/professional degree or higher: 9.2%

Housing: Homeownership rate: 51.0%; Median home value: $141,600; Median year structure built: 1971; Homeowner vacancy rate: 7.5%; Median selected monthly owner costs: $1,615 with a mortgage, $616 without a mortgage; Median gross rent: $885 per month; Rental vacancy rate: 13.2%

Health Insurance: 90.1% have insurance; 53.9% have private insurance; 51.7% have public insurance; 9.9% do not have insurance; 2.1% of children under 18 do not have insurance

Transportation: Commute: 83.3% car, 2.8% public transportation, 6.5% walk, 4.9% work from home; Mean travel time to work: 27.9 minutes

Additional Information Contacts

Town of Thompson . . . . (845) 794-2500
http://www.townofthompson.com

THOMPSONVILLE (unincorporated postal area)
ZCTA: 12784

Covers a land area of 2.261 square miles and a water area of 0.007 square miles. Located at 41.67° N. Lat; 74.64° W. Long. Elevation is 1,168 feet.

Population: 47; Growth (since 2000): -20.3%; Density: 20.8 persons per square mile; Race: 27.7% White, 72.3% Black/African American, 0.0% Asian, 0.0% American Indian/Alaska Native, 0.0% Native Hawaiian/Other Pacific Islander, 0.0% Two or more races, 0.0% Hispanic of any race; Average household size: 3.92; Median age: 14.6; Age under 18: 61.7%; Age 65 and over: 27.7%; Males per 100 females: 100.0; Marriage status: 0.0% never married, 100.0% now married, 0.0% separated, 0.0% widowed, 0.0% divorced; Foreign born: 27.7%; Speak English only: 72.3%; With disability: 27.7%; Veterans: 0.0%; Ancestry: 14.9% Czech, 14.9% Yugoslavian, 12.8% German

Employment: 0.0% management, business, and financial, 0.0% computer, engineering, and science, 0.0% education, legal, community service, arts, and media, 0.0% healthcare practitioners, 100.0% service, 0.0% sales and office, 0.0% natural resources, construction, and maintenance, 0.0% production, transportation, and material moving

Income: Per capita: $10,183; Median household: n/a; Average household: n/a; Households with income of $100,000 or more: n/a; Poverty rate: n/a

Educational Attainment: High school diploma or higher: 100.0%; Bachelor's degree or higher: n/a; Graduate/professional degree or higher: n/a

Housing: Homeownership rate: 58.3%; Median home value: n/a; Median year structure built: Before 1940; Homeowner vacancy rate: 0.0%; Median selected monthly owner costs: $0 with a mortgage, $0 without a mortgage; Median gross rent: n/a per month; Rental vacancy rate: 81.5%

Health Insurance: 100.0% have insurance; 72.3% have private insurance; 27.7% have public insurance; 0.0% do not have insurance; 0.0% of children under 18 do not have insurance

Transportation: Commute: 0.0% car, 100.0% public transportation, 0.0% walk, 0.0% work from home; Mean travel time to work: 0.0 minutes

TUSTEN (town). Covers a land area of 47.205 square miles and a water area of 1.580 square miles. Located at 41.57° N. Lat; 75.00° W. Long. Elevation is 709 feet.

Population: 1,302; Growth (since 2000): -8.0%; Density: 27.6 persons per square mile; Race: 88.4% White, 6.3% Black/African American, 2.2% Asian, 1.6% American Indian/Alaska Native, 0.0% Native Hawaiian/Other Pacific Islander, 0.6% Two or more races, 2.6% Hispanic of any race; Average household size: 2.01; Median age: 52.8; Age under 18: 13.0%; Age 65 and over: 28.3%; Males per 100 females: 109.5; Marriage status: 33.6% never married, 47.9% now married, 2.1% separated, 3.9% widowed, 14.7% divorced; Foreign born: 6.5%; Speak English only: 92.7%; With disability: 19.7%; Veterans: 11.1%; Ancestry: 28.6% German, 23.1% Irish, 9.5% Italian, 6.7% English, 6.6% Polish

Employment: 19.9% management, business, and financial, 2.6% computer, engineering, and science, 9.1% education, legal, community service, arts, and media, 4.4% healthcare practitioners, 18.8% service, 26.0% sales and office, 7.6% natural resources, construction, and maintenance, 11.6% production, transportation, and material moving

Income: Per capita: $34,071; Median household: $45,682; Average household: $67,206; Households with income of $100,000 or more: 15.9%; Poverty rate: 14.4%

Educational Attainment: High school diploma or higher: 84.8%; Bachelor's degree or higher: 32.1%; Graduate/professional degree or higher: 11.1%

Housing: Homeownership rate: 74.7%; Median home value: $172,600; Median year structure built: 1971; Homeowner vacancy rate: 6.4%; Median selected monthly owner costs: $1,609 with a mortgage, $657 without a mortgage; Median gross rent: $655 per month; Rental vacancy rate: 5.3%

Health Insurance: 91.6% have insurance; 66.0% have private insurance; 50.6% have public insurance; 8.4% do not have insurance; 2.9% of children under 18 do not have insurance

Transportation: Commute: 85.0% car, 5.9% public transportation, 2.4% walk, 6.2% work from home; Mean travel time to work: 43.9 minutes

WESTBROOKVILLE (unincorporated postal area)
ZCTA: 12785

Covers a land area of 16.666 square miles and a water area of 0.894 square miles. Located at 41.53° N. Lat; 74.56° W. Long..

Population: 855; Growth (since 2000): 359.7%; Density: 51.3 persons per square mile; Race: 90.4% White, 6.8% Black/African American, 0.0% Asian, 0.0% American Indian/Alaska Native, 0.0% Native Hawaiian/Other Pacific Islander, 2.8% Two or more races, 12.2% Hispanic of any race; Average household size: 2.37; Median age: 48.6; Age under 18: 19.5%; Age 65 and over: 27.6%; Males per 100 females: 101.6; Marriage status: 15.8% never married, 72.2% now married, 5.9% separated, 7.2% widowed, 4.8% divorced; Foreign born: 0.0%; Speak English only: 97.4%; With disability: 20.1%; Veterans: 10.0%; Ancestry: 24.7% Italian, 21.8% Irish, 19.5% German, 14.3% American, 7.6% Polish

Employment: 6.1% management, business, and financial, 0.0% computer, engineering, and science, 8.5% education, legal, community service, arts, and media, 17.6% healthcare practitioners, 20.0% service, 32.3% sales and office, 10.4% natural resources, construction, and maintenance, 5.1% production, transportation, and material moving

Income: Per capita: $34,605; Median household: $50,750; Average household: $82,638; Households with income of $100,000 or more: 31.0%; Poverty rate: 9.2%

Educational Attainment: High school diploma or higher: 94.3%; Bachelor's degree or higher: 24.8%; Graduate/professional degree or higher: 13.8%

Housing: Homeownership rate: 70.4%; Median home value: $170,300; Median year structure built: 1964; Homeowner vacancy rate: 0.0%; Median selected monthly owner costs: $1,740 with a mortgage, $769 without a mortgage; Median gross rent: $1,096 per month; Rental vacancy rate: 28.9%

Health Insurance: 95.1% have insurance; 62.2% have private insurance; 51.1% have public insurance; 4.9% do not have insurance; 0.0% of children under 18 do not have insurance

Transportation: Commute: 97.9% car, 0.0% public transportation, 0.0% walk, 2.1% work from home; Mean travel time to work: 28.7 minutes

WHITE LAKE (unincorporated postal area)
ZCTA: 12786

Covers a land area of 14.963 square miles and a water area of 2.790 square miles. Located at 41.64° N. Lat; 74.86° W. Long. Elevation is 1,335 feet.

Population: 322; Growth (since 2000): -51.6%; Density: 21.5 persons per square mile; Race: 91.6% White, 0.0% Black/African American, 0.0% Asian, 8.4% American Indian/Alaska Native, 0.0% Native Hawaiian/Other Pacific Islander, 0.0% Two or more races, 0.0% Hispanic of any race; Average household size: 1.46; Median age: 68.1; Age under 18: 0.0%; Age 65 and over: 50.6%; Males per 100 females: 97.9; Marriage status: 24.8% never married, 63.4% now married, 0.0% separated, 11.8% widowed, 0.0% divorced; Foreign born: 9.9%; Speak English only: 90.1%; With disability: 9.3%; Veterans: 31.4%; Ancestry: 28.0% English, 22.7% Italian, 18.3% American, 16.1% Irish, 6.8% German

Employment: 20.5% management, business, and financial, 0.0% computer, engineering, and science, 0.0% education, legal, community service, arts, and media, 0.0% healthcare practitioners, 17.3% service, 41.7% sales and office, 20.5% natural resources, construction, and maintenance, 0.0% production, transportation, and material moving
Income: Per capita: $48,390; Median household: $49,886; Average household: $71,428; Households with income of $100,000 or more: 29.5%; Poverty rate: 11.2%
Educational Attainment: High school diploma or higher: 100.0%; Bachelor's degree or higher: 42.5%; Graduate/professional degree or higher: 10.6%
Housing: Homeownership rate: 52.3%; Median home value: $165,400; Median year structure built: 1958; Homeowner vacancy rate: 0.0%; Median selected monthly owner costs: $1,353 with a mortgage, $0 without a mortgage; Median gross rent: $1,040 per month; Rental vacancy rate: 11.8%
Health Insurance: 93.2% have insurance; 88.2% have private insurance; 50.6% have public insurance; 6.8% do not have insurance; 0.0% of children under 18 do not have insurance
Transportation: Commute: 100.0% car, 0.0% public transportation, 0.0% walk, 0.0% work from home; Mean travel time to work: 40.1 minutes

WHITE SULPHUR SPRINGS (unincorporated postal area)
ZCTA: 12787

Covers a land area of 3.510 square miles and a water area of 0.002 square miles. Located at 41.80° N. Lat; 74.85° W. Long. Elevation is 1,362 feet.

Population: 297; Growth (since 2000): 33.2%; Density: 84.6 persons per square mile; Race: 97.6% White, 0.0% Black/African American, 2.4% Asian, 0.0% American Indian/Alaska Native, 0.0% Native Hawaiian/Other Pacific Islander, 0.0% Two or more races, 11.1% Hispanic of any race; Average household size: 2.86; Median age: 50.6; Age under 18: 16.2%; Age 65 and over: 24.6%; Males per 100 females: 97.4; Marriage status: 23.2% never married, 57.9% now married, 2.0% separated, 10.6% widowed, 8.3% divorced; Foreign born: 2.4%; Speak English only: 96.1%; With disability: 7.1%; Veterans: 14.1%; Ancestry: 33.0% German, 27.3% English, 14.5% Irish, 5.4% Italian, 5.1% American

Employment: 6.7% management, business, and financial, 2.2% computer, engineering, and science, 11.9% education, legal, community service, arts, and media, 3.7% healthcare practitioners, 27.6% service, 23.1% sales and office, 14.2% natural resources, construction, and maintenance, 10.4% production, transportation, and material moving
Income: Per capita: $27,598; Median household: $58,214; Average household: $75,815; Households with income of $100,000 or more: 26.9%; Poverty rate: 6.4%
Educational Attainment: High school diploma or higher: 95.9%; Bachelor's degree or higher: 21.2%; Graduate/professional degree or higher: 14.9%
Housing: Homeownership rate: 83.7%; Median home value: $137,500; Median year structure built: Before 1940; Homeowner vacancy rate: 25.0%; Median selected monthly owner costs: $3,145 with a mortgage, $750 without a mortgage; Median gross rent: n/a per month; Rental vacancy rate: 0.0%
Health Insurance: 95.3% have insurance; 81.5% have private insurance; 33.0% have public insurance; 4.7% do not have insurance; 0.0% of children under 18 do not have insurance

Transportation: Commute: 100.0% car, 0.0% public transportation, 0.0% walk, 0.0% work from home; Mean travel time to work: 22.2 minutes

WOODBOURNE (unincorporated postal area)
ZCTA: 12788

Covers a land area of 23.499 square miles and a water area of 0.212 square miles. Located at 41.79° N. Lat; 74.59° W. Long. Elevation is 1,188 feet.

Population: 2,926; Growth (since 2000): -0.3%; Density: 124.5 persons per square mile; Race: 69.7% White, 18.0% Black/African American, 0.4% Asian, 1.2% American Indian/Alaska Native, 0.0% Native Hawaiian/Other Pacific Islander, 6.4% Two or more races, 16.8% Hispanic of any race; Average household size: 2.62; Median age: 44.2; Age under 18: 12.0%; Age 65 and over: 11.5%; Males per 100 females: 178.3; Marriage status: 42.3% never married, 45.4% now married, 2.5% separated, 4.8% widowed, 7.5% divorced; Foreign born: 10.6%; Speak English only: 80.2%; With disability: 12.0%; Veterans: 8.2%; Ancestry: 14.8% Polish, 11.6% Italian, 11.2% Irish, 10.8% German, 4.8% Russian
Employment: 8.3% management, business, and financial, 0.0% computer, engineering, and science, 14.3% education, legal, community service, arts, and media, 8.8% healthcare practitioners, 19.7% service, 29.5% sales and office, 9.5% natural resources, construction, and maintenance, 9.9% production, transportation, and material moving
Income: Per capita: $19,874; Median household: $58,103; Average household: $68,650; Households with income of $100,000 or more: 22.4%; Poverty rate: 12.9%
Educational Attainment: High school diploma or higher: 84.0%; Bachelor's degree or higher: 18.9%; Graduate/professional degree or higher: 7.2%
Housing: Homeownership rate: 83.8%; Median home value: $168,200; Median year structure built: 1976; Homeowner vacancy rate: 5.5%; Median selected monthly owner costs: $1,195 with a mortgage, $470 without a mortgage; Median gross rent: $836 per month; Rental vacancy rate: 24.8%
Health Insurance: 96.5% have insurance; 65.7% have private insurance; 44.5% have public insurance; 3.5% do not have insurance; 2.5% of children under 18 do not have insurance
Transportation: Commute: 95.6% car, 0.0% public transportation, 2.9% walk, 1.5% work from home; Mean travel time to work: 20.4 minutes

WOODRIDGE (village).
Covers a land area of 1.603 square miles and a water area of 0.105 square miles. Located at 41.72° N. Lat; 74.58° W. Long. Elevation is 1,161 feet.

Population: 916; Growth (since 2000): 1.6%; Density: 571.3 persons per square mile; Race: 81.8% White, 7.6% Black/African American, 3.3% Asian, 0.0% American Indian/Alaska Native, 0.0% Native Hawaiian/Other Pacific Islander, 4.5% Two or more races, 25.2% Hispanic of any race; Average household size: 2.57; Median age: 32.8; Age under 18: 28.2%; Age 65 and over: 13.1%; Males per 100 females: 105.1; Marriage status: 47.4% never married, 37.2% now married, 0.7% separated, 5.8% widowed, 9.6% divorced; Foreign born: 12.6%; Speak English only: 65.2%; With disability: 16.0%; Veterans: 3.8%; Ancestry: 10.3% Irish, 9.1% German, 8.6% Italian, 6.7% Russian, 4.0% American
Employment: 7.0% management, business, and financial, 5.1% computer, engineering, and science, 9.9% education, legal, community service, arts, and media, 0.0% healthcare practitioners, 27.3% service, 34.9% sales and office, 1.6% natural resources, construction, and maintenance, 14.2% production, transportation, and material moving
Income: Per capita: $19,639; Median household: $34,722; Average household: $49,006; Households with income of $100,000 or more: 10.8%; Poverty rate: 23.2%
Educational Attainment: High school diploma or higher: 81.8%; Bachelor's degree or higher: 15.0%; Graduate/professional degree or higher: 5.5%
Housing: Homeownership rate: 36.5%; Median home value: $98,700; Median year structure built: 1978; Homeowner vacancy rate: 8.7%; Median selected monthly owner costs: $1,417 with a mortgage, $618 without a mortgage; Median gross rent: $701 per month; Rental vacancy rate: 10.1%
Health Insurance: 91.9% have insurance; 35.4% have private insurance; 67.8% have public insurance; 8.1% do not have insurance; 1.8% of children under 18 do not have insurance
Safety: Violent crime rate: 0.0 per 10,000 population; Property crime rate: 201.8 per 10,000 population

Transportation: Commute: 80.1% car, 3.6% public transportation, 2.7% walk, 3.0% work from home; Mean travel time to work: 28.5 minutes

WURTSBORO (village). Covers a land area of 1.266 square miles and a water area of 0 square miles. Located at 41.58° N. Lat; 74.49° W. Long. Elevation is 577 feet.

Population: 1,264; Growth (since 2000): 2.4%; Density: 998.2 persons per square mile; Race: 87.6% White, 8.6% Black/African American, 0.2% Asian, 0.3% American Indian/Alaska Native, 0.0% Native Hawaiian/Other Pacific Islander, 2.1% Two or more races, 9.3% Hispanic of any race; Average household size: 2.48; Median age: 41.8; Age under 18: 16.1%; Age 65 and over: 18.8%; Males per 100 females: 89.1; Marriage status: 35.3% never married, 44.8% now married, 2.5% separated, 8.5% widowed, 11.4% divorced; Foreign born: 5.5%; Speak English only: 90.9%; With disability: 17.9%; Veterans: 7.0%; Ancestry: 31.2% Irish, 21.0% Italian, 16.1% German, 8.5% English, 5.1% Polish
Employment: 7.6% management, business, and financial, 4.8% computer, engineering, and science, 6.7% education, legal, community service, arts, and media, 1.4% healthcare practitioners, 22.5% service, 29.9% sales and office, 10.1% natural resources, construction, and maintenance, 17.0% production, transportation, and material moving
Income: Per capita: $30,833; Median household: $63,281; Average household: $72,418; Households with income of $100,000 or more: 27.3%; Poverty rate: 9.1%
Educational Attainment: High school diploma or higher: 88.0%; Bachelor's degree or higher: 22.9%; Graduate/professional degree or higher: 8.0%

School District(s)
Monticello Central SD (KG-12)
   Enrollment: 3,020 . . . . (845) 794-7700
Housing: Homeownership rate: 66.9%; Median home value: $168,200; Median year structure built: 1973; Homeowner vacancy rate: 2.0%; Median selected monthly owner costs: $1,750 with a mortgage, $770 without a mortgage; Median gross rent: $940 per month; Rental vacancy rate: 12.1%
Health Insurance: 96.0% have insurance; 72.2% have private insurance; 43.3% have public insurance; 4.0% do not have insurance; 0.0% of children under 18 do not have insurance
Transportation: Commute: 88.6% car, 3.6% public transportation, 2.6% walk, 3.3% work from home; Mean travel time to work: 31.1 minutes

YOUNGSVILLE (unincorporated postal area)
ZCTA: 12791
Covers a land area of 6.558 square miles and a water area of 0.010 square miles. Located at 41.82° N. Lat; 74.89° W. Long. Elevation is 1,197 feet.
Population: 619; Growth (since 2000): 38.2%; Density: 94.4 persons per square mile; Race: 83.4% White, 2.1% Black/African American, 7.4% Asian, 0.0% American Indian/Alaska Native, 0.0% Native Hawaiian/Other Pacific Islander, 7.1% Two or more races, 0.0% Hispanic of any race; Average household size: 2.62; Median age: 36.8; Age under 18: 30.2%; Age 65 and over: 14.7%; Males per 100 females: 90.4; Marriage status: 13.2% never married, 61.1% now married, 0.0% separated, 1.6% widowed, 24.1% divorced; Foreign born: 7.4%; Speak English only: 97.5%; With disability: 8.9%; Veterans: 4.2%; Ancestry: 32.1% American, 31.7% Irish, 31.0% German, 7.9% Dutch, 5.5% English
Employment: 3.2% management, business, and financial, 2.5% computer, engineering, and science, 36.5% education, legal, community service, arts, and media, 0.0% healthcare practitioners, 9.8% service, 18.9% sales and office, 15.1% natural resources, construction, and maintenance, 14.0% production, transportation, and material moving
Income: Per capita: $29,574; Median household: $77,600; Average household: $75,232; Households with income of $100,000 or more: 27.5%; Poverty rate: 0.6%
Educational Attainment: High school diploma or higher: 98.3%; Bachelor's degree or higher: 26.7%; Graduate/professional degree or higher: 17.8%
Housing: Homeownership rate: 60.2%; Median home value: $165,400; Median year structure built: 1962; Homeowner vacancy rate: 0.0%; Median selected monthly owner costs: $1,542 with a mortgage, $807 without a mortgage; Median gross rent: $696 per month; Rental vacancy rate: 0.0%
Health Insurance: 85.9% have insurance; 69.8% have private insurance; 27.0% have public insurance; 14.1% do not have insurance; 0.0% of children under 18 do not have insurance

Transportation: Commute: 100.0% car, 0.0% public transportation, 0.0% walk, 0.0% work from home; Mean travel time to work: 35.0 minutes

YULAN (unincorporated postal area)
ZCTA: 12792
Covers a land area of 3.391 square miles and a water area of 0.002 square miles. Located at 41.51° N. Lat; 74.96° W. Long. Elevation is 1,063 feet.
Population: 180; Growth (since 2000): -39.0%; Density: 53.1 persons per square mile; Race: 98.9% White, 0.0% Black/African American, 1.1% Asian, 0.0% American Indian/Alaska Native, 0.0% Native Hawaiian/Other Pacific Islander, 0.0% Two or more races, 0.0% Hispanic of any race; Average household size: 2.90; Median age: 34.3; Age under 18: 31.1%; Age 65 and over: 13.3%; Males per 100 females: 108.1; Marriage status: 13.7% never married, 79.8% now married, 0.0% separated, 6.5% widowed, 0.0% divorced; Foreign born: 6.1%; Speak English only: 91.8%; With disability: 16.7%; Veterans: 0.0%; Ancestry: 56.1% Irish, 44.4% German, 15.0% Polish, 10.6% Italian, 5.0% Eastern European
Employment: 17.3% management, business, and financial, 0.0% computer, engineering, and science, 0.0% education, legal, community service, arts, and media, 7.7% healthcare practitioners, 7.7% service, 26.9% sales and office, 17.3% natural resources, construction, and maintenance, 23.1% production, transportation, and material moving
Income: Per capita: $17,767; Median household: $42,813; Average household: $54,365; Households with income of $100,000 or more: 14.5%; Poverty rate: 14.4%
Educational Attainment: High school diploma or higher: 86.3%; Bachelor's degree or higher: 23.4%; Graduate/professional degree or higher: 12.1%
Housing: Homeownership rate: 72.6%; Median home value: $144,800; Median year structure built: 1973; Homeowner vacancy rate: 0.0%; Median selected monthly owner costs: $1,386 with a mortgage, $0 without a mortgage; Median gross rent: n/a per month; Rental vacancy rate: 32.0%
Health Insurance: 90.6% have insurance; 71.1% have private insurance; 26.7% have public insurance; 9.4% do not have insurance; 0.0% of children under 18 do not have insurance
Transportation: Commute: 82.7% car, 0.0% public transportation, 0.0% walk, 17.3% work from home; Mean travel time to work: 35.9 minutes

Tioga County

Located in southern New York; bounded on the south by Pennsylvania; crossed by the Susquehanna River. Covers a land area of 518.602 square miles, a water area of 4.278 square miles, and is located in the Eastern Time Zone at 42.18° N. Lat., 76.30° W. Long. The county was founded in 1791. County seat is Owego.

Tioga County is part of the Binghamton, NY Metropolitan Statistical Area. The entire metro area includes: Broome County, NY; Tioga County, NY

Population: 49,322; Growth (since 2000): -4.8%; Density: 95.1 persons per square mile; Race: 96.7% White, 0.6% Black/African American, 0.8% Asian, 0.0% American Indian/Alaska Native, 0.0% Native Hawaiian/Other Pacific Islander, 1.6% two or more races, 1.8% Hispanic of any race; Average household size: 2.44; Median age: 44.0; Age under 18: 21.7%; Age 65 and over: 18.5%; Males per 100 females: 98.3; Marriage status: 25.8% never married, 57.0% now married, 2.2% separated, 6.6% widowed, 10.5% divorced; Foreign born: 2.0%; Speak English only: 97.1%; With disability: 14.0%; Veterans: 10.4%; Ancestry: 17.8% German, 14.9% Irish, 14.5% English, 8.8% Italian, 7.8% American
Religion: Six largest groups: 11.4% Catholicism, 10.3% Methodist/Pietist, 2.2% Baptist, 2.1% Non-denominational Protestant, 1.8% Holiness, 1.5% Presbyterian-Reformed
Economy: Unemployment rate: 3.7%; Leading industries: 16.5 % retail trade; 13.2 % other services (except public administration); 12.5 % construction; Farms: 536 totaling 107,873 acres; Company size: 0 employ 1,000 or more persons, 0 employ 500 to 999 persons, 10 employ 100 to 499 persons, 777 employ less than 100 persons; Business ownership: 1,020 women-owned, n/a Black-owned, 32 Hispanic-owned, 56 Asian-owned, n/a American Indian/Alaska Native-owned
Employment: 13.4% management, business, and financial, 6.8% computer, engineering, and science, 9.1% education, legal, community

service, arts, and media, 5.6% healthcare practitioners, 20.1% service, 22.2% sales and office, 9.5% natural resources, construction, and maintenance, 13.3% production, transportation, and material moving
Income: Per capita: $30,252; Median household: $57,153; Average household: $73,357; Households with income of $100,000 or more: 24.0%; Poverty rate: 11.2%
Educational Attainment: High school diploma or higher: 90.0%; Bachelor's degree or higher: 24.7%; Graduate/professional degree or higher: 9.1%
Housing: Homeownership rate: 77.1%; Median home value: $113,000; Median year structure built: 1966; Homeowner vacancy rate: 1.6%; Median selected monthly owner costs: $1,236 with a mortgage, $499 without a mortgage; Median gross rent: $695 per month; Rental vacancy rate: 4.6%
Vital Statistics: Birth rate: 94.5 per 10,000 population; Death rate: 91.4 per 10,000 population; Age-adjusted cancer mortality rate: 140.5 deaths per 100,000 population
Health Insurance: 94.3% have insurance; 71.3% have private insurance; 38.2% have public insurance; 5.7% do not have insurance; 3.6% of children under 18 do not have insurance
Health Care: Physicians: 7.0 per 10,000 population; Dentists: 1.9 per 10,000 population; Hospital beds: 0.0 per 10,000 population; Hospital admissions: 0.0 per 10,000 population
Transportation: Commute: 93.3% car, 0.9% public transportation, 1.9% walk, 2.6% work from home; Mean travel time to work: 23.0 minutes
2016 Presidential Election: 59.5% Trump, 33.8% Clinton, 4.2% Johnson, 1.5% Stein
National and State Parks: Fairfield State Forest; Ketchumville State Forest; Oakley Corners State Forest; Robinson Hollow State Forest
Additional Information Contacts
Tioga Government . . . . (607) 687-8660
http://www.tiogacountyny.com

Tioga County Communities

APALACHIN (CDP). Covers a land area of 1.459 square miles and a water area of 0 square miles. Located at 42.07° N. Lat; 76.16° W. Long. Elevation is 843 feet.
Population: 1,255; Growth (since 2000): 11.5%; Density: 860.0 persons per square mile; Race: 99.3% White, 0.0% Black/African American, 0.0% Asian, 0.0% American Indian/Alaska Native, 0.0% Native Hawaiian/Other Pacific Islander, 0.7% Two or more races, 1.7% Hispanic of any race; Average household size: 2.51; Median age: 42.9; Age under 18: 19.0%; Age 65 and over: 22.9%; Males per 100 females: 105.3; Marriage status: 22.1% never married, 52.7% now married, 1.6% separated, 10.3% widowed, 14.9% divorced; Foreign born: 2.2%; Speak English only: 94.6%; With disability: 7.9%; Veterans: 4.1%; Ancestry: 18.7% German, 18.5% Irish, 12.7% Polish, 12.0% English, 4.3% Albanian
Employment: 1.7% management, business, and financial, 6.7% computer, engineering, and science, 6.5% education, legal, community service, arts, and media, 5.7% healthcare practitioners, 30.3% service, 27.1% sales and office, 11.1% natural resources, construction, and maintenance, 10.8% production, transportation, and material moving
Income: Per capita: $28,070; Median household: $49,342; Average household: $69,691; Households with income of $100,000 or more: 22.2%; Poverty rate: 1.0%
Educational Attainment: High school diploma or higher: 93.3%; Bachelor's degree or higher: 11.2%; Graduate/professional degree or higher: 1.0%
School District(s)
Owego-Apalachin Central SD (PK-12)
    Enrollment: 2,130 . . . . (607) 687-6224
Vestal Central SD (KG-12)
    Enrollment: 3,373 . . . . (607) 757-2241
Housing: Homeownership rate: 59.4%; Median home value: $118,100; Median year structure built: 1960; Homeowner vacancy rate: 0.0%; Median selected monthly owner costs: $1,366 with a mortgage, $530 without a mortgage; Median gross rent: $617 per month; Rental vacancy rate: 0.0%
Health Insurance: 97.9% have insurance; 85.3% have private insurance; 30.8% have public insurance; 2.1% do not have insurance; 3.3% of children under 18 do not have insurance
Transportation: Commute: 96.8% car, 1.3% public transportation, 1.9% walk, 0.0% work from home; Mean travel time to work: 18.8 minutes

BARTON (town). Covers a land area of 59.275 square miles and a water area of 0.414 square miles. Located at 42.08° N. Lat; 76.50° W. Long. Elevation is 804 feet.
Population: 8,599; Growth (since 2000): -5.2%; Density: 145.1 persons per square mile; Race: 96.5% White, 0.9% Black/African American, 0.2% Asian, 0.0% American Indian/Alaska Native, 0.0% Native Hawaiian/Other Pacific Islander, 2.4% Two or more races, 1.4% Hispanic of any race; Average household size: 2.46; Median age: 39.9; Age under 18: 24.1%; Age 65 and over: 16.3%; Males per 100 females: 92.1; Marriage status: 28.5% never married, 51.6% now married, 3.9% separated, 7.2% widowed, 12.8% divorced; Foreign born: 0.8%; Speak English only: 98.8%; With disability: 16.0%; Veterans: 9.8%; Ancestry: 16.9% German, 16.7% Irish, 11.4% English, 11.1% Italian, 6.4% American
Employment: 10.4% management, business, and financial, 2.0% computer, engineering, and science, 7.9% education, legal, community service, arts, and media, 8.6% healthcare practitioners, 25.0% service, 16.7% sales and office, 6.4% natural resources, construction, and maintenance, 23.1% production, transportation, and material moving
Income: Per capita: $24,794; Median household: $41,678; Average household: $60,758; Households with income of $100,000 or more: 18.7%; Poverty rate: 20.8%
Educational Attainment: High school diploma or higher: 87.1%; Bachelor's degree or higher: 15.0%; Graduate/professional degree or higher: 6.8%
Housing: Homeownership rate: 67.6%; Median home value: $95,000; Median year structure built: 1950; Homeowner vacancy rate: 1.1%; Median selected monthly owner costs: $1,039 with a mortgage, $463 without a mortgage; Median gross rent: $666 per month; Rental vacancy rate: 2.5%
Health Insurance: 90.4% have insurance; 60.7% have private insurance; 43.4% have public insurance; 9.6% do not have insurance; 7.2% of children under 18 do not have insurance
Transportation: Commute: 92.6% car, 0.9% public transportation, 4.2% walk, 1.6% work from home; Mean travel time to work: 20.5 minutes
Additional Information Contacts
Town of Barton . . . . (607) 565-2261
http://www.townofbarton.org

BERKSHIRE (town). Covers a land area of 30.216 square miles and a water area of 0.010 square miles. Located at 42.30° N. Lat; 76.17° W. Long. Elevation is 1,047 feet.
Population: 1,213; Growth (since 2000): -11.2%; Density: 40.1 persons per square mile; Race: 99.1% White, 0.0% Black/African American, 0.7% Asian, 0.0% American Indian/Alaska Native, 0.0% Native Hawaiian/Other Pacific Islander, 0.2% Two or more races, 0.0% Hispanic of any race; Average household size: 2.58; Median age: 48.9; Age under 18: 23.9%; Age 65 and over: 21.4%; Males per 100 females: 100.9; Marriage status: 22.7% never married, 62.9% now married, 0.9% separated, 4.9% widowed, 9.4% divorced; Foreign born: 1.4%; Speak English only: 98.9%; With disability: 14.3%; Veterans: 16.7%; Ancestry: 19.8% German, 14.7% American, 13.1% English, 12.2% Irish, 10.3% Italian
Employment: 11.1% management, business, and financial, 4.8% computer, engineering, and science, 8.3% education, legal, community service, arts, and media, 7.4% healthcare practitioners, 18.7% service, 20.9% sales and office, 11.5% natural resources, construction, and maintenance, 17.2% production, transportation, and material moving
Income: Per capita: $29,195; Median household: $57,500; Average household: $73,831; Households with income of $100,000 or more: 21.9%; Poverty rate: 13.8%
Educational Attainment: High school diploma or higher: 87.0%; Bachelor's degree or higher: 15.0%; Graduate/professional degree or higher: 5.8%
Housing: Homeownership rate: 94.3%; Median home value: $97,100; Median year structure built: 1970; Homeowner vacancy rate: 6.0%; Median selected monthly owner costs: $1,132 with a mortgage, $533 without a mortgage; Median gross rent: $809 per month; Rental vacancy rate: 0.0%
Health Insurance: 95.6% have insurance; 63.1% have private insurance; 50.6% have public insurance; 4.4% do not have insurance; 1.0% of children under 18 do not have insurance
Transportation: Commute: 88.5% car, 0.8% public transportation, 4.3% walk, 4.5% work from home; Mean travel time to work: 27.7 minutes
Additional Information Contacts
Town of Berkshire . . . . (607) 657-8131
http://berkshireny.com

CANDOR (town). Covers a land area of 94.510 square miles and a water area of 0.110 square miles. Located at 42.23° N. Lat; 76.33° W. Long. Elevation is 902 feet.

Population: 5,087; Growth (since 2000): -4.3%; Density: 53.8 persons per square mile; Race: 97.4% White, 0.6% Black/African American, 0.0% Asian, 0.0% American Indian/Alaska Native, 0.2% Native Hawaiian/Other Pacific Islander, 1.8% Two or more races, 2.1% Hispanic of any race; Average household size: 2.63; Median age: 38.4; Age under 18: 26.2%; Age 65 and over: 16.1%; Males per 100 females: 95.3; Marriage status: 25.6% never married, 61.5% now married, 2.7% separated, 6.0% widowed, 6.9% divorced; Foreign born: 0.6%; Speak English only: 97.8%; With disability: 13.7%; Veterans: 13.5%; Ancestry: 11.5% German, 10.2% Irish, 9.6% American, 9.4% Italian, 8.0% English

Employment: 14.0% management, business, and financial, 2.3% computer, engineering, and science, 8.7% education, legal, community service, arts, and media, 3.2% healthcare practitioners, 24.4% service, 22.7% sales and office, 14.4% natural resources, construction, and maintenance, 10.3% production, transportation, and material moving

Income: Per capita: $24,867; Median household: $54,750; Average household: $64,598; Households with income of $100,000 or more: 19.8%; Poverty rate: 9.4%

Educational Attainment: High school diploma or higher: 91.7%; Bachelor's degree or higher: 20.8%; Graduate/professional degree or higher: 6.7%

School District(s)

Candor Central SD (KG-12)
    Enrollment: 727 . . . . (607) 659-5010

Housing: Homeownership rate: 79.7%; Median home value: $94,000; Median year structure built: 1977; Homeowner vacancy rate: 2.9%; Median selected monthly owner costs: $1,122 with a mortgage, $490 without a mortgage; Median gross rent: $763 per month; Rental vacancy rate: 12.8%

Health Insurance: 95.9% have insurance; 74.8% have private insurance; 35.2% have public insurance; 4.1% do not have insurance; 1.5% of children under 18 do not have insurance

Transportation: Commute: 91.6% car, 1.7% public transportation, 1.1% walk, 4.7% work from home; Mean travel time to work: 27.6 minutes

Additional Information Contacts

Town of Candor . . . . (607) 659-3175
    http://candorny.us

CANDOR (village). Covers a land area of 0.441 square miles and a water area of 0 square miles. Located at 42.23° N. Lat; 76.34° W. Long. Elevation is 902 feet.

Population: 727; Growth (since 2000): -15.0%; Density: 1,650.4 persons per square mile; Race: 96.6% White, 0.3% Black/African American, 0.0% Asian, 0.0% American Indian/Alaska Native, 1.7% Native Hawaiian/Other Pacific Islander, 1.5% Two or more races, 2.9% Hispanic of any race; Average household size: 2.64; Median age: 31.7; Age under 18: 28.6%; Age 65 and over: 11.1%; Males per 100 females: 88.3; Marriage status: 21.8% never married, 65.3% now married, 4.9% separated, 5.3% widowed, 7.7% divorced; Foreign born: 0.4%; Speak English only: 98.9%; With disability: 18.2%; Veterans: 11.9%; Ancestry: 18.7% Irish, 17.9% English, 15.1% Italian, 14.0% German, 4.3% American

Employment: 8.5% management, business, and financial, 5.8% computer, engineering, and science, 14.9% education, legal, community service, arts, and media, 3.5% healthcare practitioners, 21.9% service, 21.9% sales and office, 9.4% natural resources, construction, and maintenance, 14.0% production, transportation, and material moving

Income: Per capita: $21,560; Median household: $55,208; Average household: $55,765; Households with income of $100,000 or more: 9.1%; Poverty rate: 14.4%

Educational Attainment: High school diploma or higher: 92.0%; Bachelor's degree or higher: 20.9%; Graduate/professional degree or higher: 8.7%

School District(s)

Candor Central SD (KG-12)
    Enrollment: 727 . . . . (607) 659-5010

Housing: Homeownership rate: 80.0%; Median home value: $85,800; Median year structure built: Before 1940; Homeowner vacancy rate: 3.5%; Median selected monthly owner costs: $1,182 with a mortgage, $458 without a mortgage; Median gross rent: $635 per month; Rental vacancy rate: 11.3%

Health Insurance: 95.7% have insurance; 81.0% have private insurance; 31.9% have public insurance; 4.3% do not have insurance; 0.0% of children under 18 do not have insurance

Transportation: Commute: 84.8% car, 3.3% public transportation, 6.6% walk, 3.9% work from home; Mean travel time to work: 25.9 minutes

LOCKWOOD (unincorporated postal area)
ZCTA: 14859

Covers a land area of 31.161 square miles and a water area of 0.061 square miles. Located at 42.11° N. Lat; 76.54° W. Long. Elevation is 902 feet.

Population: 842; Growth (since 2000): -25.9%; Density: 27.0 persons per square mile; Race: 91.1% White, 0.0% Black/African American, 0.0% Asian, 0.0% American Indian/Alaska Native, 0.0% Native Hawaiian/Other Pacific Islander, 8.9% Two or more races, 2.0% Hispanic of any race; Average household size: 2.62; Median age: 48.2; Age under 18: 19.1%; Age 65 and over: 24.9%; Males per 100 females: 97.1; Marriage status: 29.2% never married, 56.4% now married, 1.7% separated, 6.5% widowed, 7.9% divorced; Foreign born: 0.0%; Speak English only: 99.6%; With disability: 13.2%; Veterans: 12.5%; Ancestry: 23.6% American, 14.1% German, 9.7% English, 9.1% Irish, 8.4% Italian

Employment: 12.5% management, business, and financial, 5.1% computer, engineering, and science, 0.0% education, legal, community service, arts, and media, 15.2% healthcare practitioners, 11.3% service, 14.6% sales and office, 17.9% natural resources, construction, and maintenance, 23.5% production, transportation, and material moving

Income: Per capita: $27,406; Median household: $56,750; Average household: $71,916; Households with income of $100,000 or more: 24.6%; Poverty rate: 8.1%

Educational Attainment: High school diploma or higher: 87.5%; Bachelor's degree or higher: 6.6%; Graduate/professional degree or higher: 3.1%

Housing: Homeownership rate: 91.6%; Median home value: $91,300; Median year structure built: 1958; Homeowner vacancy rate: 0.0%; Median selected monthly owner costs: $1,259 with a mortgage, $441 without a mortgage; Median gross rent: $618 per month; Rental vacancy rate: 0.0%

Health Insurance: 87.9% have insurance; 65.9% have private insurance; 41.7% have public insurance; 12.1% do not have insurance; 23.6% of children under 18 do not have insurance

Transportation: Commute: 98.5% car, 0.0% public transportation, 0.0% walk, 1.5% work from home; Mean travel time to work: 32.8 minutes

NEWARK VALLEY (town). Covers a land area of 50.295 square miles and a water area of 0.100 square miles. Located at 42.23° N. Lat; 76.16° W. Long. Elevation is 968 feet.

Population: 3,791; Growth (since 2000): -7.5%; Density: 75.4 persons per square mile; Race: 98.0% White, 0.2% Black/African American, 0.1% Asian, 0.1% American Indian/Alaska Native, 0.0% Native Hawaiian/Other Pacific Islander, 1.4% Two or more races, 0.7% Hispanic of any race; Average household size: 2.58; Median age: 45.1; Age under 18: 22.3%; Age 65 and over: 18.7%; Males per 100 females: 101.2; Marriage status: 22.1% never married, 64.2% now married, 2.5% separated, 6.2% widowed, 7.5% divorced; Foreign born: 0.7%; Speak English only: 98.7%; With disability: 14.0%; Veterans: 11.4%; Ancestry: 21.6% German, 17.9% English, 13.4% Irish, 11.2% American, 6.8% Polish

Employment: 12.8% management, business, and financial, 12.4% computer, engineering, and science, 6.1% education, legal, community service, arts, and media, 7.5% healthcare practitioners, 15.0% service, 18.3% sales and office, 11.5% natural resources, construction, and maintenance, 16.4% production, transportation, and material moving

Income: Per capita: $37,779; Median household: $65,313; Average household: $94,562; Households with income of $100,000 or more: 27.8%; Poverty rate: 5.7%

Educational Attainment: High school diploma or higher: 92.6%; Bachelor's degree or higher: 28.3%; Graduate/professional degree or higher: 12.5%

School District(s)

Newark Valley Central SD (PK-12)
    Enrollment: 1,224 . . . . (607) 642-3221

Housing: Homeownership rate: 85.1%; Median home value: $104,000; Median year structure built: 1968; Homeowner vacancy rate: 4.8%; Median selected monthly owner costs: $1,204 with a mortgage, $501 without a mortgage; Median gross rent: $662 per month; Rental vacancy rate: 5.2%

Health Insurance: 95.3% have insurance; 79.0% have private insurance; 30.4% have public insurance; 4.7% do not have insurance; 1.0% of children under 18 do not have insurance

Transportation: Commute: 94.6% car, 0.4% public transportation, 0.1% walk, 4.9% work from home; Mean travel time to work: 28.5 minutes

NEWARK VALLEY (village). Covers a land area of 0.988 square miles and a water area of 0 square miles. Located at 42.22° N. Lat; 76.19° W. Long. Elevation is 968 feet.

Population: 1,084; Growth (since 2000): 1.2%; Density: 1,097.4 persons per square mile; Race: 92.9% White, 0.6% Black/African American, 0.3% Asian, 0.5% American Indian/Alaska Native, 0.0% Native Hawaiian/Other Pacific Islander, 5.0% Two or more races, 2.4% Hispanic of any race; Average household size: 2.82; Median age: 35.2; Age under 18: 32.6%; Age 65 and over: 10.7%; Males per 100 females: 89.2; Marriage status: 33.8% never married, 50.4% now married, 4.3% separated, 5.3% widowed, 10.6% divorced; Foreign born: 1.3%; Speak English only: 96.9%; With disability: 12.1%; Veterans: 7.1%; Ancestry: 23.9% German, 15.6% Irish, 11.4% English, 7.7% American, 4.6% Polish

Employment: 15.2% management, business, and financial, 8.5% computer, engineering, and science, 7.6% education, legal, community service, arts, and media, 5.6% healthcare practitioners, 14.3% service, 18.6% sales and office, 8.7% natural resources, construction, and maintenance, 21.3% production, transportation, and material moving

Income: Per capita: $23,831; Median household: $50,938; Average household: $65,778; Households with income of $100,000 or more: 24.0%; Poverty rate: 10.2%

Educational Attainment: High school diploma or higher: 93.3%; Bachelor's degree or higher: 22.6%; Graduate/professional degree or higher: 9.9%

School District(s)
Newark Valley Central SD (PK-12)
    Enrollment: 1,224 . . . . (607) 642-3221
Housing: Homeownership rate: 70.3%; Median home value: $96,300; Median year structure built: Before 1940; Homeowner vacancy rate: 2.8%; Median selected monthly owner costs: $1,238 with a mortgage, $511 without a mortgage; Median gross rent: $638 per month; Rental vacancy rate: 9.5%

Health Insurance: 96.3% have insurance; 77.9% have private insurance; 32.8% have public insurance; 3.7% do not have insurance; 2.5% of children under 18 do not have insurance

Transportation: Commute: 95.4% car, 1.4% public transportation, 0.5% walk, 2.8% work from home; Mean travel time to work: 28.7 minutes

NICHOLS (town). Covers a land area of 33.727 square miles and a water area of 0.938 square miles. Located at 42.03° N. Lat; 76.35° W. Long. Elevation is 791 feet.

Population: 2,712; Growth (since 2000): 5.0%; Density: 80.4 persons per square mile; Race: 96.3% White, 0.6% Black/African American, 0.9% Asian, 0.0% American Indian/Alaska Native, 0.0% Native Hawaiian/Other Pacific Islander, 2.1% Two or more races, 1.5% Hispanic of any race; Average household size: 2.57; Median age: 42.1; Age under 18: 22.2%; Age 65 and over: 19.0%; Males per 100 females: 101.5; Marriage status: 25.1% never married, 53.3% now married, 1.8% separated, 7.4% widowed, 14.3% divorced; Foreign born: 1.0%; Speak English only: 99.2%; With disability: 13.3%; Veterans: 12.2%; Ancestry: 20.6% English, 19.6% German, 14.2% Irish, 5.8% Italian, 4.9% American

Employment: 16.5% management, business, and financial, 3.9% computer, engineering, and science, 8.2% education, legal, community service, arts, and media, 5.3% healthcare practitioners, 17.8% service, 19.5% sales and office, 12.5% natural resources, construction, and maintenance, 16.2% production, transportation, and material moving

Income: Per capita: $25,428; Median household: $55,208; Average household: $64,006; Households with income of $100,000 or more: 15.7%; Poverty rate: 9.1%

Educational Attainment: High school diploma or higher: 88.5%; Bachelor's degree or higher: 15.0%; Graduate/professional degree or higher: 4.7%

Housing: Homeownership rate: 85.1%; Median home value: $99,500; Median year structure built: 1961; Homeowner vacancy rate: 0.7%; Median selected monthly owner costs: $1,067 with a mortgage, $419 without a mortgage; Median gross rent: $639 per month; Rental vacancy rate: 9.8%

Health Insurance: 95.4% have insurance; 74.0% have private insurance; 42.3% have public insurance; 4.6% do not have insurance; 1.6% of children under 18 do not have insurance

Transportation: Commute: 91.3% car, 1.7% public transportation, 1.3% walk, 4.1% work from home; Mean travel time to work: 22.5 minutes

NICHOLS (village). Covers a land area of 0.518 square miles and a water area of 0 square miles. Located at 42.02° N. Lat; 76.37° W. Long. Elevation is 791 feet.

Population: 548; Growth (since 2000): -4.5%; Density: 1,057.0 persons per square mile; Race: 98.9% White, 0.0% Black/African American, 0.0% Asian, 0.0% American Indian/Alaska Native, 0.0% Native Hawaiian/Other Pacific Islander, 0.5% Two or more races, 0.0% Hispanic of any race; Average household size: 2.87; Median age: 38.2; Age under 18: 22.6%; Age 65 and over: 13.1%; Males per 100 females: 96.9; Marriage status: 34.8% never married, 48.1% now married, 0.0% separated, 5.6% widowed, 11.5% divorced; Foreign born: 0.5%; Speak English only: 100.0%; With disability: 10.4%; Veterans: 8.3%; Ancestry: 24.3% German, 13.0% Irish, 11.9% English, 10.4% Italian, 4.6% American

Employment: 7.9% management, business, and financial, 3.6% computer, engineering, and science, 11.9% education, legal, community service, arts, and media, 6.8% healthcare practitioners, 19.8% service, 23.4% sales and office, 8.6% natural resources, construction, and maintenance, 18.0% production, transportation, and material moving

Income: Per capita: $20,700; Median household: $55,536; Average household: $56,280; Households with income of $100,000 or more: 12.6%; Poverty rate: 16.0%

Educational Attainment: High school diploma or higher: 93.4%; Bachelor's degree or higher: 14.4%; Graduate/professional degree or higher: 7.4%

Housing: Homeownership rate: 69.6%; Median home value: $85,900; Median year structure built: Before 1940; Homeowner vacancy rate: 0.0%; Median selected monthly owner costs: $1,063 with a mortgage, $450 without a mortgage; Median gross rent: $664 per month; Rental vacancy rate: 22.7%

Health Insurance: 96.7% have insurance; 73.7% have private insurance; 37.8% have public insurance; 3.3% do not have insurance; 2.2% of children under 18 do not have insurance

Transportation: Commute: 94.6% car, 0.0% public transportation, 5.4% walk, 0.0% work from home; Mean travel time to work: 20.1 minutes

OWEGO (town). Covers a land area of 104.221 square miles and a water area of 1.522 square miles. Located at 42.09° N. Lat; 76.20° W. Long. Elevation is 814 feet.

History: Owego came into existence as Ah-wah-ga, "where the valley widens." Thomas C. Platt born here. Settled in 1787 and incorporated in 1827 on site of Native American village destroyed (1779) in Sullivan campaign.

Population: 19,092; Growth (since 2000): -6.3%; Density: 183.2 persons per square mile; Race: 96.4% White, 0.6% Black/African American, 1.5% Asian, 0.0% American Indian/Alaska Native, 0.0% Native Hawaiian/Other Pacific Islander, 1.2% Two or more races, 1.9% Hispanic of any race; Average household size: 2.41; Median age: 45.6; Age under 18: 19.4%; Age 65 and over: 20.2%; Males per 100 females: 100.4; Marriage status: 26.0% never married, 59.6% now married, 1.8% separated, 6.2% widowed, 8.3% divorced; Foreign born: 3.3%; Speak English only: 95.4%; With disability: 11.7%; Veterans: 9.1%; Ancestry: 19.3% German, 16.8% Irish, 13.9% English, 10.5% Italian, 6.6% Polish

Employment: 13.7% management, business, and financial, 11.2% computer, engineering, and science, 10.4% education, legal, community service, arts, and media, 5.1% healthcare practitioners, 18.3% service, 24.3% sales and office, 8.4% natural resources, construction, and maintenance, 8.5% production, transportation, and material moving

Income: Per capita: $34,618; Median household: $68,735; Average household: $84,069; Households with income of $100,000 or more: 31.0%; Poverty rate: 6.9%

Educational Attainment: High school diploma or higher: 92.2%; Bachelor's degree or higher: 33.7%; Graduate/professional degree or higher: 12.4%

School District(s)
Owego-Apalachin Central SD (PK-12)
    Enrollment: 2,130 . . . . (607) 687-6224
Housing: Homeownership rate: 77.9%; Median home value: $131,300; Median year structure built: 1963; Homeowner vacancy rate: 0.0%; Median selected monthly owner costs: $1,446 with a mortgage, $552 without a mortgage; Median gross rent: $665 per month; Rental vacancy rate: 4.4%

Health Insurance: 95.0% have insurance; 77.6% have private insurance; 33.1% have public insurance; 5.0% do not have insurance; 3.8% of children under 18 do not have insurance

Newspapers: Tioga Co Courier (weekly circulation 2,400)

Transportation: Commute: 93.6% car, 0.4% public transportation, 2.1% walk, 2.0% work from home; Mean travel time to work: 20.1 minutes
Additional Information Contacts
Town of Owego . . . . (607) 687-0123
  http://www.townofowego.com

OWEGO (village). County seat. Covers a land area of 2.454 square miles and a water area of 0.215 square miles. Located at 42.10° N. Lat; 76.26° W. Long. Elevation is 814 feet.

Population: 3,805; Growth (since 2000): -2.7%; Density: 1,550.6 persons per square mile; Race: 94.1% White, 1.3% Black/African American, 2.8% Asian, 0.0% American Indian/Alaska Native, 0.0% Native Hawaiian/Other Pacific Islander, 1.8% Two or more races, 3.7% Hispanic of any race; Average household size: 2.23; Median age: 37.8; Age under 18: 21.0%; Age 65 and over: 16.9%; Males per 100 females: 95.3; Marriage status: 34.8% never married, 43.8% now married, 2.7% separated, 9.4% widowed, 12.0% divorced; Foreign born: 6.5%; Speak English only: 89.5%; With disability: 15.5%; Veterans: 8.4%; Ancestry: 19.7% German, 16.7% English, 16.0% Irish, 6.3% Italian, 4.5% Polish
Employment: 12.6% management, business, and financial, 9.8% computer, engineering, and science, 10.7% education, legal, community service, arts, and media, 4.5% healthcare practitioners, 25.3% service, 24.1% sales and office, 3.6% natural resources, construction, and maintenance, 9.6% production, transportation, and material moving
Income: Per capita: $25,966; Median household: $46,651; Average household: $59,018; Households with income of $100,000 or more: 17.7%; Poverty rate: 16.7%
Educational Attainment: High school diploma or higher: 89.6%; Bachelor's degree or higher: 28.1%; Graduate/professional degree or higher: 11.6%

School District(s)
Owego-Apalachin Central SD (PK-12)
  Enrollment: 2,130 . . . . (607) 687-6224
Housing: Homeownership rate: 54.2%; Median home value: $92,700; Median year structure built: Before 1940; Homeowner vacancy rate: 0.0%; Median selected monthly owner costs: $1,355 with a mortgage, $569 without a mortgage; Median gross rent: $640 per month; Rental vacancy rate: 9.3%
Health Insurance: 92.2% have insurance; 63.2% have private insurance; 43.6% have public insurance; 7.8% do not have insurance; 6.6% of children under 18 do not have insurance
Safety: Violent crime rate: 26.5 per 10,000 population; Property crime rate: 405.4 per 10,000 population
Newspapers: Tioga Co Courier (weekly circulation 2,400)
Transportation: Commute: 84.9% car, 0.9% public transportation, 7.3% walk, 1.0% work from home; Mean travel time to work: 18.5 minutes

RICHFORD (town). Covers a land area of 38.187 square miles and a water area of 0.019 square miles. Located at 42.37° N. Lat; 76.19° W. Long. Elevation is 1,115 feet.

Population: 1,056; Growth (since 2000): -9.7%; Density: 27.7 persons per square mile; Race: 97.9% White, 0.0% Black/African American, 0.0% Asian, 0.9% American Indian/Alaska Native, 0.0% Native Hawaiian/Other Pacific Islander, 1.1% Two or more races, 0.8% Hispanic of any race; Average household size: 2.50; Median age: 43.2; Age under 18: 19.8%; Age 65 and over: 12.7%; Males per 100 females: 104.5; Marriage status: 32.6% never married, 53.2% now married, 2.0% separated, 4.6% widowed, 9.6% divorced; Foreign born: 0.9%; Speak English only: 98.7%; With disability: 16.2%; Veterans: 11.8%; Ancestry: 16.2% English, 15.2% American, 6.5% German, 4.4% Irish, 3.6% Italian
Employment: 6.5% management, business, and financial, 4.0% computer, engineering, and science, 5.4% education, legal, community service, arts, and media, 1.9% healthcare practitioners, 20.6% service, 27.3% sales and office, 15.8% natural resources, construction, and maintenance, 18.5% production, transportation, and material moving
Income: Per capita: $23,099; Median household: $50,313; Average household: $56,886; Households with income of $100,000 or more: 15.8%; Poverty rate: 12.0%
Educational Attainment: High school diploma or higher: 85.2%; Bachelor's degree or higher: 9.6%; Graduate/professional degree or higher: 3.4%
Housing: Homeownership rate: 85.8%; Median home value: $82,300; Median year structure built: 1981; Homeowner vacancy rate: 0.0%; Median selected monthly owner costs: $1,159 with a mortgage, $383 without a mortgage; Median gross rent: $627 per month; Rental vacancy rate: 0.0%

Health Insurance: 90.5% have insurance; 63.4% have private insurance; 39.2% have public insurance; 9.5% do not have insurance; 0.0% of children under 18 do not have insurance
Transportation: Commute: 92.5% car, 4.1% public transportation, 1.5% walk, 1.9% work from home; Mean travel time to work: 32.1 minutes

SPENCER (town). Covers a land area of 49.550 square miles and a water area of 0.326 square miles. Located at 42.22° N. Lat; 76.47° W. Long. Elevation is 994 feet.

Population: 3,014; Growth (since 2000): 1.2%; Density: 60.8 persons per square mile; Race: 91.6% White, 1.6% Black/African American, 1.5% Asian, 0.2% American Indian/Alaska Native, 0.0% Native Hawaiian/Other Pacific Islander, 2.9% Two or more races, 3.0% Hispanic of any race; Average household size: 2.30; Median age: 40.3; Age under 18: 22.1%; Age 65 and over: 19.2%; Males per 100 females: 101.6; Marriage status: 30.0% never married, 49.7% now married, 2.2% separated, 5.5% widowed, 14.8% divorced; Foreign born: 5.0%; Speak English only: 94.6%; With disability: 14.6%; Veterans: 6.8%; Ancestry: 21.0% English, 18.7% German, 18.3% Irish, 8.0% American, 5.8% Dutch
Employment: 13.4% management, business, and financial, 4.1% computer, engineering, and science, 10.8% education, legal, community service, arts, and media, 4.5% healthcare practitioners, 18.9% service, 21.6% sales and office, 14.6% natural resources, construction, and maintenance, 12.2% production, transportation, and material moving
Income: Per capita: $24,980; Median household: $46,756; Average household: $56,531; Households with income of $100,000 or more: 14.5%; Poverty rate: 12.8%
Educational Attainment: High school diploma or higher: 91.8%; Bachelor's degree or higher: 28.4%; Graduate/professional degree or higher: 8.2%

School District(s)
Spencer-Van Etten Central SD (PK-12)
  Enrollment: 933 . . . . (607) 589-7100
Housing: Homeownership rate: 71.7%; Median home value: $122,600; Median year structure built: 1973; Homeowner vacancy rate: 2.4%; Median selected monthly owner costs: $1,405 with a mortgage, $499 without a mortgage; Median gross rent: $997 per month; Rental vacancy rate: 6.8%
Health Insurance: 94.2% have insurance; 68.1% have private insurance; 43.8% have public insurance; 5.8% do not have insurance; 4.2% of children under 18 do not have insurance
Transportation: Commute: 95.5% car, 1.0% public transportation, 1.0% walk, 2.2% work from home; Mean travel time to work: 29.2 minutes

SPENCER (village). Covers a land area of 1.015 square miles and a water area of 0.014 square miles. Located at 42.21° N. Lat; 76.50° W. Long. Elevation is 994 feet.

Population: 824; Growth (since 2000): 12.7%; Density: 812.2 persons per square mile; Race: 96.2% White, 2.8% Black/African American, 1.0% Asian, 0.0% American Indian/Alaska Native, 0.0% Native Hawaiian/Other Pacific Islander, 0.0% Two or more races, 0.1% Hispanic of any race; Average household size: 2.31; Median age: 45.1; Age under 18: 24.8%; Age 65 and over: 20.9%; Males per 100 females: 88.8; Marriage status: 21.6% never married, 50.2% now married, 0.9% separated, 8.7% widowed, 19.5% divorced; Foreign born: 2.9%; Speak English only: 96.4%; With disability: 16.4%; Veterans: 6.8%; Ancestry: 22.5% English, 20.1% Irish, 15.5% German, 8.1% American, 7.4% Italian
Employment: 14.0% management, business, and financial, 5.7% computer, engineering, and science, 10.6% education, legal, community service, arts, and media, 6.0% healthcare practitioners, 17.7% service, 23.1% sales and office, 14.6% natural resources, construction, and maintenance, 8.3% production, transportation, and material moving
Income: Per capita: $24,232; Median household: $45,893; Average household: $54,942; Households with income of $100,000 or more: 15.7%; Poverty rate: 18.6%
Educational Attainment: High school diploma or higher: 88.9%; Bachelor's degree or higher: 20.4%; Graduate/professional degree or higher: 8.1%

School District(s)
Spencer-Van Etten Central SD (PK-12)
  Enrollment: 933 . . . . (607) 589-7100
Housing: Homeownership rate: 63.6%; Median home value: $111,700; Median year structure built: Before 1940; Homeowner vacancy rate: 0.0%; Median selected monthly owner costs: $1,309 with a mortgage, $513 without a mortgage; Median gross rent: $719 per month; Rental vacancy rate: 3.7%

Health Insurance: 93.8% have insurance; 64.2% have private insurance; 46.0% have public insurance; 6.2% do not have insurance; 1.9% of children under 18 do not have insurance
Transportation: Commute: 90.9% car, 1.2% public transportation, 3.2% walk, 3.5% work from home; Mean travel time to work: 29.3 minutes

---

TIOGA (town). Covers a land area of 58.620 square miles and a water area of 0.839 square miles. Located at 42.11° N. Lat; 76.37° W. Long.
History: This area of New York was settled by distinct cultures of indigenous peoples, including the Owasco, who migrated from the south, and the Point Peninsula Complex peoples. A 2011 paper by archaeologist Dr. John P. Hart argues there was no definable Owasco culture.
Population: 4,758; Growth (since 2000): -1.7%; Density: 81.2 persons per square mile; Race: 98.7% White, 0.0% Black/African American, 0.0% Asian, 0.0% American Indian/Alaska Native, 0.0% Native Hawaiian/Other Pacific Islander, 1.3% Two or more races, 2.5% Hispanic of any race; Average household size: 2.21; Median age: 47.5; Age under 18: 20.4%; Age 65 and over: 18.1%; Males per 100 females: 96.7; Marriage status: 20.8% never married, 52.1% now married, 1.1% separated, 9.5% widowed, 17.5% divorced; Foreign born: 0.8%; Speak English only: 98.9%; With disability: 19.4%; Veterans: 11.6%; Ancestry: 18.8% English, 17.4% German, 11.1% American, 11.0% Irish, 5.5% Swedish
Employment: 17.1% management, business, and financial, 1.5% computer, engineering, and science, 9.1% education, legal, community service, arts, and media, 5.0% healthcare practitioners, 21.1% service, 25.8% sales and office, 6.1% natural resources, construction, and maintenance, 14.3% production, transportation, and material moving
Income: Per capita: $30,304; Median household: $48,006; Average household: $65,716; Households with income of $100,000 or more: 20.3%; Poverty rate: 16.5%
Educational Attainment: High school diploma or higher: 84.4%; Bachelor's degree or higher: 16.0%; Graduate/professional degree or higher: 4.4%
Housing: Homeownership rate: 75.6%; Median home value: $102,500; Median year structure built: 1975; Homeowner vacancy rate: 3.2%; Median selected monthly owner costs: $1,112 with a mortgage, $471 without a mortgage; Median gross rent: $710 per month; Rental vacancy rate: 0.0%
Health Insurance: 95.8% have insurance; 59.1% have private insurance; 49.5% have public insurance; 4.2% do not have insurance; 2.5% of children under 18 do not have insurance
Transportation: Commute: 95.2% car, 1.1% public transportation, 0.0% walk, 1.9% work from home; Mean travel time to work: 24.0 minutes

---

WAVERLY (village). Covers a land area of 2.293 square miles and a water area of 0.027 square miles. Located at 42.01° N. Lat; 76.54° W. Long. Elevation is 817 feet.
History: Incorporated 1853.
Population: 4,259; Growth (since 2000): -7.6%; Density: 1,857.2 persons per square mile; Race: 96.9% White, 1.8% Black/African American, 0.1% Asian, 0.0% American Indian/Alaska Native, 0.0% Native Hawaiian/Other Pacific Islander, 1.2% Two or more races, 1.2% Hispanic of any race; Average household size: 2.31; Median age: 36.6; Age under 18: 23.2%; Age 65 and over: 17.7%; Males per 100 females: 86.0; Marriage status: 35.2% never married, 42.7% now married, 5.5% separated, 10.0% widowed, 12.1% divorced; Foreign born: 0.5%; Speak English only: 98.6%; With disability: 18.6%; Veterans: 10.9%; Ancestry: 19.4% Irish, 17.2% German, 15.3% Italian, 11.6% English, 4.5% French
Employment: 11.1% management, business, and financial, 1.6% computer, engineering, and science, 10.4% education, legal, community service, arts, and media, 7.6% healthcare practitioners, 29.6% service, 15.6% sales and office, 4.4% natural resources, construction, and maintenance, 19.6% production, transportation, and material moving
Income: Per capita: $24,001; Median household: $34,523; Average household: $55,357; Households with income of $100,000 or more: 16.0%; Poverty rate: 23.2%
Educational Attainment: High school diploma or higher: 88.1%; Bachelor's degree or higher: 15.6%; Graduate/professional degree or higher: 6.7%

School District(s)
Waverly Central SD (PK-12)
    Enrollment: 1,593 . . . . (607) 565-2841
Housing: Homeownership rate: 54.9%; Median home value: $89,400; Median year structure built: Before 1940; Homeowner vacancy rate: 0.0%; Median selected monthly owner costs: $1,031 with a mortgage, $514

without a mortgage; Median gross rent: $711 per month; Rental vacancy rate: 3.4%
Health Insurance: 89.9% have insurance; 59.1% have private insurance; 44.5% have public insurance, 10.1% do not have insurance; 5.2% of children under 18 do not have insurance
Safety: Violent crime rate: 14.5 per 10,000 population; Property crime rate: 41.0 per 10,000 population
Transportation: Commute: 90.3% car, 0.7% public transportation, 5.7% walk, 1.9% work from home; Mean travel time to work: 16.8 minutes
Additional Information Contacts
Village of Waverly . . . . (607) 565-8106
    http://www.waverlybarton.com

WILLSEYVILLE (unincorporated postal area)
ZCTA: 13864
    Covers a land area of 26.650 square miles and a water area of 0.006 square miles. Located at 42.27° N. Lat; 76.39° W. Long. Elevation is 948 feet.
Population: 1,089; Growth (since 2000): 0.4%; Density: 40.9 persons per square mile; Race: 98.3% White, 0.0% Black/African American, 0.0% Asian, 0.0% American Indian/Alaska Native, 0.0% Native Hawaiian/Other Pacific Islander, 1.7% Two or more races, 7.3% Hispanic of any race; Average household size: 2.25; Median age: 36.0; Age under 18: 22.4%; Age 65 and over: 17.6%; Males per 100 females: 100.5; Marriage status: 20.9% never married, 58.4% now married, 5.4% separated, 9.0% widowed, 11.8% divorced; Foreign born: 0.0%; Speak English only: 98.9%; With disability: 10.2%; Veterans: 12.2%; Ancestry: 22.0% Irish, 11.2% Italian, 8.9% American, 6.3% Polish, 6.2% German
Employment: 6.8% management, business, and financial, 3.9% computer, engineering, and science, 3.9% education, legal, community service, arts, and media, 0.0% healthcare practitioners, 32.2% service, 23.2% sales and office, 16.6% natural resources, construction, and maintenance, 13.4% production, transportation, and material moving
Income: Per capita: $26,185; Median household: $38,695; Average household: $57,400; Households with income of $100,000 or more: 12.8%; Poverty rate: 6.1%
Educational Attainment: High school diploma or higher: 81.5%; Bachelor's degree or higher: 22.1%; Graduate/professional degree or higher: 6.3%
Housing: Homeownership rate: 57.7%; Median home value: $128,100; Median year structure built: 1981; Homeowner vacancy rate: 0.0%; Median selected monthly owner costs: $1,375 with a mortgage, $558 without a mortgage; Median gross rent: $745 per month; Rental vacancy rate: 0.0%
Health Insurance: 93.7% have insurance; 60.2% have private insurance; 51.4% have public insurance; 6.3% do not have insurance; 0.0% of children under 18 do not have insurance
Transportation: Commute: 96.1% car, 3.9% public transportation, 0.0% walk, 0.0% work from home; Mean travel time to work: 28.1 minutes

---

Tompkins County

Located in west central New York; includes part of Cayuga Lake. Covers a land area of 474.649 square miles, a water area of 16.909 square miles, and is located in the Eastern Time Zone at 42.45° N. Lat., 76.47° W. Long. The county was founded in 1817. County seat is Ithaca.

Tompkins County is part of the Ithaca, NY Metropolitan Statistical Area. The entire metro area includes: Tompkins County, NY

Weather Station: Ithaca Cornell Univ									Elevation: 959 feet		
	Jan	Feb	Mar	Apr	May	Jun	Jul	Aug	Sep	Oct	Nov	Dec
High	31	34	41	55	67	76	80	79	71	59	47	36
Low	15	16	23	34	44	53	58	57	49	39	31	21
Precip	2.0	1.8	2.8	3.3	3.2	3.9	3.9	3.5	3.7	3.3	3.2	2.3
Snow	17.4	12.7	12.2	3.6	0.0	0.0	0.0	0.0	0.0	0.4	4.8	12.9

High and Low temperatures in degrees Fahrenheit; Precipitation and Snow in inches

Population: 104,415; Growth (since 2000): 8.2%; Density: 220.0 persons per square mile; Race: 80.4% White, 4.0% Black/African American, 10.3% Asian, 0.2% American Indian/Alaska Native, 0.0% Native Hawaiian/Other Pacific Islander, 3.9% two or more races, 4.8% Hispanic of any race; Average household size: 2.33; Median age: 30.4; Age under 18: 15.2%; Age 65 and over: 12.7%; Males per 100 females: 97.1; Marriage status: 49.7% never married, 38.8% now married, 1.4% separated, 4.0% widowed, 7.4% divorced; Foreign born: 13.2%; Speak English only: 86.2%;

With disability: 8.8%; Veterans: 4.8%; Ancestry: 14.0% German, 13.0% Irish, 11.9% English, 8.2% American, 8.1% Italian

Religion: Six largest groups: 7.2% Catholicism, 4.0% Methodist/Pietist, 2.1% Non-denominational Protestant, 2.0% Presbyterian-Reformed, 1.3% Pentecostal, 1.2% Lutheran

Economy: Unemployment rate: 3.3%; Leading industries: 15.1% retail trade; 14.0% accommodation and food services; 11.9% professional, scientific, and technical services; Farms: 558 totaling 90,774 acres; Company size: 3 employ 1,000 or more persons, 2 employ 500 to 999 persons, 38 employ 100 to 499 persons, 2,327 employ less than 100 persons; Business ownership: 2,989 women-owned, 203 Black-owned, 275 Hispanic-owned, 564 Asian-owned, 51 American Indian/Alaska Native-owned

Employment: 13.8% management, business, and financial, 9.7% computer, engineering, and science, 22.6% education, legal, community service, arts, and media, 5.4% healthcare practitioners, 17.9% service, 19.2% sales and office, 5.7% natural resources, construction, and maintenance, 5.7% production, transportation, and material moving

Income: Per capita: $29,759; Median household: $56,200; Average household: $77,086; Households with income of $100,000 or more: 24.6%; Poverty rate: 20.4%

Educational Attainment: High school diploma or higher: 94.5%; Bachelor's degree or higher: 52.6%; Graduate/professional degree or higher: 29.8%

Housing: Homeownership rate: 55.5%; Median home value: $190,100; Median year structure built: 1972; Homeowner vacancy rate: 1.8%; Median selected monthly owner costs: $1,536 with a mortgage, $647 without a mortgage; Median gross rent: $1,055 per month; Rental vacancy rate: 3.4%

Vital Statistics: Birth rate: 76.9 per 10,000 population; Death rate: 59.3 per 10,000 population; Age-adjusted cancer mortality rate: 154.4 deaths per 100,000 population

Health Insurance: 95.0% have insurance; 79.3% have private insurance; 26.4% have public insurance; 5.0% do not have insurance; 3.3% of children under 18 do not have insurance

Health Care: Physicians: 24.6 per 10,000 population; Dentists: 5.5 per 10,000 population; Hospital beds: 18.5 per 10,000 population; Hospital admissions: 626.5 per 10,000 population

Air Quality Index (AQI): Percent of Days: 95.9% good, 4.1% moderate, 0.0% unhealthy for sensitive individuals, 0.0% unhealthy, 0.0% very unhealthy; Annual median: 34; Annual maximum: 71

Transportation: Commute: 70.7% car, 6.5% public transportation, 14.2% walk, 6.3% work from home; Mean travel time to work: 18.6 minutes

2016 Presidential Election: 24.3% Trump, 67.7% Clinton, 3.3% Johnson, 3.2% Stein

National and State Parks: Alan Treman State Marine Park; Buttermilk Falls State Park; Danby State Forest; Hammond Hill State Forest; Newfield State Forest; Potato Hill State Forest; Robert H Treman State park; Shindagin Hollow State Forest; Taughannock Falls State Park; Yellow Barn State Forest

Additional Information Contacts

Tompkins Government . . . . (607) 274-5431
http://www.co.tompkins.ny.us

Tompkins County Communities

BROOKTONDALE (unincorporated postal area)
ZCTA: 14817

Covers a land area of 40.294 square miles and a water area of 0.097 square miles. Located at 42.36° N. Lat; 76.33° W. Long. Elevation is 915 feet.

Population: 2,411; Growth (since 2000): 5.7%; Density: 59.8 persons per square mile; Race: 86.4% White, 6.4% Black/African American, 1.6% Asian, 0.0% American Indian/Alaska Native, 0.0% Native Hawaiian/Other Pacific Islander, 5.6% Two or more races, 2.4% Hispanic of any race; Average household size: 2.84; Median age: 36.0; Age under 18: 22.4%; Age 65 and over: 8.3%; Males per 100 females: 101.9; Marriage status: 41.7% never married, 46.1% now married, 1.9% separated, 4.1% widowed, 8.1% divorced; Foreign born: 4.5%; Speak English only: 97.3%; With disability: 17.2%; Veterans: 4.1%; Ancestry: 18.7% English, 16.3% German, 12.3% American, 10.9% Irish, 7.9% Polish

Employment: 13.7% management, business, and financial, 14.8% computer, engineering, and science, 11.2% education, legal, community service, arts, and media, 7.8% healthcare practitioners, 23.0% service,

19.4% sales and office, 10.0% natural resources, construction, and maintenance, 0.0% production, transportation, and material moving

Income: Per capita: $23,683; Median household: $46,901; Average household: $65,533; Households with income of $100,000 or more: 11.5%; Poverty rate: 9.6%

Educational Attainment: High school diploma or higher: 94.0%; Bachelor's degree or higher: 42.7%; Graduate/professional degree or higher: 24.3%

Housing: Homeownership rate: 68.9%; Median home value: $150,400; Median year structure built: 1975; Homeowner vacancy rate: 0.0%; Median selected monthly owner costs: $1,235 with a mortgage, $557 without a mortgage; Median gross rent: $871 per month; Rental vacancy rate: 0.0%

Health Insurance: 95.7% have insurance; 77.6% have private insurance; 24.7% have public insurance; 4.3% do not have insurance; 0.0% of children under 18 do not have insurance

Transportation: Commute: 86.7% car, 4.3% public transportation, 3.0% walk, 6.0% work from home; Mean travel time to work: 22.6 minutes

CAROLINE (town). Covers a land area of 54.763 square miles and a water area of 0.130 square miles. Located at 42.36° N. Lat; 76.33° W. Long. Elevation is 968 feet.

Population: 3,419; Growth (since 2000): 17.5%; Density: 62.4 persons per square mile; Race: 89.4% White, 5.1% Black/African American, 1.1% Asian, 0.0% American Indian/Alaska Native, 0.0% Native Hawaiian/Other Pacific Islander, 4.4% Two or more races, 3.1% Hispanic of any race; Average household size: 2.74; Median age: 39.0; Age under 18: 22.4%; Age 65 and over: 9.7%; Males per 100 females: 99.9; Marriage status: 34.6% never married, 49.0% now married, 1.2% separated, 3.1% widowed, 13.3% divorced; Foreign born: 3.5%; Speak English only: 98.1%; With disability: 14.7%; Veterans: 3.5%; Ancestry: 18.4% English, 14.9% German, 14.0% Irish, 13.5% American, 8.5% Italian

Employment: 11.0% management, business, and financial, 14.3% computer, engineering, and science, 15.7% education, legal, community service, arts, and media, 5.2% healthcare practitioners, 23.2% service, 20.0% sales and office, 9.9% natural resources, construction, and maintenance, 0.8% production, transportation, and material moving

Income: Per capita: $28,593; Median household: $65,388; Average household: $76,281; Households with income of $100,000 or more: 20.5%; Poverty rate: 7.0%

Educational Attainment: High school diploma or higher: 95.4%; Bachelor's degree or higher: 48.9%; Graduate/professional degree or higher: 25.6%

Housing: Homeownership rate: 67.3%; Median home value: $164,900; Median year structure built: 1974; Homeowner vacancy rate: 0.0%; Median selected monthly owner costs: $1,329 with a mortgage, $600 without a mortgage; Median gross rent: $895 per month; Rental vacancy rate: 0.0%

Health Insurance: 95.5% have insurance; 78.7% have private insurance; 24.4% have public insurance; 4.5% do not have insurance; 0.0% of children under 18 do not have insurance

Transportation: Commute: 88.6% car, 2.9% public transportation, 2.9% walk, 5.6% work from home; Mean travel time to work: 21.4 minutes

CAYUGA HEIGHTS (village). Covers a land area of 1.767 square miles and a water area of 0.001 square miles. Located at 42.47° N. Lat; 76.49° W. Long. Elevation is 787 feet.

Population: 3,779; Growth (since 2000): 15.5%; Density: 2,139.0 persons per square mile; Race: 75.3% White, 1.7% Black/African American, 18.7% Asian, 1.1% American Indian/Alaska Native, 0.0% Native Hawaiian/Other Pacific Islander, 0.2% Two or more races, 2.8% Hispanic of any race; Average household size: 2.04; Median age: 36.4; Age under 18: 12.9%; Age 65 and over: 22.3%; Males per 100 females: 94.1; Marriage status: 41.5% never married, 50.5% now married, 0.0% separated, 4.8% widowed, 3.1% divorced; Foreign born: 25.7%; Speak English only: 77.2%; With disability: 11.6%; Veterans: 4.3%; Ancestry: 12.1% English, 10.2% German, 5.9% Irish, 5.2% Scottish, 5.1% Italian

Employment: 13.3% management, business, and financial, 17.3% computer, engineering, and science, 43.2% education, legal, community service, arts, and media, 2.0% healthcare practitioners, 10.8% service, 11.1% sales and office, 0.9% natural resources, construction, and maintenance, 1.4% production, transportation, and material moving

Income: Per capita: $54,518; Median household: $108,365; Average household: $136,812; Households with income of $100,000 or more: 52.5%; Poverty rate: 7.5%

Educational Attainment: High school diploma or higher: 98.0%; Bachelor's degree or higher: 88.7%; Graduate/professional degree or higher: 67.5%

Housing: Homeownership rate: 49.5%; Median home value: $367,900; Median year structure built: 1969; Homeowner vacancy rate: 3.4%; Median selected monthly owner costs: $3,222 with a mortgage, $1,016 without a mortgage; Median gross rent: $1,154 per month; Rental vacancy rate: 8.8%

Health Insurance: 98.3% have insurance; 92.8% have private insurance; 25.1% have public insurance; 1.7% do not have insurance; 0.3% of children under 18 do not have insurance

Safety: Violent crime rate: 0.0 per 10,000 population; Property crime rate: 70.8 per 10,000 population

Transportation: Commute: 59.0% car, 13.5% public transportation, 16.0% walk, 5.5% work from home; Mean travel time to work: 13.5 minutes

DANBY (town). Covers a land area of 53.553 square miles and a water area of 0.222 square miles. Located at 42.33° N. Lat; 76.47° W. Long. Elevation is 1,237 feet.

Population: 3,483; Growth (since 2000): 15.8%; Density: 65.0 persons per square mile; Race: 93.8% White, 3.4% Black/African American, 0.8% Asian, 0.5% American Indian/Alaska Native, 0.0% Native Hawaiian/Other Pacific Islander, 0.5% Two or more races, 1.3% Hispanic of any race; Average household size: 2.22; Median age: 50.7; Age under 18: 15.7%; Age 65 and over: 24.7%; Males per 100 females: 97.6; Marriage status: 25.9% never married, 57.2% now married, 1.3% separated, 6.6% widowed, 10.3% divorced; Foreign born: 5.6%; Speak English only: 95.7%; With disability: 13.7%; Veterans: 9.7%; Ancestry: 20.2% Irish, 19.4% English, 17.6% German, 13.1% Italian, 7.6% American

Employment: 15.4% management, business, and financial, 7.8% computer, engineering, and science, 20.3% education, legal, community service, arts, and media, 3.6% healthcare practitioners, 18.3% service, 22.9% sales and office, 10.7% natural resources, construction, and maintenance, 1.0% production, transportation, and material moving

Income: Per capita: $37,327; Median household: $56,458; Average household: $81,659; Households with income of $100,000 or more: 28.9%; Poverty rate: 17.6%

Educational Attainment: High school diploma or higher: 96.3%; Bachelor's degree or higher: 43.3%; Graduate/professional degree or higher: 22.1%

Housing: Homeownership rate: 85.8%; Median home value: $182,900; Median year structure built: 1975; Homeowner vacancy rate: 5.0%; Median selected monthly owner costs: $1,519 with a mortgage, $654 without a mortgage; Median gross rent: $866 per month; Rental vacancy rate: 0.0%

Health Insurance: 96.0% have insurance; 79.6% have private insurance; 42.2% have public insurance; 4.0% do not have insurance; 4.9% of children under 18 do not have insurance

Transportation: Commute: 94.1% car, 3.1% public transportation, 1.8% walk, 1.0% work from home; Mean travel time to work: 20.7 minutes

DRYDEN (town). Covers a land area of 93.640 square miles and a water area of 0.690 square miles. Located at 42.48° N. Lat; 76.36° W. Long. Elevation is 1,089 feet.

Population: 14,897; Growth (since 2000): 10.1%; Density: 159.1 persons per square mile; Race: 91.7% White, 3.0% Black/African American, 1.4% Asian, 0.1% American Indian/Alaska Native, 0.2% Native Hawaiian/Other Pacific Islander, 3.2% Two or more races, 3.3% Hispanic of any race; Average household size: 2.39; Median age: 38.2; Age under 18: 20.2%; Age 65 and over: 12.9%; Males per 100 females: 100.1; Marriage status: 35.0% never married, 48.8% now married, 2.6% separated, 4.5% widowed, 11.6% divorced; Foreign born: 5.7%; Speak English only: 94.0%; With disability: 11.4%; Veterans: 6.1%; Ancestry: 17.9% English, 17.5% German, 16.8% Irish, 11.7% American, 8.5% Italian

Employment: 14.2% management, business, and financial, 7.3% computer, engineering, and science, 19.3% education, legal, community service, arts, and media, 7.1% healthcare practitioners, 18.7% service, 20.0% sales and office, 5.3% natural resources, construction, and maintenance, 8.2% production, transportation, and material moving

Income: Per capita: $33,782; Median household: $62,852; Average household: $82,099; Households with income of $100,000 or more: 27.3%; Poverty rate: 14.6%

Educational Attainment: High school diploma or higher: 94.2%; Bachelor's degree or higher: 46.7%; Graduate/professional degree or higher: 26.5%

School District(s)
Dryden Central SD (KG-12)
    Enrollment: 1,554 . . . . (607) 844-5361
Two-year College(s)
Tompkins Cortland Community College (Public)
    Enrollment: 2,632 . . . . (607) 844-8211
    Tuition: In-state $6,014; Out-of-state $11,264

Housing: Homeownership rate: 67.9%; Median home value: $166,800; Median year structure built: 1976; Homeowner vacancy rate: 0.2%; Median selected monthly owner costs: $1,486 with a mortgage, $559 without a mortgage; Median gross rent: $857 per month; Rental vacancy rate: 0.7%

Health Insurance: 94.3% have insurance; 72.4% have private insurance; 34.7% have public insurance; 5.7% do not have insurance; 3.1% of children under 18 do not have insurance

Transportation: Commute: 85.9% car, 3.1% public transportation, 3.5% walk, 5.5% work from home; Mean travel time to work: 19.3 minutes

Additional Information Contacts
Town of Dryden . . . . (607) 844-8888
    http://www.dryden.ny.us

DRYDEN (village). Covers a land area of 1.756 square miles and a water area of 0.014 square miles. Located at 42.49° N. Lat; 76.30° W. Long. Elevation is 1,089 feet.

Population: 2,040; Growth (since 2000): 11.4%; Density: 1,161.6 persons per square mile; Race: 91.1% White, 3.5% Black/African American, 1.7% Asian, 0.2% American Indian/Alaska Native, 0.0% Native Hawaiian/Other Pacific Islander, 3.2% Two or more races, 10.0% Hispanic of any race; Average household size: 2.48; Median age: 39.7; Age under 18: 24.3%; Age 65 and over: 12.1%; Males per 100 females: 96.9; Marriage status: 33.2% never married, 51.4% now married, 2.2% separated, 5.9% widowed, 9.5% divorced; Foreign born: 9.6%; Speak English only: 88.2%; With disability: 12.5%; Veterans: 6.9%; Ancestry: 21.3% English, 20.9% German, 18.1% Irish, 9.4% Italian, 9.1% American

Employment: 15.9% management, business, and financial, 10.2% computer, engineering, and science, 20.1% education, legal, community service, arts, and media, 5.8% healthcare practitioners, 16.2% service, 22.8% sales and office, 2.0% natural resources, construction, and maintenance, 7.0% production, transportation, and material moving

Income: Per capita: $31,405; Median household: $64,250; Average household: $77,017; Households with income of $100,000 or more: 29.2%; Poverty rate: 15.0%

Educational Attainment: High school diploma or higher: 91.2%; Bachelor's degree or higher: 43.0%; Graduate/professional degree or higher: 21.9%

School District(s)
Dryden Central SD (KG-12)
    Enrollment: 1,554 . . . . (607) 844-5361
Two-year College(s)
Tompkins Cortland Community College (Public)
    Enrollment: 2,632 . . . . (607) 844-8211
    Tuition: In-state $6,014; Out-of-state $11,264

Housing: Homeownership rate: 65.2%; Median home value: $162,400; Median year structure built: 1967; Homeowner vacancy rate: 0.0%; Median selected monthly owner costs: $1,503 with a mortgage, $657 without a mortgage; Median gross rent: $779 per month; Rental vacancy rate: 0.0%

Health Insurance: 98.0% have insurance; 74.6% have private insurance; 35.6% have public insurance; 2.0% do not have insurance; 0.0% of children under 18 do not have insurance

Safety: Violent crime rate: 14.2 per 10,000 population; Property crime rate: 316.8 per 10,000 population

Transportation: Commute: 89.8% car, 2.6% public transportation, 2.6% walk, 2.0% work from home; Mean travel time to work: 20.3 minutes

Additional Information Contacts
Village of Dryden . . . . (607) 844-8122
    http://www.dryden-ny.org

EAST ITHACA (CDP). Covers a land area of 1.733 square miles and a water area of 0.050 square miles. Located at 42.43° N. Lat; 76.46° W. Long. Elevation is 804 feet.

Population: 2,244; Growth (since 2000): 2.4%; Density: 1,294.8 persons per square mile; Race: 59.6% White, 3.5% Black/African American, 30.2% Asian, 0.0% American Indian/Alaska Native, 0.0% Native Hawaiian/Other Pacific Islander, 3.8% Two or more races, 7.2% Hispanic of any race; Average household size: 2.08; Median age: 33.8; Age under 18: 16.0%; Age 65 and over: 9.1%; Males per 100 females: 98.3; Marriage status:

38.3% never married, 46.8% now married, 1.9% separated, 3.0% widowed, 11.9% divorced; Foreign born: 36.5%; Speak English only: 67.2%; With disability: 1.6%; Veterans: 1.3%; Ancestry: 18.7% Irish, 18.3% German, 11.4% English, 8.8% Italian, 3.5% Dutch

Employment: 12.9% management, business, and financial, 10.4% computer, engineering, and science, 34.0% education, legal, community service, arts, and media, 13.9% healthcare practitioners, 14.4% service, 8.0% sales and office, 4.9% natural resources, construction, and maintenance, 1.4% production, transportation, and material moving
Income: Per capita: $43,493; Median household: $47,176; Average household: $89,714; Households with income of $100,000 or more: 29.3%; Poverty rate: 22.2%
Educational Attainment: High school diploma or higher: 97.4%; Bachelor's degree or higher: 76.3%; Graduate/professional degree or higher: 42.0%
Housing: Homeownership rate: 52.5%; Median home value: $222,300; Median year structure built: 1982; Homeowner vacancy rate: 0.0%; Median selected monthly owner costs: $1,692 with a mortgage, $742 without a mortgage; Median gross rent: $893 per month; Rental vacancy rate: 0.0%
Health Insurance: 99.5% have insurance; 81.4% have private insurance; 24.6% have public insurance; 0.5% do not have insurance; 0.0% of children under 18 do not have insurance
Transportation: Commute: 62.5% car, 8.5% public transportation, 12.9% walk, 10.1% work from home; Mean travel time to work: 17.4 minutes

ENFIELD (town). Covers a land area of 36.732 square miles and a water area of 0.104 square miles. Located at 42.44° N. Lat; 76.62° W. Long. Elevation is 1,106 feet.
Population: 3,616; Growth (since 2000): 7.3%; Density: 98.4 persons per square mile; Race: 92.0% White, 0.6% Black/African American, 0.0% Asian, 0.0% American Indian/Alaska Native, 0.0% Native Hawaiian/Other Pacific Islander, 7.1% Two or more races, 1.5% Hispanic of any race; Average household size: 2.38; Median age: 47.4; Age under 18: 17.0%; Age 65 and over: 16.0%; Males per 100 females: 95.2; Marriage status: 29.7% never married, 54.8% now married, 0.8% separated, 6.1% widowed, 9.4% divorced; Foreign born: 1.7%; Speak English only: 99.2%; With disability: 11.4%; Veterans: 8.5%; Ancestry: 21.9% Irish, 17.1% English, 13.4% German, 7.6% Italian, 7.5% Dutch
Employment: 11.4% management, business, and financial, 4.2% computer, engineering, and science, 10.5% education, legal, community service, arts, and media, 2.2% healthcare practitioners, 32.8% service, 20.3% sales and office, 9.5% natural resources, construction, and maintenance, 9.2% production, transportation, and material moving
Income: Per capita: $31,357; Median household: $54,811; Average household: $73,148; Households with income of $100,000 or more: 17.3%; Poverty rate: 6.8%
Educational Attainment: High school diploma or higher: 90.3%; Bachelor's degree or higher: 26.4%; Graduate/professional degree or higher: 5.8%
Housing: Homeownership rate: 79.6%; Median home value: $126,300; Median year structure built: 1985; Homeowner vacancy rate: 3.8%; Median selected monthly owner costs: $1,213 with a mortgage, $519 without a mortgage; Median gross rent: $942 per month; Rental vacancy rate: 16.8%
Health Insurance: 96.5% have insurance; 73.0% have private insurance; 35.9% have public insurance; 3.5% do not have insurance; 3.0% of children under 18 do not have insurance
Transportation: Commute: 91.2% car, 0.7% public transportation, 1.0% walk, 7.1% work from home; Mean travel time to work: 22.9 minutes

ETNA (unincorporated postal area)
ZCTA: 13062
Covers a land area of 0.180 square miles and a water area of 0.007 square miles. Located at 42.48° N. Lat; 76.38° W. Long. Elevation is 1,020 feet.
Population: 63; Growth (since 2000): -51.9%; Density: 349.2 persons per square mile; Race: 100.0% White, 0.0% Black/African American, 0.0% Asian, 0.0% American Indian/Alaska Native, 0.0% Native Hawaiian/Other Pacific Islander, 0.0% Two or more races, 0.0% Hispanic of any race; Average household size: 2.86; Median age: 11.8; Age under 18: 54.0%; Age 65 and over: 0.0%; Males per 100 females: 94.4; Marriage status: 0.0% never married, 48.3% now married, 0.0% separated, 0.0% widowed, 51.7% divorced; Foreign born: 0.0%; Speak English only: 100.0%; With disability: 0.0%; Veterans: 0.0%; Ancestry: 66.7% Polish, 22.2% Italian, 11.1% Irish, 11.1% Lithuanian

Employment: 0.0% management, business, and financial, 0.0% computer, engineering, and science, 24.1% education, legal, community service, arts, and media, 0.0% healthcare practitioners, 75.9% service, 0.0% sales and office, 0.0% natural resources, construction, and maintenance, 0.0% production, transportation, and material moving
Income: Per capita: $18,924; Median household: n/a; Average household: n/a; Households with income of $100,000 or more: 31.8%; Poverty rate: n/a
Educational Attainment: High school diploma or higher: 100.0%; Bachelor's degree or higher: 48.3%; Graduate/professional degree or higher: 24.1%
Housing: Homeownership rate: 100.0%; Median home value: n/a; Median year structure built: Before 1940; Homeowner vacancy rate: 0.0%; Median selected monthly owner costs: $0 with a mortgage, $0 without a mortgage; Median gross rent: n/a per month; Rental vacancy rate: 0.0%
Health Insurance: 76.2% have insurance; 54.0% have private insurance; 22.2% have public insurance; 23.8% do not have insurance; 0.0% of children under 18 do not have insurance
Transportation: Commute: 100.0% car, 0.0% public transportation, 0.0% walk, 0.0% work from home; Mean travel time to work: 0.0 minutes

FOREST HOME (CDP). Covers a land area of 0.251 square miles and a water area of 0.023 square miles. Located at 42.45° N. Lat; 76.47° W. Long. Elevation is 922 feet.
Population: 597; Growth (since 2000): -36.6%; Density: 2,376.8 persons per square mile; Race: 45.7% White, 3.0% Black/African American, 44.7% Asian, 0.0% American Indian/Alaska Native, 0.0% Native Hawaiian/Other Pacific Islander, 6.5% Two or more races, 8.2% Hispanic of any race; Average household size: 2.12; Median age: 29.5; Age under 18: 12.7%; Age 65 and over: 7.4%; Males per 100 females: 102.8; Marriage status: 45.1% never married, 52.3% now married, 0.6% separated, 0.0% widowed, 2.7% divorced; Foreign born: 63.1%; Speak English only: 40.5%; With disability: 0.7%; Veterans: 1.3%; Ancestry: 7.5% Irish, 6.0% English, 6.0% Italian, 5.4% German, 3.5% Swedish
Employment: 5.8% management, business, and financial, 20.2% computer, engineering, and science, 55.4% education, legal, community service, arts, and media, 1.6% healthcare practitioners, 4.3% service, 12.8% sales and office, 0.0% natural resources, construction, and maintenance, 0.0% production, transportation, and material moving
Income: Per capita: $33,172; Median household: $42,250; Average household: $68,802; Households with income of $100,000 or more: 22.0%; Poverty rate: 24.6%
Educational Attainment: High school diploma or higher: 99.0%; Bachelor's degree or higher: 87.7%; Graduate/professional degree or higher: 61.0%
Housing: Homeownership rate: 28.1%; Median home value: $391,200; Median year structure built: 1969; Homeowner vacancy rate: 0.0%; Median selected monthly owner costs: $2,563 with a mortgage, $725 without a mortgage; Median gross rent: $1,157 per month; Rental vacancy rate: 10.2%
Health Insurance: 95.6% have insurance; 84.8% have private insurance; 19.8% have public insurance; 4.4% do not have insurance; 3.9% of children under 18 do not have insurance
Transportation: Commute: 20.7% car, 33.3% public transportation, 35.0% walk, 4.6% work from home; Mean travel time to work: 12.4 minutes

FREEVILLE (village). Covers a land area of 1.058 square miles and a water area of 0.037 square miles. Located at 42.51° N. Lat; 76.35° W. Long. Elevation is 1,043 feet.
Population: 399; Growth (since 2000): -21.0%; Density: 377.0 persons per square mile; Race: 96.7% White, 0.0% Black/African American, 0.5% Asian, 0.8% American Indian/Alaska Native, 0.0% Native Hawaiian/Other Pacific Islander, 2.0% Two or more races, 0.0% Hispanic of any race; Average household size: 2.19; Median age: 49.4; Age under 18: 16.8%; Age 65 and over: 18.3%; Males per 100 females: 98.5; Marriage status: 27.9% never married, 54.7% now married, 1.5% separated, 5.5% widowed, 11.9% divorced; Foreign born: 1.0%; Speak English only: 99.0%; With disability: 16.8%; Veterans: 7.8%; Ancestry: 26.3% English, 25.8% German, 12.0% Irish, 11.8% Italian, 9.5% American
Employment: 14.2% management, business, and financial, 10.0% computer, engineering, and science, 19.9% education, legal, community service, arts, and media, 3.8% healthcare practitioners, 20.4% service, 16.6% sales and office, 8.1% natural resources, construction, and maintenance, 7.1% production, transportation, and material moving

Income: Per capita: $31,769; Median household: $58,929; Average household: $69,219; Households with income of $100,000 or more: 24.1%; Poverty rate: 8.3%

Educational Attainment: High school diploma or higher: 95.1%; Bachelor's degree or higher: 44.6%; Graduate/professional degree or higher: 16.1%

School District(s)

Dryden Central SD (KG-12)
    Enrollment: 1,554 . . . . (607) 844-5361
George Junior Republic Union Free SD (07-12)
    Enrollment: 140 . . . . (607) 844-6343

Housing: Homeownership rate: 69.8%; Median home value: $149,500; Median year structure built: Before 1940; Homeowner vacancy rate: 5.2%; Median selected monthly owner costs: $1,310 with a mortgage, $470 without a mortgage; Median gross rent: $811 per month; Rental vacancy rate: 19.1%

Health Insurance: 96.5% have insurance; 73.9% have private insurance; 34.8% have public insurance; 3.5% do not have insurance; 0.0% of children under 18 do not have insurance

Transportation: Commute: 80.6% car, 2.8% public transportation, 6.2% walk, 3.8% work from home; Mean travel time to work: 20.5 minutes

GROTON (town).
Covers a land area of 49.406 square miles and a water area of 0.133 square miles. Located at 42.58° N. Lat; 76.36° W. Long. Elevation is 997 feet.

History: Incorporated 1860.

Population: 6,078; Growth (since 2000): 4.9%; Density: 123.0 persons per square mile; Race: 93.0% White, 1.4% Black/African American, 2.5% Asian, 0.1% American Indian/Alaska Native, 0.0% Native Hawaiian/Other Pacific Islander, 2.8% Two or more races, 4.5% Hispanic of any race; Average household size: 2.42; Median age: 43.2; Age under 18: 18.1%; Age 65 and over: 17.4%; Males per 100 females: 96.3; Marriage status: 33.6% never married, 51.8% now married, 1.5% separated, 6.0% widowed, 8.7% divorced; Foreign born: 3.7%; Speak English only: 95.8%; With disability: 13.9%; Veterans: 8.6%; Ancestry: 22.4% German, 16.2% Irish, 15.3% English, 13.8% American, 7.2% Dutch

Employment: 16.8% management, business, and financial, 3.3% computer, engineering, and science, 10.5% education, legal, community service, arts, and media, 5.9% healthcare practitioners, 21.4% service, 17.2% sales and office, 10.6% natural resources, construction, and maintenance, 14.3% production, transportation, and material moving

Income: Per capita: $29,743; Median household: $59,750; Average household: $71,081; Households with income of $100,000 or more: 21.9%; Poverty rate: 10.2%

Educational Attainment: High school diploma or higher: 91.7%; Bachelor's degree or higher: 22.9%; Graduate/professional degree or higher: 8.7%

School District(s)

Groton Central SD (PK-12)
    Enrollment: 843 . . . . (607) 898-5301

Housing: Homeownership rate: 73.2%; Median home value: $131,200; Median year structure built: 1948; Homeowner vacancy rate: 1.9%; Median selected monthly owner costs: $1,226 with a mortgage, $544 without a mortgage; Median gross rent: $839 per month; Rental vacancy rate: 3.4%

Health Insurance: 93.0% have insurance; 70.3% have private insurance; 36.2% have public insurance; 7.0% do not have insurance; 1.4% of children under 18 do not have insurance

Transportation: Commute: 90.3% car, 0.8% public transportation, 4.1% walk, 4.5% work from home; Mean travel time to work: 24.0 minutes

Additional Information Contacts

Town of Groton . . . . (607) 898-5035
    http://townofgrotonny.org

GROTON (village).
Covers a land area of 1.738 square miles and a water area of <.001 square miles. Located at 42.58° N. Lat; 76.36° W. Long. Elevation is 997 feet.

Population: 2,389; Growth (since 2000): -3.3%; Density: 1,374.5 persons per square mile; Race: 90.4% White, 2.4% Black/African American, 1.4% Asian, 0.3% American Indian/Alaska Native, 0.0% Native Hawaiian/Other Pacific Islander, 5.0% Two or more races, 2.7% Hispanic of any race; Average household size: 2.32; Median age: 40.3; Age under 18: 18.9%; Age 65 and over: 18.9%; Males per 100 females: 88.4; Marriage status: 35.5% never married, 45.9% now married, 1.7% separated, 10.2% widowed, 8.4% divorced; Foreign born: 3.8%; Speak English only: 94.7%;

With disability: 15.0%; Veterans: 6.9%; Ancestry: 20.3% German, 18.0% Irish, 17.1% English, 9.3% American, 8.8% Italian

Employment: 17.2% management, business, and financial, 2.5% computer, engineering, and science, 14.9% education, legal, community service, arts, and media, 4.7% healthcare practitioners, 22.2% service, 19.2% sales and office, 7.9% natural resources, construction, and maintenance, 11.5% production, transportation, and material moving

Income: Per capita: $26,312; Median household: $51,042; Average household: $62,066; Households with income of $100,000 or more: 15.4%; Poverty rate: 12.5%

Educational Attainment: High school diploma or higher: 92.1%; Bachelor's degree or higher: 24.3%; Graduate/professional degree or higher: 9.4%

School District(s)

Groton Central SD (PK-12)
    Enrollment: 843 . . . . (607) 898-5301

Housing: Homeownership rate: 63.6%; Median home value: $123,400; Median year structure built: Before 1940; Homeowner vacancy rate: 5.2%; Median selected monthly owner costs: $1,140 with a mortgage, $512 without a mortgage; Median gross rent: $643 per month; Rental vacancy rate: 6.1%

Health Insurance: 91.1% have insurance; 70.1% have private insurance; 40.3% have public insurance; 8.9% do not have insurance; 1.7% of children under 18 do not have insurance

Safety: Violent crime rate: 8.4 per 10,000 population; Property crime rate: 164.3 per 10,000 population

Transportation: Commute: 89.7% car, 2.2% public transportation, 4.1% walk, 3.0% work from home; Mean travel time to work: 22.1 minutes

ITHACA (city).
County seat. Covers a land area of 5.388 square miles and a water area of 0.684 square miles. Located at 42.44° N. Lat; 76.50° W. Long. Elevation is 410 feet.

History: Detachments of General John Sullivan's expedition crossed the site of Ithaca in 1779. The first settlers came in 1788 and 1789, but when the site was included within the Military Tract and title given to Revolutionary War veterans, these pioneers were obliged to move on. The land was later acquired by Simeon De Witt, surveyor-general of New York State, who gave the place its name. Solid growth began after the opening of Cornell University in 1868. In 1888, Ithaca became a city. For several years beginning in 1914, Ithaca was a center of the motion picture industry.

Population: 30,720; Growth (since 2000): 4.9%; Density: 5,701.4 persons per square mile; Race: 68.6% White, 6.6% Black/African American, 17.6% Asian, 0.3% American Indian/Alaska Native, 0.0% Native Hawaiian/Other Pacific Islander, 5.1% Two or more races, 7.3% Hispanic of any race; Average household size: 2.31; Median age: 21.8; Age under 18: 8.8%; Age 65 and over: 5.8%; Males per 100 females: 101.5; Marriage status: 76.8% never married, 18.0% now married, 1.1% separated, 1.4% widowed, 3.8% divorced; Foreign born: 17.5%; Speak English only: 79.7%; With disability: 5.9%; Veterans: 1.8%; Ancestry: 9.3% Irish, 8.7% German, 6.8% American, 6.7% Italian, 5.5% English

Employment: 10.7% management, business, and financial, 13.2% computer, engineering, and science, 28.3% education, legal, community service, arts, and media, 3.0% healthcare practitioners, 16.7% service, 21.0% sales and office, 3.1% natural resources, construction, and maintenance, 4.0% production, transportation, and material moving

Income: Per capita: $18,985; Median household: $31,967; Average household: $54,565; Households with income of $100,000 or more: 16.6%; Poverty rate: 43.4%

Educational Attainment: High school diploma or higher: 94.0%; Bachelor's degree or higher: 64.4%; Graduate/professional degree or higher: 37.5%

School District(s)

Ithaca City SD (PK-12)
    Enrollment: 5,360 . . . . (607) 274-2101
New Roots Charter School (09-12)
    Enrollment: 138 . . . . (607) 882-9220
Tompkins-Seneca-Tioga Boces
    Enrollment: n/a . . . . (607) 257-1551

Four-year College(s)

Cornell University (Private, Not-for-profit)
    Enrollment: 23,016 . . . . (607) 255-2000
    Tuition: In-state $52,853; Out-of-state $52,853

Ithaca College (Private, Not-for-profit)
Enrollment: 6,516 . . . . (607) 274-3011
Tuition: In-state $42,884; Out-of-state $42,884
Vocational/Technical School(s)
Finger Lakes School of Massage (Private, For-profit)
Enrollment: 22 . . . . (607) 272-9026
Tuition: $15,900
Housing: Homeownership rate: 26.1%; Median home value: $233,100; Median year structure built: 1953; Homeowner vacancy rate: 1.8%; Median selected monthly owner costs: $1,757 with a mortgage, $762 without a mortgage; Median gross rent: $1,086 per month; Rental vacancy rate: 3.2%
Health Insurance: 94.2% have insurance; 81.8% have private insurance; 17.4% have public insurance; 5.8% do not have insurance; 6.7% of children under 18 do not have insurance
Hospitals: Cayuga Medical Center at Ithaca (204 beds)
Safety: Violent crime rate: 18.1 per 10,000 population; Property crime rate: 290.9 per 10,000 population
Newspapers: Ithaca Journal (daily circulation 16,400); Ithaca Times (weekly circulation 22,000)
Transportation: Commute: 37.8% car, 12.8% public transportation, 38.4% walk, 7.7% work from home; Mean travel time to work: 16.2 minutes
Airports: Ithaca Tompkins Regional (primary service/non-hub)
Additional Information Contacts
City of Ithaca . . . . (607) 274-6570
http://www.ci.ithaca.ny.us

ITHACA (town). Covers a land area of 28.946 square miles and a water area of 1.340 square miles. Located at 42.41° N. Lat; 76.54° W. Long. Elevation is 410 feet.
History: Settled 1789, Incorporated as a city 1888.
Population: 20,372; Growth (since 2000): 11.9%; Density: 703.8 persons per square mile; Race: 72.8% White, 4.8% Black/African American, 16.4% Asian, 0.3% American Indian/Alaska Native, 0.0% Native Hawaiian/Other Pacific Islander, 3.9% Two or more races, 4.5% Hispanic of any race; Average household size: 2.23; Median age: 26.9; Age under 18: 14.0%; Age 65 and over: 13.5%; Males per 100 females: 89.1; Marriage status: 51.2% never married, 39.1% now married, 0.7% separated, 4.7% widowed, 5.0% divorced; Foreign born: 22.9%; Speak English only: 77.7%; With disability: 7.2%; Veterans: 3.6%; Ancestry: 12.3% German, 10.9% Irish, 9.3% English, 6.5% Italian, 4.8% Polish
Employment: 11.8% management, business, and financial, 12.1% computer, engineering, and science, 30.0% education, legal, community service, arts, and media, 5.8% healthcare practitioners, 16.5% service, 17.5% sales and office, 3.1% natural resources, construction, and maintenance, 3.3% production, transportation, and material moving
Income: Per capita: $33,174; Median household: $60,831; Average household: $95,062; Households with income of $100,000 or more: 30.4%; Poverty rate: 16.2%
Educational Attainment: High school diploma or higher: 97.0%; Bachelor's degree or higher: 71.7%; Graduate/professional degree or higher: 47.5%
School District(s)
Ithaca City SD (PK-12)
Enrollment: 5,360 . . . . (607) 274-2101
New Roots Charter School (09-12)
Enrollment: 138 . . . . (607) 882-9220
Tompkins-Seneca-Tioga Boces
Enrollment: n/a . . . . (607) 257-1551
Four-year College(s)
Cornell University (Private, Not-for-profit)
Enrollment: 23,016 . . . . (607) 255-2000
Tuition: In-state $52,853; Out-of-state $52,853
Ithaca College (Private, Not-for-profit)
Enrollment: 6,516 . . . . (607) 274-3011
Tuition: In-state $42,884; Out-of-state $42,884
Vocational/Technical School(s)
Finger Lakes School of Massage (Private, For-profit)
Enrollment: 22 . . . . (607) 272-9026
Tuition: $15,900
Housing: Homeownership rate: 50.9%; Median home value: $248,600; Median year structure built: 1973; Homeowner vacancy rate: 2.1%; Median selected monthly owner costs: $1,930 with a mortgage, $846 without a mortgage; Median gross rent: $1,153 per month; Rental vacancy rate: 3.9%

Health Insurance: 97.0% have insurance; 86.7% have private insurance; 21.6% have public insurance; 3.0% do not have insurance; 2.7% of children under 18 do not have insurance
Hospitals: Cayuga Medical Center at Ithaca (204 beds)
Newspapers: Ithaca Journal (daily circulation 16,400); Ithaca Times (weekly circulation 22,000)
Transportation: Commute: 62.3% car, 7.8% public transportation, 17.5% walk, 8.7% work from home; Mean travel time to work: 15.1 minutes
Airports: Ithaca Tompkins Regional (primary service/non-hub)
Additional Information Contacts
Town of Ithaca . . . . (607) 273-1721
http://www.town.ithaca.ny.us

JACKSONVILLE (unincorporated postal area)
ZCTA: 14854
Covers a land area of 0.023 square miles and a water area of 0 square miles. Located at 42.51° N. Lat; 76.61° W. Long. Elevation is 1,024 feet.
Population: 30; Growth (since 2000): n/a; Density: 1,318.0 persons per square mile; Race: 100.0% White, 0.0% Black/African American, 0.0% Asian, 0.0% American Indian/Alaska Native, 0.0% Native Hawaiian/Other Pacific Islander, 0.0% Two or more races, 0.0% Hispanic of any race; Average household size: 1.43; Median age: 57.7; Age under 18: 0.0%; Age 65 and over: 40.0%; Males per 100 females: 48.0; Marriage status: 0.0% never married, 60.0% now married, 0.0% separated, 0.0% widowed, 40.0% divorced; Foreign born: 0.0%; Speak English only: 100.0%; With disability: 0.0%; Veterans: 0.0%; Ancestry: 40.0% Italian
Employment: 0.0% management, business, and financial, 50.0% computer, engineering, and science, 0.0% education, legal, community service, arts, and media, 50.0% healthcare practitioners, 0.0% service, 0.0% sales and office, 0.0% natural resources, construction, and maintenance, 0.0% production, transportation, and material moving
Income: Per capita: $58,440; Median household: n/a; Average household: n/a; Households with income of $100,000 or more: 42.9%; Poverty rate: n/a
Educational Attainment: High school diploma or higher: 100.0%; Bachelor's degree or higher: 70.0%; Graduate/professional degree or higher: n/a
Housing: Homeownership rate: 100.0%; Median home value: n/a; Median year structure built: n/a; Homeowner vacancy rate: 0.0%; Median selected monthly owner costs: $0 with a mortgage, $0 without a mortgage; Median gross rent: n/a per month; Rental vacancy rate: 0.0%
Health Insurance: 100.0% have insurance; 100.0% have private insurance; 40.0% have public insurance; 0.0% do not have insurance; 0.0% of children under 18 do not have insurance
Transportation: Commute: 100.0% car, 0.0% public transportation, 0.0% walk, 0.0% work from home; Mean travel time to work: 0.0 minutes

LANSING (town). Covers a land area of 60.490 square miles and a water area of 9.452 square miles. Located at 42.57° N. Lat; 76.53° W. Long. Elevation is 928 feet.
Population: 11,454; Growth (since 2000): 8.9%; Density: 189.4 persons per square mile; Race: 81.4% White, 1.7% Black/African American, 13.0% Asian, 0.2% American Indian/Alaska Native, 0.0% Native Hawaiian/Other Pacific Islander, 2.8% Two or more races, 4.4% Hispanic of any race; Average household size: 2.26; Median age: 37.6; Age under 18: 21.6%; Age 65 and over: 17.9%; Males per 100 females: 101.0; Marriage status: 31.3% never married, 51.6% now married, 1.1% separated, 5.6% widowed, 11.5% divorced; Foreign born: 17.1%; Speak English only: 84.4%; With disability: 7.0%; Veterans: 8.5%; Ancestry: 17.2% German, 14.3% English, 13.5% Irish, 8.7% Italian, 8.2% American
Employment: 22.0% management, business, and financial, 9.2% computer, engineering, and science, 25.9% education, legal, community service, arts, and media, 4.5% healthcare practitioners, 11.4% service, 17.2% sales and office, 5.5% natural resources, construction, and maintenance, 4.2% production, transportation, and material moving
Income: Per capita: $41,046; Median household: $66,059; Average household: $93,085; Households with income of $100,000 or more: 31.8%; Poverty rate: 9.2%
Educational Attainment: High school diploma or higher: 95.8%; Bachelor's degree or higher: 62.3%; Graduate/professional degree or higher: 36.0%
School District(s)
Lansing Central SD (KG-12)
Enrollment: 1,179 . . . . (607) 533-3020

Housing: Homeownership rate: 57.5%; Median home value: $239,000; Median year structure built: 1979; Homeowner vacancy rate: 2.6%; Median selected monthly owner costs: $1,700 with a mortgage, $771 without a mortgage; Median gross rent: $1,278 per month; Rental vacancy rate: 0.0%
Health Insurance: 95.8% have insurance; 84.2% have private insurance; 25.4% have public insurance; 4.2% do not have insurance; 0.0% of children under 18 do not have insurance
Transportation: Commute: 84.2% car, 7.4% public transportation, 1.6% walk, 5.6% work from home; Mean travel time to work: 18.1 minutes
Additional Information Contacts
Town of Lansing . . . . (607) 533-4142
http://www.lansingtown.com

LANSING (village). Covers a land area of 4.610 square miles and a water area of 0.019 square miles. Located at 42.49° N. Lat; 76.49° W. Long. Elevation is 928 feet.
Population: 3,601; Growth (since 2000): 5.4%; Density: 781.1 persons per square mile; Race: 60.6% White, 4.1% Black/African American, 31.1% Asian, 0.5% American Indian/Alaska Native, 0.0% Native Hawaiian/Other Pacific Islander, 3.4% Two or more races, 6.9% Hispanic of any race; Average household size: 2.16; Median age: 33.0; Age under 18: 20.4%; Age 65 and over: 16.1%; Males per 100 females: 102.0; Marriage status: 38.9% never married, 46.6% now married, 0.9% separated, 6.0% widowed, 8.5% divorced; Foreign born: 39.5%; Speak English only: 65.6%; With disability: 3.0%; Veterans: 10.0%; Ancestry: 14.9% German, 9.0% English, 8.8% Irish, 8.4% Italian, 3.5% Scottish
Employment: 24.8% management, business, and financial, 11.5% computer, engineering, and science, 29.1% education, legal, community service, arts, and media, 7.4% healthcare practitioners, 10.4% service, 13.1% sales and office, 0.0% natural resources, construction, and maintenance, 3.6% production, transportation, and material moving
Income: Per capita: $36,986; Median household: $63,166; Average household: $81,172; Households with income of $100,000 or more: 26.0%; Poverty rate: 9.2%
Educational Attainment: High school diploma or higher: 96.7%; Bachelor's degree or higher: 73.2%; Graduate/professional degree or higher: 47.2%
School District(s)
Lansing Central SD (KG-12)
Enrollment: 1,179 . . . . (607) 533-3020
Housing: Homeownership rate: 30.9%; Median home value: $334,600; Median year structure built: 1977; Homeowner vacancy rate: 2.0%; Median selected monthly owner costs: $2,366 with a mortgage, $1,070 without a mortgage; Median gross rent: $1,328 per month; Rental vacancy rate: 0.0%
Health Insurance: 93.3% have insurance; 87.6% have private insurance; 16.2% have public insurance; 6.7% do not have insurance; 0.0% of children under 18 do not have insurance
Transportation: Commute: 73.1% car, 19.9% public transportation, 2.3% walk, 2.1% work from home; Mean travel time to work: 16.9 minutes
Additional Information Contacts
Village of Lansing . . . . (607) 257-0424
http://www.vlansing.org

MCLEAN (unincorporated postal area)
ZCTA: 13102
Covers a land area of 0.058 square miles and a water area of 0.001 square miles. Located at 42.55° N. Lat; 76.29° W. Long..
Population: 20; Growth (since 2000): n/a; Density: 343.6 persons per square mile; Race: 100.0% White, 0.0% Black/African American, 0.0% Asian, 0.0% American Indian/Alaska Native, 0.0% Native Hawaiian/Other Pacific Islander, 0.0% Two or more races, 0.0% Hispanic of any race; Average household size: 2.00; Median age: n/a; Age under 18: 0.0%; Age 65 and over: 100.0%; Males per 100 females: 117.9; Marriage status: 0.0% never married, 0.0% now married, 0.0% separated, 100.0% widowed, 0.0% divorced; Foreign born: 0.0%; Speak English only: 100.0%; With disability: 100.0%; Veterans: 0.0%; Ancestry: 50.0% Dutch, 50.0% German
Employment: n/a management, business, and financial, n/a computer, engineering, and science, n/a education, legal, community service, arts, and media, n/a healthcare practitioners, n/a service, n/a sales and office, n/a natural resources, construction, and maintenance, n/a production, transportation, and material moving

Income: Per capita: n/a; Median household: n/a; Average household: n/a; Households with income of $100,000 or more: n/a; Poverty rate: n/a
Educational Attainment: High school diploma or higher: 50.0%; Bachelor's degree or higher: n/a; Graduate/professional degree or higher: n/a
School District(s)
Dryden Central SD (KG-12)
Enrollment: 1,554 . . . . (607) 844-5361
Housing: Homeownership rate: 100.0%; Median home value: n/a; Median year structure built: n/a; Homeowner vacancy rate: 0.0%; Median selected monthly owner costs: $0 with a mortgage, $0 without a mortgage; Median gross rent: n/a per month; Rental vacancy rate: 0.0%
Health Insurance: 100.0% have insurance; 50.0% have private insurance; 100.0% have public insurance; 0.0% do not have insurance; 0.0% of children under 18 do not have insurance
Transportation: Commute: n/a car, n/a public transportation, n/a walk, n/a work from home; Mean travel time to work: 0.0 minutes

NEWFIELD (town). Covers a land area of 58.841 square miles and a water area of 0.127 square miles. Located at 42.34° N. Lat; 76.61° W. Long. Elevation is 1,050 feet.
Population: 5,314; Growth (since 2000): 4.0%; Density: 90.3 persons per square mile; Race: 93.4% White, 1.6% Black/African American, 1.7% Asian, 0.6% American Indian/Alaska Native, 0.0% Native Hawaiian/Other Pacific Islander, 2.8% Two or more races, 3.7% Hispanic of any race; Average household size: 2.45; Median age: 44.6; Age under 18: 17.1%; Age 65 and over: 16.1%; Males per 100 females: 94.7; Marriage status: 33.4% never married, 53.2% now married, 1.8% separated, 6.3% widowed, 7.1% divorced; Foreign born: 1.1%; Speak English only: 95.2%; With disability: 11.8%; Veterans: 8.2%; Ancestry: 19.0% German, 14.6% Italian, 12.9% American, 12.7% English, 10.0% Irish
Employment: 10.8% management, business, and financial, 5.4% computer, engineering, and science, 11.5% education, legal, community service, arts, and media, 10.1% healthcare practitioners, 20.6% service, 20.2% sales and office, 13.1% natural resources, construction, and maintenance, 8.3% production, transportation, and material moving
Income: Per capita: $29,581; Median household: $63,086; Average household: $69,999; Households with income of $100,000 or more: 20.1%; Poverty rate: 13.1%
Educational Attainment: High school diploma or higher: 90.2%; Bachelor's degree or higher: 28.1%; Graduate/professional degree or higher: 11.4%
School District(s)
Newfield Central SD (PK-12)
Enrollment: 835 . . . . (607) 564-9955
Housing: Homeownership rate: 74.7%; Median home value: $130,300; Median year structure built: 1980; Homeowner vacancy rate: 1.0%; Median selected monthly owner costs: $1,189 with a mortgage, $462 without a mortgage; Median gross rent: $799 per month; Rental vacancy rate: 11.9%
Health Insurance: 93.9% have insurance; 62.9% have private insurance; 41.6% have public insurance; 6.1% do not have insurance; 2.9% of children under 18 do not have insurance
Transportation: Commute: 91.0% car, 0.3% public transportation, 3.2% walk, 2.2% work from home; Mean travel time to work: 24.2 minutes
Additional Information Contacts
Town of Newfield . . . . (607) 564-9981
http://newfieldny.org

NEWFIELD HAMLET (CDP). Covers a land area of 1.257 square miles and a water area of <.001 square miles. Located at 42.36° N. Lat; 76.59° W. Long. Elevation is 1,050 feet.
Population: 723; Growth (since 2000): 11.7%; Density: 575.1 persons per square mile; Race: 100.0% White, 0.0% Black/African American, 0.0% Asian, 0.0% American Indian/Alaska Native, 0.0% Native Hawaiian/Other Pacific Islander, 0.0% Two or more races, 1.8% Hispanic of any race; Average household size: 2.17; Median age: 56.4; Age under 18: 3.0%; Age 65 and over: 31.1%; Males per 100 females: 89.8; Marriage status: 12.8% never married, 54.9% now married, 0.0% separated, 14.1% widowed, 18.1% divorced; Foreign born: 0.0%; Speak English only: 98.2%; With disability: 22.7%; Veterans: 0.0%; Ancestry: 32.8% German, 31.7% Dutch, 14.8% American, 11.1% English, 10.8% Irish
Employment: 15.4% management, business, and financial, 5.7% computer, engineering, and science, 4.5% education, legal, community service, arts, and media, 20.6% healthcare practitioners, 28.6% service,

20.2% sales and office, 0.0% natural resources, construction, and maintenance, 5.0% production, transportation, and material moving
Income: Per capita: $29,048; Median household: $67,917; Average household: $60,498; Households with income of $100,000 or more: 19.5%; Poverty rate: 2.5%
Educational Attainment: High school diploma or higher: 73.2%; Bachelor's degree or higher: 22.6%; Graduate/professional degree or higher: 10.0%
Housing: Homeownership rate: 75.4%; Median home value: $102,000; Median year structure built: 1953; Homeowner vacancy rate: 0.0%; Median selected monthly owner costs: $776 with a mortgage, n/a without a mortgage; Median gross rent: n/a per month; Rental vacancy rate: 0.0%
Health Insurance: 94.7% have insurance; 59.5% have private insurance; 45.0% have public insurance; 5.3% do not have insurance; 56.0% of children under 18 do not have insurance
Transportation: Commute: 84.4% car, 2.3% public transportation, 0.0% walk, 0.0% work from home; Mean travel time to work: 32.8 minutes

NORTHEAST ITHACA (CDP). Covers a land area of 1.469 square miles and a water area of 0.004 square miles. Located at 42.47° N. Lat; 76.46° W. Long.

Population: 3,186; Growth (since 2000): 20.0%; Density: 2,168.1 persons per square mile; Race: 55.6% White, 3.5% Black/African American, 34.4% Asian, 0.0% American Indian/Alaska Native, 0.0% Native Hawaiian/Other Pacific Islander, 6.4% Two or more races, 2.3% Hispanic of any race; Average household size: 2.79; Median age: 31.6; Age under 18: 27.0%; Age 65 and over: 9.5%; Males per 100 females: 98.6; Marriage status: 35.3% never married, 57.8% now married, 0.6% separated, 3.3% widowed, 3.5% divorced; Foreign born: 41.0%; Speak English only: 60.5%; With disability: 4.8%; Veterans: 4.8%; Ancestry: 12.6% German, 9.4% English, 8.9% Irish, 6.4% Polish, 4.3% American
Employment: 16.5% management, business, and financial, 20.2% computer, engineering, and science, 27.4% education, legal, community service, arts, and media, 5.3% healthcare practitioners, 11.6% service, 12.7% sales and office, 4.2% natural resources, construction, and maintenance, 2.1% production, transportation, and material moving
Income: Per capita: $31,002; Median household: $56,913; Average household: $87,428; Households with income of $100,000 or more: 24.9%; Poverty rate: 16.3%
Educational Attainment: High school diploma or higher: 98.3%; Bachelor's degree or higher: 79.2%; Graduate/professional degree or higher: 50.7%
Housing: Homeownership rate: 49.1%; Median home value: $249,900; Median year structure built: 1969; Homeowner vacancy rate: 3.1%; Median selected monthly owner costs: $2,024 with a mortgage, $849 without a mortgage; Median gross rent: $1,324 per month; Rental vacancy rate: 0.0%
Health Insurance: 94.7% have insurance; 88.5% have private insurance; 14.5% have public insurance; 5.3% do not have insurance; 9.3% of children under 18 do not have insurance
Transportation: Commute: 74.4% car, 10.7% public transportation, 3.3% walk, 6.8% work from home; Mean travel time to work: 14.4 minutes

NORTHWEST ITHACA (CDP). Covers a land area of 2.908 square miles and a water area of 0.662 square miles. Located at 42.47° N. Lat; 76.54° W. Long. Elevation is 915 feet.

Population: 1,180; Growth (since 2000): 5.8%; Density: 405.8 persons per square mile; Race: 91.6% White, 3.1% Black/African American, 0.8% Asian, 0.0% American Indian/Alaska Native, 0.0% Native Hawaiian/Other Pacific Islander, 1.4% Two or more races, 11.9% Hispanic of any race; Average household size: 2.11; Median age: 54.8; Age under 18: 14.1%; Age 65 and over: 30.6%; Males per 100 females: 82.3; Marriage status: 26.2% never married, 49.7% now married, 4.8% separated, 14.2% widowed, 9.9% divorced; Foreign born: 18.0%; Speak English only: 74.9%; With disability: 14.9%; Veterans: 10.1%; Ancestry: 13.6% German, 12.0% American, 10.6% Italian, 8.7% Irish, 7.5% English
Employment: 14.7% management, business, and financial, 7.3% computer, engineering, and science, 17.5% education, legal, community service, arts, and media, 12.7% healthcare practitioners, 18.4% service, 22.0% sales and office, 1.7% natural resources, construction, and maintenance, 5.6% production, transportation, and material moving
Income: Per capita: $47,326; Median household: $68,947; Average household: $107,335; Households with income of $100,000 or more: 31.7%; Poverty rate: 15.0%

Educational Attainment: High school diploma or higher: 92.4%; Bachelor's degree or higher: 47.6%; Graduate/professional degree or higher: 29.8%
Housing: Homeownership rate: 48.0%; Median home value: $247,800; Median year structure built: 1980; Homeowner vacancy rate: 0.0%; Median selected monthly owner costs: $2,000 with a mortgage, $1,021 without a mortgage; Median gross rent: $1,042 per month; Rental vacancy rate: 13.0%
Health Insurance: 96.1% have insurance; 76.2% have private insurance; 37.5% have public insurance; 3.9% do not have insurance; 0.0% of children under 18 do not have insurance
Transportation: Commute: 86.7% car, 1.8% public transportation, 6.2% walk, 5.3% work from home; Mean travel time to work: 20.0 minutes

SLATERVILLE SPRINGS (unincorporated postal area)
ZCTA: 14881
Covers a land area of 1.229 square miles and a water area of 0.001 square miles. Located at 42.40° N. Lat; 76.36° W. Long. Elevation is 1,112 feet.

Population: 263; Growth (since 2000): 63.4%; Density: 214.1 persons per square mile; Race: 100.0% White, 0.0% Black/African American, 0.0% Asian, 0.0% American Indian/Alaska Native, 0.0% Native Hawaiian/Other Pacific Islander, 0.0% Two or more races, 0.0% Hispanic of any race; Average household size: 2.33; Median age: 44.6; Age under 18: 0.0%; Age 65 and over: 16.7%; Males per 100 females: 90.1; Marriage status: 0.0% never married, 48.7% now married, 0.0% separated, 0.0% widowed, 51.3% divorced; Foreign born: 0.0%; Speak English only: 100.0%; With disability: 30.0%; Veterans: 0.0%; Ancestry: 46.4% American, 12.9% Italian, 12.2% Scotch-Irish, 11.8% English, 7.6% French
Employment: 0.0% management, business, and financial, 14.2% computer, engineering, and science, 0.0% education, legal, community service, arts, and media, 0.0% healthcare practitioners, 34.0% service, 51.8% sales and office, 0.0% natural resources, construction, and maintenance, 0.0% production, transportation, and material moving
Income: Per capita: $52,596; Median household: $115,495; Average household: $116,504; Households with income of $100,000 or more: 75.2%; Poverty rate: n/a
Educational Attainment: High school diploma or higher: 95.1%; Bachelor's degree or higher: 62.4%; Graduate/professional degree or higher: 16.0%

School District(s)
Ithaca City SD (PK-12)
    Enrollment: 5,360 . . . . (607) 274-2101
Housing: Homeownership rate: 41.6%; Median home value: $280,400; Median year structure built: 1974; Homeowner vacancy rate: 0.0%; Median selected monthly owner costs: $2,304 with a mortgage, $0 without a mortgage; Median gross rent: n/a per month; Rental vacancy rate: 0.0%
Health Insurance: 79.8% have insurance; 36.9% have private insurance; 53.6% have public insurance; 20.2% do not have insurance; 0.0% of children under 18 do not have insurance
Transportation: Commute: 91.9% car, 0.0% public transportation, 8.1% walk, 0.0% work from home; Mean travel time to work: 15.4 minutes

SOUTH HILL (CDP). Covers a land area of 5.896 square miles and a water area of 0.094 square miles. Located at 42.41° N. Lat; 76.49° W. Long. Elevation is 778 feet.

Population: 6,693; Growth (since 2000): 11.5%; Density: 1,135.2 persons per square mile; Race: 83.5% White, 7.4% Black/African American, 3.6% Asian, 0.4% American Indian/Alaska Native, 0.0% Native Hawaiian/Other Pacific Islander, 3.0% Two or more races, 4.0% Hispanic of any race; Average household size: 2.25; Median age: 20.0; Age under 18: 6.9%; Age 65 and over: 7.0%; Males per 100 females: 80.0; Marriage status: 78.5% never married, 16.9% now married, 0.4% separated, 3.1% widowed, 1.5% divorced; Foreign born: 7.1%; Speak English only: 91.6%; With disability: 6.4%; Veterans: 2.9%; Ancestry: 11.0% Irish, 10.6% German, 7.0% English, 5.9% Italian, 5.0% Polish
Employment: 4.7% management, business, and financial, 8.5% computer, engineering, and science, 19.5% education, legal, community service, arts, and media, 5.1% healthcare practitioners, 24.0% service, 30.2% sales and office, 2.2% natural resources, construction, and maintenance, 5.8% production, transportation, and material moving

Income: Per capita: $14,859; Median household: $50,673; Average household: $75,356; Households with income of $100,000 or more: 19.6%; Poverty rate: 21.2%

Educational Attainment: High school diploma or higher: 95.0%; Bachelor's degree or higher: 55.7%; Graduate/professional degree or higher: 38.0%

Housing: Homeownership rate: 52.7%; Median home value: $209,500; Median year structure built: 1971; Homeowner vacancy rate: 2.5%; Median selected monthly owner costs: $1,690 with a mortgage, $666 without a mortgage; Median gross rent: $1,242 per month; Rental vacancy rate: 0.5%

Health Insurance: 96.5% have insurance; 89.3% have private insurance; 13.6% have public insurance; 3.5% do not have insurance; 1.9% of children under 18 do not have insurance

Transportation: Commute: 50.6% car, 0.2% public transportation, 34.9% walk, 12.8% work from home; Mean travel time to work: 13.7 minutes

TRUMANSBURG (village). Covers a land area of 1.387 square miles and a water area of 0.004 square miles. Located at 42.54° N. Lat; 76.66° W. Long. Elevation is 965 feet.

History: Settled 1792; incorporated 1865.

Population: 1,818; Growth (since 2000): 15.0%; Density: 1,310.7 persons per square mile; Race: 94.2% White, 1.9% Black/African American, 0.8% Asian, 0.0% American Indian/Alaska Native, 0.0% Native Hawaiian/Other Pacific Islander, 3.1% Two or more races, 1.6% Hispanic of any race; Average household size: 2.14; Median age: 50.3; Age under 18: 16.6%; Age 65 and over: 25.0%; Males per 100 females: 84.3; Marriage status: 27.8% never married, 50.1% now married, 5.5% separated, 9.0% widowed, 13.1% divorced; Foreign born: 4.1%; Speak English only: 96.5%; With disability: 14.6%; Veterans: 5.5%; Ancestry: 22.3% English, 18.4% German, 17.5% Irish, 11.2% Italian, 9.6% American

Employment: 18.3% management, business, and financial, 7.1% computer, engineering, and science, 17.4% education, legal, community service, arts, and media, 7.2% healthcare practitioners, 20.6% service, 17.3% sales and office, 4.7% natural resources, construction, and maintenance, 7.4% production, transportation, and material moving

Income: Per capita: $35,804; Median household: $55,057; Average household: $74,578; Households with income of $100,000 or more: 24.1%; Poverty rate: 13.0%

Educational Attainment: High school diploma or higher: 96.6%; Bachelor's degree or higher: 51.7%; Graduate/professional degree or higher: 23.5%

School District(s)

Trumansburg Central SD (PK-12)
    Enrollment: 1,092 . . . . (607) 387-7551

Housing: Homeownership rate: 62.9%; Median home value: $205,600; Median year structure built: Before 1940; Homeowner vacancy rate: 0.0%; Median selected monthly owner costs: $1,534 with a mortgage, $695 without a mortgage; Median gross rent: $1,035 per month; Rental vacancy rate: 10.0%

Health Insurance: 94.1% have insurance; 74.9% have private insurance; 38.1% have public insurance; 5.9% do not have insurance; 0.0% of children under 18 do not have insurance

Safety: Violent crime rate: 0.0 per 10,000 population; Property crime rate: 197.4 per 10,000 population

Newspapers: Finger Lakes Community Papers (weekly circulation 7,000)

Transportation: Commute: 82.2% car, 4.0% public transportation, 3.9% walk, 9.3% work from home; Mean travel time to work: 23.1 minutes

Additional Information Contacts
Village of Trumansburg . . . . (607) 387-6501
    http://www.trumansburg-ny.gov

ULYSSES (town). Covers a land area of 32.889 square miles and a water area of 4.026 square miles. Located at 42.51° N. Lat; 76.62° W. Long.

Population: 5,062; Growth (since 2000): 6.0%; Density: 153.9 persons per square mile; Race: 95.0% White, 1.1% Black/African American, 1.0% Asian, 0.0% American Indian/Alaska Native, 0.0% Native Hawaiian/Other Pacific Islander, 3.0% Two or more races, 3.9% Hispanic of any race; Average household size: 2.23; Median age: 50.2; Age under 18: 17.2%; Age 65 and over: 22.2%; Males per 100 females: 89.8; Marriage status: 25.4% never married, 55.8% now married, 2.8% separated, 6.8% widowed, 11.9% divorced; Foreign born: 4.6%; Speak English only: 96.7%; With disability: 11.7%; Veterans: 5.3%; Ancestry: 19.2% English, 19.1% Irish, 18.0% German, 12.0% Italian, 6.8% American

Employment: 18.2% management, business, and financial, 7.7% computer, engineering, and science, 14.1% education, legal, community service, arts, and media, 9.0% healthcare practitioners, 19.6% service, 17.3% sales and office, 5.6% natural resources, construction, and maintenance, 8.4% production, transportation, and material moving

Income: Per capita: $38,657; Median household: $68,551; Average household: $85,016; Households with income of $100,000 or more: 30.5%; Poverty rate: 10.3%

Educational Attainment: High school diploma or higher: 95.6%; Bachelor's degree or higher: 45.5%; Graduate/professional degree or higher: 20.5%

Housing: Homeownership rate: 79.0%; Median home value: $206,200; Median year structure built: 1959; Homeowner vacancy rate: 1.6%; Median selected monthly owner costs: $1,371 with a mortgage, $742 without a mortgage; Median gross rent: $1,024 per month; Rental vacancy rate: 12.7%

Health Insurance: 93.8% have insurance; 77.5% have private insurance; 34.1% have public insurance; 6.2% do not have insurance; 1.1% of children under 18 do not have insurance

Transportation: Commute: 86.3% car, 4.6% public transportation, 1.4% walk, 7.0% work from home; Mean travel time to work: 21.1 minutes

Additional Information Contacts
Town of Ulysses . . . . (607) 387-5767
    http://www.ulysses.ny.us

Ulster County

Located in southeastern New York, mainly in the Catskills; bounded on the east by the Hudson River; drained by the Wallkill River; includes part of the Shawangunk Range and several small lakes. Covers a land area of 1,124.235 square miles, a water area of 36.525 square miles, and is located in the Eastern Time Zone at 41.95° N. Lat., 74.27° W. Long. The county was founded in 1683. County seat is Kingston.

Ulster County is part of the Kingston, NY Metropolitan Statistical Area. The entire metro area includes: Ulster County, NY

Weather Station: Mohonk Lake   Elevation: 1,245 feet

	Jan	Feb	Mar	Apr	May	Jun	Jul	Aug	Sep	Oct	Nov	Dec
High	32	36	45	59	69	77	81	79	71	60	48	37
Low	18	20	27	38	49	58	63	62	55	44	34	24
Precip	3.6	3.1	4.4	4.4	4.8	4.6	4.8	4.3	4.7	4.7	4.0	4.2
Snow	16.5	12.7	12.4	2.9	tr	0.0	0.0	0.0	0.0	0.1	3.2	13.4

High and Low temperatures in degrees Fahrenheit; Precipitation and Snow in inches

Weather Station: Slide Mountain   Elevation: 2,649 feet

	Jan	Feb	Mar	Apr	May	Jun	Jul	Aug	Sep	Oct	Nov	Dec
High	27	30	37	49	61	68	72	71	64	54	42	31
Low	11	12	19	31	41	50	54	53	46	36	27	16
Precip	4.4	3.9	5.3	5.5	5.5	5.5	5.5	4.9	5.8	6.0	5.7	4.9
Snow	24.3	18.9	20.0	6.3	0.3	0.0	0.0	0.0	0.0	2.0	7.5	20.1

High and Low temperatures in degrees Fahrenheit; Precipitation and Snow in inches

Population: 180,129; Growth (since 2000): 1.3%; Density: 160.2 persons per square mile; Race: 85.5% White, 5.7% Black/African American, 2.1% Asian, 0.2% American Indian/Alaska Native, 0.1% Native Hawaiian/Other Pacific Islander, 3.9% two or more races, 9.8% Hispanic of any race; Average household size: 2.42; Median age: 43.6; Age under 18: 18.3%; Age 65 and over: 18.0%; Males per 100 females: 99.0; Marriage status: 33.5% never married, 49.0% now married, 2.3% separated, 6.5% widowed, 11.0% divorced; Foreign born: 7.8%; Speak English only: 88.9%; With disability: 13.6%; Veterans: 6.4%; Ancestry: 20.4% Irish, 18.6% Italian, 18.6% German, 8.0% English, 5.0% Polish

Religion: Six largest groups: 27.5% Catholicism, 3.6% Methodist/Pietist, 3.0% Presbyterian-Reformed, 1.4% Lutheran, 0.9% Non-denominational Protestant, 0.8% Muslim Estimate

Economy: Unemployment rate: 3.4%; Leading industries: 15.5 % retail trade; 11.9 % construction; 11.8 % accommodation and food services; Farms: 486 totaling 71,222 acres; Company size: 0 employ 1,000 or more persons, 4 employ 500 to 999 persons, 58 employ 100 to 499 persons, 4,752 employ less than 100 persons; Business ownership: 6,287 women-owned, 658 Black-owned, 815 Hispanic-owned, 311 Asian-owned, 65 American Indian/Alaska Native-owned

Employment: 13.5% management, business, and financial, 4.9% computer, engineering, and science, 14.8% education, legal, community service, arts, and media, 6.4% healthcare practitioners, 18.3% service,

23.6% sales and office, 9.4% natural resources, construction, and maintenance, 9.2% production, transportation, and material moving
Income: Per capita: $32,453; Median household: $61,652; Average household: $80,754; Households with income of $100,000 or more: 27.8%; Poverty rate: 13.2%
Educational Attainment: High school diploma or higher: 90.7%; Bachelor's degree or higher: 31.4%; Graduate/professional degree or higher: 14.2%
Housing: Homeownership rate: 69.4%; Median home value: $221,600; Median year structure built: 1964; Homeowner vacancy rate: 1.9%; Median selected monthly owner costs: $1,906 with a mortgage, $739 without a mortgage; Median gross rent: $1,053 per month; Rental vacancy rate: 5.6%
Vital Statistics: Birth rate: 84.6 per 10,000 population; Death rate: 94.6 per 10,000 population; Age-adjusted cancer mortality rate: 162.3 deaths per 100,000 population
Health Insurance: 93.1% have insurance; 70.4% have private insurance; 37.4% have public insurance; 6.9% do not have insurance; 3.1% of children under 18 do not have insurance
Health Care: Physicians: 19.9 per 10,000 population; Dentists: 6.1 per 10,000 population; Hospital beds: 16.4 per 10,000 population; Hospital admissions: 641.1 per 10,000 population
Transportation: Commute: 85.6% car, 2.4% public transportation, 4.1% walk, 6.4% work from home; Mean travel time to work: 28.2 minutes
2016 Presidential Election: 41.3% Trump, 52.3% Clinton, 2.8% Johnson, 2.5% Stein
National and State Parks: Bristol Beach State Park; Catskill State Park; Senate House State Historic Site; Shawangunk Grasslands National Wildlife Refuge; Turkey Point State Open Space Area
Additional Information Contacts
Ulster Government . . . . (845) 340-3288
    http://www.co.ulster.ny.us

Ulster County Communities

ACCORD (CDP). Covers a land area of 3.400 square miles and a water area of 0.043 square miles. Located at 41.80° N. Lat; 74.23° W. Long. Elevation is 253 feet.
Population: 586; Growth (since 2000): -5.8%; Density: 172.3 persons per square mile; Race: 88.1% White, 0.0% Black/African American, 0.0% Asian, 0.0% American Indian/Alaska Native, 0.0% Native Hawaiian/Other Pacific Islander, 11.8% Two or more races, 0.2% Hispanic of any race; Average household size: 2.78; Median age: 48.8; Age under 18: 11.3%; Age 65 and over: 19.5%; Males per 100 females: 100.0; Marriage status: 28.4% never married, 54.9% now married, 5.0% separated, 7.9% widowed, 8.8% divorced; Foreign born: 0.2%; Speak English only: 98.8%; With disability: 16.8%; Veterans: 6.6%; Ancestry: 47.8% German, 29.2% Irish, 21.3% Scotch-Irish, 17.2% Italian, 6.0% English
Employment: 7.4% management, business, and financial, 2.5% computer, engineering, and science, 8.9% education, legal, community service, arts, and media, 5.3% healthcare practitioners, 34.8% service, 26.6% sales and office, 9.6% natural resources, construction, and maintenance, 5.0% production, transportation, and material moving
Income: Per capita: $34,847; Median household: n/a; Average household: $106,343; Households with income of $100,000 or more: 43.0%; Poverty rate: 4.9%
Educational Attainment: High school diploma or higher: 88.1%; Bachelor's degree or higher: 10.0%; Graduate/professional degree or higher: 5.0%
School District(s)
Rondout Valley Central SD (KG-12)
    Enrollment: 2,008 . . . . (845) 687-2400
Housing: Homeownership rate: 58.9%; Median home value: $153,600; Median year structure built: 1960; Homeowner vacancy rate: 10.9%; Median selected monthly owner costs: $1,837 with a mortgage, n/a without a mortgage; Median gross rent: $738 per month; Rental vacancy rate: 0.0%
Health Insurance: 91.7% have insurance; 63.9% have private insurance; 30.6% have public insurance; 8.3% do not have insurance; 0.0% of children under 18 do not have insurance
Transportation: Commute: 97.6% car, 0.0% public transportation, 0.0% walk, 2.4% work from home; Mean travel time to work: 22.3 minutes

BEARSVILLE (unincorporated postal area)
ZCTA: 12409
    Covers a land area of 14.268 square miles and a water area of 0.223 square miles. Located at 42.04° N. Lat; 74.18° W. Long. Elevation is 699 feet.
Population: 672; Growth (since 2000): 44.8%; Density: 47.1 persons per square mile; Race: 98.7% White, 0.4% Black/African American, 0.0% Asian, 0.0% American Indian/Alaska Native, 0.0% Native Hawaiian/Other Pacific Islander, 0.9% Two or more races, 0.6% Hispanic of any race; Average household size: 2.06; Median age: 58.6; Age under 18: 14.1%; Age 65 and over: 32.4%; Males per 100 females: 84.4; Marriage status: 24.9% never married, 54.2% now married, 0.0% separated, 4.7% widowed, 16.2% divorced; Foreign born: 11.6%; Speak English only: 88.7%; With disability: 12.9%; Veterans: 0.0%; Ancestry: 21.6% French, 13.8% German, 12.5% Russian, 11.2% Danish, 9.1% Italian
Employment: 22.3% management, business, and financial, 5.1% computer, engineering, and science, 28.0% education, legal, community service, arts, and media, 5.4% healthcare practitioners, 17.2% service, 4.1% sales and office, 17.9% natural resources, construction, and maintenance, 0.0% production, transportation, and material moving
Income: Per capita: $54,246; Median household: $88,906; Average household: $114,548; Households with income of $100,000 or more: 46.9%; Poverty rate: 13.2%
Educational Attainment: High school diploma or higher: 96.6%; Bachelor's degree or higher: 69.4%; Graduate/professional degree or higher: 39.8%
Housing: Homeownership rate: 86.9%; Median home value: $355,400; Median year structure built: 1958; Homeowner vacancy rate: 0.0%; Median selected monthly owner costs: $1,941 with a mortgage, $1,183 without a mortgage; Median gross rent: $1,422 per month; Rental vacancy rate: 0.0%
Health Insurance: 90.3% have insurance; 71.9% have private insurance; 45.8% have public insurance; 9.7% do not have insurance; 0.0% of children under 18 do not have insurance
Transportation: Commute: 75.7% car, 5.4% public transportation, 2.7% walk, 10.5% work from home; Mean travel time to work: 35.3 minutes

BIG INDIAN (unincorporated postal area)
ZCTA: 12410
    Covers a land area of 41.181 square miles and a water area of 0.036 square miles. Located at 42.07° N. Lat; 74.42° W. Long. Elevation is 1,217 feet.
Population: 571; Growth (since 2000): -30.4%; Density: 13.9 persons per square mile; Race: 98.6% White, 0.0% Black/African American, 0.0% Asian, 0.0% American Indian/Alaska Native, 0.0% Native Hawaiian/Other Pacific Islander, 0.0% Two or more races, 3.3% Hispanic of any race; Average household size: 2.17; Median age: 56.0; Age under 18: 15.2%; Age 65 and over: 25.7%; Males per 100 females: 107.9; Marriage status: 18.4% never married, 55.2% now married, 0.0% separated, 8.9% widowed, 17.6% divorced; Foreign born: 4.6%; Speak English only: 96.1%; With disability: 19.1%; Veterans: 11.8%; Ancestry: 29.9% Irish, 25.7% German, 15.9% Dutch, 8.1% Italian, 6.0% English
Employment: 33.2% management, business, and financial, 0.0% computer, engineering, and science, 22.0% education, legal, community service, arts, and media, 0.0% healthcare practitioners, 11.6% service, 4.8% sales and office, 24.8% natural resources, construction, and maintenance, 3.6% production, transportation, and material moving
Income: Per capita: $32,001; Median household: $58,000; Average household: $70,595; Households with income of $100,000 or more: 23.5%; Poverty rate: 5.3%
Educational Attainment: High school diploma or higher: 100.0%; Bachelor's degree or higher: 29.3%; Graduate/professional degree or higher: 7.8%
Housing: Homeownership rate: 95.7%; Median home value: $203,300; Median year structure built: 1958; Homeowner vacancy rate: 0.0%; Median selected monthly owner costs: $1,946 with a mortgage, $588 without a mortgage; Median gross rent: n/a per month; Rental vacancy rate: 77.1%
Health Insurance: 93.0% have insurance; 74.8% have private insurance; 28.4% have public insurance; 7.0% do not have insurance; 0.0% of children under 18 do not have insurance
Transportation: Commute: 82.5% car, 0.0% public transportation, 7.5% walk, 0.0% work from home; Mean travel time to work: 43.7 minutes

BLOOMINGTON (unincorporated postal area)
ZCTA: 12411

Covers a land area of 0.937 square miles and a water area of 0.019 square miles. Located at 41.88° N. Lat; 74.04° W. Long. Elevation is 184 feet.

Population: 318; Growth (since 2000): -16.8%; Density: 339.3 persons per square mile; Race: 100.0% White, 0.0% Black/African American, 0.0% Asian, 0.0% American Indian/Alaska Native, 0.0% Native Hawaiian/Other Pacific Islander, 0.0% Two or more races, 0.0% Hispanic of any race; Average household size: 2.45; Median age: 48.1; Age under 18: 17.9%; Age 65 and over: 21.7%; Males per 100 females: 97.2; Marriage status: 19.2% never married, 72.7% now married, 0.0% separated, 1.5% widowed, 6.6% divorced; Foreign born: 5.3%; Speak English only: 91.1%; With disability: 9.4%; Veterans: 11.5%; Ancestry: 25.5% Italian, 24.5% Irish, 17.6% German, 14.5% Polish, 11.9% English

Employment: 14.1% management, business, and financial, 7.8% computer, engineering, and science, 28.6% education, legal, community service, arts, and media, 3.9% healthcare practitioners, 4.9% service, 19.4% sales and office, 5.3% natural resources, construction, and maintenance, 16.0% production, transportation, and material moving

Income: Per capita: $30,464; Median household: $84,474; Average household: $73,216; Households with income of $100,000 or more: 22.3%; Poverty rate: n/a

Educational Attainment: High school diploma or higher: 98.4%; Bachelor's degree or higher: 43.1%; Graduate/professional degree or higher: 27.0%

Housing: Homeownership rate: 100.0%; Median home value: $262,500; Median year structure built: Before 1940; Homeowner vacancy rate: 0.0%; Median selected monthly owner costs: $2,375 with a mortgage, $744 without a mortgage; Median gross rent: n/a per month; Rental vacancy rate: 0.0%

Health Insurance: 100.0% have insurance; 90.6% have private insurance; 27.7% have public insurance; 0.0% do not have insurance; 0.0% of children under 18 do not have insurance

Transportation: Commute: 81.6% car, 0.0% public transportation, 5.3% walk, 13.1% work from home; Mean travel time to work: 24.5 minutes

BOICEVILLE (unincorporated postal area)
ZCTA: 12412

Covers a land area of 6.070 square miles and a water area of 0 square miles. Located at 42.01° N. Lat; 74.28° W. Long. Elevation is 630 feet.

Population: 548; Growth (since 2000): -40.9%; Density: 90.3 persons per square mile; Race: 81.9% White, 0.0% Black/African American, 2.9% Asian, 0.0% American Indian/Alaska Native, 0.0% Native Hawaiian/Other Pacific Islander, 3.6% Two or more races, 11.5% Hispanic of any race; Average household size: 2.12; Median age: 58.5; Age under 18: 10.6%; Age 65 and over: 42.9%; Males per 100 females: 103.3; Marriage status: 14.7% never married, 62.7% now married, 11.0% separated, 15.7% widowed, 6.9% divorced; Foreign born: 10.6%; Speak English only: 85.6%; With disability: 21.2%; Veterans: 8.4%; Ancestry: 24.3% Irish, 21.7% Italian, 20.8% German, 9.7% English, 8.4% Dutch

Employment: 16.9% management, business, and financial, 0.0% computer, engineering, and science, 64.8% education, legal, community service, arts, and media, 0.0% healthcare practitioners, 11.3% service, 7.0% sales and office, 0.0% natural resources, construction, and maintenance, 0.0% production, transportation, and material moving

Income: Per capita: $36,332; Median household: $65,676; Average household: $70,549; Households with income of $100,000 or more: 6.2%; Poverty rate: 11.5%

Educational Attainment: High school diploma or higher: 81.6%; Bachelor's degree or higher: 16.9%; Graduate/professional degree or higher: n/a

School District(s)
Onteora Central SD (KG-12)

Enrollment: 1,367 . . . . (845) 657-8851

Housing: Homeownership rate: 66.8%; Median home value: $210,300; Median year structure built: 1968; Homeowner vacancy rate: 0.0%; Median selected monthly owner costs: $0 with a mortgage, $743 without a mortgage; Median gross rent: $981 per month; Rental vacancy rate: 32.8%

Health Insurance: 93.8% have insurance; 57.8% have private insurance; 67.7% have public insurance; 6.2% do not have insurance; 0.0% of children under 18 do not have insurance

Transportation: Commute: 88.7% car, 0.0% public transportation, 0.0% walk, 11.3% work from home; Mean travel time to work: 0.0 minutes

CHICHESTER (unincorporated postal area)
ZCTA: 12416

Covers a land area of 5.085 square miles and a water area of <.001 square miles. Located at 42.10° N. Lat; 74.28° W. Long. Elevation is 965 feet.

Population: 130; Growth (since 2000): 49.4%; Density: 25.6 persons per square mile; Race: 43.8% White, 0.0% Black/African American, 0.0% Asian, 0.0% American Indian/Alaska Native, 0.0% Native Hawaiian/Other Pacific Islander, 0.0% Two or more races, 56.2% Hispanic of any race; Average household size: 2.32; Median age: 36.5; Age under 18: 29.2%; Age 65 and over: 20.0%; Males per 100 females: 102.2; Marriage status: 40.2% never married, 59.8% now married, 0.0% separated, 0.0% widowed, 0.0% divorced; Foreign born: 26.9%; Speak English only: 43.8%; With disability: 25.4%; Veterans: 0.0%; Ancestry: 20.0% Polish, 20.0% Russian

Employment: 0.0% management, business, and financial, 0.0% computer, engineering, and science, 0.0% education, legal, community service, arts, and media, 0.0% healthcare practitioners, 75.6% service, 0.0% sales and office, 0.0% natural resources, construction, and maintenance, 24.4% production, transportation, and material moving

Income: Per capita: $11,937; Median household: $25,769; Average household: $27,471; Households with income of $100,000 or more: n/a; Poverty rate: 56.2%

Educational Attainment: High school diploma or higher: 87.7%; Bachelor's degree or higher: 32.1%; Graduate/professional degree or higher: 32.1%

Housing: Homeownership rate: 64.3%; Median home value: n/a; Median year structure built: 1975; Homeowner vacancy rate: 0.0%; Median selected monthly owner costs: $0 with a mortgage, $0 without a mortgage; Median gross rent: n/a per month; Rental vacancy rate: 0.0%

Health Insurance: 88.5% have insurance; 59.2% have private insurance; 49.2% have public insurance; 11.5% do not have insurance; 0.0% of children under 18 do not have insurance

Transportation: Commute: 100.0% car, 0.0% public transportation, 0.0% walk, 0.0% work from home; Mean travel time to work: 0.0 minutes

CLINTONDALE (CDP).
Covers a land area of 5.572 square miles and a water area of 0.039 square miles. Located at 41.69° N. Lat; 74.05° W. Long. Elevation is 545 feet.

Population: 1,657; Growth (since 2000): 16.4%; Density: 297.4 persons per square mile; Race: 89.0% White, 2.5% Black/African American, 6.6% Asian, 0.0% American Indian/Alaska Native, 0.0% Native Hawaiian/Other Pacific Islander, 0.7% Two or more races, 9.1% Hispanic of any race; Average household size: 2.41; Median age: 49.6; Age under 18: 17.6%; Age 65 and over: 14.1%; Males per 100 females: 101.9; Marriage status: 30.5% never married, 54.7% now married, 0.9% separated, 12.8% widowed, 2.0% divorced; Foreign born: 13.9%; Speak English only: 89.1%; With disability: 23.9%; Veterans: 4.0%; Ancestry: 27.8% German, 20.9% Italian, 12.8% Irish, 9.7% English, 5.3% Norwegian

Employment: 19.4% management, business, and financial, 8.7% computer, engineering, and science, 21.6% education, legal, community service, arts, and media, 2.3% healthcare practitioners, 11.9% service, 18.8% sales and office, 9.7% natural resources, construction, and maintenance, 7.4% production, transportation, and material moving

Income: Per capita: $39,933; Median household: $58,393; Average household: $94,904; Households with income of $100,000 or more: 41.3%; Poverty rate: 5.6%

Educational Attainment: High school diploma or higher: 94.9%; Bachelor's degree or higher: 33.2%; Graduate/professional degree or higher: 6.2%

Housing: Homeownership rate: 53.6%; Median home value: $272,900; Median year structure built: 1967; Homeowner vacancy rate: 0.0%; Median selected monthly owner costs: $2,684 with a mortgage, $744 without a mortgage; Median gross rent: $872 per month; Rental vacancy rate: 0.0%

Health Insurance: 94.0% have insurance; 63.7% have private insurance; 35.4% have public insurance; 6.0% do not have insurance; 2.1% of children under 18 do not have insurance

Transportation: Commute: 79.3% car, 9.1% public transportation, 6.3% walk, 5.3% work from home; Mean travel time to work: 26.0 minutes

CONNELLY (unincorporated postal area)
ZCTA: 12417

Covers a land area of 0.316 square miles and a water area of 0.029 square miles. Located at 41.91° N. Lat; 73.99° W. Long. Elevation is 23 feet.

Population: 479; Growth (since 2000): n/a; Density: 1,518.2 persons per square mile; Race: 66.4% White, 4.0% Black/African American, 0.0% Asian, 0.0% American Indian/Alaska Native, 0.0% Native Hawaiian/Other Pacific Islander, 20.9% Two or more races, 8.8% Hispanic of any race; Average household size: 2.78; Median age: 35.9; Age under 18: 11.7%; Age 65 and over: 9.0%; Males per 100 females: 90.5; Marriage status: 42.1% never married, 32.2% now married, 0.0% separated, 8.0% widowed, 17.7% divorced; Foreign born: 0.0%; Speak English only: 100.0%; With disability: 14.2%; Veterans: 2.4%; Ancestry: 36.1% German, 30.5% Irish, 18.0% Swedish, 17.5% Italian, 4.8% Dutch

Employment: 22.1% management, business, and financial, 0.0% computer, engineering, and science, 2.4% education, legal, community service, arts, and media, 0.0% healthcare practitioners, 37.0% service, 19.7% sales and office, 18.7% natural resources, construction, and maintenance, 0.0% production, transportation, and material moving

Income: Per capita: $24,093; Median household: $79,063; Average household: $63,903; Households with income of $100,000 or more: 19.2%; Poverty rate: 13.6%

Educational Attainment: High school diploma or higher: 75.6%; Bachelor's degree or higher: n/a; Graduate/professional degree or higher: n/a

Housing: Homeownership rate: 70.9%; Median home value: $131,300; Median year structure built: 1960; Homeowner vacancy rate: 0.0%; Median selected monthly owner costs: $1,385 with a mortgage, $538 without a mortgage; Median gross rent: $1,316 per month; Rental vacancy rate: 25.4%

Health Insurance: 93.5% have insurance; 45.1% have private insurance; 52.0% have public insurance; 6.5% do not have insurance; 0.0% of children under 18 do not have insurance

Transportation: Commute: 92.0% car, 0.0% public transportation, 0.0% walk, 8.0% work from home; Mean travel time to work: 25.1 minutes

COTTEKILL (unincorporated postal area)
ZCTA: 12419

Covers a land area of 2.395 square miles and a water area of 0.021 square miles. Located at 41.86° N. Lat; 74.10° W. Long. Elevation is 253 feet.

Population: 629; Growth (since 2000): 99.7%; Density: 262.6 persons per square mile; Race: 89.2% White, 5.4% Black/African American, 0.0% Asian, 2.5% American Indian/Alaska Native, 0.0% Native Hawaiian/Other Pacific Islander, 2.9% Two or more races, 4.3% Hispanic of any race; Average household size: 2.27; Median age: 39.8; Age under 18: 13.4%; Age 65 and over: 16.5%; Males per 100 females: 96.2; Marriage status: 42.6% never married, 30.5% now married, 5.9% separated, 9.6% widowed, 17.4% divorced; Foreign born: 0.0%; Speak English only: 100.0%; With disability: 16.7%; Veterans: 5.9%; Ancestry: 30.4% German, 15.1% English, 11.9% Italian, 10.3% Irish, 10.2% French

Employment: 2.2% management, business, and financial, 10.8% computer, engineering, and science, 13.8% education, legal, community service, arts, and media, 18.3% healthcare practitioners, 14.9% service, 25.4% sales and office, 4.1% natural resources, construction, and maintenance, 10.4% production, transportation, and material moving

Income: Per capita: $24,538; Median household: $51,563; Average household: $55,713; Households with income of $100,000 or more: 13.4%; Poverty rate: 29.6%

Educational Attainment: High school diploma or higher: 95.4%; Bachelor's degree or higher: 35.9%; Graduate/professional degree or higher: 11.1%

School District(s)
Rondout Valley Central SD (KG-12)

    Enrollment: 2,008 . . . . (845) 687-2400

Housing: Homeownership rate: 50.2%; Median home value: $242,400; Median year structure built: 1956; Homeowner vacancy rate: 0.0%; Median selected monthly owner costs: $1,786 with a mortgage, $680 without a mortgage; Median gross rent: $974 per month; Rental vacancy rate: 0.0%

Health Insurance: 87.4% have insurance; 43.4% have private insurance; 51.5% have public insurance; 12.6% do not have insurance; 0.0% of children under 18 do not have insurance

Transportation: Commute: 98.1% car, 0.0% public transportation, 0.0% walk, 0.0% work from home; Mean travel time to work: 26.0 minutes

CRAGSMOOR (CDP).
Covers a land area of 4.351 square miles and a water area of 0 square miles. Located at 41.67° N. Lat; 74.39° W. Long. Elevation is 1,863 feet.

Population: 413; Growth (since 2000): -12.9%; Density: 94.9 persons per square mile; Race: 94.2% White, 0.0% Black/African American, 0.0% Asian, 0.0% American Indian/Alaska Native, 0.0% Native Hawaiian/Other Pacific Islander, 0.0% Two or more races, 5.8% Hispanic of any race; Average household size: 2.20; Median age: 53.7; Age under 18: 9.9%; Age 65 and over: 21.5%; Males per 100 females: 102.3; Marriage status: 23.9% never married, 55.4% now married, 2.4% separated, 7.5% widowed, 13.2% divorced; Foreign born: 5.3%; Speak English only: 94.4%; With disability: 17.7%; Veterans: 11.8%; Ancestry: 14.5% German, 14.0% Irish, 11.9% Italian, 11.6% American, 10.9% Polish

Employment: 7.8% management, business, and financial, 25.7% computer, engineering, and science, 23.3% education, legal, community service, arts, and media, 0.0% healthcare practitioners, 14.4% service, 7.0% sales and office, 10.5% natural resources, construction, and maintenance, 11.3% production, transportation, and material moving

Income: Per capita: $46,128; Median household: $93,500; Average household: $98,089; Households with income of $100,000 or more: 43.6%; Poverty rate: 6.8%

Educational Attainment: High school diploma or higher: 88.1%; Bachelor's degree or higher: 57.8%; Graduate/professional degree or higher: 31.7%

Housing: Homeownership rate: 90.4%; Median home value: $188,200; Median year structure built: 1949; Homeowner vacancy rate: 9.9%; Median selected monthly owner costs: $1,391 with a mortgage, $417 without a mortgage; Median gross rent: n/a per month; Rental vacancy rate: 0.0%

Health Insurance: 97.8% have insurance; 93.2% have private insurance; 23.7% have public insurance; 2.2% do not have insurance; 0.0% of children under 18 do not have insurance

Transportation: Commute: 62.1% car, 6.5% public transportation, 0.0% walk, 31.5% work from home; Mean travel time to work: 30.4 minutes

DENNING (town).
Covers a land area of 105.666 square miles and a water area of 0.099 square miles. Located at 41.96° N. Lat; 74.48° W. Long. Elevation is 1,959 feet.

Population: 535; Growth (since 2000): 3.7%; Density: 5.1 persons per square mile; Race: 94.6% White, 0.0% Black/African American, 1.3% Asian, 0.0% American Indian/Alaska Native, 0.0% Native Hawaiian/Other Pacific Islander, 0.0% Two or more races, 4.3% Hispanic of any race; Average household size: 2.46; Median age: 49.1; Age under 18: 20.9%; Age 65 and over: 22.4%; Males per 100 females: 106.4; Marriage status: 28.3% never married, 64.4% now married, 2.0% separated, 2.9% widowed, 4.4% divorced; Foreign born: 5.6%; Speak English only: 94.9%; With disability: 15.0%; Veterans: 7.3%; Ancestry: 29.0% German, 20.7% English, 19.8% Irish, 13.6% Italian, 10.7% Polish

Employment: 21.6% management, business, and financial, 4.3% computer, engineering, and science, 17.7% education, legal, community service, arts, and media, 6.9% healthcare practitioners, 25.4% service, 7.3% sales and office, 12.5% natural resources, construction, and maintenance, 4.3% production, transportation, and material moving

Income: Per capita: $32,478; Median household: $77,969; Average household: $83,240; Households with income of $100,000 or more: 29.3%; Poverty rate: 8.9%

Educational Attainment: High school diploma or higher: 94.9%; Bachelor's degree or higher: 44.4%; Graduate/professional degree or higher: 24.9%

Housing: Homeownership rate: 77.1%; Median home value: $214,300; Median year structure built: 1971; Homeowner vacancy rate: 7.1%; Median selected monthly owner costs: $1,568 with a mortgage, $564 without a mortgage; Median gross rent: $1,143 per month; Rental vacancy rate: 0.0%

Health Insurance: 97.6% have insurance; 80.7% have private insurance; 34.8% have public insurance; 2.4% do not have insurance; 0.0% of children under 18 do not have insurance

Transportation: Commute: 77.1% car, 3.5% public transportation, 7.9% walk, 9.7% work from home; Mean travel time to work: 26.3 minutes

EAST KINGSTON (CDP). Covers a land area of 0.674 square miles and a water area of 0.022 square miles. Located at 41.95° N. Lat; 73.97° W. Long. Elevation is 151 feet.

Population: 618; Growth (since 2000): 116.8%; Density: 917.1 persons per square mile; Race: 89.5% White, 5.8% Black/African American, 0.0% Asian, 0.0% American Indian/Alaska Native, 0.0% Native Hawaiian/Other Pacific Islander, 4.7% Two or more races, 21.8% Hispanic of any race; Average household size: 3.00; Median age: 33.9; Age under 18: 33.0%; Age 65 and over: 10.2%; Males per 100 females: 110.7; Marriage status: 33.0% never married, 44.7% now married, 11.1% separated, 11.1% widowed, 11.3% divorced; Foreign born: 0.0%; Speak English only: 100.0%; With disability: 19.3%; Veterans: 9.2%; Ancestry: 49.8% Italian, 27.0% Irish, 16.8% English, 15.4% Dutch, 6.5% German

Employment: 13.7% management, business, and financial, 0.0% computer, engineering, and science, 4.0% education, legal, community service, arts, and media, 0.0% healthcare practitioners, 30.9% service, 13.3% sales and office, 34.5% natural resources, construction, and maintenance, 3.6% production, transportation, and material moving

Income: Per capita: $15,085; Median household: $39,762; Average household: $44,226; Households with income of $100,000 or more: n/a; Poverty rate: 33.2%

Educational Attainment: High school diploma or higher: 92.8%; Bachelor's degree or higher: 2.6%; Graduate/professional degree or higher: n/a

Housing: Homeownership rate: 56.8%; Median home value: $145,500; Median year structure built: Before 1940; Homeowner vacancy rate: 0.0%; Median selected monthly owner costs: $1,150 with a mortgage, $318 without a mortgage; Median gross rent: $1,115 per month; Rental vacancy rate: 0.0%

Health Insurance: 88.7% have insurance; 47.1% have private insurance; 51.8% have public insurance; 11.3% do not have insurance; 14.7% of children under 18 do not have insurance

Transportation: Commute: 100.0% car, 0.0% public transportation, 0.0% walk, 0.0% work from home; Mean travel time to work: 26.6 minutes

ELLENVILLE (village). Covers a land area of 8.725 square miles and a water area of 0.087 square miles. Located at 41.71° N. Lat; 74.36° W. Long. Elevation is 338 feet.

History: Incorporated 1856.

Population: 4,082; Growth (since 2000): -1.2%; Density: 467.9 persons per square mile; Race: 65.1% White, 10.5% Black/African American, 5.6% Asian, 0.0% American Indian/Alaska Native, 0.0% Native Hawaiian/Other Pacific Islander, 9.5% Two or more races, 28.4% Hispanic of any race; Average household size: 2.56; Median age: 37.0; Age under 18: 25.7%; Age 65 and over: 11.5%; Males per 100 females: 94.1; Marriage status: 35.4% never married, 50.2% now married, 2.5% separated, 5.1% widowed, 9.3% divorced; Foreign born: 13.4%; Speak English only: 72.8%; With disability: 11.8%; Veterans: 3.4%; Ancestry: 19.4% Irish, 11.0% American, 8.5% Italian, 7.8% Polish, 6.5% Dutch

Employment: 4.1% management, business, and financial, 0.0% computer, engineering, and science, 10.8% education, legal, community service, arts, and media, 0.9% healthcare practitioners, 34.3% service, 23.0% sales and office, 13.2% natural resources, construction, and maintenance, 13.7% production, transportation, and material moving

Income: Per capita: $21,663; Median household: $45,531; Average household: $52,206; Households with income of $100,000 or more: 12.2%; Poverty rate: 18.9%

Educational Attainment: High school diploma or higher: 79.8%; Bachelor's degree or higher: 14.7%; Graduate/professional degree or higher: 6.9%

School District(s)

Ellenville Central SD (PK-12)
    Enrollment: 1,692 . . . . (845) 647-0100

Housing: Homeownership rate: 45.6%; Median home value: $123,600; Median year structure built: 1954; Homeowner vacancy rate: 0.0%; Median selected monthly owner costs: $1,806 with a mortgage, $535 without a mortgage; Median gross rent: $803 per month; Rental vacancy rate: 0.0%

Health Insurance: 87.4% have insurance; 48.4% have private insurance; 48.7% have public insurance; 12.6% do not have insurance; 4.9% of children under 18 do not have insurance

Hospitals: Ellenville Regional Hospital (35 beds)

Safety: Violent crime rate: 44.6 per 10,000 population; Property crime rate: 337.3 per 10,000 population

Newspapers: Shawangunk Journal (weekly circulation 3,500)

Transportation: Commute: 85.6% car, 2.9% public transportation, 7.5% walk, 2.9% work from home; Mean travel time to work: 27.8 minutes

Additional Information Contacts

Village of Ellenville . . . . (845) 647-7080
    http://villageofellenville.sharepoint.com/Pages/default.aspx

ESOPUS (town). Covers a land area of 37.312 square miles and a water area of 4.628 square miles. Located at 41.83° N. Lat; 73.99° W. Long. Elevation is 125 feet.

History: Seat of Mt. St. Alphonsus Theological Seminary. John Burroughs lived near here. Town was formed in 1811, and was partly annexed by Kingston in 1818.

Population: 8,886; Growth (since 2000): -4.8%; Density: 238.2 persons per square mile; Race: 92.6% White, 1.3% Black/African American, 0.6% Asian, 0.0% American Indian/Alaska Native, 0.0% Native Hawaiian/Other Pacific Islander, 2.9% Two or more races, 5.7% Hispanic of any race; Average household size: 2.38; Median age: 43.3; Age under 18: 18.0%; Age 65 and over: 17.8%; Males per 100 females: 93.4; Marriage status: 30.5% never married, 47.6% now married, 3.0% separated, 7.2% widowed, 14.7% divorced; Foreign born: 7.1%; Speak English only: 93.1%; With disability: 13.9%; Veterans: 4.5%; Ancestry: 28.0% Irish, 23.3% German, 18.5% Italian, 8.2% American, 6.3% Polish

Employment: 13.8% management, business, and financial, 3.0% computer, engineering, and science, 11.2% education, legal, community service, arts, and media, 7.6% healthcare practitioners, 17.3% service, 29.2% sales and office, 10.5% natural resources, construction, and maintenance, 7.3% production, transportation, and material moving

Income: Per capita: $33,443; Median household: $69,777; Average household: $84,185; Households with income of $100,000 or more: 27.0%; Poverty rate: 11.9%

Educational Attainment: High school diploma or higher: 89.9%; Bachelor's degree or higher: 26.9%; Graduate/professional degree or higher: 11.6%

Housing: Homeownership rate: 73.6%; Median home value: $198,500; Median year structure built: 1965; Homeowner vacancy rate: 1.7%; Median selected monthly owner costs: $1,865 with a mortgage, $754 without a mortgage; Median gross rent: $1,156 per month; Rental vacancy rate: 5.7%

Health Insurance: 94.3% have insurance; 68.9% have private insurance; 38.4% have public insurance; 5.7% do not have insurance; 6.1% of children under 18 do not have insurance

Transportation: Commute: 82.2% car, 2.1% public transportation, 7.2% walk, 8.2% work from home; Mean travel time to work: 23.7 minutes

Additional Information Contacts

Town of Esopus. . . . . (845) 331-3709
    http://www.esopus.com

GARDINER (CDP). Covers a land area of 3.863 square miles and a water area of 0 square miles. Located at 41.68° N. Lat; 74.15° W. Long. Elevation is 315 feet.

Population: 773; Growth (since 2000): -9.7%; Density: 200.1 persons per square mile; Race: 84.3% White, 0.0% Black/African American, 0.0% Asian, 0.0% American Indian/Alaska Native, 0.0% Native Hawaiian/Other Pacific Islander, 12.8% Two or more races, 8.0% Hispanic of any race; Average household size: 2.63; Median age: 43.6; Age under 18: 21.9%; Age 65 and over: 18.4%; Males per 100 females: 95.5; Marriage status: 18.4% never married, 73.4% now married, 0.0% separated, 3.5% widowed, 4.7% divorced; Foreign born: 0.0%; Speak English only: 100.0%; With disability: 12.7%; Veterans: 2.5%; Ancestry: 26.9% Irish, 24.1% German, 13.5% Dutch, 13.5% Italian, 11.3% English

Employment: 19.0% management, business, and financial, 6.7% computer, engineering, and science, 16.5% education, legal, community service, arts, and media, 4.4% healthcare practitioners, 8.3% service, 25.5% sales and office, 14.7% natural resources, construction, and maintenance, 5.0% production, transportation, and material moving

Income: Per capita: $29,894; Median household: $71,098; Average household: $76,393; Households with income of $100,000 or more: 19.7%; Poverty rate: n/a

Educational Attainment: High school diploma or higher: 86.6%; Bachelor's degree or higher: 40.6%; Graduate/professional degree or higher: 29.1%

Housing: Homeownership rate: 83.3%; Median home value: $221,000; Median year structure built: 1970; Homeowner vacancy rate: 0.0%; Median selected monthly owner costs: $1,914 with a mortgage, n/a without a mortgage; Median gross rent: n/a per month; Rental vacancy rate: 0.0%

Health Insurance: 93.0% have insurance; 81.8% have private insurance; 29.2% have public insurance; 7.0% do not have insurance; 0.0% of children under 18 do not have insurance
Transportation: Commute: 84.4% car, 0.0% public transportation, 11.1% walk, 4.5% work from home; Mean travel time to work: 16.5 minutes

GARDINER (town). Covers a land area of 43.435 square miles and a water area of 0.510 square miles. Located at 41.69° N. Lat; 74.19° W. Long. Elevation is 315 feet.

History: A 17th-century gristmill is here.
Population: 5,671; Growth (since 2000): 8.3%; Density: 130.6 persons per square mile; Race: 94.5% White, 2.6% Black/African American, 0.0% Asian, 0.0% American Indian/Alaska Native, 0.0% Native Hawaiian/Other Pacific Islander, 2.0% Two or more races, 6.7% Hispanic of any race; Average household size: 2.63; Median age: 44.4; Age under 18: 23.8%; Age 65 and over: 18.7%; Males per 100 females: 100.7; Marriage status: 27.0% never married, 61.9% now married, 1.1% separated, 1.8% widowed, 9.3% divorced; Foreign born: 6.3%; Speak English only: 94.2%; With disability: 12.9%; Veterans: 5.9%; Ancestry: 25.4% Irish, 19.0% German, 16.4% Italian, 6.9% American, 6.4% Polish
Employment: 23.8% management, business, and financial, 8.8% computer, engineering, and science, 15.9% education, legal, community service, arts, and media, 6.4% healthcare practitioners, 13.9% service, 13.6% sales and office, 5.5% natural resources, construction, and maintenance, 12.0% production, transportation, and material moving
Income: Per capita: $39,451; Median household: $71,853; Average household: $102,535; Households with income of $100,000 or more: 35.9%; Poverty rate: 8.0%
Educational Attainment: High school diploma or higher: 94.9%; Bachelor's degree or higher: 48.8%; Graduate/professional degree or higher: 25.0%
Housing: Homeownership rate: 79.2%; Median home value: $319,600; Median year structure built: 1980; Homeowner vacancy rate: 0.0%; Median selected monthly owner costs: $2,212 with a mortgage, $978 without a mortgage; Median gross rent: $1,192 per month; Rental vacancy rate: 0.0%
Health Insurance: 95.7% have insurance; 82.7% have private insurance; 26.3% have public insurance; 4.3% do not have insurance; 1.6% of children under 18 do not have insurance
Transportation: Commute: 86.1% car, 2.9% public transportation, 1.8% walk, 7.3% work from home; Mean travel time to work: 29.6 minutes
Additional Information Contacts
Town of Gardiner. . . . . (845) 255-9675
  http://www.townofgardiner.org

GLASCO (CDP). Covers a land area of 1.762 square miles and a water area of 0.683 square miles. Located at 42.05° N. Lat; 73.95° W. Long. Elevation is 151 feet.

Population: 2,646; Growth (since 2000): 56.4%; Density: 1,501.3 persons per square mile; Race: 84.7% White, 5.6% Black/African American, 3.3% Asian, 0.6% American Indian/Alaska Native, 0.0% Native Hawaiian/Other Pacific Islander, 2.0% Two or more races, 10.6% Hispanic of any race; Average household size: 2.81; Median age: 39.8; Age under 18: 27.4%; Age 65 and over: 17.8%; Males per 100 females: 82.0; Marriage status: 42.9% never married, 39.4% now married, 1.7% separated, 7.6% widowed, 10.1% divorced; Foreign born: 12.1%; Speak English only: 88.1%; With disability: 16.2%; Veterans: 8.3%; Ancestry: 22.6% Italian, 19.5% German, 19.5% Irish, 8.7% Dutch, 8.0% Hungarian
Employment: 14.7% management, business, and financial, 1.9% computer, engineering, and science, 12.8% education, legal, community service, arts, and media, 5.2% healthcare practitioners, 28.9% service, 17.0% sales and office, 6.6% natural resources, construction, and maintenance, 13.0% production, transportation, and material moving
Income: Per capita: $21,421; Median household: $50,000; Average household: $57,653; Households with income of $100,000 or more: 20.5%; Poverty rate: 16.3%
Educational Attainment: High school diploma or higher: 80.0%; Bachelor's degree or higher: 17.2%; Graduate/professional degree or higher: 7.1%
School District(s)
Saugerties Central SD (KG-12)
  Enrollment: 2,613 . . . . (845) 247-6501
Housing: Homeownership rate: 63.5%; Median home value: $221,800; Median year structure built: 1976; Homeowner vacancy rate: 4.4%; Median selected monthly owner costs: $1,962 with a mortgage, $791 without a

mortgage; Median gross rent: $1,150 per month; Rental vacancy rate: 0.0%
Health Insurance: 93.9% have insurance; 63.8% have private insurance; 45.1% have public insurance; 6.1% do not have insurance; 0.0% of children under 18 do not have insurance
Transportation: Commute: 96.5% car, 0.0% public transportation, 0.7% walk, 2.3% work from home; Mean travel time to work: 23.4 minutes

GLENFORD (unincorporated postal area)
ZCTA: 12433
Covers a land area of 3.820 square miles and a water area of 0.086 square miles. Located at 42.00° N. Lat; 74.16° W. Long. Elevation is 659 feet.
Population: 548; Growth (since 2000): 35.6%; Density: 143.5 persons per square mile; Race: 84.5% White, 1.8% Black/African American, 2.7% Asian, 0.0% American Indian/Alaska Native, 0.0% Native Hawaiian/Other Pacific Islander, 7.5% Two or more races, 2.7% Hispanic of any race; Average household size: 2.32; Median age: 49.0; Age under 18: 15.5%; Age 65 and over: 25.2%; Males per 100 females: 98.8; Marriage status: 16.8% never married, 74.7% now married, 2.6% separated, 4.5% widowed, 3.9% divorced; Foreign born: 7.8%; Speak English only: 88.5%; With disability: 17.3%; Veterans: 16.8%; Ancestry: 27.6% Irish, 17.3% English, 14.1% Welsh, 13.9% German, 9.7% Polish
Employment: 9.1% management, business, and financial, 0.0% computer, engineering, and science, 43.2% education, legal, community service, arts, and media, 9.1% healthcare practitioners, 6.1% service, 30.3% sales and office, 2.3% natural resources, construction, and maintenance, 0.0% production, transportation, and material moving
Income: Per capita: $54,752; Median household: $138,134; Average household: $137,012; Households with income of $100,000 or more: 64.4%; Poverty rate: 4.4%
Educational Attainment: High school diploma or higher: 100.0%; Bachelor's degree or higher: 73.0%; Graduate/professional degree or higher: 41.6%
Housing: Homeownership rate: 81.4%; Median home value: $360,000; Median year structure built: 1980; Homeowner vacancy rate: 0.0%; Median selected monthly owner costs: $3,087 with a mortgage, $581 without a mortgage; Median gross rent: n/a per month; Rental vacancy rate: 0.0%
Health Insurance: 88.5% have insurance; 76.5% have private insurance; 46.7% have public insurance; 11.5% do not have insurance; 0.0% of children under 18 do not have insurance
Transportation: Commute: 83.5% car, 2.6% public transportation, 0.0% walk, 13.9% work from home; Mean travel time to work: 22.2 minutes

GREENFIELD PARK (unincorporated postal area)
ZCTA: 12435
Covers a land area of 9.957 square miles and a water area of 0.077 square miles. Located at 41.73° N. Lat; 74.51° W. Long. Elevation is 873 feet.
Population: 327; Growth (since 2000): 25.3%; Density: 32.8 persons per square mile; Race: 100.0% White, 0.0% Black/African American, 0.0% Asian, 0.0% American Indian/Alaska Native, 0.0% Native Hawaiian/Other Pacific Islander, 0.0% Two or more races, 6.4% Hispanic of any race; Average household size: 2.95; Median age: 47.1; Age under 18: 18.7%; Age 65 and over: 11.3%; Males per 100 females: 109.0; Marriage status: 24.8% never married, 51.1% now married, 0.0% separated, 8.6% widowed, 15.4% divorced; Foreign born: 23.5%; Speak English only: 71.6%; With disability: 13.8%; Veterans: 10.5%; Ancestry: 14.7% Albanian, 11.0% German, 10.4% English, 5.8% Irish, 5.5% Italian
Employment: 3.7% management, business, and financial, 0.0% computer, engineering, and science, 16.5% education, legal, community service, arts, and media, 0.6% healthcare practitioners, 27.4% service, 12.2% sales and office, 14.0% natural resources, construction, and maintenance, 25.6% production, transportation, and material moving
Income: Per capita: $21,795; Median household: $58,958; Average household: $61,810; Households with income of $100,000 or more: 25.2%; Poverty rate: 9.5%
Educational Attainment: High school diploma or higher: 96.9%; Bachelor's degree or higher: 22.7%; Graduate/professional degree or higher: 7.4%
Housing: Homeownership rate: 60.4%; Median home value: $259,000; Median year structure built: 1969; Homeowner vacancy rate: 0.0%; Median selected monthly owner costs: $1,241 with a mortgage, $0

without a mortgage; Median gross rent: $994 per month; Rental vacancy rate: 0.0%
Health Insurance: 93.6% have insurance; 63.9% have private insurance; 37.3% have public insurance; 6.4% do not have insurance; 0.0% of children under 18 do not have insurance
Transportation: Commute: 100.0% car, 0.0% public transportation, 0.0% walk, 0.0% work from home; Mean travel time to work: 22.7 minutes

HARDENBURGH (town). Covers a land area of 80.787 square miles and a water area of 0.235 square miles. Located at 42.05° N. Lat; 74.62° W. Long.
Population: 233; Growth (since 2000): 12.0%; Density: 2.9 persons per square mile; Race: 97.9% White, 0.0% Black/African American, 0.4% Asian, 0.0% American Indian/Alaska Native, 0.0% Native Hawaiian/Other Pacific Islander, 1.7% Two or more races, 0.0% Hispanic of any race; Average household size: 2.08; Median age: 55.9; Age under 18: 17.6%; Age 65 and over: 23.6%; Males per 100 females: 116.4; Marriage status: 22.5% never married, 63.5% now married, 4.0% separated, 5.5% widowed, 8.5% divorced; Foreign born: 0.4%; Speak English only: 96.9%; With disability: 21.0%; Veterans: 11.5%; Ancestry: 36.1% German, 18.0% Italian, 15.5% Irish, 12.0% English, 9.9% Scottish
Employment: 33.9% management, business, and financial, 0.0% computer, engineering, and science, 14.7% education, legal, community service, arts, and media, 5.5% healthcare practitioners, 28.4% service, 4.6% sales and office, 5.5% natural resources, construction, and maintenance, 7.3% production, transportation, and material moving
Income: Per capita: $33,975; Median household: $43,750; Average household: $71,379; Households with income of $100,000 or more: 27.7%; Poverty rate: 22.3%
Educational Attainment: High school diploma or higher: 90.7%; Bachelor's degree or higher: 38.3%; Graduate/professional degree or higher: 12.0%
Housing: Homeownership rate: 68.8%; Median home value: $222,900; Median year structure built: 1972; Homeowner vacancy rate: 6.9%; Median selected monthly owner costs: $1,406 with a mortgage, n/a without a mortgage; Median gross rent: $763 per month; Rental vacancy rate: 0.0%
Health Insurance: 94.4% have insurance; 60.5% have private insurance; 48.1% have public insurance; 5.6% do not have insurance; 9.5% of children under 18 do not have insurance
Transportation: Commute: 50.5% car, 1.0% public transportation, 39.8% walk, 5.8% work from home; Mean travel time to work: 32.9 minutes

HIGH FALLS (CDP). Covers a land area of 1.196 square miles and a water area of 0 square miles. Located at 41.83° N. Lat; 74.12° W. Long. Elevation is 161 feet.
Population: 794; Growth (since 2000): 26.6%; Density: 663.8 persons per square mile; Race: 96.5% White, 0.3% Black/African American, 2.4% Asian, 0.1% American Indian/Alaska Native, 0.0% Native Hawaiian/Other Pacific Islander, 0.6% Two or more races, 0.5% Hispanic of any race; Average household size: 2.47; Median age: 45.4; Age under 18: 16.8%; Age 65 and over: 18.4%; Males per 100 females: 93.5; Marriage status: 42.2% never married, 49.5% now married, 8.4% separated, 2.5% widowed, 5.8% divorced; Foreign born: 0.0%; Speak English only: 99.7%; With disability: 18.1%; Veterans: 1.4%; Ancestry: 34.0% Irish, 23.9% German, 21.2% Italian, 11.2% Polish, 10.2% Scottish
Employment: 4.7% management, business, and financial, 0.0% computer, engineering, and science, 30.7% education, legal, community service, arts, and media, 0.0% healthcare practitioners, 28.4% service, 21.7% sales and office, 5.7% natural resources, construction, and maintenance, 8.8% production, transportation, and material moving
Income: Per capita: $24,762; Median household: n/a; Average household: $54,441; Households with income of $100,000 or more: 11.9%; Poverty rate: 26.2%
Educational Attainment: High school diploma or higher: 93.0%; Bachelor's degree or higher: 21.0%; Graduate/professional degree or higher: 9.4%
Housing: Homeownership rate: 66.1%; Median home value: $234,100; Median year structure built: 1954; Homeowner vacancy rate: 0.0%; Median selected monthly owner costs: $2,089 with a mortgage, n/a without a mortgage; Median gross rent: $1,704 per month; Rental vacancy rate: 0.0%
Health Insurance: 85.9% have insurance; 65.8% have private insurance; 28.4% have public insurance; 14.1% do not have insurance; 0.0% of children under 18 do not have insurance

Transportation: Commute: 95.3% car, 0.0% public transportation, 0.0% walk, 4.7% work from home; Mean travel time to work: 21.7 minutes

HIGHLAND (CDP). Covers a land area of 4.686 square miles and a water area of 0.390 square miles. Located at 41.72° N. Lat; 73.96° W. Long. Elevation is 174 feet.
Population: 5,375; Growth (since 2000): 6.2%; Density: 1,147.1 persons per square mile; Race: 87.6% White, 6.1% Black/African American, 1.0% Asian, 0.0% American Indian/Alaska Native, 0.0% Native Hawaiian/Other Pacific Islander, 3.1% Two or more races, 15.8% Hispanic of any race; Average household size: 2.43; Median age: 41.4; Age under 18: 20.5%; Age 65 and over: 17.4%; Males per 100 females: 88.7; Marriage status: 31.8% never married, 49.7% now married, 2.2% separated, 7.4% widowed, 11.1% divorced; Foreign born: 4.8%; Speak English only: 94.3%; With disability: 10.9%; Veterans: 5.4%; Ancestry: 22.8% Italian, 14.3% Irish, 12.0% German, 7.2% Polish, 6.0% English
Employment: 13.2% management, business, and financial, 10.4% computer, engineering, and science, 12.3% education, legal, community service, arts, and media, 12.2% healthcare practitioners, 19.0% service, 22.1% sales and office, 7.5% natural resources, construction, and maintenance, 3.4% production, transportation, and material moving
Income: Per capita: $30,321; Median household: $66,010; Average household: $75,314; Households with income of $100,000 or more: 24.6%; Poverty rate: 13.9%
Educational Attainment: High school diploma or higher: 90.3%; Bachelor's degree or higher: 30.4%; Graduate/professional degree or higher: 10.0%

School District(s)
Highland Central SD (KG-12)
    Enrollment: 1,800 . . . . (845) 691-1014
Housing: Homeownership rate: 61.4%; Median home value: $220,800; Median year structure built: 1975; Homeowner vacancy rate: 3.2%; Median selected monthly owner costs: $2,043 with a mortgage, $845 without a mortgage; Median gross rent: $1,192 per month; Rental vacancy rate: 13.6%
Health Insurance: 95.7% have insurance; 70.2% have private insurance; 38.9% have public insurance; 4.3% do not have insurance; 1.1% of children under 18 do not have insurance
Transportation: Commute: 89.9% car, 0.7% public transportation, 0.0% walk, 7.3% work from home; Mean travel time to work: 27.9 minutes

HIGHMOUNT (unincorporated postal area)
ZCTA: 12441
    Covers a land area of 6.327 square miles and a water area of 0.001 square miles. Located at 42.13° N. Lat; 74.51° W. Long. Elevation is 1,857 feet.
Population: 25; Growth (since 2000): n/a; Density: 4.0 persons per square mile; Race: 100.0% White, 0.0% Black/African American, 0.0% Asian, 0.0% American Indian/Alaska Native, 0.0% Native Hawaiian/Other Pacific Islander, 0.0% Two or more races, 0.0% Hispanic of any race; Average household size: 2.08; Median age: 56.8; Age under 18: 0.0%; Age 65 and over: 36.0%; Males per 100 females: 119.2; Marriage status: 0.0% never married, 100.0% now married, 0.0% separated, 0.0% widowed, 0.0% divorced; Foreign born: 0.0%; Speak English only: 100.0%; With disability: 0.0%; Veterans: 16.0%; Ancestry: 32.0% English, 32.0% German, 32.0% Norwegian, 32.0% Swedish
Employment: 100.0% management, business, and financial, 0.0% computer, engineering, and science, 0.0% education, legal, community service, arts, and media, 0.0% healthcare practitioners, 0.0% service, 0.0% sales and office, 0.0% natural resources, construction, and maintenance, 0.0% production, transportation, and material moving
Income: Per capita: $51,792; Median household: n/a; Average household: n/a; Households with income of $100,000 or more: 33.3%; Poverty rate: n/a
Educational Attainment: High school diploma or higher: 100.0%; Bachelor's degree or higher: 100.0%; Graduate/professional degree or higher: 68.0%
Housing: Homeownership rate: 100.0%; Median home value: n/a; Median year structure built: 1993; Homeowner vacancy rate: 0.0%; Median selected monthly owner costs: $0 with a mortgage, $0 without a mortgage; Median gross rent: n/a per month; Rental vacancy rate: 0.0%
Health Insurance: 100.0% have insurance; 80.0% have private insurance; 36.0% have public insurance; 0.0% do not have insurance; 0.0% of children under 18 do not have insurance

Transportation: Commute: 0.0% car, 0.0% public transportation, 0.0% walk, 100.0% work from home; Mean travel time to work: 0.0 minutes

HILLSIDE (CDP).
Covers a land area of 0.825 square miles and a water area of 0.003 square miles. Located at 41.92° N. Lat; 74.03° W. Long. Elevation is 318 feet.
Population: 915; Growth (since 2000): 3.7%; Density: 1,108.8 persons per square mile; Race: 97.7% White, 2.3% Black/African American, 0.0% Asian, 0.0% American Indian/Alaska Native, 0.0% Native Hawaiian/Other Pacific Islander, 0.0% Two or more races, 3.5% Hispanic of any race; Average household size: 2.56; Median age: 51.5; Age under 18: 20.5%; Age 65 and over: 27.2%; Males per 100 females: 98.4; Marriage status: 18.6% never married, 65.0% now married, 0.0% separated, 10.4% widowed, 6.0% divorced; Foreign born: 9.1%; Speak English only: 88.4%; With disability: 13.7%; Veterans: 9.9%; Ancestry: 25.4% German, 25.4% Italian, 23.0% Irish, 10.5% English, 7.7% Dutch
Employment: 26.6% management, business, and financial, 6.8% computer, engineering, and science, 23.8% education, legal, community service, arts, and media, 9.8% healthcare practitioners, 12.9% service, 11.9% sales and office, 6.8% natural resources, construction, and maintenance, 1.4% production, transportation, and material moving
Income: Per capita: $52,339; Median household: $100,568; Average household: $130,714; Households with income of $100,000 or more: 50.7%; Poverty rate: 2.1%
Educational Attainment: High school diploma or higher: 90.0%; Bachelor's degree or higher: 51.1%; Graduate/professional degree or higher: 34.1%
Housing: Homeownership rate: 100.0%; Median home value: $292,200; Median year structure built: 1967; Homeowner vacancy rate: 0.0%; Median selected monthly owner costs: $2,222 with a mortgage, $980 without a mortgage; Median gross rent: n/a per month; Rental vacancy rate: 0.0%
Health Insurance: 98.1% have insurance; 82.1% have private insurance; 32.8% have public insurance; 1.9% do not have insurance; 0.0% of children under 18 do not have insurance
Transportation: Commute: 87.0% car, 3.8% public transportation, 4.5% walk, 3.3% work from home; Mean travel time to work: 24.0 minutes

HURLEY (CDP).
Covers a land area of 5.486 square miles and a water area of 0.032 square miles. Located at 41.91° N. Lat; 74.06° W. Long. Elevation is 197 feet.
Population: 3,386; Growth (since 2000): -4.9%; Density: 617.2 persons per square mile; Race: 92.4% White, 2.5% Black/African American, 1.8% Asian, 0.2% American Indian/Alaska Native, 0.0% Native Hawaiian/Other Pacific Islander, 1.9% Two or more races, 4.2% Hispanic of any race; Average household size: 2.33; Median age: 50.8; Age under 18: 15.5%; Age 65 and over: 25.0%; Males per 100 females: 95.7; Marriage status: 24.6% never married, 59.6% now married, 2.9% separated, 6.7% widowed, 9.0% divorced; Foreign born: 5.4%; Speak English only: 94.3%; With disability: 11.3%; Veterans: 6.4%; Ancestry: 22.8% German, 22.1% Italian, 19.3% Irish, 12.5% English, 7.3% Polish
Employment: 12.7% management, business, and financial, 2.8% computer, engineering, and science, 16.3% education, legal, community service, arts, and media, 5.7% healthcare practitioners, 21.6% service, 27.2% sales and office, 6.8% natural resources, construction, and maintenance, 6.9% production, transportation, and material moving
Income: Per capita: $47,921; Median household: $90,529; Average household: $110,700; Households with income of $100,000 or more: 43.3%; Poverty rate: 7.7%
Educational Attainment: High school diploma or higher: 95.8%; Bachelor's degree or higher: 42.8%; Graduate/professional degree or higher: 20.3%

School District(s)
Kingston City SD (PK-12)
    Enrollment: 6,445 . . . . (845) 943-3003
Housing: Homeownership rate: 88.7%; Median home value: $236,400; Median year structure built: 1958; Homeowner vacancy rate: 0.8%; Median selected monthly owner costs: $1,884 with a mortgage, $729 without a mortgage; Median gross rent: $1,168 per month; Rental vacancy rate: 0.0%
Health Insurance: 97.3% have insurance; 80.6% have private insurance; 38.6% have public insurance; 2.7% do not have insurance; 2.6% of children under 18 do not have insurance
Transportation: Commute: 90.1% car, 2.4% public transportation, 0.0% walk, 7.1% work from home; Mean travel time to work: 23.7 minutes

HURLEY (town).
Covers a land area of 29.911 square miles and a water area of 6.056 square miles. Located at 41.96° N. Lat; 74.12° W. Long. Elevation is 197 feet.
History: In 1662, Peter Stuyvesant, Dutch Governor of Niew Amsterdam, established the village of Niew Dorp on the site of an earlier Native American Settlement. On June 7, 1663, during the Esopus Wars, the village was attacked and destroyed. On September 17, 1669, the abandoned village was resettled and renamed Hurley after Francis Lovelace, Baron Hurley of Ireland.
Population: 6,168; Growth (since 2000): -6.0%; Density: 206.2 persons per square mile; Race: 94.2% White, 1.5% Black/African American, 0.5% Asian, 0.1% American Indian/Alaska Native, 0.0% Native Hawaiian/Other Pacific Islander, 3.1% Two or more races, 2.7% Hispanic of any race; Average household size: 2.21; Median age: 52.6; Age under 18: 15.0%; Age 65 and over: 26.0%; Males per 100 females: 92.9; Marriage status: 21.9% never married, 57.5% now married, 2.7% separated, 7.5% widowed, 13.1% divorced; Foreign born: 4.1%; Speak English only: 96.2%; With disability: 12.2%; Veterans: 7.7%; Ancestry: 23.2% Irish, 22.7% German, 18.4% Italian, 12.8% English, 7.4% Polish
Employment: 11.1% management, business, and financial, 3.9% computer, engineering, and science, 23.3% education, legal, community service, arts, and media, 7.6% healthcare practitioners, 16.3% service, 25.1% sales and office, 6.5% natural resources, construction, and maintenance, 6.1% production, transportation, and material moving
Income: Per capita: $46,241; Median household: $76,696; Average household: $101,828; Households with income of $100,000 or more: 38.7%; Poverty rate: 10.4%
Educational Attainment: High school diploma or higher: 95.7%; Bachelor's degree or higher: 43.4%; Graduate/professional degree or higher: 25.2%

School District(s)
Kingston City SD (PK-12)
    Enrollment: 6,445 . . . . (845) 943-3003
Housing: Homeownership rate: 91.2%; Median home value: $235,000; Median year structure built: 1962; Homeowner vacancy rate: 0.0%; Median selected monthly owner costs: $1,821 with a mortgage, $674 without a mortgage; Median gross rent: $1,184 per month; Rental vacancy rate: 7.4%
Health Insurance: 94.9% have insurance; 77.3% have private insurance; 41.9% have public insurance; 5.1% do not have insurance; 4.4% of children under 18 do not have insurance
Transportation: Commute: 85.3% car, 3.7% public transportation, 1.3% walk, 8.7% work from home; Mean travel time to work: 25.9 minutes
Additional Information Contacts
Town of Hurley . . . . (845) 331-7474
    http://townofhurley.org/content

KERHONKSON (CDP).
Covers a land area of 5.277 square miles and a water area of 0.018 square miles. Located at 41.78° N. Lat; 74.30° W. Long. Elevation is 262 feet.
Population: 2,151; Growth (since 2000): 24.2%; Density: 407.6 persons per square mile; Race: 91.4% White, 4.6% Black/African American, 0.0% Asian, 0.0% American Indian/Alaska Native, 0.0% Native Hawaiian/Other Pacific Islander, 0.9% Two or more races, 6.6% Hispanic of any race; Average household size: 3.08; Median age: 33.6; Age under 18: 25.1%; Age 65 and over: 17.2%; Males per 100 females: 97.7; Marriage status: 35.1% never married, 41.1% now married, 1.3% separated, 9.7% widowed, 14.1% divorced; Foreign born: 7.2%; Speak English only: 89.8%; With disability: 20.6%; Veterans: 6.1%; Ancestry: 29.5% Norwegian, 25.6% Irish, 19.3% German, 11.0% Danish, 8.6% Italian
Employment: 2.0% management, business, and financial, 0.0% computer, engineering, and science, 10.2% education, legal, community service, arts, and media, 3.2% healthcare practitioners, 45.9% service, 22.7% sales and office, 13.7% natural resources, construction, and maintenance, 2.3% production, transportation, and material moving
Income: Per capita: $17,481; Median household: $45,833; Average household: $50,746; Households with income of $100,000 or more: 9.7%; Poverty rate: 12.0%
Educational Attainment: High school diploma or higher: 77.2%; Bachelor's degree or higher: 13.5%; Graduate/professional degree or higher: 6.2%

School District(s)
Rondout Valley Central SD (KG-12)
    Enrollment: 2,008 . . . . (845) 687-2400

Housing: Homeownership rate: 64.5%; Median home value: $171,100; Median year structure built: 1960; Homeowner vacancy rate: 8.8%; Median selected monthly owner costs: $1,491 with a mortgage, $496 without a mortgage; Median gross rent: $922 per month; Rental vacancy rate: 0.0%
Health Insurance: 94.1% have insurance; 43.7% have private insurance; 62.0% have public insurance; 5.9% do not have insurance; 2.0% of children under 18 do not have insurance
Transportation: Commute: 89.3% car, 3.4% public transportation, 0.0% walk, 7.2% work from home; Mean travel time to work: 30.2 minutes

KINGSTON (city). County seat. Covers a land area of 7.486 square miles and a water area of 1.287 square miles. Located at 41.93° N. Lat; 74.00° W. Long. Elevation is 197 feet.

History: In 1615, Dutch traders established a trading post at the present site of Kingston and named it Esopus. A group of Dutch colonists from Albany made the first permanent settlement in 1653. In 1658, Director General Peter Stuyvesant erected a stockade and blockhouse and in 1661 granted a charter to the village, which he called Wiltwyck. In 1669, the English Governor Francis Lovelace gave it its present name in honor of Kingston L'Isle, his family seat in England. Kingston was the site of the New York government during 1777. Boat building and the cement industry both began about 1830.
Population: 23,419; Growth (since 2000): -0.2%; Density: 3,128.2 persons per square mile; Race: 68.7% White, 16.6% Black/African American, 3.8% Asian, 0.3% American Indian/Alaska Native, 0.0% Native Hawaiian/Other Pacific Islander, 7.8% Two or more races, 14.1% Hispanic of any race; Average household size: 2.40; Median age: 38.1; Age under 18: 21.4%; Age 65 and over: 15.0%; Males per 100 females: 92.7; Marriage status: 39.9% never married, 40.6% now married, 3.5% separated, 7.0% widowed, 12.6% divorced; Foreign born: 11.2%; Speak English only: 83.5%; With disability: 14.5%; Veterans: 6.2%; Ancestry: 19.2% Irish, 16.3% German, 14.9% Italian, 6.2% English, 3.8% Dutch
Employment: 14.3% management, business, and financial, 3.1% computer, engineering, and science, 14.6% education, legal, community service, arts, and media, 5.1% healthcare practitioners, 21.2% service, 24.1% sales and office, 7.1% natural resources, construction, and maintenance, 10.5% production, transportation, and material moving
Income: Per capita: $25,785; Median household: $45,487; Average household: $60,850; Households with income of $100,000 or more: 17.7%; Poverty rate: 18.0%
Educational Attainment: High school diploma or higher: 85.9%; Bachelor's degree or higher: 26.1%; Graduate/professional degree or higher: 12.0%

School District(s)
Kingston City SD (PK-12)
    Enrollment: 6,445 . . . . (845) 943-3003
Housing: Homeownership rate: 46.7%; Median home value: $165,400; Median year structure built: Before 1940; Homeowner vacancy rate: 2.8%; Median selected monthly owner costs: $1,711 with a mortgage, $733 without a mortgage; Median gross rent: $1,034 per month; Rental vacancy rate: 4.2%
Health Insurance: 91.1% have insurance; 54.3% have private insurance; 47.9% have public insurance; 8.9% do not have insurance; 4.3% of children under 18 do not have insurance
Hospitals: Health Alliance Hospital Broadway Campus (150 beds); Health Alliance Hospital Mary's Avenue Campus (222 beds)
Safety: Violent crime rate: 31.6 per 10,000 population; Property crime rate: 194.3 per 10,000 population
Newspapers: Daily Freeman (daily circulation 19,300); Ulster Publishing (weekly circulation 5,500)
Transportation: Commute: 81.8% car, 4.2% public transportation, 5.7% walk, 5.5% work from home; Mean travel time to work: 23.7 minutes
Airports: Kingston-Ulster (general aviation)
Additional Information Contacts
City of Kingston . . . . (845) 331-0080
    http://www.ci.kingston.ny.us

KINGSTON (town). Covers a land area of 7.702 square miles and a water area of 0.048 square miles. Located at 41.98° N. Lat; 74.04° W. Long. Elevation is 197 feet.

History: First permanent settlement (Wiltwyck) was established in 1652. Served as the first capital of New York State until it was burned by the British in Oct. 1777. Many old Dutch stone houses; the Senate house (1676 meeting place of the first state legislature); the old Dutch church (1659) and cemetery (1661); and the burial place of James Clinton.

Incorporated as a village 1805, and as a city through the union (1872) of Kingston and Rondout.
Population: 1,055; Growth (since 2000): 16.2%; Density: 137.0 persons per square mile; Race: 95.9% White, 0.0% Black/African American, 1.2% Asian, 0.2% American Indian/Alaska Native, 0.8% Native Hawaiian/Other Pacific Islander, 0.8% Two or more races, 4.6% Hispanic of any race; Average household size: 2.36; Median age: 48.6; Age under 18: 15.2%; Age 65 and over: 18.4%; Males per 100 females: 101.6; Marriage status: 26.7% never married, 55.4% now married, 2.2% separated, 5.2% widowed, 12.8% divorced; Foreign born: 2.1%; Speak English only: 97.0%; With disability: 10.7%; Veterans: 10.3%; Ancestry: 25.5% German, 24.0% Irish, 21.6% Italian, 7.2% English, 7.2% French
Employment: 12.4% management, business, and financial, 2.3% computer, engineering, and science, 12.0% education, legal, community service, arts, and media, 9.5% healthcare practitioners, 17.0% service, 21.2% sales and office, 14.9% natural resources, construction, and maintenance, 10.8% production, transportation, and material moving
Income: Per capita: $41,087; Median household: $74,792; Average household: $95,627; Households with income of $100,000 or more: 29.1%; Poverty rate: 9.0%
Educational Attainment: High school diploma or higher: 89.1%; Bachelor's degree or higher: 23.6%; Graduate/professional degree or higher: 13.1%

School District(s)
Kingston City SD (PK-12)
    Enrollment: 6,445 . . . . (845) 943-3003
Housing: Homeownership rate: 88.6%; Median home value: $205,900; Median year structure built: 1977; Homeowner vacancy rate: 0.0%; Median selected monthly owner costs: $1,625 with a mortgage, $629 without a mortgage; Median gross rent: $1,139 per month; Rental vacancy rate: 0.0%
Health Insurance: 91.0% have insurance; 73.9% have private insurance; 33.6% have public insurance; 9.0% do not have insurance; 4.5% of children under 18 do not have insurance
Hospitals: Health Alliance Hospital Broadway Campus (150 beds); Health Alliance Hospital Mary's Avenue Campus (222 beds)
Newspapers: Daily Freeman (daily circulation 19,300); Ulster Publishing (weekly circulation 5,500)
Transportation: Commute: 89.1% car, 0.8% public transportation, 0.7% walk, 8.7% work from home; Mean travel time to work: 32.9 minutes
Airports: Kingston-Ulster (general aviation)
Additional Information Contacts
Town of Kingston . . . . (845) 336-8853
    http://www.townkingstonny.us

LAKE HILL (unincorporated postal area)
ZCTA: 12448
    Covers a land area of 11.661 square miles and a water area of 0.243 square miles. Located at 42.09° N. Lat; 74.16° W. Long. Elevation is 1,109 feet.
    Population: 427; Growth (since 2000): 95.9%; Density: 36.6 persons per square mile; Race: 100.0% White, 0.0% Black/African American, 0.0% Asian, 0.0% American Indian/Alaska Native, 0.0% Native Hawaiian/Other Pacific Islander, 0.0% Two or more races, 0.0% Hispanic of any race; Average household size: 1.82; Median age: 62.1; Age under 18: 8.0%; Age 65 and over: 38.6%; Males per 100 females: 103.1; Marriage status: 9.5% never married, 72.0% now married, 0.0% separated, 10.3% widowed, 8.3% divorced; Foreign born: 6.6%; Speak English only: 93.7%; With disability: 4.7%; Veterans: 8.7%; Ancestry: 23.2% Italian, 20.8% English, 20.1% Irish, 16.2% German, 15.9% Russian
    Employment: 46.7% management, business, and financial, 0.0% computer, engineering, and science, 18.2% education, legal, community service, arts, and media, 0.0% healthcare practitioners, 7.6% service, 15.1% sales and office, 6.7% natural resources, construction, and maintenance, 5.8% production, transportation, and material moving
    Income: Per capita: $122,844; Median household: $109,531; Average household: $218,956; Households with income of $100,000 or more: 55.8%; Poverty rate: n/a
    Educational Attainment: High school diploma or higher: 100.0%; Bachelor's degree or higher: 63.9%; Graduate/professional degree or higher: 29.3%
    Housing: Homeownership rate: 88.9%; Median home value: $298,800; Median year structure built: 1949; Homeowner vacancy rate: 10.7%; Median selected monthly owner costs: $1,964 with a mortgage, $916

without a mortgage; Median gross rent: n/a per month; Rental vacancy rate: 0.0%

Health Insurance: 86.7% have insurance; 68.9% have private insurance; 43.3% have public insurance; 13.3% do not have insurance; 0.0% of children under 18 do not have insurance

Transportation: Commute: 67.1% car, 2.7% public transportation, 0.0% walk, 30.2% work from home; Mean travel time to work: 40.3 minutes

LAKE KATRINE (CDP).
Covers a land area of 2.254 square miles and a water area of 0.040 square miles. Located at 41.99° N. Lat; 73.99° W. Long. Elevation is 184 feet.

Population: 2,499; Growth (since 2000): 4.3%; Density: 1,108.5 persons per square mile; Race: 81.3% White, 3.7% Black/African American, 3.6% Asian, 0.0% American Indian/Alaska Native, 0.0% Native Hawaiian/Other Pacific Islander, 9.1% Two or more races, 5.4% Hispanic of any race; Average household size: 2.23; Median age: 52.5; Age under 18: 14.4%; Age 65 and over: 28.5%; Males per 100 females: 89.6; Marriage status: 30.4% never married, 48.2% now married, 2.4% separated, 13.1% widowed, 8.3% divorced; Foreign born: 7.0%; Speak English only: 90.9%; With disability: 14.3%; Veterans: 11.9%; Ancestry: 22.2% Irish, 19.1% Italian, 14.9% German, 10.8% English, 9.0% Polish

Employment: 12.8% management, business, and financial, 8.4% computer, engineering, and science, 10.9% education, legal, community service, arts, and media, 9.4% healthcare practitioners, 18.5% service, 27.9% sales and office, 9.5% natural resources, construction, and maintenance, 2.7% production, transportation, and material moving

Income: Per capita: $31,340; Median household: $43,878; Average household: $69,998; Households with income of $100,000 or more: 18.2%; Poverty rate: 13.6%

Educational Attainment: High school diploma or higher: 88.7%; Bachelor's degree or higher: 23.4%; Graduate/professional degree or higher: 9.7%

School District(s)
Kingston City SD (PK-12)
    Enrollment: 6,445 . . . . (845) 943-3003

Vocational/Technical School(s)
Ulster BOCES School of Practical Nursing (Public)
    Enrollment: 65 . . . . (845) 331-5050
    Tuition: $13,400

Housing: Homeownership rate: 55.4%; Median home value: $179,300; Median year structure built: 1977; Homeowner vacancy rate: 0.0%; Median selected monthly owner costs: $1,879 with a mortgage, $666 without a mortgage; Median gross rent: $1,074 per month; Rental vacancy rate: 0.0%

Health Insurance: 96.2% have insurance; 72.5% have private insurance; 43.3% have public insurance; 3.8% do not have insurance; 0.0% of children under 18 do not have insurance

Transportation: Commute: 88.8% car, 0.0% public transportation, 1.7% walk, 7.2% work from home; Mean travel time to work: 18.8 minutes

LINCOLN PARK (CDP).
Covers a land area of 1.434 square miles and a water area of 0.030 square miles. Located at 41.96° N. Lat; 74.00° W. Long. Elevation is 187 feet.

Population: 2,222; Growth (since 2000): -4.9%; Density: 1,549.6 persons per square mile; Race: 88.2% White, 6.8% Black/African American, 3.7% Asian, 0.4% American Indian/Alaska Native, 0.0% Native Hawaiian/Other Pacific Islander, 1.0% Two or more races, 8.2% Hispanic of any race; Average household size: 1.93; Median age: 45.6; Age under 18: 18.0%; Age 65 and over: 28.3%; Males per 100 females: 84.1; Marriage status: 32.9% never married, 41.4% now married, 1.6% separated, 15.0% widowed, 10.7% divorced; Foreign born: 6.0%; Speak English only: 93.2%; With disability: 17.5%; Veterans: 7.9%; Ancestry: 24.6% Irish, 22.7% German, 10.4% Italian, 9.8% Dutch, 7.8% English

Employment: 8.4% management, business, and financial, 9.5% computer, engineering, and science, 9.9% education, legal, community service, arts, and media, 7.5% healthcare practitioners, 17.0% service, 32.9% sales and office, 5.6% natural resources, construction, and maintenance, 9.1% production, transportation, and material moving

Income: Per capita: $23,114; Median household: $27,039; Average household: $44,177; Households with income of $100,000 or more: 11.9%; Poverty rate: 27.1%

Educational Attainment: High school diploma or higher: 89.7%; Bachelor's degree or higher: 21.3%; Graduate/professional degree or higher: 7.4%

Housing: Homeownership rate: 42.2%; Median home value: $170,400; Median year structure built: 1965; Homeowner vacancy rate: 0.0%; Median selected monthly owner costs: $1,535 with a mortgage, $561 without a mortgage; Median gross rent: $949 per month; Rental vacancy rate: 0.0%

Health Insurance: 96.0% have insurance; 67.5% have private insurance; 51.9% have public insurance; 4.0% do not have insurance; 2.9% of children under 18 do not have insurance

Transportation: Commute: 93.5% car, 0.0% public transportation, 3.9% walk, 1.5% work from home; Mean travel time to work: 20.1 minutes

LLOYD (town).
Covers a land area of 31.266 square miles and a water area of 2.019 square miles. Located at 41.71° N. Lat; 74.00° W. Long. Elevation is 381 feet.

Population: 10,571; Growth (since 2000): 6.3%; Density: 338.1 persons per square mile; Race: 88.9% White, 5.6% Black/African American, 0.7% Asian, 0.0% American Indian/Alaska Native, 0.0% Native Hawaiian/Other Pacific Islander, 2.6% Two or more races, 13.3% Hispanic of any race; Average household size: 2.56; Median age: 41.2; Age under 18: 21.6%; Age 65 and over: 15.9%; Males per 100 females: 95.3; Marriage status: 31.5% never married, 50.0% now married, 1.7% separated, 7.3% widowed, 11.2% divorced; Foreign born: 6.4%; Speak English only: 91.8%; With disability: 12.0%; Veterans: 6.3%; Ancestry: 27.1% Italian, 16.7% Irish, 11.6% German, 6.3% English, 6.2% Polish

Employment: 12.8% management, business, and financial, 8.7% computer, engineering, and science, 14.2% education, legal, community service, arts, and media, 7.9% healthcare practitioners, 18.4% service, 21.6% sales and office, 9.5% natural resources, construction, and maintenance, 7.0% production, transportation, and material moving

Income: Per capita: $32,627; Median household: $69,363; Average household: $84,635; Households with income of $100,000 or more: 30.8%; Poverty rate: 10.1%

Educational Attainment: High school diploma or higher: 90.6%; Bachelor's degree or higher: 32.7%; Graduate/professional degree or higher: 12.8%

Housing: Homeownership rate: 68.0%; Median home value: $244,000; Median year structure built: 1974; Homeowner vacancy rate: 2.5%; Median selected monthly owner costs: $2,030 with a mortgage, $870 without a mortgage; Median gross rent: $1,152 per month; Rental vacancy rate: 12.5%

Health Insurance: 95.5% have insurance; 73.7% have private insurance; 35.0% have public insurance; 4.5% do not have insurance; 1.5% of children under 18 do not have insurance

Safety: Violent crime rate: 5.7 per 10,000 population; Property crime rate: 95.6 per 10,000 population

Transportation: Commute: 90.1% car, 1.4% public transportation, 1.5% walk, 6.0% work from home; Mean travel time to work: 26.9 minutes

Additional Information Contacts
Town of Lloyd . . . . (845) 691-8011
    http://www.townoflloyd.com

MALDEN-ON-HUDSON (CDP).
Covers a land area of 0.501 square miles and a water area of 0 square miles. Located at 42.09° N. Lat; 73.94° W. Long. Elevation is 85 feet.

Population: 235; Growth (since 2000): n/a; Density: 469.0 persons per square mile; Race: 100.0% White, 0.0% Black/African American, 0.0% Asian, 0.0% American Indian/Alaska Native, 0.0% Native Hawaiian/Other Pacific Islander, 0.0% Two or more races, 59.1% Hispanic of any race; Average household size: 2.04; Median age: 31.8; Age under 18: 19.6%; Age 65 and over: 24.7%; Males per 100 females: 88.4; Marriage status: 25.4% never married, 39.2% now married, 0.0% separated, 25.4% widowed, 10.1% divorced; Foreign born: 60.4%; Speak English only: 23.1%; With disability: 49.8%; Veterans: 0.0%; Ancestry: 20.4% French, 20.4% German, 2.1% Irish, 2.1% Italian

Employment: 0.0% management, business, and financial, 0.0% computer, engineering, and science, 0.0% education, legal, community service, arts, and media, 0.0% healthcare practitioners, 82.7% service, 0.0% sales and office, 17.3% natural resources, construction, and maintenance, 0.0% production, transportation, and material moving

Income: Per capita: $18,014; Median household: $35,755; Average household: $38,774; Households with income of $100,000 or more: n/a; Poverty rate: n/a

Educational Attainment: High school diploma or higher: 85.2%; Bachelor's degree or higher: n/a; Graduate/professional degree or higher: n/a

Housing: Homeownership rate: 46.1%; Median home value: n/a; Median year structure built: Before 1940; Homeowner vacancy rate: 0.0%; Median selected monthly owner costs: n/a with a mortgage, n/a without a mortgage; Median gross rent: n/a per month; Rental vacancy rate: 0.0%
Health Insurance: 51.9% have insurance; 28.5% have private insurance; 43.8% have public insurance; 48.1% do not have insurance; 0.0% of children under 18 do not have insurance
Transportation: Commute: 100.0% car, 0.0% public transportation, 0.0% walk, 0.0% work from home; Mean travel time to work: 0.0 minutes

MARBLETOWN (town).
Covers a land area of 54.471 square miles and a water area of 0.709 square miles. Located at 41.87° N. Lat; 74.16° W. Long. Elevation is 223 feet.

Population: 5,543; Growth (since 2000): -5.3%; Density: 101.8 persons per square mile; Race: 85.8% White, 6.9% Black/African American, 0.9% Asian, 0.0% American Indian/Alaska Native, 0.0% Native Hawaiian/Other Pacific Islander, 4.7% Two or more races, 4.0% Hispanic of any race; Average household size: 2.21; Median age: 48.4; Age under 18: 17.1%; Age 65 and over: 20.4%; Males per 100 females: 97.4; Marriage status: 27.2% never married, 54.7% now married, 0.9% separated, 6.1% widowed, 12.0% divorced; Foreign born: 7.8%; Speak English only: 96.9%; With disability: 14.9%; Veterans: 8.4%; Ancestry: 20.5% Irish, 18.6% German, 14.7% Italian, 12.6% English, 5.7% American
Employment: 18.3% management, business, and financial, 4.5% computer, engineering, and science, 18.1% education, legal, community service, arts, and media, 11.2% healthcare practitioners, 14.2% service, 20.9% sales and office, 6.1% natural resources, construction, and maintenance, 6.7% production, transportation, and material moving
Income: Per capita: $39,194; Median household: $62,635; Average household: $86,471; Households with income of $100,000 or more: 28.3%; Poverty rate: 12.2%
Educational Attainment: High school diploma or higher: 93.1%; Bachelor's degree or higher: 42.6%; Graduate/professional degree or higher: 20.2%
Housing: Homeownership rate: 79.7%; Median home value: $266,800; Median year structure built: 1965; Homeowner vacancy rate: 0.0%; Median selected monthly owner costs: $1,795 with a mortgage, $685 without a mortgage; Median gross rent: $1,181 per month; Rental vacancy rate: 0.0%
Health Insurance: 94.8% have insurance; 80.3% have private insurance; 30.4% have public insurance; 5.2% do not have insurance; 3.2% of children under 18 do not have insurance
Transportation: Commute: 81.3% car, 1.8% public transportation, 4.8% walk, 10.1% work from home; Mean travel time to work: 27.9 minutes
Additional Information Contacts
Town of Marbletown . . . . (845) 687-9673
  http://www.marbletown.net

MARLBORO (CDP).
Covers a land area of 4.456 square miles and a water area of 0.636 square miles. Located at 41.60° N. Lat; 73.98° W. Long. Elevation is 177 feet.
History: Also spelled Marlborough.
Population: 3,636; Growth (since 2000): 55.5%; Density: 816.0 persons per square mile; Race: 94.2% White, 3.2% Black/African American, 1.7% Asian, 0.0% American Indian/Alaska Native, 0.0% Native Hawaiian/Other Pacific Islander, 0.7% Two or more races, 4.7% Hispanic of any race; Average household size: 2.40; Median age: 45.4; Age under 18: 21.3%; Age 65 and over: 18.6%; Males per 100 females: 94.0; Marriage status: 27.5% never married, 52.1% now married, 4.5% separated, 3.9% widowed, 16.4% divorced; Foreign born: 4.7%; Speak English only: 94.7%; With disability: 13.1%; Veterans: 9.6%; Ancestry: 36.1% Italian, 24.1% Irish, 17.1% German, 10.9% English, 3.5% American
Employment: 18.0% management, business, and financial, 3.2% computer, engineering, and science, 8.1% education, legal, community service, arts, and media, 8.5% healthcare practitioners, 11.8% service, 28.7% sales and office, 7.6% natural resources, construction, and maintenance, 14.0% production, transportation, and material moving
Income: Per capita: $33,996; Median household: $69,088; Average household: $81,409; Households with income of $100,000 or more: 30.6%; Poverty rate: 5.8%
Educational Attainment: High school diploma or higher: 92.1%; Bachelor's degree or higher: 29.8%; Graduate/professional degree or higher: 10.7%

School District(s)
Marlboro Central SD (KG-12)
  Enrollment: 1,942 . . . . (845) 236-5802
Housing: Homeownership rate: 63.4%; Median home value: $236,100; Median year structure built: 1968; Homeowner vacancy rate: 3.9%; Median selected monthly owner costs: $1,959 with a mortgage, $915 without a mortgage; Median gross rent: $911 per month; Rental vacancy rate: 5.5%
Health Insurance: 98.4% have insurance; 78.2% have private insurance; 35.0% have public insurance; 1.6% do not have insurance; 0.9% of children under 18 do not have insurance
Transportation: Commute: 90.7% car, 1.9% public transportation, 2.1% walk, 3.8% work from home; Mean travel time to work: 29.9 minutes

MARLBOROUGH (town).
Covers a land area of 24.470 square miles and a water area of 2.029 square miles. Located at 41.64° N. Lat; 73.99° W. Long.
Population: 8,727; Growth (since 2000): 5.6%; Density: 356.6 persons per square mile; Race: 93.6% White, 2.4% Black/African American, 1.4% Asian, 0.0% American Indian/Alaska Native, 0.0% Native Hawaiian/Other Pacific Islander, 1.8% Two or more races, 5.9% Hispanic of any race; Average household size: 2.53; Median age: 43.8; Age under 18: 20.8%; Age 65 and over: 15.6%; Males per 100 females: 97.1; Marriage status: 29.4% never married, 54.2% now married, 2.8% separated, 4.0% widowed, 12.4% divorced; Foreign born: 6.4%; Speak English only: 93.4%; With disability: 12.3%; Veterans: 7.8%; Ancestry: 30.9% Italian, 21.8% German, 21.0% Irish, 8.8% English, 3.4% American
Employment: 13.0% management, business, and financial, 6.2% computer, engineering, and science, 13.2% education, legal, community service, arts, and media, 8.0% healthcare practitioners, 13.4% service, 21.9% sales and office, 11.5% natural resources, construction, and maintenance, 12.8% production, transportation, and material moving
Income: Per capita: $36,150; Median household: $77,759; Average household: $89,950; Households with income of $100,000 or more: 34.9%; Poverty rate: 6.9%
Educational Attainment: High school diploma or higher: 92.1%; Bachelor's degree or higher: 31.8%; Graduate/professional degree or higher: 14.1%
Housing: Homeownership rate: 69.4%; Median home value: $239,900; Median year structure built: 1972; Homeowner vacancy rate: 3.1%; Median selected monthly owner costs: $2,129 with a mortgage, $914 without a mortgage; Median gross rent: $962 per month; Rental vacancy rate: 3.0%
Health Insurance: 96.4% have insurance; 82.9% have private insurance; 27.2% have public insurance; 3.6% do not have insurance; 0.9% of children under 18 do not have insurance
Safety: Violent crime rate: 8.1 per 10,000 population; Property crime rate: 60.2 per 10,000 population
Transportation: Commute: 93.0% car, 0.9% public transportation, 1.2% walk, 4.3% work from home; Mean travel time to work: 29.4 minutes
Additional Information Contacts
Town of Marlborough . . . . (845) 795-5100
  http://www.townofmarlboroughny.org

MILTON (CDP).
Covers a land area of 2.962 square miles and a water area of 0.049 square miles. Located at 41.66° N. Lat; 73.97° W. Long. Elevation is 148 feet.
Population: 1,167; Growth (since 2000): -6.7%; Density: 393.9 persons per square mile; Race: 95.5% White, 0.7% Black/African American, 0.0% Asian, 0.0% American Indian/Alaska Native, 0.0% Native Hawaiian/Other Pacific Islander, 0.1% Two or more races, 6.3% Hispanic of any race; Average household size: 2.47; Median age: 46.2; Age under 18: 16.1%; Age 65 and over: 12.4%; Males per 100 females: 103.9; Marriage status: 42.9% never married, 44.5% now married, 2.7% separated, 3.9% widowed, 8.7% divorced; Foreign born: 1.5%; Speak English only: 94.5%; With disability: 5.7%; Veterans: 6.9%; Ancestry: 34.5% German, 26.0% Italian, 25.4% Irish, 12.9% English, 4.3% Polish
Employment: 11.7% management, business, and financial, 1.9% computer, engineering, and science, 13.1% education, legal, community service, arts, and media, 4.3% healthcare practitioners, 9.4% service, 24.3% sales and office, 14.0% natural resources, construction, and maintenance, 21.3% production, transportation, and material moving
Income: Per capita: $36,499; Median household: $77,969; Average household: $86,673; Households with income of $100,000 or more: 26.8%; Poverty rate: 4.4%

Educational Attainment: High school diploma or higher: 95.5%; Bachelor's degree or higher: 35.6%; Graduate/professional degree or higher: 16.0%

School District(s)
Marlboro Central SD (KG-12)

    Enrollment: 1,942 . . . . (845) 236-5802
Housing: Homeownership rate: 74.5%; Median home value: $203,000; Median year structure built: 1975; Homeowner vacancy rate: 0.0%; Median selected monthly owner costs: $2,337 with a mortgage, $768 without a mortgage; Median gross rent: $1,579 per month; Rental vacancy rate: 0.0%
Health Insurance: 97.6% have insurance; 85.5% have private insurance; 22.1% have public insurance; 2.4% do not have insurance; 0.0% of children under 18 do not have insurance
Transportation: Commute: 93.8% car, 0.0% public transportation, 1.3% walk, 5.0% work from home; Mean travel time to work: 30.5 minutes

MODENA (unincorporated postal area)
ZCTA: 12548

Covers a land area of 5.871 square miles and a water area of 0.208 square miles. Located at 41.66° N. Lat; 74.10° W. Long. Elevation is 456 feet.

Population: 1,368; Growth (since 2000): -10.5%; Density: 233.0 persons per square mile; Race: 79.2% White, 12.1% Black/African American, 0.8% Asian, 0.0% American Indian/Alaska Native, 0.0% Native Hawaiian/Other Pacific Islander, 1.5% Two or more races, 16.1% Hispanic of any race; Average household size: 2.34; Median age: 50.5; Age under 18: 13.1%; Age 65 and over: 15.0%; Males per 100 females: 102.2; Marriage status: 31.1% never married, 57.1% now married, 0.7% separated, 6.0% widowed, 5.8% divorced; Foreign born: 14.5%; Speak English only: 83.8%; With disability: 22.3%; Veterans: 3.3%; Ancestry: 19.6% Irish, 15.4% German, 10.8% Jamaican, 10.7% Italian, 8.6% American
Employment: 6.3% management, business, and financial, 2.6% computer, engineering, and science, 4.5% education, legal, community service, arts, and media, 7.2% healthcare practitioners, 28.3% service, 22.6% sales and office, 10.1% natural resources, construction, and maintenance, 18.4% production, transportation, and material moving
Income: Per capita: $30,898; Median household: $55,703; Average household: $69,669; Households with income of $100,000 or more: 27.2%; Poverty rate: 14.8%
Educational Attainment: High school diploma or higher: 94.3%; Bachelor's degree or higher: 24.3%; Graduate/professional degree or higher: 9.2%
Housing: Homeownership rate: 83.2%; Median home value: $232,100; Median year structure built: 1978; Homeowner vacancy rate: 0.0%; Median selected monthly owner costs: $2,311 with a mortgage, $489 without a mortgage; Median gross rent: $693 per month; Rental vacancy rate: 0.0%
Health Insurance: 92.5% have insurance; 77.2% have private insurance; 31.1% have public insurance; 7.5% do not have insurance; 8.1% of children under 18 do not have insurance
Transportation: Commute: 97.6% car, 0.0% public transportation, 0.0% walk, 0.0% work from home; Mean travel time to work: 33.7 minutes

MOUNT MARION (unincorporated postal area)
ZCTA: 12456

Covers a land area of 0.540 square miles and a water area of 0.020 square miles. Located at 42.03° N. Lat; 74.00° W. Long. Elevation is 174 feet.

Population: 840; Growth (since 2000): 28.6%; Density: 1,554.9 persons per square mile; Race: 90.1% White, 3.7% Black/African American, 0.0% Asian, 0.6% American Indian/Alaska Native, 0.0% Native Hawaiian/Other Pacific Islander, 5.6% Two or more races, 13.5% Hispanic of any race; Average household size: 3.94; Median age: 32.2; Age under 18: 30.2%; Age 65 and over: 12.5%; Males per 100 females: 99.7; Marriage status: 34.6% never married, 62.4% now married, 1.4% separated, 1.4% widowed, 1.6% divorced; Foreign born: 1.9%; Speak English only: 96.6%; With disability: 17.7%; Veterans: 8.9%; Ancestry: 29.2% Irish, 18.3% Italian, 13.8% German, 8.8% Dutch, 6.9% Scottish
Employment: 4.1% management, business, and financial, 0.0% computer, engineering, and science, 2.6% education, legal, community service, arts, and media, 5.5% healthcare practitioners, 25.9% service, 31.8% sales and office, 22.7% natural resources, construction, and maintenance, 7.3% production, transportation, and material moving

Income: Per capita: $16,392; Median household: $46,198; Average household: $59,564; Households with income of $100,000 or more: 14.5%; Poverty rate: 5.8%
Educational Attainment: High school diploma or higher: 76.9%; Bachelor's degree or higher: 8.7%; Graduate/professional degree or higher: 2.7%
Housing: Homeownership rate: 84.5%; Median home value: $135,100; Median year structure built: 1954; Homeowner vacancy rate: 0.0%; Median selected monthly owner costs: $1,558 with a mortgage, $807 without a mortgage; Median gross rent: $1,297 per month; Rental vacancy rate: 0.0%
Health Insurance: 91.1% have insurance; 57.4% have private insurance; 46.9% have public insurance; 8.9% do not have insurance; 9.1% of children under 18 do not have insurance
Transportation: Commute: 83.4% car, 0.0% public transportation, 5.2% walk, 7.6% work from home; Mean travel time to work: 34.7 minutes

MOUNT TREMPER (unincorporated postal area)
ZCTA: 12457

Covers a land area of 13.973 square miles and a water area of 0 square miles. Located at 42.04° N. Lat; 74.25° W. Long. Elevation is 725 feet.

Population: 742; Growth (since 2000): -33.9%; Density: 53.1 persons per square mile; Race: 95.6% White, 0.0% Black/African American, 2.0% Asian, 0.0% American Indian/Alaska Native, 0.0% Native Hawaiian/Other Pacific Islander, 2.4% Two or more races, 1.2% Hispanic of any race; Average household size: 1.77; Median age: 55.7; Age under 18: 9.0%; Age 65 and over: 27.9%; Males per 100 females: 108.5; Marriage status: 22.3% never married, 52.1% now married, 0.0% separated, 2.5% widowed, 23.2% divorced; Foreign born: 10.8%; Speak English only: 96.6%; With disability: 14.6%; Veterans: 7.0%; Ancestry: 21.8% French, 19.3% Dutch, 17.5% Irish, 15.4% German, 6.7% Swedish
Employment: 9.1% management, business, and financial, 5.2% computer, engineering, and science, 8.1% education, legal, community service, arts, and media, 5.2% healthcare practitioners, 15.3% service, 36.7% sales and office, 12.0% natural resources, construction, and maintenance, 8.4% production, transportation, and material moving
Income: Per capita: $35,586; Median household: $34,583; Average household: $65,219; Households with income of $100,000 or more: 7.9%; Poverty rate: 18.9%
Educational Attainment: High school diploma or higher: 83.7%; Bachelor's degree or higher: 39.8%; Graduate/professional degree or higher: 21.2%
Housing: Homeownership rate: 60.4%; Median home value: $264,800; Median year structure built: 1954; Homeowner vacancy rate: 0.0%; Median selected monthly owner costs: $1,721 with a mortgage, $506 without a mortgage; Median gross rent: $1,172 per month; Rental vacancy rate: 0.0%
Health Insurance: 89.9% have insurance; 67.5% have private insurance; 37.6% have public insurance; 10.1% do not have insurance; 12.2% of children under 18 do not have insurance
Transportation: Commute: 84.5% car, 0.0% public transportation, 0.0% walk, 13.1% work from home; Mean travel time to work: 33.2 minutes

NAPANOCH (CDP). Covers a land area of 1.220 square miles and a water area of 0.025 square miles. Located at 41.75° N. Lat; 74.37° W. Long. Elevation is 312 feet.

Population: 1,062; Growth (since 2000): -9.1%; Density: 870.2 persons per square mile; Race: 94.9% White, 0.0% Black/African American, 0.8% Asian, 0.0% American Indian/Alaska Native, 0.0% Native Hawaiian/Other Pacific Islander, 2.0% Two or more races, 6.9% Hispanic of any race; Average household size: 2.26; Median age: 43.8; Age under 18: 22.3%; Age 65 and over: 20.3%; Males per 100 females: 92.5; Marriage status: 23.0% never married, 52.0% now married, 2.4% separated, 9.0% widowed, 16.0% divorced; Foreign born: 2.2%; Speak English only: 94.6%; With disability: 9.8%; Veterans: 6.3%; Ancestry: 40.3% German, 15.0% Italian, 11.8% Irish, 6.5% Belgian, 4.8% English
Employment: 9.4% management, business, and financial, 1.6% computer, engineering, and science, 11.2% education, legal, community service, arts, and media, 7.4% healthcare practitioners, 21.5% service, 23.7% sales and office, 13.9% natural resources, construction, and maintenance, 11.2% production, transportation, and material moving
Income: Per capita: $29,758; Median household: $51,607; Average household: $66,537; Households with income of $100,000 or more: 19.0%; Poverty rate: 9.9%

Educational Attainment: High school diploma or higher: 99.0%; Bachelor's degree or higher: 27.1%; Graduate/professional degree or higher: 9.5%
Housing: Homeownership rate: 79.5%; Median home value: $118,000; Median year structure built: 1964; Homeowner vacancy rate: 0.0%; Median selected monthly owner costs: $1,194 with a mortgage, $616 without a mortgage; Median gross rent: $748 per month; Rental vacancy rate: 0.0%
Health Insurance: 94.4% have insurance; 73.4% have private insurance; 31.4% have public insurance; 5.6% do not have insurance; 0.0% of children under 18 do not have insurance
Transportation: Commute: 92.7% car, 0.0% public transportation, 0.0% walk, 5.6% work from home; Mean travel time to work: 29.8 minutes

NEW PALTZ (town). Covers a land area of 33.875 square miles and a water area of 0.432 square miles. Located at 41.76° N. Lat; 74.09° W. Long. Elevation is 239 feet.

History: State University of N.Y. College at New Paltz is here. Settled by Huguenots in 1677; incorporated 1887.
Population: 14,124; Growth (since 2000): 10.1%; Density: 416.9 persons per square mile; Race: 85.2% White, 4.3% Black/African American, 5.6% Asian, 0.5% American Indian/Alaska Native, 0.0% Native Hawaiian/Other Pacific Islander, 1.9% Two or more races, 11.2% Hispanic of any race; Average household size: 2.49; Median age: 24.7; Age under 18: 15.8%; Age 65 and over: 12.5%; Males per 100 females: 83.9; Marriage status: 55.0% never married, 33.9% now married, 1.3% separated, 4.6% widowed, 6.6% divorced; Foreign born: 9.5%; Speak English only: 84.0%; With disability: 9.6%; Veterans: 3.2%; Ancestry: 22.6% Italian, 18.2% Irish, 13.5% German, 8.0% English, 4.8% Russian
Employment: 10.7% management, business, and financial, 7.4% computer, engineering, and science, 22.9% education, legal, community service, arts, and media, 6.2% healthcare practitioners, 17.7% service, 26.7% sales and office, 4.1% natural resources, construction, and maintenance, 4.4% production, transportation, and material moving
Income: Per capita: $29,475; Median household: $71,806; Average household: $89,100; Households with income of $100,000 or more: 34.4%; Poverty rate: 16.1%
Educational Attainment: High school diploma or higher: 96.1%; Bachelor's degree or higher: 59.0%; Graduate/professional degree or higher: 32.9%

School District(s)
New Paltz Central SD (KG-12)
    Enrollment: 2,249 . . . . (845) 256-4020
Ulster Boces
    Enrollment: n/a . . . . (845) 255-3040

Four-year College(s)
State University of New York at New Paltz (Public)
    Enrollment: 7,565 . . . . (877) 696-7411
    Tuition: In-state $7,775; Out-of-state $17,625

Housing: Homeownership rate: 57.2%; Median home value: $304,000; Median year structure built: 1972; Homeowner vacancy rate: 4.1%; Median selected monthly owner costs: $2,404 with a mortgage, $872 without a mortgage; Median gross rent: $1,217 per month; Rental vacancy rate: 7.3%
Health Insurance: 94.7% have insurance; 80.7% have private insurance; 24.3% have public insurance; 5.3% do not have insurance; 1.5% of children under 18 do not have insurance
Safety: Violent crime rate: 15.6 per 10,000 population; Property crime rate: 116.8 per 10,000 population
Newspapers: New Paltz Times (weekly circulation 4,600)
Transportation: Commute: 72.0% car, 3.2% public transportation, 16.0% walk, 6.1% work from home; Mean travel time to work: 29.5 minutes
Additional Information Contacts
Town of New Paltz . . . . (845) 255-0604
    http://www.townofnewpaltz.org

NEW PALTZ (village). Covers a land area of 1.715 square miles and a water area of 0.037 square miles. Located at 41.75° N. Lat; 74.08° W. Long. Elevation is 239 feet.

Population: 7,040; Growth (since 2000): 16.7%; Density: 4,104.4 persons per square mile; Race: 77.3% White, 6.0% Black/African American, 9.1% Asian, 0.2% American Indian/Alaska Native, 0.0% Native Hawaiian/Other Pacific Islander, 2.7% Two or more races, 15.2% Hispanic of any race; Average household size: 2.16; Median age: 21.4; Age under 18: 8.9%; Age 65 and over: 7.4%; Males per 100 females: 71.5; Marriage status: 77.3% never married, 15.1% now married, 0.5% separated, 4.0%

widowed, 3.6% divorced; Foreign born: 12.9%; Speak English only: 76.8%; With disability: 8.4%; Veterans: 2.3%; Ancestry: 23.3% Italian, 19.5% Irish, 11.7% German, 7.2% English, 5.6% Russian
Employment: 5.0% management, business, and financial, 6.2% computer, engineering, and science, 19.8% education, legal, community service, arts, and media, 2.5% healthcare practitioners, 25.6% service, 32.8% sales and office, 2.5% natural resources, construction, and maintenance, 5.6% production, transportation, and material moving
Income: Per capita: $17,782; Median household: $39,252; Average household: $57,936; Households with income of $100,000 or more: 18.3%; Poverty rate: 33.3%
Educational Attainment: High school diploma or higher: 96.6%; Bachelor's degree or higher: 65.6%; Graduate/professional degree or higher: 38.8%

School District(s)
New Paltz Central SD (KG-12)
    Enrollment: 2,249 . . . . (845) 256-4020
Ulster Boces
    Enrollment: n/a . . . . (845) 255-3040

Four-year College(s)
State University of New York at New Paltz (Public)
    Enrollment: 7,565 . . . . (877) 696-7411
    Tuition: In-state $7,775; Out-of-state $17,625

Housing: Homeownership rate: 27.2%; Median home value: $270,800; Median year structure built: 1972; Homeowner vacancy rate: 6.3%; Median selected monthly owner costs: $2,573 with a mortgage, $793 without a mortgage; Median gross rent: $1,212 per month; Rental vacancy rate: 8.0%
Health Insurance: 93.2% have insurance; 77.8% have private insurance; 22.3% have public insurance; 6.8% do not have insurance; 2.5% of children under 18 do not have insurance
Newspapers: New Paltz Times (weekly circulation 4,600)
Transportation: Commute: 55.4% car, 1.9% public transportation, 35.3% walk, 3.9% work from home; Mean travel time to work: 23.0 minutes
Additional Information Contacts
Village of New Paltz . . . . (845) 255-0130
    http://villageofnewpaltz.org

OLIVE (town). Covers a land area of 58.450 square miles and a water area of 6.743 square miles. Located at 41.95° N. Lat; 74.27° W. Long.

Population: 4,333; Growth (since 2000): -5.4%; Density: 74.1 persons per square mile; Race: 91.2% White, 0.0% Black/African American, 1.8% Asian, 0.6% American Indian/Alaska Native, 2.2% Native Hawaiian/Other Pacific Islander, 2.7% Two or more races, 5.5% Hispanic of any race; Average household size: 2.24; Median age: 48.9; Age under 18: 15.3%; Age 65 and over: 23.3%; Males per 100 females: 99.6; Marriage status: 26.2% never married, 53.4% now married, 2.5% separated, 7.7% widowed, 12.6% divorced; Foreign born: 7.0%; Speak English only: 88.1%; With disability: 11.7%; Veterans: 6.2%; Ancestry: 23.1% Irish, 17.8% German, 15.3% Italian, 9.9% Polish, 8.2% English
Employment: 12.4% management, business, and financial, 4.7% computer, engineering, and science, 17.9% education, legal, community service, arts, and media, 8.6% healthcare practitioners, 12.7% service, 28.9% sales and office, 6.0% natural resources, construction, and maintenance, 8.7% production, transportation, and material moving
Income: Per capita: $33,779; Median household: $64,352; Average household: $73,434; Households with income of $100,000 or more: 25.7%; Poverty rate: 8.0%
Educational Attainment: High school diploma or higher: 87.8%; Bachelor's degree or higher: 38.2%; Graduate/professional degree or higher: 16.0%
Housing: Homeownership rate: 78.6%; Median home value: $248,600; Median year structure built: 1969; Homeowner vacancy rate: 0.0%; Median selected monthly owner costs: $1,936 with a mortgage, $726 without a mortgage; Median gross rent: $902 per month; Rental vacancy rate: 9.2%
Health Insurance: 94.4% have insurance; 71.3% have private insurance; 39.9% have public insurance; 5.6% do not have insurance; 0.0% of children under 18 do not have insurance
Safety: Violent crime rate: 0.0 per 10,000 population; Property crime rate: 16.2 per 10,000 population
Transportation: Commute: 87.0% car, 3.2% public transportation, 1.9% walk, 7.9% work from home; Mean travel time to work: 36.8 minutes
Additional Information Contacts
Town of Olive . . . . (845) 657-8118
    http://town.olive.ny.us

OLIVEBRIDGE (unincorporated postal area)
ZCTA: 12461

Covers a land area of 23.889 square miles and a water area of 0.023 square miles. Located at 41.90° N. Lat; 74.27° W. Long. Elevation is 571 feet.

Population: 1,771; Growth (since 2000): -0.6%; Density: 74.1 persons per square mile; Race: 86.5% White, 0.1% Black/African American, 3.6% Asian, 0.0% American Indian/Alaska Native, 5.3% Native Hawaiian/Other Pacific Islander, 4.5% Two or more races, 6.3% Hispanic of any race; Average household size: 2.28; Median age: 49.2; Age under 18: 16.1%; Age 65 and over: 20.5%; Males per 100 females: 99.8; Marriage status: 27.1% never married, 52.6% now married, 1.8% separated, 2.0% widowed, 18.3% divorced; Foreign born: 3.8%; Speak English only: 88.4%; With disability: 8.8%; Veterans: 7.8%; Ancestry: 28.3% Irish, 14.9% Italian, 14.1% German, 11.4% Polish, 9.4% English

Employment: 14.3% management, business, and financial, 3.0% computer, engineering, and science, 12.6% education, legal, community service, arts, and media, 10.7% healthcare practitioners, 15.8% service, 30.5% sales and office, 3.7% natural resources, construction, and maintenance, 9.3% production, transportation, and material moving

Income: Per capita: $34,580; Median household: $64,120; Average household: $76,986; Households with income of $100,000 or more: 33.8%; Poverty rate: 4.5%

Educational Attainment: High school diploma or higher: 90.2%; Bachelor's degree or higher: 43.1%; Graduate/professional degree or higher: 21.5%

Housing: Homeownership rate: 76.9%; Median home value: $258,900; Median year structure built: 1973; Homeowner vacancy rate: 0.0%; Median selected monthly owner costs: $2,282 with a mortgage, $670 without a mortgage; Median gross rent: $824 per month; Rental vacancy rate: 0.0%

Health Insurance: 92.6% have insurance; 63.7% have private insurance; 36.1% have public insurance; 7.4% do not have insurance; 0.0% of children under 18 do not have insurance

Transportation: Commute: 83.8% car, 7.0% public transportation, 1.7% walk, 7.4% work from home; Mean travel time to work: 45.3 minutes

PHOENICIA (CDP).
Covers a land area of 0.456 square miles and a water area of 0 square miles. Located at 42.08° N. Lat; 74.31° W. Long. Elevation is 827 feet.

Population: 256; Growth (since 2000): -32.8%; Density: 561.9 persons per square mile; Race: 100.0% White, 0.0% Black/African American, 0.0% Asian, 0.0% American Indian/Alaska Native, 0.0% Native Hawaiian/Other Pacific Islander, 0.0% Two or more races, 0.0% Hispanic of any race; Average household size: 1.41; Median age: 66.0; Age under 18: 0.0%; Age 65 and over: 62.9%; Males per 100 females: 87.3; Marriage status: 35.5% never married, 25.4% now married, 10.5% separated, 14.1% widowed, 25.0% divorced; Foreign born: 10.5%; Speak English only: 83.6%; With disability: 55.9%; Veterans: 9.0%; Ancestry: 45.7% German, 27.3% English, 13.3% Russian, 10.9% Italian, 10.5% French

Employment: 16.7% management, business, and financial, 0.0% computer, engineering, and science, 35.7% education, legal, community service, arts, and media, 0.0% healthcare practitioners, 28.6% service, 19.0% sales and office, 0.0% natural resources, construction, and maintenance, 0.0% production, transportation, and material moving

Income: Per capita: $28,187; Median household: $36,696; Average household: $38,056; Households with income of $100,000 or more: n/a; Poverty rate: 19.1%

Educational Attainment: High school diploma or higher: 100.0%; Bachelor's degree or higher: 32.5%; Graduate/professional degree or higher: 23.0%

School District(s)
Onteora Central SD (KG-12)
    Enrollment: 1,367 . . . . (845) 657-8851

Housing: Homeownership rate: 65.4%; Median home value: $228,100; Median year structure built: Before 1940; Homeowner vacancy rate: 0.0%; Median selected monthly owner costs: n/a with a mortgage, $380 without a mortgage; Median gross rent: $1,083 per month; Rental vacancy rate: 0.0%

Health Insurance: 95.3% have insurance; 67.2% have private insurance; 81.6% have public insurance; 4.7% do not have insurance; 0.0% of children under 18 do not have insurance

Transportation: Commute: 100.0% car, 0.0% public transportation, 0.0% walk, 0.0% work from home; Mean travel time to work: 0.0 minutes

PINE HILL (CDP).
Covers a land area of 2.078 square miles and a water area of 0.010 square miles. Located at 42.13° N. Lat; 74.47° W. Long. Elevation is 1,499 feet.

Population: 223; Growth (since 2000): -27.6%; Density: 107.3 persons per square mile; Race: 100.0% White, 0.0% Black/African American, 0.0% Asian, 0.0% American Indian/Alaska Native, 0.0% Native Hawaiian/Other Pacific Islander, 0.0% Two or more races, 0.0% Hispanic of any race; Average household size: 1.94; Median age: 62.3; Age under 18: 8.5%; Age 65 and over: 33.6%; Males per 100 females: 99.3; Marriage status: 16.2% never married, 43.6% now married, 4.4% separated, 5.9% widowed, 34.3% divorced; Foreign born: 14.8%; Speak English only: 90.1%; With disability: 22.4%; Veterans: 14.2%; Ancestry: 26.9% German, 23.3% Italian, 22.9% American, 20.2% Irish, 4.9% British

Employment: 0.0% management, business, and financial, 7.3% computer, engineering, and science, 19.5% education, legal, community service, arts, and media, 0.0% healthcare practitioners, 48.8% service, 11.0% sales and office, 13.4% natural resources, construction, and maintenance, 0.0% production, transportation, and material moving

Income: Per capita: $26,887; Median household: $42,969; Average household: $51,343; Households with income of $100,000 or more: 14.8%; Poverty rate: 27.5%

Educational Attainment: High school diploma or higher: 96.4%; Bachelor's degree or higher: 30.2%; Graduate/professional degree or higher: 15.4%

Housing: Homeownership rate: 95.7%; Median home value: $206,300; Median year structure built: 1955; Homeowner vacancy rate: 0.0%; Median selected monthly owner costs: $1,232 with a mortgage, $452 without a mortgage; Median gross rent: n/a per month; Rental vacancy rate: 86.5%

Health Insurance: 91.0% have insurance; 51.6% have private insurance; 55.2% have public insurance; 9.0% do not have insurance; 0.0% of children under 18 do not have insurance

Transportation: Commute: 95.1% car, 0.0% public transportation, 4.9% walk, 0.0% work from home; Mean travel time to work: 30.9 minutes

PLATTEKILL (CDP).
Covers a land area of 2.550 square miles and a water area of 0.073 square miles. Located at 41.62° N. Lat; 74.06° W. Long. Elevation is 568 feet.

Population: 798; Growth (since 2000): -24.0%; Density: 312.9 persons per square mile; Race: 71.8% White, 14.9% Black/African American, 0.0% Asian, 0.0% American Indian/Alaska Native, 0.0% Native Hawaiian/Other Pacific Islander, 0.0% Two or more races, 26.3% Hispanic of any race; Average household size: 3.05; Median age: 40.2; Age under 18: 19.0%; Age 65 and over: 16.2%; Males per 100 females: 97.8; Marriage status: 50.1% never married, 40.8% now married, 0.0% separated, 1.0% widowed, 8.1% divorced; Foreign born: 12.2%; Speak English only: 80.2%; With disability: 17.7%; Veterans: 6.2%; Ancestry: 17.0% Irish, 15.8% Italian, 11.8% European, 11.5% German, 11.0% Haitian

Employment: 4.5% management, business, and financial, 4.0% computer, engineering, and science, 19.5% education, legal, community service, arts, and media, 10.0% healthcare practitioners, 20.0% service, 19.0% sales and office, 12.6% natural resources, construction, and maintenance, 10.5% production, transportation, and material moving

Income: Per capita: $25,596; Median household: n/a; Average household: $75,761; Households with income of $100,000 or more: 32.5%; Poverty rate: 15.2%

Educational Attainment: High school diploma or higher: 72.3%; Bachelor's degree or higher: 26.7%; Graduate/professional degree or higher: 10.1%

School District(s)
Wallkill Central SD (KG-12)
    Enrollment: 2,982 . . . . (845) 895-7100

Housing: Homeownership rate: 60.7%; Median home value: $240,100; Median year structure built: 1978; Homeowner vacancy rate: 9.1%; Median selected monthly owner costs: $1,789 with a mortgage, $1,494 without a mortgage; Median gross rent: $1,107 per month; Rental vacancy rate: 14.9%

Health Insurance: 92.5% have insurance; 66.8% have private insurance; 35.7% have public insurance; 7.5% do not have insurance; 0.0% of children under 18 do not have insurance

Transportation: Commute: 87.6% car, 7.9% public transportation, 0.0% walk, 4.5% work from home; Mean travel time to work: 32.1 minutes

PLATTEKILL (town).
Covers a land area of 35.111 square miles and a water area of 0.628 square miles. Located at 41.65° N. Lat; 74.07° W. Long. Elevation is 568 feet.

History: The town was settled early in the 18th century. The Town of Plattekill was established in 1800 from part of the Town of Marlborough.

Population: 10,323; Growth (since 2000): 4.4%; Density: 294.0 persons per square mile; Race: 86.0% White, 6.3% Black/African American, 1.6% Asian, 0.0% American Indian/Alaska Native, 0.0% Native Hawaiian/Other Pacific Islander, 2.1% Two or more races, 13.4% Hispanic of any race; Average household size: 2.57; Median age: 48.2; Age under 18: 16.7%; Age 65 and over: 18.7%; Males per 100 females: 97.6; Marriage status: 31.2% never married, 52.0% now married, 2.1% separated, 7.9% widowed, 8.9% divorced; Foreign born: 7.9%; Speak English only: 85.5%; With disability: 19.9%; Veterans: 6.5%; Ancestry: 19.0% Italian, 17.1% German, 15.3% Irish, 6.8% English, 5.5% Polish

Employment: 10.0% management, business, and financial, 4.7% computer, engineering, and science, 12.8% education, legal, community service, arts, and media, 6.1% healthcare practitioners, 15.5% service, 27.1% sales and office, 9.6% natural resources, construction, and maintenance, 14.2% production, transportation, and material moving

Income: Per capita: $33,817; Median household: $61,702; Average household: $83,562; Households with income of $100,000 or more: 31.0%; Poverty rate: 10.8%

Educational Attainment: High school diploma or higher: 89.8%; Bachelor's degree or higher: 25.1%; Graduate/professional degree or higher: 8.2%

School District(s)
Wallkill Central SD (KG-12)
   Enrollment: 2,982 . . . . (845) 895-7100

Housing: Homeownership rate: 78.9%; Median home value: $198,700; Median year structure built: 1981; Homeowner vacancy rate: 2.8%; Median selected monthly owner costs: $2,156 with a mortgage, $739 without a mortgage; Median gross rent: $925 per month; Rental vacancy rate: 2.1%

Health Insurance: 91.9% have insurance; 70.2% have private insurance; 35.6% have public insurance; 8.1% do not have insurance; 10.1% of children under 18 do not have insurance

Safety: Violent crime rate: 6.9 per 10,000 population; Property crime rate: 54.1 per 10,000 population

Transportation: Commute: 92.7% car, 2.5% public transportation, 1.2% walk, 2.6% work from home; Mean travel time to work: 30.6 minutes

Additional Information Contacts
Town of Plattekill . . . . (845) 883-7331
   http://town.plattekill.ny.us

PORT EWEN (CDP).
Covers a land area of 1.973 square miles and a water area of 0.653 square miles. Located at 41.90° N. Lat; 73.98° W. Long. Elevation is 184 feet.

Population: 3,342; Growth (since 2000): -8.4%; Density: 1,693.9 persons per square mile; Race: 92.0% White, 0.8% Black/African American, 1.3% Asian, 0.0% American Indian/Alaska Native, 0.0% Native Hawaiian/Other Pacific Islander, 4.8% Two or more races, 3.5% Hispanic of any race; Average household size: 2.32; Median age: 47.9; Age under 18: 12.5%; Age 65 and over: 22.9%; Males per 100 females: 86.8; Marriage status: 31.9% never married, 46.1% now married, 2.5% separated, 8.8% widowed, 13.1% divorced; Foreign born: 5.2%; Speak English only: 94.1%; With disability: 14.3%; Veterans: 5.6%; Ancestry: 29.9% German, 29.7% Irish, 19.7% Italian, 5.5% Dutch, 5.4% English

Employment: 17.2% management, business, and financial, 2.5% computer, engineering, and science, 8.6% education, legal, community service, arts, and media, 7.2% healthcare practitioners, 19.9% service, 28.1% sales and office, 10.2% natural resources, construction, and maintenance, 6.3% production, transportation, and material moving

Income: Per capita: $36,010; Median household: $66,571; Average household: $80,274; Households with income of $100,000 or more: 27.0%; Poverty rate: 4.1%

Educational Attainment: High school diploma or higher: 90.7%; Bachelor's degree or higher: 22.1%; Graduate/professional degree or higher: 10.2%

School District(s)
Kingston City SD (PK-12)
   Enrollment: 6,445 . . . . (845) 943-3003

Housing: Homeownership rate: 74.1%; Median home value: $192,900; Median year structure built: 1968; Homeowner vacancy rate: 1.2%; Median selected monthly owner costs: $1,740 with a mortgage, $740 without a mortgage; Median gross rent: $1,083 per month; Rental vacancy rate: 12.7%

Health Insurance: 94.9% have insurance; 69.4% have private insurance; 43.2% have public insurance; 5.1% do not have insurance; 0.0% of children under 18 do not have insurance

Transportation: Commute: 90.0% car, 3.4% public transportation, 1.9% walk, 4.7% work from home; Mean travel time to work: 21.7 minutes

RIFTON (CDP).
Covers a land area of 1.175 square miles and a water area of 0 square miles. Located at 41.83° N. Lat; 74.04° W. Long. Elevation is 180 feet.

Population: 298; Growth (since 2000): -40.5%; Density: 253.5 persons per square mile; Race: 100.0% White, 0.0% Black/African American, 0.0% Asian, 0.0% American Indian/Alaska Native, 0.0% Native Hawaiian/Other Pacific Islander, 0.0% Two or more races, 0.0% Hispanic of any race; Average household size: 2.61; Median age: 34.6; Age under 18: 31.5%; Age 65 and over: 6.0%; Males per 100 females: 95.7; Marriage status: 34.8% never married, 50.5% now married, 0.0% separated, 0.0% widowed, 14.7% divorced; Foreign born: 0.0%; Speak English only: 100.0%; With disability: 9.1%; Veterans: 4.4%; Ancestry: 29.5% Polish, 22.1% Italian, 18.5% German, 17.8% Irish, 10.1% Finnish

Employment: 0.0% management, business, and financial, 14.2% computer, engineering, and science, 14.2% education, legal, community service, arts, and media, 0.0% healthcare practitioners, 0.0% service, 53.2% sales and office, 18.4% natural resources, construction, and maintenance, 0.0% production, transportation, and material moving

Income: Per capita: $42,073; Median household: $86,625; Average household: $106,709; Households with income of $100,000 or more: 43.8%; Poverty rate: 8.7%

Educational Attainment: High school diploma or higher: 100.0%; Bachelor's degree or higher: 50.5%; Graduate/professional degree or higher: 36.3%

Housing: Homeownership rate: 50.9%; Median home value: $340,800; Median year structure built: Before 1940; Homeowner vacancy rate: 0.0%; Median selected monthly owner costs: $2,250 with a mortgage, n/a without a mortgage; Median gross rent: n/a per month; Rental vacancy rate: 0.0%

Health Insurance: 100.0% have insurance; 85.2% have private insurance; 17.8% have public insurance; 0.0% do not have insurance; 0.0% of children under 18 do not have insurance

Transportation: Commute: 67.4% car, 14.2% public transportation, 18.4% walk, 0.0% work from home; Mean travel time to work: 0.0 minutes

ROCHESTER (town).
Covers a land area of 89.303 square miles and a water area of 0.416 square miles. Located at 41.81° N. Lat; 74.27° W. Long.

Population: 7,254; Growth (since 2000): 3.4%; Density: 81.2 persons per square mile; Race: 89.6% White, 1.4% Black/African American, 0.8% Asian, 0.1% American Indian/Alaska Native, 0.0% Native Hawaiian/Other Pacific Islander, 4.7% Two or more races, 4.8% Hispanic of any race; Average household size: 2.40; Median age: 46.8; Age under 18: 15.2%; Age 65 and over: 17.6%; Males per 100 females: 101.5; Marriage status: 29.5% never married, 49.1% now married, 3.6% separated, 7.6% widowed, 13.8% divorced; Foreign born: 6.7%; Speak English only: 90.2%; With disability: 15.1%; Veterans: 7.6%; Ancestry: 24.6% German, 18.7% Irish, 17.3% Italian, 11.9% Norwegian, 4.6% English

Employment: 15.2% management, business, and financial, 5.9% computer, engineering, and science, 10.5% education, legal, community service, arts, and media, 2.8% healthcare practitioners, 26.9% service, 24.8% sales and office, 9.3% natural resources, construction, and maintenance, 4.6% production, transportation, and material moving

Income: Per capita: $37,816; Median household: $62,697; Average household: $89,473; Households with income of $100,000 or more: 31.4%; Poverty rate: 8.4%

Educational Attainment: High school diploma or higher: 90.5%; Bachelor's degree or higher: 25.3%; Graduate/professional degree or higher: 10.1%

Housing: Homeownership rate: 75.5%; Median home value: $223,500; Median year structure built: 1978; Homeowner vacancy rate: 3.6%; Median selected monthly owner costs: $1,733 with a mortgage, $618 without a mortgage; Median gross rent: $934 per month; Rental vacancy rate: 12.6%

Health Insurance: 91.2% have insurance; 64.3% have private insurance; 40.2% have public insurance; 8.8% do not have insurance; 3.6% of children under 18 do not have insurance

Transportation: Commute: 86.2% car, 5.0% public transportation, 0.3% walk, 7.6% work from home; Mean travel time to work: 33.6 minutes

Additional Information Contacts

Town of Rochester . . . . (845) 626-7384
http://www.townofrochester.net/Pages/index

ROSENDALE (town). Covers a land area of 19.979 square miles and
a water area of 0.767 square miles. Located at 41.85° N. Lat; 74.08° W.
Long. Elevation is 66 feet.

History: Incorporated 1890.

Population: 5,952; Growth (since 2000): -6.3%; Density: 297.9 persons
per square mile; Race: 95.6% White, 1.3% Black/African American, 1.1%
Asian, 0.4% American Indian/Alaska Native, 0.0% Native Hawaiian/Other
Pacific Islander, 1.5% Two or more races, 2.9% Hispanic of any race;
Average household size: 2.37; Median age: 47.8; Age under 18: 13.7%;
Age 65 and over: 22.7%; Males per 100 females: 95.1; Marriage status:
36.1% never married, 47.5% now married, 2.8% separated, 5.6%
widowed, 10.8% divorced; Foreign born: 3.8%; Speak English only: 97.7%;
With disability: 14.3%; Veterans: 8.7%; Ancestry: 22.5% Irish, 20.8%
German, 18.3% Italian, 11.8% English, 7.9% Dutch

Employment: 11.5% management, business, and financial, 5.3%
computer, engineering, and science, 16.4% education, legal, community
service, arts, and media, 7.3% healthcare practitioners, 21.5% service,
20.2% sales and office, 9.3% natural resources, construction, and
maintenance, 8.6% production, transportation, and material moving

Income: Per capita: $33,576; Median household: $64,676; Average
household: $77,330; Households with income of $100,000 or more: 25.9%;
Poverty rate: 8.7%

Educational Attainment: High school diploma or higher: 92.7%;
Bachelor's degree or higher: 32.9%; Graduate/professional degree or
higher: 13.7%

Housing: Homeownership rate: 74.9%; Median home value: $218,200;
Median year structure built: 1955; Homeowner vacancy rate: 0.0%; Median
selected monthly owner costs: $1,797 with a mortgage, $696 without a
mortgage; Median gross rent: $1,100 per month; Rental vacancy rate:
4.3%

Health Insurance: 92.1% have insurance; 72.6% have private insurance;
41.3% have public insurance; 7.9% do not have insurance; 3.0% of
children under 18 do not have insurance

Safety: Violent crime rate: 1.7 per 10,000 population; Property crime rate:
49.4 per 10,000 population

Transportation: Commute: 91.9% car, 1.1% public transportation, 1.2%
walk, 4.1% work from home; Mean travel time to work: 26.5 minutes

Additional Information Contacts

Town of Rosendale . . . . (845) 658-3159
http://www.townofrosendale.com

ROSENDALE HAMLET (CDP). Covers a land area of 1.904
square miles and a water area of 0.055 square miles. Located at 41.85° N.
Lat; 74.07° W. Long.

Population: 1,212; Growth (since 2000): -11.8%; Density: 636.6 persons
per square mile; Race: 91.0% White, 1.2% Black/African American, 2.6%
Asian, 0.0% American Indian/Alaska Native, 0.0% Native Hawaiian/Other
Pacific Islander, 4.9% Two or more races, 1.6% Hispanic of any race;
Average household size: 1.98; Median age: 50.9; Age under 18: 9.7%;
Age 65 and over: 28.7%; Males per 100 females: 91.6; Marriage status:
42.6% never married, 43.2% now married, 0.0% separated, 2.4%
widowed, 11.8% divorced; Foreign born: 3.9%; Speak English only: 95.7%;
With disability: 16.0%; Veterans: 9.9%; Ancestry: 23.7% Irish, 16.2%
Italian, 15.4% German, 12.8% Dutch, 9.5% English

Employment: 7.2% management, business, and financial, 7.2% computer,
engineering, and science, 16.0% education, legal, community service, arts,
and media, 2.2% healthcare practitioners, 20.5% service, 26.5% sales and
office, 12.3% natural resources, construction, and maintenance, 8.2%
production, transportation, and material moving

Income: Per capita: $27,779; Median household: $46,447; Average
household: $53,206; Households with income of $100,000 or more: 9.9%;
Poverty rate: 6.3%

Educational Attainment: High school diploma or higher: 90.8%;
Bachelor's degree or higher: 16.3%; Graduate/professional degree or
higher: 6.2%

Housing: Homeownership rate: 69.2%; Median home value: $188,300;
Median year structure built: 1953; Homeowner vacancy rate: 0.0%; Median
selected monthly owner costs: $1,769 with a mortgage, $615 without a
mortgage; Median gross rent: $971 per month; Rental vacancy rate: 4.1%

Health Insurance: 92.0% have insurance; 70.1% have private insurance;
50.3% have public insurance; 8.0% do not have insurance; 0.0% of
children under 18 do not have insurance

Transportation: Commute: 87.6% car, 1.4% public transportation, 2.6%
walk, 2.6% work from home; Mean travel time to work: 19.0 minutes

RUBY (unincorporated postal area)
ZCTA: 12475

Covers a land area of 1.229 square miles and a water area of 0 square
miles. Located at 42.02° N. Lat; 74.02° W. Long. Elevation is 312 feet.

Population: 221; Growth (since 2000): n/a; Density: 179.8 persons per
square mile; Race: 79.2% White, 0.0% Black/African American, 0.0%
Asian, 0.0% American Indian/Alaska Native, 0.0% Native
Hawaiian/Other Pacific Islander, 20.8% Two or more races, 5.0%
Hispanic of any race; Average household size: 1.74; Median age: 59.2;
Age under 18: 28.5%; Age 65 and over: 24.0%; Males per 100 females:
108.2; Marriage status: 45.1% never married, 24.9% now married, 0.0%
separated, 5.8% widowed, 24.3% divorced; Foreign born: 3.6%; Speak
English only: 100.0%; With disability: 20.4%; Veterans: 5.7%; Ancestry:
26.7% Irish, 25.3% German, 15.4% Polish, 14.0% Jamaican, 5.0%
French Canadian

Employment: 32.2% management, business, and financial, 0.0%
computer, engineering, and science, 0.0% education, legal, community
service, arts, and media, 0.0% healthcare practitioners, 6.8% service,
35.6% sales and office, 6.8% natural resources, construction, and
maintenance, 18.6% production, transportation, and material moving

Income: Per capita: $39,243; Median household: n/a; Average
household: $66,832; Households with income of $100,000 or more:
22.0%; Poverty rate: 19.0%

Educational Attainment: High school diploma or higher: 100.0%;
Bachelor's degree or higher: 6.3%; Graduate/professional degree or
higher: 6.3%

Housing: Homeownership rate: 72.4%; Median home value: $188,200;
Median year structure built: 1955; Homeowner vacancy rate: 0.0%;
Median selected monthly owner costs: $0 with a mortgage, $0 without a
mortgage; Median gross rent: $1,514 per month; Rental vacancy rate:
0.0%

Health Insurance: 100.0% have insurance; 63.8% have private
insurance; 53.4% have public insurance; 0.0% do not have insurance;
0.0% of children under 18 do not have insurance

Transportation: Commute: 93.2% car, 0.0% public transportation, 6.8%
walk, 0.0% work from home; Mean travel time to work: 21.6 minutes

SAUGERTIES (town). Covers a land area of 64.574 square miles and
a water area of 3.386 square miles. Located at 42.09° N. Lat; 73.99° W.
Long. Elevation is 154 feet.

History: Former summer resort. Incorporated 1831.

Population: 19,192; Growth (since 2000): -3.4%; Density: 297.2 persons
per square mile; Race: 91.2% White, 2.0% Black/African American, 1.2%
Asian, 0.1% American Indian/Alaska Native, 0.0% Native Hawaiian/Other
Pacific Islander, 3.9% Two or more races, 8.0% Hispanic of any race;
Average household size: 2.51; Median age: 43.0; Age under 18: 20.7%;
Age 65 and over: 18.0%; Males per 100 females: 95.2; Marriage status:
32.2% never married, 49.4% now married, 2.0% separated, 8.2%
widowed, 10.2% divorced; Foreign born: 6.8%; Speak English only: 90.9%;
With disability: 14.4%; Veterans: 6.5%; Ancestry: 25.7% Irish, 25.6%
German, 19.1% Italian, 7.9% Dutch, 7.8% English

Employment: 14.2% management, business, and financial, 2.9%
computer, engineering, and science, 12.0% education, legal, community
service, arts, and media, 6.6% healthcare practitioners, 18.2% service,
21.6% sales and office, 14.1% natural resources, construction, and
maintenance, 10.3% production, transportation, and material moving

Income: Per capita: $29,930; Median household: $58,433; Average
household: $73,038; Households with income of $100,000 or more: 25.0%;
Poverty rate: 9.9%

Educational Attainment: High school diploma or higher: 90.4%;
Bachelor's degree or higher: 25.3%; Graduate/professional degree or
higher: 10.6%

School District(s)

Saugerties Central SD (KG-12)

    Enrollment: 2,613 . . . . (845) 247-6501

Housing: Homeownership rate: 69.7%; Median home value: $215,100;
Median year structure built: 1961; Homeowner vacancy rate: 1.4%; Median
selected monthly owner costs: $1,861 with a mortgage, $750 without a

mortgage; Median gross rent: $1,057 per month; Rental vacancy rate: 7.9%

Health Insurance: 92.5% have insurance; 71.9% have private insurance; 37.7% have public insurance; 7.5% do not have insurance; 1.3% of children under 18 do not have insurance

Safety: Violent crime rate: 12.6 per 10,000 population; Property crime rate: 111.4 per 10,000 population

Newspapers: Saugerties Post-Star (weekly circulation 2,500)

Transportation: Commute: 89.5% car, 1.1% public transportation, 2.7% walk, 5.9% work from home; Mean travel time to work: 24.9 minutes

Additional Information Contacts

Town of Saugerties . . . . (845) 246-2800
  http://www.saugerties.ny.us

SAUGERTIES (village). Covers a land area of 1.784 square miles and a water area of 0.477 square miles. Located at 42.08° N. Lat; 73.94° W. Long. Elevation is 154 feet.

Population: 3,898; Growth (since 2000): -21.3%; Density: 2,185.6 persons per square mile; Race: 90.9% White, 1.4% Black/African American, 0.0% Asian, 0.0% American Indian/Alaska Native, 0.0% Native Hawaiian/Other Pacific Islander, 4.0% Two or more races, 14.8% Hispanic of any race; Average household size: 2.18; Median age: 39.7; Age under 18: 19.9%; Age 65 and over: 20.0%; Males per 100 females: 93.9; Marriage status: 38.3% never married, 37.6% now married, 2.9% separated, 11.5% widowed, 12.6% divorced; Foreign born: 8.0%; Speak English only: 85.8%; With disability: 15.3%; Veterans: 6.6%; Ancestry: 27.2% German, 26.1% Irish, 18.8% Italian, 9.9% English, 5.3% Dutch

Employment: 10.3% management, business, and financial, 3.5% computer, engineering, and science, 14.2% education, legal, community service, arts, and media, 4.8% healthcare practitioners, 19.4% service, 23.1% sales and office, 14.0% natural resources, construction, and maintenance, 10.7% production, transportation, and material moving

Income: Per capita: $25,889; Median household: $39,760; Average household: $56,207; Households with income of $100,000 or more: 15.2%; Poverty rate: 11.3%

Educational Attainment: High school diploma or higher: 88.8%; Bachelor's degree or higher: 26.6%; Graduate/professional degree or higher: 10.9%

School District(s)

Saugerties Central SD (KG-12)
  Enrollment: 2,613 . . . . (845) 247-6501

Housing: Homeownership rate: 47.4%; Median home value: $215,800; Median year structure built: Before 1940; Homeowner vacancy rate: 0.0%; Median selected monthly owner costs: $1,898 with a mortgage, $823 without a mortgage; Median gross rent: $969 per month; Rental vacancy rate: 9.2%

Health Insurance: 89.5% have insurance; 70.4% have private insurance; 35.7% have public insurance; 10.5% do not have insurance; 0.0% of children under 18 do not have insurance

Newspapers: Saugerties Post-Star (weekly circulation 2,500)

Transportation: Commute: 80.6% car, 2.4% public transportation, 6.1% walk, 8.3% work from home; Mean travel time to work: 22.1 minutes

SAUGERTIES SOUTH (CDP). Covers a land area of 0.953 square miles and a water area of 0.210 square miles. Located at 42.06° N. Lat; 73.95° W. Long.

Population: 1,911; Growth (since 2000): -16.4%; Density: 2,006.1 persons per square mile; Race: 89.3% White, 3.9% Black/African American, 0.8% Asian, 0.0% American Indian/Alaska Native, 0.0% Native Hawaiian/Other Pacific Islander, 4.2% Two or more races, 6.3% Hispanic of any race; Average household size: 2.36; Median age: 46.9; Age under 18: 17.2%; Age 65 and over: 23.3%; Males per 100 females: 92.0; Marriage status: 31.6% never married, 48.1% now married, 0.7% separated, 11.2% widowed, 9.1% divorced; Foreign born: 4.6%; Speak English only: 94.4%; With disability: 18.3%; Veterans: 10.0%; Ancestry: 23.8% Irish, 23.1% German, 16.2% Italian, 8.1% English, 7.7% Polish

Employment: 12.4% management, business, and financial, 2.8% computer, engineering, and science, 17.3% education, legal, community service, arts, and media, 1.6% healthcare practitioners, 17.9% service, 23.6% sales and office, 14.5% natural resources, construction, and maintenance, 10.0% production, transportation, and material moving

Income: Per capita: $32,931; Median household: $68,147; Average household: $75,344; Households with income of $100,000 or more: 30.1%; Poverty rate: 7.5%

Educational Attainment: High school diploma or higher: 94.0%; Bachelor's degree or higher: 25.2%; Graduate/professional degree or higher: 10.3%

Housing: Homeownership rate: 68.3%; Median home value: $183,400; Median year structure built: 1965; Homeowner vacancy rate: 0.0%; Median selected monthly owner costs: $1,752 with a mortgage, $623 without a mortgage; Median gross rent: $1,019 per month; Rental vacancy rate: 0.0%

Health Insurance: 95.4% have insurance; 85.3% have private insurance; 37.7% have public insurance; 4.6% do not have insurance; 7.1% of children under 18 do not have insurance

Transportation: Commute: 92.1% car, 0.0% public transportation, 4.7% walk, 3.2% work from home; Mean travel time to work: 19.6 minutes

SHANDAKEN (town). Covers a land area of 119.784 square miles and a water area of 0.058 square miles. Located at 42.03° N. Lat; 74.36° W. Long. Elevation is 1,056 feet.

Population: 2,847; Growth (since 2000): -12.0%; Density: 23.8 persons per square mile; Race: 92.9% White, 0.0% Black/African American, 0.0% Asian, 0.0% American Indian/Alaska Native, 0.0% Native Hawaiian/Other Pacific Islander, 0.5% Two or more races, 4.7% Hispanic of any race; Average household size: 1.96; Median age: 57.0; Age under 18: 9.7%; Age 65 and over: 30.2%; Males per 100 females: 101.2; Marriage status: 26.5% never married, 49.2% now married, 1.4% separated, 5.8% widowed, 18.5% divorced; Foreign born: 10.0%; Speak English only: 90.7%; With disability: 20.8%; Veterans: 10.0%; Ancestry: 17.3% German, 12.4% Irish, 11.6% Italian, 11.6% Dutch, 9.9% French

Employment: 12.9% management, business, and financial, 1.4% computer, engineering, and science, 20.8% education, legal, community service, arts, and media, 1.6% healthcare practitioners, 16.3% service, 18.4% sales and office, 16.6% natural resources, construction, and maintenance, 11.9% production, transportation, and material moving

Income: Per capita: $32,211; Median household: $37,170; Average household: $61,715; Households with income of $100,000 or more: 16.3%; Poverty rate: 14.3%

Educational Attainment: High school diploma or higher: 91.6%; Bachelor's degree or higher: 31.2%; Graduate/professional degree or higher: 14.5%

Housing: Homeownership rate: 79.2%; Median home value: $203,300; Median year structure built: 1955; Homeowner vacancy rate: 4.3%; Median selected monthly owner costs: $1,567 with a mortgage, $507 without a mortgage; Median gross rent: $1,059 per month; Rental vacancy rate: 21.0%

Health Insurance: 84.3% have insurance; 63.3% have private insurance; 40.9% have public insurance; 15.7% do not have insurance; 20.0% of children under 18 do not have insurance

Safety: Violent crime rate: 3.4 per 10,000 population; Property crime rate: 104.6 per 10,000 population

Transportation: Commute: 83.1% car, 4.0% public transportation, 1.9% walk, 5.9% work from home; Mean travel time to work: 40.9 minutes

SHAWANGUNK (town). Covers a land area of 56.056 square miles and a water area of 0.494 square miles. Located at 41.63° N. Lat; 74.27° W. Long. Elevation is 299 feet.

History: The town's name comes from the Dutch translation of the Lenape's "Scha-WAN-gunk" meaning "it is smokey air" referring to the nearby Catskill Mountains, known as the "Hidden Mountains."

Population: 14,095; Growth (since 2000): 17.2%; Density: 251.4 persons per square mile; Race: 85.0% White, 7.9% Black/African American, 2.0% Asian, 0.3% American Indian/Alaska Native, 0.0% Native Hawaiian/Other Pacific Islander, 2.8% Two or more races, 13.3% Hispanic of any race; Average household size: 2.72; Median age: 39.9; Age under 18: 17.6%; Age 65 and over: 12.5%; Males per 100 females: 131.2; Marriage status: 28.3% never married, 59.9% now married, 1.9% separated, 3.6% widowed, 8.2% divorced; Foreign born: 4.6%; Speak English only: 87.0%; With disability: 7.9%; Veterans: 6.3%; Ancestry: 18.7% German, 18.4% Italian, 18.0% Irish, 8.5% English, 3.8% Dutch

Employment: 15.7% management, business, and financial, 5.1% computer, engineering, and science, 13.8% education, legal, community service, arts, and media, 5.4% healthcare practitioners, 14.0% service, 26.8% sales and office, 10.1% natural resources, construction, and maintenance, 9.0% production, transportation, and material moving

Income: Per capita: $30,395; Median household: $82,352; Average household: $100,876; Households with income of $100,000 or more: 43.0%; Poverty rate: 21.5%

Educational Attainment: High school diploma or higher: 94.6%; Bachelor's degree or higher: 23.5%; Graduate/professional degree or higher: 9.5%

Housing: Homeownership rate: 82.3%; Median home value: $249,800; Median year structure built: 1972; Homeowner vacancy rate: 1.2%; Median selected monthly owner costs: $2,102 with a mortgage, $765 without a mortgage; Median gross rent: $967 per month; Rental vacancy rate: 0.0%

Health Insurance: 91.5% have insurance; 74.4% have private insurance; 29.0% have public insurance; 8.5% do not have insurance; 0.0% of children under 18 do not have insurance

Safety: Violent crime rate: 1.4 per 10,000 population; Property crime rate: 55.6 per 10,000 population

Transportation: Commute: 87.3% car, 1.2% public transportation, 3.6% walk, 7.0% work from home; Mean travel time to work: 36.7 minutes

Additional Information Contacts

Town of Shawangunk . . . . (845) 895-2611
http://www.shawangunk.org

SHOKAN (CDP). Covers a land area of 3.891 square miles and a water area of 0 square miles. Located at 41.98° N. Lat; 74.21° W. Long. Elevation is 709 feet.

Population: 1,217; Growth (since 2000): -2.8%; Density: 312.8 persons per square mile; Race: 96.5% White, 0.0% Black/African American, 0.0% Asian, 2.1% American Indian/Alaska Native, 0.0% Native Hawaiian/Other Pacific Islander, 1.5% Two or more races, 5.1% Hispanic of any race; Average household size: 2.47; Median age: 42.3; Age under 18: 16.7%; Age 65 and over: 22.3%; Males per 100 females: 98.5; Marriage status: 28.9% never married, 57.0% now married, 1.4% separated, 9.8% widowed, 4.3% divorced; Foreign born: 10.3%; Speak English only: 87.9%; With disability: 13.7%; Veterans: 2.1%; Ancestry: 21.1% Italian, 16.4% Irish, 13.3% German, 9.5% American, 6.7% European

Employment: 0.0% management, business, and financial, 3.2% computer, engineering, and science, 20.7% education, legal, community service, arts, and media, 6.8% healthcare practitioners, 13.3% service, 34.5% sales and office, 7.8% natural resources, construction, and maintenance, 13.6% production, transportation, and material moving

Income: Per capita: $27,169; Median household: $55,114; Average household: $66,689; Households with income of $100,000 or more: 17.0%; Poverty rate: 14.2%

Educational Attainment: High school diploma or higher: 79.9%; Bachelor's degree or higher: 29.1%; Graduate/professional degree or higher: 13.0%

Housing: Homeownership rate: 79.9%; Median home value: $253,600; Median year structure built: 1962; Homeowner vacancy rate: 0.0%; Median selected monthly owner costs: $1,670 with a mortgage, $719 without a mortgage; Median gross rent: $1,231 per month; Rental vacancy rate: 0.0%

Health Insurance: 98.4% have insurance; 82.3% have private insurance; 40.5% have public insurance; 1.6% do not have insurance; 0.0% of children under 18 do not have insurance

Transportation: Commute: 92.7% car, 0.0% public transportation, 3.9% walk, 3.4% work from home; Mean travel time to work: 22.8 minutes

SPRING GLEN (unincorporated postal area)

ZCTA: 12483

Covers a land area of 3.324 square miles and a water area of 0.030 square miles. Located at 41.67° N. Lat; 74.42° W. Long. Elevation is 400 feet.

Population: 267; Growth (since 2000): n/a; Density: 80.3 persons per square mile; Race: 100.0% White, 0.0% Black/African American, 0.0% Asian, 0.0% American Indian/Alaska Native, 0.0% Native Hawaiian/Other Pacific Islander, 0.0% Two or more races, 0.0% Hispanic of any race; Average household size: 1.53; Median age: 68.4; Age under 18: 5.6%; Age 65 and over: 60.3%; Males per 100 females: 90.4; Marriage status: 8.3% never married, 51.2% now married, 7.5% separated, 27.4% widowed, 13.1% divorced; Foreign born: 11.2%; Speak English only: 91.7%; With disability: 26.6%; Veterans: 21.0%; Ancestry: 24.7% English, 22.8% Italian, 20.6% German, 16.9% Irish, 11.2% Slovene

Employment: 5.7% management, business, and financial, 0.0% computer, engineering, and science, 34.4% education, legal, community service, arts, and media, 0.0% healthcare practitioners, 26.6% service, 33.3% sales and office, 0.0% natural resources, construction, and maintenance, 0.0% production, transportation, and material moving

Income: Per capita: $36,827; Median household: n/a; Average household: $53,791; Households with income of $100,000 or more: 17.2%; Poverty rate: 7.9%

Educational Attainment: High school diploma or higher: 83.7%; Bachelor's degree or higher: 15.9%; Graduate/professional degree or higher: 15.9%

Housing: Homeownership rate: 50.9%; Median home value: $98,800; Median year structure built: 1946; Homeowner vacancy rate: 0.0%; Median selected monthly owner costs: $0 with a mortgage, $0 without a mortgage; Median gross rent: n/a per month; Rental vacancy rate: 0.0%

Health Insurance: 100.0% have insurance; 33.3% have private insurance; 73.8% have public insurance; 0.0% do not have insurance; 0.0% of children under 18 do not have insurance

Transportation: Commute: 100.0% car, 0.0% public transportation, 0.0% walk, 0.0% work from home; Mean travel time to work: 29.2 minutes

STONE RIDGE (CDP). Covers a land area of 5.190 square miles and a water area of 0.040 square miles. Located at 41.85° N. Lat; 74.15° W. Long. Elevation is 364 feet.

Population: 1,169; Growth (since 2000): -0.3%; Density: 225.2 persons per square mile; Race: 66.6% White, 17.4% Black/African American, 3.0% Asian, 0.0% American Indian/Alaska Native, 0.0% Native Hawaiian/Other Pacific Islander, 13.1% Two or more races, 1.7% Hispanic of any race; Average household size: 2.35; Median age: 55.3; Age under 18: 11.5%; Age 65 and over: 21.5%; Males per 100 females: 92.9; Marriage status: 31.0% never married, 55.5% now married, 2.8% separated, 6.0% widowed, 7.5% divorced; Foreign born: 21.5%; Speak English only: 95.1%; With disability: 6.7%; Veterans: 10.2%; Ancestry: 22.2% Irish, 17.4% Jamaican, 15.7% German, 6.8% Polish, 5.6% English

Employment: 7.3% management, business, and financial, 4.4% computer, engineering, and science, 23.0% education, legal, community service, arts, and media, 14.0% healthcare practitioners, 20.3% service, 13.7% sales and office, 15.3% natural resources, construction, and maintenance, 1.9% production, transportation, and material moving

Income: Per capita: $39,806; Median household: $88,992; Average household: $88,182; Households with income of $100,000 or more: 38.7%; Poverty rate: 7.3%

Educational Attainment: High school diploma or higher: 95.3%; Bachelor's degree or higher: 41.1%; Graduate/professional degree or higher: 23.4%

School District(s)

Rondout Valley Central SD (KG-12)

Enrollment: 2,008 . . . . (845) 687-2400

Two-year College(s)

Ulster County Community College (Public)

Enrollment: 3,560 . . . . (845) 687-5000

Tuition: In-state $5,354; Out-of-state $9,834

Housing: Homeownership rate: 81.5%; Median home value: $274,400; Median year structure built: 1966; Homeowner vacancy rate: 0.0%; Median selected monthly owner costs: $2,243 with a mortgage, $730 without a mortgage; Median gross rent: $1,189 per month; Rental vacancy rate: 0.0%

Health Insurance: 93.8% have insurance; 81.5% have private insurance; 24.1% have public insurance; 6.2% do not have insurance; 10.7% of children under 18 do not have insurance

Transportation: Commute: 90.7% car, 7.2% public transportation, 0.0% walk, 2.1% work from home; Mean travel time to work: 28.0 minutes

TILLSON (CDP). Covers a land area of 2.345 square miles and a water area of 0.024 square miles. Located at 41.83° N. Lat; 74.07° W. Long. Elevation is 233 feet.

Population: 1,778; Growth (since 2000): 4.0%; Density: 758.2 persons per square mile; Race: 99.7% White, 0.0% Black/African American, 0.3% Asian, 0.0% American Indian/Alaska Native, 0.0% Native Hawaiian/Other Pacific Islander, 0.0% Two or more races, 4.7% Hispanic of any race; Average household size: 2.65; Median age: 46.8; Age under 18: 15.9%; Age 65 and over: 19.5%; Males per 100 females: 91.5; Marriage status: 33.5% never married, 53.7% now married, 2.9% separated, 6.4% widowed, 6.4% divorced; Foreign born: 5.3%; Speak English only: 98.8%; With disability: 12.4%; Veterans: 8.8%; Ancestry: 25.5% Italian, 22.7% Irish, 19.5% German, 12.8% English, 9.4% Dutch

Employment: 19.0% management, business, and financial, 4.5% computer, engineering, and science, 12.1% education, legal, community service, arts, and media, 13.9% healthcare practitioners, 24.7% service,

18.5% sales and office, 3.8% natural resources, construction, and maintenance, 3.4% production, transportation, and material moving
Income: Per capita: $38,603; Median household: $92,898; Average household: $101,251; Households with income of $100,000 or more: 44.4%; Poverty rate: 8.2%
Educational Attainment: High school diploma or higher: 89.0%; Bachelor's degree or higher: 41.8%; Graduate/professional degree or higher: 14.7%
Housing: Homeownership rate: 87.3%; Median home value: $235,000; Median year structure built: 1964; Homeowner vacancy rate: 0.0%; Median selected monthly owner costs: $1,878 with a mortgage, $824 without a mortgage; Median gross rent: $1,606 per month; Rental vacancy rate: 0.0%
Health Insurance: 95.8% have insurance; 82.7% have private insurance; 32.3% have public insurance; 4.2% do not have insurance; 8.0% of children under 18 do not have insurance
Transportation: Commute: 98.2% car, 0.0% public transportation, 0.0% walk, 1.2% work from home; Mean travel time to work: 29.4 minutes

ULSTER (town).
Covers a land area of 26.803 square miles and a water area of 2.077 square miles. Located at 41.97° N. Lat; 74.01° W. Long.
Population: 12,335; Growth (since 2000): -1.7%; Density: 460.2 persons per square mile; Race: 86.9% White, 3.9% Black/African American, 3.9% Asian, 0.1% American Indian/Alaska Native, 0.0% Native Hawaiian/Other Pacific Islander, 3.9% Two or more races, 8.0% Hispanic of any race; Average household size: 2.31; Median age: 47.7; Age under 18: 17.6%; Age 65 and over: 23.4%; Males per 100 females: 93.8; Marriage status: 31.1% never married, 49.4% now married, 1.8% separated, 9.4% widowed, 10.1% divorced; Foreign born: 8.3%; Speak English only: 90.9%; With disability: 15.6%; Veterans: 7.7%; Ancestry: 23.3% Irish, 20.1% Italian, 17.0% German, 11.4% English, 7.5% Dutch
Employment: 13.8% management, business, and financial, 5.0% computer, engineering, and science, 10.7% education, legal, community service, arts, and media, 7.3% healthcare practitioners, 18.6% service, 26.2% sales and office, 9.1% natural resources, construction, and maintenance, 9.2% production, transportation, and material moving
Income: Per capita: $31,638; Median household: $50,941; Average household: $72,344; Households with income of $100,000 or more: 21.9%; Poverty rate: 14.1%
Educational Attainment: High school diploma or higher: 89.2%; Bachelor's degree or higher: 25.2%; Graduate/professional degree or higher: 11.2%
Housing: Homeownership rate: 67.1%; Median home value: $185,400; Median year structure built: 1967; Homeowner vacancy rate: 2.1%; Median selected monthly owner costs: $1,811 with a mortgage, $715 without a mortgage; Median gross rent: $1,020 per month; Rental vacancy rate: 1.5%
Health Insurance: 95.3% have insurance; 71.4% have private insurance; 43.4% have public insurance; 4.7% do not have insurance; 2.6% of children under 18 do not have insurance
Safety: Violent crime rate: 6.4 per 10,000 population; Property crime rate: 274.2 per 10,000 population
Transportation: Commute: 90.5% car, 0.7% public transportation, 3.1% walk, 4.6% work from home; Mean travel time to work: 21.0 minutes
Additional Information Contacts
Town of Ulster . . . . (845) 382-2455
   http://townofulster.org/content

ULSTER PARK (unincorporated postal area)
ZCTA: 12487
   Covers a land area of 15.704 square miles and a water area of 0.284 square miles. Located at 41.87° N. Lat; 74.00° W. Long. Elevation is 157 feet.
   Population: 3,460; Growth (since 2000): -10.3%; Density: 220.3 persons per square mile; Race: 90.8% White, 2.2% Black/African American, 0.2% Asian, 0.0% American Indian/Alaska Native, 0.0% Native Hawaiian/Other Pacific Islander, 1.4% Two or more races, 9.9% Hispanic of any race; Average household size: 2.30; Median age: 41.2; Age under 18: 18.4%; Age 65 and over: 17.9%; Males per 100 females: 93.7; Marriage status: 24.3% never married, 46.9% now married, 2.1% separated, 7.1% widowed, 21.7% divorced; Foreign born: 8.3%; Speak English only: 88.0%; With disability: 13.7%; Veterans: 5.8%; Ancestry: 25.0% Irish, 22.0% Italian, 16.6% German, 10.4% American, 5.6% Polish

Employment: 9.1% management, business, and financial, 4.6% computer, engineering, and science, 12.9% education, legal, community service, arts, and media, 2.7% healthcare practitioners, 14.3% service, 37.3% sales and office, 11.3% natural resources, construction, and maintenance, 7.8% production, transportation, and material moving
Income: Per capita: $35,131; Median household: $64,699; Average household: $87,182; Households with income of $100,000 or more: 24.1%; Poverty rate: 14.7%
Educational Attainment: High school diploma or higher: 92.1%; Bachelor's degree or higher: 26.4%; Graduate/professional degree or higher: 11.5%

School District(s)
Kingston City SD (PK-12)
   Enrollment: 6,445 . . . . (845) 943-3003
Housing: Homeownership rate: 65.9%; Median home value: $182,400; Median year structure built: 1968; Homeowner vacancy rate: 0.0%; Median selected monthly owner costs: $1,523 with a mortgage, $729 without a mortgage; Median gross rent: $1,223 per month; Rental vacancy rate: 3.8%
Health Insurance: 94.6% have insurance; 74.4% have private insurance; 32.3% have public insurance; 5.4% do not have insurance; 5.5% of children under 18 do not have insurance
Transportation: Commute: 80.5% car, 1.9% public transportation, 12.8% walk, 4.8% work from home; Mean travel time to work: 24.1 minutes

WALKER VALLEY (CDP).
Covers a land area of 2.120 square miles and a water area of 0.010 square miles. Located at 41.64° N. Lat; 74.38° W. Long. Elevation is 663 feet.
Population: 1,161; Growth (since 2000): 53.2%; Density: 547.5 persons per square mile; Race: 100.0% White, 0.0% Black/African American, 0.0% Asian, 0.0% American Indian/Alaska Native, 0.0% Native Hawaiian/Other Pacific Islander, 0.0% Two or more races, 0.0% Hispanic of any race; Average household size: 3.65; Median age: 26.8; Age under 18: 41.2%; Age 65 and over: 6.5%; Males per 100 females: 106.0; Marriage status: 27.3% never married, 58.7% now married, 2.2% separated, 1.3% widowed, 12.7% divorced; Foreign born: 0.0%; Speak English only: 95.6%; With disability: 12.0%; Veterans: 0.0%; Ancestry: 23.6% German, 16.6% Irish, 5.3% Polish, 5.2% French, 5.2% Yugoslavian
Employment: 40.9% management, business, and financial, 0.0% computer, engineering, and science, 0.0% education, legal, community service, arts, and media, 0.0% healthcare practitioners, 5.7% service, 43.4% sales and office, 0.0% natural resources, construction, and maintenance, 9.9% production, transportation, and material moving
Income: Per capita: $30,308; Median household: $102,375; Average household: $105,449; Households with income of $100,000 or more: 67.9%; Poverty rate: 20.4%
Educational Attainment: High school diploma or higher: 100.0%; Bachelor's degree or higher: 18.7%; Graduate/professional degree or higher: 5.2%
Housing: Homeownership rate: 85.8%; Median home value: $226,500; Median year structure built: 1972; Homeowner vacancy rate: 0.0%; Median selected monthly owner costs: $2,215 with a mortgage, $972 without a mortgage; Median gross rent: n/a per month; Rental vacancy rate: 0.0%
Health Insurance: 96.1% have insurance; 81.7% have private insurance; 15.8% have public insurance; 3.9% do not have insurance; 0.0% of children under 18 do not have insurance
Transportation: Commute: 91.9% car, 0.0% public transportation, 0.0% walk, 8.1% work from home; Mean travel time to work: 37.4 minutes

WALLKILL (CDP).
Covers a land area of 3.067 square miles and a water area of 0 square miles. Located at 41.61° N. Lat; 74.16° W. Long. Elevation is 262 feet.
Population: 2,312; Growth (since 2000): 7.9%; Density: 753.8 persons per square mile; Race: 84.3% White, 5.0% Black/African American, 7.5% Asian, 0.0% American Indian/Alaska Native, 0.0% Native Hawaiian/Other Pacific Islander, 0.0% Two or more races, 4.7% Hispanic of any race; Average household size: 2.65; Median age: 42.2; Age under 18: 22.6%; Age 65 and over: 17.6%; Males per 100 females: 97.8; Marriage status: 23.0% never married, 56.8% now married, 1.3% separated, 5.4% widowed, 14.9% divorced; Foreign born: 5.0%; Speak English only: 92.7%; With disability: 10.8%; Veterans: 4.6%; Ancestry: 23.1% German, 20.6% Italian, 19.6% Irish, 11.6% English, 11.0% American
Employment: 12.4% management, business, and financial, 3.5% computer, engineering, and science, 28.7% education, legal, community

service, arts, and media, 6.3% healthcare practitioners, 10.1% service, 25.2% sales and office, 10.5% natural resources, construction, and maintenance, 3.3% production, transportation, and material moving
Income: Per capita: $32,782; Median household: $75,938; Average household: $82,390; Households with income of $100,000 or more: 36.5%; Poverty rate: 2.6%
Educational Attainment: High school diploma or higher: 94.7%; Bachelor's degree or higher: 34.9%; Graduate/professional degree or higher: 17.3%

School District(s)
Wallkill Central SD (KG-12)
    Enrollment: 2,982 .... (845) 895-7100
Housing: Homeownership rate: 59.1%; Median home value: $216,400; Median year structure built: 1967; Homeowner vacancy rate: 6.9%; Median selected monthly owner costs: $2,074 with a mortgage, $587 without a mortgage; Median gross rent: $950 per month; Rental vacancy rate: 0.0%
Health Insurance: 97.7% have insurance; 79.2% have private insurance; 31.2% have public insurance; 2.3% do not have insurance; 0.0% of children under 18 do not have insurance
Transportation: Commute: 87.9% car, 0.0% public transportation, 6.3% walk, 2.4% work from home; Mean travel time to work: 34.3 minutes

WATCHTOWER (CDP). Covers a land area of 0.777 square miles and a water area of 0 square miles. Located at 41.64° N. Lat; 74.26° W. Long. Elevation is 344 feet.
Population: 2,090; Growth (since 2000): n/a; Density: 2,689.1 persons per square mile; Race: 65.2% White, 15.5% Black/African American, 4.9% Asian, 0.0% American Indian/Alaska Native, 0.0% Native Hawaiian/Other Pacific Islander, 7.9% Two or more races, 33.7% Hispanic of any race; Average household size: 0.00; Median age: 32.6; Age under 18: 0.0%; Age 65 and over: 3.9%; Males per 100 females: 183.5; Marriage status: 38.1% never married, 61.9% now married, 0.6% separated, 0.0% widowed, 0.0% divorced; Foreign born: 9.9%; Speak English only: 71.8%; With disability: 0.5%; Veterans: 0.0%; Ancestry: 16.6% German, 10.4% Irish, 8.5% English, 7.9% Italian, 2.8% Swedish
Employment: 0.0% management, business, and financial, 0.0% computer, engineering, and science, 0.0% education, legal, community service, arts, and media, 13.8% healthcare practitioners, 13.8% service, 13.8% sales and office, 13.8% natural resources, construction, and maintenance, 45.0% production, transportation, and material moving
Income: Per capita: $4,309; Median household: n/a; Average household: n/a; Households with income of $100,000 or more: n/a; Poverty rate: 91.7%
Educational Attainment: High school diploma or higher: 97.3%; Bachelor's degree or higher: 10.9%; Graduate/professional degree or higher: 1.4%
Housing: Homeownership rate: n/a; Median home value: n/a; Median year structure built: n/a; Homeowner vacancy rate: 0.0%; Median selected monthly owner costs: n/a with a mortgage, n/a without a mortgage; Median gross rent: n/a per month; Rental vacancy rate: 0.0%
Health Insurance: 71.7% have insurance; 40.9% have private insurance; 34.0% have public insurance; 28.3% do not have insurance; 0.0% of children under 18 do not have insurance
Transportation: Commute: 33.3% car, 0.0% public transportation, 31.9% walk, 34.8% work from home; Mean travel time to work: 0.0 minutes

WAWARSING (town). Covers a land area of 130.505 square miles and a water area of 3.358 square miles. Located at 41.75° N. Lat; 74.42° W. Long. Elevation is 295 feet.
Population: 13,004; Growth (since 2000): 0.9%; Density: 99.6 persons per square mile; Race: 71.7% White, 10.0% Black/African American, 2.2% Asian, 0.3% American Indian/Alaska Native, 0.0% Native Hawaiian/Other Pacific Islander, 8.6% Two or more races, 20.8% Hispanic of any race; Average household size: 2.44; Median age: 41.5; Age under 18: 18.8%; Age 65 and over: 15.1%; Males per 100 females: 128.3; Marriage status: 38.9% never married, 43.7% now married, 2.7% separated, 6.5% widowed, 10.9% divorced; Foreign born: 11.0%; Speak English only: 79.0%; With disability: 16.2%; Veterans: 5.6%; Ancestry: 18.0% Irish, 14.7% German, 11.0% Italian, 6.0% English, 5.7% American
Employment: 6.9% management, business, and financial, 2.1% computer, engineering, and science, 11.5% education, legal, community service, arts, and media, 3.8% healthcare practitioners, 28.6% service, 20.9% sales and office, 13.5% natural resources, construction, and maintenance, 12.7% production, transportation, and material moving

Income: Per capita: $22,784; Median household: $46,889; Average household: $60,620; Households with income of $100,000 or more: 17.2%; Poverty rate: 17.9%
Educational Attainment: High school diploma or higher: 83.8%; Bachelor's degree or higher: 18.2%; Graduate/professional degree or higher: 6.8%
Housing: Homeownership rate: 62.3%; Median home value: $138,800; Median year structure built: 1959; Homeowner vacancy rate: 1.4%; Median selected monthly owner costs: $1,487 with a mortgage, $614 without a mortgage; Median gross rent: $871 per month; Rental vacancy rate: 4.4%
Health Insurance: 90.0% have insurance; 58.9% have private insurance; 44.0% have public insurance; 10.0% do not have insurance; 3.9% of children under 18 do not have insurance
Transportation: Commute: 89.8% car, 2.2% public transportation, 3.5% walk, 4.0% work from home; Mean travel time to work: 32.6 minutes
Additional Information Contacts
Town of Wawarsing........................... (845) 647-7800
  http://www.townofwawarsing.net

WEST HURLEY (CDP). Covers a land area of 3.787 square miles and a water area of <.001 square miles. Located at 42.01° N. Lat; 74.11° W. Long. Elevation is 597 feet.
Population: 1,863; Growth (since 2000): -11.5%; Density: 491.9 persons per square mile; Race: 98.2% White, 0.4% Black/African American, 1.0% Asian, 0.0% American Indian/Alaska Native, 0.0% Native Hawaiian/Other Pacific Islander, 0.4% Two or more races, 0.2% Hispanic of any race; Average household size: 2.03; Median age: 54.2; Age under 18: 11.2%; Age 65 and over: 30.2%; Males per 100 females: 84.7; Marriage status: 17.4% never married, 54.4% now married, 2.9% separated, 9.8% widowed, 18.5% divorced; Foreign born: 3.8%; Speak English only: 98.8%; With disability: 13.7%; Veterans: 8.1%; Ancestry: 22.7% Irish, 20.9% German, 20.0% Italian, 14.1% English, 6.3% French
Employment: 10.3% management, business, and financial, 1.7% computer, engineering, and science, 24.6% education, legal, community service, arts, and media, 12.9% healthcare practitioners, 17.1% service, 25.4% sales and office, 1.9% natural resources, construction, and maintenance, 6.2% production, transportation, and material moving
Income: Per capita: $42,043; Median household: $59,107; Average household: $84,952; Households with income of $100,000 or more: 30.4%; Poverty rate: 12.1%
Educational Attainment: High school diploma or higher: 94.5%; Bachelor's degree or higher: 40.1%; Graduate/professional degree or higher: 25.4%
Housing: Homeownership rate: 88.9%; Median home value: $232,100; Median year structure built: 1964; Homeowner vacancy rate: 0.0%; Median selected monthly owner costs: $1,699 with a mortgage, $731 without a mortgage; Median gross rent: $1,081 per month; Rental vacancy rate: 0.0%
Health Insurance: 93.0% have insurance; 75.6% have private insurance; 45.5% have public insurance; 7.0% do not have insurance; 0.0% of children under 18 do not have insurance
Transportation: Commute: 77.6% car, 7.4% public transportation, 4.9% walk, 9.1% work from home; Mean travel time to work: 28.4 minutes

WEST PARK (unincorporated postal area)
ZCTA: 12493
    Covers a land area of 6.894 square miles and a water area of 0.021 square miles. Located at 41.79° N. Lat; 73.97° W. Long. Elevation is 102 feet.
Population: 316; Growth (since 2000): -42.2%; Density: 45.8 persons per square mile; Race: 95.9% White, 2.2% Black/African American, 0.0% Asian, 0.0% American Indian/Alaska Native, 0.0% Native Hawaiian/Other Pacific Islander, 1.9% Two or more races, 13.0% Hispanic of any race; Average household size: 1.99; Median age: 28.6; Age under 18: 25.9%; Age 65 and over: 9.2%; Males per 100 females: 113.4; Marriage status: 61.7% never married, 23.3% now married, 0.0% separated, 11.5% widowed, 3.6% divorced; Foreign born: 2.8%; Speak English only: 87.9%; With disability: 0.0%; Veterans: 0.0%; Ancestry: 64.2% Irish, 56.0% Italian, 18.7% German, 9.2% Polish, 2.8% European
Employment: 0.0% management, business, and financial, 0.0% computer, engineering, and science, 33.7% education, legal, community service, arts, and media, 53.0% healthcare practitioners, 0.0% service, 13.4% sales and office, 0.0% natural resources, construction, and maintenance, 0.0% production, transportation, and material moving

Income: Per capita: $36,014; Median household: $88,173; Average household: $75,512; Households with income of $100,000 or more: n/a; Poverty rate: n/a
Educational Attainment: High school diploma or higher: 83.6%; Bachelor's degree or higher: 53.7%; Graduate/professional degree or higher: 20.3%
Housing: Homeownership rate: 44.4%; Median home value: $180,200; Median year structure built: 1962; Homeowner vacancy rate: 0.0%; Median selected monthly owner costs: $0 with a mortgage, $0 without a mortgage; Median gross rent: n/a per month; Rental vacancy rate: 0.0%
Health Insurance: 100.0% have insurance; 89.9% have private insurance; 10.1% have public insurance; 0.0% do not have insurance; 0.0% of children under 18 do not have insurance
Transportation: Commute: 100.0% car, 0.0% public transportation, 0.0% walk, 0.0% work from home; Mean travel time to work: 0.0 minutes

WEST SHOKAN (unincorporated postal area)
ZCTA: 12494

Covers a land area of 18.744 square miles and a water area of 0 square miles. Located at 41.96° N. Lat; 74.29° W. Long. Elevation is 666 feet.
Population: 620; Growth (since 2000): -13.2%; Density: 33.1 persons per square mile; Race: 100.0% White, 0.0% Black/African American, 0.0% Asian, 0.0% American Indian/Alaska Native, 0.0% Native Hawaiian/Other Pacific Islander, 0.0% Two or more races, 0.0% Hispanic of any race; Average household size: 1.93; Median age: 48.9; Age under 18: 18.7%; Age 65 and over: 19.2%; Males per 100 females: 97.4; Marriage status: 30.1% never married, 39.0% now married, 0.0% separated, 13.6% widowed, 17.3% divorced; Foreign born: 7.9%; Speak English only: 87.1%; With disability: 8.7%; Veterans: 5.6%; Ancestry: 34.4% German, 28.2% Polish, 21.6% Ukrainian, 17.1% Irish, 11.8% English
Employment: 28.9% management, business, and financial, 0.0% computer, engineering, and science, 9.4% education, legal, community service, arts, and media, 12.5% healthcare practitioners, 2.7% service, 26.7% sales and office, 14.9% natural resources, construction, and maintenance, 4.9% production, transportation, and material moving
Income: Per capita: $37,216; Median household: $65,913; Average household: $70,774; Households with income of $100,000 or more: 28.5%; Poverty rate: 1.1%
Educational Attainment: High school diploma or higher: 98.0%; Bachelor's degree or higher: 56.5%; Graduate/professional degree or higher: 20.0%
Housing: Homeownership rate: 89.4%; Median home value: $248,500; Median year structure built: 1972; Homeowner vacancy rate: 0.0%; Median selected monthly owner costs: $2,041 with a mortgage, $763 without a mortgage; Median gross rent: n/a per month; Rental vacancy rate: 0.0%
Health Insurance: 96.0% have insurance; 86.3% have private insurance; 27.6% have public insurance; 4.0% do not have insurance; 0.0% of children under 18 do not have insurance
Transportation: Commute: 86.9% car, 0.0% public transportation, 0.0% walk, 13.1% work from home; Mean travel time to work: 30.6 minutes

WILLOW (unincorporated postal area)
ZCTA: 12495

Covers a land area of 9.140 square miles and a water area of 0 square miles. Located at 42.08° N. Lat; 74.24° W. Long. Elevation is 1,093 feet.
Population: 288; Growth (since 2000): 52.4%; Density: 31.5 persons per square mile; Race: 89.9% White, 4.2% Black/African American, 5.9% Asian, 0.0% American Indian/Alaska Native, 0.0% Native Hawaiian/Other Pacific Islander, 0.0% Two or more races, 6.3% Hispanic of any race; Average household size: 2.15; Median age: 52.0; Age under 18: 9.0%; Age 65 and over: 23.6%; Males per 100 females: 100.8; Marriage status: 11.1% never married, 84.0% now married, 1.9% separated, 1.9% widowed, 3.1% divorced; Foreign born: 11.1%; Speak English only: 92.0%; With disability: 5.9%; Veterans: 0.0%; Ancestry: 30.6% Italian, 25.7% Polish, 22.2% German, 8.3% English, 7.6% American
Employment: 10.4% management, business, and financial, 15.1% computer, engineering, and science, 37.5% education, legal, community service, arts, and media, 3.1% healthcare practitioners, 13.0% service, 14.6% sales and office, 6.3% natural resources, construction, and maintenance, 0.0% production, transportation, and material moving

Income: Per capita: $68,874; Median household: $130,750; Average household: $143,582; Households with income of $100,000 or more: 52.2%; Poverty rate: 5.6%
Educational Attainment: High school diploma or higher: 95.3%; Bachelor's degree or higher: 49.0%; Graduate/professional degree or higher: 28.5%
Housing: Homeownership rate: 100.0%; Median home value: $535,000; Median year structure built: 1973; Homeowner vacancy rate: 0.0%; Median selected monthly owner costs: $2,402 with a mortgage, $1,501 without a mortgage; Median gross rent: n/a per month; Rental vacancy rate: 0.0%
Health Insurance: 100.0% have insurance; 92.4% have private insurance; 26.0% have public insurance; 0.0% do not have insurance; 0.0% of children under 18 do not have insurance
Transportation: Commute: 49.0% car, 10.9% public transportation, 6.3% walk, 27.6% work from home; Mean travel time to work: 40.9 minutes

WOODSTOCK (CDP). Covers a land area of 5.916 square miles and a water area of 0.009 square miles. Located at 42.05° N. Lat; 74.11° W. Long. Elevation is 561 feet.
Population: 2,091; Growth (since 2000): -4.4%; Density: 353.4 persons per square mile; Race: 87.5% White, 4.2% Black/African American, 3.0% Asian, 0.0% American Indian/Alaska Native, 0.0% Native Hawaiian/Other Pacific Islander, 2.8% Two or more races, 3.6% Hispanic of any race; Average household size: 1.94; Median age: 55.6; Age under 18: 17.3%; Age 65 and over: 34.4%; Males per 100 females: 86.1; Marriage status: 30.0% never married, 45.8% now married, 1.6% separated, 7.3% widowed, 16.9% divorced; Foreign born: 8.7%; Speak English only: 91.8%; With disability: 13.3%; Veterans: 12.3%; Ancestry: 16.5% Italian, 14.9% German, 14.6% English, 12.6% Russian, 10.7% Irish
Employment: 17.1% management, business, and financial, 8.3% computer, engineering, and science, 20.8% education, legal, community service, arts, and media, 6.4% healthcare practitioners, 11.7% service, 26.0% sales and office, 3.3% natural resources, construction, and maintenance, 6.3% production, transportation, and material moving
Income: Per capita: $38,107; Median household: $47,478; Average household: $75,798; Households with income of $100,000 or more: 26.3%; Poverty rate: 28.1%
Educational Attainment: High school diploma or higher: 96.5%; Bachelor's degree or higher: 53.4%; Graduate/professional degree or higher: 22.0%

School District(s)
Onteora Central SD (KG-12)
    Enrollment: 1,367 . . . . (845) 657-8851
Housing: Homeownership rate: 70.2%; Median home value: $326,400; Median year structure built: 1953; Homeowner vacancy rate: 0.0%; Median selected monthly owner costs: $2,061 with a mortgage, $820 without a mortgage; Median gross rent: $1,066 per month; Rental vacancy rate: 2.5%
Health Insurance: 97.9% have insurance; 65.4% have private insurance; 52.7% have public insurance; 2.1% do not have insurance; 0.0% of children under 18 do not have insurance
Transportation: Commute: 64.7% car, 6.6% public transportation, 4.6% walk, 20.9% work from home; Mean travel time to work: 25.6 minutes

WOODSTOCK (town). Covers a land area of 67.289 square miles and a water area of 0.544 square miles. Located at 42.06° N. Lat; 74.17° W. Long. Elevation is 561 feet.
History: Best known for its association with the famous 3-day music festival in 1969, Woodstock had a reputation as an artists' colony and progressive retreat long before the 1960s. A tannery center in the 19th century, it became an art colony in 1902. In 1906 the Manhattan-based Arts Student League opened a summer school here, and the adjacent Maverick colony drew social reformers, artists, and performers. To this day the village remains a magnet for tourists, artists, and drifters.
Population: 5,862; Growth (since 2000): -6.1%; Density: 87.1 persons per square mile; Race: 90.6% White, 3.1% Black/African American, 3.1% Asian, 0.0% American Indian/Alaska Native, 0.0% Native Hawaiian/Other Pacific Islander, 2.3% Two or more races, 2.9% Hispanic of any race; Average household size: 2.03; Median age: 56.9; Age under 18: 14.4%; Age 65 and over: 31.4%; Males per 100 females: 91.3; Marriage status: 23.0% never married, 57.5% now married, 0.8% separated, 5.9% widowed, 13.6% divorced; Foreign born: 9.4%; Speak English only: 91.8%;

With disability: 11.4%; Veterans: 6.9%; Ancestry: 17.4% Italian, 14.7% German, 13.8% Irish, 12.6% English, 9.0% Russian
Employment: 17.1% management, business, and financial, 10.2% computer, engineering, and science, 23.2% education, legal, community service, arts, and media, 6.7% healthcare practitioners, 11.3% service, 17.5% sales and office, 7.7% natural resources, construction, and maintenance, 6.3% production, transportation, and material moving
Income: Per capita: $55,017; Median household: $73,227; Average household: $113,131; Households with income of $100,000 or more: 36.4%; Poverty rate: 13.4%
Educational Attainment: High school diploma or higher: 97.1%; Bachelor's degree or higher: 59.9%; Graduate/professional degree or higher: 28.6%

School District(s)
Onteora Central SD (KG-12)
   Enrollment: 1,367 . . . . (845) 657-8851
Housing: Homeownership rate: 80.5%; Median home value: $325,800; Median year structure built: 1958; Homeowner vacancy rate: 2.1%; Median selected monthly owner costs: $2,122 with a mortgage, $852 without a mortgage; Median gross rent: $1,189 per month; Rental vacancy rate: 7.2%
Health Insurance: 94.5% have insurance; 71.5% have private insurance; 43.6% have public insurance; 5.5% do not have insurance; 1.7% of children under 18 do not have insurance
Safety: Violent crime rate: 3.4 per 10,000 population; Property crime rate: 105.0 per 10,000 population
Transportation: Commute: 68.8% car, 4.6% public transportation, 3.5% walk, 20.6% work from home; Mean travel time to work: 30.8 minutes
Additional Information Contacts
Town of Woodstock. . . . . (845) 679-2113
   http://www.woodstockny.org

ZENA (CDP). Covers a land area of 2.935 square miles and a water area of 0 square miles. Located at 42.02° N. Lat; 74.09° W. Long. Elevation is 377 feet.
Population: 1,218; Growth (since 2000): 8.8%; Density: 415.0 persons per square mile; Race: 84.0% White, 5.7% Black/African American, 6.8% Asian, 0.0% American Indian/Alaska Native, 0.0% Native Hawaiian/Other Pacific Islander, 3.5% Two or more races, 6.1% Hispanic of any race; Average household size: 2.53; Median age: 52.8; Age under 18: 18.4%; Age 65 and over: 21.3%; Males per 100 females: 92.4; Marriage status: 19.3% never married, 67.4% now married, 1.3% separated, 4.0% widowed, 9.3% divorced; Foreign born: 10.4%; Speak English only: 92.6%; With disability: 13.3%; Veterans: 3.1%; Ancestry: 27.4% Italian, 21.0% Irish, 11.3% German, 6.8% Polish, 5.8% Dutch
Employment: 14.7% management, business, and financial, 14.5% computer, engineering, and science, 23.9% education, legal, community service, arts, and media, 13.1% healthcare practitioners, 5.3% service, 16.8% sales and office, 4.4% natural resources, construction, and maintenance, 7.3% production, transportation, and material moving
Income: Per capita: $39,630; Median household: $89,034; Average household: $98,926; Households with income of $100,000 or more: 33.8%; Poverty rate: 4.2%
Educational Attainment: High school diploma or higher: 98.1%; Bachelor's degree or higher: 57.8%; Graduate/professional degree or higher: 28.7%
Housing: Homeownership rate: 91.0%; Median home value: $255,800; Median year structure built: 1963; Homeowner vacancy rate: 5.0%; Median selected monthly owner costs: $2,036 with a mortgage, $873 without a mortgage; Median gross rent: n/a per month; Rental vacancy rate: 0.0%
Health Insurance: 96.6% have insurance; 78.8% have private insurance; 32.7% have public insurance; 3.4% do not have insurance; 4.8% of children under 18 do not have insurance
Transportation: Commute: 85.4% car, 0.0% public transportation, 0.0% walk, 14.6% work from home; Mean travel time to work: 29.4 minutes

Warren County

Located in eastern New York, in the Adirondacks; bounded on the east by Lake George; drained by the Hudson and Schroon Rivers. Covers a land area of 866.952 square miles, a water area of 64.652 square miles, and is located in the Eastern Time Zone at 43.56° N. Lat., 73.84° W. Long. The county was founded in 1813. County seat is Lake George.

Warren County is part of the Glens Falls, NY Metropolitan Statistical Area. The entire metro area includes: Warren County, NY; Washington County, NY

Weather Station: Glens Falls Arpt   **Elevation: 320 feet**

	Jan	Feb	Mar	Apr	May	Jun	Jul	Aug	Sep	Oct	Nov	Dec
High	29	33	42	57	68	77	81	79	71	58	46	34
Low	9	11	21	34	44	53	58	56	48	36	28	17
Precip	2.9	2.0	3.0	3.0	3.6	3.5	4.1	3.6	3.3	3.4	3.3	3.0
Snow	na	13.2	12.8	2.4	tr	0.0	tr	na	na	na	na	na

High and Low temperatures in degrees Fahrenheit; Precipitation and Snow in inches

Weather Station: Glens Falls Farm   **Elevation: 503 feet**

	Jan	Feb	Mar	Apr	May	Jun	Jul	Aug	Sep	Oct	Nov	Dec
High	31	35	44	59	70	79	82	80	73	60	48	35
Low	11	12	22	34	45	54	59	57	50	38	29	18
Precip	3.3	2.7	3.6	3.7	4.0	4.2	4.6	4.2	3.9	4.0	4.1	3.7
Snow	19.0	12.4	11.3	2.0	0.0	0.0	0.0	0.0	0.0	tr	2.5	12.4

High and Low temperatures in degrees Fahrenheit; Precipitation and Snow in inches

Population: 64,701; Growth (since 2000): 2.2%; Density: 74.6 persons per square mile; Race: 96.0% White, 1.2% Black/African American, 1.0% Asian, 0.2% American Indian/Alaska Native, 0.1% Native Hawaiian/Other Pacific Islander, 1.3% two or more races, 2.4% Hispanic of any race; Average household size: 2.34; Median age: 46.2; Age under 18: 18.8%; Age 65 and over: 20.3%; Males per 100 females: 95.4; Marriage status: 29.3% never married, 50.4% now married, 2.1% separated, 7.7% widowed, 12.5% divorced; Foreign born: 3.6%; Speak English only: 94.8%; With disability: 14.5%; Veterans: 9.5%; Ancestry: 21.1% Irish, 14.4% German, 14.0% English, 13.2% Italian, 9.8% French
Religion: Six largest groups: 22.1% Catholicism, 3.2% Methodist/Pietist, 2.1% Presbyterian-Reformed, 1.7% Episcopalianism/Anglicanism, 1.4% Holiness, 1.3% Baptist
Economy: Unemployment rate: 3.4%; Leading industries: 18.5 % accommodation and food services; 17.9 % retail trade; 12.0 % health care and social assistance; Farms: 117 totaling 9,528 acres; Company size: 1 employs 1,000 or more persons, 4 employ 500 to 999 persons, 40 employ 100 to 499 persons, 2,272 employ less than 100 persons; Business ownership: 1,902 women-owned, n/a Black-owned, 62 Hispanic-owned, 95 Asian-owned, 36 American Indian/Alaska Native-owned
Employment: 12.4% management, business, and financial, 4.0% computer, engineering, and science, 12.6% education, legal, community service, arts, and media, 6.7% healthcare practitioners, 20.0% service, 24.9% sales and office, 8.1% natural resources, construction, and maintenance, 11.2% production, transportation, and material moving
Income: Per capita: $33,127; Median household: $60,222; Average household: $76,756; Households with income of $100,000 or more: 24.5%; Poverty rate: 9.9%
Educational Attainment: High school diploma or higher: 91.7%; Bachelor's degree or higher: 29.3%; Graduate/professional degree or higher: 13.7%
Housing: Homeownership rate: 71.9%; Median home value: $192,800; Median year structure built: 1973; Homeowner vacancy rate: 1.9%; Median selected monthly owner costs: $1,433 with a mortgage, $537 without a mortgage; Median gross rent: $881 per month; Rental vacancy rate: 8.2%
Vital Statistics: Birth rate: 84.1 per 10,000 population; Death rate: 101.2 per 10,000 population; Age-adjusted cancer mortality rate: 190.2 deaths per 100,000 population
Health Insurance: 94.1% have insurance; 73.9% have private insurance; 38.3% have public insurance; 5.9% do not have insurance; 2.5% of children under 18 do not have insurance
Health Care: Physicians: 33.2 per 10,000 population; Dentists: 9.5 per 10,000 population; Hospital beds: 42.6 per 10,000 population; Hospital admissions: 2,040.2 per 10,000 population
Transportation: Commute: 90.8% car, 0.9% public transportation, 3.3% walk, 3.4% work from home; Mean travel time to work: 22.8 minutes
2016 Presidential Election: 50.1% Trump, 41.7% Clinton, 4.0% Johnson, 2.7% Stein
National and State Parks: Lake George Beach State Park
Additional Information Contacts
Warren Government . . . . (518) 761-6539
   http://www.co.warren.ny.us

Warren County Communities

ADIRONDACK (unincorporated postal area)
ZCTA: 12808

Covers a land area of 22.184 square miles and a water area of 2.850 square miles. Located at 43.76° N. Lat; 73.72° W. Long. Elevation is 814 feet.

Population: 408; Growth (since 2000): 43.2%; Density: 18.4 persons per square mile; Race: 96.1% White, 0.0% Black/African American, 0.0% Asian, 0.0% American Indian/Alaska Native, 0.0% Native Hawaiian/Other Pacific Islander, 3.9% Two or more races, 0.0% Hispanic of any race; Average household size: 2.05; Median age: 60.2; Age under 18: 9.3%; Age 65 and over: 42.4%; Males per 100 females: 104.0; Marriage status: 10.2% never married, 68.2% now married, 4.3% separated, 9.4% widowed, 12.3% divorced; Foreign born: 1.5%; Speak English only: 99.3%; With disability: 23.3%; Veterans: 15.4%; Ancestry: 25.0% American, 15.9% Italian, 15.2% English, 12.3% Irish, 9.6% German

Employment: 4.5% management, business, and financial, 3.4% computer, engineering, and science, 15.8% education, legal, community service, arts, and media, 0.0% healthcare practitioners, 29.9% service, 18.1% sales and office, 13.6% natural resources, construction, and maintenance, 14.7% production, transportation, and material moving

Income: Per capita: $41,645; Median household: $62,396; Average household: $84,419; Households with income of $100,000 or more: 25.1%; Poverty rate: 3.9%

Educational Attainment: High school diploma or higher: 88.0%; Bachelor's degree or higher: 27.8%; Graduate/professional degree or higher: 19.1%

Housing: Homeownership rate: 100.0%; Median home value: $310,600; Median year structure built: 1979; Homeowner vacancy rate: 2.5%; Median selected monthly owner costs: $1,450 with a mortgage, $456 without a mortgage; Median gross rent: n/a per month; Rental vacancy rate: 100.0%

Health Insurance: 95.6% have insurance; 80.6% have private insurance; 52.7% have public insurance; 4.4% do not have insurance; 0.0% of children under 18 do not have insurance

Transportation: Commute: 80.8% car, 0.0% public transportation, 0.0% walk, 17.5% work from home; Mean travel time to work: 34.4 minutes

ATHOL (unincorporated postal area)
ZCTA: 12810

Covers a land area of 66.404 square miles and a water area of 1.140 square miles. Located at 43.49° N. Lat; 73.99° W. Long. Elevation is 787 feet.

Population: 737; Growth (since 2000): 14.6%; Density: 11.1 persons per square mile; Race: 99.2% White, 0.0% Black/African American, 0.0% Asian, 0.0% American Indian/Alaska Native, 0.0% Native Hawaiian/Other Pacific Islander, 0.3% Two or more races, 3.1% Hispanic of any race; Average household size: 2.60; Median age: 47.1; Age under 18: 19.4%; Age 65 and over: 14.9%; Males per 100 females: 112.5; Marriage status: 22.4% never married, 52.6% now married, 2.3% separated, 9.2% widowed, 15.8% divorced; Foreign born: 1.1%; Speak English only: 96.5%; With disability: 16.0%; Veterans: 8.6%; Ancestry: 16.0% German, 15.9% English, 15.6% Irish, 7.6% American, 7.6% French

Employment: 11.2% management, business, and financial, 5.9% computer, engineering, and science, 1.5% education, legal, community service, arts, and media, 3.2% healthcare practitioners, 27.3% service, 17.1% sales and office, 13.9% natural resources, construction, and maintenance, 20.0% production, transportation, and material moving

Income: Per capita: $26,083; Median household: $58,304; Average household: $65,395; Households with income of $100,000 or more: 14.5%; Poverty rate: 7.6%

Educational Attainment: High school diploma or higher: 87.4%; Bachelor's degree or higher: 7.5%; Graduate/professional degree or higher: 1.8%

Housing: Homeownership rate: 90.1%; Median home value: $114,100; Median year structure built: 1978; Homeowner vacancy rate: 0.0%; Median selected monthly owner costs: $1,067 with a mortgage, $385 without a mortgage; Median gross rent: $680 per month; Rental vacancy rate: 0.0%

Health Insurance: 88.3% have insurance; 66.1% have private insurance; 33.1% have public insurance; 11.7% do not have insurance; 2.8% of children under 18 do not have insurance

Transportation: Commute: 94.1% car, 0.0% public transportation, 4.2% walk, 1.7% work from home; Mean travel time to work: 31.9 minutes

BAKERS MILLS (unincorporated postal area)
ZCTA: 12811

Covers a land area of 1.722 square miles and a water area of 0 square miles. Located at 43.61° N. Lat; 74.03° W. Long. Elevation is 1,594 feet.

Population: 18; Growth (since 2000): n/a; Density: 10.5 persons per square mile; Race: 83.3% White, 0.0% Black/African American, 0.0% Asian, 0.0% American Indian/Alaska Native, 0.0% Native Hawaiian/Other Pacific Islander, 16.7% Two or more races, 0.0% Hispanic of any race; Average household size: 0.00; Median age: n/a; Age under 18: 0.0%; Age 65 and over: 100.0%; Males per 100 females: 95.4; Marriage status: 0.0% never married, 0.0% now married, 0.0% separated, 0.0% widowed, 100.0% divorced; Foreign born: 0.0%; Speak English only: 100.0%; With disability: 0.0%; Veterans: 100.0%; Ancestry: 83.3% Irish, 16.7% Dutch, 16.7% Italian

Employment: n/a management, business, and financial, n/a computer, engineering, and science, n/a education, legal, community service, arts, and media, n/a healthcare practitioners, n/a service, n/a sales and office, n/a natural resources, construction, and maintenance, n/a production, transportation, and material moving

Income: Per capita: n/a; Median household: n/a; Average household: n/a; Households with income of $100,000 or more: n/a; Poverty rate: n/a

Educational Attainment: High school diploma or higher: 100.0%; Bachelor's degree or higher: 16.7%; Graduate/professional degree or higher: n/a

Housing: Homeownership rate: 83.3%; Median home value: n/a; Median year structure built: 1974; Homeowner vacancy rate: 0.0%; Median selected monthly owner costs: $0 with a mortgage, $0 without a mortgage; Median gross rent: n/a per month; Rental vacancy rate: 0.0%

Health Insurance: 100.0% have insurance; 16.7% have private insurance; 100.0% have public insurance; 0.0% do not have insurance; 0.0% of children under 18 do not have insurance

Transportation: Commute: n/a car, n/a public transportation, n/a walk, n/a work from home; Mean travel time to work: 0.0 minutes

BOLTON (town). Covers a land area of 63.270 square miles and a water area of 26.771 square miles. Located at 43.58° N. Lat; 73.66° W. Long. Elevation is 374 feet.

Population: 2,166; Growth (since 2000): 2.3%; Density: 34.2 persons per square mile; Race: 92.7% White, 3.7% Black/African American, 0.0% Asian, 0.0% American Indian/Alaska Native, 0.0% Native Hawaiian/Other Pacific Islander, 0.0% Two or more races, 3.5% Hispanic of any race; Average household size: 2.14; Median age: 53.0; Age under 18: 8.7%; Age 65 and over: 29.0%; Males per 100 females: 104.8; Marriage status: 27.3% never married, 54.2% now married, 1.9% separated, 8.1% widowed, 10.4% divorced; Foreign born: 7.8%; Speak English only: 88.8%; With disability: 15.5%; Veterans: 7.1%; Ancestry: 20.0% English, 15.3% German, 13.6% Italian, 13.4% Irish, 9.1% French

Employment: 21.6% management, business, and financial, 1.6% computer, engineering, and science, 6.0% education, legal, community service, arts, and media, 5.2% healthcare practitioners, 16.3% service, 25.8% sales and office, 13.5% natural resources, construction, and maintenance, 10.0% production, transportation, and material moving

Income: Per capita: $40,915; Median household: $61,661; Average household: $85,568; Households with income of $100,000 or more: 26.3%; Poverty rate: 3.6%

Educational Attainment: High school diploma or higher: 91.2%; Bachelor's degree or higher: 34.1%; Graduate/professional degree or higher: 12.9%

Housing: Homeownership rate: 78.4%; Median home value: $329,200; Median year structure built: 1977; Homeowner vacancy rate: 2.8%; Median selected monthly owner costs: $1,523 with a mortgage, $579 without a mortgage; Median gross rent: $888 per month; Rental vacancy rate: 9.9%

Health Insurance: 92.8% have insurance; 68.4% have private insurance; 46.4% have public insurance; 7.2% do not have insurance; 0.0% of children under 18 do not have insurance

Safety: Violent crime rate: 4.4 per 10,000 population; Property crime rate: 26.4 per 10,000 population

Transportation: Commute: 86.2% car, 0.7% public transportation, 9.5% walk, 3.0% work from home; Mean travel time to work: 24.8 minutes

BOLTON LANDING (CDP). Covers a land area of 1.062 square miles and a water area of 0.176 square miles. Located at 43.56° N. Lat; 73.66° W. Long. Elevation is 361 feet.

Population: 388; Growth (since 2000): n/a; Density: 365.2 persons per square mile; Race: 73.7% White, 20.6% Black/African American, 0.0% Asian, 0.0% American Indian/Alaska Native, 0.0% Native Hawaiian/Other Pacific Islander, 0.0% Two or more races, 5.7% Hispanic of any race; Average household size: 2.16; Median age: 40.9; Age under 18: 13.1%; Age 65 and over: 27.8%; Males per 100 females: 101.2; Marriage status: 34.7% never married, 42.4% now married, 8.6% separated, 14.8% widowed, 8.0% divorced; Foreign born: 13.9%; Speak English only: 90.6%; With disability: 13.1%; Veterans: 5.0%; Ancestry: 17.5% Italian, 15.5% American, 14.7% English, 12.1% Swiss, 9.5% German

Employment: 54.7% management, business, and financial, 0.0% computer, engineering, and science, 0.0% education, legal, community service, arts, and media, 4.7% healthcare practitioners, 14.2% service, 26.4% sales and office, 0.0% natural resources, construction, and maintenance, 0.0% production, transportation, and material moving

Income: Per capita: $30,432; Median household: $32,632; Average household: $60,976; Households with income of $100,000 or more: 8.9%; Poverty rate: n/a

Educational Attainment: High school diploma or higher: 85.2%; Bachelor's degree or higher: 22.1%; Graduate/professional degree or higher: 5.7%

School District(s)

Bolton Central SD (PK-12)

    Enrollment: 203 . . . . (518) 644-2400

Housing: Homeownership rate: 54.4%; Median home value: $268,400; Median year structure built: 1963; Homeowner vacancy rate: 13.3%; Median selected monthly owner costs: $2,453 with a mortgage, $359 without a mortgage; Median gross rent: $807 per month; Rental vacancy rate: 15.5%

Health Insurance: 85.1% have insurance; 48.2% have private insurance; 55.9% have public insurance; 14.9% do not have insurance; 0.0% of children under 18 do not have insurance

Transportation: Commute: 41.2% car, 4.7% public transportation, 54.1% walk, 0.0% work from home; Mean travel time to work: 14.1 minutes

BRANT LAKE (unincorporated postal area)

ZCTA: 12815

Covers a land area of 36.592 square miles and a water area of 2.976 square miles. Located at 43.70° N. Lat; 73.67° W. Long. Elevation is 794 feet.

Population: 986; Growth (since 2000): 3.2%; Density: 26.9 persons per square mile; Race: 96.2% White, 0.0% Black/African American, 0.0% Asian, 0.0% American Indian/Alaska Native, 0.0% Native Hawaiian/Other Pacific Islander, 3.8% Two or more races, 0.6% Hispanic of any race; Average household size: 2.23; Median age: 54.4; Age under 18: 13.6%; Age 65 and over: 27.2%; Males per 100 females: 98.9; Marriage status: 23.6% never married, 59.9% now married, 1.7% separated, 9.7% widowed, 6.8% divorced; Foreign born: 3.3%; Speak English only: 92.5%; With disability: 17.6%; Veterans: 13.7%; Ancestry: 22.8% English, 20.8% German, 17.4% Irish, 10.8% Italian, 6.3% French

Employment: 10.1% management, business, and financial, 4.0% computer, engineering, and science, 4.8% education, legal, community service, arts, and media, 5.3% healthcare practitioners, 23.5% service, 31.3% sales and office, 13.9% natural resources, construction, and maintenance, 7.1% production, transportation, and material moving

Income: Per capita: $33,697; Median household: $63,036; Average household: $72,870; Households with income of $100,000 or more: 27.3%; Poverty rate: 8.8%

Educational Attainment: High school diploma or higher: 88.9%; Bachelor's degree or higher: 30.9%; Graduate/professional degree or higher: 13.9%

Housing: Homeownership rate: 90.9%; Median home value: $195,800; Median year structure built: 1977; Homeowner vacancy rate: 2.9%; Median selected monthly owner costs: $1,330 with a mortgage, $420 without a mortgage; Median gross rent: $850 per month; Rental vacancy rate: 16.7%

Health Insurance: 97.6% have insurance; 74.5% have private insurance; 41.7% have public insurance; 2.4% do not have insurance; 0.0% of children under 18 do not have insurance

Transportation: Commute: 94.7% car, 0.0% public transportation, 1.9% walk, 3.4% work from home; Mean travel time to work: 34.5 minutes

CHESTER (town). Covers a land area of 84.190 square miles and a water area of 2.860 square miles. Located at 43.69° N. Lat; 73.87° W. Long.

Population: 3,302; Growth (since 2000): -8.6%; Density: 39.2 persons per square mile; Race: 99.8% White, 0.2% Black/African American, 0.0% Asian, 0.0% American Indian/Alaska Native, 0.0% Native Hawaiian/Other Pacific Islander, 0.0% Two or more races, 0.9% Hispanic of any race; Average household size: 2.29; Median age: 46.7; Age under 18: 19.3%; Age 65 and over: 22.0%; Males per 100 females: 99.5; Marriage status: 25.5% never married, 59.2% now married, 2.9% separated, 7.2% widowed, 8.2% divorced; Foreign born: 1.4%; Speak English only: 87.0%; With disability: 13.8%; Veterans: 6.0%; Ancestry: 30.1% Irish, 23.9% German, 17.5% English, 10.5% French, 7.5% Italian

Employment: 12.1% management, business, and financial, 0.0% computer, engineering, and science, 11.7% education, legal, community service, arts, and media, 8.7% healthcare practitioners, 23.6% service, 18.3% sales and office, 11.1% natural resources, construction, and maintenance, 14.6% production, transportation, and material moving

Income: Per capita: $28,228; Median household: $56,979; Average household: $64,186; Households with income of $100,000 or more: 19.5%; Poverty rate: 14.2%

Educational Attainment: High school diploma or higher: 93.1%; Bachelor's degree or higher: 34.0%; Graduate/professional degree or higher: 14.4%

Housing: Homeownership rate: 83.0%; Median home value: $179,500; Median year structure built: 1972; Homeowner vacancy rate: 1.9%; Median selected monthly owner costs: $1,213 with a mortgage, $481 without a mortgage; Median gross rent: $789 per month; Rental vacancy rate: 16.8%

Health Insurance: 92.0% have insurance; 64.9% have private insurance; 43.9% have public insurance; 8.0% do not have insurance; 1.1% of children under 18 do not have insurance

Transportation: Commute: 85.2% car, 0.6% public transportation, 5.2% walk, 8.0% work from home; Mean travel time to work: 24.8 minutes

CHESTERTOWN (CDP). Covers a land area of 3.843 square miles and a water area of 0.013 square miles. Located at 43.64° N. Lat; 73.78° W. Long. Elevation is 843 feet.

Population: 493; Growth (since 2000): n/a; Density: 128.3 persons per square mile; Race: 99.6% White, 0.4% Black/African American, 0.0% Asian, 0.0% American Indian/Alaska Native, 0.0% Native Hawaiian/Other Pacific Islander, 0.0% Two or more races, 0.4% Hispanic of any race; Average household size: 1.83; Median age: 51.6; Age under 18: 5.5%; Age 65 and over: 17.4%; Males per 100 females: 94.5; Marriage status: 20.9% never married, 49.2% now married, 0.0% separated, 15.6% widowed, 14.3% divorced; Foreign born: 0.0%; Speak English only: 100.0%; With disability: 20.7%; Veterans: 2.8%; Ancestry: 26.4% English, 25.8% Irish, 16.6% French, 9.7% German, 7.3% Dutch

Employment: 2.1% management, business, and financial, 0.0% computer, engineering, and science, 1.8% education, legal, community service, arts, and media, 4.7% healthcare practitioners, 27.4% service, 29.7% sales and office, 10.3% natural resources, construction, and maintenance, 24.1% production, transportation, and material moving

Income: Per capita: $27,494; Median household: $47,679; Average household: $49,276; Households with income of $100,000 or more: 4.1%; Poverty rate: 10.5%

Educational Attainment: High school diploma or higher: 92.1%; Bachelor's degree or higher: 16.5%; Graduate/professional degree or higher: 7.9%

School District(s)

North Warren Central SD (PK-12)

    Enrollment: 541 . . . . (518) 494-3015

Housing: Homeownership rate: 46.6%; Median home value: $170,500; Median year structure built: 1958; Homeowner vacancy rate: 0.0%; Median selected monthly owner costs: $1,179 with a mortgage, n/a without a mortgage; Median gross rent: $693 per month; Rental vacancy rate: 0.0%

Health Insurance: 61.3% have insurance; 47.9% have private insurance; 24.5% have public insurance; 38.7% do not have insurance; 0.0% of children under 18 do not have insurance

Transportation: Commute: 81.5% car, 0.0% public transportation, 11.8% walk, 6.8% work from home; Mean travel time to work: 18.7 minutes

DIAMOND POINT (unincorporated postal area)

ZCTA: 12824

Covers a land area of 15.164 square miles and a water area of 0.487 square miles. Located at 43.52° N. Lat; 73.73° W. Long. Elevation is 331 feet.

Population: 1,032; Growth (since 2000): 40.4%; Density: 68.1 persons per square mile; Race: 100.0% White, 0.0% Black/African American, 0.0% Asian, 0.0% American Indian/Alaska Native, 0.0% Native Hawaiian/Other Pacific Islander, 0.0% Two or more races, 2.7% Hispanic of any race; Average household size: 2.08; Median age: 57.9; Age under 18: 4.5%; Age 65 and over: 29.3%; Males per 100 females: 101.4; Marriage status: 25.1% never married, 57.8% now married, 1.0% separated, 3.4% widowed, 13.7% divorced; Foreign born: 7.1%; Speak English only: 90.5%; With disability: 14.6%; Veterans: 8.8%; Ancestry: 24.2% English, 18.5% Italian, 14.4% German, 13.4% Irish, 12.1% French

Employment: 12.8% management, business, and financial, 3.0% computer, engineering, and science, 5.4% education, legal, community service, arts, and media, 8.1% healthcare practitioners, 17.8% service, 28.1% sales and office, 10.3% natural resources, construction, and maintenance, 14.6% production, transportation, and material moving

Income: Per capita: $46,475; Median household: $64,231; Average household: $94,117; Households with income of $100,000 or more: 37.6%; Poverty rate: 3.9%

Educational Attainment: High school diploma or higher: 92.8%; Bachelor's degree or higher: 35.4%; Graduate/professional degree or higher: 11.3%

Housing: Homeownership rate: 88.3%; Median home value: $298,200; Median year structure built: 1977; Homeowner vacancy rate: 0.0%; Median selected monthly owner costs: $1,551 with a mortgage, $850 without a mortgage; Median gross rent: $1,156 per month; Rental vacancy rate: 0.0%

Health Insurance: 95.7% have insurance; 80.0% have private insurance; 37.6% have public insurance; 4.3% do not have insurance; 0.0% of children under 18 do not have insurance

Transportation: Commute: 91.0% car, 0.0% public transportation, 3.4% walk, 4.4% work from home; Mean travel time to work: 28.4 minutes

GLENS FALLS (city). Covers a land area of 3.851 square miles and a water area of 0.138 square miles. Located at 43.31° N. Lat; 73.65° W. Long. Elevation is 344 feet.

History: The site of Glens Falls was part of the Queensbury Patent, 23,000 acres of land granted in 1759 to 23 men. The water power provided by the 60-foot falls in the Hudson River determined the location of the settlement. During the Revolution the village was destroyed by the British. In 1788, Colonel John Glen of Schenectady acquired land and built mills here. There followed a succession of industrial activities, beginning with lumbering and followed by the manufacture of lime, cement, paper and cellulose.

Population: 14,428; Growth (since 2000): 0.5%; Density: 3,746.5 persons per square mile; Race: 92.4% White, 1.6% Black/African American, 2.1% Asian, 0.3% American Indian/Alaska Native, 0.2% Native Hawaiian/Other Pacific Islander, 3.0% Two or more races, 4.3% Hispanic of any race; Average household size: 2.23; Median age: 38.2; Age under 18: 20.3%; Age 65 and over: 14.0%; Males per 100 females: 94.3; Marriage status: 38.0% never married, 39.8% now married, 2.2% separated, 5.6% widowed, 16.7% divorced; Foreign born: 4.4%; Speak English only: 94.1%; With disability: 14.7%; Veterans: 8.4%; Ancestry: 22.0% Irish, 13.9% Italian, 12.4% English, 10.2% German, 9.8% French

Employment: 11.8% management, business, and financial, 4.8% computer, engineering, and science, 15.1% education, legal, community service, arts, and media, 6.6% healthcare practitioners, 20.3% service, 22.5% sales and office, 6.4% natural resources, construction, and maintenance, 12.5% production, transportation, and material moving

Income: Per capita: $28,604; Median household: $48,716; Average household: $62,656; Households with income of $100,000 or more: 18.8%; Poverty rate: 16.0%

Educational Attainment: High school diploma or higher: 91.0%; Bachelor's degree or higher: 27.0%; Graduate/professional degree or higher: 11.8%

School District(s)

Glens Falls City SD (PK-12)

Enrollment: 2,068 . . . . (518) 792-1212

Glens Falls Common SD (KG-06)

Enrollment: 157 . . . . (518) 792-3231

Vocational/Technical School(s)

Adirondack Beauty School (Private, For-profit)

Enrollment: n/a . . . . (518) 745-1646

Tuition: $10,100

Housing: Homeownership rate: 51.2%; Median home value: $149,100; Median year structure built: Before 1940; Homeowner vacancy rate: 0.6%; Median selected monthly owner costs: $1,386 with a mortgage, $543 without a mortgage; Median gross rent: $826 per month; Rental vacancy rate: 4.4%

Health Insurance: 92.8% have insurance; 67.5% have private insurance; 38.4% have public insurance; 7.2% do not have insurance; 2.2% of children under 18 do not have insurance

Hospitals: Glens Falls Hospital (410 beds)

Safety: Violent crime rate: 20.3 per 10,000 population; Property crime rate: 133.2 per 10,000 population

Newspapers: Post-Star (daily circulation 33,300); The Chronicle (weekly circulation 30,000)

Transportation: Commute: 86.5% car, 2.3% public transportation, 7.4% walk, 1.8% work from home; Mean travel time to work: 17.4 minutes; Amtrak: Train service available.

Airports: Floyd Bennett Memorial (general aviation)

Additional Information Contacts

City of Glens Falls . . . . (518) 761-3803

http://www.cityofglensfalls.com

GLENS FALLS NORTH (CDP). Covers a land area of 8.232 square miles and a water area of 0.088 square miles. Located at 43.33° N. Lat; 73.68° W. Long.

History: Glens Falls North is a census-designated place (CDP) in Warren County, New York. Its residents call it not Glens Falls North, but the Town of Queensbury.

Population: 8,490; Growth (since 2000): 5.3%; Density: 1,031.3 persons per square mile; Race: 95.9% White, 0.1% Black/African American, 2.7% Asian, 0.1% American Indian/Alaska Native, 0.0% Native Hawaiian/Other Pacific Islander, 1.2% Two or more races, 1.7% Hispanic of any race; Average household size: 2.33; Median age: 45.4; Age under 18: 20.0%; Age 65 and over: 22.0%; Males per 100 females: 87.8; Marriage status: 29.5% never married, 49.1% now married, 1.5% separated, 9.6% widowed, 11.8% divorced; Foreign born: 7.1%; Speak English only: 90.9%; With disability: 15.5%; Veterans: 9.8%; Ancestry: 20.2% Irish, 19.0% Italian, 13.8% English, 12.7% German, 6.8% French

Employment: 13.8% management, business, and financial, 2.9% computer, engineering, and science, 16.0% education, legal, community service, arts, and media, 8.2% healthcare practitioners, 17.0% service, 26.1% sales and office, 5.2% natural resources, construction, and maintenance, 10.8% production, transportation, and material moving

Income: Per capita: $35,972; Median household: $64,391; Average household: $83,968; Households with income of $100,000 or more: 27.9%; Poverty rate: 10.4%

Educational Attainment: High school diploma or higher: 96.3%; Bachelor's degree or higher: 35.6%; Graduate/professional degree or higher: 19.5%

Housing: Homeownership rate: 65.1%; Median home value: $217,400; Median year structure built: 1977; Homeowner vacancy rate: 2.1%; Median selected monthly owner costs: $1,574 with a mortgage, $506 without a mortgage; Median gross rent: $912 per month; Rental vacancy rate: 12.8%

Health Insurance: 96.8% have insurance; 83.2% have private insurance; 33.8% have public insurance; 3.2% do not have insurance; 3.6% of children under 18 do not have insurance

Transportation: Commute: 92.6% car, 0.9% public transportation, 1.5% walk, 3.7% work from home; Mean travel time to work: 22.4 minutes

HAGUE (town). Covers a land area of 63.760 square miles and a water area of 15.859 square miles. Located at 43.69° N. Lat; 73.55° W. Long. Elevation is 331 feet.

Population: 891; Growth (since 2000): 4.3%; Density: 14.0 persons per square mile; Race: 97.6% White, 0.0% Black/African American, 0.6% Asian, 0.0% American Indian/Alaska Native, 0.0% Native Hawaiian/Other Pacific Islander, 1.3% Two or more races, 1.2% Hispanic of any race; Average household size: 2.19; Median age: 58.2; Age under 18: 15.9%; Age 65 and over: 33.6%; Males per 100 females: 97.5; Marriage status: 18.1% never married, 64.8% now married, 2.0% separated, 7.0% widowed, 10.1% divorced; Foreign born: 0.7%; Speak English only: 96.5%; With disability: 14.1%; Veterans: 10.4%; Ancestry: 17.8% Irish, 15.7% English, 15.4% German, 9.9% French, 8.5% Scottish

Employment: 11.5% management, business, and financial, 2.6% computer, engineering, and science, 12.3% education, legal, community service, arts, and media, 8.6% healthcare practitioners, 22.3% service, 12.3% sales and office, 19.1% natural resources, construction, and maintenance, 11.3% production, transportation, and material moving
Income: Per capita: $33,883; Median household: $60,000; Average household: $73,976; Households with income of $100,000 or more: 25.9%; Poverty rate: 8.5%
Educational Attainment: High school diploma or higher: 93.0%; Bachelor's degree or higher: 35.0%; Graduate/professional degree or higher: 18.1%
Housing: Homeownership rate: 88.7%; Median home value: $343,500; Median year structure built: 1967; Homeowner vacancy rate: 3.8%; Median selected monthly owner costs: $1,565 with a mortgage, $674 without a mortgage; Median gross rent: $838 per month; Rental vacancy rate: 0.0%
Health Insurance: 92.4% have insurance; 70.9% have private insurance; 47.3% have public insurance; 7.6% do not have insurance; 6.3% of children under 18 do not have insurance
Transportation: Commute: 91.3% car, 1.4% public transportation, 5.2% walk, 2.2% work from home; Mean travel time to work: 25.7 minutes

HORICON (town). Covers a land area of 65.767 square miles and a water area of 6.100 square miles. Located at 43.72° N. Lat; 73.71° W. Long.
Population: 1,640; Growth (since 2000): 10.9%; Density: 24.9 persons per square mile; Race: 95.6% White, 0.0% Black/African American, 0.0% Asian, 0.0% American Indian/Alaska Native, 0.0% Native Hawaiian/Other Pacific Islander, 4.4% Two or more races, 0.4% Hispanic of any race; Average household size: 2.30; Median age: 54.7; Age under 18: 12.8%; Age 65 and over: 30.9%; Males per 100 females: 100.4; Marriage status: 21.6% never married, 60.5% now married, 2.1% separated, 9.8% widowed, 8.1% divorced; Foreign born: 2.4%; Speak English only: 94.8%; With disability: 20.5%; Veterans: 13.0%; Ancestry: 19.5% English, 17.7% German, 17.0% Irish, 11.7% Italian, 9.5% American
Employment: 8.5% management, business, and financial, 3.4% computer, engineering, and science, 8.1% education, legal, community service, arts, and media, 3.4% healthcare practitioners, 22.2% service, 30.2% sales and office, 14.3% natural resources, construction, and maintenance, 10.0% production, transportation, and material moving
Income: Per capita: $35,066; Median household: $63,600; Average household: $78,367; Households with income of $100,000 or more: 26.8%; Poverty rate: 11.5%
Educational Attainment: High school diploma or higher: 88.6%; Bachelor's degree or higher: 28.6%; Graduate/professional degree or higher: 15.0%
Housing: Homeownership rate: 93.9%; Median home value: $221,000; Median year structure built: 1978; Homeowner vacancy rate: 3.9%; Median selected monthly owner costs: $1,325 with a mortgage, $437 without a mortgage; Median gross rent: $850 per month; Rental vacancy rate: 29.5%
Health Insurance: 96.3% have insurance; 73.7% have private insurance; 46.5% have public insurance; 3.7% do not have insurance; 0.0% of children under 18 do not have insurance
Transportation: Commute: 91.1% car, 0.0% public transportation, 1.2% walk, 7.3% work from home; Mean travel time to work: 32.7 minutes

JOHNSBURG (town). Covers a land area of 203.976 square miles and a water area of 2.768 square miles. Located at 43.66° N. Lat; 74.07° W. Long. Elevation is 1,283 feet.
Population: 2,002; Growth (since 2000): -18.3%; Density: 9.8 persons per square mile; Race: 95.9% White, 0.0% Black/African American, 0.0% Asian, 0.0% American Indian/Alaska Native, 0.0% Native Hawaiian/Other Pacific Islander, 4.1% Two or more races, 0.2% Hispanic of any race; Average household size: 2.40; Median age: 53.1; Age under 18: 16.6%; Age 65 and over: 24.5%; Males per 100 females: 96.2; Marriage status: 22.0% never married, 58.7% now married, 3.0% separated, 7.6% widowed, 11.7% divorced; Foreign born: 1.4%; Speak English only: 98.5%; With disability: 22.2%; Veterans: 10.5%; Ancestry: 23.5% Irish, 20.8% English, 13.2% German, 10.6% French, 8.5% American
Employment: 6.9% management, business, and financial, 3.5% computer, engineering, and science, 9.2% education, legal, community service, arts, and media, 4.5% healthcare practitioners, 23.8% service, 29.4% sales and office, 15.2% natural resources, construction, and maintenance, 7.4% production, transportation, and material moving

Income: Per capita: $22,807; Median household: $39,500; Average household: $53,937; Households with income of $100,000 or more: 18.0%; Poverty rate: 10.3%
Educational Attainment: High school diploma or higher: 86.9%; Bachelor's degree or higher: 19.2%; Graduate/professional degree or higher: 8.6%
Housing: Homeownership rate: 78.8%; Median home value: $151,400; Median year structure built: 1973; Homeowner vacancy rate: 0.0%; Median selected monthly owner costs: $1,053 with a mortgage, $409 without a mortgage; Median gross rent: $686 per month; Rental vacancy rate: 0.0%
Health Insurance: 91.4% have insurance; 65.0% have private insurance; 44.6% have public insurance; 8.6% do not have insurance; 9.8% of children under 18 do not have insurance
Transportation: Commute: 90.1% car, 0.0% public transportation, 0.0% walk, 7.8% work from home; Mean travel time to work: 21.5 minutes

KATTSKILL BAY (unincorporated postal area) ZCTA: 12844
Covers a land area of 2.737 square miles and a water area of 0 square miles. Located at 43.49° N. Lat; 73.62° W. Long..
Population: 222; Growth (since 2000): -17.5%; Density: 81.1 persons per square mile; Race: 91.4% White, 3.6% Black/African American, 1.4% Asian, 0.0% American Indian/Alaska Native, 0.0% Native Hawaiian/Other Pacific Islander, 1.8% Two or more races, 2.3% Hispanic of any race; Average household size: 1.91; Median age: 51.3; Age under 18: 19.4%; Age 65 and over: 37.8%; Males per 100 females: 103.1; Marriage status: 18.4% never married, 63.1% now married, 0.0% separated, 4.5% widowed, 14.0% divorced; Foreign born: 4.5%; Speak English only: 96.7%; With disability: 10.4%; Veterans: 17.3%; Ancestry: 32.0% Irish, 23.0% French, 23.0% German, 13.5% American, 11.7% English
Employment: 0.0% management, business, and financial, 0.0% computer, engineering, and science, 24.7% education, legal, community service, arts, and media, 0.0% healthcare practitioners, 25.8% service, 20.2% sales and office, 29.2% natural resources, construction, and maintenance, 0.0% production, transportation, and material moving
Income: Per capita: $26,659; Median household: $60,469; Average household: $58,619; Households with income of $100,000 or more: 10.1%; Poverty rate: 16.1%
Educational Attainment: High school diploma or higher: 98.0%; Bachelor's degree or higher: 37.3%; Graduate/professional degree or higher: 11.8%
Housing: Homeownership rate: 76.8%; Median home value: n/a; Median year structure built: 1972; Homeowner vacancy rate: 0.0%; Median selected monthly owner costs: $0 with a mortgage, $1,501 without a mortgage; Median gross rent: n/a per month; Rental vacancy rate: 0.0%
Health Insurance: 96.4% have insurance; 85.1% have private insurance; 37.8% have public insurance; 3.6% do not have insurance; 2.1% of children under 18 do not have insurance
Transportation: Commute: 65.3% car, 0.0% public transportation, 25.0% walk, 9.7% work from home; Mean travel time to work: 12.8 minutes

LAKE GEORGE (town). Covers a land area of 30.069 square miles and a water area of 2.549 square miles. Located at 43.44° N. Lat; 73.72° W. Long. Elevation is 344 feet.
History: Vestiges of Fort William Henry, built by Sir William Johnson, and Fort George are in the village. Incorporated 1903.
Population: 3,454; Growth (since 2000): -3.5%; Density: 114.9 persons per square mile; Race: 97.5% White, 0.5% Black/African American, 1.0% Asian, 0.0% American Indian/Alaska Native, 0.0% Native Hawaiian/Other Pacific Islander, 0.8% Two or more races, 2.2% Hispanic of any race; Average household size: 2.29; Median age: 49.5; Age under 18: 16.6%; Age 65 and over: 23.2%; Males per 100 females: 101.9; Marriage status: 29.8% never married, 53.7% now married, 1.2% separated, 6.2% widowed, 10.3% divorced; Foreign born: 3.4%; Speak English only: 96.1%; With disability: 10.4%; Veterans: 9.9%; Ancestry: 26.7% Irish, 17.7% German, 15.7% Italian, 10.5% English, 7.2% French
Employment: 16.5% management, business, and financial, 6.2% computer, engineering, and science, 13.8% education, legal, community service, arts, and media, 6.2% healthcare practitioners, 19.1% service, 23.5% sales and office, 6.2% natural resources, construction, and maintenance, 8.5% production, transportation, and material moving

Income: Per capita: $37,093; Median household: $66,719; Average household: $83,653; Households with income of $100,000 or more: 25.3%; Poverty rate: 7.2%
Educational Attainment: High school diploma or higher: 91.2%; Bachelor's degree or higher: 31.8%; Graduate/professional degree or higher: 11.4%

School District(s)
Lake George Central SD (KG-12)
    Enrollment: 805 . . . . (518) 668-5456
Housing: Homeownership rate: 75.5%; Median home value: $254,900; Median year structure built: 1974; Homeowner vacancy rate: 4.6%; Median selected monthly owner costs: $1,520 with a mortgage, $639 without a mortgage; Median gross rent: $902 per month; Rental vacancy rate: 7.2%
Health Insurance: 93.1% have insurance; 72.4% have private insurance; 40.6% have public insurance; 6.9% do not have insurance; 3.9% of children under 18 do not have insurance
Transportation: Commute: 86.6% car, 1.6% public transportation, 6.3% walk, 4.6% work from home; Mean travel time to work: 24.1 minutes

LAKE GEORGE (village). County seat. Covers a land area of 0.586 square miles and a water area of 0 square miles. Located at 43.43° N. Lat; 73.72° W. Long. Elevation is 344 feet.

Population: 947; Growth (since 2000): -3.9%; Density: 1,615.9 persons per square mile; Race: 96.2% White, 1.4% Black/African American, 0.0% Asian, 0.0% American Indian/Alaska Native, 0.0% Native Hawaiian/Other Pacific Islander, 2.4% Two or more races, 4.2% Hispanic of any race; Average household size: 2.20; Median age: 49.5; Age under 18: 16.9%; Age 65 and over: 24.4%; Males per 100 females: 95.7; Marriage status: 36.7% never married, 41.7% now married, 1.0% separated, 6.5% widowed, 15.1% divorced; Foreign born: 5.4%; Speak English only: 94.7%; With disability: 18.3%; Veterans: 8.1%; Ancestry: 24.8% Irish, 20.7% German, 18.7% Italian, 12.2% English, 6.0% American
Employment: 12.9% management, business, and financial, 5.4% computer, engineering, and science, 10.2% education, legal, community service, arts, and media, 4.4% healthcare practitioners, 30.3% service, 26.4% sales and office, 3.5% natural resources, construction, and maintenance, 6.8% production, transportation, and material moving
Income: Per capita: $38,528; Median household: $49,306; Average household: $82,245; Households with income of $100,000 or more: 18.7%; Poverty rate: 11.0%
Educational Attainment: High school diploma or higher: 85.9%; Bachelor's degree or higher: 24.7%; Graduate/professional degree or higher: 11.1%

School District(s)
Lake George Central SD (KG-12)
    Enrollment: 805 . . . . (518) 668-5456
Housing: Homeownership rate: 49.2%; Median home value: $222,600; Median year structure built: 1956; Homeowner vacancy rate: 0.0%; Median selected monthly owner costs: $1,173 with a mortgage, $600 without a mortgage; Median gross rent: $880 per month; Rental vacancy rate: 11.5%
Health Insurance: 91.8% have insurance; 63.1% have private insurance; 48.5% have public insurance; 8.2% do not have insurance; 7.1% of children under 18 do not have insurance
Transportation: Commute: 82.7% car, 0.0% public transportation, 11.0% walk, 6.3% work from home; Mean travel time to work: 18.8 minutes

LAKE LUZERNE (town). Covers a land area of 52.519 square miles and a water area of 1.540 square miles. Located at 43.35° N. Lat; 73.79° W. Long. Elevation is 564 feet.

History: Also called Luzerne.
Population: 3,298; Growth (since 2000): 2.5%; Density: 62.8 persons per square mile; Race: 99.7% White, 0.2% Black/African American, 0.0% Asian, 0.0% American Indian/Alaska Native, 0.0% Native Hawaiian/Other Pacific Islander, 0.2% Two or more races, 2.7% Hispanic of any race; Average household size: 2.51; Median age: 48.4; Age under 18: 14.3%; Age 65 and over: 21.0%; Males per 100 females: 99.1; Marriage status: 26.9% never married, 45.0% now married, 2.4% separated, 13.4% widowed, 14.8% divorced; Foreign born: 0.6%; Speak English only: 99.0%; With disability: 22.7%; Veterans: 9.4%; Ancestry: 20.5% Irish, 19.5% German, 16.9% French, 16.6% English, 11.0% Italian
Employment: 10.4% management, business, and financial, 0.0% computer, engineering, and science, 9.5% education, legal, community service, arts, and media, 3.3% healthcare practitioners, 16.5% service, 28.3% sales and office, 13.8% natural resources, construction, and maintenance, 18.2% production, transportation, and material moving

Income: Per capita: $27,643; Median household: $53,627; Average household: $66,803; Households with income of $100,000 or more: 18.0%; Poverty rate: 7.2%
Educational Attainment: High school diploma or higher: 84.5%; Bachelor's degree or higher: 22.1%; Graduate/professional degree or higher: 7.4%

School District(s)
Hadley-Luzerne Central SD (PK-12)
    Enrollment: 740 . . . . (518) 696-2378
Housing: Homeownership rate: 82.3%; Median home value: $165,400; Median year structure built: 1980; Homeowner vacancy rate: 1.6%; Median selected monthly owner costs: $1,256 with a mortgage, $495 without a mortgage; Median gross rent: $887 per month; Rental vacancy rate: 0.0%
Health Insurance: 93.0% have insurance; 72.3% have private insurance; 42.2% have public insurance; 7.0% do not have insurance; 0.0% of children under 18 do not have insurance
Transportation: Commute: 91.0% car, 0.0% public transportation, 0.7% walk, 4.3% work from home; Mean travel time to work: 33.7 minutes

NORTH CREEK (CDP). Covers a land area of 1.595 square miles and a water area of 0.051 square miles. Located at 43.69° N. Lat; 73.99° W. Long. Elevation is 1,030 feet.

Population: 614; Growth (since 2000): n/a; Density: 385.0 persons per square mile; Race: 95.1% White, 0.0% Black/African American, 0.0% Asian, 0.0% American Indian/Alaska Native, 0.0% Native Hawaiian/Other Pacific Islander, 4.9% Two or more races, 0.0% Hispanic of any race; Average household size: 2.17; Median age: 56.1; Age under 18: 9.9%; Age 65 and over: 26.2%; Males per 100 females: 96.8; Marriage status: 25.3% never married, 50.6% now married, 0.0% separated, 14.1% widowed, 9.9% divorced; Foreign born: 1.3%; Speak English only: 97.2%; With disability: 17.4%; Veterans: 13.0%; Ancestry: 18.7% American, 18.1% English, 16.6% Irish, 12.4% German, 12.4% Italian
Employment: 8.7% management, business, and financial, 2.1% computer, engineering, and science, 9.0% education, legal, community service, arts, and media, 9.7% healthcare practitioners, 31.3% service, 21.9% sales and office, 7.3% natural resources, construction, and maintenance, 10.1% production, transportation, and material moving
Income: Per capita: $26,085; Median household: $52,708; Average household: $57,528; Households with income of $100,000 or more: 21.8%; Poverty rate: 13.1%
Educational Attainment: High school diploma or higher: 81.1%; Bachelor's degree or higher: 20.8%; Graduate/professional degree or higher: 15.6%

School District(s)
Johnsburg Central SD (PK-12)
    Enrollment: 342 . . . . (518) 251-2814
Housing: Homeownership rate: 57.5%; Median home value: $161,400; Median year structure built: 1980; Homeowner vacancy rate: 0.0%; Median selected monthly owner costs: $1,234 with a mortgage, $628 without a mortgage; Median gross rent: $711 per month; Rental vacancy rate: 0.0%
Health Insurance: 93.5% have insurance; 55.7% have private insurance; 49.0% have public insurance; 6.5% do not have insurance; 0.0% of children under 18 do not have insurance
Transportation: Commute: 87.4% car, 0.0% public transportation, 0.0% walk, 9.1% work from home; Mean travel time to work: 23.0 minutes

NORTH RIVER (unincorporated postal area)
ZCTA: 12856
    Covers a land area of 63.591 square miles and a water area of 1.073 square miles. Located at 43.67° N. Lat; 74.14° W. Long. Elevation is 1,073 feet.
Population: 144; Growth (since 2000): -35.7%; Density: 2.3 persons per square mile; Race: 100.0% White, 0.0% Black/African American, 0.0% Asian, 0.0% American Indian/Alaska Native, 0.0% Native Hawaiian/Other Pacific Islander, 0.0% Two or more races, 0.0% Hispanic of any race; Average household size: 2.88; Median age: 27.3; Age under 18: 4.2%; Age 65 and over: 4.2%; Males per 100 females: 94.8; Marriage status: 54.9% never married, 24.3% now married, 4.2% separated, 0.0% widowed, 20.8% divorced; Foreign born: 4.2%; Speak English only: 100.0%; With disability: 0.0%; Veterans: 0.0%; Ancestry: 61.1% Irish, 36.1% French, 34.7% English, 20.1% German, 9.0% Scottish
Employment: 0.0% management, business, and financial, 0.0% computer, engineering, and science, 11.6% education, legal, community service, arts, and media, 0.0% healthcare practitioners, 8.3% service,

Profiles of New York State

67.8% sales and office, 12.4% natural resources, construction, and maintenance, 0.0% production, transportation, and material moving
Income: Per capita: $23,787; Median household: n/a; Average household: $64,072; Households with income of $100,000 or more: 28.0%; Poverty rate: 4.2%
Educational Attainment: High school diploma or higher: 100.0%; Bachelor's degree or higher: 66.1%; Graduate/professional degree or higher: 4.7%
Housing: Homeownership rate: 100.0%; Median home value: $164,200; Median year structure built: 1985; Homeowner vacancy rate: 0.0%; Median selected monthly owner costs: $0 with a mortgage, $567 without a mortgage; Median gross rent: n/a per month; Rental vacancy rate: 0.0%
Health Insurance: 100.0% have insurance; 100.0% have private insurance; 4.2% have public insurance; 0.0% do not have insurance; 0.0% of children under 18 do not have insurance
Transportation: Commute: 94.2% car, 0.0% public transportation, 0.0% walk, 5.8% work from home; Mean travel time to work: 0.0 minutes

POTTERSVILLE (CDP).
Covers a land area of 2.279 square miles and a water area of 0.047 square miles. Located at 43.74° N. Lat; 73.82° W. Long. Elevation is 846 feet.
Population: 282; Growth (since 2000): n/a; Density: 123.8 persons per square mile; Race: 98.6% White, 1.4% Black/African American, 0.0% Asian, 0.0% American Indian/Alaska Native, 0.0% Native Hawaiian/Other Pacific Islander, 0.0% Two or more races, 0.0% Hispanic of any race; Average household size: 1.98; Median age: 29.9; Age under 18: 16.7%; Age 65 and over: 22.0%; Males per 100 females: 91.9; Marriage status: 61.9% never married, 35.1% now married, 2.9% separated, 0.0% widowed, 2.9% divorced; Foreign born: 2.8%; Speak English only: 98.6%; With disability: 20.9%; Veterans: 0.0%; Ancestry: 61.0% Irish, 44.0% German, 23.0% French, 9.2% English, 5.3% Russian
Employment: 0.0% management, business, and financial, 0.0% computer, engineering, and science, 0.0% education, legal, community service, arts, and media, 9.1% healthcare practitioners, 44.5% service, 12.2% sales and office, 26.8% natural resources, construction, and maintenance, 7.3% production, transportation, and material moving
Income: Per capita: $26,168; Median household: n/a; Average household: $55,531; Households with income of $100,000 or more: 19.7%; Poverty rate: 39.8%
Educational Attainment: High school diploma or higher: 100.0%; Bachelor's degree or higher: 14.1%; Graduate/professional degree or higher: n/a

Two-year College(s)
Word of Life Bible Institute (Private, Not-for-profit, Interdenominational)
    Enrollment: 522 . . . . (518) 494-4723
    Tuition: In-state $10,300; Out-of-state $10,300
Housing: Homeownership rate: 71.2%; Median home value: $103,900; Median year structure built: 1968; Homeowner vacancy rate: 0.0%; Median selected monthly owner costs: n/a with a mortgage, $390 without a mortgage; Median gross rent: n/a per month; Rental vacancy rate: 0.0%
Health Insurance: 100.0% have insurance; 63.5% have private insurance; 56.4% have public insurance; 0.0% do not have insurance; 0.0% of children under 18 do not have insurance
Transportation: Commute: 69.5% car, 0.0% public transportation, 26.2% walk, 0.0% work from home; Mean travel time to work: 24.9 minutes

QUEENSBURY (town).
Covers a land area of 62.830 square miles and a water area of 2.009 square miles. Located at 43.37° N. Lat; 73.67° W. Long. Elevation is 315 feet.
Population: 27,568; Growth (since 2000): 8.4%; Density: 438.8 persons per square mile; Race: 96.6% White, 1.3% Black/African American, 1.1% Asian, 0.4% American Indian/Alaska Native, 0.0% Native Hawaiian/Other Pacific Islander, 0.5% Two or more races, 1.5% Hispanic of any race; Average household size: 2.42; Median age: 46.8; Age under 18: 19.9%; Age 65 and over: 20.8%; Males per 100 females: 92.6; Marriage status: 28.6% never married, 51.6% now married, 1.6% separated, 8.3% widowed, 11.5% divorced; Foreign born: 3.8%; Speak English only: 95.1%; With disability: 13.1%; Veterans: 10.2%; Ancestry: 20.7% Irish, 14.5% Italian, 14.1% German, 12.9% English, 10.0% French
Employment: 12.7% management, business, and financial, 4.4% computer, engineering, and science, 13.0% education, legal, community service, arts, and media, 7.9% healthcare practitioners, 19.8% service, 26.8% sales and office, 6.3% natural resources, construction, and maintenance, 9.1% production, transportation, and material moving

Income: Per capita: $37,505; Median household: $70,431; Average household: $90,295; Households with income of $100,000 or more: 30.6%; Poverty rate: 6.8%
Educational Attainment: High school diploma or higher: 94.6%; Bachelor's degree or higher: 33.2%; Graduate/professional degree or higher: 17.2%

School District(s)
Queensbury Union Free SD (KG-12)
    Enrollment: 3,356 . . . . (518) 824-5602
Two-year College(s)
Adirondack Community College (Public)
    Enrollment: 3,892 . . . . (518) 743-2200
    Tuition: In-state $5,119; Out-of-state $9,511
Housing: Homeownership rate: 76.7%; Median home value: $223,900; Median year structure built: 1983; Homeowner vacancy rate: 1.0%; Median selected monthly owner costs: $1,548 with a mortgage, $587 without a mortgage; Median gross rent: $1,045 per month; Rental vacancy rate: 10.9%
Health Insurance: 96.0% have insurance; 82.0% have private insurance; 32.9% have public insurance; 4.0% do not have insurance; 3.1% of children under 18 do not have insurance
Transportation: Commute: 94.5% car, 0.5% public transportation, 0.6% walk, 3.2% work from home; Mean travel time to work: 22.9 minutes
Additional Information Contacts
Town of Queensbury . . . . (518) 761-8234
    http://www.queensbury.net

SILVER BAY (unincorporated postal area)
ZCTA: 12874
Covers a land area of 21.418 square miles and a water area of 0.307 square miles. Located at 43.69° N. Lat; 73.55° W. Long. Elevation is 348 feet.
Population: 148; Growth (since 2000): -15.9%; Density: 6.9 persons per square mile; Race: 98.6% White, 0.0% Black/African American, 0.0% Asian, 0.0% American Indian/Alaska Native, 0.0% Native Hawaiian/Other Pacific Islander, 1.4% Two or more races, 0.0% Hispanic of any race; Average household size: 1.70; Median age: 70.5; Age under 18: 1.4%; Age 65 and over: 60.8%; Males per 100 females: 105.8; Marriage status: 6.8% never married, 76.0% now married, 0.0% separated, 11.6% widowed, 5.5% divorced; Foreign born: 0.0%; Speak English only: 98.6%; With disability: 24.3%; Veterans: 10.3%; Ancestry: 21.6% German, 20.3% English, 9.5% Swedish, 8.8% Scottish, 8.1% Irish
Employment: 12.0% management, business, and financial, 6.0% computer, engineering, and science, 24.0% education, legal, community service, arts, and media, 14.0% healthcare practitioners, 4.0% service, 20.0% sales and office, 20.0% natural resources, construction, and maintenance, 0.0% production, transportation, and material moving
Income: Per capita: $53,741; Median household: $71,458; Average household: $90,746; Households with income of $100,000 or more: 29.9%; Poverty rate: n/a
Educational Attainment: High school diploma or higher: 100.0%; Bachelor's degree or higher: 65.1%; Graduate/professional degree or higher: 35.6%
Housing: Homeownership rate: 97.7%; Median home value: $575,000; Median year structure built: 1968; Homeowner vacancy rate: 12.4%; Median selected monthly owner costs: $2,000 with a mortgage, $850 without a mortgage; Median gross rent: n/a per month; Rental vacancy rate: 0.0%
Health Insurance: 100.0% have insurance; 91.2% have private insurance; 60.8% have public insurance; 0.0% do not have insurance; 0.0% of children under 18 do not have insurance
Transportation: Commute: 93.6% car, 0.0% public transportation, 0.0% walk, 6.4% work from home; Mean travel time to work: 31.4 minutes

STONY CREEK (town).
Covers a land area of 82.162 square miles and a water area of 1.042 square miles. Located at 43.42° N. Lat; 74.03° W. Long. Elevation is 827 feet.
Population: 660; Growth (since 2000): -11.2%; Density: 8.0 persons per square mile; Race: 96.5% White, 1.1% Black/African American, 0.5% Asian, 0.0% American Indian/Alaska Native, 0.0% Native Hawaiian/Other Pacific Islander, 2.0% Two or more races, 2.4% Hispanic of any race; Average household size: 2.25; Median age: 54.5; Age under 18: 12.9%; Age 65 and over: 28.9%; Males per 100 females: 102.9; Marriage status: 23.9% never married, 50.9% now married, 2.2% separated, 9.2%

widowed, 16.0% divorced; Foreign born: 0.5%; Speak English only: 99.1%; With disability: 16.5%; Veterans: 14.6%; Ancestry: 23.8% Irish, 22.0% English, 13.8% German, 9.1% French, 8.8% American

Employment: 12.7% management, business, and financial, 1.8% computer, engineering, and science, 13.8% education, legal, community service, arts, and media, 6.7% healthcare practitioners, 20.1% service, 18.7% sales and office, 14.8% natural resources, construction, and maintenance, 11.3% production, transportation, and material moving

Income: Per capita: $26,086; Median household: $49,583; Average household: $56,048; Households with income of $100,000 or more: 11.6%; Poverty rate: 8.2%

Educational Attainment: High school diploma or higher: 89.5%; Bachelor's degree or higher: 12.8%; Graduate/professional degree or higher: 6.9%

Housing: Homeownership rate: 88.1%; Median home value: $143,500; Median year structure built: 1963; Homeowner vacancy rate: 6.2%; Median selected monthly owner costs: $1,131 with a mortgage, $471 without a mortgage; Median gross rent: $716 per month; Rental vacancy rate: 0.0%

Health Insurance: 92.1% have insurance; 71.4% have private insurance; 47.1% have public insurance; 7.9% do not have insurance; 5.7% of children under 18 do not have insurance

Transportation: Commute: 84.5% car, 3.9% public transportation, 1.8% walk, 7.4% work from home; Mean travel time to work: 43.2 minutes

---

THURMAN (town). Covers a land area of 91.098 square miles and a water area of 1.678 square miles. Located at 43.49° N. Lat; 73.99° W. Long. Elevation is 1,316 feet.

Population: 1,267; Growth (since 2000): 5.7%; Density: 13.9 persons per square mile; Race: 98.3% White, 1.0% Black/African American, 0.0% Asian, 0.0% American Indian/Alaska Native, 0.0% Native Hawaiian/Other Pacific Islander, 0.3% Two or more races, 2.1% Hispanic of any race; Average household size: 2.63; Median age: 47.3; Age under 18: 20.7%; Age 65 and over: 19.7%; Males per 100 females: 104.9; Marriage status: 22.3% never married, 56.7% now married, 1.7% separated, 7.3% widowed, 13.7% divorced; Foreign born: 0.9%; Speak English only: 98.0%; With disability: 18.9%; Veterans: 10.6%; Ancestry: 19.3% German, 16.7% Irish, 14.7% English, 8.8% French, 7.9% American

Employment: 11.1% management, business, and financial, 4.2% computer, engineering, and science, 5.9% education, legal, community service, arts, and media, 4.0% healthcare practitioners, 22.5% service, 18.6% sales and office, 12.7% natural resources, construction, and maintenance, 21.0% production, transportation, and material moving

Income: Per capita: $25,553; Median household: $52,989; Average household: $64,477; Households with income of $100,000 or more: 16.2%; Poverty rate: 12.1%

Educational Attainment: High school diploma or higher: 87.1%; Bachelor's degree or higher: 13.1%; Graduate/professional degree or higher: 5.4%

Housing: Homeownership rate: 89.8%; Median home value: $130,800; Median year structure built: 1979; Homeowner vacancy rate: 0.0%; Median selected monthly owner costs: $1,046 with a mortgage, $446 without a mortgage; Median gross rent: $850 per month; Rental vacancy rate: 0.0%

Health Insurance: 91.6% have insurance; 65.4% have private insurance; 41.9% have public insurance; 8.4% do not have insurance; 1.5% of children under 18 do not have insurance

Transportation: Commute: 89.6% car, 0.0% public transportation, 7.1% walk, 3.2% work from home; Mean travel time to work: 30.9 minutes

---

WARRENSBURG (CDP). Covers a land area of 11.028 square miles and a water area of 0.319 square miles. Located at 43.52° N. Lat; 73.77° W. Long. Elevation is 745 feet.

Population: 3,141; Growth (since 2000): -2.1%; Density: 284.8 persons per square mile; Race: 98.8% White, 1.0% Black/African American, 0.0% Asian, 0.0% American Indian/Alaska Native, 0.0% Native Hawaiian/Other Pacific Islander, 0.2% Two or more races, 4.5% Hispanic of any race; Average household size: 2.33; Median age: 44.5; Age under 18: 20.1%; Age 65 and over: 17.9%; Males per 100 females: 92.1; Marriage status: 23.2% never married, 57.3% now married, 5.3% separated, 7.9% widowed, 11.7% divorced; Foreign born: 5.4%; Speak English only: 95.3%; With disability: 10.9%; Veterans: 6.4%; Ancestry: 15.6% Irish, 15.2% English, 12.5% German, 9.7% Italian, 7.3% American

Employment: 9.7% management, business, and financial, 5.3% computer, engineering, and science, 11.1% education, legal, community service, arts, and media, 3.3% healthcare practitioners, 20.5% service, 24.0% sales and

office, 10.7% natural resources, construction, and maintenance, 15.5% production, transportation, and material moving

Income: Per capita: $27,637; Median household: $50,778; Average household: $63,211; Households with income of $100,000 or more: 18.2%; Poverty rate: 13.1%

Educational Attainment: High school diploma or higher: 85.4%; Bachelor's degree or higher: 18.2%; Graduate/professional degree or higher: 8.3%

School District(s)

Warrensburg Central SD (PK-12)
    Enrollment: 756 . . . . (518) 623-2861

Housing: Homeownership rate: 67.1%; Median home value: $128,900; Median year structure built: 1951; Homeowner vacancy rate: 5.0%; Median selected monthly owner costs: $1,303 with a mortgage, $526 without a mortgage; Median gross rent: $750 per month; Rental vacancy rate: 16.9%

Health Insurance: 92.8% have insurance; 67.0% have private insurance; 47.6% have public insurance; 7.2% do not have insurance; 0.0% of children under 18 do not have insurance

Transportation: Commute: 92.7% car, 0.0% public transportation, 2.1% walk, 1.1% work from home; Mean travel time to work: 21.1 minutes

---

WARRENSBURG (town). Covers a land area of 63.461 square miles and a water area of 1.338 square miles. Located at 43.52° N. Lat; 73.81° W. Long. Elevation is 745 feet.

Population: 4,025; Growth (since 2000): -5.4%; Density: 63.4 persons per square mile; Race: 98.5% White, 0.8% Black/African American, 0.1% Asian, 0.0% American Indian/Alaska Native, 0.0% Native Hawaiian/Other Pacific Islander, 0.5% Two or more races, 3.9% Hispanic of any race; Average household size: 2.34; Median age: 45.5; Age under 18: 20.9%; Age 65 and over: 19.5%; Males per 100 females: 95.9; Marriage status: 22.7% never married, 58.8% now married, 4.5% separated, 7.2% widowed, 11.2% divorced; Foreign born: 4.4%; Speak English only: 95.8%; With disability: 11.8%; Veterans: 8.6%; Ancestry: 15.6% Irish, 14.8% English, 13.5% German, 12.9% Italian, 6.7% American

Employment: 10.6% management, business, and financial, 5.1% computer, engineering, and science, 10.3% education, legal, community service, arts, and media, 3.8% healthcare practitioners, 19.1% service, 24.9% sales and office, 10.4% natural resources, construction, and maintenance, 15.7% production, transportation, and material moving

Income: Per capita: $27,992; Median household: $50,778; Average household: $64,747; Households with income of $100,000 or more: 20.0%; Poverty rate: 13.2%

Educational Attainment: High school diploma or higher: 86.9%; Bachelor's degree or higher: 21.1%; Graduate/professional degree or higher: 9.6%

School District(s)

Warrensburg Central SD (PK-12)
    Enrollment: 756 . . . . (518) 623-2861

Housing: Homeownership rate: 69.9%; Median home value: $138,100; Median year structure built: 1962; Homeowner vacancy rate: 7.7%; Median selected monthly owner costs: $1,355 with a mortgage, $502 without a mortgage; Median gross rent: $767 per month; Rental vacancy rate: 16.3%

Health Insurance: 93.0% have insurance; 63.7% have private insurance; 49.6% have public insurance; 7.0% do not have insurance; 0.0% of children under 18 do not have insurance

Transportation: Commute: 92.9% car, 0.0% public transportation, 2.1% walk, 1.4% work from home; Mean travel time to work: 21.6 minutes

Additional Information Contacts

Town of Warrensburg . . . . (518) 623-4561
    http://townofwarrensburg.org

WEST GLENS FALLS (CDP). Covers a land area of 4.682 square miles and a water area of 0.131 square miles. Located at 43.30° N. Lat; 73.69° W. Long. Elevation is 381 feet.

History: West Glens Falls is a census-designated place (CDP) and hamlet in Warren County, New York.

Population: 7,208; Growth (since 2000): 7.2%; Density: 1,539.5 persons per square mile; Race: 94.1% White, 3.3% Black/African American, 0.7% Asian, 1.5% American Indian/Alaska Native, 0.0% Native Hawaiian/Other Pacific Islander, 0.3% Two or more races, 1.0% Hispanic of any race; Average household size: 2.53; Median age: 40.8; Age under 18: 23.7%; Age 65 and over: 13.7%; Males per 100 females: 93.5; Marriage status: 32.2% never married, 45.1% now married, 1.7% separated, 7.8% widowed, 15.0% divorced; Foreign born: 2.3%; Speak English only: 96.8%;

With disability: 13.1%; Veterans: 12.5%; Ancestry: 20.8% Irish, 15.8% German, 14.8% French, 10.4% English, 9.8% Italian
Employment: 11.4% management, business, and financial, 4.7% computer, engineering, and science, 11.2% education, legal, community service, arts, and media, 7.9% healthcare practitioners, 22.2% service, 28.1% sales and office, 6.4% natural resources, construction, and maintenance, 8.2% production, transportation, and material moving
Income: Per capita: $30,407; Median household: $61,875; Average household: $76,056; Households with income of $100,000 or more: 22.2%; Poverty rate: 6.7%
Educational Attainment: High school diploma or higher: 93.0%; Bachelor's degree or higher: 20.6%; Graduate/professional degree or higher: 11.3%
Housing: Homeownership rate: 83.1%; Median home value: $155,700; Median year structure built: 1986; Homeowner vacancy rate: 0.0%; Median selected monthly owner costs: $1,293 with a mortgage, $500 without a mortgage; Median gross rent: $1,134 per month; Rental vacancy rate: 0.0%
Health Insurance: 94.3% have insurance; 73.1% have private insurance; 34.8% have public insurance; 5.7% do not have insurance; 2.3% of children under 18 do not have insurance
Transportation: Commute: 94.0% car, 0.0% public transportation, 0.4% walk, 3.5% work from home; Mean travel time to work: 24.0 minutes

WEVERTOWN (unincorporated postal area)

ZCTA: 12886
Covers a land area of 14.478 square miles and a water area of 0.053 square miles. Located at 43.68° N. Lat; 73.93° W. Long. Elevation is 1,066 feet.
Population: 179; Growth (since 2000): 113.1%; Density: 12.4 persons per square mile; Race: 95.5% White, 0.0% Black/African American, 0.0% Asian, 0.0% American Indian/Alaska Native, 0.0% Native Hawaiian/Other Pacific Islander, 4.5% Two or more races, 0.0% Hispanic of any race; Average household size: 2.00; Median age: 50.8; Age under 18: 16.2%; Age 65 and over: 16.2%; Males per 100 females: 99.3; Marriage status: 7.7% never married, 74.2% now married, 0.0% separated, 4.5% widowed, 13.5% divorced; Foreign born: 5.6%; Speak English only: 100.0%; With disability: 26.3%; Veterans: 0.0%; Ancestry: 16.2% German, 15.1% French, 12.8% Dutch, 10.6% English, 10.6% Irish
Employment: 14.5% management, business, and financial, 14.5% computer, engineering, and science, 6.4% education, legal, community service, arts, and media, 0.0% healthcare practitioners, 38.2% service, 15.5% sales and office, 4.5% natural resources, construction, and maintenance, 6.4% production, transportation, and material moving
Income: Per capita: $36,599; Median household: $98,571; Average household: $77,169; Households with income of $100,000 or more: 45.3%; Poverty rate: 10.1%
Educational Attainment: High school diploma or higher: 90.7%; Bachelor's degree or higher: 13.3%; Graduate/professional degree or higher: 10.0%
Housing: Homeownership rate: 76.7%; Median home value: $108,300; Median year structure built: 1970; Homeowner vacancy rate: 0.0%; Median selected monthly owner costs: $964 with a mortgage, $353 without a mortgage; Median gross rent: n/a per month; Rental vacancy rate: 0.0%
Health Insurance: 100.0% have insurance; 64.8% have private insurance; 50.3% have public insurance; 0.0% do not have insurance; 0.0% of children under 18 do not have insurance
Transportation: Commute: 84.5% car, 0.0% public transportation, 0.0% walk, 9.1% work from home; Mean travel time to work: 25.4 minutes

Washington County

Located in eastern New York; bounded on the northwest by Lake George, on the east by Vermont, and on the west by the Hudson River; drained by the Poultney, Mettawee, and Hoosic Rivers; includes part of Lake Champlain. Covers a land area of 831.184 square miles, a water area of 14.704 square miles, and is located in the Eastern Time Zone at 43.31° N. Lat., 73.44° W. Long. The county was founded in 1772. County seat is Hudson Falls.

Washington County is part of the Glens Falls, NY Metropolitan Statistical Area. The entire metro area includes: Warren County, NY; Washington County, NY

Weather Station: Whitehall										Elevation: 119 feet		
	Jan	Feb	Mar	Apr	May	Jun	Jul	Aug	Sep	Oct	Nov	Dec
High	30	34	44	59	71	80	84	82	73	61	47	35
Low	12	14	24	36	47	57	61	60	52	41	32	20
Precip	3.0	2.5	3.0	3.2	3.7	3.9	4.5	4.2	3.7	3.7	3.6	3.2
Snow	16.6	12.0	12.5	2.2	0.0	0.0	0.0	0.0	0.0	tr	2.7	13.6

High and Low temperatures in degrees Fahrenheit; Precipitation and Snow in inches

Population: 62,183; Growth (since 2000): 1.9%; Density: 74.8 persons per square mile; Race: 93.8% White, 3.4% Black/African American, 0.5% Asian, 0.2% American Indian/Alaska Native, 0.0% Native Hawaiian/Other Pacific Islander, 1.5% two or more races, 2.6% Hispanic of any race; Average household size: 2.46; Median age: 43.6; Age under 18: 19.6%; Age 65 and over: 17.7%; Males per 100 females: 107.6; Marriage status: 30.8% never married, 51.1% now married, 2.4% separated, 6.0% widowed, 12.2% divorced; Foreign born: 2.1%; Speak English only: 96.7%; With disability: 14.2%; Veterans: 9.5%; Ancestry: 19.7% Irish, 18.3% American, 11.6% English, 11.4% German, 10.7% French
Religion: Six largest groups: 21.5% Catholicism, 5.2% Methodist/Pietist, 2.5% Baptist, 2.0% Presbyterian-Reformed, 1.2% Non-denominational Protestant, 0.8% Episcopalianism/Anglicanism
Economy: Unemployment rate: 3.3%; Leading industries: 17.8 % retail trade; 13.5 % construction; 11.1 % other services (except public administration); Farms: 851 totaling 189,391 acres; Company size: 0 employ 1,000 or more persons, 1 employs 500 to 999 persons, 16 employ 100 to 499 persons, 1,035 employ less than 100 persons; Business ownership: 1,484 women-owned, n/a Black-owned, 54 Hispanic-owned, 36 Asian-owned, 34 American Indian/Alaska Native-owned
Employment: 10.2% management, business, and financial, 3.1% computer, engineering, and science, 9.5% education, legal, community service, arts, and media, 5.2% healthcare practitioners, 19.8% service, 23.3% sales and office, 12.9% natural resources, construction, and maintenance, 16.1% production, transportation, and material moving
Income: Per capita: $26,064; Median household: $52,527; Average household: $65,798; Households with income of $100,000 or more: 18.7%; Poverty rate: 12.8%
Educational Attainment: High school diploma or higher: 88.4%; Bachelor's degree or higher: 19.8%; Graduate/professional degree or higher: 8.2%
Housing: Homeownership rate: 72.7%; Median home value: $144,900; Median year structure built: 1962; Homeowner vacancy rate: 2.0%; Median selected monthly owner costs: $1,348 with a mortgage, $530 without a mortgage; Median gross rent: $823 per month; Rental vacancy rate: 5.1%
Vital Statistics: Birth rate: 93.3 per 10,000 population; Death rate: 106.3 per 10,000 population; Age-adjusted cancer mortality rate: 189.8 deaths per 100,000 population
Health Insurance: 93.0% have insurance; 67.2% have private insurance; 42.9% have public insurance; 7.0% do not have insurance; 4.0% of children under 18 do not have insurance
Health Care: Physicians: 5.2 per 10,000 population; Dentists: 2.3 per 10,000 population; Hospital beds: 0.0 per 10,000 population; Hospital admissions: 0.0 per 10,000 population
Transportation: Commute: 90.8% car, 0.9% public transportation, 3.3% walk, 4.1% work from home; Mean travel time to work: 26.2 minutes
2016 Presidential Election: 55.5% Trump, 37.1% Clinton, 3.8% Johnson, 2.4% Stein
National and State Parks: Carters Pond State Wildlife Management Area
Additional Information Contacts
Washington Government . . . . (518) 746-2210
    http://www.co.washington.ny.us

Washington County Communities

ARGYLE (town). Covers a land area of 56.536 square miles and a water area of 1.260 square miles. Located at 43.23° N. Lat; 73.48° W. Long. Elevation is 285 feet.
Population: 3,731; Growth (since 2000): 1.2%; Density: 66.0 persons per square mile; Race: 99.0% White, 0.2% Black/African American, 0.0% Asian, 0.0% American Indian/Alaska Native, 0.0% Native Hawaiian/Other Pacific Islander, 0.8% Two or more races, 0.5% Hispanic of any race; Average household size: 2.31; Median age: 47.3; Age under 18: 16.2%; Age 65 and over: 20.2%; Males per 100 females: 100.6; Marriage status: 28.5% never married, 58.0% now married, 1.1% separated, 6.1% widowed, 7.4% divorced; Foreign born: 1.2%; Speak English only: 98.9%;

With disability: 11.2%; Veterans: 7.1%; Ancestry: 22.4% Irish, 19.4% American, 12.7% German, 12.4% English, 11.1% French

Employment: 10.5% management, business, and financial, 3.6% computer, engineering, and science, 12.3% education, legal, community service, arts, and media, 5.2% healthcare practitioners, 13.6% service, 23.7% sales and office, 9.2% natural resources, construction, and maintenance, 21.8% production, transportation, and material moving

Income: Per capita: $29,379; Median household: $52,805; Average household: $67,785; Households with income of $100,000 or more: 21.4%; Poverty rate: 17.1%

Educational Attainment: High school diploma or higher: 93.2%; Bachelor's degree or higher: 21.9%; Graduate/professional degree or higher: 10.8%

School District(s)

Argyle Central SD (KG-12)

    Enrollment: 532 . . . . (518) 638-8243

Housing: Homeownership rate: 81.2%; Median home value: $152,800; Median year structure built: 1973; Homeowner vacancy rate: 1.5%; Median selected monthly owner costs: $1,335 with a mortgage, $512 without a mortgage; Median gross rent: $787 per month; Rental vacancy rate: 7.6%

Health Insurance: 94.5% have insurance; 74.0% have private insurance; 37.4% have public insurance; 5.5% do not have insurance; 0.3% of children under 18 do not have insurance

Transportation: Commute: 94.3% car, 0.0% public transportation, 2.5% walk, 2.8% work from home; Mean travel time to work: 28.9 minutes

---

ARGYLE (village). Covers a land area of 0.350 square miles and a water area of 0 square miles. Located at 43.24° N. Lat; 73.49° W. Long. Elevation is 285 feet.

Population: 470; Growth (since 2000): 62.6%; Density: 1,343.1 persons per square mile; Race: 94.5% White, 1.1% Black/African American, 0.0% Asian, 0.0% American Indian/Alaska Native, 0.0% Native Hawaiian/Other Pacific Islander, 4.0% Two or more races, 2.6% Hispanic of any race; Average household size: 2.42; Median age: 38.6; Age under 18: 23.8%; Age 65 and over: 19.8%; Males per 100 females: 98.7; Marriage status: 33.5% never married, 46.0% now married, 0.8% separated, 13.6% widowed, 6.9% divorced; Foreign born: 1.1%; Speak English only: 98.7%; With disability: 17.9%; Veterans: 4.2%; Ancestry: 21.1% Irish, 19.8% English, 18.1% German, 12.3% American, 12.1% French

Employment: 11.2% management, business, and financial, 2.2% computer, engineering, and science, 9.0% education, legal, community service, arts, and media, 4.9% healthcare practitioners, 21.1% service, 20.6% sales and office, 13.5% natural resources, construction, and maintenance, 17.5% production, transportation, and material moving

Income: Per capita: $22,142; Median household: $36,250; Average household: $51,877; Households with income of $100,000 or more: 19.6%; Poverty rate: 13.7%

Educational Attainment: High school diploma or higher: 91.5%; Bachelor's degree or higher: 20.8%; Graduate/professional degree or higher: 10.1%

School District(s)

Argyle Central SD (KG-12)

    Enrollment: 532 . . . . (518) 638-8243

Housing: Homeownership rate: 51.0%; Median home value: $115,100; Median year structure built: Before 1940; Homeowner vacancy rate: 0.0%; Median selected monthly owner costs: $1,313 with a mortgage, $542 without a mortgage; Median gross rent: $602 per month; Rental vacancy rate: 5.9%

Health Insurance: 92.8% have insurance; 63.8% have private insurance; 44.7% have public insurance; 7.2% do not have insurance; 1.8% of children under 18 do not have insurance

Transportation: Commute: 92.4% car, 0.0% public transportation, 2.2% walk, 4.9% work from home; Mean travel time to work: 22.2 minutes

---

CAMBRIDGE (town). Covers a land area of 36.357 square miles and a water area of 0.127 square miles. Located at 43.01° N. Lat; 73.45° W. Long. Elevation is 489 feet.

History: Cambridge Historical District within the village. Its weekly, *Washington County Post,* was founded in 1787. Settled c.1761, incorporated 1866.

Population: 1,954; Growth (since 2000): -9.2%; Density: 53.7 persons per square mile; Race: 96.3% White, 0.5% Black/African American, 1.6% Asian, 0.0% American Indian/Alaska Native, 0.0% Native Hawaiian/Other Pacific Islander, 1.0% Two or more races, 1.5% Hispanic of any race; Average household size: 2.47; Median age: 42.8; Age under 18: 24.8%;

Age 65 and over: 17.7%; Males per 100 females: 108.4; Marriage status: 25.7% never married, 57.8% now married, 1.7% separated, 4.2% widowed, 12.2% divorced; Foreign born: 3.1%; Speak English only: 96.4%; With disability: 7.5%; Veterans: 6.1%; Ancestry: 21.2% English, 19.1% German, 16.9% American, 13.7% Irish, 8.2% French

Employment: 15.4% management, business, and financial, 4.1% computer, engineering, and science, 19.6% education, legal, community service, arts, and media, 4.1% healthcare practitioners, 15.5% service, 19.5% sales and office, 11.1% natural resources, construction, and maintenance, 10.6% production, transportation, and material moving

Income: Per capita: $33,651; Median household: $65,417; Average household: $81,941; Households with income of $100,000 or more: 30.9%; Poverty rate: 7.5%

Educational Attainment: High school diploma or higher: 97.9%; Bachelor's degree or higher: 46.8%; Graduate/professional degree or higher: 23.7%

School District(s)

Cambridge Central SD (PK-12)

    Enrollment: 876 . . . . (518) 677-2653

Housing: Homeownership rate: 85.0%; Median home value: $204,500; Median year structure built: 1963; Homeowner vacancy rate: 0.0%; Median selected monthly owner costs: $1,518 with a mortgage, $695 without a mortgage; Median gross rent: $793 per month; Rental vacancy rate: 9.9%

Health Insurance: 96.0% have insurance; 80.4% have private insurance; 31.5% have public insurance; 4.0% do not have insurance; 1.6% of children under 18 do not have insurance

Newspapers: Cambridge Eagle (weekly circulation 4,400)

Transportation: Commute: 89.8% car, 0.0% public transportation, 1.9% walk, 8.4% work from home; Mean travel time to work: 29.6 minutes

---

CAMBRIDGE (village). Covers a land area of 1.678 square miles and a water area of 0 square miles. Located at 43.03° N. Lat; 73.38° W. Long. Elevation is 489 feet.

Population: 1,733; Growth (since 2000): -10.0%; Density: 1,033.1 persons per square mile; Race: 96.8% White, 0.6% Black/African American, 0.0% Asian, 0.0% American Indian/Alaska Native, 0.0% Native Hawaiian/Other Pacific Islander, 2.0% Two or more races, 1.4% Hispanic of any race; Average household size: 2.17; Median age: 42.2; Age under 18: 23.8%; Age 65 and over: 17.3%; Males per 100 females: 89.5; Marriage status: 28.4% never married, 51.5% now married, 2.1% separated, 5.2% widowed, 14.9% divorced; Foreign born: 1.1%; Speak English only: 97.4%; With disability: 12.2%; Veterans: 7.5%; Ancestry: 26.9% Irish, 22.1% German, 15.4% American, 12.5% English, 10.1% Italian

Employment: 12.5% management, business, and financial, 3.7% computer, engineering, and science, 15.8% education, legal, community service, arts, and media, 6.1% healthcare practitioners, 15.9% service, 14.2% sales and office, 11.0% natural resources, construction, and maintenance, 20.8% production, transportation, and material moving

Income: Per capita: $27,637; Median household: $51,573; Average household: $59,771; Households with income of $100,000 or more: 18.8%; Poverty rate: 10.3%

Educational Attainment: High school diploma or higher: 91.9%; Bachelor's degree or higher: 35.2%; Graduate/professional degree or higher: 19.0%

School District(s)

Cambridge Central SD (PK-12)

    Enrollment: 876 . . . . (518) 677-2653

Housing: Homeownership rate: 63.5%; Median home value: $157,200; Median year structure built: Before 1940; Homeowner vacancy rate: 0.0%; Median selected monthly owner costs: $1,419 with a mortgage, $587 without a mortgage; Median gross rent: $809 per month; Rental vacancy rate: 14.1%

Health Insurance: 92.5% have insurance; 70.1% have private insurance; 41.2% have public insurance; 7.5% do not have insurance; 1.4% of children under 18 do not have insurance

Safety: Violent crime rate: 5.5 per 10,000 population; Property crime rate: 88.4 per 10,000 population

Newspapers: Cambridge Eagle (weekly circulation 4,400)

Transportation: Commute: 92.4% car, 0.0% public transportation, 1.9% walk, 4.6% work from home; Mean travel time to work: 32.3 minutes

CLEMONS (unincorporated postal area)
ZCTA: 12819

Covers a land area of 28.976 square miles and a water area of 0.464 square miles. Located at 43.59° N. Lat; 73.47° W. Long. Elevation is 377 feet.

Population: 346; Growth (since 2000): -4.9%; Density: 11.9 persons per square mile; Race: 98.6% White, 0.0% Black/African American, 0.0% Asian, 0.0% American Indian/Alaska Native, 0.0% Native Hawaiian/Other Pacific Islander, 1.4% Two or more races, 0.6% Hispanic of any race; Average household size: 2.54; Median age: 49.3; Age under 18: 17.1%; Age 65 and over: 22.0%; Males per 100 females: 97.5; Marriage status: 20.0% never married, 60.3% now married, 3.0% separated, 5.7% widowed, 14.0% divorced; Foreign born: 0.6%; Speak English only: 93.9%; With disability: 17.1%; Veterans: 12.5%; Ancestry: 26.0% American, 15.0% French, 13.6% Irish, 10.7% German, 10.1% Italian

Employment: 17.8% management, business, and financial, 4.6% computer, engineering, and science, 6.6% education, legal, community service, arts, and media, 1.3% healthcare practitioners, 23.7% service, 22.4% sales and office, 11.2% natural resources, construction, and maintenance, 12.5% production, transportation, and material moving

Income: Per capita: $28,099; Median household: $59,643; Average household: $69,207; Households with income of $100,000 or more: 16.3%; Poverty rate: 11.6%

Educational Attainment: High school diploma or higher: 89.0%; Bachelor's degree or higher: 22.3%; Graduate/professional degree or higher: 8.0%

Housing: Homeownership rate: 86.8%; Median home value: $133,300; Median year structure built: 1972; Homeowner vacancy rate: 0.0%; Median selected monthly owner costs: $1,205 with a mortgage, $470 without a mortgage; Median gross rent: $933 per month; Rental vacancy rate: 0.0%

Health Insurance: 93.4% have insurance; 77.5% have private insurance; 36.4% have public insurance; 6.6% do not have insurance; 9.0% of children under 18 do not have insurance

Transportation: Commute: 89.3% car, 0.0% public transportation, 0.7% walk, 10.1% work from home; Mean travel time to work: 42.8 minutes

COMSTOCK (unincorporated postal area)
ZCTA: 12821

Covers a land area of 5.548 square miles and a water area of 0.061 square miles. Located at 43.45° N. Lat; 73.42° W. Long. Elevation is 128 feet.

Population: 2,845; Growth (since 2000): -11.6%; Density: 512.8 persons per square mile; Race: 36.1% White, 51.1% Black/African American, 0.2% Asian, 0.3% American Indian/Alaska Native, 0.0% Native Hawaiian/Other Pacific Islander, 4.3% Two or more races, 23.6% Hispanic of any race; Average household size: 2.89; Median age: 35.4; Age under 18: 2.6%; Age 65 and over: 4.7%; Males per 100 females: ***.*; Marriage status: 62.1% never married, 24.3% now married, 2.6% separated, 2.8% widowed, 10.8% divorced; Foreign born: 6.7%; Speak English only: 80.7%; With disability: 16.2%; Veterans: 3.6%; Ancestry: 15.7% American, 7.0% Italian, 5.8% French, 5.7% Irish, 3.6% German

Employment: 26.9% management, business, and financial, 0.0% computer, engineering, and science, 6.7% education, legal, community service, arts, and media, 0.0% healthcare practitioners, 27.9% service, 0.0% sales and office, 19.2% natural resources, construction, and maintenance, 19.2% production, transportation, and material moving

Income: Per capita: $4,063; Median household: n/a; Average household: $61,928; Households with income of $100,000 or more: 12.1%; Poverty rate: 4.9%

Educational Attainment: High school diploma or higher: 72.4%; Bachelor's degree or higher: 5.1%; Graduate/professional degree or higher: 0.3%

Housing: Homeownership rate: 63.1%; Median home value: $99,300; Median year structure built: 1992; Homeowner vacancy rate: 0.0%; Median selected monthly owner costs: $950 with a mortgage, $293 without a mortgage; Median gross rent: n/a per month; Rental vacancy rate: 0.0%

Health Insurance: 77.7% have insurance; 40.0% have private insurance; 54.2% have public insurance; 22.3% do not have insurance; 0.0% of children under 18 do not have insurance

Transportation: Commute: 60.6% car, 0.0% public transportation, 26.9% walk, 0.0% work from home; Mean travel time to work: 0.0 minutes

COSSAYUNA (unincorporated postal area)
ZCTA: 12823

Covers a land area of 4.261 square miles and a water area of 0.081 square miles. Located at 43.18° N. Lat; 73.41° W. Long. Elevation is 479 feet.

Population: 420; Growth (since 2000): 121.1%; Density: 98.6 persons per square mile; Race: 100.0% White, 0.0% Black/African American, 0.0% Asian, 0.0% American Indian/Alaska Native, 0.0% Native Hawaiian/Other Pacific Islander, 0.0% Two or more races, 0.0% Hispanic of any race; Average household size: 2.78; Median age: 52.9; Age under 18: 12.4%; Age 65 and over: 3.8%; Males per 100 females: 100.0; Marriage status: 23.4% never married, 33.7% now married, 0.0% separated, 0.0% widowed, 42.9% divorced; Foreign born: 0.0%; Speak English only: 100.0%; With disability: 2.6%; Veterans: 13.9%; Ancestry: 61.7% American, 12.9% Dutch, 5.0% German, 4.8% Irish, 2.6% French

Employment: 7.9% management, business, and financial, 0.0% computer, engineering, and science, 0.0% education, legal, community service, arts, and media, 0.0% healthcare practitioners, 49.0% service, 0.0% sales and office, 43.0% natural resources, construction, and maintenance, 0.0% production, transportation, and material moving

Income: Per capita: $20,304; Median household: n/a; Average household: $56,077; Households with income of $100,000 or more: 33.8%; Poverty rate: 33.1%

Educational Attainment: High school diploma or higher: 68.9%; Bachelor's degree or higher: n/a; Graduate/professional degree or higher: n/a

Housing: Homeownership rate: 92.7%; Median home value: n/a; Median year structure built: 1990; Homeowner vacancy rate: 0.0%; Median selected monthly owner costs: $1,611 with a mortgage, $0 without a mortgage; Median gross rent: n/a per month; Rental vacancy rate: 0.0%

Health Insurance: 87.1% have insurance; 66.9% have private insurance; 38.8% have public insurance; 12.9% do not have insurance; 0.0% of children under 18 do not have insurance

Transportation: Commute: 100.0% car, 0.0% public transportation, 0.0% walk, 0.0% work from home; Mean travel time to work: 0.0 minutes

DRESDEN (town).
Covers a land area of 52.254 square miles and a water area of 2.745 square miles. Located at 43.59° N. Lat; 73.47° W. Long. Elevation is 138 feet.

Population: 567; Growth (since 2000): -16.2%; Density: 10.9 persons per square mile; Race: 99.1% White, 0.0% Black/African American, 0.0% Asian, 0.0% American Indian/Alaska Native, 0.0% Native Hawaiian/Other Pacific Islander, 0.9% Two or more races, 0.4% Hispanic of any race; Average household size: 2.21; Median age: 55.4; Age under 18: 13.4%; Age 65 and over: 28.0%; Males per 100 females: 95.2; Marriage status: 18.8% never married, 58.7% now married, 1.8% separated, 9.1% widowed, 13.3% divorced; Foreign born: 2.1%; Speak English only: 95.0%; With disability: 15.2%; Veterans: 11.8%; Ancestry: 23.5% American, 13.2% Irish, 12.9% French, 10.9% German, 8.1% English

Employment: 16.4% management, business, and financial, 2.9% computer, engineering, and science, 8.4% education, legal, community service, arts, and media, 5.0% healthcare practitioners, 18.1% service, 22.7% sales and office, 14.3% natural resources, construction, and maintenance, 12.2% production, transportation, and material moving

Income: Per capita: $32,855; Median household: $57,917; Average household: $71,479; Households with income of $100,000 or more: 13.7%; Poverty rate: 12.4%

Educational Attainment: High school diploma or higher: 85.7%; Bachelor's degree or higher: 23.6%; Graduate/professional degree or higher: 8.8%

Housing: Homeownership rate: 83.2%; Median home value: $158,200; Median year structure built: 1968; Homeowner vacancy rate: 1.4%; Median selected monthly owner costs: $1,176 with a mortgage, $633 without a mortgage; Median gross rent: $1,028 per month; Rental vacancy rate: 12.0%

Health Insurance: 94.0% have insurance; 70.5% have private insurance; 46.7% have public insurance; 6.0% do not have insurance; 7.1% of children under 18 do not have insurance

Transportation: Commute: 89.8% car, 0.0% public transportation, 0.4% walk, 7.7% work from home; Mean travel time to work: 35.1 minutes

EASTON (town). Covers a land area of 62.304 square miles and a water area of 0.934 square miles. Located at 43.03° N. Lat; 73.54° W. Long. Elevation is 436 feet.
Population: 2,491; Growth (since 2000): 10.3%; Density: 40.0 persons per square mile; Race: 98.2% White, 0.0% Black/African American, 0.4% Asian, 0.0% American Indian/Alaska Native, 0.0% Native Hawaiian/Other Pacific Islander, 1.2% Two or more races, 1.7% Hispanic of any race; Average household size: 2.59; Median age: 44.6; Age under 18: 22.0%; Age 65 and over: 18.5%; Males per 100 females: 103.1; Marriage status: 22.5% never married, 61.3% now married, 1.4% separated, 6.9% widowed, 9.2% divorced; Foreign born: 1.6%; Speak English only: 98.1%; With disability: 11.3%; Veterans: 11.3%; Ancestry: 19.2% Irish, 15.2% English, 9.9% American, 9.8% German, 8.9% Italian
Employment: 15.3% management, business, and financial, 5.1% computer, engineering, and science, 9.9% education, legal, community service, arts, and media, 5.1% healthcare practitioners, 15.7% service, 20.1% sales and office, 15.7% natural resources, construction, and maintenance, 13.0% production, transportation, and material moving
Income: Per capita: $39,782; Median household: $75,463; Average household: $102,742; Households with income of $100,000 or more: 33.4%; Poverty rate: 4.3%
Educational Attainment: High school diploma or higher: 92.2%; Bachelor's degree or higher: 33.3%; Graduate/professional degree or higher: 14.8%
Housing: Homeownership rate: 83.9%; Median home value: $200,900; Median year structure built: 1955; Homeowner vacancy rate: 0.0%; Median selected monthly owner costs: $1,470 with a mortgage, $659 without a mortgage; Median gross rent: $869 per month; Rental vacancy rate: 0.0%
Health Insurance: 95.9% have insurance; 85.0% have private insurance; 27.6% have public insurance; 4.1% do not have insurance; 0.0% of children under 18 do not have insurance
Transportation: Commute: 88.2% car, 0.0% public transportation, 4.5% walk, 6.8% work from home; Mean travel time to work: 30.6 minutes

FORT ANN (town). Covers a land area of 108.999 square miles and a water area of 1.780 square miles. Located at 43.46° N. Lat; 73.53° W. Long. Elevation is 157 feet.
Population: 6,111; Growth (since 2000): -4.8%; Density: 56.1 persons per square mile; Race: 68.4% White, 25.0% Black/African American, 0.1% Asian, 0.1% American Indian/Alaska Native, 0.0% Native Hawaiian/Other Pacific Islander, 2.5% Two or more races, 11.5% Hispanic of any race; Average household size: 2.59; Median age: 38.9; Age under 18: 10.8%; Age 65 and over: 12.7%; Males per 100 females: 237.1; Marriage status: 43.5% never married, 41.4% now married, 1.7% separated, 4.7% widowed, 10.4% divorced; Foreign born: 4.1%; Speak English only: 88.1%; With disability: 13.9%; Veterans: 6.8%; Ancestry: 19.7% American, 11.4% Irish, 9.0% French, 8.6% English, 5.9% Italian
Employment: 13.1% management, business, and financial, 1.2% computer, engineering, and science, 9.2% education, legal, community service, arts, and media, 2.9% healthcare practitioners, 21.8% service, 23.3% sales and office, 15.7% natural resources, construction, and maintenance, 12.7% production, transportation, and material moving
Income: Per capita: $17,377; Median household: $63,125; Average household: $72,087; Households with income of $100,000 or more: 19.5%; Poverty rate: 6.2%
Educational Attainment: High school diploma or higher: 82.1%; Bachelor's degree or higher: 12.1%; Graduate/professional degree or higher: 3.4%

School District(s)
Fort Ann Central SD (PK-12)
    Enrollment: 506 . . . . (518) 639-5594
Housing: Homeownership rate: 82.2%; Median home value: $151,000; Median year structure built: 1976; Homeowner vacancy rate: 2.0%; Median selected monthly owner costs: $1,366 with a mortgage, $522 without a mortgage; Median gross rent: $1,018 per month; Rental vacancy rate: 4.2%
Health Insurance: 92.5% have insurance; 73.5% have private insurance; 37.5% have public insurance; 7.5% do not have insurance; 5.7% of children under 18 do not have insurance
Transportation: Commute: 92.1% car, 0.0% public transportation, 3.8% walk, 2.8% work from home; Mean travel time to work: 23.0 minutes
Additional Information Contacts
Town of Fort Ann. . . . . (518) 639-8929
    http://www.fortann.us

FORT ANN (village). Covers a land area of 0.293 square miles and a water area of 0.015 square miles. Located at 43.42° N. Lat; 73.49° W. Long. Elevation is 157 feet.
Population: 382; Growth (since 2000): -18.9%; Density: 1,305.6 persons per square mile; Race: 95.0% White, 0.0% Black/African American, 0.0% Asian, 0.0% American Indian/Alaska Native, 0.0% Native Hawaiian/Other Pacific Islander, 5.0% Two or more races, 5.5% Hispanic of any race; Average household size: 2.62; Median age: 36.4; Age under 18: 21.7%; Age 65 and over: 15.7%; Males per 100 females: 96.0; Marriage status: 28.0% never married, 54.4% now married, 3.1% separated, 5.3% widowed, 12.3% divorced; Foreign born: 0.0%; Speak English only: 95.3%; With disability: 14.9%; Veterans: 10.4%; Ancestry: 23.3% Irish, 17.0% French, 13.6% American, 9.7% English, 8.1% German
Employment: 9.3% management, business, and financial, 1.0% computer, engineering, and science, 8.3% education, legal, community service, arts, and media, 7.4% healthcare practitioners, 17.2% service, 21.6% sales and office, 12.3% natural resources, construction, and maintenance, 23.0% production, transportation, and material moving
Income: Per capita: $27,484; Median household: $59,375; Average household: $67,130; Households with income of $100,000 or more: 23.3%; Poverty rate: 7.3%
Educational Attainment: High school diploma or higher: 95.7%; Bachelor's degree or higher: 14.0%; Graduate/professional degree or higher: 4.0%

School District(s)
Fort Ann Central SD (PK-12)
    Enrollment: 506 . . . . (518) 639-5594
Housing: Homeownership rate: 72.6%; Median home value: $129,700; Median year structure built: Before 1940; Homeowner vacancy rate: 0.0%; Median selected monthly owner costs: $1,292 with a mortgage, $508 without a mortgage; Median gross rent: $750 per month; Rental vacancy rate: 21.6%
Health Insurance: 92.4% have insurance; 75.7% have private insurance; 34.0% have public insurance; 7.6% do not have insurance; 14.9% of children under 18 do not have insurance
Transportation: Commute: 89.4% car, 0.0% public transportation, 8.0% walk, 1.6% work from home; Mean travel time to work: 22.8 minutes

FORT EDWARD (town). Covers a land area of 26.630 square miles and a water area of 0.796 square miles. Located at 43.23° N. Lat; 73.56° W. Long. Elevation is 138 feet.
History: Fort built here in 1755 to protect portage between the Hudson River and Lake Champlain; it was occupied by Burgoyne in 1777. Incorporated 1849.
Population: 6,213; Growth (since 2000): 5.4%; Density: 233.3 persons per square mile; Race: 96.1% White, 2.7% Black/African American, 0.0% Asian, 0.0% American Indian/Alaska Native, 0.0% Native Hawaiian/Other Pacific Islander, 1.0% Two or more races, 1.2% Hispanic of any race; Average household size: 2.48; Median age: 43.7; Age under 18: 21.6%; Age 65 and over: 19.1%; Males per 100 females: 98.9; Marriage status: 33.3% never married, 45.5% now married, 5.9% separated, 6.3% widowed, 14.9% divorced; Foreign born: 0.3%; Speak English only: 98.5%; With disability: 20.3%; Veterans: 10.3%; Ancestry: 21.1% Irish, 14.8% American, 14.3% French, 13.4% English, 13.1% Italian
Employment: 5.9% management, business, and financial, 3.2% computer, engineering, and science, 5.5% education, legal, community service, arts, and media, 8.2% healthcare practitioners, 19.4% service, 33.0% sales and office, 12.6% natural resources, construction, and maintenance, 12.3% production, transportation, and material moving
Income: Per capita: $25,322; Median household: $49,099; Average household: $62,637; Households with income of $100,000 or more: 12.8%; Poverty rate: 10.4%
Educational Attainment: High school diploma or higher: 85.8%; Bachelor's degree or higher: 12.4%; Graduate/professional degree or higher: 3.1%

School District(s)
Fort Edward Union Free SD (PK-12)
    Enrollment: 529 . . . . (518) 747-4594
Washington-Saratoga-Warren-Hamilton-Essex Boces
    Enrollment: n/a . . . . (518) 746-3310
Housing: Homeownership rate: 66.4%; Median home value: $111,400; Median year structure built: 1941; Homeowner vacancy rate: 0.0%; Median selected monthly owner costs: $1,267 with a mortgage, $488 without a mortgage; Median gross rent: $865 per month; Rental vacancy rate: 4.8%

Health Insurance: 93.0% have insurance; 58.8% have private insurance; 50.2% have public insurance; 7.0% do not have insurance; 1.1% of children under 18 do not have insurance
Transportation: Commute: 91.2% car, 0.6% public transportation, 3.4% walk, 3.4% work from home; Mean travel time to work: 23.4 minutes; Amtrak: Train service available.
Additional Information Contacts
Town of Fort Edward . . . . (518) 747-4023
  http://www.fortedward.net

FORT EDWARD (village). Covers a land area of 1.756 square miles and a water area of 0.180 square miles. Located at 43.27° N. Lat; 73.58° W. Long. Elevation is 138 feet.
Population: 3,321; Growth (since 2000): 5.7%; Density: 1,890.9 persons per square mile; Race: 98.5% White, 0.0% Black/African American, 0.0% Asian, 0.0% American Indian/Alaska Native, 0.0% Native Hawaiian/Other Pacific Islander, 1.1% Two or more races, 1.8% Hispanic of any race; Average household size: 2.41; Median age: 39.0; Age under 18: 25.7%; Age 65 and over: 12.9%; Males per 100 females: 95.3; Marriage status: 35.2% never married, 48.6% now married, 5.8% separated, 4.4% widowed, 11.8% divorced; Foreign born: 0.0%; Speak English only: 98.8%; With disability: 21.2%; Veterans: 9.3%; Ancestry: 17.8% Irish, 16.1% English, 15.9% French, 15.0% Italian, 10.3% German
Employment: 7.0% management, business, and financial, 3.7% computer, engineering, and science, 5.9% education, legal, community service, arts, and media, 8.6% healthcare practitioners, 23.8% service, 28.1% sales and office, 11.6% natural resources, construction, and maintenance, 11.3% production, transportation, and material moving
Income: Per capita: $21,387; Median household: $47,758; Average household: $51,077; Households with income of $100,000 or more: 7.6%; Poverty rate: 11.9%
Educational Attainment: High school diploma or higher: 88.6%; Bachelor's degree or higher: 12.2%; Graduate/professional degree or higher: 3.1%

School District(s)
Fort Edward Union Free SD (PK-12)
  Enrollment: 529 . . . . (518) 747-4594
Washington-Saratoga-Warren-Hamilton-Essex Boces
  Enrollment: n/a . . . . (518) 746-3310
Housing: Homeownership rate: 65.4%; Median home value: $98,900; Median year structure built: Before 1940; Homeowner vacancy rate: 0.0%; Median selected monthly owner costs: $1,218 with a mortgage, $423 without a mortgage; Median gross rent: $831 per month; Rental vacancy rate: 7.8%
Health Insurance: 91.1% have insurance; 58.7% have private insurance; 47.0% have public insurance; 8.9% do not have insurance; 1.7% of children under 18 do not have insurance
Safety: Violent crime rate: 9.1 per 10,000 population; Property crime rate: 51.8 per 10,000 population
Transportation: Commute: 92.2% car, 1.0% public transportation, 3.9% walk, 1.3% work from home; Mean travel time to work: 23.7 minutes; Amtrak: Train service available.

GRANVILLE (town). Covers a land area of 55.618 square miles and a water area of 0.500 square miles. Located at 43.42° N. Lat; 73.31° W. Long. Elevation is 410 feet.
History: Granville, on the eastern border of Washington County, New York, contains a village of the same name. Granville is named for John Carteret, 2nd Earl Granvilleand has been called the "Colored Slate Capital of the World" for the various colored slate mined in its quaries, including green, gray, gray black, purple, mottled green and purple, and red.
Population: 6,537; Growth (since 2000): 1.3%; Density: 117.5 persons per square mile; Race: 94.4% White, 0.8% Black/African American, 1.0% Asian, 1.0% American Indian/Alaska Native, 0.0% Native Hawaiian/Other Pacific Islander, 2.5% Two or more races, 1.3% Hispanic of any race; Average household size: 2.54; Median age: 46.3; Age under 18: 22.2%; Age 65 and over: 19.5%; Males per 100 females: 97.6; Marriage status: 29.5% never married, 48.5% now married, 2.2% separated, 5.1% widowed, 16.9% divorced; Foreign born: 3.0%; Speak English only: 96.5%; With disability: 15.6%; Veterans: 10.2%; Ancestry: 27.8% American, 12.9% Irish, 12.8% German, 9.4% English, 9.3% French
Employment: 7.2% management, business, and financial, 1.4% computer, engineering, and science, 7.3% education, legal, community service, arts, and media, 4.7% healthcare practitioners, 22.0% service, 28.6% sales and

office, 10.2% natural resources, construction, and maintenance, 18.6% production, transportation, and material moving
Income: Per capita: $22,119; Median household: $42,316; Average household: $54,885; Households with income of $100,000 or more: 13.4%; Poverty rate: 17.1%
Educational Attainment: High school diploma or higher: 84.1%; Bachelor's degree or higher: 13.1%; Graduate/professional degree or higher: 6.9%

School District(s)
Granville Central SD (PK-12)
  Enrollment: 1,119 . . . . (518) 642-1051
Housing: Homeownership rate: 66.0%; Median home value: $116,900; Median year structure built: 1963; Homeowner vacancy rate: 2.5%; Median selected monthly owner costs: $1,357 with a mortgage, $484 without a mortgage; Median gross rent: $698 per month; Rental vacancy rate: 4.5%
Health Insurance: 91.4% have insurance; 60.7% have private insurance; 48.0% have public insurance; 8.6% do not have insurance; 3.4% of children under 18 do not have insurance
Newspapers: Manchester Newspapers (weekly circulation 51,000); Northshire Free Press (weekly circulation 8,000)
Transportation: Commute: 88.6% car, 0.2% public transportation, 5.7% walk, 4.2% work from home; Mean travel time to work: 29.6 minutes
Additional Information Contacts
Town of Granville . . . . (518) 642-2640
  http://granvillevillage.com

GRANVILLE (village). Covers a land area of 1.570 square miles and a water area of <.001 square miles. Located at 43.41° N. Lat; 73.27° W. Long. Elevation is 410 feet.
Population: 2,440; Growth (since 2000): -7.7%; Density: 1,553.7 persons per square mile; Race: 94.1% White, 0.4% Black/African American, 2.6% Asian, 0.6% American Indian/Alaska Native, 0.0% Native Hawaiian/Other Pacific Islander, 1.9% Two or more races, 1.7% Hispanic of any race; Average household size: 2.23; Median age: 46.5; Age under 18: 20.5%; Age 65 and over: 19.1%; Males per 100 females: 85.9; Marriage status: 27.9% never married, 44.2% now married, 5.1% separated, 7.6% widowed, 20.3% divorced; Foreign born: 3.6%; Speak English only: 97.0%; With disability: 18.6%; Veterans: 9.4%; Ancestry: 17.7% Irish, 15.6% American, 13.3% German, 10.3% French, 9.4% Italian
Employment: 8.4% management, business, and financial, 2.4% computer, engineering, and science, 14.2% education, legal, community service, arts, and media, 6.8% healthcare practitioners, 22.7% service, 21.1% sales and office, 8.8% natural resources, construction, and maintenance, 15.5% production, transportation, and material moving
Income: Per capita: $20,603; Median household: $36,118; Average household: $44,740; Households with income of $100,000 or more: 10.5%; Poverty rate: 21.0%
Educational Attainment: High school diploma or higher: 85.5%; Bachelor's degree or higher: 15.2%; Graduate/professional degree or higher: 8.0%

School District(s)
Granville Central SD (PK-12)
  Enrollment: 1,119 . . . . (518) 642-1051
Housing: Homeownership rate: 51.3%; Median home value: $101,700; Median year structure built: Before 1940; Homeowner vacancy rate: 0.0%; Median selected monthly owner costs: $1,273 with a mortgage, $576 without a mortgage; Median gross rent: $582 per month; Rental vacancy rate: 7.1%
Health Insurance: 94.3% have insurance; 58.0% have private insurance; 47.5% have public insurance; 5.7% do not have insurance; 1.6% of children under 18 do not have insurance
Safety: Violent crime rate: 8.2 per 10,000 population; Property crime rate: 61.1 per 10,000 population
Newspapers: Manchester Newspapers (weekly circulation 51,000); Northshire Free Press (weekly circulation 8,000)
Transportation: Commute: 79.4% car, 0.6% public transportation, 13.8% walk, 4.6% work from home; Mean travel time to work: 26.4 minutes

GREENWICH (town). Covers a land area of 43.663 square miles and a water area of 0.598 square miles. Located at 43.15° N. Lat; 73.48° W. Long. Elevation is 374 feet.
History: Incorporated 1809.
Population: 4,863; Growth (since 2000): -0.7%; Density: 111.4 persons per square mile; Race: 97.5% White, 0.1% Black/African American, 1.5% Asian, 0.5% American Indian/Alaska Native, 0.0% Native Hawaiian/Other

Pacific Islander, 0.5% Two or more races, 1.9% Hispanic of any race; Average household size: 2.55; Median age: 45.8; Age under 18: 17.8%; Age 65 and over: 17.2%; Males per 100 females: 97.3; Marriage status: 27.5% never married, 52.7% now married, 1.7% separated, 6.7% widowed, 13.1% divorced; Foreign born: 2.4%; Speak English only: 97.1%; With disability: 8.0%; Veterans: 11.4%; Ancestry: 28.3% Irish, 13.3% American, 10.8% English, 10.8% French, 10.3% Italian
Employment: 11.1% management, business, and financial, 6.9% computer, engineering, and science, 11.8% education, legal, community service, arts, and media, 5.3% healthcare practitioners, 19.0% service, 18.7% sales and office, 13.1% natural resources, construction, and maintenance, 14.1% production, transportation, and material moving
Income: Per capita: $30,995; Median household: $59,609; Average household: $77,540; Households with income of $100,000 or more: 31.2%; Poverty rate: 10.0%
Educational Attainment: High school diploma or higher: 90.5%; Bachelor's degree or higher: 27.0%; Graduate/professional degree or higher: 11.9%

School District(s)
Greenwich Central SD (KG-12)
    Enrollment: 1,023 . . . . (518) 692-9542
Housing: Homeownership rate: 80.3%; Median home value: $171,500; Median year structure built: 1953; Homeowner vacancy rate: 3.5%; Median selected monthly owner costs: $1,603 with a mortgage, $595 without a mortgage; Median gross rent: $771 per month; Rental vacancy rate: 2.1%
Health Insurance: 92.8% have insurance; 70.1% have private insurance; 39.8% have public insurance; 7.2% do not have insurance; 0.7% of children under 18 do not have insurance
Newspapers: Greenwich Journal & Salem Press (weekly circulation 1,800)
Transportation: Commute: 91.3% car, 0.0% public transportation, 2.4% walk, 5.6% work from home; Mean travel time to work: 30.3 minutes
Additional Information Contacts
Town of Greenwich . . . . (518) 692-7611
    http://www.greenwichny.org

GREENWICH (village). Covers a land area of 1.477 square miles and a water area of 0 square miles. Located at 43.09° N. Lat; 73.50° W. Long. Elevation is 374 feet.
Population: 2,045; Growth (since 2000): 7.5%; Density: 1,384.6 persons per square mile; Race: 96.9% White, 0.2% Black/African American, 0.4% Asian, 0.4% American Indian/Alaska Native, 0.0% Native Hawaiian/Other Pacific Islander, 2.1% Two or more races, 4.9% Hispanic of any race; Average household size: 2.57; Median age: 37.0; Age under 18: 26.1%; Age 65 and over: 13.3%; Males per 100 females: 93.6; Marriage status: 32.7% never married, 52.1% now married, 2.6% separated, 6.0% widowed, 9.2% divorced; Foreign born: 2.2%; Speak English only: 95.5%; With disability: 8.0%; Veterans: 8.6%; Ancestry: 36.3% Irish, 11.0% German, 10.9% English, 9.7% Italian, 8.6% American
Employment: 10.2% management, business, and financial, 4.8% computer, engineering, and science, 12.3% education, legal, community service, arts, and media, 5.1% healthcare practitioners, 16.0% service, 25.1% sales and office, 15.1% natural resources, construction, and maintenance, 11.4% production, transportation, and material moving
Income: Per capita: $32,859; Median household: $65,521; Average household: $83,768; Households with income of $100,000 or more: 28.6%; Poverty rate: 10.8%
Educational Attainment: High school diploma or higher: 94.9%; Bachelor's degree or higher: 31.0%; Graduate/professional degree or higher: 12.8%

School District(s)
Greenwich Central SD (KG-12)
    Enrollment: 1,023 . . . . (518) 692-9542
Housing: Homeownership rate: 64.4%; Median home value: $164,800; Median year structure built: Before 1940; Homeowner vacancy rate: 1.5%; Median selected monthly owner costs: $1,543 with a mortgage, $770 without a mortgage; Median gross rent: $812 per month; Rental vacancy rate: 2.7%
Health Insurance: 93.7% have insurance; 74.2% have private insurance; 31.7% have public insurance; 6.3% do not have insurance; 1.1% of children under 18 do not have insurance
Safety: Violent crime rate: 17.4 per 10,000 population; Property crime rate: 127.5 per 10,000 population
Newspapers: Greenwich Journal & Salem Press (weekly circulation 1,800)

Transportation: Commute: 87.1% car, 0.0% public transportation, 5.8% walk, 5.4% work from home; Mean travel time to work: 28.7 minutes

HAMPTON (town). Covers a land area of 22.242 square miles and a water area of 0.348 square miles. Located at 43.55° N. Lat; 73.29° W. Long. Elevation is 427 feet.
Population: 852; Growth (since 2000): -2.2%; Density: 38.3 persons per square mile; Race: 99.4% White, 0.0% Black/African American, 0.0% Asian, 0.0% American Indian/Alaska Native, 0.0% Native Hawaiian/Other Pacific Islander, 0.5% Two or more races, 0.1% Hispanic of any race; Average household size: 2.37; Median age: 48.6; Age under 18: 15.6%; Age 65 and over: 21.0%; Males per 100 females: 103.0; Marriage status: 24.1% never married, 52.4% now married, 2.3% separated, 7.3% widowed, 16.2% divorced; Foreign born: 1.8%; Speak English only: 97.5%; With disability: 16.0%; Veterans: 11.7%; Ancestry: 20.8% American, 16.9% French, 10.4% Irish, 9.6% English, 9.4% German
Employment: 12.6% management, business, and financial, 1.9% computer, engineering, and science, 7.9% education, legal, community service, arts, and media, 2.3% healthcare practitioners, 22.7% service, 25.0% sales and office, 7.5% natural resources, construction, and maintenance, 20.1% production, transportation, and material moving
Income: Per capita: $27,462; Median household: $52,000; Average household: $63,793; Households with income of $100,000 or more: 19.1%; Poverty rate: 9.4%
Educational Attainment: High school diploma or higher: 88.5%; Bachelor's degree or higher: 13.2%; Graduate/professional degree or higher: 5.3%
Housing: Homeownership rate: 85.4%; Median home value: $132,800; Median year structure built: 1979; Homeowner vacancy rate: 2.3%; Median selected monthly owner costs: $1,109 with a mortgage, $476 without a mortgage; Median gross rent: $950 per month; Rental vacancy rate: 0.0%
Health Insurance: 94.8% have insurance; 73.9% have private insurance; 37.3% have public insurance; 5.2% do not have insurance; 0.0% of children under 18 do not have insurance
Transportation: Commute: 92.3% car, 0.5% public transportation, 0.5% walk, 6.1% work from home; Mean travel time to work: 24.5 minutes

HARTFORD (town). Covers a land area of 43.384 square miles and a water area of 0.105 square miles. Located at 43.36° N. Lat; 73.41° W. Long. Elevation is 390 feet.
Population: 2,092; Growth (since 2000): -8.2%; Density: 48.2 persons per square mile; Race: 95.5% White, 0.2% Black/African American, 2.6% Asian, 0.2% American Indian/Alaska Native, 0.0% Native Hawaiian/Other Pacific Islander, 1.6% Two or more races, 3.7% Hispanic of any race; Average household size: 2.52; Median age: 44.4; Age under 18: 20.5%; Age 65 and over: 16.1%; Males per 100 females: 101.9; Marriage status: 25.6% never married, 61.8% now married, 1.3% separated, 5.3% widowed, 7.2% divorced; Foreign born: 1.9%; Speak English only: 97.4%; With disability: 14.1%; Veterans: 7.3%; Ancestry: 20.8% Irish, 19.5% American, 15.3% English, 9.8% French, 6.6% German
Employment: 12.1% management, business, and financial, 2.3% computer, engineering, and science, 12.0% education, legal, community service, arts, and media, 5.7% healthcare practitioners, 20.3% service, 16.6% sales and office, 16.7% natural resources, construction, and maintenance, 14.4% production, transportation, and material moving
Income: Per capita: $27,408; Median household: $60,774; Average household: $68,981; Households with income of $100,000 or more: 24.5%; Poverty rate: 12.9%
Educational Attainment: High school diploma or higher: 88.4%; Bachelor's degree or higher: 21.6%; Graduate/professional degree or higher: 9.0%

School District(s)
Hartford Central SD (PK-12)
    Enrollment: 459 . . . . (518) 632-5931
Housing: Homeownership rate: 88.7%; Median home value: $157,700; Median year structure built: 1980; Homeowner vacancy rate: 3.5%; Median selected monthly owner costs: $1,403 with a mortgage, $487 without a mortgage; Median gross rent: $908 per month; Rental vacancy rate: 0.0%
Health Insurance: 95.9% have insurance; 75.4% have private insurance; 34.9% have public insurance; 4.1% do not have insurance; 8.9% of children under 18 do not have insurance
Transportation: Commute: 95.8% car, 0.0% public transportation, 0.9% walk, 2.6% work from home; Mean travel time to work: 24.3 minutes

HEBRON (town). Covers a land area of 56.108 square miles and a water area of 0.310 square miles. Located at 43.26° N. Lat; 73.35° W. Long.

Population: 1,814; Growth (since 2000): 2.3%; Density: 32.3 persons per square mile; Race: 97.9% White, 0.0% Black/African American, 0.7% Asian, 0.1% American Indian/Alaska Native, 0.0% Native Hawaiian/Other Pacific Islander, 1.4% Two or more races, 1.7% Hispanic of any race; Average household size: 2.35; Median age: 48.7; Age under 18: 16.4%; Age 65 and over: 19.1%; Males per 100 females: 104.1; Marriage status: 26.6% never married, 52.1% now married, 1.3% separated, 7.7% widowed, 13.7% divorced; Foreign born: 1.5%; Speak English only: 97.1%; With disability: 14.4%; Veterans: 9.9%; Ancestry: 15.4% American, 14.5% English, 11.0% Irish, 9.4% German, 9.3% French

Employment: 14.8% management, business, and financial, 1.2% computer, engineering, and science, 8.6% education, legal, community service, arts, and media, 7.3% healthcare practitioners, 18.3% service, 15.8% sales and office, 16.7% natural resources, construction, and maintenance, 17.3% production, transportation, and material moving

Income: Per capita: $26,352; Median household: $51,510; Average household: $61,122; Households with income of $100,000 or more: 14.4%; Poverty rate: 14.0%

Educational Attainment: High school diploma or higher: 84.5%; Bachelor's degree or higher: 23.3%; Graduate/professional degree or higher: 10.6%

Housing: Homeownership rate: 89.0%; Median home value: $145,700; Median year structure built: 1979; Homeowner vacancy rate: 5.5%; Median selected monthly owner costs: $1,315 with a mortgage, $495 without a mortgage; Median gross rent: $864 per month; Rental vacancy rate: 7.0%

Health Insurance: 91.9% have insurance; 58.7% have private insurance; 48.0% have public insurance; 8.1% do not have insurance; 3.3% of children under 18 do not have insurance

Transportation: Commute: 91.2% car, 0.1% public transportation, 3.4% walk, 4.0% work from home; Mean travel time to work: 32.1 minutes

HUDSON FALLS (village). County seat. Covers a land area of 1.832 square miles and a water area of 0.058 square miles. Located at 43.30° N. Lat; 73.58° W. Long. Elevation is 295 feet.

History: Settlers arrived in Hudson Falls in the 1760's and built gristmills and sawmills on the river near the 70-foot falls. The Burgoyne campaign delayed development and then the settlement was burned in 1780 by Sir Guy Carleton. In the 19th century, pulpwood, floated down the Hudson River from the Adirondack forests, helped to establish paper manufacturing as the dominant industry.

Population: 7,174; Growth (since 2000): 3.6%; Density: 3,916.1 persons per square mile; Race: 94.7% White, 2.1% Black/African American, 0.2% Asian, 0.0% American Indian/Alaska Native, 0.0% Native Hawaiian/Other Pacific Islander, 2.6% Two or more races, 1.4% Hispanic of any race; Average household size: 2.52; Median age: 37.1; Age under 18: 23.8%; Age 65 and over: 14.6%; Males per 100 females: 92.3; Marriage status: 37.7% never married, 42.8% now married, 1.8% separated, 5.1% widowed, 14.5% divorced; Foreign born: 2.1%; Speak English only: 98.6%; With disability: 15.3%; Veterans: 10.8%; Ancestry: 24.9% Irish, 16.6% American, 16.2% German, 14.4% French, 11.8% Italian

Employment: 6.6% management, business, and financial, 4.8% computer, engineering, and science, 9.7% education, legal, community service, arts, and media, 5.2% healthcare practitioners, 25.5% service, 22.6% sales and office, 11.4% natural resources, construction, and maintenance, 14.1% production, transportation, and material moving

Income: Per capita: $22,102; Median household: $44,992; Average household: $54,867; Households with income of $100,000 or more: 11.3%; Poverty rate: 20.4%

Educational Attainment: High school diploma or higher: 89.9%; Bachelor's degree or higher: 14.7%; Graduate/professional degree or higher: 4.8%

School District(s)
Hudson Falls Central SD (PK-12)
    Enrollment: 2,386 . . . . (518) 747-2121
Vocational/Technical School(s)
Washington Saratoga Warren Hamilton Essex BOCES-Practical Nursing Program (Public)
    Enrollment: 35 . . . . (518) 746-3508
    Tuition: $12,675

Housing: Homeownership rate: 48.7%; Median home value: $125,400; Median year structure built: 1940; Homeowner vacancy rate: 6.6%; Median

selected monthly owner costs: $1,148 with a mortgage, $463 without a mortgage; Median gross rent: $797 per month; Rental vacancy rate: 0.0%

Health Insurance: 90.3% have insurance; 56.4% have private insurance; 50.0% have public insurance, 9.7% do not have insurance; 7.2% of children under 18 do not have insurance

Safety: Violent crime rate: 22.6 per 10,000 population; Property crime rate: 76.1 per 10,000 population

Transportation: Commute: 90.0% car, 4.5% public transportation, 0.9% walk, 3.0% work from home; Mean travel time to work: 22.8 minutes

Additional Information Contacts
Village of Hudson Falls . . . . (518) 747-5426
    http://www.villageofhudsonfalls.com

HULETTS LANDING (unincorporated postal area)
ZCTA: 12841
    Covers a land area of 16.967 square miles and a water area of 0.041 square miles. Located at 43.61° N. Lat; 73.53° W. Long. Elevation is 371 feet.

Population: 99; Growth (since 2000): 13.8%; Density: 5.8 persons per square mile; Race: 100.0% White, 0.0% Black/African American, 0.0% Asian, 0.0% American Indian/Alaska Native, 0.0% Native Hawaiian/Other Pacific Islander, 0.0% Two or more races, 0.0% Hispanic of any race; Average household size: 1.48; Median age: 68.2; Age under 18: 0.0%; Age 65 and over: 54.5%; Males per 100 females: 87.8; Marriage status: 12.1% never married, 55.6% now married, 0.0% separated, 25.3% widowed, 7.1% divorced; Foreign born: 10.1%; Speak English only: 92.9%; With disability: 17.2%; Veterans: 11.1%; Ancestry: 21.2% German, 20.2% Irish, 15.2% Swedish, 11.1% English, 9.1% French

Employment: 15.8% management, business, and financial, 0.0% computer, engineering, and science, 18.4% education, legal, community service, arts, and media, 26.3% healthcare practitioners, 0.0% service, 0.0% sales and office, 39.5% natural resources, construction, and maintenance, 0.0% production, transportation, and material moving

Income: Per capita: $62,278; Median household: $55,208; Average household: $90,518; Households with income of $100,000 or more: 10.5%; Poverty rate: 2.0%

Educational Attainment: High school diploma or higher: 81.8%; Bachelor's degree or higher: 32.3%; Graduate/professional degree or higher: 19.2%

Housing: Homeownership rate: 77.6%; Median home value: $1,062,500; Median year structure built: 1962; Homeowner vacancy rate: 5.5%; Median selected monthly owner costs: $817 with a mortgage, $1,422 without a mortgage; Median gross rent: n/a per month; Rental vacancy rate: 0.0%

Health Insurance: 93.9% have insurance; 73.7% have private insurance; 63.6% have public insurance; 6.1% do not have insurance; 0.0% of children under 18 do not have insurance

Transportation: Commute: 92.1% car, 0.0% public transportation, 0.0% walk, 7.9% work from home; Mean travel time to work: 15.6 minutes

JACKSON (town). Covers a land area of 37.160 square miles and a water area of 0.406 square miles. Located at 43.08° N. Lat; 73.38° W. Long.

Population: 1,809; Growth (since 2000): 5.3%; Density: 48.7 persons per square mile; Race: 96.6% White, 2.9% Black/African American, 0.2% Asian, 0.0% American Indian/Alaska Native, 0.0% Native Hawaiian/Other Pacific Islander, 0.3% Two or more races, 0.8% Hispanic of any race; Average household size: 2.17; Median age: 53.4; Age under 18: 14.8%; Age 65 and over: 27.5%; Males per 100 females: 104.8; Marriage status: 20.1% never married, 58.1% now married, 2.5% separated, 8.8% widowed, 12.9% divorced; Foreign born: 1.6%; Speak English only: 97.0%; With disability: 15.0%; Veterans: 10.9%; Ancestry: 19.6% German, 18.7% Irish, 13.3% American, 10.9% English, 9.7% Polish

Employment: 13.3% management, business, and financial, 2.8% computer, engineering, and science, 11.1% education, legal, community service, arts, and media, 8.0% healthcare practitioners, 11.1% service, 20.2% sales and office, 16.1% natural resources, construction, and maintenance, 17.3% production, transportation, and material moving

Income: Per capita: $30,843; Median household: $57,404; Average household: $66,281; Households with income of $100,000 or more: 18.5%; Poverty rate: 5.2%

Educational Attainment: High school diploma or higher: 90.0%; Bachelor's degree or higher: 28.5%; Graduate/professional degree or higher: 8.2%

Housing: Homeownership rate: 79.4%; Median home value: $179,800; Median year structure built: 1967; Homeowner vacancy rate: 0.0%; Median selected monthly owner costs: $1,513 with a mortgage, $643 without a mortgage; Median gross rent: $905 per month; Rental vacancy rate: 0.0%
Health Insurance: 96.7% have insurance; 77.4% have private insurance; 44.4% have public insurance; 3.3% do not have insurance; 3.6% of children under 18 do not have insurance
Transportation: Commute: 91.8% car, 0.0% public transportation, 3.0% walk, 4.2% work from home; Mean travel time to work: 29.9 minutes

KINGSBURY (town).

Covers a land area of 39.678 square miles and a water area of 0.327 square miles. Located at 43.34° N. Lat; 73.55° W. Long. Elevation is 305 feet.
Population: 12,551; Growth (since 2000): 12.4%; Density: 316.3 persons per square mile; Race: 94.9% White, 1.9% Black/African American, 0.1% Asian, 0.1% American Indian/Alaska Native, 0.0% Native Hawaiian/Other Pacific Islander, 2.5% Two or more races, 2.5% Hispanic of any race; Average household size: 2.55; Median age: 37.4; Age under 18: 23.2%; Age 65 and over: 13.8%; Males per 100 females: 96.4; Marriage status: 34.2% never married, 48.8% now married, 2.2% separated, 5.3% widowed, 11.7% divorced; Foreign born: 2.0%; Speak English only: 98.0%; With disability: 13.2%; Veterans: 10.8%; Ancestry: 25.1% Irish, 16.8% American, 13.9% German, 12.1% Italian, 11.9% French
Employment: 8.2% management, business, and financial, 4.0% computer, engineering, and science, 8.3% education, legal, community service, arts, and media, 4.4% healthcare practitioners, 22.7% service, 25.8% sales and office, 11.7% natural resources, construction, and maintenance, 14.8% production, transportation, and material moving
Income: Per capita: $24,912; Median household: $48,771; Average household: $62,683; Households with income of $100,000 or more: 15.6%; Poverty rate: 16.0%
Educational Attainment: High school diploma or higher: 89.6%; Bachelor's degree or higher: 18.5%; Graduate/professional degree or higher: 7.4%
Housing: Homeownership rate: 55.3%; Median home value: $137,300; Median year structure built: 1960; Homeowner vacancy rate: 3.5%; Median selected monthly owner costs: $1,284 with a mortgage, $466 without a mortgage; Median gross rent: $852 per month; Rental vacancy rate: 6.3%
Health Insurance: 91.2% have insurance; 61.5% have private insurance; 44.5% have public insurance; 8.8% do not have insurance; 8.9% of children under 18 do not have insurance
Transportation: Commute: 92.2% car, 3.1% public transportation, 0.7% walk, 3.0% work from home; Mean travel time to work: 22.1 minutes

MIDDLE GRANVILLE (unincorporated postal area)
ZCTA: 12849

Covers a land area of 2.719 square miles and a water area of 0.011 square miles. Located at 43.45° N. Lat; 73.30° W. Long. Elevation is 371 feet.
Population: 359; Growth (since 2000): -19.3%; Density: 132.0 persons per square mile; Race: 99.2% White, 0.8% Black/African American, 0.0% Asian, 0.0% American Indian/Alaska Native, 0.0% Native Hawaiian/Other Pacific Islander, 0.0% Two or more races, 0.0% Hispanic of any race; Average household size: 2.37; Median age: 63.3; Age under 18: 20.6%; Age 65 and over: 42.3%; Males per 100 females: 94.4; Marriage status: 13.9% never married, 81.3% now married, 0.0% separated, 0.0% widowed, 4.7% divorced; Foreign born: 0.0%; Speak English only: 100.0%; With disability: 12.8%; Veterans: 10.5%; Ancestry: 53.5% American, 12.5% German, 8.4% French, 4.2% Danish, 4.2% Dutch
Employment: 14.0% management, business, and financial, 0.0% computer, engineering, and science, 0.0% education, legal, community service, arts, and media, 0.0% healthcare practitioners, 22.0% service, 48.4% sales and office, 5.9% natural resources, construction, and maintenance, 9.7% production, transportation, and material moving
Income: Per capita: $30,300; Median household: $66,635; Average household: $74,334; Households with income of $100,000 or more: 12.3%; Poverty rate: 0.8%
Educational Attainment: High school diploma or higher: 90.2%; Bachelor's degree or higher: n/a; Graduate/professional degree or higher: n/a

School District(s)
Granville Central SD (PK-12)
 Enrollment: 1,119 . . . . (518) 642-1051

Housing: Homeownership rate: 100.0%; Median home value: $204,900; Median year structure built: 1981; Homeowner vacancy rate: 0.0%; Median selected monthly owner costs: $1,639 with a mortgage, $1,105 without a mortgage; Median gross rent: n/a per month; Rental vacancy rate: 0.0%
Health Insurance: 100.0% have insurance; 72.7% have private insurance; 56.0% have public insurance; 0.0% do not have insurance; 0.0% of children under 18 do not have insurance
Transportation: Commute: 94.1% car, 0.0% public transportation, 5.9% walk, 0.0% work from home; Mean travel time to work: 14.8 minutes

PUTNAM (town).

Covers a land area of 32.791 square miles and a water area of 2.627 square miles. Located at 43.75° N. Lat; 73.42° W. Long. Elevation is 335 feet.
Population: 639; Growth (since 2000): -0.9%; Density: 19.5 persons per square mile; Race: 99.7% White, 0.0% Black/African American, 0.3% Asian, 0.0% American Indian/Alaska Native, 0.0% Native Hawaiian/Other Pacific Islander, 0.0% Two or more races, 0.5% Hispanic of any race; Average household size: 2.16; Median age: 55.1; Age under 18: 21.8%; Age 65 and over: 31.1%; Males per 100 females: 100.3; Marriage status: 15.5% never married, 60.4% now married, 3.1% separated, 6.8% widowed, 17.3% divorced; Foreign born: 1.9%; Speak English only: 99.2%; With disability: 14.3%; Veterans: 12.9%; Ancestry: 31.0% Irish, 18.5% American, 15.2% English, 14.7% French, 13.0% German
Employment: 14.7% management, business, and financial, 0.9% computer, engineering, and science, 15.7% education, legal, community service, arts, and media, 0.9% healthcare practitioners, 24.4% service, 12.0% sales and office, 18.4% natural resources, construction, and maintenance, 12.9% production, transportation, and material moving
Income: Per capita: $39,650; Median household: $54,333; Average household: $83,697; Households with income of $100,000 or more: 20.2%; Poverty rate: 13.9%
Educational Attainment: High school diploma or higher: 95.7%; Bachelor's degree or higher: 21.3%; Graduate/professional degree or higher: 11.4%
Housing: Homeownership rate: 89.9%; Median home value: $153,900; Median year structure built: 1957; Homeowner vacancy rate: 7.0%; Median selected monthly owner costs: $1,170 with a mortgage, $477 without a mortgage; Median gross rent: $900 per month; Rental vacancy rate: 0.0%
Health Insurance: 95.8% have insurance; 75.5% have private insurance; 48.4% have public insurance; 4.2% do not have insurance; 0.0% of children under 18 do not have insurance
Transportation: Commute: 92.2% car, 0.0% public transportation, 2.3% walk, 4.6% work from home; Mean travel time to work: 30.4 minutes

PUTNAM STATION (unincorporated postal area)
ZCTA: 12861

Covers a land area of 32.791 square miles and a water area of 0.566 square miles. Located at 43.75° N. Lat; 73.42° W. Long. Elevation is 118 feet.
Population: 639; Growth (since 2000): -0.9%; Density: 19.5 persons per square mile; Race: 99.7% White, 0.0% Black/African American, 0.3% Asian, 0.0% American Indian/Alaska Native, 0.0% Native Hawaiian/Other Pacific Islander, 0.0% Two or more races, 0.5% Hispanic of any race; Average household size: 2.16; Median age: 55.1; Age under 18: 21.8%; Age 65 and over: 31.1%; Males per 100 females: 100.3; Marriage status: 15.5% never married, 60.4% now married, 3.1% separated, 6.8% widowed, 17.3% divorced; Foreign born: 1.9%; Speak English only: 99.2%; With disability: 14.3%; Veterans: 12.9%; Ancestry: 31.0% Irish, 18.5% American, 15.2% English, 14.7% French, 13.0% German
Employment: 14.7% management, business, and financial, 0.9% computer, engineering, and science, 15.7% education, legal, community service, arts, and media, 0.9% healthcare practitioners, 24.4% service, 12.0% sales and office, 18.4% natural resources, construction, and maintenance, 12.9% production, transportation, and material moving
Income: Per capita: $39,650; Median household: $54,333; Average household: $83,697; Households with income of $100,000 or more: 20.2%; Poverty rate: 13.9%
Educational Attainment: High school diploma or higher: 95.7%; Bachelor's degree or higher: 21.3%; Graduate/professional degree or higher: 11.4%

School District(s)
Putnam Central SD (PK-06)
 Enrollment: 17 . . . . (518) 547-8266

Housing: Homeownership rate: 89.9%; Median home value: $153,900; Median year structure built: 1957; Homeowner vacancy rate: 7.0%; Median selected monthly owner costs: $1,170 with a mortgage, $477 without a mortgage; Median gross rent: $900 per month; Rental vacancy rate: 0.0%

Health Insurance: 95.8% have insurance; 75.5% have private insurance; 48.4% have public insurance; 4.2% do not have insurance; 0.0% of children under 18 do not have insurance

Transportation: Commute: 92.2% car, 0.0% public transportation, 2.3% walk, 4.6% work from home; Mean travel time to work: 30.4 minutes

---

SALEM (town). Covers a land area of 52.362 square miles and a water area of 0.058 square miles. Located at 43.16° N. Lat; 73.32° W. Long. Elevation is 482 feet.

History: Settled 1764, incorporated 1803.

Population: 2,661; Growth (since 2000): -1.5%; Density: 50.8 persons per square mile; Race: 98.5% White, 0.2% Black/African American, 0.0% Asian, 0.2% American Indian/Alaska Native, 0.0% Native Hawaiian/Other Pacific Islander, 0.3% Two or more races, 3.2% Hispanic of any race; Average household size: 2.29; Median age: 47.1; Age under 18: 20.7%; Age 65 and over: 21.9%; Males per 100 females: 100.4; Marriage status: 24.5% never married, 55.5% now married, 0.6% separated, 9.0% widowed, 11.0% divorced; Foreign born: 2.4%; Speak English only: 96.5%; With disability: 12.4%; Veterans: 8.5%; Ancestry: 17.4% Irish, 15.6% American, 14.4% German, 14.1% English, 8.6% Italian

Employment: 12.7% management, business, and financial, 1.5% computer, engineering, and science, 12.4% education, legal, community service, arts, and media, 7.8% healthcare practitioners, 10.8% service, 20.6% sales and office, 17.1% natural resources, construction, and maintenance, 17.1% production, transportation, and material moving

Income: Per capita: $26,153; Median household: $56,534; Average household: $59,669; Households with income of $100,000 or more: 14.9%; Poverty rate: 14.2%

Educational Attainment: High school diploma or higher: 94.7%; Bachelor's degree or higher: 31.3%; Graduate/professional degree or higher: 12.8%

School District(s)

Salem Central SD (KG-12)
    Enrollment: 559 . . . . (518) 854-7855

Housing: Homeownership rate: 83.9%; Median home value: $151,500; Median year structure built: 1957; Homeowner vacancy rate: 2.0%; Median selected monthly owner costs: $1,211 with a mortgage, $556 without a mortgage; Median gross rent: $747 per month; Rental vacancy rate: 11.1%

Health Insurance: 93.8% have insurance; 69.9% have private insurance; 43.4% have public insurance; 6.2% do not have insurance; 0.9% of children under 18 do not have insurance

Transportation: Commute: 84.3% car, 0.6% public transportation, 4.3% walk, 9.3% work from home; Mean travel time to work: 26.2 minutes

---

SALEM (village). Covers a land area of 2.928 square miles and a water area of 0 square miles. Located at 43.17° N. Lat; 73.33° W. Long. Elevation is 482 feet.

Population: 713; Growth (since 2000): -26.0%; Density: 243.5 persons per square mile; Race: 96.1% White, 0.4% Black/African American, 0.0% Asian, 0.7% American Indian/Alaska Native, 0.0% Native Hawaiian/Other Pacific Islander, 0.0% Two or more races, 5.0% Hispanic of any race; Average household size: 2.18; Median age: 47.0; Age under 18: 19.1%; Age 65 and over: 22.7%; Males per 100 females: 93.1; Marriage status: 27.2% never married, 49.3% now married, 0.8% separated, 12.7% widowed, 10.8% divorced; Foreign born: 3.4%; Speak English only: 95.2%; With disability: 14.3%; Veterans: 7.3%; Ancestry: 16.1% American, 15.7% Irish, 14.0% German, 8.8% Italian, 8.1% French

Employment: 9.3% management, business, and financial, 4.3% computer, engineering, and science, 10.7% education, legal, community service, arts, and media, 7.0% healthcare practitioners, 16.8% service, 28.4% sales and office, 9.9% natural resources, construction, and maintenance, 13.6% production, transportation, and material moving

Income: Per capita: $27,691; Median household: $60,667; Average household: $59,960; Households with income of $100,000 or more: 12.8%; Poverty rate: 11.9%

Educational Attainment: High school diploma or higher: 92.7%; Bachelor's degree or higher: 27.5%; Graduate/professional degree or higher: 14.4%

School District(s)

Salem Central SD (KG-12)
    Enrollment: 559 . . . . (518) 854-7855

Housing: Homeownership rate: 73.9%; Median home value: $116,500; Median year structure built: Before 1940; Homeowner vacancy rate: 2.5%; Median selected monthly owner costs: $1,397 with a mortgage, $608 without a mortgage; Median gross rent: $581 per month; Rental vacancy rate: 8.7%

Health Insurance: 93.3% have insurance; 63.4% have private insurance; 48.2% have public insurance; 6.7% do not have insurance; 0.0% of children under 18 do not have insurance

Transportation: Commute: 87.8% car, 0.0% public transportation, 8.2% walk, 4.1% work from home; Mean travel time to work: 23.7 minutes

---

SHUSHAN (unincorporated postal area)

ZCTA: 12873

Covers a land area of 21.118 square miles and a water area of <.001 square miles. Located at 43.12° N. Lat; 73.31° W. Long. Elevation is 469 feet.

Population: 784; Growth (since 2000): -3.0%; Density: 37.1 persons per square mile; Race: 99.9% White, 0.1% Black/African American, 0.0% Asian, 0.0% American Indian/Alaska Native, 0.0% Native Hawaiian/Other Pacific Islander, 0.0% Two or more races, 0.0% Hispanic of any race; Average household size: 2.25; Median age: 50.0; Age under 18: 16.8%; Age 65 and over: 26.1%; Males per 100 females: 100.5; Marriage status: 25.6% never married, 54.5% now married, 0.6% separated, 6.4% widowed, 13.5% divorced; Foreign born: 1.1%; Speak English only: 96.6%; With disability: 14.2%; Veterans: 7.8%; Ancestry: 26.4% English, 15.8% Irish, 14.9% French, 14.8% Italian, 12.6% German

Employment: 17.5% management, business, and financial, 1.7% computer, engineering, and science, 7.3% education, legal, community service, arts, and media, 9.0% healthcare practitioners, 8.0% service, 18.2% sales and office, 26.2% natural resources, construction, and maintenance, 12.1% production, transportation, and material moving

Income: Per capita: $25,903; Median household: $47,917; Average household: $57,932; Households with income of $100,000 or more: 14.2%; Poverty rate: 5.2%

Educational Attainment: High school diploma or higher: 93.2%; Bachelor's degree or higher: 36.8%; Graduate/professional degree or higher: 14.0%

Housing: Homeownership rate: 93.9%; Median home value: $166,800; Median year structure built: 1955; Homeowner vacancy rate: 0.0%; Median selected monthly owner costs: $1,305 with a mortgage, $515 without a mortgage; Median gross rent: $1,031 per month; Rental vacancy rate: 0.0%

Health Insurance: 95.3% have insurance; 74.4% have private insurance; 43.5% have public insurance; 4.7% do not have insurance; 3.2% of children under 18 do not have insurance

Transportation: Commute: 86.6% car, 1.8% public transportation, 0.0% walk, 9.4% work from home; Mean travel time to work: 29.0 minutes

---

WHITE CREEK (town). Covers a land area of 47.923 square miles and a water area of 0.053 square miles. Located at 42.99° N. Lat; 73.32° W. Long. Elevation is 656 feet.

Population: 3,325; Growth (since 2000): -2.5%; Density: 69.4 persons per square mile; Race: 97.0% White, 0.0% Black/African American, 1.8% Asian, 0.2% American Indian/Alaska Native, 0.0% Native Hawaiian/Other Pacific Islander, 1.0% Two or more races, 0.4% Hispanic of any race; Average household size: 2.20; Median age: 49.8; Age under 18: 16.2%; Age 65 and over: 23.1%; Males per 100 females: 93.5; Marriage status: 27.1% never married, 52.9% now married, 3.9% separated, 4.9% widowed, 15.1% divorced; Foreign born: 1.2%; Speak English only: 99.4%; With disability: 16.8%; Veterans: 8.9%; Ancestry: 24.5% Irish, 20.9% American, 17.4% German, 10.6% English, 7.7% Italian

Employment: 12.3% management, business, and financial, 2.0% computer, engineering, and science, 10.2% education, legal, community service, arts, and media, 6.2% healthcare practitioners, 21.6% service, 12.1% sales and office, 11.0% natural resources, construction, and maintenance, 24.7% production, transportation, and material moving

Income: Per capita: $26,819; Median household: $52,969; Average household: $58,350; Households with income of $100,000 or more: 15.6%; Poverty rate: 6.7%

Educational Attainment: High school diploma or higher: 90.2%; Bachelor's degree or higher: 21.2%; Graduate/professional degree or higher: 10.1%

Housing: Homeownership rate: 78.8%; Median home value: $157,700; Median year structure built: 1965; Homeowner vacancy rate: 0.0%; Median selected monthly owner costs: $1,190 with a mortgage, $627 without a mortgage; Median gross rent: $731 per month; Rental vacancy rate: 9.4%

Health Insurance: 95.6% have insurance; 73.9% have private insurance; 44.8% have public insurance; 4.4% do not have insurance; 1.0% of children under 18 do not have insurance

Transportation: Commute: 88.1% car, 0.0% public transportation, 6.6% walk, 4.8% work from home; Mean travel time to work: 26.8 minutes

WHITEHALL (town).
Covers a land area of 57.176 square miles and a water area of 1.729 square miles. Located at 43.54° N. Lat; 73.39° W. Long. Elevation is 157 feet.

History: Settled 1759, incorporated 1806.

Population: 3,973; Growth (since 2000): -1.5%; Density: 69.5 persons per square mile; Race: 98.6% White, 0.6% Black/African American, 0.0% Asian, 0.0% American Indian/Alaska Native, 0.0% Native Hawaiian/Other Pacific Islander, 0.0% Two or more races, 1.0% Hispanic of any race; Average household size: 2.49; Median age: 39.1; Age under 18: 21.9%; Age 65 and over: 14.9%; Males per 100 females: 103.9; Marriage status: 33.5% never married, 51.8% now married, 2.3% separated, 6.7% widowed, 8.0% divorced; Foreign born: 1.6%; Speak English only: 96.7%; With disability: 19.2%; Veterans: 8.9%; Ancestry: 22.9% American, 17.4% Irish, 15.8% French, 12.7% Italian, 9.6% English

Employment: 7.4% management, business, and financial, 0.9% computer, engineering, and science, 5.4% education, legal, community service, arts, and media, 3.6% healthcare practitioners, 25.6% service, 23.5% sales and office, 14.9% natural resources, construction, and maintenance, 18.8% production, transportation, and material moving

Income: Per capita: $22,070; Median household: $41,463; Average household: $53,870; Households with income of $100,000 or more: 16.7%; Poverty rate: 20.8%

Educational Attainment: High school diploma or higher: 85.2%; Bachelor's degree or higher: 9.7%; Graduate/professional degree or higher: 2.1%

School District(s)
Whitehall Central SD (PK-12)
    Enrollment: 805 . . . . (518) 499-1772

Housing: Homeownership rate: 65.9%; Median home value: $98,200; Median year structure built: 1943; Homeowner vacancy rate: 0.0%; Median selected monthly owner costs: $1,267 with a mortgage, $494 without a mortgage; Median gross rent: $782 per month; Rental vacancy rate: 0.0%

Health Insurance: 91.3% have insurance; 58.8% have private insurance; 46.6% have public insurance; 8.7% do not have insurance; 4.1% of children under 18 do not have insurance

Transportation: Commute: 87.4% car, 0.9% public transportation, 10.1% walk, 1.2% work from home; Mean travel time to work: 25.2 minutes; Amtrak: Train service available.

Additional Information Contacts
Town of Whitehall . . . . (518) 499-1535
   http://www.whitehallny.info/Town.html

WHITEHALL (village).
Covers a land area of 4.703 square miles and a water area of 0.212 square miles. Located at 43.56° N. Lat; 73.42° W. Long. Elevation is 157 feet.

Population: 2,550; Growth (since 2000): -4.4%; Density: 542.2 persons per square mile; Race: 98.3% White, 1.0% Black/African American, 0.0% Asian, 0.0% American Indian/Alaska Native, 0.0% Native Hawaiian/Other Pacific Islander, 0.0% Two or more races, 1.2% Hispanic of any race; Average household size: 2.39; Median age: 36.6; Age under 18: 23.6%; Age 65 and over: 15.3%; Males per 100 females: 104.1; Marriage status: 35.5% never married, 46.1% now married, 3.7% separated, 7.2% widowed, 11.2% divorced; Foreign born: 1.1%; Speak English only: 98.6%; With disability: 19.9%; Veterans: 8.9%; Ancestry: 25.0% American, 18.3% Irish, 14.8% Italian, 14.5% French, 8.0% English

Employment: 8.5% management, business, and financial, 1.6% computer, engineering, and science, 6.4% education, legal, community service, arts, and media, 5.4% healthcare practitioners, 26.5% service, 23.0% sales and office, 10.9% natural resources, construction, and maintenance, 17.7% production, transportation, and material moving

Income: Per capita: $19,764; Median household: $34,559; Average household: $46,091; Households with income of $100,000 or more: 11.0%; Poverty rate: 26.5%

Educational Attainment: High school diploma or higher: 83.6%; Bachelor's degree or higher: 8.7%; Graduate/professional degree or higher: 2.1%

School District(s)
Whitehall Central SD (PK-12)
    Enrollment: 805 . . . . (518) 499-1772

Housing: Homeownership rate: 55.9%; Median home value: $84,400; Median year structure built: Before 1940; Homeowner vacancy rate: 0.0%; Median selected monthly owner costs: $1,139 with a mortgage, $521 without a mortgage; Median gross rent: $780 per month; Rental vacancy rate: 0.0%

Health Insurance: 87.9% have insurance; 46.8% have private insurance; 55.1% have public insurance; 12.1% do not have insurance; 6.6% of children under 18 do not have insurance

Transportation: Commute: 91.4% car, 1.6% public transportation, 4.3% walk, 2.0% work from home; Mean travel time to work: 23.0 minutes; Amtrak: Train service available.

Wayne County

Located in western New York; bounded on the north by Lake Ontario; drained by the Clyde River. Covers a land area of 603.826 square miles, a water area of 779.225 square miles, and is located in the Eastern Time Zone at 43.46° N. Lat., 77.06° W. Long. The county was founded in 1823. County seat is Lyons.

Wayne County is part of the Rochester, NY Metropolitan Statistical Area. The entire metro area includes: Livingston County, NY; Monroe County, NY; Ontario County, NY; Orleans County, NY; Wayne County, NY; Yates County, NY

Weather Station: Sodus Center										Elevation: 419 feet	
	Jan	Feb	Mar	Apr	May	Jun	Jul	Aug	Sep	Oct	Nov	Dec
High	33	35	44	57	69	78	81	80	73	60	49	37
Low	18	19	26	37	46	55	61	60	53	42	34	24
Precip	2.7	2.1	2.7	3.1	3.2	3.5	3.3	3.3	3.7	4.0	4.0	3.2
Snow	29.7	16.3	12.9	2.8	0.1	0.0	0.0	0.0	0.0	0.1	7.1	23.7

High and Low temperatures in degrees Fahrenheit; Precipitation and Snow in inches

Population: 91,442; Growth (since 2000): -2.5%; Density: 151.4 persons per square mile; Race: 93.1% White, 3.0% Black/African American, 0.7% Asian, 0.2% American Indian/Alaska Native, 0.1% Native Hawaiian/Other Pacific Islander, 2.0% two or more races, 4.2% Hispanic of any race; Average household size: 2.45; Median age: 43.6; Age under 18: 21.9%; Age 65 and over: 17.2%; Males per 100 females: 98.5; Marriage status: 28.1% never married, 54.0% now married, 2.3% separated, 6.3% widowed, 11.6% divorced; Foreign born: 2.9%; Speak English only: 94.9%; With disability: 14.7%; Veterans: 8.8%; Ancestry: 22.6% German, 16.1% Irish, 13.9% Italian, 13.1% English, 12.1% Dutch

Religion: Six largest groups: 16.4% Catholicism, 5.2% Methodist/Pietist, 3.1% Presbyterian-Reformed, 2.4% Baptist, 2.1% Non-denominational Protestant, 1.3% Holiness

Economy: Unemployment rate: 3.4%; Leading industries: 16.1 % construction; 15.4 % retail trade; 11.4 % other services (except public administration); Farms: 873 totaling 179,109 acres; Company size: 0 employ 1,000 or more persons, 2 employ 500 to 999 persons, 29 employ 100 to 499 persons, 1,695 employ less than 100 persons; Business ownership: 1,837 women-owned, 50 Black-owned, 170 Hispanic-owned, 132 Asian-owned, 37 American Indian/Alaska Native-owned

Employment: 11.7% management, business, and financial, 5.0% computer, engineering, and science, 10.7% education, legal, community service, arts, and media, 6.1% healthcare practitioners, 15.5% service, 23.9% sales and office, 10.7% natural resources, construction, and maintenance, 16.5% production, transportation, and material moving

Income: Per capita: $27,318; Median household: $53,693; Average household: $66,991; Households with income of $100,000 or more: 19.5%; Poverty rate: 11.7%

Educational Attainment: High school diploma or higher: 89.6%; Bachelor's degree or higher: 21.7%; Graduate/professional degree or higher: 8.9%

Housing: Homeownership rate: 76.8%; Median home value: $118,900; Median year structure built: 1965; Homeowner vacancy rate: 1.5%; Median

selected monthly owner costs: $1,235 with a mortgage, $532 without a mortgage; Median gross rent: $742 per month; Rental vacancy rate: 6.2%
Vital Statistics: Birth rate: 106.1 per 10,000 population; Death rate: 92.5 per 10,000 population; Age-adjusted cancer mortality rate: 177.9 deaths per 100,000 population
Health Insurance: 94.1% have insurance; 71.5% have private insurance; 37.5% have public insurance; 5.9% do not have insurance; 4.5% of children under 18 do not have insurance
Health Care: Physicians: 6.3 per 10,000 population; Dentists: 5.0 per 10,000 population; Hospital beds: 30.8 per 10,000 population; Hospital admissions: 643.4 per 10,000 population
Air Quality Index (AQI): Percent of Days: 93.8% good, 5.9% moderate, 0.3% unhealthy for sensitive individuals, 0.0% unhealthy, 0.0% very unhealthy; Annual median: 36; Annual maximum: 101
Transportation: Commute: 92.7% car, 0.7% public transportation, 2.2% walk, 3.2% work from home; Mean travel time to work: 24.9 minutes
2016 Presidential Election: 58.9% Trump, 33.9% Clinton, 4.8% Johnson, 1.4% Stein
Additional Information Contacts
Wayne Government . . . . (315) 946-5400
  http://www.co.wayne.ny.us

Wayne County Communities

ARCADIA (town). Covers a land area of 52.033 square miles and a water area of 0.111 square miles. Located at 43.10° N. Lat; 77.08° W. Long.
Population: 13,822; Growth (since 2000): -7.2%; Density: 265.6 persons per square mile; Race: 87.8% White, 5.2% Black/African American, 1.3% Asian, 0.3% American Indian/Alaska Native, 0.2% Native Hawaiian/Other Pacific Islander, 3.4% Two or more races, 5.1% Hispanic of any race; Average household size: 2.27; Median age: 46.2; Age under 18: 18.2%; Age 65 and over: 18.4%; Males per 100 females: 93.6; Marriage status: 33.1% never married, 43.4% now married, 3.1% separated, 7.4% widowed, 16.1% divorced; Foreign born: 3.1%; Speak English only: 94.0%; With disability: 18.9%; Veterans: 9.8%; Ancestry: 18.8% German, 16.1% Irish, 15.4% Dutch, 12.8% Italian, 12.1% English
Employment: 10.7% management, business, and financial, 3.1% computer, engineering, and science, 10.6% education, legal, community service, arts, and media, 5.5% healthcare practitioners, 15.6% service, 25.1% sales and office, 9.1% natural resources, construction, and maintenance, 20.2% production, transportation, and material moving
Income: Per capita: $24,532; Median household: $43,729; Average household: $55,642; Households with income of $100,000 or more: 12.3%; Poverty rate: 15.9%
Educational Attainment: High school diploma or higher: 90.0%; Bachelor's degree or higher: 17.9%; Graduate/professional degree or higher: 7.3%
Housing: Homeownership rate: 63.8%; Median home value: $96,700; Median year structure built: 1956; Homeowner vacancy rate: 0.7%; Median selected monthly owner costs: $1,143 with a mortgage, $512 without a mortgage; Median gross rent: $717 per month; Rental vacancy rate: 7.0%
Health Insurance: 94.1% have insurance; 65.3% have private insurance; 45.7% have public insurance; 5.9% do not have insurance; 3.7% of children under 18 do not have insurance
Transportation: Commute: 89.7% car, 1.5% public transportation, 4.9% walk, 3.0% work from home; Mean travel time to work: 20.3 minutes
Additional Information Contacts
Town of Arcadia . . . . (315) 331-1222

BUTLER (town). Covers a land area of 37.090 square miles and a water area of 0.079 square miles. Located at 43.18° N. Lat; 76.77° W. Long.
Population: 1,891; Growth (since 2000): -17.0%; Density: 51.0 persons per square mile; Race: 95.9% White, 1.4% Black/African American, 0.0% Asian, 0.0% American Indian/Alaska Native, 0.0% Native Hawaiian/Other Pacific Islander, 2.2% Two or more races, 0.8% Hispanic of any race; Average household size: 2.51; Median age: 41.1; Age under 18: 23.0%; Age 65 and over: 15.5%; Males per 100 females: 108.9; Marriage status: 32.3% never married, 51.6% now married, 3.3% separated, 8.0% widowed, 8.1% divorced; Foreign born: 0.3%; Speak English only: 98.0%; With disability: 13.0%; Veterans: 8.9%; Ancestry: 23.0% German, 16.1% Irish, 13.5% English, 9.8% Dutch, 7.3% American
Employment: 9.7% management, business, and financial, 2.3% computer, engineering, and science, 7.8% education, legal, community service, arts,

and media, 3.7% healthcare practitioners, 9.4% service, 28.1% sales and office, 17.4% natural resources, construction, and maintenance, 21.5% production, transportation, and material moving
Income: Per capita: $21,617; Median household: $44,423; Average household: $55,220; Households with income of $100,000 or more: 12.9%; Poverty rate: 17.1%
Educational Attainment: High school diploma or higher: 84.2%; Bachelor's degree or higher: 8.5%; Graduate/professional degree or higher: 3.9%
Housing: Homeownership rate: 80.8%; Median home value: $88,400; Median year structure built: 1961; Homeowner vacancy rate: 0.0%; Median selected monthly owner costs: $1,085 with a mortgage, $434 without a mortgage; Median gross rent: $608 per month; Rental vacancy rate: 0.0%
Health Insurance: 86.7% have insurance; 58.8% have private insurance; 40.9% have public insurance; 13.3% do not have insurance; 16.7% of children under 18 do not have insurance
Transportation: Commute: 89.3% car, 0.0% public transportation, 6.1% walk, 3.5% work from home; Mean travel time to work: 27.6 minutes

CLYDE (village). Covers a land area of 2.198 square miles and a water area of 0.059 square miles. Located at 43.08° N. Lat; 76.87° W. Long. Elevation is 400 feet.
History: Incorporated 1835.
Population: 1,991; Growth (since 2000): -12.3%; Density: 905.8 persons per square mile; Race: 93.6% White, 2.5% Black/African American, 0.1% Asian, 0.1% American Indian/Alaska Native, 0.0% Native Hawaiian/Other Pacific Islander, 3.7% Two or more races, 8.3% Hispanic of any race; Average household size: 2.93; Median age: 29.6; Age under 18: 33.1%; Age 65 and over: 12.4%; Males per 100 females: 94.7; Marriage status: 35.2% never married, 48.1% now married, 4.7% separated, 4.2% widowed, 12.5% divorced; Foreign born: 1.2%; Speak English only: 96.0%; With disability: 16.8%; Veterans: 4.3%; Ancestry: 23.2% Italian, 18.5% Irish, 14.0% German, 12.0% English, 8.1% Dutch
Employment: 6.3% management, business, and financial, 3.6% computer, engineering, and science, 9.3% education, legal, community service, arts, and media, 8.7% healthcare practitioners, 22.0% service, 23.5% sales and office, 14.1% natural resources, construction, and maintenance, 12.7% production, transportation, and material moving
Income: Per capita: $19,593; Median household: $44,844; Average household: $55,704; Households with income of $100,000 or more: 13.2%; Poverty rate: 15.9%
Educational Attainment: High school diploma or higher: 82.8%; Bachelor's degree or higher: 10.8%; Graduate/professional degree or higher: 7.5%
School District(s)
Clyde-Savannah Central SD (PK-12)
  Enrollment: 845 . . . . (315) 902-3000
Housing: Homeownership rate: 71.7%; Median home value: $68,600; Median year structure built: Before 1940; Homeowner vacancy rate: 4.5%; Median selected monthly owner costs: $968 with a mortgage, $519 without a mortgage; Median gross rent: $777 per month; Rental vacancy rate: 25.1%
Health Insurance: 95.3% have insurance; 70.1% have private insurance; 37.3% have public insurance; 4.7% do not have insurance; 0.9% of children under 18 do not have insurance
Safety: Violent crime rate: 5.1 per 10,000 population; Property crime rate: 208.0 per 10,000 population
Transportation: Commute: 91.8% car, 0.1% public transportation, 2.9% walk, 3.2% work from home; Mean travel time to work: 27.0 minutes

GALEN (town). Covers a land area of 59.477 square miles and a water area of 0.581 square miles. Located at 43.07° N. Lat; 76.88° W. Long.
Population: 4,176; Growth (since 2000): -5.9%; Density: 70.2 persons per square mile; Race: 94.6% White, 1.2% Black/African American, 1.0% Asian, 0.8% American Indian/Alaska Native, 0.0% Native Hawaiian/Other Pacific Islander, 1.9% Two or more races, 5.4% Hispanic of any race; Average household size: 2.94; Median age: 33.3; Age under 18: 32.2%; Age 65 and over: 13.4%; Males per 100 females: 99.8; Marriage status: 33.1% never married, 50.6% now married, 3.7% separated, 5.2% widowed, 11.1% divorced; Foreign born: 1.3%; Speak English only: 93.0%; With disability: 15.9%; Veterans: 5.2%; Ancestry: 17.7% German, 17.6% Italian, 13.6% Irish, 10.4% English, 9.0% Dutch
Employment: 8.3% management, business, and financial, 2.4% computer, engineering, and science, 10.5% education, legal, community service, arts, and media, 4.8% healthcare practitioners, 16.6% service, 21.3% sales and

office, 16.2% natural resources, construction, and maintenance, 20.0% production, transportation, and material moving
Income: Per capita: $20,240; Median household: $53,750; Average household: $58,893; Households with income of $100,000 or more: 13.6%; Poverty rate: 12.0%
Educational Attainment: High school diploma or higher: 82.0%; Bachelor's degree or higher: 10.9%; Graduate/professional degree or higher: 6.8%
Housing: Homeownership rate: 80.7%; Median home value: $83,900; Median year structure built: 1942; Homeowner vacancy rate: 4.0%; Median selected monthly owner costs: $985 with a mortgage, $501 without a mortgage; Median gross rent: $788 per month; Rental vacancy rate: 19.0%
Health Insurance: 84.6% have insurance; 58.1% have private insurance; 37.9% have public insurance; 15.4% do not have insurance; 20.2% of children under 18 do not have insurance
Transportation: Commute: 88.4% car, 1.1% public transportation, 3.0% walk, 6.2% work from home; Mean travel time to work: 25.7 minutes

HURON (town). Covers a land area of 39.392 square miles and a water area of 3.710 square miles. Located at 43.25° N. Lat; 76.90° W. Long. Elevation is 390 feet.
Population: 2,257; Growth (since 2000): 6.6%; Density: 57.3 persons per square mile; Race: 88.3% White, 6.2% Black/African American, 1.8% Asian, 0.2% American Indian/Alaska Native, 0.0% Native Hawaiian/Other Pacific Islander, 0.6% Two or more races, 9.2% Hispanic of any race; Average household size: 2.48; Median age: 47.2; Age under 18: 18.8%; Age 65 and over: 19.6%; Males per 100 females: 107.6; Marriage status: 24.9% never married, 62.1% now married, 1.7% separated, 4.0% widowed, 9.0% divorced; Foreign born: 4.7%; Speak English only: 90.4%; With disability: 11.4%; Veterans: 8.3%; Ancestry: 20.6% German, 15.2% Irish, 14.4% English, 8.6% Dutch, 4.1% French
Employment: 20.8% management, business, and financial, 4.7% computer, engineering, and science, 6.1% education, legal, community service, arts, and media, 3.8% healthcare practitioners, 16.4% service, 17.2% sales and office, 16.2% natural resources, construction, and maintenance, 14.8% production, transportation, and material moving
Income: Per capita: $32,345; Median household: $65,850; Average household: $83,575; Households with income of $100,000 or more: 28.5%; Poverty rate: 14.5%
Educational Attainment: High school diploma or higher: 91.7%; Bachelor's degree or higher: 27.2%; Graduate/professional degree or higher: 10.5%
Housing: Homeownership rate: 81.1%; Median home value: $184,600; Median year structure built: 1965; Homeowner vacancy rate: 1.7%; Median selected monthly owner costs: $1,228 with a mortgage, $705 without a mortgage; Median gross rent: $533 per month; Rental vacancy rate: 3.0%
Health Insurance: 90.8% have insurance; 69.2% have private insurance; 38.1% have public insurance; 9.2% do not have insurance; 3.2% of children under 18 do not have insurance
Transportation: Commute: 92.2% car, 0.0% public transportation, 1.6% walk, 6.2% work from home; Mean travel time to work: 35.5 minutes

LYONS (town). Covers a land area of 37.485 square miles and a water area of 0.111 square miles. Located at 43.09° N. Lat; 77.00° W. Long. Elevation is 410 feet.
History: Settled 1800; incorporated 1831.
Population: 5,504; Growth (since 2000): -5.6%; Density: 146.8 persons per square mile; Race: 88.5% White, 6.5% Black/African American, 0.5% Asian, 0.0% American Indian/Alaska Native, 0.0% Native Hawaiian/Other Pacific Islander, 2.7% Two or more races, 5.3% Hispanic of any race; Average household size: 2.36; Median age: 42.1; Age under 18: 20.0%; Age 65 and over: 19.6%; Males per 100 females: 96.0; Marriage status: 32.3% never married, 49.2% now married, 2.5% separated, 7.3% widowed, 11.2% divorced; Foreign born: 2.1%; Speak English only: 97.0%; With disability: 19.3%; Veterans: 9.2%; Ancestry: 26.1% German, 14.4% Irish, 14.0% Italian, 12.3% English, 9.9% Dutch
Employment: 8.7% management, business, and financial, 2.2% computer, engineering, and science, 18.2% education, legal, community service, arts, and media, 7.0% healthcare practitioners, 17.0% service, 24.3% sales and office, 8.1% natural resources, construction, and maintenance, 14.6% production, transportation, and material moving
Income: Per capita: $22,250; Median household: $49,266; Average household: $53,579; Households with income of $100,000 or more: 10.6%; Poverty rate: 18.0%

Educational Attainment: High school diploma or higher: 88.1%; Bachelor's degree or higher: 18.2%; Graduate/professional degree or higher: 9.0%

School District(s)
Lyons Central SD (PK-12)
    Enrollment: 971 . . . . (315) 946-2200
Housing: Homeownership rate: 69.3%; Median home value: $81,000; Median year structure built: Before 1940; Homeowner vacancy rate: 3.9%; Median selected monthly owner costs: $1,042 with a mortgage, $479 without a mortgage; Median gross rent: $706 per month; Rental vacancy rate: 8.3%
Health Insurance: 95.2% have insurance; 69.6% have private insurance; 41.9% have public insurance; 4.8% do not have insurance; 2.2% of children under 18 do not have insurance
Transportation: Commute: 96.6% car, 0.9% public transportation, 2.2% walk, 0.4% work from home; Mean travel time to work: 24.2 minutes
Additional Information Contacts
Town of Lyons . . . . (315) 946-6252
    http://www.lyonsny.com/thetown

LYONS (village). County seat. Covers a land area of 4.074 square miles and a water area of 0.077 square miles. Located at 43.06° N. Lat; 76.99° W. Long. Elevation is 410 feet.
Population: 3,367; Growth (since 2000): -8.9%; Density: 826.5 persons per square mile; Race: 84.9% White, 7.3% Black/African American, 0.8% Asian, 0.0% American Indian/Alaska Native, 0.0% Native Hawaiian/Other Pacific Islander, 4.5% Two or more races, 6.7% Hispanic of any race; Average household size: 2.22; Median age: 42.1; Age under 18: 20.6%; Age 65 and over: 19.2%; Males per 100 females: 92.4; Marriage status: 37.2% never married, 39.9% now married, 3.6% separated, 7.7% widowed, 15.2% divorced; Foreign born: 1.1%; Speak English only: 98.8%; With disability: 21.5%; Veterans: 9.1%; Ancestry: 20.5% German, 15.8% Irish, 13.0% French, 12.9% Italian, 9.2% English
Employment: 5.0% management, business, and financial, 2.3% computer, engineering, and science, 11.2% education, legal, community service, arts, and media, 8.3% healthcare practitioners, 22.1% service, 27.8% sales and office, 6.6% natural resources, construction, and maintenance, 16.7% production, transportation, and material moving
Income: Per capita: $21,958; Median household: $40,603; Average household: $47,289; Households with income of $100,000 or more: 8.1%; Poverty rate: 20.0%
Educational Attainment: High school diploma or higher: 87.6%; Bachelor's degree or higher: 12.3%; Graduate/professional degree or higher: 7.2%

School District(s)
Lyons Central SD (PK-12)
    Enrollment: 971 . . . . (315) 946-2200
Housing: Homeownership rate: 60.7%; Median home value: $72,000; Median year structure built: Before 1940; Homeowner vacancy rate: 2.6%; Median selected monthly owner costs: $981 with a mortgage, $454 without a mortgage; Median gross rent: $694 per month; Rental vacancy rate: 9.1%
Health Insurance: 95.5% have insurance; 62.5% have private insurance; 47.4% have public insurance; 4.5% do not have insurance; 0.0% of children under 18 do not have insurance
Transportation: Commute: 95.4% car, 1.4% public transportation, 2.5% walk, 0.6% work from home; Mean travel time to work: 19.7 minutes

MACEDON (town). Covers a land area of 38.681 square miles and a water area of 0.177 square miles. Located at 43.08° N. Lat; 77.31° W. Long. Elevation is 472 feet.
Population: 9,010; Growth (since 2000): 3.7%; Density: 232.9 persons per square mile; Race: 97.2% White, 0.5% Black/African American, 0.4% Asian, 0.0% American Indian/Alaska Native, 0.0% Native Hawaiian/Other Pacific Islander, 1.7% Two or more races, 3.3% Hispanic of any race; Average household size: 2.46; Median age: 43.2; Age under 18: 21.9%; Age 65 and over: 16.1%; Males per 100 females: 99.5; Marriage status: 28.7% never married, 55.9% now married, 1.4% separated, 5.9% widowed, 9.6% divorced; Foreign born: 2.4%; Speak English only: 96.1%; With disability: 14.0%; Veterans: 6.3%; Ancestry: 24.4% German, 18.8% Irish, 15.3% Italian, 11.9% English, 7.3% Dutch
Employment: 12.0% management, business, and financial, 6.9% computer, engineering, and science, 10.1% education, legal, community service, arts, and media, 8.1% healthcare practitioners, 18.8% service,

20.7% sales and office, 10.9% natural resources, construction, and maintenance, 12.5% production, transportation, and material moving
Income: Per capita: $30,786; Median household: $59,549; Average household: $75,622; Households with income of $100,000 or more: 22.9%; Poverty rate: 6.2%
Educational Attainment: High school diploma or higher: 92.2%; Bachelor's degree or higher: 26.4%; Graduate/professional degree or higher: 11.2%

School District(s)
Palmyra-Macedon Central SD (KG-12)
    Enrollment: 1,922 . . . . (315) 597-3401
Housing: Homeownership rate: 79.8%; Median home value: $143,700; Median year structure built: 1981; Homeowner vacancy rate: 1.7%; Median selected monthly owner costs: $1,373 with a mortgage, $648 without a mortgage; Median gross rent: $766 per month; Rental vacancy rate: 6.4%
Health Insurance: 95.6% have insurance; 78.5% have private insurance; 31.1% have public insurance; 4.4% do not have insurance; 0.4% of children under 18 do not have insurance
Safety: Violent crime rate: 10.0 per 10,000 population; Property crime rate: 132.6 per 10,000 population
Newspapers: Times of Wayne County (weekly circulation 12,500)
Transportation: Commute: 93.8% car, 0.1% public transportation, 0.2% walk, 4.4% work from home; Mean travel time to work: 24.4 minutes
Additional Information Contacts
Town of Macedon . . . . (315) 986-5932
    http://www.macedontown.net/s2

MACEDON (village). Covers a land area of 1.225 square miles and a water area of 0.007 square miles. Located at 43.07° N. Lat; 77.30° W. Long. Elevation is 472 feet.
Population: 1,659; Growth (since 2000): 10.9%; Density: 1,354.1 persons per square mile; Race: 97.1% White, 2.2% Black/African American, 0.1% Asian, 0.0% American Indian/Alaska Native, 0.2% Native Hawaiian/Other Pacific Islander, 0.4% Two or more races, 3.9% Hispanic of any race; Average household size: 2.72; Median age: 44.5; Age under 18: 25.0%; Age 65 and over: 12.5%; Males per 100 females: 101.2; Marriage status: 22.6% never married, 64.5% now married, 2.0% separated, 4.1% widowed, 8.8% divorced; Foreign born: 4.0%; Speak English only: 91.7%; With disability: 11.8%; Veterans: 5.8%; Ancestry: 20.7% German, 20.0% Italian, 19.0% Irish, 14.0% English, 7.4% American
Employment: 16.0% management, business, and financial, 6.6% computer, engineering, and science, 13.8% education, legal, community service, arts, and media, 7.9% healthcare practitioners, 17.0% service, 19.3% sales and office, 9.1% natural resources, construction, and maintenance, 10.2% production, transportation, and material moving
Income: Per capita: $30,716; Median household: $72,500; Average household: $82,451; Households with income of $100,000 or more: 29.9%; Poverty rate: 3.2%
Educational Attainment: High school diploma or higher: 93.9%; Bachelor's degree or higher: 36.0%; Graduate/professional degree or higher: 17.0%

School District(s)
Palmyra-Macedon Central SD (KG-12)
    Enrollment: 1,922 . . . . (315) 597-3401
Housing: Homeownership rate: 83.6%; Median home value: $132,400; Median year structure built: 1969; Homeowner vacancy rate: 1.9%; Median selected monthly owner costs: $1,419 with a mortgage, $592 without a mortgage; Median gross rent: $768 per month; Rental vacancy rate: 12.3%
Health Insurance: 96.6% have insurance; 81.7% have private insurance; 26.0% have public insurance; 3.4% do not have insurance; 0.0% of children under 18 do not have insurance
Newspapers: Times of Wayne County (weekly circulation 12,500)
Transportation: Commute: 95.9% car, 0.0% public transportation, 1.0% walk, 2.2% work from home; Mean travel time to work: 26.3 minutes

MARION (CDP). Covers a land area of 3.053 square miles and a water area of 0.006 square miles. Located at 43.14° N. Lat; 77.19° W. Long. Elevation is 459 feet.
Population: 1,433; Growth (since 2000): n/a; Density: 469.4 persons per square mile; Race: 95.3% White, 4.7% Black/African American, 0.0% Asian, 0.0% American Indian/Alaska Native, 0.0% Native Hawaiian/Other Pacific Islander, 0.0% Two or more races, 1.6% Hispanic of any race; Average household size: 2.33; Median age: 41.4; Age under 18: 24.8%; Age 65 and over: 12.8%; Males per 100 females: 92.2; Marriage status: 23.8% never married, 51.7% now married, 2.0% separated, 5.9%

widowed, 18.7% divorced; Foreign born: 1.6%; Speak English only: 97.6%; With disability: 20.9%; Veterans: 3.1%; Ancestry: 20.1% Dutch, 18.5% German, 17.9% Irish, 16.3% Italian, 12.0% English
Employment: 9.6% management, business, and financial, 8.3% computer, engineering, and science, 16.9% education, legal, community service, arts, and media, 4.6% healthcare practitioners, 7.6% service, 21.2% sales and office, 9.6% natural resources, construction, and maintenance, 22.3% production, transportation, and material moving
Income: Per capita: $24,096; Median household: $42,969; Average household: $55,506; Households with income of $100,000 or more: 11.9%; Poverty rate: 14.0%
Educational Attainment: High school diploma or higher: 90.4%; Bachelor's degree or higher: 23.9%; Graduate/professional degree or higher: 9.0%

School District(s)
Marion Central SD (PK-12)
    Enrollment: 773 . . . . (315) 926-2300
Housing: Homeownership rate: 70.0%; Median home value: $101,700; Median year structure built: 1959; Homeowner vacancy rate: 0.0%; Median selected monthly owner costs: $1,106 with a mortgage, $429 without a mortgage; Median gross rent: $758 per month; Rental vacancy rate: 0.0%
Health Insurance: 95.5% have insurance; 61.0% have private insurance; 48.0% have public insurance; 4.5% do not have insurance; 0.0% of children under 18 do not have insurance
Transportation: Commute: 98.5% car, 0.2% public transportation, 1.3% walk, 0.0% work from home; Mean travel time to work: 26.5 minutes

MARION (town). Covers a land area of 29.147 square miles and a water area of 0.103 square miles. Located at 43.17° N. Lat; 77.19° W. Long. Elevation is 459 feet.
Population: 4,651; Growth (since 2000): -6.5%; Density: 159.6 persons per square mile; Race: 94.4% White, 2.5% Black/African American, 0.0% Asian, 0.0% American Indian/Alaska Native, 0.0% Native Hawaiian/Other Pacific Islander, 3.0% Two or more races, 1.8% Hispanic of any race; Average household size: 2.50; Median age: 43.6; Age under 18: 21.5%; Age 65 and over: 15.3%; Males per 100 females: 95.1; Marriage status: 25.5% never married, 58.2% now married, 2.3% separated, 4.7% widowed, 11.5% divorced; Foreign born: 2.0%; Speak English only: 97.7%; With disability: 12.8%; Veterans: 8.1%; Ancestry: 24.4% German, 22.9% Dutch, 12.9% Irish, 11.9% English, 9.3% Italian
Employment: 14.4% management, business, and financial, 4.5% computer, engineering, and science, 8.9% education, legal, community service, arts, and media, 6.3% healthcare practitioners, 10.8% service, 26.5% sales and office, 7.9% natural resources, construction, and maintenance, 20.7% production, transportation, and material moving
Income: Per capita: $28,515; Median household: $63,393; Average household: $70,265; Households with income of $100,000 or more: 23.0%; Poverty rate: 9.1%
Educational Attainment: High school diploma or higher: 91.2%; Bachelor's degree or higher: 21.7%; Graduate/professional degree or higher: 7.9%

School District(s)
Marion Central SD (PK-12)
    Enrollment: 773 . . . . (315) 926-2300
Housing: Homeownership rate: 86.9%; Median home value: $112,900; Median year structure built: 1969; Homeowner vacancy rate: 0.0%; Median selected monthly owner costs: $1,123 with a mortgage, $541 without a mortgage; Median gross rent: $768 per month; Rental vacancy rate: 9.0%
Health Insurance: 95.0% have insurance; 73.8% have private insurance; 34.5% have public insurance; 5.0% do not have insurance; 2.7% of children under 18 do not have insurance
Transportation: Commute: 95.4% car, 0.0% public transportation, 2.9% walk, 1.6% work from home; Mean travel time to work: 26.6 minutes
Additional Information Contacts
Town of Marion . . . . (315) 926-4271
    http://www.townofmarionny.com

NEWARK (village). Covers a land area of 5.406 square miles and a water area of 0.005 square miles. Located at 43.04° N. Lat; 77.09° W. Long. Elevation is 443 feet.
History: Incorporated 1839.
Population: 9,029; Growth (since 2000): -6.7%; Density: 1,670.1 persons per square mile; Race: 84.6% White, 7.7% Black/African American, 1.3% Asian, 0.3% American Indian/Alaska Native, 0.3% Native Hawaiian/Other Pacific Islander, 3.0% Two or more races, 7.0% Hispanic of any race;

Average household size: 2.23; Median age: 43.7; Age under 18: 19.3%; Age 65 and over: 15.9%; Males per 100 females: 90.5; Marriage status: 36.4% never married, 41.2% now married, 4.3% separated, 7.0% widowed, 15.3% divorced; Foreign born: 3.5%; Speak English only: 93.9%; With disability: 22.5%; Veterans: 6.8%; Ancestry: 18.0% German, 16.7% Irish, 13.7% English, 13.7% Italian, 11.2% Dutch
Employment: 9.1% management, business, and financial, 1.5% computer, engineering, and science, 10.6% education, legal, community service, arts, and media, 3.2% healthcare practitioners, 19.3% service, 27.1% sales and office, 8.3% natural resources, construction, and maintenance, 21.0% production, transportation, and material moving
Income: Per capita: $24,175; Median household: $38,445; Average household: $54,258; Households with income of $100,000 or more: 11.2%; Poverty rate: 18.3%
Educational Attainment: High school diploma or higher: 87.7%; Bachelor's degree or higher: 16.2%; Graduate/professional degree or higher: 6.7%

School District(s)
Newark Central SD (PK-12)
    Enrollment: 2,227 . . . . (315) 332-3217
Ontario-Seneca-Yates-Cayuga-Wayne Boces
    Enrollment: n/a . . . . (315) 332-7284
Vocational/Technical School(s)
Wayne Finger Lakes BOCES-Practical Nursing Program (Public)
    Enrollment: 228. . . . . (315) 332-7375
    Tuition: $17,350
Housing: Homeownership rate: 50.4%; Median home value: $86,000; Median year structure built: 1952; Homeowner vacancy rate: 1.4%; Median selected monthly owner costs: $1,076 with a mortgage, $519 without a mortgage; Median gross rent: $717 per month; Rental vacancy rate: 7.8%
Health Insurance: 93.3% have insurance; 56.3% have private insurance; 48.8% have public insurance; 6.7% do not have insurance; 0.7% of children under 18 do not have insurance
Hospitals: Newark - Wayne Community Hospital
Newspapers: Newark Courier-Gazette (weekly circulation 3,600)
Transportation: Commute: 88.3% car, 2.3% public transportation, 7.6% walk, 0.8% work from home; Mean travel time to work: 19.6 minutes
Additional Information Contacts
Village of Newark . . . . (315) 331-4770
    http://www.villageofnewark.com

NORTH ROSE (CDP).
Covers a land area of 1.690 square miles and a water area of 0 square miles. Located at 43.19° N. Lat; 76.89° W. Long. Elevation is 387 feet.
Population: 402; Growth (since 2000): n/a; Density: 237.8 persons per square mile; Race: 94.3% White, 1.5% Black/African American, 0.7% Asian, 0.0% American Indian/Alaska Native, 0.0% Native Hawaiian/Other Pacific Islander, 2.5% Two or more races, 9.0% Hispanic of any race; Average household size: 1.89; Median age: 58.0; Age under 18: 16.9%; Age 65 and over: 33.6%; Males per 100 females: 88.7; Marriage status: 21.6% never married, 33.2% now married, 3.2% separated, 20.4% widowed, 24.8% divorced; Foreign born: 7.5%; Speak English only: 91.1%; With disability: 23.4%; Veterans: 5.7%; Ancestry: 23.9% German, 17.2% English, 16.9% Irish, 7.7% Italian, 6.5% Dutch
Employment: 4.7% management, business, and financial, 4.7% computer, engineering, and science, 4.7% education, legal, community service, arts, and media, 6.5% healthcare practitioners, 15.9% service, 27.1% sales and office, 18.7% natural resources, construction, and maintenance, 17.8% production, transportation, and material moving
Income: Per capita: $22,967; Median household: $34,435; Average household: $41,542; Households with income of $100,000 or more: 6.6%; Poverty rate: 14.2%
Educational Attainment: High school diploma or higher: 80.6%; Bachelor's degree or higher: 8.4%; Graduate/professional degree or higher: 4.1%
School District(s)
North Rose-Wolcott Central SD (PK-12)
    Enrollment: 1,293 . . . . (315) 594-3141
Housing: Homeownership rate: 76.1%; Median home value: $85,600; Median year structure built: 1941; Homeowner vacancy rate: 7.9%; Median selected monthly owner costs: $730 with a mortgage, $404 without a mortgage; Median gross rent: $622 per month; Rental vacancy rate: 22.7%
Health Insurance: 100.0% have insurance; 46.3% have private insurance; 66.2% have public insurance; 0.0% do not have insurance; 0.0% of children under 18 do not have insurance

Transportation: Commute: 90.1% car, 0.0% public transportation, 0.0% walk, 9.9% work from home; Mean travel time to work: 22.7 minutes

ONTARIO (CDP).
Covers a land area of 3.796 square miles and a water area of 0 square miles. Located at 43.22° N. Lat; 77.28° W. Long. Elevation is 440 feet.
Population: 1,901; Growth (since 2000): n/a; Density: 500.8 persons per square mile; Race: 99.4% White, 0.6% Black/African American, 0.0% Asian, 0.0% American Indian/Alaska Native, 0.0% Native Hawaiian/Other Pacific Islander, 0.0% Two or more races, 6.8% Hispanic of any race; Average household size: 1.96; Median age: 47.9; Age under 18: 9.2%; Age 65 and over: 17.3%; Males per 100 females: 92.9; Marriage status: 32.1% never married, 45.4% now married, 3.9% separated, 7.6% widowed, 14.9% divorced; Foreign born: 6.8%; Speak English only: 92.2%; With disability: 11.6%; Veterans: 7.2%; Ancestry: 23.0% Italian, 20.4% German, 17.8% English, 11.6% Dutch, 10.6% Irish
Employment: 8.5% management, business, and financial, 8.0% computer, engineering, and science, 8.4% education, legal, community service, arts, and media, 3.6% healthcare practitioners, 14.0% service, 28.1% sales and office, 8.7% natural resources, construction, and maintenance, 20.7% production, transportation, and material moving
Income: Per capita: $27,514; Median household: $38,977; Average household: $53,039; Households with income of $100,000 or more: 15.1%; Poverty rate: 13.2%
Educational Attainment: High school diploma or higher: 86.8%; Bachelor's degree or higher: 23.2%; Graduate/professional degree or higher: 8.0%
Housing: Homeownership rate: 70.4%; Median home value: $85,400; Median year structure built: 1969; Homeowner vacancy rate: 0.0%; Median selected monthly owner costs: $1,290 with a mortgage, $554 without a mortgage; Median gross rent: $498 per month; Rental vacancy rate: 0.0%
Health Insurance: 85.7% have insurance; 66.9% have private insurance; 35.2% have public insurance; 14.3% do not have insurance; 0.0% of children under 18 do not have insurance
Transportation: Commute: 98.4% car, 0.0% public transportation, 1.6% walk, 0.0% work from home; Mean travel time to work: 23.9 minutes

ONTARIO (town).
Covers a land area of 32.412 square miles and a water area of 0.086 square miles. Located at 43.25° N. Lat; 77.32° W. Long. Elevation is 440 feet.
Population: 10,093; Growth (since 2000): 3.2%; Density: 311.4 persons per square mile; Race: 94.7% White, 2.6% Black/African American, 1.1% Asian, 0.0% American Indian/Alaska Native, 0.0% Native Hawaiian/Other Pacific Islander, 1.5% Two or more races, 2.3% Hispanic of any race; Average household size: 2.31; Median age: 46.1; Age under 18: 19.1%; Age 65 and over: 17.4%; Males per 100 females: 98.1; Marriage status: 25.4% never married, 58.6% now married, 1.5% separated, 5.9% widowed, 10.2% divorced; Foreign born: 3.4%; Speak English only: 96.4%; With disability: 11.2%; Veterans: 9.0%; Ancestry: 29.1% German, 20.3% Italian, 16.1% Irish, 12.8% English, 9.9% Dutch
Employment: 10.7% management, business, and financial, 6.2% computer, engineering, and science, 11.1% education, legal, community service, arts, and media, 9.6% healthcare practitioners, 14.8% service, 22.6% sales and office, 8.6% natural resources, construction, and maintenance, 16.4% production, transportation, and material moving
Income: Per capita: $33,063; Median household: $61,951; Average household: $76,064; Households with income of $100,000 or more: 26.0%; Poverty rate: 4.7%
Educational Attainment: High school diploma or higher: 93.8%; Bachelor's degree or higher: 26.1%; Graduate/professional degree or higher: 10.2%
Housing: Homeownership rate: 79.3%; Median home value: $151,800; Median year structure built: 1974; Homeowner vacancy rate: 0.9%; Median selected monthly owner costs: $1,406 with a mortgage, $586 without a mortgage; Median gross rent: $833 per month; Rental vacancy rate: 0.0%
Health Insurance: 95.7% have insurance; 83.4% have private insurance; 27.7% have public insurance; 4.3% do not have insurance; 1.6% of children under 18 do not have insurance
Transportation: Commute: 96.6% car, 0.4% public transportation, 1.1% walk, 1.8% work from home; Mean travel time to work: 25.2 minutes
Additional Information Contacts
Town of Ontario. . . . . (315) 524-7105
    http://www.ontariotown.org

PALMYRA (town)

PALMYRA (town). Covers a land area of 33.435 square miles and a water area of 0.234 square miles. Located at 43.08° N. Lat; 77.19° W. Long. Elevation is 486 feet.

History: Joseph Smith, founder and first president of the Mormon Church, lived and published *The Book of Mormon* here. Hill Cumorah Center pageant held each August atop the glacial drumlin where Smith buried his tablets four miles south of villlage.

Population: 7,702; Growth (since 2000): 0.4%; Density: 230.4 persons per square mile; Race: 96.2% White, 0.5% Black/African American, 1.1% Asian, 0.1% American Indian/Alaska Native, 0.0% Native Hawaiian/Other Pacific Islander, 1.5% Two or more races, 4.4% Hispanic of any race; Average household size: 2.33; Median age: 43.2; Age under 18: 22.6%; Age 65 and over: 16.3%; Males per 100 females: 98.2; Marriage status: 27.5% never married, 52.9% now married, 2.9% separated, 7.4% widowed, 12.2% divorced; Foreign born: 2.0%; Speak English only: 96.7%; With disability: 12.2%; Veterans: 9.9%; Ancestry: 22.3% Irish, 19.2% German, 15.0% Italian, 12.2% English, 11.1% Dutch

Employment: 10.6% management, business, and financial, 5.8% computer, engineering, and science, 8.9% education, legal, community service, arts, and media, 3.7% healthcare practitioners, 15.7% service, 28.5% sales and office, 10.2% natural resources, construction, and maintenance, 16.6% production, transportation, and material moving

Income: Per capita: $27,145; Median household: $49,537; Average household: $63,075; Households with income of $100,000 or more: 17.3%; Poverty rate: 16.8%

Educational Attainment: High school diploma or higher: 87.6%; Bachelor's degree or higher: 21.4%; Graduate/professional degree or higher: 7.3%

School District(s)
Palmyra-Macedon Central SD (KG-12)
    Enrollment: 1,922 . . . . (315) 597-3401

Housing: Homeownership rate: 67.9%; Median home value: $113,900; Median year structure built: 1959; Homeowner vacancy rate: 4.3%; Median selected monthly owner costs: $1,227 with a mortgage, $498 without a mortgage; Median gross rent: $745 per month; Rental vacancy rate: 1.6%

Health Insurance: 94.4% have insurance; 67.8% have private insurance; 39.6% have public insurance; 5.6% do not have insurance; 0.4% of children under 18 do not have insurance

Newspapers: Palmyra Courier-Journal (weekly circulation 2,700)

Transportation: Commute: 93.7% car, 1.2% public transportation, 1.3% walk, 3.3% work from home; Mean travel time to work: 25.5 minutes

Additional Information Contacts
Town of Palmyra . . . . (315) 597-5521
    http://www.palmyrany.com

PALMYRA (village)

PALMYRA (village). Covers a land area of 1.347 square miles and a water area of 0 square miles. Located at 43.06° N. Lat; 77.23° W. Long. Elevation is 486 feet.

Population: 3,417; Growth (since 2000): -2.1%; Density: 2,537.0 persons per square mile; Race: 95.6% White, 0.7% Black/African American, 0.0% Asian, 0.0% American Indian/Alaska Native, 0.0% Native Hawaiian/Other Pacific Islander, 2.8% Two or more races, 6.0% Hispanic of any race; Average household size: 2.29; Median age: 36.1; Age under 18: 23.1%; Age 65 and over: 12.9%; Males per 100 females: 95.9; Marriage status: 32.0% never married, 43.9% now married, 2.3% separated, 7.3% widowed, 16.8% divorced; Foreign born: 0.5%; Speak English only: 97.7%; With disability: 12.4%; Veterans: 8.6%; Ancestry: 23.5% Irish, 20.2% Italian, 19.1% German, 10.6% English, 9.9% Dutch

Employment: 11.7% management, business, and financial, 3.9% computer, engineering, and science, 7.9% education, legal, community service, arts, and media, 3.4% healthcare practitioners, 20.8% service, 27.8% sales and office, 8.8% natural resources, construction, and maintenance, 15.7% production, transportation, and material moving

Income: Per capita: $25,127; Median household: $41,835; Average household: $57,526; Households with income of $100,000 or more: 13.9%; Poverty rate: 19.9%

Educational Attainment: High school diploma or higher: 88.7%; Bachelor's degree or higher: 22.4%; Graduate/professional degree or higher: 7.2%

School District(s)
Palmyra-Macedon Central SD (KG-12)
    Enrollment: 1,922 . . . . (315) 597-3401

Housing: Homeownership rate: 54.4%; Median home value: $99,900; Median year structure built: 1944; Homeowner vacancy rate: 3.4%; Median selected monthly owner costs: $1,222 with a mortgage, $602 without a mortgage; Median gross rent: $748 per month; Rental vacancy rate: 2.5%

Health Insurance: 92.7% have insurance; 64.4% have private insurance; 38.4% have public insurance; 7.3% do not have insurance; 0.0% of children under 18 do not have insurance

Newspapers: Palmyra Courier-Journal (weekly circulation 2,700)

Transportation: Commute: 91.6% car, 0.9% public transportation, 2.4% walk, 4.0% work from home; Mean travel time to work: 27.0 minutes

Additional Information Contacts
Village of Palmyra . . . . (315) 597-4849
    http://www.palmyrany.com

PULTNEYVILLE (CDP)

PULTNEYVILLE (CDP). Covers a land area of 2.242 square miles and a water area of <.001 square miles. Located at 43.27° N. Lat; 77.17° W. Long. Elevation is 272 feet.

Population: 741; Growth (since 2000): n/a; Density: 330.5 persons per square mile; Race: 100.0% White, 0.0% Black/African American, 0.0% Asian, 0.0% American Indian/Alaska Native, 0.0% Native Hawaiian/Other Pacific Islander, 0.0% Two or more races, 0.0% Hispanic of any race; Average household size: 2.53; Median age: 44.8; Age under 18: 20.9%; Age 65 and over: 23.6%; Males per 100 females: 94.4; Marriage status: 25.7% never married, 63.0% now married, 1.4% separated, 6.8% widowed, 4.6% divorced; Foreign born: 0.0%; Speak English only: 97.2%; With disability: 10.7%; Veterans: 6.0%; Ancestry: 37.9% Dutch, 30.9% Irish, 26.9% English, 23.8% German, 12.8% American

Employment: 9.9% management, business, and financial, 5.2% computer, engineering, and science, 11.3% education, legal, community service, arts, and media, 13.2% healthcare practitioners, 9.6% service, 22.3% sales and office, 10.2% natural resources, construction, and maintenance, 18.2% production, transportation, and material moving

Income: Per capita: $37,391; Median household: $76,875; Average household: $94,670; Households with income of $100,000 or more: 27.9%; Poverty rate: n/a

Educational Attainment: High school diploma or higher: 91.6%; Bachelor's degree or higher: 37.8%; Graduate/professional degree or higher: 18.9%

Housing: Homeownership rate: 97.6%; Median home value: $155,600; Median year structure built: 1946; Homeowner vacancy rate: 8.0%; Median selected monthly owner costs: $1,672 with a mortgage, $638 without a mortgage; Median gross rent: n/a per month; Rental vacancy rate: 0.0%

Health Insurance: 97.3% have insurance; 87.2% have private insurance; 28.5% have public insurance; 2.7% do not have insurance; 0.0% of children under 18 do not have insurance

Transportation: Commute: 84.4% car, 0.0% public transportation, 3.4% walk, 12.2% work from home; Mean travel time to work: 34.9 minutes

RED CREEK (village)

RED CREEK (village). Covers a land area of 0.909 square miles and a water area of 0.027 square miles. Located at 43.25° N. Lat; 76.72° W. Long. Elevation is 341 feet.

Population: 658; Growth (since 2000): 26.3%; Density: 724.2 persons per square mile; Race: 100.0% White, 0.0% Black/African American, 0.0% Asian, 0.0% American Indian/Alaska Native, 0.0% Native Hawaiian/Other Pacific Islander, 0.0% Two or more races, 2.6% Hispanic of any race; Average household size: 2.95; Median age: 28.8; Age under 18: 37.2%; Age 65 and over: 7.9%; Males per 100 females: 102.3; Marriage status: 41.8% never married, 45.3% now married, 3.7% separated, 5.9% widowed, 6.9% divorced; Foreign born: 0.0%; Speak English only: 97.5%; With disability: 20.4%; Veterans: 13.1%; Ancestry: 17.3% German, 13.2% Irish, 10.6% English, 7.8% Dutch, 5.0% French

Employment: 9.6% management, business, and financial, 2.0% computer, engineering, and science, 12.0% education, legal, community service, arts, and media, 3.2% healthcare practitioners, 14.0% service, 26.0% sales and office, 12.0% natural resources, construction, and maintenance, 21.2% production, transportation, and material moving

Income: Per capita: $16,916; Median household: $34,236; Average household: $48,774; Households with income of $100,000 or more: 9.8%; Poverty rate: 22.2%

Educational Attainment: High school diploma or higher: 87.1%; Bachelor's degree or higher: 10.7%; Graduate/professional degree or higher: 5.5%

School District(s)
Red Creek Central SD (PK-12)
    Enrollment: 960 . . . . (315) 754-2010

Housing: Homeownership rate: 60.5%; Median home value: $73,200; Median year structure built: Before 1940; Homeowner vacancy rate: 0.0%;

Median selected monthly owner costs: $1,040 with a mortgage, $450 without a mortgage; Median gross rent: $615 per month; Rental vacancy rate: 6.4%
Health Insurance: 82.5% have insurance; 38.0% have private insurance; 49.8% have public insurance; 17.5% do not have insurance; 23.1% of children under 18 do not have insurance
Newspapers: The Lakeshore News (weekly circulation 3,500)
Transportation: Commute: 87.9% car, 0.0% public transportation, 11.2% walk, 0.0% work from home; Mean travel time to work: 32.8 minutes

ROSE (town). Covers a land area of 33.896 square miles and a water area of 0.006 square miles. Located at 43.16° N. Lat; 76.90° W. Long. Elevation is 420 feet.
Population: 2,204; Growth (since 2000): -9.7%; Density: 65.0 persons per square mile; Race: 97.8% White, 0.7% Black/African American, 0.1% Asian, 0.1% American Indian/Alaska Native, 0.0% Native Hawaiian/Other Pacific Islander, 0.9% Two or more races, 3.7% Hispanic of any race; Average household size: 2.59; Median age: 44.7; Age under 18: 23.9%; Age 65 and over: 23.3%; Males per 100 females: 93.2; Marriage status: 27.5% never married, 48.7% now married, 1.5% separated, 10.4% widowed, 13.4% divorced; Foreign born: 2.4%; Speak English only: 95.5%; With disability: 20.6%; Veterans: 10.8%; Ancestry: 27.2% German, 15.0% Irish, 13.2% English, 10.8% Dutch, 8.0% French
Employment: 6.6% management, business, and financial, 3.5% computer, engineering, and science, 7.4% education, legal, community service, arts, and media, 8.8% healthcare practitioners, 14.3% service, 26.4% sales and office, 11.2% natural resources, construction, and maintenance, 21.7% production, transportation, and material moving
Income: Per capita: $23,680; Median household: $45,859; Average household: $62,211; Households with income of $100,000 or more: 11.1%; Poverty rate: 9.9%
Educational Attainment: High school diploma or higher: 84.4%; Bachelor's degree or higher: 15.4%; Graduate/professional degree or higher: 7.1%
Housing: Homeownership rate: 86.0%; Median home value: $85,400; Median year structure built: 1946; Homeowner vacancy rate: 2.0%; Median selected monthly owner costs: $1,089 with a mortgage, $455 without a mortgage; Median gross rent: $859 per month; Rental vacancy rate: 11.4%
Health Insurance: 89.7% have insurance; 60.1% have private insurance; 43.1% have public insurance; 10.3% do not have insurance; 13.3% of children under 18 do not have insurance
Transportation: Commute: 93.0% car, 0.0% public transportation, 3.8% walk, 2.4% work from home; Mean travel time to work: 27.9 minutes

SAVANNAH (CDP). Covers a land area of 1.180 square miles and a water area of 0 square miles. Located at 43.07° N. Lat; 76.76° W. Long. Elevation is 420 feet.
Population: 509; Growth (since 2000): n/a; Density: 431.5 persons per square mile; Race: 92.7% White, 0.2% Black/African American, 0.0% Asian, 1.2% American Indian/Alaska Native, 0.0% Native Hawaiian/Other Pacific Islander, 5.9% Two or more races, 5.7% Hispanic of any race; Average household size: 2.66; Median age: 44.5; Age under 18: 23.6%; Age 65 and over: 19.8%; Males per 100 females: 88.5; Marriage status: 29.4% never married, 50.5% now married, 4.3% separated, 6.2% widowed, 14.0% divorced; Foreign born: 0.0%; Speak English only: 100.0%; With disability: 21.6%; Veterans: 10.8%; Ancestry: 21.6% Dutch, 20.6% German, 20.4% Irish, 13.8% English, 7.7% Italian
Employment: 6.7% management, business, and financial, 1.6% computer, engineering, and science, 3.1% education, legal, community service, arts, and media, 7.3% healthcare practitioners, 8.3% service, 29.5% sales and office, 17.6% natural resources, construction, and maintenance, 25.9% production, transportation, and material moving
Income: Per capita: $25,303; Median household: $53,482; Average household: $62,736; Households with income of $100,000 or more: 14.4%; Poverty rate: 13.9%
Educational Attainment: High school diploma or higher: 82.9%; Bachelor's degree or higher: 11.2%; Graduate/professional degree or higher: 1.5%
Housing: Homeownership rate: 79.7%; Median home value: $60,300; Median year structure built: Before 1940; Homeowner vacancy rate: 0.0%; Median selected monthly owner costs: $974 with a mortgage, $506 without a mortgage; Median gross rent: $652 per month; Rental vacancy rate: 0.0%

Health Insurance: 97.4% have insurance; 62.9% have private insurance; 49.7% have public insurance; 2.6% do not have insurance; 0.0% of children under 18 do not have insurance
Transportation: Commute: 94.2% car, 1.1% public transportation, 0.0% walk, 3.2% work from home; Mean travel time to work: 25.5 minutes

SAVANNAH (town). Covers a land area of 35.968 square miles and a water area of 0.211 square miles. Located at 43.08° N. Lat; 76.75° W. Long. Elevation is 420 feet.
Population: 1,643; Growth (since 2000): -10.6%; Density: 45.7 persons per square mile; Race: 93.9% White, 0.4% Black/African American, 0.5% Asian, 1.0% American Indian/Alaska Native, 0.0% Native Hawaiian/Other Pacific Islander, 4.3% Two or more races, 4.6% Hispanic of any race; Average household size: 2.68; Median age: 46.1; Age under 18: 24.0%; Age 65 and over: 21.2%; Males per 100 females: 99.1; Marriage status: 26.7% never married, 55.6% now married, 3.2% separated, 6.1% widowed, 11.7% divorced; Foreign born: 0.5%; Speak English only: 92.9%; With disability: 21.4%; Veterans: 12.1%; Ancestry: 19.4% German, 19.2% English, 12.1% Dutch, 11.7% Irish, 8.2% French
Employment: 9.7% management, business, and financial, 1.4% computer, engineering, and science, 6.1% education, legal, community service, arts, and media, 6.9% healthcare practitioners, 8.6% service, 23.1% sales and office, 18.2% natural resources, construction, and maintenance, 25.9% production, transportation, and material moving
Income: Per capita: $23,128; Median household: $49,722; Average household: $60,016; Households with income of $100,000 or more: 13.4%; Poverty rate: 9.7%
Educational Attainment: High school diploma or higher: 80.0%; Bachelor's degree or higher: 8.6%; Graduate/professional degree or higher: 3.3%
Housing: Homeownership rate: 85.9%; Median home value: $84,500; Median year structure built: 1962; Homeowner vacancy rate: 1.8%; Median selected monthly owner costs: $1,063 with a mortgage, $528 without a mortgage; Median gross rent: $757 per month; Rental vacancy rate: 0.0%
Health Insurance: 88.9% have insurance; 61.9% have private insurance; 43.0% have public insurance; 11.1% do not have insurance; 22.2% of children under 18 do not have insurance
Transportation: Commute: 92.7% car, 1.1% public transportation, 0.0% walk, 3.8% work from home; Mean travel time to work: 31.4 minutes

SODUS (town). Covers a land area of 67.268 square miles and a water area of 1.979 square miles. Located at 43.22° N. Lat; 77.05° W. Long. Elevation is 436 feet.
History: The raising of silkworms was attempted in Sodus in the 1830s. The attempt failed because mulberry trees could not withstand the severe winters. The lotuses of nearby Sodus Bay are famous. Incorporated in 1918.
Population: 8,175; Growth (since 2000): -8.6%; Density: 121.5 persons per square mile; Race: 90.4% White, 5.7% Black/African American, 0.4% Asian, 0.3% American Indian/Alaska Native, 0.0% Native Hawaiian/Other Pacific Islander, 1.7% Two or more races, 5.5% Hispanic of any race; Average household size: 2.55; Median age: 43.1; Age under 18: 21.9%; Age 65 and over: 19.9%; Males per 100 females: 98.3; Marriage status: 28.1% never married, 52.5% now married, 3.3% separated, 6.4% widowed, 13.1% divorced; Foreign born: 2.9%; Speak English only: 93.9%; With disability: 15.5%; Veterans: 8.5%; Ancestry: 20.3% German, 19.1% Dutch, 14.0% Irish, 13.9% English, 12.2% Italian
Employment: 8.3% management, business, and financial, 2.3% computer, engineering, and science, 7.3% education, legal, community service, arts, and media, 4.3% healthcare practitioners, 22.7% service, 25.6% sales and office, 12.5% natural resources, construction, and maintenance, 17.1% production, transportation, and material moving
Income: Per capita: $23,344; Median household: $47,636; Average household: $58,483; Households with income of $100,000 or more: 16.7%; Poverty rate: 21.6%
Educational Attainment: High school diploma or higher: 88.0%; Bachelor's degree or higher: 14.2%; Graduate/professional degree or higher: 6.5%

School District(s)
Sodus Central SD (PK-12)
    Enrollment: 1,103 . . . . (315) 483-5201
Housing: Homeownership rate: 77.0%; Median home value: $98,500; Median year structure built: 1955; Homeowner vacancy rate: 0.2%; Median selected monthly owner costs: $1,133 with a mortgage, $528 without a mortgage; Median gross rent: $767 per month; Rental vacancy rate: 9.3%

Health Insurance: 94.7% have insurance; 62.4% have private insurance; 50.2% have public insurance; 5.3% do not have insurance; 2.0% of children under 18 do not have insurance
Transportation: Commute: 88.1% car, 1.6% public transportation, 1.9% walk, 3.9% work from home; Mean travel time to work: 25.4 minutes
Additional Information Contacts
Town of Sodus . . . . (315) 576-3818
  http://sodusny.org

SODUS (village). Covers a land area of 0.941 square miles and a water area of 0 square miles. Located at 43.24° N. Lat; 77.06° W. Long. Elevation is 436 feet.
Population: 1,943; Growth (since 2000): 12.0%; Density: 2,065.0 persons per square mile; Race: 78.8% White, 16.9% Black/African American, 0.0% Asian, 0.9% American Indian/Alaska Native, 0.0% Native Hawaiian/Other Pacific Islander, 2.2% Two or more races, 8.9% Hispanic of any race; Average household size: 2.54; Median age: 33.5; Age under 18: 27.6%; Age 65 and over: 14.1%; Males per 100 females: 89.5; Marriage status: 40.3% never married, 40.7% now married, 3.9% separated, 8.0% widowed, 11.0% divorced; Foreign born: 1.9%; Speak English only: 94.8%; With disability: 17.1%; Veterans: 10.7%; Ancestry: 17.7% German, 15.5% Dutch, 13.0% Irish, 11.2% English, 5.8% Italian
Employment: 5.8% management, business, and financial, 3.2% computer, engineering, and science, 6.1% education, legal, community service, arts, and media, 6.8% healthcare practitioners, 26.6% service, 21.0% sales and office, 7.7% natural resources, construction, and maintenance, 22.8% production, transportation, and material moving
Income: Per capita: $20,245; Median household: $36,250; Average household: $48,837; Households with income of $100,000 or more: 8.3%; Poverty rate: 22.0%
Educational Attainment: High school diploma or higher: 86.3%; Bachelor's degree or higher: 11.8%; Graduate/professional degree or higher: 3.9%
School District(s)
Sodus Central SD (PK-12)
  Enrollment: 1,103 . . . . (315) 483-5201
Housing: Homeownership rate: 57.3%; Median home value: $74,300; Median year structure built: Before 1940; Homeowner vacancy rate: 0.0%; Median selected monthly owner costs: $930 with a mortgage, $416 without a mortgage; Median gross rent: $701 per month; Rental vacancy rate: 7.7%
Health Insurance: 91.6% have insurance; 53.5% have private insurance; 52.8% have public insurance; 8.4% do not have insurance; 6.5% of children under 18 do not have insurance
Safety: Violent crime rate: 0.0 per 10,000 population; Property crime rate: 29.0 per 10,000 population
Transportation: Commute: 86.4% car, 2.7% public transportation, 7.2% walk, 2.0% work from home; Mean travel time to work: 25.6 minutes

SODUS POINT (village). Covers a land area of 1.468 square miles and a water area of 0.006 square miles. Located at 43.26° N. Lat; 77.00° W. Long. Elevation is 276 feet.
History: Fired upon by British in War of 1812.
Population: 951; Growth (since 2000): -18.0%; Density: 647.9 persons per square mile; Race: 97.0% White, 0.8% Black/African American, 0.3% Asian, 0.0% American Indian/Alaska Native, 0.0% Native Hawaiian/Other Pacific Islander, 1.9% Two or more races, 0.3% Hispanic of any race; Average household size: 2.17; Median age: 51.7; Age under 18: 22.5%; Age 65 and over: 30.8%; Males per 100 females: 105.0; Marriage status: 19.5% never married, 59.9% now married, 5.4% separated, 7.5% widowed, 13.0% divorced; Foreign born: 1.6%; Speak English only: 98.0%; With disability: 12.4%; Veterans: 13.4%; Ancestry: 26.2% Irish, 22.0% German, 16.4% English, 13.4% Dutch, 11.7% Italian
Employment: 12.3% management, business, and financial, 6.0% computer, engineering, and science, 9.7% education, legal, community service, arts, and media, 5.8% healthcare practitioners, 14.4% service, 21.5% sales and office, 12.8% natural resources, construction, and maintenance, 17.5% production, transportation, and material moving
Income: Per capita: $29,161; Median household: $43,417; Average household: $62,513; Households with income of $100,000 or more: 21.8%; Poverty rate: 20.6%
Educational Attainment: High school diploma or higher: 96.5%; Bachelor's degree or higher: 26.4%; Graduate/professional degree or higher: 12.8%

Housing: Homeownership rate: 81.5%; Median home value: $142,600; Median year structure built: 1952; Homeowner vacancy rate: 1.6%; Median selected monthly owner costs: $1,234 with a mortgage, $553 without a mortgage; Median gross rent: $783 per month; Rental vacancy rate: 12.9%
Health Insurance: 96.6% have insurance; 65.5% have private insurance; 50.1% have public insurance; 3.4% do not have insurance; 0.0% of children under 18 do not have insurance
Safety: Violent crime rate: 0.0 per 10,000 population; Property crime rate: 0.0 per 10,000 population
Transportation: Commute: 90.3% car, 0.0% public transportation, 1.6% walk, 6.2% work from home; Mean travel time to work: 30.8 minutes
Additional Information Contacts
Village of Sodus Point . . . . (315) 483-9881
  http://www.soduspoint.info

WALWORTH (town). Covers a land area of 33.853 square miles and a water area of 0.043 square miles. Located at 43.16° N. Lat; 77.31° W. Long. Elevation is 541 feet.
Population: 9,296; Growth (since 2000): 10.6%; Density: 274.6 persons per square mile; Race: 96.4% White, 1.4% Black/African American, 0.5% Asian, 0.1% American Indian/Alaska Native, 0.0% Native Hawaiian/Other Pacific Islander, 1.3% Two or more races, 2.6% Hispanic of any race; Average household size: 2.73; Median age: 40.8; Age under 18: 26.4%; Age 65 and over: 13.3%; Males per 100 females: 99.3; Marriage status: 23.7% never married, 65.3% now married, 1.2% separated, 4.8% widowed, 6.3% divorced; Foreign born: 4.7%; Speak English only: 95.1%; With disability: 8.9%; Veterans: 10.0%; Ancestry: 27.5% German, 20.5% Italian, 17.4% Irish, 17.0% English, 5.8% Polish
Employment: 15.7% management, business, and financial, 9.9% computer, engineering, and science, 15.6% education, legal, community service, arts, and media, 5.5% healthcare practitioners, 11.9% service, 25.4% sales and office, 6.6% natural resources, construction, and maintenance, 9.4% production, transportation, and material moving
Income: Per capita: $33,311; Median household: $76,212; Average household: $90,875; Households with income of $100,000 or more: 36.6%; Poverty rate: 2.8%
Educational Attainment: High school diploma or higher: 96.7%; Bachelor's degree or higher: 41.1%; Graduate/professional degree or higher: 16.2%
School District(s)
Gananda Central SD (KG-12)
  Enrollment: 1,003 . . . . (315) 986-3521
Housing: Homeownership rate: 93.4%; Median home value: $162,200; Median year structure built: 1982; Homeowner vacancy rate: 0.7%; Median selected monthly owner costs: $1,564 with a mortgage, $582 without a mortgage; Median gross rent: $728 per month; Rental vacancy rate: 0.0%
Health Insurance: 97.2% have insurance; 86.5% have private insurance; 22.7% have public insurance; 2.8% do not have insurance; 2.4% of children under 18 do not have insurance
Transportation: Commute: 96.5% car, 0.3% public transportation, 0.4% walk, 2.3% work from home; Mean travel time to work: 25.5 minutes
Additional Information Contacts
Town of Walworth . . . . (315) 986-1400
  http://www.townwalworthny.com

WILLIAMSON (CDP). Covers a land area of 3.840 square miles and a water area of 0.004 square miles. Located at 43.22° N. Lat; 77.18° W. Long. Elevation is 443 feet.
Population: 2,376; Growth (since 2000): n/a; Density: 618.7 persons per square mile; Race: 95.9% White, 0.3% Black/African American, 0.3% Asian, 0.0% American Indian/Alaska Native, 0.0% Native Hawaiian/Other Pacific Islander, 0.0% Two or more races, 3.5% Hispanic of any race; Average household size: 2.28; Median age: 47.1; Age under 18: 20.6%; Age 65 and over: 16.9%; Males per 100 females: 93.3; Marriage status: 24.8% never married, 46.3% now married, 3.1% separated, 8.2% widowed, 20.7% divorced; Foreign born: 1.3%; Speak English only: 96.0%; With disability: 13.8%; Veterans: 5.1%; Ancestry: 21.6% German, 16.1% Dutch, 13.6% Irish, 10.5% English, 8.1% Italian
Employment: 14.4% management, business, and financial, 2.5% computer, engineering, and science, 11.7% education, legal, community service, arts, and media, 5.8% healthcare practitioners, 12.0% service, 23.5% sales and office, 13.5% natural resources, construction, and maintenance, 16.6% production, transportation, and material moving

Income: Per capita: $23,180; Median household: $46,000; Average household: $52,699; Households with income of $100,000 or more: 9.7%; Poverty rate: 9.0%

Educational Attainment: High school diploma or higher: 89.1%; Bachelor's degree or higher: 11.6%; Graduate/professional degree or higher: 7.6%

School District(s)
Williamson Central SD (PK-12)
   Enrollment: 1,132 . . . . (315) 589-9661

Housing: Homeownership rate: 59.3%; Median home value: $97,700; Median year structure built: 1966; Homeowner vacancy rate: 0.0%; Median selected monthly owner costs: $1,116 with a mortgage, $554 without a mortgage; Median gross rent: $563 per month; Rental vacancy rate: 2.6%

Health Insurance: 96.9% have insurance; 65.9% have private insurance; 43.2% have public insurance; 3.1% do not have insurance; 0.0% of children under 18 do not have insurance

Newspapers: Sun & Record (weekly circulation 3,500)

Transportation: Commute: 99.4% car, 0.0% public transportation, 0.0% walk, 0.0% work from home; Mean travel time to work: 25.5 minutes

---

WILLIAMSON (town). Covers a land area of 34.640 square miles and a water area of 0.015 square miles. Located at 43.25° N. Lat; 77.19° W. Long. Elevation is 443 feet.

Population: 6,806; Growth (since 2000): 0.4%; Density: 196.5 persons per square mile; Race: 90.8% White, 3.5% Black/African American, 0.1% Asian, 0.6% American Indian/Alaska Native, 0.5% Native Hawaiian/Other Pacific Islander, 1.9% Two or more races, 7.7% Hispanic of any race; Average household size: 2.44; Median age: 46.4; Age under 18: 20.3%; Age 65 and over: 18.5%; Males per 100 females: 100.0; Marriage status: 25.8% never married, 56.2% now married, 1.6% separated, 6.1% widowed, 11.9% divorced; Foreign born: 5.2%; Speak English only: 89.6%; With disability: 14.7%; Veterans: 7.6%; Ancestry: 18.2% German, 17.6% Dutch, 14.9% Irish, 12.0% English, 10.2% Italian

Employment: 12.2% management, business, and financial, 5.6% computer, engineering, and science, 10.1% education, legal, community service, arts, and media, 6.1% healthcare practitioners, 11.5% service, 21.5% sales and office, 16.4% natural resources, construction, and maintenance, 16.6% production, transportation, and material moving

Income: Per capita: $30,056; Median household: $58,977; Average household: $73,648; Households with income of $100,000 or more: 21.1%; Poverty rate: 9.1%

Educational Attainment: High school diploma or higher: 87.1%; Bachelor's degree or higher: 22.2%; Graduate/professional degree or higher: 9.5%

School District(s)
Williamson Central SD (PK-12)
   Enrollment: 1,132 . . . . (315) 589-9661

Housing: Homeownership rate: 78.4%; Median home value: $128,600; Median year structure built: 1962; Homeowner vacancy rate: 1.6%; Median selected monthly owner costs: $1,338 with a mortgage, $542 without a mortgage; Median gross rent: $689 per month; Rental vacancy rate: 9.2%

Health Insurance: 96.5% have insurance; 77.9% have private insurance; 35.0% have public insurance; 3.5% do not have insurance; 2.7% of children under 18 do not have insurance

Newspapers: Sun & Record (weekly circulation 3,500)

Transportation: Commute: 89.8% car, 0.0% public transportation, 1.8% walk, 5.9% work from home; Mean travel time to work: 24.3 minutes

Additional Information Contacts
Town of Williamson . . . . (315) 589-8100
   http://town.williamson.ny.us

WOLCOTT (town). Covers a land area of 39.050 square miles and a water area of 0.901 square miles. Located at 43.27° N. Lat; 76.77° W. Long. Elevation is 371 feet.

History: Incorporated 1873.

Population: 4,212; Growth (since 2000): -10.2%; Density: 107.9 persons per square mile; Race: 95.0% White, 3.0% Black/African American, 0.3% Asian, 0.0% American Indian/Alaska Native, 0.0% Native Hawaiian/Other Pacific Islander, 1.2% Two or more races, 2.0% Hispanic of any race; Average household size: 2.39; Median age: 41.0; Age under 18: 24.2%; Age 65 and over: 15.2%; Males per 100 females: 109.4; Marriage status: 25.1% never married, 56.1% now married, 1.8% separated, 5.6% widowed, 13.1% divorced; Foreign born: 1.3%; Speak English only: 96.9%; With disability: 19.3%; Veterans: 10.2%; Ancestry: 20.2% German, 14.8% English, 12.8% Irish, 8.7% American, 7.6% Dutch

Employment: 17.3% management, business, and financial, 1.6% computer, engineering, and science, 10.1% education, legal, community service, arts, and media, 3.1% healthcare practitioners, 19.2% service, 17.1% sales and office, 14.2% natural resources, construction, and maintenance, 17.4% production, transportation, and material moving

Income: Per capita: $21,369; Median household: $43,631; Average household: $51,409; Households with income of $100,000 or more: 8.4%; Poverty rate: 15.8%

Educational Attainment: High school diploma or higher: 82.1%; Bachelor's degree or higher: 11.2%; Graduate/professional degree or higher: 4.9%

School District(s)
North Rose-Wolcott Central SD (PK-12)
   Enrollment: 1,293 . . . . (315) 594-3141

Housing: Homeownership rate: 74.8%; Median home value: $80,500; Median year structure built: 1958; Homeowner vacancy rate: 0.7%; Median selected monthly owner costs: $986 with a mortgage, $437 without a mortgage; Median gross rent: $605 per month; Rental vacancy rate: 7.4%

Health Insurance: 91.7% have insurance; 57.2% have private insurance; 47.4% have public insurance; 8.3% do not have insurance; 6.7% of children under 18 do not have insurance

Transportation: Commute: 87.7% car, 0.0% public transportation, 5.8% walk, 1.8% work from home; Mean travel time to work: 26.4 minutes

Additional Information Contacts
Town of Wolcott . . . . (315) 594-9431
   http://www.wolcottny.org/townindex.php

WOLCOTT (village). Covers a land area of 1.948 square miles and a water area of 0.019 square miles. Located at 43.22° N. Lat; 76.81° W. Long. Elevation is 371 feet.

Population: 1,755; Growth (since 2000): 2.5%; Density: 901.1 persons per square mile; Race: 95.6% White, 1.9% Black/African American, 0.0% Asian, 0.0% American Indian/Alaska Native, 0.0% Native Hawaiian/Other Pacific Islander, 2.3% Two or more races, 2.1% Hispanic of any race; Average household size: 2.26; Median age: 38.5; Age under 18: 24.6%; Age 65 and over: 15.4%; Males per 100 females: 97.8; Marriage status: 34.2% never married, 39.7% now married, 3.0% separated, 9.1% widowed, 16.9% divorced; Foreign born: 1.5%; Speak English only: 98.7%; With disability: 21.3%; Veterans: 8.2%; Ancestry: 18.1% German, 13.9% English, 13.3% Irish, 12.2% Dutch, 10.5% American

Employment: 9.7% management, business, and financial, 1.8% computer, engineering, and science, 12.4% education, legal, community service, arts, and media, 2.8% healthcare practitioners, 23.0% service, 23.0% sales and office, 9.3% natural resources, construction, and maintenance, 17.9% production, transportation, and material moving

Income: Per capita: $18,858; Median household: $31,905; Average household: $42,877; Households with income of $100,000 or more: 7.9%; Poverty rate: 25.7%

Educational Attainment: High school diploma or higher: 84.0%; Bachelor's degree or higher: 11.7%; Graduate/professional degree or higher: 5.4%

School District(s)
North Rose-Wolcott Central SD (PK-12)
   Enrollment: 1,293 . . . . (315) 594-3141

Housing: Homeownership rate: 61.3%; Median home value: $76,100; Median year structure built: 1945; Homeowner vacancy rate: 0.0%; Median selected monthly owner costs: $925 with a mortgage, $443 without a mortgage; Median gross rent: $515 per month; Rental vacancy rate: 8.8%

Health Insurance: 94.4% have insurance; 54.1% have private insurance; 53.3% have public insurance; 5.6% do not have insurance; 2.6% of children under 18 do not have insurance

Safety: Violent crime rate: 0.0 per 10,000 population; Property crime rate: 31.0 per 10,000 population

Transportation: Commute: 87.1% car, 0.0% public transportation, 9.8% walk, 1.0% work from home; Mean travel time to work: 22.1 minutes

---

Westchester County

Located in southeastern New York; bounded on the west by the Hudson River, on the southeast by Long Island Sound, and on the east by Connecticut; drained by the Byram, Mianus, and Rippowam Rivers. Covers a land area of 430.497 square miles, a water area of 69.498 square miles, and is located in the Eastern Time Zone at 41.15° N. Lat., 73.75° W. Long. The county was founded in 1683. County seat is White Plains.

Westchester County is part of the New York-Newark-Jersey City, NY-NJ-PA Metropolitan Statistical Area. The entire metro area includes: Dutchess County-Putnam County, NY Metropolitan Division (Dutchess County, NY; Putnam County, NY); Nassau County-Suffolk County, NY Metropolitan Division (Nassau County, NY; Suffolk County, NY); Newark, NJ-PA Metropolitan Division (Essex County, NJ; Hunterdon County, NJ; Morris County, NJ; Somerset County, NJ; Sussex County, NJ; Union County, NJ; Pike County, PA); New York-Jersey City-White Plains, NY-NJ Metropolitan Division (Bergen County, NJ; Hudson County, NJ; Middlesex County, NJ; Monmouth County, NJ; Ocean County, NJ; Passaic County, NJ; Bronx County, NY; Kings County, NY; New York County, NY; Orange County, NY; Queens County, NY; Richmond County, NY; Rockland County, NY; Westchester County, NY)

Weather Station: Dobbs Ferry Ardsley   Elevation: 200 feet

	Jan	Feb	Mar	Apr	May	Jun	Jul	Aug	Sep	Oct	Nov	Dec
High	39	42	50	62	72	81	85	84	76	65	54	43
Low	23	25	31	40	50	59	64	64	56	45	36	28
Precip	3.8	3.0	4.5	4.7	4.5	4.4	4.6	4.2	4.6	4.5	4.4	4.3
Snow	9.0	8.4	5.7	0.9	tr	0.0	0.0	0.0	0.0	0.1	0.7	5.8

High and Low temperatures in degrees Fahrenheit; Precipitation and Snow in inches

Weather Station: Yorktown Heights 1 W   Elevation: 669 feet

	Jan	Feb	Mar	Apr	May	Jun	Jul	Aug	Sep	Oct	Nov	Dec
High	34	38	47	59	69	78	82	81	73	62	51	40
Low	19	21	28	39	49	58	63	62	54	43	35	25
Precip	3.6	3.0	4.0	4.6	4.4	4.8	4.8	4.4	4.5	4.5	4.4	3.9
Snow	11.0	10.3	7.7	2.1	0.0	0.0	0.0	0.0	0.0	tr	1.3	7.6

High and Low temperatures in degrees Fahrenheit; Precipitation and Snow in inches

Population: 975,321; Growth (since 2000): 5.6%; Density: 2,265.6 persons per square mile; Race: 65.4% White, 14.6% Black/African American, 5.9% Asian, 0.4% American Indian/Alaska Native, 0.0% Native Hawaiian/Other Pacific Islander, 3.0% two or more races, 24.0% Hispanic of any race; Average household size: 2.74; Median age: 40.6; Age under 18: 22.6%; Age 65 and over: 16.0%; Males per 100 females: 92.7; Marriage status: 33.9% never married, 52.4% now married, 2.2% separated, 5.6% widowed, 8.0% divorced; Foreign born: 25.4%; Speak English only: 66.7%; With disability: 9.2%; Veterans: 4.0%; Ancestry: 17.5% Italian, 11.9% Irish, 6.6% German, 5.0% American, 3.4% English
Religion: Six largest groups: 45.9% Catholicism, 5.2% Judaism, 1.7% Methodist/Pietist, 1.6% Baptist, 1.5% Episcopalianism/Anglicanism, 1.4% Presbyterian-Reformed
Economy: Unemployment rate: 3.6%; Leading industries: 13.0 % professional, scientific, and technical services; 11.9 % retail trade; 11.1 % construction; Farms: 131 totaling 7,752 acres; Company size: 22 employ 1,000 or more persons, 47 employ 500 to 999 persons, 530 employ 100 to 499 persons, 31,342 employ less than 100 persons; Business ownership: 39,870 women-owned, 9,982 Black-owned, 16,965 Hispanic-owned, 7,206 Asian-owned, 698 American Indian/Alaska Native-owned
Employment: 19.4% management, business, and financial, 4.7% computer, engineering, and science, 16.5% education, legal, community service, arts, and media, 6.7% healthcare practitioners, 18.6% service, 21.3% sales and office, 6.8% natural resources, construction, and maintenance, 6.0% production, transportation, and material moving
Income: Per capita: $52,049; Median household: $89,968; Average household: $143,304; Households with income of $100,000 or more: 46.2%; Poverty rate: 9.4%
Educational Attainment: High school diploma or higher: 87.6%; Bachelor's degree or higher: 47.7%; Graduate/professional degree or higher: 23.8%
Housing: Homeownership rate: 61.5%; Median home value: $513,300; Median year structure built: 1956; Homeowner vacancy rate: 1.7%; Median selected monthly owner costs: $3,340 with a mortgage, $1,391 without a mortgage; Median gross rent: $1,444 per month; Rental vacancy rate: 5.5%
Vital Statistics: Birth rate: 106.8 per 10,000 population; Death rate: 75.3 per 10,000 population; Age-adjusted cancer mortality rate: 124.4 deaths per 100,000 population
Health Insurance: 92.2% have insurance; 73.9% have private insurance; 30.0% have public insurance; 7.8% do not have insurance; 2.6% of children under 18 do not have insurance
Health Care: Physicians: 67.1 per 10,000 population; Dentists: 10.9 per 10,000 population; Hospital beds: 41.3 per 10,000 population; Hospital admissions: 1,261.4 per 10,000 population

Air Quality Index (AQI): Percent of Days: 90.1% good, 8.5% moderate, 1.4% unhealthy for sensitive individuals, 0.0% unhealthy, 0.0% very unhealthy; Annual median: 36; Annual maximum: 112
Transportation: Commute: 65.7% car, 22.7% public transportation, 4.8% walk, 5.2% work from home; Mean travel time to work: 34.1 minutes
2016 Presidential Election: 31.2% Trump, 64.9% Clinton, 1.9% Johnson, 1.0% Stein
National and State Parks: Brinton Brook National Audubon Society Sanctuary; Echo Lake State Park; John Jay Homestead State Historic Site; Mohansic State Park; Saint Pauls Church National Historic Site; Titus Mill Pond State Tidal Wetlands
Additional Information Contacts
Westchester Government . . . . (914) 995-2900
http://www3.westchestergov.com

Westchester County Communities

AMAWALK (unincorporated postal area)
ZCTA: 10501
    Covers a land area of 1.399 square miles and a water area of 0.001 square miles. Located at 41.30° N. Lat; 73.76° W. Long. Elevation is 413 feet.
Population: 1,239; Growth (since 2000): 47.0%; Density: 885.4 persons per square mile; Race: 92.3% White, 1.2% Black/African American, 0.4% Asian, 0.0% American Indian/Alaska Native, 0.0% Native Hawaiian/Other Pacific Islander, 2.9% Two or more races, 8.7% Hispanic of any race; Average household size: 3.07; Median age: 47.9; Age under 18: 21.4%; Age 65 and over: 18.4%; Males per 100 females: 103.8; Marriage status: 23.1% never married, 68.9% now married, 0.0% separated, 3.1% widowed, 5.0% divorced; Foreign born: 12.8%; Speak English only: 80.5%; With disability: 13.1%; Veterans: 3.9%; Ancestry: 39.5% Italian, 22.6% Irish, 13.0% American, 8.0% German, 5.8% Albanian
Employment: 23.6% management, business, and financial, 5.2% computer, engineering, and science, 17.9% education, legal, community service, arts, and media, 3.8% healthcare practitioners, 8.0% service, 27.4% sales and office, 6.4% natural resources, construction, and maintenance, 7.7% production, transportation, and material moving
Income: Per capita: $58,472; Median household: $146,250; Average household: $178,051; Households with income of $100,000 or more: 69.2%; Poverty rate: 0.6%
Educational Attainment: High school diploma or higher: 93.9%; Bachelor's degree or higher: 48.1%; Graduate/professional degree or higher: 16.5%
Housing: Homeownership rate: 98.0%; Median home value: $668,200; Median year structure built: 1974; Homeowner vacancy rate: 0.0%; Median selected monthly owner costs: $4,000 with a mortgage, $1,501 without a mortgage; Median gross rent: n/a per month; Rental vacancy rate: 0.0%
Health Insurance: 98.2% have insurance; 91.5% have private insurance; 21.2% have public insurance; 1.8% do not have insurance; 0.0% of children under 18 do not have insurance
Transportation: Commute: 92.3% car, 6.1% public transportation, 0.0% walk, 1.6% work from home; Mean travel time to work: 41.4 minutes

ARDSLEY (village). Covers a land area of 1.323 square miles and a water area of 0 square miles. Located at 41.01° N. Lat; 73.84° W. Long. Elevation is 210 feet.
History: The town took the name "Ardsley" after the name of a local baron's estate, and the first village postmaster was appointed in 1883. Incorporated in 1896, Ardsley would continue to grow at a steady pace, until a fire destroyed the village center in 1914.
Population: 4,557; Growth (since 2000): 6.7%; Density: 3,445.6 persons per square mile; Race: 71.5% White, 1.9% Black/African American, 18.9% Asian, 0.2% American Indian/Alaska Native, 0.0% Native Hawaiian/Other Pacific Islander, 3.2% Two or more races, 9.1% Hispanic of any race; Average household size: 2.81; Median age: 47.8; Age under 18: 21.7%; Age 65 and over: 21.0%; Males per 100 females: 88.4; Marriage status: 27.9% never married, 58.7% now married, 0.0% separated, 6.7% widowed, 6.7% divorced; Foreign born: 27.9%; Speak English only: 67.6%; With disability: 10.9%; Veterans: 3.0%; Ancestry: 18.6% Irish, 12.7% Italian, 6.9% American, 5.6% Russian, 5.0% Polish
Employment: 27.9% management, business, and financial, 7.9% computer, engineering, and science, 20.8% education, legal, community service, arts, and media, 8.1% healthcare practitioners, 9.1% service,

19.6% sales and office, 3.0% natural resources, construction, and maintenance, 3.6% production, transportation, and material moving
Income: Per capita: $68,138; Median household: $130,586; Average household: $186,431; Households with income of $100,000 or more: 66.4%; Poverty rate: 2.7%
Educational Attainment: High school diploma or higher: 95.9%; Bachelor's degree or higher: 64.7%; Graduate/professional degree or higher: 35.5%

School District(s)
Ardsley Union Free SD (KG-12)
    Enrollment: 2,074 . . . . (914) 295-5510
Housing: Homeownership rate: 81.2%; Median home value: $620,200; Median year structure built: 1957; Homeowner vacancy rate: 0.0%; Median selected monthly owner costs: $3,687 with a mortgage, $1,501 without a mortgage; Median gross rent: $1,313 per month; Rental vacancy rate: 11.6%
Health Insurance: 95.6% have insurance; 84.6% have private insurance; 28.5% have public insurance; 4.4% do not have insurance; 0.0% of children under 18 do not have insurance
Safety: Violent crime rate: 4.3 per 10,000 population; Property crime rate: 75.1 per 10,000 population
Transportation: Commute: 70.4% car, 19.4% public transportation, 3.3% walk, 5.5% work from home; Mean travel time to work: 33.2 minutes
Additional Information Contacts
Village of Ardsley . . . . (914) 693-1550
    http://www.ardsleyvillage.com

ARDSLEY ON HUDSON (unincorporated postal area)
ZCTA: 10503
    Covers a land area of 0.015 square miles and a water area of 0 square miles. Located at 41.03° N. Lat; 73.88° W. Long..
    Population: 137; Growth (since 2000): 19.1%; Density: 9,216.9 persons per square mile; Race: 89.8% White, 0.0% Black/African American, 10.2% Asian, 0.0% American Indian/Alaska Native, 0.0% Native Hawaiian/Other Pacific Islander, 0.0% Two or more races, 11.7% Hispanic of any race; Average household size: 1.44; Median age: 61.0; Age under 18: 0.0%; Age 65 and over: 40.1%; Males per 100 females: 63.6; Marriage status: 21.9% never married, 47.4% now married, 9.5% separated, 10.9% widowed, 19.7% divorced; Foreign born: 10.2%; Speak English only: 70.8%; With disability: 9.5%; Veterans: 0.0%; Ancestry: 19.0% German, 11.7% Irish, 10.9% Polish, 10.2% American, 9.5% French
    Employment: 30.2% management, business, and financial, 0.0% computer, engineering, and science, 41.7% education, legal, community service, arts, and media, 0.0% healthcare practitioners, 0.0% service, 28.1% sales and office, 0.0% natural resources, construction, and maintenance, 0.0% production, transportation, and material moving
    Income: Per capita: $108,945; Median household: n/a; Average household: $151,294; Households with income of $100,000 or more: 42.1%; Poverty rate: 9.5%
    Educational Attainment: High school diploma or higher: 100.0%; Bachelor's degree or higher: 81.0%; Graduate/professional degree or higher: 48.2%
    Housing: Homeownership rate: 100.0%; Median home value: $525,900; Median year structure built: Before 1940; Homeowner vacancy rate: 0.0%; Median selected monthly owner costs: $0 with a mortgage, $453 without a mortgage; Median gross rent: n/a per month; Rental vacancy rate: 0.0%
    Health Insurance: 100.0% have insurance; 80.3% have private insurance; 40.1% have public insurance; 0.0% do not have insurance; 0.0% of children under 18 do not have insurance
    Transportation: Commute: 55.2% car, 44.8% public transportation, 0.0% walk, 0.0% work from home; Mean travel time to work: 38.6 minutes

ARMONK (CDP). Covers a land area of 5.966 square miles and a water area of 0.093 square miles. Located at 41.13° N. Lat; 73.72° W. Long. Elevation is 387 feet.
History: The Indians of North Castle were the Siwanoys, who belonged to the Wappinger Confederacy, and were part of the Algonkian-speaking group. They gave the name of Armonck (the name the Indians called Byram River) undoubtedly gave us thw hamlet name of Armonk.
Population: 4,537; Growth (since 2000): 31.1%; Density: 760.4 persons per square mile; Race: 92.2% White, 0.7% Black/African American, 4.7% Asian, 0.0% American Indian/Alaska Native, 0.0% Native Hawaiian/Other

Pacific Islander, 1.2% Two or more races, 8.2% Hispanic of any race; Average household size: 3.17; Median age: 42.2; Age under 18: 27.8%; Age 65 and over: 12.8%; Males per 100 females: 97.0; Marriage status: 25.6% never married, 67.0% now married, 0.3% separated, 2.0% widowed, 5.4% divorced; Foreign born: 8.4%; Speak English only: 81.8%; With disability: 6.1%; Veterans: 4.7%; Ancestry: 19.9% Italian, 9.9% Irish, 9.6% German, 8.2% Eastern European, 7.3% Russian
Employment: 31.4% management, business, and financial, 9.2% computer, engineering, and science, 17.3% education, legal, community service, arts, and media, 8.2% healthcare practitioners, 11.4% service, 19.7% sales and office, 2.4% natural resources, construction, and maintenance, 0.4% production, transportation, and material moving
Income: Per capita: $99,791; Median household: $211,389; Average household: $311,447; Households with income of $100,000 or more: 82.5%; Poverty rate: 1.4%
Educational Attainment: High school diploma or higher: 96.7%; Bachelor's degree or higher: 79.6%; Graduate/professional degree or higher: 42.0%

School District(s)
Byram Hills Central SD (KG-12)
    Enrollment: 2,393 . . . . (914) 273-4082
Housing: Homeownership rate: 92.4%; Median home value: $888,900; Median year structure built: 1979; Homeowner vacancy rate: 1.3%; Median selected monthly owner costs: $4,000+ with a mortgage, $1,501 without a mortgage; Median gross rent: $3,500+ per month; Rental vacancy rate: 9.2%
Health Insurance: 96.4% have insurance; 91.7% have private insurance; 13.3% have public insurance; 3.6% do not have insurance; 3.1% of children under 18 do not have insurance
Transportation: Commute: 75.5% car, 16.3% public transportation, 2.1% walk, 5.4% work from home; Mean travel time to work: 32.9 minutes

BALDWIN PLACE (unincorporated postal area)
ZCTA: 10505
    Covers a land area of 0.652 square miles and a water area of 0 square miles. Located at 41.34° N. Lat; 73.75° W. Long..
    Population: 960; Growth (since 2000): n/a; Density: 1,471.6 persons per square mile; Race: 83.0% White, 2.0% Black/African American, 15.0% Asian, 0.0% American Indian/Alaska Native, 0.0% Native Hawaiian/Other Pacific Islander, 0.0% Two or more races, 9.3% Hispanic of any race; Average household size: 3.21; Median age: 38.0; Age under 18: 35.7%; Age 65 and over: 13.3%; Males per 100 females: 98.4; Marriage status: 33.5% never married, 58.3% now married, 0.0% separated, 2.1% widowed, 6.1% divorced; Foreign born: 6.4%; Speak English only: 83.7%; With disability: 15.3%; Veterans: 5.8%; Ancestry: 24.2% Italian, 22.4% Irish, 17.1% American, 4.2% Polish, 4.1% Russian
    Employment: 28.6% management, business, and financial, 1.8% computer, engineering, and science, 16.1% education, legal, community service, arts, and media, 8.2% healthcare practitioners, 17.3% service, 20.2% sales and office, 3.3% natural resources, construction, and maintenance, 4.6% production, transportation, and material moving
    Income: Per capita: $53,019; Median household: n/a; Average household: $162,763; Households with income of $100,000 or more: 53.2%; Poverty rate: 2.3%
    Educational Attainment: High school diploma or higher: 100.0%; Bachelor's degree or higher: 55.3%; Graduate/professional degree or higher: 39.7%
    Housing: Homeownership rate: 58.6%; Median home value: $721,300; Median year structure built: 2003; Homeowner vacancy rate: 0.0%; Median selected monthly owner costs: $4,000 with a mortgage, $1,501 without a mortgage; Median gross rent: $1,273 per month; Rental vacancy rate: 0.0%
    Health Insurance: 94.4% have insurance; 78.0% have private insurance; 27.8% have public insurance; 5.6% do not have insurance; 4.2% of children under 18 do not have insurance
    Transportation: Commute: 79.1% car, 12.2% public transportation, 3.1% walk, 5.6% work from home; Mean travel time to work: 37.4 minutes

BEDFORD (CDP). Covers a land area of 3.507 square miles and a water area of 0.048 square miles. Located at 41.20° N. Lat; 73.65° W. Long. Elevation is 377 feet.
Population: 1,898; Growth (since 2000): 10.1%; Density: 541.2 persons per square mile; Race: 95.7% White, 0.3% Black/African American, 1.9% Asian, 0.0% American Indian/Alaska Native, 0.0% Native Hawaiian/Other

Pacific Islander, 1.6% Two or more races, 3.7% Hispanic of any race; Average household size: 2.92; Median age: 47.3; Age under 18: 28.0%; Age 65 and over: 17.0%; Males per 100 females: 99.1; Marriage status: 20.5% never married, 64.9% now married, 0.0% separated, 6.3% widowed, 8.2% divorced; Foreign born: 6.6%; Speak English only: 97.1%; With disability: 4.8%; Veterans: 4.2%; Ancestry: 34.8% Irish, 23.9% Italian, 18.4% German, 18.1% English, 7.5% American

Employment: 29.8% management, business, and financial, 7.5% computer, engineering, and science, 14.7% education, legal, community service, arts, and media, 5.3% healthcare practitioners, 16.3% service, 22.9% sales and office, 3.6% natural resources, construction, and maintenance, 0.0% production, transportation, and material moving

Income: Per capita: $89,519; Median household: $190,556; Average household: $259,764; Households with income of $100,000 or more: 74.0%; Poverty rate: 3.6%

Educational Attainment: High school diploma or higher: 96.7%; Bachelor's degree or higher: 66.9%; Graduate/professional degree or higher: 30.5%

School District(s)

Bedford Central SD (PK-12)
    Enrollment: 4,187 . . . . (914) 241-6010
Housing: Homeownership rate: 99.1%; Median home value: $881,800; Median year structure built: 1961; Homeowner vacancy rate: 4.5%; Median selected monthly owner costs: $4,000+ with a mortgage, $1,501 without a mortgage; Median gross rent: n/a per month; Rental vacancy rate: 77.8%
Health Insurance: 99.5% have insurance; 96.0% have private insurance; 16.6% have public insurance; 0.5% do not have insurance; 1.6% of children under 18 do not have insurance
Transportation: Commute: 59.9% car, 14.9% public transportation, 3.3% walk, 22.0% work from home; Mean travel time to work: 41.4 minutes

BEDFORD (town). Covers a land area of 37.173 square miles and a water area of 2.247 square miles. Located at 41.23° N. Lat; 73.66° W. Long. Elevation is 377 feet.

History: Caramoor Art and Music Center. Maximum-security Tacoma Correctional Facility for Women is at nearby Bedford Hills village. Also known as Bedford Village.

Population: 17,955; Growth (since 2000): -1.0%; Density: 483.0 persons per square mile; Race: 81.6% White, 4.1% Black/African American, 3.2% Asian, 0.2% American Indian/Alaska Native, 0.0% Native Hawaiian/Other Pacific Islander, 2.1% Two or more races, 15.8% Hispanic of any race; Average household size: 2.85; Median age: 40.0; Age under 18: 24.5%; Age 65 and over: 14.0%; Males per 100 females: 84.3; Marriage status: 30.1% never married, 58.5% now married, 1.2% separated, 4.2% widowed, 7.2% divorced; Foreign born: 17.1%; Speak English only: 79.2%; With disability: 6.5%; Veterans: 4.2%; Ancestry: 18.7% Irish, 18.4% Italian, 12.5% German, 9.4% English, 4.9% Polish

Employment: 25.5% management, business, and financial, 5.9% computer, engineering, and science, 17.9% education, legal, community service, arts, and media, 4.8% healthcare practitioners, 19.0% service, 19.1% sales and office, 5.7% natural resources, construction, and maintenance, 2.1% production, transportation, and material moving

Income: Per capita: $73,830; Median household: $121,797; Average household: $224,836; Households with income of $100,000 or more: 57.9%; Poverty rate: 5.3%

Educational Attainment: High school diploma or higher: 88.2%; Bachelor's degree or higher: 58.5%; Graduate/professional degree or higher: 28.5%

School District(s)

Bedford Central SD (PK-12)
    Enrollment: 4,187 . . . . (914) 241-6010
Housing: Homeownership rate: 72.1%; Median home value: $733,300; Median year structure built: 1962; Homeowner vacancy rate: 5.1%; Median selected monthly owner costs: $3,907 with a mortgage, $1,501 without a mortgage; Median gross rent: $1,585 per month; Rental vacancy rate: 2.6%
Health Insurance: 93.1% have insurance; 80.2% have private insurance; 24.2% have public insurance; 6.9% do not have insurance; 0.4% of children under 18 do not have insurance
Safety: Violent crime rate: 2.8 per 10,000 population; Property crime rate: 20.6 per 10,000 population
Transportation: Commute: 65.4% car, 20.7% public transportation, 3.1% walk, 10.1% work from home; Mean travel time to work: 38.5 minutes

Additional Information Contacts
Town of Bedford . . . . (914) 666-4534
    http://www.bedfordny.info

BEDFORD HILLS (CDP). Covers a land area of 1.006 square miles and a water area of 0 square miles. Located at 41.24° N. Lat; 73.69° W. Long. Elevation is 341 feet.

Population: 3,738; Growth (since 2000): n/a; Density: 3,715.4 persons per square mile; Race: 60.9% White, 1.4% Black/African American, 2.4% Asian, 0.0% American Indian/Alaska Native, 0.0% Native Hawaiian/Other Pacific Islander, 0.4% Two or more races, 48.5% Hispanic of any race; Average household size: 2.67; Median age: 34.4; Age under 18: 30.5%; Age 65 and over: 8.8%; Males per 100 females: 97.8; Marriage status: 38.3% never married, 52.6% now married, 0.0% separated, 2.0% widowed, 7.1% divorced; Foreign born: 41.7%; Speak English only: 45.3%; With disability: 5.6%; Veterans: 3.4%; Ancestry: 17.0% Italian, 8.8% German, 7.0% Irish, 5.8% Hungarian, 4.4% Israeli

Employment: 12.6% management, business, and financial, 7.3% computer, engineering, and science, 7.4% education, legal, community service, arts, and media, 3.4% healthcare practitioners, 37.9% service, 14.7% sales and office, 14.6% natural resources, construction, and maintenance, 2.0% production, transportation, and material moving

Income: Per capita: $29,428; Median household: $48,125; Average household: $78,947; Households with income of $100,000 or more: 26.8%; Poverty rate: 11.6%

Educational Attainment: High school diploma or higher: 68.5%; Bachelor's degree or higher: 38.8%; Graduate/professional degree or higher: 21.4%

School District(s)

Bedford Central SD (PK-12)
    Enrollment: 4,187 . . . . (914) 241-6010
Housing: Homeownership rate: 36.5%; Median home value: $493,100; Median year structure built: 1963; Homeowner vacancy rate: 0.0%; Median selected monthly owner costs: $2,760 with a mortgage, $1,077 without a mortgage; Median gross rent: $1,374 per month; Rental vacancy rate: 0.0%
Health Insurance: 80.0% have insurance; 47.3% have private insurance; 36.5% have public insurance; 20.0% do not have insurance; 0.0% of children under 18 do not have insurance
Newspapers: Record-Review (weekly circulation 4,000)
Transportation: Commute: 79.2% car, 15.8% public transportation, 1.9% walk, 3.0% work from home; Mean travel time to work: 34.5 minutes

BRIARCLIFF MANOR (village). Covers a land area of 5.962 square miles and a water area of 0.850 square miles. Located at 41.14° N. Lat; 73.85° W. Long. Elevation is 249 feet.

History: Settled 1896, incorporated 1902.

Population: 7,864; Growth (since 2000): 2.2%; Density: 1,319.1 persons per square mile; Race: 82.7% White, 3.3% Black/African American, 8.5% Asian, 0.0% American Indian/Alaska Native, 0.1% Native Hawaiian/Other Pacific Islander, 3.1% Two or more races, 8.2% Hispanic of any race; Average household size: 2.74; Median age: 46.1; Age under 18: 22.6%; Age 65 and over: 18.7%; Males per 100 females: 92.3; Marriage status: 25.4% never married, 62.5% now married, 0.5% separated, 6.9% widowed, 5.2% divorced; Foreign born: 13.1%; Speak English only: 83.4%; With disability: 7.5%; Veterans: 5.5%; Ancestry: 24.2% Italian, 14.6% Irish, 8.2% German, 6.9% American, 6.1% Russian

Employment: 28.2% management, business, and financial, 7.9% computer, engineering, and science, 21.7% education, legal, community service, arts, and media, 11.3% healthcare practitioners, 7.3% service, 19.4% sales and office, 2.5% natural resources, construction, and maintenance, 1.7% production, transportation, and material moving

Income: Per capita: $79,476; Median household: $157,963; Average household: $231,624; Households with income of $100,000 or more: 68.7%; Poverty rate: 2.6%

Educational Attainment: High school diploma or higher: 94.9%; Bachelor's degree or higher: 71.2%; Graduate/professional degree or higher: 40.5%

School District(s)

Briarcliff Manor Union Free SD (KG-12)
    Enrollment: 1,487 . . . . (914) 432-8115
Housing: Homeownership rate: 83.1%; Median home value: $686,200; Median year structure built: 1964; Homeowner vacancy rate: 0.4%; Median selected monthly owner costs: $4,000+ with a mortgage, $1,501 without a

mortgage; Median gross rent: $1,500 per month; Rental vacancy rate: 0.0%

Health Insurance: 98.0% have insurance; 90.4% have private insurance; 21.5% have public insurance; 2.0% do not have insurance; 0.0% of children under 18 do not have insurance

Safety: Violent crime rate: 2.5 per 10,000 population; Property crime rate: 24.8 per 10,000 population

Transportation: Commute: 55.4% car, 29.1% public transportation, 2.7% walk, 11.9% work from home; Mean travel time to work: 39.6 minutes

Additional Information Contacts

Village of Briarcliff Manor . . . . (914) 941-4800
  http://www.briarcliffmanor.org/pages/index

BRONXVILLE (village).

Covers a land area of 0.962 square miles and a water area of 0 square miles. Located at 40.94° N. Lat; 73.83° W. Long. Elevation is 92 feet.

History: Seat of Sarah Lawrence College. Settled 1664, incorporated 1898.

Population: 6,428; Growth (since 2000): -1.8%; Density: 6,682.0 persons per square mile; Race: 89.6% White, 1.0% Black/African American, 4.6% Asian, 0.0% American Indian/Alaska Native, 0.0% Native Hawaiian/Other Pacific Islander, 2.5% Two or more races, 5.3% Hispanic of any race; Average household size: 2.81; Median age: 41.4; Age under 18: 29.2%; Age 65 and over: 13.6%; Males per 100 females: 88.7; Marriage status: 26.4% never married, 61.0% now married, 1.0% separated, 8.1% widowed, 4.5% divorced; Foreign born: 12.5%; Speak English only: 84.2%; With disability: 6.6%; Veterans: 3.3%; Ancestry: 26.1% Irish, 17.9% Italian, 17.3% German, 12.1% English, 5.5% American

Employment: 35.1% management, business, and financial, 3.4% computer, engineering, and science, 21.0% education, legal, community service, arts, and media, 7.7% healthcare practitioners, 8.4% service, 22.5% sales and office, 1.3% natural resources, construction, and maintenance, 0.6% production, transportation, and material moving

Income: Per capita: $116,698; Median household: $205,781; Average household: $340,448; Households with income of $100,000 or more: 70.1%; Poverty rate: 2.9%

Educational Attainment: High school diploma or higher: 97.2%; Bachelor's degree or higher: 80.5%; Graduate/professional degree or higher: 47.8%

School District(s)

Bronxville Union Free SD (KG-12)
  Enrollment: 1,661 . . . . (914) 395-0500

Four-year College(s)

Concordia College-New York (Private, Not-for-profit, Lutheran Church - Missouri Synod)
  Enrollment: 1,597 . . . . (914) 337-9300
    Tuition: In-state $31,600; Out-of-state $31,600
Sarah Lawrence College (Private, Not-for-profit)
  Enrollment: 1,696 . . . . (914) 337-0700
    Tuition: In-state $54,010; Out-of-state $54,010

Housing: Homeownership rate: 82.0%; Median home value: $1,077,200; Median year structure built: Before 1940; Homeowner vacancy rate: 2.3%; Median selected monthly owner costs: $4,000+ with a mortgage, $1,501 without a mortgage; Median gross rent: $2,745 per month; Rental vacancy rate: 0.0%

Health Insurance: 97.7% have insurance; 91.8% have private insurance; 17.5% have public insurance; 2.3% do not have insurance; 1.9% of children under 18 do not have insurance

Hospitals: Lawrence Hospital Center (281 beds)

Safety: Violent crime rate: 0.0 per 10,000 population; Property crime rate: 45.2 per 10,000 population

Transportation: Commute: 37.5% car, 46.6% public transportation, 5.7% walk, 8.4% work from home; Mean travel time to work: 40.0 minutes

Additional Information Contacts

Village of Bronxville . . . . (914) 337-6500
  http://villageofbronxville.com

BUCHANAN (village).

Covers a land area of 1.382 square miles and a water area of 0.339 square miles. Located at 41.26° N. Lat; 73.95° W. Long. Elevation is 39 feet.

History: Incorporated 1928.

Population: 2,255; Growth (since 2000): 3.0%; Density: 1,632.1 persons per square mile; Race: 77.7% White, 4.3% Black/African American, 1.8% Asian, 0.0% American Indian/Alaska Native, 0.0% Native Hawaiian/Other Pacific Islander, 3.5% Two or more races, 16.4% Hispanic of any race;

Average household size: 2.99; Median age: 40.9; Age under 18: 22.0%; Age 65 and over: 12.6%; Males per 100 females: 101.1; Marriage status: 29.6% never married, 61.6% now married, 2.1% separated, 4.0% widowed, 4.9% divorced; Foreign born: 14.1%; Speak English only: 80.1%; With disability: 11.5%; Veterans: 6.0%; Ancestry: 24.2% Irish, 21.2% Italian, 13.9% German, 6.4% Polish, 6.3% English

Employment: 18.3% management, business, and financial, 6.7% computer, engineering, and science, 11.0% education, legal, community service, arts, and media, 4.5% healthcare practitioners, 16.3% service, 25.3% sales and office, 7.7% natural resources, construction, and maintenance, 10.4% production, transportation, and material moving

Income: Per capita: $39,108; Median household: $107,418; Average household: $114,357; Households with income of $100,000 or more: 58.1%; Poverty rate: 6.7%

Educational Attainment: High school diploma or higher: 92.7%; Bachelor's degree or higher: 33.5%; Graduate/professional degree or higher: 13.4%

School District(s)

Hendrick Hudson Central SD (KG-12)
  Enrollment: 2,345 . . . . (914) 257-5100

Housing: Homeownership rate: 77.8%; Median home value: $390,800; Median year structure built: 1952; Homeowner vacancy rate: 2.6%; Median selected monthly owner costs: $2,604 with a mortgage, $1,186 without a mortgage; Median gross rent: $1,447 per month; Rental vacancy rate: 8.2%

Health Insurance: 95.7% have insurance; 85.5% have private insurance; 21.1% have public insurance; 4.3% do not have insurance; 2.4% of children under 18 do not have insurance

Safety: Violent crime rate: 0.0 per 10,000 population; Property crime rate: 8.8 per 10,000 population

Transportation: Commute: 85.6% car, 10.4% public transportation, 0.0% walk, 4.0% work from home; Mean travel time to work: 31.8 minutes

Additional Information Contacts

Village of Buchanan . . . . (914) 737-1033
  http://villageofbuchanan.com

CHAPPAQUA (CDP).

Covers a land area of 0.450 square miles and a water area of 0 square miles. Located at 41.16° N. Lat; 73.77° W. Long. Elevation is 492 feet.

History: Originally a Quaker community; later estate area. Horace Greeley lived here.

Population: 1,298; Growth (since 2000): -86.3%; Density: 2,884.3 persons per square mile; Race: 84.5% White, 0.0% Black/African American, 13.5% Asian, 0.0% American Indian/Alaska Native, 0.0% Native Hawaiian/Other Pacific Islander, 2.0% Two or more races, 0.0% Hispanic of any race; Average household size: 2.63; Median age: 40.9; Age under 18: 22.6%; Age 65 and over: 20.7%; Males per 100 females: 88.2; Marriage status: 27.4% never married, 59.2% now married, 0.0% separated, 5.7% widowed, 7.7% divorced; Foreign born: 14.7%; Speak English only: 86.6%; With disability: 5.2%; Veterans: 9.6%; Ancestry: 25.7% Italian, 10.9% Irish, 8.5% English, 7.6% Ukrainian, 7.3% German

Employment: 24.4% management, business, and financial, 7.5% computer, engineering, and science, 27.0% education, legal, community service, arts, and media, 9.5% healthcare practitioners, 10.8% service, 17.4% sales and office, 0.0% natural resources, construction, and maintenance, 3.4% production, transportation, and material moving

Income: Per capita: $85,313; Median household: $213,040; Average household: $219,804; Households with income of $100,000 or more: 77.8%; Poverty rate: 2.7%

Educational Attainment: High school diploma or higher: 100.0%; Bachelor's degree or higher: 87.8%; Graduate/professional degree or higher: 44.9%

School District(s)

Chappaqua Central SD (KG-12)
  Enrollment: 3,839 . . . . (914) 238-7200

Housing: Homeownership rate: 80.5%; Median home value: $602,500; Median year structure built: 1941; Homeowner vacancy rate: 0.0%; Median selected monthly owner costs: $3,301 with a mortgage, $1,267 without a mortgage; Median gross rent: $1,933 per month; Rental vacancy rate: 0.0%

Health Insurance: 100.0% have insurance; 93.7% have private insurance; 20.4% have public insurance; 0.0% do not have insurance; 0.0% of children under 18 do not have insurance

Transportation: Commute: 63.8% car, 33.8% public transportation, 0.0% walk, 2.3% work from home; Mean travel time to work: 46.1 minutes

CORTLANDT (town). Covers a land area of 39.255 square miles and a water area of 10.761 square miles. Located at 41.26° N. Lat; 73.90° W. Long.

History: The Bear Mountain Bridge Road and Toll House, and the site of Old Croton Dam, both in Cortlandt, are listed on the National Register of Historic Places.

Population: 42,816; Growth (since 2000): 11.3%; Density: 1,090.7 persons per square mile; Race: 78.5% White, 6.5% Black/African American, 3.9% Asian, 0.2% American Indian/Alaska Native, 0.0% Native Hawaiian/Other Pacific Islander, 2.7% Two or more races, 16.5% Hispanic of any race; Average household size: 2.76; Median age: 44.2; Age under 18: 23.0%; Age 65 and over: 16.4%; Males per 100 females: 96.4; Marriage status: 29.1% never married, 56.5% now married, 1.5% separated, 5.3% widowed, 9.1% divorced; Foreign born: 15.0%; Speak English only: 80.5%; With disability: 10.0%; Veterans: 5.7%; Ancestry: 23.3% Italian, 20.1% Irish, 11.4% German, 4.9% English, 4.1% American

Employment: 19.5% management, business, and financial, 6.4% computer, engineering, and science, 20.0% education, legal, community service, arts, and media, 5.7% healthcare practitioners, 15.6% service, 21.0% sales and office, 5.7% natural resources, construction, and maintenance, 6.1% production, transportation, and material moving

Income: Per capita: $49,381; Median household: $103,266; Average household: $136,721; Households with income of $100,000 or more: 51.5%; Poverty rate: 5.5%

Educational Attainment: High school diploma or higher: 93.5%; Bachelor's degree or higher: 49.2%; Graduate/professional degree or higher: 22.4%

Housing: Homeownership rate: 75.2%; Median home value: $407,100; Median year structure built: 1961; Homeowner vacancy rate: 1.4%; Median selected monthly owner costs: $3,032 with a mortgage, $1,342 without a mortgage; Median gross rent: $1,436 per month; Rental vacancy rate: 4.0%

Health Insurance: 95.9% have insurance; 84.0% have private insurance; 24.2% have public insurance; 4.1% do not have insurance; 2.6% of children under 18 do not have insurance

Transportation: Commute: 75.6% car, 15.6% public transportation, 2.0% walk, 5.7% work from home; Mean travel time to work: 39.8 minutes

Additional Information Contacts

Town of Cortlandt . . . . (914) 734-1020
http://www.townofcortlandt.com

CORTLANDT MANOR (unincorporated postal area)
ZCTA: 10567

Covers a land area of 22.137 square miles and a water area of 0.453 square miles. Located at 41.29° N. Lat; 73.90° W. Long..

Population: 20,778; Growth (since 2000): 16.7%; Density: 938.6 persons per square mile; Race: 76.3% White, 6.4% Black/African American, 3.0% Asian, 0.1% American Indian/Alaska Native, 0.0% Native Hawaiian/Other Pacific Islander, 3.3% Two or more races, 20.6% Hispanic of any race; Average household size: 2.94; Median age: 44.1; Age under 18: 23.8%; Age 65 and over: 16.2%; Males per 100 females: 97.6; Marriage status: 27.7% never married, 59.7% now married, 0.9% separated, 5.5% widowed, 7.1% divorced; Foreign born: 15.6%; Speak English only: 78.3%; With disability: 8.5%; Veterans: 5.0%; Ancestry: 24.1% Italian, 17.0% Irish, 11.2% German, 4.5% English, 3.7% American

Employment: 20.8% management, business, and financial, 5.1% computer, engineering, and science, 20.7% education, legal, community service, arts, and media, 6.0% healthcare practitioners, 13.9% service, 22.2% sales and office, 5.4% natural resources, construction, and maintenance, 6.0% production, transportation, and material moving

Income: Per capita: $50,080; Median household: $114,207; Average household: $147,949; Households with income of $100,000 or more: 55.7%; Poverty rate: 5.0%

Educational Attainment: High school diploma or higher: 93.7%; Bachelor's degree or higher: 48.1%; Graduate/professional degree or higher: 21.1%

School District(s)

Hendrick Hudson Central SD (KG-12)
Enrollment: 2,345 . . . . (914) 257-5100
Lakeland Central SD (PK-12)
Enrollment: 5,728 . . . . (914) 245-1700

Housing: Homeownership rate: 88.7%; Median home value: $385,800; Median year structure built: 1964; Homeowner vacancy rate: 2.0%; Median selected monthly owner costs: $3,025 with a mortgage, $1,358

without a mortgage; Median gross rent: $1,816 per month; Rental vacancy rate: 3.1%

Health Insurance: 96.1% have insurance; 85.6% have private insurance; 22.8% have public insurance; 3.9% do not have insurance; 1.3% of children under 18 do not have insurance

Hospitals: Hudson Valley Hospital Center (120 beds)

Transportation: Commute: 78.6% car, 13.0% public transportation, 1.1% walk, 5.8% work from home; Mean travel time to work: 42.4 minutes

CROMPOND (CDP). Covers a land area of 2.420 square miles and a water area of 0.020 square miles. Located at 41.30° N. Lat; 73.84° W. Long. Elevation is 420 feet.

Population: 2,333; Growth (since 2000): 13.8%; Density: 964.2 persons per square mile; Race: 71.9% White, 12.6% Black/African American, 2.6% Asian, 0.0% American Indian/Alaska Native, 0.0% Native Hawaiian/Other Pacific Islander, 4.5% Two or more races, 16.2% Hispanic of any race; Average household size: 2.70; Median age: 43.4; Age under 18: 23.7%; Age 65 and over: 17.4%; Males per 100 females: 85.1; Marriage status: 23.0% never married, 64.0% now married, 0.0% separated, 6.1% widowed, 6.9% divorced; Foreign born: 9.9%; Speak English only: 89.8%; With disability: 10.5%; Veterans: 6.1%; Ancestry: 38.8% Italian, 18.2% Irish, 5.5% German, 4.9% American, 4.8% Polish

Employment: 24.4% management, business, and financial, 4.3% computer, engineering, and science, 18.8% education, legal, community service, arts, and media, 10.8% healthcare practitioners, 16.3% service, 16.5% sales and office, 5.1% natural resources, construction, and maintenance, 3.9% production, transportation, and material moving

Income: Per capita: $53,902; Median household: $128,462; Average household: $154,141; Households with income of $100,000 or more: 70.6%; Poverty rate: 0.4%

Educational Attainment: High school diploma or higher: 92.2%; Bachelor's degree or higher: 46.8%; Graduate/professional degree or higher: 24.4%

School District(s)

Lakeland Central SD (PK-12)
Enrollment: 5,728 . . . . (914) 245-1700

Housing: Homeownership rate: 89.7%; Median home value: $513,300; Median year structure built: 1972; Homeowner vacancy rate: 0.0%; Median selected monthly owner costs: $3,390 with a mortgage, $1,461 without a mortgage; Median gross rent: $1,688 per month; Rental vacancy rate: 0.0%

Health Insurance: 96.0% have insurance; 88.3% have private insurance; 16.8% have public insurance; 4.0% do not have insurance; 0.0% of children under 18 do not have insurance

Transportation: Commute: 85.5% car, 4.8% public transportation, 1.3% walk, 7.7% work from home; Mean travel time to work: 34.2 minutes

CROSS RIVER (unincorporated postal area)
ZCTA: 10518

Covers a land area of 3.448 square miles and a water area of 0.054 square miles. Located at 41.27° N. Lat; 73.59° W. Long. Elevation is 338 feet.

Population: 1,246; Growth (since 2000): -19.7%; Density: 361.4 persons per square mile; Race: 95.2% White, 0.0% Black/African American, 4.8% Asian, 0.0% American Indian/Alaska Native, 0.0% Native Hawaiian/Other Pacific Islander, 0.0% Two or more races, 0.0% Hispanic of any race; Average household size: 2.93; Median age: 51.9; Age under 18: 16.3%; Age 65 and over: 25.9%; Males per 100 females: 90.4; Marriage status: 27.2% never married, 58.3% now married, 0.0% separated, 9.3% widowed, 5.2% divorced; Foreign born: 10.5%; Speak English only: 93.5%; With disability: 8.6%; Veterans: 7.6%; Ancestry: 29.1% Italian, 23.8% Irish, 13.6% English, 12.3% American, 8.9% Polish

Employment: 31.2% management, business, and financial, 9.8% computer, engineering, and science, 26.8% education, legal, community service, arts, and media, 3.8% healthcare practitioners, 6.9% service, 21.6% sales and office, 0.0% natural resources, construction, and maintenance, 0.0% production, transportation, and material moving

Income: Per capita: $74,590; Median household: $193,472; Average household: $213,463; Households with income of $100,000 or more: 73.2%; Poverty rate: 9.1%

Educational Attainment: High school diploma or higher: 98.4%; Bachelor's degree or higher: 81.5%; Graduate/professional degree or higher: 33.7%

School District(s)
Katonah-Lewisboro Union Free SD (KG-12)
  Enrollment: 3,135 . . . . (914) 763-7003
Housing: Homeownership rate: 95.5%; Median home value: $784,200; Median year structure built: 1986; Homeowner vacancy rate: 8.4%; Median selected monthly owner costs: $4,000 with a mortgage, $1,501 without a mortgage; Median gross rent: n/a per month; Rental vacancy rate: 0.0%
Health Insurance: 97.6% have insurance; 89.0% have private insurance; 29.2% have public insurance; 2.4% do not have insurance; 4.8% of children under 18 do not have insurance
Newspapers: Lewisboro Ledger (weekly circulation 2,100)
Transportation: Commute: 61.3% car, 20.1% public transportation, 6.9% walk, 11.8% work from home; Mean travel time to work: 42.5 minutes

CROTON FALLS (unincorporated postal area)
ZCTA: 10519

Covers a land area of 0.744 square miles and a water area of 0.025 square miles. Located at 41.35° N. Lat; 73.65° W. Long. Elevation is 269 feet.
Population: 185; Growth (since 2000): 18.6%; Density: 248.6 persons per square mile; Race: 79.5% White, 0.0% Black/African American, 20.5% Asian, 0.0% American Indian/Alaska Native, 0.0% Native Hawaiian/Other Pacific Islander, 0.0% Two or more races, 0.0% Hispanic of any race; Average household size: 1.88; Median age: 45.4; Age under 18: 10.8%; Age 65 and over: 23.8%; Males per 100 females: 91.5; Marriage status: 12.4% never married, 70.8% now married, 0.0% separated, 16.8% widowed, 0.0% divorced; Foreign born: 37.3%; Speak English only: 82.7%; With disability: 16.8%; Veterans: 6.7%; Ancestry: 30.8% German, 14.1% Dutch, 7.0% Irish, 5.9% English, 5.9% Italian
Employment: 0.0% management, business, and financial, 33.6% computer, engineering, and science, 0.0% education, legal, community service, arts, and media, 42.9% healthcare practitioners, 23.5% service, 0.0% sales and office, 0.0% natural resources, construction, and maintenance, 0.0% production, transportation, and material moving
Income: Per capita: $97,884; Median household: n/a; Average household: $189,487; Households with income of $100,000 or more: 56.7%; Poverty rate: 1.6%
Educational Attainment: High school diploma or higher: 100.0%; Bachelor's degree or higher: 57.0%; Graduate/professional degree or higher: 56.4%
Housing: Homeownership rate: 100.0%; Median home value: n/a; Median year structure built: 1944; Homeowner vacancy rate: 0.0%; Median selected monthly owner costs: $3,816 with a mortgage, $0 without a mortgage; Median gross rent: n/a per month; Rental vacancy rate: 0.0%
Health Insurance: 100.0% have insurance; 98.9% have private insurance; 23.8% have public insurance; 0.0% do not have insurance; 0.0% of children under 18 do not have insurance
Transportation: Commute: 58.0% car, 16.0% public transportation, 0.0% walk, 26.1% work from home; Mean travel time to work: 0.0 minutes

CROTON-ON-HUDSON (village). Covers a land area of 4.642 square miles and a water area of 6.038 square miles. Located at 41.21° N. Lat; 73.90° W. Long. Elevation is 161 feet.
History: During 1920s, fashionable haven for intellectuals such as Edna St. Vincent Millay, Doris Stevens, Stuart Chase and John Reed. Van Cortlandt Manor, a restored 18th-century Dutch-English manorhouse on 20 acres of what was once 86,000-acre estate is located here. Settled 1609, Incorporated 1898.
Population: 8,257; Growth (since 2000): 8.6%; Density: 1,778.6 persons per square mile; Race: 80.6% White, 6.8% Black/African American, 5.0% Asian, 0.5% American Indian/Alaska Native, 0.0% Native Hawaiian/Other Pacific Islander, 2.3% Two or more races, 11.2% Hispanic of any race; Average household size: 2.66; Median age: 43.7; Age under 18: 25.9%; Age 65 and over: 15.2%; Males per 100 females: 92.3; Marriage status: 24.0% never married, 60.9% now married, 2.2% separated, 5.9% widowed, 9.3% divorced; Foreign born: 15.4%; Speak English only: 82.3%; With disability: 6.7%; Veterans: 4.8%; Ancestry: 22.5% Italian, 20.0% Irish, 12.7% German, 5.1% English, 4.5% Polish
Employment: 19.4% management, business, and financial, 10.4% computer, engineering, and science, 23.5% education, legal, community service, arts, and media, 6.3% healthcare practitioners, 14.7% service,

17.5% sales and office, 4.2% natural resources, construction, and maintenance, 4.0% production, transportation, and material moving
Income: Per capita: $57,880; Median household: $124,708; Average household: $154,544; Households with income of $100,000 or more: 57.6%; Poverty rate: 3.9%
Educational Attainment: High school diploma or higher: 94.0%; Bachelor's degree or higher: 62.5%; Graduate/professional degree or higher: 33.0%

School District(s)
Croton-Harmon Union Free SD (KG-12)
  Enrollment: 1,650 . . . . (914) 271-4793
Housing: Homeownership rate: 72.2%; Median home value: $507,600; Median year structure built: 1955; Homeowner vacancy rate: 0.0%; Median selected monthly owner costs: $3,276 with a mortgage, $1,466 without a mortgage; Median gross rent: $1,597 per month; Rental vacancy rate: 1.3%
Health Insurance: 94.2% have insurance; 84.6% have private insurance; 20.1% have public insurance; 5.8% do not have insurance; 6.9% of children under 18 do not have insurance
Safety: Violent crime rate: 4.8 per 10,000 population; Property crime rate: 45.9 per 10,000 population
Newspapers: The Gazette (weekly circulation 3,000)
Transportation: Commute: 64.2% car, 24.2% public transportation, 4.3% walk, 6.4% work from home; Mean travel time to work: 39.7 minutes; Amtrak: Train service available.

CRUGERS (CDP). Covers a land area of 0.661 square miles and a water area of 0.574 square miles. Located at 41.23° N. Lat; 73.93° W. Long. Elevation is 98 feet.
Population: 1,541; Growth (since 2000): -12.0%; Density: 2,332.6 persons per square mile; Race: 85.2% White, 4.5% Black/African American, 4.0% Asian, 0.0% American Indian/Alaska Native, 0.0% Native Hawaiian/Other Pacific Islander, 0.6% Two or more races, 12.9% Hispanic of any race; Average household size: 1.65; Median age: 65.9; Age under 18: 10.6%; Age 65 and over: 51.1%; Males per 100 females: 81.3; Marriage status: 28.2% never married, 40.0% now married, 2.2% separated, 16.2% widowed, 15.6% divorced; Foreign born: 17.5%; Speak English only: 88.0%; With disability: 23.1%; Veterans: 11.6%; Ancestry: 18.8% Irish, 17.8% Italian, 14.4% Norwegian, 13.3% Danish, 8.8% German
Employment: 13.3% management, business, and financial, 0.0% computer, engineering, and science, 19.6% education, legal, community service, arts, and media, 0.0% healthcare practitioners, 29.5% service, 21.5% sales and office, 6.8% natural resources, construction, and maintenance, 9.3% production, transportation, and material moving
Income: Per capita: $35,014; Median household: $42,955; Average household: $61,371; Households with income of $100,000 or more: 17.2%; Poverty rate: 7.0%
Educational Attainment: High school diploma or higher: 81.6%; Bachelor's degree or higher: 35.1%; Graduate/professional degree or higher: 14.8%
Housing: Homeownership rate: 20.0%; Median home value: $415,100; Median year structure built: 1961; Homeowner vacancy rate: 0.0%; Median selected monthly owner costs: $3,190 with a mortgage, $1,367 without a mortgage; Median gross rent: $1,143 per month; Rental vacancy rate: 0.0%
Health Insurance: 100.0% have insurance; 78.7% have private insurance; 52.5% have public insurance; 0.0% do not have insurance; 0.0% of children under 18 do not have insurance
Transportation: Commute: 73.4% car, 15.7% public transportation, 3.8% walk, 5.7% work from home; Mean travel time to work: 35.2 minutes

DOBBS FERRY (village). Covers a land area of 2.429 square miles and a water area of 0.752 square miles. Located at 41.01° N. Lat; 73.87° W. Long. Elevation is 210 feet.
History: Named for Jeremiah Dobbs, who operated a ferry across the Hudson River. Site of Livingston Manor, where George Washington and Marshal Rochambeau of France are said to have planned the Yorktown Campaign. Seat of Mercy College. Incorporated 1873.
Population: 11,141; Growth (since 2000): 4.9%; Density: 4,586.2 persons per square mile; Race: 80.3% White, 6.1% Black/African American, 6.7% Asian, 0.3% American Indian/Alaska Native, 0.0% Native Hawaiian/Other Pacific Islander, 3.6% Two or more races, 11.1% Hispanic of any race; Average household size: 2.72; Median age: 40.2; Age under 18: 21.8%; Age 65 and over: 14.9%; Males per 100 females: 91.4; Marriage status: 34.9% never married, 53.6% now married, 1.1% separated, 4.4%

widowed, 7.1% divorced; Foreign born: 17.3%; Speak English only: 79.0%; With disability: 7.4%; Veterans: 4.7%; Ancestry: 23.0% Italian, 18.4% Irish, 10.2% German, 7.4% Polish, 4.7% English
Employment: 20.1% management, business, and financial, 7.2% computer, engineering, and science, 24.2% education, legal, community service, arts, and media, 8.5% healthcare practitioners, 13.3% service, 19.0% sales and office, 2.7% natural resources, construction, and maintenance, 5.0% production, transportation, and material moving
Income: Per capita: $60,490; Median household: $126,988; Average household: $177,255; Households with income of $100,000 or more: 63.6%; Poverty rate: 2.9%
Educational Attainment: High school diploma or higher: 94.7%; Bachelor's degree or higher: 60.0%; Graduate/professional degree or higher: 31.3%

School District(s)
Dobbs Ferry Union Free SD (KG-12)
    Enrollment: 1,499 . . . . (914) 693-1506
Greenburgh Eleven Union Free SD (KG-12)
    Enrollment: 98 . . . . (914) 693-8500
Greenburgh-North Castle Union Free SD (07-12)
    Enrollment: 28 . . . . (914) 693-4309

Four-year College(s)
Mercy College (Private, Not-for-profit)
    Enrollment: 9,506 . . . . (800) 637-2969
    Tuition: In-state $18,714; Out-of-state $18,714
Housing: Homeownership rate: 60.6%; Median home value: $617,700; Median year structure built: 1954; Homeowner vacancy rate: 1.2%; Median selected monthly owner costs: $3,733 with a mortgage, $1,501 without a mortgage; Median gross rent: $1,875 per month; Rental vacancy rate: 5.8%
Health Insurance: 94.7% have insurance; 84.2% have private insurance; 21.2% have public insurance; 5.3% do not have insurance; 2.0% of children under 18 do not have insurance
Safety: Violent crime rate: 3.6 per 10,000 population; Property crime rate: 80.0 per 10,000 population
Newspapers: Rivertowns Enterprise (weekly circulation 6,200)
Transportation: Commute: 64.0% car, 24.7% public transportation, 5.2% walk, 5.4% work from home; Mean travel time to work: 31.1 minutes
Additional Information Contacts
Village of Dobbs Ferry . . . . (914) 231-8504
    http://www.dobbsferry.com

EASTCHESTER (CDP).
Covers a land area of 3.294 square miles and a water area of 0.088 square miles. Located at 40.96° N. Lat; 73.81° W. Long. Elevation is 23 feet.
History: Laws for the region (of which Eastchester CDP is a part) were established in 1665, under an agreement called the "Eastchester Covenant." The covenant was a rare document for this period. It contained 26 provisions, such items as: education of children, disposition and upkeep of property, and support of a minister.
Population: 20,099; Growth (since 2000): 8.3%; Density: 6,102.6 persons per square mile; Race: 87.1% White, 1.5% Black/African American, 7.2% Asian, 0.3% American Indian/Alaska Native, 0.0% Native Hawaiian/Other Pacific Islander, 2.1% Two or more races, 6.1% Hispanic of any race; Average household size: 2.57; Median age: 43.9; Age under 18: 21.9%; Age 65 and over: 19.5%; Males per 100 females: 89.4; Marriage status: 28.1% never married, 59.0% now married, 1.0% separated, 6.8% widowed, 6.1% divorced; Foreign born: 17.2%; Speak English only: 80.2%; With disability: 8.3%; Veterans: 4.8%; Ancestry: 39.6% Italian, 17.8% Irish, 7.7% German, 6.8% American, 3.7% Russian
Employment: 26.0% management, business, and financial, 4.8% computer, engineering, and science, 20.5% education, legal, community service, arts, and media, 6.0% healthcare practitioners, 11.3% service, 24.2% sales and office, 5.1% natural resources, construction, and maintenance, 2.2% production, transportation, and material moving
Income: Per capita: $62,109; Median household: $119,531; Average household: $156,863; Households with income of $100,000 or more: 57.0%; Poverty rate: 2.7%
Educational Attainment: High school diploma or higher: 93.9%; Bachelor's degree or higher: 59.8%; Graduate/professional degree or higher: 30.4%

School District(s)
Eastchester Union Free SD (KG-12)
    Enrollment: 3,210 . . . . (914) 793-6130

Tuckahoe Union Free SD (KG-12)
    Enrollment: 1,178 . . . . (914) 337-6600
Housing: Homeownership rate: 80.4%; Median home value: $583,100; Median year structure built: 1951; Homeowner vacancy rate: 2.1%; Median selected monthly owner costs: $3,287 with a mortgage, $1,501 without a mortgage; Median gross rent: $1,775 per month; Rental vacancy rate: 3.1%
Health Insurance: 97.5% have insurance; 88.5% have private insurance; 23.3% have public insurance; 2.5% do not have insurance; 0.2% of children under 18 do not have insurance
Transportation: Commute: 67.8% car, 23.6% public transportation, 3.2% walk, 5.1% work from home; Mean travel time to work: 33.1 minutes

EASTCHESTER (town).
Covers a land area of 4.853 square miles and a water area of 0.088 square miles. Located at 40.95° N. Lat; 73.81° W. Long. Elevation is 23 feet.
History: Named for the town of Chester in England. Once a township (formed 1788) extending from the present Bronx North to Scarsdale; Mt. Vernon city was separated from it in 1892; the section South of Mt. Vernon was annexed by N.Y. city in 1895.
Population: 33,183; Growth (since 2000): 6.0%; Density: 6,837.5 persons per square mile; Race: 85.0% White, 2.7% Black/African American, 6.5% Asian, 0.2% American Indian/Alaska Native, 0.0% Native Hawaiian/Other Pacific Islander, 2.7% Two or more races, 7.4% Hispanic of any race; Average household size: 2.57; Median age: 42.5; Age under 18: 22.5%; Age 65 and over: 17.7%; Males per 100 females: 88.7; Marriage status: 29.9% never married, 56.3% now married, 1.6% separated, 6.4% widowed, 7.4% divorced; Foreign born: 18.2%; Speak English only: 78.1%; With disability: 8.2%; Veterans: 4.5%; Ancestry: 32.9% Italian, 19.8% Irish, 9.2% German, 6.1% American, 4.9% English
Employment: 25.9% management, business, and financial, 4.3% computer, engineering, and science, 20.4% education, legal, community service, arts, and media, 6.5% healthcare practitioners, 12.9% service, 22.2% sales and office, 5.6% natural resources, construction, and maintenance, 2.1% production, transportation, and material moving
Income: Per capita: $70,816; Median household: $116,014; Average household: $181,054; Households with income of $100,000 or more: 55.3%; Poverty rate: 3.2%
Educational Attainment: High school diploma or higher: 94.2%; Bachelor's degree or higher: 60.5%; Graduate/professional degree or higher: 31.7%

School District(s)
Eastchester Union Free SD (KG-12)
    Enrollment: 3,210 . . . . (914) 793-6130
Tuckahoe Union Free SD (KG-12)
    Enrollment: 1,178 . . . . (914) 337-6600
Housing: Homeownership rate: 73.4%; Median home value: $606,400; Median year structure built: 1950; Homeowner vacancy rate: 1.9%; Median selected monthly owner costs: $3,461 with a mortgage, $1,501 without a mortgage; Median gross rent: $1,788 per month; Rental vacancy rate: 3.8%
Health Insurance: 96.1% have insurance; 86.9% have private insurance; 23.0% have public insurance; 3.9% do not have insurance; 0.6% of children under 18 do not have insurance
Safety: Violent crime rate: 2.5 per 10,000 population; Property crime rate: 85.3 per 10,000 population
Transportation: Commute: 60.1% car, 28.9% public transportation, 4.2% walk, 5.9% work from home; Mean travel time to work: 35.4 minutes
Additional Information Contacts
Town of Eastchester . . . . (914) 771-3351
    http://www.eastchester.org

ELMSFORD (village).
Covers a land area of 1.027 square miles and a water area of 0 square miles. Located at 41.05° N. Lat; 73.81° W. Long. Elevation is 177 feet.
History: Incorporated 1910.
Population: 4,942; Growth (since 2000): 5.7%; Density: 4,813.4 persons per square mile; Race: 41.1% White, 21.8% Black/African American, 7.1% Asian, 0.5% American Indian/Alaska Native, 0.0% Native Hawaiian/Other Pacific Islander, 2.8% Two or more races, 44.4% Hispanic of any race; Average household size: 3.29; Median age: 35.5; Age under 18: 18.9%; Age 65 and over: 11.4%; Males per 100 females: 103.8; Marriage status: 41.3% never married, 45.8% now married, 1.6% separated, 3.9% widowed, 9.0% divorced; Foreign born: 42.0%; Speak English only: 44.9%;

With disability: 8.8%; Veterans: 3.1%; Ancestry: 8.7% Italian, 7.4% Irish, 6.3% Haitian, 4.0% German, 2.6% American
Employment: 10.7% management, business, and financial, 8.2% computer, engineering, and science, 12.5% education, legal, community service, arts, and media, 4.5% healthcare practitioners, 31.4% service, 14.0% sales and office, 11.2% natural resources, construction, and maintenance, 7.5% production, transportation, and material moving
Income: Per capita: $35,728; Median household: $86,066; Average household: $112,669; Households with income of $100,000 or more: 38.1%; Poverty rate: 15.3%
Educational Attainment: High school diploma or higher: 77.2%; Bachelor's degree or higher: 35.9%; Graduate/professional degree or higher: 18.2%

School District(s)
Elmsford Union Free SD (PK-12)
    Enrollment: 1,023 . . . . (914) 592-6632
Vocational/Technical School(s)
Westchester School for Dental Assistant (Private, For-profit)
    Enrollment: 66 . . . . (914) 682-9001
    Tuition: $10,500
Housing: Homeownership rate: 47.7%; Median home value: $420,400; Median year structure built: 1955; Homeowner vacancy rate: 3.8%; Median selected monthly owner costs: $3,261 with a mortgage, $1,317 without a mortgage; Median gross rent: $1,694 per month; Rental vacancy rate: 3.4%
Health Insurance: 82.7% have insurance; 65.9% have private insurance; 26.1% have public insurance; 17.3% do not have insurance; 5.2% of children under 18 do not have insurance
Safety: Violent crime rate: 9.9 per 10,000 population; Property crime rate: 27.6 per 10,000 population
Transportation: Commute: 72.1% car, 13.9% public transportation, 8.0% walk, 3.7% work from home; Mean travel time to work: 24.5 minutes
Additional Information Contacts
Village of Elmsford . . . . (914) 592-6555
    http://www.elmsfordny.org

FAIRVIEW (CDP). Covers a land area of 0.428 square miles and a water area of 0.003 square miles. Located at 41.04° N. Lat; 73.80° W. Long. Elevation is 217 feet.
Population: 3,013; Growth (since 2000): 4.4%; Density: 7,037.5 persons per square mile; Race: 26.8% White, 61.7% Black/African American, 3.8% Asian, 2.0% American Indian/Alaska Native, 0.0% Native Hawaiian/Other Pacific Islander, 1.2% Two or more races, 24.9% Hispanic of any race; Average household size: 3.00; Median age: 30.9; Age under 18: 25.8%; Age 65 and over: 10.0%; Males per 100 females: 88.0; Marriage status: 51.6% never married, 35.3% now married, 1.6% separated, 3.5% widowed, 9.6% divorced; Foreign born: 35.0%; Speak English only: 61.3%; With disability: 6.0%; Veterans: 1.9%; Ancestry: 9.6% Haitian, 4.7% African, 3.9% Jamaican, 3.3% Guyanese, 3.2% American
Employment: 6.0% management, business, and financial, 2.5% computer, engineering, and science, 4.3% education, legal, community service, arts, and media, 2.5% healthcare practitioners, 36.8% service, 27.8% sales and office, 5.8% natural resources, construction, and maintenance, 14.4% production, transportation, and material moving
Income: Per capita: $25,774; Median household: $39,722; Average household: $72,155; Households with income of $100,000 or more: 26.2%; Poverty rate: 11.9%
Educational Attainment: High school diploma or higher: 83.2%; Bachelor's degree or higher: 14.8%; Graduate/professional degree or higher: 6.3%
Housing: Homeownership rate: 35.3%; Median home value: $359,200; Median year structure built: 1964; Homeowner vacancy rate: 0.0%; Median selected monthly owner costs: $3,000 with a mortgage, $1,205 without a mortgage; Median gross rent: $1,116 per month; Rental vacancy rate: 4.0%
Health Insurance: 89.8% have insurance; 45.2% have private insurance; 51.0% have public insurance; 10.2% do not have insurance; 2.7% of children under 18 do not have insurance
Transportation: Commute: 76.3% car, 11.2% public transportation, 7.5% walk, 4.3% work from home; Mean travel time to work: 22.5 minutes

GOLDEN'S BRIDGE (CDP). Covers a land area of 2.430 square miles and a water area of 0.133 square miles. Located at 41.28° N. Lat; 73.67° W. Long. Elevation is 217 feet.
Population: 1,724; Growth (since 2000): 9.3%; Density: 709.6 persons per square mile; Race: 90.6% White, 2.1% Black/African American, 2.8% Asian, 0.0% American Indian/Alaska Native, 0.0% Native Hawaiian/Other Pacific Islander, 1.0% Two or more races, 4.5% Hispanic of any race; Average household size: 2.68; Median age: 46.6; Age under 18: 25.6%; Age 65 and over: 19.1%; Males per 100 females: 92.4; Marriage status: 19.6% never married, 64.7% now married, 0.5% separated, 7.6% widowed, 8.1% divorced; Foreign born: 9.9%; Speak English only: 88.7%; With disability: 5.7%; Veterans: 1.9%; Ancestry: 19.3% Irish, 17.9% Italian, 12.4% German, 11.7% Eastern European, 7.3% English
Employment: 36.7% management, business, and financial, 4.1% computer, engineering, and science, 14.5% education, legal, community service, arts, and media, 9.1% healthcare practitioners, 16.3% service, 16.3% sales and office, 1.9% natural resources, construction, and maintenance, 1.0% production, transportation, and material moving
Income: Per capita: $75,300; Median household: $133,462; Average household: $200,371; Households with income of $100,000 or more: 66.9%; Poverty rate: 3.4%
Educational Attainment: High school diploma or higher: 100.0%; Bachelor's degree or higher: 72.1%; Graduate/professional degree or higher: 36.0%

School District(s)
Katonah-Lewisboro Union Free SD (KG-12)
    Enrollment: 3,135 . . . . (914) 763-7003
Housing: Homeownership rate: 89.9%; Median home value: $596,100; Median year structure built: 1970; Homeowner vacancy rate: 0.0%; Median selected monthly owner costs: $3,468 with a mortgage, $1,432 without a mortgage; Median gross rent: n/a per month; Rental vacancy rate: 0.0%
Health Insurance: 98.4% have insurance; 88.9% have private insurance; 25.7% have public insurance; 1.6% do not have insurance; 4.4% of children under 18 do not have insurance
Transportation: Commute: 80.2% car, 11.9% public transportation, 1.1% walk, 6.8% work from home; Mean travel time to work: 39.3 minutes

GRANITE SPRINGS (unincorporated postal area)
ZCTA: 10527
    Covers a land area of 2.444 square miles and a water area of 0.008 square miles. Located at 41.32° N. Lat; 73.77° W. Long. Elevation is 515 feet.
Population: 821; Growth (since 2000): -25.2%; Density: 335.9 persons per square mile; Race: 97.1% White, 0.4% Black/African American, 2.6% Asian, 0.0% American Indian/Alaska Native, 0.0% Native Hawaiian/Other Pacific Islander, 0.0% Two or more races, 0.2% Hispanic of any race; Average household size: 3.20; Median age: 46.2; Age under 18: 30.0%; Age 65 and over: 18.3%; Males per 100 females: 102.2; Marriage status: 21.6% never married, 68.0% now married, 4.5% separated, 2.0% widowed, 8.5% divorced; Foreign born: 2.8%; Speak English only: 96.2%; With disability: 6.1%; Veterans: 1.2%; Ancestry: 30.7% Italian, 24.8% Irish, 10.6% German, 8.9% English, 3.7% Russian
Employment: 20.9% management, business, and financial, 4.1% computer, engineering, and science, 20.4% education, legal, community service, arts, and media, 13.7% healthcare practitioners, 10.1% service, 22.5% sales and office, 4.3% natural resources, construction, and maintenance, 4.1% production, transportation, and material moving
Income: Per capita: $54,136; Median household: $158,977; Average household: $173,620; Households with income of $100,000 or more: 80.5%; Poverty rate: 1.2%
Educational Attainment: High school diploma or higher: 94.9%; Bachelor's degree or higher: 67.5%; Graduate/professional degree or higher: 50.0%
Housing: Homeownership rate: 100.0%; Median home value: $636,900; Median year structure built: 1975; Homeowner vacancy rate: 0.0%; Median selected monthly owner costs: $3,324 with a mortgage, $1,501 without a mortgage; Median gross rent: n/a per month; Rental vacancy rate: 0.0%
Health Insurance: 98.5% have insurance; 91.5% have private insurance; 18.6% have public insurance; 1.5% do not have insurance; 0.0% of children under 18 do not have insurance
Transportation: Commute: 84.5% car, 11.8% public transportation, 0.0% walk, 2.3% work from home; Mean travel time to work: 39.3 minutes

GREENBURGH (town). Covers a land area of 30.309 square miles and a water area of 5.805 square miles. Located at 41.03° N. Lat; 73.84° W. Long. Elevation is 348 feet.

History: The Romer-Van Tassel House served as the first town hall from 1793 to the early 19th century. It was added to the National Register of Historic Places in 1994.

Population: 91,799; Growth (since 2000): 5.8%; Density: 3,028.8 persons per square mile; Race: 68.2% White, 13.1% Black/African American, 9.9% Asian, 0.4% American Indian/Alaska Native, 0.0% Native Hawaiian/Other Pacific Islander, 2.8% Two or more races, 15.2% Hispanic of any race; Average household size: 2.69; Median age: 42.4; Age under 18: 22.0%; Age 65 and over: 17.1%; Males per 100 females: 89.5; Marriage status: 31.9% never married, 55.2% now married, 1.4% separated, 5.1% widowed, 7.8% divorced; Foreign born: 22.8%; Speak English only: 71.9%; With disability: 7.6%; Veterans: 3.8%; Ancestry: 14.9% Italian, 12.4% Irish, 7.8% German, 5.4% American, 4.7% Polish

Employment: 21.8% management, business, and financial, 7.2% computer, engineering, and science, 21.5% education, legal, community service, arts, and media, 8.1% healthcare practitioners, 14.3% service, 18.8% sales and office, 3.9% natural resources, construction, and maintenance, 4.5% production, transportation, and material moving

Income: Per capita: $62,358; Median household: $120,256; Average household: $168,520; Households with income of $100,000 or more: 59.0%; Poverty rate: 4.8%

Educational Attainment: High school diploma or higher: 93.4%; Bachelor's degree or higher: 61.4%; Graduate/professional degree or higher: 33.8%

Housing: Homeownership rate: 72.7%; Median home value: $552,200; Median year structure built: 1958; Homeowner vacancy rate: 0.7%; Median selected monthly owner costs: $3,537 with a mortgage, $1,501 without a mortgage; Median gross rent: $1,721 per month; Rental vacancy rate: 5.0%

Health Insurance: 94.8% have insurance; 83.0% have private insurance; 23.8% have public insurance; 5.2% do not have insurance; 2.3% of children under 18 do not have insurance

Safety: Violent crime rate: 10.9 per 10,000 population; Property crime rate: 133.5 per 10,000 population

Transportation: Commute: 66.4% car, 22.9% public transportation, 3.4% walk, 6.2% work from home; Mean travel time to work: 33.5 minutes

Additional Information Contacts
Town of Greenburgh . . . . (914) 993-1500
  http://www.greenburghny.com

GREENVILLE (CDP). Covers a land area of 2.562 square miles and a water area of 0.035 square miles. Located at 41.00° N. Lat; 73.82° W. Long. Elevation is 249 feet.

History: Residents popularly refer to the Greenville area as "Edgemont". Edgemont was originally a development designed by different architects for summer homes for Manhattanites.

Population: 7,087; Growth (since 2000): -18.1%; Density: 2,765.9 persons per square mile; Race: 67.4% White, 3.0% Black/African American, 25.3% Asian, 0.0% American Indian/Alaska Native, 0.0% Native Hawaiian/Other Pacific Islander, 4.0% Two or more races, 4.2% Hispanic of any race; Average household size: 3.21; Median age: 42.9; Age under 18: 29.3%; Age 65 and over: 15.1%; Males per 100 females: 94.4; Marriage status: 25.8% never married, 64.2% now married, 0.6% separated, 4.3% widowed, 5.6% divorced; Foreign born: 22.5%; Speak English only: 69.5%; With disability: 3.8%; Veterans: 1.6%; Ancestry: 8.4% Italian, 7.5% Russian, 7.3% Polish, 6.3% German, 5.6% American

Employment: 27.2% management, business, and financial, 10.3% computer, engineering, and science, 25.4% education, legal, community service, arts, and media, 11.4% healthcare practitioners, 5.6% service, 14.8% sales and office, 2.9% natural resources, construction, and maintenance, 2.4% production, transportation, and material moving

Income: Per capita: $87,077; Median household: $212,042; Average household: $279,820; Households with income of $100,000 or more: 79.5%; Poverty rate: 3.8%

Educational Attainment: High school diploma or higher: 95.9%; Bachelor's degree or higher: 79.1%; Graduate/professional degree or higher: 52.2%

Housing: Homeownership rate: 93.9%; Median home value: $905,200; Median year structure built: 1959; Homeowner vacancy rate: 0.0%; Median selected monthly owner costs: $4,000+ with a mortgage, $1,501 without a mortgage; Median gross rent: $1,744 per month; Rental vacancy rate: 0.0%

Health Insurance: 97.9% have insurance; 90.9% have private insurance; 16.3% have public insurance; 2.1% do not have insurance; 0.7% of children under 18 do not have insurance

Transportation: Commute: 48.6% car, 41.2% public transportation, 0.8% walk, 8.7% work from home; Mean travel time to work: 45.5 minutes

HARRISON (town/village). Covers a land area of 16.766 square miles and a water area of 0.603 square miles. Located at 41.03° N. Lat; 73.72° W. Long. Elevation is 69 feet.

History: Harrison was established in 1696 by John Harrison, who was given 24 hours to ride his horse around an area which would become his as payment to a debt owed him by the King. The town was named for Harrison, and was incorporated as a town on March 7, 1788.

Population: 28,319; Growth (since 2000): 17.2%; Density: 1,689.1 persons per square mile; Race: 78.6% White, 4.5% Black/African American, 8.9% Asian, 0.5% American Indian/Alaska Native, 0.0% Native Hawaiian/Other Pacific Islander, 3.3% Two or more races, 12.4% Hispanic of any race; Average household size: 2.88; Median age: 34.9; Age under 18: 21.6%; Age 65 and over: 13.8%; Males per 100 females: 88.5; Marriage status: 39.0% never married, 49.0% now married, 1.5% separated, 5.0% widowed, 7.0% divorced; Foreign born: 23.1%; Speak English only: 69.5%; With disability: 8.5%; Veterans: 2.9%; Ancestry: 29.4% Italian, 12.0% Irish, 7.6% German, 6.8% American, 4.5% Russian

Employment: 23.2% management, business, and financial, 4.6% computer, engineering, and science, 16.1% education, legal, community service, arts, and media, 4.6% healthcare practitioners, 17.2% service, 25.2% sales and office, 6.5% natural resources, construction, and maintenance, 2.5% production, transportation, and material moving

Income: Per capita: $64,519; Median household: $117,453; Average household: $209,774; Households with income of $100,000 or more: 60.2%; Poverty rate: 6.6%

Educational Attainment: High school diploma or higher: 91.7%; Bachelor's degree or higher: 54.0%; Graduate/professional degree or higher: 24.4%

School District(s)
Harrison Central SD (KG-12)
  Enrollment: 3,600 . . . . (914) 630-3021
Vocational/Technical School(s)
Southern Westchester BOCES-Practical Nursing Program (Public)
  Enrollment: 121 . . . . (914) 592-0849
  Tuition: $13,800

Housing: Homeownership rate: 63.8%; Median home value: $824,300; Median year structure built: 1958; Homeowner vacancy rate: 0.2%; Median selected monthly owner costs: $4,000+ with a mortgage, $1,501 without a mortgage; Median gross rent: $2,138 per month; Rental vacancy rate: 2.2%

Health Insurance: 95.7% have insurance; 82.6% have private insurance; 22.4% have public insurance; 4.3% do not have insurance; 2.7% of children under 18 do not have insurance

Safety: Violent crime rate: 0.4 per 10,000 population; Property crime rate: 40.7 per 10,000 population

Transportation: Commute: 63.4% car, 20.9% public transportation, 8.2% walk, 6.6% work from home; Mean travel time to work: 30.5 minutes

Additional Information Contacts
Village and Town of Harrison . . . . (914) 670-3000
  http://www.harrison-ny.gov

HARTSDALE (CDP). Covers a land area of 0.895 square miles and a water area of 0 square miles. Located at 41.02° N. Lat; 73.80° W. Long. Elevation is 184 feet.

History: The intersection of Central Park Avenue and Hartsdale Avenue was named "Hart's Corners" after Robert Hart, one of these farmers who successfully bid for the land, and in the mid 1800s the entire area became known as "Hartsdale".

Population: 5,114; Growth (since 2000): -48.0%; Density: 5,713.6 persons per square mile; Race: 60.1% White, 6.3% Black/African American, 19.5% Asian, 0.0% American Indian/Alaska Native, 0.0% Native Hawaiian/Other Pacific Islander, 3.5% Two or more races, 16.9% Hispanic of any race; Average household size: 1.96; Median age: 50.1; Age under 18: 14.0%; Age 65 and over: 26.0%; Males per 100 females: 80.9; Marriage status: 31.1% never married, 51.1% now married, 0.9% separated, 4.9% widowed, 12.8% divorced; Foreign born: 31.6%; Speak English only: 63.0%; With disability: 7.7%; Veterans: 1.9%; Ancestry: 17.3% Italian, 11.1% Irish, 7.3% American, 6.0% German, 5.3% Polish

Employment: 23.4% management, business, and financial, 7.9% computer, engineering, and science, 26.4% education, legal, community service, arts, and media, 9.1% healthcare practitioners, 4.9% service, 21.4% sales and office, 3.3% natural resources, construction, and maintenance, 3.6% production, transportation, and material moving
Income: Per capita: $59,169; Median household: $81,467; Average household: $115,504; Households with income of $100,000 or more: 43.6%; Poverty rate: 8.9%
Educational Attainment: High school diploma or higher: 96.2%; Bachelor's degree or higher: 69.2%; Graduate/professional degree or higher: 40.8%

School District(s)
Greenburgh Central SD (PK-12)
    Enrollment: 1,894 . . . . (914) 761-6000
Housing: Homeownership rate: 74.2%; Median home value: $246,700; Median year structure built: 1960; Homeowner vacancy rate: 1.2%; Median selected monthly owner costs: $1,877 with a mortgage, $363 without a mortgage; Median gross rent: $1,735 per month; Rental vacancy rate: 13.5%
Health Insurance: 96.5% have insurance; 80.7% have private insurance; 31.9% have public insurance; 3.5% do not have insurance; 0.0% of children under 18 do not have insurance
Transportation: Commute: 53.0% car, 31.5% public transportation, 3.3% walk, 10.3% work from home; Mean travel time to work: 37.6 minutes

HASTINGS-ON-HUDSON (village). Covers a land area of 1.952 square miles and a water area of 0.961 square miles. Located at 40.99° N. Lat; 73.88° W. Long. Elevation is 125 feet.
History: Incorporated 1879.
Population: 7,993; Growth (since 2000): 4.5%; Density: 4,094.0 persons per square mile; Race: 90.0% White, 4.2% Black/African American, 2.4% Asian, 0.0% American Indian/Alaska Native, 0.0% Native Hawaiian/Other Pacific Islander, 1.8% Two or more races, 6.0% Hispanic of any race; Average household size: 2.60; Median age: 44.9; Age under 18: 24.6%; Age 65 and over: 18.9%; Males per 100 females: 89.4; Marriage status: 30.2% never married, 56.9% now married, 1.4% separated, 4.4% widowed, 8.5% divorced; Foreign born: 11.1%; Speak English only: 86.8%; With disability: 7.0%; Veterans: 4.7%; Ancestry: 17.7% Irish, 11.6% Italian, 10.8% German, 8.3% English, 6.2% Russian
Employment: 21.8% management, business, and financial, 9.6% computer, engineering, and science, 30.7% education, legal, community service, arts, and media, 8.3% healthcare practitioners, 9.7% service, 14.6% sales and office, 2.5% natural resources, construction, and maintenance, 2.8% production, transportation, and material moving
Income: Per capita: $68,407; Median household: $127,143; Average household: $184,200; Households with income of $100,000 or more: 61.3%; Poverty rate: 4.1%
Educational Attainment: High school diploma or higher: 97.6%; Bachelor's degree or higher: 71.8%; Graduate/professional degree or higher: 42.0%

School District(s)
Greenburgh-Graham Union Free SD (KG-12)
    Enrollment: 100 . . . . (914) 478-1106
Hastings-On-Hudson Union Free SD (KG-12)
    Enrollment: 1,608 . . . . (914) 478-6205
Housing: Homeownership rate: 73.8%; Median home value: $612,900; Median year structure built: 1942; Homeowner vacancy rate: 1.3%; Median selected monthly owner costs: $3,651 with a mortgage, $1,501 without a mortgage; Median gross rent: $1,855 per month; Rental vacancy rate: 3.3%
Health Insurance: 96.2% have insurance; 85.1% have private insurance; 23.2% have public insurance; 3.8% do not have insurance; 3.8% of children under 18 do not have insurance
Safety: Violent crime rate: 3.8 per 10,000 population; Property crime rate: 82.6 per 10,000 population
Transportation: Commute: 53.5% car, 31.5% public transportation, 3.9% walk, 9.8% work from home; Mean travel time to work: 39.1 minutes
Additional Information Contacts
Village of Hastings-on-Hudson . . . . (914) 478-3400
    http://www.hastingsgov.org

HAWTHORNE (CDP). Covers a land area of 1.093 square miles and a water area of 0 square miles. Located at 41.10° N. Lat; 73.80° W. Long. Elevation is 282 feet.
Population: 4,644; Growth (since 2000): -8.6%; Density: 4,249.0 persons per square mile; Race: 85.1% White, 1.1% Black/African American, 5.0% Asian, 0.0% American Indian/Alaska Native, 0.0% Native Hawaiian/Other Pacific Islander, 1.0% Two or more races, 12.3% Hispanic of any race; Average household size: 2.93; Median age: 45.1; Age under 18: 22.0%; Age 65 and over: 18.8%; Males per 100 females: 95.8; Marriage status: 26.3% never married, 62.3% now married, 0.8% separated, 4.5% widowed, 7.0% divorced; Foreign born: 13.3%; Speak English only: 79.4%; With disability: 12.4%; Veterans: 5.8%; Ancestry: 45.0% Italian, 18.8% Irish, 8.2% German, 3.9% American, 2.9% Croatian
Employment: 23.1% management, business, and financial, 4.0% computer, engineering, and science, 15.3% education, legal, community service, arts, and media, 6.3% healthcare practitioners, 18.4% service, 19.3% sales and office, 8.2% natural resources, construction, and maintenance, 5.4% production, transportation, and material moving
Income: Per capita: $42,236; Median household: $94,135; Average household: $122,393; Households with income of $100,000 or more: 48.4%; Poverty rate: 3.9%
Educational Attainment: High school diploma or higher: 90.8%; Bachelor's degree or higher: 46.0%; Graduate/professional degree or higher: 22.5%

School District(s)
Hawthorne-Cedar Knolls Union Free SD (KG-12)
    Enrollment: 240 . . . . (914) 749-2903
Mount Pleasant Central SD (KG-12)
    Enrollment: 1,901 . . . . (914) 769-5500
Housing: Homeownership rate: 84.4%; Median home value: $504,400; Median year structure built: 1956; Homeowner vacancy rate: 0.0%; Median selected monthly owner costs: $3,395 with a mortgage, $1,348 without a mortgage; Median gross rent: $1,529 per month; Rental vacancy rate: 2.8%
Health Insurance: 97.8% have insurance; 83.1% have private insurance; 28.6% have public insurance; 2.2% do not have insurance; 0.0% of children under 18 do not have insurance
Transportation: Commute: 81.9% car, 11.9% public transportation, 1.5% walk, 4.6% work from home; Mean travel time to work: 29.6 minutes

HERITAGE HILLS (CDP). Covers a land area of 1.864 square miles and a water area of 0.039 square miles. Located at 41.34° N. Lat; 73.70° W. Long. Elevation is 587 feet.
History: This community in Northern Westchester is located in the town of Somers, N.Y. and was designed to enhance the quality of living for its residents. It is a self contained complex of over 2,500 units on 1,100 acres of beautiful countryside, 40% of which will remain as open space.
Population: 4,481; Growth (since 2000): 21.7%; Density: 2,404.6 persons per square mile; Race: 96.1% White, 1.3% Black/African American, 0.7% Asian, 1.0% American Indian/Alaska Native, 0.0% Native Hawaiian/Other Pacific Islander, 0.0% Two or more races, 5.5% Hispanic of any race; Average household size: 1.84; Median age: 69.8; Age under 18: 6.1%; Age 65 and over: 63.6%; Males per 100 females: 65.0; Marriage status: 11.2% never married, 62.0% now married, 0.1% separated, 16.1% widowed, 10.7% divorced; Foreign born: 10.9%; Speak English only: 90.5%; With disability: 19.3%; Veterans: 13.6%; Ancestry: 29.4% Italian, 19.0% Irish, 9.5% German, 8.4% English, 7.3% Russian
Employment: 21.5% management, business, and financial, 3.9% computer, engineering, and science, 22.0% education, legal, community service, arts, and media, 4.8% healthcare practitioners, 6.7% service, 29.4% sales and office, 10.0% natural resources, construction, and maintenance, 1.6% production, transportation, and material moving
Income: Per capita: $53,224; Median household: $75,682; Average household: $97,947; Households with income of $100,000 or more: 36.8%; Poverty rate: 5.2%
Educational Attainment: High school diploma or higher: 96.4%; Bachelor's degree or higher: 53.0%; Graduate/professional degree or higher: 23.2%
Housing: Homeownership rate: 88.5%; Median home value: $421,100; Median year structure built: 1985; Homeowner vacancy rate: 1.8%; Median selected monthly owner costs: $2,266 with a mortgage, $1,099 without a mortgage; Median gross rent: $2,341 per month; Rental vacancy rate: 0.0%

Health Insurance: 98.6% have insurance; 80.6% have private insurance; 69.6% have public insurance; 1.4% do not have insurance; 0.0% of children under 18 do not have insurance
Transportation: Commute: 86.4% car, 7.7% public transportation, 0.0% walk, 5.9% work from home; Mean travel time to work: 37.2 minutes

IRVINGTON (village). Covers a land area of 2.773 square miles and a water area of 1.290 square miles. Located at 41.03° N. Lat; 73.87° W. Long. Elevation is 125 feet.
History: Here at Nevis, once the estate of Alexander Hamilton's son, are a Columbia University arboretum and a children's Museum. Originally called Dearman; renamed (1857) for Washington Irving, who bought the estate Sunnyside (extant) here in 1835. Settled c.1655, Incorporated 1872.
Population: 6,588; Growth (since 2000): -0.6%; Density: 2,375.5 persons per square mile; Race: 88.5% White, 0.4% Black/African American, 7.8% Asian, 0.0% American Indian/Alaska Native, 0.1% Native Hawaiian/Other Pacific Islander, 1.9% Two or more races, 6.6% Hispanic of any race; Average household size: 2.80; Median age: 42.7; Age under 18: 28.5%; Age 65 and over: 14.9%; Males per 100 females: 90.6; Marriage status: 25.7% never married, 62.3% now married, 2.5% separated, 5.6% widowed, 6.4% divorced; Foreign born: 11.4%; Speak English only: 84.4%; With disability: 6.2%; Veterans: 4.6%; Ancestry: 19.5% Irish, 17.1% Italian, 10.4% German, 6.2% Polish, 5.9% American
Employment: 28.4% management, business, and financial, 8.4% computer, engineering, and science, 26.2% education, legal, community service, arts, and media, 8.3% healthcare practitioners, 7.3% service, 15.1% sales and office, 5.0% natural resources, construction, and maintenance, 1.3% production, transportation, and material moving
Income: Per capita: $81,137; Median household: $133,194; Average household: $227,642; Households with income of $100,000 or more: 64.8%; Poverty rate: 5.7%
Educational Attainment: High school diploma or higher: 97.1%; Bachelor's degree or higher: 71.6%; Graduate/professional degree or higher: 40.6%

School District(s)
Irvington Union Free SD (KG-12)
    Enrollment: 1,770 . . . . (914) 591-8501
Housing: Homeownership rate: 81.4%; Median home value: $670,200; Median year structure built: 1955; Homeowner vacancy rate: 2.1%; Median selected monthly owner costs: $4,000+ with a mortgage, $1,411 without a mortgage; Median gross rent: $1,495 per month; Rental vacancy rate: 7.3%
Health Insurance: 98.3% have insurance; 90.0% have private insurance; 17.9% have public insurance; 1.7% do not have insurance; 0.0% of children under 18 do not have insurance
Safety: Violent crime rate: 4.5 per 10,000 population; Property crime rate: 24.2 per 10,000 population
Transportation: Commute: 61.6% car, 26.4% public transportation, 3.2% walk, 8.7% work from home; Mean travel time to work: 36.3 minutes
Additional Information Contacts
Village of Irvington . . . . (914) 591-7070
    http://www.irvingtonny.gov

JEFFERSON VALLEY-YORKTOWN (CDP). Covers a land area of 6.926 square miles and a water area of 0.096 square miles. Located at 41.32° N. Lat; 73.80° W. Long.
Population: 14,533; Growth (since 2000): -2.4%; Density: 2,098.4 persons per square mile; Race: 87.2% White, 3.9% Black/African American, 4.4% Asian, 1.0% American Indian/Alaska Native, 0.0% Native Hawaiian/Other Pacific Islander, 2.1% Two or more races, 10.3% Hispanic of any race; Average household size: 2.78; Median age: 45.9; Age under 18: 23.8%; Age 65 and over: 20.5%; Males per 100 females: 91.3; Marriage status: 23.9% never married, 61.6% now married, 0.8% separated, 7.7% widowed, 6.8% divorced; Foreign born: 10.4%; Speak English only: 85.2%; With disability: 9.6%; Veterans: 5.8%; Ancestry: 35.9% Italian, 23.6% Irish, 12.9% German, 4.8% Polish, 4.3% American
Employment: 18.3% management, business, and financial, 4.6% computer, engineering, and science, 19.8% education, legal, community service, arts, and media, 7.6% healthcare practitioners, 12.7% service, 25.8% sales and office, 6.3% natural resources, construction, and maintenance, 4.9% production, transportation, and material moving
Income: Per capita: $50,230; Median household: $121,543; Average household: $136,386; Households with income of $100,000 or more: 61.0%; Poverty rate: 1.9%

Educational Attainment: High school diploma or higher: 95.1%; Bachelor's degree or higher: 50.3%; Graduate/professional degree or higher: 26.0%
Housing: Homeownership rate: 91.1%; Median home value: $416,000; Median year structure built: 1968; Homeowner vacancy rate: 0.0%; Median selected monthly owner costs: $3,122 with a mortgage, $1,046 without a mortgage; Median gross rent: $1,538 per month; Rental vacancy rate: 0.0%
Health Insurance: 99.0% have insurance; 89.4% have private insurance; 25.1% have public insurance; 1.0% do not have insurance; 0.0% of children under 18 do not have insurance
Transportation: Commute: 89.1% car, 6.2% public transportation, 0.5% walk, 3.1% work from home; Mean travel time to work: 37.7 minutes

KATONAH (CDP). Covers a land area of 0.725 square miles and a water area of 0.079 square miles. Located at 41.26° N. Lat; 73.69° W. Long. Elevation is 236 feet.
Population: 2,091; Growth (since 2000): n/a; Density: 2,882.3 persons per square mile; Race: 86.7% White, 3.1% Black/African American, 2.9% Asian, 0.0% American Indian/Alaska Native, 0.0% Native Hawaiian/Other Pacific Islander, 2.8% Two or more races, 7.5% Hispanic of any race; Average household size: 3.21; Median age: 41.6; Age under 18: 26.5%; Age 65 and over: 11.0%; Males per 100 females: 88.0; Marriage status: 29.9% never married, 58.0% now married, 4.2% separated, 2.9% widowed, 9.3% divorced; Foreign born: 11.0%; Speak English only: 89.6%; With disability: 5.7%; Veterans: 4.0%; Ancestry: 24.3% Irish, 20.6% German, 15.7% Italian, 13.2% English, 9.0% Dutch
Employment: 26.5% management, business, and financial, 5.2% computer, engineering, and science, 22.4% education, legal, community service, arts, and media, 5.9% healthcare practitioners, 15.9% service, 16.8% sales and office, 1.8% natural resources, construction, and maintenance, 5.7% production, transportation, and material moving
Income: Per capita: $66,661; Median household: $136,250; Average household: $208,040; Households with income of $100,000 or more: 65.2%; Poverty rate: 2.2%
Educational Attainment: High school diploma or higher: 98.4%; Bachelor's degree or higher: 79.1%; Graduate/professional degree or higher: 41.1%

School District(s)
Katonah-Lewisboro Union Free SD (KG-12)
    Enrollment: 3,135 . . . . (914) 763-7003
Housing: Homeownership rate: 81.6%; Median home value: $714,400; Median year structure built: Before 1940; Homeowner vacancy rate: 0.0%; Median selected monthly owner costs: $3,494 with a mortgage, $1,501 without a mortgage; Median gross rent: $2,152 per month; Rental vacancy rate: 16.1%
Health Insurance: 96.8% have insurance; 89.8% have private insurance; 15.5% have public insurance; 3.2% do not have insurance; 0.0% of children under 18 do not have insurance
Transportation: Commute: 66.4% car, 20.1% public transportation, 1.7% walk, 10.9% work from home; Mean travel time to work: 37.8 minutes

LAKE MOHEGAN (CDP). Covers a land area of 2.876 square miles and a water area of 0.199 square miles. Located at 41.31° N. Lat; 73.85° W. Long. Elevation is 522 feet.
History: Lake Mohegan is a census-designated place (CDP) located in the town of Yorktown in Westchester County, New York.
Population: 5,921; Growth (since 2000): -1.0%; Density: 2,058.9 persons per square mile; Race: 77.9% White, 3.8% Black/African American, 4.4% Asian, 0.0% American Indian/Alaska Native, 0.0% Native Hawaiian/Other Pacific Islander, 0.7% Two or more races, 29.0% Hispanic of any race; Average household size: 2.84; Median age: 44.1; Age under 18: 20.4%; Age 65 and over: 11.3%; Males per 100 females: 95.2; Marriage status: 35.2% never married, 47.6% now married, 2.1% separated, 6.1% widowed, 11.2% divorced; Foreign born: 19.3%; Speak English only: 74.0%; With disability: 8.3%; Veterans: 3.1%; Ancestry: 28.8% Italian, 18.6% Irish, 5.5% German, 4.8% English, 3.2% American
Employment: 10.7% management, business, and financial, 2.6% computer, engineering, and science, 14.0% education, legal, community service, arts, and media, 4.2% healthcare practitioners, 29.1% service, 25.0% sales and office, 7.4% natural resources, construction, and maintenance, 7.0% production, transportation, and material moving
Income: Per capita: $37,013; Median household: $105,428; Average household: $106,497; Households with income of $100,000 or more: 51.0%; Poverty rate: 2.8%

Educational Attainment: High school diploma or higher: 94.1%; Bachelor's degree or higher: 44.7%; Graduate/professional degree or higher: 18.8%
Housing: Homeownership rate: 79.3%; Median home value: $336,500; Median year structure built: 1968; Homeowner vacancy rate: 0.0%; Median selected monthly owner costs: $2,495 with a mortgage, $1,083 without a mortgage; Median gross rent: $2,097 per month; Rental vacancy rate: 0.0%
Health Insurance: 95.1% have insurance; 77.0% have private insurance; 27.2% have public insurance; 4.9% do not have insurance; 9.2% of children under 18 do not have insurance
Transportation: Commute: 78.7% car, 8.9% public transportation, 7.6% walk, 4.3% work from home; Mean travel time to work: 36.4 minutes

LARCHMONT (village).
Covers a land area of 1.077 square miles and a water area of 0.002 square miles. Located at 40.93° N. Lat; 73.75° W. Long. Elevation is 52 feet.
History: Joyce Kilmer lived here. Developed c.1845, incorporated 1891.
Population: 6,111; Growth (since 2000): -5.8%; Density: 5,672.2 persons per square mile; Race: 87.6% White, 2.4% Black/African American, 3.4% Asian, 0.3% American Indian/Alaska Native, 0.0% Native Hawaiian/Other Pacific Islander, 4.5% Two or more races, 10.2% Hispanic of any race; Average household size: 2.93; Median age: 36.3; Age under 18: 33.3%; Age 65 and over: 10.8%; Males per 100 females: 95.5; Marriage status: 20.2% never married, 70.5% now married, 1.1% separated, 3.6% widowed, 5.7% divorced; Foreign born: 15.5%; Speak English only: 81.5%; With disability: 2.9%; Veterans: 3.7%; Ancestry: 15.7% American, 15.5% Italian, 11.8% Irish, 11.3% English, 10.7% German
Employment: 32.7% management, business, and financial, 12.0% computer, engineering, and science, 22.6% education, legal, community service, arts, and media, 6.9% healthcare practitioners, 7.8% service, 15.2% sales and office, 2.0% natural resources, construction, and maintenance, 0.8% production, transportation, and material moving
Income: Per capita: $107,512; Median household: $198,661; Average household: $313,586; Households with income of $100,000 or more: 74.7%; Poverty rate: 1.9%
Educational Attainment: High school diploma or higher: 99.3%; Bachelor's degree or higher: 88.0%; Graduate/professional degree or higher: 49.3%

School District(s)
Mamaroneck Union Free SD (PK-12)
    Enrollment: 5,484 . . . . (914) 220-3005
Housing: Homeownership rate: 73.2%; Median home value: $1,183,700; Median year structure built: Before 1940; Homeowner vacancy rate: 0.0%; Median selected monthly owner costs: $4,000+ with a mortgage, $1,501 without a mortgage; Median gross rent: $1,922 per month; Rental vacancy rate: 0.0%
Health Insurance: 98.9% have insurance; 93.1% have private insurance; 15.7% have public insurance; 1.1% do not have insurance; 0.0% of children under 18 do not have insurance
Safety: Violent crime rate: 4.9 per 10,000 population; Property crime rate: 167.2 per 10,000 population
Transportation: Commute: 43.7% car, 44.4% public transportation, 1.7% walk, 9.7% work from home; Mean travel time to work: 45.6 minutes
Additional Information Contacts
Village of Larchmont . . . . (914) 834-6230
    http://www.villageoflarchmont.org

LEWISBORO (town).
Covers a land area of 27.746 square miles and a water area of 1.416 square miles. Located at 41.27° N. Lat; 73.59° W. Long. Elevation is 728 feet.
History: The town was formed in 1747 as the "Town of Salem." John Lewis, a financier, requested that the town be given his name and established a fund for the town, though he did not follow through on his promise of a railroad link.
Population: 12,741; Growth (since 2000): 3.4%; Density: 459.2 persons per square mile; Race: 90.9% White, 3.3% Black/African American, 2.5% Asian, 0.2% American Indian/Alaska Native, 0.0% Native Hawaiian/Other Pacific Islander, 0.9% Two or more races, 5.8% Hispanic of any race; Average household size: 2.71; Median age: 46.3; Age under 18: 22.7%; Age 65 and over: 17.0%; Males per 100 females: 96.7; Marriage status: 24.5% never married, 63.7% now married, 0.4% separated, 4.4% widowed, 7.4% divorced; Foreign born: 11.5%; Speak English only: 87.9%; With disability: 6.3%; Veterans: 4.9%; Ancestry: 19.3% Italian, 17.7% Irish, 9.9% German, 7.5% English, 7.0% Russian

Employment: 29.1% management, business, and financial, 8.4% computer, engineering, and science, 20.6% education, legal, community service, arts, and media, 7.9% healthcare practitioners, 9.9% service, 17.2% sales and office, 4.6% natural resources, construction, and maintenance, 2.4% production, transportation, and material moving
Income: Per capita: $78,922; Median household: $148,824; Average household: $212,240; Households with income of $100,000 or more: 68.7%; Poverty rate: 3.7%
Educational Attainment: High school diploma or higher: 97.1%; Bachelor's degree or higher: 71.0%; Graduate/professional degree or higher: 36.3%
Housing: Homeownership rate: 91.0%; Median home value: $648,100; Median year structure built: 1975; Homeowner vacancy rate: 1.5%; Median selected monthly owner costs: $3,777 with a mortgage, $1,501 without a mortgage; Median gross rent: $1,979 per month; Rental vacancy rate: 0.0%
Health Insurance: 97.2% have insurance; 87.4% have private insurance; 23.2% have public insurance; 2.8% do not have insurance; 3.9% of children under 18 do not have insurance
Safety: Violent crime rate: 0.0 per 10,000 population; Property crime rate: 0.8 per 10,000 population
Transportation: Commute: 74.0% car, 12.9% public transportation, 2.4% walk, 10.6% work from home; Mean travel time to work: 43.5 minutes
Additional Information Contacts
Town of Lewisboro . . . . (914) 763-3511
    http://www.lewisborogov.com

LINCOLNDALE (CDP).
Covers a land area of 0.958 square miles and a water area of 0.041 square miles. Located at 41.33° N. Lat; 73.72° W. Long. Elevation is 338 feet.
Population: 1,651; Growth (since 2000): -18.2%; Density: 1,724.2 persons per square mile; Race: 96.5% White, 0.7% Black/African American, 0.8% Asian, 0.0% American Indian/Alaska Native, 0.7% Native Hawaiian/Other Pacific Islander, 0.0% Two or more races, 9.8% Hispanic of any race; Average household size: 2.90; Median age: 36.9; Age under 18: 24.5%; Age 65 and over: 13.9%; Males per 100 females: 95.5; Marriage status: 23.1% never married, 62.1% now married, 0.6% separated, 6.6% widowed, 8.2% divorced; Foreign born: 5.2%; Speak English only: 91.9%; With disability: 7.5%; Veterans: 7.6%; Ancestry: 43.5% Irish, 30.0% Italian, 17.1% American, 5.6% German, 5.1% English
Employment: 19.6% management, business, and financial, 1.0% computer, engineering, and science, 25.6% education, legal, community service, arts, and media, 0.0% healthcare practitioners, 19.1% service, 28.1% sales and office, 5.4% natural resources, construction, and maintenance, 1.3% production, transportation, and material moving
Income: Per capita: $46,371; Median household: $105,625; Average household: $133,712; Households with income of $100,000 or more: 51.5%; Poverty rate: 2.5%
Educational Attainment: High school diploma or higher: 97.3%; Bachelor's degree or higher: 56.9%; Graduate/professional degree or higher: 30.7%

School District(s)
Somers Central SD (KG-12)
    Enrollment: 3,103 . . . . (914) 277-2400
Housing: Homeownership rate: 91.9%; Median home value: $376,700; Median year structure built: 1976; Homeowner vacancy rate: 0.0%; Median selected monthly owner costs: $2,840 with a mortgage, $1,185 without a mortgage; Median gross rent: $1,720 per month; Rental vacancy rate: 0.0%
Health Insurance: 96.2% have insurance; 90.8% have private insurance; 18.9% have public insurance; 3.8% do not have insurance; 0.0% of children under 18 do not have insurance
Transportation: Commute: 90.5% car, 5.5% public transportation, 0.8% walk, 2.6% work from home; Mean travel time to work: 35.3 minutes

MAMARONECK (town).
Covers a land area of 6.654 square miles and a water area of 7.410 square miles. Located at 40.92° N. Lat; 73.74° W. Long. Elevation is 47 feet.
History: Initially a farming community. Settled 1661, incorporated 1895.
Population: 29,945; Growth (since 2000): 3.4%; Density: 4,500.2 persons per square mile; Race: 81.7% White, 3.9% Black/African American, 4.6% Asian, 0.1% American Indian/Alaska Native, 0.0% Native Hawaiian/Other Pacific Islander, 2.9% Two or more races, 17.7% Hispanic of any race; Average household size: 2.77; Median age: 40.0; Age under 18: 26.3%; Age 65 and over: 14.7%; Males per 100 females: 93.9; Marriage status:

28.3% never married, 59.3% now married, 0.7% separated, 4.7% widowed, 7.7% divorced; Foreign born: 23.0%; Speak English only: 71.8%; With disability: 6.7%; Veterans: 3.4%; Ancestry: 15.7% Italian, 12.2% Irish, 8.6% German, 7.6% American, 6.1% English

Employment: 28.8% management, business, and financial, 4.8% computer, engineering, and science, 20.7% education, legal, community service, arts, and media, 4.5% healthcare practitioners, 16.8% service, 17.5% sales and office, 4.8% natural resources, construction, and maintenance, 2.0% production, transportation, and material moving

Income: Per capita: $81,382; Median household: $121,261; Average household: $225,891; Households with income of $100,000 or more: 57.6%; Poverty rate: 5.5%

Educational Attainment: High school diploma or higher: 92.0%; Bachelor's degree or higher: 67.3%; Graduate/professional degree or higher: 37.1%

School District(s)
Mamaroneck Union Free SD (PK-12)
    Enrollment: 5,484 . . . . (914) 220-3005
Rye Neck Union Free SD (KG-12)
    Enrollment: 1,637 . . . . (914) 777-5200

Housing: Homeownership rate: 67.4%; Median home value: $878,000; Median year structure built: 1944; Homeowner vacancy rate: 0.5%; Median selected monthly owner costs: $4,000+ with a mortgage, $1,501 without a mortgage; Median gross rent: $1,759 per month; Rental vacancy rate: 0.0%

Health Insurance: 95.9% have insurance; 84.0% have private insurance; 22.7% have public insurance; 4.1% do not have insurance; 1.2% of children under 18 do not have insurance

Safety: Violent crime rate: 0.8 per 10,000 population; Property crime rate: 49.1 per 10,000 population

Transportation: Commute: 49.2% car, 33.7% public transportation, 6.3% walk, 9.0% work from home; Mean travel time to work: 37.5 minutes

Additional Information Contacts
Town of Mamaroneck . . . . (914) 381-7870
    http://www.townofmamaroneck.org

MAMARONECK (village). Covers a land area of 3.170 square miles and a water area of 3.407 square miles. Located at 40.93° N. Lat; 73.73° W. Long. Elevation is 47 feet.

Population: 19,327; Growth (since 2000): 3.1%; Density: 6,097.4 persons per square mile; Race: 75.5% White, 7.0% Black/African American, 4.8% Asian, 0.0% American Indian/Alaska Native, 0.0% Native Hawaiian/Other Pacific Islander, 2.2% Two or more races, 24.6% Hispanic of any race; Average household size: 2.68; Median age: 40.9; Age under 18: 23.1%; Age 65 and over: 15.7%; Males per 100 females: 95.1; Marriage status: 32.3% never married, 51.6% now married, 1.4% separated, 6.0% widowed, 10.2% divorced; Foreign born: 30.6%; Speak English only: 61.8%; With disability: 7.2%; Veterans: 3.6%; Ancestry: 21.6% Italian, 12.2% Irish, 6.5% German, 6.0% American, 3.3% French

Employment: 23.4% management, business, and financial, 2.9% computer, engineering, and science, 15.6% education, legal, community service, arts, and media, 5.0% healthcare practitioners, 20.4% service, 20.2% sales and office, 7.7% natural resources, construction, and maintenance, 5.0% production, transportation, and material moving

Income: Per capita: $56,404; Median household: $91,161; Average household: $151,854; Households with income of $100,000 or more: 47.4%; Poverty rate: 7.5%

Educational Attainment: High school diploma or higher: 86.8%; Bachelor's degree or higher: 51.1%; Graduate/professional degree or higher: 25.6%

School District(s)
Mamaroneck Union Free SD (PK-12)
    Enrollment: 5,484 . . . . (914) 220-3005
Rye Neck Union Free SD (KG-12)
    Enrollment: 1,637 . . . . (914) 777-5200

Housing: Homeownership rate: 54.8%; Median home value: $611,100; Median year structure built: 1951; Homeowner vacancy rate: 2.4%; Median selected monthly owner costs: $3,422 with a mortgage, $1,481 without a mortgage; Median gross rent: $1,820 per month; Rental vacancy rate: 0.0%

Health Insurance: 92.4% have insurance; 75.4% have private insurance; 28.2% have public insurance; 7.6% do not have insurance; 2.1% of children under 18 do not have insurance

Safety: Violent crime rate: 9.8 per 10,000 population; Property crime rate: 67.4 per 10,000 population

Transportation: Commute: 62.4% car, 24.0% public transportation, 5.1% walk, 5.7% work from home; Mean travel time to work: 32.8 minutes

Additional Information Contacts
Village of Mamaroneck . . . . (914) 777-7722
    http://www.village.mamaroneck.ny.us

MARYKNOLL (unincorporated postal area)

ZCTA: 10545

Covers a land area of 0.126 square miles and a water area of 0 square miles. Located at 41.18° N. Lat; 73.84° W. Long..

Population: 128; Growth (since 2000): n/a; Density: 1,016.4 persons per square mile; Race: 84.4% White, 15.6% Black/African American, 0.0% Asian, 0.0% American Indian/Alaska Native, 0.0% Native Hawaiian/Other Pacific Islander, 0.0% Two or more races, 15.6% Hispanic of any race; Average household size: 0.00; Median age: 52.2; Age under 18: 0.0%; Age 65 and over: 23.4%; Males per 100 females: ***.*; Marriage status: 69.5% never married, 30.5% now married, 0.0% separated, 0.0% widowed, 0.0% divorced; Foreign born: 14.1%; Speak English only: 62.5%; With disability: 7.0%; Veterans: 0.0%; Ancestry: 39.1% Irish, 24.2% American, 8.6% German, 8.6% Italian, 7.0% Armenian

Employment: 0.0% management, business, and financial, 0.0% computer, engineering, and science, 40.4% education, legal, community service, arts, and media, 0.0% healthcare practitioners, 38.3% service, 0.0% sales and office, 0.0% natural resources, construction, and maintenance, 21.3% production, transportation, and material moving

Income: Per capita: $20,855; Median household: n/a; Average household: n/a; Households with income of $100,000 or more: n/a; Poverty rate: 63.3%

Educational Attainment: High school diploma or higher: 100.0%; Bachelor's degree or higher: 57.6%; Graduate/professional degree or higher: 33.1%

Housing: Homeownership rate: n/a; Median home value: n/a; Median year structure built: n/a; Homeowner vacancy rate: 0.0%; Median selected monthly owner costs: $0 with a mortgage, $0 without a mortgage; Median gross rent: n/a per month; Rental vacancy rate: 0.0%

Health Insurance: 83.6% have insurance; 36.7% have private insurance; 46.9% have public insurance; 16.4% do not have insurance; 0.0% of children under 18 do not have insurance

Transportation: Commute: 19.1% car, 0.0% public transportation, 59.6% walk, 21.3% work from home; Mean travel time to work: 16.6 minutes

---

MILLWOOD (unincorporated postal area)

ZCTA: 10546

Covers a land area of 1.123 square miles and a water area of 0.005 square miles. Located at 41.20° N. Lat; 73.80° W. Long. Elevation is 361 feet.

Population: 1,494; Growth (since 2000): 22.1%; Density: 1,330.4 persons per square mile; Race: 73.7% White, 0.3% Black/African American, 15.9% Asian, 0.0% American Indian/Alaska Native, 0.0% Native Hawaiian/Other Pacific Islander, 1.3% Two or more races, 8.5% Hispanic of any race; Average household size: 3.10; Median age: 44.0; Age under 18: 26.6%; Age 65 and over: 14.7%; Males per 100 females: 97.1; Marriage status: 22.6% never married, 69.6% now married, 0.7% separated, 3.2% widowed, 4.7% divorced; Foreign born: 19.9%; Speak English only: 81.3%; With disability: 6.8%; Veterans: 2.0%; Ancestry: 12.7% Polish, 12.2% Italian, 8.9% Irish, 6.7% Trinidadian and Tobagonian, 6.4% Hungarian

Employment: 40.6% management, business, and financial, 8.9% computer, engineering, and science, 17.0% education, legal, community service, arts, and media, 9.2% healthcare practitioners, 6.6% service, 10.7% sales and office, 1.2% natural resources, construction, and maintenance, 5.7% production, transportation, and material moving

Income: Per capita: $72,709; Median household: $178,611; Average household: $222,743; Households with income of $100,000 or more: 78.2%; Poverty rate: 0.3%

Educational Attainment: High school diploma or higher: 95.5%; Bachelor's degree or higher: 73.7%; Graduate/professional degree or higher: 46.5%

Housing: Homeownership rate: 89.2%; Median home value: $675,600; Median year structure built: 1974; Homeowner vacancy rate: 1.4%; Median selected monthly owner costs: $3,852 with a mortgage, $1,501 without a mortgage; Median gross rent: $3,242 per month; Rental vacancy rate: 0.0%

Health Insurance: 100.0% have insurance; 96.0% have private insurance; 17.1% have public insurance; 0.0% do not have insurance; 0.0% of children under 18 do not have insurance
Transportation: Commute: 78.7% car, 16.1% public transportation, 0.0% walk, 5.2% work from home; Mean travel time to work: 34.3 minutes

MOHEGAN LAKE (unincorporated postal area)
ZCTA: 10547
Covers a land area of 5.066 square miles and a water area of 0.199 square miles. Located at 41.31° N. Lat; 73.85° W. Long. Elevation is 472 feet.

Population: 7,709; Growth (since 2000): -9.8%; Density: 1,521.7 persons per square mile; Race: 75.9% White, 8.0% Black/African American, 3.9% Asian, 0.0% American Indian/Alaska Native, 0.0% Native Hawaiian/Other Pacific Islander, 0.8% Two or more races, 25.5% Hispanic of any race; Average household size: 2.90; Median age: 43.4; Age under 18: 19.2%; Age 65 and over: 10.8%; Males per 100 females: 96.6; Marriage status: 39.7% never married, 45.5% now married, 2.0% separated, 4.0% widowed, 10.9% divorced; Foreign born: 17.0%; Speak English only: 73.4%; With disability: 11.1%; Veterans: 3.6%; Ancestry: 28.6% Italian, 21.1% Irish, 6.7% German, 4.6% American, 4.6% English
Employment: 13.0% management, business, and financial, 3.5% computer, engineering, and science, 11.2% education, legal, community service, arts, and media, 3.9% healthcare practitioners, 27.8% service, 25.1% sales and office, 7.8% natural resources, construction, and maintenance, 7.7% production, transportation, and material moving
Income: Per capita: $35,977; Median household: $97,708; Average household: $106,960; Households with income of $100,000 or more: 49.3%; Poverty rate: 6.4%
Educational Attainment: High school diploma or higher: 91.9%; Bachelor's degree or higher: 41.0%; Graduate/professional degree or higher: 17.9%

School District(s)
Lakeland Central SD (PK-12)
    Enrollment: 5,728 . . . . (914) 245-1700
Housing: Homeownership rate: 75.6%; Median home value: $339,500; Median year structure built: 1965; Homeowner vacancy rate: 0.0%; Median selected monthly owner costs: $2,671 with a mortgage, $1,053 without a mortgage; Median gross rent: $1,773 per month; Rental vacancy rate: 2.2%
Health Insurance: 95.0% have insurance; 76.9% have private insurance; 27.5% have public insurance; 5.0% do not have insurance; 8.7% of children under 18 do not have insurance
Transportation: Commute: 80.9% car, 9.2% public transportation, 7.5% walk, 2.0% work from home; Mean travel time to work: 35.1 minutes

MONTROSE (CDP). Covers a land area of 1.614 square miles and a water area of 0.052 square miles. Located at 41.24° N. Lat; 73.94° W. Long. Elevation is 115 feet.
Population: 3,036; Growth (since 2000): n/a; Density: 1,880.8 persons per square mile; Race: 86.9% White, 2.1% Black/African American, 1.9% Asian, 0.0% American Indian/Alaska Native, 0.0% Native Hawaiian/Other Pacific Islander, 1.4% Two or more races, 15.7% Hispanic of any race; Average household size: 2.60; Median age: 43.5; Age under 18: 18.4%; Age 65 and over: 16.0%; Males per 100 females: 97.0; Marriage status: 30.3% never married, 51.9% now married, 1.6% separated, 5.7% widowed, 12.2% divorced; Foreign born: 10.5%; Speak English only: 86.6%; With disability: 11.8%; Veterans: 8.4%; Ancestry: 36.0% Irish, 33.8% Italian, 8.5% German, 5.2% American, 4.8% English
Employment: 14.9% management, business, and financial, 7.8% computer, engineering, and science, 19.0% education, legal, community service, arts, and media, 3.9% healthcare practitioners, 19.5% service, 20.7% sales and office, 10.6% natural resources, construction, and maintenance, 3.5% production, transportation, and material moving
Income: Per capita: $40,868; Median household: $80,625; Average household: $104,670; Households with income of $100,000 or more: 39.3%; Poverty rate: 8.6%
Educational Attainment: High school diploma or higher: 95.9%; Bachelor's degree or higher: 37.7%; Graduate/professional degree or higher: 13.5%

School District(s)
Hendrick Hudson Central SD (KG-12)
    Enrollment: 2,345 . . . . (914) 257-5100

Housing: Homeownership rate: 71.6%; Median home value: $359,700; Median year structure built: 1960; Homeowner vacancy rate: 2.7%; Median selected monthly owner costs: $2,670 with a mortgage, $1,043 without a mortgage; Median gross rent: $1,280 per month; Rental vacancy rate: 9.8%
Health Insurance: 96.3% have insurance; 83.9% have private insurance; 29.1% have public insurance; 3.7% do not have insurance; 0.0% of children under 18 do not have insurance
Hospitals: VA Hudson Valley Healthcare System
Transportation: Commute: 72.9% car, 22.5% public transportation, 0.4% walk, 4.2% work from home; Mean travel time to work: 41.0 minutes

MOUNT KISCO (town/village). Covers a land area of 3.035 square miles and a water area of 0.030 square miles. Located at 41.20° N. Lat; 73.73° W. Long. Elevation is 305 feet.
Population: 10,994; Growth (since 2000): 10.1%; Density: 3,622.1 persons per square mile; Race: 66.1% White, 5.5% Black/African American, 3.3% Asian, 0.0% American Indian/Alaska Native, 0.0% Native Hawaiian/Other Pacific Islander, 2.4% Two or more races, 43.4% Hispanic of any race; Average household size: 2.74; Median age: 40.3; Age under 18: 21.9%; Age 65 and over: 13.6%; Males per 100 females: 107.4; Marriage status: 33.9% never married, 54.9% now married, 2.2% separated, 5.0% widowed, 6.3% divorced; Foreign born: 37.7%; Speak English only: 49.9%; With disability: 8.4%; Veterans: 3.8%; Ancestry: 14.1% Irish, 13.9% Italian, 5.8% German, 3.5% English, 3.0% Polish
Employment: 15.2% management, business, and financial, 5.0% computer, engineering, and science, 10.5% education, legal, community service, arts, and media, 3.9% healthcare practitioners, 33.0% service, 18.5% sales and office, 7.6% natural resources, construction, and maintenance, 6.3% production, transportation, and material moving
Income: Per capita: $41,183; Median household: $77,801; Average household: $111,470; Households with income of $100,000 or more: 40.6%; Poverty rate: 9.5%
Educational Attainment: High school diploma or higher: 81.7%; Bachelor's degree or higher: 40.9%; Graduate/professional degree or higher: 19.5%

School District(s)
Bedford Central SD (PK-12)
    Enrollment: 4,187 . . . . (914) 241-6010
Four-year College(s)
Yeshiva of Nitra Rabbinical College (Private, Not-for-profit)
    Enrollment: 209 . . . . (718) 384-5460
    Tuition: In-state $8,500; Out-of-state $8,500
Vocational/Technical School(s)
Finger Lakes School of Massage (Private, For-profit)
    Enrollment: 39 . . . . (914) 241-7363
    Tuition: $17,900
Housing: Homeownership rate: 57.0%; Median home value: $402,500; Median year structure built: 1967; Homeowner vacancy rate: 0.7%; Median selected monthly owner costs: $2,423 with a mortgage, $1,054 without a mortgage; Median gross rent: $1,483 per month; Rental vacancy rate: 1.5%
Health Insurance: 84.8% have insurance; 65.7% have private insurance; 29.2% have public insurance; 15.2% do not have insurance; 1.4% of children under 18 do not have insurance
Hospitals: Northern Westchester Hospital (233 beds)
Transportation: Commute: 72.5% car, 9.9% public transportation, 8.9% walk, 3.9% work from home; Mean travel time to work: 25.1 minutes
Additional Information Contacts
Village and Town of Mount Kisco . . . . (914) 241-0500
    http://www.mountkisco.org

MOUNT PLEASANT (town). Covers a land area of 27.423 square miles and a water area of 5.335 square miles. Located at 41.10° N. Lat; 73.82° W. Long. Elevation is 259 feet.
History: Mount Pleasant is home to the John D. Rockefeller Estate which was added to the National Register of Historic Places in 1976 as a National Historic Landmark.
Population: 44,635; Growth (since 2000): 3.3%; Density: 1,627.7 persons per square mile; Race: 77.8% White, 4.2% Black/African American, 4.7% Asian, 0.1% American Indian/Alaska Native, 0.0% Native Hawaiian/Other Pacific Islander, 2.4% Two or more races, 21.5% Hispanic of any race; Average household size: 2.90; Median age: 40.1; Age under 18: 23.1%; Age 65 and over: 14.9%; Males per 100 females: 101.8; Marriage status: 33.0% never married, 56.2% now married, 1.8% separated, 4.6%

widowed, 6.2% divorced; Foreign born: 20.4%; Speak English only: 70.7%; With disability: 8.4%; Veterans: 4.0%; Ancestry: 26.1% Italian, 15.0% Irish, 8.3% German, 5.5% American, 4.0% English
Employment: 21.5% management, business, and financial, 4.9% computer, engineering, and science, 17.7% education, legal, community service, arts, and media, 7.0% healthcare practitioners, 16.7% service, 19.1% sales and office, 7.3% natural resources, construction, and maintenance, 5.7% production, transportation, and material moving
Income: Per capita: $51,700; Median household: $111,023; Average household: $157,185; Households with income of $100,000 or more: 53.9%; Poverty rate: 8.3%
Educational Attainment: High school diploma or higher: 88.3%; Bachelor's degree or higher: 51.3%; Graduate/professional degree or higher: 26.1%
Housing: Homeownership rate: 70.1%; Median home value: $629,000; Median year structure built: 1956; Homeowner vacancy rate: 1.7%; Median selected monthly owner costs: $3,792 with a mortgage, $1,501 without a mortgage; Median gross rent: $1,482 per month; Rental vacancy rate: 2.6%
Health Insurance: 94.4% have insurance; 80.8% have private insurance; 24.7% have public insurance; 5.6% do not have insurance; 2.1% of children under 18 do not have insurance
Transportation: Commute: 71.2% car, 16.4% public transportation, 6.1% walk, 5.8% work from home; Mean travel time to work: 29.9 minutes
Additional Information Contacts
Town of Mount Pleasant . . . . (914) 742-2300
   http://www.mtpleasantny.com

MOUNT VERNON (city). Covers a land area of 4.386 square miles and a water area of 0.017 square miles. Located at 40.91° N. Lat; 73.83° W. Long. Elevation is 112 feet.
History: Named for George Washington's estate on the Potomac River, which was named for Edward Vernon, British admiral. John Peter Zenger was arrested here for libel in 1733. The city itself was not founded until 1851, when a cooperative group, the Industrial Home Association, bought the land and built a planned community. St. Paul's Church (c.1761), a national historic site, is here. The city, which has a large French-American population, has been the scene of a great deal of controversy over school and housing integration in the 1970s, 1980s, and 1990s.
Population: 68,671; Growth (since 2000): 0.4%; Density: 15,658.0 persons per square mile; Race: 22.1% White, 66.7% Black/African American, 2.1% Asian, 0.5% American Indian/Alaska Native, 0.0% Native Hawaiian/Other Pacific Islander, 2.6% Two or more races, 15.4% Hispanic of any race; Average household size: 2.70; Median age: 38.5; Age under 18: 20.9%; Age 65 and over: 15.1%; Males per 100 females: 83.3; Marriage status: 44.9% never married, 38.0% now married, 3.7% separated, 6.5% widowed, 10.6% divorced; Foreign born: 33.0%; Speak English only: 75.7%; With disability: 11.3%; Veterans: 3.2%; Ancestry: 19.8% Jamaican, 6.3% Italian, 3.2% American, 2.9% Irish, 2.9% Haitian
Employment: 12.7% management, business, and financial, 2.5% computer, engineering, and science, 12.4% education, legal, community service, arts, and media, 7.4% healthcare practitioners, 25.8% service, 23.6% sales and office, 7.3% natural resources, construction, and maintenance, 8.2% production, transportation, and material moving
Income: Per capita: $29,826; Median household: $54,573; Average household: $76,753; Households with income of $100,000 or more: 25.1%; Poverty rate: 14.8%
Educational Attainment: High school diploma or higher: 84.1%; Bachelor's degree or higher: 28.4%; Graduate/professional degree or higher: 11.3%

School District(s)
Amani Public Charter School (05-08)
   Enrollment: 343 . . . . (914) 668-2553
Mount Vernon SD (PK-12)
   Enrollment: 8,290 . . . . (914) 665-5000
Vocational/Technical School(s)
Westchester School of Beauty Culture (Private, For-profit)
   Enrollment: 78 . . . . (914) 699-2344
   Tuition: $12,550
Housing: Homeownership rate: 39.7%; Median home value: $355,600; Median year structure built: 1942; Homeowner vacancy rate: 3.6%; Median selected monthly owner costs: $2,928 with a mortgage, $1,146 without a mortgage; Median gross rent: $1,291 per month; Rental vacancy rate: 4.4%

Health Insurance: 90.2% have insurance; 62.6% have private insurance; 40.0% have public insurance; 9.8% do not have insurance; 2.8% of children under 18 do not have insurance
Hospitals: Montefiore Mount Vernon Hospital (228 beds)
Safety: Violent crime rate: 63.8 per 10,000 population; Property crime rate: 188.9 per 10,000 population
Transportation: Commute: 60.4% car, 30.0% public transportation, 5.5% walk, 2.7% work from home; Mean travel time to work: 34.8 minutes
Additional Information Contacts
City of Mount Vernon . . . . (914) 665-2300
   http://www.cmvny.com

NEW CASTLE (town). Covers a land area of 23.236 square miles and a water area of 0.383 square miles. Located at 41.18° N. Lat; 73.77° W. Long.
History: In 1696 Caleb Heathcote purchases a large tract of land including what is now New Castle from Wampus and other Native American sachems. In 1730 Quakers begin settling in the northern and western parts of North Castle, which will become New Castle.
Population: 18,035; Growth (since 2000): 3.1%; Density: 776.2 persons per square mile; Race: 86.8% White, 1.8% Black/African American, 8.8% Asian, 0.3% American Indian/Alaska Native, 0.0% Native Hawaiian/Other Pacific Islander, 1.3% Two or more races, 3.3% Hispanic of any race; Average household size: 3.04; Median age: 43.2; Age under 18: 28.6%; Age 65 and over: 13.7%; Males per 100 females: 99.2; Marriage status: 23.1% never married, 69.3% now married, 0.3% separated, 2.4% widowed, 5.2% divorced; Foreign born: 13.1%; Speak English only: 86.1%; With disability: 5.5%; Veterans: 3.6%; Ancestry: 15.4% Italian, 13.0% Irish, 12.2% German, 7.9% Polish, 6.9% Russian
Employment: 33.3% management, business, and financial, 5.0% computer, engineering, and science, 26.0% education, legal, community service, arts, and media, 9.0% healthcare practitioners, 4.0% service, 18.7% sales and office, 1.5% natural resources, construction, and maintenance, 2.4% production, transportation, and material moving
Income: Per capita: $99,067; Median household: $211,105; Average household: $300,864; Households with income of $100,000 or more: 80.7%; Poverty rate: 2.0%
Educational Attainment: High school diploma or higher: 98.2%; Bachelor's degree or higher: 83.5%; Graduate/professional degree or higher: 49.1%
Housing: Homeownership rate: 92.9%; Median home value: $884,500; Median year structure built: 1964; Homeowner vacancy rate: 1.5%; Median selected monthly owner costs: $4,000+ with a mortgage, $1,501 without a mortgage; Median gross rent: $1,978 per month; Rental vacancy rate: 0.0%
Health Insurance: 99.1% have insurance; 93.9% have private insurance; 15.8% have public insurance; 0.9% do not have insurance; 0.2% of children under 18 do not have insurance
Transportation: Commute: 59.4% car, 30.3% public transportation, 2.3% walk, 7.9% work from home; Mean travel time to work: 43.2 minutes
Additional Information Contacts
Town of New Castle . . . . (914) 238-7269
   http://www.mynewcastle.org

NEW ROCHELLE (city). Covers a land area of 10.350 square miles and a water area of 2.885 square miles. Located at 40.92° N. Lat; 73.78° W. Long. Elevation is 85 feet.
History: New Rochelle occupies the site of the villages of the Siwanoy, principal nation of the Wappinger confederacy. In 1689, a group of Huguenot refugees purchased a tract of 6,000 acres and named the settlement for their old home in France, La Rochelle. New Rochelle was incorporated as a village in 1857 and as a city in 1899.
Population: 79,877; Growth (since 2000): 10.7%; Density: 7,717.4 persons per square mile; Race: 60.0% White, 20.0% Black/African American, 4.5% Asian, 0.1% American Indian/Alaska Native, 0.0% Native Hawaiian/Other Pacific Islander, 3.5% Two or more races, 29.4% Hispanic of any race; Average household size: 2.69; Median age: 39.4; Age under 18: 20.8%; Age 65 and over: 16.5%; Males per 100 females: 92.3; Marriage status: 36.1% never married, 49.3% now married, 2.5% separated, 6.5% widowed, 8.1% divorced; Foreign born: 29.6%; Speak English only: 60.1%; With disability: 9.9%; Veterans: 3.9%; Ancestry: 16.3% Italian, 7.7% Irish, 4.8% American, 4.2% German, 3.3% Jamaican
Employment: 16.1% management, business, and financial, 4.1% computer, engineering, and science, 15.4% education, legal, community service, arts, and media, 7.8% healthcare practitioners, 21.1% service,

20.0% sales and office, 8.9% natural resources, construction, and maintenance, 6.6% production, transportation, and material moving
Income: Per capita: $44,440; Median household: $77,320; Average household: $121,268; Households with income of $100,000 or more: 40.2%; Poverty rate: 11.2%
Educational Attainment: High school diploma or higher: 82.8%; Bachelor's degree or higher: 44.0%; Graduate/professional degree or higher: 23.1%

School District(s)
New Rochelle City SD (PK-12)
    Enrollment: 10,864 . . . . (914) 576-4200

Four-year College(s)
Iona College (Private, Not-for-profit, Roman Catholic)
    Enrollment: 3,792 . . . . (914) 633-2000
    Tuition: In-state $37,682; Out-of-state $37,682
The College of New Rochelle (Private, Not-for-profit)
    Enrollment: 3,234 . . . . (914) 654-5000
    Tuition: In-state $36,618; Out-of-state $36,618

Housing: Homeownership rate: 50.9%; Median home value: $552,700; Median year structure built: 1951; Homeowner vacancy rate: 1.6%; Median selected monthly owner costs: $3,637 with a mortgage, $1,501 without a mortgage; Median gross rent: $1,432 per month; Rental vacancy rate: 3.8%
Health Insurance: 89.6% have insurance; 68.3% have private insurance; 32.7% have public insurance; 10.4% do not have insurance; 4.2% of children under 18 do not have insurance
Hospitals: Montefiore New Rochelle Hospital (476 beds)
Safety: Violent crime rate: 22.8 per 10,000 population; Property crime rate: 143.7 per 10,000 population
Newspapers: Westchester Guardian (weekly circulation 15,000)
Transportation: Commute: 62.6% car, 23.5% public transportation, 6.8% walk, 5.1% work from home; Mean travel time to work: 32.1 minutes; Amtrak: Train service available.
Additional Information Contacts
City of New Rochelle . . . . (914) 654-2000
    http://www.newrochelleny.com

NORTH CASTLE (town).
Covers a land area of 23.757 square miles and a water area of 2.604 square miles. Located at 41.14° N. Lat; 73.69° W. Long. Elevation is 597 feet.
History: Town got its name from a barrier built by the Mohicans to protect themselves from attack.
Population: 12,309; Growth (since 2000): 13.5%; Density: 518.1 persons per square mile; Race: 89.0% White, 2.2% Black/African American, 4.4% Asian, 0.2% American Indian/Alaska Native, 0.0% Native Hawaiian/Other Pacific Islander, 1.8% Two or more races, 9.9% Hispanic of any race; Average household size: 3.01; Median age: 44.3; Age under 18: 27.0%; Age 65 and over: 13.6%; Males per 100 females: 98.2; Marriage status: 23.7% never married, 67.9% now married, 0.9% separated, 2.6% widowed, 5.8% divorced; Foreign born: 13.0%; Speak English only: 79.3%; With disability: 5.7%; Veterans: 4.3%; Ancestry: 21.0% Italian, 9.9% Irish, 9.4% German, 7.0% Polish, 6.4% Eastern European
Employment: 30.0% management, business, and financial, 6.2% computer, engineering, and science, 19.4% education, legal, community service, arts, and media, 9.2% healthcare practitioners, 11.8% service, 18.8% sales and office, 3.5% natural resources, construction, and maintenance, 1.1% production, transportation, and material moving
Income: Per capita: $97,689; Median household: $180,859; Average household: $290,004; Households with income of $100,000 or more: 73.5%; Poverty rate: 2.0%
Educational Attainment: High school diploma or higher: 97.1%; Bachelor's degree or higher: 74.3%; Graduate/professional degree or higher: 40.7%
Housing: Homeownership rate: 88.8%; Median home value: $927,200; Median year structure built: 1967; Homeowner vacancy rate: 0.9%; Median selected monthly owner costs: $4,000+ with a mortgage, $1,501 without a mortgage; Median gross rent: $2,034 per month; Rental vacancy rate: 8.0%
Health Insurance: 96.1% have insurance; 89.1% have private insurance; 16.5% have public insurance; 3.9% do not have insurance; 2.1% of children under 18 do not have insurance
Transportation: Commute: 71.8% car, 17.1% public transportation, 0.8% walk, 9.5% work from home; Mean travel time to work: 34.6 minutes

Additional Information Contacts
Town of North Castle . . . . (914) 273-3321
    http://www.northcastleny.com

NORTH SALEM (town).
Covers a land area of 21.326 square miles and a water area of 1.519 square miles. Located at 41.34° N. Lat; 73.60° W. Long. Elevation is 505 feet.
History: DeLancey Town Hall, a restored 18th-century Georgian manor, is on the National Register of Historic Places; Museum, Japanese Stroll Garden also here.
Population: 5,205; Growth (since 2000): 0.6%; Density: 244.1 persons per square mile; Race: 87.6% White, 3.5% Black/African American, 2.5% Asian, 0.6% American Indian/Alaska Native, 0.0% Native Hawaiian/Other Pacific Islander, 3.4% Two or more races, 8.0% Hispanic of any race; Average household size: 2.70; Median age: 48.5; Age under 18: 20.7%; Age 65 and over: 20.3%; Males per 100 females: 94.1; Marriage status: 23.6% never married, 62.4% now married, 1.8% separated, 6.8% widowed, 7.3% divorced; Foreign born: 14.7%; Speak English only: 85.6%; With disability: 5.9%; Veterans: 5.3%; Ancestry: 22.7% Italian, 14.6% Irish, 13.4% German, 9.1% English, 3.8% Polish
Employment: 24.3% management, business, and financial, 6.6% computer, engineering, and science, 17.4% education, legal, community service, arts, and media, 7.3% healthcare practitioners, 8.7% service, 27.4% sales and office, 5.2% natural resources, construction, and maintenance, 3.1% production, transportation, and material moving
Income: Per capita: $70,398; Median household: $137,414; Average household: $195,815; Households with income of $100,000 or more: 65.1%; Poverty rate: 5.2%
Educational Attainment: High school diploma or higher: 96.1%; Bachelor's degree or higher: 59.9%; Graduate/professional degree or higher: 23.9%

School District(s)
North Salem Central SD (KG-12)
    Enrollment: 1,118 . . . . (914) 669-5414
Housing: Homeownership rate: 83.3%; Median home value: $582,400; Median year structure built: 1963; Homeowner vacancy rate: 3.8%; Median selected monthly owner costs: $3,340 with a mortgage, $1,475 without a mortgage; Median gross rent: $1,697 per month; Rental vacancy rate: 0.0%
Health Insurance: 94.0% have insurance; 83.1% have private insurance; 22.8% have public insurance; 6.0% do not have insurance; 12.2% of children under 18 do not have insurance
Transportation: Commute: 74.8% car, 9.5% public transportation, 1.6% walk, 13.5% work from home; Mean travel time to work: 37.1 minutes
Additional Information Contacts
Town of North Salem . . . . (914) 669-5577
    http://www.northsalemny.org

OSSINING (town).
Covers a land area of 11.556 square miles and a water area of 4.168 square miles. Located at 41.16° N. Lat; 73.86° W. Long. Elevation is 161 feet.
History: Ossining is the site of Sing Sing state prison (built 1825—1828). This prison was long known for its extreme discipline, but under Thomas Mott Osborne and Lewis Edward Lawes, notable reforms were introduced. By end of 19th century, second-largest industrial center in Westchester. Brickyards produced bricks for Old Croton Aqueduct. Maryknoll, the headquarters of the Catholic Foreign Mission Society, is nearby. Settled c.1750, Incorporated 1813 as Sing Sing, renamed 1901.
Population: 38,257; Growth (since 2000): 4.7%; Density: 3,310.5 persons per square mile; Race: 56.0% White, 12.4% Black/African American, 5.1% Asian, 1.6% American Indian/Alaska Native, 0.0% Native Hawaiian/Other Pacific Islander, 3.2% Two or more races, 35.0% Hispanic of any race; Average household size: 2.82; Median age: 39.6; Age under 18: 22.4%; Age 65 and over: 14.4%; Males per 100 females: 104.3; Marriage status: 34.1% never married, 52.7% now married, 2.0% separated, 5.0% widowed, 8.3% divorced; Foreign born: 30.8%; Speak English only: 58.1%; With disability: 8.3%; Veterans: 4.0%; Ancestry: 14.0% Italian, 10.7% Irish, 6.1% German, 3.8% English, 3.4% American
Employment: 17.7% management, business, and financial, 4.2% computer, engineering, and science, 14.8% education, legal, community service, arts, and media, 5.2% healthcare practitioners, 21.4% service, 19.8% sales and office, 11.6% natural resources, construction, and maintenance, 5.3% production, transportation, and material moving

Income: Per capita: $43,217; Median household: $82,645; Average household: $128,103; Households with income of $100,000 or more: 44.7%; Poverty rate: 8.9%

Educational Attainment: High school diploma or higher: 82.5%; Bachelor's degree or higher: 43.5%; Graduate/professional degree or higher: 21.9%

School District(s)

Ossining Union Free SD (PK-12)
  Enrollment: 5,060 . . . . (914) 941-7700

Four-year College(s)

Kehilath Yakov Rabbinical Seminary (Private, Not-for-profit, Jewish)
  Enrollment: 159 . . . . (718) 963-1212
  Tuition: In-state $9,700; Out-of-state $9,700

Housing: Homeownership rate: 61.8%; Median home value: $440,300; Median year structure built: 1962; Homeowner vacancy rate: 1.2%; Median selected monthly owner costs: $3,207 with a mortgage, $1,501 without a mortgage; Median gross rent: $1,484 per month; Rental vacancy rate: 2.5%

Health Insurance: 86.9% have insurance; 67.3% have private insurance; 30.0% have public insurance; 13.1% do not have insurance; 1.7% of children under 18 do not have insurance

Transportation: Commute: 69.0% car, 16.7% public transportation, 6.2% walk, 6.3% work from home; Mean travel time to work: 33.5 minutes

Additional Information Contacts
Town of Ossining . . . . (914) 762-6000
  http://www.townofossining.com

OSSINING (village). Covers a land area of 3.149 square miles and a water area of 3.283 square miles. Located at 41.16° N. Lat; 73.87° W. Long. Elevation is 161 feet.

Population: 25,386; Growth (since 2000): 5.7%; Density: 8,060.9 persons per square mile; Race: 43.8% White, 15.8% Black/African American, 4.2% Asian, 2.4% American Indian/Alaska Native, 0.0% Native Hawaiian/Other Pacific Islander, 3.4% Two or more races, 47.5% Hispanic of any race; Average household size: 2.93; Median age: 36.7; Age under 18: 23.7%; Age 65 and over: 11.1%; Males per 100 females: 113.0; Marriage status: 37.1% never married, 48.4% now married, 2.5% separated, 4.7% widowed, 9.8% divorced; Foreign born: 39.6%; Speak English only: 46.9%; With disability: 8.3%; Veterans: 3.2%; Ancestry: 9.4% Italian, 8.0% Irish, 4.1% German, 3.5% Jamaican, 3.0% English

Employment: 13.4% management, business, and financial, 3.0% computer, engineering, and science, 11.0% education, legal, community service, arts, and media, 3.9% healthcare practitioners, 27.2% service, 19.0% sales and office, 15.6% natural resources, construction, and maintenance, 6.8% production, transportation, and material moving

Income: Per capita: $30,906; Median household: $63,918; Average household: $93,771; Households with income of $100,000 or more: 33.5%; Poverty rate: 10.9%

Educational Attainment: High school diploma or higher: 75.8%; Bachelor's degree or higher: 31.4%; Graduate/professional degree or higher: 14.3%

School District(s)

Ossining Union Free SD (PK-12)
  Enrollment: 5,060 . . . . (914) 941-7700

Four-year College(s)

Kehilath Yakov Rabbinical Seminary (Private, Not-for-profit, Jewish)
  Enrollment: 159 . . . . (718) 963-1212
  Tuition: In-state $9,700; Out-of-state $9,700

Housing: Homeownership rate: 49.3%; Median home value: $368,200; Median year structure built: 1958; Homeowner vacancy rate: 1.4%; Median selected monthly owner costs: $2,825 with a mortgage, $1,326 without a mortgage; Median gross rent: $1,482 per month; Rental vacancy rate: 3.0%

Health Insurance: 81.3% have insurance; 56.8% have private insurance; 32.9% have public insurance; 18.7% do not have insurance; 2.5% of children under 18 do not have insurance

Safety: Violent crime rate: 7.9 per 10,000 population; Property crime rate: 96.4 per 10,000 population

Transportation: Commute: 72.7% car, 13.0% public transportation, 7.7% walk, 4.3% work from home; Mean travel time to work: 30.8 minutes

Additional Information Contacts
Village of Ossining . . . . (914) 762-8428
  http://www.villageofossining.org

PEEKSKILL (city). Covers a land area of 4.368 square miles and a water area of 1.230 square miles. Located at 41.29° N. Lat; 73.92° W. Long. Elevation is 128 feet.

History: Named for Jan Peeck, a Dutch trader from New Amsterdam. In the American Revolution, Peekskill was attacked and burned (1777) by the British; after the war the city became a prominent trade center. In 19th century had foundries based on Putnam County iron deposits. Peter Cooper and Henry Ward Beecher born here. St. Peter's Church, dedicated in 1767, has been restored. Settled 1665. Incorporated as a village 1816, as a city 1940.

Population: 24,111; Growth (since 2000): 7.4%; Density: 5,520.5 persons per square mile; Race: 41.8% White, 21.4% Black/African American, 3.1% Asian, 0.7% American Indian/Alaska Native, 0.0% Native Hawaiian/Other Pacific Islander, 7.3% Two or more races, 39.5% Hispanic of any race; Average household size: 2.54; Median age: 39.6; Age under 18: 22.6%; Age 65 and over: 15.7%; Males per 100 females: 95.6; Marriage status: 36.5% never married, 45.6% now married, 2.7% separated, 6.1% widowed, 11.8% divorced; Foreign born: 27.2%; Speak English only: 63.1%; With disability: 13.3%; Veterans: 6.7%; Ancestry: 12.4% Italian, 10.2% Irish, 6.7% German, 3.0% English, 2.7% American

Employment: 10.9% management, business, and financial, 4.5% computer, engineering, and science, 12.6% education, legal, community service, arts, and media, 5.3% healthcare practitioners, 21.8% service, 19.8% sales and office, 12.4% natural resources, construction, and maintenance, 12.8% production, transportation, and material moving

Income: Per capita: $32,413; Median household: $54,839; Average household: $80,127; Households with income of $100,000 or more: 26.9%; Poverty rate: 13.0%

Educational Attainment: High school diploma or higher: 78.4%; Bachelor's degree or higher: 27.1%; Graduate/professional degree or higher: 11.7%

School District(s)

Peekskill City SD (PK-12)
  Enrollment: 3,529 . . . . (914) 737-3300

Four-year College(s)

Ohr Hameir Theological Seminary (Private, Not-for-profit)
  Enrollment: 101 . . . . (914) 736-1500
  Tuition: In-state $11,250; Out-of-state $11,250

Vocational/Technical School(s)

Empire Beauty School-Peekskill (Private, For-profit)
  Enrollment: 33 . . . . (800) 920-4593
  Tuition: $12,500

Housing: Homeownership rate: 48.6%; Median home value: $286,200; Median year structure built: 1959; Homeowner vacancy rate: 2.9%; Median selected monthly owner costs: $2,366 with a mortgage, $920 without a mortgage; Median gross rent: $1,352 per month; Rental vacancy rate: 1.7%

Health Insurance: 88.1% have insurance; 60.5% have private insurance; 39.6% have public insurance; 11.9% do not have insurance; 3.6% of children under 18 do not have insurance

Safety: Violent crime rate: 14.1 per 10,000 population; Property crime rate: 74.2 per 10,000 population

Transportation: Commute: 71.9% car, 17.4% public transportation, 4.7% walk, 3.8% work from home; Mean travel time to work: 37.2 minutes

Additional Information Contacts
City of Peekskill . . . . (914) 737-3400
  http://www.cityofpeekskill.com

PELHAM (town). Covers a land area of 2.172 square miles and a water area of 0.046 square miles. Located at 40.90° N. Lat; 73.81° W. Long. Elevation is 72 feet.

History: Settled in 17th century; incorporated 1896.

Population: 12,650; Growth (since 2000): 6.6%; Density: 5,824.3 persons per square mile; Race: 78.8% White, 7.9% Black/African American, 5.9% Asian, 0.0% American Indian/Alaska Native, 0.0% Native Hawaiian/Other Pacific Islander, 4.9% Two or more races, 11.5% Hispanic of any race; Average household size: 3.14; Median age: 39.7; Age under 18: 28.4%; Age 65 and over: 13.7%; Males per 100 females: 96.4; Marriage status: 29.9% never married, 58.8% now married, 1.5% separated, 4.9% widowed, 6.4% divorced; Foreign born: 15.2%; Speak English only: 81.3%; With disability: 4.6%; Veterans: 5.4%; Ancestry: 24.5% Italian, 17.5% Irish, 10.7% German, 7.1% English, 5.5% American

Employment: 30.3% management, business, and financial, 4.4% computer, engineering, and science, 21.6% education, legal, community service, arts, and media, 7.2% healthcare practitioners, 11.1% service,

17.4% sales and office, 4.9% natural resources, construction, and maintenance, 3.1% production, transportation, and material moving
Income: Per capita: $77,330; Median household: $146,833; Average household: $238,344; Households with income of $100,000 or more: 64.7%; Poverty rate: 3.6%
Educational Attainment: High school diploma or higher: 94.8%; Bachelor's degree or higher: 63.3%; Graduate/professional degree or higher: 33.5%

School District(s)
Pelham Union Free SD (KG-12)
   Enrollment: 2,876 . . . . (914) 738-3434
Housing: Homeownership rate: 77.1%; Median home value: $751,600; Median year structure built: Before 1940; Homeowner vacancy rate: 1.5%; Median selected monthly owner costs: $4,000+ with a mortgage, $1,501 without a mortgage; Median gross rent: $1,812 per month; Rental vacancy rate: 9.9%
Health Insurance: 96.6% have insurance; 88.4% have private insurance; 17.9% have public insurance; 3.4% do not have insurance; 3.4% of children under 18 do not have insurance
Newspapers: Norway Times (weekly circulation 7,000); Pelham Weekly (weekly circulation 2,100)
Transportation: Commute: 55.6% car, 34.2% public transportation, 2.8% walk, 5.9% work from home; Mean travel time to work: 35.0 minutes
Additional Information Contacts
Town of Pelham . . . . (914) 738-0777
   http://townofpelham.com

PELHAM (village). Covers a land area of 0.829 square miles and a water area of 0.005 square miles. Located at 40.91° N. Lat; 73.81° W. Long. Elevation is 72 feet.
History: On June 27, 1654, Thomas Pell purchased 9,166 acres (37.09 sq. km.) from the Native American tribe of the Siwanoys. Among the land that he purchased, of course, was all the land that constitutes today's Village of Pelham. Upon his death in 1669, Thomas Pell left the land to his nephew and sole heir, John Pell.
Population: 7,016; Growth (since 2000): 9.6%; Density: 8,460.7 persons per square mile; Race: 71.6% White, 11.9% Black/African American, 7.5% Asian, 0.0% American Indian/Alaska Native, 0.0% Native Hawaiian/Other Pacific Islander, 5.6% Two or more races, 14.3% Hispanic of any race; Average household size: 3.09; Median age: 40.1; Age under 18: 26.7%; Age 65 and over: 13.5%; Males per 100 females: 95.8; Marriage status: 29.9% never married, 58.4% now married, 2.4% separated, 4.1% widowed, 7.6% divorced; Foreign born: 18.8%; Speak English only: 80.0%; With disability: 5.3%; Veterans: 6.6%; Ancestry: 23.5% Italian, 15.8% Irish, 10.2% German, 6.9% English, 5.8% Jamaican
Employment: 27.5% management, business, and financial, 4.1% computer, engineering, and science, 19.1% education, legal, community service, arts, and media, 6.7% healthcare practitioners, 13.3% service, 18.9% sales and office, 6.0% natural resources, construction, and maintenance, 4.4% production, transportation, and material moving
Income: Per capita: $71,486; Median household: $127,470; Average household: $216,895; Households with income of $100,000 or more: 60.4%; Poverty rate: 3.0%
Educational Attainment: High school diploma or higher: 93.3%; Bachelor's degree or higher: 54.7%; Graduate/professional degree or higher: 29.6%

School District(s)
Pelham Union Free SD (KG-12)
   Enrollment: 2,876 . . . . (914) 738-3434
Housing: Homeownership rate: 67.5%; Median home value: $647,000; Median year structure built: Before 1940; Homeowner vacancy rate: 3.0%; Median selected monthly owner costs: $4,000+ with a mortgage, $1,501 without a mortgage; Median gross rent: $1,743 per month; Rental vacancy rate: 9.2%
Health Insurance: 94.9% have insurance; 85.4% have private insurance; 19.4% have public insurance; 5.1% do not have insurance; 6.5% of children under 18 do not have insurance
Safety: Violent crime rate: 0.0 per 10,000 population; Property crime rate: 98.1 per 10,000 population
Newspapers: Norway Times (weekly circulation 7,000); Pelham Weekly (weekly circulation 2,100)
Transportation: Commute: 54.9% car, 34.8% public transportation, 4.4% walk, 4.6% work from home; Mean travel time to work: 34.4 minutes

Additional Information Contacts
Village of Pelham . . . . (914) 738-2015
   http://www.pelhamgov.com

PELHAM MANOR (village). Covers a land area of 1.343 square miles and a water area of 0.041 square miles. Located at 40.89° N. Lat; 73.81° W. Long. Elevation is 62 feet.
History: Settled in mid-17th century; incorporated 1891.
Population: 5,634; Growth (since 2000): 3.1%; Density: 4,196.1 persons per square mile; Race: 87.8% White, 3.0% Black/African American, 3.9% Asian, 0.0% American Indian/Alaska Native, 0.0% Native Hawaiian/Other Pacific Islander, 4.1% Two or more races, 8.1% Hispanic of any race; Average household size: 3.20; Median age: 39.2; Age under 18: 30.6%; Age 65 and over: 14.0%; Males per 100 females: 97.1; Marriage status: 30.0% never married, 59.2% now married, 0.3% separated, 5.9% widowed, 4.9% divorced; Foreign born: 10.8%; Speak English only: 82.9%; With disability: 3.9%; Veterans: 4.0%; Ancestry: 25.7% Italian, 19.6% Irish, 11.3% German, 7.4% English, 6.5% American
Employment: 34.2% management, business, and financial, 4.9% computer, engineering, and science, 25.2% education, legal, community service, arts, and media, 7.8% healthcare practitioners, 8.2% service, 15.3% sales and office, 3.2% natural resources, construction, and maintenance, 1.2% production, transportation, and material moving
Income: Per capita: $84,608; Median household: $158,417; Average household: $266,138; Households with income of $100,000 or more: 70.5%; Poverty rate: 4.2%
Educational Attainment: High school diploma or higher: 96.8%; Bachelor's degree or higher: 75.1%; Graduate/professional degree or higher: 38.8%
Housing: Homeownership rate: 89.5%; Median home value: $858,900; Median year structure built: Before 1940; Homeowner vacancy rate: 0.0%; Median selected monthly owner costs: $4,000+ with a mortgage, $1,501 without a mortgage; Median gross rent: $2,223 per month; Rental vacancy rate: 12.4%
Health Insurance: 98.6% have insurance; 92.1% have private insurance; 16.0% have public insurance; 1.4% do not have insurance; 0.0% of children under 18 do not have insurance
Safety: Violent crime rate: 7.2 per 10,000 population; Property crime rate: 290.5 per 10,000 population
Transportation: Commute: 56.7% car, 33.4% public transportation, 0.6% walk, 7.7% work from home; Mean travel time to work: 35.9 minutes
Additional Information Contacts
Village of Pelham Manor . . . . (914) 738-8820
   http://www.pelhammanor.org

PLEASANTVILLE (village). Covers a land area of 1.824 square miles and a water area of 0.002 square miles. Located at 41.13° N. Lat; 73.78° W. Long. Elevation is 292 feet.
History: French Huguenot Isaac See (sometimes spelled Sie) settled here as an agent for Dutch landowner Frederick Philipse in 1695, thus beginning the modern history of Pleasantville.
Population: 7,275; Growth (since 2000): 1.4%; Density: 3,987.4 persons per square mile; Race: 84.2% White, 3.5% Black/African American, 4.0% Asian, 0.0% American Indian/Alaska Native, 0.0% Native Hawaiian/Other Pacific Islander, 1.2% Two or more races, 12.4% Hispanic of any race; Average household size: 2.66; Median age: 41.2; Age under 18: 25.9%; Age 65 and over: 14.7%; Males per 100 females: 95.4; Marriage status: 32.0% never married, 54.1% now married, 1.0% separated, 5.1% widowed, 8.9% divorced; Foreign born: 11.9%; Speak English only: 82.8%; With disability: 6.8%; Veterans: 3.8%; Ancestry: 24.7% Irish, 23.1% Italian, 15.1% German, 7.2% English, 6.5% Polish
Employment: 26.8% management, business, and financial, 5.2% computer, engineering, and science, 27.8% education, legal, community service, arts, and media, 5.2% healthcare practitioners, 10.0% service, 17.7% sales and office, 3.9% natural resources, construction, and maintenance, 3.6% production, transportation, and material moving
Income: Per capita: $53,142; Median household: $113,071; Average household: $147,272; Households with income of $100,000 or more: 56.7%; Poverty rate: 3.4%
Educational Attainment: High school diploma or higher: 96.3%; Bachelor's degree or higher: 60.7%; Graduate/professional degree or higher: 33.5%

School District(s)
Mount Pleasant-Cottage Union Free SD (KG-12)
   Enrollment: 180 . . . . (914) 769-0456

Pleasantville Union Free SD (KG-12)
Enrollment: 1,687 . . . . (914) 741-1400
Housing: Homeownership rate: 77.8%; Median home value: $571,300; Median year structure built: 1952; Homeowner vacancy rate: 3.9%; Median selected monthly owner costs: $3,232 with a mortgage, $1,501 without a mortgage; Median gross rent: $1,465 per month; Rental vacancy rate: 2.7%
Health Insurance: 96.5% have insurance; 90.0% have private insurance; 19.2% have public insurance; 3.5% do not have insurance; 2.8% of children under 18 do not have insurance
Safety: Violent crime rate: 1.4 per 10,000 population; Property crime rate: 69.7 per 10,000 population
Transportation: Commute: 75.8% car, 16.2% public transportation, 4.5% walk, 3.5% work from home; Mean travel time to work: 30.6 minutes
Additional Information Contacts
Village of Pleasantville . . . . (914) 769-1900
http://www.pleasantville-ny.gov

PORT CHESTER (village). Covers a land area of 2.331 square miles and a water area of 0.071 square miles. Located at 41.00° N. Lat; 73.67° W. Long. Elevation is 43 feet.

History: Named for Chester, England, and for its location as a port on Long Island Sound. Gen. Israel Putnam had his headquarters here 1777—1778. Several Colonial homes remain. Previously called Saw Pits, village was renamed in 1837. Settled after 1660. Incorporated 1868.
Population: 29,623; Growth (since 2000): 6.3%; Density: 12,710.3 persons per square mile; Race: 55.0% White, 4.7% Black/African American, 1.5% Asian, 1.4% American Indian/Alaska Native, 0.0% Native Hawaiian/Other Pacific Islander, 2.3% Two or more races, 64.8% Hispanic of any race; Average household size: 3.29; Median age: 36.4; Age under 18: 23.9%; Age 65 and over: 11.1%; Males per 100 females: 110.3; Marriage status: 38.7% never married, 49.9% now married, 4.0% separated, 4.3% widowed, 7.1% divorced; Foreign born: 45.3%; Speak English only: 35.4%; With disability: 9.5%; Veterans: 2.4%; Ancestry: 12.9% Italian, 4.7% Irish, 4.5% American, 3.1% German, 2.1% English
Employment: 9.4% management, business, and financial, 1.3% computer, engineering, and science, 6.7% education, legal, community service, arts, and media, 3.8% healthcare practitioners, 34.2% service, 21.8% sales and office, 12.0% natural resources, construction, and maintenance, 10.7% production, transportation, and material moving
Income: Per capita: $27,488; Median household: $60,041; Average household: $86,645; Households with income of $100,000 or more: 31.3%; Poverty rate: 12.4%
Educational Attainment: High school diploma or higher: 70.7%; Bachelor's degree or higher: 23.2%; Graduate/professional degree or higher: 9.1%
School District(s)
Port Chester-Rye Union Free SD (KG-12)
Enrollment: 4,984 . . . . (914) 934-7901
Housing: Homeownership rate: 42.2%; Median home value: $445,200; Median year structure built: 1949; Homeowner vacancy rate: 1.5%; Median selected monthly owner costs: $3,179 with a mortgage, $1,285 without a mortgage; Median gross rent: $1,475 per month; Rental vacancy rate: 3.3%
Health Insurance: 78.8% have insurance; 50.6% have private insurance; 35.0% have public insurance; 21.2% do not have insurance; 3.3% of children under 18 do not have insurance
Safety: Violent crime rate: 16.5 per 10,000 population; Property crime rate: 108.7 per 10,000 population
Newspapers: Hometown Media (weekly circulation 38,000); Westmore News (weekly circulation 3,500)
Transportation: Commute: 65.5% car, 17.3% public transportation, 9.0% walk, 2.5% work from home; Mean travel time to work: 25.7 minutes
Additional Information Contacts
Village of Port Chester . . . . (914) 939-5202
http://www.portchesterny.com

POUND RIDGE (town). Covers a land area of 22.638 square miles and a water area of 0.803 square miles. Located at 41.21° N. Lat; 73.58° W. Long. Elevation is 620 feet.

History: Originally home to the Siwanoy and Kitchawong Indians (Mohican tribes, a subgroup of the Algonquians), the town takes its name from a tribal "pound" or enclosure for game that was on one of the area's many "ridges". The Indians led a relatively peaceful life of planting, hunting, and fishing.

Population: 5,230; Growth (since 2000): 10.7%; Density: 231.0 persons per square mile; Race: 93.2% White, 1.5% Black/African American, 3.5% Asian, 0.0% American Indian/Alaska Native, 0.0% Native Hawaiian/Other Pacific Islander, 1.7% Two or more races, 2.0% Hispanic of any race; Average household size: 2.63; Median age: 50.6; Age under 18: 20.7%; Age 65 and over: 22.5%; Males per 100 females: 96.7; Marriage status: 20.2% never married, 68.7% now married, 0.8% separated, 4.8% widowed, 6.4% divorced; Foreign born: 9.2%; Speak English only: 90.7%; With disability: 7.1%; Veterans: 5.7%; Ancestry: 27.6% Italian, 13.3% German, 13.1% Irish, 8.7% English, 7.1% European
Employment: 32.9% management, business, and financial, 4.3% computer, engineering, and science, 24.2% education, legal, community service, arts, and media, 7.6% healthcare practitioners, 7.8% service, 17.4% sales and office, 1.7% natural resources, construction, and maintenance, 4.1% production, transportation, and material moving
Income: Per capita: $128,800; Median household: $198,500; Average household: $339,521; Households with income of $100,000 or more: 77.3%; Poverty rate: 0.7%
Educational Attainment: High school diploma or higher: 99.3%; Bachelor's degree or higher: 75.5%; Graduate/professional degree or higher: 36.8%
School District(s)
Bedford Central SD (PK-12)
Enrollment: 4,187 . . . . (914) 241-6010
Housing: Homeownership rate: 89.7%; Median home value: $923,700; Median year structure built: 1972; Homeowner vacancy rate: 1.3%; Median selected monthly owner costs: $4,000+ with a mortgage, $1,501 without a mortgage; Median gross rent: $3,442 per month; Rental vacancy rate: 0.0%
Health Insurance: 98.1% have insurance; 91.9% have private insurance; 24.7% have public insurance; 1.9% do not have insurance; 1.0% of children under 18 do not have insurance
Safety: Violent crime rate: 9.5 per 10,000 population; Property crime rate: 62.8 per 10,000 population
Transportation: Commute: 59.7% car, 19.8% public transportation, 3.8% walk, 15.2% work from home; Mean travel time to work: 44.3 minutes
Additional Information Contacts
Town of Pound Ridge . . . . (914) 764-5511
http://www.townofpoundridge.com

PURCHASE (unincorporated postal area)
ZCTA: 10577
Covers a land area of 6.717 square miles and a water area of 0.033 square miles. Located at 41.04° N. Lat; 73.71° W. Long. Elevation is 351 feet.
Population: 6,332; Growth (since 2000): 83.3%; Density: 942.7 persons per square mile; Race: 72.7% White, 12.6% Black/African American, 5.7% Asian, 0.3% American Indian/Alaska Native, 0.2% Native Hawaiian/Other Pacific Islander, 5.6% Two or more races, 13.1% Hispanic of any race; Average household size: 3.04; Median age: 20.3; Age under 18: 11.0%; Age 65 and over: 6.5%; Males per 100 females: 78.3; Marriage status: 73.7% never married, 24.1% now married, 0.4% separated, 1.7% widowed, 0.5% divorced; Foreign born: 15.7%; Speak English only: 75.5%; With disability: 8.9%; Veterans: 1.7%; Ancestry: 17.9% Italian, 16.1% Irish, 12.9% German, 5.8% Polish, 4.6% Russian
Employment: 20.0% management, business, and financial, 1.4% computer, engineering, and science, 14.4% education, legal, community service, arts, and media, 5.0% healthcare practitioners, 22.9% service, 33.2% sales and office, 1.7% natural resources, construction, and maintenance, 1.4% production, transportation, and material moving
Income: Per capita: $54,963; Median household: $213,173; Average household: $412,271; Households with income of $100,000 or more: 76.9%; Poverty rate: 11.8%
Educational Attainment: High school diploma or higher: 94.8%; Bachelor's degree or higher: 71.8%; Graduate/professional degree or higher: 38.7%
School District(s)
Harrison Central SD (KG-12)
Enrollment: 3,600 . . . . (914) 630-3021
Four-year College(s)
LIU Hudson at Westchester (Private, Not-for-profit)
Enrollment: 325 . . . . (914) 831-2700
Manhattanville College (Private, Not-for-profit)
Enrollment: 2,690 . . . . (914) 694-2200
Tuition: In-state $37,910; Out-of-state $37,910

SUNY at Purchase College (Public)
 Enrollment: 4,167 . . . . (914) 251-6000
 Tuition: In-state $8,498; Out-of-state $18,148
Two-year College(s)
LIU Hudson at Westchester (Private, Not-for-profit)
 Enrollment: 325. . . . . (914) 831-2700
Manhattanville College (Private, Not-for-profit)
 Enrollment: 2,690 . . . . (914) 694-2200
 Tuition: In-state $37,910; Out-of-state $37,910
SUNY at Purchase College (Public)
 Enrollment: 4,167 . . . . (914) 251-6000
 Tuition: In-state $8,498; Out-of-state $18,148
Vocational/Technical School(s)
LIU Hudson at Westchester (Private, Not-for-profit)
 Enrollment: 325. . . . . (914) 831-2700
Manhattanville College (Private, Not-for-profit)
 Enrollment: 2,690 . . . . (914) 694-2200
 2016-17 Tuition: In-state $37,910; Out-of-state $37,910
SUNY at Purchase College (Public)
 Enrollment: 4,167 . . . . (914) 251-6000
 2016-17 Tuition: In-state $8,498; Out-of-state $18,148
Housing: Homeownership rate: 88.1%; Median home value: $1,116,200; Median year structure built: 1975; Homeowner vacancy rate: 1.6%; Median selected monthly owner costs: $4,000 with a mortgage, $1,501 without a mortgage; Median gross rent: $3,500+ per month; Rental vacancy rate: 0.0%
Health Insurance: 95.4% have insurance; 86.1% have private insurance; 17.0% have public insurance; 4.6% do not have insurance; 3.3% of children under 18 do not have insurance
Transportation: Commute: 49.3% car, 12.1% public transportation, 25.3% walk, 12.9% work from home; Mean travel time to work: 23.5 minutes

PURDYS (unincorporated postal area)
ZCTA: 10578
Covers a land area of 1.584 square miles and a water area of 0.168 square miles. Located at 41.32° N. Lat; 73.68° W. Long. Elevation is 253 feet.
Population: 851; Growth (since 2000): 28.7%; Density: 537.3 persons per square mile; Race: 85.7% White, 0.0% Black/African American, 4.0% Asian, 0.0% American Indian/Alaska Native, 0.0% Native Hawaiian/Other Pacific Islander, 0.0% Two or more races, 19.5% Hispanic of any race; Average household size: 3.08; Median age: 37.9; Age under 18: 21.4%; Age 65 and over: 2.2%; Males per 100 females: 92.9; Marriage status: 39.3% never married, 50.2% now married, 1.0% separated, 2.5% widowed, 8.1% divorced; Foreign born: 21.3%; Speak English only: 74.5%; With disability: 2.0%; Veterans: 2.5%; Ancestry: 24.0% Italian, 17.0% German, 11.3% English, 9.8% Irish, 8.1% Russian
Employment: 12.2% management, business, and financial, 9.8% computer, engineering, and science, 24.7% education, legal, community service, arts, and media, 3.7% healthcare practitioners, 7.7% service, 28.6% sales and office, 8.9% natural resources, construction, and maintenance, 4.4% production, transportation, and material moving
Income: Per capita: $38,378; Median household: $105,625; Average household: $114,040; Households with income of $100,000 or more: 50.7%; Poverty rate: 3.6%
Educational Attainment: High school diploma or higher: 100.0%; Bachelor's degree or higher: 51.1%; Graduate/professional degree or higher: 20.7%
Housing: Homeownership rate: 77.2%; Median home value: $479,200; Median year structure built: 1956; Homeowner vacancy rate: 0.0%; Median selected monthly owner costs: $3,266 with a mortgage, $996 without a mortgage; Median gross rent: $1,786 per month; Rental vacancy rate: 0.0%
Health Insurance: 91.7% have insurance; 85.2% have private insurance; 8.3% have public insurance; 8.3% do not have insurance; 0.0% of children under 18 do not have insurance
Transportation: Commute: 85.5% car, 14.5% public transportation, 0.0% walk, 0.0% work from home; Mean travel time to work: 40.1 minutes

RYE (city).
Covers a land area of 5.848 square miles and a water area of 14.173 square miles. Located at 40.94° N. Lat; 73.69° W. Long. Elevation is 26 feet.
History: Named for Rye in Sussex, England. In colonial times, Rye was the first stop on the Boston Post Road after N.Y. city. The old Square House, an inn where many Revolutionary notables stayed, is now a museum. Playland, a large county-owned amusement park, is on the beach here. Chief Justice John Jay is buried in Rye. Settled 1660. Incorporated as a city 1942.
Population: 16,004; Growth (since 2000): 7.0%; Density: 2,736.5 persons per square mile; Race: 90.0% White, 0.9% Black/African American, 4.8% Asian, 0.7% American Indian/Alaska Native, 0.0% Native Hawaiian/Other Pacific Islander, 2.1% Two or more races, 6.1% Hispanic of any race; Average household size: 2.91; Median age: 42.9; Age under 18: 30.2%; Age 65 and over: 15.4%; Males per 100 females: 92.7; Marriage status: 20.9% never married, 67.6% now married, 1.6% separated, 5.8% widowed, 5.7% divorced; Foreign born: 16.2%; Speak English only: 81.7%; With disability: 8.6%; Veterans: 4.8%; Ancestry: 19.9% Irish, 16.9% Italian, 12.1% German, 9.6% American, 8.8% English
Employment: 30.9% management, business, and financial, 3.8% computer, engineering, and science, 17.0% education, legal, community service, arts, and media, 6.7% healthcare practitioners, 10.7% service, 25.0% sales and office, 2.9% natural resources, construction, and maintenance, 3.0% production, transportation, and material moving
Income: Per capita: $95,000; Median household: $172,422; Average household: $276,177; Households with income of $100,000 or more: 68.1%; Poverty rate: 3.2%
Educational Attainment: High school diploma or higher: 95.9%; Bachelor's degree or higher: 73.5%; Graduate/professional degree or higher: 37.8%
School District(s)
Rye City SD (KG-12)
 Enrollment: 3,452 . . . . (914) 967-6108
Housing: Homeownership rate: 76.3%; Median home value: $1,094,500; Median year structure built: 1954; Homeowner vacancy rate: 0.0%; Median selected monthly owner costs: $4,000+ with a mortgage, $1,501 without a mortgage; Median gross rent: $2,137 per month; Rental vacancy rate: 0.0%
Health Insurance: 98.0% have insurance; 89.9% have private insurance; 17.6% have public insurance; 2.0% do not have insurance; 0.8% of children under 18 do not have insurance
Safety: Violent crime rate: 3.1 per 10,000 population; Property crime rate: 45.6 per 10,000 population
Transportation: Commute: 52.1% car, 33.5% public transportation, 3.6% walk, 9.6% work from home; Mean travel time to work: 37.7 minutes
Additional Information Contacts
City of Rye. . . . . (914) 967-5400
 http://www.ryeny.gov

RYE (town).
Covers a land area of 6.919 square miles and a water area of 0.435 square miles. Located at 41.01° N. Lat; 73.69° W. Long. Elevation is 26 feet.
Population: 46,978; Growth (since 2000): 7.1%; Density: 6,789.9 persons per square mile; Race: 64.8% White, 4.5% Black/African American, 3.3% Asian, 0.9% American Indian/Alaska Native, 0.0% Native Hawaiian/Other Pacific Islander, 2.2% Two or more races, 46.1% Hispanic of any race; Average household size: 3.07; Median age: 38.5; Age under 18: 24.5%; Age 65 and over: 13.4%; Males per 100 females: 102.9; Marriage status: 34.4% never married, 53.2% now married, 2.9% separated, 4.8% widowed, 7.6% divorced; Foreign born: 37.2%; Speak English only: 48.1%; With disability: 8.5%; Veterans: 3.1%; Ancestry: 16.7% Italian, 6.8% Irish, 6.2% American, 4.4% German, 2.5% Russian
Employment: 15.4% management, business, and financial, 2.1% computer, engineering, and science, 10.9% education, legal, community service, arts, and media, 4.7% healthcare practitioners, 27.1% service, 21.8% sales and office, 9.6% natural resources, construction, and maintenance, 8.5% production, transportation, and material moving
Income: Per capita: $40,709; Median household: $78,245; Average household: $122,268; Households with income of $100,000 or more: 41.9%; Poverty rate: 10.0%
Educational Attainment: High school diploma or higher: 78.0%; Bachelor's degree or higher: 36.9%; Graduate/professional degree or higher: 16.9%

School District(s)
Rye City SD (KG-12)
    Enrollment: 3,452 . . . . (914) 967-6108
Housing: Homeownership rate: 54.1%; Median home value: $558,900; Median year structure built: 1953; Homeowner vacancy rate: 3.0%; Median selected monthly owner costs: $3,572 with a mortgage, $1,396 without a mortgage; Median gross rent: $1,570 per month; Rental vacancy rate: 3.4%
Health Insurance: 84.1% have insurance; 62.0% have private insurance; 31.1% have public insurance; 15.9% do not have insurance; 2.1% of children under 18 do not have insurance
Transportation: Commute: 66.4% car, 19.8% public transportation, 6.2% walk, 3.5% work from home; Mean travel time to work: 28.5 minutes
Additional Information Contacts
Town of Rye . . . . (914) 939-3570
    http://www.townofryeny.com

RYE BROOK (village). Covers a land area of 3.433 square miles and a water area of 0.031 square miles. Located at 41.03° N. Lat; 73.69° W. Long. Elevation is 249 feet.
History: Prior to the village's establishment on July 7, 1982, the area was an unincorporated section of the Town of Rye. The population was 8,602 according to the 2000 census. Rye Brook has been designated as a Tree City USA for 14 years.
Population: 9,543; Growth (since 2000): 10.9%; Density: 2,780.0 persons per square mile; Race: 82.6% White, 2.2% Black/African American, 6.7% Asian, 0.2% American Indian/Alaska Native, 0.0% Native Hawaiian/Other Pacific Islander, 1.4% Two or more races, 14.6% Hispanic of any race; Average household size: 2.75; Median age: 42.9; Age under 18: 26.1%; Age 65 and over: 20.1%; Males per 100 females: 88.4; Marriage status: 24.6% never married, 61.4% now married, 0.2% separated, 6.3% widowed, 7.7% divorced; Foreign born: 20.9%; Speak English only: 71.4%; With disability: 8.0%; Veterans: 4.7%; Ancestry: 19.4% Italian, 9.3% American, 8.4% Russian, 7.0% Irish, 5.9% Polish
Employment: 28.3% management, business, and financial, 4.1% computer, engineering, and science, 20.6% education, legal, community service, arts, and media, 7.1% healthcare practitioners, 12.5% service, 20.7% sales and office, 4.8% natural resources, construction, and maintenance, 2.0% production, transportation, and material moving
Income: Per capita: $70,486; Median household: $131,818; Average household: $192,907; Households with income of $100,000 or more: 61.3%; Poverty rate: 7.7%
Educational Attainment: High school diploma or higher: 90.2%; Bachelor's degree or higher: 65.5%; Graduate/professional degree or higher: 32.3%
School District(s)
Blind Brook-Rye Union Free SD (KG-12)
    Enrollment: 1,501 . . . . (914) 937-3600
Westchester Boces
    Enrollment: n/a . . . . (914) 937-3820
Housing: Homeownership rate: 77.0%; Median home value: $746,800; Median year structure built: 1963; Homeowner vacancy rate: 3.7%; Median selected monthly owner costs: $4,000+ with a mortgage, $1,501 without a mortgage; Median gross rent: $1,669 per month; Rental vacancy rate: 8.1%
Health Insurance: 92.1% have insurance; 79.7% have private insurance; 26.3% have public insurance; 7.9% do not have insurance; 0.0% of children under 18 do not have insurance
Safety: Violent crime rate: 0.0 per 10,000 population; Property crime rate: 95.8 per 10,000 population
Transportation: Commute: 64.6% car, 27.8% public transportation, 0.8% walk, 6.2% work from home; Mean travel time to work: 36.0 minutes
Additional Information Contacts
Village of Rye Brook . . . . (914) 939-1121
    http://www.ryebrook.org

SCARSDALE (town/village). Covers a land area of 6.660 square miles and a water area of 0.008 square miles. Located at 40.99° N. Lat; 73.78° W. Long. Elevation is 217 feet.
Population: 17,856; Growth (since 2000): 0.2%; Density: 2,680.9 persons per square mile; Race: 80.4% White, 0.9% Black/African American, 15.1% Asian, 0.1% American Indian/Alaska Native, 0.1% Native Hawaiian/Other Pacific Islander, 3.1% Two or more races, 4.4% Hispanic of any race; Average household size: 3.20; Median age: 43.0; Age under 18: 31.5%; Age 65 and over: 14.5%; Males per 100 females: 95.1; Marriage status:

20.3% never married, 73.1% now married, 0.6% separated, 3.6% widowed, 3.0% divorced; Foreign born: 22.8%; Speak English only: 75.8%; With disability: 5.3%; Veterans: 3.3%; Ancestry: 10.4% Russian, 9.1% Italian, 7.9% American, 6.8% German, 6.6% Polish
Employment: 35.2% management, business, and financial, 7.2% computer, engineering, and science, 23.2% education, legal, community service, arts, and media, 8.8% healthcare practitioners, 4.1% service, 20.2% sales and office, 0.6% natural resources, construction, and maintenance, 0.7% production, transportation, and material moving
Income: Per capita: $131,067; Median household: $250,000+; Average household: $417,335; Households with income of $100,000 or more: 85.1%; Poverty rate: 2.5%
Educational Attainment: High school diploma or higher: 98.4%; Bachelor's degree or higher: 89.0%; Graduate/professional degree or higher: 58.3%
School District(s)
Eastchester Union Free SD (KG-12)
    Enrollment: 3,210 . . . . (914) 793-6130
Edgemont Union Free SD (KG-12)
    Enrollment: 1,979 . . . . (914) 472-7768
Scarsdale Union Free SD (KG-12)
    Enrollment: 4,826 . . . . (914) 721-2410
Housing: Homeownership rate: 90.8%; Median home value: $1,337,800; Median year structure built: 1941; Homeowner vacancy rate: 0.7%; Median selected monthly owner costs: $4,000+ with a mortgage, $1,501 without a mortgage; Median gross rent: $3,087 per month; Rental vacancy rate: 4.5%
Health Insurance: 99.1% have insurance; 92.7% have private insurance; 15.6% have public insurance; 0.9% do not have insurance; 0.7% of children under 18 do not have insurance
Safety: Violent crime rate: 3.3 per 10,000 population; Property crime rate: 71.0 per 10,000 population
Newspapers: Scarsdale Inquirer (weekly circulation 6,500)
Transportation: Commute: 43.9% car, 43.5% public transportation, 1.3% walk, 9.8% work from home; Mean travel time to work: 43.7 minutes
Additional Information Contacts
Village and Town of Scarsdale . . . . (914) 722-1175
    http://www.scarsdale.com

SCOTTS CORNERS (CDP). Covers a land area of 1.773 square miles and a water area of 0 square miles. Located at 41.19° N. Lat; 73.56° W. Long. Elevation is 397 feet.
Population: 567; Growth (since 2000): -9.1%; Density: 319.8 persons per square mile; Race: 92.9% White, 0.0% Black/African American, 7.1% Asian, 0.0% American Indian/Alaska Native, 0.0% Native Hawaiian/Other Pacific Islander, 0.0% Two or more races, 0.0% Hispanic of any race; Average household size: 2.30; Median age: 53.9; Age under 18: 14.3%; Age 65 and over: 34.4%; Males per 100 females: 95.9; Marriage status: 20.1% never married, 70.1% now married, 0.0% separated, 1.9% widowed, 8.0% divorced; Foreign born: 15.5%; Speak English only: 70.2%; With disability: 6.0%; Veterans: 15.4%; Ancestry: 31.7% Italian, 21.2% American, 11.8% German, 10.8% European, 10.6% Irish
Employment: 29.2% management, business, and financial, 7.2% computer, engineering, and science, 25.8% education, legal, community service, arts, and media, 17.5% healthcare practitioners, 0.0% service, 13.4% sales and office, 6.9% natural resources, construction, and maintenance, 0.0% production, transportation, and material moving
Income: Per capita: $123,090; Median household: $172,222; Average household: $275,838; Households with income of $100,000 or more: 71.6%; Poverty rate: n/a
Educational Attainment: High school diploma or higher: 98.1%; Bachelor's degree or higher: 70.1%; Graduate/professional degree or higher: 48.0%
Housing: Homeownership rate: 83.7%; Median home value: $877,500; Median year structure built: 1970; Homeowner vacancy rate: 0.0%; Median selected monthly owner costs: $4,000+ with a mortgage, $1,501 without a mortgage; Median gross rent: n/a per month; Rental vacancy rate: 0.0%
Health Insurance: 100.0% have insurance; 97.0% have private insurance; 33.7% have public insurance; 0.0% do not have insurance; 0.0% of children under 18 do not have insurance
Transportation: Commute: 30.1% car, 24.6% public transportation, 7.0% walk, 34.6% work from home; Mean travel time to work: 53.2 minutes

SHENOROCK (CDP). Covers a land area of 0.700 square miles and a water area of 0.029 square miles. Located at 41.33° N. Lat; 73.74° W. Long. Elevation is 509 feet.
Population: 2,071; Growth (since 2000): 9.8%; Density: 2,959.1 persons per square mile; Race: 90.1% White, 1.6% Black/African American, 5.0% Asian, 0.7% American Indian/Alaska Native, 0.0% Native Hawaiian/Other Pacific Islander, 1.3% Two or more races, 14.1% Hispanic of any race; Average household size: 2.90; Median age: 39.8; Age under 18: 26.8%; Age 65 and over: 9.8%; Males per 100 females: 94.9; Marriage status: 23.9% never married, 64.8% now married, 2.0% separated, 4.0% widowed, 7.3% divorced; Foreign born: 13.9%; Speak English only: 86.3%; With disability: 6.7%; Veterans: 9.0%; Ancestry: 29.5% Italian, 19.5% Irish, 8.5% German, 8.4% Polish, 4.6% American
Employment: 16.8% management, business, and financial, 6.2% computer, engineering, and science, 17.2% education, legal, community service, arts, and media, 9.7% healthcare practitioners, 17.1% service, 18.6% sales and office, 9.7% natural resources, construction, and maintenance, 4.7% production, transportation, and material moving
Income: Per capita: $39,907; Median household: $105,179; Average household: $111,442; Households with income of $100,000 or more: 54.1%; Poverty rate: 0.3%
Educational Attainment: High school diploma or higher: 96.4%; Bachelor's degree or higher: 34.8%; Graduate/professional degree or higher: 15.6%
Housing: Homeownership rate: 86.5%; Median home value: $375,500; Median year structure built: 1950; Homeowner vacancy rate: 0.0%; Median selected monthly owner costs: $2,623 with a mortgage, $827 without a mortgage; Median gross rent: $1,772 per month; Rental vacancy rate: 0.0%
Health Insurance: 98.8% have insurance; 94.8% have private insurance; 16.6% have public insurance; 1.2% do not have insurance; 0.0% of children under 18 do not have insurance
Transportation: Commute: 86.4% car, 6.2% public transportation, 0.9% walk, 6.5% work from home; Mean travel time to work: 31.4 minutes

SHRUB OAK (CDP). Covers a land area of 1.580 square miles and a water area of 0.027 square miles. Located at 41.33° N. Lat; 73.83° W. Long. Elevation is 440 feet.
Population: 2,356; Growth (since 2000): 30.0%; Density: 1,490.8 persons per square mile; Race: 73.3% White, 4.6% Black/African American, 2.0% Asian, 0.0% American Indian/Alaska Native, 0.0% Native Hawaiian/Other Pacific Islander, 0.0% Two or more races, 29.0% Hispanic of any race; Average household size: 2.52; Median age: 52.8; Age under 18: 15.6%; Age 65 and over: 26.6%; Males per 100 females: 89.2; Marriage status: 24.4% never married, 65.7% now married, 0.9% separated, 4.3% widowed, 5.6% divorced; Foreign born: 23.2%; Speak English only: 73.8%; With disability: 16.7%; Veterans: 12.8%; Ancestry: 31.2% Italian, 23.3% Irish, 18.6% German, 4.2% Russian, 3.7% American
Employment: 13.1% management, business, and financial, 6.6% computer, engineering, and science, 10.9% education, legal, community service, arts, and media, 10.1% healthcare practitioners, 20.1% service, 19.7% sales and office, 12.6% natural resources, construction, and maintenance, 6.7% production, transportation, and material moving
Income: Per capita: $37,723; Median household: $78,529; Average household: $94,263; Households with income of $100,000 or more: 43.9%; Poverty rate: 9.6%
Educational Attainment: High school diploma or higher: 89.9%; Bachelor's degree or higher: 36.1%; Graduate/professional degree or higher: 14.7%

School District(s)
Lakeland Central SD (PK-12)
    Enrollment: 5,728 . . . . (914) 245-1700
Housing: Homeownership rate: 78.7%; Median home value: $343,000; Median year structure built: 1962; Homeowner vacancy rate: 0.0%; Median selected monthly owner costs: $3,342 with a mortgage, $1,431 without a mortgage; Median gross rent: $1,742 per month; Rental vacancy rate: 0.0%
Health Insurance: 92.2% have insurance; 78.5% have private insurance; 43.3% have public insurance; 7.8% do not have insurance; 0.0% of children under 18 do not have insurance
Transportation: Commute: 82.5% car, 8.9% public transportation, 7.3% walk, 1.4% work from home; Mean travel time to work: 26.8 minutes

SLEEPY HOLLOW (village). Covers a land area of 2.161 square miles and a water area of 2.919 square miles. Located at 41.10° N. Lat; 73.87° W. Long. Elevation is 89 feet.
History: Sleepy Hollow is a village in the town of Mount Pleasant in Westchester County, New York. It is known as the setting of "The Legend of Sleepy Hollow," a short story by Washington Irving, who lived in neighboring Tarrytown and is buried in Sleepy Hollow Cemetery.
Population: 10,190; Growth (since 2000): 10.6%; Density: 4,716.1 persons per square mile; Race: 57.7% White, 4.1% Black/African American, 2.0% Asian, 0.1% American Indian/Alaska Native, 0.0% Native Hawaiian/Other Pacific Islander, 4.5% Two or more races, 54.5% Hispanic of any race; Average household size: 2.70; Median age: 38.7; Age under 18: 23.2%; Age 65 and over: 15.6%; Males per 100 females: 94.2; Marriage status: 33.4% never married, 53.4% now married, 3.2% separated, 6.0% widowed, 7.1% divorced; Foreign born: 41.0%; Speak English only: 40.7%; With disability: 11.1%; Veterans: 3.1%; Ancestry: 8.4% Italian, 6.8% Irish, 4.8% American, 4.0% German, 3.2% English
Employment: 14.1% management, business, and financial, 3.1% computer, engineering, and science, 12.0% education, legal, community service, arts, and media, 4.3% healthcare practitioners, 26.0% service, 18.8% sales and office, 12.4% natural resources, construction, and maintenance, 9.3% production, transportation, and material moving
Income: Per capita: $39,840; Median household: $55,368; Average household: $106,298; Households with income of $100,000 or more: 32.3%; Poverty rate: 19.8%
Educational Attainment: High school diploma or higher: 73.8%; Bachelor's degree or higher: 35.1%; Graduate/professional degree or higher: 17.9%

School District(s)
Pocantico Hills Central SD (PK-08)
    Enrollment: 321 . . . . (914) 631-2440
Union Free SD of the Tarrytowns (KG-12)
    Enrollment: 2,730 . . . . (914) 631-9404
Housing: Homeownership rate: 35.3%; Median home value: $634,000; Median year structure built: 1947; Homeowner vacancy rate: 2.2%; Median selected monthly owner costs: $4,000+ with a mortgage, $1,501 without a mortgage; Median gross rent: $1,439 per month; Rental vacancy rate: 0.0%
Health Insurance: 85.7% have insurance; 56.7% have private insurance; 37.9% have public insurance; 14.3% do not have insurance; 3.2% of children under 18 do not have insurance
Hospitals: Phelps Memorial Hospital Assn (235 beds)
Transportation: Commute: 60.6% car, 19.4% public transportation, 14.3% walk, 4.6% work from home; Mean travel time to work: 25.9 minutes
Additional Information Contacts
Village of Sleepy Hollow . . . . (914) 366-5106
    http://www.sleepyhollowny.gov

SOMERS (town). Covers a land area of 29.642 square miles and a water area of 2.518 square miles. Located at 41.30° N. Lat; 73.72° W. Long. Elevation is 279 feet.
History: Formerly a rural, summer lake community. Early Dutch settlement, it was incorporated 1778 as Stephentown. Renamed Somerstown for US naval hero Captain Richard Somers.
Population: 21,448; Growth (since 2000): 16.9%; Density: 723.6 persons per square mile; Race: 92.0% White, 1.2% Black/African American, 3.3% Asian, 0.5% American Indian/Alaska Native, 0.1% Native Hawaiian/Other Pacific Islander, 0.9% Two or more races, 8.0% Hispanic of any race; Average household size: 2.69; Median age: 48.5; Age under 18: 22.0%; Age 65 and over: 25.5%; Males per 100 females: 91.0; Marriage status: 22.6% never married, 61.5% now married, 0.8% separated, 8.0% widowed, 7.9% divorced; Foreign born: 11.2%; Speak English only: 87.8%; With disability: 10.3%; Veterans: 7.1%; Ancestry: 32.7% Italian, 23.0% Irish, 10.3% German, 6.5% English, 5.7% Polish
Employment: 25.3% management, business, and financial, 4.6% computer, engineering, and science, 19.3% education, legal, community service, arts, and media, 6.2% healthcare practitioners, 10.7% service, 23.3% sales and office, 6.3% natural resources, construction, and maintenance, 4.2% production, transportation, and material moving
Income: Per capita: $58,600; Median household: $118,098; Average household: $158,197; Households with income of $100,000 or more: 56.4%; Poverty rate: 2.3%
Educational Attainment: High school diploma or higher: 95.9%; Bachelor's degree or higher: 55.1%; Graduate/professional degree or higher: 26.2%

School District(s)
Somers Central SD (KG-12)

Enrollment: 3,103 . . . . (914) 277-2400

Housing: Homeownership rate: 89.8%; Median home value: $494,600; Median year structure built: 1978; Homeowner vacancy rate: 1.6%; Median selected monthly owner costs: $3,037 with a mortgage, $1,225 without a mortgage; Median gross rent: $2,011 per month; Rental vacancy rate: 0.0%

Health Insurance: 97.1% have insurance; 87.5% have private insurance; 30.4% have public insurance; 2.9% do not have insurance; 0.6% of children under 18 do not have insurance

Transportation: Commute: 84.1% car, 8.0% public transportation, 1.1% walk, 6.3% work from home; Mean travel time to work: 37.1 minutes

Additional Information Contacts

Town of Somers . . . . (914) 277-3323

http://www.somersny.com

SOUTH SALEM (unincorporated postal area)
ZCTA: 10590

Covers a land area of 13.497 square miles and a water area of 0.520 square miles. Located at 41.26° N. Lat; 73.54° W. Long. Elevation is 541 feet.

Population: 7,047; Growth (since 2000): -2.3%; Density: 522.1 persons per square mile; Race: 90.9% White, 4.1% Black/African American, 2.7% Asian, 0.4% American Indian/Alaska Native, 0.0% Native Hawaiian/Other Pacific Islander, 0.5% Two or more races, 6.4% Hispanic of any race; Average household size: 2.71; Median age: 45.2; Age under 18: 23.4%; Age 65 and over: 15.3%; Males per 100 females: 98.2; Marriage status: 27.0% never married, 62.1% now married, 0.6% separated, 3.8% widowed, 7.1% divorced; Foreign born: 9.8%; Speak English only: 88.9%; With disability: 6.6%; Veterans: 5.4%; Ancestry: 16.7% Irish, 16.5% Italian, 8.9% German, 8.1% American, 7.5% English

Employment: 29.8% management, business, and financial, 11.0% computer, engineering, and science, 16.3% education, legal, community service, arts, and media, 7.5% healthcare practitioners, 7.5% service, 17.6% sales and office, 6.6% natural resources, construction, and maintenance, 3.8% production, transportation, and material moving

Income: Per capita: $70,172; Median household: $135,000; Average household: $188,738; Households with income of $100,000 or more: 64.7%; Poverty rate: 3.8%

Educational Attainment: High school diploma or higher: 97.6%; Bachelor's degree or higher: 65.4%; Graduate/professional degree or higher: 30.2%

School District(s)
Katonah-Lewisboro Union Free SD (KG-12)

Enrollment: 3,135 . . . . (914) 763-7003

Housing: Homeownership rate: 93.1%; Median home value: $574,900; Median year structure built: 1974; Homeowner vacancy rate: 1.1%; Median selected monthly owner costs: $3,415 with a mortgage, $1,367 without a mortgage; Median gross rent: $1,867 per month; Rental vacancy rate: 0.0%

Health Insurance: 96.9% have insurance; 86.5% have private insurance; 21.5% have public insurance; 3.1% do not have insurance; 4.6% of children under 18 do not have insurance

Transportation: Commute: 77.5% car, 10.5% public transportation, 2.8% walk, 9.2% work from home; Mean travel time to work: 42.6 minutes

TARRYTOWN (village).
Covers a land area of 2.926 square miles and a water area of 2.753 square miles. Located at 41.07° N. Lat; 73.87° W. Long. Elevation is 121 feet.

History: Named for a variation of the Dutch translation of "wheat". Of interest are Sunnyside, the home of Washington Irving; Sleepy Hollow cemetery, where Irving is buried; Philipsburg Manor, an estate; and Lyndhurst (1838), a Gothic Revival mansion. Philipsburg Manor, an early trading center complex northwest of village center, includes a Dutch farmhouse (c.1683) and a restored operating gristmill. Settled in the 17th century by Dutch. Incorporated 1870.

Population: 11,534; Growth (since 2000): 4.0%; Density: 3,941.5 persons per square mile; Race: 76.2% White, 5.4% Black/African American, 6.4% Asian, 0.0% American Indian/Alaska Native, 0.0% Native Hawaiian/Other Pacific Islander, 1.2% Two or more races, 28.4% Hispanic of any race; Average household size: 2.49; Median age: 40.3; Age under 18: 20.4%; Age 65 and over: 15.5%; Males per 100 females: 87.7; Marriage status: 33.4% never married, 52.2% now married, 0.7% separated, 5.3%

widowed, 9.2% divorced; Foreign born: 23.5%; Speak English only: 68.8%; With disability: 8.2%; Veterans: 4.1%; Ancestry: 13.8% Irish, 13.0% Italian, 9.7% German, 5.4% American, 5.1% English

Employment: 25.8% management, business, and financial, 6.9% computer, engineering, and science, 18.0% education, legal, community service, arts, and media, 6.9% healthcare practitioners, 15.9% service, 17.0% sales and office, 3.9% natural resources, construction, and maintenance, 5.6% production, transportation, and material moving

Income: Per capita: $59,870; Median household: $111,031; Average household: $150,144; Households with income of $100,000 or more: 55.8%; Poverty rate: 2.8%

Educational Attainment: High school diploma or higher: 91.8%; Bachelor's degree or higher: 54.8%; Graduate/professional degree or higher: 28.9%

School District(s)
Union Free SD of the Tarrytowns (KG-12)

Enrollment: 2,730 . . . . (914) 631-9404

Housing: Homeownership rate: 60.7%; Median home value: $582,800; Median year structure built: 1953; Homeowner vacancy rate: 0.0%; Median selected monthly owner costs: $3,464 with a mortgage, $1,501 without a mortgage; Median gross rent: $1,628 per month; Rental vacancy rate: 0.0%

Health Insurance: 95.2% have insurance; 85.6% have private insurance; 22.2% have public insurance; 4.8% do not have insurance; 1.5% of children under 18 do not have insurance

Safety: Violent crime rate: 7.8 per 10,000 population; Property crime rate: 42.3 per 10,000 population

Newspapers: The Hudson Independent (weekly circulation 13,700)

Transportation: Commute: 66.0% car, 21.8% public transportation, 4.8% walk, 6.0% work from home; Mean travel time to work: 32.0 minutes

Additional Information Contacts

Village of Tarrytown . . . . (914) 631-1652

http://www.tarrytowngov.com/pages/index

THORNWOOD (CDP).
Covers a land area of 1.107 square miles and a water area of 0 square miles. Located at 41.12° N. Lat; 73.78° W. Long. Elevation is 269 feet.

History: Thornwood once had a large and thriving marble quarry near its heart, the intersection of Route 141 and Kensico Road (known as Four Corners). The quarry pit was filled in the mid 1980s and the Town Center shopping center constructed over it.

Population: 3,956; Growth (since 2000): -33.8%; Density: 3,573.1 persons per square mile; Race: 91.7% White, 1.2% Black/African American, 2.0% Asian, 0.0% American Indian/Alaska Native, 0.0% Native Hawaiian/Other Pacific Islander, 0.3% Two or more races, 15.1% Hispanic of any race; Average household size: 3.06; Median age: 41.4; Age under 18: 20.1%; Age 65 and over: 16.9%; Males per 100 females: 98.7; Marriage status: 26.5% never married, 60.2% now married, 1.4% separated, 4.4% widowed, 8.8% divorced; Foreign born: 14.7%; Speak English only: 77.9%; With disability: 5.1%; Veterans: 4.7%; Ancestry: 47.3% Italian, 17.8% Irish, 9.3% German, 3.6% Albanian, 3.3% Polish

Employment: 18.0% management, business, and financial, 5.6% computer, engineering, and science, 15.6% education, legal, community service, arts, and media, 5.6% healthcare practitioners, 12.4% service, 25.8% sales and office, 7.2% natural resources, construction, and maintenance, 9.8% production, transportation, and material moving

Income: Per capita: $49,638; Median household: $135,688; Average household: $150,504; Households with income of $100,000 or more: 62.3%; Poverty rate: 3.2%

Educational Attainment: High school diploma or higher: 89.0%; Bachelor's degree or higher: 49.5%; Graduate/professional degree or higher: 20.5%

School District(s)
Mount Pleasant Central SD (KG-12)

Enrollment: 1,901 . . . . (914) 769-5500

Housing: Homeownership rate: 76.6%; Median home value: $599,200; Median year structure built: 1954; Homeowner vacancy rate: 0.0%; Median selected monthly owner costs: $3,340 with a mortgage, $1,328 without a mortgage; Median gross rent: $1,813 per month; Rental vacancy rate: 23.4%

Health Insurance: 97.0% have insurance; 86.6% have private insurance; 21.8% have public insurance; 3.0% do not have insurance; 2.8% of children under 18 do not have insurance

Transportation: Commute: 87.1% car, 10.1% public transportation, 0.0% walk, 2.8% work from home; Mean travel time to work: 28.7 minutes

TUCKAHOE (village).

Covers a land area of 0.598 square miles and a water area of 0 square miles. Located at 40.95° N. Lat; 73.82° W. Long. Elevation is 112 feet.

History: Settled 1684; incorporated 1903.

Population: 6,656; Growth (since 2000): 7.2%; Density: 11,138.8 persons per square mile; Race: 74.0% White, 8.1% Black/African American, 6.3% Asian, 0.0% American Indian/Alaska Native, 0.0% Native Hawaiian/Other Pacific Islander, 4.7% Two or more races, 13.6% Hispanic of any race; Average household size: 2.38; Median age: 39.5; Age under 18: 17.6%; Age 65 and over: 16.2%; Males per 100 females: 86.6; Marriage status: 38.1% never married, 44.3% now married, 3.7% separated, 4.0% widowed, 13.6% divorced; Foreign born: 26.9%; Speak English only: 65.8%; With disability: 9.5%; Veterans: 4.4%; Ancestry: 27.2% Italian, 19.7% Irish, 7.2% Portuguese, 5.9% German, 4.8% American

Employment: 18.1% management, business, and financial, 3.3% computer, engineering, and science, 19.8% education, legal, community service, arts, and media, 7.3% healthcare practitioners, 21.8% service, 15.9% sales and office, 11.0% natural resources, construction, and maintenance, 2.9% production, transportation, and material moving

Income: Per capita: $52,798; Median household: $70,354; Average household: $123,364; Households with income of $100,000 or more: 38.4%; Poverty rate: 5.1%

Educational Attainment: High school diploma or higher: 92.6%; Bachelor's degree or higher: 46.1%; Graduate/professional degree or higher: 22.3%

Housing: Homeownership rate: 47.0%; Median home value: $450,600; Median year structure built: 1957; Homeowner vacancy rate: 0.0%; Median selected monthly owner costs: $3,128 with a mortgage, $1,501 without a mortgage; Median gross rent: $1,722 per month; Rental vacancy rate: 5.4%

Health Insurance: 90.5% have insurance; 77.6% have private insurance; 27.2% have public insurance; 9.5% do not have insurance; 0.0% of children under 18 do not have insurance

Safety: Violent crime rate: 1.5 per 10,000 population; Property crime rate: 51.2 per 10,000 population

Transportation: Commute: 54.4% car, 31.1% public transportation, 6.2% walk, 6.2% work from home; Mean travel time to work: 39.1 minutes

Additional Information Contacts

Village of Tuckahoe............................... (914) 961-3100
    http://www.tuckahoe.com

VALHALLA (CDP).

Covers a land area of 0.830 square miles and a water area of 0 square miles. Located at 41.08° N. Lat; 73.78° W. Long. Elevation is 256 feet.

Population: 3,304; Growth (since 2000): -38.6%; Density: 3,980.8 persons per square mile; Race: 88.4% White, 2.1% Black/African American, 3.2% Asian, 0.0% American Indian/Alaska Native, 0.0% Native Hawaiian/Other Pacific Islander, 3.3% Two or more races, 19.6% Hispanic of any race; Average household size: 2.97; Median age: 43.6; Age under 18: 19.2%; Age 65 and over: 16.5%; Males per 100 females: 94.1; Marriage status: 33.7% never married, 54.1% now married, 4.9% separated, 7.5% widowed, 4.7% divorced; Foreign born: 23.6%; Speak English only: 68.0%; With disability: 11.4%; Veterans: 3.5%; Ancestry: 29.3% Italian, 16.3% Irish, 10.5% German, 5.1% American, 4.4% Croatian

Employment: 16.9% management, business, and financial, 4.2% computer, engineering, and science, 13.9% education, legal, community service, arts, and media, 5.5% healthcare practitioners, 24.0% service, 19.2% sales and office, 10.1% natural resources, construction, and maintenance, 6.2% production, transportation, and material moving

Income: Per capita: $44,903; Median household: $104,205; Average household: $130,638; Households with income of $100,000 or more: 51.4%; Poverty rate: 3.2%

Educational Attainment: High school diploma or higher: 90.9%; Bachelor's degree or higher: 44.4%; Graduate/professional degree or higher: 19.1%

School District(s)

Greenburgh-North Castle Union Free SD (07-12)
    Enrollment: 28........................... (914) 693-4309
Mount Pleasant-Blythedale Union Free SD (KG-12)
    Enrollment: 110........................... (914) 347-1800
Valhalla Union Free SD (KG-12)
    Enrollment: 1,480........................... (914) 683-5040

Four-year College(s)

New York Medical College (Private, Not-for-profit, Jewish)
    Enrollment: 1,498........................... (914) 594-4000

Two-year College(s)

SUNY Westchester Community College (Public)
    Enrollment: 12,571........................... (914) 606-6600
    Tuition: In-state $4,743; Out-of-state $12,233

Housing: Homeownership rate: 75.7%; Median home value: $565,300; Median year structure built: 1954; Homeowner vacancy rate: 0.0%; Median selected monthly owner costs: $3,631 with a mortgage, $1,455 without a mortgage; Median gross rent: $1,896 per month; Rental vacancy rate: 0.0%

Health Insurance: 94.8% have insurance; 81.7% have private insurance; 27.1% have public insurance; 5.2% do not have insurance; 0.0% of children under 18 do not have insurance

Hospitals: Westchester Medical Center (635 beds)

Transportation: Commute: 72.9% car, 18.1% public transportation, 2.7% walk, 5.7% work from home; Mean travel time to work: 31.3 minutes

VERPLANCK (CDP).

Covers a land area of 0.622 square miles and a water area of 0.104 square miles. Located at 41.26° N. Lat; 73.96° W. Long. Elevation is 59 feet.

Population: 1,462; Growth (since 2000): 88.2%; Density: 2,349.4 persons per square mile; Race: 86.7% White, 0.9% Black/African American, 2.5% Asian, 0.0% American Indian/Alaska Native, 0.0% Native Hawaiian/Other Pacific Islander, 2.3% Two or more races, 20.2% Hispanic of any race; Average household size: 3.00; Median age: 36.7; Age under 18: 25.2%; Age 65 and over: 7.2%; Males per 100 females: 92.1; Marriage status: 35.4% never married, 47.3% now married, 2.2% separated, 4.9% widowed, 12.4% divorced; Foreign born: 16.1%; Speak English only: 85.8%; With disability: 11.5%; Veterans: 3.0%; Ancestry: 31.8% Irish, 26.7% Italian, 11.4% English, 8.8% German, 4.9% European

Employment: 18.3% management, business, and financial, 0.7% computer, engineering, and science, 12.3% education, legal, community service, arts, and media, 4.2% healthcare practitioners, 31.2% service, 15.9% sales and office, 10.4% natural resources, construction, and maintenance, 7.0% production, transportation, and material moving

Income: Per capita: $35,586; Median household: $92,283; Average household: $104,610; Households with income of $100,000 or more: 41.3%; Poverty rate: 3.4%

Educational Attainment: High school diploma or higher: 89.9%; Bachelor's degree or higher: 26.9%; Graduate/professional degree or higher: 10.9%

Housing: Homeownership rate: 57.8%; Median home value: $296,300; Median year structure built: 1951; Homeowner vacancy rate: 0.0%; Median selected monthly owner costs: $2,733 with a mortgage, $972 without a mortgage; Median gross rent: $1,458 per month; Rental vacancy rate: 10.9%

Health Insurance: 96.6% have insurance; 77.2% have private insurance; 25.7% have public insurance; 3.4% do not have insurance; 0.0% of children under 18 do not have insurance

Transportation: Commute: 81.4% car, 12.3% public transportation, 3.1% walk, 2.0% work from home; Mean travel time to work: 36.0 minutes

WACCABUC (unincorporated postal area)

ZCTA: 10597

Covers a land area of 3.339 square miles and a water area of 0.249 square miles. Located at 41.29° N. Lat; 73.60° W. Long. Elevation is 554 feet.

Population: 919; Growth (since 2000): 106.5%; Density: 275.2 persons per square mile; Race: 100.0% White, 0.0% Black/African American, 0.0% Asian, 0.0% American Indian/Alaska Native, 0.0% Native Hawaiian/Other Pacific Islander, 0.0% Two or more races, 0.0% Hispanic of any race; Average household size: 2.60; Median age: 52.1; Age under 18: 21.0%; Age 65 and over: 27.7%; Males per 100 females: 100.4; Marriage status: 14.8% never married, 73.1% now married, 0.0% separated, 3.7% widowed, 8.3% divorced; Foreign born: 13.7%; Speak English only: 82.6%; With disability: 2.6%; Veterans: 9.9%; Ancestry: 31.9% Russian, 22.3% German, 15.6% Irish, 14.9% Italian, 11.8% Estonian

Employment: 33.3% management, business, and financial, 7.6% computer, engineering, and science, 43.5% education, legal, community service, arts, and media, 9.5% healthcare practitioners, 0.0% service, 6.1% sales and office, 0.0% natural resources, construction, and maintenance, 0.0% production, transportation, and material moving

Income: Per capita: $121,502; Median household: $250,000+; Average household: $311,804; Households with income of $100,000 or more: 88.3%; Poverty rate: n/a

Educational Attainment: High school diploma or higher: 100.0%; Bachelor's degree or higher: 94.2%; Graduate/professional degree or higher: 58.7%

Housing: Homeownership rate: 100.0%; Median home value: $931,200; Median year structure built: 1979; Homeowner vacancy rate: 0.0%; Median selected monthly owner costs: $4,000 with a mortgage, $1,501 without a mortgage; Median gross rent: n/a per month; Rental vacancy rate: 0.0%

Health Insurance: 100.0% have insurance; 97.0% have private insurance; 33.7% have public insurance; 0.0% do not have insurance; 0.0% of children under 18 do not have insurance

Transportation: Commute: 80.1% car, 12.1% public transportation, 0.0% walk, 7.8% work from home; Mean travel time to work: 53.3 minutes

WEST HARRISON (unincorporated postal area)

ZCTA: 10604

Covers a land area of 6.813 square miles and a water area of 1.252 square miles. Located at 41.06° N. Lat; 73.74° W. Long..

Population: 11,153; Growth (since 2000): 6.9%; Density: 1,637.0 persons per square mile; Race: 77.6% White, 6.1% Black/African American, 5.9% Asian, 0.4% American Indian/Alaska Native, 0.0% Native Hawaiian/Other Pacific Islander, 2.4% Two or more races, 22.8% Hispanic of any race; Average household size: 2.92; Median age: 40.4; Age under 18: 21.9%; Age 65 and over: 15.0%; Males per 100 females: 92.0; Marriage status: 32.7% never married, 51.1% now married, 1.4% separated, 5.4% widowed, 10.8% divorced; Foreign born: 29.2%; Speak English only: 63.2%; With disability: 9.5%; Veterans: 3.5%; Ancestry: 29.4% Italian, 7.8% American, 7.5% Irish, 5.2% German, 3.4% English

Employment: 16.4% management, business, and financial, 6.4% computer, engineering, and science, 14.3% education, legal, community service, arts, and media, 5.6% healthcare practitioners, 22.2% service, 22.5% sales and office, 7.5% natural resources, construction, and maintenance, 5.0% production, transportation, and material moving

Income: Per capita: $51,097; Median household: $88,750; Average household: $144,593; Households with income of $100,000 or more: 46.4%; Poverty rate: 8.2%

Educational Attainment: High school diploma or higher: 89.3%; Bachelor's degree or higher: 43.3%; Graduate/professional degree or higher: 19.0%

School District(s)

Harrison Central SD (KG-12)

    Enrollment: 3,600 . . . . (914) 630-3021

Housing: Homeownership rate: 55.0%; Median home value: $650,800; Median year structure built: 1958; Homeowner vacancy rate: 1.2%; Median selected monthly owner costs: $3,430 with a mortgage, $1,501 without a mortgage; Median gross rent: $1,820 per month; Rental vacancy rate: 2.6%

Health Insurance: 91.6% have insurance; 72.9% have private insurance; 28.6% have public insurance; 8.4% do not have insurance; 3.3% of children under 18 do not have insurance

Transportation: Commute: 77.8% car, 12.3% public transportation, 4.1% walk, 4.8% work from home; Mean travel time to work: 24.8 minutes

WHITE PLAINS (city). County seat. Covers a land area of 9.768 square miles and a water area of 0.117 square miles. Located at 41.03° N. Lat; 73.75° W. Long. Elevation is 213 feet.

History: Named for the Weckquaeskeck word "quaropas," meaning "white marshes or plains". Settled by Puritans in 1683. The state convention that ratified the Declaration of Independence met (1776) here. The battle of White Plains (1776), a principal engagement of the American Revolution occurred here. Gen. George Washington briefly made his headquarters here at Elijah Miller House, which still stands. Other buildings from the revolutionary period are also preserved. Incorporated as a village 1866 (originally named Quarrapas by Siwanoy people), as a city 1916.

Population: 58,404; Growth (since 2000): 10.0%; Density: 5,979.2 persons per square mile; Race: 59.7% White, 12.5% Black/African American, 7.8% Asian, 0.8% American Indian/Alaska Native, 0.0% Native Hawaiian/Other Pacific Islander, 2.3% Two or more races, 33.2% Hispanic of any race; Average household size: 2.58; Median age: 38.1; Age under 18: 20.3%; Age 65 and over: 15.6%; Males per 100 females: 92.7; Marriage status: 36.1% never married, 49.9% now married, 2.6% separated, 5.9% widowed, 8.2% divorced; Foreign born: 30.8%; Speak

English only: 56.6%; With disability: 9.1%; Veterans: 3.5%; Ancestry: 13.9% Italian, 9.1% Irish, 5.7% German, 5.0% American, 2.9% Russian

Employment: 20.9% management, business, and financial, 5.3% computer, engineering, and science, 16.7% education, legal, community service, arts, and media, 5.5% healthcare practitioners, 21.9% service, 19.8% sales and office, 5.0% natural resources, construction, and maintenance, 4.8% production, transportation, and material moving

Income: Per capita: $47,907; Median household: $87,550; Average household: $123,588; Households with income of $100,000 or more: 45.6%; Poverty rate: 11.9%

Educational Attainment: High school diploma or higher: 86.6%; Bachelor's degree or higher: 50.3%; Graduate/professional degree or higher: 24.9%

School District(s)

Greenburgh Central SD (PK-12)

    Enrollment: 1,894 . . . . (914) 761-6000

Valhalla Union Free SD (KG-12)

    Enrollment: 1,480 . . . . (914) 683-5040

White Plains City SD (KG-12)

    Enrollment: 7,105 . . . . (914) 422-2019

Four-year College(s)

The College of Westchester (Private, For-profit)

    Enrollment: 916 . . . . (914) 948-4442

    Tuition: In-state $21,015; Out-of-state $21,015

Two-year College(s)

Center for Ultrasound Research & Education (Private, For-profit)

    Enrollment: 37 . . . . (855) 843-2873

Vocational/Technical School(s)

New York School of Esthetics & Day Spa (Private, For-profit)

    Enrollment: 105 . . . . (914) 631-4432

    Tuition: $7,375

Housing: Homeownership rate: 52.1%; Median home value: $526,100; Median year structure built: 1958; Homeowner vacancy rate: 2.0%; Median selected monthly owner costs: $3,146 with a mortgage, $1,324 without a mortgage; Median gross rent: $1,687 per month; Rental vacancy rate: 2.3%

Health Insurance: 88.3% have insurance; 68.8% have private insurance; 30.3% have public insurance; 11.7% do not have insurance; 3.3% of children under 18 do not have insurance

Hospitals: White Plains Hospital Center (307 beds); Winifred Masterson Burke Rehabilitation Hospital (150 beds)

Safety: Violent crime rate: 17.6 per 10,000 population; Property crime rate: 168.0 per 10,000 population

Newspapers: Journal News (daily circulation 122,000); Review Press (weekly circulation 5,500); White Plains Times (weekly circulation 25,000)

Transportation: Commute: 67.9% car, 17.7% public transportation, 7.9% walk, 4.5% work from home; Mean travel time to work: 27.4 minutes

Airports: Westchester County (primary service/small hub)

Additional Information Contacts

City of White Plains . . . . (914) 422-1200

    http://www.ci.white-plains.ny.us

YONKERS (city). Covers a land area of 18.012 square miles and a water area of 2.285 square miles. Located at 40.95° N. Lat; 73.87° W. Long. Elevation is 82 feet.

History: Named for Adriaen Van der Donck, whose title was "jonkheer," purchaser of the land. The village of Nappeckamack stood on the site of Yonkers before the Kekeskick Purchase (1639) made by the Dutch West India Company. The city site was included in a grant of land made in 1646 by the company to Adriaen Cornelissen Van der Donck, the first lawyer and first historian of New Netherland. By reason of his wealth and social position, Van der Donck enjoyed the courtesy title of "jonker," the Dutch equivalent of "his young lordship," from which was derived the name of the city.

Population: 200,999; Growth (since 2000): 2.5%; Density: 11,159.2 persons per square mile; Race: 56.3% White, 17.8% Black/African American, 7.2% Asian, 0.4% American Indian/Alaska Native, 0.0% Native Hawaiian/Other Pacific Islander, 3.8% Two or more races, 36.3% Hispanic of any race; Average household size: 2.66; Median age: 38.8; Age under 18: 21.7%; Age 65 and over: 16.4%; Males per 100 females: 90.0; Marriage status: 39.2% never married, 45.9% now married, 3.2% separated, 6.3% widowed, 8.6% divorced; Foreign born: 30.6%; Speak English only: 53.1%; With disability: 11.3%; Veterans: 3.7%; Ancestry: 14.1% Italian, 10.9% Irish, 4.4% American, 3.3% German, 2.3% Polish

Employment: 13.8% management, business, and financial, 3.8% computer, engineering, and science, 12.6% education, legal, community service, arts, and media, 7.0% healthcare practitioners, 21.2% service, 24.2% sales and office, 7.9% natural resources, construction, and maintenance, 9.4% production, transportation, and material moving
Income: Per capita: $32,521; Median household: $62,399; Average household: $84,764; Households with income of $100,000 or more: 30.6%; Poverty rate: 16.4%
Educational Attainment: High school diploma or higher: 82.5%; Bachelor's degree or higher: 32.6%; Graduate/professional degree or higher: 14.2%

School District(s)
Charter School of Educational Excellence (KG-08)
 Enrollment: 699 . . . . (914) 476-5070
Greenburgh-North Castle Union Free SD (07-12)
 Enrollment: 28 . . . . (914) 693-4309
Yonkers City SD (PK-12)
 Enrollment: 27,006 . . . . (914) 376-8100
Four-year College(s)
Saint Vladimirs Orthodox Theological Seminary (Private, Not-for-profit, Russian Orthodox)
 Enrollment: 89 . . . . (914) 961-8313
Two-year College(s)
Cochran School of Nursing (Private, Not-for-profit)
 Enrollment: 120 . . . . (914) 964-4296
Housing: Homeownership rate: 47.3%; Median home value: $380,100; Median year structure built: 1955; Homeowner vacancy rate: 2.2%; Median selected monthly owner costs: $2,585 with a mortgage, $1,030 without a mortgage; Median gross rent: $1,292 per month; Rental vacancy rate: 10.6%
Health Insurance: 90.3% have insurance; 62.5% have private insurance; 39.6% have public insurance; 9.7% do not have insurance; 3.5% of children under 18 do not have insurance
Hospitals: Saint John's Riverside Hospital (407 beds); Saint Joseph's Medical Center (194 beds)
Safety: Violent crime rate: 40.2 per 10,000 population; Property crime rate: 100.4 per 10,000 population
Newspapers: Martinelli Publications (weekly circulation 52,000)
Transportation: Commute: 63.3% car, 27.5% public transportation, 4.7% walk, 2.9% work from home; Mean travel time to work: 34.3 minutes; Amtrak: Train service available.
Additional Information Contacts
City of Yonkers . . . . (914) 377-6020
 http://www.cityofyonkers.com

YORKTOWN (town).
Covers a land area of 36.645 square miles and a water area of 2.612 square miles. Located at 41.27° N. Lat; 73.82° W. Long. Elevation is 505 feet.
History: Nearby, at Crompound (2.5 miles east of Peekskill), is the former anarchist Mohegan colony designed by Lewis Mumford in 1923 and led by American Harry Kelly and Englishmen Joseph Cohen and Leonard Abbott. Also known as the twelve Mohegan Colony and the Modern School Movement, the colony flourished both here and in the Stetton colony in N.J.
Population: 36,900; Growth (since 2000): 1.6%; Density: 1,007.0 persons per square mile; Race: 83.9% White, 4.3% Black/African American, 4.7% Asian, 0.4% American Indian/Alaska Native, 0.0% Native Hawaiian/Other Pacific Islander, 1.5% Two or more races, 15.0% Hispanic of any race; Average household size: 2.79; Median age: 45.5; Age under 18: 22.0%; Age 65 and over: 18.4%; Males per 100 females: 93.0; Marriage status: 26.6% never married, 58.9% now married, 1.6% separated, 6.6% widowed, 7.9% divorced; Foreign born: 14.9%; Speak English only: 80.7%; With disability: 9.6%; Veterans: 5.1%; Ancestry: 32.4% Italian, 19.4% Irish, 10.7% German, 4.9% American, 4.7% English
Employment: 18.0% management, business, and financial, 5.3% computer, engineering, and science, 19.9% education, legal, community service, arts, and media, 6.5% healthcare practitioners, 16.0% service, 22.1% sales and office, 7.0% natural resources, construction, and maintenance, 5.3% production, transportation, and material moving
Income: Per capita: $49,205; Median household: $115,732; Average household: $136,238; Households with income of $100,000 or more: 56.8%; Poverty rate: 3.3%
Educational Attainment: High school diploma or higher: 94.2%; Bachelor's degree or higher: 49.5%; Graduate/professional degree or higher: 24.5%

Housing: Homeownership rate: 84.9%; Median home value: $413,000; Median year structure built: 1967; Homeowner vacancy rate: 0.5%; Median selected monthly owner costs: $3,090 with a mortgage, $1,193 without a mortgage; Median gross rent: $1,418 per month; Rental vacancy rate: 0.0%
Health Insurance: 97.1% have insurance; 84.6% have private insurance; 26.5% have public insurance; 2.9% do not have insurance; 1.8% of children under 18 do not have insurance
Safety: Violent crime rate: 3.2 per 10,000 population; Property crime rate: 58.4 per 10,000 population
Transportation: Commute: 85.4% car, 7.1% public transportation, 2.7% walk, 4.1% work from home; Mean travel time to work: 35.8 minutes
Additional Information Contacts
Town of Yorktown . . . . (914) 962-5722
 http://www.yorktownny.org

YORKTOWN HEIGHTS (CDP).
Covers a land area of 0.914 square miles and a water area of 0.003 square miles. Located at 41.27° N. Lat; 73.77° W. Long. Elevation is 492 feet.
Population: 1,623; Growth (since 2000): -79.6%; Density: 1,775.3 persons per square mile; Race: 94.7% White, 0.9% Black/African American, 2.3% Asian, 0.0% American Indian/Alaska Native, 0.0% Native Hawaiian/Other Pacific Islander, 0.9% Two or more races, 4.6% Hispanic of any race; Average household size: 2.68; Median age: 46.7; Age under 18: 16.0%; Age 65 and over: 23.5%; Males per 100 females: 94.9; Marriage status: 34.2% never married, 49.9% now married, 2.1% separated, 3.9% widowed, 12.1% divorced; Foreign born: 13.9%; Speak English only: 84.3%; With disability: 13.2%; Veterans: 3.2%; Ancestry: 55.1% Italian, 10.8% German, 8.1% Irish, 5.7% English, 5.4% Danish
Employment: 13.4% management, business, and financial, 5.4% computer, engineering, and science, 16.8% education, legal, community service, arts, and media, 10.9% healthcare practitioners, 19.0% service, 20.5% sales and office, 9.5% natural resources, construction, and maintenance, 4.5% production, transportation, and material moving
Income: Per capita: $55,299; Median household: $75,634; Average household: $146,516; Households with income of $100,000 or more: 37.4%; Poverty rate: 6.3%
Educational Attainment: High school diploma or higher: 98.5%; Bachelor's degree or higher: 43.9%; Graduate/professional degree or higher: 15.0%

School District(s)
Lakeland Central SD (PK-12)
 Enrollment: 5,728 . . . . (914) 245-1700
Putnam-Northern Westchester Boces
 Enrollment: n/a . . . . (914) 245-2700
Yorktown Central SD (KG-12)
 Enrollment: 3,466 . . . . (914) 243-8000
Vocational/Technical School(s)
Putnam Westchester BOCES-Practical Nursing Program (Public)
 Enrollment: 22 . . . . (914) 245-2700
 Tuition: $13,000
Housing: Homeownership rate: 83.3%; Median home value: $369,200; Median year structure built: 1965; Homeowner vacancy rate: 0.0%; Median selected monthly owner costs: $2,961 with a mortgage, $1,131 without a mortgage; Median gross rent: $1,068 per month; Rental vacancy rate: 0.0%
Health Insurance: 97.5% have insurance; 76.0% have private insurance; 40.9% have public insurance; 2.5% do not have insurance; 9.0% of children under 18 do not have insurance
Newspapers: North County News (weekly circulation 10,000)
Transportation: Commute: 94.3% car, 0.0% public transportation, 2.6% walk, 3.0% work from home; Mean travel time to work: 27.6 minutes

Wyoming County

Located in western New York; drained by the Genesee River. Covers a land area of 592.746 square miles, a water area of 3.541 square miles, and is located in the Eastern Time Zone at 42.70° N. Lat., 78.23° W. Long. The county was founded in 1841. County seat is Warsaw.

Weather Station: Warsaw 6 SW   Elevation: 1,819 feet

	Jan	Feb	Mar	Apr	May	Jun	Jul	Aug	Sep	Oct	Nov	Dec
High	28	30	38	52	64	72	76	75	68	56	44	32
Low	13	14	20	33	43	53	57	56	49	38	29	19
Precip	3.2	2.5	3.2	3.4	4.0	4.6	4.5	3.7	4.6	4.0	3.9	3.7
Snow	35.3	25.5	20.7	6.1	0.2	0.0	0.0	0.0	0.0	0.6	12.4	29.7

High and Low temperatures in degrees Fahrenheit; Precipitation and Snow in inches

Population: 40,886; Growth (since 2000): -5.8%; Density: 69.0 persons per square mile; Race: 91.9% White, 5.2% Black/African American, 0.4% Asian, 0.4% American Indian/Alaska Native, 0.0% Native Hawaiian/Other Pacific Islander, 1.4% two or more races, 3.3% Hispanic of any race; Average household size: 2.39; Median age: 41.8; Age under 18: 19.9%; Age 65 and over: 16.1%; Males per 100 females: 119.5; Marriage status: 30.3% never married, 53.0% now married, 2.0% separated, 5.3% widowed, 11.4% divorced; Foreign born: 1.8%; Speak English only: 95.9%; With disability: 13.4%; Veterans: 8.4%; Ancestry: 30.9% German, 15.2% Irish, 11.8% English, 11.4% Polish, 7.9% Italian
Religion: Six largest groups: 18.9% Catholicism, 4.7% Methodist/Pietist, 4.3% Presbyterian-Reformed, 1.6% Baptist, 1.2% Non-denominational Protestant, 1.0% Episcopalianism/Anglicanism
Economy: Unemployment rate: 3.2%; Leading industries: 15.9 % retail trade; 13.6 % other services (except public administration); 13.1 % construction; Farms: 713 totaling 225,864 acres; Company size: 0 employ 1,000 or more persons, 1 employs 500 to 999 persons, 12 employ 100 to 499 persons, 766 employ less than 100 persons; Business ownership: 799 women-owned, n/a Black-owned, n/a Hispanic-owned, n/a Asian-owned, n/a American Indian/Alaska Native-owned
Employment: 11.7% management, business, and financial, 2.9% computer, engineering, and science, 8.3% education, legal, community service, arts, and media, 5.2% healthcare practitioners, 18.6% service, 22.4% sales and office, 15.1% natural resources, construction, and maintenance, 15.9% production, transportation, and material moving
Income: Per capita: $25,635; Median household: $55,459; Average household: $65,699; Households with income of $100,000 or more: 17.0%; Poverty rate: 11.4%
Educational Attainment: High school diploma or higher: 88.3%; Bachelor's degree or higher: 15.4%; Graduate/professional degree or higher: 5.8%
Housing: Homeownership rate: 75.8%; Median home value: $108,500; Median year structure built: 1952; Homeowner vacancy rate: 1.3%; Median selected monthly owner costs: $1,135 with a mortgage, $486 without a mortgage; Median gross rent: $634 per month; Rental vacancy rate: 2.7%
Vital Statistics: Birth rate: 87.2 per 10,000 population; Death rate: 82.0 per 10,000 population; Age-adjusted cancer mortality rate: 173.0 deaths per 100,000 population
Health Insurance: 95.1% have insurance; 74.5% have private insurance; 36.8% have public insurance; 4.9% do not have insurance; 3.5% of children under 18 do not have insurance
Health Care: Physicians: 8.7 per 10,000 population; Dentists: 4.7 per 10,000 population; Hospital beds: 18.5 per 10,000 population; Hospital admissions: 592.7 per 10,000 population
Transportation: Commute: 91.6% car, 0.4% public transportation, 3.7% walk, 3.1% work from home; Mean travel time to work: 24.7 minutes
2016 Presidential Election: 71.9% Trump, 22.6% Clinton, 3.9% Johnson, 1.0% Stein
National and State Parks: Letchworth State Park; Silver Lake State Park
Additional Information Contacts
Wyoming Government. . . . . (716) 786-8810
  http://www.wyomingco.net

Wyoming County Communities

ARCADE (town). Covers a land area of 47.004 square miles and a water area of 0.106 square miles. Located at 42.57° N. Lat; 78.37° W. Long. Elevation is 1,476 feet.
Population: 4,108; Growth (since 2000): -1.8%; Density: 87.4 persons per square mile; Race: 96.2% White, 1.5% Black/African American, 0.8% Asian, 0.0% American Indian/Alaska Native, 0.0% Native Hawaiian/Other Pacific Islander, 0.2% Two or more races, 3.9% Hispanic of any race; Average household size: 2.26; Median age: 41.1; Age under 18: 22.0%; Age 65 and over: 16.1%; Males per 100 females: 95.3; Marriage status: 31.2% never married, 49.8% now married, 2.0% separated, 8.0% widowed, 11.0% divorced; Foreign born: 1.1%; Speak English only: 97.6%;

With disability: 14.0%; Veterans: 6.4%; Ancestry: 36.5% German, 14.8% English, 13.3% Irish, 12.1% Polish, 10.9% Italian
Employment: 11.0% management, business, and financial, 3.6% computer, engineering, and science, 9.2% education, legal, community service, arts, and media, 4.3% healthcare practitioners, 18.2% service, 26.1% sales and office, 12.0% natural resources, construction, and maintenance, 15.6% production, transportation, and material moving
Income: Per capita: $24,187; Median household: $41,875; Average household: $54,986; Households with income of $100,000 or more: 13.2%; Poverty rate: 17.8%
Educational Attainment: High school diploma or higher: 89.1%; Bachelor's degree or higher: 14.6%; Graduate/professional degree or higher: 4.6%
School District(s)
Yorkshire-Pioneer Central SD (PK-12)
  Enrollment: 2,544 . . . . (716) 492-9304
Housing: Homeownership rate: 74.6%; Median home value: $111,200; Median year structure built: 1971; Homeowner vacancy rate: 1.7%; Median selected monthly owner costs: $1,126 with a mortgage, $382 without a mortgage; Median gross rent: $623 per month; Rental vacancy rate: 4.4%
Health Insurance: 96.6% have insurance; 69.3% have private insurance; 39.5% have public insurance; 3.4% do not have insurance; 1.7% of children under 18 do not have insurance
Newspapers: Arcade Herald (weekly circulation 5,000)
Transportation: Commute: 91.7% car, 0.0% public transportation, 3.8% walk, 2.7% work from home; Mean travel time to work: 22.8 minutes

ARCADE (village). Covers a land area of 2.649 square miles and a water area of 0.003 square miles. Located at 42.53° N. Lat; 78.44° W. Long. Elevation is 1,476 feet.
Population: 2,159; Growth (since 2000): 6.6%; Density: 814.9 persons per square mile; Race: 96.1% White, 0.0% Black/African American, 1.0% Asian, 0.0% American Indian/Alaska Native, 0.0% Native Hawaiian/Other Pacific Islander, 0.5% Two or more races, 3.2% Hispanic of any race; Average household size: 2.29; Median age: 35.3; Age under 18: 27.3%; Age 65 and over: 12.8%; Males per 100 females: 90.5; Marriage status: 32.2% never married, 47.9% now married, 2.4% separated, 7.2% widowed, 12.7% divorced; Foreign born: 1.3%; Speak English only: 96.5%; With disability: 13.6%; Veterans: 7.8%; Ancestry: 37.0% German, 14.4% English, 13.1% Polish, 12.0% Irish, 10.8% Italian
Employment: 8.0% management, business, and financial, 6.0% computer, engineering, and science, 10.9% education, legal, community service, arts, and media, 4.9% healthcare practitioners, 18.6% service, 28.4% sales and office, 7.8% natural resources, construction, and maintenance, 15.4% production, transportation, and material moving
Income: Per capita: $24,169; Median household: $40,691; Average household: $55,857; Households with income of $100,000 or more: 14.1%; Poverty rate: 19.5%
Educational Attainment: High school diploma or higher: 89.4%; Bachelor's degree or higher: 17.5%; Graduate/professional degree or higher: 7.1%
School District(s)
Yorkshire-Pioneer Central SD (PK-12)
  Enrollment: 2,544 . . . . (716) 492-9304
Housing: Homeownership rate: 64.0%; Median home value: $103,700; Median year structure built: 1945; Homeowner vacancy rate: 0.0%; Median selected monthly owner costs: $1,029 with a mortgage, $559 without a mortgage; Median gross rent: $563 per month; Rental vacancy rate: 3.6%
Health Insurance: 94.5% have insurance; 67.3% have private insurance; 36.8% have public insurance; 5.5% do not have insurance; 2.7% of children under 18 do not have insurance
Safety: Violent crime rate: 10.2 per 10,000 population; Property crime rate: 102.2 per 10,000 population
Newspapers: Arcade Herald (weekly circulation 5,000)
Transportation: Commute: 90.4% car, 0.0% public transportation, 5.5% walk, 2.3% work from home; Mean travel time to work: 22.2 minutes
Additional Information Contacts
Village of Arcade. . . . . (585) 492-1111
  http://www.villageofarcade.org

ATTICA (town). Covers a land area of 35.712 square miles and a water area of 0.315 square miles. Located at 42.82° N. Lat; 78.25° W. Long. Elevation is 981 feet.
Population: 7,364; Growth (since 2000): 22.2%; Density: 206.2 persons per square mile; Race: 70.5% White, 24.5% Black/African American, 0.3%

Asian, 0.8% American Indian/Alaska Native, 0.0% Native Hawaiian/Other Pacific Islander, 2.5% Two or more races, 9.0% Hispanic of any race; Average household size: 2.57; Median age: 36.4; Age under 18: 14.1%; Age 65 and over: 8.1%; Males per 100 females: 283.4; Marriage status: 47.7% never married, 38.7% now married, 2.9% separated, 3.3% widowed, 10.3% divorced; Foreign born: 2.8%; Speak English only: 90.5%; With disability: 8.5%; Veterans: 6.3%; Ancestry: 22.6% German, 9.7% Irish, 7.5% Polish, 6.9% English, 6.6% Italian

Employment: 10.5% management, business, and financial, 3.5% computer, engineering, and science, 5.5% education, legal, community service, arts, and media, 8.3% healthcare practitioners, 24.3% service, 22.6% sales and office, 8.0% natural resources, construction, and maintenance, 17.3% production, transportation, and material moving

Income: Per capita: $15,913; Median household: $61,951; Average household: $68,049; Households with income of $100,000 or more: 20.7%; Poverty rate: 7.1%

Educational Attainment: High school diploma or higher: 80.2%; Bachelor's degree or higher: 9.3%; Graduate/professional degree or higher: 3.7%

School District(s)

Attica Central SD (KG-12)
    Enrollment: 1,290 . . . . (585) 591-2173

Housing: Homeownership rate: 70.4%; Median home value: $113,600; Median year structure built: 1947; Homeowner vacancy rate: 1.4%; Median selected monthly owner costs: $1,178 with a mortgage, $471 without a mortgage; Median gross rent: $664 per month; Rental vacancy rate: 6.9%

Health Insurance: 96.3% have insurance; 82.1% have private insurance; 28.8% have public insurance; 3.7% do not have insurance; 0.0% of children under 18 do not have insurance

Transportation: Commute: 90.6% car, 0.3% public transportation, 4.0% walk, 4.4% work from home; Mean travel time to work: 23.4 minutes

Additional Information Contacts

Town of Attica . . . . (585) 591-2920
    http://www.townofattica.net

ATTICA (village). Covers a land area of 1.691 square miles and a water area of 0 square miles. Located at 42.86° N. Lat; 78.28° W. Long. Elevation is 981 feet.

Population: 2,790; Growth (since 2000): 7.4%; Density: 1,649.4 persons per square mile; Race: 95.1% White, 0.0% Black/African American, 0.3% Asian, 0.9% American Indian/Alaska Native, 0.0% Native Hawaiian/Other Pacific Islander, 3.8% Two or more races, 0.3% Hispanic of any race; Average household size: 2.50; Median age: 33.2; Age under 18: 28.5%; Age 65 and over: 11.2%; Males per 100 females: 93.7; Marriage status: 33.4% never married, 46.5% now married, 3.3% separated, 5.3% widowed, 14.9% divorced; Foreign born: 0.5%; Speak English only: 99.1%; With disability: 7.8%; Veterans: 8.3%; Ancestry: 30.5% German, 13.1% Polish, 11.9% Irish, 10.1% English, 8.2% Italian

Employment: 5.9% management, business, and financial, 2.6% computer, engineering, and science, 5.1% education, legal, community service, arts, and media, 7.2% healthcare practitioners, 25.9% service, 27.3% sales and office, 6.8% natural resources, construction, and maintenance, 19.2% production, transportation, and material moving

Income: Per capita: $26,172; Median household: $57,653; Average household: $66,000; Households with income of $100,000 or more: 15.8%; Poverty rate: 12.0%

Educational Attainment: High school diploma or higher: 90.6%; Bachelor's degree or higher: 17.7%; Graduate/professional degree or higher: 6.5%

School District(s)

Attica Central SD (KG-12)
    Enrollment: 1,290 . . . . (585) 591-2173

Housing: Homeownership rate: 59.0%; Median home value: $95,700; Median year structure built: Before 1940; Homeowner vacancy rate: 2.5%; Median selected monthly owner costs: $1,036 with a mortgage, $464 without a mortgage; Median gross rent: $666 per month; Rental vacancy rate: 7.3%

Health Insurance: 96.7% have insurance; 79.0% have private insurance; 33.3% have public insurance; 3.3% do not have insurance; 0.0% of children under 18 do not have insurance

Transportation: Commute: 90.9% car, 0.5% public transportation, 5.7% walk, 1.7% work from home; Mean travel time to work: 21.9 minutes

Additional Information Contacts

Village of Attica . . . . (585) 591-0898
    http://attica.org

BENNINGTON (town). Covers a land area of 55.049 square miles and a water area of 0.215 square miles. Located at 42.82° N. Lat; 78.39° W. Long. Elevation is 1,207 feet.

Population: 3,261; Growth (since 2000): -2.6%; Density: 59.2 persons per square mile; Race: 99.4% White, 0.0% Black/African American, 0.3% Asian, 0.0% American Indian/Alaska Native, 0.0% Native Hawaiian/Other Pacific Islander, 0.0% Two or more races, 1.5% Hispanic of any race; Average household size: 2.38; Median age: 47.0; Age under 18: 17.2%; Age 65 and over: 20.2%; Males per 100 females: 107.0; Marriage status: 24.5% never married, 58.5% now married, 1.1% separated, 6.1% widowed, 10.8% divorced; Foreign born: 1.3%; Speak English only: 98.0%; With disability: 11.0%; Veterans: 9.9%; Ancestry: 36.0% German, 31.9% Polish, 13.0% Irish, 10.0% English, 7.7% Italian

Employment: 10.6% management, business, and financial, 2.2% computer, engineering, and science, 10.1% education, legal, community service, arts, and media, 4.0% healthcare practitioners, 18.6% service, 23.1% sales and office, 14.5% natural resources, construction, and maintenance, 16.9% production, transportation, and material moving

Income: Per capita: $31,341; Median household: $65,192; Average household: $72,404; Households with income of $100,000 or more: 22.0%; Poverty rate: 4.2%

Educational Attainment: High school diploma or higher: 91.9%; Bachelor's degree or higher: 19.9%; Graduate/professional degree or higher: 8.1%

Housing: Homeownership rate: 89.1%; Median home value: $147,300; Median year structure built: 1962; Homeowner vacancy rate: 0.7%; Median selected monthly owner costs: $1,297 with a mortgage, $580 without a mortgage; Median gross rent: $618 per month; Rental vacancy rate: 0.0%

Health Insurance: 95.3% have insurance; 81.6% have private insurance; 33.1% have public insurance; 4.7% do not have insurance; 3.2% of children under 18 do not have insurance

Transportation: Commute: 93.6% car, 0.7% public transportation, 2.9% walk, 1.2% work from home; Mean travel time to work: 31.6 minutes

BLISS (CDP). Covers a land area of 9.792 square miles and a water area of 0 square miles. Located at 42.58° N. Lat; 78.25° W. Long. Elevation is 1,745 feet.

Population: 597; Growth (since 2000): n/a; Density: 61.0 persons per square mile; Race: 98.8% White, 1.2% Black/African American, 0.0% Asian, 0.0% American Indian/Alaska Native, 0.0% Native Hawaiian/Other Pacific Islander, 0.0% Two or more races, 0.0% Hispanic of any race; Average household size: 2.63; Median age: 38.6; Age under 18: 22.4%; Age 65 and over: 12.9%; Males per 100 females: 92.3; Marriage status: 29.5% never married, 44.2% now married, 3.1% separated, 8.1% widowed, 18.3% divorced; Foreign born: 0.0%; Speak English only: 99.3%; With disability: 13.6%; Veterans: 7.6%; Ancestry: 32.8% German, 26.6% Irish, 12.6% European, 11.2% Italian, 9.5% Polish

Employment: 14.9% management, business, and financial, 2.3% computer, engineering, and science, 1.0% education, legal, community service, arts, and media, 2.6% healthcare practitioners, 14.9% service, 25.2% sales and office, 17.2% natural resources, construction, and maintenance, 21.9% production, transportation, and material moving

Income: Per capita: $25,726; Median household: $61,250; Average household: $66,978; Households with income of $100,000 or more: 20.7%; Poverty rate: 17.9%

Educational Attainment: High school diploma or higher: 92.0%; Bachelor's degree or higher: 15.8%; Graduate/professional degree or higher: 3.9%

Housing: Homeownership rate: 91.2%; Median home value: $87,400; Median year structure built: 1942; Homeowner vacancy rate: 0.0%; Median selected monthly owner costs: $980 with a mortgage, $465 without a mortgage; Median gross rent: n/a per month; Rental vacancy rate: 0.0%

Health Insurance: 96.5% have insurance; 73.5% have private insurance; 35.3% have public insurance; 3.5% do not have insurance; 5.0% of children under 18 do not have insurance

Transportation: Commute: 92.9% car, 0.0% public transportation, 0.0% walk, 3.4% work from home; Mean travel time to work: 37.2 minutes

CASTILE (town). Covers a land area of 36.980 square miles and a water area of 1.415 square miles. Located at 42.66° N. Lat; 78.02° W. Long. Elevation is 1,355 feet.

Population: 2,829; Growth (since 2000): -1.5%; Density: 76.5 persons per square mile; Race: 96.8% White, 1.1% Black/African American, 0.0% Asian, 0.7% American Indian/Alaska Native, 0.0% Native Hawaiian/Other Pacific Islander, 1.4% Two or more races, 4.7% Hispanic of any race;

Average household size: 2.42; Median age: 48.3; Age under 18: 22.6%; Age 65 and over: 22.6%; Males per 100 females: 99.0; Marriage status: 21.6% never married, 63.3% now married, 3.9% separated, 7.1% widowed, 8.0% divorced; Foreign born: 3.7%; Speak English only: 95.3%; With disability: 20.7%; Veterans: 10.9%; Ancestry: 31.3% German, 19.4% English, 16.5% Irish, 7.6% Polish, 7.1% Italian
Employment: 17.9% management, business, and financial, 1.8% computer, engineering, and science, 8.4% education, legal, community service, arts, and media, 2.5% healthcare practitioners, 16.5% service, 24.1% sales and office, 15.2% natural resources, construction, and maintenance, 13.6% production, transportation, and material moving
Income: Per capita: $27,680; Median household: $52,417; Average household: $65,996; Households with income of $100,000 or more: 16.0%; Poverty rate: 15.0%
Educational Attainment: High school diploma or higher: 91.3%; Bachelor's degree or higher: 21.7%; Graduate/professional degree or higher: 8.7%
Housing: Homeownership rate: 83.7%; Median home value: $97,300; Median year structure built: 1941; Homeowner vacancy rate: 0.0%; Median selected monthly owner costs: $1,076 with a mortgage, $456 without a mortgage; Median gross rent: $641 per month; Rental vacancy rate: 7.4%
Health Insurance: 96.0% have insurance; 72.3% have private insurance; 43.5% have public insurance; 4.0% do not have insurance; 5.6% of children under 18 do not have insurance
Transportation: Commute: 91.2% car, 0.0% public transportation, 4.0% walk, 4.8% work from home; Mean travel time to work: 22.7 minutes

CASTILE (village). Covers a land area of 1.352 square miles and a water area of 0 square miles. Located at 42.63° N. Lat; 78.05° W. Long. Elevation is 1,355 feet.
Population: 951; Growth (since 2000): -9.5%; Density: 703.5 persons per square mile; Race: 98.3% White, 0.0% Black/African American, 0.0% Asian, 0.0% American Indian/Alaska Native, 0.0% Native Hawaiian/Other Pacific Islander, 1.7% Two or more races, 0.4% Hispanic of any race; Average household size: 2.52; Median age: 39.0; Age under 18: 27.9%; Age 65 and over: 19.0%; Males per 100 females: 93.0; Marriage status: 26.6% never married, 59.2% now married, 8.5% separated, 5.5% widowed, 8.8% divorced; Foreign born: 1.1%; Speak English only: 96.1%; With disability: 19.8%; Veterans: 9.6%; Ancestry: 26.5% German, 24.7% English, 17.1% Irish, 7.7% Italian, 5.0% Polish
Employment: 14.7% management, business, and financial, 4.7% computer, engineering, and science, 5.8% education, legal, community service, arts, and media, 3.1% healthcare practitioners, 21.3% service, 26.8% sales and office, 11.5% natural resources, construction, and maintenance, 12.1% production, transportation, and material moving
Income: Per capita: $21,149; Median household: $39,018; Average household: $52,951; Households with income of $100,000 or more: 8.7%; Poverty rate: 24.6%
Educational Attainment: High school diploma or higher: 93.5%; Bachelor's degree or higher: 16.9%; Graduate/professional degree or higher: 7.0%
Housing: Homeownership rate: 74.5%; Median home value: $82,200; Median year structure built: Before 1940; Homeowner vacancy rate: 0.0%; Median selected monthly owner costs: $1,000 with a mortgage, $411 without a mortgage; Median gross rent: $624 per month; Rental vacancy rate: 0.0%
Health Insurance: 97.1% have insurance; 65.2% have private insurance; 51.4% have public insurance; 2.9% do not have insurance; 3.6% of children under 18 do not have insurance
Transportation: Commute: 96.4% car, 0.0% public transportation, 0.0% walk, 3.6% work from home; Mean travel time to work: 22.5 minutes

COVINGTON (town). Covers a land area of 26.138 square miles and a water area of 0 square miles. Located at 42.83° N. Lat; 78.01° W. Long. Elevation is 1,102 feet.
Population: 1,045; Growth (since 2000): -23.0%; Density: 40.0 persons per square mile; Race: 97.6% White, 0.3% Black/African American, 0.0% Asian, 1.2% American Indian/Alaska Native, 0.0% Native Hawaiian/Other Pacific Islander, 0.9% Two or more races, 1.0% Hispanic of any race; Average household size: 2.41; Median age: 45.6; Age under 18: 21.1%; Age 65 and over: 16.5%; Males per 100 females: 105.0; Marriage status: 25.8% never married, 61.1% now married, 2.0% separated, 6.6% widowed, 6.5% divorced; Foreign born: 0.6%; Speak English only: 97.8%; With disability: 10.5%; Veterans: 6.2%; Ancestry: 31.5% Irish, 26.4% German, 18.3% English, 11.9% Italian, 11.2% American

Employment: 11.8% management, business, and financial, 0.7% computer, engineering, and science, 7.8% education, legal, community service, arts, and media, 5.1% healthcare practitioners, 11.2% service, 23.5% sales and office, 21.9% natural resources, construction, and maintenance, 18.1% production, transportation, and material moving
Income: Per capita: $27,557; Median household: $59,048; Average household: $65,250; Households with income of $100,000 or more: 18.0%; Poverty rate: 9.0%
Educational Attainment: High school diploma or higher: 89.4%; Bachelor's degree or higher: 17.8%; Graduate/professional degree or higher: 8.3%
Housing: Homeownership rate: 83.4%; Median home value: $111,800; Median year structure built: 1973; Homeowner vacancy rate: 1.9%; Median selected monthly owner costs: $1,152 with a mortgage, $469 without a mortgage; Median gross rent: $646 per month; Rental vacancy rate: 0.0%
Health Insurance: 95.0% have insurance; 74.1% have private insurance; 38.0% have public insurance; 5.0% do not have insurance; 3.1% of children under 18 do not have insurance
Transportation: Commute: 96.9% car, 0.0% public transportation, 0.6% walk, 2.6% work from home; Mean travel time to work: 23.9 minutes

COWLESVILLE (unincorporated postal area)
ZCTA: 14037
Covers a land area of 17.307 square miles and a water area of 0.008 square miles. Located at 42.80° N. Lat; 78.45° W. Long. Elevation is 945 feet.
Population: 1,006; Growth (since 2000): -5.7%; Density: 58.1 persons per square mile; Race: 98.9% White, 0.0% Black/African American, 0.0% Asian, 0.0% American Indian/Alaska Native, 0.0% Native Hawaiian/Other Pacific Islander, 0.0% Two or more races, 3.0% Hispanic of any race; Average household size: 2.41; Median age: 44.9; Age under 18: 17.1%; Age 65 and over: 16.5%; Males per 100 females: 105.3; Marriage status: 24.8% never married, 56.5% now married, 0.9% separated, 3.3% widowed, 15.5% divorced; Foreign born: 0.8%; Speak English only: 96.1%; With disability: 9.7%; Veterans: 10.3%; Ancestry: 32.0% German, 23.1% Polish, 7.3% Irish, 7.2% American, 6.2% English
Employment: 11.9% management, business, and financial, 0.0% computer, engineering, and science, 10.7% education, legal, community service, arts, and media, 4.9% healthcare practitioners, 27.9% service, 17.2% sales and office, 14.6% natural resources, construction, and maintenance, 12.8% production, transportation, and material moving
Income: Per capita: $30,440; Median household: $70,000; Average household: $70,800; Households with income of $100,000 or more: 28.7%; Poverty rate: 8.1%
Educational Attainment: High school diploma or higher: 95.9%; Bachelor's degree or higher: 20.3%; Graduate/professional degree or higher: 9.4%
Housing: Homeownership rate: 83.3%; Median home value: $157,000; Median year structure built: 1955; Homeowner vacancy rate: 2.5%; Median selected monthly owner costs: $1,392 with a mortgage, $573 without a mortgage; Median gross rent: $523 per month; Rental vacancy rate: 0.0%
Health Insurance: 94.5% have insurance; 79.6% have private insurance; 31.8% have public insurance; 5.5% do not have insurance; 0.0% of children under 18 do not have insurance
Transportation: Commute: 90.8% car, 0.0% public transportation, 3.1% walk, 1.7% work from home; Mean travel time to work: 26.4 minutes

DALE (unincorporated postal area)
ZCTA: 14039
Covers a land area of 1.868 square miles and a water area of 0 square miles. Located at 42.85° N. Lat; 78.17° W. Long. Elevation is 1,201 feet.
Population: 102; Growth (since 2000): -12.8%; Density: 54.6 persons per square mile; Race: 100.0% White, 0.0% Black/African American, 0.0% Asian, 0.0% American Indian/Alaska Native, 0.0% Native Hawaiian/Other Pacific Islander, 0.0% Two or more races, 0.0% Hispanic of any race; Average household size: 2.37; Median age: 29.9; Age under 18: 33.3%; Age 65 and over: 6.9%; Males per 100 females: 102.0; Marriage status: 25.4% never married, 66.2% now married, 0.0% separated, 0.0% widowed, 8.5% divorced; Foreign born: 0.0%; Speak English only: 100.0%; With disability: 9.8%; Veterans: 11.8%; Ancestry: 21.6% English, 17.6% German, 14.7% Irish, 8.8% Polish, 7.8% Scottish
Employment: 6.0% management, business, and financial, 0.0% computer, engineering, and science, 0.0% education, legal, community service, arts, and media, 0.0% healthcare practitioners, 12.0% service,

34.0% sales and office, 40.0% natural resources, construction, and maintenance, 8.0% production, transportation, and material moving
Income: Per capita: $22,730; Median household: $55,313; Average household: $55,065; Households with income of $100,000 or more: 20.9%; Poverty rate: 17.6%
Educational Attainment: High school diploma or higher: 95.2%; Bachelor's degree or higher: 16.1%; Graduate/professional degree or higher: n/a
Housing: Homeownership rate: 72.1%; Median home value: $83,000; Median year structure built: Before 1940; Homeowner vacancy rate: 0.0%; Median selected monthly owner costs: $900 with a mortgage, $0 without a mortgage; Median gross rent: $550 per month; Rental vacancy rate: 0.0%
Health Insurance: 94.1% have insurance; 79.4% have private insurance; 18.6% have public insurance; 5.9% do not have insurance; 0.0% of children under 18 do not have insurance
Transportation: Commute: 100.0% car, 0.0% public transportation, 0.0% walk, 0.0% work from home; Mean travel time to work: 30.9 minutes

EAGLE (town). Covers a land area of 36.283 square miles and a water area of 0.187 square miles. Located at 42.56° N. Lat; 78.25° W. Long. Elevation is 1,768 feet.
Population: 1,336; Growth (since 2000): 11.9%; Density: 36.8 persons per square mile; Race: 98.0% White, 0.5% Black/African American, 0.7% Asian, 0.0% American Indian/Alaska Native, 0.0% Native Hawaiian/Other Pacific Islander, 0.8% Two or more races, 1.0% Hispanic of any race; Average household size: 2.68; Median age: 38.5; Age under 18: 25.1%; Age 65 and over: 14.2%; Males per 100 females: 101.4; Marriage status: 24.9% never married, 55.0% now married, 1.6% separated, 6.6% widowed, 13.6% divorced; Foreign born: 1.6%; Speak English only: 94.3%; With disability: 12.4%; Veterans: 7.1%; Ancestry: 31.9% German, 16.8% Irish, 10.6% Polish, 7.6% Italian, 7.3% English
Employment: 12.8% management, business, and financial, 1.5% computer, engineering, and science, 2.5% education, legal, community service, arts, and media, 4.5% healthcare practitioners, 16.5% service, 22.1% sales and office, 20.8% natural resources, construction, and maintenance, 19.3% production, transportation, and material moving
Income: Per capita: $23,588; Median household: $57,188; Average household: $63,660; Households with income of $100,000 or more: 16.2%; Poverty rate: 14.2%
Educational Attainment: High school diploma or higher: 88.6%; Bachelor's degree or higher: 12.0%; Graduate/professional degree or higher: 2.3%
Housing: Homeownership rate: 88.4%; Median home value: $94,200; Median year structure built: 1966; Homeowner vacancy rate: 2.4%; Median selected monthly owner costs: $1,012 with a mortgage, $476 without a mortgage; Median gross rent: $764 per month; Rental vacancy rate: 0.0%
Health Insurance: 93.3% have insurance; 72.8% have private insurance; 35.3% have public insurance; 6.7% do not have insurance; 13.6% of children under 18 do not have insurance
Transportation: Commute: 92.3% car, 0.0% public transportation, 2.2% walk, 2.5% work from home; Mean travel time to work: 35.1 minutes

GAINESVILLE (town). Covers a land area of 35.570 square miles and a water area of 0.138 square miles. Located at 42.65° N. Lat; 78.13° W. Long. Elevation is 1,617 feet.
Population: 2,269; Growth (since 2000): -2.7%; Density: 63.8 persons per square mile; Race: 95.3% White, 0.2% Black/African American, 0.8% Asian, 1.5% American Indian/Alaska Native, 0.0% Native Hawaiian/Other Pacific Islander, 1.8% Two or more races, 1.2% Hispanic of any race; Average household size: 2.54; Median age: 38.9; Age under 18: 25.0%; Age 65 and over: 15.6%; Males per 100 females: 102.8; Marriage status: 28.8% never married, 50.1% now married, 0.6% separated, 7.2% widowed, 13.9% divorced; Foreign born: 1.7%; Speak English only: 99.0%; With disability: 15.8%; Veterans: 8.7%; Ancestry: 30.5% German, 12.3% Irish, 11.7% English, 9.7% Polish, 9.3% Italian
Employment: 10.5% management, business, and financial, 3.1% computer, engineering, and science, 5.5% education, legal, community service, arts, and media, 3.0% healthcare practitioners, 19.8% service, 23.4% sales and office, 15.7% natural resources, construction, and maintenance, 18.9% production, transportation, and material moving
Income: Per capita: $22,554; Median household: $48,884; Average household: $57,168; Households with income of $100,000 or more: 13.5%; Poverty rate: 14.4%

Educational Attainment: High school diploma or higher: 85.9%; Bachelor's degree or higher: 11.9%; Graduate/professional degree or higher: 4.1%
School District(s)
Letchworth Central SD (PK-12)
    Enrollment: 963 . . . . (585) 493-5450
Housing: Homeownership rate: 78.9%; Median home value: $78,600; Median year structure built: 1945; Homeowner vacancy rate: 0.0%; Median selected monthly owner costs: $892 with a mortgage, $441 without a mortgage; Median gross rent: $641 per month; Rental vacancy rate: 2.1%
Health Insurance: 93.3% have insurance; 67.8% have private insurance; 39.1% have public insurance; 6.7% do not have insurance; 8.1% of children under 18 do not have insurance
Transportation: Commute: 95.1% car, 0.8% public transportation, 2.3% walk, 0.9% work from home; Mean travel time to work: 22.4 minutes

GAINESVILLE (village). Covers a land area of 0.856 square miles and a water area of 0 square miles. Located at 42.64° N. Lat; 78.13° W. Long. Elevation is 1,617 feet.
Population: 215; Growth (since 2000): -29.3%; Density: 251.2 persons per square mile; Race: 96.3% White, 0.0% Black/African American, 0.0% Asian, 3.7% American Indian/Alaska Native, 0.0% Native Hawaiian/Other Pacific Islander, 0.0% Two or more races, 0.0% Hispanic of any race; Average household size: 2.50; Median age: 40.3; Age under 18: 23.3%; Age 65 and over: 19.5%; Males per 100 females: 110.1; Marriage status: 27.3% never married, 57.6% now married, 2.3% separated, 4.1% widowed, 11.0% divorced; Foreign born: 0.9%; Speak English only: 99.5%; With disability: 14.9%; Veterans: 11.5%; Ancestry: 32.1% German, 17.2% English, 11.2% Dutch, 9.8% Irish, 9.8% Polish
Employment: 5.3% management, business, and financial, 1.1% computer, engineering, and science, 3.2% education, legal, community service, arts, and media, 5.3% healthcare practitioners, 29.5% service, 31.6% sales and office, 11.6% natural resources, construction, and maintenance, 12.6% production, transportation, and material moving
Income: Per capita: $19,820; Median household: $46,250; Average household: $48,783; Households with income of $100,000 or more: 10.5%; Poverty rate: 18.6%
Educational Attainment: High school diploma or higher: 89.6%; Bachelor's degree or higher: 10.4%; Graduate/professional degree or higher: 0.7%
School District(s)
Letchworth Central SD (PK-12)
    Enrollment: 963 . . . . (585) 493-5450
Housing: Homeownership rate: 74.4%; Median home value: $71,100; Median year structure built: Before 1940; Homeowner vacancy rate: 0.0%; Median selected monthly owner costs: $675 with a mortgage, $436 without a mortgage; Median gross rent: $663 per month; Rental vacancy rate: 15.4%
Health Insurance: 97.2% have insurance; 67.4% have private insurance; 48.4% have public insurance; 2.8% do not have insurance; 0.0% of children under 18 do not have insurance
Transportation: Commute: 100.0% car, 0.0% public transportation, 0.0% walk, 0.0% work from home; Mean travel time to work: 23.6 minutes

GENESEE FALLS (town). Covers a land area of 15.615 square miles and a water area of 0.086 square miles. Located at 42.57° N. Lat; 78.06° W. Long.
Population: 388; Growth (since 2000): -15.7%; Density: 24.8 persons per square mile; Race: 95.1% White, 0.0% Black/African American, 1.5% Asian, 0.0% American Indian/Alaska Native, 0.0% Native Hawaiian/Other Pacific Islander, 3.4% Two or more races, 0.0% Hispanic of any race; Average household size: 2.18; Median age: 46.6; Age under 18: 14.2%; Age 65 and over: 14.9%; Males per 100 females: 96.4; Marriage status: 34.5% never married, 48.5% now married, 1.5% separated, 7.0% widowed, 9.9% divorced; Foreign born: 0.3%; Speak English only: 99.5%; With disability: 15.7%; Veterans: 6.9%; Ancestry: 24.7% German, 19.1% Irish, 17.5% English, 12.1% Dutch, 9.0% Italian
Employment: 4.3% management, business, and financial, 1.6% computer, engineering, and science, 6.4% education, legal, community service, arts, and media, 5.9% healthcare practitioners, 22.9% service, 14.9% sales and office, 14.9% natural resources, construction, and maintenance, 29.3% production, transportation, and material moving
Income: Per capita: $24,269; Median household: $43,500; Average household: $51,189; Households with income of $100,000 or more: 10.1%; Poverty rate: 15.7%

Educational Attainment: High school diploma or higher: 88.2%; Bachelor's degree or higher: 17.0%; Graduate/professional degree or higher: 4.2%

Housing: Homeownership rate: 73.6%; Median home value: $74,000; Median year structure built: 1953; Homeowner vacancy rate: 1.5%; Median selected monthly owner costs: $977 with a mortgage, $368 without a mortgage; Median gross rent: $679 per month; Rental vacancy rate: 0.0%

Health Insurance: 89.4% have insurance; 62.6% have private insurance; 39.2% have public insurance; 10.6% do not have insurance; 0.0% of children under 18 do not have insurance

Transportation: Commute: 95.2% car, 0.5% public transportation, 0.5% walk, 2.7% work from home; Mean travel time to work: 31.3 minutes

---

JAVA (town). Covers a land area of 47.128 square miles and a water area of 0.202 square miles. Located at 42.65° N. Lat; 78.39° W. Long. Elevation is 1,522 feet.

Population: 1,952; Growth (since 2000): -12.2%; Density: 41.4 persons per square mile; Race: 100.0% White, 0.0% Black/African American, 0.0% Asian, 0.0% American Indian/Alaska Native, 0.0% Native Hawaiian/Other Pacific Islander, 0.0% Two or more races, 0.0% Hispanic of any race; Average household size: 2.27; Median age: 45.3; Age under 18: 17.7%; Age 65 and over: 18.3%; Males per 100 females: 106.5; Marriage status: 22.2% never married, 62.2% now married, 1.0% separated, 5.0% widowed, 10.6% divorced; Foreign born: 0.5%; Speak English only: 99.1%; With disability: 9.7%; Veterans: 10.5%; Ancestry: 46.6% German, 18.8% Irish, 14.0% Polish, 9.9% English, 8.7% American

Employment: 10.7% management, business, and financial, 2.6% computer, engineering, and science, 7.2% education, legal, community service, arts, and media, 3.6% healthcare practitioners, 17.1% service, 22.8% sales and office, 16.5% natural resources, construction, and maintenance, 19.4% production, transportation, and material moving

Income: Per capita: $27,034; Median household: $53,981; Average household: $61,416; Households with income of $100,000 or more: 14.4%; Poverty rate: 4.5%

Educational Attainment: High school diploma or higher: 89.8%; Bachelor's degree or higher: 14.3%; Graduate/professional degree or higher: 3.6%

Housing: Homeownership rate: 83.3%; Median home value: $131,600; Median year structure built: 1948; Homeowner vacancy rate: 0.7%; Median selected monthly owner costs: $1,206 with a mortgage, $461 without a mortgage; Median gross rent: $832 per month; Rental vacancy rate: 0.0%

Health Insurance: 95.2% have insurance; 83.3% have private insurance; 28.3% have public insurance; 4.8% do not have insurance; 0.0% of children under 18 do not have insurance

Transportation: Commute: 94.9% car, 0.0% public transportation, 3.0% walk, 2.1% work from home; Mean travel time to work: 26.3 minutes

---

JAVA CENTER (unincorporated postal area)
ZCTA: 14082

Covers a land area of 9.929 square miles and a water area of 0.111 square miles. Located at 42.66° N. Lat; 78.38° W. Long. Elevation is 1,522 feet.

Population: 474; Growth (since 2000): 10.7%; Density: 47.7 persons per square mile; Race: 100.0% White, 0.0% Black/African American, 0.0% Asian, 0.0% American Indian/Alaska Native, 0.0% Native Hawaiian/Other Pacific Islander, 0.0% Two or more races, 0.0% Hispanic of any race; Average household size: 2.19; Median age: 51.9; Age under 18: 9.1%; Age 65 and over: 16.9%; Males per 100 females: 105.8; Marriage status: 21.2% never married, 68.4% now married, 0.9% separated, 3.2% widowed, 7.1% divorced; Foreign born: 0.0%; Speak English only: 100.0%; With disability: 6.8%; Veterans: 9.3%; Ancestry: 60.3% German, 19.4% Irish, 16.0% Polish, 15.6% English, 11.6% Italian

Employment: 14.7% management, business, and financial, 0.0% computer, engineering, and science, 5.4% education, legal, community service, arts, and media, 3.0% healthcare practitioners, 5.0% service, 32.4% sales and office, 14.0% natural resources, construction, and maintenance, 25.4% production, transportation, and material moving

Income: Per capita: $31,881; Median household: $57,857; Average household: $69,219; Households with income of $100,000 or more: 17.5%; Poverty rate: 2.1%

Educational Attainment: High school diploma or higher: 85.6%; Bachelor's degree or higher: 11.8%; Graduate/professional degree or higher: 1.5%

Housing: Homeownership rate: 88.0%; Median home value: $151,600; Median year structure built: 1956; Homeowner vacancy rate: 0.0%;

Median selected monthly owner costs: $1,286 with a mortgage, $500 without a mortgage; Median gross rent: n/a per month; Rental vacancy rate: 0.0%

Health Insurance: 98.3% have insurance; 86.1% have private insurance; 26.4% have public insurance; 1.7% do not have insurance; 0.0% of children under 18 do not have insurance

Transportation: Commute: 95.0% car, 0.0% public transportation, 3.3% walk, 1.7% work from home; Mean travel time to work: 26.6 minutes

---

MIDDLEBURY (town). Covers a land area of 35.643 square miles and a water area of 0.025 square miles. Located at 42.82° N. Lat; 78.13° W. Long.

Population: 1,381; Growth (since 2000): -8.4%; Density: 38.7 persons per square mile; Race: 98.3% White, 1.5% Black/African American, 0.0% Asian, 0.0% American Indian/Alaska Native, 0.0% Native Hawaiian/Other Pacific Islander, 0.0% Two or more races, 0.4% Hispanic of any race; Average household size: 2.43; Median age: 45.0; Age under 18: 20.9%; Age 65 and over: 18.2%; Males per 100 females: 105.6; Marriage status: 24.8% never married, 63.2% now married, 1.1% separated, 4.8% widowed, 7.3% divorced; Foreign born: 1.4%; Speak English only: 99.7%; With disability: 17.5%; Veterans: 7.3%; Ancestry: 28.0% German, 21.7% Irish, 19.4% English, 7.7% American, 4.8% Polish

Employment: 14.1% management, business, and financial, 1.9% computer, engineering, and science, 12.7% education, legal, community service, arts, and media, 6.0% healthcare practitioners, 15.2% service, 20.3% sales and office, 14.8% natural resources, construction, and maintenance, 15.1% production, transportation, and material moving

Income: Per capita: $28,739; Median household: $59,792; Average household: $69,996; Households with income of $100,000 or more: 24.1%; Poverty rate: 10.9%

Educational Attainment: High school diploma or higher: 93.7%; Bachelor's degree or higher: 26.2%; Graduate/professional degree or higher: 11.0%

Housing: Homeownership rate: 86.3%; Median home value: $105,700; Median year structure built: Before 1940; Homeowner vacancy rate: 2.9%; Median selected monthly owner costs: $1,266 with a mortgage, $471 without a mortgage; Median gross rent: $621 per month; Rental vacancy rate: 0.0%

Health Insurance: 95.7% have insurance; 73.6% have private insurance; 40.0% have public insurance; 4.3% do not have insurance; 1.0% of children under 18 do not have insurance

Transportation: Commute: 92.5% car, 0.3% public transportation, 1.6% walk, 4.5% work from home; Mean travel time to work: 27.7 minutes

---

NORTH JAVA (unincorporated postal area)
ZCTA: 14113

Covers a land area of 17.021 square miles and a water area of <.001 square miles. Located at 42.67° N. Lat; 78.34° W. Long. Elevation is 1,562 feet.

Population: 621; Growth (since 2000): -19.9%; Density: 36.5 persons per square mile; Race: 100.0% White, 0.0% Black/African American, 0.0% Asian, 0.0% American Indian/Alaska Native, 0.0% Native Hawaiian/Other Pacific Islander, 0.0% Two or more races, 1.3% Hispanic of any race; Average household size: 2.15; Median age: 43.4; Age under 18: 16.1%; Age 65 and over: 17.4%; Males per 100 females: 109.2; Marriage status: 20.9% never married, 55.1% now married, 0.4% separated, 10.3% widowed, 13.7% divorced; Foreign born: 2.7%; Speak English only: 96.6%; With disability: 12.1%; Veterans: 15.0%; Ancestry: 42.0% German, 24.5% Irish, 19.3% Polish, 9.2% Italian, 8.9% English

Employment: 3.5% management, business, and financial, 0.0% computer, engineering, and science, 6.4% education, legal, community service, arts, and media, 3.2% healthcare practitioners, 25.0% service, 22.8% sales and office, 19.6% natural resources, construction, and maintenance, 19.6% production, transportation, and material moving

Income: Per capita: $28,036; Median household: $44,886; Average household: $61,733; Households with income of $100,000 or more: 10.7%; Poverty rate: 7.7%

Educational Attainment: High school diploma or higher: 97.9%; Bachelor's degree or higher: 16.5%; Graduate/professional degree or higher: 5.1%

Housing: Homeownership rate: 78.5%; Median home value: $134,400; Median year structure built: 1950; Homeowner vacancy rate: 0.0%; Median selected monthly owner costs: $1,196 with a mortgage, $538 without a mortgage; Median gross rent: $669 per month; Rental vacancy rate: 0.0%

Health Insurance: 86.8% have insurance; 76.3% have private insurance; 29.5% have public insurance; 13.2% do not have insurance; 0.0% of children under 18 do not have insurance
Transportation: Commute: 90.1% car, 1.6% public transportation, 4.8% walk, 3.5% work from home; Mean travel time to work: 29.4 minutes

ORANGEVILLE (town). Covers a land area of 35.560 square miles and a water area of 0.082 square miles. Located at 42.74° N. Lat; 78.25° W. Long.

Population: 1,546; Growth (since 2000): 18.8%; Density: 43.5 persons per square mile; Race: 98.3% White, 0.0% Black/African American, 0.0% Asian, 0.0% American Indian/Alaska Native, 0.0% Native Hawaiian/Other Pacific Islander, 1.1% Two or more races, 1.2% Hispanic of any race; Average household size: 2.55; Median age: 39.5; Age under 18: 19.9%; Age 65 and over: 13.8%; Males per 100 females: 108.5; Marriage status: 27.4% never married, 61.1% now married, 1.1% separated, 2.8% widowed, 8.7% divorced; Foreign born: 1.0%; Speak English only: 99.0%; With disability: 10.9%; Veterans: 7.4%; Ancestry: 45.1% German, 14.2% Polish, 11.7% Irish, 8.3% English, 8.3% Italian
Employment: 11.0% management, business, and financial, 6.3% computer, engineering, and science, 7.4% education, legal, community service, arts, and media, 4.7% healthcare practitioners, 21.5% service, 18.5% sales and office, 18.7% natural resources, construction, and maintenance, 12.0% production, transportation, and material moving
Income: Per capita: $26,332; Median household: $60,119; Average household: $66,392; Households with income of $100,000 or more: 20.1%; Poverty rate: 6.8%
Educational Attainment: High school diploma or higher: 96.4%; Bachelor's degree or higher: 20.6%; Graduate/professional degree or higher: 4.8%
Housing: Homeownership rate: 88.1%; Median home value: $133,000; Median year structure built: 1973; Homeowner vacancy rate: 0.0%; Median selected monthly owner costs: $1,260 with a mortgage, $580 without a mortgage; Median gross rent: n/a per month; Rental vacancy rate: 0.0%
Health Insurance: 96.8% have insurance; 82.9% have private insurance; 30.1% have public insurance; 3.2% do not have insurance; 1.8% of children under 18 do not have insurance
Transportation: Commute: 89.5% car, 0.4% public transportation, 2.8% walk, 7.3% work from home; Mean travel time to work: 26.6 minutes

PERRY (town). Covers a land area of 36.405 square miles and a water area of 0.242 square miles. Located at 42.75° N. Lat; 78.01° W. Long. Elevation is 1,371 feet.

History: In 1833, the Reverend William Arthur became pastor of the First Baptist Church in Perry. His son, Chester Alan Arthur, then four yeas old, was destined to become the 21st President of the United States.
Population: 4,429; Growth (since 2000): -33.4%; Density: 121.7 persons per square mile; Race: 94.8% White, 0.7% Black/African American, 0.3% Asian, 0.0% American Indian/Alaska Native, 0.0% Native Hawaiian/Other Pacific Islander, 2.3% Two or more races, 3.0% Hispanic of any race; Average household size: 2.48; Median age: 39.7; Age under 18: 22.3%; Age 65 and over: 16.5%; Males per 100 females: 94.8; Marriage status: 25.9% never married, 59.7% now married, 2.0% separated, 3.8% widowed, 10.6% divorced; Foreign born: 2.4%; Speak English only: 93.7%; With disability: 15.5%; Veterans: 11.7%; Ancestry: 20.1% Irish, 18.6% German, 11.5% English, 9.5% American, 8.1% Polish
Employment: 10.2% management, business, and financial, 3.3% computer, engineering, and science, 9.5% education, legal, community service, arts, and media, 6.2% healthcare practitioners, 15.4% service, 19.5% sales and office, 16.8% natural resources, construction, and maintenance, 19.0% production, transportation, and material moving
Income: Per capita: $26,160; Median household: $53,789; Average household: $64,311; Households with income of $100,000 or more: 11.6%; Poverty rate: 10.1%
Educational Attainment: High school diploma or higher: 90.9%; Bachelor's degree or higher: 15.7%; Graduate/professional degree or higher: 3.9%
School District(s)
Perry Central SD (PK-12)
    Enrollment: 870 . . . . (585) 237-0270
Housing: Homeownership rate: 66.1%; Median home value: $85,900; Median year structure built: Before 1940; Homeowner vacancy rate: 1.9%; Median selected monthly owner costs: $1,048 with a mortgage, $522 without a mortgage; Median gross rent: $705 per month; Rental vacancy rate: 4.3%

Health Insurance: 94.9% have insurance; 70.6% have private insurance; 43.6% have public insurance; 5.1% do not have insurance; 2.5% of children under 18 do not have insurance
Newspapers: Perry Herald (weekly circulation 900)
Transportation: Commute: 89.0% car, 0.9% public transportation, 7.1% walk, 1.5% work from home; Mean travel time to work: 20.5 minutes
Additional Information Contacts
Town of Perry . . . . (585) 237-2241
    http://www.townofperryny.com

PERRY (village). Covers a land area of 2.337 square miles and a water area of 0.112 square miles. Located at 42.72° N. Lat; 78.01° W. Long. Elevation is 1,371 feet.

Population: 3,570; Growth (since 2000): -9.5%; Density: 1,527.3 persons per square mile; Race: 95.1% White, 1.0% Black/African American, 0.4% Asian, 0.0% American Indian/Alaska Native, 0.0% Native Hawaiian/Other Pacific Islander, 3.5% Two or more races, 1.4% Hispanic of any race; Average household size: 2.50; Median age: 38.1; Age under 18: 25.8%; Age 65 and over: 16.1%; Males per 100 females: 91.0; Marriage status: 28.6% never married, 55.6% now married, 2.2% separated, 4.8% widowed, 11.0% divorced; Foreign born: 1.0%; Speak English only: 95.7%; With disability: 17.4%; Veterans: 12.9%; Ancestry: 20.3% Irish, 18.2% German, 15.7% English, 10.4% American, 9.1% Polish
Employment: 10.8% management, business, and financial, 3.3% computer, engineering, and science, 11.5% education, legal, community service, arts, and media, 6.1% healthcare practitioners, 18.8% service, 19.3% sales and office, 9.7% natural resources, construction, and maintenance, 20.4% production, transportation, and material moving
Income: Per capita: $22,321; Median household: $45,969; Average household: $55,981; Households with income of $100,000 or more: 10.0%; Poverty rate: 10.7%
Educational Attainment: High school diploma or higher: 89.9%; Bachelor's degree or higher: 17.8%; Graduate/professional degree or higher: 3.7%
School District(s)
Perry Central SD (PK-12)
    Enrollment: 870 . . . . (585) 237-0270
Housing: Homeownership rate: 62.6%; Median home value: $84,300; Median year structure built: Before 1940; Homeowner vacancy rate: 2.6%; Median selected monthly owner costs: $997 with a mortgage, $544 without a mortgage; Median gross rent: $707 per month; Rental vacancy rate: 4.9%
Health Insurance: 95.6% have insurance; 67.0% have private insurance; 47.6% have public insurance; 4.4% do not have insurance; 1.7% of children under 18 do not have insurance
Safety: Violent crime rate: 11.5 per 10,000 population; Property crime rate: 167.3 per 10,000 population
Newspapers: Perry Herald (weekly circulation 900)
Transportation: Commute: 93.9% car, 1.2% public transportation, 1.9% walk, 1.2% work from home; Mean travel time to work: 20.8 minutes
Additional Information Contacts
Village of Perry . . . . (585) 237-2216
    http://www.villageofperry.com

PIKE (CDP). Covers a land area of 1.494 square miles and a water area of <.001 square miles. Located at 42.55° N. Lat; 78.15° W. Long. Elevation is 1,545 feet.

Population: 207; Growth (since 2000): -45.8%; Density: 138.6 persons per square mile; Race: 90.3% White, 9.7% Black/African American, 0.0% Asian, 0.0% American Indian/Alaska Native, 0.0% Native Hawaiian/Other Pacific Islander, 0.0% Two or more races, 3.9% Hispanic of any race; Average household size: 1.88; Median age: 59.1; Age under 18: 13.5%; Age 65 and over: 28.0%; Males per 100 females: 101.6; Marriage status: 24.7% never married, 60.5% now married, 0.0% separated, 3.2% widowed, 11.6% divorced; Foreign born: 0.0%; Speak English only: 100.0%; With disability: 19.8%; Veterans: 12.8%; Ancestry: 33.3% German, 30.4% English, 6.3% Scottish, 4.3% Dutch, 3.9% Swedish
Employment: 10.8% management, business, and financial, 0.0% computer, engineering, and science, 15.7% education, legal, community service, arts, and media, 14.5% healthcare practitioners, 21.7% service, 10.8% sales and office, 14.5% natural resources, construction, and maintenance, 12.0% production, transportation, and material moving
Income: Per capita: $21,048; Median household: $36,042; Average household: $40,523; Households with income of $100,000 or more: n/a; Poverty rate: 7.2%

Educational Attainment: High school diploma or higher: 89.1%; Bachelor's degree or higher: 11.5%; Graduate/professional degree or higher: 3.6%
Housing: Homeownership rate: 90.9%; Median home value: $57,900; Median year structure built: Before 1940; Homeowner vacancy rate: 0.0%; Median selected monthly owner costs: $953 with a mortgage, $468 without a mortgage; Median gross rent: n/a per month; Rental vacancy rate: 0.0%
Health Insurance: 96.1% have insurance; 61.4% have private insurance; 53.6% have public insurance; 3.9% do not have insurance; 0.0% of children under 18 do not have insurance
Transportation: Commute: 100.0% car, 0.0% public transportation, 0.0% walk, 0.0% work from home; Mean travel time to work: 25.8 minutes

PIKE (town). Covers a land area of 31.084 square miles and a water area of 0.145 square miles. Located at 42.57° N. Lat; 78.14° W. Long. Elevation is 1,545 feet.
Population: 940; Growth (since 2000): -13.4%; Density: 30.2 persons per square mile; Race: 96.3% White, 2.1% Black/African American, 1.5% Asian, 0.0% American Indian/Alaska Native, 0.0% Native Hawaiian/Other Pacific Islander, 0.1% Two or more races, 2.4% Hispanic of any race; Average household size: 2.36; Median age: 46.4; Age under 18: 22.4%; Age 65 and over: 17.9%; Males per 100 females: 104.4; Marriage status: 24.2% never married, 62.0% now married, 2.2% separated, 2.6% widowed, 11.2% divorced; Foreign born: 1.0%; Speak English only: 93.9%; With disability: 11.4%; Veterans: 13.3%; Ancestry: 29.5% German, 13.3% English, 12.4% Irish, 10.9% American, 5.0% Dutch
Employment: 13.2% management, business, and financial, 3.8% computer, engineering, and science, 10.1% education, legal, community service, arts, and media, 7.1% healthcare practitioners, 11.1% service, 16.5% sales and office, 23.8% natural resources, construction, and maintenance, 14.4% production, transportation, and material moving
Income: Per capita: $25,871; Median household: $52,159; Average household: $61,519; Households with income of $100,000 or more: 15.6%; Poverty rate: 10.4%
Educational Attainment: High school diploma or higher: 90.5%; Bachelor's degree or higher: 14.6%; Graduate/professional degree or higher: 8.1%
Housing: Homeownership rate: 91.0%; Median home value: $81,900; Median year structure built: 1963; Homeowner vacancy rate: 0.0%; Median selected monthly owner costs: $1,149 with a mortgage, $472 without a mortgage; Median gross rent: $715 per month; Rental vacancy rate: 0.0%
Health Insurance: 88.7% have insurance; 68.9% have private insurance; 36.6% have public insurance; 11.3% do not have insurance; 21.2% of children under 18 do not have insurance
Transportation: Commute: 93.8% car, 1.4% public transportation, 1.2% walk, 1.9% work from home; Mean travel time to work: 29.1 minutes

PORTAGEVILLE (unincorporated postal area)
ZCTA: 14536
Covers a land area of 18.222 square miles and a water area of 0.164 square miles. Located at 42.54° N. Lat; 78.08° W. Long. Elevation is 1,115 feet.
Population: 556; Growth (since 2000): -16.3%; Density: 30.5 persons per square mile; Race: 96.0% White, 0.0% Black/African American, 1.1% Asian, 0.0% American Indian/Alaska Native, 0.0% Native Hawaiian/Other Pacific Islander, 2.9% Two or more races, 3.1% Hispanic of any race; Average household size: 2.22; Median age: 43.7; Age under 18: 21.0%; Age 65 and over: 17.6%; Males per 100 females: 103.3; Marriage status: 29.3% never married, 51.4% now married, 1.6% separated, 6.4% widowed, 12.9% divorced; Foreign born: 0.5%; Speak English only: 97.0%; With disability: 16.4%; Veterans: 9.3%; Ancestry: 24.3% German, 16.2% American, 16.0% Irish, 15.6% Dutch, 15.5% English
Employment: 10.9% management, business, and financial, 2.9% computer, engineering, and science, 9.6% education, legal, community service, arts, and media, 4.6% healthcare practitioners, 17.6% service, 18.8% sales and office, 14.6% natural resources, construction, and maintenance, 20.9% production, transportation, and material moving
Income: Per capita: $23,247; Median household: $42,813; Average household: $51,466; Households with income of $100,000 or more: 9.6%; Poverty rate: 19.2%
Educational Attainment: High school diploma or higher: 88.3%; Bachelor's degree or higher: 13.9%; Graduate/professional degree or higher: 4.0%

Housing: Homeownership rate: 80.1%; Median home value: $76,800; Median year structure built: 1942; Homeowner vacancy rate: 4.3%; Median selected monthly owner costs: $958 with a mortgage, $438 without a mortgage; Median gross rent: $650 per month; Rental vacancy rate: 0.0%
Health Insurance: 91.5% have insurance; 59.0% have private insurance; 48.9% have public insurance; 8.5% do not have insurance; 0.0% of children under 18 do not have insurance
Transportation: Commute: 95.0% car, 0.4% public transportation, 0.4% walk, 2.5% work from home; Mean travel time to work: 34.8 minutes

SHELDON (town). Covers a land area of 47.348 square miles and a water area of 0.025 square miles. Located at 42.75° N. Lat; 78.38° W. Long. Elevation is 1,512 feet.
Population: 2,352; Growth (since 2000): -8.2%; Density: 49.7 persons per square mile; Race: 95.8% White, 2.5% Black/African American, 0.1% Asian, 1.6% American Indian/Alaska Native, 0.0% Native Hawaiian/Other Pacific Islander, 0.0% Two or more races, 0.3% Hispanic of any race; Average household size: 2.36; Median age: 48.3; Age under 18: 19.6%; Age 65 and over: 21.6%; Males per 100 females: 110.9; Marriage status: 25.8% never married, 61.7% now married, 1.9% separated, 4.6% widowed, 7.9% divorced; Foreign born: 0.5%; Speak English only: 97.6%; With disability: 12.8%; Veterans: 10.3%; Ancestry: 49.1% German, 15.2% Irish, 14.7% Polish, 8.2% English, 5.9% Italian
Employment: 11.6% management, business, and financial, 3.0% computer, engineering, and science, 11.5% education, legal, community service, arts, and media, 2.9% healthcare practitioners, 17.0% service, 22.8% sales and office, 17.8% natural resources, construction, and maintenance, 13.3% production, transportation, and material moving
Income: Per capita: $30,306; Median household: $62,222; Average household: $71,609; Households with income of $100,000 or more: 18.9%; Poverty rate: 7.9%
Educational Attainment: High school diploma or higher: 93.6%; Bachelor's degree or higher: 18.1%; Graduate/professional degree or higher: 8.6%
Housing: Homeownership rate: 80.6%; Median home value: $144,200; Median year structure built: 1964; Homeowner vacancy rate: 0.0%; Median selected monthly owner costs: $1,231 with a mortgage, $533 without a mortgage; Median gross rent: $743 per month; Rental vacancy rate: 0.0%
Health Insurance: 96.2% have insurance; 81.5% have private insurance; 33.4% have public insurance; 3.8% do not have insurance; 0.8% of children under 18 do not have insurance
Transportation: Commute: 92.0% car, 1.3% public transportation, 0.8% walk, 5.2% work from home; Mean travel time to work: 29.5 minutes

SILVER LAKE (unincorporated postal area)
ZCTA: 14549
Covers a land area of 0.112 square miles and a water area of 0 square miles. Located at 42.70° N. Lat; 78.02° W. Long. Elevation is 1,375 feet.
Population: 41; Growth (since 2000): n/a; Density: 364.8 persons per square mile; Race: 100.0% White, 0.0% Black/African American, 0.0% Asian, 0.0% American Indian/Alaska Native, 0.0% Native Hawaiian/Other Pacific Islander, 0.0% Two or more races, 0.0% Hispanic of any race; Average household size: 1.78; Median age: 56.7; Age under 18: 19.5%; Age 65 and over: 34.1%; Males per 100 females: 71.7; Marriage status: 19.5% never married, 48.8% now married, 0.0% separated, 9.8% widowed, 22.0% divorced; Foreign born: 0.0%; Speak English only: 100.0%; With disability: 9.8%; Veterans: 0.0%; Ancestry: 36.6% English, 22.0% Irish, 12.2% German, 12.2% Italian, 12.2% Polish
Employment: 20.8% management, business, and financial, 0.0% computer, engineering, and science, 20.8% education, legal, community service, arts, and media, 20.8% healthcare practitioners, 0.0% service, 37.5% sales and office, 0.0% natural resources, construction, and maintenance, 0.0% production, transportation, and material moving
Income: Per capita: $31,932; Median household: n/a; Average household: $56,922; Households with income of $100,000 or more: 21.7%; Poverty rate: n/a
Educational Attainment: High school diploma or higher: 100.0%; Bachelor's degree or higher: 45.5%; Graduate/professional degree or higher: 30.3%
Housing: Homeownership rate: 43.5%; Median home value: n/a; Median year structure built: 1949; Homeowner vacancy rate: 0.0%; Median selected monthly owner costs: $0 with a mortgage, $0 without a mortgage; Median gross rent: $514 per month; Rental vacancy rate: 0.0%

Health Insurance: 100.0% have insurance; 100.0% have private insurance; 34.1% have public insurance; 0.0% do not have insurance; 0.0% of children under 18 do not have insurance
Transportation: Commute: 100.0% car, 0.0% public transportation, 0.0% walk, 0.0% work from home; Mean travel time to work: 0.0 minutes

SILVER SPRINGS (village).
Covers a land area of 0.952 square miles and a water area of 0.027 square miles. Located at 42.66° N. Lat; 78.08° W. Long. Elevation is 1,414 feet.
Population: 911; Growth (since 2000): 7.9%; Density: 956.6 persons per square mile; Race: 93.6% White, 0.5% Black/African American, 0.7% Asian, 2.7% American Indian/Alaska Native, 0.0% Native Hawaiian/Other Pacific Islander, 2.0% Two or more races, 2.2% Hispanic of any race; Average household size: 2.32; Median age: 40.6; Age under 18: 26.0%; Age 65 and over: 16.7%; Males per 100 females: 89.3; Marriage status: 34.8% never married, 32.2% now married, 0.8% separated, 12.2% widowed, 20.8% divorced; Foreign born: 2.1%; Speak English only: 98.3%; With disability: 22.0%; Veterans: 5.2%; Ancestry: 32.8% German, 13.2% Irish, 11.3% English, 8.9% Polish, 6.0% American
Employment: 11.0% management, business, and financial, 1.0% computer, engineering, and science, 2.6% education, legal, community service, arts, and media, 2.8% healthcare practitioners, 17.9% service, 27.4% sales and office, 16.4% natural resources, construction, and maintenance, 21.0% production, transportation, and material moving
Income: Per capita: $20,252; Median household: $40,000; Average household: $47,285; Households with income of $100,000 or more: 9.5%; Poverty rate: 23.4%
Educational Attainment: High school diploma or higher: 80.3%; Bachelor's degree or higher: 5.4%; Graduate/professional degree or higher: 1.3%
Housing: Homeownership rate: 67.3%; Median home value: $73,200; Median year structure built: 1943; Homeowner vacancy rate: 0.0%; Median selected monthly owner costs: $894 with a mortgage, $467 without a mortgage; Median gross rent: $593 per month; Rental vacancy rate: 0.0%
Health Insurance: 90.9% have insurance; 58.3% have private insurance; 49.3% have public insurance; 9.1% do not have insurance; 9.8% of children under 18 do not have insurance
Transportation: Commute: 89.2% car, 2.1% public transportation, 5.0% walk, 2.4% work from home; Mean travel time to work: 18.4 minutes

STRYKERSVILLE (CDP).
Covers a land area of 3.420 square miles and a water area of 0 square miles. Located at 42.71° N. Lat; 78.45° W. Long. Elevation is 1,083 feet.
Population: 689; Growth (since 2000): n/a; Density: 201.4 persons per square mile; Race: 98.0% White, 2.0% Black/African American, 0.0% Asian, 0.0% American Indian/Alaska Native, 0.0% Native Hawaiian/Other Pacific Islander, 0.0% Two or more races, 0.0% Hispanic of any race; Average household size: 2.58; Median age: 45.1; Age under 18: 24.8%; Age 65 and over: 19.9%; Males per 100 females: 93.1; Marriage status: 27.1% never married, 58.5% now married, 0.0% separated, 7.1% widowed, 7.3% divorced; Foreign born: 0.0%; Speak English only: 98.2%; With disability: 8.6%; Veterans: 8.1%; Ancestry: 44.3% German, 22.1% Irish, 20.5% Polish, 8.1% French, 5.8% Ukrainian
Employment: 13.9% management, business, and financial, 0.0% computer, engineering, and science, 12.5% education, legal, community service, arts, and media, 0.0% healthcare practitioners, 21.4% service, 19.2% sales and office, 20.3% natural resources, construction, and maintenance, 12.5% production, transportation, and material moving
Income: Per capita: $27,682; Median household: $63,583; Average household: $70,142; Households with income of $100,000 or more: 17.2%; Poverty rate: 5.8%
Educational Attainment: High school diploma or higher: 91.8%; Bachelor's degree or higher: 21.5%; Graduate/professional degree or higher: 10.8%
Housing: Homeownership rate: 77.2%; Median home value: $145,700; Median year structure built: 1965; Homeowner vacancy rate: 0.0%; Median selected monthly owner costs: $1,203 with a mortgage, $516 without a mortgage; Median gross rent: $782 per month; Rental vacancy rate: 0.0%
Health Insurance: 95.6% have insurance; 83.9% have private insurance; 30.8% have public insurance; 4.4% do not have insurance; 0.0% of children under 18 do not have insurance
Transportation: Commute: 96.0% car, 0.0% public transportation, 2.6% walk, 0.0% work from home; Mean travel time to work: 30.1 minutes

VARYSBURG (unincorporated postal area)
ZCTA: 14167
Covers a land area of 37.669 square miles and a water area of 0.004 square miles. Located at 42.75° N. Lat; 78.32° W. Long. Elevation is 1,158 feet.
Population: 1,718; Growth (since 2000): 4.4%; Density: 45.6 persons per square mile; Race: 96.7% White, 2.6% Black/African American, 0.2% Asian, 0.0% American Indian/Alaska Native, 0.0% Native Hawaiian/Other Pacific Islander, 0.0% Two or more races, 0.8% Hispanic of any race; Average household size: 2.45; Median age: 45.1; Age under 18: 18.9%; Age 65 and over: 17.9%; Males per 100 females: 117.1; Marriage status: 27.3% never married, 62.0% now married, 3.0% separated, 2.7% widowed, 8.0% divorced; Foreign born: 0.8%; Speak English only: 97.5%; With disability: 11.4%; Veterans: 10.7%; Ancestry: 49.6% German, 19.8% Polish, 10.9% Irish, 10.7% English, 9.3% Italian
Employment: 9.7% management, business, and financial, 3.5% computer, engineering, and science, 8.4% education, legal, community service, arts, and media, 4.3% healthcare practitioners, 19.1% service, 24.5% sales and office, 18.6% natural resources, construction, and maintenance, 11.9% production, transportation, and material moving
Income: Per capita: $28,525; Median household: $60,714; Average household: $69,064; Households with income of $100,000 or more: 22.1%; Poverty rate: 6.4%
Educational Attainment: High school diploma or higher: 95.9%; Bachelor's degree or higher: 14.9%; Graduate/professional degree or higher: 5.2%

School District(s)
Attica Central SD (KG-12)
    Enrollment: 1,290 . . . . (585) 591-2173
Housing: Homeownership rate: 83.6%; Median home value: $141,000; Median year structure built: 1968; Homeowner vacancy rate: 0.0%; Median selected monthly owner costs: $1,306 with a mortgage, $589 without a mortgage; Median gross rent: $635 per month; Rental vacancy rate: 0.0%
Health Insurance: 95.6% have insurance; 78.9% have private insurance; 34.7% have public insurance; 4.4% do not have insurance; 1.8% of children under 18 do not have insurance
Transportation: Commute: 87.2% car, 0.6% public transportation, 1.2% walk, 10.4% work from home; Mean travel time to work: 28.9 minutes

WARSAW (town).
Covers a land area of 35.416 square miles and a water area of 0.050 square miles. Located at 42.74° N. Lat; 78.13° W. Long. Elevation is 1,014 feet.
Population: 4,938; Growth (since 2000): -8.9%; Density: 139.4 persons per square mile; Race: 94.2% White, 1.6% Black/African American, 0.3% Asian, 0.0% American Indian/Alaska Native, 0.0% Native Hawaiian/Other Pacific Islander, 3.0% Two or more races, 1.6% Hispanic of any race; Average household size: 2.18; Median age: 43.5; Age under 18: 20.9%; Age 65 and over: 18.6%; Males per 100 females: 91.4; Marriage status: 26.5% never married, 46.1% now married, 2.0% separated, 6.2% widowed, 21.2% divorced; Foreign born: 1.4%; Speak English only: 97.8%; With disability: 14.5%; Veterans: 6.5%; Ancestry: 28.4% German, 16.0% Irish, 13.7% English, 10.6% Polish, 9.3% Italian
Employment: 11.9% management, business, and financial, 2.4% computer, engineering, and science, 7.8% education, legal, community service, arts, and media, 6.8% healthcare practitioners, 21.3% service, 23.8% sales and office, 14.7% natural resources, construction, and maintenance, 11.2% production, transportation, and material moving
Income: Per capita: $33,566; Median household: $54,821; Average household: $73,247; Households with income of $100,000 or more: 18.3%; Poverty rate: 17.1%
Educational Attainment: High school diploma or higher: 85.9%; Bachelor's degree or higher: 14.7%; Graduate/professional degree or higher: 7.2%

School District(s)
Warsaw Central SD (KG-12)
    Enrollment: 875 . . . . (585) 786-8000
Housing: Homeownership rate: 57.5%; Median home value: $111,500; Median year structure built: Before 1940; Homeowner vacancy rate: 3.5%; Median selected monthly owner costs: $1,101 with a mortgage, $555 without a mortgage; Median gross rent: $539 per month; Rental vacancy rate: 0.0%
Health Insurance: 94.5% have insurance; 69.7% have private insurance; 39.4% have public insurance; 5.5% do not have insurance; 2.7% of children under 18 do not have insurance

Hospitals: Wyoming County Community Hospital (264 beds)
Newspapers: Warsaw's Country Courier (weekly circulation 2,000)
Transportation: Commute: 89.6% car, 0.0% public transportation, 5.4% walk, 2.5% work from home; Mean travel time to work: 19.8 minutes

WARSAW (village). County seat. Covers a land area of 4.106 square miles and a water area of 0 square miles. Located at 42.74° N. Lat; 78.14° W. Long. Elevation is 1,014 feet.

Population: 3,548; Growth (since 2000): -7.0%; Density: 864.1 persons per square mile; Race: 91.9% White, 2.3% Black/African American, 0.4% Asian, 0.0% American Indian/Alaska Native, 0.0% Native Hawaiian/Other Pacific Islander, 4.2% Two or more races, 1.9% Hispanic of any race; Average household size: 2.11; Median age: 43.5; Age under 18: 19.4%; Age 65 and over: 19.4%; Males per 100 females: 90.5; Marriage status: 31.6% never married, 35.3% now married, 2.7% separated, 7.8% widowed, 25.3% divorced; Foreign born: 2.0%; Speak English only: 97.2%; With disability: 16.0%; Veterans: 6.9%; Ancestry: 24.7% German, 14.6% Irish, 14.1% English, 11.2% Polish, 9.8% American
Employment: 13.3% management, business, and financial, 1.9% computer, engineering, and science, 6.3% education, legal, community service, arts, and media, 6.9% healthcare practitioners, 20.3% service, 26.2% sales and office, 13.6% natural resources, construction, and maintenance, 11.5% production, transportation, and material moving
Income: Per capita: $25,918; Median household: $41,466; Average household: $54,762; Households with income of $100,000 or more: 13.8%; Poverty rate: 22.6%
Educational Attainment: High school diploma or higher: 83.7%; Bachelor's degree or higher: 13.0%; Graduate/professional degree or higher: 5.3%

School District(s)
Warsaw Central SD (KG-12)
    Enrollment: 875 . . . . (585) 786-8000
Housing: Homeownership rate: 46.6%; Median home value: $105,700; Median year structure built: Before 1940; Homeowner vacancy rate: 0.0%; Median selected monthly owner costs: $1,071 with a mortgage, $503 without a mortgage; Median gross rent: $499 per month; Rental vacancy rate: 0.0%
Health Insurance: 94.2% have insurance; 65.5% have private insurance; 44.1% have public insurance; 5.8% do not have insurance; 0.0% of children under 18 do not have insurance
Hospitals: Wyoming County Community Hospital (264 beds)
Safety: Violent crime rate: 12.0 per 10,000 population; Property crime rate: 108.2 per 10,000 population
Newspapers: Warsaw's Country Courier (weekly circulation 2,000)
Transportation: Commute: 85.5% car, 0.1% public transportation, 7.1% walk, 3.7% work from home; Mean travel time to work: 19.0 minutes

WETHERSFIELD (town). Covers a land area of 35.810 square miles and a water area of 0.307 square miles. Located at 42.65° N. Lat; 78.24° W. Long.

Population: 748; Growth (since 2000): -16.0%; Density: 20.9 persons per square mile; Race: 99.5% White, 0.0% Black/African American, 0.5% Asian, 0.0% American Indian/Alaska Native, 0.0% Native Hawaiian/Other Pacific Islander, 0.0% Two or more races, 1.6% Hispanic of any race; Average household size: 2.47; Median age: 40.9; Age under 18: 23.5%; Age 65 and over: 11.4%; Males per 100 females: 112.8; Marriage status: 24.6% never married, 63.2% now married, 0.3% separated, 5.3% widowed, 7.0% divorced; Foreign born: 2.7%; Speak English only: 97.3%; With disability: 11.1%; Veterans: 9.1%; Ancestry: 33.2% German, 21.3% Irish, 15.8% English, 13.0% Polish, 12.7% Italian
Employment: 15.0% management, business, and financial, 1.1% computer, engineering, and science, 9.4% education, legal, community service, arts, and media, 5.9% healthcare practitioners, 20.1% service, 16.6% sales and office, 16.9% natural resources, construction, and maintenance, 15.0% production, transportation, and material moving
Income: Per capita: $26,447; Median household: $53,750; Average household: $65,489; Households with income of $100,000 or more: 19.2%; Poverty rate: 19.5%
Educational Attainment: High school diploma or higher: 92.8%; Bachelor's degree or higher: 15.6%; Graduate/professional degree or higher: 6.0%
Housing: Homeownership rate: 73.6%; Median home value: $91,800; Median year structure built: 1972; Homeowner vacancy rate: 0.0%; Median selected monthly owner costs: $993 with a mortgage, $434 without a mortgage; Median gross rent: $844 per month; Rental vacancy rate: 0.0%

Health Insurance: 91.8% have insurance; 66.3% have private insurance; 36.6% have public insurance; 8.2% do not have insurance; 4.3% of children under 18 do not have insurance
Transportation: Commute: 86.1% car, 0.0% public transportation, 4.8% walk, 7.0% work from home; Mean travel time to work: 28.2 minutes

WYOMING (village). Covers a land area of 0.669 square miles and a water area of 0 square miles. Located at 42.82° N. Lat; 78.08° W. Long. Elevation is 988 feet.

Population: 361; Growth (since 2000): -29.6%; Density: 539.7 persons per square mile; Race: 99.4% White, 0.0% Black/African American, 0.0% Asian, 0.0% American Indian/Alaska Native, 0.0% Native Hawaiian/Other Pacific Islander, 0.0% Two or more races, 0.6% Hispanic of any race; Average household size: 2.54; Median age: 44.3; Age under 18: 22.2%; Age 65 and over: 17.5%; Males per 100 females: 100.9; Marriage status: 27.9% never married, 58.7% now married, 2.0% separated, 5.2% widowed, 8.2% divorced; Foreign born: 1.1%; Speak English only: 98.9%; With disability: 20.2%; Veterans: 10.3%; Ancestry: 21.9% English, 20.8% Irish, 18.6% German, 10.5% American, 5.5% Italian
Employment: 10.9% management, business, and financial, 3.0% computer, engineering, and science, 15.8% education, legal, community service, arts, and media, 9.1% healthcare practitioners, 12.7% service, 20.6% sales and office, 11.5% natural resources, construction, and maintenance, 16.4% production, transportation, and material moving
Income: Per capita: $25,265; Median household: $57,917; Average household: $63,159; Households with income of $100,000 or more: 15.5%; Poverty rate: 13.6%
Educational Attainment: High school diploma or higher: 94.6%; Bachelor's degree or higher: 19.8%; Graduate/professional degree or higher: 6.6%

School District(s)
Wyoming Central SD (KG-08)
    Enrollment: 111 . . . . (585) 495-6222
Housing: Homeownership rate: 76.8%; Median home value: $94,600; Median year structure built: Before 1940; Homeowner vacancy rate: 3.5%; Median selected monthly owner costs: $1,056 with a mortgage, $456 without a mortgage; Median gross rent: $615 per month; Rental vacancy rate: 0.0%
Health Insurance: 97.5% have insurance; 79.2% have private insurance; 36.6% have public insurance; 2.5% do not have insurance; 3.5% of children under 18 do not have insurance
Transportation: Commute: 92.4% car, 1.3% public transportation, 1.9% walk, 0.0% work from home; Mean travel time to work: 27.5 minutes

Yates County

Located in west central New York; bounded on the east by Seneca Lake; includes parts of Keuka and Canandaigua Lakes. Covers a land area of 338.143 square miles, a water area of 37.647 square miles, and is located in the Eastern Time Zone at 42.64° N. Lat., 77.10° W. Long. The county was founded in 1823. County seat is Penn Yan.

Yates County is part of the Rochester, NY Metropolitan Statistical Area. The entire metro area includes: Livingston County, NY; Monroe County, NY; Ontario County, NY; Orleans County, NY; Wayne County, NY; Yates County, NY

Population: 25,083; Growth (since 2000): 1.9%; Density: 74.2 persons per square mile; Race: 96.3% White, 1.1% Black/African American, 0.7% Asian, 0.2% American Indian/Alaska Native, 0.0% Native Hawaiian/Other Pacific Islander, 1.2% two or more races, 2.2% Hispanic of any race; Average household size: 2.55; Median age: 41.7; Age under 18: 22.5%; Age 65 and over: 19.0%; Males per 100 females: 93.9; Marriage status: 29.6% never married, 55.0% now married, 2.9% separated, 5.4% widowed, 10.0% divorced; Foreign born: 1.9%; Speak English only: 85.8%; With disability: 12.0%; Veterans: 8.3%; Ancestry: 24.0% German, 14.7% Irish, 14.5% English, 8.4% American, 6.2% Italian
Religion: Six largest groups: 11.3% Catholicism, 8.3% Methodist/Pietist, 4.0% Baptist, 2.0% Presbyterian-Reformed, 1.9% Lutheran, 0.8% Non-denominational Protestant
Economy: Unemployment rate: 3.1%; Leading industries: 16.4 % construction; 15.3 % retail trade; 12.7 % other services (except public administration); Farms: 919 totaling 126,946 acres; Company size: 0 employ 1,000 or more persons, 1 employs 500 to 999 persons, 4 employ 100 to 499 persons, 513 employ less than 100 persons; Business

ownership: 557 women-owned, n/a Black-owned, n/a Hispanic-owned, n/a Asian-owned, n/a American Indian/Alaska Native-owned
Employment: 12.9% management, business, and financial, 2.9% computer, engineering, and science, 10.6% education, legal, community service, arts, and media, 4.2% healthcare practitioners, 19.8% service, 20.6% sales and office, 13.9% natural resources, construction, and maintenance, 15.1% production, transportation, and material moving
Income: Per capita: $26,608; Median household: $51,758; Average household: $69,970; Households with income of $100,000 or more: 21.3%; Poverty rate: 13.1%
Educational Attainment: High school diploma or higher: 86.1%; Bachelor's degree or higher: 23.9%; Graduate/professional degree or higher: 10.6%
Housing: Homeownership rate: 77.1%; Median home value: $128,900; Median year structure built: 1963; Homeowner vacancy rate: 1.4%; Median selected monthly owner costs: $1,144 with a mortgage, $514 without a mortgage; Median gross rent: $732 per month; Rental vacancy rate: 5.8%
Vital Statistics: Birth rate: 130.6 per 10,000 population; Death rate: 103.4 per 10,000 population; Age-adjusted cancer mortality rate: 165.8 deaths per 100,000 population
Health Insurance: 80.4% have insurance; 59.1% have private insurance; 36.5% have public insurance; 19.6% do not have insurance; 35.5% of children under 18 do not have insurance
Health Care: Physicians: 8.0 per 10,000 population; Dentists: 4.8 per 10,000 population; Hospital beds: 74.3 per 10,000 population; Hospital admissions: 374.1 per 10,000 population
Transportation: Commute: 77.5% car, 0.3% public transportation, 8.1% walk, 10.0% work from home; Mean travel time to work: 22.5 minutes
2016 Presidential Election: 56.2% Trump, 36.4% Clinton, 4.9% Johnson, 1.5% Stein
National and State Parks: Keuka Lake State Park
Additional Information Contacts
Yates Government . . . . (315) 536-5120
  http://www.yatescounty.org

Yates County Communities

BARRINGTON (town). Covers a land area of 35.753 square miles and a water area of 1.378 square miles. Located at 42.52° N. Lat; 77.05° W. Long. Elevation is 1,565 feet.
Population: 1,545; Growth (since 2000): 10.7%; Density: 43.2 persons per square mile; Race: 97.7% White, 1.2% Black/African American, 0.1% Asian, 0.0% American Indian/Alaska Native, 0.0% Native Hawaiian/Other Pacific Islander, 0.6% Two or more races, 1.2% Hispanic of any race; Average household size: 2.64; Median age: 44.9; Age under 18: 25.3%; Age 65 and over: 25.0%; Males per 100 females: 93.4; Marriage status: 23.1% never married, 63.9% now married, 1.1% separated, 6.6% widowed, 6.4% divorced; Foreign born: 0.5%; Speak English only: 68.4%; With disability: 11.8%; Veterans: 8.1%; Ancestry: 23.6% German, 19.1% American, 14.1% Swiss, 10.1% English, 6.9% Irish
Employment: 19.0% management, business, and financial, 2.4% computer, engineering, and science, 7.8% education, legal, community service, arts, and media, 4.9% healthcare practitioners, 12.1% service, 18.9% sales and office, 18.9% natural resources, construction, and maintenance, 16.0% production, transportation, and material moving
Income: Per capita: $31,021; Median household: $56,250; Average household: $82,908; Households with income of $100,000 or more: 27.2%; Poverty rate: 8.3%
Educational Attainment: High school diploma or higher: 74.4%; Bachelor's degree or higher: 23.9%; Graduate/professional degree or higher: 11.0%
Housing: Homeownership rate: 92.5%; Median home value: $169,000; Median year structure built: 1981; Homeowner vacancy rate: 0.0%; Median selected monthly owner costs: $1,464 with a mortgage, $506 without a mortgage; Median gross rent: $683 per month; Rental vacancy rate: 22.8%
Health Insurance: 61.6% have insurance; 47.1% have private insurance; 33.1% have public insurance; 38.4% do not have insurance; 69.5% of children under 18 do not have insurance
Transportation: Commute: 61.6% car, 0.0% public transportation, 7.4% walk, 17.4% work from home; Mean travel time to work: 22.0 minutes

BELLONA (unincorporated postal area)
ZCTA: 14415
  Covers a land area of 1.452 square miles and a water area of 0 square miles. Located at 42.76° N. Lat; 77.02° W. Long. Elevation is 725 feet.

Population: 161; Growth (since 2000): 159.7%; Density: 110.9 persons per square mile; Race: 85.1% White, 0.0% Black/African American, 0.0% Asian, 0.0% American Indian/Alaska Native, 0.0% Native Hawaiian/Other Pacific Islander, 14.9% Two or more races, 0.0% Hispanic of any race; Average household size: 2.12; Median age: 51.3; Age under 18: 5.0%; Age 65 and over: 13.7%; Males per 100 females: 83.3; Marriage status: 40.4% never married, 53.2% now married, 2.6% separated, 3.2% widowed, 3.2% divorced; Foreign born: 0.0%; Speak English only: 78.3%; With disability: 0.0%; Veterans: 0.0%; Ancestry: 22.4% English, 21.7% German, 16.1% American, 11.2% Irish, 9.9% French Canadian
Employment: 12.3% management, business, and financial, 0.0% computer, engineering, and science, 19.6% education, legal, community service, arts, and media, 0.0% healthcare practitioners, 26.8% service, 10.1% sales and office, 13.8% natural resources, construction, and maintenance, 17.4% production, transportation, and material moving
Income: Per capita: $27,337; Median household: n/a; Average household: $56,762; Households with income of $100,000 or more: 19.7%; Poverty rate: n/a
Educational Attainment: High school diploma or higher: 71.1%; Bachelor's degree or higher: 9.6%; Graduate/professional degree or higher: 5.3%
Housing: Homeownership rate: 81.6%; Median home value: $113,600; Median year structure built: Before 1940; Homeowner vacancy rate: 0.0%; Median selected monthly owner costs: $1,131 with a mortgage, $334 without a mortgage; Median gross rent: n/a per month; Rental vacancy rate: 0.0%
Health Insurance: 80.1% have insurance; 51.6% have private insurance; 28.6% have public insurance; 19.9% do not have insurance; 0.0% of children under 18 do not have insurance
Transportation: Commute: 90.8% car, 0.0% public transportation, 0.0% walk, 9.2% work from home; Mean travel time to work: 20.0 minutes

BENTON (town). Covers a land area of 41.473 square miles and a water area of 2.964 square miles. Located at 42.72° N. Lat; 77.05° W. Long. Elevation is 837 feet.
Population: 2,792; Growth (since 2000): 5.8%; Density: 67.3 persons per square mile; Race: 96.8% White, 1.4% Black/African American, 0.2% Asian, 0.0% American Indian/Alaska Native, 0.0% Native Hawaiian/Other Pacific Islander, 1.2% Two or more races, 0.8% Hispanic of any race; Average household size: 3.00; Median age: 43.4; Age under 18: 23.9%; Age 65 and over: 19.8%; Males per 100 females: 94.6; Marriage status: 27.3% never married, 57.1% now married, 0.8% separated, 9.1% widowed, 6.6% divorced; Foreign born: 1.2%; Speak English only: 67.5%; With disability: 7.2%; Veterans: 4.4%; Ancestry: 24.9% German, 14.6% English, 14.4% Swiss, 12.2% Irish, 11.6% American
Employment: 18.8% management, business, and financial, 4.4% computer, engineering, and science, 8.4% education, legal, community service, arts, and media, 2.5% healthcare practitioners, 16.4% service, 21.5% sales and office, 13.8% natural resources, construction, and maintenance, 14.2% production, transportation, and material moving
Income: Per capita: $26,993; Median household: $67,375; Average household: $83,247; Households with income of $100,000 or more: 29.1%; Poverty rate: 7.3%
Educational Attainment: High school diploma or higher: 75.3%; Bachelor's degree or higher: 17.2%; Graduate/professional degree or higher: 8.5%
Housing: Homeownership rate: 86.1%; Median home value: $157,000; Median year structure built: 1943; Homeowner vacancy rate: 0.8%; Median selected monthly owner costs: $1,244 with a mortgage, $525 without a mortgage; Median gross rent: $711 per month; Rental vacancy rate: 17.4%
Health Insurance: 61.9% have insurance; 49.1% have private insurance; 24.0% have public insurance; 38.1% do not have insurance; 67.3% of children under 18 do not have insurance
Transportation: Commute: 75.3% car, 0.0% public transportation, 6.2% walk, 13.9% work from home; Mean travel time to work: 20.6 minutes

BRANCHPORT (unincorporated postal area)
ZCTA: 14418
  Covers a land area of 37.364 square miles and a water area of 0.040 square miles. Located at 42.60° N. Lat; 77.22° W. Long. Elevation is 741 feet.
Population: 1,376; Growth (since 2000): -7.1%; Density: 36.8 persons per square mile; Race: 99.7% White, 0.0% Black/African American, 0.0% Asian, 0.0% American Indian/Alaska Native, 0.0% Native

Hawaiian/Other Pacific Islander, 0.3% Two or more races, 4.4% Hispanic of any race; Average household size: 2.63; Median age: 45.9; Age under 18: 20.1%; Age 65 and over: 18.2%; Males per 100 females: 99.5; Marriage status: 28.5% never married, 63.6% now married, 6.4% separated, 0.9% widowed, 7.0% divorced; Foreign born: 1.7%; Speak English only: 97.5%; With disability: 11.0%; Veterans: 10.9%; Ancestry: 23.7% German, 20.9% English, 18.7% Irish, 11.2% Polish, 10.8% Italian
Employment: 8.0% management, business, and financial, 8.6% computer, engineering, and science, 5.4% education, legal, community service, arts, and media, 11.3% healthcare practitioners, 5.7% service, 19.5% sales and office, 12.1% natural resources, construction, and maintenance, 29.4% production, transportation, and material moving
Income: Per capita: $32,967; Median household: $71,458; Average household: $85,775; Households with income of $100,000 or more: 29.3%; Poverty rate: 11.8%
Educational Attainment: High school diploma or higher: 92.8%; Bachelor's degree or higher: 28.3%; Graduate/professional degree or higher: 12.7%
Housing: Homeownership rate: 90.1%; Median home value: $149,000; Median year structure built: 1977; Homeowner vacancy rate: 1.7%; Median selected monthly owner costs: $1,326 with a mortgage, $633 without a mortgage; Median gross rent: $1,155 per month; Rental vacancy rate: 0.0%
Health Insurance: 92.0% have insurance; 76.7% have private insurance; 28.9% have public insurance; 8.0% do not have insurance; 23.9% of children under 18 do not have insurance
Transportation: Commute: 88.2% car, 0.0% public transportation, 1.7% walk, 9.7% work from home; Mean travel time to work: 28.0 minutes

DRESDEN (village).
Covers a land area of 0.302 square miles and a water area of 0.006 square miles. Located at 42.68° N. Lat; 76.96° W. Long. Elevation is 509 feet.
Population: 418; Growth (since 2000): 36.2%; Density: 1,385.2 persons per square mile; Race: 96.4% White, 0.0% Black/African American, 0.0% Asian, 0.0% American Indian/Alaska Native, 0.0% Native Hawaiian/Other Pacific Islander, 3.6% Two or more races, 19.4% Hispanic of any race; Average household size: 2.90; Median age: 34.8; Age under 18: 23.4%; Age 65 and over: 8.4%; Males per 100 females: 115.4; Marriage status: 22.8% never married, 58.9% now married, 5.6% separated, 5.6% widowed, 12.7% divorced; Foreign born: 12.0%; Speak English only: 80.0%; With disability: 10.0%; Veterans: 5.6%; Ancestry: 20.1% German, 16.3% Irish, 9.1% Dutch, 7.7% Danish, 6.5% English
Employment: 7.6% management, business, and financial, 0.0% computer, engineering, and science, 10.3% education, legal, community service, arts, and media, 1.8% healthcare practitioners, 16.1% service, 21.9% sales and office, 24.6% natural resources, construction, and maintenance, 17.9% production, transportation, and material moving
Income: Per capita: $25,000; Median household: $55,417; Average household: $69,528; Households with income of $100,000 or more: 20.9%; Poverty rate: 11.2%
Educational Attainment: High school diploma or higher: 80.5%; Bachelor's degree or higher: 21.2%; Graduate/professional degree or higher: 9.2%
Housing: Homeownership rate: 72.9%; Median home value: $90,400; Median year structure built: Before 1940; Homeowner vacancy rate: 0.0%; Median selected monthly owner costs: $892 with a mortgage, $545 without a mortgage; Median gross rent: $860 per month; Rental vacancy rate: 11.4%
Health Insurance: 79.4% have insurance; 58.1% have private insurance; 27.0% have public insurance; 20.6% do not have insurance; 8.5% of children under 18 do not have insurance
Transportation: Commute: 91.9% car, 0.0% public transportation, 0.9% walk, 0.0% work from home; Mean travel time to work: 25.1 minutes

DUNDEE (village).
Covers a land area of 1.124 square miles and a water area of 0 square miles. Located at 42.52° N. Lat; 76.98° W. Long. Elevation is 984 feet.
History: Incorporated 1847.
Population: 1,655; Growth (since 2000): -2.1%; Density: 1,472.4 persons per square mile; Race: 95.9% White, 0.6% Black/African American, 0.4% Asian, 0.0% American Indian/Alaska Native, 0.0% Native Hawaiian/Other Pacific Islander, 2.0% Two or more races, 1.7% Hispanic of any race; Average household size: 2.22; Median age: 38.9; Age under 18: 23.7%; Age 65 and over: 14.0%; Males per 100 females: 93.2; Marriage status: 25.6% never married, 50.4% now married, 5.0% separated, 8.5%

widowed, 15.5% divorced; Foreign born: 1.0%; Speak English only: 98.2%; With disability: 11.5%; Veterans: 7.8%; Ancestry: 19.0% American, 16.5% German, 14.8% English, 12.3% Irish, 5.7% French
Employment: 6.7% management, business, and financial, 3.5% computer, engineering, and science, 14.7% education, legal, community service, arts, and media, 3.9% healthcare practitioners, 23.5% service, 18.9% sales and office, 3.8% natural resources, construction, and maintenance, 25.1% production, transportation, and material moving
Income: Per capita: $24,470; Median household: $36,696; Average household: $55,534; Households with income of $100,000 or more: 10.6%; Poverty rate: 16.3%
Educational Attainment: High school diploma or higher: 89.6%; Bachelor's degree or higher: 14.0%; Graduate/professional degree or higher: 6.0%

School District(s)
Dundee Central SD (PK-12)
    Enrollment: 731 . . . . (607) 243-5533
Housing: Homeownership rate: 54.2%; Median home value: $79,300; Median year structure built: Before 1940; Homeowner vacancy rate: 6.3%; Median selected monthly owner costs: $959 with a mortgage, $437 without a mortgage; Median gross rent: $594 per month; Rental vacancy rate: 0.0%
Health Insurance: 89.2% have insurance; 55.4% have private insurance; 44.8% have public insurance; 10.8% do not have insurance; 3.0% of children under 18 do not have insurance
Newspapers: The Observer (weekly circulation 2,100); Watkins Glen Review/Express (weekly circulation 3,000)
Transportation: Commute: 80.6% car, 0.0% public transportation, 12.0% walk, 5.8% work from home; Mean travel time to work: 20.5 minutes

HIMROD (unincorporated postal area)
ZCTA: 14842
    Covers a land area of 16.731 square miles and a water area of 0.007 square miles. Located at 42.60° N. Lat; 76.98° W. Long. Elevation is 797 feet.
Population: 838; Growth (since 2000): -7.8%; Density: 50.1 persons per square mile; Race: 100.0% White, 0.0% Black/African American, 0.0% Asian, 0.0% American Indian/Alaska Native, 0.0% Native Hawaiian/Other Pacific Islander, 0.0% Two or more races, 0.0% Hispanic of any race; Average household size: 2.54; Median age: 51.7; Age under 18: 27.7%; Age 65 and over: 22.9%; Males per 100 females: 100.9; Marriage status: 26.7% never married, 45.8% now married, 2.5% separated, 9.2% widowed, 18.3% divorced; Foreign born: 4.2%; Speak English only: 75.3%; With disability: 6.9%; Veterans: 9.1%; Ancestry: 30.2% German, 21.5% Irish, 17.9% English, 11.1% American, 6.9% Swiss
Employment: 10.2% management, business, and financial, 3.7% computer, engineering, and science, 28.5% education, legal, community service, arts, and media, 0.0% healthcare practitioners, 32.8% service, 9.0% sales and office, 11.6% natural resources, construction, and maintenance, 4.2% production, transportation, and material moving
Income: Per capita: $17,496; Median household: $39,483; Average household: $44,157; Households with income of $100,000 or more: n/a; Poverty rate: 25.2%
Educational Attainment: High school diploma or higher: 89.5%; Bachelor's degree or higher: 38.3%; Graduate/professional degree or higher: 15.6%
Housing: Homeownership rate: 96.7%; Median home value: $146,100; Median year structure built: 1983; Homeowner vacancy rate: 0.0%; Median selected monthly owner costs: $888 with a mortgage, $478 without a mortgage; Median gross rent: n/a per month; Rental vacancy rate: 0.0%
Health Insurance: 72.7% have insurance; 64.2% have private insurance; 34.8% have public insurance; 27.3% do not have insurance; 58.4% of children under 18 do not have insurance
Transportation: Commute: 66.8% car, 0.0% public transportation, 11.1% walk, 13.8% work from home; Mean travel time to work: 19.2 minutes

ITALY (town).
Covers a land area of 40.140 square miles and a water area of 0.122 square miles. Located at 42.62° N. Lat; 77.31° W. Long. Elevation is 1,109 feet.
Population: 1,036; Growth (since 2000): -4.7%; Density: 25.8 persons per square mile; Race: 97.2% White, 0.0% Black/African American, 0.0% Asian, 0.0% American Indian/Alaska Native, 0.0% Native Hawaiian/Other

Pacific Islander, 2.8% Two or more races, 4.1% Hispanic of any race; Average household size: 2.42; Median age: 46.9; Age under 18: 20.3%; Age 65 and over: 19.1%; Males per 100 females: 103.0; Marriage status: 17.1% never married, 65.5% now married, 4.3% separated, 4.1% widowed, 13.2% divorced; Foreign born: 2.2%; Speak English only: 97.3%; With disability: 13.2%; Veterans: 6.4%; Ancestry: 20.8% German, 16.8% English, 14.4% Irish, 9.0% American, 8.0% Polish

Employment: 7.4% management, business, and financial, 2.5% computer, engineering, and science, 8.5% education, legal, community service, arts, and media, 7.6% healthcare practitioners, 20.1% service, 22.0% sales and office, 18.2% natural resources, construction, and maintenance, 13.7% production, transportation, and material moving

Income: Per capita: $26,771; Median household: $56,346; Average household: $64,071; Households with income of $100,000 or more: 15.1%; Poverty rate: 17.7%

Educational Attainment: High school diploma or higher: 89.6%; Bachelor's degree or higher: 23.5%; Graduate/professional degree or higher: 9.5%

Housing: Homeownership rate: 93.2%; Median home value: $95,000; Median year structure built: 1973; Homeowner vacancy rate: 1.9%; Median selected monthly owner costs: $1,211 with a mortgage, $434 without a mortgage; Median gross rent: $690 per month; Rental vacancy rate: 0.0%

Health Insurance: 92.8% have insurance; 58.3% have private insurance; 47.9% have public insurance; 7.2% do not have insurance; 5.3% of children under 18 do not have insurance

Transportation: Commute: 93.4% car, 0.0% public transportation, 0.7% walk, 5.3% work from home; Mean travel time to work: 38.4 minutes

---

JERUSALEM (town). Covers a land area of 58.639 square miles and a water area of 6.762 square miles. Located at 42.61° N. Lat; 77.16° W. Long.

Population: 4,455; Growth (since 2000): -1.5%; Density: 76.0 persons per square mile; Race: 93.4% White, 1.4% Black/African American, 2.9% Asian, 0.7% American Indian/Alaska Native, 0.0% Native Hawaiian/Other Pacific Islander, 0.4% Two or more races, 2.4% Hispanic of any race; Average household size: 2.51; Median age: 38.4; Age under 18: 17.4%; Age 65 and over: 17.2%; Males per 100 females: 82.1; Marriage status: 37.2% never married, 55.0% now married, 2.8% separated, 1.2% widowed, 6.6% divorced; Foreign born: 3.7%; Speak English only: 94.1%; With disability: 8.5%; Veterans: 9.2%; Ancestry: 22.5% German, 20.4% English, 17.1% Irish, 9.7% Italian, 7.2% Polish

Employment: 9.9% management, business, and financial, 4.1% computer, engineering, and science, 7.3% education, legal, community service, arts, and media, 5.0% healthcare practitioners, 18.3% service, 27.8% sales and office, 10.5% natural resources, construction, and maintenance, 17.2% production, transportation, and material moving

Income: Per capita: $28,200; Median household: $69,671; Average household: $85,618; Households with income of $100,000 or more: 32.1%; Poverty rate: 13.0%

Educational Attainment: High school diploma or higher: 89.8%; Bachelor's degree or higher: 30.2%; Graduate/professional degree or higher: 13.3%

Housing: Homeownership rate: 87.4%; Median home value: $169,900; Median year structure built: 1971; Homeowner vacancy rate: 2.2%; Median selected monthly owner costs: $1,289 with a mortgage, $615 without a mortgage; Median gross rent: $1,132 per month; Rental vacancy rate: 0.0%

Health Insurance: 92.4% have insurance; 76.6% have private insurance; 29.1% have public insurance; 7.6% do not have insurance; 16.0% of children under 18 do not have insurance

Transportation: Commute: 74.2% car, 0.9% public transportation, 14.7% walk, 8.7% work from home; Mean travel time to work: 19.8 minutes

Additional Information Contacts

Town of Jerusalem . . . . (315) 595-6668
    http://www.jerusalem-ny.org

KEUKA PARK (CDP). Covers a land area of 0.678 square miles and a water area of 0.559 square miles. Located at 42.61° N. Lat; 77.09° W. Long. Elevation is 774 feet.

Population: 972; Growth (since 2000): n/a; Density: 1,434.0 persons per square mile; Race: 78.2% White, 6.5% Black/African American, 12.4% Asian, 1.9% American Indian/Alaska Native, 0.0% Native Hawaiian/Other Pacific Islander, 1.0% Two or more races, 0.8% Hispanic of any race; Average household size: 2.06; Median age: 20.0; Age under 18: 2.2%; Age 65 and over: 7.8%; Males per 100 females: 50.6; Marriage status:

86.2% never married, 13.4% now married, 0.0% separated, 0.0% widowed, 0.4% divorced; Foreign born: 13.5%; Speak English only: 92.8%; With disability: 7.9%; Veterans: 3.9%; Ancestry: 17.6% Italian, 14.7% German, 11.4% Irish, 6.1% Polish, 5.5% English

Employment: 4.1% management, business, and financial, 1.1% computer, engineering, and science, 8.1% education, legal, community service, arts, and media, 0.0% healthcare practitioners, 43.5% service, 39.9% sales and office, 0.0% natural resources, construction, and maintenance, 3.4% production, transportation, and material moving

Income: Per capita: $9,560; Median household: $59,464; Average household: $90,993; Households with income of $100,000 or more: 28.4%; Poverty rate: n/a

Educational Attainment: High school diploma or higher: 100.0%; Bachelor's degree or higher: 49.6%; Graduate/professional degree or higher: 44.5%

Four-year College(s)
Keuka College (Private, Not-for-profit, Baptist)
    Enrollment: 1,953 . . . . (315) 279-5000
    Tuition: In-state $30,946; Out-of-state $30,946

Housing: Homeownership rate: 58.0%; Median home value: n/a; Median year structure built: 1953; Homeowner vacancy rate: 0.0%; Median selected monthly owner costs: n/a with a mortgage, n/a without a mortgage; Median gross rent: $989 per month; Rental vacancy rate: 0.0%

Health Insurance: 96.1% have insurance; 84.6% have private insurance; 17.6% have public insurance; 3.9% do not have insurance; 0.0% of children under 18 do not have insurance

Transportation: Commute: 20.2% car, 4.1% public transportation, 60.2% walk, 15.4% work from home; Mean travel time to work: 9.3 minutes

---

MIDDLESEX (town). Covers a land area of 30.875 square miles and a water area of 3.229 square miles. Located at 42.72° N. Lat; 77.29° W. Long. Elevation is 771 feet.

Population: 1,378; Growth (since 2000): 2.5%; Density: 44.6 persons per square mile; Race: 96.2% White, 1.9% Black/African American, 0.1% Asian, 0.0% American Indian/Alaska Native, 0.1% Native Hawaiian/Other Pacific Islander, 1.1% Two or more races, 2.5% Hispanic of any race; Average household size: 2.54; Median age: 46.8; Age under 18: 19.4%; Age 65 and over: 17.6%; Males per 100 females: 99.6; Marriage status: 21.3% never married, 62.1% now married, 2.0% separated, 6.4% widowed, 10.2% divorced; Foreign born: 0.4%; Speak English only: 97.8%; With disability: 10.5%; Veterans: 8.3%; Ancestry: 23.1% German, 15.9% Irish, 13.4% English, 12.6% Italian, 5.4% Dutch

Employment: 12.1% management, business, and financial, 2.8% computer, engineering, and science, 11.2% education, legal, community service, arts, and media, 5.4% healthcare practitioners, 19.1% service, 20.0% sales and office, 16.1% natural resources, construction, and maintenance, 13.2% production, transportation, and material moving

Income: Per capita: $29,850; Median household: $62,000; Average household: $75,560; Households with income of $100,000 or more: 21.5%; Poverty rate: 10.4%

Educational Attainment: High school diploma or higher: 94.7%; Bachelor's degree or higher: 29.5%; Graduate/professional degree or higher: 11.1%

Housing: Homeownership rate: 89.2%; Median home value: $136,700; Median year structure built: 1978; Homeowner vacancy rate: 0.0%; Median selected monthly owner costs: $1,166 with a mortgage, $503 without a mortgage; Median gross rent: $691 per month; Rental vacancy rate: 12.0%

Health Insurance: 94.3% have insurance; 72.6% have private insurance; 35.3% have public insurance; 5.7% do not have insurance; 5.7% of children under 18 do not have insurance

Transportation: Commute: 95.3% car, 0.0% public transportation, 0.5% walk, 3.5% work from home; Mean travel time to work: 31.4 minutes

---

MILO (town). Covers a land area of 38.434 square miles and a water area of 5.901 square miles. Located at 42.61° N. Lat; 77.01° W. Long.

Population: 6,900; Growth (since 2000): -1.8%; Density: 179.5 persons per square mile; Race: 97.7% White, 1.1% Black/African American, 0.3% Asian, 0.0% American Indian/Alaska Native, 0.0% Native Hawaiian/Other Pacific Islander, 0.8% Two or more races, 0.9% Hispanic of any race; Average household size: 2.32; Median age: 44.8; Age under 18: 22.3%; Age 65 and over: 21.2%; Males per 100 females: 92.3; Marriage status: 32.6% never married, 46.2% now married, 4.2% separated, 6.5% widowed, 14.7% divorced; Foreign born: 1.5%; Speak English only: 89.4%; With disability: 17.0%; Veterans: 9.8%; Ancestry: 24.7% German, 18.9% Irish, 13.9% English, 6.5% American, 6.0% Italian

Employment: 12.0% management, business, and financial, 2.4% computer, engineering, and science, 11.5% education, legal, community service, arts, and media, 3.6% healthcare practitioners, 24.7% service, 19.6% sales and office, 12.5% natural resources, construction, and maintenance, 13.6% production, transportation, and material moving
Income: Per capita: $22,399; Median household: $37,054; Average household: $51,591; Households with income of $100,000 or more: 11.4%; Poverty rate: 17.8%
Educational Attainment: High school diploma or higher: 87.9%; Bachelor's degree or higher: 23.7%; Graduate/professional degree or higher: 9.8%
Housing: Homeownership rate: 63.4%; Median home value: $113,600; Median year structure built: 1950; Homeowner vacancy rate: 0.5%; Median selected monthly owner costs: $1,016 with a mortgage, $490 without a mortgage; Median gross rent: $729 per month; Rental vacancy rate: 6.5%
Health Insurance: 83.3% have insurance; 56.3% have private insurance; 45.7% have public insurance; 16.7% do not have insurance; 34.6% of children under 18 do not have insurance
Transportation: Commute: 74.8% car, 0.0% public transportation, 10.2% walk, 10.5% work from home; Mean travel time to work: 19.4 minutes
Additional Information Contacts
Town of Milo . . . . (315) 536-8911
    http://www.townofmilo.com

PENN YAN (village). County seat. Covers a land area of 2.381 square miles and a water area of 0.056 square miles. Located at 42.66° N. Lat; 77.05° W. Long. Elevation is 728 feet.
History: Controversy between the settlers from Pennsylvania and New England over a name for this place was compromised by combining the first syllables of Pennsylvania and Yankee.
Population: 4,784; Growth (since 2000): -8.3%; Density: 2,008.9 persons per square mile; Race: 96.3% White, 1.9% Black/African American, 0.3% Asian, 0.0% American Indian/Alaska Native, 0.0% Native Hawaiian/Other Pacific Islander, 1.2% Two or more races, 1.5% Hispanic of any race; Average household size: 2.16; Median age: 45.8; Age under 18: 20.9%; Age 65 and over: 23.0%; Males per 100 females: 86.7; Marriage status: 32.4% never married, 41.8% now married, 3.9% separated, 9.6% widowed, 16.2% divorced; Foreign born: 1.5%; Speak English only: 98.3%; With disability: 18.2%; Veterans: 10.1%; Ancestry: 18.9% Irish, 16.9% German, 15.1% English, 7.6% Italian, 6.0% Danish
Employment: 9.8% management, business, and financial, 3.4% computer, engineering, and science, 11.6% education, legal, community service, arts, and media, 3.5% healthcare practitioners, 28.1% service, 22.5% sales and office, 8.7% natural resources, construction, and maintenance, 12.3% production, transportation, and material moving
Income: Per capita: $20,989; Median household: $31,700; Average household: $45,437; Households with income of $100,000 or more: 11.6%; Poverty rate: 19.7%
Educational Attainment: High school diploma or higher: 87.8%; Bachelor's degree or higher: 19.4%; Graduate/professional degree or higher: 6.3%

School District(s)
Penn Yan Central SD (PK-12)
    Enrollment: 1,460 . . . . (315) 536-3371
Housing: Homeownership rate: 49.9%; Median home value: $99,800; Median year structure built: Before 1940; Homeowner vacancy rate: 0.0%; Median selected monthly owner costs: $967 with a mortgage, $471 without a mortgage; Median gross rent: $730 per month; Rental vacancy rate: 6.8%
Health Insurance: 91.9% have insurance; 59.7% have private insurance; 50.6% have public insurance; 8.1% do not have insurance; 14.7% of children under 18 do not have insurance
Hospitals: Soldiers & Sailors Memorial Hospital of Yates (186 beds)
Safety: Violent crime rate: 6.0 per 10,000 population; Property crime rate: 116.9 per 10,000 population
Newspapers: The Chronicle-Express (weekly circulation 3,900)
Transportation: Commute: 77.6% car, 0.0% public transportation, 13.7% walk, 8.3% work from home; Mean travel time to work: 17.5 minutes
Airports: Penn Yan (general aviation)
Additional Information Contacts
Village of Penn Yan. . . . . (315) 536-3015
    http://www.villageofpennyan.com

POTTER (town). Covers a land area of 37.238 square miles and a water area of 0 square miles. Located at 42.71° N. Lat; 77.18° W. Long. Elevation is 896 feet.
Population: 1,973; Growth (since 2000): 7.8%; Density: 53.0 persons per square mile; Race: 96.6% White, 0.4% Black/African American, 0.1% Asian, 0.7% American Indian/Alaska Native, 0.0% Native Hawaiian/Other Pacific Islander, 2.3% Two or more races, 5.0% Hispanic of any race; Average household size: 3.01; Median age: 32.4; Age under 18: 31.7%; Age 65 and over: 11.9%; Males per 100 females: 99.5; Marriage status: 32.2% never married, 53.8% now married, 2.7% separated, 5.4% widowed, 8.5% divorced; Foreign born: 2.5%; Speak English only: 78.9%; With disability: 8.3%; Veterans: 5.1%; Ancestry: 24.6% German, 14.5% English, 10.3% Irish, 8.4% Swiss, 8.1% Italian
Employment: 16.3% management, business, and financial, 1.5% computer, engineering, and science, 11.1% education, legal, community service, arts, and media, 2.7% healthcare practitioners, 16.9% service, 18.2% sales and office, 19.0% natural resources, construction, and maintenance, 14.3% production, transportation, and material moving
Income: Per capita: $22,200; Median household: $48,438; Average household: $67,015; Households with income of $100,000 or more: 19.4%; Poverty rate: 16.5%
Educational Attainment: High school diploma or higher: 80.3%; Bachelor's degree or higher: 13.5%; Graduate/professional degree or higher: 6.0%
Housing: Homeownership rate: 79.6%; Median home value: $117,300; Median year structure built: 1971; Homeowner vacancy rate: 2.6%; Median selected monthly owner costs: $1,153 with a mortgage, $523 without a mortgage; Median gross rent: $798 per month; Rental vacancy rate: 4.7%
Health Insurance: 70.0% have insurance; 51.5% have private insurance; 28.8% have public insurance; 30.0% do not have insurance; 41.5% of children under 18 do not have insurance
Transportation: Commute: 80.0% car, 0.0% public transportation, 3.9% walk, 10.2% work from home; Mean travel time to work: 27.2 minutes

RUSHVILLE (village). Covers a land area of 0.639 square miles and a water area of 0 square miles. Located at 42.76° N. Lat; 77.23° W. Long. Elevation is 876 feet.
Population: 597; Growth (since 2000): -3.9%; Density: 933.8 persons per square mile; Race: 96.1% White, 1.2% Black/African American, 0.0% Asian, 0.7% American Indian/Alaska Native, 0.0% Native Hawaiian/Other Pacific Islander, 2.0% Two or more races, 6.9% Hispanic of any race; Average household size: 2.22; Median age: 44.2; Age under 18: 25.8%; Age 65 and over: 20.6%; Males per 100 females: 91.8; Marriage status: 36.3% never married, 38.5% now married, 3.9% separated, 12.0% widowed, 13.3% divorced; Foreign born: 1.5%; Speak English only: 98.9%; With disability: 21.4%; Veterans: 4.7%; Ancestry: 20.9% English, 20.9% German, 20.6% Irish, 13.2% Italian, 5.5% French
Employment: 6.3% management, business, and financial, 0.0% computer, engineering, and science, 8.2% education, legal, community service, arts, and media, 2.4% healthcare practitioners, 24.5% service, 17.8% sales and office, 14.9% natural resources, construction, and maintenance, 26.0% production, transportation, and material moving
Income: Per capita: $22,858; Median household: $37,875; Average household: $53,260; Households with income of $100,000 or more: 10.7%; Poverty rate: 29.3%
Educational Attainment: High school diploma or higher: 80.6%; Bachelor's degree or higher: 10.1%; Graduate/professional degree or higher: 4.4%

School District(s)
Gorham-Middlesex Central SD (Marcus Whitman) (PK-12)
    Enrollment: 1,229 . . . . (585) 554-4848
Housing: Homeownership rate: 63.0%; Median home value: $101,800; Median year structure built: Before 1940; Homeowner vacancy rate: 8.0%; Median selected monthly owner costs: $1,134 with a mortgage, $515 without a mortgage; Median gross rent: $539 per month; Rental vacancy rate: 0.0%
Health Insurance: 96.5% have insurance; 55.6% have private insurance; 55.9% have public insurance; 3.5% do not have insurance; 1.9% of children under 18 do not have insurance
Transportation: Commute: 92.3% car, 0.0% public transportation, 3.4% walk, 2.9% work from home; Mean travel time to work: 29.8 minutes

STARKEY (town). Covers a land area of 32.831 square miles and a water area of 6.375 square miles. Located at 42.52° N. Lat; 76.94° W. Long. Elevation is 804 feet.

Population: 3,504; Growth (since 2000): 1.1%; Density: 106.7 persons per square mile; Race: 95.7% White, 1.1% Black/African American, 0.3% Asian, 0.0% American Indian/Alaska Native, 0.0% Native Hawaiian/Other Pacific Islander, 1.3% Two or more races, 1.0% Hispanic of any race; Average household size: 2.48; Median age: 38.7; Age under 18: 23.6%; Age 65 and over: 18.3%; Males per 100 females: 101.1; Marriage status: 26.9% never married, 57.2% now married, 2.7% separated, 5.5% widowed, 10.4% divorced; Foreign born: 0.6%; Speak English only: 89.1%; With disability: 12.9%; Veterans: 9.4%; Ancestry: 23.2% German, 14.9% American, 12.2% English, 11.5% Irish, 9.2% Dutch

Employment: 8.5% management, business, and financial, 2.5% computer, engineering, and science, 16.3% education, legal, community service, arts, and media, 4.3% healthcare practitioners, 24.2% service, 14.8% sales and office, 11.3% natural resources, construction, and maintenance, 18.1% production, transportation, and material moving

Income: Per capita: $30,524; Median household: $48,750; Average household: $76,757; Households with income of $100,000 or more: 26.0%; Poverty rate: 11.3%

Educational Attainment: High school diploma or higher: 90.3%; Bachelor's degree or higher: 24.6%; Graduate/professional degree or higher: 12.7%

Housing: Homeownership rate: 68.2%; Median home value: $103,700; Median year structure built: 1945; Homeowner vacancy rate: 2.8%; Median selected monthly owner costs: $1,071 with a mortgage, $453 without a mortgage; Median gross rent: $651 per month; Rental vacancy rate: 0.0%

Health Insurance: 82.6% have insurance; 55.9% have private insurance; 43.5% have public insurance; 17.4% do not have insurance; 28.1% of children under 18 do not have insurance

Transportation: Commute: 80.2% car, 0.9% public transportation, 7.8% walk, 8.6% work from home; Mean travel time to work: 20.2 minutes

TORREY (town). Covers a land area of 22.760 square miles and a water area of 10.915 square miles. Located at 42.67° N. Lat; 76.95° W. Long. Elevation is 509 feet.

Population: 1,500; Growth (since 2000): 14.8%; Density: 65.9 persons per square mile; Race: 96.7% White, 0.0% Black/African American, 0.0% Asian, 0.0% American Indian/Alaska Native, 0.0% Native Hawaiian/Other Pacific Islander, 2.9% Two or more races, 8.0% Hispanic of any race; Average household size: 2.81; Median age: 39.0; Age under 18: 22.4%; Age 65 and over: 18.4%; Males per 100 females: 105.4; Marriage status: 22.4% never married, 66.1% now married, 2.6% separated, 5.3% widowed, 6.3% divorced; Foreign born: 4.0%; Speak English only: 77.6%; With disability: 11.1%; Veterans: 7.6%; Ancestry: 27.2% German, 13.3% Irish, 8.7% Danish, 8.5% American, 8.3% English

Employment: 19.5% management, business, and financial, 2.2% computer, engineering, and science, 10.1% education, legal, community service, arts, and media, 4.9% healthcare practitioners, 11.0% service, 19.2% sales and office, 19.5% natural resources, construction, and maintenance, 13.6% production, transportation, and material moving

Income: Per capita: $29,540; Median household: $59,091; Average household: $78,794; Households with income of $100,000 or more: 24.4%; Poverty rate: 5.9%

Educational Attainment: High school diploma or higher: 84.5%; Bachelor's degree or higher: 26.1%; Graduate/professional degree or higher: 11.0%

Housing: Homeownership rate: 87.6%; Median home value: $161,400; Median year structure built: 1966; Homeowner vacancy rate: 1.7%; Median selected monthly owner costs: $1,086 with a mortgage, $558 without a mortgage; Median gross rent: $825 per month; Rental vacancy rate: 6.2%

Health Insurance: 70.0% have insurance; 54.6% have private insurance; 29.3% have public insurance; 30.0% do not have insurance; 43.6% of children under 18 do not have insurance

Transportation: Commute: 80.3% car, 0.0% public transportation, 2.6% walk, 9.8% work from home; Mean travel time to work: 25.9 minutes

Place Name Index

Accord (CDP) Ulster County, 684
Acra (unincorporated) Greene County, 253
Adams (town) Jefferson County, 279
Adams (village) Jefferson County, 279
Adams Center (CDP) Jefferson County, 279
Addison (town) Steuben County, 593
Addison (village) Steuben County, 593
Adirondack (unincorporated) Warren County, 705
Afton (town) Chenango County, 131
Afton (village) Chenango County, 131
Airmont (village) Rockland County, 528
Akron (village) Erie County, 199
Alabama (town) Genesee County, 246
Albany (city) Albany County, 49
Albany County, 49
Albertson (CDP) Nassau County, 345
Albion (town) Orleans County, 484
Albion (village) Orleans County, 484
Albion (town) Oswego County, 488
Alden (town) Erie County, 199
Alden (village) Erie County, 200
Alder Creek (unincorporated) Oneida County, 418
Alexander (town) Genesee County, 246
Alexander (village) Genesee County, 246
Alexandria (town) Jefferson County, 280
Alexandria Bay (village) Jefferson County, 280
Alfred (town) Allegany County, 59
Alfred (village) Allegany County, 59
Alfred Station (unincorporated) Allegany County, 60
Allegany (town) Cattaraugus County, 83
Allegany (village) Cattaraugus County, 83
Allegany County, 58
Allegany Reservation (reservation) Cattaraugus County, 83
Allen (town) Allegany County, 60
Allentown (unincorporated) Allegany County, 60
Alma (town) Allegany County, 60
Almond (town) Allegany County, 61
Almond (village) Allegany County, 61
Alpine (unincorporated) Schuyler County, 583
Alplaus (unincorporated) Schenectady County, 571
Altamont (village) Albany County, 50
Altmar (village) Oswego County, 488
Altona (town) Clinton County, 141
Altona (CDP) Clinton County, 141
Amagansett (CDP) Suffolk County, 608
Amawalk (unincorporated) Westchester County, 730
Amboy (town) Oswego County, 489
Amenia (town) Dutchess County, 181
Amenia (CDP) Dutchess County, 181
Ames (village) Montgomery County, 338
Amherst (town) Erie County, 200
Amity (town) Allegany County, 61
Amityville (village) Suffolk County, 608
Amsterdam (town) Montgomery County, 339
Amsterdam (city) Montgomery County, 338
Ancram (town) Columbia County, 151
Ancramdale (unincorporated) Columbia County, 151
Andes (town) Delaware County, 168
Andes (CDP) Delaware County, 168
Andover (town) Allegany County, 61
Andover (village) Allegany County, 62
Angelica (town) Allegany County, 62
Angelica (village) Allegany County, 62
Angola (village) Erie County, 200
Angola on the Lake (CDP) Erie County, 201
Annandale on Hudson (unincorporated) Dutchess County, 182

Annsville (town) Oneida County, 419
Antwerp (town) Jefferson County, 280
Antwerp (village) Jefferson County, 280
Apalachin (CDP) Tioga County, 671
Appleton (unincorporated) Niagara County, 409
Apulia Station (unincorporated) Onondaga County, 438
Aquebogue (CDP) Suffolk County, 608
Arcade (town) Wyoming County, 756
Arcade (village) Wyoming County, 756
Arcadia (town) Wayne County, 722
Arden (unincorporated) Orange County, 462
Ardsley (village) Westchester County, 730
Ardsley on Hudson (unincorporated) Westchester County, 731
Argyle (town) Washington County, 712
Argyle (village) Washington County, 713
Arietta (town) Hamilton County, 265
Arkport (village) Steuben County, 593
Arkville (unincorporated) Delaware County, 168
Arkwright (town) Chautauqua County, 108
Arlington (CDP) Dutchess County, 182
Armonk (CDP) Westchester County, 731
Arverne (unincorporated) Queens County, 393
Asharoken (village) Suffolk County, 608
Ashford (town) Cattaraugus County, 84
Ashland (town) Chemung County, 123
Ashland (town) Greene County, 253
Ashville (unincorporated) Chautauqua County, 109
Astoria (unincorporated) Queens County, 393
Athens (town) Greene County, 253
Athens (village) Greene County, 253
Athol (unincorporated) Warren County, 705
Atlanta (unincorporated) Steuben County, 593
Atlantic Beach (village) Nassau County, 345
Attica (town) Wyoming County, 756
Attica (village) Wyoming County, 757
Au Sable (town) Clinton County, 141
Au Sable Forks (CDP) Clinton County, 141
Auburn (city) Cayuga County, 98
Augusta (town) Oneida County, 419
Aurelius (town) Cayuga County, 99
Aurora (village) Cayuga County, 99
Aurora (town) Erie County, 201
Austerlitz (town) Columbia County, 151
Ava (town) Oneida County, 419
Averill Park (CDP) Rensselaer County, 518
Avoca (town) Steuben County, 594
Avoca (village) Steuben County, 594
Avon (town) Livingston County, 304
Avon (village) Livingston County, 304
Babylon (town) Suffolk County, 609
Babylon (village) Suffolk County, 609
Bainbridge (town) Chenango County, 131
Bainbridge (village) Chenango County, 132
Baiting Hollow (CDP) Suffolk County, 609
Bakers Mills (unincorporated) Warren County, 705
Baldwin (town) Chemung County, 124
Baldwin (CDP) Nassau County, 345
Baldwin Harbor (CDP) Nassau County, 346
Baldwin Place (unincorporated) Westchester County, 731
Baldwinsville (village) Onondaga County, 438
Ballston (town) Saratoga County, 559
Ballston Lake (unincorporated) Saratoga County, 559
Ballston Spa (village) Saratoga County, 559
Balmville (CDP) Orange County, 462
Bangor (town) Franklin County, 231
Bardonia (CDP) Rockland County, 528
Barker (town) Broome County, 73
Barker (village) Niagara County, 410

Barneveld (village) Oneida County, 419
Barnum Island (CDP) Nassau County, 346
Barre (town) Orleans County, 484
Barrington (town) Yates County, 765
Barrytown (unincorporated) Dutchess County, 182
Barryville (unincorporated) Sullivan County, 654
Barton (town) Tioga County, 671
Basom (unincorporated) Genesee County, 246
Batavia (town) Genesee County, 247
Batavia (city) Genesee County, 247
Bath (town) Steuben County, 594
Bath (village) Steuben County, 594
Baxter Estates (village) Nassau County, 346
Bay Park (CDP) Nassau County, 346
Bay Shore (CDP) Suffolk County, 610
Bayport (CDP) Suffolk County, 610
Bayside (unincorporated) Queens County, 394
Bayville (village) Nassau County, 346
Baywood (CDP) Suffolk County, 610
Beacon (city) Dutchess County, 183
Bearsville (unincorporated) Ulster County, 684
Beaver Dam Lake (CDP) Orange County, 462
Beaver Dams (unincorporated) Schuyler County, 584
Beaver Falls (unincorporated) Lewis County, 296
Bedford (town) Westchester County, 732
Bedford (CDP) Westchester County, 731
Bedford Hills (CDP) Westchester County, 732
Beekman (town) Dutchess County, 183
Beekmantown (town) Clinton County, 142
Belfast (town) Allegany County, 63
Belfast (CDP) Allegany County, 62
Belle Terre (village) Suffolk County, 610
Bellerose (village) Nassau County, 347
Bellerose Terrace (CDP) Nassau County, 347
Belleville (CDP) Jefferson County, 281
Bellmont (town) Franklin County, 231
Bellmore (CDP) Nassau County, 347
Bellona (unincorporated) Yates County, 765
Bellport (village) Suffolk County, 611
Belmont (village) Allegany County, 63
Bemus Point (village) Chautauqua County, 109
Bennington (town) Wyoming County, 757
Benson (town) Hamilton County, 265
Benton (town) Yates County, 765
Bergen (town) Genesee County, 247
Bergen (village) Genesee County, 248
Berkshire (town) Tioga County, 671
Berlin (town) Rensselaer County, 518
Berne (town) Albany County, 50
Bernhards Bay (unincorporated) Oswego County, 489
Bethany (town) Genesee County, 248
Bethel (town) Sullivan County, 654
Bethlehem (town) Albany County, 51
Bethpage (CDP) Nassau County, 348
Big Flats (town) Chemung County, 124
Big Flats (CDP) Chemung County, 124
Big Indian (unincorporated) Ulster County, 684
Billington Heights (CDP) Erie County, 201
Binghamton (town) Broome County, 74
Binghamton (city) Broome County, 74
Binghamton University (CDP) Broome County, 75
Birdsall (town) Allegany County, 63
Black Brook (town) Clinton County, 142
Black Creek (unincorporated) Allegany County, 63
Black River (village) Jefferson County, 281
Blasdell (village) Erie County, 201
Blauvelt (CDP) Rockland County, 528
Bleecker (town) Fulton County, 241
Blenheim (town) Schoharie County, 575

CDP = Census Designated Place

CDP = Census Designated Place

CDP = Census Designated Place

Forest Hills (unincorporated) Queens County, 398

Forest Home (CDP) Tompkins County, 678

Forestburgh (town) Sullivan County, 657

Forestport (town) Oneida County, 424

Forestville (village) Chautauqua County, 114

Fort Ann (town) Washington County, 715

Fort Ann (village) Washington County, 715

Fort Covington (town) Franklin County, 234

Fort Covington Hamlet (CDP) Franklin County, 235

Fort Drum (CDP) Jefferson County, 286

Fort Edward (town) Washington County, 715

Fort Edward (village) Washington County, 716

Fort Hunter (unincorporated) Montgomery County, 340

Fort Johnson (village) Montgomery County, 340

Fort Montgomery (CDP) Orange County, 466

Fort Plain (village) Montgomery County, 341

Fort Salonga (CDP) Suffolk County, 621

Fowler (town) Saint Lawrence County, 545

Fowlerville (CDP) Livingston County, 307

Frankfort (town) Herkimer County, 271

Frankfort (village) Herkimer County, 271

Franklin (town) Delaware County, 173

Franklin (village) Delaware County, 173

Franklin (town) Franklin County, 235

Franklin County, 230

Franklin Springs (unincorporated) Oneida County, 424

Franklin Square (CDP) Nassau County, 352

Franklinville (town) Cattaraugus County, 87

Franklinville (village) Cattaraugus County, 87

Fredonia (village) Chautauqua County, 115

Freedom (town) Cattaraugus County, 88

Freedom Plains (CDP) Dutchess County, 186

Freehold (unincorporated) Greene County, 257

Freeport (village) Nassau County, 353

Freetown (town) Cortland County, 163

Freeville (village) Tompkins County, 678

Fremont (town) Steuben County, 599

Fremont (town) Sullivan County, 658

Fremont Center (unincorporated) Sullivan County, 658

French Creek (town) Chautauqua County, 115

Fresh Meadows (unincorporated) Queens County, 398

Frewsburg (CDP) Chautauqua County, 115

Friendship (town) Allegany County, 67

Friendship (CDP) Allegany County, 67

Fulton (city) Oswego County, 490

Fulton (town) Schoharie County, 578

Fulton County, 240

Fultonham (unincorporated) Schoharie County, 578

Fultonville (village) Montgomery County, 341

Gabriels (unincorporated) Franklin County, 235

Gaines (town) Orleans County, 485

Gainesville (town) Wyoming County, 759

Gainesville (village) Wyoming County, 759

Galen (town) Wayne County, 722

Galeville (CDP) Onondaga County, 442

Gallatin (town) Columbia County, 154

Galway (town) Saratoga County, 562

Galway (village) Saratoga County, 562

Gang Mills (CDP) Steuben County, 599

Gansevoort (unincorporated) Saratoga County, 562

Garden City (village) Nassau County, 353

Garden City Park (CDP) Nassau County, 353

Garden City South (CDP) Nassau County, 354

Gardiner (town) Ulster County, 688

Gardiner (CDP) Ulster County, 687

Gardnertown (CDP) Orange County, 467

Garnerville (unincorporated) Rockland County, 529

Garrattsville (unincorporated) Otsego County, 503

Garrison (unincorporated) Putnam County, 514

Gasport (CDP) Niagara County, 410

Gates (town) Monroe County, 329

Gates (CDP) Monroe County, 329

Geddes (town) Onondaga County, 442

Genesee (town) Allegany County, 67

Genesee County, 245

Genesee Falls (town) Wyoming County, 759

Geneseo (town) Livingston County, 307

Geneseo (village) Livingston County, 308

Geneva (town) Ontario County, 455

Geneva (city) Ontario County, 455

Genoa (town) Cayuga County, 101

Georgetown (town) Madison County, 320

German (town) Chenango County, 132

German Flatts (town) Herkimer County, 271

Germantown (town) Columbia County, 155

Germantown (CDP) Columbia County, 155

Gerry (town) Chautauqua County, 115

Getzville (unincorporated) Erie County, 209

Ghent (town) Columbia County, 155

Ghent (CDP) Columbia County, 155

Gilbertsville (village) Otsego County, 503

Gilboa (town) Schoharie County, 578

Gilgo (CDP) Suffolk County, 621

Glasco (CDP) Ulster County, 688

Glen (town) Montgomery County, 341

Glen Aubrey (CDP) Broome County, 77

Glen Cove (city) Nassau County, 354

Glen Head (CDP) Nassau County, 354

Glen Oaks (unincorporated) Queens County, 399

Glen Park (village) Jefferson County, 286

Glen Spey (unincorporated) Sullivan County, 658

Glen Wild (unincorporated) Sullivan County, 658

Glenfield (unincorporated) Lewis County, 298

Glenford (unincorporated) Ulster County, 688

Glenmont (unincorporated) Albany County, 53

Glens Falls (city) Warren County, 707

Glens Falls North (CDP) Warren County, 707

Glenville (town) Schenectady County, 572

Glenwood (unincorporated) Erie County, 210

Glenwood Landing (CDP) Nassau County, 354

Gloversville (city) Fulton County, 242

Golden's Bridge (CDP) Westchester County, 737

Gordon Heights (CDP) Suffolk County, 622

Gorham (town) Ontario County, 456

Gorham (CDP) Ontario County, 456

Goshen (town) Orange County, 467

Goshen (village) Orange County, 467

Gouverneur (town) Saint Lawrence County, 546

Gouverneur (village) Saint Lawrence County, 546

Gowanda (village) Cattaraugus County, 88

Grafton (town) Rensselaer County, 521

Grahamsville (unincorporated) Sullivan County, 659

Granby (town) Oswego County, 491

Grand Gorge (unincorporated) Delaware County, 173

Grand Island (town) Erie County, 210

Grand View-on-Hudson (village) Rockland County, 530

Grandyle Village (CDP) Erie County, 210

Granger (town) Allegany County, 67

Granite Springs (unincorporated) Westchester County, 737

Granville (town) Washington County, 716

Granville (village) Washington County, 716

Great Bend (CDP) Jefferson County, 286

Great Neck (village) Nassau County, 355

Great Neck Estates (village) Nassau County, 355

Great Neck Gardens (CDP) Nassau County, 355

Great Neck Plaza (village) Nassau County, 355

Great River (CDP) Suffolk County, 622

Great Valley (town) Cattaraugus County, 88

Greece (town) Monroe County, 330

Greece (CDP) Monroe County, 329

Green Island (town/village) Albany County, 53

Greenburgh (town) Westchester County, 738

Greene (town) Chenango County, 133

Greene (village) Chenango County, 133

Greene County, 252

Greenfield (town) Saratoga County, 562

Greenfield Center (unincorporated) Saratoga County, 563

Greenfield Park (unincorporated) Ulster County, 688

Greenhurst (unincorporated) Chautauqua County, 116

Greenlawn (CDP) Suffolk County, 622

Greenport (town) Columbia County, 156

Greenport (village) Suffolk County, 622

Greenport West (CDP) Suffolk County, 623

Greenvale (CDP) Nassau County, 356

Greenville (town) Greene County, 258

Greenville (CDP) Greene County, 257

Greenville (town) Orange County, 467

Greenville (CDP) Westchester County, 738

Greenwich (town) Washington County, 716

Greenwich (village) Washington County, 717

Greenwood (town) Steuben County, 599

Greenwood Lake (village) Orange County, 468

Greig (town) Lewis County, 298

Greigsville (CDP) Livingston County, 308

Groton (town) Tompkins County, 679

Groton (village) Tompkins County, 679

Grove (town) Allegany County, 68

Groveland (town) Livingston County, 308

Groveland Station (CDP) Livingston County, 308

Guilderland (town) Albany County, 54

Guilderland Center (unincorporated) Albany County, 54

Guilford (town) Chenango County, 133

Guilford (CDP) Chenango County, 133

Hadley (town) Saratoga County, 563

Hadley (CDP) Saratoga County, 563

Hagaman (village) Montgomery County, 341

Hague (town) Warren County, 707

Hailesboro (CDP) Saint Lawrence County, 546

Haines Falls (unincorporated) Greene County, 258

Halcott (town) Greene County, 258

Halcottsville (unincorporated) Delaware County, 174

Halesite (CDP) Suffolk County, 623

Halfmoon (town) Saratoga County, 563

Hall (CDP) Ontario County, 456

Hamburg (town) Erie County, 210

Hamburg (village) Erie County, 211

Hamden (town) Delaware County, 174

Hamilton (town) Madison County, 320

Hamilton (village) Madison County, 321

Hamilton County, 264

Hamlin (town) Monroe County, 330

Hamlin (CDP) Monroe County, 330

Hammond (town) Saint Lawrence County, 546

Hammond (village) Saint Lawrence County, 547

Hammondsport (village) Steuben County, 599

Hampton (town) Washington County, 717

Hampton Bays (CDP) Suffolk County, 623

CDP = Census Designated Place

Hampton Manor (CDP) Rensselaer County, 521
Hamptonburgh (town) Orange County, 468
Hancock (town) Delaware County, 174
Hancock (village) Delaware County, 174
Hankins (unincorporated) Sullivan County, 659
Hannacroix (unincorporated) Greene County, 258
Hannawa Falls (CDP) Saint Lawrence County, 547
Hannibal (town) Oswego County, 491
Hannibal (village) Oswego County, 491
Hanover (town) Chautauqua County, 116
Harbor Hills (CDP) Nassau County, 356
Harbor Isle (CDP) Nassau County, 356
Hardenburgh (town) Ulster County, 689
Harford (town) Cortland County, 163
Harmony (town) Chautauqua County, 116
Harpersfield (town) Delaware County, 175
Harpursville (unincorporated) Broome County, 78
Harrietstown (town) Franklin County, 235
Harriman (village) Orange County, 468
Harris (unincorporated) Sullivan County, 659
Harris Hill (CDP) Erie County, 211
Harrisburg (town) Lewis County, 298
Harrison (town/village) Westchester County, 738
Harrisville (village) Lewis County, 299
Hartford (town) Washington County, 717
Hartland (town) Niagara County, 411
Hartsdale (CDP) Westchester County, 738
Hartsville (town) Steuben County, 600
Hartwick (town) Otsego County, 503
Hartwick (CDP) Otsego County, 503
Hastings (town) Oswego County, 492
Hastings-on-Hudson (village) Westchester County, 739
Hauppauge (CDP) Suffolk County, 623
Haverstraw (town) Rockland County, 530
Haverstraw (village) Rockland County, 530
Haviland (CDP) Dutchess County, 186
Hawthorne (CDP) Westchester County, 739
Head of the Harbor (village) Suffolk County, 624
Hebron (town) Washington County, 718
Hector (town) Schuyler County, 585
Hemlock (CDP) Livingston County, 309
Hempstead (town) Nassau County, 356
Hempstead (village) Nassau County, 357
Henderson (town) Jefferson County, 287
Henderson (CDP) Jefferson County, 287
Henderson Harbor (unincorporated) Jefferson County, 287
Henrietta (town) Monroe County, 330
Hensonville (unincorporated) Greene County, 259
Heritage Hills (CDP) Westchester County, 739
Herkimer (town) Herkimer County, 272
Herkimer (village) Herkimer County, 272
Herkimer County, 269
Hermon (town) Saint Lawrence County, 547
Hermon (village) Saint Lawrence County, 547
Herricks (CDP) Nassau County, 357
Herrings (village) Jefferson County, 287
Heuvelton (village) Saint Lawrence County, 548
Hewlett (CDP) Nassau County, 358
Hewlett Bay Park (village) Nassau County, 358
Hewlett Harbor (village) Nassau County, 358
Hewlett Neck (village) Nassau County, 358
Hicksville (CDP) Nassau County, 359
High Falls (CDP) Ulster County, 689
Highland (town) Sullivan County, 659
Highland (CDP) Ulster County, 689
Highland Falls (village) Orange County, 469
Highland Lake (unincorporated) Sullivan County, 660

Highland Mills (unincorporated) Orange County, 469
Highlands (town) Orange County, 469
Highmount (unincorporated) Ulster County, 689
Hillburn (village) Rockland County, 530
Hillcrest (CDP) Rockland County, 531
Hillsdale (town) Columbia County, 156
Hillside (CDP) Ulster County, 690
Hillside Lake (CDP) Dutchess County, 186
Hilton (village) Monroe County, 331
Himrod (unincorporated) Yates County, 766
Hinckley (unincorporated) Oneida County, 424
Hinsdale (town) Cattaraugus County, 88
Hobart (village) Delaware County, 175
Hoffmeister (unincorporated) Hamilton County, 266
Hogansburg (unincorporated) Franklin County, 236
Holbrook (CDP) Suffolk County, 624
Holland (town) Erie County, 212
Holland (CDP) Erie County, 211
Holland Patent (village) Oneida County, 425
Holley (village) Orleans County, 485
Hollis (unincorporated) Queens County, 399
Hollowville (unincorporated) Columbia County, 156
Holmes (unincorporated) Dutchess County, 187
Holtsville (CDP) Suffolk County, 624
Homer (town) Cortland County, 164
Homer (village) Cortland County, 164
Honeoye (CDP) Ontario County, 457
Honeoye Falls (village) Monroe County, 331
Hoosick (town) Rensselaer County, 521
Hoosick Falls (village) Rensselaer County, 521
Hope (town) Hamilton County, 266
Hopewell (town) Ontario County, 457
Hopewell Junction (CDP) Dutchess County, 187
Hopkinton (town) Saint Lawrence County, 548
Horicon (town) Warren County, 708
Hornby (town) Steuben County, 600
Hornell (city) Steuben County, 600
Hornellsville (town) Steuben County, 600
Horseheads (town) Chemung County, 127
Horseheads (village) Chemung County, 127
Horseheads North (CDP) Chemung County, 127
Hortonville (CDP) Sullivan County, 660
Houghton (CDP) Allegany County, 68
Hounsfield (town) Jefferson County, 287
Howard (town) Steuben County, 601
Howard Beach (unincorporated) Queens County, 399
Howells (unincorporated) Orange County, 469
Howes Cave (unincorporated) Schoharie County, 579
Hubbardsville (unincorporated) Madison County, 321
Hudson (city) Columbia County, 156
Hudson Falls (village) Washington County, 718
Huguenot (unincorporated) Orange County, 470
Huletts Landing (unincorporated) Washington County, 718
Hume (town) Allegany County, 68
Humphrey (town) Cattaraugus County, 89
Hunt (CDP) Livingston County, 309
Hunter (town) Greene County, 259
Hunter (village) Greene County, 259
Huntington (town) Suffolk County, 625
Huntington (CDP) Suffolk County, 624
Huntington Bay (village) Suffolk County, 625
Huntington Station (CDP) Suffolk County, 625
Hurley (town) Ulster County, 690
Hurley (CDP) Ulster County, 690
Hurleyville (unincorporated) Sullivan County, 660

Huron (town) Wayne County, 723
Hyde Park (town) Dutchess County, 187
Hyde Park (CDP) Dutchess County, 187
Ilion (village) Herkimer County, 272
Independence (town) Allegany County, 68
Indian Lake (town) Hamilton County, 266
Inlet (town) Hamilton County, 266
Interlaken (village) Seneca County, 588
Inwood (CDP) Nassau County, 359
Ionia (unincorporated) Ontario County, 457
Ira (town) Cayuga County, 101
Irondequoit (CDP) Monroe County, 331
Irving (unincorporated) Erie County, 212
Irvington (village) Westchester County, 740
Ischua (town) Cattaraugus County, 89
Island Park (village) Nassau County, 359
Islandia (village) Suffolk County, 626
Islip (town) Suffolk County, 626
Islip (CDP) Suffolk County, 626
Islip Terrace (CDP) Suffolk County, 627
Italy (town) Yates County, 766
Ithaca (town) Tompkins County, 680
Ithaca (city) Tompkins County, 679
Jackson (town) Washington County, 718
Jackson Heights (unincorporated) Queens County, 399
Jacksonville (unincorporated) Tompkins County, 680
Jamaica (unincorporated) Queens County, 400
Jamesport (CDP) Suffolk County, 627
Jamestown (city) Chautauqua County, 116
Jamestown West (CDP) Chautauqua County, 117
Jamesville (unincorporated) Onondaga County, 442
Jasper (town) Steuben County, 601
Java (town) Wyoming County, 760
Java Center (unincorporated) Wyoming County, 760
Jay (town) Essex County, 222
Jefferson (town) Schoharie County, 579
Jefferson County, 278
Jefferson Heights (CDP) Greene County, 259
Jefferson Valley-Yorktown (CDP) Westchester County, 740
Jeffersonville (village) Sullivan County, 660
Jericho (CDP) Nassau County, 360
Jerusalem (town) Yates County, 767
Jewett (town) Greene County, 260
Johnsburg (town) Warren County, 708
Johnson (unincorporated) Orange County, 470
Johnson City (village) Broome County, 78
Johnsonville (unincorporated) Rensselaer County, 522
Johnstown (town) Fulton County, 243
Johnstown (city) Fulton County, 243
Jordan (village) Onondaga County, 443
Jordanville (unincorporated) Herkimer County, 273
Junius (town) Seneca County, 588
Kanona (unincorporated) Steuben County, 601
Kaser (village) Rockland County, 531
Katonah (CDP) Westchester County, 740
Kattskill Bay (unincorporated) Warren County, 708
Kauneonga Lake (unincorporated) Sullivan County, 661
Keene (town) Essex County, 223
Keene Valley (unincorporated) Essex County, 223
Keeseville (village) Clinton County, 145
Kendall (town) Orleans County, 485
Kenmore (village) Erie County, 212
Kennedy (CDP) Chautauqua County, 117

CDP = Census Designated Place

Kenoza Lake (unincorporated) Sullivan County, 661

Kensington (village) Nassau County, 360

Kent (town) Putnam County, 514

Kerhonkson (CDP) Ulster County, 690

Keuka Park (CDP) Yates County, 767

Kew Gardens (unincorporated) Queens County, 401

Kiamesha Lake (unincorporated) Sullivan County, 661

Kiantone (town) Chautauqua County, 117

Kill Buck (unincorporated) Cattaraugus County, 89

Killawog (unincorporated) Broome County, 78

Kinderhook (town) Columbia County, 157

Kinderhook (village) Columbia County, 157

King Ferry (unincorporated) Cayuga County, 101

Kings Park (CDP) Suffolk County, 627

Kings Point (village) Nassau County, 360

Kingsbury (town) Washington County, 719

Kingston (town) Ulster County, 691

Kingston (city) Ulster County, 691

Kirkland (town) Oneida County, 425

Kirkville (unincorporated) Madison County, 321

Kirkwood (town) Broome County, 78

Kiryas Joel (village) Orange County, 470

Knowlesville (unincorporated) Orleans County, 486

Knox (town) Albany County, 54

Knoxboro (unincorporated) Oneida County, 425

Kortright (town) Delaware County, 175

Kysorville (CDP) Livingston County, 309

La Fargeville (CDP) Jefferson County, 288

La Grange (town) Dutchess County, 188

Lackawanna (city) Erie County, 212

Lacona (village) Oswego County, 492

LaFayette (town) Onondaga County, 443

Lagrangeville (unincorporated) Dutchess County, 188

Lake Carmel (CDP) Putnam County, 514

Lake Clear (unincorporated) Franklin County, 236

Lake Erie Beach (CDP) Erie County, 213

Lake George (town) Warren County, 708

Lake George (village) Warren County, 709

Lake Grove (village) Suffolk County, 627

Lake Hill (unincorporated) Ulster County, 691

Lake Huntington (unincorporated) Sullivan County, 661

Lake Katrine (CDP) Ulster County, 692

Lake Luzerne (town) Warren County, 709

Lake Mohegan (CDP) Westchester County, 740

Lake Peekskill (unincorporated) Putnam County, 514

Lake Placid (village) Essex County, 223

Lake Pleasant (town) Hamilton County, 267

Lake Ronkonkoma (CDP) Suffolk County, 628

Lake Success (village) Nassau County, 360

Lake View (unincorporated) Erie County, 213

Lakeland (CDP) Onondaga County, 443

Lakeview (CDP) Nassau County, 361

Lakeville (CDP) Livingston County, 309

Lakewood (village) Chautauqua County, 118

Lancaster (town) Erie County, 213

Lancaster (village) Erie County, 213

Lanesville (unincorporated) Greene County, 260

Lansing (town) Tompkins County, 680

Lansing (village) Tompkins County, 681

Lapeer (town) Cortland County, 164

Larchmont (village) Westchester County, 741

Latham (unincorporated) Albany County, 54

Lattingtown (village) Nassau County, 361

Laurel (CDP) Suffolk County, 628

Laurel Hollow (village) Nassau County, 361

Laurens (town) Otsego County, 504

Laurens (village) Otsego County, 504

Lawrence (village) Nassau County, 361

Lawrence (town) Saint Lawrence County, 548

Lawtons (unincorporated) Erie County, 214

Le Ray (town) Jefferson County, 288

Le Roy (town) Genesee County, 250

Le Roy (village) Genesee County, 250

Lebanon (town) Madison County, 321

Ledyard (town) Cayuga County, 102

Lee (town) Oneida County, 425

Lee Center (unincorporated) Oneida County, 426

Leeds (CDP) Greene County, 260

Leicester (town) Livingston County, 309

Leicester (village) Livingston County, 310

Lenox (town) Madison County, 322

Leon (town) Cattaraugus County, 89

Leonardsville (unincorporated) Madison County, 322

Levittown (CDP) Nassau County, 362

Lewis (town) Essex County, 223

Lewis (town) Lewis County, 299

Lewis County, 295

Lewisboro (town) Westchester County, 741

Lewiston (town) Niagara County, 411

Lewiston (village) Niagara County, 411

Lexington (town) Greene County, 260

Leyden (town) Lewis County, 299

Liberty (town) Sullivan County, 662

Liberty (village) Sullivan County, 662

Lido Beach (CDP) Nassau County, 362

Lily Dale (unincorporated) Chautauqua County, 118

Lima (town) Livingston County, 310

Lima (village) Livingston County, 310

Lime Lake (CDP) Cattaraugus County, 90

Limestone (CDP) Cattaraugus County, 90

Lincklaen (town) Chenango County, 134

Lincoln (town) Madison County, 322

Lincoln Park (CDP) Ulster County, 692

Lincolndale (CDP) Westchester County, 741

Lindenhurst (village) Suffolk County, 628

Lindley (town) Steuben County, 601

Linwood (CDP) Livingston County, 311

Lisbon (town) Saint Lawrence County, 548

Lisle (town) Broome County, 79

Lisle (village) Broome County, 79

Litchfield (town) Herkimer County, 273

Little Falls (town) Herkimer County, 273

Little Falls (city) Herkimer County, 273

Little Genesee (unincorporated) Allegany County, 69

Little Neck (unincorporated) Queens County, 401

Little Valley (town) Cattaraugus County, 90

Little Valley (village) Cattaraugus County, 90

Little York (unincorporated) Cortland County, 164

Liverpool (village) Onondaga County, 444

Livingston (town) Columbia County, 157

Livingston County, 303

Livingston Manor (CDP) Sullivan County, 662

Livonia (town) Livingston County, 311

Livonia (village) Livingston County, 311

Livonia Center (CDP) Livingston County, 311

Lloyd (town) Ulster County, 692

Lloyd Harbor (village) Suffolk County, 628

Loch Sheldrake (CDP) Sullivan County, 662

Locke (town) Cayuga County, 102

Lockport (town) Niagara County, 412

Lockport (city) Niagara County, 411

Lockwood (unincorporated) Tioga County, 672

Locust Valley (CDP) Nassau County, 362

Lodi (town) Seneca County, 589

Lodi (village) Seneca County, 589

Long Beach (city) Nassau County, 363

Long Eddy (unincorporated) Delaware County, 175

Long Island City (unincorporated) Queens County, 402

Long Lake (town) Hamilton County, 267

Long Lake (CDP) Hamilton County, 267

Lorenz Park (CDP) Columbia County, 157

Lorraine (town) Jefferson County, 288

Lorraine (CDP) Jefferson County, 288

Louisville (town) Saint Lawrence County, 549

Lowman (unincorporated) Chemung County, 128

Lowville (town) Lewis County, 299

Lowville (village) Lewis County, 300

Lumberland (town) Sullivan County, 663

Lyme (town) Jefferson County, 289

Lynbrook (village) Nassau County, 363

Lyncourt (CDP) Onondaga County, 444

Lyndon (town) Cattaraugus County, 91

Lyndonville (village) Orleans County, 486

Lyon Mountain (CDP) Clinton County, 146

Lyons (town) Wayne County, 723

Lyons (village) Wayne County, 723

Lyons Falls (village) Lewis County, 300

Lyonsdale (town) Lewis County, 300

Lysander (town) Onondaga County, 444

Macedon (town) Wayne County, 723

Macedon (village) Wayne County, 724

Machias (town) Cattaraugus County, 91

Machias (CDP) Cattaraugus County, 91

Macomb (town) Saint Lawrence County, 549

Madison (town) Madison County, 322

Madison (village) Madison County, 323

Madison County, 316

Madrid (town) Saint Lawrence County, 549

Madrid (CDP) Saint Lawrence County, 549

Mahopac (CDP) Putnam County, 515

Maine (town) Broome County, 79

Malden Bridge (unincorporated) Columbia County, 158

Malden-on-Hudson (CDP) Ulster County, 692

Mallory (unincorporated) Oswego County, 492

Malone (town) Franklin County, 236

Malone (village) Franklin County, 236

Malta (town) Saratoga County, 564

Malverne (village) Nassau County, 363

Malverne Park Oaks (CDP) Nassau County, 364

Mamakating (town) Sullivan County, 663

Mamaroneck (town) Westchester County, 741

Mamaroneck (village) Westchester County, 742

Manchester (town) Ontario County, 457

Manchester (village) Ontario County, 458

Manhasset (CDP) Nassau County, 364

Manhasset Hills (CDP) Nassau County, 364

Manhattan (borough) New York County, 388

Manheim (town) Herkimer County, 274

Manlius (town) Onondaga County, 444

Manlius (village) Onondaga County, 445

Mannsville (village) Jefferson County, 289

Manorhaven (village) Nassau County, 364

Manorville (CDP) Suffolk County, 629

Mansfield (town) Cattaraugus County, 91

Maple Springs (unincorporated) Chautauqua County, 118

Maplecrest (unincorporated) Greene County, 261

Marathon (town) Cortland County, 165

Marathon (village) Cortland County, 165

Marbletown (town) Ulster County, 693

Marcellus (town) Onondaga County, 445

Marcellus (village) Onondaga County, 445

Marcy (town) Oneida County, 426

Margaretville (village) Delaware County, 176

CDP = Census Designated Place

CDP = Census Designated Place

Newfield (town) Tompkins County, 681
Newfield Hamlet (CDP) Tompkins County, 681
Newport (town) Herkimer County, 274
Newport (village) Herkimer County, 275
Newstead (town) Erie County, 214
Newton Falls (unincorporated) Saint Lawrence County, 551
Niagara (town) Niagara County, 413
Niagara County, 409
Niagara Falls (city) Niagara County, 413
Niagara University (unincorporated) Niagara County, 414
Nichols (town) Tioga County, 673
Nichols (village) Tioga County, 673
Nicholville (unincorporated) Saint Lawrence County, 551
Niles (town) Cayuga County, 104
Nineveh (unincorporated) Broome County, 80
Niskayuna (town) Schenectady County, 573
Nissequogue (village) Suffolk County, 632
Niverville (CDP) Columbia County, 158
Norfolk (town) Saint Lawrence County, 551
Norfolk (CDP) Saint Lawrence County, 551
North Amityville (CDP) Suffolk County, 633
North Babylon (CDP) Suffolk County, 633
North Ballston Spa (CDP) Saratoga County, 565
North Bangor (unincorporated) Franklin County, 237
North Bay (unincorporated) Oneida County, 427
North Bay Shore (CDP) Suffolk County, 633
North Bellmore (CDP) Nassau County, 367
North Bellport (CDP) Suffolk County, 635
North Blenheim (unincorporated) Schoharie County, 580
North Boston (CDP) Erie County, 215
North Branch (unincorporated) Sullivan County, 664
North Brookfield (unincorporated) Madison County, 324
North Castle (town) Westchester County, 745
North Chatham (unincorporated) Columbia County, 158
North Chili (unincorporated) Monroe County, 332
North Collins (town) Erie County, 215
North Collins (village) Erie County, 215
North Creek (CDP) Warren County, 709
North Dansville (town) Livingston County, 312
North East (town) Dutchess County, 190
North Elba (town) Essex County, 225
North Gates (CDP) Monroe County, 332
North Great River (CDP) Suffolk County, 634
North Greenbush (town) Rensselaer County, 523
North Harmony (town) Chautauqua County, 119
North Haven (village) Suffolk County, 634
North Hempstead (town) Nassau County, 368
North Hills (village) Nassau County, 368
North Hornell (village) Steuben County, 602
North Hudson (town) Essex County, 225
North Java (unincorporated) Wyoming County, 760
North Lawrence (unincorporated) Saint Lawrence County, 552
North Lindenhurst (CDP) Suffolk County, 634
North Lynbrook (CDP) Nassau County, 368
North Massapequa (CDP) Nassau County, 368
North Merrick (CDP) Nassau County, 369
North New Hyde Park (CDP) Nassau County, 369
North Norwich (town) Chenango County, 135
North Patchogue (CDP) Suffolk County, 634
North Pitcher (unincorporated) Chenango County, 135

North River (unincorporated) Warren County, 709
North Rose (CDP) Wayne County, 725
North Salem (town) Westchester County, 745
North Sea (CDP) Suffolk County, 635
North Syracuse (village) Onondaga County, 447
North Tonawanda (city) Niagara County, 414
North Valley Stream (CDP) Nassau County, 369
North Wantagh (CDP) Nassau County, 369
Northampton (town) Fulton County, 244
Northampton (CDP) Suffolk County, 635
Northeast Ithaca (CDP) Tompkins County, 682
Northport (village) Suffolk County, 635
Northumberland (town) Saratoga County, 566
Northville (village) Fulton County, 244
Northville (CDP) Suffolk County, 636
Northwest Harbor (CDP) Suffolk County, 636
Northwest Ithaca (CDP) Tompkins County, 682
Norway (town) Herkimer County, 275
Norwich (town) Chenango County, 136
Norwich (city) Chenango County, 135
Norwood (village) Saint Lawrence County, 552
Noyack (CDP) Suffolk County, 636
Nunda (town) Livingston County, 312
Nunda (village) Livingston County, 313
Nyack (village) Rockland County, 533
Oak Beach-Captree (CDP) Suffolk County, 636
Oak Hill (unincorporated) Greene County, 261
Oakdale (CDP) Suffolk County, 636
Oakfield (town) Genesee County, 250
Oakfield (village) Genesee County, 251
Oakland Gardens (unincorporated) Queens County, 403
Obernburg (unincorporated) Sullivan County, 665
Ocean Beach (village) Suffolk County, 637
Oceanside (CDP) Nassau County, 370
Odessa (village) Schuyler County, 586
Ogden (town) Monroe County, 332
Ogdensburg (city) Saint Lawrence County, 552
Ohio (town) Herkimer County, 275
Oil Springs Reservation (reservation) Allegany County, 69
Olcott (CDP) Niagara County, 414
Old Bethpage (CDP) Nassau County, 370
Old Brookville (village) Nassau County, 370
Old Chatham (unincorporated) Columbia County, 159
Old Field (village) Suffolk County, 637
Old Forge (CDP) Herkimer County, 275
Old Westbury (village) Nassau County, 371
Olean (town) Cattaraugus County, 92
Olean (city) Cattaraugus County, 92
Olive (town) Ulster County, 695
Olivebridge (unincorporated) Ulster County, 696
Olmstedville (unincorporated) Essex County, 226
Oneida (city) Madison County, 324
Oneida Castle (village) Oneida County, 428
Oneida County, 418
Oneonta (town) Otsego County, 506
Oneonta (city) Otsego County, 506
Onondaga (town) Onondaga County, 447
Onondaga County, 437
Onondaga Nation Reservation (reservation) Onondaga County, 447
Ontario (town) Wayne County, 725
Ontario (CDP) Wayne County, 725
Ontario County, 452
Oppenheim (town) Fulton County, 244
Orange (town) Schuyler County, 586
Orange County, 461
Orange Lake (CDP) Orange County, 475
Orangeburg (CDP) Rockland County, 534

Orangetown (town) Rockland County, 534
Orangeville (town) Wyoming County, 761
Orchard Park (town) Erie County, 215
Orchard Park (village) Erie County, 216
Orient (CDP) Suffolk County, 637
Oriskany (village) Oneida County, 428
Oriskany Falls (village) Oneida County, 428
Orleans (town) Jefferson County, 289
Orleans County, 483
Orwell (town) Oswego County, 494
Osceola (town) Lewis County, 301
Ossian (town) Livingston County, 313
Ossining (town) Westchester County, 745
Ossining (village) Westchester County, 746
Oswegatchie (town) Saint Lawrence County, 553
Oswego (town) Oswego County, 494
Oswego (city) Oswego County, 494
Oswego County, 488
Otego (town) Otsego County, 507
Otego (village) Otsego County, 507
Otisco (town) Onondaga County, 448
Otisville (village) Orange County, 476
Otsego (town) Otsego County, 507
Otsego County, 499
Otselic (town) Chenango County, 136
Otto (town) Cattaraugus County, 93
Ovid (town) Seneca County, 589
Ovid (village) Seneca County, 589
Owasco (town) Cayuga County, 104
Owego (town) Tioga County, 673
Owego (village) Tioga County, 674
Owls Head (unincorporated) Franklin County, 237
Oxbow (CDP) Jefferson County, 290
Oxford (town) Chenango County, 136
Oxford (village) Chenango County, 136
Oyster Bay (town) Nassau County, 371
Oyster Bay (CDP) Nassau County, 371
Oyster Bay Cove (village) Nassau County, 371
Ozone Park (unincorporated) Queens County, 403
Painted Post (village) Steuben County, 602
Palatine (town) Montgomery County, 342
Palatine Bridge (village) Montgomery County, 343
Palenville (CDP) Greene County, 261
Palermo (town) Oswego County, 495
Palisades (unincorporated) Rockland County, 534
Palmyra (town) Wayne County, 726
Palmyra (village) Wayne County, 726
Pamelia (town) Jefferson County, 290
Pamelia Center (CDP) Jefferson County, 290
Panama (village) Chautauqua County, 119
Paradox (unincorporated) Essex County, 226
Parc (CDP) Clinton County, 147
Paris (town) Oneida County, 428
Parish (town) Oswego County, 495
Parish (village) Oswego County, 495
Parishville (town) Saint Lawrence County, 553
Parishville (CDP) Saint Lawrence County, 553
Parksville (unincorporated) Sullivan County, 665
Parma (town) Monroe County, 333
Patchogue (village) Suffolk County, 638
Patterson (town) Putnam County, 515
Pattersonville (unincorporated) Schenectady County, 573
Paul Smiths (CDP) Franklin County, 238
Pavilion (town) Genesee County, 251
Pavilion (CDP) Genesee County, 251
Pawling (town) Dutchess County, 190
Pawling (village) Dutchess County, 190
Peach Lake (CDP) Putnam County, 516

CDP = Census Designated Place

Pearl River (CDP) Rockland County, 534
Peconic (CDP) Suffolk County, 638
Peekskill (city) Westchester County, 746
Pelham (town) Westchester County, 746
Pelham (village) Westchester County, 747
Pelham Manor (village) Westchester County, 747
Pembroke (town) Genesee County, 252
Pendleton (town) Niagara County, 414
Penfield (town) Monroe County, 333
Penn Yan (village) Yates County, 768
Pennellville (unincorporated) Oswego County, 495
Perinton (town) Monroe County, 333
Perkinsville (unincorporated) Steuben County, 602
Perry (town) Wyoming County, 761
Perry (village) Wyoming County, 761
Perrysburg (town) Cattaraugus County, 93
Perrysburg (CDP) Cattaraugus County, 93
Persia (town) Cattaraugus County, 93
Perth (town) Fulton County, 245
Peru (town) Clinton County, 147
Peru (CDP) Clinton County, 147
Peterboro (unincorporated) Madison County, 324
Petersburgh (town) Rensselaer County, 523
Pharsalia (town) Chenango County, 137
Phelps (town) Ontario County, 458
Phelps (village) Ontario County, 459
Philadelphia (town) Jefferson County, 290
Philadelphia (village) Jefferson County, 291
Philipstown (town) Putnam County, 516
Phillipsport (unincorporated) Sullivan County, 665
Philmont (village) Columbia County, 159
Phoenicia (CDP) Ulster County, 696
Phoenix (village) Oswego County, 496
Piercefield (town) Saint Lawrence County, 553
Piermont (village) Rockland County, 535
Pierrepont (town) Saint Lawrence County, 554
Pierrepont Manor (CDP) Jefferson County, 291
Piffard (CDP) Livingston County, 313
Pike (town) Wyoming County, 762
Pike (CDP) Wyoming County, 761
Pinckney (town) Lewis County, 301
Pine Bush (CDP) Orange County, 476
Pine City (unincorporated) Chemung County, 128
Pine Hill (CDP) Ulster County, 696
Pine Island (unincorporated) Orange County, 476
Pine Plains (town) Dutchess County, 191
Pine Plains (CDP) Dutchess County, 190
Pine Valley (CDP) Chemung County, 128
Piseco (unincorporated) Hamilton County, 268
Pitcairn (town) Saint Lawrence County, 554
Pitcher (town) Chenango County, 137
Pittsfield (town) Otsego County, 508
Pittsford (town) Monroe County, 333
Pittsford (village) Monroe County, 334
Pittstown (town) Rensselaer County, 523
Plainedge (CDP) Nassau County, 372
Plainfield (town) Otsego County, 508
Plainview (CDP) Nassau County, 372
Plandome (village) Nassau County, 372
Plandome Heights (village) Nassau County, 373
Plandome Manor (village) Nassau County, 373
Plattekill (town) Ulster County, 697
Plattekill (CDP) Ulster County, 696
Plattsburgh (town) Clinton County, 148
Plattsburgh (city) Clinton County, 148
Plattsburgh West (CDP) Clinton County, 148
Pleasant Valley (town) Dutchess County, 191

Pleasant Valley (CDP) Dutchess County, 191
Pleasantville (village) Westchester County, 747
Plessis (CDP) Jefferson County, 291
Plymouth (town) Chenango County, 137
Poestenkill (town) Rensselaer County, 524
Poestenkill (CDP) Rensselaer County, 523
Point Lookout (CDP) Nassau County, 373
Poland (town) Chautauqua County, 119
Poland (village) Herkimer County, 276
Pomfret (town) Chautauqua County, 119
Pomona (village) Rockland County, 535
Pompey (town) Onondaga County, 448
Pond Eddy (unincorporated) Sullivan County, 666
Poospatuck Reservation (reservation) Suffolk County, 638
Poquott (village) Suffolk County, 638
Port Byron (village) Cayuga County, 104
Port Chester (village) Westchester County, 748
Port Crane (unincorporated) Broome County, 80
Port Dickinson (village) Broome County, 80
Port Ewen (CDP) Ulster County, 697
Port Gibson (CDP) Ontario County, 459
Port Henry (village) Essex County, 226
Port Jefferson (village) Suffolk County, 639
Port Jefferson Station (CDP) Suffolk County, 639
Port Jervis (city) Orange County, 476
Port Kent (unincorporated) Essex County, 226
Port Leyden (village) Lewis County, 302
Port Washington (CDP) Nassau County, 373
Port Washington North (village) Nassau County, 374
Portage (town) Livingston County, 313
Portageville (unincorporated) Wyoming County, 762
Porter (town) Niagara County, 415
Porter Corners (unincorporated) Saratoga County, 566
Portland (town) Chautauqua County, 120
Portlandville (unincorporated) Otsego County, 508
Portville (town) Cattaraugus County, 94
Portville (village) Cattaraugus County, 94
Potsdam (town) Saint Lawrence County, 554
Potsdam (village) Saint Lawrence County, 554
Potter (town) Yates County, 768
Pottersville (CDP) Warren County, 710
Poughkeepsie (town) Dutchess County, 192
Poughkeepsie (city) Dutchess County, 192
Poughquag (unincorporated) Dutchess County, 193
Pound Ridge (town) Westchester County, 748
Prattsburgh (town) Steuben County, 603
Prattsburgh (CDP) Steuben County, 602
Prattsville (town) Greene County, 262
Prattsville (CDP) Greene County, 262
Preble (town) Cortland County, 166
Preston (town) Chenango County, 137
Preston Hollow (unincorporated) Albany County, 56
Preston-Potter Hollow (CDP) Albany County, 56
Princetown (town) Schenectady County, 573
Prospect (village) Oneida County, 429
Providence (town) Saratoga County, 566
Pulaski (village) Oswego County, 496
Pulteney (town) Steuben County, 603
Pultneyville (CDP) Wayne County, 726
Purchase (unincorporated) Westchester County, 748
Purdys (unincorporated) Westchester County, 749
Purling (unincorporated) Greene County, 262
Putnam (town) Washington County, 719

Putnam County, 512
Putnam Lake (CDP) Putnam County, 516
Putnam Station (unincorporated) Washington County, 719
Putnam Valley (town) Putnam County, 516
Pyrites (unincorporated) Saint Lawrence County, 555
Queens (borough) Queens County, 391
Queens Village (unincorporated) Queens County, 404
Queensbury (town) Warren County, 710
Quiogue (CDP) Suffolk County, 639
Quogue (village) Suffolk County, 639
Rainbow Lake (unincorporated) Franklin County, 238
Ramapo (town) Rockland County, 535
Randolph (town) Cattaraugus County, 94
Ransomville (CDP) Niagara County, 415
Rapids (CDP) Niagara County, 415
Raquette Lake (unincorporated) Hamilton County, 268
Rathbone (town) Steuben County, 603
Ravena (village) Albany County, 56
Ray Brook (unincorporated) Essex County, 227
Raymondville (unincorporated) Saint Lawrence County, 555
Reading (town) Schuyler County, 586
Red Creek (village) Wayne County, 726
Red Hook (town) Dutchess County, 193
Red Hook (village) Dutchess County, 193
Red House (town) Cattaraugus County, 94
Red Oaks Mill (CDP) Dutchess County, 193
Redfield (town) Oswego County, 496
Redford (CDP) Clinton County, 149
Redwood (CDP) Jefferson County, 291
Rego Park (unincorporated) Queens County, 405
Remsen (town) Oneida County, 429
Remsen (village) Oneida County, 429
Remsenburg-Speonk (CDP) Suffolk County, 640
Rensselaer (city) Rensselaer County, 524
Rensselaer County, 517
Rensselaer Falls (village) Saint Lawrence County, 555
Rensselaerville (town) Albany County, 56
Retsof (CDP) Livingston County, 314
Rexford (unincorporated) Saratoga County, 566
Rexville (unincorporated) Steuben County, 603
Rhinebeck (town) Dutchess County, 194
Rhinebeck (village) Dutchess County, 194
Rhinecliff (CDP) Dutchess County, 194
Richburg (village) Allegany County, 69
Richfield (town) Otsego County, 508
Richfield Springs (village) Otsego County, 509
Richford (town) Tioga County, 674
Richland (town) Oswego County, 496
Richmond (town) Ontario County, 459
Richmond Hill (unincorporated) Queens County, 405
Richmondville (town) Schoharie County, 580
Richmondville (village) Schoharie County, 580
Richville (village) Saint Lawrence County, 556
Ridge (CDP) Suffolk County, 640
Ridgeway (town) Orleans County, 487
Ridgewood (unincorporated) Queens County, 405
Rifton (CDP) Ulster County, 697
Riga (town) Monroe County, 334
Ripley (town) Chautauqua County, 120
Ripley (CDP) Chautauqua County, 120
Riverhead (town) Suffolk County, 641
Riverhead (CDP) Suffolk County, 640
Riverside (village) Steuben County, 604
Riverside (CDP) Suffolk County, 641

CDP = Census Designated Place

Rochester (city) Monroe County, 334
Rochester (town) Ulster County, 697
Rock City Falls (unincorporated) Saratoga County, 567
Rock Hill (CDP) Sullivan County, 666
Rock Stream (unincorporated) Schuyler County, 586
Rock Tavern (unincorporated) Orange County, 477
Rockaway Park (unincorporated) Queens County, 405
Rockland (town) Sullivan County, 666
Rockland County, 527
Rockville Centre (village) Nassau County, 374
Rocky Point (CDP) Suffolk County, 641
Rodman (town) Jefferson County, 292
Rodman (CDP) Jefferson County, 292
Rome (city) Oneida County, 429
Romulus (town) Seneca County, 590
Romulus (CDP) Seneca County, 589
Ronkonkoma (CDP) Suffolk County, 641
Roosevelt (CDP) Nassau County, 374
Root (town) Montgomery County, 343
Roscoe (CDP) Sullivan County, 666
Rose (town) Wayne County, 727
Roseboom (town) Otsego County, 509
Rosedale (unincorporated) Queens County, 406
Rosendale (town) Ulster County, 698
Rosendale Hamlet (CDP) Ulster County, 698
Roslyn (village) Nassau County, 374
Roslyn Estates (village) Nassau County, 375
Roslyn Harbor (village) Nassau County, 375
Roslyn Heights (CDP) Nassau County, 375
Rossie (town) Saint Lawrence County, 556
Rotterdam (town) Schenectady County, 573
Rotterdam (CDP) Schenectady County, 573
Rotterdam Junction (unincorporated) Schenectady County, 574
Round Lake (village) Saratoga County, 567
Round Top (unincorporated) Greene County, 262
Rouses Point (village) Clinton County, 149
Roxbury (town) Delaware County, 177
Royalton (town) Niagara County, 415
Ruby (unincorporated) Ulster County, 698
Rush (town) Monroe County, 335
Rushford (town) Allegany County, 70
Rushford (CDP) Allegany County, 70
Rushville (village) Yates County, 768
Russell (town) Saint Lawrence County, 556
Russell Gardens (village) Nassau County, 375
Russia (town) Herkimer County, 276
Rutland (town) Jefferson County, 292
Rye (town) Westchester County, 749
Rye (city) Westchester County, 749
Rye Brook (village) Westchester County, 750
Sabael (unincorporated) Hamilton County, 268
Sackets Harbor (village) Jefferson County, 292
Saddle Rock (village) Nassau County, 376
Saddle Rock Estates (CDP) Nassau County, 376
Sag Harbor (village) Suffolk County, 642
Sagaponack (village) Suffolk County, 642
Saint Albans (unincorporated) Queens County, 406
Saint Armand (town) Essex County, 227
Saint Bonaventure (CDP) Cattaraugus County, 95
Saint James (CDP) Suffolk County, 642
Saint Johnsville (town) Montgomery County, 343
Saint Johnsville (village) Montgomery County, 343
Saint Lawrence County, 540

Saint Regis Falls (CDP) Franklin County, 238
Saint Regis Mohawk Reservation (reservation) Franklin County, 238
Salamanca (town) Cattaraugus County, 95
Salamanca (city) Cattaraugus County, 95
Salem (town) Washington County, 720
Salem (village) Washington County, 720
Salina (town) Onondaga County, 448
Salisbury (town) Herkimer County, 276
Salisbury (CDP) Nassau County, 376
Salisbury Center (unincorporated) Herkimer County, 276
Salisbury Mills (CDP) Orange County, 477
Salt Point (CDP) Dutchess County, 195
Saltaire (village) Suffolk County, 642
Sanborn (CDP) Niagara County, 416
Sand Lake (town) Rensselaer County, 524
Sand Ridge (CDP) Oswego County, 497
Sands Point (village) Nassau County, 376
Sandy Creek (town) Oswego County, 497
Sandy Creek (village) Oswego County, 497
Sanford (town) Broome County, 80
Sangerfield (town) Oneida County, 430
Santa Clara (town) Franklin County, 239
Saranac (town) Clinton County, 149
Saranac Lake (village) Franklin County, 239
Saratoga (town) Saratoga County, 567
Saratoga County, 558
Saratoga Springs (city) Saratoga County, 567
Sardinia (town) Erie County, 216
Saugerties (town) Ulster County, 698
Saugerties (village) Ulster County, 699
Saugerties South (CDP) Ulster County, 699
Sauquoit (unincorporated) Oneida County, 430
Savannah (town) Wayne County, 727
Savannah (CDP) Wayne County, 727
Savona (village) Steuben County, 604
Sayville (CDP) Suffolk County, 643
Scarsdale (town/village) Westchester County, 750
Schaghticoke (town) Rensselaer County, 525
Schaghticoke (village) Rensselaer County, 525
Schenectady (city) Schenectady County, 574
Schenectady County, 570
Schenevus (CDP) Otsego County, 509
Schodack (town) Rensselaer County, 525
Schodack Landing (unincorporated) Rensselaer County, 525
Schoharie (town) Schoharie County, 580
Schoharie (village) Schoharie County, 581
Schoharie County, 575
Schroeppel (town) Oswego County, 497
Schroon (town) Essex County, 227
Schroon Lake (CDP) Essex County, 227
Schuyler (town) Herkimer County, 277
Schuyler County, 583
Schuyler Falls (town) Clinton County, 149
Schuylerville (village) Saratoga County, 568
Scio (town) Allegany County, 70
Scio (CDP) Allegany County, 70
Scipio (town) Cayuga County, 105
Scipio Center (unincorporated) Cayuga County, 105
Scotchtown (CDP) Orange County, 477
Scotia (village) Schenectady County, 575
Scott (town) Cortland County, 166
Scotts Corners (CDP) Westchester County, 750
Scottsburg (CDP) Livingston County, 314
Scottsville (village) Monroe County, 336
Scriba (town) Oswego County, 498
Sea Cliff (village) Nassau County, 377
Seaford (CDP) Nassau County, 377
Searingtown (CDP) Nassau County, 377
Selden (CDP) Suffolk County, 643

Selkirk (unincorporated) Albany County, 57
Sempronius (town) Cayuga County, 105
Seneca (town) Ontario County, 459
Seneca County, 587
Seneca Falls (town) Seneca County, 590
Seneca Falls (CDP) Seneca County, 590
Seneca Knolls (CDP) Onondaga County, 448
Sennett (town) Cayuga County, 105
Setauket-East Setauket (CDP) Suffolk County, 643
Severance (unincorporated) Essex County, 228
Seward (town) Schoharie County, 581
Shandaken (town) Ulster County, 699
Sharon (town) Schoharie County, 581
Sharon Springs (village) Schoharie County, 581
Shawangunk (town) Ulster County, 699
Shelby (town) Orleans County, 487
Sheldon (town) Wyoming County, 762
Shelter Island (town) Suffolk County, 644
Shelter Island (CDP) Suffolk County, 644
Shelter Island Heights (CDP) Suffolk County, 644
Shenorock (CDP) Westchester County, 751
Sherburne (town) Chenango County, 138
Sherburne (village) Chenango County, 138
Sheridan (town) Chautauqua County, 120
Sherman (town) Chautauqua County, 121
Sherman (village) Chautauqua County, 121
Sherrill (city) Oneida County, 430
Shinnecock Hills (CDP) Suffolk County, 644
Shinnecock Reservation (reservation) Suffolk County, 645
Shirley (CDP) Suffolk County, 645
Shokan (CDP) Ulster County, 700
Shoreham (village) Suffolk County, 645
Shortsville (village) Ontario County, 459
Shrub Oak (CDP) Westchester County, 751
Shushan (unincorporated) Washington County, 720
Sidney (town) Delaware County, 177
Sidney (village) Delaware County, 178
Sidney Center (unincorporated) Delaware County, 178
Silver Bay (unincorporated) Warren County, 710
Silver Creek (village) Chautauqua County, 121
Silver Lake (unincorporated) Wyoming County, 762
Silver Springs (village) Wyoming County, 763
Sinclairville (village) Chautauqua County, 121
Skaneateles (town) Onondaga County, 448
Skaneateles (village) Onondaga County, 449
Skaneateles Falls (unincorporated) Onondaga County, 449
Slate Hill (unincorporated) Orange County, 477
Slaterville Springs (unincorporated) Tompkins County, 682
Sleepy Hollow (village) Westchester County, 751
Slingerlands (unincorporated) Albany County, 57
Sloan (village) Erie County, 216
Sloansville (unincorporated) Schoharie County, 582
Sloatsburg (village) Rockland County, 536
Smallwood (CDP) Sullivan County, 667
Smithfield (town) Madison County, 325
Smithtown (town) Suffolk County, 646
Smithtown (CDP) Suffolk County, 645
Smithville (town) Chenango County, 138
Smithville Flats (CDP) Chenango County, 138
Smyrna (town) Chenango County, 139
Smyrna (village) Chenango County, 139
Sodus (town) Wayne County, 727
Sodus (village) Wayne County, 728

CDP = Census Designated Place

CDP = Census Designated Place

CDP = Census Designated Place

CDP = Census Designated Place

Comparative Statistics

This section compares the 100 largest incorporated places, townships, and CDPs (Census Designated Places) by population in the state, by the following data points:

Population

Place	2000 Census	2010 Census	Current Estimate[1]	Population Growth Since 2000 (%)
Albany city *Albany Co.*	95,658	97,856	98,498	2.9
Amherst town *Erie Co.*	116,510	122,366	125,024	7.3
Babylon town *Suffolk Co.*	211,792	213,603	213,199	0.6
Bay Shore CDP *Suffolk Co.*	23,852	26,337	30,392	27.4
Bethlehem town *Albany Co.*	31,304	33,656	34,912	11.5
Binghamton city *Broome Co.*	47,380	47,376	45,964	-2.9
Brentwood CDP *Suffolk Co.*	53,917	60,664	63,115	17.0
Brighton CDP *Monroe Co.*	35,584	36,609	36,753	3.2
Bronx borough *Bronx Co.*	1,332,650	1,385,108	1,455,846	9.2
Brookhaven town *Suffolk Co.*	448,248	486,040	487,731	8.8
Brooklyn borough *Kings Co.*	2,465,326	2,504,700	2,635,121	6.8
Buffalo city *Erie Co.*	292,648	261,310	259,574	-11.3
Carmel town *Putnam Co.*	33,006	34,305	34,328	4.0
Centereach CDP *Suffolk Co.*	27,285	31,578	31,953	17.1
Central Islip CDP *Suffolk Co.*	31,950	34,450	33,253	4.0
Cheektowaga town *Erie Co.*	94,019	88,226	87,484	-6.9
Cicero town *Onondaga Co.*	27,982	31,632	31,326	11.9
Clarence town *Erie Co.*	26,123	30,673	31,954	22.3
Clarkstown town *Rockland Co.*	82,082	84,187	87,224	6.2
Clay town *Onondaga Co.*	58,805	58,206	59,626	1.4
Clifton Park town *Saratoga Co.*	32,995	36,705	36,884	11.7
Colonie town *Albany Co.*	79,258	81,591	83,051	4.7
Commack CDP *Suffolk Co.*	36,367	36,124	37,117	2.0
Coram CDP *Suffolk Co.*	34,923	39,113	40,713	16.5
Cortlandt town *Westchester Co.*	38,467	41,592	42,816	11.3
East Meadow CDP *Nassau Co.*	37,461	38,132	37,195	-0.7
Eastchester town *Westchester Co.*	31,318	32,363	33,183	5.9
Elmont CDP *Nassau Co.*	32,657	33,198	36,636	12.1
Franklin Square CDP *Nassau Co.*	29,342	29,320	32,482	10.7
Freeport village *Nassau Co.*	43,783	42,860	43,380	-0.9
Glenville town *Schenectady Co.*	28,183	29,480	29,506	4.6
Greece town *Monroe Co.*	94,141	96,095	96,842	2.8
Greenburgh town *Westchester Co.*	86,764	88,400	91,799	5.8
Guilderland town *Albany Co.*	32,688	35,303	35,745	9.3
Hamburg town *Erie Co.*	56,259	56,936	58,147	3.3
Haverstraw town *Rockland Co.*	33,811	36,634	37,497	10.9
Hempstead town *Nassau Co.*	755,924	759,757	772,296	2.1
Hempstead village *Nassau Co.*	56,554	53,891	55,698	-1.5
Henrietta town *Monroe Co.*	39,028	42,581	43,609	11.7
Hicksville CDP *Nassau Co.*	41,260	41,547	42,368	2.6
Huntington town *Suffolk Co.*	195,289	203,264	204,011	4.4
Huntington Station CDP *Suffolk Co.*	29,910	33,029	33,338	11.4
Irondequoit CDP *Monroe Co.*	52,354	51,692	50,890	-2.8
Islip town *Suffolk Co.*	322,612	335,543	335,302	3.9
Ithaca city *Tompkins Co.*	29,287	30,014	30,720	4.8
Jamestown city *Chautauqua Co.*	31,730	31,146	30,094	-5.1
Lancaster town *Erie Co.*	39,019	41,604	42,942	10.0
Levittown CDP *Nassau Co.*	53,067	51,881	51,839	-2.3
Long Beach city *Nassau Co.*	35,462	33,275	33,657	-5.0
Mamaroneck town *Westchester Co.*	28,967	29,156	29,945	3.3

Place	2000 Census	2010 Census	Current Estimate[1]	Population Growth Since 2000 (%)
Manhattan borough *New York Co.*	1,537,195	1,585,873	1,653,877	7.5
Manlius town *Onondaga Co.*	31,872	32,370	32,282	1.2
Monroe town *Orange Co.*	31,407	39,912	42,913	36.6
Mount Pleasant town *Westchester Co.*	43,221	43,724	44,635	3.2
Mount Vernon city *Westchester Co.*	68,381	67,292	68,671	0.4
New City CDP *Rockland Co.*	34,038	33,559	34,338	0.8
New Rochelle city *Westchester Co.*	72,182	77,062	79,877	10.6
New York city *New York Co.*	8,008,278	8,175,133	8,560,072	6.8
Newburgh town *Orange Co.*	27,568	29,801	30,697	11.3
Niagara Falls city *Niagara Co.*	55,593	50,193	48,976	-11.9
North Hempstead town *Nassau Co.*	222,611	226,322	231,085	3.8
North Tonawanda city *Niagara Co.*	33,262	31,568	30,752	-7.5
Oceanside CDP *Nassau Co.*	32,733	32,109	30,710	-6.1
Orangetown town *Rockland Co.*	47,711	49,212	50,365	5.5
Orchard Park town *Erie Co.*	27,637	29,054	29,545	6.9
Ossining town *Westchester Co.*	36,534	37,674	38,257	4.7
Oyster Bay town *Nassau Co.*	293,925	293,214	298,655	1.6
Penfield town *Monroe Co.*	34,645	36,242	37,245	7.5
Perinton town *Monroe Co.*	46,090	46,462	46,660	1.2
Pittsford town *Monroe Co.*	27,219	29,405	29,507	8.4
Port Chester village *Westchester Co.*	27,867	28,967	29,623	6.3
Poughkeepsie town *Dutchess Co.*	42,777	43,341	44,513	4.0
Poughkeepsie city *Dutchess Co.*	29,871	32,736	30,505	2.1
Queens borough *Queens Co.*	2,229,379	2,230,722	2,339,280	4.9
Ramapo town *Rockland Co.*	108,905	126,595	134,440	23.4
Riverhead town *Suffolk Co.*	27,680	33,506	33,839	22.2
Rochester city *Monroe Co.*	219,773	210,565	209,463	-4.6
Rome city *Oneida Co.*	34,950	33,725	32,589	-6.7
Rye town *Westchester Co.*	43,880	45,928	46,978	7.0
Salina town *Onondaga Co.*	33,290	33,710	33,307	0.0
Schenectady city *Schenectady Co.*	61,821	66,135	65,705	6.2
Smithtown town *Suffolk Co.*	115,715	117,801	117,863	1.8
Southampton town *Suffolk Co.*	54,712	56,790	58,024	6.0
Spring Valley village *Rockland Co.*	25,464	31,347	32,538	27.7
Staten Island borough *Richmond Co.*	443,728	468,730	475,948	7.2
Syracuse city *Onondaga Co.*	147,306	145,170	144,405	-1.9
Tonawanda town *Erie Co.*	78,155	73,567	73,044	-6.5
Tonawanda CDP *Erie Co.*	61,729	58,144	57,725	-6.4
Troy city *Rensselaer Co.*	49,170	50,129	49,826	1.3
Union town *Broome Co.*	56,298	56,346	54,817	-2.6
Uniondale CDP *Nassau Co.*	23,011	24,759	31,597	37.3
Utica city *Oneida Co.*	60,651	62,235	61,114	0.7
Valley Stream village *Nassau Co.*	36,368	37,511	37,843	4.0
Warwick town *Orange Co.*	30,764	32,065	31,305	1.7
Webster town *Monroe Co.*	37,926	42,641	44,224	16.6
West Babylon CDP *Suffolk Co.*	43,452	43,213	43,168	-0.6
West Seneca CDP *Erie Co.*	45,943	44,711	45,340	-1.3
White Plains city *Westchester Co.*	53,077	56,853	58,404	10.0
Yonkers city *Westchester Co.*	196,086	195,976	200,999	2.5
Yorktown town *Westchester Co.*	36,318	36,081	36,900	1.6

NOTE: (1) Current population is based on the American Community Survey's 2013-2017 Five-Year Estimate.
SOURCE: U.S. Census Bureau, Census 2010, Census 2000; U.S. Census Bureau, American Community Survey, 2013-2017 Five-Year Estimates

Physical Characteristics

Place	Density (persons per square mile)	Land Area (square miles)	Water Area (square miles)	Elevation (feet)
Albany city *Albany Co.*	4,605.2	21.39	0.55	148
Amherst town *Erie Co.*	2,350.0	53.20	0.39	597
Babylon town *Suffolk Co.*	4,075.0	52.32	61.86	7
Bay Shore CDP *Suffolk Co.*	5,662.1	5.37	0.16	16
Bethlehem town *Albany Co.*	712.1	49.03	0.83	210
Binghamton city *Broome Co.*	4,382.1	10.49	0.65	866
Brentwood CDP *Suffolk Co.*	5,747.9	10.98	0.00	79
Brighton CDP *Monroe Co.*	2,384.1	15.42	0.17	446
Bronx borough *Bronx Co.*	34,583.7	42.10	15.38	49
Brookhaven town *Suffolk Co.*	1,879.9	259.44	272.10	10
Brooklyn borough *Kings Co.*	37,210.9	70.82	26.10	49
Buffalo city *Erie Co.*	6,427.6	40.38	12.11	600
Carmel town *Putnam Co.*	956.0	35.91	4.79	561
Centereach CDP *Suffolk Co.*	3,666.7	8.71	0.00	98
Central Islip CDP *Suffolk Co.*	4,676.2	7.11	0.00	89
Cheektowaga town *Erie Co.*	2,973.4	29.42	0.06	650
Cicero town *Onondaga Co.*	648.9	48.27	0.19	394
Clarence town *Erie Co.*	597.2	53.50	0.13	738
Clarkstown town *Rockland Co.*	2,267.0	38.48	8.59	n/a
Clay town *Onondaga Co.*	1,243.3	47.96	0.90	394
Clifton Park town *Saratoga Co.*	765.2	48.20	2.00	344
Colonie town *Albany Co.*	1,484.6	55.94	1.90	312
Commack CDP *Suffolk Co.*	3,101.2	11.97	0.00	131
Coram CDP *Suffolk Co.*	2,945.0	13.82	0.00	95
Cortlandt town *Westchester Co.*	1,090.7	39.25	10.76	n/a
East Meadow CDP *Nassau Co.*	5,900.2	6.30	0.02	72
Eastchester town *Westchester Co.*	6,837.5	4.85	0.09	23
Elmont CDP *Nassau Co.*	10,875.4	3.37	0.01	39
Franklin Square CDP *Nassau Co.*	11,287.6	2.88	0.00	66
Freeport village *Nassau Co.*	9,372.9	4.63	0.24	20
Glenville town *Schenectady Co.*	599.9	49.19	1.49	705
Greece town *Monroe Co.*	2,038.0	47.52	3.87	430
Greenburgh town *Westchester Co.*	3,028.8	30.31	5.81	348
Guilderland town *Albany Co.*	617.3	57.90	0.88	207
Hamburg town *Erie Co.*	1,407.2	41.32	0.03	820
Haverstraw town *Rockland Co.*	1,692.5	22.16	5.26	33
Hempstead town *Nassau Co.*	6,512.5	118.59	73.00	56
Hempstead village *Nassau Co.*	15,127.0	3.68	0.00	56
Henrietta town *Monroe Co.*	1,233.6	35.35	0.30	600
Hicksville CDP *Nassau Co.*	6,238.9	6.79	0.02	148
Huntington town *Suffolk Co.*	2,167.5	94.12	42.99	75
Huntington Station CDP *Suffolk Co.*	6,090.1	5.47	0.00	217
Irondequoit CDP *Monroe Co.*	3,392.4	15.00	1.83	381
Islip town *Suffolk Co.*	3,220.5	104.11	58.89	13
Ithaca city *Tompkins Co.*	5,701.4	5.39	0.68	410
Jamestown city *Chautauqua Co.*	3,368.3	8.93	0.13	1,378
Lancaster town *Erie Co.*	1,139.0	37.70	0.23	669
Levittown CDP *Nassau Co.*	7,611.0	6.81	0.02	85
Long Beach city *Nassau Co.*	15,197.3	2.21	1.68	7
Mamaroneck town *Westchester Co.*	4,500.2	6.65	7.41	47

Place	Density (persons per square mile)	Land Area (square miles)	Water Area (square miles)	Elevation (feet)
Manhattan borough *New York Co.*	72,447.3	22.83	10.76	115
Manlius town *Onondaga Co.*	655.9	49.22	0.74	591
Monroe town *Orange Co.*	2,148.2	19.98	1.28	643
Mount Pleasant town *Westchester Co.*	1,627.7	27.42	5.33	259
Mount Vernon city *Westchester Co.*	15,658.0	4.39	0.02	112
New City CDP *Rockland Co.*	2,203.7	15.58	0.79	157
New Rochelle city *Westchester Co.*	7,717.4	10.35	2.89	85
New York city *New York Co.*	28,284.4	302.64	165.84	87
Newburgh town *Orange Co.*	719.3	42.68	4.27	131
Niagara Falls city *Niagara Co.*	3,476.9	14.09	2.74	614
North Hempstead town *Nassau Co.*	4,318.4	53.51	15.60	102
North Tonawanda city *Niagara Co.*	3,044.7	10.10	0.80	574
Oceanside CDP *Nassau Co.*	6,212.0	4.94	0.47	13
Orangetown town *Rockland Co.*	2,090.0	24.10	7.27	200
Orchard Park town *Erie Co.*	768.6	38.44	0.08	863
Ossining town *Westchester Co.*	3,310.5	11.56	4.17	161
Oyster Bay town *Nassau Co.*	2,878.7	103.75	65.65	49
Penfield town *Monroe Co.*	1,000.9	37.21	0.63	423
Perinton town *Monroe Co.*	1,364.9	34.19	0.36	n/a
Pittsford town *Monroe Co.*	1,272.9	23.18	0.21	492
Port Chester village *Westchester Co.*	12,710.3	2.33	0.07	43
Poughkeepsie town *Dutchess Co.*	1,561.1	28.51	2.63	200
Poughkeepsie city *Dutchess Co.*	5,930.4	5.14	0.57	200
Queens borough *Queens Co.*	21,553.8	108.53	69.68	43
Ramapo town *Rockland Co.*	2,196.8	61.20	0.70	331
Riverhead town *Suffolk Co.*	501.9	67.43	133.84	13
Rochester city *Monroe Co.*	5,854.1	35.78	1.37	505
Rome city *Oneida Co.*	435.7	74.79	0.81	456
Rye town *Westchester Co.*	6,789.9	6.92	0.43	26
Salina town *Onondaga Co.*	2,422.3	13.75	1.31	n/a
Schenectady city *Schenectady Co.*	6,095.4	10.78	0.19	243
Smithtown town *Suffolk Co.*	2,194.9	53.70	57.75	59
Southampton town *Suffolk Co.*	416.9	139.19	154.51	26
Spring Valley village *Rockland Co.*	16,142.0	2.02	0.00	446
Staten Island borough *Richmond Co.*	8,153.9	58.37	43.92	161
Syracuse city *Onondaga Co.*	5,766.2	25.04	0.56	397
Tonawanda town *Erie Co.*	3,898.8	18.73	1.54	574
Tonawanda CDP *Erie Co.*	3,336.8	17.30	1.34	574
Troy city *Rensselaer Co.*	4,810.8	10.36	0.70	33
Union town *Broome Co.*	1,546.2	35.45	0.54	846
Uniondale CDP *Nassau Co.*	11,674.3	2.71	0.00	52
Utica city *Oneida Co.*	3,646.7	16.76	0.26	456
Valley Stream village *Nassau Co.*	10,867.8	3.48	0.02	16
Warwick town *Orange Co.*	308.9	101.34	3.55	518
Webster town *Monroe Co.*	1,318.9	33.53	1.71	446
West Babylon CDP *Suffolk Co.*	5,557.9	7.77	0.31	39
West Seneca CDP *Erie Co.*	2,122.9	21.36	0.06	597
White Plains city *Westchester Co.*	5,979.2	9.77	0.12	213
Yonkers city *Westchester Co.*	11,159.2	18.01	2.28	82
Yorktown town *Westchester Co.*	1,007.0	36.64	2.61	505

SOURCE: U.S. Census Bureau, Census 2010; U.S. Census Bureau, American Community Survey, 2013-2017 Five-Year Estimates

Population by Race/Hispanic Origin

Place	White[1] (%)	Black[1] (%)	Asian[1] (%)	AIAN[1,2] (%)	NHOPI[1,3] (%)	Two or More Races (%)	Hispanic[4] (%)
Albany city *Albany Co.*	55.1	28.7	7.4	0.3	0.0	5.6	9.8
Amherst town *Erie Co.*	80.6	6.5	8.9	0.2	0.0	2.6	3.7
Babylon town *Suffolk Co.*	67.6	16.5	3.4	0.2	0.0	3.5	22.1
Bay Shore CDP *Suffolk Co.*	51.7	24.0	3.5	0.7	0.0	6.3	38.3
Bethlehem town *Albany Co.*	91.6	2.1	4.1	0.0	0.0	1.9	1.5
Binghamton city *Broome Co.*	75.0	13.3	4.6	0.4	0.0	4.9	7.1
Brentwood CDP *Suffolk Co.*	58.8	14.6	1.6	0.5	0.0	5.1	66.7
Brighton CDP *Monroe Co.*	79.3	6.4	10.8	0.3	0.0	2.5	4.1
Bronx borough *Bronx Co.*	21.0	33.6	3.7	0.7	0.1	3.5	55.7
Brookhaven town *Suffolk Co.*	85.4	5.7	4.8	0.2	0.0	2.1	15.4
Brooklyn borough *Kings Co.*	43.2	33.0	11.9	0.3	0.0	2.7	19.3
Buffalo city *Erie Co.*	47.6	37.1	5.2	0.4	0.0	3.8	11.3
Carmel town *Putnam Co.*	90.8	1.1	2.9	0.0	0.0	2.1	10.9
Centereach CDP *Suffolk Co.*	88.6	2.7	5.2	0.2	0.2	1.8	15.3
Central Islip CDP *Suffolk Co.*	48.3	27.2	2.7	0.2	0.0	6.5	45.6
Cheektowaga town *Erie Co.*	84.4	10.4	2.3	0.2	0.1	2.0	2.6
Cicero town *Onondaga Co.*	94.7	1.7	1.3	0.4	0.0	1.6	1.9
Clarence town *Erie Co.*	93.0	0.7	4.4	0.0	0.1	1.6	1.8
Clarkstown town *Rockland Co.*	70.9	11.2	10.4	0.2	0.0	3.3	14.0
Clay town *Onondaga Co.*	89.5	5.4	1.9	0.2	0.0	2.8	3.1
Clifton Park town *Saratoga Co.*	88.4	3.0	5.7	0.1	0.1	1.6	3.3
Colonie town *Albany Co.*	80.9	5.9	8.6	0.2	0.1	3.5	4.5
Commack CDP *Suffolk Co.*	90.6	1.7	4.6	0.0	0.0	2.2	5.9
Coram CDP *Suffolk Co.*	78.6	10.4	6.5	0.3	0.1	2.0	18.9
Cortlandt town *Westchester Co.*	78.5	6.5	3.9	0.2	0.0	2.7	16.5
East Meadow CDP *Nassau Co.*	74.0	5.6	11.0	0.4	0.0	2.8	14.5
Eastchester town *Westchester Co.*	85.0	2.7	6.5	0.2	0.0	2.7	7.4
Elmont CDP *Nassau Co.*	21.1	47.4	13.9	0.2	0.0	5.6	21.4
Franklin Square CDP *Nassau Co.*	69.2	2.8	13.1	0.0	0.0	3.4	20.4
Freeport village *Nassau Co.*	40.5	31.2	1.0	1.3	0.0	16.1	42.9
Glenville town *Schenectady Co.*	94.7	1.6	1.5	0.0	0.1	1.8	3.0
Greece town *Monroe Co.*	86.7	6.5	2.6	0.2	0.0	2.4	5.3
Greenburgh town *Westchester Co.*	68.2	13.1	9.9	0.4	0.0	2.8	15.2
Guilderland town *Albany Co.*	84.3	4.5	8.2	0.0	0.0	1.8	4.0
Hamburg town *Erie Co.*	96.3	1.1	0.4	0.3	0.0	1.2	1.9
Haverstraw town *Rockland Co.*	54.5	15.7	4.6	0.0	0.0	3.8	45.1
Hempstead town *Nassau Co.*	63.9	17.0	6.0	0.3	0.0	4.4	20.1
Hempstead village *Nassau Co.*	13.8	46.3	1.7	0.8	0.0	5.0	46.6
Henrietta town *Monroe Co.*	77.3	9.1	8.9	0.4	0.1	2.7	4.0
Hicksville CDP *Nassau Co.*	65.5	4.3	23.2	0.2	0.0	3.3	15.6
Huntington town *Suffolk Co.*	82.9	4.8	5.6	0.1	0.0	1.4	12.2
Huntington Station CDP *Suffolk Co.*	62.8	9.4	3.1	0.2	0.0	1.8	37.8
Irondequoit CDP *Monroe Co.*	84.8	9.1	1.3	0.1	0.0	2.5	8.7
Islip town *Suffolk Co.*	72.5	10.5	2.6	0.3	0.1	3.9	30.8
Ithaca city *Tompkins Co.*	68.6	6.6	17.6	0.3	0.0	5.1	7.3
Jamestown city *Chautauqua Co.*	86.9	5.2	0.5	0.4	0.0	3.7	8.6
Lancaster town *Erie Co.*	96.6	1.3	0.6	0.4	0.0	0.7	2.1
Levittown CDP *Nassau Co.*	84.1	1.4	7.3	0.0	0.0	2.2	14.6
Long Beach city *Nassau Co.*	80.9	6.3	3.1	0.1	0.0	3.0	14.5
Mamaroneck town *Westchester Co.*	81.7	3.9	4.6	0.1	0.0	2.9	17.7

Place	White[1] (%)	Black[1] (%)	Asian[1] (%)	AIAN[1,2] (%)	NHOPI[1,3] (%)	Two or More Races (%)	Hispanic[4] (%)
Manhattan borough *New York Co.*	56.4	14.9	12.0	0.4	0.1	4.4	26.1
Manlius town *Onondaga Co.*	89.9	3.1	3.5	0.3	0.0	2.6	1.4
Monroe town *Orange Co.*	86.6	3.2	2.8	0.3	0.0	1.8	11.3
Mount Pleasant town *Westchester Co.*	77.8	4.2	4.7	0.1	0.0	2.4	21.5
Mount Vernon city *Westchester Co.*	22.1	66.7	2.1	0.5	0.0	2.6	15.4
New City CDP *Rockland Co.*	74.6	9.3	10.1	0.1	0.0	3.1	10.1
New Rochelle city *Westchester Co.*	60.0	20.0	4.5	0.1	0.0	3.5	29.4
New York city *New York Co.*	42.8	24.3	14.0	0.4	0.1	3.3	29.1
Newburgh town *Orange Co.*	74.5	12.8	2.0	0.1	0.0	4.4	18.8
Niagara Falls city *Niagara Co.*	69.5	22.6	1.0	1.5	0.1	4.6	3.6
North Hempstead town *Nassau Co.*	66.9	6.0	18.2	0.2	0.1	2.2	13.8
North Tonawanda city *Niagara Co.*	95.2	1.5	0.4	0.4	0.0	1.9	2.1
Oceanside CDP *Nassau Co.*	92.6	1.0	2.3	0.5	0.0	1.0	10.6
Orangetown town *Rockland Co.*	81.2	6.0	7.3	0.6	0.0	2.3	10.6
Orchard Park town *Erie Co.*	96.2	0.7	1.9	0.1	0.0	0.6	2.6
Ossining town *Westchester Co.*	56.0	12.4	5.1	1.6	0.0	3.2	35.0
Oyster Bay town *Nassau Co.*	82.5	2.7	11.1	0.1	0.0	1.6	8.2
Penfield town *Monroe Co.*	91.1	2.7	3.1	0.1	0.0	2.5	4.4
Perinton town *Monroe Co.*	92.3	1.7	3.9	0.1	0.0	1.6	3.4
Pittsford town *Monroe Co.*	87.7	1.2	8.7	0.0	0.0	1.7	2.4
Port Chester village *Westchester Co.*	55.0	4.7	1.5	1.4	0.0	2.3	64.8
Poughkeepsie town *Dutchess Co.*	72.9	13.3	6.0	0.3	0.1	3.4	12.7
Poughkeepsie city *Dutchess Co.*	48.1	37.6	1.3	0.4	0.0	5.2	17.8
Queens borough *Queens Co.*	39.7	18.2	25.3	0.4	0.1	3.4	28.0
Ramapo town *Rockland Co.*	70.5	15.4	3.7	0.1	0.0	1.7	14.1
Riverhead town *Suffolk Co.*	85.6	9.7	1.0	0.9	0.0	1.5	13.5
Rochester city *Monroe Co.*	46.6	40.7	3.3	1.0	0.0	4.5	17.8
Rome city *Oneida Co.*	88.3	6.6	1.3	0.1	0.0	2.5	6.3
Rye town *Westchester Co.*	64.8	4.5	3.3	0.9	0.0	2.2	46.1
Salina town *Onondaga Co.*	88.6	4.9	2.4	0.2	0.0	3.5	3.3
Schenectady city *Schenectady Co.*	59.4	20.9	6.4	0.5	0.0	5.4	10.3
Smithtown town *Suffolk Co.*	91.9	1.1	4.3	0.0	0.0	1.3	5.2
Southampton town *Suffolk Co.*	87.4	5.7	2.5	0.1	0.0	2.4	20.2
Spring Valley village *Rockland Co.*	34.8	37.6	2.5	0.0	0.0	2.0	29.9
Staten Island borough *Richmond Co.*	74.8	10.3	8.5	0.3	0.0	2.3	18.2
Syracuse city *Onondaga Co.*	55.2	29.0	7.0	0.9	0.0	5.5	9.1
Tonawanda town *Erie Co.*	90.0	4.6	2.0	0.3	0.0	2.2	3.7
Tonawanda CDP *Erie Co.*	89.4	4.3	2.4	0.3	0.0	2.4	4.0
Troy city *Rensselaer Co.*	69.8	17.1	4.1	0.1	0.0	7.3	9.7
Union town *Broome Co.*	86.2	5.7	3.9	0.1	0.1	3.0	3.6
Uniondale CDP *Nassau Co.*	34.1	38.2	3.2	0.7	0.0	11.6	35.4
Utica city *Oneida Co.*	63.4	15.8	11.9	0.3	0.0	4.6	12.3
Valley Stream village *Nassau Co.*	44.5	25.1	15.0	0.0	0.0	4.7	25.2
Warwick town *Orange Co.*	84.8	5.8	1.3	0.7	0.2	4.4	11.0
Webster town *Monroe Co.*	91.0	2.2	3.8	0.0	0.0	2.7	2.3
West Babylon CDP *Suffolk Co.*	76.8	11.1	3.5	0.1	0.1	2.3	18.3
West Seneca CDP *Erie Co.*	96.3	1.7	0.3	0.1	0.0	0.8	1.9
White Plains city *Westchester Co.*	59.7	12.5	7.8	0.8	0.0	2.3	33.2
Yonkers city *Westchester Co.*	56.3	17.8	7.2	0.4	0.0	3.8	36.3
Yorktown town *Westchester Co.*	83.9	4.3	4.7	0.4	0.0	1.5	15.0

NOTE: (1) Exclude multiple race combinations; (2) American Indian/Alaska Native; (3) Native Hawaiian/Other Pacific Islander; (4) May be of any race
SOURCE: U.S. Census Bureau, American Community Survey, 2013-2017 Five-Year Estimates

Average Household Size, Age, and Male/Female Ratio

Place	Average Household Size (persons)	Median Age (years)	Age Under 18 (%)	Age 65 and Over (%)	Males per 100 Females
Albany city *Albany Co.*	2.14	30.9	17.3	12.6	88.5
Amherst town *Erie Co.*	2.34	40.1	19.3	19.2	93.4
Babylon town *Suffolk Co.*	3.18	39.7	21.4	14.0	93.6
Bay Shore CDP *Suffolk Co.*	3.32	34.7	25.9	10.8	98.1
Bethlehem town *Albany Co.*	2.51	42.8	22.8	17.2	93.5
Binghamton city *Broome Co.*	2.21	36.4	19.3	17.0	93.1
Brentwood CDP *Suffolk Co.*	4.56	32.6	26.4	8.6	96.5
Brighton CDP *Monroe Co.*	2.18	39.7	17.6	19.8	85.6
Bronx borough *Bronx Co.*	2.85	33.6	25.2	11.8	89.0
Brookhaven town *Suffolk Co.*	2.94	39.5	22.2	14.5	98.0
Brooklyn borough *Kings Co.*	2.75	34.8	23.1	12.8	89.9
Buffalo city *Erie Co.*	2.26	32.8	22.9	12.2	91.3
Carmel town *Putnam Co.*	2.89	43.9	20.8	15.9	103.2
Centereach CDP *Suffolk Co.*	3.28	38.0	22.2	14.1	95.4
Central Islip CDP *Suffolk Co.*	3.57	34.2	24.4	9.7	108.1
Cheektowaga town *Erie Co.*	2.20	42.7	17.7	19.1	93.0
Cicero town *Onondaga Co.*	2.56	41.0	22.9	14.1	93.3
Clarence town *Erie Co.*	2.65	44.8	24.3	16.9	93.6
Clarkstown town *Rockland Co.*	2.89	44.3	21.8	18.9	94.5
Clay town *Onondaga Co.*	2.50	39.5	22.1	14.5	95.3
Clifton Park town *Saratoga Co.*	2.55	42.8	23.0	17.4	95.9
Colonie town *Albany Co.*	2.45	41.1	18.6	17.2	97.2
Commack CDP *Suffolk Co.*	3.03	46.2	21.2	18.7	96.2
Coram CDP *Suffolk Co.*	2.77	40.3	22.4	13.4	96.0
Cortlandt town *Westchester Co.*	2.76	44.2	23.0	16.4	95.3
East Meadow CDP *Nassau Co.*	2.91	42.7	18.0	18.8	100.7
Eastchester town *Westchester Co.*	2.57	42.5	22.5	17.7	88.5
Elmont CDP *Nassau Co.*	3.73	39.1	19.9	13.2	94.3
Franklin Square CDP *Nassau Co.*	3.36	39.5	21.6	16.9	98.2
Freeport village *Nassau Co.*	3.14	37.7	21.7	15.0	90.6
Glenville town *Schenectady Co.*	2.69	42.8	21.4	18.9	84.9
Greece town *Monroe Co.*	2.37	43.8	19.8	19.5	92.7
Greenburgh town *Westchester Co.*	2.69	42.4	22.0	17.1	94.4
Guilderland town *Albany Co.*	2.36	40.0	20.0	16.2	97.8
Hamburg town *Erie Co.*	2.37	43.5	20.4	18.6	89.8
Haverstraw town *Rockland Co.*	3.05	36.8	23.7	13.5	94.4
Hempstead town *Nassau Co.*	3.14	40.1	22.2	15.6	94.3
Hempstead village *Nassau Co.*	3.50	33.9	27.0	10.3	90.6
Henrietta town *Monroe Co.*	2.56	33.6	18.9	13.8	106.3
Hicksville CDP *Nassau Co.*	3.19	43.9	18.1	17.2	94.6
Huntington town *Suffolk Co.*	2.93	44.3	22.8	17.7	96.3
Huntington Station CDP *Suffolk Co.*	3.32	36.9	26.8	11.0	105.4
Irondequoit CDP *Monroe Co.*	2.28	44.2	19.8	20.3	88.6
Islip town *Suffolk Co.*	3.35	38.0	23.6	12.6	97.6
Ithaca city *Tompkins Co.*	2.31	21.8	8.8	5.8	101.4
Jamestown city *Chautauqua Co.*	2.29	38.1	23.9	16.3	96.1
Lancaster town *Erie Co.*	2.39	42.8	21.4	16.2	96.3
Levittown CDP *Nassau Co.*	3.16	42.0	20.1	16.3	93.2
Long Beach city *Nassau Co.*	2.26	44.3	15.4	17.9	86.0
Mamaroneck town *Westchester Co.*	2.77	40.0	26.3	14.7	97.2

Place	Average Household Size (persons)	Median Age (years)	Age Under 18 (%)	Age 65 and Over (%)	Males per 100 Females
Manhattan borough *New York Co.*	2.10	37.1	14.5	15.3	89.7
Manlius town *Onondaga Co.*	2.46	44.7	24.1	20.0	90.4
Monroe town *Orange Co.*	4.10	21.2	44.9	5.8	100.3
Mount Pleasant town *Westchester Co.*	2.90	40.1	23.1	14.9	98.9
Mount Vernon city *Westchester Co.*	2.70	38.5	20.9	15.1	83.4
New City CDP *Rockland Co.*	3.02	44.4	22.6	18.6	95.2
New Rochelle city *Westchester Co.*	2.69	39.4	20.8	16.5	97.2
New York city *New York Co.*	2.67	36.2	21.0	13.6	91.1
Newburgh town *Orange Co.*	2.79	41.2	21.6	15.0	94.9
Niagara Falls city *Niagara Co.*	2.28	38.6	22.3	15.4	89.7
North Hempstead town *Nassau Co.*	2.95	42.6	22.8	19.3	93.8
North Tonawanda city *Niagara Co.*	2.24	44.3	18.6	18.5	97.3
Oceanside CDP *Nassau Co.*	2.85	44.3	20.2	17.1	96.2
Orangetown town *Rockland Co.*	2.65	43.0	20.1	18.8	97.1
Orchard Park town *Erie Co.*	2.54	45.6	21.6	20.3	95.0
Ossining town *Westchester Co.*	2.82	39.6	22.4	14.4	105.1
Oyster Bay town *Nassau Co.*	2.95	44.2	21.1	17.7	95.5
Penfield town *Monroe Co.*	2.43	46.0	23.0	20.8	85.9
Perinton town *Monroe Co.*	2.44	45.9	21.6	20.0	91.3
Pittsford town *Monroe Co.*	2.56	43.4	22.7	19.2	91.2
Port Chester village *Westchester Co.*	3.29	36.4	23.9	11.1	107.8
Poughkeepsie town *Dutchess Co.*	2.57	36.9	19.3	15.7	90.3
Poughkeepsie city *Dutchess Co.*	2.34	37.7	20.8	15.0	98.6
Queens borough *Queens Co.*	2.97	38.3	20.2	14.3	94.1
Ramapo town *Rockland Co.*	3.79	28.0	36.2	11.5	97.2
Riverhead town *Suffolk Co.*	2.47	48.7	16.5	23.9	93.0
Rochester city *Monroe Co.*	2.32	31.7	23.3	10.3	94.9
Rome city *Oneida Co.*	2.36	39.5	20.8	17.3	106.0
Rye town *Westchester Co.*	3.07	38.5	24.5	13.4	101.8
Salina town *Onondaga Co.*	2.25	42.4	20.0	19.9	90.0
Schenectady city *Schenectady Co.*	2.73	36.4	20.7	13.4	93.6
Smithtown town *Suffolk Co.*	2.88	45.5	21.7	18.8	94.3
Southampton town *Suffolk Co.*	2.55	45.3	19.0	20.0	105.7
Spring Valley village *Rockland Co.*	3.62	29.6	33.1	8.1	99.4
Staten Island borough *Richmond Co.*	2.82	39.9	22.1	15.1	93.8
Syracuse city *Onondaga Co.*	2.34	30.6	21.9	12.0	89.4
Tonawanda town *Erie Co.*	2.19	43.4	18.9	20.2	87.4
Tonawanda CDP *Erie Co.*	2.20	43.8	19.3	20.8	86.1
Troy city *Rensselaer Co.*	2.25	30.6	20.0	10.9	99.8
Union town *Broome Co.*	2.23	41.6	20.0	19.7	93.8
Uniondale CDP *Nassau Co.*	3.47	32.9	19.8	14.4	90.3
Utica city *Oneida Co.*	2.48	34.0	24.9	15.3	92.8
Valley Stream village *Nassau Co.*	3.16	40.8	22.0	13.9	95.9
Warwick town *Orange Co.*	2.65	45.9	21.8	17.0	101.2
Webster town *Monroe Co.*	2.47	43.7	21.4	18.6	88.5
West Babylon CDP *Suffolk Co.*	3.15	41.0	20.6	16.0	93.6
West Seneca CDP *Erie Co.*	2.29	45.0	18.4	20.3	93.1
White Plains city *Westchester Co.*	2.58	38.1	20.3	15.6	92.3
Yonkers city *Westchester Co.*	2.66	38.8	21.7	16.4	89.5
Yorktown town *Westchester Co.*	2.79	45.5	22.0	18.4	96.1

SOURCE: U.S. Census Bureau, American Community Survey, 2013-2017 Five-Year Estimates

Foreign Born, Language Spoken, Disabled Persons, and Veterans

Place	Foreign Born (%)	Speak English Only at Home (%)	With a Disability (%)	Veterans (%)
Albany city *Albany Co.*	12.70	83.3	12.1	4.2
Amherst town *Erie Co.*	13.10	84.2	10.5	6.5
Babylon town *Suffolk Co.*	19.80	73.2	10.5	5.3
Bay Shore CDP *Suffolk Co.*	22.40	65.5	11.0	4.1
Bethlehem town *Albany Co.*	6.60	92.3	8.9	6.4
Binghamton city *Broome Co.*	9.50	86.5	20.3	6.3
Brentwood CDP *Suffolk Co.*	42.00	29.2	8.2	3.5
Brighton CDP *Monroe Co.*	17.00	81.3	11.1	5.8
Bronx borough *Bronx Co.*	35.30	40.7	14.6	2.5
Brookhaven town *Suffolk Co.*	12.50	80.8	9.7	5.9
Brooklyn borough *Kings Co.*	36.90	54.1	10.3	2.0
Buffalo city *Erie Co.*	9.50	82.4	16.2	6.0
Carmel town *Putnam Co.*	13.90	81.3	10.5	4.9
Centereach CDP *Suffolk Co.*	11.30	83.7	10.0	5.7
Central Islip CDP *Suffolk Co.*	34.20	48.6	9.5	4.1
Cheektowaga town *Erie Co.*	5.00	93.0	13.6	8.9
Cicero town *Onondaga Co.*	3.20	95.2	10.8	6.3
Clarence town *Erie Co.*	6.50	92.3	8.5	6.5
Clarkstown town *Rockland Co.*	21.30	71.1	9.8	4.3
Clay town *Onondaga Co.*	5.10	93.8	10.2	8.2
Clifton Park town *Saratoga Co.*	8.30	88.9	7.5	8.2
Colonie town *Albany Co.*	12.00	84.9	10.5	6.8
Commack CDP *Suffolk Co.*	9.40	87.1	8.6	6.4
Coram CDP *Suffolk Co.*	17.00	78.1	8.8	5.2
Cortlandt town *Westchester Co.*	15.00	80.5	10.0	5.7
East Meadow CDP *Nassau Co.*	19.00	72.3	10.9	5.4
Eastchester town *Westchester Co.*	18.20	78.1	8.2	4.5
Elmont CDP *Nassau Co.*	45.10	52.3	7.5	2.4
Franklin Square CDP *Nassau Co.*	25.20	60.5	7.2	4.4
Freeport village *Nassau Co.*	29.00	57.6	7.9	3.3
Glenville town *Schenectady Co.*	3.30	95.4	11.9	9.4
Greece town *Monroe Co.*	6.90	90.0	13.3	7.4
Greenburgh town *Westchester Co.*	22.80	71.9	7.6	3.8
Guilderland town *Albany Co.*	9.00	88.8	8.9	6.1
Hamburg town *Erie Co.*	2.60	96.7	11.2	8.4
Haverstraw town *Rockland Co.*	29.90	52.2	11.5	3.8
Hempstead town *Nassau Co.*	22.20	72.1	8.4	4.4
Hempstead village *Nassau Co.*	41.00	50.1	6.1	3.0
Henrietta town *Monroe Co.*	13.70	83.2	13.0	6.1
Hicksville CDP *Nassau Co.*	30.50	62.8	9.0	5.4
Huntington town *Suffolk Co.*	13.90	80.7	7.7	5.2
Huntington Station CDP *Suffolk Co.*	25.80	56.9	7.3	3.7
Irondequoit CDP *Monroe Co.*	7.60	87.1	13.7	7.9
Islip town *Suffolk Co.*	20.60	67.9	9.3	5.3
Ithaca city *Tompkins Co.*	17.50	79.7	5.9	1.8
Jamestown city *Chautauqua Co.*	1.80	91.2	20.5	8.5
Lancaster town *Erie Co.*	3.40	94.9	9.2	8.3
Levittown CDP *Nassau Co.*	14.10	82.0	10.1	5.2
Long Beach city *Nassau Co.*	14.60	82.0	10.9	5.0
Mamaroneck town *Westchester Co.*	23.00	71.8	6.7	3.4

Place	Foreign Born (%)	Speak English Only at Home (%)	With a Disability (%)	Veterans (%)
Manhattan borough *New York Co.*	28.90	60.0	10.2	2.3
Manlius town *Onondaga Co.*	6.20	92.4	10.6	8.1
Monroe town *Orange Co.*	10.40	39.0	6.7	3.9
Mount Pleasant town *Westchester Co.*	20.40	70.7	8.4	4.0
Mount Vernon city *Westchester Co.*	33.00	75.7	11.3	3.2
New City CDP *Rockland Co.*	18.40	75.2	8.7	5.1
New Rochelle city *Westchester Co.*	29.60	60.1	9.9	3.9
New York city *New York Co.*	37.20	51.1	10.8	2.4
Newburgh town *Orange Co.*	9.50	81.0	10.4	7.9
Niagara Falls city *Niagara Co.*	4.80	95.0	16.2	8.5
North Hempstead town *Nassau Co.*	29.30	61.9	7.7	3.8
North Tonawanda city *Niagara Co.*	3.00	96.1	17.1	9.2
Oceanside CDP *Nassau Co.*	11.30	85.1	8.5	4.8
Orangetown town *Rockland Co.*	16.10	81.3	10.4	4.6
Orchard Park town *Erie Co.*	3.90	95.8	9.6	8.3
Ossining town *Westchester Co.*	30.80	58.1	8.3	4.0
Oyster Bay town *Nassau Co.*	15.80	79.7	8.8	5.3
Penfield town *Monroe Co.*	7.60	91.3	9.9	7.4
Perinton town *Monroe Co.*	7.60	92.5	9.2	7.3
Pittsford town *Monroe Co.*	10.40	88.4	8.0	5.9
Port Chester village *Westchester Co.*	45.30	35.4	9.5	2.4
Poughkeepsie town *Dutchess Co.*	13.30	81.2	12.0	5.4
Poughkeepsie city *Dutchess Co.*	19.10	78.8	16.2	5.4
Queens borough *Queens Co.*	47.50	44.0	9.6	2.4
Ramapo town *Rockland Co.*	22.40	47.5	7.8	3.0
Riverhead town *Suffolk Co.*	13.40	80.6	13.8	9.1
Rochester city *Monroe Co.*	8.70	80.4	17.9	4.2
Rome city *Oneida Co.*	2.90	92.5	16.3	11.0
Rye town *Westchester Co.*	37.20	48.1	8.5	3.1
Salina town *Onondaga Co.*	5.30	92.3	13.1	8.6
Schenectady city *Schenectady Co.*	15.90	87.4	16.1	5.7
Smithtown town *Suffolk Co.*	8.10	88.6	8.9	6.0
Southampton town *Suffolk Co.*	19.00	76.6	9.2	5.9
Spring Valley village *Rockland Co.*	42.30	32.9	7.3	1.8
Staten Island borough *Richmond Co.*	22.20	68.7	10.0	4.6
Syracuse city *Onondaga Co.*	12.50	81.7	16.2	5.4
Tonawanda town *Erie Co.*	5.40	92.6	14.4	8.2
Tonawanda CDP *Erie Co.*	5.70	92.3	14.8	8.1
Troy city *Rensselaer Co.*	7.40	87.1	15.5	5.3
Union town *Broome Co.*	7.00	91.8	15.0	8.2
Uniondale CDP *Nassau Co.*	34.50	56.5	7.5	3.6
Utica city *Oneida Co.*	19.40	70.8	18.4	6.1
Valley Stream village *Nassau Co.*	34.90	61.7	9.3	4.7
Warwick town *Orange Co.*	6.30	89.2	12.7	8.9
Webster town *Monroe Co.*	9.80	88.7	10.5	6.9
West Babylon CDP *Suffolk Co.*	14.60	79.8	11.1	6.0
West Seneca CDP *Erie Co.*	2.50	96.0	12.7	8.5
White Plains city *Westchester Co.*	30.80	56.6	9.1	3.5
Yonkers city *Westchester Co.*	30.60	53.1	11.3	3.7
Yorktown town *Westchester Co.*	14.90	80.7	9.6	5.1

SOURCE: U.S. Census Bureau, American Community Survey, 2013-2017 Five-Year Estimates

Five Largest Ancestry Groups

Place	Group 1	Group 2	Group 3	Group 4	Group 5
Albany city *Albany Co.*	Irish (14.8%)	Italian (12.3%)	German (10.2%)	English (5.2%)	Polish (3.9%)
Amherst town *Erie Co.*	German (24.7%)	Italian (19.0%)	Irish (15.9%)	Polish (13.8%)	English (8.1%)
Babylon town *Suffolk Co.*	Italian (24.6%)	Irish (16.7%)	German (11.6%)	Polish (5.0%)	American (3.4%)
Bay Shore CDP *Suffolk Co.*	Italian (15.3%)	Irish (14.6%)	German (8.6%)	Haitian (3.2%)	English (2.9%)
Bethlehem town *Albany Co.*	Irish (25.7%)	German (18.7%)	Italian (17.0%)	English (12.8%)	Polish (6.5%)
Binghamton city *Broome Co.*	Irish (19.2%)	German (13.8%)	Italian (11.5%)	English (8.9%)	Polish (4.8%)
Brentwood CDP *Suffolk Co.*	Italian (4.2%)	Haitian (3.5%)	Irish (2.9%)	German (1.6%)	American (1.3%)
Brighton CDP *Monroe Co.*	German (17.8%)	Irish (14.1%)	Italian (12.4%)	English (11.0%)	Polish (5.3%)
Bronx borough *Bronx Co.*	Jamaican (4.7%)	Italian (3.0%)	American (2.8%)	African (2.6%)	Irish (1.9%)
Brookhaven town *Suffolk Co.*	Italian (27.8%)	Irish (20.2%)	German (16.5%)	American (5.2%)	Polish (4.6%)
Brooklyn borough *Kings Co.*	American (6.0%)	Italian (5.1%)	Irish (3.4%)	Jamaican (3.3%)	Haitian (3.0%)
Buffalo city *Erie Co.*	Irish (12.1%)	German (12.0%)	Italian (10.7%)	Polish (9.0%)	English (3.6%)
Carmel town *Putnam Co.*	Italian (31.1%)	Irish (23.5%)	German (11.9%)	American (4.9%)	Polish (4.7%)
Centereach CDP *Suffolk Co.*	Italian (32.6%)	Irish (23.4%)	German (18.5%)	Polish (4.2%)	American (3.7%)
Central Islip CDP *Suffolk Co.*	Italian (5.8%)	Irish (5.4%)	German (4.8%)	African (4.1%)	Haitian (3.1%)
Cheektowaga town *Erie Co.*	Polish (31.3%)	German (26.4%)	Italian (15.5%)	Irish (14.7%)	English (5.3%)
Cicero town *Onondaga Co.*	Irish (24.9%)	Italian (21.7%)	German (19.5%)	English (12.1%)	Polish (8.0%)
Clarence town *Erie Co.*	German (33.9%)	Italian (25.0%)	Irish (18.2%)	Polish (15.8%)	English (8.9%)
Clarkstown town *Rockland Co.*	Italian (20.6%)	Irish (17.1%)	German (6.8%)	American (5.2%)	Haitian (4.6%)
Clay town *Onondaga Co.*	Irish (25.2%)	Italian (21.3%)	German (20.2%)	English (10.5%)	Polish (7.2%)
Clifton Park town *Saratoga Co.*	Irish (24.2%)	Italian (19.5%)	German (18.2%)	English (11.5%)	Polish (7.3%)
Colonie town *Albany Co.*	Irish (23.8%)	Italian (19.1%)	German (14.8%)	English (7.3%)	Polish (6.5%)
Commack CDP *Suffolk Co.*	Italian (34.6%)	Irish (19.2%)	German (13.0%)	Polish (6.7%)	Russian (4.7%)
Coram CDP *Suffolk Co.*	Italian (24.0%)	Irish (15.3%)	German (12.0%)	American (8.4%)	English (4.3%)
Cortlandt town *Westchester Co.*	Italian (23.3%)	Irish (20.1%)	German (11.4%)	English (4.9%)	American (4.1%)
East Meadow CDP *Nassau Co.*	Italian (21.7%)	Irish (12.7%)	German (8.4%)	Polish (5.3%)	American (4.0%)
Eastchester town *Westchester Co.*	Italian (32.9%)	Irish (19.8%)	German (9.2%)	American (6.1%)	English (4.9%)
Elmont CDP *Nassau Co.*	Haitian (15.6%)	Jamaican (9.9%)	Italian (7.1%)	German (3.0%)	Irish (2.5%)
Franklin Square CDP *Nassau Co.*	Italian (33.3%)	Irish (12.6%)	German (8.0%)	Polish (4.1%)	Greek (2.7%)
Freeport village *Nassau Co.*	Irish (7.5%)	Italian (6.6%)	German (4.8%)	Jamaican (4.0%)	American (2.9%)
Glenville town *Schenectady Co.*	Irish (23.5%)	Italian (20.9%)	German (19.4%)	English (12.9%)	Polish (9.9%)
Greece town *Monroe Co.*	Italian (26.0%)	German (21.7%)	Irish (17.5%)	English (10.5%)	Polish (4.9%)
Greenburgh town *Westchester Co.*	Italian (14.9%)	Irish (12.4%)	German (7.8%)	American (5.4%)	Polish (4.7%)
Guilderland town *Albany Co.*	Irish (23.1%)	Italian (19.4%)	German (15.6%)	English (10.5%)	Polish (6.3%)
Hamburg town *Erie Co.*	German (31.5%)	Irish (25.7%)	Polish (22.6%)	Italian (17.4%)	English (7.8%)
Haverstraw town *Rockland Co.*	Irish (12.0%)	Italian (12.0%)	German (5.5%)	Haitian (4.7%)	American (3.3%)
Hempstead town *Nassau Co.*	Italian (18.3%)	Irish (13.5%)	German (8.3%)	American (4.0%)	Polish (4.0%)
Hempstead village *Nassau Co.*	Jamaican (8.4%)	Haitian (3.6%)	(a) (1.7%)	Italian (1.7%)	Guyanese (1.4%)
Henrietta town *Monroe Co.*	German (18.5%)	Italian (13.4%)	Irish (12.5%)	English (8.4%)	American (7.3%)
Hicksville CDP *Nassau Co.*	Italian (17.9%)	Irish (16.6%)	German (10.5%)	Polish (3.9%)	English (3.5%)
Huntington town *Suffolk Co.*	Italian (24.8%)	Irish (18.2%)	German (13.5%)	Polish (5.4%)	American (5.4%)
Huntington Station CDP *Suffolk Co.*	Italian (15.0%)	Irish (11.4%)	German (10.2%)	American (4.9%)	Polish (4.2%)
Irondequoit CDP *Monroe Co.*	Italian (20.9%)	German (20.8%)	Irish (15.1%)	English (9.9%)	Polish (6.0%)
Islip town *Suffolk Co.*	Italian (20.7%)	Irish (17.2%)	German (12.1%)	Polish (3.1%)	English (3.1%)
Ithaca city *Tompkins Co.*	Irish (9.3%)	German (8.7%)	American (6.8%)	Italian (6.7%)	English (5.5%)
Jamestown city *Chautauqua Co.*	Italian (16.4%)	German (15.6%)	Swedish (15.5%)	Irish (13.4%)	English (9.4%)
Lancaster town *Erie Co.*	Polish (32.0%)	German (31.3%)	Italian (19.9%)	Irish (15.0%)	English (6.6%)
Levittown CDP *Nassau Co.*	Italian (26.5%)	Irish (21.2%)	German (12.9%)	Polish (4.3%)	English (4.2%)
Long Beach city *Nassau Co.*	Irish (20.5%)	Italian (17.5%)	German (10.1%)	American (7.3%)	Russian (5.9%)
Mamaroneck town *Westchester Co.*	Italian (15.7%)	Irish (12.2%)	German (8.6%)	American (7.6%)	English (6.1%)

Place	Group 1	Group 2	Group 3	Group 4	Group 5
Manhattan borough *New York Co.*	Irish (6.7%)	German (6.1%)	Italian (6.1%)	American (5.2%)	English (4.2%)
Manlius town *Onondaga Co.*	Irish (26.4%)	German (18.5%)	Italian (15.8%)	English (13.7%)	Polish (5.6%)
Monroe town *Orange Co.*	American (18.9%)	Hungarian (10.0%)	Italian (9.2%)	Irish (8.3%)	German (4.5%)
Mount Pleasant town *Westchester Co.*	Italian (26.1%)	Irish (15.0%)	German (8.3%)	American (5.5%)	English (4.0%)
Mount Vernon city *Westchester Co.*	Jamaican (19.8%)	Italian (6.3%)	American (3.2%)	Irish (2.9%)	Haitian (2.9%)
New City CDP *Rockland Co.*	Italian (17.8%)	Irish (15.2%)	German (7.3%)	Russian (6.5%)	Polish (6.1%)
New Rochelle city *Westchester Co.*	Italian (16.3%)	Irish (7.7%)	American (4.8%)	German (4.2%)	Jamaican (3.3%)
New York city *New York Co.*	Italian (6.4%)	American (4.7%)	Irish (4.4%)	German (3.0%)	Jamaican (2.7%)
Newburgh town *Orange Co.*	Italian (23.0%)	Irish (18.2%)	German (9.6%)	American (9.0%)	English (5.9%)
Niagara Falls city *Niagara Co.*	Italian (18.0%)	American (12.9%)	German (12.8%)	Irish (12.2%)	Polish (7.4%)
North Hempstead town *Nassau Co.*	Italian (13.8%)	Irish (10.0%)	German (6.6%)	American (5.8%)	Polish (4.8%)
North Tonawanda city *Niagara Co.*	German (30.5%)	Italian (19.5%)	Polish (18.7%)	Irish (18.5%)	English (10.2%)
Oceanside CDP *Nassau Co.*	Italian (30.6%)	Irish (16.8%)	German (9.3%)	Polish (7.2%)	Russian (6.0%)
Orangetown town *Rockland Co.*	Irish (30.4%)	Italian (17.0%)	German (10.0%)	American (5.7%)	English (4.3%)
Orchard Park town *Erie Co.*	German (27.8%)	Irish (27.6%)	Polish (20.4%)	Italian (17.0%)	English (8.5%)
Ossining town *Westchester Co.*	Italian (14.0%)	Irish (10.7%)	German (6.1%)	English (3.8%)	American (3.4%)
Oyster Bay town *Nassau Co.*	Italian (27.6%)	Irish (18.7%)	German (12.3%)	Polish (5.8%)	Russian (4.3%)
Penfield town *Monroe Co.*	Italian (22.6%)	German (20.5%)	Irish (18.2%)	English (14.3%)	Polish (6.5%)
Perinton town *Monroe Co.*	German (23.3%)	Italian (20.2%)	Irish (19.8%)	English (14.8%)	Polish (6.4%)
Pittsford town *Monroe Co.*	Irish (18.7%)	German (17.4%)	Italian (16.5%)	English (14.8%)	Polish (6.1%)
Port Chester village *Westchester Co.*	Italian (12.9%)	Irish (4.7%)	American (4.5%)	German (3.1%)	English (2.1%)
Poughkeepsie town *Dutchess Co.*	Italian (20.0%)	Irish (17.0%)	German (12.4%)	English (6.6%)	Polish (5.3%)
Poughkeepsie city *Dutchess Co.*	Irish (12.4%)	Italian (11.8%)	German (7.3%)	Jamaican (6.8%)	American (5.3%)
Queens borough *Queens Co.*	Italian (5.5%)	American (3.8%)	Irish (3.7%)	Jamaican (2.8%)	Guyanese (2.8%)
Ramapo town *Rockland Co.*	American (12.5%)	Hungarian (7.6%)	European (7.1%)	Haitian (6.3%)	Italian (6.1%)
Riverhead town *Suffolk Co.*	Irish (18.5%)	Italian (17.6%)	German (13.8%)	Polish (10.8%)	American (5.5%)
Rochester city *Monroe Co.*	German (9.0%)	Irish (8.7%)	Italian (8.1%)	English (5.1%)	Polish (2.6%)
Rome city *Oneida Co.*	American (22.6%)	Italian (20.5%)	Irish (14.0%)	German (12.1%)	English (7.0%)
Rye town *Westchester Co.*	Italian (16.7%)	Irish (6.8%)	American (6.2%)	German (4.4%)	Russian (2.5%)
Salina town *Onondaga Co.*	Italian (25.3%)	Irish (22.8%)	German (20.3%)	English (11.5%)	Polish (7.9%)
Schenectady city *Schenectady Co.*	Italian (13.9%)	Irish (11.7%)	German (9.7%)	Guyanese (5.5%)	Polish (5.5%)
Smithtown town *Suffolk Co.*	Italian (34.7%)	Irish (23.2%)	German (18.1%)	Polish (6.2%)	English (5.4%)
Southampton town *Suffolk Co.*	Irish (17.8%)	Italian (14.4%)	German (13.4%)	English (8.1%)	Polish (6.8%)
Spring Valley village *Rockland Co.*	Haitian (19.1%)	American (8.1%)	Hungarian (3.7%)	Jamaican (3.5%)	Polish (3.1%)
Staten Island borough *Richmond Co.*	Italian (30.2%)	Irish (11.8%)	American (6.1%)	German (4.2%)	Polish (3.6%)
Syracuse city *Onondaga Co.*	Irish (14.1%)	Italian (11.7%)	German (10.6%)	English (5.2%)	Polish (4.0%)
Tonawanda town *Erie Co.*	German (28.6%)	Italian (24.1%)	Irish (19.6%)	Polish (15.2%)	English (8.8%)
Tonawanda CDP *Erie Co.*	German (28.2%)	Italian (23.3%)	Irish (19.1%)	Polish (15.8%)	English (8.9%)
Troy city *Rensselaer Co.*	Irish (21.7%)	Italian (14.7%)	German (9.9%)	French (6.5%)	English (6.0%)
Union town *Broome Co.*	Irish (17.1%)	Italian (15.6%)	German (13.9%)	English (10.6%)	Polish (6.9%)
Uniondale CDP *Nassau Co.*	Jamaican (6.2%)	Italian (5.6%)	Haitian (5.6%)	Irish (4.0%)	American (2.9%)
Utica city *Oneida Co.*	Italian (16.9%)	Irish (9.8%)	German (7.3%)	American (6.4%)	Yugoslavian (5.6%)
Valley Stream village *Nassau Co.*	Italian (12.4%)	Irish (7.1%)	German (5.6%)	American (4.1%)	Haitian (3.1%)
Warwick town *Orange Co.*	Irish (24.1%)	Italian (18.5%)	German (15.9%)	American (13.5%)	English (6.8%)
Webster town *Monroe Co.*	Italian (25.7%)	German (23.4%)	Irish (16.9%)	English (11.9%)	Polish (7.1%)
West Babylon CDP *Suffolk Co.*	Italian (31.4%)	Irish (18.3%)	German (13.5%)	Polish (6.0%)	English (3.3%)
West Seneca CDP *Erie Co.*	German (30.3%)	Polish (27.1%)	Irish (24.7%)	Italian (19.4%)	English (5.2%)
White Plains city *Westchester Co.*	Italian (13.9%)	Irish (9.1%)	German (5.7%)	American (5.0%)	Russian (2.9%)
Yonkers city *Westchester Co.*	Italian (14.1%)	Irish (10.9%)	American (4.4%)	German (3.3%)	Polish (2.3%)
Yorktown town *Westchester Co.*	Italian (32.4%)	Irish (19.4%)	German (10.7%)	American (4.9%)	English (4.7%)

NOTE: "French" excludes Basque; (a) Trinidadian and Tobagonian; Please refer to the User Guide for more information.
SOURCE: U.S. Census Bureau, American Community Survey, 2013-2017 Five-Year Estimates

Marriage Status

Place	Never Married (%)	Now Married[1] (%)	Separated (%)	Widowed (%)	Divorced (%)
Albany city *Albany Co.*	59.4	26.5	1.9	5.5	8.5
Amherst town *Erie Co.*	35.0	49.9	1.4	6.6	8.4
Babylon town *Suffolk Co.*	35.5	49.5	2.0	6.5	8.5
Bay Shore CDP *Suffolk Co.*	38.1	47.1	3.1	5.0	9.8
Bethlehem town *Albany Co.*	27.9	58.1	0.7	6.6	7.5
Binghamton city *Broome Co.*	46.4	32.6	2.6	7.8	13.2
Brentwood CDP *Suffolk Co.*	45.2	42.0	2.8	4.5	8.3
Brighton CDP *Monroe Co.*	35.9	47.6	1.3	7.3	9.2
Bronx borough *Bronx Co.*	48.8	36.5	5.2	5.6	9.2
Brookhaven town *Suffolk Co.*	33.7	52.0	1.7	5.9	8.5
Brooklyn borough *Kings Co.*	44.1	43.3	3.1	5.4	7.1
Buffalo city *Erie Co.*	51.5	31.9	3.1	6.3	10.3
Carmel town *Putnam Co.*	27.9	59.9	1.2	5.2	7.0
Centereach CDP *Suffolk Co.*	32.2	53.7	2.0	6.9	7.3
Central Islip CDP *Suffolk Co.*	46.1	39.3	2.1	5.5	9.2
Cheektowaga town *Erie Co.*	35.4	45.3	1.4	7.8	11.5
Cicero town *Onondaga Co.*	27.0	56.9	1.7	5.9	10.3
Clarence town *Erie Co.*	24.4	61.5	1.4	6.9	7.3
Clarkstown town *Rockland Co.*	28.9	57.3	1.4	6.8	7.1
Clay town *Onondaga Co.*	30.9	53.0	2.0	5.0	11.1
Clifton Park town *Saratoga Co.*	24.3	62.0	1.5	4.8	8.9
Colonie town *Albany Co.*	35.3	49.4	1.8	5.8	9.5
Commack CDP *Suffolk Co.*	27.1	60.2	0.7	7.1	5.6
Coram CDP *Suffolk Co.*	33.4	50.6	1.6	6.0	10.0
Cortlandt town *Westchester Co.*	29.1	56.5	1.5	5.3	9.1
East Meadow CDP *Nassau Co.*	30.9	53.0	2.3	8.5	7.6
Eastchester town *Westchester Co.*	29.9	56.3	1.6	6.4	7.4
Elmont CDP *Nassau Co.*	39.0	47.0	2.7	6.1	7.9
Franklin Square CDP *Nassau Co.*	33.4	53.9	0.6	6.6	6.1
Freeport village *Nassau Co.*	43.5	41.8	3.3	6.5	8.2
Glenville town *Schenectady Co.*	29.9	51.4	1.5	7.4	11.3
Greece town *Monroe Co.*	29.5	51.0	1.6	7.9	11.6
Greenburgh town *Westchester Co.*	31.9	55.2	1.4	5.1	7.8
Guilderland town *Albany Co.*	34.9	50.3	1.7	6.0	8.7
Hamburg town *Erie Co.*	28.5	52.0	1.1	7.1	12.4
Haverstraw town *Rockland Co.*	36.2	48.4	2.6	5.3	10.1
Hempstead town *Nassau Co.*	34.3	52.8	1.7	6.2	6.7
Hempstead village *Nassau Co.*	49.4	37.7	3.3	4.9	8.0
Henrietta town *Monroe Co.*	41.0	45.3	1.5	4.1	9.6
Hicksville CDP *Nassau Co.*	31.5	56.7	1.3	6.6	5.3
Huntington town *Suffolk Co.*	28.0	58.4	1.3	6.5	7.1
Huntington Station CDP *Suffolk Co.*	36.2	50.7	2.2	4.9	8.1
Irondequoit CDP *Monroe Co.*	30.6	50.4	1.9	7.0	12.0
Islip town *Suffolk Co.*	36.3	49.6	2.0	5.9	8.2
Ithaca city *Tompkins Co.*	76.8	18.0	1.1	1.4	3.8
Jamestown city *Chautauqua Co.*	35.4	41.7	3.7	6.8	16.1
Lancaster town *Erie Co.*	27.7	56.6	2.0	6.4	9.3
Levittown CDP *Nassau Co.*	30.5	56.0	1.7	6.8	6.6
Long Beach city *Nassau Co.*	37.7	43.5	2.4	6.5	12.3
Mamaroneck town *Westchester Co.*	28.3	59.3	0.7	4.7	7.7

Place	Never Married (%)	Now Married[1] (%)	Separated (%)	Widowed (%)	Divorced (%)
Manhattan borough *New York Co.*	50.0	36.8	2.6	4.8	8.4
Manlius town *Onondaga Co.*	22.9	58.6	1.3	7.5	11.0
Monroe town *Orange Co.*	29.2	63.2	1.0	3.1	4.4
Mount Pleasant town *Westchester Co.*	33.0	56.2	1.8	4.6	6.2
Mount Vernon city *Westchester Co.*	44.9	38.0	3.7	6.5	10.6
New City CDP *Rockland Co.*	27.7	61.3	1.0	5.4	5.7
New Rochelle city *Westchester Co.*	36.1	49.3	2.5	6.5	8.1
New York city *New York Co.*	43.9	42.7	3.1	5.6	7.8
Newburgh town *Orange Co.*	28.4	55.8	2.1	6.2	9.7
Niagara Falls city *Niagara Co.*	41.4	39.2	3.0	7.3	12.1
North Hempstead town *Nassau Co.*	28.2	59.3	1.1	6.5	6.0
North Tonawanda city *Niagara Co.*	31.8	48.2	2.1	8.0	12.1
Oceanside CDP *Nassau Co.*	29.3	59.6	1.2	6.6	4.6
Orangetown town *Rockland Co.*	34.6	52.2	1.4	6.3	6.9
Orchard Park town *Erie Co.*	25.9	59.6	1.4	5.9	8.6
Ossining town *Westchester Co.*	34.1	52.7	2.0	5.0	8.3
Oyster Bay town *Nassau Co.*	28.0	59.4	1.2	6.8	5.8
Penfield town *Monroe Co.*	22.7	60.5	1.4	7.3	9.5
Perinton town *Monroe Co.*	24.2	59.9	1.2	5.4	10.4
Pittsford town *Monroe Co.*	28.8	59.0	0.7	6.1	6.1
Port Chester village *Westchester Co.*	38.7	49.9	4.0	4.3	7.1
Poughkeepsie town *Dutchess Co.*	40.1	46.0	2.2	6.0	7.9
Poughkeepsie city *Dutchess Co.*	47.6	36.2	3.7	5.8	10.3
Queens borough *Queens Co.*	38.5	47.9	2.6	6.1	7.5
Ramapo town *Rockland Co.*	33.5	55.7	1.9	5.0	5.8
Riverhead town *Suffolk Co.*	29.8	52.7	2.0	8.5	9.0
Rochester city *Monroe Co.*	56.2	27.5	3.9	5.2	11.1
Rome city *Oneida Co.*	37.0	42.3	3.4	7.6	13.1
Rye town *Westchester Co.*	34.4	53.2	2.9	4.8	7.6
Salina town *Onondaga Co.*	33.0	46.9	2.3	6.9	13.2
Schenectady city *Schenectady Co.*	45.7	36.2	3.3	7.2	10.9
Smithtown town *Suffolk Co.*	26.9	59.6	0.9	7.1	6.4
Southampton town *Suffolk Co.*	31.5	51.7	1.4	7.2	9.7
Spring Valley village *Rockland Co.*	40.0	48.2	4.2	4.6	7.2
Staten Island borough *Richmond Co.*	33.3	53.3	1.8	6.5	6.9
Syracuse city *Onondaga Co.*	54.0	30.2	2.9	5.8	10.0
Tonawanda town *Erie Co.*	29.9	49.8	1.6	8.5	11.8
Tonawanda CDP *Erie Co.*	29.6	49.0	1.7	9.2	12.2
Troy city *Rensselaer Co.*	55.0	30.7	2.3	4.9	9.5
Union town *Broome Co.*	33.0	47.3	2.4	7.4	12.3
Uniondale CDP *Nassau Co.*	47.4	39.7	2.2	5.8	7.0
Utica city *Oneida Co.*	43.8	37.0	2.6	7.8	11.4
Valley Stream village *Nassau Co.*	32.9	53.4	1.7	5.4	8.3
Warwick town *Orange Co.*	26.2	56.6	1.9	6.7	10.5
Webster town *Monroe Co.*	25.5	59.0	1.4	6.8	8.7
West Babylon CDP *Suffolk Co.*	31.2	51.8	1.8	7.9	9.1
West Seneca CDP *Erie Co.*	30.7	51.0	0.9	8.3	10.0
White Plains city *Westchester Co.*	36.1	49.9	2.6	5.9	8.2
Yonkers city *Westchester Co.*	39.2	45.9	3.2	6.3	8.6
Yorktown town *Westchester Co.*	26.6	58.9	1.6	6.6	7.9

NOTE: (1) Includes separated.
SOURCE: U.S. Census Bureau, American Community Survey, 2013-2017 Five-Year Estimates

Employment by Occupation

Place	MBF[1] (%)	CES[2] (%)	ELCAM[3] (%)	HPT[4] (%)	S[5] (%)	SO[6] (%)	NRCM[7] (%)	PTMM[8] (%)
Albany city *Albany Co.*	13.2	7.2	13.5	6.8	23.6	24.9	4.4	6.4
Amherst town *Erie Co.*	18.8	7.2	17.1	9.2	14.8	23.4	4.2	5.3
Babylon town *Suffolk Co.*	12.1	4.0	10.8	5.4	19.2	27.0	9.8	11.8
Bay Shore CDP *Suffolk Co.*	12.1	1.6	11.0	5.0	23.9	26.2	7.8	12.3
Bethlehem town *Albany Co.*	21.5	8.8	20.6	7.4	10.6	21.4	4.7	5.0
Binghamton city *Broome Co.*	10.2	3.9	14.8	4.6	25.1	27.1	4.7	9.6
Brentwood CDP *Suffolk Co.*	6.2	2.1	5.0	3.4	26.6	22.8	10.7	23.2
Brighton CDP *Monroe Co.*	17.2	12.4	23.5	10.6	11.2	17.0	2.7	5.4
Bronx borough *Bronx Co.*	8.6	2.0	10.1	4.3	33.4	23.5	7.1	11.1
Brookhaven town *Suffolk Co.*	14.1	5.2	12.5	7.4	16.6	25.6	9.7	8.9
Brooklyn borough *Kings Co.*	14.2	4.5	17.2	4.9	23.1	21.5	6.2	8.5
Buffalo city *Erie Co.*	11.1	3.3	12.9	5.5	24.1	25.3	5.2	12.7
Carmel town *Putnam Co.*	14.6	4.7	14.6	7.4	16.4	24.2	12.7	5.4
Centereach CDP *Suffolk Co.*	15.9	4.6	9.2	7.0	18.5	27.6	8.6	8.6
Central Islip CDP *Suffolk Co.*	7.0	1.9	6.5	5.4	23.3	25.6	9.4	20.8
Cheektowaga town *Erie Co.*	12.3	4.1	8.7	6.6	17.7	29.1	6.9	14.7
Cicero town *Onondaga Co.*	15.0	6.0	10.6	8.0	15.6	27.2	6.9	10.7
Clarence town *Erie Co.*	22.8	5.2	16.6	7.7	12.6	22.2	6.8	5.9
Clarkstown town *Rockland Co.*	18.7	5.9	14.5	10.3	16.0	23.0	5.7	5.9
Clay town *Onondaga Co.*	15.6	6.1	10.8	8.8	14.7	27.4	7.1	9.6
Clifton Park town *Saratoga Co.*	22.4	12.6	14.2	7.7	8.9	22.5	6.3	5.4
Colonie town *Albany Co.*	19.3	8.1	11.6	7.3	15.4	26.0	5.0	7.2
Commack CDP *Suffolk Co.*	20.2	5.2	16.5	8.0	12.5	26.9	5.4	5.3
Coram CDP *Suffolk Co.*	12.6	4.1	13.6	6.7	17.1	27.0	9.5	9.4
Cortlandt town *Westchester Co.*	19.5	6.4	20.0	5.7	15.6	21.0	5.7	6.1
East Meadow CDP *Nassau Co.*	14.6	3.8	14.5	8.6	16.2	28.4	7.5	6.5
Eastchester town *Westchester Co.*	25.9	4.3	20.4	6.5	12.9	22.2	5.6	2.1
Elmont CDP *Nassau Co.*	10.3	3.1	9.1	9.1	24.5	25.4	8.3	10.1
Franklin Square CDP *Nassau Co.*	12.5	4.5	11.7	8.6	17.6	27.7	8.9	8.5
Freeport village *Nassau Co.*	10.8	2.9	12.4	6.0	24.0	23.7	8.5	11.7
Glenville town *Schenectady Co.*	16.1	6.9	13.3	7.0	15.3	28.6	5.9	6.8
Greece town *Monroe Co.*	14.2	6.1	10.0	6.7	18.5	25.1	6.8	12.5
Greenburgh town *Westchester Co.*	21.8	7.2	21.5	8.1	14.3	18.8	3.9	4.5
Guilderland town *Albany Co.*	18.7	10.1	15.1	7.2	12.9	25.9	4.5	5.6
Hamburg town *Erie Co.*	13.5	4.7	12.3	7.6	18.4	25.1	7.2	11.2
Haverstraw town *Rockland Co.*	8.5	3.5	10.0	7.3	26.9	23.7	8.0	12.1
Hempstead town *Nassau Co.*	15.8	3.8	14.5	7.4	18.1	25.2	7.2	8.0
Hempstead village *Nassau Co.*	7.4	2.1	6.7	3.8	35.2	21.7	10.4	12.7
Henrietta town *Monroe Co.*	14.0	10.9	11.0	7.1	17.1	23.8	6.0	10.2
Hicksville CDP *Nassau Co.*	14.1	4.3	12.0	7.4	17.2	28.6	7.6	8.8
Huntington town *Suffolk Co.*	20.0	5.3	17.0	7.2	13.2	25.0	6.4	5.9
Huntington Station CDP *Suffolk Co.*	11.8	3.8	13.3	4.9	24.6	21.1	9.2	11.4
Irondequoit CDP *Monroe Co.*	16.1	7.5	12.8	6.8	17.8	23.5	5.8	9.7
Islip town *Suffolk Co.*	12.1	3.3	11.3	5.0	19.9	26.1	9.2	13.2
Ithaca city *Tompkins Co.*	10.7	13.2	28.3	3.0	16.7	21.0	3.1	4.0
Jamestown city *Chautauqua Co.*	9.4	2.6	10.9	4.6	18.6	26.1	7.5	20.3
Lancaster town *Erie Co.*	17.4	4.5	9.7	7.4	16.5	26.8	5.3	12.3
Levittown CDP *Nassau Co.*	15.0	3.9	13.5	5.8	16.8	28.5	7.0	9.5
Long Beach city *Nassau Co.*	20.3	3.6	17.3	5.2	15.9	26.7	6.2	4.8
Mamaroneck town *Westchester Co.*	28.8	4.8	20.7	4.5	16.8	17.5	4.8	2.0

Place	MBF[1] (%)	CES[2] (%)	ELCAM[3] (%)	HPT[4] (%)	S[5] (%)	SO[6] (%)	NRCM[7] (%)	PTMM[8] (%)
Manhattan borough *New York Co.*	27.1	6.5	21.1	5.3	13.9	20.0	2.2	3.8
Manlius town *Onondaga Co.*	18.9	5.6	19.2	9.9	11.5	23.7	5.7	5.5
Monroe town *Orange Co.*	13.8	5.0	17.0	4.5	16.0	29.4	5.9	8.3
Mount Pleasant town *Westchester Co.*	21.5	4.9	17.7	7.0	16.7	19.1	7.3	5.7
Mount Vernon city *Westchester Co.*	12.7	2.5	12.4	7.4	25.8	23.6	7.3	8.2
New City CDP *Rockland Co.*	20.7	6.4	14.9	11.2	12.7	23.8	4.7	5.5
New Rochelle city *Westchester Co.*	16.1	4.1	15.4	7.8	21.1	20.0	8.9	6.6
New York city *New York Co.*	15.9	4.4	15.2	5.2	22.8	22.0	6.1	8.4
Newburgh town *Orange Co.*	13.3	4.1	13.0	6.3	17.5	26.6	9.0	10.2
Niagara Falls city *Niagara Co.*	8.9	2.8	10.8	4.6	25.1	27.9	7.0	13.0
North Hempstead town *Nassau Co.*	20.7	5.5	14.4	10.8	12.3	24.6	5.2	6.5
North Tonawanda city *Niagara Co.*	11.3	4.5	10.5	6.0	16.9	28.0	7.9	14.9
Oceanside CDP *Nassau Co.*	20.0	3.7	19.2	4.0	14.5	28.4	5.6	4.6
Orangetown town *Rockland Co.*	17.8	5.4	19.7	7.5	17.6	21.7	6.5	3.8
Orchard Park town *Erie Co.*	19.9	6.5	13.8	8.5	14.6	22.7	5.2	8.7
Ossining town *Westchester Co.*	17.7	4.2	14.8	5.2	21.4	19.8	11.6	5.3
Oyster Bay town *Nassau Co.*	20.3	5.3	15.0	8.0	13.5	26.5	5.8	5.6
Penfield town *Monroe Co.*	21.1	8.9	14.4	9.7	11.4	24.5	4.0	6.0
Perinton town *Monroe Co.*	20.4	9.9	16.3	7.3	13.4	23.5	4.6	4.6
Pittsford town *Monroe Co.*	22.8	7.5	21.3	10.6	10.4	21.4	2.0	4.0
Port Chester village *Westchester Co.*	9.4	1.3	6.7	3.8	34.2	21.8	12.0	10.7
Poughkeepsie town *Dutchess Co.*	12.2	7.7	15.3	5.7	19.4	24.9	5.7	9.2
Poughkeepsie city *Dutchess Co.*	7.8	4.3	11.9	5.3	29.0	24.2	8.0	9.5
Queens borough *Queens Co.*	12.9	4.0	11.1	5.3	24.6	23.3	8.2	10.7
Ramapo town *Rockland Co.*	14.8	3.8	17.5	7.1	20.3	23.2	6.9	6.5
Riverhead town *Suffolk Co.*	15.0	5.6	8.8	5.1	18.3	28.2	11.8	7.2
Rochester city *Monroe Co.*	9.5	4.6	12.8	6.6	24.9	24.2	4.7	12.7
Rome city *Oneida Co.*	12.1	5.4	11.0	7.7	21.7	24.9	4.8	12.5
Rye town *Westchester Co.*	15.4	2.1	10.9	4.7	27.1	21.8	9.6	8.5
Salina town *Onondaga Co.*	14.9	5.2	12.0	6.2	17.1	28.2	5.7	10.8
Schenectady city *Schenectady Co.*	10.7	4.6	10.5	6.1	23.4	25.5	5.9	13.2
Smithtown town *Suffolk Co.*	19.6	5.7	16.8	7.6	12.5	25.9	6.7	5.2
Southampton town *Suffolk Co.*	15.3	2.6	12.6	6.3	18.3	22.3	17.2	5.4
Spring Valley village *Rockland Co.*	8.7	2.0	8.3	4.1	35.0	22.0	10.0	9.9
Staten Island borough *Richmond Co.*	14.4	4.1	14.3	7.9	19.3	23.2	8.7	8.1
Syracuse city *Onondaga Co.*	9.4	4.3	15.5	5.9	24.0	25.2	5.1	10.6
Tonawanda town *Erie Co.*	15.2	5.1	12.8	6.5	17.1	28.6	5.6	9.1
Tonawanda CDP *Erie Co.*	14.8	5.5	12.3	6.6	17.5	28.1	6.0	9.2
Troy city *Rensselaer Co.*	12.0	7.8	13.8	4.5	20.6	24.2	6.1	11.0
Union town *Broome Co.*	11.8	7.2	11.9	8.1	19.1	26.0	5.2	10.7
Uniondale CDP *Nassau Co.*	9.5	2.2	11.2	7.4	25.9	23.8	8.3	11.7
Utica city *Oneida Co.*	9.2	3.2	11.0	5.6	26.7	23.9	6.4	14.1
Valley Stream village *Nassau Co.*	12.4	3.8	11.4	9.7	19.0	27.4	7.9	8.4
Warwick town *Orange Co.*	15.5	5.5	12.7	5.4	17.4	24.8	7.5	11.3
Webster town *Monroe Co.*	18.4	10.3	11.9	7.8	12.2	23.1	6.9	9.5
West Babylon CDP *Suffolk Co.*	13.8	3.7	11.2	4.8	15.2	29.8	10.4	11.0
West Seneca CDP *Erie Co.*	14.0	5.6	10.1	7.7	15.4	27.0	6.6	13.6
White Plains city *Westchester Co.*	20.9	5.3	16.7	5.5	21.9	19.8	5.0	4.8
Yonkers city *Westchester Co.*	13.8	3.8	12.6	7.0	21.2	24.2	7.9	9.4
Yorktown town *Westchester Co.*	18.0	5.3	19.9	6.5	16.0	22.1	7.0	5.3

NOTES: (1) Management, business, and financial occupations; (2) Computer, engineering, and science occupations; (3) Education, legal, community service, arts, and media occupations; (4) Healthcare practitioners and technical occupations; (5) Service occupations; (6) Sales and office occupations; (7) Natural resources, construction, and maintenance occupations; (8) Production, transportation, and material moving occupations
SOURCE: U.S. Census Bureau, American Community Survey, 2013-2017 Five-Year Estimates

Educational Attainment

	Percent of Population 25 Years and Over with:		
Place	High School Diploma or Higher[1]	Bachelor's Degree or Higher	Graduate/Professional Degree
Albany city *Albany Co.*	89.6	38.1	18.4
Amherst town *Erie Co.*	95.4	55.3	28.6
Babylon town *Suffolk Co.*	88.0	25.8	9.7
Bay Shore CDP *Suffolk Co.*	85.0	30.6	14.1
Bethlehem town *Albany Co.*	97.0	58.6	33.0
Binghamton city *Broome Co.*	85.1	23.5	10.7
Brentwood CDP *Suffolk Co.*	69.5	13.0	4.0
Brighton CDP *Monroe Co.*	95.9	65.3	37.0
Bronx borough *Bronx Co.*	71.5	19.4	6.9
Brookhaven town *Suffolk Co.*	91.3	32.4	15.2
Brooklyn borough *Kings Co.*	80.7	35.2	13.9
Buffalo city *Erie Co.*	83.9	25.8	11.0
Carmel town *Putnam Co.*	93.2	37.1	15.5
Centereach CDP *Suffolk Co.*	91.8	29.1	12.2
Central Islip CDP *Suffolk Co.*	74.3	15.8	5.7
Cheektowaga town *Erie Co.*	91.5	22.2	8.0
Cicero town *Onondaga Co.*	94.9	31.9	12.8
Clarence town *Erie Co.*	96.3	50.1	25.3
Clarkstown town *Rockland Co.*	91.4	49.8	22.7
Clay town *Onondaga Co.*	94.5	35.1	13.3
Clifton Park town *Saratoga Co.*	97.5	55.7	26.0
Colonie town *Albany Co.*	92.8	41.0	18.2
Commack CDP *Suffolk Co.*	96.7	48.9	22.6
Coram CDP *Suffolk Co.*	92.5	34.2	14.3
Cortlandt town *Westchester Co.*	93.5	49.2	22.4
East Meadow CDP *Nassau Co.*	91.1	38.1	17.6
Eastchester town *Westchester Co.*	94.2	60.5	31.7
Elmont CDP *Nassau Co.*	87.5	28.0	9.7
Franklin Square CDP *Nassau Co.*	89.3	32.1	10.8
Freeport village *Nassau Co.*	80.8	27.8	11.2
Glenville town *Schenectady Co.*	95.9	36.9	16.5
Greece town *Monroe Co.*	92.2	28.4	10.2
Greenburgh town *Westchester Co.*	93.4	61.4	33.8
Guilderland town *Albany Co.*	97.8	50.3	26.5
Hamburg town *Erie Co.*	94.5	32.6	13.7
Haverstraw town *Rockland Co.*	82.5	28.4	11.3
Hempstead town *Nassau Co.*	89.6	39.4	17.3
Hempstead village *Nassau Co.*	69.5	18.9	7.5
Henrietta town *Monroe Co.*	90.0	37.0	15.5
Hicksville CDP *Nassau Co.*	90.9	35.0	12.5
Huntington town *Suffolk Co.*	93.4	51.4	24.4
Huntington Station CDP *Suffolk Co.*	79.6	34.3	14.8
Irondequoit CDP *Monroe Co.*	92.3	34.9	13.6
Islip town *Suffolk Co.*	85.2	28.3	12.4
Ithaca city *Tompkins Co.*	94.0	64.4	37.5
Jamestown city *Chautauqua Co.*	86.3	17.5	7.3
Lancaster town *Erie Co.*	95.1	33.4	12.9
Levittown CDP *Nassau Co.*	91.7	32.1	12.7
Long Beach city *Nassau Co.*	93.8	48.5	23.2
Mamaroneck town *Westchester Co.*	92.0	67.3	37.1

Place	Percent of Population 25 Years and Over with:		
	High School Diploma or Higher[1]	Bachelor's Degree or Higher	Graduate/Professional Degree
Manhattan borough *New York Co.*	86.8	60.7	29.1
Manlius town *Onondaga Co.*	96.7	52.2	26.9
Monroe town *Orange Co.*	82.5	29.3	11.3
Mount Pleasant town *Westchester Co.*	88.3	51.3	26.1
Mount Vernon city *Westchester Co.*	84.1	28.4	11.3
New City CDP *Rockland Co.*	94.6	58.4	28.3
New Rochelle city *Westchester Co.*	82.8	44.0	23.1
New York city *New York Co.*	81.1	36.7	15.2
Newburgh town *Orange Co.*	93.2	30.4	12.2
Niagara Falls city *Niagara Co.*	87.8	17.5	7.1
North Hempstead town *Nassau Co.*	91.2	54.3	26.3
North Tonawanda city *Niagara Co.*	92.7	24.5	9.9
Oceanside CDP *Nassau Co.*	95.0	44.6	19.5
Orangetown town *Rockland Co.*	91.3	51.2	23.4
Orchard Park town *Erie Co.*	96.2	45.8	21.1
Ossining town *Westchester Co.*	82.5	43.5	21.9
Oyster Bay town *Nassau Co.*	94.7	49.1	21.8
Penfield town *Monroe Co.*	94.0	53.0	24.8
Perinton town *Monroe Co.*	96.5	57.1	26.5
Pittsford town *Monroe Co.*	98.2	73.5	40.1
Port Chester village *Westchester Co.*	70.7	23.2	9.1
Poughkeepsie town *Dutchess Co.*	91.5	37.2	18.3
Poughkeepsie city *Dutchess Co.*	81.7	23.6	9.7
Queens borough *Queens Co.*	81.1	30.8	11.3
Ramapo town *Rockland Co.*	82.6	32.1	15.2
Riverhead town *Suffolk Co.*	88.0	27.0	11.9
Rochester city *Monroe Co.*	80.8	24.0	9.9
Rome city *Oneida Co.*	87.1	20.5	8.1
Rye town *Westchester Co.*	78.0	36.9	16.9
Salina town *Onondaga Co.*	91.4	28.1	11.0
Schenectady city *Schenectady Co.*	83.9	22.3	8.0
Smithtown town *Suffolk Co.*	95.5	48.0	22.9
Southampton town *Suffolk Co.*	91.7	39.7	17.1
Spring Valley village *Rockland Co.*	68.3	15.4	5.1
Staten Island borough *Richmond Co.*	88.7	32.1	13.0
Syracuse city *Onondaga Co.*	81.5	27.4	12.4
Tonawanda town *Erie Co.*	93.7	35.4	15.6
Tonawanda CDP *Erie Co.*	93.4	35.5	15.3
Troy city *Rensselaer Co.*	87.2	25.7	9.8
Union town *Broome Co.*	91.6	30.3	11.9
Uniondale CDP *Nassau Co.*	79.8	26.4	10.5
Utica city *Oneida Co.*	78.6	17.6	6.2
Valley Stream village *Nassau Co.*	90.8	37.4	15.3
Warwick town *Orange Co.*	94.2	37.1	15.6
Webster town *Monroe Co.*	95.4	44.9	20.0
West Babylon CDP *Suffolk Co.*	89.7	24.5	8.6
West Seneca CDP *Erie Co.*	93.9	28.3	11.1
White Plains city *Westchester Co.*	86.6	50.3	24.9
Yonkers city *Westchester Co.*	82.5	32.6	14.2
Yorktown town *Westchester Co.*	94.2	49.5	24.5

NOTE: (1) Includes General Equivalency Diploma (GED)
SOURCE: U.S. Census Bureau, American Community Survey, 2013-2017 Five-Year Estimates

Health Insurance

Place	Percent of Total Population with:				Percent of Population[1] Under Age 18 without Health Insurance
	Any Insurance	Private Insurance	Public Insurance	No Insurance	
Albany city *Albany Co.*	92.8	66.8	38.1	7.2	2.4
Amherst town *Erie Co.*	97.6	83.5	30.2	2.4	1.4
Babylon town *Suffolk Co.*	92.4	74.2	30.3	7.6	3.2
Bay Shore CDP *Suffolk Co.*	91.4	71.9	27.8	8.6	2.1
Bethlehem town *Albany Co.*	97.6	91.4	22.3	2.4	1.4
Binghamton city *Broome Co.*	93.7	52.7	54.7	6.3	1.3
Brentwood CDP *Suffolk Co.*	84.8	60.6	32.6	15.2	6.5
Brighton CDP *Monroe Co.*	96.2	83.4	26.5	3.8	2.9
Bronx borough *Bronx Co.*	88.9	44.1	54.6	11.1	3.2
Brookhaven town *Suffolk Co.*	94.4	78.4	28.7	5.6	1.8
Brooklyn borough *Kings Co.*	90.5	53.4	44.5	9.5	2.8
Buffalo city *Erie Co.*	93.7	49.5	54.1	6.3	1.9
Carmel town *Putnam Co.*	94.9	83.3	23.8	5.1	2.4
Centereach CDP *Suffolk Co.*	94.8	82.4	24.4	5.2	1.8
Central Islip CDP *Suffolk Co.*	85.6	61.1	33.1	14.4	4.5
Cheektowaga town *Erie Co.*	95.3	75.4	37.1	4.7	2.5
Cicero town *Onondaga Co.*	95.6	80.2	28.2	4.4	2.9
Clarence town *Erie Co.*	97.7	88.9	22.4	2.3	2.6
Clarkstown town *Rockland Co.*	95.3	80.1	29.0	4.7	2.6
Clay town *Onondaga Co.*	96.3	81.4	29.8	3.7	1.5
Clifton Park town *Saratoga Co.*	98.1	89.1	24.0	1.9	0.5
Colonie town *Albany Co.*	96.6	83.5	29.6	3.4	1.8
Commack CDP *Suffolk Co.*	97.4	87.2	23.9	2.6	1.6
Coram CDP *Suffolk Co.*	95.5	77.5	28.6	4.5	1.4
Cortlandt town *Westchester Co.*	95.9	84.0	24.2	4.1	2.6
East Meadow CDP *Nassau Co.*	93.9	80.1	29.9	6.1	2.8
Eastchester town *Westchester Co.*	96.1	86.9	23.0	3.9	0.6
Elmont CDP *Nassau Co.*	92.5	71.6	30.3	7.5	3.4
Franklin Square CDP *Nassau Co.*	94.4	77.3	28.5	5.6	1.9
Freeport village *Nassau Co.*	87.9	66.2	32.8	12.1	7.9
Glenville town *Schenectady Co.*	95.9	81.6	29.5	4.1	3.4
Greece town *Monroe Co.*	95.7	75.0	37.2	4.3	2.0
Greenburgh town *Westchester Co.*	94.8	83.0	23.8	5.2	2.3
Guilderland town *Albany Co.*	96.8	86.9	25.1	3.2	0.9
Hamburg town *Erie Co.*	96.7	82.8	29.4	3.3	1.9
Haverstraw town *Rockland Co.*	89.9	61.5	39.3	10.1	2.6
Hempstead town *Nassau Co.*	93.5	78.2	27.6	6.5	2.9
Hempstead village *Nassau Co.*	81.3	48.5	41.9	18.7	4.5
Henrietta town *Monroe Co.*	96.8	80.4	29.6	3.2	1.3
Hicksville CDP *Nassau Co.*	94.4	79.6	27.3	5.6	2.6
Huntington town *Suffolk Co.*	95.0	82.5	26.2	5.0	3.1
Huntington Station CDP *Suffolk Co.*	84.7	64.7	28.8	15.3	9.1
Irondequoit CDP *Monroe Co.*	96.4	76.4	36.4	3.6	2.6
Islip town *Suffolk Co.*	91.8	75.1	27.6	8.2	3.3
Ithaca city *Tompkins Co.*	94.2	81.8	17.4	5.8	6.7
Jamestown city *Chautauqua Co.*	93.4	53.6	54.2	6.6	6.1
Lancaster town *Erie Co.*	97.1	84.4	27.8	2.9	1.7
Levittown CDP *Nassau Co.*	96.3	84.7	25.3	3.7	2.4
Long Beach city *Nassau Co.*	92.7	76.8	29.4	7.3	0.4
Mamaroneck town *Westchester Co.*	95.9	84.0	22.7	4.1	1.2

Place	Percent of Total Population with:				Percent of Population[1] Under Age 18 without Health Insurance
	Any Insurance	Private Insurance	Public Insurance	No Insurance	
Manhattan borough *New York Co.*	93.3	68.3	33.3	6.7	2.1
Manlius town *Onondaga Co.*	96.9	80.8	32.7	3.1	3.2
Monroe town *Orange Co.*	96.4	50.2	54.6	3.6	1.3
Mount Pleasant town *Westchester Co.*	94.4	80.8	24.7	5.6	2.1
Mount Vernon city *Westchester Co.*	90.2	62.6	40.0	9.8	2.8
New City CDP *Rockland Co.*	96.9	85.9	25.4	3.1	1.3
New Rochelle city *Westchester Co.*	89.6	68.3	32.7	10.4	4.2
New York city *New York Co.*	90.2	56.6	42.0	9.8	3.0
Newburgh town *Orange Co.*	94.2	77.7	30.5	5.8	5.4
Niagara Falls city *Niagara Co.*	94.5	57.0	52.4	5.5	1.8
North Hempstead town *Nassau Co.*	93.9	81.6	25.8	6.1	3.6
North Tonawanda city *Niagara Co.*	95.8	76.0	37.9	4.2	1.5
Oceanside CDP *Nassau Co.*	96.6	85.0	24.0	3.4	2.3
Orangetown town *Rockland Co.*	95.0	81.4	27.9	5.0	6.1
Orchard Park town *Erie Co.*	98.1	87.4	27.4	1.9	0.7
Ossining town *Westchester Co.*	86.9	67.3	30.0	13.1	1.7
Oyster Bay town *Nassau Co.*	96.8	86.0	24.5	3.2	1.6
Penfield town *Monroe Co.*	97.7	83.5	30.6	2.3	1.7
Perinton town *Monroe Co.*	97.3	86.0	27.5	2.7	1.6
Pittsford town *Monroe Co.*	98.8	92.8	22.0	1.2	0.9
Port Chester village *Westchester Co.*	78.8	50.6	35.0	21.2	3.3
Poughkeepsie town *Dutchess Co.*	96.2	80.1	29.3	3.8	2.4
Poughkeepsie city *Dutchess Co.*	89.0	52.9	49.2	11.0	2.8
Queens borough *Queens Co.*	87.8	56.8	39.2	12.2	3.7
Ramapo town *Rockland Co.*	90.6	48.9	50.8	9.4	4.0
Riverhead town *Suffolk Co.*	92.2	72.9	38.2	7.8	2.4
Rochester city *Monroe Co.*	92.6	51.2	52.0	7.4	3.0
Rome city *Oneida Co.*	95.4	65.3	46.7	4.6	0.5
Rye town *Westchester Co.*	84.1	62.0	31.1	15.9	2.1
Salina town *Onondaga Co.*	95.8	76.9	38.2	4.2	2.4
Schenectady city *Schenectady Co.*	92.2	56.7	48.3	7.8	3.6
Smithtown town *Suffolk Co.*	97.7	88.7	23.5	2.3	1.4
Southampton town *Suffolk Co.*	87.2	70.3	33.0	12.8	4.4
Spring Valley village *Rockland Co.*	80.0	34.3	51.6	20.0	6.6
Staten Island borough *Richmond Co.*	94.1	70.8	33.0	5.9	2.5
Syracuse city *Onondaga Co.*	92.8	57.8	47.9	7.2	3.6
Tonawanda town *Erie Co.*	97.4	77.6	37.3	2.6	0.7
Tonawanda CDP *Erie Co.*	97.3	77.1	38.0	2.7	0.9
Troy city *Rensselaer Co.*	93.9	62.1	42.4	6.1	2.8
Union town *Broome Co.*	94.6	68.8	42.6	5.4	2.7
Uniondale CDP *Nassau Co.*	86.7	68.1	28.7	13.3	9.1
Utica city *Oneida Co.*	93.4	46.2	59.2	6.6	2.9
Valley Stream village *Nassau Co.*	92.6	75.7	27.4	7.4	4.9
Warwick town *Orange Co.*	96.9	83.8	27.0	3.1	2.0
Webster town *Monroe Co.*	96.8	83.6	28.9	3.2	2.3
West Babylon CDP *Suffolk Co.*	93.5	77.6	29.4	6.5	2.3
West Seneca CDP *Erie Co.*	96.6	80.5	34.0	3.4	0.5
White Plains city *Westchester Co.*	88.3	68.8	30.3	11.7	3.3
Yonkers city *Westchester Co.*	90.3	62.5	39.6	9.7	3.5
Yorktown town *Westchester Co.*	97.1	84.6	26.5	2.9	1.8

NOTE: (1) Civilian noninstitutionalized population.
SOURCE: U.S. Census Bureau, American Community Survey, 2013-2017 Five-Year Estimates

Income and Poverty

Place	Average Household Income ($)	Median Household Income ($)	Per Capita Income ($)	Households w/$100,000+ Income (%)	Poverty Rate (%)
Albany city *Albany Co.*	63,120	43,790	27,632	18.6	24.5
Amherst town *Erie Co.*	98,705	72,459	40,124	35.8	10.8
Babylon town *Suffolk Co.*	102,521	86,339	33,875	42.5	7.4
Bay Shore CDP *Suffolk Co.*	98,001	80,123	31,036	38.5	9.7
Bethlehem town *Albany Co.*	125,738	96,384	49,794	48.2	5.0
Binghamton city *Broome Co.*	48,530	31,103	21,710	10.1	33.3
Brentwood CDP *Suffolk Co.*	93,756	74,127	22,661	34.5	12.3
Brighton CDP *Monroe Co.*	97,641	70,567	43,174	33.9	10.8
Bronx borough *Bronx Co.*	53,730	36,593	19,721	13.9	29.7
Brookhaven town *Suffolk Co.*	108,666	89,594	37,341	44.1	7.5
Brooklyn borough *Kings Co.*	80,782	52,782	29,928	26.2	21.9
Buffalo city *Erie Co.*	50,456	34,268	22,294	12.1	30.9
Carmel town *Putnam Co.*	125,607	100,790	44,260	50.4	3.3
Centereach CDP *Suffolk Co.*	113,562	98,025	35,887	49.4	5.5
Central Islip CDP *Suffolk Co.*	81,255	67,804	24,830	29.1	13.0
Cheektowaga town *Erie Co.*	61,361	50,868	28,100	16.0	10.7
Cicero town *Onondaga Co.*	88,139	76,740	34,949	34.6	6.9
Clarence town *Erie Co.*	124,321	95,315	46,960	47.6	3.9
Clarkstown town *Rockland Co.*	135,868	111,025	47,603	55.9	6.1
Clay town *Onondaga Co.*	81,627	69,227	33,102	28.4	9.3
Clifton Park town *Saratoga Co.*	117,191	101,738	45,870	51.3	3.6
Colonie town *Albany Co.*	93,422	74,244	37,295	34.7	6.6
Commack CDP *Suffolk Co.*	143,371	124,461	48,513	60.8	3.9
Coram CDP *Suffolk Co.*	96,453	82,151	35,967	37.4	4.6
Cortlandt town *Westchester Co.*	136,721	103,266	49,381	51.5	5.5
East Meadow CDP *Nassau Co.*	116,731	94,513	39,549	48.1	4.6
Eastchester town *Westchester Co.*	181,054	116,014	70,816	55.3	3.2
Elmont CDP *Nassau Co.*	109,837	94,353	31,076	47.8	7.7
Franklin Square CDP *Nassau Co.*	111,068	99,919	34,193	50.0	5.7
Freeport village *Nassau Co.*	90,199	71,184	29,899	35.1	12.6
Glenville town *Schenectady Co.*	86,440	75,018	34,732	33.2	5.8
Greece town *Monroe Co.*	70,569	57,202	30,496	21.8	8.4
Greenburgh town *Westchester Co.*	168,520	120,256	62,358	59.0	4.8
Guilderland town *Albany Co.*	106,519	78,194	43,336	41.5	4.9
Hamburg town *Erie Co.*	80,594	65,349	34,327	27.9	6.8
Haverstraw town *Rockland Co.*	92,842	73,619	31,234	37.6	11.1
Hempstead town *Nassau Co.*	126,525	102,002	41,052	50.8	6.6
Hempstead village *Nassau Co.*	75,726	58,476	22,825	27.5	20.2
Henrietta town *Monroe Co.*	77,095	62,883	29,181	27.4	13.0
Hicksville CDP *Nassau Co.*	121,098	104,188	39,289	51.7	4.6
Huntington town *Suffolk Co.*	151,755	112,790	52,523	55.5	6.4
Huntington Station CDP *Suffolk Co.*	101,856	82,077	32,140	40.5	14.5
Irondequoit CDP *Monroe Co.*	70,493	56,986	31,341	21.2	8.6
Islip town *Suffolk Co.*	109,660	90,278	34,222	44.7	8.0
Ithaca city *Tompkins Co.*	54,565	31,967	18,985	16.6	43.4
Jamestown city *Chautauqua Co.*	43,076	31,875	18,983	6.8	29.7
Lancaster town *Erie Co.*	84,713	68,647	35,588	32.9	5.7
Levittown CDP *Nassau Co.*	118,657	108,179	38,792	53.8	4.6
Long Beach city *Nassau Co.*	110,820	85,619	49,055	44.5	7.7
Mamaroneck town *Westchester Co.*	225,891	121,261	81,382	57.6	5.5

Place	Average Household Income ($)	Median Household Income ($)	Per Capita Income ($)	Households w/$100,000+ Income (%)	Poverty Rate (%)
Manhattan borough *New York Co.*	146,019	79,781	69,529	42.4	17.3
Manlius town *Onondaga Co.*	109,217	79,158	44,864	38.5	4.3
Monroe town *Orange Co.*	87,250	66,482	21,622	34.2	28.6
Mount Pleasant town *Westchester Co.*	157,185	111,023	51,700	53.9	8.3
Mount Vernon city *Westchester Co.*	76,753	54,573	29,826	25.1	14.8
New City CDP *Rockland Co.*	153,966	124,765	51,569	63.2	4.2
New Rochelle city *Westchester Co.*	121,268	77,320	44,440	40.2	11.2
New York city *New York Co.*	93,196	57,782	35,761	29.3	19.6
Newburgh town *Orange Co.*	103,151	86,010	37,686	41.3	7.0
Niagara Falls city *Niagara Co.*	47,744	33,965	21,368	10.5	27.5
North Hempstead town *Nassau Co.*	165,932	111,570	56,755	55.3	4.9
North Tonawanda city *Niagara Co.*	64,678	53,002	29,344	19.1	8.8
Oceanside CDP *Nassau Co.*	127,670	109,484	45,731	53.9	5.5
Orangetown town *Rockland Co.*	136,220	98,782	49,876	49.5	6.5
Orchard Park town *Erie Co.*	115,888	89,955	45,698	43.3	4.0
Ossining town *Westchester Co.*	128,103	82,645	43,217	44.7	8.9
Oyster Bay town *Nassau Co.*	159,880	120,826	54,532	58.5	3.9
Penfield town *Monroe Co.*	99,734	80,879	41,096	40.3	4.3
Perinton town *Monroe Co.*	102,790	83,036	42,555	40.1	5.2
Pittsford town *Monroe Co.*	162,778	110,544	58,334	54.6	3.3
Port Chester village *Westchester Co.*	86,645	60,041	27,488	31.3	12.4
Poughkeepsie town *Dutchess Co.*	94,389	74,349	33,498	35.7	8.5
Poughkeepsie city *Dutchess Co.*	59,148	40,840	26,105	14.6	22.4
Queens borough *Queens Co.*	81,335	62,008	28,814	28.6	13.7
Ramapo town *Rockland Co.*	96,306	69,245	26,148	34.9	24.0
Riverhead town *Suffolk Co.*	92,089	66,147	37,970	31.1	9.5
Rochester city *Monroe Co.*	47,352	32,347	21,055	10.0	33.1
Rome city *Oneida Co.*	59,662	45,570	24,970	15.1	19.4
Rye town *Westchester Co.*	122,268	78,245	40,709	41.9	10.0
Salina town *Onondaga Co.*	66,440	53,708	30,097	17.9	10.7
Schenectady city *Schenectady Co.*	55,574	43,174	22,874	14.0	21.0
Smithtown town *Suffolk Co.*	142,682	118,836	50,255	58.8	3.2
Southampton town *Suffolk Co.*	128,721	83,150	49,374	43.7	7.8
Spring Valley village *Rockland Co.*	67,677	43,434	20,518	17.0	25.9
Staten Island borough *Richmond Co.*	95,885	76,244	33,922	38.3	12.9
Syracuse city *Onondaga Co.*	50,825	34,716	21,187	12.0	32.6
Tonawanda town *Erie Co.*	67,462	55,936	31,137	21.1	8.5
Tonawanda CDP *Erie Co.*	67,042	55,247	30,794	20.0	8.7
Troy city *Rensselaer Co.*	55,043	40,911	22,955	14.6	26.1
Union town *Broome Co.*	63,147	47,824	28,166	19.4	13.4
Uniondale CDP *Nassau Co.*	98,706	76,157	26,436	37.2	12.0
Utica city *Oneida Co.*	49,957	33,873	20,153	10.5	30.4
Valley Stream village *Nassau Co.*	115,558	99,439	37,726	49.8	4.4
Warwick town *Orange Co.*	115,147	89,788	43,990	44.7	4.6
Webster town *Monroe Co.*	87,522	75,552	36,005	33.0	4.9
West Babylon CDP *Suffolk Co.*	105,362	86,611	35,234	43.2	5.5
West Seneca CDP *Erie Co.*	73,617	62,705	32,413	23.2	7.0
White Plains city *Westchester Co.*	123,588	87,550	47,907	45.6	11.9
Yonkers city *Westchester Co.*	84,764	62,399	32,521	30.6	16.4
Yorktown town *Westchester Co.*	136,238	115,732	49,205	56.8	3.3

SOURCE: U.S. Census Bureau, American Community Survey, 2013-2017 Five-Year Estimates

Housing

Place	Homeownership Rate (%)	Median Home Value ($)	Median Year Structure Built	Homeowner Vacancy Rate (%)	Median Gross Rent ($/month)	Rental Vacancy Rate (%)
Albany city *Albany Co.*	37.2	171,900	Before 1940	2.7	924	4.8
Amherst town *Erie Co.*	70.6	186,600	1970	1.0	1,020	3.0
Babylon town *Suffolk Co.*	76.2	343,700	1960	1.6	1,603	5.1
Bay Shore CDP *Suffolk Co.*	62.5	323,000	1959	0.5	1,477	4.2
Bethlehem town *Albany Co.*	75.8	275,000	1975	1.4	1,122	5.1
Binghamton city *Broome Co.*	45.0	87,500	1941	3.7	702	8.5
Brentwood CDP *Suffolk Co.*	72.8	285,500	1963	0.9	1,348	4.5
Brighton CDP *Monroe Co.*	57.1	171,800	1961	0.8	982	6.0
Bronx borough *Bronx Co.*	19.7	371,800	1950	2.0	1,133	2.2
Brookhaven town *Suffolk Co.*	79.1	332,200	1974	1.4	1,670	4.5
Brooklyn borough *Kings Co.*	30.0	623,900	Before 1940	1.8	1,314	3.4
Buffalo city *Erie Co.*	41.0	77,800	Before 1940	0.9	735	4.9
Carmel town *Putnam Co.*	81.3	376,300	1969	0.3	1,292	4.8
Centereach CDP *Suffolk Co.*	84.9	335,400	1968	0.5	1,891	4.8
Central Islip CDP *Suffolk Co.*	66.2	254,900	1973	0.7	1,553	3.4
Cheektowaga town *Erie Co.*	70.2	104,800	1959	1.0	802	4.7
Cicero town *Onondaga Co.*	80.7	151,000	1978	1.3	831	4.4
Clarence town *Erie Co.*	84.7	271,300	1985	0.0	942	0.7
Clarkstown town *Rockland Co.*	79.7	445,100	1970	0.8	1,564	7.8
Clay town *Onondaga Co.*	73.7	142,300	1976	1.4	898	5.9
Clifton Park town *Saratoga Co.*	82.0	280,700	1982	0.3	1,174	7.2
Colonie town *Albany Co.*	68.8	226,600	1968	0.7	1,089	1.6
Commack CDP *Suffolk Co.*	92.0	471,300	1964	0.8	1,683	5.5
Coram CDP *Suffolk Co.*	69.0	308,600	1979	2.0	1,839	5.5
Cortlandt town *Westchester Co.*	75.2	407,100	1961	1.4	1,436	4.0
East Meadow CDP *Nassau Co.*	87.9	414,200	1956	0.6	1,921	3.0
Eastchester town *Westchester Co.*	73.4	606,400	1950	1.9	1,788	3.8
Elmont CDP *Nassau Co.*	79.1	374,900	1953	3.0	1,680	2.4
Franklin Square CDP *Nassau Co.*	83.1	447,600	1953	1.2	1,473	0.5
Freeport village *Nassau Co.*	67.6	317,400	1953	1.6	1,385	0.7
Glenville town *Schenectady Co.*	77.2	185,500	1957	1.2	995	7.4
Greece town *Monroe Co.*	72.2	130,500	1971	0.8	909	7.3
Greenburgh town *Westchester Co.*	72.7	552,200	1958	0.7	1,721	5.0
Guilderland town *Albany Co.*	65.8	251,500	1976	0.7	1,145	6.6
Hamburg town *Erie Co.*	74.6	153,200	1969	0.6	809	3.1
Haverstraw town *Rockland Co.*	60.4	295,800	1971	1.7	1,425	1.6
Hempstead town *Nassau Co.*	80.8	421,300	1953	1.1	1,554	3.9
Hempstead village *Nassau Co.*	43.4	308,800	1956	2.0	1,350	8.6
Henrietta town *Monroe Co.*	69.4	141,300	1974	1.0	979	4.2
Hicksville CDP *Nassau Co.*	86.7	421,900	1954	0.5	1,820	12.3
Huntington town *Suffolk Co.*	85.4	520,600	1962	1.7	1,767	7.8
Huntington Station CDP *Suffolk Co.*	73.1	356,900	1958	2.3	1,703	8.8
Irondequoit CDP *Monroe Co.*	77.9	118,600	1955	1.8	878	6.2
Islip town *Suffolk Co.*	78.0	352,200	1965	1.0	1,620	4.6
Ithaca city *Tompkins Co.*	26.1	233,100	1953	1.8	1,086	3.2
Jamestown city *Chautauqua Co.*	50.3	63,900	Before 1940	2.2	593	10.3
Lancaster town *Erie Co.*	77.0	176,300	1974	0.7	742	1.5
Levittown CDP *Nassau Co.*	92.3	367,700	1952	0.6	1,944	4.2
Long Beach city *Nassau Co.*	57.7	463,200	1957	4.3	1,806	3.5
Mamaroneck town *Westchester Co.*	67.4	878,000	1944	0.5	1,759	0.0

Place	Homeownership Rate (%)	Median Home Value ($)	Median Year Structure Built	Homeowner Vacancy Rate (%)	Median Gross Rent ($/month)	Rental Vacancy Rate (%)
Manhattan borough *New York Co.*	24.1	915,300	1950	2.3	1,615	4.6
Manlius town *Onondaga Co.*	77.1	184,200	1971	0.1	938	3.5
Monroe town *Orange Co.*	58.2	330,600	1985	2.8	1,228	1.2
Mount Pleasant town *Westchester Co.*	70.1	629,000	1956	1.7	1,482	2.6
Mount Vernon city *Westchester Co.*	39.7	355,600	1942	3.6	1,291	4.4
New City CDP *Rockland Co.*	89.4	472,800	1969	1.1	1,366	10.2
New Rochelle city *Westchester Co.*	50.9	552,700	1951	1.6	1,432	3.8
New York city *New York Co.*	32.6	538,700	1949	1.8	1,340	3.4
Newburgh town *Orange Co.*	81.2	250,600	1969	2.8	1,438	5.3
Niagara Falls city *Niagara Co.*	57.2	69,900	1942	12.4	645	17.8
North Hempstead town *Nassau Co.*	78.3	662,600	1954	1.0	1,766	4.5
North Tonawanda city *Niagara Co.*	68.9	112,600	1954	0.5	666	9.5
Oceanside CDP *Nassau Co.*	88.0	443,900	1955	0.9	1,355	2.1
Orangetown town *Rockland Co.*	73.5	472,800	1961	1.8	1,470	5.4
Orchard Park town *Erie Co.*	76.9	228,100	1973	0.0	947	8.9
Ossining town *Westchester Co.*	61.8	440,300	1962	1.2	1,484	2.5
Oyster Bay town *Nassau Co.*	88.1	485,900	1957	1.1	1,856	6.9
Penfield town *Monroe Co.*	82.7	193,800	1976	0.5	891	10.9
Perinton town *Monroe Co.*	79.5	196,600	1975	0.3	963	8.6
Pittsford town *Monroe Co.*	86.6	270,400	1972	1.3	1,167	7.3
Port Chester village *Westchester Co.*	42.2	445,200	1949	1.5	1,475	3.3
Poughkeepsie town *Dutchess Co.*	69.3	241,900	1966	3.0	1,158	4.2
Poughkeepsie city *Dutchess Co.*	35.2	190,400	1954	5.5	1,095	6.0
Queens borough *Queens Co.*	44.5	481,300	1951	1.4	1,456	2.7
Ramapo town *Rockland Co.*	57.9	417,300	1970	1.2	1,354	2.5
Riverhead town *Suffolk Co.*	79.0	350,000	1982	2.4	1,372	4.2
Rochester city *Monroe Co.*	36.5	79,400	Before 1940	1.3	807	7.6
Rome city *Oneida Co.*	55.1	94,900	1951	1.6	748	3.0
Rye town *Westchester Co.*	54.1	558,900	1953	3.0	1,570	3.4
Salina town *Onondaga Co.*	67.1	110,900	1960	2.1	871	5.8
Schenectady city *Schenectady Co.*	51.9	110,800	Before 1940	2.8	854	8.7
Smithtown town *Suffolk Co.*	88.9	466,700	1967	0.8	1,653	6.9
Southampton town *Suffolk Co.*	78.1	626,400	1974	2.7	1,779	2.2
Spring Valley village *Rockland Co.*	28.0	278,600	1968	3.0	1,293	3.6
Staten Island borough *Richmond Co.*	69.5	460,200	1972	2.0	1,229	6.5
Syracuse city *Onondaga Co.*	38.3	91,100	1945	3.1	769	7.5
Tonawanda town *Erie Co.*	72.8	124,200	1953	0.5	792	4.8
Tonawanda CDP *Erie Co.*	74.0	125,500	1955	0.5	810	4.8
Troy city *Rensselaer Co.*	36.8	144,400	Before 1940	2.4	879	4.3
Union town *Broome Co.*	60.7	110,500	1954	1.5	733	8.6
Uniondale CDP *Nassau Co.*	70.1	337,900	1955	2.1	1,649	6.0
Utica city *Oneida Co.*	47.9	89,400	Before 1940	2.4	689	7.3
Valley Stream village *Nassau Co.*	81.8	385,400	1949	0.8	1,642	3.2
Warwick town *Orange Co.*	77.8	303,100	1968	2.6	1,107	1.5
Webster town *Monroe Co.*	76.2	180,200	1980	1.1	1,015	1.2
West Babylon CDP *Suffolk Co.*	75.9	343,000	1962	1.1	1,694	3.9
West Seneca CDP *Erie Co.*	76.9	141,500	1964	0.2	780	2.2
White Plains city *Westchester Co.*	52.1	526,100	1958	2.0	1,687	2.3
Yonkers city *Westchester Co.*	47.3	380,100	1955	2.2	1,292	10.6
Yorktown town *Westchester Co.*	84.9	413,000	1967	0.5	1,418	0.0

SOURCE: U.S. Census Bureau, American Community Survey, 2013-2017 Five-Year Estimates

Commute to Work

Place	Automobile (%)	Public Transportation (%)	Walk (%)	Work from Home (%)	Mean Travel Time to Work (minutes)
Albany city *Albany Co.*	70.6	14.3	10.6	2.5	18.6
Amherst town *Erie Co.*	90.1	1.9	2.9	4.2	19.2
Babylon town *Suffolk Co.*	86.0	8.3	1.8	2.4	30.9
Bay Shore CDP *Suffolk Co.*	81.1	11.2	2.6	3.6	33.8
Bethlehem town *Albany Co.*	90.4	1.3	1.7	5.7	21.4
Binghamton city *Broome Co.*	80.7	7.9	6.2	2.8	17.0
Brentwood CDP *Suffolk Co.*	91.9	3.6	1.6	1.4	26.8
Brighton CDP *Monroe Co.*	87.3	3.3	2.6	4.9	16.6
Bronx borough *Bronx Co.*	27.4	60.2	7.6	3.1	44.2
Brookhaven town *Suffolk Co.*	90.5	4.1	1.3	3.2	33.2
Brooklyn borough *Kings Co.*	22.6	61.8	8.6	4.3	42.4
Buffalo city *Erie Co.*	78.3	11.5	5.7	2.5	20.9
Carmel town *Putnam Co.*	87.4	6.6	1.1	4.4	38.0
Centereach CDP *Suffolk Co.*	94.0	3.2	0.4	1.8	29.1
Central Islip CDP *Suffolk Co.*	90.7	6.2	1.1	0.8	27.9
Cheektowaga town *Erie Co.*	94.9	1.5	1.1	1.7	19.5
Cicero town *Onondaga Co.*	93.5	0.6	1.2	3.5	19.2
Clarence town *Erie Co.*	92.6	0.4	0.6	6.0	22.0
Clarkstown town *Rockland Co.*	85.3	7.9	1.2	4.6	33.2
Clay town *Onondaga Co.*	93.5	0.8	1.2	3.9	20.0
Clifton Park town *Saratoga Co.*	91.9	1.0	0.5	5.7	25.4
Colonie town *Albany Co.*	89.8	2.8	2.2	3.7	19.6
Commack CDP *Suffolk Co.*	87.4	6.7	1.1	3.8	33.4
Coram CDP *Suffolk Co.*	90.5	3.7	0.8	2.9	35.5
Cortlandt town *Westchester Co.*	75.6	15.6	2.0	5.7	39.8
East Meadow CDP *Nassau Co.*	87.3	8.1	0.8	3.3	31.2
Eastchester town *Westchester Co.*	60.1	28.9	4.2	5.9	35.4
Elmont CDP *Nassau Co.*	72.9	22.1	2.5	1.7	40.2
Franklin Square CDP *Nassau Co.*	82.5	11.9	2.1	3.1	35.0
Freeport village *Nassau Co.*	77.1	13.2	5.8	3.4	32.2
Glenville town *Schenectady Co.*	94.4	1.3	1.7	2.3	23.5
Greece town *Monroe Co.*	94.8	0.7	1.2	2.6	20.0
Greenburgh town *Westchester Co.*	66.4	22.9	3.4	6.2	33.5
Guilderland town *Albany Co.*	89.9	1.4	2.2	4.6	21.4
Hamburg town *Erie Co.*	94.6	1.1	1.5	2.3	22.8
Haverstraw town *Rockland Co.*	82.7	8.1	2.8	4.4	30.0
Hempstead town *Nassau Co.*	76.0	17.1	2.6	3.5	35.8
Hempstead village *Nassau Co.*	68.5	23.3	4.0	2.1	32.1
Henrietta town *Monroe Co.*	88.1	3.0	4.9	3.2	18.5
Hicksville CDP *Nassau Co.*	79.7	12.3	2.6	3.2	33.8
Huntington town *Suffolk Co.*	81.7	10.3	1.3	5.5	34.6
Huntington Station CDP *Suffolk Co.*	81.1	9.9	2.7	4.2	30.3
Irondequoit CDP *Monroe Co.*	92.0	1.8	1.2	3.6	20.1
Islip town *Suffolk Co.*	88.8	6.6	1.2	2.3	30.7
Ithaca city *Tompkins Co.*	37.8	12.8	38.4	7.7	16.2
Jamestown city *Chautauqua Co.*	88.1	0.8	7.2	2.2	14.7
Lancaster town *Erie Co.*	95.6	0.6	0.4	2.9	21.9
Levittown CDP *Nassau Co.*	83.5	11.4	1.6	1.9	32.8
Long Beach city *Nassau Co.*	71.3	19.1	4.4	3.2	41.2
Mamaroneck town *Westchester Co.*	49.2	33.7	6.3	9.0	37.5

Place	Automobile (%)	Public Trans-portation (%)	Walk (%)	Work from Home (%)	Mean Travel Time to Work (minutes)
Manhattan borough *New York Co.*	7.8	59.4	20.4	6.7	31.8
Manlius town *Onondaga Co.*	91.1	0.6	1.3	6.5	22.0
Monroe town *Orange Co.*	69.1	13.9	10.4	4.2	32.9
Mount Pleasant town *Westchester Co.*	71.2	16.4	6.1	5.8	29.9
Mount Vernon city *Westchester Co.*	60.4	30.0	5.5	2.7	34.8
New City CDP *Rockland Co.*	85.0	8.5	0.7	4.8	35.5
New Rochelle city *Westchester Co.*	62.6	23.5	6.8	5.1	32.1
New York city *New York Co.*	26.6	56.5	10.0	4.1	40.8
Newburgh town *Orange Co.*	89.8	4.8	0.5	4.4	31.0
Niagara Falls city *Niagara Co.*	89.9	2.6	3.6	1.5	18.3
North Hempstead town *Nassau Co.*	71.0	19.7	3.1	4.9	36.1
North Tonawanda city *Niagara Co.*	94.7	0.5	0.9	2.4	20.9
Oceanside CDP *Nassau Co.*	76.9	15.8	1.6	5.1	36.9
Orangetown town *Rockland Co.*	81.9	9.0	3.0	5.4	32.8
Orchard Park town *Erie Co.*	94.4	0.4	1.1	3.4	21.8
Ossining town *Westchester Co.*	69.0	16.7	6.2	6.3	33.5
Oyster Bay town *Nassau Co.*	78.8	14.2	1.7	4.1	35.3
Penfield town *Monroe Co.*	91.7	0.8	0.7	6.1	20.0
Perinton town *Monroe Co.*	90.8	0.7	1.4	6.2	20.9
Pittsford town *Monroe Co.*	85.1	0.2	4.5	8.7	18.3
Port Chester village *Westchester Co.*	65.5	17.3	9.0	2.5	25.7
Poughkeepsie town *Dutchess Co.*	78.6	4.8	9.7	5.6	26.4
Poughkeepsie city *Dutchess Co.*	75.1	9.7	10.8	1.6	25.8
Queens borough *Queens Co.*	38.5	51.7	5.8	2.6	43.5
Ramapo town *Rockland Co.*	75.8	9.9	6.1	5.6	28.5
Riverhead town *Suffolk Co.*	89.6	1.5	2.0	5.6	27.6
Rochester city *Monroe Co.*	79.3	9.2	6.7	2.7	20.1
Rome city *Oneida Co.*	90.3	0.3	3.1	4.5	17.5
Rye town *Westchester Co.*	66.4	19.8	6.2	3.5	28.5
Salina town *Onondaga Co.*	92.5	1.5	2.2	2.6	18.1
Schenectady city *Schenectady Co.*	81.8	8.5	5.1	2.7	22.2
Smithtown town *Suffolk Co.*	87.8	6.4	0.6	4.3	33.6
Southampton town *Suffolk Co.*	82.8	6.1	2.6	7.4	26.5
Spring Valley village *Rockland Co.*	72.9	14.2	5.2	2.2	26.1
Staten Island borough *Richmond Co.*	64.0	29.9	2.5	2.5	44.0
Syracuse city *Onondaga Co.*	73.7	9.6	11.3	3.3	18.4
Tonawanda town *Erie Co.*	93.0	2.1	1.9	1.9	20.0
Tonawanda CDP *Erie Co.*	93.3	2.1	1.8	2.0	19.7
Troy city *Rensselaer Co.*	77.8	7.9	10.4	2.9	22.3
Union town *Broome Co.*	87.4	2.8	4.9	3.7	18.1
Uniondale CDP *Nassau Co.*	78.7	10.9	6.5	2.8	30.0
Utica city *Oneida Co.*	85.8	3.5	6.5	3.6	17.4
Valley Stream village *Nassau Co.*	70.0	24.9	1.9	2.2	42.9
Warwick town *Orange Co.*	84.5	5.8	1.5	7.4	40.1
Webster town *Monroe Co.*	93.6	0.2	1.3	4.1	20.3
West Babylon CDP *Suffolk Co.*	87.5	8.4	0.8	2.7	32.6
West Seneca CDP *Erie Co.*	95.7	1.0	1.2	1.8	20.9
White Plains city *Westchester Co.*	67.9	17.7	7.9	4.5	27.4
Yonkers city *Westchester Co.*	63.3	27.5	4.7	2.9	34.3
Yorktown town *Westchester Co.*	85.4	7.1	2.7	4.1	35.8

SOURCE: U.S. Census Bureau, American Community Survey, 2013-2017 Five-Year Estimates

Crime

Place	Violent Crime Rate (crimes per 10,000 population)	Property Crime Rate (crimes per 10,000 population)
Albany city *Albany Co.*	89.2	345.7
Amherst town *Erie Co.*	10.2	154.2
Babylon town *Suffolk Co.*	n/a	n/a
Bay Shore CDP *Suffolk Co.*	n/a	n/a
Bethlehem town *Albany Co.*	5.3	136.8
Binghamton city *Broome Co.*	79.7	436.8
Brentwood CDP *Suffolk Co.*	n/a	n/a
Brighton CDP *Monroe Co.*	7.7	213.4
Bronx borough *Bronx Co.*	n/a	n/a
Brookhaven town *Suffolk Co.*	n/a	n/a
Brooklyn borough *Kings Co.*	n/a	n/a
Buffalo city *Erie Co.*	101.9	383.6
Carmel town *Putnam Co.*	2.6	36.5
Centereach CDP *Suffolk Co.*	n/a	n/a
Central Islip CDP *Suffolk Co.*	n/a	n/a
Cheektowaga town *Erie Co.*	24.1	296.0
Cicero town *Onondaga Co.*	4.1	93.7
Clarence town *Erie Co.*	n/a	n/a
Clarkstown town *Rockland Co.*	10.9	137.5
Clay town *Onondaga Co.*	n/a	n/a
Clifton Park town *Saratoga Co.*	n/a	n/a
Colonie town *Albany Co.*	10.6	239.2
Commack CDP *Suffolk Co.*	n/a	n/a
Coram CDP *Suffolk Co.*	n/a	n/a
Cortlandt town *Westchester Co.*	n/a	n/a
East Meadow CDP *Nassau Co.*	n/a	n/a
Eastchester town *Westchester Co.*	2.5	85.3
Elmont CDP *Nassau Co.*	n/a	n/a
Franklin Square CDP *Nassau Co.*	n/a	n/a
Freeport village *Nassau Co.*	21.7	93.9
Glenville town *Schenectady Co.*	6.5	214.3
Greece town *Monroe Co.*	18.1	201.1
Greenburgh town *Westchester Co.*	10.9	133.5
Guilderland town *Albany Co.*	7.9	200.9
Hamburg town *Erie Co.*	8.0	189.8
Haverstraw town *Rockland Co.*	11.2	79.4
Hempstead town *Nassau Co.*	n/a	n/a
Hempstead village *Nassau Co.*	59.5	106.3
Henrietta town *Monroe Co.*	n/a	n/a
Hicksville CDP *Nassau Co.*	n/a	n/a
Huntington town *Suffolk Co.*	n/a	n/a
Huntington Station CDP *Suffolk Co.*	n/a	n/a
Irondequoit CDP *Monroe Co.*	21.6	221.9
Islip town *Suffolk Co.*	n/a	n/a
Ithaca city *Tompkins Co.*	18.1	290.9
Jamestown city *Chautauqua Co.*	66.3	297.3
Lancaster town *Erie Co.*	6.1	108.4
Levittown CDP *Nassau Co.*	n/a	n/a
Long Beach city *Nassau Co.*	6.2	58.9
Mamaroneck town *Westchester Co.*	0.8	49.1

Place	Violent Crime Rate (crimes per 10,000 population)	Property Crime Rate (crimes per 10,000 population)
Manhattan borough *New York Co.*	n/a	n/a
Manlius town *Onondaga Co.*	6.9	138.9
Monroe town *Orange Co.*	n/a	n/a
Mount Pleasant town *Westchester Co.*	n/a	n/a
Mount Vernon city *Westchester Co.*	63.8	188.9
New City CDP *Rockland Co.*	n/a	n/a
New Rochelle city *Westchester Co.*	22.8	143.7
New York city *New York Co.*	53.9	144.9
Newburgh town *Orange Co.*	7.8	343.1
Niagara Falls city *Niagara Co.*	112.4	482.8
North Hempstead town *Nassau Co.*	n/a	n/a
North Tonawanda city *Niagara Co.*	12.2	166.5
Oceanside CDP *Nassau Co.*	n/a	n/a
Orangetown town *Rockland Co.*	12.2	80.2
Orchard Park town *Erie Co.*	9.8	85.8
Ossining town *Westchester Co.*	n/a	n/a
Oyster Bay town *Nassau Co.*	n/a	n/a
Penfield town *Monroe Co.*	n/a	n/a
Perinton town *Monroe Co.*	n/a	n/a
Pittsford town *Monroe Co.*	n/a	n/a
Port Chester village *Westchester Co.*	16.5	108.7
Poughkeepsie town *Dutchess Co.*	n/a	n/a
Poughkeepsie city *Dutchess Co.*	70.6	199.9
Queens borough *Queens Co.*	n/a	n/a
Ramapo town *Rockland Co.*	4.7	73.7
Riverhead town *Suffolk Co.*	n/a	n/a
Rochester city *Monroe Co.*	89.7	380.4
Rome city *Oneida Co.*	22.1	174.8
Rye town *Westchester Co.*	n/a	n/a
Salina town *Onondaga Co.*	n/a	n/a
Schenectady city *Schenectady Co.*	89.2	317.9
Smithtown town *Suffolk Co.*	n/a	n/a
Southampton town *Suffolk Co.*	12.2	119.8
Spring Valley village *Rockland Co.*	40.6	118.9
Staten Island borough *Richmond Co.*	n/a	n/a
Syracuse city *Onondaga Co.*	70.5	336.7
Tonawanda town *Erie Co.*	17.5	159.4
Tonawanda CDP *Erie Co.*	n/a	n/a
Troy city *Rensselaer Co.*	70.7	348.9
Union town *Broome Co.*	n/a	n/a
Uniondale CDP *Nassau Co.*	n/a	n/a
Utica city *Oneida Co.*	55.8	328.8
Valley Stream village *Nassau Co.*	n/a	n/a
Warwick town *Orange Co.*	7.1	56.6
Webster town *Monroe Co.*	7.1	91.1
West Babylon CDP *Suffolk Co.*	n/a	n/a
West Seneca CDP *Erie Co.*	9.7	123.5
White Plains city *Westchester Co.*	17.6	168.0
Yonkers city *Westchester Co.*	40.2	100.4
Yorktown town *Westchester Co.*	3.2	58.4

NOTE: n/a not available.
SOURCE: Federal Bureau of Investigation, Uniform Crime Reports, 2017

Community Rankings

This section ranks incorporated places and CDPs (Census Designated Places) with populations of 2,500 or more. Unincorporated postal areas were not considered. For each topic below, you will find two tables, one in Descending Order—highest to lowest, and one in Ascending Order—lowest to highest. Six topics are exceptions to this rule, and only include Descending Order—Water Area, Ancestry (five tables), American Indian/Alaska Native Population, Native Hawaiian/Other Pacific Islander, Homeowner Vacancy Rate, and Commute to Work: Public Transportation. This is because there are an extraordinarily large number of places that place at the bottom of these topics with zero numbers.

Land Area

Top 150 Places Ranked in *Descending* Order

State Rank	Sq. Miles	Place	State Rank	Sq. Miles	Place
1	302.643	**New York** (city)	76	65.498	**Oswegatchie** (town) Saint Lawrence County
2	259.439	**Brookhaven** (town) Suffolk County	77	64.951	**Phelps** (town) Ontario County
3	196.866	**Harrietstown** (town) Franklin County	78	64.943	**Theresa** (town) Jefferson County
4	179.182	**Croghan** (town) Lewis County	79	64.574	**Saugerties** (town) Ulster County
5	158.822	**Hancock** (town) Delaware County	80	64.491	**Moriah** (town) Essex County
6	151.654	**North Elba** (town) Essex County	81	64.198	**Delhi** (town) Delaware County
7	139.195	**Southampton** (town) Suffolk County	82	64.030	**Berne** (town) Albany County
8	130.505	**Wawarsing** (town) Ulster County	83	63.461	**Warrensburg** (town) Warren County
9	119.784	**Shandaken** (town) Ulster County	84	63.032	**Hoosick** (town) Rensselaer County
10	118.587	**Hempstead** (town) Nassau County	85	62.830	**Queensbury** (town) Warren County
11	117.348	**Tupper Lake** (town) Franklin County	86	62.107	**Wallkill** (town) Orange County
12	115.286	**Saranac** (town) Clinton County	87	61.927	**Schodack** (town) Rensselaer County
13	108.999	**Fort Ann** (town) Washington County	88	61.716	**Guilford** (town) Chenango County
14	108.532	**Queens** (borough) Queens County	89	61.715	**Lysander** (town) Onondaga County
15	108.280	**Lisbon** (town) Saint Lawrence County	90	61.628	**Pittstown** (town) Rensselaer County
16	104.765	**Canton** (town) Saint Lawrence County	91	61.448	**Vienna** (town) Oneida County
17	104.221	**Owego** (town) Tioga County	92	61.198	**Ramapo** (town) Rockland County
18	104.114	**Islip** (town) Suffolk County	93	60.490	**Lansing** (town) Tompkins County
19	103.747	**Oyster Bay** (town) Nassau County	94	60.439	**Catskill** (town) Greene County
20	102.369	**Hector** (town) Schuyler County	95	60.425	**Beekmantown** (town) Clinton County
21	101.519	**Malone** (town) Franklin County	96	60.252	**Pierrepont** (town) Saint Lawrence County
22	101.403	**Potsdam** (town) Saint Lawrence County	97	60.167	**Annsville** (town) Oneida County
23	101.340	**Warwick** (town) Orange County	98	60.063	**Oxford** (town) Chenango County
24	100.983	**Altona** (town) Clinton County	99	59.828	**Cairo** (town) Greene County
25	96.837	**Walton** (town) Delaware County	100	59.477	**Galen** (town) Wayne County
26	96.674	**Middletown** (town) Delaware County	101	59.275	**Barton** (town) Tioga County
27	96.108	**Mamakating** (town) Sullivan County	102	59.132	**Brownville** (town) Jefferson County
28	95.319	**Bath** (town) Steuben County	103	59.080	**Dannemora** (town) Clinton County
29	94.510	**Candor** (town) Tioga County	104	58.841	**Newfield** (town) Tompkins County
30	94.156	**Rockland** (town) Sullivan County	105	58.639	**Jerusalem** (town) Yates County
31	94.123	**Huntington** (town) Suffolk County	106	58.620	**Tioga** (town) Tioga County
32	93.897	**Stockholm** (town) Saint Lawrence County	107	58.450	**Olive** (town) Ulster County
33	93.640	**Dryden** (town) Tompkins County	108	58.385	**Mayfield** (town) Fulton County
34	91.743	**Windsor** (town) Broome County	109	58.370	**Staten Island** (borough) Richmond County
35	91.103	**Brasher** (town) Saint Lawrence County	110	58.170	**Washington** (town) Dutchess County
36	90.419	**Hunter** (town) Greene County	111	57.902	**Guilderland** (town) Albany County
37	89.303	**Rochester** (town) Ulster County	112	57.880	**Stephentown** (town) Rensselaer County
38	87.632	**Mooers** (town) Clinton County	113	57.791	**Westerlo** (town) Albany County
39	85.265	**Bethel** (town) Sullivan County	114	57.741	**Onondaga** (town) Onondaga County
40	85.146	**Ellisburg** (town) Jefferson County	115	57.499	**New Scotland** (town) Albany County
41	84.190	**Chester** (town) Warren County	116	57.248	**Richland** (town) Oswego County
42	84.089	**Thompson** (town) Sullivan County	117	57.176	**Whitehall** (town) Washington County
43	82.773	**Neversink** (town) Sullivan County	118	56.962	**Russia** (town) Herkimer County
44	82.360	**Clayton** (town) Jefferson County	119	56.796	**Canandaigua** (town) Ontario County
45	81.433	**Ticonderoga** (town) Essex County	120	56.765	**Constantia** (town) Oswego County
46	79.579	**Liberty** (town) Sullivan County	121	56.763	**Corinth** (town) Saratoga County
47	79.036	**Chesterfield** (town) Essex County	122	56.740	**Norfolk** (town) Saint Lawrence County
48	78.887	**Peru** (town) Clinton County	123	56.536	**Argyle** (town) Washington County
49	78.623	**Wilna** (town) Jefferson County	124	56.503	**East Fishkill** (town) Dutchess County
50	78.347	**Colesville** (town) Broome County	125	56.353	**Cape Vincent** (town) Jefferson County
51	77.622	**Fallsburg** (town) Sullivan County	126	56.056	**Shawangunk** (town) Ulster County
52	75.077	**Greene** (town) Chenango County	127	55.943	**Colonie** (town) Albany County
53	74.791	**Rome** (city) Oneida County	128	55.618	**Granville** (town) Washington County
54	74.328	**East Hampton** (town) Suffolk County	129	55.589	**New Bremen** (town) Lewis County
55	73.643	**Le Ray** (town) Jefferson County	130	55.190	**Dover** (town) Dutchess County
56	73.163	**Sullivan** (town) Madison County	131	55.049	**Bennington** (town) Wyoming County
57	72.657	**Alexandria** (town) Jefferson County	132	54.819	**Fayette** (town) Seneca County
58	71.878	**Boonville** (town) Oneida County	133	54.763	**Caroline** (town) Tompkins County
59	71.423	**Orleans** (town) Jefferson County	134	54.471	**Marbletown** (town) Ulster County
60	71.217	**Gouverneur** (town) Saint Lawrence County	135	54.351	**Canisteo** (town) Steuben County
61	70.923	**Allegany** (town) Cattaraugus County	136	54.153	**Chazy** (town) Clinton County
62	70.816	**Brooklyn** (borough) Kings County	137	54.013	**Camden** (town) Oneida County
63	70.782	**Duanesburg** (town) Schenectady County	138	53.890	**Otsego** (town) Otsego County
64	70.214	**Johnstown** (town) Fulton County	139	53.783	**Southold** (town) Suffolk County
65	69.966	**Royalton** (town) Niagara County	140	53.698	**Smithtown** (town) Suffolk County
66	69.934	**Concord** (town) Erie County	141	53.553	**Danby** (town) Tompkins County
67	69.230	**Verona** (town) Oneida County	142	53.512	**North Hempstead** (town) Nassau County
68	67.688	**Jay** (town) Essex County	143	53.503	**Clarence** (town) Erie County
69	67.426	**Riverhead** (town) Suffolk County	144	53.227	**Chatham** (town) Columbia County
70	67.388	**Greenfield** (town) Saratoga County	145	53.203	**Amherst** (town) Erie County
71	67.289	**Woodstock** (town) Ulster County	146	52.519	**Lake Luzerne** (town) Warren County
72	67.268	**Sodus** (town) Wayne County	147	52.378	**Hartland** (town) Niagara County
73	67.099	**Chautauqua** (town) Chautauqua County	148	52.362	**Salem** (town) Washington County
74	66.502	**Deerpark** (town) Orange County	149	52.319	**Babylon** (town) Suffolk County
75	66.378	**Pompey** (town) Onondaga County	150	52.033	**Arcadia** (town) Wayne County

Note: This section ranks incorporated places and CDPs (Census Designated Places) with populations of 2,500 or more. Unincorporated postal areas were not considered. Please refer to the User Guide for additional information.

Land Area

Top 150 Places Ranked in *Ascending* Order

State Rank	Sq. Miles	Place
1	0.172	**Kaser** (village) Rockland County
2	0.312	**Great Neck Plaza** (village) Nassau County
3	0.324	**SUNY Oswego** (CDP) Oswego County
4	0.356	**New Square** (village) Rockland County
5	0.404	**Garden City South** (CDP) Nassau County
6	0.408	**Thomaston** (village) Nassau County
7	0.428	**Fairview** (CDP) Westchester County
8	0.445	**Island Park** (village) Nassau County
9	0.465	**Manorhaven** (village) Nassau County
10	0.478	**Port Washington North** (village) Nassau County
11	0.518	**Munsey Park** (village) Nassau County
12	0.533	**University Gardens** (CDP) Nassau County
13	0.569	**East Williston** (village) Nassau County
14	0.573	**Herricks** (CDP) Nassau County
15	0.578	**South Hempstead** (CDP) Nassau County
16	0.591	**Manhasset Hills** (CDP) Nassau County
17	0.598	**Tuckahoe** (village) Westchester County
18	0.605	**South Nyack** (village) Rockland County
19	0.626	**Williston Park** (village) Nassau County
20	0.645	**Roslyn** (village) Nassau County
21	0.668	**Arlington** (CDP) Dutchess County
22	0.671	**Yorkville** (village) Oneida County
23	0.675	**Cedarhurst** (village) Nassau County
24	0.679	**Piermont** (village) Rockland County
25	0.680	**Albertson** (CDP) Nassau County
26	0.747	**Green Island** (town/village) Albany County
27	0.757	**Great Neck Estates** (village) Nassau County
28	0.770	**Nyack** (village) Rockland County
29	0.775	**Binghamton University** (CDP) Broome County
30	0.786	**Sloan** (village) Erie County
31	0.829	**Pelham** (village) Westchester County
32	0.830	**Valhalla** (CDP) Westchester County
33	0.841	**Mechanicville** (city) Saratoga County
34	0.844	**Crown Heights** (CDP) Dutchess County
35	0.860	**New Hyde Park** (village) Nassau County
36	0.873	**South Valley Stream** (CDP) Nassau County
37	0.876	**Mohawk** (village) Herkimer County
38	0.881	**Hewlett** (CDP) Nassau County
39	0.889	**Halesite** (CDP) Suffolk County
40	0.895	**Hartsdale** (CDP) Westchester County
41	0.914	**Locust Valley** (CDP) Nassau County
42	0.929	**Searingtown** (CDP) Nassau County
43	0.935	**Carle Place** (CDP) Nassau County
44	0.962	**Bronxville** (village) Westchester County
45	0.972	**Glenwood Landing** (CDP) Nassau County
46	0.976	**Brightwaters** (village) Suffolk County
47	0.984	**Garden City Park** (CDP) Nassau County
48	1.000	**Lakeview** (CDP) Nassau County
49	1.004	**Harriman** (village) Orange County
50	1.006	**Bedford Hills** (CDP) Westchester County
51	1.014	**Frankfort** (village) Herkimer County
52	1.017	**East Rockaway** (village) Nassau County
53	1.027	**Elmsford** (village) Westchester County
54	1.047	**East Norwich** (CDP) Nassau County
55	1.050	**Whitesboro** (village) Oneida County
56	1.058	**Malverne** (village) Nassau County
57	1.061	**Vails Gate** (CDP) Orange County
58	1.067	**Corinth** (village) Saratoga County
59	1.077	**Larchmont** (village) Westchester County
60	1.090	**Highland Falls** (village) Orange County
61	1.093	**Hawthorne** (CDP) Westchester County
62	1.097	**Lewiston** (village) Niagara County
63	1.107	**Thornwood** (CDP) Westchester County
64	1.108	**Wappingers Falls** (village) Dutchess County
65	1.109	**Kiryas Joel** (village) Orange County
66	1.115	**Sea Cliff** (village) Nassau County
67	1.121	**Farmingdale** (village) Nassau County
68	1.123	**Blasdell** (village) Erie County
69	1.146	**Elmira Heights** (village) Chemung County
70	1.148	**Dannemora** (village) Clinton County
71	1.152	**Galeville** (CDP) Onondaga County
72	1.154	**Village Green** (CDP) Onondaga County
73	1.160	**Silver Creek** (village) Chautauqua County
74	1.173	**Keeseville** (village) Clinton County
75	1.180	**New York Mills** (village) Oneida County
76	1.190	**Alfred** (village) Allegany County
77	1.204	**Wanakah** (CDP) Erie County
78	1.205	**Baldwin Harbor** (CDP) Nassau County
79	1.233	**Oyster Bay** (CDP) Nassau County
80	1.243	**Lyncourt** (CDP) Onondaga County
81	1.260	**Williamsville** (village) Erie County
82	1.273	**Minoa** (village) Onondaga County
83	1.297	**Hillcrest** (CDP) Rockland County
84	1.302	**Wheatley Heights** (CDP) Suffolk County
85	1.323	**Ardsley** (village) Westchester County
86	1.325	**East Rochester** (town/village) Monroe County
87	1.329	**Great Neck** (village) Nassau County
88	1.337	**Spencerport** (village) Monroe County
89	1.343	**Pelham Manor** (village) Westchester County
90	1.345	**Watervliet** (city) Albany County
91	1.346	**Orchard Park** (village) Erie County
92	1.347	**Palmyra** (village) Wayne County
93	1.347	**Islip Terrace** (CDP) Suffolk County
94	1.354	**Maybrook** (village) Orange County
95	1.358	**South Glens Falls** (village) Saratoga County
96	1.364	**Westvale** (CDP) Onondaga County
97	1.371	**Lake Placid** (village) Essex County
98	1.373	**Victor** (village) Ontario County
99	1.373	**University at Buffalo** (CDP) Erie County
100	1.404	**Plainedge** (CDP) Nassau County
101	1.406	**Montgomery** (village) Orange County
102	1.417	**Floral Park** (village) Nassau County
103	1.435	**Kenmore** (village) Erie County
104	1.450	**Bayville** (village) Nassau County
105	1.467	**Mount Ivy** (CDP) Rockland County
106	1.467	**Ravena** (village) Albany County
107	1.469	**Northeast Ithaca** (CDP) Tompkins County
108	1.476	**Roslyn Heights** (CDP) Nassau County
109	1.479	**New Cassel** (CDP) Nassau County
110	1.483	**Lakeland** (CDP) Onondaga County
111	1.487	**Milton** (CDP) Saratoga County
112	1.519	**West Haverstraw** (village) Rockland County
113	1.523	**Rhinebeck** (village) Dutchess County
114	1.541	**Walton** (village) Delaware County
115	1.581	**Inwood** (CDP) Nassau County
116	1.589	**Fairport** (village) Monroe County
117	1.593	**Gowanda** (village) Cattaraugus County
118	1.598	**Hoosick Falls** (village) Rensselaer County
119	1.599	**Ballston Spa** (village) Saratoga County
120	1.614	**Montrose** (CDP) Westchester County
121	1.618	**Flower Hill** (village) Nassau County
122	1.622	**East Syracuse** (village) Onondaga County
123	1.637	**Sound Beach** (CDP) Suffolk County
124	1.639	**Glen Head** (CDP) Nassau County
125	1.654	**Solvay** (village) Onondaga County
126	1.685	**Scotia** (village) Schenectady County
127	1.691	**Attica** (village) Wyoming County
128	1.697	**Stony Brook University** (CDP) Suffolk County
129	1.705	**Gordon Heights** (CDP) Suffolk County
130	1.715	**New Paltz** (village) Ulster County
131	1.719	**North Merrick** (CDP) Nassau County
132	1.737	**Salisbury** (CDP) Nassau County
133	1.739	**Lido Beach** (CDP) Nassau County
134	1.746	**Fayetteville** (village) Onondaga County
135	1.756	**Fort Edward** (village) Washington County
136	1.762	**Glasco** (CDP) Ulster County
137	1.767	**Cayuga Heights** (village) Tompkins County
138	1.770	**Roosevelt** (CDP) Nassau County
139	1.775	**Spackenkill** (CDP) Dutchess County
140	1.780	**Hilton** (village) Monroe County
141	1.784	**Saugerties** (village) Ulster County
142	1.785	**Manlius** (village) Onondaga County
143	1.791	**Dolgeville** (village) Herkimer County
144	1.794	**Blue Point** (CDP) Suffolk County
145	1.824	**Pleasantville** (village) Westchester County
146	1.827	**Thiells** (CDP) Rockland County
147	1.832	**Hudson Falls** (village) Washington County
148	1.845	**Lake Success** (village) Nassau County
149	1.864	**Heritage Hills** (CDP) Westchester County
150	1.864	**North Valley Stream** (CDP) Nassau County

Note: This section ranks incorporated places and CDPs (Census Designated Places) with populations of 2,500 or more. Unincorporated postal areas were not considered. Please refer to the User Guide for additional information.

Water Area

Top 150 Places Ranked in *Descending* Order

State Rank	Sq. Miles	Place	State Rank	Sq. Miles	Place
1	349.917	**Southold** (town) Suffolk County	76	4.693	**Bethel** (town) Sullivan County
2	312.224	**East Hampton** (town) Suffolk County	77	4.659	**Porter** (town) Niagara County
3	272.097	**Brookhaven** (town) Suffolk County	78	4.655	**Fishkill** (town) Dutchess County
4	165.841	**New York** (city)	79	4.628	**Esopus** (town) Ulster County
5	154.510	**Southampton** (town) Suffolk County	80	4.315	**Gorham** (town) Ontario County
6	133.841	**Riverhead** (town) Suffolk County	81	4.265	**Newburgh** (town) Orange County
7	73.000	**Hempstead** (town) Nassau County	82	4.168	**Ossining** (town) Westchester County
8	71.488	**Hounsfield** (town) Jefferson County	83	4.157	**Sandy Creek** (town) Oswego County
9	69.675	**Queens** (borough) Queens County	84	4.068	**Rhinebeck** (town) Dutchess County
10	65.652	**Oyster Bay** (town) Nassau County	85	4.026	**Ulysses** (town) Tompkins County
11	61.861	**Babylon** (town) Suffolk County	86	4.010	**Lewiston** (town) Niagara County
12	58.891	**Islip** (town) Suffolk County	87	3.975	**Stony Point** (town) Rockland County
13	57.752	**Smithtown** (town) Suffolk County	88	3.875	**Greece** (town) Monroe County
14	43.921	**Staten Island** (borough) Richmond County	89	3.871	**Red Hook** (town) Dutchess County
15	42.988	**Huntington** (town) Suffolk County	90	3.726	**Catskill** (town) Greene County
16	42.915	**Constantia** (town) Oswego County	91	3.614	**Oswego** (city) Oswego County
17	33.628	**Vienna** (town) Oneida County	92	3.546	**Warwick** (town) Orange County
18	33.499	**Cape Vincent** (town) Jefferson County	93	3.532	**Malta** (town) Saratoga County
19	26.336	**Chesterfield** (town) Essex County	94	3.491	**Neversink** (town) Sullivan County
20	26.102	**Brooklyn** (borough) Kings County	95	3.456	**Russia** (town) Herkimer County
21	22.288	**Plattsburgh** (town) Clinton County	96	3.408	**Thompson** (town) Sullivan County
22	21.671	**Clayton** (town) Jefferson County	97	3.407	**Mamaroneck** (village) Westchester County
23	16.944	**Shelter Island** (town) Suffolk County	98	3.386	**Saugerties** (town) Ulster County
24	16.814	**Harrietstown** (town) Franklin County	99	3.358	**Wawarsing** (town) Ulster County
25	15.598	**North Hempstead** (town) Nassau County	100	3.342	**Scriba** (town) Oswego County
26	15.382	**Bronx** (borough) Bronx County	101	3.283	**Ossining** (village) Westchester County
27	15.342	**Louisville** (town) Saint Lawrence County	102	3.245	**Southeast** (town) Putnam County
28	14.173	**Rye** (city) Westchester County	103	3.242	**Seneca Falls** (town) Seneca County
29	13.613	**Northampton** (town) Fulton County	104	3.216	**Pittstown** (town) Rensselaer County
30	13.591	**Romulus** (town) Seneca County	105	3.195	**Hyde Park** (town) Dutchess County
31	13.492	**Peru** (town) Clinton County	106	3.181	**Ogdensburg** (city) Saint Lawrence County
32	12.754	**Tupper Lake** (town) Franklin County	107	3.104	**Geddes** (town) Onondaga County
33	12.589	**Glen Cove** (city) Nassau County	108	3.060	**Highlands** (town) Orange County
34	12.110	**Buffalo** (city) Erie County	109	3.057	**Haverstraw** (village) Rockland County
35	11.900	**Alexandria** (town) Jefferson County	110	3.038	**Coeymans** (town) Albany County
36	11.774	**Massena** (town) Saint Lawrence County	111	2.994	**New Windsor** (town) Orange County
37	11.583	**Fayette** (town) Seneca County	112	2.994	**Hancock** (town) Delaware County
38	10.762	**Manhattan** (borough) New York County	113	2.964	**Benton** (town) Yates County
39	10.761	**Cortlandt** (town) Westchester County	114	2.919	**Sleepy Hollow** (village) Westchester County
40	10.214	**Hector** (town) Schuyler County	115	2.894	**Lysander** (town) Onondaga County
41	9.452	**Lansing** (town) Tompkins County	116	2.885	**New Rochelle** (city) Westchester County
42	9.202	**Beekmantown** (town) Clinton County	117	2.860	**Chester** (town) Warren County
43	8.593	**Clarkstown** (town) Rockland County	118	2.849	**Croghan** (town) Lewis County
44	8.059	**Broadalbin** (town) Fulton County	119	2.822	**Kent** (town) Putnam County
45	7.585	**Champlain** (town) Clinton County	120	2.812	**Livonia** (town) Livingston County
46	7.410	**Mamaroneck** (town) Westchester County	121	2.801	**Richland** (town) Oswego County
47	7.320	**Brownville** (town) Jefferson County	122	2.785	**Philipstown** (town) Putnam County
48	7.268	**Orangetown** (town) Rockland County	123	2.753	**Tarrytown** (village) Westchester County
49	7.163	**Chazy** (town) Clinton County	124	2.742	**Niagara Falls** (city) Niagara County
50	7.012	**Ticonderoga** (town) Essex County	125	2.685	**East Quogue** (CDP) Suffolk County
51	6.762	**Jerusalem** (town) Yates County	126	2.630	**Poughkeepsie** (town) Dutchess County
52	6.759	**Dannemora** (town) Clinton County	127	2.622	**Athens** (town) Greene County
53	6.743	**Olive** (town) Ulster County	128	2.612	**Yorktown** (town) Westchester County
54	6.620	**Orleans** (town) Jefferson County	129	2.604	**North Castle** (town) Westchester County
55	6.619	**Moriah** (town) Essex County	130	2.594	**Owasco** (town) Cayuga County
56	6.375	**Starkey** (town) Yates County	131	2.561	**Mamakating** (town) Sullivan County
57	6.299	**Mayfield** (town) Fulton County	132	2.549	**Lake George** (town) Warren County
58	6.220	**Skaneateles** (town) Onondaga County	133	2.518	**Somers** (town) Westchester County
59	6.056	**Hurley** (town) Ulster County	134	2.487	**Lido Beach** (CDP) Nassau County
60	6.038	**Croton-on-Hudson** (village) Westchester County	135	2.480	**Fleming** (town) Cayuga County
61	5.901	**Milo** (town) Yates County	136	2.383	**Stillwater** (town) Saratoga County
62	5.805	**Greenburgh** (town) Westchester County	137	2.339	**Saratoga** (town) Saratoga County
63	5.735	**Canandaigua** (town) Ontario County	138	2.315	**New Haven** (town) Oswego County
64	5.705	**Oswegatchie** (town) Saint Lawrence County	139	2.299	**Tuxedo** (town) Orange County
65	5.636	**Lisbon** (town) Saint Lawrence County	140	2.285	**Yonkers** (city) Westchester County
66	5.335	**Mount Pleasant** (town) Westchester County	141	2.252	**Montauk** (CDP) Suffolk County
67	5.260	**Haverstraw** (town) Rockland County	142	2.247	**Bedford** (town) Westchester County
68	5.174	**Hampton Bays** (CDP) Suffolk County	143	2.191	**Westhampton** (CDP) Suffolk County
69	5.162	**Otsego** (town) Otsego County	144	2.114	**Schaghticoke** (town) Rensselaer County
70	5.020	**Grand Island** (town) Erie County	145	2.077	**Ulster** (town) Ulster County
71	4.841	**West Monroe** (town) Oswego County	146	2.057	**Wilson** (town) Niagara County
72	4.789	**Theresa** (town) Jefferson County	147	2.055	**Carmel Hamlet** (CDP) Putnam County
73	4.786	**Carmel** (town) Putnam County	148	2.049	**Potsdam** (town) Saint Lawrence County
74	4.740	**Au Sable** (town) Clinton County	149	2.049	**Saint Regis Mohawk Reservation** (reservation) Franklin County
75	4.737	**North Elba** (town) Essex County	150	2.029	**Marlborough** (town) Ulster County

Note: This section ranks incorporated places and CDPs (Census Designated Places) with populations of 2,500 or more. Unincorporated postal areas were not considered. Please refer to the User Guide for additional information.

Elevation

Top 150 Places Ranked in *Descending* Order

State Rank	Feet	Place
1	1,965	**North Elba** (town) Essex County
2	1,854	**Harrietstown** (town) Franklin County
3	1,801	**Lake Placid** (village) Essex County
4	1,765	**Alfred** (town) Allegany County
4	1,765	**Alfred** (village) Allegany County
6	1,673	**Pompey** (town) Onondaga County
7	1,634	**Neversink** (town) Sullivan County
8	1,598	**Tupper Lake** (town) Franklin County
8	1,598	**Tupper Lake** (village) Franklin County
10	1,591	**Franklinville** (town) Cattaraugus County
11	1,588	**Hunter** (town) Greene County
12	1,545	**Saranac Lake** (village) Franklin County
13	1,512	**Monticello** (village) Sullivan County
13	1,512	**Wellsville** (town) Allegany County
13	1,512	**Wellsville** (village) Allegany County
16	1,506	**Liberty** (town) Sullivan County
16	1,506	**Liberty** (village) Sullivan County
18	1,496	**Cuba** (town) Allegany County
19	1,489	**Paris** (town) Oneida County
20	1,486	**Guilford** (town) Chenango County
21	1,480	**Otisco** (town) Onondaga County
22	1,476	**Arcade** (town) Wyoming County
23	1,447	**Olean** (city) Cattaraugus County
24	1,434	**Yorkshire** (town) Cattaraugus County
25	1,430	**Portville** (town) Cattaraugus County
26	1,421	**Allegany** (town) Cattaraugus County
27	1,414	**Dannemora** (town) Clinton County
27	1,414	**Dannemora** (village) Clinton County
29	1,404	**Virgil** (town) Cortland County
30	1,394	**Sardinia** (town) Erie County
31	1,381	**Salamanca** (city) Cattaraugus County
32	1,378	**Jamestown** (city) Chautauqua County
33	1,375	**Wayland** (town) Steuben County
34	1,371	**Delhi** (town) Delaware County
34	1,371	**Delhi** (village) Delaware County
34	1,371	**Perry** (town) Wyoming County
34	1,371	**Perry** (village) Wyoming County
38	1,365	**Busti** (town) Chautauqua County
39	1,362	**Chautauqua** (town) Chautauqua County
40	1,355	**Castile** (town) Wyoming County
40	1,355	**Oswegatchie** (town) Saint Lawrence County
42	1,352	**Concord** (town) Erie County
43	1,329	**Springville** (village) Erie County
44	1,325	**Bethel** (town) Sullivan County
44	1,325	**Lakewood** (village) Chautauqua County
46	1,306	**Davenport** (town) Delaware County
47	1,293	**Rockland** (town) Sullivan County
48	1,276	**Randolph** (town) Cattaraugus County
49	1,250	**Tully** (town) Onondaga County
50	1,247	**Sangerfield** (town) Oneida County
51	1,237	**Danby** (town) Tompkins County
52	1,234	**Knox** (town) Albany County
53	1,224	**Cazenovia** (town) Madison County
53	1,224	**Cazenovia** (village) Madison County
55	1,207	**Bennington** (town) Wyoming County
55	1,207	**Fallsburg** (town) Sullivan County
55	1,207	**Milford** (town) Otsego County
55	1,207	**Walton** (town) Delaware County
55	1,207	**Walton** (village) Delaware County
60	1,204	**Eaton** (town) Madison County
60	1,204	**Madison** (town) Madison County
62	1,178	**Munsons Corners** (CDP) Cortland County
63	1,165	**Westerlo** (town) Albany County
64	1,161	**Hornell** (city) Steuben County
65	1,148	**Boonville** (town) Oneida County
66	1,135	**Canisteo** (town) Steuben County
67	1,132	**LaFayette** (town) Onondaga County
68	1,129	**Cortland** (city) Cortland County
68	1,129	**Russia** (town) Herkimer County
70	1,125	**Homer** (town) Cortland County
70	1,125	**Homer** (village) Cortland County
72	1,122	**Hamilton** (town) Madison County
72	1,122	**Hamilton** (village) Madison County
74	1,112	**Laurens** (town) Otsego County
74	1,112	**New Berlin** (town) Chenango County
74	1,112	**Oneonta** (city) Otsego County
74	1,112	**Oneonta** (town) Otsego County
78	1,109	**Bath** (town) Steuben County
78	1,109	**Bath** (village) Steuben County
80	1,106	**Enfield** (town) Tompkins County
80	1,106	**Holland** (town) Erie County
82	1,089	**Dryden** (town) Tompkins County
83	1,079	**Colden** (town) Erie County
84	1,070	**East Bloomfield** (town) Ontario County
84	1,070	**Otego** (town) Otsego County
84	1,070	**Triangle** (town) Broome County
87	1,056	**Shandaken** (town) Ulster County
88	1,050	**Newfield** (town) Tompkins County
89	1,047	**Sherburne** (town) Chenango County
90	1,037	**Greenville** (town) Orange County
91	1,033	**Livonia** (town) Livingston County
92	1,014	**Campbell** (town) Steuben County
92	1,014	**Norwich** (city) Chenango County
92	1,014	**Norwich** (town) Chenango County
92	1,014	**Warsaw** (town) Wyoming County
92	1,014	**Warsaw** (village) Wyoming County
97	1,010	**Unadilla** (town) Otsego County
98	1,001	**Afton** (town) Chenango County
98	1,001	**Darien** (town) Genesee County
100	997	**Addison** (town) Steuben County
100	997	**Champion** (town) Jefferson County
100	997	**Groton** (town) Tompkins County
103	994	**Bainbridge** (town) Chenango County
103	994	**Spencer** (town) Tioga County
105	991	**Sidney** (town) Delaware County
105	991	**Sidney** (village) Delaware County
107	981	**Attica** (town) Wyoming County
107	981	**Attica** (village) Wyoming County
109	974	**Lisle** (town) Broome County
110	971	**Berne** (town) Albany County
110	971	**Denmark** (town) Lewis County
110	971	**Oxford** (town) Chenango County
113	968	**Caroline** (town) Tompkins County
113	968	**Newark Valley** (town) Tioga County
115	955	**Augusta** (town) Oneida County
115	955	**Pavilion** (town) Genesee County
117	948	**West Bloomfield** (town) Ontario County
117	948	**Windsor** (town) Broome County
119	942	**Boston** (town) Erie County
119	942	**Nunda** (town) Livingston County
121	935	**Gang Mills** (CDP) Steuben County
122	932	**Alexander** (town) Genesee County
122	932	**Corning** (city) Steuben County
122	932	**Corning** (town) Steuben County
125	928	**Lansing** (town) Tompkins County
125	928	**Lansing** (village) Tompkins County
127	922	**Cobleskill** (town) Schoharie County
127	922	**Cobleskill** (village) Schoharie County
127	922	**Hancock** (town) Delaware County
130	919	**East Aurora** (village) Erie County
130	919	**Greene** (town) Chenango County
132	912	**Maine** (town) Broome County
133	902	**Big Flats** (CDP) Chemung County
133	902	**Big Flats** (town) Chemung County
133	902	**Candor** (town) Tioga County
133	902	**Fleming** (town) Cayuga County
137	896	**Chenango Bridge** (CDP) Broome County
137	896	**Horseheads** (town) Chemung County
137	896	**Horseheads** (village) Chemung County
137	896	**Le Roy** (town) Genesee County
137	896	**Le Roy** (village) Genesee County
142	892	**Batavia** (city) Genesee County
142	892	**Batavia** (town) Genesee County
142	892	**Kirkwood** (town) Broome County
142	892	**Owasco** (town) Cayuga County
146	889	**Gorham** (town) Ontario County
146	889	**Southport** (CDP) Chemung County
146	889	**Southport** (town) Chemung County
149	886	**West Elmira** (CDP) Chemung County
150	883	**Lowville** (town) Lewis County

Note: This section ranks incorporated places and CDPs (Census Designated Places) with populations of 2,500 or more. Unincorporated postal areas were not considered. Please refer to the User Guide for additional information.

Elevation

Top 150 Places Ranked in *Ascending* Order

State Rank	Feet	Place	State Rank	Feet	Place
1	3	**Port Jefferson** (village) Suffolk County	73	30	**East Moriches** (CDP) Suffolk County
2	7	**Babylon** (town) Suffolk County	73	30	**Lindenhurst** (village) Suffolk County
2	7	**Babylon** (village) Suffolk County	73	30	**Mastic** (CDP) Suffolk County
2	7	**Flanders** (CDP) Suffolk County	73	30	**North Great River** (CDP) Suffolk County
2	7	**Inwood** (CDP) Nassau County	73	30	**Port Washington North** (village) Nassau County
2	7	**Island Park** (village) Nassau County	73	30	**Watervliet** (city) Albany County
2	7	**Lido Beach** (CDP) Nassau County	82	33	**Cold Spring Harbor** (CDP) Suffolk County
2	7	**Long Beach** (city) Nassau County	82	33	**East Hampton** (town) Suffolk County
2	7	**Mastic Beach** (village) Suffolk County	82	33	**Fort Salonga** (CDP) Suffolk County
10	10	**Blue Point** (CDP) Suffolk County	82	33	**Hampton Bays** (CDP) Suffolk County
10	10	**Brookhaven** (CDP) Suffolk County	82	33	**Haverstraw** (town) Rockland County
10	10	**Brookhaven** (town) Suffolk County	82	33	**Haverstraw** (village) Rockland County
10	10	**East Rockaway** (village) Nassau County	82	33	**Montauk** (CDP) Suffolk County
10	10	**Oakdale** (CDP) Suffolk County	82	33	**Mount Sinai** (CDP) Suffolk County
10	10	**Seaford** (CDP) Nassau County	82	33	**North Amityville** (CDP) Suffolk County
10	10	**South Valley Stream** (CDP) Nassau County	82	33	**Troy** (city) Rensselaer County
10	10	**Springs** (CDP) Suffolk County	92	36	**Menands** (village) Albany County
18	13	**Baldwin Harbor** (CDP) Nassau County	92	36	**North Bay Shore** (CDP) Suffolk County
18	13	**East Quogue** (CDP) Suffolk County	92	36	**North Wantagh** (CDP) Nassau County
18	13	**Islip** (CDP) Suffolk County	92	36	**Westhampton** (CDP) Suffolk County
18	13	**Islip** (town) Suffolk County	96	39	**Bayville** (village) Nassau County
18	13	**Manorhaven** (village) Nassau County	96	39	**Elmont** (CDP) Nassau County
18	13	**Oceanside** (CDP) Nassau County	96	39	**Lakeview** (CDP) Nassau County
18	13	**Riverhead** (CDP) Suffolk County	96	39	**Malverne** (village) Nassau County
18	13	**Riverhead** (town) Suffolk County	96	39	**North Valley Stream** (CDP) Nassau County
18	13	**West Bay Shore** (CDP) Suffolk County	96	39	**Roosevelt** (CDP) Nassau County
18	13	**West Sayville** (CDP) Suffolk County	96	39	**Roslyn** (village) Nassau County
28	16	**Bay Shore** (CDP) Suffolk County	96	39	**West Babylon** (CDP) Suffolk County
28	16	**Bayport** (CDP) Suffolk County	96	39	**Yaphank** (CDP) Suffolk County
28	16	**East Islip** (CDP) Suffolk County	105	43	**Catskill** (town) Greene County
28	16	**East Massapequa** (CDP) Nassau County	105	43	**Catskill** (village) Greene County
28	16	**Mattituck** (CDP) Suffolk County	105	43	**North Lindenhurst** (CDP) Suffolk County
28	16	**Merrick** (CDP) Nassau County	105	43	**Port Chester** (village) Westchester County
28	16	**North Sea** (CDP) Suffolk County	105	43	**Queens** (borough) Queens County
28	16	**Rensselaer** (city) Rensselaer County	105	43	**Sands Point** (village) Nassau County
28	16	**Valley Stream** (village) Nassau County	105	43	**South Hempstead** (CDP) Nassau County
37	20	**Amityville** (village) Suffolk County	105	43	**Tappan** (CDP) Rockland County
37	20	**Bellmore** (CDP) Nassau County	113	46	**North Bellmore** (CDP) Nassau County
37	20	**Freeport** (village) Nassau County	113	46	**North Bellport** (CDP) Suffolk County
37	20	**Lynbrook** (village) Nassau County	113	46	**North Merrick** (CDP) Nassau County
37	20	**Patchogue** (village) Suffolk County	116	47	**Mamaroneck** (town) Westchester County
37	20	**Sayville** (CDP) Suffolk County	116	47	**Mamaroneck** (village) Westchester County
37	20	**West Islip** (CDP) Suffolk County	118	49	**Bronx** (borough) Bronx County
44	23	**Baldwin** (CDP) Nassau County	118	49	**Brooklyn** (borough) Kings County
44	23	**Brightwaters** (village) Suffolk County	118	49	**Centerport** (CDP) Suffolk County
44	23	**Copiague** (CDP) Suffolk County	118	49	**North Massapequa** (CDP) Nassau County
44	23	**East Patchogue** (CDP) Suffolk County	118	49	**North Patchogue** (CDP) Suffolk County
44	23	**Eastchester** (CDP) Westchester County	118	49	**Oyster Bay** (CDP) Nassau County
44	23	**Eastchester** (town) Westchester County	118	49	**Oyster Bay** (town) Nassau County
44	23	**Glen Cove** (city) Nassau County	125	52	**Larchmont** (village) Westchester County
44	23	**Green Island** (town/village) Albany County	125	52	**Manorville** (CDP) Suffolk County
44	23	**Hewlett** (CDP) Nassau County	125	52	**Shelter Island** (town) Suffolk County
44	23	**Islip Terrace** (CDP) Suffolk County	125	52	**Shirley** (CDP) Suffolk County
44	23	**Lawrence** (village) Nassau County	125	52	**Uniondale** (CDP) Nassau County
44	23	**Massapequa** (CDP) Nassau County	130	56	**Hempstead** (town) Nassau County
44	23	**Massapequa Park** (village) Nassau County	130	56	**Hempstead** (village) Nassau County
44	23	**Moriches** (CDP) Suffolk County	130	56	**Wyandanch** (CDP) Suffolk County
44	23	**North Babylon** (CDP) Suffolk County	133	59	**Baywood** (CDP) Suffolk County
44	23	**Southold** (CDP) Suffolk County	133	59	**Coeymans** (town) Albany County
44	23	**Southold** (town) Suffolk County	133	59	**Northport** (village) Suffolk County
44	23	**Woodmere** (CDP) Nassau County	133	59	**Smithtown** (CDP) Suffolk County
62	26	**Athens** (town) Greene County	133	59	**Smithtown** (town) Suffolk County
62	26	**Center Moriches** (CDP) Suffolk County	133	59	**South Farmingdale** (CDP) Nassau County
62	26	**Halesite** (CDP) Suffolk County	139	62	**Hauppauge** (CDP) Suffolk County
62	26	**Kings Point** (village) Nassau County	139	62	**Pelham Manor** (village) Westchester County
62	26	**Noyack** (CDP) Suffolk County	141	66	**Bohemia** (CDP) Suffolk County
62	26	**Rockville Centre** (village) Nassau County	141	66	**Franklin Square** (CDP) Nassau County
62	26	**Rye** (city) Westchester County	141	66	**Islandia** (village) Suffolk County
62	26	**Rye** (town) Westchester County	141	66	**Plainedge** (CDP) Nassau County
62	26	**Southampton** (town) Suffolk County	141	66	**Rosendale** (town) Ulster County
62	26	**Southampton** (village) Suffolk County	146	69	**East Farmingdale** (CDP) Suffolk County
62	26	**Wantagh** (CDP) Nassau County	146	69	**Harrison** (town/village) Westchester County
73	30	**Calverton** (CDP) Suffolk County	146	69	**Waterford** (town) Saratoga County
73	30	**Cedarhurst** (village) Nassau County	146	69	**West Hempstead** (CDP) Nassau County
73	30	**Cutchogue** (CDP) Suffolk County	150	72	**East Meadow** (CDP) Nassau County

Note: This section ranks incorporated places and CDPs (Census Designated Places) with populations of 2,500 or more. Unincorporated postal areas were not considered. Please refer to the User Guide for additional information.

Population

Top 150 Places Ranked in *Descending* Order

State Rank	Number	Place	State Rank	Number	Place
1	8,560,072	New York (city)	76	33,657	Long Beach (city) Nassau County
2	2,635,121	Brooklyn (borough) Kings County	77	33,338	Huntington Station (CDP) Suffolk County
3	2,339,280	Queens (borough) Queens County	78	33,307	Salina (town) Onondaga County
4	1,653,877	Manhattan (borough) New York County	79	33,253	Central Islip (CDP) Suffolk County
5	1,455,846	Bronx (borough) Bronx County	80	33,183	Eastchester (town) Westchester County
6	772,296	Hempstead (town) Nassau County	81	32,589	Rome (city) Oneida County
7	487,731	Brookhaven (town) Suffolk County	82	32,538	Spring Valley (village) Rockland County
8	475,948	Staten Island (borough) Richmond County	83	32,482	Franklin Square (CDP) Nassau County
9	335,302	Islip (town) Suffolk County	84	32,282	Manlius (town) Onondaga County
10	298,655	Oyster Bay (town) Nassau County	85	31,954	Clarence (town) Erie County
11	259,574	Buffalo (city) Erie County	86	31,953	Centereach (CDP) Suffolk County
12	231,085	North Hempstead (town) Nassau County	87	31,597	Uniondale (CDP) Nassau County
13	213,199	Babylon (town) Suffolk County	88	31,326	Cicero (town) Onondaga County
14	209,463	Rochester (city) Monroe County	89	31,305	Warwick (town) Orange County
15	204,011	Huntington (town) Suffolk County	90	30,752	North Tonawanda (city) Niagara County
16	200,999	Yonkers (city) Westchester County	91	30,720	Ithaca (city) Tompkins County
17	144,405	Syracuse (city) Onondaga County	92	30,710	Oceanside (CDP) Nassau County
18	134,440	Ramapo (town) Rockland County	93	30,697	Newburgh (town) Orange County
19	125,024	Amherst (town) Erie County	94	30,505	Poughkeepsie (city) Dutchess County
20	117,863	Smithtown (town) Suffolk County	95	30,392	Bay Shore (CDP) Suffolk County
21	98,498	Albany (city) Albany County	96	30,094	Jamestown (city) Chautauqua County
22	96,842	Greece (town) Monroe County	97	29,945	Mamaroneck (town) Westchester County
23	91,799	Greenburgh (town) Westchester County	98	29,623	Port Chester (village) Westchester County
24	87,484	Cheektowaga (town) Erie County	99	29,545	Orchard Park (town) Erie County
25	87,224	Clarkstown (town) Rockland County	100	29,507	Pittsford (town) Monroe County
26	83,051	Colonie (town) Albany County	101	29,506	Glenville (town) Schenectady County
27	79,877	New Rochelle (city) Westchester County	102	29,415	Rotterdam (town) Schenectady County
28	74,597	Cheektowaga (CDP) Erie County	103	29,312	East Fishkill (town) Dutchess County
29	73,044	Tonawanda (town) Erie County	104	28,742	Chili (town) Monroe County
30	68,671	Mount Vernon (city) Westchester County	105	28,653	Gates (town) Monroe County
31	65,705	Schenectady (city) Schenectady County	106	28,540	Wallkill (town) Orange County
32	63,115	Brentwood (CDP) Suffolk County	107	28,444	Newburgh (city) Orange County
33	61,114	Utica (city) Oneida County	108	28,319	Harrison (town/village) Westchester County
34	59,626	Clay (town) Onondaga County	109	28,302	Elmira (city) Chemung County
35	58,404	White Plains (city) Westchester County	110	28,232	Vestal (town) Broome County
36	58,147	Hamburg (town) Erie County	111	27,729	Middletown (city) Orange County
37	58,024	Southampton (town) Suffolk County	112	27,682	Saratoga Springs (city) Saratoga County
38	57,725	Tonawanda (CDP) Erie County	113	27,653	Deer Park (CDP) Suffolk County
39	55,698	Hempstead (village) Nassau County	114	27,647	Dix Hills (CDP) Suffolk County
40	54,817	Union (town) Broome County	115	27,568	Queensbury (town) Warren County
41	51,839	Levittown (CDP) Nassau County	116	27,376	Glen Cove (city) Nassau County
42	50,890	Irondequoit (CDP) Monroe County	117	27,257	Lindenhurst (village) Suffolk County
43	50,365	Orangetown (town) Rockland County	118	27,186	Shirley (CDP) Suffolk County
44	49,826	Troy (city) Rensselaer County	119	27,117	West Islip (CDP) Suffolk County
45	48,976	Niagara Falls (city) Niagara County	120	26,962	Auburn (city) Cayuga County
46	46,978	Rye (town) Westchester County	121	26,906	Wappinger (town) Dutchess County
47	46,660	Perinton (town) Monroe County	122	26,799	New Windsor (town) Orange County
48	45,964	Binghamton (city) Broome County	123	26,437	Watertown (city) Jefferson County
49	45,340	West Seneca (CDP) Erie County	124	26,340	Smithtown (CDP) Suffolk County
50	44,635	Mount Pleasant (town) Westchester County	125	26,141	Plainview (CDP) Nassau County
51	44,513	Poughkeepsie (town) Dutchess County	126	26,117	Holbrook (CDP) Suffolk County
52	44,224	Webster (town) Monroe County	127	25,617	De Witt (town) Onondaga County
53	43,609	Henrietta (town) Monroe County	128	25,386	Ossining (village) Westchester County
54	43,380	Freeport (village) Nassau County	129	25,214	Baldwin (CDP) Nassau County
55	43,168	West Babylon (CDP) Suffolk County	130	24,485	Rockville Centre (village) Nassau County
56	42,942	Lancaster (town) Erie County	131	24,408	Camillus (town) Onondaga County
57	42,913	Monroe (town) Orange County	132	24,129	Medford (CDP) Suffolk County
58	42,816	Cortlandt (town) Westchester County	133	24,111	Peekskill (city) Westchester County
59	42,368	Hicksville (CDP) Nassau County	134	23,664	Montgomery (town) Orange County
60	40,713	Coram (CDP) Suffolk County	135	23,660	Halfmoon (town) Saratoga County
61	38,257	Ossining (town) Westchester County	136	23,508	Fishkill (town) Dutchess County
62	37,843	Valley Stream (village) Nassau County	137	23,419	Kingston (city) Ulster County
63	37,497	Haverstraw (town) Rockland County	138	23,020	Onondaga (town) Onondaga County
64	37,245	Penfield (town) Monroe County	139	22,926	Copiague (CDP) Suffolk County
65	37,195	East Meadow (CDP) Nassau County	140	22,796	East Patchogue (CDP) Suffolk County
66	37,117	Commack (CDP) Suffolk County	141	22,794	Kiryas Joel (village) Orange County
67	36,900	Yorktown (town) Westchester County	142	22,699	Garden City (village) Nassau County
68	36,884	Clifton Park (town) Saratoga County	143	22,658	Lysander (town) Onondaga County
69	36,753	Brighton (CDP) Monroe County	144	22,473	Le Ray (town) Jefferson County
70	36,636	Elmont (CDP) Nassau County	145	22,243	Niskayuna (town) Schenectady County
71	35,745	Guilderland (town) Albany County	146	22,241	Southold (town) Suffolk County
72	34,912	Bethlehem (town) Albany County	147	22,102	Massapequa (CDP) Nassau County
73	34,338	New City (CDP) Rockland County	148	22,043	Monsey (CDP) Rockland County
74	34,328	Carmel (town) Putnam County	149	21,992	New Hartford (town) Oneida County
75	33,839	Riverhead (town) Suffolk County	150	21,935	East Hampton (town) Suffolk County

Note: This section ranks incorporated places and CDPs (Census Designated Places) with populations of 2,500 or more. Unincorporated postal areas were not considered. Please refer to the User Guide for additional information.

Population

Top 150 Places Ranked in *Ascending* Order

State Rank	Number	Place
1	2,502	**Frankfort** (village) Herkimer County
2	2,504	**Pine Plains** (town) Dutchess County
3	2,509	**Parish** (town) Oswego County
4	2,511	**Mount Morris** (village) Livingston County
5	2,512	**Lakeland** (CDP) Onondaga County
6	2,516	**West Bloomfield** (town) Ontario County
7	2,517	**Sangerfield** (town) Oneida County
8	2,526	**Augusta** (town) Oneida County
9	2,535	**Randolph** (town) Cattaraugus County
9	2,535	**Yates** (town) Orleans County
11	2,537	**Addison** (town) Steuben County
11	2,537	**Virgil** (town) Cortland County
13	2,540	**Pavilion** (town) Genesee County
14	2,542	**Saint Johnsville** (town) Montgomery County
15	2,544	**Dolgeville** (village) Herkimer County
15	2,544	**Russia** (town) Herkimer County
17	2,546	**Pierrepont** (town) Saint Lawrence County
18	2,550	**Whitehall** (village) Washington County
19	2,551	**Mohawk** (village) Herkimer County
20	2,557	**Silver Creek** (village) Chautauqua County
21	2,558	**Otisco** (town) Onondaga County
22	2,570	**New Berlin** (town) Chenango County
23	2,574	**Piermont** (village) Rockland County
24	2,578	**Catlin** (town) Chemung County
25	2,582	**East Williston** (village) Nassau County
26	2,584	**Northampton** (town) Fulton County
27	2,587	**Alden** (village) Erie County
28	2,590	**Sheridan** (town) Chautauqua County
29	2,594	**Delaware** (town) Sullivan County
29	2,594	**Lewiston** (village) Niagara County
31	2,597	**Brasher** (town) Saint Lawrence County
31	2,597	**Fleming** (town) Cayuga County
33	2,606	**Lake Placid** (village) Essex County
34	2,608	**Rhinebeck** (village) Dutchess County
35	2,611	**Alexander** (town) Genesee County
36	2,621	**Green Island** (town/village) Albany County
37	2,629	**Yorkville** (village) Oneida County
38	2,631	**Blasdell** (village) Erie County
39	2,633	**Chesterfield** (town) Essex County
40	2,637	**Laurens** (town) Otsego County
41	2,643	**Shelter Island** (town) Suffolk County
42	2,646	**Glasco** (CDP) Ulster County
43	2,650	**Hunter** (town) Greene County
44	2,651	**Corinth** (village) Saratoga County
45	2,655	**Horseheads North** (CDP) Chemung County
46	2,659	**Kendall** (town) Orleans County
47	2,661	**Salem** (town) Washington County
48	2,671	**Clarence Center** (CDP) Erie County
49	2,672	**Westhampton** (CDP) Suffolk County
50	2,678	**Barker** (town) Broome County
51	2,681	**Durham** (town) Greene County
52	2,685	**New Bremen** (town) Lewis County
53	2,703	**Seneca** (town) Ontario County
54	2,705	**Coxsackie** (village) Greene County
55	2,706	**Somerset** (town) Niagara County
56	2,707	**Lisle** (town) Broome County
57	2,709	**Jay** (town) Essex County
58	2,712	**Nichols** (town) Tioga County
59	2,718	**Aurelius** (town) Cayuga County
59	2,718	**Florida** (town) Montgomery County
59	2,718	**Tully** (town) Onondaga County
62	2,725	**Stockport** (town) Columbia County
63	2,735	**Thomaston** (village) Nassau County
64	2,739	**Munsey Park** (village) Nassau County
65	2,740	**Clarence** (CDP) Erie County
66	2,752	**Honeoye Falls** (village) Monroe County
67	2,757	**Victor** (village) Ontario County
68	2,770	**Halesite** (CDP) Suffolk County
69	2,773	**Afton** (town) Chenango County
70	2,790	**Attica** (village) Wyoming County
71	2,792	**Benton** (town) Yates County
71	2,792	**Sardinia** (town) Erie County
73	2,805	**Davenport** (town) Delaware County
74	2,811	**Berne** (town) Albany County
75	2,818	**Knox** (town) Albany County
76	2,828	**Orleans** (town) Jefferson County
77	2,829	**Castile** (town) Wyoming County
77	2,829	**Voorheesville** (village) Albany County
79	2,835	**Elma Center** (CDP) Erie County
79	2,835	**Northwest Harbor** (CDP) Suffolk County
81	2,837	**Cape Vincent** (town) Jefferson County
82	2,840	**Great Neck Estates** (village) Nassau County
83	2,841	**Denmark** (town) Lewis County
84	2,845	**Florida** (village) Orange County
85	2,847	**Guilford** (town) Chenango County
85	2,847	**Shandaken** (town) Ulster County
87	2,849	**Roslyn** (village) Nassau County
88	2,851	**Cazenovia** (village) Madison County
89	2,856	**Sands Point** (village) Nassau County
90	2,859	**New Haven** (town) Oswego County
91	2,861	**Moira** (town) Franklin County
92	2,864	**Gowanda** (village) Cattaraugus County
93	2,868	**Triangle** (town) Broome County
94	2,870	**North Boston** (CDP) Erie County
95	2,877	**Crown Heights** (CDP) Dutchess County
96	2,888	**East Norwich** (CDP) Nassau County
96	2,888	**Lakewood** (village) Chautauqua County
98	2,889	**Franklinville** (town) Cattaraugus County
99	2,890	**Munsons Corners** (CDP) Cortland County
100	2,893	**Akron** (village) Erie County
101	2,897	**Theresa** (town) Jefferson County
102	2,901	**Carlton** (town) Orleans County
103	2,902	**Wanakah** (CDP) Erie County
104	2,906	**Stephentown** (town) Rensselaer County
105	2,907	**West Sand Lake** (CDP) Rensselaer County
106	2,915	**Altona** (town) Clinton County
107	2,934	**Chenango Bridge** (CDP) Broome County
108	2,936	**Cornwall-on-Hudson** (village) Orange County
109	2,937	**Milford** (town) Otsego County
110	2,946	**Madison** (town) Madison County
111	2,947	**Walton** (village) Delaware County
112	2,955	**Balmville** (CDP) Orange County
113	2,961	**Otego** (town) Otsego County
114	2,964	**Callicoon** (town) Sullivan County
115	2,965	**Harriman** (village) Orange County
115	2,965	**Nunda** (town) Livingston County
117	2,979	**Annsville** (town) Oneida County
118	2,987	**Keeseville** (village) Clinton County
119	2,997	**North East** (town) Dutchess County
120	3,010	**Bergen** (town) Genesee County
121	3,013	**Fairview** (CDP) Westchester County
122	3,014	**Spencer** (town) Tioga County
123	3,017	**East Syracuse** (village) Onondaga County
124	3,032	**Wales** (town) Erie County
125	3,036	**Montrose** (CDP) Westchester County
126	3,039	**Schoharie** (town) Schoharie County
127	3,042	**Sterling** (town) Cayuga County
128	3,044	**South Hempstead** (CDP) Nassau County
129	3,054	**Sherrill** (city) Oneida County
130	3,065	**Rutland** (town) Jefferson County
131	3,072	**Darien** (town) Genesee County
132	3,073	**Lido Beach** (CDP) Nassau County
133	3,077	**Wynantskill** (CDP) Rensselaer County
134	3,078	**Pamelia** (town) Jefferson County
135	3,080	**Croghan** (town) Lewis County
136	3,084	**Ticonderoga** (CDP) Essex County
137	3,085	**Au Sable** (town) Clinton County
138	3,092	**Hancock** (town) Delaware County
138	3,092	**Moriches** (CDP) Suffolk County
140	3,096	**Brightwaters** (village) Suffolk County
141	3,103	**Pomona** (village) Rockland County
142	3,108	**Louisville** (town) Saint Lawrence County
143	3,112	**Lake Success** (village) Nassau County
144	3,116	**Greenwood Lake** (village) Orange County
145	3,141	**Warrensburg** (CDP) Warren County
146	3,142	**Sloatsburg** (village) Rockland County
147	3,151	**Oakfield** (town) Genesee County
148	3,167	**Cuba** (town) Allegany County
149	3,174	**Locust Valley** (CDP) Nassau County
150	3,176	**Delhi** (village) Delaware County

Note: This section ranks incorporated places and CDPs (Census Designated Places) with populations of 2,500 or more. Unincorporated postal areas were not considered. Please refer to the User Guide for additional information.

Population Growth Since 2000

Top 150 Places Ranked in *Descending* Order

State Rank	Percent	Place
1	120.1	**Big Flats** (CDP) Chemung County
2	113.5	**Romulus** (town) Seneca County
3	73.5	**Kiryas Joel** (village) Orange County
4	72.9	**New Square** (village) Rockland County
5	68.2	**Brookville** (village) Nassau County
6	61.5	**Keeseville** (village) Clinton County
7	56.4	**Glasco** (CDP) Ulster County
8	55.5	**Marlboro** (CDP) Ulster County
9	54.9	**Kaser** (village) Rockland County
10	52.9	**Clarence Center** (CDP) Erie County
11	52.0	**Monsey** (CDP) Rockland County
12	47.1	**Victor** (town) Ontario County
13	46.0	**North Bay Shore** (CDP) Suffolk County
14	45.6	**Springs** (CDP) Suffolk County
15	41.5	**Riverside** (CDP) Suffolk County
16	41.2	**Noyack** (CDP) Suffolk County
17	41.1	**Flanders** (CDP) Suffolk County
18	40.3	**Canandaigua** (town) Ontario County
19	37.3	**Uniondale** (CDP) Nassau County
20	37.1	**Mount Sinai** (CDP) Suffolk County
21	36.6	**Monroe** (town) Orange County
22	34.5	**Wilton** (town) Saratoga County
23	34.4	**Riverhead** (CDP) Suffolk County
24	33.3	**Moriches** (CDP) Suffolk County
25	31.7	**Harriman** (village) Orange County
26	31.4	**Center Moriches** (CDP) Suffolk County
27	31.1	**Armonk** (CDP) Westchester County
28	30.5	**Manorville** (CDP) Suffolk County
29	29.5	**Wheatfield** (town) Niagara County
30	28.8	**Gang Mills** (CDP) Steuben County
31	28.7	**East Hampton North** (CDP) Suffolk County
32	28.6	**Mastic Beach** (village) Suffolk County
32	28.6	**Newfane** (CDP) Niagara County
32	28.6	**Rocky Point** (CDP) Suffolk County
35	28.5	**Augusta** (town) Oneida County
36	28.4	**North Bellport** (CDP) Suffolk County
36	28.4	**North Hills** (village) Nassau County
38	28.1	**Halfmoon** (town) Saratoga County
39	27.8	**Spring Valley** (village) Rockland County
40	27.4	**Bay Shore** (CDP) Suffolk County
41	26.7	**Melville** (CDP) Suffolk County
42	26.3	**Montebello** (village) Rockland County
43	26.0	**Beekman** (town) Dutchess County
44	25.9	**Minisink** (town) Orange County
45	25.5	**Wading River** (CDP) Suffolk County
45	25.5	**Yaphank** (CDP) Suffolk County
47	24.5	**Montgomery** (village) Orange County
47	24.5	**Orangeburg** (CDP) Rockland County
49	23.6	**Greenville** (town) Orange County
50	23.4	**Milton** (CDP) Saratoga County
50	23.4	**Ramapo** (town) Rockland County
52	23.1	**Calcium** (CDP) Jefferson County
53	23.0	**Delhi** (village) Delaware County
54	22.9	**Woodbury** (town) Orange County
55	22.8	**South Valley Stream** (CDP) Nassau County
56	22.3	**Clarence** (town) Erie County
56	22.3	**Riverhead** (town) Suffolk County
58	22.2	**Attica** (town) Wyoming County
59	22.0	**Saint Regis Mohawk Reservation** (reservation) Franklin County
60	21.8	**Farmington** (town) Ontario County
61	21.7	**Heritage Hills** (CDP) Westchester County
62	21.5	**Wesley Hills** (village) Rockland County
63	21.3	**North Valley Stream** (CDP) Nassau County
64	21.2	**Ballston** (town) Saratoga County
65	21.1	**Myers Corner** (CDP) Dutchess County
66	20.8	**Rensselaer** (city) Rensselaer County
67	20.5	**Lakeview** (CDP) Nassau County
68	20.4	**Haverstraw** (village) Rockland County
69	20.3	**West Nyack** (CDP) Rockland County
70	20.0	**Northeast Ithaca** (CDP) Tompkins County
70	20.0	**Theresa** (town) Jefferson County
72	19.7	**Port Washington North** (village) Nassau County
73	19.3	**North Amityville** (CDP) Suffolk County
74	19.2	**West Sand Lake** (CDP) Rensselaer County
75	19.1	**Munsons Corners** (CDP) Cortland County
76	18.9	**Pompey** (town) Onondaga County
77	18.8	**Holtsville** (CDP) Suffolk County
78	18.6	**Shelter Island** (town) Suffolk County
79	18.5	**Southold** (CDP) Suffolk County
80	18.2	**Malta** (town) Saratoga County
81	17.5	**Caroline** (town) Tompkins County
81	17.5	**Dolgeville** (village) Herkimer County
81	17.5	**Hamptonburgh** (town) Orange County
81	17.5	**Jay** (town) Essex County
81	17.5	**Lysander** (town) Onondaga County
86	17.3	**Crawford** (town) Orange County
87	17.2	**Harrison** (town/village) Westchester County
87	17.2	**New Windsor** (town) Orange County
87	17.2	**Shawangunk** (town) Ulster County
90	17.1	**Brentwood** (CDP) Suffolk County
90	17.1	**Centereach** (CDP) Suffolk County
92	16.9	**East Shoreham** (CDP) Suffolk County
92	16.9	**Somers** (town) Westchester County
92	16.9	**Terryville** (CDP) Suffolk County
95	16.7	**New Paltz** (village) Ulster County
96	16.6	**Coram** (CDP) Suffolk County
96	16.6	**Webster** (town) Monroe County
98	16.2	**Brewerton** (CDP) Onondaga County
98	16.2	**Wawayanda** (town) Orange County
100	16.1	**Batavia** (town) Genesee County
100	16.1	**Erwin** (town) Steuben County
102	16.0	**Fishkill** (town) Dutchess County
103	15.8	**Danby** (town) Tompkins County
103	15.8	**Thiells** (CDP) Rockland County
105	15.7	**Wallkill** (town) Orange County
106	15.6	**Clarkson** (town) Monroe County
107	15.5	**Cayuga Heights** (village) Tompkins County
107	15.5	**Gordon Heights** (CDP) Suffolk County
109	15.2	**East Farmingdale** (CDP) Suffolk County
110	15.1	**Chester** (village) Orange County
110	15.1	**Green Island** (town/village) Albany County
110	15.1	**Harris Hill** (CDP) Erie County
113	14.8	**East Quogue** (CDP) Suffolk County
113	14.8	**Mattituck** (CDP) Suffolk County
115	14.7	**Orleans** (town) Jefferson County
116	14.5	**East Fishkill** (town) Dutchess County
117	14.4	**Hamilton** (village) Madison County
118	14.3	**Calverton** (CDP) Suffolk County
119	14.1	**Hamilton** (town) Madison County
119	14.1	**Stillwater** (town) Saratoga County
121	14.0	**Fort Drum** (CDP) Jefferson County
121	14.0	**Nesconset** (CDP) Suffolk County
123	13.9	**Mechanicstown** (CDP) Orange County
124	13.8	**East Moriches** (CDP) Suffolk County
124	13.8	**Elma Center** (CDP) Erie County
124	13.8	**Pomona** (village) Rockland County
127	13.7	**Airmont** (village) Rockland County
128	13.5	**North Castle** (town) Westchester County
129	13.3	**Le Ray** (town) Jefferson County
129	13.3	**Montgomery** (town) Orange County
129	13.3	**Victor** (village) Ontario County
132	13.2	**Duanesburg** (town) Schenectady County
133	13.1	**Carmel Hamlet** (CDP) Putnam County
134	12.9	**Gorham** (town) Ontario County
135	12.8	**Cutchogue** (CDP) Suffolk County
136	12.5	**Saranac Lake** (village) Franklin County
137	12.4	**Kingsbury** (town) Washington County
137	12.4	**New Hempstead** (village) Rockland County
137	12.4	**North Greenbush** (town) Rensselaer County
140	12.2	**East Greenbush** (CDP) Rensselaer County
140	12.2	**Elmont** (CDP) Nassau County
140	12.2	**New York Mills** (village) Oneida County
143	12.0	**Cicero** (town) Onondaga County
143	12.0	**Grand Island** (town) Erie County
145	11.9	**Ithaca** (town) Tompkins County
146	11.8	**Clifton Park** (town) Saratoga County
146	11.8	**Glenwood Landing** (CDP) Nassau County
146	11.8	**Milton** (town) Saratoga County
149	11.7	**Henrietta** (town) Monroe County
149	11.7	**Hopewell** (town) Ontario County

Note: *This section ranks incorporated places and CDPs (Census Designated Places) with populations of 2,500 or more. Unincorporated postal areas were not considered. Please refer to the User Guide for additional information.*

Population Growth Since 2000

Top 150 Places Ranked in *Ascending* Order

State Rank	Percent	Place
1	-69.8	**Arlington** (CDP) Dutchess County
2	-48.0	**Hartsdale** (CDP) Westchester County
3	-38.6	**Valhalla** (CDP) Westchester County
4	-33.8	**Thornwood** (CDP) Westchester County
5	-33.4	**Perry** (town) Wyoming County
6	-28.7	**Red Oaks Mill** (CDP) Dutchess County
7	-24.5	**Albion** (village) Orleans County
8	-23.6	**Murray** (town) Orleans County
9	-23.1	**Mount Morris** (village) Livingston County
10	-21.3	**Saugerties** (village) Ulster County
11	-20.8	**Collins** (town) Erie County
12	-18.1	**Greenville** (CDP) Westchester County
13	-18.0	**Sound Beach** (CDP) Suffolk County
14	-17.9	**Southampton** (village) Suffolk County
15	-15.4	**Bardonia** (CDP) Rockland County
16	-15.2	**Cape Vincent** (town) Jefferson County
16	-15.2	**Rhinebeck** (village) Dutchess County
18	-14.3	**Setauket-East Setauket** (CDP) Suffolk County
19	-14.2	**Hudson** (city) Columbia County
20	-13.4	**Moravia** (town) Cayuga County
21	-13.2	**Groveland** (town) Livingston County
21	-13.2	**Portland** (town) Chautauqua County
23	-12.9	**Gaines** (town) Orleans County
24	-12.7	**Wellsville** (village) Allegany County
25	-12.4	**Lake Erie Beach** (CDP) Erie County
26	-12.2	**North Patchogue** (CDP) Suffolk County
26	-12.2	**Ogdensburg** (city) Saint Lawrence County
28	-12.0	**Shandaken** (town) Ulster County
29	-11.9	**Lakeland** (CDP) Onondaga County
29	-11.9	**Niagara Falls** (city) Niagara County
31	-11.7	**Silver Creek** (village) Chautauqua County
32	-11.6	**Middletown** (town) Delaware County
33	-11.5	**Balmville** (CDP) Orange County
34	-11.4	**Lakewood** (village) Chautauqua County
34	-11.4	**Sterling** (town) Cayuga County
36	-11.3	**Buffalo** (city) Erie County
36	-11.3	**Catskill** (village) Greene County
36	-11.3	**Eden** (CDP) Erie County
36	-11.3	**Islip** (CDP) Suffolk County
40	-11.2	**Hewlett** (CDP) Nassau County
41	-11.0	**Gouverneur** (village) Saint Lawrence County
42	-10.9	**Conklin** (town) Broome County
43	-10.6	**Oyster Bay** (CDP) Nassau County
44	-10.5	**South Lockport** (CDP) Niagara County
44	-10.5	**Spackenkill** (CDP) Dutchess County
46	-10.4	**Hancock** (town) Delaware County
47	-10.2	**Wolcott** (town) Wayne County
48	-10.1	**Campbell** (town) Steuben County
48	-10.1	**Seneca Falls** (CDP) Seneca County
50	-10.0	**Baldwin Harbor** (CDP) Nassau County
51	-9.9	**Locust Valley** (CDP) Nassau County
51	-9.9	**Oakdale** (CDP) Suffolk County
51	-9.9	**Yorkshire** (town) Cattaraugus County
54	-9.8	**Westfield** (town) Chautauqua County
55	-9.7	**Dannemora** (town) Clinton County
56	-9.6	**Hanover** (town) Chautauqua County
56	-9.6	**Haviland** (CDP) Dutchess County
58	-9.5	**Perry** (village) Wyoming County
59	-9.4	**Medina** (village) Orleans County
59	-9.4	**Olean** (city) Cattaraugus County
61	-9.2	**Merrick** (CDP) Nassau County
61	-9.2	**Niagara** (town) Niagara County
61	-9.2	**Searingtown** (CDP) Nassau County
61	-9.2	**Sidney** (town) Delaware County
65	-9.1	**Putnam Lake** (CDP) Putnam County
65	-9.1	**Scriba** (town) Oswego County
67	-9.0	**Claverack** (town) Columbia County
68	-8.9	**Lyons** (village) Wayne County
68	-8.9	**Warsaw** (town) Wyoming County
70	-8.8	**Brutus** (town) Cayuga County
70	-8.8	**Coeymans** (town) Albany County
70	-8.8	**Lancaster** (village) Erie County
70	-8.8	**Selden** (CDP) Suffolk County
74	-8.7	**Lyncourt** (CDP) Onondaga County
74	-8.7	**Sheridan** (town) Chautauqua County

State Rank	Percent	Place
76	-8.6	**Chester** (town) Warren County
76	-8.6	**Greenwood Lake** (village) Orange County
76	-8.6	**Hawthorne** (CDP) Westchester County
76	-8.6	**Portville** (town) Cattaraugus County
76	-8.6	**Sodus** (town) Wayne County
81	-8.5	**Batavia** (city) Genesee County
81	-8.5	**Caledonia** (town) Livingston County
81	-8.5	**Elmira** (city) Chemung County
81	-8.5	**Lowville** (village) Lewis County
85	-8.4	**Ellicott** (town) Chautauqua County
85	-8.4	**Port Ewen** (CDP) Ulster County
85	-8.4	**West Point** (CDP) Orange County
88	-8.3	**New Berlin** (town) Chenango County
88	-8.3	**North Lindenhurst** (CDP) Suffolk County
88	-8.3	**Penn Yan** (village) Yates County
91	-8.2	**Lima** (town) Livingston County
91	-8.2	**Salamanca** (city) Cattaraugus County
93	-8.1	**Depew** (village) Erie County
93	-8.1	**Dunkirk** (city) Chautauqua County
95	-8.0	**Canisteo** (town) Steuben County
96	-7.9	**Ilion** (village) Herkimer County
96	-7.9	**Schoharie** (town) Schoharie County
98	-7.8	**Altona** (town) Clinton County
99	-7.7	**Canandaigua** (city) Ontario County
99	-7.7	**Little Falls** (city) Herkimer County
99	-7.7	**Wheatland** (town) Monroe County
102	-7.6	**Franklinville** (town) Cattaraugus County
102	-7.6	**Hornell** (city) Steuben County
102	-7.6	**Southport** (CDP) Chemung County
102	-7.6	**Waverly** (village) Tioga County
102	-7.6	**Wayland** (town) Steuben County
107	-7.5	**Fairmount** (CDP) Onondaga County
107	-7.5	**Greene** (town) Chenango County
107	-7.5	**Newark Valley** (town) Tioga County
107	-7.5	**North Tonawanda** (city) Niagara County
111	-7.4	**Aurelius** (town) Cayuga County
111	-7.4	**Evans** (town) Erie County
111	-7.4	**Westfield** (village) Chautauqua County
114	-7.3	**Farmingville** (CDP) Suffolk County
114	-7.3	**Northwest Harbor** (CDP) Suffolk County
116	-7.2	**Arcadia** (town) Wayne County
116	-7.2	**Lockport** (city) Niagara County
118	-7.1	**Dix** (town) Schuyler County
118	-7.1	**Stockport** (town) Columbia County
118	-7.1	**Tonawanda** (city) Erie County
118	-7.1	**Unadilla** (town) Otsego County
122	-7.0	**Cheektowaga** (town) Erie County
122	-7.0	**Otego** (town) Otsego County
122	-7.0	**Ronkonkoma** (CDP) Suffolk County
122	-7.0	**Warsaw** (village) Wyoming County
126	-6.9	**Afton** (town) Chenango County
126	-6.9	**Dansville** (village) Livingston County
126	-6.9	**Horseheads North** (CDP) Chemung County
126	-6.9	**Parish** (town) Oswego County
126	-6.9	**Wellsville** (town) Allegany County
126	-6.9	**Westhampton** (CDP) Suffolk County
132	-6.8	**Rome** (city) Oneida County
133	-6.7	**Cheektowaga** (CDP) Erie County
133	-6.7	**Kenmore** (village) Erie County
133	-6.7	**Lewiston** (village) Niagara County
133	-6.7	**Newark** (village) Wayne County
133	-6.7	**Tupper Lake** (village) Franklin County
138	-6.6	**Coxsackie** (village) Greene County
138	-6.6	**Cuba** (town) Allegany County
138	-6.6	**East Aurora** (village) Erie County
138	-6.6	**East Northport** (CDP) Suffolk County
142	-6.5	**Chautauqua** (town) Chautauqua County
142	-6.5	**Elmira** (town) Chemung County
142	-6.5	**Guilford** (town) Chenango County
142	-6.5	**Marion** (town) Wayne County
142	-6.5	**Southport** (town) Chemung County
142	-6.5	**Tonawanda** (CDP) Erie County
142	-6.5	**Tonawanda** (town) Erie County
142	-6.5	**Village Green** (CDP) Onondaga County
150	-6.4	**Chatham** (town) Columbia County

Note: *This section ranks incorporated places and CDPs (Census Designated Places) with populations of 2,500 or more. Unincorporated postal areas were not considered. Please refer to the User Guide for additional information.*

Population Density

Top 150 Places Ranked in *Descending* Order

State Rank	Pop./ Sq. Mi.	Place	State Rank	Pop./ Sq. Mi.	Place
1	72,447.3	**Manhattan** (borough) New York County	76	6,710.9	**Thomaston** (village) Nassau County
2	37,210.9	**Brooklyn** (borough) Kings County	77	6,685.1	**Bellmore** (CDP) Nassau County
3	34,583.7	**Bronx** (borough) Bronx County	78	6,682.0	**Bronxville** (village) Westchester County
4	29,823.0	**Kaser** (village) Rockland County	79	6,571.5	**Plainedge** (CDP) Nassau County
5	28,284.4	**New York** (city)	80	6,515.4	**Inwood** (CDP) Nassau County
6	22,438.6	**New Square** (village) Rockland County	81	6,512.5	**Hempstead** (town) Nassau County
7	22,308.3	**Great Neck Plaza** (village) Nassau County	82	6,485.5	**Westbury** (village) Nassau County
8	21,553.8	**Queens** (borough) Queens County	83	6,427.6	**Buffalo** (city) Erie County
9	20,561.2	**Kiryas Joel** (village) Orange County	84	6,318.5	**North Wantagh** (CDP) Nassau County
10	16,142.0	**Spring Valley** (village) Rockland County	85	6,238.9	**Hicksville** (CDP) Nassau County
11	15,658.0	**Mount Vernon** (city) Westchester County	86	6,212.4	**Massapequa** (CDP) Nassau County
12	15,197.3	**Long Beach** (city) Nassau County	87	6,212.0	**Oceanside** (CDP) Nassau County
13	15,127.0	**Hempstead** (village) Nassau County	88	6,206.7	**North Massapequa** (CDP) Nassau County
14	14,256.5	**Manorhaven** (village) Nassau County	89	6,158.4	**Mechanicville** (city) Saratoga County
15	12,710.3	**Port Chester** (village) Westchester County	90	6,151.8	**Haverstraw** (village) Rockland County
16	11,723.9	**Williston Park** (village) Nassau County	91	6,102.6	**Eastchester** (CDP) Westchester County
17	11,674.3	**Uniondale** (CDP) Nassau County	92	6,097.4	**Mamaroneck** (village) Westchester County
18	11,523.8	**New Hyde Park** (village) Nassau County	93	6,095.4	**Schenectady** (city) Schenectady County
19	11,505.8	**SUNY Oswego** (CDP) Oswego County	94	6,090.1	**Huntington Station** (CDP) Suffolk County
20	11,478.5	**Floral Park** (village) Nassau County	95	6,084.9	**Baldwin Harbor** (CDP) Nassau County
21	11,287.6	**Franklin Square** (CDP) Nassau County	96	6,053.6	**Manhasset Hills** (CDP) Nassau County
22	11,159.2	**Yonkers** (city) Westchester County	97	5,979.2	**White Plains** (city) Westchester County
23	11,138.8	**Tuckahoe** (village) Westchester County	98	5,932.6	**Hillcrest** (CDP) Rockland County
24	10,875.4	**Elmont** (CDP) Nassau County	99	5,930.4	**Poughkeepsie** (city) Dutchess County
25	10,867.8	**Valley Stream** (village) Nassau County	100	5,901.0	**Seaford** (CDP) Nassau County
26	10,707.5	**Island Park** (village) Nassau County	101	5,900.2	**East Meadow** (CDP) Nassau County
27	10,672.5	**Kenmore** (village) Erie County	102	5,861.1	**South Nyack** (village) Rockland County
28	10,272.9	**North Valley Stream** (CDP) Nassau County	103	5,854.1	**Rochester** (city) Monroe County
29	10,227.6	**Mineola** (village) Nassau County	104	5,824.3	**Pelham** (town) Westchester County
30	10,132.4	**Garden City South** (CDP) Nassau County	105	5,766.2	**Syracuse** (city) Onondaga County
31	9,904.4	**Cedarhurst** (village) Nassau County	106	5,747.9	**Brentwood** (CDP) Suffolk County
32	9,785.5	**Lynbrook** (village) Nassau County	107	5,713.6	**Hartsdale** (CDP) Westchester County
33	9,698.9	**Monsey** (CDP) Rockland County	108	5,701.4	**Ithaca** (city) Tompkins County
34	9,682.0	**New Cassel** (CDP) Nassau County	109	5,672.2	**Larchmont** (village) Westchester County
35	9,678.9	**East Rockaway** (village) Nassau County	110	5,662.1	**Bay Shore** (CDP) Suffolk County
36	9,372.9	**Freeport** (village) Nassau County	111	5,639.0	**Arlington** (CDP) Dutchess County
37	9,168.8	**Nyack** (village) Rockland County	112	5,619.9	**North Lindenhurst** (CDP) Suffolk County
38	9,089.0	**Roosevelt** (CDP) Nassau County	113	5,557.9	**West Babylon** (CDP) Suffolk County
39	8,509.2	**Baldwin** (CDP) Nassau County	114	5,520.5	**Peekskill** (city) Westchester County
40	8,463.6	**Garden City Park** (CDP) Nassau County	115	5,508.9	**Patchogue** (village) Suffolk County
41	8,460.7	**Pelham** (village) Westchester County	116	5,462.9	**Middletown** (city) Orange County
42	8,399.6	**North Amityville** (CDP) Suffolk County	117	5,433.2	**East Massapequa** (CDP) Nassau County
43	8,153.9	**Staten Island** (borough) Richmond County	118	5,388.3	**Eggertsville** (CDP) Erie County
44	8,114.0	**Malverne** (village) Nassau County	119	5,336.9	**Stony Brook University** (CDP) Suffolk County
45	8,060.9	**Ossining** (village) Westchester County	120	5,284.6	**Munsey Park** (village) Nassau County
46	8,046.5	**Binghamton University** (CDP) Broome County	121	5,263.2	**South Hempstead** (CDP) Nassau County
47	7,932.8	**South Valley Stream** (CDP) Nassau County	122	5,260.3	**Carle Place** (CDP) Nassau County
48	7,900.5	**North New Hyde Park** (CDP) Nassau County	123	5,258.9	**Suffern** (village) Rockland County
49	7,892.0	**University Gardens** (CDP) Nassau County	124	5,144.8	**Merrick** (CDP) Nassau County
50	7,793.8	**Massapequa Park** (village) Nassau County	125	5,098.8	**North Babylon** (CDP) Suffolk County
51	7,790.3	**Albertson** (CDP) Nassau County	126	5,017.2	**East Rochester** (town/village) Monroe County
52	7,780.0	**Farmingdale** (village) Nassau County	127	4,980.5	**Babylon** (village) Suffolk County
53	7,729.3	**Great Neck** (village) Nassau County	128	4,948.7	**Oyster Bay** (CDP) Nassau County
54	7,717.4	**New Rochelle** (city) Westchester County	129	4,923.5	**Searingtown** (CDP) Nassau County
55	7,630.6	**North Bellmore** (CDP) Nassau County	130	4,912.5	**Sound Beach** (CDP) Suffolk County
56	7,611.0	**Levittown** (CDP) Nassau County	131	4,887.5	**Wappingers Falls** (village) Dutchess County
57	7,581.6	**Watervliet** (city) Albany County	132	4,857.2	**Cortland** (city) Cortland County
58	7,540.3	**Rockville Centre** (village) Nassau County	133	4,836.4	**Wantagh** (CDP) Nassau County
59	7,476.6	**Newburgh** (city) Orange County	134	4,813.4	**Elmsford** (village) Westchester County
60	7,471.6	**West Hempstead** (CDP) Nassau County	135	4,810.8	**Troy** (city) Rensselaer County
61	7,248.8	**Lindenhurst** (village) Suffolk County	136	4,758.6	**Bethpage** (CDP) Nassau County
62	7,235.0	**North Merrick** (CDP) Nassau County	137	4,716.1	**Sleepy Hollow** (village) Westchester County
63	7,197.5	**Herricks** (CDP) Nassau County	138	4,676.2	**Central Islip** (CDP) Suffolk County
64	7,181.8	**Salisbury** (CDP) Nassau County	139	4,656.7	**Bayville** (village) Nassau County
65	7,123.5	**Copiague** (CDP) Suffolk County	140	4,641.1	**Mount Ivy** (CDP) Rockland County
66	7,113.5	**Hewlett** (CDP) Nassau County	141	4,613.1	**Scotia** (village) Schenectady County
67	7,037.5	**Fairview** (CDP) Westchester County	142	4,611.6	**Selden** (CDP) Suffolk County
68	6,896.6	**South Farmingdale** (CDP) Nassau County	143	4,609.0	**Roslyn Heights** (CDP) Nassau County
69	6,837.5	**Eastchester** (town) Westchester County	144	4,605.2	**Albany** (city) Albany County
70	6,813.7	**West Haverstraw** (village) Rockland County	145	4,598.9	**Sloan** (village) Erie County
71	6,812.7	**Woodmere** (CDP) Nassau County	146	4,586.2	**Dobbs Ferry** (village) Westchester County
72	6,789.9	**Rye** (town) Westchester County	147	4,584.9	**University at Buffalo** (CDP) Erie County
73	6,769.8	**Port Washington North** (village) Nassau County	148	4,561.2	**Sea Cliff** (village) Nassau County
74	6,756.5	**Lakeview** (CDP) Nassau County	149	4,559.9	**Plainview** (CDP) Nassau County
75	6,730.1	**North Bay Shore** (CDP) Suffolk County	150	4,540.4	**East Williston** (village) Nassau County

Note: This section ranks incorporated places and CDPs (Census Designated Places) with populations of 2,500 or more. Unincorporated postal areas were not considered. Please refer to the User Guide for additional information.

Population Density

Top 150 Places Ranked in *Ascending* Order

State Rank	Pop./ Sq. Mi.	Place	State Rank	Pop./ Sq. Mi.	Place
1	17.2	**Croghan** (town) Lewis County	76	66.9	**Sterling** (town) Cayuga County
2	19.5	**Hancock** (town) Delaware County	77	67.3	**Benton** (town) Yates County
3	23.8	**Shandaken** (town) Ulster County	78	67.5	**Knox** (town) Albany County
4	28.5	**Brasher** (town) Saint Lawrence County	79	67.6	**York** (town) Livingston County
4	28.5	**Harrietstown** (town) Franklin County	80	67.8	**Yates** (town) Orleans County
6	28.9	**Altona** (town) Clinton County	81	67.9	**Catlin** (town) Chemung County
7	29.3	**Hunter** (town) Greene County	82	68.0	**Rutland** (town) Jefferson County
8	33.3	**Chesterfield** (town) Essex County	83	69.4	**North East** (town) Dutchess County
9	34.4	**Saranac** (town) Clinton County	83	69.4	**White Creek** (town) Washington County
10	37.0	**Middletown** (town) Delaware County	85	69.5	**Sheridan** (town) Chautauqua County
11	37.7	**Lisbon** (town) Saint Lawrence County	85	69.5	**Whitehall** (town) Washington County
12	38.8	**Stockholm** (town) Saint Lawrence County	87	70.2	**Galen** (town) Wayne County
13	38.9	**Rockland** (town) Sullivan County	88	70.3	**Randolph** (town) Cattaraugus County
14	39.2	**Chester** (town) Warren County	89	70.4	**Otsego** (town) Otsego County
15	39.6	**Orleans** (town) Jefferson County	90	70.6	**Greene** (town) Chenango County
16	40.0	**Jay** (town) Essex County	91	70.8	**Fayette** (town) Seneca County
17	41.1	**Ellisburg** (town) Jefferson County	92	71.1	**Hounsfield** (town) Jefferson County
17	41.1	**Mooers** (town) Clinton County	93	71.3	**Pavilion** (town) Genesee County
19	41.8	**Neversink** (town) Sullivan County	94	72.2	**Madison** (town) Madison County
20	42.3	**Pierrepont** (town) Saint Lawrence County	95	72.9	**Somerset** (town) Niagara County
21	43.9	**Berne** (town) Albany County	96	73.0	**Moriah** (town) Essex County
22	44.6	**Theresa** (town) Jefferson County	97	73.2	**Middleburgh** (town) Schoharie County
23	44.7	**Russia** (town) Herkimer County	98	73.6	**Alexander** (town) Genesee County
24	46.1	**Guilford** (town) Chenango County	99	74.1	**Olive** (town) Ulster County
25	48.2	**Hector** (town) Schuyler County	100	74.2	**Delaware** (town) Sullivan County
26	48.3	**New Bremen** (town) Lewis County	101	74.7	**Chatham** (town) Columbia County
27	48.7	**Bethel** (town) Sullivan County	102	75.4	**Newark Valley** (town) Tioga County
28	49.5	**Annsville** (town) Oneida County	103	75.5	**Tuxedo** (town) Orange County
29	49.9	**Tupper Lake** (town) Franklin County	104	75.7	**Triangle** (town) Broome County
30	50.2	**Stephentown** (town) Rensselaer County	105	76.0	**Jerusalem** (town) Yates County
31	50.3	**Cape Vincent** (town) Jefferson County	106	76.2	**Stanford** (town) Dutchess County
32	50.8	**Salem** (town) Washington County	107	76.5	**Castile** (town) Wyoming County
33	53.6	**Seneca** (town) Ontario County	108	76.9	**Delhi** (town) Delaware County
33	53.6	**Virgil** (town) Cortland County	109	77.1	**Hartland** (town) Niagara County
35	53.8	**Candor** (town) Tioga County	110	77.6	**Richmond** (town) Ontario County
36	54.2	**Florida** (town) Montgomery County	111	77.8	**Chazy** (town) Clinton County
37	54.4	**Davenport** (town) Delaware County	112	78.7	**Dannemora** (town) Clinton County
37	54.4	**Durham** (town) Greene County	112	78.7	**Palatine** (town) Montgomery County
39	54.7	**Walton** (town) Delaware County	114	78.9	**Au Sable** (town) Clinton County
40	55.6	**Sardinia** (town) Erie County	115	79.2	**New Baltimore** (town) Greene County
41	55.7	**New Berlin** (town) Chenango County	116	79.9	**Nunda** (town) Livingston County
42	55.8	**Franklinville** (town) Cattaraugus County	117	80.2	**Wilna** (town) Jefferson County
43	55.9	**North Elba** (town) Essex County	118	80.4	**Nichols** (town) Tioga County
44	56.1	**Denmark** (town) Lewis County	119	80.7	**Norfolk** (town) Saint Lawrence County
44	56.1	**Fort Ann** (town) Washington County	119	80.7	**Washington** (town) Dutchess County
46	56.2	**Alexandria** (town) Jefferson County	121	80.9	**Galway** (town) Saratoga County
47	57.7	**Lisle** (town) Broome County	121	80.9	**Kendall** (town) Orleans County
48	58.5	**Westerlo** (town) Albany County	123	81.2	**Rochester** (town) Ulster County
49	59.2	**Bennington** (town) Wyoming County	123	81.2	**Tioga** (town) Tioga County
50	60.1	**Parish** (town) Oswego County	125	81.6	**Campbell** (town) Steuben County
51	60.5	**Afton** (town) Chenango County	126	81.7	**Sangerfield** (town) Oneida County
51	60.5	**Ticonderoga** (town) Essex County	127	81.9	**Minden** (town) Montgomery County
53	60.7	**Canisteo** (town) Steuben County	127	81.9	**Pine Plains** (town) Dutchess County
54	60.8	**Spencer** (town) Tioga County	129	82.1	**North Collins** (town) Erie County
55	61.0	**Callicoon** (town) Sullivan County	130	84.7	**Veteran** (town) Chemung County
56	61.4	**Clayton** (town) Jefferson County	131	84.8	**Schuyler** (town) Herkimer County
57	62.4	**Caroline** (town) Tompkins County	132	85.2	**Wales** (town) Erie County
58	62.7	**Laurens** (town) Otsego County	133	85.3	**Canajoharie** (town) Montgomery County
59	62.8	**Lake Luzerne** (town) Warren County	134	85.5	**Groveland** (town) Livingston County
60	63.3	**Boonville** (town) Oneida County	135	86.4	**Constantia** (town) Oswego County
60	63.3	**Moira** (town) Franklin County	135	86.4	**Copake** (town) Columbia County
60	63.3	**Oxford** (town) Chenango County	135	86.4	**Mount Morris** (town) Livingston County
63	63.4	**Warrensburg** (town) Warren County	138	86.6	**Otisco** (town) Onondaga County
64	63.7	**Milford** (town) Otsego County	139	87.1	**Woodstock** (town) Ulster County
65	64.0	**Louisville** (town) Saint Lawrence County	140	87.2	**Gorham** (town) Ontario County
66	64.7	**Barker** (town) Broome County	141	87.4	**Arcade** (town) Wyoming County
67	64.8	**Darien** (town) Genesee County	142	88.4	**Peru** (town) Clinton County
68	64.9	**Otego** (town) Otsego County	143	88.6	**Vienna** (town) Oneida County
69	65.0	**Chautauqua** (town) Chautauqua County	144	89.2	**Palermo** (town) Oswego County
69	65.0	**Danby** (town) Tompkins County	145	89.9	**Aurelius** (town) Cayuga County
71	65.5	**Colesville** (town) Broome County	146	90.1	**Sherburne** (town) Chenango County
72	66.0	**Argyle** (town) Washington County	147	90.2	**Cuba** (town) Allegany County
73	66.5	**Carlton** (town) Orleans County	148	90.3	**Newfield** (town) Tompkins County
74	66.6	**Windsor** (town) Broome County	148	90.3	**Sandy Creek** (town) Oswego County
75	66.8	**Oswegatchie** (town) Saint Lawrence County	150	90.6	**Verona** (town) Oneida County

Note: This section ranks incorporated places and CDPs (Census Designated Places) with populations of 2,500 or more. Unincorporated postal areas were not considered. Please refer to the User Guide for additional information.

White Population

Top 150 Places Ranked in *Descending* Order

State Rank	Percent	Place	State Rank	Percent	Place
1	100.0	**Yorkshire** (town) Cattaraugus County	71	98.2	**Holland** (town) Erie County
2	99.8	**Chester** (town) Warren County	71	98.2	**Nunda** (town) Livingston County
3	99.7	**Lake Luzerne** (town) Warren County	71	98.2	**Parish** (town) Oswego County
3	99.7	**Schuyler** (town) Herkimer County	71	98.2	**Poestenkill** (town) Rensselaer County
5	99.6	**Darien** (town) Genesee County	71	98.2	**Sullivan** (town) Madison County
5	99.6	**Eden** (CDP) Erie County	71	98.2	**West Bloomfield** (town) Ontario County
5	99.6	**Elma** (town) Erie County	82	98.1	**Amsterdam** (town) Montgomery County
5	99.6	**Kaser** (village) Rockland County	82	98.1	**Skaneateles** (town) Onondaga County
5	99.6	**North Boston** (CDP) Erie County	82	98.1	**Wellsville** (village) Allegany County
5	99.6	**Owasco** (town) Cayuga County	82	98.1	**Yorkville** (village) Oneida County
5	99.6	**Stephentown** (town) Rensselaer County	86	98.0	**Bainbridge** (town) Chenango County
12	99.5	**Kiryas Joel** (village) Orange County	86	98.0	**Chittenango** (village) Madison County
12	99.5	**Sardinia** (town) Erie County	86	98.0	**Croghan** (town) Lewis County
12	99.5	**Stockholm** (town) Saint Lawrence County	86	98.0	**Jay** (town) Essex County
12	99.5	**Whitesboro** (village) Oneida County	86	98.0	**Mooers** (town) Clinton County
16	99.4	**Alexander** (town) Genesee County	86	98.0	**New Baltimore** (town) Greene County
16	99.4	**Bennington** (town) Wyoming County	86	98.0	**Newark Valley** (town) Tioga County
16	99.4	**Pittstown** (town) Rensselaer County	86	98.0	**Pine Plains** (town) Dutchess County
16	99.4	**Walton** (village) Delaware County	86	98.0	**Sandy Creek** (town) Oswego County
20	99.3	**New Square** (village) Rockland County	95	97.9	**Lee** (town) Oneida County
20	99.3	**Sangerfield** (town) Oneida County	95	97.9	**Moira** (town) Franklin County
20	99.3	**Windsor** (town) Broome County	95	97.9	**Sherrill** (city) Oneida County
23	99.2	**Eden** (town) Erie County	95	97.9	**Triangle** (town) Broome County
24	99.1	**Newfane** (CDP) Niagara County	99	97.8	**Hector** (town) Schuyler County
25	99.0	**Argyle** (town) Washington County	99	97.8	**Lisbon** (town) Saint Lawrence County
25	99.0	**Vienna** (town) Oneida County	99	97.8	**Lisle** (town) Broome County
27	98.9	**Charlton** (town) Saratoga County	99	97.8	**Sand Lake** (town) Rensselaer County
27	98.9	**Knox** (town) Albany County	99	97.8	**Scriba** (town) Oswego County
27	98.9	**Madison** (town) Madison County	99	97.8	**Ticonderoga** (town) Essex County
27	98.9	**Marilla** (town) Erie County	105	97.7	**Campbell** (town) Steuben County
27	98.9	**Sterling** (town) Cayuga County	105	97.7	**Fleming** (town) Cayuga County
32	98.8	**Blue Point** (CDP) Suffolk County	105	97.7	**Floyd** (town) Oneida County
32	98.8	**Elma Center** (CDP) Erie County	105	97.7	**Milo** (town) Yates County
32	98.8	**Mohawk** (village) Herkimer County	105	97.7	**Newfane** (town) Niagara County
32	98.8	**Portville** (town) Cattaraugus County	105	97.7	**Otisco** (town) Onondaga County
32	98.8	**Southold** (CDP) Suffolk County	105	97.7	**Trenton** (town) Oneida County
32	98.8	**Warrensburg** (CDP) Warren County	112	97.6	**Clarence** (CDP) Erie County
32	98.8	**Wayland** (town) Steuben County	112	97.6	**Ellery** (town) Chautauqua County
39	98.7	**Colden** (town) Erie County	112	97.6	**Westerlo** (town) Albany County
39	98.7	**Laurens** (town) Otsego County	115	97.5	**Greenwich** (town) Washington County
39	98.7	**Northampton** (town) Fulton County	115	97.5	**Lake George** (town) Warren County
39	98.7	**Oswegatchie** (town) Saint Lawrence County	115	97.5	**Mayfield** (town) Fulton County
39	98.7	**Pendleton** (town) Niagara County	115	97.5	**Middleburgh** (town) Schoharie County
39	98.7	**Tioga** (town) Tioga County	115	97.5	**Milford** (town) Otsego County
39	98.7	**Walton** (town) Delaware County	115	97.5	**Riga** (town) Monroe County
46	98.6	**Boston** (town) Erie County	115	97.5	**Seneca** (town) Ontario County
46	98.6	**Gorham** (town) Ontario County	115	97.5	**Shelter Island** (town) Suffolk County
46	98.6	**Orleans** (town) Jefferson County	115	97.5	**Westfield** (village) Chautauqua County
46	98.6	**Whitehall** (town) Washington County	124	97.4	**Big Flats** (town) Chemung County
50	98.5	**Constantia** (town) Oswego County	124	97.4	**Candor** (town) Tioga County
50	98.5	**Fort Edward** (village) Washington County	124	97.4	**Champlain** (town) Clinton County
50	98.5	**Lakewood** (village) Chautauqua County	124	97.4	**Guilford** (town) Chenango County
50	98.5	**Lido Beach** (CDP) Nassau County	124	97.4	**Milton** (CDP) Saratoga County
50	98.5	**Salem** (town) Washington County	124	97.4	**New Berlin** (town) Chenango County
50	98.5	**Volney** (town) Oswego County	124	97.4	**New Haven** (town) Oswego County
50	98.5	**Warrensburg** (town) Warren County	124	97.4	**West Elmira** (CDP) Chemung County
57	98.4	**Barker** (town) Broome County	132	97.3	**Boonville** (town) Oneida County
57	98.4	**Canisteo** (town) Steuben County	132	97.3	**Busti** (town) Chautauqua County
57	98.4	**East Bloomfield** (town) Ontario County	132	97.3	**Centerport** (CDP) Suffolk County
57	98.4	**Hoosick** (town) Rensselaer County	132	97.3	**Franklinville** (town) Cattaraugus County
57	98.4	**Manheim** (town) Herkimer County	132	97.3	**Granby** (town) Oswego County
57	98.4	**Richland** (town) Oswego County	132	97.3	**Kendall** (town) Orleans County
63	98.3	**Adams** (town) Jefferson County	132	97.3	**Malone** (village) Franklin County
63	98.3	**Broadalbin** (town) Fulton County	132	97.3	**Ticonderoga** (CDP) Essex County
63	98.3	**Clayton** (town) Jefferson County	132	97.3	**West Monroe** (town) Oswego County
63	98.3	**Hoosick Falls** (village) Rensselaer County	132	97.3	**West Sand Lake** (CDP) Rensselaer County
63	98.3	**Peru** (town) Clinton County	142	97.2	**Afton** (town) Chenango County
63	98.3	**Somerset** (town) Niagara County	142	97.2	**Aurora** (town) Erie County
63	98.3	**Westfield** (town) Chautauqua County	142	97.2	**Canastota** (village) Madison County
63	98.3	**Whitehall** (village) Washington County	142	97.2	**Corinth** (town) Saratoga County
71	98.2	**Aurelius** (town) Cayuga County	142	97.2	**Greenville** (town) Greene County
71	98.2	**Carroll** (town) Chautauqua County	142	97.2	**Macedon** (town) Wayne County
71	98.2	**Chenango Bridge** (CDP) Broome County	142	97.2	**Norfolk** (town) Saint Lawrence County
71	98.2	**Conklin** (town) Broome County	149	97.1	**Cambria** (town) Niagara County
71	98.2	**Dolgeville** (village) Herkimer County	149	97.1	**East Moriches** (CDP) Suffolk County

Note: *This section ranks incorporated places and CDPs (Census Designated Places) with populations of 2,500 or more. Unincorporated postal areas were not considered. Please refer to the User Guide for additional information.*

White Population

Top 150 Places Ranked in *Ascending* Order

State Rank	Percent	Place
1	5.3	**Saint Regis Mohawk Reservation** (reservation) Franklin County
2	13.2	**Lakeview** (CDP) Nassau County
3	13.8	**Hempstead** (village) Nassau County
4	13.9	**North Amityville** (CDP) Suffolk County
5	16.0	**Roosevelt** (CDP) Nassau County
6	19.9	**New Cassel** (CDP) Nassau County
7	20.3	**Wyandanch** (CDP) Suffolk County
8	21.0	**Bronx** (borough) Bronx County
9	21.1	**Elmont** (CDP) Nassau County
10	22.1	**Mount Vernon** (city) Westchester County
11	24.0	**North Valley Stream** (CDP) Nassau County
12	26.8	**Fairview** (CDP) Westchester County
13	28.2	**Hillcrest** (CDP) Rockland County
14	29.2	**North Bay Shore** (CDP) Suffolk County
15	30.0	**Wheatley Heights** (CDP) Suffolk County
16	34.1	**Uniondale** (CDP) Nassau County
17	34.8	**Spring Valley** (village) Rockland County
18	35.1	**Newburgh** (city) Orange County
18	35.1	**Stony Brook University** (CDP) Suffolk County
20	37.6	**Inwood** (CDP) Nassau County
21	39.7	**Queens** (borough) Queens County
22	40.4	**Garden City Park** (CDP) Nassau County
23	40.5	**Freeport** (village) Nassau County
24	41.1	**Elmsford** (village) Westchester County
25	41.8	**Peekskill** (city) Westchester County
26	41.9	**South Valley Stream** (CDP) Nassau County
27	42.8	**New York** (city)
28	43.2	**Brooklyn** (borough) Kings County
29	43.8	**Ossining** (village) Westchester County
30	44.5	**Dannemora** (village) Clinton County
30	44.5	**Valley Stream** (village) Nassau County
32	45.3	**Haverstraw** (village) Rockland County
33	46.2	**Baldwin** (CDP) Nassau County
34	46.6	**Rochester** (city) Monroe County
35	47.4	**Westbury** (village) Nassau County
36	47.6	**Buffalo** (city) Erie County
37	47.7	**Monticello** (village) Sullivan County
38	48.1	**Poughkeepsie** (city) Dutchess County
39	48.3	**Central Islip** (CDP) Suffolk County
40	48.5	**Herricks** (CDP) Nassau County
41	48.7	**Middletown** (city) Orange County
42	49.1	**Manhasset Hills** (CDP) Nassau County
43	49.2	**Gordon Heights** (CDP) Suffolk County
44	49.8	**Lake Success** (village) Nassau County
45	50.9	**Searingtown** (CDP) Nassau County
46	51.5	**Harriman** (village) Orange County
47	51.7	**Bay Shore** (CDP) Suffolk County
48	52.0	**West Haverstraw** (village) Rockland County
49	52.1	**Riverside** (CDP) Suffolk County
50	52.4	**Dannemora** (town) Clinton County
51	52.6	**Scotchtown** (CDP) Orange County
52	52.7	**Arlington** (CDP) Dutchess County
53	53.0	**University Gardens** (CDP) Nassau County
54	53.4	**University at Buffalo** (CDP) Erie County
55	53.5	**New Hyde Park** (village) Nassau County
56	54.5	**Haverstraw** (town) Rockland County
56	54.5	**Mechanicstown** (CDP) Orange County
58	55.0	**Port Chester** (village) Westchester County
59	55.1	**Albany** (city) Albany County
60	55.2	**Syracuse** (city) Onondaga County
61	55.4	**Calcium** (CDP) Jefferson County
62	55.6	**Northeast Ithaca** (CDP) Tompkins County
63	56.0	**Ossining** (town) Westchester County
64	56.3	**Yonkers** (city) Westchester County
65	56.4	**Manhattan** (borough) New York County
66	57.0	**North New Hyde Park** (CDP) Nassau County
67	57.4	**Menands** (village) Albany County
68	57.6	**Mount Ivy** (CDP) Rockland County
69	57.7	**Sleepy Hollow** (village) Westchester County
70	58.7	**Orange Lake** (CDP) Orange County
71	58.8	**Brentwood** (CDP) Suffolk County
72	59.0	**Baldwin Harbor** (CDP) Nassau County
73	59.2	**East Farmingdale** (CDP) Suffolk County
74	59.4	**Schenectady** (city) Schenectady County
75	59.5	**Vails Gate** (CDP) Orange County
76	59.7	**White Plains** (city) Westchester County
77	60.0	**New Rochelle** (city) Westchester County
78	60.1	**Hartsdale** (CDP) Westchester County
79	60.6	**Lansing** (village) Tompkins County
80	60.9	**Bedford Hills** (CDP) Westchester County
80	60.9	**Wallkill** (town) Orange County
82	61.1	**Baywood** (CDP) Suffolk County
83	61.6	**Chestnut Ridge** (village) Rockland County
84	61.7	**Jericho** (CDP) Nassau County
85	62.0	**Nanuet** (CDP) Rockland County
86	62.2	**New Hempstead** (village) Rockland County
87	62.5	**Glen Cove** (city) Nassau County
88	62.8	**Huntington Station** (CDP) Suffolk County
89	62.9	**Hudson** (city) Columbia County
90	63.3	**Islandia** (village) Suffolk County
90	63.3	**Nyack** (village) Rockland County
90	63.3	**Romulus** (town) Seneca County
93	63.4	**Utica** (city) Oneida County
94	63.5	**Thomaston** (village) Nassau County
95	63.7	**Wappingers Falls** (village) Dutchess County
96	63.9	**Hempstead** (town) Nassau County
97	64.0	**Binghamton University** (CDP) Broome County
98	64.8	**Rye** (town) Westchester County
99	65.1	**Ellenville** (village) Ulster County
100	65.5	**Hicksville** (CDP) Nassau County
101	65.6	**Chester** (village) Orange County
102	66.1	**Mount Kisco** (town/village) Westchester County
102	66.1	**Roslyn Heights** (CDP) Nassau County
104	66.2	**Thompson** (town) Sullivan County
105	66.4	**Fort Drum** (CDP) Jefferson County
106	66.7	**Beacon** (city) Dutchess County
107	66.9	**North Hempstead** (town) Nassau County
108	67.2	**Old Westbury** (village) Nassau County
109	67.3	**West Hempstead** (CDP) Nassau County
110	67.4	**Greenville** (CDP) Westchester County
111	67.6	**Babylon** (town) Suffolk County
111	67.6	**Copiague** (CDP) Suffolk County
113	67.9	**Salamanca** (city) Cattaraugus County
114	68.2	**Greenburgh** (town) Westchester County
115	68.3	**Le Ray** (town) Jefferson County
115	68.3	**Monroe** (village) Orange County
115	68.3	**Syosset** (CDP) Nassau County
118	68.4	**Fort Ann** (town) Washington County
119	68.5	**Groveland** (town) Livingston County
120	68.6	**Ithaca** (city) Tompkins County
121	68.7	**Kingston** (city) Ulster County
122	68.9	**North Bellport** (CDP) Suffolk County
123	69.2	**Franklin Square** (CDP) Nassau County
124	69.5	**Highland Falls** (village) Orange County
124	69.5	**Niagara Falls** (city) Niagara County
126	69.6	**New Windsor** (town) Orange County
127	69.7	**Fishkill** (town) Dutchess County
128	69.8	**Troy** (city) Rensselaer County
129	70.4	**Valley Cottage** (CDP) Rockland County
130	70.5	**Attica** (town) Wyoming County
130	70.5	**Deer Park** (CDP) Suffolk County
130	70.5	**Ramapo** (town) Rockland County
133	70.9	**Clarkstown** (town) Rockland County
134	71.0	**Maybrook** (village) Orange County
134	71.0	**Pomona** (village) Rockland County
134	71.0	**South Nyack** (village) Rockland County
137	71.5	**Albertson** (CDP) Nassau County
137	71.5	**Ardsley** (village) Westchester County
139	71.6	**Pelham** (village) Westchester County
140	71.7	**North Hills** (village) Nassau County
140	71.7	**Wawarsing** (town) Ulster County
142	71.9	**Muttontown** (village) Nassau County
143	72.0	**Mount Hope** (town) Orange County
144	72.2	**Fallsburg** (town) Sullivan County
144	72.2	**Greenlawn** (CDP) Suffolk County
144	72.2	**Manorhaven** (village) Nassau County
147	72.3	**Balmville** (CDP) Orange County
148	72.5	**Collins** (town) Erie County
148	72.5	**Islip** (town) Suffolk County
150	72.7	**Eggertsville** (CDP) Erie County

Note: This section ranks incorporated places and CDPs (Census Designated Places) with populations of 2,500 or more. Unincorporated postal areas were not considered. Please refer to the User Guide for additional information.

Black/African American Population

Top 150 Places Ranked in *Descending* Order

State Rank	Percent	Place
1	74.6	**Lakeview** (CDP) Nassau County
2	66.7	**Mount Vernon** (city) Westchester County
3	61.7	**Fairview** (CDP) Westchester County
4	59.5	**Wyandanch** (CDP) Suffolk County
5	56.0	**Roosevelt** (CDP) Nassau County
6	55.6	**North Amityville** (CDP) Suffolk County
7	50.8	**Wheatley Heights** (CDP) Suffolk County
8	48.1	**Hillcrest** (CDP) Rockland County
8	48.1	**North Valley Stream** (CDP) Nassau County
10	47.4	**Elmont** (CDP) Nassau County
11	46.3	**Hempstead** (village) Nassau County
12	42.6	**Gordon Heights** (CDP) Suffolk County
13	42.1	**Dannemora** (village) Clinton County
14	40.7	**Rochester** (city) Monroe County
15	39.7	**New Cassel** (CDP) Nassau County
16	38.2	**Uniondale** (CDP) Nassau County
17	37.6	**Poughkeepsie** (city) Dutchess County
17	37.6	**Spring Valley** (village) Rockland County
19	37.1	**Buffalo** (city) Erie County
20	35.8	**Dannemora** (town) Clinton County
21	35.5	**Baldwin** (CDP) Nassau County
22	33.6	**Bronx** (borough) Bronx County
23	33.0	**Brooklyn** (borough) Kings County
24	32.8	**Riverside** (CDP) Suffolk County
25	31.5	**South Valley Stream** (CDP) Nassau County
26	31.2	**Freeport** (village) Nassau County
26	31.2	**Monticello** (village) Sullivan County
28	30.9	**Romulus** (town) Seneca County
29	29.0	**Syracuse** (city) Onondaga County
30	28.7	**Albany** (city) Albany County
31	27.2	**Central Islip** (CDP) Suffolk County
32	27.0	**Baldwin Harbor** (CDP) Nassau County
32	27.0	**Newburgh** (city) Orange County
34	26.1	**Arlington** (CDP) Dutchess County
35	25.7	**Groveland** (town) Livingston County
35	25.7	**Mechanicstown** (CDP) Orange County
37	25.2	**Westbury** (village) Nassau County
38	25.1	**Valley Stream** (village) Nassau County
39	25.0	**Fort Ann** (town) Washington County
39	25.0	**Scotchtown** (CDP) Orange County
41	24.6	**Nyack** (village) Rockland County
42	24.5	**Attica** (town) Wyoming County
43	24.3	**New York** (city)
44	24.0	**Bay Shore** (CDP) Suffolk County
45	23.9	**Calcium** (CDP) Jefferson County
45	23.9	**Chestnut Ridge** (CDP) Rockland County
47	23.8	**Inwood** (CDP) Nassau County
48	23.0	**North Bellport** (CDP) Suffolk County
49	22.8	**Orange Lake** (CDP) Orange County
50	22.6	**Niagara Falls** (city) Niagara County
51	22.2	**Harriman** (village) Orange County
51	22.2	**Hudson** (city) Columbia County
53	21.8	**Elmsford** (village) Westchester County
54	21.6	**Middletown** (city) Orange County
55	21.5	**Catskill** (village) Greene County
55	21.5	**Mount Ivy** (CDP) Rockland County
57	21.4	**Peekskill** (city) Westchester County
57	21.4	**Riverhead** (CDP) Suffolk County
59	20.9	**Schenectady** (city) Schenectady County
60	20.1	**Vails Gate** (CDP) Orange County
61	20.0	**New Rochelle** (city) Westchester County
62	19.7	**Thompson** (town) Sullivan County
63	19.5	**Coxsackie** (village) Greene County
64	19.4	**Maybrook** (village) Orange County
65	18.7	**Albion** (town) Orleans County
65	18.7	**New Hempstead** (village) Rockland County
65	18.7	**Wallkill** (town) Orange County
68	18.2	**Highland Falls** (village) Orange County
68	18.2	**Queens** (borough) Queens County
70	18.1	**Beacon** (city) Dutchess County
71	18.0	**North Bay Shore** (CDP) Suffolk County
72	17.8	**Yonkers** (city) Westchester County
73	17.6	**West Haverstraw** (village) Rockland County
74	17.1	**Troy** (city) Rensselaer County
75	17.0	**Hempstead** (town) Nassau County
76	16.6	**Kingston** (city) Ulster County
76	16.6	**Mount Hope** (town) Orange County
76	16.6	**Nanuet** (CDP) Rockland County
79	16.5	**Babylon** (town) Suffolk County
79	16.5	**Baywood** (CDP) Suffolk County
79	16.5	**Greenlawn** (CDP) Suffolk County
79	16.5	**Malone** (town) Franklin County
83	16.3	**Collins** (town) Erie County
84	16.0	**Fairview** (CDP) Dutchess County
84	16.0	**Menands** (village) Albany County
86	15.9	**South Nyack** (village) Rockland County
87	15.8	**Ossining** (village) Westchester County
87	15.8	**Utica** (city) Oneida County
89	15.7	**Haverstraw** (town) Rockland County
90	15.6	**Fort Drum** (CDP) Jefferson County
90	15.6	**Pomona** (village) Rockland County
92	15.4	**Ramapo** (town) Rockland County
93	15.1	**Middle Island** (CDP) Suffolk County
94	15.0	**Elmira** (city) Chemung County
95	14.9	**Eggertsville** (CDP) Erie County
95	14.9	**Manhattan** (borough) New York County
97	14.7	**Le Ray** (town) Jefferson County
97	14.7	**Port Jervis** (city) Orange County
99	14.6	**Brentwood** (CDP) Suffolk County
100	14.5	**Delhi** (village) Delaware County
101	14.2	**Cape Vincent** (town) Jefferson County
102	13.7	**Deer Park** (CDP) Suffolk County
103	13.5	**East Massapequa** (CDP) Nassau County
103	13.5	**Southampton** (village) Suffolk County
105	13.3	**Binghamton** (city) Broome County
105	13.3	**Poughkeepsie** (town) Dutchess County
107	13.2	**Chester** (village) Orange County
107	13.2	**Moravia** (town) Cayuga County
107	13.2	**SUNY Oswego** (CDP) Oswego County
110	13.1	**Greenburgh** (town) Westchester County
111	13.0	**North Gates** (CDP) Monroe County
112	12.9	**Fishkill** (town) Dutchess County
113	12.8	**Islandia** (village) Suffolk County
113	12.8	**New Windsor** (town) Orange County
113	12.8	**Newburgh** (town) Orange County
116	12.7	**Balmville** (CDP) Orange County
117	12.5	**White Plains** (city) Westchester County
118	12.4	**Ossining** (town) Westchester County
119	12.3	**Alden** (town) Erie County
119	12.3	**Mastic Beach** (village) Suffolk County
121	11.9	**Fallsburg** (town) Sullivan County
121	11.9	**Pelham** (village) Westchester County
123	11.8	**Cheektowaga** (CDP) Erie County
123	11.8	**Gates** (town) Monroe County
125	11.5	**Marcy** (town) Oneida County
126	11.4	**North Elba** (town) Essex County
127	11.3	**East Farmingdale** (CDP) Suffolk County
127	11.3	**University at Buffalo** (CDP) Erie County
129	11.2	**Albion** (village) Orleans County
129	11.2	**Clarkstown** (town) Rockland County
129	11.2	**Haverstraw** (village) Rockland County
132	11.1	**West Babylon** (CDP) Suffolk County
133	10.7	**Mastic** (CDP) Suffolk County
134	10.6	**Thiells** (CDP) Rockland County
134	10.6	**Watervliet** (city) Albany County
136	10.5	**Ellenville** (village) Ulster County
136	10.5	**Islip** (town) Suffolk County
138	10.4	**Cheektowaga** (town) Erie County
138	10.4	**Coram** (CDP) Suffolk County
140	10.3	**Staten Island** (borough) Richmond County
140	10.3	**Wappingers Falls** (village) Dutchess County
140	10.3	**West Hempstead** (CDP) Nassau County
143	10.2	**Chili** (town) Monroe County
143	10.2	**Geneva** (city) Ontario County
143	10.2	**New Windsor** (CDP) Orange County
143	10.2	**Stony Brook University** (CDP) Suffolk County
147	10.1	**South Blooming Grove** (village) Orange County
148	10.0	**Gates** (CDP) Monroe County
148	10.0	**Stony Point** (CDP) Rockland County
148	10.0	**Wawarsing** (town) Ulster County

Note: This section ranks incorporated places and CDPs (Census Designated Places) with populations of 2,500 or more. Unincorporated postal areas were not considered. Please refer to the User Guide for additional information.

Black/African American Population

Top 150 Places Ranked in *Ascending* Order

State Rank	Percent	Place
1	0.0	**Attica** (village) Wyoming County
1	0.0	**Barker** (town) Broome County
1	0.0	**Bennington** (town) Wyoming County
1	0.0	**Bergen** (town) Genesee County
1	0.0	**Brewerton** (CDP) Onondaga County
1	0.0	**Canastota** (village) Madison County
1	0.0	**Cedarhurst** (village) Nassau County
1	0.0	**Clarence Center** (CDP) Erie County
1	0.0	**Clarkson** (CDP) Monroe County
1	0.0	**Constantia** (town) Oswego County
1	0.0	**Cornwall-on-Hudson** (village) Orange County
1	0.0	**Darien** (town) Genesee County
1	0.0	**Elma** (town) Erie County
1	0.0	**Elma Center** (CDP) Erie County
1	0.0	**Fayette** (town) Seneca County
1	0.0	**Florida** (town) Montgomery County
1	0.0	**Fort Edward** (village) Washington County
1	0.0	**Great Neck Estates** (village) Nassau County
1	0.0	**Hector** (town) Schuyler County
1	0.0	**Holland** (town) Erie County
1	0.0	**Hoosick** (town) Rensselaer County
1	0.0	**Hoosick Falls** (village) Rensselaer County
1	0.0	**Horseheads North** (CDP) Chemung County
1	0.0	**Kaser** (village) Rockland County
1	0.0	**Kiryas Joel** (village) Orange County
1	0.0	**Lewiston** (village) Niagara County
1	0.0	**Lisle** (town) Broome County
1	0.0	**Louisville** (town) Saint Lawrence County
1	0.0	**Mahopac** (CDP) Putnam County
1	0.0	**Manhasset Hills** (CDP) Nassau County
1	0.0	**Mattituck** (CDP) Suffolk County
1	0.0	**Milton** (CDP) Saratoga County
1	0.0	**Minden** (town) Montgomery County
1	0.0	**Mooers** (town) Clinton County
1	0.0	**Munsey Park** (village) Nassau County
1	0.0	**New Berlin** (town) Chenango County
1	0.0	**North Boston** (CDP) Erie County
1	0.0	**Olive** (town) Ulster County
1	0.0	**Otisco** (town) Onondaga County
1	0.0	**Owasco** (town) Cayuga County
1	0.0	**Palermo** (town) Oswego County
1	0.0	**Parish** (town) Oswego County
1	0.0	**Pendleton** (town) Niagara County
1	0.0	**Pittstown** (town) Rensselaer County
1	0.0	**Plainedge** (CDP) Nassau County
1	0.0	**Portville** (town) Cattaraugus County
1	0.0	**Richmond** (town) Ontario County
1	0.0	**Sardinia** (town) Erie County
1	0.0	**Scriba** (town) Oswego County
1	0.0	**Seaford** (CDP) Nassau County
1	0.0	**Shandaken** (town) Ulster County
1	0.0	**Shelter Island** (town) Suffolk County
1	0.0	**Skaneateles** (town) Onondaga County
1	0.0	**Stephentown** (town) Rensselaer County
1	0.0	**Sterling** (town) Cayuga County
1	0.0	**Stockholm** (town) Saint Lawrence County
1	0.0	**Tioga** (town) Tioga County
1	0.0	**Trenton** (town) Oneida County
1	0.0	**Village Green** (CDP) Onondaga County
1	0.0	**Wales** (town) Erie County
1	0.0	**Walton** (village) Delaware County
1	0.0	**Wanakah** (CDP) Erie County
1	0.0	**West Bloomfield** (town) Ontario County
1	0.0	**Westfield** (town) Chautauqua County
1	0.0	**Westfield** (village) Chautauqua County
1	0.0	**White Creek** (town) Washington County
1	0.0	**Whitesboro** (village) Oneida County
1	0.0	**Yorkshire** (town) Cattaraugus County
69	0.1	**Batavia** (town) Genesee County
69	0.1	**Bayville** (village) Nassau County
69	0.1	**Berne** (town) Albany County
69	0.1	**Blue Point** (CDP) Suffolk County
69	0.1	**East Norwich** (CDP) Nassau County
69	0.1	**East Quogue** (CDP) Suffolk County
69	0.1	**Eden** (CDP) Erie County
69	0.1	**Eden** (town) Erie County
69	0.1	**Fairport** (village) Monroe County
69	0.1	**Franklinville** (town) Cattaraugus County
69	0.1	**Glens Falls North** (CDP) Warren County
69	0.1	**Greenwich** (town) Washington County
69	0.1	**Hartland** (town) Niagara County
69	0.1	**Hornellsville** (town) Steuben County
69	0.1	**Madison** (town) Madison County
69	0.1	**Manorhaven** (village) Nassau County
69	0.1	**Old Bethpage** (CDP) Nassau County
69	0.1	**Saint Regis Mohawk Reservation** (reservation) Franklin County
69	0.1	**Schroeppel** (town) Oswego County
69	0.1	**Schuyler** (town) Herkimer County
69	0.1	**Seneca** (town) Ontario County
69	0.1	**Somerset** (town) Niagara County
69	0.1	**Southold** (CDP) Suffolk County
69	0.1	**Volney** (town) Oswego County
69	0.1	**Waterloo** (village) Seneca County
69	0.1	**Windsor** (town) Broome County
95	0.2	**Adams** (town) Jefferson County
95	0.2	**Argyle** (town) Washington County
95	0.2	**Avon** (town) Livingston County
95	0.2	**Bainbridge** (town) Chenango County
95	0.2	**Boonville** (town) Oneida County
95	0.2	**Chester** (town) Warren County
95	0.2	**Cold Spring Harbor** (CDP) Suffolk County
95	0.2	**Cornwall** (town) Orange County
95	0.2	**Fleming** (town) Cayuga County
95	0.2	**Gorham** (town) Ontario County
95	0.2	**Lake Luzerne** (town) Warren County
95	0.2	**Lenox** (town) Madison County
95	0.2	**Lido Beach** (CDP) Nassau County
95	0.2	**Marilla** (town) Erie County
95	0.2	**Massena** (town) Saint Lawrence County
95	0.2	**Massena** (village) Saint Lawrence County
95	0.2	**Mayfield** (town) Fulton County
95	0.2	**Miller Place** (CDP) Suffolk County
95	0.2	**Mohawk** (town) Montgomery County
95	0.2	**New Scotland** (town) Albany County
95	0.2	**New Square** (village) Rockland County
95	0.2	**Newark Valley** (town) Tioga County
95	0.2	**Northampton** (town) Fulton County
95	0.2	**Palatine** (town) Montgomery County
95	0.2	**Saint James** (CDP) Suffolk County
95	0.2	**Salem** (town) Washington County
95	0.2	**Sandy Creek** (town) Oswego County
95	0.2	**Sidney** (town) Delaware County
95	0.2	**Victor** (village) Ontario County
95	0.2	**Walton** (town) Delaware County
95	0.2	**Wayland** (town) Steuben County
95	0.2	**West Sayville** (CDP) Suffolk County
95	0.2	**York** (town) Livingston County
128	0.3	**Champlain** (town) Clinton County
128	0.3	**Chenango Bridge** (CDP) Broome County
128	0.3	**Clarkson** (town) Monroe County
128	0.3	**Copake** (town) Columbia County
128	0.3	**Cuba** (town) Allegany County
128	0.3	**East Glenville** (CDP) Schenectady County
128	0.3	**Elbridge** (town) Onondaga County
128	0.3	**Fenton** (town) Broome County
128	0.3	**Fulton** (city) Oswego County
128	0.3	**Garden City South** (CDP) Nassau County
128	0.3	**Guilford** (town) Chenango County
128	0.3	**Herricks** (CDP) Nassau County
128	0.3	**Hunter** (town) Greene County
128	0.3	**Jay** (town) Essex County
128	0.3	**Lake Placid** (village) Essex County
128	0.3	**Lawrence** (village) Nassau County
128	0.3	**Lloyd Harbor** (village) Suffolk County
128	0.3	**Malone** (village) Franklin County
128	0.3	**Manheim** (town) Herkimer County
128	0.3	**Mohawk** (village) Herkimer County
128	0.3	**Moira** (town) Franklin County
128	0.3	**Newfane** (town) Niagara County
128	0.3	**Otego** (town) Otsego County

Note: This section ranks incorporated places and CDPs (Census Designated Places) with populations of 2,500 or more. Unincorporated postal areas were not considered. Please refer to the User Guide for additional information.

Asian Population

Top 150 Places Ranked in *Descending* Order

State Rank	Percent	Place		State Rank	Percent	Place
1	45.0	Stony Brook University (CDP) Suffolk County		76	9.9	Greenburgh (town) Westchester County
2	44.5	Garden City Park (CDP) Nassau County		76	9.9	Hewlett (CDP) Nassau County
3	43.8	Herricks (CDP) Nassau County		78	9.8	Congers (CDP) Rockland County
4	43.1	Searingtown (CDP) Nassau County		78	9.8	Elwood (CDP) Suffolk County
5	42.9	Manhasset Hills (CDP) Nassau County		80	9.7	Brookville (village) Nassau County
6	39.7	Lake Success (village) Nassau County		81	9.6	Chester (village) Orange County
7	36.7	University Gardens (CDP) Nassau County		81	9.6	Erwin (town) Steuben County
8	35.6	North New Hyde Park (CDP) Nassau County		81	9.6	Niskayuna (town) Schenectady County
9	34.4	Northeast Ithaca (CDP) Tompkins County		84	9.5	Arlington (CDP) Dutchess County
10	33.3	Thomaston (village) Nassau County		84	9.5	Munsey Park (village) Nassau County
11	32.5	New Hyde Park (village) Nassau County		84	9.5	Sands Point (village) Nassau County
12	31.9	Jericho (CDP) Nassau County		87	9.2	Westbury (village) Nassau County
13	31.1	Lansing (village) Tompkins County		88	9.1	East Farmingdale (CDP) Suffolk County
14	27.8	Syosset (CDP) Nassau County		88	9.1	New Paltz (village) Ulster County
15	25.6	University at Buffalo (CDP) Erie County		90	8.9	Amherst (town) Erie County
16	25.3	Greenville (CDP) Westchester County		90	8.9	East Hills (village) Nassau County
16	25.3	Queens (borough) Queens County		90	8.9	Harrison (town/village) Westchester County
18	24.5	North Hills (village) Nassau County		90	8.9	Henrietta (town) Monroe County
19	23.7	Albertson (CDP) Nassau County		94	8.8	Calcium (CDP) Jefferson County
20	23.2	Binghamton University (CDP) Broome County		94	8.8	Great Neck (village) Nassau County
20	23.2	Hicksville (CDP) Nassau County		94	8.8	Johnson City (village) Broome County
22	23.0	Muttontown (village) Nassau County		94	8.8	New Castle (town) Westchester County
23	21.9	Roslyn Heights (CDP) Nassau County		94	8.8	Setauket-East Setauket (CDP) Suffolk County
24	20.1	Manorhaven (village) Nassau County		99	8.7	Eggertsville (CDP) Erie County
25	19.5	Hartsdale (CDP) Westchester County		99	8.7	Pittsford (town) Monroe County
26	18.9	Ardsley (village) Westchester County		101	8.6	Colonie (town) Albany County
27	18.7	Cayuga Heights (village) Tompkins County		101	8.6	Montebello (village) Rockland County
28	18.2	Flower Hill (village) Nassau County		101	8.6	West Nyack (CDP) Rockland County
28	18.2	North Hempstead (town) Nassau County		104	8.5	Briarcliff Manor (village) Westchester County
30	17.8	Old Westbury (village) Nassau County		104	8.5	Garden City South (CDP) Nassau County
31	17.6	Ithaca (city) Tompkins County		104	8.5	Staten Island (borough) Richmond County
32	17.2	Menands (village) Albany County		107	8.4	Colonie (village) Albany County
33	16.7	Gang Mills (CDP) Steuben County		107	8.4	Farmingdale (village) Nassau County
34	16.4	Ithaca (town) Tompkins County		107	8.4	West Hempstead (CDP) Nassau County
34	16.4	Tappan (CDP) Rockland County		110	8.2	Deer Park (CDP) Suffolk County
36	16.1	Dix Hills (CDP) Suffolk County		110	8.2	Guilderland (town) Albany County
36	16.1	South Valley Stream (CDP) Nassau County		110	8.2	Port Washington (CDP) Nassau County
38	15.4	Great Neck Plaza (village) Nassau County		113	8.1	Port Jefferson Station (CDP) Suffolk County
39	15.3	Salisbury (CDP) Nassau County		114	7.9	Rensselaer (city) Rensselaer County
40	15.1	Scarsdale (town/village) Westchester County		115	7.8	Hudson (city) Columbia County
41	15.0	Valley Stream (village) Nassau County		115	7.8	Irvington (village) Westchester County
42	14.8	Plainview (CDP) Nassau County		115	7.8	White Plains (city) Westchester County
43	14.4	Valley Cottage (CDP) Rockland County		118	7.6	Floral Park (village) Nassau County
44	14.0	New York (city)		118	7.6	Port Jefferson (village) Suffolk County
45	13.9	Elmont (CDP) Nassau County		118	7.6	Watertown (town) Jefferson County
46	13.4	Williston Park (village) Nassau County		121	7.5	Pelham (village) Westchester County
47	13.3	Vestal (town) Broome County		121	7.5	Thiells (CDP) Rockland County
48	13.1	Franklin Square (CDP) Nassau County		123	7.4	Albany (city) Albany County
48	13.1	North Valley Stream (CDP) Nassau County		124	7.3	Geneva (town) Ontario County
50	13.0	Lansing (town) Tompkins County		124	7.3	Levittown (CDP) Nassau County
50	13.0	Nanuet (CDP) Rockland County		124	7.3	Melville (CDP) Suffolk County
52	12.6	Myers Corner (CDP) Dutchess County		124	7.3	Orangetown (town) Rockland County
52	12.6	Westmere (CDP) Albany County		124	7.3	Piermont (village) Rockland County
54	12.5	Roslyn (village) Nassau County		124	7.3	Spackenkill (CDP) Dutchess County
55	12.4	Manhasset (CDP) Nassau County		124	7.3	Vails Gate (CDP) Orange County
56	12.1	Webster (village) Monroe County		131	7.2	Eastchester (CDP) Westchester County
57	12.0	Manhattan (borough) New York County		131	7.2	Yonkers (city) Westchester County
58	11.9	Brooklyn (borough) Kings County		133	7.1	Elmsford (village) Westchester County
58	11.9	Stony Brook (CDP) Suffolk County		133	7.1	Hamilton (village) Madison County
58	11.9	Utica (city) Oneida County		133	7.1	Suffern (village) Rockland County
61	11.8	Carle Place (CDP) Nassau County		136	7.0	Syracuse (city) Onondaga County
62	11.4	Islandia (village) Suffolk County		137	6.9	Fishkill (town) Dutchess County
63	11.2	Mineola (village) Nassau County		137	6.9	Plainedge (CDP) Nassau County
64	11.1	Oyster Bay (town) Nassau County		137	6.9	Selden (CDP) Suffolk County
64	11.1	Woodbury (CDP) Nassau County		137	6.9	South Huntington (CDP) Suffolk County
66	11.0	East Meadow (CDP) Nassau County		141	6.8	Great Neck Estates (village) Nassau County
67	10.8	Brighton (CDP) Monroe County		142	6.7	Dobbs Ferry (village) Westchester County
67	10.8	East Williston (village) Nassau County		142	6.7	Galeville (CDP) Onondaga County
69	10.5	Orangeburg (CDP) Rockland County		142	6.7	Moriches (CDP) Suffolk County
70	10.4	Clarkstown (town) Rockland County		142	6.7	Rye Brook (village) Westchester County
70	10.4	Wheatley Heights (CDP) Suffolk County		146	6.5	Airmont (village) Rockland County
72	10.2	Bardonia (CDP) Rockland County		146	6.5	Coram (CDP) Suffolk County
72	10.2	Hillcrest (CDP) Rockland County		146	6.5	De Witt (town) Onondaga County
74	10.1	New City (CDP) Rockland County		146	6.5	Eastchester (town) Westchester County
75	10.0	Pomona (village) Rockland County		150	6.4	Bethpage (CDP) Nassau County

Note: This section ranks incorporated places and CDPs (Census Designated Places) with populations of 2,500 or more. Unincorporated postal areas were not considered. Please refer to the User Guide for additional information.

Asian Population

Top 150 Places Ranked in *Ascending* Order

State Rank	Percent	Place		State Rank	Percent	Place
1	0.0	**Albion** (town) Orleans County		1	0.0	**Niagara** (town) Niagara County
1	0.0	**Albion** (village) Orleans County		1	0.0	**Norfolk** (town) Saint Lawrence County
1	0.0	**Alden** (town) Erie County		1	0.0	**North Boston** (CDP) Erie County
1	0.0	**Alden** (village) Erie County		1	0.0	**North Dansville** (town) Livingston County
1	0.0	**Alexander** (town) Genesee County		1	0.0	**North Syracuse** (village) Onondaga County
1	0.0	**Amsterdam** (town) Montgomery County		1	0.0	**Northampton** (town) Fulton County
1	0.0	**Argyle** (town) Washington County		1	0.0	**Orleans** (town) Jefferson County
1	0.0	**Augusta** (town) Oneida County		1	0.0	**Otisco** (town) Onondaga County
1	0.0	**Balmville** (CDP) Orange County		1	0.0	**Oxford** (town) Chenango County
1	0.0	**Blasdell** (village) Erie County		1	0.0	**Palmyra** (village) Wayne County
1	0.0	**Boston** (town) Erie County		1	0.0	**Pavilion** (town) Genesee County
1	0.0	**Canastota** (village) Madison County		1	0.0	**Peru** (town) Clinton County
1	0.0	**Candor** (town) Tioga County		1	0.0	**Pittstown** (town) Rensselaer County
1	0.0	**Carroll** (town) Chautauqua County		1	0.0	**Poestenkill** (town) Rensselaer County
1	0.0	**Carthage** (village) Jefferson County		1	0.0	**Portville** (town) Cattaraugus County
1	0.0	**Castile** (town) Wyoming County		1	0.0	**Ravena** (village) Albany County
1	0.0	**Charlton** (town) Saratoga County		1	0.0	**Richmond** (town) Ontario County
1	0.0	**Chester** (town) Warren County		1	0.0	**Salem** (town) Washington County
1	0.0	**Chesterfield** (town) Essex County		1	0.0	**Sand Lake** (town) Rensselaer County
1	0.0	**Clarendon** (town) Orleans County		1	0.0	**Sangerfield** (town) Oneida County
1	0.0	**Clayton** (town) Jefferson County		1	0.0	**Sardinia** (town) Erie County
1	0.0	**Colesville** (town) Broome County		1	0.0	**Saugerties** (village) Ulster County
1	0.0	**Conklin** (town) Broome County		1	0.0	**Shandaken** (town) Ulster County
1	0.0	**Constantia** (town) Oswego County		1	0.0	**Sherrill** (city) Oneida County
1	0.0	**Corinth** (town) Saratoga County		1	0.0	**Silver Creek** (village) Chautauqua County
1	0.0	**Corinth** (village) Saratoga County		1	0.0	**Stockholm** (town) Saint Lawrence County
1	0.0	**Croghan** (town) Lewis County		1	0.0	**Stockport** (town) Columbia County
1	0.0	**Cuba** (town) Allegany County		1	0.0	**Tioga** (town) Tioga County
1	0.0	**Dannemora** (village) Clinton County		1	0.0	**Tupper Lake** (village) Franklin County
1	0.0	**Dansville** (village) Livingston County		1	0.0	**Unadilla** (town) Otsego County
1	0.0	**Darien** (town) Genesee County		1	0.0	**Verona** (town) Oneida County
1	0.0	**Dolgeville** (village) Herkimer County		1	0.0	**Vienna** (town) Oneida County
1	0.0	**East Bloomfield** (town) Ontario County		1	0.0	**Virgil** (town) Cortland County
1	0.0	**Eden** (CDP) Erie County		1	0.0	**Volney** (town) Oswego County
1	0.0	**Elbridge** (town) Onondaga County		1	0.0	**Walton** (town) Delaware County
1	0.0	**Ellery** (town) Chautauqua County		1	0.0	**Walton** (village) Delaware County
1	0.0	**Enfield** (town) Tompkins County		1	0.0	**Warrensburg** (CDP) Warren County
1	0.0	**Floyd** (town) Oneida County		1	0.0	**Waterloo** (town) Seneca County
1	0.0	**Fort Edward** (town) Washington County		1	0.0	**Waterloo** (village) Seneca County
1	0.0	**Fort Edward** (village) Washington County		1	0.0	**Wayland** (town) Steuben County
1	0.0	**Galway** (town) Saratoga County		1	0.0	**Wellsville** (village) Allegany County
1	0.0	**Gardiner** (town) Ulster County		1	0.0	**West Bloomfield** (town) Ontario County
1	0.0	**Gouverneur** (town) Saint Lawrence County		1	0.0	**West Monroe** (town) Oswego County
1	0.0	**Gouverneur** (village) Saint Lawrence County		1	0.0	**West Sand Lake** (CDP) Rensselaer County
1	0.0	**Granby** (town) Oswego County		1	0.0	**Westvale** (CDP) Onondaga County
1	0.0	**Greenwood Lake** (village) Orange County		1	0.0	**Whitehall** (town) Washington County
1	0.0	**Guilford** (town) Chenango County		1	0.0	**Whitehall** (village) Washington County
1	0.0	**Hanover** (town) Chautauqua County		1	0.0	**Whitesboro** (village) Oneida County
1	0.0	**Harrietstown** (town) Franklin County		1	0.0	**Wynantskill** (CDP) Rensselaer County
1	0.0	**Holland** (town) Erie County		1	0.0	**Yorkshire** (town) Cattaraugus County
1	0.0	**Hopewell** (town) Ontario County		126	0.1	**Altona** (town) Clinton County
1	0.0	**Kendall** (town) Orleans County		126	0.1	**Aurelius** (town) Cayuga County
1	0.0	**Kirkwood** (town) Broome County		126	0.1	**Brookhaven** (CDP) Suffolk County
1	0.0	**Kiryas Joel** (village) Orange County		126	0.1	**Coeymans** (town) Albany County
1	0.0	**Lake Luzerne** (town) Warren County		126	0.1	**Denmark** (town) Lewis County
1	0.0	**Le Roy** (town) Genesee County		126	0.1	**Eden** (town) Erie County
1	0.0	**Le Roy** (village) Genesee County		126	0.1	**Ellisburg** (town) Jefferson County
1	0.0	**Lisbon** (town) Saint Lawrence County		126	0.1	**Fort Ann** (town) Washington County
1	0.0	**Lisle** (town) Broome County		126	0.1	**Frankfort** (town) Herkimer County
1	0.0	**Malone** (village) Franklin County		126	0.1	**Fulton** (city) Oswego County
1	0.0	**Manchester** (town) Ontario County		126	0.1	**Hoosick** (town) Rensselaer County
1	0.0	**Manheim** (town) Herkimer County		126	0.1	**Jay** (town) Essex County
1	0.0	**Marilla** (town) Erie County		126	0.1	**Kingsbury** (town) Washington County
1	0.0	**Marion** (town) Wayne County		126	0.1	**Lenox** (town) Madison County
1	0.0	**Minoa** (village) Onondaga County		126	0.1	**Madison** (town) Madison County
1	0.0	**Mohawk** (village) Herkimer County		126	0.1	**Mayfield** (town) Fulton County
1	0.0	**Moira** (town) Franklin County		126	0.1	**Monsey** (CDP) Rockland County
1	0.0	**Mooers** (town) Clinton County		126	0.1	**Newark Valley** (town) Tioga County
1	0.0	**Mount Morris** (town) Livingston County		126	0.1	**Owasco** (town) Cayuga County
1	0.0	**Mount Morris** (village) Livingston County		126	0.1	**Portland** (town) Chautauqua County
1	0.0	**Neversink** (town) Sullivan County		126	0.1	**Rockland** (town) Sullivan County
1	0.0	**New Baltimore** (town) Greene County		126	0.1	**Romulus** (town) Seneca County
1	0.0	**New Square** (village) Rockland County		126	0.1	**Roosevelt** (CDP) Nassau County
1	0.0	**Newfane** (CDP) Niagara County		126	0.1	**Russia** (town) Herkimer County
1	0.0	**Newfane** (town) Niagara County		126	0.1	**Schuyler** (town) Herkimer County

Note: This section ranks incorporated places and CDPs (Census Designated Places) with populations of 2,500 or more. Unincorporated postal areas were not considered. Please refer to the User Guide for additional information.

American Indian/Alaska Native Population

Top 150 Places Ranked in *Descending* Order

State Rank	Percent	Place	State Rank	Percent	Place
1	81.2	Saint Regis Mohawk Reservation (reservation) Franklin County	66	1.0	Rochester (city) Monroe County
2	17.6	Salamanca (city) Cattaraugus County	66	1.0	Watertown (city) Jefferson County
3	4.6	Southport (CDP) Chemung County	78	0.9	Attica (village) Wyoming County
4	3.2	Niagara (town) Niagara County	78	0.9	Frankfort (town) Herkimer County
5	3.1	Catskill (village) Greene County	78	0.9	North Bay Shore (CDP) Suffolk County
5	3.1	Southport (town) Chemung County	78	0.9	Riverhead (town) Suffolk County
7	3.0	Sound Beach (CDP) Suffolk County	78	0.9	Rye (town) Westchester County
7	3.0	Wappingers Falls (village) Dutchess County	78	0.9	Syracuse (city) Onondaga County
9	2.8	Greenwood Lake (village) Orange County	78	0.9	Wallkill (town) Orange County
9	2.8	Mattituck (CDP) Suffolk County	85	0.8	Attica (town) Wyoming County
9	2.8	Wanakah (CDP) Erie County	85	0.8	Chester (village) Orange County
12	2.7	Gowanda (village) Cattaraugus County	85	0.8	Clarendon (town) Orleans County
13	2.4	Ossining (village) Westchester County	85	0.8	Depew (village) Erie County
14	2.3	Oneida (city) Madison County	85	0.8	Frankfort (village) Herkimer County
15	2.2	Fort Drum (CDP) Jefferson County	85	0.8	Galen (town) Wayne County
16	2.1	Russia (town) Herkimer County	85	0.8	Glen Cove (city) Nassau County
17	2.0	Fairview (CDP) Westchester County	85	0.8	Hancock (town) Delaware County
17	2.0	Massena (town) Saint Lawrence County	85	0.8	Hempstead (village) Nassau County
17	2.0	Riverhead (CDP) Suffolk County	85	0.8	Lewiston (village) Niagara County
20	1.9	LaFayette (town) Onondaga County	85	0.8	Marilla (town) Erie County
21	1.8	Florida (village) Orange County	85	0.8	Milton (town) Saratoga County
21	1.8	Galway (town) Saratoga County	85	0.8	Port Jervis (city) Orange County
21	1.8	Massena (village) Saint Lawrence County	85	0.8	Porter (town) Niagara County
21	1.8	North Gates (CDP) Monroe County	85	0.8	Silver Creek (village) Chautauqua County
21	1.8	Richmond (town) Ontario County	85	0.8	South Nyack (village) Rockland County
21	1.8	Yates (town) Orleans County	85	0.8	Tonawanda (city) Erie County
27	1.6	Blasdell (village) Erie County	85	0.8	White Plains (city) Westchester County
27	1.6	Ossining (town) Westchester County	103	0.7	Alden (town) Erie County
27	1.6	Springville (village) Erie County	103	0.7	Batavia (town) Genesee County
30	1.5	Albertson (CDP) Nassau County	103	0.7	Bay Shore (CDP) Suffolk County
30	1.5	Le Ray (town) Jefferson County	103	0.7	Bronx (borough) Bronx County
30	1.5	Niagara Falls (city) Niagara County	103	0.7	Castile (town) Wyoming County
30	1.5	West Glens Falls (CDP) Warren County	103	0.7	Evans (town) Erie County
30	1.5	Wyandanch (CDP) Suffolk County	103	0.7	Farmington (town) Ontario County
35	1.4	Ballston Spa (village) Saratoga County	103	0.7	Gates (town) Monroe County
35	1.4	Catskill (town) Greene County	103	0.7	Gloversville (city) Fulton County
35	1.4	Geneva (city) Ontario County	103	0.7	Inwood (CDP) Nassau County
35	1.4	Great Neck Plaza (village) Nassau County	103	0.7	Jerusalem (town) Yates County
35	1.4	Hanover (town) Chautauqua County	103	0.7	Madison (town) Madison County
35	1.4	Norfolk (town) Saint Lawrence County	103	0.7	Minisink (town) Orange County
35	1.4	Pearl River (CDP) Rockland County	103	0.7	North Syracuse (village) Onondaga County
35	1.4	Port Chester (village) Westchester County	103	0.7	Oakfield (town) Genesee County
35	1.4	Roosevelt (CDP) Nassau County	103	0.7	Peekskill (city) Westchester County
35	1.4	Warwick (village) Orange County	103	0.7	Potsdam (village) Saint Lawrence County
45	1.3	Baywood (CDP) Suffolk County	103	0.7	Rye (city) Westchester County
45	1.3	Brasher (town) Saint Lawrence County	103	0.7	Saranac Lake (village) Franklin County
45	1.3	Collins (town) Erie County	103	0.7	Solvay (village) Onondaga County
45	1.3	Fairview (CDP) Dutchess County	103	0.7	Uniondale (CDP) Nassau County
45	1.3	Freeport (village) Nassau County	103	0.7	Wappinger (town) Dutchess County
45	1.3	Hartland (town) Niagara County	103	0.7	Warwick (town) Orange County
45	1.3	Scotchtown (CDP) Orange County	103	0.7	Wellsville (town) Allegany County
45	1.3	Tully (town) Onondaga County	127	0.6	Batavia (city) Genesee County
53	1.2	Colesville (town) Broome County	127	0.6	Bayport (CDP) Suffolk County
53	1.2	Fenton (town) Broome County	127	0.6	Canton (village) Saint Lawrence County
53	1.2	Onondaga (town) Onondaga County	127	0.6	Chester (town) Orange County
53	1.2	Romulus (town) Seneca County	127	0.6	Cobleskill (village) Schoharie County
53	1.2	Sand Lake (town) Rensselaer County	127	0.6	Copiague (CDP) Suffolk County
53	1.2	Williston Park (village) Nassau County	127	0.6	Dolgeville (village) Herkimer County
59	1.1	Beacon (city) Dutchess County	127	0.6	Glasco (CDP) Ulster County
59	1.1	Bethel (town) Sullivan County	127	0.6	Groveland (town) Livingston County
59	1.1	Cayuga Heights (village) Tompkins County	127	0.6	Harrietstown (town) Franklin County
59	1.1	Mattydale (CDP) Onondaga County	127	0.6	Hopewell (town) Ontario County
59	1.1	Somerset (town) Niagara County	127	0.6	Kendall (town) Orleans County
59	1.1	Virgil (town) Cortland County	127	0.6	Kent (town) Putnam County
59	1.1	Washington (town) Dutchess County	127	0.6	Lake Success (village) Nassau County
66	1.0	Alden (village) Erie County	127	0.6	Manorhaven (village) Nassau County
66	1.0	Beekman (town) Dutchess County	127	0.6	New Windsor (CDP) Orange County
66	1.0	Concord (town) Erie County	127	0.6	Newburgh (city) Orange County
66	1.0	Granville (town) Washington County	127	0.6	Newfield (town) Tompkins County
66	1.0	Heritage Hills (CDP) Westchester County	127	0.6	North Salem (town) Westchester County
66	1.0	Jefferson Valley-Yorktown (CDP) Westchester County	127	0.6	Ogdensburg (city) Saint Lawrence County
66	1.0	Lake Carmel (CDP) Putnam County	127	0.6	Olean (city) Cattaraugus County
66	1.0	Louisville (town) Saint Lawrence County	127	0.6	Olive (town) Ulster County
66	1.0	Monroe (village) Orange County	127	0.6	Orangetown (town) Rockland County
66	1.0	North Collins (town) Erie County	127	0.6	Potsdam (town) Saint Lawrence County

Note: *This section ranks incorporated places and CDPs (Census Designated Places) with populations of 2,500 or more. Unincorporated postal areas were not considered. Please refer to the User Guide for additional information.*

Native Hawaiian/Other Pacific Islander Population

Top 150 Places Ranked in *Descending* Order

State Rank	Percent	Place	State Rank	Percent	Place
1	2.2	**Olive** (town) Ulster County	64	0.1	**Collins** (town) Erie County
2	2.1	**Saint Regis Mohawk Reservation** (reservation) Franklin County	64	0.1	**Colonie** (town) Albany County
3	2.0	**Fort Drum** (CDP) Jefferson County	64	0.1	**Coram** (CDP) Suffolk County
4	1.3	**Gordon Heights** (CDP) Suffolk County	64	0.1	**Dix Hills** (CDP) Suffolk County
4	1.3	**Montgomery** (village) Orange County	64	0.1	**East Northport** (CDP) Suffolk County
6	1.2	**Le Ray** (town) Jefferson County	64	0.1	**Ellisburg** (town) Jefferson County
7	1.1	**Cornwall-on-Hudson** (village) Orange County	64	0.1	**Farmington** (town) Ontario County
8	1.0	**Warwick** (village) Orange County	64	0.1	**Fishkill** (town) Dutchess County
9	0.9	**Canandaigua** (city) Ontario County	64	0.1	**Gates** (town) Monroe County
10	0.8	**Frankfort** (village) Herkimer County	64	0.1	**Geddes** (town) Onondaga County
10	0.8	**Herricks** (CDP) Nassau County	64	0.1	**Glenville** (town) Schenectady County
10	0.8	**Ilion** (village) Herkimer County	64	0.1	**Gowanda** (village) Cattaraugus County
13	0.7	**Alden** (village) Erie County	64	0.1	**Halfmoon** (town) Saratoga County
13	0.7	**Lowville** (village) Lewis County	64	0.1	**Henrietta** (town) Monroe County
15	0.6	**Berne** (town) Albany County	64	0.1	**Irvington** (village) Westchester County
16	0.5	**German Flatts** (town) Herkimer County	64	0.1	**Islip** (town) Suffolk County
16	0.5	**Lowville** (town) Lewis County	64	0.1	**Keeseville** (village) Clinton County
16	0.5	**New Hyde Park** (village) Nassau County	64	0.1	**Lackawanna** (city) Erie County
16	0.5	**Ronkonkoma** (CDP) Suffolk County	64	0.1	**Lima** (town) Livingston County
16	0.5	**Williamson** (town) Wayne County	64	0.1	**Manhattan** (borough) New York County
21	0.4	**Champion** (town) Jefferson County	64	0.1	**Manorhaven** (village) Nassau County
21	0.4	**Mechanicstown** (CDP) Orange County	64	0.1	**Murray** (town) Orleans County
21	0.4	**Oneida** (city) Madison County	64	0.1	**New Cassel** (CDP) Nassau County
21	0.4	**Royalton** (town) Niagara County	64	0.1	**New Hartford** (town) Oneida County
21	0.4	**Shelby** (town) Orleans County	64	0.1	**New York** (city)
21	0.4	**Wappingers Falls** (village) Dutchess County	64	0.1	**Niagara Falls** (city) Niagara County
27	0.3	**Canandaigua** (town) Ontario County	64	0.1	**North Hempstead** (town) Nassau County
27	0.3	**Canton** (village) Saint Lawrence County	64	0.1	**North Valley Stream** (CDP) Nassau County
27	0.3	**Cornwall** (town) Orange County	64	0.1	**Norwich** (city) Chenango County
27	0.3	**Frankfort** (town) Herkimer County	64	0.1	**Ogdensburg** (city) Saint Lawrence County
27	0.3	**Maybrook** (village) Orange County	64	0.1	**Oswego** (city) Oswego County
27	0.3	**Montgomery** (town) Orange County	64	0.1	**Plattsburgh** (town) Clinton County
27	0.3	**Newark** (village) Wayne County	64	0.1	**Pomfret** (town) Chautauqua County
27	0.3	**Northampton** (town) Fulton County	64	0.1	**Poughkeepsie** (town) Dutchess County
27	0.3	**South Nyack** (village) Rockland County	64	0.1	**Queens** (borough) Queens County
36	0.2	**Airmont** (village) Rockland County	64	0.1	**Scarsdale** (town/village) Westchester County
36	0.2	**Alden** (town) Erie County	64	0.1	**Schodack** (town) Rensselaer County
36	0.2	**Arcadia** (town) Wayne County	64	0.1	**Somers** (town) Westchester County
36	0.2	**Ballston** (town) Saratoga County	64	0.1	**South Valley Stream** (CDP) Nassau County
36	0.2	**Candor** (town) Tioga County	64	0.1	**Union** (town) Broome County
36	0.2	**Canton** (town) Saint Lawrence County	64	0.1	**University at Buffalo** (CDP) Erie County
36	0.2	**Centereach** (CDP) Suffolk County	64	0.1	**Wallkill** (town) Orange County
36	0.2	**Chautauqua** (town) Chautauqua County	64	0.1	**Wappinger** (town) Dutchess County
36	0.2	**Cobleskill** (town) Schoharie County	64	0.1	**Watertown** (city) Jefferson County
36	0.2	**Cobleskill** (village) Schoharie County	64	0.1	**West Babylon** (CDP) Suffolk County
36	0.2	**Dryden** (town) Tompkins County	64	0.1	**Westbury** (village) Nassau County
36	0.2	**Fredonia** (village) Chautauqua County	122	0.0	**Adams** (town) Jefferson County
36	0.2	**Glens Falls** (city) Warren County	122	0.0	**Addison** (town) Steuben County
36	0.2	**Holbrook** (CDP) Suffolk County	122	0.0	**Afton** (town) Chenango County
36	0.2	**Hudson** (city) Columbia County	122	0.0	**Akron** (village) Erie County
36	0.2	**Johnson City** (village) Broome County	122	0.0	**Albany** (city) Albany County
36	0.2	**Livonia** (town) Livingston County	122	0.0	**Albertson** (CDP) Nassau County
36	0.2	**Melville** (CDP) Suffolk County	122	0.0	**Albion** (town) Orleans County
36	0.2	**North Gates** (CDP) Monroe County	122	0.0	**Albion** (village) Orleans County
36	0.2	**Oswegatchie** (town) Saint Lawrence County	122	0.0	**Alexander** (town) Genesee County
36	0.2	**Patterson** (town) Putnam County	122	0.0	**Alexandria** (town) Jefferson County
36	0.2	**Pierrepont** (town) Saint Lawrence County	122	0.0	**Alfred** (town) Allegany County
36	0.2	**Sayville** (CDP) Suffolk County	122	0.0	**Alfred** (village) Allegany County
36	0.2	**Skaneateles** (town) Onondaga County	122	0.0	**Allegany** (town) Cattaraugus County
36	0.2	**Stony Brook** (CDP) Suffolk County	122	0.0	**Amenia** (town) Dutchess County
36	0.2	**Triangle** (town) Broome County	122	0.0	**Amherst** (town) Erie County
36	0.2	**Warwick** (town) Orange County	122	0.0	**Amityville** (village) Suffolk County
36	0.2	**Westmoreland** (town) Oneida County	122	0.0	**Amsterdam** (city) Montgomery County
64	0.1	**Altona** (town) Clinton County	122	0.0	**Amsterdam** (town) Montgomery County
64	0.1	**Baldwin** (CDP) Nassau County	122	0.0	**Annsville** (town) Oneida County
64	0.1	**Beacon** (city) Dutchess County	122	0.0	**Arcade** (town) Wyoming County
64	0.1	**Briarcliff Manor** (village) Westchester County	122	0.0	**Ardsley** (village) Westchester County
64	0.1	**Bronx** (borough) Bronx County	122	0.0	**Argyle** (town) Washington County
64	0.1	**Camillus** (town) Onondaga County	122	0.0	**Arlington** (CDP) Dutchess County
64	0.1	**Champlain** (town) Clinton County	122	0.0	**Armonk** (CDP) Westchester County
64	0.1	**Cheektowaga** (CDP) Erie County	122	0.0	**Athens** (town) Greene County
64	0.1	**Cheektowaga** (town) Erie County	122	0.0	**Attica** (town) Wyoming County
64	0.1	**Chesterfield** (town) Essex County	122	0.0	**Attica** (village) Wyoming County
64	0.1	**Clarence** (town) Erie County	122	0.0	**Au Sable** (town) Clinton County
64	.0.1	**Clifton Park** (town) Saratoga County	122	0.0	**Auburn** (city) Cayuga County

Note: This section ranks incorporated places and CDPs (Census Designated Places) with populations of 2,500 or more. Unincorporated postal areas were not considered. Please refer to the User Guide for additional information.

Two or More Races

Top 150 Places Ranked in *Descending* Order

State Rank	Percent	Place
1	16.4	**Greenwood Lake** (village) Orange County
2	16.1	**Freeport** (village) Nassau County
3	13.7	**Roosevelt** (CDP) Nassau County
4	13.0	**Monticello** (village) Sullivan County
5	12.2	**North Bay Shore** (CDP) Suffolk County
6	11.7	**Riverside** (CDP) Suffolk County
7	11.6	**Uniondale** (CDP) Nassau County
8	11.2	**Solvay** (village) Onondaga County
9	9.7	**Balmville** (CDP) Orange County
10	9.5	**Ellenville** (village) Ulster County
11	8.7	**Menands** (village) Albany County
12	8.6	**Salamanca** (city) Cattaraugus County
12	8.6	**Wawarsing** (town) Ulster County
14	8.4	**Pamelia** (town) Jefferson County
15	7.9	**Mount Ivy** (CDP) Rockland County
16	7.8	**Kingston** (city) Ulster County
16	7.8	**Lyncourt** (CDP) Onondaga County
18	7.7	**Fort Drum** (CDP) Jefferson County
19	7.6	**Thompson** (town) Sullivan County
20	7.5	**Bergen** (town) Genesee County
20	7.5	**East Farmingdale** (CDP) Suffolk County
22	7.3	**Baldwin** (CDP) Nassau County
22	7.3	**Calcium** (CDP) Jefferson County
22	7.3	**Le Ray** (town) Jefferson County
22	7.3	**Peekskill** (city) Westchester County
22	7.3	**Troy** (city) Rensselaer County
27	7.2	**Wyandanch** (CDP) Suffolk County
28	7.1	**Enfield** (town) Tompkins County
28	7.1	**Webster** (village) Monroe County
30	7.0	**Orange Lake** (CDP) Orange County
31	6.9	**Calverton** (CDP) Suffolk County
31	6.9	**Greenport** (town) Columbia County
33	6.7	**Amsterdam** (city) Montgomery County
33	6.7	**Rensselaer** (city) Rensselaer County
35	6.6	**Lakeview** (CDP) Nassau County
36	6.5	**Central Islip** (CDP) Suffolk County
36	6.5	**Elmira** (city) Chemung County
36	6.5	**North Amityville** (CDP) Suffolk County
36	6.5	**Scotchtown** (CDP) Orange County
40	6.4	**Florida** (village) Orange County
40	6.4	**Northeast Ithaca** (CDP) Tompkins County
42	6.3	**Bay Shore** (CDP) Suffolk County
42	6.3	**Gowanda** (village) Cattaraugus County
42	6.3	**Moriches** (CDP) Suffolk County
42	6.3	**Stony Brook University** (CDP) Suffolk County
42	6.3	**West Point** (CDP) Orange County
47	6.1	**Mechanicstown** (CDP) Orange County
48	6.0	**Beacon** (city) Dutchess County
48	6.0	**Hamilton** (village) Madison County
48	6.0	**Hudson** (city) Columbia County
51	5.9	**Crown Heights** (CDP) Dutchess County
52	5.8	**Lake Placid** (village) Essex County
52	5.8	**Watervliet** (city) Albany County
52	5.8	**Westmoreland** (town) Oneida County
55	5.7	**Carle Place** (CDP) Nassau County
55	5.7	**Elmira Heights** (village) Chemung County
55	5.7	**Maybrook** (village) Orange County
55	5.7	**Watertown** (city) Jefferson County
59	5.6	**Albany** (city) Albany County
59	5.6	**Elmont** (CDP) Nassau County
59	5.6	**Goshen** (village) Orange County
59	5.6	**Pelham** (village) Westchester County
59	5.6	**Saint Regis Mohawk Reservation** (reservation) Franklin County
64	5.5	**Chatham** (town) Columbia County
64	5.5	**Le Roy** (village) Genesee County
64	5.5	**Syracuse** (city) Onondaga County
67	5.4	**North Syracuse** (village) Onondaga County
67	5.4	**Schenectady** (city) Schenectady County
69	5.3	**Lackawanna** (city) Erie County
69	5.3	**South Nyack** (village) Rockland County
69	5.3	**Wallkill** (town) Orange County
72	5.2	**Copiague** (CDP) Suffolk County
72	5.2	**Poughkeepsie** (city) Dutchess County
74	5.1	**Brentwood** (CDP) Suffolk County
74	5.1	**Highlands** (town) Orange County
74	5.1	**Ithaca** (city) Tompkins County
74	5.1	**Port Jervis** (city) Orange County
74	5.1	**SUNY Oswego** (CDP) Oswego County
74	5.1	**Valley Cottage** (CDP) Rockland County
80	5.0	**Cape Vincent** (town) Jefferson County
80	5.0	**Geddes** (town) Onondaga County
80	5.0	**Hempstead** (village) Nassau County
80	5.0	**Herricks** (CDP) Nassau County
80	5.0	**Middletown** (city) Orange County
85	4.9	**Binghamton** (city) Broome County
85	4.9	**Binghamton University** (CDP) Broome County
85	4.9	**Carmel Hamlet** (CDP) Putnam County
85	4.9	**Hillcrest** (CDP) Rockland County
85	4.9	**Pelham** (town) Westchester County
85	4.9	**Rockland** (town) Sullivan County
91	4.8	**Babylon** (village) Suffolk County
91	4.8	**Mastic Beach** (village) Suffolk County
91	4.8	**Nyack** (village) Rockland County
91	4.8	**Port Ewen** (CDP) Ulster County
95	4.7	**Marbletown** (town) Ulster County
95	4.7	**Rochester** (town) Ulster County
95	4.7	**Tuckahoe** (village) Westchester County
95	4.7	**Valley Stream** (village) Nassau County
95	4.7	**Westbury** (village) Nassau County
100	4.6	**Copake** (town) Columbia County
100	4.6	**East Rochester** (town/village) Monroe County
100	4.6	**Mount Hope** (town) Orange County
100	4.6	**Niagara Falls** (city) Niagara County
100	4.6	**Utica** (city) Oneida County
100	4.6	**West Hempstead** (CDP) Nassau County
106	4.5	**Baywood** (CDP) Suffolk County
106	4.5	**Greenville** (town) Orange County
106	4.5	**Larchmont** (village) Westchester County
106	4.5	**Lyons** (village) Wayne County
106	4.5	**Newburgh** (city) Orange County
106	4.5	**Rochester** (city) Monroe County
106	4.5	**Sleepy Hollow** (village) Westchester County
106	4.5	**West Haverstraw** (village) Rockland County
106	4.5	**Wilna** (town) Jefferson County
115	4.4	**Caroline** (town) Tompkins County
115	4.4	**Carthage** (village) Jefferson County
115	4.4	**Greece** (town) Monroe County
115	4.4	**Hempstead** (town) Nassau County
115	4.4	**Manhattan** (borough) New York County
115	4.4	**Mattydale** (CDP) Onondaga County
115	4.4	**Newburgh** (town) Orange County
115	4.4	**Piermont** (village) Rockland County
115	4.4	**Warwick** (town) Orange County
124	4.3	**Brookville** (village) Nassau County
124	4.3	**Corinth** (village) Saratoga County
124	4.3	**Fishkill** (town) Dutchess County
124	4.3	**Minoa** (village) Onondaga County
124	4.3	**Theresa** (town) Jefferson County
124	4.3	**West Bay Shore** (CDP) Suffolk County
130	4.2	**Baldwin Harbor** (CDP) Nassau County
130	4.2	**Endicott** (village) Broome County
130	4.2	**Highland Falls** (village) Orange County
130	4.2	**North Valley Stream** (CDP) Nassau County
130	4.2	**Putnam Lake** (CDP) Putnam County
130	4.2	**Randolph** (town) Cattaraugus County
130	4.2	**University at Buffalo** (CDP) Erie County
130	4.2	**Warsaw** (village) Wyoming County
138	4.1	**Arlington** (CDP) Dutchess County
138	4.1	**Cohoes** (city) Albany County
138	4.1	**Fallsburg** (town) Sullivan County
138	4.1	**Homer** (village) Cortland County
138	4.1	**Montgomery** (village) Orange County
138	4.1	**New Cassel** (CDP) Nassau County
138	4.1	**New Windsor** (town) Orange County
138	4.1	**Pelham Manor** (village) Westchester County
146	4.0	**Auburn** (city) Cayuga County
146	4.0	**Avon** (village) Livingston County
146	4.0	**Fairview** (CDP) Dutchess County
146	4.0	**Greenville** (CDP) Westchester County
146	4.0	**Inwood** (CDP) Nassau County

Note: This section ranks incorporated places and CDPs (Census Designated Places) with populations of 2,500 or more. Unincorporated postal areas were not considered. Please refer to the User Guide for additional information.

Two or More Races

Top 150 Places Ranked in *Ascending* Order

State Rank	Percent	Place
1	0.0	**Bennington** (town) Wyoming County
1	0.0	**Big Flats** (CDP) Chemung County
1	0.0	**Big Flats** (town) Chemung County
1	0.0	**Carroll** (town) Chautauqua County
1	0.0	**Catskill** (village) Greene County
1	0.0	**Chester** (town) Warren County
1	0.0	**Clarence** (CDP) Erie County
1	0.0	**Clarence Center** (CDP) Erie County
1	0.0	**Colden** (town) Erie County
1	0.0	**Cutchogue** (CDP) Suffolk County
1	0.0	**Durham** (town) Greene County
1	0.0	**Eden** (CDP) Erie County
1	0.0	**Ghent** (town) Columbia County
1	0.0	**Grandyle Village** (CDP) Erie County
1	0.0	**Halesite** (CDP) Suffolk County
1	0.0	**Heritage Hills** (CDP) Westchester County
1	0.0	**Lakewood** (village) Chautauqua County
1	0.0	**Lawrence** (village) Nassau County
1	0.0	**Marilla** (town) Erie County
1	0.0	**Newfane** (CDP) Niagara County
1	0.0	**North Sea** (CDP) Suffolk County
1	0.0	**Shelter Island** (town) Suffolk County
1	0.0	**West Sand Lake** (CDP) Rensselaer County
1	0.0	**Westerlo** (town) Albany County
1	0.0	**Westfield** (town) Chautauqua County
1	0.0	**Westfield** (village) Chautauqua County
1	0.0	**Whitehall** (town) Washington County
1	0.0	**Whitehall** (village) Washington County
1	0.0	**Whitesboro** (village) Oneida County
1	0.0	**Yorkshire** (town) Cattaraugus County
31	0.1	**East Islip** (CDP) Suffolk County
31	0.1	**Elma** (town) Erie County
31	0.1	**Kaser** (village) Rockland County
31	0.1	**Knox** (town) Albany County
31	0.1	**Madison** (town) Madison County
31	0.1	**Middleburgh** (town) Schoharie County
31	0.1	**Mount Morris** (village) Livingston County
31	0.1	**Sand Lake** (town) Rensselaer County
31	0.1	**Schuyler** (town) Herkimer County
31	0.1	**Sherrill** (city) Oneida County
31	0.1	**Stephentown** (town) Rensselaer County
42	0.2	**Alexander** (town) Genesee County
42	0.2	**Arcade** (town) Wyoming County
42	0.2	**Broadalbin** (town) Fulton County
42	0.2	**Cambria** (town) Niagara County
42	0.2	**Cayuga Heights** (village) Tompkins County
42	0.2	**Chazy** (town) Clinton County
42	0.2	**Coxsackie** (town) Greene County
42	0.2	**Eden** (town) Erie County
42	0.2	**Kiryas Joel** (village) Orange County
42	0.2	**Lake Luzerne** (town) Warren County
42	0.2	**Monsey** (CDP) Rockland County
42	0.2	**Southampton** (village) Suffolk County
42	0.2	**Southold** (CDP) Suffolk County
42	0.2	**Warrensburg** (CDP) Warren County
42	0.2	**Windsor** (town) Broome County
57	0.3	**Aurelius** (town) Cayuga County
57	0.3	**Barker** (town) Broome County
57	0.3	**Cazenovia** (town) Madison County
57	0.3	**Cedarhurst** (village) Nassau County
57	0.3	**Chenango Bridge** (CDP) Broome County
57	0.3	**Coxsackie** (village) Greene County
57	0.3	**Darien** (town) Genesee County
57	0.3	**East Hampton North** (CDP) Suffolk County
57	0.3	**Fleming** (town) Cayuga County
57	0.3	**Floyd** (town) Oneida County
57	0.3	**Hamptonburgh** (town) Orange County
57	0.3	**Hewlett** (CDP) Nassau County
57	0.3	**Laurens** (town) Otsego County
57	0.3	**Munsons Corners** (CDP) Cortland County
57	0.3	**Niagara** (town) Niagara County
57	0.3	**Oneida** (city) Madison County
57	0.3	**Orchard Park** (village) Erie County
57	0.3	**Oswegatchie** (town) Saint Lawrence County
57	0.3	**Owasco** (town) Cayuga County
57	0.3	**Salem** (town) Washington County
57	0.3	**Saranac** (town) Clinton County
57	0.3	**Sardinia** (town) Erie County
57	0.3	**Somerset** (town) Niagara County
57	0.3	**Sound Beach** (CDP) Suffolk County
57	0.3	**South Glens Falls** (village) Saratoga County
57	0.3	**Springs** (CDP) Suffolk County
57	0.3	**Stillwater** (town) Saratoga County
57	0.3	**Thornwood** (CDP) Westchester County
57	0.3	**Wellsville** (town) Allegany County
57	0.3	**West Glens Falls** (CDP) Warren County
87	0.4	**Bedford Hills** (CDP) Westchester County
87	0.4	**Blue Point** (CDP) Suffolk County
87	0.4	**Boston** (town) Erie County
87	0.4	**Canisteo** (town) Steuben County
87	0.4	**Catlin** (town) Chemung County
87	0.4	**Conklin** (town) Broome County
87	0.4	**East Moriches** (CDP) Suffolk County
87	0.4	**Elma Center** (CDP) Erie County
87	0.4	**Haviland** (CDP) Dutchess County
87	0.4	**Jerusalem** (town) Yates County
87	0.4	**Lido Beach** (CDP) Nassau County
87	0.4	**Massapequa Park** (village) Nassau County
87	0.4	**Mount Morris** (town) Livingston County
87	0.4	**New Square** (village) Rockland County
87	0.4	**North Boston** (CDP) Erie County
87	0.4	**Noyack** (CDP) Suffolk County
87	0.4	**Portland** (town) Chautauqua County
87	0.4	**Sangerfield** (town) Oneida County
87	0.4	**Sullivan** (town) Madison County
106	0.5	**Amsterdam** (town) Montgomery County
106	0.5	**Augusta** (town) Oneida County
106	0.5	**Batavia** (town) Genesee County
106	0.5	**Canandaigua** (city) Ontario County
106	0.5	**Charlton** (town) Saratoga County
106	0.5	**Danby** (town) Tompkins County
106	0.5	**Frankfort** (town) Herkimer County
106	0.5	**Garden City South** (CDP) Nassau County
106	0.5	**Gorham** (town) Ontario County
106	0.5	**Greenwich** (town) Washington County
106	0.5	**Massapequa** (CDP) Nassau County
106	0.5	**Nunda** (town) Livingston County
106	0.5	**Pavilion** (town) Genesee County
106	0.5	**Pine Plains** (town) Dutchess County
106	0.5	**Queensbury** (town) Warren County
106	0.5	**Rush** (town) Monroe County
106	0.5	**Shandaken** (town) Ulster County
106	0.5	**Stockholm** (town) Saint Lawrence County
106	0.5	**Ticonderoga** (town) Essex County
106	0.5	**Triangle** (town) Broome County
106	0.5	**Warrensburg** (town) Warren County
106	0.5	**Wellsville** (village) Allegany County
106	0.5	**Yorkville** (village) Oneida County
129	0.6	**Addison** (town) Steuben County
129	0.6	**Bohemia** (CDP) Suffolk County
129	0.6	**Croghan** (town) Lewis County
129	0.6	**Dannemora** (town) Clinton County
129	0.6	**Dannemora** (village) Clinton County
129	0.6	**East Bloomfield** (town) Ontario County
129	0.6	**Fayetteville** (village) Onondaga County
129	0.6	**Glen Head** (CDP) Nassau County
129	0.6	**Harris Hill** (CDP) Erie County
129	0.6	**Horseheads North** (CDP) Chemung County
129	0.6	**Kings Park** (CDP) Suffolk County
129	0.6	**La Grange** (town) Dutchess County
129	0.6	**Lee** (town) Oneida County
129	0.6	**Little Falls** (city) Herkimer County
129	0.6	**Manheim** (town) Herkimer County
129	0.6	**Montauk** (CDP) Suffolk County
129	0.6	**Orchard Park** (town) Erie County
129	0.6	**Pittstown** (town) Rensselaer County
129	0.6	**Plattsburgh** (town) Clinton County
129	0.6	**Saint Johnsville** (town) Montgomery County
129	0.6	**Stockport** (town) Columbia County
129	0.6	**Ticonderoga** (CDP) Essex County

Note: This section ranks incorporated places and CDPs (Census Designated Places) with populations of 2,500 or more. Unincorporated postal areas were not considered. Please refer to the User Guide for additional information.

Hispanic Population

Top 150 Places Ranked in *Descending* Order

State Rank	Percent	Place
1	68.7	**Haverstraw** (village) Rockland County
2	66.7	**Brentwood** (CDP) Suffolk County
3	66.3	**North Bay Shore** (CDP) Suffolk County
4	64.8	**Port Chester** (village) Westchester County
5	58.1	**Flanders** (CDP) Suffolk County
6	55.7	**Bronx** (borough) Bronx County
7	54.5	**Sleepy Hollow** (village) Westchester County
8	51.9	**New Cassel** (CDP) Nassau County
9	50.7	**Newburgh** (city) Orange County
10	50.0	**West Haverstraw** (village) Rockland County
11	48.5	**Bedford Hills** (CDP) Westchester County
12	47.5	**Ossining** (village) Westchester County
13	46.6	**Hempstead** (village) Nassau County
14	46.1	**Rye** (town) Westchester County
15	45.6	**Central Islip** (CDP) Suffolk County
16	45.1	**Haverstraw** (town) Rockland County
16	45.1	**Inwood** (CDP) Nassau County
18	44.4	**Elmsford** (village) Westchester County
19	43.4	**Mount Kisco** (town/village) Westchester County
20	42.9	**Freeport** (village) Nassau County
21	42.1	**Roosevelt** (CDP) Nassau County
22	41.2	**Middletown** (city) Orange County
23	39.5	**Peekskill** (city) Westchester County
24	38.3	**Bay Shore** (CDP) Suffolk County
25	37.8	**Huntington Station** (CDP) Suffolk County
26	37.0	**Copiague** (CDP) Suffolk County
27	36.3	**Yonkers** (city) Westchester County
28	35.4	**Uniondale** (CDP) Nassau County
29	35.3	**Baywood** (CDP) Suffolk County
30	35.0	**Ossining** (town) Westchester County
31	34.8	**North Amityville** (CDP) Suffolk County
32	34.1	**Wyandanch** (CDP) Suffolk County
33	33.9	**Patchogue** (village) Suffolk County
34	33.2	**White Plains** (city) Westchester County
35	33.0	**Gordon Heights** (CDP) Suffolk County
36	32.7	**North Bellport** (CDP) Suffolk County
37	32.2	**Monticello** (village) Sullivan County
38	31.8	**East Hampton North** (CDP) Suffolk County
39	31.4	**Chester** (village) Orange County
40	31.0	**Island Park** (village) Nassau County
41	30.9	**Dunkirk** (city) Chautauqua County
42	30.8	**Islip** (town) Suffolk County
43	30.1	**Harriman** (village) Orange County
44	29.9	**Spring Valley** (village) Rockland County
45	29.7	**Amsterdam** (city) Montgomery County
46	29.4	**New Rochelle** (city) Westchester County
47	29.1	**New York** (city)
48	29.0	**Lake Mohegan** (CDP) Westchester County
48	29.0	**Mechanicstown** (CDP) Orange County
50	28.6	**Hampton Bays** (CDP) Suffolk County
51	28.4	**Ellenville** (village) Ulster County
51	28.4	**Liberty** (village) Sullivan County
51	28.4	**Tarrytown** (village) Westchester County
54	28.1	**Wappingers Falls** (village) Dutchess County
55	28.0	**Queens** (borough) Queens County
56	27.8	**New Windsor** (CDP) Orange County
57	27.5	**Westbury** (village) Nassau County
58	27.2	**Mount Ivy** (CDP) Rockland County
59	26.9	**Glen Cove** (city) Nassau County
60	26.8	**Monroe** (village) Orange County
61	26.4	**Balmville** (CDP) Orange County
62	26.1	**Manhattan** (borough) New York County
63	25.9	**Hillcrest** (CDP) Rockland County
64	25.5	**Islandia** (village) Suffolk County
64	25.5	**North Patchogue** (CDP) Suffolk County
66	25.2	**Valley Stream** (village) Nassau County
67	25.0	**Baldwin** (CDP) Nassau County
67	25.0	**Mastic** (CDP) Suffolk County
69	24.9	**Fairview** (CDP) Westchester County
69	24.9	**Scotchtown** (CDP) Orange County
71	24.7	**East Farmingdale** (CDP) Suffolk County
72	24.6	**Mamaroneck** (village) Westchester County
73	24.3	**Springs** (CDP) Suffolk County
74	24.2	**Washingtonville** (village) Orange County
75	24.0	**Orange Lake** (CDP) Orange County
76	23.6	**Greenwood Lake** (village) Orange County
76	23.6	**Thompson** (town) Sullivan County
78	23.5	**Wallkill** (town) Orange County
79	23.4	**New Windsor** (town) Orange County
80	23.1	**Thiells** (CDP) Rockland County
81	23.0	**Amityville** (village) Suffolk County
82	22.6	**Fort Drum** (CDP) Jefferson County
83	22.4	**Liberty** (town) Sullivan County
83	22.4	**Manorhaven** (village) Nassau County
85	22.1	**Babylon** (town) Suffolk County
85	22.1	**North Lindenhurst** (CDP) Suffolk County
87	21.6	**Beacon** (city) Dutchess County
87	21.6	**Fallsburg** (town) Sullivan County
87	21.6	**Medford** (CDP) Suffolk County
90	21.5	**Mount Pleasant** (town) Westchester County
91	21.4	**Elmont** (CDP) Nassau County
92	21.2	**Shirley** (CDP) Suffolk County
93	21.1	**Lake Carmel** (CDP) Putnam County
94	21.0	**Arlington** (CDP) Dutchess County
94	21.0	**Vails Gate** (CDP) Orange County
96	20.9	**East Hampton** (town) Suffolk County
97	20.8	**Wawarsing** (town) Ulster County
98	20.6	**Calcium** (CDP) Jefferson County
99	20.5	**Cedarhurst** (village) Nassau County
100	20.4	**Franklin Square** (CDP) Nassau County
101	20.3	**Riverhead** (CDP) Suffolk County
101	20.3	**West Hempstead** (CDP) Nassau County
103	20.2	**Southampton** (town) Suffolk County
103	20.2	**Southeast** (town) Putnam County
105	20.1	**Hempstead** (town) Nassau County
105	20.1	**New Hyde Park** (village) Nassau County
107	19.9	**Northwest Harbor** (CDP) Suffolk County
108	19.8	**Riverside** (CDP) Suffolk County
109	19.6	**Baldwin Harbor** (CDP) Nassau County
109	19.6	**Maybrook** (village) Orange County
109	19.6	**Suffern** (village) Rockland County
109	19.6	**Valhalla** (CDP) Westchester County
113	19.5	**Lynbrook** (village) Nassau County
114	19.4	**East Patchogue** (CDP) Suffolk County
114	19.4	**Le Ray** (town) Jefferson County
114	19.4	**Mineola** (village) Nassau County
114	19.4	**Stony Point** (CDP) Rockland County
118	19.3	**Brooklyn** (borough) Kings County
118	19.3	**Nyack** (village) Rockland County
120	19.1	**Goshen** (village) Orange County
120	19.1	**New Hempstead** (village) Rockland County
120	19.1	**Woodbury** (town) Orange County
123	18.9	**Coram** (CDP) Suffolk County
123	18.9	**Terryville** (CDP) Suffolk County
123	18.9	**Valley Cottage** (CDP) Rockland County
126	18.8	**Newburgh** (town) Orange County
127	18.6	**Mount Morris** (village) Livingston County
128	18.5	**Lindenhurst** (village) Suffolk County
129	18.4	**Lakeview** (CDP) Nassau County
130	18.3	**Chester** (town) Orange County
130	18.3	**West Babylon** (CDP) Suffolk County
132	18.2	**Selden** (CDP) Suffolk County
132	18.2	**Staten Island** (borough) Richmond County
134	18.1	**Florida** (village) Orange County
134	18.1	**Woodbury** (village) Orange County
136	18.0	**Patterson** (town) Putnam County
137	17.9	**South Blooming Grove** (village) Orange County
137	17.9	**Stony Point** (town) Rockland County
139	17.8	**Carle Place** (CDP) Nassau County
139	17.8	**Poughkeepsie** (city) Dutchess County
139	17.8	**Rochester** (city) Monroe County
142	17.7	**Mamaroneck** (town) Westchester County
143	17.4	**Geneva** (city) Ontario County
143	17.4	**West Bay Shore** (CDP) Suffolk County
145	17.1	**Islip** (CDP) Suffolk County
146	16.9	**Hartsdale** (CDP) Westchester County
147	16.7	**East Rockaway** (village) Nassau County
148	16.6	**Blooming Grove** (town) Orange County
148	16.6	**Gardnertown** (CDP) Orange County
148	16.6	**Mastic Beach** (village) Suffolk County

Note: This section ranks incorporated places and CDPs (Census Designated Places) with populations of 2,500 or more. Unincorporated postal areas were not considered. Please refer to the User Guide for additional information.

Hispanic Population

Top 150 Places Ranked in *Ascending* Order

State Rank	Percent	Place
1	0.0	**Beekmantown** (town) Clinton County
1	0.0	**Cambria** (town) Niagara County
1	0.0	**Canastota** (village) Madison County
1	0.0	**Clarence Center** (CDP) Erie County
1	0.0	**Constantia** (town) Oswego County
1	0.0	**Fenton** (town) Broome County
1	0.0	**Galeville** (CDP) Onondaga County
1	0.0	**Kaser** (village) Rockland County
1	0.0	**Knox** (town) Albany County
1	0.0	**New Haven** (town) Oswego County
1	0.0	**New York Mills** (village) Oneida County
1	0.0	**North Boston** (CDP) Erie County
1	0.0	**Stockholm** (town) Saint Lawrence County
1	0.0	**Vienna** (town) Oneida County
1	0.0	**Village Green** (CDP) Onondaga County
16	0.1	**Aurelius** (town) Cayuga County
16	0.1	**Elma** (town) Erie County
16	0.1	**Jay** (town) Essex County
16	0.1	**Lenox** (town) Madison County
16	0.1	**Lisle** (town) Broome County
16	0.1	**North Hills** (village) Nassau County
16	0.1	**Oswegatchie** (town) Saint Lawrence County
16	0.1	**Otego** (town) Otsego County
24	0.2	**Alden** (village) Erie County
24	0.2	**Alexander** (town) Genesee County
24	0.2	**Clarendon** (town) Orleans County
24	0.2	**Ellery** (town) Chautauqua County
24	0.2	**LaFayette** (town) Onondaga County
24	0.2	**Lisbon** (town) Saint Lawrence County
24	0.2	**Owasco** (town) Cayuga County
24	0.2	**Ticonderoga** (CDP) Essex County
32	0.3	**Attica** (village) Wyoming County
32	0.3	**Chenango Bridge** (CDP) Broome County
32	0.3	**Newfane** (CDP) Niagara County
32	0.3	**Newfane** (town) Niagara County
32	0.3	**Palermo** (town) Oswego County
32	0.3	**Pendleton** (town) Niagara County
32	0.3	**Sterling** (town) Cayuga County
32	0.3	**Ticonderoga** (town) Essex County
32	0.3	**Verona** (town) Oneida County
41	0.4	**Elma Center** (CDP) Erie County
41	0.4	**Honeoye Falls** (village) Monroe County
41	0.4	**Lowville** (town) Lewis County
41	0.4	**Lowville** (village) Lewis County
41	0.4	**Moira** (town) Franklin County
41	0.4	**Northampton** (town) Fulton County
41	0.4	**Norwich** (town) Chenango County
41	0.4	**Nunda** (town) Livingston County
41	0.4	**Sandy Creek** (town) Oswego County
41	0.4	**Skaneateles** (town) Onondaga County
41	0.4	**Stephentown** (town) Rensselaer County
41	0.4	**White Creek** (town) Washington County
41	0.4	**York** (town) Livingston County
54	0.5	**Argyle** (town) Washington County
54	0.5	**Bainbridge** (town) Chenango County
54	0.5	**Carroll** (town) Chautauqua County
54	0.5	**Charlton** (town) Saratoga County
54	0.5	**Chenango** (town) Broome County
54	0.5	**Colesville** (town) Broome County
54	0.5	**Elmira Heights** (village) Chemung County
54	0.5	**Hastings** (town) Oswego County
54	0.5	**Lewiston** (village) Niagara County
54	0.5	**Milford** (town) Otsego County
54	0.5	**Norfolk** (town) Saint Lawrence County
54	0.5	**Spencerport** (village) Monroe County
54	0.5	**Trenton** (town) Oneida County
54	0.5	**Victor** (town) Ontario County
68	0.6	**Chazy** (town) Clinton County
68	0.6	**Elmira** (town) Chemung County
68	0.6	**Hamburg** (village) Erie County
68	0.6	**Madison** (town) Madison County
68	0.6	**Massena** (town) Saint Lawrence County
68	0.6	**Massena** (village) Saint Lawrence County
68	0.6	**Pittstown** (town) Rensselaer County
68	0.6	**Sangerfield** (town) Oneida County
68	0.6	**Wayland** (town) Steuben County
68	0.6	**Wilson** (town) Niagara County
78	0.7	**Brownville** (town) Jefferson County
78	0.7	**Brutus** (town) Cayuga County
78	0.7	**Canisteo** (town) Steuben County
78	0.7	**Deerfield** (town) Oneida County
78	0.7	**East Greenbush** (CDP) Rensselaer County
78	0.7	**Gouverneur** (village) Saint Lawrence County
78	0.7	**Lee** (town) Oneida County
78	0.7	**Livonia** (town) Livingston County
78	0.7	**Newark Valley** (town) Tioga County
78	0.7	**Newstead** (town) Erie County
78	0.7	**Russia** (town) Herkimer County
78	0.7	**Wellsville** (town) Allegany County
78	0.7	**Wellsville** (village) Allegany County
78	0.7	**West Elmira** (CDP) Chemung County
78	0.7	**Whitesboro** (village) Oneida County
93	0.8	**Benton** (town) Yates County
93	0.8	**Clarence** (CDP) Erie County
93	0.8	**Harrietstown** (town) Franklin County
93	0.8	**Lakeland** (CDP) Onondaga County
93	0.8	**Mexico** (town) Oswego County
93	0.8	**Parish** (town) Oswego County
93	0.8	**Phelps** (town) Ontario County
93	0.8	**Saranac Lake** (village) Franklin County
93	0.8	**Sherburne** (town) Chenango County
102	0.9	**Bergen** (town) Genesee County
102	0.9	**Camden** (town) Oneida County
102	0.9	**Champlain** (town) Clinton County
102	0.9	**Chester** (town) Warren County
102	0.9	**Cuba** (town) Allegany County
102	0.9	**Holland** (town) Erie County
102	0.9	**Milo** (town) Yates County
102	0.9	**Richland** (town) Oswego County
102	0.9	**Schuyler** (town) Herkimer County
102	0.9	**Virgil** (town) Cortland County
102	0.9	**Wales** (town) Erie County
102	0.9	**West Monroe** (town) Oswego County
102	0.9	**Westmoreland** (town) Oneida County
115	1.0	**Big Flats** (town) Chemung County
115	1.0	**Boston** (town) Erie County
115	1.0	**Corning** (town) Steuben County
115	1.0	**Coxsackie** (village) Greene County
115	1.0	**Croghan** (town) Lewis County
115	1.0	**Hartland** (town) Niagara County
115	1.0	**Lakewood** (village) Chautauqua County
115	1.0	**Manheim** (town) Herkimer County
115	1.0	**New Berlin** (town) Chenango County
115	1.0	**New Square** (village) Rockland County
115	1.0	**North Dansville** (town) Livingston County
115	1.0	**Starkey** (town) Yates County
115	1.0	**Waterloo** (village) Seneca County
115	1.0	**West Glens Falls** (CDP) Warren County
115	1.0	**Whitehall** (town) Washington County
130	1.1	**Afton** (town) Chenango County
130	1.1	**Binghamton** (town) Broome County
130	1.1	**Coeymans** (town) Albany County
130	1.1	**Pembroke** (town) Genesee County
130	1.1	**Pierrepont** (town) Saint Lawrence County
130	1.1	**Victor** (village) Ontario County
130	1.1	**Wanakah** (CDP) Erie County
137	1.2	**Avon** (town) Livingston County
137	1.2	**Big Flats** (CDP) Chemung County
137	1.2	**Busti** (town) Chautauqua County
137	1.2	**Clayton** (town) Jefferson County
137	1.2	**Concord** (town) Erie County
137	1.2	**Dansville** (village) Livingston County
137	1.2	**East Aurora** (village) Erie County
137	1.2	**Fort Edward** (town) Washington County
137	1.2	**Gowanda** (village) Cattaraugus County
137	1.2	**Greenfield** (town) Saratoga County
137	1.2	**Hector** (town) Schuyler County
137	1.2	**Lawrence** (village) Nassau County
137	1.2	**Mendon** (town) Monroe County
137	1.2	**New Bremen** (town) Lewis County

Note: This section ranks incorporated places and CDPs (Census Designated Places) with populations of 2,500 or more. Unincorporated postal areas were not considered. Please refer to the User Guide for additional information.

Average Household Size

Top 150 Places Ranked in *Descending* Order

State Rank	Persons	Place		State Rank	Persons	Place
1	5.96	**New Square** (village) Rockland County		73	3.20	**Scarsdale** (town/village) Westchester County
2	5.50	**Kiryas Joel** (village) Orange County		77	3.19	**Hicksville** (CDP) Nassau County
3	5.48	**Kaser** (village) Rockland County		77	3.19	**Old Westbury** (village) Nassau County
4	5.41	**Monsey** (CDP) Rockland County		77	3.19	**Plainedge** (CDP) Nassau County
5	4.95	**North Bay Shore** (CDP) Suffolk County		80	3.18	**Babylon** (town) Suffolk County
6	4.56	**Brentwood** (CDP) Suffolk County		80	3.18	**Baldwin** (CDP) Nassau County
7	4.51	**New Hempstead** (village) Rockland County		80	3.18	**Chestnut Ridge** (village) Rockland County
8	4.47	**New Cassel** (CDP) Nassau County		80	3.18	**Searingtown** (CDP) Nassau County
9	4.33	**Lakeview** (CDP) Nassau County		84	3.17	**Armonk** (CDP) Westchester County
10	4.10	**Monroe** (town) Orange County		84	3.17	**East Islip** (CDP) Suffolk County
11	4.05	**Hillcrest** (CDP) Rockland County		86	3.16	**Levittown** (CDP) Nassau County
12	4.03	**Wyandanch** (CDP) Suffolk County		86	3.16	**Valley Stream** (village) Nassau County
13	3.87	**North Amityville** (CDP) Suffolk County		88	3.15	**Elwood** (CDP) Suffolk County
14	3.84	**West Point** (CDP) Orange County		88	3.15	**Wantagh** (CDP) Nassau County
15	3.79	**Ramapo** (town) Rockland County		88	3.15	**West Babylon** (CDP) Suffolk County
16	3.75	**Roosevelt** (CDP) Nassau County		88	3.15	**Westbury** (village) Nassau County
16	3.75	**Wheatley Heights** (CDP) Suffolk County		92	3.14	**Center Moriches** (CDP) Suffolk County
18	3.73	**Elmont** (CDP) Nassau County		92	3.14	**Chester** (town) Orange County
19	3.66	**Flanders** (CDP) Suffolk County		92	3.14	**Freeport** (village) Nassau County
20	3.63	**Wesley Hills** (village) Rockland County		92	3.14	**Hempstead** (town) Nassau County
21	3.62	**Spring Valley** (village) Rockland County		92	3.14	**Manhasset Hills** (CDP) Nassau County
22	3.61	**Viola** (CDP) Rockland County		92	3.14	**Pelham** (town) Westchester County
23	3.57	**Central Islip** (CDP) Suffolk County		98	3.13	**South Farmingdale** (CDP) Nassau County
24	3.52	**Mastic** (CDP) Suffolk County		99	3.12	**Deer Park** (CDP) Suffolk County
25	3.50	**Hempstead** (village) Nassau County		99	3.12	**West Islip** (CDP) Suffolk County
26	3.49	**Munsey Park** (village) Nassau County		101	3.11	**East Farmingdale** (CDP) Suffolk County
27	3.48	**Lake Success** (village) Nassau County		101	3.11	**Massapequa** (CDP) Nassau County
27	3.48	**North Valley Stream** (CDP) Nassau County		103	3.10	**Garden City South** (CDP) Nassau County
29	3.47	**Kings Point** (village) Nassau County		103	3.10	**Pomona** (village) Rockland County
29	3.47	**Uniondale** (CDP) Nassau County		105	3.09	**Pelham** (village) Westchester County
31	3.46	**Cedarhurst** (village) Nassau County		105	3.09	**Spackenkill** (CDP) Dutchess County
31	3.46	**Shirley** (CDP) Suffolk County		107	3.08	**Lindenhurst** (village) Suffolk County
33	3.43	**New Hyde Park** (village) Nassau County		107	3.08	**Muttontown** (village) Nassau County
34	3.42	**Islip Terrace** (CDP) Suffolk County		107	3.08	**Syosset** (CDP) Nassau County
35	3.41	**Thiells** (CDP) Rockland County		110	3.07	**Brookville** (village) Nassau County
36	3.40	**Duanesburg** (town) Schenectady County		110	3.07	**Flower Hill** (village) Nassau County
37	3.39	**Airmont** (village) Rockland County		110	3.07	**Greenlawn** (CDP) Suffolk County
37	3.39	**South Valley Stream** (CDP) Nassau County		110	3.07	**Greenville** (town) Orange County
39	3.37	**Hamptonburgh** (town) Orange County		110	3.07	**Lawrence** (village) Nassau County
40	3.36	**Franklin Square** (CDP) Nassau County		110	3.07	**Massapequa Park** (village) Nassau County
40	3.36	**West Hempstead** (CDP) Nassau County		110	3.07	**Rye** (town) Westchester County
42	3.35	**Islip** (CDP) Suffolk County		117	3.06	**Clarence Center** (CDP) Erie County
42	3.35	**West Haverstraw** (village) Rockland County		117	3.06	**North Bellmore** (CDP) Nassau County
42	3.35	**Woodmere** (CDP) Nassau County		117	3.06	**Thornwood** (CDP) Westchester County
45	3.34	**Gordon Heights** (CDP) Suffolk County		120	3.05	**East Fishkill** (town) Dutchess County
46	3.32	**Bay Shore** (CDP) Suffolk County		120	3.05	**Haverstraw** (town) Rockland County
46	3.32	**Garden City Park** (CDP) Nassau County		120	3.05	**North Lindenhurst** (CDP) Suffolk County
46	3.32	**Huntington Station** (CDP) Suffolk County		120	3.05	**Ronkonkoma** (CDP) Suffolk County
46	3.32	**Islandia** (village) Suffolk County		120	3.05	**Stony Brook University** (CDP) Suffolk County
50	3.31	**North Bellport** (CDP) Suffolk County		125	3.04	**New Castle** (town) Westchester County
50	3.31	**Terryville** (CDP) Suffolk County		126	3.03	**Commack** (CDP) Suffolk County
52	3.30	**Dix Hills** (CDP) Suffolk County		126	3.03	**Islip** (CDP) Suffolk County
52	3.30	**Inwood** (CDP) Nassau County		126	3.03	**Minisink** (town) Orange County
52	3.30	**North New Hyde Park** (CDP) Nassau County		129	3.02	**Congers** (CDP) Rockland County
55	3.29	**Elmsford** (village) Westchester County		129	3.02	**Fort Drum** (CDP) Jefferson County
55	3.29	**Port Chester** (village) Westchester County		129	3.02	**New City** (CDP) Rockland County
57	3.28	**Centereach** (CDP) Suffolk County		129	3.02	**Seaford** (CDP) Nassau County
58	3.27	**Blauvelt** (CDP) Rockland County		133	3.01	**Great Neck Estates** (village) Nassau County
58	3.27	**East Shoreham** (CDP) Suffolk County		133	3.01	**Holtsville** (CDP) Suffolk County
58	3.27	**Farmingville** (CDP) Suffolk County		133	3.01	**Manorville** (CDP) Suffolk County
58	3.27	**Herricks** (CDP) Nassau County		133	3.01	**North Castle** (town) Westchester County
62	3.26	**Woodbury** (town) Orange County		133	3.01	**North Massapequa** (CDP) Nassau County
63	3.25	**Baywood** (CDP) Suffolk County		138	3.00	**Baldwin Harbor** (CDP) Nassau County
64	3.24	**Roslyn Heights** (CDP) Nassau County		138	3.00	**Benton** (town) Yates County
64	3.24	**Selden** (CDP) Suffolk County		138	3.00	**Fairview** (CDP) Westchester County
66	3.23	**Woodbury** (village) Orange County		138	3.00	**Medford** (CDP) Suffolk County
67	3.22	**Copiague** (CDP) Suffolk County		138	3.00	**Newburgh** (city) Orange County
67	3.22	**Great Neck** (village) Nassau County		138	3.00	**Walden** (village) Orange County
69	3.21	**East Williston** (village) Nassau County		144	2.99	**Lloyd Harbor** (village) Suffolk County
69	3.21	**Greenville** (CDP) Westchester County		144	2.99	**Orleans** (town) Jefferson County
69	3.21	**Haverstraw** (village) Rockland County		144	2.99	**South Hempstead** (CDP) Nassau County
69	3.21	**Salisbury** (CDP) Nassau County		144	2.99	**Stony Point** (CDP) Rockland County
73	3.20	**Monroe** (village) Orange County		148	2.98	**East Norwich** (CDP) Nassau County
73	3.20	**North Merrick** (CDP) Nassau County		148	2.98	**Miller Place** (CDP) Suffolk County
73	3.20	**Pelham Manor** (village) Westchester County		148	2.98	**Montebello** (village) Rockland County

Note: This section ranks incorporated places and CDPs (Census Designated Places) with populations of 2,500 or more. Unincorporated postal areas were not considered. Please refer to the User Guide for additional information.

Average Household Size

Top 150 Places Ranked in *Ascending* Order

State Rank	Persons	Place
1	1.77	**Great Neck Plaza** (village) Nassau County
2	1.84	**Heritage Hills** (CDP) Westchester County
3	1.85	**Lewiston** (village) Niagara County
4	1.88	**Binghamton University** (CDP) Broome County
5	1.89	**Riverside** (CDP) Suffolk County
6	1.92	**Canton** (village) Saint Lawrence County
7	1.96	**Alfred** (village) Allegany County
7	1.96	**Hartsdale** (CDP) Westchester County
7	1.96	**Shandaken** (town) Ulster County
7	1.96	**Village Green** (CDP) Onondaga County
11	1.97	**Middletown** (town) Delaware County
11	1.97	**Rhinebeck** (village) Dutchess County
13	2.01	**Hunter** (town) Greene County
14	2.03	**Calverton** (CDP) Suffolk County
14	2.03	**Lakewood** (village) Chautauqua County
14	2.03	**Saratoga Springs** (city) Saratoga County
14	2.03	**Woodstock** (town) Ulster County
18	2.04	**Cayuga Heights** (village) Tompkins County
19	2.05	**Bath** (village) Steuben County
19	2.05	**Claverack** (town) Columbia County
21	2.06	**Cazenovia** (village) Madison County
21	2.06	**Hudson** (city) Columbia County
21	2.06	**North Hills** (village) Nassau County
21	2.06	**South Glens Falls** (village) Saratoga County
25	2.07	**Corning** (city) Steuben County
26	2.08	**Whitesboro** (village) Oneida County
26	2.08	**Williamsville** (village) Erie County
28	2.09	**Otsego** (town) Otsego County
28	2.09	**Potsdam** (village) Saint Lawrence County
28	2.09	**Roslyn** (village) Nassau County
28	2.09	**Wellsville** (village) Allegany County
32	2.10	**Delhi** (village) Delaware County
32	2.10	**Gowanda** (village) Cattaraugus County
32	2.10	**Manhattan** (borough) New York County
32	2.10	**Northwest Harbor** (CDP) Suffolk County
36	2.11	**Medina** (village) Orleans County
36	2.11	**Moriches** (CDP) Suffolk County
36	2.11	**Warsaw** (village) Wyoming County
39	2.12	**Alfred** (town) Allegany County
39	2.12	**Cohoes** (city) Albany County
39	2.12	**Plattsburgh** (city) Clinton County
39	2.12	**Wellsville** (town) Allegany County
43	2.13	**Auburn** (city) Cayuga County
43	2.13	**Canandaigua** (city) Ontario County
43	2.13	**Horseheads** (village) Chemung County
43	2.13	**New York Mills** (village) Oneida County
43	2.13	**Shelby** (town) Orleans County
48	2.14	**Albany** (city) Albany County
48	2.14	**Endicott** (village) Broome County
48	2.14	**Highland Falls** (village) Orange County
48	2.14	**Nyack** (village) Rockland County
48	2.14	**Piermont** (village) Rockland County
53	2.15	**Delhi** (town) Delaware County
53	2.15	**Guilford** (town) Chenango County
53	2.15	**Hornellsville** (town) Steuben County
53	2.15	**Mooers** (town) Clinton County
53	2.15	**North Dansville** (town) Livingston County
53	2.15	**Tonawanda** (city) Erie County
59	2.16	**Alden** (village) Erie County
59	2.16	**Dickinson** (town) Broome County
59	2.16	**Geneva** (town) Ontario County
59	2.16	**Kenmore** (village) Erie County
59	2.16	**Lansing** (village) Tompkins County
59	2.16	**Mount Morris** (village) Livingston County
59	2.16	**New Paltz** (village) Ulster County
59	2.16	**Penn Yan** (village) Yates County
59	2.16	**Saranac Lake** (village) Franklin County
68	2.17	**Batavia** (town) Genesee County
68	2.17	**Green Island** (town/village) Albany County
68	2.17	**Herkimer** (village) Herkimer County
68	2.17	**Rhinebeck** (town) Dutchess County
72	2.18	**Brighton** (CDP) Monroe County
72	2.18	**Greenport** (town) Columbia County
72	2.18	**North Elba** (town) Essex County
72	2.18	**Saugerties** (village) Ulster County
72	2.18	**Shelter Island** (town) Suffolk County
72	2.18	**Southport** (CDP) Chemung County
72	2.18	**Warsaw** (town) Wyoming County
79	2.19	**Amsterdam** (town) Montgomery County
79	2.19	**Cheektowaga** (CDP) Erie County
79	2.19	**Hamilton** (village) Madison County
79	2.19	**Massena** (town) Saint Lawrence County
79	2.19	**Mechanicville** (city) Saratoga County
79	2.19	**Solvay** (village) Onondaga County
79	2.19	**Tonawanda** (town) Erie County
79	2.19	**Tupper Lake** (village) Franklin County
87	2.20	**Cheektowaga** (town) Erie County
87	2.20	**Dansville** (village) Livingston County
87	2.20	**Herkimer** (town) Herkimer County
87	2.20	**Malone** (village) Franklin County
87	2.20	**Tonawanda** (CDP) Erie County
87	2.20	**Webster** (village) Monroe County
87	2.20	**White Creek** (town) Washington County
94	2.21	**Ballston Spa** (village) Saratoga County
94	2.21	**Binghamton** (city) Broome County
94	2.21	**Canton** (town) Saint Lawrence County
94	2.21	**Hurley** (town) Ulster County
94	2.21	**Marbletown** (town) Ulster County
94	2.21	**Massena** (village) Saint Lawrence County
94	2.21	**North Gates** (CDP) Monroe County
94	2.21	**Oneonta** (city) Otsego County
94	2.21	**Tioga** (town) Tioga County
103	2.22	**Allegany** (town) Cattaraugus County
103	2.22	**Blasdell** (village) Erie County
103	2.22	**Danby** (town) Tompkins County
103	2.22	**Fairport** (village) Monroe County
103	2.22	**Kirkland** (town) Oneida County
103	2.22	**Lyons** (village) Wayne County
103	2.22	**Ogdensburg** (city) Saint Lawrence County
103	2.22	**Olean** (city) Cattaraugus County
103	2.22	**Watervliet** (city) Albany County
103	2.22	**Westmere** (CDP) Albany County
113	2.23	**Bath** (town) Steuben County
113	2.23	**Cobleskill** (village) Schoharie County
113	2.23	**Glens Falls** (city) Warren County
113	2.23	**Hector** (town) Schuyler County
113	2.23	**Ithaca** (town) Tompkins County
113	2.23	**Louisville** (town) Saint Lawrence County
113	2.23	**Middleburgh** (town) Schoharie County
113	2.23	**Newark** (village) Wayne County
113	2.23	**Owego** (village) Tioga County
113	2.23	**Oxford** (town) Chenango County
113	2.23	**Seneca Falls** (town) Seneca County
113	2.23	**Sloan** (village) Erie County
113	2.23	**Ulysses** (town) Tompkins County
113	2.23	**Union** (town) Broome County
113	2.23	**Whitestown** (town) Oneida County
128	2.24	**Akron** (village) Erie County
128	2.24	**East Syracuse** (village) Onondaga County
128	2.24	**Elmira** (town) Chemung County
128	2.24	**Johnson City** (village) Broome County
128	2.24	**Munsons Corners** (CDP) Cortland County
128	2.24	**New Berlin** (town) Chenango County
128	2.24	**North Tonawanda** (city) Niagara County
128	2.24	**Olive** (town) Ulster County
128	2.24	**Van Buren** (town) Onondaga County
128	2.24	**Wanakah** (CDP) Erie County
138	2.25	**Busti** (town) Chautauqua County
138	2.25	**Campbell** (town) Steuben County
138	2.25	**Cape Vincent** (town) Jefferson County
138	2.25	**Endwell** (CDP) Broome County
138	2.25	**Galeville** (CDP) Onondaga County
138	2.25	**Geneva** (city) Ontario County
138	2.25	**Lancaster** (village) Erie County
138	2.25	**Oswego** (city) Oswego County
138	2.25	**Rensselaer** (city) Rensselaer County
138	2.25	**Salina** (town) Onondaga County
138	2.25	**South Hill** (CDP) Tompkins County
138	2.25	**Southampton** (village) Suffolk County
138	2.25	**Springville** (village) Erie County

Note: This section ranks incorporated places and CDPs (Census Designated Places) with populations of 2,500 or more. Unincorporated postal areas were not considered. Please refer to the User Guide for additional information.

Median Age

Top 150 Places Ranked in *Descending* Order

State Rank	Years	Place	State Rank	Years	Place
1	69.8	**Heritage Hills** (CDP) Westchester County	74	49.0	**Campbell** (town) Steuben County
2	62.6	**North Hills** (village) Nassau County	74	49.0	**Muttontown** (village) Nassau County
3	57.0	**Shandaken** (town) Ulster County	74	49.0	**Warwick** (village) Orange County
4	56.9	**Southampton** (village) Suffolk County	79	48.9	**Gorham** (town) Ontario County
4	56.9	**Woodstock** (town) Ulster County	79	48.9	**Guilford** (town) Chenango County
6	56.0	**Montauk** (CDP) Suffolk County	79	48.9	**Olive** (town) Ulster County
7	55.8	**Middletown** (town) Delaware County	79	48.9	**Wayland** (town) Steuben County
8	55.6	**Northwest Harbor** (CDP) Suffolk County	83	48.8	**Clarendon** (town) Orleans County
9	55.2	**Elma Center** (CDP) Erie County	83	48.8	**Copake** (town) Columbia County
10	54.2	**Rhinebeck** (village) Dutchess County	83	48.8	**Greenwood Lake** (village) Orange County
11	54.0	**Calverton** (CDP) Suffolk County	86	48.7	**Riverhead** (town) Suffolk County
11	54.0	**Carroll** (town) Chautauqua County	87	48.6	**Callicoon** (town) Sullivan County
13	53.9	**Madison** (town) Madison County	87	48.6	**Hornellsville** (town) Steuben County
14	53.5	**Rhinebeck** (town) Dutchess County	87	48.6	**Westerlo** (town) Albany County
15	53.2	**Lewiston** (village) Niagara County	90	48.5	**Athens** (town) Greene County
16	53.0	**Southold** (town) Suffolk County	90	48.5	**Melville** (CDP) Suffolk County
17	52.7	**Lido Beach** (CDP) Nassau County	90	48.5	**New Baltimore** (town) Greene County
18	52.6	**Hurley** (town) Ulster County	90	48.5	**North Salem** (town) Westchester County
18	52.6	**Oxford** (town) Chenango County	90	48.5	**Somers** (town) Westchester County
20	52.5	**Great Neck Plaza** (village) Nassau County	90	48.5	**Washington** (town) Dutchess County
21	52.4	**Fleming** (town) Cayuga County	96	48.4	**Eden** (town) Erie County
21	52.4	**Hunter** (town) Greene County	96	48.4	**Lake Luzerne** (town) Warren County
23	52.3	**Cutchogue** (CDP) Suffolk County	96	48.4	**Malverne** (village) Nassau County
23	52.3	**Skaneateles** (town) Onondaga County	96	48.4	**Marbletown** (town) Ulster County
25	52.0	**Mattituck** (CDP) Suffolk County	96	48.4	**Searingtown** (CDP) Nassau County
26	51.9	**Amsterdam** (town) Montgomery County	96	48.4	**West Hills** (CDP) Suffolk County
26	51.9	**Veteran** (town) Chemung County	102	48.3	**Castile** (town) Wyoming County
28	51.8	**Southold** (CDP) Suffolk County	102	48.3	**Colden** (town) Erie County
29	51.7	**Westhampton** (CDP) Suffolk County	102	48.3	**Galway** (town) Saratoga County
30	51.5	**Batavia** (town) Genesee County	102	48.3	**Northport** (village) Suffolk County
31	51.4	**Bardonia** (CDP) Rockland County	102	48.3	**Porter** (town) Niagara County
31	51.4	**Otsego** (town) Otsego County	102	48.3	**Williamsville** (village) Erie County
33	51.0	**East Hampton** (town) Suffolk County	108	48.2	**Kinderhook** (town) Columbia County
34	50.9	**Shelter Island** (town) Suffolk County	108	48.2	**Lake Erie Beach** (CDP) Erie County
34	50.9	**Stanford** (town) Dutchess County	108	48.2	**Plattekill** (town) Ulster County
36	50.8	**Hurley** (CDP) Ulster County	111	48.1	**North Sea** (CDP) Suffolk County
37	50.7	**Danby** (town) Tompkins County	112	48.0	**Bethel** (town) Sullivan County
37	50.7	**Louisville** (town) Saint Lawrence County	112	48.0	**Carmel Hamlet** (CDP) Putnam County
39	50.6	**Claverack** (town) Columbia County	112	48.0	**Montebello** (village) Rockland County
39	50.6	**Lake Success** (village) Nassau County	115	47.9	**Hancock** (town) Delaware County
39	50.6	**Pound Ridge** (town) Westchester County	115	47.9	**Hartland** (town) Niagara County
39	50.6	**Richmond** (town) Ontario County	115	47.9	**Lakewood** (village) Chautauqua County
43	50.5	**Owasco** (town) Cayuga County	115	47.9	**Mayfield** (town) Fulton County
44	50.4	**Elma** (town) Erie County	115	47.9	**New Berlin** (town) Chenango County
44	50.4	**Lakeland** (CDP) Onondaga County	115	47.9	**Port Ewen** (CDP) Ulster County
44	50.4	**Ridge** (CDP) Suffolk County	115	47.9	**Sangerfield** (town) Oneida County
47	50.3	**North Boston** (CDP) Erie County	115	47.9	**Schoharie** (town) Schoharie County
48	50.2	**Ulysses** (town) Tompkins County	115	47.9	**West Nyack** (CDP) Rockland County
49	50.1	**Brookhaven** (CDP) Suffolk County	124	47.8	**Ardsley** (village) Westchester County
49	50.1	**Hartsdale** (CDP) Westchester County	124	47.8	**Binghamton** (town) Broome County
51	50.0	**Sheridan** (town) Chautauqua County	124	47.8	**Ghent** (town) Columbia County
51	50.0	**West Bloomfield** (town) Ontario County	124	47.8	**Riga** (town) Monroe County
53	49.9	**Woodbury** (CDP) Nassau County	124	47.8	**Rosendale** (town) Ulster County
54	49.8	**Livingston** (town) Columbia County	124	47.8	**Union Vale** (town) Dutchess County
54	49.8	**White Creek** (town) Washington County	130	47.7	**Balmville** (CDP) Orange County
56	49.7	**Roslyn** (village) Nassau County	130	47.7	**Berne** (town) Albany County
56	49.7	**West Elmira** (CDP) Chemung County	130	47.7	**Chatham** (town) Columbia County
58	49.6	**Otego** (town) Otsego County	130	47.7	**Elmira** (town) Chemung County
59	49.5	**Carlton** (town) Orleans County	130	47.7	**Sands Point** (village) Nassau County
59	49.5	**Ellery** (town) Chautauqua County	130	47.7	**Ulster** (town) Ulster County
59	49.5	**Fayette** (town) Seneca County	136	47.6	**Baldwinsville** (village) Onondaga County
59	49.5	**Lake George** (town) Warren County	136	47.6	**Bayville** (village) Nassau County
59	49.5	**Marilla** (town) Erie County	136	47.6	**Fort Salonga** (CDP) Suffolk County
64	49.4	**Afton** (town) Chenango County	139	47.5	**Brunswick** (town) Rensselaer County
64	49.4	**Greenport** (town) Columbia County	139	47.5	**Geneva** (town) Ontario County
66	49.3	**Rush** (town) Monroe County	139	47.5	**Mooers** (town) Clinton County
67	49.2	**Florida** (town) Montgomery County	139	47.5	**New Hartford** (town) Oneida County
67	49.2	**Wanakah** (CDP) Erie County	139	47.5	**Philipstown** (town) Putnam County
67	49.2	**Westfield** (town) Chautauqua County	139	47.5	**Sennett** (town) Cayuga County
70	49.1	**Charlton** (town) Saratoga County	139	47.5	**Tioga** (town) Tioga County
70	49.1	**Hector** (town) Schuyler County	139	47.5	**Wellsville** (town) Allegany County
70	49.1	**Middleburgh** (town) Schoharie County	147	47.4	**Chesterfield** (town) Essex County
70	49.1	**Piermont** (village) Rockland County	147	47.4	**Clarence** (CDP) Erie County
74	49.0	**Boston** (town) Erie County	147	47.4	**Enfield** (town) Tompkins County
74	49.0	**Busti** (town) Chautauqua County	147	47.4	**Laurens** (town) Otsego County

Note: This section ranks incorporated places and CDPs (Census Designated Places) with populations of 2,500 or more. Unincorporated postal areas were not considered. Please refer to the User Guide for additional information.

Median Age

Top 150 Places Ranked in *Ascending* Order

State Rank	Years	Place
1	13.8	**Kiryas Joel** (village) Orange County
2	13.9	**New Square** (village) Rockland County
3	15.7	**Kaser** (village) Rockland County
4	16.2	**Monsey** (CDP) Rockland County
5	19.6	**Binghamton University** (CDP) Broome County
5	19.6	**SUNY Oswego** (CDP) Oswego County
7	19.7	**University at Buffalo** (CDP) Erie County
8	20.0	**South Hill** (CDP) Tompkins County
9	20.1	**Alfred** (village) Allegany County
10	20.3	**Alfred** (town) Allegany County
11	20.4	**Stony Brook University** (CDP) Suffolk County
12	20.6	**Delhi** (village) Delaware County
13	20.7	**Oswego** (town) Oswego County
14	20.8	**Geneseo** (village) Livingston County
15	21.0	**Potsdam** (village) Saint Lawrence County
16	21.2	**Monroe** (town) Orange County
16	21.2	**West Point** (CDP) Orange County
18	21.3	**Hamilton** (village) Madison County
19	21.4	**New Paltz** (village) Ulster County
20	21.8	**Geneseo** (town) Livingston County
20	21.8	**Ithaca** (city) Tompkins County
22	21.9	**Canton** (village) Saint Lawrence County
22	21.9	**Fort Drum** (CDP) Jefferson County
22	21.9	**Oneonta** (city) Otsego County
25	22.0	**Brockport** (village) Monroe County
26	22.5	**Arlington** (CDP) Dutchess County
27	22.7	**Hamilton** (town) Madison County
28	22.9	**Brookville** (village) Nassau County
29	23.2	**Highlands** (town) Orange County
30	23.3	**Le Ray** (town) Jefferson County
31	23.7	**Eaton** (town) Madison County
32	24.0	**Old Westbury** (village) Nassau County
33	24.3	**Potsdam** (town) Saint Lawrence County
34	24.7	**New Paltz** (town) Ulster County
35	24.8	**Sweden** (town) Monroe County
36	24.9	**Cobleskill** (village) Schoharie County
37	25.2	**Delhi** (town) Delaware County
38	25.4	**Fredonia** (village) Chautauqua County
39	26.1	**Calcium** (CDP) Jefferson County
40	26.4	**Vestal** (town) Broome County
41	26.6	**Viola** (CDP) Rockland County
42	26.9	**Ithaca** (town) Tompkins County
43	27.6	**Cedarhurst** (village) Nassau County
44	27.8	**Canton** (town) Saint Lawrence County
45	27.9	**Cortland** (city) Cortland County
45	27.9	**Newburgh** (city) Orange County
47	28.0	**Ramapo** (town) Rockland County
48	28.4	**Plattsburgh** (city) Clinton County
49	29.1	**Wilna** (town) Jefferson County
50	29.3	**Carthage** (village) Jefferson County
51	29.5	**Gordon Heights** (CDP) Suffolk County
52	29.6	**Geneva** (city) Ontario County
52	29.6	**Spring Valley** (village) Rockland County
54	30.0	**Wesley Hills** (village) Rockland County
55	30.5	**North Bay Shore** (CDP) Suffolk County
56	30.6	**Syracuse** (city) Onondaga County
56	30.6	**Troy** (city) Rensselaer County
58	30.9	**Albany** (city) Albany County
58	30.9	**Fairview** (CDP) Westchester County
60	31.0	**Munsons Corners** (CDP) Cortland County
61	31.1	**Watertown** (city) Jefferson County
62	31.3	**Pomfret** (town) Chautauqua County
63	31.4	**Fairview** (CDP) Dutchess County
64	31.6	**Northeast Ithaca** (CDP) Tompkins County
65	31.7	**Rochester** (city) Monroe County
66	31.9	**New Hempstead** (village) Rockland County
67	32.1	**New Cassel** (CDP) Nassau County
67	32.1	**Wyandanch** (CDP) Suffolk County
69	32.6	**Brentwood** (CDP) Suffolk County
69	32.6	**Yorkville** (village) Oneida County
71	32.8	**Buffalo** (city) Erie County
72	32.9	**Uniondale** (CDP) Nassau County
73	33.0	**Lansing** (village) Tompkins County
74	33.1	**Cobleskill** (town) Schoharie County
74	33.1	**East Farmingdale** (CDP) Suffolk County
74	33.1	**North Bellport** (CDP) Suffolk County
77	33.2	**Attica** (village) Wyoming County
78	33.3	**Galen** (town) Wayne County
78	33.3	**Salamanca** (city) Cattaraugus County
80	33.4	**Elmira** (city) Chemung County
81	33.5	**Haverstraw** (village) Rockland County
81	33.5	**Hounsfield** (town) Jefferson County
83	33.6	**Bronx** (borough) Bronx County
83	33.6	**Henrietta** (town) Monroe County
85	33.7	**Wheatland** (town) Monroe County
86	33.8	**West Haverstraw** (village) Rockland County
87	33.9	**Hempstead** (village) Nassau County
87	33.9	**New Bremen** (town) Lewis County
89	34.0	**North Amityville** (CDP) Suffolk County
89	34.0	**Utica** (city) Oneida County
91	34.1	**Kings Point** (village) Nassau County
92	34.2	**Central Islip** (CDP) Suffolk County
92	34.2	**Menands** (village) Albany County
92	34.2	**Rutland** (town) Jefferson County
95	34.4	**Bedford Hills** (CDP) Westchester County
95	34.4	**Lakeview** (CDP) Nassau County
97	34.6	**Canastota** (village) Madison County
97	34.6	**Wappingers Falls** (village) Dutchess County
99	34.7	**Bay Shore** (CDP) Suffolk County
99	34.7	**Woodmere** (CDP) Nassau County
101	34.8	**Brooklyn** (borough) Kings County
101	34.8	**Harriman** (village) Orange County
101	34.8	**Monticello** (village) Sullivan County
101	34.8	**Norwich** (city) Chenango County
105	34.9	**Harrison** (town/village) Westchester County
105	34.9	**Inwood** (CDP) Nassau County
105	34.9	**Norfolk** (town) Saint Lawrence County
105	34.9	**Oswego** (city) Oswego County
105	34.9	**Rensselaer** (city) Rensselaer County
110	35.0	**Roosevelt** (CDP) Nassau County
111	35.1	**Monroe** (village) Orange County
112	35.2	**Elmira Heights** (village) Chemung County
113	35.3	**Mastic** (CDP) Suffolk County
113	35.3	**Shirley** (CDP) Suffolk County
115	35.5	**Elmsford** (village) Westchester County
115	35.5	**Johnson City** (village) Broome County
117	35.7	**Gouverneur** (village) Saint Lawrence County
117	35.7	**Mattydale** (CDP) Onondaga County
117	35.7	**South Valley Stream** (CDP) Nassau County
120	35.8	**Adams** (town) Jefferson County
120	35.8	**Dolgeville** (village) Herkimer County
120	35.8	**Mechanicville** (city) Saratoga County
120	35.8	**Middletown** (city) Orange County
120	35.8	**Walton** (village) Delaware County
125	35.9	**East Rochester** (town/village) Monroe County
125	35.9	**Walden** (village) Orange County
127	36.0	**Riverside** (CDP) Suffolk County
128	36.1	**Dannemora** (village) Clinton County
128	36.1	**Flanders** (CDP) Suffolk County
128	36.1	**Hamlin** (town) Monroe County
128	36.1	**Palmyra** (village) Wayne County
128	36.1	**Sidney** (village) Delaware County
133	36.2	**Great Neck** (village) Nassau County
133	36.2	**New York** (city)
133	36.2	**Romulus** (town) Seneca County
136	36.3	**Brewerton** (CDP) Onondaga County
136	36.3	**East Syracuse** (village) Onondaga County
136	36.3	**Gouverneur** (town) Saint Lawrence County
136	36.3	**Larchmont** (village) Westchester County
136	36.3	**Malone** (town) Franklin County
141	36.4	**Attica** (town) Wyoming County
141	36.4	**Binghamton** (city) Broome County
141	36.4	**Cayuga Heights** (village) Tompkins County
141	36.4	**Pamelia** (town) Jefferson County
141	36.4	**Patchogue** (village) Suffolk County
141	36.4	**Port Chester** (village) Westchester County
141	36.4	**Schenectady** (city) Schenectady County
148	36.5	**Airmont** (village) Rockland County
148	36.5	**Brasher** (town) Saint Lawrence County
148	36.5	**Saint Johnsville** (town) Montgomery County

Note: This section ranks incorporated places and CDPs (Census Designated Places) with populations of 2,500 or more. Unincorporated postal areas were not considered. Please refer to the User Guide for additional information.

Population Under Age 18

Top 150 Places Ranked in *Descending* Order

State Rank	Percent	Place
1	61.2	**New Square** (village) Rockland County
2	60.4	**Kiryas Joel** (village) Orange County
3	56.7	**Kaser** (village) Rockland County
4	54.5	**Monsey** (CDP) Rockland County
5	44.9	**Monroe** (town) Orange County
6	36.2	**Ramapo** (town) Rockland County
7	35.4	**Wesley Hills** (village) Rockland County
8	34.8	**Viola** (CDP) Rockland County
9	34.5	**Flanders** (CDP) Suffolk County
10	33.4	**Woodmere** (CDP) Nassau County
11	33.3	**Larchmont** (village) Westchester County
12	33.1	**Spring Valley** (village) Rockland County
13	33.0	**Newburgh** (city) Orange County
14	32.2	**Galen** (town) Wayne County
15	31.5	**Carthage** (village) Jefferson County
15	31.5	**Scarsdale** (town/village) Westchester County
17	31.4	**Munsey Park** (village) Nassau County
18	31.2	**Gordon Heights** (CDP) Suffolk County
19	30.9	**Walton** (village) Delaware County
20	30.7	**Lawrence** (village) Nassau County
21	30.6	**Pelham Manor** (village) Westchester County
22	30.5	**Bedford Hills** (CDP) Westchester County
22	30.5	**New Hempstead** (village) Rockland County
24	30.2	**Rye** (city) Westchester County
24	30.2	**Salamanca** (city) Cattaraugus County
26	30.1	**Clarence Center** (CDP) Erie County
27	29.9	**Great Neck** (village) Nassau County
28	29.7	**Cedarhurst** (village) Nassau County
28	29.7	**Fort Drum** (CDP) Jefferson County
28	29.7	**Randolph** (town) Cattaraugus County
31	29.6	**Rutland** (town) Jefferson County
32	29.5	**New Bremen** (town) Lewis County
33	29.4	**Hounsfield** (town) Jefferson County
34	29.3	**Airmont** (village) Rockland County
34	29.3	**Greenville** (CDP) Westchester County
36	29.2	**Bronxville** (village) Westchester County
37	29.1	**Brasher** (town) Saint Lawrence County
37	29.1	**East Hills** (village) Nassau County
37	29.1	**Wilna** (town) Jefferson County
40	29.0	**Clarkson** (CDP) Monroe County
41	28.8	**Great Neck Estates** (village) Nassau County
42	28.6	**New Castle** (town) Westchester County
43	28.5	**Attica** (village) Wyoming County
43	28.5	**Irvington** (village) Westchester County
43	28.5	**Manorhaven** (village) Nassau County
46	28.4	**Lloyd Harbor** (village) Suffolk County
46	28.4	**Pelham** (town) Westchester County
46	28.4	**Richland** (town) Oswego County
49	28.3	**Dolgeville** (village) Herkimer County
49	28.3	**North Bay Shore** (CDP) Suffolk County
51	27.9	**East Shoreham** (CDP) Suffolk County
51	27.9	**Monroe** (village) Orange County
53	27.8	**Armonk** (CDP) Westchester County
54	27.7	**North Bellport** (CDP) Suffolk County
55	27.6	**Hilton** (village) Monroe County
55	27.6	**Le Ray** (town) Jefferson County
55	27.6	**Mastic** (CDP) Suffolk County
55	27.6	**Woodbury** (town) Orange County
59	27.5	**Manheim** (town) Herkimer County
59	27.5	**Sidney** (village) Delaware County
59	27.5	**Victor** (village) Ontario County
62	27.4	**Glasco** (CDP) Ulster County
63	27.3	**Port Jervis** (city) Orange County
63	27.3	**Woodbury** (village) Orange County
65	27.2	**Augusta** (town) Oneida County
65	27.2	**Grandyle Village** (CDP) Erie County
67	27.1	**Adams** (town) Jefferson County
67	27.1	**New Cassel** (CDP) Nassau County
69	27.0	**Bainbridge** (town) Chenango County
69	27.0	**Hempstead** (village) Nassau County
69	27.0	**North Castle** (town) Westchester County
69	27.0	**Northeast Ithaca** (CDP) Tompkins County
69	27.0	**Wyandanch** (CDP) Suffolk County
74	26.9	**East Williston** (village) Nassau County
74	26.9	**Minden** (town) Montgomery County
76	26.8	**Chestnut Ridge** (village) Rockland County
76	26.8	**Haverstraw** (village) Rockland County
76	26.8	**Huntington Station** (CDP) Suffolk County
76	26.8	**Walton** (town) Delaware County
80	26.7	**Pelham** (village) Westchester County
81	26.6	**Neversink** (town) Sullivan County
81	26.6	**Theresa** (town) Jefferson County
83	26.5	**Monticello** (village) Sullivan County
83	26.5	**Sands Point** (village) Nassau County
85	26.4	**Brentwood** (CDP) Suffolk County
85	26.4	**Miller Place** (CDP) Suffolk County
85	26.4	**Walworth** (town) Wayne County
88	26.3	**Mamaroneck** (town) Westchester County
88	26.3	**Norfolk** (town) Saint Lawrence County
90	26.2	**Candor** (town) Tioga County
90	26.2	**Manorville** (CDP) Suffolk County
90	26.2	**Pamelia** (town) Jefferson County
90	26.2	**Spackenkill** (CDP) Dutchess County
90	26.2	**Walden** (village) Orange County
95	26.1	**Chittenango** (village) Madison County
95	26.1	**Kendall** (town) Orleans County
95	26.1	**Menands** (village) Albany County
95	26.1	**Rye Brook** (village) Westchester County
99	26.0	**Center Moriches** (CDP) Suffolk County
99	26.0	**Flower Hill** (village) Nassau County
99	26.0	**Minoa** (village) Onondaga County
99	26.0	**Saint Johnsville** (town) Montgomery County
103	25.9	**Bay Shore** (CDP) Suffolk County
103	25.9	**Croton-on-Hudson** (village) Westchester County
103	25.9	**Ilion** (village) Herkimer County
103	25.9	**Mattydale** (CDP) Onondaga County
103	25.9	**Pleasantville** (village) Westchester County
103	25.9	**Stockholm** (town) Saint Lawrence County
103	25.9	**Thomaston** (village) Nassau County
110	25.8	**Catlin** (town) Chemung County
110	25.8	**Ellisburg** (town) Jefferson County
110	25.8	**Fairview** (CDP) Westchester County
110	25.8	**Perry** (town) Wyoming County
114	25.7	**Ellenville** (village) Ulster County
114	25.7	**Fort Edward** (village) Washington County
114	25.7	**Inwood** (CDP) Nassau County
114	25.7	**Niskayuna** (town) Schenectady County
114	25.7	**Ridgeway** (town) Orleans County
114	25.7	**West Sand Lake** (CDP) Rensselaer County
120	25.6	**Pompey** (town) Onondaga County
120	25.6	**West Haverstraw** (village) Rockland County
122	25.5	**Canajoharie** (town) Montgomery County
122	25.5	**Farmington** (town) Ontario County
122	25.5	**Greenlawn** (CDP) Suffolk County
122	25.5	**Lakeview** (CDP) Nassau County
126	25.4	**Addison** (town) Steuben County
126	25.4	**Corinth** (village) Saratoga County
126	25.4	**Orleans** (town) Jefferson County
126	25.4	**Rocky Point** (CDP) Suffolk County
126	25.4	**Victor** (town) Ontario County
131	25.3	**Brewerton** (CDP) Onondaga County
131	25.3	**Calcium** (CDP) Jefferson County
131	25.3	**Elmira Heights** (village) Chemung County
131	25.3	**Gang Mills** (CDP) Steuben County
131	25.3	**Oswegatchie** (town) Saint Lawrence County
131	25.3	**Somerset** (town) Niagara County
131	25.3	**Spencerport** (village) Monroe County
131	25.3	**Triangle** (town) Broome County
139	25.2	**Bronx** (borough) Bronx County
139	25.2	**Garden City** (village) Nassau County
139	25.2	**North Collins** (town) Erie County
139	25.2	**Syosset** (CDP) Nassau County
143	25.1	**Cornwall-on-Hudson** (village) Orange County
143	25.1	**Kings Point** (village) Nassau County
145	25.0	**Firthcliffe** (CDP) Orange County
145	25.0	**Florida** (village) Orange County
145	25.0	**Manhasset** (CDP) Nassau County
145	25.0	**Minisink** (town) Orange County
145	25.0	**South Hempstead** (CDP) Nassau County
150	24.9	**Cornwall** (town) Orange County

Note: This section ranks incorporated places and CDPs (Census Designated Places) with populations of 2,500 or more. Unincorporated postal areas were not considered. Please refer to the User Guide for additional information.

Population Under Age 18

Top 150 Places Ranked in *Ascending* Order

State Rank	Percent	Place
1	1.2	**SUNY Oswego** (CDP) Oswego County
2	1.6	**Binghamton University** (CDP) Broome County
3	1.7	**Stony Brook University** (CDP) Suffolk County
4	2.0	**University at Buffalo** (CDP) Erie County
5	2.5	**Alfred** (village) Allegany County
6	4.3	**Riverside** (CDP) Suffolk County
7	5.1	**Dannemora** (village) Clinton County
8	5.6	**Dannemora** (town) Clinton County
9	6.1	**Heritage Hills** (CDP) Westchester County
10	6.2	**Alfred** (town) Allegany County
11	6.9	**South Hill** (CDP) Tompkins County
12	7.7	**Canton** (village) Saint Lawrence County
13	8.1	**Hamilton** (village) Madison County
14	8.5	**Potsdam** (village) Saint Lawrence County
15	8.8	**Ithaca** (city) Tompkins County
16	8.9	**New Paltz** (village) Ulster County
17	9.1	**Northwest Harbor** (CDP) Suffolk County
18	9.5	**Groveland** (town) Livingston County
19	9.6	**Calverton** (CDP) Suffolk County
20	9.7	**Shandaken** (town) Ulster County
21	10.4	**Delhi** (village) Delaware County
21	10.4	**Geneseo** (village) Livingston County
21	10.4	**Montauk** (CDP) Suffolk County
24	10.8	**Fort Ann** (town) Washington County
24	10.8	**Geneseo** (town) Livingston County
24	10.8	**Romulus** (town) Seneca County
27	11.1	**Oneonta** (city) Otsego County
28	11.2	**Cazenovia** (village) Madison County
29	11.3	**Collins** (town) Erie County
30	11.8	**Middletown** (town) Delaware County
30	11.8	**Oswego** (town) Oswego County
32	12.2	**North Hills** (village) Nassau County
33	12.5	**Brockport** (village) Monroe County
33	12.5	**Port Ewen** (CDP) Ulster County
35	12.6	**Delhi** (town) Delaware County
35	12.6	**North Elba** (town) Essex County
37	12.9	**Cayuga Heights** (village) Tompkins County
38	13.0	**Canton** (town) Saint Lawrence County
39	13.2	**Madison** (town) Madison County
40	13.6	**Potsdam** (town) Saint Lawrence County
41	13.7	**Cobleskill** (village) Schoharie County
41	13.7	**Rosendale** (town) Ulster County
43	13.9	**Cape Vincent** (town) Jefferson County
44	14.0	**Great Neck Plaza** (village) Nassau County
44	14.0	**Hartsdale** (CDP) Westchester County
44	14.0	**Hunter** (town) Greene County
44	14.0	**Ithaca** (town) Tompkins County
44	14.0	**Otsego** (town) Otsego County
49	14.1	**Attica** (town) Wyoming County
49	14.1	**Hamilton** (town) Madison County
49	14.1	**Hector** (town) Schuyler County
52	14.2	**Lewiston** (village) Niagara County
52	14.2	**Plattsburgh** (city) Clinton County
54	14.3	**Lake Luzerne** (town) Warren County
54	14.3	**New Baltimore** (town) Greene County
54	14.3	**Orangeburg** (CDP) Rockland County
57	14.4	**Woodstock** (town) Ulster County
58	14.5	**Kirkland** (town) Oneida County
58	14.5	**Manhattan** (borough) New York County
60	14.6	**South Nyack** (village) Rockland County
61	14.7	**Fleming** (town) Cayuga County
62	14.8	**Clarendon** (town) Orleans County
63	14.9	**Eaton** (town) Madison County
64	15.0	**Hurley** (town) Ulster County
64	15.0	**Lakeland** (CDP) Onondaga County
64	15.0	**Lewiston** (town) Niagara County
67	15.1	**Allegany** (town) Cattaraugus County
67	15.1	**Ghent** (town) Columbia County
67	15.1	**Otego** (town) Otsego County
70	15.2	**Davenport** (town) Delaware County
70	15.2	**Rhinebeck** (village) Dutchess County
70	15.2	**Rochester** (town) Ulster County
70	15.2	**Stanford** (town) Dutchess County
74	15.3	**Dickinson** (town) Broome County
74	15.3	**Olive** (town) Ulster County
74	15.3	**Southampton** (village) Suffolk County
77	15.4	**Cobleskill** (town) Schoharie County
77	15.4	**Elma Center** (CDP) Erie County
77	15.4	**Greenport** (town) Columbia County
77	15.4	**Long Beach** (city) Nassau County
77	15.4	**Marcy** (town) Oneida County
77	15.4	**Saratoga Springs** (city) Saratoga County
77	15.4	**Veteran** (town) Chemung County
84	15.5	**Athens** (town) Greene County
84	15.5	**Brunswick** (town) Rensselaer County
84	15.5	**Hurley** (CDP) Ulster County
84	15.5	**Richmond** (town) Ontario County
84	15.5	**Village Green** (CDP) Onondaga County
89	15.6	**Batavia** (town) Genesee County
89	15.6	**Fredonia** (village) Chautauqua County
89	15.6	**Williamsville** (village) Erie County
92	15.7	**Amsterdam** (town) Montgomery County
92	15.7	**Bethel** (town) Sullivan County
92	15.7	**Danby** (town) Tompkins County
92	15.7	**Louisville** (town) Saint Lawrence County
92	15.7	**Maybrook** (village) Orange County
92	15.7	**Middleburgh** (town) Schoharie County
92	15.7	**Piermont** (village) Rockland County
92	15.7	**Vails Gate** (CDP) Orange County
100	15.8	**Albion** (town) Orleans County
100	15.8	**New Paltz** (town) Ulster County
102	15.9	**Southold** (town) Suffolk County
102	15.9	**Sweden** (town) Monroe County
102	15.9	**Vestal** (town) Broome County
105	16.0	**Afton** (town) Chenango County
105	16.0	**Guilford** (town) Chenango County
107	16.1	**Mattituck** (CDP) Suffolk County
108	16.2	**Argyle** (town) Washington County
108	16.2	**Fairport** (village) Monroe County
108	16.2	**Florida** (town) Montgomery County
108	16.2	**Herkimer** (town) Herkimer County
108	16.2	**Herkimer** (village) Herkimer County
108	16.2	**White Creek** (town) Washington County
114	16.3	**Westerlo** (town) Albany County
115	16.4	**East Hampton** (town) Suffolk County
115	16.4	**North East** (town) Dutchess County
117	16.5	**Cohoes** (city) Albany County
117	16.5	**Cortland** (city) Cortland County
117	16.5	**Oxford** (town) Chenango County
117	16.5	**Riverhead** (town) Suffolk County
121	16.6	**Carlton** (town) Orleans County
121	16.6	**Lake George** (town) Warren County
121	16.6	**Livingston** (town) Columbia County
121	16.6	**Moravia** (town) Cayuga County
125	16.7	**Colonie** (village) Albany County
125	16.7	**Eden** (town) Erie County
125	16.7	**Plattekill** (town) Ulster County
125	16.7	**Roslyn** (village) Nassau County
125	16.7	**Wynantskill** (CDP) Rensselaer County
130	16.8	**Chester** (village) Orange County
130	16.8	**Gaines** (town) Orleans County
130	16.8	**Rhinebeck** (town) Dutchess County
130	16.8	**West Bloomfield** (town) Ontario County
134	16.9	**Aurelius** (town) Cayuga County
134	16.9	**Farmingdale** (village) Nassau County
134	16.9	**Gorham** (town) Ontario County
134	16.9	**Green Island** (town/village) Albany County
134	16.9	**Mount Hope** (town) Orange County
134	16.9	**Munsons Corners** (CDP) Cortland County
140	17.0	**Amenia** (town) Dutchess County
140	17.0	**Delaware** (town) Sullivan County
140	17.0	**Enfield** (town) Tompkins County
140	17.0	**Mayfield** (town) Fulton County
140	17.0	**North Sea** (CDP) Suffolk County
140	17.0	**Oakdale** (CDP) Suffolk County
140	17.0	**Pomfret** (town) Chautauqua County
140	17.0	**Wappingers Falls** (village) Dutchess County
148	17.1	**Carroll** (town) Chautauqua County
148	17.1	**Chautauqua** (town) Chautauqua County
148	17.1	**Highland Falls** (village) Orange County

Note: This section ranks incorporated places and CDPs (Census Designated Places) with populations of 2,500 or more. Unincorporated postal areas were not considered. Please refer to the User Guide for additional information.

Population Age 65 and Over

Top 150 Places Ranked in *Descending* Order

State Rank	Percent	Place
1	63.6	**Heritage Hills** (CDP) Westchester County
2	46.0	**North Hills** (village) Nassau County
3	34.9	**Calverton** (CDP) Suffolk County
4	33.2	**Middletown** (town) Delaware County
5	33.1	**Shelter Island** (town) Suffolk County
6	32.9	**Montauk** (CDP) Suffolk County
7	32.6	**Rhinebeck** (village) Dutchess County
8	32.5	**Southampton** (village) Suffolk County
9	31.9	**Great Neck Plaza** (village) Nassau County
10	31.6	**Northwest Harbor** (CDP) Suffolk County
11	31.4	**Woodstock** (town) Ulster County
12	31.0	**Lake Success** (village) Nassau County
13	30.3	**Rhinebeck** (town) Dutchess County
14	30.2	**Shandaken** (town) Ulster County
15	30.1	**Bardonia** (CDP) Rockland County
16	29.6	**Hunter** (town) Greene County
16	29.6	**Lewiston** (village) Niagara County
18	29.2	**Clarence** (CDP) Erie County
18	29.2	**Ridge** (CDP) Suffolk County
20	29.1	**Southold** (CDP) Suffolk County
21	28.9	**Southold** (town) Suffolk County
21	28.9	**Veteran** (town) Chemung County
23	28.6	**Cutchogue** (CDP) Suffolk County
23	28.6	**West Elmira** (CDP) Chemung County
25	27.7	**Roslyn** (village) Nassau County
26	27.6	**Woodbury** (CDP) Nassau County
27	27.5	**Lido Beach** (CDP) Nassau County
28	27.2	**Elma Center** (CDP) Erie County
28	27.2	**Warwick** (village) Orange County
30	27.1	**Lakewood** (village) Chautauqua County
31	26.6	**Melville** (CDP) Suffolk County
32	26.5	**Westhampton** (CDP) Suffolk County
33	26.2	**Madison** (town) Madison County
34	26.1	**Livingston** (town) Columbia County
35	26.0	**Amsterdam** (town) Montgomery County
35	26.0	**Hartsdale** (CDP) Westchester County
35	26.0	**Hurley** (town) Ulster County
35	26.0	**North Sea** (CDP) Suffolk County
39	25.9	**East Hampton** (town) Suffolk County
39	25.9	**Ellery** (town) Chautauqua County
41	25.6	**New Hartford** (town) Oneida County
42	25.5	**Somers** (town) Westchester County
43	25.3	**Orangeburg** (CDP) Rockland County
44	25.2	**Geneva** (town) Ontario County
44	25.2	**Skaneateles** (town) Onondaga County
46	25.1	**Hornellsville** (town) Steuben County
46	25.1	**New Berlin** (town) Chenango County
48	25.0	**Hurley** (CDP) Ulster County
49	24.8	**Claverack** (town) Columbia County
49	24.8	**Middleburgh** (town) Schoharie County
51	24.7	**Danby** (town) Tompkins County
52	24.6	**Busti** (town) Chautauqua County
52	24.6	**Otsego** (town) Otsego County
54	24.5	**Ghent** (town) Columbia County
55	24.3	**Campbell** (town) Steuben County
55	24.3	**West Bloomfield** (town) Ontario County
57	24.2	**Newfane** (CDP) Niagara County
58	24.1	**Bainbridge** (town) Chenango County
58	24.1	**Callicoon** (town) Sullivan County
58	24.1	**Greenport** (town) Columbia County
61	24.0	**Chatham** (town) Columbia County
61	24.0	**Elmira** (town) Chemung County
61	24.0	**Horseheads** (village) Chemung County
61	24.0	**Williamsville** (village) Erie County
65	23.9	**Riverhead** (town) Suffolk County
66	23.8	**Baldwinsville** (village) Onondaga County
67	23.7	**Wanakah** (CDP) Erie County
68	23.6	**Carlton** (town) Chautauqua County
69	23.4	**Marilla** (town) Erie County
69	23.4	**Sherrill** (city) Oneida County
69	23.4	**Ulster** (town) Ulster County
72	23.3	**Milford** (town) Otsego County
72	23.3	**Olive** (town) Ulster County
74	23.2	**Lake George** (town) Warren County
74	23.2	**Westfield** (town) Chautauqua County

State Rank	Percent	Place
76	23.1	**Chautauqua** (town) Chautauqua County
76	23.1	**Fayetteville** (village) Onondaga County
76	23.1	**Otego** (town) Otsego County
76	23.1	**Searingtown** (CDP) Nassau County
76	23.1	**White Creek** (town) Washington County
81	23.0	**Penn Yan** (village) Yates County
81	23.0	**Piermont** (village) Rockland County
83	22.9	**Carlton** (town) Orleans County
83	22.9	**Lakeland** (CDP) Onondaga County
83	22.9	**Port Ewen** (CDP) Ulster County
86	22.8	**Fleming** (town) Cayuga County
86	22.8	**Lewiston** (town) Niagara County
88	22.7	**Gates** (CDP) Monroe County
88	22.7	**Johnstown** (town) Fulton County
88	22.7	**Rosendale** (town) Ulster County
88	22.7	**Schuyler** (town) Herkimer County
92	22.6	**Castile** (town) Wyoming County
92	22.6	**Schoharie** (town) Schoharie County
94	22.5	**East Glenville** (CDP) Schenectady County
94	22.5	**Mattituck** (CDP) Suffolk County
94	22.5	**Oxford** (town) Chenango County
94	22.5	**Oyster Bay** (CDP) Nassau County
94	22.5	**Port Washington** (CDP) Nassau County
94	22.5	**Port Washington North** (village) Nassau County
94	22.5	**Pound Ridge** (town) Westchester County
101	22.4	**Tappan** (CDP) Rockland County
101	22.4	**Washington** (town) Dutchess County
103	22.3	**Cayuga Heights** (village) Tompkins County
103	22.3	**Wellsville** (town) Allegany County
103	22.3	**West Bay Shore** (CDP) Suffolk County
103	22.3	**Westfield** (village) Chautauqua County
107	22.2	**Galway** (town) Saratoga County
107	22.2	**North Greenbush** (town) Rensselaer County
107	22.2	**Northport** (village) Suffolk County
107	22.2	**Oneonta** (town) Otsego County
107	22.2	**Owasco** (town) Cayuga County
107	22.2	**Port Jefferson** (village) Suffolk County
107	22.2	**Tuxedo** (town) Orange County
107	22.2	**Ulysses** (town) Tompkins County
115	22.1	**Copake** (town) Columbia County
115	22.1	**Gorham** (town) Ontario County
115	22.1	**Herkimer** (village) Herkimer County
115	22.1	**Hewlett** (CDP) Nassau County
115	22.1	**Mount Morris** (town) Livingston County
120	22.0	**Chester** (town) Warren County
120	22.0	**Galeville** (CDP) Onondaga County
120	22.0	**Glens Falls North** (CDP) Warren County
120	22.0	**Herkimer** (town) Herkimer County
120	22.0	**Lawrence** (village) Nassau County
120	22.0	**Middle Island** (CDP) Suffolk County
120	22.0	**Portville** (town) Cattaraugus County
127	21.9	**Coxsackie** (village) Greene County
127	21.9	**Elma** (town) Erie County
127	21.9	**Salem** (town) Washington County
130	21.8	**Brookhaven** (CDP) Suffolk County
130	21.8	**Mechanicstown** (CDP) Orange County
130	21.8	**Thomaston** (village) Nassau County
130	21.8	**Unadilla** (town) Otsego County
134	21.7	**Boston** (town) Erie County
134	21.7	**Carmel Hamlet** (CDP) Putnam County
134	21.7	**Malverne** (village) Nassau County
134	21.7	**Manhasset Hills** (CDP) Nassau County
134	21.7	**Moira** (town) Franklin County
139	21.6	**Delaware** (town) Sullivan County
139	21.6	**Laurens** (town) Otsego County
139	21.6	**Wheatfield** (town) Niagara County
142	21.5	**Canandaigua** (town) Ontario County
142	21.5	**Catskill** (town) Greene County
142	21.5	**Stony Brook** (CDP) Suffolk County
145	21.4	**Bayville** (village) Nassau County
145	21.4	**Hector** (town) Schuyler County
145	21.4	**Lee** (town) Oneida County
145	21.4	**Riverhead** (CDP) Suffolk County
149	21.3	**Bethpage** (CDP) Nassau County
149	21.3	**Davenport** (town) Delaware County

Note: This section ranks incorporated places and CDPs (Census Designated Places) with populations of 2,500 or more. Unincorporated postal areas were not considered. Please refer to the User Guide for additional information.

Population Age 65 and Over

Top 150 Places Ranked in *Ascending* Order

State Rank	Percent	Place
1	0.0	**SUNY Oswego** (CDP) Oswego County
1	0.0	**University at Buffalo** (CDP) Erie County
3	0.1	**Fort Drum** (CDP) Jefferson County
4	0.2	**Binghamton University** (CDP) Broome County
5	0.5	**West Point** (CDP) Orange County
6	1.8	**New Square** (village) Rockland County
7	2.1	**Alfred** (village) Allegany County
7	2.1	**Le Ray** (town) Jefferson County
9	2.2	**Kiryas Joel** (village) Orange County
10	2.5	**Calcium** (CDP) Jefferson County
11	2.7	**Kaser** (village) Rockland County
12	4.1	**Stony Brook University** (CDP) Suffolk County
13	4.2	**Dannemora** (village) Clinton County
14	4.3	**Alfred** (town) Allegany County
15	4.9	**Harriman** (village) Orange County
16	5.8	**Ithaca** (city) Tompkins County
16	5.8	**Monroe** (town) Orange County
16	5.8	**Monsey** (CDP) Rockland County
19	6.0	**Geneseo** (village) Livingston County
19	6.0	**Groveland** (town) Livingston County
21	6.2	**Gordon Heights** (CDP) Suffolk County
21	6.2	**North Bay Shore** (CDP) Suffolk County
23	6.5	**Dannemora** (town) Clinton County
24	7.0	**Clarence Center** (CDP) Erie County
24	7.0	**Highlands** (town) Orange County
24	7.0	**South Hill** (CDP) Tompkins County
27	7.3	**Potsdam** (village) Saint Lawrence County
28	7.4	**New Paltz** (village) Ulster County
29	7.7	**Flanders** (CDP) Suffolk County
30	7.8	**North Bellport** (CDP) Suffolk County
31	7.9	**Greenwood Lake** (village) Orange County
32	8.1	**Attica** (town) Wyoming County
32	8.1	**Spring Valley** (village) Rockland County
34	8.2	**Mastic** (CDP) Suffolk County
35	8.4	**Oswego** (town) Oswego County
36	8.6	**Brentwood** (CDP) Suffolk County
36	8.6	**Newburgh** (city) Orange County
38	8.8	**Bedford Hills** (CDP) Westchester County
39	9.3	**Romulus** (town) Seneca County
40	9.5	**Northeast Ithaca** (CDP) Tompkins County
41	9.7	**Caroline** (town) Tompkins County
41	9.7	**Central Islip** (CDP) Suffolk County
41	9.7	**Watertown** (town) Jefferson County
44	9.8	**Riverside** (CDP) Suffolk County
44	9.8	**Wyandanch** (CDP) Suffolk County
46	9.9	**Mastic Beach** (village) Suffolk County
46	9.9	**West Sand Lake** (CDP) Rensselaer County
48	10.0	**Baywood** (CDP) Suffolk County
48	10.0	**Fairview** (CDP) Westchester County
48	10.0	**New Hempstead** (village) Rockland County
48	10.0	**Walden** (village) Orange County
52	10.1	**New Cassel** (CDP) Nassau County
53	10.2	**Duanesburg** (town) Schenectady County
53	10.2	**West Haverstraw** (village) Rockland County
55	10.3	**Hempstead** (village) Nassau County
55	10.3	**Monroe** (village) Orange County
55	10.3	**Rochester** (city) Monroe County
55	10.3	**Wheatley Heights** (CDP) Suffolk County
59	10.5	**Catlin** (town) Chemung County
59	10.5	**Hilton** (village) Monroe County
61	10.6	**Center Moriches** (CDP) Suffolk County
61	10.6	**Rocky Point** (CDP) Suffolk County
63	10.7	**Hamilton** (village) Madison County
64	10.8	**Bay Shore** (CDP) Suffolk County
64	10.8	**Delhi** (village) Delaware County
64	10.8	**Larchmont** (village) Westchester County
64	10.8	**Shirley** (CDP) Suffolk County
68	10.9	**Manorhaven** (village) Nassau County
68	10.9	**New Haven** (town) Oswego County
68	10.9	**Troy** (city) Rensselaer County
71	11.0	**Huntington Station** (CDP) Suffolk County
71	11.0	**Potsdam** (town) Saint Lawrence County
71	11.0	**Yaphank** (CDP) Suffolk County
74	11.1	**Gouverneur** (town) Saint Lawrence County
74	11.1	**Islip Terrace** (CDP) Suffolk County
74	11.1	**Ossining** (village) Westchester County
74	11.1	**Port Chester** (village) Westchester County
78	11.2	**Attica** (village) Wyoming County
78	11.2	**East Shoreham** (CDP) Suffolk County
78	11.2	**East Syracuse** (village) Onondaga County
78	11.2	**Fairview** (CDP) Dutchess County
78	11.2	**Hamlin** (CDP) Monroe County
78	11.2	**Northumberland** (town) Saratoga County
84	11.3	**Glenwood Landing** (CDP) Nassau County
84	11.3	**Lake Mohegan** (CDP) Westchester County
86	11.4	**Canastota** (village) Madison County
86	11.4	**Chester** (town) Orange County
86	11.4	**Elmsford** (village) Westchester County
86	11.4	**Wawayanda** (town) Orange County
86	11.4	**Woodbury** (town) Orange County
91	11.5	**Ellenville** (village) Ulster County
91	11.5	**Elmira** (city) Chemung County
91	11.5	**Maybrook** (village) Orange County
91	11.5	**Minisink** (town) Orange County
91	11.5	**Ramapo** (town) Rockland County
96	11.6	**Brockport** (village) Monroe County
96	11.6	**Brookville** (village) Nassau County
96	11.6	**North Amityville** (CDP) Suffolk County
96	11.6	**Oneonta** (city) Otsego County
100	11.7	**Arlington** (CDP) Dutchess County
100	11.7	**Brewerton** (CDP) Onondaga County
100	11.7	**Knox** (town) Albany County
100	11.7	**Marcy** (town) Oneida County
100	11.7	**Patchogue** (village) Suffolk County
105	11.8	**Bronx** (borough) Bronx County
105	11.8	**Chester** (village) Orange County
105	11.8	**Lakeview** (CDP) Nassau County
105	11.8	**Roosevelt** (CDP) Nassau County
105	11.8	**Theresa** (town) Jefferson County
105	11.8	**Wilna** (town) Jefferson County
111	11.9	**Brasher** (town) Saint Lawrence County
111	11.9	**Rutland** (town) Jefferson County
113	12.0	**Beekman** (town) Dutchess County
113	12.0	**Eaton** (town) Madison County
113	12.0	**Farmingville** (CDP) Suffolk County
113	12.0	**Horseheads North** (CDP) Chemung County
113	12.0	**Menands** (village) Albany County
113	12.0	**Syracuse** (city) Onondaga County
119	12.1	**Malone** (town) Franklin County
119	12.1	**Mount Hope** (town) Orange County
119	12.1	**Sweden** (town) Monroe County
122	12.2	**Buffalo** (city) Erie County
122	12.2	**North Lindenhurst** (CDP) Suffolk County
122	12.2	**Watertown** (city) Jefferson County
122	12.2	**Woodbury** (village) Orange County
126	12.3	**Hamilton** (town) Madison County
126	12.3	**Lake Placid** (village) Essex County
128	12.4	**Canton** (village) Saint Lawrence County
128	12.4	**Geneseo** (town) Livingston County
130	12.5	**East Farmingdale** (CDP) Suffolk County
130	12.5	**Grandyle Village** (CDP) Erie County
130	12.5	**New Paltz** (town) Ulster County
130	12.5	**Shawangunk** (town) Ulster County
130	12.5	**Watervliet** (city) Albany County
135	12.6	**Albany** (city) Albany County
135	12.6	**Islip** (town) Suffolk County
137	12.7	**Copiague** (CDP) Suffolk County
137	12.7	**Fort Ann** (town) Washington County
137	12.7	**Inwood** (CDP) Nassau County
140	12.8	**Armonk** (CDP) Westchester County
140	12.8	**Brooklyn** (borough) Kings County
140	12.8	**Greenville** (town) Orange County
140	12.8	**Haverstraw** (village) Rockland County
140	12.8	**Hudson** (city) Columbia County
140	12.8	**Mamakating** (town) Sullivan County
140	12.8	**Mattydale** (CDP) Onondaga County
140	12.8	**Old Westbury** (village) Nassau County
148	12.9	**Adams** (town) Jefferson County
148	12.9	**Collins** (town) Erie County
148	12.9	**Denmark** (town) Lewis County

Note: This section ranks incorporated places and CDPs (Census Designated Places) with populations of 2,500 or more. Unincorporated postal areas were not considered. Please refer to the User Guide for additional information.

Males per 100 Females

Top 150 Places Ranked in *Descending* Order

State Rank	Ratio	Place		State Rank	Ratio	Place
1	578.6	Dannemora (village) Clinton County		76	105.5	Kaser (village) Rockland County
2	380.2	Dannemora (town) Clinton County		77	105.4	Croghan (town) Lewis County
3	334.9	Groveland (town) Livingston County		78	105.3	Galway (town) Saratoga County
4	283.4	Attica (town) Wyoming County		78	105.3	Moriah (town) Essex County
5	264.2	Romulus (town) Seneca County		80	105.1	Richmond (town) Ontario County
6	261.1	West Point (CDP) Orange County		81	104.9	Stockholm (town) Saint Lawrence County
7	237.1	Fort Ann (town) Washington County		82	104.7	Granby (town) Oswego County
8	228.6	Collins (town) Erie County		83	104.6	Barker (town) Broome County
9	208.9	Marcy (town) Oneida County		83	104.6	Southampton (town) Suffolk County
10	184.3	Coxsackie (town) Greene County		85	104.4	Huntington Station (CDP) Suffolk County
11	178.0	Riverside (CDP) Suffolk County		86	104.3	Ossining (town) Westchester County
12	177.1	Cape Vincent (town) Jefferson County		87	104.2	Sloatsburg (village) Rockland County
13	175.8	Malone (town) Franklin County		88	104.1	University at Buffalo (CDP) Erie County
14	173.7	Moravia (town) Cayuga County		88	104.1	Whitehall (village) Washington County
15	165.2	Mount Hope (town) Orange County		90	103.9	Harrietstown (town) Franklin County
16	163.2	Highlands (town) Orange County		90	103.9	Sardinia (town) Erie County
17	154.7	Alfred (village) Allegany County		90	103.9	Whitehall (town) Washington County
18	143.2	Alfred (town) Allegany County		90	103.9	Yates (town) Orleans County
19	139.9	North Elba (town) Essex County		94	103.8	Dickinson (town) Broome County
20	135.8	Alden (town) Erie County		94	103.8	Elmsford (village) Westchester County
21	135.5	Fort Drum (CDP) Jefferson County		96	103.7	Hartland (town) Niagara County
22	134.7	Altona (town) Clinton County		96	103.7	North Bay Shore (CDP) Suffolk County
23	131.2	Shawangunk (town) Ulster County		96	103.7	North Sea (CDP) Suffolk County
24	131.0	Beekman (town) Dutchess County		99	103.6	Brentwood (CDP) Suffolk County
25	128.4	Watertown (town) Jefferson County		99	103.6	Randolph (town) Cattaraugus County
26	128.3	Wawarsing (town) Ulster County		101	103.5	Fishkill (town) Dutchess County
27	127.8	Gouverneur (town) Saint Lawrence County		101	103.5	New Cassel (CDP) Nassau County
28	126.6	Portland (town) Chautauqua County		101	103.5	Northumberland (town) Saratoga County
29	124.0	Fallsburg (town) Sullivan County		101	103.5	Riverhead (CDP) Suffolk County
30	123.9	Kings Point (village) Nassau County		105	103.4	Bath (town) Steuben County
31	123.5	Le Ray (town) Jefferson County		105	103.4	Russia (town) Herkimer County
32	120.6	Ogdensburg (city) Saint Lawrence County		107	103.3	North East (town) Dutchess County
33	119.4	Yaphank (CDP) Suffolk County		107	103.3	Norwich (town) Chenango County
34	119.1	Delhi (village) Delaware County		109	103.2	Clinton (town) Dutchess County
35	114.6	Flanders (CDP) Suffolk County		109	103.2	Knox (town) Albany County
36	113.9	Potsdam (village) Saint Lawrence County		109	103.2	Monroe (town) Orange County
37	113.5	Beacon (city) Dutchess County		109	103.2	Pierrepont (town) Saint Lawrence County
38	113.0	Ossining (village) Westchester County		113	103.1	Greenville (town) Orange County
39	112.8	Hopewell (town) Ontario County		113	103.1	Spring Valley (village) Rockland County
40	112.0	Batavia (town) Genesee County		115	103.0	Rush (town) Monroe County
41	111.5	Southport (town) Chemung County		115	103.0	Virgil (town) Cortland County
42	111.3	Johnstown (town) Fulton County		117	102.9	Auburn (city) Cayuga County
43	111.2	Tupper Lake (town) Franklin County		117	102.9	Rye (town) Westchester County
44	110.7	Henrietta (town) Monroe County		117	102.9	Sandy Creek (town) Oswego County
45	110.6	Bethel (town) Sullivan County		117	102.9	Sterling (town) Cayuga County
46	110.3	Hancock (town) Delaware County		121	102.8	Dover (town) Dutchess County
46	110.3	Port Chester (village) Westchester County		121	102.8	Sennett (town) Cayuga County
48	110.1	Seneca (town) Ontario County		121	102.8	Windsor (town) Broome County
49	110.0	Stony Brook University (CDP) Suffolk County		124	102.7	Westerlo (town) Albany County
50	109.8	Delhi (town) Delaware County		125	102.6	Fleming (town) Cayuga County
51	109.4	Wolcott (town) Wayne County		125	102.6	Floyd (town) Oneida County
52	109.3	Constantia (town) Oswego County		127	102.5	Calcium (CDP) Jefferson County
53	109.1	Binghamton University (CDP) Broome County		127	102.5	Eaton (town) Madison County
54	108.5	Springs (CDP) Suffolk County		127	102.5	Hannibal (town) Oswego County
55	108.3	Chautauqua (town) Chautauqua County		127	102.5	Southeast (town) Putnam County
55	108.3	Pamelia (town) Jefferson County		131	102.4	Annsville (town) Oneida County
57	108.1	Pavilion (town) Genesee County		131	102.4	Elmira (city) Chemung County
58	107.9	Potsdam (town) Saint Lawrence County		131	102.4	Fairview (CDP) Dutchess County
58	107.9	York (town) Livingston County		131	102.4	Hunter (town) Greene County
60	107.5	New Square (village) Rockland County		131	102.4	Patterson (town) Putnam County
61	107.4	Mount Kisco (town/village) Westchester County		131	102.4	Putnam Lake (CDP) Putnam County
62	107.3	Colesville (town) Broome County		131	102.4	Verona (town) Oneida County
62	107.3	Kiryas Joel (village) Orange County		138	102.3	Berne (town) Albany County
64	107.0	Bennington (town) Wyoming County		138	102.3	Carlton (town) Orleans County
65	106.7	Hudson (city) Columbia County		140	102.2	Goshen (town) Orange County
66	106.4	West Monroe (town) Oswego County		140	102.2	Hector (town) Schuyler County
67	106.2	Stockport (town) Columbia County		140	102.2	Mamakating (town) Sullivan County
68	106.0	Hampton Bays (CDP) Suffolk County		143	102.1	Monroe (town) Orange County
68	106.0	Monsey (CDP) Rockland County		143	102.1	New Haven (town) Oswego County
70	105.9	Pawling (town) Dutchess County		143	102.1	Troy (city) Rensselaer County
70	105.9	Theresa (town) Jefferson County		146	102.0	Center Moriches (CDP) Suffolk County
72	105.7	Darien (town) Genesee County		146	102.0	Cutchogue (CDP) Suffolk County
72	105.7	Otisco (town) Onondaga County		146	102.0	Lansing (village) Tompkins County
72	105.7	Oxford (town) Chenango County		146	102.0	Munsey Park (village) Nassau County
75	105.6	Rome (city) Oneida County		146	102.0	Nassau (town) Rensselaer County

Note: This section ranks incorporated places and CDPs (Census Designated Places) with populations of 2,500 or more. Unincorporated postal areas were not considered. Please refer to the User Guide for additional information.

Males per 100 Females

Top 150 Places Ranked in *Ascending* Order

State Rank	Ratio	Place
1	65.0	**Heritage Hills** (CDP) Westchester County
2	67.4	**Cazenovia** (village) Madison County
3	71.5	**New Paltz** (village) Ulster County
4	73.8	**Orangeburg** (CDP) Rockland County
5	75.4	**Great Neck Plaza** (village) Nassau County
6	77.7	**Williamsville** (village) Erie County
7	78.8	**Lake Success** (village) Nassau County
8	79.4	**Clarence** (CDP) Erie County
9	80.0	**South Hill** (CDP) Tompkins County
10	80.5	**Lewiston** (village) Niagara County
10	80.5	**Rhinebeck** (village) Dutchess County
12	80.9	**Hartsdale** (CDP) Westchester County
13	81.5	**Geneseo** (village) Livingston County
14	82.0	**Glasco** (CDP) Ulster County
15	82.1	**Jerusalem** (town) Yates County
16	82.4	**Galeville** (CDP) Onondaga County
17	82.7	**Roslyn** (village) Nassau County
18	82.8	**Horseheads** (village) Chemung County
18	82.8	**Warwick** (village) Orange County
20	83.3	**Arlington** (CDP) Dutchess County
20	83.3	**Mount Vernon** (city) Westchester County
20	83.3	**Rhinebeck** (town) Dutchess County
23	83.7	**Hamilton** (village) Madison County
24	83.9	**New Paltz** (town) Ulster County
24	83.9	**Oneonta** (city) Otsego County
26	84.0	**Geneseo** (town) Livingston County
27	84.1	**Brookville** (village) Nassau County
28	84.3	**Bedford** (town) Westchester County
29	84.5	**Norwich** (city) Chenango County
30	84.7	**Mechanicstown** (CDP) Orange County
31	85.0	**Malone** (village) Franklin County
31	85.0	**Ridge** (CDP) Suffolk County
33	85.6	**Otsego** (town) Otsego County
34	85.7	**East Aurora** (village) Erie County
34	85.7	**North Amityville** (CDP) Suffolk County
36	85.8	**Westvale** (CDP) Onondaga County
37	85.9	**Cazenovia** (town) Madison County
38	86.0	**Maybrook** (village) Orange County
38	86.0	**Waverly** (village) Tioga County
40	86.1	**Homer** (village) Cortland County
41	86.3	**Nyack** (village) Rockland County
42	86.5	**Waterloo** (village) Seneca County
43	86.6	**Irondequoit** (CDP) Monroe County
43	86.6	**New Hartford** (town) Oneida County
43	86.6	**Tuckahoe** (village) Westchester County
46	86.7	**Penn Yan** (village) Yates County
46	86.7	**Pittsford** (town) Monroe County
46	86.7	**Whitesboro** (village) Oneida County
49	86.8	**Port Ewen** (CDP) Ulster County
50	87.0	**Lakeview** (CDP) Nassau County
50	87.0	**Mechanicville** (city) Saratoga County
50	87.0	**Munsons Corners** (CDP) Cortland County
50	87.0	**Vails Gate** (CDP) Orange County
54	87.1	**South Nyack** (village) Rockland County
55	87.4	**Firthcliffe** (CDP) Orange County
55	87.4	**Geddes** (town) Onondaga County
55	87.4	**Kenmore** (village) Erie County
55	87.4	**Manlius** (village) Onondaga County
55	87.4	**Woodbury** (CDP) Nassau County
60	87.5	**Hoosick Falls** (village) Rensselaer County
61	87.6	**Goshen** (village) Orange County
61	87.6	**North Hills** (village) Nassau County
61	87.6	**North Valley Stream** (CDP) Nassau County
64	87.7	**Tarrytown** (village) Westchester County
65	87.8	**Geneva** (city) Ontario County
65	87.8	**Glens Falls North** (CDP) Warren County
65	87.8	**Medina** (village) Orleans County
68	88.0	**Fairview** (CDP) Westchester County
68	88.0	**Minoa** (village) Onondaga County
70	88.1	**Fredonia** (village) Chautauqua County
70	88.1	**Islandia** (village) Suffolk County
72	88.2	**Rockville Centre** (village) Nassau County
73	88.3	**Brockport** (village) Monroe County
73	88.3	**Bronx** (borough) Bronx County
73	88.3	**Little Falls** (city) Herkimer County

State Rank	Ratio	Place
76	88.4	**Ardsley** (village) Westchester County
76	88.4	**Rye Brook** (village) Westchester County
78	88.5	**Cheektowaga** (CDP) Erie County
78	88.5	**Fairmount** (CDP) Onondaga County
78	88.5	**Harrison** (town/village) Westchester County
78	88.5	**Manhattan** (borough) New York County
82	88.6	**Herkimer** (village) Herkimer County
82	88.6	**Honeoye Falls** (village) Monroe County
84	88.7	**Bronxville** (village) Westchester County
84	88.7	**Eastchester** (town) Westchester County
84	88.7	**Highland** (CDP) Ulster County
84	88.7	**Lewiston** (town) Niagara County
88	88.8	**Canandaigua** (city) Ontario County
88	88.8	**Greece** (CDP) Monroe County
88	88.8	**North Greenbush** (town) Rensselaer County
88	88.8	**Tonawanda** (town) Erie County
92	88.9	**Cheektowaga** (town) Erie County
92	88.9	**Sidney** (village) Delaware County
92	88.9	**Wellsville** (village) Allegany County
95	89.0	**Chittenango** (village) Madison County
95	89.0	**Manhasset** (CDP) Nassau County
97	89.1	**Glenwood Landing** (CDP) Nassau County
97	89.1	**Ithaca** (town) Tompkins County
97	89.1	**Plattsburgh** (city) Clinton County
97	89.1	**Tonawanda** (CDP) Erie County
101	89.2	**Dansville** (village) Livingston County
102	89.3	**Brighton** (CDP) Monroe County
102	89.3	**Brooklyn** (borough) Kings County
102	89.3	**Carthage** (village) Jefferson County
102	89.3	**East Rockaway** (village) Nassau County
102	89.3	**Horseheads North** (CDP) Chemung County
102	89.3	**Westfield** (village) Chautauqua County
108	89.4	**Blasdell** (village) Erie County
108	89.4	**Eastchester** (CDP) Westchester County
108	89.4	**Hastings-on-Hudson** (village) Westchester County
108	89.4	**Johnstown** (city) Fulton County
108	89.4	**Nanuet** (CDP) Rockland County
108	89.4	**Webster** (village) Monroe County
108	89.4	**West Elmira** (CDP) Chemung County
115	89.5	**Bethpage** (CDP) Nassau County
115	89.5	**Greenburgh** (town) Westchester County
115	89.5	**North Dansville** (town) Livingston County
115	89.5	**Sayville** (CDP) Suffolk County
119	89.6	**Newfane** (CDP) Niagara County
120	89.7	**Cohoes** (city) Albany County
120	89.7	**Green Island** (town/village) Albany County
120	89.7	**Hornellsville** (town) Steuben County
123	89.8	**Baldwinsville** (village) Onondaga County
123	89.8	**Saint Johnsville** (town) Montgomery County
123	89.8	**Ulysses** (town) Tompkins County
123	89.8	**Wellsville** (town) Allegany County
127	89.9	**Amherst** (town) Erie County
127	89.9	**Batavia** (city) Genesee County
127	89.9	**Coxsackie** (village) Greene County
127	89.9	**Melville** (CDP) Suffolk County
127	89.9	**Piermont** (village) Rockland County
127	89.9	**Thomaston** (village) Nassau County
133	90.0	**Amsterdam** (city) Montgomery County
133	90.0	**Elmira** (town) Chemung County
133	90.0	**Hamilton** (town) Madison County
133	90.0	**Yonkers** (city) Westchester County
137	90.1	**Garden City** (village) Nassau County
137	90.1	**Hamburg** (village) Erie County
139	90.2	**Lowville** (village) Lewis County
139	90.2	**Lynbrook** (village) Nassau County
139	90.2	**Mount Ivy** (CDP) Rockland County
139	90.2	**South Glens Falls** (village) Saratoga County
139	90.2	**Wynantskill** (CDP) Rensselaer County
144	90.3	**Horseheads** (town) Chemung County
145	90.4	**Great Neck Estates** (village) Nassau County
145	90.4	**Greece** (town) Monroe County
145	90.4	**New York** (city)
145	90.4	**Salina** (town) Onondaga County
149	90.5	**Herkimer** (town) Herkimer County
149	90.5	**Kirkland** (town) Oneida County

Note: *This section ranks incorporated places and CDPs (Census Designated Places) with populations of 2,500 or more. Unincorporated postal areas were not considered. Please refer to the User Guide for additional information.*

Marriage Status: Never Married

Top 150 Places Ranked in *Descending* Order

State Rank	Percent	Place	State Rank	Percent	Place
1	99.7	**SUNY Oswego** (CDP) Oswego County	76	45.4	**Pomfret** (town) Chautauqua County
2	99.4	**Binghamton University** (CDP) Broome County	77	45.3	**New Cassel** (CDP) Nassau County
3	98.7	**University at Buffalo** (CDP) Erie County	78	45.2	**Brentwood** (CDP) Suffolk County
4	93.5	**Stony Brook University** (CDP) Suffolk County	78	45.2	**North Bellport** (CDP) Suffolk County
5	93.4	**Alfred** (village) Allegany County	80	44.9	**Mount Vernon** (city) Westchester County
6	84.3	**Alfred** (town) Allegany County	81	44.6	**Collins** (town) Erie County
7	79.1	**Geneseo** (village) Livingston County	81	44.6	**Groveland** (town) Livingston County
8	78.5	**South Hill** (CDP) Tompkins County	83	44.5	**Saint Regis Mohawk Reservation** (reservation) Franklin County
9	77.3	**New Paltz** (village) Ulster County	84	44.2	**Malone** (town) Franklin County
10	76.8	**Ithaca** (city) Tompkins County	85	44.1	**Brooklyn** (borough) Kings County
11	75.7	**Hamilton** (village) Madison County	86	43.9	**New York** (city)
12	75.1	**Potsdam** (village) Saint Lawrence County	87	43.8	**Utica** (city) Oneida County
13	70.8	**West Point** (CDP) Orange County	88	43.5	**Fort Ann** (town) Washington County
14	68.8	**Delhi** (village) Delaware County	88	43.5	**Freeport** (village) Nassau County
15	68.2	**Canton** (village) Saint Lawrence County	90	43.4	**Dickinson** (town) Broome County
16	67.4	**Riverside** (CDP) Suffolk County	90	43.4	**Lackawanna** (city) Erie County
17	67.1	**Brockport** (village) Monroe County	90	43.4	**Orangeburg** (CDP) Rockland County
18	64.0	**Arlington** (CDP) Dutchess County	93	43.2	**Inwood** (CDP) Nassau County
19	63.9	**Oneonta** (city) Otsego County	94	43.1	**Lakeview** (CDP) Nassau County
20	63.5	**Geneseo** (town) Livingston County	95	42.9	**East Syracuse** (village) Onondaga County
21	62.7	**Oswego** (town) Oswego County	95	42.9	**Glasco** (CDP) Ulster County
22	61.4	**Dannemora** (village) Clinton County	97	42.8	**North Bay Shore** (CDP) Suffolk County
23	59.4	**Albany** (city) Albany County	98	42.6	**Mastic Beach** (village) Suffolk County
24	58.0	**Potsdam** (town) Saint Lawrence County	98	42.6	**North Elba** (town) Essex County
25	57.2	**Cobleskill** (village) Schoharie County	100	42.3	**Red Hook** (town) Dutchess County
25	57.2	**Hamilton** (town) Madison County	101	42.0	**Portland** (town) Chautauqua County
27	56.2	**Rochester** (city) Monroe County	102	41.7	**Kirkland** (town) Oneida County
28	56.0	**Cortland** (city) Cortland County	103	41.5	**Cayuga Heights** (village) Tompkins County
29	55.7	**Highlands** (town) Orange County	104	41.4	**Mohawk** (village) Herkimer County
30	55.1	**Eaton** (town) Madison County	104	41.4	**Niagara Falls** (city) Niagara County
31	55.0	**New Paltz** (town) Ulster County	106	41.3	**Allegany** (town) Cattaraugus County
31	55.0	**Troy** (city) Rensselaer County	106	41.3	**Elmsford** (village) Westchester County
33	54.7	**Dannemora** (town) Clinton County	106	41.3	**Highland Falls** (village) Orange County
34	54.2	**Gordon Heights** (CDP) Suffolk County	106	41.3	**Thompson** (town) Sullivan County
35	54.0	**Canton** (town) Saint Lawrence County	110	41.1	**Fort Drum** (CDP) Jefferson County
35	54.0	**Syracuse** (city) Onondaga County	110	41.1	**Middletown** (city) Orange County
37	53.9	**Sweden** (town) Monroe County	110	41.1	**Oswego** (city) Oswego County
38	53.7	**Wyandanch** (CDP) Suffolk County	113	41.0	**Albion** (town) Orleans County
39	53.6	**Delhi** (town) Delaware County	113	41.0	**Amsterdam** (city) Montgomery County
40	53.4	**Plattsburgh** (city) Clinton County	113	41.0	**Henrietta** (town) Monroe County
41	51.9	**Geneva** (city) Ontario County	116	40.8	**New Hempstead** (village) Rockland County
42	51.7	**Romulus** (town) Seneca County	117	40.6	**Ticonderoga** (CDP) Essex County
43	51.6	**Fairview** (CDP) Westchester County	118	40.3	**Mattydale** (CDP) Onondaga County
44	51.5	**Buffalo** (city) Erie County	119	40.1	**Poughkeepsie** (town) Dutchess County
45	51.2	**Ithaca** (town) Tompkins County	120	40.0	**Spring Valley** (village) Rockland County
46	50.6	**Fredonia** (village) Chautauqua County	121	39.9	**Cohoes** (city) Albany County
47	50.1	**Newburgh** (city) Orange County	121	39.9	**Kingston** (city) Ulster County
48	50.0	**Manhattan** (borough) New York County	121	39.9	**Wheatley Heights** (CDP) Suffolk County
49	49.5	**Brookville** (village) Nassau County	124	39.8	**Stockport** (town) Columbia County
50	49.4	**Hempstead** (village) Nassau County	124	39.8	**Wappingers Falls** (village) Dutchess County
50	49.4	**Roosevelt** (CDP) Nassau County	126	39.4	**Lyncourt** (CDP) Onondaga County
52	49.3	**North Amityville** (CDP) Suffolk County	126	39.4	**West Haverstraw** (village) Rockland County
53	48.8	**Bronx** (borough) Bronx County	128	39.3	**Chester** (village) Orange County
54	48.5	**Cazenovia** (village) Madison County	128	39.3	**Solvay** (village) Onondaga County
55	47.8	**Catskill** (village) Greene County	128	39.3	**Yaphank** (CDP) Suffolk County
56	47.7	**Attica** (town) Wyoming County	131	39.2	**Yonkers** (city) Westchester County
57	47.6	**Old Westbury** (village) Nassau County	132	39.1	**Maybrook** (village) Orange County
57	47.6	**Poughkeepsie** (city) Dutchess County	133	39.0	**Elmont** (CDP) Nassau County
57	47.6	**Vestal** (town) Broome County	133	39.0	**Harrison** (town/village) Westchester County
60	47.4	**Uniondale** (CDP) Nassau County	133	39.0	**Hillcrest** (CDP) Rockland County
61	47.3	**Coxsackie** (town) Greene County	136	38.9	**Lansing** (village) Tompkins County
62	47.0	**Fairview** (CDP) Dutchess County	136	38.9	**Liberty** (village) Sullivan County
63	46.9	**Monticello** (village) Sullivan County	136	38.9	**Mechanicville** (city) Saratoga County
64	46.8	**Elmira** (city) Chemung County	136	38.9	**Moravia** (town) Cayuga County
65	46.6	**Cobleskill** (town) Schoharie County	136	38.9	**Wawarsing** (town) Ulster County
65	46.6	**Hudson** (city) Columbia County	141	38.8	**Copiague** (CDP) Suffolk County
67	46.5	**Munsons Corners** (CDP) Cortland County	141	38.8	**Fallsburg** (town) Sullivan County
68	46.4	**Binghamton** (city) Broome County	141	38.8	**Rensselaer** (city) Rensselaer County
68	46.4	**Green Island** (town/village) Albany County	144	38.7	**Delaware** (town) Sullivan County
70	46.1	**Central Islip** (CDP) Suffolk County	144	38.7	**Port Chester** (village) Westchester County
71	45.8	**Watervliet** (city) Albany County	144	38.7	**Wawayanda** (town) Orange County
72	45.7	**Schenectady** (city) Schenectady County	147	38.6	**Nyack** (village) Rockland County
73	45.6	**South Nyack** (village) Rockland County	148	38.5	**East Farmingdale** (CDP) Suffolk County
73	45.6	**Yorkville** (village) Oneida County	148	38.5	**Gowanda** (village) Cattaraugus County
75	45.5	**Marcy** (town) Oneida County	148	38.5	**Queens** (borough) Queens County

Note: This section ranks incorporated places and CDPs (Census Designated Places) with populations of 2,500 or more. Unincorporated postal areas were not considered. Please refer to the User Guide for additional information.

Marriage Status: Never Married

Top 150 Places Ranked in *Ascending* Order

State Rank	Percent	Place
1	11.2	**Heritage Hills** (CDP) Westchester County
2	13.0	**North Hills** (village) Nassau County
3	15.1	**West Elmira** (CDP) Chemung County
4	16.1	**East Hills** (village) Nassau County
5	16.8	**Woodbury** (CDP) Nassau County
6	17.3	**Wanakah** (CDP) Erie County
7	18.5	**Elma Center** (CDP) Erie County
7	18.5	**Halesite** (CDP) Suffolk County
9	18.8	**Skaneateles** (town) Onondaga County
10	18.9	**Wales** (town) Erie County
11	19.2	**Elmira** (town) Chemung County
12	19.5	**Campbell** (town) Steuben County
13	19.6	**Hartland** (town) Niagara County
14	19.7	**Northwest Harbor** (CDP) Suffolk County
15	19.8	**Lido Beach** (CDP) Nassau County
16	19.9	**Colesville** (town) Broome County
16	19.9	**Ellisburg** (town) Jefferson County
16	19.9	**Fayette** (town) Seneca County
19	20.0	**Rutland** (town) Jefferson County
19	20.0	**Sands Point** (village) Nassau County
21	20.2	**Larchmont** (village) Westchester County
21	20.2	**Palatine** (town) Montgomery County
21	20.2	**Pound Ridge** (town) Westchester County
24	20.3	**Scarsdale** (town/village) Westchester County
25	20.4	**Lake Success** (village) Nassau County
26	20.8	**Red Oaks Mill** (CDP) Dutchess County
26	20.8	**Stockholm** (town) Saint Lawrence County
26	20.8	**Tioga** (town) Tioga County
26	20.8	**Westhampton** (CDP) Suffolk County
30	20.9	**Galway** (town) Saratoga County
30	20.9	**Madison** (town) Madison County
30	20.9	**Rye** (city) Westchester County
30	20.9	**Scriba** (town) Oswego County
34	21.0	**Unadilla** (town) Otsego County
35	21.1	**Marilla** (town) Erie County
35	21.1	**Thomaston** (village) Nassau County
37	21.3	**Louisville** (town) Saint Lawrence County
37	21.3	**Pittstown** (town) Rensselaer County
37	21.3	**Plainview** (CDP) Nassau County
40	21.5	**Middletown** (town) Delaware County
40	21.5	**Shelter Island** (town) Suffolk County
40	21.5	**Veteran** (town) Chemung County
43	21.6	**Castile** (town) Wyoming County
43	21.6	**Jay** (town) Essex County
45	21.7	**Greenfield** (town) Saratoga County
45	21.7	**New Baltimore** (town) Greene County
45	21.7	**New Berlin** (town) Chenango County
45	21.7	**Port Washington** (CDP) Nassau County
45	21.7	**Seneca** (town) Ontario County
50	21.9	**Hurley** (town) Ulster County
51	22.0	**Myers Corner** (CDP) Dutchess County
51	22.0	**Newfane** (CDP) Niagara County
53	22.1	**Newark Valley** (town) Tioga County
54	22.2	**Brownville** (town) Jefferson County
54	22.2	**Calcium** (CDP) Jefferson County
54	22.2	**Charlton** (town) Saratoga County
54	22.2	**Minoa** (village) Onondaga County
54	22.2	**Saranac** (town) Clinton County
59	22.3	**Busti** (town) Chautauqua County
59	22.3	**Claverack** (town) Columbia County
59	22.3	**Oxford** (town) Chenango County
59	22.3	**Springville** (village) Erie County
59	22.3	**West Bay Shore** (CDP) Suffolk County
64	22.5	**Callicoon** (town) Sullivan County
64	22.5	**Calverton** (CDP) Suffolk County
64	22.5	**Floyd** (town) Oneida County
64	22.5	**Munsey Park** (village) Nassau County
64	22.5	**Westerlo** (town) Albany County
69	22.6	**Fleming** (town) Cayuga County
69	22.6	**Laurens** (town) Otsego County
69	22.6	**Manhasset Hills** (CDP) Nassau County
69	22.6	**North Boston** (CDP) Erie County
69	22.6	**Somers** (town) Westchester County
69	22.6	**Windsor** (town) Broome County
75	22.7	**Centerport** (CDP) Suffolk County
75	22.7	**Penfield** (town) Monroe County
75	22.7	**Warrensburg** (town) Warren County
78	22.8	**Brightwaters** (village) Suffolk County
78	22.8	**Owasco** (town) Cayuga County
80	22.9	**Manlius** (town) Onondaga County
80	22.9	**Victor** (town) Ontario County
82	23.0	**Westfield** (town) Chautauqua County
82	23.0	**Woodstock** (town) Ulster County
84	23.1	**Flower Hill** (village) Nassau County
84	23.1	**Gorham** (town) Ontario County
84	23.1	**Haviland** (CDP) Dutchess County
84	23.1	**New Castle** (town) Westchester County
84	23.1	**Pavilion** (town) Genesee County
84	23.1	**Vienna** (town) Oneida County
84	23.1	**Yates** (town) Orleans County
91	23.2	**Gang Mills** (CDP) Steuben County
91	23.2	**Lysander** (town) Onondaga County
91	23.2	**Rush** (town) Monroe County
91	23.2	**Warrensburg** (CDP) Warren County
91	23.2	**Warwick** (village) Orange County
91	23.2	**Wheatfield** (town) Niagara County
97	23.3	**Barker** (town) Broome County
97	23.3	**Carroll** (town) Chautauqua County
97	23.3	**Fayetteville** (village) Onondaga County
97	23.3	**Melville** (CDP) Suffolk County
101	23.4	**Great Neck Plaza** (village) Nassau County
101	23.4	**Neversink** (town) Sullivan County
101	23.4	**North Wantagh** (CDP) Nassau County
101	23.4	**Putnam Valley** (town) Putnam County
105	23.5	**Davenport** (town) Delaware County
105	23.5	**Great Neck Estates** (village) Nassau County
105	23.5	**Montauk** (CDP) Suffolk County
105	23.5	**Northport** (village) Suffolk County
105	23.5	**Stillwater** (town) Saratoga County
110	23.6	**Broadalbin** (town) Fulton County
110	23.6	**East Aurora** (village) Erie County
110	23.6	**Minden** (town) Montgomery County
110	23.6	**North Salem** (town) Westchester County
110	23.6	**Northumberland** (town) Saratoga County
110	23.6	**Nunda** (town) Livingston County
110	23.6	**Pembroke** (town) Genesee County
110	23.6	**West Bloomfield** (town) Ontario County
118	23.7	**Champion** (town) Jefferson County
118	23.7	**Hamburg** (village) Erie County
118	23.7	**North Castle** (town) Westchester County
118	23.7	**Walworth** (town) Wayne County
122	23.8	**Erwin** (town) Steuben County
122	23.8	**Kendall** (town) Orleans County
122	23.8	**La Grange** (town) Dutchess County
122	23.8	**Lee** (town) Oneida County
122	23.8	**Nesconset** (CDP) Suffolk County
122	23.8	**Oswegatchie** (town) Saint Lawrence County
122	23.8	**Sheridan** (town) Chautauqua County
129	23.9	**Big Flats** (CDP) Chemung County
129	23.9	**Clarendon** (town) Orleans County
129	23.9	**Cutchogue** (CDP) Suffolk County
129	23.9	**Jefferson Valley-Yorktown** (CDP) Westchester County
129	23.9	**Springs** (CDP) Suffolk County
134	24.0	**Croton-on-Hudson** (village) Westchester County
134	24.0	**Elma** (town) Erie County
134	24.0	**Lisbon** (town) Saint Lawrence County
134	24.0	**Lloyd Harbor** (village) Suffolk County
134	24.0	**Manlius** (village) Onondaga County
134	24.0	**Pompey** (town) Onondaga County
134	24.0	**Ridge** (CDP) Suffolk County
134	24.0	**Spackenkill** (CDP) Dutchess County
134	24.0	**Volney** (town) Oswego County
143	24.1	**Greenwood Lake** (village) Orange County
143	24.1	**Hewlett** (CDP) Nassau County
143	24.1	**Phelps** (town) Ontario County
143	24.1	**Voorheesville** (village) Albany County
147	24.2	**Alexander** (town) Genesee County
147	24.2	**Horseheads North** (CDP) Chemung County
147	24.2	**Orange Lake** (CDP) Orange County
147	24.2	**Perinton** (town) Monroe County

Note: This section ranks incorporated places and CDPs (Census Designated Places) with populations of 2,500 or more. Unincorporated postal areas were not considered. Please refer to the User Guide for additional information.

Marriage Status: Now Married

Top 150 Places Ranked in *Descending* Order

State Rank	Percent	Place
1	76.4	East Hills (village) Nassau County
2	73.1	Scarsdale (town/village) Westchester County
3	72.2	Kiryas Joel (village) Orange County
4	71.4	Munsey Park (village) Nassau County
5	70.5	Larchmont (village) Westchester County
6	69.8	Calcium (CDP) Jefferson County
6	69.8	Sands Point (village) Nassau County
8	69.5	Wesley Hills (village) Rockland County
9	69.4	Lido Beach (CDP) Nassau County
10	69.3	New Castle (town) Westchester County
11	69.2	New Square (village) Rockland County
11	69.2	North Hills (village) Nassau County
13	68.7	Pound Ridge (town) Westchester County
14	68.2	Horseheads North (CDP) Chemung County
15	68.0	West Elmira (CDP) Chemung County
16	67.9	North Castle (town) Westchester County
17	67.8	Lloyd Harbor (village) Suffolk County
18	67.6	Rye (city) Westchester County
19	67.5	Manhasset Hills (CDP) Nassau County
20	67.3	Myers Corner (CDP) Dutchess County
21	67.2	Brownville (town) Jefferson County
22	67.1	Great Neck Estates (village) Nassau County
22	67.1	Plainview (CDP) Nassau County
24	67.0	Armonk (CDP) Westchester County
24	67.0	Hartland (town) Niagara County
24	67.0	Marilla (town) Erie County
24	67.0	Muttontown (village) Nassau County
28	66.9	Kaser (village) Rockland County
29	66.8	Neversink (town) Sullivan County
30	66.7	Ellisburg (town) Jefferson County
31	66.6	Springs (CDP) Suffolk County
32	66.3	Dix Hills (CDP) Suffolk County
33	66.1	Wading River (CDP) Suffolk County
34	66.0	East Shoreham (CDP) Suffolk County
35	65.8	Galway (town) Saratoga County
35	65.8	Red Oaks Mill (CDP) Dutchess County
37	65.6	Elmira (town) Chemung County
38	65.4	Searingtown (CDP) Nassau County
39	65.3	Walworth (town) Wayne County
40	65.1	Northumberland (town) Saratoga County
40	65.1	Union Vale (town) Dutchess County
40	65.1	Victor (town) Ontario County
43	65.0	Jericho (CDP) Nassau County
44	64.9	Lake Success (village) Nassau County
45	64.8	Mount Sinai (CDP) Suffolk County
46	64.7	Syosset (CDP) Nassau County
47	64.6	Woodmere (CDP) Nassau County
48	64.5	Clarence Center (CDP) Erie County
48	64.5	West Hills (CDP) Suffolk County
50	64.4	Brightwaters (village) Suffolk County
50	64.4	Flower Hill (village) Nassau County
52	64.2	Greenville (CDP) Westchester County
52	64.2	Newark Valley (town) Tioga County
52	64.2	Pompey (town) Onondaga County
52	64.2	Stillwater (town) Saratoga County
56	64.1	Charlton (town) Saratoga County
56	64.1	Mendon (town) Monroe County
56	64.1	Richmond (town) Ontario County
59	64.0	Haviland (CDP) Dutchess County
60	63.8	Monsey (CDP) Rockland County
61	63.7	Kendall (town) Orleans County
61	63.7	Lewisboro (town) Westchester County
61	63.7	Rutland (town) Jefferson County
61	63.7	Veteran (town) Chemung County
65	63.6	Garden City Park (CDP) Nassau County
65	63.6	Skaneateles (town) Onondaga County
67	63.5	Putnam Valley (town) Putnam County
68	63.4	Montauk (CDP) Suffolk County
68	63.4	New Baltimore (town) Greene County
68	63.4	Pierrepont (town) Saint Lawrence County
68	63.4	Port Washington (CDP) Nassau County
72	63.3	Castile (town) Wyoming County
72	63.3	Old Bethpage (CDP) Nassau County
72	63.3	West Bay Shore (CDP) Suffolk County
75	63.2	Glen Head (CDP) Nassau County
75	63.2	Monroe (town) Orange County
77	63.1	Fleming (town) Cayuga County
78	63.0	Fayette (town) Seneca County
79	62.9	Bellmore (CDP) Nassau County
79	62.9	East Fishkill (town) Dutchess County
79	62.9	Greenfield (town) Saratoga County
79	62.9	Merrick (CDP) Nassau County
79	62.9	Seneca (town) Ontario County
84	62.8	Cold Spring Harbor (CDP) Suffolk County
84	62.8	La Grange (town) Dutchess County
84	62.8	Spackenkill (CDP) Dutchess County
84	62.8	Thomaston (village) Nassau County
88	62.6	Big Flats (town) Chemung County
88	62.6	Pittstown (town) Rensselaer County
90	62.5	Briarcliff Manor (village) Westchester County
90	62.5	Pamelia (town) Jefferson County
90	62.5	Windsor (town) Broome County
93	62.4	Airmont (village) Rockland County
93	62.4	Deerfield (town) Oneida County
93	62.4	Great Neck (village) Nassau County
93	62.4	North Salem (town) Westchester County
93	62.4	Northwest Harbor (CDP) Suffolk County
98	62.3	Hawthorne (CDP) Westchester County
98	62.3	Irvington (village) Westchester County
98	62.3	Nesconset (CDP) Suffolk County
101	62.1	Barker (town) Broome County
101	62.1	Big Flats (CDP) Chemung County
101	62.1	Colesville (town) Broome County
101	62.1	Wales (town) Erie County
101	62.1	Woodbury (CDP) Nassau County
106	62.0	Campbell (town) Steuben County
106	62.0	Clifton Park (town) Saratoga County
106	62.0	Fort Salonga (CDP) Suffolk County
106	62.0	Halesite (CDP) Suffolk County
106	62.0	Heritage Hills (CDP) Westchester County
106	62.0	Lawrence (village) Nassau County
112	61.9	Catlin (town) Chemung County
112	61.9	Colden (town) Erie County
112	61.9	Gardiner (town) Ulster County
112	61.9	West Sand Lake (CDP) Rensselaer County
116	61.8	Clayton (town) Jefferson County
117	61.6	Jefferson Valley-Yorktown (CDP) Westchester County
118	61.5	Candor (town) Tioga County
118	61.5	Clarence (town) Erie County
118	61.5	Croghan (town) Lewis County
118	61.5	Somers (town) Westchester County
118	61.5	South Farmingdale (CDP) Nassau County
118	61.5	Stony Brook (CDP) Suffolk County
124	61.4	Grand Island (town) Erie County
124	61.4	Rye Brook (village) Westchester County
124	61.4	Volney (town) Oswego County
127	61.3	New City (CDP) Rockland County
127	61.3	Philipstown (town) Putnam County
129	61.2	Lysander (town) Onondaga County
129	61.2	New Bremen (town) Lewis County
129	61.2	Sand Lake (town) Rensselaer County
129	61.2	Voorheesville (village) Albany County
129	61.2	Wanakah (CDP) Erie County
134	61.1	Berne (town) Albany County
134	61.1	North Merrick (CDP) Nassau County
134	61.1	Rush (town) Monroe County
134	61.1	Saranac (town) Clinton County
138	61.0	Bronxville (village) Westchester County
138	61.0	Elwood (CDP) Suffolk County
138	61.0	Pavilion (town) Genesee County
141	60.9	Centerport (CDP) Suffolk County
141	60.9	Croton-on-Hudson (village) Westchester County
141	60.9	Hewlett (CDP) Nassau County
141	60.9	Melville (CDP) Suffolk County
141	60.9	Monroe (village) Orange County
141	60.9	Pembroke (town) Genesee County
141	60.9	Wheatfield (town) Niagara County
148	60.8	Binghamton (town) Broome County
148	60.8	Center Moriches (CDP) Suffolk County
148	60.8	Fayetteville (village) Onondaga County

Note: This section ranks incorporated places and CDPs (Census Designated Places) with populations of 2,500 or more. Unincorporated postal areas were not considered. Please refer to the User Guide for additional information.

Marriage Status: Now Married

Top 150 Places Ranked in *Ascending* Order

State Rank	Percent	Place
1	0.3	**SUNY Oswego** (CDP) Oswego County
2	0.6	**Binghamton University** (CDP) Broome County
3	1.2	**University at Buffalo** (CDP) Erie County
4	3.9	**Stony Brook University** (CDP) Suffolk County
5	5.8	**Alfred** (village) Allegany County
6	13.0	**Alfred** (town) Allegany County
7	15.1	**New Paltz** (village) Ulster County
8	15.7	**Geneseo** (village) Livingston County
9	15.9	**Hamilton** (village) Madison County
10	16.4	**Potsdam** (village) Saint Lawrence County
11	16.9	**South Hill** (CDP) Tompkins County
12	18.0	**Ithaca** (city) Tompkins County
13	20.5	**Delhi** (village) Delaware County
14	20.8	**Riverside** (CDP) Suffolk County
15	20.9	**Brockport** (village) Monroe County
16	22.2	**Canton** (village) Saint Lawrence County
17	24.8	**Arlington** (CDP) Dutchess County
18	25.9	**Cobleskill** (village) Schoharie County
19	26.0	**Oneonta** (city) Otsego County
20	26.5	**Albany** (city) Albany County
21	26.7	**West Point** (CDP) Orange County
22	26.9	**Geneseo** (town) Livingston County
23	27.5	**Rochester** (city) Monroe County
24	28.4	**Dannemora** (village) Clinton County
25	30.0	**Cortland** (city) Cortland County
26	30.2	**Oswego** (town) Oswego County
26	30.2	**Syracuse** (city) Onondaga County
28	30.4	**Plattsburgh** (city) Clinton County
29	30.7	**Gordon Heights** (CDP) Suffolk County
29	30.7	**Troy** (city) Rensselaer County
31	30.9	**Potsdam** (town) Saint Lawrence County
32	31.6	**Hamilton** (town) Madison County
33	31.7	**Delhi** (town) Delaware County
33	31.7	**Eaton** (town) Madison County
35	31.9	**Buffalo** (city) Erie County
36	32.1	**Canton** (town) Saint Lawrence County
37	32.6	**Binghamton** (city) Broome County
38	32.9	**Hudson** (city) Columbia County
39	33.0	**Saint Regis Mohawk Reservation** (reservation) Franklin County
40	33.3	**Cazenovia** (village) Madison County
40	33.3	**Geneva** (city) Ontario County
42	33.4	**Cobleskill** (town) Schoharie County
42	33.4	**Whitesboro** (village) Oneida County
44	33.9	**New Paltz** (town) Ulster County
45	34.2	**Dannemora** (town) Clinton County
45	34.2	**Wyandanch** (CDP) Suffolk County
47	34.3	**Sweden** (town) Monroe County
48	34.5	**Munsons Corners** (CDP) Cortland County
48	34.5	**New York Mills** (village) Oneida County
48	34.5	**Romulus** (town) Seneca County
51	34.8	**Catskill** (village) Greene County
51	34.8	**Green Island** (town/village) Albany County
53	35.3	**Fairview** (CDP) Westchester County
53	35.3	**Warsaw** (village) Wyoming County
55	35.4	**Portland** (town) Chautauqua County
56	35.5	**Monticello** (village) Sullivan County
57	35.7	**Blasdell** (village) Erie County
57	35.7	**Elmira** (city) Chemung County
59	36.1	**Gowanda** (village) Cattaraugus County
60	36.2	**Poughkeepsie** (city) Dutchess County
60	36.2	**Schenectady** (city) Schenectady County
62	36.3	**Mattydale** (CDP) Onondaga County
63	36.5	**Bronx** (borough) Bronx County
63	36.5	**North Amityville** (CDP) Suffolk County
65	36.8	**Lackawanna** (city) Erie County
65	36.8	**Manhattan** (borough) New York County
67	36.9	**Dickinson** (town) Broome County
67	36.9	**Newburgh** (city) Orange County
69	37.0	**Utica** (city) Oneida County
70	37.1	**Mechanicville** (city) Saratoga County
71	37.2	**Highlands** (town) Orange County
71	37.2	**Mohawk** (village) Herkimer County
73	37.6	**Saugerties** (village) Ulster County
74	37.7	**Hempstead** (village) Nassau County
75	37.9	**Collins** (town) Erie County
76	38.0	**Mount Vernon** (city) Westchester County
77	38.2	**Liberty** (village) Sullivan County
77	38.2	**Watervliet** (city) Albany County
79	38.5	**Yorkville** (village) Oneida County
80	38.7	**Attica** (town) Wyoming County
81	38.8	**Lyncourt** (CDP) Onondaga County
81	38.8	**Roosevelt** (CDP) Nassau County
83	38.9	**Amsterdam** (city) Montgomery County
83	38.9	**Auburn** (city) Cayuga County
85	39.1	**Ithaca** (town) Tompkins County
86	39.2	**Fredonia** (village) Chautauqua County
86	39.2	**Niagara Falls** (city) Niagara County
88	39.3	**Central Islip** (CDP) Suffolk County
89	39.4	**Glasco** (CDP) Ulster County
89	39.4	**Kirkland** (town) Oneida County
91	39.6	**Fairview** (CDP) Dutchess County
92	39.7	**Uniondale** (CDP) Nassau County
93	39.8	**Glens Falls** (city) Warren County
94	39.9	**East Rochester** (town/village) Monroe County
94	39.9	**Gouverneur** (village) Saint Lawrence County
94	39.9	**Little Falls** (city) Herkimer County
94	39.9	**Lyons** (village) Wayne County
94	39.9	**Malone** (town) Franklin County
94	39.9	**Salamanca** (city) Cattaraugus County
100	40.1	**Endicott** (village) Broome County
100	40.1	**Groveland** (town) Livingston County
102	40.3	**Cohoes** (city) Albany County
102	40.3	**South Nyack** (village) Rockland County
104	40.4	**East Syracuse** (village) Onondaga County
104	40.4	**Solvay** (village) Onondaga County
106	40.6	**Kingston** (city) Ulster County
106	40.6	**Vestal** (town) Broome County
108	40.8	**Sloan** (village) Erie County
108	40.8	**South Glens Falls** (village) Saratoga County
110	41.0	**Albion** (town) Orleans County
110	41.0	**Johnson City** (village) Broome County
110	41.0	**Sidney** (village) Delaware County
110	41.0	**Webster** (village) Monroe County
114	41.1	**North Elba** (town) Essex County
115	41.2	**Akron** (village) Erie County
115	41.2	**Newark** (village) Wayne County
117	41.3	**Noyack** (CDP) Suffolk County
118	41.4	**Coxsackie** (town) Greene County
118	41.4	**Fort Ann** (town) Washington County
118	41.4	**Vails Gate** (CDP) Orange County
121	41.5	**North Bellport** (CDP) Suffolk County
121	41.5	**Thompson** (town) Sullivan County
123	41.6	**Chester** (village) Orange County
123	41.6	**Oswego** (city) Oswego County
123	41.6	**Port Jervis** (city) Orange County
126	41.7	**Jamestown** (city) Chautauqua County
127	41.8	**Freeport** (village) Nassau County
127	41.8	**Marcy** (town) Oneida County
127	41.8	**Penn Yan** (village) Yates County
127	41.8	**Williamsville** (village) Erie County
131	41.9	**Olean** (city) Cattaraugus County
132	42.0	**Brentwood** (CDP) Suffolk County
132	42.0	**Wappingers Falls** (village) Dutchess County
134	42.1	**Lakeview** (CDP) Nassau County
135	42.3	**Rome** (city) Oneida County
136	42.5	**Hornell** (city) Steuben County
136	42.5	**Island Park** (village) Nassau County
136	42.5	**Rensselaer** (city) Rensselaer County
139	42.6	**Maybrook** (village) Orange County
140	42.7	**Bath** (village) Steuben County
140	42.7	**New York** (city)
140	42.7	**Norwich** (city) Chenango County
140	42.7	**Riverhead** (CDP) Suffolk County
140	42.7	**Waverly** (village) Tioga County
145	42.8	**Hudson Falls** (village) Washington County
145	42.8	**Malone** (village) Franklin County
145	42.8	**Orangeburg** (CDP) Rockland County
145	42.8	**Pomfret** (town) Chautauqua County
145	42.8	**Waterloo** (town) Seneca County
150	43.2	**Lockport** (city) Niagara County

Note: This section ranks incorporated places and CDPs (Census Designated Places) with populations of 2,500 or more. Unincorporated postal areas were not considered. Please refer to the User Guide for additional information.

Marriage Status: Separated

Top 150 Places Ranked in *Descending* Order

State Rank	Percent	Place	State Rank	Percent	Place
1	8.7	**Moriches** (CDP) Suffolk County	71	3.9	**Mamakating** (town) Sullivan County
2	8.3	**Rockland** (town) Sullivan County	71	3.9	**Penn Yan** (village) Yates County
3	7.6	**Walton** (village) Delaware County	71	3.9	**Randolph** (town) Cattaraugus County
4	7.1	**Rutland** (town) Jefferson County	71	3.9	**Rochester** (city) Monroe County
5	6.3	**Hoosick Falls** (village) Rensselaer County	71	3.9	**Sheridan** (town) Chautauqua County
6	6.2	**Addison** (town) Steuben County	71	3.9	**Wellsville** (village) Allegany County
7	6.0	**Arlington** (CDP) Dutchess County	71	3.9	**White Creek** (town) Washington County
8	5.9	**Dix** (town) Schuyler County	83	3.8	**Champlain** (town) Clinton County
8	5.9	**Fort Edward** (town) Washington County	83	3.8	**Corinth** (village) Saratoga County
10	5.8	**Fort Edward** (village) Washington County	83	3.8	**Oswego** (city) Oswego County
11	5.6	**Saint Regis Mohawk Reservation** (reservation) Franklin County	83	3.8	**Vienna** (town) Oneida County
11	5.6	**Whitesboro** (village) Oneida County	83	3.8	**Volney** (town) Oswego County
13	5.5	**Waverly** (village) Tioga County	83	3.8	**Watertown** (city) Jefferson County
14	5.3	**Liberty** (village) Sullivan County	83	3.8	**Westfield** (town) Chautauqua County
14	5.3	**Warrensburg** (CDP) Warren County	83	3.8	**Wilna** (town) Jefferson County
16	5.2	**Bronx** (borough) Bronx County	91	3.7	**Alexandria** (town) Jefferson County
16	5.2	**Norwich** (city) Chenango County	91	3.7	**Auburn** (city) Cayuga County
18	5.1	**Green Island** (town/village) Albany County	91	3.7	**Dolgeville** (village) Herkimer County
18	5.1	**North Syracuse** (village) Onondaga County	91	3.7	**Florida** (town) Montgomery County
20	5.0	**Athens** (town) Greene County	91	3.7	**Galen** (town) Wayne County
20	5.0	**Newburgh** (city) Orange County	91	3.7	**Hopewell** (town) Ontario County
22	4.9	**Carthage** (village) Jefferson County	91	3.7	**Jamestown** (city) Chautauqua County
22	4.9	**Valhalla** (CDP) Westchester County	91	3.7	**Johnstown** (town) Fulton County
24	4.8	**Malone** (village) Franklin County	91	3.7	**Kirkwood** (town) Broome County
24	4.8	**Walton** (town) Delaware County	91	3.7	**Mechanicstown** (CDP) Orange County
24	4.8	**Windsor** (town) Broome County	91	3.7	**Mount Vernon** (city) Westchester County
27	4.7	**Walden** (village) Orange County	91	3.7	**Murray** (town) Orleans County
27	4.7	**Wayland** (town) Steuben County	91	3.7	**Poughkeepsie** (city) Dutchess County
29	4.6	**Adams** (town) Jefferson County	91	3.7	**Richland** (town) Oswego County
29	4.6	**Hoosick** (town) Rensselaer County	91	3.7	**Schroeppel** (town) Oswego County
29	4.6	**Mechanicville** (city) Saratoga County	91	3.7	**Southport** (CDP) Chemung County
32	4.5	**Canastota** (village) Madison County	91	3.7	**Tuckahoe** (village) Westchester County
32	4.5	**Constantia** (town) Oswego County	91	3.7	**Watervliet** (city) Albany County
32	4.5	**Marlboro** (CDP) Ulster County	91	3.7	**Whitehall** (village) Washington County
32	4.5	**Mount Morris** (village) Livingston County	91	3.7	**Wyandanch** (CDP) Suffolk County
32	4.5	**Warrensburg** (town) Warren County	111	3.6	**Au Sable** (town) Clinton County
32	4.5	**Washington** (town) Dutchess County	111	3.6	**Calcium** (CDP) Jefferson County
38	4.4	**Dannemora** (village) Clinton County	111	3.6	**Chester** (town) Orange County
38	4.4	**Davenport** (town) Delaware County	111	3.6	**Claverack** (town) Columbia County
38	4.4	**Fulton** (city) Oswego County	111	3.6	**Elmira** (city) Chemung County
41	4.3	**Le Roy** (village) Genesee County	111	3.6	**Endicott** (village) Broome County
41	4.3	**Newark** (village) Wayne County	111	3.6	**Gordon Heights** (CDP) Suffolk County
41	4.3	**North Bellport** (CDP) Suffolk County	111	3.6	**Ilion** (village) Herkimer County
41	4.3	**Ogdensburg** (city) Saint Lawrence County	111	3.6	**Lyons** (village) Wayne County
41	4.3	**Spencerport** (village) Monroe County	111	3.6	**Nassau** (town) Rensselaer County
41	4.3	**Westmoreland** (town) Oneida County	111	3.6	**New Berlin** (town) Chenango County
47	4.2	**Gardnertown** (CDP) Orange County	111	3.6	**Nyack** (village) Rockland County
47	4.2	**Gloversville** (city) Fulton County	111	3.6	**Rochester** (town) Ulster County
47	4.2	**Milo** (town) Yates County	111	3.6	**Unadilla** (town) Otsego County
47	4.2	**Minden** (town) Montgomery County	125	3.5	**Brewerton** (CDP) Onondaga County
47	4.2	**Spring Valley** (village) Rockland County	125	3.5	**Cazenovia** (town) Madison County
52	4.1	**Dunkirk** (city) Chautauqua County	125	3.5	**Florida** (village) Orange County
52	4.1	**Groveland** (town) Livingston County	125	3.5	**Kingston** (city) Ulster County
52	4.1	**Hancock** (town) Delaware County	125	3.5	**North Bay Shore** (CDP) Suffolk County
52	4.1	**Haverstraw** (town) Rockland County	130	3.4	**Canisteo** (town) Steuben County
52	4.1	**Keeseville** (village) Clinton County	130	3.4	**Collins** (town) Erie County
52	4.1	**Liberty** (town) Sullivan County	130	3.4	**Johnson City** (village) Broome County
52	4.1	**Moravia** (town) Cayuga County	130	3.4	**Rome** (city) Oneida County
52	4.1	**North Dansville** (town) Livingston County	130	3.4	**Solvay** (village) Onondaga County
52	4.1	**Northampton** (town) Fulton County	130	3.4	**Wellsville** (town) Allegany County
52	4.1	**Tupper Lake** (village) Franklin County	136	3.3	**Amsterdam** (city) Montgomery County
62	4.0	**Dannemora** (town) Clinton County	136	3.3	**Attica** (village) Wyoming County
62	4.0	**Dansville** (village) Livingston County	136	3.3	**Carroll** (town) Chautauqua County
62	4.0	**Geneva** (town) Ontario County	136	3.3	**Clarence** (CDP) Erie County
62	4.0	**Lakeview** (CDP) Nassau County	136	3.3	**Denmark** (town) Lewis County
62	4.0	**Malone** (town) Franklin County	136	3.3	**Durham** (town) Greene County
62	4.0	**North Gates** (CDP) Monroe County	136	3.3	**Fishkill** (town) Dutchess County
62	4.0	**Port Chester** (village) Westchester County	136	3.3	**Freeport** (village) Nassau County
62	4.0	**Rensselaer** (city) Rensselaer County	136	3.3	**Hanover** (town) Chautauqua County
62	4.0	**Saint Johnsville** (town) Montgomery County	136	3.3	**Hempstead** (village) Nassau County
71	3.9	**Albion** (town) Orleans County	136	3.3	**Honeoye Falls** (village) Monroe County
71	3.9	**Barton** (town) Tioga County	136	3.3	**Lenox** (town) Madison County
71	3.9	**Castile** (town) Wyoming County	136	3.3	**Little Falls** (city) Herkimer County
71	3.9	**Elbridge** (town) Onondaga County	136	3.3	**Romulus** (town) Seneca County
71	3.9	**Louisville** (town) Saint Lawrence County	136	3.3	**Schenectady** (city) Schenectady County

Note: *This section ranks incorporated places and CDPs (Census Designated Places) with populations of 2,500 or more. Unincorporated postal areas were not considered. Please refer to the User Guide for additional information.*

Marriage Status: Separated
Top 150 Places Ranked in *Ascending* Order

State Rank	Percent	Place
1	0.0	**Akron** (village) Erie County
1	0.0	**Ardsley** (village) Westchester County
1	0.0	**Bedford Hills** (CDP) Westchester County
1	0.0	**Binghamton University** (CDP) Broome County
1	0.0	**Cayuga Heights** (village) Tompkins County
1	0.0	**Deerfield** (town) Oneida County
1	0.0	**East Norwich** (CDP) Nassau County
1	0.0	**Elma Center** (CDP) Erie County
1	0.0	**Greenville** (town) Orange County
1	0.0	**Greenwood Lake** (village) Orange County
1	0.0	**Hamptonburgh** (town) Orange County
1	0.0	**Mattituck** (CDP) Suffolk County
1	0.0	**Montauk** (CDP) Suffolk County
1	0.0	**Munsey Park** (village) Nassau County
1	0.0	**New Square** (village) Rockland County
1	0.0	**North Hills** (village) Nassau County
1	0.0	**SUNY Oswego** (CDP) Oswego County
1	0.0	**Sands Point** (village) Nassau County
1	0.0	**Shelter Island** (town) Suffolk County
1	0.0	**Stony Brook University** (CDP) Suffolk County
1	0.0	**University at Buffalo** (CDP) Erie County
1	0.0	**West Sand Lake** (CDP) Rensselaer County
1	0.0	**Westerlo** (town) Albany County
24	0.1	**Alfred** (town) Allegany County
24	0.1	**Alfred** (village) Allegany County
24	0.1	**Heritage Hills** (CDP) Westchester County
24	0.1	**Manhasset Hills** (CDP) Nassau County
24	0.1	**Otego** (town) Otsego County
24	0.1	**West Point** (CDP) Orange County
24	0.1	**Woodbury** (CDP) Nassau County
31	0.2	**Bardonia** (CDP) Rockland County
31	0.2	**Callicoon** (town) Sullivan County
31	0.2	**East Hills** (village) Nassau County
31	0.2	**Elma** (town) Erie County
31	0.2	**Garden City South** (CDP) Nassau County
31	0.2	**Kiryas Joel** (village) Orange County
31	0.2	**Lloyd Harbor** (village) Suffolk County
31	0.2	**Rye Brook** (village) Westchester County
31	0.2	**Searingtown** (CDP) Nassau County
40	0.3	**Armonk** (CDP) Westchester County
40	0.3	**Bergen** (town) Genesee County
40	0.3	**Cambria** (town) Niagara County
40	0.3	**Canton** (village) Saint Lawrence County
40	0.3	**Coxsackie** (village) Greene County
40	0.3	**Eaton** (town) Madison County
40	0.3	**Herricks** (CDP) Nassau County
40	0.3	**Kaser** (village) Rockland County
40	0.3	**Lisbon** (town) Saint Lawrence County
40	0.3	**Malta** (town) Saratoga County
40	0.3	**Marilla** (town) Erie County
40	0.3	**Monsey** (CDP) Rockland County
40	0.3	**New Castle** (town) Westchester County
40	0.3	**Old Westbury** (village) Nassau County
40	0.3	**Pelham Manor** (village) Westchester County
40	0.3	**Springs** (CDP) Suffolk County
56	0.4	**Beekmantown** (town) Clinton County
56	0.4	**Clarence Center** (CDP) Erie County
56	0.4	**Clinton** (town) Dutchess County
56	0.4	**East Hampton North** (CDP) Suffolk County
56	0.4	**Gang Mills** (CDP) Steuben County
56	0.4	**Garden City** (village) Nassau County
56	0.4	**Kings Point** (village) Nassau County
56	0.4	**Lewisboro** (town) Westchester County
56	0.4	**North Great River** (CDP) Suffolk County
56	0.4	**Pendleton** (town) Niagara County
56	0.4	**Port Washington North** (village) Nassau County
56	0.4	**Somerset** (town) Niagara County
56	0.4	**South Hill** (CDP) Tompkins County
56	0.4	**Wanakah** (CDP) Erie County
70	0.5	**Albertson** (CDP) Nassau County
70	0.5	**Briarcliff Manor** (village) Westchester County
70	0.5	**Brookville** (village) Nassau County
70	0.5	**East Hampton** (town) Suffolk County
70	0.5	**East Williston** (village) Nassau County
70	0.5	**Fayetteville** (village) Onondaga County
70	0.5	**Great Neck** (village) Nassau County
70	0.5	**Harris Hill** (CDP) Erie County
70	0.5	**Lowville** (town) Lewis County
70	0.5	**Mount Ivy** (CDP) Rockland County
70	0.5	**Muttontown** (village) Nassau County
70	0.5	**New Paltz** (village) Ulster County
70	0.5	**Newfane** (CDP) Niagara County
70	0.5	**North New Hyde Park** (CDP) Nassau County
70	0.5	**North Patchogue** (CDP) Suffolk County
70	0.5	**Norwich** (town) Chenango County
70	0.5	**Noyack** (CDP) Suffolk County
70	0.5	**Roslyn** (village) Nassau County
70	0.5	**Sardinia** (town) Erie County
70	0.5	**South Nyack** (village) Rockland County
90	0.6	**Bethpage** (CDP) Nassau County
90	0.6	**Chenango Bridge** (CDP) Broome County
90	0.6	**Ellery** (town) Chautauqua County
90	0.6	**Fort Salonga** (CDP) Suffolk County
90	0.6	**Franklin Square** (CDP) Nassau County
90	0.6	**Greenville** (CDP) Westchester County
90	0.6	**Holland** (town) Erie County
90	0.6	**Lawrence** (village) Nassau County
90	0.6	**Mooers** (town) Clinton County
90	0.6	**North Bellmore** (CDP) Nassau County
90	0.6	**Northeast Ithaca** (CDP) Tompkins County
90	0.6	**Old Bethpage** (CDP) Nassau County
90	0.6	**Oswego** (town) Oswego County
90	0.6	**Salem** (town) Washington County
90	0.6	**Salisbury** (CDP) Nassau County
90	0.6	**Scarsdale** (town/village) Westchester County
90	0.6	**South Valley Stream** (CDP) Nassau County
90	0.6	**Trenton** (town) Oneida County
90	0.6	**Vestal** (town) Broome County
90	0.6	**Westvale** (CDP) Onondaga County
110	0.7	**Bethlehem** (town) Albany County
110	0.7	**Boston** (town) Erie County
110	0.7	**Carle Place** (CDP) Nassau County
110	0.7	**Center Moriches** (CDP) Suffolk County
110	0.7	**Commack** (CDP) Suffolk County
110	0.7	**Elwood** (CDP) Suffolk County
110	0.7	**Fleming** (town) Cayuga County
110	0.7	**Greenville** (town) Greene County
110	0.7	**Ithaca** (town) Tompkins County
110	0.7	**Lake Success** (village) Nassau County
110	0.7	**Lido Beach** (CDP) Nassau County
110	0.7	**Lowville** (village) Lewis County
110	0.7	**Lysander** (town) Onondaga County
110	0.7	**Malverne** (village) Nassau County
110	0.7	**Mamaroneck** (town) Westchester County
110	0.7	**Manhasset** (CDP) Nassau County
110	0.7	**Montebello** (village) Rockland County
110	0.7	**Myers Corner** (CDP) Dutchess County
110	0.7	**Nesconset** (CDP) Suffolk County
110	0.7	**North Boston** (CDP) Erie County
110	0.7	**North Wantagh** (CDP) Nassau County
110	0.7	**Pawling** (town) Dutchess County
110	0.7	**Peru** (town) Clinton County
110	0.7	**Pittsford** (town) Monroe County
110	0.7	**Tarrytown** (village) Westchester County
110	0.7	**Tully** (town) Onondaga County
110	0.7	**Virgil** (town) Cortland County
110	0.7	**Wantagh** (CDP) Nassau County
110	0.7	**Woodmere** (CDP) Nassau County
110	0.7	**York** (town) Livingston County
140	0.8	**Baldwinsville** (village) Onondaga County
140	0.8	**Benton** (town) Yates County
140	0.8	**Clarkson** (town) Monroe County
140	0.8	**Colonie** (village) Albany County
140	0.8	**East Fishkill** (town) Dutchess County
140	0.8	**East Northport** (CDP) Suffolk County
140	0.8	**Enfield** (town) Tompkins County
140	0.8	**Franklinville** (town) Cattaraugus County
140	0.8	**Hamilton** (town) Madison County
140	0.8	**Hamilton** (village) Madison County
140	0.8	**Hawthorne** (CDP) Westchester County

Note: This section ranks incorporated places and CDPs (Census Designated Places) with populations of 2,500 or more. Unincorporated postal areas were not considered. Please refer to the User Guide for additional information.

Marriage Status: Widowed

Top 150 Places Ranked in *Descending* Order

State Rank	Percent	Place	State Rank	Percent	Place
1	16.1	**Heritage Hills** (CDP) Westchester County	72	9.6	**Saint James** (CDP) Suffolk County
2	15.1	**Hornellsville** (town) Steuben County	72	9.6	**Westmoreland** (town) Oneida County
3	14.8	**Great Neck Plaza** (village) Nassau County	78	9.5	**Greenlawn** (CDP) Suffolk County
4	14.7	**Woodbury** (CDP) Nassau County	78	9.5	**Oxford** (town) Chenango County
5	14.4	**Roslyn** (village) Nassau County	78	9.5	**Port Jervis** (city) Orange County
6	14.2	**Calverton** (CDP) Suffolk County	78	9.5	**Tioga** (town) Tioga County
7	13.4	**Clarence** (CDP) Erie County	78	9.5	**West Elmira** (CDP) Chemung County
7	13.4	**Lake Luzerne** (town) Warren County	83	9.4	**Greece** (CDP) Monroe County
9	13.2	**Westfield** (village) Chautauqua County	83	9.4	**Middleburgh** (town) Schoharie County
10	13.0	**Lewiston** (village) Niagara County	83	9.4	**New York Mills** (village) Oneida County
11	12.8	**Lakewood** (village) Chautauqua County	83	9.4	**Owego** (village) Tioga County
11	12.8	**Oyster Bay** (CDP) Nassau County	83	9.4	**Ulster** (town) Ulster County
13	12.7	**Elma Center** (CDP) Erie County	83	9.4	**Warwick** (village) Orange County
13	12.7	**Middletown** (town) Delaware County	89	9.3	**Orangeburg** (CDP) Rockland County
15	12.0	**Rockland** (town) Sullivan County	89	9.3	**Springville** (village) Erie County
16	11.9	**Newfane** (CDP) Niagara County	91	9.2	**Bayport** (CDP) Suffolk County
17	11.7	**Hunter** (town) Greene County	91	9.2	**Canandaigua** (town) Ontario County
17	11.7	**Lake Success** (village) Nassau County	91	9.2	**Herkimer** (town) Herkimer County
19	11.6	**Geneva** (town) Ontario County	91	9.2	**Johnson City** (village) Broome County
20	11.5	**Horseheads** (village) Chemung County	91	9.2	**Lowville** (town) Lewis County
20	11.5	**Munsons Corners** (CDP) Cortland County	91	9.2	**North Wantagh** (CDP) Nassau County
20	11.5	**North Hills** (village) Nassau County	91	9.2	**Rhinebeck** (town) Dutchess County
20	11.5	**Saugerties** (village) Ulster County	91	9.2	**Seneca Falls** (CDP) Seneca County
24	11.4	**Guilford** (town) Chenango County	91	9.2	**Tonawanda** (CDP) Erie County
24	11.4	**Ridge** (CDP) Suffolk County	100	9.1	**Benton** (town) Yates County
26	11.3	**Carroll** (town) Chautauqua County	100	9.1	**East Glenville** (CDP) Schenectady County
27	11.2	**Livingston** (town) Columbia County	100	9.1	**Fulton** (city) Oswego County
27	11.2	**Vails Gate** (CDP) Orange County	103	9.0	**Champlain** (town) Clinton County
27	11.2	**Wanakah** (CDP) Erie County	103	9.0	**Orange Lake** (CDP) Orange County
30	11.1	**Carmel Hamlet** (CDP) Putnam County	103	9.0	**Salem** (town) Washington County
31	11.0	**Westfield** (town) Chautauqua County	106	8.9	**Busti** (town) Chautauqua County
32	10.9	**Pine Plains** (town) Dutchess County	106	8.9	**Lackawanna** (city) Erie County
32	10.9	**Wellsville** (town) Allegany County	106	8.9	**Riverhead** (CDP) Suffolk County
34	10.7	**Herkimer** (village) Herkimer County	109	8.8	**Auburn** (city) Cayuga County
34	10.7	**Saint Johnsville** (town) Montgomery County	109	8.8	**Coxsackie** (village) Greene County
34	10.7	**Ticonderoga** (town) Essex County	109	8.8	**Island Park** (village) Nassau County
37	10.6	**Minoa** (village) Onondaga County	109	8.8	**Lee** (town) Oneida County
37	10.6	**Montauk** (CDP) Suffolk County	109	8.8	**Mechanicstown** (CDP) Orange County
37	10.6	**New Hartford** (town) Oneida County	109	8.8	**Middle Island** (CDP) Suffolk County
37	10.6	**Oswegatchie** (town) Saint Lawrence County	109	8.8	**Port Ewen** (CDP) Ulster County
41	10.5	**Baldwinsville** (village) Onondaga County	109	8.8	**Webster** (village) Monroe County
42	10.4	**Akron** (village) Erie County	117	8.7	**Elmira** (town) Chemung County
42	10.4	**Galeville** (CDP) Onondaga County	117	8.7	**Gloversville** (city) Fulton County
44	10.3	**Amsterdam** (town) Montgomery County	117	8.7	**Madison** (town) Madison County
44	10.3	**Ballston Spa** (village) Saratoga County	117	8.7	**Mayfield** (town) Fulton County
44	10.3	**Palatine** (town) Montgomery County	117	8.7	**Portville** (town) Cattaraugus County
44	10.3	**Sennett** (town) Cayuga County	117	8.7	**Rensselaer** (city) Rensselaer County
48	10.2	**Montebello** (village) Rockland County	117	8.7	**Van Buren** (town) Onondaga County
49	10.1	**Gowanda** (village) Cattaraugus County	124	8.6	**Albertson** (CDP) Nassau County
49	10.1	**Johnstown** (town) Fulton County	124	8.6	**Chesterfield** (town) Essex County
49	10.1	**Melville** (CDP) Suffolk County	124	8.6	**Clarkson** (CDP) Monroe County
49	10.1	**Otsego** (town) Otsego County	124	8.6	**Greenport** (town) Columbia County
53	10.0	**Bath** (village) Steuben County	124	8.6	**Horseheads** (town) Chemung County
53	10.0	**Goshen** (village) Orange County	124	8.6	**Jay** (town) Essex County
53	10.0	**Manchester** (town) Ontario County	124	8.6	**Liberty** (village) Sullivan County
53	10.0	**Mohawk** (town) Montgomery County	124	8.6	**Lyncourt** (CDP) Onondaga County
53	10.0	**North Great River** (CDP) Suffolk County	124	8.6	**Medina** (village) Orleans County
53	10.0	**Viola** (CDP) Rockland County	124	8.6	**Niagara** (town) Niagara County
53	10.0	**Waverly** (village) Tioga County	124	8.6	**Sangerfield** (town) Oneida County
60	9.9	**Wellsville** (village) Allegany County	124	8.6	**Sheridan** (town) Chautauqua County
60	9.9	**Westhampton** (CDP) Suffolk County	124	8.6	**Sterling** (town) Cayuga County
62	9.8	**Boonville** (town) Oneida County	137	8.5	**Bethpage** (CDP) Nassau County
62	9.8	**Lewiston** (town) Niagara County	137	8.5	**Brookhaven** (CDP) Suffolk County
62	9.8	**North Greenbush** (town) Rensselaer County	137	8.5	**Clarkson** (town) Monroe County
62	9.8	**Otego** (town) Otsego County	137	8.5	**Cohoes** (city) Albany County
62	9.8	**Sayville** (CDP) Suffolk County	137	8.5	**East Meadow** (CDP) Nassau County
62	9.8	**Westerlo** (town) Albany County	137	8.5	**Ellicott** (town) Chautauqua County
68	9.7	**Claverack** (town) Columbia County	137	8.5	**Farmingdale** (village) Nassau County
68	9.7	**Gouverneur** (village) Saint Lawrence County	137	8.5	**Kirkland** (town) Oneida County
68	9.7	**Southampton** (village) Suffolk County	137	8.5	**Manheim** (town) Herkimer County
68	9.7	**Valley Cottage** (CDP) Rockland County	137	8.5	**Massena** (village) Saint Lawrence County
72	9.6	**Blasdell** (village) Erie County	137	8.5	**Riverhead** (town) Suffolk County
72	9.6	**Glens Falls North** (CDP) Warren County	137	8.5	**Salamanca** (city) Cattaraugus County
72	9.6	**Little Falls** (city) Herkimer County	137	8.5	**Skaneateles** (town) Onondaga County
72	9.6	**Penn Yan** (village) Yates County	137	8.5	**Sloan** (village) Erie County

Note: This section ranks incorporated places and CDPs (Census Designated Places) with populations of 2,500 or more. Unincorporated postal areas were not considered. Please refer to the User Guide for additional information.

Marriage Status: Widowed

Top 150 Places Ranked in *Ascending* Order

State Rank	Percent	Place	State Rank	Percent	Place
1	0.0	**Binghamton University** (CDP) Broome County	73	3.6	**Larchmont** (village) Westchester County
1	0.0	**SUNY Oswego** (CDP) Oswego County	73	3.6	**Potsdam** (town) Saint Lawrence County
1	0.0	**University at Buffalo** (CDP) Erie County	73	3.6	**Sands Point** (village) Nassau County
4	0.4	**West Point** (CDP) Orange County	73	3.6	**Scarsdale** (town/village) Westchester County
5	0.5	**Alfred** (village) Allegany County	73	3.6	**Shawangunk** (town) Ulster County
5	0.5	**Fort Drum** (CDP) Jefferson County	81	3.7	**Fleming** (town) Cayuga County
7	0.6	**Calcium** (CDP) Jefferson County	81	3.7	**North Bellport** (CDP) Suffolk County
7	0.6	**Kaser** (village) Rockland County	83	3.8	**Greenwood Lake** (village) Orange County
9	1.0	**New Square** (village) Rockland County	83	3.8	**Perry** (town) Wyoming County
10	1.1	**Alfred** (town) Allegany County	83	3.8	**Rocky Point** (CDP) Suffolk County
11	1.2	**Jerusalem** (town) Yates County	83	3.8	**Scotchtown** (CDP) Orange County
11	1.2	**Kiryas Joel** (village) Orange County	87	3.9	**Alexander** (town) Genesee County
13	1.3	**Horseheads North** (CDP) Chemung County	87	3.9	**Center Moriches** (CDP) Suffolk County
14	1.4	**Highlands** (town) Orange County	87	3.9	**East Shoreham** (CDP) Suffolk County
14	1.4	**Ithaca** (city) Tompkins County	87	3.9	**East Syracuse** (village) Onondaga County
16	1.5	**Le Ray** (town) Jefferson County	87	3.9	**Ellisburg** (town) Jefferson County
17	1.7	**Groveland** (town) Livingston County	87	3.9	**Elmsford** (village) Westchester County
17	1.7	**Saint Regis Mohawk Reservation** (reservation) Franklin County	87	3.9	**Marlboro** (CDP) Ulster County
17	1.7	**Wesley Hills** (village) Rockland County	87	3.9	**Pompey** (town) Onondaga County
20	1.8	**Gardiner** (town) Ulster County	87	3.9	**South Valley Stream** (CDP) Nassau County
20	1.8	**Highland Falls** (village) Orange County	87	3.9	**Sweden** (town) Monroe County
22	1.9	**Knox** (town) Albany County	97	4.0	**Annsville** (town) Oneida County
22	1.9	**Monsey** (CDP) Rockland County	97	4.0	**Canton** (village) Saint Lawrence County
24	2.0	**Armonk** (CDP) Westchester County	97	4.0	**Grandyle Village** (CDP) Erie County
24	2.0	**Bedford Hills** (CDP) Westchester County	97	4.0	**Marlborough** (town) Ulster County
26	2.1	**Dannemora** (village) Clinton County	97	4.0	**New Paltz** (village) Ulster County
27	2.2	**Dannemora** (town) Clinton County	97	4.0	**New Scotland** (town) Albany County
28	2.3	**Harriman** (village) Orange County	97	4.0	**Tuckahoe** (village) Westchester County
28	2.3	**Stony Brook University** (CDP) Suffolk County	104	4.1	**Baldwin Harbor** (CDP) Nassau County
30	2.4	**Geneseo** (village) Livingston County	104	4.1	**Chittenango** (village) Madison County
30	2.4	**Kings Point** (village) Nassau County	104	4.1	**Haviland** (CDP) Dutchess County
30	2.4	**New Castle** (town) Westchester County	104	4.1	**Henrietta** (town) Monroe County
30	2.4	**Old Westbury** (village) Nassau County	104	4.1	**Hudson** (city) Columbia County
30	2.4	**Piermont** (village) Rockland County	104	4.1	**Mastic** (CDP) Suffolk County
30	2.4	**Yaphank** (CDP) Suffolk County	104	4.1	**Mohawk** (village) Herkimer County
36	2.5	**Milford** (town) Otsego County	104	4.1	**Pelham** (village) Westchester County
36	2.5	**Springs** (CDP) Suffolk County	104	4.1	**Richmond** (town) Ontario County
38	2.6	**North Castle** (town) Westchester County	113	4.2	**Bedford** (town) Westchester County
38	2.6	**Oswego** (town) Oswego County	113	4.2	**Dix Hills** (CDP) Suffolk County
40	2.7	**Marilla** (town) Erie County	113	4.2	**Dover** (town) Dutchess County
41	2.8	**Brookville** (village) Nassau County	113	4.2	**Great Neck Estates** (village) Nassau County
41	2.8	**Conklin** (town) Broome County	113	4.2	**Hamptonburgh** (town) Orange County
41	2.8	**Cornwall-on-Hudson** (village) Orange County	113	4.2	**Putnam Valley** (town) Putnam County
41	2.8	**Duanesburg** (town) Schenectady County	113	4.2	**Shirley** (CDP) Suffolk County
41	2.8	**Menands** (village) Albany County	113	4.2	**Thiells** (CDP) Rockland County
41	2.8	**Wading River** (CDP) Suffolk County	113	4.2	**Tully** (town) Onondaga County
47	2.9	**Chester** (town) Orange County	113	4.2	**West Haverstraw** (village) Rockland County
47	2.9	**Gordon Heights** (CDP) Suffolk County	123	4.3	**Greenville** (CDP) Westchester County
49	3.0	**Mount Hope** (town) Orange County	123	4.3	**Lloyd Harbor** (village) Suffolk County
49	3.0	**Stephentown** (town) Rensselaer County	123	4.3	**Marcy** (town) Oneida County
51	3.1	**Brownville** (town) Jefferson County	123	4.3	**Miller Place** (CDP) Suffolk County
51	3.1	**Caroline** (town) Tompkins County	123	4.3	**Milton** (CDP) Saratoga County
51	3.1	**Monroe** (town) Orange County	123	4.3	**Milton** (town) Saratoga County
51	3.1	**South Hill** (CDP) Tompkins County	123	4.3	**Oneonta** (city) Otsego County
55	3.2	**Delhi** (village) Delaware County	123	4.3	**Pierrepont** (town) Saint Lawrence County
55	3.2	**East Bloomfield** (town) Ontario County	123	4.3	**Port Chester** (village) Westchester County
55	3.2	**Potsdam** (village) Saint Lawrence County	123	4.3	**Scriba** (town) Oswego County
58	3.3	**Attica** (town) Wyoming County	123	4.3	**Stockport** (town) Columbia County
58	3.3	**Mahopac** (CDP) Putnam County	123	4.3	**Wilton** (town) Saratoga County
58	3.3	**Munsey Park** (village) Nassau County	135	4.4	**Cedarhurst** (village) Nassau County
58	3.3	**Northeast Ithaca** (CDP) Tompkins County	135	4.4	**Chester** (village) Orange County
58	3.3	**Stanford** (town) Dutchess County	135	4.4	**Chili** (town) Monroe County
58	3.3	**Walton** (village) Delaware County	135	4.4	**Dobbs Ferry** (village) Westchester County
64	3.4	**Hamlin** (CDP) Monroe County	135	4.4	**Fairport** (village) Monroe County
64	3.4	**Hamlin** (town) Monroe County	135	4.4	**Fort Edward** (village) Washington County
64	3.4	**North Bay Shore** (CDP) Suffolk County	135	4.4	**Hastings-on-Hudson** (village) Westchester County
64	3.4	**Pamelia** (town) Jefferson County	135	4.4	**Lakeland** (CDP) Onondaga County
64	3.4	**Romulus** (town) Seneca County	135	4.4	**Lewisboro** (town) Westchester County
69	3.5	**Binghamton** (town) Broome County	135	4.4	**Rush** (town) Monroe County
69	3.5	**Fairview** (CDP) Westchester County	135	4.4	**Saratoga** (town) Saratoga County
69	3.5	**Greenville** (town) Orange County	135	4.4	**Southeast** (town) Putnam County
69	3.5	**Jericho** (CDP) Nassau County	135	4.4	**Thornwood** (CDP) Westchester County
73	3.6	**Constantia** (town) Oswego County	148	4.5	**Augusta** (town) Oneida County
73	3.6	**Darien** (town) Genesee County	148	4.5	**Brentwood** (CDP) Suffolk County
73	3.6	**Glen Head** (CDP) Nassau County	148	4.5	**Catlin** (town) Chemung County

Note: This section ranks incorporated places and CDPs (Census Designated Places) with populations of 2,500 or more. Unincorporated postal areas were not considered. Please refer to the User Guide for additional information.

Marriage Status: Divorced

Top 150 Places Ranked in *Descending* Order

State Rank	Percent	Place	State Rank	Percent	Place
1	25.3	**Warsaw** (village) Wyoming County	73	14.6	**Moriah** (town) Essex County
2	23.8	**Whitesboro** (village) Oneida County	73	14.6	**Noyack** (CDP) Suffolk County
3	21.2	**Warsaw** (town) Wyoming County	73	14.6	**Scriba** (town) Oswego County
4	21.1	**Greenwood Lake** (village) Orange County	73	14.6	**Southampton** (village) Suffolk County
5	20.8	**Saint Regis Mohawk Reservation** (reservation) Franklin County	80	14.5	**Hudson Falls** (village) Washington County
6	20.4	**New York Mills** (village) Oneida County	80	14.5	**Medina** (village) Orleans County
7	19.2	**Bath** (village) Steuben County	80	14.5	**Mount Morris** (town) Livingston County
8	18.5	**Shandaken** (town) Ulster County	80	14.5	**Van Buren** (town) Onondaga County
8	18.5	**South Glens Falls** (village) Saratoga County	80	14.5	**Walton** (village) Delaware County
10	18.3	**Mattydale** (CDP) Onondaga County	85	14.4	**Baldwinsville** (village) Onondaga County
11	18.2	**Afton** (town) Chenango County	85	14.4	**Carthage** (village) Jefferson County
12	18.1	**Stockholm** (town) Saint Lawrence County	85	14.4	**Lockport** (city) Niagara County
12	18.1	**Waterloo** (town) Seneca County	85	14.4	**Scotia** (village) Schenectady County
14	17.5	**Bath** (town) Steuben County	85	14.4	**Sheridan** (town) Chautauqua County
14	17.5	**Tioga** (town) Tioga County	85	14.4	**Warwick** (village) Orange County
16	17.3	**Mohawk** (village) Herkimer County	85	14.4	**Wellsville** (village) Allegany County
16	17.3	**West Monroe** (town) Oswego County	92	14.3	**Alden** (town) Erie County
18	16.9	**Granville** (town) Washington County	92	14.3	**Claverack** (town) Columbia County
18	16.9	**Murray** (town) Orleans County	92	14.3	**Elbridge** (town) Onondaga County
18	16.9	**North Syracuse** (village) Onondaga County	92	14.3	**Firthcliffe** (CDP) Orange County
18	16.9	**Village Green** (CDP) Onondaga County	92	14.3	**Liberty** (village) Sullivan County
22	16.8	**Palmyra** (village) Wayne County	92	14.3	**Lisbon** (town) Saint Lawrence County
23	16.7	**Glens Falls** (city) Warren County	92	14.3	**Nichols** (town) Tioga County
23	16.7	**Mechanicville** (city) Saratoga County	99	14.2	**Guilford** (town) Chenango County
25	16.6	**Augusta** (town) Oneida County	99	14.2	**Roslyn** (village) Nassau County
25	16.6	**Williamsville** (village) Erie County	99	14.2	**Wayland** (town) Steuben County
27	16.5	**Blasdell** (village) Erie County	102	14.1	**Green Island** (town/village) Albany County
28	16.4	**Hudson** (city) Columbia County	102	14.1	**Little Falls** (city) Herkimer County
28	16.4	**Marlboro** (CDP) Ulster County	102	14.1	**Tonawanda** (city) Erie County
28	16.4	**Sidney** (village) Delaware County	105	14.0	**Rotterdam** (CDP) Schenectady County
28	16.4	**Southport** (CDP) Chemung County	105	14.0	**Sherburne** (town) Chenango County
32	16.3	**East Rochester** (town/village) Monroe County	105	14.0	**Sidney** (town) Delaware County
33	16.2	**Conklin** (town) Broome County	108	13.9	**Canandaigua** (city) Ontario County
33	16.2	**Manchester** (town) Ontario County	108	13.9	**Floyd** (town) Oneida County
33	16.2	**Norwich** (town) Chenango County	108	13.9	**Ghent** (town) Columbia County
33	16.2	**Penn Yan** (village) Yates County	108	13.9	**Webster** (village) Monroe County
37	16.1	**Arcadia** (town) Wayne County	112	13.8	**Ballston Spa** (village) Saratoga County
37	16.1	**Jamestown** (city) Chautauqua County	112	13.8	**Batavia** (city) Genesee County
39	16.0	**Olean** (city) Cattaraugus County	112	13.8	**Canandaigua** (town) Ontario County
40	15.9	**Frankfort** (village) Herkimer County	112	13.8	**Corning** (city) Steuben County
41	15.8	**Mount Ivy** (CDP) Rockland County	112	13.8	**Le Roy** (town) Genesee County
42	15.7	**South Lockport** (CDP) Niagara County	112	13.8	**Piermont** (village) Rockland County
43	15.6	**Portland** (town) Chautauqua County	112	13.8	**Rochester** (town) Ulster County
44	15.5	**Gaines** (town) Orleans County	119	13.7	**Laurens** (town) Otsego County
44	15.5	**Mount Morris** (village) Livingston County	119	13.7	**Norwich** (city) Chenango County
44	15.5	**Waterloo** (village) Seneca County	121	13.6	**Groveland** (town) Livingston County
47	15.4	**Salamanca** (city) Cattaraugus County	121	13.6	**Herkimer** (village) Herkimer County
48	15.3	**Akron** (village) Erie County	121	13.6	**Lakewood** (village) Chautauqua County
48	15.3	**East Aurora** (village) Erie County	121	13.6	**Massena** (town) Saint Lawrence County
48	15.3	**Gowanda** (village) Cattaraugus County	121	13.6	**Southport** (town) Chemung County
48	15.3	**Lake Placid** (village) Essex County	121	13.6	**Tuckahoe** (village) Westchester County
48	15.3	**Newark** (village) Wayne County	121	13.6	**Woodstock** (town) Ulster County
48	15.3	**Springville** (village) Erie County	128	13.5	**Greece** (CDP) Monroe County
54	15.2	**Lyons** (village) Wayne County	128	13.5	**Manlius** (village) Onondaga County
54	15.2	**Middletown** (town) Delaware County	128	13.5	**Rotterdam** (town) Schenectady County
54	15.2	**New Haven** (town) Oswego County	131	13.4	**Fairport** (village) Monroe County
54	15.2	**Oneida** (city) Madison County	131	13.4	**Hanover** (town) Chautauqua County
58	15.1	**Hannibal** (town) Oswego County	131	13.4	**Homer** (village) Cortland County
58	15.1	**White Creek** (town) Washington County	131	13.4	**Le Roy** (village) Genesee County
60	15.0	**West Glens Falls** (CDP) Warren County	131	13.4	**Solvay** (village) Onondaga County
61	14.9	**Attica** (village) Wyoming County	131	13.4	**Whitestown** (town) Oneida County
61	14.9	**Auburn** (city) Cayuga County	131	13.4	**Wilson** (town) Niagara County
61	14.9	**Fort Edward** (town) Washington County	138	13.3	**Caroline** (town) Tompkins County
61	14.9	**Great Neck Plaza** (village) Nassau County	138	13.3	**Chittenango** (village) Madison County
65	14.8	**Lake Luzerne** (town) Warren County	140	13.2	**Avon** (town) Livingston County
65	14.8	**Spencer** (town) Tioga County	140	13.2	**Binghamton** (city) Broome County
67	14.7	**Callicoon** (town) Sullivan County	140	13.2	**Lyncourt** (CDP) Onondaga County
67	14.7	**Chester** (village) Orange County	140	13.2	**Rhinebeck** (village) Dutchess County
67	14.7	**Endicott** (village) Broome County	140	13.2	**Salina** (town) Onondaga County
67	14.7	**Esopus** (town) Ulster County	140	13.2	**Stanford** (town) Dutchess County
67	14.7	**Milo** (town) Yates County	140	13.2	**Sterling** (town) Cayuga County
67	14.7	**Yates** (town) Orleans County	140	13.2	**Sullivan** (town) Madison County
73	14.6	**Bainbridge** (town) Chenango County	148	13.1	**Dunkirk** (city) Chautauqua County
73	14.6	**Fulton** (city) Oswego County	148	13.1	**Greenwich** (town) Washington County
73	14.6	**Malone** (village) Franklin County	148	13.1	**Hurley** (town) Ulster County

Note: This section ranks incorporated places and CDPs (Census Designated Places) with populations of 2,500 or more. Unincorporated postal areas were not considered. Please refer to the User Guide for additional information.

Marriage Status: Divorced

Top 150 Places Ranked in *Ascending* Order

State Rank	Percent	Place
1	0.0	**Binghamton University** (CDP) Broome County
1	0.0	**SUNY Oswego** (CDP) Oswego County
3	0.1	**New Square** (village) Rockland County
3	0.1	**University at Buffalo** (CDP) Erie County
5	0.3	**Alfred** (village) Allegany County
5	0.3	**Stony Brook University** (CDP) Suffolk County
7	0.9	**Kiryas Joel** (village) Orange County
8	1.2	**Brookville** (village) Nassau County
9	1.5	**Kaser** (village) Rockland County
9	1.5	**Monsey** (CDP) Rockland County
9	1.5	**South Hill** (CDP) Tompkins County
12	1.7	**Alfred** (town) Allegany County
13	1.8	**New Hempstead** (village) Rockland County
13	1.8	**Old Westbury** (village) Nassau County
15	1.9	**Fort Drum** (CDP) Jefferson County
16	2.0	**Kings Point** (village) Nassau County
17	2.1	**Wesley Hills** (village) Rockland County
18	2.2	**West Point** (CDP) Orange County
19	2.3	**Lawrence** (village) Nassau County
20	2.6	**East Hills** (village) Nassau County
20	2.6	**Montauk** (CDP) Suffolk County
22	2.8	**Geneseo** (village) Livingston County
22	2.8	**Munsey Park** (village) Nassau County
24	2.9	**Manhasset Hills** (CDP) Nassau County
25	3.0	**Lake Success** (village) Nassau County
25	3.0	**Muttontown** (village) Nassau County
25	3.0	**North New Hyde Park** (CDP) Nassau County
25	3.0	**Scarsdale** (town/village) Westchester County
29	3.1	**Blauvelt** (CDP) Rockland County
29	3.1	**Cayuga Heights** (village) Tompkins County
31	3.4	**Clarence Center** (CDP) Erie County
31	3.4	**New Cassel** (CDP) Nassau County
33	3.5	**Northeast Ithaca** (CDP) Tompkins County
34	3.6	**Hamilton** (village) Madison County
34	3.6	**New Paltz** (village) Ulster County
36	3.7	**Garden City** (village) Nassau County
36	3.7	**Garden City Park** (CDP) Nassau County
38	3.8	**Ithaca** (city) Tompkins County
38	3.8	**Le Ray** (town) Jefferson County
38	3.8	**Lloyd Harbor** (village) Suffolk County
38	3.8	**Old Bethpage** (CDP) Nassau County
38	3.8	**Plainview** (CDP) Nassau County
38	3.8	**Woodmere** (CDP) Nassau County
44	4.0	**Dix Hills** (CDP) Suffolk County
44	4.0	**Hamptonburgh** (town) Orange County
44	4.0	**New Hyde Park** (village) Nassau County
47	4.1	**Cedarhurst** (village) Nassau County
47	4.1	**Monroe** (village) Orange County
47	4.1	**Searingtown** (CDP) Nassau County
50	4.4	**Monroe** (town) Orange County
50	4.4	**Syosset** (CDP) Nassau County
50	4.4	**Wynantskill** (CDP) Rensselaer County
53	4.5	**Airmont** (village) Rockland County
53	4.5	**Bronxville** (village) Westchester County
53	4.5	**Neversink** (town) Sullivan County
53	4.5	**Orangeburg** (CDP) Rockland County
53	4.5	**Oswego** (town) Oswego County
53	4.5	**Stony Point** (CDP) Rockland County
53	4.5	**Viola** (CDP) Rockland County
60	4.6	**Geneseo** (town) Livingston County
60	4.6	**Greenville** (town) Orange County
60	4.6	**Oceanside** (CDP) Nassau County
60	4.6	**Wading River** (CDP) Suffolk County
64	4.7	**Fort Salonga** (CDP) Suffolk County
64	4.7	**Great Neck** (village) Nassau County
64	4.7	**Valhalla** (CDP) Westchester County
67	4.8	**Bellmore** (CDP) Nassau County
67	4.8	**Salisbury** (CDP) Nassau County
69	4.9	**Merrick** (CDP) Nassau County
69	4.9	**Pelham Manor** (village) Westchester County
71	5.0	**Ithaca** (town) Tompkins County
71	5.0	**Lido Beach** (CDP) Nassau County
71	5.0	**West Hills** (CDP) Suffolk County
74	5.1	**Herricks** (CDP) Nassau County
74	5.1	**North Merrick** (CDP) Nassau County
74	5.1	**Riverside** (CDP) Suffolk County
74	5.1	**Roslyn Heights** (CDP) Nassau County
78	5.2	**Briarcliff Manor** (village) Westchester County
78	5.2	**Fredonia** (village) Chautauqua County
78	5.2	**Great Neck Estates** (village) Nassau County
78	5.2	**New Castle** (town) Westchester County
78	5.2	**Pomona** (village) Rockland County
78	5.2	**South Farmingdale** (CDP) Nassau County
84	5.3	**East Williston** (village) Nassau County
84	5.3	**Hicksville** (CDP) Nassau County
84	5.3	**Mount Sinai** (CDP) Suffolk County
84	5.3	**Potsdam** (village) Saint Lawrence County
88	5.4	**Armonk** (CDP) Westchester County
88	5.4	**Hamilton** (town) Madison County
90	5.5	**Massapequa** (CDP) Nassau County
90	5.5	**North Bellmore** (CDP) Nassau County
90	5.5	**Union Vale** (town) Dutchess County
90	5.5	**Wantagh** (CDP) Nassau County
94	5.6	**Canton** (village) Saint Lawrence County
94	5.6	**Commack** (CDP) Suffolk County
94	5.6	**Greenville** (CDP) Westchester County
94	5.6	**Highlands** (town) Orange County
94	5.6	**Jericho** (CDP) Nassau County
94	5.6	**Massapequa Park** (village) Nassau County
94	5.6	**Mendon** (town) Monroe County
94	5.6	**Stony Point** (town) Rockland County
102	5.7	**Amenia** (town) Dutchess County
102	5.7	**Baldwin Harbor** (CDP) Nassau County
102	5.7	**East Shoreham** (CDP) Suffolk County
102	5.7	**Elwood** (CDP) Suffolk County
102	5.7	**Larchmont** (village) Westchester County
102	5.7	**Melville** (CDP) Suffolk County
102	5.7	**New City** (CDP) Rockland County
102	5.7	**Rye** (city) Westchester County
110	5.8	**North Castle** (town) Westchester County
110	5.8	**Oyster Bay** (town) Nassau County
110	5.8	**Ramapo** (town) Rockland County
110	5.8	**West Hempstead** (CDP) Nassau County
110	5.8	**West Sand Lake** (CDP) Rensselaer County
115	5.9	**Bayville** (village) Nassau County
115	5.9	**Myers Corner** (CDP) Dutchess County
115	5.9	**Oneonta** (city) Otsego County
115	5.9	**Terryville** (CDP) Suffolk County
115	5.9	**Wheatley Heights** (CDP) Suffolk County
120	6.0	**Arlington** (CDP) Dutchess County
120	6.0	**Bethpage** (CDP) Nassau County
120	6.0	**Clinton** (town) Dutchess County
120	6.0	**Cold Spring Harbor** (CDP) Suffolk County
120	6.0	**Deerfield** (town) Oneida County
120	6.0	**Granby** (town) Oswego County
120	6.0	**North Hempstead** (town) Nassau County
120	6.0	**Northumberland** (town) Saratoga County
120	6.0	**Paris** (town) Oneida County
120	6.0	**Patterson** (town) Putnam County
120	6.0	**Seaford** (CDP) Nassau County
131	6.1	**Albertson** (CDP) Nassau County
131	6.1	**Eastchester** (CDP) Westchester County
131	6.1	**Franklin Square** (CDP) Nassau County
131	6.1	**Pendleton** (town) Niagara County
131	6.1	**Pittsford** (town) Monroe County
136	6.2	**Carle Place** (CDP) Nassau County
136	6.2	**Duanesburg** (town) Schenectady County
136	6.2	**East Rockaway** (village) Nassau County
136	6.2	**Geneva** (town) Ontario County
136	6.2	**Glen Head** (CDP) Nassau County
136	6.2	**Horseheads North** (CDP) Chemung County
136	6.2	**Mount Pleasant** (town) Westchester County
136	6.2	**Port Washington North** (village) Nassau County
144	6.3	**East Islip** (CDP) Suffolk County
144	6.3	**Floral Park** (village) Nassau County
144	6.3	**Hauppauge** (CDP) Suffolk County
144	6.3	**Mount Kisco** (town/village) Westchester County
144	6.3	**North Hills** (village) Nassau County
144	6.3	**Pearl River** (CDP) Rockland County
144	6.3	**Plainedge** (CDP) Nassau County

Note: *This section ranks incorporated places and CDPs (Census Designated Places) with populations of 2,500 or more. Unincorporated postal areas were not considered. Please refer to the User Guide for additional information.*

Foreign Born

Top 150 Places Ranked in *Descending* Order

State Rank	Percent	Place	State Rank	Percent	Place
1	47.5	**Queens** (borough) Queens County	76	25.8	**Huntington Station** (CDP) Suffolk County
2	45.8	**Garden City Park** (CDP) Nassau County	77	25.7	**Cayuga Heights** (village) Tompkins County
3	45.7	**Hillcrest** (CDP) Rockland County	78	25.6	**Salisbury** (CDP) Nassau County
4	45.6	**New Cassel** (CDP) Nassau County	79	25.2	**Franklin Square** (CDP) Nassau County
5	45.3	**Port Chester** (village) Westchester County	79	25.2	**Saint Regis Mohawk Reservation** (reservation) Franklin County
6	45.1	**Elmont** (CDP) Nassau County	79	25.2	**Wyandanch** (CDP) Suffolk County
7	42.3	**Spring Valley** (village) Rockland County	82	25.1	**Baldwin** (CDP) Nassau County
8	42.0	**Brentwood** (CDP) Suffolk County	82	25.1	**Lakeview** (CDP) Nassau County
8	42.0	**Elmsford** (village) Westchester County	84	24.9	**Mount Ivy** (CDP) Rockland County
10	41.8	**North Bay Shore** (CDP) Suffolk County	85	24.6	**East Farmingdale** (CDP) Suffolk County
11	41.7	**Bedford Hills** (CDP) Westchester County	86	24.2	**Springs** (CDP) Suffolk County
12	41.0	**Hempstead** (village) Nassau County	87	24.1	**Newburgh** (city) Orange County
12	41.0	**Northeast Ithaca** (CDP) Tompkins County	88	24.0	**Noyack** (CDP) Suffolk County
12	41.0	**Sleepy Hollow** (village) Westchester County	88	24.0	**Syosset** (CDP) Nassau County
15	39.6	**Ossining** (village) Westchester County	90	23.9	**Cedarhurst** (village) Nassau County
16	39.5	**Lansing** (village) Tompkins County	91	23.8	**Wheatley Heights** (CDP) Suffolk County
17	38.3	**Haverstraw** (village) Rockland County	92	23.6	**Baldwin Harbor** (CDP) Nassau County
18	37.7	**Mount Kisco** (town/village) Westchester County	92	23.6	**Valhalla** (CDP) Westchester County
19	37.2	**New York** (city)	94	23.5	**Harriman** (village) Orange County
19	37.2	**Rye** (town) Westchester County	94	23.5	**Tarrytown** (village) Westchester County
21	37.0	**Manhasset Hills** (CDP) Nassau County	96	23.4	**Hewlett** (CDP) Nassau County
21	37.0	**North Valley Stream** (CDP) Nassau County	97	23.1	**Harrison** (town/village) Westchester County
23	36.9	**Brooklyn** (borough) Kings County	98	23.0	**Mamaroneck** (town) Westchester County
24	36.8	**Roosevelt** (CDP) Nassau County	99	22.9	**Ithaca** (town) Tompkins County
25	36.7	**New Hyde Park** (village) Nassau County	100	22.8	**Flower Hill** (village) Nassau County
26	36.4	**Herricks** (CDP) Nassau County	100	22.8	**Greenburgh** (town) Westchester County
27	35.3	**Bronx** (borough) Bronx County	100	22.8	**Scarsdale** (town/village) Westchester County
28	35.1	**Great Neck** (village) Nassau County	103	22.7	**Mahopac** (CDP) Putnam County
29	35.0	**Fairview** (CDP) Westchester County	104	22.5	**Greenville** (CDP) Westchester County
30	34.9	**Valley Stream** (village) Nassau County	104	22.5	**New Hempstead** (village) Rockland County
31	34.7	**Westbury** (village) Nassau County	106	22.4	**Bay Shore** (CDP) Suffolk County
32	34.5	**Uniondale** (CDP) Nassau County	106	22.4	**Ramapo** (town) Rockland County
33	34.3	**Lake Success** (village) Nassau County	108	22.2	**Hempstead** (town) Nassau County
33	34.3	**Searingtown** (CDP) Nassau County	108	22.2	**Menands** (village) Albany County
35	34.2	**Central Islip** (CDP) Suffolk County	108	22.2	**Staten Island** (borough) Richmond County
36	34.1	**South Valley Stream** (CDP) Nassau County	108	22.2	**West Hempstead** (CDP) Nassau County
36	34.1	**University Gardens** (CDP) Nassau County	112	22.0	**Nyack** (village) Rockland County
38	34.0	**Flanders** (CDP) Suffolk County	113	21.6	**Webster** (village) Monroe County
39	33.2	**Manorhaven** (village) Nassau County	114	21.5	**Riverhead** (CDP) Suffolk County
40	33.0	**Mount Vernon** (city) Westchester County	115	21.4	**Old Westbury** (village) Nassau County
41	32.6	**Inwood** (CDP) Nassau County	115	21.4	**Vails Gate** (CDP) Orange County
42	32.5	**North New Hyde Park** (CDP) Nassau County	117	21.3	**Clarkstown** (town) Rockland County
43	32.4	**Stony Brook University** (CDP) Suffolk County	118	21.2	**Muttontown** (village) Nassau County
44	31.7	**North Amityville** (CDP) Suffolk County	119	21.0	**East Hampton** (town) Suffolk County
44	31.7	**Thomaston** (village) Nassau County	119	21.0	**Pomona** (village) Rockland County
46	31.6	**Hartsdale** (CDP) Westchester County	121	20.9	**Carle Place** (CDP) Nassau County
47	31.4	**West Haverstraw** (village) Rockland County	121	20.9	**North Bellport** (CDP) Suffolk County
48	30.8	**Ossining** (town) Westchester County	121	20.9	**Roslyn** (village) Nassau County
48	30.8	**White Plains** (city) Westchester County	121	20.9	**Rye Brook** (village) Westchester County
50	30.6	**Mamaroneck** (village) Westchester County	125	20.8	**Port Washington North** (village) Nassau County
50	30.6	**Yonkers** (city) Westchester County	125	20.8	**Tappan** (CDP) Rockland County
52	30.5	**Hicksville** (CDP) Nassau County	127	20.7	**Suffern** (village) Rockland County
53	30.0	**Roslyn Heights** (CDP) Nassau County	128	20.6	**Islip** (town) Suffolk County
54	29.9	**Haverstraw** (town) Rockland County	129	20.4	**Manhasset** (CDP) Nassau County
55	29.7	**Glen Cove** (city) Nassau County	129	20.4	**Mount Pleasant** (town) Westchester County
55	29.7	**Kings Point** (village) Nassau County	129	20.4	**Wappingers Falls** (village) Dutchess County
57	29.6	**New Rochelle** (city) Westchester County	132	19.8	**Babylon** (town) Suffolk County
58	29.3	**Mineola** (village) Nassau County	132	19.8	**Port Washington** (CDP) Nassau County
58	29.3	**North Hempstead** (town) Nassau County	134	19.4	**Utica** (city) Oneida County
60	29.1	**Nanuet** (CDP) Rockland County	135	19.3	**Lake Mohegan** (CDP) Westchester County
61	29.0	**Freeport** (village) Nassau County	136	19.2	**Williston Park** (village) Nassau County
62	28.9	**Copiague** (CDP) Suffolk County	137	19.1	**Poughkeepsie** (city) Dutchess County
62	28.9	**Manhattan** (borough) New York County	138	19.0	**Arlington** (CDP) Dutchess County
64	28.1	**East Hampton North** (CDP) Suffolk County	138	19.0	**East Meadow** (CDP) Nassau County
64	28.1	**Great Neck Plaza** (village) Nassau County	138	19.0	**Southampton** (town) Suffolk County
66	27.9	**Ardsley** (village) Westchester County	141	18.9	**Deer Park** (CDP) Suffolk County
67	27.7	**North Lindenhurst** (CDP) Suffolk County	141	18.9	**University at Buffalo** (CDP) Erie County
68	27.2	**Peekskill** (city) Westchester County	143	18.8	**Hudson** (city) Columbia County
69	27.0	**North Hills** (village) Nassau County	143	18.8	**Pelham** (village) Westchester County
70	26.9	**Tuckahoe** (village) Westchester County	145	18.6	**Glen Head** (CDP) Nassau County
71	26.7	**Jericho** (CDP) Nassau County	145	18.6	**Northwest Harbor** (CDP) Suffolk County
72	26.5	**Albertson** (CDP) Nassau County	147	18.4	**Chestnut Ridge** (village) Rockland County
73	26.2	**Islandia** (village) Suffolk County	147	18.4	**New City** (CDP) Rockland County
74	26.1	**Great Neck Estates** (village) Nassau County	149	18.3	**Locust Valley** (CDP) Nassau County
75	26.0	**Hampton Bays** (CDP) Suffolk County	150	18.2	**Dix Hills** (CDP) Suffolk County

Note: This section ranks incorporated places and CDPs (Census Designated Places) with populations of 2,500 or more. Unincorporated postal areas were not considered. Please refer to the User Guide for additional information.

Foreign Born

Top 150 Places Ranked in *Ascending* Order

State Rank	Percent	Place	State Rank	Percent	Place
1	0.0	**Canastota** (village) Madison County	76	1.2	**Argyle** (town) Washington County
1	0.0	**Carroll** (town) Chautauqua County	76	1.2	**Benton** (town) Yates County
1	0.0	**Fort Edward** (village) Washington County	76	1.2	**Canisteo** (town) Steuben County
4	0.2	**Ellery** (town) Chautauqua County	76	1.2	**Charlton** (town) Saratoga County
4	0.2	**Sangerfield** (town) Oneida County	76	1.2	**Constantia** (town) Oswego County
4	0.2	**Sardinia** (town) Erie County	76	1.2	**Dolgeville** (village) Herkimer County
4	0.2	**West Monroe** (town) Oswego County	76	1.2	**Fenton** (town) Broome County
4	0.2	**Yorkshire** (town) Cattaraugus County	76	1.2	**Greene** (town) Chenango County
9	0.3	**Fort Edward** (town) Washington County	76	1.2	**Le Roy** (town) Genesee County
9	0.3	**Verona** (town) Oneida County	76	1.2	**Lee** (town) Oneida County
11	0.4	**Clarendon** (town) Orleans County	76	1.2	**Sandy Creek** (town) Oswego County
11	0.4	**East Bloomfield** (town) Ontario County	76	1.2	**Sherrill** (city) Oneida County
11	0.4	**Otisco** (town) Onondaga County	76	1.2	**Sterling** (town) Cayuga County
11	0.4	**Southport** (CDP) Chemung County	76	1.2	**White Creek** (town) Washington County
11	0.4	**Wayland** (town) Steuben County	90	1.3	**Adams** (town) Jefferson County
16	0.5	**Attica** (village) Wyoming County	90	1.3	**Bennington** (town) Wyoming County
16	0.5	**Lenox** (town) Madison County	90	1.3	**Brasher** (town) Saint Lawrence County
16	0.5	**Moriah** (town) Essex County	90	1.3	**Clayton** (town) Jefferson County
16	0.5	**New Haven** (town) Oswego County	90	1.3	**Coeymans** (town) Albany County
16	0.5	**Palmyra** (village) Wayne County	90	1.3	**Ellisburg** (town) Jefferson County
16	0.5	**Waverly** (village) Tioga County	90	1.3	**Galen** (town) Wayne County
22	0.6	**Candor** (town) Tioga County	90	1.3	**Gouverneur** (village) Saint Lawrence County
22	0.6	**Ilion** (village) Herkimer County	90	1.3	**Hannibal** (town) Oswego County
22	0.6	**Lake Luzerne** (town) Warren County	90	1.3	**Jay** (town) Essex County
22	0.6	**Lisle** (town) Broome County	90	1.3	**Kendall** (town) Orleans County
22	0.6	**Starkey** (town) Yates County	90	1.3	**Middleburgh** (town) Schoharie County
22	0.6	**York** (town) Livingston County	90	1.3	**Milford** (town) Otsego County
28	0.7	**Alexander** (town) Genesee County	90	1.3	**New Bremen** (town) Lewis County
28	0.7	**Conklin** (town) Broome County	90	1.3	**Pembroke** (town) Genesee County
28	0.7	**Holland** (town) Erie County	90	1.3	**South Glens Falls** (village) Saratoga County
28	0.7	**Newark Valley** (town) Tioga County	90	1.3	**Wolcott** (town) Wayne County
28	0.7	**Waterloo** (village) Seneca County	107	1.4	**Alexandria** (town) Jefferson County
33	0.8	**Barton** (town) Tioga County	107	1.4	**Busti** (town) Chautauqua County
33	0.8	**Camden** (town) Oneida County	107	1.4	**Chester** (town) Warren County
33	0.8	**Franklinville** (town) Cattaraugus County	107	1.4	**Hartland** (town) Niagara County
33	0.8	**Parish** (town) Oswego County	107	1.4	**Lakewood** (village) Chautauqua County
33	0.8	**Portville** (town) Cattaraugus County	107	1.4	**Le Roy** (village) Genesee County
33	0.8	**Southport** (town) Chemung County	107	1.4	**Mexico** (town) Oswego County
33	0.8	**Tioga** (town) Tioga County	107	1.4	**Scotia** (village) Schenectady County
33	0.8	**Trenton** (town) Oneida County	107	1.4	**Sennett** (town) Cayuga County
33	0.8	**Whitesboro** (village) Oneida County	107	1.4	**Wales** (town) Erie County
42	0.9	**Annsville** (town) Oneida County	107	1.4	**Warsaw** (town) Wyoming County
42	0.9	**Campbell** (town) Steuben County	118	1.5	**Broadalbin** (town) Fulton County
42	0.9	**Mayfield** (town) Fulton County	118	1.5	**Ellicott** (town) Chautauqua County
42	0.9	**North Dansville** (town) Livingston County	118	1.5	**Granby** (town) Oswego County
42	0.9	**Nunda** (town) Livingston County	118	1.5	**Johnstown** (town) Fulton County
42	0.9	**Pavilion** (town) Genesee County	118	1.5	**Milo** (town) Yates County
42	0.9	**Ravena** (village) Albany County	118	1.5	**Moreau** (town) Saratoga County
42	0.9	**Stephentown** (town) Rensselaer County	118	1.5	**Penn Yan** (village) Yates County
42	0.9	**Yates** (town) Orleans County	118	1.5	**Portland** (town) Chautauqua County
51	1.0	**Carthage** (village) Jefferson County	118	1.5	**Sullivan** (town) Madison County
51	1.0	**Croghan** (town) Lewis County	118	1.5	**Tupper Lake** (village) Franklin County
51	1.0	**Cuba** (town) Allegany County	118	1.5	**Volney** (town) Oswego County
51	1.0	**Darien** (town) Genesee County	118	1.5	**Wellsville** (village) Allegany County
51	1.0	**Gaines** (town) Orleans County	130	1.6	**Chittenango** (village) Madison County
51	1.0	**Guilford** (town) Chenango County	130	1.6	**Dix** (town) Schuyler County
51	1.0	**Hastings** (town) Oswego County	130	1.6	**Hoosick** (town) Rensselaer County
51	1.0	**Manheim** (town) Herkimer County	130	1.6	**Maine** (town) Broome County
51	1.0	**Moravia** (town) Cayuga County	130	1.6	**Malone** (village) Franklin County
51	1.0	**Nichols** (town) Tioga County	130	1.6	**Norwich** (town) Chenango County
51	1.0	**Perry** (village) Wyoming County	130	1.6	**Orleans** (town) Jefferson County
51	1.0	**Poestenkill** (town) Rensselaer County	130	1.6	**Richland** (town) Oswego County
51	1.0	**Windsor** (town) Broome County	130	1.6	**Saranac Lake** (village) Franklin County
64	1.1	**Arcade** (town) Wyoming County	130	1.6	**Whitehall** (village) Washington County
64	1.1	**Boonville** (town) Oneida County	140	1.7	**Au Sable** (town) Clinton County
64	1.1	**Dansville** (village) Livingston County	140	1.7	**Brownville** (town) Jefferson County
64	1.1	**Denmark** (town) Lewis County	140	1.7	**Eden** (town) Erie County
64	1.1	**Lyons** (village) Wayne County	140	1.7	**Enfield** (town) Tompkins County
64	1.1	**Mooers** (town) Clinton County	140	1.7	**Hamburg** (village) Erie County
64	1.1	**Newfield** (town) Tompkins County	140	1.7	**Hanover** (town) Chautauqua County
64	1.1	**Northumberland** (town) Saratoga County	140	1.7	**Harrietstown** (town) Franklin County
64	1.1	**Schroeppel** (town) Oswego County	140	1.7	**Mount Morris** (town) Livingston County
64	1.1	**Walton** (village) Delaware County	140	1.7	**Newfane** (town) Niagara County
64	1.1	**Waterloo** (town) Seneca County	140	1.7	**Norfolk** (town) Saint Lawrence County
64	1.1	**Whitehall** (village) Washington County	140	1.7	**Orchard Park** (village) Erie County

Note: This section ranks incorporated places and CDPs (Census Designated Places) with populations of 2,500 or more. Unincorporated postal areas were not considered. Please refer to the User Guide for additional information.

Speak English Only at Home

Top 150 Places Ranked in *Descending* Order

State Rank	Percent	Place	State Rank	Percent	Place
1	100.0	**Carroll** (town) Chautauqua County	73	98.3	**Penn Yan** (village) Yates County
2	99.9	**Croghan** (town) Lewis County	73	98.3	**Wilson** (town) Niagara County
3	99.7	**Constantia** (town) Oswego County	78	98.2	**Duanesburg** (town) Schenectady County
3	99.7	**Yorkshire** (town) Cattaraugus County	78	98.2	**Eden** (town) Erie County
5	99.6	**Newfane** (CDP) Niagara County	78	98.2	**Elma Center** (CDP) Erie County
6	99.5	**Newfane** (town) Niagara County	78	98.2	**Pembroke** (town) Genesee County
7	99.4	**Otisco** (town) Onondaga County	78	98.2	**Pittstown** (town) Rensselaer County
7	99.4	**White Creek** (town) Washington County	78	98.2	**Ravena** (village) Albany County
9	99.3	**Canisteo** (town) Steuben County	78	98.2	**Scotia** (village) Schenectady County
9	99.3	**Ellery** (town) Chautauqua County	85	98.1	**Aurelius** (town) Cayuga County
9	99.3	**Sangerfield** (town) Oneida County	85	98.1	**Caroline** (town) Tompkins County
12	99.2	**Alexander** (town) Genesee County	85	98.1	**Coxsackie** (village) Greene County
12	99.2	**Enfield** (town) Tompkins County	85	98.1	**Lake Erie Beach** (CDP) Erie County
12	99.2	**Nichols** (town) Tioga County	85	98.1	**Lee** (town) Oneida County
12	99.2	**Sandy Creek** (town) Oswego County	85	98.1	**Saranac Lake** (village) Franklin County
12	99.2	**Southport** (CDP) Chemung County	85	98.1	**Stephentown** (town) Rensselaer County
17	99.1	**Afton** (town) Chenango County	92	98.0	**Aurora** (town) Erie County
17	99.1	**Attica** (village) Wyoming County	92	98.0	**Bennington** (town) Wyoming County
17	99.1	**Eden** (CDP) Erie County	92	98.0	**Berne** (town) Albany County
17	99.1	**Mohawk** (village) Herkimer County	92	98.0	**Brutus** (town) Cayuga County
17	99.1	**Nunda** (town) Livingston County	92	98.0	**Dix** (town) Schuyler County
22	99.0	**Cambria** (town) Niagara County	92	98.0	**East Aurora** (village) Erie County
22	99.0	**Kendall** (town) Orleans County	92	98.0	**Kingsbury** (town) Washington County
22	99.0	**Lake Luzerne** (town) Warren County	92	98.0	**Lisle** (town) Broome County
22	99.0	**Pendleton** (town) Niagara County	92	98.0	**Malone** (village) Franklin County
22	99.0	**Pierrepont** (town) Saint Lawrence County	92	98.0	**Mexico** (town) Oswego County
22	99.0	**Sterling** (town) Cayuga County	92	98.0	**Sullivan** (town) Madison County
28	98.9	**Argyle** (town) Washington County	103	97.9	**Athens** (town) Greene County
28	98.9	**Clarendon** (town) Orleans County	103	97.9	**Boston** (town) Erie County
28	98.9	**Ilion** (village) Herkimer County	103	97.9	**Lenox** (town) Madison County
28	98.9	**Tioga** (town) Tioga County	103	97.9	**Moira** (town) Franklin County
28	98.9	**Vienna** (town) Oneida County	103	97.9	**New Bremen** (town) Lewis County
33	98.8	**Barton** (town) Tioga County	103	97.9	**Parish** (town) Oswego County
33	98.8	**Fort Edward** (village) Washington County	103	97.9	**Volney** (town) Oswego County
33	98.8	**Franklinville** (town) Cattaraugus County	110	97.8	**Candor** (town) Tioga County
33	98.8	**Jay** (town) Essex County	110	97.8	**Carthage** (village) Jefferson County
33	98.8	**Lyons** (village) Wayne County	110	97.8	**Lewiston** (village) Niagara County
38	98.7	**Alden** (village) Erie County	110	97.8	**Mayfield** (town) Fulton County
38	98.7	**Canastota** (village) Madison County	110	97.8	**New Berlin** (town) Chenango County
38	98.7	**Fenton** (town) Broome County	110	97.8	**North Collins** (town) Erie County
38	98.7	**Hartland** (town) Niagara County	110	97.8	**Otego** (town) Otsego County
38	98.7	**Newark Valley** (town) Tioga County	110	97.8	**Silver Creek** (village) Chautauqua County
38	98.7	**Northampton** (town) Fulton County	110	97.8	**Warsaw** (town) Wyoming County
38	98.7	**Wayland** (town) Steuben County	110	97.8	**York** (town) Livingston County
45	98.6	**Adams** (town) Jefferson County	120	97.7	**Addison** (town) Steuben County
45	98.6	**Chittenango** (village) Madison County	120	97.7	**Big Flats** (CDP) Chemung County
45	98.6	**Dansville** (village) Livingston County	120	97.7	**Brownville** (town) Jefferson County
45	98.6	**Hastings** (town) Oswego County	120	97.7	**Cuba** (town) Allegany County
45	98.6	**Hudson Falls** (village) Washington County	120	97.7	**Greene** (town) Chenango County
45	98.6	**Munsons Corners** (CDP) Cortland County	120	97.7	**Guilford** (town) Chenango County
45	98.6	**Nassau** (town) Rensselaer County	120	97.7	**Johnstown** (town) Fulton County
45	98.6	**Waverly** (village) Tioga County	120	97.7	**Marion** (town) Wayne County
45	98.6	**Whitehall** (village) Washington County	120	97.7	**North Boston** (CDP) Erie County
45	98.6	**Whitesboro** (village) Oneida County	120	97.7	**Palmyra** (town) Wayne County
55	98.5	**Alexandria** (town) Jefferson County	120	97.7	**Rosendale** (town) Ulster County
55	98.5	**Fort Edward** (town) Washington County	120	97.7	**Royalton** (town) Niagara County
55	98.5	**Gouverneur** (village) Saint Lawrence County	120	97.7	**South Glens Falls** (village) Saratoga County
55	98.5	**Mohawk** (town) Montgomery County	120	97.7	**Unadilla** (town) Otsego County
55	98.5	**North Dansville** (town) Livingston County	134	97.6	**Arcade** (town) Wyoming County
55	98.5	**Schroeppel** (town) Oswego County	134	97.6	**Broadalbin** (town) Fulton County
55	98.5	**Sennett** (town) Cayuga County	134	97.6	**Chenango Bridge** (CDP) Broome County
55	98.5	**Southport** (town) Chemung County	134	97.6	**Claverack** (town) Columbia County
55	98.5	**Wales** (town) Erie County	134	97.6	**Conklin** (town) Broome County
55	98.5	**Wellsville** (village) Allegany County	134	97.6	**Cortlandville** (town) Cortland County
65	98.4	**Clayton** (town) Jefferson County	134	97.6	**East Bloomfield** (town) Ontario County
65	98.4	**Gaines** (town) Orleans County	134	97.6	**Floyd** (town) Oneida County
65	98.4	**German Flatts** (town) Herkimer County	134	97.6	**Moreau** (town) Saratoga County
65	98.4	**Saranac** (town) Clinton County	134	97.6	**Ticonderoga** (CDP) Essex County
65	98.4	**Spencerport** (village) Monroe County	144	97.5	**Blasdell** (village) Erie County
65	98.4	**Verona** (town) Oneida County	144	97.5	**Coeymans** (town) Albany County
65	98.4	**Waterloo** (village) Seneca County	144	97.5	**Holland** (town) Erie County
65	98.4	**Windsor** (town) Broome County	144	97.5	**Le Roy** (village) Genesee County
73	98.3	**Camden** (town) Oneida County	144	97.5	**Mechanicville** (city) Saratoga County
73	98.3	**Charlton** (town) Saratoga County	144	97.5	**Mooers** (town) Clinton County
73	98.3	**Le Roy** (town) Genesee County	144	97.5	**Sardinia** (town) Erie County

Note: *This section ranks incorporated places and CDPs (Census Designated Places) with populations of 2,500 or more. Unincorporated postal areas were not considered. Please refer to the User Guide for additional information.*

Speak English Only at Home

Top 150 Places Ranked in *Ascending* Order

State Rank	Percent	Place
1	4.0	**Kaser** (village) Rockland County
2	4.5	**Kiryas Joel** (village) Orange County
3	5.8	**New Square** (village) Rockland County
4	22.7	**Monsey** (CDP) Rockland County
5	29.2	**Brentwood** (CDP) Suffolk County
6	32.9	**Spring Valley** (village) Rockland County
7	34.0	**North Bay Shore** (CDP) Suffolk County
8	35.0	**Haverstraw** (village) Rockland County
9	35.4	**Port Chester** (village) Westchester County
10	36.5	**New Cassel** (CDP) Nassau County
11	39.0	**Monroe** (town) Orange County
12	39.4	**Flanders** (CDP) Suffolk County
13	40.7	**Bronx** (borough) Bronx County
13	40.7	**Sleepy Hollow** (village) Westchester County
15	41.6	**Stony Brook University** (CDP) Suffolk County
16	41.7	**Garden City Park** (CDP) Nassau County
17	44.0	**Queens** (borough) Queens County
18	44.9	**Elmsford** (village) Westchester County
19	45.3	**Bedford Hills** (CDP) Westchester County
20	46.9	**Ossining** (village) Westchester County
21	47.2	**Manhasset Hills** (CDP) Nassau County
22	47.5	**Ramapo** (town) Rockland County
23	48.1	**Rye** (town) Westchester County
24	48.6	**Central Islip** (CDP) Suffolk County
25	48.7	**Great Neck** (village) Nassau County
25	48.7	**West Haverstraw** (village) Rockland County
27	49.5	**Hillcrest** (CDP) Rockland County
28	49.9	**Mount Kisco** (town/village) Westchester County
29	50.1	**Hempstead** (village) Nassau County
30	51.1	**New York** (city)
31	52.2	**Haverstraw** (town) Rockland County
31	52.2	**Herricks** (CDP) Nassau County
33	52.3	**Elmont** (CDP) Nassau County
34	53.1	**Inwood** (CDP) Nassau County
34	53.1	**Yonkers** (city) Westchester County
36	53.2	**Searingtown** (CDP) Nassau County
37	53.4	**Lake Success** (village) Nassau County
38	53.7	**New Hyde Park** (village) Nassau County
39	54.1	**Brooklyn** (borough) Kings County
40	54.3	**Newburgh** (city) Orange County
41	55.1	**Thomaston** (village) Nassau County
42	55.4	**Manorhaven** (village) Nassau County
43	55.8	**North New Hyde Park** (CDP) Nassau County
44	56.3	**Westbury** (village) Nassau County
45	56.5	**Uniondale** (CDP) Nassau County
46	56.6	**White Plains** (city) Westchester County
47	56.9	**Huntington Station** (CDP) Suffolk County
48	57.0	**Roosevelt** (CDP) Nassau County
49	57.6	**Freeport** (village) Nassau County
50	58.1	**Ossining** (town) Westchester County
51	58.4	**Glen Cove** (city) Nassau County
52	59.1	**Viola** (CDP) Rockland County
53	59.2	**University Gardens** (CDP) Nassau County
54	60.0	**Manhattan** (borough) New York County
55	60.1	**New Rochelle** (city) Westchester County
56	60.5	**Copiague** (CDP) Suffolk County
56	60.5	**Franklin Square** (CDP) Nassau County
56	60.5	**Northeast Ithaca** (CDP) Tompkins County
59	60.8	**Roslyn Heights** (CDP) Nassau County
60	61.2	**North Amityville** (CDP) Suffolk County
61	61.3	**Fairview** (CDP) Westchester County
61	61.3	**Mineola** (village) Nassau County
63	61.4	**Kings Point** (village) Nassau County
64	61.7	**Valley Stream** (village) Nassau County
65	61.8	**Mamaroneck** (village) Westchester County
66	61.9	**North Hempstead** (town) Nassau County
67	62.2	**Islandia** (village) Suffolk County
68	62.8	**Hicksville** (CDP) Nassau County
69	62.9	**East Hampton North** (CDP) Suffolk County
70	63.0	**Hartsdale** (CDP) Westchester County
70	63.0	**Middletown** (city) Orange County
70	63.0	**Wyandanch** (CDP) Suffolk County
73	63.1	**Nanuet** (CDP) Rockland County
73	63.1	**Peekskill** (city) Westchester County
75	63.8	**Wappingers Falls** (village) Dutchess County
76	64.1	**North Lindenhurst** (CDP) Suffolk County
77	64.2	**Mount Ivy** (CDP) Rockland County
78	64.3	**Airmont** (village) Rockland County
79	64.4	**Albertson** (CDP) Nassau County
80	64.7	**Jericho** (CDP) Nassau County
80	64.7	**Saint Regis Mohawk Reservation** (reservation) Franklin County
82	64.8	**South Valley Stream** (CDP) Nassau County
83	65.5	**Bay Shore** (CDP) Suffolk County
84	65.6	**Lansing** (village) Tompkins County
85	65.8	**Tuckahoe** (village) Westchester County
86	66.0	**University at Buffalo** (CDP) Erie County
87	66.1	**Great Neck Plaza** (village) Nassau County
87	66.1	**Syosset** (CDP) Nassau County
89	66.8	**North Bellport** (CDP) Suffolk County
89	66.8	**Salisbury** (CDP) Nassau County
91	67.0	**Hewlett** (CDP) Nassau County
92	67.2	**Harriman** (village) Orange County
93	67.4	**New Hempstead** (village) Rockland County
93	67.4	**Patchogue** (village) Suffolk County
95	67.5	**Benton** (town) Yates County
96	67.6	**Ardsley** (village) Westchester County
97	67.8	**Old Westbury** (village) Nassau County
98	67.9	**Islip** (town) Suffolk County
99	68.0	**Valhalla** (CDP) Westchester County
100	68.1	**Carle Place** (CDP) Nassau County
101	68.2	**East Farmingdale** (CDP) Suffolk County
102	68.3	**Hampton Bays** (CDP) Suffolk County
103	68.4	**North Valley Stream** (CDP) Nassau County
104	68.5	**Cedarhurst** (village) Nassau County
105	68.7	**Staten Island** (borough) Richmond County
106	68.8	**Tarrytown** (village) Westchester County
106	68.8	**Vails Gate** (CDP) Orange County
108	69.5	**Greenville** (CDP) Westchester County
108	69.5	**Harrison** (town/village) Westchester County
110	69.6	**Springs** (CDP) Suffolk County
111	70.1	**Binghamton University** (CDP) Broome County
112	70.4	**Mechanicstown** (CDP) Orange County
113	70.5	**Great Neck Estates** (village) Nassau County
113	70.5	**West Hempstead** (CDP) Nassau County
115	70.7	**Mount Pleasant** (town) Westchester County
116	70.8	**Utica** (city) Oneida County
117	71.0	**Baldwin** (CDP) Nassau County
117	71.0	**Thiells** (CDP) Rockland County
119	71.1	**Clarkstown** (town) Rockland County
120	71.2	**Riverhead** (CDP) Suffolk County
121	71.3	**Manhasset** (CDP) Nassau County
121	71.3	**Muttontown** (village) Nassau County
123	71.4	**Baywood** (CDP) Suffolk County
123	71.4	**Rye Brook** (village) Westchester County
125	71.6	**Balmville** (CDP) Orange County
126	71.8	**Mahopac** (CDP) Putnam County
126	71.8	**Mamaroneck** (town) Westchester County
128	71.9	**Greenburgh** (town) Westchester County
129	72.1	**Flower Hill** (village) Nassau County
129	72.1	**Hempstead** (town) Nassau County
131	72.3	**East Meadow** (CDP) Nassau County
132	72.4	**Gordon Heights** (CDP) Suffolk County
133	72.5	**Mastic** (CDP) Suffolk County
133	72.5	**Monroe** (village) Orange County
133	72.5	**Valley Cottage** (CDP) Rockland County
136	72.6	**Island Park** (village) Nassau County
137	72.8	**Amsterdam** (city) Montgomery County
137	72.8	**Ellenville** (village) Ulster County
139	73.0	**Lakeview** (CDP) Nassau County
140	73.1	**Suffern** (village) Rockland County
141	73.2	**Babylon** (town) Suffolk County
141	73.2	**Deer Park** (CDP) Suffolk County
143	73.4	**Glen Head** (CDP) Nassau County
143	73.4	**Pomona** (village) Rockland County
143	73.4	**Wheatley Heights** (CDP) Suffolk County
146	73.5	**Scotchtown** (CDP) Orange County
146	73.5	**South Blooming Grove** (village) Orange County
148	73.6	**East Hampton** (town) Suffolk County
148	73.6	**Nyack** (village) Rockland County
150	73.8	**Chestnut Ridge** (village) Rockland County

Note: This section ranks incorporated places and CDPs (Census Designated Places) with populations of 2,500 or more. Unincorporated postal areas were not considered. Please refer to the User Guide for additional information.

Individuals with a Disability

Top 150 Places Ranked in *Descending* Order

State Rank	Percent	Place	State Rank	Percent	Place
1	25.9	Middleburgh (town) Schoharie County	73	19.2	Riverside (CDP) Suffolk County
2	25.5	Albion (village) Orleans County	73	19.2	Southport (CDP) Chemung County
3	25.2	Liberty (village) Sullivan County	73	19.2	Whitehall (town) Washington County
4	24.2	Oxford (town) Chenango County	79	19.1	Pine Plains (town) Dutchess County
5	24.1	Stockholm (town) Saint Lawrence County	80	19.0	Massena (village) Saint Lawrence County
6	23.3	New Berlin (town) Chenango County	80	19.0	Sheridan (town) Chautauqua County
7	23.1	Catskill (village) Greene County	82	18.9	Arcadia (town) Wayne County
8	22.9	Mohawk (village) Herkimer County	82	18.9	Athens (town) Greene County
9	22.7	Lake Luzerne (town) Warren County	82	18.9	Liberty (town) Sullivan County
9	22.7	Mooers (town) Clinton County	82	18.9	Malone (village) Franklin County
11	22.6	Corinth (village) Saratoga County	86	18.6	Saint Regis Mohawk Reservation (reservation) Franklin County
12	22.5	Newark (village) Wayne County	86	18.6	Sherburne (town) Chenango County
13	22.4	Bath (village) Steuben County	86	18.6	Waverly (village) Tioga County
14	22.1	Albion (town) Orleans County	89	18.4	Bergen (town) Genesee County
15	21.9	Copake (town) Columbia County	89	18.4	Lisle (town) Broome County
15	21.9	Wellsville (village) Allegany County	89	18.4	Utica (city) Oneida County
17	21.8	Keeseville (village) Clinton County	92	18.3	Hanover (town) Chautauqua County
17	21.8	Medina (village) Orleans County	92	18.3	Sandy Creek (town) Oswego County
19	21.6	Carthage (village) Jefferson County	94	18.2	Cobleskill (village) Schoharie County
20	21.5	Gaines (town) Orleans County	94	18.2	Greenport (town) Columbia County
20	21.5	Lyons (village) Wayne County	94	18.2	Penn Yan (village) Yates County
20	21.5	Moriah (town) Essex County	97	18.1	Alden (village) Erie County
23	21.4	Collins (town) Erie County	97	18.1	Elmira (city) Chemung County
23	21.4	Herkimer (town) Herkimer County	97	18.1	Endicott (village) Broome County
25	21.3	Altona (town) Clinton County	100	18.0	Amenia (town) Dutchess County
25	21.3	Ticonderoga (CDP) Essex County	100	18.0	Canisteo (town) Steuben County
27	21.2	Fort Edward (village) Washington County	100	18.0	Shelby (town) Orleans County
27	21.2	Ticonderoga (town) Essex County	100	18.0	Sidney (town) Delaware County
29	21.1	Kirkwood (town) Broome County	100	18.0	Whitesboro (village) Oneida County
29	21.1	Livingston (town) Columbia County	105	17.9	Campbell (town) Steuben County
31	21.0	Fallsburg (town) Sullivan County	105	17.9	Manchester (town) Ontario County
32	20.9	Herkimer (village) Herkimer County	105	17.9	Rochester (city) Monroe County
33	20.8	Shandaken (town) Ulster County	108	17.8	Beekmantown (town) Clinton County
34	20.7	Castile (town) Wyoming County	108	17.8	Mechanicstown (CDP) Orange County
34	20.7	Champion (town) Jefferson County	108	17.8	Montauk (CDP) Suffolk County
34	20.7	Yorkshire (town) Cattaraugus County	108	17.8	Port Jervis (city) Orange County
37	20.6	Monticello (village) Sullivan County	108	17.8	Silver Creek (village) Chautauqua County
38	20.5	Jamestown (city) Chautauqua County	108	17.8	Vails Gate (CDP) Orange County
39	20.3	Afton (town) Chenango County	114	17.7	Carroll (town) Chautauqua County
39	20.3	Binghamton (city) Broome County	114	17.7	Mount Morris (town) Livingston County
39	20.3	Fort Edward (town) Washington County	116	17.6	Cohoes (city) Albany County
39	20.3	Hannibal (town) Oswego County	116	17.6	Fulton (city) Oswego County
39	20.3	Little Falls (city) Herkimer County	116	17.6	Guilford (town) Chenango County
44	20.2	Hoosick Falls (village) Rensselaer County	116	17.6	Hancock (town) Delaware County
44	20.2	Wayland (town) Steuben County	116	17.6	Hornell (city) Steuben County
44	20.2	Wellsville (town) Allegany County	116	17.6	Verona (town) Oneida County
47	20.1	Catskill (town) Greene County	116	17.6	Watervliet (city) Albany County
48	20.0	Au Sable (town) Clinton County	123	17.5	Lackawanna (city) Erie County
48	20.0	Middletown (town) Delaware County	123	17.5	North Gates (CDP) Monroe County
48	20.0	Norwich (city) Chenango County	123	17.5	North Syracuse (village) Onondaga County
51	19.9	Amsterdam (city) Montgomery County	126	17.4	Dix (town) Schuyler County
51	19.9	Colesville (town) Broome County	126	17.4	Perry (village) Wyoming County
51	19.9	Dannemora (village) Clinton County	126	17.4	Richland (town) Oswego County
51	19.9	Norwich (town) Chenango County	126	17.4	Southport (town) Chemung County
51	19.9	Plattekill (town) Ulster County	126	17.4	Tonawanda (city) Erie County
51	19.9	Waterloo (town) Seneca County	131	17.3	Brasher (town) Saint Lawrence County
51	19.9	Whitehall (village) Washington County	131	17.3	Croghan (town) Lewis County
58	19.8	Corinth (town) Saratoga County	131	17.3	Floyd (town) Oneida County
58	19.8	Deerpark (town) Orange County	131	17.3	Johnstown (city) Fulton County
58	19.8	Dunkirk (city) Chautauqua County	131	17.3	Johnstown (town) Fulton County
58	19.8	Wappingers Falls (village) Dutchess County	131	17.3	Portland (town) Chautauqua County
62	19.7	Hornellsville (town) Steuben County	131	17.3	Ridge (CDP) Suffolk County
62	19.7	Ridgeway (town) Orleans County	131	17.3	Schroeppel (town) Oswego County
64	19.6	Claverack (town) Columbia County	131	17.3	Warwick (village) Orange County
65	19.5	Dover (town) Dutchess County	140	17.2	Mount Morris (village) Livingston County
65	19.5	Gowanda (village) Cattaraugus County	140	17.2	Wilna (town) Jefferson County
67	19.4	Massena (town) Saint Lawrence County	142	17.1	Brownville (town) Jefferson County
67	19.4	Tioga (town) Tioga County	142	17.1	Hudson (city) Columbia County
69	19.3	Heritage Hills (CDP) Westchester County	142	17.1	Nassau (town) Rensselaer County
69	19.3	Louisville (town) Saint Lawrence County	142	17.1	North Tonawanda (city) Niagara County
69	19.3	Lyons (town) Wayne County	146	17.0	Barker (town) Broome County
69	19.3	Wolcott (town) Wayne County	146	17.0	Camden (town) Oneida County
73	19.2	Bath (town) Steuben County	146	17.0	Elmira Heights (village) Chemung County
73	19.2	Gloversville (city) Fulton County	146	17.0	Milo (town) Yates County
73	19.2	Ogdensburg (city) Saint Lawrence County	146	17.0	Minisink (town) Orange County

Note: *This section ranks incorporated places and CDPs (Census Designated Places) with populations of 2,500 or more. Unincorporated postal areas were not considered. Please refer to the User Guide for additional information.*

Individuals with a Disability

Top 150 Places Ranked in *Ascending* Order

State Rank	Percent	Place		State Rank	Percent	Place
1	2.7	**New Square** (village) Rockland County		74	6.7	**Mamaroneck** (town) Westchester County
2	2.9	**Kiryas Joel** (village) Orange County		74	6.7	**Monroe** (town) Orange County
2	2.9	**Larchmont** (village) Westchester County		74	6.7	**South Valley Stream** (CDP) Nassau County
4	3.0	**Lansing** (village) Tompkins County		74	6.7	**Syosset** (CDP) Nassau County
5	3.3	**Calcium** (CDP) Jefferson County		74	6.7	**Thomaston** (village) Nassau County
5	3.3	**Clarence Center** (CDP) Erie County		81	6.8	**Canton** (village) Saint Lawrence County
7	3.4	**Alfred** (village) Allegany County		81	6.8	**Hamilton** (village) Madison County
7	3.4	**Kaser** (village) Rockland County		81	6.8	**Pleasantville** (village) Westchester County
9	3.6	**University at Buffalo** (CDP) Erie County		81	6.8	**Roosevelt** (CDP) Nassau County
10	3.8	**Greenville** (CDP) Westchester County		85	6.9	**Garden City** (village) Nassau County
10	3.8	**West Point** (CDP) Orange County		85	6.9	**Huntington** (CDP) Suffolk County
12	3.9	**Pelham Manor** (village) Westchester County		85	6.9	**Jericho** (CDP) Nassau County
13	4.0	**Alfred** (town) Allegany County		85	6.9	**New Cassel** (CDP) Nassau County
13	4.0	**Stony Brook University** (CDP) Suffolk County		89	7.0	**Hastings-on-Hudson** (village) Westchester County
15	4.2	**SUNY Oswego** (CDP) Oswego County		89	7.0	**Lake Success** (village) Nassau County
16	4.3	**Munsey Park** (village) Nassau County		89	7.0	**Lansing** (town) Tompkins County
17	4.4	**East Williston** (village) Nassau County		89	7.0	**North Boston** (CDP) Erie County
18	4.5	**Old Westbury** (village) Nassau County		89	7.0	**Piermont** (village) Rockland County
19	4.6	**Binghamton University** (CDP) Broome County		94	7.1	**Crown Heights** (CDP) Dutchess County
19	4.6	**Pelham** (town) Westchester County		94	7.1	**LaFayette** (town) Onondaga County
21	4.7	**New Hempstead** (village) Rockland County		94	7.1	**Pound Ridge** (town) Westchester County
22	4.8	**Northeast Ithaca** (CDP) Tompkins County		97	7.2	**Baldwin** (CDP) Nassau County
23	4.9	**Manhasset** (CDP) Nassau County		97	7.2	**Benton** (town) Yates County
24	5.0	**Halesite** (CDP) Suffolk County		97	7.2	**East Norwich** (CDP) Nassau County
25	5.1	**Glenwood Landing** (CDP) Nassau County		97	7.2	**Franklin Square** (CDP) Nassau County
25	5.1	**Thornwood** (CDP) Westchester County		97	7.2	**Greenville** (town) Greene County
27	5.2	**Fort Drum** (CDP) Jefferson County		97	7.2	**Ithaca** (town) Tompkins County
28	5.3	**Cedarhurst** (village) Nassau County		97	7.2	**Mamaroneck** (village) Westchester County
28	5.3	**Lawrence** (village) Nassau County		97	7.2	**Manhasset Hills** (CDP) Nassau County
28	5.3	**Muttontown** (village) Nassau County		105	7.3	**Huntington Station** (CDP) Suffolk County
28	5.3	**Pelham** (village) Westchester County		105	7.3	**Pomona** (village) Rockland County
28	5.3	**Scarsdale** (town/village) Westchester County		105	7.3	**Spring Valley** (village) Rockland County
33	5.4	**Flanders** (CDP) Suffolk County		108	7.4	**Dobbs Ferry** (village) Westchester County
33	5.4	**Great Neck Estates** (village) Nassau County		108	7.4	**Kings Point** (village) Nassau County
33	5.4	**Hunter** (town) Greene County		110	7.5	**Briarcliff Manor** (village) Westchester County
33	5.4	**Manorhaven** (village) Nassau County		110	7.5	**Clifton Park** (town) Saratoga County
37	5.5	**New Castle** (town) Westchester County		110	7.5	**Cornwall-on-Hudson** (village) Orange County
38	5.6	**Bedford Hills** (CDP) Westchester County		110	7.5	**East Hills** (village) Nassau County
38	5.6	**North Great River** (CDP) Suffolk County		110	7.5	**Elmont** (CDP) Nassau County
40	5.7	**Glen Head** (CDP) Nassau County		110	7.5	**South Farmingdale** (CDP) Nassau County
40	5.7	**Monsey** (CDP) Rockland County		110	7.5	**Uniondale** (CDP) Nassau County
40	5.7	**North Castle** (town) Westchester County		117	7.6	**Center Moriches** (CDP) Suffolk County
40	5.7	**West Hills** (CDP) Suffolk County		117	7.6	**Grandyle Village** (CDP) Erie County
44	5.8	**University Gardens** (CDP) Nassau County		117	7.6	**Great Neck** (village) Nassau County
45	5.9	**Ithaca** (city) Tompkins County		117	7.6	**Greenburgh** (town) Westchester County
45	5.9	**North Salem** (town) Westchester County		117	7.6	**Hewlett** (CDP) Nassau County
45	5.9	**Springs** (CDP) Suffolk County		117	7.6	**Manorville** (CDP) Suffolk County
45	5.9	**West Sand Lake** (CDP) Rensselaer County		117	7.6	**Merrick** (CDP) Nassau County
49	6.0	**Brookville** (village) Nassau County		117	7.6	**Port Jefferson** (village) Suffolk County
49	6.0	**Fairview** (CDP) Westchester County		125	7.7	**Fort Salonga** (CDP) Suffolk County
51	6.1	**Armonk** (CDP) Westchester County		125	7.7	**Hartsdale** (CDP) Westchester County
51	6.1	**East Islip** (CDP) Suffolk County		125	7.7	**Huntington** (town) Suffolk County
51	6.1	**Hempstead** (village) Nassau County		125	7.7	**Moriches** (CDP) Suffolk County
54	6.2	**Blue Point** (CDP) Suffolk County		125	7.7	**North Hempstead** (town) Nassau County
54	6.2	**Centerport** (CDP) Suffolk County		125	7.7	**Otsego** (town) Otsego County
54	6.2	**Flower Hill** (village) Nassau County		131	7.8	**Attica** (village) Wyoming County
54	6.2	**Irvington** (village) Westchester County		131	7.8	**New Hyde Park** (village) Nassau County
54	6.2	**Lloyd Harbor** (village) Suffolk County		131	7.8	**Poestenkill** (town) Rensselaer County
59	6.3	**Lewisboro** (town) Westchester County		131	7.8	**Ramapo** (town) Rockland County
60	6.4	**Mineola** (village) Nassau County		131	7.8	**Wantagh** (CDP) Nassau County
60	6.4	**South Hill** (CDP) Tompkins County		131	7.8	**West Hempstead** (CDP) Nassau County
60	6.4	**Wesley Hills** (village) Rockland County		137	7.9	**Floral Park** (village) Nassau County
60	6.4	**West Nyack** (CDP) Rockland County		137	7.9	**Freeport** (village) Nassau County
64	6.5	**Bedford** (town) Westchester County		137	7.9	**Nesconset** (CDP) Suffolk County
64	6.5	**Cold Spring Harbor** (CDP) Suffolk County		137	7.9	**Noyack** (CDP) Suffolk County
64	6.5	**Islandia** (village) Suffolk County		137	7.9	**Setauket-East Setauket** (CDP) Suffolk County
64	6.5	**Le Ray** (town) Jefferson County		137	7.9	**Shawangunk** (town) Ulster County
64	6.5	**Sands Point** (village) Nassau County		137	7.9	**Woodmere** (CDP) Nassau County
69	6.6	**Bronxville** (village) Westchester County		144	8.0	**Greenlawn** (CDP) Suffolk County
69	6.6	**East Shoreham** (CDP) Suffolk County		144	8.0	**Greenwich** (town) Washington County
69	6.6	**Islip Terrace** (CDP) Suffolk County		144	8.0	**Lake Grove** (village) Suffolk County
69	6.6	**North Merrick** (CDP) Nassau County		144	8.0	**Mount Ivy** (CDP) Rockland County
69	6.6	**South Hempstead** (CDP) Nassau County		144	8.0	**New Scotland** (town) Albany County
74	6.7	**Croton-on-Hudson** (village) Westchester County		144	8.0	**Northport** (village) Suffolk County
74	6.7	**Dix Hills** (CDP) Suffolk County		144	8.0	**Orchard Park** (village) Erie County

Note: This section ranks incorporated places and CDPs (Census Designated Places) with populations of 2,500 or more. Unincorporated postal areas were not considered. Please refer to the User Guide for additional information.

Veterans

Top 150 Places Ranked in *Descending* Order

State Rank	Percent	Place
1	50.1	**West Point** (CDP) Orange County
2	21.4	**Highlands** (town) Orange County
3	20.4	**Champion** (town) Jefferson County
4	19.9	**Pamelia** (town) Jefferson County
5	18.9	**Rutland** (town) Jefferson County
6	18.8	**Shelter Island** (town) Suffolk County
7	18.6	**Theresa** (town) Jefferson County
8	18.4	**Le Ray** (town) Jefferson County
9	16.5	**Fort Drum** (CDP) Jefferson County
10	16.4	**Calcium** (CDP) Jefferson County
11	15.6	**Bath** (village) Steuben County
12	15.3	**Adams** (town) Jefferson County
12	15.3	**Volney** (town) Oswego County
14	15.1	**Bath** (town) Steuben County
15	14.9	**Ticonderoga** (CDP) Essex County
16	14.7	**Franklinville** (town) Cattaraugus County
17	14.6	**West Bloomfield** (town) Ontario County
18	14.4	**Orleans** (town) Jefferson County
19	14.2	**Cuba** (town) Allegany County
19	14.2	**Hornellsville** (town) Steuben County
21	14.0	**Scriba** (town) Oswego County
22	13.9	**Hounsfield** (town) Jefferson County
23	13.7	**Au Sable** (town) Clinton County
23	13.7	**Campbell** (town) Steuben County
23	13.7	**Elma Center** (CDP) Erie County
26	13.6	**Beekmantown** (town) Clinton County
26	13.6	**Heritage Hills** (CDP) Westchester County
28	13.5	**Candor** (town) Tioga County
29	13.3	**Watertown** (city) Jefferson County
30	13.2	**Calverton** (CDP) Suffolk County
30	13.2	**Oxford** (town) Chenango County
32	13.1	**Cornwall-on-Hudson** (village) Orange County
33	13.0	**Wilna** (town) Jefferson County
34	12.9	**Perry** (village) Wyoming County
35	12.8	**Ticonderoga** (town) Essex County
35	12.8	**Warwick** (village) Orange County
37	12.7	**Corning** (town) Steuben County
37	12.7	**Veteran** (town) Chemung County
39	12.6	**Brutus** (town) Cayuga County
39	12.6	**Colesville** (town) Broome County
39	12.6	**Gouverneur** (village) Saint Lawrence County
39	12.6	**Middleburgh** (town) Schoharie County
39	12.6	**Village Green** (CDP) Onondaga County
44	12.5	**Sterling** (town) Cayuga County
44	12.5	**West Glens Falls** (CDP) Warren County
46	12.4	**Carthage** (village) Jefferson County
46	12.4	**Chesterfield** (town) Essex County
46	12.4	**Mechanicville** (city) Saratoga County
46	12.4	**New York Mills** (village) Oneida County
50	12.3	**Brownville** (town) Jefferson County
50	12.3	**Corinth** (town) Saratoga County
50	12.3	**Hamlin** (CDP) Monroe County
50	12.3	**Manchester** (town) Ontario County
50	12.3	**Vienna** (town) Oneida County
55	12.2	**Gaines** (town) Orleans County
55	12.2	**Nichols** (town) Tioga County
57	12.1	**Carroll** (town) Chautauqua County
57	12.1	**Corinth** (village) Saratoga County
57	12.1	**Portville** (town) Cattaraugus County
57	12.1	**Ridgeway** (town) Orleans County
57	12.1	**Stockholm** (town) Saint Lawrence County
62	12.0	**New Berlin** (town) Chenango County
63	11.9	**Hornell** (city) Steuben County
63	11.9	**Phelps** (town) Ontario County
63	11.9	**Yorkshire** (town) Cattaraugus County
66	11.8	**Herkimer** (town) Herkimer County
66	11.8	**Manheim** (town) Herkimer County
68	11.7	**Batavia** (town) Genesee County
68	11.7	**Perry** (town) Wyoming County
68	11.7	**Springville** (village) Erie County
71	11.6	**Milford** (town) Otsego County
71	11.6	**Saratoga** (town) Saratoga County
71	11.6	**Somerset** (town) Niagara County
71	11.6	**Tioga** (town) Tioga County
75	11.5	**Annsville** (town) Oneida County
75	11.5	**Firthcliffe** (CDP) Orange County
75	11.5	**Neversink** (town) Sullivan County
75	11.5	**Oswegatchie** (town) Saint Lawrence County
79	11.4	**Greenwich** (town) Washington County
79	11.4	**Newark Valley** (town) Tioga County
79	11.4	**Southport** (CDP) Chemung County
79	11.4	**West Monroe** (town) Oswego County
83	11.3	**Camden** (town) Oneida County
83	11.3	**Concord** (town) Erie County
83	11.3	**Dix** (town) Schuyler County
83	11.3	**Ellery** (town) Chautauqua County
83	11.3	**Herkimer** (village) Herkimer County
88	11.2	**Boonville** (town) Oneida County
88	11.2	**Fayette** (town) Seneca County
88	11.2	**Lee** (town) Oneida County
88	11.2	**Whitestown** (town) Oneida County
92	11.1	**Bainbridge** (town) Chenango County
92	11.1	**Elma** (town) Erie County
92	11.1	**Tully** (town) Onondaga County
95	11.0	**Claverack** (town) Columbia County
95	11.0	**Hamlin** (town) Monroe County
95	11.0	**Hanover** (town) Chautauqua County
95	11.0	**Madison** (town) Madison County
95	11.0	**Palermo** (town) Oswego County
95	11.0	**Rome** (city) Oneida County
95	11.0	**Trenton** (town) Oneida County
102	10.9	**Castile** (town) Wyoming County
102	10.9	**Chazy** (town) Clinton County
102	10.9	**Duanesburg** (town) Schenectady County
102	10.9	**East Greenbush** (CDP) Rensselaer County
102	10.9	**Keeseville** (village) Clinton County
102	10.9	**Norwich** (town) Chenango County
102	10.9	**Peru** (town) Clinton County
102	10.9	**Richland** (town) Oswego County
102	10.9	**Saint Johnsville** (town) Montgomery County
102	10.9	**Southport** (town) Chemung County
102	10.9	**Waverly** (village) Tioga County
113	10.8	**Broadalbin** (town) Fulton County
113	10.8	**East Glenville** (CDP) Schenectady County
113	10.8	**Guilford** (town) Chenango County
113	10.8	**Hudson Falls** (village) Washington County
113	10.8	**Kingsbury** (town) Washington County
113	10.8	**Marilla** (town) Erie County
113	10.8	**Wellsville** (town) Allegany County
120	10.7	**Galway** (town) Saratoga County
120	10.7	**Geneva** (town) Ontario County
120	10.7	**Greenville** (town) Greene County
120	10.7	**Harrietstown** (town) Franklin County
120	10.7	**Oneida** (city) Madison County
120	10.7	**Stanford** (town) Dutchess County
120	10.7	**Stockport** (town) Columbia County
120	10.7	**Walton** (village) Delaware County
120	10.7	**Wanakah** (CDP) Erie County
129	10.6	**Afton** (town) Chenango County
129	10.6	**Clayton** (town) Jefferson County
129	10.6	**Cornwall** (town) Orange County
129	10.6	**Eden** (CDP) Erie County
129	10.6	**Lisbon** (town) Saint Lawrence County
129	10.6	**Norfolk** (town) Saint Lawrence County
129	10.6	**Sandy Creek** (town) Oswego County
129	10.6	**Wayland** (town) Steuben County
137	10.5	**Deerpark** (town) Orange County
137	10.5	**Elmira** (town) Chemung County
137	10.5	**Highland Falls** (village) Orange County
137	10.5	**Hoosick** (town) Rensselaer County
137	10.5	**Medina** (village) Orleans County
137	10.5	**Milton** (CDP) Saratoga County
137	10.5	**Sennett** (town) Cayuga County
137	10.5	**Sullivan** (town) Madison County
137	10.5	**Tonawanda** (city) Erie County
137	10.5	**Wheatfield** (town) Niagara County
147	10.4	**Catskill** (village) Greene County
147	10.4	**Ellisburg** (town) Jefferson County
147	10.4	**Hastings** (town) Oswego County
147	10.4	**New Baltimore** (town) Greene County

Note: *This section ranks incorporated places and CDPs (Census Designated Places) with populations of 2,500 or more. Unincorporated postal areas were not considered. Please refer to the User Guide for additional information.*

Veterans

Top 150 Places Ranked in *Ascending* Order

State Rank	Percent	Place	State Rank	Percent	Place
1	0.0	Binghamton University (CDP) Broome County	70	3.3	Nesconset (CDP) Suffolk County
1	0.0	SUNY Oswego (CDP) Oswego County	70	3.3	Scarsdale (town/village) Westchester County
3	0.3	Kaser (village) Rockland County	78	3.4	Bardonia (CDP) Rockland County
3	0.3	University at Buffalo (CDP) Erie County	78	3.4	Bedford Hills (CDP) Westchester County
5	0.4	New Square (village) Rockland County	78	3.4	Delhi (village) Delaware County
6	0.5	Alfred (village) Allegany County	78	3.4	Ellenville (village) Ulster County
6	0.5	Kiryas Joel (village) Orange County	78	3.4	Kings Point (village) Nassau County
8	0.7	Monsey (CDP) Rockland County	78	3.4	Mamaroneck (town) Westchester County
9	1.4	Hamilton (village) Madison County	78	3.4	Newburgh (city) Orange County
9	1.4	Old Westbury (village) Nassau County	85	3.5	Brentwood (CDP) Suffolk County
11	1.6	Greenville (CDP) Westchester County	85	3.5	Caroline (town) Tompkins County
12	1.7	Alfred (town) Allegany County	85	3.5	Flower Hill (village) Nassau County
12	1.7	New Cassel (CDP) Nassau County	85	3.5	Manorhaven (village) Nassau County
14	1.8	Brookville (village) Nassau County	85	3.5	Patchogue (village) Suffolk County
14	1.8	Ithaca (city) Tompkins County	85	3.5	South Valley Stream (CDP) Nassau County
14	1.8	Spring Valley (village) Rockland County	85	3.5	Valhalla (CDP) Westchester County
17	1.9	Fairview (CDP) Westchester County	85	3.5	White Plains (city) Westchester County
17	1.9	Hartsdale (CDP) Westchester County	93	3.6	Harriman (village) Orange County
17	1.9	New Hyde Park (village) Nassau County	93	3.6	Hillcrest (CDP) Rockland County
20	2.0	Brooklyn (borough) Kings County	93	3.6	Ithaca (town) Tompkins County
21	2.1	Flanders (CDP) Suffolk County	93	3.6	Mamaroneck (village) Westchester County
21	2.1	Great Neck Estates (village) Nassau County	93	3.6	New Castle (town) Westchester County
21	2.1	Muttontown (village) Nassau County	93	3.6	Port Washington North (village) Nassau County
21	2.1	Viola (CDP) Rockland County	93	3.6	Uniondale (CDP) Nassau County
25	2.2	Geneseo (village) Livingston County	93	3.6	Westbury (village) Nassau County
25	2.2	Lawrence (village) Nassau County	101	3.7	Copiague (CDP) Suffolk County
25	2.2	Sands Point (village) Nassau County	101	3.7	Eaton (town) Madison County
28	2.3	Manhattan (borough) New York County	101	3.7	Huntington Station (CDP) Suffolk County
28	2.3	Mount Ivy (CDP) Rockland County	101	3.7	Larchmont (village) Westchester County
28	2.3	New Paltz (village) Ulster County	101	3.7	Merrick (CDP) Nassau County
28	2.3	Roosevelt (CDP) Nassau County	101	3.7	Yonkers (city) Westchester County
32	2.4	Elmont (CDP) Nassau County	107	3.8	Cedarhurst (village) Nassau County
32	2.4	New York (city)	107	3.8	East Farmingdale (CDP) Suffolk County
32	2.4	Port Chester (village) Westchester County	107	3.8	Great Neck Plaza (village) Nassau County
32	2.4	Queens (borough) Queens County	107	3.8	Greenburgh (town) Westchester County
32	2.4	Wesley Hills (village) Rockland County	107	3.8	Hamilton (town) Madison County
37	2.5	Bronx (borough) Bronx County	107	3.8	Haverstraw (town) Rockland County
37	2.5	Thomaston (village) Nassau County	107	3.8	Haverstraw (village) Rockland County
39	2.6	Clarence Center (CDP) Erie County	107	3.8	Mount Kisco (town/village) Westchester County
39	2.6	Inwood (CDP) Nassau County	107	3.8	Nanuet (CDP) Rockland County
41	2.7	Munsey Park (village) Nassau County	107	3.8	North Hempstead (town) Nassau County
41	2.7	Woodmere (CDP) Nassau County	107	3.8	Pleasantville (village) Westchester County
43	2.8	Jericho (CDP) Nassau County	107	3.8	South Nyack (village) Rockland County
43	2.8	New Hempstead (village) Rockland County	107	3.8	Syosset (CDP) Nassau County
45	2.9	East Williston (village) Nassau County	120	3.9	Canton (village) Saint Lawrence County
45	2.9	Harrison (town/village) Westchester County	120	3.9	Fairview (CDP) Dutchess County
45	2.9	Manhasset Hills (CDP) Nassau County	120	3.9	Monroe (town) Orange County
45	2.9	North Bay Shore (CDP) Suffolk County	120	3.9	Munsons Corners (CDP) Cortland County
45	2.9	South Hill (CDP) Tompkins County	120	3.9	New Rochelle (city) Westchester County
45	2.9	University Gardens (CDP) Nassau County	120	3.9	Sea Cliff (village) Nassau County
51	3.0	Ardsley (village) Westchester County	126	4.0	Centerport (CDP) Suffolk County
51	3.0	Great Neck (village) Nassau County	126	4.0	Mount Pleasant (town) Westchester County
51	3.0	Hempstead (village) Nassau County	126	4.0	North Boston (CDP) Erie County
51	3.0	Ramapo (town) Rockland County	126	4.0	Ossining (town) Westchester County
55	3.1	East Hampton North (CDP) Suffolk County	126	4.0	Pelham Manor (village) Westchester County
55	3.1	Elmsford (village) Westchester County	126	4.0	Roslyn (village) Nassau County
55	3.1	Lake Mohegan (CDP) Westchester County	126	4.0	Salisbury (CDP) Nassau County
55	3.1	North Amityville (CDP) Suffolk County	126	4.0	Stony Brook University (CDP) Suffolk County
55	3.1	Rye (town) Westchester County	134	4.1	Bay Shore (CDP) Suffolk County
55	3.1	Sleepy Hollow (village) Westchester County	134	4.1	Central Islip (CDP) Suffolk County
61	3.2	Dix Hills (CDP) Suffolk County	134	4.1	Oswego (town) Oswego County
61	3.2	Mahopac (CDP) Putnam County	134	4.1	Tarrytown (village) Westchester County
61	3.2	Mineola (village) Nassau County	134	4.1	Wheatley Heights (CDP) Suffolk County
61	3.2	Mount Vernon (city) Westchester County	139	4.2	Albany (city) Albany County
61	3.2	New Paltz (town) Ulster County	139	4.2	Bedford (town) Westchester County
61	3.2	Nyack (village) Rockland County	139	4.2	Dannemora (village) Clinton County
61	3.2	Ossining (village) Westchester County	139	4.2	Herricks (CDP) Nassau County
61	3.2	Potsdam (village) Saint Lawrence County	139	4.2	Putnam Valley (town) Putnam County
61	3.2	Roslyn Heights (CDP) Nassau County	139	4.2	Rochester (city) Monroe County
70	3.3	Baldwin (CDP) Nassau County	145	4.3	Baldwin Harbor (CDP) Nassau County
70	3.3	Bronxville (village) Westchester County	145	4.3	Cayuga Heights (village) Tompkins County
70	3.3	Freeport (village) Nassau County	145	4.3	Clarkstown (town) Rockland County
70	3.3	Gordon Heights (CDP) Suffolk County	145	4.3	East Hills (village) Nassau County
70	3.3	Lakeview (CDP) Nassau County	145	4.3	Garden City Park (CDP) Nassau County
70	3.3	Montebello (village) Rockland County	145	4.3	Mastic (CDP) Suffolk County

Note: This section ranks incorporated places and CDPs (Census Designated Places) with populations of 2,500 or more. Unincorporated postal areas were not considered. Please refer to the User Guide for additional information.

Ancestry: German

Top 150 Places Ranked in *Descending* Order

State Rank	Percent	Place
1	49.1	**Sardinia** (town) Erie County
2	48.3	**Alden** (village) Erie County
3	45.0	**Marilla** (town) Erie County
4	44.7	**Alexander** (town) Genesee County
5	42.7	**Colden** (town) Erie County
6	41.7	**Holland** (town) Erie County
7	41.4	**Akron** (village) Erie County
8	41.0	**Bennington** (town) Wyoming County
8	41.0	**Eden** (town) Erie County
8	41.0	**North Collins** (town) Erie County
11	40.7	**Boston** (town) Erie County
12	40.3	**East Aurora** (village) Erie County
12	40.3	**Wales** (town) Erie County
14	39.8	**Clarence** (CDP) Erie County
14	39.8	**Lancaster** (village) Erie County
16	39.2	**Arcade** (town) Wyoming County
16	39.2	**Blasdell** (village) Erie County
16	39.2	**Newstead** (town) Erie County
19	39.1	**Alden** (town) Erie County
19	39.1	**Hartland** (town) Niagara County
21	39.0	**Tonawanda** (city) Erie County
22	38.3	**New Bremen** (town) Lewis County
23	38.0	**Oakfield** (town) Genesee County
24	37.9	**Yorkshire** (town) Cattaraugus County
25	37.6	**Aurora** (town) Erie County
25	37.6	**Hancock** (town) Delaware County
27	37.4	**Darien** (town) Genesee County
28	37.3	**Pembroke** (town) Genesee County
29	37.2	**Claverack** (town) Columbia County
29	37.2	**Concord** (town) Erie County
29	37.2	**Silver Creek** (village) Chautauqua County
32	37.1	**Portville** (town) Cattaraugus County
33	36.9	**Franklinville** (town) Cattaraugus County
34	36.6	**East Bloomfield** (town) Ontario County
34	36.6	**Hanover** (town) Chautauqua County
34	36.6	**Warsaw** (town) Wyoming County
37	36.4	**Croghan** (town) Lewis County
38	36.1	**Wanakah** (CDP) Erie County
39	35.9	**Wayland** (town) Steuben County
40	35.8	**Pendleton** (town) Niagara County
41	35.5	**Elma Center** (CDP) Erie County
42	35.4	**Middleburgh** (town) Schoharie County
43	35.3	**Attica** (village) Wyoming County
44	35.2	**Dansville** (village) Livingston County
44	35.2	**Warsaw** (village) Wyoming County
46	35.0	**Hamlin** (CDP) Monroe County
47	34.8	**Springville** (village) Erie County
48	34.3	**Hamburg** (village) Erie County
49	34.1	**Collins** (town) Erie County
50	34.0	**Delaware** (town) Sullivan County
50	34.0	**Gowanda** (village) Cattaraugus County
52	33.9	**Richmond** (town) Ontario County
53	33.8	**Harris Hill** (CDP) Erie County
54	33.6	**Eden** (CDP) Erie County
54	33.6	**Le Roy** (village) Genesee County
56	33.5	**North Dansville** (town) Livingston County
57	33.4	**Lancaster** (town) Erie County
57	33.4	**Naples** (town) Ontario County
59	33.3	**Depew** (village) Erie County
60	33.2	**North Tonawanda** (city) Niagara County
60	33.2	**Perry** (town) Wyoming County
62	33.1	**Hamlin** (town) Monroe County
63	32.9	**Newfane** (town) Niagara County
64	32.8	**Lima** (town) Livingston County
65	32.7	**Evans** (town) Erie County
66	32.5	**Westfield** (town) Chautauqua County
67	32.4	**Batavia** (town) Genesee County
67	32.4	**Cambria** (town) Niagara County
69	32.3	**Elma** (town) Erie County
69	32.3	**Lake Erie Beach** (CDP) Erie County
69	32.3	**Newfane** (CDP) Niagara County
72	32.1	**Hamburg** (town) Erie County
73	32.0	**Lockport** (town) Niagara County
73	32.0	**Royalton** (town) Niagara County
75	31.9	**Pavilion** (town) Genesee County
75	31.9	**West Seneca** (CDP) Erie County
77	31.3	**Allegany** (town) Cattaraugus County
77	31.3	**Clarence** (town) Erie County
79	31.1	**Rush** (town) Monroe County
80	31.0	**Kendall** (town) Orleans County
81	30.9	**Westfield** (village) Chautauqua County
82	30.8	**Cato** (town) Cayuga County
83	30.7	**Lockport** (city) Niagara County
84	30.6	**Westerlo** (town) Albany County
85	30.5	**Orchard Park** (town) Erie County
86	30.3	**Cohocton** (town) Steuben County
86	30.3	**Orchard Park** (village) Erie County
86	30.3	**Tonawanda** (CDP) Erie County
89	30.1	**Caledonia** (town) Livingston County
89	30.1	**Nunda** (town) Livingston County
89	30.1	**SUNY Oswego** (CDP) Oswego County
89	30.1	**Southold** (CDP) Suffolk County
89	30.1	**Tonawanda** (town) Erie County
94	30.0	**Spencerport** (village) Monroe County
95	29.9	**Livonia** (town) Livingston County
96	29.8	**Clarkson** (town) Monroe County
96	29.8	**Schoharie** (town) Schoharie County
96	29.8	**Shelby** (town) Orleans County
99	29.7	**Clarendon** (town) Orleans County
99	29.7	**Riga** (town) Monroe County
99	29.7	**Rockland** (town) Sullivan County
102	29.6	**Benton** (town) Yates County
102	29.6	**Big Flats** (CDP) Chemung County
102	29.6	**Blue Point** (CDP) Suffolk County
102	29.6	**Hilton** (village) Monroe County
102	29.6	**Parma** (town) Monroe County
102	29.6	**South Lockport** (CDP) Niagara County
108	29.5	**Castile** (town) Wyoming County
109	29.3	**Fairport** (village) Monroe County
109	29.3	**Stamford** (town) Delaware County
111	29.2	**Mount Morris** (town) Livingston County
111	29.2	**Ridgeway** (town) Orleans County
113	29.1	**Carlton** (town) Orleans County
113	29.1	**Wilson** (town) Niagara County
115	29.0	**Kenmore** (village) Erie County
115	29.0	**Le Roy** (town) Genesee County
115	29.0	**Mount Morris** (village) Livingston County
118	28.9	**Honeoye Falls** (village) Monroe County
118	28.9	**Port Ewen** (CDP) Ulster County
120	28.8	**Callicoon** (town) Sullivan County
120	28.8	**Perry** (village) Wyoming County
122	28.7	**Berne** (town) Albany County
122	28.7	**Clarkson** (CDP) Monroe County
122	28.7	**Knox** (town) Albany County
125	28.6	**Hounsfield** (town) Jefferson County
125	28.6	**Ontario** (town) Wayne County
127	28.5	**Ogden** (town) Monroe County
128	28.3	**Chili** (town) Monroe County
128	28.3	**Porter** (town) Niagara County
130	28.2	**Olean** (city) Cattaraugus County
130	28.2	**Unadilla** (town) Otsego County
132	28.1	**Canandaigua** (town) Ontario County
132	28.1	**Farmington** (town) Ontario County
132	28.1	**Manheim** (town) Herkimer County
135	28.0	**Brewerton** (CDP) Onondaga County
135	28.0	**Grand Island** (town) Erie County
135	28.0	**Victor** (village) Ontario County
138	27.8	**Chatham** (town) Columbia County
138	27.8	**Jerusalem** (town) Yates County
138	27.8	**Phelps** (town) Ontario County
138	27.8	**West Bloomfield** (town) Ontario County
142	27.7	**Portland** (town) Chautauqua County
142	27.7	**Somerset** (town) Niagara County
144	27.6	**Clinton** (town) Dutchess County
144	27.6	**West Monroe** (town) Oswego County
146	27.5	**Gorham** (town) Ontario County
147	27.4	**Wellsville** (village) Allegany County
148	27.3	**Palatine** (town) Montgomery County
148	27.3	**Saugerties** (village) Ulster County
150	27.2	**Wheatfield** (town) Niagara County

Note: This section ranks incorporated places and CDPs (Census Designated Places) with populations of 2,500 or more. Unincorporated postal areas were not considered. Please refer to the User Guide for additional information.

Ancestry: English

Top 150 Places Ranked in *Descending* Order

State Rank	Percent	Place
1	27.7	**East Bloomfield** (town) Ontario County
2	26.2	**Pavilion** (town) Genesee County
3	25.3	**Otsego** (town) Otsego County
4	25.0	**Marcellus** (town) Onondaga County
5	24.9	**Caroline** (town) Tompkins County
5	24.9	**Greene** (town) Chenango County
7	24.4	**Homer** (town) Cortland County
8	23.7	**Otisco** (town) Onondaga County
9	23.4	**Hopewell** (town) Ontario County
9	23.4	**Sandy Creek** (town) Oswego County
11	23.3	**Pierrepont** (town) Saint Lawrence County
12	23.2	**Triangle** (town) Broome County
13	23.1	**Skaneateles** (town) Onondaga County
14	23.0	**Homer** (village) Cortland County
14	23.0	**Nunda** (town) Livingston County
16	22.9	**Conklin** (town) Broome County
17	22.7	**Aurelius** (town) Cayuga County
18	22.5	**Batavia** (town) Genesee County
19	22.3	**New Berlin** (town) Chenango County
20	21.8	**Honeoye Falls** (village) Monroe County
20	21.8	**Newark Valley** (town) Tioga County
22	21.3	**Milford** (town) Otsego County
23	21.2	**Clarkson** (CDP) Monroe County
23	21.2	**Sidney** (village) Delaware County
25	21.1	**Gaines** (town) Orleans County
26	20.9	**Bergen** (town) Genesee County
26	20.9	**Norwich** (town) Chenango County
28	20.8	**Sennett** (town) Cayuga County
29	20.7	**Danby** (town) Tompkins County
29	20.7	**Elbridge** (town) Onondaga County
31	20.5	**Chester** (town) Warren County
31	20.5	**Skaneateles** (village) Onondaga County
33	20.4	**Caneadea** (town) Allegany County
33	20.4	**Scriba** (town) Oswego County
35	20.2	**Seneca** (town) Ontario County
35	20.2	**Sheridan** (town) Chautauqua County
37	20.1	**Ellery** (town) Chautauqua County
38	20.0	**Canisteo** (town) Steuben County
39	19.8	**Brutus** (town) Cayuga County
39	19.8	**Chautauqua** (town) Chautauqua County
39	19.8	**Ellisburg** (town) Jefferson County
39	19.8	**Owasco** (town) Cayuga County
39	19.8	**Riga** (town) Monroe County
44	19.7	**Ballston** (town) Saratoga County
45	19.6	**Mendon** (town) Monroe County
46	19.5	**Laurens** (town) Otsego County
47	19.4	**Cortlandville** (town) Cortland County
47	19.4	**Ridgeway** (town) Orleans County
47	19.4	**Walworth** (town) Wayne County
47	19.4	**West Bloomfield** (town) Ontario County
51	19.3	**Hartland** (town) Niagara County
51	19.3	**Hilton** (village) Monroe County
51	19.3	**Jerusalem** (town) Yates County
54	19.2	**Brewerton** (CDP) Onondaga County
54	19.2	**Clarkson** (town) Monroe County
54	19.2	**Sidney** (town) Delaware County
57	19.1	**East Aurora** (village) Erie County
57	19.1	**Fort Edward** (village) Washington County
57	19.1	**Hornellsville** (town) Steuben County
57	19.1	**Tioga** (town) Tioga County
61	19.0	**Caledonia** (town) Livingston County
62	18.9	**Castile** (town) Wyoming County
62	18.9	**Newfane** (CDP) Niagara County
62	18.9	**Virgil** (town) Cortland County
65	18.8	**Richmond** (town) Ontario County
66	18.7	**Manchester** (town) Ontario County
67	18.5	**Benton** (town) Yates County
67	18.5	**Canandaigua** (town) Ontario County
67	18.5	**Geneva** (town) Ontario County
67	18.5	**Milton** (CDP) Saratoga County
67	18.5	**Waterloo** (village) Seneca County
67	18.5	**West Monroe** (town) Oswego County
73	18.4	**Farmington** (town) Ontario County
73	18.4	**Kendall** (town) Orleans County
73	18.4	**Ulysses** (town) Tompkins County
76	18.3	**Somerset** (town) Niagara County
76	18.3	**Unadilla** (town) Otsego County
76	18.3	**Volney** (town) Oswego County
79	18.2	**Moira** (town) Franklin County
79	18.2	**Salem** (town) Washington County
81	18.1	**Clarendon** (town) Orleans County
81	18.1	**Silver Creek** (village) Chautauqua County
81	18.1	**Veteran** (town) Chemung County
81	18.1	**York** (town) Livingston County
85	18.0	**Westfield** (village) Chautauqua County
86	17.9	**Fenton** (town) Broome County
86	17.9	**Medina** (village) Orleans County
88	17.8	**Guilford** (town) Chenango County
89	17.7	**Fleming** (town) Cayuga County
89	17.7	**Norfolk** (town) Saint Lawrence County
89	17.7	**Stephentown** (town) Rensselaer County
92	17.6	**Norwich** (city) Chenango County
92	17.6	**Oxford** (town) Chenango County
92	17.6	**Portville** (town) Cattaraugus County
95	17.5	**Marbletown** (town) Ulster County
95	17.5	**Penn Yan** (village) Yates County
95	17.5	**Phelps** (town) Ontario County
95	17.5	**Windsor** (town) Broome County
99	17.4	**Alexander** (town) Genesee County
99	17.4	**Barton** (town) Tioga County
99	17.4	**Chatham** (town) Columbia County
99	17.4	**Cohocton** (town) Steuben County
99	17.4	**Westmoreland** (town) Oneida County
104	17.3	**Bath** (village) Steuben County
104	17.3	**Cato** (town) Cayuga County
104	17.3	**Fort Edward** (town) Washington County
104	17.3	**LaFayette** (town) Onondaga County
104	17.3	**New Haven** (town) Oswego County
104	17.3	**Shelby** (town) Orleans County
104	17.3	**Wolcott** (town) Wayne County
111	17.2	**Pembroke** (town) Genesee County
112	17.1	**Village Green** (CDP) Onondaga County
113	17.0	**Randolph** (town) Cattaraugus County
113	17.0	**Richland** (town) Oswego County
113	17.0	**Wheatland** (town) Monroe County
116	16.9	**Hamlin** (town) Monroe County
116	16.9	**Lima** (town) Livingston County
116	16.9	**Livonia** (town) Livingston County
116	16.9	**Marion** (town) Wayne County
120	16.8	**Charlton** (town) Saratoga County
120	16.8	**Hamlin** (CDP) Monroe County
120	16.8	**Holland** (town) Erie County
120	16.8	**Ontario** (town) Wayne County
120	16.8	**Tully** (town) Onondaga County
125	16.7	**Hastings** (town) Oswego County
125	16.7	**Knox** (town) Albany County
125	16.7	**Naples** (town) Ontario County
125	16.7	**Ticonderoga** (CDP) Essex County
125	16.7	**Ticonderoga** (town) Essex County
130	16.6	**Fayette** (town) Seneca County
130	16.6	**Mexico** (town) Oswego County
130	16.6	**Sherburne** (town) Chenango County
130	16.6	**Vienna** (town) Oneida County
134	16.5	**Hanover** (town) Chautauqua County
134	16.5	**Murray** (town) Orleans County
134	16.5	**Nichols** (town) Tioga County
134	16.5	**Pittsford** (town) Monroe County
134	16.5	**Wilson** (town) Niagara County
139	16.4	**Newark** (village) Wayne County
139	16.4	**Spencer** (town) Tioga County
141	16.3	**Addison** (town) Steuben County
141	16.3	**Glen** (town) Montgomery County
141	16.3	**Wellsville** (village) Allegany County
144	16.2	**Busti** (town) Chautauqua County
144	16.2	**Saranac Lake** (village) Franklin County
144	16.2	**Schoharie** (town) Schoharie County
144	16.2	**Westfield** (town) Chautauqua County
148	16.1	**Akron** (village) Erie County
148	16.1	**Cuba** (town) Allegany County
148	16.1	**North East** (town) Dutchess County

Note: This section ranks incorporated places and CDPs (Census Designated Places) with populations of 2,500 or more. Unincorporated postal areas were not considered. Please refer to the User Guide for additional information.

Ancestry: American

Top 150 Places Ranked in *Descending* Order

State Rank	Percent	Place
1	44.4	**Eaton** (town) Madison County
2	34.5	**Madison** (town) Madison County
3	31.3	**Hamilton** (town) Madison County
4	27.6	**Chittenango** (village) Madison County
5	27.3	**Oneida** (city) Madison County
6	26.7	**Sangerfield** (town) Oneida County
7	26.0	**Coxsackie** (village) Greene County
8	24.9	**Cazenovia** (village) Madison County
9	24.8	**Cazenovia** (town) Madison County
10	24.1	**Granville** (town) Washington County
10	24.1	**Hamilton** (village) Madison County
12	23.9	**Dix** (town) Schuyler County
12	23.9	**Vernon** (town) Oneida County
14	23.8	**Whitehall** (village) Washington County
15	23.7	**Watchtower** (CDP) Ulster County
16	23.4	**Corinth** (town) Saratoga County
17	22.9	**Camden** (town) Oneida County
18	22.6	**Vienna** (town) Oneida County
19	22.5	**Lenox** (town) Madison County
19	22.5	**White Creek** (town) Washington County
21	22.2	**Catlin** (town) Chemung County
22	22.1	**Granville** (village) Washington County
22	22.1	**New Baltimore** (town) Greene County
24	22.0	**Deerpark** (town) Orange County
25	21.6	**Bath** (village) Steuben County
26	21.3	**Beekmantown** (town) Clinton County
27	21.2	**Verona** (town) Oneida County
28	21.1	**Bath** (town) Steuben County
28	21.1	**Sullivan** (town) Madison County
28	21.1	**Whitehall** (town) Washington County
31	21.0	**New York Mills** (village) Oneida County
32	20.5	**Corinth** (village) Saratoga County
32	20.5	**Somerset** (town) Niagara County
34	19.6	**Canastota** (village) Madison County
35	19.4	**Hector** (town) Schuyler County
36	19.3	**Minisink** (town) Orange County
37	19.1	**Greenville** (town) Greene County
38	18.6	**Walton** (town) Delaware County
39	18.4	**Mooers** (town) Clinton County
39	18.4	**Salem** (town) Washington County
39	18.4	**Starkey** (town) Yates County
42	18.3	**Hudson Falls** (village) Washington County
42	18.3	**Newfane** (CDP) Niagara County
44	18.1	**Norwich** (town) Chenango County
45	18.0	**West Monroe** (town) Oswego County
46	17.9	**Campbell** (town) Steuben County
46	17.9	**Southport** (CDP) Chemung County
48	17.8	**Chemung** (town) Chemung County
48	17.8	**Kirkland** (town) Oneida County
50	17.7	**Roslyn** (village) Nassau County
51	17.5	**Newfane** (town) Niagara County
52	17.4	**Fort Ann** (town) Washington County
52	17.4	**Niagara** (town) Niagara County
54	17.3	**Saranac** (town) Clinton County
55	17.1	**Wawayanda** (town) Orange County
56	16.7	**Copake** (town) Columbia County
57	16.3	**Addison** (town) Steuben County
58	16.2	**Firthcliffe** (CDP) Orange County
58	16.2	**Northumberland** (town) Saratoga County
58	16.2	**Rye** (city) Westchester County
61	16.1	**Kings Point** (village) Nassau County
61	16.1	**Moreau** (town) Saratoga County
61	16.1	**Port Jervis** (city) Orange County
61	16.1	**Ravena** (village) Albany County
65	16.0	**Larchmont** (village) Westchester County
65	16.0	**Lee** (town) Oneida County
65	16.0	**Sands Point** (village) Nassau County
65	16.0	**Southport** (town) Chemung County
69	15.9	**Cairo** (town) Greene County
70	15.8	**Schuyler Falls** (town) Clinton County
71	15.7	**Elmira** (city) Chemung County
72	15.6	**Trenton** (town) Oneida County
72	15.6	**Tuxedo** (town) Orange County
74	15.5	**Hunter** (town) Greene County
74	15.5	**Kingsbury** (town) Washington County
76	15.4	**Chazy** (town) Clinton County
76	15.4	**Glens Falls** (city) Warren County
78	15.2	**Coxsackie** (town) Greene County
79	15.1	**Greenwood Lake** (village) Orange County
80	15.0	**Lewiston** (village) Niagara County
81	14.9	**Groton** (town) Tompkins County
82	14.8	**Floyd** (town) Oneida County
83	14.7	**South Glens Falls** (village) Saratoga County
84	14.5	**Annsville** (town) Oneida County
84	14.5	**Colesville** (town) Broome County
86	14.4	**Caroline** (town) Tompkins County
87	14.3	**Gardnertown** (CDP) Orange County
88	14.1	**Hewlett** (CDP) Nassau County
88	14.1	**Walton** (village) Delaware County
90	14.0	**Dryden** (town) Tompkins County
90	14.0	**Newfield** (town) Tompkins County
92	13.9	**Mexico** (town) Oswego County
92	13.9	**West Glens Falls** (CDP) Warren County
94	13.8	**Minden** (town) Montgomery County
95	13.7	**Greenwich** (town) Washington County
95	13.7	**Wesley Hills** (village) Rockland County
97	13.6	**Balmville** (CDP) Orange County
97	13.6	**Ulysses** (town) Tompkins County
99	13.5	**Crawford** (town) Orange County
100	13.4	**Paris** (town) Oneida County
100	13.4	**Veteran** (town) Chemung County
102	13.3	**Kiryas Joel** (village) Orange County
102	13.3	**Rye Brook** (village) Westchester County
102	13.3	**Wilton** (town) Saratoga County
105	13.2	**Canajoharie** (town) Montgomery County
105	13.2	**Queensbury** (town) Warren County
107	13.1	**Schoharie** (town) Schoharie County
108	13.0	**Coeymans** (town) Albany County
108	13.0	**Cornwall** (town) Orange County
108	13.0	**Danby** (town) Tompkins County
108	13.0	**Greene** (town) Chenango County
112	12.9	**Woodbury** (town) Orange County
113	12.8	**Milford** (town) Otsego County
114	12.7	**Elmira Heights** (village) Chemung County
114	12.7	**Esopus** (town) Ulster County
114	12.7	**Woodbury** (village) Orange County
117	12.6	**Glens Falls North** (CDP) Warren County
117	12.6	**Rome** (city) Oneida County
119	12.5	**Boonville** (town) Oneida County
119	12.5	**Manlius** (village) Onondaga County
119	12.5	**Mechanicstown** (CDP) Orange County
119	12.5	**Royalton** (town) Niagara County
123	12.4	**Barker** (town) Broome County
123	12.4	**Johnstown** (town) Fulton County
123	12.4	**Mayfield** (town) Fulton County
123	12.4	**Plattsburgh** (town) Clinton County
127	12.3	**Greenville** (town) Orange County
128	12.2	**Gloversville** (city) Fulton County
128	12.2	**Highland Falls** (village) Orange County
128	12.2	**Otego** (town) Otsego County
128	12.2	**Vails Gate** (CDP) Orange County
132	12.1	**Benton** (town) Yates County
132	12.1	**Erwin** (town) Steuben County
132	12.1	**Wallkill** (town) Orange County
135	12.0	**North Hills** (village) Nassau County
136	11.9	**Hoosick Falls** (village) Rensselaer County
136	11.9	**Hopewell** (town) Ontario County
138	11.8	**Corning** (town) Steuben County
138	11.8	**New Hartford** (town) Oneida County
138	11.8	**Westerlo** (town) Albany County
141	11.7	**Saint Johnsville** (town) Montgomery County
142	11.6	**Hornell** (city) Steuben County
142	11.6	**Horseheads** (village) Chemung County
142	11.6	**Horseheads North** (CDP) Chemung County
142	11.6	**Saratoga** (town) Saratoga County
142	11.6	**Warwick** (village) Orange County
142	11.6	**Woodmere** (CDP) Nassau County
148	11.5	**Blooming Grove** (town) Orange County
148	11.5	**Chesterfield** (town) Essex County
148	11.5	**Goshen** (village) Orange County

Note: This section ranks incorporated places and CDPs (Census Designated Places) with populations of 2,500 or more. Unincorporated postal areas were not considered. Please refer to the User Guide for additional information.

Ancestry: Irish

Top 150 Places Ranked in *Descending* Order

State Rank	Percent	Place
1	49.2	**Pearl River** (CDP) Rockland County
2	40.1	**Wynantskill** (CDP) Rensselaer County
3	39.9	**Sayville** (CDP) Suffolk County
4	36.9	**Garden City** (village) Nassau County
5	35.8	**Westvale** (CDP) Onondaga County
6	35.7	**East Greenbush** (CDP) Rensselaer County
7	35.4	**Green Island** (town/village) Albany County
8	34.9	**Blue Point** (CDP) Suffolk County
9	34.7	**Skaneateles** (village) Onondaga County
10	34.5	**East Islip** (CDP) Suffolk County
10	34.5	**Washington** (town) Dutchess County
12	34.1	**Rockville Centre** (village) Nassau County
13	34.0	**Wanakah** (CDP) Erie County
13	34.0	**West Sayville** (CDP) Suffolk County
15	33.9	**Clinton** (town) Dutchess County
16	33.8	**Marcellus** (town) Onondaga County
17	33.4	**Williston Park** (village) Nassau County
18	33.2	**Brightwaters** (village) Suffolk County
18	33.2	**Massapequa Park** (village) Nassau County
20	33.1	**Blauvelt** (CDP) Rockland County
21	32.8	**East Quogue** (CDP) Suffolk County
22	32.7	**Rocky Point** (CDP) Suffolk County
23	32.6	**Schaghticoke** (town) Rensselaer County
24	32.5	**North Patchogue** (CDP) Suffolk County
25	32.3	**Watervliet** (city) Albany County
26	32.0	**Islip Terrace** (CDP) Suffolk County
26	32.0	**West Islip** (CDP) Suffolk County
28	31.8	**Floral Park** (village) Nassau County
28	31.8	**Schuyler** (town) Herkimer County
30	31.7	**Orleans** (town) Jefferson County
31	31.6	**East Greenbush** (town) Rensselaer County
32	31.5	**Cornwall** (town) Orange County
32	31.5	**Mentz** (town) Cayuga County
34	31.4	**Babylon** (village) Suffolk County
35	31.3	**North Great River** (CDP) Suffolk County
36	31.2	**East Shoreham** (CDP) Suffolk County
36	31.2	**Fayetteville** (village) Onondaga County
38	31.1	**Chenango Bridge** (CDP) Broome County
38	31.1	**Colonie** (village) Albany County
38	31.1	**East Williston** (village) Nassau County
38	31.1	**Orangetown** (town) Rockland County
42	31.0	**Malverne** (village) Nassau County
42	31.0	**Pamelia** (town) Jefferson County
42	31.0	**Rensselaer** (city) Rensselaer County
45	30.8	**Mechanicville** (city) Saratoga County
46	30.7	**Ridge** (CDP) Suffolk County
47	30.6	**Blooming Grove** (town) Orange County
47	30.6	**LaFayette** (town) Onondaga County
49	30.5	**Centerport** (CDP) Suffolk County
49	30.5	**Cornwall-on-Hudson** (village) Orange County
49	30.5	**Massapequa** (CDP) Nassau County
49	30.5	**Shelter Island** (town) Suffolk County
53	30.4	**Orchard Park** (village) Erie County
54	30.3	**South Hempstead** (CDP) Nassau County
54	30.3	**Warwick** (village) Orange County
56	30.2	**Fort Salonga** (CDP) Suffolk County
56	30.2	**SUNY Oswego** (CDP) Oswego County
58	30.0	**Blasdell** (village) Erie County
58	30.0	**Southold** (CDP) Suffolk County
58	30.0	**Waterford** (town) Saratoga County
58	30.0	**West Nyack** (CDP) Rockland County
62	29.9	**Firthcliffe** (CDP) Orange County
63	29.8	**Bayport** (CDP) Suffolk County
63	29.8	**Greenville** (town) Orange County
63	29.8	**Rosendale** (town) Ulster County
66	29.7	**Bayville** (village) Nassau County
67	29.6	**Center Moriches** (CDP) Suffolk County
67	29.6	**Oswego** (city) Oswego County
69	29.5	**Amenia** (town) Dutchess County
69	29.5	**Miller Place** (CDP) Suffolk County
69	29.5	**Wantagh** (CDP) Nassau County
72	29.4	**Owasco** (town) Cayuga County
72	29.4	**Seaford** (CDP) Nassau County
74	29.3	**Skaneateles** (town) Onondaga County
75	29.2	**Cold Spring Harbor** (CDP) Suffolk County
75	29.2	**East Northport** (CDP) Suffolk County
75	29.2	**North Greenbush** (town) Rensselaer County
78	29.1	**Esopus** (town) Ulster County
78	29.1	**Galway** (town) Saratoga County
78	29.1	**Lake Ronkonkoma** (CDP) Suffolk County
78	29.1	**Philipstown** (town) Putnam County
82	28.9	**Camillus** (town) Onondaga County
82	28.9	**Mohawk** (village) Herkimer County
82	28.9	**West Bay Shore** (CDP) Suffolk County
85	28.8	**Glenwood Landing** (CDP) Nassau County
86	28.7	**Kings Park** (CDP) Suffolk County
86	28.7	**Montgomery** (village) Orange County
88	28.6	**Bethlehem** (town) Albany County
88	28.6	**Bohemia** (CDP) Suffolk County
88	28.6	**Brunswick** (town) Rensselaer County
88	28.6	**Dover** (town) Dutchess County
88	28.6	**Geddes** (town) Onondaga County
88	28.6	**Halesite** (CDP) Suffolk County
88	28.6	**Manorville** (CDP) Suffolk County
88	28.6	**Oswego** (town) Oswego County
88	28.6	**Saint James** (CDP) Suffolk County
88	28.6	**Stillwater** (town) Saratoga County
98	28.5	**East Moriches** (CDP) Suffolk County
98	28.5	**Maine** (town) Broome County
98	28.5	**Nesconset** (CDP) Suffolk County
98	28.5	**Putnam Lake** (CDP) Putnam County
102	28.3	**Nassau** (town) Rensselaer County
103	28.2	**Chenango** (town) Broome County
103	28.2	**North Merrick** (CDP) Nassau County
105	28.1	**Fairmount** (CDP) Onondaga County
105	28.1	**Manlius** (village) Onondaga County
107	28.0	**Bardonia** (CDP) Rockland County
107	28.0	**East Syracuse** (village) Onondaga County
107	28.0	**Monroe** (village) Orange County
110	27.9	**Islip** (CDP) Suffolk County
110	27.9	**North East** (town) Dutchess County
112	27.7	**East Patchogue** (CDP) Suffolk County
112	27.7	**Onondaga** (town) Onondaga County
114	27.6	**Caledonia** (town) Livingston County
114	27.6	**Saranac Lake** (village) Franklin County
116	27.5	**Hamburg** (village) Erie County
117	27.3	**Ballston Spa** (village) Saratoga County
118	27.2	**Kirkwood** (town) Broome County
118	27.2	**Lloyd Harbor** (village) Suffolk County
118	27.2	**South Farmingdale** (CDP) Nassau County
121	27.1	**Colonie** (town) Albany County
122	27.0	**Clayton** (town) Jefferson County
122	27.0	**Congers** (CDP) Rockland County
122	27.0	**West Elmira** (CDP) Chemung County
122	27.0	**Yaphank** (CDP) Suffolk County
126	26.9	**Ballston** (town) Saratoga County
126	26.9	**Plainedge** (CDP) Nassau County
126	26.9	**Sand Lake** (town) Rensselaer County
129	26.8	**South Blooming Grove** (village) Orange County
129	26.8	**Voorheesville** (village) Albany County
129	26.8	**Windsor** (town) Broome County
132	26.7	**Hornellsville** (town) Steuben County
132	26.7	**Kinderhook** (town) Columbia County
132	26.7	**Richmondville** (town) Schoharie County
135	26.6	**Fairport** (village) Monroe County
135	26.6	**Holbrook** (CDP) Suffolk County
137	26.5	**East Rockaway** (village) Nassau County
137	26.5	**Livonia** (town) Livingston County
139	26.4	**Catskill** (village) Greene County
139	26.4	**East Bloomfield** (town) Ontario County
139	26.4	**Sound Beach** (CDP) Suffolk County
139	26.4	**Union Vale** (town) Dutchess County
143	26.3	**Callicoon** (town) Sullivan County
143	26.3	**Ghent** (town) Columbia County
143	26.3	**Holtsville** (CDP) Suffolk County
143	26.3	**Milton** (town) Saratoga County
147	26.2	**Hyde Park** (town) Dutchess County
147	26.2	**Lake George** (town) Warren County
147	26.2	**Mastic Beach** (village) Suffolk County
147	26.2	**Middleburgh** (town) Schoharie County

Note: This section ranks incorporated places and CDPs (Census Designated Places) with populations of 2,500 or more. Unincorporated postal areas were not considered. Please refer to the User Guide for additional information.

Ancestry: Italian

Top 150 Places Ranked in *Descending* Order

State Rank	Percent	Place
1	47.8	**North Massapequa** (CDP) Nassau County
2	46.9	**Thornwood** (CDP) Westchester County
3	46.7	**Halesite** (CDP) Suffolk County
4	45.8	**Eastchester** (CDP) Westchester County
5	45.6	**Massapequa** (CDP) Nassau County
6	44.4	**Massapequa Park** (village) Nassau County
7	43.7	**Hawthorne** (CDP) Westchester County
8	42.3	**West Islip** (CDP) Suffolk County
9	42.1	**Frankfort** (village) Herkimer County
10	41.3	**East Norwich** (CDP) Nassau County
11	41.2	**Islip Terrace** (CDP) Suffolk County
12	40.8	**Jefferson Valley-Yorktown** (CDP) Westchester County
12	40.8	**Miller Place** (CDP) Suffolk County
14	40.7	**Marlboro** (CDP) Ulster County
15	40.4	**Franklin Square** (CDP) Nassau County
16	40.3	**Nesconset** (CDP) Suffolk County
17	40.0	**Bayville** (village) Nassau County
18	39.6	**Saint James** (CDP) Suffolk County
19	39.1	**Lake Grove** (village) Suffolk County
20	38.3	**South Farmingdale** (CDP) Nassau County
21	38.0	**East Islip** (CDP) Suffolk County
21	38.0	**Seaford** (CDP) Nassau County
23	37.8	**Smithtown** (CDP) Suffolk County
24	37.4	**Plainedge** (CDP) Nassau County
25	37.3	**Manorville** (CDP) Suffolk County
26	36.4	**Smithtown** (town) Suffolk County
27	36.1	**Hauppauge** (CDP) Suffolk County
27	36.1	**Ronkonkoma** (CDP) Suffolk County
29	36.0	**Lyncourt** (CDP) Onondaga County
30	35.9	**Eastchester** (town) Westchester County
30	35.9	**Frankfort** (town) Herkimer County
32	35.8	**Centerport** (CDP) Suffolk County
33	35.7	**North Great River** (CDP) Suffolk County
33	35.7	**Oakdale** (CDP) Suffolk County
35	35.4	**North Babylon** (CDP) Suffolk County
35	35.4	**Pelham Manor** (village) Westchester County
37	35.2	**Bohemia** (CDP) Suffolk County
37	35.2	**Union Vale** (town) Dutchess County
37	35.2	**Yorktown** (town) Westchester County
40	35.1	**Center Moriches** (CDP) Suffolk County
40	35.1	**Selden** (CDP) Suffolk County
42	34.8	**Holbrook** (CDP) Suffolk County
42	34.8	**Holtsville** (CDP) Suffolk County
42	34.8	**Port Jefferson Station** (CDP) Suffolk County
45	34.7	**Oyster Bay** (CDP) Nassau County
46	34.6	**Malverne** (village) Nassau County
47	34.5	**Brightwaters** (village) Suffolk County
48	34.4	**Bethpage** (CDP) Nassau County
48	34.4	**East Fishkill** (town) Dutchess County
48	34.4	**Kenmore** (village) Erie County
51	34.2	**Farmingville** (CDP) Suffolk County
52	34.1	**Glen Head** (CDP) Nassau County
53	33.9	**Bayport** (CDP) Suffolk County
53	33.9	**Deer Park** (CDP) Suffolk County
53	33.9	**Garden City South** (CDP) Nassau County
53	33.9	**West Babylon** (CDP) Suffolk County
57	33.8	**Carmel** (town) Putnam County
57	33.8	**Commack** (CDP) Suffolk County
57	33.8	**Old Brookville** (village) Nassau County
60	33.7	**Blue Point** (CDP) Suffolk County
60	33.7	**Centereach** (CDP) Suffolk County
60	33.7	**Fort Salonga** (CDP) Suffolk County
60	33.7	**Kings Park** (CDP) Suffolk County
60	33.7	**Putnam Lake** (CDP) Putnam County
65	33.6	**Lindenhurst** (village) Suffolk County
65	33.6	**Mechanicville** (city) Saratoga County
65	33.6	**Shirley** (CDP) Suffolk County
68	33.3	**Elwood** (CDP) Suffolk County
68	33.3	**Somers** (town) Westchester County
70	33.2	**Marlborough** (town) Ulster County
71	33.1	**Babylon** (village) Suffolk County
72	33.0	**Lake Ronkonkoma** (CDP) Suffolk County
72	33.0	**Rotterdam** (CDP) Schenectady County
74	32.9	**East Massapequa** (CDP) Nassau County
75	32.8	**North Patchogue** (CDP) Suffolk County
76	32.6	**Greece** (CDP) Monroe County
76	32.6	**Mount Sinai** (CDP) Suffolk County
76	32.6	**Terryville** (CDP) Suffolk County
76	32.6	**Yaphank** (CDP) Suffolk County
80	32.2	**Garden City** (village) Nassau County
81	31.8	**Bellmore** (CDP) Nassau County
81	31.8	**Heritage Hills** (CDP) Westchester County
83	31.7	**Munsey Park** (village) Nassau County
84	31.6	**Mahopac** (CDP) Putnam County
84	31.6	**Staten Island** (borough) Richmond County
86	31.5	**East Williston** (village) Nassau County
86	31.5	**Wantagh** (CDP) Nassau County
88	31.4	**Mastic** (CDP) Suffolk County
88	31.4	**Rotterdam** (town) Schenectady County
88	31.4	**Sayville** (CDP) Suffolk County
88	31.4	**Sound Beach** (CDP) Suffolk County
92	31.3	**East Northport** (CDP) Suffolk County
93	31.2	**North Gates** (CDP) Monroe County
93	31.2	**Ridge** (CDP) Suffolk County
95	31.1	**Cold Spring Harbor** (CDP) Suffolk County
95	31.1	**Levittown** (CDP) Nassau County
97	31.0	**South Huntington** (CDP) Suffolk County
98	30.9	**Putnam Valley** (town) Putnam County
99	30.8	**Montrose** (CDP) Westchester County
99	30.8	**Owasco** (town) Cayuga County
99	30.8	**West Bay Shore** (CDP) Suffolk County
102	30.7	**Lynbrook** (village) Nassau County
102	30.7	**North Merrick** (CDP) Nassau County
104	30.6	**Stillwater** (town) Saratoga County
104	30.6	**West Sayville** (CDP) Suffolk County
106	30.5	**Middle Island** (CDP) Suffolk County
107	30.4	**Beekman** (town) Dutchess County
107	30.4	**Brookhaven** (town) Suffolk County
107	30.4	**Lloyd** (town) Ulster County
107	30.4	**Southeast** (town) Putnam County
111	30.2	**Congers** (CDP) Rockland County
112	30.1	**East Shoreham** (CDP) Suffolk County
112	30.1	**Medford** (CDP) Suffolk County
112	30.1	**North Wantagh** (CDP) Nassau County
115	29.7	**Locust Valley** (CDP) Nassau County
115	29.7	**Mastic Beach** (village) Suffolk County
115	29.7	**Pleasantville** (village) Westchester County
118	29.6	**Rocky Point** (CDP) Suffolk County
119	29.5	**Stony Point** (CDP) Rockland County
120	29.4	**Islip** (CDP) Suffolk County
120	29.4	**Monroe** (village) Orange County
120	29.4	**Oceanside** (CDP) Nassau County
120	29.4	**SUNY Oswego** (CDP) Oswego County
124	29.2	**Farmingdale** (village) Nassau County
125	29.0	**Oyster Bay** (town) Nassau County
125	29.0	**Stony Point** (town) Rockland County
127	28.9	**Myers Corner** (CDP) Dutchess County
128	28.8	**Wappinger** (town) Dutchess County
129	28.4	**Solvay** (village) Onondaga County
129	28.4	**Westvale** (CDP) Onondaga County
131	28.3	**East Patchogue** (CDP) Suffolk County
132	28.2	**Fredonia** (village) Chautauqua County
132	28.2	**Greenport** (town) Columbia County
132	28.2	**Mount Morris** (village) Livingston County
135	28.1	**Hilton** (village) Monroe County
135	28.1	**Montgomery** (village) Orange County
135	28.1	**Patterson** (town) Putnam County
138	28.0	**Lakeland** (CDP) Onondaga County
138	28.0	**Salina** (town) Onondaga County
138	28.0	**West Hills** (CDP) Suffolk County
141	27.9	**Carle Place** (CDP) Nassau County
142	27.7	**Coram** (CDP) Suffolk County
142	27.7	**East Moriches** (CDP) Suffolk County
142	27.7	**Gates** (CDP) Monroe County
142	27.7	**Pawling** (town) Dutchess County
146	27.6	**Hurley** (CDP) Ulster County
146	27.6	**Stony Brook** (CDP) Suffolk County
148	27.5	**Geddes** (town) Onondaga County
149	27.4	**Seneca Falls** (CDP) Seneca County
149	27.4	**Webster** (town) Monroe County

Note: *This section ranks incorporated places and CDPs (Census Designated Places) with populations of 2,500 or more. Unincorporated postal areas were not considered. Please refer to the User Guide for additional information.*

Employment: Management, Business, and Financial Occupations
Top 150 Places Ranked in *Descending* Order

State Rank	Percent	Place	State Rank	Percent	Place
1	36.3	**Munsey Park** (village) Nassau County	75	23.3	**Dix Hills** (CDP) Suffolk County
2	35.8	**Sands Point** (village) Nassau County	77	23.2	**Harrison** (town/village) Westchester County
3	35.4	**Cold Spring Harbor** (CDP) Suffolk County	78	23.1	**Clarence Center** (CDP) Erie County
4	35.2	**Scarsdale** (town/village) Westchester County	78	23.1	**East Greenbush** (CDP) Rensselaer County
5	35.1	**Bronxville** (village) Westchester County	78	23.1	**Hawthorne** (CDP) Westchester County
6	34.2	**Pelham Manor** (village) Westchester County	81	23.0	**Great Neck Plaza** (village) Nassau County
7	33.3	**New Castle** (town) Westchester County	81	23.0	**Wilton** (town) Saratoga County
8	32.9	**Pound Ridge** (town) Westchester County	83	22.9	**Malverne** (village) Nassau County
9	32.7	**Larchmont** (village) Westchester County	84	22.8	**Clarence** (town) Erie County
10	31.4	**Armonk** (CDP) Westchester County	84	22.8	**Pittsford** (town) Monroe County
11	30.9	**Rye** (city) Westchester County	86	22.7	**Glenwood Landing** (CDP) Nassau County
12	30.3	**Pelham** (town) Westchester County	86	22.7	**New Scotland** (town) Albany County
13	30.2	**Woodbury** (CDP) Nassau County	88	22.6	**Kinderhook** (town) Columbia County
14	30.0	**Flower Hill** (village) Nassau County	88	22.6	**Skaneateles** (town) Onondaga County
14	30.0	**North Castle** (town) Westchester County	90	22.4	**Clifton Park** (town) Saratoga County
16	29.8	**Garden City** (village) Nassau County	90	22.4	**Herricks** (CDP) Nassau County
16	29.8	**Montebello** (village) Rockland County	90	22.4	**Pompey** (town) Onondaga County
18	29.1	**Lewisboro** (town) Westchester County	90	22.4	**Viola** (CDP) Rockland County
19	28.8	**Jericho** (CDP) Nassau County	94	22.3	**Kings Point** (village) Nassau County
19	28.8	**Mamaroneck** (town) Westchester County	94	22.3	**Woodmere** (CDP) Nassau County
21	28.7	**Clarence** (CDP) Erie County	96	22.2	**Fort Salonga** (CDP) Suffolk County
22	28.5	**Centerport** (CDP) Suffolk County	96	22.2	**Great Neck Estates** (village) Nassau County
23	28.4	**Irvington** (village) Westchester County	98	22.1	**Airmont** (village) Rockland County
24	28.3	**Rye Brook** (village) Westchester County	98	22.1	**Schoharie** (town) Schoharie County
25	28.2	**Briarcliff Manor** (village) Westchester County	100	22.0	**Lansing** (town) Tompkins County
25	28.2	**Thomaston** (village) Nassau County	101	21.9	**Cornwall-on-Hudson** (village) Orange County
27	27.9	**Ardsley** (village) Westchester County	101	21.9	**South Hempstead** (CDP) Nassau County
27	27.9	**East Norwich** (CDP) Nassau County	101	21.9	**Wales** (town) Erie County
29	27.8	**Harris Hill** (CDP) Erie County	101	21.9	**Wesley Hills** (village) Rockland County
30	27.7	**Muttontown** (village) Nassau County	105	21.8	**Greenburgh** (town) Westchester County
30	27.7	**Noyack** (CDP) Suffolk County	105	21.8	**Hastings-on-Hudson** (village) Westchester County
32	27.5	**Pelham** (village) Westchester County	105	21.8	**Saratoga Springs** (city) Saratoga County
33	27.2	**Greenville** (CDP) Westchester County	108	21.7	**Myers Corner** (CDP) Dutchess County
34	27.1	**East Williston** (village) Nassau County	109	21.5	**Bardonia** (CDP) Rockland County
34	27.1	**Manhattan** (borough) New York County	109	21.5	**Bethlehem** (town) Albany County
36	27.0	**East Hills** (village) Nassau County	109	21.5	**Heritage Hills** (CDP) Westchester County
36	27.0	**West Hills** (CDP) Suffolk County	109	21.5	**Lynbrook** (village) Nassau County
38	26.8	**Pleasantville** (village) Westchester County	109	21.5	**Mount Pleasant** (town) Westchester County
39	26.7	**Brookville** (village) Nassau County	114	21.4	**Tappan** (CDP) Rockland County
40	26.6	**Glen Head** (CDP) Nassau County	114	21.4	**Washington** (town) Dutchess County
41	26.5	**Searingtown** (CDP) Nassau County	116	21.3	**Congers** (CDP) Rockland County
42	26.3	**Manhasset** (CDP) Nassau County	116	21.3	**Lido Beach** (CDP) Nassau County
43	26.0	**Eastchester** (CDP) Westchester County	118	21.2	**Firthcliffe** (CDP) Orange County
44	25.9	**Eastchester** (town) Westchester County	118	21.2	**Southampton** (village) Suffolk County
45	25.8	**Tarrytown** (village) Westchester County	120	21.1	**Northport** (village) Suffolk County
45	25.8	**University Gardens** (CDP) Nassau County	120	21.1	**Penfield** (town) Monroe County
47	25.6	**North Hills** (village) Nassau County	120	21.1	**Wantagh** (CDP) Nassau County
48	25.5	**Bedford** (town) Westchester County	123	21.0	**Menands** (village) Albany County
48	25.5	**Syosset** (CDP) Nassau County	124	20.9	**Niskayuna** (town) Schenectady County
50	25.3	**Elma Center** (CDP) Erie County	124	20.9	**Tuxedo** (town) Orange County
50	25.3	**Roslyn** (village) Nassau County	124	20.9	**White Plains** (city) Westchester County
50	25.3	**Somers** (town) Westchester County	127	20.8	**Cornwall** (town) Orange County
53	25.2	**Rockville Centre** (village) Nassau County	127	20.8	**Melville** (CDP) Suffolk County
54	25.1	**East Aurora** (village) Erie County	129	20.7	**Big Flats** (town) Chemung County
54	25.1	**Locust Valley** (CDP) Nassau County	129	20.7	**New City** (CDP) Rockland County
56	25.0	**Oyster Bay** (CDP) Nassau County	129	20.7	**North Hempstead** (town) Nassau County
57	24.9	**Victor** (town) Ontario County	129	20.7	**Piermont** (village) Rockland County
58	24.8	**Huntington** (CDP) Suffolk County	133	20.6	**Marcellus** (town) Onondaga County
58	24.8	**Lansing** (village) Tompkins County	133	20.6	**Putnam Valley** (town) Putnam County
60	24.6	**Manorhaven** (village) Nassau County	135	20.5	**Baldwin Harbor** (CDP) Nassau County
61	24.5	**Port Washington** (CDP) Nassau County	135	20.5	**Mendon** (town) Monroe County
62	24.3	**North Salem** (town) Westchester County	135	20.5	**Smithtown** (CDP) Suffolk County
63	24.2	**Manhasset Hills** (CDP) Nassau County	138	20.4	**Big Flats** (CDP) Chemung County
64	24.1	**Lloyd Harbor** (village) Suffolk County	138	20.4	**Perinton** (town) Monroe County
65	24.0	**Shelter Island** (town) Suffolk County	140	20.3	**Goshen** (village) Orange County
66	23.9	**Lake Success** (village) Nassau County	140	20.3	**Long Beach** (city) Nassau County
66	23.9	**Old Bethpage** (CDP) Nassau County	140	20.3	**North Greenbush** (town) Rensselaer County
68	23.8	**Gardiner** (town) Ulster County	140	20.3	**North Merrick** (CDP) Nassau County
68	23.8	**Roslyn Heights** (CDP) Nassau County	140	20.3	**Oyster Bay** (town) Nassau County
70	23.7	**Merrick** (CDP) Nassau County	145	20.2	**Commack** (CDP) Suffolk County
70	23.7	**Plainview** (CDP) Nassau County	145	20.2	**West Elmira** (CDP) Chemung County
72	23.5	**Voorheesville** (village) Albany County	147	20.1	**Dobbs Ferry** (village) Westchester County
73	23.4	**Hartsdale** (CDP) Westchester County	148	20.0	**Elwood** (CDP) Suffolk County
73	23.4	**Mamaroneck** (village) Westchester County	148	20.0	**Huntington** (town) Suffolk County
75	23.3	**Albertson** (CDP) Nassau County	148	20.0	**Oceanside** (CDP) Nassau County

Note: *This section ranks incorporated places and CDPs (Census Designated Places) with populations of 2,500 or more. Unincorporated postal areas were not considered. Please refer to the User Guide for additional information.*

Employment: Management, Business, and Financial Occupations

Top 150 Places Ranked in *Ascending* Order

State Rank	Percent	Place	State Rank	Percent	Place
1	1.0	**Dannemora** (village) Clinton County	75	7.4	**Gouverneur** (town) Saint Lawrence County
2	2.0	**Flanders** (CDP) Suffolk County	75	7.4	**Hempstead** (village) Nassau County
3	2.9	**Riverside** (CDP) Suffolk County	75	7.4	**Whitehall** (town) Washington County
4	3.5	**SUNY Oswego** (CDP) Oswego County	79	7.5	**Mount Morris** (town) Livingston County
5	3.6	**Alfred** (village) Allegany County	80	7.6	**Dolgeville** (village) Herkimer County
6	4.1	**Ellenville** (village) Ulster County	80	7.6	**Fulton** (city) Oswego County
7	4.5	**Binghamton University** (CDP) Broome County	80	7.6	**Hornell** (city) Steuben County
7	4.5	**Mohawk** (village) Herkimer County	80	7.6	**Liberty** (town) Sullivan County
9	4.7	**South Hill** (CDP) Tompkins County	80	7.6	**Malone** (village) Franklin County
9	4.7	**Whitesboro** (village) Oneida County	80	7.6	**North Lindenhurst** (CDP) Suffolk County
11	4.9	**Darien** (town) Genesee County	86	7.7	**Saint Johnsville** (town) Montgomery County
12	5.0	**Lyons** (village) Wayne County	87	7.8	**Geneseo** (village) Livingston County
12	5.0	**New Paltz** (village) Ulster County	87	7.8	**Liberty** (village) Sullivan County
12	5.0	**North Amityville** (CDP) Suffolk County	87	7.8	**Parish** (town) Oswego County
15	5.1	**Bath** (village) Steuben County	87	7.8	**Poughkeepsie** (city) Dutchess County
16	5.5	**Haverstraw** (village) Rockland County	91	7.9	**Baldwinsville** (village) Onondaga County
16	5.5	**Tupper Lake** (village) Franklin County	91	7.9	**Brasher** (town) Saint Lawrence County
18	5.7	**Moira** (town) Franklin County	91	7.9	**Vienna** (town) Oneida County
18	5.7	**University at Buffalo** (CDP) Erie County	94	8.0	**Cortland** (city) Cortland County
20	5.8	**Gordon Heights** (CDP) Suffolk County	94	8.0	**Maybrook** (village) Orange County
20	5.8	**Ticonderoga** (CDP) Essex County	94	8.0	**Stony Brook University** (CDP) Suffolk County
20	5.8	**West Haverstraw** (village) Rockland County	97	8.1	**Lake Erie Beach** (CDP) Erie County
23	5.9	**Arlington** (CDP) Dutchess County	97	8.1	**Marilla** (town) Erie County
23	5.9	**Attica** (village) Wyoming County	97	8.1	**North Collins** (town) Erie County
23	5.9	**Corinth** (town) Saratoga County	97	8.1	**North Dansville** (town) Livingston County
23	5.9	**Fort Edward** (town) Washington County	101	8.2	**Akron** (village) Erie County
27	6.0	**Fairview** (CDP) Westchester County	101	8.2	**Kingsbury** (town) Washington County
27	6.0	**Herkimer** (village) Herkimer County	103	8.3	**Deerpark** (town) Orange County
27	6.0	**Minden** (town) Montgomery County	103	8.3	**Galen** (town) Wayne County
30	6.1	**Ticonderoga** (town) Essex County	103	8.3	**Lisle** (town) Broome County
30	6.1	**Wappingers Falls** (village) Dutchess County	103	8.3	**Schuyler** (town) Herkimer County
32	6.2	**Brentwood** (CDP) Suffolk County	103	8.3	**Sodus** (town) Wayne County
32	6.2	**Colesville** (town) Broome County	103	8.3	**Sound Beach** (CDP) Suffolk County
32	6.2	**Elmira** (city) Chemung County	109	8.4	**Gouverneur** (village) Saint Lawrence County
35	6.3	**Alfred** (town) Allegany County	109	8.4	**Harriman** (village) Orange County
35	6.3	**Dix** (town) Schuyler County	109	8.4	**Lakeview** (CDP) Nassau County
35	6.3	**Inwood** (CDP) Nassau County	109	8.4	**Mastic** (CDP) Suffolk County
35	6.3	**Little Falls** (city) Herkimer County	109	8.4	**Port Jervis** (city) Orange County
35	6.3	**Riverhead** (CDP) Suffolk County	109	8.4	**Wellsville** (village) Allegany County
35	6.3	**Roosevelt** (CDP) Nassau County	115	8.5	**Hamlin** (CDP) Monroe County
41	6.4	**Hillcrest** (CDP) Rockland County	115	8.5	**Haverstraw** (town) Rockland County
41	6.4	**Watertown** (town) Jefferson County	115	8.5	**Herkimer** (town) Herkimer County
43	6.5	**Wyandanch** (CDP) Suffolk County	115	8.5	**Manheim** (town) Herkimer County
44	6.6	**Hudson Falls** (village) Washington County	115	8.5	**Moriah** (town) Essex County
45	6.7	**Elmira Heights** (village) Chemung County	115	8.5	**Mount Morris** (village) Livingston County
45	6.7	**Saranac** (town) Clinton County	115	8.5	**Newburgh** (city) Orange County
47	6.8	**North Bay Shore** (CDP) Suffolk County	115	8.5	**Starkey** (town) Yates County
47	6.8	**Pierrepont** (town) Saint Lawrence County	115	8.5	**Whitehall** (village) Washington County
47	6.8	**Yorkshire** (town) Cattaraugus County	124	8.6	**Bergen** (town) Genesee County
50	6.9	**Corinth** (village) Saratoga County	124	8.6	**Bronx** (borough) Bronx County
50	6.9	**Galeville** (CDP) Onondaga County	124	8.6	**Kirkwood** (town) Broome County
50	6.9	**Munsons Corners** (CDP) Cortland County	124	8.6	**Marcy** (town) Oneida County
50	6.9	**New Haven** (town) Oswego County	124	8.6	**New Cassel** (CDP) Nassau County
50	6.9	**Waterloo** (town) Seneca County	124	8.6	**Rockland** (town) Sullivan County
50	6.9	**Wawarsing** (town) Ulster County	124	8.6	**Thompson** (town) Sullivan County
56	7.0	**Alexandria** (town) Jefferson County	131	8.7	**Cobleskill** (village) Schoharie County
56	7.0	**Au Sable** (town) Clinton County	131	8.7	**Lowville** (town) Lewis County
56	7.0	**Carroll** (town) Chautauqua County	131	8.7	**Lyons** (town) Wayne County
56	7.0	**Central Islip** (CDP) Suffolk County	131	8.7	**Sloan** (village) Erie County
56	7.0	**Collins** (town) Erie County	131	8.7	**Spring Valley** (village) Rockland County
56	7.0	**Dansville** (village) Livingston County	131	8.7	**Tupper Lake** (town) Franklin County
56	7.0	**Fort Edward** (village) Washington County	137	8.8	**Athens** (town) Greene County
56	7.0	**Monticello** (village) Sullivan County	137	8.8	**Southport** (CDP) Chemung County
56	7.0	**Niagara** (town) Niagara County	139	8.9	**Clarendon** (town) Orleans County
56	7.0	**Volney** (town) Oswego County	139	8.9	**Cortlandville** (town) Cortland County
66	7.1	**Bath** (town) Steuben County	139	8.9	**East Rochester** (town/village) Monroe County
67	7.2	**Granville** (town) Washington County	139	8.9	**Elbridge** (town) Onondaga County
67	7.2	**Wayland** (town) Steuben County	139	8.9	**Greenville** (town) Greene County
69	7.3	**Dannemora** (town) Clinton County	139	8.9	**Niagara Falls** (city) Niagara County
69	7.3	**Delaware** (town) Sullivan County	139	8.9	**Ogdensburg** (city) Saint Lawrence County
69	7.3	**Dunkirk** (city) Chautauqua County	139	8.9	**Orleans** (town) Jefferson County
69	7.3	**Hannibal** (town) Oswego County	139	8.9	**Sidney** (town) Delaware County
69	7.3	**Johnson City** (village) Broome County	148	9.0	**Alexander** (town) Genesee County
69	7.3	**Nunda** (town) Livingston County	148	9.0	**Hounsfield** (town) Jefferson County
75	7.4	**Catskill** (village) Greene County	148	9.0	**Lisbon** (town) Saint Lawrence County

Note: This section ranks incorporated places and CDPs (Census Designated Places) with populations of 2,500 or more. Unincorporated postal areas were not considered. Please refer to the User Guide for additional information.

Employment: Computer, Engineering, and Science Occupations

Top 150 Places Ranked in *Descending* Order

State Rank	Percent	Place
1	22.3	**Gang Mills** (CDP) Steuben County
2	20.2	**Northeast Ithaca** (CDP) Tompkins County
3	17.5	**Greenwood Lake** (village) Orange County
4	17.3	**Cayuga Heights** (village) Tompkins County
5	15.9	**Menands** (village) Albany County
6	15.8	**Erwin** (town) Steuben County
7	15.3	**Niskayuna** (town) Schenectady County
8	14.3	**Caroline** (town) Tompkins County
9	14.2	**East Greenbush** (CDP) Rensselaer County
10	13.6	**Herricks** (CDP) Nassau County
11	13.4	**Webster** (village) Monroe County
12	13.2	**Ithaca** (city) Tompkins County
13	12.7	**Honeoye Falls** (village) Monroe County
14	12.6	**Clifton Park** (town) Saratoga County
15	12.5	**Mendon** (town) Monroe County
16	12.4	**Brighton** (CDP) Monroe County
16	12.4	**Newark Valley** (town) Tioga County
16	12.4	**Stony Brook University** (CDP) Suffolk County
19	12.3	**Spackenkill** (CDP) Dutchess County
20	12.1	**Ithaca** (town) Tompkins County
21	12.0	**Larchmont** (village) Westchester County
22	11.7	**Malta** (town) Saratoga County
23	11.5	**Lansing** (village) Tompkins County
24	11.4	**Ballston Spa** (village) Saratoga County
25	11.2	**Halfmoon** (town) Saratoga County
25	11.2	**Owego** (town) Tioga County
27	11.1	**Richmond** (town) Ontario County
28	11.0	**Stony Brook** (CDP) Suffolk County
29	10.9	**Henrietta** (town) Monroe County
29	10.9	**Port Jefferson Station** (CDP) Suffolk County
31	10.5	**Pomona** (village) Rockland County
32	10.4	**Croton-on-Hudson** (village) Westchester County
32	10.4	**Highland** (CDP) Ulster County
34	10.3	**Greenville** (CDP) Westchester County
34	10.3	**Veteran** (town) Chemung County
34	10.3	**Webster** (town) Monroe County
37	10.2	**Woodstock** (town) Ulster County
38	10.1	**Guilderland** (town) Albany County
39	10.0	**Rush** (town) Monroe County
40	9.9	**Perinton** (town) Monroe County
40	9.9	**Thomaston** (village) Nassau County
40	9.9	**Walworth** (town) Wayne County
43	9.8	**Farmington** (town) Ontario County
43	9.8	**Owego** (village) Tioga County
43	9.8	**Port Jefferson** (village) Suffolk County
46	9.7	**Corning** (town) Steuben County
46	9.7	**Saratoga Springs** (city) Saratoga County
46	9.7	**Triangle** (town) Broome County
46	9.7	**West Nyack** (CDP) Rockland County
50	9.6	**Hastings-on-Hudson** (village) Westchester County
51	9.5	**Riverside** (CDP) Suffolk County
51	9.5	**Syosset** (CDP) Nassau County
51	9.5	**Tuxedo** (town) Orange County
54	9.3	**East Greenbush** (town) Rensselaer County
55	9.2	**Armonk** (CDP) Westchester County
55	9.2	**Lansing** (town) Tompkins County
57	9.1	**Chili** (town) Monroe County
58	9.0	**Colonie** (village) Albany County
58	9.0	**Sand Lake** (town) Rensselaer County
60	8.9	**Minoa** (village) Onondaga County
60	8.9	**Penfield** (town) Monroe County
62	8.8	**Bethlehem** (town) Albany County
62	8.8	**East Glenville** (CDP) Schenectady County
62	8.8	**Gardiner** (town) Ulster County
62	8.8	**Lowville** (village) Lewis County
66	8.7	**Lloyd** (town) Ulster County
66	8.7	**Pompey** (town) Onondaga County
66	8.7	**Wilton** (town) Saratoga County
69	8.6	**Huntington** (CDP) Suffolk County
70	8.5	**Endwell** (CDP) Broome County
70	8.5	**Fishkill** (town) Dutchess County
70	8.5	**South Hill** (CDP) Tompkins County
70	8.5	**Wading River** (CDP) Suffolk County
74	8.4	**Binghamton** (town) Broome County
74	8.4	**Fairport** (village) Monroe County
74	8.4	**Irvington** (village) Westchester County
74	8.4	**Lewisboro** (town) Westchester County
78	8.3	**Amityville** (village) Suffolk County
79	8.2	**Broadalbin** (town) Fulton County
79	8.2	**Charlton** (town) Saratoga County
79	8.2	**Cortlandville** (town) Cortland County
79	8.2	**Elmsford** (village) Westchester County
79	8.2	**Great Neck Plaza** (village) Nassau County
79	8.2	**Poestenkill** (town) Rensselaer County
79	8.2	**West Sayville** (CDP) Suffolk County
86	8.1	**Colonie** (town) Albany County
86	8.1	**Flower Hill** (village) Nassau County
86	8.1	**Jericho** (CDP) Nassau County
86	8.1	**Lima** (town) Livingston County
90	8.0	**Brunswick** (town) Rensselaer County
90	8.0	**Fairview** (CDP) Dutchess County
90	8.0	**Milton** (town) Saratoga County
90	8.0	**Ogden** (town) Monroe County
90	8.0	**Westmere** (CDP) Albany County
95	7.9	**Ardsley** (village) Westchester County
95	7.9	**Baldwinsville** (village) Onondaga County
95	7.9	**Briarcliff Manor** (village) Westchester County
95	7.9	**Hartsdale** (CDP) Westchester County
95	7.9	**University Gardens** (CDP) Nassau County
95	7.9	**Vestal** (town) Broome County
101	7.8	**Chenango Bridge** (CDP) Broome County
101	7.8	**Colden** (town) Erie County
101	7.8	**Danby** (town) Tompkins County
101	7.8	**Homer** (town) Cortland County
101	7.8	**Montrose** (CDP) Westchester County
101	7.8	**Schodack** (town) Rensselaer County
101	7.8	**Troy** (city) Rensselaer County
101	7.8	**West Sand Lake** (CDP) Rensselaer County
109	7.7	**Ballston** (town) Saratoga County
109	7.7	**Piermont** (village) Rockland County
109	7.7	**Poughkeepsie** (town) Dutchess County
109	7.7	**Red Hook** (town) Dutchess County
109	7.7	**Setauket-East Setauket** (CDP) Suffolk County
109	7.7	**Ulysses** (town) Tompkins County
109	7.7	**Washingtonville** (village) Orange County
116	7.6	**Boston** (town) Erie County
116	7.6	**La Grange** (town) Dutchess County
116	7.6	**North Greenbush** (town) Rensselaer County
119	7.5	**Irondequoit** (CDP) Monroe County
119	7.5	**Pittsford** (town) Monroe County
121	7.4	**Coeymans** (town) Albany County
121	7.4	**Corning** (city) Steuben County
121	7.4	**Delhi** (town) Delaware County
121	7.4	**Hauppauge** (CDP) Suffolk County
121	7.4	**New Paltz** (town) Ulster County
121	7.4	**Putnam Valley** (town) Putnam County
121	7.4	**Ravena** (village) Albany County
128	7.3	**Bedford Hills** (CDP) Westchester County
128	7.3	**Chittenango** (village) Madison County
128	7.3	**Dryden** (town) Tompkins County
128	7.3	**South Nyack** (village) Rockland County
128	7.3	**Suffern** (village) Rockland County
128	7.3	**Union Vale** (town) Dutchess County
134	7.2	**Albany** (city) Albany County
134	7.2	**Amherst** (town) Erie County
134	7.2	**Dobbs Ferry** (village) Westchester County
134	7.2	**Farmingdale** (village) Nassau County
134	7.2	**Greenburgh** (town) Westchester County
134	7.2	**Hunter** (town) Greene County
134	7.2	**Lyncourt** (CDP) Onondaga County
134	7.2	**New York Mills** (village) Oneida County
134	7.2	**North Great River** (CDP) Suffolk County
134	7.2	**Scarsdale** (town/village) Westchester County
134	7.2	**Union** (town) Broome County
134	7.2	**Williamsville** (village) Erie County
146	7.1	**Bayville** (village) Nassau County
146	7.1	**Livonia** (town) Livingston County
146	7.1	**Wynantskill** (CDP) Rensselaer County
149	7.0	**Great Neck Estates** (village) Nassau County
149	7.0	**Victor** (village) Ontario County

Note: This section ranks incorporated places and CDPs (Census Designated Places) with populations of 2,500 or more. Unincorporated postal areas were not considered. Please refer to the User Guide for additional information.

Employment: Computer, Engineering, and Science Occupations

Top 150 Places Ranked in *Ascending* Order

State Rank	Percent	Place	State Rank	Percent	Place
1	0.0	**Carroll** (town) Chautauqua County	74	1.6	**Bay Shore** (CDP) Suffolk County
1	0.0	**Carthage** (village) Jefferson County	74	1.6	**Beekmantown** (town) Clinton County
1	0.0	**Chester** (town) Warren County	74	1.6	**Dolgeville** (village) Herkimer County
1	0.0	**Dannemora** (village) Clinton County	74	1.6	**Hannibal** (town) Oswego County
1	0.0	**Dansville** (village) Livingston County	74	1.6	**Lake Placid** (village) Essex County
1	0.0	**Ellenville** (village) Ulster County	74	1.6	**Springs** (CDP) Suffolk County
1	0.0	**Flanders** (CDP) Suffolk County	74	1.6	**Waterloo** (town) Seneca County
1	0.0	**Lake Luzerne** (town) Warren County	74	1.6	**Waverly** (village) Tioga County
1	0.0	**Rockland** (town) Sullivan County	74	1.6	**Whitehall** (village) Washington County
1	0.0	**Walton** (village) Delaware County	74	1.6	**Wolcott** (town) Wayne County
11	0.2	**Sidney** (village) Delaware County	86	1.7	**Brasher** (town) Saint Lawrence County
12	0.3	**Greenport** (town) Columbia County	86	1.7	**Gloversville** (city) Fulton County
13	0.5	**Gouverneur** (town) Saint Lawrence County	86	1.7	**Hanover** (town) Chautauqua County
13	0.5	**Yorkshire** (town) Cattaraugus County	86	1.7	**Lido Beach** (CDP) Nassau County
15	0.6	**Lisbon** (town) Saint Lawrence County	86	1.7	**Malone** (town) Franklin County
16	0.7	**Bainbridge** (town) Chenango County	86	1.7	**Mount Morris** (village) Livingston County
16	0.7	**Mechanicstown** (CDP) Orange County	86	1.7	**New Haven** (town) Oswego County
16	0.7	**North Dansville** (town) Livingston County	86	1.7	**Vails Gate** (CDP) Orange County
16	0.7	**Sloan** (village) Erie County	86	1.7	**Westfield** (town) Chautauqua County
20	0.8	**Croghan** (town) Lewis County	95	1.8	**Adams** (town) Jefferson County
20	0.8	**Monticello** (village) Sullivan County	95	1.8	**Batavia** (town) Genesee County
20	0.8	**Tupper Lake** (village) Franklin County	95	1.8	**Castile** (town) Wyoming County
23	0.9	**Jay** (town) Essex County	95	1.8	**Frankfort** (village) Herkimer County
23	0.9	**Portland** (town) Chautauqua County	95	1.8	**Le Roy** (village) Genesee County
23	0.9	**Whitehall** (town) Washington County	95	1.8	**Mastic** (CDP) Suffolk County
26	1.0	**Brownville** (town) Jefferson County	95	1.8	**Oneida** (city) Madison County
26	1.0	**Dannemora** (town) Clinton County	95	1.8	**Otsego** (town) Otsego County
26	1.0	**Gouverneur** (village) Saint Lawrence County	95	1.8	**Palatine** (town) Montgomery County
26	1.0	**Hillcrest** (CDP) Rockland County	95	1.8	**South Lockport** (CDP) Niagara County
26	1.0	**Oswegatchie** (town) Saint Lawrence County	105	1.9	**Albion** (village) Orleans County
26	1.0	**Sidney** (town) Delaware County	105	1.9	**Central Islip** (CDP) Suffolk County
32	1.1	**Chesterfield** (town) Essex County	105	1.9	**Deerpark** (town) Orange County
32	1.1	**Inwood** (CDP) Nassau County	105	1.9	**Glasco** (CDP) Ulster County
32	1.1	**Mohawk** (village) Herkimer County	105	1.9	**Louisville** (town) Saint Lawrence County
32	1.1	**Mount Morris** (town) Livingston County	105	1.9	**Madison** (town) Madison County
32	1.1	**Ogdensburg** (city) Saint Lawrence County	105	1.9	**Milford** (town) Otsego County
32	1.1	**Tupper Lake** (town) Franklin County	105	1.9	**Montauk** (CDP) Suffolk County
32	1.1	**Unadilla** (town) Otsego County	105	1.9	**Otego** (town) Otsego County
32	1.1	**Verona** (town) Oneida County	105	1.9	**Royalton** (town) Niagara County
40	1.2	**Alexandria** (town) Jefferson County	105	1.9	**Saranac** (town) Clinton County
40	1.2	**Davenport** (town) Delaware County	105	1.9	**Seneca** (town) Ontario County
40	1.2	**Fort Ann** (town) Washington County	105	1.9	**Warsaw** (village) Wyoming County
40	1.2	**Livingston** (town) Columbia County	105	1.9	**Wellsville** (village) Allegany County
40	1.2	**Orange Lake** (CDP) Orange County	119	2.0	**Barton** (town) Tioga County
40	1.2	**Southold** (CDP) Suffolk County	119	2.0	**Bronx** (borough) Bronx County
46	1.3	**Delaware** (town) Sullivan County	119	2.0	**Canisteo** (town) Steuben County
46	1.3	**Oakfield** (town) Genesee County	119	2.0	**Haverstraw** (village) Rockland County
46	1.3	**Port Chester** (village) Westchester County	119	2.0	**Lackawanna** (city) Erie County
46	1.3	**Shelby** (town) Orleans County	119	2.0	**Mattydale** (CDP) Onondaga County
46	1.3	**Westfield** (village) Chautauqua County	119	2.0	**Mayfield** (town) Fulton County
51	1.4	**Amenia** (town) Dutchess County	119	2.0	**North Amityville** (CDP) Suffolk County
51	1.4	**Colesville** (town) Broome County	119	2.0	**Sandy Creek** (town) Oswego County
51	1.4	**Granville** (town) Washington County	119	2.0	**Sherrill** (city) Oneida County
51	1.4	**Hancock** (town) Delaware County	119	2.0	**Spring Valley** (village) Rockland County
51	1.4	**Liberty** (town) Sullivan County	119	2.0	**Ticonderoga** (town) Essex County
51	1.4	**Manheim** (town) Herkimer County	119	2.0	**White Creek** (town) Washington County
51	1.4	**North Bay Shore** (CDP) Suffolk County	132	2.1	**Brentwood** (CDP) Suffolk County
51	1.4	**Roosevelt** (CDP) Nassau County	132	2.1	**Denmark** (town) Lewis County
51	1.4	**Saint Johnsville** (town) Montgomery County	132	2.1	**East Quogue** (CDP) Suffolk County
51	1.4	**Salamanca** (city) Cattaraugus County	132	2.1	**Fayette** (town) Seneca County
51	1.4	**Shandaken** (town) Ulster County	132	2.1	**Goshen** (village) Orange County
51	1.4	**Solvay** (village) Onondaga County	132	2.1	**Hempstead** (village) Nassau County
51	1.4	**West Elmira** (CDP) Chemung County	132	2.1	**Kiryas Joel** (village) Orange County
64	1.5	**Elmira** (town) Chemung County	132	2.1	**Liberty** (village) Sullivan County
64	1.5	**Hoosick Falls** (village) Rensselaer County	132	2.1	**Mamakating** (town) Sullivan County
64	1.5	**Malone** (village) Franklin County	132	2.1	**Minden** (town) Montgomery County
64	1.5	**Moira** (town) Franklin County	132	2.1	**New Hempstead** (village) Rockland County
64	1.5	**Moriah** (town) Essex County	132	2.1	**Randolph** (town) Cattaraugus County
64	1.5	**Newark** (village) Wayne County	132	2.1	**Rocky Point** (CDP) Suffolk County
64	1.5	**Salem** (town) Washington County	132	2.1	**Rye** (town) Westchester County
64	1.5	**Stockport** (town) Columbia County	132	2.1	**Schuyler** (town) Herkimer County
64	1.5	**Thompson** (town) Sullivan County	132	2.1	**Sherburne** (town) Chenango County
64	1.5	**Tioga** (town) Tioga County	132	2.1	**Wawarsing** (town) Ulster County
74	1.6	**Albion** (town) Orleans County	132	2.1	**Yorkville** (village) Oneida County
74	1.6	**Annsville** (town) Oneida County	150	2.2	**Bennington** (town) Wyoming County

Note: *This section ranks incorporated places and CDPs (Census Designated Places) with populations of 2,500 or more. Unincorporated postal areas were not considered. Please refer to the User Guide for additional information.*

Employment: Education, Legal, Community Service, Arts, and Media Occupations

Top 150 Places Ranked in *Descending* Order

State Rank	Percent	Place
1	48.4	**Kaser** (village) Rockland County
2	43.2	**Cayuga Heights** (village) Tompkins County
3	38.3	**Hamilton** (village) Madison County
4	36.9	**Canton** (village) Saint Lawrence County
5	34.7	**New Square** (village) Rockland County
6	34.3	**Monsey** (CDP) Rockland County
7	31.3	**Clarence Center** (CDP) Erie County
7	31.3	**Hamilton** (town) Madison County
9	30.7	**Hastings-on-Hudson** (village) Westchester County
10	30.5	**Halesite** (CDP) Suffolk County
11	30.3	**West Point** (CDP) Orange County
12	30.0	**Ithaca** (town) Tompkins County
13	29.8	**Potsdam** (village) Saint Lawrence County
14	29.1	**Lansing** (village) Tompkins County
15	29.0	**Sea Cliff** (village) Nassau County
16	28.9	**Saint Regis Mohawk Reservation** (reservation) Franklin County
17	28.3	**Ithaca** (city) Tompkins County
18	27.8	**Pleasantville** (village) Westchester County
19	27.4	**Northeast Ithaca** (CDP) Tompkins County
20	27.2	**Lawrence** (village) Nassau County
21	26.4	**Hartsdale** (CDP) Westchester County
22	26.2	**Irvington** (village) Westchester County
23	26.0	**New Castle** (town) Westchester County
24	25.9	**Canton** (town) Saint Lawrence County
24	25.9	**Hewlett** (CDP) Nassau County
24	25.9	**Lansing** (town) Tompkins County
24	25.9	**Port Washington North** (village) Nassau County
28	25.4	**Cornwall-on-Hudson** (village) Orange County
28	25.4	**Greenville** (CDP) Westchester County
28	25.4	**Viola** (CDP) Rockland County
31	25.2	**Pelham Manor** (village) Westchester County
32	24.6	**Potsdam** (town) Saint Lawrence County
33	24.5	**South Nyack** (village) Rockland County
34	24.2	**Dobbs Ferry** (village) Westchester County
34	24.2	**Pound Ridge** (town) Westchester County
36	23.9	**Woodmere** (CDP) Nassau County
37	23.5	**Brighton** (CDP) Monroe County
37	23.5	**Croton-on-Hudson** (village) Westchester County
37	23.5	**Lloyd Harbor** (village) Suffolk County
40	23.4	**West Bay Shore** (CDP) Suffolk County
41	23.3	**Hurley** (town) Ulster County
42	23.2	**Scarsdale** (town/village) Westchester County
42	23.2	**Woodstock** (town) Ulster County
44	23.1	**Blauvelt** (CDP) Rockland County
45	23.0	**Manlius** (village) Onondaga County
45	23.0	**Rhinebeck** (village) Dutchess County
47	22.9	**Cazenovia** (village) Madison County
47	22.9	**New Paltz** (town) Ulster County
49	22.6	**Larchmont** (village) Westchester County
50	22.5	**Babylon** (village) Suffolk County
50	22.5	**Great Neck Estates** (village) Nassau County
50	22.5	**West Elmira** (CDP) Chemung County
53	22.4	**Bellmore** (CDP) Nassau County
53	22.4	**Huntington** (CDP) Suffolk County
55	22.2	**Lowville** (village) Lewis County
55	22.2	**Williamsville** (village) Erie County
57	22.1	**Setauket-East Setauket** (CDP) Suffolk County
57	22.1	**Stony Brook** (CDP) Suffolk County
59	22.0	**Heritage Hills** (CDP) Westchester County
59	22.0	**Rockville Centre** (village) Nassau County
61	21.9	**Fredonia** (village) Chautauqua County
61	21.9	**Merrick** (CDP) Nassau County
63	21.8	**West Hills** (CDP) Suffolk County
64	21.7	**Briarcliff Manor** (village) Westchester County
64	21.7	**Centerport** (CDP) Suffolk County
64	21.7	**Cold Spring Harbor** (CDP) Suffolk County
67	21.6	**Pelham** (town) Westchester County
68	21.5	**Greenburgh** (town) Westchester County
69	21.3	**Pittsford** (town) Monroe County
70	21.1	**Fort Salonga** (CDP) Suffolk County
70	21.1	**Manhattan** (borough) New York County
72	21.0	**Bronxville** (village) Westchester County
72	21.0	**Elmira** (town) Chemung County
74	20.8	**Ardsley** (village) Westchester County
74	20.8	**Shandaken** (town) Ulster County
76	20.7	**Mamaroneck** (town) Westchester County
77	20.6	**Bethlehem** (town) Albany County
77	20.6	**Flower Hill** (village) Nassau County
77	20.6	**Lewisboro** (town) Westchester County
77	20.6	**Nyack** (village) Rockland County
77	20.6	**Rye Brook** (village) Westchester County
77	20.6	**Sloatsburg** (village) Rockland County
77	20.6	**Thomaston** (village) Nassau County
84	20.5	**East Hills** (village) Nassau County
84	20.5	**Eastchester** (CDP) Westchester County
84	20.5	**Stony Brook University** (CDP) Suffolk County
87	20.4	**East Shoreham** (CDP) Suffolk County
87	20.4	**Eastchester** (town) Westchester County
89	20.3	**Danby** (town) Tompkins County
89	20.3	**Homer** (village) Cortland County
89	20.3	**Port Washington** (CDP) Nassau County
92	20.2	**Delaware** (town) Sullivan County
93	20.1	**Kiryas Joel** (village) Orange County
93	20.1	**Sayville** (CDP) Suffolk County
95	20.0	**Cortlandt** (town) Westchester County
95	20.0	**Floral Park** (village) Nassau County
95	20.0	**Garden City South** (CDP) Nassau County
95	20.0	**Marcy** (town) Oneida County
95	20.0	**Old Bethpage** (CDP) Nassau County
95	20.0	**Philipstown** (town) Putnam County
101	19.9	**Yorktown** (town) Westchester County
102	19.8	**Alfred** (town) Allegany County
102	19.8	**Geneseo** (village) Livingston County
102	19.8	**Jefferson Valley-Yorktown** (CDP) Westchester County
102	19.8	**New Paltz** (village) Ulster County
102	19.8	**Port Jefferson** (village) Suffolk County
102	19.8	**Tuckahoe** (village) Westchester County
108	19.7	**Orangetown** (town) Rockland County
109	19.6	**Pearl River** (CDP) Rockland County
109	19.6	**Rhinebeck** (town) Dutchess County
111	19.5	**Calcium** (CDP) Jefferson County
111	19.5	**Glenwood Landing** (CDP) Nassau County
111	19.5	**South Hill** (CDP) Tompkins County
114	19.4	**Catskill** (village) Greene County
114	19.4	**Great Neck Plaza** (village) Nassau County
114	19.4	**North Castle** (town) Westchester County
117	19.3	**Dryden** (town) Tompkins County
117	19.3	**Oneonta** (city) Otsego County
117	19.3	**Red Hook** (town) Dutchess County
117	19.3	**Somers** (town) Westchester County
117	19.3	**Stanford** (town) Dutchess County
122	19.2	**East Aurora** (village) Erie County
122	19.2	**Lowville** (town) Lewis County
122	19.2	**Manlius** (town) Onondaga County
122	19.2	**Oceanside** (CDP) Nassau County
126	19.1	**Kirkland** (town) Oneida County
126	19.1	**Nesconset** (CDP) Suffolk County
126	19.1	**Pelham** (village) Westchester County
129	19.0	**Bayville** (village) Nassau County
129	19.0	**Montrose** (CDP) Westchester County
129	19.0	**Pomfret** (town) Chautauqua County
132	18.9	**East Norwich** (CDP) Nassau County
133	18.8	**East Greenbush** (CDP) Rensselaer County
133	18.8	**Garden City** (village) Nassau County
133	18.8	**Goshen** (village) Orange County
133	18.8	**Skaneateles** (town) Onondaga County
137	18.7	**Highlands** (town) Orange County
137	18.7	**Oakdale** (CDP) Suffolk County
137	18.7	**Otsego** (town) Otsego County
137	18.7	**Sands Point** (village) Nassau County
141	18.6	**East Williston** (village) Nassau County
141	18.6	**Lido Beach** (CDP) Nassau County
141	18.6	**North Merrick** (CDP) Nassau County
141	18.6	**Westvale** (CDP) Onondaga County
145	18.4	**Brightwaters** (village) Suffolk County
145	18.4	**Munsons Corners** (CDP) Cortland County
145	18.4	**Plainview** (CDP) Nassau County
148	18.3	**Athens** (town) Greene County
148	18.3	**Cornwall** (town) Orange County
150	18.2	**Callicoon** (town) Sullivan County

Note: This section ranks incorporated places and CDPs (Census Designated Places) with populations of 2,500 or more. Unincorporated postal areas were not considered. Please refer to the User Guide for additional information.

Employment: Education, Legal, Community Service, Arts, and Media Occupations

Top 150 Places Ranked in *Ascending* Order

State Rank	Percent	Place	State Rank	Percent	Place
1	3.1	Maybrook (village) Orange County	76	7.2	Calverton (CDP) Suffolk County
2	3.3	Mohawk (town) Montgomery County	76	7.2	Evans (town) Erie County
3	3.9	Vienna (town) Oneida County	76	7.2	Gouverneur (village) Saint Lawrence County
4	4.0	Vails Gate (CDP) Orange County	76	7.2	Hastings (town) Oswego County
5	4.1	Moriches (CDP) Suffolk County	76	7.2	Newburgh (city) Orange County
6	4.2	North Bay Shore (CDP) Suffolk County	81	7.3	Altona (town) Clinton County
7	4.3	Constantia (town) Oswego County	81	7.3	Farmingville (CDP) Suffolk County
7	4.3	Fairview (CDP) Westchester County	81	7.3	Granby (town) Oswego County
7	4.3	Whitesboro (village) Oneida County	81	7.3	Granville (town) Washington County
10	4.6	Verona (town) Oneida County	81	7.3	Jerusalem (town) Yates County
11	4.7	Holland (town) Erie County	81	7.3	Mastic Beach (village) Suffolk County
12	4.9	Cambria (town) Niagara County	81	7.3	Shelby (town) Orleans County
12	4.9	Newfane (town) Niagara County	81	7.3	Sodus (town) Wayne County
14	5.0	Brentwood (CDP) Suffolk County	81	7.3	Westmoreland (town) Oneida County
15	5.1	Attica (village) Wyoming County	90	7.4	Bedford Hills (CDP) Westchester County
15	5.1	Wilna (town) Jefferson County	90	7.4	Fort Drum (CDP) Jefferson County
17	5.3	Clarendon (town) Orleans County	90	7.4	Newfane (CDP) Niagara County
17	5.3	Mattydale (CDP) Onondaga County	90	7.4	South Glens Falls (village) Saratoga County
17	5.3	Riverhead (CDP) Suffolk County	94	7.5	Cobleskill (village) Schoharie County
17	5.3	Sloan (village) Erie County	95	7.6	Akron (village) Erie County
21	5.4	Whitehall (town) Washington County	95	7.6	Minden (town) Montgomery County
22	5.5	Attica (town) Wyoming County	95	7.6	Village Green (CDP) Onondaga County
22	5.5	Fort Edward (town) Washington County	95	7.6	Watervliet (city) Albany County
24	5.6	Albion (village) Orleans County	99	7.7	Blasdell (village) Erie County
24	5.6	Champlain (town) Clinton County	99	7.7	Brewerton (CDP) Onondaga County
24	5.6	Lake Placid (village) Essex County	99	7.7	Dannemora (village) Clinton County
24	5.6	New Cassel (CDP) Nassau County	99	7.7	Greenwood Lake (village) Orange County
24	5.6	Southport (CDP) Chemung County	99	7.7	Haverstraw (village) Rockland County
29	5.7	Hannibal (town) Oswego County	99	7.7	Seneca (town) Ontario County
29	5.7	Pavilion (town) Genesee County	99	7.7	Somerset (town) Niagara County
29	5.7	SUNY Oswego (CDP) Oswego County	99	7.7	Wyandanch (CDP) Suffolk County
32	5.8	Guilford (town) Chenango County	107	7.8	Poestenkill (town) Rensselaer County
33	5.9	Fort Edward (village) Washington County	107	7.8	Roosevelt (CDP) Nassau County
34	6.0	Lyncourt (CDP) Onondaga County	107	7.8	Warsaw (town) Wyoming County
35	6.1	Newark Valley (town) Tioga County	107	7.8	Waterford (town) Saratoga County
35	6.1	North Bellport (CDP) Suffolk County	111	7.9	Barton (town) Tioga County
35	6.1	Pittstown (town) Rensselaer County	111	7.9	Charlton (town) Saratoga County
38	6.2	Alexander (town) Genesee County	111	7.9	Colonie (village) Albany County
38	6.2	Barker (town) Broome County	111	7.9	Kirkwood (town) Broome County
38	6.2	Brutus (town) Cayuga County	111	7.9	Mooers (town) Clinton County
38	6.2	Yorkshire (town) Cattaraugus County	111	7.9	Palmyra (village) Wayne County
42	6.3	Lenox (town) Madison County	111	7.9	Schodack (town) Rensselaer County
42	6.3	Mastic (CDP) Suffolk County	111	7.9	Westerlo (town) Albany County
42	6.3	Warsaw (village) Wyoming County	119	8.0	Hoosick Falls (village) Rensselaer County
45	6.4	Murray (town) Orleans County	119	8.0	Mayfield (town) Fulton County
45	6.4	Whitehall (village) Washington County	119	8.0	Niagara (town) Niagara County
47	6.5	Carthage (village) Jefferson County	119	8.0	Sardinia (town) Erie County
47	6.5	Central Islip (CDP) Suffolk County	119	8.0	Scotchtown (CDP) Orange County
47	6.5	Copiague (CDP) Suffolk County	119	8.0	Solvay (village) Onondaga County
47	6.5	Eden (town) Erie County	125	8.1	Colden (town) Erie County
47	6.5	Flanders (CDP) Suffolk County	125	8.1	Gloversville (city) Fulton County
47	6.5	Stockport (town) Columbia County	125	8.1	Greenville (town) Orange County
47	6.5	West Haverstraw (village) Rockland County	125	8.1	Marlboro (CDP) Ulster County
54	6.6	Canastota (village) Madison County	125	8.1	Selden (CDP) Suffolk County
54	6.6	Keeseville (village) Clinton County	130	8.2	Campbell (town) Steuben County
54	6.6	Oswegatchie (town) Saint Lawrence County	130	8.2	Endicott (village) Broome County
54	6.6	Riverside (CDP) Suffolk County	130	8.2	Islandia (village) Suffolk County
54	6.6	Wappingers Falls (village) Dutchess County	130	8.2	New Haven (town) Oswego County
59	6.7	Hempstead (village) Nassau County	130	8.2	Nichols (town) Tioga County
59	6.7	Oakfield (town) Genesee County	130	8.2	Triangle (town) Broome County
59	6.7	Port Chester (village) Westchester County	136	8.3	Au Sable (town) Clinton County
62	6.8	Annsville (town) Oneida County	136	8.3	Kingsbury (town) Washington County
62	6.8	Liberty (village) Sullivan County	136	8.3	Le Roy (village) Genesee County
64	6.9	East Syracuse (village) Onondaga County	136	8.3	New Berlin (town) Chenango County
64	6.9	Hoosick (town) Rensselaer County	136	8.3	Pamelia (town) Jefferson County
64	6.9	LaFayette (town) Onondaga County	136	8.3	Spring Valley (village) Rockland County
64	6.9	North Amityville (CDP) Suffolk County	136	8.3	Stephentown (town) Rensselaer County
68	7.0	Albion (town) Orleans County	143	8.4	Benton (town) Yates County
68	7.0	Depew (village) Erie County	143	8.4	Castile (town) Wyoming County
68	7.0	Inwood (CDP) Nassau County	143	8.4	Corinth (town) Saratoga County
68	7.0	York (town) Livingston County	143	8.4	Deerpark (town) Orange County
72	7.1	Galeville (CDP) Onondaga County	143	8.4	Duanesburg (town) Schenectady County
72	7.1	Monticello (village) Sullivan County	143	8.4	East Bloomfield (town) Ontario County
72	7.1	Schaghticoke (town) Rensselaer County	143	8.4	Livingston (town) Columbia County
72	7.1	Southport (town) Chemung County	143	8.4	Manchester (town) Ontario County

Note: This section ranks incorporated places and CDPs (Census Designated Places) with populations of 2,500 or more. Unincorporated postal areas were not considered. Please refer to the User Guide for additional information.

Employment: Healthcare Practitioners

Top 150 Places Ranked in *Descending* Order

State Rank	Percent	Place	State Rank	Percent	Place
1	24.3	**Manhasset Hills** (CDP) Nassau County	76	10.4	**Munsey Park** (village) Nassau County
2	24.2	**North Hills** (village) Nassau County	76	10.4	**Syosset** (CDP) Nassau County
3	19.8	**Otsego** (town) Otsego County	76	10.4	**Tappan** (CDP) Rockland County
4	18.5	**Montebello** (village) Rockland County	79	10.3	**Clarkstown** (town) Rockland County
5	17.5	**Old Westbury** (village) Nassau County	79	10.3	**Fairmount** (CDP) Onondaga County
6	17.3	**Great Neck Estates** (village) Nassau County	79	10.3	**Woodbury** (village) Orange County
7	17.0	**Woodbury** (CDP) Nassau County	82	10.2	**Carle Place** (CDP) Nassau County
8	16.4	**Wesley Hills** (village) Rockland County	82	10.2	**Lysander** (town) Onondaga County
9	15.7	**Bardonia** (CDP) Rockland County	82	10.2	**Pompey** (town) Onondaga County
10	15.5	**East Hills** (village) Nassau County	82	10.2	**Valley Cottage** (CDP) Rockland County
11	15.3	**Herricks** (CDP) Nassau County	86	10.1	**Marcy** (town) Oneida County
12	14.9	**Muttontown** (village) Nassau County	86	10.1	**Newfield** (town) Tompkins County
13	14.8	**East Williston** (village) Nassau County	86	10.1	**Ogdensburg** (city) Saint Lawrence County
14	14.5	**Lake Success** (village) Nassau County	86	10.1	**Victor** (village) Ontario County
15	14.4	**Lido Beach** (CDP) Nassau County	90	10.0	**Hamburg** (village) Erie County
16	14.2	**Rhinebeck** (village) Dutchess County	90	10.0	**Sherburne** (town) Chenango County
17	14.1	**Garden City Park** (CDP) Nassau County	90	10.0	**Van Buren** (town) Onondaga County
17	14.1	**Roslyn Heights** (CDP) Nassau County	93	9.9	**Canisteo** (town) Steuben County
19	14.0	**Searingtown** (CDP) Nassau County	93	9.9	**Chester** (village) Orange County
20	13.9	**Great Neck** (village) Nassau County	93	9.9	**Fayetteville** (village) Onondaga County
21	13.6	**Roslyn** (village) Nassau County	93	9.9	**Glen Head** (CDP) Nassau County
22	13.5	**Brightwaters** (village) Suffolk County	93	9.9	**Manlius** (town) Onondaga County
22	13.5	**Chestnut Ridge** (village) Rockland County	93	9.9	**Orchard Park** (village) Erie County
22	13.5	**Rhinebeck** (town) Dutchess County	93	9.9	**West Elmira** (CDP) Chemung County
25	13.4	**Pomona** (village) Rockland County	100	9.8	**Brookville** (village) Nassau County
25	13.4	**Port Jefferson** (village) Suffolk County	100	9.8	**Catskill** (village) Greene County
27	13.2	**North New Hyde Park** (CDP) Nassau County	100	9.8	**Gordon Heights** (CDP) Suffolk County
28	13.1	**Hounsfield** (town) Jefferson County	100	9.8	**Hilton** (village) Monroe County
28	13.1	**Lawrence** (village) Nassau County	100	9.8	**Pierrepont** (town) Saint Lawrence County
28	13.1	**Sherrill** (city) Oneida County	100	9.8	**Schuyler Falls** (town) Clinton County
31	13.0	**New Hyde Park** (village) Nassau County	100	9.8	**Vernon** (town) Oneida County
32	12.8	**Dix Hills** (CDP) Suffolk County	100	9.8	**Woodbury** (town) Orange County
33	12.7	**Stony Brook** (CDP) Suffolk County	108	9.7	**Mohawk** (village) Herkimer County
34	12.4	**Clarence** (CDP) Erie County	108	9.7	**Penfield** (town) Monroe County
35	12.3	**Jericho** (CDP) Nassau County	108	9.7	**Piermont** (village) Rockland County
35	12.3	**Malverne** (village) Nassau County	108	9.7	**Rocky Point** (CDP) Suffolk County
37	12.2	**Highland** (CDP) Ulster County	108	9.7	**Saranac Lake** (village) Franklin County
37	12.2	**Johnstown** (town) Fulton County	108	9.7	**Valley Stream** (village) Nassau County
39	12.1	**Horseheads North** (CDP) Chemung County	108	9.7	**Wheatley Heights** (CDP) Suffolk County
40	12.0	**Rutland** (town) Jefferson County	115	9.6	**Camillus** (town) Onondaga County
40	12.0	**Watertown** (town) Jefferson County	115	9.6	**Deerfield** (town) Oneida County
42	11.9	**Galway** (town) Saratoga County	115	9.6	**Floyd** (town) Oneida County
42	11.9	**Hewlett** (CDP) Nassau County	115	9.6	**Gouverneur** (town) Saint Lawrence County
44	11.7	**Horseheads** (village) Chemung County	115	9.6	**Newfane** (CDP) Niagara County
44	11.7	**Setauket-East Setauket** (CDP) Suffolk County	115	9.6	**Ontario** (town) Wayne County
46	11.6	**Woodmere** (CDP) Nassau County	115	9.6	**Sangerfield** (town) Oneida County
47	11.5	**Cambria** (town) Niagara County	122	9.5	**East Glenville** (CDP) Schenectady County
47	11.5	**Great Neck Plaza** (village) Nassau County	122	9.5	**Greenville** (town) Greene County
49	11.4	**Dix** (town) Schuyler County	122	9.5	**Kings Point** (village) Nassau County
49	11.4	**Greenville** (CDP) Westchester County	122	9.5	**Lakewood** (village) Chautauqua County
49	11.4	**Horseheads** (town) Chemung County	122	9.5	**Red Oaks Mill** (CDP) Dutchess County
52	11.3	**Briarcliff Manor** (village) Westchester County	122	9.5	**Skaneateles** (town) Onondaga County
52	11.3	**Brookhaven** (CDP) Suffolk County	122	9.5	**Vails Gate** (CDP) Orange County
52	11.3	**Mohawk** (town) Montgomery County	129	9.4	**Elma Center** (CDP) Erie County
55	11.2	**Marbletown** (town) Ulster County	129	9.4	**Saranac** (town) Clinton County
55	11.2	**New City** (CDP) Rockland County	129	9.4	**West Nyack** (CDP) Rockland County
55	11.2	**New Hartford** (town) Oneida County	129	9.4	**Westerlo** (town) Albany County
58	11.1	**North Valley Stream** (CDP) Nassau County	129	9.4	**Westfield** (village) Chautauqua County
58	11.1	**South Valley Stream** (CDP) Nassau County	134	9.3	**Broadalbin** (town) Fulton County
60	11.0	**Manorville** (CDP) Suffolk County	134	9.3	**Canandaigua** (city) Ontario County
61	10.9	**Johnson City** (village) Broome County	134	9.3	**Hillcrest** (CDP) Rockland County
61	10.9	**Lowville** (town) Lewis County	137	9.2	**Amherst** (town) Erie County
63	10.8	**North Hempstead** (town) Nassau County	137	9.2	**Baldwin Harbor** (CDP) Nassau County
63	10.8	**Village Green** (CDP) Onondaga County	137	9.2	**Bayport** (CDP) Suffolk County
65	10.7	**Miller Place** (CDP) Suffolk County	137	9.2	**Chenango** (town) Broome County
65	10.7	**Mineola** (village) Nassau County	137	9.2	**Chenango Bridge** (CDP) Broome County
65	10.7	**Orange Lake** (CDP) Orange County	137	9.2	**Glenwood Landing** (CDP) Nassau County
68	10.6	**Baldwin** (CDP) Nassau County	137	9.2	**Kirkland** (town) Oneida County
68	10.6	**Brighton** (CDP) Monroe County	137	9.2	**Manhasset** (CDP) Nassau County
68	10.6	**Mount Ivy** (CDP) Rockland County	137	9.2	**Moriches** (CDP) Suffolk County
68	10.6	**Pittsford** (town) Monroe County	137	9.2	**North Castle** (town) Westchester County
68	10.6	**Pittstown** (town) Rensselaer County	137	9.2	**Portville** (town) Cattaraugus County
73	10.5	**Florida** (town) Montgomery County	137	9.2	**Salisbury** (CDP) Nassau County
73	10.5	**Lowville** (village) Lewis County	137	9.2	**Spackenkill** (CDP) Dutchess County
73	10.5	**Nanuet** (CDP) Rockland County	137	9.2	**Viola** (CDP) Rockland County

Note: *This section ranks incorporated places and CDPs (Census Designated Places) with populations of 2,500 or more. Unincorporated postal areas were not considered. Please refer to the User Guide for additional information.*

Employment: Healthcare Practitioners

Top 150 Places Ranked in *Ascending* Order

State Rank	Percent	Place		State Rank	Percent	Place
1	0.0	**Binghamton University** (CDP) Broome County		72	3.1	**Oswego** (town) Oswego County
1	0.0	**Kaser** (village) Rockland County		72	3.1	**Wolcott** (town) Wayne County
1	0.0	**Riverside** (CDP) Suffolk County		78	3.2	**Candor** (town) Tioga County
1	0.0	**SUNY Oswego** (CDP) Oswego County		78	3.2	**Cornwall-on-Hudson** (village) Orange County
5	0.4	**Alfred** (village) Allegany County		78	3.2	**Dannemora** (village) Clinton County
6	0.6	**Alfred** (town) Allegany County		78	3.2	**Florida** (village) Orange County
6	0.6	**Kiryas Joel** (village) Orange County		78	3.2	**Newark** (village) Wayne County
8	0.7	**New Square** (village) Rockland County		78	3.2	**Ridgeway** (town) Orleans County
9	0.9	**Ellenville** (village) Ulster County		78	3.2	**Romulus** (town) Seneca County
10	1.0	**Mooers** (town) Clinton County		78	3.2	**Salamanca** (city) Cattaraugus County
11	1.1	**Calcium** (CDP) Jefferson County		86	3.3	**Avon** (village) Livingston County
12	1.2	**Noyack** (CDP) Suffolk County		86	3.3	**Hamilton** (town) Madison County
13	1.4	**University at Buffalo** (CDP) Erie County		86	3.3	**Lake Luzerne** (town) Warren County
14	1.6	**East Hampton North** (CDP) Suffolk County		86	3.3	**Locust Valley** (CDP) Nassau County
14	1.6	**Gardnertown** (CDP) Orange County		86	3.3	**Warrensburg** (CDP) Warren County
14	1.6	**Shandaken** (town) Ulster County		91	3.4	**Akron** (village) Erie County
17	1.7	**Ghent** (town) Columbia County		91	3.4	**Bedford Hills** (CDP) Westchester County
18	1.8	**Mount Morris** (village) Livingston County		91	3.4	**Brentwood** (CDP) Suffolk County
18	1.8	**Potsdam** (village) Saint Lawrence County		91	3.4	**Callicoon** (town) Sullivan County
20	1.9	**Mattituck** (CDP) Suffolk County		91	3.4	**Delhi** (village) Delaware County
20	1.9	**Otego** (town) Otsego County		91	3.4	**Hunter** (town) Greene County
22	2.0	**Cayuga Heights** (village) Tompkins County		91	3.4	**Palmyra** (village) Wayne County
22	2.0	**Monsey** (CDP) Rockland County		91	3.4	**Perth** (town) Fulton County
24	2.1	**North East** (town) Dutchess County		91	3.4	**Ravena** (village) Albany County
25	2.2	**Enfield** (town) Tompkins County		91	3.4	**Stony Brook University** (CDP) Suffolk County
26	2.3	**Mount Morris** (town) Livingston County		101	3.5	**Catlin** (town) Chemung County
26	2.3	**Richmond** (town) Ontario County		101	3.5	**Clarendon** (town) Orleans County
28	2.4	**Calverton** (CDP) Suffolk County		101	3.5	**Geneseo** (village) Livingston County
28	2.4	**Ellisburg** (town) Jefferson County		101	3.5	**Penn Yan** (village) Yates County
28	2.4	**Island Park** (village) Nassau County		101	3.5	**Unadilla** (town) Otsego County
28	2.4	**Munsons Corners** (CDP) Cortland County		101	3.5	**Wappingers Falls** (village) Dutchess County
28	2.4	**North Bay Shore** (CDP) Suffolk County		107	3.6	**Danby** (town) Tompkins County
28	2.4	**Southampton** (village) Suffolk County		107	3.6	**Duanesburg** (town) Schenectady County
34	2.5	**Benton** (town) Yates County		107	3.6	**Hancock** (town) Delaware County
34	2.5	**Castile** (town) Wyoming County		107	3.6	**Milo** (town) Yates County
34	2.5	**Fairview** (CDP) Westchester County		107	3.6	**Montgomery** (village) Orange County
34	2.5	**Mechanicville** (city) Saratoga County		107	3.6	**Niagara** (town) Niagara County
34	2.5	**New Paltz** (village) Ulster County		107	3.6	**Vienna** (town) Oneida County
39	2.6	**Franklinville** (town) Cattaraugus County		107	3.6	**West Bloomfield** (town) Ontario County
39	2.6	**Liberty** (village) Sullivan County		107	3.6	**Whitehall** (town) Washington County
39	2.6	**Schroeppel** (town) Oswego County		107	3.6	**Whitesboro** (village) Oneida County
42	2.7	**Alexandria** (town) Jefferson County		117	3.7	**Annsville** (town) Oneida County
42	2.7	**Brockport** (village) Monroe County		117	3.7	**Lisle** (town) Broome County
42	2.7	**Camden** (town) Oneida County		117	3.7	**Medina** (village) Orleans County
42	2.7	**Mattydale** (CDP) Onondaga County		117	3.7	**Minden** (town) Montgomery County
42	2.7	**Norfolk** (town) Saint Lawrence County		117	3.7	**Norwich** (city) Chenango County
42	2.7	**Oxford** (town) Chenango County		117	3.7	**Palmyra** (town) Wayne County
42	2.7	**Pembroke** (town) Genesee County		117	3.7	**Saint Regis Mohawk Reservation** (reservation) Franklin County
42	2.7	**Riverhead** (CDP) Suffolk County		117	3.7	**Shelby** (town) Orleans County
50	2.8	**Cazenovia** (village) Madison County		125	3.8	**Carlton** (town) Orleans County
50	2.8	**Erwin** (town) Steuben County		125	3.8	**Hempstead** (village) Nassau County
50	2.8	**Fredonia** (village) Chautauqua County		125	3.8	**Hudson** (city) Columbia County
50	2.8	**Hamilton** (village) Madison County		125	3.8	**Islip Terrace** (CDP) Suffolk County
50	2.8	**Norwich** (town) Chenango County		125	3.8	**Johnstown** (city) Fulton County
50	2.8	**Rochester** (town) Ulster County		125	3.8	**Port Chester** (village) Westchester County
56	2.9	**Albion** (village) Orleans County		125	3.8	**Schoharie** (town) Schoharie County
56	2.9	**Clarence Center** (CDP) Erie County		125	3.8	**Tupper Lake** (town) Franklin County
56	2.9	**Copake** (town) Columbia County		125	3.8	**Warrensburg** (town) Warren County
56	2.9	**Fort Ann** (town) Washington County		125	3.8	**Wawarsing** (town) Ulster County
56	2.9	**Mechanicstown** (CDP) Orange County		125	3.8	**Windsor** (town) Broome County
56	2.9	**Portland** (town) Chautauqua County		136	3.9	**Albion** (town) Orleans County
56	2.9	**Sloan** (village) Erie County		136	3.9	**Babylon** (village) Suffolk County
56	2.9	**Voorheesville** (village) Albany County		136	3.9	**Deerpark** (town) Orange County
56	2.9	**West Monroe** (town) Oswego County		136	3.9	**Menands** (village) Albany County
65	3.0	**Canastota** (village) Madison County		136	3.9	**Middleburgh** (town) Schoharie County
65	3.0	**Ithaca** (city) Tompkins County		136	3.9	**Montrose** (CDP) Westchester County
65	3.0	**Newburgh** (city) Orange County		136	3.9	**Moravia** (town) Cayuga County
65	3.0	**Somerset** (town) Niagara County		136	3.9	**Mount Kisco** (town/village) Westchester County
65	3.0	**Walden** (village) Orange County		136	3.9	**New Scotland** (town) Albany County
65	3.0	**West Sand Lake** (CDP) Rensselaer County		136	3.9	**North Lindenhurst** (CDP) Suffolk County
65	3.0	**Westmoreland** (town) Oneida County		136	3.9	**Oakfield** (town) Genesee County
72	3.1	**Copiague** (CDP) Suffolk County		136	3.9	**Olean** (city) Cattaraugus County
72	3.1	**Gloversville** (city) Fulton County		136	3.9	**Ossining** (village) Westchester County
72	3.1	**Inwood** (CDP) Nassau County		136	3.9	**Pawling** (town) Dutchess County
72	3.1	**New Haven** (town) Oswego County		150	4.0	**Bennington** (town) Wyoming County

Note: This section ranks incorporated places and CDPs (Census Designated Places) with populations of 2,500 or more. Unincorporated postal areas were not considered. Please refer to the User Guide for additional information.

Employment: Service Occupations

Top 150 Places Ranked in *Descending* Order

State Rank	Percent	Place	State Rank	Percent	Place
1	42.4	SUNY Oswego (CDP) Oswego County	74	27.4	Glen Cove (city) Nassau County
2	40.9	Alfred (village) Allegany County	74	27.4	Wellsville (town) Allegany County
3	40.0	Binghamton University (CDP) Broome County	78	27.3	Portland (town) Chautauqua County
4	37.9	Bedford Hills (CDP) Westchester County	79	27.2	Oneida (city) Madison County
5	37.2	Cobleskill (village) Schoharie County	79	27.2	Oneonta (city) Otsego County
6	36.9	Tupper Lake (village) Franklin County	79	27.2	Ossining (village) Westchester County
7	36.8	Fairview (CDP) Westchester County	82	27.1	Au Sable (town) Clinton County
8	36.0	Alfred (town) Allegany County	82	27.1	Blasdell (village) Erie County
9	35.8	North East (town) Dutchess County	82	27.1	Rye (town) Westchester County
10	35.2	Hempstead (village) Nassau County	85	27.0	Salamanca (city) Cattaraugus County
11	35.1	Wappingers Falls (village) Dutchess County	86	26.9	Haverstraw (town) Rockland County
12	35.0	Arlington (CDP) Dutchess County	86	26.9	Rochester (town) Ulster County
12	35.0	Spring Valley (village) Rockland County	86	26.9	Rockland (town) Sullivan County
14	34.9	Tupper Lake (town) Franklin County	89	26.7	Utica (city) Oneida County
15	34.5	Dannemora (village) Clinton County	90	26.6	Brentwood (CDP) Suffolk County
16	34.3	Ellenville (village) Ulster County	90	26.6	Geneseo (town) Livingston County
17	34.2	Port Chester (village) Westchester County	90	26.6	Wilna (town) Jefferson County
18	34.1	Norfolk (town) Saint Lawrence County	93	26.5	Beekmantown (town) Clinton County
19	33.4	Bronx (borough) Bronx County	93	26.5	Whitehall (village) Washington County
19	33.4	Monticello (village) Sullivan County	95	26.4	Collins (town) Erie County
21	33.0	Mount Kisco (town/village) Westchester County	95	26.4	Harriman (village) Orange County
22	32.9	Jay (town) Essex County	97	26.3	Lackawanna (city) Erie County
22	32.9	Oswego (town) Oswego County	98	26.2	Fort Drum (CDP) Jefferson County
24	32.8	Enfield (town) Tompkins County	98	26.2	Malone (town) Franklin County
24	32.8	Inwood (CDP) Nassau County	100	26.0	Hornell (city) Steuben County
26	32.7	Haverstraw (village) Rockland County	100	26.0	Sleepy Hollow (village) Westchester County
27	32.3	North Amityville (CDP) Suffolk County	102	25.9	Attica (village) Wyoming County
28	32.0	Mount Morris (village) Livingston County	102	25.9	Thompson (town) Sullivan County
29	31.8	Munsons Corners (CDP) Cortland County	102	25.9	Uniondale (CDP) Nassau County
29	31.8	Whitesboro (village) Oneida County	105	25.8	Middletown (city) Orange County
31	31.6	Wellsville (village) Allegany County	105	25.8	Mount Vernon (city) Westchester County
32	31.5	Greenport (town) Columbia County	105	25.8	Vails Gate (CDP) Orange County
32	31.5	Hillcrest (CDP) Rockland County	108	25.7	Dickinson (town) Broome County
34	31.4	Elmsford (village) Westchester County	108	25.7	Watertown (city) Jefferson County
34	31.4	Lisbon (town) Saint Lawrence County	110	25.6	Corinth (village) Saratoga County
36	31.2	Geneseo (village) Livingston County	110	25.6	New Paltz (village) Ulster County
36	31.2	West Haverstraw (village) Rockland County	110	25.6	Whitehall (town) Washington County
38	30.9	Moira (town) Franklin County	113	25.5	Hudson Falls (village) Washington County
38	30.9	Montauk (CDP) Suffolk County	113	25.5	Maybrook (village) Orange County
40	30.5	Hancock (town) Delaware County	115	25.4	Dix (town) Schuyler County
41	30.2	Hudson (city) Columbia County	115	25.4	Dunkirk (city) Chautauqua County
41	30.2	Mohawk (village) Herkimer County	115	25.4	Hampton Bays (CDP) Suffolk County
43	30.1	Albion (village) Orleans County	115	25.4	Solvay (village) Onondaga County
44	29.8	Roosevelt (CDP) Nassau County	119	25.3	Dover (town) Dutchess County
45	29.6	Waverly (village) Tioga County	119	25.3	Granby (town) Oswego County
46	29.5	Carthage (village) Jefferson County	119	25.3	Le Roy (village) Genesee County
47	29.4	Cobleskill (town) Schoharie County	119	25.3	New Cassel (CDP) Nassau County
48	29.3	Dannemora (town) Clinton County	119	25.3	Owego (village) Tioga County
49	29.2	Gowanda (village) Cattaraugus County	124	25.1	Binghamton (city) Broome County
50	29.1	Lake Mohegan (CDP) Westchester County	124	25.1	Deerpark (town) Orange County
50	29.1	Stockholm (town) Saint Lawrence County	124	25.1	Galeville (CDP) Onondaga County
52	29.0	Mount Morris (town) Livingston County	124	25.1	Niagara Falls (city) Niagara County
52	29.0	Poughkeepsie (city) Dutchess County	128	25.0	Barton (town) Tioga County
54	28.9	Glasco (CDP) Ulster County	128	25.0	East Rochester (town/village) Monroe County
55	28.7	Wyandanch (CDP) Suffolk County	128	25.0	Harrietstown (town) Franklin County
56	28.6	Lakeview (CDP) Nassau County	128	25.0	Mooers (town) Clinton County
56	28.6	Wawarsing (town) Ulster County	132	24.9	Conklin (town) Broome County
58	28.4	Elmira (city) Chemung County	132	24.9	Corinth (town) Saratoga County
59	28.3	Newburgh (city) Orange County	132	24.9	Rochester (city) Monroe County
60	28.1	Malone (village) Franklin County	132	24.9	Saint Johnsville (town) Montgomery County
60	28.1	Penn Yan (village) Yates County	132	24.9	Shelter Island (town) Suffolk County
62	28.0	Albion (town) Orleans County	132	24.9	Verona (town) Oneida County
62	28.0	Port Jervis (city) Orange County	138	24.8	Gordon Heights (CDP) Suffolk County
64	27.9	Neversink (town) Sullivan County	139	24.7	Liberty (town) Sullivan County
64	27.9	North Bay Shore (CDP) Suffolk County	139	24.7	Milo (town) Yates County
64	27.9	Southport (CDP) Chemung County	139	24.7	Plattsburgh (city) Clinton County
67	27.8	Schuyler (town) Herkimer County	142	24.6	Brownville (town) Jefferson County
68	27.7	University at Buffalo (CDP) Erie County	142	24.6	Delhi (town) Delaware County
69	27.6	Herkimer (village) Herkimer County	142	24.6	Ghent (town) Columbia County
70	27.5	Alexandria (town) Jefferson County	142	24.6	Gloversville (city) Fulton County
70	27.5	Keeseville (village) Clinton County	142	24.6	Huntington Station (CDP) Suffolk County
70	27.5	Moriah (town) Essex County	142	24.6	Lee (town) Oneida County
70	27.5	Oswegatchie (town) Saint Lawrence County	142	24.6	Norwich (town) Chenango County
74	27.4	Delhi (village) Delaware County	142	24.6	Queens (borough) Queens County
74	27.4	Frankfort (village) Herkimer County	142	24.6	Southport (town) Chemung County

Note: This section ranks incorporated places and CDPs (Census Designated Places) with populations of 2,500 or more. Unincorporated postal areas were not considered. Please refer to the User Guide for additional information.

Employment: Service Occupations

Top 150 Places Ranked in *Ascending* Order

State Rank	Percent	Place
1	2.6	Riverside (CDP) Suffolk County
2	3.4	Lawrence (village) Nassau County
3	3.5	East Hills (village) Nassau County
4	3.8	Munsey Park (village) Nassau County
5	4.0	New Castle (town) Westchester County
6	4.1	Scarsdale (town/village) Westchester County
7	4.3	North Hills (village) Nassau County
8	4.6	Kaser (village) Rockland County
9	4.9	Hartsdale (CDP) Westchester County
9	4.9	Muttontown (village) Nassau County
11	5.3	Woodbury (CDP) Nassau County
12	5.4	Great Neck Estates (village) Nassau County
13	5.6	Greenville (CDP) Westchester County
14	5.7	Centerport (CDP) Suffolk County
15	5.8	Cold Spring Harbor (CDP) Suffolk County
16	6.0	Flower Hill (village) Nassau County
17	6.1	Manhasset Hills (CDP) Nassau County
17	6.1	Schoharie (town) Schoharie County
17	6.1	Viola (CDP) Rockland County
20	6.3	Sands Point (village) Nassau County
21	6.4	East Williston (village) Nassau County
21	6.4	Lake Success (village) Nassau County
21	6.4	Syosset (CDP) Nassau County
24	6.5	Jericho (CDP) Nassau County
25	6.6	Elma Center (CDP) Erie County
26	6.7	Gang Mills (CDP) Steuben County
26	6.7	Heritage Hills (CDP) Westchester County
28	6.9	Halesite (CDP) Suffolk County
29	7.3	Briarcliff Manor (village) Westchester County
29	7.3	Irvington (village) Westchester County
31	7.4	Montebello (village) Rockland County
31	7.4	Niskayuna (town) Schenectady County
31	7.4	West Hills (CDP) Suffolk County
34	7.6	Searingtown (CDP) Nassau County
35	7.8	Carmel Hamlet (CDP) Putnam County
35	7.8	Larchmont (village) Westchester County
35	7.8	Pound Ridge (town) Westchester County
35	7.8	Thomaston (village) Nassau County
39	7.9	Kings Point (village) Nassau County
40	8.0	Tuxedo (town) Orange County
41	8.1	Dix Hills (CDP) Suffolk County
41	8.1	Wesley Hills (village) Rockland County
43	8.2	East Greenbush (CDP) Rensselaer County
43	8.2	Pelham Manor (village) Westchester County
43	8.2	Woodmere (CDP) Nassau County
46	8.3	Lloyd Harbor (village) Suffolk County
47	8.4	Bronxville (village) Westchester County
48	8.6	Pompey (town) Onondaga County
49	8.7	North Salem (town) Westchester County
50	8.9	Clifton Park (town) Saratoga County
50	8.9	Northport (village) Suffolk County
52	9.0	Huntington (CDP) Suffolk County
53	9.1	Ardsley (village) Westchester County
53	9.1	Malverne (village) Nassau County
55	9.3	Berne (town) Albany County
55	9.3	Stony Brook (CDP) Suffolk County
57	9.4	Melville (CDP) Suffolk County
57	9.4	Monsey (CDP) Rockland County
57	9.4	Old Bethpage (CDP) Nassau County
57	9.4	University Gardens (CDP) Nassau County
61	9.5	Albertson (CDP) Nassau County
61	9.5	Lowville (village) Lewis County
63	9.6	North New Hyde Park (CDP) Nassau County
64	9.7	East Norwich (CDP) Nassau County
64	9.7	Hastings-on-Hudson (village) Westchester County
64	9.7	Plainview (CDP) Nassau County
67	9.8	Chenango Bridge (CDP) Broome County
68	9.9	Great Neck (village) Nassau County
68	9.9	Lewisboro (town) Westchester County
68	9.9	Voorheesville (village) Albany County
71	10.0	Erwin (town) Steuben County
71	10.0	Fayetteville (village) Onondaga County
71	10.0	Garden City (village) Nassau County
71	10.0	Pleasantville (village) Westchester County
75	10.2	Hounsfield (town) Jefferson County

State Rank	Percent	Place
75	10.2	Menands (village) Albany County
75	10.2	North Bellmore (CDP) Nassau County
75	10.2	Port Washington North (village) Nassau County
75	10.2	Setauket-East Setauket (CDP) Suffolk County
75	10.2	West Elmira (CDP) Chemung County
81	10.3	East Islip (CDP) Suffolk County
81	10.3	Manhasset (CDP) Nassau County
83	10.4	Lansing (village) Tompkins County
83	10.4	Lido Beach (CDP) Nassau County
83	10.4	Pittsford (town) Monroe County
83	10.4	Port Jefferson Station (CDP) Suffolk County
83	10.4	Sea Cliff (village) Nassau County
83	10.4	Sterling (town) Cayuga County
89	10.5	Manorhaven (village) Nassau County
89	10.5	New Scotland (town) Albany County
91	10.6	Bethlehem (town) Albany County
91	10.6	East Greenbush (town) Rensselaer County
91	10.6	Fort Salonga (CDP) Suffolk County
91	10.6	Merrick (CDP) Nassau County
91	10.6	Yates (town) Orleans County
96	10.7	Richmond (town) Ontario County
96	10.7	Rush (town) Monroe County
96	10.7	Rye (city) Westchester County
96	10.7	Somers (town) Westchester County
96	10.7	South Nyack (village) Rockland County
96	10.7	West Bloomfield (town) Ontario County
102	10.8	Bellmore (CDP) Nassau County
102	10.8	Cayuga Heights (village) Tompkins County
102	10.8	Clarence (CDP) Erie County
102	10.8	Marion (town) Wayne County
102	10.8	Roslyn (village) Nassau County
102	10.8	Salem (town) Washington County
108	10.9	Babylon (village) Suffolk County
108	10.9	East Aurora (village) Erie County
108	10.9	Orchard Park (village) Erie County
111	11.0	Cornwall-on-Hudson (village) Orange County
112	11.1	Canajoharie (town) Montgomery County
112	11.1	Cutchogue (CDP) Suffolk County
112	11.1	Pelham (town) Westchester County
115	11.2	Brighton (CDP) Monroe County
115	11.2	Kendall (town) Orleans County
115	11.2	Spackenkill (CDP) Dutchess County
118	11.3	Eastchester (CDP) Westchester County
118	11.3	Garden City South (CDP) Nassau County
118	11.3	Lysander (town) Onondaga County
118	11.3	West Sayville (CDP) Suffolk County
118	11.3	Woodstock (town) Ulster County
123	11.4	Armonk (CDP) Westchester County
123	11.4	Elmira (town) Chemung County
123	11.4	Lansing (town) Tompkins County
123	11.4	Penfield (town) Monroe County
127	11.5	Clarence Center (CDP) Erie County
127	11.5	Guilford (town) Chenango County
127	11.5	Manlius (town) Onondaga County
127	11.5	Plainedge (CDP) Nassau County
127	11.5	Williamson (town) Wayne County
127	11.5	Williston Park (village) Nassau County
133	11.6	Great Neck Plaza (village) Nassau County
133	11.6	Malta (town) Saratoga County
133	11.6	Northeast Ithaca (CDP) Tompkins County
133	11.6	Pomona (village) Rockland County
133	11.6	Saint James (CDP) Suffolk County
138	11.7	West Bay Shore (CDP) Suffolk County
139	11.8	Baldwin Harbor (CDP) Nassau County
139	11.8	Marlboro (CDP) Ulster County
139	11.8	North Castle (town) Westchester County
139	11.8	North Merrick (CDP) Nassau County
139	11.8	Pembroke (town) Genesee County
139	11.8	Victor (town) Ontario County
145	11.9	Afton (town) Chenango County
145	11.9	Carroll (town) Chautauqua County
145	11.9	Kiryas Joel (village) Orange County
145	11.9	Walworth (town) Wayne County
149	12.0	Manorville (CDP) Suffolk County
149	12.0	Pendleton (town) Niagara County

Note: This section ranks incorporated places and CDPs (Census Designated Places) with populations of 2,500 or more. Unincorporated postal areas were not considered. Please refer to the User Guide for additional information.

Employment: Sales and Office Occupations

Top 150 Places Ranked in *Descending* Order

State Rank	Percent	Place
1	45.3	**University at Buffalo** (CDP) Erie County
2	40.6	**SUNY Oswego** (CDP) Oswego County
3	39.8	**Lake Placid** (village) Essex County
4	37.8	**Kiryas Joel** (village) Orange County
5	37.2	**Lewiston** (village) Niagara County
6	36.4	**Moriches** (CDP) Suffolk County
7	36.2	**Stony Brook University** (CDP) Suffolk County
8	36.0	**Perth** (town) Fulton County
9	35.9	**Scotia** (village) Schenectady County
10	35.4	**Melville** (CDP) Suffolk County
11	34.9	**Galeville** (CDP) Onondaga County
12	34.7	**North Lindenhurst** (CDP) Suffolk County
13	34.6	**Carmel Hamlet** (CDP) Putnam County
13	34.6	**Colonie** (village) Albany County
15	34.4	**Kings Point** (village) Nassau County
15	34.4	**Tuxedo** (town) Orange County
17	33.3	**Brewerton** (CDP) Onondaga County
18	33.0	**Fort Edward** (town) Washington County
19	32.9	**East Farmingdale** (CDP) Suffolk County
20	32.8	**New Paltz** (village) Ulster County
20	32.8	**North Syracuse** (village) Onondaga County
20	32.8	**Port Washington North** (village) Nassau County
23	32.6	**Vails Gate** (CDP) Orange County
24	32.5	**Haviland** (CDP) Dutchess County
25	32.4	**Herkimer** (village) Herkimer County
25	32.4	**Lawrence** (village) Nassau County
27	32.2	**Brockport** (village) Monroe County
28	32.1	**Riverhead** (CDP) Suffolk County
29	31.9	**Selden** (CDP) Suffolk County
30	31.8	**Canastota** (village) Madison County
31	31.7	**Duanesburg** (town) Schenectady County
32	31.6	**Brutus** (town) Cayuga County
33	31.4	**North Great River** (CDP) Suffolk County
34	31.3	**Mamakating** (town) Sullivan County
35	31.2	**Walden** (village) Orange County
36	31.1	**Mechanicstown** (CDP) Orange County
37	31.0	**East Syracuse** (village) Onondaga County
38	30.9	**Chester** (village) Orange County
39	30.8	**Minoa** (village) Onondaga County
40	30.7	**Calverton** (CDP) Suffolk County
41	30.6	**Lido Beach** (CDP) Nassau County
41	30.6	**Washingtonville** (village) Orange County
43	30.5	**Kenmore** (village) Erie County
43	30.5	**Lake Carmel** (CDP) Putnam County
45	30.4	**Crown Heights** (CDP) Dutchess County
45	30.4	**Scotchtown** (CDP) Orange County
45	30.4	**South Farmingdale** (CDP) Nassau County
48	30.3	**Mattydale** (CDP) Onondaga County
48	30.3	**Searingtown** (CDP) Nassau County
48	30.3	**University Gardens** (CDP) Nassau County
48	30.3	**Whitesboro** (village) Oneida County
52	30.2	**Holbrook** (CDP) Suffolk County
52	30.2	**Lake Success** (village) Nassau County
52	30.2	**Liberty** (village) Sullivan County
52	30.2	**North Elba** (town) Essex County
52	30.2	**Patterson** (town) Putnam County
52	30.2	**Schroeppel** (town) Oswego County
52	30.2	**South Hill** (CDP) Tompkins County
52	30.2	**Wheatley Heights** (CDP) Suffolk County
60	30.1	**Niagara** (town) Niagara County
60	30.1	**Schoharie** (town) Schoharie County
62	30.0	**Baywood** (CDP) Suffolk County
62	30.0	**Binghamton University** (CDP) Broome County
62	30.0	**Fairview** (CDP) Dutchess County
62	30.0	**Islip Terrace** (CDP) Suffolk County
62	30.0	**Maybrook** (village) Orange County
62	30.0	**Menands** (village) Albany County
62	30.0	**Trenton** (town) Oneida County
69	29.9	**Fayetteville** (village) Onondaga County
69	29.9	**Gates** (CDP) Monroe County
69	29.9	**Yorkville** (village) Oneida County
72	29.8	**Allegany** (town) Cattaraugus County
72	29.8	**Mechanicville** (city) Saratoga County
72	29.8	**Tonawanda** (city) Erie County
72	29.8	**West Babylon** (CDP) Suffolk County
76	29.7	**Great Neck** (village) Nassau County
76	29.7	**Porter** (town) Niagara County
76	29.7	**West Islip** (CDP) Suffolk County
79	29.6	**Lake Grove** (village) Suffolk County
79	29.6	**Wallkill** (town) Orange County
81	29.5	**Cheektowaga** (CDP) Erie County
81	29.5	**Gardnertown** (CDP) Orange County
81	29.5	**Hamlin** (town) Monroe County
81	29.5	**Sweden** (town) Monroe County
85	29.4	**Heritage Hills** (CDP) Westchester County
85	29.4	**Monroe** (town) Orange County
85	29.4	**Olean** (city) Cattaraugus County
85	29.4	**Sloan** (village) Erie County
89	29.3	**North Hills** (village) Nassau County
90	29.2	**Esopus** (town) Ulster County
91	29.1	**Cheektowaga** (town) Erie County
91	29.1	**Harriman** (village) Orange County
93	29.0	**Garden City South** (CDP) Nassau County
93	29.0	**Johnson City** (village) Broome County
95	28.9	**Fairport** (village) Monroe County
95	28.9	**Herkimer** (town) Herkimer County
95	28.9	**Olive** (town) Ulster County
95	28.9	**Orchard Park** (village) Erie County
95	28.9	**Village Green** (CDP) Onondaga County
95	28.9	**Westhampton** (CDP) Suffolk County
101	28.8	**South Lockport** (CDP) Niagara County
101	28.8	**Thiells** (CDP) Rockland County
103	28.7	**Carroll** (town) Chautauqua County
103	28.7	**Clarendon** (town) Orleans County
103	28.7	**Firthcliffe** (CDP) Orange County
103	28.7	**Kings Park** (CDP) Suffolk County
103	28.7	**Marlboro** (CDP) Ulster County
103	28.7	**North New Hyde Park** (CDP) Nassau County
109	28.6	**Dickinson** (town) Broome County
109	28.6	**Glenville** (town) Schenectady County
109	28.6	**Granville** (town) Washington County
109	28.6	**Hicksville** (CDP) Nassau County
109	28.6	**Laurens** (town) Otsego County
109	28.6	**Pendleton** (town) Niagara County
109	28.6	**Southold** (CDP) Suffolk County
109	28.6	**Tonawanda** (town) Erie County
117	28.5	**Homer** (town) Cortland County
117	28.5	**Levittown** (CDP) Nassau County
117	28.5	**North Babylon** (CDP) Suffolk County
117	28.5	**Palmyra** (town) Wayne County
121	28.4	**East Meadow** (CDP) Nassau County
121	28.4	**Islandia** (village) Suffolk County
121	28.4	**Oceanside** (CDP) Nassau County
121	28.4	**Plattsburgh** (city) Clinton County
121	28.4	**Poestenkill** (town) Rensselaer County
126	28.3	**Canandaigua** (town) Ontario County
126	28.3	**Lake Luzerne** (town) Warren County
126	28.3	**Montgomery** (village) Orange County
126	28.3	**Putnam Lake** (CDP) Putnam County
130	28.2	**Riverhead** (town) Suffolk County
130	28.2	**Rotterdam** (CDP) Schenectady County
130	28.2	**Salina** (town) Onondaga County
133	28.1	**East Bloomfield** (town) Ontario County
133	28.1	**East Greenbush** (town) Rensselaer County
133	28.1	**Fort Edward** (village) Washington County
133	28.1	**Lancaster** (village) Erie County
133	28.1	**Mohawk** (village) Herkimer County
133	28.1	**Port Ewen** (CDP) Ulster County
133	28.1	**Tonawanda** (CDP) Erie County
133	28.1	**West Glens Falls** (CDP) Warren County
141	28.0	**Blooming Grove** (town) Orange County
141	28.0	**Cuba** (town) Allegany County
141	28.0	**Greece** (CDP) Monroe County
141	28.0	**Hamlin** (CDP) Monroe County
141	28.0	**Homer** (village) Cortland County
141	28.0	**North Tonawanda** (city) Niagara County
141	28.0	**Nunda** (town) Livingston County
141	28.0	**Sound Beach** (CDP) Suffolk County
141	28.0	**Watervliet** (city) Albany County
150	27.9	**Annsville** (town) Oneida County

Note: This section ranks incorporated places and CDPs (Census Designated Places) with populations of 2,500 or more. Unincorporated postal areas were not considered. Please refer to the User Guide for additional information.

Employment: Sales and Office Occupations

Top 150 Places Ranked in *Ascending* Order

State Rank	Percent	Place
1	0.0	**Saint Regis Mohawk Reservation** (reservation) Franklin County
2	10.0	**Campbell** (town) Steuben County
3	11.1	**Cayuga Heights** (village) Tompkins County
4	12.0	**Stockholm** (town) Saint Lawrence County
5	12.1	**White Creek** (town) Washington County
6	12.7	**Northeast Ithaca** (CDP) Tompkins County
7	13.0	**Newfane** (CDP) Niagara County
8	13.1	**Lansing** (village) Tompkins County
9	13.4	**North East** (town) Dutchess County
10	13.5	**Westfield** (village) Chautauqua County
11	13.6	**Gardiner** (town) Ulster County
12	13.7	**Shelter Island** (town) Suffolk County
13	14.0	**Elmsford** (village) Westchester County
14	14.4	**Colden** (town) Erie County
14	14.4	**Livonia** (town) Livingston County
16	14.6	**Hastings-on-Hudson** (village) Westchester County
17	14.7	**Bedford Hills** (CDP) Westchester County
17	14.7	**Washington** (town) Dutchess County
19	14.8	**Greenville** (CDP) Westchester County
19	14.8	**Hamilton** (village) Madison County
19	14.8	**Starkey** (town) Yates County
22	14.9	**Croghan** (town) Lewis County
22	14.9	**Johnstown** (town) Fulton County
24	15.0	**Moriah** (town) Essex County
25	15.1	**Irvington** (village) Westchester County
25	15.1	**Verona** (town) Oneida County
27	15.2	**Larchmont** (village) Westchester County
27	15.2	**Virgil** (town) Cortland County
29	15.3	**Pelham Manor** (village) Westchester County
30	15.5	**Royalton** (town) Niagara County
31	15.6	**Waverly** (village) Tioga County
31	15.6	**Westfield** (town) Chautauqua County
33	15.7	**Lowville** (town) Lewis County
34	15.8	**Avon** (village) Livingston County
35	15.9	**Colesville** (town) Broome County
35	15.9	**Tuckahoe** (village) Westchester County
37	16.0	**Wellsville** (village) Allegany County
38	16.1	**Greenville** (town) Greene County
38	16.1	**Madison** (town) Madison County
38	16.1	**Phelps** (town) Ontario County
41	16.2	**Gowanda** (village) Cattaraugus County
41	16.2	**Wellsville** (town) Allegany County
43	16.3	**Guilford** (town) Chenango County
43	16.3	**Norwich** (town) Chenango County
43	16.3	**Stephentown** (town) Rensselaer County
46	16.5	**Delaware** (town) Sullivan County
46	16.5	**Jay** (town) Essex County
46	16.5	**Lisbon** (town) Saint Lawrence County
46	16.5	**Pamelia** (town) Jefferson County
50	16.6	**Flanders** (CDP) Suffolk County
50	16.6	**Mexico** (town) Oswego County
52	16.7	**Barton** (town) Tioga County
52	16.7	**Corning** (town) Steuben County
52	16.7	**Galway** (town) Saratoga County
52	16.7	**Mendon** (town) Monroe County
52	16.7	**Shelby** (town) Orleans County
57	16.8	**Chatham** (town) Columbia County
57	16.8	**Eaton** (town) Madison County
57	16.8	**Montebello** (village) Rockland County
57	16.8	**Orleans** (town) Jefferson County
61	16.9	**Otsego** (town) Otsego County
62	17.0	**Brighton** (CDP) Monroe County
62	17.0	**Carthage** (village) Jefferson County
62	17.0	**Glasco** (CDP) Ulster County
62	17.0	**Munsons Corners** (CDP) Cortland County
62	17.0	**Tarrytown** (village) Westchester County
62	17.0	**Tupper Lake** (village) Franklin County
68	17.1	**Otisco** (town) Onondaga County
68	17.1	**Sherrill** (city) Oneida County
68	17.1	**Wolcott** (town) Wayne County
68	17.1	**Wyandanch** (CDP) Suffolk County
72	17.2	**Groton** (town) Tompkins County
72	17.2	**Lansing** (town) Tompkins County
72	17.2	**Lewisboro** (town) Westchester County
72	17.2	**Windsor** (town) Broome County
76	17.3	**Hamilton** (town) Madison County
76	17.3	**Hillcrest** (CDP) Rockland County
76	17.3	**Ulysses** (town) Tompkins County
79	17.4	**Albion** (village) Orleans County
79	17.4	**Darien** (town) Genesee County
79	17.4	**Pelham** (town) Westchester County
79	17.4	**Pound Ridge** (town) Westchester County
79	17.4	**Walton** (village) Delaware County
79	17.4	**West Point** (CDP) Orange County
85	17.5	**Beekmantown** (town) Clinton County
85	17.5	**Croton-on-Hudson** (village) Westchester County
85	17.5	**Harris Hill** (CDP) Erie County
85	17.5	**Herricks** (CDP) Nassau County
85	17.5	**Ithaca** (town) Tompkins County
85	17.5	**Mamaroneck** (town) Westchester County
85	17.5	**Sheridan** (town) Chautauqua County
85	17.5	**Woodstock** (town) Ulster County
93	17.7	**Copake** (town) Columbia County
93	17.7	**Locust Valley** (CDP) Nassau County
93	17.7	**Pleasantville** (village) Westchester County
96	17.8	**Conklin** (town) Broome County
96	17.8	**Dansville** (village) Livingston County
96	17.8	**Hopewell** (town) Ontario County
96	17.8	**Kinderhook** (town) Columbia County
100	17.9	**Greenwood Lake** (village) Orange County
100	17.9	**Northwest Harbor** (CDP) Suffolk County
100	17.9	**Tupper Lake** (town) Franklin County
103	18.0	**Albion** (town) Orleans County
103	18.0	**Geneva** (town) Ontario County
103	18.0	**Palermo** (town) Oswego County
106	18.1	**Ghent** (town) Columbia County
106	18.1	**Vernon** (town) Oneida County
108	18.2	**Elma** (town) Erie County
108	18.2	**Tully** (town) Onondaga County
108	18.2	**Unadilla** (town) Otsego County
111	18.3	**Chester** (town) Warren County
111	18.3	**Hornellsville** (town) Steuben County
111	18.3	**Mattituck** (CDP) Suffolk County
111	18.3	**Medina** (village) Orleans County
111	18.3	**Newark Valley** (town) Tioga County
116	18.4	**Blue Point** (CDP) Suffolk County
116	18.4	**Groveland** (town) Livingston County
116	18.4	**Lee** (town) Oneida County
116	18.4	**New Bremen** (town) Lewis County
116	18.4	**Roslyn Heights** (CDP) Nassau County
116	18.4	**Shandaken** (town) Ulster County
122	18.5	**Montauk** (CDP) Suffolk County
122	18.5	**Mount Kisco** (town/village) Westchester County
122	18.5	**Spackenkill** (CDP) Dutchess County
125	18.6	**Florida** (town) Montgomery County
125	18.6	**Lima** (town) Livingston County
125	18.6	**Sangerfield** (town) Oneida County
125	18.6	**Stanford** (town) Dutchess County
129	18.7	**Granby** (town) Oswego County
129	18.7	**Greenwich** (town) Washington County
129	18.7	**New Castle** (town) Westchester County
132	18.8	**Greenburgh** (town) Westchester County
132	18.8	**Middleburgh** (town) Schoharie County
132	18.8	**North Castle** (town) Westchester County
132	18.8	**Noyack** (CDP) Suffolk County
132	18.8	**Nyack** (village) Rockland County
132	18.8	**Sleepy Hollow** (village) Westchester County
138	18.9	**Arlington** (CDP) Dutchess County
138	18.9	**Augusta** (town) Oneida County
138	18.9	**Pelham** (village) Westchester County
138	18.9	**Theresa** (town) Jefferson County
142	19.0	**Chenango Bridge** (CDP) Broome County
142	19.0	**Dobbs Ferry** (village) Westchester County
142	19.0	**Ossining** (village) Westchester County
142	19.0	**Sherburne** (town) Chenango County
142	19.0	**Somerset** (town) Niagara County
147	19.1	**Bedford** (town) Westchester County
147	19.1	**Clarkson** (town) Monroe County
147	19.1	**Hancock** (town) Delaware County
147	19.1	**Honeoye Falls** (village) Monroe County

Note: This section ranks incorporated places and CDPs (Census Designated Places) with populations of 2,500 or more. Unincorporated postal areas were not considered. Please refer to the User Guide for additional information.

Employment: Natural Resources, Construction, and Maintenance Occupations

Top 150 Places Ranked in *Descending* Order

State Rank	Percent	Place
1	44.7	**Riverside** (CDP) Suffolk County
2	40.4	**Flanders** (CDP) Suffolk County
3	23.2	**Brasher** (town) Saint Lawrence County
4	22.7	**Springs** (CDP) Suffolk County
5	22.4	**Groveland** (town) Livingston County
6	21.8	**Carthage** (village) Jefferson County
6	21.8	**Gouverneur** (village) Saint Lawrence County
8	21.6	**New Haven** (town) Oswego County
9	20.7	**East Hampton North** (CDP) Suffolk County
10	19.6	**Sterling** (town) Cayuga County
11	19.4	**Ellisburg** (town) Jefferson County
12	19.2	**Gouverneur** (town) Saint Lawrence County
13	19.1	**New Bremen** (town) Lewis County
14	18.9	**Berne** (town) Albany County
15	18.8	**Vienna** (town) Oneida County
16	18.7	**Riverhead** (CDP) Suffolk County
16	18.7	**West Bloomfield** (town) Ontario County
18	18.6	**Copake** (town) Columbia County
18	18.6	**Delaware** (town) Sullivan County
18	18.6	**Mattituck** (CDP) Suffolk County
21	18.3	**Hampton Bays** (CDP) Suffolk County
22	18.0	**Darien** (town) Genesee County
22	18.0	**Pamelia** (town) Jefferson County
24	17.9	**Chazy** (town) Clinton County
24	17.9	**Constantia** (town) Oswego County
26	17.8	**Lisle** (town) Broome County
27	17.5	**Adams** (town) Jefferson County
27	17.5	**Augusta** (town) Oneida County
29	17.3	**Albion** (village) Orleans County
30	17.2	**Guilford** (town) Chenango County
30	17.2	**Southampton** (town) Suffolk County
30	17.2	**Volney** (town) Oswego County
33	17.1	**Bethel** (town) Sullivan County
33	17.1	**Denmark** (town) Lewis County
33	17.1	**Hopewell** (town) Ontario County
33	17.1	**Orleans** (town) Jefferson County
33	17.1	**Salem** (town) Washington County
38	17.0	**North East** (town) Dutchess County
39	16.9	**Carlton** (town) Orleans County
39	16.9	**East Hampton** (town) Suffolk County
39	16.9	**North Patchogue** (CDP) Suffolk County
42	16.8	**Perry** (town) Wyoming County
43	16.6	**Shandaken** (town) Ulster County
44	16.5	**Clarkson** (town) Monroe County
45	16.4	**Schroeppel** (town) Oswego County
45	16.4	**Williamson** (town) Wayne County
47	16.3	**West Monroe** (town) Oswego County
47	16.3	**Wilna** (town) Jefferson County
49	16.2	**Galen** (town) Wayne County
50	16.1	**Oakfield** (town) Genesee County
50	16.1	**Sardinia** (town) Erie County
52	16.0	**Cape Vincent** (town) Jefferson County
53	15.9	**Westhampton** (CDP) Suffolk County
54	15.8	**Holland** (town) Erie County
55	15.7	**Albion** (town) Orleans County
55	15.7	**Duanesburg** (town) Schenectady County
55	15.7	**Fort Ann** (town) Washington County
55	15.7	**Gorham** (town) Ontario County
59	15.6	**Ossining** (village) Westchester County
59	15.6	**Stockholm** (town) Saint Lawrence County
61	15.4	**Callicoon** (town) Sullivan County
61	15.4	**Floyd** (town) Oneida County
61	15.4	**Kendall** (town) Orleans County
61	15.4	**Pavilion** (town) Genesee County
65	15.2	**Castile** (town) Wyoming County
65	15.2	**Croghan** (town) Lewis County
65	15.2	**Fleming** (town) Cayuga County
65	15.2	**Otisco** (town) Onondaga County
65	15.2	**Richland** (town) Oswego County
65	15.2	**Sheridan** (town) Chautauqua County
71	15.1	**Alexandria** (town) Jefferson County
71	15.1	**Eden** (town) Erie County
71	15.1	**North Collins** (town) Erie County
74	15.0	**Greenville** (town) Greene County
74	15.0	**Hounsfield** (town) Jefferson County
74	15.0	**Mooers** (town) Clinton County
74	15.0	**Westerlo** (town) Albany County
78	14.9	**Elbridge** (town) Onondaga County
78	14.9	**Nunda** (town) Livingston County
78	14.9	**Whitehall** (town) Washington County
81	14.8	**Bergen** (town) Genesee County
82	14.7	**Warsaw** (town) Wyoming County
83	14.6	**Bedford Hills** (CDP) Westchester County
83	14.6	**Clinton** (town) Dutchess County
83	14.6	**Colden** (town) Erie County
83	14.6	**Spencer** (town) Tioga County
83	14.6	**Walton** (town) Delaware County
83	14.6	**York** (town) Livingston County
89	14.5	**Bennington** (town) Wyoming County
89	14.5	**Cambria** (town) Niagara County
89	14.5	**Florida** (town) Montgomery County
89	14.5	**Inwood** (CDP) Nassau County
89	14.5	**Middleburgh** (town) Schoharie County
94	14.4	**Candor** (town) Tioga County
94	14.4	**Canisteo** (town) Steuben County
94	14.4	**Mastic Beach** (village) Suffolk County
94	14.4	**New Baltimore** (town) Greene County
94	14.4	**Yorkshire** (town) Cattaraugus County
99	14.3	**Cedarhurst** (village) Nassau County
99	14.3	**Palatine** (town) Montgomery County
99	14.3	**Palermo** (town) Oswego County
99	14.3	**Sandy Creek** (town) Oswego County
99	14.3	**Theresa** (town) Jefferson County
99	14.3	**Westmoreland** (town) Oneida County
105	14.2	**Caledonia** (town) Livingston County
105	14.2	**Gaines** (town) Orleans County
105	14.2	**Moriah** (town) Essex County
105	14.2	**Mount Hope** (town) Orange County
105	14.2	**Wolcott** (town) Wayne County
110	14.1	**East Patchogue** (CDP) Suffolk County
110	14.1	**Saugerties** (town) Ulster County
110	14.1	**Somerset** (town) Niagara County
113	14.0	**East Islip** (CDP) Suffolk County
113	14.0	**Neversink** (town) Sullivan County
113	14.0	**Saugerties** (village) Ulster County
113	14.0	**Sherburne** (town) Chenango County
113	14.0	**Virgil** (town) Cortland County
118	13.9	**Dannemora** (village) Clinton County
118	13.9	**Gates** (CDP) Monroe County
118	13.9	**Verona** (town) Oneida County
121	13.8	**Benton** (town) Yates County
121	13.8	**Lake Luzerne** (town) Warren County
121	13.8	**Lowville** (town) Lewis County
121	13.8	**Montauk** (CDP) Suffolk County
121	13.8	**Windsor** (town) Broome County
126	13.7	**Campbell** (town) Steuben County
126	13.7	**Southold** (town) Suffolk County
128	13.6	**Warsaw** (village) Wyoming County
129	13.5	**Alexander** (town) Genesee County
129	13.5	**Madison** (town) Madison County
129	13.5	**North Bellport** (CDP) Suffolk County
129	13.5	**Seneca** (town) Ontario County
129	13.5	**Wawarsing** (town) Ulster County
134	13.4	**Center Moriches** (CDP) Suffolk County
134	13.4	**Louisville** (town) Saint Lawrence County
134	13.4	**Murray** (town) Orleans County
134	13.4	**Noyack** (CDP) Suffolk County
134	13.4	**Pleasant Valley** (town) Dutchess County
134	13.4	**Waterloo** (town) Seneca County
140	13.3	**Eden** (CDP) Erie County
140	13.3	**Rensselaer** (city) Rensselaer County
140	13.3	**Southold** (CDP) Suffolk County
143	13.2	**Ellenville** (village) Ulster County
143	13.2	**Paris** (town) Oneida County
145	13.1	**Collins** (town) Erie County
145	13.1	**Ghent** (town) Columbia County
145	13.1	**Greenwich** (town) Washington County
145	13.1	**Hanover** (town) Chautauqua County
145	13.1	**Newfield** (town) Tompkins County
145	13.1	**Sangerfield** (town) Oneida County

Note: This section ranks incorporated places and CDPs (Census Designated Places) with populations of 2,500 or more. Unincorporated postal areas were not considered. Please refer to the User Guide for additional information.

Employment: Natural Resources, Construction, and Maintenance Occupations

Top 150 Places Ranked in *Ascending* Order

State Rank	Percent	Place
1	0.0	Binghamton University (CDP) Broome County
1	0.0	Lake Success (village) Nassau County
1	0.0	Lansing (village) Tompkins County
4	0.1	North Hills (village) Nassau County
5	0.5	Lawrence (village) Nassau County
6	0.6	Lido Beach (CDP) Nassau County
6	0.6	Rhinebeck (village) Dutchess County
6	0.6	Scarsdale (town/village) Westchester County
9	0.8	Kaser (village) Rockland County
10	0.9	Cayuga Heights (village) Tompkins County
10	0.9	University at Buffalo (CDP) Erie County
12	1.2	Flower Hill (village) Nassau County
13	1.3	Bronxville (village) Westchester County
14	1.4	Brookville (village) Nassau County
15	1.5	East Norwich (CDP) Nassau County
15	1.5	Garden City (village) Nassau County
15	1.5	New Castle (town) Westchester County
15	1.5	Thomaston (village) Nassau County
15	1.5	Woodbury (CDP) Nassau County
20	1.6	Arlington (CDP) Dutchess County
20	1.6	Herkimer (village) Herkimer County
20	1.6	Hewlett (CDP) Nassau County
23	1.7	Old Westbury (village) Nassau County
23	1.7	Pound Ridge (town) Westchester County
23	1.7	SUNY Oswego (CDP) Oswego County
26	1.8	Great Neck Estates (village) Nassau County
26	1.8	Jericho (CDP) Nassau County
28	1.9	Menands (village) Albany County
28	1.9	Victor (village) Ontario County
30	2.0	Larchmont (village) Westchester County
30	2.0	Pittsford (town) Monroe County
30	2.0	Roslyn (village) Nassau County
30	2.0	Stony Brook University (CDP) Suffolk County
30	2.0	Viola (CDP) Rockland County
35	2.2	Manhattan (borough) New York County
35	2.2	South Hill (CDP) Tompkins County
37	2.3	Canton (village) Saint Lawrence County
37	2.3	Nyack (village) Rockland County
37	2.3	Port Washington North (village) Nassau County
37	2.3	West Nyack (CDP) Rockland County
41	2.4	Armonk (CDP) Westchester County
41	2.4	East Hills (village) Nassau County
41	2.4	Great Neck Plaza (village) Nassau County
41	2.4	Munsey Park (village) Nassau County
45	2.5	Briarcliff Manor (village) Westchester County
45	2.5	Hastings-on-Hudson (village) Westchester County
45	2.5	New Paltz (village) Ulster County
48	2.6	Melville (CDP) Suffolk County
48	2.6	Monsey (CDP) Rockland County
48	2.6	Roslyn Heights (CDP) Nassau County
51	2.7	Brighton (CDP) Monroe County
51	2.7	Dobbs Ferry (village) Westchester County
51	2.7	East Williston (village) Nassau County
51	2.7	Great Neck (village) Nassau County
51	2.7	University Gardens (CDP) Nassau County
56	2.8	Sands Point (village) Nassau County
56	2.8	Veteran (town) Chemung County
56	2.8	West Point (CDP) Orange County
56	2.8	Williamsville (village) Erie County
60	2.9	Bath (village) Steuben County
60	2.9	Greenville (CDP) Westchester County
60	2.9	Rye (city) Westchester County
63	3.0	Ardsley (village) Westchester County
63	3.0	Montebello (village) Rockland County
65	3.1	Brewerton (CDP) Onondaga County
65	3.1	Fairport (village) Monroe County
65	3.1	Ithaca (city) Tompkins County
65	3.1	Ithaca (town) Tompkins County
65	3.1	Tappan (CDP) Rockland County
70	3.2	Cold Spring Harbor (CDP) Suffolk County
70	3.2	Lewiston (village) Niagara County
70	3.2	Pelham Manor (village) Westchester County
70	3.2	Village Green (CDP) Onondaga County
74	3.3	Hartsdale (CDP) Westchester County
74	3.3	Muttontown (village) Nassau County
74	3.3	Stony Brook (CDP) Suffolk County
77	3.4	Halesite (CDP) Suffolk County
77	3.4	Victor (town) Ontario County
79	3.5	Clarence Center (CDP) Erie County
79	3.5	Dix Hills (CDP) Suffolk County
79	3.5	North Castle (town) Westchester County
79	3.5	Old Bethpage (CDP) Nassau County
79	3.5	Syosset (CDP) Nassau County
84	3.6	Olean (city) Cattaraugus County
84	3.6	Owego (village) Tioga County
86	3.7	Garden City Park (CDP) Nassau County
86	3.7	Hudson (city) Columbia County
86	3.7	Johnson City (village) Broome County
86	3.7	Kings Point (village) Nassau County
86	3.7	Kirkland (town) Oneida County
86	3.7	Plainview (CDP) Nassau County
86	3.7	Pomona (village) Rockland County
86	3.7	Potsdam (village) Saint Lawrence County
94	3.9	Greenburgh (town) Westchester County
94	3.9	Pleasantville (village) Westchester County
94	3.9	Ravena (village) Albany County
94	3.9	Tarrytown (village) Westchester County
98	4.0	Penfield (town) Monroe County
99	4.1	Geneseo (village) Livingston County
99	4.1	Lloyd Harbor (village) Suffolk County
99	4.1	Manhasset (CDP) Nassau County
99	4.1	New Paltz (town) Ulster County
99	4.1	Searingtown (CDP) Nassau County
104	4.2	Amherst (town) Erie County
104	4.2	Chestnut Ridge (village) Rockland County
104	4.2	Croton-on-Hudson (village) Westchester County
104	4.2	Kenmore (village) Erie County
104	4.2	Northeast Ithaca (CDP) Tompkins County
104	4.2	Plattsburgh (city) Clinton County
104	4.2	South Nyack (village) Rockland County
104	4.2	Woodmere (CDP) Nassau County
112	4.3	Bardonia (CDP) Rockland County
112	4.3	Eggertsville (CDP) Erie County
112	4.3	Kiryas Joel (village) Orange County
112	4.3	Oneonta (city) Otsego County
112	4.3	Sea Cliff (village) Nassau County
117	4.4	Albany (city) Albany County
117	4.4	Allegany (town) Cattaraugus County
117	4.4	Mount Morris (village) Livingston County
117	4.4	Waverly (village) Tioga County
121	4.5	Centerport (CDP) Suffolk County
121	4.5	Cuba (town) Allegany County
121	4.5	Firthcliffe (CDP) Orange County
121	4.5	Galeville (CDP) Onondaga County
121	4.5	Guilderland (town) Albany County
121	4.5	Johnstown (city) Fulton County
121	4.5	Monroe (village) Orange County
121	4.5	Rockville Centre (village) Nassau County
121	4.5	Saratoga Springs (city) Saratoga County
121	4.5	Wading River (CDP) Suffolk County
121	4.5	Wheatley Heights (CDP) Suffolk County
132	4.6	Bellmore (CDP) Nassau County
132	4.6	Glenwood Landing (CDP) Nassau County
132	4.6	Herkimer (town) Herkimer County
132	4.6	Lewisboro (town) Westchester County
132	4.6	Liberty (village) Sullivan County
132	4.6	Perinton (town) Monroe County
132	4.6	Rhinebeck (town) Dutchess County
132	4.6	Tuxedo (town) Orange County
140	4.7	Bethlehem (town) Albany County
140	4.7	Binghamton (city) Broome County
140	4.7	New City (CDP) Rockland County
140	4.7	Rochester (city) Monroe County
140	4.7	Watervliet (city) Albany County
145	4.8	Frankfort (village) Herkimer County
145	4.8	Hamburg (village) Erie County
145	4.8	Mamaroneck (town) Westchester County
145	4.8	Orchard Park (village) Erie County
145	4.8	Port Jefferson (village) Suffolk County
145	4.8	Rome (city) Oneida County

Note: This section ranks incorporated places and CDPs (Census Designated Places) with populations of 2,500 or more. Unincorporated postal areas were not considered. Please refer to the User Guide for additional information.

Employment: Production, Transportation, and Material Moving Occupations

Top 150 Places Ranked in *Descending* Order

State Rank	Percent	Place	State Rank	Percent	Place
1	29.0	**Liberty** (village) Sullivan County	76	18.8	**Altona** (town) Clinton County
2	27.7	**Guilford** (town) Chenango County	76	18.8	**Moravia** (town) Cayuga County
3	27.5	**Yates** (town) Orleans County	76	18.8	**Whitehall** (town) Washington County
4	26.6	**Colesville** (town) Broome County	79	18.7	**Canajoharie** (town) Montgomery County
5	26.2	**Westfield** (town) Chautauqua County	79	18.7	**Lake Erie Beach** (CDP) Erie County
6	26.1	**Pembroke** (town) Genesee County	79	18.7	**Oakfield** (town) Genesee County
7	26.0	**Unadilla** (town) Otsego County	82	18.6	**Granville** (town) Washington County
8	25.9	**Croghan** (town) Lewis County	82	18.6	**Richmond** (town) Ontario County
8	25.9	**Ellicott** (town) Chautauqua County	84	18.5	**Bath** (village) Steuben County
10	24.9	**Minden** (town) Montgomery County	85	18.4	**Lackawanna** (city) Erie County
11	24.7	**White Creek** (town) Washington County	85	18.4	**Marilla** (town) Erie County
12	24.5	**Sloan** (village) Erie County	85	18.4	**Mattydale** (CDP) Onondaga County
13	24.3	**Yorkshire** (town) Cattaraugus County	88	18.3	**Kirkwood** (town) Broome County
14	24.0	**Campbell** (town) Steuben County	88	18.3	**North Dansville** (town) Livingston County
15	23.7	**Westfield** (village) Chautauqua County	90	18.2	**Lake Luzerne** (town) Warren County
16	23.2	**Brentwood** (CDP) Suffolk County	91	18.1	**Copiague** (CDP) Suffolk County
17	23.1	**Barton** (town) Tioga County	91	18.1	**Hastings** (town) Oswego County
17	23.1	**South Glens Falls** (village) Saratoga County	91	18.1	**Hoosick** (town) Rensselaer County
19	22.9	**Darien** (town) Genesee County	91	18.1	**Newfane** (CDP) Niagara County
19	22.9	**North Bay Shore** (CDP) Suffolk County	91	18.1	**Starkey** (town) Yates County
19	22.9	**Royalton** (town) Niagara County	91	18.1	**Walton** (town) Delaware County
22	22.5	**Wayland** (town) Steuben County	97	18.0	**Bergen** (town) Genesee County
23	22.1	**Somerset** (town) Niagara County	97	18.0	**Lockport** (city) Niagara County
24	22.0	**Carroll** (town) Chautauqua County	97	18.0	**Waterloo** (village) Seneca County
24	22.0	**Hoosick Falls** (village) Rensselaer County	97	18.0	**Wellsville** (town) Allegany County
24	22.0	**Wyandanch** (CDP) Suffolk County	101	17.8	**Barker** (town) Broome County
27	21.8	**Argyle** (town) Washington County	101	17.8	**Madison** (town) Madison County
27	21.8	**Au Sable** (town) Clinton County	101	17.8	**Port Jervis** (city) Orange County
29	21.5	**Verona** (town) Oneida County	104	17.7	**Addison** (town) Steuben County
30	21.4	**Champlain** (town) Clinton County	104	17.7	**Mechanicstown** (CDP) Orange County
30	21.4	**Phelps** (town) Ontario County	104	17.7	**Whitehall** (village) Washington County
32	21.3	**Afton** (town) Chenango County	107	17.6	**Evans** (town) Erie County
33	21.2	**Shelby** (town) Orleans County	107	17.6	**Lima** (town) Livingston County
34	21.1	**Bainbridge** (town) Chenango County	107	17.6	**Mohawk** (town) Montgomery County
35	21.0	**Newark** (village) Wayne County	107	17.6	**New Berlin** (town) Chenango County
36	20.9	**Ridgeway** (town) Orleans County	107	17.6	**New York Mills** (village) Oneida County
37	20.8	**Catlin** (town) Chemung County	107	17.6	**West Monroe** (town) Oswego County
37	20.8	**Central Islip** (CDP) Suffolk County	107	17.6	**Wilson** (town) Niagara County
39	20.7	**Marion** (town) Wayne County	114	17.5	**Akron** (village) Erie County
40	20.6	**Hannibal** (town) Oswego County	114	17.5	**Greene** (town) Chenango County
41	20.5	**Kendall** (town) Orleans County	114	17.5	**Greenwood Lake** (village) Orange County
42	20.4	**Perry** (village) Wyoming County	114	17.5	**New Cassel** (CDP) Nassau County
43	20.3	**Camden** (town) Oneida County	114	17.5	**Roosevelt** (CDP) Nassau County
43	20.3	**Dunkirk** (city) Chautauqua County	119	17.4	**Bath** (town) Steuben County
43	20.3	**Jamestown** (city) Chautauqua County	119	17.4	**Wolcott** (town) Wayne County
43	20.3	**Randolph** (town) Cattaraugus County	121	17.3	**Alden** (village) Erie County
47	20.2	**Arcadia** (town) Wayne County	121	17.3	**Attica** (town) Wyoming County
48	20.1	**Dansville** (village) Livingston County	121	17.3	**Newfane** (town) Niagara County
48	20.1	**Norwich** (town) Chenango County	121	17.3	**Sterling** (town) Cayuga County
48	20.1	**Parish** (town) Oswego County	125	17.2	**Jerusalem** (town) Yates County
48	20.1	**Pavilion** (town) Genesee County	125	17.2	**Walton** (village) Delaware County
48	20.1	**Saint Regis Mohawk Reservation** (reservation) Franklin County	125	17.2	**West Bloomfield** (town) Ontario County
53	20.0	**Galen** (town) Wayne County	128	17.1	**Carlton** (town) Orleans County
53	20.0	**Manheim** (town) Herkimer County	128	17.1	**Durham** (town) Greene County
53	20.0	**Newburgh** (city) Orange County	128	17.1	**Hornell** (city) Steuben County
53	20.0	**Portland** (town) Chautauqua County	128	17.1	**Salem** (town) Washington County
57	19.8	**Clarendon** (town) Orleans County	128	17.1	**Sodus** (town) Wayne County
57	19.8	**Gloversville** (city) Fulton County	133	17.0	**Elmira Heights** (village) Chemung County
57	19.8	**Vienna** (town) Oneida County	133	17.0	**Fayette** (town) Seneca County
60	19.7	**Conklin** (town) Broome County	135	16.9	**Batavia** (town) Genesee County
61	19.6	**Mayfield** (town) Fulton County	135	16.9	**Bennington** (town) Wyoming County
61	19.6	**Waverly** (village) Tioga County	135	16.9	**Hancock** (town) Delaware County
63	19.5	**Ravena** (village) Albany County	135	16.9	**Hanover** (town) Chautauqua County
64	19.4	**Medina** (village) Orleans County	135	16.9	**Waterloo** (town) Seneca County
65	19.3	**Palermo** (town) Oswego County	140	16.8	**Cairo** (town) Greene County
66	19.2	**Attica** (village) Wyoming County	140	16.8	**Corinth** (village) Saratoga County
66	19.2	**Mount Morris** (town) Livingston County	140	16.8	**Florida** (town) Montgomery County
68	19.1	**Annsville** (town) Oneida County	140	16.8	**Sheridan** (town) Chautauqua County
68	19.1	**Coeymans** (town) Albany County	140	16.8	**Vernon** (town) Oneida County
68	19.1	**Fulton** (city) Oswego County	145	16.7	**Haverstraw** (village) Rockland County
71	19.0	**Amsterdam** (city) Montgomery County	145	16.7	**Lyons** (village) Wayne County
71	19.0	**Otego** (town) Otsego County	147	16.6	**Alexander** (town) Genesee County
71	19.0	**Perry** (town) Wyoming County	147	16.6	**Avon** (village) Livingston County
74	18.9	**Dolgeville** (village) Herkimer County	147	16.6	**Le Roy** (town) Genesee County
74	18.9	**Windsor** (town) Broome County	147	16.6	**New Bremen** (town) Lewis County

Note: This section ranks incorporated places and CDPs (Census Designated Places) with populations of 2,500 or more. Unincorporated postal areas were not considered. Please refer to the User Guide for additional information.

Employment: Production, Transportation, and Material Moving Occupations

Top 150 Places Ranked in *Ascending* Order

State Rank	Percent	Place
1	0.0	Great Neck Estates (village) Nassau County
1	0.0	Southampton (village) Suffolk County
3	0.4	Armonk (CDP) Westchester County
4	0.5	Muttontown (village) Nassau County
5	0.6	Bronxville (village) Westchester County
5	0.6	East Hills (village) Nassau County
7	0.7	Sands Point (village) Nassau County
7	0.7	Scarsdale (town/village) Westchester County
7	0.7	Springs (CDP) Suffolk County
10	0.8	Caroline (town) Tompkins County
10	0.8	Larchmont (village) Westchester County
12	0.9	North Hills (village) Nassau County
13	1.0	Danby (town) Tompkins County
13	1.0	Manhasset Hills (CDP) Nassau County
15	1.1	Brookville (village) Nassau County
15	1.1	North Castle (town) Westchester County
17	1.2	Pelham Manor (village) Westchester County
18	1.3	Irvington (village) Westchester County
18	1.3	Roslyn (village) Nassau County
18	1.3	Wesley Hills (village) Rockland County
21	1.4	Cayuga Heights (village) Tompkins County
21	1.4	Searingtown (CDP) Nassau County
23	1.5	Clarence Center (CDP) Erie County
23	1.5	Menands (village) Albany County
25	1.6	Heritage Hills (CDP) Westchester County
25	1.6	Woodbury (CDP) Nassau County
27	1.7	Briarcliff Manor (village) Westchester County
27	1.7	Piermont (village) Rockland County
27	1.7	Stony Brook University (CDP) Suffolk County
30	1.8	Pearl River (CDP) Rockland County
31	1.9	Flanders (CDP) Suffolk County
31	1.9	Flower Hill (village) Nassau County
33	2.0	Bedford Hills (CDP) Westchester County
33	2.0	East Williston (village) Nassau County
33	2.0	Mamaroneck (town) Westchester County
33	2.0	Rye Brook (village) Westchester County
37	2.1	Bedford (town) Westchester County
37	2.1	Cold Spring Harbor (CDP) Suffolk County
37	2.1	Eastchester (town) Westchester County
37	2.1	Lawrence (village) Nassau County
37	2.1	Lloyd Harbor (village) Suffolk County
37	2.1	Northeast Ithaca (CDP) Tompkins County
43	2.2	Alfred (village) Allegany County
43	2.2	Eastchester (CDP) Westchester County
43	2.2	Noyack (CDP) Suffolk County
46	2.3	Lido Beach (CDP) Nassau County
46	2.3	Port Jefferson (village) Suffolk County
46	2.3	SUNY Oswego (CDP) Oswego County
49	2.4	Fort Salonga (CDP) Suffolk County
49	2.4	Greenville (CDP) Westchester County
49	2.4	Lewisboro (town) Westchester County
49	2.4	New Castle (town) Westchester County
53	2.5	Harrison (town/village) Westchester County
53	2.5	Pomona (village) Rockland County
55	2.6	Great Neck Plaza (village) Nassau County
56	2.7	Airmont (village) Rockland County
56	2.7	Malverne (village) Nassau County
56	2.7	Munsey Park (village) Nassau County
56	2.7	Tuxedo (town) Orange County
56	2.7	Valley Cottage (CDP) Rockland County
61	2.8	Hastings-on-Hudson (village) Westchester County
61	2.8	Herricks (CDP) Nassau County
63	2.9	Tuckahoe (village) Westchester County
64	3.0	Clarence (CDP) Erie County
64	3.0	East Glenville (CDP) Schenectady County
64	3.0	Minoa (village) Onondaga County
64	3.0	Old Westbury (village) Nassau County
64	3.0	Rye (city) Westchester County
64	3.0	South Hempstead (CDP) Nassau County
70	3.1	North Salem (town) Westchester County
70	3.1	Pelham (town) Westchester County
72	3.2	Blauvelt (CDP) Rockland County
72	3.2	Stony Brook (CDP) Suffolk County
74	3.3	Ithaca (town) Tompkins County
74	3.3	Lake Success (village) Nassau County

State Rank	Percent	Place
74	3.3	Melville (CDP) Suffolk County
74	3.3	Sea Cliff (village) Nassau County
78	3.4	Garden City (village) Nassau County
78	3.4	Highland (CDP) Ulster County
80	3.5	Brightwaters (village) Suffolk County
80	3.5	Montrose (CDP) Westchester County
80	3.5	Setauket-East Setauket (CDP) Suffolk County
80	3.5	South Huntington (CDP) Suffolk County
84	3.6	Ardsley (village) Westchester County
84	3.6	Charlton (town) Saratoga County
84	3.6	Hartsdale (CDP) Westchester County
84	3.6	Lansing (village) Tompkins County
84	3.6	Merrick (CDP) Nassau County
84	3.6	North Sea (CDP) Suffolk County
84	3.6	Pleasantville (village) Westchester County
84	3.6	Rockville Centre (village) Nassau County
84	3.6	Syosset (CDP) Nassau County
93	3.7	Adams (town) Jefferson County
93	3.7	Jericho (CDP) Nassau County
93	3.7	Louisville (town) Saint Lawrence County
93	3.7	Montebello (village) Rockland County
97	3.8	Carthage (village) Jefferson County
97	3.8	Manhattan (borough) New York County
97	3.8	Orangetown (town) Rockland County
100	3.9	Massapequa Park (village) Nassau County
100	3.9	Neversink (town) Sullivan County
102	4.0	Croton-on-Hudson (village) Westchester County
102	4.0	Ithaca (city) Tompkins County
102	4.0	New Square (village) Rockland County
102	4.0	Otsego (town) Otsego County
102	4.0	Pittsford (town) Monroe County
102	4.0	West Hills (CDP) Suffolk County
102	4.0	Westvale (CDP) Onondaga County
109	4.1	Nesconset (CDP) Suffolk County
109	4.1	New Hempstead (village) Rockland County
109	4.1	Nyack (village) Rockland County
109	4.1	Port Washington (CDP) Nassau County
109	4.1	Pound Ridge (town) Westchester County
109	4.1	Putnam Valley (town) Putnam County
109	4.1	University at Buffalo (CDP) Erie County
109	4.1	Viola (CDP) Rockland County
117	4.2	Clarkson (CDP) Monroe County
117	4.2	Kaser (village) Rockland County
117	4.2	Lansing (town) Tompkins County
117	4.2	Mount Sinai (CDP) Suffolk County
117	4.2	Smithtown (CDP) Suffolk County
117	4.2	Somers (town) Westchester County
123	4.3	Centerport (CDP) Suffolk County
123	4.3	Port Washington North (village) Nassau County
123	4.3	Thiells (CDP) Rockland County
123	4.3	Thomaston (village) Nassau County
127	4.4	Alfred (town) Allegany County
127	4.4	Mahopac (CDP) Putnam County
127	4.4	New Paltz (town) Ulster County
127	4.4	Pelham (village) Westchester County
127	4.4	Woodmere (CDP) Nassau County
132	4.5	Greenburgh (town) Westchester County
132	4.5	Oneonta (city) Otsego County
132	4.5	Saratoga Springs (city) Saratoga County
135	4.6	East Greenbush (CDP) Rensselaer County
135	4.6	Fort Drum (CDP) Jefferson County
135	4.6	Hamilton (village) Madison County
135	4.6	Huntington (CDP) Suffolk County
135	4.6	Oceanside (CDP) Nassau County
135	4.6	Perinton (town) Monroe County
135	4.6	Rochester (town) Ulster County
135	4.6	University Gardens (CDP) Nassau County
143	4.7	Niskayuna (town) Schenectady County
143	4.7	Plainview (CDP) Nassau County
143	4.7	Rhinebeck (village) Dutchess County
146	4.8	East Hampton (town) Suffolk County
146	4.8	East Northport (CDP) Suffolk County
146	4.8	Glenwood Landing (CDP) Nassau County
146	4.8	Long Beach (city) Nassau County
146	4.8	South Nyack (village) Rockland County

Note: This section ranks incorporated places and CDPs (Census Designated Places) with populations of 2,500 or more. Unincorporated postal areas were not considered. Please refer to the User Guide for additional information.

Per Capita Income

Top 150 Places Ranked in *Descending* Order

State Rank	Dollars	Place
1	136,542	**Sands Point** (village) Nassau County
2	131,067	**Scarsdale** (town/village) Westchester County
3	128,800	**Pound Ridge** (town) Westchester County
4	125,610	**Muttontown** (village) Nassau County
5	116,698	**Bronxville** (village) Westchester County
6	114,928	**Lloyd Harbor** (village) Suffolk County
7	110,733	**Northwest Harbor** (CDP) Suffolk County
8	107,512	**Larchmont** (village) Westchester County
9	100,537	**Munsey Park** (village) Nassau County
10	99,791	**Armonk** (CDP) Westchester County
11	99,067	**New Castle** (town) Westchester County
12	97,689	**North Castle** (town) Westchester County
13	95,137	**Flower Hill** (village) Nassau County
14	95,000	**Rye** (city) Westchester County
15	94,367	**Brookville** (village) Nassau County
16	89,604	**East Hills** (village) Nassau County
17	89,325	**Lido Beach** (CDP) Nassau County
18	87,282	**North Hills** (village) Nassau County
19	87,077	**Greenville** (CDP) Westchester County
20	84,608	**Pelham Manor** (village) Westchester County
21	84,161	**Woodbury** (CDP) Nassau County
22	83,447	**Lawrence** (village) Nassau County
23	81,382	**Mamaroneck** (town) Westchester County
24	81,137	**Irvington** (village) Westchester County
25	81,109	**Cold Spring Harbor** (CDP) Suffolk County
26	79,476	**Briarcliff Manor** (village) Westchester County
27	79,432	**Piermont** (village) Rockland County
28	79,366	**Great Neck Estates** (village) Nassau County
29	78,922	**Lewisboro** (town) Westchester County
30	77,330	**Pelham** (town) Westchester County
31	75,045	**Old Westbury** (village) Nassau County
32	73,940	**Roslyn** (village) Nassau County
33	73,830	**Bedford** (town) Westchester County
34	73,275	**East Williston** (village) Nassau County
35	72,044	**Kings Point** (village) Nassau County
36	71,613	**Jericho** (CDP) Nassau County
37	71,486	**Pelham** (village) Westchester County
38	70,816	**Eastchester** (town) Westchester County
39	70,486	**Rye Brook** (village) Westchester County
40	70,398	**North Salem** (town) Westchester County
41	69,529	**Manhattan** (borough) New York County
42	69,203	**Montebello** (village) Rockland County
43	68,789	**Garden City** (village) Nassau County
44	68,407	**Hastings-on-Hudson** (village) Westchester County
45	68,138	**Ardsley** (village) Westchester County
46	68,125	**Manhasset** (CDP) Nassau County
47	65,997	**North Sea** (CDP) Suffolk County
48	65,020	**East Norwich** (CDP) Nassau County
49	64,903	**Port Washington** (CDP) Nassau County
50	64,519	**Harrison** (town/village) Westchester County
51	64,325	**Thomaston** (village) Nassau County
52	64,172	**Lake Success** (village) Nassau County
53	64,157	**Melville** (CDP) Suffolk County
54	64,061	**Syosset** (CDP) Nassau County
55	63,154	**Manhasset Hills** (CDP) Nassau County
56	62,904	**East Hampton** (town) Suffolk County
57	62,701	**Southampton** (village) Suffolk County
58	62,445	**Huntington** (CDP) Suffolk County
59	62,358	**Greenburgh** (town) Westchester County
60	62,166	**Oyster Bay** (CDP) Nassau County
61	62,114	**Centerport** (CDP) Suffolk County
62	62,109	**Eastchester** (CDP) Westchester County
63	61,452	**Setauket-East Setauket** (CDP) Suffolk County
63	61,452	**Skaneateles** (town) Onondaga County
65	61,356	**Searingtown** (CDP) Nassau County
66	61,348	**Halesite** (CDP) Suffolk County
67	61,288	**West Hills** (CDP) Suffolk County
68	61,176	**Dix Hills** (CDP) Suffolk County
69	60,678	**Brightwaters** (village) Suffolk County
70	60,490	**Dobbs Ferry** (village) Westchester County
71	60,471	**Fort Salonga** (CDP) Suffolk County
72	60,361	**Tuxedo** (town) Orange County
73	59,965	**Merrick** (CDP) Nassau County
74	59,870	**Tarrytown** (village) Westchester County
75	59,454	**Bardonia** (CDP) Rockland County
76	59,382	**University Gardens** (CDP) Nassau County
77	59,169	**Hartsdale** (CDP) Westchester County
78	58,600	**Somers** (town) Westchester County
79	58,408	**Locust Valley** (CDP) Nassau County
80	58,334	**Pittsford** (town) Monroe County
81	58,026	**Rockville Centre** (village) Nassau County
82	57,880	**Croton-on-Hudson** (village) Westchester County
83	56,892	**Northport** (village) Suffolk County
84	56,873	**Plainview** (CDP) Nassau County
85	56,755	**North Hempstead** (town) Nassau County
86	56,688	**Sea Cliff** (village) Nassau County
87	56,503	**Shelter Island** (town) Suffolk County
88	56,419	**Philipstown** (town) Putnam County
89	56,404	**Mamaroneck** (village) Westchester County
90	56,189	**West Nyack** (CDP) Rockland County
91	55,648	**Port Washington North** (village) Nassau County
92	55,511	**Glen Head** (CDP) Nassau County
93	55,412	**Springs** (CDP) Suffolk County
94	55,348	**Old Bethpage** (CDP) Nassau County
95	55,188	**Stony Brook** (CDP) Suffolk County
96	55,017	**Woodstock** (town) Ulster County
97	54,934	**Glenwood Landing** (CDP) Nassau County
98	54,532	**Oyster Bay** (town) Nassau County
99	54,518	**Cayuga Heights** (village) Tompkins County
100	53,963	**Babylon** (village) Suffolk County
101	53,896	**Tappan** (CDP) Rockland County
102	53,888	**Great Neck Plaza** (village) Nassau County
103	53,711	**Roslyn Heights** (CDP) Nassau County
104	53,604	**Westhampton** (CDP) Suffolk County
105	53,224	**Heritage Hills** (CDP) Westchester County
106	53,142	**Pleasantville** (village) Westchester County
107	53,135	**Port Jefferson** (village) Suffolk County
108	53,046	**Mendon** (town) Monroe County
109	52,798	**Tuckahoe** (village) Westchester County
110	52,703	**Victor** (town) Ontario County
111	52,589	**Pompey** (town) Onondaga County
112	52,523	**Huntington** (town) Suffolk County
113	52,369	**Stanford** (town) Dutchess County
114	51,700	**Mount Pleasant** (town) Westchester County
115	51,667	**Wantagh** (CDP) Nassau County
116	51,569	**New City** (CDP) Rockland County
117	51,334	**Fayetteville** (village) Onondaga County
118	50,921	**Woodmere** (CDP) Nassau County
119	50,696	**Rhinebeck** (town) Dutchess County
120	50,656	**Southold** (CDP) Suffolk County
121	50,255	**Smithtown** (town) Suffolk County
122	50,230	**Jefferson Valley-Yorktown** (CDP) Westchester County
123	50,216	**West Bay Shore** (CDP) Suffolk County
124	50,116	**Pearl River** (CDP) Rockland County
125	49,983	**Smithtown** (CDP) Suffolk County
126	49,876	**Orangetown** (town) Rockland County
127	49,794	**Bethlehem** (town) Albany County
128	49,690	**Bayville** (village) Nassau County
129	49,638	**Thornwood** (CDP) Westchester County
130	49,608	**South Nyack** (village) Rockland County
131	49,481	**Saratoga Springs** (city) Saratoga County
132	49,381	**Cortlandt** (town) Westchester County
133	49,374	**Southampton** (town) Suffolk County
134	49,281	**Massapequa** (CDP) Nassau County
135	49,205	**Yorktown** (town) Westchester County
136	49,055	**Long Beach** (city) Nassau County
137	48,798	**Herricks** (CDP) Nassau County
138	48,723	**Bellmore** (CDP) Nassau County
139	48,513	**Commack** (CDP) Suffolk County
140	48,480	**Noyack** (CDP) Suffolk County
141	48,444	**Southold** (town) Suffolk County
142	48,303	**Farmingdale** (village) Nassau County
143	48,255	**Malverne** (village) Nassau County
144	48,116	**Cutchogue** (CDP) Suffolk County
145	48,070	**North Wantagh** (CDP) Nassau County
146	47,921	**Hurley** (CDP) Ulster County
147	47,920	**East Hampton North** (CDP) Suffolk County
148	47,907	**White Plains** (city) Westchester County
149	47,888	**East Rockaway** (village) Nassau County
150	47,840	**Bayport** (CDP) Suffolk County

Note: This section ranks incorporated places and CDPs (Census Designated Places) with populations of 2,500 or more. Unincorporated postal areas were not considered. Please refer to the User Guide for additional information.

Per Capita Income

Top 150 Places Ranked in *Ascending* Order

State Rank	Dollars	Place
1	3,100	Binghamton University (CDP) Broome County
2	3,638	University at Buffalo (CDP) Erie County
3	4,639	Dannemora (village) Clinton County
4	5,389	Stony Brook University (CDP) Suffolk County
5	5,463	Kaser (village) Rockland County
6	6,568	New Square (village) Rockland County
7	7,007	SUNY Oswego (CDP) Oswego County
8	8,376	Alfred (village) Allegany County
9	8,425	Kiryas Joel (village) Orange County
10	9,445	Dannemora (town) Clinton County
11	11,507	Alfred (town) Allegany County
12	12,356	Monsey (CDP) Rockland County
13	12,436	Groveland (town) Livingston County
14	14,780	Romulus (town) Seneca County
15	14,859	South Hill (CDP) Tompkins County
16	15,359	Potsdam (village) Saint Lawrence County
17	15,562	Geneseo (village) Livingston County
18	15,755	Delhi (village) Delaware County
19	15,913	Attica (town) Wyoming County
20	16,839	Salamanca (city) Cattaraugus County
21	16,923	Monticello (village) Sullivan County
22	17,023	Gouverneur (town) Saint Lawrence County
23	17,288	Elmira (city) Chemung County
24	17,340	Brockport (village) Monroe County
25	17,377	Fort Ann (town) Washington County
26	17,712	Walton (village) Delaware County
27	17,782	New Paltz (village) Ulster County
28	17,797	Carthage (village) Jefferson County
29	18,194	Albion (town) Orleans County
30	18,235	Malone (town) Franklin County
31	18,240	Eaton (town) Madison County
32	18,312	Newburgh (city) Orange County
33	18,366	Gouverneur (village) Saint Lawrence County
34	18,442	Fort Drum (CDP) Jefferson County
35	18,643	Collins (town) Erie County
36	18,819	Riverside (CDP) Suffolk County
37	18,824	Cobleskill (village) Schoharie County
38	18,983	Jamestown (city) Chautauqua County
39	18,985	Ithaca (city) Tompkins County
40	19,104	Canton (village) Saint Lawrence County
41	19,408	Oneonta (city) Otsego County
42	19,588	Arlington (CDP) Dutchess County
43	19,702	Saint Johnsville (town) Montgomery County
44	19,721	Bronx (borough) Bronx County
45	19,764	Whitehall (village) Washington County
46	19,851	Minden (town) Montgomery County
47	19,854	West Point (CDP) Orange County
48	19,871	Lackawanna (city) Erie County
49	19,899	Altona (town) Clinton County
50	19,902	Liberty (village) Sullivan County
51	20,001	Hannibal (town) Oswego County
52	20,006	Hamilton (village) Madison County
53	20,052	Dunkirk (city) Chautauqua County
54	20,120	Moravia (town) Cayuga County
55	20,153	Utica (city) Oneida County
56	20,230	Wyandanch (CDP) Suffolk County
57	20,240	Galen (town) Wayne County
58	20,353	Gloversville (city) Fulton County
59	20,424	Fallsburg (town) Sullivan County
60	20,443	Portland (town) Chautauqua County
61	20,518	Spring Valley (village) Rockland County
62	20,531	Hornell (city) Steuben County
63	20,615	Oswego (town) Oswego County
64	20,681	Mohawk (village) Herkimer County
65	20,925	Wilna (town) Jefferson County
66	20,951	Yorkshire (town) Cattaraugus County
67	20,953	Cortland (city) Cortland County
68	20,989	Penn Yan (village) Yates County
69	21,044	Corinth (village) Saratoga County
70	21,055	Rochester (city) Monroe County
71	21,081	Mount Morris (town) Livingston County
72	21,133	Le Ray (town) Jefferson County
73	21,163	Randolph (town) Cattaraugus County
74	21,187	Syracuse (city) Onondaga County
75	21,252	Keeseville (village) Clinton County
76	21,261	Manheim (town) Herkimer County
77	21,321	Munsons Corners (CDP) Cortland County
78	21,345	Stockholm (town) Saint Lawrence County
79	21,359	Sidney (village) Delaware County
80	21,368	Niagara Falls (city) Niagara County
81	21,369	Wolcott (town) Wayne County
82	21,387	Fort Edward (village) Washington County
83	21,421	Glasco (CDP) Ulster County
84	21,449	Cape Vincent (town) Jefferson County
85	21,469	Mount Morris (village) Livingston County
86	21,470	Geneva (city) Ontario County
87	21,622	Monroe (town) Orange County
88	21,663	Ellenville (village) Ulster County
89	21,704	Endicott (village) Broome County
90	21,710	Binghamton (city) Broome County
91	21,837	Potsdam (town) Saint Lawrence County
92	21,897	Walton (town) Delaware County
93	21,914	Geneseo (town) Livingston County
94	21,917	Herkimer (village) Herkimer County
95	21,931	Amsterdam (city) Montgomery County
96	21,958	Lyons (village) Wayne County
97	22,001	Catskill (village) Greene County
98	22,024	Fulton (city) Oswego County
99	22,070	Whitehall (town) Washington County
100	22,100	Sidney (town) Delaware County
101	22,102	Hudson Falls (village) Washington County
102	22,113	Au Sable (town) Clinton County
103	22,119	Granville (town) Washington County
104	22,133	Colesville (town) Broome County
105	22,162	Augusta (town) Oneida County
106	22,250	Lyons (town) Wayne County
107	22,263	Dolgeville (village) Herkimer County
108	22,294	Buffalo (city) Erie County
109	22,321	Perry (town) Wyoming County
110	22,398	Watertown (city) Jefferson County
111	22,399	Milo (town) Yates County
112	22,415	Annsville (town) Oneida County
113	22,482	Canton (town) Saint Lawrence County
114	22,517	Brasher (town) Saint Lawrence County
115	22,528	Medina (village) Orleans County
116	22,651	Calcium (CDP) Jefferson County
117	22,661	Brentwood (CDP) Suffolk County
118	22,683	Norwich (city) Chenango County
119	22,693	Richland (town) Oswego County
120	22,711	Shelby (town) Orleans County
121	22,784	Wawarsing (town) Ulster County
122	22,810	Ilion (village) Herkimer County
123	22,825	Hempstead (village) Nassau County
124	22,874	Schenectady (city) Schenectady County
125	22,902	North Bay Shore (CDP) Suffolk County
126	22,955	Troy (city) Rensselaer County
127	23,018	Ridgeway (town) Orleans County
128	23,026	Elmira Heights (village) Chemung County
129	23,081	Little Falls (city) Herkimer County
130	23,111	Vienna (town) Oneida County
131	23,142	Inwood (CDP) Nassau County
132	23,187	Auburn (city) Cayuga County
133	23,192	Frankfort (village) Herkimer County
134	23,241	Ogdensburg (city) Saint Lawrence County
135	23,292	Massena (town) Saint Lawrence County
136	23,293	Massena (village) Saint Lawrence County
137	23,313	Hudson (city) Columbia County
138	23,341	Plattsburgh (city) Clinton County
139	23,344	Sodus (town) Wayne County
140	23,428	Malone (village) Franklin County
141	23,440	Cobleskill (town) Schoharie County
142	23,483	Franklinville (town) Cattaraugus County
143	23,487	Coxsackie (town) Greene County
144	23,495	Lisle (town) Broome County
145	23,515	New Bremen (town) Lewis County
146	23,544	Hamilton (town) Madison County
147	23,554	North Amityville (CDP) Suffolk County
148	23,589	Hopewell (town) Ontario County
149	23,601	Norfolk (town) Saint Lawrence County
150	23,694	Allegany (town) Cattaraugus County

Note: This section ranks incorporated places and CDPs (Census Designated Places) with populations of 2,500 or more. Unincorporated postal areas were not considered. Please refer to the User Guide for additional information.

Median Household Income

Top 150 Places Ranked in *Descending* Order

State Rank	Dollars	Place
1	250,000+	**Brookville** (village) Nassau County
1	250,000+	**Munsey Park** (village) Nassau County
1	250,000+	**Scarsdale** (town/village) Westchester County
4	231,607	**Sands Point** (village) Nassau County
5	221,250	**Muttontown** (village) Nassau County
6	212,042	**Greenville** (CDP) Westchester County
7	211,389	**Armonk** (CDP) Westchester County
8	211,105	**New Castle** (town) Westchester County
9	211,087	**Lloyd Harbor** (village) Suffolk County
10	205,781	**Bronxville** (village) Westchester County
11	199,000	**East Hills** (village) Nassau County
12	198,661	**Larchmont** (village) Westchester County
13	198,500	**Pound Ridge** (town) Westchester County
14	180,859	**North Castle** (town) Westchester County
15	178,750	**Flower Hill** (village) Nassau County
16	173,088	**Cold Spring Harbor** (CDP) Suffolk County
17	172,422	**Rye** (city) Westchester County
18	167,083	**Lake Success** (village) Nassau County
19	166,568	**Woodbury** (CDP) Nassau County
20	163,958	**Old Westbury** (village) Nassau County
21	161,163	**Garden City** (village) Nassau County
22	161,111	**Lido Beach** (CDP) Nassau County
23	158,417	**Pelham Manor** (village) Westchester County
24	158,182	**Great Neck Estates** (village) Nassau County
25	157,963	**Briarcliff Manor** (village) Westchester County
26	157,798	**Montebello** (village) Rockland County
27	157,708	**Northwest Harbor** (CDP) Suffolk County
28	156,397	**East Williston** (village) Nassau County
29	156,029	**Jericho** (CDP) Nassau County
30	155,661	**Syosset** (CDP) Nassau County
31	155,234	**Manhasset Hills** (CDP) Nassau County
32	155,179	**Stony Brook University** (CDP) Suffolk County
33	154,570	**Searingtown** (CDP) Nassau County
34	152,263	**Dix Hills** (CDP) Suffolk County
35	150,208	**East Norwich** (CDP) Nassau County
36	148,824	**Lewisboro** (town) Westchester County
37	147,572	**Merrick** (CDP) Nassau County
38	146,833	**Pelham** (town) Westchester County
39	141,863	**Setauket-East Setauket** (CDP) Suffolk County
40	140,185	**West Nyack** (CDP) Rockland County
41	137,414	**North Salem** (town) Westchester County
42	136,214	**Wantagh** (CDP) Nassau County
43	135,688	**Thornwood** (CDP) Westchester County
44	134,688	**Herricks** (CDP) Nassau County
45	133,194	**Irvington** (village) Westchester County
46	132,635	**Plainview** (CDP) Nassau County
47	132,619	**South Valley Stream** (CDP) Nassau County
48	132,553	**Woodmere** (CDP) Nassau County
49	131,818	**Fort Salonga** (CDP) Suffolk County
49	131,818	**Rye Brook** (village) Westchester County
51	131,308	**Stony Brook** (CDP) Suffolk County
52	130,586	**Ardsley** (village) Westchester County
53	130,433	**Manhasset** (CDP) Nassau County
54	129,609	**Lawrence** (village) Nassau County
55	127,998	**North Bellmore** (CDP) Nassau County
56	127,470	**Pelham** (village) Westchester County
57	127,143	**Hastings-on-Hudson** (village) Westchester County
58	126,988	**Dobbs Ferry** (village) Westchester County
59	126,651	**Halesite** (CDP) Suffolk County
60	126,410	**Blauvelt** (CDP) Rockland County
61	126,402	**Smithtown** (CDP) Suffolk County
62	125,736	**Bellmore** (CDP) Nassau County
63	125,603	**East Shoreham** (CDP) Suffolk County
64	125,589	**Woodbury** (village) Orange County
65	124,907	**North Merrick** (CDP) Nassau County
66	124,765	**New City** (CDP) Rockland County
67	124,708	**Croton-on-Hudson** (village) Westchester County
68	124,461	**Commack** (CDP) Suffolk County
69	124,167	**West Hills** (CDP) Suffolk County
70	123,951	**North Wantagh** (CDP) Nassau County
71	123,655	**Melville** (CDP) Suffolk County
72	123,484	**Woodbury** (town) Orange County
73	123,454	**Glenwood Landing** (CDP) Nassau County
74	123,384	**Massapequa** (CDP) Nassau County
75	123,177	**Seaford** (CDP) Nassau County
76	123,152	**Brightwaters** (village) Suffolk County
77	123,110	**Babylon** (village) Suffolk County
78	123,102	**Massapequa Park** (village) Nassau County
79	122,614	**Thiells** (CDP) Rockland County
80	122,083	**Kings Point** (village) Nassau County
81	121,797	**Bedford** (town) Westchester County
82	121,543	**Jefferson Valley-Yorktown** (CDP) Westchester County
83	121,261	**Mamaroneck** (town) Westchester County
84	121,184	**North Hills** (village) Nassau County
85	120,826	**Oyster Bay** (town) Nassau County
86	120,528	**East Islip** (CDP) Suffolk County
87	120,391	**Centerport** (CDP) Suffolk County
88	120,256	**Greenburgh** (town) Westchester County
89	120,233	**Port Washington** (CDP) Nassau County
90	119,963	**Miller Place** (CDP) Suffolk County
91	119,833	**Spackenkill** (CDP) Dutchess County
92	119,531	**Eastchester** (CDP) Westchester County
93	119,453	**Nesconset** (CDP) Suffolk County
94	119,396	**North New Hyde Park** (CDP) Nassau County
95	118,917	**Plainedge** (CDP) Nassau County
96	118,836	**Smithtown** (town) Suffolk County
97	118,654	**Baldwin Harbor** (CDP) Nassau County
98	118,246	**Pomona** (village) Rockland County
99	118,098	**Somers** (town) Westchester County
100	117,453	**Harrison** (town/village) Westchester County
101	117,313	**Blue Point** (CDP) Suffolk County
102	117,279	**Thomaston** (village) Nassau County
103	117,021	**Huntington** (CDP) Suffolk County
104	117,015	**New Hyde Park** (village) Nassau County
105	116,709	**Wading River** (CDP) Suffolk County
106	116,014	**Eastchester** (town) Westchester County
107	115,750	**Lakeview** (CDP) Nassau County
108	115,732	**Yorktown** (town) Westchester County
109	115,691	**Sea Cliff** (village) Nassau County
110	115,500	**North Massapequa** (CDP) Nassau County
111	115,250	**Wesley Hills** (village) Rockland County
112	115,133	**Putnam Valley** (town) Putnam County
113	114,375	**Old Bethpage** (CDP) Nassau County
114	114,364	**Bethpage** (CDP) Nassau County
115	114,310	**Mount Sinai** (CDP) Suffolk County
116	114,205	**New Hempstead** (village) Rockland County
117	114,088	**Garden City South** (CDP) Nassau County
118	113,913	**Roslyn Heights** (CDP) Nassau County
119	113,889	**Albertson** (CDP) Nassau County
120	113,750	**South Hempstead** (CDP) Nassau County
121	113,333	**Congers** (CDP) Rockland County
122	113,224	**South Farmingdale** (CDP) Nassau County
123	113,071	**Pleasantville** (village) Westchester County
124	112,790	**Huntington** (town) Suffolk County
125	112,554	**Bardonia** (CDP) Rockland County
126	112,257	**West Bay Shore** (CDP) Suffolk County
127	112,143	**Tappan** (CDP) Rockland County
128	111,687	**West Islip** (CDP) Suffolk County
129	111,675	**Elwood** (CDP) Suffolk County
130	111,641	**Wheatley Heights** (CDP) Suffolk County
131	111,570	**North Hempstead** (town) Nassau County
132	111,250	**Salisbury** (CDP) Nassau County
133	111,049	**Pompey** (town) Onondaga County
134	111,031	**Tarrytown** (village) Westchester County
135	111,025	**Clarkstown** (town) Rockland County
136	111,023	**Mount Pleasant** (town) Westchester County
137	110,544	**Pittsford** (town) Monroe County
138	110,530	**Shelter Island** (town) Suffolk County
139	109,484	**Oceanside** (CDP) Nassau County
140	109,232	**La Grange** (town) Dutchess County
141	108,850	**Northport** (village) Suffolk County
142	108,654	**Garden City Park** (CDP) Nassau County
143	108,547	**Hauppauge** (CDP) Suffolk County
144	108,438	**Islip Terrace** (CDP) Suffolk County
145	108,365	**Cayuga Heights** (village) Tompkins County
146	108,179	**Levittown** (CDP) Nassau County
147	108,103	**Philipstown** (town) Putnam County
148	107,986	**West Hempstead** (CDP) Nassau County
149	107,917	**Floral Park** (village) Nassau County
150	107,222	**Clarence Center** (CDP) Erie County

Note: *This section ranks incorporated places and CDPs (Census Designated Places) with populations of 2,500 or more. Unincorporated postal areas were not considered. Please refer to the User Guide for additional information.*

Median Household Income

Top 150 Places Ranked in *Ascending* Order

State Rank	Dollars	Place
1	17,564	**Kaser** (village) Rockland County
2	23,924	**New Square** (village) Rockland County
3	29,688	**Liberty** (village) Sullivan County
4	30,319	**Salamanca** (city) Cattaraugus County
5	30,525	**Kiryas Joel** (village) Orange County
6	30,907	**Walton** (village) Delaware County
7	31,103	**Binghamton** (city) Broome County
8	31,169	**Monticello** (village) Sullivan County
9	31,667	**Potsdam** (village) Saint Lawrence County
10	31,700	**Penn Yan** (village) Yates County
11	31,875	**Alfred** (village) Allegany County
11	31,875	**Jamestown** (city) Chautauqua County
13	31,967	**Ithaca** (city) Tompkins County
14	32,259	**Albion** (village) Orleans County
15	32,347	**Rochester** (city) Monroe County
16	32,646	**Elmira** (city) Chemung County
17	33,873	**Utica** (city) Oneida County
18	33,965	**Niagara Falls** (city) Niagara County
19	34,217	**Gouverneur** (village) Saint Lawrence County
20	34,268	**Buffalo** (city) Erie County
21	34,495	**Cobleskill** (village) Schoharie County
22	34,523	**Waverly** (village) Tioga County
23	34,559	**Whitehall** (village) Washington County
24	34,651	**Gouverneur** (town) Saint Lawrence County
25	34,707	**Dunkirk** (city) Chautauqua County
26	34,716	**Syracuse** (city) Onondaga County
27	34,877	**Bath** (village) Steuben County
28	35,024	**Catskill** (village) Greene County
29	35,038	**Geneseo** (village) Livingston County
30	35,371	**Endicott** (village) Broome County
31	35,397	**Gloversville** (city) Fulton County
32	35,439	**Hudson** (city) Columbia County
33	35,482	**Lackawanna** (city) Erie County
34	35,616	**Gowanda** (village) Cattaraugus County
35	36,200	**Saint Johnsville** (town) Montgomery County
36	36,250	**Sidney** (town) Delaware County
37	36,424	**Sidney** (village) Delaware County
38	36,593	**Bronx** (borough) Bronx County
39	36,621	**Malone** (village) Franklin County
40	36,810	**North Dansville** (town) Livingston County
41	36,922	**Newburgh** (city) Orange County
42	37,054	**Milo** (town) Yates County
43	37,170	**Shandaken** (town) Ulster County
44	37,225	**East Syracuse** (village) Onondaga County
45	37,553	**Dansville** (village) Livingston County
46	37,736	**New York Mills** (village) Oneida County
47	37,925	**Monsey** (CDP) Rockland County
48	38,098	**Mount Morris** (village) Livingston County
49	38,445	**Newark** (village) Wayne County
50	38,464	**Oswego** (city) Oswego County
51	38,859	**Randolph** (town) Cattaraugus County
52	38,889	**Riverside** (CDP) Suffolk County
53	38,901	**Ogdensburg** (city) Saint Lawrence County
54	39,252	**New Paltz** (village) Ulster County
55	39,375	**Alfred** (town) Allegany County
56	39,500	**Whitesboro** (village) Oneida County
57	39,534	**Little Falls** (city) Herkimer County
58	39,706	**Albion** (town) Orleans County
59	39,722	**Fairview** (CDP) Westchester County
60	39,741	**Medina** (village) Orleans County
61	39,760	**Saugerties** (village) Ulster County
62	39,992	**Johnson City** (village) Broome County
63	40,136	**Amsterdam** (city) Montgomery County
64	40,216	**South Glens Falls** (village) Saratoga County
65	40,291	**Olean** (city) Cattaraugus County
66	40,313	**Cobleskill** (town) Schoharie County
67	40,331	**Saint Regis Mohawk Reservation** (reservation) Franklin County
68	40,400	**Hornell** (city) Steuben County
69	40,603	**Lyons** (village) Wayne County
70	40,614	**Norwich** (city) Chenango County
71	40,615	**Vails Gate** (CDP) Orange County
72	40,708	**Auburn** (city) Cayuga County
73	40,767	**Watertown** (city) Jefferson County
74	40,795	**Delhi** (village) Delaware County
75	40,804	**Stockholm** (town) Saint Lawrence County
76	40,840	**Poughkeepsie** (city) Dutchess County
77	40,875	**Altona** (town) Clinton County
78	40,911	**Troy** (city) Rensselaer County
79	40,914	**Munsons Corners** (CDP) Cortland County
80	40,920	**Geneva** (city) Ontario County
81	40,927	**Fulton** (city) Oswego County
82	40,970	**Massena** (village) Saint Lawrence County
83	41,048	**Liberty** (town) Sullivan County
84	41,066	**Massena** (town) Saint Lawrence County
85	41,176	**Bath** (town) Steuben County
86	41,199	**Westfield** (village) Chautauqua County
87	41,227	**Herkimer** (village) Herkimer County
88	41,278	**Minden** (town) Montgomery County
89	41,359	**Brockport** (village) Monroe County
90	41,377	**Oneonta** (city) Otsego County
91	41,463	**Whitehall** (town) Washington County
92	41,466	**Warsaw** (village) Wyoming County
93	41,477	**Lockport** (city) Niagara County
94	41,584	**Fallsburg** (town) Sullivan County
95	41,678	**Barton** (town) Tioga County
96	41,835	**Palmyra** (village) Wayne County
97	41,875	**Arcade** (town) Wyoming County
98	41,906	**Keeseville** (village) Clinton County
99	42,031	**Yorkshire** (town) Cattaraugus County
100	42,115	**Mooers** (town) Clinton County
101	42,175	**Thompson** (town) Sullivan County
102	42,316	**Granville** (town) Washington County
103	42,500	**Croghan** (town) Lewis County
104	42,616	**Dix** (town) Schuyler County
105	42,623	**Fort Drum** (CDP) Jefferson County
106	42,976	**Cortland** (city) Cortland County
107	43,013	**Sherburne** (town) Chenango County
108	43,074	**Carthage** (village) Jefferson County
109	43,152	**Wellsville** (village) Allegany County
110	43,174	**Schenectady** (city) Schenectady County
111	43,182	**Au Sable** (town) Clinton County
112	43,407	**North Gates** (CDP) Monroe County
113	43,434	**Spring Valley** (village) Rockland County
114	43,465	**Niagara** (town) Niagara County
115	43,472	**Blasdell** (village) Erie County
115	43,472	**Portland** (town) Chautauqua County
117	43,477	**Plattsburgh** (city) Clinton County
118	43,533	**Elmira Heights** (village) Chemung County
119	43,631	**Wolcott** (town) Wayne County
120	43,729	**Arcadia** (town) Wayne County
121	43,750	**Webster** (village) Monroe County
122	43,756	**Wellsville** (town) Allegany County
123	43,790	**Albany** (city) Albany County
124	43,839	**Murray** (town) Orleans County
125	43,844	**North Syracuse** (village) Onondaga County
126	43,899	**Carroll** (town) Chautauqua County
127	43,958	**Manheim** (town) Herkimer County
128	43,981	**Catskill** (town) Greene County
129	44,167	**Mohawk** (village) Herkimer County
130	44,263	**Geneseo** (town) Livingston County
131	44,342	**Batavia** (city) Genesee County
132	44,388	**Oneida** (city) Madison County
133	44,408	**Le Roy** (village) Genesee County
134	44,527	**Richland** (town) Oswego County
135	44,572	**Alexandria** (town) Jefferson County
136	44,625	**Mechanicville** (city) Saratoga County
137	44,774	**South Lockport** (CDP) Niagara County
138	44,813	**Ilion** (village) Herkimer County
139	44,992	**Hudson Falls** (village) Washington County
140	45,250	**Corinth** (village) Saratoga County
141	45,313	**Dolgeville** (village) Herkimer County
142	45,326	**Middletown** (town) Delaware County
143	45,487	**Kingston** (city) Ulster County
144	45,531	**Ellenville** (village) Ulster County
145	45,542	**Hancock** (town) Delaware County
146	45,570	**Rome** (city) Oneida County
147	45,644	**Sloan** (village) Erie County
148	45,653	**Shelby** (town) Orleans County
149	45,726	**German Flatts** (town) Herkimer County
150	45,733	**Oxford** (town) Chenango County

Note: This section ranks incorporated places and CDPs (Census Designated Places) with populations of 2,500 or more. Unincorporated postal areas were not considered. Please refer to the User Guide for additional information.

Average Household Income
Top 150 Places Ranked in *Descending* Order

State Rank	Dollars	Place
1	425,300	**Brookville** (village) Nassau County
2	417,335	**Scarsdale** (town/village) Westchester County
3	405,772	**Sands Point** (village) Nassau County
4	387,953	**Muttontown** (village) Nassau County
5	350,541	**Munsey Park** (village) Nassau County
6	345,588	**Lloyd Harbor** (village) Suffolk County
7	340,448	**Bronxville** (village) Westchester County
8	339,521	**Pound Ridge** (town) Westchester County
9	325,450	**Old Westbury** (village) Nassau County
10	313,586	**Larchmont** (village) Westchester County
11	311,447	**Armonk** (CDP) Westchester County
12	300,864	**New Castle** (town) Westchester County
13	292,151	**Flower Hill** (village) Nassau County
14	290,004	**North Castle** (town) Westchester County
15	279,820	**Greenville** (CDP) Westchester County
16	277,635	**Kings Point** (village) Nassau County
17	276,177	**Rye** (city) Westchester County
18	266,138	**Pelham Manor** (village) Westchester County
19	263,894	**East Hills** (village) Nassau County
20	255,262	**Lawrence** (village) Nassau County
21	252,898	**Lake Success** (village) Nassau County
22	240,848	**Cold Spring Harbor** (CDP) Suffolk County
23	239,946	**Woodbury** (CDP) Nassau County
24	238,344	**Pelham** (town) Westchester County
25	237,515	**Great Neck Estates** (village) Nassau County
26	233,941	**East Williston** (village) Nassau County
27	231,624	**Briarcliff Manor** (village) Westchester County
28	231,216	**Northwest Harbor** (CDP) Suffolk County
29	229,067	**Lido Beach** (CDP) Nassau County
30	227,642	**Irvington** (village) Westchester County
31	225,891	**Mamaroneck** (town) Westchester County
32	224,836	**Bedford** (town) Westchester County
33	216,895	**Pelham** (village) Westchester County
34	212,240	**Lewisboro** (town) Westchester County
35	211,804	**Jericho** (CDP) Nassau County
36	209,774	**Harrison** (town/village) Westchester County
37	208,773	**Garden City** (village) Nassau County
38	204,380	**Montebello** (village) Rockland County
39	201,530	**Manhasset** (CDP) Nassau County
40	199,642	**Dix Hills** (CDP) Suffolk County
41	195,815	**North Salem** (town) Westchester County
42	195,781	**Syosset** (CDP) Nassau County
43	194,622	**Manhasset Hills** (CDP) Nassau County
44	193,247	**East Norwich** (CDP) Nassau County
45	192,907	**Rye Brook** (village) Westchester County
46	192,583	**Searingtown** (CDP) Nassau County
47	186,431	**Ardsley** (village) Westchester County
48	184,200	**Hastings-on-Hudson** (village) Westchester County
49	181,054	**Eastchester** (town) Westchester County
50	178,709	**North Hills** (village) Nassau County
51	178,194	**Port Washington** (CDP) Nassau County
52	177,255	**Dobbs Ferry** (village) Westchester County
53	175,105	**Fort Salonga** (CDP) Suffolk County
54	173,814	**Merrick** (CDP) Nassau County
55	173,330	**Thomaston** (village) Nassau County
56	171,141	**Melville** (CDP) Suffolk County
57	171,065	**Woodmere** (CDP) Nassau County
58	169,639	**Roslyn Heights** (CDP) Nassau County
59	169,325	**Piermont** (village) Rockland County
60	168,802	**West Hills** (CDP) Suffolk County
61	168,520	**Greenburgh** (town) Westchester County
62	168,017	**Setauket-East Setauket** (CDP) Suffolk County
63	166,987	**Centerport** (CDP) Suffolk County
64	165,932	**North Hempstead** (town) Nassau County
65	165,299	**Brightwaters** (village) Suffolk County
66	164,122	**Roslyn** (village) Nassau County
67	163,557	**Stony Brook University** (CDP) Suffolk County
68	163,355	**Plainview** (CDP) Nassau County
69	162,778	**Pittsford** (town) Monroe County
70	160,928	**Old Bethpage** (CDP) Nassau County
71	160,581	**Wantagh** (CDP) Nassau County
72	160,240	**Bardonia** (CDP) Rockland County
73	159,880	**Oyster Bay** (town) Nassau County
74	159,539	**Blauvelt** (CDP) Rockland County
75	158,282	**Tappan** (CDP) Rockland County
76	158,197	**Somers** (town) Westchester County
77	157,901	**Glen Head** (CDP) Nassau County
78	157,473	**Herricks** (CDP) Nassau County
79	157,185	**Mount Pleasant** (town) Westchester County
80	156,968	**Halesite** (CDP) Suffolk County
81	156,863	**Eastchester** (CDP) Westchester County
82	156,051	**Stony Brook** (CDP) Suffolk County
83	155,280	**North Sea** (CDP) Suffolk County
84	154,544	**Croton-on-Hudson** (village) Westchester County
85	153,966	**New City** (CDP) Rockland County
86	152,620	**Huntington** (CDP) Suffolk County
87	152,092	**Locust Valley** (CDP) Nassau County
88	151,854	**Mamaroneck** (village) Westchester County
89	151,755	**Huntington** (town) Suffolk County
90	151,194	**Philipstown** (town) Putnam County
91	151,011	**North New Hyde Park** (CDP) Nassau County
92	150,535	**Rockville Centre** (village) Nassau County
93	150,504	**Thornwood** (CDP) Westchester County
94	150,244	**Sea Cliff** (village) Nassau County
95	150,235	**Pompey** (town) Onondaga County
96	150,144	**Tarrytown** (village) Westchester County
97	149,434	**East Hampton** (town) Suffolk County
98	149,371	**West Nyack** (CDP) Rockland County
99	149,323	**Massapequa** (CDP) Nassau County
100	148,931	**University Gardens** (CDP) Nassau County
101	148,540	**Glenwood Landing** (CDP) Nassau County
102	148,494	**Southampton** (village) Suffolk County
103	147,288	**Port Washington North** (village) Nassau County
104	147,272	**Pleasantville** (village) Westchester County
105	147,236	**North Merrick** (CDP) Nassau County
106	147,206	**Babylon** (village) Suffolk County
107	146,578	**South Valley Stream** (CDP) Nassau County
108	146,019	**Manhattan** (borough) New York County
109	145,128	**Smithtown** (CDP) Suffolk County
110	144,592	**Tuxedo** (town) Orange County
111	143,371	**Commack** (CDP) Suffolk County
112	142,862	**Pomona** (village) Rockland County
113	142,682	**Smithtown** (town) Suffolk County
114	142,135	**Springs** (CDP) Suffolk County
115	141,872	**Garden City South** (CDP) Nassau County
116	141,664	**Seaford** (CDP) Nassau County
117	141,605	**Elwood** (CDP) Suffolk County
118	140,352	**North Bellmore** (CDP) Nassau County
119	140,114	**Westhampton** (CDP) Suffolk County
120	139,556	**Mendon** (town) Monroe County
121	139,501	**West Bay Shore** (CDP) Suffolk County
122	139,491	**Oyster Bay** (CDP) Nassau County
123	139,259	**Wesley Hills** (village) Rockland County
124	139,191	**East Shoreham** (CDP) Suffolk County
125	138,864	**East Islip** (CDP) Suffolk County
126	138,522	**Skaneateles** (town) Onondaga County
127	138,119	**Pearl River** (CDP) Rockland County
128	138,110	**Mount Sinai** (CDP) Suffolk County
129	137,811	**Northport** (village) Suffolk County
130	137,239	**Wading River** (CDP) Suffolk County
131	137,196	**North Wantagh** (CDP) Nassau County
132	137,195	**Bellmore** (CDP) Nassau County
133	136,812	**Cayuga Heights** (village) Tompkins County
134	136,721	**Cortlandt** (town) Westchester County
135	136,386	**Jefferson Valley-Yorktown** (CDP) Westchester County
136	136,238	**Yorktown** (town) Westchester County
137	136,220	**Orangetown** (town) Rockland County
138	136,173	**Massapequa Park** (village) Nassau County
139	136,040	**Nesconset** (CDP) Suffolk County
140	135,868	**Clarkstown** (town) Rockland County
141	135,853	**Spackenkill** (CDP) Dutchess County
142	135,814	**South Nyack** (village) Rockland County
143	135,394	**Congers** (CDP) Rockland County
144	134,923	**Baldwin Harbor** (CDP) Nassau County
145	134,715	**Victor** (town) Ontario County
146	133,966	**Port Jefferson** (village) Suffolk County
147	133,939	**New Hempstead** (village) Rockland County
148	133,936	**South Hempstead** (CDP) Nassau County
149	133,450	**Bayville** (village) Nassau County
150	133,285	**Miller Place** (CDP) Suffolk County

Note: This section ranks incorporated places and CDPs (Census Designated Places) with populations of 2,500 or more. Unincorporated postal areas were not considered. Please refer to the User Guide for additional information.

Average Household Income

Top 150 Places Ranked in *Ascending* Order

State Rank	Dollars	Place	State Rank	Dollars	Place
1	14,650	University at Buffalo (CDP) Erie County	76	54,258	Newark (village) Wayne County
2	29,520	Kaser (village) Rockland County	77	54,275	Blasdell (village) Erie County
3	38,543	New Square (village) Rockland County	78	54,455	Randolph (town) Cattaraugus County
4	41,114	Salamanca (city) Cattaraugus County	79	54,518	Calcium (CDP) Jefferson County
5	41,296	Monticello (village) Sullivan County	80	54,565	Dannemora (village) Clinton County
6	43,076	Jamestown (city) Chautauqua County	80	54,565	Ithaca (city) Tompkins County
7	43,518	Walton (village) Delaware County	82	54,590	Webster (village) Monroe County
8	44,791	Dunkirk (city) Chautauqua County	83	54,728	Riverside (CDP) Suffolk County
9	45,315	Gouverneur (village) Saint Lawrence County	84	54,742	Portland (town) Chautauqua County
10	45,437	Penn Yan (village) Yates County	85	54,762	Warsaw (village) Wyoming County
11	46,074	Elmira (city) Chemung County	86	54,848	Galeville (CDP) Onondaga County
12	46,091	Whitehall (village) Washington County	87	54,867	Hudson Falls (village) Washington County
13	46,096	Mount Morris (village) Livingston County	88	54,885	Granville (town) Washington County
14	46,506	Kiryas Joel (village) Orange County	89	54,986	Arcade (town) Wyoming County
15	46,616	Lackawanna (city) Erie County	90	55,043	Troy (city) Rensselaer County
16	46,981	Endicott (village) Broome County	91	55,061	Hannibal (town) Oswego County
17	47,289	Lyons (village) Wayne County	92	55,229	Cortland (city) Cortland County
18	47,352	Rochester (city) Monroe County	93	55,279	Westfield (town) Chautauqua County
19	47,543	Mohawk (village) Herkimer County	94	55,310	Wellsville (village) Allegany County
20	47,676	Gouverneur (town) Saint Lawrence County	95	55,357	Waverly (village) Tioga County
21	47,744	Niagara Falls (city) Niagara County	96	55,369	Catskill (village) Greene County
22	47,954	Gloversville (city) Fulton County	97	55,412	Corinth (village) Saratoga County
23	48,369	Medina (village) Orleans County	98	55,494	Frankfort (village) Herkimer County
24	48,528	Liberty (village) Sullivan County	99	55,496	Au Sable (town) Clinton County
25	48,530	Binghamton (city) Broome County	100	55,574	Schenectady (city) Schenectady County
26	49,167	Carthage (village) Jefferson County	101	55,642	Arcadia (town) Wayne County
27	49,193	Shelby (town) Orleans County	102	55,651	Altona (town) Clinton County
28	49,474	Stockholm (town) Saint Lawrence County	103	55,733	Hancock (town) Delaware County
29	49,815	Hornell (city) Steuben County	104	55,766	Sloan (village) Erie County
30	49,957	Utica (city) Oneida County	105	55,878	Geneva (city) Ontario County
31	50,031	Herkimer (village) Herkimer County	106	55,932	Wellsville (town) Allegany County
32	50,081	Sidney (town) Delaware County	107	55,933	Dolgeville (village) Herkimer County
33	50,456	Buffalo (city) Erie County	108	55,981	Perry (village) Wyoming County
34	50,513	Yorkshire (town) Cattaraugus County	109	56,034	Dansville (village) Livingston County
35	50,735	South Glens Falls (village) Saratoga County	110	56,207	Saugerties (village) Ulster County
36	50,773	Watertown (city) Jefferson County	111	56,280	Ilion (village) Herkimer County
37	50,785	Sidney (village) Delaware County	112	56,283	Silver Creek (village) Chautauqua County
38	50,825	Syracuse (city) Onondaga County	113	56,313	Oswego (city) Oswego County
39	50,910	Massena (town) Saint Lawrence County	114	56,339	Ridgeway (town) Orleans County
40	51,077	Fort Edward (village) Washington County	115	56,436	Albion (village) Orleans County
41	51,092	Walton (town) Delaware County	116	56,504	Herkimer (town) Herkimer County
42	51,147	New York Mills (village) Oneida County	117	56,524	Mechanicville (city) Saratoga County
43	51,170	Saint Regis Mohawk Reservation (reservation) Franklin County	118	56,531	Spencer (town) Tioga County
44	51,375	Saint Johnsville (town) Montgomery County	119	56,613	Plattsburgh (city) Clinton County
45	51,409	Wolcott (town) Wayne County	120	56,650	Little Falls (city) Herkimer County
46	51,422	Massena (village) Saint Lawrence County	121	56,689	Sherburne (village) Chenango County
47	51,459	Keeseville (village) Clinton County	122	56,746	Bath (town) Steuben County
48	51,482	Minden (town) Montgomery County	123	56,886	North Gates (CDP) Monroe County
49	51,499	Fort Drum (CDP) Jefferson County	124	56,902	Batavia (city) Genesee County
50	51,591	Milo (town) Yates County	125	56,980	Colesville (town) Broome County
51	51,692	Brockport (village) Monroe County	126	56,998	Westfield (village) Chautauqua County
52	51,779	Munsons Corners (CDP) Cortland County	127	57,086	Niagara (town) Niagara County
53	51,856	Mount Morris (town) Livingston County	128	57,190	Wilna (town) Jefferson County
54	51,878	Bath (village) Steuben County	129	57,526	Palmyra (village) Wayne County
55	52,119	Elmira Heights (village) Chemung County	130	57,549	Watervliet (city) Albany County
56	52,206	Ellenville (village) Ulster County	131	57,568	Le Ray (town) Jefferson County
57	52,356	Hudson (city) Columbia County	132	57,622	Annsville (town) Oneida County
58	52,481	Fulton (city) Oswego County	133	57,624	Fallsburg (town) Sullivan County
59	52,553	Cobleskill (village) Schoharie County	134	57,653	Glasco (CDP) Ulster County
60	52,670	Whitesboro (village) Oneida County	135	57,698	Southport (CDP) Chemung County
61	52,687	Auburn (city) Cayuga County	136	57,728	German Flatts (town) Herkimer County
62	52,746	Malone (village) Franklin County	137	57,793	Tonawanda (city) Erie County
63	53,025	Solvay (village) Onondaga County	138	57,794	Vienna (town) Oneida County
64	53,230	Geneseo (village) Livingston County	139	57,802	Olean (city) Cattaraugus County
65	53,271	Amsterdam (city) Montgomery County	140	57,862	Lockport (city) Niagara County
66	53,401	Lyncourt (CDP) Onondaga County	141	57,936	New Paltz (village) Ulster County
67	53,579	Lyons (town) Wayne County	142	57,971	South Lockport (CDP) Niagara County
68	53,721	Manheim (town) Herkimer County	143	57,974	Franklinville (town) Cattaraugus County
69	53,730	Bronx (borough) Bronx County	144	58,242	Arlington (CDP) Dutchess County
70	53,775	Norwich (city) Chenango County	144	58,242	Mooers (town) Clinton County
71	53,870	Whitehall (town) Washington County	146	58,350	White Creek (town) Washington County
72	53,935	East Syracuse (village) Onondaga County	147	58,417	North Dansville (town) Livingston County
73	53,987	Alfred (village) Allegany County	148	58,441	Wayland (town) Steuben County
74	54,121	Newburgh (city) Orange County	149	58,483	Sodus (town) Wayne County
75	54,147	Johnson City (village) Broome County	150	58,506	Potsdam (village) Saint Lawrence County

Note: This section ranks incorporated places and CDPs (Census Designated Places) with populations of 2,500 or more. Unincorporated postal areas were not considered. Please refer to the User Guide for additional information.

Households with Income of $100,000 or More

Top 150 Places Ranked in *Descending* Order

State Rank	Percent	Place	State Rank	Percent	Place
1	86.4	**Munsey Park** (village) Nassau County	76	60.1	**Kings Point** (village) Nassau County
2	85.1	**Scarsdale** (town/village) Westchester County	77	60.0	**Glen Head** (CDP) Nassau County
3	84.2	**Sands Point** (village) Nassau County	77	60.0	**Nesconset** (CDP) Suffolk County
4	82.5	**Armonk** (CDP) Westchester County	77	60.0	**Plainedge** (CDP) Nassau County
5	81.8	**Muttontown** (village) Nassau County	77	60.0	**Spackenkill** (CDP) Dutchess County
6	80.7	**New Castle** (town) Westchester County	81	59.7	**Mount Sinai** (CDP) Suffolk County
7	79.5	**Greenville** (CDP) Westchester County	82	59.4	**Glenwood Landing** (CDP) Nassau County
8	77.8	**East Hills** (village) Nassau County	82	59.4	**Sea Cliff** (village) Nassau County
9	77.3	**Pound Ridge** (town) Westchester County	84	59.3	**Massapequa** (CDP) Nassau County
10	77.2	**Lake Success** (village) Nassau County	85	59.0	**Baldwin Harbor** (CDP) Nassau County
11	77.0	**Brookville** (village) Nassau County	85	59.0	**Greenburgh** (town) Westchester County
12	75.3	**Old Westbury** (village) Nassau County	87	58.9	**Thomaston** (village) Nassau County
13	75.2	**East Williston** (village) Nassau County	88	58.8	**Centerport** (CDP) Suffolk County
14	74.7	**Larchmont** (village) Westchester County	88	58.8	**Smithtown** (town) Suffolk County
15	74.5	**Flower Hill** (village) Nassau County	90	58.7	**West Bay Shore** (CDP) Suffolk County
16	73.7	**Lloyd Harbor** (village) Suffolk County	91	58.5	**Bellmore** (CDP) Nassau County
17	73.5	**North Castle** (town) Westchester County	91	58.5	**Oyster Bay** (town) Nassau County
18	73.3	**Cold Spring Harbor** (CDP) Suffolk County	93	58.4	**Babylon** (village) Suffolk County
19	71.7	**Jericho** (CDP) Nassau County	94	58.3	**New Hyde Park** (village) Nassau County
20	71.3	**Stony Brook University** (CDP) Suffolk County	94	58.3	**South Valley Stream** (CDP) Nassau County
21	70.5	**Pelham Manor** (village) Westchester County	96	58.2	**North Wantagh** (CDP) Nassau County
22	70.3	**Halesite** (CDP) Suffolk County	97	58.1	**North Massapequa** (CDP) Nassau County
23	70.2	**Dix Hills** (CDP) Suffolk County	98	58.0	**Manhasset** (CDP) Nassau County
23	70.2	**Manhasset Hills** (CDP) Nassau County	99	57.9	**Bedford** (town) Westchester County
25	70.1	**Bronxville** (village) Westchester County	100	57.8	**Congers** (CDP) Rockland County
26	69.9	**Merrick** (CDP) Nassau County	101	57.7	**Lawrence** (village) Nassau County
27	69.4	**Syosset** (CDP) Nassau County	102	57.6	**Croton-on-Hudson** (village) Westchester County
28	69.0	**Garden City** (village) Nassau County	102	57.6	**Mamaroneck** (town) Westchester County
29	68.7	**Briarcliff Manor** (village) Westchester County	104	57.4	**Miller Place** (CDP) Suffolk County
29	68.7	**Lewisboro** (town) Westchester County	105	57.2	**La Grange** (town) Dutchess County
31	68.1	**East Norwich** (CDP) Nassau County	106	57.0	**Eastchester** (CDP) Westchester County
31	68.1	**Rye** (city) Westchester County	106	57.0	**Wesley Hills** (village) Rockland County
33	67.9	**Great Neck Estates** (village) Nassau County	108	56.8	**Bardonia** (CDP) Rockland County
34	67.4	**East Shoreham** (CDP) Suffolk County	108	56.8	**Port Washington** (CDP) Nassau County
35	66.6	**Wantagh** (CDP) Nassau County	108	56.8	**Yorktown** (town) Westchester County
36	66.4	**Ardsley** (village) Westchester County	111	56.7	**Pleasantville** (village) Westchester County
37	66.3	**Fort Salonga** (CDP) Suffolk County	112	56.6	**Old Bethpage** (CDP) Nassau County
38	66.2	**Woodbury** (CDP) Nassau County	113	56.5	**West Islip** (CDP) Suffolk County
39	65.9	**Montebello** (village) Rockland County	114	56.4	**Somers** (town) Westchester County
40	65.1	**North Salem** (town) Westchester County	114	56.4	**Wheatley Heights** (CDP) Suffolk County
41	64.8	**Irvington** (village) Westchester County	116	56.2	**South Farmingdale** (CDP) Nassau County
42	64.7	**Pelham** (town) Westchester County	117	56.0	**Salisbury** (CDP) Nassau County
43	64.4	**Setauket-East Setauket** (CDP) Suffolk County	118	55.9	**Clarkstown** (town) Rockland County
44	64.0	**Searingtown** (CDP) Nassau County	118	55.9	**Roslyn Heights** (CDP) Nassau County
45	63.8	**Woodbury** (village) Orange County	118	55.9	**Shelter Island** (town) Suffolk County
46	63.7	**Herricks** (CDP) Nassau County	118	55.9	**South Hempstead** (CDP) Nassau County
47	63.6	**Dobbs Ferry** (village) Westchester County	118	55.9	**Wading River** (CDP) Suffolk County
48	63.2	**New City** (CDP) Rockland County	123	55.8	**Elwood** (CDP) Suffolk County
49	62.9	**North New Hyde Park** (CDP) Nassau County	123	55.8	**Tarrytown** (village) Westchester County
50	62.8	**North Bellmore** (CDP) Nassau County	125	55.7	**Garden City South** (CDP) Nassau County
50	62.8	**West Nyack** (CDP) Rockland County	126	55.5	**Huntington** (town) Suffolk County
52	62.7	**Seaford** (CDP) Nassau County	127	55.4	**Albertson** (CDP) Nassau County
52	62.7	**Woodmere** (CDP) Nassau County	127	55.4	**Philipstown** (town) Putnam County
54	62.5	**Blauvelt** (CDP) Rockland County	129	55.3	**Clarence Center** (CDP) Erie County
55	62.3	**Smithtown** (CDP) Suffolk County	129	55.3	**Eastchester** (town) Westchester County
55	62.3	**Thornwood** (CDP) Westchester County	129	55.3	**North Hempstead** (town) Nassau County
57	62.2	**East Islip** (CDP) Suffolk County	132	55.2	**Bethpage** (CDP) Nassau County
58	62.1	**Plainview** (CDP) Nassau County	132	55.2	**Huntington** (CDP) Suffolk County
58	62.1	**Woodbury** (town) Orange County	132	55.2	**Melville** (CDP) Suffolk County
60	61.8	**Lido Beach** (CDP) Nassau County	132	55.2	**North Hills** (village) Nassau County
60	61.8	**Stony Brook** (CDP) Suffolk County	132	55.2	**Pompey** (town) Onondaga County
62	61.6	**Thiells** (CDP) Rockland County	137	55.0	**Hauppauge** (CDP) Suffolk County
63	61.3	**Hastings-on-Hudson** (village) Westchester County	138	54.9	**Blue Point** (CDP) Suffolk County
63	61.3	**Rye Brook** (village) Westchester County	138	54.9	**Lakeview** (CDP) Nassau County
65	61.2	**Brightwaters** (village) Suffolk County	140	54.8	**Putnam Valley** (town) Putnam County
65	61.2	**Massapequa Park** (village) Nassau County	141	54.7	**Floral Park** (village) Nassau County
65	61.2	**Pomona** (village) Rockland County	142	54.6	**Malverne** (village) Nassau County
68	61.0	**Jefferson Valley-Yorktown** (CDP) Westchester County	142	54.6	**Pittsford** (town) Monroe County
69	60.8	**Commack** (CDP) Suffolk County	144	54.5	**Tappan** (CDP) Rockland County
69	60.8	**North Merrick** (CDP) Nassau County	145	54.3	**East Moriches** (CDP) Suffolk County
71	60.5	**New Hempstead** (village) Rockland County	146	54.0	**Garden City Park** (CDP) Nassau County
72	60.4	**Northwest Harbor** (CDP) Suffolk County	147	53.9	**Mount Pleasant** (town) Westchester County
72	60.4	**Pelham** (village) Westchester County	147	53.9	**Niskayuna** (town) Schenectady County
74	60.2	**Harrison** (town/village) Westchester County	147	53.9	**Oceanside** (CDP) Nassau County
74	60.2	**West Hills** (CDP) Suffolk County	150	53.8	**Islip Terrace** (CDP) Suffolk County

Note: This section ranks incorporated places and CDPs (Census Designated Places) with populations of 2,500 or more. Unincorporated postal areas were not considered. Please refer to the User Guide for additional information.

Households with Income of $100,000 or More

Top 150 Places Ranked in *Ascending* Order

State Rank	Percent	Place
1	3.5	**Kaser** (village) Rockland County
2	4.8	**Whitesboro** (village) Oneida County
3	6.0	**Mohawk** (village) Herkimer County
4	6.5	**Calcium** (CDP) Jefferson County
4	6.5	**Yorkshire** (town) Cattaraugus County
6	6.6	**Bath** (village) Steuben County
7	6.8	**Jamestown** (city) Chautauqua County
7	6.8	**Monticello** (village) Sullivan County
7	6.8	**Salamanca** (city) Cattaraugus County
10	7.2	**Gouverneur** (town) Saint Lawrence County
11	7.6	**Fort Edward** (village) Washington County
12	7.9	**Lackawanna** (city) Erie County
13	8.0	**Walton** (village) Delaware County
14	8.1	**Dannemora** (village) Clinton County
14	8.1	**Lyons** (village) Wayne County
16	8.2	**Dunkirk** (city) Chautauqua County
17	8.3	**Shelby** (town) Orleans County
18	8.4	**Wolcott** (town) Wayne County
19	8.5	**Fort Drum** (CDP) Jefferson County
20	8.9	**Sloan** (village) Erie County
21	9.0	**Gouverneur** (village) Saint Lawrence County
21	9.0	**New Square** (village) Rockland County
21	9.0	**Schuyler** (town) Herkimer County
24	9.1	**Hornell** (city) Steuben County
25	9.2	**Minden** (town) Montgomery County
26	9.4	**Yorkville** (village) Oneida County
27	9.5	**Endicott** (village) Broome County
27	9.5	**Mattydale** (CDP) Onondaga County
29	9.7	**Medina** (village) Orleans County
29	9.7	**Munsons Corners** (CDP) Cortland County
31	9.8	**Keeseville** (village) Clinton County
32	9.9	**Hannibal** (town) Oswego County
32	9.9	**Portland** (town) Chautauqua County
32	9.9	**Solvay** (village) Onondaga County
35	10.0	**Elmira** (city) Chemung County
35	10.0	**Perry** (village) Wyoming County
35	10.0	**Rochester** (city) Monroe County
38	10.1	**Binghamton** (city) Broome County
39	10.2	**Gloversville** (city) Fulton County
39	10.2	**Watertown** (city) Jefferson County
41	10.5	**Niagara Falls** (city) Niagara County
41	10.5	**Utica** (city) Oneida County
43	10.6	**Blasdell** (village) Erie County
43	10.6	**Herkimer** (village) Herkimer County
43	10.6	**Lyons** (town) Wayne County
43	10.6	**South Glens Falls** (village) Saratoga County
47	10.7	**Stockholm** (town) Saint Lawrence County
48	10.8	**Mount Morris** (village) Livingston County
48	10.8	**New York Mills** (village) Oneida County
48	10.8	**Walton** (town) Delaware County
48	10.8	**Wellsville** (village) Allegany County
52	11.0	**Le Ray** (town) Jefferson County
52	11.0	**Whitehall** (village) Washington County
54	11.1	**Catskill** (village) Greene County
54	11.1	**Kiryas Joel** (village) Orange County
54	11.1	**Little Falls** (city) Herkimer County
57	11.2	**Bath** (town) Steuben County
57	11.2	**Newark** (village) Wayne County
59	11.3	**Hudson Falls** (village) Washington County
59	11.3	**Wellsville** (town) Allegany County
61	11.4	**Milo** (town) Yates County
61	11.4	**Saint Johnsville** (town) Montgomery County
61	11.4	**Watervliet** (city) Albany County
64	11.5	**Colesville** (town) Broome County
64	11.5	**Hudson** (city) Columbia County
66	11.6	**Brasher** (town) Saint Lawrence County
66	11.6	**Elmira Heights** (village) Chemung County
66	11.6	**Gowanda** (village) Cattaraugus County
66	11.6	**Penn Yan** (village) Yates County
66	11.6	**Perry** (town) Wyoming County
71	11.8	**Silver Creek** (village) Chautauqua County
72	11.9	**Hanover** (town) Chautauqua County
72	11.9	**Massena** (town) Saint Lawrence County
74	12.0	**Ogdensburg** (city) Saint Lawrence County
74	12.0	**Syracuse** (city) Onondaga County
76	12.1	**Buffalo** (city) Erie County
76	12.1	**Fulton** (city) Oswego County
76	12.1	**Saint Regis Mohawk Reservation** (reservation) Franklin County
79	12.2	**Auburn** (city) Cayuga County
79	12.2	**Cortland** (city) Cortland County
79	12.2	**Ellenville** (village) Ulster County
79	12.2	**Liberty** (village) Sullivan County
79	12.2	**Norfolk** (town) Saint Lawrence County
84	12.3	**Arcadia** (town) Wayne County
84	12.3	**Carthage** (village) Jefferson County
84	12.3	**Massena** (village) Saint Lawrence County
87	12.4	**Vienna** (town) Oneida County
88	12.5	**Niagara** (town) Niagara County
88	12.5	**Sidney** (town) Delaware County
90	12.6	**Au Sable** (town) Clinton County
90	12.6	**Sidney** (village) Delaware County
92	12.7	**Southport** (CDP) Chemung County
93	12.8	**Fort Edward** (town) Washington County
93	12.8	**Hancock** (town) Delaware County
93	12.8	**Waterloo** (town) Seneca County
96	12.9	**Arlington** (CDP) Dutchess County
96	12.9	**Mount Morris** (town) Livingston County
98	13.1	**Amsterdam** (city) Montgomery County
98	13.1	**Brockport** (village) Monroe County
98	13.1	**Davenport** (town) Delaware County
98	13.1	**Lyncourt** (CDP) Onondaga County
102	13.2	**Altona** (town) Clinton County
102	13.2	**Arcade** (town) Wyoming County
102	13.2	**Bainbridge** (town) Chenango County
105	13.3	**Westfield** (town) Chautauqua County
106	13.4	**Granville** (town) Washington County
106	13.4	**Guilford** (town) Chenango County
106	13.4	**Webster** (village) Monroe County
109	13.6	**Galen** (town) Wayne County
109	13.6	**Herkimer** (town) Herkimer County
109	13.6	**New Berlin** (town) Chenango County
109	13.6	**North Dansville** (town) Livingston County
113	13.7	**Albion** (town) Orleans County
113	13.7	**Geneva** (city) Ontario County
113	13.7	**North Syracuse** (village) Onondaga County
116	13.8	**Augusta** (town) Oneida County
116	13.8	**Johnson City** (village) Broome County
116	13.8	**Warsaw** (village) Wyoming County
119	13.9	**Bronx** (borough) Bronx County
119	13.9	**Palmyra** (village) Wayne County
121	14.0	**Lockport** (city) Niagara County
121	14.0	**Ravena** (village) Albany County
121	14.0	**Schenectady** (city) Schenectady County
124	14.1	**Frankfort** (village) Herkimer County
125	14.3	**Batavia** (city) Genesee County
125	14.3	**East Syracuse** (village) Onondaga County
125	14.3	**Green Island** (town/village) Albany County
125	14.3	**Kendall** (town) Orleans County
125	14.3	**Malone** (village) Franklin County
130	14.4	**Canisteo** (town) Steuben County
130	14.4	**Dansville** (village) Livingston County
130	14.4	**Galeville** (CDP) Onondaga County
133	14.5	**Manheim** (town) Herkimer County
133	14.5	**Spencer** (town) Tioga County
135	14.6	**Poughkeepsie** (city) Dutchess County
135	14.6	**Sherburne** (town) Chenango County
135	14.6	**Troy** (city) Rensselaer County
138	14.7	**Le Roy** (village) Genesee County
138	14.7	**Rutland** (town) Jefferson County
140	14.8	**Cohoes** (city) Albany County
140	14.8	**Lisle** (town) Broome County
140	14.8	**Westfield** (village) Chautauqua County
143	14.9	**Cobleskill** (village) Schoharie County
143	14.9	**Frankfort** (town) Herkimer County
143	14.9	**Hartland** (town) Niagara County
143	14.9	**Salem** (town) Washington County
143	14.9	**Tonawanda** (city) Erie County
148	15.0	**Claverack** (town) Columbia County
148	15.0	**Geneva** (town) Ontario County
148	15.0	**Hornellsville** (town) Steuben County

Note: This section ranks incorporated places and CDPs (Census Designated Places) with populations of 2,500 or more. Unincorporated postal areas were not considered. Please refer to the User Guide for additional information.

Poverty Rate

Top 150 Places Ranked in *Descending* Order

State Rank	Percent	Place
1	76.1	**Kaser** (village) Rockland County
2	64.4	**New Square** (village) Rockland County
3	48.0	**Kiryas Joel** (village) Orange County
4	44.1	**Monsey** (CDP) Rockland County
5	43.4	**Ithaca** (city) Tompkins County
6	41.4	**Geneseo** (village) Livingston County
7	38.1	**Alfred** (village) Allegany County
8	33.3	**Binghamton** (city) Broome County
8	33.3	**New Paltz** (village) Ulster County
10	33.1	**Rochester** (city) Monroe County
11	32.6	**Syracuse** (city) Onondaga County
12	32.3	**Malone** (village) Franklin County
13	31.5	**Carthage** (village) Jefferson County
14	31.3	**Walton** (village) Delaware County
15	31.2	**Newburgh** (city) Orange County
16	30.9	**Buffalo** (city) Erie County
16	30.9	**Elmira** (city) Chemung County
18	30.8	**Gouverneur** (village) Saint Lawrence County
19	30.5	**Mount Morris** (village) Livingston County
20	30.4	**Utica** (city) Oneida County
21	29.7	**Bronx** (borough) Bronx County
21	29.7	**Jamestown** (city) Chautauqua County
23	29.6	**Geneseo** (town) Livingston County
24	29.2	**Catskill** (village) Greene County
25	29.1	**Little Falls** (city) Herkimer County
26	28.8	**Alfred** (town) Allegany County
27	28.6	**Monroe** (town) Orange County
28	28.4	**Gloversville** (city) Fulton County
29	28.0	**Brockport** (village) Monroe County
29	28.0	**Oswego** (city) Oswego County
31	27.5	**Niagara Falls** (city) Niagara County
31	27.5	**Potsdam** (village) Saint Lawrence County
33	27.3	**Fallsburg** (town) Sullivan County
34	27.2	**Monticello** (village) Sullivan County
34	27.2	**Salamanca** (city) Cattaraugus County
36	27.0	**Walton** (town) Delaware County
37	26.6	**Gouverneur** (town) Saint Lawrence County
38	26.5	**Whitehall** (village) Washington County
39	26.4	**Delhi** (village) Delaware County
39	26.4	**Fulton** (city) Oswego County
39	26.4	**Liberty** (village) Sullivan County
42	26.3	**Saint Johnsville** (town) Montgomery County
43	26.1	**Troy** (city) Rensselaer County
44	25.9	**Albion** (village) Orleans County
44	25.9	**Spring Valley** (village) Rockland County
46	25.6	**Amsterdam** (city) Montgomery County
46	25.6	**Oneonta** (city) Otsego County
48	25.5	**Dansville** (village) Livingston County
49	25.4	**Lackawanna** (city) Erie County
50	25.3	**North Dansville** (town) Livingston County
51	25.1	**Albion** (town) Orleans County
52	24.9	**Cobleskill** (village) Schoharie County
52	24.9	**Moira** (town) Franklin County
54	24.8	**Oswegatchie** (town) Saint Lawrence County
55	24.7	**Watertown** (city) Jefferson County
56	24.5	**Albany** (city) Albany County
57	24.4	**Cortland** (city) Cortland County
57	24.4	**Massena** (town) Saint Lawrence County
59	24.3	**Plattsburgh** (city) Clinton County
60	24.2	**Norwich** (city) Chenango County
61	24.1	**Sidney** (village) Delaware County
62	24.0	**Malone** (town) Franklin County
62	24.0	**Massena** (village) Saint Lawrence County
62	24.0	**Ramapo** (town) Rockland County
65	23.7	**Gowanda** (village) Cattaraugus County
65	23.7	**Portland** (town) Chautauqua County
67	23.2	**Waverly** (village) Tioga County
68	22.8	**Olean** (city) Cattaraugus County
69	22.7	**Dunkirk** (city) Chautauqua County
70	22.6	**Warsaw** (village) Wyoming County
71	22.4	**Poughkeepsie** (city) Dutchess County
72	22.3	**Richland** (town) Oswego County
73	22.2	**Oneonta** (town) Otsego County
73	22.2	**Wyandanch** (CDP) Suffolk County
75	22.1	**Granby** (town) Oswego County

State Rank	Percent	Place
76	22.0	**Lowville** (town) Lewis County
76	22.0	**Mount Morris** (town) Livingston County
78	21.9	**Brooklyn** (borough) Kings County
79	21.8	**Batavia** (city) Genesee County
80	21.6	**Sodus** (town) Wayne County
81	21.5	**Shawangunk** (town) Ulster County
82	21.4	**Sidney** (town) Delaware County
82	21.4	**Wilna** (town) Jefferson County
84	21.2	**South Hill** (CDP) Tompkins County
85	21.1	**Canajoharie** (town) Montgomery County
85	21.1	**Minden** (town) Montgomery County
87	21.0	**Schenectady** (city) Schenectady County
88	20.9	**Hornell** (city) Steuben County
88	20.9	**Ilion** (village) Herkimer County
88	20.9	**Norfolk** (town) Saint Lawrence County
91	20.8	**Barton** (town) Tioga County
91	20.8	**Fredonia** (village) Chautauqua County
91	20.8	**Mattydale** (CDP) Onondaga County
91	20.8	**Ogdensburg** (city) Saint Lawrence County
91	20.8	**Whitehall** (town) Washington County
96	20.7	**East Syracuse** (village) Onondaga County
97	20.5	**Westfield** (village) Chautauqua County
98	20.4	**Hudson Falls** (village) Washington County
98	20.4	**Rockland** (town) Sullivan County
100	20.3	**Dolgeville** (village) Herkimer County
101	20.2	**Hempstead** (village) Nassau County
102	20.0	**Lyons** (village) Wayne County
103	19.9	**Palmyra** (village) Wayne County
104	19.8	**Geneva** (town) Ontario County
104	19.8	**Sleepy Hollow** (village) Westchester County
106	19.7	**Penn Yan** (village) Yates County
107	19.6	**Canton** (village) Saint Lawrence County
107	19.6	**Endicott** (village) Broome County
107	19.6	**New York** (city)
107	19.6	**Saint Regis Mohawk Reservation** (reservation) Franklin County
107	19.6	**Thompson** (town) Sullivan County
107	19.6	**Wellsville** (village) Allegany County
113	19.5	**Mohawk** (village) Herkimer County
114	19.4	**Augusta** (town) Oneida County
114	19.4	**Durham** (town) Greene County
114	19.4	**Harrietstown** (town) Franklin County
114	19.4	**Mechanicstown** (CDP) Orange County
114	19.4	**Munsons Corners** (CDP) Cortland County
114	19.4	**Rome** (city) Oneida County
120	19.3	**Palatine** (town) Montgomery County
120	19.3	**Potsdam** (town) Saint Lawrence County
120	19.3	**Vienna** (town) Oneida County
123	19.2	**Hudson** (city) Columbia County
124	19.1	**Murray** (town) Orleans County
125	19.0	**Oneida** (city) Madison County
126	18.9	**Ellenville** (village) Ulster County
126	18.9	**Geneva** (city) Ontario County
126	18.9	**German Flatts** (town) Herkimer County
129	18.8	**Herkimer** (village) Herkimer County
130	18.7	**Mechanicville** (city) Saratoga County
130	18.7	**Pomfret** (town) Chautauqua County
132	18.6	**Johnson City** (village) Broome County
132	18.6	**Keeseville** (village) Clinton County
132	18.6	**Webster** (village) Monroe County
135	18.5	**Saranac Lake** (village) Franklin County
135	18.5	**Sweden** (town) Monroe County
137	18.4	**Hannibal** (town) Oswego County
138	18.3	**Fairview** (CDP) Dutchess County
138	18.3	**Newark** (village) Wayne County
140	18.2	**Cobleskill** (town) Schoharie County
141	18.1	**Bath** (village) Steuben County
142	18.0	**Hounsfield** (town) Jefferson County
142	18.0	**Kingston** (city) Ulster County
142	18.0	**Lyons** (town) Wayne County
142	18.0	**Port Jervis** (city) Orange County
142	18.0	**Verona** (town) Oneida County
147	17.9	**Dannemora** (town) Clinton County
147	17.9	**North Bellport** (CDP) Suffolk County
147	17.9	**Wawarsing** (town) Ulster County
150	17.8	**Arcade** (town) Wyoming County

Note: This section ranks incorporated places and CDPs (Census Designated Places) with populations of 2,500 or more. Unincorporated postal areas were not considered. Please refer to the User Guide for additional information.

Poverty Rate

Top 150 Places Ranked in *Ascending* Order

State Rank	Percent	Place
1	0.5	**Clarence Center** (CDP) Erie County
1	0.5	**Manhasset Hills** (CDP) Nassau County
3	0.7	**Pound Ridge** (town) Westchester County
4	1.0	**Brightwaters** (village) Suffolk County
4	1.0	**North Hills** (village) Nassau County
4	1.0	**Red Oaks Mill** (CDP) Dutchess County
7	1.1	**Milton** (CDP) Saratoga County
8	1.2	**Halesite** (CDP) Suffolk County
9	1.3	**New Hempstead** (village) Rockland County
9	1.3	**West Point** (CDP) Orange County
11	1.4	**Armonk** (CDP) Westchester County
11	1.4	**East Hills** (village) Nassau County
11	1.4	**Orchard Park** (village) Erie County
14	1.5	**Massapequa Park** (village) Nassau County
15	1.6	**Putnam Lake** (CDP) Putnam County
16	1.7	**Bardonia** (CDP) Rockland County
17	1.8	**Sands Point** (village) Nassau County
17	1.8	**Setauket-East Setauket** (CDP) Suffolk County
17	1.8	**Wesley Hills** (village) Rockland County
20	1.9	**Elma Center** (CDP) Erie County
20	1.9	**Flower Hill** (village) Nassau County
20	1.9	**Jefferson Valley-Yorktown** (CDP) Westchester County
20	1.9	**Larchmont** (village) Westchester County
20	1.9	**Wantagh** (CDP) Nassau County
25	2.0	**Bethpage** (CDP) Nassau County
25	2.0	**New Castle** (town) Westchester County
25	2.0	**North Boston** (CDP) Erie County
25	2.0	**North Castle** (town) Westchester County
25	2.0	**Spackenkill** (CDP) Dutchess County
25	2.0	**West Hills** (CDP) Suffolk County
31	2.1	**Cold Spring Harbor** (CDP) Suffolk County
31	2.1	**Floral Park** (village) Nassau County
31	2.1	**Glen Head** (CDP) Nassau County
31	2.1	**Lido Beach** (CDP) Nassau County
31	2.1	**Munsey Park** (village) Nassau County
36	2.2	**North Wantagh** (CDP) Nassau County
36	2.2	**Richmond** (town) Ontario County
36	2.2	**Wynantskill** (CDP) Rensselaer County
39	2.3	**Cutchogue** (CDP) Suffolk County
39	2.3	**Glenwood Landing** (CDP) Nassau County
39	2.3	**Old Westbury** (village) Nassau County
39	2.3	**Port Washington** (CDP) Nassau County
39	2.3	**Shelter Island** (town) Suffolk County
39	2.3	**Somers** (town) Westchester County
39	2.3	**Victor** (town) Ontario County
46	2.4	**Firthcliffe** (CDP) Orange County
46	2.4	**Fleming** (town) Cayuga County
46	2.4	**Massapequa** (CDP) Nassau County
46	2.4	**Myers Corner** (CDP) Dutchess County
50	2.5	**Albertson** (CDP) Nassau County
50	2.5	**Bellmore** (CDP) Nassau County
50	2.5	**Harris Hill** (CDP) Erie County
50	2.5	**North New Hyde Park** (CDP) Nassau County
50	2.5	**Plainedge** (CDP) Nassau County
50	2.5	**Scarsdale** (town/village) Westchester County
56	2.6	**Briarcliff Manor** (village) Westchester County
56	2.6	**Minoa** (village) Onondaga County
56	2.6	**North Bellmore** (CDP) Nassau County
56	2.6	**Wheatley Heights** (CDP) Suffolk County
56	2.6	**Williston Park** (village) Nassau County
61	2.7	**Ardsley** (village) Westchester County
61	2.7	**East Quogue** (CDP) Suffolk County
61	2.7	**Eastchester** (CDP) Westchester County
61	2.7	**Florida** (village) Orange County
65	2.8	**Centerport** (CDP) Suffolk County
65	2.8	**Charlton** (town) Saratoga County
65	2.8	**Garden City** (village) Nassau County
65	2.8	**Lake Mohegan** (CDP) Westchester County
65	2.8	**Malverne** (village) Nassau County
65	2.8	**Tarrytown** (village) Westchester County
65	2.8	**Thiells** (CDP) Rockland County
65	2.8	**Walworth** (town) Wayne County
73	2.9	**Bronxville** (village) Westchester County
73	2.9	**Dobbs Ferry** (village) Westchester County
73	2.9	**La Grange** (town) Dutchess County
73	2.9	**Monroe** (village) Orange County
73	2.9	**Montebello** (village) Rockland County
73	2.9	**Nesconset** (CDP) Suffolk County
73	2.9	**Oyster Bay** (CDP) Nassau County
73	2.9	**Smithtown** (CDP) Suffolk County
73	2.9	**Tuxedo** (town) Orange County
73	2.9	**West Bay Shore** (CDP) Suffolk County
83	3.0	**Gardnertown** (CDP) Orange County
83	3.0	**Malta** (town) Saratoga County
83	3.0	**Pelham** (village) Westchester County
83	3.0	**South Valley Stream** (CDP) Nassau County
87	3.1	**Brookville** (village) Nassau County
87	3.1	**Fairport** (village) Monroe County
87	3.1	**Holbrook** (CDP) Suffolk County
87	3.1	**Islandia** (village) Suffolk County
87	3.1	**Lakeland** (CDP) Onondaga County
87	3.1	**Sennett** (town) Cayuga County
87	3.1	**Tappan** (CDP) Rockland County
94	3.2	**Eastchester** (town) Westchester County
94	3.2	**Hauppauge** (CDP) Suffolk County
94	3.2	**Highlands** (town) Orange County
94	3.2	**Merrick** (CDP) Nassau County
94	3.2	**North Merrick** (CDP) Nassau County
94	3.2	**Rye** (city) Westchester County
94	3.2	**Searingtown** (CDP) Nassau County
94	3.2	**Smithtown** (town) Suffolk County
94	3.2	**Syosset** (CDP) Nassau County
94	3.2	**Thornwood** (CDP) Westchester County
94	3.2	**Valhalla** (CDP) Westchester County
94	3.2	**Wanakah** (CDP) Erie County
106	3.3	**Carmel** (town) Putnam County
106	3.3	**East Shoreham** (CDP) Suffolk County
106	3.3	**North Greenbush** (town) Rensselaer County
106	3.3	**Pittsford** (town) Monroe County
106	3.3	**Seaford** (CDP) Nassau County
106	3.3	**Skaneateles** (town) Onondaga County
106	3.3	**Yorktown** (town) Westchester County
113	3.4	**Blue Point** (CDP) Suffolk County
113	3.4	**Brunswick** (town) Rensselaer County
113	3.4	**Oakdale** (CDP) Suffolk County
113	3.4	**Old Bethpage** (CDP) Nassau County
113	3.4	**Pleasantville** (village) Westchester County
118	3.5	**Boston** (town) Erie County
118	3.5	**East Norwich** (CDP) Nassau County
118	3.5	**Mattituck** (CDP) Suffolk County
118	3.5	**Pompey** (town) Onondaga County
118	3.5	**Salisbury** (CDP) Nassau County
118	3.5	**Woodbury** (CDP) Nassau County
124	3.6	**Blauvelt** (CDP) Rockland County
124	3.6	**Clifton Park** (town) Saratoga County
124	3.6	**Jay** (town) Essex County
124	3.6	**Kings Point** (village) Nassau County
124	3.6	**Pelham** (town) Westchester County
124	3.6	**Schodack** (town) Rensselaer County
124	3.6	**South Farmingdale** (CDP) Nassau County
124	3.6	**South Hempstead** (CDP) Nassau County
132	3.7	**Cornwall-on-Hudson** (village) Orange County
132	3.7	**East Rockaway** (village) Nassau County
132	3.7	**Kings Park** (CDP) Suffolk County
132	3.7	**Lewisboro** (town) Westchester County
132	3.7	**New Scotland** (town) Albany County
132	3.7	**Voorheesville** (village) Albany County
138	3.8	**Center Moriches** (CDP) Suffolk County
138	3.8	**East Fishkill** (town) Dutchess County
138	3.8	**Greenville** (CDP) Westchester County
138	3.8	**Knox** (town) Albany County
138	3.8	**North Valley Stream** (CDP) Nassau County
138	3.8	**Owasco** (town) Cayuga County
138	3.8	**Plainview** (CDP) Nassau County
138	3.8	**Rocky Point** (CDP) Suffolk County
146	3.9	**Clarence** (town) Erie County
146	3.9	**Commack** (CDP) Suffolk County
146	3.9	**Cornwall** (town) Orange County
146	3.9	**Croton-on-Hudson** (village) Westchester County
146	3.9	**Hawthorne** (CDP) Westchester County

Note: This section ranks incorporated places and CDPs (Census Designated Places) with populations of 2,500 or more. Unincorporated postal areas were not considered. Please refer to the User Guide for additional information.

Educational Attainment: High School Diploma or Higher

Top 150 Places Ranked in *Descending* Order

State Rank	Percent	Place	State Rank	Percent	Place
1	100.0	**Alfred** (village) Allegany County	76	96.9	**Alden** (village) Erie County
1	100.0	**University at Buffalo** (CDP) Erie County	76	96.9	**Babylon** (village) Suffolk County
1	100.0	**West Point** (CDP) Orange County	76	96.9	**Brightwaters** (village) Suffolk County
4	99.7	**Horseheads North** (CDP) Chemung County	76	96.9	**Dix Hills** (CDP) Suffolk County
5	99.5	**Clarence Center** (CDP) Erie County	76	96.9	**Fayetteville** (village) Onondaga County
5	99.5	**Glenwood Landing** (CDP) Nassau County	76	96.9	**Harris Hill** (CDP) Erie County
7	99.3	**Larchmont** (village) Westchester County	76	96.9	**Stony Brook** (CDP) Suffolk County
7	99.3	**Pound Ridge** (town) Westchester County	83	96.8	**Jericho** (CDP) Nassau County
9	99.2	**Shelter Island** (town) Suffolk County	83	96.8	**Pelham Manor** (village) Westchester County
10	99.1	**Milton** (CDP) Saratoga County	83	96.8	**Pompey** (town) Onondaga County
11	98.9	**Orchard Park** (village) Erie County	83	96.8	**Wantagh** (CDP) Nassau County
12	98.8	**Minoa** (village) Onondaga County	87	96.7	**Armonk** (CDP) Westchester County
13	98.7	**Munsey Park** (village) Nassau County	87	96.7	**Commack** (CDP) Suffolk County
13	98.7	**Skaneateles** (town) Onondaga County	87	96.7	**Lansing** (village) Tompkins County
15	98.6	**Brookville** (village) Nassau County	87	96.7	**Manlius** (town) Onondaga County
15	98.6	**North Boston** (CDP) Erie County	87	96.7	**Philipstown** (town) Putnam County
17	98.5	**Lawrence** (village) Nassau County	87	96.7	**Seaford** (CDP) Nassau County
17	98.5	**Northwest Harbor** (CDP) Suffolk County	87	96.7	**South Hempstead** (CDP) Nassau County
19	98.4	**East Williston** (village) Nassau County	87	96.7	**Victor** (town) Ontario County
19	98.4	**Halesite** (CDP) Suffolk County	87	96.7	**Walworth** (town) Wayne County
19	98.4	**Lloyd Harbor** (village) Suffolk County	96	96.6	**Greenville** (town) Orange County
19	98.4	**Scarsdale** (town/village) Westchester County	96	96.6	**Hauppauge** (CDP) Suffolk County
23	98.3	**Northeast Ithaca** (CDP) Tompkins County	96	96.6	**Manlius** (village) Onondaga County
23	98.3	**West Elmira** (CDP) Chemung County	96	96.6	**Massapequa** (CDP) Nassau County
25	98.2	**Fort Salonga** (CDP) Suffolk County	96	96.6	**New Paltz** (village) Ulster County
25	98.2	**Muttontown** (village) Nassau County	96	96.6	**Niskayuna** (town) Schenectady County
25	98.2	**New Castle** (town) Westchester County	96	96.6	**Otsego** (town) Otsego County
25	98.2	**Old Westbury** (village) Nassau County	96	96.6	**Rush** (town) Monroe County
25	98.2	**Pittsford** (town) Monroe County	104	96.5	**Menands** (village) Albany County
30	98.1	**East Hills** (village) Nassau County	104	96.5	**Perinton** (town) Monroe County
30	98.1	**North Hills** (village) Nassau County	104	96.5	**Tuxedo** (town) Orange County
30	98.1	**Spencerport** (village) Monroe County	107	96.4	**East Norwich** (CDP) Nassau County
33	98.0	**Cayuga Heights** (village) Tompkins County	107	96.4	**Heritage Hills** (CDP) Westchester County
33	98.0	**Eden** (CDP) Erie County	107	96.4	**Rockville Centre** (village) Nassau County
33	98.0	**Garden City** (village) Nassau County	110	96.3	**Avon** (village) Livingston County
33	98.0	**Marcellus** (town) Onondaga County	110	96.3	**Brunswick** (town) Rensselaer County
33	98.0	**Westvale** (CDP) Onondaga County	110	96.3	**Clarence** (town) Erie County
38	97.9	**Fredonia** (village) Chautauqua County	110	96.3	**Danby** (town) Tompkins County
38	97.9	**Port Jefferson** (village) Suffolk County	110	96.3	**Farmington** (town) Ontario County
38	97.9	**Sea Cliff** (village) Nassau County	110	96.3	**Glens Falls North** (CDP) Warren County
38	97.9	**Voorheesville** (village) Albany County	110	96.3	**Pleasantville** (village) Westchester County
38	97.9	**Williamsville** (village) Erie County	117	96.2	**Boston** (town) Erie County
43	97.8	**Cold Spring Harbor** (CDP) Suffolk County	117	96.2	**Floyd** (town) Oneida County
43	97.8	**East Greenbush** (CDP) Rensselaer County	117	96.2	**Hartsdale** (CDP) Westchester County
43	97.8	**Guilderland** (town) Albany County	117	96.2	**Massapequa Park** (village) Nassau County
46	97.7	**Centerport** (CDP) Suffolk County	117	96.2	**Merrick** (CDP) Nassau County
46	97.7	**Miller Place** (CDP) Suffolk County	117	96.2	**Orchard Park** (town) Erie County
46	97.7	**Westmere** (CDP) Albany County	117	96.2	**Sands Point** (village) Nassau County
49	97.6	**Hamburg** (village) Erie County	117	96.2	**Southold** (CDP) Suffolk County
49	97.6	**Hastings-on-Hudson** (village) Westchester County	117	96.2	**West Hills** (CDP) Suffolk County
49	97.6	**West Nyack** (CDP) Rockland County	126	96.1	**Cazenovia** (town) Madison County
52	97.5	**Clifton Park** (town) Saratoga County	126	96.1	**East Aurora** (village) Erie County
52	97.5	**Mendon** (town) Monroe County	126	96.1	**East Moriches** (CDP) Suffolk County
54	97.4	**Richmond** (town) Ontario County	126	96.1	**Lewiston** (village) Niagara County
55	97.3	**Elmira** (town) Chemung County	126	96.1	**New Paltz** (town) Ulster County
55	97.3	**South Nyack** (village) Rockland County	126	96.1	**North Salem** (town) Westchester County
57	97.2	**Bronxville** (village) Westchester County	126	96.1	**Pendleton** (town) Niagara County
57	97.2	**Cambria** (town) Niagara County	126	96.1	**Stephentown** (town) Rensselaer County
57	97.2	**Northport** (village) Suffolk County	134	96.0	**North Massapequa** (CDP) Nassau County
60	97.1	**Canastota** (village) Madison County	134	96.0	**North Sea** (CDP) Suffolk County
60	97.1	**Elma** (town) Erie County	136	95.9	**Ardsley** (village) Westchester County
60	97.1	**Elma Center** (CDP) Erie County	136	95.9	**Brighton** (CDP) Monroe County
60	97.1	**Hunter** (town) Greene County	136	95.9	**Cutchogue** (CDP) Suffolk County
60	97.1	**Irvington** (village) Westchester County	136	95.9	**East Glenville** (CDP) Schenectady County
60	97.1	**Lewisboro** (town) Westchester County	136	95.9	**East Rockaway** (village) Nassau County
60	97.1	**Malta** (town) Saratoga County	136	95.9	**Gang Mills** (CDP) Steuben County
60	97.1	**North Castle** (town) Westchester County	136	95.9	**Glenville** (town) Schenectady County
60	97.1	**Red Oaks Mill** (CDP) Dutchess County	136	95.9	**Greenville** (CDP) Westchester County
60	97.1	**Scotia** (village) Schenectady County	136	95.9	**Montrose** (CDP) Westchester County
60	97.1	**Setauket-East Setauket** (CDP) Suffolk County	136	95.9	**Roslyn** (village) Nassau County
60	97.1	**Spackenkill** (CDP) Dutchess County	136	95.9	**Rye** (city) Westchester County
60	97.1	**Woodstock** (town) Ulster County	136	95.9	**Somers** (town) Westchester County
73	97.0	**Bethlehem** (town) Albany County	148	95.8	**Baldwin Harbor** (CDP) Nassau County
73	97.0	**Huntington** (CDP) Suffolk County	148	95.8	**Camillus** (town) Onondaga County
73	97.0	**Ithaca** (town) Tompkins County	148	95.8	**Canandaigua** (town) Ontario County

Note: This section ranks incorporated places and CDPs (Census Designated Places) with populations of 2,500 or more. Unincorporated postal areas were not considered. Please refer to the User Guide for additional information.

Educational Attainment: High School Diploma or Higher

Top 150 Places Ranked in *Ascending* Order

State Rank	Percent	Place
1	63.8	**Kiryas Joel** (village) Orange County
2	67.4	**North Bay Shore** (CDP) Suffolk County
3	68.3	**Spring Valley** (village) Rockland County
4	68.5	**Bedford Hills** (CDP) Westchester County
4	68.5	**Romulus** (town) Seneca County
6	68.9	**Kaser** (village) Rockland County
7	69.5	**Brentwood** (CDP) Suffolk County
7	69.5	**Hempstead** (village) Nassau County
9	70.2	**Riverside** (CDP) Suffolk County
10	70.3	**New Square** (village) Rockland County
11	70.7	**Port Chester** (village) Westchester County
12	71.5	**Bronx** (borough) Bronx County
13	72.0	**Newburgh** (city) Orange County
14	72.2	**Roosevelt** (CDP) Nassau County
15	72.5	**Haverstraw** (village) Rockland County
16	73.6	**Coxsackie** (town) Greene County
17	73.8	**Sleepy Hollow** (village) Westchester County
18	74.3	**Central Islip** (CDP) Suffolk County
19	74.7	**New Cassel** (CDP) Nassau County
20	74.8	**Inwood** (CDP) Nassau County
21	75.3	**Benton** (town) Yates County
21	75.3	**Dannemora** (village) Clinton County
23	75.8	**Ossining** (village) Westchester County
24	77.2	**Elmsford** (village) Westchester County
25	77.5	**Albion** (village) Orleans County
25	77.5	**Dannemora** (town) Clinton County
27	77.9	**Wyandanch** (CDP) Suffolk County
28	78.0	**Rye** (town) Westchester County
29	78.4	**Peekskill** (city) Westchester County
30	78.6	**Minden** (town) Montgomery County
30	78.6	**Utica** (city) Oneida County
32	78.7	**Albion** (town) Orleans County
33	78.8	**Monsey** (CDP) Rockland County
34	78.9	**West Haverstraw** (village) Rockland County
35	79.0	**Malone** (town) Franklin County
36	79.2	**North Amityville** (CDP) Suffolk County
37	79.5	**Riverhead** (CDP) Suffolk County
38	79.6	**Huntington Station** (CDP) Suffolk County
38	79.6	**Liberty** (village) Sullivan County
40	79.8	**Ellenville** (village) Ulster County
40	79.8	**Uniondale** (CDP) Nassau County
42	80.0	**Glasco** (CDP) Ulster County
43	80.2	**Attica** (town) Wyoming County
44	80.3	**Fallsburg** (town) Sullivan County
44	80.3	**Groveland** (town) Livingston County
46	80.4	**Copiague** (CDP) Suffolk County
46	80.4	**Lackawanna** (city) Erie County
48	80.5	**Portland** (town) Chautauqua County
49	80.7	**Brooklyn** (borough) Kings County
50	80.8	**Freeport** (village) Nassau County
50	80.8	**Rochester** (city) Monroe County
50	80.8	**Wappingers Falls** (village) Dutchess County
53	81.1	**New York** (city)
53	81.1	**Queens** (borough) Queens County
55	81.2	**Dansville** (village) Livingston County
55	81.2	**Marcy** (town) Oneida County
57	81.3	**Malone** (village) Franklin County
58	81.5	**Cape Vincent** (town) Jefferson County
58	81.5	**Syracuse** (city) Onondaga County
60	81.6	**Glen Cove** (city) Nassau County
60	81.6	**North Bellport** (CDP) Suffolk County
62	81.7	**Gloversville** (city) Fulton County
62	81.7	**Hillcrest** (CDP) Rockland County
62	81.7	**Mount Kisco** (town/village) Westchester County
62	81.7	**Poughkeepsie** (city) Dutchess County
66	81.9	**Altona** (town) Clinton County
66	81.9	**Monticello** (village) Sullivan County
66	81.9	**Moravia** (town) Cayuga County
69	82.0	**Galen** (town) Wayne County
70	82.1	**Fort Ann** (town) Washington County
70	82.1	**Mount Morris** (town) Livingston County
70	82.1	**Wolcott** (town) Wayne County
73	82.2	**Liberty** (town) Sullivan County
74	82.3	**North Dansville** (town) Livingston County
75	82.4	**Collins** (town) Erie County
76	82.5	**Amsterdam** (city) Montgomery County
76	82.5	**Haverstraw** (town) Rockland County
76	82.5	**Monroe** (town) Orange County
76	82.5	**Ossining** (town) Westchester County
76	82.5	**Yonkers** (city) Westchester County
81	82.6	**Ramapo** (town) Rockland County
82	82.7	**North Gates** (CDP) Monroe County
83	82.8	**New Rochelle** (city) Westchester County
83	82.8	**Walton** (village) Delaware County
85	83.1	**Colesville** (town) Broome County
86	83.2	**Fairview** (CDP) Westchester County
86	83.2	**Granby** (town) Oswego County
86	83.2	**Middletown** (city) Orange County
89	83.3	**Brookhaven** (CDP) Suffolk County
89	83.3	**Yorkshire** (town) Cattaraugus County
91	83.5	**Ogdensburg** (city) Saint Lawrence County
91	83.5	**Scriba** (town) Oswego County
93	83.6	**Whitehall** (village) Washington County
94	83.7	**Hancock** (town) Delaware County
94	83.7	**North East** (town) Dutchess County
94	83.7	**Warsaw** (village) Wyoming County
97	83.8	**Amenia** (town) Dutchess County
97	83.8	**Wawarsing** (town) Ulster County
99	83.9	**Buffalo** (city) Erie County
99	83.9	**Gouverneur** (town) Saint Lawrence County
99	83.9	**Schenectady** (city) Schenectady County
102	84.0	**Croghan** (town) Lewis County
102	84.0	**Eaton** (town) Madison County
102	84.0	**Gaines** (town) Orleans County
102	84.0	**Keeseville** (village) Clinton County
102	84.0	**New Berlin** (town) Chenango County
107	84.1	**Cobleskill** (village) Schoharie County
107	84.1	**Granville** (town) Washington County
107	84.1	**Mount Vernon** (city) Westchester County
110	84.2	**Elmira** (city) Chemung County
110	84.2	**Salamanca** (city) Cattaraugus County
112	84.3	**Bethel** (town) Sullivan County
113	84.4	**Champlain** (town) Clinton County
113	84.4	**Port Jervis** (city) Orange County
113	84.4	**Tioga** (town) Tioga County
113	84.4	**Westbury** (village) Nassau County
117	84.5	**Fulton** (city) Oswego County
117	84.5	**Lake Luzerne** (town) Warren County
117	84.5	**Mastic** (CDP) Suffolk County
120	84.6	**Auburn** (city) Cayuga County
120	84.6	**Norwich** (town) Chenango County
122	84.7	**Dover** (town) Dutchess County
122	84.7	**Hannibal** (town) Oswego County
124	84.8	**Flanders** (CDP) Suffolk County
124	84.8	**Galeville** (CDP) Onondaga County
126	84.9	**Geneva** (city) Ontario County
127	85.0	**Bay Shore** (CDP) Suffolk County
127	85.0	**Constantia** (town) Oswego County
127	85.0	**Corinth** (village) Saratoga County
127	85.0	**Hudson** (city) Columbia County
127	85.0	**Shirley** (CDP) Suffolk County
132	85.1	**Binghamton** (city) Broome County
132	85.1	**Catskill** (town) Greene County
132	85.1	**North Lindenhurst** (CDP) Suffolk County
132	85.1	**Sloan** (village) Erie County
132	85.1	**Stockport** (town) Columbia County
137	85.2	**Dunkirk** (city) Chautauqua County
137	85.2	**Islip** (town) Suffolk County
137	85.2	**Palatine** (town) Montgomery County
137	85.2	**Westfield** (village) Chautauqua County
137	85.2	**Whitehall** (town) Washington County
142	85.3	**Canajoharie** (town) Montgomery County
143	85.4	**Cairo** (town) Greene County
143	85.4	**Claverack** (town) Columbia County
143	85.4	**Mooers** (town) Clinton County
143	85.4	**Oswegatchie** (town) Saint Lawrence County
143	85.4	**Warrensburg** (CDP) Warren County
148	85.5	**Thompson** (town) Sullivan County
149	85.6	**Manheim** (town) Herkimer County
149	85.6	**Sidney** (town) Delaware County

Note: This section ranks incorporated places and CDPs (Census Designated Places) with populations of 2,500 or more. Unincorporated postal areas were not considered. Please refer to the User Guide for additional information.

Educational Attainment: Bachelor's Degree or Higher

Top 150 Places Ranked in *Descending* Order

State Rank	Percent	Place	State Rank	Percent	Place
1	89.0	**Scarsdale** (town/village) Westchester County	76	60.7	**Manhattan** (borough) New York County
2	88.7	**Cayuga Heights** (village) Tompkins County	76	60.7	**Merrick** (CDP) Nassau County
3	88.0	**Larchmont** (village) Westchester County	76	60.7	**Pleasantville** (village) Westchester County
4	84.2	**Munsey Park** (village) Nassau County	79	60.5	**Eastchester** (town) Westchester County
5	83.5	**New Castle** (town) Westchester County	80	60.4	**Williamsville** (village) Erie County
6	82.2	**Sands Point** (village) Nassau County	81	60.1	**East Norwich** (CDP) Nassau County
7	80.9	**East Hills** (village) Nassau County	81	60.1	**Gang Mills** (CDP) Steuben County
8	80.5	**Bronxville** (village) Westchester County	83	60.0	**Dobbs Ferry** (village) Westchester County
9	79.6	**Armonk** (CDP) Westchester County	83	60.0	**Manhasset** (CDP) Nassau County
10	79.2	**Northeast Ithaca** (CDP) Tompkins County	85	59.9	**North Salem** (town) Westchester County
11	79.1	**Greenville** (CDP) Westchester County	85	59.9	**Port Jefferson** (village) Suffolk County
12	76.6	**Old Westbury** (village) Nassau County	85	59.9	**Shelter Island** (town) Suffolk County
13	76.3	**Flower Hill** (village) Nassau County	85	59.9	**South Nyack** (village) Rockland County
14	76.1	**Brookville** (village) Nassau County	85	59.9	**Woodstock** (town) Ulster County
15	75.5	**Pound Ridge** (town) Westchester County	90	59.8	**Eastchester** (CDP) Westchester County
16	75.3	**Lawrence** (village) Nassau County	91	59.4	**Centerport** (CDP) Suffolk County
17	75.1	**Pelham Manor** (village) Westchester County	92	59.2	**Rockville Centre** (village) Nassau County
18	74.9	**Lloyd Harbor** (village) Suffolk County	93	59.1	**Great Neck Plaza** (village) Nassau County
19	74.3	**North Castle** (town) Westchester County	94	59.0	**New Paltz** (town) Ulster County
20	74.0	**University at Buffalo** (CDP) Erie County	95	58.9	**Mendon** (town) Monroe County
21	73.6	**Great Neck Estates** (village) Nassau County	96	58.7	**Brightwaters** (village) Suffolk County
22	73.5	**Pittsford** (town) Monroe County	96	58.7	**Port Washington North** (village) Nassau County
22	73.5	**Rye** (city) Westchester County	98	58.6	**Bethlehem** (town) Albany County
24	73.4	**Muttontown** (village) Nassau County	98	58.6	**Halesite** (CDP) Suffolk County
25	73.3	**Alfred** (village) Allegany County	98	58.6	**Niskayuna** (town) Schenectady County
26	73.2	**Lansing** (village) Tompkins County	101	58.5	**Bedford** (town) Westchester County
27	72.0	**Garden City** (village) Nassau County	102	58.4	**Glen Head** (CDP) Nassau County
28	71.8	**Hastings-on-Hudson** (village) Westchester County	102	58.4	**New City** (CDP) Rockland County
29	71.7	**Ithaca** (town) Tompkins County	104	57.7	**Noyack** (CDP) Suffolk County
30	71.6	**Irvington** (village) Westchester County	105	57.2	**West Hills** (CDP) Suffolk County
31	71.2	**Briarcliff Manor** (village) Westchester County	106	57.1	**Perinton** (town) Monroe County
32	71.0	**Lewisboro** (town) Westchester County	106	57.1	**South Valley Stream** (CDP) Nassau County
33	70.0	**Jericho** (CDP) Nassau County	108	57.0	**Lake Success** (village) Nassau County
33	70.0	**West Point** (CDP) Orange County	109	56.8	**Old Bethpage** (CDP) Nassau County
35	69.8	**Cold Spring Harbor** (CDP) Suffolk County	110	56.4	**Melville** (CDP) Suffolk County
36	69.7	**Lido Beach** (CDP) Nassau County	111	56.3	**Northwest Harbor** (CDP) Suffolk County
37	69.5	**East Williston** (village) Nassau County	112	56.0	**Manlius** (village) Onondaga County
37	69.5	**Thomaston** (village) Nassau County	113	55.8	**Blauvelt** (CDP) Rockland County
39	69.3	**Clarence Center** (CDP) Erie County	113	55.8	**Kings Point** (village) Nassau County
40	69.2	**Hartsdale** (CDP) Westchester County	115	55.7	**Clifton Park** (town) Saratoga County
41	68.4	**Piermont** (village) Rockland County	115	55.7	**South Hill** (CDP) Tompkins County
42	67.9	**Menands** (village) Albany County	117	55.6	**Fayetteville** (village) Onondaga County
43	67.5	**Roslyn** (village) Nassau County	118	55.5	**Bardonia** (CDP) Rockland County
44	67.3	**Mamaroneck** (town) Westchester County	118	55.5	**Rhinebeck** (village) Dutchess County
45	67.2	**Stony Brook** (CDP) Suffolk County	120	55.4	**Alfred** (town) Allegany County
46	66.3	**Glenwood Landing** (CDP) Nassau County	121	55.3	**Amherst** (town) Erie County
47	65.6	**Montebello** (village) Rockland County	122	55.2	**Saratoga Springs** (city) Saratoga County
47	65.6	**New Paltz** (village) Ulster County	123	55.1	**Somers** (town) Westchester County
49	65.5	**Rye Brook** (village) Westchester County	124	55.0	**Victor** (town) Ontario County
50	65.4	**Sea Cliff** (village) Nassau County	125	54.8	**Tarrytown** (village) Westchester County
51	65.3	**Brighton** (CDP) Monroe County	126	54.7	**Pelham** (village) Westchester County
52	65.2	**Woodbury** (CDP) Nassau County	127	54.6	**Herricks** (CDP) Nassau County
53	64.7	**Ardsley** (village) Westchester County	128	54.4	**Skaneateles** (town) Onondaga County
54	64.5	**Manhasset Hills** (CDP) Nassau County	129	54.3	**North Hempstead** (town) Nassau County
55	64.4	**Ithaca** (city) Tompkins County	130	54.1	**Voorheesville** (village) Albany County
56	64.1	**Syosset** (CDP) Nassau County	131	54.0	**Harrison** (town/village) Westchester County
57	63.8	**Woodmere** (CDP) Nassau County	132	53.9	**Spackenkill** (CDP) Dutchess County
58	63.6	**Roslyn Heights** (CDP) Nassau County	133	53.7	**Potsdam** (village) Saint Lawrence County
58	63.6	**Setauket-East Setauket** (CDP) Suffolk County	134	53.2	**Canton** (village) Saint Lawrence County
60	63.5	**University Gardens** (CDP) Nassau County	135	53.1	**Great Neck** (village) Nassau County
61	63.3	**Pelham** (town) Westchester County	136	53.0	**Heritage Hills** (CDP) Westchester County
62	63.2	**Plainview** (CDP) Nassau County	136	53.0	**Penfield** (town) Monroe County
63	63.0	**Port Washington** (CDP) Nassau County	138	52.9	**Tuxedo** (town) Orange County
64	62.9	**Searingtown** (CDP) Nassau County	139	52.7	**Fort Salonga** (CDP) Suffolk County
65	62.7	**Hamilton** (village) Madison County	140	52.3	**Philipstown** (town) Putnam County
66	62.5	**Croton-on-Hudson** (village) Westchester County	140	52.3	**Southampton** (village) Suffolk County
67	62.4	**Huntington** (CDP) Suffolk County	142	52.2	**Manlius** (town) Onondaga County
68	62.3	**Lansing** (town) Tompkins County	143	51.9	**West Elmira** (CDP) Chemung County
69	62.1	**North Hills** (village) Nassau County	144	51.8	**Tappan** (CDP) Rockland County
70	61.9	**Orchard Park** (village) Erie County	145	51.7	**Eggertsville** (CDP) Erie County
71	61.8	**Dix Hills** (CDP) Suffolk County	146	51.4	**Huntington** (town) Suffolk County
72	61.6	**Northport** (village) Suffolk County	146	51.4	**Manorhaven** (village) Nassau County
73	61.4	**Greenburgh** (town) Westchester County	148	51.3	**Mount Pleasant** (town) Westchester County
74	61.0	**Wesley Hills** (village) Rockland County	149	51.2	**Orangetown** (town) Rockland County
75	60.8	**Pomona** (village) Rockland County	150	51.1	**Malverne** (village) Nassau County

Note: This section ranks incorporated places and CDPs (Census Designated Places) with populations of 2,500 or more. Unincorporated postal areas were not considered. Please refer to the User Guide for additional information.

Educational Attainment: Bachelor's Degree or Higher

Top 150 Places Ranked in *Ascending* Order

State Rank	Percent	Place	State Rank	Percent	Place
1	2.9	**Dannemora** (village) Clinton County	76	14.7	**Ellenville** (village) Ulster County
2	3.9	**New Square** (village) Rockland County	76	14.7	**Hudson Falls** (village) Washington County
3	4.4	**Dannemora** (town) Clinton County	76	14.7	**Mastic** (CDP) Suffolk County
3	4.4	**Kaser** (village) Rockland County	76	14.7	**Warsaw** (town) Wyoming County
5	6.3	**Riverside** (CDP) Suffolk County	80	14.8	**Fairview** (CDP) Westchester County
6	6.6	**Kiryas Joel** (village) Orange County	80	14.8	**Moira** (town) Franklin County
7	8.2	**Hannibal** (town) Oswego County	82	14.9	**Champlain** (town) Clinton County
8	8.6	**Romulus** (town) Seneca County	82	14.9	**Verona** (town) Oneida County
9	8.7	**Whitehall** (village) Washington County	84	15.0	**Barton** (town) Tioga County
10	9.2	**Gouverneur** (village) Saint Lawrence County	84	15.0	**Bath** (village) Steuben County
11	9.3	**Attica** (town) Wyoming County	84	15.0	**Gowanda** (village) Cattaraugus County
12	9.5	**Groveland** (town) Livingston County	84	15.0	**Nichols** (town) Tioga County
13	9.7	**Whitehall** (town) Washington County	88	15.1	**Carroll** (town) Chautauqua County
14	9.8	**Albion** (village) Orleans County	88	15.1	**Keeseville** (village) Clinton County
15	10.3	**Lisle** (town) Broome County	88	15.1	**Norwich** (town) Chenango County
16	10.4	**Annsville** (town) Oneida County	88	15.1	**Stockport** (town) Columbia County
16	10.4	**Gouverneur** (town) Saint Lawrence County	92	15.2	**Blasdell** (village) Erie County
18	10.9	**Galen** (town) Wayne County	92	15.2	**Parish** (town) Oswego County
19	11.1	**Carthage** (village) Jefferson County	92	15.2	**Sardinia** (town) Erie County
19	11.1	**Vienna** (town) Oneida County	95	15.3	**Clarendon** (town) Orleans County
21	11.2	**Wolcott** (town) Wayne County	95	15.3	**Colesville** (town) Broome County
22	11.5	**Albion** (town) Orleans County	95	15.3	**Richland** (town) Oswego County
22	11.5	**Collins** (town) Erie County	98	15.4	**Niagara** (town) Niagara County
22	11.5	**Hancock** (town) Delaware County	98	15.4	**Southport** (CDP) Chemung County
22	11.5	**North Bay Shore** (CDP) Suffolk County	98	15.4	**Spring Valley** (village) Rockland County
26	11.6	**Altona** (town) Clinton County	101	15.5	**Elmira** (city) Chemung County
26	11.6	**Palermo** (town) Oswego County	101	15.5	**Moriah** (town) Essex County
28	11.7	**West Monroe** (town) Oswego County	101	15.5	**Norfolk** (town) Saint Lawrence County
29	12.1	**Fort Ann** (town) Washington County	104	15.6	**Darien** (town) Genesee County
29	12.1	**Saint Johnsville** (town) Montgomery County	104	15.6	**Somerset** (town) Niagara County
31	12.2	**Fort Edward** (village) Washington County	104	15.6	**Waverly** (village) Tioga County
32	12.3	**Constantia** (town) Oswego County	104	15.6	**Yates** (town) Orleans County
32	12.3	**Lyons** (village) Wayne County	108	15.7	**Perry** (town) Wyoming County
34	12.4	**Fort Edward** (town) Washington County	108	15.7	**Whitesboro** (village) Oneida County
34	12.4	**Minden** (town) Montgomery County	110	15.8	**Central Islip** (CDP) Suffolk County
34	12.4	**Moravia** (town) Cayuga County	110	15.8	**Guilford** (town) Chenango County
34	12.4	**Wilna** (town) Jefferson County	110	15.8	**Inwood** (CDP) Nassau County
38	12.6	**New Haven** (town) Oswego County	110	15.8	**Murray** (town) Orleans County
38	12.6	**Wayland** (town) Steuben County	114	15.9	**Portland** (town) Chautauqua County
40	12.7	**Denmark** (town) Lewis County	114	15.9	**Randolph** (town) Cattaraugus County
40	12.7	**Mayfield** (town) Fulton County	116	16.0	**Mount Morris** (village) Livingston County
42	12.8	**Au Sable** (town) Clinton County	116	16.0	**Tioga** (town) Tioga County
42	12.8	**Sloan** (village) Erie County	118	16.1	**Manchester** (town) Ontario County
44	12.9	**Liberty** (village) Sullivan County	118	16.1	**New Berlin** (town) Chenango County
45	13.0	**Brentwood** (CDP) Suffolk County	120	16.2	**Bath** (town) Steuben County
45	13.0	**Mount Morris** (town) Livingston County	120	16.2	**Mastic Beach** (CDP) Suffolk County
45	13.0	**Warsaw** (village) Wyoming County	120	16.2	**Newark** (village) Wayne County
48	13.1	**Corinth** (village) Saratoga County	123	16.3	**Fulton** (city) Oswego County
48	13.1	**Granville** (town) Washington County	123	16.3	**Walton** (village) Delaware County
50	13.2	**Deerpark** (town) Orange County	125	16.4	**Palatine** (town) Montgomery County
50	13.2	**Gloversville** (city) Fulton County	125	16.4	**Roosevelt** (CDP) Nassau County
52	13.3	**Sandy Creek** (town) Oswego County	125	16.4	**Sidney** (town) Delaware County
53	13.5	**Wyandanch** (CDP) Suffolk County	128	16.5	**Coxsackie** (town) Greene County
54	13.6	**Croghan** (town) Lewis County	128	16.5	**Monsey** (CDP) Rockland County
54	13.6	**Yorkshire** (town) Cattaraugus County	130	16.6	**Liberty** (town) Sullivan County
56	13.7	**Lackawanna** (city) Erie County	130	16.6	**Lyncourt** (CDP) Onondaga County
56	13.7	**Unadilla** (town) Otsego County	130	16.6	**North Dansville** (town) Livingston County
58	13.8	**Oakfield** (town) Genesee County	133	16.7	**Calverton** (CDP) Suffolk County
59	13.9	**Brasher** (town) Saint Lawrence County	133	16.7	**New Bremen** (town) Lewis County
59	13.9	**Dunkirk** (city) Chautauqua County	133	16.7	**South Lockport** (CDP) Niagara County
59	13.9	**Salamanca** (city) Cattaraugus County	136	16.8	**Ogdensburg** (city) Saint Lawrence County
62	14.2	**Hastings** (town) Oswego County	136	16.8	**South Glens Falls** (village) Saratoga County
62	14.2	**Newburgh** (city) Orange County	138	17.0	**Alexander** (town) Genesee County
62	14.2	**Sodus** (town) Wayne County	138	17.0	**Canajoharie** (town) Montgomery County
62	14.2	**Waterloo** (town) Seneca County	138	17.0	**Ellisburg** (town) Jefferson County
66	14.3	**Hartland** (town) Niagara County	141	17.1	**Barker** (town) Broome County
66	14.3	**Theresa** (town) Jefferson County	141	17.1	**Lisbon** (town) Saint Lawrence County
68	14.4	**Afton** (town) Chenango County	143	17.2	**Benton** (town) Yates County
68	14.4	**Dix** (town) Schuyler County	143	17.2	**Dansville** (village) Livingston County
68	14.4	**Tupper Lake** (village) Franklin County	143	17.2	**Glasco** (CDP) Ulster County
71	14.5	**Galeville** (CDP) Onondaga County	146	17.3	**Ridgeway** (town) Orleans County
71	14.5	**Mattydale** (CDP) Onondaga County	146	17.3	**Walton** (town) Delaware County
73	14.6	**Amsterdam** (city) Montgomery County	148	17.4	**Camden** (town) Oneida County
73	14.6	**Arcade** (town) Wyoming County	148	17.4	**Cape Vincent** (town) Jefferson County
73	14.6	**Malone** (town) Franklin County	148	17.4	**North Lindenhurst** (CDP) Suffolk County

Note: *This section ranks incorporated places and CDPs (Census Designated Places) with populations of 2,500 or more. Unincorporated postal areas were not considered. Please refer to the User Guide for additional information.*

Educational Attainment: Graduate/Professional Degree or Higher

Top 150 Places Ranked in *Descending* Order

State Rank	Percent	Place	State Rank	Percent	Place
1	67.5	**Cayuga Heights** (village) Tompkins County	76	31.8	**Fayetteville** (village) Onondaga County
2	58.3	**Scarsdale** (town/village) Westchester County	76	31.8	**Hamilton** (town) Madison County
3	52.2	**Greenville** (CDP) Westchester County	78	31.7	**Eastchester** (town) Westchester County
4	50.7	**Northeast Ithaca** (CDP) Tompkins County	79	31.3	**Dobbs Ferry** (village) Westchester County
5	49.3	**Larchmont** (village) Westchester County	80	31.1	**Dix Hills** (CDP) Suffolk County
6	49.1	**New Castle** (town) Westchester County	80	31.1	**Merrick** (CDP) Nassau County
7	47.8	**Bronxville** (village) Westchester County	82	31.0	**Clarence Center** (CDP) Erie County
8	47.5	**Ithaca** (town) Tompkins County	82	31.0	**Glen Head** (CDP) Nassau County
9	47.2	**Lansing** (village) Tompkins County	84	30.9	**Syosset** (CDP) Nassau County
10	46.9	**Alfred** (village) Allegany County	85	30.8	**Orchard Park** (village) Erie County
11	45.9	**East Hills** (village) Nassau County	85	30.8	**Plainview** (CDP) Nassau County
12	45.0	**West Point** (CDP) Orange County	85	30.8	**University Gardens** (CDP) Nassau County
13	44.8	**Lawrence** (village) Nassau County	88	30.4	**Eastchester** (CDP) Westchester County
14	44.7	**Great Neck Estates** (village) Nassau County	89	30.2	**Roslyn Heights** (CDP) Nassau County
15	43.4	**Old Westbury** (village) Nassau County	90	30.1	**Canton** (village) Saint Lawrence County
16	43.3	**Hamilton** (village) Madison County	91	29.6	**Centerport** (CDP) Suffolk County
17	43.0	**Munsey Park** (village) Nassau County	91	29.6	**Pelham** (village) Westchester County
18	42.9	**Thomaston** (village) Nassau County	93	29.4	**Mendon** (town) Monroe County
19	42.6	**Sands Point** (village) Nassau County	94	29.3	**Pomona** (village) Rockland County
20	42.0	**Armonk** (CDP) Westchester County	95	29.2	**Brightwaters** (village) Suffolk County
20	42.0	**Hastings-on-Hudson** (village) Westchester County	96	29.1	**Manhattan** (borough) New York County
22	41.0	**Port Jefferson** (village) Suffolk County	97	29.0	**Northwest Harbor** (CDP) Suffolk County
23	40.9	**Lloyd Harbor** (village) Suffolk County	97	29.0	**Port Washington** (CDP) Nassau County
24	40.8	**Hartsdale** (CDP) Westchester County	97	29.0	**Rockville Centre** (village) Nassau County
25	40.7	**North Castle** (town) Westchester County	100	28.9	**Tarrytown** (village) Westchester County
26	40.6	**Irvington** (village) Westchester County	101	28.8	**South Nyack** (village) Rockland County
27	40.5	**Briarcliff Manor** (village) Westchester County	101	28.8	**University at Buffalo** (CDP) Erie County
27	40.5	**Muttontown** (village) Nassau County	103	28.7	**East Norwich** (CDP) Nassau County
29	40.4	**Lido Beach** (CDP) Nassau County	103	28.7	**Manhasset** (CDP) Nassau County
30	40.1	**Pittsford** (town) Monroe County	105	28.6	**Amherst** (town) Erie County
31	39.8	**Montebello** (village) Rockland County	105	28.6	**Woodstock** (town) Ulster County
32	39.7	**Stony Brook** (CDP) Suffolk County	107	28.5	**Bedford** (town) Westchester County
33	38.8	**New Paltz** (village) Ulster County	108	28.4	**Old Bethpage** (CDP) Nassau County
33	38.8	**Pelham Manor** (village) Westchester County	109	28.3	**New City** (CDP) Rockland County
35	38.7	**Brookville** (village) Nassau County	109	28.3	**Williamsville** (village) Erie County
36	38.5	**East Williston** (village) Nassau County	111	28.1	**East Greenbush** (CDP) Rensselaer County
37	38.3	**Wesley Hills** (village) Rockland County	111	28.1	**Northport** (village) Suffolk County
38	38.2	**Manhasset Hills** (CDP) Nassau County	111	28.1	**Otsego** (town) Otsego County
39	38.0	**South Hill** (CDP) Tompkins County	111	28.1	**Rhinebeck** (town) Dutchess County
40	37.8	**Rye** (city) Westchester County	115	27.8	**Melville** (CDP) Suffolk County
41	37.5	**Ithaca** (city) Tompkins County	115	27.8	**Skaneateles** (town) Onondaga County
42	37.4	**Woodmere** (CDP) Nassau County	117	27.3	**Shelter Island** (town) Suffolk County
43	37.1	**Mamaroneck** (town) Westchester County	118	27.2	**Great Neck Plaza** (village) Nassau County
44	37.0	**Brighton** (CDP) Monroe County	118	27.2	**Lake Success** (village) Nassau County
44	37.0	**Piermont** (village) Rockland County	120	26.9	**Manlius** (town) Onondaga County
46	36.8	**Pound Ridge** (town) Westchester County	121	26.8	**Highlands** (town) Orange County
47	36.6	**Setauket-East Setauket** (CDP) Suffolk County	122	26.5	**Dryden** (town) Tompkins County
48	36.3	**Lewisboro** (town) Westchester County	122	26.5	**Eggertsville** (CDP) Erie County
49	36.2	**North Hills** (village) Nassau County	122	26.5	**Guilderland** (town) Albany County
50	36.0	**Lansing** (town) Tompkins County	122	26.5	**Perinton** (town) Monroe County
51	35.9	**Flower Hill** (village) Nassau County	126	26.4	**East Shoreham** (CDP) Suffolk County
52	35.5	**Alfred** (town) Allegany County	126	26.4	**South Valley Stream** (CDP) Nassau County
52	35.5	**Ardsley** (village) Westchester County	126	26.4	**West Bay Shore** (CDP) Suffolk County
54	35.3	**Potsdam** (village) Saint Lawrence County	129	26.3	**North Hempstead** (town) Nassau County
55	35.0	**Jericho** (CDP) Nassau County	130	26.2	**Saratoga Springs** (city) Saratoga County
56	34.9	**Glenwood Landing** (CDP) Nassau County	130	26.2	**Somers** (town) Westchester County
57	34.4	**Gang Mills** (CDP) Steuben County	130	26.2	**West Nyack** (CDP) Rockland County
57	34.4	**Sea Cliff** (village) Nassau County	133	26.1	**Erwin** (town) Steuben County
59	34.2	**Cold Spring Harbor** (CDP) Suffolk County	133	26.1	**Mount Pleasant** (town) Westchester County
60	34.1	**Searingtown** (CDP) Nassau County	135	26.0	**Clifton Park** (town) Saratoga County
61	34.0	**Halesite** (CDP) Suffolk County	135	26.0	**Jefferson Valley-Yorktown** (CDP) Westchester County
62	33.8	**Garden City** (village) Nassau County	137	25.9	**Albertson** (CDP) Nassau County
62	33.8	**Greenburgh** (town) Westchester County	137	25.9	**West Hills** (CDP) Suffolk County
62	33.8	**Woodbury** (CDP) Nassau County	139	25.8	**Victor** (town) Ontario County
65	33.5	**Pelham** (town) Westchester County	139	25.8	**West Elmira** (CDP) Chemung County
65	33.5	**Pleasantville** (village) Westchester County	141	25.7	**Port Washington North** (village) Nassau County
67	33.0	**Bethlehem** (town) Albany County	141	25.7	**Potsdam** (town) Saint Lawrence County
67	33.0	**Croton-on-Hudson** (village) Westchester County	141	25.7	**Spackenkill** (CDP) Dutchess County
67	33.0	**Niskayuna** (town) Schenectady County	144	25.6	**Caroline** (town) Tompkins County
70	32.9	**New Paltz** (town) Ulster County	144	25.6	**Mamaroneck** (village) Westchester County
70	32.9	**Rhinebeck** (village) Dutchess County	146	25.4	**Fort Salonga** (CDP) Suffolk County
72	32.6	**Huntington** (CDP) Suffolk County	147	25.3	**Clarence** (town) Erie County
73	32.3	**Rye Brook** (village) Westchester County	148	25.2	**Cedarhurst** (village) Nassau County
74	32.1	**Menands** (village) Albany County	148	25.2	**Hurley** (town) Ulster County
75	32.0	**Roslyn** (village) Nassau County	150	25.0	**Gardiner** (town) Ulster County

Note: *This section ranks incorporated places and CDPs (Census Designated Places) with populations of 2,500 or more. Unincorporated postal areas were not considered. Please refer to the User Guide for additional information.*

Educational Attainment: Graduate/Professional Degree or Higher

Top 150 Places Ranked in *Ascending* Order

State Rank	Percent	Place	State Rank	Percent	Place
1	0.4	**Riverside** (CDP) Suffolk County	76	5.3	**Afton** (town) Chenango County
2	0.5	**Kiryas Joel** (village) Orange County	76	5.3	**Champlain** (town) Clinton County
3	0.9	**New Square** (village) Rockland County	76	5.3	**Moriah** (town) Essex County
4	1.3	**Dannemora** (village) Clinton County	76	5.3	**Warsaw** (village) Wyoming County
5	2.0	**Dannemora** (town) Clinton County	80	5.4	**Carroll** (town) Chautauqua County
5	2.0	**Kaser** (village) Rockland County	81	5.5	**Amsterdam** (city) Montgomery County
7	2.1	**Whitehall** (town) Washington County	81	5.5	**Ellisburg** (town) Jefferson County
7	2.1	**Whitehall** (village) Washington County	81	5.5	**Mooers** (town) Clinton County
9	2.2	**Albion** (village) Orleans County	84	5.6	**Constantia** (town) Oswego County
9	2.2	**Hannibal** (town) Oswego County	84	5.6	**Gates** (CDP) Monroe County
11	2.5	**Sloan** (village) Erie County	84	5.6	**Guilford** (town) Chenango County
12	2.9	**Groveland** (town) Livingston County	84	5.6	**Lackawanna** (city) Erie County
13	3.1	**Fort Edward** (town) Washington County	84	5.6	**Manchester** (town) Ontario County
13	3.1	**Fort Edward** (village) Washington County	84	5.6	**Niagara** (town) Niagara County
15	3.4	**Fort Ann** (town) Washington County	84	5.6	**Roosevelt** (CDP) Nassau County
15	3.4	**Hoosick** (town) Rensselaer County	84	5.6	**Verona** (town) Oneida County
15	3.4	**Whitesboro** (village) Oneida County	84	5.6	**Yates** (town) Orleans County
18	3.5	**Green Island** (town/village) Albany County	93	5.7	**Baywood** (CDP) Suffolk County
19	3.6	**Mastic** (CDP) Suffolk County	93	5.7	**Central Islip** (CDP) Suffolk County
20	3.7	**Albion** (town) Orleans County	93	5.7	**Dix** (town) Schuyler County
20	3.7	**Attica** (town) Wyoming County	93	5.7	**Hopewell** (town) Ontario County
20	3.7	**Corinth** (village) Saratoga County	93	5.7	**Sandy Creek** (town) Oswego County
20	3.7	**North Bay Shore** (CDP) Suffolk County	98	5.8	**Broadalbin** (town) Fulton County
20	3.7	**Perry** (village) Wyoming County	98	5.8	**Enfield** (town) Tompkins County
25	3.8	**Lyncourt** (CDP) Onondaga County	98	5.8	**Inwood** (CDP) Nassau County
25	3.8	**Palermo** (town) Oswego County	98	5.8	**Newfane** (town) Niagara County
27	3.9	**East Syracuse** (village) Onondaga County	98	5.8	**North Patchogue** (CDP) Suffolk County
27	3.9	**Mattydale** (CDP) Onondaga County	98	5.8	**Sidney** (town) Delaware County
27	3.9	**Perry** (town) Wyoming County	98	5.8	**Wayland** (town) Steuben County
27	3.9	**Romulus** (town) Seneca County	105	5.9	**Calcium** (CDP) Jefferson County
31	4.0	**Brentwood** (CDP) Suffolk County	105	5.9	**Croghan** (town) Lewis County
31	4.0	**Stockport** (town) Columbia County	105	5.9	**Murray** (town) Orleans County
33	4.2	**Lisle** (town) Broome County	105	5.9	**Ravena** (village) Albany County
33	4.2	**Mechanicville** (city) Saratoga County	109	6.0	**Au Sable** (town) Clinton County
33	4.2	**Salamanca** (city) Cattaraugus County	109	6.0	**Carthage** (village) Jefferson County
33	4.2	**Vienna** (town) Oneida County	109	6.0	**Hastings** (town) Oswego County
33	4.2	**Wyandanch** (CDP) Suffolk County	109	6.0	**Newfane** (CDP) Niagara County
38	4.3	**Deerpark** (town) Orange County	109	6.0	**Parish** (town) Oswego County
38	4.3	**Floyd** (town) Oneida County	109	6.0	**Southport** (CDP) Chemung County
38	4.3	**Somerset** (town) Niagara County	109	6.0	**Unadilla** (town) Otsego County
38	4.3	**South Glens Falls** (village) Saratoga County	116	6.1	**Bethel** (town) Sullivan County
42	4.4	**Tioga** (town) Tioga County	116	6.1	**Fulton** (city) Oswego County
43	4.5	**Schaghticoke** (town) Rensselaer County	116	6.1	**Mastic Beach** (village) Suffolk County
44	4.6	**Altona** (town) Clinton County	116	6.1	**Mayfield** (town) Fulton County
44	4.6	**Arcade** (town) Wyoming County	116	6.1	**Mount Morris** (town) Livingston County
44	4.6	**Clarendon** (town) Orleans County	121	6.2	**Brasher** (town) Saint Lawrence County
44	4.6	**Denmark** (town) Lewis County	121	6.2	**Gloversville** (city) Fulton County
44	4.6	**New York Mills** (village) Oneida County	121	6.2	**North Amityville** (CDP) Suffolk County
44	4.6	**West Monroe** (town) Oswego County	121	6.2	**Port Jervis** (city) Orange County
50	4.7	**Collins** (town) Erie County	121	6.2	**Sardinia** (town) Erie County
50	4.7	**Galeville** (CDP) Onondaga County	121	6.2	**Utica** (city) Oneida County
50	4.7	**Monticello** (village) Sullivan County	127	6.3	**Barker** (town) Broome County
50	4.7	**Nichols** (town) Tioga County	127	6.3	**Dunkirk** (city) Chautauqua County
50	4.7	**Waterloo** (village) Seneca County	127	6.3	**Fairview** (CDP) Westchester County
55	4.8	**Blasdell** (village) Erie County	127	6.3	**Hamlin** (town) Monroe County
55	4.8	**Corinth** (town) Saratoga County	127	6.3	**Newburgh** (city) Orange County
55	4.8	**Gouverneur** (town) Saint Lawrence County	127	6.3	**Penn Yan** (village) Yates County
55	4.8	**Hudson Falls** (village) Washington County	127	6.3	**Theresa** (town) Jefferson County
55	4.8	**Keeseville** (village) Clinton County	134	6.4	**Bath** (town) Steuben County
55	4.8	**Liberty** (village) Sullivan County	134	6.4	**Camden** (town) Oneida County
55	4.8	**Saint Johnsville** (town) Montgomery County	134	6.4	**Copiague** (CDP) Suffolk County
62	4.9	**Augusta** (town) Oneida County	134	6.4	**Hartland** (town) Niagara County
62	4.9	**Hoosick Falls** (village) Rensselaer County	134	6.4	**Moreau** (town) Saratoga County
62	4.9	**Minden** (town) Montgomery County	134	6.4	**North Lindenhurst** (CDP) Suffolk County
62	4.9	**New Haven** (town) Oswego County	134	6.4	**Oakfield** (town) Genesee County
62	4.9	**Wilna** (town) Jefferson County	134	6.4	**Waterloo** (town) Seneca County
62	4.9	**Wolcott** (town) Wayne County	142	6.5	**Attica** (village) Wyoming County
68	5.0	**Moravia** (town) Cayuga County	142	6.5	**Norwich** (town) Chenango County
68	5.0	**Scriba** (town) Oswego County	142	6.5	**Sodus** (town) Wayne County
68	5.0	**Yorkshire** (town) Cattaraugus County	142	6.5	**Tupper Lake** (village) Franklin County
71	5.1	**Spring Valley** (village) Rockland County	142	6.5	**Walton** (town) Delaware County
72	5.2	**Annsville** (town) Oneida County	147	6.6	**Alexander** (town) Genesee County
72	5.2	**Calverton** (CDP) Suffolk County	147	6.6	**Champion** (town) Jefferson County
72	5.2	**Riverhead** (CDP) Suffolk County	147	6.6	**Depew** (village) Erie County
72	5.2	**Vernon** (town) Oneida County	147	6.6	**Oneida** (city) Madison County

Note: This section ranks incorporated places and CDPs (Census Designated Places) with populations of 2,500 or more. Unincorporated postal areas were not considered. Please refer to the User Guide for additional information.

Homeownership Rate

Top 150 Places Ranked in *Descending* Order

State Rank	Percent	Place
1	99.4	**East Hills** (village) Nassau County
2	99.0	**Clarence Center** (CDP) Erie County
3	98.5	**Red Oaks Mill** (CDP) Dutchess County
4	98.2	**Manhasset Hills** (CDP) Nassau County
5	98.1	**Searingtown** (CDP) Nassau County
6	97.6	**Kings Point** (village) Nassau County
7	97.4	**Massapequa Park** (village) Nassau County
7	97.4	**Muttontown** (village) Nassau County
9	96.8	**Lake Success** (village) Nassau County
10	96.5	**East Williston** (village) Nassau County
11	96.4	**Blauvelt** (CDP) Rockland County
12	96.0	**Albertson** (CDP) Nassau County
13	95.8	**Malverne** (village) Nassau County
13	95.8	**New Baltimore** (town) Greene County
15	95.6	**Barker** (town) Broome County
15	95.6	**West Bay Shore** (CDP) Suffolk County
17	95.4	**East Norwich** (CDP) Nassau County
18	95.2	**Charlton** (town) Saratoga County
18	95.2	**Herricks** (CDP) Nassau County
20	95.1	**Westvale** (CDP) Onondaga County
21	95.0	**North Massapequa** (CDP) Nassau County
22	94.7	**Dix Hills** (CDP) Suffolk County
23	94.6	**Brightwaters** (village) Suffolk County
23	94.6	**West Islip** (CDP) Suffolk County
25	94.5	**Miller Place** (CDP) Suffolk County
25	94.5	**Munsey Park** (village) Nassau County
25	94.5	**North Merrick** (CDP) Nassau County
25	94.5	**Wading River** (CDP) Suffolk County
29	94.4	**La Grange** (town) Dutchess County
29	94.4	**Spackenkill** (CDP) Dutchess County
29	94.4	**West Hills** (CDP) Suffolk County
29	94.4	**West Nyack** (CDP) Rockland County
33	94.3	**Wantagh** (CDP) Nassau County
34	94.2	**Garden City** (village) Nassau County
34	94.2	**Old Westbury** (village) Nassau County
36	94.1	**Massapequa** (CDP) Nassau County
36	94.1	**Merrick** (CDP) Nassau County
38	94.0	**Lloyd Harbor** (village) Suffolk County
38	94.0	**Marilla** (town) Erie County
38	94.0	**Northwest Harbor** (CDP) Suffolk County
38	94.0	**Pendleton** (town) Niagara County
38	94.0	**Veteran** (town) Chemung County
38	94.0	**Wesley Hills** (village) Rockland County
44	93.9	**Greenville** (CDP) Westchester County
44	93.9	**North Wantagh** (CDP) Nassau County
44	93.9	**Tappan** (CDP) Rockland County
47	93.7	**Hamptonburgh** (town) Orange County
48	93.6	**Brookville** (village) Nassau County
49	93.4	**Walworth** (town) Wayne County
50	93.3	**Owasco** (town) Cayuga County
51	93.2	**North New Hyde Park** (CDP) Nassau County
52	93.1	**Lakeview** (CDP) Nassau County
52	93.1	**Myers Corner** (CDP) Dutchess County
52	93.1	**Sennett** (town) Cayuga County
52	93.1	**Setauket-East Setauket** (CDP) Suffolk County
52	93.1	**Sound Beach** (CDP) Suffolk County
57	93.0	**Fort Salonga** (CDP) Suffolk County
58	92.9	**Centerport** (CDP) Suffolk County
58	92.9	**New Castle** (town) Westchester County
58	92.9	**Sands Point** (village) Nassau County
58	92.9	**South Farmingdale** (CDP) Nassau County
62	92.8	**Elwood** (CDP) Suffolk County
63	92.7	**East Shoreham** (CDP) Suffolk County
64	92.6	**West Sand Lake** (CDP) Rensselaer County
64	92.6	**Windsor** (town) Broome County
66	92.4	**Armonk** (CDP) Westchester County
67	92.3	**Levittown** (CDP) Nassau County
68	92.2	**Baldwin Harbor** (CDP) Nassau County
68	92.2	**Elma Center** (CDP) Erie County
68	92.2	**Mount Sinai** (CDP) Suffolk County
71	92.1	**Berne** (town) Albany County
72	92.0	**Commack** (CDP) Suffolk County
72	92.0	**Pompey** (town) Onondaga County
74	91.9	**Deerfield** (town) Oneida County
74	91.9	**Gates** (CDP) Monroe County
74	91.9	**Old Bethpage** (CDP) Nassau County
74	91.9	**Salisbury** (CDP) Nassau County
78	91.8	**Wanakah** (CDP) Erie County
79	91.6	**Binghamton** (town) Broome County
79	91.6	**Great Neck Estates** (village) Nassau County
79	91.6	**Montebello** (village) Rockland County
79	91.6	**Wales** (town) Erie County
83	91.5	**Syosset** (CDP) Nassau County
84	91.4	**Flower Hill** (village) Nassau County
84	91.4	**Stony Brook** (CDP) Suffolk County
86	91.3	**Plainview** (CDP) Nassau County
87	91.2	**Hurley** (town) Ulster County
88	91.1	**Cutchogue** (CDP) Suffolk County
88	91.1	**Greenville** (town) Orange County
88	91.1	**Jefferson Valley-Yorktown** (CDP) Westchester County
88	91.1	**New Hempstead** (village) Rockland County
88	91.1	**Pomona** (village) Rockland County
88	91.1	**Saint James** (CDP) Suffolk County
94	91.0	**Bethpage** (CDP) Nassau County
94	91.0	**Garden City South** (CDP) Nassau County
94	91.0	**Lewisboro** (town) Westchester County
97	90.8	**Putnam Valley** (town) Putnam County
97	90.8	**Scarsdale** (town/village) Westchester County
99	90.6	**Haviland** (CDP) Dutchess County
100	90.5	**Thiells** (CDP) Rockland County
101	90.3	**Lido Beach** (CDP) Nassau County
101	90.3	**Northumberland** (town) Saratoga County
101	90.3	**Rush** (town) Monroe County
101	90.3	**Sand Lake** (town) Rensselaer County
105	90.2	**Oswego** (town) Oswego County
106	90.1	**East Islip** (CDP) Suffolk County
106	90.1	**Johnstown** (town) Fulton County
108	89.9	**East Fishkill** (town) Dutchess County
109	89.8	**Grandyle Village** (CDP) Erie County
109	89.8	**Oswegatchie** (town) Saint Lawrence County
109	89.8	**Seaford** (CDP) Nassau County
109	89.8	**Somers** (town) Westchester County
113	89.7	**Knox** (town) Albany County
113	89.7	**North Bellmore** (CDP) Nassau County
113	89.7	**Pound Ridge** (town) Westchester County
113	89.7	**West Bloomfield** (town) Ontario County
117	89.6	**Hopewell** (town) Ontario County
118	89.5	**Cambria** (town) Niagara County
118	89.5	**Islip Terrace** (CDP) Suffolk County
118	89.5	**Pelham Manor** (village) Westchester County
118	89.5	**West Elmira** (CDP) Chemung County
122	89.4	**New City** (CDP) Rockland County
123	89.3	**Orleans** (town) Jefferson County
123	89.3	**Shelter Island** (town) Suffolk County
125	89.2	**Hamlin** (CDP) Monroe County
125	89.2	**Islandia** (village) Suffolk County
127	89.1	**Bennington** (town) Wyoming County
127	89.1	**Glenwood Landing** (CDP) Nassau County
127	89.1	**Westerlo** (town) Albany County
130	89.0	**Beekman** (town) Dutchess County
130	89.0	**Plainedge** (CDP) Nassau County
132	88.9	**Bellmore** (CDP) Nassau County
132	88.9	**Halesite** (CDP) Suffolk County
132	88.9	**Lake Erie Beach** (CDP) Erie County
132	88.9	**Smithtown** (town) Suffolk County
132	88.9	**Woodmere** (CDP) Nassau County
137	88.8	**Eaton** (town) Madison County
137	88.8	**North Castle** (town) Westchester County
139	88.7	**Floyd** (town) Oneida County
139	88.7	**Hurley** (CDP) Ulster County
139	88.7	**North Valley Stream** (CDP) Nassau County
142	88.5	**Fleming** (town) Cayuga County
142	88.5	**Heritage Hills** (CDP) Westchester County
142	88.5	**Riga** (town) Monroe County
145	88.4	**Wilson** (town) Niagara County
145	88.4	**Woodbury** (village) Orange County
147	88.2	**Sheridan** (town) Chautauqua County
148	88.1	**Oyster Bay** (town) Nassau County
149	88.0	**Galway** (town) Saratoga County
149	88.0	**Oceanside** (CDP) Nassau County

Note: This section ranks incorporated places and CDPs (Census Designated Places) with populations of 2,500 or more. Unincorporated postal areas were not considered. Please refer to the User Guide for additional information.

Homeownership Rate

Top 150 Places Ranked in *Ascending* Order

State Rank	Percent	Place
1	1.1	**Fort Drum** (CDP) Jefferson County
1	1.1	**West Point** (CDP) Orange County
3	5.4	**Kaser** (village) Rockland County
4	13.5	**New Square** (village) Rockland County
5	17.4	**Le Ray** (town) Jefferson County
6	17.5	**Calcium** (CDP) Jefferson County
7	19.7	**Bronx** (borough) Bronx County
8	24.1	**Manhattan** (borough) New York County
9	26.1	**Ithaca** (city) Tompkins County
10	26.7	**Monticello** (village) Sullivan County
11	27.1	**Arlington** (CDP) Dutchess County
12	27.2	**New Paltz** (village) Ulster County
13	28.0	**Spring Valley** (village) Rockland County
14	28.4	**Kiryas Joel** (village) Orange County
15	28.9	**Alfred** (village) Allegany County
16	30.0	**Brooklyn** (borough) Kings County
17	30.5	**Nyack** (village) Rockland County
18	30.9	**Lansing** (village) Tompkins County
19	32.0	**Newburgh** (city) Orange County
20	32.4	**Green Island** (town/village) Albany County
21	32.6	**New York** (city)
22	33.4	**Cobleskill** (village) Schoharie County
23	34.1	**Hudson** (city) Columbia County
24	34.3	**Manorhaven** (village) Nassau County
25	35.2	**Poughkeepsie** (city) Dutchess County
26	35.3	**Fairview** (CDP) Westchester County
26	35.3	**Sleepy Hollow** (village) Westchester County
28	35.7	**Watervliet** (city) Albany County
29	36.5	**Bedford Hills** (CDP) Westchester County
29	36.5	**Mechanicville** (city) Saratoga County
29	36.5	**Rochester** (city) Monroe County
32	36.7	**Wappingers Falls** (village) Dutchess County
33	36.8	**Troy** (city) Rensselaer County
34	37.2	**Albany** (city) Albany County
35	37.3	**Menands** (village) Albany County
36	37.4	**Plattsburgh** (city) Clinton County
37	37.8	**Liberty** (village) Sullivan County
38	38.0	**Lake Placid** (village) Essex County
39	38.3	**Syracuse** (city) Onondaga County
40	39.2	**Geneseo** (village) Livingston County
41	39.4	**Rensselaer** (city) Rensselaer County
42	39.5	**Monsey** (CDP) Rockland County
42	39.5	**Potsdam** (village) Saint Lawrence County
44	39.7	**Mount Vernon** (city) Westchester County
45	40.1	**Brockport** (village) Monroe County
46	40.2	**Haverstraw** (village) Rockland County
47	40.3	**Watertown** (city) Jefferson County
48	40.7	**Webster** (village) Monroe County
49	41.0	**Buffalo** (city) Erie County
50	41.1	**Carthage** (village) Jefferson County
51	41.2	**Highlands** (town) Orange County
52	41.6	**Herkimer** (village) Herkimer County
53	42.0	**Cohoes** (city) Albany County
54	42.2	**Port Chester** (village) Westchester County
55	42.7	**New York Mills** (village) Oneida County
56	43.3	**Mechanicstown** (CDP) Orange County
57	43.4	**Hempstead** (village) Nassau County
58	43.7	**Endicott** (village) Broome County
59	44.5	**Queens** (borough) Queens County
60	44.8	**Harriman** (village) Orange County
61	45.0	**Binghamton** (city) Broome County
62	45.1	**Elmira** (city) Chemung County
63	45.6	**Ellenville** (village) Ulster County
64	45.7	**Moriches** (CDP) Suffolk County
65	45.9	**South Glens Falls** (village) Saratoga County
66	46.0	**Oneonta** (city) Otsego County
67	46.1	**Norwich** (city) Chenango County
68	46.5	**Gouverneur** (village) Saint Lawrence County
69	46.6	**Inwood** (CDP) Nassau County
69	46.6	**Warsaw** (village) Wyoming County
71	46.7	**Kingston** (city) Ulster County
72	46.9	**Auburn** (city) Cayuga County
73	47.0	**Tuckahoe** (village) Westchester County
74	47.3	**Munsons Corners** (CDP) Cortland County
74	47.3	**Yonkers** (city) Westchester County
76	47.4	**Saugerties** (village) Ulster County
77	47.7	**Cortland** (city) Cortland County
77	47.7	**East Syracuse** (village) Onondaga County
77	47.7	**Elmsford** (village) Westchester County
80	47.9	**Utica** (city) Oneida County
81	48.1	**Highland Falls** (village) Orange County
82	48.6	**Peekskill** (city) Westchester County
82	48.6	**Vails Gate** (CDP) Orange County
84	48.7	**Hudson Falls** (village) Washington County
85	49.0	**Geneseo** (town) Livingston County
86	49.1	**Geneva** (city) Ontario County
86	49.1	**Northeast Ithaca** (CDP) Tompkins County
88	49.2	**Catskill** (village) Greene County
89	49.3	**Ossining** (village) Westchester County
90	49.4	**Elmira Heights** (village) Chemung County
91	49.5	**Cayuga Heights** (village) Tompkins County
92	49.7	**Batavia** (city) Genesee County
93	49.8	**Alfred** (town) Allegany County
93	49.8	**Cobleskill** (town) Schoharie County
95	49.9	**Penn Yan** (village) Yates County
96	50.0	**Olean** (city) Cattaraugus County
97	50.3	**Jamestown** (city) Chautauqua County
97	50.3	**Wellsville** (village) Allegany County
99	50.4	**Newark** (village) Wayne County
100	50.9	**Ithaca** (town) Tompkins County
100	50.9	**New Rochelle** (city) Westchester County
102	51.0	**Gloversville** (city) Fulton County
102	51.0	**Rhinebeck** (village) Dutchess County
102	51.0	**Thompson** (town) Sullivan County
105	51.1	**Glen Cove** (city) Nassau County
106	51.2	**Glens Falls** (city) Warren County
107	51.3	**Bath** (village) Steuben County
108	51.4	**Canton** (village) Saint Lawrence County
109	51.9	**Corning** (city) Steuben County
109	51.9	**Herkimer** (town) Herkimer County
109	51.9	**Schenectady** (city) Schenectady County
112	52.0	**Sidney** (village) Delaware County
113	52.1	**Hounsfield** (town) Jefferson County
113	52.1	**White Plains** (city) Westchester County
115	52.2	**Ballston Spa** (village) Saratoga County
116	52.3	**Patchogue** (village) Suffolk County
116	52.3	**Salamanca** (city) Cattaraugus County
118	52.4	**Lackawanna** (city) Erie County
119	52.5	**Wilna** (town) Jefferson County
120	52.6	**Viola** (CDP) Rockland County
121	52.7	**Oswego** (city) Oswego County
121	52.7	**South Hill** (CDP) Tompkins County
123	53.1	**Delhi** (village) Delaware County
123	53.1	**Goshen** (village) Orange County
123	53.1	**Malone** (village) Franklin County
126	53.2	**Amsterdam** (city) Montgomery County
127	53.4	**Port Jervis** (city) Orange County
128	53.8	**Walton** (village) Delaware County
128	53.8	**Whitesboro** (village) Oneida County
130	54.1	**Rye** (town) Westchester County
131	54.2	**Owego** (village) Tioga County
132	54.4	**Mohawk** (village) Herkimer County
132	54.4	**Palmyra** (village) Wayne County
134	54.6	**Great Neck Plaza** (village) Nassau County
134	54.6	**Solvay** (village) Onondaga County
136	54.8	**Johnson City** (village) Broome County
136	54.8	**Mamaroneck** (village) Westchester County
136	54.8	**Saranac Lake** (village) Franklin County
136	54.8	**Saratoga Springs** (city) Saratoga County
140	54.9	**Waverly** (village) Tioga County
141	55.0	**Blasdell** (village) Erie County
141	55.0	**Middletown** (city) Orange County
143	55.1	**Rome** (city) Oneida County
144	55.3	**Kingsbury** (town) Washington County
145	55.9	**Sweden** (town) Monroe County
145	55.9	**Whitehall** (village) Washington County
147	56.0	**Liberty** (town) Sullivan County
147	56.0	**Westmere** (CDP) Albany County
149	56.1	**Albion** (village) Orleans County
149	56.1	**Fulton** (city) Oswego County

Note: This section ranks incorporated places and CDPs (Census Designated Places) with populations of 2,500 or more. Unincorporated postal areas were not considered. Please refer to the User Guide for additional information.

Median Home Value

Top 150 Places Ranked in *Descending* Order

State Rank	Dollars	Place	State Rank	Dollars	Place
1	2 million+	**Kings Point** (village) Nassau County	76	619,100	**Glen Head** (CDP) Nassau County
1	2 million+	**Sands Point** (village) Nassau County	77	617,700	**Dobbs Ferry** (village) Westchester County
3	1,815,600	**Brookville** (village) Nassau County	78	617,400	**Monsey** (CDP) Rockland County
4	1,729,800	**Old Westbury** (village) Nassau County	79	615,100	**Rockville Centre** (village) Nassau County
5	1,632,500	**Muttontown** (village) Nassau County	80	612,900	**Hastings-on-Hudson** (village) Westchester County
6	1,505,700	**Munsey Park** (village) Nassau County	81	611,100	**Mamaroneck** (village) Westchester County
7	1,403,900	**Lloyd Harbor** (village) Suffolk County	82	609,100	**Glenwood Landing** (CDP) Nassau County
8	1,337,800	**Scarsdale** (town/village) Westchester County	83	606,400	**Eastchester** (town) Westchester County
9	1,247,100	**Great Neck Estates** (village) Nassau County	84	599,200	**Thornwood** (CDP) Westchester County
10	1,237,700	**Flower Hill** (village) Nassau County	85	595,600	**Centerport** (CDP) Suffolk County
11	1,195,700	**Southampton** (village) Suffolk County	86	595,200	**West Hills** (CDP) Suffolk County
12	1,183,700	**Larchmont** (village) Westchester County	87	590,100	**Garden City Park** (CDP) Nassau County
13	1,156,900	**Lake Success** (village) Nassau County	88	583,100	**Eastchester** (CDP) Westchester County
14	1,094,500	**Rye** (city) Westchester County	89	582,800	**Tarrytown** (village) Westchester County
15	1,077,200	**Bronxville** (village) Westchester County	90	582,400	**North Salem** (town) Westchester County
16	1,019,300	**Manhasset** (CDP) Nassau County	91	578,100	**Stony Brook University** (CDP) Suffolk County
17	979,500	**North Hills** (village) Nassau County	92	575,400	**Piermont** (village) Rockland County
18	970,100	**East Hills** (village) Nassau County	93	574,200	**Locust Valley** (CDP) Nassau County
19	927,200	**North Castle** (town) Westchester County	94	573,600	**Huntington** (CDP) Suffolk County
20	923,700	**Pound Ridge** (town) Westchester County	95	571,300	**Pleasantville** (village) Westchester County
21	915,300	**Manhattan** (borough) New York County	96	570,900	**Halesite** (CDP) Suffolk County
22	905,200	**Greenville** (CDP) Westchester County	97	570,000	**Old Bethpage** (CDP) Nassau County
23	901,700	**Northwest Harbor** (CDP) Suffolk County	98	567,600	**Wesley Hills** (village) Rockland County
24	889,100	**Lawrence** (village) Nassau County	99	565,300	**Valhalla** (CDP) Westchester County
25	888,900	**Armonk** (CDP) Westchester County	100	563,700	**North New Hyde Park** (CDP) Nassau County
26	884,500	**New Castle** (town) Westchester County	101	562,600	**Northport** (village) Suffolk County
27	878,000	**Mamaroneck** (town) Westchester County	101	562,600	**Oyster Bay** (CDP) Nassau County
28	871,300	**Montauk** (CDP) Suffolk County	103	560,600	**Mattituck** (CDP) Suffolk County
29	858,900	**Pelham Manor** (village) Westchester County	104	558,900	**Rye** (town) Westchester County
30	835,000	**Manhasset Hills** (CDP) Nassau County	105	557,000	**Manorhaven** (village) Nassau County
31	831,100	**Woodbury** (CDP) Nassau County	106	552,700	**New Rochelle** (city) Westchester County
32	829,500	**Searingtown** (CDP) Nassau County	107	552,200	**Greenburgh** (town) Westchester County
33	824,300	**Harrison** (town/village) Westchester County	108	548,600	**Albertson** (CDP) Nassau County
34	817,200	**North Sea** (CDP) Suffolk County	109	546,600	**Floral Park** (village) Nassau County
35	815,900	**East Williston** (village) Nassau County	110	544,400	**Southold** (town) Suffolk County
36	812,500	**Kaser** (village) Rockland County	111	543,400	**Merrick** (CDP) Nassau County
37	811,800	**Garden City** (village) Nassau County	112	542,800	**Bardonia** (CDP) Rockland County
38	809,700	**Thomaston** (village) Nassau County	113	538,700	**New York** (city)
39	807,500	**East Hampton** (town) Suffolk County	114	538,100	**Bayville** (village) Nassau County
40	795,100	**Great Neck** (village) Nassau County	115	536,600	**Plainview** (CDP) Nassau County
41	785,600	**Shelter Island** (town) Suffolk County	116	526,900	**East Quogue** (CDP) Suffolk County
42	771,400	**Port Washington** (CDP) Nassau County	117	526,100	**White Plains** (city) Westchester County
43	771,100	**Roslyn Heights** (CDP) Nassau County	118	524,400	**Southold** (CDP) Suffolk County
44	766,300	**Port Washington North** (village) Nassau County	119	524,000	**Cedarhurst** (village) Nassau County
45	763,900	**Cold Spring Harbor** (CDP) Suffolk County	120	520,600	**Huntington** (town) Suffolk County
46	751,600	**Pelham** (town) Westchester County	121	514,400	**Cutchogue** (CDP) Suffolk County
47	746,800	**Rye Brook** (village) Westchester County	122	514,200	**Port Jefferson** (village) Suffolk County
48	733,300	**Bedford** (town) Westchester County	123	510,900	**Garden City South** (CDP) Nassau County
49	732,100	**Jericho** (CDP) Nassau County	124	507,600	**Croton-on-Hudson** (village) Westchester County
50	721,600	**Westhampton** (CDP) Suffolk County	125	504,400	**Hawthorne** (CDP) Westchester County
51	714,900	**Noyack** (CDP) Suffolk County	126	503,400	**Brightwaters** (village) Suffolk County
52	694,600	**Dix Hills** (CDP) Suffolk County	127	499,000	**New Hyde Park** (village) Nassau County
53	686,200	**Briarcliff Manor** (village) Westchester County	128	498,700	**Williston Park** (village) Nassau County
54	680,700	**East Hampton North** (CDP) Suffolk County	129	498,600	**Pomona** (village) Rockland County
55	678,300	**Fort Salonga** (CDP) Suffolk County	130	497,700	**Blauvelt** (CDP) Rockland County
56	674,000	**Springs** (CDP) Suffolk County	131	497,300	**Massapequa** (CDP) Nassau County
57	670,200	**Irvington** (village) Westchester County	132	494,600	**Somers** (town) Westchester County
58	666,900	**Lido Beach** (CDP) Nassau County	133	494,100	**Elwood** (CDP) Suffolk County
59	662,600	**North Hempstead** (town) Nassau County	134	493,100	**Bedford Hills** (CDP) Westchester County
60	658,000	**Sea Cliff** (village) Nassau County	135	486,000	**Carle Place** (CDP) Nassau County
61	648,100	**Lewisboro** (town) Westchester County	136	485,900	**Oyster Bay** (town) Nassau County
62	647,000	**Pelham** (village) Westchester County	137	485,200	**New Hempstead** (village) Rockland County
63	641,000	**University Gardens** (CDP) Nassau County	138	483,900	**Smithtown** (CDP) Suffolk County
64	640,000	**East Norwich** (CDP) Nassau County	139	483,800	**West Nyack** (CDP) Rockland County
65	638,400	**Viola** (CDP) Rockland County	140	481,300	**Queens** (borough) Queens County
66	635,000	**Melville** (CDP) Suffolk County	141	480,300	**Glen Cove** (city) Nassau County
67	634,000	**Sleepy Hollow** (village) Westchester County	142	479,900	**Philipstown** (town) Putnam County
68	629,000	**Mount Pleasant** (town) Westchester County	143	479,400	**Wantagh** (CDP) Nassau County
69	627,000	**Syosset** (CDP) Nassau County	144	478,600	**Tappan** (CDP) Rockland County
70	626,400	**Southampton** (town) Suffolk County	145	472,800	**New City** (CDP) Rockland County
71	624,000	**Montebello** (village) Rockland County	145	472,800	**Orangetown** (town) Rockland County
72	623,900	**Brooklyn** (borough) Kings County	147	471,300	**Commack** (CDP) Suffolk County
73	623,000	**Woodmere** (CDP) Nassau County	148	470,600	**Airmont** (village) Rockland County
74	620,600	**Herricks** (CDP) Nassau County	149	468,400	**Roslyn** (village) Nassau County
75	620,200	**Ardsley** (village) Westchester County	150	467,500	**North Merrick** (CDP) Nassau County

Note: This section ranks incorporated places and CDPs (Census Designated Places) with populations of 2,500 or more. Unincorporated postal areas were not considered. Please refer to the User Guide for additional information.

Median Home Value

Top 150 Places Ranked in *Ascending* Order

State Rank	Dollars	Place	State Rank	Dollars	Place
1	60,500	**Wellsville** (village) Allegany County	76	87,500	**Binghamton** (city) Broome County
2	63,900	**Jamestown** (city) Chautauqua County	77	87,600	**Ellicott** (town) Chautauqua County
3	64,300	**Dunkirk** (city) Chautauqua County	78	87,800	**Campbell** (town) Steuben County
4	65,700	**Salamanca** (city) Cattaraugus County	79	88,500	**Colesville** (town) Broome County
5	66,200	**Hornell** (city) Steuben County	79	88,500	**Lockport** (city) Niagara County
6	67,500	**Mount Morris** (village) Livingston County	81	88,600	**Altona** (town) Clinton County
7	68,100	**Ogdensburg** (city) Saint Lawrence County	81	88,600	**Johnstown** (city) Fulton County
8	68,700	**Wellsville** (town) Allegany County	83	88,700	**Hanover** (town) Chautauqua County
9	69,900	**Niagara Falls** (city) Niagara County	84	88,800	**Lisle** (town) Broome County
10	70,900	**Franklinville** (town) Cattaraugus County	85	89,000	**Portville** (town) Cattaraugus County
11	71,300	**Medina** (village) Orleans County	86	89,300	**Frankfort** (village) Herkimer County
12	72,000	**Lyons** (village) Wayne County	86	89,300	**Yorkshire** (town) Cattaraugus County
13	72,800	**Elmira** (city) Chemung County	88	89,400	**Granby** (town) Oswego County
14	74,900	**Sloan** (village) Erie County	88	89,400	**Herkimer** (town) Herkimer County
15	75,100	**Cuba** (town) Allegany County	88	89,400	**Utica** (city) Oneida County
15	75,100	**Little Falls** (city) Herkimer County	88	89,400	**Waverly** (village) Tioga County
15	75,100	**Massena** (village) Saint Lawrence County	92	89,600	**Ridgeway** (town) Orleans County
18	76,600	**Massena** (town) Saint Lawrence County	93	89,700	**Albion** (town) Orleans County
19	77,100	**Minden** (town) Montgomery County	93	89,700	**Lisbon** (town) Saint Lawrence County
20	77,200	**Gowanda** (village) Cattaraugus County	95	89,800	**Endicott** (village) Broome County
21	77,400	**Gloversville** (city) Fulton County	95	89,800	**Schuyler** (town) Herkimer County
22	77,500	**Stockholm** (town) Saint Lawrence County	97	89,900	**Newfane** (CDP) Niagara County
23	77,600	**Albion** (village) Orleans County	97	89,900	**Nunda** (town) Livingston County
23	77,600	**Olean** (city) Cattaraugus County	97	89,900	**Westfield** (town) Chautauqua County
25	77,800	**Buffalo** (city) Erie County	100	90,100	**Lackawanna** (city) Erie County
25	77,800	**Ilion** (village) Herkimer County	101	90,400	**Moira** (town) Franklin County
25	77,800	**Waterloo** (town) Seneca County	102	91,100	**Gouverneur** (town) Saint Lawrence County
28	78,200	**Fulton** (city) Oswego County	102	91,100	**Syracuse** (city) Onondaga County
29	78,500	**Bath** (village) Steuben County	104	91,200	**Seneca Falls** (CDP) Seneca County
30	78,600	**Norfolk** (town) Saint Lawrence County	105	91,800	**Brasher** (town) Saint Lawrence County
31	78,900	**Riverside** (CDP) Suffolk County	105	91,800	**Southport** (town) Chemung County
32	79,400	**Rochester** (city) Monroe County	107	92,200	**Keeseville** (village) Clinton County
33	79,900	**Mohawk** (village) Herkimer County	107	92,200	**South Lockport** (CDP) Niagara County
34	80,500	**Wolcott** (town) Wayne County	109	92,500	**Yorkville** (village) Oneida County
35	80,600	**Saint Johnsville** (town) Montgomery County	110	92,600	**Lyncourt** (CDP) Onondaga County
36	80,800	**Manheim** (town) Herkimer County	111	92,700	**Owego** (village) Tioga County
37	81,000	**Lyons** (town) Wayne County	112	93,100	**Le Roy** (village) Genesee County
38	81,900	**Herkimer** (village) Herkimer County	113	93,500	**Gouverneur** (village) Saint Lawrence County
39	82,000	**Dolgeville** (village) Herkimer County	114	93,600	**Au Sable** (town) Clinton County
40	82,100	**Silver Creek** (village) Chautauqua County	115	93,700	**Geneva** (city) Ontario County
41	82,200	**Malone** (village) Franklin County	115	93,700	**Palatine** (town) Montgomery County
42	82,500	**German Flatts** (town) Herkimer County	117	93,800	**Wayland** (town) Steuben County
43	82,600	**Shelby** (town) Orleans County	118	93,900	**Unadilla** (town) Otsego County
44	82,800	**Hannibal** (town) Oswego County	119	94,000	**Blasdell** (village) Erie County
45	83,000	**Norwich** (town) Chenango County	119	94,000	**Candor** (town) Tioga County
46	83,200	**Waterloo** (village) Seneca County	121	94,100	**Oakfield** (town) Genesee County
47	83,400	**Elmira Heights** (village) Chemung County	121	94,100	**Whitesboro** (village) Oneida County
48	83,500	**Mount Morris** (town) Livingston County	123	94,200	**Batavia** (city) Genesee County
49	83,600	**Niagara** (town) Niagara County	124	94,300	**Allegany** (town) Cattaraugus County
50	83,700	**Monticello** (village) Sullivan County	124	94,300	**Palermo** (town) Oswego County
51	83,800	**Randolph** (town) Cattaraugus County	126	94,900	**Rome** (city) Oneida County
52	83,900	**Bath** (town) Steuben County	127	95,000	**Barton** (town) Tioga County
52	83,900	**Galen** (town) Wayne County	127	95,000	**Murray** (town) Orleans County
54	84,000	**Southport** (CDP) Chemung County	129	95,300	**Bainbridge** (town) Chenango County
55	84,200	**Oswego** (city) Oswego County	129	95,300	**Guilford** (town) Chenango County
55	84,200	**Portland** (town) Chautauqua County	131	95,600	**Tupper Lake** (village) Franklin County
57	84,300	**Perry** (village) Wyoming County	132	95,700	**Attica** (village) Wyoming County
58	84,400	**Whitehall** (village) Washington County	133	96,100	**Malone** (town) Franklin County
59	84,500	**New Haven** (town) Oswego County	134	96,200	**Walton** (village) Delaware County
60	84,700	**New Berlin** (town) Chenango County	135	96,400	**Yates** (town) Orleans County
61	84,800	**Addison** (town) Steuben County	136	96,700	**Arcadia** (town) Wayne County
61	84,800	**Canisteo** (town) Steuben County	137	96,900	**Oxford** (town) Chenango County
63	85,200	**North Dansville** (town) Livingston County	138	97,300	**Castile** (town) Wyoming County
63	85,200	**Sidney** (town) Delaware County	138	97,300	**East Rochester** (town/village) Monroe County
65	85,300	**Carroll** (town) Chautauqua County	140	97,400	**Mooers** (town) Clinton County
66	85,400	**Mattydale** (CDP) Onondaga County	141	97,600	**Manchester** (town) Ontario County
67	85,800	**Amsterdam** (city) Montgomery County	142	97,800	**Auburn** (city) Cayuga County
67	85,800	**Johnson City** (village) Broome County	143	98,200	**Cortland** (city) Cortland County
67	85,800	**Sidney** (village) Delaware County	143	98,200	**Tonawanda** (city) Erie County
70	85,900	**Perry** (town) Wyoming County	143	98,200	**Whitehall** (town) Washington County
70	85,900	**Westfield** (village) Chautauqua County	146	98,500	**Sodus** (town) Wayne County
72	86,000	**Newark** (village) Wayne County	147	98,600	**Lake Erie Beach** (CDP) Erie County
73	86,100	**Norwich** (city) Chenango County	148	98,900	**Fort Edward** (village) Washington County
74	86,200	**Gaines** (town) Orleans County	149	99,000	**Sterling** (town) Cayuga County
75	86,800	**Dansville** (village) Livingston County	150	99,300	**Canajoharie** (town) Montgomery County

Note: *This section ranks incorporated places and CDPs (Census Designated Places) with populations of 2,500 or more. Unincorporated postal areas were not considered. Please refer to the User Guide for additional information.*

Median Year Structure Built

Top 150 Places Ranked in *Descending* Order

State Rank	Year	Place
1	1998	**Fort Drum** (CDP) Jefferson County
2	1997	**Calcium** (CDP) Jefferson County
2	1997	**Kiryas Joel** (village) Orange County
4	1996	**Kaser** (village) Rockland County
4	1996	**New Square** (village) Rockland County
6	1994	**Le Ray** (town) Jefferson County
6	1994	**University at Buffalo** (CDP) Erie County
6	1994	**Wilton** (town) Saratoga County
9	1993	**Manorville** (CDP) Suffolk County
10	1992	**Victor** (town) Ontario County
11	1991	**Canandaigua** (town) Ontario County
11	1991	**Milton** (CDP) Saratoga County
13	1990	**Gordon Heights** (CDP) Suffolk County
13	1990	**Halfmoon** (town) Saratoga County
13	1990	**Monsey** (CDP) Rockland County
13	1990	**Saint Regis Mohawk Reservation** (reservation) Franklin County
17	1989	**Wheatfield** (town) Niagara County
18	1987	**Moriches** (CDP) Suffolk County
18	1987	**Northumberland** (town) Saratoga County
20	1986	**Malta** (town) Saratoga County
20	1986	**North Hills** (village) Nassau County
20	1986	**South Lockport** (CDP) Niagara County
20	1986	**West Glens Falls** (CDP) Warren County
24	1985	**Calverton** (CDP) Suffolk County
24	1985	**Clarence** (town) Erie County
24	1985	**Enfield** (town) Tompkins County
24	1985	**Greenfield** (town) Saratoga County
24	1985	**Greenville** (town) Orange County
24	1985	**Heritage Hills** (CDP) Westchester County
24	1985	**Monroe** (town) Orange County
31	1984	**Altona** (town) Clinton County
31	1984	**Beekman** (town) Dutchess County
31	1984	**Beekmantown** (town) Clinton County
31	1984	**Stillwater** (town) Saratoga County
35	1983	**Annsville** (town) Oneida County
35	1983	**Crawford** (town) Orange County
35	1983	**Davenport** (town) Delaware County
35	1983	**East Hampton North** (CDP) Suffolk County
35	1983	**Queensbury** (town) Warren County
40	1982	**Clarence Center** (CDP) Erie County
40	1982	**Clifton Park** (town) Saratoga County
40	1982	**Fallsburg** (town) Sullivan County
40	1982	**Farmington** (town) Ontario County
40	1982	**Hastings** (town) Oswego County
40	1982	**Hounsfield** (town) Jefferson County
40	1982	**Milton** (town) Saratoga County
40	1982	**Peru** (town) Clinton County
40	1982	**Riverhead** (town) Suffolk County
40	1982	**Stephentown** (town) Rensselaer County
40	1982	**Walworth** (town) Wayne County
40	1982	**Washingtonville** (village) Orange County
40	1982	**West Monroe** (town) Oswego County
40	1982	**Yaphank** (CDP) Suffolk County
54	1981	**Chester** (town) Orange County
54	1981	**Chester** (village) Orange County
54	1981	**Gang Mills** (CDP) Steuben County
54	1981	**Harriman** (village) Orange County
54	1981	**Lockport** (town) Niagara County
54	1981	**Macedon** (town) Wayne County
54	1981	**Melville** (CDP) Suffolk County
54	1981	**Perth** (town) Fulton County
54	1981	**Plattekill** (town) Ulster County
54	1981	**Schuyler** (town) Herkimer County
54	1981	**Scriba** (town) Oswego County
54	1981	**Volney** (town) Oswego County
54	1981	**Woodbury** (town) Orange County
67	1980	**East Fishkill** (town) Dutchess County
67	1980	**East Moriches** (CDP) Suffolk County
67	1980	**Fishkill** (town) Dutchess County
67	1980	**Gardiner** (town) Ulster County
67	1980	**Hamlin** (CDP) Monroe County
67	1980	**Hannibal** (town) Oswego County
67	1980	**Lake Luzerne** (town) Warren County
67	1980	**Lysander** (town) Onondaga County
67	1980	**Mechanicstown** (CDP) Orange County
67	1980	**Mexico** (town) Oswego County
67	1980	**Middle Island** (CDP) Suffolk County
67	1980	**Minisink** (town) Orange County
67	1980	**Mooers** (town) Clinton County
67	1980	**Newfield** (town) Tompkins County
67	1980	**Webster** (town) Monroe County
67	1980	**Westhampton** (CDP) Suffolk County
67	1980	**Woodbury** (village) Orange County
84	1979	**Armonk** (CDP) Westchester County
84	1979	**Brewerton** (CDP) Onondaga County
84	1979	**Clarkson** (CDP) Monroe County
84	1979	**Clarkson** (town) Monroe County
84	1979	**Coram** (CDP) Suffolk County
84	1979	**Hilton** (village) Monroe County
84	1979	**Hopewell** (town) Ontario County
84	1979	**Lansing** (town) Tompkins County
84	1979	**Mount Sinai** (CDP) Suffolk County
84	1979	**North Sea** (CDP) Suffolk County
84	1979	**Northwest Harbor** (CDP) Suffolk County
84	1979	**Plattsburgh** (town) Clinton County
84	1979	**Schuyler Falls** (town) Clinton County
84	1979	**Union Vale** (town) Dutchess County
84	1979	**Viola** (CDP) Rockland County
99	1978	**Cicero** (town) Onondaga County
99	1978	**East Hampton** (town) Suffolk County
99	1978	**Montauk** (CDP) Suffolk County
99	1978	**Montebello** (village) Rockland County
99	1978	**New Haven** (town) Oswego County
99	1978	**North Bellport** (CDP) Suffolk County
99	1978	**Otego** (town) Otsego County
99	1978	**Pierrepont** (town) Saint Lawrence County
99	1978	**Ridge** (CDP) Suffolk County
99	1978	**Rochester** (town) Ulster County
99	1978	**Shelter Island** (town) Suffolk County
99	1978	**Somers** (town) Westchester County
99	1978	**Springs** (CDP) Suffolk County
99	1978	**Woodbury** (CDP) Nassau County
113	1977	**Candor** (town) Tioga County
113	1977	**East Greenbush** (CDP) Rensselaer County
113	1977	**Glens Falls North** (CDP) Warren County
113	1977	**Hamptonburgh** (town) Orange County
113	1977	**Lansing** (village) Tompkins County
113	1977	**Montgomery** (village) Orange County
113	1977	**Mount Ivy** (CDP) Rockland County
113	1977	**Neversink** (town) Sullivan County
113	1977	**New Windsor** (town) Orange County
113	1977	**Ogden** (town) Monroe County
113	1977	**Otisco** (town) Onondaga County
113	1977	**Palermo** (town) Oswego County
113	1977	**Riverhead** (CDP) Suffolk County
113	1977	**Shirley** (CDP) Suffolk County
113	1977	**Wading River** (CDP) Suffolk County
113	1977	**Wallkill** (town) Orange County
113	1977	**Watertown** (town) Jefferson County
113	1977	**Westerlo** (town) Albany County
131	1976	**Afton** (town) Chenango County
131	1976	**Au Sable** (town) Clinton County
131	1976	**Ballston** (town) Saratoga County
131	1976	**Cape Vincent** (town) Jefferson County
131	1976	**Chili** (town) Monroe County
131	1976	**Clay** (town) Onondaga County
131	1976	**Clinton** (town) Dutchess County
131	1976	**Dryden** (town) Tompkins County
131	1976	**Fort Ann** (town) Washington County
131	1976	**Glasco** (CDP) Ulster County
131	1976	**Guilderland** (town) Albany County
131	1976	**Holtsville** (CDP) Suffolk County
131	1976	**Lisle** (town) Broome County
131	1976	**Livingston** (town) Columbia County
131	1976	**Noyack** (CDP) Suffolk County
131	1976	**Penfield** (town) Monroe County
131	1976	**Pomona** (village) Rockland County
131	1976	**Scotchtown** (CDP) Orange County
131	1976	**Southeast** (town) Putnam County
131	1976	**Tully** (town) Onondaga County

Note: *This section ranks incorporated places and CDPs (Census Designated Places) with populations of 2,500 or more. Unincorporated postal areas were not considered. Please refer to the User Guide for additional information.*

Median Year Structure Built

Top 150 Places Ranked in *Ascending* Order

State Rank	Year	Place
1	<1940	**Albany** (city) Albany County
1	<1940	**Albion** (town) Orleans County
1	<1940	**Albion** (village) Orleans County
1	<1940	**Amsterdam** (city) Montgomery County
1	<1940	**Attica** (village) Wyoming County
1	<1940	**Auburn** (city) Cayuga County
1	<1940	**Augusta** (town) Oneida County
1	<1940	**Ballston Spa** (village) Saratoga County
1	<1940	**Batavia** (city) Genesee County
1	<1940	**Bronxville** (village) Westchester County
1	<1940	**Brooklyn** (borough) Kings County
1	<1940	**Buffalo** (city) Erie County
1	<1940	**Canajoharie** (town) Montgomery County
1	<1940	**Carthage** (village) Jefferson County
1	<1940	**Catskill** (village) Greene County
1	<1940	**Cohoes** (city) Albany County
1	<1940	**Corinth** (village) Saratoga County
1	<1940	**Corning** (city) Steuben County
1	<1940	**Cornwall-on-Hudson** (village) Orange County
1	<1940	**Cortland** (city) Cortland County
1	<1940	**Dannemora** (village) Clinton County
1	<1940	**Dansville** (village) Livingston County
1	<1940	**Delhi** (village) Delaware County
1	<1940	**Dolgeville** (village) Herkimer County
1	<1940	**Dunkirk** (city) Chautauqua County
1	<1940	**East Aurora** (village) Erie County
1	<1940	**East Syracuse** (village) Onondaga County
1	<1940	**Elmira** (city) Chemung County
1	<1940	**Endicott** (village) Broome County
1	<1940	**Floral Park** (village) Nassau County
1	<1940	**Fort Edward** (village) Washington County
1	<1940	**Frankfort** (village) Herkimer County
1	<1940	**Geneva** (city) Ontario County
1	<1940	**German Flatts** (town) Herkimer County
1	<1940	**Glens Falls** (city) Warren County
1	<1940	**Gloversville** (city) Fulton County
1	<1940	**Gouverneur** (village) Saint Lawrence County
1	<1940	**Gowanda** (village) Cattaraugus County
1	<1940	**Great Neck Estates** (village) Nassau County
1	<1940	**Green Island** (town/village) Albany County
1	<1940	**Hamilton** (town) Madison County
1	<1940	**Hamilton** (village) Madison County
1	<1940	**Harrietstown** (town) Franklin County
1	<1940	**Herkimer** (town) Herkimer County
1	<1940	**Herkimer** (village) Herkimer County
1	<1940	**Homer** (town) Cortland County
1	<1940	**Homer** (village) Cortland County
1	<1940	**Hoosick** (town) Rensselaer County
1	<1940	**Hoosick Falls** (village) Rensselaer County
1	<1940	**Hornell** (city) Steuben County
1	<1940	**Hudson** (city) Columbia County
1	<1940	**Ilion** (village) Herkimer County
1	<1940	**Jamestown** (city) Chautauqua County
1	<1940	**Johnstown** (city) Fulton County
1	<1940	**Kenmore** (village) Erie County
1	<1940	**Kingston** (city) Ulster County
1	<1940	**Larchmont** (village) Westchester County
1	<1940	**Le Roy** (village) Genesee County
1	<1940	**Little Falls** (city) Herkimer County
1	<1940	**Lockport** (city) Niagara County
1	<1940	**Locust Valley** (CDP) Nassau County
1	<1940	**Lowville** (town) Lewis County
1	<1940	**Lowville** (village) Lewis County
1	<1940	**Lyons** (town) Wayne County
1	<1940	**Lyons** (village) Wayne County
1	<1940	**Manhasset** (CDP) Nassau County
1	<1940	**Manheim** (town) Herkimer County
1	<1940	**Mechanicville** (city) Saratoga County
1	<1940	**Medina** (village) Orleans County
1	<1940	**Mohawk** (village) Herkimer County
1	<1940	**Mount Morris** (town) Livingston County
1	<1940	**Mount Morris** (village) Livingston County
1	<1940	**Newburgh** (city) Orange County
1	<1940	**Norwich** (city) Chenango County
1	<1940	**Oakfield** (town) Genesee County
1	<1940	**Ogdensburg** (city) Saint Lawrence County
1	<1940	**Olean** (city) Cattaraugus County
1	<1940	**Oneida** (city) Madison County
1	<1940	**Oneonta** (city) Otsego County
1	<1940	**Oswego** (city) Oswego County
1	<1940	**Otsego** (town) Otsego County
1	<1940	**Owego** (village) Tioga County
1	<1940	**Pelham** (town) Westchester County
1	<1940	**Pelham** (village) Westchester County
1	<1940	**Pelham Manor** (village) Westchester County
1	<1940	**Penn Yan** (village) Yates County
1	<1940	**Perry** (town) Wyoming County
1	<1940	**Perry** (village) Wyoming County
1	<1940	**Port Jervis** (city) Orange County
1	<1940	**Ridgeway** (town) Orleans County
1	<1940	**Rochester** (city) Monroe County
1	<1940	**Saint Johnsville** (town) Montgomery County
1	<1940	**Salamanca** (city) Cattaraugus County
1	<1940	**Sangerfield** (town) Oneida County
1	<1940	**Saranac Lake** (village) Franklin County
1	<1940	**Saugerties** (village) Ulster County
1	<1940	**Schenectady** (city) Schenectady County
1	<1940	**Scotia** (village) Schenectady County
1	<1940	**Sea Cliff** (village) Nassau County
1	<1940	**Seneca Falls** (CDP) Seneca County
1	<1940	**Silver Creek** (village) Chautauqua County
1	<1940	**Somerset** (town) Niagara County
1	<1940	**South Nyack** (village) Rockland County
1	<1940	**Ticonderoga** (CDP) Essex County
1	<1940	**Troy** (city) Rensselaer County
1	<1940	**Utica** (city) Oneida County
1	<1940	**Walton** (village) Delaware County
1	<1940	**Warsaw** (town) Wyoming County
1	<1940	**Warsaw** (village) Wyoming County
1	<1940	**Watertown** (city) Jefferson County
1	<1940	**Watervliet** (city) Albany County
1	<1940	**Waverly** (village) Tioga County
1	<1940	**Wellsville** (village) Allegany County
1	<1940	**Whitehall** (village) Washington County
1	<1940	**Williston Park** (village) Nassau County
116	1940	**Hudson Falls** (village) Washington County
117	1941	**Addison** (town) Steuben County
117	1941	**Binghamton** (city) Broome County
117	1941	**Castile** (town) Wyoming County
117	1941	**Fort Edward** (town) Washington County
117	1941	**Malone** (town) Franklin County
117	1941	**Scarsdale** (town/village) Westchester County
117	1941	**Westfield** (village) Chautauqua County
117	1941	**York** (town) Livingston County
125	1942	**Canton** (village) Saint Lawrence County
125	1942	**Fulton** (city) Oswego County
125	1942	**Galen** (town) Wayne County
125	1942	**Hastings-on-Hudson** (village) Westchester County
125	1942	**Minden** (town) Montgomery County
125	1942	**Mount Vernon** (city) Westchester County
125	1942	**Niagara Falls** (city) Niagara County
125	1942	**Royalton** (town) Niagara County
125	1942	**Yorkville** (village) Oneida County
134	1943	**Benton** (town) Yates County
134	1943	**Canisteo** (town) Steuben County
134	1943	**Munsey Park** (village) Nassau County
134	1943	**Whitehall** (town) Washington County
138	1944	**Lynbrook** (village) Nassau County
138	1944	**Malverne** (village) Nassau County
138	1944	**Mamaroneck** (town) Westchester County
138	1944	**Moriah** (town) Essex County
138	1944	**Palmyra** (village) Wayne County
138	1944	**Seneca** (town) Ontario County
144	1945	**Cedarhurst** (village) Nassau County
144	1945	**Fredonia** (village) Chautauqua County
144	1945	**Randolph** (town) Cattaraugus County
144	1945	**Starkey** (town) Yates County
144	1945	**Syracuse** (city) Onondaga County
144	1945	**Wellsville** (town) Allegany County
150	1946	**Baldwin** (CDP) Nassau County

Note: This section ranks incorporated places and CDPs (Census Designated Places) with populations of 2,500 or more. Unincorporated postal areas were not considered. Please refer to the User Guide for additional information.

Homeowner Vacancy Rate

Top 150 Places Ranked in *Descending* Order

State Rank	Percent	Place		State Rank	Percent	Place
1	19.0	Kaser (village) Rockland County		74	4.5	Lewiston (town) Niagara County
2	13.2	Copake (town) Columbia County		74	4.5	Port Jervis (city) Orange County
3	12.4	Niagara Falls (city) Niagara County		74	4.5	Rhinebeck (village) Dutchess County
4	10.8	Canton (village) Saint Lawrence County		74	4.5	Yorkshire (town) Cattaraugus County
5	9.4	Lewiston (village) Niagara County		80	4.4	Glasco (CDP) Ulster County
6	9.1	Little Falls (city) Herkimer County		80	4.4	Granby (town) Oswego County
7	8.8	Wilson (town) Niagara County		80	4.4	Hancock (town) Delaware County
8	8.6	Gouverneur (village) Saint Lawrence County		80	4.4	Horseheads North (CDP) Chemung County
9	8.2	Bethel (town) Sullivan County		80	4.4	Liberty (village) Sullivan County
9	8.2	Chittenango (village) Madison County		80	4.4	Lockport (town) Niagara County
11	7.9	Rockland (town) Sullivan County		80	4.4	Northampton (town) Fulton County
12	7.8	Manorhaven (village) Nassau County		87	4.3	Big Flats (CDP) Chemung County
12	7.8	Ticonderoga (CDP) Essex County		87	4.3	Long Beach (city) Nassau County
14	7.7	East Syracuse (village) Onondaga County		87	4.3	Moriah (town) Essex County
14	7.7	Lockport (city) Niagara County		87	4.3	Newfane (town) Niagara County
14	7.7	Newburgh (city) Orange County		87	4.3	Palmyra (town) Wayne County
14	7.7	Warrensburg (town) Warren County		87	4.3	Shandaken (town) Ulster County
18	7.6	Alfred (village) Allegany County		93	4.2	Clarendon (town) Orleans County
19	7.5	Delhi (village) Delaware County		93	4.2	Gouverneur (town) Saint Lawrence County
19	7.5	Thompson (town) Sullivan County		93	4.2	Islandia (village) Suffolk County
21	7.4	Lakewood (village) Chautauqua County		93	4.2	Mount Hope (town) Orange County
22	7.3	Fallsburg (town) Sullivan County		93	4.2	Stockholm (town) Saint Lawrence County
23	7.2	Cairo (town) Greene County		93	4.2	Watertown (city) Jefferson County
23	7.2	Chatham (town) Columbia County		93	4.2	Webster (village) Monroe County
25	7.1	Lake Placid (village) Essex County		100	4.1	Center Moriches (CDP) Suffolk County
26	7.0	Nyack (village) Rockland County		100	4.1	Coxsackie (village) Greene County
27	6.8	Ticonderoga (town) Essex County		100	4.1	Gordon Heights (CDP) Suffolk County
28	6.6	Hudson Falls (village) Washington County		100	4.1	Keeseville (village) Clinton County
28	6.6	Myers Corner (CDP) Dutchess County		100	4.1	New Paltz (town) Ulster County
28	6.6	South Lockport (CDP) Niagara County		100	4.1	North Gates (CDP) Monroe County
28	6.6	Wyandanch (CDP) Suffolk County		100	4.1	Saranac (town) Clinton County
32	6.5	Monticello (village) Sullivan County		100	4.1	Sidney (village) Delaware County
32	6.5	Richmond (town) Ontario County		108	4.0	Cape Vincent (town) Jefferson County
34	6.3	Fairview (CDP) Dutchess County		108	4.0	Galen (town) Wayne County
34	6.3	New Paltz (village) Ulster County		108	4.0	Sterling (town) Cayuga County
36	6.2	Dunkirk (city) Chautauqua County		111	3.9	Cornwall (town) Orange County
37	6.1	Tupper Lake (village) Franklin County		111	3.9	Lyons (town) Wayne County
38	6.0	Alexandria (town) Jefferson County		111	3.9	Marlboro (CDP) Ulster County
39	5.9	Canton (town) Saint Lawrence County		111	3.9	Middleburgh (town) Schoharie County
40	5.8	Herkimer (village) Herkimer County		111	3.9	New Baltimore (town) Greene County
40	5.8	Olean (city) Cattaraugus County		111	3.9	Pleasantville (village) Westchester County
40	5.8	Richland (town) Oswego County		111	3.9	Pomfret (town) Chautauqua County
40	5.8	Westhampton (CDP) Suffolk County		111	3.9	Tupper Lake (town) Franklin County
44	5.7	Gloversville (city) Fulton County		111	3.9	Wappinger (town) Dutchess County
44	5.7	Porter (town) Niagara County		111	3.9	Wheatley Heights (CDP) Suffolk County
46	5.6	Mamakating (town) Sullivan County		121	3.8	Delhi (town) Delaware County
47	5.5	Catskill (village) Greene County		121	3.8	Elmsford (village) Westchester County
47	5.5	Lido Beach (CDP) Nassau County		121	3.8	Enfield (town) Tompkins County
47	5.5	Poughkeepsie (city) Dutchess County		121	3.8	North Salem (town) Westchester County
47	5.5	Washington (town) Dutchess County		125	3.7	Alfred (town) Allegany County
51	5.3	West Sand Lake (CDP) Rensselaer County		125	3.7	Batavia (city) Genesee County
52	5.2	East Massapequa (CDP) Nassau County		125	3.7	Binghamton (city) Broome County
52	5.2	New Windsor (CDP) Orange County		125	3.7	Catskill (town) Greene County
52	5.2	Niagara (town) Niagara County		125	3.7	Lawrence (village) Nassau County
52	5.2	Sullivan (town) Madison County		125	3.7	Rotterdam (CDP) Schenectady County
56	5.1	Bedford (town) Westchester County		125	3.7	Rye Brook (village) Westchester County
56	5.1	Deerpark (town) Orange County		125	3.7	Watertown (town) Jefferson County
58	5.0	Danby (town) Tompkins County		133	3.6	Minisink (town) Orange County
58	5.0	East Rochester (town/village) Monroe County		133	3.6	Mount Vernon (city) Westchester County
58	5.0	Fredonia (village) Chautauqua County		133	3.6	Plattsburgh (city) Clinton County
58	5.0	Mount Ivy (CDP) Rockland County		133	3.6	Pleasant Valley (town) Dutchess County
58	5.0	Somerset (town) Niagara County		133	3.6	Rochester (town) Ulster County
58	5.0	Warrensburg (CDP) Warren County		133	3.6	Scotchtown (CDP) Orange County
64	4.9	Denmark (town) Lewis County		139	3.5	Carroll (town) Chautauqua County
65	4.8	Berne (town) Albany County		139	3.5	Chester (village) Orange County
65	4.8	Guilford (town) Chenango County		139	3.5	Dannemora (village) Clinton County
65	4.8	Newark Valley (town) Tioga County		139	3.5	Greenwich (town) Washington County
68	4.7	Herkimer (town) Herkimer County		139	3.5	Johnstown (city) Fulton County
68	4.7	Riverside (CDP) Suffolk County		139	3.5	Kingsbury (town) Washington County
70	4.6	Afton (town) Chenango County		139	3.5	Maybrook (village) Orange County
70	4.6	Firthcliffe (CDP) Orange County		139	3.5	Melville (CDP) Suffolk County
70	4.6	Franklinville (town) Cattaraugus County		139	3.5	Mooers (town) Clinton County
70	4.6	Lake George (town) Warren County		139	3.5	North Sea (CDP) Suffolk County
74	4.5	Chautauqua (town) Chautauqua County		139	3.5	Southampton (village) Suffolk County
74	4.5	East Quogue (CDP) Suffolk County		139	3.5	Warsaw (town) Wyoming County

Note: *This section ranks incorporated places and CDPs (Census Designated Places) with populations of 2,500 or more. Unincorporated postal areas were not considered. Please refer to the User Guide for additional information.*

Median Selected Monthly Owner Costs: With Mortgage

Top 150 Places Ranked in *Descending* Order

State Rank	Dollars	Place	State Rank	Dollars	Place
1	4,000+	**Armonk** (CDP) Westchester County	76	3,422	**Mamaroneck** (village) Westchester County
1	4,000+	**Briarcliff Manor** (village) Westchester County	77	3,413	**Oyster Bay** (CDP) Nassau County
1	4,000+	**Bronxville** (village) Westchester County	78	3,400	**Sea Cliff** (village) Nassau County
1	4,000+	**Brookville** (village) Nassau County	79	3,395	**Hawthorne** (CDP) Westchester County
1	4,000+	**Cold Spring Harbor** (CDP) Suffolk County	80	3,392	**Centerport** (CDP) Suffolk County
1	4,000+	**Dix Hills** (CDP) Suffolk County	81	3,391	**Brightwaters** (village) Suffolk County
1	4,000+	**East Hills** (village) Nassau County	82	3,381	**Merrick** (CDP) Nassau County
1	4,000+	**East Williston** (village) Nassau County	83	3,371	**Bardonia** (CDP) Rockland County
1	4,000+	**Flower Hill** (village) Nassau County	84	3,361	**Roslyn** (village) Nassau County
1	4,000+	**Garden City** (village) Nassau County	85	3,345	**Huntington** (CDP) Suffolk County
1	4,000+	**Great Neck Estates** (village) Nassau County	86	3,340	**North Salem** (town) Westchester County
1	4,000+	**Greenville** (CDP) Westchester County	86	3,340	**Thornwood** (CDP) Westchester County
1	4,000+	**Harrison** (town/village) Westchester County	88	3,331	**Elwood** (CDP) Suffolk County
1	4,000+	**Irvington** (village) Westchester County	89	3,330	**Plainview** (CDP) Nassau County
1	4,000+	**Jericho** (CDP) Nassau County	90	3,320	**Glenwood Landing** (CDP) Nassau County
1	4,000+	**Kaser** (village) Rockland County	91	3,317	**Airmont** (village) Rockland County
1	4,000+	**Kings Point** (village) Nassau County	92	3,316	**Glen Head** (CDP) Nassau County
1	4,000+	**Lake Success** (village) Nassau County	93	3,306	**Manorville** (CDP) Suffolk County
1	4,000+	**Larchmont** (village) Westchester County	94	3,305	**Wantagh** (CDP) Nassau County
1	4,000+	**Lawrence** (village) Nassau County	95	3,287	**Eastchester** (CDP) Westchester County
1	4,000+	**Lloyd Harbor** (village) Suffolk County	96	3,284	**Congers** (CDP) Rockland County
1	4,000+	**Mamaroneck** (town) Westchester County	97	3,283	**East Norwich** (CDP) Nassau County
1	4,000+	**Manhasset Hills** (CDP) Nassau County	98	3,276	**Croton-on-Hudson** (village) Westchester County
1	4,000+	**Montebello** (village) Rockland County	98	3,276	**Monsey** (CDP) Rockland County
1	4,000+	**Munsey Park** (village) Nassau County	100	3,273	**East Rockaway** (village) Nassau County
1	4,000+	**Muttontown** (village) Nassau County	101	3,267	**Halesite** (CDP) Suffolk County
1	4,000+	**New Castle** (town) Westchester County	102	3,261	**Elmsford** (village) Westchester County
1	4,000+	**North Castle** (town) Westchester County	103	3,253	**Massapequa** (CDP) Nassau County
1	4,000+	**North Hills** (village) Nassau County	104	3,250	**Herricks** (CDP) Nassau County
1	4,000+	**Old Westbury** (village) Nassau County	104	3,250	**Saint James** (CDP) Suffolk County
1	4,000+	**Pelham** (town) Westchester County	106	3,248	**Bayport** (CDP) Suffolk County
1	4,000+	**Pelham** (village) Westchester County	106	3,248	**Carmel Hamlet** (CDP) Putnam County
1	4,000+	**Pelham Manor** (village) Westchester County	108	3,242	**Stony Brook** (CDP) Suffolk County
1	4,000+	**Pound Ridge** (town) Westchester County	109	3,238	**West Hills** (CDP) Suffolk County
1	4,000+	**Rye** (city) Westchester County	110	3,237	**North Merrick** (CDP) Nassau County
1	4,000+	**Rye Brook** (village) Westchester County	111	3,232	**Pleasantville** (village) Westchester County
1	4,000+	**Sands Point** (village) Nassau County	112	3,222	**Cayuga Heights** (village) Tompkins County
1	4,000+	**Scarsdale** (town/village) Westchester County	113	3,218	**Orangetown** (town) Rockland County
1	4,000+	**Searingtown** (CDP) Nassau County	114	3,215	**South Valley Stream** (CDP) Nassau County
1	4,000+	**Sleepy Hollow** (village) Westchester County	115	3,214	**Miller Place** (CDP) Suffolk County
1	4,000+	**Woodbury** (CDP) Nassau County	116	3,213	**North New Hyde Park** (CDP) Nassau County
42	3,996	**Port Washington** (CDP) Nassau County	117	3,208	**Huntington** (town) Suffolk County
43	3,987	**Manhasset** (CDP) Nassau County	118	3,207	**Ossining** (town) Westchester County
44	3,952	**Great Neck** (village) Nassau County	119	3,202	**Oyster Bay** (town) Nassau County
45	3,947	**Roslyn Heights** (CDP) Nassau County	120	3,192	**Commack** (CDP) Suffolk County
46	3,928	**Viola** (CDP) Rockland County	121	3,183	**Mount Sinai** (CDP) Suffolk County
47	3,907	**Bedford** (town) Westchester County	122	3,179	**Port Chester** (village) Westchester County
48	3,882	**Lido Beach** (CDP) Nassau County	123	3,174	**Floral Park** (village) Nassau County
49	3,802	**Old Bethpage** (CDP) Nassau County	124	3,173	**Lynbrook** (village) Nassau County
50	3,792	**Mount Pleasant** (town) Westchester County	124	3,173	**Seaford** (CDP) Nassau County
51	3,777	**Lewisboro** (town) Westchester County	126	3,170	**Cedarhurst** (village) Nassau County
52	3,753	**Port Washington North** (village) Nassau County	127	3,164	**Smithtown** (CDP) Suffolk County
53	3,733	**Dobbs Ferry** (village) Westchester County	128	3,158	**New City** (CDP) Rockland County
54	3,687	**Ardsley** (village) Westchester County	129	3,154	**Piermont** (village) Rockland County
55	3,677	**Syosset** (CDP) Nassau County	130	3,148	**Babylon** (village) Suffolk County
56	3,671	**Fort Salonga** (CDP) Suffolk County	131	3,146	**White Plains** (city) Westchester County
57	3,651	**Hastings-on-Hudson** (village) Westchester County	132	3,145	**Pearl River** (CDP) Rockland County
58	3,637	**New Rochelle** (city) Westchester County	133	3,142	**Bellmore** (CDP) Nassau County
59	3,631	**Valhalla** (CDP) Westchester County	133	3,142	**Chestnut Ridge** (village) Rockland County
60	3,596	**South Nyack** (village) Rockland County	133	3,142	**Smithtown** (town) Suffolk County
61	3,572	**Rye** (town) Westchester County	136	3,128	**Tuckahoe** (village) Westchester County
62	3,551	**Rockville Centre** (village) Nassau County	137	3,126	**Baldwin Harbor** (CDP) Nassau County
63	3,548	**North Hempstead** (town) Nassau County	138	3,123	**New Hempstead** (village) Rockland County
64	3,542	**Southampton** (village) Suffolk County	139	3,122	**Jefferson Valley-Yorktown** (CDP) Westchester County
65	3,538	**Blauvelt** (CDP) Rockland County	140	3,116	**Noyack** (CDP) Suffolk County
66	3,537	**Greenburgh** (town) Westchester County	141	3,112	**Manhattan** (borough) New York County
67	3,482	**Thomaston** (village) Nassau County	142	3,110	**Orangeburg** (CDP) Rockland County
68	3,473	**Woodmere** (CDP) Nassau County	143	3,098	**Malverne** (village) Nassau County
69	3,469	**Pomona** (village) Rockland County	144	3,095	**Locust Valley** (CDP) Nassau County
70	3,464	**Tarrytown** (village) Westchester County	144	3,095	**Port Jefferson** (village) Suffolk County
71	3,463	**Hewlett** (CDP) Nassau County	146	3,092	**Clarkstown** (town) Rockland County
72	3,461	**Eastchester** (town) Westchester County	147	3,090	**Yorktown** (town) Westchester County
73	3,457	**Wesley Hills** (village) Rockland County	148	3,086	**Oceanside** (CDP) Nassau County
74	3,443	**Melville** (CDP) Suffolk County	149	3,076	**North Massapequa** (CDP) Nassau County
75	3,438	**Garden City Park** (CDP) Nassau County	150	3,074	**Moriches** (CDP) Suffolk County

Note: This section ranks incorporated places and CDPs (Census Designated Places) with populations of 2,500 or more. Unincorporated postal areas were not considered. Please refer to the User Guide for additional information.

Median Selected Monthly Owner Costs: With Mortgage

Top 150 Places Ranked in *Ascending* Order

State Rank	Dollars	Place	State Rank	Dollars	Place
1	810	**Salamanca** (city) Cattaraugus County	76	1,051	**Endicott** (village) Broome County
2	835	**Dunkirk** (city) Chautauqua County	77	1,052	**Malone** (village) Franklin County
3	841	**Wellsville** (village) Allegany County	78	1,053	**Yorkshire** (town) Cattaraugus County
4	850	**Jamestown** (city) Chautauqua County	79	1,055	**Springville** (village) Erie County
5	877	**Westfield** (village) Chautauqua County	79	1,055	**Yorkville** (village) Oneida County
6	883	**Gowanda** (village) Cattaraugus County	81	1,057	**Fulton** (city) Oswego County
7	900	**Southport** (CDP) Chemung County	82	1,061	**Medina** (village) Orleans County
8	908	**Sloan** (village) Erie County	83	1,063	**Gouverneur** (town) Saint Lawrence County
9	915	**Canisteo** (town) Steuben County	84	1,064	**Johnson City** (village) Broome County
10	923	**Hornell** (city) Steuben County	85	1,067	**Nichols** (town) Tioga County
11	928	**Niagara Falls** (city) Niagara County	86	1,068	**Syracuse** (city) Onondaga County
12	932	**Elmira** (city) Chemung County	87	1,069	**Blasdell** (village) Erie County
13	933	**Massena** (village) Saint Lawrence County	88	1,071	**Starkey** (town) Yates County
13	933	**Mooers** (town) Clinton County	88	1,071	**Tupper Lake** (town) Franklin County
15	934	**Massena** (town) Saint Lawrence County	88	1,071	**Warsaw** (village) Wyoming County
16	941	**Saint Regis Mohawk Reservation** (reservation) Franklin County	91	1,073	**Binghamton** (city) Broome County
17	947	**Buffalo** (city) Erie County	92	1,074	**North Syracuse** (village) Onondaga County
18	954	**Wellsville** (town) Allegany County	92	1,074	**Utica** (city) Oneida County
19	959	**Gouverneur** (village) Saint Lawrence County	94	1,076	**Castile** (town) Wyoming County
20	960	**Little Falls** (city) Herkimer County	94	1,076	**Champlain** (town) Clinton County
21	963	**Niagara** (town) Niagara County	94	1,076	**Newark** (village) Wayne County
22	965	**Mohawk** (village) Herkimer County	94	1,076	**Seneca Falls** (CDP) Seneca County
23	967	**Penn Yan** (village) Yates County	98	1,077	**Johnstown** (city) Fulton County
24	971	**Ellicott** (town) Chautauqua County	99	1,078	**Oswego** (city) Oswego County
25	974	**Tupper Lake** (village) Franklin County	100	1,080	**Geneva** (city) Ontario County
25	974	**Westfield** (town) Chautauqua County	100	1,080	**Ridgeway** (town) Orleans County
27	975	**Ilion** (village) Herkimer County	102	1,082	**Batavia** (city) Genesee County
28	976	**Hanover** (town) Chautauqua County	102	1,082	**Brasher** (town) Saint Lawrence County
28	976	**Saint Johnsville** (town) Montgomery County	104	1,085	**Allegany** (town) Cattaraugus County
30	979	**Randolph** (town) Cattaraugus County	104	1,085	**Collins** (town) Erie County
31	981	**Lyons** (village) Wayne County	104	1,085	**New York Mills** (village) Oneida County
31	981	**Silver Creek** (village) Chautauqua County	104	1,085	**Nunda** (town) Livingston County
33	983	**Wayland** (town) Steuben County	104	1,085	**Solvay** (village) Onondaga County
34	985	**Chautauqua** (town) Chautauqua County	109	1,086	**Bath** (town) Steuben County
34	985	**Galen** (town) Wayne County	109	1,086	**Cuba** (town) Allegany County
36	986	**Franklinville** (town) Cattaraugus County	109	1,086	**Frankfort** (village) Herkimer County
36	986	**Mattydale** (CDP) Onondaga County	109	1,086	**Lisbon** (town) Saint Lawrence County
36	986	**Wolcott** (town) Wayne County	109	1,086	**Lockport** (city) Niagara County
39	987	**Oswegatchie** (town) Saint Lawrence County	114	1,087	**Whitesboro** (village) Oneida County
40	989	**Carroll** (town) Chautauqua County	115	1,088	**Champion** (town) Jefferson County
41	990	**Ogdensburg** (city) Saint Lawrence County	115	1,088	**Dansville** (village) Livingston County
42	992	**Gloversville** (city) Fulton County	115	1,088	**Lyncourt** (CDP) Onondaga County
43	993	**Waterloo** (town) Seneca County	115	1,088	**North Dansville** (town) Livingston County
44	994	**Au Sable** (town) Clinton County	119	1,089	**Herkimer** (village) Herkimer County
45	997	**Perry** (village) Wyoming County	120	1,092	**Horseheads** (village) Chemung County
46	1,003	**Lackawanna** (city) Erie County	121	1,094	**Augusta** (town) Oneida County
47	1,011	**Addison** (town) Steuben County	121	1,094	**Gaines** (town) Orleans County
47	1,011	**Altona** (town) Clinton County	123	1,095	**Watertown** (city) Jefferson County
49	1,012	**Boonville** (town) Oneida County	124	1,096	**Camden** (town) Oneida County
50	1,016	**Dolgeville** (village) Herkimer County	125	1,097	**Eaton** (town) Madison County
50	1,016	**Milo** (town) Yates County	126	1,101	**Tonawanda** (city) Erie County
52	1,017	**Keeseville** (village) Clinton County	126	1,101	**Warsaw** (town) Wyoming County
52	1,017	**Village Green** (CDP) Onondaga County	128	1,103	**Norwich** (town) Chenango County
54	1,022	**Stockholm** (town) Saint Lawrence County	129	1,104	**Newfane** (CDP) Niagara County
55	1,024	**Schuyler** (town) Herkimer County	130	1,109	**Somerset** (town) Niagara County
55	1,024	**Southport** (town) Chemung County	131	1,110	**Johnstown** (town) Fulton County
57	1,025	**Norfolk** (town) Saint Lawrence County	132	1,111	**Lisle** (town) Broome County
57	1,025	**Olean** (city) Cattaraugus County	132	1,111	**Manchester** (town) Ontario County
59	1,026	**Romulus** (town) Seneca County	134	1,112	**Cheektowaga** (town) Erie County
60	1,028	**German Flatts** (town) Herkimer County	134	1,112	**Tioga** (town) Tioga County
61	1,031	**Waverly** (village) Tioga County	136	1,114	**Middleburgh** (town) Schoharie County
62	1,032	**Dix** (town) Schuyler County	136	1,114	**Sheridan** (town) Chautauqua County
62	1,032	**Rochester** (city) Monroe County	138	1,116	**Oakfield** (town) Genesee County
64	1,033	**Galeville** (CDP) Onondaga County	139	1,118	**Lakeland** (CDP) Onondaga County
65	1,035	**Elmira Heights** (village) Chemung County	140	1,120	**Cheektowaga** (CDP) Erie County
66	1,036	**Attica** (village) Wyoming County	140	1,120	**Dannemora** (town) Clinton County
66	1,036	**New Berlin** (town) Chenango County	140	1,120	**Walton** (town) Delaware County
68	1,039	**Barton** (town) Tioga County	143	1,121	**Akron** (village) Erie County
69	1,042	**Lyons** (town) Wayne County	144	1,122	**Albion** (village) Orleans County
70	1,044	**Hornellsville** (town) Steuben County	144	1,122	**Candor** (town) Tioga County
71	1,047	**Manheim** (town) Herkimer County	144	1,122	**Lake Erie Beach** (CDP) Erie County
72	1,048	**Bath** (village) Steuben County	144	1,122	**Unadilla** (town) Otsego County
72	1,048	**Perry** (town) Wyoming County	148	1,123	**Marion** (town) Wayne County
72	1,048	**Portland** (town) Chautauqua County	148	1,123	**Mount Morris** (village) Livingston County
75	1,049	**Waterloo** (village) Seneca County	150	1,124	**Sandy Creek** (town) Oswego County

Note: This section ranks incorporated places and CDPs (Census Designated Places) with populations of 2,500 or more. Unincorporated postal areas were not considered. Please refer to the User Guide for additional information.

Median Selected Monthly Owner Costs: Without Mortgage

Top 150 Places Ranked in *Descending* Order

State Rank	Dollars	Place	State Rank	Dollars	Place
1	1,500+	**Ardsley** (village) Westchester County	1	1,500+	**Woodbury** (CDP) Nassau County
1	1,500+	**Armonk** (CDP) Westchester County	1	1,500+	**Woodmere** (CDP) Nassau County
1	1,500+	**Bedford** (town) Westchester County	78	1,499	**Pomona** (village) Rockland County
1	1,500+	**Briarcliff Manor** (village) Westchester County	79	1,492	**Piermont** (village) Rockland County
1	1,500+	**Brightwaters** (village) Suffolk County	80	1,483	**Blauvelt** (CDP) Rockland County
1	1,500+	**Bronxville** (village) Westchester County	81	1,481	**Mamaroneck** (village) Westchester County
1	1,500+	**Brookville** (village) Nassau County	82	1,475	**North Salem** (town) Westchester County
1	1,500+	**Cold Spring Harbor** (CDP) Suffolk County	83	1,466	**Baldwin Harbor** (CDP) Nassau County
1	1,500+	**Dix Hills** (CDP) Suffolk County	83	1,466	**Croton-on-Hudson** (village) Westchester County
1	1,500+	**Dobbs Ferry** (village) Westchester County	85	1,463	**Setauket-East Setauket** (CDP) Suffolk County
1	1,500+	**East Hills** (village) Nassau County	86	1,461	**Plainview** (CDP) Nassau County
1	1,500+	**East Williston** (village) Nassau County	87	1,455	**Valhalla** (CDP) Westchester County
1	1,500+	**Eastchester** (CDP) Westchester County	88	1,451	**Elwood** (CDP) Suffolk County
1	1,500+	**Eastchester** (town) Westchester County	89	1,449	**Glenwood Landing** (CDP) Nassau County
1	1,500+	**Flower Hill** (village) Nassau County	89	1,449	**West Hills** (CDP) Suffolk County
1	1,500+	**Fort Salonga** (CDP) Suffolk County	91	1,443	**Nesconset** (CDP) Suffolk County
1	1,500+	**Garden City** (village) Nassau County	92	1,439	**Airmont** (village) Rockland County
1	1,500+	**Great Neck** (village) Nassau County	93	1,437	**Stony Brook** (CDP) Suffolk County
1	1,500+	**Great Neck Estates** (village) Nassau County	94	1,433	**Lakeview** (CDP) Nassau County
1	1,500+	**Greenburgh** (town) Westchester County	95	1,429	**Sea Cliff** (village) Nassau County
1	1,500+	**Greenville** (CDP) Westchester County	96	1,426	**Bardonia** (CDP) Rockland County
1	1,500+	**Harrison** (town/village) Westchester County	97	1,422	**New City** (CDP) Rockland County
1	1,500+	**Hastings-on-Hudson** (village) Westchester County	98	1,411	**Irvington** (village) Westchester County
1	1,500+	**Herricks** (CDP) Nassau County	99	1,405	**Babylon** (village) Suffolk County
1	1,500+	**Huntington** (CDP) Suffolk County	99	1,405	**Centerport** (CDP) Suffolk County
1	1,500+	**Jericho** (CDP) Nassau County	101	1,404	**Congers** (CDP) Rockland County
1	1,500+	**Kings Point** (village) Nassau County	102	1,402	**Amityville** (village) Suffolk County
1	1,500+	**Lake Success** (village) Nassau County	103	1,400	**East Shoreham** (CDP) Suffolk County
1	1,500+	**Larchmont** (village) Westchester County	104	1,396	**Rye** (town) Westchester County
1	1,500+	**Lawrence** (village) Nassau County	105	1,387	**Floral Park** (village) Nassau County
1	1,500+	**Lewisboro** (town) Westchester County	106	1,384	**Huntington** (town) Suffolk County
1	1,500+	**Lido Beach** (CDP) Nassau County	107	1,379	**Tuxedo** (town) Orange County
1	1,500+	**Lloyd Harbor** (village) Suffolk County	108	1,377	**Massapequa** (CDP) Nassau County
1	1,500+	**Mamaroneck** (town) Westchester County	108	1,377	**Oakdale** (CDP) Suffolk County
1	1,500+	**Manhasset** (CDP) Nassau County	110	1,374	**Nyack** (village) Rockland County
1	1,500+	**Manhasset Hills** (CDP) Nassau County	111	1,373	**West Islip** (CDP) Suffolk County
1	1,500+	**Merrick** (CDP) Nassau County	112	1,372	**Bayport** (CDP) Suffolk County
1	1,500+	**Monsey** (CDP) Rockland County	113	1,367	**South Hempstead** (CDP) Nassau County
1	1,500+	**Montebello** (village) Rockland County	114	1,366	**Miller Place** (CDP) Suffolk County
1	1,500+	**Mount Pleasant** (town) Westchester County	115	1,364	**University Gardens** (CDP) Nassau County
1	1,500+	**Munsey Park** (village) Nassau County	116	1,362	**Tappan** (CDP) Rockland County
1	1,500+	**Muttontown** (village) Nassau County	117	1,357	**Clarkstown** (town) Rockland County
1	1,500+	**New Castle** (town) Westchester County	118	1,356	**East Moriches** (CDP) Suffolk County
1	1,500+	**New Hempstead** (village) Rockland County	119	1,348	**Hawthorne** (CDP) Westchester County
1	1,500+	**New Rochelle** (city) Westchester County	119	1,348	**Westbury** (village) Nassau County
1	1,500+	**North Castle** (town) Westchester County	121	1,347	**Mount Sinai** (CDP) Suffolk County
1	1,500+	**North Hempstead** (town) Nassau County	122	1,343	**North Merrick** (CDP) Nassau County
1	1,500+	**North Hills** (village) Nassau County	123	1,342	**Cortlandt** (town) Westchester County
1	1,500+	**Old Bethpage** (CDP) Nassau County	124	1,341	**Malverne** (village) Nassau County
1	1,500+	**Old Westbury** (village) Nassau County	125	1,338	**Roslyn** (village) Nassau County
1	1,500+	**Ossining** (town) Westchester County	125	1,338	**Thiells** (CDP) Rockland County
1	1,500+	**Pelham** (town) Westchester County	127	1,337	**Wantagh** (CDP) Nassau County
1	1,500+	**Pelham** (village) Westchester County	128	1,335	**Smithtown** (CDP) Suffolk County
1	1,500+	**Pelham Manor** (village) Westchester County	129	1,334	**Hewlett** (CDP) Nassau County
1	1,500+	**Pleasantville** (village) Westchester County	130	1,332	**Commack** (CDP) Suffolk County
1	1,500+	**Port Washington** (CDP) Nassau County	131	1,331	**Halesite** (CDP) Suffolk County
1	1,500+	**Port Washington North** (village) Nassau County	131	1,331	**Ramapo** (town) Rockland County
1	1,500+	**Pound Ridge** (town) Westchester County	133	1,329	**Bellmore** (CDP) Nassau County
1	1,500+	**Rockville Centre** (village) Nassau County	134	1,328	**Thornwood** (CDP) Westchester County
1	1,500+	**Roslyn Heights** (CDP) Nassau County	135	1,326	**Center Moriches** (CDP) Suffolk County
1	1,500+	**Rye** (city) Westchester County	135	1,326	**Ossining** (village) Westchester County
1	1,500+	**Rye Brook** (village) Westchester County	137	1,324	**White Plains** (city) Westchester County
1	1,500+	**Sands Point** (village) Nassau County	138	1,322	**North Bellmore** (CDP) Nassau County
1	1,500+	**Scarsdale** (town/village) Westchester County	139	1,321	**East Massapequa** (CDP) Nassau County
1	1,500+	**Searingtown** (CDP) Nassau County	140	1,317	**Elmsford** (village) Westchester County
1	1,500+	**Sleepy Hollow** (village) Westchester County	141	1,316	**Glen Cove** (city) Nassau County
1	1,500+	**South Nyack** (village) Rockland County	142	1,313	**North Great River** (CDP) Suffolk County
1	1,500+	**South Valley Stream** (CDP) Nassau County	143	1,311	**North Wantagh** (CDP) Nassau County
1	1,500+	**Syosset** (CDP) Nassau County	143	1,311	**Oyster Bay** (town) Nassau County
1	1,500+	**Tarrytown** (village) Westchester County	145	1,310	**Brookhaven** (CDP) Suffolk County
1	1,500+	**Thomaston** (village) Nassau County	146	1,308	**Moriches** (CDP) Suffolk County
1	1,500+	**Tuckahoe** (village) Westchester County	146	1,308	**Sloatsburg** (village) Rockland County
1	1,500+	**Viola** (CDP) Rockland County	148	1,304	**West Nyack** (CDP) Rockland County
1	1,500+	**Wesley Hills** (village) Rockland County	149	1,302	**Northwest Harbor** (CDP) Suffolk County
1	1,500+	**West Bay Shore** (CDP) Suffolk County	150	1,299	**Smithtown** (town) Suffolk County

Note: This section ranks incorporated places and CDPs (Census Designated Places) with populations of 2,500 or more. Unincorporated postal areas were not considered. Please refer to the User Guide for additional information.

Median Selected Monthly Owner Costs: Without Mortgage

Top 150 Places Ranked in *Ascending* Order

State Rank	Dollars	Place	State Rank	Dollars	Place
1	251	**Saint Regis Mohawk Reservation** (reservation) Franklin County	76	444	**Granby** (town) Oswego County
2	284	**Calcium** (CDP) Jefferson County	77	445	**Horseheads** (village) Chemung County
3	333	**Salamanca** (city) Cattaraugus County	78	446	**Dannemora** (town) Clinton County
4	348	**Au Sable** (town) Clinton County	79	447	**Champion** (town) Jefferson County
5	351	**Altona** (town) Clinton County	79	447	**Ellery** (town) Chautauqua County
6	362	**Keeseville** (village) Clinton County	79	447	**Massena** (town) Saint Lawrence County
7	363	**Hartsdale** (CDP) Westchester County	82	448	**Orleans** (town) Jefferson County
8	366	**Mohawk** (village) Herkimer County	83	449	**Oneonta** (town) Otsego County
9	375	**Mattydale** (CDP) Onondaga County	84	450	**Ilion** (village) Herkimer County
10	378	**Buffalo** (city) Erie County	84	450	**Portland** (town) Chautauqua County
11	381	**Sloan** (village) Erie County	86	453	**Beekmantown** (town) Clinton County
11	381	**Yorkshire** (town) Cattaraugus County	86	453	**Colesville** (town) Broome County
13	382	**Arcade** (town) Wyoming County	86	453	**Oswegatchie** (town) Saint Lawrence County
14	384	**Norwich** (town) Chenango County	86	453	**Oxford** (town) Chenango County
15	389	**Hornell** (city) Steuben County	86	453	**Starkey** (town) Yates County
16	395	**Gowanda** (village) Cattaraugus County	91	454	**Lyons** (village) Wayne County
16	395	**Jamestown** (city) Chautauqua County	92	455	**Batavia** (city) Genesee County
18	396	**Moira** (town) Franklin County	92	455	**Le Roy** (village) Genesee County
19	397	**Canisteo** (town) Steuben County	94	456	**Castile** (town) Wyoming County
20	398	**Lisbon** (town) Saint Lawrence County	95	457	**Watertown** (city) Jefferson County
20	398	**Sidney** (town) Delaware County	96	458	**Annsville** (town) Oneida County
22	400	**Hannibal** (town) Oswego County	96	458	**Campbell** (town) Steuben County
23	403	**New York Mills** (village) Oneida County	98	459	**Dix** (town) Schuyler County
24	409	**North Dansville** (town) Livingston County	98	459	**Hancock** (town) Delaware County
24	409	**Unadilla** (town) Otsego County	98	459	**New Bremen** (town) Lewis County
26	412	**Sherburne** (town) Chenango County	101	460	**Randolph** (town) Cattaraugus County
27	413	**Blasdell** (village) Erie County	101	460	**Theresa** (town) Jefferson County
27	413	**Le Ray** (town) Jefferson County	103	462	**Newfield** (town) Tompkins County
29	414	**German Flatts** (town) Herkimer County	103	462	**Sherrill** (city) Oneida County
29	414	**Pavilion** (town) Genesee County	105	463	**Barton** (town) Tioga County
31	415	**Westfield** (town) Chautauqua County	105	463	**Hudson Falls** (village) Washington County
32	416	**Collins** (town) Erie County	105	463	**Lisle** (town) Broome County
32	416	**Lyncourt** (CDP) Onondaga County	105	463	**Verona** (town) Oneida County
34	417	**Galeville** (CDP) Onondaga County	109	464	**Attica** (village) Wyoming County
34	417	**Wellsville** (town) Allegany County	109	464	**Bath** (village) Steuben County
34	417	**Westfield** (village) Chautauqua County	111	465	**New Haven** (town) Oswego County
37	418	**Manheim** (town) Herkimer County	112	466	**Chesterfield** (town) Essex County
38	419	**Nichols** (town) Tioga County	112	466	**Dannemora** (village) Clinton County
38	419	**Southport** (CDP) Chemung County	112	466	**Kingsbury** (town) Washington County
40	420	**Boonville** (town) Oneida County	112	466	**Little Falls** (city) Herkimer County
41	421	**Chautauqua** (town) Chautauqua County	112	466	**Oneonta** (city) Otsego County
41	421	**Johnstown** (town) Fulton County	117	467	**Fenton** (town) Broome County
41	421	**Romulus** (town) Seneca County	117	467	**Gaines** (town) Orleans County
44	422	**Cape Vincent** (town) Jefferson County	117	467	**Rochester** (city) Monroe County
45	423	**Dansville** (village) Livingston County	117	467	**Sardinia** (town) Erie County
45	423	**Fort Edward** (village) Washington County	117	467	**Tonawanda** (city) Erie County
45	423	**Pamelia** (town) Jefferson County	122	468	**Lee** (town) Oneida County
45	423	**Vernon** (town) Oneida County	122	468	**Madison** (town) Madison County
49	426	**Dunkirk** (city) Chautauqua County	122	468	**Niagara** (town) Niagara County
49	426	**Windsor** (town) Broome County	122	468	**Northumberland** (town) Saratoga County
51	427	**East Syracuse** (village) Onondaga County	126	469	**Corinth** (village) Saratoga County
51	427	**Elmira** (city) Chemung County	126	469	**Kirkwood** (town) Broome County
51	427	**Norfolk** (town) Saint Lawrence County	126	469	**Lakewood** (village) Chautauqua County
51	427	**Stockholm** (town) Saint Lawrence County	129	470	**Brownville** (town) Jefferson County
55	428	**Akron** (village) Erie County	129	470	**Massena** (village) Saint Lawrence County
55	428	**Camden** (town) Oneida County	129	470	**Palermo** (town) Oswego County
55	428	**Croghan** (town) Lewis County	129	470	**Plattsburgh** (town) Clinton County
55	428	**Frankfort** (village) Herkimer County	129	470	**Tupper Lake** (town) Franklin County
55	428	**Mooers** (town) Clinton County	134	471	**Attica** (town) Wyoming County
60	429	**Southport** (town) Chemung County	134	471	**Guilford** (town) Chenango County
61	433	**Ellicott** (town) Chautauqua County	134	471	**Horseheads** (town) Chemung County
62	435	**Wellsville** (village) Allegany County	134	471	**Laurens** (town) Otsego County
63	436	**Dickinson** (town) Broome County	134	471	**Newfane** (CDP) Niagara County
63	436	**Lackawanna** (city) Erie County	134	471	**Penn Yan** (village) Yates County
63	436	**Niagara Falls** (city) Niagara County	134	471	**Tioga** (town) Tioga County
63	436	**Portville** (town) Cattaraugus County	141	472	**New Baltimore** (town) Greene County
63	436	**Sandy Creek** (town) Oswego County	141	472	**Solvay** (village) Onondaga County
68	437	**Mohawk** (town) Montgomery County	143	473	**Hanover** (town) Chautauqua County
68	437	**Wolcott** (town) Wayne County	143	473	**Jay** (town) Essex County
70	438	**Gouverneur** (town) Saint Lawrence County	143	473	**Lowville** (town) Lewis County
71	440	**Brasher** (town) Saint Lawrence County	143	473	**Seneca Falls** (CDP) Seneca County
71	440	**Chazy** (town) Clinton County	147	474	**Gouverneur** (village) Saint Lawrence County
73	442	**Adams** (town) Jefferson County	148	475	**Alexandria** (town) Jefferson County
73	442	**Tupper Lake** (village) Franklin County	148	475	**Nunda** (town) Livingston County
75	443	**Village Green** (CDP) Onondaga County	148	475	**Olean** (city) Cattaraugus County

Note: *This section ranks incorporated places and CDPs (Census Designated Places) with populations of 2,500 or more. Unincorporated postal areas were not considered. Please refer to the User Guide for additional information.*

Median Gross Rent

Top 150 Places Ranked in *Descending* Order

State Rank	Dollars	Place
1	3,500+	**Armonk** (CDP) Westchester County
1	3,500+	**East Williston** (village) Nassau County
1	3,500+	**Great Neck Estates** (village) Nassau County
1	3,500+	**Lake Success** (village) Nassau County
5	3,442	**Pound Ridge** (town) Westchester County
6	3,250	**Herricks** (CDP) Nassau County
7	3,224	**Sands Point** (village) Nassau County
8	3,159	**Brookville** (village) Nassau County
9	3,113	**West Point** (CDP) Orange County
10	3,087	**Scarsdale** (town/village) Westchester County
11	3,009	**Baldwin Harbor** (CDP) Nassau County
12	2,889	**Cold Spring Harbor** (CDP) Suffolk County
13	2,862	**Lido Beach** (CDP) Nassau County
14	2,762	**Syosset** (CDP) Nassau County
15	2,745	**Bronxville** (village) Westchester County
16	2,677	**Garden City** (village) Nassau County
17	2,639	**West Hills** (CDP) Suffolk County
18	2,621	**Lakeview** (CDP) Nassau County
19	2,617	**Albertson** (CDP) Nassau County
20	2,515	**East Shoreham** (CDP) Suffolk County
21	2,497	**Stony Brook** (CDP) Suffolk County
22	2,368	**East Norwich** (CDP) Nassau County
23	2,367	**Woodbury** (CDP) Nassau County
24	2,341	**Heritage Hills** (CDP) Westchester County
25	2,306	**North Merrick** (CDP) Nassau County
26	2,271	**Roslyn** (village) Nassau County
27	2,265	**Manorhaven** (village) Nassau County
28	2,262	**Pomona** (village) Rockland County
29	2,245	**Massapequa Park** (village) Nassau County
30	2,227	**Tappan** (CDP) Rockland County
31	2,223	**Pelham Manor** (village) Westchester County
32	2,161	**Spackenkill** (CDP) Dutchess County
33	2,144	**Terryville** (CDP) Suffolk County
34	2,142	**Elwood** (CDP) Suffolk County
35	2,140	**Yaphank** (CDP) Suffolk County
36	2,138	**Harrison** (town/village) Westchester County
37	2,137	**Rye** (city) Westchester County
38	2,127	**Flanders** (CDP) Suffolk County
39	2,125	**South Farmingdale** (CDP) Nassau County
40	2,122	**Noyack** (CDP) Suffolk County
41	2,097	**Lake Mohegan** (CDP) Westchester County
42	2,092	**Shelter Island** (town) Suffolk County
43	2,087	**Merrick** (CDP) Nassau County
44	2,079	**Melville** (CDP) Suffolk County
45	2,067	**North Bellport** (CDP) Suffolk County
46	2,065	**Massapequa** (CDP) Nassau County
47	2,050	**Springs** (CDP) Suffolk County
48	2,048	**Montauk** (CDP) Suffolk County
49	2,038	**Westhampton** (CDP) Suffolk County
50	2,034	**North Castle** (town) Westchester County
51	2,032	**Shirley** (CDP) Suffolk County
52	2,012	**Glen Head** (CDP) Nassau County
53	2,011	**Somers** (town) Westchester County
54	1,995	**Halesite** (CDP) Suffolk County
55	1,988	**Thomaston** (village) Nassau County
56	1,979	**Lewisboro** (town) Westchester County
57	1,978	**New Castle** (town) Westchester County
58	1,972	**Hauppauge** (CDP) Suffolk County
59	1,963	**New Hempstead** (village) Rockland County
60	1,954	**Sea Cliff** (village) Nassau County
61	1,950	**Seaford** (CDP) Nassau County
62	1,946	**East Rockaway** (village) Nassau County
63	1,945	**Plainedge** (CDP) Nassau County
64	1,944	**Levittown** (CDP) Nassau County
65	1,938	**West Bay Shore** (CDP) Suffolk County
66	1,935	**Jericho** (CDP) Nassau County
67	1,934	**North Sea** (CDP) Suffolk County
68	1,933	**North New Hyde Park** (CDP) Nassau County
69	1,925	**Thiells** (CDP) Rockland County
70	1,922	**Larchmont** (village) Westchester County
71	1,921	**East Meadow** (CDP) Nassau County
72	1,916	**Dix Hills** (CDP) Suffolk County
73	1,913	**Myers Corner** (CDP) Dutchess County
74	1,908	**Port Washington North** (village) Nassau County
75	1,900	**Nesconset** (CDP) Suffolk County
76	1,896	**Valhalla** (CDP) Westchester County
77	1,893	**Huntington** (CDP) Suffolk County
78	1,891	**Centereach** (CDP) Suffolk County
79	1,890	**Holbrook** (CDP) Suffolk County
80	1,885	**Setauket-East Setauket** (CDP) Suffolk County
81	1,875	**Dobbs Ferry** (village) Westchester County
82	1,865	**Nanuet** (CDP) Rockland County
83	1,864	**North Babylon** (CDP) Suffolk County
84	1,860	**East Quogue** (CDP) Suffolk County
85	1,856	**Calverton** (CDP) Suffolk County
85	1,856	**Oyster Bay** (town) Nassau County
87	1,855	**Hastings-on-Hudson** (village) Westchester County
88	1,854	**Islandia** (village) Suffolk County
89	1,850	**East Northport** (CDP) Suffolk County
89	1,850	**South Hempstead** (CDP) Nassau County
91	1,849	**North Great River** (CDP) Suffolk County
92	1,845	**Bellmore** (CDP) Nassau County
93	1,843	**Cedarhurst** (village) Nassau County
94	1,842	**Centerport** (CDP) Suffolk County
95	1,841	**Oyster Bay** (CDP) Nassau County
96	1,839	**Coram** (CDP) Suffolk County
96	1,839	**Great Neck Plaza** (village) Nassau County
98	1,820	**Hicksville** (CDP) Nassau County
98	1,820	**Mamaroneck** (village) Westchester County
100	1,819	**Locust Valley** (CDP) Nassau County
101	1,816	**Bethpage** (CDP) Nassau County
102	1,814	**South Huntington** (CDP) Suffolk County
102	1,814	**West Hempstead** (CDP) Nassau County
104	1,813	**Thornwood** (CDP) Westchester County
105	1,812	**Pelham** (town) Westchester County
106	1,808	**Port Washington** (CDP) Nassau County
107	1,806	**Long Beach** (city) Nassau County
108	1,805	**Babylon** (village) Suffolk County
108	1,805	**Westbury** (village) Nassau County
110	1,799	**North Massapequa** (CDP) Nassau County
111	1,791	**Woodmere** (CDP) Nassau County
112	1,788	**Eastchester** (town) Westchester County
113	1,787	**Mastic Beach** (village) Suffolk County
114	1,779	**Medford** (CDP) Suffolk County
114	1,779	**Southampton** (town) Suffolk County
116	1,777	**East Hampton** (town) Suffolk County
116	1,777	**Fort Salonga** (CDP) Suffolk County
118	1,775	**Eastchester** (CDP) Westchester County
119	1,772	**East Islip** (CDP) Suffolk County
120	1,768	**Great Neck** (village) Nassau County
121	1,767	**Huntington** (town) Suffolk County
122	1,766	**Lake Grove** (village) Suffolk County
122	1,766	**North Hempstead** (town) Nassau County
122	1,766	**Roosevelt** (CDP) Nassau County
125	1,762	**Sayville** (CDP) Suffolk County
126	1,759	**Mamaroneck** (town) Westchester County
127	1,756	**Wantagh** (CDP) Nassau County
128	1,755	**East Moriches** (CDP) Suffolk County
129	1,750	**Farmingville** (CDP) Suffolk County
130	1,744	**Greenville** (CDP) Westchester County
131	1,743	**Lynbrook** (village) Nassau County
131	1,743	**Pelham** (village) Westchester County
133	1,742	**Glen Cove** (city) Nassau County
134	1,739	**Orange Lake** (CDP) Orange County
135	1,738	**North Valley Stream** (CDP) Nassau County
136	1,735	**Hartsdale** (CDP) Westchester County
137	1,725	**Carle Place** (CDP) Nassau County
138	1,723	**Williston Park** (village) Nassau County
139	1,722	**Tuckahoe** (village) Westchester County
140	1,721	**Greenburgh** (town) Westchester County
141	1,718	**Southampton** (village) Suffolk County
142	1,717	**Munsey Park** (village) Nassau County
143	1,715	**Montebello** (village) Rockland County
144	1,713	**Garden City Park** (CDP) Nassau County
145	1,711	**Riverside** (CDP) Suffolk County
146	1,709	**Moriches** (CDP) Suffolk County
147	1,705	**Hampton Bays** (CDP) Suffolk County
148	1,703	**Huntington Station** (CDP) Suffolk County
148	1,703	**North Bay Shore** (CDP) Suffolk County
150	1,701	**Gordon Heights** (CDP) Suffolk County

Note: *This section ranks incorporated places and CDPs (Census Designated Places) with populations of 2,500 or more. Unincorporated postal areas were not considered. Please refer to the User Guide for additional information.*

Median Gross Rent

Top 150 Places Ranked in *Ascending* Order

State Rank	Dollars	Place
1	446	**Saint Regis Mohawk Reservation** (reservation) Franklin County
2	491	**Madison** (town) Madison County
3	493	**Portville** (town) Cattaraugus County
4	499	**Warsaw** (village) Wyoming County
5	530	**Clarence** (CDP) Erie County
6	537	**Holland** (town) Erie County
7	539	**Warsaw** (town) Wyoming County
8	544	**Guilford** (town) Chenango County
9	547	**Mohawk** (village) Herkimer County
10	554	**Boonville** (town) Oneida County
10	554	**Lockport** (town) Niagara County
12	558	**Palatine** (town) Montgomery County
12	558	**Randolph** (town) Cattaraugus County
14	563	**Chautauqua** (town) Chautauqua County
14	563	**Mooers** (town) Clinton County
16	564	**Afton** (town) Chenango County
17	565	**Cuba** (town) Allegany County
18	568	**Nunda** (town) Livingston County
19	574	**Eden** (CDP) Erie County
20	579	**Manheim** (town) Herkimer County
21	582	**Greene** (town) Chenango County
22	583	**Collins** (town) Erie County
22	583	**South Lockport** (CDP) Niagara County
24	584	**Addison** (town) Steuben County
25	586	**Canisteo** (town) Steuben County
26	592	**Little Falls** (city) Herkimer County
27	593	**Jamestown** (city) Chautauqua County
27	593	**Veteran** (town) Chemung County
29	594	**Hartland** (town) Niagara County
30	596	**Conklin** (town) Broome County
30	596	**Frankfort** (village) Herkimer County
32	597	**Bath** (village) Steuben County
33	602	**Ogdensburg** (city) Saint Lawrence County
34	605	**Concord** (town) Erie County
34	605	**Wolcott** (town) Wayne County
36	606	**Floyd** (town) Oneida County
37	611	**Portland** (town) Chautauqua County
37	611	**Wellsville** (village) Allegany County
39	612	**Gowanda** (village) Cattaraugus County
39	612	**Springville** (village) Erie County
41	614	**Wheatfield** (town) Niagara County
42	615	**Bath** (town) Steuben County
43	616	**Hornell** (city) Steuben County
44	617	**Franklinville** (town) Cattaraugus County
45	618	**Bennington** (town) Wyoming County
46	620	**Murray** (town) Orleans County
46	620	**Salamanca** (city) Cattaraugus County
46	620	**Tupper Lake** (village) Franklin County
49	621	**Brownville** (town) Jefferson County
49	621	**Croghan** (town) Lewis County
49	621	**Lackawanna** (city) Erie County
52	622	**German Flatts** (town) Herkimer County
52	622	**Wellsville** (town) Allegany County
54	623	**Arcade** (town) Wyoming County
54	623	**Olean** (city) Cattaraugus County
56	624	**Batavia** (town) Genesee County
56	624	**North Collins** (town) Erie County
58	625	**Dolgeville** (village) Herkimer County
59	626	**Colden** (town) Erie County
59	626	**Oswegatchie** (town) Saint Lawrence County
61	627	**Dix** (town) Schuyler County
61	627	**Hornellsville** (town) Steuben County
61	627	**Moravia** (town) Cayuga County
64	628	**Sherburne** (town) Chenango County
65	629	**Camden** (town) Oneida County
65	629	**Ilion** (village) Herkimer County
67	631	**Norwich** (town) Chenango County
68	632	**Windsor** (town) Broome County
69	633	**Cape Vincent** (town) Jefferson County
70	634	**Ellicott** (town) Chautauqua County
71	635	**Akron** (village) Erie County
72	636	**Gorham** (town) Ontario County
72	636	**Sloan** (village) Erie County
74	638	**Sangerfield** (town) Oneida County
75	639	**Lowville** (village) Lewis County
75	639	**Nichols** (town) Tioga County
77	640	**Dunkirk** (city) Chautauqua County
77	640	**Endwell** (CDP) Broome County
77	640	**Owego** (village) Tioga County
77	640	**Pavilion** (town) Genesee County
81	641	**Castile** (town) Wyoming County
81	641	**Yorkshire** (town) Cattaraugus County
83	644	**Hancock** (town) Delaware County
83	644	**Saint Johnsville** (town) Montgomery County
85	645	**Fredonia** (village) Chautauqua County
85	645	**Niagara Falls** (city) Niagara County
87	646	**Albion** (village) Orleans County
87	646	**Au Sable** (town) Clinton County
87	646	**Gouverneur** (village) Saint Lawrence County
87	646	**Newfane** (CDP) Niagara County
91	647	**Lowville** (town) Lewis County
92	648	**Norwich** (city) Chenango County
92	648	**Russia** (town) Herkimer County
92	648	**Whitesboro** (village) Oneida County
95	649	**Elbridge** (town) Onondaga County
95	649	**Lancaster** (village) Erie County
95	649	**Waterloo** (village) Seneca County
98	650	**Westfield** (town) Chautauqua County
99	651	**Medina** (village) Orleans County
99	651	**Mount Morris** (village) Livingston County
99	651	**Starkey** (town) Yates County
102	652	**Tupper Lake** (town) Franklin County
103	653	**Marilla** (town) Erie County
104	656	**Minden** (town) Montgomery County
104	656	**Wayland** (town) Steuben County
106	658	**Allegany** (town) Cattaraugus County
106	658	**Malone** (town) Franklin County
106	658	**Triangle** (town) Broome County
109	662	**Newark Valley** (town) Tioga County
110	664	**Attica** (town) Wyoming County
111	665	**Elmira Heights** (village) Chemung County
111	665	**Owego** (town) Tioga County
113	666	**Attica** (village) Wyoming County
113	666	**Barton** (town) Tioga County
113	666	**North Tonawanda** (city) Niagara County
116	667	**Ridgeway** (town) Orleans County
117	668	**Mexico** (town) Oswego County
118	669	**Moriah** (town) Essex County
118	669	**Sherrill** (city) Oneida County
118	669	**Vernon** (town) Oneida County
121	671	**Ellery** (town) Chautauqua County
122	672	**Busti** (town) Chautauqua County
122	672	**Dansville** (village) Livingston County
122	672	**Sandy Creek** (town) Oswego County
125	673	**Albion** (town) Orleans County
125	673	**Champlain** (town) Clinton County
127	674	**Frankfort** (town) Herkimer County
127	674	**Malone** (village) Franklin County
127	674	**Oxford** (town) Chenango County
127	674	**Sidney** (village) Delaware County
131	675	**North Dansville** (town) Livingston County
131	675	**Sidney** (town) Delaware County
133	676	**Canastota** (village) Madison County
134	677	**Colesville** (town) Broome County
134	677	**Le Roy** (village) Genesee County
136	679	**Eaton** (town) Madison County
137	680	**Lakewood** (village) Chautauqua County
138	682	**New Berlin** (town) Chenango County
139	684	**Avon** (village) Livingston County
139	684	**Greenlawn** (CDP) Suffolk County
139	684	**Solvay** (village) Onondaga County
139	684	**Westfield** (village) Chautauqua County
143	686	**Endicott** (village) Broome County
144	687	**Chittenango** (village) Madison County
145	688	**Trenton** (town) Oneida County
146	689	**Maine** (town) Broome County
146	689	**Manchester** (town) Ontario County
146	689	**Oneida** (city) Madison County
146	689	**Utica** (city) Oneida County
146	689	**Williamson** (town) Wayne County

Note: This section ranks incorporated places and CDPs (Census Designated Places) with populations of 2,500 or more. Unincorporated postal areas were not considered. Please refer to the User Guide for additional information.

Rental Vacancy Rate

Top 150 Places Ranked in *Descending* Order

State Rank	Percent	Place
1	49.7	**Montauk** (CDP) Suffolk County
2	41.5	**Kings Point** (village) Nassau County
3	35.4	**Muttontown** (village) Nassau County
4	28.6	**West Bloomfield** (town) Ontario County
5	26.9	**Otego** (town) Otsego County
6	25.6	**Wilson** (town) Niagara County
7	25.3	**Pierrepont** (town) Saint Lawrence County
8	24.7	**West Sand Lake** (CDP) Rensselaer County
9	24.1	**East Norwich** (CDP) Nassau County
10	23.7	**Marilla** (town) Erie County
10	23.7	**Myers Corner** (CDP) Dutchess County
12	23.4	**Thornwood** (CDP) Westchester County
13	23.0	**South Lockport** (CDP) Niagara County
14	22.6	**Sennett** (town) Cayuga County
15	21.4	**Perth** (town) Fulton County
16	21.1	**Lockport** (town) Niagara County
16	21.1	**Sandy Creek** (town) Oswego County
18	21.0	**Shandaken** (town) Ulster County
19	20.7	**Setauket-East Setauket** (CDP) Suffolk County
20	20.5	**Hartland** (town) Niagara County
20	20.5	**Newfane** (town) Niagara County
22	20.2	**Catskill** (village) Greene County
23	19.9	**Chesterfield** (town) Essex County
24	19.7	**Nesconset** (CDP) Suffolk County
25	19.4	**Pompey** (town) Onondaga County
26	19.3	**Eaton** (town) Madison County
27	19.1	**Lockport** (city) Niagara County
28	19.0	**Galen** (town) Wayne County
29	18.9	**Northport** (village) Suffolk County
30	18.8	**Pendleton** (town) Niagara County
31	18.7	**Rocky Point** (CDP) Suffolk County
32	18.6	**Mamakating** (town) Sullivan County
32	18.6	**Tappan** (CDP) Rockland County
34	18.4	**Minden** (town) Montgomery County
35	18.3	**Wading River** (CDP) Suffolk County
36	18.1	**Richmond** (town) Ontario County
37	17.8	**Niagara Falls** (city) Niagara County
38	17.6	**Durham** (town) Greene County
38	17.6	**Lloyd Harbor** (village) Suffolk County
40	17.4	**Benton** (town) Yates County
41	17.2	**Lakeview** (CDP) Nassau County
42	17.0	**Catskill** (town) Greene County
43	16.9	**Warrensburg** (CDP) Warren County
44	16.8	**Chester** (town) Warren County
44	16.8	**Enfield** (town) Tompkins County
46	16.3	**Warrensburg** (town) Warren County
47	16.2	**Royalton** (town) Niagara County
48	16.0	**Chenango Bridge** (CDP) Broome County
49	15.9	**Barker** (town) Broome County
50	15.8	**Fallsburg** (town) Sullivan County
51	15.7	**Berne** (town) Albany County
51	15.7	**Hector** (town) Schuyler County
51	15.7	**Mattituck** (CDP) Suffolk County
51	15.7	**Southold** (CDP) Suffolk County
55	15.6	**Alfred** (town) Allegany County
56	15.5	**Dix Hills** (CDP) Suffolk County
57	15.4	**Carle Place** (CDP) Nassau County
58	15.1	**Clayton** (town) Jefferson County
59	14.8	**Bethpage** (CDP) Nassau County
60	14.6	**Nassau** (town) Rensselaer County
60	14.6	**New Haven** (town) Oswego County
62	14.5	**East Hampton** (town) Suffolk County
63	14.4	**Chenango** (town) Broome County
63	14.4	**Rockland** (town) Sullivan County
65	14.3	**Sound Beach** (CDP) Suffolk County
66	14.2	**Keeseville** (village) Clinton County
66	14.2	**Southport** (CDP) Chemung County
68	14.0	**Southold** (town) Suffolk County
68	14.0	**Southport** (town) Chemung County
70	13.9	**Newfane** (CDP) Niagara County
70	13.9	**Plainedge** (CDP) Nassau County
72	13.7	**Dix** (town) Schuyler County
72	13.7	**Stony Point** (CDP) Rockland County
72	13.7	**Unadilla** (town) Otsego County
75	13.6	**East Islip** (CDP) Suffolk County
75	13.6	**Ghent** (town) Columbia County
75	13.6	**Highland** (CDP) Ulster County
75	13.6	**Little Falls** (city) Herkimer County
79	13.5	**Gouverneur** (village) Saint Lawrence County
79	13.5	**Hartsdale** (CDP) Westchester County
79	13.5	**Hunter** (town) Greene County
82	13.3	**Delhi** (town) Delaware County
82	13.3	**Horseheads North** (CDP) Chemung County
84	13.2	**Somerset** (town) Niagara County
84	13.2	**Thompson** (town) Sullivan County
86	13.1	**Amsterdam** (town) Montgomery County
86	13.1	**Greenfield** (town) Saratoga County
88	13.0	**Middleburgh** (town) Schoharie County
88	13.0	**Silver Creek** (village) Chautauqua County
90	12.9	**Great Neck** (village) Nassau County
91	12.8	**Candor** (town) Tioga County
91	12.8	**Glens Falls North** (CDP) Warren County
93	12.7	**Oneonta** (town) Otsego County
93	12.7	**Port Ewen** (CDP) Ulster County
93	12.7	**Ulysses** (town) Tompkins County
96	12.6	**Fredonia** (village) Chautauqua County
96	12.6	**Rochester** (town) Ulster County
98	12.5	**Lloyd** (town) Ulster County
98	12.5	**New Hartford** (town) Oneida County
98	12.5	**South Farmingdale** (CDP) Nassau County
98	12.5	**Union Vale** (town) Dutchess County
102	12.4	**Pelham Manor** (village) Westchester County
103	12.3	**Hicksville** (CDP) Nassau County
103	12.3	**Lakeland** (CDP) Onondaga County
103	12.3	**Stony Point** (town) Rockland County
106	12.2	**Knox** (town) Albany County
107	12.1	**Galeville** (CDP) Onondaga County
107	12.1	**Gouverneur** (town) Saint Lawrence County
109	12.0	**Champion** (town) Jefferson County
109	12.0	**Otsego** (town) Otsego County
111	11.9	**Newfield** (town) Tompkins County
112	11.8	**Gardnertown** (CDP) Orange County
113	11.7	**Clinton** (town) Dutchess County
113	11.7	**Cold Spring Harbor** (CDP) Suffolk County
115	11.6	**Ardsley** (village) Westchester County
115	11.6	**Seneca Falls** (CDP) Seneca County
115	11.6	**Wheatfield** (town) Niagara County
118	11.5	**Melville** (CDP) Suffolk County
118	11.5	**Orchard Park** (village) Erie County
118	11.5	**Vienna** (town) Oneida County
121	11.4	**Orleans** (town) Jefferson County
122	11.3	**Ellicott** (town) Chautauqua County
122	11.3	**Hornell** (city) Steuben County
122	11.3	**North Merrick** (CDP) Nassau County
125	11.2	**Deerpark** (town) Orange County
125	11.2	**Denmark** (town) Lewis County
125	11.2	**Firthcliffe** (CDP) Orange County
125	11.2	**Floyd** (town) Oneida County
125	11.2	**Islandia** (village) Suffolk County
125	11.2	**LaFayette** (town) Onondaga County
131	11.1	**Alfred** (village) Allegany County
131	11.1	**Salem** (town) Washington County
131	11.1	**Trenton** (town) Oneida County
134	11.0	**Massapequa** (CDP) Nassau County
134	11.0	**Wappingers Falls** (village) Dutchess County
136	10.9	**Penfield** (town) Monroe County
136	10.9	**Queensbury** (town) Warren County
136	10.9	**Watertown** (city) Jefferson County
139	10.8	**Volney** (town) Oswego County
140	10.7	**East Glenville** (CDP) Schenectady County
140	10.7	**Lowville** (village) Lewis County
140	10.7	**New Berlin** (town) Chenango County
140	10.7	**Westfield** (village) Chautauqua County
144	10.6	**Davenport** (town) Delaware County
144	10.6	**Middle Island** (CDP) Suffolk County
144	10.6	**Pomfret** (town) Chautauqua County
144	10.6	**Yonkers** (city) Westchester County
148	10.5	**Verona** (town) Oneida County
149	10.4	**Big Flats** (CDP) Chemung County
149	10.4	**Farmingdale** (village) Nassau County

Note: *This section ranks incorporated places and CDPs (Census Designated Places) with populations of 2,500 or more. Unincorporated postal areas were not considered. Please refer to the User Guide for additional information.*

Population with Health Insurance
Top 150 Places Ranked in *Descending* Order

State Rank	Percent	Place
1	100.0	**Clarence Center** (CDP) Erie County
1	100.0	**Hilton** (village) Monroe County
1	100.0	**Minoa** (village) Onondaga County
1	100.0	**West Point** (CDP) Orange County
5	99.8	**New Square** (village) Rockland County
5	99.8	**Sands Point** (village) Nassau County
7	99.7	**Woodbury** (CDP) Nassau County
8	99.4	**Lido Beach** (CDP) Nassau County
8	99.4	**Triangle** (town) Broome County
8	99.4	**University at Buffalo** (CDP) Erie County
11	99.3	**Charlton** (town) Saratoga County
12	99.2	**Clarkson** (CDP) Monroe County
12	99.2	**East Norwich** (CDP) Nassau County
12	99.2	**Gang Mills** (CDP) Steuben County
15	99.1	**Carroll** (town) Chautauqua County
15	99.1	**Halesite** (CDP) Suffolk County
15	99.1	**New Castle** (town) Westchester County
15	99.1	**SUNY Oswego** (CDP) Oswego County
15	99.1	**Scarsdale** (town/village) Westchester County
15	99.1	**Schoharie** (town) Schoharie County
21	99.0	**Bardonia** (CDP) Rockland County
21	99.0	**Cold Spring Harbor** (CDP) Suffolk County
21	99.0	**Coxsackie** (village) Greene County
21	99.0	**Elma Center** (CDP) Erie County
21	99.0	**Jefferson Valley-Yorktown** (CDP) Westchester County
21	99.0	**Wesley Hills** (village) Rockland County
27	98.9	**Galway** (town) Saratoga County
27	98.9	**Larchmont** (village) Westchester County
27	98.9	**Melville** (CDP) Suffolk County
27	98.9	**Miller Place** (CDP) Suffolk County
31	98.8	**Kiryas Joel** (village) Orange County
31	98.8	**Lawrence** (village) Nassau County
31	98.8	**Pendleton** (town) Niagara County
31	98.8	**Pittsford** (town) Monroe County
31	98.8	**Westerlo** (town) Albany County
36	98.7	**Nesconset** (CDP) Suffolk County
37	98.6	**Heritage Hills** (CDP) Westchester County
37	98.6	**Lloyd Harbor** (village) Suffolk County
37	98.6	**Menands** (village) Albany County
37	98.6	**New Scotland** (town) Albany County
37	98.6	**Pelham Manor** (village) Westchester County
37	98.6	**Poestenkill** (town) Rensselaer County
37	98.6	**Royalton** (town) Niagara County
37	98.6	**Spackenkill** (CDP) Dutchess County
37	98.6	**Westvale** (CDP) Onondaga County
46	98.5	**Amenia** (town) Dutchess County
46	98.5	**Munsey Park** (village) Nassau County
46	98.5	**Nunda** (town) Livingston County
46	98.5	**Plainedge** (CDP) Nassau County
46	98.5	**Sayville** (CDP) Suffolk County
46	98.5	**Stony Brook** (CDP) Suffolk County
46	98.5	**West Hills** (CDP) Suffolk County
53	98.4	**Lowville** (town) Lewis County
53	98.4	**Marlboro** (CDP) Ulster County
53	98.4	**University Gardens** (CDP) Nassau County
53	98.4	**Voorheesville** (village) Albany County
57	98.3	**Bethpage** (CDP) Nassau County
57	98.3	**Brutus** (town) Cayuga County
57	98.3	**Cayuga Heights** (village) Tompkins County
57	98.3	**Galeville** (CDP) Onondaga County
57	98.3	**Glenwood Landing** (CDP) Nassau County
57	98.3	**Irvington** (village) Westchester County
57	98.3	**Kaser** (village) Rockland County
57	98.3	**Malta** (town) Saratoga County
57	98.3	**North Hills** (village) Nassau County
57	98.3	**North Wantagh** (CDP) Nassau County
57	98.3	**Norwich** (town) Chenango County
57	98.3	**Rush** (town) Monroe County
69	98.2	**Orchard Park** (village) Erie County
69	98.2	**Putnam Valley** (town) Putnam County
69	98.2	**Seaford** (CDP) Nassau County
69	98.2	**Wantagh** (CDP) Nassau County
73	98.1	**Clarendon** (town) Orleans County
73	98.1	**Clifton Park** (town) Saratoga County
73	98.1	**Florida** (village) Orange County
73	98.1	**Garden City** (village) Nassau County
73	98.1	**Geneseo** (town) Livingston County
73	98.1	**Mendon** (town) Monroe County
73	98.1	**New York Mills** (village) Oneida County
73	98.1	**Orchard Park** (town) Erie County
73	98.1	**Pound Ridge** (town) Westchester County
73	98.1	**Red Oaks Mill** (CDP) Dutchess County
73	98.1	**Riga** (town) Monroe County
84	98.0	**Ballston** (town) Saratoga County
84	98.0	**Briarcliff Manor** (village) Westchester County
84	98.0	**Copake** (town) Columbia County
84	98.0	**East Williston** (village) Nassau County
84	98.0	**Hartland** (town) Niagara County
84	98.0	**Massapequa** (CDP) Nassau County
84	98.0	**Montebello** (village) Rockland County
84	98.0	**Northport** (village) Suffolk County
84	98.0	**Rockville Centre** (village) Nassau County
84	98.0	**Rye** (city) Westchester County
84	98.0	**Smithtown** (CDP) Suffolk County
84	98.0	**Woodmere** (CDP) Nassau County
96	97.9	**East Hills** (village) Nassau County
96	97.9	**Fleming** (town) Cayuga County
96	97.9	**Gates** (CDP) Monroe County
96	97.9	**Greenville** (CDP) Westchester County
96	97.9	**Huntington** (CDP) Suffolk County
96	97.9	**North Great River** (CDP) Suffolk County
96	97.9	**Setauket-East Setauket** (CDP) Suffolk County
96	97.9	**Victor** (town) Ontario County
96	97.9	**Wynantskill** (CDP) Rensselaer County
105	97.8	**Brightwaters** (village) Suffolk County
105	97.8	**Canastota** (village) Madison County
105	97.8	**Erwin** (town) Steuben County
105	97.8	**Hawthorne** (CDP) Westchester County
105	97.8	**Lowville** (village) Lewis County
105	97.8	**Schuyler Falls** (town) Clinton County
105	97.8	**Wanakah** (CDP) Erie County
105	97.8	**Wheatfield** (town) Niagara County
113	97.7	**Bronxville** (village) Westchester County
113	97.7	**Centerport** (CDP) Suffolk County
113	97.7	**Clarence** (town) Erie County
113	97.7	**Colonie** (village) Albany County
113	97.7	**East Greenbush** (CDP) Rensselaer County
113	97.7	**Eggertsville** (CDP) Erie County
113	97.7	**Hamburg** (village) Erie County
113	97.7	**Hamilton** (town) Madison County
113	97.7	**Nassau** (town) Rensselaer County
113	97.7	**New Hartford** (town) Oneida County
113	97.7	**North Massapequa** (CDP) Nassau County
113	97.7	**Northumberland** (town) Saratoga County
113	97.7	**Parma** (town) Monroe County
113	97.7	**Penfield** (town) Monroe County
113	97.7	**Smithtown** (town) Suffolk County
113	97.7	**Washingtonville** (village) Orange County
129	97.6	**Alfred** (village) Allegany County
129	97.6	**Amherst** (town) Erie County
129	97.6	**Bayport** (CDP) Suffolk County
129	97.6	**Bellmore** (CDP) Nassau County
129	97.6	**Bethlehem** (town) Albany County
129	97.6	**Jericho** (CDP) Nassau County
129	97.6	**Kenmore** (village) Erie County
129	97.6	**Plainview** (CDP) Nassau County
129	97.6	**Tappan** (CDP) Rockland County
129	97.6	**Wading River** (CDP) Suffolk County
129	97.6	**Wales** (town) Erie County
129	97.6	**Williamsville** (village) Erie County
141	97.5	**Cazenovia** (village) Madison County
141	97.5	**East Islip** (CDP) Suffolk County
141	97.5	**East Shoreham** (CDP) Suffolk County
141	97.5	**Eastchester** (CDP) Westchester County
141	97.5	**Fairport** (village) Monroe County
141	97.5	**Geneseo** (village) Livingston County
141	97.5	**Merrick** (CDP) Nassau County
141	97.5	**Neversink** (town) Sullivan County
149	97.4	**Allegany** (town) Cattaraugus County
149	97.4	**Beekmantown** (town) Clinton County

Note: This section ranks incorporated places and CDPs (Census Designated Places) with populations of 2,500 or more. Unincorporated postal areas were not considered. Please refer to the User Guide for additional information.

Population with Health Insurance

Top 150 Places Ranked in *Ascending* Order

State Rank	Percent	Place	State Rank	Percent	Place
1	61.9	**Benton** (town) Yates County	74	89.1	**Yates** (town) Orleans County
2	69.4	**Riverside** (CDP) Suffolk County	77	89.2	**Chautauqua** (town) Chautauqua County
3	71.3	**Flanders** (CDP) Suffolk County	77	89.2	**Wellsville** (town) Allegany County
4	78.8	**Port Chester** (village) Westchester County	79	89.3	**Corinth** (village) Saratoga County
5	80.0	**Bedford Hills** (CDP) Westchester County	80	89.4	**New Bremen** (town) Lewis County
5	80.0	**Spring Valley** (village) Rockland County	80	89.4	**Russia** (town) Herkimer County
7	80.4	**Romulus** (town) Seneca County	82	89.5	**Saugerties** (village) Ulster County
8	81.3	**Hempstead** (village) Nassau County	83	89.6	**Maybrook** (village) Orange County
8	81.3	**Ossining** (village) Westchester County	83	89.6	**Middletown** (town) Delaware County
10	81.4	**Saint Regis Mohawk Reservation** (reservation) Franklin County	83	89.6	**New Rochelle** (city) Westchester County
11	81.5	**New Cassel** (CDP) Nassau County	86	89.7	**Middletown** (city) Orange County
12	82.5	**Minden** (town) Montgomery County	86	89.7	**Minisink** (town) Orange County
13	82.6	**Starkey** (town) Yates County	86	89.7	**Wappingers Falls** (village) Dutchess County
14	82.7	**Elmsford** (village) Westchester County	89	89.8	**Fairview** (CDP) Westchester County
15	83.1	**Oswegatchie** (town) Saint Lawrence County	89	89.8	**Gouverneur** (town) Saint Lawrence County
16	83.3	**Milo** (town) Yates County	89	89.8	**Gowanda** (village) Cattaraugus County
17	83.7	**Noyack** (CDP) Suffolk County	89	89.8	**Seneca** (town) Ontario County
18	84.1	**Rye** (town) Westchester County	89	89.8	**Trenton** (town) Oneida County
19	84.2	**New Hempstead** (village) Rockland County	94	89.9	**Haverstraw** (town) Rockland County
19	84.2	**Roosevelt** (CDP) Nassau County	94	89.9	**Oneonta** (town) Otsego County
21	84.3	**Shandaken** (town) Ulster County	94	89.9	**Waverly** (village) Tioga County
22	84.4	**Viola** (CDP) Rockland County	97	90.0	**Ravena** (village) Albany County
23	84.6	**Galen** (town) Wayne County	97	90.0	**Wawarsing** (town) Ulster County
24	84.7	**Huntington Station** (CDP) Suffolk County	99	90.1	**Cape Vincent** (town) Jefferson County
25	84.8	**Brentwood** (CDP) Suffolk County	99	90.1	**Glen Cove** (city) Nassau County
25	84.8	**Hampton Bays** (CDP) Suffolk County	99	90.1	**Thompson** (town) Sullivan County
25	84.8	**Mount Kisco** (town/village) Westchester County	102	90.2	**Mount Vernon** (city) Westchester County
28	84.9	**Orleans** (town) Jefferson County	102	90.2	**New York** (city)
29	85.4	**Pamelia** (town) Jefferson County	104	90.3	**Gouverneur** (village) Saint Lawrence County
30	85.5	**Newburgh** (city) Orange County	104	90.3	**Hudson Falls** (village) Washington County
30	85.5	**Palatine** (town) Montgomery County	104	90.3	**Southeast** (town) Putnam County
32	85.6	**Central Islip** (CDP) Suffolk County	104	90.3	**Yonkers** (city) Westchester County
33	85.7	**Sleepy Hollow** (village) Westchester County	108	90.4	**Barton** (town) Tioga County
34	85.9	**North Amityville** (CDP) Suffolk County	108	90.4	**Harriman** (village) Orange County
35	86.0	**Fayette** (town) Seneca County	108	90.4	**Lake Erie Beach** (CDP) Erie County
36	86.3	**Monticello** (village) Sullivan County	108	90.4	**North Bellport** (CDP) Suffolk County
37	86.6	**Manorhaven** (village) Nassau County	112	90.5	**Brooklyn** (borough) Kings County
38	86.7	**Uniondale** (CDP) Nassau County	112	90.5	**North Lindenhurst** (CDP) Suffolk County
39	86.8	**Ellisburg** (town) Jefferson County	112	90.5	**Tuckahoe** (village) Westchester County
39	86.8	**Saint Johnsville** (town) Montgomery County	115	90.6	**Calcium** (CDP) Jefferson County
41	86.9	**Ossining** (town) Westchester County	115	90.6	**Glen Head** (CDP) Nassau County
41	86.9	**Wyandanch** (CDP) Suffolk County	115	90.6	**Ramapo** (town) Rockland County
43	87.1	**Bainbridge** (town) Chenango County	115	90.6	**Salamanca** (city) Cattaraugus County
44	87.2	**Inwood** (CDP) Nassau County	119	90.7	**East Hampton** (town) Suffolk County
44	87.2	**Southampton** (town) Suffolk County	119	90.7	**Johnstown** (town) Fulton County
46	87.3	**Patchogue** (village) Suffolk County	119	90.7	**North Boston** (CDP) Erie County
47	87.4	**Ellenville** (village) Ulster County	119	90.7	**Somerset** (town) Niagara County
48	87.5	**Mount Morris** (town) Livingston County	119	90.7	**Sterling** (town) Cayuga County
48	87.5	**Wellsville** (village) Allegany County	119	90.7	**Vails Gate** (CDP) Orange County
50	87.6	**Springs** (CDP) Suffolk County	125	90.8	**Copiague** (CDP) Suffolk County
51	87.7	**North Bay Shore** (CDP) Suffolk County	126	90.9	**East Hampton North** (CDP) Suffolk County
51	87.7	**North East** (town) Dutchess County	126	90.9	**Shelby** (town) Orleans County
51	87.7	**Riverhead** (CDP) Suffolk County	126	90.9	**Village Green** (CDP) Onondaga County
54	87.8	**Haverstraw** (village) Rockland County	129	91.0	**Augusta** (town) Oneida County
54	87.8	**Liberty** (village) Sullivan County	129	91.0	**Mechanicstown** (CDP) Orange County
54	87.8	**Queens** (borough) Queens County	129	91.0	**Nyack** (village) Rockland County
57	87.9	**Freeport** (village) Nassau County	129	91.0	**Volney** (town) Oswego County
57	87.9	**Locust Valley** (CDP) Nassau County	133	91.1	**Dix** (town) Schuyler County
57	87.9	**West Haverstraw** (village) Rockland County	133	91.1	**East Patchogue** (CDP) Suffolk County
57	87.9	**Whitehall** (village) Washington County	133	91.1	**Fort Edward** (village) Washington County
61	88.0	**LaFayette** (town) Onondaga County	133	91.1	**Hancock** (town) Delaware County
62	88.1	**Hillcrest** (CDP) Rockland County	133	91.1	**Kingston** (city) Ulster County
62	88.1	**Peekskill** (city) Westchester County	138	91.2	**Kingsbury** (town) Washington County
62	88.1	**Westbury** (village) Nassau County	138	91.2	**Liberty** (town) Sullivan County
65	88.3	**White Plains** (city) Westchester County	138	91.2	**New Hyde Park** (village) Nassau County
66	88.5	**Newfane** (CDP) Niagara County	138	91.2	**Rochester** (town) Ulster County
67	88.9	**Bronx** (borough) Bronx County	142	91.3	**Addison** (town) Steuben County
67	88.9	**Mastic Beach** (village) Suffolk County	142	91.3	**Mount Ivy** (CDP) Rockland County
69	89.0	**Baywood** (CDP) Suffolk County	142	91.3	**Whitehall** (town) Washington County
69	89.0	**Croghan** (town) Lewis County	145	91.4	**Bay Shore** (CDP) Suffolk County
69	89.0	**Lake Placid** (village) Essex County	145	91.4	**Calverton** (CDP) Suffolk County
69	89.0	**Mastic** (CDP) Suffolk County	145	91.4	**Conklin** (town) Broome County
69	89.0	**Poughkeepsie** (city) Dutchess County	145	91.4	**Dover** (town) Dutchess County
74	89.1	**Norfolk** (town) Saint Lawrence County	145	91.4	**Endicott** (village) Broome County
74	89.1	**Richland** (town) Oswego County	145	91.4	**Ghent** (town) Columbia County

Note: *This section ranks incorporated places and CDPs (Census Designated Places) with populations of 2,500 or more. Unincorporated postal areas were not considered. Please refer to the User Guide for additional information.*

Population with Private Health Insurance

Top 150 Places Ranked in *Descending* Order

State Rank	Percent	Place
1	97.4	**Clarence Center** (CDP) Erie County
2	97.1	**West Point** (CDP) Orange County
3	93.9	**New Castle** (town) Westchester County
4	93.8	**Woodbury** (CDP) Nassau County
5	93.1	**Larchmont** (village) Westchester County
6	93.0	**Fort Drum** (CDP) Jefferson County
7	92.8	**Cayuga Heights** (village) Tompkins County
7	92.8	**Pittsford** (town) Monroe County
9	92.7	**Scarsdale** (town/village) Westchester County
10	92.4	**Cold Spring Harbor** (CDP) Suffolk County
10	92.4	**Sands Point** (village) Nassau County
12	92.3	**Nesconset** (CDP) Suffolk County
13	92.2	**Garden City** (village) Nassau County
13	92.2	**Plainedge** (CDP) Nassau County
15	92.1	**Pelham Manor** (village) Westchester County
16	92.0	**Lloyd Harbor** (village) Suffolk County
17	91.9	**East Hills** (village) Nassau County
17	91.9	**Pound Ridge** (town) Westchester County
17	91.9	**Seaford** (CDP) Nassau County
20	91.8	**Bronxville** (village) Westchester County
21	91.7	**Armonk** (CDP) Westchester County
21	91.7	**Lawrence** (village) Nassau County
23	91.6	**East Norwich** (CDP) Nassau County
24	91.5	**Brightwaters** (village) Suffolk County
24	91.5	**Charlton** (town) Saratoga County
26	91.4	**Bethlehem** (town) Albany County
27	91.1	**Poestenkill** (town) Rensselaer County
28	91.0	**Glenwood Landing** (CDP) Nassau County
28	91.0	**Wantagh** (CDP) Nassau County
30	90.9	**Greenville** (CDP) Westchester County
31	90.5	**East Shoreham** (CDP) Suffolk County
31	90.5	**East Williston** (village) Nassau County
31	90.5	**Gang Mills** (CDP) Steuben County
31	90.5	**Manhasset Hills** (CDP) Nassau County
35	90.4	**Briarcliff Manor** (village) Westchester County
36	90.3	**Setauket-East Setauket** (CDP) Suffolk County
37	90.2	**Flower Hill** (village) Nassau County
37	90.2	**Sea Cliff** (village) Nassau County
37	90.2	**Williston Park** (village) Nassau County
40	90.0	**Irvington** (village) Westchester County
40	90.0	**Munsey Park** (village) Nassau County
40	90.0	**Pleasantville** (village) Westchester County
40	90.0	**Wading River** (CDP) Suffolk County
44	89.9	**Fairport** (village) Monroe County
44	89.9	**Rye** (city) Westchester County
46	89.8	**Massapequa Park** (village) Nassau County
46	89.8	**North Wantagh** (CDP) Nassau County
46	89.8	**Wanakah** (CDP) Erie County
49	89.7	**New Scotland** (town) Albany County
49	89.7	**Smithtown** (CDP) Suffolk County
49	89.7	**Stony Brook** (CDP) Suffolk County
52	89.5	**East Islip** (CDP) Suffolk County
52	89.5	**Floral Park** (village) Nassau County
52	89.5	**Malta** (town) Saratoga County
55	89.4	**Halesite** (CDP) Suffolk County
55	89.4	**Hamilton** (village) Madison County
55	89.4	**Harris Hill** (CDP) Erie County
55	89.4	**Jefferson Valley-Yorktown** (CDP) Westchester County
59	89.3	**Centerport** (CDP) Suffolk County
59	89.3	**SUNY Oswego** (CDP) Oswego County
59	89.3	**South Hill** (CDP) Tompkins County
62	89.2	**Lido Beach** (CDP) Nassau County
62	89.2	**Manhasset** (CDP) Nassau County
62	89.2	**University Gardens** (CDP) Nassau County
65	89.1	**Clifton Park** (town) Saratoga County
65	89.1	**Mendon** (town) Monroe County
65	89.1	**Merrick** (CDP) Nassau County
65	89.1	**North Castle** (town) Westchester County
65	89.1	**Voorheesville** (village) Albany County
70	89.0	**Malverne** (village) Nassau County
70	89.0	**North Merrick** (CDP) Nassau County
72	88.9	**Bardonia** (CDP) Rockland County
72	88.9	**Clarence** (town) Erie County
74	88.8	**Clarence** (CDP) Erie County
74	88.8	**Fleming** (town) Cayuga County
74	88.8	**Sayville** (CDP) Suffolk County
77	88.7	**Haviland** (CDP) Dutchess County
77	88.7	**Lake Success** (village) Nassau County
77	88.7	**Smithtown** (town) Suffolk County
80	88.6	**Brookville** (village) Nassau County
80	88.6	**Huntington** (CDP) Suffolk County
80	88.6	**Miller Place** (CDP) Suffolk County
80	88.6	**North Bellmore** (CDP) Nassau County
80	88.6	**Southampton** (village) Suffolk County
80	88.6	**Syosset** (CDP) Nassau County
80	88.6	**Wesley Hills** (village) Rockland County
87	88.5	**Bellmore** (CDP) Nassau County
87	88.5	**Eastchester** (CDP) Westchester County
87	88.5	**Northeast Ithaca** (CDP) Tompkins County
90	88.4	**Blue Point** (CDP) Suffolk County
90	88.4	**Minoa** (village) Onondaga County
90	88.4	**Pelham** (town) Westchester County
93	88.3	**University at Buffalo** (CDP) Erie County
94	88.2	**Babylon** (village) Suffolk County
94	88.2	**Montebello** (village) Rockland County
94	88.2	**Orchard Park** (village) Erie County
94	88.2	**Pendleton** (town) Niagara County
94	88.2	**Sand Lake** (town) Rensselaer County
99	88.1	**East Greenbush** (CDP) Rensselaer County
100	88.0	**East Greenbush** (town) Rensselaer County
100	88.0	**Hamilton** (town) Madison County
100	88.0	**Red Oaks Mill** (CDP) Dutchess County
100	88.0	**West Hills** (CDP) Suffolk County
104	87.9	**Highlands** (town) Orange County
105	87.8	**Muttontown** (village) Nassau County
106	87.7	**North Great River** (CDP) Suffolk County
106	87.7	**Putnam Valley** (town) Putnam County
106	87.7	**Victor** (town) Ontario County
109	87.6	**Alfred** (village) Allegany County
109	87.6	**Lansing** (village) Tompkins County
111	87.5	**Bethpage** (CDP) Nassau County
111	87.5	**Plainview** (CDP) Nassau County
111	87.5	**Skaneateles** (town) Onondaga County
111	87.5	**Somers** (town) Westchester County
111	87.5	**Spackenkill** (CDP) Dutchess County
116	87.4	**Lewisboro** (town) Westchester County
116	87.4	**Orchard Park** (town) Erie County
118	87.3	**Kings Point** (village) Nassau County
118	87.3	**Westerlo** (town) Albany County
120	87.2	**Commack** (CDP) Suffolk County
120	87.2	**Shelter Island** (town) Suffolk County
120	87.2	**Westmere** (CDP) Albany County
123	87.1	**Holbrook** (CDP) Suffolk County
123	87.1	**Massapequa** (CDP) Nassau County
123	87.1	**Old Westbury** (village) Nassau County
126	87.0	**Saint James** (CDP) Suffolk County
127	86.9	**Blooming Grove** (town) Orange County
127	86.9	**Eastchester** (town) Westchester County
127	86.9	**Guilderland** (town) Albany County
130	86.8	**Bayport** (CDP) Suffolk County
130	86.8	**Elma Center** (CDP) Erie County
132	86.7	**Ithaca** (town) Tompkins County
132	86.7	**Jericho** (CDP) Nassau County
132	86.7	**Myers Corner** (CDP) Dutchess County
135	86.6	**Dix Hills** (CDP) Suffolk County
135	86.6	**Hauppauge** (CDP) Suffolk County
135	86.6	**La Grange** (town) Dutchess County
135	86.6	**North Massapequa** (CDP) Nassau County
135	86.6	**Owasco** (town) Cayuga County
135	86.6	**Thornwood** (CDP) Westchester County
141	86.5	**Cornwall-on-Hudson** (village) Orange County
141	86.5	**Crown Heights** (CDP) Dutchess County
141	86.5	**Kings Park** (CDP) Suffolk County
141	86.5	**Walworth** (town) Wayne County
145	86.4	**Gates** (CDP) Monroe County
145	86.4	**Melville** (CDP) Suffolk County
145	86.4	**Spencerport** (village) Monroe County
145	86.4	**Woodbury** (town) Orange County
149	86.3	**Pittstown** (town) Rensselaer County
149	86.3	**West Sand Lake** (CDP) Rensselaer County

Note: *This section ranks incorporated places and CDPs (Census Designated Places) with populations of 2,500 or more. Unincorporated postal areas were not considered. Please refer to the User Guide for additional information.*

Population with Private Health Insurance

Top 150 Places Ranked in *Ascending* Order

State Rank	Percent	Place	State Rank	Percent	Place
1	6.4	**Kaser** (village) Rockland County	76	58.1	**Galen** (town) Wayne County
2	13.6	**New Square** (village) Rockland County	76	58.1	**Palatine** (town) Montgomery County
3	25.2	**Kiryas Joel** (village) Orange County	78	58.5	**Hornell** (city) Steuben County
4	26.6	**Monsey** (CDP) Rockland County	79	58.7	**Fort Edward** (village) Washington County
5	32.1	**Liberty** (village) Sullivan County	80	58.8	**Fort Edward** (town) Washington County
6	34.3	**Spring Valley** (village) Rockland County	80	58.8	**Whitehall** (town) Washington County
7	35.5	**Monticello** (village) Sullivan County	82	58.9	**Wawarsing** (town) Ulster County
8	37.3	**Flanders** (CDP) Suffolk County	83	59.0	**Hudson** (city) Columbia County
9	40.4	**Newburgh** (city) Orange County	83	59.0	**Manheim** (town) Herkimer County
10	44.1	**Bronx** (borough) Bronx County	83	59.0	**Richland** (town) Oswego County
11	44.7	**Gouverneur** (village) Saint Lawrence County	83	59.0	**Saint Regis Mohawk Reservation** (reservation) Franklin County
12	45.2	**Fairview** (CDP) Westchester County	87	59.1	**Tioga** (town) Tioga County
13	46.2	**Utica** (city) Oneida County	87	59.1	**Waverly** (village) Tioga County
14	46.5	**Haverstraw** (village) Rockland County	89	59.2	**Granby** (town) Oswego County
15	46.8	**Whitehall** (village) Washington County	90	59.5	**Mount Morris** (village) Livingston County
16	47.3	**Bedford Hills** (CDP) Westchester County	90	59.5	**Watertown** (city) Jefferson County
17	48.0	**Riverside** (CDP) Suffolk County	92	59.6	**Oswegatchie** (town) Saint Lawrence County
18	48.4	**Ellenville** (village) Ulster County	93	59.7	**Penn Yan** (village) Yates County
19	48.5	**Hempstead** (village) Nassau County	94	59.9	**Ticonderoga** (CDP) Essex County
20	48.9	**Elmira** (city) Chemung County	95	60.1	**Keeseville** (village) Clinton County
20	48.9	**Ramapo** (town) Rockland County	95	60.1	**Middletown** (town) Delaware County
22	49.1	**Benton** (town) Yates County	97	60.4	**Herkimer** (village) Herkimer County
23	49.2	**Gouverneur** (town) Saint Lawrence County	98	60.5	**Peekskill** (city) Westchester County
24	49.5	**Buffalo** (city) Erie County	99	60.6	**Brentwood** (CDP) Suffolk County
25	49.6	**Saint Johnsville** (town) Montgomery County	99	60.6	**Port Jervis** (city) Orange County
26	50.2	**Gloversville** (city) Fulton County	101	60.7	**Barton** (town) Tioga County
26	50.2	**Monroe** (town) Orange County	101	60.7	**Granville** (town) Washington County
28	50.6	**Port Chester** (village) Westchester County	101	60.7	**Roosevelt** (CDP) Nassau County
29	51.2	**Rochester** (city) Monroe County	104	61.0	**Bath** (town) Steuben County
30	51.5	**Fallsburg** (town) Sullivan County	105	61.1	**Central Islip** (CDP) Suffolk County
31	51.7	**Minden** (town) Montgomery County	105	61.1	**Wellsville** (town) Allegany County
32	51.8	**Wyandanch** (CDP) Suffolk County	105	61.1	**Wilna** (town) Jefferson County
33	52.6	**Amsterdam** (city) Montgomery County	108	61.2	**Malone** (village) Franklin County
34	52.7	**Binghamton** (city) Broome County	108	61.2	**North Amityville** (CDP) Suffolk County
35	52.9	**Poughkeepsie** (city) Dutchess County	108	61.2	**West Monroe** (town) Oswego County
36	53.0	**Wellsville** (village) Allegany County	111	61.4	**Canajoharie** (town) Montgomery County
37	53.4	**Brooklyn** (borough) Kings County	112	61.5	**Haverstraw** (town) Rockland County
38	53.5	**Salamanca** (city) Cattaraugus County	112	61.5	**Kingsbury** (town) Washington County
39	53.6	**Jamestown** (city) Chautauqua County	112	61.5	**North Bay Shore** (CDP) Suffolk County
40	53.8	**Liberty** (town) Sullivan County	115	61.6	**Volney** (town) Oswego County
40	53.8	**Little Falls** (city) Herkimer County	116	61.8	**Palermo** (town) Oswego County
40	53.8	**Mohawk** (village) Herkimer County	116	61.8	**Ridgeway** (town) Orleans County
43	53.9	**Carthage** (village) Jefferson County	118	61.9	**Walton** (town) Delaware County
43	53.9	**Thompson** (town) Sullivan County	118	61.9	**West Haverstraw** (village) Rockland County
45	54.1	**Ilion** (village) Herkimer County	120	62.0	**East Hampton North** (CDP) Suffolk County
46	54.3	**Kingston** (city) Ulster County	120	62.0	**New Hempstead** (village) Rockland County
47	54.9	**Lackawanna** (city) Erie County	120	62.0	**Rye** (town) Westchester County
48	55.0	**Inwood** (CDP) Nassau County	123	62.1	**Troy** (city) Rensselaer County
49	55.3	**Viola** (CDP) Rockland County	124	62.2	**Stockport** (town) Columbia County
50	55.8	**Hannibal** (town) Oswego County	125	62.3	**Schroeppel** (town) Oswego County
51	55.9	**Starkey** (town) Yates County	126	62.4	**New Berlin** (town) Chenango County
52	56.0	**Dunkirk** (city) Chautauqua County	126	62.4	**Sodus** (town) Wayne County
53	56.1	**Bath** (village) Steuben County	128	62.5	**Hancock** (town) Delaware County
54	56.2	**Mount Morris** (town) Livingston County	128	62.5	**Lyons** (village) Wayne County
55	56.3	**Fulton** (city) Oswego County	128	62.5	**Yonkers** (city) Westchester County
55	56.3	**Milo** (town) Yates County	131	62.6	**Mount Vernon** (city) Westchester County
55	56.3	**Newark** (village) Wayne County	131	62.6	**Sterling** (town) Cayuga County
58	56.4	**Hudson Falls** (village) Washington County	133	62.7	**Sidney** (village) Delaware County
59	56.6	**Endicott** (village) Broome County	134	62.8	**Romulus** (town) Seneca County
59	56.6	**New York** (city)	135	62.9	**Massena** (town) Saint Lawrence County
61	56.7	**Schenectady** (city) Schenectady County	135	62.9	**Newfield** (town) Tompkins County
61	56.7	**Sleepy Hollow** (village) Westchester County	137	63.1	**Addison** (town) Steuben County
63	56.8	**Ossining** (village) Westchester County	137	63.1	**Afton** (town) Chenango County
63	56.8	**Queens** (borough) Queens County	137	63.1	**New Cassel** (CDP) Nassau County
65	56.9	**Walton** (village) Delaware County	137	63.1	**Vienna** (town) Oneida County
66	57.0	**Niagara Falls** (city) Niagara County	141	63.2	**Altona** (town) Clinton County
67	57.1	**Corinth** (village) Saratoga County	141	63.2	**Owego** (village) Tioga County
67	57.1	**German Flatts** (town) Herkimer County	141	63.2	**Vails Gate** (CDP) Orange County
69	57.2	**Wolcott** (town) Wayne County	144	63.3	**Johnson City** (village) Broome County
70	57.4	**Albion** (town) Orleans County	144	63.3	**Shandaken** (town) Ulster County
70	57.4	**Riverhead** (CDP) Suffolk County	146	63.4	**Colesville** (town) Broome County
72	57.5	**Dolgeville** (village) Herkimer County	146	63.4	**South Glens Falls** (village) Saratoga County
73	57.6	**Albion** (village) Orleans County	146	63.4	**Stockholm** (town) Saint Lawrence County
74	57.8	**Syracuse** (city) Onondaga County	149	63.5	**Massena** (village) Saint Lawrence County
75	58.0	**Gordon Heights** (CDP) Suffolk County	150	63.6	**North Bellport** (CDP) Suffolk County

Note: This section ranks incorporated places and CDPs (Census Designated Places) with populations of 2,500 or more. Unincorporated postal areas were not considered. Please refer to the User Guide for additional information.

Population with Public Health Insurance

Top 150 Places Ranked in *Descending* Order

State Rank	Percent	Place
1	94.1	**Kaser** (village) Rockland County
2	89.5	**New Square** (village) Rockland County
3	80.3	**Kiryas Joel** (village) Orange County
4	72.9	**Monsey** (CDP) Rockland County
5	69.6	**Heritage Hills** (CDP) Westchester County
6	63.5	**Liberty** (village) Sullivan County
7	62.5	**Monticello** (village) Sullivan County
8	59.7	**Gouverneur** (village) Saint Lawrence County
9	59.6	**Hannibal** (town) Oswego County
10	59.2	**Utica** (city) Oneida County
11	57.1	**Walton** (village) Delaware County
12	57.0	**Malone** (village) Franklin County
13	55.6	**Bath** (village) Steuben County
13	55.6	**Little Falls** (city) Herkimer County
15	55.3	**Fallsburg** (town) Sullivan County
16	55.1	**Whitehall** (village) Washington County
17	54.9	**Elmira** (city) Chemung County
18	54.7	**Binghamton** (city) Broome County
19	54.6	**Bronx** (borough) Bronx County
19	54.6	**Monroe** (town) Orange County
21	54.4	**Amsterdam** (city) Montgomery County
22	54.3	**Gloversville** (city) Fulton County
23	54.2	**Jamestown** (city) Chautauqua County
24	54.1	**Buffalo** (city) Erie County
25	53.7	**Lackawanna** (city) Erie County
26	53.3	**Dunkirk** (city) Chautauqua County
27	53.1	**New York Mills** (village) Oneida County
28	53.0	**Middletown** (town) Delaware County
29	52.8	**Newburgh** (city) Orange County
30	52.4	**Mohawk** (village) Herkimer County
30	52.4	**Niagara Falls** (city) Niagara County
32	52.2	**Vienna** (town) Oneida County
33	52.0	**Hornell** (city) Steuben County
33	52.0	**Rochester** (city) Monroe County
35	51.7	**Thompson** (town) Sullivan County
35	51.7	**West Monroe** (town) Oswego County
37	51.6	**Herkimer** (village) Herkimer County
37	51.6	**Ilion** (village) Herkimer County
37	51.6	**Spring Valley** (village) Rockland County
40	51.5	**Dolgeville** (village) Herkimer County
41	51.2	**Bath** (town) Steuben County
41	51.2	**Gouverneur** (town) Saint Lawrence County
43	51.1	**Albion** (village) Orleans County
44	51.0	**Fairview** (CDP) Westchester County
45	50.9	**Fulton** (city) Oswego County
45	50.9	**Granby** (town) Oswego County
45	50.9	**Stockholm** (town) Saint Lawrence County
48	50.8	**Davenport** (town) Delaware County
48	50.8	**Medina** (village) Orleans County
48	50.8	**Ramapo** (town) Rockland County
51	50.7	**Catskill** (village) Greene County
52	50.6	**Penn Yan** (village) Yates County
53	50.3	**Albion** (town) Orleans County
54	50.2	**Carlton** (town) Orleans County
54	50.2	**Fort Edward** (town) Washington County
54	50.2	**Sodus** (town) Wayne County
57	50.1	**Ticonderoga** (CDP) Essex County
58	50.0	**Carthage** (village) Jefferson County
58	50.0	**Hudson Falls** (village) Washington County
60	49.8	**Geneva** (town) Ontario County
60	49.8	**Middleburgh** (town) Schoharie County
60	49.8	**Salamanca** (city) Cattaraugus County
63	49.7	**German Flatts** (town) Herkimer County
63	49.7	**Mount Morris** (village) Livingston County
65	49.6	**Herkimer** (town) Herkimer County
65	49.6	**Saint Johnsville** (town) Montgomery County
65	49.6	**Warrensburg** (town) Warren County
68	49.5	**Calverton** (CDP) Suffolk County
68	49.5	**Tioga** (town) Tioga County
70	49.4	**Carroll** (town) Chautauqua County
70	49.4	**Massena** (town) Saint Lawrence County
70	49.4	**New Berlin** (town) Chenango County
73	49.2	**Haverstraw** (village) Rockland County
73	49.2	**Keeseville** (village) Clinton County
73	49.2	**Moira** (town) Franklin County
73	49.2	**Poughkeepsie** (city) Dutchess County
73	49.2	**Wellsville** (village) Allegany County
78	48.8	**Newark** (village) Wayne County
79	48.7	**Ellenville** (village) Ulster County
80	48.6	**Watertown** (city) Jefferson County
81	48.4	**Massena** (village) Saint Lawrence County
81	48.4	**Mount Morris** (town) Livingston County
81	48.4	**Ticonderoga** (town) Essex County
84	48.3	**Schenectady** (city) Schenectady County
85	48.2	**Endicott** (village) Broome County
85	48.2	**Malone** (town) Franklin County
87	48.1	**Altona** (town) Clinton County
88	48.0	**Granville** (town) Washington County
88	48.0	**Sidney** (town) Delaware County
90	47.9	**Kingston** (city) Ulster County
90	47.9	**Syracuse** (city) Onondaga County
92	47.8	**Liberty** (town) Sullivan County
92	47.8	**Mooers** (town) Clinton County
94	47.7	**Olean** (city) Cattaraugus County
95	47.6	**Perry** (village) Wyoming County
95	47.6	**Warrensburg** (CDP) Warren County
97	47.5	**Milford** (town) Otsego County
98	47.4	**Lyons** (village) Wayne County
98	47.4	**Norwich** (city) Chenango County
98	47.4	**Wolcott** (town) Wayne County
101	47.3	**Portland** (town) Chautauqua County
102	47.1	**Coxsackie** (village) Greene County
103	47.0	**Dansville** (village) Livingston County
103	47.0	**Fort Edward** (village) Washington County
105	46.9	**Batavia** (city) Genesee County
105	46.9	**Yorkshire** (town) Cattaraugus County
107	46.8	**Saranac Lake** (village) Franklin County
108	46.7	**Johnson City** (village) Broome County
108	46.7	**Manheim** (town) Herkimer County
108	46.7	**Minden** (town) Montgomery County
108	46.7	**North Dansville** (town) Livingston County
108	46.7	**Rome** (city) Oneida County
108	46.7	**South Glens Falls** (village) Saratoga County
114	46.6	**Afton** (town) Chenango County
114	46.6	**Florida** (town) Montgomery County
114	46.6	**Harrietstown** (town) Franklin County
114	46.6	**Verona** (town) Oneida County
114	46.6	**Whitehall** (town) Washington County
119	46.5	**Galeville** (CDP) Onondaga County
120	46.3	**Annsville** (town) Oneida County
121	46.2	**Oneida** (city) Madison County
122	46.1	**Dannemora** (village) Clinton County
122	46.1	**Sandy Creek** (town) Oswego County
122	46.1	**Wellsville** (town) Allegany County
125	46.0	**Collins** (town) Erie County
125	46.0	**Oxford** (town) Chenango County
127	45.7	**Arcadia** (town) Wayne County
127	45.7	**Milo** (town) Yates County
129	45.6	**Brasher** (town) Saint Lawrence County
129	45.6	**Colesville** (town) Broome County
131	45.5	**South Lockport** (CDP) Niagara County
132	45.4	**Corinth** (village) Saratoga County
132	45.4	**Hudson** (city) Columbia County
132	45.4	**North Hills** (village) Nassau County
132	45.4	**Schroeppel** (town) Oswego County
132	45.4	**Sherburne** (town) Chenango County
132	45.4	**Theresa** (town) Jefferson County
132	45.4	**Wyandanch** (CDP) Suffolk County
139	45.3	**Walton** (town) Delaware County
140	45.2	**Nunda** (town) Livingston County
140	45.2	**Randolph** (town) Cattaraugus County
142	45.1	**Canisteo** (town) Steuben County
142	45.1	**Glasco** (CDP) Ulster County
144	45.0	**Catskill** (town) Greene County
144	45.0	**Hunter** (town) Greene County
144	45.0	**Madison** (town) Madison County
147	44.8	**Ogdensburg** (city) Saint Lawrence County
147	44.8	**White Creek** (town) Washington County
149	44.7	**Claverack** (town) Columbia County
149	44.7	**Greenport** (town) Columbia County

Note: This section ranks incorporated places and CDPs (Census Designated Places) with populations of 2,500 or more. Unincorporated postal areas were not considered. Please refer to the User Guide for additional information.

Population with Public Health Insurance

Top 150 Places Ranked in *Ascending* Order

State Rank	Percent	Place	State Rank	Percent	Place
1	4.9	**West Point** (CDP) Orange County	75	21.7	**Poestenkill** (town) Rensselaer County
2	7.9	**Clarence Center** (CDP) Erie County	75	21.7	**Potsdam** (village) Saint Lawrence County
3	8.1	**Fort Drum** (CDP) Jefferson County	78	21.8	**Mahopac** (CDP) Putnam County
4	11.5	**SUNY Oswego** (CDP) Oswego County	78	21.8	**Thornwood** (CDP) Westchester County
5	11.7	**Binghamton University** (CDP) Broome County	78	21.8	**Woodbury** (village) Orange County
6	12.5	**University at Buffalo** (CDP) Erie County	81	21.9	**Seaford** (CDP) Nassau County
7	13.3	**Armonk** (CDP) Westchester County	81	21.9	**Washingtonville** (village) Orange County
8	13.6	**South Hill** (CDP) Tompkins County	83	22.0	**Blauvelt** (CDP) Rockland County
9	14.5	**Northeast Ithaca** (CDP) Tompkins County	83	22.0	**Pittsford** (town) Monroe County
10	15.1	**Brookville** (village) Nassau County	85	22.1	**Brightwaters** (village) Suffolk County
11	15.2	**Alfred** (village) Allegany County	85	22.1	**Horseheads North** (CDP) Chemung County
12	15.6	**Scarsdale** (town/village) Westchester County	85	22.1	**Wheatley Heights** (CDP) Suffolk County
13	15.7	**Larchmont** (village) Westchester County	88	22.2	**Gang Mills** (CDP) Steuben County
14	15.8	**Munsey Park** (village) Nassau County	88	22.2	**Holtsville** (CDP) Suffolk County
14	15.8	**New Castle** (town) Westchester County	88	22.2	**Tarrytown** (village) Westchester County
16	16.0	**Pelham Manor** (village) Westchester County	91	22.3	**Bethlehem** (town) Albany County
16	16.0	**Stony Brook University** (CDP) Suffolk County	91	22.3	**New Paltz** (village) Ulster County
18	16.2	**Lansing** (village) Tompkins County	93	22.4	**Clarence** (town) Erie County
19	16.3	**Greenville** (CDP) Westchester County	93	22.4	**Eden** (CDP) Erie County
20	16.5	**North Castle** (town) Westchester County	93	22.4	**Hamilton** (town) Madison County
21	16.6	**Greenwood Lake** (village) Orange County	93	22.4	**Harrison** (village) Westchester County
21	16.6	**Le Ray** (town) Jefferson County	93	22.4	**Montebello** (village) Rockland County
23	17.2	**Old Westbury** (village) Nassau County	93	22.4	**Smithtown** (CDP) Suffolk County
24	17.4	**Ithaca** (city) Tompkins County	99	22.5	**East Moriches** (CDP) Suffolk County
25	17.5	**Bronxville** (village) Westchester County	99	22.5	**Nesconset** (CDP) Suffolk County
26	17.6	**East Shoreham** (CDP) Suffolk County	99	22.5	**West Hills** (CDP) Suffolk County
26	17.6	**Rye** (city) Westchester County	102	22.7	**Baldwin Harbor** (CDP) Nassau County
28	17.9	**Irvington** (village) Westchester County	102	22.7	**East Greenbush** (CDP) Rensselaer County
28	17.9	**Pelham** (town) Westchester County	102	22.7	**Mamaroneck** (town) Westchester County
30	18.1	**Cold Spring Harbor** (CDP) Suffolk County	102	22.7	**Walworth** (town) Wayne County
31	18.4	**East Hills** (village) Nassau County	102	22.7	**West Islip** (CDP) Suffolk County
31	18.4	**Muttontown** (village) Nassau County	102	22.7	**Woodmere** (CDP) Nassau County
33	18.5	**Alfred** (town) Allegany County	108	22.8	**Haviland** (CDP) Dutchess County
33	18.5	**Hamilton** (town) Madison County	108	22.8	**Knox** (town) Albany County
35	18.7	**Glenwood Landing** (CDP) Nassau County	108	22.8	**Miller Place** (CDP) Suffolk County
35	18.7	**Great Neck Estates** (village) Nassau County	108	22.8	**North Salem** (town) Westchester County
37	19.2	**Flower Hill** (village) Nassau County	108	22.8	**Woodbury** (CDP) Nassau County
37	19.2	**Glen Head** (CDP) Nassau County	113	22.9	**Bohemia** (CDP) Suffolk County
37	19.2	**Pleasantville** (village) Westchester County	114	23.0	**Dix Hills** (CDP) Suffolk County
40	19.3	**Plainedge** (CDP) Nassau County	114	23.0	**Eastchester** (town) Westchester County
41	19.4	**East Islip** (CDP) Suffolk County	114	23.0	**Myers Corner** (CDP) Dutchess County
41	19.4	**Pelham** (village) Westchester County	114	23.0	**Roslyn Heights** (CDP) Nassau County
43	19.6	**Halesite** (CDP) Suffolk County	114	23.0	**University Gardens** (CDP) Nassau County
44	19.7	**Blue Point** (CDP) Suffolk County	119	23.1	**Putnam Valley** (town) Putnam County
45	19.9	**Lloyd Harbor** (village) Suffolk County	120	23.2	**Hastings-on-Hudson** (village) Westchester County
46	20.0	**Wading River** (CDP) Suffolk County	120	23.2	**Lewisboro** (town) Westchester County
47	20.1	**Croton-on-Hudson** (village) Westchester County	120	23.2	**Malta** (town) Saratoga County
47	20.1	**East Williston** (village) Nassau County	123	23.3	**Eastchester** (CDP) Westchester County
49	20.2	**Highlands** (town) Orange County	123	23.3	**Pendleton** (town) Niagara County
49	20.2	**Sands Point** (village) Nassau County	123	23.3	**Wynantskill** (CDP) Rensselaer County
49	20.2	**Sea Cliff** (village) Nassau County	126	23.4	**Red Oaks Mill** (CDP) Dutchess County
49	20.2	**West Sand Lake** (CDP) Rensselaer County	127	23.5	**Bellmore** (CDP) Nassau County
53	20.3	**Wantagh** (CDP) Nassau County	127	23.5	**Blooming Grove** (town) Orange County
54	20.4	**Center Moriches** (CDP) Suffolk County	127	23.5	**Cedarhurst** (village) Nassau County
55	20.7	**Harriman** (village) Orange County	127	23.5	**Garden City South** (CDP) Nassau County
56	20.8	**Babylon** (village) Suffolk County	127	23.5	**Massapequa Park** (village) Nassau County
57	20.9	**Manhasset** (CDP) Nassau County	127	23.5	**Mineola** (village) Nassau County
58	21.0	**Syosset** (CDP) Nassau County	127	23.5	**Smithtown** (town) Suffolk County
58	21.0	**Woodbury** (town) Orange County	127	23.5	**Spencerport** (village) Monroe County
60	21.1	**North Merrick** (CDP) Nassau County	135	23.6	**Baldwin** (CDP) Nassau County
60	21.1	**Setauket-East Setauket** (CDP) Suffolk County	135	23.6	**Centerport** (CDP) Suffolk County
62	21.2	**Canton** (village) Saint Lawrence County	135	23.6	**East Norwich** (CDP) Nassau County
62	21.2	**Dobbs Ferry** (village) Westchester County	135	23.6	**Kings Point** (village) Nassau County
62	21.2	**Geneseo** (village) Livingston County	135	23.6	**Watertown** (town) Jefferson County
65	21.3	**Islip Terrace** (CDP) Suffolk County	140	23.7	**Beekman** (town) Dutchess County
65	21.3	**Williston Park** (village) Nassau County	140	23.7	**Lynbrook** (village) Nassau County
67	21.4	**Garden City** (village) Nassau County	140	23.7	**Manorhaven** (village) Nassau County
67	21.4	**Lake Success** (village) Nassau County	140	23.7	**North Massapequa** (CDP) Nassau County
67	21.4	**Mendon** (town) Monroe County	140	23.7	**South Valley Stream** (CDP) Nassau County
70	21.5	**Briarcliff Manor** (village) Westchester County	145	23.8	**Carmel** (town) Putnam County
70	21.5	**Floral Park** (village) Nassau County	145	23.8	**Greenburgh** (town) Westchester County
70	21.5	**Jericho** (CDP) Nassau County	145	23.8	**Hamptonburgh** (town) Orange County
70	21.5	**Merrick** (CDP) Nassau County	145	23.8	**North Bellmore** (CDP) Nassau County
74	21.6	**Ithaca** (town) Tompkins County	145	23.8	**Pittstown** (town) Rensselaer County
75	21.7	**Manhasset Hills** (CDP) Nassau County	145	23.8	**Southeast** (town) Putnam County

Note: *This section ranks incorporated places and CDPs (Census Designated Places) with populations of 2,500 or more. Unincorporated postal areas were not considered. Please refer to the User Guide for additional information.*

Population with No Health Insurance

Top 150 Places Ranked in *Descending* Order

State Rank	Percent	Place	State Rank	Percent	Place
1	38.1	**Benton** (town) Yates County	74	10.9	**Yates** (town) Orleans County
2	30.6	**Riverside** (CDP) Suffolk County	77	10.8	**Chautauqua** (town) Chautauqua County
3	28.7	**Flanders** (CDP) Suffolk County	77	10.8	**Wellsville** (town) Allegany County
4	21.2	**Port Chester** (village) Westchester County	79	10.7	**Corinth** (village) Saratoga County
5	20.0	**Bedford Hills** (CDP) Westchester County	80	10.6	**New Bremen** (town) Lewis County
5	20.0	**Spring Valley** (village) Rockland County	80	10.6	**Russia** (town) Herkimer County
7	19.6	**Romulus** (town) Seneca County	82	10.5	**Saugerties** (village) Ulster County
8	18.7	**Hempstead** (village) Nassau County	83	10.4	**Maybrook** (village) Orange County
8	18.7	**Ossining** (village) Westchester County	83	10.4	**Middletown** (town) Delaware County
10	18.6	**Saint Regis Mohawk Reservation** (reservation) Franklin County	83	10.4	**New Rochelle** (city) Westchester County
11	18.5	**New Cassel** (CDP) Nassau County	86	10.3	**Middletown** (city) Orange County
12	17.5	**Minden** (town) Montgomery County	86	10.3	**Minisink** (town) Orange County
13	17.4	**Starkey** (town) Yates County	86	10.3	**Wappingers Falls** (village) Dutchess County
14	17.3	**Elmsford** (village) Westchester County	89	10.2	**Fairview** (CDP) Westchester County
15	16.9	**Oswegatchie** (town) Saint Lawrence County	89	10.2	**Gouverneur** (town) Saint Lawrence County
16	16.7	**Milo** (town) Yates County	89	10.2	**Gowanda** (village) Cattaraugus County
17	16.3	**Noyack** (CDP) Suffolk County	89	10.2	**Seneca** (town) Ontario County
18	15.9	**Rye** (town) Westchester County	89	10.2	**Trenton** (town) Oneida County
19	15.8	**New Hempstead** (village) Rockland County	94	10.1	**Haverstraw** (town) Rockland County
19	15.8	**Roosevelt** (CDP) Nassau County	94	10.1	**Oneonta** (town) Otsego County
21	15.7	**Shandaken** (town) Ulster County	94	10.1	**Waverly** (village) Tioga County
22	15.6	**Viola** (CDP) Rockland County	97	10.0	**Ravena** (village) Albany County
23	15.4	**Galen** (town) Wayne County	97	10.0	**Wawarsing** (town) Ulster County
24	15.3	**Huntington Station** (CDP) Suffolk County	99	9.9	**Cape Vincent** (town) Jefferson County
25	15.2	**Brentwood** (CDP) Suffolk County	99	9.9	**Glen Cove** (city) Nassau County
25	15.2	**Hampton Bays** (CDP) Suffolk County	99	9.9	**Thompson** (town) Sullivan County
25	15.2	**Mount Kisco** (town/village) Westchester County	102	9.8	**Mount Vernon** (city) Westchester County
28	15.1	**Orleans** (town) Jefferson County	102	9.8	**New York** (city)
29	14.6	**Pamelia** (town) Jefferson County	104	9.7	**Gouverneur** (village) Saint Lawrence County
30	14.5	**Newburgh** (city) Orange County	104	9.7	**Hudson Falls** (village) Washington County
30	14.5	**Palatine** (town) Montgomery County	104	9.7	**Southeast** (town) Putnam County
32	14.4	**Central Islip** (CDP) Suffolk County	104	9.7	**Yonkers** (city) Westchester County
33	14.3	**Sleepy Hollow** (village) Westchester County	108	9.6	**Barton** (town) Tioga County
34	14.1	**North Amityville** (CDP) Suffolk County	108	9.6	**Harriman** (village) Orange County
35	14.0	**Fayette** (town) Seneca County	108	9.6	**Lake Erie Beach** (CDP) Erie County
36	13.7	**Monticello** (village) Sullivan County	108	9.6	**North Bellport** (CDP) Suffolk County
37	13.4	**Manorhaven** (village) Nassau County	112	9.5	**Brooklyn** (borough) Kings County
38	13.3	**Uniondale** (CDP) Nassau County	112	9.5	**North Lindenhurst** (CDP) Suffolk County
39	13.2	**Ellisburg** (town) Jefferson County	112	9.5	**Tuckahoe** (village) Westchester County
39	13.2	**Saint Johnsville** (town) Montgomery County	115	9.4	**Calcium** (CDP) Jefferson County
41	13.1	**Ossining** (town) Westchester County	115	9.4	**Glen Head** (CDP) Nassau County
41	13.1	**Wyandanch** (CDP) Suffolk County	115	9.4	**Ramapo** (town) Rockland County
43	12.9	**Bainbridge** (town) Chenango County	115	9.4	**Salamanca** (city) Cattaraugus County
44	12.8	**Inwood** (CDP) Nassau County	119	9.3	**East Hampton** (town) Suffolk County
44	12.8	**Southampton** (town) Suffolk County	119	9.3	**Johnstown** (town) Fulton County
46	12.7	**Patchogue** (village) Suffolk County	119	9.3	**North Boston** (CDP) Erie County
47	12.6	**Ellenville** (village) Ulster County	119	9.3	**Somerset** (town) Niagara County
48	12.5	**Mount Morris** (town) Livingston County	119	9.3	**Sterling** (town) Cayuga County
48	12.5	**Wellsville** (village) Allegany County	119	9.3	**Vails Gate** (CDP) Orange County
50	12.4	**Springs** (CDP) Suffolk County	125	9.2	**Copiague** (CDP) Suffolk County
51	12.3	**North Bay Shore** (CDP) Suffolk County	126	9.1	**East Hampton North** (CDP) Suffolk County
51	12.3	**North East** (town) Dutchess County	126	9.1	**Shelby** (town) Orleans County
51	12.3	**Riverhead** (CDP) Suffolk County	126	9.1	**Village Green** (CDP) Onondaga County
54	12.2	**Haverstraw** (village) Rockland County	129	9.0	**Augusta** (town) Oneida County
54	12.2	**Liberty** (village) Sullivan County	129	9.0	**Mechanicstown** (CDP) Orange County
54	12.2	**Queens** (borough) Queens County	129	9.0	**Nyack** (village) Rockland County
57	12.1	**Freeport** (village) Nassau County	129	9.0	**Volney** (town) Oswego County
57	12.1	**Locust Valley** (CDP) Nassau County	133	8.9	**Dix** (town) Schuyler County
57	12.1	**West Haverstraw** (village) Rockland County	133	8.9	**East Patchogue** (CDP) Suffolk County
57	12.1	**Whitehall** (village) Washington County	133	8.9	**Fort Edward** (village) Washington County
61	12.0	**LaFayette** (town) Onondaga County	133	8.9	**Hancock** (town) Delaware County
62	11.9	**Hillcrest** (CDP) Rockland County	133	8.9	**Kingston** (city) Ulster County
62	11.9	**Peekskill** (city) Westchester County	138	8.8	**Kingsbury** (town) Washington County
62	11.9	**Westbury** (village) Nassau County	138	8.8	**Liberty** (town) Sullivan County
65	11.7	**White Plains** (city) Westchester County	138	8.8	**New Hyde Park** (village) Nassau County
66	11.5	**Newfane** (CDP) Niagara County	138	8.8	**Rochester** (town) Ulster County
67	11.1	**Bronx** (borough) Bronx County	142	8.7	**Addison** (town) Steuben County
67	11.1	**Mastic Beach** (village) Suffolk County	142	8.7	**Mount Ivy** (CDP) Rockland County
69	11.0	**Baywood** (CDP) Suffolk County	142	8.7	**Whitehall** (town) Washington County
69	11.0	**Croghan** (town) Lewis County	145	8.6	**Bay Shore** (CDP) Suffolk County
69	11.0	**Lake Placid** (village) Essex County	145	8.6	**Calverton** (CDP) Suffolk County
69	11.0	**Mastic** (CDP) Suffolk County	145	8.6	**Conklin** (town) Broome County
69	11.0	**Poughkeepsie** (city) Dutchess County	145	8.6	**Dover** (town) Dutchess County
74	10.9	**Norfolk** (town) Saint Lawrence County	145	8.6	**Endicott** (village) Broome County
74	10.9	**Richland** (town) Oswego County	145	8.6	**Ghent** (town) Columbia County

Note: This section ranks incorporated places and CDPs (Census Designated Places) with populations of 2,500 or more. Unincorporated postal areas were not considered. Please refer to the User Guide for additional information.

Population with No Health Insurance

Top 150 Places Ranked in *Ascending* Order

State Rank	Percent	Place	State Rank	Percent	Place
1	0.0	Clarence Center (CDP) Erie County	73	1.9	Garden City (village) Nassau County
1	0.0	Hilton (village) Monroe County	73	1.9	Geneseo (town) Livingston County
1	0.0	Minoa (village) Onondaga County	73	1.9	Mendon (town) Monroe County
1	0.0	West Point (CDP) Orange County	73	1.9	New York Mills (village) Oneida County
5	0.2	New Square (village) Rockland County	73	1.9	Orchard Park (town) Erie County
5	0.2	Sands Point (village) Nassau County	73	1.9	Pound Ridge (town) Westchester County
7	0.3	Woodbury (CDP) Nassau County	73	1.9	Red Oaks Mill (CDP) Dutchess County
8	0.6	Lido Beach (CDP) Nassau County	73	1.9	Riga (town) Monroe County
8	0.6	Triangle (town) Broome County	84	2.0	Ballston (town) Saratoga County
8	0.6	University at Buffalo (CDP) Erie County	84	2.0	Briarcliff Manor (village) Westchester County
11	0.7	Charlton (town) Saratoga County	84	2.0	Copake (town) Columbia County
12	0.8	Clarkson (CDP) Monroe County	84	2.0	East Williston (village) Nassau County
12	0.8	East Norwich (CDP) Nassau County	84	2.0	Hartland (town) Niagara County
12	0.8	Gang Mills (CDP) Steuben County	84	2.0	Massapequa (CDP) Nassau County
15	0.9	Carroll (town) Chautauqua County	84	2.0	Montebello (village) Rockland County
15	0.9	Halesite (CDP) Suffolk County	84	2.0	Northport (village) Suffolk County
15	0.9	New Castle (town) Westchester County	84	2.0	Rockville Centre (village) Nassau County
15	0.9	SUNY Oswego (CDP) Oswego County	84	2.0	Rye (city) Westchester County
15	0.9	Scarsdale (town/village) Westchester County	84	2.0	Smithtown (CDP) Suffolk County
15	0.9	Schoharie (town) Schoharie County	84	2.0	Woodmere (CDP) Nassau County
21	1.0	Bardonia (CDP) Rockland County	96	2.1	East Hills (village) Nassau County
21	1.0	Cold Spring Harbor (CDP) Suffolk County	96	2.1	Fleming (town) Cayuga County
21	1.0	Coxsackie (village) Greene County	96	2.1	Gates (CDP) Monroe County
21	1.0	Elma Center (CDP) Erie County	96	2.1	Greenville (CDP) Westchester County
21	1.0	Jefferson Valley-Yorktown (CDP) Westchester County	96	2.1	Huntington (town) Suffolk County
21	1.0	Wesley Hills (village) Rockland County	96	2.1	North Great River (CDP) Suffolk County
27	1.1	Galway (town) Saratoga County	96	2.1	Setauket-East Setauket (CDP) Suffolk County
27	1.1	Larchmont (village) Westchester County	96	2.1	Victor (town) Ontario County
27	1.1	Melville (CDP) Suffolk County	96	2.1	Wynantskill (CDP) Rensselaer County
27	1.1	Miller Place (CDP) Suffolk County	105	2.2	Brightwaters (village) Suffolk County
31	1.2	Kiryas Joel (village) Orange County	105	2.2	Canastota (village) Madison County
31	1.2	Lawrence (village) Nassau County	105	2.2	Erwin (town) Steuben County
31	1.2	Pendleton (town) Niagara County	105	2.2	Hawthorne (CDP) Westchester County
31	1.2	Pittsford (town) Monroe County	105	2.2	Lowville (village) Lewis County
31	1.2	Westerlo (town) Albany County	105	2.2	Schuyler Falls (town) Clinton County
36	1.3	Nesconset (CDP) Suffolk County	105	2.2	Wanakah (CDP) Erie County
37	1.4	Heritage Hills (CDP) Westchester County	105	2.2	Wheatfield (town) Niagara County
37	1.4	Lloyd Harbor (village) Suffolk County	113	2.3	Bronxville (village) Westchester County
37	1.4	Menands (village) Albany County	113	2.3	Centerport (CDP) Suffolk County
37	1.4	New Scotland (town) Albany County	113	2.3	Clarence (town) Erie County
37	1.4	Pelham Manor (village) Westchester County	113	2.3	Colonie (village) Albany County
37	1.4	Poestenkill (town) Rensselaer County	113	2.3	East Greenbush (CDP) Rensselaer County
37	1.4	Royalton (town) Niagara County	113	2.3	Eggertsville (CDP) Erie County
37	1.4	Spackenkill (CDP) Dutchess County	113	2.3	Hamburg (village) Erie County
37	1.4	Westvale (CDP) Onondaga County	113	2.3	Hamilton (town) Madison County
46	1.5	Amenia (town) Dutchess County	113	2.3	Nassau (town) Rensselaer County
46	1.5	Munsey Park (village) Nassau County	113	2.3	New Hartford (town) Oneida County
46	1.5	Nunda (town) Livingston County	113	2.3	North Massapequa (CDP) Nassau County
46	1.5	Plainedge (CDP) Nassau County	113	2.3	Northumberland (town) Saratoga County
46	1.5	Sayville (CDP) Suffolk County	113	2.3	Parma (town) Monroe County
46	1.5	Stony Brook (CDP) Suffolk County	113	2.3	Penfield (town) Monroe County
46	1.5	West Hills (CDP) Suffolk County	113	2.3	Smithtown (town) Suffolk County
53	1.6	Lowville (town) Lewis County	113	2.3	Washingtonville (village) Orange County
53	1.6	Marlboro (CDP) Ulster County	129	2.4	Alfred (village) Allegany County
53	1.6	University Gardens (CDP) Nassau County	129	2.4	Amherst (town) Erie County
53	1.6	Voorheesville (village) Albany County	129	2.4	Bayport (CDP) Suffolk County
57	1.7	Bethpage (CDP) Nassau County	129	2.4	Bellmore (CDP) Nassau County
57	1.7	Brutus (town) Cayuga County	129	2.4	Bethlehem (town) Albany County
57	1.7	Cayuga Heights (village) Tompkins County	129	2.4	Jericho (CDP) Nassau County
57	1.7	Galeville (CDP) Onondaga County	129	2.4	Kenmore (village) Erie County
57	1.7	Glenwood Landing (CDP) Nassau County	129	2.4	Plainview (CDP) Nassau County
57	1.7	Irvington (village) Westchester County	129	2.4	Tappan (CDP) Rockland County
57	1.7	Kaser (village) Rockland County	129	2.4	Wading River (CDP) Suffolk County
57	1.7	Malta (town) Saratoga County	129	2.4	Wales (town) Erie County
57	1.7	North Hills (village) Nassau County	129	2.4	Williamsville (village) Erie County
57	1.7	North Wantagh (CDP) Nassau County	141	2.5	Cazenovia (village) Madison County
57	1.7	Norwich (town) Chenango County	141	2.5	East Islip (CDP) Suffolk County
57	1.7	Rush (town) Monroe County	141	2.5	East Shoreham (CDP) Suffolk County
69	1.8	Orchard Park (village) Erie County	141	2.5	Eastchester (CDP) Westchester County
69	1.8	Putnam Valley (town) Putnam County	141	2.5	Fairport (village) Monroe County
69	1.8	Seaford (CDP) Nassau County	141	2.5	Merrick (CDP) Nassau County
69	1.8	Wantagh (CDP) Nassau County	141	2.5	Neversink (town) Sullivan County
73	1.9	Clarendon (town) Orleans County	148	2.6	Allegany (town) Cattaraugus County
73	1.9	Clifton Park (town) Saratoga County	148	2.6	Beekmantown (town) Clinton County
73	1.9	Florida (village) Orange County	148	2.6	Big Flats (town) Chemung County

Note: *This section ranks incorporated places and CDPs (Census Designated Places) with populations of 2,500 or more. Unincorporated postal areas were not considered. Please refer to the User Guide for additional information.*

Population Under 18 Years Old with No Health Insurance

Top 150 Places Ranked in *Descending* Order

State Rank	Percent	Place
1	67.3	**Benton** (town) Yates County
2	36.1	**Oswegatchie** (town) Saint Lawrence County
3	34.6	**Milo** (town) Yates County
3	34.6	**Minden** (town) Montgomery County
5	28.1	**Starkey** (town) Yates County
6	26.7	**Saint Regis Mohawk Reservation** (reservation) Franklin County
7	26.5	**Orleans** (town) Jefferson County
8	25.5	**Romulus** (town) Seneca County
9	24.9	**Bainbridge** (town) Chenango County
10	24.0	**Trenton** (town) Oneida County
11	23.4	**Owasco** (town) Cayuga County
12	22.1	**Palatine** (town) Montgomery County
12	22.1	**Pamelia** (town) Jefferson County
14	21.7	**Conklin** (town) Broome County
15	21.4	**Richland** (town) Oswego County
16	21.1	**Saint Johnsville** (town) Montgomery County
17	20.8	**Fayette** (town) Seneca County
18	20.3	**Seneca** (town) Ontario County
19	20.2	**Galen** (town) Wayne County
20	20.0	**Shandaken** (town) Ulster County
21	18.7	**Viola** (CDP) Rockland County
22	18.2	**Chautauqua** (town) Chautauqua County
23	16.5	**Russia** (town) Herkimer County
24	16.2	**Wellsville** (village) Allegany County
25	16.0	**Jerusalem** (town) Yates County
26	15.8	**Lakeland** (CDP) Onondaga County
27	15.7	**Ellisburg** (town) Jefferson County
28	15.4	**Ridgeway** (town) Orleans County
29	15.3	**Yates** (town) Orleans County
30	14.7	**Penn Yan** (village) Yates County
31	14.6	**New Cassel** (CDP) Nassau County
32	14.1	**Croghan** (town) Lewis County
32	14.1	**Norfolk** (town) Saint Lawrence County
34	13.7	**Lake Erie Beach** (CDP) Erie County
34	13.7	**Manorhaven** (village) Nassau County
36	13.5	**Moriches** (CDP) Suffolk County
37	13.4	**West Elmira** (CDP) Chemung County
38	13.1	**Wellsville** (town) Allegany County
39	12.9	**Campbell** (town) Steuben County
40	12.6	**Lake Placid** (village) Essex County
41	12.5	**Alden** (village) Erie County
41	12.5	**Arlington** (CDP) Dutchess County
43	12.2	**North Salem** (town) Westchester County
44	12.1	**Chesterfield** (town) Essex County
44	12.1	**New Bremen** (town) Lewis County
46	12.0	**Evans** (town) Erie County
46	12.0	**Mattituck** (CDP) Suffolk County
48	11.5	**Corning** (town) Steuben County
49	11.3	**Saratoga** (town) Saratoga County
50	11.2	**Gouverneur** (town) Saint Lawrence County
50	11.2	**Waterford** (town) Saratoga County
52	10.8	**Lyncourt** (CDP) Onondaga County
53	10.7	**LaFayette** (town) Onondaga County
54	10.6	**Shelby** (town) Orleans County
55	10.5	**Vails Gate** (CDP) Orange County
56	10.1	**Blauvelt** (CDP) Rockland County
56	10.1	**Elmira** (town) Chemung County
56	10.1	**Manheim** (town) Herkimer County
56	10.1	**Plattekill** (town) Ulster County
60	10.0	**Durham** (town) Greene County
60	10.0	**Johnstown** (town) Fulton County
62	9.8	**Flanders** (CDP) Suffolk County
63	9.6	**Aurelius** (town) Cayuga County
64	9.5	**Middletown** (town) Delaware County
65	9.4	**Davenport** (town) Delaware County
65	9.4	**Lisbon** (town) Saint Lawrence County
67	9.3	**Northeast Ithaca** (CDP) Tompkins County
68	9.2	**Lake Mohegan** (CDP) Westchester County
69	9.1	**Huntington Station** (CDP) Suffolk County
69	9.1	**Mount Morris** (town) Livingston County
69	9.1	**Uniondale** (CDP) Nassau County
72	8.9	**Kingsbury** (town) Washington County
73	8.8	**Kirkwood** (town) Broome County
74	8.5	**North Elba** (town) Essex County
75	8.4	**Cape Vincent** (town) Jefferson County
75	8.4	**Springs** (CDP) Suffolk County
77	8.2	**Walton** (town) Delaware County
78	8.1	**Locust Valley** (CDP) Nassau County
79	8.0	**Gorham** (town) Ontario County
79	8.0	**Valley Cottage** (CDP) Rockland County
81	7.9	**Freeport** (village) Nassau County
81	7.9	**Hillcrest** (CDP) Rockland County
81	7.9	**Marcellus** (town) Onondaga County
84	7.8	**Southold** (CDP) Suffolk County
85	7.6	**Carmel Hamlet** (CDP) Putnam County
85	7.6	**Homer** (town) Cortland County
87	7.4	**Coxsackie** (town) Greene County
87	7.4	**Cuba** (town) Allegany County
87	7.4	**Williamsville** (village) Erie County
90	7.3	**Gowanda** (village) Cattaraugus County
91	7.2	**Barton** (town) Tioga County
91	7.2	**Floyd** (town) Oneida County
91	7.2	**Hudson Falls** (village) Washington County
91	7.2	**Salamanca** (city) Cattaraugus County
91	7.2	**Westbury** (village) Nassau County
96	7.1	**North Collins** (town) Erie County
97	7.0	**Alfred** (town) Allegany County
97	7.0	**Pearl River** (CDP) Rockland County
97	7.0	**Roosevelt** (CDP) Nassau County
100	6.9	**Augusta** (town) Oneida County
100	6.9	**Baldwin Harbor** (CDP) Nassau County
100	6.9	**Blasdell** (village) Erie County
100	6.9	**Boonville** (town) Oneida County
100	6.9	**Croton-on-Hudson** (village) Westchester County
105	6.8	**Ellicott** (town) Chautauqua County
105	6.8	**Yorkshire** (town) Cattaraugus County
107	6.7	**Gloversville** (city) Fulton County
107	6.7	**Ithaca** (city) Tompkins County
107	6.7	**Wolcott** (town) Wayne County
110	6.6	**Harriman** (village) Orange County
110	6.6	**Minisink** (town) Orange County
110	6.6	**Owego** (village) Tioga County
110	6.6	**Spring Valley** (village) Rockland County
110	6.6	**Whitehall** (village) Washington County
115	6.5	**Bayville** (village) Nassau County
115	6.5	**Brentwood** (CDP) Suffolk County
115	6.5	**Fairmount** (CDP) Onondaga County
115	6.5	**Newfane** (CDP) Niagara County
115	6.5	**Pelham** (village) Westchester County
115	6.5	**Somerset** (town) Niagara County
121	6.4	**Eaton** (town) Madison County
121	6.4	**North Sea** (CDP) Suffolk County
123	6.3	**Nyack** (village) Rockland County
124	6.2	**Fenton** (town) Broome County
125	6.1	**Blue Point** (CDP) Suffolk County
125	6.1	**Esopus** (town) Ulster County
125	6.1	**Jamestown** (city) Chautauqua County
125	6.1	**New Berlin** (town) Chenango County
125	6.1	**Northwest Harbor** (CDP) Suffolk County
125	6.1	**Orangetown** (town) Rockland County
125	6.1	**Patterson** (town) Putnam County
125	6.1	**Shelter Island** (town) Suffolk County
125	6.1	**Volney** (town) Oswego County
134	6.0	**Addison** (town) Steuben County
134	6.0	**Mohawk** (village) Herkimer County
134	6.0	**Montauk** (CDP) Suffolk County
137	5.9	**Cornwall-on-Hudson** (village) Orange County
137	5.9	**Lee** (town) Oneida County
137	5.9	**Mastic Beach** (village) Suffolk County
137	5.9	**New Hempstead** (village) Rockland County
141	5.8	**Lisle** (town) Broome County
141	5.8	**Moira** (town) Franklin County
141	5.8	**Roslyn** (village) Nassau County
144	5.7	**Champion** (town) Jefferson County
144	5.7	**Fort Ann** (town) Washington County
144	5.7	**Glen Cove** (city) Nassau County
144	5.7	**Tupper Lake** (village) Franklin County
148	5.6	**Castile** (town) Wyoming County
148	5.6	**East Glenville** (CDP) Schenectady County
150	5.5	**Northampton** (town) Fulton County

Note: *This section ranks incorporated places and CDPs (Census Designated Places) with populations of 2,500 or more. Unincorporated postal areas were not considered. Please refer to the User Guide for additional information.*

Population Under 18 Years Old with No Health Insurance

Top 150 Places Ranked in *Ascending* Order

State Rank	Percent	Place		State Rank	Percent	Place
1	0.0	**Allegany** (town) Cattaraugus County		1	0.0	**Homer** (village) Cortland County
1	0.0	**Amenia** (town) Dutchess County		1	0.0	**Honeoye Falls** (village) Monroe County
1	0.0	**Amityville** (village) Suffolk County		1	0.0	**Hoosick Falls** (village) Rensselaer County
1	0.0	**Ardsley** (village) Westchester County		1	0.0	**Horseheads North** (CDP) Chemung County
1	0.0	**Attica** (town) Wyoming County		1	0.0	**Irvington** (village) Westchester County
1	0.0	**Attica** (village) Wyoming County		1	0.0	**Islandia** (village) Suffolk County
1	0.0	**Avon** (town) Livingston County		1	0.0	**Islip Terrace** (CDP) Suffolk County
1	0.0	**Avon** (village) Livingston County		1	0.0	**Jefferson Valley-Yorktown** (CDP) Westchester County
1	0.0	**Ballston** (town) Saratoga County		1	0.0	**Kenmore** (village) Erie County
1	0.0	**Bardonia** (CDP) Rockland County		1	0.0	**Lake Luzerne** (town) Warren County
1	0.0	**Barker** (town) Broome County		1	0.0	**Lakewood** (village) Chautauqua County
1	0.0	**Batavia** (town) Genesee County		1	0.0	**Lansing** (town) Tompkins County
1	0.0	**Bedford Hills** (CDP) Westchester County		1	0.0	**Lansing** (village) Tompkins County
1	0.0	**Beekmantown** (town) Clinton County		1	0.0	**Larchmont** (village) Westchester County
1	0.0	**Binghamton** (town) Broome County		1	0.0	**Lawrence** (village) Nassau County
1	0.0	**Boston** (town) Erie County		1	0.0	**Lewiston** (town) Niagara County
1	0.0	**Brasher** (town) Saint Lawrence County		1	0.0	**Lewiston** (village) Niagara County
1	0.0	**Briarcliff Manor** (village) Westchester County		1	0.0	**Lido Beach** (CDP) Nassau County
1	0.0	**Brookville** (village) Nassau County		1	0.0	**Livingston** (town) Columbia County
1	0.0	**Cairo** (town) Greene County		1	0.0	**Livonia** (town) Livingston County
1	0.0	**Callicoon** (town) Sullivan County		1	0.0	**Louisville** (town) Saint Lawrence County
1	0.0	**Calverton** (CDP) Suffolk County		1	0.0	**Lyons** (village) Wayne County
1	0.0	**Canastota** (village) Madison County		1	0.0	**Madison** (town) Madison County
1	0.0	**Caroline** (town) Tompkins County		1	0.0	**Malone** (village) Franklin County
1	0.0	**Carroll** (town) Chautauqua County		1	0.0	**Mechanicstown** (CDP) Orange County
1	0.0	**Carthage** (village) Jefferson County		1	0.0	**Medina** (village) Orleans County
1	0.0	**Centerport** (CDP) Suffolk County		1	0.0	**Melville** (CDP) Suffolk County
1	0.0	**Charlton** (town) Saratoga County		1	0.0	**Menands** (village) Albany County
1	0.0	**Chittenango** (village) Madison County		1	0.0	**Mendon** (town) Monroe County
1	0.0	**Clarence Center** (CDP) Erie County		1	0.0	**Milton** (CDP) Saratoga County
1	0.0	**Clarendon** (town) Orleans County		1	0.0	**Minoa** (village) Onondaga County
1	0.0	**Clarkson** (CDP) Monroe County		1	0.0	**Montebello** (village) Rockland County
1	0.0	**Clarkson** (town) Monroe County		1	0.0	**Montrose** (CDP) Westchester County
1	0.0	**Cold Spring Harbor** (CDP) Suffolk County		1	0.0	**Mooers** (town) Clinton County
1	0.0	**Copake** (town) Columbia County		1	0.0	**Mount Morris** (village) Livingston County
1	0.0	**Coxsackie** (village) Greene County		1	0.0	**Nanuet** (CDP) Rockland County
1	0.0	**Crown Heights** (CDP) Dutchess County		1	0.0	**Neversink** (town) Sullivan County
1	0.0	**Cutchogue** (CDP) Suffolk County		1	0.0	**New Baltimore** (town) Greene County
1	0.0	**Dannemora** (town) Clinton County		1	0.0	**New Scotland** (town) Albany County
1	0.0	**Dannemora** (village) Clinton County		1	0.0	**New Windsor** (CDP) Orange County
1	0.0	**Dansville** (village) Livingston County		1	0.0	**New York Mills** (village) Oneida County
1	0.0	**East Hampton North** (CDP) Suffolk County		1	0.0	**North Boston** (CDP) Erie County
1	0.0	**East Moriches** (CDP) Suffolk County		1	0.0	**North Dansville** (town) Livingston County
1	0.0	**East Northport** (CDP) Suffolk County		1	0.0	**North Hills** (village) Nassau County
1	0.0	**East Norwich** (CDP) Nassau County		1	0.0	**North Wantagh** (CDP) Nassau County
1	0.0	**East Syracuse** (village) Onondaga County		1	0.0	**Norwich** (city) Chenango County
1	0.0	**Eden** (CDP) Erie County		1	0.0	**Nunda** (town) Livingston County
1	0.0	**Elma Center** (CDP) Erie County		1	0.0	**Olean** (city) Cattaraugus County
1	0.0	**Fairport** (village) Monroe County		1	0.0	**Olive** (town) Ulster County
1	0.0	**Fleming** (town) Cayuga County		1	0.0	**Orange Lake** (CDP) Orange County
1	0.0	**Florida** (town) Montgomery County		1	0.0	**Orangeburg** (CDP) Rockland County
1	0.0	**Florida** (village) Orange County		1	0.0	**Orchard Park** (village) Erie County
1	0.0	**Frankfort** (town) Herkimer County		1	0.0	**Otego** (town) Otsego County
1	0.0	**Frankfort** (village) Herkimer County		1	0.0	**Otsego** (town) Otsego County
1	0.0	**Galeville** (CDP) Onondaga County		1	0.0	**Oxford** (town) Chenango County
1	0.0	**Gang Mills** (CDP) Steuben County		1	0.0	**Palmyra** (village) Wayne County
1	0.0	**Garden City Park** (CDP) Nassau County		1	0.0	**Pavilion** (town) Genesee County
1	0.0	**Gates** (CDP) Monroe County		1	0.0	**Pelham Manor** (village) Westchester County
1	0.0	**Glasco** (CDP) Ulster County		1	0.0	**Pembroke** (town) Genesee County
1	0.0	**Gordon Heights** (CDP) Suffolk County		1	0.0	**Piermont** (village) Rockland County
1	0.0	**Great Neck Plaza** (village) Nassau County		1	0.0	**Pierrepont** (town) Saint Lawrence County
1	0.0	**Greenville** (town) Greene County		1	0.0	**Pine Plains** (town) Dutchess County
1	0.0	**Greenwood Lake** (village) Orange County		1	0.0	**Plainedge** (CDP) Nassau County
1	0.0	**Guilford** (town) Chenango County		1	0.0	**Pompey** (town) Onondaga County
1	0.0	**Halesite** (CDP) Suffolk County		1	0.0	**Port Ewen** (CDP) Ulster County
1	0.0	**Hamptonburgh** (town) Orange County		1	0.0	**Putnam Lake** (CDP) Putnam County
1	0.0	**Hartland** (town) Niagara County		1	0.0	**Putnam Valley** (town) Putnam County
1	0.0	**Hartsdale** (CDP) Westchester County		1	0.0	**Red Oaks Mill** (CDP) Dutchess County
1	0.0	**Haviland** (CDP) Dutchess County		1	0.0	**Richmond** (town) Ontario County
1	0.0	**Hawthorne** (CDP) Westchester County		1	0.0	**Riverside** (CDP) Suffolk County
1	0.0	**Heritage Hills** (CDP) Westchester County		1	0.0	**Rockville Centre** (village) Nassau County
1	0.0	**Hewlett** (CDP) Nassau County		1	0.0	**Rush** (town) Monroe County
1	0.0	**Highland Falls** (village) Orange County		1	0.0	**Rye Brook** (village) Westchester County
1	0.0	**Hilton** (village) Monroe County		1	0.0	**Sands Point** (village) Nassau County
1	0.0	**Holland** (town) Erie County		1	0.0	**Saranac** (town) Clinton County

Note: This section ranks incorporated places and CDPs (Census Designated Places) with populations of 2,500 or more. Unincorporated postal areas were not considered. Please refer to the User Guide for additional information.

Commute to Work: Car

Top 150 Places Ranked in *Descending* Order

State Rank	Percent	Place	State Rank	Percent	Place
1	100.0	**North Boston** (CDP) Erie County	75	95.5	**Bethel** (town) Sullivan County
2	99.5	**Conklin** (town) Broome County	75	95.5	**Franklinville** (town) Cattaraugus County
3	98.9	**Horseheads North** (CDP) Chemung County	75	95.5	**Hanover** (town) Chautauqua County
4	98.8	**Newfane** (CDP) Niagara County	75	95.5	**Kirkwood** (town) Broome County
5	98.4	**Canastota** (village) Madison County	75	95.5	**Spencer** (town) Tioga County
6	98.2	**Veteran** (town) Chemung County	81	95.4	**Canandaigua** (town) Ontario County
7	98.1	**Lakeland** (CDP) Onondaga County	81	95.4	**Coxsackie** (town) Greene County
7	98.1	**Village Green** (CDP) Onondaga County	81	95.4	**Lyons** (village) Wayne County
9	97.9	**Colesville** (town) Broome County	81	95.4	**Marion** (town) Wayne County
9	97.9	**Palermo** (town) Oswego County	85	95.3	**Brutus** (town) Cayuga County
11	97.8	**Fenton** (town) Broome County	85	95.3	**Frankfort** (town) Herkimer County
11	97.8	**Neversink** (town) Sullivan County	85	95.3	**Moreau** (town) Saratoga County
13	97.7	**Broadalbin** (town) Fulton County	85	95.3	**Ravena** (village) Albany County
14	97.6	**Milton** (CDP) Saratoga County	89	95.2	**Elma Center** (CDP) Erie County
14	97.6	**Saranac** (town) Clinton County	89	95.2	**Haviland** (CDP) Dutchess County
16	97.4	**Riga** (town) Monroe County	89	95.2	**Pembroke** (town) Genesee County
17	97.2	**Alden** (town) Erie County	89	95.2	**Pompey** (town) Onondaga County
18	97.1	**Lake Erie Beach** (CDP) Erie County	89	95.2	**Tioga** (town) Tioga County
18	97.1	**Paris** (town) Oneida County	89	95.2	**West Sand Lake** (CDP) Rensselaer County
18	97.1	**Schuyler** (town) Herkimer County	95	95.1	**Coeymans** (town) Albany County
21	97.0	**Clarendon** (town) Orleans County	95	95.1	**Concord** (town) Erie County
21	97.0	**Schaghticoke** (town) Rensselaer County	95	95.1	**East Shoreham** (CDP) Suffolk County
21	97.0	**Windsor** (town) Broome County	95	95.1	**Wanakah** (CDP) Erie County
24	96.9	**Poestenkill** (town) Rensselaer County	99	95.0	**Charlton** (town) Saratoga County
25	96.8	**Chenango Bridge** (CDP) Broome County	99	95.0	**Gouverneur** (village) Saint Lawrence County
25	96.8	**Gates** (CDP) Monroe County	99	95.0	**Sterling** (town) Cayuga County
25	96.8	**Hoosick Falls** (village) Rensselaer County	102	94.9	**Cheektowaga** (CDP) Erie County
25	96.8	**Lenox** (town) Madison County	102	94.9	**Cheektowaga** (town) Erie County
25	96.8	**Livonia** (town) Livingston County	102	94.9	**East Glenville** (CDP) Schenectady County
25	96.8	**Newfane** (town) Niagara County	102	94.9	**Gang Mills** (CDP) Steuben County
25	96.8	**Pendleton** (town) Niagara County	102	94.9	**Mayfield** (town) Fulton County
32	96.7	**Bainbridge** (town) Chenango County	102	94.9	**New Haven** (town) Oswego County
32	96.7	**Madison** (town) Madison County	102	94.9	**Theresa** (town) Jefferson County
34	96.6	**Horseheads** (village) Chemung County	102	94.9	**Wheatfield** (town) Niagara County
34	96.6	**Lyons** (town) Wayne County	110	94.8	**Greece** (town) Monroe County
34	96.6	**Ontario** (town) Wayne County	110	94.8	**Terryville** (CDP) Suffolk County
37	96.5	**Clarkson** (CDP) Monroe County	110	94.8	**West Elmira** (CDP) Chemung County
37	96.5	**Glasco** (CDP) Ulster County	113	94.7	**Grand Island** (town) Erie County
37	96.5	**LaFayette** (town) Onondaga County	113	94.7	**Hamburg** (village) Erie County
37	96.5	**Owasco** (town) Cayuga County	113	94.7	**Homer** (village) Cortland County
37	96.5	**Walworth** (town) Wayne County	113	94.7	**Horseheads** (town) Chemung County
42	96.4	**Binghamton** (town) Broome County	113	94.7	**New Hartford** (town) Oneida County
42	96.4	**Cambria** (town) Niagara County	113	94.7	**North Tonawanda** (city) Niagara County
42	96.4	**Evans** (town) Erie County	113	94.7	**Wawayanda** (town) Orange County
45	96.3	**Constantia** (town) Oswego County	113	94.7	**Yaphank** (CDP) Suffolk County
45	96.3	**Corning** (town) Steuben County	121	94.6	**Busti** (town) Chautauqua County
45	96.3	**Coxsackie** (village) Greene County	121	94.6	**Grandyle Village** (CDP) Erie County
48	96.2	**Boston** (town) Erie County	121	94.6	**Hamburg** (town) Erie County
49	96.1	**Floyd** (town) Oneida County	121	94.6	**Hamlin** (town) Monroe County
49	96.1	**Lisbon** (town) Saint Lawrence County	121	94.6	**Minoa** (village) Onondaga County
49	96.1	**Nassau** (town) Rensselaer County	121	94.6	**New Bremen** (town) Lewis County
52	96.0	**Elbridge** (town) Onondaga County	121	94.6	**Newark Valley** (town) Tioga County
52	96.0	**Lyncourt** (CDP) Onondaga County	128	94.5	**Adams** (town) Jefferson County
52	96.0	**Norwich** (town) Chenango County	128	94.5	**Galeville** (CDP) Onondaga County
52	96.0	**Pittstown** (town) Rensselaer County	128	94.5	**Laurens** (town) Otsego County
52	96.0	**West Bloomfield** (town) Ontario County	128	94.5	**Lee** (town) Oneida County
57	95.9	**Big Flats** (town) Chemung County	128	94.5	**Liberty** (town) Sullivan County
57	95.9	**Depew** (village) Erie County	128	94.5	**Liberty** (village) Sullivan County
59	95.8	**Brownville** (town) Jefferson County	128	94.5	**Marilla** (town) Erie County
59	95.8	**Deerfield** (town) Oneida County	128	94.5	**Phelps** (town) Ontario County
59	95.8	**Portville** (town) Cattaraugus County	128	94.5	**Queensbury** (town) Warren County
59	95.8	**Wheatland** (town) Monroe County	128	94.5	**Rutland** (town) Jefferson County
63	95.7	**Big Flats** (CDP) Chemung County	138	94.4	**Brasher** (town) Saint Lawrence County
63	95.7	**Darien** (town) Genesee County	138	94.4	**Collins** (town) Erie County
63	95.7	**Deerpark** (town) Orange County	138	94.4	**Glenville** (town) Schenectady County
63	95.7	**Lakewood** (village) Chautauqua County	138	94.4	**Hamlin** (CDP) Monroe County
63	95.7	**Lancaster** (village) Erie County	138	94.4	**Lockport** (town) Niagara County
63	95.7	**Norfolk** (town) Saint Lawrence County	138	94.4	**Orchard Park** (town) Erie County
63	95.7	**Sandy Creek** (town) Oswego County	138	94.4	**Pamelia** (town) Jefferson County
63	95.7	**West Seneca** (CDP) Erie County	138	94.4	**Rocky Point** (CDP) Suffolk County
71	95.6	**Chenango** (town) Broome County	138	94.4	**Rotterdam** (CDP) Schenectady County
71	95.6	**Chittenango** (village) Madison County	138	94.4	**Rush** (town) Monroe County
71	95.6	**Lancaster** (town) Erie County	138	94.4	**Schoharie** (town) Schoharie County
71	95.6	**Wilson** (town) Niagara County	138	94.4	**Vienna** (town) Oneida County
75	95.5	**Altona** (town) Clinton County	138	94.4	**Westerlo** (town) Albany County

Note: This section ranks incorporated places and CDPs (Census Designated Places) with populations of 2,500 or more. Unincorporated postal areas were not considered. Please refer to the User Guide for additional information.

Commute to Work: Car

Top 150 Places Ranked in *Ascending* Order

State Rank	Percent	Place
1	7.8	**Manhattan** (borough) New York County
2	22.2	**Stony Brook University** (CDP) Suffolk County
3	22.6	**Brooklyn** (borough) Kings County
4	25.7	**West Point** (CDP) Orange County
5	26.4	**Alfred** (village) Allegany County
6	26.6	**New York** (city)
7	27.2	**SUNY Oswego** (CDP) Oswego County
8	27.4	**Bronx** (borough) Bronx County
9	32.7	**Binghamton University** (CDP) Broome County
10	34.0	**Kaser** (village) Rockland County
11	36.4	**New Square** (village) Rockland County
12	37.3	**Alfred** (town) Allegany County
13	37.5	**Bronxville** (village) Westchester County
14	37.8	**Ithaca** (city) Tompkins County
15	38.5	**Queens** (borough) Queens County
16	40.5	**Munsey Park** (village) Nassau County
17	43.7	**Larchmont** (village) Westchester County
18	43.8	**University at Buffalo** (CDP) Erie County
19	43.9	**Scarsdale** (town/village) Westchester County
20	44.2	**Great Neck Plaza** (village) Nassau County
21	44.9	**Kiryas Joel** (village) Orange County
22	46.5	**Hamilton** (village) Madison County
23	48.6	**Greenville** (CDP) Westchester County
24	49.2	**Mamaroneck** (town) Westchester County
25	50.6	**South Hill** (CDP) Tompkins County
26	52.0	**Thomaston** (village) Nassau County
27	52.1	**Rye** (city) Westchester County
28	52.2	**Potsdam** (village) Saint Lawrence County
29	52.6	**Canton** (village) Saint Lawrence County
30	52.8	**Sands Point** (village) Nassau County
31	53.0	**Hartsdale** (CDP) Westchester County
32	53.5	**Hastings-on-Hudson** (village) Westchester County
33	54.4	**Tuckahoe** (village) Westchester County
34	54.9	**Pelham** (village) Westchester County
35	55.1	**Flower Hill** (village) Nassau County
36	55.4	**Briarcliff Manor** (village) Westchester County
36	55.4	**New Paltz** (village) Ulster County
38	55.6	**Pelham** (town) Westchester County
39	55.8	**Highlands** (town) Orange County
39	55.8	**Port Washington** (CDP) Nassau County
41	56.7	**Pelham Manor** (village) Westchester County
42	56.9	**Lido Beach** (CDP) Nassau County
43	57.2	**Arlington** (CDP) Dutchess County
44	57.4	**Manhasset** (CDP) Nassau County
45	57.5	**Great Neck Estates** (village) Nassau County
46	57.8	**Geneseo** (village) Livingston County
47	58.3	**Old Westbury** (village) Nassau County
48	58.8	**Fort Drum** (CDP) Jefferson County
49	59.0	**Brookville** (village) Nassau County
49	59.0	**Cayuga Heights** (village) Tompkins County
51	59.4	**New Castle** (town) Westchester County
52	59.7	**Pound Ridge** (town) Westchester County
53	60.1	**Eastchester** (town) Westchester County
54	60.4	**Mount Vernon** (city) Westchester County
54	60.4	**University Gardens** (CDP) Nassau County
56	60.6	**Sleepy Hollow** (village) Westchester County
57	61.6	**Irvington** (village) Westchester County
58	62.0	**Northwest Harbor** (CDP) Suffolk County
59	62.3	**Ithaca** (town) Tompkins County
60	62.4	**Mamaroneck** (village) Westchester County
61	62.6	**New Rochelle** (city) Westchester County
62	62.7	**Rockville Centre** (village) Nassau County
63	63.2	**Oneonta** (city) Otsego County
64	63.3	**Yonkers** (city) Westchester County
65	63.4	**Harrison** (town/village) Westchester County
66	64.0	**Dobbs Ferry** (village) Westchester County
66	64.0	**Staten Island** (borough) Richmond County
68	64.2	**Croton-on-Hudson** (village) Westchester County
68	64.2	**South Valley Stream** (CDP) Nassau County
70	64.5	**Hamilton** (town) Madison County
71	64.6	**Cazenovia** (village) Madison County
71	64.6	**Rye Brook** (village) Westchester County
73	64.9	**Brockport** (village) Monroe County
74	65.0	**Delhi** (village) Delaware County
75	65.4	**Bedford** (town) Westchester County
75	65.4	**Kings Point** (village) Nassau County
77	65.5	**Great Neck** (village) Nassau County
77	65.5	**Port Chester** (village) Westchester County
79	65.6	**Monsey** (CDP) Rockland County
80	65.7	**Garden City** (village) Nassau County
81	65.9	**Cobleskill** (village) Schoharie County
82	66.0	**Tarrytown** (village) Westchester County
83	66.4	**Greenburgh** (town) Westchester County
83	66.4	**Rye** (town) Westchester County
85	66.5	**Philipstown** (town) Putnam County
86	67.8	**Eastchester** (CDP) Westchester County
87	67.9	**White Plains** (city) Westchester County
88	68.1	**Inwood** (CDP) Nassau County
88	68.1	**Lawrence** (village) Nassau County
90	68.5	**Hempstead** (village) Nassau County
91	68.8	**Geneseo** (town) Livingston County
91	68.8	**Woodstock** (town) Ulster County
93	68.9	**Lloyd Harbor** (village) Suffolk County
94	69.0	**Ossining** (town) Westchester County
94	69.0	**Port Washington North** (village) Nassau County
96	69.1	**Monroe** (town) Orange County
97	69.3	**Cold Spring Harbor** (CDP) Suffolk County
98	69.5	**Otsego** (town) Otsego County
98	69.5	**Roslyn Heights** (CDP) Nassau County
98	69.5	**Woodmere** (CDP) Nassau County
101	69.6	**Jericho** (CDP) Nassau County
102	69.7	**Merrick** (CDP) Nassau County
103	70.0	**Valley Stream** (village) Nassau County
104	70.2	**Muttontown** (village) Nassau County
105	70.4	**Ardsley** (village) Westchester County
105	70.4	**Le Ray** (town) Jefferson County
107	70.6	**Albany** (city) Albany County
107	70.6	**Viola** (CDP) Rockland County
109	70.8	**East Williston** (village) Nassau County
110	70.9	**Hudson** (city) Columbia County
111	71.0	**Lake Success** (village) Nassau County
111	71.0	**North Hempstead** (town) Nassau County
113	71.2	**Manorhaven** (village) Nassau County
113	71.2	**Mount Pleasant** (town) Westchester County
115	71.3	**Long Beach** (city) Nassau County
116	71.4	**Stanford** (town) Dutchess County
117	71.7	**Eaton** (town) Madison County
117	71.7	**Red Hook** (town) Dutchess County
119	71.8	**North Castle** (town) Westchester County
120	71.9	**Newburgh** (city) Orange County
120	71.9	**Peekskill** (city) Westchester County
122	72.0	**New Paltz** (town) Ulster County
123	72.1	**Elmsford** (village) Westchester County
124	72.2	**Canton** (town) Saint Lawrence County
125	72.5	**Mount Kisco** (town/village) Westchester County
126	72.6	**Centerport** (CDP) Suffolk County
127	72.7	**Ossining** (village) Westchester County
127	72.7	**Potsdam** (town) Saint Lawrence County
129	72.8	**Cobleskill** (town) Schoharie County
129	72.8	**Lakeview** (CDP) Nassau County
129	72.8	**Syosset** (CDP) Nassau County
132	72.9	**Elmont** (CDP) Nassau County
132	72.9	**Herricks** (CDP) Nassau County
132	72.9	**Montrose** (CDP) Westchester County
132	72.9	**Southampton** (village) Suffolk County
132	72.9	**Spring Valley** (village) Rockland County
132	72.9	**Valhalla** (CDP) Westchester County
138	73.0	**Cedarhurst** (village) Nassau County
139	73.1	**Lansing** (village) Tompkins County
140	73.3	**East Hills** (village) Nassau County
140	73.3	**South Nyack** (village) Rockland County
142	73.4	**Lynbrook** (village) Nassau County
143	73.5	**Oswego** (city) Oswego County
144	73.7	**Sea Cliff** (village) Nassau County
144	73.7	**Syracuse** (city) Onondaga County
146	73.9	**Rhinebeck** (village) Dutchess County
147	74.0	**Lewisboro** (town) Westchester County
148	74.2	**Jerusalem** (town) Yates County
148	74.2	**Malverne** (village) Nassau County
150	74.3	**Plainview** (CDP) Nassau County

Note: This section ranks incorporated places and CDPs (Census Designated Places) with populations of 2,500 or more. Unincorporated postal areas were not considered. Please refer to the User Guide for additional information.

Commute to Work: Public Transportation

Top 150 Places Ranked in *Descending* Order

State Rank	Percent	Place
1	61.8	**Brooklyn** (borough) Kings County
2	60.2	**Bronx** (borough) Bronx County
3	59.4	**Manhattan** (borough) New York County
4	56.5	**New York** (city)
5	51.7	**Queens** (borough) Queens County
6	51.2	**Munsey Park** (village) Nassau County
7	46.6	**Bronxville** (village) Westchester County
8	44.4	**Larchmont** (village) Westchester County
9	43.5	**Scarsdale** (town/village) Westchester County
10	41.2	**Greenville** (CDP) Westchester County
11	36.8	**Great Neck Plaza** (village) Nassau County
12	35.8	**Thomaston** (village) Nassau County
13	34.8	**Pelham** (village) Westchester County
13	34.8	**University Gardens** (CDP) Nassau County
15	34.2	**Pelham** (town) Westchester County
16	33.7	**Mamaroneck** (town) Westchester County
17	33.5	**Rye** (city) Westchester County
18	33.4	**Pelham Manor** (village) Westchester County
19	31.5	**Hartsdale** (CDP) Westchester County
19	31.5	**Hastings-on-Hudson** (village) Westchester County
21	31.2	**Sands Point** (village) Nassau County
22	31.1	**Flower Hill** (village) Nassau County
22	31.1	**Tuckahoe** (village) Westchester County
24	30.3	**New Castle** (town) Westchester County
25	30.0	**Mount Vernon** (city) Westchester County
26	29.9	**Staten Island** (borough) Richmond County
27	29.1	**Briarcliff Manor** (village) Westchester County
28	28.9	**Eastchester** (town) Westchester County
29	28.6	**Port Washington** (CDP) Nassau County
30	27.8	**Rye Brook** (village) Westchester County
31	27.5	**Yonkers** (city) Westchester County
32	26.4	**Irvington** (village) Westchester County
33	26.0	**Rockville Centre** (village) Nassau County
34	25.9	**Manhasset** (CDP) Nassau County
35	25.5	**Great Neck Estates** (village) Nassau County
36	25.1	**East Williston** (village) Nassau County
37	24.9	**Valley Stream** (village) Nassau County
38	24.7	**Dobbs Ferry** (village) Westchester County
39	24.4	**Garden City** (village) Nassau County
39	24.4	**Lakeview** (CDP) Nassau County
41	24.2	**Croton-on-Hudson** (village) Westchester County
41	24.2	**South Valley Stream** (CDP) Nassau County
43	24.0	**Mamaroneck** (village) Westchester County
44	23.9	**Port Washington North** (village) Nassau County
45	23.6	**Eastchester** (CDP) Westchester County
46	23.5	**New Rochelle** (city) Westchester County
47	23.3	**Hempstead** (village) Nassau County
48	23.0	**Merrick** (CDP) Nassau County
49	22.9	**Greenburgh** (town) Westchester County
50	22.7	**Jericho** (CDP) Nassau County
51	22.5	**Montrose** (CDP) Westchester County
52	22.3	**Herricks** (CDP) Nassau County
53	22.1	**Elmont** (CDP) Nassau County
54	21.9	**Great Neck** (village) Nassau County
55	21.8	**Tarrytown** (village) Westchester County
56	21.7	**Roslyn Heights** (CDP) Nassau County
57	21.5	**Muttontown** (village) Nassau County
58	21.4	**Lido Beach** (CDP) Nassau County
59	21.2	**Cold Spring Harbor** (CDP) Suffolk County
60	20.9	**Harrison** (town/village) Westchester County
61	20.7	**Bedford** (town) Westchester County
62	20.6	**Inwood** (CDP) Nassau County
63	20.5	**Manorhaven** (village) Nassau County
64	20.3	**Woodmere** (CDP) Nassau County
65	20.1	**New Hyde Park** (village) Nassau County
66	20.0	**Lynbrook** (village) Nassau County
67	19.9	**Lansing** (village) Tompkins County
68	19.8	**Pound Ridge** (town) Westchester County
68	19.8	**Rye** (town) Westchester County
70	19.7	**North Hempstead** (town) Nassau County
70	19.7	**Plainview** (CDP) Nassau County
72	19.5	**Philipstown** (town) Putnam County
73	19.4	**Ardsley** (village) Westchester County
73	19.4	**Sleepy Hollow** (village) Westchester County
75	19.2	**Kiryas Joel** (village) Orange County
76	19.1	**Long Beach** (city) Nassau County
76	19.1	**Woodbury** (CDP) Nassau County
78	18.8	**Floral Park** (village) Nassau County
79	18.7	**Garden City Park** (CDP) Nassau County
80	18.6	**Hewlett** (CDP) Nassau County
81	18.5	**Syosset** (CDP) Nassau County
82	18.3	**Malverne** (village) Nassau County
83	18.2	**Baldwin Harbor** (CDP) Nassau County
84	18.1	**Lake Success** (village) Nassau County
84	18.1	**Valhalla** (CDP) Westchester County
86	18.0	**East Hills** (village) Nassau County
87	17.7	**North Valley Stream** (CDP) Nassau County
87	17.7	**White Plains** (city) Westchester County
89	17.6	**Wantagh** (CDP) Nassau County
90	17.5	**East Rockaway** (village) Nassau County
90	17.5	**North New Hyde Park** (CDP) Nassau County
92	17.4	**Lawrence** (village) Nassau County
92	17.4	**Peekskill** (city) Westchester County
94	17.3	**Port Chester** (village) Westchester County
95	17.1	**Hempstead** (town) Nassau County
95	17.1	**Lloyd Harbor** (village) Suffolk County
95	17.1	**North Castle** (town) Westchester County
98	17.0	**Northwest Harbor** (CDP) Suffolk County
99	16.8	**Kings Point** (village) Nassau County
100	16.7	**Ossining** (town) Westchester County
101	16.6	**Island Park** (village) Nassau County
102	16.4	**Baldwin** (CDP) Nassau County
102	16.4	**Mount Pleasant** (town) Westchester County
102	16.4	**Williston Park** (village) Nassau County
105	16.3	**Armonk** (CDP) Westchester County
106	16.2	**Centerport** (CDP) Suffolk County
106	16.2	**Pleasantville** (village) Westchester County
108	15.8	**Bedford Hills** (CDP) Westchester County
108	15.8	**Oceanside** (CDP) Nassau County
110	15.7	**North Merrick** (CDP) Nassau County
110	15.7	**University at Buffalo** (CDP) Erie County
112	15.6	**Cortlandt** (town) Westchester County
113	15.2	**Massapequa** (CDP) Nassau County
113	15.2	**Roosevelt** (CDP) Nassau County
113	15.2	**Searingtown** (CDP) Nassau County
116	14.9	**West Hills** (CDP) Suffolk County
117	14.8	**Seaford** (CDP) Nassau County
118	14.7	**Farmingdale** (village) Nassau County
118	14.7	**Garden City South** (CDP) Nassau County
120	14.6	**North Bellmore** (CDP) Nassau County
121	14.4	**Sea Cliff** (village) Nassau County
122	14.3	**Albany** (city) Albany County
122	14.3	**Massapequa Park** (village) Nassau County
122	14.3	**South Nyack** (village) Rockland County
125	14.2	**Babylon** (village) Suffolk County
125	14.2	**Oyster Bay** (town) Nassau County
125	14.2	**Spring Valley** (village) Rockland County
128	14.1	**East Norwich** (CDP) Nassau County
128	14.1	**Glenwood Landing** (CDP) Nassau County
130	13.9	**Amityville** (village) Suffolk County
130	13.9	**Elmsford** (village) Westchester County
130	13.9	**Monroe** (town) Orange County
133	13.8	**Mineola** (village) Nassau County
134	13.6	**Haverstraw** (village) Rockland County
134	13.6	**Manhasset Hills** (CDP) Nassau County
136	13.5	**Cayuga Heights** (village) Tompkins County
137	13.2	**Freeport** (village) Nassau County
137	13.2	**West Hempstead** (CDP) Nassau County
139	13.1	**Albertson** (CDP) Nassau County
139	13.1	**Huntington** (CDP) Suffolk County
141	13.0	**Bellmore** (CDP) Nassau County
141	13.0	**Ossining** (village) Westchester County
143	12.9	**Harriman** (village) Orange County
143	12.9	**Lewisboro** (town) Westchester County
143	12.9	**Locust Valley** (CDP) Nassau County
146	12.8	**Ithaca** (city) Tompkins County
146	12.8	**Westbury** (village) Nassau County
148	12.5	**East Massapequa** (CDP) Nassau County
149	12.4	**Maybrook** (village) Orange County
150	12.3	**East Farmingdale** (CDP) Suffolk County

Note: This section ranks incorporated places and CDPs (Census Designated Places) with populations of 2,500 or more. Unincorporated postal areas were not considered. Please refer to the User Guide for additional information.

Commute to Work: Walk

Top 150 Places Ranked in *Descending* Order

State Rank	Percent	Place	State Rank	Percent	Place
1	71.2	**Alfred** (village) Allegany County	75	10.0	**Red Hook** (town) Dutchess County
2	61.1	**SUNY Oswego** (CDP) Oswego County	77	9.8	**Pomfret** (town) Chautauqua County
3	59.8	**Alfred** (town) Allegany County	78	9.7	**Poughkeepsie** (town) Dutchess County
4	57.1	**Stony Brook University** (CDP) Suffolk County	79	9.5	**Bath** (village) Steuben County
5	47.5	**Binghamton University** (CDP) Broome County	79	9.5	**Newburgh** (city) Orange County
6	44.8	**Kaser** (village) Rockland County	81	9.3	**Cazenovia** (town) Madison County
7	44.4	**New Square** (village) Rockland County	81	9.3	**Olean** (city) Cattaraugus County
8	38.4	**Ithaca** (city) Tompkins County	83	9.2	**Allegany** (town) Cattaraugus County
9	37.5	**Potsdam** (village) Saint Lawrence County	83	9.2	**Harrietstown** (town) Franklin County
10	37.0	**West Point** (CDP) Orange County	83	9.2	**Sidney** (town) Delaware County
11	35.3	**New Paltz** (village) Ulster County	86	9.0	**Port Chester** (village) Westchester County
12	34.9	**South Hill** (CDP) Tompkins County	87	8.9	**Mount Kisco** (town/village) Westchester County
13	33.8	**Hamilton** (village) Madison County	87	8.9	**Port Jervis** (city) Orange County
14	33.7	**Geneseo** (village) Livingston County	89	8.8	**Great Neck Plaza** (village) Nassau County
15	33.0	**University at Buffalo** (CDP) Erie County	89	8.8	**Oswego** (city) Oswego County
16	32.9	**Canton** (village) Saint Lawrence County	89	8.8	**Rhinebeck** (town) Dutchess County
17	28.4	**Arlington** (CDP) Dutchess County	92	8.7	**Nyack** (village) Rockland County
18	28.3	**Cobleskill** (village) Schoharie County	93	8.6	**Brooklyn** (borough) Kings County
19	27.3	**Kiryas Joel** (village) Orange County	93	8.6	**Catskill** (village) Greene County
20	26.6	**Brockport** (village) Monroe County	93	8.6	**Endicott** (village) Broome County
21	25.3	**Fort Drum** (CDP) Jefferson County	96	8.5	**Corning** (city) Steuben County
22	24.2	**Oneonta** (city) Otsego County	96	8.5	**Hunter** (town) Greene County
23	23.9	**Cazenovia** (village) Madison County	96	8.5	**Walton** (village) Delaware County
23	23.9	**Geneseo** (town) Livingston County	99	8.4	**Augusta** (town) Oneida County
25	22.3	**Delhi** (village) Delaware County	99	8.4	**Westfield** (village) Chautauqua County
26	21.2	**Highlands** (town) Orange County	101	8.3	**Hornell** (city) Steuben County
27	21.1	**Hamilton** (town) Madison County	101	8.3	**Romulus** (town) Seneca County
28	20.4	**Cobleskill** (town) Schoharie County	103	8.2	**Harrison** (town/village) Westchester County
28	20.4	**Manhattan** (borough) New York County	103	8.2	**Northwest Harbor** (CDP) Suffolk County
30	19.6	**Oswego** (town) Oswego County	105	8.1	**Auburn** (city) Cayuga County
31	19.5	**Potsdam** (town) Saint Lawrence County	105	8.1	**Inwood** (CDP) Nassau County
32	18.8	**Otsego** (town) Otsego County	105	8.1	**Malone** (village) Franklin County
33	18.2	**Eaton** (town) Madison County	105	8.1	**Westfield** (town) Chautauqua County
34	18.1	**Hudson** (city) Columbia County	109	8.0	**Elmsford** (village) Westchester County
35	17.5	**Ithaca** (town) Tompkins County	110	7.9	**Boonville** (town) Oneida County
36	17.4	**Le Ray** (town) Jefferson County	110	7.9	**Dix** (town) Schuyler County
37	16.6	**Canton** (town) Saint Lawrence County	110	7.9	**Hancock** (town) Delaware County
38	16.4	**Brookville** (village) Nassau County	110	7.9	**White Plains** (city) Westchester County
39	16.1	**Delhi** (town) Delaware County	114	7.8	**Saratoga Springs** (city) Saratoga County
40	16.0	**Cayuga Heights** (village) Tompkins County	114	7.8	**Starkey** (town) Yates County
40	16.0	**New Paltz** (town) Ulster County	116	7.7	**Ossining** (village) Westchester County
42	15.4	**Sweden** (town) Monroe County	116	7.7	**Wellsville** (town) Allegany County
43	14.7	**Jerusalem** (town) Yates County	118	7.6	**Batavia** (city) Genesee County
44	14.5	**Monsey** (CDP) Rockland County	118	7.6	**Bronx** (borough) Bronx County
45	14.4	**Geneva** (city) Ontario County	118	7.6	**Lake Mohegan** (CDP) Westchester County
46	14.3	**Sleepy Hollow** (village) Westchester County	118	7.6	**Newark** (village) Wayne County
47	14.2	**Old Westbury** (village) Nassau County	118	7.6	**Sherburne** (town) Chenango County
48	14.0	**Cortland** (city) Cortland County	123	7.5	**Dannemora** (village) Clinton County
49	13.7	**Penn Yan** (village) Yates County	123	7.5	**Ellenville** (village) Ulster County
50	12.9	**Kirkland** (town) Oneida County	123	7.5	**Elmira** (city) Chemung County
51	12.8	**Rhinebeck** (village) Dutchess County	123	7.5	**Fairview** (CDP) Westchester County
52	12.7	**Fredonia** (village) Chautauqua County	127	7.4	**Glens Falls** (city) Warren County
53	12.6	**Dansville** (village) Livingston County	127	7.4	**North East** (town) Dutchess County
54	12.1	**Cedarhurst** (village) Nassau County	129	7.3	**Owego** (village) Tioga County
55	11.9	**Saint Johnsville** (town) Montgomery County	129	7.3	**Richmond** (town) Ontario County
56	11.7	**Sidney** (village) Delaware County	131	7.2	**Esopus** (town) Ulster County
57	11.6	**Norwich** (city) Chenango County	131	7.2	**Jamestown** (city) Chautauqua County
58	11.5	**Monticello** (village) Sullivan County	131	7.2	**Pine Plains** (town) Dutchess County
59	11.4	**Lowville** (town) Lewis County	134	7.1	**Perry** (town) Wyoming County
60	11.3	**Syracuse** (city) Onondaga County	134	7.1	**Stanford** (town) Dutchess County
61	10.8	**Poughkeepsie** (city) Dutchess County	134	7.1	**Warsaw** (village) Wyoming County
62	10.7	**North Dansville** (town) Livingston County	137	7.0	**Fairview** (CDP) Dutchess County
62	10.7	**Saranac Lake** (village) Franklin County	137	7.0	**Johnson City** (village) Broome County
64	10.6	**Albany** (city) Albany County	137	7.0	**Mattydale** (CDP) Onondaga County
64	10.6	**Herkimer** (village) Herkimer County	140	6.8	**New Rochelle** (city) Westchester County
66	10.5	**Herkimer** (town) Herkimer County	141	6.7	**Rochester** (city) Monroe County
66	10.5	**Riverside** (CDP) Suffolk County	142	6.6	**White Creek** (town) Washington County
68	10.4	**Monroe** (town) Orange County	143	6.5	**Corinth** (village) Saratoga County
68	10.4	**Plattsburgh** (city) Clinton County	143	6.5	**Davenport** (town) Delaware County
68	10.4	**Troy** (city) Rensselaer County	143	6.5	**Port Washington** (CDP) Nassau County
68	10.4	**Wellsville** (village) Allegany County	143	6.5	**Thompson** (town) Sullivan County
72	10.2	**Milo** (town) Yates County	143	6.5	**Uniondale** (CDP) Nassau County
73	10.1	**Lowville** (village) Lewis County	143	6.5	**Utica** (city) Oneida County
73	10.1	**Whitehall** (town) Washington County	149	6.3	**Lake George** (town) Warren County
75	10.0	**New York** (city)	149	6.3	**Mamaroneck** (town) Westchester County

Note: This section ranks incorporated places and CDPs (Census Designated Places) with populations of 2,500 or more. Unincorporated postal areas were not considered. Please refer to the User Guide for additional information.

Commute to Work: Walk

Top 150 Places Ranked in *Ascending* Order

State Rank	Percent	Place
1	0.0	**Altona** (town) Clinton County
1	0.0	**Bardonia** (CDP) Rockland County
1	0.0	**Bayport** (CDP) Suffolk County
1	0.0	**Bethel** (town) Sullivan County
1	0.0	**Binghamton** (town) Broome County
1	0.0	**Calcium** (CDP) Jefferson County
1	0.0	**Canastota** (village) Madison County
1	0.0	**Champion** (town) Jefferson County
1	0.0	**Charlton** (town) Saratoga County
1	0.0	**Chesterfield** (town) Essex County
1	0.0	**Clarendon** (town) Orleans County
1	0.0	**Clarkson** (CDP) Monroe County
1	0.0	**Conklin** (town) Broome County
1	0.0	**Coxsackie** (village) Greene County
1	0.0	**East Hills** (village) Nassau County
1	0.0	**East Moriches** (CDP) Suffolk County
1	0.0	**East Shoreham** (CDP) Suffolk County
1	0.0	**Elma Center** (CDP) Erie County
1	0.0	**Farmington** (town) Ontario County
1	0.0	**Fenton** (town) Broome County
1	0.0	**Fort Salonga** (CDP) Suffolk County
1	0.0	**Garden City South** (CDP) Nassau County
1	0.0	**Gardnertown** (CDP) Orange County
1	0.0	**Gordon Heights** (CDP) Suffolk County
1	0.0	**Grand Island** (town) Erie County
1	0.0	**Grandyle Village** (CDP) Erie County
1	0.0	**Greenville** (town) Orange County
1	0.0	**Haviland** (CDP) Dutchess County
1	0.0	**Heritage Hills** (CDP) Westchester County
1	0.0	**Highland** (CDP) Ulster County
1	0.0	**Horseheads North** (CDP) Chemung County
1	0.0	**Hurley** (CDP) Ulster County
1	0.0	**Johnstown** (town) Fulton County
1	0.0	**Kirkwood** (town) Broome County
1	0.0	**Lake Carmel** (CDP) Putnam County
1	0.0	**Lakeland** (CDP) Onondaga County
1	0.0	**Lewiston** (village) Niagara County
1	0.0	**Liberty** (village) Sullivan County
1	0.0	**Milton** (CDP) Saratoga County
1	0.0	**Minisink** (town) Orange County
1	0.0	**Minoa** (village) Onondaga County
1	0.0	**Mohawk** (village) Herkimer County
1	0.0	**Moira** (town) Franklin County
1	0.0	**Montebello** (village) Rockland County
1	0.0	**Nesconset** (CDP) Suffolk County
1	0.0	**New Baltimore** (town) Greene County
1	0.0	**New Hempstead** (village) Rockland County
1	0.0	**Newfane** (town) Niagara County
1	0.0	**North Boston** (CDP) Erie County
1	0.0	**Noyack** (CDP) Suffolk County
1	0.0	**Orange Lake** (CDP) Orange County
1	0.0	**Paris** (town) Oneida County
1	0.0	**Pittstown** (town) Rensselaer County
1	0.0	**Ridge** (CDP) Suffolk County
1	0.0	**Rush** (town) Monroe County
1	0.0	**Saint Regis Mohawk Reservation** (reservation) Franklin County
1	0.0	**Schuyler** (town) Herkimer County
1	0.0	**Thornwood** (CDP) Westchester County
1	0.0	**Tioga** (town) Tioga County
1	0.0	**Village Green** (CDP) Onondaga County
1	0.0	**Volney** (town) Oswego County
1	0.0	**Wanakah** (CDP) Erie County
1	0.0	**West Nyack** (CDP) Rockland County
1	0.0	**West Sayville** (CDP) Suffolk County
1	0.0	**Yorkville** (village) Oneida County
66	0.1	**Broadalbin** (town) Fulton County
66	0.1	**Coxsackie** (town) Greene County
66	0.1	**Newark Valley** (town) Tioga County
66	0.1	**Red Oaks Mill** (CDP) Dutchess County
66	0.1	**Schaghticoke** (town) Rensselaer County
66	0.1	**Schodack** (town) Rensselaer County
72	0.2	**Coeymans** (town) Albany County
72	0.2	**Greenlawn** (CDP) Suffolk County
72	0.2	**Islandia** (village) Suffolk County
72	0.2	**La Grange** (town) Dutchess County
72	0.2	**Lancaster** (village) Erie County
72	0.2	**Macedon** (town) Wayne County
72	0.2	**Middle Island** (CDP) Suffolk County
72	0.2	**Moriah** (town) Essex County
72	0.2	**Piermont** (village) Rockland County
72	0.2	**Plainedge** (CDP) Nassau County
72	0.2	**Selden** (CDP) Suffolk County
72	0.2	**Stony Point** (CDP) Rockland County
72	0.2	**Woodbury** (CDP) Nassau County
85	0.3	**Airmont** (village) Rockland County
85	0.3	**Brookhaven** (CDP) Suffolk County
85	0.3	**Canandaigua** (town) Ontario County
85	0.3	**Congers** (CDP) Rockland County
85	0.3	**East Glenville** (CDP) Schenectady County
85	0.3	**East Quogue** (CDP) Suffolk County
85	0.3	**Miller Place** (CDP) Suffolk County
85	0.3	**Mount Hope** (town) Orange County
85	0.3	**Otisco** (town) Onondaga County
85	0.3	**Pomona** (village) Rockland County
85	0.3	**Rochester** (town) Ulster County
85	0.3	**Scotchtown** (CDP) Orange County
85	0.3	**Seneca** (town) Ontario County
85	0.3	**Shelter Island** (town) Suffolk County
85	0.3	**South Blooming Grove** (village) Orange County
85	0.3	**Stillwater** (town) Saratoga County
85	0.3	**Stony Point** (town) Rockland County
85	0.3	**Terryville** (CDP) Suffolk County
103	0.4	**Alexander** (town) Genesee County
103	0.4	**Amsterdam** (town) Montgomery County
103	0.4	**Bethpage** (CDP) Nassau County
103	0.4	**Blue Point** (CDP) Suffolk County
103	0.4	**Boston** (town) Erie County
103	0.4	**Carmel Hamlet** (CDP) Putnam County
103	0.4	**Centereach** (CDP) Suffolk County
103	0.4	**Chenango** (town) Broome County
103	0.4	**Clarkson** (town) Monroe County
103	0.4	**Dix Hills** (CDP) Suffolk County
103	0.4	**Hamptonburgh** (town) Orange County
103	0.4	**Hauppauge** (CDP) Suffolk County
103	0.4	**Lancaster** (town) Erie County
103	0.4	**Manhasset Hills** (CDP) Nassau County
103	0.4	**Manorville** (CDP) Suffolk County
103	0.4	**Montgomery** (village) Orange County
103	0.4	**Montrose** (CDP) Westchester County
103	0.4	**Mount Sinai** (CDP) Suffolk County
103	0.4	**New Windsor** (CDP) Orange County
103	0.4	**North Bellmore** (CDP) Nassau County
103	0.4	**North Wantagh** (CDP) Nassau County
103	0.4	**Pembroke** (town) Genesee County
103	0.4	**Pierrepont** (town) Saint Lawrence County
103	0.4	**Pompey** (town) Onondaga County
103	0.4	**Walworth** (town) Wayne County
103	0.4	**West Glens Falls** (CDP) Warren County
129	0.5	**Baldwin Harbor** (CDP) Nassau County
129	0.5	**Baywood** (CDP) Suffolk County
129	0.5	**Brasher** (town) Saint Lawrence County
129	0.5	**Clifton Park** (town) Saratoga County
129	0.5	**East Fishkill** (town) Dutchess County
129	0.5	**East Massapequa** (CDP) Nassau County
129	0.5	**Gates** (CDP) Monroe County
129	0.5	**Greenfield** (town) Saratoga County
129	0.5	**Hewlett** (CDP) Nassau County
129	0.5	**Holtsville** (CDP) Suffolk County
129	0.5	**Islip** (CDP) Suffolk County
129	0.5	**Jefferson Valley-Yorktown** (CDP) Westchester County
129	0.5	**Keeseville** (village) Clinton County
129	0.5	**Louisville** (town) Saint Lawrence County
129	0.5	**Malta** (town) Saratoga County
129	0.5	**Mastic Beach** (village) Suffolk County
129	0.5	**Mattituck** (CDP) Suffolk County
129	0.5	**Medford** (CDP) Suffolk County
129	0.5	**Nassau** (town) Rensselaer County
129	0.5	**Neversink** (town) Sullivan County
129	0.5	**Newburgh** (town) Orange County
129	0.5	**North Hills** (village) Nassau County

Note: *This section ranks incorporated places and CDPs (Census Designated Places) with populations of 2,500 or more. Unincorporated postal areas were not considered. Please refer to the User Guide for additional information.*

Commute to Work: Work from Home

Top 150 Places Ranked in *Descending* Order

State Rank	Percent	Place	State Rank	Percent	Place
1	34.9	**West Point** (CDP) Orange County	76	8.7	**Greenville** (CDP) Westchester County
2	20.6	**Woodstock** (town) Ulster County	76	8.7	**Hurley** (town) Ulster County
3	20.1	**Highlands** (town) Orange County	76	8.7	**Irvington** (village) Westchester County
4	19.9	**Lido Beach** (CDP) Nassau County	76	8.7	**Ithaca** (town) Tompkins County
5	16.5	**Stanford** (town) Dutchess County	76	8.7	**Jerusalem** (town) Yates County
6	15.6	**Afton** (town) Chenango County	76	8.7	**Pittsford** (town) Monroe County
7	15.2	**Pound Ridge** (town) Westchester County	82	8.6	**Bardonia** (CDP) Rockland County
8	14.4	**Southampton** (village) Suffolk County	82	8.6	**Cutchogue** (CDP) Suffolk County
9	14.1	**Noyack** (CDP) Suffolk County	82	8.6	**Ellisburg** (town) Jefferson County
10	14.0	**Great Neck Estates** (village) Nassau County	82	8.6	**Greenwood Lake** (village) Orange County
11	13.9	**Benton** (town) Yates County	82	8.6	**Hamilton** (town) Madison County
12	13.7	**Old Westbury** (village) Nassau County	82	8.6	**Mattituck** (CDP) Suffolk County
13	13.5	**North Salem** (town) Westchester County	82	8.6	**Starkey** (town) Yates County
14	13.3	**Binghamton University** (CDP) Broome County	89	8.5	**Marcellus** (town) Onondaga County
14	13.3	**Viola** (CDP) Rockland County	89	8.5	**Palatine** (town) Montgomery County
16	12.9	**Kings Point** (village) Nassau County	91	8.4	**Bronxville** (village) Westchester County
17	12.8	**Northwest Harbor** (CDP) Suffolk County	91	8.4	**Chesterfield** (town) Essex County
17	12.8	**South Hill** (CDP) Tompkins County	91	8.4	**Schroeppel** (town) Oswego County
17	12.8	**Stockholm** (town) Saint Lawrence County	94	8.3	**Cazenovia** (town) Madison County
20	12.6	**Westhampton** (CDP) Suffolk County	94	8.3	**Otsego** (town) Otsego County
21	12.5	**Wesley Hills** (village) Rockland County	94	8.3	**Penn Yan** (village) Yates County
22	12.4	**Brookville** (village) Nassau County	94	8.3	**Saugerties** (village) Ulster County
22	12.4	**Delaware** (town) Sullivan County	98	8.2	**Esopus** (town) Ulster County
24	12.3	**Chatham** (town) Columbia County	99	8.1	**Fairport** (village) Monroe County
25	12.2	**Fort Drum** (CDP) Jefferson County	100	8.0	**Bellmore** (CDP) Nassau County
26	12.1	**Clinton** (town) Dutchess County	100	8.0	**Callicoon** (town) Sullivan County
26	12.1	**Tully** (town) Onondaga County	100	8.0	**Chester** (town) Warren County
28	12.0	**Red Hook** (town) Dutchess County	100	8.0	**East Moriches** (CDP) Suffolk County
28	12.0	**Saratoga Springs** (city) Saratoga County	100	8.0	**Lloyd Harbor** (village) Suffolk County
30	11.9	**Briarcliff Manor** (village) Westchester County	100	8.0	**Victor** (town) Ontario County
31	11.8	**Flower Hill** (village) Nassau County	106	7.9	**Cornwall** (town) Orange County
32	11.7	**Hunter** (town) Greene County	106	7.9	**Greenfield** (town) Saratoga County
33	11.6	**Chautauqua** (town) Chautauqua County	106	7.9	**Manhasset** (CDP) Nassau County
34	11.5	**Philipstown** (town) Putnam County	106	7.9	**Monsey** (CDP) Rockland County
35	11.3	**Balmville** (CDP) Orange County	106	7.9	**Mount Ivy** (CDP) Rockland County
36	11.1	**Sands Point** (village) Nassau County	106	7.9	**New Castle** (town) Westchester County
37	11.0	**Middletown** (town) Delaware County	106	7.9	**Olive** (town) Ulster County
38	10.8	**Rhinebeck** (town) Dutchess County	106	7.9	**Russia** (town) Herkimer County
39	10.7	**Red Oaks Mill** (CDP) Dutchess County	114	7.8	**Greenville** (town) Orange County
40	10.6	**Lewisboro** (town) Westchester County	114	7.8	**Shelter Island** (town) Suffolk County
41	10.5	**Hamilton** (village) Madison County	114	7.8	**Stony Brook University** (CDP) Suffolk County
41	10.5	**Milo** (town) Yates County	117	7.7	**East Syracuse** (village) Onondaga County
43	10.4	**Montauk** (CDP) Suffolk County	117	7.7	**Ithaca** (city) Tompkins County
44	10.3	**Hartsdale** (CDP) Westchester County	117	7.7	**Jay** (town) Essex County
45	10.2	**Lawrence** (village) Nassau County	117	7.7	**Pelham Manor** (village) Westchester County
46	10.1	**Bedford** (town) Westchester County	117	7.7	**SUNY Oswego** (CDP) Oswego County
46	10.1	**Marbletown** (town) Ulster County	122	7.6	**Hamptonburgh** (town) Orange County
48	10.0	**Delhi** (village) Delaware County	122	7.6	**Munsey Park** (village) Nassau County
48	10.0	**Westmoreland** (town) Oneida County	122	7.6	**Potsdam** (village) Saint Lawrence County
50	9.8	**Hastings-on-Hudson** (village) Westchester County	122	7.6	**Rochester** (town) Ulster County
50	9.8	**Oneonta** (town) Otsego County	126	7.5	**Airmont** (village) Rockland County
50	9.8	**Scarsdale** (town/village) Westchester County	126	7.5	**Arlington** (CDP) Dutchess County
50	9.8	**Thomaston** (village) Nassau County	126	7.5	**Cape Vincent** (town) Jefferson County
54	9.7	**Larchmont** (village) Westchester County	126	7.5	**Somerset** (town) Niagara County
54	9.7	**Piermont** (village) Rockland County	126	7.5	**South Nyack** (village) Rockland County
56	9.6	**Otisco** (town) Onondaga County	131	7.4	**Boonville** (town) Oneida County
56	9.6	**Pomona** (village) Rockland County	131	7.4	**Eaton** (town) Madison County
56	9.6	**Rye** (city) Westchester County	131	7.4	**Great Neck** (village) Nassau County
59	9.5	**North Castle** (town) Westchester County	131	7.4	**Melville** (CDP) Suffolk County
60	9.3	**Le Ray** (town) Jefferson County	131	7.4	**Rhinebeck** (village) Dutchess County
60	9.3	**Pine Plains** (town) Dutchess County	131	7.4	**Southampton** (town) Suffolk County
60	9.3	**Salem** (town) Washington County	131	7.4	**Warwick** (town) Orange County
63	9.2	**Cazenovia** (village) Madison County	138	7.3	**Ballston Spa** (village) Saratoga County
63	9.2	**Washington** (town) Dutchess County	138	7.3	**Davenport** (town) Delaware County
65	9.1	**Centerport** (CDP) Suffolk County	138	7.3	**Gardiner** (town) Ulster County
65	9.1	**East Hampton** (town) Suffolk County	138	7.3	**Goshen** (town) Orange County
65	9.1	**Mendon** (town) Monroe County	138	7.3	**Guilford** (town) Chenango County
65	9.1	**Westfield** (town) Chautauqua County	138	7.3	**Highland** (CDP) Ulster County
69	9.0	**Huntington** (CDP) Suffolk County	138	7.3	**New Hempstead** (village) Rockland County
69	9.0	**Mamaroneck** (town) Westchester County	145	7.2	**Chestnut Ridge** (village) Rockland County
71	8.9	**Firthcliffe** (CDP) Orange County	145	7.2	**Whitesboro** (village) Oneida County
72	8.8	**East Hills** (village) Nassau County	147	7.1	**Enfield** (town) Tompkins County
72	8.8	**Lake Success** (village) Nassau County	147	7.1	**Harris Hill** (CDP) Erie County
72	8.8	**Marcy** (town) Oneida County	147	7.1	**Hurley** (CDP) Ulster County
72	8.8	**Minisink** (town) Orange County	150	7.0	**Clarence Center** (CDP) Erie County

Note: This section ranks incorporated places and CDPs (Census Designated Places) with populations of 2,500 or more. Unincorporated postal areas were not considered. Please refer to the User Guide for additional information.

Commute to Work: Work from Home

Top 150 Places Ranked in *Ascending* Order

State Rank	Percent	Place	State Rank	Percent	Place
1	0.0	**Mount Morris** (village) Livingston County	76	1.4	**Brentwood** (CDP) Suffolk County
1	0.0	**North Boston** (CDP) Erie County	76	1.4	**Carle Place** (CDP) Nassau County
1	0.0	**Palermo** (town) Oswego County	76	1.4	**Coxsackie** (town) Greene County
1	0.0	**Riverside** (CDP) Suffolk County	76	1.4	**Deerpark** (town) Orange County
1	0.0	**Saint Regis Mohawk Reservation** (reservation) Franklin County	76	1.4	**Evans** (town) Erie County
6	0.2	**Bainbridge** (town) Chenango County	76	1.4	**Horseheads** (village) Chemung County
7	0.3	**Lackawanna** (city) Erie County	76	1.4	**Livonia** (town) Livingston County
7	0.3	**Veteran** (town) Chemung County	76	1.4	**Mineola** (village) Nassau County
9	0.4	**Bohemia** (CDP) Suffolk County	76	1.4	**Norwich** (town) Chenango County
9	0.4	**Clarendon** (town) Orleans County	76	1.4	**Nunda** (town) Livingston County
9	0.4	**Hamburg** (village) Erie County	76	1.4	**Vernon** (town) Oneida County
9	0.4	**Lyons** (town) Wayne County	76	1.4	**Warrensburg** (town) Warren County
13	0.5	**Conklin** (town) Broome County	88	1.5	**Au Sable** (town) Clinton County
13	0.5	**Neversink** (town) Sullivan County	88	1.5	**Copiague** (CDP) Suffolk County
13	0.5	**Pamelia** (town) Jefferson County	88	1.5	**Coxsackie** (village) Greene County
16	0.6	**Lyons** (village) Wayne County	88	1.5	**Darien** (town) Genesee County
16	0.6	**Madison** (town) Madison County	88	1.5	**Depew** (village) Erie County
16	0.6	**Perth** (town) Fulton County	88	1.5	**Dunkirk** (city) Chautauqua County
19	0.7	**Blasdell** (village) Erie County	88	1.5	**Gordon Heights** (CDP) Suffolk County
19	0.7	**Gaines** (town) Orleans County	88	1.5	**LaFayette** (town) Onondaga County
19	0.7	**Mount Morris** (town) Livingston County	88	1.5	**Lindenhurst** (village) Suffolk County
22	0.8	**Canastota** (village) Madison County	88	1.5	**Middle Island** (CDP) Suffolk County
22	0.8	**Central Islip** (CDP) Suffolk County	88	1.5	**Niagara Falls** (city) Niagara County
22	0.8	**Mattydale** (CDP) Onondaga County	88	1.5	**Perry** (town) Wyoming County
22	0.8	**Newark** (village) Wayne County	88	1.5	**Portville** (town) Cattaraugus County
22	0.8	**Sidney** (village) Delaware County	88	1.5	**Randolph** (town) Cattaraugus County
27	0.9	**Colesville** (town) Broome County	88	1.5	**Scotchtown** (CDP) Orange County
27	0.9	**Gloversville** (city) Fulton County	88	1.5	**Washingtonville** (village) Orange County
27	0.9	**Hoosick Falls** (village) Rensselaer County	104	1.6	**Albion** (village) Orleans County
27	0.9	**Hornell** (city) Steuben County	104	1.6	**Alden** (town) Erie County
27	0.9	**Schuyler** (town) Herkimer County	104	1.6	**Barton** (town) Tioga County
27	0.9	**Wellsville** (town) Allegany County	104	1.6	**Batavia** (city) Genesee County
33	1.0	**Broadalbin** (village) Fulton County	104	1.6	**Catskill** (village) Greene County
33	1.0	**Danby** (town) Tompkins County	104	1.6	**Clarkson** (town) Monroe County
33	1.0	**Deer Park** (CDP) Suffolk County	104	1.6	**Dolgeville** (village) Herkimer County
33	1.0	**Gouverneur** (village) Saint Lawrence County	104	1.6	**Floyd** (town) Oneida County
33	1.0	**Hillcrest** (CDP) Rockland County	104	1.6	**Lake Erie Beach** (CDP) Erie County
33	1.0	**Mechanicstown** (CDP) Orange County	104	1.6	**Marion** (town) Wayne County
33	1.0	**Owego** (village) Tioga County	104	1.6	**North Lindenhurst** (CDP) Suffolk County
33	1.0	**Ravena** (village) Albany County	104	1.6	**Oakfield** (town) Genesee County
33	1.0	**Schoharie** (town) Schoharie County	104	1.6	**Oneida** (city) Madison County
33	1.0	**Vails Gate** (CDP) Orange County	104	1.6	**Poughkeepsie** (city) Dutchess County
33	1.0	**Wellsville** (village) Allegany County	104	1.6	**Saint Johnsville** (town) Montgomery County
44	1.1	**Horseheads North** (CDP) Chemung County	104	1.6	**Schaghticoke** (town) Rensselaer County
44	1.1	**New Haven** (town) Oswego County	104	1.6	**Schuyler Falls** (town) Clinton County
44	1.1	**North Bay Shore** (CDP) Suffolk County	104	1.6	**Scotia** (village) Schenectady County
44	1.1	**Owasco** (town) Cayuga County	104	1.6	**Southport** (CDP) Chemung County
44	1.1	**Sloan** (village) Erie County	123	1.7	**Albion** (town) Orleans County
44	1.1	**South Lockport** (CDP) Niagara County	123	1.7	**Attica** (village) Wyoming County
44	1.1	**Village Green** (CDP) Onondaga County	123	1.7	**Cheektowaga** (town) Erie County
44	1.1	**Warrensburg** (CDP) Warren County	123	1.7	**Corning** (city) Steuben County
44	1.1	**Yorkshire** (town) Cattaraugus County	123	1.7	**Corning** (town) Steuben County
53	1.2	**Albertson** (CDP) Nassau County	123	1.7	**Dannemora** (town) Clinton County
53	1.2	**Bennington** (town) Wyoming County	123	1.7	**Elmira Heights** (village) Chemung County
53	1.2	**Brutus** (town) Cayuga County	123	1.7	**Elmont** (CDP) Nassau County
53	1.2	**East Rockaway** (village) Nassau County	123	1.7	**Frankfort** (town) Herkimer County
53	1.2	**Lyncourt** (CDP) Onondaga County	123	1.7	**Franklinville** (town) Cattaraugus County
53	1.2	**Newfane** (CDP) Niagara County	123	1.7	**Mayfield** (town) Fulton County
53	1.2	**North Amityville** (CDP) Suffolk County	123	1.7	**Middleburgh** (town) Schoharie County
53	1.2	**Oswego** (city) Oswego County	123	1.7	**Nassau** (town) Rensselaer County
53	1.2	**Perry** (village) Wyoming County	123	1.7	**New Cassel** (CDP) Nassau County
53	1.2	**Plainedge** (CDP) Nassau County	123	1.7	**North Bellport** (CDP) Suffolk County
53	1.2	**Ronkonkoma** (CDP) Suffolk County	123	1.7	**North Valley Stream** (CDP) Nassau County
53	1.2	**South Blooming Grove** (village) Orange County	123	1.7	**Riga** (town) Monroe County
53	1.2	**Springville** (village) Erie County	123	1.7	**Rocky Point** (CDP) Suffolk County
53	1.2	**Whitehall** (town) Washington County	123	1.7	**Salamanca** (city) Cattaraugus County
53	1.2	**Williston Park** (village) Nassau County	123	1.7	**Saranac** (town) Clinton County
68	1.3	**Big Flats** (CDP) Chemung County	123	1.7	**Watervliet** (city) Albany County
68	1.3	**Colonie** (village) Albany County	123	1.7	**West Bay Shore** (CDP) Suffolk County
68	1.3	**Fort Edward** (village) Washington County	145	1.8	**Altona** (town) Clinton County
68	1.3	**Galeville** (CDP) Onondaga County	145	1.8	**Centereach** (CDP) Suffolk County
68	1.3	**Lakeland** (CDP) Onondaga County	145	1.8	**Cheektowaga** (CDP) Erie County
68	1.3	**Otego** (town) Otsego County	145	1.8	**Clarkson** (CDP) Monroe County
68	1.3	**Poestenkill** (town) Rensselaer County	145	1.8	**Fenton** (town) Broome County
68	1.3	**Southport** (town) Chemung County	145	1.8	**Glens Falls** (city) Warren County

Note: This section ranks incorporated places and CDPs (Census Designated Places) with populations of 2,500 or more. Unincorporated postal areas were not considered. Please refer to the User Guide for additional information.

Mean Travel Time to Work

Top 150 Places Ranked in *Descending* Order

State Rank	Minutes	Place
1	49.7	**Greenwood Lake** (village) Orange County
2	47.0	**Sands Point** (village) Nassau County
3	46.5	**Munsey Park** (village) Nassau County
4	45.6	**Larchmont** (village) Westchester County
5	45.5	**Greenville** (CDP) Westchester County
6	45.4	**Manorhaven** (village) Nassau County
7	44.3	**Pound Ridge** (town) Westchester County
8	44.2	**Bronx** (borough) Bronx County
9	44.0	**Philipstown** (town) Putnam County
9	44.0	**Staten Island** (borough) Richmond County
11	43.8	**University Gardens** (CDP) Nassau County
12	43.7	**Scarsdale** (town/village) Westchester County
13	43.5	**Lewisboro** (town) Westchester County
13	43.5	**Lloyd Harbor** (village) Suffolk County
13	43.5	**Queens** (borough) Queens County
16	43.3	**Muttontown** (village) Nassau County
17	43.2	**New Castle** (town) Westchester County
18	42.9	**Lake Carmel** (CDP) Putnam County
18	42.9	**Valley Stream** (village) Nassau County
20	42.4	**Brooklyn** (borough) Kings County
20	42.4	**Roslyn Heights** (CDP) Nassau County
22	42.3	**Flower Hill** (village) Nassau County
22	42.3	**North Valley Stream** (CDP) Nassau County
22	42.3	**Putnam Valley** (town) Putnam County
22	42.3	**South Valley Stream** (CDP) Nassau County
26	42.1	**Mount Hope** (town) Orange County
27	41.7	**Woodbury** (CDP) Nassau County
28	41.6	**Herricks** (CDP) Nassau County
29	41.4	**Lido Beach** (CDP) Nassau County
30	41.3	**Kent** (town) Putnam County
31	41.2	**Long Beach** (city) Nassau County
31	41.2	**Pawling** (town) Dutchess County
33	41.0	**Montrose** (CDP) Westchester County
33	41.0	**Thomaston** (village) Nassau County
35	40.9	**Shandaken** (town) Ulster County
35	40.9	**Woodmere** (CDP) Nassau County
37	40.8	**East Norwich** (CDP) Nassau County
37	40.8	**Greenville** (town) Orange County
37	40.8	**New York** (city)
40	40.7	**Tuxedo** (town) Orange County
41	40.2	**Elmont** (CDP) Nassau County
41	40.2	**Woodbury** (town) Orange County
43	40.1	**Mechanicstown** (CDP) Orange County
43	40.1	**Warwick** (town) Orange County
45	40.0	**Bronxville** (village) Westchester County
45	40.0	**Garden City Park** (CDP) Nassau County
47	39.8	**Cold Spring Harbor** (CDP) Suffolk County
47	39.8	**Cortlandt** (town) Westchester County
49	39.7	**Croton-on-Hudson** (village) Westchester County
49	39.7	**Fort Salonga** (CDP) Suffolk County
49	39.7	**Woodbury** (village) Orange County
52	39.6	**Briarcliff Manor** (village) Westchester County
52	39.6	**East Hills** (village) Nassau County
54	39.5	**Miller Place** (CDP) Suffolk County
55	39.4	**Merrick** (CDP) Nassau County
56	39.3	**Dover** (town) Dutchess County
57	39.2	**Blooming Grove** (town) Orange County
57	39.2	**Rockville Centre** (village) Nassau County
57	39.2	**Washingtonville** (village) Orange County
60	39.1	**Baldwin Harbor** (CDP) Nassau County
60	39.1	**Hastings-on-Hudson** (village) Westchester County
60	39.1	**Tuckahoe** (village) Westchester County
63	39.0	**Searingtown** (CDP) Nassau County
64	38.9	**Carmel Hamlet** (CDP) Putnam County
64	38.9	**Patterson** (town) Putnam County
66	38.7	**Harriman** (village) Orange County
66	38.7	**Port Washington** (CDP) Nassau County
68	38.6	**Manhasset Hills** (CDP) Nassau County
69	38.5	**Bedford** (town) Westchester County
69	38.5	**Plainview** (CDP) Nassau County
69	38.5	**Syosset** (CDP) Nassau County
72	38.4	**Beekman** (town) Dutchess County
72	38.4	**Mastic Beach** (village) Suffolk County
74	38.1	**South Blooming Grove** (village) Orange County
75	38.0	**Carmel** (town) Putnam County
75	38.0	**Crawford** (town) Orange County
77	37.7	**Jefferson Valley-Yorktown** (CDP) Westchester County
77	37.7	**Rye** (city) Westchester County
79	37.6	**East Fishkill** (town) Dutchess County
79	37.6	**Hartsdale** (CDP) Westchester County
79	37.6	**Myers Corner** (CDP) Dutchess County
79	37.6	**Port Washington North** (village) Nassau County
83	37.5	**Garden City** (village) Nassau County
83	37.5	**Malverne** (village) Nassau County
83	37.5	**Mamaroneck** (town) Westchester County
83	37.5	**Nunda** (town) Livingston County
87	37.4	**Fishkill** (town) Dutchess County
87	37.4	**North Bellmore** (CDP) Nassau County
87	37.4	**North New Hyde Park** (CDP) Nassau County
90	37.3	**Chester** (town) Orange County
90	37.3	**Huntington** (town) Suffolk County
90	37.3	**Lawrence** (village) Nassau County
93	37.2	**Heritage Hills** (CDP) Westchester County
93	37.2	**Massapequa Park** (village) Nassau County
93	37.2	**Peekskill** (city) Westchester County
93	37.2	**Putnam Lake** (CDP) Putnam County
93	37.2	**West Hills** (CDP) Suffolk County
98	37.1	**Centerport** (CDP) Suffolk County
98	37.1	**Jericho** (CDP) Nassau County
98	37.1	**Mamakating** (town) Sullivan County
98	37.1	**New Hempstead** (village) Rockland County
98	37.1	**North Salem** (town) Westchester County
98	37.1	**Somers** (town) Westchester County
104	37.0	**East Shoreham** (CDP) Suffolk County
105	36.9	**Glenwood Landing** (CDP) Nassau County
105	36.9	**Lynbrook** (village) Nassau County
105	36.9	**Oceanside** (CDP) Nassau County
108	36.8	**Olive** (town) Ulster County
109	36.7	**Dix Hills** (CDP) Suffolk County
109	36.7	**Lake Success** (village) Nassau County
109	36.7	**Shawangunk** (town) Ulster County
112	36.6	**Florida** (village) Orange County
113	36.5	**Pittstown** (town) Rensselaer County
113	36.5	**Port Jefferson Station** (CDP) Suffolk County
113	36.5	**Seaford** (CDP) Nassau County
116	36.4	**Baldwin** (CDP) Nassau County
116	36.4	**Lake Mohegan** (CDP) Westchester County
118	36.3	**Beacon** (city) Dutchess County
118	36.3	**Irvington** (village) Westchester County
118	36.3	**Massapequa** (CDP) Nassau County
118	36.3	**Wappinger** (town) Dutchess County
122	36.2	**Great Neck Plaza** (village) Nassau County
122	36.2	**Lakeview** (CDP) Nassau County
122	36.2	**Montebello** (village) Rockland County
122	36.2	**Rocky Point** (CDP) Suffolk County
122	36.2	**Sound Beach** (CDP) Suffolk County
127	36.1	**Garden City South** (CDP) Nassau County
127	36.1	**North Hempstead** (town) Nassau County
127	36.1	**Southeast** (town) Putnam County
130	36.0	**Bellmore** (CDP) Nassau County
130	36.0	**Goshen** (town) Orange County
130	36.0	**Kings Park** (CDP) Suffolk County
130	36.0	**Rye Brook** (village) Westchester County
134	35.9	**East Rockaway** (village) Nassau County
134	35.9	**Pelham Manor** (village) Westchester County
134	35.9	**Saint Regis Mohawk Reservation** (reservation) Franklin County
134	35.9	**Union Vale** (town) Dutchess County
138	35.8	**Glen Head** (CDP) Nassau County
138	35.8	**Hempstead** (town) Nassau County
138	35.8	**Mahopac** (CDP) Putnam County
138	35.8	**Middleburgh** (town) Schoharie County
138	35.8	**Yorktown** (town) Westchester County
143	35.7	**Bayville** (village) Nassau County
143	35.7	**Cutchogue** (CDP) Suffolk County
143	35.7	**Lake Grove** (village) Suffolk County
146	35.6	**East Williston** (village) Nassau County
146	35.6	**North Massapequa** (CDP) Nassau County
146	35.6	**North Merrick** (CDP) Nassau County
146	35.6	**North Wantagh** (CDP) Nassau County
150	35.5	**Clinton** (town) Dutchess County

Note: *This section ranks incorporated places and CDPs (Census Designated Places) with populations of 2,500 or more. Unincorporated postal areas were not considered. Please refer to the User Guide for additional information.*

Mean Travel Time to Work

Top 150 Places Ranked in *Ascending* Order

State Rank	Minutes	Place
1	8.6	**Fort Drum** (CDP) Jefferson County
2	9.5	**West Point** (CDP) Orange County
3	9.6	**SUNY Oswego** (CDP) Oswego County
4	9.7	**Alfred** (village) Allegany County
5	10.6	**Le Ray** (town) Jefferson County
6	10.9	**Alfred** (town) Allegany County
7	11.9	**Hamilton** (village) Madison County
8	12.6	**Binghamton University** (CDP) Broome County
9	12.9	**Potsdam** (village) Saint Lawrence County
10	13.1	**Dunkirk** (city) Chautauqua County
10	13.1	**Tupper Lake** (village) Franklin County
12	13.5	**Cayuga Heights** (village) Tompkins County
13	13.6	**Ellicott** (town) Chautauqua County
13	13.6	**Ogdensburg** (city) Saint Lawrence County
13	13.6	**University at Buffalo** (CDP) Erie County
16	13.7	**South Hill** (CDP) Tompkins County
17	13.8	**Pamelia** (town) Jefferson County
17	13.8	**Tupper Lake** (town) Franklin County
19	13.9	**Calcium** (CDP) Jefferson County
19	13.9	**Fredonia** (village) Chautauqua County
19	13.9	**Whitesboro** (village) Oneida County
22	14.1	**Plattsburgh** (city) Clinton County
23	14.2	**Kaser** (village) Rockland County
24	14.4	**Northeast Ithaca** (CDP) Tompkins County
25	14.5	**East Syracuse** (village) Onondaga County
25	14.5	**New York Mills** (village) Oneida County
27	14.6	**Lyncourt** (CDP) Onondaga County
28	14.7	**Jamestown** (city) Chautauqua County
29	14.8	**Watertown** (city) Jefferson County
30	14.9	**Oneonta** (city) Otsego County
30	14.9	**Pomfret** (town) Chautauqua County
32	15.0	**Lakewood** (village) Chautauqua County
33	15.1	**Corning** (city) Steuben County
33	15.1	**Ithaca** (town) Tompkins County
35	15.2	**New Square** (village) Rockland County
36	15.3	**Hamilton** (town) Madison County
37	15.5	**Wellsville** (village) Allegany County
38	15.6	**Gang Mills** (CDP) Steuben County
39	15.7	**Bath** (village) Steuben County
40	15.9	**Galeville** (CDP) Onondaga County
40	15.9	**Otsego** (town) Otsego County
40	15.9	**Wellsville** (town) Allegany County
43	16.0	**De Witt** (town) Onondaga County
43	16.0	**Johnson City** (village) Broome County
43	16.0	**Olean** (city) Cattaraugus County
46	16.1	**Norwich** (city) Chenango County
46	16.1	**Saranac Lake** (village) Franklin County
48	16.2	**Elmira** (town) Chemung County
48	16.2	**Geneseo** (village) Livingston County
48	16.2	**Ithaca** (city) Tompkins County
48	16.2	**Lake Placid** (village) Essex County
48	16.2	**Whitestown** (town) Oneida County
53	16.3	**Dickinson** (town) Broome County
53	16.3	**Kirkland** (town) Oneida County
53	16.3	**Mohawk** (village) Herkimer County
53	16.3	**North Elba** (town) Essex County
53	16.3	**Potsdam** (town) Saint Lawrence County
53	16.3	**West Elmira** (CDP) Chemung County
59	16.4	**Busti** (town) Chautauqua County
60	16.5	**Geneva** (town) Ontario County
60	16.5	**Menands** (village) Albany County
62	16.6	**Brighton** (CDP) Monroe County
62	16.6	**Horseheads** (village) Chemung County
62	16.6	**Marcy** (town) Oneida County
65	16.7	**Cortland** (city) Cortland County
65	16.7	**Gates** (CDP) Monroe County
67	16.8	**Eggertsville** (CDP) Erie County
67	16.8	**Malone** (village) Franklin County
67	16.8	**Massena** (village) Saint Lawrence County
67	16.8	**New Hartford** (town) Oneida County
67	16.8	**Waverly** (village) Tioga County
72	16.9	**Canton** (village) Saint Lawrence County
72	16.9	**Delhi** (village) Delaware County
72	16.9	**East Rochester** (town/village) Monroe County
72	16.9	**Green Island** (town/village) Albany County
72	16.9	**Lansing** (village) Tompkins County
77	17.0	**Binghamton** (city) Broome County
77	17.0	**Harrietstown** (town) Franklin County
79	17.2	**Colonie** (village) Albany County
79	17.2	**Mattydale** (CDP) Onondaga County
79	17.2	**Mount Morris** (town) Livingston County
79	17.2	**Niagara** (town) Niagara County
83	17.3	**Erwin** (town) Steuben County
83	17.3	**Hornell** (city) Steuben County
83	17.3	**Rutland** (town) Jefferson County
86	17.4	**Gaines** (town) Orleans County
86	17.4	**Glens Falls** (city) Warren County
86	17.4	**Munsons Corners** (CDP) Cortland County
86	17.4	**Utica** (city) Oneida County
90	17.5	**Alexandria** (town) Jefferson County
90	17.5	**Penn Yan** (village) Yates County
90	17.5	**Rome** (city) Oneida County
90	17.5	**Williamsville** (village) Erie County
94	17.6	**Corning** (town) Steuben County
95	17.7	**Massena** (town) Saint Lawrence County
95	17.7	**Southport** (CDP) Chemung County
97	17.8	**Cortlandville** (town) Cortland County
97	17.8	**Malone** (town) Franklin County
97	17.8	**Oswego** (city) Oswego County
97	17.8	**Plattsburgh** (town) Clinton County
97	17.8	**Schuyler Falls** (town) Clinton County
97	17.8	**Stony Brook University** (CDP) Suffolk County
103	17.9	**Allegany** (town) Cattaraugus County
104	18.0	**Auburn** (city) Cayuga County
104	18.0	**Mount Morris** (village) Livingston County
104	18.0	**North Syracuse** (village) Onondaga County
107	18.1	**Endwell** (CDP) Broome County
107	18.1	**Lansing** (town) Tompkins County
107	18.1	**Salamanca** (city) Cattaraugus County
107	18.1	**Salina** (town) Onondaga County
107	18.1	**Union** (town) Broome County
112	18.2	**Webster** (village) Monroe County
113	18.3	**Highlands** (town) Orange County
113	18.3	**Niagara Falls** (city) Niagara County
113	18.3	**Pittsford** (town) Monroe County
116	18.4	**Albion** (village) Orleans County
116	18.4	**Syracuse** (city) Onondaga County
116	18.4	**Vestal** (town) Broome County
119	18.5	**Batavia** (city) Genesee County
119	18.5	**Elmira** (city) Chemung County
119	18.5	**Gates** (town) Monroe County
119	18.5	**Henrietta** (town) Monroe County
119	18.5	**Horseheads** (town) Chemung County
119	18.5	**Owego** (village) Tioga County
119	18.5	**Watervliet** (city) Albany County
119	18.5	**Yorkville** (village) Oneida County
127	18.6	**Albany** (city) Albany County
127	18.6	**Blasdell** (village) Erie County
127	18.6	**Eaton** (town) Madison County
127	18.6	**Ellery** (town) Chautauqua County
127	18.6	**Elmira Heights** (village) Chemung County
127	18.6	**Herkimer** (village) Herkimer County
127	18.6	**Johnstown** (city) Fulton County
127	18.6	**Spencerport** (village) Monroe County
135	18.7	**Fairport** (village) Monroe County
135	18.7	**Watertown** (town) Jefferson County
137	18.8	**Herkimer** (town) Herkimer County
138	18.9	**Chenango Bridge** (CDP) Broome County
138	18.9	**Geneva** (city) Ontario County
138	18.9	**Riverside** (CDP) Suffolk County
138	18.9	**Southport** (town) Chemung County
138	18.9	**Verona** (town) Oneida County
143	19.0	**Brockport** (village) Monroe County
143	19.0	**Oswegatchie** (town) Saint Lawrence County
143	19.0	**Warsaw** (village) Wyoming County
143	19.0	**Wilna** (town) Jefferson County
147	19.1	**Canton** (town) Saint Lawrence County
147	19.1	**East Greenbush** (town) Rensselaer County
147	19.1	**Sloan** (village) Erie County
150	19.2	**Amherst** (town) Erie County

Note: This section ranks incorporated places and CDPs (Census Designated Places) with populations of 2,500 or more. Unincorporated postal areas were not considered. Please refer to the User Guide for additional information.

Violent Crime Rate per 10,000 Population

Top 150 Places Ranked in *Descending* Order

State Rank	Rate	Place	State Rank	Rate	Place
1	123.6	**Newburgh** (city) Orange County	76	19.2	**Yorkville** (village) Oneida County
2	112.4	**Niagara Falls** (city) Niagara County	77	19.1	**Sidney** (village) Delaware County
3	101.9	**Buffalo** (city) Erie County	78	18.9	**De Witt** (town) Onondaga County
4	89.7	**Rochester** (city) Monroe County	79	18.1	**Greece** (town) Monroe County
5	89.2	**Albany** (city) Albany County	79	18.1	**Ithaca** (city) Tompkins County
5	89.2	**Schenectady** (city) Schenectady County	81	17.7	**Ellicott** (town) Chautauqua County
7	79.7	**Binghamton** (city) Broome County	82	17.6	**Cazenovia** (village) Madison County
8	72.4	**Hudson** (city) Columbia County	82	17.6	**White Plains** (city) Westchester County
9	70.7	**Troy** (city) Rensselaer County	84	17.5	**Amsterdam** (city) Montgomery County
10	70.6	**Poughkeepsie** (city) Dutchess County	84	17.5	**Tonawanda** (town) Erie County
11	70.5	**Syracuse** (city) Onondaga County	86	16.5	**Port Chester** (village) Westchester County
12	67.5	**Herkimer** (village) Herkimer County	87	16.3	**Salamanca** (city) Cattaraugus County
13	66.3	**Jamestown** (city) Chautauqua County	88	15.9	**Delhi** (village) Delaware County
14	64.2	**Liberty** (village) Sullivan County	88	15.9	**Fulton** (city) Oswego County
15	63.9	**Batavia** (city) Genesee County	90	15.7	**Plattsburgh** (city) Clinton County
16	63.8	**Mount Vernon** (city) Westchester County	90	15.7	**Scotia** (village) Schenectady County
17	62.4	**Johnson City** (village) Broome County	92	15.6	**New Paltz** (town) Ulster County
18	59.5	**Hempstead** (village) Nassau County	93	15.4	**Green Island** (town/village) Albany County
19	57.2	**Endicott** (village) Broome County	94	15.2	**Chester** (village) Orange County
20	56.5	**Monticello** (village) Sullivan County	95	14.5	**Waverly** (village) Tioga County
21	55.8	**Utica** (city) Oneida County	96	14.2	**Le Roy** (village) Genesee County
22	54.0	**Watertown** (city) Jefferson County	96	14.2	**Tupper Lake** (village) Franklin County
23	53.9	**New York** (city)	98	14.1	**Peekskill** (city) Westchester County
24	52.2	**Albion** (village) Orleans County	99	14.0	**Akron** (village) Erie County
25	47.8	**Malone** (village) Franklin County	100	13.9	**Rensselaer** (city) Rensselaer County
26	44.6	**Ellenville** (village) Ulster County	101	13.3	**Johnstown** (city) Fulton County
27	43.2	**Gloversville** (city) Fulton County	102	13.3	**Cobleskill** (village) Schoharie County
28	42.1	**Lackawanna** (city) Erie County	102	13.2	**North Syracuse** (village) Onondaga County
29	41.8	**Medina** (village) Orleans County	104	12.6	**Saugerties** (village) Ulster County
30	41.6	**Watervliet** (city) Albany County	105	12.5	**Rotterdam** (town) Schenectady County
31	41.0	**Ilion** (village) Herkimer County	105	12.5	**Seneca Falls** (town) Seneca County
32	40.6	**Spring Valley** (village) Rockland County	107	12.3	**Fredonia** (village) Chautauqua County
33	40.2	**Yonkers** (city) Westchester County	108	12.2	**North Tonawanda** (city) Niagara County
34	38.2	**Norwich** (city) Chenango County	108	12.2	**Orangetown** (town) Rockland County
35	37.3	**Middletown** (city) Orange County	108	12.2	**Southampton** (town) Suffolk County
36	37.2	**Corning** (city) Steuben County	111	12.0	**Warsaw** (village) Wyoming County
37	36.3	**Dunkirk** (city) Chautauqua County	112	11.8	**Lowville** (village) Lewis County
38	34.0	**Little Falls** (city) Herkimer County	113	11.6	**Amityville** (village) Suffolk County
39	31.9	**Canandaigua** (city) Ontario County	114	11.5	**Perry** (village) Wyoming County
40	31.6	**Kingston** (city) Ulster County	115	11.2	**Depew** (village) Erie County
41	31.0	**Beacon** (city) Dutchess County	115	11.2	**Haverstraw** (town) Rockland County
42	30.5	**Port Jervis** (city) Orange County	115	11.2	**Niagara** (town) Niagara County
43	30.4	**Saranac Lake** (village) Franklin County	118	11.1	**Evans** (town) Erie County
43	30.4	**Tonawanda** (city) Erie County	119	10.9	**Clarkstown** (town) Rockland County
45	28.8	**Elmira** (city) Chemung County	119	10.9	**Greenburgh** (town) Westchester County
46	28.0	**South Glens Falls** (village) Saratoga County	119	10.9	**Suffern** (village) Rockland County
47	27.1	**Ogdensburg** (city) Saint Lawrence County	122	10.8	**Fallsburg** (town) Sullivan County
48	27.0	**Bath** (village) Steuben County	123	10.6	**Colonie** (town) Albany County
49	26.5	**Owego** (village) Tioga County	124	10.5	**Walden** (village) Orange County
50	25.6	**Mechanicville** (city) Saratoga County	125	10.4	**Monroe** (village) Orange County
51	25.3	**Menands** (village) Albany County	126	10.3	**Cornwall-on-Hudson** (village) Orange County
51	25.3	**Solvay** (village) Onondaga County	127	10.2	**Amherst** (town) Erie County
53	24.7	**Wellsville** (village) Allegany County	127	10.2	**Chittenango** (village) Madison County
54	24.1	**Brockport** (village) Monroe County	127	10.2	**Potsdam** (village) Saint Lawrence County
54	24.1	**Cheektowaga** (town) Erie County	130	10.0	**Macedon** (village) Wayne County
54	24.1	**Cohoes** (city) Albany County	130	10.0	**Waterloo** (village) Seneca County
57	22.8	**New Rochelle** (city) Westchester County	132	9.9	**Elmsford** (village) Westchester County
58	22.7	**Oneida** (city) Madison County	132	9.9	**Westfield** (village) Chautauqua County
59	22.6	**Hudson Falls** (village) Washington County	134	9.8	**Crawford** (town) Orange County
59	22.6	**Olean** (city) Cattaraugus County	134	9.8	**Mamaroneck** (village) Westchester County
61	22.5	**Wallkill** (town) Orange County	134	9.8	**Orchard Park** (town) Erie County
62	22.1	**Rome** (city) Oneida County	137	9.7	**Rockville Centre** (village) Nassau County
63	21.7	**Freeport** (village) Nassau County	137	9.7	**West Seneca** (CDP) Erie County
64	21.6	**Geneva** (city) Ontario County	139	9.5	**Dolgeville** (village) Herkimer County
64	21.6	**Irondequoit** (CDP) Monroe County	139	9.5	**Pound Ridge** (town) Westchester County
66	21.1	**Mount Morris** (village) Livingston County	141	9.4	**New Windsor** (town) Orange County
67	20.9	**Gates** (town) Monroe County	142	9.3	**Blooming Grove** (town) Orange County
68	20.6	**Oswego** (city) Oswego County	143	9.2	**Lynbrook** (village) Nassau County
69	20.5	**Ticonderoga** (town) Essex County	144	9.1	**Deerpark** (town) Orange County
70	20.4	**Carthage** (village) Jefferson County	144	9.1	**Fort Edward** (village) Washington County
71	20.3	**Glens Falls** (city) Warren County	146	8.9	**Dansville** (village) Livingston County
72	20.0	**Saratoga Springs** (city) Saratoga County	147	8.8	**Chester** (town) Orange County
73	19.9	**Addison** (town) Steuben County	148	8.6	**Kenmore** (village) Erie County
74	19.6	**Cuba** (town) Allegany County	149	8.5	**Cortland** (city) Cortland County
75	19.3	**Oneonta** (city) Otsego County	149	8.5	**East Hampton** (town) Suffolk County

Note: This section ranks incorporated places and CDPs (Census Designated Places) with populations of 2,500 or more. Unincorporated postal areas were not considered. Please refer to the User Guide for additional information.

Violent Crime Rate per 10,000 Population

Top 150 Places Ranked in *Ascending* Order

State Rank	Rate	Place	State Rank	Rate	Place
1	0.0	**Avon** (village) Livingston County	76	5.2	**Washingtonville** (village) Orange County
1	0.0	**Bronxville** (village) Westchester County	77	5.3	**Bethlehem** (town) Albany County
1	0.0	**Carroll** (town) Chautauqua County	78	5.4	**Lloyd Harbor** (village) Suffolk County
1	0.0	**Cayuga Heights** (village) Tompkins County	79	5.5	**Fairport** (village) Monroe County
1	0.0	**Durham** (town) Greene County	79	5.5	**Northport** (village) Suffolk County
1	0.0	**Greenport** (town) Columbia County	81	5.6	**Floral Park** (village) Nassau County
1	0.0	**Hamilton** (village) Madison County	82	5.7	**Lloyd** (town) Ulster County
1	0.0	**Homer** (village) Cortland County	82	5.7	**Moriah** (town) Essex County
1	0.0	**Horseheads** (village) Chemung County	84	5.8	**Stony Point** (town) Rockland County
1	0.0	**Kirkland** (town) Oneida County	85	5.9	**Hoosick Falls** (village) Rensselaer County
1	0.0	**Lewisboro** (town) Westchester County	85	5.9	**Waterford** (town) Saratoga County
1	0.0	**Malverne** (village) Nassau County	87	6.0	**East Rochester** (town/village) Monroe County
1	0.0	**Montgomery** (village) Orange County	87	6.0	**Penn Yan** (village) Yates County
1	0.0	**Mount Hope** (town) Orange County	87	6.0	**Southampton** (village) Suffolk County
1	0.0	**New Berlin** (town) Chenango County	90	6.1	**Lancaster** (town) Erie County
1	0.0	**Norfolk** (town) Saint Lawrence County	90	6.1	**New York Mills** (village) Oneida County
1	0.0	**Old Westbury** (village) Nassau County	92	6.2	**Cairo** (town) Greene County
1	0.0	**Olive** (town) Ulster County	92	6.2	**Long Beach** (city) Nassau County
1	0.0	**Pelham** (village) Westchester County	94	6.4	**Ogden** (town) Monroe County
1	0.0	**Piermont** (village) Rockland County	94	6.4	**Ulster** (town) Ulster County
1	0.0	**Pine Plains** (town) Dutchess County	96	6.5	**Camillus** (town) Onondaga County
1	0.0	**Rye Brook** (village) Westchester County	96	6.5	**Eden** (town) Erie County
1	0.0	**Sands Point** (village) Nassau County	96	6.5	**Glenville** (town) Schenectady County
1	0.0	**Sherrill** (city) Oneida County	96	6.5	**North Greenbush** (town) Rensselaer County
1	0.0	**Tuxedo** (town) Orange County	100	6.7	**Niskayuna** (town) Schenectady County
1	0.0	**Whitesboro** (village) Oneida County	101	6.8	**Coeymans** (town) Albany County
27	0.4	**Harrison** (town/village) Westchester County	101	6.8	**East Fishkill** (town) Dutchess County
28	0.8	**Kent** (town) Putnam County	101	6.8	**Geddes** (town) Onondaga County
28	0.8	**Mamaroneck** (town) Westchester County	104	6.9	**Manlius** (town) Onondaga County
30	0.9	**Garden City** (village) Nassau County	104	6.9	**Plattekill** (town) Ulster County
31	1.1	**Whitestown** (town) Oneida County	106	7.1	**Warwick** (town) Orange County
32	1.4	**Pleasantville** (village) Westchester County	106	7.1	**Webster** (town) Monroe County
32	1.4	**Shawangunk** (town) Ulster County	108	7.2	**Pelham Manor** (village) Westchester County
34	1.5	**Canton** (village) Saint Lawrence County	109	7.5	**Goshen** (village) Orange County
34	1.5	**Stillwater** (town) Saratoga County	110	7.7	**Brighton** (CDP) Monroe County
34	1.5	**Tuckahoe** (village) Westchester County	110	7.7	**Elmira Heights** (village) Chemung County
37	1.7	**Rosendale** (town) Ulster County	110	7.7	**Rhinebeck** (village) Dutchess County
38	1.8	**Elmira** (town) Chemung County	113	7.8	**Baldwinsville** (village) Onondaga County
39	1.9	**Ballston Spa** (village) Saratoga County	113	7.8	**Newburgh** (town) Orange County
40	2.1	**Cornwall** (town) Orange County	113	7.8	**Tarrytown** (village) Westchester County
41	2.4	**Geneseo** (village) Livingston County	113	7.8	**Vestal** (town) Broome County
41	2.4	**Highlands** (town) Orange County	117	7.9	**Guilderland** (town) Albany County
43	2.5	**Briarcliff Manor** (village) Westchester County	117	7.9	**Highland Falls** (village) Orange County
43	2.5	**Eastchester** (town) Westchester County	117	7.9	**New Hartford** (town) Oneida County
45	2.6	**Carmel** (town) Putnam County	117	7.9	**Ossining** (village) Westchester County
45	2.6	**Port Washington** (CDP) Nassau County	121	8.0	**Hamburg** (town) Erie County
45	2.6	**Schodack** (town) Rensselaer County	122	8.1	**Marlborough** (town) Ulster County
48	2.8	**Bedford** (town) Westchester County	123	8.3	**Lake Placid** (village) Essex County
49	2.9	**Glen Cove** (city) Nassau County	124	8.5	**Cortland** (city) Cortland County
50	3.1	**Rye** (city) Westchester County	124	8.5	**East Hampton** (town) Suffolk County
51	3.2	**Greenwood Lake** (village) Orange County	124	8.5	**Maybrook** (village) Orange County
51	3.2	**Lake Success** (village) Nassau County	124	8.5	**South Nyack** (village) Rockland County
51	3.2	**Yorktown** (town) Westchester County	124	8.5	**Southold** (town) Suffolk County
54	3.3	**Fishkill** (town) Dutchess County	129	8.6	**Kenmore** (village) Erie County
54	3.3	**Scarsdale** (town/village) Westchester County	130	8.8	**Chester** (town) Orange County
56	3.4	**Nunda** (town) Livingston County	131	8.9	**Dansville** (village) Livingston County
56	3.4	**Shandaken** (town) Ulster County	132	9.1	**Deerpark** (town) Orange County
56	3.4	**Woodstock** (town) Ulster County	132	9.1	**Fort Edward** (village) Washington County
59	3.5	**Florida** (village) Orange County	134	9.2	**Lynbrook** (village) Nassau County
60	3.6	**Dobbs Ferry** (village) Westchester County	135	9.3	**Blooming Grove** (town) Orange County
60	3.6	**Woodbury** (town) Orange County	136	9.4	**New Windsor** (town) Orange County
62	3.8	**Hastings-on-Hudson** (village) Westchester County	137	9.5	**Dolgeville** (village) Herkimer County
62	3.8	**Kings Point** (village) Nassau County	137	9.5	**Pound Ridge** (town) Westchester County
64	4.1	**Cicero** (town) Onondaga County	139	9.7	**Rockville Centre** (village) Nassau County
64	4.1	**Harriman** (village) Orange County	139	9.7	**West Seneca** (CDP) Erie County
66	4.3	**Ardsley** (village) Westchester County	141	9.8	**Crawford** (town) Orange County
66	4.3	**East Greenbush** (town) Rensselaer County	141	9.8	**Mamaroneck** (village) Westchester County
68	4.4	**Canastota** (village) Madison County	141	9.8	**Orchard Park** (town) Erie County
69	4.5	**Irvington** (village) Westchester County	144	9.9	**Elmsford** (village) Westchester County
70	4.6	**Goshen** (town) Orange County	144	9.9	**Westfield** (village) Chautauqua County
71	4.7	**Ramapo** (town) Rockland County	146	10.0	**Macedon** (town) Wayne County
72	4.8	**Croton-on-Hudson** (village) Westchester County	146	10.0	**Waterloo** (village) Seneca County
72	4.8	**Hyde Park** (town) Dutchess County	148	10.2	**Amherst** (town) Erie County
74	4.9	**Hornell** (city) Steuben County	148	10.2	**Chittenango** (village) Madison County
74	4.9	**Larchmont** (village) Westchester County	148	10.2	**Potsdam** (village) Saint Lawrence County

Note: *This section ranks incorporated places and CDPs (Census Designated Places) with populations of 2,500 or more. Unincorporated postal areas were not considered. Please refer to the User Guide for additional information.*

Property Crime Rate per 10,000 Population

Top 150 Places Ranked in *Descending* Order

State Rank	Rate	Place	State Rank	Rate	Place
1	518.0	**Johnson City** (village) Broome County	76	199.9	**Poughkeepsie** (city) Dutchess County
2	482.8	**Niagara Falls** (city) Niagara County	77	199.3	**Canandaigua** (city) Ontario County
3	458.4	**Woodbury** (town) Orange County	77	199.3	**Geneseo** (village) Livingston County
4	445.8	**Niagara** (town) Niagara County	79	196.2	**South Glens Falls** (village) Saratoga County
5	437.2	**Herkimer** (village) Herkimer County	80	194.3	**Kingston** (city) Ulster County
6	436.8	**Binghamton** (city) Broome County	81	191.7	**Amsterdam** (city) Montgomery County
7	409.4	**Watertown** (city) Jefferson County	82	189.8	**Hamburg** (town) Erie County
8	405.4	**Owego** (village) Tioga County	83	188.9	**Mount Vernon** (city) Westchester County
9	383.6	**Buffalo** (city) Erie County	84	182.3	**Niskayuna** (town) Schenectady County
10	381.3	**Menands** (village) Albany County	85	179.8	**Plattsburgh** (city) Clinton County
11	380.4	**Rochester** (city) Monroe County	86	174.8	**Rome** (city) Oneida County
12	363.2	**Ellicott** (town) Chautauqua County	87	170.3	**Cortland** (city) Cortland County
13	356.6	**Ogdensburg** (city) Saint Lawrence County	88	168.9	**Beacon** (city) Dutchess County
14	348.9	**Troy** (city) Rensselaer County	89	168.7	**Salamanca** (city) Cattaraugus County
15	345.7	**Albany** (city) Albany County	90	168.0	**White Plains** (city) Westchester County
16	344.6	**Oneida** (city) Madison County	91	167.5	**Oneonta** (city) Otsego County
17	343.1	**Newburgh** (town) Orange County	92	167.3	**Perry** (village) Wyoming County
18	340.7	**Liberty** (village) Sullivan County	93	167.2	**Larchmont** (village) Westchester County
19	337.3	**Ellenville** (village) Ulster County	94	166.5	**North Tonawanda** (city) Niagara County
20	336.7	**Syracuse** (city) Onondaga County	95	166.4	**Carthage** (village) Jefferson County
21	331.0	**Endicott** (village) Broome County	96	165.5	**Dunkirk** (city) Chautauqua County
22	329.0	**Batavia** (city) Genesee County	97	164.2	**Saratoga Springs** (city) Saratoga County
23	328.8	**Utica** (city) Oneida County	98	162.4	**Depew** (village) Erie County
24	324.3	**Ilion** (village) Herkimer County	99	159.4	**Tonawanda** (town) Erie County
25	323.0	**Albion** (village) Orleans County	100	154.9	**Wellsville** (village) Allegany County
26	318.0	**Hudson** (city) Columbia County	101	154.2	**Amherst** (town) Erie County
27	317.9	**Schenectady** (city) Schenectady County	102	154.0	**Monroe** (village) Orange County
28	311.1	**Elmira** (city) Chemung County	103	153.1	**Kenmore** (village) Erie County
29	309.6	**Bath** (village) Steuben County	104	152.1	**Waterloo** (village) Seneca County
30	297.3	**Jamestown** (city) Chautauqua County	105	151.0	**Rhinebeck** (village) Dutchess County
31	296.0	**Cheektowaga** (town) Erie County	106	150.3	**Cuba** (town) Allegany County
32	292.9	**New Hartford** (town) Oneida County	107	148.9	**Fredonia** (village) Chautauqua County
33	292.8	**Gates** (town) Monroe County	108	145.7	**North Syracuse** (village) Onondaga County
34	290.9	**Ithaca** (city) Tompkins County	109	144.9	**New York** (city)
35	290.6	**Fulton** (city) Oswego County	110	143.7	**New Rochelle** (city) Westchester County
36	290.5	**Pelham Manor** (village) Westchester County	111	143.3	**Elmira Heights** (village) Chemung County
37	285.6	**Monticello** (village) Sullivan County	112	139.6	**Canastota** (village) Madison County
38	281.4	**De Witt** (town) Onondaga County	113	138.9	**Manlius** (town) Onondaga County
39	278.2	**Olean** (city) Cattaraugus County	114	137.5	**Clarkstown** (town) Rockland County
39	278.2	**Rotterdam** (town) Schenectady County	115	136.8	**Bethlehem** (town) Albany County
41	277.8	**Norwich** (city) Chenango County	116	133.8	**Chester** (village) Orange County
42	274.2	**Ulster** (town) Ulster County	117	133.5	**Greenburgh** (town) Westchester County
43	271.3	**Seneca Falls** (town) Seneca County	118	133.3	**Scotia** (village) Schenectady County
44	271.2	**Greenport** (town) Columbia County	119	133.2	**Glens Falls** (city) Warren County
45	266.0	**Newburgh** (city) Orange County	120	133.1	**East Rochester** (town/village) Monroe County
46	261.2	**Little Falls** (city) Herkimer County	121	133.0	**Evans** (town) Erie County
47	260.3	**Port Jervis** (city) Orange County	122	132.7	**Amityville** (village) Suffolk County
48	259.6	**Medina** (village) Orleans County	123	132.6	**Macedon** (town) Wayne County
49	254.5	**Johnstown** (city) Fulton County	124	132.0	**Lake Placid** (village) Essex County
50	253.9	**Southampton** (village) Suffolk County	125	131.5	**New Windsor** (town) Orange County
51	253.3	**Sidney** (village) Delaware County	126	129.9	**Cazenovia** (village) Madison County
52	249.9	**Tupper Lake** (village) Franklin County	127	125.4	**Rensselaer** (city) Rensselaer County
53	246.5	**Corning** (city) Steuben County	128	124.2	**North Greenbush** (town) Rensselaer County
54	244.5	**Cobleskill** (village) Schoharie County	129	123.5	**West Seneca** (CDP) Erie County
55	244.1	**Gloversville** (city) Fulton County	130	121.8	**Hornell** (city) Steuben County
56	239.2	**Colonie** (town) Albany County	131	120.9	**Highland Falls** (village) Orange County
57	238.9	**Malone** (village) Franklin County	132	120.3	**Camillus** (town) Onondaga County
58	238.3	**Middletown** (city) Orange County	133	119.8	**Southampton** (town) Suffolk County
59	236.5	**Dansville** (village) Livingston County	134	119.5	**Walden** (village) Orange County
60	235.1	**Mount Morris** (village) Livingston County	135	118.9	**Spring Valley** (village) Rockland County
61	224.4	**Solvay** (village) Onondaga County	136	117.6	**Cohoes** (city) Albany County
62	223.1	**Geneva** (city) Ontario County	137	116.9	**Penn Yan** (village) Yates County
63	221.9	**Irondequoit** (CDP) Monroe County	138	116.8	**New Paltz** (village) Ulster County
64	218.8	**Wallkill** (town) Orange County	139	115.6	**Green Island** (town/village) Albany County
65	218.7	**Oswego** (city) Oswego County	140	114.5	**Hoosick Falls** (village) Rensselaer County
66	214.3	**Glenville** (town) Schenectady County	141	113.6	**Le Roy** (village) Genesee County
67	213.4	**Brighton** (CDP) Monroe County	142	113.4	**East Hampton** (town) Suffolk County
68	210.0	**Tonawanda** (city) Erie County	143	112.9	**New York Mills** (village) Oneida County
69	209.9	**Geddes** (town) Onondaga County	144	111.7	**New Berlin** (town) Chenango County
70	204.0	**Vestal** (town) Broome County	145	111.4	**Saugerties** (town) Ulster County
71	203.5	**East Greenbush** (town) Rensselaer County	146	111.3	**Coeymans** (town) Albany County
72	203.0	**Watervliet** (city) Albany County	147	108.9	**Lowville** (village) Lewis County
73	201.1	**Greece** (town) Monroe County	148	108.7	**Port Chester** (village) Westchester County
74	200.9	**Guilderland** (town) Albany County	149	108.4	**Lancaster** (town) Erie County
75	200.3	**Lackawanna** (city) Erie County	150	108.2	**Warsaw** (village) Wyoming County

Note: This section ranks incorporated places and CDPs (Census Designated Places) with populations of 2,500 or more. Unincorporated postal areas were not considered. Please refer to the User Guide for additional information.

Property Crime Rate per 10,000 Population

Top 150 Places Ranked in *Ascending* Order

State Rank	Rate	Place	State Rank	Rate	Place
1	0.0	**Carroll** (town) Chautauqua County	76	65.6	**Horseheads** (village) Chemung County
1	0.0	**Moriah** (town) Essex County	77	67.4	**Mamaroneck** (village) Westchester County
1	0.0	**Pine Plains** (town) Dutchess County	78	67.9	**Greenwood Lake** (village) Orange County
4	0.8	**Lewisboro** (town) Westchester County	79	69.0	**Sherrill** (city) Oneida County
5	1.8	**Elmira** (town) Chemung County	80	69.7	**Pleasantville** (village) Westchester County
6	2.2	**Norfolk** (town) Saint Lawrence County	81	70.8	**Cayuga Heights** (village) Tompkins County
7	7.2	**Mount Hope** (town) Orange County	82	71.0	**Scarsdale** (town/village) Westchester County
8	8.8	**Chester** (town) Orange County	83	73.7	**Ramapo** (town) Rockland County
9	9.7	**Highlands** (town) Orange County	84	74.2	**Peekskill** (city) Westchester County
10	10.2	**Tuxedo** (town) Orange County	85	75.1	**Ardsley** (village) Westchester County
11	14.0	**Florida** (village) Orange County	86	75.4	**Rockville Centre** (village) Nassau County
12	14.6	**Hamilton** (village) Madison County	87	75.5	**Cornwall-on-Hudson** (village) Orange County
13	16.2	**Olive** (town) Ulster County	88	76.1	**Hudson Falls** (village) Washington County
14	19.1	**Kings Point** (village) Nassau County	89	76.2	**Dolgeville** (village) Herkimer County
15	20.6	**Bedford** (town) Westchester County	90	76.3	**Delhi** (village) Delaware County
16	22.0	**Cornwall** (town) Orange County	91	77.0	**Harriman** (village) Orange County
17	22.8	**Maybrook** (village) Orange County	92	77.7	**Ticonderoga** (town) Essex County
18	24.2	**Irvington** (village) Westchester County	93	79.4	**Haverstraw** (town) Rockland County
19	24.4	**Kirkland** (town) Oneida County	94	80.0	**Dobbs Ferry** (village) Westchester County
19	24.4	**Lloyd Harbor** (village) Suffolk County	95	80.2	**Orangetown** (town) Rockland County
21	24.6	**Akron** (village) Erie County	96	81.3	**Fairport** (village) Monroe County
22	24.8	**Briarcliff Manor** (village) Westchester County	97	82.6	**Hastings-on-Hudson** (village) Westchester County
23	25.6	**Homer** (village) Cortland County	98	85.3	**Eastchester** (town) Westchester County
24	25.7	**Malverne** (village) Nassau County	99	85.8	**Orchard Park** (town) Erie County
25	26.3	**Floral Park** (village) Nassau County	100	87.3	**Saranac Lake** (village) Franklin County
26	27.6	**Elmsford** (village) Westchester County	101	87.5	**Baldwinsville** (village) Onondaga County
27	32.0	**Canton** (village) Saint Lawrence County	102	88.9	**Fallsburg** (town) Sullivan County
28	32.6	**Whitestown** (town) Oneida County	103	90.5	**Ballston Spa** (village) Saratoga County
29	33.0	**Westfield** (village) Chautauqua County	104	91.1	**Webster** (town) Monroe County
30	33.8	**Durham** (town) Greene County	105	92.1	**Yorkville** (village) Oneida County
31	34.4	**Sands Point** (village) Nassau County	106	92.2	**Potsdam** (village) Saint Lawrence County
32	36.5	**Carmel** (town) Putnam County	107	93.7	**Cicero** (town) Onondaga County
33	36.8	**Schodack** (town) Rensselaer County	108	93.9	**Freeport** (village) Nassau County
34	39.7	**Avon** (village) Livingston County	109	94.8	**Garden City** (village) Nassau County
35	40.3	**Montgomery** (village) Orange County	110	95.6	**Lloyd** (town) Ulster County
36	40.7	**Harrison** (town/village) Westchester County	111	95.8	**Rye Brook** (village) Westchester County
36	40.7	**Nunda** (town) Livingston County	112	96.4	**Ossining** (village) Westchester County
38	41.0	**Waverly** (village) Tioga County	113	97.1	**Goshen** (village) Orange County
39	42.3	**Tarrytown** (village) Westchester County	114	98.1	**Pelham** (village) Westchester County
40	42.5	**South Nyack** (village) Rockland County	115	98.5	**Deerpark** (town) Orange County
41	45.2	**Bronxville** (village) Westchester County	116	98.6	**Whitesboro** (village) Oneida County
42	45.6	**Rye** (city) Westchester County	117	100.4	**Yonkers** (city) Westchester County
43	45.9	**Croton-on-Hudson** (village) Westchester County	118	102.8	**Goshen** (town) Orange County
44	46.5	**Stillwater** (town) Saratoga County	119	103.3	**Ogden** (town) Monroe County
45	46.6	**Piermont** (village) Rockland County	120	103.5	**Brockport** (village) Monroe County
46	46.8	**Kent** (town) Putnam County	121	104.6	**Shandaken** (town) Ulster County
47	48.2	**Waterford** (town) Saratoga County	122	105.0	**Woodstock** (town) Ulster County
48	48.4	**Eden** (town) Erie County	123	106.3	**Hempstead** (village) Nassau County
49	48.5	**East Fishkill** (town) Dutchess County	123	106.3	**Mechanicville** (city) Saratoga County
49	48.5	**Old Westbury** (village) Nassau County	125	106.7	**Crawford** (town) Orange County
51	48.9	**Stony Point** (town) Rockland County	126	107.1	**Southold** (town) Suffolk County
52	49.1	**Mamaroneck** (town) Westchester County	127	108.2	**Warsaw** (village) Wyoming County
53	49.4	**Rosendale** (town) Ulster County	128	108.4	**Lancaster** (town) Erie County
54	50.6	**Hyde Park** (town) Dutchess County	129	108.7	**Port Chester** (village) Westchester County
55	51.1	**Chittenango** (village) Madison County	130	108.9	**Lowville** (village) Lewis County
55	51.1	**Port Washington** (CDP) Nassau County	131	111.3	**Coeymans** (town) Albany County
57	51.2	**Tuckahoe** (village) Westchester County	132	111.4	**Saugerties** (town) Ulster County
58	51.6	**Addison** (town) Steuben County	133	111.7	**New Berlin** (town) Chenango County
59	51.8	**Fort Edward** (village) Washington County	134	112.9	**New York Mills** (village) Oneida County
60	52.1	**Lynbrook** (village) Nassau County	135	113.4	**East Hampton** (town) Suffolk County
61	52.3	**Blooming Grove** (town) Orange County	136	113.6	**Le Roy** (village) Genesee County
62	54.1	**Plattekill** (town) Ulster County	137	114.5	**Hoosick Falls** (village) Rensselaer County
63	54.5	**Cairo** (town) Greene County	138	115.6	**Green Island** (town/village) Albany County
64	55.1	**Glen Cove** (city) Nassau County	139	116.8	**New Paltz** (town) Ulster County
65	55.5	**Suffern** (village) Rockland County	140	116.9	**Penn Yan** (village) Yates County
66	55.6	**Shawangunk** (town) Ulster County	141	117.6	**Cohoes** (city) Albany County
67	56.2	**Fishkill** (town) Dutchess County	142	118.9	**Spring Valley** (village) Rockland County
68	56.6	**Warwick** (town) Orange County	143	119.5	**Walden** (village) Orange County
69	57.3	**Northport** (village) Suffolk County	144	119.8	**Southampton** (town) Suffolk County
70	57.4	**Washingtonville** (village) Orange County	145	120.3	**Camillus** (town) Onondaga County
71	58.4	**Yorktown** (town) Westchester County	146	120.9	**Highland Falls** (village) Orange County
72	58.9	**Long Beach** (city) Nassau County	147	121.8	**Hornell** (city) Steuben County
73	60.2	**Marlborough** (town) Ulster County	148	123.5	**West Seneca** (CDP) Erie County
74	60.8	**Lake Success** (village) Nassau County	149	124.2	**North Greenbush** (town) Rensselaer County
75	62.8	**Pound Ridge** (town) Westchester County	150	125.4	**Rensselaer** (city) Rensselaer County

Note: This section ranks incorporated places and CDPs (Census Designated Places) with populations of 2,500 or more. Unincorporated postal areas were not considered. Please refer to the User Guide for additional information.

Education

New York Public School Educational Profile

Category	Value	Category	Value
Schools *(2015-2016)*	4,824	**Status Dropout Rate** *(%) (2014)*	
Instructional Level		All Students	6.0
Primary	2,560	White	3.6
Middle	817	Black	7.9
High	1,025	Asian	3.3
Other/Not Reported	422	American Indian/Alaska Native	11.3
Curriculum		Hispanic	11.6
Regular	4,618	**Staff** *(2015-2016)*	
Special Education	131	Teachers (FTE)	205,958.3
Vocational	21	Average Salary in 2017 ($)	81,902
Alternative	54	Librarians/Media Specialists (FTE)	2,410.2
Type		Guidance Counselors (FTE)	6,920.7
Magnet	110	**Ratios** *(2015-2016)*	
Charter	256	Number of Students per Teacher	13.2 to 1
Title I Eligible	3,578	Number of Students per Librarian	1,125.1 to 1
School-wide Title I	2,937	Number of Students per Guidance Counselor	391.8 to 1
Students *(2015-2016)*	2,711,626	**Finances** *(2014-2015)*	
Gender (%)		Expenditures ($ per student)	
Male	51.4	Total Expenditures	22,745
Female	48.6	Current Expenditures	20,744
Race/Ethnicity (%)		Instruction	14,571
White, Non-Hispanic	44.7	Support Services	5,756
Black, Non-Hispanic	17.7	Non-Instruction	417
Asian, Non-Hispanic	9.1	Net Current per Attendance for Title I	22,232
American Indian/Alaska Native, Non-Hispanic	0.6	Revenue ($ per student)	
Hawaiian Native/Pacific Islander, Non-Hispanic	n/a	Total Revenue	23,060
Two or More Races, Non-Hispanic	2.0	From Federal Sources	1,033
Hispanic of Any Race	25.9	From State Sources	9,463
Special Programs (%)		From Local Sources	12,565
Individual Education Program (IEP)	18.4	From Intermediate Sources	125
English Language Learner (ELL)	8.0	**College Entrance Exam Scores**	
Eligible for Free Lunch Program	43.7	New SAT Test *(2017)*	
Eligible for Reduced-Price Lunch Program	4.8	Participation Rate (%)	67
Adjusted Cohort Graduation Rate *(%) (2015-2016)*		Mean Combined Score	1,051
All Students	80.4	Mean Evidence-based Reading & Writing Score	528
White, Non-Hispanic	89.3	Mean Math Score	523
Black, Non-Hispanic	68.5	ACT *(2017)*	
Asian/Pacific Islander, Non-Hispanic	86.7	Participation Rate (%)	31
American Indian/Alaska Native, Non-Hispanic	68.0	Mean Composite Score	24.2
Hispanic of Any Race	68.1	Mean English Score	23.8
Students with Disabilities	52.6	Mean Math Score	24.0
Limited English Proficient	37.8	Mean Reading Score	24.6
Economically Disadvantaged	72.8	Mean Science Score	23.9

Note: *For an explanation of data, please refer to the User Guide in the front of the book*

Number of Schools

Rank	Number	District Name	City
1	1,833	New York City Chancellor's Office	New York
2	118	NYC Geographic District # 2	New York
3	85	NYC Geographic District #10	Bronx
4	73	NYC Geographic District # 9	Bronx
5	71	NYC Geographic District #31	Staten Island
6	64	NYC Geographic District #11	Bronx
7	62	NYC Geographic District #27	Ozone Park
8	57	Buffalo City SD	Buffalo
8	57	NYC Geographic District # 8	Bronx
8	57	NYC Geographic District #24	Corona
11	52	NYC Geographic District #12	Bronx
11	52	NYC Geographic District #17	Brooklyn
11	52	Rochester City SD	Rochester
14	50	NYC Geographic District #19	Brooklyn
14	50	NYC Geographic District #28	Jamaica
16	49	NYC Geographic District # 6	New York
17	48	NYC Geographic District #29	Queens Village
17	48	NYC Geographic District #30	Long Isl City
19	47	NYC Geographic District #15	Brooklyn
20	45	NYC Geographic District # 3	New York
20	45	NYC Geographic District #25	Flushing
22	44	NYC Geographic District # 7	Bronx
23	43	NYC Geographic District #20	Brooklyn
24	42	NYC Geographic District #13	Brooklyn
25	41	NYC Geographic District #14	Brooklyn
26	40	NYC Geographic District #21	Brooklyn
26	40	NYC Geographic District #22	Brooklyn
26	40	Yonkers City SD	Yonkers
29	35	NYC Geographic District #18	Brooklyn
30	34	Syracuse City SD	Syracuse
31	32	NYC Geographic District # 4	New York
31	32	NYC Geographic District # 5	New York
31	32	NYC Geographic District #26	Bayside
34	31	NYC Geographic District # 1	New York
35	30	NYC Geographic District #23	Brooklyn
36	29	NYC Geographic District #16	Brooklyn
37	27	NYC Geographic District #32	Brooklyn
38	18	Sachem Central SD	Lake Ronkonkoma
39	17	Albany City SD	Albany
39	17	Brentwood UFSD	Brentwood
39	17	Greece Central SD	Rochester
39	17	Schenectady City SD	Schenectady
43	16	Clarkstown Central SD	New City
43	16	Mount Vernon SD	Mount Vernon
45	15	Wappingers Central SD	Hopewell Junction
46	14	East Ramapo CSD (Spring Valley)	Spring Valley
46	14	Middle Country Central SD	Centereach
48	13	Liverpool Central SD	Liverpool
48	13	Smithtown Central SD	Smithtown
48	13	Utica City SD	Utica
48	13	Williamsville Central SD	East Amherst
52	12	Ithaca City SD	Ithaca
52	12	Kenmore-Tonawanda UFSD	Buffalo
52	12	Newburgh City SD	Newburgh
52	12	Shenendehowa Central SD	Clifton Park
56	11	Arlington Central SD	Lagrangeville
56	11	Elmira City SD	Elmira
56	11	Niagara Falls City SD	Niagara Falls
56	11	North Syracuse Central SD	North Syracuse
56	11	Patchogue-Medford UFSD	Patchogue
56	11	Webster Central SD	Webster
62	10	Binghamton City SD	Binghamton
62	10	Connetquot Central SD	Bohemia
62	10	East Meadow UFSD	Westbury
62	10	Great Neck UFSD	Great Neck
62	10	Hempstead UFSD	Hempstead
62	10	Kingston City SD	Kingston
62	10	Levittown UFSD	Levittown
62	10	New Rochelle City SD	New Rochelle
62	10	Oceanside UFSD	Oceanside
62	10	Rome City SD	Rome
62	10	Syosset Central SD	Syosset
62	10	West Irondequoit Central SD	Rochester
74	9	Corning City SD	Painted Post
74	9	Half Hollow Hills Central SD	Dix Hills
74	9	Hicksville UFSD	Hicksville
74	9	Jamestown City SD	Jamestown
74	9	Massapequa UFSD	Massapequa
74	9	Northport-East Northport UFSD	Northport
74	9	Pittsford Central SD	Pittsford
74	9	Rush-Henrietta Central SD	Henrietta
74	9	West Seneca Central SD	West Seneca
83	8	Baldwinsville Central SD	Baldwinsville
83	8	Central Islip UFSD	Central Islip
83	8	Commack UFSD	East Northport
83	8	Fairport Central SD	Fairport
83	8	Freeport UFSD	Freeport
83	8	Haverstraw-Stony Point CSD	Garnerville
83	8	Huntington UFSD	Huntington Stn
83	8	Indian River Central SD	Philadelphia
83	8	Lakeland Central SD	Shrub Oak
83	8	Lindenhurst UFSD	Lindenhurst
83	8	Niskayuna Central SD	Schenectady
83	8	North Colonie CSD	Latham
83	8	Plainview-Old Bethpage CSD	Plainview
83	8	Saratoga Spgs City SD	Saratoga Spgs
83	8	South Colonie Central SD	Albany
83	8	Three Village Central SD	Stony Brook
83	8	Troy City SD	Troy
83	8	Uniondale UFSD	Uniondale
83	8	Watertown City SD	Watertown
83	8	William Floyd UFSD	Mastic Beach
103	7	Auburn City SD	Auburn
103	7	Baldwin UFSD	Baldwin
103	7	Bay Shore UFSD	Bay Shore
103	7	Bedford Central SD	Bedford
103	7	Bethlehem Central SD	Delmar
103	7	Central Square Central SD	Central Square
103	7	East Greenbush Central SD	East Greenbush
103	7	East Syracuse Minoa Central SD	East Syracuse
103	7	Garden City UFSD	Garden City
103	7	Guilderland Central SD	Guilderland Center
103	7	Horseheads Central SD	Horseheads
103	7	Lancaster Central SD	Lancaster
103	7	Lockport City SD	Lockport
103	7	Longwood Central SD	Middle Island
103	7	Lynbrook UFSD	Lynbrook
103	7	Monroe-Woodbury Central SD	Central Valley
103	7	North Babylon UFSD	North Babylon
103	7	Oswego City SD	Oswego
103	7	Pine Bush Central SD	Pine Bush
103	7	Port Washington UFSD	Port Washington
103	7	Poughkeepsie City SD	Poughkeepsie
103	7	Ramapo Central SD (Suffern)	Hillburn
103	7	Riverhead Central SD	Riverhead
103	7	Rockville Ctr UFSD	Rockville Ctr
103	7	Scarsdale UFSD	Scarsdale
103	7	South Huntington UFSD	Huntington Stn
103	7	Vestal Central SD	Vestal
103	7	West Babylon UFSD	West Babylon
103	7	West Genesee Central SD	Camillus
103	7	West Islip UFSD	West Islip
103	7	Westbury UFSD	Old Westbury
103	7	White Plains City SD	White Plains
103	7	Whitesboro Central SD	Whitesboro
136	6	Amsterdam City SD	Amsterdam
136	6	Ballston Spa Central SD	Ballston Spa
136	6	Beacon City SD	Beacon
136	6	Brookhaven-Comsewogue UFSD	Port Jeff Stn
136	6	Chappaqua Central SD	Chappaqua
136	6	Clarence Central SD	Clarence
136	6	Copiague UFSD	Copiague
136	6	Cortland City SD	Cortland
136	6	Dunkirk City SD	Dunkirk
136	6	East Irondequoit Central SD	Rochester
136	6	East Islip UFSD	Islip Terrace
136	6	Elmont UFSD	Elmont
136	6	Farmingdale UFSD	Farmingdale
136	6	Fayetteville-Manlius Central SD	Manlius
136	6	Frontier Central SD	Hamburg
136	6	Fulton City SD	Fulton
136	6	Gates-Chili Central SD	Rochester
136	6	Glen Cove City SD	Glen Cove
136	6	Gloversville City SD	Gloversville
136	6	Greenburgh Central SD	Hartsdale
136	6	Hamburg Central SD	Hamburg
136	6	Harrison Central SD	Harrison
136	6	Hyde Park Central SD	Hyde Park
136	6	Iroquois Central SD	Elma
136	6	Long Beach City SD	Long Beach
136	6	Mamaroneck UFSD	Mamaroneck
136	6	Middletown City SD	Middletown
136	6	Niagara-Wheatfield Central SD	Niagara Falls
136	6	North Tonawanda City SD	North Tonawanda
136	6	Oneida City SD	Oneida
136	6	Orchard Park Central SD	West Seneca
136	6	Ossining UFSD	Ossining
136	6	Peekskill City SD	Peekskill
136	6	Pelham UFSD	Pelham
136	6	Penfield Central SD	Rochester
136	6	Port Chester-Rye UFSD	Port Chester
136	6	Saugerties Central SD	Saugerties
136	6	Scotia-Glenville Central SD	Scotia
136	6	South Country Central SD	East Patchogue
136	6	S Glens Fls Central SD	S Glens Fls
136	6	Spencerport Central SD	Spencerport
136	6	Sweet Home Central SD	Amherst
136	6	Union-Endicott Central SD	Endicott
136	6	Valley Central SD (Montgomery)	Montgomery
180	5	Amityville UFSD	Amityville
180	5	Averill Park Central SD	Averill Park
180	5	Bayport-Blue Point UFSD	Bayport
180	5	Beekmantown Central SD	West Chazy
180	5	Bellmore-Merrick Central High SD	North Merrick
180	5	Bethpage UFSD	Bethpage
180	5	Brockport Central SD	Brockport
180	5	Burnt Hills-Ballston Lake Central SD	Scotia
180	5	Camden Central SD	Camden
180	5	Carmel Central SD	Patterson
180	5	Carthage Central SD	Carthage
180	5	Churchville-Chili Central SD	Churchville
180	5	Cohoes City SD	Cohoes
180	5	Cornwall Central SD	Cornwall on Hdsn
180	5	Deer Park UFSD	Deer Park
180	5	Dryden Central SD	Dryden
180	5	Eastchester UFSD	Eastchester
180	5	Eastport-South Manor CSD	Manorville
180	5	Evans-Brant Central SD (Lake Shore)	Angola
180	5	Glens Falls City SD	Glens Falls
180	5	Grand Island Central SD	Grand Island
180	5	Hauppauge UFSD	Hauppauge
180	5	Hendrick Hudson Central SD	Montrose
180	5	Herricks UFSD	New Hyde Park
180	5	Hewlett-Woodmere UFSD	Woodmere
180	5	Hilton Central SD	Hilton
180	5	Hornell City SD	Hornell
180	5	Hudson Falls Central SD	Fort Edward
180	5	Islip UFSD	Islip
180	5	Jamesville-Dewitt Central SD	Dewitt
180	5	Jericho UFSD	Jericho
180	5	Johnstown City SD	Johnstown
180	5	Katonah-Lewisboro UFSD	South Salem
180	5	Kings Park Central SD	Kings Park
180	5	Lawrence UFSD	Cedarhurst
180	5	Mahopac Central SD	Mahopac
180	5	Malone Central SD	Malone
180	5	Massena Central SD	Massena
180	5	Mexico Central SD	Mexico
180	5	Mineola UFSD	Mineola
180	5	Minisink Valley Central SD	Slate Hill
180	5	Monticello Central SD	Monticello
180	5	Nanuet UFSD	Nanuet
180	5	New Hartford Central SD	New Hartford
180	5	Newark Central SD	Newark
180	5	North Bellmore UFSD	Bellmore
180	5	North Shore Central SD	Sea Cliff
180	5	Nyack UFSD	Nyack
180	5	Oneonta City SD	Oneonta
180	5	Pearl River UFSD	Pearl River
180	5	Plainedge UFSD	N Massapequa
180	5	Plattsburgh City SD	Plattsburgh
180	5	Rondout Valley Central SD	Accord
180	5	Roosevelt UFSD	Roosevelt
180	5	Roslyn UFSD	Roslyn
180	5	Rye City SD	Rye
180	5	Sayville UFSD	Sayville
180	5	Sewanhaka Central High SD	Floral Park
180	5	Sherrill City SD	Verona
180	5	UFSD of the Tarrytowns	Sleepy Hollow
180	5	Victor Central SD	Victor
180	5	Wallkill Central SD	Wallkill
180	5	Wantagh UFSD	Wantagh
180	5	Washingtonville Central SD	Washingtonville
180	5	Waverly Central SD	Waverly
180	5	Wayne Central SD	Ontario Center
180	5	West Hempstead UFSD	West Hempstead
180	5	Yorktown Central SD	Yorktown Hgts
248	4	Amherst Central SD	Amherst
248	4	Batavia City SD	Batavia

Note: This section only includes districts with 1,500 or more students; All categories are ranked from high to low

Rank	Value	District Name	City
248	4	Brewster Central SD	Brewster
248	4	Brighton Central SD	Rochester
248	4	Broadalbin-Perth Central SD	Broadalbin
248	4	Byram Hills Central SD	Armonk
248	4	Central Valley CSD at Ilion-Mohawk	Ilion
248	4	Cheektowaga Central SD	Cheektowaga
248	4	Cheektowaga-Maryvale UFSD	Cheektowaga
248	4	Chenango Valley Central SD	Binghamton
248	4	Chittenango Central SD	Chittenango
248	4	Cobleskill-Richmondville CSD	Cobleskill
248	4	Cold Spring Hrbr Central SD	Cold Spring Hrbr
248	4	Elwood UFSD	Greenlawn
248	4	Geneva City SD	Geneva
248	4	Goshen Central SD	Goshen
248	4	Harborfields Central SD	Greenlawn
248	4	Homer Central SD	Homer
248	4	Honeoye Falls-Lima Central SD	Honeoye Falls
248	4	Irvington UFSD	Irvington
248	4	Island Trees UFSD	Levittown
248	4	Johnson City Central SD	Johnson City
248	4	Kinderhook Central SD	Valatie
248	4	Lackawanna City SD	Lackawanna
248	4	Lansingburgh Central SD	Troy
248	4	Lewiston-Porter Central SD	Youngstown
248	4	Locust Valley Central SD	Locust Valley
248	4	Maine-Endwell Central SD	Endwell
248	4	Malverne UFSD	Malverne
248	4	Manhasset UFSD	Manhasset
248	4	Miller Place UFSD	Miller Place
248	4	Mount Pleasant Central SD	Thornwood
248	4	New Hyde Pk-Garden City Pk UFSD	New Hyde Park
248	4	New Paltz Central SD	New Paltz
248	4	Newfane Central SD	Burt
248	4	Norwich City SD	Norwich
248	4	Olean City SD	Olean
248	4	Owego-Apalachin Central SD	Owego
248	4	Palmyra-Macedon Central SD	Palmyra
248	4	Phelps-Clifton Springs Central SD	Clifton Springs
248	4	Port Jervis City SD	Port Jervis
248	4	Queensbury UFSD	Queensbury
248	4	Ravena-Coeymans-Selkirk Cent SD	Ravena
248	4	Red Hook Central SD	Red Hook
248	4	Rocky Point UFSD	Rocky Point
248	4	Rotterdam-Mohonasen Central SD	Schenectady
248	4	Rye Neck UFSD	Mamaroneck
248	4	Salmon River Central SD	Fort Covington
248	4	Seaford UFSD	Seaford
248	4	Shoreham-Wading River Central SD	Shoreham
248	4	Somers Central SD	Somers
248	4	South Jefferson Central SD	Adams Center
248	4	South Orangetown Central SD	Blauvelt
248	4	Springville-Griffith Institute CSD	Springville
248	4	Starpoint Central SD	Lockport
248	4	Susquehanna Valley Central SD	Conklin
248	4	Tonawanda City SD	Tonawanda
248	4	Valley Stream 13 UFSD	Valley Stream
248	4	Valley Stream Central High SD	Valley Stream
248	4	Warwick Valley Central SD	Warwick
248	4	Waterloo Central SD	Waterloo
248	4	Westhill Central SD	Syracuse
248	4	Windsor Central SD	Windsor
248	4	Wyandanch UFSD	Wyandanch
248	4	Yorkshire-Pioneer Central SD	Yorkshire
313	3	Albion Central SD	Albion
313	3	Alden Central SD	Alden
313	3	Ardsley UFSD	Ardsley
313	3	Babylon UFSD	Babylon
313	3	Bath Central SD	Bath
313	3	Blind Brook-Rye UFSD	Rye Brook
313	3	Bronxville UFSD	Bronxville
313	3	Canandaigua City SD	Canandaigua
313	3	Catskill Central SD	Catskill
313	3	Center Moriches UFSD	Center Moriches
313	3	Chenango Forks Central SD	Binghamton
313	3	Croton-Harmon UFSD	Croton on Hdsn
313	3	Dansville Central SD	Dansville
313	3	Depew UFSD	Depew
313	3	East Aurora UFSD	East Aurora
313	3	East Hampton UFSD	East Hampton
313	3	East Williston UFSD	Old Westbury
313	3	Edgemont UFSD	Scarsdale
313	3	Ellenville Central SD	Ellenville
313	3	Franklin Square UFSD	Franklin Square
313	3	Fredonia Central SD	Fredonia
313	3	General Brown Central SD	Dexter
313	3	Gouverneur Central SD	Gouverneur
313	3	Hampton Bays UFSD	Hampton Bays
313	3	Hastings-On-Hudson UFSD	Hastings on Hdsn
313	3	Highland Central SD	Highland
313	3	Hudson City SD	Hudson
313	3	Livonia Central SD	Livonia
313	3	Marcellus Central SD	Marcellus
313	3	Marlboro Central SD	Milton
313	3	Medina Central SD	Medina
313	3	Mount Sinai UFSD	Mount Sinai
313	3	Ogdensburg City SD	Ogdensburg
313	3	Oyster Bay-East Norwich Central SD	Oyster Bay
313	3	Phoenix Central SD	Phoenix
313	3	Pleasantville UFSD	Pleasantville
313	3	Putnam Valley Central SD	Putnam Valley
313	3	Schalmont Central SD	Schenectady
313	3	Schuylerville Central SD	Schuylerville
313	3	Southampton UFSD	Southampton
313	3	Valley Stream 30 UFSD	Valley Stream
313	3	Westhampton Bch UFSD	Westhampton Bch
355	2	Liberty Central SD	Liberty
355	2	Peru Central SD	Peru
357	1	Charter School for Applied Techs	Buffalo

Number of Teachers

Rank	Number	District Name	City
1	75,065.0	New York City Chancellor's Office	New York
2	3,951.8	NYC Geographic District # 2	New York
3	3,933.5	NYC Geographic District #31	Staten Island
4	3,781.5	NYC Geographic District #10	Bronx
5	3,547.8	NYC Geographic District #24	Corona
6	3,134.5	NYC Geographic District #20	Brooklyn
7	2,898.7	NYC Geographic District #27	Ozone Park
8	2,646.2	Buffalo City SD	Buffalo
9	2,528.5	NYC Geographic District #11	Bronx
10	2,506.9	NYC Geographic District # 9	Bronx
11	2,505.9	NYC Geographic District #30	Long Isl City
12	2,388.7	NYC Geographic District #28	Jamaica
13	2,361.9	Rochester City SD	Rochester
14	2,315.7	NYC Geographic District #25	Flushing
15	2,251.1	NYC Geographic District #15	Brooklyn
16	2,224.7	NYC Geographic District #21	Brooklyn
17	2,106.0	NYC Geographic District #22	Brooklyn
18	2,043.7	NYC Geographic District # 8	Bronx
19	1,767.0	NYC Geographic District #26	Bayside
20	1,704.6	NYC Geographic District #12	Bronx
21	1,699.8	NYC Geographic District #29	Queens Village
22	1,609.0	NYC Geographic District # 6	New York
23	1,552.5	NYC Geographic District #19	Brooklyn
24	1,548.6	NYC Geographic District #17	Brooklyn
25	1,529.6	Syracuse City SD	Syracuse
26	1,526.1	Yonkers City SD	Yonkers
27	1,497.6	NYC Geographic District # 3	New York
28	1,455.3	NYC Geographic District # 7	Bronx
29	1,355.5	NYC Geographic District #14	Brooklyn
30	1,293.2	NYC Geographic District #13	Brooklyn
31	1,131.7	NYC Geographic District #18	Brooklyn
32	1,080.4	Brentwood UFSD	Brentwood
33	1,050.6	NYC Geographic District # 4	New York
34	947.3	Sachem Central SD	Lake Ronkonkoma
35	941.1	Greece Central SD	Rochester
36	886.1	Newburgh City SD	Newburgh
37	878.8	NYC Geographic District # 5	New York
38	878.5	NYC Geographic District # 1	New York
39	875.5	NYC Geographic District #32	Brooklyn
40	762.2	Wappingers Central SD	Hopewell Junction
41	759.4	Williamsville Central SD	East Amherst
42	727.9	New Rochelle City SD	New Rochelle
43	712.5	Middle Country Central SD	Centereach
44	691.4	NYC Geographic District #23	Brooklyn
45	669.9	Schenectady City SD	Schenectady
46	669.1	Smithtown Central SD	Smithtown
47	664.7	Half Hollow Hills Central SD	Dix Hills
48	662.5	Albany City SD	Albany
49	658.6	Great Neck UFSD	Great Neck
50	652.1	Clarkstown Central SD	New City
51	638.0	Shenendehowa Central SD	Clifton Park
52	633.8	Utica City SD	Utica
53	633.2	Longwood Central SD	Middle Island
54	629.6	North Syracuse Central SD	North Syracuse
55	625.8	Webster Central SD	Webster
56	621.9	Mount Vernon SD	Mount Vernon
57	619.0	Levittown UFSD	Levittown
58	617.2	Kenmore-Tonawanda UFSD	Buffalo
59	616.5	Massapequa UFSD	Massapequa
60	615.8	Arlington Central SD	Lagrangeville
61	603.7	Syosset Central SD	Syosset
62	603.0	East Meadow UFSD	Westbury
63	597.3	East Ramapo CSD (Spring Valley)	Spring Valley
64	590.6	William Floyd UFSD	Mastic Beach
65	561.8	Uniondale UFSD	Uniondale
66	554.2	Liverpool Central SD	Liverpool
67	548.9	NYC Geographic District #16	Brooklyn
68	543.5	Haverstraw-Stony Point CSD	Garnerville
69	538.9	Commack UFSD	East Northport
70	529.0	White Plains City SD	White Plains
71	518.1	Connetquot Central SD	Bohemia
72	515.4	Kingston City SD	Kingston
73	514.3	Fairport Central SD	Fairport
74	511.1	Middletown City SD	Middletown
75	509.2	Patchogue-Medford UFSD	Patchogue
76	506.4	Freeport UFSD	Freeport
77	503.9	Sewanhaka Central High SD	Floral Park
78	502.8	Binghamton City SD	Binghamton
79	500.0	Lindenhurst UFSD	Lindenhurst
80	498.8	Central Islip UFSD	Central Islip
81	489.0	Three Village Central SD	Stony Brook
82	483.1	South Huntington UFSD	Huntington Stn
83	483.0	Monroe-Woodbury Central SD	Central Valley
84	478.0	Rush-Henrietta Central SD	Henrietta
85	472.6	Saratoga Spgs City SD	Saratoga Spgs
86	463.0	Northport-East Northport UFSD	Northport
87	454.4	West Seneca Central SD	West Seneca
88	454.0	Plainview-Old Bethpage CSD	Plainview
89	452.6	Farmingdale UFSD	Farmingdale
90	452.5	Pittsford Central SD	Pittsford
91	451.4	Ithaca City SD	Ithaca
92	448.4	Bay Shore UFSD	Bay Shore
93	444.0	North Colonie CSD	Latham
94	443.7	Lakeland Central SD	Shrub Oak
95	433.0	Oceanside UFSD	Oceanside
96	430.9	Port Washington UFSD	Port Washington
97	428.9	Bellmore-Merrick Central High SD	North Merrick
98	428.6	Niagara Falls City SD	Niagara Falls
99	425.4	Rome City SD	Rome
100	418.3	Elmira City SD	Elmira
101	415.2	Lancaster Central SD	Lancaster
102	404.5	Corning City SD	Painted Post
103	402.2	Jamestown City SD	Jamestown
104	399.2	Scarsdale UFSD	Scarsdale
105	390.1	Guilderland Central SD	Guilderland Center
106	389.0	Hicksville UFSD	Hicksville
107	387.7	Mamaroneck UFSD	Mamaroneck
108	384.9	Baldwinsville Central SD	Baldwinsville
109	383.0	Orchard Park Central SD	West Seneca
110	382.6	South Colonie Central SD	Albany
111	382.1	Baldwin UFSD	Baldwin
112	377.8	Ramapo Central SD (Suffern)	Hillburn
113	377.7	South Country Central SD	East Patchogue
114	376.6	Penfield Central SD	Rochester
115	374.5	Pine Bush Central SD	Pine Bush
116	371.3	Lockport City SD	Lockport
117	367.3	Mahopac Central SD	Mahopac
118	366.4	Valley Central SD (Montgomery)	Montgomery
119	365.7	Bedford Central SD	Bedford
120	364.1	West Islip UFSD	West Islip
121	363.8	Deer Park UFSD	Deer Park
122	360.5	Huntington UFSD	Huntington Stn
123	359.9	Gates-Chili Central SD	Rochester
124	355.6	Frontier Central SD	Hamburg
125	355.5	Riverhead Central SD	Riverhead
126	355.2	Ossining UFSD	Ossining
127	350.8	Valley Stream Central High SD	Valley Stream
128	346.8	Hilton Central SD	Hilton
129	345.2	Herricks UFSD	New Hyde Park
130	344.1	North Babylon UFSD	North Babylon
131	344.0	West Genesee Central SD	Camillus
132	342.4	Auburn City SD	Auburn
133	339.7	West Babylon UFSD	West Babylon
134	334.9	Troy City SD	Troy
135	332.9	Victor Central SD	Victor
136	331.4	East Islip UFSD	Islip Terrace
137	329.5	Clarence Central SD	Clarence
138	328.8	Bethlehem Central SD	Delmar
139	327.8	Port Chester-Rye UFSD	Port Chester

Note: This section only includes districts with 1,500 or more students; All categories are ranked from high to low

Rank	Value	District Name	City
140	326.0	Fayetteville-Manlius Central SD	Manlius
141	323.8	Ballston Spa Central SD	Ballston Spa
142	323.1	Rockville Ctr UFSD	Rockville Ctr
143	322.8	Spencerport Central SD	Spencerport
144	318.6	Carmel Central SD	Patterson
145	318.2	Chappaqua Central SD	Chappaqua
146	316.4	Union-Endicott Central SD	Endicott
147	313.9	Hempstead UFSD	Hempstead
147	313.9	Niskayuna Central SD	Schenectady
149	313.7	Jericho UFSD	Jericho
150	313.6	Brighton Central SD	Rochester
151	313.1	Harrison Central SD	Harrison
152	311.3	Long Beach City SD	Long Beach
153	310.8	East Greenbush Central SD	East Greenbush
154	310.6	Oswego City SD	Oswego
155	308.9	Elmont UFSD	Elmont
156	307.9	Copiague UFSD	Copiague
157	307.8	Brockport Central SD	Brockport
158	306.6	Washingtonville Central SD	Washingtonville
159	306.1	Canandaigua City SD	Canandaigua
160	304.9	Westbury UFSD	Old Westbury
161	304.7	Indian River Central SD	Philadelphia
162	302.0	Garden City UFSD	Garden City
163	301.7	Churchville-Chili Central SD	Churchville
164	299.1	Hauppauge UFSD	Hauppauge
165	298.6	Poughkeepsie City SD	Poughkeepsie
166	298.1	East Syracuse Minoa Central SD	East Syracuse
167	296.0	Central Square Central SD	Central Square
168	286.7	North Shore Central SD	Sea Cliff
169	285.6	Horseheads Central SD	Horseheads
170	285.5	Hamburg Central SD	Hamburg
171	284.4	Amsterdam City SD	Amsterdam
172	283.9	Watertown City SD	Watertown
173	282.1	Hyde Park Central SD	Hyde Park
174	281.7	Fulton City SD	Fulton
175	280.6	Minisink Valley Central SD	Slate Hill
176	279.3	Yorktown Central SD	Yorktown Hgts
177	277.7	Eastport-South Manor CSD	Manorville
178	276.3	Hewlett-Woodmere UFSD	Woodmere
179	273.2	Vestal Central SD	Vestal
180	272.9	East Irondequoit Central SD	Rochester
181	271.9	Amityville UFSD	Amityville
182	270.4	Sweet Home Central SD	Amherst
183	269.7	Monticello Central SD	Monticello
184	267.8	Brookhaven-Comsewogue UFSD	Port Jeff Stn
185	267.4	Roslyn UFSD	Roslyn
186	266.2	Manhasset UFSD	Manhasset
187	265.5	Katonah-Lewisboro UFSD	South Salem
188	265.2	West Irondequoit Central SD	Rochester
189	265.1	Lynbrook UFSD	Lynbrook
190	264.2	Lawrence UFSD	Cedarhurst
191	263.8	Kings Park Central SD	Kings Park
192	261.1	Bethpage UFSD	Bethpage
193	260.5	Wantagh UFSD	Wantagh
194	258.6	Carthage Central SD	Carthage
195	257.9	Warwick Valley Central SD	Warwick
196	257.7	Queensbury UFSD	Queensbury
197	257.6	Plainedge UFSD	N Massapequa
198	255.6	Burnt Hills-Ballston Lake Central SD	Scotia
199	254.6	Rye City SD	Rye
200	252.7	Glen Cove City SD	Glen Cove
201	252.2	North Tonawanda City SD	North Tonawanda
202	251.4	South Orangetown Central SD	Blauvelt
203	251.3	Whitesboro Central SD	Whitesboro
204	250.0	Nyack UFSD	Nyack
205	246.5	Harborfields Central SD	Greenlawn
206	246.3	Niagara-Wheatfield Central SD	Niagara Falls
207	246.0	Somers Central SD	Somers
208	242.8	Rocky Point UFSD	Rocky Point
209	242.5	Mineola UFSD	Mineola
210	242.1	Wallkill Central SD	Wallkill
211	241.9	S Glens Fls Central SD	S Glens Fls
212	241.6	Amherst Central SD	Amherst
213	240.9	Islip UFSD	Islip
214	238.4	Eastchester UFSD	Eastchester
215	237.7	Sayville UFSD	Sayville
216	235.5	Brewster Central SD	Brewster
217	233.7	Beacon City SD	Beacon
218	233.2	Wayne Central SD	Ontario Center
219	230.4	Roosevelt UFSD	Roosevelt
220	228.8	Grand Island Central SD	Grand Island
221	228.0	Gloversville City SD	Gloversville
222	227.9	Cortland City SD	Cortland
223	223.6	Bayport-Blue Point UFSD	Bayport
224	222.8	Port Jervis City SD	Port Jervis
225	222.6	Byram Hills Central SD	Armonk
226	222.0	Pelham UFSD	Pelham
227	221.8	Peekskill City SD	Peekskill
228	221.7	Yorkshire-Pioneer Central SD	Yorkshire
229	219.9	Jamesville-Dewitt Central SD	Dewitt
230	219.4	Goshen Central SD	Goshen
231	218.8	UFSD of the Tarrytowns	Sleepy Hollow
232	216.2	Cornwall Central SD	Cornwall on Hdsn
233	212.2	Miller Place UFSD	Miller Place
234	211.2	Averill Park Central SD	Averill Park
234	211.2	Batavia City SD	Batavia
236	210.4	New Hartford Central SD	New Hartford
237	206.3	Evans-Brant Central SD (Lake Shore)	Angola
238	206.1	Geneva City SD	Geneva
239	206.0	Hendrick Hudson Central SD	Montrose
240	204.9	Johnson City Central SD	Johnson City
241	203.9	Saugerties Central SD	Saugerties
241	203.9	Seaford UFSD	Seaford
243	201.4	Starpoint Central SD	Lockport
244	198.7	Rotterdam-Mohonasen Central SD	Schenectady
245	197.5	Dunkirk City SD	Dunkirk
246	197.3	Mexico Central SD	Mexico
247	196.8	Ravena-Coeymans-Selkirk Cent SD	Ravena
248	196.6	Iroquois Central SD	Elma
249	194.3	Malone Central SD	Malone
250	194.1	Massena Central SD	Massena
250	194.1	Newark Central SD	Newark
252	192.4	Pearl River UFSD	Pearl River
253	192.3	Lansingburgh Central SD	Troy
254	191.9	Scotia-Glenville Central SD	Scotia
255	191.4	Island Trees UFSD	Levittown
256	190.7	Camden Central SD	Camden
257	190.3	Locust Valley Central SD	Locust Valley
258	190.1	Plattsburgh City SD	Plattsburgh
259	189.9	Rondout Valley Central SD	Accord
260	188.2	Central Valley CSD at Ilion-Mohawk	Ilion
261	187.7	Maine-Endwell Central SD	Endwell
262	187.2	Mount Pleasant Central SD	Thornwood
263	187.0	Nanuet UFSD	Nanuet
264	186.2	Shoreham-Wading River Central SD	Shoreham
265	186.1	North Bellmore UFSD	Bellmore
266	184.0	Cheektowaga Central SD	Cheektowaga
267	182.2	Honeoye Falls-Lima Central SD	Honeoye Falls
268	179.4	Ardsley UFSD	Ardsley
269	179.1	Olean City SD	Olean
270	177.6	New Paltz Central SD	New Paltz
271	175.9	Elwood UFSD	Greenlawn
272	175.6	Homer Central SD	Homer
273	175.4	Mount Sinai UFSD	Mount Sinai
274	174.8	East Hampton UFSD	East Hampton
274	174.8	Hudson Falls Central SD	Fort Edward
276	174.7	Palmyra-Macedon Central SD	Palmyra
277	174.2	Greenburgh Central SD	Hartsdale
278	172.1	Valley Stream 13 UFSD	Valley Stream
279	171.8	Westhampton Bch UFSD	Westhampton Bch
280	169.1	West Hempstead UFSD	West Hempstead
281	168.9	Norwich City SD	Norwich
282	166.5	Oneida City SD	Oneida
283	166.2	Lewiston-Porter Central SD	Youngstown
283	166.2	Red Hook Central SD	Red Hook
285	166.0	Hampton Bays UFSD	Hampton Bays
286	165.6	Dryden Central SD	Dryden
287	165.1	Southampton UFSD	Southampton
288	164.7	Wyandanch UFSD	Wyandanch
289	164.5	Irvington UFSD	Irvington
290	162.9	Beekmantown Central SD	West Chazy
291	162.7	Chittenango Central SD	Chittenango
292	161.3	Cohoes City SD	Cohoes
293	161.2	East Williston UFSD	Old Westbury
294	160.9	Phoenix Central SD	Phoenix
295	159.5	Depew UFSD	Depew
296	158.7	Owego-Apalachin Central SD	Owego
297	158.6	Cold Spring Hrbr Central SD	Cold Spring Hrbr
298	156.4	Hudson City SD	Hudson
299	156.2	Windsor Central SD	Windsor
300	154.5	Cheektowaga-Maryvale UFSD	Cheektowaga
300	154.5	Peru Central SD	Peru
302	154.1	Pleasantville UFSD	Pleasantville
303	153.5	Kinderhook Central SD	Valatie
303	153.5	Oneonta City SD	Oneonta
305	153.4	Malverne UFSD	Malverne
306	151.8	Edgemont UFSD	Scarsdale
307	150.9	Salmon River Central SD	Fort Covington
308	150.1	Sherrill City SD	Verona
309	149.0	Glens Falls City SD	Glens Falls
310	148.6	Albion Central SD	Albion
311	148.2	Susquehanna Valley Central SD	Conklin
312	147.7	Cobleskill-Richmondville CSD	Cobleskill
313	145.7	Marlboro Central SD	Milton
314	145.5	Waterloo Central SD	Waterloo
315	145.3	Babylon UFSD	Babylon
316	145.2	Lackawanna City SD	Lackawanna
317	144.0	Phelps-Clifton Springs Central SD	Clifton Springs
318	143.8	Tonawanda City SD	Tonawanda
319	143.1	Oyster Bay-East Norwich Central SD	Oyster Bay
320	142.6	Springville-Griffith Institute CSD	Springville
321	142.2	Livonia Central SD	Livonia
322	142.1	Hastings-On-Hudson UFSD	Hastings on Hdsn
323	141.9	Franklin Square UFSD	Franklin Square
324	141.5	Bath Central SD	Bath
325	141.1	Schalmont Central SD	Schenectady
326	138.5	Medina Central SD	Medina
327	138.3	Johnstown City SD	Johnstown
328	137.8	New Hyde Pk-Garden City Pk UFSD	New Hyde Park
329	137.0	Bronxville UFSD	Bronxville
329	137.0	South Jefferson Central SD	Adams Center
331	136.6	Fredonia Central SD	Fredonia
332	136.4	Marcellus Central SD	Marcellus
333	136.3	Ogdensburg City SD	Ogdensburg
334	136.1	Highland Central SD	Highland
335	135.4	Dansville Central SD	Dansville
335	135.4	Liberty Central SD	Liberty
337	135.3	Broadalbin-Perth Central SD	Broadalbin
338	135.0	Westhill Central SD	Syracuse
339	134.7	Hornell City SD	Hornell
339	134.7	Putnam Valley Central SD	Putnam Valley
341	134.5	Chenango Valley Central SD	Binghamton
342	134.3	Schuylerville Central SD	Schuylerville
343	134.1	Charter School for Applied Techs	Buffalo
344	132.8	Catskill Central SD	Catskill
345	132.5	Alden Central SD	Alden
346	131.3	Croton-Harmon UFSD	Croton on Hdsn
347	125.9	Blind Brook-Rye UFSD	Rye Brook
348	123.1	Ellenville Central SD	Ellenville
349	122.2	Newfane Central SD	Burt
350	121.7	Gouverneur Central SD	Gouverneur
350	121.7	Rye Neck UFSD	Mamaroneck
352	119.8	Center Moriches UFSD	Center Moriches
353	119.0	Chenango Forks Central SD	Binghamton
354	118.7	East Aurora UFSD	East Aurora
355	117.4	Waverly Central SD	Waverly
356	111.5	Valley Stream 30 UFSD	Valley Stream
357	94.5	General Brown Central SD	Dexter

Number of Students

Rank	Number	District Name	City
1	11,076,080	New York City Chancellor's Office	New York
2	61,899	NYC Geographic District #31	Staten Island
3	61,702	NYC Geographic District # 2	New York
4	58,907	NYC Geographic District #24	Corona
5	56,031	NYC Geographic District #10	Bronx
6	49,749	NYC Geographic District #20	Brooklyn
7	45,845	NYC Geographic District #27	Ozone Park
8	41,096	NYC Geographic District #28	Jamaica
9	40,204	NYC Geographic District #11	Bronx
10	39,993	NYC Geographic District #30	Long Isl City
11	37,209	NYC Geographic District # 9	Bronx
12	36,647	NYC Geographic District #25	Flushing
13	35,305	NYC Geographic District #22	Brooklyn
14	34,757	NYC Geographic District #21	Brooklyn
15	33,345	Buffalo City SD	Buffalo
16	31,868	NYC Geographic District #26	Bayside
17	31,036	NYC Geographic District #15	Brooklyn
18	29,413	NYC Geographic District # 8	Bronx
19	28,886	Rochester City SD	Rochester
20	27,809	NYC Geographic District #29	Queens Village
21	26,728	Yonkers City SD	Yonkers
22	24,581	NYC Geographic District #12	Bronx
23	23,873	NYC Geographic District #19	Brooklyn
24	23,477	NYC Geographic District # 6	New York
25	23,325	NYC Geographic District #17	Brooklyn
26	21,988	NYC Geographic District # 3	New York
27	21,514	NYC Geographic District #13	Brooklyn
28	20,934	Syracuse City SD	Syracuse

Note: This section only includes districts with 1,500 or more students; All categories are ranked from high to low

Rank	Students	District	Location
29	20,197	NYC Geographic District # 7	Bronx
30	19,050	NYC Geographic District #14	Brooklyn
31	18,941	Brentwood UFSD	Brentwood
32	16,571	NYC Geographic District #18	Brooklyn
33	13,627	Sachem Central SD	Lake Ronkonkoma
34	13,522	NYC Geographic District # 4	New York
35	12,590	NYC Geographic District #32	Brooklyn
36	12,586	NYC Geographic District # 5	New York
37	11,393	Newburgh City SD	Newburgh
38	11,286	NYC Geographic District # 1	New York
39	11,232	Greece Central SD	Rochester
40	11,168	Wappingers Central SD	Hopewell Junction
41	10,958	New Rochelle City SD	New Rochelle
42	10,037	NYC Geographic District #23	Brooklyn
43	10,008	Middle Country Central SD	Centereach
44	9,972	Williamsville Central SD	East Amherst
45	9,966	Utica City SD	Utica
46	9,792	Shenendehowa Central SD	Clifton Park
47	9,706	Schenectady City SD	Schenectady
48	9,464	Smithtown Central SD	Smithtown
49	9,121	Longwood Central SD	Middle Island
50	9,055	Albany City SD	Albany
51	9,011	North Syracuse Central SD	North Syracuse
52	8,818	William Floyd UFSD	Mastic Beach
53	8,697	East Ramapo CSD (Spring Valley)	Spring Valley
54	8,572	Arlington Central SD	Lagrangeville
55	8,542	Half Hollow Hills Central SD	Dix Hills
56	8,442	Webster Central SD	Webster
57	8,195	Sewanhaka Central High SD	Floral Park
58	8,172	Clarkstown Central SD	New City
59	8,043	Mount Vernon SD	Mount Vernon
60	8,029	Hempstead UFSD	Hempstead
61	7,949	Haverstraw-Stony Point CSD	Garnerville
62	7,653	Patchogue-Medford UFSD	Patchogue
63	7,600	NYC Geographic District #16	Brooklyn
64	7,366	Central Islip UFSD	Central Islip
65	7,334	Middletown City SD	Middletown
66	7,295	Liverpool Central SD	Liverpool
67	7,169	Massapequa UFSD	Massapequa
68	7,148	East Meadow UFSD	Westbury
69	7,098	Levittown UFSD	Levittown
70	7,070	White Plains City SD	White Plains
71	7,061	Niagara Falls City SD	Niagara Falls
72	6,963	Freeport UFSD	Freeport
73	6,949	Kenmore-Tonawanda UFSD	Buffalo
74	6,947	Monroe-Woodbury Central SD	Central Valley
75	6,834	Uniondale UFSD	Uniondale
76	6,700	West Seneca Central SD	West Seneca
77	6,627	Great Neck UFSD	Great Neck
78	6,550	Commack UFSD	East Northport
79	6,481	Three Village Central SD	Stony Brook
80	6,399	Saratoga Spgs City SD	Saratoga Spgs
81	6,312	Kingston City SD	Kingston
82	6,270	Syosset Central SD	Syosset
83	6,260	Elmira City SD	Elmira
84	6,106	Lindenhurst UFSD	Lindenhurst
85	6,100	Connetquot Central SD	Bohemia
86	6,037	Fairport Central SD	Fairport
87	6,036	South Huntington UFSD	Huntington Stn
88	5,931	Bay Shore UFSD	Bay Shore
89	5,836	Farmingdale UFSD	Farmingdale
90	5,786	Binghamton City SD	Binghamton
91	5,778	Lakeland Central SD	Shrub Oak
92	5,764	Lancaster Central SD	Lancaster
93	5,707	Pittsford Central SD	Pittsford
94	5,642	Northport-East Northport UFSD	Northport
95	5,611	Baldwinsville Central SD	Baldwinsville
96	5,585	Oceanside UFSD	Oceanside
97	5,513	North Colonie CSD	Latham
98	5,480	Rome City SD	Rome
99	5,472	Rush-Henrietta Central SD	Henrietta
100	5,456	Bellmore-Merrick Central High SD	North Merrick
101	5,397	Port Washington UFSD	Port Washington
102	5,367	Riverhead Central SD	Riverhead
103	5,356	Ithaca City SD	Ithaca
104	5,339	Mamaroneck UFSD	Mamaroneck
105	5,338	Pine Bush Central SD	Pine Bush
106	5,275	Hicksville UFSD	Hicksville
107	5,171	Copiague UFSD	Copiague
108	5,048	Westbury UFSD	Old Westbury
109	4,964	Ossining UFSD	Ossining
110	4,929	Frontier Central SD	Hamburg
111	4,918	Jamestown City SD	Jamestown
112	4,906	Guilderland Central SD	Guilderland Center
113	4,889	Plainview-Old Bethpage CSD	Plainview
114	4,879	South Colonie Central SD	Albany
115	4,861	Orchard Park Central SD	West Seneca
116	4,801	Scarsdale UFSD	Scarsdale
117	4,798	Corning City SD	Painted Post
118	4,768	Baldwin UFSD	Baldwin
119	4,745	North Babylon UFSD	North Babylon
120	4,710	West Genesee Central SD	Camillus
121	4,699	Lockport City SD	Lockport
122	4,682	Port Chester-Rye UFSD	Port Chester
123	4,622	Bethlehem Central SD	Delmar
124	4,545	Huntington UFSD	Huntington Stn
125	4,523	Valley Stream Central High SD	Valley Stream
126	4,521	South Country Central SD	East Patchogue
127	4,512	West Islip UFSD	West Islip
128	4,484	Clarence Central SD	Clarence
129	4,476	Penfield Central SD	Rochester
130	4,458	Victor Central SD	Victor
131	4,454	Poughkeepsie City SD	Poughkeepsie
132	4,443	Hilton Central SD	Hilton
133	4,416	Ramapo Central SD (Suffern)	Hillburn
134	4,367	Bedford Central SD	Bedford
135	4,355	Mahopac Central SD	Mahopac
136	4,323	Valley Central SD (Montgomery)	Montgomery
137	4,293	Auburn City SD	Auburn
138	4,210	Fayetteville-Manlius Central SD	Manlius
139	4,207	Washingtonville Central SD	Washingtonville
140	4,196	Carmel Central SD	Patterson
141	4,192	Horseheads Central SD	Horseheads
142	4,173	Gates-Chili Central SD	Rochester
143	4,170	Deer Park UFSD	Deer Park
144	4,140	Ballston Spa Central SD	Ballston Spa
145	4,133	Niskayuna Central SD	Schenectady
146	4,071	Troy City SD	Troy
147	4,027	West Babylon UFSD	West Babylon
148	4,014	East Greenbush Central SD	East Greenbush
149	3,967	Central Square Central SD	Central Square
150	3,962	Watertown City SD	Watertown
151	3,915	Indian River Central SD	Philadelphia
152	3,914	Long Beach City SD	Long Beach
153	3,902	Churchville-Chili Central SD	Churchville
154	3,894	Herricks UFSD	New Hyde Park
155	3,890	Minisink Valley Central SD	Slate Hill
156	3,878	Union-Endicott Central SD	Endicott
157	3,874	East Islip UFSD	Islip Terrace
158	3,866	Chappaqua Central SD	Chappaqua
159	3,861	Garden City UFSD	Garden City
160	3,843	Amsterdam City SD	Amsterdam
161	3,816	Elmont UFSD	Elmont
162	3,789	Oswego City SD	Oswego
163	3,751	Brookhaven-Comsewogue UFSD	Port Jeff Stn
164	3,704	Niagara-Wheatfield Central SD	Niagara Falls
165	3,675	Warwick Valley Central SD	Warwick
166	3,649	Hauppauge UFSD	Hauppauge
167	3,623	Spencerport Central SD	Spencerport
168	3,600	Hyde Park Central SD	Hyde Park
169	3,579	Canandaigua City SD	Canandaigua
170	3,575	West Irondequoit Central SD	Rochester
171	3,572	Hamburg Central SD	Hamburg
172	3,554	North Tonawanda City SD	North Tonawanda
173	3,535	Harrison Central SD	Harrison
174	3,531	Brockport Central SD	Brockport
175	3,528	Eastport-South Manor CSD	Manorville
176	3,523	Brighton Central SD	Rochester
177	3,520	Rockville Ctr UFSD	Rockville Ctr
178	3,500	East Syracuse Minoa Central SD	East Syracuse
179	3,486	Yorktown Central SD	Yorktown Hgts
180	3,443	Fulton City SD	Fulton
181	3,430	Kings Park Central SD	Kings Park
182	3,405	Peekskill City SD	Peekskill
183	3,353	Vestal Central SD	Vestal
184	3,349	Queensbury UFSD	Queensbury
185	3,338	Manhasset UFSD	Manhasset
185	3,338	Roosevelt UFSD	Roosevelt
187	3,332	Rye City SD	Rye
188	3,277	Glen Cove City SD	Glen Cove
189	3,251	Carthage Central SD	Carthage
190	3,248	Rocky Point UFSD	Rocky Point
191	3,245	Harborfields Central SD	Greenlawn
192	3,242	Whitesboro Central SD	Whitesboro
193	3,220	Cornwall Central SD	Cornwall on Hdsn
194	3,189	Amityville UFSD	Amityville
195	3,187	Eastchester UFSD	Eastchester
196	3,186	S Glens Fls Central SD	S Glens Fls
197	3,179	Brewster Central SD	Brewster
198	3,176	Somers Central SD	Somers
199	3,165	South Orangetown Central SD	Blauvelt
200	3,156	Katonah-Lewisboro UFSD	South Salem
200	3,156	Sweet Home Central SD	Amherst
202	3,147	Roslyn UFSD	Roslyn
203	3,108	East Irondequoit Central SD	Rochester
204	3,076	Burnt Hills-Ballston Lake Central SD	Scotia
204	3,076	Hewlett-Woodmere UFSD	Woodmere
206	3,044	Plainedge UFSD	N Massapequa
207	3,038	Wantagh UFSD	Wantagh
208	3,027	Beacon City SD	Beacon
209	3,025	Wallkill Central SD	Wallkill
210	3,015	Sayville UFSD	Sayville
211	3,007	Jericho UFSD	Jericho
212	3,002	Monticello Central SD	Monticello
213	2,995	Nyack UFSD	Nyack
214	2,970	Amherst Central SD	Amherst
215	2,958	Grand Island Central SD	Grand Island
215	2,958	Jamesville-Dewitt Central SD	Dewitt
217	2,931	Goshen Central SD	Goshen
218	2,902	Bethpage UFSD	Bethpage
219	2,890	Islip UFSD	Islip
220	2,855	Averill Park Central SD	Averill Park
221	2,831	Gloversville City SD	Gloversville
222	2,822	Pelham UFSD	Pelham
223	2,812	Rotterdam-Mohonasen Central SD	Schenectady
224	2,810	Mineola UFSD	Mineola
225	2,793	Lynbrook UFSD	Lynbrook
226	2,768	Massena Central SD	Massena
227	2,762	UFSD of the Tarrytowns	Sleepy Hollow
228	2,749	Miller Place UFSD	Miller Place
229	2,719	North Shore Central SD	Sea Cliff
230	2,685	Starpoint Central SD	Lockport
231	2,684	Port Jervis City SD	Port Jervis
232	2,680	Lawrence UFSD	Cedarhurst
233	2,603	New Hartford Central SD	New Hartford
234	2,577	Saugerties Central SD	Saugerties
235	2,562	Johnson City Central SD	Johnson City
236	2,545	Wyandanch UFSD	Wyandanch
237	2,544	Pearl River UFSD	Pearl River
238	2,515	Yorkshire-Pioneer Central SD	Yorkshire
239	2,514	Scotia-Glenville Central SD	Scotia
240	2,498	Cortland City SD	Cortland
241	2,476	Byram Hills Central SD	Armonk
242	2,469	Evans-Brant Central SD (Lake Shore)	Angola
243	2,468	Maine-Endwell Central SD	Endwell
244	2,413	Hudson Falls Central SD	Fort Edward
245	2,381	Mount Sinai UFSD	Mount Sinai
246	2,378	Hendrick Hudson Central SD	Montrose
247	2,372	Central Valley CSD at Ilion-Mohawk	Ilion
248	2,357	Lansingburgh Central SD	Troy
249	2,334	Malone Central SD	Malone
250	2,317	Shoreham-Wading River Central SD	Shoreham
251	2,315	Batavia City SD	Batavia
252	2,314	Iroquois Central SD	Elma
253	2,305	Bayport-Blue Point UFSD	Bayport
254	2,289	Elwood UFSD	Greenlawn
255	2,285	Seaford UFSD	Seaford
256	2,282	Geneva City SD	Geneva
257	2,265	Camden Central SD	Camden
258	2,254	Island Trees UFSD	Levittown
259	2,242	Wayne Central SD	Ontario Center
260	2,237	Honeoye Falls-Lima Central SD	Honeoye Falls
261	2,230	Cheektowaga-Maryvale UFSD	Cheektowaga
262	2,229	New Paltz Central SD	New Paltz
263	2,224	Nanuet UFSD	Nanuet
264	2,209	Newark Central SD	Newark
265	2,203	Oneida City SD	Oneida
266	2,186	Olean City SD	Olean
267	2,171	Mexico Central SD	Mexico
268	2,161	Owego-Apalachin Central SD	Owego
269	2,113	North Bellmore UFSD	Bellmore
270	2,111	Cheektowaga Central SD	Cheektowaga
271	2,110	Hampton Bays UFSD	Hampton Bays
272	2,103	Locust Valley Central SD	Locust Valley
273	2,095	Dunkirk City SD	Dunkirk
274	2,078	Lewiston-Porter Central SD	Youngstown
275	2,077	West Hempstead UFSD	West Hempstead
276	2,058	Valley Stream 13 UFSD	Valley Stream
277	2,055	Glens Falls City SD	Glens Falls
278	2,047	Ardsley UFSD	Ardsley
279	2,039	Charter School for Applied Techs	Buffalo
280	2,023	Homer Central SD	Homer

Note: This section only includes districts with 1,500 or more students; All categories are ranked from high to low

Rank	Number	District Name	City
281	2,014	Franklin Square UFSD	Franklin Square
282	1,981	Marlboro Central SD	Milton
282	1,981	Sherrill City SD	Verona
284	1,968	Albion Central SD	Albion
285	1,946	South Jefferson Central SD	Adams Center
286	1,940	Rondout Valley Central SD	Accord
287	1,927	Chittenango Central SD	Chittenango
288	1,923	Edgemont UFSD	Scarsdale
289	1,904	Red Hook Central SD	Red Hook
290	1,894	Mount Pleasant Central SD	Thornwood
291	1,893	Palmyra-Macedon Central SD	Palmyra
292	1,891	Peru Central SD	Peru
293	1,883	Norwich City SD	Norwich
294	1,882	Beekmantown Central SD	West Chazy
295	1,878	Ravena-Coeymans-Selkirk Cent SD	Ravena
296	1,873	Plattsburgh City SD	Plattsburgh
297	1,871	Greenburgh Central SD	Hartsdale
298	1,870	Cohoes City SD	Cohoes
299	1,869	Kinderhook Central SD	Valatie
300	1,862	Phoenix Central SD	Phoenix
301	1,859	Depew UFSD	Depew
302	1,850	Hudson City SD	Hudson
303	1,842	Schalmont Central SD	Schenectady
304	1,836	Broadalbin-Perth Central SD	Broadalbin
305	1,813	Westhampton Bch UFSD	Westhampton Bch
306	1,811	Chenango Valley Central SD	Binghamton
307	1,809	East Hampton UFSD	East Hampton
308	1,805	Cold Spring Hrbr Central SD	Cold Spring Hrbr
309	1,801	Highland Central SD	Highland
310	1,800	East Aurora UFSD	East Aurora
311	1,779	Westhill Central SD	Syracuse
312	1,775	Irvington UFSD	Irvington
313	1,772	Lackawanna City SD	Lackawanna
314	1,771	Johnstown City SD	Johnstown
315	1,759	Springville-Griffith Institute CSD	Springville
316	1,751	Ellenville Central SD	Ellenville
317	1,743	Hornell City SD	Hornell
318	1,736	Tonawanda City SD	Tonawanda
319	1,722	Putnam Valley Central SD	Putnam Valley
320	1,721	Cobleskill-Richmondville CSD	Cobleskill
321	1,715	East Williston UFSD	Old Westbury
322	1,701	Ogdensburg City SD	Ogdensburg
323	1,700	Malverne UFSD	Malverne
323	1,700	Oneonta City SD	Oneonta
325	1,694	Pleasantville UFSD	Pleasantville
326	1,693	Windsor Central SD	Windsor
327	1,691	Marcellus Central SD	Marcellus
328	1,683	New Hyde Pk-Garden City Pk UFSD	New Hyde Park
329	1,665	Bronxville UFSD	Bronxville
330	1,658	Southampton UFSD	Southampton
331	1,651	Medina Central SD	Medina
332	1,650	Croton-Harmon UFSD	Croton on Hdsn
333	1,648	Center Moriches UFSD	Center Moriches
334	1,647	Schuylerville Central SD	Schuylerville
335	1,642	Alden Central SD	Alden
336	1,626	Liberty Central SD	Liberty
337	1,623	Waterloo Central SD	Waterloo
338	1,620	Livonia Central SD	Livonia
339	1,614	Oyster Bay-East Norwich Central SD	Oyster Bay
339	1,614	Waverly Central SD	Waverly
341	1,610	Newfane Central SD	Burt
342	1,609	Catskill Central SD	Catskill
342	1,609	Gouverneur Central SD	Gouverneur
344	1,608	Dryden Central SD	Dryden
345	1,604	Babylon UFSD	Babylon
346	1,599	Salmon River Central SD	Fort Covington
347	1,591	Rye Neck UFSD	Mamaroneck
348	1,585	Chenango Forks Central SD	Binghamton
349	1,584	Bath Central SD	Bath
350	1,578	Hastings-On-Hudson UFSD	Hastings on Hdsn
351	1,575	Phelps-Clifton Springs Central SD	Clifton Springs
352	1,547	Valley Stream 30 UFSD	Valley Stream
353	1,543	Dansville Central SD	Dansville
354	1,539	Susquehanna Valley Central SD	Conklin
355	1,535	General Brown Central SD	Dexter
356	1,519	Fredonia Central SD	Fredonia
357	1,515	Blind Brook-Rye UFSD	Rye Brook

Male Students

Rank	Percent	District Name	City
1	55.4	Lansingburgh Central SD	Troy
2	54.8	NYC Geographic District #23	Brooklyn
3	54.5	Susquehanna Valley Central SD	Conklin
4	54.4	Chenango Forks Central SD	Binghamton
4	54.4	Westhampton Bch UFSD	Westhampton Bch
6	54.2	NYC Geographic District #16	Brooklyn
7	54.0	Southampton UFSD	Southampton
8	53.9	West Hempstead UFSD	West Hempstead
9	53.8	Amityville UFSD	Amityville
9	53.8	NYC Geographic District # 7	Bronx
9	53.8	Olean City SD	Olean
12	53.7	Ardsley UFSD	Ardsley
12	53.7	NYC Geographic District #24	Corona
12	53.7	Roosevelt UFSD	Roosevelt
15	53.6	Malone Central SD	Malone
15	53.6	Valley Stream 30 UFSD	Valley Stream
17	53.5	NYC Geographic District # 5	New York
17	53.5	Wallkill Central SD	Wallkill
19	53.4	NYC Geographic District #19	Brooklyn
20	53.3	Hempstead UFSD	Hempstead
20	53.3	Ogdensburg City SD	Ogdensburg
22	53.2	Deer Park UFSD	Deer Park
22	53.2	Jericho UFSD	Jericho
22	53.2	Lackawanna City SD	Lackawanna
22	53.2	Sherrill City SD	Verona
26	53.1	Cortland City SD	Cortland
26	53.1	Fredonia Central SD	Fredonia
26	53.1	Irvington UFSD	Irvington
29	53.0	Dryden Central SD	Dryden
29	53.0	Edgemont UFSD	Scarsdale
29	53.0	Lawrence UFSD	Cedarhurst
29	53.0	Malverne UFSD	Malverne
29	53.0	NYC Geographic District #11	Bronx
29	53.0	NYC Geographic District #14	Brooklyn
29	53.0	Shoreham-Wading River Central SD	Shoreham
36	52.9	Beekmantown Central SD	West Chazy
36	52.9	East Williston UFSD	Old Westbury
36	52.9	Kinderhook Central SD	Valatie
36	52.9	NYC Geographic District #27	Ozone Park
36	52.9	Rye Neck UFSD	Mamaroneck
41	52.8	General Brown Central SD	Dexter
41	52.8	Hewlett-Woodmere UFSD	Woodmere
41	52.8	Waterloo Central SD	Waterloo
44	52.7	Amherst Central SD	Amherst
44	52.7	Farmingdale UFSD	Farmingdale
44	52.7	Hauppauge UFSD	Hauppauge
44	52.7	Mineola UFSD	Mineola
44	52.7	Pine Bush Central SD	Pine Bush
44	52.7	Pleasantville UFSD	Pleasantville
50	52.6	East Ramapo CSD (Spring Valley)	Spring Valley
50	52.6	Hampton Bays UFSD	Hampton Bays
50	52.6	Herricks UFSD	New Hyde Park
50	52.6	Marlboro Central SD	Milton
50	52.6	Miller Place UFSD	Miller Place
50	52.6	NYC Geographic District # 8	Bronx
50	52.6	Northport-East Northport UFSD	Northport
50	52.6	Ossining UFSD	Ossining
50	52.6	Oyster Bay-East Norwich Central SD	Oyster Bay
50	52.6	Pelham UFSD	Pelham
50	52.6	Poughkeepsie City SD	Poughkeepsie
50	52.6	Scotia-Glenville Central SD	Scotia
62	52.5	Gouverneur Central SD	Gouverneur
62	52.5	Mount Sinai UFSD	Mount Sinai
62	52.5	NYC Geographic District #13	Brooklyn
62	52.5	Phoenix Central SD	Phoenix
62	52.5	Port Jervis City SD	Port Jervis
62	52.5	Rondout Valley Central SD	Accord
62	52.5	Syosset Central SD	Syosset
69	52.4	Brockport Central SD	Brockport
69	52.4	Central Islip UFSD	Central Islip
69	52.4	Fulton City SD	Fulton
69	52.4	NYC Geographic District #20	Brooklyn
69	52.4	NYC Geographic District #29	Queens Village
69	52.4	Oceanside UFSD	Oceanside
69	52.4	Peekskill City SD	Peekskill
69	52.4	Peru Central SD	Peru
69	52.4	Plainview-Old Bethpage CSD	Plainview
69	52.4	Windsor Central SD	Windsor
79	52.3	Canandaigua City SD	Canandaigua
79	52.3	Freeport UFSD	Freeport
79	52.3	Half Hollow Hills Central SD	Dix Hills
79	52.3	Marcellus Central SD	Marcellus
79	52.3	Newfane Central SD	Burt
79	52.3	South Huntington UFSD	Huntington Stn
79	52.3	Spencerport Central SD	Spencerport
79	52.3	Syracuse City SD	Syracuse
87	52.2	Auburn City SD	Auburn
87	52.2	Batavia City SD	Batavia
87	52.2	Bedford Central SD	Bedford
87	52.2	Clarkstown Central SD	New City
87	52.2	Dunkirk City SD	Dunkirk
87	52.2	Homer Central SD	Homer
87	52.2	Monticello Central SD	Monticello
87	52.2	NYC Geographic District # 9	Bronx
87	52.2	North Syracuse Central SD	North Syracuse
87	52.2	Queensbury UFSD	Queensbury
87	52.2	Valley Stream Central High SD	Valley Stream
98	52.1	Chappaqua Central SD	Chappaqua
98	52.1	Chenango Valley Central SD	Binghamton
98	52.1	Cold Spring Hrbr Central SD	Cold Spring Hrbr
98	52.1	Ithaca City SD	Ithaca
98	52.1	Lynbrook UFSD	Lynbrook
98	52.1	Middletown City SD	Middletown
98	52.1	Mount Vernon City SD	Mount Vernon
98	52.1	Plattsburgh City SD	Plattsburgh
98	52.1	Riverhead Central SD	Riverhead
107	52.0	Bay Shore UFSD	Bay Shore
107	52.0	Cheektowaga Central SD	Cheektowaga
107	52.0	Connetquot Central SD	Bohemia
107	52.0	Elmira City SD	Elmira
107	52.0	Hudson City SD	Hudson
107	52.0	Levittown UFSD	Levittown
107	52.0	NYC Geographic District #31	Staten Island
107	52.0	Newburgh City SD	Newburgh
107	52.0	Owego-Apalachin Central SD	Owego
107	52.0	Vestal Central SD	Vestal
107	52.0	West Irondequoit Central SD	Rochester
107	52.0	West Islip UFSD	West Islip
119	51.9	Ballston Spa Central SD	Ballston Spa
119	51.9	Binghamton City SD	Binghamton
119	51.9	East Islip UFSD	Islip Terrace
119	51.9	East Syracuse Minoa Central SD	East Syracuse
119	51.9	Ellenville Central SD	Ellenville
119	51.9	Hicksville UFSD	Hicksville
119	51.9	Manhasset UFSD	Manhasset
119	51.9	Mexico Central SD	Mexico
119	51.9	Mount Pleasant Central SD	Thornwood
119	51.9	New Hartford Central SD	New Hartford
119	51.9	NYC Geographic District # 6	New York
119	51.9	NYC Geographic District #10	Bronx
119	51.9	NYC Geographic District #12	Bronx
132	51.8	Broadalbin-Perth Central SD	Broadalbin
132	51.8	Burnt Hills-Ballston Lake Central SD	Scotia
132	51.8	Dansville Central SD	Dansville
132	51.8	Fairport Central SD	Fairport
132	51.8	Geneva City SD	Geneva
132	51.8	Great Neck UFSD	Great Neck
132	51.8	Haverstraw-Stony Point CSD	Garnerville
132	51.8	Honeoye Falls-Lima Central SD	Honeoye Falls
132	51.8	Horseheads Central SD	Horseheads
132	51.8	Jamestown City SD	Jamestown
132	51.8	Jamesville-Dewitt Central SD	Dewitt
132	51.8	Johnstown City SD	Johnstown
132	51.8	Mamaroneck UFSD	Mamaroneck
132	51.8	Middle Country Central SD	Centereach
132	51.8	Oswego City SD	Oswego
132	51.8	Putnam Valley Central SD	Putnam Valley
132	51.8	Red Hook Central SD	Red Hook
132	51.8	Schalmont Central SD	Schenectady
132	51.8	Schenectady City SD	Schenectady
151	51.7	Amsterdam City SD	Amsterdam
151	51.7	East Irondequoit Central SD	Rochester
151	51.7	Glen Cove City SD	Glen Cove
151	51.7	Gloversville City SD	Gloversville
151	51.7	North Babylon UFSD	North Babylon
151	51.7	Rye City SD	Rye
151	51.7	Washingtonville Central SD	Washingtonville
158	51.6	Bayport-Blue Point UFSD	Bayport
158	51.6	Brentwood UFSD	Brentwood
158	51.6	Churchville-Chili Central SD	Churchville
158	51.6	Copiague UFSD	Copiague
158	51.6	Eastchester UFSD	Eastchester
158	51.6	Hyde Park Central SD	Hyde Park
158	51.6	Iroquois Central SD	Elma
158	51.6	NYC Geographic District #18	Brooklyn
158	51.6	NYC Geographic District #32	Brooklyn
158	51.6	Port Chester-Rye UFSD	Port Chester
158	51.6	Rochester City SD	Rochester
158	51.6	Rockville Ctr UFSD	Rockville Ctr
158	51.6	Rome City SD	Rome

Note: This section only includes districts with 1,500 or more students; All categories are ranked from high to low

Rank	Percent	District Name	City
158	51.6	Somers Central SD	Somers
158	51.6	Sweet Home Central SD	Amherst
158	51.6	William Floyd UFSD	Mastic Beach
158	51.6	Yonkers City SD	Yonkers
175	51.5	Albion Central SD	Albion
175	51.5	Baldwinsville Central SD	Baldwinsville
175	51.5	Depew UFSD	Depew
175	51.5	Elwood UFSD	Greenlawn
175	51.5	Long Beach City SD	Long Beach
175	51.5	New Rochelle City SD	New Rochelle
175	51.5	NYC Geographic District #21	Brooklyn
175	51.5	Newark Central SD	Newark
175	51.5	North Shore Central SD	Sea Cliff
175	51.5	Norwich City SD	Norwich
175	51.5	South Country Central SD	East Patchogue
175	51.5	S Glens Fls Central SD	S Glens Fls
175	51.5	Starpoint Central SD	Lockport
175	51.5	Watertown City SD	Watertown
175	51.5	Yorktown Central SD	Yorktown Hgts
175	51.5	New York City Chancellor's Office	New York
191	51.4	Babylon UFSD	Babylon
191	51.4	Brewster Central SD	Brewster
191	51.4	Carthage Central SD	Carthage
191	51.4	Central Valley CSD at Ilion-Mohawk	Ilion
191	51.4	Charter School for Applied Techs	Buffalo
191	51.4	Hornell City SD	Hornell
191	51.4	Lewiston-Porter Central SD	Youngstown
191	51.4	Longwood Central SD	Middle Island
191	51.4	Minisink Valley Central SD	Slate Hill
191	51.4	NYC Geographic District #26	Bayside
191	51.4	NYC Geographic District #28	Jamaica
191	51.4	Sewanhaka Central High SD	Floral Park
191	51.4	Shenendehowa Central SD	Clifton Park
191	51.4	Union-Endicott Central SD	Endicott
191	51.4	Uniondale UFSD	Uniondale
191	51.4	Waverly Central SD	Waverly
191	51.4	Wayne Central SD	Ontario Center
191	51.4	West Genesee Central SD	Camillus
191	51.4	Westbury UFSD	Old Westbury
191	51.4	Wyandanch UFSD	Wyandanch
211	51.3	Baldwin UFSD	Baldwin
211	51.3	Bronxville UFSD	Bronxville
211	51.3	Islip UFSD	Islip
211	51.3	Mahopac Central SD	Mahopac
211	51.3	Nanuet UFSD	Nanuet
211	51.3	NYC Geographic District #22	Brooklyn
211	51.3	Nyack UFSD	Nyack
211	51.3	Port Washington UFSD	Port Washington
211	51.3	Ravena-Coeymans-Selkirk Cent SD	Ravena
211	51.3	Wappingers Central SD	Hopewell Junction
211	51.3	West Seneca Central SD	West Seneca
211	51.3	Whitesboro Central SD	Whitesboro
223	51.2	Alden Central SD	Alden
223	51.2	Central Square Central SD	Central Square
223	51.2	Cohoes City SD	Cohoes
223	51.2	Cornwall Central SD	Cornwall on Hdsn
223	51.2	New Hyde Pk-Garden City Pk UFSD	New Hyde Park
223	51.2	North Tonawanda City SD	North Tonawanda
223	51.2	Patchogue-Medford UFSD	Patchogue
223	51.2	Scarsdale UFSD	Scarsdale
223	51.2	Warwick Valley Central SD	Warwick
232	51.1	Albany City SD	Albany
232	51.1	Bethlehem Central SD	Delmar
232	51.1	Carmel Central SD	Patterson
232	51.1	Cobleskill-Richmondville CSD	Cobleskill
232	51.1	Corning City SD	Painted Post
232	51.1	Indian River Central SD	Philadelphia
232	51.1	Kings Park Central SD	Kings Park
232	51.1	Lindenhurst UFSD	Lindenhurst
232	51.1	Monroe-Woodbury Central SD	Central Valley
232	51.1	New Paltz Central SD	New Paltz
232	51.1	NYC Geographic District # 1	New York
232	51.1	NYC Geographic District #30	Long Isl City
232	51.1	Plainedge UFSD	N Massapequa
245	51.0	Bath Central SD	Bath
245	51.0	Commack UFSD	East Northport
245	51.0	Huntington UFSD	Huntington Stn
245	51.0	Lancaster Central SD	Lancaster
245	51.0	NYC Geographic District #25	Flushing
245	51.0	Sayville UFSD	Sayville
245	51.0	Yorkshire-Pioneer Central SD	Yorkshire
252	50.9	Bethpage UFSD	Bethpage
252	50.9	Glens Falls City SD	Glens Falls
252	50.9	Greece Central SD	Rochester
252	50.9	Hudson Falls Central SD	Fort Edward
252	50.9	Island Trees UFSD	Levittown
252	50.9	Liberty Central SD	Liberty
252	50.9	Three Village Central SD	Stony Brook
252	50.9	Webster Central SD	Webster
260	50.8	Byram Hills Central SD	Armonk
260	50.8	Liverpool Central SD	Liverpool
260	50.8	Locust Valley Central SD	Locust Valley
260	50.8	NYC Geographic District #17	Brooklyn
260	50.8	North Colonie CSD	Latham
260	50.8	Orchard Park Central SD	West Seneca
260	50.8	Palmyra-Macedon Central SD	Palmyra
260	50.8	Roslyn UFSD	Roslyn
260	50.8	Rush-Henrietta Central SD	Henrietta
260	50.8	Williamsville Central SD	East Amherst
270	50.7	Averill Park Central SD	Averill Park
270	50.7	Blind Brook-Rye UFSD	Rye Brook
270	50.7	East Aurora UFSD	East Aurora
270	50.7	Goshen Central SD	Goshen
270	50.7	Hilton Central SD	Hilton
270	50.7	Kenmore-Tonawanda UFSD	Buffalo
270	50.7	Lakeland Central SD	Shrub Oak
270	50.7	Lockport City SD	Lockport
270	50.7	Niagara Falls City SD	Niagara Falls
270	50.7	Pearl River UFSD	Pearl River
270	50.7	Phelps-Clifton Springs Central SD	Clifton Springs
270	50.7	Schuylerville Central SD	Schuylerville
270	50.7	Smithtown Central SD	Smithtown
270	50.7	South Colonie Central SD	Albany
270	50.7	Springville-Griffith Institute CSD	Springville
270	50.7	Victor Central SD	Victor
286	50.6	Cheektowaga-Maryvale UFSD	Cheektowaga
286	50.6	Eastport-South Manor CSD	Manorville
286	50.6	Elmont UFSD	Elmont
286	50.6	Fayetteville-Manlius Central SD	Manlius
286	50.6	Frontier Central SD	Hamburg
286	50.6	Hamburg Central SD	Hamburg
286	50.6	Harborfields Central SD	Greenlawn
286	50.6	Hastings-On-Hudson UFSD	Hastings on Hdsn
286	50.6	Hendrick Hudson Central SD	Montrose
286	50.6	Highland Central SD	Highland
286	50.6	Tonawanda City SD	Tonawanda
286	50.6	Troy City SD	Troy
298	50.5	Buffalo City SD	Buffalo
298	50.5	Camden Central SD	Camden
298	50.5	Clarence Central SD	Clarence
298	50.5	Guilderland Central SD	Guilderland Center
298	50.5	Livonia Central SD	Livonia
298	50.5	Niagara-Wheatfield Central SD	Niagara Falls
298	50.5	Seaford UFSD	Seaford
305	50.4	Arlington Central SD	Lagrangeville
305	50.4	Brighton Central SD	Rochester
305	50.4	Center Moriches UFSD	Center Moriches
305	50.4	Chittenango Central SD	Chittenango
305	50.4	Franklin Square UFSD	Franklin Square
305	50.4	Massapequa UFSD	Massapequa
305	50.4	North Bellmore UFSD	Bellmore
305	50.4	Sachem Central SD	Lake Ronkonkoma
305	50.4	Utica City SD	Utica
314	50.3	Catskill Central SD	Catskill
314	50.3	Evans-Brant Central SD (Lake Shore)	Angola
314	50.3	Johnson City Central SD	Johnson City
314	50.3	Medina Central SD	Medina
314	50.3	Penfield Central SD	Rochester
314	50.3	Salmon River Central SD	Fort Covington
320	50.2	Grand Island Central SD	Grand Island
320	50.2	Rotterdam-Mohonasen Central SD	Schenectady
320	50.2	Saratoga Spgs City SD	Saratoga Spgs
320	50.2	South Jefferson Central SD	Adams Center
320	50.2	Valley Central SD (Montgomery)	Montgomery
320	50.2	Valley Stream 13 UFSD	Valley Stream
326	50.1	Brookhaven-Comsewogue UFSD	Port Jeff Stn
326	50.1	Croton-Harmon UFSD	Croton on Hdsn
326	50.1	East Meadow UFSD	Westbury
326	50.1	Gates-Chili Central SD	Rochester
326	50.1	Kingston City SD	Kingston
326	50.1	Niskayuna Central SD	Schenectady
326	50.1	South Orangetown Central SD	Blauvelt
333	50.0	East Hampton UFSD	East Hampton
333	50.0	Greenburgh Central SD	Hartsdale
333	50.0	Harrison Central SD	Harrison
333	50.0	NYC Geographic District #15	Brooklyn
333	50.0	UFSD of the Tarrytowns	Sleepy Hollow
338	49.9	Bellmore-Merrick Central High SD	North Merrick
338	49.9	Katonah-Lewisboro UFSD	South Salem
338	49.9	Oneonta City SD	Oneonta
338	49.9	Wantagh UFSD	Wantagh
338	49.9	West Babylon UFSD	West Babylon
343	49.8	East Greenbush Central SD	East Greenbush
344	49.6	Maine-Endwell Central SD	Endwell
344	49.6	Ramapo Central SD (Suffern)	Hillburn
344	49.6	White Plains City SD	White Plains
347	49.5	Beacon City SD	Beacon
347	49.5	Rocky Point UFSD	Rocky Point
349	49.4	Oneida City SD	Oneida
350	49.3	Garden City UFSD	Garden City
350	49.3	Massena Central SD	Massena
350	49.3	Pittsford Central SD	Pittsford
350	49.3	Saugerties Central SD	Saugerties
354	49.2	NYC Geographic District # 4	New York
355	48.6	Westhill Central SD	Syracuse
356	47.6	NYC Geographic District # 2	New York
357	46.3	NYC Geographic District # 3	New York

Female Students

Rank	Percent	District Name	City
1	53.7	NYC Geographic District # 3	New York
2	52.4	NYC Geographic District # 2	New York
3	51.4	Westhill Central SD	Syracuse
4	50.8	NYC Geographic District # 4	New York
5	50.7	Garden City UFSD	Garden City
5	50.7	Massena Central SD	Massena
5	50.7	Pittsford Central SD	Pittsford
5	50.7	Saugerties Central SD	Saugerties
9	50.6	Oneida City SD	Oneida
10	50.5	Beacon City SD	Beacon
10	50.5	Rocky Point UFSD	Rocky Point
12	50.4	Maine-Endwell Central SD	Endwell
12	50.4	Ramapo Central SD (Suffern)	Hillburn
12	50.4	White Plains City SD	White Plains
15	50.2	East Greenbush Central SD	East Greenbush
16	50.1	Bellmore-Merrick Central High SD	North Merrick
16	50.1	Katonah-Lewisboro UFSD	South Salem
16	50.1	Oneonta City SD	Oneonta
16	50.1	Wantagh UFSD	Wantagh
16	50.1	West Babylon UFSD	West Babylon
21	50.0	East Hampton UFSD	East Hampton
21	50.0	Greenburgh Central SD	Hartsdale
21	50.0	Harrison Central SD	Harrison
21	50.0	NYC Geographic District #15	Brooklyn
21	50.0	UFSD of the Tarrytowns	Sleepy Hollow
26	49.9	Brookhaven-Comsewogue UFSD	Port Jeff Stn
26	49.9	Croton-Harmon UFSD	Croton on Hdsn
26	49.9	East Meadow UFSD	Westbury
26	49.9	Gates-Chili Central SD	Rochester
26	49.9	Kingston City SD	Kingston
26	49.9	Niskayuna Central SD	Schenectady
26	49.9	South Orangetown Central SD	Blauvelt
33	49.8	Grand Island Central SD	Grand Island
33	49.8	Rotterdam-Mohonasen Central SD	Schenectady
33	49.8	Saratoga Spgs City SD	Saratoga Spgs
33	49.8	South Jefferson Central SD	Adams Center
33	49.8	Valley Central SD (Montgomery)	Montgomery
33	49.8	Valley Stream 13 UFSD	Valley Stream
39	49.7	Arlington Central SD	Lagrangeville
39	49.7	Catskill Central SD	Catskill
39	49.7	Evans-Brant Central SD (Lake Shore)	Angola
39	49.7	Johnson City Central SD	Johnson City
39	49.7	Medina Central SD	Medina
39	49.7	Penfield Central SD	Rochester
39	49.7	Salmon River Central SD	Fort Covington
46	49.6	Brighton Central SD	Rochester
46	49.6	Center Moriches UFSD	Center Moriches
46	49.6	Chittenango Central SD	Chittenango
46	49.6	Franklin Square UFSD	Franklin Square
46	49.6	Massapequa UFSD	Massapequa
46	49.6	North Bellmore UFSD	Bellmore
46	49.6	Sachem Central SD	Lake Ronkonkoma
46	49.6	Utica City SD	Utica
54	49.5	Buffalo City SD	Buffalo
54	49.5	Camden Central SD	Camden
54	49.5	Clarence Central SD	Clarence
54	49.5	Guilderland Central SD	Guilderland Center
54	49.5	Livonia Central SD	Livonia
54	49.5	Niagara-Wheatfield Central SD	Niagara Falls
54	49.5	Seaford UFSD	Seaford

Note: This section only includes districts with 1,500 or more students; All categories are ranked from high to low

Rank	Score	District	Location
61	49.4	Cheektowaga-Maryvale UFSD	Cheektowaga
61	49.4	Eastport-South Manor CSD	Manorville
61	49.4	Elmont UFSD	Elmont
61	49.4	Fayetteville-Manlius Central SD	Manlius
61	49.4	Frontier Central SD	Hamburg
61	49.4	Hamburg Central SD	Hamburg
61	49.4	Harborfields Central SD	Greenlawn
61	49.4	Hastings-On-Hudson UFSD	Hastings on Hdsn
61	49.4	Hendrick Hudson Central SD	Montrose
61	49.4	Highland Central SD	Highland
61	49.4	Tonawanda City SD	Tonawanda
61	49.4	Troy City SD	Troy
73	49.3	Averill Park Central SD	Averill Park
73	49.3	Blind Brook-Rye UFSD	Rye Brook
73	49.3	East Aurora UFSD	East Aurora
73	49.3	Goshen Central SD	Goshen
73	49.3	Hilton Central SD	Hilton
73	49.3	Kenmore-Tonawanda UFSD	Buffalo
73	49.3	Lakeland Central SD	Shrub Oak
73	49.3	Lockport City SD	Lockport
73	49.3	Niagara Falls City SD	Niagara Falls
73	49.3	Pearl River UFSD	Pearl River
73	49.3	Phelps-Clifton Springs Central SD	Clifton Springs
73	49.3	Schuylerville Central SD	Schuylerville
73	49.3	Smithtown Central SD	Smithtown
73	49.3	South Colonie Central SD	Albany
73	49.3	Springville-Griffith Institute CSD	Springville
73	49.3	Victor Central SD	Victor
89	49.2	Byram Hills Central SD	Armonk
89	49.2	Liverpool Central SD	Liverpool
89	49.2	Locust Valley Central SD	Locust Valley
89	49.2	NYC Geographic District #17	Brooklyn
89	49.2	North Colonie CSD	Latham
89	49.2	Orchard Park Central SD	West Seneca
89	49.2	Palmyra-Macedon Central SD	Palmyra
89	49.2	Roslyn UFSD	Roslyn
89	49.2	Rush-Henrietta Central SD	Henrietta
89	49.2	Williamsville Central SD	East Amherst
99	49.1	Bethpage UFSD	Bethpage
99	49.1	Glens Falls City SD	Glens Falls
99	49.1	Greece Central SD	Rochester
99	49.1	Hudson Falls Central SD	Fort Edward
99	49.1	Island Trees UFSD	Levittown
99	49.1	Liberty Central SD	Liberty
99	49.1	Three Village Central SD	Stony Brook
99	49.1	Webster Central SD	Webster
107	49.0	Bath Central SD	Bath
107	49.0	Commack UFSD	East Northport
107	49.0	Huntington UFSD	Huntington Stn
107	49.0	Lancaster Central SD	Lancaster
107	49.0	NYC Geographic District #25	Flushing
107	49.0	Sayville UFSD	Sayville
107	49.0	Yorkshire-Pioneer Central SD	Yorkshire
114	48.9	Albany City SD	Albany
114	48.9	Bethlehem Central SD	Delmar
114	48.9	Carmel Central SD	Patterson
114	48.9	Cobleskill-Richmondville CSD	Cobleskill
114	48.9	Corning City SD	Painted Post
114	48.9	Indian River Central SD	Philadelphia
114	48.9	Kings Park Central SD	Kings Park
114	48.9	Lindenhurst UFSD	Lindenhurst
114	48.9	Monroe-Woodbury Central SD	Central Valley
114	48.9	New Paltz Central SD	New Paltz
114	48.9	NYC Geographic District # 1	New York
114	48.9	NYC Geographic District #30	Long Isl City
114	48.9	Plainedge UFSD	N Massapequa
127	48.8	Alden Central SD	Alden
127	48.8	Central Square Central SD	Central Square
127	48.8	Cohoes City SD	Cohoes
127	48.8	Cornwall Central SD	Cornwall on Hdsn
127	48.8	New Hyde Pk-Garden City Pk UFSD	New Hyde Park
127	48.8	North Tonawanda City SD	North Tonawanda
127	48.8	Patchogue-Medford UFSD	Patchogue
127	48.8	Scarsdale UFSD	Scarsdale
127	48.8	Warwick Valley Central SD	Warwick
136	48.7	Baldwin UFSD	Baldwin
136	48.7	Bronxville UFSD	Bronxville
136	48.7	Islip UFSD	Islip
136	48.7	Mahopac Central SD	Mahopac
136	48.7	Nanuet UFSD	Nanuet
136	48.7	NYC Geographic District #22	Brooklyn
136	48.7	Nyack UFSD	Nyack
136	48.7	Port Washington UFSD	Port Washington
136	48.7	Ravena-Coeymans-Selkirk Cent SD	Ravena
136	48.7	Wappingers Central SD	Hopewell Junction
136	48.7	West Seneca Central SD	West Seneca
136	48.7	Whitesboro Central SD	Whitesboro
148	48.6	Babylon UFSD	Babylon
148	48.6	Brewster Central SD	Brewster
148	48.6	Carthage Central SD	Carthage
148	48.6	Central Valley CSD at Ilion-Mohawk	Ilion
148	48.6	Charter School for Applied Techs	Buffalo
148	48.6	Hornell City SD	Hornell
148	48.6	Lewiston-Porter Central SD	Youngstown
148	48.6	Longwood Central SD	Middle Island
148	48.6	Minisink Valley Central SD	Slate Hill
148	48.6	NYC Geographic District #26	Bayside
148	48.6	NYC Geographic District #28	Jamaica
148	48.6	Sewanhaka Central High SD	Floral Park
148	48.6	Shenendehowa Central SD	Clifton Park
148	48.6	Union-Endicott Central SD	Endicott
148	48.6	Uniondale UFSD	Uniondale
148	48.6	Waverly Central SD	Waverly
148	48.6	Wayne Central SD	Ontario Center
148	48.6	West Genesee Central SD	Camillus
148	48.6	Westbury UFSD	Old Westbury
148	48.6	Wyandanch UFSD	Wyandanch
168	48.5	Albion Central SD	Albion
168	48.5	Baldwinsville Central SD	Baldwinsville
168	48.5	Depew UFSD	Depew
168	48.5	Elwood UFSD	Greenlawn
168	48.5	Long Beach City SD	Long Beach
168	48.5	New Rochelle City SD	New Rochelle
168	48.5	NYC Geographic District #21	Brooklyn
168	48.5	Newark Central SD	Newark
168	48.5	North Shore Central SD	Sea Cliff
168	48.5	Norwich City SD	Norwich
168	48.5	South Country Central SD	East Patchogue
168	48.5	S Glens Fls Central SD	S Glens Fls
168	48.5	Starpoint Central SD	Lockport
168	48.5	Watertown City SD	Watertown
168	48.5	Yorktown Central SD	Yorktown Hgts
168	48.5	New York City Chancellor's Office	New York
184	48.4	Bayport-Blue Point UFSD	Bayport
184	48.4	Brentwood UFSD	Brentwood
184	48.4	Churchville-Chili Central SD	Churchville
184	48.4	Copiague UFSD	Copiague
184	48.4	Eastchester UFSD	Eastchester
184	48.4	Hyde Park Central SD	Hyde Park
184	48.4	Iroquois Central SD	Elma
184	48.4	NYC Geographic District #18	Brooklyn
184	48.4	NYC Geographic District #32	Brooklyn
184	48.4	Port Chester-Rye UFSD	Port Chester
184	48.4	Rochester City SD	Rochester
184	48.4	Rockville Ctr UFSD	Rockville Ctr
184	48.4	Rome City SD	Rome
184	48.4	Somers Central SD	Somers
184	48.4	Sweet Home Central SD	Amherst
184	48.4	William Floyd UFSD	Mastic Beach
184	48.4	Yonkers City SD	Yonkers
201	48.3	Amsterdam City SD	Amsterdam
201	48.3	East Irondequoit Central SD	Rochester
201	48.3	Glen Cove City SD	Glen Cove
201	48.3	Gloversville City SD	Gloversville
201	48.3	North Babylon UFSD	North Babylon
201	48.3	Rye City SD	Rye
201	48.3	Washingtonville Central SD	Washingtonville
208	48.2	Broadalbin-Perth Central SD	Broadalbin
208	48.2	Burnt Hills-Ballston Lake Central SD	Scotia
208	48.2	Dansville Central SD	Dansville
208	48.2	Fairport Central SD	Fairport
208	48.2	Geneva City SD	Geneva
208	48.2	Great Neck UFSD	Great Neck
208	48.2	Haverstraw-Stony Point CSD	Garnerville
208	48.2	Honeoye Falls-Lima Central SD	Honeoye Falls
208	48.2	Horseheads Central SD	Horseheads
208	48.2	Jamestown City SD	Jamestown
208	48.2	Jamesville-Dewitt Central SD	Dewitt
208	48.2	Johnstown City SD	Johnstown
208	48.2	Mamaroneck UFSD	Mamaroneck
208	48.2	Middle Country Central SD	Centereach
208	48.2	Oswego City SD	Oswego
208	48.2	Putnam Valley Central SD	Putnam Valley
208	48.2	Red Hook Central SD	Red Hook
208	48.2	Schalmont Central SD	Schenectady
208	48.2	Schenectady City SD	Schenectady
227	48.1	Ballston Spa Central SD	Ballston Spa
227	48.1	Binghamton City SD	Binghamton
227	48.1	East Islip UFSD	Islip Terrace
227	48.1	East Syracuse Minoa Central SD	East Syracuse
227	48.1	Ellenville Central SD	Ellenville
227	48.1	Hicksville UFSD	Hicksville
227	48.1	Manhasset UFSD	Manhasset
227	48.1	Mexico Central SD	Mexico
227	48.1	Mount Pleasant Central SD	Thornwood
227	48.1	New Hartford Central SD	New Hartford
227	48.1	NYC Geographic District # 6	New York
227	48.1	NYC Geographic District #10	Bronx
227	48.1	NYC Geographic District #12	Bronx
240	48.0	Bay Shore UFSD	Bay Shore
240	48.0	Cheektowaga Central SD	Cheektowaga
240	48.0	Connetquot Central SD	Bohemia
240	48.0	Elmira City SD	Elmira
240	48.0	Hudson City SD	Hudson
240	48.0	Levittown UFSD	Levittown
240	48.0	NYC Geographic District #31	Staten Island
240	48.0	Newburgh City SD	Newburgh
240	48.0	Owego-Apalachin Central SD	Owego
240	48.0	Vestal Central SD	Vestal
240	48.0	West Irondequoit Central SD	Rochester
240	48.0	West Islip UFSD	West Islip
252	47.9	Chappaqua Central SD	Chappaqua
252	47.9	Chenango Valley Central SD	Binghamton
252	47.9	Cold Spring Hrbr Central SD	Cold Spring Hrbr
252	47.9	Ithaca City SD	Ithaca
252	47.9	Lynbrook UFSD	Lynbrook
252	47.9	Middletown City SD	Middletown
252	47.9	Mount Vernon City SD	Mount Vernon
252	47.9	Plattsburgh City SD	Plattsburgh
252	47.9	Riverhead Central SD	Riverhead
261	47.8	Auburn City SD	Auburn
261	47.8	Batavia City SD	Batavia
261	47.8	Bedford Central SD	Bedford
261	47.8	Clarkstown Central SD	New City
261	47.8	Dunkirk City SD	Dunkirk
261	47.8	Homer Central SD	Homer
261	47.8	Monticello Central SD	Monticello
261	47.8	NYC Geographic District # 9	Bronx
261	47.8	North Syracuse Central SD	North Syracuse
261	47.8	Queensbury UFSD	Queensbury
261	47.8	Valley Stream Central High SD	Valley Stream
272	47.7	Canandaigua City SD	Canandaigua
272	47.7	Freeport UFSD	Freeport
272	47.7	Half Hollow Hills Central SD	Dix Hills
272	47.7	Marcellus Central SD	Marcellus
272	47.7	Newfane Central SD	Burt
272	47.7	South Huntington UFSD	Huntington Stn
272	47.7	Spencerport Central SD	Spencerport
272	47.7	Syracuse City SD	Syracuse
280	47.6	Brockport Central SD	Brockport
280	47.6	Central Islip UFSD	Central Islip
280	47.6	Fulton City SD	Fulton
280	47.6	NYC Geographic District #20	Brooklyn
280	47.6	NYC Geographic District #29	Queens Village
280	47.6	Oceanside UFSD	Oceanside
280	47.6	Peekskill City SD	Peekskill
280	47.6	Peru Central SD	Peru
280	47.6	Plainview-Old Bethpage CSD	Plainview
280	47.6	Windsor Central SD	Windsor
290	47.5	Gouverneur Central SD	Gouverneur
290	47.5	Mount Sinai UFSD	Mount Sinai
290	47.5	NYC Geographic District #13	Brooklyn
290	47.5	Phoenix Central SD	Phoenix
290	47.5	Port Jervis City SD	Port Jervis
290	47.5	Rondout Valley Central SD	Accord
290	47.5	Syosset Central SD	Syosset
297	47.4	East Ramapo CSD (Spring Valley)	Spring Valley
297	47.4	Hampton Bays UFSD	Hampton Bays
297	47.4	Herricks UFSD	New Hyde Park
297	47.4	Marlboro Central SD	Milton
297	47.4	Miller Place UFSD	Miller Place
297	47.4	NYC Geographic District # 8	Bronx
297	47.4	Northport-East Northport UFSD	Northport
297	47.4	Ossining UFSD	Ossining
297	47.4	Oyster Bay-East Norwich Central SD	Oyster Bay
297	47.4	Pelham UFSD	Pelham
297	47.4	Poughkeepsie City SD	Poughkeepsie
297	47.4	Scotia-Glenville Central SD	Scotia
309	47.3	Amherst Central SD	Amherst
309	47.3	Farmingdale UFSD	Farmingdale
309	47.3	Hauppauge UFSD	Hauppauge
309	47.3	Mineola UFSD	Mineola

Note: This section only includes districts with 1,500 or more students; All categories are ranked from high to low

309	47.3	Pine Bush Central SD	Pine Bush
309	47.3	Pleasantville UFSD	Pleasantville
315	47.2	General Brown Central SD	Dexter
315	47.2	Hewlett-Woodmere UFSD	Woodmere
315	47.2	Waterloo Central SD	Waterloo
318	47.1	Beekmantown Central SD	West Chazy
318	47.1	East Williston UFSD	Old Westbury
318	47.1	Kinderhook Central SD	Valatie
318	47.1	NYC Geographic District #27	Ozone Park
318	47.1	Rye Neck UFSD	Mamaroneck
323	47.0	Dryden Central SD	Dryden
323	47.0	Edgemont UFSD	Scarsdale
323	47.0	Lawrence UFSD	Cedarhurst
323	47.0	Malverne UFSD	Malverne
323	47.0	NYC Geographic District #11	Bronx
323	47.0	NYC Geographic District #14	Brooklyn
323	47.0	Shoreham-Wading River Central SD	Shoreham
330	46.9	Cortland City SD	Cortland
330	46.9	Fredonia Central SD	Fredonia
330	46.9	Irvington UFSD	Irvington
333	46.8	Deer Park UFSD	Deer Park
333	46.8	Jericho UFSD	Jericho
333	46.8	Lackawanna City SD	Lackawanna
333	46.8	Sherrill City SD	Verona
337	46.7	Hempstead UFSD	Hempstead
337	46.7	Ogdensburg City SD	Ogdensburg
339	46.6	NYC Geographic District #19	Brooklyn
340	46.5	NYC Geographic District # 5	New York
340	46.5	Wallkill Central SD	Wallkill
342	46.4	Malone Central SD	Malone
342	46.4	Valley Stream 30 UFSD	Valley Stream
344	46.3	Ardsley UFSD	Ardsley
344	46.3	NYC Geographic District #24	Corona
344	46.3	Roosevelt UFSD	Roosevelt
347	46.2	Amityville UFSD	Amityville
347	46.2	NYC Geographic District # 7	Bronx
347	46.2	Olean City SD	Olean
350	46.1	West Hempstead UFSD	West Hempstead
351	46.0	Southampton UFSD	Southampton
352	45.8	NYC Geographic District #16	Brooklyn
353	45.6	Chenango Forks Central SD	Binghamton
353	45.6	Westhampton Bch UFSD	Westhampton Bch
355	45.5	Susquehanna Valley Central SD	Conklin
356	45.2	NYC Geographic District #23	Brooklyn
357	44.6	Lansingburgh Central SD	Troy

White Students

Rank	Percent	District Name	City
1	98.2	Ogdensburg City SD	Ogdensburg
2	97.7	Bath Central SD	Bath
3	97.2	Gouverneur Central SD	Gouverneur
4	96.9	Waverly Central SD	Waverly
5	96.7	Marcellus Central SD	Marcellus
6	96.5	Alden Central SD	Alden
7	96.4	Malone Central SD	Malone
8	96.0	Sherrill City SD	Verona
9	95.9	Livonia Central SD	Livonia
9	95.9	South Jefferson Central SD	Adams Center
9	95.9	Yorkshire-Pioneer Central SD	Yorkshire
12	95.6	Beekmantown Central SD	West Chazy
13	95.5	Camden Central SD	Camden
14	95.4	Homer Central SD	Homer
15	95.3	Broadalbin-Perth Central SD	Broadalbin
16	95.2	Mexico Central SD	Mexico
17	95.0	General Brown Central SD	Dexter
18	94.9	Central Valley CSD at Ilion-Mohawk	Ilion
18	94.9	Hamburg Central SD	Hamburg
20	94.8	Iroquois Central SD	Elma
21	94.7	Schuylerville Central SD	Schuylerville
22	94.6	Central Square Central SD	Central Square
22	94.6	East Aurora UFSD	East Aurora
22	94.6	Phoenix Central SD	Phoenix
25	94.5	S Glens Fls Central SD	S Glens Fls
26	94.4	Owego-Apalachin Central SD	Owego
26	94.4	Queensbury UFSD	Queensbury
28	94.3	Ballston Spa Central SD	Ballston Spa
29	94.2	Wayne Central SD	Ontario Center
30	94.1	Peru Central SD	Peru
30	94.1	Starpoint Central SD	Lockport
32	93.9	Springville-Griffith Institute CSD	Springville
33	93.8	Johnstown City SD	Johnstown
34	93.7	Averill Park Central SD	Averill Park
34	93.7	Burnt Hills-Ballston Lake Central SD	Scotia
36	93.6	Chenango Forks Central SD	Binghamton
36	93.6	Orchard Park Central SD	West Seneca
38	93.4	Massapequa UFSD	Massapequa
39	93.3	Dansville Central SD	Dansville
40	93.0	Newfane Central SD	Burt
41	92.8	Lancaster Central SD	Lancaster
42	92.7	Chittenango Central SD	Chittenango
43	92.5	Whitesboro Central SD	Whitesboro
44	92.4	Honeoye Falls-Lima Central SD	Honeoye Falls
45	92.0	North Tonawanda City SD	North Tonawanda
45	92.0	Windsor Central SD	Windsor
47	91.5	Cobleskill-Richmondville CSD	Cobleskill
47	91.5	Kinderhook Central SD	Valatie
49	91.4	Fulton City SD	Fulton
49	91.4	Scotia-Glenville Central SD	Scotia
51	91.3	Susquehanna Valley Central SD	Conklin
52	91.2	Lewiston-Porter Central SD	Youngstown
52	91.2	Phelps-Clifton Springs Central SD	Clifton Springs
54	91.0	Plainedge UFSD	N Massapequa
55	90.9	Chenango Valley Central SD	Binghamton
55	90.9	Norwich City SD	Norwich
57	90.6	Eastport-South Manor CSD	Manorville
57	90.6	Palmyra-Macedon Central SD	Palmyra
59	90.4	Clarence Central SD	Clarence
59	90.4	Dryden Central SD	Dryden
59	90.4	Garden City UFSD	Garden City
59	90.4	West Genesee Central SD	Camillus
63	90.3	Saratoga Spgs City SD	Saratoga Spgs
64	90.2	Cold Spring Hrbr Central SD	Cold Spring Hrbr
65	90.1	Frontier Central SD	Hamburg
65	90.1	Oswego City SD	Oswego
65	90.1	Seaford UFSD	Seaford
68	90.0	Tonawanda City SD	Tonawanda
69	89.9	Hudson Falls Central SD	Fort Edward
69	89.9	Maine-Endwell Central SD	Endwell
71	89.7	Hilton Central SD	Hilton
71	89.7	Oneida City SD	Oneida
71	89.7	Wantagh UFSD	Wantagh
74	89.6	Plattsburgh City SD	Plattsburgh
74	89.6	West Seneca Central SD	West Seneca
76	89.4	Kings Park Central SD	Kings Park
77	89.3	Somers Central SD	Somers
78	89.2	Hornell City SD	Hornell
79	88.9	Sayville UFSD	Sayville
79	88.9	Shoreham-Wading River Central SD	Shoreham
81	88.8	Canandaigua City SD	Canandaigua
82	88.7	Baldwinsville Central SD	Baldwinsville
83	88.6	Schalmont Central SD	Schenectady
84	88.5	Bayport-Blue Point UFSD	Bayport
84	88.5	Horseheads Central SD	Horseheads
86	88.4	Depew UFSD	Depew
86	88.4	Westhill Central SD	Syracuse
88	88.3	Glens Falls City SD	Glens Falls
89	88.0	Miller Place UFSD	Miller Place
90	87.9	Cortland City SD	Cortland
90	87.9	Waterloo Central SD	Waterloo
92	87.7	Red Hook Central SD	Red Hook
93	87.6	Byram Hills Central SD	Armonk
94	87.5	Rondout Valley Central SD	Accord
95	87.3	Corning City SD	Painted Post
95	87.3	East Syracuse Minoa Central SD	East Syracuse
95	87.3	Victor Central SD	Victor
98	87.1	Bethlehem Central SD	Delmar
98	87.1	Massena Central SD	Massena
100	87.0	West Islip UFSD	West Islip
101	86.8	Grand Island Central SD	Grand Island
102	86.7	Northport-East Northport UFSD	Northport
103	86.5	Fairport Central SD	Fairport
104	86.4	Gloversville City SD	Gloversville
105	86.0	Smithtown Central SD	Smithtown
106	85.8	Rotterdam-Mohonasen Central SD	Schenectady
107	85.7	Webster Central SD	Webster
108	85.5	Blind Brook-Rye UFSD	Rye Brook
109	85.2	Mount Sinai UFSD	Mount Sinai
110	85.1	New Hartford Central SD	New Hartford
111	84.5	North Syracuse Central SD	North Syracuse
112	84.4	Penfield Central SD	Rochester
113	84.3	Rocky Point UFSD	Rocky Point
114	84.2	Rye City SD	Rye
115	84.1	Bellmore-Merrick Central High SD	North Merrick
116	84.0	Bronxville UFSD	Bronxville
117	83.9	Fredonia Central SD	Fredonia
118	83.7	Mount Pleasant Central SD	Thornwood
118	83.7	Ravena-Coeymans-Selkirk Cent SD	Ravena
120	83.3	Commack UFSD	East Northport
120	83.3	Katonah-Lewisboro UFSD	South Salem
122	83.1	Spencerport Central SD	Spencerport
123	83.0	Fayetteville-Manlius Central SD	Manlius
124	82.9	Three Village Central SD	Stony Brook
125	82.7	Rome City SD	Rome
126	82.6	Brockport Central SD	Brockport
127	82.4	Pearl River UFSD	Pearl River
127	82.4	Vestal Central SD	Vestal
129	82.3	North Shore Central SD	Sea Cliff
130	81.8	Niagara-Wheatfield Central SD	Niagara Falls
131	81.6	East Greenbush Central SD	East Greenbush
132	81.5	Pleasantville UFSD	Pleasantville
133	81.2	Churchville-Chili Central SD	Churchville
133	81.2	Olean City SD	Olean
133	81.2	Saugerties Central SD	Saugerties
136	80.9	Auburn City SD	Auburn
137	80.6	Oneonta City SD	Oneonta
138	80.5	Connetquot Central SD	Bohemia
139	80.0	Babylon UFSD	Babylon
140	79.7	Jamesville-Dewitt Central SD	Dewitt
141	79.6	Evans-Brant Central SD (Lake Shore)	Angola
141	79.6	Kenmore-Tonawanda UFSD	Buffalo
143	79.4	Chappaqua Central SD	Chappaqua
143	79.4	Mahopac Central SD	Mahopac
145	79.1	Medina Central SD	Medina
145	79.1	Putnam Valley Central SD	Putnam Valley
147	79.0	Hauppauge UFSD	Hauppauge
147	79.0	Warwick Valley Central SD	Warwick
149	78.9	Shenendehowa Central SD	Clifton Park
150	78.4	New Paltz Central SD	New Paltz
151	78.3	Harborfields Central SD	Greenlawn
152	78.0	Cheektowaga-Maryvale UFSD	Cheektowaga
152	78.0	Minisink Valley Central SD	Slate Hill
152	78.0	Sachem Central SD	Lake Ronkonkoma
155	77.9	East Islip UFSD	Islip Terrace
156	77.6	Guilderland Central SD	Guilderland Center
156	77.6	Pittsford Central SD	Pittsford
158	77.5	Cohoes City SD	Cohoes
159	77.0	Williamsville Central SD	East Amherst
160	76.9	Center Moriches UFSD	Center Moriches
160	76.9	Locust Valley Central SD	Locust Valley
160	76.9	Rockville Ctr UFSD	Rockville Ctr
163	76.4	Liverpool Central SD	Liverpool
164	76.3	Oceanside UFSD	Oceanside
165	75.9	Albion Central SD	Albion
166	75.6	Plainview-Old Bethpage CSD	Plainview
167	75.3	Yorktown Central SD	Yorktown Hgts
168	75.2	North Bellmore UFSD	Bellmore
169	75.1	Hastings-On-Hudson UFSD	Hastings on Hdsn
170	74.9	Carthage Central SD	Carthage
171	74.7	Batavia City SD	Batavia
172	74.5	Newark Central SD	Newark
173	74.4	Niskayuna Central SD	Schenectady
174	74.1	Catskill Central SD	Catskill
175	73.9	Lynbrook UFSD	Lynbrook
176	73.8	South Orangetown Central SD	Blauvelt
177	73.5	Arlington Central SD	Lagrangeville
177	73.5	Elmira City SD	Elmira
179	73.4	Bethpage UFSD	Bethpage
180	73.0	Lindenhurst UFSD	Lindenhurst
180	73.0	Lockport City SD	Lockport
180	73.0	West Irondequoit Central SD	Rochester
183	72.9	Union-Endicott Central SD	Endicott
183	72.9	Wappingers Central SD	Hopewell Junction
185	72.8	Croton-Harmon UFSD	Croton on Hdsn
185	72.8	Port Jervis City SD	Port Jervis
187	72.6	Roslyn UFSD	Roslyn
188	72.3	Goshen Central SD	Goshen
189	72.1	Levittown UFSD	Levittown
189	72.1	Watertown City SD	Watertown
191	71.9	Island Trees UFSD	Levittown
191	71.9	Marlboro Central SD	Milton
193	71.8	Highland Central SD	Highland
193	71.8	Irvington UFSD	Irvington
195	71.6	East Williston UFSD	Old Westbury
196	71.3	Manhasset UFSD	Manhasset
197	71.1	Cornwall Central SD	Cornwall on Hdsn
197	71.1	North Colonie CSD	Latham
199	70.7	Brighton Central SD	Rochester
200	70.6	Lakeland Central SD	Shrub Oak
200	70.6	Oyster Bay-East Norwich Central SD	Oyster Bay
202	70.2	South Colonie Central SD	Albany

Note: This section only includes districts with 1,500 or more students; All categories are ranked from high to low

203	70.1	Eastchester UFSD	Eastchester
203	70.1	Westhampton Bch UFSD	Westhampton Bch
205	70.0	Carmel Central SD	Patterson
205	70.0	Mamaroneck UFSD	Mamaroneck
207	69.5	Middle Country Central SD	Centereach
208	69.3	Amherst Central SD	Amherst
209	69.0	Wallkill Central SD	Wallkill
210	68.9	Pine Bush Central SD	Pine Bush
211	68.3	Scarsdale UFSD	Scarsdale
212	68.1	Hyde Park Central SD	Hyde Park
213	67.9	Pelham UFSD	Pelham
214	67.9	Franklin Square UFSD	Franklin Square
215	67.7	Elwood UFSD	Greenlawn
216	67.6	Sweet Home Central SD	Amherst
217	67.5	Harrison Central SD	Harrison
218	66.9	West Babylon UFSD	West Babylon
219	66.6	Farmingdale UFSD	Farmingdale
220	66.5	Washingtonville Central SD	Washingtonville
221	66.3	Islip UFSD	Islip
222	65.9	Rye Neck UFSD	Mamaroneck
223	65.8	Brookhaven-Comsewogue UFSD	Port Jeff Stn
224	65.6	Jamestown City SD	Jamestown
224	65.6	Valley Central SD (Montgomery)	Montgomery
226	65.5	Indian River Central SD	Philadelphia
226	65.5	Ithaca City SD	Ithaca
228	65.4	Clarkstown Central SD	New City
229	65.3	Greece Central SD	Rochester
230	65.2	Hewlett-Woodmere UFSD	Woodmere
231	65.0	Lackawanna City SD	Lackawanna
232	64.3	Ardsley UFSD	Ardsley
233	63.8	Ramapo Central SD (Suffern)	Hillburn
234	63.7	Rush-Henrietta Central SD	Henrietta
235	63.4	Port Washington UFSD	Port Washington
236	63.3	Brewster Central SD	Brewster
237	63.2	Lansingburgh Central SD	Troy
238	62.9	Syosset Central SD	Syosset
239	62.1	Johnson City Central SD	Johnson City
240	61.8	Monroe-Woodbury Central SD	Central Valley
241	61.0	Gates-Chili Central SD	Rochester
241	61.0	Half Hollow Hills Central SD	Dix Hills
243	60.9	Hendrick Hudson Central SD	Montrose
244	59.8	Nanuet UFSD	Nanuet
245	58.6	Long Beach City SD	Long Beach
246	58.4	Mineola UFSD	Mineola
247	57.7	Bedford Central SD	Bedford
248	56.5	Kingston City SD	Kingston
249	56.2	East Meadow UFSD	Westbury
250	54.4	Edgemont UFSD	Scarsdale
251	52.8	Patchogue-Medford UFSD	Patchogue
252	52.7	Great Neck UFSD	Great Neck
253	51.9	East Irondequoit Central SD	Rochester
254	51.4	William Floyd UFSD	Mastic Beach
255	50.8	Longwood Central SD	Middle Island
256	49.4	Southampton UFSD	Southampton
257	49.0	Liberty Central SD	Liberty
258	48.6	NYC Geographic District #31	Staten Island
259	48.5	Ellenville Central SD	Ellenville
260	47.7	Cheektowaga Central SD	Cheektowaga
261	47.6	Binghamton City SD	Binghamton
261	47.6	Nyack UFSD	Nyack
263	47.4	Geneva City SD	Geneva
264	47.1	Amsterdam City SD	Amsterdam
264	47.1	Monticello Central SD	Monticello
266	46.7	Deer Park UFSD	Deer Park
267	46.2	North Babylon UFSD	North Babylon
268	45.9	Hudson City SD	Hudson
269	45.6	Beacon City SD	Beacon
270	45.3	Troy City SD	Troy
271	45.1	South Huntington UFSD	Huntington Stn
272	44.9	Jericho UFSD	Jericho
272	44.9	Niagara Falls City SD	Niagara Falls
274	43.0	Hampton Bays UFSD	Hampton Bays
274	43.0	Riverhead Central SD	Riverhead
276	42.5	East Hampton UFSD	East Hampton
277	42.1	South Country Central SD	East Patchogue
278	41.2	Huntington UFSD	Huntington Stn
279	38.4	Dunkirk City SD	Dunkirk
280	36.5	Sewanhaka Central High SD	Floral Park
281	35.2	Hicksville UFSD	Hicksville
282	33.7	New Hyde Pk-Garden City Pk UFSD	New Hyde Park
283	33.0	Bay Shore UFSD	Bay Shore
284	32.9	Herricks UFSD	New Hyde Park
285	32.8	Utica City SD	Utica
285	32.8	West Hempstead UFSD	West Hempstead

287	32.1	UFSD of the Tarrytowns	Sleepy Hollow
288	32.0	NYC Geographic District #21	Brooklyn
289	31.8	NYC Geographic District # 3	New York
290	31.6	Salmon River Central SD	Fort Covington
291	29.8	Valley Stream 13 UFSD	Valley Stream
292	29.7	NYC Geographic District #22	Brooklyn
293	29.2	Glen Cove City SD	Glen Cove
294	28.4	Haverstraw-Stony Point CSD	Garnerville
295	27.9	NYC Geographic District #15	Brooklyn
296	27.4	New Rochelle City SD	New Rochelle
297	26.7	Schenectady City SD	Schenectady
298	26.5	NYC Geographic District #20	Brooklyn
299	25.5	Charter School for Applied Techs	Buffalo
300	24.8	NYC Geographic District # 2	New York
301	24.6	Ossining UFSD	Ossining
301	24.6	White Plains City SD	White Plains
303	23.1	Syracuse City SD	Syracuse
304	22.9	Valley Stream Central High SD	Valley Stream
305	21.0	Newburgh City SD	Newburgh
306	20.2	Buffalo City SD	Buffalo
307	19.9	Albany City SD	Albany
308	19.3	Lawrence UFSD	Cedarhurst
309	17.9	Malverne UFSD	Malverne
310	17.8	Baldwin UFSD	Baldwin
311	17.5	NYC Geographic District # 1	New York
311	17.5	NYC Geographic District #26	Bayside
313	17.3	Middletown City SD	Middletown
313	17.3	Yonkers City SD	Yonkers
315	15.9	Port Chester-Rye UFSD	Port Chester
316	15.8	Copiague UFSD	Copiague
316	15.8	NYC Geographic District #28	Jamaica
318	15.6	NYC Geographic District #30	Long Isl City
319	14.6	New York City Chancellor's Office	New York
320	14.1	NYC Geographic District #24	Corona
321	14.0	NYC Geographic District #13	Brooklyn
322	13.7	NYC Geographic District #25	Flushing
323	12.9	NYC Geographic District #14	Brooklyn
324	12.7	Greenburgh Central SD	Hartsdale
325	10.4	NYC Geographic District #27	Ozone Park
326	10.0	Rochester City SD	Rochester
327	9.4	Freeport UFSD	Freeport
328	9.0	Peekskill City SD	Peekskill
329	8.6	Poughkeepsie City SD	Poughkeepsie
330	7.9	NYC Geographic District #11	Bronx
331	7.2	Elmont UFSD	Elmont
332	6.0	Amityville UFSD	Amityville
333	5.8	NYC Geographic District # 8	Bronx
334	5.7	NYC Geographic District #10	Bronx
335	5.4	East Ramapo CSD (Spring Valley)	Spring Valley
336	5.1	Central Islip UFSD	Central Islip
337	4.9	Mount Vernon SD	Mount Vernon
338	4.5	NYC Geographic District # 5	New York
338	4.5	NYC Geographic District # 6	New York
340	4.4	Brentwood UFSD	Brentwood
340	4.4	NYC Geographic District # 4	New York
342	4.1	Valley Stream 30 UFSD	Valley Stream
343	2.8	Hempstead UFSD	Hempstead
344	2.7	NYC Geographic District #17	Brooklyn
345	2.0	NYC Geographic District #29	Queens Village
346	1.9	NYC Geographic District #18	Brooklyn
347	1.8	NYC Geographic District #16	Brooklyn
347	1.8	NYC Geographic District #32	Brooklyn
349	1.6	NYC Geographic District #19	Brooklyn
349	1.6	Westbury UFSD	Old Westbury
351	1.4	NYC Geographic District # 7	Bronx
352	1.3	NYC Geographic District #12	Bronx
352	1.3	NYC Geographic District #23	Brooklyn
354	1.1	NYC Geographic District # 9	Bronx
355	0.9	Uniondale UFSD	Uniondale
356	0.8	Wyandanch UFSD	Wyandanch
357	0.0	Roosevelt UFSD	Roosevelt

Black Students

Rank	Percent	District Name	City
1	87.9	NYC Geographic District #18	Brooklyn
2	77.4	NYC Geographic District #17	Brooklyn
3	74.9	NYC Geographic District #23	Brooklyn
4	74.7	NYC Geographic District #16	Brooklyn
5	72.2	Mount Vernon SD	Mount Vernon
6	65.0	NYC Geographic District #29	Queens Village
7	58.3	Rochester City SD	Rochester
8	52.8	Roosevelt UFSD	Roosevelt

9	52.4	Wyandanch UFSD	Wyandanch
10	52.3	Malverne UFSD	Malverne
11	52.0	Poughkeepsie City SD	Poughkeepsie
12	49.7	Albany City SD	Albany
13	49.4	NYC Geographic District # 5	New York
14	49.1	Syracuse City SD	Syracuse
15	48.1	Buffalo City SD	Buffalo
15	48.1	NYC Geographic District #19	Brooklyn
17	47.2	Baldwin UFSD	Baldwin
18	46.8	NYC Geographic District #13	Brooklyn
19	45.3	Elmont UFSD	Elmont
20	43.9	Amityville UFSD	Amityville
21	42.5	Uniondale UFSD	Uniondale
22	41.2	NYC Geographic District #11	Bronx
23	40.7	Greenburgh Central SD	Hartsdale
24	38.7	Valley Stream 30 UFSD	Valley Stream
25	36.9	East Ramapo CSD (Spring Valley)	Spring Valley
26	36.2	Charter School for Applied Techs	Buffalo
27	35.5	Cheektowaga Central SD	Cheektowaga
28	34.8	Niagara Falls City SD	Niagara Falls
29	34.6	NYC Geographic District #22	Brooklyn
30	32.7	Schenectady City SD	Schenectady
31	31.2	Troy City SD	Troy
32	30.8	Valley Stream Central High SD	Valley Stream
33	29.5	NYC Geographic District # 9	Bronx
34	29.1	Hempstead UFSD	Hempstead
35	27.2	New York City Chancellor's Office	New York
36	26.8	NYC Geographic District # 7	Bronx
37	26.4	Binghamton City SD	Binghamton
38	26.2	Sewanhaka Central High SD	Floral Park
39	26.0	Utica City SD	Utica
40	25.9	NYC Geographic District #12	Bronx
41	25.5	NYC Geographic District # 4	New York
41	25.5	Westbury UFSD	Old Westbury
43	24.9	Middletown City SD	Middletown
43	24.9	NYC Geographic District #27	Ozone Park
45	24.8	Newburgh City SD	Newburgh
46	24.6	Peekskill City SD	Peekskill
47	24.1	Copiague UFSD	Copiague
48	24.0	NYC Geographic District #28	Jamaica
49	23.6	Freeport UFSD	Freeport
50	23.4	Valley Stream 13 UFSD	Valley Stream
51	23.3	NYC Geographic District # 8	Bronx
52	23.1	NYC Geographic District #14	Brooklyn
53	22.7	NYC Geographic District # 3	New York
54	22.4	North Babylon UFSD	North Babylon
55	22.0	Hudson City SD	Hudson
56	21.7	Lawrence UFSD	Cedarhurst
57	21.5	New Rochelle City SD	New Rochelle
58	20.3	Bay Shore UFSD	Bay Shore
59	20.1	South Country Central SD	East Patchogue
60	20.0	Monticello Central SD	Monticello
61	19.9	Central Islip UFSD	Central Islip
62	19.5	West Hempstead UFSD	West Hempstead
62	19.5	Yonkers City SD	Yonkers
64	19.2	Sweet Home Central SD	Amherst
65	19.1	Nyack UFSD	Nyack
66	18.9	East Irondequoit Central SD	Rochester
67	17.9	Beacon City SD	Beacon
67	17.9	Longwood Central SD	Middle Island
69	17.8	NYC Geographic District #32	Brooklyn
70	17.6	Deer Park UFSD	Deer Park
71	17.2	Lackawanna City SD	Lackawanna
72	17.0	Gates-Chili Central SD	Rochester
72	17.0	NYC Geographic District # 1	New York
74	16.9	Lansingburgh Central SD	Troy
75	16.8	NYC Geographic District #10	Bronx
76	16.1	NYC Geographic District #21	Brooklyn
77	15.7	NYC Geographic District # 2	New York
78	15.1	Amherst Central SD	Amherst
79	14.7	Elmira City SD	Elmira
80	14.5	Rush-Henrietta Central SD	Henrietta
81	14.4	Kingston City SD	Kingston
81	14.4	NYC Geographic District #15	Brooklyn
81	14.4	William Floyd UFSD	Mastic Beach
84	14.2	Greece Central SD	Rochester
85	14.0	White Plains City SD	White Plains
86	13.5	NYC Geographic District #31	Staten Island
87	13.4	Johnson City Central SD	Johnson City
88	13.3	Riverhead Central SD	Riverhead
89	12.7	Geneva City SD	Geneva
90	12.4	Lockport City SD	Lockport
91	12.3	Haverstraw-Stony Point CSD	Garnerville
92	11.9	NYC Geographic District #26	Bayside

Note: This section only includes districts with 1,500 or more students; All categories are ranked from high to low

Rank	Value	School District	Location
93	11.8	Half Hollow Hills Central SD	Dix Hills
94	11.7	Hyde Park Central SD	Hyde Park
95	11.6	Ossining UFSD	Ossining
96	11.4	Indian River Central SD	Philadelphia
97	11.1	Ellenville Central SD	Ellenville
98	10.9	Albion Central SD	Albion
99	10.6	Brentwood UFSD	Brentwood
99	10.6	Long Beach City SD	Long Beach
101	9.9	Catskill Central SD	Catskill
102	9.8	Pine Bush Central SD	Pine Bush
103	9.7	Liberty Central SD	Liberty
103	9.7	Rome City SD	Rome
105	9.6	Cheektowaga-Maryvale UFSD	Cheektowaga
105	9.6	Glen Cove City SD	Glen Cove
107	9.5	West Irondequoit Central SD	Rochester
108	9.2	Huntington UFSD	Huntington Stn
109	9.0	Ithaca City SD	Ithaca
109	9.0	Valley Central SD (Montgomery)	Montgomery
111	8.8	Cohoes City SD	Cohoes
111	8.8	Liverpool Central SD	Liverpool
111	8.8	Union-Endicott Central SD	Endicott
114	8.5	Watertown City SD	Watertown
115	8.1	NYC Geographic District #25	Flushing
116	7.9	South Huntington UFSD	Huntington Stn
117	7.8	NYC Geographic District # 6	New York
118	7.7	Newark Central SD	Newark
118	7.7	Port Jervis City SD	Port Jervis
120	7.5	Churchville-Chili Central SD	Churchville
121	7.4	Arlington Central SD	Lagrangeville
122	7.3	Highland Central SD	Highland
123	7.2	Hewlett-Woodmere UFSD	Woodmere
123	7.2	Washingtonville Central SD	Washingtonville
125	7.1	Brighton Central SD	Rochester
125	7.1	NYC Geographic District #30	Long Isl City
127	7.0	Monroe-Woodbury Central SD	Central Valley
128	6.9	Auburn City SD	Auburn
128	6.9	Marlboro Central SD	Milton
130	6.8	West Babylon UFSD	West Babylon
131	6.7	Plattsburgh City SD	Plattsburgh
131	6.7	South Colonie Central SD	Albany
133	6.6	Batavia City SD	Batavia
133	6.6	Elwood UFSD	Greenlawn
133	6.6	Oneonta City SD	Oneonta
136	6.5	Jamesville-Dewitt Central SD	Dewitt
136	6.5	Kenmore-Tonawanda UFSD	Buffalo
138	6.4	Cornwall Central SD	Cornwall on Hdsn
139	6.3	Dunkirk City SD	Dunkirk
139	6.3	Rockville Ctr UFSD	Rockville Ctr
139	6.3	Wallkill Central SD	Wallkill
142	6.1	Carthage Central SD	Carthage
142	6.1	Olean City SD	Olean
142	6.1	Ramapo Central SD (Suffern)	Hillburn
145	5.9	Islip UFSD	Islip
145	5.9	Pelham UFSD	Pelham
147	5.8	Amsterdam City SD	Amsterdam
147	5.8	Farmingdale UFSD	Farmingdale
147	5.8	Lakeland Central SD	Shrub Oak
147	5.8	Nanuet UFSD	Nanuet
147	5.8	Wappingers Central SD	Hopewell Junction
152	5.6	Hendrick Hudson Central SD	Montrose
153	5.1	Port Chester-Rye UFSD	Port Chester
154	5.0	Fairport Central SD	Fairport
154	5.0	Medina Central SD	Medina
156	4.9	Irvington UFSD	Irvington
156	4.9	Southampton UFSD	Southampton
158	4.8	North Colonie CSD	Latham
159	4.7	Spencerport Central SD	Spencerport
159	4.7	Warwick Valley Central SD	Warwick
161	4.5	Center Moriches UFSD	Center Moriches
161	4.5	East Syracuse Minoa Central SD	East Syracuse
161	4.5	Gloversville City SD	Gloversville
161	4.5	Harborfields Central SD	Greenlawn
161	4.5	Patchogue-Medford UFSD	Patchogue
166	4.4	Minisink Valley Central SD	Slate Hill
167	4.3	Brockport Central SD	Brockport
167	4.3	UFSD of the Tarrytowns	Sleepy Hollow
167	4.3	Waterloo Central SD	Waterloo
167	4.3	Westhill Central SD	Syracuse
171	4.2	Goshen Central SD	Goshen
172	4.1	New Paltz Central SD	New Paltz
172	4.1	North Syracuse Central SD	North Syracuse
174	4.0	East Meadow UFSD	Westbury
174	4.0	Hornell City SD	Hornell
174	4.0	Middle Country Central SD	Centereach
174	4.0	Penfield Central SD	Rochester
174	4.0	Ravena-Coeymans-Selkirk Cent SD	Ravena
179	3.9	Ardsley UFSD	Ardsley
179	3.9	Jamestown City SD	Jamestown
181	3.8	East Hampton UFSD	East Hampton
181	3.8	Williamsville Central SD	East Amherst
183	3.7	Niskayuna Central SD	Schenectady
184	3.6	Clarkstown Central SD	New City
184	3.6	Guilderland Central SD	Guilderland Center
184	3.6	Rondout Valley Central SD	Accord
184	3.6	Scotia-Glenville Central SD	Scotia
188	3.5	Croton-Harmon UFSD	Croton on Hdsn
189	3.4	Cortland City SD	Cortland
189	3.4	Norwich City SD	Norwich
189	3.4	Roslyn UFSD	Roslyn
192	3.3	Bedford Central SD	Bedford
192	3.3	NYC Geographic District #24	Corona
192	3.3	Rye Neck Central SD	Mamaroneck
192	3.3	Webster Central SD	Webster
196	3.2	Babylon UFSD	Babylon
196	3.2	Lynbrook UFSD	Lynbrook
198	3.1	NYC Geographic District #20	Brooklyn
198	3.1	Pittsford Central SD	Pittsford
198	3.1	Rotterdam-Mohonasen Central SD	Schenectady
201	3.0	Fayetteville-Manlius Central SD	Manlius
201	3.0	Hauppauge UFSD	Hauppauge
203	2.9	West Seneca Central SD	West Seneca
204	2.8	Yorktown Central SD	Yorktown Hgts
205	2.7	Central Valley CSD at Ilion-Mohawk	Ilion
205	2.7	Hicksville UFSD	Hicksville
205	2.7	Mamaroneck UFSD	Mamaroneck
205	2.7	Mineola UFSD	Mineola
205	2.7	Susquehanna Valley Central SD	Conklin
205	2.7	Vestal Central SD	Vestal
211	2.6	Bethlehem Central SD	Delmar
211	2.6	Carmel Central SD	Patterson
211	2.6	Corning City SD	Painted Post
211	2.6	Lindenhurst UFSD	Lindenhurst
211	2.6	Manhasset UFSD	Manhasset
211	2.6	Niagara-Wheatfield Central SD	Niagara Falls
211	2.6	Putnam Valley Central SD	Putnam Valley
211	2.6	Sachem Central SD	Lake Ronkonkoma
211	2.6	West Genesee Central SD	Camillus
220	2.5	Hastings-On-Hudson UFSD	Hastings on Hdsn
220	2.5	Maine-Endwell Central SD	Endwell
220	2.5	Oyster Bay-East Norwich Central SD	Oyster Bay
223	2.4	Depew UFSD	Depew
223	2.4	East Greenbush Central SD	East Greenbush
223	2.4	Red Hook Central SD	Red Hook
223	2.4	Shenendehowa Central SD	Clifton Park
227	2.3	Brewster Central SD	Brewster
227	2.3	Victor Central SD	Victor
229	2.2	Glens Falls City SD	Glens Falls
229	2.2	Jericho UFSD	Jericho
231	2.1	Harrison Central SD	Harrison
231	2.1	Kinderhook Central SD	Valatie
231	2.1	North Bellmore UFSD	Bellmore
231	2.1	Tonawanda City SD	Tonawanda
235	2.0	Grand Island Central SD	Grand Island
235	2.0	Windsor Central SD	Windsor
237	1.9	Bellmore-Merrick Central High SD	North Merrick
237	1.9	Brookhaven-Comsewogue UFSD	Port Jeff Stn
237	1.9	Connetquot Central SD	Bohemia
237	1.9	East Islip UFSD	Islip Terrace
237	1.9	Horseheads Central SD	Horseheads
237	1.9	Saugerties Central SD	Saugerties
243	1.8	Baldwinsville Central SD	Baldwinsville
243	1.8	Canandaigua City SD	Canandaigua
243	1.8	Hilton Central SD	Hilton
243	1.8	Mount Sinai UFSD	Mount Sinai
243	1.8	Oceanside UFSD	Oceanside
243	1.8	Saratoga Spgs City SD	Saratoga Spgs
243	1.8	South Orangetown Central SD	Blauvelt
250	1.7	Ballston Spa Central SD	Ballston Spa
250	1.7	Broadalbin-Perth Central SD	Broadalbin
250	1.7	Eastchester UFSD	Eastchester
250	1.7	Oswego City SD	Oswego
250	1.7	Peru Central SD	Peru
250	1.7	Port Washington UFSD	Port Washington
250	1.7	Westhampton Bch UFSD	Westhampton Bch
257	1.6	Cobleskill-Richmondville CSD	Cobleskill
257	1.6	Eastport-South Manor CSD	Manorville
257	1.6	New Hartford Central SD	New Hartford
257	1.6	Rocky Point UFSD	Rocky Point
257	1.6	Schalmont Central SD	Schenectady
262	1.5	Beekmantown Central SD	West Chazy
262	1.5	Edgemont UFSD	Scarsdale
262	1.5	Evans-Brant Central SD (Lake Shore)	Angola
262	1.5	Franklin Square UFSD	Franklin Square
262	1.5	Fulton City SD	Fulton
262	1.5	Island Trees UFSD	Levittown
262	1.5	Oneida City SD	Oneida
262	1.5	Owego-Apalachin Central SD	Owego
262	1.5	Pleasantville UFSD	Pleasantville
262	1.5	Schuylerville Central SD	Schuylerville
262	1.5	Three Village Central SD	Stony Brook
273	1.4	Dansville Central SD	Dansville
273	1.4	General Brown Central SD	Dexter
273	1.4	Lewiston-Porter Central SD	Youngstown
273	1.4	Mahopac Central SD	Mahopac
273	1.4	Massena Central SD	Massena
273	1.4	Miller Place UFSD	Miller Place
273	1.4	North Tonawanda City SD	North Tonawanda
280	1.3	Fredonia Central SD	Fredonia
280	1.3	Great Neck UFSD	Great Neck
280	1.3	Hudson Falls Central SD	Fort Edward
280	1.3	Johnstown City SD	Johnstown
280	1.3	Rye City SD	Rye
280	1.3	Shoreham-Wading River Central SD	Shoreham
280	1.3	Starpoint Central SD	Lockport
287	1.2	Burnt Hills-Ballston Lake Central SD	Scotia
287	1.2	Newfane Central SD	Burt
287	1.2	Orchard Park Central SD	West Seneca
287	1.2	Pearl River UFSD	Pearl River
287	1.2	Phelps-Clifton Springs Central SD	Clifton Springs
287	1.2	Somers Central SD	Somers
287	1.2	Wayne Central SD	Ontario Center
287	1.2	Whitesboro Central SD	Whitesboro
295	1.1	Bath Central SD	Bath
295	1.1	Bayport-Blue Point UFSD	Bayport
295	1.1	Chenango Valley Central SD	Binghamton
295	1.1	Chittenango Central SD	Chittenango
295	1.1	Frontier Central SD	Hamburg
295	1.1	Hampton Bays UFSD	Hampton Bays
295	1.1	Lancaster Central SD	Lancaster
295	1.1	Queensbury UFSD	Queensbury
295	1.1	Sayville UFSD	Sayville
304	1.0	Alden Central SD	Alden
304	1.0	Chenango Forks Central SD	Binghamton
304	1.0	Commack UFSD	East Northport
304	1.0	Levittown UFSD	Levittown
304	1.0	Locust Valley Central SD	Locust Valley
304	1.0	Scarsdale UFSD	Scarsdale
304	1.0	Smithtown Central SD	Smithtown
304	1.0	Yorkshire-Pioneer Central SD	Yorkshire
312	0.9	Clarence Central SD	Clarence
312	0.9	Palmyra-Macedon Central SD	Palmyra
312	0.9	S Glens Fls Central SD	S Glens Fls
315	0.8	Chappaqua Central SD	Chappaqua
315	0.8	Cold Spring Hrbr Central SD	Cold Spring Hrbr
315	0.8	East Aurora UFSD	East Aurora
315	0.8	East Williston UFSD	Old Westbury
315	0.8	Honeoye Falls-Lima Central SD	Honeoye Falls
315	0.8	Katonah-Lewisboro UFSD	South Salem
315	0.8	Livonia Central SD	Livonia
315	0.8	Malone Central SD	Malone
315	0.8	Northport-East Northport UFSD	Northport
324	0.7	Averill Park Central SD	Averill Park
324	0.7	Central Square Central SD	Central Square
324	0.7	Dryden Central SD	Dryden
324	0.7	Garden City UFSD	Garden City
324	0.7	Gouverneur Central SD	Gouverneur
324	0.7	Mexico Central SD	Mexico
324	0.7	Ogdensburg City SD	Ogdensburg
324	0.7	Phoenix Central SD	Phoenix
324	0.7	Sherrill City SD	Verona
333	0.6	Bethpage UFSD	Bethpage
333	0.6	New Hyde Pk-Garden City Pk UFSD	New Hyde Park
333	0.6	North Shore Central SD	Sea Cliff
333	0.6	Syosset Central SD	Syosset
337	0.5	Camden Central SD	Camden
337	0.5	Hamburg Central SD	Hamburg
337	0.5	Herricks UFSD	New Hyde Park
337	0.5	Mount Pleasant Central SD	Thornwood
337	0.5	Seaford UFSD	Seaford
337	0.5	South Jefferson Central SD	Adams Center
337	0.5	Waverly Central SD	Waverly
344	0.4	Byram Hills Central SD	Armonk

Note: This section only includes districts with 1,500 or more students; All categories are ranked from high to low

Rank	Percent	District Name	City
344	0.4	Homer Central SD	Homer
344	0.4	Iroquois Central SD	Elma
344	0.4	Kings Park Central SD	Kings Park
344	0.4	Plainedge UFSD	N Massapequa
349	0.3	Blind Brook-Rye UFSD	Rye Brook
349	0.3	Massapequa UFSD	Massapequa
349	0.3	Springville-Griffith Institute CSD	Springville
352	0.2	Bronxville UFSD	Bronxville
352	0.2	Marcellus Central SD	Marcellus
352	0.2	Plainview-Old Bethpage CSD	Plainview
352	0.2	Wantagh UFSD	Wantagh
352	0.2	West Islip UFSD	West Islip
357	0.1	Salmon River Central SD	Fort Covington

Asian Students

Rank	Percent	District Name	City
1	59.2	Herricks UFSD	New Hyde Park
2	51.7	NYC Geographic District #26	Bayside
3	49.4	Jericho UFSD	Jericho
4	47.7	NYC Geographic District #25	Flushing
5	46.9	New Hyde Pk-Garden City Pk UFSD	New Hyde Park
6	42.9	NYC Geographic District #20	Brooklyn
7	35.6	Great Neck UFSD	Great Neck
8	31.4	Edgemont UFSD	Scarsdale
8	31.4	Syosset Central SD	Syosset
10	30.6	Hicksville UFSD	Hicksville
11	28.6	NYC Geographic District #28	Jamaica
12	24.8	NYC Geographic District #21	Brooklyn
13	24.6	Valley Stream 30 UFSD	Valley Stream
14	22.9	NYC Geographic District #2	New York
15	22.5	NYC Geographic District #27	Ozone Park
16	22.1	NYC Geographic District #30	Long Isl City
17	21.1	NYC Geographic District #1	New York
18	20.9	East Williston UFSD	Old Westbury
19	19.5	Sewanhaka Central High SD	Floral Park
20	19.4	NYC Geographic District #13	Brooklyn
20	19.4	NYC Geographic District #24	Corona
22	18.9	Valley Stream Central High SD	Valley Stream
23	18.8	East Meadow UFSD	Westbury
24	18.7	NYC Geographic District #22	Brooklyn
25	18.6	Manhasset UFSD	Manhasset
26	18.5	Ardsley UFSD	Ardsley
27	18.3	Scarsdale UFSD	Scarsdale
28	17.6	Plainview-Old Bethpage CSD	Plainview
29	17.5	Utica City SD	Utica
30	17.0	Valley Stream 13 UFSD	Valley Stream
31	16.6	Schenectady City SD	Schenectady
32	16.5	Elmont UFSD	Elmont
33	16.3	Roslyn UFSD	Roslyn
34	16.1	Niskayuna Central SD	Schenectady
35	15.9	NYC Geographic District #15	Brooklyn
36	15.5	New York City Chancellor's Office	New York
37	15.4	North Colonie CSD	Latham
38	15.1	Nanuet UFSD	Nanuet
39	14.5	NYC Geographic District #29	Queens Village
40	14.0	Clarkstown Central SD	New City
41	13.7	Half Hollow Hills Central SD	Dix Hills
42	13.3	Eastchester UFSD	Eastchester
43	12.4	Harrison Central SD	Harrison
44	12.3	Guilderland Central SD	Guilderland Center
45	11.9	Ithaca City SD	Ithaca
45	11.9	Mineola UFSD	Mineola
47	11.6	Deer Park UFSD	Deer Park
48	11.5	Williamsville Central SD	East Amherst
49	11.3	Rush-Henrietta Central SD	Henrietta
50	11.2	Brighton Central SD	Rochester
50	11.2	Irvington UFSD	Irvington
52	11.1	Chappaqua Central SD	Chappaqua
53	11.0	Port Washington UFSD	Port Washington
54	10.7	Bethpage UFSD	Bethpage
55	10.6	Hewlett-Woodmere UFSD	Woodmere
56	10.3	Hudson City SD	Hudson
57	10.1	Pittsford Central SD	Pittsford
58	9.4	Shenendehowa Central SD	Clifton Park
59	9.3	South Colonie Central SD	Albany
59	9.3	Three Village Central SD	Stony Brook
61	9.1	Fayetteville-Manlius Central SD	Manlius
61	9.1	Franklin Square UFSD	Franklin Square
61	9.1	Island Trees UFSD	Levittown
64	8.8	Albany City SD	Albany
64	8.8	Vestal Central SD	Vestal
66	8.6	Buffalo City SD	Buffalo
67	8.5	Elwood UFSD	Greenlawn
67	8.5	Levittown UFSD	Levittown
67	8.5	South Orangetown Central SD	Blauvelt
70	8.4	Hauppauge UFSD	Hauppauge
70	8.4	NYC Geographic District #31	Staten Island
72	8.1	Syracuse City SD	Syracuse
73	7.9	Greenburgh Central SD	Hartsdale
73	7.9	NYC Geographic District #3	New York
75	7.7	Ramapo Central SD (Suffern)	Hillburn
76	7.6	Commack UFSD	East Northport
76	7.6	Rye City SD	Rye
78	7.5	Rye Neck UFSD	Mamaroneck
79	7.3	NYC Geographic District #4	New York
79	7.3	NYC Geographic District #10	Bronx
79	7.3	North Bellmore UFSD	Bellmore
79	7.3	Nyack UFSD	Nyack
79	7.3	West Hempstead UFSD	West Hempstead
84	7.2	NYC Geographic District #11	Bronx
85	6.9	Bronxville UFSD	Bronxville
86	6.8	Amherst Central SD	Amherst
86	6.8	Monroe-Woodbury Central SD	Central Valley
88	6.6	Jamesville-Dewitt Central SD	Dewitt
88	6.6	NYC Geographic District #19	Brooklyn
90	6.5	Bethlehem Central SD	Delmar
91	6.4	Pleasantville UFSD	Pleasantville
92	6.3	Blind Brook-Rye UFSD	Rye Brook
92	6.3	Hastings-On-Hudson UFSD	Hastings on Hdsn
94	6.2	South Huntington UFSD	Huntington Stn
95	6.1	Yorktown Central SD	Yorktown Hgts
96	5.9	Byram Hills Central SD	Armonk
96	5.9	Middle Country Central SD	Centereach
98	5.7	Croton-Harmon UFSD	Croton on Hdsn
98	5.7	Sachem Central SD	Lake Ronkonkoma
98	5.7	Sweet Home Central SD	Amherst
101	5.6	Bellmore-Merrick Central High SD	North Merrick
101	5.6	Johnson City Central SD	Johnson City
101	5.6	Mount Sinai UFSD	Mount Sinai
101	5.6	New Hartford Central SD	New Hartford
105	5.5	Connetquot Central SD	Bohemia
105	5.5	Lawrence UFSD	Cedarhurst
107	5.4	Cheektowaga Central SD	Cheektowaga
107	5.4	Farmingdale UFSD	Farmingdale
107	5.4	North Babylon UFSD	North Babylon
107	5.4	Yonkers City SD	Yonkers
111	5.3	Lynbrook UFSD	Lynbrook
111	5.3	North Shore Central SD	Sea Cliff
113	5.2	NYC Geographic District #8	Bronx
113	5.2	Pearl River UFSD	Pearl River
113	5.2	Pelham UFSD	Pelham
116	5.1	Cornwall Central SD	Cornwall on Hdsn
116	5.1	East Greenbush Central SD	East Greenbush
116	5.1	Gates-Chili Central SD	Rochester
116	5.1	Wappingers Central SD	Hopewell Junction
120	4.9	Malverne UFSD	Malverne
121	4.8	Smithtown Central SD	Smithtown
122	4.6	Mount Pleasant Central SD	Thornwood
122	4.6	New Rochelle City SD	New Rochelle
124	4.5	Bedford Central SD	Bedford
124	4.5	East Ramapo CSD (Spring Valley)	Spring Valley
124	4.5	Lakeland Central SD	Shrub Oak
124	4.5	NYC Geographic District #14	Brooklyn
124	4.5	Ossining UFSD	Ossining
129	4.3	Highland Central SD	Highland
130	4.3	Bay Shore UFSD	Bay Shore
130	4.3	Liverpool Central SD	Liverpool
130	4.3	Mamaroneck UFSD	Mamaroneck
133	4.2	Baldwin UFSD	Baldwin
133	4.2	West Babylon UFSD	West Babylon
135	4.1	Arlington Central SD	Lagrangeville
136	4.0	Cold Spring Hrbr Central SD	Cold Spring Hrbr
136	4.0	Garden City UFSD	Garden City
136	4.0	Glen Cove City SD	Glen Cove
136	4.0	Harborfields Central SD	Greenlawn
136	4.0	Hendrick Hudson Central SD	Montrose
141	3.9	Corning City SD	Painted Post
141	3.9	Goshen Central SD	Goshen
141	3.9	Haverstraw-Stony Point CSD	Garnerville
144	3.8	Clarence Central SD	Clarence
144	3.8	Longwood Central SD	Middle Island
144	3.8	Somers Central SD	Somers
147	3.7	Oneonta City SD	Oneonta
147	3.7	Rochester City SD	Rochester
149	3.6	Horseheads Central SD	Horseheads
149	3.6	NYC Geographic District #5	New York
149	3.6	Webster Central SD	Webster
149	3.6	White Plains City SD	White Plains
153	3.5	Locust Valley Central SD	Locust Valley
153	3.5	Oceanside UFSD	Oceanside
155	3.4	Babylon UFSD	Babylon
155	3.4	Brookhaven-Comsewogue UFSD	Port Jeff Stn
155	3.4	Lindenhurst UFSD	Lindenhurst
155	3.4	Long Beach City SD	Long Beach
159	3.3	Cheektowaga-Maryvale UFSD	Cheektowaga
159	3.3	Oyster Bay-East Norwich Central SD	Oyster Bay
161	3.2	Binghamton City SD	Binghamton
161	3.2	Fairport Central SD	Fairport
163	3.1	Greece Central SD	Rochester
163	3.1	New Paltz Central SD	New Paltz
165	2.9	Grand Island Central SD	Grand Island
165	2.9	Islip UFSD	Islip
165	2.9	Washingtonville Central SD	Washingtonville
165	2.9	West Irondequoit Central SD	Rochester
169	2.8	Beacon City SD	Beacon
169	2.8	Northport-East Northport UFSD	Northport
169	2.8	Patchogue-Medford UFSD	Patchogue
169	2.8	Penfield Central SD	Rochester
169	2.8	Victor Central SD	Victor
174	2.7	Brewster Central SD	Brewster
174	2.7	Miller Place UFSD	Miller Place
174	2.7	Plainedge UFSD	N Massapequa
174	2.7	William Floyd UFSD	Mastic Beach
178	2.6	Carmel Central SD	Patterson
178	2.6	Indian River Central SD	Philadelphia
178	2.6	Katonah-Lewisboro UFSD	South Salem
178	2.6	Kings Park Central SD	Kings Park
178	2.6	UFSD of the Tarrytowns	Sleepy Hollow
183	2.5	Central Islip UFSD	Central Islip
183	2.5	East Hampton UFSD	East Hampton
183	2.5	Ellenville Central SD	Ellenville
183	2.5	Middletown City SD	Middletown
183	2.5	NYC Geographic District #17	Brooklyn
183	2.5	Olean City SD	Olean
183	2.5	Pine Bush Central SD	Pine Bush
190	2.4	Kingston City SD	Kingston
190	2.4	Newburgh City SD	Newburgh
190	2.4	Red Hook Central SD	Red Hook
190	2.4	Rockville Ctr UFSD	Rockville Ctr
190	2.4	Southampton UFSD	Southampton
190	2.4	Wantagh UFSD	Wantagh
196	2.3	Charter School for Applied Techs	Buffalo
196	2.3	Churchville-Chili Central SD	Churchville
196	2.3	East Islip UFSD	Islip Terrace
196	2.3	East Syracuse Minoa Central SD	East Syracuse
196	2.3	NYC Geographic District #12	Bronx
196	2.3	Shoreham-Wading River Central SD	Shoreham
202	2.2	Brentwood UFSD	Brentwood
202	2.2	Copiague UFSD	Copiague
202	2.2	Depew UFSD	Depew
202	2.2	Plattsburgh City SD	Plattsburgh
202	2.2	Rotterdam-Mohonasen Central SD	Schenectady
202	2.2	Seaford UFSD	Seaford
208	2.1	Bayport-Blue Point UFSD	Bayport
208	2.1	Scotia-Glenville Central SD	Scotia
208	2.1	Union-Endicott Central SD	Endicott
208	2.1	Warwick Valley Central SD	Warwick
208	2.1	Watertown City SD	Watertown
208	2.1	Westhampton Bch UFSD	Westhampton Bch
208	2.1	Westhill Central SD	Syracuse
215	2.0	Hyde Park Central SD	Hyde Park
215	2.0	Lewiston-Porter Central SD	Youngstown
215	2.0	NYC Geographic District #32	Brooklyn
215	2.0	Niagara-Wheatfield Central SD	Niagara Falls
215	2.0	North Syracuse Central SD	North Syracuse
215	2.0	Saugerties Central SD	Saugerties
215	2.0	Schalmont Central SD	Schenectady
215	2.0	South Country Central SD	East Patchogue
215	2.0	Spencerport Central SD	Spencerport
215	2.0	Troy City SD	Troy
225	1.9	East Irondequoit Central SD	Rochester
225	1.9	Huntington UFSD	Huntington Stn
225	1.9	Mahopac Central SD	Mahopac
225	1.9	Rondout Valley Central SD	Accord
225	1.9	Saratoga Spgs City SD	Saratoga Spgs
225	1.9	Sayville UFSD	Sayville
225	1.9	West Islip UFSD	West Islip
232	1.8	Carthage Central SD	Carthage
232	1.8	Geneva City SD	Geneva
232	1.8	Honeoye Falls-Lima Central SD	Honeoye Falls

Note: This section only includes districts with 1,500 or more students; All categories are ranked from high to low

232	1.8	Kenmore-Tonawanda UFSD	Buffalo
232	1.8	Minisink Valley Central SD	Slate Hill
232	1.8	Orchard Park Central SD	West Seneca
238	1.7	Burnt Hills-Ballston Lake Central SD	Scotia
238	1.7	Massapequa UFSD	Massapequa
238	1.7	Monticello Central SD	Monticello
238	1.7	Port Chester-Rye UFSD	Port Chester
238	1.7	Putnam Valley Central SD	Putnam Valley
238	1.7	Valley Central SD (Montgomery)	Montgomery
238	1.7	West Seneca Central SD	West Seneca
245	1.6	Canandaigua City SD	Canandaigua
245	1.6	Center Moriches UFSD	Center Moriches
245	1.6	Lackawanna City SD	Lackawanna
245	1.6	NYC Geographic District #16	Brooklyn
245	1.6	Niagara Falls City SD	Niagara Falls
245	1.6	Peekskill City SD	Peekskill
251	1.5	Maine-Endwell Central SD	Endwell
251	1.5	Mount Vernon City SD	Mount Vernon
253	1.4	Ballston Spa Central SD	Ballston Spa
253	1.4	Glens Falls City SD	Glens Falls
253	1.4	Marcellus Central SD	Marcellus
253	1.4	Marlboro Central SD	Milton
253	1.4	NYC Geographic District # 9	Bronx
253	1.4	Port Jervis City SD	Port Jervis
253	1.4	Riverhead Central SD	Riverhead
253	1.4	Rome City SD	Rome
253	1.4	Whitesboro Central SD	Whitesboro
253	1.4	Windsor Central SD	Windsor
263	1.3	Averill Park Central SD	Averill Park
263	1.3	Baldwinsville Central SD	Baldwinsville
263	1.3	Hilton Central SD	Hilton
263	1.3	Kinderhook Central SD	Valatie
263	1.3	NYC Geographic District # 6	New York
263	1.3	Oswego City SD	Oswego
263	1.3	Rocky Point UFSD	Rocky Point
263	1.3	Wallkill Central SD	Wallkill
263	1.3	West Genesee Central SD	Camillus
263	1.3	Westbury UFSD	Old Westbury
273	1.2	Brockport Central SD	Brockport
273	1.2	Eastport-South Manor CSD	Manorville
273	1.2	Fredonia Central SD	Fredonia
273	1.2	Freeport UFSD	Freeport
273	1.2	Lancaster Central SD	Lancaster
273	1.2	NYC Geographic District #18	Brooklyn
273	1.2	Oneida City SD	Oneida
273	1.2	Uniondale UFSD	Uniondale
281	1.1	Chenango Valley Central SD	Binghamton
281	1.1	Dryden Central SD	Dryden
281	1.1	East Aurora UFSD	East Aurora
281	1.1	Johnstown City SD	Johnstown
281	1.1	NYC Geographic District # 7	Bronx
281	1.1	Queensbury UFSD	Queensbury
287	1.0	Batavia City SD	Batavia
287	1.0	Cohoes City SD	Cohoes
287	1.0	Frontier Central SD	Hamburg
287	1.0	Lansingburgh Central SD	Troy
287	1.0	NYC Geographic District #23	Brooklyn
287	1.0	North Tonawanda City SD	North Tonawanda
287	1.0	Ravena-Coeymans-Selkirk Cent SD	Ravena
287	1.0	Starpoint Central SD	Lockport
287	1.0	Susquehanna Valley Central SD	Conklin
296	0.9	Amsterdam City SD	Amsterdam
296	0.9	Hampton Bays UFSD	Hampton Bays
296	0.9	Norwich City SD	Norwich
296	0.9	Phelps-Clifton Springs Central SD	Clifton Springs
296	0.9	Poughkeepsie City SD	Poughkeepsie
296	0.9	Schuylerville Central SD	Schuylerville
302	0.8	Albion Central SD	Albion
302	0.8	Amityville UFSD	Amityville
302	0.8	Auburn City SD	Auburn
302	0.8	Catskill Central SD	Catskill
302	0.8	Chittenango Central SD	Chittenango
302	0.8	Cortland City SD	Cortland
302	0.8	Fulton City SD	Fulton
302	0.8	Hamburg Central SD	Hamburg
302	0.8	Iroquois Central SD	Elma
302	0.8	Liberty Central SD	Liberty
302	0.8	Lockport City SD	Lockport
302	0.8	Malone Central SD	Malone
302	0.8	South Jefferson Central SD	Adams Center
302	0.8	Wayne Central SD	Ontario Center
302	0.8	Yorkshire-Pioneer Central SD	Yorkshire
317	0.7	Beekmantown Central SD	West Chazy
317	0.7	Broadalbin-Perth Central SD	Broadalbin
317	0.7	Central Square Central SD	Central Square
317	0.7	Central Valley CSD at Ilion-Mohawk	Ilion
317	0.7	Cobleskill-Richmondville CSD	Cobleskill
317	0.7	General Brown Central SD	Dexter
317	0.7	Hornell City SD	Hornell
317	0.7	Hudson Falls Central SD	Fort Edward
317	0.7	S Glens Fls Central SD	S Glens Fls
317	0.7	Springville-Griffith Institute CSD	Springville
317	0.7	Waterloo Central SD	Waterloo
317	0.7	Waverly Central SD	Waverly
329	0.6	Chenango Forks Central SD	Binghamton
329	0.6	Dansville Central SD	Dansville
329	0.6	Evans-Brant Central SD (Lake Shore)	Angola
329	0.6	Homer Central SD	Homer
329	0.6	Medina Central SD	Medina
329	0.6	Newark Central SD	Newark
329	0.6	Palmyra-Macedon Central SD	Palmyra
329	0.6	Peru Central SD	Peru
337	0.5	Alden Central SD	Alden
337	0.5	Elmira City SD	Elmira
337	0.5	Gloversville City SD	Gloversville
337	0.5	Hempstead UFSD	Hempstead
337	0.5	Jamestown City SD	Jamestown
337	0.5	Massena Central SD	Massena
337	0.5	Ogdensburg City SD	Ogdensburg
337	0.5	Owego-Apalachin Central SD	Owego
337	0.5	Sherrill City SD	Verona
337	0.5	Tonawanda City SD	Tonawanda
347	0.4	Wyandanch UFSD	Wyandanch
348	0.3	Livonia Central SD	Livonia
348	0.3	Newfane Central SD	Burt
348	0.3	Phoenix Central SD	Phoenix
351	0.2	Camden Central SD	Camden
351	0.2	Dunkirk City SD	Dunkirk
351	0.2	Gouverneur Central SD	Gouverneur
351	0.2	Mexico Central SD	Mexico
355	0.1	Bath Central SD	Bath
355	0.1	Salmon River Central SD	Fort Covington
357	0.0	Roosevelt UFSD	Roosevelt

American Indian/Alaska Native Students

Rank	Percent	District Name	City
1	63.9	Salmon River Central SD	Fort Covington
2	13.6	Evans-Brant Central SD (Lake Shore)	Angola
3	9.2	Massena Central SD	Massena
4	7.2	Southampton UFSD	Southampton
5	7.0	Niagara-Wheatfield Central SD	Niagara Falls
6	3.5	Center Moriches UFSD	Center Moriches
6	3.5	NYC Geographic District #27	Ozone Park
8	3.1	NYC Geographic District #28	Jamaica
9	2.8	Niagara Falls City SD	Niagara Falls
10	2.7	NYC Geographic District #29	Queens Village
11	2.4	Oneida City SD	Oneida
12	1.7	North Tonawanda City SD	North Tonawanda
13	1.3	NYC Geographic District #11	Bronx
13	1.3	NYC Geographic District #17	Brooklyn
15	1.2	NYC Geographic District #19	Brooklyn
16	1.1	NYC Geographic District #23	Brooklyn
16	1.1	Syracuse City SD	Syracuse
18	1.0	NYC Geographic District #12	Bronx
18	1.0	NYC Geographic District #16	Brooklyn
20	0.9	Albion Central SD	Albion
20	0.9	NYC Geographic District # 4	New York
20	0.9	NYC Geographic District #18	Brooklyn
20	0.9	New York City Chancellor's Office	New York
24	0.8	Buffalo City SD	Buffalo
24	0.8	Freeport UFSD	Freeport
24	0.8	Malone Central SD	Malone
24	0.8	NYC Geographic District # 5	New York
24	0.8	NYC Geographic District # 8	Bronx
24	0.8	South Country Central SD	East Patchogue
24	0.8	West Genesee Central SD	Camillus
31	0.7	East Syracuse Minoa Central SD	East Syracuse
31	0.7	Kenmore-Tonawanda UFSD	Buffalo
31	0.7	Lawrence UFSD	Cedarhurst
31	0.7	Lewiston-Porter Central SD	Youngstown
31	0.7	NYC Geographic District # 1	New York
31	0.7	NYC Geographic District #10	Bronx
31	0.7	NYC Geographic District #13	Brooklyn
31	0.7	NYC Geographic District #26	Bayside
31	0.7	NYC Geographic District #30	Long Isl City
31	0.7	Springville-Griffith Institute CSD	Springville
41	0.6	Central Square Central SD	Central Square
41	0.6	Chenango Valley Central SD	Binghamton
41	0.6	Franklin Square UFSD	Franklin Square
41	0.6	Indian River Central SD	Philadelphia
41	0.6	Lackawanna City SD	Lackawanna
41	0.6	Lockport City SD	Lockport
41	0.6	Medina Central SD	Medina
41	0.6	NYC Geographic District # 2	New York
41	0.6	NYC Geographic District # 3	New York
41	0.6	NYC Geographic District # 7	Bronx
41	0.6	NYC Geographic District #22	Brooklyn
41	0.6	Tonawanda City SD	Tonawanda
53	0.5	Canandaigua City SD	Canandaigua
53	0.5	Charter School for Applied Techs	Buffalo
53	0.5	Dunkirk City SD	Dunkirk
53	0.5	Frontier Central SD	Hamburg
53	0.5	Grand Island Central SD	Grand Island
53	0.5	Iroquois Central SD	Elma
53	0.5	Liverpool Central SD	Liverpool
53	0.5	NYC Geographic District # 9	Bronx
53	0.5	NYC Geographic District #14	Brooklyn
53	0.5	NYC Geographic District #21	Brooklyn
53	0.5	NYC Geographic District #24	Corona
53	0.5	NYC Geographic District #25	Flushing
53	0.5	NYC Geographic District #32	Brooklyn
53	0.5	North Syracuse Central SD	North Syracuse
53	0.5	Olean City SD	Olean
53	0.5	Phoenix Central SD	Phoenix
53	0.5	Rondout Valley Central SD	Accord
53	0.5	Rotterdam-Mohonasen Central SD	Schenectady
53	0.5	Sherrill City SD	Verona
53	0.5	William Floyd UFSD	Mastic Beach
73	0.4	Albany City SD	Albany
73	0.4	Baldwinsville Central SD	Baldwinsville
73	0.4	Bayport-Blue Point UFSD	Bayport
73	0.4	Carthage Central SD	Carthage
73	0.4	Cheektowaga Central SD	Cheektowaga
73	0.4	Chittenango Central SD	Chittenango
73	0.4	Corning City SD	Painted Post
73	0.4	Dryden Central SD	Dryden
73	0.4	Ellenville Central SD	Ellenville
73	0.4	Fulton City SD	Fulton
73	0.4	General Brown Central SD	Dexter
73	0.4	Johnson City Central SD	Johnson City
73	0.4	Longwood Central SD	Middle Island
73	0.4	Lynbrook UFSD	Lynbrook
73	0.4	Maine-Endwell Central SD	Endwell
73	0.4	Mexico Central SD	Mexico
73	0.4	Minisink Valley Central SD	Slate Hill
73	0.4	NYC Geographic District #31	Staten Island
73	0.4	North Bellmore UFSD	Bellmore
73	0.4	Palmyra-Macedon Central SD	Palmyra
73	0.4	Pine Bush Central SD	Pine Bush
73	0.4	Ramapo Central SD (Suffern)	Hillburn
73	0.4	Susquehanna Valley Central SD	Conklin
73	0.4	Victor Central SD	Victor
73	0.4	Watertown City SD	Watertown
73	0.4	West Seneca Central SD	West Seneca
73	0.4	Westhill Central SD	Syracuse
100	0.3	Alden Central SD	Alden
100	0.3	Amherst Central SD	Amherst
100	0.3	Amityville UFSD	Amityville
100	0.3	Beekmantown Central SD	West Chazy
100	0.3	Bellmore-Merrick Central High SD	North Merrick
100	0.3	Binghamton City SD	Binghamton
100	0.3	Central Valley CSD at Ilion-Mohawk	Ilion
100	0.3	Cheektowaga-Maryvale UFSD	Cheektowaga
100	0.3	Chenango Forks Central SD	Binghamton
100	0.3	Clarence Central SD	Clarence
100	0.3	Cohoes City SD	Cohoes
100	0.3	Cornwall Central SD	Cornwall on Hdsn
100	0.3	Depew UFSD	Depew
100	0.3	Eastchester UFSD	Eastchester
100	0.3	Irvington UFSD	Irvington
100	0.3	Ithaca City SD	Ithaca
100	0.3	Jamestown City SD	Jamestown
100	0.3	Jamesville-Dewitt Central SD	Dewitt
100	0.3	Kingston City SD	Kingston
100	0.3	Lancaster Central SD	Lancaster
100	0.3	New Paltz Central SD	New Paltz
100	0.3	NYC Geographic District #15	Brooklyn
100	0.3	NYC Geographic District #20	Brooklyn
100	0.3	North Shore Central SD	Sea Cliff
100	0.3	Norwich City SD	Norwich

Note: This section only includes districts with 1,500 or more students; All categories are ranked from high to low

Rank	Percent	District Name	City
100	0.3	Orchard Park Central SD	West Seneca
100	0.3	Peru Central SD	Peru
100	0.3	Plattsburgh City SD	Plattsburgh
100	0.3	Port Jervis City SD	Port Jervis
100	0.3	Red Hook Central SD	Red Hook
100	0.3	Riverhead Central SD	Riverhead
100	0.3	Rush-Henrietta Central SD	Henrietta
100	0.3	Rye Neck UFSD	Mamaroneck
100	0.3	South Jefferson Central SD	Adams Center
100	0.3	Valley Stream 13 UFSD	Valley Stream
100	0.3	Vestal Central SD	Vestal
100	0.3	Washingtonville Central SD	Washingtonville
100	0.3	Waterloo Central SD	Waterloo
100	0.3	West Irondequoit Central SD	Rochester
100	0.3	Williamsville Central SD	East Amherst
100	0.3	Yorkshire-Pioneer Central SD	Yorkshire
141	0.2	Brentwood UFSD	Brentwood
141	0.2	Brewster Central SD	Brewster
141	0.2	Broadalbin-Perth Central SD	Broadalbin
141	0.2	Brockport Central SD	Brockport
141	0.2	Brookhaven-Comsewogue UFSD	Port Jeff Stn
141	0.2	Camden Central SD	Camden
141	0.2	Carmel Central SD	Patterson
141	0.2	Catskill Central SD	Catskill
141	0.2	East Greenbush Central SD	East Greenbush
141	0.2	East Irondequoit Central SD	Rochester
141	0.2	Elmira City SD	Elmira
141	0.2	Farmingdale UFSD	Farmingdale
141	0.2	Fayetteville-Manlius Central SD	Manlius
141	0.2	Gates-Chili Central SD	Rochester
141	0.2	Half Hollow Hills Central SD	Dix Hills
141	0.2	Hamburg Central SD	Hamburg
141	0.2	Hampton Bays UFSD	Hampton Bays
141	0.2	Haverstraw-Stony Point CSD	Garnerville
141	0.2	Hempstead UFSD	Hempstead
141	0.2	Hewlett-Woodmere UFSD	Woodmere
141	0.2	Highland Central SD	Highland
141	0.2	Hilton Central SD	Hilton
141	0.2	Honeoye Falls-Lima Central SD	Honeoye Falls
141	0.2	Hyde Park Central SD	Hyde Park
141	0.2	Katonah-Lewisboro UFSD	South Salem
141	0.2	Lakeland Central SD	Shrub Oak
141	0.2	Marcellus Central SD	Marcellus
141	0.2	Middletown City SD	Middletown
141	0.2	New Hyde Pk-Garden City Pk UFSD	New Hyde Park
141	0.2	NYC Geographic District # 6	New York
141	0.2	Newark Central SD	Newark
141	0.2	Newburgh City SD	Newburgh
141	0.2	Newfane Central SD	Burt
141	0.2	North Babylon UFSD	North Babylon
141	0.2	North Colonie CSD	Latham
141	0.2	Oswego City SD	Oswego
141	0.2	Oyster Bay-East Norwich Central SD	Oyster Bay
141	0.2	Plainedge UFSD	N Massapequa
141	0.2	Queensbury UFSD	Queensbury
141	0.2	Rochester City SD	Rochester
141	0.2	Rocky Point UFSD	Rocky Point
141	0.2	Rome City SD	Rome
141	0.2	Rye City SD	Rye
141	0.2	Sachem Central SD	Lake Ronkonkoma
141	0.2	Sayville UFSD	Sayville
141	0.2	Schalmont Central SD	Schenectady
141	0.2	Scotia-Glenville Central SD	Scotia
141	0.2	Smithtown Central SD	Smithtown
141	0.2	South Huntington UFSD	Huntington Stn
141	0.2	Spencerport Central SD	Spencerport
141	0.2	Sweet Home Central SD	Amherst
141	0.2	Troy City SD	Troy
141	0.2	Valley Central SD (Montgomery)	Montgomery
141	0.2	Wallkill Central SD	Wallkill
141	0.2	West Hempstead UFSD	West Hempstead
141	0.2	Yonkers City SD	Yonkers
197	0.1	Amsterdam City SD	Amsterdam
197	0.1	Arlington Central SD	Lagrangeville
197	0.1	Auburn City SD	Auburn
197	0.1	Baldwin UFSD	Baldwin
197	0.1	Batavia City SD	Batavia
197	0.1	Bath Central SD	Bath
197	0.1	Bay Shore UFSD	Bay Shore
197	0.1	Bethpage UFSD	Bethpage
197	0.1	Blind Brook-Rye UFSD	Rye Brook
197	0.1	Brighton Central SD	Rochester
197	0.1	Burnt Hills-Ballston Lake Central SD	Scotia
197	0.1	Byram Hills Central SD	Armonk
197	0.1	Central Islip UFSD	Central Islip
197	0.1	Chappaqua Central SD	Chappaqua
197	0.1	Churchville-Chili Central SD	Churchville
197	0.1	Clarkstown Central SD	New City
197	0.1	Commack UFSD	East Northport
197	0.1	Connetquot Central SD	Bohemia
197	0.1	Cortland City SD	Cortland
197	0.1	Croton-Harmon UFSD	Croton on Hdsn
197	0.1	Dansville Central SD	Dansville
197	0.1	Deer Park UFSD	Deer Park
197	0.1	East Aurora UFSD	East Aurora
197	0.1	East Hampton UFSD	East Hampton
197	0.1	East Islip UFSD	Islip Terrace
197	0.1	East Meadow UFSD	Westbury
197	0.1	East Williston UFSD	Old Westbury
197	0.1	Eastport-South Manor CSD	Manorville
197	0.1	Edgemont UFSD	Scarsdale
197	0.1	Elmont UFSD	Elmont
197	0.1	Fairport Central SD	Fairport
197	0.1	Fredonia Central SD	Fredonia
197	0.1	Geneva City SD	Geneva
197	0.1	Gloversville City SD	Gloversville
197	0.1	Goshen Central SD	Goshen
197	0.1	Gouverneur Central SD	Gouverneur
197	0.1	Greece Central SD	Rochester
197	0.1	Greenburgh Central SD	Hartsdale
197	0.1	Guilderland Central SD	Guilderland Center
197	0.1	Harborfields Central SD	Greenlawn
197	0.1	Harrison Central SD	Harrison
197	0.1	Hauppauge UFSD	Hauppauge
197	0.1	Hicksville UFSD	Hicksville
197	0.1	Hornell City SD	Hornell
197	0.1	Horseheads Central SD	Horseheads
197	0.1	Hudson City SD	Hudson
197	0.1	Hudson Falls Central SD	Fort Edward
197	0.1	Island Trees UFSD	Levittown
197	0.1	Islip UFSD	Islip
197	0.1	Jericho UFSD	Jericho
197	0.1	Kinderhook Central SD	Valatie
197	0.1	Lansingburgh Central SD	Troy
197	0.1	Levittown UFSD	Levittown
197	0.1	Liberty Central SD	Liberty
197	0.1	Lindenhurst UFSD	Lindenhurst
197	0.1	Livonia Central SD	Livonia
197	0.1	Massapequa UFSD	Massapequa
197	0.1	Miller Place UFSD	Miller Place
197	0.1	Mineola UFSD	Mineola
197	0.1	Monroe-Woodbury Central SD	Central Valley
197	0.1	Monticello Central SD	Monticello
197	0.1	Mount Vernon City SD	Mount Vernon
197	0.1	New Rochelle City SD	New Rochelle
197	0.1	Niskayuna Central SD	Schenectady
197	0.1	Northport-East Northport UFSD	Northport
197	0.1	Nyack UFSD	Nyack
197	0.1	Oceanside UFSD	Oceanside
197	0.1	Ogdensburg City SD	Ogdensburg
197	0.1	Patchogue-Medford UFSD	Patchogue
197	0.1	Peekskill City SD	Peekskill
197	0.1	Penfield Central SD	Rochester
197	0.1	Phelps-Clifton Springs Central SD	Clifton Springs
197	0.1	Plainview-Old Bethpage CSD	Plainview
197	0.1	Pleasantville Central SD	Pleasantville
197	0.1	Port Chester-Rye UFSD	Port Chester
197	0.1	Port Washington UFSD	Port Washington
197	0.1	Poughkeepsie City SD	Poughkeepsie
197	0.1	Putnam Valley Central SD	Putnam Valley
197	0.1	Ravena-Coeymans-Selkirk Cent SD	Ravena
197	0.1	Saratoga Spgs City SD	Saratoga Spgs
197	0.1	Saugerties Central SD	Saugerties
197	0.1	Scarsdale UFSD	Scarsdale
197	0.1	Schenectady City SD	Schenectady
197	0.1	Schuylerville Central SD	Schuylerville
197	0.1	Shenendehowa Central SD	Clifton Park
197	0.1	South Colonie Central SD	Albany
197	0.1	South Orangetown Central SD	Blauvelt
197	0.1	Starpoint Central SD	Lockport
197	0.1	Syosset Central SD	Syosset
197	0.1	Three Village Central SD	Stony Brook
197	0.1	Union-Endicott Central SD	Endicott
197	0.1	Uniondale UFSD	Uniondale
197	0.1	Utica City SD	Utica
197	0.1	Valley Stream 30 UFSD	Valley Stream
197	0.1	Valley Stream Central High SD	Valley Stream
197	0.1	Warwick Valley Central SD	Warwick
197	0.1	Webster Central SD	Webster
197	0.1	Westbury UFSD	Old Westbury
197	0.1	Westhampton Bch UFSD	Westhampton Bch
197	0.1	Yorktown Central SD	Yorktown Hgts
297	0.0	Ardsley UFSD	Ardsley
297	0.0	Averill Park Central SD	Averill Park
297	0.0	Babylon UFSD	Babylon
297	0.0	Ballston Spa Central SD	Ballston Spa
297	0.0	Beacon City SD	Beacon
297	0.0	Bedford Central SD	Bedford
297	0.0	Bethlehem Central SD	Delmar
297	0.0	Bronxville UFSD	Bronxville
297	0.0	Cobleskill-Richmondville CSD	Cobleskill
297	0.0	Cold Spring Hrbr Central SD	Cold Spring Hrbr
297	0.0	Copiague UFSD	Copiague
297	0.0	East Ramapo CSD (Spring Valley)	Spring Valley
297	0.0	Elwood UFSD	Greenlawn
297	0.0	Garden City UFSD	Garden City
297	0.0	Glen Cove City SD	Glen Cove
297	0.0	Glens Falls City SD	Glens Falls
297	0.0	Great Neck UFSD	Great Neck
297	0.0	Hastings-On-Hudson UFSD	Hastings on Hdsn
297	0.0	Hendrick Hudson Central SD	Montrose
297	0.0	Herricks UFSD	New Hyde Park
297	0.0	Homer Central SD	Homer
297	0.0	Huntington UFSD	Huntington Stn
297	0.0	Johnstown City SD	Johnstown
297	0.0	Kings Park Central SD	Kings Park
297	0.0	Locust Valley Central SD	Locust Valley
297	0.0	Long Beach City SD	Long Beach
297	0.0	Mahopac Central SD	Mahopac
297	0.0	Malverne UFSD	Malverne
297	0.0	Mamaroneck UFSD	Mamaroneck
297	0.0	Manhasset UFSD	Manhasset
297	0.0	Marlboro Central SD	Milton
297	0.0	Middle Country Central SD	Centereach
297	0.0	Mount Pleasant Central SD	Thornwood
297	0.0	Mount Sinai UFSD	Mount Sinai
297	0.0	Nanuet UFSD	Nanuet
297	0.0	New Hartford Central SD	New Hartford
297	0.0	Oneonta City SD	Oneonta
297	0.0	Ossining UFSD	Ossining
297	0.0	Owego-Apalachin Central SD	Owego
297	0.0	Pearl River UFSD	Pearl River
297	0.0	Pelham UFSD	Pelham
297	0.0	Pittsford Central SD	Pittsford
297	0.0	Rockville Ctr UFSD	Rockville Ctr
297	0.0	Roosevelt UFSD	Roosevelt
297	0.0	Roslyn UFSD	Roslyn
297	0.0	Seaford UFSD	Seaford
297	0.0	Sewanhaka Central High SD	Floral Park
297	0.0	Shoreham-Wading River Central SD	Shoreham
297	0.0	Somers Central SD	Somers
297	0.0	S Glens Fls Central SD	S Glens Fls
297	0.0	UFSD of the Tarrytowns	Sleepy Hollow
297	0.0	Wantagh UFSD	Wantagh
297	0.0	Wappingers Central SD	Hopewell Junction
297	0.0	Waverly Central SD	Waverly
297	0.0	Wayne Central SD	Ontario Center
297	0.0	West Babylon UFSD	West Babylon
297	0.0	West Islip UFSD	West Islip
297	0.0	White Plains City SD	White Plains
297	0.0	Whitesboro Central SD	Whitesboro
297	0.0	Windsor Central SD	Windsor
297	0.0	Wyandanch UFSD	Wyandanch

Native Hawaiian/Pacific Islander Students

Rank	Percent	District Name	City
n/a	n/a	Albany City SD	Albany
n/a	n/a	Albion Central SD	Albion
n/a	n/a	Alden Central SD	Alden
n/a	n/a	Amherst Central SD	Amherst
n/a	n/a	Amityville UFSD	Amityville
n/a	n/a	Amsterdam City SD	Amsterdam
n/a	n/a	Ardsley UFSD	Ardsley
n/a	n/a	Arlington Central SD	Lagrangeville
n/a	n/a	Auburn City SD	Auburn
n/a	n/a	Averill Park Central SD	Averill Park
n/a	n/a	Babylon UFSD	Babylon
n/a	n/a	Baldwin UFSD	Baldwin
n/a	n/a	Baldwinsville Central SD	Baldwinsville

Note: This section only includes districts with 1,500 or more students; All categories are ranked from high to low

		District	Location
n/a	n/a	Ballston Spa Central SD	Ballston Spa
n/a	n/a	Batavia City SD	Batavia
n/a	n/a	Bath Central SD	Bath
n/a	n/a	Bay Shore UFSD	Bay Shore
n/a	n/a	Bayport-Blue Point UFSD	Bayport
n/a	n/a	Beacon City SD	Beacon
n/a	n/a	Bedford Central SD	Bedford
n/a	n/a	Beekmantown Central SD	West Chazy
n/a	n/a	Bellmore-Merrick Central High SD	North Merrick
n/a	n/a	Bethlehem Central SD	Delmar
n/a	n/a	Bethpage UFSD	Bethpage
n/a	n/a	Binghamton City SD	Binghamton
n/a	n/a	Blind Brook-Rye UFSD	Rye Brook
n/a	n/a	Brentwood UFSD	Brentwood
n/a	n/a	Brewster Central SD	Brewster
n/a	n/a	Brighton Central SD	Rochester
n/a	n/a	Broadalbin-Perth Central SD	Broadalbin
n/a	n/a	Brockport Central SD	Brockport
n/a	n/a	Bronxville UFSD	Bronxville
n/a	n/a	Brookhaven-Comsewogue UFSD	Port Jeff Stn
n/a	n/a	Buffalo City SD	Buffalo
n/a	n/a	Burnt Hills-Ballston Lake Central SD	Scotia
n/a	n/a	Byram Hills Central SD	Armonk
n/a	n/a	Camden Central SD	Camden
n/a	n/a	Canandaigua City SD	Canandaigua
n/a	n/a	Carmel Central SD	Patterson
n/a	n/a	Carthage Central SD	Carthage
n/a	n/a	Catskill Central SD	Catskill
n/a	n/a	Center Moriches UFSD	Center Moriches
n/a	n/a	Central Islip UFSD	Central Islip
n/a	n/a	Central Square Central SD	Central Square
n/a	n/a	Central Valley CSD at Ilion-Mohawk	Ilion
n/a	n/a	Chappaqua Central SD	Chappaqua
n/a	n/a	Charter School for Applied Techs	Buffalo
n/a	n/a	Cheektowaga Central SD	Cheektowaga
n/a	n/a	Cheektowaga-Maryvale UFSD	Cheektowaga
n/a	n/a	Chenango Forks Central SD	Binghamton
n/a	n/a	Chenango Valley Central SD	Binghamton
n/a	n/a	Chittenango Central SD	Chittenango
n/a	n/a	Churchville-Chili Central SD	Churchville
n/a	n/a	Clarence Central SD	Clarence
n/a	n/a	Clarkstown Central SD	New City
n/a	n/a	Cobleskill-Richmondville CSD	Cobleskill
n/a	n/a	Cohoes City SD	Cohoes
n/a	n/a	Cold Spring Hrbr Central SD	Cold Spring Hrbr
n/a	n/a	Commack UFSD	East Northport
n/a	n/a	Connetquot Central SD	Bohemia
n/a	n/a	Copiague UFSD	Copiague
n/a	n/a	Corning City SD	Painted Post
n/a	n/a	Cornwall Central SD	Cornwall on Hdsn
n/a	n/a	Cortland City SD	Cortland
n/a	n/a	Croton-Harmon UFSD	Croton on Hdsn
n/a	n/a	Dansville Central SD	Dansville
n/a	n/a	Deer Park UFSD	Deer Park
n/a	n/a	Depew UFSD	Depew
n/a	n/a	Dryden Central SD	Dryden
n/a	n/a	Dunkirk City SD	Dunkirk
n/a	n/a	East Aurora UFSD	East Aurora
n/a	n/a	East Greenbush Central SD	East Greenbush
n/a	n/a	East Hampton UFSD	East Hampton
n/a	n/a	East Irondequoit Central SD	Rochester
n/a	n/a	East Islip UFSD	Islip Terrace
n/a	n/a	East Meadow UFSD	Westbury
n/a	n/a	East Ramapo CSD (Spring Valley)	Spring Valley
n/a	n/a	East Syracuse Minoa Central SD	East Syracuse
n/a	n/a	East Williston UFSD	Old Westbury
n/a	n/a	Eastchester UFSD	Eastchester
n/a	n/a	Eastport-South Manor CSD	Manorville
n/a	n/a	Edgemont UFSD	Scarsdale
n/a	n/a	Ellenville Central SD	Ellenville
n/a	n/a	Elmira City SD	Elmira
n/a	n/a	Elmont UFSD	Elmont
n/a	n/a	Elwood UFSD	Greenlawn
n/a	n/a	Evans-Brant Central SD (Lake Shore)	Angola
n/a	n/a	Fairport Central SD	Fairport
n/a	n/a	Farmingdale UFSD	Farmingdale
n/a	n/a	Fayetteville-Manlius Central SD	Manlius
n/a	n/a	Franklin Square UFSD	Franklin Square
n/a	n/a	Fredonia Central SD	Fredonia
n/a	n/a	Freeport UFSD	Freeport
n/a	n/a	Frontier Central SD	Hamburg
n/a	n/a	Fulton City SD	Fulton
n/a	n/a	Garden City UFSD	Garden City
n/a	n/a	Gates-Chili Central SD	Rochester
n/a	n/a	General Brown Central SD	Dexter
n/a	n/a	Geneva City SD	Geneva
n/a	n/a	Glen Cove City SD	Glen Cove
n/a	n/a	Glens Falls City SD	Glens Falls
n/a	n/a	Gloversville City SD	Gloversville
n/a	n/a	Goshen Central SD	Goshen
n/a	n/a	Gouverneur Central SD	Gouverneur
n/a	n/a	Grand Island Central SD	Grand Island
n/a	n/a	Great Neck UFSD	Great Neck
n/a	n/a	Greece Central SD	Rochester
n/a	n/a	Greenburgh Central SD	Hartsdale
n/a	n/a	Guilderland Central SD	Guilderland Center
n/a	n/a	Half Hollow Hills Central SD	Dix Hills
n/a	n/a	Hamburg Central SD	Hamburg
n/a	n/a	Hampton Bays UFSD	Hampton Bays
n/a	n/a	Harborfields Central SD	Greenlawn
n/a	n/a	Harrison Central SD	Harrison
n/a	n/a	Hastings-On-Hudson UFSD	Hastings on Hdsn
n/a	n/a	Hauppauge UFSD	Hauppauge
n/a	n/a	Haverstraw-Stony Point CSD	Garnerville
n/a	n/a	Hempstead UFSD	Hempstead
n/a	n/a	Hendrick Hudson Central SD	Montrose
n/a	n/a	Herricks UFSD	New Hyde Park
n/a	n/a	Hewlett-Woodmere UFSD	Woodmere
n/a	n/a	Hicksville UFSD	Hicksville
n/a	n/a	Highland Central SD	Highland
n/a	n/a	Hilton Central SD	Hilton
n/a	n/a	Homer Central SD	Homer
n/a	n/a	Honeoye Falls-Lima Central SD	Honeoye Falls
n/a	n/a	Hornell City SD	Hornell
n/a	n/a	Horseheads Central SD	Horseheads
n/a	n/a	Hudson City SD	Hudson
n/a	n/a	Hudson Falls Central SD	Fort Edward
n/a	n/a	Huntington UFSD	Huntington Stn
n/a	n/a	Hyde Park Central SD	Hyde Park
n/a	n/a	Indian River Central SD	Philadelphia
n/a	n/a	Iroquois Central SD	Elma
n/a	n/a	Irvington UFSD	Irvington
n/a	n/a	Island Trees UFSD	Levittown
n/a	n/a	Islip UFSD	Islip
n/a	n/a	Ithaca City SD	Ithaca
n/a	n/a	Jamestown City SD	Jamestown
n/a	n/a	Jamesville-Dewitt Central SD	Dewitt
n/a	n/a	Jericho UFSD	Jericho
n/a	n/a	Johnson City Central SD	Johnson City
n/a	n/a	Johnstown City SD	Johnstown
n/a	n/a	Katonah-Lewisboro UFSD	South Salem
n/a	n/a	Kenmore-Tonawanda UFSD	Buffalo
n/a	n/a	Kinderhook Central SD	Valatie
n/a	n/a	Kings Park Central SD	Kings Park
n/a	n/a	Kingston City SD	Kingston
n/a	n/a	Lackawanna City SD	Lackawanna
n/a	n/a	Lakeland Central SD	Shrub Oak
n/a	n/a	Lancaster Central SD	Lancaster
n/a	n/a	Lansingburgh Central SD	Troy
n/a	n/a	Lawrence UFSD	Cedarhurst
n/a	n/a	Levittown UFSD	Levittown
n/a	n/a	Lewiston-Porter Central SD	Youngstown
n/a	n/a	Liberty Central SD	Liberty
n/a	n/a	Lindenhurst UFSD	Lindenhurst
n/a	n/a	Liverpool Central SD	Liverpool
n/a	n/a	Livonia Central SD	Livonia
n/a	n/a	Lockport City SD	Lockport
n/a	n/a	Locust Valley Central SD	Locust Valley
n/a	n/a	Long Beach City SD	Long Beach
n/a	n/a	Longwood Central SD	Middle Island
n/a	n/a	Lynbrook UFSD	Lynbrook
n/a	n/a	Mahopac Central SD	Mahopac
n/a	n/a	Maine-Endwell Central SD	Endwell
n/a	n/a	Malone Central SD	Malone
n/a	n/a	Malverne UFSD	Malverne
n/a	n/a	Mamaroneck UFSD	Mamaroneck
n/a	n/a	Manhasset UFSD	Manhasset
n/a	n/a	Marcellus Central SD	Marcellus
n/a	n/a	Marlboro Central SD	Milton
n/a	n/a	Massapequa UFSD	Massapequa
n/a	n/a	Massena Central SD	Massena
n/a	n/a	Medina Central SD	Medina
n/a	n/a	Mexico Central SD	Mexico
n/a	n/a	Middle Country Central SD	Centereach
n/a	n/a	Middletown City SD	Middletown
n/a	n/a	Miller Place UFSD	Miller Place
n/a	n/a	Mineola UFSD	Mineola
n/a	n/a	Minisink Valley Central SD	Slate Hill
n/a	n/a	Monroe-Woodbury Central SD	Central Valley
n/a	n/a	Monticello Central SD	Monticello
n/a	n/a	Mount Pleasant Central SD	Thornwood
n/a	n/a	Mount Sinai UFSD	Mount Sinai
n/a	n/a	Mount Vernon SD	Mount Vernon
n/a	n/a	Nanuet UFSD	Nanuet
n/a	n/a	New Hartford Central SD	New Hartford
n/a	n/a	New Hyde Pk-Garden City Pk UFSD	New Hyde Park
n/a	n/a	New Paltz Central SD	New Paltz
n/a	n/a	New Rochelle City SD	New Rochelle
n/a	n/a	NYC Geographic District # 1	New York
n/a	n/a	NYC Geographic District # 2	New York
n/a	n/a	NYC Geographic District # 3	New York
n/a	n/a	NYC Geographic District # 4	New York
n/a	n/a	NYC Geographic District # 5	New York
n/a	n/a	NYC Geographic District # 6	New York
n/a	n/a	NYC Geographic District # 7	Bronx
n/a	n/a	NYC Geographic District # 8	Bronx
n/a	n/a	NYC Geographic District # 9	Bronx
n/a	n/a	NYC Geographic District #10	Bronx
n/a	n/a	NYC Geographic District #11	Bronx
n/a	n/a	NYC Geographic District #12	Bronx
n/a	n/a	NYC Geographic District #13	Brooklyn
n/a	n/a	NYC Geographic District #14	Brooklyn
n/a	n/a	NYC Geographic District #15	Brooklyn
n/a	n/a	NYC Geographic District #16	Brooklyn
n/a	n/a	NYC Geographic District #17	Brooklyn
n/a	n/a	NYC Geographic District #18	Brooklyn
n/a	n/a	NYC Geographic District #19	Brooklyn
n/a	n/a	NYC Geographic District #20	Brooklyn
n/a	n/a	NYC Geographic District #21	Brooklyn
n/a	n/a	NYC Geographic District #22	Brooklyn
n/a	n/a	NYC Geographic District #23	Brooklyn
n/a	n/a	NYC Geographic District #24	Corona
n/a	n/a	NYC Geographic District #25	Flushing
n/a	n/a	NYC Geographic District #26	Bayside
n/a	n/a	NYC Geographic District #27	Ozone Park
n/a	n/a	NYC Geographic District #28	Jamaica
n/a	n/a	NYC Geographic District #29	Queens Village
n/a	n/a	NYC Geographic District #30	Long Isl City
n/a	n/a	NYC Geographic District #31	Staten Island
n/a	n/a	NYC Geographic District #32	Brooklyn
n/a	n/a	Newark Central SD	Newark
n/a	n/a	Newburgh City SD	Newburgh
n/a	n/a	Newfane Central SD	Burt
n/a	n/a	Niagara Falls City SD	Niagara Falls
n/a	n/a	Niagara-Wheatfield Central SD	Niagara Falls
n/a	n/a	Niskayuna Central SD	Schenectady
n/a	n/a	North Babylon UFSD	North Babylon
n/a	n/a	North Bellmore UFSD	Bellmore
n/a	n/a	North Colonie CSD	Latham
n/a	n/a	North Shore Central SD	Sea Cliff
n/a	n/a	North Syracuse Central SD	North Syracuse
n/a	n/a	North Tonawanda City SD	North Tonawanda
n/a	n/a	Northport-East Northport UFSD	Northport
n/a	n/a	Norwich City SD	Norwich
n/a	n/a	Nyack UFSD	Nyack
n/a	n/a	Oceanside UFSD	Oceanside
n/a	n/a	Ogdensburg City SD	Ogdensburg
n/a	n/a	Olean City SD	Olean
n/a	n/a	Oneida City SD	Oneida
n/a	n/a	Oneonta City SD	Oneonta
n/a	n/a	Orchard Park Central SD	West Seneca
n/a	n/a	Ossining UFSD	Ossining
n/a	n/a	Oswego City SD	Oswego
n/a	n/a	Owego-Apalachin Central SD	Owego
n/a	n/a	Oyster Bay-East Norwich Central SD	Oyster Bay
n/a	n/a	Palmyra-Macedon Central SD	Palmyra
n/a	n/a	Patchogue-Medford UFSD	Patchogue
n/a	n/a	Pearl River UFSD	Pearl River
n/a	n/a	Peekskill City SD	Peekskill
n/a	n/a	Pelham UFSD	Pelham
n/a	n/a	Penfield Central SD	Rochester
n/a	n/a	Peru Central SD	Peru
n/a	n/a	Phelps-Clifton Springs Central SD	Clifton Springs
n/a	n/a	Phoenix Central SD	Phoenix
n/a	n/a	Pine Bush Central SD	Pine Bush
n/a	n/a	Pittsford Central SD	Pittsford
n/a	n/a	Plainedge UFSD	N Massapequa
n/a	n/a	Plainview-Old Bethpage CSD	Plainview
n/a	n/a	Plattsburgh City SD	Plattsburgh
n/a	n/a	Pleasantville UFSD	Pleasantville
n/a	n/a	Port Chester-Rye UFSD	Port Chester
n/a	n/a	Port Jervis City SD	Port Jervis

Note: This section only includes districts with 1,500 or more students; All categories are ranked from high to low

		District Name	City
n/a	n/a	Port Washington UFSD	Port Washington
n/a	n/a	Poughkeepsie City SD	Poughkeepsie
n/a	n/a	Putnam Valley Central SD	Putnam Valley
n/a	n/a	Queensbury UFSD	Queensbury
n/a	n/a	Ramapo Central SD (Suffern)	Hillburn
n/a	n/a	Ravena-Coeymans-Selkirk Cent SD	Ravena
n/a	n/a	Red Hook Central SD	Red Hook
n/a	n/a	Riverhead Central SD	Riverhead
n/a	n/a	Rochester City SD	Rochester
n/a	n/a	Rockville Ctr UFSD	Rockville Ctr
n/a	n/a	Rocky Point UFSD	Rocky Point
n/a	n/a	Rome City SD	Rome
n/a	n/a	Rondout Valley Central SD	Accord
n/a	n/a	Roosevelt UFSD	Roosevelt
n/a	n/a	Roslyn UFSD	Roslyn
n/a	n/a	Rotterdam-Mohonasen Central SD	Schenectady
n/a	n/a	Rush-Henrietta Central SD	Henrietta
n/a	n/a	Rye City SD	Rye
n/a	n/a	Rye Neck UFSD	Mamaroneck
n/a	n/a	Sachem Central SD	Lake Ronkonkoma
n/a	n/a	Salmon River Central SD	Fort Covington
n/a	n/a	Saratoga Spgs City SD	Saratoga Spgs
n/a	n/a	Saugerties Central SD	Saugerties
n/a	n/a	Sayville UFSD	Sayville
n/a	n/a	Scarsdale UFSD	Scarsdale
n/a	n/a	Schalmont Central SD	Schenectady
n/a	n/a	Schenectady City SD	Schenectady
n/a	n/a	Schuylerville Central SD	Schuylerville
n/a	n/a	Scotia-Glenville Central SD	Scotia
n/a	n/a	Seaford UFSD	Seaford
n/a	n/a	Sewanhaka Central High SD	Floral Park
n/a	n/a	Shenendehowa Central SD	Clifton Park
n/a	n/a	Sherrill City SD	Verona
n/a	n/a	Shoreham-Wading River Central SD	Shoreham
n/a	n/a	Smithtown Central SD	Smithtown
n/a	n/a	Somers Central SD	Somers
n/a	n/a	South Colonie Central SD	Albany
n/a	n/a	South Country Central SD	East Patchogue
n/a	n/a	S Glens Fls Central SD	S Glens Fls
n/a	n/a	South Huntington UFSD	Huntington Stn
n/a	n/a	South Jefferson Central SD	Adams Center
n/a	n/a	South Orangetown Central SD	Blauvelt
n/a	n/a	Southampton UFSD	Southampton
n/a	n/a	Spencerport Central SD	Spencerport
n/a	n/a	Springville-Griffith Institute CSD	Springville
n/a	n/a	Starpoint Central SD	Lockport
n/a	n/a	Susquehanna Valley Central SD	Conklin
n/a	n/a	Sweet Home Central SD	Amherst
n/a	n/a	Syosset Central SD	Syosset
n/a	n/a	Syracuse City SD	Syracuse
n/a	n/a	Three Village Central SD	Stony Brook
n/a	n/a	Tonawanda City SD	Tonawanda
n/a	n/a	Troy City SD	Troy
n/a	n/a	UFSD of the Tarrytowns	Sleepy Hollow
n/a	n/a	Union-Endicott Central SD	Endicott
n/a	n/a	Uniondale UFSD	Uniondale
n/a	n/a	Utica City SD	Utica
n/a	n/a	Valley Central SD (Montgomery)	Montgomery
n/a	n/a	Valley Stream 13 UFSD	Valley Stream
n/a	n/a	Valley Stream 30 UFSD	Valley Stream
n/a	n/a	Valley Stream Central High SD	Valley Stream
n/a	n/a	Vestal Central SD	Vestal
n/a	n/a	Victor Central SD	Victor
n/a	n/a	Wallkill Central SD	Wallkill
n/a	n/a	Wantagh UFSD	Wantagh
n/a	n/a	Wappingers Central SD	Hopewell Junction
n/a	n/a	Warwick Valley Central SD	Warwick
n/a	n/a	Washingtonville Central SD	Washingtonville
n/a	n/a	Waterloo Central SD	Waterloo
n/a	n/a	Watertown City SD	Watertown
n/a	n/a	Waverly Central SD	Waverly
n/a	n/a	Wayne Central SD	Ontario Center
n/a	n/a	Webster Central SD	Webster
n/a	n/a	West Babylon UFSD	West Babylon
n/a	n/a	West Genesee Central SD	Camillus
n/a	n/a	West Hempstead UFSD	West Hempstead
n/a	n/a	West Irondequoit Central SD	Rochester
n/a	n/a	West Islip UFSD	West Islip
n/a	n/a	West Seneca Central SD	West Seneca
n/a	n/a	Westbury UFSD	Old Westbury
n/a	n/a	Westhampton Bch UFSD	Westhampton Bch
n/a	n/a	Westhill Central SD	Syracuse
n/a	n/a	White Plains City SD	White Plains
n/a	n/a	Whitesboro Central SD	Whitesboro
n/a	n/a	William Floyd UFSD	Mastic Beach
n/a	n/a	Williamsville Central SD	East Amherst
n/a	n/a	Windsor Central SD	Windsor
n/a	n/a	Wyandanch UFSD	Wyandanch
n/a	n/a	Yonkers City SD	Yonkers
n/a	n/a	Yorkshire-Pioneer Central SD	Yorkshire
n/a	n/a	Yorktown Central SD	Yorktown Hgts
n/a	n/a	New York City Chancellor's Office	New York

Students who are Two or More Races

Rank	Percent	District Name	City
1	10.4	Geneva City SD	Geneva
2	10.1	Batavia City SD	Batavia
2	10.1	Niagara Falls City SD	Niagara Falls
4	9.7	Binghamton City SD	Binghamton
4	9.7	Jamestown City SD	Jamestown
6	8.8	Elmira City SD	Elmira
7	8.5	Johnson City Central SD	Johnson City
8	8.4	Medina Central SD	Medina
9	8.3	Charter School for Applied Techs	Buffalo
9	8.3	Union-Endicott Central SD	Endicott
11	7.8	Watertown City SD	Watertown
12	7.7	Auburn City SD	Auburn
13	7.6	Ithaca City SD	Ithaca
14	7.5	Hudson City SD	Hudson
15	7.3	Kingston City SD	Kingston
16	6.7	Carthage Central SD	Carthage
17	6.7	Lansingburgh Central SD	Troy
18	6.5	Olean City SD	Olean
19	6.1	South Colonie Central SD	Albany
20	6.0	East Irondequoit Central SD	Rochester
20	6.0	Gates-Chili Central SD	Rochester
22	5.9	Edgemont UFSD	Scarsdale
22	5.9	Indian River Central SD	Philadelphia
22	5.9	Poughkeepsie City SD	Poughkeepsie
25	5.8	Lockport City SD	Lockport
26	5.7	Scarsdale UFSD	Scarsdale
26	5.7	Troy City SD	Troy
28	5.6	Brighton Central SD	Rochester
29	5.4	Beacon City SD	Beacon
29	5.4	Hastings-On-Hudson UFSD	Hastings on Hdsn
29	5.4	Syracuse City SD	Syracuse
32	5.3	Catskill Central SD	Catskill
32	5.3	East Greenbush Central SD	East Greenbush
34	5.2	Cohoes City SD	Cohoes
35	5.1	North Syracuse Central SD	North Syracuse
36	5.0	Pelham UFSD	Pelham
36	5.0	Rye Neck UFSD	Mamaroneck
36	5.0	Schenectady City SD	Schenectady
39	4.9	Albany City SD	Albany
39	4.9	Dryden Central SD	Dryden
39	4.9	Hendrick Hudson Central SD	Montrose
39	4.9	Newark Central SD	Newark
39	4.9	Utica City SD	Utica
44	4.7	Ravena-Coeymans-Selkirk Cent SD	Ravena
45	4.6	Brockport Central SD	Brockport
45	4.6	Katonah-Lewisboro UFSD	South Salem
45	4.6	Liverpool Central SD	Liverpool
45	4.6	Port Jervis City SD	Port Jervis
49	4.5	Cheektowaga Central SD	Cheektowaga
49	4.5	Westhampton Bch UFSD	Westhampton Bch
51	4.4	Monticello Central SD	Monticello
52	4.3	Chenango Valley Central SD	Binghamton
52	4.3	Nyack UFSD	Nyack
54	4.2	Cheektowaga-Maryvale UFSD	Cheektowaga
54	4.2	Cortland City SD	Cortland
54	4.2	Glens Falls City SD	Glens Falls
54	4.2	Greece Central SD	Rochester
54	4.2	Hyde Park Central SD	Hyde Park
59	4.1	Gloversville City SD	Gloversville
59	4.1	Hudson Falls Central SD	Fort Edward
59	4.1	Kenmore-Tonawanda UFSD	Buffalo
59	4.1	Pittsford Central SD	Pittsford
59	4.1	Saugerties Central SD	Saugerties
64	4.0	Amherst Central SD	Amherst
64	4.0	Irvington UFSD	Irvington
64	4.0	Spencerport Central SD	Spencerport
67	3.9	Highland Central SD	Highland
67	3.9	Longwood Central SD	Middle Island
67	3.9	Niagara-Wheatfield Central SD	Niagara Falls
67	3.9	Rush-Henrietta Central SD	Henrietta
67	3.9	William Floyd UFSD	Mastic Beach
72	3.8	Baldwinsville Central SD	Baldwinsville
72	3.8	Williamsville Central SD	East Amherst
74	3.7	Corning City SD	Painted Post
74	3.7	Dunkirk City SD	Dunkirk
74	3.7	Eastchester UFSD	Eastchester
74	3.7	Hornell City SD	Hornell
74	3.7	Valley Stream 30 UFSD	Valley Stream
79	3.6	Bronxville UFSD	Bronxville
79	3.6	Chappaqua Central SD	Chappaqua
79	3.6	Half Hollow Hills Central SD	Dix Hills
79	3.6	NYC Geographic District # 3	New York
79	3.6	North Colonie CSD	Latham
79	3.6	Shenendehowa Central SD	Clifton Park
85	3.5	Buffalo City SD	Buffalo
85	3.5	Canandaigua City SD	Canandaigua
85	3.5	Penfield Central SD	Rochester
88	3.4	Baldwin UFSD	Baldwin
88	3.4	Grand Island Central SD	Grand Island
88	3.4	Jamesville-Dewitt Central SD	Dewitt
88	3.4	Palmyra-Macedon Central SD	Palmyra
92	3.3	Churchville-Chili Central SD	Churchville
92	3.3	Ellenville Central SD	Ellenville
92	3.3	Schalmont Central SD	Schenectady
92	3.3	West Irondequoit Central SD	Rochester
96	3.2	Frontier Central SD	Hamburg
96	3.2	Horseheads Central SD	Horseheads
96	3.2	Liberty Central SD	Liberty
96	3.2	NYC Geographic District # 2	New York
100	3.1	Maine-Endwell Central SD	Endwell
100	3.1	Middletown City SD	Middletown
100	3.1	New Hartford Central SD	New Hartford
100	3.1	Oneida City SD	Oneida
100	3.1	Rotterdam-Mohonasen Central SD	Schenectady
105	3.0	Amsterdam City SD	Amsterdam
105	3.0	Guilderland Central SD	Guilderland Center
107	2.9	Newfane Central SD	Burt
107	2.9	Niskayuna Central SD	Schenectady
107	2.9	Ossining UFSD	Ossining
107	2.9	Port Washington UFSD	Port Washington
107	2.9	Salmon River Central SD	Fort Covington
107	2.9	Waterloo Central SD	Waterloo
113	2.8	Arlington Central SD	Lagrangeville
113	2.8	Fredonia Central SD	Fredonia
113	2.8	Harborfields Central SD	Greenlawn
113	2.8	Huntington UFSD	Huntington Stn
113	2.8	Newburgh City SD	Newburgh
113	2.8	Ramapo Central SD (Suffern)	Hillburn
119	2.7	Amityville UFSD	Amityville
119	2.7	Bedford Central SD	Bedford
119	2.7	Depew UFSD	Depew
119	2.7	Hilton Central SD	Hilton
119	2.7	New Paltz Central SD	New Paltz
119	2.7	Oyster Bay-East Norwich Central SD	Oyster Bay
119	2.7	South Country Central SD	East Patchogue
119	2.7	Valley Central SD (Montgomery)	Montgomery
119	2.7	Vestal Central SD	Vestal
119	2.7	West Hempstead UFSD	West Hempstead
119	2.7	Yorktown Central SD	Yorktown Hgts
130	2.6	Deer Park UFSD	Deer Park
130	2.6	East Syracuse Minoa Central SD	East Syracuse
130	2.6	Islip UFSD	Islip
130	2.6	NYC Geographic District #13	Brooklyn
130	2.6	NYC Geographic District #15	Brooklyn
130	2.6	Saratoga Spgs City SD	Saratoga Spgs
130	2.6	South Orangetown Central SD	Blauvelt
130	2.6	Susquehanna Valley Central SD	Conklin
130	2.6	Valley Stream 13 UFSD	Valley Stream
139	2.5	Brewster Central SD	Brewster
139	2.5	Carmel Central SD	Patterson
139	2.5	Mamaroneck UFSD	Mamaroneck
139	2.5	Marlboro Central SD	Milton
139	2.5	Oceanside UFSD	Oceanside
139	2.5	Phoenix Central SD	Phoenix
139	2.5	South Huntington UFSD	Huntington Stn
139	2.5	Tonawanda City SD	Tonawanda
147	2.4	Chittenango Central SD	Chittenango
147	2.4	North Shore Central SD	Sea Cliff
147	2.4	Rockville Ctr UFSD	Rockville Ctr
147	2.4	UFSD of the Tarrytowns	Sleepy Hollow
147	2.4	Whitesboro Central SD	Whitesboro
152	2.3	Lackawanna City SD	Lackawanna
152	2.3	Long Beach City SD	Long Beach
152	2.3	New Hyde Pk-Garden City Pk UFSD	New Hyde Park
155	2.2	Clarence Central SD	Clarence

Note: This section only includes districts with 1,500 or more students; All categories are ranked from high to low

155	2.2	East Islip UFSD	Islip Terrace
155	2.2	Hewlett-Woodmere UFSD	Woodmere
155	2.2	Honeoye Falls-Lima Central SD	Honeoye Falls
155	2.2	Victor Central SD	Victor
155	2.2	Washingtonville Central SD	Washingtonville
155	2.2	White Plains City SD	White Plains
162	2.1	Averill Park Central SD	Averill Park
162	2.1	Blind Brook-Rye UFSD	Rye Brook
162	2.1	Croton-Harmon UFSD	Croton on Hdsn
162	2.1	Elmont UFSD	Elmont
162	2.1	Elwood UFSD	Greenlawn
162	2.1	NYC Geographic District # 1	New York
162	2.1	North Bellmore UFSD	Bellmore
162	2.1	Oneonta City SD	Oneonta
162	2.1	Peru Central SD	Peru
162	2.1	Pine Bush Central SD	Pine Bush
162	2.1	Webster Central SD	Webster
162	2.1	West Genesee Central SD	Camillus
162	2.1	West Seneca Central SD	West Seneca
162	2.1	Windsor Central SD	Windsor
176	2.0	Bay Shore UFSD	Bay Shore
176	2.0	Evans-Brant Central SD (Lake Shore)	Angola
176	2.0	Iroquois Central SD	Elma
176	2.0	Middle Country Central SD	Centereach
176	2.0	North Babylon UFSD	North Babylon
176	2.0	Northport-East Northport UFSD	Northport
176	2.0	West Islip UFSD	West Islip
183	1.9	Cornwall Central SD	Cornwall on Hdsn
183	1.9	Fayetteville-Manlius Central SD	Manlius
183	1.9	Great Neck UFSD	Great Neck
183	1.9	Peekskill City SD	Peekskill
183	1.9	Westhill Central SD	Syracuse
188	1.8	Burnt Hills-Ballston Lake Central SD	Scotia
188	1.8	Chenango Forks Central SD	Binghamton
188	1.8	Clarkstown Central SD	New City
188	1.8	East Hampton UFSD	East Hampton
188	1.8	Fairport Central SD	Fairport
188	1.8	Lancaster Central SD	Lancaster
188	1.8	Lewiston-Porter Central SD	Youngstown
188	1.8	Lynbrook UFSD	Lynbrook
188	1.8	Mahopac Central SD	Mahopac
188	1.8	Malverne UFSD	Malverne
188	1.8	Rocky Point UFSD	Rocky Point
188	1.8	Starpoint Central SD	Lockport
188	1.8	Wallkill Central SD	Wallkill
188	1.8	Wantagh UFSD	Wantagh
188	1.8	Warwick Valley Central SD	Warwick
203	1.7	Babylon UFSD	Babylon
203	1.7	Homer Central SD	Homer
203	1.7	NYC Geographic District #28	Jamaica
203	1.7	Oswego City SD	Oswego
203	1.7	Patchogue-Medford UFSD	Patchogue
203	1.7	Pleasantville UFSD	Pleasantville
203	1.7	Sachem Central SD	Lake Ronkonkoma
203	1.7	Sayville UFSD	Sayville
203	1.7	S Glens Fls Central SD	S Glens Fls
203	1.7	Sweet Home Central SD	Amherst
213	1.6	Brookhaven-Comsewogue UFSD	Port Jeff Stn
213	1.6	Camden Central SD	Camden
213	1.6	Central Square Central SD	Central Square
213	1.6	Fulton City SD	Fulton
213	1.6	Hicksville UFSD	Hicksville
213	1.6	Miller Place UFSD	Miller Place
219	1.5	Ardsley UFSD	Ardsley
219	1.5	Commack UFSD	East Northport
219	1.5	Hamburg Central SD	Hamburg
219	1.5	Hauppauge UFSD	Hauppauge
219	1.5	Haverstraw-Stony Point CSD	Garnerville
219	1.5	Livonia Central SD	Livonia
219	1.5	Manhasset UFSD	Manhasset
219	1.5	Mexico Central SD	Mexico
219	1.5	Putnam Valley Central SD	Putnam Valley
219	1.5	Queensbury UFSD	Queensbury
219	1.5	Riverhead Central SD	Riverhead
219	1.5	Shoreham-Wading River Central SD	Shoreham
219	1.5	Springville-Griffith Institute CSD	Springville
219	1.5	West Babylon UFSD	West Babylon
233	1.4	Cold Spring Hrbr Central SD	Cold Spring Hrbr
233	1.4	Dansville Central SD	Dansville
233	1.4	Farmingdale UFSD	Farmingdale
233	1.4	Franklin Square UFSD	Franklin Square
233	1.4	Freeport UFSD	Freeport
233	1.4	Garden City UFSD	Garden City
233	1.4	Goshen Central SD	Goshen
233	1.4	Mineola UFSD	Mineola
233	1.4	NYC Geographic District #31	Staten Island
233	1.4	Norwich City SD	Norwich
233	1.4	Syosset Central SD	Syosset
233	1.4	Wappingers Central SD	Hopewell Junction
233	1.4	Wayne Central SD	Ontario Center
246	1.3	Byram Hills Central SD	Armonk
246	1.3	Cobleskill-Richmondville CSD	Cobleskill
246	1.3	Copiague UFSD	Copiague
246	1.3	East Williston UFSD	Old Westbury
246	1.3	Locust Valley Central SD	Locust Valley
246	1.3	NYC Geographic District # 5	New York
246	1.3	NYC Geographic District #14	Brooklyn
246	1.3	Orchard Park Central SD	West Seneca
246	1.3	Owego-Apalachin Central SD	Owego
246	1.3	Sherrill City SD	Verona
246	1.3	South Jefferson Central SD	Adams Center
246	1.3	Yonkers City SD	Yonkers
258	1.2	Bayport-Blue Point UFSD	Bayport
258	1.2	Bethpage UFSD	Bethpage
258	1.2	Lakeland Central SD	Shrub Oak
258	1.2	Nanuet UFSD	Nanuet
258	1.2	NYC Geographic District #26	Bayside
258	1.2	Three Village Central SD	Stony Brook
258	1.2	New York City Chancellor's Office	New York
265	1.1	East Aurora UFSD	East Aurora
265	1.1	Harrison Central SD	Harrison
265	1.1	Herricks UFSD	New Hyde Park
265	1.1	Monroe-Woodbury Central SD	Central Valley
265	1.1	NYC Geographic District # 4	New York
265	1.1	NYC Geographic District #21	Brooklyn
265	1.1	NYC Geographic District #30	Long Isl City
265	1.1	Smithtown Central SD	Smithtown
273	1.0	Johnstown City SD	Johnstown
273	1.0	Levittown UFSD	Levittown
273	1.0	NYC Geographic District #22	Brooklyn
273	1.0	NYC Geographic District #29	Queens Village
273	1.0	Plainview-Old Bethpage CSD	Plainview
278	0.9	Ballston Spa Central SD	Ballston Spa
278	0.9	Bethlehem Central SD	Delmar
278	0.9	East Ramapo CSD (Spring Valley)	Spring Valley
278	0.9	Hampton Bays UFSD	Hampton Bays
278	0.9	Kinderhook Central SD	Valatie
278	0.9	Kings Park Central SD	Kings Park
278	0.9	Lindenhurst UFSD	Lindenhurst
278	0.9	NYC Geographic District #10	Bronx
278	0.9	NYC Geographic District #25	Flushing
278	0.9	NYC Geographic District #27	Ozone Park
278	0.9	North Tonawanda City SD	North Tonawanda
278	0.9	Rondout Valley Central SD	Accord
290	0.8	Connetquot Central SD	Bohemia
290	0.8	General Brown Central SD	Dexter
290	0.8	Glen Cove City SD	Glen Cove
290	0.8	Greenburgh Central SD	Hartsdale
290	0.8	Lawrence UFSD	Cedarhurst
290	0.8	Marcellus Central SD	Marcellus
290	0.8	New Rochelle City SD	New Rochelle
290	0.8	NYC Geographic District #17	Brooklyn
290	0.8	Phelps-Clifton Springs Central SD	Clifton Springs
290	0.8	Rye City SD	Rye
290	0.8	Waverly Central SD	Waverly
301	0.7	Eastport-South Manor CSD	Manorville
301	0.7	NYC Geographic District #20	Brooklyn
301	0.7	Seaford UFSD	Seaford
304	0.6	Alden Central SD	Alden
304	0.6	Central Valley CSD at Ilion-Mohawk	Ilion
304	0.6	Massapequa UFSD	Massapequa
304	0.6	NYC Geographic District # 6	New York
304	0.6	NYC Geographic District #11	Bronx
304	0.6	NYC Geographic District #18	Brooklyn
304	0.6	NYC Geographic District #24	Corona
304	0.6	Roslyn UFSD	Roslyn
304	0.6	Valley Stream Central High SD	Valley Stream
304	0.6	Yorkshire-Pioneer Central SD	Yorkshire
314	0.5	Broadalbin-Perth Central SD	Broadalbin
314	0.5	East Meadow UFSD	Westbury
314	0.5	Jericho UFSD	Jericho
314	0.5	Mount Pleasant Central SD	Thornwood
314	0.5	Mount Sinai UFSD	Mount Sinai
314	0.5	Mount Vernon SD	Mount Vernon
314	0.5	NYC Geographic District #16	Brooklyn
314	0.5	Pearl River UFSD	Pearl River
314	0.5	Plattsburgh City SD	Plattsburgh
314	0.5	Schuylerville Central SD	Schuylerville
314	0.5	Wyandanch UFSD	Wyandanch
325	0.4	Bellmore-Merrick Central High SD	North Merrick
325	0.4	Brentwood UFSD	Brentwood
325	0.4	Malone Central SD	Malone
325	0.4	NYC Geographic District # 7	Bronx
325	0.4	NYC Geographic District # 8	Bronx
325	0.4	Red Hook Central SD	Red Hook
325	0.4	Rome City SD	Rome
325	0.4	Uniondale UFSD	Uniondale
333	0.3	Hempstead UFSD	Hempstead
333	0.3	NYC Geographic District # 9	Bronx
333	0.3	NYC Geographic District #19	Brooklyn
333	0.3	NYC Geographic District #23	Brooklyn
333	0.3	Port Chester-Rye UFSD	Port Chester
333	0.3	Scotia-Glenville Central SD	Scotia
333	0.3	Sewanhaka Central High SD	Floral Park
333	0.3	Somers Central SD	Somers
341	0.2	Massena Central SD	Massena
341	0.2	NYC Geographic District #12	Bronx
341	0.2	NYC Geographic District #32	Brooklyn
341	0.2	Ogdensburg City SD	Ogdensburg
341	0.2	Westbury UFSD	Old Westbury
346	0.1	Albion Central SD	Albion
346	0.1	Bath Central SD	Bath
346	0.1	Central Islip UFSD	Central Islip
346	0.1	Gouverneur Central SD	Gouverneur
346	0.1	Island Trees UFSD	Levittown
346	0.1	Plainedge UFSD	N Massapequa
346	0.1	Rochester City SD	Rochester
346	0.1	Roosevelt UFSD	Roosevelt
354	0.0	Beekmantown Central SD	West Chazy
354	0.0	Center Moriches UFSD	Center Moriches
354	0.0	Minisink Valley Central SD	Slate Hill
354	0.0	Southampton UFSD	Southampton

Hispanic Students

Rank	Percent	District Name	City
1	85.7	NYC Geographic District # 6	New York
2	82.2	Brentwood UFSD	Brentwood
3	77.7	NYC Geographic District #32	Brooklyn
4	76.9	Port Chester-Rye UFSD	Port Chester
5	72.3	Central Islip UFSD	Central Islip
6	71.4	Westbury UFSD	Old Westbury
7	69.7	NYC Geographic District # 7	Bronx
8	69.3	NYC Geographic District #12	Bronx
9	68.6	NYC Geographic District #10	Bronx
10	67.3	NYC Geographic District # 9	Bronx
11	67.1	Hempstead UFSD	Hempstead
12	64.4	NYC Geographic District # 8	Bronx
13	63.6	Freeport UFSD	Freeport
14	62.8	Peekskill City SD	Peekskill
15	62.1	NYC Geographic District #24	Corona
16	60.9	NYC Geographic District # 4	New York
17	58.5	UFSD of the Tarrytowns	Sleepy Hollow
18	57.8	NYC Geographic District #14	Brooklyn
19	56.5	Copiague UFSD	Copiague
20	56.4	Glen Cove City SD	Glen Cove
21	56.3	Ossining UFSD	Ossining
22	56.3	Yonkers City SD	Yonkers
23	55.5	White Plains City SD	White Plains
24	54.9	Uniondale UFSD	Uniondale
25	53.9	Hampton Bays UFSD	Hampton Bays
26	53.6	Haverstraw-Stony Point CSD	Garnerville
27	53.5	NYC Geographic District #30	Long Isl City
28	52.2	East Ramapo CSD (Spring Valley)	Spring Valley
29	52.1	Middletown City SD	Middletown
30	52.0	Lawrence UFSD	Cedarhurst
31	50.8	Dunkirk City SD	Dunkirk
32	49.4	East Hampton UFSD	East Hampton
33	48.8	Newburgh City SD	Newburgh
34	47.1	Roosevelt UFSD	Roosevelt
35	46.3	Amityville UFSD	Amityville
36	46.0	Wyandanch UFSD	Wyandanch
37	45.6	New Rochelle City SD	New Rochelle
38	44.8	Huntington UFSD	Huntington Stn
39	43.1	Amsterdam City SD	Amsterdam
40	42.1	NYC Geographic District #19	Brooklyn
41	41.8	NYC Geographic District #11	Bronx
42	41.5	NYC Geographic District # 1	New York
43	40.6	New York City Chancellor's Office	New York
44	40.4	NYC Geographic District # 5	New York
44	40.4	Riverhead Central SD	Riverhead

Note: This section only includes districts with 1,500 or more students; All categories are ranked from high to low

Rank	Value	District	City
46	40.3	Bay Shore UFSD	Bay Shore
47	38.8	NYC Geographic District #15	Brooklyn
48	38.1	Patchogue-Medford UFSD	Patchogue
48	38.1	South Huntington UFSD	Huntington Stn
50	37.8	Greenburgh Central SD	Hartsdale
50	37.8	NYC Geographic District #27	Ozone Park
52	37.5	West Hempstead UFSD	West Hempstead
53	37.3	Liberty Central SD	Liberty
54	36.1	Southampton UFSD	Southampton
55	34.3	Ellenville Central SD	Ellenville
56	33.3	NYC Geographic District # 3	New York
57	32.8	NYC Geographic District # 2	New York
58	32.6	Poughkeepsie City SD	Poughkeepsie
59	32.3	South Country Central SD	East Patchogue
60	31.8	Bedford Central SD	Bedford
61	29.8	Hicksville UFSD	Hicksville
62	29.1	NYC Geographic District #25	Flushing
63	28.9	Brewster Central SD	Brewster
64	28.8	Elmont UFSD	Elmont
65	28.7	Valley Stream 30 UFSD	Valley Stream
66	28.3	Beacon City SD	Beacon
67	27.7	Geneva City SD	Geneva
67	27.7	NYC Geographic District #31	Staten Island
67	27.7	Rochester City SD	Rochester
70	27.4	Baldwin UFSD	Baldwin
71	27.2	Charter School for Applied Techs	Buffalo
72	27.1	Brookhaven-Comsewogue UFSD	Port Jeff Stn
72	27.1	William Floyd UFSD	Mastic Beach
74	26.9	Valley Stream 13 UFSD	Valley Stream
75	26.8	NYC Geographic District #28	Jamaica
76	26.7	Valley Stream Central High SD	Valley Stream
77	26.6	Monticello Central SD	Monticello
77	26.6	NYC Geographic District #20	Brooklyn
79	25.6	Mineola UFSD	Mineola
79	25.6	NYC Geographic District #21	Brooklyn
81	25.1	Long Beach City SD	Long Beach
82	24.6	Hendrick Hudson Central SD	Montrose
83	23.7	North Babylon UFSD	North Babylon
84	23.2	Longwood Central SD	Middle Island
85	23.1	Malverne UFSD	Malverne
85	23.1	Monroe-Woodbury Central SD	Central Valley
87	22.1	Islip UFSD	Islip
88	22.0	Carmel Central SD	Patterson
89	21.7	Nyack UFSD	Nyack
90	21.5	Wallkill Central SD	Wallkill
90	21.5	Westhampton Bch UFSD	Westhampton Bch
92	21.4	Deer Park UFSD	Deer Park
92	21.4	NYC Geographic District #23	Brooklyn
94	21.1	East Irondequoit Central SD	Rochester
95	20.8	Port Washington UFSD	Port Washington
95	20.8	Valley Central SD (Montgomery)	Montgomery
95	20.8	Washingtonville Central SD	Washingtonville
98	20.7	Mount Vernon SD	Mount Vernon
99	20.6	Farmingdale UFSD	Farmingdale
99	20.6	Oyster Bay-East Norwich Central SD	Oyster Bay
101	20.5	Mamaroneck UFSD	Mamaroneck
102	20.4	West Babylon UFSD	West Babylon
103	20.3	East Meadow UFSD	Westbury
103	20.3	NYC Geographic District #16	Brooklyn
105	19.9	Jamestown City SD	Jamestown
105	19.9	Lindenhurst UFSD	Lindenhurst
107	19.5	Franklin Square UFSD	Franklin Square
108	19.1	Kingston City SD	Kingston
108	19.1	Ramapo Central SD (Suffern)	Hillburn
110	18.9	Schenectady City SD	Schenectady
111	18.8	Buffalo City SD	Buffalo
112	18.7	Utica City SD	Utica
113	18.6	Middle Country Central SD	Centereach
114	18.1	Goshen Central SD	Goshen
114	18.1	Nanuet UFSD	Nanuet
116	17.9	Rye Neck UFSD	Mamaroneck
117	17.7	Lakeland Central SD	Shrub Oak
118	17.5	Sewanhaka Central High SD	Floral Park
119	17.4	Levittown UFSD	Levittown
119	17.4	Locust Valley Central SD	Locust Valley
121	17.3	Island Trees UFSD	Levittown
121	17.3	Marlboro Central SD	Milton
123	17.0	NYC Geographic District #26	Bayside
124	16.9	Harrison Central SD	Harrison
125	16.5	NYC Geographic District #13	Brooklyn
126	16.4	Albany City SD	Albany
126	16.4	Pine Bush Central SD	Pine Bush
128	16.3	New Hyde Pk-Garden City Pk UFSD	New Hyde Park
129	15.9	Pelham UFSD	Pelham
130	15.8	Croton-Harmon UFSD	Croton on Hdsn
130	15.8	Oceanside UFSD	Oceanside
132	15.7	Troy City SD	Troy
133	15.6	East Islip UFSD	Islip Terrace
134	15.5	Mahopac Central SD	Mahopac
135	15.4	Lynbrook UFSD	Lynbrook
135	15.4	NYC Geographic District #17	Brooklyn
137	15.3	Cornwall Central SD	Cornwall on Hdsn
137	15.3	Minisink Valley Central SD	Slate Hill
137	15.3	NYC Geographic District #22	Brooklyn
140	15.1	Elwood UFSD	Greenlawn
141	15.0	Clarkstown Central SD	New City
142	14.9	Putnam Valley Central SD	Putnam Valley
143	14.8	Wappingers Central SD	Hopewell Junction
144	14.7	NYC Geographic District #29	Queens Village
145	14.6	Hewlett-Woodmere UFSD	Woodmere
146	14.2	Hudson City SD	Hudson
147	14.0	Bethpage UFSD	Bethpage
148	13.9	Indian River Central SD	Philadelphia
149	13.8	Hyde Park Central SD	Hyde Park
150	13.5	Center Moriches UFSD	Center Moriches
151	13.3	Lackawanna City SD	Lackawanna
152	13.2	Port Jervis City SD	Port Jervis
152	13.2	South Orangetown Central SD	Blauvelt
152	13.2	Syracuse City SD	Syracuse
155	13.1	Yorktown Central SD	Yorktown Hgts
156	13.0	Greece Central SD	Rochester
157	12.9	Binghamton City SD	Binghamton
157	12.9	North Bellmore UFSD	Bellmore
159	12.4	Highland Central SD	Highland
159	12.4	Warwick Valley Central SD	Warwick
161	12.4	Arlington Central SD	Lagrangeville
161	12.1	Lansingburgh Central SD	Troy
163	12.0	Newark Central SD	Newark
164	11.9	Rockville Ctr UFSD	Rockville Ctr
164	11.9	Sachem Central SD	Lake Ronkonkoma
166	11.8	Ardsley UFSD	Ardsley
166	11.8	Babylon UFSD	Babylon
168	11.4	New Paltz Central SD	New Paltz
169	11.3	Albion Central SD	Albion
170	11.2	Connetquot Central SD	Bohemia
171	11.0	West Irondequoit Central SD	Rochester
172	10.9	Eastchester UFSD	Eastchester
173	10.8	Gates-Chili Central SD	Rochester
173	10.8	Saugerties Central SD	Saugerties
175	10.7	Fredonia Central SD	Fredonia
175	10.7	Mount Pleasant Central SD	Thornwood
175	10.7	Pearl River UFSD	Pearl River
175	10.7	Rocky Point UFSD	Rocky Point
179	10.6	Hastings-On-Hudson UFSD	Hastings on Hdsn
180	10.3	Harborfields Central SD	Greenlawn
181	10.0	Johnson City Central SD	Johnson City
182	9.9	Carthage Central SD	Carthage
183	9.8	Half Hollow Hills Central SD	Dix Hills
184	9.7	Catskill Central SD	Catskill
185	9.2	North Shore Central SD	Sea Cliff
186	9.1	Watertown City SD	Watertown
187	8.9	Pleasantville UFSD	Pleasantville
187	8.9	West Islip UFSD	West Islip
189	8.7	Katonah-Lewisboro UFSD	South Salem
190	8.5	Great Neck UFSD	Great Neck
191	8.0	Hauppauge UFSD	Hauppauge
192	7.8	Irvington UFSD	Irvington
193	7.7	Union-Endicott Central SD	Endicott
194	7.6	Bellmore-Merrick Central High SD	North Merrick
194	7.6	South Colonie Central SD	Albany
196	7.5	Batavia City SD	Batavia
196	7.5	Northport-East Northport UFSD	Northport
198	7.4	Lockport City SD	Lockport
198	7.4	NYC Geographic District #18	Brooklyn
200	7.3	Kenmore-Tonawanda UFSD	Buffalo
201	7.2	Brockport Central SD	Brockport
202	7.1	Cohoes City SD	Cohoes
202	7.1	Oneonta City SD	Oneonta
202	7.1	Roslyn UFSD	Roslyn
205	6.9	Smithtown Central SD	Smithtown
206	6.8	Mount Sinai UFSD	Mount Sinai
206	6.8	Red Hook Central SD	Red Hook
208	6.7	Edgemont UFSD	Scarsdale
209	6.6	Bayport-Blue Point UFSD	Bayport
209	6.6	Kings Park Central SD	Kings Park
209	6.6	Ravena-Coeymans-Selkirk Cent SD	Ravena
209	6.6	Scarsdale UFSD	Scarsdale
213	6.5	Commack UFSD	East Northport
213	6.5	Seaford UFSD	Seaford
215	6.4	Cheektowaga Central SD	Cheektowaga
215	6.4	Rush-Henrietta Central SD	Henrietta
217	6.3	Medina Central SD	Medina
217	6.3	Sayville UFSD	Sayville
219	6.2	Herricks UFSD	New Hyde Park
219	6.2	Miller Place UFSD	Miller Place
221	6.0	Manhasset UFSD	Manhasset
221	6.0	Shoreham-Wading River Central SD	Shoreham
221	6.0	Spencerport Central SD	Spencerport
221	6.0	Wantagh UFSD	Wantagh
225	5.9	Eastport-South Manor CSD	Manorville
225	5.9	Phelps-Clifton Springs Central SD	Clifton Springs
225	5.9	Rye City SD	Rye
228	5.8	Ithaca City SD	Ithaca
228	5.8	Niagara Falls City SD	Niagara Falls
230	5.7	Blind Brook-Rye UFSD	Rye Brook
230	5.7	Plainedge UFSD	N Massapequa
230	5.7	Rondout Valley Central SD	Accord
233	5.6	Churchville-Chili Central SD	Churchville
233	5.6	Rome City SD	Rome
233	5.6	Sweet Home Central SD	Amherst
236	5.5	Plainview-Old Bethpage CSD	Plainview
236	5.5	Shenendehowa Central SD	Clifton Park
238	5.4	East Greenbush Central SD	East Greenbush
239	5.3	Brighton Central SD	Rochester
239	5.3	East Williston UFSD	Old Westbury
239	5.3	Liverpool Central SD	Liverpool
239	5.3	Penfield Central SD	Rochester
239	5.3	Rotterdam-Mohonasen Central SD	Schenectady
239	5.3	Somers Central SD	Somers
245	5.2	Bronxville UFSD	Bronxville
245	5.2	Webster Central SD	Webster
247	5.1	Pittsford Central SD	Pittsford
248	5.0	Chappaqua Central SD	Chappaqua
248	5.0	North Colonie CSD	Latham
248	5.0	Oswego City SD	Oswego
248	5.0	Three Village Central SD	Stony Brook
252	4.9	Cobleskill-Richmondville CSD	Cobleskill
253	4.8	Victor Central SD	Victor
254	4.6	Byram Hills Central SD	Armonk
254	4.6	Cheektowaga-Maryvale UFSD	Cheektowaga
254	4.6	New Hartford Central SD	New Hartford
257	4.5	Gloversville City SD	Gloversville
258	4.4	Amherst Central SD	Amherst
258	4.4	Grand Island Central SD	Grand Island
260	4.3	Fulton City SD	Fulton
260	4.3	Hilton Central SD	Hilton
260	4.3	Schalmont Central SD	Schenectady
260	4.3	Tonawanda City SD	Tonawanda
264	4.2	Frontier Central SD	Hamburg
265	4.1	Kinderhook Central SD	Valatie
265	4.1	Palmyra-Macedon Central SD	Palmyra
267	4.0	Baldwinsville Central SD	Baldwinsville
267	4.0	Depew UFSD	Depew
269	3.9	Massapequa UFSD	Massapequa
269	3.9	North Syracuse Central SD	North Syracuse
269	3.9	Waterloo Central SD	Waterloo
272	3.8	Canandaigua City SD	Canandaigua
272	3.8	Glens Falls City SD	Glens Falls
272	3.8	Hudson Falls Central SD	Fort Edward
275	3.6	Auburn City SD	Auburn
275	3.6	Cortland City SD	Cortland
275	3.6	Syosset Central SD	Syosset
275	3.6	Williamsville Central SD	East Amherst
279	3.5	Cold Spring Hrbr Central SD	Cold Spring Hrbr
279	3.5	Fairport Central SD	Fairport
279	3.5	Garden City UFSD	Garden City
279	3.5	Jamesville-Dewitt Central SD	Dewitt
283	3.4	Guilderland Central SD	Guilderland Center
284	3.2	Dansville Central SD	Dansville
284	3.2	Olean City SD	Olean
284	3.2	Saratoga Spgs City SD	Saratoga Spgs
284	3.2	West Seneca Central SD	West Seneca
288	3.1	Norwich City SD	Norwich
289	3.0	Vestal Central SD	Vestal
290	2.9	Bethlehem Central SD	Delmar
290	2.9	Jericho UFSD	Jericho
290	2.9	Niskayuna Central SD	Schenectady
290	2.9	North Tonawanda City SD	North Tonawanda
290	2.9	Westhill Central SD	Syracuse
295	2.8	Chenango Forks Central SD	Binghamton
295	2.8	Johnstown City SD	Johnstown
295	2.8	Lancaster Central SD	Lancaster

Note: This section only includes districts with 1,500 or more students; All categories are ranked from high to low

Rank	Percent	District Name	City
295	2.8	Lewiston-Porter Central SD	Youngstown
295	2.8	Niagara-Wheatfield Central SD	Niagara Falls
295	2.8	West Genesee Central SD	Camillus
301	2.7	Evans-Brant Central SD (Lake Shore)	Angola
301	2.7	Fayetteville-Manlius Central SD	Manlius
301	2.7	Horseheads Central SD	Horseheads
301	2.7	Springville-Griffith Institute CSD	Springville
305	2.6	Chittenango Central SD	Chittenango
305	2.6	Dryden Central SD	Dryden
305	2.6	East Syracuse Minoa Central SD	East Syracuse
305	2.6	Honeoye Falls-Lima Central SD	Honeoye Falls
305	2.6	Maine-Endwell Central SD	Endwell
310	2.5	Whitesboro Central SD	Whitesboro
310	2.5	Windsor Central SD	Windsor
312	2.4	Clarence Central SD	Clarence
312	2.4	Newfane Central SD	Burt
312	2.4	Wayne Central SD	Ontario Center
315	2.3	Averill Park Central SD	Averill Park
315	2.3	East Aurora UFSD	East Aurora
315	2.3	Elmira City SD	Elmira
315	2.3	Schuylerville Central SD	Schuylerville
315	2.3	Scotia-Glenville Central SD	Scotia
320	2.2	Corning City SD	Painted Post
320	2.2	Hornell City SD	Hornell
320	2.2	Owego-Apalachin Central SD	Owego
320	2.2	S Glens Fls Central SD	S Glens Fls
324	2.1	Hamburg Central SD	Hamburg
324	2.1	Mexico Central SD	Mexico
324	2.1	Oneida City SD	Oneida
327	2.0	Susquehanna Valley Central SD	Conklin
328	1.9	Beekmantown Central SD	West Chazy
328	1.9	Camden Central SD	Camden
328	1.9	Chenango Valley Central SD	Binghamton
328	1.9	Orchard Park Central SD	West Seneca
332	1.8	Central Square Central SD	Central Square
332	1.8	Homer Central SD	Homer
334	1.7	Ballston Spa Central SD	Ballston Spa
334	1.7	Queensbury UFSD	Queensbury
336	1.6	Broadalbin-Perth Central SD	Broadalbin
336	1.6	General Brown Central SD	Dexter
336	1.6	Gouverneur Central SD	Gouverneur
336	1.6	Starpoint Central SD	Lockport
340	1.5	Burnt Hills-Ballston Lake Central SD	Scotia
340	1.5	Iroquois Central SD	Elma
340	1.5	Livonia Central SD	Livonia
340	1.5	Massena Central SD	Massena
340	1.5	Phoenix Central SD	Phoenix
340	1.5	Yorkshire-Pioneer Central SD	Yorkshire
346	1.3	Salmon River Central SD	Fort Covington
346	1.3	South Jefferson Central SD	Adams Center
348	1.1	Alden Central SD	Alden
348	1.1	Peru Central SD	Peru
348	1.1	Sherrill City SD	Verona
348	1.1	Waverly Central SD	Waverly
352	0.9	Bath Central SD	Bath
353	0.8	Central Valley CSD at Ilion-Mohawk	Ilion
353	0.8	Malone Central SD	Malone
355	0.7	Marcellus Central SD	Marcellus
355	0.7	Plattsburgh City SD	Plattsburgh
357	0.3	Ogdensburg City SD	Ogdensburg

Individual Education Program Students

Rank	Percent	District Name	City
1	39.7	Lawrence UFSD	Cedarhurst
2	37.5	NYC Geographic District #16	Brooklyn
3	35.5	NYC Geographic District # 5	New York
4	33.1	NYC Geographic District #23	Brooklyn
5	33.0	East Ramapo CSD (Spring Valley)	Spring Valley
6	31.1	NYC Geographic District #17	Brooklyn
7	30.9	NYC Geographic District # 7	Bronx
7	30.9	NYC Geographic District # 8	Bronx
9	29.9	NYC Geographic District #21	Brooklyn
10	29.7	NYC Geographic District # 4	New York
11	28.2	NYC Geographic District #22	Brooklyn
12	27.9	NYC Geographic District #19	Brooklyn
13	27.6	Buffalo City SD	Buffalo
14	27.5	NYC Geographic District # 9	Bronx
14	27.5	NYC Geographic District #31	Staten Island
16	26.6	NYC Geographic District #12	Bronx
17	26.5	Lackawanna City SD	Lackawanna
18	26.0	Kingston City SD	Kingston
19	25.7	NYC Geographic District #11	Bronx
20	25.4	NYC Geographic District #14	Brooklyn
21	24.9	NYC Geographic District #32	Brooklyn
22	24.7	Kenmore-Tonawanda UFSD	Buffalo
22	24.7	NYC Geographic District #18	Brooklyn
24	24.5	NYC Geographic District #20	Brooklyn
25	24.2	NYC Geographic District #10	Bronx
26	24.0	Plattsburgh City SD	Plattsburgh
27	23.8	NYC Geographic District # 6	New York
28	23.7	North Tonawanda City SD	North Tonawanda
29	23.3	Port Jervis City SD	Port Jervis
30	23.0	NYC Geographic District #27	Ozone Park
31	22.9	Rochester City SD	Rochester
32	22.6	NYC Geographic District # 1	New York
33	21.9	Troy City SD	Troy
34	21.7	NYC Geographic District #15	Brooklyn
34	21.7	NYC Geographic District #29	Queens Village
34	21.7	New York City Chancellor's Office	New York
37	21.6	Saugerties Central SD	Saugerties
38	21.1	Greenburgh Central SD	Hartsdale
39	21.0	Lockport City SD	Lockport
39	21.0	Mount Vernon	Mount Vernon
39	21.0	Valley Central SD (Montgomery)	Montgomery
42	20.9	North Bellmore UFSD	Bellmore
42	20.9	Syracuse City SD	Syracuse
44	20.7	Hudson City SD	Hudson
44	20.7	Malverne UFSD	Malverne
46	20.5	Ellenville Central SD	Ellenville
46	20.5	Schenectady City SD	Schenectady
48	20.4	Hewlett-Woodmere UFSD	Woodmere
48	20.4	Locust Valley Central SD	Locust Valley
50	20.3	Catskill Central SD	Catskill
50	20.3	Monticello Central SD	Monticello
50	20.3	West Islip UFSD	West Islip
53	20.2	Gloversville City SD	Gloversville
54	20.1	Norwich City SD	Norwich
55	20.0	Lansingburgh Central SD	Troy
55	20.0	Oneonta City SD	Oneonta
55	20.0	Rondout Valley Central SD	Accord
58	19.9	Beacon City SD	Beacon
58	19.9	Longwood Central SD	Middle Island
58	19.9	NYC Geographic District # 3	New York
61	19.7	Liverpool Central SD	Liverpool
61	19.7	Poughkeepsie City SD	Poughkeepsie
63	19.6	Half Hollow Hills Central SD	Dix Hills
64	19.4	Frontier Central SD	Hamburg
64	19.4	Niagara Falls City SD	Niagara Falls
64	19.4	Wyandanch UFSD	Wyandanch
67	19.3	Corning City SD	Painted Post
67	19.3	Evans-Brant Central SD (Lake Shore)	Angola
67	19.3	Long Beach City SD	Long Beach
67	19.3	West Hempstead UFSD	West Hempstead
71	19.2	Depew UFSD	Depew
71	19.2	NYC Geographic District #24	Corona
73	19.1	Mahopac Central SD	Mahopac
74	19.0	Dryden Central SD	Dryden
74	19.0	Lewiston-Porter Central SD	Youngstown
76	18.9	Commack UFSD	East Northport
77	18.8	Hudson Falls Central SD	Fort Edward
77	18.8	Yorkshire-Pioneer Central SD	Yorkshire
79	18.7	Gates-Chili Central SD	Rochester
79	18.7	Gouverneur Central SD	Gouverneur
79	18.7	Oswego City SD	Oswego
82	18.6	Glen Cove City SD	Glen Cove
82	18.6	Hornell City SD	Hornell
84	18.5	Mount Pleasant Central SD	Thornwood
84	18.5	Peru Central SD	Peru
84	18.5	Yonkers City SD	Yonkers
87	18.4	Averill Park Central SD	Averill Park
87	18.4	Cheektowaga Central SD	Cheektowaga
87	18.4	Owego-Apalachin Central SD	Owego
87	18.4	Peekskill City SD	Peekskill
91	18.3	Baldwin UFSD	Baldwin
91	18.3	Beekmantown Central SD	West Chazy
91	18.3	Dansville Central SD	Dansville
91	18.3	East Greenbush Central SD	East Greenbush
91	18.3	NYC Geographic District #28	Jamaica
96	18.2	Hyde Park Central SD	Hyde Park
97	18.1	Glens Falls City SD	Glens Falls
97	18.1	Maine-Endwell Central SD	Endwell
97	18.1	Minisink Valley Central SD	Slate Hill
97	18.1	Rocky Point UFSD	Rocky Point
101	18.0	Kings Park Central SD	Kings Park
101	18.0	Newburgh City SD	Newburgh
103	17.9	Connetquot Central SD	Bohemia
103	17.9	Monroe-Woodbury Central SD	Central Valley
105	17.8	Fulton City SD	Fulton
105	17.8	Goshen Central SD	Goshen
105	17.8	Lindenhurst UFSD	Lindenhurst
105	17.8	Olean City SD	Olean
105	17.8	Seaford UFSD	Seaford
105	17.8	Watertown City SD	Watertown
111	17.7	Bayport-Blue Point UFSD	Bayport
111	17.7	Lancaster Central SD	Lancaster
111	17.7	Marlboro Central SD	Milton
111	17.7	NYC Geographic District #30	Long Isl City
115	17.6	Clarkstown Central SD	New City
115	17.6	East Syracuse Minoa Central SD	East Syracuse
115	17.6	Middletown City SD	Middletown
115	17.6	NYC Geographic District # 2	New York
115	17.6	Wappingers Central SD	Hopewell Junction
120	17.5	Kinderhook Central SD	Valatie
120	17.5	North Shore Central SD	Sea Cliff
120	17.5	Whitesboro Central SD	Whitesboro
123	17.4	Huntington UFSD	Huntington Stn
123	17.4	Oneida City SD	Oneida
123	17.4	Scotia-Glenville Central SD	Scotia
123	17.4	South Huntington UFSD	Huntington Stn
127	17.3	Amityville UFSD	Amityville
127	17.3	NYC Geographic District #13	Brooklyn
127	17.3	Waterloo Central SD	Waterloo
127	17.3	West Babylon UFSD	West Babylon
131	17.2	Deer Park UFSD	Deer Park
131	17.2	New Paltz Central SD	New Paltz
131	17.2	Riverhead Central SD	Riverhead
134	17.1	Binghamton City SD	Binghamton
134	17.1	Eastport-South Manor CSD	Manorville
134	17.1	Massena Central SD	Massena
134	17.1	Mineola UFSD	Mineola
134	17.1	Newfane Central SD	Burt
134	17.1	Orchard Park Central SD	West Seneca
134	17.1	Shoreham-Wading River Central SD	Shoreham
141	17.0	Cohoes City SD	Cohoes
141	17.0	North Babylon UFSD	North Babylon
141	17.0	Ogdensburg City SD	Ogdensburg
141	17.0	Utica City SD	Utica
141	17.0	White Plains City SD	White Plains
146	16.9	Arlington Central SD	Lagrangeville
146	16.9	Lakeland Central SD	Shrub Oak
148	16.8	Carthage Central SD	Carthage
148	16.8	Katonah-Lewisboro UFSD	South Salem
148	16.8	Port Washington UFSD	Port Washington
148	16.8	Southampton UFSD	Southampton
152	16.7	Center Moriches UFSD	Center Moriches
152	16.7	Hamburg Central SD	Hamburg
152	16.7	Somers Central SD	Somers
155	16.6	NYC Geographic District #25	Flushing
155	16.6	Smithtown Central SD	Smithtown
157	16.5	Albany City SD	Albany
157	16.5	Chenango Valley Central SD	Binghamton
157	16.5	Johnson City Central SD	Johnson City
157	16.5	Pine Bush Central SD	Pine Bush
157	16.5	South Jefferson Central SD	Adams Center
157	16.5	Union-Endicott Central SD	Endicott
163	16.4	Auburn City SD	Auburn
163	16.4	Bath Central SD	Bath
163	16.4	Brighton Central SD	Rochester
163	16.4	Elmira City SD	Elmira
163	16.4	Harborfields Central SD	Greenlawn
163	16.4	Mexico Central SD	Mexico
163	16.4	Middle Country Central SD	Centereach
163	16.4	Northport-East Northport UFSD	Northport
163	16.4	Phelps-Clifton Springs Central SD	Clifton Springs
163	16.4	Pleasantville UFSD	Pleasantville
163	16.4	Rome City SD	Rome
174	16.3	Babylon UFSD	Babylon
174	16.3	Ballston Spa Central SD	Ballston Spa
174	16.3	General Brown Central SD	Dexter
174	16.3	Warwick Valley Central SD	Warwick
178	16.2	Brookhaven-Comsewogue UFSD	Port Jeff Stn
178	16.2	Highland Central SD	Highland
178	16.2	Ramapo Central SD (Suffern)	Hillburn
178	16.2	South Colonie Central SD	Albany
182	16.1	Great Neck UFSD	Great Neck
182	16.1	Oyster Bay-East Norwich Central SD	Oyster Bay
182	16.1	Sachem Central SD	Lake Ronkonkoma
185	16.0	Iroquois Central SD	Elma
185	16.0	Ravena-Coeymans-Selkirk Cent SD	Ravena
185	16.0	Yorktown Central SD	Yorktown Hgts

Note: This section only includes districts with 1,500 or more students; All categories are ranked from high to low

188	15.9	Cheektowaga-Maryvale UFSD	Cheektowaga
188	15.9	Jericho UFSD	Jericho
188	15.9	North Syracuse Central SD	North Syracuse
188	15.9	Plainview-Old Bethpage CSD	Plainview
192	15.8	Amherst Central SD	Amherst
192	15.8	Bay Shore UFSD	Bay Shore
192	15.8	Byram Hills Central SD	Armonk
192	15.8	Central Square Central SD	Central Square
192	15.8	Guilderland Central SD	Guilderland Center
192	15.8	New Rochelle City SD	New Rochelle
192	15.8	South Country Central SD	East Patchogue
199	15.7	Amsterdam City SD	Amsterdam
199	15.7	Geneva City SD	Geneva
199	15.7	Tonawanda City SD	Tonawanda
199	15.7	West Seneca Central SD	West Seneca
199	15.7	Westhill Central SD	Syracuse
204	15.6	Carmel Central SD	Patterson
204	15.6	East Islip UFSD	Islip Terrace
204	15.6	Malone Central SD	Malone
204	15.6	Miller Place UFSD	Miller Place
208	15.5	Brewster Central SD	Brewster
208	15.5	Putnam Valley Central SD	Putnam Valley
210	15.4	Canandaigua City SD	Canandaigua
210	15.4	Farmingdale UFSD	Farmingdale
210	15.4	Nyack UFSD	Nyack
210	15.4	Queensbury UFSD	Queensbury
210	15.4	Rockville Ctr UFSD	Rockville Ctr
215	15.3	Baldwinsville Central SD	Baldwinsville
215	15.3	Copiague UFSD	Copiague
215	15.3	Hauppauge UFSD	Hauppauge
215	15.3	Islip UFSD	Islip
215	15.3	Mamaroneck UFSD	Mamaroneck
215	15.3	Wantagh UFSD	Wantagh
215	15.3	William Floyd UFSD	Mastic Beach
222	15.2	Central Valley CSD at Ilion-Mohawk	Ilion
222	15.2	Chittenango Central SD	Chittenango
222	15.2	East Aurora UFSD	East Aurora
222	15.2	Eastchester UFSD	Eastchester
222	15.2	North Colonie CSD	Latham
222	15.2	Rotterdam-Mohonasen Central SD	Schenectady
222	15.2	Wallkill Central SD	Wallkill
222	15.2	West Genesee Central SD	Camillus
230	15.1	Cortland City SD	Cortland
230	15.1	Freeport UFSD	Freeport
230	15.1	Lynbrook UFSD	Lynbrook
233	15.0	Levittown UFSD	Levittown
233	15.0	Niagara-Wheatfield Central SD	Niagara Falls
233	15.0	Valley Stream Central High SD	Valley Stream
236	14.9	Bethpage UFSD	Bethpage
236	14.9	Haverstraw-Stony Point CSD	Garnerville
236	14.9	Indian River Central SD	Philadelphia
236	14.9	Palmyra-Macedon Central SD	Palmyra
240	14.8	Hendrick Hudson Central SD	Montrose
240	14.8	Herricks UFSD	New Hyde Park
240	14.8	Liberty Central SD	Liberty
240	14.8	NYC Geographic District #26	Bayside
240	14.8	S Glens Fls Central SD	S Glens Fls
240	14.8	Three Village Central SD	Stony Brook
240	14.8	Valley Stream 13 UFSD	Valley Stream
247	14.7	Grand Island Central SD	Grand Island
247	14.7	Red Hook Central SD	Red Hook
247	14.7	Sayville UFSD	Sayville
250	14.6	Alden Central SD	Alden
250	14.6	Camden Central SD	Camden
250	14.6	Fairport Central SD	Fairport
250	14.6	Hicksville UFSD	Hicksville
254	14.5	Bellmore-Merrick Central High SD	North Merrick
254	14.5	Clarence Central SD	Clarence
256	14.4	Brockport Central SD	Brockport
256	14.4	Ithaca City SD	Ithaca
256	14.4	Medina Central SD	Medina
256	14.4	Salmon River Central SD	Fort Covington
256	14.4	Spencerport Central SD	Spencerport
256	14.4	Starpoint Central SD	Lockport
262	14.3	Brentwood UFSD	Brentwood
262	14.3	Cornwall Central SD	Cornwall on Hdsn
262	14.3	Honeoye Falls-Lima Central SD	Honeoye Falls
262	14.3	Wayne Central SD	Ontario Center
266	14.2	Manhasset UFSD	Manhasset
266	14.2	Port Chester-Rye UFSD	Port Chester
268	14.1	Washingtonville Central SD	Washingtonville
269	14.0	Pearl River UFSD	Pearl River
269	14.0	Roosevelt UFSD	Roosevelt
269	14.0	Schalmont Central SD	Schenectady
269	14.0	Vestal Central SD	Vestal
273	13.9	Burnt Hills-Ballston Lake Central SD	Scotia
273	13.9	Chenango Forks Central SD	Binghamton
273	13.9	Churchville-Chili Central SD	Churchville
273	13.9	Greece Central SD	Rochester
273	13.9	Hempstead UFSD	Hempstead
273	13.9	Irvington UFSD	Irvington
273	13.9	Uniondale UFSD	Uniondale
273	13.9	Waverly Central SD	Waverly
281	13.8	Jamesville-Dewitt Central SD	Dewitt
281	13.8	Oceanside UFSD	Oceanside
281	13.8	Patchogue-Medford UFSD	Patchogue
284	13.6	East Meadow UFSD	Westbury
284	13.6	Garden City UFSD	Garden City
284	13.6	Nanuet UFSD	Nanuet
284	13.6	Susquehanna Valley Central SD	Conklin
288	13.5	Westbury UFSD	Old Westbury
288	13.5	Windsor Central SD	Windsor
290	13.4	Ardsley UFSD	Ardsley
291	13.3	Homer Central SD	Homer
291	13.3	New Hyde Pk-Garden City Pk UFSD	New Hyde Park
291	13.3	Westhampton Bch UFSD	Westhampton Bch
294	13.2	Jamestown City SD	Jamestown
295	13.1	Batavia City SD	Batavia
295	13.1	Bedford Central SD	Bedford
295	13.1	Hastings-On-Hudson UFSD	Hastings on Hdsn
295	13.1	Horseheads Central SD	Horseheads
295	13.1	UFSD of the Tarrytowns	Sleepy Hollow
300	13.0	Albion Central SD	Albion
300	13.0	Croton-Harmon UFSD	Croton on Hdsn
300	13.0	Island Trees UFSD	Levittown
300	13.0	Newark Central SD	Newark
300	13.0	Springville-Griffith Institute CSD	Springville
305	12.8	Central Islip UFSD	Central Islip
305	12.8	Franklin Square UFSD	Franklin Square
305	12.8	Mount Sinai UFSD	Mount Sinai
308	12.7	East Irondequoit Central SD	Rochester
308	12.7	Johnstown City SD	Johnstown
308	12.7	Sewanhaka Central High SD	Floral Park
311	12.6	Bethlehem Central SD	Delmar
311	12.6	Edgemont UFSD	Scarsdale
311	12.6	Plainedge UFSD	N Massapequa
314	12.5	Harrison Central SD	Harrison
314	12.5	Marcellus Central SD	Marcellus
314	12.5	Saratoga Spgs City SD	Saratoga Spgs
317	12.4	Fredonia Central SD	Fredonia
317	12.4	Ossining UFSD	Ossining
317	12.4	South Orangetown Central SD	Blauvelt
320	12.3	Pelham UFSD	Pelham
320	12.3	Syosset Central SD	Syosset
322	12.2	Elwood UFSD	Greenlawn
322	12.2	Sherrill City SD	Verona
324	12.1	New Hartford Central SD	New Hartford
324	12.1	West Irondequoit Central SD	Rochester
324	12.1	Williamsville Central SD	East Amherst
327	12.0	Hampton Bays UFSD	Hampton Bays
328	11.9	Dunkirk City SD	Dunkirk
328	11.9	Niskayuna Central SD	Schenectady
328	11.9	Rye Neck UFSD	Mamaroneck
331	11.8	Massapequa UFSD	Massapequa
331	11.8	Valley Stream 30 UFSD	Valley Stream
333	11.7	Rush-Henrietta Central SD	Henrietta
334	11.5	East Hampton UFSD	East Hampton
334	11.5	Elmont UFSD	Elmont
334	11.5	Phoenix Central SD	Phoenix
337	11.3	Pittsford Central SD	Pittsford
338	11.2	East Williston UFSD	Old Westbury
339	11.1	Broadalbin-Perth Central SD	Broadalbin
339	11.1	Hilton Central SD	Hilton
339	11.1	Shenendehowa Central SD	Clifton Park
342	10.9	Cold Spring Hrbr Central SD	Cold Spring Hrbr
343	10.8	Chappaqua Central SD	Chappaqua
344	10.7	Schuylerville Central SD	Schuylerville
345	10.6	Fayetteville-Manlius Central SD	Manlius
345	10.6	Webster Central SD	Webster
347	10.4	Penfield Central SD	Rochester
348	10.3	Victor Central SD	Victor
349	10.1	Roslyn UFSD	Roslyn
350	10.0	Cobleskill-Richmondville CSD	Cobleskill
350	10.0	Scarsdale UFSD	Scarsdale
352	9.9	Livonia Central SD	Livonia
352	9.9	Rye City SD	Rye
354	9.8	Sweet Home Central SD	Amherst
355	9.1	Bronxville UFSD	Bronxville
n/a	n/a	Blind Brook-Rye UFSD	Rye Brook
n/a	n/a	Charter School for Applied Techs	Buffalo

English Language Learner Students

Rank	Percent	District Name	City
1	33.7	Hempstead UFSD	Hempstead
2	31.1	Westbury UFSD	Old Westbury
3	29.6	Brentwood UFSD	Brentwood
4	29.1	East Ramapo CSD (Spring Valley)	Spring Valley
5	28.0	NYC Geographic District # 6	New York
6	26.0	Central Islip UFSD	Central Islip
7	25.8	Port Chester-Rye UFSD	Port Chester
8	24.6	NYC Geographic District #20	Brooklyn
9	23.1	NYC Geographic District # 9	Bronx
10	23.0	Roosevelt UFSD	Roosevelt
11	22.6	NYC Geographic District #24	Corona
12	20.7	Riverhead Central SD	Riverhead
13	20.5	Hampton Bays UFSD	Hampton Bays
13	20.5	Wyandanch UFSD	Wyandanch
15	20.2	Peekskill City SD	Peekskill
16	20.0	NYC Geographic District #10	Bronx
17	19.9	NYC Geographic District #32	Brooklyn
18	18.6	Amityville UFSD	Amityville
18	18.6	NYC Geographic District #12	Bronx
20	18.1	Freeport UFSD	Freeport
20	18.1	Uniondale UFSD	Uniondale
22	18.0	NYC Geographic District #25	Flushing
23	17.6	NYC Geographic District #30	Long Isl City
24	17.3	NYC Geographic District #15	Brooklyn
25	16.9	Lackawanna City SD	Lackawanna
25	16.9	NYC Geographic District # 7	Bronx
27	16.5	Utica City SD	Utica
28	16.2	Lawrence UFSD	Cedarhurst
29	16.1	Huntington UFSD	Huntington Stn
30	16.0	NYC Geographic District #21	Brooklyn
31	15.1	East Hampton UFSD	East Hampton
32	15.0	Glen Cove City SD	Glen Cove
33	14.8	White Plains City SD	White Plains
34	14.6	Syracuse City SD	Syracuse
34	14.6	UFSD of the Tarrytowns	Sleepy Hollow
36	14.2	South Huntington UFSD	Huntington Stn
37	14.1	Copiague UFSD	Copiague
38	13.7	Buffalo City SD	Buffalo
39	13.0	Newburgh City SD	Newburgh
39	13.0	New York City Chancellor's Office	New York
41	12.7	Rochester City SD	Rochester
42	12.5	NYC Geographic District # 8	Bronx
42	12.5	Southampton UFSD	Southampton
44	12.1	Middletown City SD	Middletown
45	11.9	Dunkirk City SD	Dunkirk
46	11.8	Bedford Central SD	Bedford
46	11.8	NYC Geographic District #19	Brooklyn
48	11.2	Patchogue-Medford UFSD	Patchogue
48	11.2	Yonkers City SD	Yonkers
50	10.4	New Rochelle City SD	New Rochelle
50	10.4	NYC Geographic District # 4	New York
50	10.4	NYC Geographic District #14	Brooklyn
53	10.2	NYC Geographic District #22	Brooklyn
54	10.0	NYC Geographic District #11	Bronx
55	9.9	NYC Geographic District #27	Ozone Park
56	9.8	Poughkeepsie City SD	Poughkeepsie
57	9.7	NYC Geographic District # 5	New York
57	9.5	NYC Geographic District #17	Brooklyn
58	9.5	NYC Geographic District #28	Jamaica
58	9.5	Ossining UFSD	Ossining
61	9.3	Mineola UFSD	Mineola
61	9.3	NYC Geographic District # 1	New York
63	9.1	Albany City SD	Albany
64	9.0	South Country Central SD	East Patchogue
65	8.9	Hicksville UFSD	Hicksville
66	8.5	Valley Stream 30 UFSD	Valley Stream
67	8.4	Port Washington UFSD	Port Washington
68	8.3	Geneva City SD	Geneva
68	8.3	Mount Vernon SD	Mount Vernon
68	8.3	NYC Geographic District # 2	New York
71	7.7	Hudson City SD	Hudson
72	7.6	West Hempstead UFSD	West Hempstead
73	7.3	NYC Geographic District #29	Queens Village
74	7.2	Harrison Central SD	Harrison
75	7.0	Bay Shore UFSD	Bay Shore
75	7.0	Brewster Central SD	Brewster
77	6.7	NYC Geographic District #26	Bayside

Note: This section only includes districts with 1,500 or more students; All categories are ranked from high to low

Rank	Value	District	City	Rank	Value	District	City	Rank	Value	District	City
78	6.6	Liberty Central SD	Liberty	159	2.2	Clarkstown Central SD	New City	245	0.9	Brockport Central SD	Brockport
79	6.5	Nyack UFSD	Nyack	159	2.2	Edgemont UFSD	Scarsdale	245	0.9	Carthage Central SD	Carthage
80	6.4	Oyster Bay-East Norwich Central SD	Oyster Bay	159	2.2	Mahopac Central SD	Mahopac	245	0.9	Corning City SD	Painted Post
81	5.9	Brookhaven-Comsewogue UFSD	Port Jeff Stn	159	2.2	New Paltz Central SD	New Paltz	245	0.9	East Greenbush Central SD	East Greenbush
81	5.9	Greenburgh Central SD	Hartsdale	159	2.2	Niskayuna Central SD	Schenectady	245	0.9	Highland Central SD	Highland
81	5.9	New Hyde Pk-Garden City Pk UFSD	New Hyde Park	159	2.2	South Colonie Central SD	Albany	245	0.9	Katonah-Lewisboro UFSD	South Salem
84	5.8	Westhampton Bch UFSD	Westhampton Bch	159	2.2	Williamsville Central SD	East Amherst	245	0.9	Kings Park Central SD	Kings Park
85	5.7	Elmont UFSD	Elmont	169	2.1	East Syracuse Minoa Central SD	East Syracuse	245	0.9	North Tonawanda City SD	North Tonawanda
86	5.6	Eastchester UFSD	Eastchester	169	2.1	Harborfields Central SD	Greenlawn	245	0.9	Port Jervis City SD	Port Jervis
87	5.2	NYC Geographic District # 3	New York	169	2.1	Hyde Park Central SD	Hyde Park	245	0.9	Smithtown Central SD	Smithtown
87	5.2	NYC Geographic District #31	Staten Island	169	2.1	Pine Bush Central SD	Pine Bush	245	0.9	Somers Central SD	Somers
89	5.1	NYC Geographic District #23	Brooklyn	169	2.1	Pleasantville UFSD	Pleasantville	245	0.9	Three Village Central SD	Stony Brook
89	5.1	Rush-Henrietta Central SD	Henrietta	174	2.0	Ardsley UFSD	Ardsley	245	0.9	Whitesboro Central SD	Whitesboro
91	5.0	NYC Geographic District #16	Brooklyn	174	2.0	Lansingburgh Central SD	Troy	259	0.8	Cornwall Central SD	Cornwall on Hdsn
92	4.9	Baldwin UFSD	Baldwin	174	2.0	North Shore Central SD	Sea Cliff	259	0.8	Dansville Central SD	Dansville
93	4.7	NYC Geographic District #18	Brooklyn	174	2.0	Phelps-Clifton Springs Central SD	Clifton Springs	259	0.8	Pittsford Central SD	Pittsford
94	4.6	Herricks UFSD	New Hyde Park	174	2.0	Syosset Central SD	Syosset	259	0.8	Rondout Valley Central SD	Accord
94	4.6	NYC Geographic District #13	Brooklyn	174	2.0	Wallkill Central SD	Wallkill	263	0.7	Bronxville UFSD	Bronxville
94	4.6	Sweet Home Central SD	Amherst	180	1.9	Hauppauge UFSD	Hauppauge	263	0.7	Frontier Central SD	Hamburg
97	4.5	Great Neck UFSD	Great Neck	180	1.9	Mount Pleasant Central SD	Thornwood	263	0.7	North Syracuse Central SD	North Syracuse
97	4.5	Ithaca City SD	Ithaca	180	1.9	Sachem Central SD	Lake Ronkonkoma	263	0.7	Plattsburgh City SD	Plattsburgh
97	4.5	Kingston City SD	Kingston	180	1.9	Scarsdale UFSD	Scarsdale	263	0.7	Schuylerville Central SD	Schuylerville
97	4.5	Longwood Central SD	Middle Island	180	1.9	Spencerport Central SD	Spencerport	263	0.7	Union-Endicott Central SD	Endicott
101	4.4	Deer Park UFSD	Deer Park	185	1.8	Catskill Central SD	Catskill	263	0.7	Wantagh UFSD	Wantagh
101	4.4	Jamestown City SD	Jamestown	185	1.8	Fredonia Central SD	Fredonia	263	0.7	West Seneca Central SD	West Seneca
101	4.4	Mamaroneck UFSD	Mamaroneck	185	1.8	Half Hollow Hills Central SD	Dix Hills	271	0.6	Canandaigua City SD	Canandaigua
101	4.4	Valley Stream 13 UFSD	Valley Stream	185	1.8	Hendrick Hudson Central SD	Montrose	271	0.6	Cold Spring Hrbr Central SD	Cold Spring Hrbr
101	4.4	William Floyd UFSD	Mastic Beach	185	1.8	Liverpool Central SD	Liverpool	271	0.6	Fayetteville-Manlius Central SD	Manlius
106	4.3	Binghamton City SD	Binghamton	185	1.8	North Bellmore UFSD	Bellmore	271	0.6	Gouverneur Central SD	Gouverneur
106	4.3	Ellenville Central SD	Ellenville	185	1.8	Northport-East Northport UFSD	Northport	271	0.6	Haverstraw-Stony Point CSD	Garnerville
106	4.3	West Babylon UFSD	West Babylon	185	1.8	Yorktown Central SD	Yorktown Hgts	271	0.6	Hudson Falls Central SD	Fort Edward
109	4.2	Amherst Central SD	Amherst	193	1.7	Arlington Central SD	Lagrangeville	271	0.6	Mount Sinai UFSD	Mount Sinai
109	4.2	Amsterdam City SD	Amsterdam	193	1.7	Connetquot Central SD	Bohemia	271	0.6	Niagara-Wheatfield Central SD	Niagara Falls
109	4.2	Islip UFSD	Islip	193	1.7	Jamesville-Dewitt Central SD	Dewitt	271	0.6	Ravena-Coeymans-Selkirk Cent SD	Ravena
109	4.2	Long Beach City SD	Long Beach	193	1.7	Levittown UFSD	Levittown	271	0.6	Shoreham-Wading River Central SD	Shoreham
113	4.1	Kinderhook Central SD	Valatie	193	1.7	Manhasset UFSD	Manhasset	271	0.6	Tonawanda City SD	Tonawanda
113	4.1	Middle Country Central SD	Centereach	193	1.7	Webster Central SD	Webster	271	0.6	West Islip UFSD	West Islip
113	4.1	Nanuet UFSD	Nanuet	199	1.6	Grand Island Central SD	Grand Island	283	0.5	Auburn City SD	Auburn
113	4.1	North Babylon UFSD	North Babylon	199	1.6	Lynbrook UFSD	Lynbrook	283	0.5	Baldwinsville Central SD	Baldwinsville
117	4.0	Ramapo Central SD (Suffern)	Hillburn	199	1.6	Plainedge UFSD	N Massapequa	283	0.5	Bellmore-Merrick Central High SD	North Merrick
118	3.9	East Irondequoit Central SD	Rochester	199	1.6	Rockville Ctr UFSD	Rockville Ctr	283	0.5	Dryden Central SD	Dryden
118	3.9	Elwood UFSD	Greenlawn	199	1.6	Vestal Central SD	Vestal	283	0.5	Fulton City SD	Fulton
118	3.9	Lindenhurst UFSD	Lindenhurst	204	1.5	Blind Brook-Rye UFSD	Rye Brook	283	0.5	Horseheads Central SD	Horseheads
118	3.9	Locust Valley Central SD	Locust Valley	204	1.5	East Islip UFSD	Islip Terrace	283	0.5	Maine-Endwell Central SD	Endwell
122	3.8	Oceanside UFSD	Oceanside	204	1.5	Hastings-On-Hudson UFSD	Hastings on Hdsn	283	0.5	Marcellus Central SD	Marcellus
123	3.7	Center Moriches UFSD	Center Moriches	204	1.5	Pearl River UFSD	Pearl River	283	0.5	Oneida City SD	Oneida
123	3.7	Guilderland Central SD	Guilderland Center	204	1.5	Red Hook Central SD	Red Hook	283	0.5	Sayville UFSD	Sayville
125	3.6	Jericho UFSD	Jericho	204	1.5	West Irondequoit Central SD	Rochester	283	0.5	Windsor Central SD	Windsor
126	3.5	East Meadow UFSD	Westbury	210	1.4	Babylon UFSD	Babylon	294	0.4	Ballston Spa Central SD	Ballston Spa
126	3.5	Schenectady City SD	Schenectady	210	1.4	Lakeland Central SD	Shrub Oak	294	0.4	Chenango Valley Central SD	Binghamton
128	3.4	Farmingdale UFSD	Farmingdale	210	1.4	Watertown City SD	Watertown	294	0.4	Clarence Central SD	Clarence
128	3.4	Island Trees UFSD	Levittown	213	1.3	Cohoes City SD	Cohoes	294	0.4	Garden City UFSD	Garden City
130	3.3	Monticello Central SD	Monticello	213	1.3	Fairport Central SD	Fairport	294	0.4	Gloversville City SD	Gloversville
131	3.2	Goshen Central SD	Goshen	213	1.3	Irvington UFSD	Irvington	294	0.4	Homer Central SD	Homer
131	3.2	Hewlett-Woodmere UFSD	Woodmere	213	1.3	Penfield Central SD	Rochester	294	0.4	Hornell City SD	Hornell
131	3.2	North Colonie CSD	Latham	213	1.3	Shenendehowa Central SD	Clifton Park	294	0.4	Oneonta City SD	Oneonta
134	3.1	Johnson City Central SD	Johnson City	218	1.2	Bethlehem Central SD	Delmar	294	0.4	Scotia-Glenville Central SD	Scotia
134	3.1	Rye Neck UFSD	Mamaroneck	218	1.2	Churchville-Chili Central SD	Churchville	294	0.4	Sherrill City SD	Verona
134	3.1	South Orangetown Central SD	Blauvelt	218	1.2	Eastport-South Manor CSD	Manorville	294	0.4	Starpoint Central SD	Lockport
137	3.0	Cheektowaga-Maryvale UFSD	Cheektowaga	218	1.2	Minisink Valley Central SD	Slate Hill	294	0.4	Waterloo Central SD	Waterloo
137	3.0	Indian River Central SD	Philadelphia	218	1.2	Niagara Falls City SD	Niagara Falls	294	0.4	Wayne Central SD	Ontario Center
139	2.8	Greece Central SD	Rochester	218	1.2	Oswego City SD	Oswego	307	0.3	Averill Park Central SD	Averill Park
140	2.7	Putnam Valley Central SD	Putnam Valley	218	1.2	Plainview-Old Bethpage CSD	Plainview	307	0.3	Bayport-Blue Point UFSD	Bayport
140	2.7	Rocky Point UFSD	Rocky Point	218	1.2	Rome City SD	Rome	307	0.3	Burnt Hills-Ballston Lake Central SD	Scotia
140	2.7	Roslyn UFSD	Roslyn	218	1.2	Saratoga Spgs City SD	Saratoga Spgs	307	0.3	Cobleskill-Richmondville CSD	Cobleskill
143	2.6	Albion Central SD	Albion	218	1.2	Valley Central SD (Montgomery)	Montgomery	307	0.3	Hilton Central SD	Hilton
143	2.6	Carmel Central SD	Patterson	218	1.2	Warwick Valley Central SD	Warwick	307	0.3	Massapequa UFSD	Massapequa
143	2.6	Charter School for Applied Techs	Buffalo	218	1.2	Westhill Central SD	Syracuse	307	0.3	Olean City SD	Olean
143	2.6	Croton-Harmon UFSD	Croton on Hdsn	230	1.1	Commack UFSD	East Northport	307	0.3	Orchard Park Central SD	West Seneca
143	2.6	Kenmore-Tonawanda UFSD	Buffalo	230	1.1	Depew UFSD	Depew	307	0.3	Owego-Apalachin Central SD	Owego
148	2.5	Brighton Central SD	Rochester	230	1.1	Lockport City SD	Lockport	307	0.3	Palmyra-Macedon Central SD	Palmyra
148	2.5	Malverne UFSD	Malverne	230	1.1	Miller Place UFSD	Miller Place	307	0.3	Queensbury UFSD	Queensbury
148	2.5	Troy City SD	Troy	230	1.1	New Hartford Central SD	New Hartford	307	0.3	Susquehanna Valley Central SD	Conklin
151	2.4	East Williston UFSD	Old Westbury	230	1.1	Newark Central SD	Newark	319	0.2	Alden Central SD	Alden
151	2.4	Franklin Square UFSD	Franklin Square	230	1.1	Seaford UFSD	Seaford	319	0.2	Bath Central SD	Bath
151	2.4	Gates-Chili Central SD	Rochester	230	1.1	Victor Central SD	Victor	319	0.2	Broadalbin-Perth Central SD	Broadalbin
151	2.4	Monroe-Woodbury Central SD	Central Valley	230	1.1	West Genesee Central SD	Camillus	319	0.2	Byram Hills Central SD	Armonk
151	2.4	Saugerties Central SD	Saugerties	239	1.0	Chappaqua Central SD	Chappaqua	319	0.2	Central Valley CSD at Ilion-Mohawk	Ilion
151	2.4	Sewanhaka Central High SD	Floral Park	239	1.0	Medina Central SD	Medina	319	0.2	Chenango Forks Central SD	Binghamton
157	2.3	Marlboro Central SD	Milton	239	1.0	Pelham UFSD	Pelham	319	0.2	Chittenango Central SD	Chittenango
157	2.3	Valley Stream Central High SD	Valley Stream	239	1.0	Rotterdam-Mohonasen Central SD	Schenectady	319	0.2	Cortland City SD	Cortland
159	2.2	Beacon City SD	Beacon	239	1.0	Wappingers Central SD	Hopewell Junction	319	0.2	East Aurora UFSD	East Aurora
159	2.2	Bethpage UFSD	Bethpage	239	1.0	Washingtonville Central SD	Washingtonville	319	0.2	Elmira City SD	Elmira
159	2.2	Cheektowaga Central SD	Cheektowaga	245	0.9	Batavia City SD	Batavia	319	0.2	General Brown Central SD	Dexter

Note: This section only includes districts with 1,500 or more students; All categories are ranked from high to low

Rank	Percent	District Name	City
319	0.2	Glens Falls City SD	Glens Falls
319	0.2	Honeoye Falls-Lima Central SD	Honeoye Falls
319	0.2	Iroquois Central SD	Elma
319	0.2	Johnstown City SD	Johnstown
319	0.2	Lewiston-Porter Central SD	Youngstown
319	0.2	Livonia Central SD	Livonia
319	0.2	Norwich City SD	Norwich
319	0.2	Ogdensburg City SD	Ogdensburg
319	0.2	Peru Central SD	Peru
319	0.2	Schalmont Central SD	Schenectady
319	0.2	S Glens Fls Central SD	S Glens Fls
319	0.2	South Jefferson Central SD	Adams Center
319	0.2	Springville-Griffith Institute CSD	Springville
319	0.2	Waverly Central SD	Waverly
319	0.2	Yorkshire-Pioneer Central SD	Yorkshire
345	0.1	Camden Central SD	Camden
345	0.1	Central Square Central SD	Central Square
345	0.1	Evans-Brant Central SD (Lake Shore)	Angola
345	0.1	Hamburg Central SD	Hamburg
345	0.1	Lancaster Central SD	Lancaster
n/a	n/a	Beekmantown Central SD	West Chazy
n/a	n/a	Malone Central SD	Malone
n/a	n/a	Massena Central SD	Massena
n/a	n/a	Mexico Central SD	Mexico
n/a	n/a	Newfane Central SD	Burt
n/a	n/a	Phoenix Central SD	Phoenix
n/a	n/a	Rye City SD	Rye
n/a	n/a	Salmon River Central SD	Fort Covington

Students Eligible for Free Lunch

Rank	Percent	District Name	City
1	88.4	NYC Geographic District # 7	Bronx
2	86.4	NYC Geographic District # 9	Bronx
3	85.2	NYC Geographic District #12	Bronx
4	84.3	Rochester City SD	Rochester
5	83.3	Westbury UFSD	Old Westbury
6	83.0	NYC Geographic District #23	Brooklyn
7	81.6	NYC Geographic District #32	Brooklyn
8	81.5	Wyandanch UFSD	Wyandanch
9	79.2	NYC Geographic District # 6	New York
10	78.7	Lackawanna City SD	Lackawanna
10	78.7	NYC Geographic District #19	Brooklyn
12	78.2	Utica City SD	Utica
13	78.0	NYC Geographic District #16	Brooklyn
14	77.4	NYC Geographic District # 5	New York
15	76.9	NYC Geographic District #10	Bronx
16	75.4	NYC Geographic District # 4	New York
17	74.3	Poughkeepsie City SD	Poughkeepsie
18	73.8	Hempstead UFSD	Hempstead
18	73.8	NYC Geographic District # 8	Bronx
20	73.6	Syracuse City SD	Syracuse
21	73.2	NYC Geographic District #17	Brooklyn
22	72.8	Peekskill City SD	Peekskill
23	72.6	Brentwood UFSD	Brentwood
24	71.8	Yonkers City SD	Yonkers
25	70.3	Salmon River Central SD	Fort Covington
26	70.0	Niagara Falls City SD	Niagara Falls
27	68.9	NYC Geographic District #18	Brooklyn
28	68.0	Amityville UFSD	Amityville
29	67.7	Buffalo City SD	Buffalo
30	67.5	Jamestown City SD	Jamestown
30	67.5	NYC Geographic District #11	Bronx
32	67.3	Troy City SD	Troy
33	67.2	NYC Geographic District #27	Ozone Park
34	67.0	NYC Geographic District #20	Brooklyn
35	65.6	Copiague UFSD	Copiague
36	65.4	Newburgh City SD	Newburgh
37	65.3	Freeport UFSD	Freeport
38	65.2	East Ramapo CSD (Spring Valley)	Spring Valley
39	64.2	Lawrence UFSD	Cedarhurst
40	64.1	Hudson City SD	Hudson
40	64.1	Mount Vernon SD	Mount Vernon
42	63.9	Binghamton City SD	Binghamton
42	63.9	NYC Geographic District #14	Brooklyn
42	63.9	NYC Geographic District #29	Queens Village
45	63.6	NYC Geographic District #24	Corona
46	63.1	Gloversville City SD	Gloversville
47	63.0	Central Islip UFSD	Central Islip
48	62.8	NYC Geographic District #30	Long Isl City
49	62.7	Uniondale UFSD	Uniondale
50	62.6	NYC Geographic District #21	Brooklyn
51	62.5	Middletown City SD	Middletown
52	61.2	Johnson City Central SD	Johnson City
52	61.2	Schenectady City SD	Schenectady
54	61.1	Ellenville Central SD	Ellenville
55	60.6	Elmira City SD	Elmira
56	60.2	Port Chester-Rye UFSD	Port Chester
57	59.5	Amsterdam City SD	Amsterdam
58	58.9	Cohoes City SD	Cohoes
59	58.8	New York City Chancellor's Office	New York
60	58.6	NYC Geographic District #22	Brooklyn
61	58.4	Dunkirk City SD	Dunkirk
62	58.2	NYC Geographic District #28	Jamaica
63	58.1	NYC Geographic District #25	Flushing
64	57.5	NYC Geographic District # 1	New York
65	57.3	NYC Geographic District #13	Brooklyn
65	57.3	Port Jervis City SD	Port Jervis
67	57.1	Lansingburgh Central SD	Troy
68	56.7	Cheektowaga Central SD	Cheektowaga
69	56.5	Watertown City SD	Watertown
70	55.8	Geneva City SD	Geneva
71	54.5	Plattsburgh City SD	Plattsburgh
71	54.5	Rome City SD	Rome
73	53.9	Fulton City SD	Fulton
74	53.7	Hornell City SD	Hornell
75	53.5	Glen Cove City SD	Glen Cove
76	53.3	Olean City SD	Olean
77	53.1	Albany City SD	Albany
78	51.9	NYC Geographic District #15	Brooklyn
79	51.4	Batavia City SD	Batavia
80	51.3	Gouverneur Central SD	Gouverneur
80	51.3	Kingston City SD	Kingston
82	51.1	Massena Central SD	Massena
82	51.1	William Floyd UFSD	Mastic Beach
84	50.4	Ogdensburg City SD	Ogdensburg
85	50.3	Central Valley CSD at Ilion-Mohawk	Ilion
86	50.1	Elmont UFSD	Elmont
87	49.2	South Country Central SD	East Patchogue
87	49.2	UFSD of the Tarrytowns	Sleepy Hollow
89	49.1	Catskill Central SD	Catskill
89	49.1	Lockport City SD	Lockport
91	48.9	Medina Central SD	Medina
92	48.4	Auburn City SD	Auburn
93	48.1	Bath Central SD	Bath
94	47.6	Albion Central SD	Albion
95	47.5	Mexico Central SD	Mexico
96	47.4	Greenburgh Central SD	Hartsdale
97	47.3	NYC Geographic District #31	Staten Island
97	47.3	Union-Endicott Central SD	Endicott
99	47.1	Newark Central SD	Newark
100	46.9	Haverstraw-Stony Point CSD	Garnerville
100	46.9	Huntington UFSD	Huntington Stn
102	46.7	Hampton Bays UFSD	Hampton Bays
102	46.7	NYC Geographic District # 2	New York
104	46.6	New Rochelle City SD	New Rochelle
105	46.3	Malone Central SD	Malone
106	46.2	Liberty Central SD	Liberty
107	46.1	Camden Central SD	Camden
108	46.0	Cortland City SD	Cortland
108	46.0	Phoenix Central SD	Phoenix
110	45.8	NYC Geographic District #26	Bayside
111	45.6	Waverly Central SD	Waverly
112	45.3	East Irondequoit Central SD	Rochester
113	44.9	Dansville Central SD	Dansville
114	44.8	Oneida City SD	Oneida
115	44.5	Bay Shore UFSD	Bay Shore
116	44.4	Beekmantown Central SD	West Chazy
117	43.9	Oswego City SD	Oswego
118	43.5	NYC Geographic District # 3	New York
119	43.3	Riverhead Central SD	Riverhead
120	43.0	Yorkshire-Pioneer Central SD	Yorkshire
121	42.5	Dryden Central SD	Dryden
122	42.4	Tonawanda City SD	Tonawanda
123	42.3	Windsor Central SD	Windsor
124	41.8	South Huntington UFSD	Huntington Stn
125	41.7	Cheektowaga-Maryvale UFSD	Cheektowaga
126	41.6	Hudson Falls Central SD	Fort Edward
126	41.6	Longwood Central SD	Middle Island
128	41.4	Patchogue-Medford UFSD	Patchogue
129	41.2	Cobleskill-Richmondville CSD	Cobleskill
130	40.0	Beacon City SD	Beacon
130	40.0	Johnstown City SD	Johnstown
130	40.0	White Plains City SD	White Plains
133	39.0	Sweet Home Central SD	Amherst
134	38.8	Owego-Apalachin Central SD	Owego
135	38.5	Rondout Valley Central SD	Accord
136	38.4	South Jefferson Central SD	Adams Center
137	38.3	Glens Falls City SD	Glens Falls
138	38.2	Oneonta City SD	Oneonta
139	38.1	Pine Bush Central SD	Pine Bush
140	37.8	West Hempstead UFSD	West Hempstead
141	37.2	North Tonawanda City SD	North Tonawanda
142	36.8	Norwich City SD	Norwich
142	36.8	Saugerties Central SD	Saugerties
144	36.6	Depew UFSD	Depew
144	36.6	Southampton UFSD	Southampton
146	36.2	Peru Central SD	Peru
147	35.9	Hyde Park Central SD	Hyde Park
147	35.9	Malverne UFSD	Malverne
149	35.8	Greece Central SD	Rochester
149	35.8	Ravena-Coeymans-Selkirk Cent SD	Ravena
151	35.7	Central Square Central SD	Central Square
152	35.6	Brockport Central SD	Brockport
153	35.2	Kenmore-Tonawanda UFSD	Buffalo
154	35.0	Deer Park UFSD	Deer Park
155	34.4	Chenango Valley Central SD	Binghamton
155	34.4	General Brown Central SD	Dexter
157	34.3	Susquehanna Valley Central SD	Conklin
158	33.9	Broadalbin-Perth Central SD	Broadalbin
158	33.9	Homer Central SD	Homer
160	33.8	Evans-Brant Central SD (Lake Shore)	Angola
161	32.9	Ithaca City SD	Ithaca
162	32.4	Fredonia Central SD	Fredonia
163	32.3	Palmyra-Macedon Central SD	Palmyra
164	32.2	Hicksville UFSD	Hicksville
165	32.1	East Syracuse Minoa Central SD	East Syracuse
166	32.0	Corning City SD	Painted Post
166	32.0	Liverpool Central SD	Liverpool
168	31.9	West Babylon UFSD	West Babylon
169	31.8	Gates-Chili Central SD	Rochester
169	31.8	Valley Stream 30 UFSD	Valley Stream
171	31.4	Highland Central SD	Highland
172	31.2	Maine-Endwell Central SD	Endwell
173	31.1	Chenango Forks Central SD	Binghamton
174	31.0	Chittenango Central SD	Chittenango
175	30.5	East Hampton UFSD	East Hampton
176	30.4	Rotterdam-Mohonasen Central SD	Schenectady
177	30.0	Long Beach City SD	Long Beach
178	29.8	West Seneca Central SD	West Seneca
179	29.7	Carthage Central SD	Carthage
180	29.4	Valley Central SD (Montgomery)	Montgomery
181	29.2	Queensbury UFSD	Queensbury
182	29.0	Canandaigua City SD	Canandaigua
183	28.9	Phelps-Clifton Springs Central SD	Clifton Springs
184	28.8	Livonia Central SD	Livonia
185	28.4	Middle Country Central SD	Centereach
186	28.3	Kinderhook Central SD	Valatie
186	28.3	Lindenhurst UFSD	Lindenhurst
188	28.2	Marlboro Central SD	Milton
188	28.2	North Syracuse Central SD	North Syracuse
190	28.1	Rush-Henrietta Central SD	Henrietta
190	28.1	Wallkill Central SD	Wallkill
190	28.1	Whitesboro Central SD	Whitesboro
193	28.0	Ballston Spa Central SD	Ballston Spa
194	27.7	Springville-Griffith Institute CSD	Springville
195	27.5	Indian River Central SD	Philadelphia
195	27.5	Nyack UFSD	Nyack
197	27.0	Ossining UFSD	Ossining
198	26.2	Horseheads Central SD	Horseheads
199	26.1	S Glens Fls Central SD	S Glens Fls
200	26.0	Sherrill City SD	Verona
201	24.9	Westhampton Bch UFSD	Westhampton Bch
202	24.7	North Babylon UFSD	North Babylon
203	24.4	Wayne Central SD	Ontario Center
204	24.3	Islip UFSD	Islip
205	24.0	Brewster Central SD	Brewster
206	23.6	Brookhaven-Comsewogue UFSD	Port Jeff Stn
206	23.6	Rocky Point UFSD	Rocky Point
208	23.3	Niagara-Wheatfield Central SD	Niagara Falls
208	23.3	Spencerport Central SD	Spencerport
208	23.3	Valley Stream Central High SD	Valley Stream
211	23.1	Frontier Central SD	Hamburg
212	23.0	Schuylerville Central SD	Schuylerville
213	22.5	Schalmont Central SD	Schenectady
214	22.4	Baldwinsville Central SD	Baldwinsville
214	22.4	Sewanhaka Central High SD	Floral Park
216	22.2	Churchville-Chili Central SD	Churchville
217	22.1	Scotia-Glenville Central SD	Scotia
218	21.7	Amherst Central SD	Amherst
218	21.7	Farmingdale UFSD	Farmingdale

Note: This section only includes districts with 1,500 or more students; All categories are ranked from high to low

Rank	Percent	District Name	City
220	21.2	Goshen Central SD	Goshen
221	21.1	Ramapo Central SD (Suffern)	Hillburn
222	20.7	Vestal Central SD	Vestal
223	20.2	Valley Stream 13 UFSD	Valley Stream
224	20.1	Arlington Central SD	Lagrangeville
224	20.1	New Paltz Central SD	New Paltz
226	19.9	South Colonie Central SD	Albany
227	19.8	Carmel Central SD	Patterson
228	19.4	Mineola UFSD	Mineola
229	19.0	Sachem Central SD	Lake Ronkonkoma
229	19.0	West Irondequoit Central SD	Rochester
231	18.9	Grand Island Central SD	Grand Island
232	18.8	Hendrick Hudson Central SD	Montrose
233	18.6	Baldwin UFSD	Baldwin
233	18.6	Connetquot Central SD	Bohemia
235	18.4	Center Moriches UFSD	Center Moriches
235	18.4	East Islip UFSD	Islip Terrace
237	18.3	Alden Central SD	Alden
237	18.3	Oyster Bay-East Norwich Central SD	Oyster Bay
239	18.2	Lancaster Central SD	Lancaster
240	17.9	Lewiston-Porter Central SD	Youngstown
240	17.9	West Genesee Central SD	Camillus
242	17.8	Saratoga Spgs City SD	Saratoga Spgs
243	17.3	Wappingers Central SD	Hopewell Junction
244	17.1	East Meadow UFSD	Westbury
244	17.1	Elwood UFSD	Greenlawn
246	16.9	East Greenbush Central SD	East Greenbush
246	16.9	Nanuet UFSD	Nanuet
248	16.7	Hilton Central SD	Hilton
249	16.5	Fairport Central SD	Fairport
250	16.4	New Hartford Central SD	New Hartford
251	16.3	Port Washington UFSD	Port Washington
252	16.2	Hamburg Central SD	Hamburg
252	16.2	Washingtonville Central SD	Washingtonville
254	16.0	Hewlett-Woodmere UFSD	Woodmere
255	15.9	Minisink Valley Central SD	Slate Hill
256	15.8	Levittown UFSD	Levittown
257	15.7	Island Trees UFSD	Levittown
258	15.5	Lakeland Central SD	Shrub Oak
259	15.4	Averill Park Central SD	Averill Park
260	15.2	Starpoint Central SD	Lockport
261	15.0	Harrison Central SD	Harrison
261	15.0	Mamaroneck UFSD	Mamaroneck
263	14.8	Victor Central SD	Victor
264	14.7	Bedford Central SD	Bedford
265	14.5	New Hyde Pk-Garden City Pk UFSD	New Hyde Park
266	14.3	Half Hollow Hills Central SD	Dix Hills
266	14.3	Locust Valley Central SD	Locust Valley
266	14.3	North Colonie CSD	Latham
269	14.1	Jamesville-Dewitt Central SD	Dewitt
270	14.0	Westhill Central SD	Syracuse
271	13.8	Guilderland Central SD	Guilderland Center
271	13.8	Iroquois Central SD	Elma
273	13.4	Bethpage UFSD	Bethpage
273	13.4	Marcellus Central SD	Marcellus
275	13.2	Putnam Valley Central SD	Putnam Valley
275	13.2	Webster Central SD	Webster
277	13.0	Warwick Valley Central SD	Warwick
278	12.9	Monroe-Woodbury Central SD	Central Valley
279	12.5	Honeoye Falls-Lima Central SD	Honeoye Falls
280	12.4	Brighton Central SD	Rochester
280	12.4	Oceanside UFSD	Oceanside
282	12.1	Penfield Central SD	Rochester
283	12.0	Franklin Square UFSD	Franklin Square
284	11.9	Eastport-South Manor CSD	Manorville
284	11.9	North Bellmore UFSD	Bellmore
286	11.8	Babylon UFSD	Babylon
286	11.8	Red Hook Central SD	Red Hook
288	11.7	Rye Neck UFSD	Mamaroneck
288	11.7	West Islip UFSD	West Islip
290	11.6	Lynbrook UFSD	Lynbrook
291	11.5	Shenendehowa Central SD	Clifton Park
291	11.5	South Orangetown Central SD	Blauvelt
293	11.4	Great Neck UFSD	Great Neck
294	11.1	Mahopac Central SD	Mahopac
294	11.1	Orchard Park Central SD	West Seneca
296	10.9	Rockville Ctr UFSD	Rockville Ctr
297	10.6	Cornwall Central SD	Cornwall on Hdsn
297	10.6	Williamsville Central SD	East Amherst
299	10.4	Harborfields Central SD	Greenlawn
299	10.4	Pearl River UFSD	Pearl River
301	10.3	Clarkstown Central SD	New City
302	10.2	Northport-East Northport UFSD	Northport
303	10.0	Niskayuna Central SD	Schenectady
304	9.5	Miller Place UFSD	Miller Place
305	9.4	Bayport-Blue Point UFSD	Bayport
305	9.4	East Aurora UFSD	East Aurora
307	9.2	Hauppauge UFSD	Hauppauge
308	9.0	Bethlehem Central SD	Delmar
308	9.0	Sayville UFSD	Sayville
310	8.7	Fayetteville-Manlius Central SD	Manlius
311	8.6	Pleasantville UFSD	Pleasantville
312	8.5	Plainedge UFSD	N Massapequa
313	8.4	Bellmore-Merrick Central High SD	North Merrick
314	8.2	Commack UFSD	East Northport
315	8.1	Burnt Hills-Ballston Lake Central SD	Scotia
316	8.0	Pelham UFSD	Pelham
317	7.9	Kings Park Central SD	Kings Park
318	7.5	Clarence Central SD	Clarence
319	7.4	Mount Pleasant Central SD	Thornwood
320	7.2	Roslyn UFSD	Roslyn
321	7.0	Seaford UFSD	Seaford
322	6.9	Somers Central SD	Somers
323	6.8	Herricks UFSD	New Hyde Park
324	6.6	Irvington UFSD	Irvington
325	6.4	Smithtown Central SD	Smithtown
325	6.4	Yorktown Central SD	Yorktown Hgts
327	6.3	Massapequa UFSD	Massapequa
328	6.2	Plainview-Old Bethpage CSD	Plainview
329	5.6	Ardsley UFSD	Ardsley
330	5.5	Mount Sinai UFSD	Mount Sinai
331	5.1	Manhasset UFSD	Manhasset
332	5.0	Wantagh UFSD	Wantagh
333	4.9	Jericho UFSD	Jericho
333	4.9	Katonah-Lewisboro UFSD	South Salem
335	4.8	Three Village Central SD	Stony Brook
336	4.7	East Williston UFSD	Old Westbury
337	4.0	Shoreham-Wading River Central SD	Shoreham
338	3.8	Hastings-On-Hudson UFSD	Hastings on Hdsn
338	3.8	Syosset Central SD	Syosset
340	2.6	Pittsford Central SD	Pittsford
341	2.5	Byram Hills Central SD	Armonk
341	2.5	North Shore Central SD	Sea Cliff
343	2.3	Chappaqua Central SD	Chappaqua
344	1.9	Rye City SD	Rye
345	1.7	Garden City UFSD	Garden City
346	1.5	Cold Spring Hrbr Central SD	Cold Spring Hrbr
347	0.3	Blind Brook-Rye UFSD	Rye Brook
348	0.2	Bronxville UFSD	Bronxville
349	0.0	Croton-Harmon UFSD	Croton on Hdsn
349	0.0	Eastchester UFSD	Eastchester
349	0.0	Edgemont UFSD	Scarsdale
349	0.0	Roosevelt UFSD	Roosevelt
349	0.0	Scarsdale UFSD	Scarsdale
n/a	n/a	Charter School for Applied Techs	Buffalo
n/a	n/a	Monticello Central SD	Monticello
n/a	n/a	Newfane Central SD	Burt
n/a	n/a	Waterloo Central SD	Waterloo

Students Eligible for Reduced-Price Lunch

Rank	Percent	District Name	City
1	18.0	Indian River Central SD	Philadelphia
2	13.4	Middletown City SD	Middletown
3	13.3	Bedford Central SD	Bedford
4	11.5	NYC Geographic District #26	Bayside
5	11.3	Camden Central SD	Camden
6	11.0	Yorkshire-Pioneer Central SD	Yorkshire
7	10.8	Carthage Central SD	Carthage
8	10.7	Liberty Central SD	Liberty
9	10.0	NYC Geographic District #25	Flushing
10	9.8	Newark Central SD	Newark
11	9.7	Peekskill City SD	Peekskill
11	9.7	Uniondale UFSD	Uniondale
13	9.6	Elmont UFSD	Elmont
13	9.6	Hornell City SD	Hornell
15	9.4	Evans-Brant Central SD (Lake Shore)	Angola
15	9.4	Phelps-Clifton Springs Central SD	Clifton Springs
17	9.2	Patchogue-Medford UFSD	Patchogue
17	9.2	Saugerties Central SD	Saugerties
17	9.2	Susquehanna Valley Central SD	Conklin
20	9.0	Port Chester-Rye UFSD	Port Chester
21	8.9	Bath Central SD	Bath
21	8.9	Depew UFSD	Depew
21	8.9	South Jefferson Central SD	Adams Center
24	8.8	Brentwood UFSD	Brentwood
25	8.7	Ogdensburg City SD	Ogdensburg
26	8.6	Lawrence UFSD	Cedarhurst
27	8.5	Corning City SD	Painted Post
27	8.5	East Irondequoit Central SD	Rochester
29	8.4	NYC Geographic District #29	Queens Village
30	8.3	Hyde Park Central SD	Hyde Park
30	8.3	NYC Geographic District #28	Jamaica
32	8.2	Gates-Chili Central SD	Rochester
33	8.1	Salmon River Central SD	Fort Covington
33	8.1	Valley Stream 30 UFSD	Valley Stream
35	8.0	Glen Cove City SD	Glen Cove
35	8.0	Greenburgh Central SD	Hartsdale
35	8.0	Johnstown City SD	Johnstown
35	8.0	New Rochelle City SD	New Rochelle
39	7.9	Central Islip UFSD	Central Islip
39	7.9	Gouverneur Central SD	Gouverneur
39	7.9	North Babylon UFSD	North Babylon
42	7.7	Cheektowaga-Maryvale UFSD	Cheektowaga
42	7.7	Chenango Forks Central SD	Binghamton
42	7.7	NYC Geographic District #27	Ozone Park
45	7.6	Albion Central SD	Albion
45	7.6	Amityville UFSD	Amityville
45	7.6	Beacon City SD	Beacon
45	7.6	Deer Park UFSD	Deer Park
49	7.5	Cortland City SD	Cortland
49	7.5	Dansville Central SD	Dansville
49	7.5	East Syracuse Minoa Central SD	East Syracuse
49	7.5	Schuylerville Central SD	Schuylerville
49	7.5	Watertown City SD	Watertown
54	7.4	Cheektowaga Central SD	Cheektowaga
54	7.4	Malone Central SD	Malone
54	7.4	NYC Geographic District #13	Brooklyn
54	7.4	NYC Geographic District #31	Staten Island
58	7.3	Brockport Central SD	Brockport
58	7.3	Hampton Bays UFSD	Hampton Bays
58	7.3	Highland Central SD	Highland
58	7.3	Kenmore-Tonawanda UFSD	Buffalo
58	7.3	Mexico Central SD	Mexico
63	7.2	Freeport UFSD	Freeport
63	7.2	Tonawanda City SD	Tonawanda
65	7.1	Central Square Central SD	Central Square
65	7.1	Greece Central SD	Rochester
65	7.1	Lackawanna City SD	Lackawanna
65	7.1	Pine Bush Central SD	Pine Bush
69	7.0	Chittenango Central SD	Chittenango
69	7.0	Johnson City Central SD	Johnson City
69	7.0	NYC Geographic District #18	Brooklyn
69	7.0	Newburgh City SD	Newburgh
69	7.0	Sherrill City SD	Verona
69	7.0	Spencerport Central SD	Spencerport
75	6.9	Alden Central SD	Alden
75	6.9	Homer Central SD	Homer
75	6.9	Lindenhurst UFSD	Lindenhurst
75	6.9	Longwood Central SD	Middle Island
75	6.9	NYC Geographic District #22	Brooklyn
75	6.9	North Tonawanda City SD	North Tonawanda
75	6.9	Peru Central SD	Peru
75	6.9	West Hempstead UFSD	West Hempstead
83	6.8	General Brown Central SD	Dexter
83	6.8	William Floyd UFSD	Mastic Beach
85	6.7	Broadalbin-Perth Central SD	Broadalbin
85	6.7	Lockport City SD	Lockport
87	6.6	Dryden Central SD	Dryden
87	6.6	Frontier Central SD	Hamburg
87	6.6	Middle Country Central SD	Centereach
87	6.6	Oswego City SD	Oswego
87	6.6	Sweet Home Central SD	Amherst
92	6.5	Bay Shore UFSD	Bay Shore
92	6.5	Malverne UFSD	Malverne
92	6.5	Wallkill Central SD	Wallkill
95	6.4	Rondout Valley Central SD	Accord
96	6.3	Oneida City SD	Oneida
96	6.3	Rome City SD	Rome
96	6.3	Wayne Central SD	Ontario Center
99	6.2	Churchville-Chili Central SD	Churchville
99	6.2	Haverstraw-Stony Point CSD	Garnerville
99	6.2	Massena Central SD	Massena
99	6.2	Ossining UFSD	Ossining
99	6.2	Port Jervis City SD	Port Jervis
99	6.2	West Irondequoit Central SD	Rochester
105	6.1	NYC Geographic District #24	Corona
105	6.1	Springville-Griffith Institute CSD	Springville
105	6.1	Windsor Central SD	Windsor
108	6.0	Ithaca City SD	Ithaca

Note: This section only includes districts with 1,500 or more students; All categories are ranked from high to low

Rank	Score	District	City
108	6.0	NYC Geographic District #30	Long Isl City
108	6.0	Niagara-Wheatfield Central SD	Niagara Falls
108	6.0	Valley Central SD (Montgomery)	Montgomery
112	5.9	Copiague UFSD	Copiague
112	5.9	Marlboro Central SD	Milton
112	5.9	Rotterdam-Mohonasen Central SD	Schenectady
112	5.9	West Babylon UFSD	West Babylon
116	5.8	Liverpool Central SD	Liverpool
116	5.8	UFSD of the Tarrytowns	Sleepy Hollow
116	5.8	Whitesboro Central SD	Whitesboro
119	5.7	Hicksville UFSD	Hicksville
119	5.7	Horseheads Central SD	Horseheads
119	5.7	NYC Geographic District #17	Brooklyn
119	5.7	Washingtonville Central SD	Washingtonville
119	5.7	West Genesee Central SD	Camillus
124	5.6	Cobleskill-Richmondville CSD	Cobleskill
124	5.6	Geneva City SD	Geneva
124	5.6	Hendrick Hudson Central SD	Montrose
124	5.6	Phoenix Central SD	Phoenix
124	5.6	Rush-Henrietta Central SD	Henrietta
124	5.6	Waverly Central SD	Waverly
124	5.6	West Seneca Central SD	West Seneca
131	5.5	Beekmantown Central SD	West Chazy
131	5.5	NYC Geographic District #20	Brooklyn
131	5.5	Olean City SD	Olean
134	5.4	Amherst Central SD	Amherst
134	5.4	Fulton City SD	Fulton
134	5.4	Hudson Falls Central SD	Fort Edward
134	5.4	Kingston City SD	Kingston
134	5.4	Medina Central SD	Medina
134	5.4	North Syracuse Central SD	North Syracuse
134	5.4	Palmyra-Macedon Central SD	Palmyra
141	5.3	Chenango Valley Central SD	Binghamton
141	5.3	NYC Geographic District #2	New York
141	5.3	NYC Geographic District #21	Brooklyn
141	5.3	South Country Central SD	East Patchogue
141	5.3	Valley Stream 13 UFSD	Valley Stream
146	5.2	Mount Vernon SD	Mount Vernon
146	5.2	S Glens Fls Central SD	S Glens Fls
146	5.2	Troy City SD	Troy
146	5.2	New York City Chancellor's Office	New York
150	5.1	Cohoes City SD	Cohoes
150	5.1	Norwich City SD	Norwich
150	5.1	Owego-Apalachin Central SD	Owego
150	5.1	Scotia-Glenville Central SD	Scotia
150	5.1	Sewanhaka Central High SD	Floral Park
155	5.0	Glens Falls City SD	Glens Falls
155	5.0	Grand Island Central SD	Grand Island
155	5.0	NYC Geographic District #1	New York
155	5.0	NYC Geographic District #11	Bronx
155	5.0	Yonkers City SD	Yonkers
160	4.9	Mineola UFSD	Mineola
160	4.9	Southampton UFSD	Southampton
162	4.8	East Ramapo CSD (Spring Valley)	Spring Valley
162	4.8	Lancaster Central SD	Lancaster
162	4.8	Niagara Falls City SD	Niagara Falls
162	4.8	Riverhead Central SD	Riverhead
162	4.8	Valley Stream Central High SD	Valley Stream
167	4.7	Union-Endicott Central SD	Endicott
168	4.6	Central Valley CSD at Ilion-Mohawk	Ilion
168	4.6	East Meadow UFSD	Westbury
170	4.5	Hewlett-Woodmere UFSD	Woodmere
170	4.5	Islip UFSD	Islip
170	4.5	Levittown UFSD	Levittown
170	4.5	Westbury UFSD	Old Westbury
174	4.4	Batavia City SD	Batavia
174	4.4	Ellenville Central SD	Ellenville
174	4.4	Rocky Point UFSD	Rocky Point
177	4.3	Island Trees UFSD	Levittown
177	4.3	Lansingburgh Central SD	Troy
177	4.3	NYC Geographic District #4	New York
177	4.3	Wyandanch UFSD	Wyandanch
181	4.2	Lakeland Central SD	Shrub Oak
181	4.2	Lewiston-Porter Central SD	Youngstown
181	4.2	NYC Geographic District #3	New York
181	4.2	NYC Geographic District #14	Brooklyn
185	4.1	Minisink Valley Central SD	Slate Hill
185	4.1	NYC Geographic District #8	Bronx
185	4.1	NYC Geographic District #10	Bronx
188	4.0	Center Moriches UFSD	Center Moriches
188	4.0	Goshen Central SD	Goshen
188	4.0	NYC Geographic District #5	New York
188	4.0	NYC Geographic District #6	New York
188	4.0	Nyack UFSD	Nyack
188	4.0	Ravena-Coeymans-Selkirk Cent SD	Ravena
188	4.0	White Plains City SD	White Plains
195	3.9	Arlington Central SD	Lagrangeville
195	3.9	Livonia Central SD	Livonia
195	3.9	Marcellus Central SD	Marcellus
195	3.9	Wappingers Central SD	Hopewell Junction
199	3.8	East Greenbush Central SD	East Greenbush
199	3.8	Fredonia Central SD	Fredonia
199	3.8	Gloversville City SD	Gloversville
199	3.8	Hilton Central SD	Hilton
199	3.8	Maine-Endwell Central SD	Endwell
204	3.7	Averill Park Central SD	Averill Park
204	3.7	Catskill Central SD	Catskill
204	3.7	Connetquot Central SD	Bohemia
204	3.7	Farmingdale UFSD	Farmingdale
204	3.7	Hamburg Central SD	Hamburg
204	3.7	Kinderhook Central SD	Valatie
204	3.7	NYC Geographic District #19	Brooklyn
204	3.7	Plattsburgh City SD	Plattsburgh
204	3.7	Red Hook Central SD	Red Hook
204	3.7	Sachem Central SD	Lake Ronkonkoma
204	3.7	Westhampton Bch UFSD	Westhampton Bch
215	3.6	Auburn City SD	Auburn
215	3.6	NYC Geographic District #7	Bronx
215	3.6	Oneonta City SD	Oneonta
215	3.6	Poughkeepsie City SD	Poughkeepsie
215	3.6	Roslyn UFSD	Roslyn
220	3.5	Brookhaven-Comsewogue UFSD	Port Jeff Stn
220	3.5	Burnt Hills-Ballston Lake Central SD	Scotia
220	3.5	East Islip UFSD	Islip Terrace
220	3.5	Elwood UFSD	Greenlawn
220	3.5	NYC Geographic District #23	Brooklyn
220	3.5	NYC Geographic District #32	Brooklyn
226	3.4	Baldwinsville Central SD	Baldwinsville
226	3.4	Bethpage UFSD	Bethpage
226	3.4	Brewster Central SD	Brewster
226	3.4	Canandaigua City SD	Canandaigua
226	3.4	Iroquois Central SD	Elma
231	3.3	Carmel Central SD	Patterson
231	3.3	Vestal Central SD	Vestal
233	3.2	New Hyde Pk-Garden City Pk UFSD	New Hyde Park
233	3.2	NYC Geographic District #15	Brooklyn
233	3.2	Schalmont Central SD	Schenectady
233	3.2	Utica City SD	Utica
237	3.1	Cornwall Central SD	Cornwall on Hdsn
237	3.1	Great Neck UFSD	Great Neck
237	3.1	NYC Geographic District #16	Brooklyn
240	3.0	Ballston Spa Central SD	Ballston Spa
240	3.0	Monroe-Woodbury Central SD	Central Valley
240	3.0	NYC Geographic District #9	Bronx
240	3.0	NYC Geographic District #12	Bronx
240	3.0	Putnam Valley Central SD	Putnam Valley
245	2.9	North Colonie CSD	Latham
245	2.9	Penfield Central SD	Rochester
245	2.9	South Colonie Central SD	Albany
248	2.8	Hauppauge UFSD	Hauppauge
248	2.8	Huntington UFSD	Huntington Stn
248	2.8	Oyster Bay-East Norwich Central SD	Oyster Bay
248	2.8	Saratoga Spgs City SD	Saratoga Spgs
252	2.7	Guilderland Central SD	Guilderland Center
252	2.7	Harrison Central SD	Harrison
252	2.7	Honeoye Falls-Lima Central SD	Honeoye Falls
252	2.7	Schenectady City SD	Schenectady
252	2.7	South Huntington UFSD	Huntington Stn
257	2.6	East Hampton UFSD	East Hampton
257	2.6	Jamesville-Dewitt Central SD	Dewitt
257	2.6	New Paltz Central SD	New Paltz
257	2.6	Starpoint Central SD	Lockport
261	2.5	Dunkirk City SD	Dunkirk
261	2.5	Franklin Square UFSD	Franklin Square
261	2.5	Queensbury UFSD	Queensbury
264	2.4	Half Hollow Hills Central SD	Dix Hills
264	2.4	Irvington UFSD	Irvington
264	2.4	Ramapo Central SD (Suffern)	Hillburn
267	2.3	Baldwin UFSD	Baldwin
267	2.3	Locust Valley Central SD	Locust Valley
267	2.3	Mahopac Central SD	Mahopac
267	2.3	Nanuet UFSD	Nanuet
267	2.3	Oceanside UFSD	Oceanside
272	2.2	Binghamton City SD	Binghamton
272	2.2	Miller Place UFSD	Miller Place
272	2.2	New Hartford Central SD	New Hartford
272	2.2	North Bellmore UFSD	Bellmore
272	2.2	Syracuse City SD	Syracuse
272	2.2	Webster Central SD	Webster
278	2.1	Fayetteville-Manlius Central SD	Manlius
278	2.1	West Islip UFSD	West Islip
280	2.0	Eastport-South Manor CSD	Manorville
280	2.0	Fairport Central SD	Fairport
280	2.0	Plainedge UFSD	N Massapequa
280	2.0	Seaford UFSD	Seaford
280	2.0	Victor Central SD	Victor
280	2.0	Westhill Central SD	Syracuse
280	2.0	Williamsville Central SD	East Amherst
287	1.9	Babylon UFSD	Babylon
287	1.9	East Aurora UFSD	East Aurora
287	1.9	Sayville UFSD	Sayville
287	1.9	Shenendehowa Central SD	Clifton Park
287	1.9	South Orangetown Central SD	Blauvelt
292	1.8	Pelham UFSD	Pelham
292	1.8	Rye Neck UFSD	Mamaroneck
294	1.7	Herricks UFSD	New Hyde Park
294	1.7	Jamestown City SD	Jamestown
294	1.7	Massapequa UFSD	Massapequa
294	1.7	Mount Pleasant Central SD	Thornwood
298	1.6	Brighton Central SD	Rochester
298	1.6	Elmira City SD	Elmira
298	1.6	Niskayuna Central SD	Schenectady
298	1.6	Northport-East Northport UFSD	Northport
298	1.6	Orchard Park Central SD	West Seneca
298	1.6	Plainview-Old Bethpage CSD	Plainview
298	1.6	Rockville Ctr UFSD	Rockville Ctr
298	1.6	Warwick Valley Central SD	Warwick
298	1.6	Yorktown Central SD	Yorktown Hgts
307	1.5	Hastings-On-Hudson UFSD	Hastings on Hdsn
307	1.5	Mamaroneck UFSD	Mamaroneck
307	1.5	Port Washington UFSD	Port Washington
310	1.4	Bellmore-Merrick Central High SD	North Merrick
310	1.4	Clarkstown Central SD	New City
310	1.4	Hempstead UFSD	Hempstead
313	1.3	Bayport-Blue Point UFSD	Bayport
313	1.3	Clarence Central SD	Clarence
313	1.3	Commack UFSD	East Northport
313	1.3	Harborfields Central SD	Greenlawn
313	1.3	Three Village Central SD	Stony Brook
318	1.2	Ardsley UFSD	Ardsley
318	1.2	Bethlehem Central SD	Delmar
318	1.2	Long Beach City SD	Long Beach
318	1.2	Smithtown Central SD	Smithtown
322	1.1	Kings Park Central SD	Kings Park
322	1.1	North Shore Central SD	Sea Cliff
324	1.0	Albany City SD	Albany
324	1.0	Pearl River UFSD	Pearl River
324	1.0	Pittsford Central SD	Pittsford
324	1.0	Wantagh UFSD	Wantagh
328	0.9	Rochester City SD	Rochester
328	0.9	Shoreham-Wading River Central SD	Shoreham
330	0.8	Pleasantville UFSD	Pleasantville
331	0.7	Amsterdam City SD	Amsterdam
331	0.7	Lynbrook UFSD	Lynbrook
333	0.6	Mount Sinai UFSD	Mount Sinai
334	0.5	Blind Brook-Rye UFSD	Rye Brook
334	0.5	Chappaqua Central SD	Chappaqua
334	0.5	East Williston UFSD	Old Westbury
334	0.5	Rye City SD	Rye
334	0.5	Syosset Central SD	Syosset
339	0.4	Katonah-Lewisboro UFSD	South Salem
339	0.4	Manhasset UFSD	Manhasset
339	0.4	Somers Central SD	Somers
342	0.3	Hudson City SD	Hudson
342	0.3	Jericho UFSD	Jericho
344	0.2	Byram Hills Central SD	Armonk
345	0.1	Garden City UFSD	Garden City
346	0.0	Bronxville UFSD	Bronxville
346	0.0	Buffalo City SD	Buffalo
346	0.0	Cold Spring Hrbr Central SD	Cold Spring Hrbr
346	0.0	Croton-Harmon UFSD	Croton on Hdsn
346	0.0	Eastchester UFSD	Eastchester
346	0.0	Edgemont UFSD	Scarsdale
346	0.0	Roosevelt UFSD	Roosevelt
346	0.0	Scarsdale UFSD	Scarsdale
n/a	n/a	Charter School for Applied Techs	Buffalo
n/a	n/a	Monticello Central SD	Monticello
n/a	n/a	Newfane Central SD	Burt
n/a	n/a	Waterloo Central SD	Waterloo

Note: This section only includes districts with 1,500 or more students; All categories are ranked from high to low

Student/Teacher Ratio

(number of students per teacher)

Rank	Number	District Name	City
1	9.5	North Shore Central SD	Sea Cliff
1	9.5	Ravena-Coeymans-Selkirk Cent SD	Ravena
3	9.6	Jericho UFSD	Jericho
3	9.6	Wayne Central SD	Ontario Center
5	9.7	Dryden Central SD	Dryden
6	9.9	Plattsburgh City SD	Plattsburgh
7	10.0	Southampton UFSD	Southampton
8	10.1	Great Neck UFSD	Great Neck
8	10.1	Lawrence UFSD	Cedarhurst
8	10.1	Mount Pleasant Central SD	Thornwood
11	10.2	Rondout Valley Central SD	Accord
12	10.3	Bayport-Blue Point UFSD	Bayport
12	10.3	East Hampton UFSD	East Hampton
14	10.4	Susquehanna Valley Central SD	Conklin
14	10.4	Syosset Central SD	Syosset
16	10.5	Lynbrook UFSD	Lynbrook
17	10.6	Dunkirk City SD	Dunkirk
17	10.6	East Williston UFSD	Old Westbury
17	10.6	Salmon River Central SD	Fort Covington
17	10.6	Westhampton Bch UFSD	Westhampton Bch
21	10.8	Irvington UFSD	Irvington
21	10.8	Palmyra-Macedon Central SD	Palmyra
21	10.8	Plainview-Old Bethpage CSD	Plainview
21	10.8	Windsor Central SD	Windsor
25	10.9	Greenburgh Central SD	Hartsdale
25	10.9	Phelps-Clifton Springs Central SD	Clifton Springs
25	10.9	Rockville Ctr UFSD	Rockville Ctr
28	11.0	Babylon UFSD	Babylon
28	11.0	Batavia City SD	Batavia
28	11.0	Cortland City SD	Cortland
28	11.0	Mexico Central SD	Mexico
28	11.0	Pleasantville UFSD	Pleasantville
33	11.1	Bethpage UFSD	Bethpage
33	11.1	Byram Hills Central SD	Armonk
33	11.1	Fredonia Central SD	Fredonia
33	11.1	Geneva City SD	Geneva
33	11.1	Hastings-On-Hudson UFSD	Hastings on Hdsn
33	11.1	Hewlett-Woodmere UFSD	Woodmere
33	11.1	Locust Valley Central SD	Locust Valley
33	11.1	Malverne UFSD	Malverne
33	11.1	Monticello Central SD	Monticello
33	11.1	Norwich City SD	Norwich
33	11.1	Oneonta City SD	Oneonta
44	11.2	Bath Central SD	Bath
44	11.2	Brighton Central SD	Rochester
44	11.2	Seaford UFSD	Seaford
44	11.2	Spencerport Central SD	Spencerport
44	11.2	Waterloo Central SD	Waterloo
49	11.3	Harrison Central SD	Harrison
49	11.3	Herricks UFSD	New Hyde Park
49	11.3	Kenmore-Tonawanda UFSD	Buffalo
49	11.3	Oyster Bay-East Norwich Central SD	Oyster Bay
49	11.3	Yorkshire-Pioneer Central SD	Yorkshire
54	11.4	Ardsley UFSD	Ardsley
54	11.4	Cold Spring Hrbr Central SD	Cold Spring Hrbr
54	11.4	Dansville Central SD	Dansville
54	11.4	East Irondequoit Central SD	Rochester
54	11.4	Livonia Central SD	Livonia
54	11.4	Newark Central SD	Newark
54	11.4	North Bellmore UFSD	Bellmore
54	11.4	Rush-Henrietta Central SD	Henrietta
62	11.5	Binghamton City SD	Binghamton
62	11.5	Brockport Central SD	Brockport
62	11.5	Cheektowaga Central SD	Cheektowaga
62	11.5	Deer Park UFSD	Deer Park
62	11.5	Hendrick Hudson Central SD	Montrose
62	11.5	Homer Central SD	Homer
62	11.5	Levittown UFSD	Levittown
62	11.5	Red Hook Central SD	Red Hook
70	11.6	Beekmantown Central SD	West Chazy
70	11.6	Cohoes City SD	Cohoes
70	11.6	Gates-Chili Central SD	Rochester
70	11.6	Massapequa UFSD	Massapequa
70	11.6	Mineola UFSD	Mineola
70	11.6	Phoenix Central SD	Phoenix
76	11.7	Amityville UFSD	Amityville
76	11.7	Canandaigua City SD	Canandaigua
76	11.7	Cobleskill-Richmondville CSD	Cobleskill
76	11.7	Depew UFSD	Depew
76	11.7	East Islip UFSD	Islip Terrace
76	11.7	East Syracuse Minoa Central SD	East Syracuse
76	11.7	Fairport Central SD	Fairport
76	11.7	Ramapo Central SD (Suffern)	Hillburn
76	11.7	Sweet Home Central SD	Amherst
76	11.7	Wantagh UFSD	Wantagh
86	11.8	Chittenango Central SD	Chittenango
86	11.8	Connetquot Central SD	Bohemia
86	11.8	Hudson City SD	Hudson
86	11.8	Iroquois Central SD	Elma
86	11.8	Island Trees UFSD	Levittown
86	11.8	Plainedge UFSD	N Massapequa
86	11.8	Roslyn UFSD	Roslyn
86	11.8	Valley Central SD (Montgomery)	Montgomery
94	11.9	Bedford Central SD	Bedford
94	11.9	Camden Central SD	Camden
94	11.9	Corning City SD	Painted Post
94	11.9	East Meadow UFSD	Westbury
94	11.9	Greece Central SD	Rochester
94	11.9	Ithaca City SD	Ithaca
94	11.9	Katonah-Lewisboro UFSD	South Salem
94	11.9	Mahopac Central SD	Mahopac
94	11.9	Medina Central SD	Medina
94	11.9	Nanuet UFSD	Nanuet
94	11.9	Penfield Central SD	Rochester
94	11.9	West Babylon UFSD	West Babylon
106	12.0	Blind Brook-Rye UFSD	Rye Brook
106	12.0	Burnt Hills-Ballston Lake Central SD	Scotia
106	12.0	Evans-Brant Central SD (Lake Shore)	Angola
106	12.0	Islip UFSD	Islip
106	12.0	Liberty Central SD	Liberty
106	12.0	Malone Central SD	Malone
106	12.0	Nyack UFSD	Nyack
106	12.0	Port Jervis City SD	Port Jervis
106	12.0	Scarsdale UFSD	Scarsdale
106	12.0	South Country Central SD	East Patchogue
106	12.0	Valley Stream 13 UFSD	Valley Stream
117	12.1	Catskill Central SD	Catskill
117	12.1	Chappaqua Central SD	Chappaqua
117	12.1	Tonawanda City SD	Tonawanda
120	12.2	Bronxville UFSD	Bronxville
120	12.2	Commack UFSD	East Northport
120	12.2	Fulton City SD	Fulton
120	12.2	Hauppauge UFSD	Hauppauge
120	12.2	Jamestown City SD	Jamestown
120	12.2	Kinderhook Central SD	Valatie
120	12.2	Kingston City SD	Kingston
120	12.2	Lackawanna City SD	Lackawanna
120	12.2	Lindenhurst UFSD	Lindenhurst
120	12.2	New Hyde Pk-Garden City Pk UFSD	New Hyde Park
120	12.2	Northport-East Northport UFSD	Northport
120	12.2	Olean City SD	Olean
120	12.2	Oswego City SD	Oswego
120	12.2	Peru Central SD	Peru
120	12.2	Rochester City SD	Rochester
120	12.2	Troy City SD	Troy
120	12.2	Uniondale UFSD	Uniondale
137	12.3	Amherst Central SD	Amherst
137	12.3	Honeoye Falls-Lima Central SD	Honeoye Falls
137	12.3	Lansingburgh Central SD	Troy
137	12.3	Schuylerville Central SD	Schuylerville
137	12.3	Springville-Griffith Institute CSD	Springville
137	12.3	Union-Endicott Central SD	Endicott
137	12.3	Vestal Central SD	Vestal
137	12.3	West Hempstead UFSD	West Hempstead
145	12.4	Alden Central SD	Alden
145	12.4	Elmont UFSD	Elmont
145	12.4	Gloversville City SD	Gloversville
145	12.4	Marcellus Central SD	Marcellus
145	12.4	New Hartford Central SD	New Hartford
145	12.4	North Colonie CSD	Latham
145	12.4	Shoreham-Wading River Central SD	Shoreham
145	12.4	West Islip UFSD	West Islip
153	12.5	Auburn City SD	Auburn
153	12.5	Baldwin UFSD	Baldwin
153	12.5	Clarkstown Central SD	New City
153	12.5	Hamburg Central SD	Hamburg
153	12.5	Johnson City Central SD	Johnson City
153	12.5	Lewiston-Porter Central SD	Youngstown
153	12.5	Manhasset UFSD	Manhasset
153	12.5	Ogdensburg City SD	Ogdensburg
153	12.5	Port Washington UFSD	Port Washington
153	12.5	South Huntington UFSD	Huntington Stn
153	12.5	Wallkill Central SD	Wallkill
153	12.5	Yorktown Central SD	Yorktown Hgts
165	12.6	Buffalo City SD	Buffalo
165	12.6	Carthage Central SD	Carthage
165	12.6	Central Valley CSD at Ilion-Mohawk	Ilion
165	12.6	Croton-Harmon UFSD	Croton on Hdsn
165	12.6	Guilderland Central SD	Guilderland Center
165	12.6	Huntington UFSD	Huntington Stn
165	12.6	Long Beach City SD	Long Beach
165	12.6	New Paltz Central SD	New Paltz
165	12.6	Pittsford Central SD	Pittsford
165	12.6	Saugerties Central SD	Saugerties
165	12.6	South Orangetown Central SD	Blauvelt
165	12.6	UFSD of the Tarrytowns	Sleepy Hollow
177	12.7	Bellmore-Merrick Central High SD	North Merrick
177	12.7	Eastport-South Manor CSD	Manorville
177	12.7	Edgemont UFSD	Scarsdale
177	12.7	Hampton Bays UFSD	Hampton Bays
177	12.7	Lockport City SD	Lockport
177	12.7	Orchard Park Central SD	West Seneca
177	12.7	Pelham UFSD	Pelham
177	12.7	Sayville UFSD	Sayville
185	12.8	Ballston Spa Central SD	Ballston Spa
185	12.8	Garden City UFSD	Garden City
185	12.8	Hilton Central SD	Hilton
185	12.8	Hyde Park Central SD	Hyde Park
185	12.8	Indian River Central SD	Philadelphia
185	12.8	Johnstown City SD	Johnstown
185	12.8	NYC Geographic District # 1	New York
185	12.8	Putnam Valley Central SD	Putnam Valley
185	12.8	South Colonie Central SD	Albany
194	12.9	Churchville-Chili Central SD	Churchville
194	12.9	East Greenbush Central SD	East Greenbush
194	12.9	Farmingdale UFSD	Farmingdale
194	12.9	Fayetteville-Manlius Central SD	Manlius
194	12.9	Grand Island Central SD	Grand Island
194	12.9	Half Hollow Hills Central SD	Dix Hills
194	12.9	Hornell City SD	Hornell
194	12.9	Mount Vernon SD	Mount Vernon
194	12.9	NYC Geographic District # 4	New York
194	12.9	Newburgh City SD	Newburgh
194	12.9	Oceanside UFSD	Oceanside
194	12.9	Rome City SD	Rome
194	12.9	Somers Central SD	Somers
194	12.9	Valley Stream Central High SD	Valley Stream
194	12.9	Whitesboro Central SD	Whitesboro
209	13.0	Beacon City SD	Beacon
209	13.0	Elwood UFSD	Greenlawn
209	13.0	Glen Cove City SD	Glen Cove
209	13.0	Kings Park Central SD	Kings Park
209	13.0	Lakeland Central SD	Shrub Oak
209	13.0	Miller Place UFSD	Miller Place
209	13.0	Queensbury UFSD	Queensbury
216	13.1	Rye City SD	Rye
216	13.1	Rye Neck UFSD	Mamaroneck
216	13.1	Schalmont Central SD	Schenectady
216	13.1	Scotia-Glenville Central SD	Scotia
216	13.1	Williamsville Central SD	East Amherst
221	13.2	Albion Central SD	Albion
221	13.2	Bay Shore UFSD	Bay Shore
221	13.2	Carmel Central SD	Patterson
221	13.2	Gouverneur Central SD	Gouverneur
221	13.2	Harborfields Central SD	Greenlawn
221	13.2	Highland Central SD	Highland
221	13.2	Liverpool Central SD	Liverpool
221	13.2	Maine-Endwell Central SD	Endwell
221	13.2	Newfane Central SD	Burt
221	13.2	Niskayuna Central SD	Schenectady
221	13.2	Oneida City SD	Oneida
221	13.2	Pearl River UFSD	Pearl River
221	13.2	Sherrill City SD	Verona
221	13.2	S Glens Fls Central SD	S Glens Fls
221	13.2	Westhill Central SD	Syracuse
236	13.3	Chenango Forks Central SD	Binghamton
236	13.3	Starpoint Central SD	Lockport
236	13.3	Three Village Central SD	Stony Brook
239	13.4	Central Square Central SD	Central Square
239	13.4	Eastchester UFSD	Eastchester
239	13.4	Goshen Central SD	Goshen
239	13.4	Rocky Point UFSD	Rocky Point
239	13.4	Victor Central SD	Victor
239	13.4	White Plains City SD	White Plains
245	13.5	Amsterdam City SD	Amsterdam
245	13.5	Averill Park Central SD	Averill Park
245	13.5	Brewster Central SD	Brewster
245	13.5	Chenango Valley Central SD	Binghamton

Note: This section only includes districts with 1,500 or more students; All categories are ranked from high to low

Rank	Number	District Name	City
245	13.5	Jamesville-Dewitt Central SD	Dewitt
245	13.5	Saratoga Spgs City SD	Saratoga Spgs
245	13.5	Webster Central SD	Webster
245	13.5	West Irondequoit Central SD	Rochester
253	13.6	Broadalbin-Perth Central SD	Broadalbin
253	13.6	Clarence Central SD	Clarence
253	13.6	Hicksville UFSD	Hicksville
253	13.6	Marlboro Central SD	Milton
253	13.6	Mount Sinai UFSD	Mount Sinai
253	13.6	Owego-Apalachin Central SD	Owego
259	13.7	Albany City SD	Albany
259	13.7	Syracuse City SD	Syracuse
259	13.7	Washingtonville Central SD	Washingtonville
259	13.7	West Genesee Central SD	Camillus
263	13.8	Center Moriches UFSD	Center Moriches
263	13.8	Freeport UFSD	Freeport
263	13.8	Glens Falls City SD	Glens Falls
263	13.8	Hudson Falls Central SD	Fort Edward
263	13.8	Mamaroneck UFSD	Mamaroneck
263	13.8	NYC Geographic District #15	Brooklyn
263	13.8	NYC Geographic District #16	Brooklyn
263	13.8	North Babylon UFSD	North Babylon
263	13.8	Waverly Central SD	Waverly
272	13.9	Arlington Central SD	Lagrangeville
272	13.9	Frontier Central SD	Hamburg
272	13.9	Lancaster Central SD	Lancaster
272	13.9	Minisink Valley Central SD	Slate Hill
272	13.9	NYC Geographic District # 7	Bronx
272	13.9	Valley Stream 30 UFSD	Valley Stream
278	14.0	Brookhaven-Comsewogue UFSD	Port Jeff Stn
278	14.0	Middle Country Central SD	Centereach
278	14.0	Ossining UFSD	Ossining
278	14.0	Watertown City SD	Watertown
282	14.1	Bethlehem Central SD	Delmar
282	14.1	NYC Geographic District #14	Brooklyn
282	14.1	North Tonawanda City SD	North Tonawanda
282	14.1	Smithtown Central SD	Smithtown
286	14.2	Ellenville Central SD	Ellenville
286	14.2	Franklin Square UFSD	Franklin Square
286	14.2	Rotterdam-Mohonasen Central SD	Schenectady
286	14.2	South Jefferson Central SD	Adams Center
290	14.3	Massena Central SD	Massena
290	14.3	Middletown City SD	Middletown
290	14.3	NYC Geographic District # 5	New York
290	14.3	North Syracuse Central SD	North Syracuse
290	14.3	Pine Bush Central SD	Pine Bush
290	14.3	Port Chester-Rye UFSD	Port Chester
290	14.3	Warwick Valley Central SD	Warwick
290	14.3	New York City Chancellor's Office	New York
298	14.4	Cheektowaga-Maryvale UFSD	Cheektowaga
298	14.4	Longwood Central SD	Middle Island
298	14.4	Monroe-Woodbury Central SD	Central Valley
298	14.4	NYC Geographic District # 8	Bronx
298	14.4	NYC Geographic District #12	Bronx
298	14.4	NYC Geographic District #32	Brooklyn
298	14.4	Sachem Central SD	Lake Ronkonkoma
305	14.5	NYC Geographic District #23	Brooklyn
305	14.5	Roosevelt UFSD	Roosevelt
305	14.5	Schenectady City SD	Schenectady
308	14.6	Baldwinsville Central SD	Baldwinsville
308	14.6	East Ramapo CSD (Spring Valley)	Spring Valley
308	14.6	Haverstraw-Stony Point CSD	Garnerville
308	14.6	NYC Geographic District # 6	New York
308	14.6	NYC Geographic District #18	Brooklyn
313	14.7	Horseheads Central SD	Horseheads
313	14.7	NYC Geographic District # 3	New York
313	14.7	Wappingers Central SD	Hopewell Junction
313	14.7	West Seneca Central SD	West Seneca
317	14.8	Central Islip UFSD	Central Islip
317	14.8	NYC Geographic District # 9	Bronx
317	14.8	NYC Geographic District #10	Bronx
320	14.9	Cornwall Central SD	Cornwall on Hdsn
320	14.9	Poughkeepsie City SD	Poughkeepsie
320	14.9	William Floyd UFSD	Mastic Beach
323	15.0	Elmira City SD	Elmira
323	15.0	Niagara-Wheatfield Central SD	Niagara Falls
323	15.0	Patchogue-Medford UFSD	Patchogue
326	15.1	New Rochelle City SD	New Rochelle
326	15.1	NYC Geographic District #17	Brooklyn
326	15.1	Riverhead Central SD	Riverhead
329	15.2	Charter School for Applied Techs	Buffalo
329	15.2	East Aurora UFSD	East Aurora
331	15.3	Shenendehowa Central SD	Clifton Park
332	15.4	NYC Geographic District #19	Brooklyn
332	15.4	Peekskill City SD	Peekskill
334	15.5	Wyandanch UFSD	Wyandanch
335	15.6	NYC Geographic District # 2	New York
335	15.6	NYC Geographic District #21	Brooklyn
337	15.7	NYC Geographic District #31	Staten Island
337	15.7	Utica City SD	Utica
339	15.8	NYC Geographic District #25	Flushing
339	15.8	NYC Geographic District #27	Ozone Park
341	15.9	NYC Geographic District #11	Bronx
341	15.9	NYC Geographic District #20	Brooklyn
343	16.0	NYC Geographic District #30	Long Isl City
344	16.3	General Brown Central SD	Dexter
344	16.3	Sewanhaka Central High SD	Floral Park
346	16.4	NYC Geographic District #29	Queens Village
347	16.5	Niagara Falls City SD	Niagara Falls
348	16.6	NYC Geographic District #13	Brooklyn
348	16.6	NYC Geographic District #24	Corona
348	16.6	Westbury UFSD	Old Westbury
351	16.8	Copiague UFSD	Copiague
351	16.8	NYC Geographic District #22	Brooklyn
353	17.2	NYC Geographic District #28	Jamaica
354	17.5	Brentwood UFSD	Brentwood
354	17.5	Yonkers City SD	Yonkers
356	18.0	NYC Geographic District #26	Bayside
357	25.6	Hempstead UFSD	Hempstead

Student/Librarian Ratio

(number of students per librarian)

Rank	Number	District Name	City
1	312.5	Locust Valley Central SD	Locust Valley
2	362.9	Oneida City SD	Oneida
3	378.3	Seaford UFSD	Seaford
4	385.1	Fulton City SD	Fulton
5	386.6	North Colonie CSD	Latham
6	397.8	Sherrill City SD	Verona
7	400.9	Oneonta City SD	Oneonta
8	412.0	Ithaca City SD	Ithaca
9	414.9	Scotia-Glenville Central SD	Scotia
10	423.8	Wayne Central SD	Ontario Center
11	431.3	Cobleskill-Richmondville CSD	Cobleskill
12	445.9	East Irondequoit Central SD	Rochester
12	445.9	Westhill Central SD	Syracuse
14	450.0	Lindenhurst UFSD	Lindenhurst
15	455.9	Rye Neck UFSD	Mamaroneck
16	456.7	Camden Central SD	Camden
17	461.4	Valley Stream 13 UFSD	Valley Stream
18	470.1	Greenburgh Central SD	Hartsdale
19	472.0	Kinderhook Central SD	Valatie
20	472.8	Peru Central SD	Peru
21	477.2	Red Hook Central SD	Red Hook
22	487.4	Rondout Valley Central SD	Accord
23	488.8	Uniondale UFSD	Uniondale
24	489.9	Evans-Brant Central SD (Lake Shore)	Angola
25	497.8	West Babylon UFSD	West Babylon
26	499.0	Yorkshire-Pioneer Central SD	Yorkshire
27	505.7	Cortland City SD	Cortland
28	506.9	New Hyde Pk-Garden City Pk UFSD	New Hyde Park
29	508.3	Homer Central SD	Homer
30	508.4	Blind Brook-Rye UFSD	Rye Brook
31	509.1	Mount Pleasant Central SD	Thornwood
32	511.6	Palmyra-Macedon Central SD	Palmyra
33	514.3	Dansville Central SD	Dansville
34	519.1	Sweet Home Central SD	Amherst
35	526.2	Valley Stream 30 UFSD	Valley Stream
36	533.5	Ravena-Coeymans-Selkirk Cent SD	Ravena
37	536.4	Liverpool Central SD	Liverpool
38	538.0	Oyster Bay-East Norwich Central SD	Oyster Bay
39	539.4	Whitesboro Central SD	Whitesboro
40	540.0	Livonia Central SD	Livonia
41	542.1	South Colonie Central SD	Albany
42	549.0	Schuylerville Central SD	Schuylerville
43	549.1	Oswego City SD	Oswego
44	550.0	Croton-Harmon UFSD	Croton on Hdsn
45	550.3	Medina Central SD	Medina
46	552.5	Chappaqua UFSD	Chappaqua
47	552.7	Southampton UFSD	Southampton
48	554.2	Burnt Hills-Ballston Lake Central SD	Scotia
49	556.0	Nanuet UFSD	Nanuet
50	556.7	Penfield Central SD	Rochester
51	559.3	Honeoye Falls-Lima Central SD	Honeoye Falls
52	559.6	Hastings-On-Hudson UFSD	Hastings on Hdsn
53	571.0	Averill Park Central SD	Averill Park
54	571.8	Guilderland Central SD	Guilderland Center
55	573.5	Massapequa UFSD	Massapequa
56	574.8	Tonawanda City SD	Tonawanda
57	575.7	East Syracuse Minoa Central SD	East Syracuse
58	576.3	Bayport-Blue Point UFSD	Bayport
59	578.5	Iroquois Central SD	Elma
60	579.3	S Glens Fls Central SD	S Glens Fls
61	580.4	Bethpage UFSD	Bethpage
62	580.9	Hicksville UFSD	Hicksville
63	587.1	Niskayuna Central SD	Schenectady
64	591.6	Grand Island Central SD	Grand Island
64	591.6	New Hartford Central SD	New Hartford
66	591.7	Lynbrook UFSD	Lynbrook
67	595.0	Bedford Central SD	Bedford
68	595.4	Jericho UFSD	Jericho
69	595.8	West Irondequoit Central SD	Rochester
70	596.1	Gates-Chili Central SD	Rochester
71	596.6	Nyack UFSD	Nyack
72	597.7	Cold Spring Hrbr Central SD	Cold Spring Hrbr
73	598.6	Scarsdale UFSD	Scarsdale
74	600.0	East Aurora UFSD	East Aurora
75	600.3	Great Neck UFSD	Great Neck
76	600.5	Indian River Central SD	Philadelphia
77	602.1	Hauppauge UFSD	Hauppauge
78	605.3	Kenmore-Tonawanda UFSD	Buffalo
79	607.6	Plainedge UFSD	N Massapequa
80	608.3	Eastport-South Manor CSD	Manorville
81	609.9	Schalmont Central SD	Schenectady
82	610.6	Hudson City SD	Hudson
83	611.1	Plainview-Old Bethpage CSD	Plainview
84	614.1	Syosset Central SD	Syosset
85	615.0	Auburn City SD	Auburn
86	619.2	Island Trees UFSD	Levittown
87	621.1	Valley Central SD (Montgomery)	Montgomery
88	623.7	Central Square Central SD	Central Square
89	624.3	Plattsburgh City SD	Plattsburgh
90	625.6	Port Jervis City SD	Port Jervis
91	626.2	Brookhaven-Comsewogue UFSD	Port Jeff Stn
92	628.1	Roslyn UFSD	Roslyn
93	631.2	Katonah-Lewisboro UFSD	South Salem
94	632.8	Elmont UFSD	Elmont
95	634.8	Johnstown City SD	Johnstown
96	638.4	Brewster Central SD	Brewster
97	639.4	Elwood UFSD	Greenlawn
98	642.3	Chittenango Central SD	Chittenango
99	647.5	Edgemont UFSD	Scarsdale
100	649.1	Saugerties Central SD	Saugerties
101	649.8	East Meadow UFSD	Westbury
102	649.9	Orchard Park Central SD	West Seneca
103	651.5	Longwood Central SD	Middle Island
104	652.2	Hyde Park Central SD	Hyde Park
105	657.1	Rochester City SD	Rochester
106	658.2	Albion Central SD	Albion
107	658.4	Bethlehem Central SD	Delmar
108	659.0	Saratoga Spgs City SD	Saratoga Spgs
109	659.6	East Williston UFSD	Old Westbury
110	662.7	Greece Central SD	Rochester
111	671.1	East Ramapo CSD (Spring Valley)	Spring Valley
112	672.0	Syracuse City SD	Syracuse
113	672.8	Binghamton City SD	Binghamton
114	673.0	Roosevelt UFSD	Roosevelt
115	680.6	Rush-Henrietta Central SD	Henrietta
116	683.5	Corning City SD	Painted Post
117	685.5	Malverne UFSD	Malverne
118	686.6	Farmingdale UFSD	Farmingdale
119	687.5	Spencerport Central SD	Spencerport
120	694.2	West Islip UFSD	West Islip
121	697.3	Mineola UFSD	Mineola
122	698.6	Yorktown Central SD	Yorktown Hgts
123	699.6	Baldwinsville Central SD	Baldwinsville
124	701.7	Fayetteville-Manlius Central SD	Manlius
125	706.0	Brighton Central SD	Rochester
126	707.4	Byram Hills Central SD	Armonk
127	709.0	Brockport Central SD	Brockport
128	709.1	North Bellmore UFSD	Bellmore
129	710.5	Sachem Central SD	Lake Ronkonkoma
130	710.8	Kingston City SD	Kingston
131	711.6	Hamburg Central SD	Hamburg
131	711.6	Long Beach City SD	Long Beach
133	718.3	Beekmantown Central SD	West Chazy
134	718.7	Lakeland Central SD	Shrub Oak
135	720.3	Owego-Apalachin Central SD	Owego
136	721.7	Three Village Central SD	Stony Brook
137	723.6	Monroe-Woodbury Central SD	Central Valley

Note: This section only includes districts with 1,500 or more students; All categories are ranked from high to low

138	723.7	Mexico Central SD	Mexico
139	725.5	Hewlett-Woodmere UFSD	Woodmere
140	735.4	Garden City UFSD	Garden City
141	738.7	Williamsville Central SD	East Amherst
142	739.0	Arlington Central SD	Lagrangeville
143	739.4	Monticello Central SD	Monticello
144	740.9	Cheektowaga-Maryvale UFSD	Cheektowaga
145	742.5	Amherst Central SD	Amherst
146	744.4	West Seneca Central SD	West Seneca
147	747.4	Patchogue-Medford UFSD	Patchogue
148	748.5	Springville-Griffith Institute CSD	Springville
149	749.8	Clarence Central SD	Clarence
150	750.0	Sayville UFSD	Sayville
151	753.0	Newburgh City SD	Newburgh
152	753.5	South Country Central SD	East Patchogue
153	755.7	Wantagh UFSD	Wantagh
154	759.9	General Brown Central SD	Dexter
155	761.5	Connetquot Central SD	Bohemia
156	767.0	Pine Bush Central SD	Pine Bush
157	767.1	Starpoint Central SD	Lockport
158	767.3	Hampton Bays UFSD	Hampton Bays
159	768.8	Port Washington UFSD	Port Washington
160	768.9	Massena Central SD	Massena
161	771.7	Batavia City SD	Batavia
162	771.8	Harrison Central SD	Harrison
163	772.6	Herricks UFSD	New Hyde Park
164	773.4	Susquehanna Valley Central SD	Conklin
165	778.0	Minisink Valley Central SD	Slate Hill
166	780.4	North Babylon UFSD	North Babylon
167	780.6	Rome City SD	Rome
168	783.7	Wappingers Central SD	Hopewell Junction
169	784.7	Chenango Forks Central SD	Binghamton
170	785.6	White Plains City SD	White Plains
171	787.5	Phelps-Clifton Springs Central SD	Clifton Springs
172	788.7	Smithtown Central SD	Smithtown
173	788.8	Clarkstown Central SD	New City
174	796.0	Bath Central SD	Bath
175	796.5	Gouverneur Central SD	Gouverneur
176	797.9	Webster Central SD	Webster
177	798.0	Babylon UFSD	Babylon
177	798.0	Hendrick Hudson Central SD	Montrose
177	798.0	Somers Central SD	Somers
180	799.5	Salmon River Central SD	Fort Covington
181	809.0	Cornwall Central SD	Cornwall on Hdsn
182	810.8	Mount Vernon SD	Mount Vernon
183	811.5	Amityville UFSD	Amityville
184	812.8	Carthage Central SD	Carthage
185	813.0	Liberty Central SD	Liberty
186	813.1	Phoenix Central SD	Phoenix
187	816.1	Frontier Central SD	Hamburg
188	818.4	North Syracuse Central SD	North Syracuse
189	824.0	Center Moriches UFSD	Center Moriches
190	825.1	Alden Central SD	Alden
191	828.0	Ballston Spa Central SD	Ballston Spa
192	837.3	Queensbury UFSD	Queensbury
193	838.4	Horseheads Central SD	Horseheads
194	845.3	Waterloo Central SD	Waterloo
195	846.5	Windsor Central SD	Windsor
196	856.9	Wyandanch UFSD	Wyandanch
197	862.4	Fairport Central SD	Fairport
198	866.8	Ellenville Central SD	Ellenville
199	872.2	Commack UFSD	East Northport
200	877.5	Hudson Falls Central SD	Fort Edward
201	883.8	Shenendehowa Central SD	Clifton Park
202	885.6	Riverhead Central SD	Riverhead
203	886.0	Huntington UFSD	Huntington Stn
203	886.0	Lackawanna City SD	Lackawanna
205	887.5	Irvington UFSD	Irvington
206	888.6	Hilton Central SD	Hilton
207	893.4	Victor Central SD	Victor
208	900.5	Rye City SD	Rye
209	901.3	Rotterdam-Mohonasen Central SD	Schenectady
210	904.5	East Hampton UFSD	East Hampton
211	906.3	North Shore Central SD	Sea Cliff
212	915.8	Jamestown City SD	Jamestown
213	918.4	Albany City SD	Albany
214	918.5	Utica City SD	Utica
215	918.8	Warwick Valley Central SD	Warwick
216	919.9	West Genesee Central SD	Camillus
217	932.6	Northport-East Northport UFSD	Northport
218	934.2	Depew UFSD	Depew
219	934.4	Pelham UFSD	Pelham
220	941.5	Norwich City SD	Norwich
221	943.9	Half Hollow Hills Central SD	Dix Hills
222	944.9	Pittsford Central SD	Pittsford
223	956.0	Amsterdam City SD	Amsterdam
224	968.0	Pleasantville UFSD	Pleasantville
225	968.7	Dryden Central SD	Dryden
226	970.6	Churchville-Chili Central SD	Churchville
227	971.9	Union-Endicott Central SD	Endicott
228	979.8	William Floyd UFSD	Mastic Beach
229	980.0	Kings Park Central SD	Kings Park
230	980.3	Goshen Central SD	Goshen
231	986.0	Jamesville-Dewitt Central SD	Dewitt
232	990.5	Watertown City SD	Watertown
233	992.4	Haverstraw-Stony Point CSD	Garnerville
234	994.7	Freeport UFSD	Freeport
235	1,003.5	East Greenbush Central SD	East Greenbush
236	1,007.0	Franklin Square UFSD	Franklin Square
237	1,012.8	South Huntington UFSD	Huntington Stn
238	1,015.8	Beacon City SD	Beacon
239	1,019.5	Charter School for Applied Techs	Buffalo
240	1,028.7	Lewiston-Porter Central SD	Youngstown
241	1,043.7	West Hempstead UFSD	West Hempstead
242	1,046.3	Central Islip UFSD	Central Islip
243	1,059.2	Maine-Endwell Central SD	Endwell
244	1,062.3	Eastchester UFSD	Eastchester
245	1,078.4	Bay Shore UFSD	Bay Shore
246	1,082.7	Rocky Point UFSD	Rocky Point
247	1,091.2	Bellmore-Merrick Central High SD	North Merrick
248	1,112.7	Manhasset UFSD	Manhasset
249	1,114.6	Mamaroneck UFSD	Mamaroneck
250	1,115.7	Newark Central SD	Newark
251	1,119.1	Ogdensburg City SD	Ogdensburg
252	1,121.4	Vestal Central SD	Vestal
253	1,130.8	Valley Stream Central High SD	Valley Stream
254	1,141.0	Geneva City SD	Geneva
255	1,164.3	Shoreham-Wading River Central SD	Shoreham
256	1,174.8	Lockport City SD	Lockport
257	1,190.5	Mount Sinai UFSD	Mount Sinai
258	1,244.1	Ossining UFSD	Ossining
259	1,262.0	Westbury UFSD	Old Westbury
260	1,271.1	South Orangetown Central SD	Blauvelt
261	1,281.0	Johnson City Central SD	Johnson City
262	1,291.3	East Islip UFSD	Islip Terrace
263	1,331.1	North Tonawanda City SD	North Tonawanda
264	1,340.0	Lawrence UFSD	Cedarhurst
265	1,357.0	Troy City SD	Troy
266	1,366.6	Buffalo City SD	Buffalo
267	1,370.0	Glens Falls City SD	Glens Falls
268	1,381.4	Miller Place UFSD	Miller Place
269	1,386.6	Schenectady City SD	Schenectady
270	1,393.0	Washingtonville Central SD	Washingtonville
271	1,411.4	Catskill Central SD	Catskill
272	1,415.5	Gloversville City SD	Gloversville
273	1,417.6	Carmel Central SD	Patterson
274	1,423.1	New Rochelle City SD	New Rochelle
275	1,445.0	Islip UFSD	Islip
276	1,466.8	Middletown City SD	Middletown
277	1,512.5	Wallkill Central SD	Wallkill
278	1,534.3	Fredonia Central SD	Fredonia
279	1,541.7	Bronxville UFSD	Bronxville
280	1,589.3	Baldwin UFSD	Baldwin
281	1,606.4	Harborfields Central SD	Greenlawn
282	1,610.0	Newfane Central SD	Burt
283	1,614.0	Waverly Central SD	Waverly
284	1,641.3	Pearl River UFSD	Pearl River
285	1,668.0	Deer Park UFSD	Deer Park
286	1,671.9	Glen Cove City SD	Glen Cove
287	1,722.0	Putnam Valley Central SD	Putnam Valley
288	1,760.0	Rockville Ctr UFSD	Rockville Ctr
289	1,765.3	Niagara Falls City SD	Niagara Falls
290	1,765.7	Highland Central SD	Highland
291	1,774.5	Levittown UFSD	Levittown
292	1,777.5	Westhampton Bch UFSD	Westhampton Bch
293	1,798.5	Canandaigua City SD	Canandaigua
294	1,811.0	Chenango Valley Central SD	Binghamton
295	1,836.0	Broadalbin-Perth Central SD	Broadalbin
296	1,870.0	Cohoes City SD	Cohoes
297	1,894.1	Brentwood UFSD	Brentwood
298	1,981.0	Marlboro Central SD	Milton
299	2,001.6	Middle Country Central SD	Centereach
300	2,014.4	NYC Geographic District #32	Brooklyn
301	2,047.0	Ardsley UFSD	Ardsley
302	2,086.7	Elmira City SD	Elmira
303	2,095.0	Dunkirk City SD	Dunkirk
304	2,111.0	Cheektowaga Central SD	Cheektowaga
305	2,122.8	NYC Geographic District # 4	New York
306	2,172.7	Copiague UFSD	Copiague
307	2,185.3	New Paltz Central SD	New Paltz
308	2,186.0	Olean City SD	Olean
309	2,205.0	Poughkeepsie City SD	Poughkeepsie
310	2,219.1	Ramapo Central SD (Suffern)	Hillburn
311	2,248.2	NYC Geographic District # 1	New York
312	2,334.0	Malone Central SD	Malone
313	2,357.0	Lansingburgh Central SD	Troy
314	2,372.0	Central Valley CSD at Ilion-Mohawk	Ilion
315	2,395.8	NYC Geographic District #13	Brooklyn
316	2,451.4	NYC Geographic District #26	Bayside
317	2,695.7	Sewanhaka Central High SD	Floral Park
318	2,761.8	NYC Geographic District # 8	Bronx
319	2,762.0	UFSD of the Tarrytowns	Sleepy Hollow
320	2,812.8	NYC Geographic District #10	Bronx
321	2,938.5	NYC Geographic District #30	Long Isl City
322	2,951.9	NYC Geographic District #22	Brooklyn
323	3,101.2	NYC Geographic District #31	Staten Island
324	3,121.3	Port Chester-Rye UFSD	Port Chester
325	3,143.4	NYC Geographic District #24	Corona
326	3,144.7	NYC Geographic District #20	Brooklyn
327	3,165.5	NYC Geographic District #21	Brooklyn
328	3,273.1	NYC Geographic District #12	Bronx
329	3,409.0	NYC Geographic District # 3	New York
330	3,410.5	NYC Geographic District #28	Jamaica
331	3,476.8	NYC Geographic District # 5	New York
332	3,480.2	Yonkers City SD	Yonkers
333	3,549.1	New York City Chancellor's Office	New York
334	3,642.4	NYC Geographic District # 2	New York
335	3,704.0	Niagara-Wheatfield Central SD	Niagara Falls
336	3,800.0	NYC Geographic District #16	Brooklyn
337	3,833.0	NYC Geographic District #14	Brooklyn
338	3,894.0	NYC Geographic District #17	Brooklyn
339	3,938.6	NYC Geographic District #27	Ozone Park
340	4,014.5	Hempstead UFSD	Hempstead
341	4,355.0	Mahopac Central SD	Mahopac
342	4,658.1	NYC Geographic District #29	Queens Village
343	4,674.4	NYC Geographic District #25	Flushing
344	4,695.4	NYC Geographic District # 6	New York
345	4,832.6	NYC Geographic District #19	Brooklyn
346	5,061.9	NYC Geographic District # 7	Bronx
347	5,090.2	NYC Geographic District # 9	Bronx
348	5,120.9	NYC Geographic District #23	Brooklyn
349	5,129.9	NYC Geographic District #15	Brooklyn
350	5,346.3	NYC Geographic District #11	Bronx
351	5,542.1	NYC Geographic District #18	Brooklyn
n/a	n/a	Hornell City SD	Hornell
n/a	n/a	Lancaster Central SD	Lancaster
n/a	n/a	Marcellus Central SD	Marcellus
n/a	n/a	Oceanside UFSD	Oceanside
n/a	n/a	Peekskill City SD	Peekskill
n/a	n/a	South Jefferson Central SD	Adams Center

Student/Counselor Ratio

(number of students per counselor)

Rank	Number	District Name	City
1	185.4	Charter School for Applied Techs	Buffalo
2	206.6	Depew UFSD	Depew
3	209.1	Beekmantown Central SD	West Chazy
4	209.2	Norwich City SD	Norwich
5	210.5	Batavia City SD	Batavia
6	211.1	Cheektowaga Central SD	Cheektowaga
7	212.2	Malone Central SD	Malone
8	214.4	East Williston UFSD	Old Westbury
9	216.4	Blind Brook-Rye UFSD	Rye Brook
9	216.4	Valley Stream Central High SD	Valley Stream
11	218.6	Olean City SD	Olean
12	222.7	Palmyra-Macedon Central SD	Palmyra
13	224.2	Wayne Central SD	Ontario Center
14	224.5	Evans-Brant Central SD (Lake Shore)	Angola
15	226.3	Bath Central SD	Bath
16	231.9	Waterloo Central SD	Waterloo
17	233.2	Bellmore-Merrick Central High SD	North Merrick
18	236.9	Southampton UFSD	Southampton
19	237.9	Bronxville UFSD	Bronxville
20	238.3	West Irondequoit Central SD	Rochester
21	240.9	Chittenango Central SD	Chittenango
22	241.9	Windsor Central SD	Windsor
23	242.5	Rondout Valley Central SD	Accord
24	242.9	Oneonta City SD	Oneonta
25	244.0	Port Jervis City SD	Port Jervis
26	244.3	Somers Central SD	Somers

Note: This section only includes districts with 1,500 or more students; All categories are ranked from high to low

Rank	Score	District	Location
27	245.9	Cobleskill-Richmondville CSD	Cobleskill
28	246.0	Salmon River Central SD	Fort Covington
29	248.7	Penfield Central SD	Rochester
30	254.6	West Genesee Central SD	Camillus
31	255.9	Ardsley UFSD	Ardsley
32	257.2	Dansville Central SD	Dansville
33	257.7	Chappaqua Central SD	Chappaqua
34	259.0	Westhampton Bch UFSD	Westhampton Bch
35	262.5	NYC Geographic District # 1	New York
36	263.0	Hastings-On-Hudson UFSD	Hastings on Hdsn
36	263.0	Katonah-Lewisboro UFSD	South Salem
38	265.2	Rye Neck UFSD	Mamaroneck
39	268.2	Gouverneur Central SD	Gouverneur
40	268.3	Ravena-Coeymans-Selkirk Cent SD	Ravena
41	270.6	Mount Pleasant Central SD	Thornwood
42	271.0	Liberty Central SD	Liberty
43	275.1	Byram Hills Central SD	Armonk
44	275.2	Medina Central SD	Medina
45	275.7	North Colonie CSD	Latham
46	279.3	Lynbrook UFSD	Lynbrook
47	279.6	Honeoye Falls-Lima Central SD	Honeoye Falls
48	280.8	Greece Central SD	Rochester
48	280.8	Troy City SD	Troy
50	281.1	Albion Central SD	Albion
51	284.9	Niagara-Wheatfield Central SD	Niagara Falls
52	286.1	Roslyn UFSD	Roslyn
53	286.3	Canandaigua City SD	Canandaigua
54	286.9	Sweet Home Central SD	Amherst
55	287.6	Plainview-Old Bethpage CSD	Plainview
56	290.5	Hornell City SD	Hornell
57	291.2	Brighton Central SD	Rochester
58	291.7	East Syracuse Minoa Central SD	East Syracuse
59	293.2	Springville-Griffith Institute CSD	Springville
60	294.3	Brockport Central SD	Brockport
61	296.7	West Hempstead UFSD	West Hempstead
62	297.3	Hendrick Hudson Central SD	Montrose
63	297.9	Mount Vernon SD	Mount Vernon
64	300.5	Niagara Falls City SD	Niagara Falls
65	300.7	Fayetteville-Manlius Central SD	Manlius
66	300.8	Cold Spring Hrbr Central SD	Cold Spring Hrbr
67	301.9	Spencerport Central SD	Spencerport
68	304.5	Queensbury UFSD	Queensbury
69	304.8	Vestal Central SD	Vestal
70	306.0	NYC Geographic District # 7	Bronx
71	307.6	Massena Central SD	Massena
72	308.1	Bethlehem Central SD	Delmar
73	310.4	Liverpool Central SD	Liverpool
74	312.2	Plattsburgh City SD	Plattsburgh
75	312.4	Rotterdam-Mohonasen Central SD	Schenectady
76	313.6	Pelham UFSD	Pelham
76	313.6	Pittsford Central SD	Pittsford
78	314.6	Gloversville City SD	Gloversville
79	315.2	Peru Central SD	Peru
80	317.3	Red Hook Central SD	Red Hook
81	317.7	Nanuet UFSD	Nanuet
82	319.5	NYC Geographic District #17	Brooklyn
83	320.8	Babylon UFSD	Babylon
84	321.4	Harrison Central SD	Harrison
85	321.6	Dryden Central SD	Dryden
86	322.0	Island Trees UFSD	Levittown
86	322.0	Newfane Central SD	Burt
88	322.4	Rome City SD	Rome
89	322.7	Irvington UFSD	Irvington
90	322.8	Oyster Bay-East Norwich Central SD	Oyster Bay
91	326.2	Long Beach City SD	Long Beach
92	326.3	Indian River Central SD	Philadelphia
93	326.4	Shenendehowa Central SD	Clifton Park
94	327.0	NYC Geographic District # 9	Bronx
95	328.5	Half Hollow Hills Central SD	Dix Hills
96	329.4	Schuylerville Central SD	Schuylerville
97	331.2	NYC Geographic District # 5	New York
98	331.4	Great Neck UFSD	Great Neck
99	331.7	Hauppauge UFSD	Hauppauge
100	333.6	Monticello Central SD	Monticello
101	334.1	Jericho UFSD	Jericho
101	334.1	Warwick Valley Central SD	Warwick
103	335.0	Lawrence UFSD	Cedarhurst
104	335.6	Starpoint Central SD	Lockport
105	336.1	Wallkill Central SD	Wallkill
106	336.2	NYC Geographic District #13	Brooklyn
107	337.6	Wantagh UFSD	Wantagh
108	338.2	Marcellus Central SD	Marcellus
109	338.8	Pleasantville UFSD	Pleasantville
110	339.8	Newark Central SD	Newark
111	340.2	Ogdensburg City SD	Ogdensburg
112	341.4	Massapequa UFSD	Massapequa
113	341.6	Harborfields Central SD	Greenlawn
114	341.7	Uniondale UFSD	Uniondale
115	341.8	Hewlett-Woodmere UFSD	Woodmere
116	342.0	Rush-Henrietta Central SD	Henrietta
117	344.5	Oswego City SD	Oswego
118	344.7	Commack UFSD	East Northport
118	344.7	Three Village Central SD	Stony Brook
120	345.3	East Irondequoit Central SD	Rochester
121	345.5	NYC Geographic District #16	Brooklyn
122	346.1	NYC Geographic District #23	Brooklyn
123	347.2	Tonawanda City SD	Tonawanda
124	348.6	Yorktown Central SD	Yorktown Hgts
125	349.9	Williamsville Central SD	East Amherst
126	350.2	Ellenville Central SD	Ellenville
127	350.5	Locust Valley Central SD	Locust Valley
128	350.6	Washingtonville Central SD	Washingtonville
129	351.0	Kenmore-Tonawanda UFSD	Buffalo
130	351.3	Jamestown City SD	Jamestown
131	354.7	Churchville-Chili Central SD	Churchville
132	354.9	Levittown UFSD	Levittown
133	355.4	Hilton Central SD	Hilton
133	355.4	North Tonawanda City SD	North Tonawanda
135	355.8	Westhill Central SD	Syracuse
136	357.4	East Meadow UFSD	Westbury
137	357.8	Cornwall Central SD	Cornwall on Hdsn
138	358.7	NYC Geographic District # 8	Bronx
139	359.8	Port Washington UFSD	Port Washington
140	360.0	East Aurora UFSD	East Aurora
141	360.2	NYC Geographic District #18	Brooklyn
142	360.6	Westbury UFSD	Old Westbury
143	361.2	NYC Geographic District # 6	New York
144	361.3	Islip UFSD	Islip
145	361.7	NYC Geographic District #19	Brooklyn
146	361.8	Mexico Central SD	Mexico
147	362.4	Fulton City SD	Fulton
148	362.8	Bethpage UFSD	Bethpage
149	362.9	Mahopac Central SD	Mahopac
150	363.2	Ballston Spa Central SD	Ballston Spa
151	366.3	Mount Sinai UFSD	Mount Sinai
152	367.2	NYC Geographic District #10	Bronx
153	368.4	Schalmont Central SD	Schenectady
154	369.1	Corning City SD	Painted Post
155	369.2	East Hampton UFSD	East Hampton
156	369.3	Scarsdale UFSD	Scarsdale
157	369.8	Jamesville-Dewitt Central SD	Dewitt
158	370.2	Rye City SD	Rye
159	370.3	NYC Geographic District #32	Brooklyn
160	370.9	Herricks UFSD	New Hyde Park
160	370.9	Manhasset UFSD	Manhasset
162	372.4	Phoenix Central SD	Phoenix
163	372.7	Arlington Central SD	Lagrangeville
163	372.7	NYC Geographic District # 3	New York
165	373.8	Kinderhook Central SD	Valatie
166	374.0	NYC Geographic District #11	Bronx
167	375.0	Croton-Harmon UFSD	Croton on Hdsn
168	375.7	Niskayuna Central SD	Schenectady
169	375.8	NYC Geographic District #27	Ozone Park
170	377.5	Camden Central SD	Camden
171	379.8	Fredonia Central SD	Fredonia
172	381.0	NYC Geographic District #14	Brooklyn
173	383.2	NYC Geographic District # 2	New York
174	384.2	Bayport-Blue Point UFSD	Bayport
175	384.6	Edgemont UFSD	Scarsdale
176	384.8	Susquehanna Valley Central SD	Conklin
177	385.2	Lakeland Central SD	Shrub Oak
178	386.1	Garden City UFSD	Garden City
179	388.4	North Shore Central SD	Sea Cliff
180	389.2	South Jefferson Central SD	Adams Center
181	389.5	Fairport Central SD	Fairport
182	391.1	Rockville Ctr UFSD	Rockville Ctr
183	392.8	Lansingburgh Central SD	Troy
184	393.8	Phelps-Clifton Springs Central SD	Clifton Springs
185	394.6	UFSD of the Tarrytowns	Sleepy Hollow
186	396.2	Marlboro Central SD	Milton
186	396.2	Watertown City SD	Watertown
188	396.3	Chenango Forks Central SD	Binghamton
189	396.5	NYC Geographic District #12	Bronx
190	396.6	Longwood Central SD	Middle Island
191	396.9	Hamburg Central SD	Hamburg
192	397.0	Bedford Central SD	Bedford
193	397.4	Brewster Central SD	Brewster
194	398.6	Amityville UFSD	Amityville
195	399.1	Broadalbin-Perth Central SD	Broadalbin
196	399.6	Carmel Central SD	Patterson
197	401.3	Rochester City SD	Rochester
198	401.4	East Greenbush Central SD	East Greenbush
198	401.4	Mineola UFSD	Mineola
200	402.3	Catskill Central SD	Catskill
201	406.0	Rocky Point UFSD	Rocky Point
202	407.9	Averill Park Central SD	Averill Park
203	409.6	Glen Cove City SD	Glen Cove
204	410.5	Alden Central SD	Alden
205	410.7	Mamaroneck UFSD	Mamaroneck
206	411.0	Glens Falls City SD	Glens Falls
207	412.0	Center Moriches UFSD	Center Moriches
208	414.9	Geneva City SD	Geneva
209	415.6	Lewiston-Porter Central SD	Youngstown
210	416.4	NYC Geographic District #25	Flushing
211	417.0	Copiague UFSD	Copiague
212	417.3	Elmira City SD	Elmira
213	418.7	Goshen Central SD	Goshen
214	419.0	Scotia-Glenville Central SD	Scotia
215	420.8	Kingston City SD	Kingston
216	421.4	New York City Chancellor's Office	New York
217	421.8	Valley Central SD (Montgomery)	Montgomery
218	422.0	Hampton Bays UFSD	Hampton Bays
219	422.1	Webster Central SD	Webster
220	422.6	NYC Geographic District # 4	New York
221	422.9	Miller Place UFSD	Miller Place
222	423.6	Bay Shore UFSD	Bay Shore
223	424.0	Pearl River UFSD	Pearl River
224	424.3	Amherst Central SD	Amherst
225	425.6	Peekskill City SD	Peekskill
226	427.0	Johnson City Central SD	Johnson City
227	427.2	Lockport City SD	Lockport
228	427.9	Nyack UFSD	Nyack
229	429.1	North Syracuse Central SD	North Syracuse
230	429.5	Saugerties Central SD	Saugerties
231	429.6	Oceanside UFSD	Oceanside
232	430.2	Smithtown Central SD	Smithtown
233	430.4	East Islip UFSD	Islip Terrace
234	430.5	Putnam Valley Central SD	Putnam Valley
235	430.7	Sayville UFSD	Sayville
236	432.4	Syosset Central SD	Syosset
237	433.5	Baldwin UFSD	Baldwin
237	433.5	Carthage Central SD	Carthage
239	433.8	New Hartford Central SD	New Hartford
240	436.1	Lindenhurst UFSD	Lindenhurst
241	439.4	Burnt Hills-Ballston Lake Central SD	Scotia
242	441.0	Eastport-South Manor CSD	Manorville
243	441.6	Haverstraw-Stony Point CSD	Garnerville
243	441.6	Ramapo Central SD (Suffern)	Hillburn
245	441.7	Clarkstown Central SD	New City
246	441.9	White Plains City SD	White Plains
247	442.8	Johnstown City SD	Johnstown
248	444.8	Pine Bush Central SD	Pine Bush
249	445.8	New Paltz Central SD	New Paltz
250	446.0	Cheektowaga-Maryvale UFSD	Cheektowaga
251	450.0	Hyde Park Central SD	Hyde Park
252	450.3	Highland Central SD	Highland
253	455.1	S Glens Fls Central SD	S Glens Fls
254	457.0	Seaford UFSD	Seaford
255	457.1	Saratoga Spgs City SD	Saratoga Spgs
256	457.8	Elwood UFSD	Greenlawn
256	457.8	Ithaca City SD	Ithaca
258	459.0	West Islip UFSD	West Islip
259	461.8	NYC Geographic District #28	Jamaica
260	463.1	Whitesboro Central SD	Whitesboro
261	463.3	Deer Park UFSD	Deer Park
262	463.4	NYC Geographic District #21	Brooklyn
262	463.4	Shoreham-Wading River Central SD	Shoreham
264	463.7	Gates-Chili Central SD	Rochester
265	466.9	Farmingdale UFSD	Farmingdale
266	467.5	Cohoes City SD	Cohoes
266	467.5	NYC Geographic District #24	Corona
268	467.6	Baldwinsville Central SD	Baldwinsville
269	467.8	Greenburgh Central SD	Hartsdale
270	468.2	Port Chester-Rye UFSD	Port Chester
271	470.2	Northport-East Northport UFSD	Northport
272	473.5	Schenectady City SD	Schenectady
273	481.8	NYC Geographic District #30	Long Isl City
274	482.2	Binghamton City SD	Binghamton
275	482.6	Hudson Falls Central SD	Fort Edward
276	485.6	Wappingers Central SD	Hopewell Junction
277	486.3	Minisink Valley Central SD	Slate Hill
278	490.0	Kings Park Central SD	Kings Park

Note: This section only includes districts with 1,500 or more students; All categories are ranked from high to low

Rank	Value	District Name	City
279	490.6	Guilderland Central SD	Guilderland Center
280	493.0	Grand Island Central SD	Grand Island
281	493.6	Maine-Endwell Central SD	Endwell
282	494.8	Chenango Valley Central SD	Binghamton
283	495.3	Sherrill City SD	Verona
284	495.9	Central Square Central SD	Central Square
285	496.4	Ossining UFSD	Ossining
286	497.3	NYC Geographic District #22	Brooklyn
287	497.5	NYC Geographic District #20	Brooklyn
288	498.1	New Rochelle City SD	New Rochelle
289	499.6	Cortland City SD	Cortland
290	500.4	Middle Country Central SD	Centereach
291	503.0	South Huntington UFSD	Huntington Stn
291	503.0	Yorkshire-Pioneer Central SD	Yorkshire
293	503.4	West Babylon UFSD	West Babylon
294	504.5	Beacon City SD	Beacon
295	504.7	Sachem Central SD	Lake Ronkonkoma
296	505.0	Huntington UFSD	Huntington Stn
297	505.8	Homer Central SD	Homer
298	508.3	Connetquot Central SD	Bohemia
299	508.8	NYC Geographic District #15	Brooklyn
300	509.0	Wyandanch UFSD	Wyandanch
301	511.7	General Brown Central SD	Dexter
302	514.2	Iroquois Central SD	Elma
303	523.4	Syracuse City SD	Syracuse
304	523.8	Dunkirk City SD	Dunkirk
305	527.5	Hicksville UFSD	Hicksville
305	527.5	South Orangetown Central SD	Blauvelt
307	535.6	Freeport UFSD	Freeport
308	543.0	NYC Geographic District #31	Staten Island
309	546.6	Patchogue-Medford UFSD	Patchogue
310	549.4	NYC Geographic District #26	Bayside
311	550.8	Oneida City SD	Oneida
312	554.0	Union-Endicott Central SD	Endicott
313	556.2	NYC Geographic District #29	Queens Village
314	556.3	Roosevelt UFSD	Roosevelt
315	557.3	Victor Central SD	Victor
316	560.5	Clarence Central SD	Clarence
317	565.9	Albany City SD	Albany
318	566.7	Malverne UFSD	Malverne
319	569.7	Newburgh City SD	Newburgh
320	572.4	Auburn City SD	Auburn
321	576.4	Lancaster Central SD	Lancaster
322	578.9	Monroe-Woodbury Central SD	Central Valley
323	579.8	East Ramapo CSD (Spring Valley)	Spring Valley
324	593.0	Central Valley CSD at Ilion-Mohawk	Ilion
325	593.1	North Babylon UFSD	North Babylon
326	602.8	South Country Central SD	East Patchogue
327	608.8	Plainedge UFSD	N Massapequa
328	609.9	South Colonie Central SD	Albany
329	617.5	Buffalo City SD	Buffalo
330	625.2	Brookhaven-Comsewogue UFSD	Port Jeff Stn
331	636.3	Poughkeepsie City SD	Poughkeepsie
332	637.7	Middletown City SD	Middletown
333	640.5	Amsterdam City SD	Amsterdam
334	666.2	Lackawanna City SD	Lackawanna
335	670.0	West Seneca Central SD	West Seneca
336	678.3	William Floyd UFSD	Mastic Beach
337	704.1	Frontier Central SD	Hamburg
338	720.3	Owego-Apalachin Central SD	Owego
339	728.5	Brentwood UFSD	Brentwood
340	740.0	Hudson City SD	Hudson
341	807.0	Waverly Central SD	Waverly
342	818.4	Central Islip UFSD	Central Islip
343	830.5	Utica City SD	Utica
344	894.5	Riverhead Central SD	Riverhead
345	906.0	Yonkers City SD	Yonkers
346	1,003.6	Hempstead UFSD	Hempstead
347	1,215.3	Orchard Park Central SD	West Seneca
n/a	n/a	Eastchester UFSD	Eastchester
n/a	n/a	Elmont UFSD	Elmont
n/a	n/a	Franklin Square UFSD	Franklin Square
n/a	n/a	Horseheads Central SD	Horseheads
n/a	n/a	Livonia Central SD	Livonia
n/a	n/a	New Hyde Pk-Garden City Pk UFSD	New Hyde Park
n/a	n/a	North Bellmore UFSD	Bellmore
n/a	n/a	Sewanhaka Central High SD	Floral Park
n/a	n/a	Valley Stream 13 UFSD	Valley Stream
n/a	n/a	Valley Stream 30 UFSD	Valley Stream

Current Expenditures per Student

Rank	Dollars	District Name	City
1	34,704	Southampton UFSD	Southampton
2	33,851	Greenburgh Central SD	Hartsdale
3	33,841	Jericho UFSD	Jericho
4	33,484	Lawrence UFSD	Cedarhurst
5	33,160	Long Beach City SD	Long Beach
6	33,053	Locust Valley Central SD	Locust Valley
7	31,359	North Shore Central SD	Sea Cliff
8	31,156	Katonah-Lewisboro UFSD	South Salem
9	31,002	Syosset Central SD	Syosset
10	30,549	East Hampton UFSD	East Hampton
11	30,373	Great Neck UFSD	Great Neck
12	30,337	Hewlett-Woodmere UFSD	Woodmere
13	29,733	Cold Spring Hrbr Central SD	Cold Spring Hrbr
14	29,609	Mineola UFSD	Mineola
15	29,216	Byram Hills Central SD	Armonk
16	29,049	Roslyn UFSD	Roslyn
17	28,999	Oyster Bay-East Norwich Central SD	Oyster Bay
18	28,720	Harrison Central SD	Harrison
19	28,314	Malverne UFSD	Malverne
20	28,295	Chappaqua Central SD	Chappaqua
21	28,106	East Williston UFSD	Old Westbury
22	27,829	Nanuet UFSD	Nanuet
23	27,240	Scarsdale UFSD	Scarsdale
24	27,132	Hendrick Hudson Central SD	Montrose
25	27,130	Central Islip UFSD	Central Islip
26	27,124	Wyandanch UFSD	Wyandanch
27	27,056	Irvington UFSD	Irvington
28	27,054	Rockville Ctr UFSD	Rockville Ctr
29	26,897	Bedford Central SD	Bedford
30	26,544	Plainview-Old Bethpage CSD	Plainview
31	26,290	East Ramapo CSD (Spring Valley)	Spring Valley
32	26,276	Ardsley UFSD	Ardsley
33	26,148	White Plains City SD	White Plains
34	26,036	West Hempstead UFSD	West Hempstead
35	25,953	Sayville UFSD	Sayville
36	25,786	Babylon UFSD	Babylon
37	25,699	Rondout Valley Central SD	Accord
38	25,612	Uniondale UFSD	Uniondale
39	25,507	Westhampton Bch UFSD	Westhampton Bch
40	25,491	Bayport-Blue Point UFSD	Bayport
41	25,490	Herricks UFSD	New Hyde Park
42	25,332	Levittown UFSD	Levittown
43	25,318	Bethpage UFSD	Bethpage
44	25,303	Huntington UFSD	Huntington Stn
45	25,288	Northport-East Northport UFSD	Northport
46	25,236	Port Washington UFSD	Port Washington
47	25,154	Mount Pleasant Central SD	Thornwood
48	25,147	Hastings-On-Hudson UFSD	Hastings on Hdsn
49	25,113	Ramapo Central SD (Suffern)	Hillburn
50	25,081	Lynbrook UFSD	Lynbrook
51	25,055	Blind Brook-Rye UFSD	Rye Brook
52	24,934	Farmingdale UFSD	Farmingdale
53	24,923	Mount Vernon SD	Mount Vernon
54	24,864	Bronxville UFSD	Bronxville
55	24,776	Hempstead UFSD	Hempstead
56	24,769	Carmel Central SD	Patterson
57	24,766	Edgemont UFSD	Scarsdale
58	24,649	Connetquot Central SD	Bohemia
59	24,617	East Islip UFSD	Islip Terrace
60	24,605	Brewster Central SD	Brewster
61	24,579	Manhasset UFSD	Manhasset
62	24,433	Shoreham-Wading River Central SD	Shoreham
63	24,365	Yorktown Central SD	Yorktown Hgts
64	24,196	Three Village Central SD	Stony Brook
65	24,146	East Meadow UFSD	Westbury
66	24,139	Monticello Central SD	Monticello
67	24,093	South Orangetown Central SD	Blauvelt
68	24,044	Garden City UFSD	Garden City
69	24,000	Amityville UFSD	Amityville
70	23,955	Seaford UFSD	Seaford
71	23,951	Oceanside UFSD	Oceanside
72	23,763	Nyack UFSD	Nyack
73	23,718	Putnam Valley Central SD	Putnam Valley
74	23,645	Lakeland Central SD	Shrub Oak
75	23,575	Haverstraw-Stony Point CSD	Garnerville
76	23,513	Mahopac Central SD	Mahopac
77	23,445	Eastchester UFSD	Eastchester
78	23,387	Ellenville Central SD	Ellenville
79	23,369	Westbury UFSD	Old Westbury
80	23,316	Peekskill City SD	Peekskill
81	23,304	Plainedge UFSD	N Massapequa
82	23,297	Hauppauge UFSD	Hauppauge
83	23,287	Liberty Central SD	Liberty
84	23,275	Commack UFSD	East Northport
85	23,258	South Country Central SD	East Patchogue
86	23,190	West Babylon UFSD	West Babylon
87	23,080	Island Trees UFSD	Levittown
88	23,063	Pleasantville UFSD	Pleasantville
89	23,041	South Huntington UFSD	Huntington Stn
90	22,954	Half Hollow Hills Central SD	Dix Hills
91	22,790	Massapequa UFSD	Massapequa
92	22,785	North Bellmore UFSD	Bellmore
93	22,752	Roosevelt UFSD	Roosevelt
94	22,729	Somers Central SD	Somers
95	22,687	Bellmore-Merrick Central High SD	North Merrick
96	22,621	Baldwin UFSD	Baldwin
97	22,607	Pearl River UFSD	Pearl River
98	22,579	Elwood UFSD	Greenlawn
99	22,490	Pelham UFSD	Pelham
100	22,442	Hicksville UFSD	Hicksville
101	22,431	UFSD of the Tarrytowns	Sleepy Hollow
102	22,351	Lindenhurst UFSD	Lindenhurst
103	22,248	Rye Neck UFSD	Mamaroneck
104	22,232	Center Moriches UFSD	Center Moriches
105	22,155	Islip UFSD	Islip
106	22,127	Copiague UFSD	Copiague
107	22,097	Glen Cove City SD	Glen Cove
108	21,946	New Paltz Central SD	New Paltz
109	21,924	Deer Park UFSD	Deer Park
110	21,916	Mexico Central SD	Mexico
111	21,855	Longwood Central SD	Middle Island
112	21,853	Bay Shore UFSD	Bay Shore
112	21,853	Mamaroneck UFSD	Mamaroneck
114	21,777	Freeport UFSD	Freeport
115	21,776	West Islip UFSD	West Islip
116	21,742	Croton-Harmon UFSD	Croton on Hdsn
116	21,742	Riverhead Central SD	Riverhead
118	21,733	Ossining UFSD	Ossining
119	21,510	Hyde Park Central SD	Hyde Park
120	21,493	Salmon River Central SD	Fort Covington
121	21,476	Red Hook Central SD	Red Hook
122	21,457	Rocky Point UFSD	Rocky Point
123	21,427	Eastport-South Manor CSD	Manorville
124	21,420	Monroe-Woodbury Central SD	Central Valley
125	21,415	Marlboro Central SD	Milton
126	21,322	Rye City SD	Rye
127	21,248	Lackawanna City SD	Lackawanna
128	21,233	North Babylon UFSD	North Babylon
129	21,200	New Rochelle City SD	New Rochelle
130	21,174	Smithtown Central SD	Smithtown
131	21,156	Valley Stream Central High SD	Valley Stream
132	21,105	Geneva City SD	Geneva
133	21,073	Schalmont Central SD	Schenectady
134	21,027	Rochester City SD	Rochester
135	20,930	Plattsburgh City SD	Plattsburgh
136	20,922	William Floyd UFSD	Mastic Beach
137	20,884	Miller Place UFSD	Miller Place
138	20,881	Clarkstown Central SD	New City
139	20,878	Kings Park Central SD	Kings Park
140	20,876	Kingston City SD	Kingston
141	20,813	Port Jervis City SD	Port Jervis
142	20,728	Wantagh UFSD	Wantagh
143	20,702	Gates-Chili Central SD	Rochester
144	20,672	Ogdensburg City SD	Ogdensburg
145	20,630	Harborfields Central SD	Greenlawn
146	20,616	Hudson City SD	Hudson
147	20,610	Mount Sinai UFSD	Mount Sinai
148	20,506	Catskill Central SD	Catskill
149	20,456	Hampton Bays UFSD	Hampton Bays
150	20,416	Valley Stream 30 UFSD	Valley Stream
151	20,380	Newburgh City SD	Newburgh
152	20,346	Albany City SD	Albany
153	20,331	Susquehanna Valley Central SD	Conklin
154	20,328	Warwick Valley Central SD	Warwick
155	20,281	Troy City SD	Troy
156	20,210	Poughkeepsie City SD	Poughkeepsie
157	20,155	Sewanhaka Central High SD	Floral Park
158	19,975	Ithaca City SD	Ithaca
159	19,765	East Irondequoit Central SD	Rochester
160	19,761	Brookhaven-Comsewogue UFSD	Port Jeff Stn
161	19,733	Dryden Central SD	Dryden
162	19,698	Yonkers City SD	Yonkers
163	19,631	Middle Country Central SD	Centereach
164	19,615	Patchogue-Medford UFSD	Patchogue
164	19,615	Ravena-Coeymans-Selkirk Cent SD	Ravena
166	19,589	Valley Stream 13 UFSD	Valley Stream
167	19,576	Rush-Henrietta Central SD	Henrietta
168	19,562	Evans-Brant Central SD (Lake Shore)	Angola

Note: This section only includes districts with 1,500 or more students; All categories are ranked from high to low

Rank	Dollars	District Name	City
169	19,495	Goshen Central SD	Goshen
170	19,452	Middletown City SD	Middletown
171	19,444	Phoenix Central SD	Phoenix
172	19,400	New Hyde Pk-Garden City Pk UFSD	New Hyde Park
173	19,291	Wallkill Central SD	Wallkill
174	19,246	Elmont UFSD	Elmont
175	19,243	Arlington Central SD	Lagrangeville
176	19,023	New York City Chancellor's Office	New York
177	18,943	Sweet Home Central SD	Amherst
178	18,940	Valley Central SD (Montgomery)	Montgomery
179	18,936	Saugerties Central SD	Saugerties
180	18,913	Buffalo City SD	Buffalo
181	18,845	Norwich City SD	Norwich
182	18,781	Kenmore-Tonawanda UFSD	Buffalo
183	18,776	Sachem Central SD	Lake Ronkonkoma
184	18,662	East Syracuse Minoa Central SD	East Syracuse
185	18,632	Highland Central SD	Highland
186	18,588	Oswego City SD	Oswego
187	18,547	Depew UFSD	Depew
188	18,415	Brentwood UFSD	Brentwood
189	18,387	Vestal Central SD	Vestal
190	18,293	Minisink Valley Central SD	Slate Hill
191	18,290	Washingtonville Central SD	Washingtonville
192	18,208	Pittsford Central SD	Pittsford
193	18,195	Ballston Spa Central SD	Ballston Spa
194	18,081	Pine Bush Central SD	Pine Bush
195	18,057	Union-Endicott Central SD	Endicott
196	18,056	Dunkirk City SD	Dunkirk
197	18,050	Phelps-Clifton Springs Central SD	Clifton Springs
198	18,048	Rome City SD	Rome
199	18,039	Newark Central SD	Newark
200	18,031	Oneonta City SD	Oneonta
201	18,001	Syracuse City SD	Syracuse
202	17,999	Peru Central SD	Peru
203	17,990	Malone Central SD	Malone
204	17,984	Port Chester-Rye UFSD	Port Chester
205	17,929	Fulton City SD	Fulton
206	17,860	Brighton Central SD	Rochester
207	17,829	Penfield Central SD	Rochester
208	17,747	East Greenbush Central SD	East Greenbush
209	17,745	Windsor Central SD	Windsor
210	17,718	Cobleskill-Richmondville CSD	Cobleskill
211	17,689	Owego-Apalachin Central SD	Owego
211	17,689	Springville-Griffith Institute CSD	Springville
213	17,688	Corning City SD	Painted Post
214	17,658	Kinderhook Central SD	Valatie
215	17,614	Batavia City SD	Batavia
216	17,613	Bath Central SD	Bath
217	17,532	Johnson City Central SD	Johnson City
218	17,522	Hornell City SD	Hornell
219	17,521	Cornwall Central SD	Cornwall on Hdsn
220	17,496	Glens Falls City SD	Glens Falls
221	17,480	Camden Central SD	Camden
222	17,370	Spencerport Central SD	Spencerport
223	17,368	Beacon City SD	Beacon
224	17,367	Beekmantown Central SD	West Chazy
225	17,333	Wappingers Central SD	Hopewell Junction
226	17,314	Gloversville City SD	Gloversville
227	17,312	Gouverneur Central SD	Gouverneur
228	17,295	Brockport Central SD	Brockport
229	17,294	Wayne Central SD	Ontario Center
230	17,292	South Colonie Central SD	Albany
231	17,278	Cohoes City SD	Cohoes
232	17,192	North Colonie CSD	Latham
233	17,167	Palmyra-Macedon Central SD	Palmyra
233	17,167	Yorkshire-Pioneer Central SD	Yorkshire
235	17,153	Newfane Central SD	Burt
236	17,134	Liverpool Central SD	Liverpool
237	17,097	Binghamton City SD	Binghamton
238	17,084	Lewiston-Porter Central SD	Youngstown
239	17,074	Iroquois Central SD	Elma
240	17,060	Greece Central SD	Rochester
241	17,041	Scotia-Glenville Central SD	Scotia
242	17,001	Chenango Valley Central SD	Binghamton
243	16,962	Fairport Central SD	Fairport
243	16,962	Waterloo Central SD	Waterloo
245	16,944	Burnt Hills-Ballston Lake Central SD	Scotia
246	16,939	Fayetteville-Manlius Central SD	Manlius
247	16,851	Fredonia Central SD	Fredonia
248	16,724	Guilderland Central SD	Guilderland Center
249	16,702	Schuylerville Central SD	Schuylerville
250	16,666	Dansville Central SD	Dansville
251	16,581	Chenango Forks Central SD	Binghamton
252	16,566	Indian River Central SD	Philadelphia
253	16,555	Churchville-Chili Central SD	Churchville
254	16,550	Homer Central SD	Homer
254	16,550	New Hartford Central SD	New Hartford
256	16,512	Cheektowaga Central SD	Cheektowaga
257	16,430	Franklin Square UFSD	Franklin Square
258	16,400	Bethlehem Central SD	Delmar
258	16,400	Schenectady City SD	Schenectady
260	16,388	Orchard Park Central SD	West Seneca
261	16,376	Niagara Falls City SD	Niagara Falls
262	16,330	Medina Central SD	Medina
263	16,302	West Irondequoit Central SD	Rochester
264	16,299	Cortland City SD	Cortland
265	16,224	North Tonawanda City SD	North Tonawanda
266	16,147	Lockport City SD	Lockport
267	16,125	Livonia Central SD	Livonia
268	16,121	Jamesville-Dewitt Central SD	Dewitt
269	16,050	Honeoye Falls-Lima Central SD	Honeoye Falls
270	16,002	Canandaigua City SD	Canandaigua
271	15,976	Webster Central SD	Webster
272	15,953	Amherst Central SD	Amherst
273	15,938	Maine-Endwell Central SD	Endwell
274	15,849	S Glens Fls Central SD	S Glens Fls
275	15,847	Oneida City SD	Oneida
276	15,760	Chittenango Central SD	Chittenango
277	15,754	Averill Park Central SD	Averill Park
278	15,743	Grand Island Central SD	Grand Island
279	15,735	North Syracuse Central SD	North Syracuse
280	15,734	Central Square Central SD	Central Square
280	15,734	Whitesboro Central SD	Whitesboro
282	15,697	Westhill Central SD	Syracuse
283	15,661	Auburn City SD	Auburn
284	15,563	Horseheads Central SD	Horseheads
285	15,501	Olean City SD	Olean
286	15,432	Marcellus Central SD	Marcellus
287	15,388	Alden Central SD	Alden
288	15,275	Baldwinsville Central SD	Baldwinsville
289	15,258	Waverly Central SD	Waverly
290	15,254	Broadalbin-Perth Central SD	Broadalbin
291	15,235	Niagara-Wheatfield Central SD	Niagara Falls
292	15,209	East Aurora UFSD	East Aurora
293	15,206	Amsterdam City SD	Amsterdam
294	15,172	Starpoint Central SD	Lockport
295	15,162	Niskayuna Central SD	Schenectady
296	15,122	Carthage Central SD	Carthage
296	15,122	Saratoga Spgs City SD	Saratoga Spgs
298	15,081	Hamburg Central SD	Hamburg
299	15,026	Massena Central SD	Massena
300	15,018	Cheektowaga-Maryvale UFSD	Cheektowaga
301	14,997	Johnstown City SD	Johnstown
302	14,937	Hudson Falls Central SD	Fort Edward
303	14,845	Hilton Central SD	Hilton
304	14,836	West Genesee Central SD	Camillus
305	14,816	Williamsville Central SD	East Amherst
306	14,806	Elmira City SD	Elmira
307	14,663	Utica City SD	Utica
308	14,602	Rotterdam-Mohonasen Central SD	Schenectady
309	14,573	Watertown City SD	Watertown
310	14,565	Lansingburgh Central SD	Troy
311	14,501	Shenendehowa Central SD	Clifton Park
312	14,431	Tonawanda City SD	Tonawanda
313	14,382	Sherrill City SD	Verona
314	14,294	West Seneca Central SD	West Seneca
315	14,251	Queensbury UFSD	Queensbury
316	14,118	Jamestown City SD	Jamestown
317	13,859	Lancaster Central SD	Lancaster
318	13,714	Frontier Central SD	Hamburg
319	13,368	Albion Central SD	Albion
320	13,367	South Jefferson Central SD	Adams Center
321	13,105	Clarence Central SD	Clarence
322	12,512	Victor Central SD	Victor
323	11,986	General Brown Central SD	Dexter
n/a	n/a	Central Valley CSD at Ilion-Mohawk	Ilion
n/a	n/a	Charter School for Applied Techs	Buffalo
n/a	n/a	NYC Geographic District # 1	New York
n/a	n/a	NYC Geographic District # 2	New York
n/a	n/a	NYC Geographic District # 3	New York
n/a	n/a	NYC Geographic District # 4	New York
n/a	n/a	NYC Geographic District # 5	New York
n/a	n/a	NYC Geographic District # 6	New York
n/a	n/a	NYC Geographic District # 7	Bronx
n/a	n/a	NYC Geographic District # 8	Bronx
n/a	n/a	NYC Geographic District # 9	Bronx
n/a	n/a	NYC Geographic District #10	Bronx
n/a	n/a	NYC Geographic District #11	Bronx
n/a	n/a	NYC Geographic District #12	Bronx
n/a	n/a	NYC Geographic District #13	Brooklyn
n/a	n/a	NYC Geographic District #14	Brooklyn
n/a	n/a	NYC Geographic District #15	Brooklyn
n/a	n/a	NYC Geographic District #16	Brooklyn
n/a	n/a	NYC Geographic District #17	Brooklyn
n/a	n/a	NYC Geographic District #18	Brooklyn
n/a	n/a	NYC Geographic District #19	Brooklyn
n/a	n/a	NYC Geographic District #20	Brooklyn
n/a	n/a	NYC Geographic District #21	Brooklyn
n/a	n/a	NYC Geographic District #22	Brooklyn
n/a	n/a	NYC Geographic District #23	Brooklyn
n/a	n/a	NYC Geographic District #24	Corona
n/a	n/a	NYC Geographic District #25	Flushing
n/a	n/a	NYC Geographic District #26	Bayside
n/a	n/a	NYC Geographic District #27	Ozone Park
n/a	n/a	NYC Geographic District #28	Jamaica
n/a	n/a	NYC Geographic District #29	Queens Village
n/a	n/a	NYC Geographic District #30	Long Isl City
n/a	n/a	NYC Geographic District #31	Staten Island
n/a	n/a	NYC Geographic District #32	Brooklyn

Total General Revenue per Student

Rank	Dollars	District Name	City
1	39,907	Southampton UFSD	Southampton
2	39,067	Long Beach City SD	Long Beach
3	38,821	Jericho UFSD	Jericho
4	37,123	Locust Valley Central SD	Locust Valley
5	36,240	Greenburgh Central SD	Hartsdale
6	35,765	North Shore Central SD	Sea Cliff
7	35,504	Hewlett-Woodmere UFSD	Woodmere
8	35,037	East Hampton UFSD	East Hampton
9	34,038	Lawrence UFSD	Cedarhurst
10	34,032	Katonah-Lewisboro UFSD	South Salem
11	33,245	Cold Spring Hrbr Central SD	Cold Spring Hrbr
12	33,149	Roslyn UFSD	Roslyn
13	32,383	Oyster Bay-East Norwich Central SD	Oyster Bay
14	32,260	Byram Hills Central SD	Armonk
15	32,148	Syosset Central SD	Syosset
16	32,139	Great Neck UFSD	Great Neck
17	32,057	Mineola UFSD	Mineola
18	31,774	Malverne UFSD	Malverne
19	31,694	Roosevelt UFSD	Roosevelt
20	31,436	East Williston UFSD	Old Westbury
21	31,435	Irvington UFSD	Irvington
22	30,614	Ardsley UFSD	Ardsley
23	30,174	Harrison Central SD	Harrison
24	30,133	Hendrick Hudson Central SD	Montrose
25	29,785	Nanuet UFSD	Nanuet
26	29,451	Scarsdale UFSD	Scarsdale
27	29,398	Chappaqua Central SD	Chappaqua
28	29,353	Central Islip UFSD	Central Islip
29	29,090	Bronxville UFSD	Bronxville
30	29,000	White Plains City SD	White Plains
31	28,860	Rondout Valley Central SD	Accord
32	28,859	Plainview-Old Bethpage CSD	Plainview
33	28,843	Rockville Ctr UFSD	Rockville Ctr
34	28,499	Bedford Central SD	Bedford
35	28,408	Ramapo Central SD (Suffern)	Hillburn
36	28,359	Babylon UFSD	Babylon
37	28,330	Westhampton Bch UFSD	Westhampton Bch
38	28,207	Shoreham-Wading River Central SD	Shoreham
39	28,017	East Ramapo CSD (Spring Valley)	Spring Valley
40	27,941	Mount Pleasant Central SD	Thornwood
41	27,795	Sayville UFSD	Sayville
42	27,779	Wyandanch UFSD	Wyandanch
43	27,755	Monticello Central SD	Monticello
44	27,605	Bayport-Blue Point UFSD	Bayport
45	27,580	Bethpage UFSD	Bethpage
46	27,566	Albany City SD	Albany
47	27,553	Herricks UFSD	New Hyde Park
48	27,447	Connetquot Central SD	Bohemia
49	27,435	Yorktown Central SD	Yorktown Hgts
50	27,422	Port Washington UFSD	Port Washington
51	27,414	Blind Brook-Rye UFSD	Rye Brook
52	27,296	Mount Vernon City SD	Mount Vernon
53	27,204	Garden City UFSD	Garden City
54	27,114	Manhasset UFSD	Manhasset
55	27,064	Lynbrook UFSD	Lynbrook
56	27,019	Hastings-On-Hudson UFSD	Hastings on Hdsn
57	27,001	Brewster Central SD	Brewster
58	26,967	Putnam Valley Central SD	Putnam Valley

Note: This section only includes districts with 1,500 or more students; All categories are ranked from high to low

Rank	Value	District	Location	Rank	Value	District	Location	Rank	Value	District	Location
59	26,944	Lackawanna City SD	Lackawanna	143	23,235	Port Jervis City SD	Port Jervis	227	19,540	Chenango Valley Central SD	Binghamton
60	26,914	Uniondale UFSD	Uniondale	144	23,152	Lindenhurst UFSD	Lindenhurst	228	19,505	Fulton City SD	Fulton
61	26,909	Edgemont UFSD	Scarsdale	145	23,021	Dryden Central SD	Dryden	229	19,483	Bethlehem Central SD	Delmar
62	26,840	Hempstead UFSD	Hempstead	146	23,012	Gates-Chili Central SD	Rochester	229	19,483	Lewiston-Porter Central SD	Youngstown
63	26,773	Liberty Central SD	Liberty	147	22,936	Harborfields Central SD	Greenlawn	231	19,478	Elmira City SD	Elmira
64	26,693	Huntington UFSD	Huntington Stn	148	22,925	Phoenix Central SD	Phoenix	232	19,457	Spencerport Central SD	Spencerport
65	26,681	West Hempstead UFSD	West Hempstead	149	22,893	Rocky Point UFSD	Rocky Point	233	19,423	Maine-Endwell Central SD	Endwell
66	26,667	Troy City SD	Troy	150	22,881	North Babylon UFSD	North Babylon	234	19,413	Churchville-Chili Central SD	Churchville
67	26,552	South Orangetown Central SD	Blauvelt	151	22,868	Newburgh City SD	Newburgh	235	19,354	Brighton Central SD	Rochester
68	26,517	Three Village Central SD	Stony Brook	152	22,837	New Rochelle City SD	New Rochelle	236	19,310	Greece Central SD	Rochester
69	26,485	Lakeland Central SD	Shrub Oak	153	22,803	Smithtown Central SD	Smithtown	237	19,189	South Colonie Central SD	Albany
70	26,442	East Islip UFSD	Islip Terrace	154	22,774	Wantagh UFSD	Wantagh	238	19,163	Gouverneur Central SD	Gouverneur
71	26,434	Nyack UFSD	Nyack	155	22,690	Valley Stream 30 UFSD	Valley Stream	239	19,107	Honeoye Falls-Lima Central SD	Honeoye Falls
72	26,423	Plainedge UFSD	N Massapequa	156	22,565	Miller Place UFSD	Miller Place	240	19,049	Springville-Griffith Institute CSD	Springville
73	26,374	Carmel Central SD	Patterson	157	22,556	Copiague UFSD	Copiague	241	18,982	Cornwall Central SD	Cornwall on Hdsn
74	26,348	Levittown UFSD	Levittown	158	22,542	Mount Sinai UFSD	Mount Sinai	242	18,942	Kinderhook Central SD	Valatie
75	26,317	Buffalo City SD	Buffalo	159	22,357	Rush-Henrietta Central SD	Henrietta	242	18,942	Liverpool Central SD	Liverpool
76	26,085	Northport-East Northport UFSD	Northport	160	22,206	Poughkeepsie City SD	Poughkeepsie	244	18,909	Cortland City SD	Cortland
77	25,985	Pleasantville UFSD	Pleasantville	161	22,148	Clarkstown Central SD	New City	245	18,908	Schuylerville Central SD	Schuylerville
78	25,852	UFSD of the Tarrytowns	Sleepy Hollow	162	22,097	Patchogue-Medford UFSD	Patchogue	246	18,883	Johnson City Central SD	Johnson City
79	25,843	Farmingdale UFSD	Farmingdale	163	22,069	Goshen Central SD	Goshen	247	18,869	Pine Bush Central SD	Pine Bush
80	25,777	South Country Central SD	East Patchogue	164	22,039	Ravena-Coeymans-Selkirk Cent SD	Ravena	248	18,801	Scotia-Glenville Central SD	Scotia
81	25,696	Seaford UFSD	Seaford	165	22,014	Middletown City SD	Middletown	249	18,772	Palmyra-Macedon Central SD	Palmyra
82	25,656	Marlboro Central SD	Milton	166	21,993	Kings Park Central SD	Kings Park	250	18,761	Niskayuna Central SD	Schenectady
83	25,629	Somers Central SD	Somers	167	21,968	Warwick Valley Central SD	Warwick	251	18,737	Fredonia Central SD	Fredonia
84	25,571	Hauppauge UFSD	Hauppauge	168	21,887	Plattsburgh City SD	Plattsburgh	252	18,728	Amsterdam City SD	Amsterdam
85	25,423	Westbury UFSD	Old Westbury	169	21,682	New Hyde Pk-Garden City Pk UFSD	New Hyde Park	253	18,710	Cheektowaga Central SD	Cheektowaga
86	25,306	Mahopac Central SD	Mahopac	170	21,641	Evans-Brant Central SD (Lake Shore)	Angola	254	18,681	Alden Central SD	Alden
87	25,268	Amityville UFSD	Amityville	171	21,594	Hornell City SD	Hornell	255	18,679	Livonia Central SD	Livonia
88	25,242	Haverstraw-Stony Point CSD	Garnerville	172	21,455	Minisink Valley Central SD	Slate Hill	256	18,659	Schenectady City SD	Schenectady
89	25,226	Massapequa UFSD	Massapequa	173	21,409	Cohoes City SD	Cohoes	257	18,651	Burnt Hills-Ballston Lake Central SD	Scotia
90	25,206	Salmon River Central SD	Fort Covington	174	21,367	Sweet Home Central SD	Amherst	258	18,629	Glens Falls City SD	Glens Falls
91	25,158	Croton-Harmon UFSD	Croton on Hdsn	175	21,287	Arlington Central SD	Lagrangeville	259	18,625	Homer Central SD	Homer
92	25,076	East Meadow UFSD	Westbury	176	21,258	Corning City SD	Painted Post	260	18,617	Westhill Central SD	Syracuse
93	24,996	Commack UFSD	East Northport	177	21,255	Highland Central SD	Highland	261	18,611	Guilderland Central SD	Guilderland Center
94	24,979	South Huntington UFSD	Huntington Stn	178	21,231	Syracuse City SD	Syracuse	262	18,575	North Colonie CSD	Latham
95	24,973	Rochester City SD	Rochester	179	21,219	Bath Central SD	Bath	263	18,568	Canandaigua City SD	Canandaigua
96	24,943	Hudson City SD	Hudson	180	21,197	Newark Central SD	Newark	264	18,515	West Irondequoit Central SD	Rochester
97	24,887	Baldwin UFSD	Baldwin	180	21,197	Saugerties Central SD	Saugerties	265	18,371	Batavia City SD	Batavia
98	24,845	Mexico Central SD	Mexico	182	21,147	Valley Central SD (Montgomery)	Montgomery	266	18,345	Fayetteville-Manlius Central SD	Manlius
99	24,799	Half Hollow Hills Central SD	Dix Hills	183	21,121	Wallkill Central SD	Wallkill	267	18,339	New Hartford Central SD	New Hartford
100	24,798	Oceanside UFSD	Oceanside	184	21,095	Malone Central SD	Malone	268	18,153	Iroquois Central SD	Elma
101	24,797	Island Trees UFSD	Levittown	185	21,090	Vestal Central SD	Vestal	269	18,123	Averill Park Central SD	Averill Park
102	24,781	Bay Shore UFSD	Bay Shore	186	21,070	Middle Country Central SD	Centereach	270	18,092	Fairport Central SD	Fairport
103	24,749	Peekskill City SD	Peekskill	187	20,957	Dunkirk City SD	Dunkirk	271	18,080	Olean City SD	Olean
104	24,636	Pearl River UFSD	Pearl River	188	20,922	Ithaca City SD	Ithaca	272	18,012	Wayne Central SD	Ontario Center
105	24,604	Islip UFSD	Islip	189	20,862	Kenmore-Tonawanda UFSD	Buffalo	273	18,002	Cheektowaga-Maryvale UFSD	Cheektowaga
106	24,547	Ellenville Central SD	Ellenville	190	20,843	Union-Endicott Central SD	Endicott	274	17,941	Wappingers Central SD	Hopewell Junction
106	24,547	Riverhead Central SD	Riverhead	191	20,833	Brookhaven-Comsewogue UFSD	Port Jeff Stn	275	17,930	Jamesville-Dewitt Central SD	Dewitt
108	24,522	Mamaroneck UFSD	Mamaroneck	192	20,828	Camden Central SD	Camden	276	17,857	Webster Central SD	Webster
109	24,484	New York City Chancellor's Office	New York	193	20,697	Gloversville City SD	Gloversville	277	17,803	North Tonawanda City SD	North Tonawanda
110	24,417	Red Hook Central SD	Red Hook	194	20,647	Norwich City SD	Norwich	278	17,765	Oneida City SD	Oneida
111	24,396	Glen Cove City SD	Glen Cove	195	20,631	Pittsford Central SD	Pittsford	279	17,742	Amherst Central SD	Amherst
112	24,303	Eastchester UFSD	Eastchester	196	20,623	Sachem Central SD	Lake Ronkonkoma	280	17,732	Lansingburgh Central SD	Troy
113	24,262	East Irondequoit Central SD	Rochester	197	20,620	Sewanhaka Central High SD	Floral Park	281	17,731	Auburn City SD	Auburn
114	24,260	Ossining UFSD	Ossining	198	20,614	Phelps-Clifton Springs Central SD	Clifton Springs	282	17,730	Starpoint Central SD	Lockport
115	24,242	William Floyd UFSD	Mastic Beach	199	20,610	Peru Central SD	Peru	283	17,721	Franklin Square UFSD	Franklin Square
116	24,218	Geneva City SD	Geneva	200	20,601	Elmont UFSD	Elmont	284	17,702	Niagara-Wheatfield Central SD	Niagara Falls
117	24,203	Rye Neck UFSD	Mamaroneck	201	20,594	Binghamton City SD	Binghamton	285	17,664	Orchard Park Central SD	West Seneca
118	24,084	West Babylon UFSD	West Babylon	202	20,590	East Syracuse Minoa Central SD	East Syracuse	286	17,596	Broadalbin-Perth Central SD	Broadalbin
119	24,067	Owego-Apalachin Central SD	Owego	203	20,589	Depew UFSD	Depew	287	17,578	Chittenango Central SD	Chittenango
120	23,964	Center Moriches UFSD	Center Moriches	204	20,478	Beekmantown Central SD	West Chazy	288	17,559	Marcellus Central SD	Marcellus
121	23,947	Hicksville UFSD	Hicksville	204	20,478	Valley Stream 13 UFSD	Valley Stream	289	17,557	Lockport City SD	Lockport
122	23,937	West Islip UFSD	West Islip	206	20,465	East Greenbush Central SD	East Greenbush	290	17,534	Whitesboro Central SD	Whitesboro
123	23,868	North Bellmore UFSD	Bellmore	207	20,354	Oneonta City SD	Oneonta	291	17,325	Central Square Central SD	Central Square
124	23,861	Catskill Central SD	Catskill	208	20,340	Cobleskill-Richmondville CSD	Cobleskill	292	17,291	Hudson Falls Central SD	Fort Edward
125	23,843	Eastport-South Manor CSD	Manorville	209	20,245	Penfield Central SD	Rochester	293	17,205	East Aurora UFSD	East Aurora
126	23,826	Hampton Bays UFSD	Hampton Bays	210	20,067	Ballston Spa Central SD	Ballston Spa	294	17,190	Albion Central SD	Albion
127	23,763	Pelham UFSD	Pelham	211	20,055	Windsor Central SD	Windsor	295	17,148	S Glens Fls Central SD	S Glens Fls
128	23,746	Schalmont Central SD	Schenectady	212	19,956	Indian River Central SD	Philadelphia	296	17,131	North Syracuse Central SD	North Syracuse
129	23,712	Freeport UFSD	Freeport	213	19,954	Oswego City SD	Oswego	297	17,037	Baldwinsville Central SD	Baldwinsville
130	23,695	Longwood Central SD	Middle Island	214	19,927	Medina Central SD	Medina	298	17,023	Saratoga Spgs City SD	Saratoga Spgs
131	23,680	Deer Park UFSD	Deer Park	215	19,913	Dansville Central SD	Dansville	299	17,014	Grand Island Central SD	Grand Island
132	23,666	Elwood UFSD	Greenlawn	216	19,908	Port Chester-Rye UFSD	Port Chester	300	16,980	Utica City SD	Utica
133	23,617	Monroe-Woodbury Central SD	Central Valley	217	19,906	Beacon City SD	Beacon	301	16,929	Tonawanda City SD	Tonawanda
134	23,589	Rye City SD	Rye	218	19,851	Niagara Falls City SD	Niagara Falls	302	16,873	Horseheads Central SD	Horseheads
135	23,492	Bellmore-Merrick Central High SD	North Merrick	219	19,835	Brockport Central SD	Brockport	303	16,803	Hilton Central SD	Hilton
136	23,481	Kingston City SD	Kingston	220	19,823	Washingtonville Central SD	Washingtonville	304	16,725	Hamburg Central SD	Hamburg
137	23,432	Waterloo Central SD	Waterloo	221	19,774	Brentwood UFSD	Brentwood	305	16,598	Waverly Central SD	Waverly
138	23,421	New Paltz Central SD	New Paltz	222	19,725	Newfane Central SD	Burt	306	16,490	Williamsville Central SD	East Amherst
139	23,406	Hyde Park Central SD	Hyde Park	222	19,725	Rome City SD	Rome	307	16,428	Rotterdam-Mohonasen Central SD	Schenectady
140	23,331	Ogdensburg City SD	Ogdensburg	224	19,606	Chenango Forks Central SD	Binghamton	308	16,408	Johnstown City SD	Johnstown
141	23,298	Valley Stream Central High SD	Valley Stream	225	19,580	Yonkers City SD	Yonkers	309	16,355	Carthage Central SD	Carthage
142	23,297	Susquehanna Valley Central SD	Conklin	226	19,578	Yorkshire-Pioneer Central SD	Yorkshire	310	16,284	Shenendehowa Central SD	Clifton Park

Note: This section only includes districts with 1,500 or more students; All categories are ranked from high to low

Rank	Dollars	District Name	City
311	16,183	Massena Central SD	Massena
312	16,146	Sherrill City SD	Verona
313	16,054	Watertown City SD	Watertown
314	15,902	West Genesee Central SD	Camillus
315	15,886	West Seneca Central SD	West Seneca
316	15,812	Queensbury UFSD	Queensbury
317	15,688	Jamestown City SD	Jamestown
318	15,256	Clarence Central SD	Clarence
319	15,089	Lancaster Central SD	Lancaster
320	15,068	South Jefferson Central SD	Adams Center
321	14,919	Frontier Central SD	Hamburg
322	14,227	General Brown Central SD	Dexter
323	13,758	Victor Central SD	Victor
n/a	n/a	Central Valley CSD at Ilion-Mohawk	Ilion
n/a	n/a	Charter School for Applied Techs	Buffalo
n/a	n/a	NYC Geographic District # 1	New York
n/a	n/a	NYC Geographic District # 2	New York
n/a	n/a	NYC Geographic District # 3	New York
n/a	n/a	NYC Geographic District # 4	New York
n/a	n/a	NYC Geographic District # 5	New York
n/a	n/a	NYC Geographic District # 6	New York
n/a	n/a	NYC Geographic District # 7	Bronx
n/a	n/a	NYC Geographic District # 8	Bronx
n/a	n/a	NYC Geographic District # 9	Bronx
n/a	n/a	NYC Geographic District #10	Bronx
n/a	n/a	NYC Geographic District #11	Bronx
n/a	n/a	NYC Geographic District #12	Bronx
n/a	n/a	NYC Geographic District #13	Brooklyn
n/a	n/a	NYC Geographic District #14	Brooklyn
n/a	n/a	NYC Geographic District #15	Brooklyn
n/a	n/a	NYC Geographic District #16	Brooklyn
n/a	n/a	NYC Geographic District #17	Brooklyn
n/a	n/a	NYC Geographic District #18	Brooklyn
n/a	n/a	NYC Geographic District #19	Brooklyn
n/a	n/a	NYC Geographic District #20	Brooklyn
n/a	n/a	NYC Geographic District #21	Brooklyn
n/a	n/a	NYC Geographic District #22	Brooklyn
n/a	n/a	NYC Geographic District #23	Brooklyn
n/a	n/a	NYC Geographic District #24	Corona
n/a	n/a	NYC Geographic District #25	Flushing
n/a	n/a	NYC Geographic District #26	Bayside
n/a	n/a	NYC Geographic District #27	Ozone Park
n/a	n/a	NYC Geographic District #28	Jamaica
n/a	n/a	NYC Geographic District #29	Queens Village
n/a	n/a	NYC Geographic District #30	Long Isl City
n/a	n/a	NYC Geographic District #31	Staten Island
n/a	n/a	NYC Geographic District #32	Brooklyn

Long-Term Debt per Student (end of FY)

Rank	Dollars	District Name	City
1	58,421	Roosevelt UFSD	Roosevelt
2	36,045	Eastport-South Manor CSD	Manorville
3	33,145	East Hampton UFSD	East Hampton
4	31,365	Buffalo City SD	Buffalo
5	30,390	Pleasantville UFSD	Pleasantville
6	28,932	Marlboro Central SD	Milton
7	28,113	Camden Central SD	Camden
8	27,137	Haverstraw-Stony Point CSD	Garnerville
9	26,987	Southampton UFSD	Southampton
10	26,129	Hornell City SD	Hornell
11	25,899	Waterloo Central SD	Waterloo
12	23,900	Long Beach City SD	Long Beach
13	23,741	East Irondequoit Central SD	Rochester
14	23,340	Phoenix Central SD	Phoenix
15	22,483	Irvington UFSD	Irvington
16	22,322	Catskill Central SD	Catskill
17	21,850	Hudson City SD	Hudson
18	20,708	South Country Central SD	East Patchogue
19	19,208	Gloversville City SD	Gloversville
20	18,847	Susquehanna Valley Central SD	Conklin
21	18,795	Westhill Central SD	Syracuse
22	18,615	Westhampton Bch UFSD	Westhampton Bch
23	18,588	Niskayuna Central SD	Schenectady
24	18,544	Depew UFSD	Depew
25	18,323	Peekskill City SD	Peekskill
26	17,836	Bath Central SD	Bath
27	17,713	Minisink Valley Central SD	Slate Hill
28	17,662	Hampton Bays UFSD	Hampton Bays
29	17,473	Cohoes City SD	Cohoes
30	17,375	Byram Hills Central SD	Armonk
31	17,025	Newark Central SD	Newark
32	16,931	Maine-Endwell Central SD	Endwell
33	16,832	Hudson Falls Central SD	Fort Edward
34	16,635	Albany City SD	Albany
35	16,191	Salmon River Central SD	Fort Covington
36	15,780	Medina Central SD	Medina
37	15,613	Nanuet UFSD	Nanuet
38	15,460	Geneva City SD	Geneva
39	15,433	Elmira City SD	Elmira
40	15,307	Johnson City Central SD	Johnson City
41	15,014	Malone Central SD	Malone
42	14,887	Liberty Central SD	Liberty
43	14,640	Pelham UFSD	Pelham
44	14,543	Phelps-Clifton Springs Central SD	Clifton Springs
45	14,362	Bayport-Blue Point UFSD	Bayport
46	14,225	Ithaca City SD	Ithaca
47	14,197	Patchogue-Medford UFSD	Patchogue
48	13,983	Schuylerville Central SD	Schuylerville
49	13,957	Somers Central SD	Somers
50	13,936	Cobleskill-Richmondville CSD	Cobleskill
51	13,881	New York City Chancellor's Office	New York
52	13,849	Dunkirk City SD	Dunkirk
53	13,805	Norwich City SD	Norwich
54	13,661	Bethlehem Central SD	Delmar
55	13,596	Three Village Central SD	Stony Brook
56	13,144	Yorktown Central SD	Yorktown Hgts
57	13,003	UFSD of the Tarrytowns	Sleepy Hollow
58	12,920	Churchville-Chili Central SD	Churchville
59	12,854	Beacon City SD	Beacon
60	12,836	Hendrick Hudson Central SD	Montrose
61	12,755	Ardsley UFSD	Ardsley
62	12,666	Rondout Valley Central SD	Accord
63	12,520	Waverly Central SD	Waverly
64	12,517	Rochester City SD	Rochester
65	12,504	Oswego City SD	Oswego
66	12,476	Gates-Chili Central SD	Rochester
67	12,382	Sachem Central SD	Lake Ronkonkoma
68	12,345	Homer Central SD	Homer
69	12,247	Cheektowaga-Maryvale UFSD	Cheektowaga
70	12,242	Blind Brook-Rye UFSD	Rye Brook
71	12,212	Broadalbin-Perth Central SD	Broadalbin
72	12,193	Niagara-Wheatfield Central SD	Niagara Falls
73	11,935	Mount Pleasant Central SD	Thornwood
74	11,916	Union-Endicott Central SD	Endicott
75	11,827	South Jefferson Central SD	Adams Center
76	11,807	Oneida City SD	Oneida
77	11,787	Marcellus Central SD	Marcellus
78	11,774	Pittsford Central SD	Pittsford
79	11,742	Bedford Central SD	Bedford
80	11,702	Peru Central SD	Peru
81	11,534	Honeoye Falls-Lima Central SD	Honeoye Falls
82	11,447	Spencerport Central SD	Spencerport
83	11,416	Eastchester UFSD	Eastchester
84	11,392	Starpoint Central SD	Lockport
85	11,382	Vestal Central SD	Vestal
86	11,370	Cornwall Central SD	Cornwall on Hdsn
87	11,350	Rye City SD	Rye
88	11,268	Sweet Home Central SD	Amherst
89	11,255	Lewiston-Porter Central SD	Youngstown
90	11,188	Miller Place UFSD	Miller Place
91	11,127	Ramapo Central SD (Suffern)	Hillburn
92	11,114	Owego-Apalachin Central SD	Owego
93	11,051	Cortland City SD	Cortland
94	10,992	Indian River Central SD	Philadelphia
95	10,989	Evans-Brant Central SD (Lake Shore)	Angola
96	10,941	Whitesboro Central SD	Whitesboro
97	10,929	Garden City UFSD	Garden City
98	10,924	Mount Vernon SD	Mount Vernon
99	10,854	Ballston Spa Central SD	Ballston Spa
100	10,714	Arlington Central SD	Lagrangeville
101	10,564	Wyandanch UFSD	Wyandanch
102	10,535	Olean City SD	Olean
103	10,532	Cold Spring Hrbr Central SD	Cold Spring Hrbr
104	10,316	East Aurora UFSD	East Aurora
105	10,313	Windsor Central SD	Windsor
106	10,311	New Hyde Pk-Garden City Pk UFSD	New Hyde Park
107	10,298	Utica City SD	Utica
108	10,292	Canandaigua City SD	Canandaigua
109	10,275	William Floyd UFSD	Mastic Beach
110	10,134	Croton-Harmon UFSD	Croton on Hdsn
111	10,133	Schalmont Central SD	Schenectady
112	10,125	Riverhead Central SD	Riverhead
113	9,989	Oneonta City SD	Oneonta
114	9,933	Dansville Central SD	Dansville
115	9,924	Chenango Forks Central SD	Binghamton
116	9,809	Mamaroneck UFSD	Mamaroneck
117	9,805	Chenango Valley Central SD	Binghamton
118	9,718	Rye Neck UFSD	Mamaroneck
119	9,710	Putnam Valley Central SD	Putnam Valley
120	9,688	Commack UFSD	East Northport
121	9,597	Mexico Central SD	Mexico
122	9,578	Red Hook Central SD	Red Hook
123	9,567	Hewlett-Woodmere UFSD	Woodmere
124	9,555	New Hartford Central SD	New Hartford
125	9,553	Yorkshire-Pioneer Central SD	Yorkshire
126	9,551	Jamestown City SD	Jamestown
127	9,498	Chappaqua Central SD	Chappaqua
128	9,403	White Plains City SD	White Plains
129	9,293	East Islip UFSD	Islip Terrace
130	9,275	Warwick Valley Central SD	Warwick
131	9,273	Carthage Central SD	Carthage
132	9,271	Watertown City SD	Watertown
133	9,268	Livonia Central SD	Livonia
134	9,159	Tonawanda City SD	Tonawanda
135	9,147	Lackawanna City SD	Lackawanna
136	9,100	Oyster Bay-East Norwich Central SD	Oyster Bay
137	9,084	Malverne UFSD	Malverne
138	9,075	Queensbury UFSD	Queensbury
139	9,024	Connetquot Central SD	Bohemia
140	8,973	Binghamton City SD	Binghamton
141	8,851	Amsterdam City SD	Amsterdam
142	8,784	Bay Shore UFSD	Bay Shore
143	8,781	Newfane Central SD	Burt
144	8,692	Dryden Central SD	Dryden
145	8,670	Sayville UFSD	Sayville
146	8,624	Hauppauge UFSD	Hauppauge
147	8,567	Syosset Central SD	Syosset
148	8,540	Jamesville-Dewitt Central SD	Dewitt
149	8,515	Rome City SD	Rome
150	8,494	Port Jervis City SD	Port Jervis
151	8,487	Burnt Hills-Ballston Lake Central SD	Scotia
152	8,485	Batavia City SD	Batavia
153	8,453	Auburn City SD	Auburn
154	8,424	Clarence Central SD	Clarence
155	8,376	Middletown City SD	Middletown
156	8,282	Smithtown Central SD	Smithtown
157	8,203	Newburgh City SD	Newburgh
158	8,182	Brentwood UFSD	Brentwood
159	8,175	Rotterdam-Mohonasen Central SD	Schenectady
160	8,080	Springville-Griffith Institute CSD	Springville
161	8,066	Lansingburgh Central SD	Troy
162	7,995	Syracuse City SD	Syracuse
163	7,976	Plainedge UFSD	N Massapequa
164	7,954	Bronxville UFSD	Bronxville
165	7,927	Troy City SD	Troy
166	7,920	South Huntington UFSD	Huntington Stn
167	7,918	West Islip UFSD	West Islip
168	7,914	Monticello Central SD	Monticello
169	7,733	Massena Central SD	Massena
170	7,680	Poughkeepsie City SD	Poughkeepsie
171	7,664	Port Washington UFSD	Port Washington
172	7,642	Penfield Central SD	Rochester
173	7,620	Guilderland Central SD	Guilderland Center
174	7,601	Harborfields Central SD	Greenlawn
175	7,439	Greece Central SD	Rochester
176	7,431	Fredonia Central SD	Fredonia
177	7,411	Webster Central SD	Webster
178	7,381	Orchard Park Central SD	West Seneca
179	7,375	Center Moriches UFSD	Center Moriches
180	7,358	Glens Falls City SD	Glens Falls
181	7,241	Plattsburgh City SD	Plattsburgh
182	7,199	Katonah-Lewisboro UFSD	South Salem
183	7,141	North Babylon UFSD	North Babylon
184	7,128	Scarsdale UFSD	Scarsdale
185	7,115	Hilton Central SD	Hilton
186	7,093	West Irondequoit Central SD	Rochester
187	7,089	Liverpool Central SD	Liverpool
188	7,088	General Brown Central SD	Dexter
189	7,067	Chittenango Central SD	Chittenango
190	7,066	South Orangetown Central SD	Blauvelt
191	7,004	Manhasset UFSD	Manhasset
192	6,928	Fulton City SD	Fulton
193	6,879	East Syracuse Minoa Central SD	East Syracuse
194	6,867	Babylon UFSD	Babylon
195	6,805	Shenendehowa Central SD	Clifton Park
196	6,746	Central Square Central SD	Central Square
197	6,721	North Shore Central SD	Sea Cliff
198	6,651	Ossining UFSD	Ossining
199	6,552	Gouverneur Central SD	Gouverneur
200	6,501	Carmel Central SD	Patterson

Note: This section only includes districts with 1,500 or more students; All categories are ranked from high to low

Rank	Value	District	Location
201	6,490	Beekmantown Central SD	West Chazy
202	6,447	East Williston UFSD	Old Westbury
203	6,439	Lakeland Central SD	Shrub Oak
204	6,438	Sherrill City SD	Verona
205	6,433	Longwood Central SD	Middle Island
206	6,432	Bethpage UFSD	Bethpage
207	6,393	Averill Park Central SD	Averill Park
208	6,343	Seaford UFSD	Seaford
209	6,264	East Greenbush Central SD	East Greenbush
210	6,214	Monroe-Woodbury Central SD	Central Valley
211	6,155	Niagara Falls City SD	Niagara Falls
212	6,139	Lockport City SD	Lockport
213	6,136	Victor Central SD	Victor
214	6,117	Highland Central SD	Highland
215	6,097	West Seneca Central SD	West Seneca
216	6,096	Ravena-Coeymans-Selkirk Cent SD	Ravena
217	6,091	Brockport Central SD	Brockport
218	6,001	Baldwinsville Central SD	Baldwinsville
219	5,978	North Syracuse Central SD	North Syracuse
220	5,907	Saugerties Central SD	Saugerties
221	5,805	Amherst Central SD	Amherst
222	5,804	Saratoga Spgs City SD	Saratoga Spgs
223	5,800	Kings Park Central SD	Kings Park
224	5,781	Wantagh UFSD	Wantagh
225	5,778	Pearl River UFSD	Pearl River
226	5,756	Islip UFSD	Islip
227	5,700	Cheektowaga Central SD	Cheektowaga
228	5,698	Mineola UFSD	Mineola
229	5,655	Palmyra-Macedon Central SD	Palmyra
230	5,597	Fairport Central SD	Fairport
231	5,565	Freeport UFSD	Freeport
232	5,508	West Babylon UFSD	West Babylon
233	5,485	Half Hollow Hills Central SD	Dix Hills
234	5,460	West Genesee Central SD	Camillus
235	5,446	Clarkstown Central SD	New City
236	5,395	S Glens Fls Central SD	S Glens Fls
237	5,325	Rocky Point UFSD	Rocky Point
238	5,311	Central Islip UFSD	Central Islip
238	5,311	Yonkers City SD	Yonkers
240	5,290	Middle Country Central SD	Centereach
241	5,268	Lancaster Central SD	Lancaster
242	5,154	Kinderhook Central SD	Valatie
243	5,138	Iroquois Central SD	Elma
244	5,126	Albion Central SD	Albion
245	5,095	Pine Bush Central SD	Pine Bush
246	5,083	New Rochelle City SD	New Rochelle
247	5,074	South Colonie Central SD	Albany
248	4,977	Island Trees UFSD	Levittown
249	4,964	Johnstown City SD	Johnstown
250	4,953	Edgemont UFSD	Scarsdale
250	4,953	Fayetteville-Manlius Central SD	Manlius
252	4,942	Alden Central SD	Alden
253	4,903	Elwood UFSD	Greenlawn
254	4,861	Mount Sinai UFSD	Mount Sinai
255	4,800	Hyde Park Central SD	Hyde Park
256	4,724	Hempstead UFSD	Hempstead
257	4,685	North Colonie CSD	Latham
258	4,657	Washingtonville Central SD	Washingtonville
259	4,561	Scotia-Glenville Central SD	Scotia
260	4,541	Herricks UFSD	New Hyde Park
261	4,476	Port Chester-Rye UFSD	Port Chester
262	4,352	Kenmore-Tonawanda UFSD	Buffalo
263	4,347	North Bellmore UFSD	Bellmore
264	4,228	Roslyn UFSD	Roslyn
264	4,228	Valley Central SD (Montgomery)	Montgomery
266	4,215	Brewster Central SD	Brewster
267	4,208	New Paltz Central SD	New Paltz
268	4,161	Brookhaven-Comsewogue UFSD	Port Jeff Stn
269	4,153	Wallkill Central SD	Wallkill
270	4,085	Locust Valley Central SD	Locust Valley
271	4,056	Ogdensburg City SD	Ogdensburg
272	3,975	Franklin Square UFSD	Franklin Square
273	3,828	Baldwin UFSD	Baldwin
274	3,775	West Hempstead UFSD	West Hempstead
275	3,755	Elmont UFSD	Elmont
276	3,693	Lindenhurst UFSD	Lindenhurst
277	3,689	Mahopac Central SD	Mahopac
278	3,607	Horseheads Central SD	Horseheads
279	3,517	East Meadow UFSD	Westbury
280	3,459	Hamburg Central SD	Hamburg
281	3,395	Rush-Henrietta Central SD	Henrietta
281	3,395	Schenectady City SD	Schenectady
283	3,269	Grand Island Central SD	Grand Island
284	3,265	Westbury UFSD	Old Westbury
285	3,239	Oceanside UFSD	Oceanside
286	3,206	Northport-East Northport UFSD	Northport
287	3,024	Plainview-Old Bethpage CSD	Plainview
288	2,984	Wayne Central SD	Ontario Center
289	2,929	Rockville Ctr UFSD	Rockville Ctr
290	2,846	Ellenville Central SD	Ellenville
291	2,788	Frontier Central SD	Hamburg
292	2,776	Amityville UFSD	Amityville
293	2,627	Levittown UFSD	Levittown
294	2,616	Jericho UFSD	Jericho
295	2,564	Farmingdale UFSD	Farmingdale
296	2,558	Massapequa UFSD	Massapequa
297	2,549	Goshen Central SD	Goshen
298	2,448	Hicksville UFSD	Hicksville
299	2,399	Kingston City SD	Kingston
300	2,302	Copiague UFSD	Copiague
301	2,296	Brighton Central SD	Rochester
302	2,156	Wappingers Central SD	Hopewell Junction
303	1,969	Williamsville Central SD	East Amherst
304	1,791	Hastings-On-Hudson UFSD	Hastings on Hdsn
305	1,769	Nyack UFSD	Nyack
306	1,665	Greenburgh Central SD	Hartsdale
307	1,515	Corning City SD	Painted Post
308	1,408	Great Neck UFSD	Great Neck
309	1,323	East Ramapo CSD (Spring Valley)	Spring Valley
310	920	Valley Stream 30 UFSD	Valley Stream
311	763	Deer Park UFSD	Deer Park
312	714	North Tonawanda City SD	North Tonawanda
313	532	Huntington UFSD	Huntington Stn
314	496	Harrison Central SD	Harrison
315	385	Uniondale UFSD	Uniondale
316	343	Glen Cove City SD	Glen Cove
317	0	Bellmore-Merrick Central High SD	North Merrick
317	0	Central Valley CSD at Ilion-Mohawk	Ilion
317	0	Charter School for Applied Techs	Buffalo
317	0	Lawrence UFSD	Cedarhurst
317	0	Lynbrook UFSD	Lynbrook
317	0	Sewanhaka Central High SD	Floral Park
317	0	Shoreham-Wading River Central SD	Shoreham
317	0	Valley Stream 13 UFSD	Valley Stream
317	0	Valley Stream Central High SD	Valley Stream
n/a	n/a	NYC Geographic District # 1	New York
n/a	n/a	NYC Geographic District # 2	New York
n/a	n/a	NYC Geographic District # 3	New York
n/a	n/a	NYC Geographic District # 4	New York
n/a	n/a	NYC Geographic District # 5	New York
n/a	n/a	NYC Geographic District # 6	New York
n/a	n/a	NYC Geographic District # 7	Bronx
n/a	n/a	NYC Geographic District # 8	Bronx
n/a	n/a	NYC Geographic District # 9	Bronx
n/a	n/a	NYC Geographic District #10	Bronx
n/a	n/a	NYC Geographic District #11	Bronx
n/a	n/a	NYC Geographic District #12	Bronx
n/a	n/a	NYC Geographic District #13	Brooklyn
n/a	n/a	NYC Geographic District #14	Brooklyn
n/a	n/a	NYC Geographic District #15	Brooklyn
n/a	n/a	NYC Geographic District #16	Brooklyn
n/a	n/a	NYC Geographic District #17	Brooklyn
n/a	n/a	NYC Geographic District #18	Brooklyn
n/a	n/a	NYC Geographic District #19	Brooklyn
n/a	n/a	NYC Geographic District #20	Brooklyn
n/a	n/a	NYC Geographic District #21	Brooklyn
n/a	n/a	NYC Geographic District #22	Brooklyn
n/a	n/a	NYC Geographic District #23	Brooklyn
n/a	n/a	NYC Geographic District #24	Corona
n/a	n/a	NYC Geographic District #25	Flushing
n/a	n/a	NYC Geographic District #26	Bayside
n/a	n/a	NYC Geographic District #27	Ozone Park
n/a	n/a	NYC Geographic District #28	Jamaica
n/a	n/a	NYC Geographic District #29	Queens Village
n/a	n/a	NYC Geographic District #30	Long Isl City
n/a	n/a	NYC Geographic District #31	Staten Island
n/a	n/a	NYC Geographic District #32	Brooklyn

Note: This section only includes districts with 1,500 or more students; All categories are ranked from high to low

2017 Mathematics State Snapshot Report
New York · Grade 4 · Public Schools

Overall Results

- In 2017, the average score of fourth-grade students in New York was 236. This was lower than the average score of 239 for public school students in the nation.
- The average score for students in New York in 2017 (236) was not significantly different from their average score in 2015 (237) and was higher than their average score in 2000 (225).
- The percentage of students in New York who performed at or above the NAEP *Proficient* level was 35 percent in 2017. This percentage was not significantly different from that in 2015 (35 percent) and was greater than that in 2000 (21 percent).
- The percentage of students in New York who performed at or above the NAEP *Basic* level was 76 percent in 2017. This percentage was not significantly different from that in 2015 (79 percent) and was greater than that in 2000 (66 percent).

Compare the Average Score in 2017 to Other States/Jurisdictions

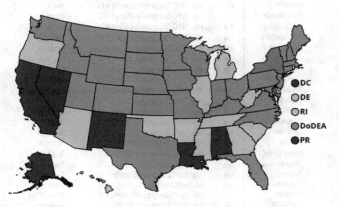

In 2017, the average score in New York (236) was
- ■ lower than those in 30 states/jurisdictions
- ■ higher than those in 8 states/jurisdictions
- ☐ not significantly different from those in 14 states/jurisdictions

DoDEA = Department of Defense Education Activity (overseas and domestic schools)

Results for Student Groups in 2017

Reporting Groups	Percentage of students	Avg. score	Percentage at or above		Percentage at
			Basic	*Proficient*	*Advanced*
Race/Ethnicity					
White	45	244	86	45	7
Black	16	224	64	22	2
Hispanic	28	223	64	20	2
Asian	8	252	88	59	15
American Indian/Alaska Native	1	‡	‡	‡	‡
Native Hawaiian/Pacific Islander	#	‡	‡	‡	‡
Two or more races	2	‡	‡	‡	‡
Gender					
Male	51	238	77	38	7
Female	49	233	75	32	4
National School Lunch Program					
Eligible	52	226	66	23	2
Not eligible	47	246	87	49	9

\# Rounds to zero.
‡ Reporting standards not met.
NOTE: Detail may not sum to totals because of rounding, and because the "Information not available" category for the National School Lunch Program, which provides free/reduced-price lunches, is not displayed. Black includes African American and Hispanic includes Latino. Race categories exclude Hispanic origin.

Achievement-Level Percentages and Average Score Results

Percent below *Basic* | Percent at *Proficient* or at *Basic* | or *Advanced*

■ Below *Basic*   ■ *Basic*   ■ *Proficient*   ■ *Advanced*

* Significantly different (*p* < .05) from state's results in 2017. Significance tests were performed using unrounded numbers.
NOTE: Detail may not sum to totals because of rounding.

Average Scores for State/Jurisdiction and Nation (public)

□ Nation (public)   ○ New York

* Significantly different (*p* < .05) from 2017. Significance tests were performed using unrounded numbers.

Score Gaps for Student Groups

- In 2017, Black students had an average score that was 19 points lower than that for White students. This performance gap was narrower than that in 2000 (27 points).
- In 2017, Hispanic students had an average score that was 20 points lower than that for White students. This performance gap was narrower than that in 2000 (30 points).
- In 2017, male students in New York had an average score that was higher than that for female students by 4 points.
- In 2017, students who were eligible for free/reduced-price school lunch, an indicator of low family income, had an average score that was 20 points lower than that for students who were not eligible. This performance gap was not significantly different from that in 2000 (26 points).

NOTE: The NAEP mathematics scale ranges from 0 to 500. Statistical comparisons are calculated on the basis of unrounded scale scores or percentages. Read more about how to interpret NAEP results from the mathematics assessment at https://nces.ed.gov/nationsreportcard/mathematics/interpret_results.aspx.
SOURCE: U.S. Department of Education, Institute of Education Sciences, National Center for Education Statistics, National Assessment of Educational Progress (NAEP), various years, 2000-2017 Mathematics Assessments.

The Nation's Report Card

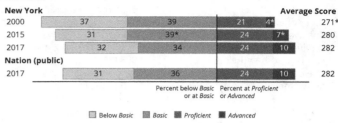

2017 Mathematics State Snapshot Report
New York · Grade 8 · Public Schools

Overall Results

- In 2017, the average score of eighth-grade students in New York was 282. This was not significantly different from the average score of 282 for public school students in the nation.
- The average score for students in New York in 2017 (282) was not significantly different from their average score in 2015 (280) and was higher than their average score in 2000 (271).
- The percentage of students in New York who performed at or above the NAEP *Proficient* level was 34 percent in 2017. This percentage was not significantly different from that in 2015 (31 percent) and was greater than that in 2000 (24 percent).
- The percentage of students in New York who performed at or above the NAEP *Basic* level was 68 percent in 2017. This percentage was not significantly different from that in 2015 (69 percent) and in 2000 (63 percent).

Compare the Average Score in 2017 to Other States/Jurisdictions

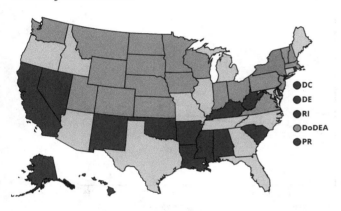

In 2017, the average score in New York (282) was
- lower than those in 21 states/jurisdictions
- higher than those in 17 states/jurisdictions
- not significantly different from those in 14 states/jurisdictions

DoDEA = Department of Defense Education Activity (overseas and domestic schools)

Achievement-Level Percentages and Average Score Results

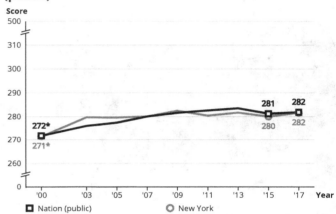

* Significantly different (*p* < .05) from state's results in 2017. Significance tests were performed using unrounded numbers.
NOTE: Detail may not sum to totals because of rounding.

Average Scores for State/Jurisdiction and Nation (public)

* Significantly different (*p* < .05) from 2017. Significance tests were performed using unrounded numbers.

Results for Student Groups in 2017

Reporting Groups	Percentage of students	Avg. score	Percentage at or above Basic	Percentage at or above Proficient	Percentage at Advanced
Race/Ethnicity					
White	49	292	79	42	13
Black	17	260	47	16	2
Hispanic	23	265	52	19	4
Asian	9	309	86	62	30
American Indian/Alaska Native	#	‡	‡	‡	‡
Native Hawaiian/Pacific Islander	#	‡	‡	‡	‡
Two or more races	1	‡	‡	‡	‡
Gender					
Male	51	281	67	33	11
Female	49	282	69	34	10
National School Lunch Program					
Eligible	49	269	56	21	4
Not eligible	49	294	80	45	16

\# Rounds to zero.
‡ Reporting standards not met.
NOTE: Detail may not sum to totals because of rounding, and because the "Information not available" category for the National School Lunch Program, which provides free/reduced-price lunches, is not displayed. Black includes African American and Hispanic includes Latino. Race categories exclude Hispanic origin.

Score Gaps for Student Groups

- In 2017, Black students had an average score that was 31 points lower than that for White students. This performance gap was not significantly different from that in 2000 (33 points).
- In 2017, Hispanic students had an average score that was 26 points lower than that for White students. This performance gap was not significantly different from that in 2000 (34 points).
- In 2017, male students in New York had an average score that was not significantly different from that for female students.
- In 2017, students who were eligible for free/reduced-price school lunch, an indicator of low family income, had an average score that was 26 points lower than that for students who were not eligible. This performance gap was not significantly different from that in 2000 (29 points).

NOTE: The NAEP mathematics scale ranges from 0 to 500. Statistical comparisons are calculated on the basis of unrounded scale scores or percentages. Read more about how to interpret NAEP results from the mathematics assessment at https://nces.ed.gov/nationsreportcard/mathematics/interpret_results.aspx.
SOURCE: U.S. Department of Education, Institute of Education Sciences, National Center for Education Statistics, National Assessment of Educational Progress (NAEP), various years, 2000-2017 Mathematics Assessments.

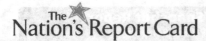

Overall Results

- In 2017, the average score of fourth-grade students in New York was 222. This was not significantly different from the average score of 221 for public school students in the nation.
- The average score for students in New York in 2017 (222) was not significantly different from their average score in 2015 (223) and was higher than their average score in 1998 (215).
- The percentage of students in New York who performed at or above the NAEP *Proficient* level was 36 percent in 2017. This percentage was not significantly different from that in 2015 (36 percent) and was greater than that in 1998 (29 percent).
- The percentage of students in New York who performed at or above the NAEP *Basic* level was 68 percent in 2017. This percentage was not significantly different from that in 2015 (68 percent) and was greater than that in 1998 (62 percent).

Achievement-Level Percentages and Average Score Results

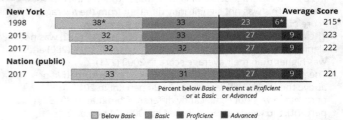

* Significantly different (*p* < .05) from state's results in 2017. Significance tests were performed using unrounded numbers.
NOTE: Detail may not sum to totals because of rounding.

Compare the Average Score in 2017 to Other States/Jurisdictions

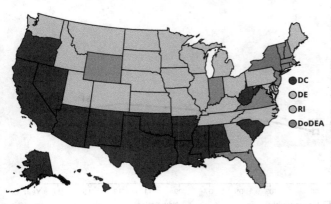

In 2017, the average score in New York (222) was
- lower than those in 10 states/jurisdictions
- higher than those in 16 states/jurisdictions
- not significantly different from those in 25 states/jurisdictions

DoDEA = Department of Defense Education Activity (overseas and domestic schools)

Average Scores for State/Jurisdiction and Nation (public)

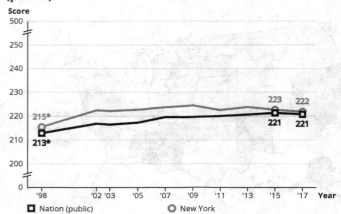

* Significantly different (*p* < .05) from 2017. Significance tests were performed using unrounded numbers.

Results for Student Groups in 2017

Reporting Groups	Percentage of students	Avg. score	Percentage at or above		Percentage at
			Basic	*Proficient*	*Advanced*
Race/Ethnicity					
White	45	232	78	47	13
Black	16	208	52	19	3
Hispanic	27	208	55	21	4
Asian	8	238	83	53	19
American Indian/Alaska Native	#	‡	‡	‡	‡
Native Hawaiian/Pacific Islander	#	‡	‡	‡	‡
Two or more races	2	‡	‡	‡	‡
Gender					
Male	50	219	65	33	8
Female	50	225	71	39	10
National School Lunch Program					
Eligible	52	211	56	24	4
Not eligible	48	234	80	49	14

Rounds to zero.
‡ Reporting standards not met.
NOTE: Detail may not sum to totals because of rounding, and because the "Information not available" category for the National School Lunch Program, which provides free/reduced-price lunches, is not displayed. Black includes African American and Hispanic includes Latino. Race categories exclude Hispanic origin.

Score Gaps for Student Groups

- In 2017, Black students had an average score that was 25 points lower than that for White students. This performance gap was narrower than that in 1998 (37 points).
- In 2017, Hispanic students had an average score that was 25 points lower than that for White students. This performance gap was narrower than that in 1998 (40 points).
- In 2017, female students in New York had an average score that was higher than that for male students by 6 points.
- In 2017, students who were eligible for free/reduced-price school lunch, an indicator of low family income, had an average score that was 23 points lower than that for students who were not eligible. This performance gap was narrower than that in 1998 (35 points).

NOTE: The NAEP reading scale ranges from 0 to 500. Statistical comparisons are calculated on the basis of unrounded scale scores or percentages. Read more about how to interpret NAEP results from the reading assessment at https://nces.ed.gov/nationsreportcard/reading/interpret_results.aspx.
SOURCE: U.S. Department of Education, Institute of Education Sciences, National Center for Education Statistics, National Assessment of Educational Progress (NAEP), various years, 1998-2017 Reading Assessments.

The Nation's Report Card

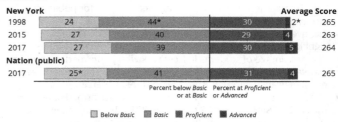

2017 Reading State Snapshot Report
New York · Grade 8 · Public Schools

Overall Results

- In 2017, the average score of eighth-grade students in New York was 264. This was not significantly different from the average score of 265 for public school students in the nation.
- The average score for students in New York in 2017 (264) was not significantly different from their average score in 2015 (263) and in 1998 (265).
- The percentage of students in New York who performed at or above the NAEP *Proficient* level was 34 percent in 2017. This percentage was not significantly different from that in 2015 (33 percent) and in 1998 (32 percent).
- The percentage of students in New York who performed at or above the NAEP *Basic* level was 73 percent in 2017. This percentage was not significantly different from that in 2015 (73 percent) and in 1998 (76 percent).

Compare the Average Score in 2017 to Other States/Jurisdictions

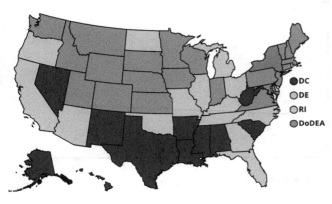

In 2017, the average score in New York (264) was
- lower than those in 23 states/jurisdictions
- higher than those in 12 states/jurisdictions
- not significantly different from those in 16 states/jurisdictions

DoDEA = Department of Defense Education Activity (overseas and domestic schools)

Results for Student Groups in 2017

Reporting Groups	Percentage of students	Avg. score	Percentage at or above Basic	Percentage at or above Proficient	Percentage at Advanced
Race/Ethnicity					
White	49	272	80	42	6
Black	17	251	61	20	1
Hispanic	23	253	65	22	1
Asian	9	277	79	49	12
American Indian/Alaska Native	#	‡	‡	‡	‡
Native Hawaiian/Pacific Islander	#	‡	‡	‡	‡
Two or more races	1	‡	‡	‡	‡
Gender					
Male	51	258	68	29	3
Female	49	270	78	40	6
National School Lunch Program					
Eligible	51	253	63	22	2
Not eligible	48	275	83	46	7

\# Rounds to zero.
‡ Reporting standards not met.
NOTE: Detail may not sum to totals because of rounding, and because the "Information not available" category for the National School Lunch Program, which provides free/reduced-price lunches, is not displayed. Black includes African American and Hispanic includes Latino. Race categories exclude Hispanic origin.

Achievement-Level Percentages and Average Score Results

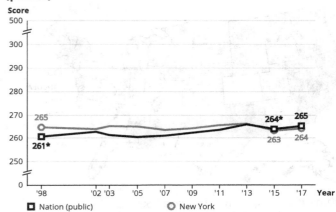

* Significantly different (*p* < .05) from state's results in 2017. Significance tests were performed using unrounded numbers.
NOTE: Detail may not sum to totals because of rounding.

Average Scores for State/Jurisdiction and Nation (public)

* Significantly different (*p* < .05) from 2017. Significance tests were performed using unrounded numbers.

Score Gaps for Student Groups

- In 2017, Black students had an average score that was 20 points lower than that for White students. This performance gap was narrower than that in 1998 (28 points).
- In 2017, Hispanic students had an average score that was 19 points lower than that for White students. This performance gap was narrower than that in 1998 (28 points).
- In 2017, female students in New York had an average score that was higher than that for male students by 12 points.
- In 2017, students who were eligible for free/reduced-price school lunch, an indicator of low family income, had an average score that was 23 points lower than that for students who were not eligible. This performance gap was not significantly different from that in 1998 (25 points).

NATIONAL CENTER for EDUCATION STATISTICS
Institute of Education Sciences

NOTE: The NAEP reading scale ranges from 0 to 500. Statistical comparisons are calculated on the basis of unrounded scale scores or percentages. Read more about how to interpret NAEP results from the reading assessment at https://nces.ed.gov/nationsreportcard/reading/interpret_results.aspx.
SOURCE: U.S. Department of Education, Institute of Education Sciences, National Center for Education Statistics, National Assessment of Educational Progress (NAEP), various years, 1998-2017 Reading Assessments.

2015 Science State Snapshot Report
New York · Grade 4 · Public Schools

Overall Results

- In 2015, the average score of fourth-grade students in New York was 150. This was lower than the average score of 153 for public school students in the nation.
- The average score for students in New York in 2015 (150) was not significantly different from their average score in 2009 (148).
- The percentage of students in New York who performed at or above the NAEP *Proficient* level was 33 percent in 2015. This percentage was not significantly different from that in 2009 (30 percent).
- The percentage of students in New York who performed at or above the NAEP *Basic* level was 72 percent in 2015. This percentage was not significantly different from that in 2009 (70 percent).

Achievement-Level Percentages and Average Score Results

Rounds to zero.
* Significantly different (*p* < .05) from state's results in 2015. Significance tests were performed using unrounded numbers.
NOTE: Detail may not sum to totals because of rounding.

Compare the Average Score in 2015 to Other States/Jurisdictions

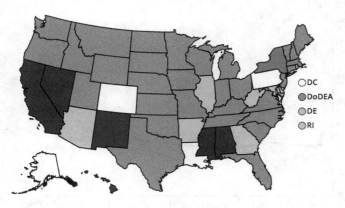

In 2015, the average score in New York (150) was
▨ lower than those in 32 states/jurisdictions
■ higher than those in 6 states/jurisdictions
▢ not significantly different from those in 8 states/jurisdictions

☐ 5 states/jurisdictions did not participate in 2015

DoDEA = Department of Defense Education Activity (overseas and domestic schools)

Average Scores for State/Jurisdiction and Nation (public)

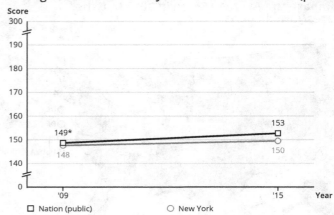

* Significantly different (*p* < .05) from 2015. Significance tests were performed using unrounded numbers.

Results for Student Groups in 2015

Reporting Groups	Percentage of students	Avg. score	Percentage at or above		Percentage at Advanced
			Basic	Proficient	
Race/Ethnicity					
White	45	164	87	49	1
Black	19	130	49	12	#
Hispanic	26	135	58	16	#
Asian	8	159	81	46	1
American Indian/Alaska Native	1	‡	‡	‡	‡
Native Hawaiian/Pacific Islander	#	‡	‡	‡	‡
Two or more races	1	‡	‡	‡	‡
Gender					
Male	52	150	72	35	1
Female	48	149	71	32	1
National School Lunch Program					
Eligible	56	138	59	20	#
Not eligible	41	164	87	49	1

Rounds to zero.
‡ Reporting standards not met.
NOTE: Detail may not sum to totals because of rounding, and because the "Information not available" category for the National School Lunch Program, which provides free/reduced-price lunches, is not displayed. Black includes African American and Hispanic includes Latino. Race categories exclude Hispanic origin.

Score Gaps for Student Groups

- In 2015, Black students had an average score that was 34 points lower than that for White students. This performance gap was not significantly different from that in 2009 (34 points).
- In 2015, Hispanic students had an average score that was 28 points lower than that for White students. This performance gap was not significantly different from that in 2009 (31 points).
- In 2015, male students in New York had an average score that was not significantly different from that for female students.
- In 2015, students who were eligible for free/reduced-price school lunch, an indicator of low family income, had an average score that was 26 points lower than that for students who were not eligible. This performance gap was not significantly different from that in 2009 (27 points).

NOTE: The NAEP science scale ranges from 0 to 300. Statistical comparisons are calculated on the basis of unrounded scale scores or percentages.
SOURCE: U.S. Department of Education, Institute of Education Sciences, National Center for Education Statistics, National Assessment of Educational Progress (NAEP), 2009 and 2015 Science Assessments.

Overall Results

- In 2015, the average score of eighth-grade students in New York was 150. This was lower than the average score of 153 for public school students in the nation.
- The average score for students in New York in 2015 (150) was not significantly different from their average score in 2011 (149) and in 2009 (149).
- The percentage of students in New York who performed at or above the NAEP *Proficient* level was 30 percent in 2015. This percentage was not significantly different from that in 2011 (29 percent) and in 2009 (31 percent).
- The percentage of students in New York who performed at or above the NAEP *Basic* level was 63 percent in 2015. This percentage was not significantly different from that in 2011 (62 percent) and in 2009 (61 percent).

Achievement-Level Percentages and Average Score Results

* Significantly different (*p* < .05) from state's results in 2015. Significance tests were performed using unrounded numbers.
NOTE: Detail may not sum to totals because of rounding.

Compare the Average Score in 2015 to Other States/Jurisdictions

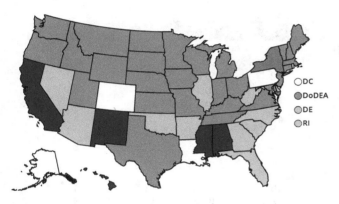

In 2015, the average score in New York (150) was
- ■ lower than those in 29 states/jurisdictions
- ■ higher than those in 5 states/jurisdictions
- ■ not significantly different from those in 12 states/jurisdictions

☐ 5 states/jurisdictions did not participate in 2015

DoDEA = Department of Defense Education Activity (overseas and domestic schools)

Average Scores for State/Jurisdiction and Nation (public)

* Significantly different (*p* < .05) from 2015. Significance tests were performed using unrounded numbers.

Results for Student Groups in 2015

Reporting Groups	Percentage of students	Avg. score	Percentage at or above Basic	Percentage at or above Proficient	Percentage at Advanced
Race/Ethnicity					
White	47	164	79	45	2
Black	20	129	38	9	#
Hispanic	23	134	46	13	#
Asian	9	158	73	39	3
American Indian/Alaska Native	#	‡	‡	‡	‡
Native Hawaiian/Pacific Islander	#	‡	‡	‡	‡
Two or more races	1	‡	‡	‡	‡
Gender					
Male	51	150	63	32	2
Female	49	149	62	28	1
National School Lunch Program					
Eligible	56	139	50	17	#
Not eligible	42	163	78	45	3

Rounds to zero.
‡ Reporting standards not met.
NOTE: Detail may not sum to totals because of rounding, and because the "Information not available" category for the National School Lunch Program, which provides free/reduced-price lunches, is not displayed. Black includes African American and Hispanic includes Latino. Race categories exclude Hispanic origin.

Score Gaps for Student Groups

- In 2015, Black students had an average score that was 35 points lower than that for White students. This performance gap was not significantly different from that in 2009 (41 points).
- In 2015, Hispanic students had an average score that was 30 points lower than that for White students. This performance gap was narrower than that in 2009 (39 points).
- In 2015, male students in New York had an average score that was not significantly different from that for female students.
- In 2015, students who were eligible for free/reduced-price school lunch, an indicator of low family income, had an average score that was 24 points lower than that for students who were not eligible. This performance gap was narrower than that in 2009 (33 points).

NOTE: The NAEP science scale ranges from 0 to 300. Statistical comparisons are calculated on the basis of unrounded scale scores or percentages.
SOURCE: U.S. Department of Education, Institute of Education Sciences, National Center for Education Statistics, National Assessment of Educational Progress (NAEP), various years, 2009-2015 Science Assessments.

The Nation's Report Card
State **Writing** 2002
Snapshot Report

New York
Grade 4
Public School

NCES 2003-532NY4

The writing assessment of the National Assessment of Educational Progress (NAEP) measures narrative, informative, and persuasive writing–three purposes identified in the NAEP framework. The NAEP writing scale ranges from 0 to 300.

Overall Writing Results for New York

- The average scale score for fourth-grade students in New York was 163.
- New York's average score (163) was higher[1] than that of the nation's public schools (153).
- Students' average scale scores in New York were higher than those in 42 jurisdictions[2], not significantly different from those in 3 jurisdictions, and lower than those in 2 jurisdictions.
- The percentage of students who performed at or above the NAEP *Proficient* level was 37 percent. The percentage of students who performed at or above the *Basic* level was 91 percent.

Student Percentage at Each Achievement Level

New York
2002   9   54   34   3

Nation (Public)
2002   15*   59*   25*   2

Percentage below *Basic* and *Basic*   Percentage *Proficient* and *Advanced*
● below *Basic*   ○ *Basic*   ◑ *Proficient*   ● *Advanced*

Performance of NAEP Reporting Groups in New York

Reporting groups	Percentage of students	Average Score	Percentage of students at			
			Below *Basic*	*Basic*	*Proficient*	*Advanced*
Male	51	156 ↑	12 ↓	58	28 ↑	2
Female	49	170 ↑	6 ↓	50 ↓	40 ↑	4
White	54	172 ↑	4 ↓	49 ↓	42 ↑	4
Black	19	148 ↑	16 ↓	63	20 ↑	1
Hispanic	21	149	16	61	22	1
Asian/Pacific Islander	6	176	4	44	47	5
American Indian/Alaska Native	#	---	---	---	---	---
Free/reduced-priced school lunch						
Eligible	44	150 ↑	16 ↓	61	22 ↑	1
Not eligible	49	172 ↑	4 ↓	49 ↓	43 ↑	4
Information not available	7	175 ↑	5 ↓	43	46 ↑	6

Average Score Gaps Between Selected Groups

- Female students in New York had an average score that was higher than that of male students (14 points). This performance gap was not significantly different from that of the Nation (18 points).
- White students had an average score that was higher than that of Black students (24 points). This performance gap was not significantly different from that of the Nation (20 points).
- White students had an average score that was higher than that of Hispanic students (23 points). This performance gap was not significantly different from that of the Nation (19 points).
- Students who were not eligible for free/reduced-price school lunch had an average score that was higher than that of students who were eligible (22 points). This performance gap was not significantly different from that of the Nation (22 points).

Writing Scale Scores at Selected Percentiles

Scale Score Distribution

	25th Percentile	50th Percentile	75th Percentile
New York	139 ↑	164 ↑	187 ↑
Nation (Public)	128	153	178

An examination of scores at different percentiles on the 0-300 NAEP writing scale at each grade indicates how well students at lower, middle, and higher levels of the distribution performed. For example, the data above shows that 75 percent of students in public schools nationally scored below *178*, while 75 percent of students in New York scored below *187*.

Percentage rounds to zero.   --- Reporting standards not met; sample size insufficient to permit a reliable estimate.
* Significantly different from New York.   ↑ Significantly higher than, ↓ lower than appropriate subgroup in the nation (public).
[1] Comparisons (higher/lower/not different) are based on statistical tests. The .05 level was used for testing statistical significance.
[2] "Jurisdictions" includes participating states and other jurisdictions (such as Guam or the District of Columbia).
NOTE: Detail may not sum to totals because of rounding. Score gaps are calculated based on differences between unrounded average scale scores.
Visit http://nces.ed.gov/nationsreportcard/states/ for additional results and detailed information.
SOURCE: U.S. Department of Education, Institute of Education Sciences, National Center for Education Statistics, National Assessment of Educational Progress (NAEP), 2002 Writing Assessment.

The National Assessment of Educational Progress (NAEP) assesses writing for three purposes identified in the NAEP framework: narrative, informative, and persuasive. The NAEP writing scale ranges from 0 to 300.

Overall Writing Results for New York

- In 2007, the average scale score for eighth-grade students in New York was 154. This was not significantly different from their average score in 2002 (151) and was higher than their average score in 1998 (146).[1]
- New York's average score (154) in 2007 was not significantly different from that of the nation's public schools (154).
- Of the 45 states and one other jurisdiction that participated in the 2007 eighth-grade assessment, students' average scale score in New York was higher than those in 11 jurisdictions, not significantly different from those in 21 jurisdictions, and lower than those in 13 jurisdictions.[2]
- The percentage of students in New York who performed at or above the NAEP *Proficient* level was 31 percent in 2007. This percentage was not significantly different from that in 2002 (30 percent) and was greater than that in 1998 (21 percent).
- The percentage of students in New York who performed at or above the NAEP *Basic* level was 87 percent in 2007. This percentage was not significantly different from that in 2002 (84 percent) and was not significantly different from that in 1998 (84 percent).

Percentages at NAEP Achievement Levels and Average Score

NOTE: The NAEP grade 8 writing achievement levels correspond to the following scale points: Below *Basic*, 113 or lower; *Basic*, 114–172; *Proficient*, 173–223; *Advanced*, 224 or above.

Performance of NAEP Reporting Groups in New York: 2007

Reporting groups	Percent of students	Average score	Percent below *Basic*	Percent of students at or above *Basic*	*Proficient*	Percent *Advanced*
Male	50	145	19	81	22	1
Female	50	163	8	92	41	2
White	56	161	8	92	38	2
Black	19	140	20	80	15	#
Hispanic	18	140	25	75	20	1
Asian/Pacific Islander	7	170	9	91	52	5
American Indian/Alaska Native	#	‡	‡	‡	‡	‡
Eligible for National School Lunch Program	47↑	145↑	20	80	22↑	1
Not eligible for National School Lunch Program	51	164	7	93	40	2

Average Score Gaps Between Selected Groups

- In 2007, male students in New York had an average score that was lower than that of female students by 18 points. This performance gap was not significantly different from that of 1998 (15 points).
- In 2007, Black students had an average score that was lower than that of White students by 21 points. This performance gap was not significantly different from that of 1998 (25 points).
- In 2007, Hispanic students had an average score that was lower than that of White students by 21 points. This performance gap was narrower than that of 1998 (31 points).
- In 2007, students who were eligible for free/reduced-price school lunch, an indicator of poverty, had an average score that was lower than that of students who were not eligible for free/reduced-price school lunch by 19 points. This performance gap was not significantly different from that of 1998 (26 points).
- In 2007, the score gap between students at the 75th percentile and students at the 25th percentile was 47 points. This performance gap was not significantly different from that of 1998 (44 points).

Writing Scores at Selected Percentiles in New York

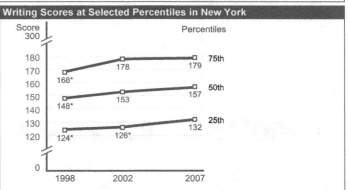

NOTE: Scores at selected percentiles on the NAEP writing scale indicate how well students at lower, middle, and higher levels performed.

Rounds to zero.   ‡ Reporting standards not met.
* Significantly different from 2007.   ↑ Significantly higher than 2002. ↓ Significantly lower than 2002.
[1] Comparisons (higher/lower/narrower/wider/not different) are based on statistical tests. The .05 level with appropriate adjustments for multiple comparisons was used for testing statistical significance. Statistical comparisons are calculated on the basis of unrounded scale scores or percentages. Comparisons across jurisdictions and comparisons with the nation or within a jurisdiction across years may be affected by differences in exclusion rates for students with disabilities (SD) and English language learners (ELL). The exclusion rates for SD and ELL in New York were 2 percent and 1 percent in 2007, respectively. For more information on NAEP significance testing, see http://nces.ed.gov/nationsreportcard/writing/interpret-results.asp#statistical.
[2] "Jurisdiction" refers to states, the District of Columbia, and the Department of Defense Education Activity schools.
NOTE: Detail may not sum to totals because of rounding and because the "Information not available" category for the National School Lunch Program, which provides free and reduced-price lunches, and the "Unclassified" category for race/ethnicity are not displayed. Visit http://nces.ed.gov/nationsreportcard/states/ for additional results and detailed information.
SOURCE: U.S. Department of Education, Institute of Education Sciences, National Center for Education Statistics, National Assessment of Educational Progress (NAEP), 1998, 2002, and 2007 Writing Assessments.

NY STATE GRADES 3-8 ELA ASSESSMENT DATA

The grades 3-8 English Language Arts (ELA) and mathematics assessments measure the higher learning standards that were adopted by the State Board of Regents in 2010, which more accurately reflect students' progress toward college and career readiness. Data are available statewide and at the county, district, and school level.

Data available on this site are based on those reported by schools and districts to the State as of August 22, 2018 via the Student Information Repository System (SIRS). The New York State School Report Card 3-8 English Language Arts (ELA) and mathematics assessment data will be based on those data reported as of the final school year reporting deadline.

For more information and additional files, please view the NYSED press release

> Due to the State's new two-session test design and performance standards, the 2018 Grades 3-8 ELA and math results cannot be compared with prior-year results. The new baseline established this year will enable comparisons with student scores in 2019 and 2020

Assessment Data - Glossary of Terms | Assessment Data - Business Rules

■ NY STATE (2017)   ■ NY STATE (2018)

Percentage Scoring at Levels

2017

ALL STUDENTS

PROFICIENT

374,234
40%

TOTAL TESTED: 939,983

LEVEL 1		LEVEL 2	
247,087	26%	318,662	34%

LEVEL 3		LEVEL 4	
249,824	27%	124,410	13%

2018

ALL STUDENTS

PROFICIENT

437,130
45%

TOTAL TESTED: 966,661

LEVEL 1		LEVEL 2	
234,445	24%	295,086	31%

LEVEL 3		LEVEL 4	
279,241	29%	157,889	16%

BY GENDER

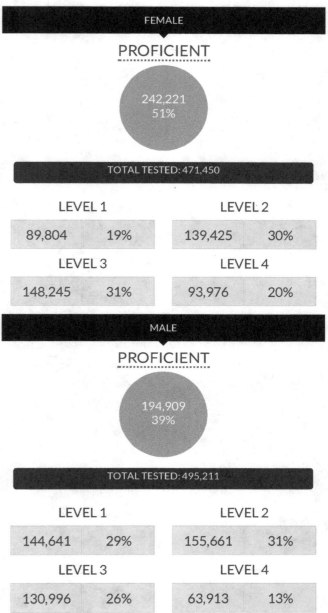

FEMALE

PROFICIENT

210,911
46%

TOTAL TESTED: 458,431

LEVEL 1		LEVEL 2	
95,923	21%	151,597	33%

LEVEL 3		LEVEL 4	
134,138	29%	76,773	17%

MALE

PROFICIENT

163,323
34%

TOTAL TESTED: 481,552

LEVEL 1		LEVEL 2	
151,164	31%	167,065	35%

LEVEL 3		LEVEL 4	
115,686	24%	47,637	10%

FEMALE

PROFICIENT

242,221
51%

TOTAL TESTED: 471,450

LEVEL 1		LEVEL 2	
89,804	19%	139,425	30%

LEVEL 3		LEVEL 4	
148,245	31%	93,976	20%

MALE

PROFICIENT

194,909
39%

TOTAL TESTED: 495,211

LEVEL 1		LEVEL 2	
144,641	29%	155,661	31%

LEVEL 3		LEVEL 4	
130,996	26%	63,913	13%

BY ETHNICITY

MULTIRACIAL

PROFICIENT

8,690
43%

TOTAL TESTED: 20,139

LEVEL 1		LEVEL 2	
5,233	26%	6,216	31%

LEVEL 3		LEVEL 4	
5,407	27%	3,283	16%

AMERICAN INDIAN OR ALASKA NATIVE

PROFICIENT

2,287
33%

TOTAL TESTED: 6,984

LEVEL 1		LEVEL 2	
2,180	31%	2,517	36%

LEVEL 3		LEVEL 4	
1,603	23%	684	10%

MULTIRACIAL

PROFICIENT

11,202
48%

TOTAL TESTED: 23,156

LEVEL 1		LEVEL 2	
5,404	23%	6,550	28%

LEVEL 3		LEVEL 4	
6,852	30%	4,350	19%

AMERICAN INDIAN OR ALASKA NATIVE

PROFICIENT

2,819
39%

TOTAL TESTED: 7,314

LEVEL 1		LEVEL 2	
2,123	29%	2,372	32%

LEVEL 3		LEVEL 4	
1,868	26%	951	13%

ASIAN OR NATIVE HAWAIIAN/OTHER PACIFIC ISLANDER

PROFICIENT

63,839
61%

TOTAL TESTED: 105,040

LEVEL 1		LEVEL 2	
14,068	13%	27,133	26%

LEVEL 3		LEVEL 4	
34,800	33%	29,039	28%

ASIAN OR NATIVE HAWAIIAN/OTHER PACIFIC ISLANDER

PROFICIENT

71,801
67%

TOTAL TESTED: 107,652

LEVEL 1		LEVEL 2	
13,083	12%	22,768	21%

LEVEL 3		LEVEL 4	
36,079	34%	35,722	33%

WHITE

PROFICIENT

168,292
47%

TOTAL TESTED: 357,585

LEVEL 1		LEVEL 2	
71,298	20%	117,995	33%

LEVEL 3		LEVEL 4	
110,097	31%	58,195	16%

WHITE

PROFICIENT

191,241
52%

TOTAL TESTED: 369,336

LEVEL 1		LEVEL 2	
69,391	19%	108,704	29%

LEVEL 3		LEVEL 4	
120,782	33%	70,459	19%

OTHER GROUPS

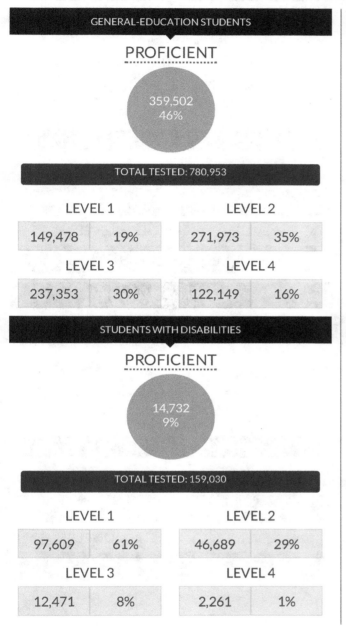

GENERAL-EDUCATION STUDENTS

PROFICIENT

359,502
46%

TOTAL TESTED: 780,953

LEVEL 1		LEVEL 2	
149,478	19%	271,973	35%

LEVEL 3		LEVEL 4	
237,353	30%	122,149	16%

STUDENTS WITH DISABILITIES

PROFICIENT

14,732
9%

TOTAL TESTED: 159,030

LEVEL 1		LEVEL 2	
97,609	61%	46,689	29%

LEVEL 3		LEVEL 4	
12,471	8%	2,261	1%

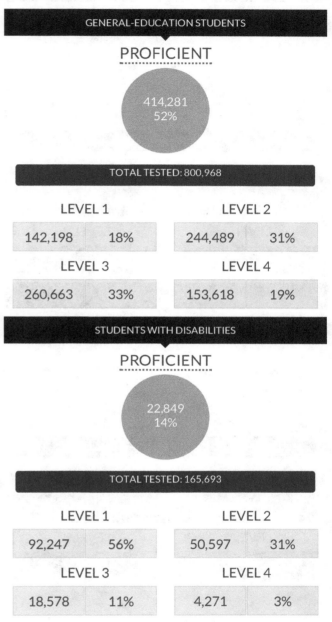

GENERAL-EDUCATION STUDENTS

PROFICIENT

414,281
52%

TOTAL TESTED: 800,968

LEVEL 1		LEVEL 2	
142,198	18%	244,489	31%

LEVEL 3		LEVEL 4	
260,663	33%	153,618	19%

STUDENTS WITH DISABILITIES

PROFICIENT

22,849
14%

TOTAL TESTED: 165,693

LEVEL 1		LEVEL 2	
92,247	56%	50,597	31%

LEVEL 3		LEVEL 4	
18,578	11%	4,271	3%

NON-ENGLISH LANGUAGE LEARNERS

PROFICIENT

370,256
43%

TOTAL TESTED: 863,424

LEVEL 1		LEVEL 2	
195,304	23%	297,864	34%

LEVEL 3		LEVEL 4	
246,110	29%	124,146	14%

ENGLISH LANGUAGE LEARNERS

PROFICIENT

3,978
5%

TOTAL TESTED: 76,559

LEVEL 1		LEVEL 2	
51,783	68%	20,798	27%

LEVEL 3		LEVEL 4	
3,714	5%	264	0%

NON-ENGLISH LANGUAGE LEARNERS

PROFICIENT

429,272
49%

TOTAL TESTED: 881,296

LEVEL 1		LEVEL 2	
182,855	21%	269,169	31%

LEVEL 3		LEVEL 4	
271,966	31%	157,306	18%

ENGLISH LANGUAGE LEARNERS

PROFICIENT

7,858
9%

TOTAL TESTED: 85,365

LEVEL 1		LEVEL 2	
51,590	60%	25,917	30%

LEVEL 3		LEVEL 4	
7,275	9%	583	1%

NOT ECONOMICALLY DISADVANTAGED

PROFICIENT

211,868
54%

TOTAL TESTED: 389,468

LEVEL 1		LEVEL 2	
57,693	15%	119,907	31%

LEVEL 3		LEVEL 4	
131,872	34%	79,996	21%

ECONOMICALLY DISADVANTAGED

PROFICIENT

162,366
29%

TOTAL TESTED: 550,515

LEVEL 1		LEVEL 2	
189,394	34%	198,755	36%

LEVEL 3		LEVEL 4	
117,952	21%	44,414	8%

NOT ECONOMICALLY DISADVANTAGED

PROFICIENT

226,403
61%

TOTAL TESTED: 373,036

LEVEL 1		LEVEL 2	
47,559	13%	99,074	27%

LEVEL 3		LEVEL 4	
133,861	36%	92,542	25%

ECONOMICALLY DISADVANTAGED

PROFICIENT

210,727
35%

TOTAL TESTED: 593,625

LEVEL 1		LEVEL 2	
186,886	31%	196,012	33%

LEVEL 3		LEVEL 4	
145,380	24%	65,347	11%

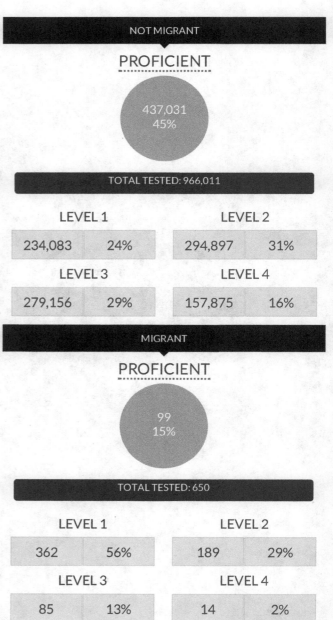

NOT MIGRANT

PROFICIENT

374,162
40%

TOTAL TESTED: 939,340

LEVEL 1		LEVEL 2	
246,690	26%	318,488	34%

LEVEL 3		LEVEL 4	
249,764	27%	124,398	13%

MIGRANT

PROFICIENT

72
11%

TOTAL TESTED: 643

LEVEL 1		LEVEL 2	
397	62%	174	27%

LEVEL 3		LEVEL 4	
60	9%	12	2%

NOT MIGRANT

PROFICIENT

437,031
45%

TOTAL TESTED: 966,011

LEVEL 1		LEVEL 2	
234,083	24%	294,897	31%

LEVEL 3		LEVEL 4	
279,156	29%	157,875	16%

MIGRANT

PROFICIENT

99
15%

TOTAL TESTED: 650

LEVEL 1		LEVEL 2	
362	56%	189	29%

LEVEL 3		LEVEL 4	
85	13%	14	2%

NY STATE GRADES 3-8 MATHEMATICS ASSESSMENT DATA

The grades 3-8 English Language Arts (ELA) and mathematics assessments measure the higher learning standards that were adopted by the State Board of Regents in 2010, which more accurately reflect students' progress toward college and career readiness. Data are available statewide and at the county, district, and school level.

Data available on this site are based on those reported by schools and districts to the State as of August 22, 2018 via the Student Information Repository System (SIRS). The New York State School Report Card 3-8 English Language Arts (ELA) and mathematics assessment data will be based on those data reported as of the final school year reporting deadline.

For more information and additional files, please view the NYSED press release

> Due to the State's new two-session test design and performance standards, the 2018 Grades 3-8 ELA and math results cannot be compared with prior-year results. The new baseline established this year will enable comparisons with student scores in 2019 and 2020

Assessment Data - Glossary of Terms | Assessment Data - Business Rules

■ NY STATE (2017)   ▨ NY STATE (2018)

Percentage Scoring at Levels

## 2017	## 2018

2017 ALL STUDENTS	2018 ALL STUDENTS
PROFICIENT	PROFICIENT
365,102 — 40%	414,857 — 45%
TOTAL TESTED: 909,106	TOTAL TESTED: 931,449

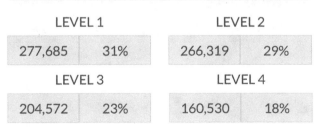

2017

LEVEL 1		LEVEL 2	
277,685	31%	266,319	29%

LEVEL 3		LEVEL 4	
204,572	23%	160,530	18%

2018

LEVEL 1		LEVEL 2	
282,460	30%	234,132	25%

LEVEL 3		LEVEL 4	
221,419	24%	193,438	21%

BY GENDER

FEMALE

PROFICIENT

178,929
41%

TOTAL TESTED: 439,877

LEVEL 1		LEVEL 2	
127,280	29%	133,668	30%

LEVEL 3		LEVEL 4	
101,206	23%	77,723	18%

FEMALE

PROFICIENT

203,203
45%

TOTAL TESTED: 450,977

LEVEL 1		LEVEL 2	
130,482	29%	117,292	26%

LEVEL 3		LEVEL 4	
109,759	24%	93,444	21%

MALE

PROFICIENT

186,173
40%

TOTAL TESTED: 469,229

LEVEL 1		LEVEL 2	
150,405	32%	132,651	28%

LEVEL 3		LEVEL 4	
103,366	22%	82,807	18%

MALE

PROFICIENT

211,654
44%

TOTAL TESTED: 480,472

LEVEL 1		LEVEL 2	
151,978	32%	116,840	24%

LEVEL 3		LEVEL 4	
111,660	23%	99,994	21%

BY ETHNICITY

MULTIRACIAL

PROFICIENT

8,538
45%

TOTAL TESTED: 19,077

LEVEL 1		LEVEL 2	
5,419	28%	5,120	27%

LEVEL 3		LEVEL 4	
4,374	23%	4,164	22%

AMERICAN INDIAN OR ALASKA NATIVE

PROFICIENT

2,121
31%

TOTAL TESTED: 6,786

LEVEL 1		LEVEL 2	
2,557	38%	2,108	31%

LEVEL 3		LEVEL 4	
1,296	19%	825	12%

MULTIRACIAL

PROFICIENT

10,677
48%

TOTAL TESTED: 22,194

LEVEL 1		LEVEL 2	
6,324	28%	5,193	23%

LEVEL 3		LEVEL 4	
5,367	24%	5,310	24%

AMERICAN INDIAN OR ALASKA NATIVE

PROFICIENT

2,550
36%

TOTAL TESTED: 7,031

LEVEL 1		LEVEL 2	
2,643	38%	1,838	26%

LEVEL 3		LEVEL 4	
1,507	21%	1,043	15%

ASIAN OR NATIVE HAWAIIAN/OTHER PACIFIC ISLANDER

PROFICIENT

68,976
67%

TOTAL TESTED: 102,664

LEVEL 1		LEVEL 2	
12,548	12%	21,140	21%

LEVEL 3		LEVEL 4	
27,853	27%	41,123	40%

WHITE

PROFICIENT

170,594
50%

TOTAL TESTED: 338,571

LEVEL 1		LEVEL 2	
68,219	20%	99,758	29%

LEVEL 3		LEVEL 4	
96,222	28%	74,372	22%

ASIAN OR NATIVE HAWAIIAN/OTHER PACIFIC ISLANDER

PROFICIENT

73,355
71%

TOTAL TESTED: 103,008

LEVEL 1		LEVEL 2	
12,343	12%	17,310	17%

LEVEL 3		LEVEL 4	
26,462	26%	46,893	46%

WHITE

PROFICIENT

189,900
54%

TOTAL TESTED: 350,520

LEVEL 1		LEVEL 2	
72,122	21%	88,498	25%

LEVEL 3		LEVEL 4	
102,664	29%	87,236	25%

BLACK OR AFRICAN AMERICAN

PROFICIENT

42,849
24%

TOTAL TESTED: 175,515

LEVEL 1		LEVEL 2	
79,996	46%	52,670	30%

LEVEL 3		LEVEL 4	
27,551	16%	15,298	9%

HISPANIC OR LATINO

PROFICIENT

72,024
27%

TOTAL TESTED: 266,493

LEVEL 1		LEVEL 2	
108,946	41%	85,523	32%

LEVEL 3		LEVEL 4	
47,276	18%	24,748	9%

BLACK OR AFRICAN AMERICAN

PROFICIENT

51,529
29%

TOTAL TESTED: 175,579

LEVEL 1		LEVEL 2	
78,672	45%	45,378	26%

LEVEL 3		LEVEL 4	
30,963	18%	20,566	12%

HISPANIC OR LATINO

PROFICIENT

86,846
32%

TOTAL TESTED: 273,117

LEVEL 1		LEVEL 2	
110,356	40%	75,915	28%

LEVEL 3		LEVEL 4	
54,456	20%	32,390	12%

OTHER GROUPS

NON-ENGLISH LANGUAGE LEARNERS

PROFICIENT

353,209
43%

TOTAL TESTED: 818,877

LEVEL 1		LEVEL 2	
222,153	27%	243,515	30%

LEVEL 3		LEVEL 4	
196,261	24%	156,948	19%

ENGLISH LANGUAGE LEARNERS

PROFICIENT

11,893
13%

TOTAL TESTED: 90,229

LEVEL 1		LEVEL 2	
55,532	62%	22,804	25%

LEVEL 3		LEVEL 4	
8,311	9%	3,582	4%

NON-ENGLISH LANGUAGE LEARNERS

PROFICIENT

399,519
48%

TOTAL TESTED: 836,316

LEVEL 1		LEVEL 2	
224,611	27%	212,186	25%

LEVEL 3		LEVEL 4	
210,626	25%	188,893	23%

ENGLISH LANGUAGE LEARNERS

PROFICIENT

15,338
16%

TOTAL TESTED: 95,133

LEVEL 1		LEVEL 2	
57,849	61%	21,946	23%

LEVEL 3		LEVEL 4	
10,793	11%	4,545	5%

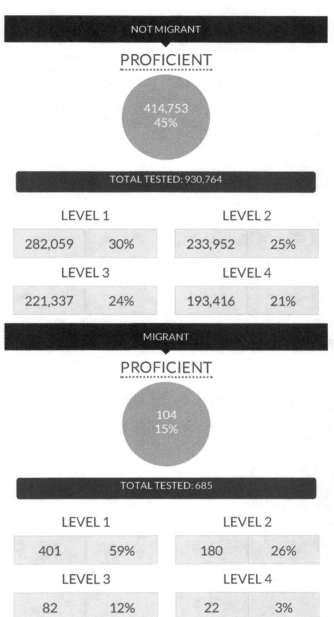

NOT MIGRANT

PROFICIENT

365,012
40%

TOTAL TESTED: 908,419

LEVEL 1		LEVEL 2	
277,275	31%	266,132	29%

LEVEL 3		LEVEL 4	
204,497	23%	160,515	18%

MIGRANT

PROFICIENT

90
13%

TOTAL TESTED: 687

LEVEL 1		LEVEL 2	
410	60%	187	27%

LEVEL 3		LEVEL 4	
75	11%	15	2%

NOT MIGRANT

PROFICIENT

414,753
45%

TOTAL TESTED: 930,764

LEVEL 1		LEVEL 2	
282,059	30%	233,952	25%

LEVEL 3		LEVEL 4	
221,337	24%	193,416	21%

MIGRANT

PROFICIENT

104
15%

TOTAL TESTED: 685

LEVEL 1		LEVEL 2	
401	59%	180	26%

LEVEL 3		LEVEL 4	
82	12%	22	3%

Ancestry and Ethnicity

New York State Profile

Population: 19,378,102

Ancestry	Population	%
Afghan (9,904)	10,755	0.06
African, Sub-Saharan (178,451)	240,909	1.25
African (90,390)	142,623	0.74
Cape Verdean (463)	844	<0.01
Ethiopian (4,371)	5,107	0.03
Ghanaian (22,113)	23,006	0.12
Kenyan (1,138)	1,324	0.01
Liberian (2,675)	3,006	0.02
Nigerian (25,852)	28,991	0.15
Senegalese (2,893)	3,166	0.02
Sierra Leonean (1,672)	1,711	0.01
Somalian (2,764)	3,053	0.02
South African (2,838)	3,993	0.02
Sudanese (1,819)	2,137	0.01
Ugandan (388)	464	<0.01
Zimbabwean (607)	646	<0.01
Other Sub-Saharan African (18,468)	20,838	0.11
Albanian (41,939)	46,223	0.24
Alsatian (202)	882	<0.01
American (689,298)	689,298	3.58
Arab (103,238)	145,746	0.76
Arab (20,874)	25,231	0.13
Egyptian (21,344)	25,478	0.13
Iraqi (1,882)	3,013	0.02
Jordanian (3,956)	4,623	0.02
Lebanese (16,431)	32,642	0.17
Moroccan (9,220)	12,364	0.06
Palestinian (4,397)	5,501	0.03
Syrian (7,544)	14,535	0.08
Other Arab (17,590)	22,359	0.12
Armenian (15,331)	24,803	0.13
Assyrian/Chaldean/Syriac (384)	644	<0.01
Australian (4,252)	7,418	0.04
Austrian (22,923)	91,260	0.47
Basque (570)	1,514	0.01
Belgian (4,380)	13,929	0.07
Brazilian (19,433)	26,401	0.14
British (29,032)	58,548	0.30
Bulgarian (6,409)	8,210	0.04
Cajun (295)	897	<0.01
Canadian (23,228)	50,059	0.26
Carpatho Rusyn (474)	741	<0.01
Celtic (1,106)	2,324	0.01
Croatian (15,221)	26,607	0.14
Cypriot (1,402)	1,721	0.01
Czech (13,656)	57,264	0.30
Czechoslovakian (9,727)	22,547	0.12
Danish (8,961)	35,247	0.18
Dutch (50,011)	277,731	1.44
Eastern European (82,212)	89,540	0.47
English (307,176)	1,180,365	6.14
Estonian (1,710)	3,462	0.02
European (142,136)	157,939	0.82
Finnish (5,117)	16,941	0.09
French, ex. Basque (93,941)	505,680	2.63
French Canadian (52,040)	134,420	0.70
German (532,432)	2,238,521	11.64
German Russian (196)	587	<0.01
Greek (102,342)	163,796	0.85
Guyanese (109,285)	123,809	0.64
Hungarian (61,925)	154,481	0.80
Icelander (753)	1,528	0.01
Iranian (23,356)	27,773	0.14
Irish (763,450)	2,565,928	13.34
Israeli (25,337)	36,808	0.19
Italian (1,405,357)	2,731,316	14.20
Latvian (4,261)	9,194	0.05
Lithuanian (15,565)	48,825	0.25
Luxemburger (158)	582	<0.01
Macedonian (6,414)	7,783	0.04
Maltese (3,431)	7,645	0.04
New Zealander (484)	1,002	0.01
Northern European (8,610)	10,116	0.05

Ancestry	Population	%
Norwegian (23,292)	85,859	0.45
Pennsylvania German (8,537)	13,519	0.07
Polish (396,502)	1,007,597	5.24
Portuguese (28,735)	52,967	0.28
Romanian (28,352)	56,605	0.29
Russian (241,898)	474,184	2.47
Scandinavian (4,984)	12,891	0.07
Scotch-Irish (58,045)	164,725	0.86
Scottish (53,369)	227,255	1.18
Serbian (5,585)	8,499	0.04
Slavic (3,865)	9,898	0.05
Slovak (14,038)	35,389	0.18
Slovene (1,922)	4,802	0.02
Soviet Union (317)	458	<0.01
Swedish (29,980)	132,781	0.69
Swiss (9,956)	39,241	0.20
Turkish (22,814)	29,907	0.16
Ukrainian (73,876)	133,633	0.69
Welsh (15,842)	88,255	0.46
West Indian, ex. Hispanic (665,395)	790,170	4.11
Bahamian (1,110)	1,796	0.01
Barbadian (22,928)	27,200	0.14
Belizean (5,612)	7,037	0.04
Bermudan (433)	672	<0.01
British West Indian (42,984)	49,916	0.26
Dutch West Indian (1,177)	1,887	0.01
Haitian (164,815)	179,024	0.93
Jamaican (265,516)	300,094	1.56
Trinidadian/Tobagonian (76,788)	89,490	0.47
U.S. Virgin Islander (2,037)	2,873	0.01
West Indian (80,923)	128,763	0.67
Other West Indian (1,072)	1,418	0.01
Yugoslavian (20,521)	28,253	0.15

Hispanic Origin	Population	%
Hispanic or Latino (of any race)	3,416,922	17.63
Central American, ex. Mexican	353,589	1.82
Costa Rican	11,576	0.06
Guatemalan	73,806	0.38
Honduran	71,919	0.37
Nicaraguan	13,006	0.07
Panamanian	28,200	0.15
Salvadoran	152,130	0.79
Other Central American	2,952	0.02
Cuban	70,803	0.37
Dominican Republic	674,787	3.48
Mexican	457,288	2.36
Puerto Rican	1,070,558	5.52
South American	513,417	2.65
Argentinean	24,969	0.13
Bolivian	7,122	0.04
Chilean	15,050	0.08
Colombian	141,879	0.73
Ecuadorian	228,216	1.18
Paraguayan	5,940	0.03
Peruvian	66,318	0.34
Uruguayan	6,021	0.03
Venezuelan	13,910	0.07
Other South American	3,992	0.02
Other Hispanic or Latino	276,480	1.43

Race*	Population	%
African-American/Black (3,073,800)	3,334,550	17.21
Not Hispanic (2,783,857)	2,946,880	15.21
Hispanic (289,943)	387,670	2.00
American Indian/Alaska Native (106,906)	221,058	1.14
Not Hispanic (53,908)	128,049	0.66
Hispanic (52,998)	93,009	0.48
Alaska Athabascan (Ala. Nat.) (57)	116	<0.01
Aleut (Alaska Native) (48)	82	<0.01
Apache (337)	1,080	0.01
Arapaho (24)	65	<0.01
Blackfeet (606)	4,496	0.02
Canadian/French Am. Ind. (530)	1,022	0.01
Central American Ind. (4,475)	8,602	0.04
Cherokee (2,714)	16,947	0.09

Race*	Population	%
Cheyenne (47)	163	<0.01
Chickasaw (68)	215	<0.01
Chippewa (548)	1,125	0.01
Choctaw (263)	1,052	0.01
Colville (11)	22	<0.01
Comanche (69)	199	<0.01
Cree (50)	263	<0.01
Creek (155)	624	<0.01
Crow (52)	181	<0.01
Delaware (598)	1,384	0.01
Hopi (39)	115	<0.01
Houma (35)	48	<0.01
Inupiat (Alaska Native) (91)	169	<0.01
Iroquois (16,957)	26,567	0.14
Kiowa (24)	44	<0.01
Lumbee (127)	304	<0.01
Menominee (19)	41	<0.01
Mexican American Ind. (5,344)	7,439	0.04
Navajo (347)	788	<0.01
Osage (31)	86	<0.01
Ottawa (24)	52	<0.01
Paiute (25)	49	<0.01
Pima (13)	40	<0.01
Potawatomi (83)	166	<0.01
Pueblo (556)	1,096	0.01
Puget Sound Salish (14)	33	<0.01
Seminole (107)	848	<0.01
Shoshone (22)	96	<0.01
Sioux (628)	1,758	0.01
South American Ind. (6,294)	13,078	0.07
Spanish American Ind. (2,563)	3,506	0.02
Tlingit-Haida (Alaska Native) (60)	169	<0.01
Tohono O'Odham (59)	103	<0.01
Tsimshian (Alaska Native) (4)	5	<0.01
Ute (13)	36	<0.01
Yakama (8)	18	<0.01
Yaqui (48)	104	<0.01
Yuman (24)	45	<0.01
Yup'ik (Alaska Native) (20)	39	<0.01
Asian (1,420,244)	1,579,494	8.15
Not Hispanic (1,406,194)	1,545,106	7.97
Hispanic (14,050)	34,388	0.18
Bangladeshi (57,761)	67,063	0.35
Bhutanese (1,534)	1,824	0.01
Burmese (11,214)	12,174	0.06
Cambodian (4,212)	5,114	0.03
Chinese, ex. Taiwanese (559,516)	598,597	3.09
Filipino (104,287)	126,129	0.65
Hmong (227)	296	<0.01
Indian (313,620)	368,767	1.90
Indonesian (4,568)	6,122	0.03
Japanese (37,780)	51,781	0.27
Korean (140,994)	153,609	0.79
Laotian (3,420)	4,471	0.02
Malaysian (2,537)	3,908	0.02
Nepalese (6,844)	7,625	0.04
Pakistani (63,696)	70,622	0.36
Sri Lankan (5,196)	6,153	0.03
Taiwanese (16,023)	18,868	0.10
Thai (9,258)	11,763	0.06
Vietnamese (28,764)	34,510	0.18
Hawaii Native/Pacific Islander (8,766)	36,423	0.19
Not Hispanic (5,320)	21,768	0.11
Hispanic (3,446)	14,655	0.08
Fijian (157)	321	<0.01
Guamanian/Chamorro (2,235)	3,407	0.02
Marshallese (32)	37	<0.01
Native Hawaiian (1,802)	5,108	0.03
Samoan (685)	1,654	0.01
Tongan (80)	138	<0.01
White (12,740,974)	13,155,274	67.89
Not Hispanic (11,304,247)	11,534,988	59.53
Hispanic (1,436,727)	1,620,286	8.36

Notes: † The Census 2010 population figure is used to calculate the percentages in the Hispanic Origin and Race categories. Ancestry percentages are based on the 2006-2010 American Community Survey population (not shown); ‡ Numbers in parentheses indicate the number of people reporting a single ancestry; * Numbers in parentheses indicate the number of persons reporting this race alone, not in combination with any other race; Please refer to the Explanation of Data for more information.

County Profiles

Albany County
Population: 304,204

Ancestry	Population	%
Afghan (14)	14	<0.01
African, Sub-Saharan (1,796)	2,330	0.77
African (1,075)	1,506	0.50
Cape Verdean (0)	13	<0.01
Ethiopian (34)	34	0.01
Ghanaian (167)	167	0.05
Kenyan (101)	101	0.03
Liberian (0)	0	<0.01
Nigerian (241)	300	0.10
Senegalese (0)	0	<0.01
Sierra Leonean (0)	0	<0.01
Somalian (0)	0	<0.01
South African (9)	32	0.01
Sudanese (25)	25	0.01
Ugandan (0)	0	<0.01
Zimbabwean (0)	8	<0.01
Other Sub-Saharan African (144)	144	0.05
Albanian (934)	1,000	0.33
Alsatian (19)	61	0.02
American (8,399)	8,399	2.76
Arab (1,379)	2,384	0.78
Arab (329)	357	0.12
Egyptian (190)	273	0.09
Iraqi (0)	0	<0.01
Jordanian (76)	76	0.02
Lebanese (222)	571	0.19
Moroccan (64)	111	0.04
Palestinian (207)	312	0.10
Syrian (102)	451	0.15
Other Arab (189)	233	0.08
Armenian (309)	621	0.20
Assyrian/Chaldean/Syriac (0)	0	<0.01
Australian (68)	126	0.04
Austrian (202)	1,353	0.45
Basque (0)	38	0.01
Belgian (59)	109	0.04
Brazilian (195)	249	0.08
British (584)	1,052	0.35
Bulgarian (22)	31	0.01
Cajun (0)	0	<0.01
Canadian (471)	996	0.33
Carpatho Rusyn (12)	26	<0.01
Celtic (15)	15	<0.01
Croatian (48)	163	0.05
Cypriot (0)	0	<0.01
Czech (334)	1,289	0.42
Czechoslovakian (52)	232	0.08
Danish (187)	869	0.29
Dutch (1,770)	11,451	3.77
Eastern European (648)	757	0.25
English (5,861)	28,025	9.22
Estonian (0)	0	<0.01
European (3,073)	3,521	1.16
Finnish (55)	316	0.10
French, ex. Basque (3,090)	19,696	6.48
French Canadian (2,042)	5,377	1.77
German (10,142)	50,507	16.61
German Russian (0)	0	<0.01
Greek (1,010)	2,365	0.78
Guyanese (716)	764	0.25
Hungarian (553)	2,084	0.69
Icelander (10)	10	<0.01
Iranian (186)	219	0.07
Irish (20,997)	72,953	24.00
Israeli (84)	117	0.04
Italian (20,747)	52,353	17.22
Latvian (111)	198	0.07
Lithuanian (160)	1,067	0.35
Luxemburger (9)	22	0.01
Macedonian (0)	0	<0.01
Maltese (11)	24	0.01
New Zealander (0)	0	<0.01

Ancestry	Population	%
Northern European (252)	356	0.12
Norwegian (574)	1,786	0.59
Pennsylvania German (52)	88	0.03
Polish (6,313)	20,711	6.81
Portuguese (208)	613	0.20
Romanian (81)	470	0.15
Russian (2,189)	5,714	1.88
Scandinavian (132)	581	0.19
Scotch-Irish (1,469)	4,121	1.36
Scottish (1,196)	5,513	1.81
Serbian (19)	19	0.01
Slavic (81)	189	0.06
Slovak (245)	780	0.26
Slovene (40)	133	0.04
Soviet Union (0)	0	<0.01
Swedish (521)	2,885	0.95
Swiss (190)	646	0.21
Turkish (35)	84	0.03
Ukrainian (1,078)	2,985	0.98
Welsh (221)	2,282	0.75
West Indian, ex. Hispanic (3,212)	4,660	1.53
Bahamian (0)	0	<0.01
Barbadian (14)	45	0.01
Belizean (0)	0	<0.01
Bermudan (36)	49	0.02
British West Indian (133)	210	0.07
Dutch West Indian (39)	90	0.03
Haitian (669)	825	0.27
Jamaican (1,592)	2,172	0.71
Trinidadian/Tobagonian (215)	329	0.11
U.S. Virgin Islander (0)	0	<0.01
West Indian (447)	873	0.29
Other West Indian (67)	67	0.02
Yugoslavian (245)	282	0.09

Hispanic Origin	Population	%
Hispanic or Latino (of any race)	14,917	4.90
Central American, ex. Mexican	735	0.24
Costa Rican	84	0.03
Guatemalan	117	0.04
Honduran	114	0.04
Nicaraguan	57	0.02
Panamanian	137	0.05
Salvadoran	208	0.07
Other Central American	18	0.01
Cuban	548	0.18
Dominican Republic	1,622	0.53
Mexican	1,540	0.51
Puerto Rican	7,633	2.51
South American	1,278	0.42
Argentinean	119	0.04
Bolivian	25	0.01
Chilean	72	0.02
Colombian	431	0.14
Ecuadorian	256	0.08
Paraguayan	12	<0.01
Peruvian	228	0.07
Uruguayan	21	0.01
Venezuelan	84	0.03
Other South American	30	0.01
Other Hispanic or Latino	1,561	0.51

Race*	Population	%
African-American/Black (38,609)	43,076	14.16
Not Hispanic (36,396)	40,017	13.15
Hispanic (2,213)	3,059	1.01
American Indian/Alaska Native (654)	2,326	0.76
Not Hispanic (453)	1,830	0.60
Hispanic (201)	496	0.16
Alaska Athabascan (Ala. Nat.) (1)	2	<0.01
Aleut (Alaska Native) (0)	0	<0.01
Apache (1)	13	<0.01
Arapaho (0)	1	<0.01
Blackfeet (11)	103	0.03
Canadian/French Am. Ind. (11)	23	0.01
Central American Ind. (13)	22	0.01

Race*	Population	%
Cherokee (39)	312	0.10
Cheyenne (0)	1	<0.01
Chickasaw (5)	5	<0.01
Chippewa (2)	6	<0.01
Choctaw (3)	15	<0.01
Colville (0)	0	<0.01
Comanche (0)	5	<0.01
Cree (1)	9	<0.01
Creek (0)	7	<0.01
Crow (2)	2	<0.01
Delaware (2)	12	<0.01
Hopi (1)	1	<0.01
Houma (0)	0	<0.01
Inupiat (Alaska Native) (1)	1	<0.01
Iroquois (80)	278	0.09
Kiowa (0)	0	<0.01
Lumbee (0)	0	<0.01
Menominee (0)	0	<0.01
Mexican American Ind. (43)	54	0.02
Navajo (2)	9	<0.01
Osage (0)	1	<0.01
Ottawa (0)	1	<0.01
Paiute (0)	0	<0.01
Pima (0)	0	<0.01
Potawatomi (1)	3	<0.01
Pueblo (1)	1	<0.01
Puget Sound Salish (0)	0	<0.01
Seminole (4)	17	0.01
Shoshone (0)	3	<0.01
Sioux (15)	32	0.01
South American Ind. (37)	85	0.03
Spanish American Ind. (8)	14	<0.01
Tlingit-Haida (Alaska Native) (2)	4	<0.01
Tohono O'Odham (0)	0	<0.01
Tsimshian (Alaska Native) (0)	0	<0.01
Ute (0)	0	<0.01
Yakama (1)	1	<0.01
Yaqui (0)	0	<0.01
Yuman (0)	0	<0.01
Yup'ik (Alaska Native) (2)	2	<0.01
Asian (14,579)	16,511	5.43
Not Hispanic (14,500)	16,300	5.36
Hispanic (79)	211	0.07
Bangladeshi (273)	305	0.10
Bhutanese (62)	62	0.02
Burmese (313)	342	0.11
Cambodian (21)	30	0.01
Chinese, ex. Taiwanese (3,552)	3,908	1.28
Filipino (1,147)	1,460	0.48
Hmong (0)	0	<0.01
Indian (4,600)	5,085	1.67
Indonesian (32)	43	0.01
Japanese (315)	520	0.17
Korean (1,329)	1,531	0.50
Laotian (5)	14	<0.01
Malaysian (11)	23	0.01
Nepalese (70)	78	0.03
Pakistani (1,377)	1,520	0.50
Sri Lankan (68)	75	0.02
Taiwanese (160)	189	0.06
Thai (93)	125	0.04
Vietnamese (610)	717	0.24
Hawaii Native/Pacific Islander (98)	333	0.11
Not Hispanic (88)	270	0.09
Hispanic (10)	63	0.02
Fijian (3)	4	<0.01
Guamanian/Chamorro (13)	31	0.01
Marshallese (0)	0	<0.01
Native Hawaiian (16)	71	0.02
Samoan (16)	29	0.01
Tongan (6)	6	<0.01
White (237,873)	244,245	80.29
Not Hispanic (231,152)	236,400	77.71
Hispanic (6,721)	7,845	2.58

*Notes: † The Census 2010 population figure is used to calculate the percentages in the Hispanic Origin and Race categories. Ancestry percentages are based on the 2006-2010 American Community Survey population (not shown); ‡ Numbers in parentheses indicate the number of people reporting a single ancestry; * Numbers in parentheses indicate the number of persons reporting this race alone, not in combination with any other race; Please refer to the Explanation of Data for more information.*

Allegany County

Population: 48,946

Ancestry	Population	%
Afghan (0)	0	<0.01
African, Sub-Saharan (22)	37	0.08
African (0)	15	0.03
Cape Verdean (0)	0	<0.01
Ethiopian (0)	0	<0.01
Ghanaian (0)	0	<0.01
Kenyan (22)	22	0.04
Liberian (0)	0	<0.01
Nigerian (0)	0	<0.01
Senegalese (0)	0	<0.01
Sierra Leonean (0)	0	<0.01
Somalian (0)	0	<0.01
South African (0)	0	<0.01
Sudanese (0)	0	<0.01
Ugandan (0)	0	<0.01
Zimbabwean (0)	0	<0.01
Other Sub-Saharan African (0)	0	<0.01
Albanian (0)	0	<0.01
Alsatian (4)	4	0.01
American (2,579)	2,579	5.25
Arab (59)	104	0.21
Arab (0)	0	<0.01
Egyptian (2)	2	<0.01
Iraqi (0)	0	<0.01
Jordanian (0)	0	<0.01
Lebanese (54)	83	0.17
Moroccan (0)	0	<0.01
Palestinian (0)	0	<0.01
Syrian (0)	13	0.03
Other Arab (3)	6	0.01
Armenian (3)	3	0.01
Assyrian/Chaldean/Syriac (0)	0	<0.01
Australian (0)	4	0.01
Austrian (16)	132	0.27
Basque (0)	0	<0.01
Belgian (8)	15	0.03
Brazilian (0)	10	0.02
British (101)	249	0.51
Bulgarian (0)	0	<0.01
Cajun (0)	2	<0.01
Canadian (23)	135	0.27
Carpatho Rusyn (0)	0	<0.01
Celtic (19)	19	0.04
Croatian (0)	39	0.08
Cypriot (0)	0	<0.01
Czech (34)	138	0.28
Czechoslovakian (34)	63	0.13
Danish (18)	87	0.18
Dutch (292)	1,775	3.61
Eastern European (8)	8	0.02
English (3,179)	8,971	18.27
Estonian (0)	0	<0.01
European (191)	255	0.52
Finnish (0)	59	0.12
French, ex. Basque (258)	1,883	3.83
French Canadian (212)	508	1.03
German (3,788)	14,728	29.99
German Russian (0)	0	<0.01
Greek (29)	74	0.15
Guyanese (0)	18	0.04
Hungarian (71)	224	0.46
Icelander (0)	0	<0.01
Iranian (0)	0	<0.01
Irish (2,480)	9,350	19.04
Israeli (0)	9	0.02
Italian (1,381)	3,451	7.03
Latvian (0)	0	<0.01
Lithuanian (42)	108	0.22
Luxemburger (0)	0	<0.01
Macedonian (0)	0	<0.01
Maltese (12)	27	0.05
New Zealander (0)	0	<0.01
Northern European (23)	23	0.05
Norwegian (64)	214	0.44
Pennsylvania German (320)	409	0.83

Ancestry (cont.)	Population	%
Polish (892)	2,591	5.28
Portuguese (0)	38	0.08
Romanian (11)	45	0.09
Russian (48)	234	0.48
Scandinavian (29)	69	0.14
Scotch-Irish (332)	1,044	2.13
Scottish (411)	1,397	2.84
Serbian (0)	6	0.01
Slavic (8)	87	0.18
Slovak (7)	41	0.08
Slovene (20)	30	0.06
Soviet Union (0)	0	<0.01
Swedish (178)	789	1.61
Swiss (55)	225	0.46
Turkish (0)	0	<0.01
Ukrainian (49)	123	0.25
Welsh (116)	581	1.18
West Indian, ex. Hispanic (26)	68	0.14
Bahamian (0)	0	<0.01
Barbadian (0)	0	<0.01
Belizean (0)	0	<0.01
Bermudan (0)	0	<0.01
British West Indian (7)	19	0.04
Dutch West Indian (0)	0	<0.01
Haitian (0)	12	0.02
Jamaican (0)	12	0.02
Trinidadian/Tobagonian (14)	20	0.04
U.S. Virgin Islander (0)	0	<0.01
West Indian (5)	5	0.01
Other West Indian (0)	0	<0.01
Yugoslavian (0)	7	0.01

Hispanic Origin	Population	%
Hispanic or Latino (of any race)	670	1.37
Central American, ex. Mexican	47	0.10
Costa Rican	1	<0.01
Guatemalan	15	0.03
Honduran	5	0.01
Nicaraguan	4	0.01
Panamanian	8	0.02
Salvadoran	14	0.03
Other Central American	0	<0.01
Cuban	17	0.03
Dominican Republic	58	0.12
Mexican	182	0.37
Puerto Rican	203	0.41
South American	78	0.16
Argentinean	1	<0.01
Bolivian	6	0.01
Chilean	5	0.01
Colombian	28	0.06
Ecuadorian	13	0.03
Paraguayan	1	<0.01
Peruvian	13	0.03
Uruguayan	0	<0.01
Venezuelan	4	0.01
Other South American	7	0.01
Other Hispanic or Latino	85	0.17

Race*	Population	%
African-American/Black (524)	732	1.50
Not Hispanic (494)	677	1.38
Hispanic (30)	55	0.11
American Indian/Alaska Native (113)	332	0.68
Not Hispanic (97)	295	0.60
Hispanic (16)	37	0.08
Alaska Athabascan (Ala. Nat.) (0)	0	<0.01
Aleut (Alaska Native) (0)	0	<0.01
Apache (2)	5	0.01
Arapaho (0)	0	<0.01
Blackfeet (0)	7	0.01
Canadian/French Am. Ind. (2)	3	0.01
Central American Ind. (0)	0	<0.01
Cherokee (11)	32	0.07
Cheyenne (0)	0	<0.01
Chickasaw (0)	0	<0.01
Chippewa (2)	4	0.01
Choctaw (0)	3	0.01
Colville (0)	0	<0.01

Race* (cont.)	Population	%
Comanche (0)	0	<0.01
Cree (0)	0	<0.01
Creek (1)	1	<0.01
Crow (1)	2	<0.01
Delaware (0)	3	0.01
Hopi (0)	0	<0.01
Houma (1)	1	<0.01
Inupiat (Alaska Native) (0)	0	<0.01
Iroquois (38)	84	0.17
Kiowa (0)	0	<0.01
Lumbee (1)	1	<0.01
Menominee (1)	1	<0.01
Mexican American Ind. (2)	3	0.01
Navajo (0)	3	0.01
Osage (0)	0	<0.01
Ottawa (0)	0	<0.01
Paiute (0)	0	<0.01
Pima (0)	0	<0.01
Potawatomi (0)	0	<0.01
Pueblo (0)	0	<0.01
Puget Sound Salish (0)	0	<0.01
Seminole (0)	0	<0.01
Shoshone (0)	0	<0.01
Sioux (0)	1	<0.01
South American Ind. (2)	7	0.01
Spanish American Ind. (0)	0	<0.01
Tlingit-Haida (Alaska Native) (0)	0	<0.01
Tohono O'Odham (0)	0	<0.01
Tsimshian (Alaska Native) (0)	0	<0.01
Ute (0)	0	<0.01
Yakama (0)	0	<0.01
Yaqui (0)	0	<0.01
Yuman (0)	0	<0.01
Yup'ik (Alaska Native) (0)	0	<0.01
Asian (452)	603	1.23
Not Hispanic (451)	591	1.21
Hispanic (1)	12	0.02
Bangladeshi (0)	0	<0.01
Bhutanese (0)	0	<0.01
Burmese (0)	0	<0.01
Cambodian (2)	3	0.01
Chinese, ex. Taiwanese (172)	205	0.42
Filipino (22)	58	0.12
Hmong (0)	0	<0.01
Indian (52)	71	0.15
Indonesian (3)	3	0.01
Japanese (59)	88	0.18
Korean (82)	111	0.23
Laotian (3)	3	0.01
Malaysian (0)	0	<0.01
Nepalese (0)	0	<0.01
Pakistani (3)	3	0.01
Sri Lankan (3)	3	0.01
Taiwanese (9)	11	0.02
Thai (9)	12	0.02
Vietnamese (12)	22	0.04
Hawaii Native/Pacific Islander (9)	20	0.04
Not Hispanic (7)	16	0.03
Hispanic (2)	4	0.01
Fijian (0)	0	<0.01
Guamanian/Chamorro (1)	2	<0.01
Marshallese (0)	0	<0.01
Native Hawaiian (7)	15	0.03
Samoan (1)	4	0.01
Tongan (0)	0	<0.01
White (47,085)	47,605	97.26
Not Hispanic (46,701)	47,175	96.38
Hispanic (384)	430	0.88

Notes: † The Census 2010 population figure is used to calculate the percentages in the Hispanic Origin and Race categories. Ancestry percentages are based on the 2006-2010 American Community Survey population (not shown); ‡ Numbers in parentheses indicate the number of people reporting a single ancestry; * Numbers in parentheses indicate the number of persons reporting this race alone, not in combination with any other race; Please refer to the Explanation of Data for more information.

Bronx County

Population: 1,385,108

Ancestry	Population	%
Afghan (14)	14	<0.01
African, Sub-Saharan (50,131)	55,928	4.10
African (19,345)	22,647	1.66
Cape Verdean (49)	108	0.01
Ethiopian (790)	945	0.07
Ghanaian (13,163)	13,490	0.99
Kenyan (12)	24	<0.01
Liberian (365)	450	0.03
Nigerian (4,896)	5,538	0.41
Senegalese (956)	1,068	0.08
Sierra Leonean (759)	759	0.06
Somalian (11)	35	<0.01
South African (29)	68	0.01
Sudanese (88)	149	0.01
Ugandan (0)	0	<0.01
Zimbabwean (108)	108	0.01
Other Sub-Saharan African (9,560)	10,539	0.77
Albanian (7,460)	7,835	0.57
Alsatian (0)	0	<0.01
American (16,297)	16,297	1.19
Arab (4,063)	5,008	0.37
Arab (1,481)	1,719	0.13
Egyptian (495)	718	0.05
Iraqi (64)	73	0.01
Jordanian (8)	8	<0.01
Lebanese (229)	347	0.03
Moroccan (526)	667	0.05
Palestinian (28)	28	<0.01
Syrian (44)	192	0.01
Other Arab (1,188)	1,256	0.09
Armenian (128)	237	0.02
Assyrian/Chaldean/Syriac (0)	18	<0.01
Australian (8)	21	<0.01
Austrian (539)	1,868	0.14
Basque (66)	109	0.01
Belgian (52)	131	0.01
Brazilian (276)	397	0.03
British (517)	1,115	0.08
Bulgarian (506)	521	0.04
Cajun (0)	0	<0.01
Canadian (197)	375	0.03
Carpatho Rusyn (0)	12	<0.01
Celtic (1)	13	<0.01
Croatian (91)	219	0.02
Cypriot (12)	38	<0.01
Czech (99)	388	0.03
Czechoslovakian (90)	226	0.02
Danish (17)	385	0.03
Dutch (314)	1,920	0.14
Eastern European (1,425)	1,646	0.12
English (1,821)	7,038	0.52
Estonian (70)	85	0.01
European (1,845)	2,270	0.17
Finnish (89)	291	0.02
French, ex. Basque (909)	4,971	0.36
French Canadian (102)	403	0.03
German (3,729)	16,487	1.21
German Russian (7)	30	<0.01
Greek (2,499)	3,607	0.26
Guyanese (10,276)	11,837	0.87
Hungarian (966)	2,427	0.18
Icelander (6)	6	<0.01
Iranian (187)	248	0.02
Irish (18,712)	38,479	2.82
Israeli (427)	618	0.05
Italian (38,592)	57,527	4.21
Latvian (92)	103	0.01
Lithuanian (167)	547	0.04
Luxemburger (0)	0	<0.01
Macedonian (628)	628	0.05
Maltese (16)	45	<0.01
New Zealander (23)	23	<0.01
Northern European (25)	25	<0.01
Norwegian (260)	773	0.06
Pennsylvania German (0)	0	<0.01

Ancestry	Population	%
Polish (3,429)	7,834	0.57
Portuguese (474)	1,113	0.08
Romanian (691)	1,164	0.09
Russian (4,351)	8,064	0.59
Scandinavian (102)	155	0.01
Scotch-Irish (516)	1,601	0.12
Scottish (388)	1,570	0.11
Serbian (154)	187	0.01
Slavic (15)	90	0.01
Slovak (87)	226	0.02
Slovene (10)	45	<0.01
Soviet Union (12)	12	<0.01
Swedish (119)	549	0.04
Swiss (24)	166	0.01
Turkish (589)	686	0.05
Ukrainian (970)	1,608	0.12
Welsh (101)	530	0.04
West Indian, ex. Hispanic (93,323)	107,527	7.87
Bahamian (165)	208	0.02
Barbadian (1,285)	1,612	0.12
Belizean (1,253)	1,493	0.11
Bermudan (101)	198	0.01
British West Indian (5,959)	7,136	0.52
Dutch West Indian (127)	172	0.01
Haitian (3,891)	4,652	0.34
Jamaican (58,387)	64,222	4.70
Trinidadian/Tobagonian (3,695)	4,811	0.35
U.S. Virgin Islander (737)	952	0.07
West Indian (17,683)	21,941	1.61
Other West Indian (40)	130	0.01
Yugoslavian (1,275)	1,480	0.11

Hispanic Origin	Population	%
Hispanic or Latino (of any race)	741,413	53.53
Central American, ex. Mexican	34,492	2.49
Costa Rican	1,095	0.08
Guatemalan	4,645	0.34
Honduran	17,990	1.30
Nicaraguan	2,342	0.17
Panamanian	2,372	0.17
Salvadoran	5,469	0.39
Other Central American	579	0.04
Cuban	8,785	0.63
Dominican Republic	240,987	17.40
Mexican	71,194	5.14
Puerto Rican	298,921	21.58
South American	35,463	2.56
Argentinean	1,117	0.08
Bolivian	227	0.02
Chilean	646	0.05
Colombian	4,635	0.33
Ecuadorian	23,206	1.68
Paraguayan	223	0.02
Peruvian	3,596	0.26
Uruguayan	148	0.01
Venezuelan	1,296	0.09
Other South American	369	0.03
Other Hispanic or Latino	51,571	3.72

Race*	Population	%
African-American/Black (505,200)	541,622	39.10
Not Hispanic (416,695)	427,134	30.84
Hispanic (88,505)	114,488	8.27
American Indian/Alaska Native (18,260)	32,011	2.31
Not Hispanic (3,460)	7,638	0.55
Hispanic (14,800)	24,373	1.76
Alaska Athabascan (Ala. Nat.) (4)	8	<0.01
Aleut (Alaska Native) (0)	3	<0.01
Apache (30)	99	0.01
Arapaho (2)	3	<0.01
Blackfeet (43)	310	0.02
Canadian/French Am. Ind. (13)	25	<0.01
Central American Ind. (2,274)	4,520	0.33
Cherokee (247)	1,312	0.09
Cheyenne (2)	5	<0.01
Chickasaw (6)	16	<0.01
Chippewa (25)	38	<0.01
Choctaw (4)	43	<0.01
Colville (0)	2	<0.01

	Population	%
Comanche (8)	26	<0.01
Cree (1)	16	<0.01
Creek (7)	47	<0.01
Crow (1)	16	<0.01
Delaware (1)	10	<0.01
Hopi (0)	2	<0.01
Houma (12)	12	<0.01
Inupiat (Alaska Native) (11)	15	<0.01
Iroquois (81)	170	0.01
Kiowa (1)	1	<0.01
Lumbee (3)	6	<0.01
Menominee (1)	3	<0.01
Mexican American Ind. (714)	963	0.07
Navajo (24)	42	<0.01
Osage (2)	3	<0.01
Ottawa (1)	1	<0.01
Paiute (0)	5	<0.01
Pima (0)	1	<0.01
Potawatomi (1)	2	<0.01
Pueblo (177)	382	0.03
Puget Sound Salish (0)	0	<0.01
Seminole (6)	50	<0.01
Shoshone (0)	8	<0.01
Sioux (46)	82	0.01
South American Ind. (1,568)	2,938	0.21
Spanish American Ind. (709)	992	0.07
Tlingit-Haida (Alaska Native) (1)	11	<0.01
Tohono O'Odham (4)	9	<0.01
Tsimshian (Alaska Native) (0)	0	<0.01
Ute (2)	5	<0.01
Yakama (3)	3	<0.01
Yaqui (4)	5	<0.01
Yuman (1)	2	<0.01
Yup'ik (Alaska Native) (1)	6	<0.01
Asian (49,609)	59,085	4.27
Not Hispanic (47,335)	53,458	3.86
Hispanic (2,274)	5,627	0.41
Bangladeshi (7,323)	8,623	0.62
Bhutanese (74)	104	0.01
Burmese (71)	81	0.01
Cambodian (1,055)	1,188	0.09
Chinese, ex. Taiwanese (6,644)	8,112	0.59
Filipino (5,576)	6,456	0.47
Hmong (1)	3	<0.01
Indian (15,865)	20,357	1.47
Indonesian (50)	96	0.01
Japanese (562)	1,027	0.07
Korean (2,840)	3,101	0.22
Laotian (99)	148	0.01
Malaysian (11)	30	<0.01
Nepalese (129)	159	0.01
Pakistani (2,399)	2,728	0.20
Sri Lankan (174)	234	0.02
Taiwanese (98)	130	0.01
Thai (326)	414	0.03
Vietnamese (3,215)	3,526	0.25
Hawaii Native/Pacific Islander (1,288)	6,213	0.45
Not Hispanic (398)	1,854	0.13
Hispanic (890)	4,359	0.31
Fijian (13)	13	<0.01
Guamanian/Chamorro (251)	376	0.03
Marshallese (3)	3	<0.01
Native Hawaiian (371)	669	0.05
Samoan (70)	160	0.01
Tongan (5)	7	<0.01
White (386,497)	427,659	30.88
Not Hispanic (151,209)	158,245	11.42
Hispanic (235,288)	269,414	19.45

*Notes: † The Census 2010 population figure is used to calculate the percentages in the Hispanic Origin and Race categories. Ancestry percentages are based on the 2006-2010 American Community Survey population (not shown); ‡ Numbers in parentheses indicate the number of people reporting a single ancestry; * Numbers in parentheses indicate the number of persons reporting this race alone, not in combination with any other race; Please refer to the Explanation of Data for more information.*

Broome County

Population: 200,600

Ancestry	Population	%
Afghan (0)	0	<0.01
African, Sub-Saharan (397)	646	0.32
African (262)	488	0.24
Cape Verdean (11)	11	0.01
Ethiopian (0)	0	<0.01
Ghanaian (43)	43	0.02
Kenyan (6)	6	<0.01
Liberian (0)	0	<0.01
Nigerian (17)	17	0.01
Senegalese (0)	0	<0.01
Sierra Leonean (0)	0	<0.01
Somalian (0)	0	<0.01
South African (9)	32	0.02
Sudanese (0)	0	<0.01
Ugandan (0)	0	<0.01
Zimbabwean (0)	0	<0.01
Other Sub-Saharan African (49)	49	0.02
Albanian (13)	20	0.01
Alsatian (13)	13	0.01
American (8,398)	8,398	4.18
Arab (1,042)	1,422	0.71
Arab (115)	132	0.07
Egyptian (106)	155	0.08
Iraqi (6)	6	<0.01
Jordanian (12)	12	0.01
Lebanese (255)	459	0.23
Moroccan (0)	8	<0.01
Palestinian (13)	25	0.01
Syrian (19)	20	0.01
Other Arab (516)	605	0.30
Armenian (139)	329	0.16
Assyrian/Chaldean/Syriac (0)	0	<0.01
Australian (39)	39	0.02
Austrian (155)	882	0.44
Basque (0)	0	<0.01
Belgian (15)	133	0.07
Brazilian (13)	13	0.01
British (355)	1,018	0.51
Bulgarian (62)	62	0.03
Cajun (3)	12	0.01
Canadian (134)	338	0.17
Carpatho Rusyn (64)	126	0.06
Celtic (30)	67	0.03
Croatian (21)	68	0.03
Cypriot (0)	0	<0.01
Czech (788)	2,348	1.17
Czechoslovakian (509)	872	0.43
Danish (163)	449	0.22
Dutch (1,265)	6,844	3.41
Eastern European (314)	386	0.19
English (7,900)	26,062	12.98
Estonian (21)	42	0.02
European (1,586)	1,795	0.89
Finnish (10)	181	0.09
French, ex. Basque (644)	6,871	3.42
French Canadian (488)	1,377	0.69
German (9,379)	36,306	18.08
German Russian (0)	0	<0.01
Greek (606)	1,245	0.62
Guyanese (171)	251	0.12
Hungarian (238)	903	0.45
Icelander (46)	46	0.02
Iranian (36)	70	0.03
Irish (12,853)	43,809	21.82
Israeli (0)	26	0.01
Italian (10,921)	27,706	13.80
Latvian (35)	125	0.06
Lithuanian (314)	1,211	0.60
Luxemburger (0)	0	<0.01
Macedonian (55)	55	0.03
Maltese (0)	24	0.01
New Zealander (0)	0	<0.01
Northern European (59)	59	0.03
Norwegian (303)	987	0.49
Pennsylvania German (541)	938	0.47

Ancestry (cont.)	Population	%
Polish (4,815)	14,217	7.08
Portuguese (77)	128	0.06
Romanian (214)	387	0.19
Russian (1,876)	5,545	2.76
Scandinavian (32)	187	0.09
Scotch-Irish (1,024)	2,833	1.41
Scottish (1,085)	4,355	2.17
Serbian (10)	65	0.03
Slavic (439)	618	0.31
Slovak (2,653)	6,570	3.27
Slovene (51)	137	0.07
Soviet Union (0)	0	<0.01
Swedish (473)	1,729	0.86
Swiss (119)	522	0.26
Turkish (189)	212	0.11
Ukrainian (1,127)	2,148	1.07
Welsh (762)	4,482	2.23
West Indian, ex. Hispanic (716)	973	0.48
Bahamian (0)	0	<0.01
Barbadian (0)	0	<0.01
Belizean (5)	5	<0.01
Bermudan (0)	0	<0.01
British West Indian (29)	55	0.03
Dutch West Indian (0)	0	<0.01
Haitian (210)	222	0.11
Jamaican (338)	478	0.24
Trinidadian/Tobagonian (54)	54	0.03
U.S. Virgin Islander (0)	0	<0.01
West Indian (80)	159	0.08
Other West Indian (0)	0	<0.01
Yugoslavian (273)	310	0.15

Hispanic Origin	Population	%
Hispanic or Latino (of any race)	6,778	3.38
Central American, ex. Mexican	420	0.21
Costa Rican	44	0.02
Guatemalan	112	0.06
Honduran	87	0.04
Nicaraguan	31	0.02
Panamanian	65	0.03
Salvadoran	81	0.04
Other Central American	0	<0.01
Cuban	322	0.16
Dominican Republic	505	0.25
Mexican	765	0.38
Puerto Rican	3,442	1.72
South American	606	0.30
Argentinean	92	0.05
Bolivian	14	0.01
Chilean	45	0.02
Colombian	181	0.09
Ecuadorian	128	0.06
Paraguayan	5	<0.01
Peruvian	94	0.05
Uruguayan	9	<0.01
Venezuelan	33	0.02
Other South American	5	<0.01
Other Hispanic or Latino	718	0.36

Race*	Population	%
African-American/Black (9,614)	12,499	6.23
Not Hispanic (8,850)	11,278	5.62
Hispanic (764)	1,221	0.61
American Indian/Alaska Native (396)	1,664	0.83
Not Hispanic (328)	1,445	0.72
Hispanic (68)	219	0.11
Alaska Athabascan *(Ala. Nat.)* (1)	4	<0.01
Aleut *(Alaska Native)* (0)	0	<0.01
Apache (7)	34	0.02
Arapaho (0)	0	<0.01
Blackfeet (8)	75	0.04
Canadian/French Am. Ind. (4)	10	<0.01
Central American Ind. (1)	1	<0.01
Cherokee (37)	248	0.12
Cheyenne (0)	0	<0.01
Chickasaw (0)	1	<0.01
Chippewa (7)	15	0.01
Choctaw (3)	14	0.01
Colville (0)	1	<0.01

Race* (cont.)	Population	%
Comanche (0)	3	<0.01
Cree (2)	6	<0.01
Creek (2)	7	<0.01
Crow (0)	5	<0.01
Delaware (2)	29	0.01
Hopi (0)	0	<0.01
Houma (0)	1	<0.01
Inupiat *(Alaska Native)* (0)	0	<0.01
Iroquois (74)	254	0.13
Kiowa (0)	1	<0.01
Lumbee (0)	1	<0.01
Menominee (0)	0	<0.01
Mexican American Ind. (7)	21	0.01
Navajo (0)	11	0.01
Osage (0)	1	<0.01
Ottawa (0)	0	<0.01
Paiute (0)	2	<0.01
Pima (0)	1	<0.01
Potawatomi (1)	3	<0.01
Pueblo (0)	2	<0.01
Puget Sound Salish (0)	0	<0.01
Seminole (0)	5	<0.01
Shoshone (0)	0	<0.01
Sioux (12)	39	0.02
South American Ind. (15)	31	0.02
Spanish American Ind. (4)	5	<0.01
Tlingit-Haida *(Alaska Native)* (0)	0	<0.01
Tohono O'Odham (0)	0	<0.01
Tsimshian *(Alaska Native)* (0)	0	<0.01
Ute (0)	0	<0.01
Yakama (0)	0	<0.01
Yaqui (2)	2	<0.01
Yuman (0)	0	<0.01
Yup'ik *(Alaska Native)* (0)	0	<0.01
Asian (7,065)	8,193	4.08
Not Hispanic (7,019)	8,072	4.02
Hispanic (46)	121	0.06
Bangladeshi (56)	67	0.03
Bhutanese (0)	0	<0.01
Burmese (12)	14	0.01
Cambodian (9)	16	0.01
Chinese, ex. Taiwanese (2,135)	2,397	1.19
Filipino (329)	515	0.26
Hmong (0)	0	<0.01
Indian (1,487)	1,683	0.84
Indonesian (24)	34	0.02
Japanese (127)	227	0.11
Korean (980)	1,117	0.56
Laotian (541)	667	0.33
Malaysian (8)	17	0.01
Nepalese (15)	18	0.01
Pakistani (233)	241	0.12
Sri Lankan (14)	22	0.01
Taiwanese (82)	103	0.05
Thai (42)	69	0.03
Vietnamese (716)	838	0.42
Hawaii Native/Pacific Islander (82)	243	0.12
Not Hispanic (60)	191	0.10
Hispanic (22)	52	0.03
Fijian (0)	3	<0.01
Guamanian/Chamorro (25)	43	0.02
Marshallese (0)	0	<0.01
Native Hawaiian (16)	48	0.02
Samoan (6)	12	0.01
Tongan (1)	1	<0.01
White (176,444)	181,009	90.23
Not Hispanic (173,074)	176,969	88.22
Hispanic (3,370)	4,040	2.01

*Notes: † The Census 2010 population figure is used to calculate the percentages in the Hispanic Origin and Race categories. Ancestry percentages are based on the 2006-2010 American Community Survey population (not shown); ‡ Numbers in parentheses indicate the number of people reporting a single ancestry; * Numbers in parentheses indicate the number of persons reporting this race alone, not in combination with any other race; Please refer to the Explanation of Data for more information.*

Cattaraugus County

Population: 80,317

Ancestry	Population	%
Afghan (0)	0	<0.01
African, Sub-Saharan (11)	52	0.06
African (11)	52	0.06
Cape Verdean (0)	0	<0.01
Ethiopian (0)	0	<0.01
Ghanaian (0)	0	<0.01
Kenyan (0)	0	<0.01
Liberian (0)	0	<0.01
Nigerian (0)	0	<0.01
Senegalese (0)	0	<0.01
Sierra Leonean (0)	0	<0.01
Somalian (0)	0	<0.01
South African (0)	0	<0.01
Sudanese (0)	0	<0.01
Ugandan (0)	0	<0.01
Zimbabwean (0)	0	<0.01
Other Sub-Saharan African (0)	0	<0.01
Albanian (0)	0	<0.01
Alsatian (0)	7	0.01
American (3,710)	3,710	4.59
Arab (161)	452	0.56
Arab (23)	23	0.03
Egyptian (0)	0	<0.01
Iraqi (0)	0	<0.01
Jordanian (0)	0	<0.01
Lebanese (138)	429	0.53
Moroccan (0)	0	<0.01
Palestinian (0)	0	<0.01
Syrian (0)	0	<0.01
Other Arab (0)	0	<0.01
Armenian (2)	6	0.01
Assyrian/Chaldean/Syriac (0)	0	<0.01
Australian (0)	0	<0.01
Austrian (28)	215	0.27
Basque (0)	4	<0.01
Belgian (51)	95	0.12
Brazilian (6)	6	0.01
British (90)	213	0.26
Bulgarian (3)	13	0.02
Cajun (0)	0	<0.01
Canadian (99)	253	0.31
Carpatho Rusyn (0)	5	<0.01
Celtic (0)	0	<0.01
Croatian (39)	61	0.08
Cypriot (0)	0	<0.01
Czech (29)	225	0.28
Czechoslovakian (59)	251	0.31
Danish (37)	157	0.19
Dutch (265)	2,195	2.72
Eastern European (51)	51	0.06
English (2,780)	10,168	12.59
Estonian (3)	3	<0.01
European (246)	375	0.46
Finnish (9)	40	0.05
French, ex. Basque (257)	2,353	2.91
French Canadian (241)	614	0.76
German (8,573)	25,659	31.77
German Russian (0)	0	<0.01
Greek (60)	178	0.22
Guyanese (0)	13	0.02
Hungarian (111)	421	0.52
Icelander (0)	0	<0.01
Iranian (0)	0	<0.01
Irish (4,105)	16,140	19.98
Israeli (6)	6	0.01
Italian (3,226)	8,276	10.25
Latvian (0)	0	<0.01
Lithuanian (44)	117	0.14
Luxemburger (0)	4	<0.01
Macedonian (8)	26	0.03
Maltese (0)	0	<0.01
New Zealander (0)	0	<0.01
Northern European (107)	107	0.13
Norwegian (102)	302	0.37
Pennsylvania German (745)	922	1.14

Ancestry (cont.)	Population	%
Polish (3,395)	9,202	11.39
Portuguese (24)	72	0.09
Romanian (38)	88	0.11
Russian (56)	311	0.39
Scandinavian (44)	87	0.11
Scotch-Irish (498)	1,255	1.55
Scottish (474)	1,632	2.02
Serbian (6)	22	0.03
Slavic (10)	78	0.10
Slovak (22)	62	0.08
Slovene (80)	102	0.13
Soviet Union (0)	0	<0.01
Swedish (581)	2,178	2.70
Swiss (52)	379	0.47
Turkish (0)	8	0.01
Ukrainian (51)	270	0.33
Welsh (171)	821	1.02
West Indian, ex. Hispanic (45)	73	0.09
Bahamian (0)	0	<0.01
Barbadian (0)	0	<0.01
Belizean (0)	0	<0.01
Bermudan (0)	0	<0.01
British West Indian (0)	0	<0.01
Dutch West Indian (0)	0	<0.01
Haitian (11)	11	0.01
Jamaican (11)	17	0.02
Trinidadian/Tobagonian (0)	0	<0.01
U.S. Virgin Islander (0)	0	<0.01
West Indian (23)	45	0.06
Other West Indian (0)	0	<0.01
Yugoslavian (37)	56	0.07

Hispanic Origin	Population	%
Hispanic or Latino (of any race)	1,345	1.67
Central American, ex. Mexican	44	0.05
Costa Rican	3	<0.01
Guatemalan	12	0.01
Honduran	9	0.01
Nicaraguan	2	<0.01
Panamanian	5	0.01
Salvadoran	13	0.02
Other Central American	0	<0.01
Cuban	37	0.05
Dominican Republic	30	0.04
Mexican	308	0.38
Puerto Rican	690	0.86
South American	70	0.09
Argentinean	8	0.01
Bolivian	2	<0.01
Chilean	5	0.01
Colombian	21	0.03
Ecuadorian	12	0.01
Paraguayan	0	<0.01
Peruvian	9	0.01
Uruguayan	1	<0.01
Venezuelan	12	0.01
Other South American	0	<0.01
Other Hispanic or Latino	166	0.21

Race*	Population	%
African-American/Black (1,024)	1,619	2.02
Not Hispanic (966)	1,519	1.89
Hispanic (58)	100	0.12
American Indian/Alaska Native (2,443)	3,079	3.83
Not Hispanic (2,361)	2,945	3.67
Hispanic (82)	134	0.17
Alaska Athabascan (Ala. Nat.) (10)	15	0.02
Aleut (Alaska Native) (1)	1	<0.01
Apache (1)	4	<0.01
Arapaho (0)	1	<0.01
Blackfeet (4)	17	0.02
Canadian/French Am. Ind. (9)	15	0.02
Central American Ind. (7)	7	0.01
Cherokee (17)	46	0.06
Cheyenne (1)	5	0.01
Chickasaw (0)	0	<0.01
Chippewa (5)	11	0.01
Choctaw (3)	4	<0.01
Colville (0)	0	<0.01

Race* (cont.)	Population	%
Comanche (0)	0	<0.01
Cree (0)	0	<0.01
Creek (7)	7	0.01
Crow (3)	4	<0.01
Delaware (8)	10	0.01
Hopi (0)	0	<0.01
Houma (0)	0	<0.01
Inupiat (Alaska Native) (1)	1	<0.01
Iroquois (1,961)	2,291	2.85
Kiowa (2)	2	<0.01
Lumbee (4)	7	0.01
Menominee (2)	2	<0.01
Mexican American Ind. (2)	3	<0.01
Navajo (4)	6	0.01
Osage (0)	0	<0.01
Ottawa (0)	0	<0.01
Paiute (6)	9	0.01
Pima (0)	0	<0.01
Potawatomi (0)	0	<0.01
Pueblo (0)	0	<0.01
Puget Sound Salish (0)	0	<0.01
Seminole (0)	5	0.01
Shoshone (2)	2	<0.01
Sioux (19)	25	0.03
South American Ind. (12)	14	0.02
Spanish American Ind. (0)	0	<0.01
Tlingit-Haida (Alaska Native) (0)	0	<0.01
Tohono O'Odham (1)	1	<0.01
Tsimshian (Alaska Native) (0)	0	<0.01
Ute (0)	0	<0.01
Yakama (0)	0	<0.01
Yaqui (1)	1	<0.01
Yuman (0)	0	<0.01
Yup'ik (Alaska Native) (0)	0	<0.01
Asian (528)	688	0.86
Not Hispanic (524)	675	0.84
Hispanic (4)	13	0.02
Bangladeshi (1)	1	<0.01
Bhutanese (0)	0	<0.01
Burmese (0)	0	<0.01
Cambodian (2)	4	<0.01
Chinese, ex. Taiwanese (109)	138	0.17
Filipino (61)	92	0.11
Hmong (0)	0	<0.01
Indian (171)	205	0.26
Indonesian (0)	5	0.01
Japanese (23)	46	0.06
Korean (42)	61	0.08
Laotian (13)	21	0.03
Malaysian (2)	2	<0.01
Nepalese (4)	4	<0.01
Pakistani (50)	50	0.06
Sri Lankan (8)	8	0.01
Taiwanese (2)	2	<0.01
Thai (3)	8	0.01
Vietnamese (27)	31	0.04
Hawaii Native/Pacific Islander (15)	36	0.04
Not Hispanic (14)	35	0.04
Hispanic (1)	1	<0.01
Fijian (5)	5	0.01
Guamanian/Chamorro (0)	0	<0.01
Marshallese (0)	0	<0.01
Native Hawaiian (7)	18	0.02
Samoan (0)	1	<0.01
Tongan (0)	0	<0.01
White (74,639)	75,918	94.52
Not Hispanic (73,849)	75,003	93.38
Hispanic (790)	915	1.14

Notes: † The Census 2010 population figure is used to calculate the percentages in the Hispanic Origin and Race categories. Ancestry percentages are based on the 2006-2010 American Community Survey population (not shown); ‡ Numbers in parentheses indicate the number of people reporting a single ancestry; * Numbers in parentheses indicate the number of persons reporting this race alone, not in combination with any other race; Please refer to the Explanation of Data for more information.

Cayuga County

Population: 80,026

Ancestry	Population	%
Afghan (0)	0	<0.01
African, Sub-Saharan (110)	224	0.28
African (110)	206	0.26
Cape Verdean (0)	0	<0.01
Ethiopian (0)	0	<0.01
Ghanaian (0)	0	<0.01
Kenyan (0)	0	<0.01
Liberian (0)	0	<0.01
Nigerian (0)	0	<0.01
Senegalese (0)	0	<0.01
Sierra Leonean (0)	0	<0.01
Somalian (0)	0	<0.01
South African (0)	0	<0.01
Sudanese (0)	0	<0.01
Ugandan (0)	0	<0.01
Zimbabwean (0)	0	<0.01
Other Sub-Saharan African (0)	18	0.02
Albanian (36)	36	0.04
Alsatian (0)	7	0.01
American (3,805)	3,805	4.73
Arab (39)	115	0.14
Arab (2)	5	0.01
Egyptian (0)	0	<0.01
Iraqi (0)	0	<0.01
Jordanian (0)	0	<0.01
Lebanese (20)	65	0.08
Moroccan (0)	0	<0.01
Palestinian (0)	0	<0.01
Syrian (7)	35	0.04
Other Arab (10)	10	0.01
Armenian (0)	11	0.01
Assyrian/Chaldean/Syriac (0)	0	<0.01
Australian (0)	10	0.01
Austrian (57)	197	0.24
Basque (0)	0	<0.01
Belgian (2)	41	0.05
Brazilian (37)	40	0.05
British (120)	275	0.34
Bulgarian (0)	0	<0.01
Cajun (0)	0	<0.01
Canadian (92)	175	0.22
Carpatho Rusyn (0)	0	<0.01
Celtic (6)	6	0.01
Croatian (0)	0	<0.01
Cypriot (0)	0	<0.01
Czech (49)	207	0.26
Czechoslovakian (72)	117	0.15
Danish (65)	201	0.25
Dutch (736)	3,758	4.67
Eastern European (24)	26	0.03
English (4,214)	14,572	18.12
Estonian (0)	0	<0.01
European (439)	513	0.64
Finnish (25)	62	0.08
French, ex. Basque (604)	3,973	4.94
French Canadian (555)	1,669	2.08
German (3,317)	14,518	18.05
German Russian (0)	0	<0.01
Greek (39)	204	0.25
Guyanese (20)	20	0.02
Hungarian (39)	187	0.23
Icelander (0)	3	<0.01
Iranian (0)	0	<0.01
Irish (5,999)	19,589	24.36
Israeli (0)	0	<0.01
Italian (4,906)	11,827	14.70
Latvian (3)	6	0.01
Lithuanian (30)	71	0.09
Luxemburger (0)	0	<0.01
Macedonian (0)	0	<0.01
Maltese (0)	0	<0.01
New Zealander (0)	0	<0.01
Northern European (42)	42	0.05
Norwegian (86)	467	0.58
Pennsylvania German (77)	112	0.14
Polish (1,970)	5,462	6.79
Portuguese (8)	74	0.09
Romanian (0)	37	0.05
Russian (179)	482	0.60
Scandinavian (30)	50	0.06
Scotch-Irish (477)	1,048	1.30
Scottish (433)	1,739	2.16
Serbian (0)	4	<0.01
Slavic (37)	37	0.05
Slovak (8)	120	0.15
Slovene (0)	0	<0.01
Soviet Union (0)	0	<0.01
Swedish (100)	712	0.89
Swiss (53)	429	0.53
Turkish (0)	20	0.02
Ukrainian (910)	2,400	2.98
Welsh (214)	839	1.04
West Indian, ex. Hispanic (140)	413	0.51
Bahamian (0)	0	<0.01
Barbadian (0)	8	0.01
Belizean (0)	0	<0.01
Bermudan (0)	0	<0.01
British West Indian (0)	1	<0.01
Dutch West Indian (8)	8	0.01
Haitian (26)	38	0.05
Jamaican (37)	118	0.15
Trinidadian/Tobagonian (34)	45	0.06
U.S. Virgin Islander (0)	0	<0.01
West Indian (35)	195	0.24
Other West Indian (0)	0	<0.01
Yugoslavian (13)	18	0.02

Hispanic Origin	Population	%
Hispanic or Latino (of any race)	1,896	2.37
Central American, ex. Mexican	331	0.41
Costa Rican	6	0.01
Guatemalan	249	0.31
Honduran	17	0.02
Nicaraguan	12	0.01
Panamanian	36	0.04
Salvadoran	10	0.01
Other Central American	1	<0.01
Cuban	75	0.09
Dominican Republic	87	0.11
Mexican	340	0.42
Puerto Rican	799	1.00
South American	85	0.11
Argentinean	2	<0.01
Bolivian	2	<0.01
Chilean	6	0.01
Colombian	29	0.04
Ecuadorian	23	0.03
Paraguayan	1	<0.01
Peruvian	10	0.01
Uruguayan	1	<0.01
Venezuelan	9	0.01
Other South American	2	<0.01
Other Hispanic or Latino	179	0.22

Race*	Population	%
African-American/Black (3,195)	4,052	5.06
Not Hispanic (3,009)	3,782	4.73
Hispanic (186)	270	0.34
American Indian/Alaska Native (283)	703	0.88
Not Hispanic (252)	636	0.79
Hispanic (31)	67	0.08
Alaska Athabascan (Ala. Nat.) (0)	0	<0.01
Aleut (Alaska Native) (1)	1	<0.01
Apache (2)	8	0.01
Arapaho (0)	1	<0.01
Blackfeet (2)	21	0.03
Canadian/French Am. Ind. (5)	6	0.01
Central American Ind. (1)	3	<0.01
Cherokee (13)	62	0.08
Cheyenne (0)	1	<0.01
Chickasaw (0)	0	<0.01
Chippewa (3)	13	0.02
Choctaw (9)	11	0.01
Colville (0)	0	<0.01
Comanche (0)	3	<0.01
Cree (0)	0	<0.01
Creek (1)	1	<0.01
Crow (0)	1	<0.01
Delaware (0)	0	<0.01
Hopi (0)	0	<0.01
Houma (0)	0	<0.01
Inupiat (Alaska Native) (0)	0	<0.01
Iroquois (107)	224	0.28
Kiowa (0)	0	<0.01
Lumbee (5)	5	0.01
Menominee (0)	0	<0.01
Mexican American Ind. (8)	15	0.02
Navajo (4)	5	0.01
Osage (0)	3	<0.01
Ottawa (5)	5	0.01
Paiute (0)	0	<0.01
Pima (0)	0	<0.01
Potawatomi (0)	0	<0.01
Pueblo (2)	2	<0.01
Puget Sound Salish (0)	0	<0.01
Seminole (0)	0	<0.01
Shoshone (0)	0	<0.01
Sioux (6)	13	0.02
South American Ind. (1)	7	0.01
Spanish American Ind. (1)	1	<0.01
Tlingit-Haida (Alaska Native) (0)	0	<0.01
Tohono O'Odham (0)	0	<0.01
Tsimshian (Alaska Native) (0)	0	<0.01
Ute (0)	0	<0.01
Yakama (0)	0	<0.01
Yaqui (0)	0	<0.01
Yuman (0)	0	<0.01
Yup'ik (Alaska Native) (0)	0	<0.01
Asian (390)	544	0.68
Not Hispanic (387)	531	0.66
Hispanic (3)	13	0.02
Bangladeshi (0)	0	<0.01
Bhutanese (0)	0	<0.01
Burmese (10)	10	0.01
Cambodian (3)	4	<0.01
Chinese, ex. Taiwanese (87)	99	0.12
Filipino (55)	98	0.12
Hmong (0)	0	<0.01
Indian (70)	92	0.11
Indonesian (1)	1	<0.01
Japanese (18)	42	0.05
Korean (51)	64	0.08
Laotian (14)	15	0.02
Malaysian (0)	0	<0.01
Nepalese (0)	0	<0.01
Pakistani (13)	13	0.02
Sri Lankan (0)	0	<0.01
Taiwanese (1)	2	<0.01
Thai (13)	20	0.02
Vietnamese (29)	59	0.07
Hawaii Native/Pacific Islander (31)	67	0.08
Not Hispanic (26)	53	0.07
Hispanic (5)	14	0.02
Fijian (1)	1	<0.01
Guamanian/Chamorro (8)	10	0.01
Marshallese (0)	0	<0.01
Native Hawaiian (10)	22	0.03
Samoan (11)	21	0.03
Tongan (0)	0	<0.01
White (74,042)	75,378	94.19
Not Hispanic (73,098)	74,281	92.82
Hispanic (944)	1,097	1.37

Notes: † The Census 2010 population figure is used to calculate the percentages in the Hispanic Origin and Race categories. Ancestry percentages are based on the 2006-2010 American Community Survey population (not shown); ‡ Numbers in parentheses indicate the number of people reporting a single ancestry; * Numbers in parentheses indicate the number of persons reporting this race alone, not in combination with any other race; Please refer to the Explanation of Data for more information.

Chautauqua County

Population: 134,905

Ancestry	Population	%
Afghan (0)	0	<0.01
African, Sub-Saharan (28)	147	0.11
African (13)	129	0.10
Cape Verdean (0)	0	<0.01
Ethiopian (0)	0	<0.01
Ghanaian (0)	0	<0.01
Kenyan (0)	0	<0.01
Liberian (0)	0	<0.01
Nigerian (8)	11	0.01
Senegalese (0)	0	<0.01
Sierra Leonean (0)	0	<0.01
Somalian (0)	0	<0.01
South African (0)	0	<0.01
Sudanese (7)	7	0.01
Ugandan (0)	0	<0.01
Zimbabwean (0)	0	<0.01
Other Sub-Saharan African (0)	0	<0.01
Albanian (107)	158	0.12
Alsatian (0)	0	<0.01
American (4,291)	4,291	3.17
Arab (100)	450	0.33
Arab (0)	44	0.03
Egyptian (11)	36	0.03
Iraqi (0)	0	<0.01
Jordanian (0)	0	<0.01
Lebanese (55)	212	0.16
Moroccan (0)	0	<0.01
Palestinian (7)	23	0.02
Syrian (27)	135	0.10
Other Arab (0)	0	<0.01
Armenian (23)	32	0.02
Assyrian/Chaldean/Syriac (0)	0	<0.01
Australian (0)	3	<0.01
Austrian (62)	422	0.31
Basque (0)	0	<0.01
Belgian (33)	45	0.03
Brazilian (19)	28	0.02
British (140)	373	0.28
Bulgarian (13)	13	0.01
Cajun (0)	0	<0.01
Canadian (98)	277	0.20
Carpatho Rusyn (0)	0	<0.01
Celtic (0)	31	0.02
Croatian (97)	210	0.16
Cypriot (0)	0	<0.01
Czech (88)	400	0.30
Czechoslovakian (43)	151	0.11
Danish (203)	649	0.48
Dutch (960)	4,144	3.06
Eastern European (31)	31	0.02
English (6,689)	21,635	15.99
Estonian (3)	3	<0.01
European (588)	620	0.46
Finnish (16)	163	0.12
French, ex. Basque (460)	3,331	2.46
French Canadian (337)	870	0.64
German (10,307)	33,780	24.97
German Russian (0)	0	<0.01
Greek (75)	159	0.12
Guyanese (0)	0	<0.01
Hungarian (273)	948	0.70
Icelander (0)	0	<0.01
Iranian (4)	4	<0.01
Irish (5,085)	20,147	14.89
Israeli (0)	16	0.01
Italian (9,579)	21,679	16.03
Latvian (5)	21	0.02
Lithuanian (11)	59	0.04
Luxemburger (0)	0	<0.01
Macedonian (50)	50	0.04
Maltese (0)	0	<0.01
New Zealander (0)	6	<0.01
Northern European (72)	80	0.06
Norwegian (298)	684	0.51
Pennsylvania German (636)	967	0.71

Ancestry	Population	%
Polish (5,698)	14,377	10.63
Portuguese (0)	28	0.02
Romanian (1)	88	0.07
Russian (127)	667	0.49
Scandinavian (88)	145	0.11
Scotch-Irish (567)	2,235	1.65
Scottish (497)	2,598	1.92
Serbian (0)	0	<0.01
Slavic (95)	169	0.12
Slovak (110)	254	0.19
Slovene (10)	38	0.03
Soviet Union (0)	0	<0.01
Swedish (6,798)	17,330	12.81
Swiss (191)	536	0.40
Turkish (0)	5	<0.01
Ukrainian (171)	372	0.28
Welsh (176)	1,038	0.77
West Indian, ex. Hispanic (99)	225	0.17
Bahamian (0)	0	<0.01
Barbadian (0)	3	<0.01
Belizean (0)	6	<0.01
Bermudan (0)	0	<0.01
British West Indian (3)	3	<0.01
Dutch West Indian (0)	3	<0.01
Haitian (36)	67	0.05
Jamaican (12)	85	0.06
Trinidadian/Tobagonian (23)	31	0.02
U.S. Virgin Islander (0)	0	<0.01
West Indian (25)	27	0.02
Other West Indian (0)	0	<0.01
Yugoslavian (28)	79	0.06

Hispanic Origin	Population	%
Hispanic or Latino (of any race)	8,241	6.11
Central American, ex. Mexican	148	0.11
Costa Rican	14	0.01
Guatemalan	56	0.04
Honduran	20	0.01
Nicaraguan	7	0.01
Panamanian	7	0.01
Salvadoran	44	0.03
Other Central American	0	<0.01
Cuban	101	0.07
Dominican Republic	167	0.12
Mexican	851	0.63
Puerto Rican	6,401	4.74
South American	180	0.13
Argentinean	26	0.02
Bolivian	5	<0.01
Chilean	5	<0.01
Colombian	70	0.05
Ecuadorian	30	0.02
Paraguayan	1	<0.01
Peruvian	22	0.02
Uruguayan	3	<0.01
Venezuelan	18	0.01
Other South American	0	<0.01
Other Hispanic or Latino	393	0.29

Race*	Population	%
African-American/Black (3,197)	4,710	3.49
Not Hispanic (2,763)	4,006	2.97
Hispanic (434)	704	0.52
American Indian/Alaska Native (689)	1,462	1.08
Not Hispanic (576)	1,258	0.93
Hispanic (113)	204	0.15
Alaska Athabascan (Ala. Nat.) (1)	1	<0.01
Aleut (Alaska Native) (0)	0	<0.01
Apache (0)	2	<0.01
Arapaho (1)	1	<0.01
Blackfeet (7)	46	0.03
Canadian/French Am. Ind. (4)	9	0.01
Central American Ind. (1)	1	<0.01
Cherokee (26)	116	0.09
Cheyenne (0)	2	<0.01
Chickasaw (0)	0	<0.01
Chippewa (5)	20	0.01
Choctaw (1)	1	<0.01
Colville (0)	0	<0.01

Race* (cont.)	Population	%
Comanche (0)	0	<0.01
Cree (0)	0	<0.01
Creek (2)	2	<0.01
Crow (1)	1	<0.01
Delaware (4)	5	<0.01
Hopi (0)	0	<0.01
Houma (1)	1	<0.01
Inupiat (Alaska Native) (5)	6	<0.01
Iroquois (365)	615	0.46
Kiowa (0)	0	<0.01
Lumbee (0)	0	<0.01
Menominee (0)	0	<0.01
Mexican American Ind. (22)	27	0.02
Navajo (3)	3	<0.01
Osage (0)	0	<0.01
Ottawa (0)	0	<0.01
Paiute (0)	0	<0.01
Pima (0)	0	<0.01
Potawatomi (0)	2	<0.01
Pueblo (3)	4	<0.01
Puget Sound Salish (0)	0	<0.01
Seminole (0)	2	<0.01
Shoshone (0)	0	<0.01
Sioux (3)	6	<0.01
South American Ind. (6)	18	0.01
Spanish American Ind. (0)	0	<0.01
Tlingit-Haida (Alaska Native) (0)	0	<0.01
Tohono O'Odham (0)	0	<0.01
Tsimshian (Alaska Native) (0)	0	<0.01
Ute (0)	0	<0.01
Yakama (0)	0	<0.01
Yaqui (0)	0	<0.01
Yuman (0)	0	<0.01
Yup'ik (Alaska Native) (0)	1	<0.01
Asian (688)	945	0.70
Not Hispanic (676)	892	0.66
Hispanic (12)	53	0.04
Bangladeshi (1)	1	<0.01
Bhutanese (0)	0	<0.01
Burmese (5)	5	<0.01
Cambodian (5)	6	<0.01
Chinese, ex. Taiwanese (169)	203	0.15
Filipino (105)	176	0.13
Hmong (1)	1	<0.01
Indian (130)	152	0.11
Indonesian (5)	15	0.01
Japanese (33)	71	0.05
Korean (105)	142	0.11
Laotian (1)	9	0.01
Malaysian (0)	3	<0.01
Nepalese (0)	0	<0.01
Pakistani (41)	42	0.03
Sri Lankan (3)	5	<0.01
Taiwanese (4)	7	0.01
Thai (22)	29	0.02
Vietnamese (36)	49	0.04
Hawaii Native/Pacific Islander (36)	100	0.07
Not Hispanic (31)	73	0.05
Hispanic (5)	27	0.02
Fijian (2)	2	<0.01
Guamanian/Chamorro (8)	16	0.01
Marshallese (0)	0	<0.01
Native Hawaiian (8)	24	0.02
Samoan (5)	8	0.01
Tongan (0)	0	<0.01
White (124,875)	127,434	94.46
Not Hispanic (120,463)	122,474	90.79
Hispanic (4,412)	4,960	3.68

Notes: † The Census 2010 population figure is used to calculate the percentages in the Hispanic Origin and Race categories. Ancestry percentages are based on the 2006-2010 American Community Survey population (not shown); ‡ Numbers in parentheses indicate the number of people reporting a single ancestry; * Numbers in parentheses indicate the number of persons reporting this race alone, not in combination with any other race; Please refer to the Explanation of Data for more information.

Chemung County

Population: 88,830

Ancestry	Population	%
Afghan (0)	0	<0.01
African, Sub-Saharan (234)	248	0.28
African (172)	186	0.21
Cape Verdean (0)	0	<0.01
Ethiopian (11)	11	0.01
Ghanaian (11)	11	0.01
Kenyan (39)	39	0.04
Liberian (0)	0	<0.01
Nigerian (1)	1	<0.01
Senegalese (0)	0	<0.01
Sierra Leonean (0)	0	<0.01
Somalian (0)	0	<0.01
South African (0)	0	<0.01
Sudanese (0)	0	<0.01
Ugandan (0)	0	<0.01
Zimbabwean (0)	0	<0.01
Other Sub-Saharan African (0)	0	<0.01
Albanian (0)	0	<0.01
Alsatian (0)	10	0.01
American (7,001)	7,001	7.89
Arab (185)	293	0.33
Arab (0)	0	<0.01
Egyptian (4)	4	<0.01
Iraqi (0)	0	<0.01
Jordanian (0)	0	<0.01
Lebanese (151)	245	0.28
Moroccan (0)	0	<0.01
Palestinian (18)	18	0.02
Syrian (14)	14	0.02
Other Arab (12)	12	0.01
Armenian (0)	37	0.04
Assyrian/Chaldean/Syriac (0)	0	<0.01
Australian (0)	0	<0.01
Austrian (60)	214	0.24
Basque (0)	0	<0.01
Belgian (37)	62	0.07
Brazilian (0)	0	<0.01
British (82)	151	0.17
Bulgarian (12)	12	0.01
Cajun (0)	0	<0.01
Canadian (175)	269	0.30
Carpatho Rusyn (0)	0	<0.01
Celtic (2)	12	0.01
Croatian (15)	62	0.07
Cypriot (0)	0	<0.01
Czech (142)	369	0.42
Czechoslovakian (104)	259	0.29
Danish (78)	202	0.23
Dutch (764)	3,692	4.16
Eastern European (32)	32	0.04
English (3,931)	12,489	14.08
Estonian (12)	12	0.01
European (260)	282	0.32
Finnish (144)	475	0.54
French, ex. Basque (455)	2,813	3.17
French Canadian (291)	894	1.01
German (5,023)	18,529	20.89
German Russian (0)	0	<0.01
Greek (134)	312	0.35
Guyanese (0)	0	<0.01
Hungarian (110)	267	0.30
Icelander (0)	0	<0.01
Iranian (12)	12	0.01
Irish (5,564)	17,907	20.19
Israeli (0)	20	0.02
Italian (3,852)	10,020	11.30
Latvian (0)	55	0.06
Lithuanian (78)	183	0.21
Luxemburger (0)	0	<0.01
Macedonian (0)	0	<0.01
Maltese (9)	9	0.01
New Zealander (0)	0	<0.01
Northern European (13)	13	0.01
Norwegian (99)	591	0.67
Pennsylvania German (229)	522	0.59

Ancestry	Population	%
Polish (2,122)	6,087	6.86
Portuguese (35)	115	0.13
Romanian (0)	43	0.05
Russian (129)	600	0.68
Scandinavian (4)	23	0.03
Scotch-Irish (616)	1,482	1.67
Scottish (456)	1,673	1.89
Serbian (11)	11	0.01
Slavic (4)	84	0.09
Slovak (44)	201	0.23
Slovene (15)	41	0.05
Soviet Union (0)	0	<0.01
Swedish (364)	1,326	1.49
Swiss (26)	166	0.19
Turkish (10)	21	0.02
Ukrainian (548)	1,369	1.54
Welsh (366)	1,410	1.59
West Indian, ex. Hispanic (228)	300	0.34
Bahamian (31)	31	0.03
Barbadian (26)	26	0.03
Belizean (0)	0	<0.01
Bermudan (0)	0	<0.01
British West Indian (14)	41	0.05
Dutch West Indian (0)	0	<0.01
Haitian (51)	51	0.06
Jamaican (72)	107	0.12
Trinidadian/Tobagonian (0)	0	<0.01
U.S. Virgin Islander (0)	0	<0.01
West Indian (23)	33	0.04
Other West Indian (11)	11	0.01
Yugoslavian (139)	193	0.22

Hispanic Origin	Population	%
Hispanic or Latino (of any race)	2,240	2.52
Central American, ex. Mexican	121	0.14
Costa Rican	18	0.02
Guatemalan	35	0.04
Honduran	15	0.02
Nicaraguan	5	0.01
Panamanian	31	0.03
Salvadoran	17	0.02
Other Central American	0	<0.01
Cuban	82	0.09
Dominican Republic	100	0.11
Mexican	404	0.45
Puerto Rican	1,156	1.30
South American	119	0.13
Argentinean	15	0.02
Bolivian	8	0.01
Chilean	2	<0.01
Colombian	26	0.03
Ecuadorian	23	0.03
Paraguayan	0	<0.01
Peruvian	27	0.03
Uruguayan	3	<0.01
Venezuelan	6	0.01
Other South American	9	0.01
Other Hispanic or Latino	258	0.29

Race*	Population	%
African-American/Black (5,828)	7,391	8.32
Not Hispanic (5,528)	6,946	7.82
Hispanic (300)	445	0.50
American Indian/Alaska Native (233)	812	0.91
Not Hispanic (206)	713	0.80
Hispanic (27)	99	0.11
Alaska Athabascan (Ala. Nat.) (0)	0	<0.01
Aleut (Alaska Native) (0)	0	<0.01
Apache (6)	8	0.01
Arapaho (0)	0	<0.01
Blackfeet (6)	44	0.05
Canadian/French Am. Ind. (0)	5	0.01
Central American Ind. (0)	1	<0.01
Cherokee (21)	121	0.14
Cheyenne (0)	0	<0.01
Chickasaw (0)	1	<0.01
Chippewa (2)	3	<0.01
Choctaw (0)	0	<0.01
Colville (0)	0	<0.01

	Population	%
Comanche (0)	0	<0.01
Cree (0)	3	<0.01
Creek (0)	1	<0.01
Crow (0)	0	<0.01
Delaware (0)	1	<0.01
Hopi (0)	0	<0.01
Houma (2)	2	<0.01
Inupiat (Alaska Native) (0)	0	<0.01
Iroquois (74)	153	0.17
Kiowa (1)	1	<0.01
Lumbee (0)	0	<0.01
Menominee (0)	0	<0.01
Mexican American Ind. (2)	8	0.01
Navajo (0)	11	0.01
Osage (0)	0	<0.01
Ottawa (0)	0	<0.01
Paiute (0)	0	<0.01
Pima (0)	0	<0.01
Potawatomi (0)	1	<0.01
Pueblo (1)	1	<0.01
Puget Sound Salish (0)	2	<0.01
Seminole (0)	6	0.01
Shoshone (0)	0	<0.01
Sioux (1)	16	0.02
South American Ind. (3)	7	0.01
Spanish American Ind. (0)	1	<0.01
Tlingit-Haida (Alaska Native) (3)	3	<0.01
Tohono O'Odham (0)	1	<0.01
Tsimshian (Alaska Native) (0)	0	<0.01
Ute (0)	0	<0.01
Yakama (0)	1	<0.01
Yaqui (0)	0	<0.01
Yuman (0)	0	<0.01
Yup'ik (Alaska Native) (0)	0	<0.01
Asian (1,057)	1,334	1.50
Not Hispanic (1,041)	1,296	1.46
Hispanic (16)	38	0.04
Bangladeshi (20)	20	0.02
Bhutanese (0)	0	<0.01
Burmese (0)	0	<0.01
Cambodian (2)	2	<0.01
Chinese, ex. Taiwanese (279)	312	0.35
Filipino (95)	164	0.18
Hmong (0)	0	<0.01
Indian (261)	310	0.35
Indonesian (4)	5	0.01
Japanese (53)	100	0.11
Korean (79)	128	0.14
Laotian (12)	32	0.04
Malaysian (2)	3	<0.01
Nepalese (3)	3	<0.01
Pakistani (97)	108	0.12
Sri Lankan (11)	12	0.01
Taiwanese (15)	21	0.02
Thai (9)	18	0.02
Vietnamese (63)	68	0.08
Hawaii Native/Pacific Islander (20)	56	0.06
Not Hispanic (14)	44	0.05
Hispanic (6)	12	0.01
Fijian (0)	0	<0.01
Guamanian/Chamorro (5)	12	0.01
Marshallese (0)	0	<0.01
Native Hawaiian (8)	17	0.02
Samoan (6)	11	0.01
Tongan (0)	1	<0.01
White (78,771)	81,009	91.20
Not Hispanic (77,643)	79,627	89.64
Hispanic (1,128)	1,382	1.56

*Notes: † The Census 2010 population figure is used to calculate the percentages in the Hispanic Origin and Race categories. Ancestry percentages are based on the 2006-2010 American Community Survey population (not shown); ‡ Numbers in parentheses indicate the number of people reporting a single ancestry; * Numbers in parentheses indicate the number of persons reporting this race alone, not in combination with any other race; Please refer to the Explanation of Data for more information.*

Chenango County

Population: 50,477

Ancestry	Population	%
Afghan (0)	0	<0.01
African, Sub-Saharan (11)	53	0.10
African (2)	31	0.06
Cape Verdean (0)	0	<0.01
Ethiopian (0)	0	<0.01
Ghanaian (5)	5	0.01
Kenyan (0)	0	<0.01
Liberian (4)	4	0.01
Nigerian (0)	13	0.03
Senegalese (0)	0	<0.01
Sierra Leonean (0)	0	<0.01
Somalian (0)	0	<0.01
South African (0)	0	<0.01
Sudanese (0)	0	<0.01
Ugandan (0)	0	<0.01
Zimbabwean (0)	0	<0.01
Other Sub-Saharan African (0)	0	<0.01
Albanian (0)	0	<0.01
Alsatian (0)	13	0.03
American (3,611)	3,611	7.07
Arab (39)	94	0.18
Arab (0)	0	<0.01
Egyptian (2)	2	<0.01
Iraqi (0)	0	<0.01
Jordanian (0)	0	<0.01
Lebanese (33)	88	0.17
Moroccan (0)	0	<0.01
Palestinian (0)	0	<0.01
Syrian (4)	4	0.01
Other Arab (0)	0	<0.01
Armenian (3)	5	0.01
Assyrian/Chaldean/Syriac (0)	0	<0.01
Australian (0)	12	0.02
Austrian (37)	147	0.29
Basque (0)	0	<0.01
Belgian (0)	7	0.01
Brazilian (3)	3	0.01
British (91)	185	0.36
Bulgarian (0)	0	<0.01
Cajun (0)	0	<0.01
Canadian (47)	133	0.26
Carpatho Rusyn (0)	0	<0.01
Celtic (3)	3	0.01
Croatian (0)	0	<0.01
Cypriot (0)	0	<0.01
Czech (43)	169	0.33
Czechoslovakian (36)	60	0.12
Danish (89)	225	0.44
Dutch (506)	2,167	4.25
Eastern European (109)	109	0.21
English (3,435)	9,260	18.14
Estonian (9)	14	0.03
European (423)	486	0.95
Finnish (7)	41	0.08
French, ex. Basque (426)	2,237	4.38
French Canadian (225)	653	1.28
German (2,635)	8,972	17.58
German Russian (0)	0	<0.01
Greek (27)	71	0.14
Guyanese (0)	0	<0.01
Hungarian (103)	456	0.89
Icelander (0)	0	<0.01
Iranian (48)	48	0.09
Irish (2,193)	8,509	16.67
Israeli (0)	0	<0.01
Italian (1,990)	4,673	9.15
Latvian (0)	0	<0.01
Lithuanian (116)	196	0.38
Luxemburger (0)	0	<0.01
Macedonian (0)	0	<0.01
Maltese (0)	0	<0.01
New Zealander (0)	0	<0.01
Northern European (173)	173	0.34
Norwegian (108)	432	0.85
Pennsylvania German (24)	86	0.17

Ancestry	Population	%
Polish (664)	1,903	3.73
Portuguese (56)	98	0.19
Romanian (2)	18	0.04
Russian (204)	337	0.66
Scandinavian (21)	75	0.15
Scotch-Irish (337)	1,126	2.21
Scottish (250)	1,081	2.12
Serbian (0)	0	<0.01
Slavic (0)	11	0.02
Slovak (80)	166	0.33
Slovene (0)	0	<0.01
Soviet Union (0)	0	<0.01
Swedish (120)	522	1.02
Swiss (182)	301	0.59
Turkish (7)	7	0.01
Ukrainian (40)	117	0.23
Welsh (230)	1,011	1.98
West Indian, ex. Hispanic (39)	50	0.10
Bahamian (0)	0	<0.01
Barbadian (0)	0	<0.01
Belizean (0)	0	<0.01
Bermudan (0)	0	<0.01
British West Indian (0)	0	<0.01
Dutch West Indian (3)	6	0.01
Haitian (0)	3	0.01
Jamaican (36)	41	0.08
Trinidadian/Tobagonian (0)	0	<0.01
U.S. Virgin Islander (0)	0	<0.01
West Indian (0)	0	<0.01
Other West Indian (0)	0	<0.01
Yugoslavian (10)	51	0.10

Hispanic Origin	Population	%
Hispanic or Latino (of any race)	929	1.84
Central American, ex. Mexican	43	0.09
Costa Rican	6	0.01
Guatemalan	23	0.05
Honduran	7	0.01
Nicaraguan	0	<0.01
Panamanian	4	0.01
Salvadoran	3	0.01
Other Central American	0	<0.01
Cuban	44	0.09
Dominican Republic	27	0.05
Mexican	175	0.35
Puerto Rican	450	0.89
South American	55	0.11
Argentinean	2	<0.01
Bolivian	0	<0.01
Chilean	4	0.01
Colombian	26	0.05
Ecuadorian	17	0.03
Paraguayan	4	0.01
Peruvian	2	<0.01
Uruguayan	0	<0.01
Venezuelan	0	<0.01
Other South American	0	<0.01
Other Hispanic or Latino	135	0.27

Race*	Population	%
African-American/Black (345)	562	1.11
Not Hispanic (323)	527	1.04
Hispanic (22)	35	0.07
American Indian/Alaska Native (172)	453	0.90
Not Hispanic (151)	426	0.84
Hispanic (21)	27	0.05
Alaska Athabascan (Ala. Nat.) (0)	0	<0.01
Aleut (Alaska Native) (1)	1	<0.01
Apache (1)	5	0.01
Arapaho (0)	0	<0.01
Blackfeet (3)	25	0.05
Canadian/French Am. Ind. (0)	0	<0.01
Central American Ind. (3)	3	0.01
Cherokee (12)	43	0.09
Cheyenne (1)	1	<0.01
Chickasaw (0)	0	<0.01
Chippewa (1)	1	<0.01
Choctaw (4)	6	0.01
Colville (0)	0	<0.01

Race* (cont.)	Population	%
Comanche (0)	1	<0.01
Cree (1)	1	<0.01
Creek (0)	0	<0.01
Crow (0)	0	<0.01
Delaware (5)	6	0.01
Hopi (0)	0	<0.01
Houma (1)	1	<0.01
Inupiat (Alaska Native) (0)	0	<0.01
Iroquois (40)	85	0.17
Kiowa (0)	0	<0.01
Lumbee (3)	3	0.01
Menominee (0)	0	<0.01
Mexican American Ind. (2)	3	0.01
Navajo (1)	1	<0.01
Osage (0)	0	<0.01
Ottawa (0)	0	<0.01
Paiute (0)	0	<0.01
Pima (0)	0	<0.01
Potawatomi (0)	0	<0.01
Pueblo (1)	2	<0.01
Puget Sound Salish (0)	0	<0.01
Seminole (0)	0	<0.01
Shoshone (0)	2	<0.01
Sioux (4)	12	0.02
South American Ind. (0)	3	0.01
Spanish American Ind. (2)	2	<0.01
Tlingit-Haida (Alaska Native) (2)	2	<0.01
Tohono O'Odham (0)	0	<0.01
Tsimshian (Alaska Native) (0)	0	<0.01
Ute (0)	0	<0.01
Yakama (0)	0	<0.01
Yaqui (0)	0	<0.01
Yuman (0)	0	<0.01
Yup'ik (Alaska Native) (0)	0	<0.01
Asian (204)	315	0.62
Not Hispanic (200)	306	0.61
Hispanic (4)	9	0.02
Bangladeshi (0)	0	<0.01
Bhutanese (0)	0	<0.01
Burmese (0)	0	<0.01
Cambodian (0)	0	<0.01
Chinese, ex. Taiwanese (58)	65	0.13
Filipino (40)	82	0.16
Hmong (0)	0	<0.01
Indian (33)	43	0.09
Indonesian (3)	3	0.01
Japanese (13)	22	0.04
Korean (29)	47	0.09
Laotian (2)	5	0.01
Malaysian (2)	5	0.01
Nepalese (0)	0	<0.01
Pakistani (0)	0	<0.01
Sri Lankan (0)	0	<0.01
Taiwanese (7)	10	0.02
Thai (3)	6	0.01
Vietnamese (10)	17	0.03
Hawaii Native/Pacific Islander (6)	27	0.05
Not Hispanic (4)	24	0.05
Hispanic (2)	3	0.01
Fijian (0)	0	<0.01
Guamanian/Chamorro (0)	3	0.01
Marshallese (0)	0	<0.01
Native Hawaiian (4)	12	0.02
Samoan (1)	1	<0.01
Tongan (0)	0	<0.01
White (48,896)	49,525	98.11
Not Hispanic (48,265)	48,823	96.72
Hispanic (631)	702	1.39

*Notes: † The Census 2010 population figure is used to calculate the percentages in the Hispanic Origin and Race categories. Ancestry percentages are based on the 2006-2010 American Community Survey population (not shown); ‡ Numbers in parentheses indicate the number of people reporting a single ancestry; * Numbers in parentheses indicate the number of persons reporting this race alone, not in combination with any other race; Please refer to the Explanation of Data for more information.*

Clinton County

Population: 82,128

Ancestry	Population	%
Afghan (0)	0	<0.01
African, Sub-Saharan (153)	172	0.21
African (85)	104	0.13
Cape Verdean (0)	0	<0.01
Ethiopian (8)	8	0.01
Ghanaian (13)	13	0.02
Kenyan (0)	0	<0.01
Liberian (0)	0	<0.01
Nigerian (0)	0	<0.01
Senegalese (0)	0	<0.01
Sierra Leonean (0)	0	<0.01
Somalian (0)	0	<0.01
South African (0)	0	<0.01
Sudanese (0)	0	<0.01
Ugandan (0)	0	<0.01
Zimbabwean (0)	0	<0.01
Other Sub-Saharan African (47)	47	0.06
Albanian (70)	70	0.08
Alsatian (0)	0	<0.01
American (7,652)	7,652	9.29
Arab (114)	350	0.42
Arab (12)	18	0.02
Egyptian (13)	19	0.02
Iraqi (0)	0	<0.01
Jordanian (0)	2	<0.01
Lebanese (59)	257	0.31
Moroccan (10)	10	0.01
Palestinian (0)	0	<0.01
Syrian (19)	43	0.05
Other Arab (1)	1	<0.01
Armenian (25)	130	0.16
Assyrian/Chaldean/Syriac (0)	0	<0.01
Australian (0)	27	0.03
Austrian (5)	234	0.28
Basque (0)	0	<0.01
Belgian (0)	39	0.05
Brazilian (22)	22	0.03
British (97)	286	0.35
Bulgarian (0)	0	<0.01
Cajun (21)	21	0.03
Canadian (602)	893	1.08
Carpatho Rusyn (0)	0	<0.01
Celtic (0)	10	0.01
Croatian (0)	48	0.06
Cypriot (0)	0	<0.01
Czech (48)	189	0.23
Czechoslovakian (0)	19	0.02
Danish (42)	149	0.18
Dutch (124)	1,267	1.54
Eastern European (39)	58	0.07
English (3,020)	9,045	10.98
Estonian (14)	31	0.04
European (370)	388	0.47
Finnish (54)	150	0.18
French, ex. Basque (7,155)	20,474	24.85
French Canadian (4,464)	6,631	8.05
German (1,440)	7,220	8.76
German Russian (0)	0	<0.01
Greek (76)	174	0.21
Guyanese (5)	19	0.02
Hungarian (30)	225	0.27
Icelander (7)	23	0.03
Iranian (167)	167	0.20
Irish (3,162)	13,491	16.38
Israeli (0)	0	<0.01
Italian (2,215)	6,104	7.41
Latvian (0)	2	<0.01
Lithuanian (61)	362	0.44
Luxemburger (0)	0	<0.01
Macedonian (0)	0	<0.01
Maltese (28)	28	0.03
New Zealander (0)	0	<0.01
Northern European (17)	17	0.02
Norwegian (77)	411	0.50
Pennsylvania German (4)	27	0.03

Ancestry	Population	%
Polish (720)	2,685	3.26
Portuguese (74)	164	0.20
Romanian (0)	80	0.10
Russian (266)	688	0.84
Scandinavian (9)	33	0.04
Scotch-Irish (620)	1,300	1.58
Scottish (519)	1,860	2.26
Serbian (0)	14	0.02
Slavic (0)	27	0.03
Slovak (32)	118	0.14
Slovene (0)	47	0.06
Soviet Union (0)	0	<0.01
Swedish (83)	585	0.71
Swiss (39)	106	0.13
Turkish (34)	34	0.04
Ukrainian (140)	255	0.31
Welsh (80)	406	0.49
West Indian, ex. Hispanic (140)	248	0.30
Bahamian (0)	0	<0.01
Barbadian (0)	4	<0.01
Belizean (0)	0	<0.01
Bermudan (0)	0	<0.01
British West Indian (43)	56	0.07
Dutch West Indian (0)	0	<0.01
Haitian (0)	14	0.02
Jamaican (35)	39	0.05
Trinidadian/Tobagonian (26)	48	0.06
U.S. Virgin Islander (0)	0	<0.01
West Indian (36)	87	0.11
Other West Indian (0)	0	<0.01
Yugoslavian (0)	10	0.01

Hispanic Origin	Population	%
Hispanic or Latino (of any race)	2,054	2.50
Central American, ex. Mexican	155	0.19
Costa Rican	12	0.01
Guatemalan	27	0.03
Honduran	31	0.04
Nicaraguan	15	0.02
Panamanian	25	0.03
Salvadoran	44	0.05
Other Central American	1	<0.01
Cuban	95	0.12
Dominican Republic	207	0.25
Mexican	302	0.37
Puerto Rican	928	1.13
South American	151	0.18
Argentinean	10	0.01
Bolivian	2	<0.01
Chilean	11	0.01
Colombian	58	0.07
Ecuadorian	24	0.03
Paraguayan	8	0.01
Peruvian	24	0.03
Uruguayan	2	<0.01
Venezuelan	10	0.01
Other South American	2	<0.01
Other Hispanic or Latino	216	0.26

Race*	Population	%
African-American/Black (3,209)	3,704	4.51
Not Hispanic (2,953)	3,383	4.12
Hispanic (256)	321	0.39
American Indian/Alaska Native (286)	747	0.91
Not Hispanic (266)	685	0.83
Hispanic (20)	62	0.08
Alaska Athabascan (Ala. Nat.) (2)	2	<0.01
Aleut (Alaska Native) (0)	1	<0.01
Apache (0)	10	0.01
Arapaho (1)	1	<0.01
Blackfeet (6)	29	0.04
Canadian/French Am. Ind. (11)	22	0.03
Central American Ind. (1)	3	<0.01
Cherokee (13)	79	0.10
Cheyenne (0)	1	<0.01
Chickasaw (0)	2	<0.01
Chippewa (5)	9	0.01
Choctaw (2)	2	<0.01
Colville (0)	0	<0.01

Race*	Population	%
Comanche (1)	3	<0.01
Cree (2)	2	<0.01
Creek (0)	1	<0.01
Crow (1)	3	<0.01
Delaware (0)	0	<0.01
Hopi (0)	0	<0.01
Houma (0)	0	<0.01
Inupiat (Alaska Native) (2)	2	<0.01
Iroquois (73)	136	0.17
Kiowa (0)	0	<0.01
Lumbee (0)	0	<0.01
Menominee (0)	0	<0.01
Mexican American Ind. (2)	4	<0.01
Navajo (0)	1	<0.01
Osage (0)	0	<0.01
Ottawa (0)	0	<0.01
Paiute (0)	0	<0.01
Pima (0)	0	<0.01
Potawatomi (1)	2	<0.01
Pueblo (1)	1	<0.01
Puget Sound Salish (0)	1	<0.01
Seminole (0)	0	<0.01
Shoshone (0)	0	<0.01
Sioux (12)	22	0.03
South American Ind. (1)	7	0.01
Spanish American Ind. (0)	0	<0.01
Tlingit-Haida (Alaska Native) (0)	0	<0.01
Tohono O'Odham (0)	0	<0.01
Tsimshian (Alaska Native) (0)	0	<0.01
Ute (0)	0	<0.01
Yakama (0)	0	<0.01
Yaqui (0)	0	<0.01
Yuman (0)	0	<0.01
Yup'ik (Alaska Native) (1)	1	<0.01
Asian (898)	1,147	1.40
Not Hispanic (890)	1,121	1.36
Hispanic (8)	26	0.03
Bangladeshi (2)	2	<0.01
Bhutanese (0)	0	<0.01
Burmese (1)	2	<0.01
Cambodian (2)	3	<0.01
Chinese, ex. Taiwanese (238)	273	0.33
Filipino (114)	185	0.23
Hmong (0)	0	<0.01
Indian (160)	182	0.22
Indonesian (0)	3	<0.01
Japanese (91)	125	0.15
Korean (96)	139	0.17
Laotian (0)	5	0.01
Malaysian (2)	4	<0.01
Nepalese (9)	9	0.01
Pakistani (30)	35	0.04
Sri Lankan (8)	13	0.02
Taiwanese (10)	11	0.01
Thai (20)	38	0.05
Vietnamese (66)	74	0.09
Hawaii Native/Pacific Islander (19)	58	0.07
Not Hispanic (15)	42	0.05
Hispanic (4)	16	0.02
Fijian (0)	0	<0.01
Guamanian/Chamorro (6)	9	0.01
Marshallese (0)	0	<0.01
Native Hawaiian (5)	17	0.02
Samoan (2)	7	0.01
Tongan (0)	0	<0.01
White (75,997)	77,099	93.88
Not Hispanic (74,832)	75,785	92.28
Hispanic (1,165)	1,314	1.60

Notes: † The Census 2010 population figure is used to calculate the percentages in the Hispanic Origin and Race categories. Ancestry percentages are based on the 2006-2010 American Community Survey population (not shown); ‡ Numbers in parentheses indicate the number of people reporting a single ancestry; * Numbers in parentheses indicate the number of persons reporting this race alone, not in combination with any other race; Please refer to the Explanation of Data for more information.

Columbia County
Population: 63,096

Ancestry	Population	%
Afghan (0)	0	<0.01
African, Sub-Saharan (171)	200	0.32
African (102)	130	0.21
Cape Verdean (0)	0	<0.01
Ethiopian (0)	0	<0.01
Ghanaian (0)	0	<0.01
Kenyan (0)	0	<0.01
Liberian (16)	16	0.03
Nigerian (29)	29	0.05
Senegalese (0)	0	<0.01
Sierra Leonean (0)	0	<0.01
Somalian (0)	0	<0.01
South African (24)	25	0.04
Sudanese (0)	0	<0.01
Ugandan (0)	0	<0.01
Zimbabwean (0)	0	<0.01
Other Sub-Saharan African (0)	0	<0.01
Albanian (0)	0	<0.01
Alsatian (0)	0	<0.01
American (5,649)	5,649	8.93
Arab (200)	246	0.39
Arab (127)	127	0.20
Egyptian (0)	3	<0.01
Iraqi (0)	0	<0.01
Jordanian (0)	0	<0.01
Lebanese (17)	32	0.05
Moroccan (43)	43	0.07
Palestinian (0)	24	0.04
Syrian (2)	6	0.01
Other Arab (11)	11	0.02
Armenian (39)	60	0.09
Assyrian/Chaldean/Syriac (0)	0	<0.01
Australian (4)	11	0.02
Austrian (60)	369	0.58
Basque (0)	4	0.01
Belgian (3)	46	0.07
Brazilian (72)	74	0.12
British (174)	400	0.63
Bulgarian (0)	0	<0.01
Cajun (0)	14	0.02
Canadian (25)	166	0.26
Carpatho Rusyn (0)	0	<0.01
Celtic (21)	21	0.03
Croatian (7)	14	0.02
Cypriot (0)	0	<0.01
Czech (52)	291	0.46
Czechoslovakian (41)	99	0.16
Danish (57)	236	0.37
Dutch (631)	4,629	7.32
Eastern European (176)	176	0.28
English (1,608)	6,951	10.99
Estonian (4)	4	0.01
European (411)	498	0.79
Finnish (68)	92	0.15
French, ex. Basque (285)	3,225	5.10
French Canadian (304)	695	1.10
German (3,377)	14,502	22.93
German Russian (0)	0	<0.01
Greek (62)	410	0.65
Guyanese (0)	0	<0.01
Hungarian (217)	681	1.08
Icelander (0)	0	<0.01
Iranian (18)	44	0.07
Irish (3,234)	12,327	19.49
Israeli (2)	2	<0.01
Italian (3,909)	10,205	16.14
Latvian (3)	55	0.09
Lithuanian (123)	309	0.49
Luxemburger (0)	0	<0.01
Macedonian (0)	0	<0.01
Maltese (0)	3	<0.01
New Zealander (0)	0	<0.01
Northern European (20)	20	0.03
Norwegian (130)	496	0.78
Pennsylvania German (9)	11	0.02

Ancestry (cont.)	Population	%
Polish (1,145)	3,588	5.67
Portuguese (20)	46	0.07
Romanian (67)	185	0.29
Russian (312)	1,220	1.93
Scandinavian (54)	78	0.12
Scotch-Irish (308)	1,127	1.78
Scottish (333)	1,672	2.64
Serbian (10)	14	0.02
Slavic (24)	89	0.14
Slovak (74)	131	0.21
Slovene (8)	16	0.03
Soviet Union (0)	0	<0.01
Swedish (112)	872	1.38
Swiss (44)	227	0.36
Turkish (20)	26	0.04
Ukrainian (304)	720	1.14
Welsh (49)	424	0.67
West Indian, ex. Hispanic (372)	418	0.66
Bahamian (0)	0	<0.01
Barbadian (0)	0	<0.01
Belizean (0)	0	<0.01
Bermudan (0)	3	<0.01
British West Indian (11)	11	0.02
Dutch West Indian (0)	0	<0.01
Haitian (93)	100	0.16
Jamaican (256)	277	0.44
Trinidadian/Tobagonian (12)	24	0.04
U.S. Virgin Islander (0)	0	<0.01
West Indian (0)	3	<0.01
Other West Indian (0)	0	<0.01
Yugoslavian (0)	11	0.02

Hispanic Origin	Population	%
Hispanic or Latino (of any race)	2,454	3.89
Central American, ex. Mexican	253	0.40
Costa Rican	11	0.02
Guatemalan	112	0.18
Honduran	34	0.05
Nicaraguan	25	0.04
Panamanian	16	0.03
Salvadoran	55	0.09
Other Central American	0	<0.01
Cuban	93	0.15
Dominican Republic	77	0.12
Mexican	732	1.16
Puerto Rican	931	1.48
South American	162	0.26
Argentinean	12	0.02
Bolivian	0	<0.01
Chilean	17	0.03
Colombian	70	0.11
Ecuadorian	41	0.06
Paraguayan	0	<0.01
Peruvian	9	0.01
Uruguayan	4	0.01
Venezuelan	8	0.01
Other South American	1	<0.01
Other Hispanic or Latino	206	0.33

Race*	Population	%
African-American/Black (2,855)	3,570	5.66
Not Hispanic (2,691)	3,327	5.27
Hispanic (164)	243	0.39
American Indian/Alaska Native (123)	476	0.75
Not Hispanic (85)	401	0.64
Hispanic (38)	75	0.12
Alaska Athabascan (Ala. Nat.) (0)	0	<0.01
Aleut (Alaska Native) (0)	0	<0.01
Apache (0)	7	0.01
Arapaho (0)	0	<0.01
Blackfeet (0)	25	0.04
Canadian/French Am. Ind. (2)	3	<0.01
Central American Ind. (0)	0	<0.01
Cherokee (10)	76	0.12
Cheyenne (0)	0	<0.01
Chickasaw (0)	5	0.01
Chippewa (1)	9	0.01
Choctaw (0)	1	<0.01
Colville (0)	0	<0.01

Race* (cont.)	Population	%
Comanche (0)	0	<0.01
Cree (0)	3	<0.01
Creek (0)	1	<0.01
Crow (0)	0	<0.01
Delaware (1)	1	<0.01
Hopi (0)	0	<0.01
Houma (0)	0	<0.01
Inupiat (Alaska Native) (0)	1	<0.01
Iroquois (21)	61	0.10
Kiowa (0)	0	<0.01
Lumbee (0)	2	<0.01
Menominee (0)	0	<0.01
Mexican American Ind. (8)	8	0.01
Navajo (0)	0	<0.01
Osage (0)	0	<0.01
Ottawa (0)	0	<0.01
Paiute (0)	0	<0.01
Pima (0)	0	<0.01
Potawatomi (1)	3	<0.01
Pueblo (0)	0	<0.01
Puget Sound Salish (0)	0	<0.01
Seminole (1)	5	0.01
Shoshone (0)	0	<0.01
Sioux (4)	11	0.02
South American Ind. (12)	17	0.03
Spanish American Ind. (0)	0	<0.01
Tlingit-Haida (Alaska Native) (0)	0	<0.01
Tohono O'Odham (0)	0	<0.01
Tsimshian (Alaska Native) (0)	0	<0.01
Ute (0)	0	<0.01
Yakama (0)	1	<0.01
Yaqui (0)	0	<0.01
Yuman (0)	0	<0.01
Yup'ik (Alaska Native) (0)	0	<0.01
Asian (1,002)	1,220	1.93
Not Hispanic (998)	1,192	1.89
Hispanic (4)	28	0.04
Bangladeshi (248)	279	0.44
Bhutanese (0)	0	<0.01
Burmese (0)	0	<0.01
Cambodian (3)	3	<0.01
Chinese, ex. Taiwanese (152)	198	0.31
Filipino (72)	105	0.17
Hmong (0)	0	<0.01
Indian (256)	315	0.50
Indonesian (4)	4	0.01
Japanese (59)	97	0.15
Korean (65)	82	0.13
Laotian (0)	1	<0.01
Malaysian (0)	0	<0.01
Nepalese (11)	11	0.02
Pakistani (28)	30	0.05
Sri Lankan (2)	2	<0.01
Taiwanese (0)	2	<0.01
Thai (7)	8	0.01
Vietnamese (33)	48	0.08
Hawaii Native/Pacific Islander (18)	45	0.07
Not Hispanic (15)	39	0.06
Hispanic (3)	6	0.01
Fijian (1)	1	<0.01
Guamanian/Chamorro (2)	3	<0.01
Marshallese (0)	0	<0.01
Native Hawaiian (2)	12	0.02
Samoan (3)	8	0.01
Tongan (0)	0	<0.01
White (57,136)	58,319	92.43
Not Hispanic (55,672)	56,690	89.85
Hispanic (1,464)	1,629	2.58

*Notes: † The Census 2010 population figure is used to calculate the percentages in the Hispanic Origin and Race categories. Ancestry percentages are based on the 2006-2010 American Community Survey population (not shown); ‡ Numbers in parentheses indicate the number of people reporting a single ancestry; * Numbers in parentheses indicate the number of persons reporting this race alone, not in combination with any other race; Please refer to the Explanation of Data for more information.*

Cortland County

Population: 49,336

Ancestry	Population	%
Afghan (0)	0	<0.01
African, Sub-Saharan (0)	0	<0.01
African (0)	0	<0.01
Cape Verdean (0)	0	<0.01
Ethiopian (0)	0	<0.01
Ghanaian (0)	0	<0.01
Kenyan (0)	0	<0.01
Liberian (0)	0	<0.01
Nigerian (0)	0	<0.01
Senegalese (0)	0	<0.01
Sierra Leonean (0)	0	<0.01
Somalian (0)	0	<0.01
South African (0)	0	<0.01
Sudanese (0)	0	<0.01
Ugandan (0)	0	<0.01
Zimbabwean (0)	0	<0.01
Other Sub-Saharan African (0)	0	<0.01
Albanian (0)	0	<0.01
Alsatian (0)	0	<0.01
American (2,591)	2,591	5.24
Arab (86)	252	0.51
Arab (5)	18	0.04
Egyptian (0)	0	<0.01
Iraqi (0)	0	<0.01
Jordanian (0)	0	<0.01
Lebanese (81)	207	0.42
Moroccan (0)	0	<0.01
Palestinian (0)	0	<0.01
Syrian (0)	27	0.05
Other Arab (0)	0	<0.01
Armenian (0)	0	<0.01
Assyrian/Chaldean/Syriac (3)	3	0.01
Australian (0)	0	<0.01
Austrian (9)	124	0.25
Basque (0)	0	<0.01
Belgian (16)	19	0.04
Brazilian (0)	13	0.03
British (49)	93	0.19
Bulgarian (0)	0	<0.01
Cajun (0)	0	<0.01
Canadian (72)	149	0.30
Carpatho Rusyn (0)	0	<0.01
Celtic (8)	19	0.04
Croatian (0)	39	0.08
Cypriot (0)	0	<0.01
Czech (15)	111	0.22
Czechoslovakian (4)	34	0.07
Danish (21)	78	0.16
Dutch (304)	1,860	3.76
Eastern European (30)	30	0.06
English (3,066)	7,856	15.89
Estonian (7)	7	0.01
European (795)	812	1.64
Finnish (0)	92	0.19
French, ex. Basque (326)	1,886	3.81
French Canadian (226)	647	1.31
German (2,599)	8,405	17.00
German Russian (0)	0	<0.01
Greek (49)	190	0.38
Guyanese (0)	0	<0.01
Hungarian (39)	146	0.30
Icelander (10)	10	0.02
Iranian (0)	2	<0.01
Irish (2,679)	8,790	17.77
Israeli (0)	0	<0.01
Italian (2,049)	5,160	10.43
Latvian (0)	2	<0.01
Lithuanian (8)	55	0.11
Luxemburger (6)	6	0.01
Macedonian (0)	0	<0.01
Maltese (3)	25	0.05
New Zealander (0)	0	<0.01
Northern European (176)	239	0.48
Norwegian (51)	265	0.54
Pennsylvania German (70)	97	0.20

	Population	%
Polish (615)	1,744	3.53
Portuguese (15)	28	0.06
Romanian (35)	75	0.15
Russian (75)	434	0.88
Scandinavian (25)	39	0.08
Scotch-Irish (176)	635	1.28
Scottish (356)	1,046	2.12
Serbian (0)	6	0.01
Slavic (18)	36	0.07
Slovak (13)	54	0.11
Slovene (0)	0	<0.01
Soviet Union (0)	0	<0.01
Swedish (71)	327	0.66
Swiss (24)	126	0.25
Turkish (50)	77	0.16
Ukrainian (151)	231	0.47
Welsh (95)	464	0.94
West Indian, ex. Hispanic (12)	34	0.07
Bahamian (0)	0	<0.01
Barbadian (0)	0	<0.01
Belizean (0)	0	<0.01
Bermudan (0)	0	<0.01
British West Indian (0)	0	<0.01
Dutch West Indian (0)	0	<0.01
Haitian (12)	25	0.05
Jamaican (0)	0	<0.01
Trinidadian/Tobagonian (0)	9	0.02
U.S. Virgin Islander (0)	0	<0.01
West Indian (0)	0	<0.01
Other West Indian (0)	0	<0.01
Yugoslavian (6)	13	0.03

Hispanic Origin	Population	%
Hispanic or Latino (of any race)	1,094	2.22
Central American, ex. Mexican	64	0.13
Costa Rican	3	0.01
Guatemalan	40	0.08
Honduran	4	0.01
Nicaraguan	1	<0.01
Panamanian	4	0.01
Salvadoran	11	0.02
Other Central American	1	<0.01
Cuban	60	0.12
Dominican Republic	66	0.13
Mexican	207	0.42
Puerto Rican	458	0.93
South American	94	0.19
Argentinean	3	0.01
Bolivian	4	0.01
Chilean	6	0.01
Colombian	40	0.08
Ecuadorian	23	0.05
Paraguayan	0	<0.01
Peruvian	11	0.02
Uruguayan	4	0.01
Venezuelan	3	0.01
Other South American	0	<0.01
Other Hispanic or Latino	145	0.29

Race*	Population	%
African-American/Black (760)	1,131	2.29
Not Hispanic (705)	1,033	2.09
Hispanic (55)	98	0.20
American Indian/Alaska Native (137)	454	0.92
Not Hispanic (126)	405	0.82
Hispanic (11)	49	0.10
Alaska Athabascan (Ala. Nat.) (0)	0	<0.01
Aleut (Alaska Native) (0)	0	<0.01
Apache (1)	1	<0.01
Arapaho (0)	0	<0.01
Blackfeet (2)	15	0.03
Canadian/French Am. Ind. (2)	10	0.02
Central American Ind. (0)	0	<0.01
Cherokee (4)	47	0.10
Cheyenne (1)	1	<0.01
Chickasaw (0)	0	<0.01
Chippewa (0)	0	<0.01
Choctaw (0)	2	<0.01
Colville (0)	0	<0.01

	Population	%
Comanche (0)	0	<0.01
Cree (1)	2	<0.01
Creek (0)	0	<0.01
Crow (0)	0	<0.01
Delaware (0)	4	0.01
Hopi (0)	0	<0.01
Houma (0)	0	<0.01
Inupiat (Alaska Native) (0)	0	<0.01
Iroquois (43)	118	0.24
Kiowa (0)	0	<0.01
Lumbee (1)	1	<0.01
Menominee (0)	0	<0.01
Mexican American Ind. (2)	4	0.01
Navajo (2)	4	0.01
Osage (0)	0	<0.01
Ottawa (0)	0	<0.01
Paiute (0)	0	<0.01
Pima (0)	0	<0.01
Potawatomi (1)	2	<0.01
Pueblo (0)	0	<0.01
Puget Sound Salish (0)	0	<0.01
Seminole (0)	0	<0.01
Shoshone (0)	0	<0.01
Sioux (3)	8	0.02
South American Ind. (1)	1	<0.01
Spanish American Ind. (0)	0	<0.01
Tlingit-Haida (Alaska Native) (0)	0	<0.01
Tohono O'Odham (0)	0	<0.01
Tsimshian (Alaska Native) (0)	0	<0.01
Ute (0)	0	<0.01
Yakama (0)	0	<0.01
Yaqui (0)	0	<0.01
Yuman (0)	0	<0.01
Yup'ik (Alaska Native) (0)	0	<0.01
Asian (416)	575	1.17
Not Hispanic (412)	558	1.13
Hispanic (4)	17	0.03
Bangladeshi (7)	13	0.03
Bhutanese (0)	0	<0.01
Burmese (0)	0	<0.01
Cambodian (1)	1	<0.01
Chinese, ex. Taiwanese (104)	136	0.28
Filipino (40)	84	0.17
Hmong (0)	0	<0.01
Indian (109)	126	0.26
Indonesian (5)	9	0.02
Japanese (26)	60	0.12
Korean (61)	83	0.17
Laotian (9)	11	0.02
Malaysian (0)	1	<0.01
Nepalese (0)	0	<0.01
Pakistani (6)	6	0.01
Sri Lankan (2)	2	<0.01
Taiwanese (2)	3	0.01
Thai (1)	3	0.01
Vietnamese (22)	24	0.05
Hawaii Native/Pacific Islander (5)	30	0.06
Not Hispanic (3)	23	0.05
Hispanic (2)	7	0.01
Fijian (0)	0	<0.01
Guamanian/Chamorro (2)	2	<0.01
Marshallese (0)	0	<0.01
Native Hawaiian (0)	12	0.02
Samoan (0)	1	<0.01
Tongan (0)	1	<0.01
White (46,901)	47,697	96.68
Not Hispanic (46,252)	46,953	95.17
Hispanic (649)	744	1.51

Notes: † The Census 2010 population figure is used to calculate the percentages in the Hispanic Origin and Race categories. Ancestry percentages are based on the 2006-2010 American Community Survey population (not shown); ‡ Numbers in parentheses indicate the number of people reporting a single ancestry; * Numbers in parentheses indicate the number of persons reporting this race alone, not in combination with any other race; Please refer to the Explanation of Data for more information.

Delaware County

Population: 47,980

Ancestry	Population	%
Afghan (0)	0	<0.01
African, Sub-Saharan (16)	45	0.09
African (16)	45	0.09
Cape Verdean (0)	0	<0.01
Ethiopian (0)	0	<0.01
Ghanaian (0)	0	<0.01
Kenyan (0)	0	<0.01
Liberian (0)	0	<0.01
Nigerian (0)	0	<0.01
Senegalese (0)	0	<0.01
Sierra Leonean (0)	0	<0.01
Somalian (0)	0	<0.01
South African (0)	0	<0.01
Sudanese (0)	0	<0.01
Ugandan (0)	0	<0.01
Zimbabwean (0)	0	<0.01
Other Sub-Saharan African (0)	0	<0.01
Albanian (0)	0	<0.01
Alsatian (0)	0	<0.01
American (1,873)	1,873	3.88
Arab (15)	15	0.03
Arab (0)	0	<0.01
Egyptian (0)	0	<0.01
Iraqi (0)	0	<0.01
Jordanian (0)	0	<0.01
Lebanese (5)	5	0.01
Moroccan (0)	0	<0.01
Palestinian (0)	0	<0.01
Syrian (8)	8	0.02
Other Arab (2)	2	<0.01
Armenian (0)	24	0.05
Assyrian/Chaldean/Syriac (0)	0	<0.01
Australian (18)	23	0.05
Austrian (30)	217	0.45
Basque (0)	0	<0.01
Belgian (5)	19	0.04
Brazilian (9)	9	0.02
British (84)	152	0.32
Bulgarian (0)	3	0.01
Cajun (0)	0	<0.01
Canadian (40)	139	0.29
Carpatho Rusyn (0)	0	<0.01
Celtic (0)	0	<0.01
Croatian (11)	11	0.02
Cypriot (0)	0	<0.01
Czech (49)	235	0.49
Czechoslovakian (46)	88	0.18
Danish (93)	274	0.57
Dutch (498)	2,859	5.93
Eastern European (53)	69	0.14
English (2,101)	7,882	16.35
Estonian (16)	16	0.03
European (124)	124	0.26
Finnish (12)	76	0.16
French, ex. Basque (281)	2,275	4.72
French Canadian (73)	414	0.86
German (3,517)	13,135	27.24
German Russian (0)	0	<0.01
Greek (82)	197	0.41
Guyanese (0)	0	<0.01
Hungarian (61)	507	1.05
Icelander (0)	8	0.02
Iranian (10)	10	0.02
Irish (2,940)	10,183	21.12
Israeli (0)	0	<0.01
Italian (2,129)	5,867	12.17
Latvian (4)	16	0.03
Lithuanian (27)	117	0.24
Luxemburger (0)	0	<0.01
Macedonian (4)	7	0.01
Maltese (5)	5	0.01
New Zealander (0)	0	<0.01
Northern European (61)	61	0.13
Norwegian (144)	542	1.12
Pennsylvania German (6)	43	0.09

Ancestry	Population	%
Polish (605)	2,189	4.54
Portuguese (22)	108	0.22
Romanian (77)	113	0.23
Russian (143)	490	1.02
Scandinavian (26)	87	0.18
Scotch-Irish (505)	1,432	2.97
Scottish (756)	2,831	5.87
Serbian (0)	0	<0.01
Slavic (13)	65	0.13
Slovak (63)	285	0.59
Slovene (20)	26	0.05
Soviet Union (0)	0	<0.01
Swedish (94)	1,011	2.10
Swiss (28)	176	0.36
Turkish (73)	78	0.16
Ukrainian (49)	124	0.26
Welsh (112)	628	1.30
West Indian, ex. Hispanic (113)	189	0.39
Bahamian (0)	0	<0.01
Barbadian (0)	9	0.02
Belizean (0)	0	<0.01
Bermudan (0)	0	<0.01
British West Indian (0)	29	0.06
Dutch West Indian (0)	0	<0.01
Haitian (30)	33	0.07
Jamaican (40)	65	0.13
Trinidadian/Tobagonian (0)	0	<0.01
U.S. Virgin Islander (28)	28	0.06
West Indian (15)	25	0.05
Other West Indian (0)	0	<0.01
Yugoslavian (53)	103	0.21

Hispanic Origin	Population	%
Hispanic or Latino (of any race)	1,560	3.25
Central American, ex. Mexican	66	0.14
Costa Rican	7	0.01
Guatemalan	19	0.04
Honduran	11	0.02
Nicaraguan	2	<0.01
Panamanian	9	0.02
Salvadoran	18	0.04
Other Central American	0	<0.01
Cuban	70	0.15
Dominican Republic	95	0.20
Mexican	381	0.79
Puerto Rican	659	1.37
South American	104	0.22
Argentinean	18	0.04
Bolivian	0	<0.01
Chilean	15	0.03
Colombian	38	0.08
Ecuadorian	14	0.03
Paraguayan	0	<0.01
Peruvian	9	0.02
Uruguayan	4	0.01
Venezuelan	6	0.01
Other South American	0	<0.01
Other Hispanic or Latino	185	0.39

Race*	Population	%
African-American/Black (779)	1,040	2.17
Not Hispanic (691)	923	1.92
Hispanic (88)	117	0.24
American Indian/Alaska Native (131)	366	0.76
Not Hispanic (102)	314	0.65
Hispanic (29)	52	0.11
Alaska Athabascan (Ala. Nat.) (0)	0	<0.01
Aleut (Alaska Native) (0)	0	<0.01
Apache (0)	0	<0.01
Arapaho (0)	0	<0.01
Blackfeet (1)	14	0.03
Canadian/French Am. Ind. (0)	0	<0.01
Central American Ind. (3)	3	0.01
Cherokee (7)	49	0.10
Cheyenne (1)	1	<0.01
Chickasaw (0)	0	<0.01
Chippewa (8)	8	0.02
Choctaw (0)	4	0.01
Colville (0)	1	<0.01

	Population	%
Comanche (0)	0	<0.01
Cree (0)	1	<0.01
Creek (0)	1	<0.01
Crow (0)	1	<0.01
Delaware (2)	8	0.02
Hopi (0)	0	<0.01
Houma (0)	0	<0.01
Inupiat (Alaska Native) (0)	1	<0.01
Iroquois (18)	41	0.09
Kiowa (0)	2	<0.01
Lumbee (0)	0	<0.01
Menominee (0)	0	<0.01
Mexican American Ind. (1)	4	0.01
Navajo (3)	5	0.01
Osage (0)	0	<0.01
Ottawa (0)	0	<0.01
Paiute (0)	0	<0.01
Pima (0)	0	<0.01
Potawatomi (0)	1	<0.01
Pueblo (0)	0	<0.01
Puget Sound Salish (0)	0	<0.01
Seminole (0)	2	<0.01
Shoshone (1)	2	<0.01
Sioux (4)	7	0.01
South American Ind. (4)	7	0.01
Spanish American Ind. (0)	0	<0.01
Tlingit-Haida (Alaska Native) (1)	1	<0.01
Tohono O'Odham (0)	0	<0.01
Tsimshian (Alaska Native) (0)	0	<0.01
Ute (0)	0	<0.01
Yakama (0)	0	<0.01
Yaqui (0)	1	<0.01
Yuman (0)	0	<0.01
Yup'ik (Alaska Native) (0)	1	<0.01
Asian (367)	500	1.04
Not Hispanic (363)	483	1.01
Hispanic (4)	17	0.04
Bangladeshi (2)	2	<0.01
Bhutanese (3)	3	0.01
Burmese (2)	2	<0.01
Cambodian (2)	2	<0.01
Chinese, ex. Taiwanese (104)	136	0.28
Filipino (70)	101	0.21
Hmong (0)	0	<0.01
Indian (74)	101	0.21
Indonesian (1)	4	0.01
Japanese (45)	69	0.14
Korean (24)	29	0.06
Laotian (2)	8	0.02
Malaysian (0)	0	<0.01
Nepalese (1)	1	<0.01
Pakistani (9)	9	0.02
Sri Lankan (3)	3	0.01
Taiwanese (6)	6	0.01
Thai (0)	1	<0.01
Vietnamese (5)	11	0.02
Hawaii Native/Pacific Islander (12)	35	0.07
Not Hispanic (6)	24	0.05
Hispanic (6)	11	0.02
Fijian (0)	0	<0.01
Guamanian/Chamorro (6)	8	0.02
Marshallese (0)	0	<0.01
Native Hawaiian (2)	6	0.01
Samoan (0)	5	0.01
Tongan (0)	0	<0.01
White (45,675)	46,241	96.38
Not Hispanic (44,706)	45,191	94.19
Hispanic (969)	1,050	2.19

Notes: † The Census 2010 population figure is used to calculate the percentages in the Hispanic Origin and Race categories. Ancestry percentages are based on the 2006-2010 American Community Survey population (not shown); ‡ Numbers in parentheses indicate the number of people reporting a single ancestry; * Numbers in parentheses indicate the number of persons reporting this race alone, not in combination with any other race; Please refer to the Explanation of Data for more information.

Dutchess County

Population: 297,488

Ancestry	Population	%
Afghan (18)	18	0.01
African, Sub-Saharan (1,645)	2,652	0.90
African (874)	1,553	0.52
Cape Verdean (0)	0	<0.01
Ethiopian (0)	0	<0.01
Ghanaian (121)	121	0.04
Kenyan (32)	32	0.01
Liberian (0)	0	<0.01
Nigerian (383)	632	0.21
Senegalese (0)	12	<0.01
Sierra Leonean (0)	0	<0.01
Somalian (0)	0	<0.01
South African (50)	84	0.03
Sudanese (0)	0	<0.01
Ugandan (0)	0	<0.01
Zimbabwean (0)	0	<0.01
Other Sub-Saharan African (185)	218	0.07
Albanian (700)	799	0.27
Alsatian (0)	10	<0.01
American (7,260)	7,260	2.45
Arab (1,145)	2,373	0.80
Arab (118)	335	0.11
Egyptian (43)	131	0.04
Iraqi (0)	0	<0.01
Jordanian (552)	808	0.27
Lebanese (257)	562	0.19
Moroccan (65)	65	0.02
Palestinian (0)	183	0.06
Syrian (11)	53	0.02
Other Arab (99)	236	0.08
Armenian (116)	253	0.09
Assyrian/Chaldean/Syriac (0)	0	<0.01
Australian (40)	134	0.05
Austrian (398)	1,727	0.58
Basque (19)	32	0.01
Belgian (53)	345	0.12
Brazilian (93)	184	0.06
British (511)	1,357	0.46
Bulgarian (106)	139	0.05
Cajun (30)	61	0.02
Canadian (222)	656	0.22
Carpatho Rusyn (27)	38	0.01
Celtic (8)	46	0.02
Croatian (57)	338	0.11
Cypriot (9)	9	<0.01
Czech (443)	1,985	0.67
Czechoslovakian (129)	515	0.17
Danish (110)	914	0.31
Dutch (1,356)	8,775	2.96
Eastern European (414)	596	0.20
English (5,208)	28,099	9.49
Estonian (32)	50	0.02
European (1,482)	1,666	0.56
Finnish (113)	488	0.16
French, ex. Basque (1,230)	9,725	3.28
French Canadian (1,021)	2,977	1.01
German (9,511)	51,637	17.44
German Russian (0)	0	<0.01
Greek (1,086)	2,738	0.92
Guyanese (233)	263	0.09
Hungarian (969)	3,435	1.16
Icelander (7)	32	0.01
Iranian (97)	203	0.07
Irish (18,790)	70,744	23.89
Israeli (127)	217	0.07
Italian (29,305)	69,349	23.42
Latvian (212)	328	0.11
Lithuanian (335)	957	0.32
Luxemburger (0)	0	<0.01
Macedonian (57)	57	0.02
Maltese (53)	92	0.03
New Zealander (21)	53	0.02
Northern European (137)	198	0.07
Norwegian (521)	2,307	0.78
Pennsylvania German (16)	188	0.06
Polish (3,538)	14,799	5.00
Portuguese (589)	1,539	0.52
Romanian (130)	592	0.20
Russian (1,673)	5,793	1.96
Scandinavian (100)	252	0.09
Scotch-Irish (1,448)	4,218	1.42
Scottish (1,334)	5,831	1.97
Serbian (45)	132	0.04
Slavic (128)	319	0.11
Slovak (349)	888	0.30
Slovene (36)	94	0.03
Soviet Union (0)	0	<0.01
Swedish (627)	3,518	1.19
Swiss (289)	1,231	0.42
Turkish (67)	226	0.08
Ukrainian (470)	1,586	0.54
Welsh (180)	1,432	0.48
West Indian, ex. Hispanic (5,456)	7,721	2.61
Bahamian (0)	0	<0.01
Barbadian (0)	36	0.01
Belizean (53)	83	0.03
Bermudan (0)	0	<0.01
British West Indian (89)	117	0.04
Dutch West Indian (0)	0	<0.01
Haitian (257)	507	0.17
Jamaican (4,473)	5,581	1.88
Trinidadian/Tobagonian (250)	356	0.12
U.S. Virgin Islander (7)	55	0.02
West Indian (327)	986	0.33
Other West Indian (0)	0	<0.01
Yugoslavian (315)	617	0.21

Hispanic Origin	Population	%
Hispanic or Latino (of any race)	31,267	10.51
Central American, ex. Mexican	2,115	0.71
Costa Rican	135	0.05
Guatemalan	1,032	0.35
Honduran	333	0.11
Nicaraguan	86	0.03
Panamanian	159	0.05
Salvadoran	361	0.12
Other Central American	9	<0.01
Cuban	1,069	0.36
Dominican Republic	1,860	0.63
Mexican	7,575	2.55
Puerto Rican	11,984	4.03
South American	4,140	1.39
Argentinean	293	0.10
Bolivian	55	0.02
Chilean	179	0.06
Colombian	1,096	0.37
Ecuadorian	1,531	0.51
Paraguayan	48	0.02
Peruvian	576	0.19
Uruguayan	163	0.05
Venezuelan	149	0.05
Other South American	50	0.02
Other Hispanic or Latino	2,524	0.85

Race*	Population	%
African-American/Black (29,518)	33,599	11.29
Not Hispanic (27,395)	30,458	10.24
Hispanic (2,123)	3,141	1.06
American Indian/Alaska Native (893)	2,648	0.89
Not Hispanic (465)	1,829	0.61
Hispanic (428)	819	0.28
Alaska Athabascan (Ala. Nat.) (0)	0	<0.01
Aleut (Alaska Native) (3)	4	<0.01
Apache (4)	24	0.01
Arapaho (0)	0	<0.01
Blackfeet (20)	109	0.04
Canadian/French Am. Ind. (4)	7	<0.01
Central American Ind. (9)	32	0.01
Cherokee (43)	401	0.13
Cheyenne (2)	3	<0.01
Chickasaw (1)	4	<0.01
Chippewa (9)	18	0.01
Choctaw (4)	13	<0.01
Colville (1)	1	<0.01
Comanche (1)	2	<0.01
Cree (0)	3	<0.01
Creek (4)	13	<0.01
Crow (0)	5	<0.01
Delaware (1)	5	<0.01
Hopi (0)	2	<0.01
Houma (0)	0	<0.01
Inupiat (Alaska Native) (3)	3	<0.01
Iroquois (72)	215	0.07
Kiowa (0)	0	<0.01
Lumbee (5)	12	<0.01
Menominee (3)	4	<0.01
Mexican American Ind. (157)	200	0.07
Navajo (4)	17	0.01
Osage (3)	3	<0.01
Ottawa (2)	2	<0.01
Paiute (0)	1	<0.01
Pima (0)	0	<0.01
Potawatomi (0)	2	<0.01
Pueblo (0)	8	<0.01
Puget Sound Salish (0)	0	<0.01
Seminole (3)	24	0.01
Shoshone (0)	3	<0.01
Sioux (11)	45	0.02
South American Ind. (53)	115	0.04
Spanish American Ind. (3)	8	<0.01
Tlingit-Haida (Alaska Native) (0)	1	<0.01
Tohono O'Odham (2)	4	<0.01
Tsimshian (Alaska Native) (0)	0	<0.01
Ute (1)	2	<0.01
Yakama (2)	2	<0.01
Yaqui (0)	0	<0.01
Yuman (0)	0	<0.01
Yup'ik (Alaska Native) (0)	0	<0.01
Asian (10,437)	12,220	4.11
Not Hispanic (10,330)	11,925	4.01
Hispanic (107)	295	0.10
Bangladeshi (166)	190	0.06
Bhutanese (0)	0	<0.01
Burmese (51)	54	0.02
Cambodian (34)	49	0.02
Chinese, ex. Taiwanese (2,733)	3,188	1.07
Filipino (869)	1,215	0.41
Hmong (0)	0	<0.01
Indian (3,531)	3,939	1.32
Indonesian (26)	53	0.02
Japanese (367)	560	0.19
Korean (1,167)	1,331	0.45
Laotian (37)	44	0.01
Malaysian (14)	25	0.01
Nepalese (42)	43	0.01
Pakistani (370)	429	0.14
Sri Lankan (43)	59	0.02
Taiwanese (127)	144	0.05
Thai (74)	115	0.04
Vietnamese (450)	527	0.18
Hawaii Native/Pacific Islander (108)	356	0.12
Not Hispanic (80)	253	0.09
Hispanic (28)	103	0.03
Fijian (0)	1	<0.01
Guamanian/Chamorro (23)	44	0.01
Marshallese (0)	1	<0.01
Native Hawaiian (26)	79	0.03
Samoan (7)	17	0.01
Tongan (3)	8	<0.01
White (238,387)	244,919	82.33
Not Hispanic (221,812)	226,434	76.12
Hispanic (16,575)	18,485	6.21

*Notes: † The Census 2010 population figure is used to calculate the percentages in the Hispanic Origin and Race categories. Ancestry percentages are based on the 2006-2010 American Community Survey population (not shown); ‡ Numbers in parentheses indicate the number of people reporting a single ancestry; * Numbers in parentheses indicate the number of persons reporting this race alone, not in combination with any other race; Please refer to the Explanation of Data for more information.*

Erie County

Population: 919,040

Ancestry	Population	%
Afghan (430)	430	0.05
African, Sub-Saharan (6,954)	7,909	0.86
African (4,615)	5,206	0.57
Cape Verdean (95)	95	0.01
Ethiopian (307)	307	0.03
Ghanaian (83)	83	0.01
Kenyan (74)	136	0.01
Liberian (92)	107	0.01
Nigerian (302)	313	0.03
Senegalese (0)	18	<0.01
Sierra Leonean (17)	17	<0.01
Somalian (706)	858	0.09
South African (79)	92	0.01
Sudanese (259)	268	0.03
Ugandan (24)	33	<0.01
Zimbabwean (45)	45	<0.01
Other Sub-Saharan African (256)	331	0.04
Albanian (515)	763	0.08
Alsatian (50)	188	0.02
American (23,171)	23,171	2.52
Arab (5,684)	8,086	0.88
Arab (2,321)	2,545	0.28
Egyptian (73)	158	0.02
Iraqi (316)	318	0.03
Jordanian (95)	108	0.01
Lebanese (1,316)	3,012	0.33
Moroccan (34)	96	0.01
Palestinian (42)	42	<0.01
Syrian (116)	306	0.03
Other Arab (1,371)	1,501	0.16
Armenian (282)	517	0.06
Assyrian/Chaldean/Syriac (0)	0	<0.01
Australian (57)	153	0.02
Austrian (952)	4,008	0.44
Basque (9)	9	<0.01
Belgian (77)	354	0.04
Brazilian (323)	370	0.04
British (1,012)	2,544	0.28
Bulgarian (530)	715	0.08
Cajun (15)	26	<0.01
Canadian (1,587)	3,446	0.37
Carpatho Rusyn (6)	19	<0.01
Celtic (80)	132	0.01
Croatian (914)	2,803	0.30
Cypriot (17)	17	<0.01
Czech (414)	2,207	0.24
Czechoslovakian (396)	1,048	0.11
Danish (250)	1,162	0.13
Dutch (1,341)	9,750	1.06
Eastern European (1,072)	1,169	0.13
English (16,244)	70,914	7.70
Estonian (110)	316	0.03
European (3,832)	4,225	0.46
Finnish (213)	883	0.10
French, ex. Basque (2,539)	25,048	2.72
French Canadian (1,843)	6,635	0.72
German (68,487)	245,605	26.66
German Russian (61)	86	0.01
Greek (1,933)	4,465	0.48
Guyanese (616)	628	0.07
Hungarian (2,785)	9,692	1.05
Icelander (25)	37	<0.01
Iranian (318)	403	0.04
Irish (39,231)	163,985	17.80
Israeli (179)	302	0.03
Italian (65,466)	152,676	16.57
Latvian (130)	237	0.03
Lithuanian (369)	1,275	0.14
Luxemburger (0)	45	<0.01
Macedonian (326)	486	0.05
Maltese (21)	58	0.01
New Zealander (11)	37	<0.01
Northern European (318)	441	0.05
Norwegian (767)	2,897	0.31
Pennsylvania German (296)	680	0.07

Ancestry	Population	%
Polish (80,210)	174,651	18.96
Portuguese (349)	1,172	0.13
Romanian (392)	909	0.10
Russian (3,531)	8,992	0.98
Scandinavian (71)	489	0.05
Scotch-Irish (3,515)	10,370	1.13
Scottish (2,997)	14,392	1.56
Serbian (785)	1,550	0.17
Slavic (286)	741	0.08
Slovak (407)	1,584	0.17
Slovene (86)	261	0.03
Soviet Union (0)	0	<0.01
Swedish (1,594)	8,485	0.92
Swiss (267)	1,342	0.15
Turkish (457)	687	0.07
Ukrainian (3,183)	7,778	0.84
Welsh (957)	5,167	0.56
West Indian, ex. Hispanic (3,504)	4,339	0.47
Bahamian (34)	34	<0.01
Barbadian (38)	64	0.01
Belizean (0)	50	0.01
Bermudan (0)	0	<0.01
British West Indian (128)	141	0.02
Dutch West Indian (0)	17	<0.01
Haitian (679)	864	0.09
Jamaican (1,863)	2,179	0.24
Trinidadian/Tobagonian (299)	349	0.04
U.S. Virgin Islander (0)	0	<0.01
West Indian (463)	641	0.07
Other West Indian (0)	0	<0.01
Yugoslavian (890)	1,263	0.14

Hispanic Origin	Population	%
Hispanic or Latino (of any race)	41,731	4.54
Central American, ex. Mexican	1,034	0.11
Costa Rican	89	0.01
Guatemalan	305	0.03
Honduran	140	0.02
Nicaraguan	58	0.01
Panamanian	200	0.02
Salvadoran	224	0.02
Other Central American	18	<0.01
Cuban	1,214	0.13
Dominican Republic	1,179	0.13
Mexican	3,992	0.43
Puerto Rican	29,400	3.20
South American	1,831	0.20
Argentinean	229	0.02
Bolivian	77	0.01
Chilean	113	0.01
Colombian	684	0.07
Ecuadorian	282	0.03
Paraguayan	27	<0.01
Peruvian	245	0.03
Uruguayan	13	<0.01
Venezuelan	136	0.01
Other South American	25	<0.01
Other Hispanic or Latino	3,081	0.34

Race*	Population	%
African-American/Black (123,931)	133,049	14.48
Not Hispanic (119,916)	127,397	13.86
Hispanic (4,015)	5,652	0.61
American Indian/Alaska Native (5,908)	10,110	1.10
Not Hispanic (5,199)	8,799	0.96
Hispanic (709)	1,311	0.14
Alaska Athabascan (Ala. Nat.) (1)	3	<0.01
Aleut (Alaska Native) (0)	0	<0.01
Apache (7)	26	<0.01
Arapaho (1)	2	<0.01
Blackfeet (22)	188	0.02
Canadian/French Am. Ind. (84)	141	0.02
Central American Ind. (14)	24	<0.01
Cherokee (87)	579	0.06
Cheyenne (0)	5	<0.01
Chickasaw (2)	3	<0.01
Chippewa (60)	105	0.01
Choctaw (12)	44	<0.01
Colville (0)	0	<0.01

	Population	%
Comanche (2)	6	<0.01
Cree (2)	9	<0.01
Creek (8)	23	<0.01
Crow (4)	12	<0.01
Delaware (13)	24	<0.01
Hopi (4)	9	<0.01
Houma (1)	2	<0.01
Inupiat (Alaska Native) (3)	9	<0.01
Iroquois (3,416)	4,481	0.49
Kiowa (1)	1	<0.01
Lumbee (3)	10	<0.01
Menominee (3)	8	<0.01
Mexican American Ind. (63)	90	0.01
Navajo (25)	43	<0.01
Osage (6)	6	<0.01
Ottawa (1)	4	<0.01
Paiute (7)	9	<0.01
Pima (1)	4	<0.01
Potawatomi (8)	16	<0.01
Pueblo (5)	12	<0.01
Puget Sound Salish (1)	2	<0.01
Seminole (3)	40	<0.01
Shoshone (0)	0	<0.01
Sioux (39)	78	0.01
South American Ind. (41)	110	0.01
Spanish American Ind. (20)	27	<0.01
Tlingit-Haida (Alaska Native) (3)	6	<0.01
Tohono O'Odham (3)	5	<0.01
Tsimshian (Alaska Native) (0)	0	<0.01
Ute (0)	0	<0.01
Yakama (0)	0	<0.01
Yaqui (3)	3	<0.01
Yuman (2)	2	<0.01
Yup'ik (Alaska Native) (1)	3	<0.01
Asian (23,789)	27,624	3.01
Not Hispanic (23,621)	27,176	2.96
Hispanic (168)	448	0.05
Bangladeshi (217)	260	0.03
Bhutanese (298)	370	0.04
Burmese (2,313)	2,414	0.26
Cambodian (88)	102	0.01
Chinese, ex. Taiwanese (4,978)	5,566	0.61
Filipino (928)	1,490	0.16
Hmong (6)	8	<0.01
Indian (6,796)	7,576	0.82
Indonesian (65)	103	0.01
Japanese (490)	838	0.09
Korean (2,356)	2,775	0.30
Laotian (369)	445	0.05
Malaysian (82)	97	0.01
Nepalese (140)	185	0.02
Pakistani (1,014)	1,159	0.13
Sri Lankan (198)	219	0.02
Taiwanese (241)	285	0.03
Thai (176)	281	0.03
Vietnamese (2,037)	2,256	0.25
Hawaii Native/Pacific Islander (219)	714	0.08
Not Hispanic (165)	552	0.06
Hispanic (54)	162	0.02
Fijian (6)	6	<0.01
Guamanian/Chamorro (40)	88	0.01
Marshallese (1)	1	<0.01
Native Hawaiian (46)	185	0.02
Samoan (45)	112	0.01
Tongan (3)	4	<0.01
White (735,244)	749,229	81.52
Not Hispanic (714,156)	725,671	78.96
Hispanic (21,088)	23,558	2.56

*Notes: † The Census 2010 population figure is used to calculate the percentages in the Hispanic Origin and Race categories. Ancestry percentages are based on the 2006-2010 American Community Survey population (not shown); ‡ Numbers in parentheses indicate the number of people reporting a single ancestry; * Numbers in parentheses indicate the number of persons reporting this race alone, not in combination with any other race; Please refer to the Explanation of Data for more information.*

Essex County

Population: 39,370

Ancestry	Population	%
Afghan (0)	0	<0.01
African, Sub-Saharan (83)	96	0.24
African (55)	67	0.17
Cape Verdean (17)	18	0.05
Ethiopian (11)	11	0.03
Ghanaian (0)	0	<0.01
Kenyan (0)	0	<0.01
Liberian (0)	0	<0.01
Nigerian (0)	0	<0.01
Senegalese (0)	0	<0.01
Sierra Leonean (0)	0	<0.01
Somalian (0)	0	<0.01
South African (0)	0	<0.01
Sudanese (0)	0	<0.01
Ugandan (0)	0	<0.01
Zimbabwean (0)	0	<0.01
Other Sub-Saharan African (0)	0	<0.01
Albanian (35)	35	0.09
Alsatian (0)	0	<0.01
American (1,715)	1,715	4.35
Arab (110)	330	0.84
Arab (0)	0	<0.01
Egyptian (0)	0	<0.01
Iraqi (0)	0	<0.01
Jordanian (0)	0	<0.01
Lebanese (83)	157	0.40
Moroccan (21)	56	0.14
Palestinian (0)	74	0.19
Syrian (3)	22	0.06
Other Arab (3)	21	0.05
Armenian (35)	43	0.11
Assyrian/Chaldean/Syriac (0)	0	<0.01
Australian (0)	0	<0.01
Austrian (19)	86	0.22
Basque (0)	0	<0.01
Belgian (0)	18	0.05
Brazilian (0)	0	<0.01
British (94)	137	0.35
Bulgarian (0)	0	<0.01
Cajun (0)	0	<0.01
Canadian (156)	231	0.59
Carpatho Rusyn (0)	0	<0.01
Celtic (44)	60	0.15
Croatian (0)	0	<0.01
Cypriot (0)	0	<0.01
Czech (95)	225	0.57
Czechoslovakian (5)	28	0.07
Danish (34)	93	0.24
Dutch (213)	940	2.38
Eastern European (64)	82	0.21
English (1,732)	5,580	14.16
Estonian (0)	0	<0.01
European (206)	216	0.55
Finnish (4)	15	0.04
French, ex. Basque (2,335)	8,236	20.90
French Canadian (573)	921	2.34
German (1,511)	5,372	13.63
German Russian (0)	0	<0.01
Greek (83)	199	0.50
Guyanese (0)	10	0.03
Hungarian (171)	308	0.78
Icelander (0)	0	<0.01
Iranian (0)	0	<0.01
Irish (2,945)	8,753	22.21
Israeli (0)	40	0.10
Italian (1,513)	3,545	8.99
Latvian (5)	5	<0.01
Lithuanian (17)	44	0.11
Luxemburger (0)	0	<0.01
Macedonian (0)	0	<0.01
Maltese (0)	0	<0.01
New Zealander (0)	0	<0.01
Northern European (4)	4	0.01
Norwegian (33)	268	0.68
Pennsylvania German (0)	11	0.03

Ancestry	Population	%
Polish (383)	1,483	3.76
Portuguese (23)	27	0.07
Romanian (126)	183	0.46
Russian (310)	688	1.75
Scandinavian (9)	41	0.10
Scotch-Irish (249)	998	2.53
Scottish (340)	1,350	3.43
Serbian (9)	29	0.07
Slavic (0)	14	0.04
Slovak (75)	106	0.27
Slovene (0)	0	<0.01
Soviet Union (0)	0	<0.01
Swedish (112)	634	1.61
Swiss (13)	108	0.27
Turkish (0)	0	<0.01
Ukrainian (11)	53	0.13
Welsh (37)	424	1.08
West Indian, ex. Hispanic (75)	114	0.29
Bahamian (0)	0	<0.01
Barbadian (0)	0	<0.01
Belizean (0)	0	<0.01
Bermudan (0)	0	<0.01
British West Indian (0)	10	0.03
Dutch West Indian (0)	0	<0.01
Haitian (0)	0	<0.01
Jamaican (17)	17	0.04
Trinidadian/Tobagonian (11)	11	0.03
U.S. Virgin Islander (0)	0	<0.01
West Indian (47)	76	0.19
Other West Indian (0)	0	<0.01
Yugoslavian (0)	0	<0.01

Hispanic Origin	Population	%
Hispanic or Latino (of any race)	993	2.52
Central American, ex. Mexican	92	0.23
Costa Rican	7	0.02
Guatemalan	29	0.07
Honduran	15	0.04
Nicaraguan	3	0.01
Panamanian	7	0.02
Salvadoran	31	0.08
Other Central American	0	<0.01
Cuban	25	0.06
Dominican Republic	83	0.21
Mexican	355	0.90
Puerto Rican	296	0.75
South American	42	0.11
Argentinean	3	0.01
Bolivian	0	<0.01
Chilean	4	0.01
Colombian	16	0.04
Ecuadorian	0	<0.01
Paraguayan	0	<0.01
Peruvian	8	0.02
Uruguayan	4	0.01
Venezuelan	7	0.02
Other South American	0	<0.01
Other Hispanic or Latino	100	0.25

Race*	Population	%
African-American/Black (1,073)	1,213	3.08
Not Hispanic (982)	1,101	2.80
Hispanic (91)	112	0.28
American Indian/Alaska Native (126)	370	0.94
Not Hispanic (99)	327	0.83
Hispanic (27)	43	0.11
Alaska Athabascan (Ala. Nat.) (1)	3	0.01
Aleut (Alaska Native) (0)	0	<0.01
Apache (1)	2	0.01
Arapaho (0)	0	<0.01
Blackfeet (4)	19	0.05
Canadian/French Am. Ind. (3)	8	0.02
Central American Ind. (0)	1	<0.01
Cherokee (2)	22	0.06
Cheyenne (0)	1	<0.01
Chickasaw (0)	0	<0.01
Chippewa (1)	1	<0.01
Choctaw (2)	2	0.01
Colville (0)	0	<0.01

Race*	Population	%
Comanche (0)	6	0.02
Cree (0)	6	0.02
Creek (0)	0	<0.01
Crow (0)	0	<0.01
Delaware (0)	1	<0.01
Hopi (0)	1	<0.01
Houma (0)	0	<0.01
Inupiat (Alaska Native) (1)	1	<0.01
Iroquois (33)	101	0.26
Kiowa (0)	0	<0.01
Lumbee (2)	7	0.02
Menominee (0)	0	<0.01
Mexican American Ind. (13)	14	0.04
Navajo (3)	3	0.01
Osage (0)	0	<0.01
Ottawa (0)	0	<0.01
Paiute (0)	0	<0.01
Pima (0)	0	<0.01
Potawatomi (0)	0	<0.01
Pueblo (0)	1	<0.01
Puget Sound Salish (0)	0	<0.01
Seminole (0)	0	<0.01
Shoshone (0)	0	<0.01
Sioux (1)	8	0.02
South American Ind. (0)	1	<0.01
Spanish American Ind. (0)	0	<0.01
Tlingit-Haida (Alaska Native) (0)	0	<0.01
Tohono O'Odham (0)	0	<0.01
Tsimshian (Alaska Native) (0)	0	<0.01
Ute (0)	0	<0.01
Yakama (0)	0	<0.01
Yaqui (0)	1	<0.01
Yuman (0)	0	<0.01
Yup'ik (Alaska Native) (0)	0	<0.01
Asian (263)	324	0.82
Not Hispanic (260)	316	0.80
Hispanic (3)	8	0.02
Bangladeshi (0)	0	<0.01
Bhutanese (0)	0	<0.01
Burmese (0)	0	<0.01
Cambodian (5)	5	0.01
Chinese, ex. Taiwanese (63)	73	0.19
Filipino (36)	54	0.14
Hmong (0)	0	<0.01
Indian (33)	41	0.10
Indonesian (0)	0	<0.01
Japanese (21)	31	0.08
Korean (38)	46	0.12
Laotian (1)	1	<0.01
Malaysian (1)	1	<0.01
Nepalese (0)	0	<0.01
Pakistani (29)	30	0.08
Sri Lankan (0)	0	<0.01
Taiwanese (0)	0	<0.01
Thai (3)	6	0.02
Vietnamese (17)	19	0.05
Hawaii Native/Pacific Islander (9)	31	0.08
Not Hispanic (8)	28	0.07
Hispanic (1)	3	0.01
Fijian (0)	0	<0.01
Guamanian/Chamorro (1)	3	0.01
Marshallese (0)	0	<0.01
Native Hawaiian (5)	15	0.04
Samoan (0)	1	<0.01
Tongan (3)	3	0.01
White (37,100)	37,536	95.34
Not Hispanic (36,588)	36,969	93.90
Hispanic (512)	567	1.44

*Notes: † The Census 2010 population figure is used to calculate the percentages in the Hispanic Origin and Race categories. Ancestry percentages are based on the 2006-2010 American Community Survey population (not shown); ‡ Numbers in parentheses indicate the number of people reporting a single ancestry; * Numbers in parentheses indicate the number of persons reporting this race alone, not in combination with any other race; Please refer to the Explanation of Data for more information.*

Franklin County

Population: 51,599

Ancestry	Population	%
Afghan (0)	0	<0.01
African, Sub-Saharan (46)	191	0.37
African (46)	182	0.35
Cape Verdean (0)	0	<0.01
Ethiopian (0)	0	<0.01
Ghanaian (0)	0	<0.01
Kenyan (0)	0	<0.01
Liberian (0)	0	<0.01
Nigerian (0)	0	<0.01
Senegalese (0)	0	<0.01
Sierra Leonean (0)	0	<0.01
Somalian (0)	0	<0.01
South African (0)	9	0.02
Sudanese (0)	0	<0.01
Ugandan (0)	0	<0.01
Zimbabwean (0)	0	<0.01
Other Sub-Saharan African (0)	0	<0.01
Albanian (74)	74	0.14
Alsatian (0)	0	<0.01
American (3,069)	3,069	5.94
Arab (243)	285	0.55
Arab (12)	12	0.02
Egyptian (0)	0	<0.01
Iraqi (0)	0	<0.01
Jordanian (0)	0	<0.01
Lebanese (59)	82	0.16
Moroccan (80)	80	0.15
Palestinian (0)	0	<0.01
Syrian (13)	22	0.04
Other Arab (79)	89	0.17
Armenian (8)	8	0.02
Assyrian/Chaldean/Syriac (0)	0	<0.01
Australian (0)	14	0.03
Austrian (21)	143	0.28
Basque (0)	0	<0.01
Belgian (5)	22	0.04
Brazilian (5)	5	0.01
British (82)	128	0.25
Bulgarian (15)	15	0.03
Cajun (0)	0	<0.01
Canadian (249)	431	0.83
Carpatho Rusyn (0)	0	<0.01
Celtic (0)	7	0.01
Croatian (0)	14	0.03
Cypriot (0)	0	<0.01
Czech (10)	73	0.14
Czechoslovakian (0)	6	0.01
Danish (23)	138	0.27
Dutch (163)	1,095	2.12
Eastern European (13)	20	0.04
English (1,709)	5,133	9.93
Estonian (0)	0	<0.01
European (179)	191	0.37
Finnish (6)	18	0.03
French, ex. Basque (3,834)	11,336	21.93
French Canadian (1,852)	2,810	5.44
German (937)	4,795	9.28
German Russian (0)	0	<0.01
Greek (63)	144	0.28
Guyanese (99)	187	0.36
Hungarian (32)	205	0.40
Icelander (0)	0	<0.01
Iranian (0)	0	<0.01
Irish (2,541)	9,398	18.18
Israeli (0)	21	0.04
Italian (794)	2,508	4.85
Latvian (0)	0	<0.01
Lithuanian (12)	94	0.18
Luxemburger (0)	6	0.01
Macedonian (0)	0	<0.01
Maltese (0)	0	<0.01
New Zealander (0)	0	<0.01
Northern European (23)	38	0.07
Norwegian (35)	145	0.28
Pennsylvania German (58)	115	0.22

Ancestry	Population	%
Polish (407)	1,135	2.20
Portuguese (30)	60	0.12
Romanian (2)	18	0.03
Russian (101)	306	0.59
Scandinavian (22)	38	0.07
Scotch-Irish (293)	865	1.67
Scottish (326)	1,124	2.17
Serbian (0)	0	<0.01
Slavic (0)	0	<0.01
Slovak (18)	37	0.07
Slovene (9)	15	0.03
Soviet Union (0)	0	<0.01
Swedish (40)	285	0.55
Swiss (59)	159	0.31
Turkish (16)	22	0.04
Ukrainian (85)	200	0.39
Welsh (41)	336	0.65
West Indian, ex. Hispanic (27)	65	0.13
Bahamian (0)	0	<0.01
Barbadian (0)	0	<0.01
Belizean (0)	0	<0.01
Bermudan (0)	0	<0.01
British West Indian (0)	0	<0.01
Dutch West Indian (0)	0	<0.01
Haitian (0)	14	0.03
Jamaican (19)	35	0.07
Trinidadian/Tobagonian (8)	8	0.02
U.S. Virgin Islander (0)	0	<0.01
West Indian (0)	8	0.02
Other West Indian (0)	0	<0.01
Yugoslavian (0)	25	0.05

Hispanic Origin	Population	%
Hispanic or Latino (of any race)	1,506	2.92
Central American, ex. Mexican	123	0.24
Costa Rican	7	0.01
Guatemalan	25	0.05
Honduran	37	0.07
Nicaraguan	1	<0.01
Panamanian	26	0.05
Salvadoran	27	0.05
Other Central American	0	<0.01
Cuban	55	0.11
Dominican Republic	209	0.41
Mexican	211	0.41
Puerto Rican	730	1.41
South American	79	0.15
Argentinean	2	<0.01
Bolivian	0	<0.01
Chilean	2	<0.01
Colombian	24	0.05
Ecuadorian	24	0.05
Paraguayan	0	<0.01
Peruvian	18	0.03
Uruguayan	1	<0.01
Venezuelan	8	0.02
Other South American	0	<0.01
Other Hispanic or Latino	99	0.19

Race*	Population	%
African-American/Black (3,127)	3,262	6.32
Not Hispanic (2,834)	2,957	5.73
Hispanic (293)	305	0.59
American Indian/Alaska Native (3,797)	4,187	8.11
Not Hispanic (3,753)	4,124	7.99
Hispanic (44)	63	0.12
Alaska Athabascan (Ala. Nat.) (0)	0	<0.01
Aleut (Alaska Native) (0)	0	<0.01
Apache (3)	4	0.01
Arapaho (0)	1	<0.01
Blackfeet (2)	6	0.01
Canadian/French Am. Ind. (5)	10	0.02
Central American Ind. (0)	0	<0.01
Cherokee (17)	36	0.07
Cheyenne (0)	0	<0.01
Chickasaw (0)	0	<0.01
Chippewa (8)	10	0.02
Choctaw (0)	0	<0.01
Colville (1)	1	<0.01

	Population	%
Comanche (0)	0	<0.01
Cree (4)	4	0.01
Creek (1)	2	<0.01
Crow (0)	6	0.01
Delaware (7)	11	0.02
Hopi (0)	0	<0.01
Houma (0)	0	<0.01
Inupiat (Alaska Native) (0)	0	<0.01
Iroquois (2,928)	3,130	6.07
Kiowa (0)	0	<0.01
Lumbee (1)	1	<0.01
Menominee (0)	0	<0.01
Mexican American Ind. (8)	9	0.02
Navajo (6)	6	0.01
Osage (0)	0	<0.01
Ottawa (0)	0	<0.01
Paiute (1)	1	<0.01
Pima (0)	0	<0.01
Potawatomi (0)	0	<0.01
Pueblo (1)	1	<0.01
Puget Sound Salish (0)	0	<0.01
Seminole (0)	0	<0.01
Shoshone (1)	1	<0.01
Sioux (1)	1	<0.01
South American Ind. (13)	17	0.03
Spanish American Ind. (8)	8	0.02
Tlingit-Haida (Alaska Native) (0)	1	<0.01
Tohono O'Odham (0)	0	<0.01
Tsimshian (Alaska Native) (0)	0	<0.01
Ute (0)	0	<0.01
Yakama (0)	0	<0.01
Yaqui (1)	1	<0.01
Yuman (0)	0	<0.01
Yup'ik (Alaska Native) (1)	1	<0.01
Asian (219)	323	0.63
Not Hispanic (215)	307	0.59
Hispanic (4)	16	0.03
Bangladeshi (2)	2	<0.01
Bhutanese (0)	0	<0.01
Burmese (0)	0	<0.01
Cambodian (2)	2	<0.01
Chinese, ex. Taiwanese (61)	70	0.14
Filipino (36)	83	0.16
Hmong (0)	0	<0.01
Indian (51)	64	0.12
Indonesian (0)	8	0.02
Japanese (6)	11	0.02
Korean (18)	34	0.07
Laotian (0)	3	0.01
Malaysian (0)	0	<0.01
Nepalese (0)	0	<0.01
Pakistani (2)	2	<0.01
Sri Lankan (0)	0	<0.01
Taiwanese (0)	0	<0.01
Thai (3)	6	0.01
Vietnamese (4)	13	0.03
Hawaii Native/Pacific Islander (10)	23	0.04
Not Hispanic (8)	19	0.04
Hispanic (2)	4	0.01
Fijian (0)	0	<0.01
Guamanian/Chamorro (1)	5	0.01
Marshallese (0)	0	<0.01
Native Hawaiian (0)	3	0.01
Samoan (1)	2	<0.01
Tongan (7)	7	0.01
White (43,437)	44,021	85.31
Not Hispanic (42,640)	43,177	83.68
Hispanic (797)	844	1.64

Notes: † The Census 2010 population figure is used to calculate the percentages in the Hispanic Origin and Race categories. Ancestry percentages are based on the 2006-2010 American Community Survey population (not shown); ‡ Numbers in parentheses indicate the number of people reporting a single ancestry; * Numbers in parentheses indicate the number of persons reporting this race alone, not in combination with any other race; Please refer to the Explanation of Data for more information.

Fulton County
Population: 55,531

Ancestry	Population	%
Afghan (0)	0	<0.01
African, Sub-Saharan (23)	23	0.04
African (23)	23	0.04
Cape Verdean (0)	0	<0.01
Ethiopian (0)	0	<0.01
Ghanaian (0)	0	<0.01
Kenyan (0)	0	<0.01
Liberian (0)	0	<0.01
Nigerian (0)	0	<0.01
Senegalese (0)	0	<0.01
Sierra Leonean (0)	0	<0.01
Somalian (0)	0	<0.01
South African (0)	0	<0.01
Sudanese (0)	0	<0.01
Ugandan (0)	0	<0.01
Zimbabwean (0)	0	<0.01
Other Sub-Saharan African (0)	0	<0.01
Albanian (0)	0	<0.01
Alsatian (0)	0	<0.01
American (5,287)	5,287	9.53
Arab (38)	86	0.15
Arab (0)	0	<0.01
Egyptian (0)	0	<0.01
Iraqi (0)	0	<0.01
Jordanian (0)	0	<0.01
Lebanese (18)	57	0.10
Moroccan (0)	0	<0.01
Palestinian (0)	9	0.02
Syrian (0)	0	<0.01
Other Arab (20)	20	0.04
Armenian (37)	88	0.16
Assyrian/Chaldean/Syriac (0)	0	<0.01
Australian (0)	0	<0.01
Austrian (21)	81	0.15
Basque (0)	0	<0.01
Belgian (11)	35	0.06
Brazilian (2)	8	0.01
British (61)	162	0.29
Bulgarian (0)	15	0.03
Cajun (0)	0	<0.01
Canadian (162)	220	0.40
Carpatho Rusyn (0)	0	<0.01
Celtic (0)	0	<0.01
Croatian (0)	0	<0.01
Cypriot (0)	0	<0.01
Czech (67)	239	0.43
Czechoslovakian (74)	146	0.26
Danish (36)	125	0.23
Dutch (358)	3,774	6.80
Eastern European (32)	32	0.06
English (2,859)	7,912	14.26
Estonian (13)	13	0.02
European (146)	153	0.28
Finnish (13)	26	0.05
French, ex. Basque (486)	3,837	6.91
French Canadian (261)	694	1.25
German (2,540)	12,273	22.11
German Russian (0)	0	<0.01
Greek (34)	142	0.26
Guyanese (0)	0	<0.01
Hungarian (47)	284	0.51
Icelander (0)	0	<0.01
Iranian (142)	145	0.26
Irish (2,348)	10,129	18.25
Israeli (0)	0	<0.01
Italian (3,386)	8,675	15.63
Latvian (0)	25	0.05
Lithuanian (187)	469	0.85
Luxemburger (0)	0	<0.01
Macedonian (0)	0	<0.01
Maltese (0)	0	<0.01
New Zealander (0)	0	<0.01
Northern European (36)	36	0.06
Norwegian (33)	279	0.50
Pennsylvania German (15)	46	0.08

Ancestry (cont.)	Population	%
Polish (1,314)	4,092	7.37
Portuguese (17)	101	0.18
Romanian (0)	0	<0.01
Russian (78)	190	0.34
Scandinavian (0)	6	0.01
Scotch-Irish (155)	653	1.18
Scottish (226)	1,178	2.12
Serbian (0)	0	<0.01
Slavic (3)	40	0.07
Slovak (328)	666	1.20
Slovene (0)	4	0.01
Soviet Union (0)	0	<0.01
Swedish (84)	410	0.74
Swiss (0)	131	0.24
Turkish (0)	15	0.03
Ukrainian (248)	510	0.92
Welsh (55)	422	0.76
West Indian, ex. Hispanic (36)	72	0.13
Bahamian (0)	0	<0.01
Barbadian (0)	0	<0.01
Belizean (0)	0	<0.01
Bermudan (0)	0	<0.01
British West Indian (0)	0	<0.01
Dutch West Indian (0)	0	<0.01
Haitian (0)	0	<0.01
Jamaican (27)	36	0.06
Trinidadian/Tobagonian (0)	27	0.05
U.S. Virgin Islander (0)	0	<0.01
West Indian (9)	9	0.02
Other West Indian (0)	0	<0.01
Yugoslavian (98)	109	0.20

Hispanic Origin	Population	%
Hispanic or Latino (of any race)	1,263	2.27
Central American, ex. Mexican	51	0.09
Costa Rican	22	0.04
Guatemalan	5	0.01
Honduran	9	0.02
Nicaraguan	2	<0.01
Panamanian	11	0.02
Salvadoran	2	<0.01
Other Central American	0	<0.01
Cuban	30	0.05
Dominican Republic	68	0.12
Mexican	138	0.25
Puerto Rican	782	1.41
South American	54	0.10
Argentinean	8	0.01
Bolivian	1	<0.01
Chilean	1	<0.01
Colombian	19	0.03
Ecuadorian	13	0.02
Paraguayan	0	<0.01
Peruvian	11	0.02
Uruguayan	0	<0.01
Venezuelan	1	<0.01
Other South American	0	<0.01
Other Hispanic or Latino	140	0.25

Race*	Population	%
African-American/Black (1,060)	1,433	2.58
Not Hispanic (981)	1,315	2.37
Hispanic (79)	118	0.21
American Indian/Alaska Native (116)	356	0.64
Not Hispanic (104)	331	0.60
Hispanic (12)	25	0.05
Alaska Athabascan (Ala. Nat.) (0)	0	<0.01
Aleut (Alaska Native) (0)	0	<0.01
Apache (4)	7	0.01
Arapaho (0)	0	<0.01
Blackfeet (3)	18	0.03
Canadian/French Am. Ind. (3)	7	0.01
Central American Ind. (0)	0	<0.01
Cherokee (5)	29	0.05
Cheyenne (0)	0	<0.01
Chickasaw (1)	1	<0.01
Chippewa (0)	4	0.01
Choctaw (0)	0	<0.01
Colville (0)	0	<0.01

Race* (cont.)	Population	%
Comanche (0)	1	<0.01
Cree (0)	1	<0.01
Creek (1)	1	<0.01
Crow (0)	0	<0.01
Delaware (1)	2	<0.01
Hopi (0)	0	<0.01
Houma (0)	0	<0.01
Inupiat (Alaska Native) (0)	0	<0.01
Iroquois (37)	86	0.15
Kiowa (0)	0	<0.01
Lumbee (0)	0	<0.01
Menominee (0)	0	<0.01
Mexican American Ind. (3)	3	0.01
Navajo (3)	6	0.01
Osage (0)	0	<0.01
Ottawa (0)	0	<0.01
Paiute (0)	0	<0.01
Pima (0)	0	<0.01
Potawatomi (0)	0	<0.01
Pueblo (0)	0	<0.01
Puget Sound Salish (0)	0	<0.01
Seminole (0)	4	0.01
Shoshone (0)	0	<0.01
Sioux (0)	5	0.01
South American Ind. (0)	0	<0.01
Spanish American Ind. (0)	0	<0.01
Tlingit-Haida (Alaska Native) (0)	0	<0.01
Tohono O'Odham (0)	0	<0.01
Tsimshian (Alaska Native) (0)	0	<0.01
Ute (0)	0	<0.01
Yakama (0)	0	<0.01
Yaqui (0)	0	<0.01
Yuman (0)	0	<0.01
Yup'ik (Alaska Native) (0)	0	<0.01
Asian (321)	454	0.82
Not Hispanic (320)	444	0.80
Hispanic (1)	10	0.02
Bangladeshi (0)	0	<0.01
Bhutanese (0)	0	<0.01
Burmese (0)	0	<0.01
Cambodian (0)	1	<0.01
Chinese, ex. Taiwanese (71)	88	0.16
Filipino (44)	80	0.14
Hmong (0)	0	<0.01
Indian (82)	100	0.18
Indonesian (3)	7	0.01
Japanese (32)	47	0.08
Korean (45)	65	0.12
Laotian (0)	0	<0.01
Malaysian (1)	2	<0.01
Nepalese (0)	0	<0.01
Pakistani (3)	5	0.01
Sri Lankan (0)	0	<0.01
Taiwanese (2)	6	0.01
Thai (2)	2	<0.01
Vietnamese (20)	29	0.05
Hawaii Native/Pacific Islander (13)	61	0.11
Not Hispanic (11)	46	0.08
Hispanic (2)	15	0.03
Fijian (0)	0	<0.01
Guamanian/Chamorro (0)	0	<0.01
Marshallese (0)	0	<0.01
Native Hawaiian (4)	34	0.06
Samoan (0)	7	0.01
Tongan (0)	0	<0.01
White (52,948)	53,684	96.67
Not Hispanic (52,110)	52,773	95.03
Hispanic (838)	911	1.64

*Notes: † The Census 2010 population figure is used to calculate the percentages in the Hispanic Origin and Race categories. Ancestry percentages are based on the 2006-2010 American Community Survey population (not shown); ‡ Numbers in parentheses indicate the number of people reporting a single ancestry; * Numbers in parentheses indicate the number of persons reporting this race alone, not in combination with any other race; Please refer to the Explanation of Data for more information.*

Genesee County

Population: 60,079

Ancestry	Population	%
Afghan (0)	0	<0.01
African, Sub-Saharan (46)	142	0.24
African (46)	142	0.24
Cape Verdean (0)	0	<0.01
Ethiopian (0)	0	<0.01
Ghanaian (0)	0	<0.01
Kenyan (0)	0	<0.01
Liberian (0)	0	<0.01
Nigerian (0)	0	<0.01
Senegalese (0)	0	<0.01
Sierra Leonean (0)	0	<0.01
Somalian (0)	0	<0.01
South African (0)	0	<0.01
Sudanese (0)	0	<0.01
Ugandan (0)	0	<0.01
Zimbabwean (0)	0	<0.01
Other Sub-Saharan African (0)	0	<0.01
Albanian (0)	0	<0.01
Alsatian (0)	0	<0.01
American (2,398)	2,398	4.00
Arab (49)	75	0.13
Arab (17)	36	0.06
Egyptian (0)	0	<0.01
Iraqi (0)	0	<0.01
Jordanian (0)	0	<0.01
Lebanese (0)	0	<0.01
Moroccan (0)	0	<0.01
Palestinian (22)	22	0.04
Syrian (0)	0	<0.01
Other Arab (10)	17	0.03
Armenian (0)	0	<0.01
Assyrian/Chaldean/Syriac (0)	0	<0.01
Australian (0)	0	<0.01
Austrian (53)	141	0.24
Basque (0)	0	<0.01
Belgian (22)	55	0.09
Brazilian (0)	0	<0.01
British (84)	183	0.31
Bulgarian (0)	83	0.14
Cajun (0)	0	<0.01
Canadian (128)	244	0.41
Carpatho Rusyn (0)	0	<0.01
Celtic (0)	0	<0.01
Croatian (10)	61	0.10
Cypriot (0)	0	<0.01
Czech (36)	194	0.32
Czechoslovakian (38)	63	0.11
Danish (47)	85	0.14
Dutch (172)	1,821	3.04
Eastern European (7)	32	0.05
English (2,539)	10,461	17.45
Estonian (0)	0	<0.01
European (240)	272	0.45
Finnish (32)	56	0.09
French, ex. Basque (314)	2,447	4.08
French Canadian (213)	453	0.76
German (5,537)	19,568	32.64
German Russian (0)	0	<0.01
Greek (151)	285	0.48
Guyanese (172)	229	0.38
Hungarian (55)	370	0.62
Icelander (0)	2	<0.01
Iranian (0)	0	<0.01
Irish (2,577)	11,417	19.04
Israeli (0)	0	<0.01
Italian (4,677)	10,953	18.27
Latvian (0)	0	<0.01
Lithuanian (12)	71	0.12
Luxemburger (0)	0	<0.01
Macedonian (0)	0	<0.01
Maltese (0)	0	<0.01
New Zealander (0)	0	<0.01
Northern European (32)	32	0.05
Norwegian (46)	168	0.28
Pennsylvania German (6)	33	0.06

	Population	%
Polish (2,200)	6,848	11.42
Portuguese (26)	33	0.06
Romanian (26)	35	0.06
Russian (39)	181	0.30
Scandinavian (7)	14	0.02
Scotch-Irish (365)	1,105	1.84
Scottish (446)	1,321	2.20
Serbian (0)	19	0.03
Slavic (9)	30	0.05
Slovak (73)	123	0.21
Slovene (0)	9	0.02
Soviet Union (0)	0	<0.01
Swedish (135)	398	0.66
Swiss (37)	114	0.19
Turkish (21)	29	0.05
Ukrainian (75)	230	0.38
Welsh (81)	480	0.80
West Indian, ex. Hispanic (62)	94	0.16
Bahamian (0)	0	<0.01
Barbadian (0)	0	<0.01
Belizean (0)	0	<0.01
Bermudan (0)	0	<0.01
British West Indian (0)	0	<0.01
Dutch West Indian (0)	0	<0.01
Haitian (0)	16	0.03
Jamaican (17)	17	0.03
Trinidadian/Tobagonian (0)	16	0.03
U.S. Virgin Islander (0)	0	<0.01
West Indian (45)	45	0.08
Other West Indian (0)	0	<0.01
Yugoslavian (0)	11	0.02

Hispanic Origin	Population	%
Hispanic or Latino (of any race)	1,616	2.69
Central American, ex. Mexican	66	0.11
Costa Rican	0	<0.01
Guatemalan	36	0.06
Honduran	10	0.02
Nicaraguan	5	0.01
Panamanian	6	0.01
Salvadoran	9	0.01
Other Central American	0	<0.01
Cuban	24	0.04
Dominican Republic	49	0.08
Mexican	683	1.14
Puerto Rican	620	1.03
South American	65	0.11
Argentinean	6	0.01
Bolivian	7	0.01
Chilean	5	0.01
Colombian	21	0.03
Ecuadorian	14	0.02
Paraguayan	0	<0.01
Peruvian	5	0.01
Uruguayan	0	<0.01
Venezuelan	7	0.01
Other South American	0	<0.01
Other Hispanic or Latino	109	0.18

Race*	Population	%
African-American/Black (1,612)	2,243	3.73
Not Hispanic (1,491)	2,053	3.42
Hispanic (121)	190	0.32
American Indian/Alaska Native (679)	997	1.66
Not Hispanic (661)	949	1.58
Hispanic (18)	48	0.08
Alaska Athabascan (Ala. Nat.) (0)	0	<0.01
Aleut (Alaska Native) (0)	0	<0.01
Apache (1)	5	0.01
Arapaho (0)	0	<0.01
Blackfeet (0)	19	0.03
Canadian/French Am. Ind. (7)	9	0.01
Central American Ind. (1)	1	<0.01
Cherokee (10)	42	0.07
Cheyenne (0)	0	<0.01
Chickasaw (0)	0	<0.01
Chippewa (5)	8	0.01
Choctaw (3)	7	0.01
Colville (0)	0	<0.01

	Population	%
Comanche (1)	1	<0.01
Cree (0)	5	0.01
Creek (4)	4	0.01
Crow (0)	0	<0.01
Delaware (1)	2	<0.01
Hopi (1)	1	<0.01
Houma (0)	0	<0.01
Inupiat (Alaska Native) (0)	0	<0.01
Iroquois (267)	344	0.57
Kiowa (0)	0	<0.01
Lumbee (0)	0	<0.01
Menominee (0)	0	<0.01
Mexican American Ind. (1)	2	<0.01
Navajo (3)	4	0.01
Osage (0)	4	0.01
Ottawa (0)	0	<0.01
Paiute (0)	0	<0.01
Pima (0)	0	<0.01
Potawatomi (0)	0	<0.01
Pueblo (0)	0	<0.01
Puget Sound Salish (0)	0	<0.01
Seminole (0)	10	0.02
Shoshone (0)	0	<0.01
Sioux (3)	5	0.01
South American Ind. (2)	2	<0.01
Spanish American Ind. (0)	0	<0.01
Tlingit-Haida (Alaska Native) (0)	0	<0.01
Tohono O'Odham (0)	0	<0.01
Tsimshian (Alaska Native) (0)	0	<0.01
Ute (0)	0	<0.01
Yakama (0)	0	<0.01
Yaqui (0)	5	0.01
Yuman (0)	0	<0.01
Yup'ik (Alaska Native) (0)	0	<0.01
Asian (357)	494	0.82
Not Hispanic (355)	481	0.80
Hispanic (2)	13	0.02
Bangladeshi (2)	4	0.01
Bhutanese (0)	0	<0.01
Burmese (0)	0	<0.01
Cambodian (0)	1	<0.01
Chinese, ex. Taiwanese (72)	95	0.16
Filipino (50)	83	0.14
Hmong (0)	0	<0.01
Indian (84)	103	0.17
Indonesian (1)	3	<0.01
Japanese (43)	57	0.09
Korean (52)	76	0.13
Laotian (14)	17	0.03
Malaysian (0)	0	<0.01
Nepalese (0)	0	<0.01
Pakistani (10)	10	0.02
Sri Lankan (0)	0	<0.01
Taiwanese (0)	0	<0.01
Thai (5)	12	0.02
Vietnamese (6)	10	0.02
Hawaii Native/Pacific Islander (4)	27	0.04
Not Hispanic (2)	17	0.03
Hispanic (2)	10	0.02
Fijian (0)	0	<0.01
Guamanian/Chamorro (2)	4	0.01
Marshallese (0)	0	<0.01
Native Hawaiian (2)	12	0.02
Samoan (0)	1	<0.01
Tongan (0)	0	<0.01
White (55,787)	56,763	94.48
Not Hispanic (54,990)	55,842	92.95
Hispanic (797)	921	1.53

*Notes: † The Census 2010 population figure is used to calculate the percentages in the Hispanic Origin and Race categories. Ancestry percentages are based on the 2006-2010 American Community Survey population (not shown); ‡ Numbers in parentheses indicate the number of people reporting a single ancestry; * Numbers in parentheses indicate the number of persons reporting this race alone, not in combination with any other race; Please refer to the Explanation of Data for more information.*

Greene County

Population: 49,221

Ancestry	Population	%
Afghan (0)	0	<0.01
African, Sub-Saharan (114)	121	0.24
African (57)	64	0.13
Cape Verdean (5)	5	0.01
Ethiopian (8)	8	0.02
Ghanaian (44)	44	0.09
Kenyan (0)	0	<0.01
Liberian (0)	0	<0.01
Nigerian (0)	0	<0.01
Senegalese (0)	0	<0.01
Sierra Leonean (0)	0	<0.01
Somalian (0)	0	<0.01
South African (0)	0	<0.01
Sudanese (0)	0	<0.01
Ugandan (0)	0	<0.01
Zimbabwean (0)	0	<0.01
Other Sub-Saharan African (0)	0	<0.01
Albanian (80)	85	0.17
Alsatian (0)	0	<0.01
American (5,920)	5,920	11.98
Arab (66)	96	0.19
Arab (0)	0	<0.01
Egyptian (0)	0	<0.01
Iraqi (0)	0	<0.01
Jordanian (0)	0	<0.01
Lebanese (11)	30	0.06
Moroccan (0)	0	<0.01
Palestinian (0)	0	<0.01
Syrian (55)	66	0.13
Other Arab (0)	0	<0.01
Armenian (26)	46	0.09
Assyrian/Chaldean/Syriac (0)	0	<0.01
Australian (25)	25	0.05
Austrian (150)	313	0.63
Basque (0)	0	<0.01
Belgian (6)	6	0.01
Brazilian (10)	10	0.02
British (176)	231	0.47
Bulgarian (0)	0	<0.01
Cajun (0)	62	0.13
Canadian (123)	223	0.45
Carpatho Rusyn (0)	0	<0.01
Celtic (0)	0	<0.01
Croatian (41)	125	0.25
Cypriot (0)	0	<0.01
Czech (31)	170	0.34
Czechoslovakian (130)	181	0.37
Danish (75)	163	0.33
Dutch (675)	2,970	6.01
Eastern European (125)	134	0.27
English (1,220)	4,245	8.59
Estonian (0)	0	<0.01
European (695)	806	1.63
Finnish (1)	84	0.17
French, ex. Basque (341)	1,780	3.60
French Canadian (221)	536	1.08
German (2,656)	8,675	17.56
German Russian (0)	0	<0.01
Greek (180)	294	0.60
Guyanese (8)	8	0.02
Hungarian (183)	448	0.91
Icelander (0)	0	<0.01
Iranian (15)	15	0.03
Irish (3,244)	9,113	18.44
Israeli (9)	9	0.02
Italian (4,020)	8,909	18.03
Latvian (0)	31	0.06
Lithuanian (48)	98	0.20
Luxemburger (0)	3	0.01
Macedonian (0)	0	<0.01
Maltese (0)	0	<0.01
New Zealander (0)	0	<0.01
Northern European (10)	16	0.03
Norwegian (206)	423	0.86
Pennsylvania German (5)	18	0.04

Ancestry	Population	%
Polish (718)	2,469	5.00
Portuguese (32)	148	0.30
Romanian (67)	83	0.17
Russian (160)	484	0.98
Scandinavian (54)	87	0.18
Scotch-Irish (163)	554	1.12
Scottish (153)	674	1.36
Serbian (68)	86	0.17
Slavic (8)	79	0.16
Slovak (110)	155	0.31
Slovene (0)	0	<0.01
Soviet Union (0)	0	<0.01
Swedish (74)	340	0.69
Swiss (31)	103	0.21
Turkish (0)	0	<0.01
Ukrainian (279)	465	0.94
Welsh (19)	225	0.46
West Indian, ex. Hispanic (82)	118	0.24
Bahamian (0)	0	<0.01
Barbadian (0)	0	<0.01
Belizean (0)	0	<0.01
Bermudan (0)	0	<0.01
British West Indian (0)	0	<0.01
Dutch West Indian (0)	0	<0.01
Haitian (8)	8	0.02
Jamaican (57)	70	0.14
Trinidadian/Tobagonian (17)	17	0.03
U.S. Virgin Islander (0)	0	<0.01
West Indian (0)	23	0.05
Other West Indian (0)	0	<0.01
Yugoslavian (36)	106	0.21

Hispanic Origin	Population	%
Hispanic or Latino (of any race)	2,419	4.91
Central American, ex. Mexican	162	0.33
Costa Rican	10	0.02
Guatemalan	30	0.06
Honduran	22	0.04
Nicaraguan	5	0.01
Panamanian	12	0.02
Salvadoran	83	0.17
Other Central American	0	<0.01
Cuban	74	0.15
Dominican Republic	148	0.30
Mexican	343	0.70
Puerto Rican	1,298	2.64
South American	189	0.38
Argentinean	17	0.03
Bolivian	0	<0.01
Chilean	22	0.04
Colombian	72	0.15
Ecuadorian	28	0.06
Paraguayan	1	<0.01
Peruvian	26	0.05
Uruguayan	4	0.01
Venezuelan	17	0.03
Other South American	2	<0.01
Other Hispanic or Latino	205	0.42

Race*	Population	%
African-American/Black (2,826)	3,272	6.65
Not Hispanic (2,606)	3,010	6.12
Hispanic (220)	262	0.53
American Indian/Alaska Native (145)	406	0.82
Not Hispanic (122)	360	0.73
Hispanic (23)	46	0.09
Alaska Athabascan (Ala. Nat.) (0)	0	<0.01
Aleut (Alaska Native) (0)	0	<0.01
Apache (2)	10	0.02
Arapaho (0)	2	<0.01
Blackfeet (0)	5	0.01
Canadian/French Am. Ind. (0)	0	<0.01
Central American Ind. (1)	2	<0.01
Cherokee (5)	45	0.09
Cheyenne (0)	0	<0.01
Chickasaw (0)	0	<0.01
Chippewa (4)	6	0.01
Choctaw (2)	6	0.01
Colville (0)	0	<0.01

	Population	%
Comanche (0)	1	<0.01
Cree (0)	0	<0.01
Creek (0)	2	<0.01
Crow (0)	0	<0.01
Delaware (1)	4	0.01
Hopi (0)	0	<0.01
Houma (0)	0	<0.01
Inupiat (Alaska Native) (1)	2	<0.01
Iroquois (19)	46	0.09
Kiowa (0)	0	<0.01
Lumbee (1)	2	<0.01
Menominee (0)	0	<0.01
Mexican American Ind. (8)	8	0.02
Navajo (1)	1	<0.01
Osage (0)	0	<0.01
Ottawa (0)	0	<0.01
Paiute (0)	0	<0.01
Pima (0)	0	<0.01
Potawatomi (0)	0	<0.01
Pueblo (0)	0	<0.01
Puget Sound Salish (0)	0	<0.01
Seminole (1)	1	<0.01
Shoshone (0)	0	<0.01
Sioux (4)	14	0.03
South American Ind. (0)	1	<0.01
Spanish American Ind. (0)	0	<0.01
Tlingit-Haida (Alaska Native) (0)	0	<0.01
Tohono O'Odham (1)	2	<0.01
Tsimshian (Alaska Native) (0)	0	<0.01
Ute (0)	0	<0.01
Yakama (0)	1	<0.01
Yaqui (0)	0	<0.01
Yuman (0)	0	<0.01
Yup'ik (Alaska Native) (0)	0	<0.01
Asian (391)	523	1.06
Not Hispanic (382)	507	1.03
Hispanic (9)	16	0.03
Bangladeshi (0)	0	<0.01
Bhutanese (0)	0	<0.01
Burmese (5)	5	0.01
Cambodian (0)	0	<0.01
Chinese, ex. Taiwanese (127)	143	0.29
Filipino (45)	78	0.16
Hmong (0)	0	<0.01
Indian (72)	106	0.22
Indonesian (0)	0	<0.01
Japanese (23)	39	0.08
Korean (20)	27	0.05
Laotian (1)	1	<0.01
Malaysian (0)	0	<0.01
Nepalese (6)	6	0.01
Pakistani (25)	31	0.06
Sri Lankan (0)	3	0.01
Taiwanese (3)	3	0.01
Thai (6)	13	0.03
Vietnamese (20)	25	0.05
Hawaii Native/Pacific Islander (19)	43	0.09
Not Hispanic (15)	39	0.08
Hispanic (4)	4	0.01
Fijian (0)	0	<0.01
Guamanian/Chamorro (6)	8	0.02
Marshallese (0)	0	<0.01
Native Hawaiian (3)	11	0.02
Samoan (1)	2	<0.01
Tongan (0)	0	<0.01
White (44,440)	45,212	91.86
Not Hispanic (42,857)	43,514	88.41
Hispanic (1,583)	1,698	3.45

Hamilton County

Population: 4,836

Ancestry	Population	%
Afghan (0)	0	<0.01
African, Sub-Saharan (5)	5	0.10
African (5)	5	0.10
Cape Verdean (0)	0	<0.01
Ethiopian (0)	0	<0.01
Ghanaian (0)	0	<0.01
Kenyan (0)	0	<0.01
Liberian (0)	0	<0.01
Nigerian (0)	0	<0.01
Senegalese (0)	0	<0.01
Sierra Leonean (0)	0	<0.01
Somalian (0)	0	<0.01
South African (0)	0	<0.01
Sudanese (0)	0	<0.01
Ugandan (0)	0	<0.01
Zimbabwean (0)	0	<0.01
Other Sub-Saharan African (0)	0	<0.01
Albanian (10)	10	0.20
Alsatian (0)	0	<0.01
American (263)	263	5.36
Arab (7)	25	0.51
Arab (0)	11	0.22
Egyptian (0)	0	<0.01
Iraqi (0)	0	<0.01
Jordanian (0)	0	<0.01
Lebanese (3)	6	0.12
Moroccan (0)	0	<0.01
Palestinian (0)	0	<0.01
Syrian (4)	8	0.16
Other Arab (0)	0	<0.01
Armenian (0)	0	<0.01
Assyrian/Chaldean/Syriac (0)	0	<0.01
Australian (5)	10	0.20
Austrian (0)	18	0.37
Basque (0)	0	<0.01
Belgian (0)	0	<0.01
Brazilian (0)	0	<0.01
British (0)	5	0.10
Bulgarian (0)	0	<0.01
Cajun (0)	0	<0.01
Canadian (15)	30	0.61
Carpatho Rusyn (0)	0	<0.01
Celtic (0)	0	<0.01
Croatian (5)	5	0.10
Cypriot (0)	0	<0.01
Czech (5)	5	0.10
Czechoslovakian (2)	3	0.06
Danish (0)	5	0.10
Dutch (64)	275	5.60
Eastern European (3)	3	0.06
English (246)	1,011	20.60
Estonian (0)	0	<0.01
European (13)	13	0.26
Finnish (7)	7	0.14
French, ex. Basque (144)	524	10.68
French Canadian (77)	133	2.71
German (276)	1,057	21.54
German Russian (0)	0	<0.01
Greek (4)	9	0.18
Guyanese (21)	21	0.43
Hungarian (10)	14	0.29
Icelander (0)	0	<0.01
Iranian (0)	0	<0.01
Irish (506)	1,117	22.76
Israeli (0)	0	<0.01
Italian (176)	421	8.58
Latvian (3)	3	0.06
Lithuanian (2)	10	0.20
Luxemburger (0)	0	<0.01
Macedonian (0)	0	<0.01
Maltese (0)	0	<0.01
New Zealander (0)	0	<0.01
Northern European (21)	21	0.43
Norwegian (32)	79	1.61
Pennsylvania German (0)	4	0.08

Ancestry (cont.)	Population	%
Polish (118)	274	5.58
Portuguese (6)	6	0.12
Romanian (11)	11	0.22
Russian (18)	53	1.08
Scandinavian (0)	2	0.04
Scotch-Irish (50)	114	2.32
Scottish (70)	286	5.83
Serbian (0)	0	<0.01
Slavic (6)	6	0.12
Slovak (7)	7	0.14
Slovene (0)	0	<0.01
Soviet Union (0)	0	<0.01
Swedish (12)	64	1.30
Swiss (12)	19	0.39
Turkish (0)	0	<0.01
Ukrainian (2)	13	0.26
Welsh (19)	57	1.16
West Indian, ex. Hispanic (0)	0	<0.01
Bahamian (0)	0	<0.01
Barbadian (0)	0	<0.01
Belizean (0)	0	<0.01
Bermudan (0)	0	<0.01
British West Indian (0)	0	<0.01
Dutch West Indian (0)	0	<0.01
Haitian (0)	0	<0.01
Jamaican (0)	0	<0.01
Trinidadian/Tobagonian (0)	0	<0.01
U.S. Virgin Islander (0)	0	<0.01
West Indian (0)	0	<0.01
Other West Indian (0)	0	<0.01
Yugoslavian (0)	0	<0.01

Hispanic Origin	Population	%
Hispanic or Latino (of any race)	51	1.05
Central American, ex. Mexican	0	<0.01
Costa Rican	0	<0.01
Guatemalan	0	<0.01
Honduran	0	<0.01
Nicaraguan	0	<0.01
Panamanian	0	<0.01
Salvadoran	0	<0.01
Other Central American	0	<0.01
Cuban	2	0.04
Dominican Republic	3	0.06
Mexican	5	0.10
Puerto Rican	30	0.62
South American	5	0.10
Argentinean	0	<0.01
Bolivian	0	<0.01
Chilean	0	<0.01
Colombian	3	0.06
Ecuadorian	0	<0.01
Paraguayan	0	<0.01
Peruvian	0	<0.01
Uruguayan	0	<0.01
Venezuelan	0	<0.01
Other South American	2	0.04
Other Hispanic or Latino	6	0.12

Race*	Population	%
African-American/Black (35)	40	0.83
Not Hispanic (33)	38	0.79
Hispanic (2)	2	0.04
American Indian/Alaska Native (11)	58	1.20
Not Hispanic (11)	53	1.10
Hispanic (0)	5	0.10
Alaska Athabascan (Ala. Nat.) (0)	0	<0.01
Aleut (Alaska Native) (0)	0	<0.01
Apache (0)	1	0.02
Arapaho (0)	0	<0.01
Blackfeet (0)	2	0.04
Canadian/French Am. Ind. (0)	0	<0.01
Central American Ind. (0)	0	<0.01
Cherokee (1)	6	0.12
Cheyenne (0)	0	<0.01
Chickasaw (0)	0	<0.01
Chippewa (0)	0	<0.01
Choctaw (0)	1	0.02
Colville (0)	0	<0.01

Race* (cont.)	Population	%
Comanche (0)	0	<0.01
Cree (0)	0	<0.01
Creek (0)	0	<0.01
Crow (0)	1	0.02
Delaware (0)	0	<0.01
Hopi (0)	0	<0.01
Houma (0)	0	<0.01
Inupiat (Alaska Native) (0)	0	<0.01
Iroquois (5)	17	0.35
Kiowa (0)	0	<0.01
Lumbee (0)	0	<0.01
Menominee (0)	0	<0.01
Mexican American Ind. (0)	0	<0.01
Navajo (0)	0	<0.01
Osage (0)	0	<0.01
Ottawa (0)	0	<0.01
Paiute (0)	0	<0.01
Pima (0)	0	<0.01
Potawatomi (0)	0	<0.01
Pueblo (0)	0	<0.01
Puget Sound Salish (0)	0	<0.01
Seminole (0)	0	<0.01
Shoshone (0)	0	<0.01
Sioux (0)	1	0.02
South American Ind. (0)	2	0.04
Spanish American Ind. (0)	0	<0.01
Tlingit-Haida (Alaska Native) (0)	0	<0.01
Tohono O'Odham (0)	0	<0.01
Tsimshian (Alaska Native) (0)	0	<0.01
Ute (0)	0	<0.01
Yakama (0)	0	<0.01
Yaqui (0)	0	<0.01
Yuman (0)	0	<0.01
Yup'ik (Alaska Native) (0)	0	<0.01
Asian (24)	29	0.60
Not Hispanic (24)	27	0.56
Hispanic (0)	2	0.04
Bangladeshi (0)	0	<0.01
Bhutanese (0)	0	<0.01
Burmese (0)	0	<0.01
Cambodian (0)	0	<0.01
Chinese, ex. Taiwanese (4)	5	0.10
Filipino (7)	11	0.23
Hmong (0)	0	<0.01
Indian (3)	3	0.06
Indonesian (0)	0	<0.01
Japanese (1)	1	0.02
Korean (3)	3	0.06
Laotian (0)	0	<0.01
Malaysian (0)	0	<0.01
Nepalese (0)	0	<0.01
Pakistani (6)	6	0.12
Sri Lankan (0)	0	<0.01
Taiwanese (0)	0	<0.01
Thai (0)	0	<0.01
Vietnamese (0)	0	<0.01
Hawaii Native/Pacific Islander (4)	4	0.08
Not Hispanic (4)	4	0.08
Hispanic (0)	0	<0.01
Fijian (0)	0	<0.01
Guamanian/Chamorro (0)	0	<0.01
Marshallese (0)	0	<0.01
Native Hawaiian (4)	4	0.08
Samoan (0)	0	<0.01
Tongan (0)	0	<0.01
White (4,705)	4,755	98.33
Not Hispanic (4,664)	4,711	97.42
Hispanic (41)	44	0.91

*Notes: † The Census 2010 population figure is used to calculate the percentages in the Hispanic Origin and Race categories. Ancestry percentages are based on the 2006-2010 American Community Survey population (not shown); ‡ Numbers in parentheses indicate the number of people reporting a single ancestry; * Numbers in parentheses indicate the number of persons reporting this race alone, not in combination with any other race; Please refer to the Explanation of Data for more information.*

Herkimer County
Population: 64,519

Ancestry	Population	%
Afghan (0)	0	<0.01
African, Sub-Saharan (42)	131	0.20
African (42)	131	0.20
Cape Verdean (0)	0	<0.01
Ethiopian (0)	0	<0.01
Ghanaian (0)	0	<0.01
Kenyan (0)	0	<0.01
Liberian (0)	0	<0.01
Nigerian (0)	0	<0.01
Senegalese (0)	0	<0.01
Sierra Leonean (0)	0	<0.01
Somalian (0)	0	<0.01
South African (0)	0	<0.01
Sudanese (0)	0	<0.01
Ugandan (0)	0	<0.01
Zimbabwean (0)	0	<0.01
Other Sub-Saharan African (0)	0	<0.01
Albanian (0)	4	0.01
Alsatian (0)	11	0.02
American (3,518)	3,518	5.47
Arab (112)	348	0.54
Arab (53)	53	0.08
Egyptian (0)	0	<0.01
Iraqi (0)	0	<0.01
Jordanian (0)	0	<0.01
Lebanese (59)	276	0.43
Moroccan (0)	0	<0.01
Palestinian (0)	0	<0.01
Syrian (0)	19	0.03
Other Arab (0)	0	<0.01
Armenian (5)	12	0.02
Assyrian/Chaldean/Syriac (0)	5	0.01
Australian (0)	26	0.04
Austrian (66)	243	0.38
Basque (0)	0	<0.01
Belgian (4)	26	0.04
Brazilian (0)	0	<0.01
British (77)	170	0.26
Bulgarian (5)	42	0.07
Cajun (0)	0	<0.01
Canadian (49)	189	0.29
Carpatho Rusyn (8)	8	0.01
Celtic (0)	19	0.03
Croatian (0)	0	<0.01
Cypriot (0)	0	<0.01
Czech (165)	257	0.40
Czechoslovakian (70)	167	0.26
Danish (103)	365	0.57
Dutch (443)	2,912	4.53
Eastern European (38)	56	0.09
English (2,785)	8,608	13.38
Estonian (36)	36	0.06
European (176)	209	0.32
Finnish (3)	32	0.05
French, ex. Basque (681)	4,581	7.12
French Canadian (802)	1,567	2.44
German (3,471)	14,484	22.51
German Russian (0)	0	<0.01
Greek (99)	160	0.25
Guyanese (0)	0	<0.01
Hungarian (47)	187	0.29
Icelander (0)	6	0.01
Iranian (0)	0	<0.01
Irish (3,812)	14,052	21.84
Israeli (0)	7	0.01
Italian (5,689)	11,059	17.19
Latvian (0)	3	<0.01
Lithuanian (102)	219	0.34
Luxemburger (0)	0	<0.01
Macedonian (0)	6	0.01
Maltese (0)	0	<0.01
New Zealander (0)	0	<0.01
Northern European (27)	27	0.04
Norwegian (23)	152	0.24
Pennsylvania German (138)	141	0.22

Ancestry (cont.)	Population	%
Polish (1,884)	5,302	8.24
Portuguese (12)	36	0.06
Romanian (17)	51	0.08
Russian (242)	562	0.87
Scandinavian (9)	13	0.02
Scotch-Irish (171)	559	0.87
Scottish (231)	970	1.51
Serbian (0)	0	<0.01
Slavic (17)	48	0.07
Slovak (105)	255	0.40
Slovene (87)	165	0.26
Soviet Union (0)	0	<0.01
Swedish (89)	356	0.55
Swiss (155)	302	0.47
Turkish (0)	0	<0.01
Ukrainian (534)	990	1.54
Welsh (496)	2,032	3.16
West Indian, ex. Hispanic (3)	137	0.21
Bahamian (0)	0	<0.01
Barbadian (0)	0	<0.01
Belizean (0)	0	<0.01
Bermudan (0)	0	<0.01
British West Indian (0)	0	<0.01
Dutch West Indian (0)	0	<0.01
Haitian (0)	20	0.03
Jamaican (0)	108	0.17
Trinidadian/Tobagonian (3)	9	0.01
U.S. Virgin Islander (0)	0	<0.01
West Indian (0)	0	<0.01
Other West Indian (0)	0	<0.01
Yugoslavian (81)	129	0.20

Hispanic Origin	Population	%
Hispanic or Latino (of any race)	1,040	1.61
Central American, ex. Mexican	51	0.08
Costa Rican	12	0.02
Guatemalan	17	0.03
Honduran	4	0.01
Nicaraguan	2	<0.01
Panamanian	8	0.01
Salvadoran	8	0.01
Other Central American	0	<0.01
Cuban	32	0.05
Dominican Republic	48	0.07
Mexican	180	0.28
Puerto Rican	514	0.80
South American	76	0.12
Argentinean	9	0.01
Bolivian	9	0.01
Chilean	7	0.01
Colombian	12	0.02
Ecuadorian	10	0.02
Paraguayan	0	<0.01
Peruvian	15	0.02
Uruguayan	6	0.01
Venezuelan	3	<0.01
Other South American	5	0.01
Other Hispanic or Latino	139	0.22

Race*	Population	%
African-American/Black (700)	1,079	1.67
Not Hispanic (640)	976	1.51
Hispanic (60)	103	0.16
American Indian/Alaska Native (157)	398	0.62
Not Hispanic (137)	340	0.53
Hispanic (20)	58	0.09
Alaska Athabascan *(Ala. Nat.)* (0)	0	<0.01
Aleut *(Alaska Native)* (0)	0	<0.01
Apache (0)	1	<0.01
Arapaho (0)	0	<0.01
Blackfeet (2)	6	0.01
Canadian/French Am. Ind. (0)	2	<0.01
Central American Ind. (1)	1	<0.01
Cherokee (3)	33	0.05
Cheyenne (0)	0	<0.01
Chickasaw (0)	0	<0.01
Chippewa (2)	3	<0.01
Choctaw (0)	0	<0.01
Colville (0)	0	<0.01

Race* (cont.)	Population	%
Comanche (0)	0	<0.01
Cree (0)	0	<0.01
Creek (2)	2	<0.01
Crow (0)	1	<0.01
Delaware (1)	6	0.01
Hopi (0)	0	<0.01
Houma (0)	0	<0.01
Inupiat *(Alaska Native)* (4)	4	0.01
Iroquois (40)	89	0.14
Kiowa (0)	1	<0.01
Lumbee (0)	1	<0.01
Menominee (0)	0	<0.01
Mexican American Ind. (7)	7	0.01
Navajo (3)	3	<0.01
Osage (0)	0	<0.01
Ottawa (0)	0	<0.01
Paiute (0)	0	<0.01
Pima (0)	0	<0.01
Potawatomi (3)	3	<0.01
Pueblo (0)	0	<0.01
Puget Sound Salish (0)	0	<0.01
Seminole (0)	0	<0.01
Shoshone (0)	0	<0.01
Sioux (2)	13	0.02
South American Ind. (5)	6	0.01
Spanish American Ind. (0)	1	<0.01
Tlingit-Haida *(Alaska Native)* (3)	3	<0.01
Tohono O'Odham (1)	1	<0.01
Tsimshian *(Alaska Native)* (0)	0	<0.01
Ute (0)	1	<0.01
Yakama (0)	0	<0.01
Yaqui (4)	4	0.01
Yuman (0)	0	<0.01
Yup'ik *(Alaska Native)* (0)	0	<0.01
Asian (332)	445	0.69
Not Hispanic (325)	433	0.67
Hispanic (7)	12	0.02
Bangladeshi (0)	0	<0.01
Bhutanese (0)	0	<0.01
Burmese (0)	0	<0.01
Cambodian (3)	8	0.01
Chinese, ex. Taiwanese (68)	77	0.12
Filipino (73)	108	0.17
Hmong (0)	0	<0.01
Indian (76)	98	0.15
Indonesian (1)	1	<0.01
Japanese (35)	54	0.08
Korean (29)	40	0.06
Laotian (4)	6	0.01
Malaysian (0)	0	<0.01
Nepalese (0)	0	<0.01
Pakistani (1)	1	<0.01
Sri Lankan (0)	0	<0.01
Taiwanese (0)	0	<0.01
Thai (10)	13	0.02
Vietnamese (13)	18	0.03
Hawaii Native/Pacific Islander (11)	23	0.04
Not Hispanic (8)	18	0.03
Hispanic (3)	5	0.01
Fijian (0)	0	<0.01
Guamanian/Chamorro (4)	5	0.01
Marshallese (0)	0	<0.01
Native Hawaiian (4)	9	0.01
Samoan (1)	3	<0.01
Tongan (0)	0	<0.01
White (62,320)	63,066	97.75
Not Hispanic (61,690)	62,311	96.58
Hispanic (630)	755	1.17

*Notes: † The Census 2010 population figure is used to calculate the percentages in the Hispanic Origin and Race categories. Ancestry percentages are based on the 2006-2010 American Community Survey population (not shown); ‡ Numbers in parentheses indicate the number of people reporting a single ancestry; * Numbers in parentheses indicate the number of persons reporting this race alone, not in combination with any other race; Please refer to the Explanation of Data for more information.*

Jefferson County
Population: 116,229

Ancestry	Population	%
Afghan (0)	0	<0.01
African, Sub-Saharan (367)	470	0.41
African (316)	409	0.36
Cape Verdean (0)	0	<0.01
Ethiopian (7)	7	0.01
Ghanaian (15)	15	0.01
Kenyan (0)	0	<0.01
Liberian (0)	0	<0.01
Nigerian (0)	0	<0.01
Senegalese (14)	23	0.02
Sierra Leonean (0)	0	<0.01
Somalian (0)	0	<0.01
South African (15)	16	0.01
Sudanese (0)	0	<0.01
Ugandan (0)	0	<0.01
Zimbabwean (0)	0	<0.01
Other Sub-Saharan African (0)	0	<0.01
Albanian (0)	3	<0.01
Alsatian (0)	0	<0.01
American (6,079)	6,079	5.28
Arab (229)	384	0.33
Arab (0)	0	<0.01
Egyptian (80)	80	0.07
Iraqi (6)	6	0.01
Jordanian (6)	6	0.01
Lebanese (18)	129	0.11
Moroccan (99)	99	0.09
Palestinian (14)	14	0.01
Syrian (6)	50	0.04
Other Arab (0)	0	<0.01
Armenian (15)	50	0.04
Assyrian/Chaldean/Syriac (0)	0	<0.01
Australian (52)	56	0.05
Austrian (37)	208	0.18
Basque (0)	0	<0.01
Belgian (67)	246	0.21
Brazilian (31)	99	0.09
British (177)	345	0.30
Bulgarian (0)	0	<0.01
Cajun (8)	8	0.01
Canadian (624)	1,138	0.99
Carpatho Rusyn (0)	0	<0.01
Celtic (0)	11	0.01
Croatian (25)	94	0.08
Cypriot (0)	0	<0.01
Czech (40)	199	0.17
Czechoslovakian (84)	122	0.11
Danish (54)	172	0.15
Dutch (642)	3,044	2.65
Eastern European (60)	76	0.07
English (4,695)	14,861	12.91
Estonian (0)	0	<0.01
European (540)	609	0.53
Finnish (20)	51	0.04
French, ex. Basque (2,381)	12,941	11.25
French Canadian (1,909)	4,176	3.63
German (5,792)	22,170	19.27
German Russian (17)	17	0.01
Greek (191)	351	0.31
Guyanese (205)	228	0.20
Hungarian (305)	700	0.61
Icelander (0)	0	<0.01
Iranian (9)	9	0.01
Irish (7,451)	23,186	20.15
Israeli (0)	9	0.01
Italian (4,621)	12,267	10.66
Latvian (0)	0	<0.01
Lithuanian (18)	114	0.10
Luxemburger (0)	0	<0.01
Macedonian (7)	9	0.01
Maltese (0)	0	<0.01
New Zealander (0)	0	<0.01
Northern European (64)	73	0.06
Norwegian (299)	657	0.57
Pennsylvania German (42)	75	0.07

Ancestry	Population	%
Polish (1,233)	3,949	3.43
Portuguese (111)	356	0.31
Romanian (60)	107	0.09
Russian (277)	600	0.52
Scandinavian (51)	77	0.07
Scotch-Irish (698)	1,943	1.69
Scottish (1,255)	3,937	3.42
Serbian (0)	7	0.01
Slavic (35)	58	0.05
Slovak (22)	90	0.08
Slovene (0)	0	<0.01
Soviet Union (0)	0	<0.01
Swedish (200)	883	0.77
Swiss (32)	371	0.32
Turkish (94)	104	0.09
Ukrainian (205)	366	0.32
Welsh (99)	860	0.75
West Indian, ex. Hispanic (927)	1,171	1.02
Bahamian (0)	0	<0.01
Barbadian (197)	220	0.19
Belizean (35)	40	0.03
Bermudan (0)	0	<0.01
British West Indian (2)	2	<0.01
Dutch West Indian (0)	74	0.06
Haitian (154)	158	0.14
Jamaican (349)	401	0.35
Trinidadian/Tobagonian (30)	76	0.07
U.S. Virgin Islander (7)	7	0.01
West Indian (153)	193	0.17
Other West Indian (0)	0	<0.01
Yugoslavian (26)	31	0.03

Hispanic Origin	Population	%
Hispanic or Latino (of any race)	6,143	5.29
Central American, ex. Mexican	421	0.36
Costa Rican	20	0.02
Guatemalan	84	0.07
Honduran	56	0.05
Nicaraguan	43	0.04
Panamanian	143	0.12
Salvadoran	75	0.06
Other Central American	0	<0.01
Cuban	186	0.16
Dominican Republic	252	0.22
Mexican	2,211	1.90
Puerto Rican	2,202	1.89
South American	339	0.29
Argentinean	17	0.01
Bolivian	5	<0.01
Chilean	20	0.02
Colombian	115	0.10
Ecuadorian	84	0.07
Paraguayan	9	0.01
Peruvian	60	0.05
Uruguayan	1	<0.01
Venezuelan	24	0.02
Other South American	4	<0.01
Other Hispanic or Latino	532	0.46

Race*	Population	%
African-American/Black (5,876)	7,366	6.34
Not Hispanic (5,475)	6,724	5.79
Hispanic (401)	642	0.55
American Indian/Alaska Native (586)	1,483	1.28
Not Hispanic (500)	1,288	1.11
Hispanic (86)	195	0.17
Alaska Athabascan (Ala. Nat.) (5)	11	0.01
Aleut (Alaska Native) (6)	6	0.01
Apache (8)	29	0.02
Arapaho (0)	0	<0.01
Blackfeet (14)	49	0.04
Canadian/French Am. Ind. (5)	11	0.01
Central American Ind. (2)	4	<0.01
Cherokee (47)	201	0.17
Cheyenne (0)	1	<0.01
Chickasaw (3)	3	<0.01
Chippewa (9)	19	0.02
Choctaw (15)	34	0.03
Colville (0)	0	<0.01

	Population	%
Comanche (1)	1	<0.01
Cree (1)	5	<0.01
Creek (5)	10	0.01
Crow (0)	1	<0.01
Delaware (2)	7	0.01
Hopi (0)	1	<0.01
Houma (0)	0	<0.01
Inupiat (Alaska Native) (6)	8	0.01
Iroquois (154)	320	0.28
Kiowa (0)	0	<0.01
Lumbee (3)	3	<0.01
Menominee (1)	1	<0.01
Mexican American Ind. (11)	23	0.02
Navajo (25)	42	0.04
Osage (0)	3	<0.01
Ottawa (0)	0	<0.01
Paiute (0)	0	<0.01
Pima (0)	0	<0.01
Potawatomi (6)	6	0.01
Pueblo (9)	14	0.01
Puget Sound Salish (0)	1	<0.01
Seminole (2)	2	<0.01
Shoshone (0)	0	<0.01
Sioux (15)	40	0.03
South American Ind. (3)	14	0.01
Spanish American Ind. (2)	4	<0.01
Tlingit-Haida (Alaska Native) (0)	2	<0.01
Tohono O'Odham (0)	0	<0.01
Tsimshian (Alaska Native) (0)	0	<0.01
Ute (0)	1	<0.01
Yakama (0)	0	<0.01
Yaqui (0)	1	<0.01
Yuman (0)	0	<0.01
Yup'ik (Alaska Native) (4)	4	<0.01
Asian (1,518)	2,253	1.94
Not Hispanic (1,464)	2,110	1.82
Hispanic (54)	143	0.12
Bangladeshi (10)	10	0.01
Bhutanese (1)	4	<0.01
Burmese (1)	1	<0.01
Cambodian (17)	27	0.02
Chinese, ex. Taiwanese (171)	242	0.21
Filipino (496)	777	0.67
Hmong (2)	4	<0.01
Indian (133)	179	0.15
Indonesian (3)	11	0.01
Japanese (71)	190	0.16
Korean (357)	558	0.48
Laotian (7)	16	0.01
Malaysian (0)	0	<0.01
Nepalese (0)	0	<0.01
Pakistani (25)	31	0.03
Sri Lankan (1)	1	<0.01
Taiwanese (3)	3	<0.01
Thai (32)	69	0.06
Vietnamese (82)	125	0.11
Hawaii Native/Pacific Islander (298)	529	0.46
Not Hispanic (273)	464	0.40
Hispanic (25)	65	0.06
Fijian (3)	4	<0.01
Guamanian/Chamorro (103)	133	0.11
Marshallese (15)	15	0.01
Native Hawaiian (52)	157	0.14
Samoan (68)	99	0.09
Tongan (2)	2	<0.01
White (103,047)	105,977	91.18
Not Hispanic (99,682)	102,062	87.81
Hispanic (3,365)	3,915	3.37

Notes: † The Census 2010 population figure is used to calculate the percentages in the Hispanic Origin and Race categories. Ancestry percentages are based on the 2006-2010 American Community Survey population (not shown); ‡ Numbers in parentheses indicate the number of people reporting a single ancestry; * Numbers in parentheses indicate the number of persons reporting this race alone, not in combination with any other race; Please refer to the Explanation of Data for more information.

Kings County

Population: 2,504,700

Ancestry	Population	%
Afghan (335)	344	0.01
African, Sub-Saharan (30,768)	63,004	2.55
African (17,256)	48,168	1.95
Cape Verdean (106)	153	0.01
Ethiopian (283)	330	0.01
Ghanaian (3,692)	3,898	0.16
Kenyan (65)	77	<0.01
Liberian (392)	452	0.02
Nigerian (5,499)	6,033	0.24
Senegalese (401)	401	0.02
Sierra Leonean (147)	147	0.01
Somalian (234)	260	0.01
South African (204)	320	0.01
Sudanese (693)	731	0.03
Ugandan (29)	54	<0.01
Zimbabwean (99)	99	<0.01
Other Sub-Saharan African (1,668)	1,881	0.08
Albanian (6,490)	6,871	0.28
Alsatian (0)	27	<0.01
American (78,858)	78,858	3.20
Arab (29,346)	34,840	1.41
Arab (6,779)	7,609	0.31
Egyptian (4,705)	5,231	0.21
Iraqi (71)	134	0.01
Jordanian (714)	752	0.03
Lebanese (3,425)	4,757	0.19
Moroccan (2,156)	2,648	0.11
Palestinian (1,372)	1,482	0.06
Syrian (4,854)	5,890	0.24
Other Arab (5,270)	6,337	0.26
Armenian (1,798)	2,300	0.09
Assyrian/Chaldean/Syriac (22)	44	<0.01
Australian (539)	832	0.03
Austrian (1,677)	5,123	0.21
Basque (69)	129	0.01
Belgian (498)	1,012	0.04
Brazilian (1,257)	1,719	0.07
British (2,002)	4,749	0.19
Bulgarian (970)	1,128	0.05
Cajun (99)	175	0.01
Canadian (1,814)	3,116	0.13
Carpatho Rusyn (46)	53	<0.01
Celtic (16)	32	<0.01
Croatian (488)	998	0.04
Cypriot (37)	62	<0.01
Czech (759)	3,393	0.14
Czechoslovakian (793)	1,684	0.07
Danish (380)	1,267	0.05
Dutch (1,616)	5,664	0.23
Eastern European (11,912)	12,941	0.52
English (9,927)	32,407	1.31
Estonian (209)	340	0.01
European (25,194)	27,499	1.11
Finnish (303)	692	0.03
French, ex. Basque (3,484)	14,137	0.57
French Canadian (1,082)	2,974	0.12
German (12,299)	52,798	2.14
German Russian (29)	55	<0.01
Greek (10,688)	14,075	0.57
Guyanese (36,322)	38,963	1.58
Hungarian (17,858)	26,607	1.08
Icelander (69)	103	<0.01
Iranian (1,520)	1,822	0.07
Irish (32,255)	84,945	3.44
Israeli (7,062)	9,707	0.39
Italian (108,743)	152,814	6.19
Latvian (418)	667	0.03
Lithuanian (938)	2,676	0.11
Luxemburger (41)	58	<0.01
Macedonian (389)	498	0.02
Maltese (197)	362	0.01
New Zealander (71)	140	0.01
Northern European (905)	961	0.04
Norwegian (2,042)	5,982	0.24
Pennsylvania German (19)	59	<0.01

Ancestry	Population	%
Polish (41,882)	66,792	2.71
Portuguese (1,106)	2,882	0.12
Romanian (4,537)	8,046	0.33
Russian (69,188)	88,579	3.59
Scandinavian (512)	882	0.04
Scotch-Irish (1,997)	6,090	0.25
Scottish (2,407)	8,809	0.36
Serbian (288)	520	0.02
Slavic (289)	564	0.02
Slovak (1,164)	1,826	0.07
Slovene (55)	160	0.01
Soviet Union (185)	219	0.01
Swedish (1,240)	5,185	0.21
Swiss (473)	1,491	0.06
Turkish (4,449)	5,164	0.21
Ukrainian (21,703)	25,046	1.02
Welsh (345)	2,606	0.11
West Indian, ex. Hispanic (257,579)	306,541	12.43
Bahamian (195)	266	0.01
Barbadian (13,358)	14,916	0.60
Belizean (1,610)	2,026	0.08
Bermudan (16)	16	<0.01
British West Indian (28,123)	30,607	1.24
Dutch West Indian (289)	424	0.02
Haitian (67,083)	69,941	2.84
Jamaican (74,216)	80,999	3.28
Trinidadian/Tobagonian (42,450)	46,490	1.88
U.S. Virgin Islander (470)	558	0.02
West Indian (29,404)	59,844	2.43
Other West Indian (365)	454	0.02
Yugoslavian (2,305)	2,800	0.11

Hispanic Origin	Population	%
Hispanic or Latino (of any race)	496,285	19.81
Central American, ex. Mexican	46,119	1.84
Costa Rican	2,576	0.10
Guatemalan	9,160	0.37
Honduran	10,071	0.40
Nicaraguan	2,407	0.10
Panamanian	13,681	0.55
Salvadoran	7,737	0.31
Other Central American	487	0.02
Cuban	7,581	0.30
Dominican Republic	86,764	3.46
Mexican	94,585	3.78
Puerto Rican	176,528	7.05
South American	49,003	1.96
Argentinean	2,760	0.11
Bolivian	310	0.01
Chilean	1,026	0.04
Colombian	8,861	0.35
Ecuadorian	28,684	1.15
Paraguayan	230	0.01
Peruvian	4,222	0.17
Uruguayan	488	0.02
Venezuelan	1,916	0.08
Other South American	506	0.02
Other Hispanic or Latino	35,705	1.43

Race*	Population	%
African-American/Black (860,083)	896,165	35.78
Not Hispanic (799,066)	820,437	32.76
Hispanic (61,017)	75,728	3.02
American Indian/Alaska Native (13,524)	26,571	1.06
Not Hispanic (4,638)	12,062	0.48
Hispanic (8,886)	14,509	0.58
Alaska Athabascan (Ala. Nat.) (1)	5	<0.01
Aleut (Alaska Native) (4)	8	<0.01
Apache (46)	122	<0.01
Arapaho (2)	10	<0.01
Blackfeet (89)	531	0.02
Canadian/French Am. Ind. (42)	62	<0.01
Central American Ind. (616)	1,263	0.05
Cherokee (289)	1,903	0.08
Cheyenne (0)	10	<0.01
Chickasaw (9)	30	<0.01
Chippewa (23)	65	<0.01
Choctaw (30)	104	<0.01
Colville (1)	1	<0.01

	Population	%
Comanche (5)	19	<0.01
Cree (3)	15	<0.01
Creek (20)	81	<0.01
Crow (5)	19	<0.01
Delaware (5)	35	<0.01
Hopi (7)	12	<0.01
Houma (1)	3	<0.01
Inupiat (Alaska Native) (7)	21	<0.01
Iroquois (194)	381	0.02
Kiowa (1)	2	<0.01
Lumbee (6)	24	<0.01
Menominee (1)	4	<0.01
Mexican American Ind. (1,022)	1,363	0.05
Navajo (41)	93	<0.01
Osage (1)	3	<0.01
Ottawa (2)	5	<0.01
Paiute (0)	1	<0.01
Pima (0)	2	<0.01
Potawatomi (3)	11	<0.01
Pueblo (93)	169	0.01
Puget Sound Salish (1)	1	<0.01
Seminole (18)	92	<0.01
Shoshone (6)	23	<0.01
Sioux (29)	121	<0.01
South American Ind. (874)	1,855	0.07
Spanish American Ind. (290)	382	0.02
Tlingit-Haida (Alaska Native) (4)	28	<0.01
Tohono O'Odham (9)	10	<0.01
Tsimshian (Alaska Native) (0)	0	<0.01
Ute (0)	4	<0.01
Yakama (1)	3	<0.01
Yaqui (11)	19	<0.01
Yuman (5)	8	<0.01
Yup'ik (Alaska Native) (0)	1	<0.01
Asian (262,276)	284,489	11.36
Not Hispanic (260,129)	279,499	11.16
Hispanic (2,147)	4,990	0.20
Bangladeshi (10,667)	12,408	0.50
Bhutanese (5)	8	<0.01
Burmese (1,055)	1,260	0.05
Cambodian (613)	751	0.03
Chinese, ex. Taiwanese (171,214)	178,214	7.12
Filipino (7,930)	10,208	0.41
Hmong (14)	22	<0.01
Indian (26,144)	33,490	1.34
Indonesian (383)	564	0.02
Japanese (3,938)	5,917	0.24
Korean (6,904)	8,201	0.33
Laotian (82)	131	0.01
Malaysian (478)	708	0.03
Nepalese (355)	393	0.02
Pakistani (18,296)	19,840	0.79
Sri Lankan (219)	270	0.01
Taiwanese (857)	1,075	0.04
Thai (636)	883	0.04
Vietnamese (3,944)	5,041	0.20
Hawaii Native/Pacific Islander (1,243)	5,784	0.23
Not Hispanic (633)	3,463	0.14
Hispanic (610)	2,321	0.09
Fijian (20)	45	<0.01
Guamanian/Chamorro (386)	568	0.02
Marshallese (1)	2	<0.01
Native Hawaiian (208)	564	0.02
Samoan (72)	216	0.01
Tongan (5)	10	<0.01
White (1,072,041)	1,120,592	44.74
Not Hispanic (893,306)	917,717	36.64
Hispanic (178,735)	202,875	8.10

*Notes: † The Census 2010 population figure is used to calculate the percentages in the Hispanic Origin and Race categories. Ancestry percentages are based on the 2006-2010 American Community Survey population (not shown); ‡ Numbers in parentheses indicate the number of people reporting a single ancestry; * Numbers in parentheses indicate the number of persons reporting this race alone, not in combination with any other race; Please refer to the Explanation of Data for more information.*

Lewis County

Population: 27,087

Ancestry	Population	%
Afghan (0)	0	<0.01
African, Sub-Saharan (17)	30	0.11
African (17)	26	0.10
Cape Verdean (0)	0	<0.01
Ethiopian (0)	0	<0.01
Ghanaian (0)	0	<0.01
Kenyan (0)	0	<0.01
Liberian (0)	0	<0.01
Nigerian (0)	0	<0.01
Senegalese (0)	0	<0.01
Sierra Leonean (0)	0	<0.01
Somalian (0)	0	<0.01
South African (0)	4	0.01
Sudanese (0)	0	<0.01
Ugandan (0)	0	<0.01
Zimbabwean (0)	0	<0.01
Other Sub-Saharan African (0)	0	<0.01
Albanian (25)	25	0.09
Alsatian (13)	50	0.19
American (1,155)	1,155	4.28
Arab (79)	83	0.31
Arab (0)	0	<0.01
Egyptian (45)	45	0.17
Iraqi (0)	0	<0.01
Jordanian (0)	0	<0.01
Lebanese (13)	13	0.05
Moroccan (0)	0	<0.01
Palestinian (0)	0	<0.01
Syrian (0)	4	0.01
Other Arab (21)	21	0.08
Armenian (7)	7	0.03
Assyrian/Chaldean/Syriac (0)	0	<0.01
Australian (0)	0	<0.01
Austrian (5)	61	0.23
Basque (0)	0	<0.01
Belgian (0)	2	0.01
Brazilian (0)	0	<0.01
British (20)	58	0.21
Bulgarian (0)	0	<0.01
Cajun (4)	4	0.01
Canadian (61)	140	0.52
Carpatho Rusyn (0)	0	<0.01
Celtic (0)	0	<0.01
Croatian (24)	24	0.09
Cypriot (0)	0	<0.01
Czech (3)	14	0.05
Czechoslovakian (6)	8	0.03
Danish (30)	71	0.26
Dutch (146)	882	3.26
Eastern European (37)	37	0.14
English (757)	2,702	10.00
Estonian (0)	0	<0.01
European (62)	71	0.26
Finnish (0)	10	0.04
French, ex. Basque (708)	3,633	13.45
French Canadian (484)	788	2.92
German (2,964)	8,378	31.01
German Russian (0)	0	<0.01
Greek (7)	12	0.04
Guyanese (39)	39	0.14
Hungarian (212)	307	1.14
Icelander (0)	0	<0.01
Iranian (9)	9	0.03
Irish (1,034)	4,543	16.82
Israeli (0)	0	<0.01
Italian (617)	1,963	7.27
Latvian (0)	0	<0.01
Lithuanian (23)	26	0.10
Luxemburger (0)	0	<0.01
Macedonian (0)	0	<0.01
Maltese (0)	0	<0.01
New Zealander (0)	0	<0.01
Northern European (22)	22	0.08
Norwegian (51)	93	0.34
Pennsylvania German (0)	0	<0.01

Ancestry	Population	%
Polish (623)	1,338	4.95
Portuguese (0)	31	0.11
Romanian (5)	5	0.02
Russian (44)	98	0.36
Scandinavian (0)	0	<0.01
Scotch-Irish (205)	396	1.47
Scottish (161)	521	1.93
Serbian (0)	0	<0.01
Slavic (0)	0	<0.01
Slovak (5)	5	0.02
Slovene (0)	20	0.07
Soviet Union (0)	0	<0.01
Swedish (52)	137	0.51
Swiss (202)	630	2.33
Turkish (0)	0	<0.01
Ukrainian (6)	29	0.11
Welsh (128)	377	1.40
West Indian, ex. Hispanic (6)	41	0.15
Bahamian (0)	0	<0.01
Barbadian (0)	0	<0.01
Belizean (0)	0	<0.01
Bermudan (0)	0	<0.01
British West Indian (0)	0	<0.01
Dutch West Indian (0)	0	<0.01
Haitian (0)	0	<0.01
Jamaican (0)	35	0.13
Trinidadian/Tobagonian (0)	0	<0.01
U.S. Virgin Islander (0)	0	<0.01
West Indian (6)	6	0.02
Other West Indian (0)	0	<0.01
Yugoslavian (15)	18	0.07

Hispanic Origin	Population	%
Hispanic or Latino (of any race)	357	1.32
Central American, ex. Mexican	22	0.08
Costa Rican	1	<0.01
Guatemalan	8	0.03
Honduran	8	0.03
Nicaraguan	2	0.01
Panamanian	3	0.01
Salvadoran	0	<0.01
Other Central American	0	<0.01
Cuban	5	0.02
Dominican Republic	5	0.02
Mexican	171	0.63
Puerto Rican	98	0.36
South American	10	0.04
Argentinean	2	0.01
Bolivian	0	<0.01
Chilean	1	<0.01
Colombian	4	0.01
Ecuadorian	3	0.01
Paraguayan	0	<0.01
Peruvian	0	<0.01
Uruguayan	0	<0.01
Venezuelan	0	<0.01
Other South American	0	<0.01
Other Hispanic or Latino	46	0.17

Race*	Population	%
African-American/Black (184)	265	0.98
Not Hispanic (170)	230	0.85
Hispanic (14)	35	0.13
American Indian/Alaska Native (53)	157	0.58
Not Hispanic (44)	146	0.54
Hispanic (9)	11	0.04
Alaska Athabascan (Ala. Nat.) (0)	0	<0.01
Aleut (Alaska Native) (4)	4	0.01
Apache (2)	3	0.01
Arapaho (0)	0	<0.01
Blackfeet (1)	9	0.03
Canadian/French Am. Ind. (0)	2	0.01
Central American Ind. (2)	3	0.01
Cherokee (2)	17	0.06
Cheyenne (0)	0	<0.01
Chickasaw (0)	0	<0.01
Chippewa (0)	2	0.01
Choctaw (0)	0	<0.01
Colville (0)	0	<0.01

Race*	Population	%
Comanche (0)	0	<0.01
Cree (0)	1	<0.01
Creek (0)	0	<0.01
Crow (0)	0	<0.01
Delaware (0)	0	<0.01
Hopi (0)	0	<0.01
Houma (0)	0	<0.01
Inupiat (Alaska Native) (0)	0	<0.01
Iroquois (19)	37	0.14
Kiowa (0)	0	<0.01
Lumbee (0)	2	0.01
Menominee (0)	0	<0.01
Mexican American Ind. (0)	0	<0.01
Navajo (0)	1	<0.01
Osage (0)	0	<0.01
Ottawa (0)	0	<0.01
Paiute (0)	0	<0.01
Pima (0)	0	<0.01
Potawatomi (0)	0	<0.01
Pueblo (0)	0	<0.01
Puget Sound Salish (0)	0	<0.01
Seminole (0)	1	<0.01
Shoshone (0)	0	<0.01
Sioux (0)	3	0.01
South American Ind. (0)	0	<0.01
Spanish American Ind. (0)	0	<0.01
Tlingit-Haida (Alaska Native) (0)	0	<0.01
Tohono O'Odham (0)	0	<0.01
Tsimshian (Alaska Native) (0)	0	<0.01
Ute (0)	0	<0.01
Yakama (0)	0	<0.01
Yaqui (0)	0	<0.01
Yuman (0)	0	<0.01
Yup'ik (Alaska Native) (0)	0	<0.01
Asian (75)	114	0.42
Not Hispanic (72)	107	0.40
Hispanic (3)	7	0.03
Bangladeshi (0)	0	<0.01
Bhutanese (0)	0	<0.01
Burmese (0)	0	<0.01
Cambodian (3)	5	0.02
Chinese, ex. Taiwanese (14)	16	0.06
Filipino (25)	38	0.14
Hmong (0)	0	<0.01
Indian (8)	13	0.05
Indonesian (0)	0	<0.01
Japanese (3)	11	0.04
Korean (14)	22	0.08
Laotian (0)	0	<0.01
Malaysian (0)	0	<0.01
Nepalese (0)	0	<0.01
Pakistani (3)	4	0.01
Sri Lankan (1)	1	<0.01
Taiwanese (0)	0	<0.01
Thai (2)	5	0.02
Vietnamese (0)	1	<0.01
Hawaii Native/Pacific Islander (16)	30	0.11
Not Hispanic (16)	27	0.10
Hispanic (0)	3	0.01
Fijian (0)	0	<0.01
Guamanian/Chamorro (4)	4	0.01
Marshallese (0)	0	<0.01
Native Hawaiian (0)	7	0.03
Samoan (1)	3	0.01
Tongan (0)	0	<0.01
White (26,465)	26,686	98.52
Not Hispanic (26,225)	26,416	97.52
Hispanic (240)	270	1.00

*Notes: † The Census 2010 population figure is used to calculate the percentages in the Hispanic Origin and Race categories. Ancestry percentages are based on the 2006-2010 American Community Survey population (not shown); ‡ Numbers in parentheses indicate the number of people reporting a single ancestry; * Numbers in parentheses indicate the number of persons reporting this race alone, not in combination with any other race; Please refer to the Explanation of Data for more information.*

Livingston County

Population: 65,393

Ancestry	Population	%
Afghan (0)	0	<0.01
African, Sub-Saharan (206)	240	0.37
African (99)	132	0.20
Cape Verdean (0)	0	<0.01
Ethiopian (27)	27	0.04
Ghanaian (0)	0	<0.01
Kenyan (0)	0	<0.01
Liberian (0)	0	<0.01
Nigerian (0)	0	<0.01
Senegalese (12)	12	0.02
Sierra Leonean (0)	0	<0.01
Somalian (0)	0	<0.01
South African (64)	64	0.10
Sudanese (0)	0	<0.01
Ugandan (0)	0	<0.01
Zimbabwean (0)	0	<0.01
Other Sub-Saharan African (4)	5	0.01
Albanian (9)	9	0.01
Alsatian (0)	0	<0.01
American (3,367)	3,367	5.15
Arab (33)	163	0.25
Arab (3)	3	<0.01
Egyptian (0)	0	<0.01
Iraqi (0)	0	<0.01
Jordanian (0)	0	<0.01
Lebanese (17)	90	0.14
Moroccan (0)	0	<0.01
Palestinian (0)	0	<0.01
Syrian (13)	70	0.11
Other Arab (0)	0	<0.01
Armenian (0)	0	<0.01
Assyrian/Chaldean/Syriac (0)	0	<0.01
Australian (21)	24	0.04
Austrian (54)	201	0.31
Basque (0)	0	<0.01
Belgian (65)	105	0.16
Brazilian (0)	88	0.13
British (86)	243	0.37
Bulgarian (0)	0	<0.01
Cajun (0)	0	<0.01
Canadian (135)	235	0.36
Carpatho Rusyn (0)	0	<0.01
Celtic (0)	0	<0.01
Croatian (0)	6	0.01
Cypriot (0)	0	<0.01
Czech (46)	179	0.27
Czechoslovakian (10)	15	0.02
Danish (11)	137	0.21
Dutch (415)	2,843	4.34
Eastern European (71)	71	0.11
English (2,964)	11,436	17.48
Estonian (0)	0	<0.01
European (506)	606	0.93
Finnish (4)	28	0.04
French, ex. Basque (318)	2,864	4.38
French Canadian (260)	668	1.02
German (5,115)	19,312	29.51
German Russian (0)	0	<0.01
Greek (41)	112	0.17
Guyanese (14)	14	0.02
Hungarian (113)	436	0.67
Icelander (0)	2	<0.01
Iranian (6)	6	0.01
Irish (3,826)	15,027	22.96
Israeli (0)	0	<0.01
Italian (3,398)	8,851	13.53
Latvian (21)	32	0.05
Lithuanian (26)	190	0.29
Luxemburger (0)	0	<0.01
Macedonian (5)	5	0.01
Maltese (0)	13	0.02
New Zealander (0)	0	<0.01
Northern European (19)	37	0.06
Norwegian (60)	173	0.26
Pennsylvania German (103)	162	0.25

Ancestry (cont.)	Population	%
Polish (973)	3,039	4.64
Portuguese (12)	189	0.29
Romanian (23)	64	0.10
Russian (65)	403	0.62
Scandinavian (44)	124	0.19
Scotch-Irish (465)	1,278	1.95
Scottish (497)	1,873	2.86
Serbian (0)	20	0.03
Slavic (0)	2	<0.01
Slovak (48)	168	0.26
Slovene (0)	12	0.02
Soviet Union (0)	0	<0.01
Swedish (160)	678	1.04
Swiss (13)	253	0.39
Turkish (0)	0	<0.01
Ukrainian (198)	491	0.75
Welsh (97)	523	0.80
West Indian, ex. Hispanic (107)	154	0.24
Bahamian (0)	0	<0.01
Barbadian (0)	0	<0.01
Belizean (0)	0	<0.01
Bermudan (0)	0	<0.01
British West Indian (8)	8	0.01
Dutch West Indian (0)	0	<0.01
Haitian (13)	14	0.02
Jamaican (52)	80	0.12
Trinidadian/Tobagonian (17)	17	0.03
U.S. Virgin Islander (0)	0	<0.01
West Indian (17)	35	0.05
Other West Indian (0)	0	<0.01
Yugoslavian (19)	43	0.07

Hispanic Origin	Population	%
Hispanic or Latino (of any race)	1,802	2.76
Central American, ex. Mexican	86	0.13
Costa Rican	8	0.01
Guatemalan	19	0.03
Honduran	17	0.03
Nicaraguan	8	0.01
Panamanian	15	0.02
Salvadoran	19	0.03
Other Central American	0	<0.01
Cuban	82	0.13
Dominican Republic	76	0.12
Mexican	327	0.50
Puerto Rican	1,006	1.54
South American	102	0.16
Argentinean	7	0.01
Bolivian	1	<0.01
Chilean	23	0.04
Colombian	36	0.06
Ecuadorian	12	0.02
Paraguayan	4	0.01
Peruvian	13	0.02
Uruguayan	2	<0.01
Venezuelan	3	<0.01
Other South American	1	<0.01
Other Hispanic or Latino	123	0.19

Race*	Population	%
African-American/Black (1,598)	1,932	2.95
Not Hispanic (1,491)	1,786	2.73
Hispanic (107)	146	0.22
American Indian/Alaska Native (187)	527	0.81
Not Hispanic (158)	474	0.72
Hispanic (29)	53	0.08
Alaska Athabascan (Ala. Nat.) (0)	0	<0.01
Aleut (Alaska Native) (0)	0	<0.01
Apache (0)	2	<0.01
Arapaho (0)	0	<0.01
Blackfeet (3)	17	0.03
Canadian/French Am. Ind. (2)	8	0.01
Central American Ind. (0)	0	<0.01
Cherokee (5)	33	0.05
Cheyenne (0)	0	<0.01
Chickasaw (0)	1	<0.01
Chippewa (4)	9	0.01
Choctaw (1)	3	<0.01
Colville (0)	0	<0.01

Race* (cont.)	Population	%
Comanche (0)	3	<0.01
Cree (0)	1	<0.01
Creek (0)	1	<0.01
Crow (0)	1	<0.01
Delaware (0)	0	<0.01
Hopi (0)	0	<0.01
Houma (0)	0	<0.01
Inupiat (Alaska Native) (0)	1	<0.01
Iroquois (66)	166	0.25
Kiowa (0)	0	<0.01
Lumbee (0)	0	<0.01
Menominee (0)	0	<0.01
Mexican American Ind. (3)	4	0.01
Navajo (2)	6	0.01
Osage (0)	0	<0.01
Ottawa (0)	0	<0.01
Paiute (0)	0	<0.01
Pima (0)	0	<0.01
Potawatomi (0)	0	<0.01
Pueblo (0)	0	<0.01
Puget Sound Salish (0)	0	<0.01
Seminole (0)	6	0.01
Shoshone (0)	0	<0.01
Sioux (0)	5	0.01
South American Ind. (4)	10	0.02
Spanish American Ind. (0)	0	<0.01
Tlingit-Haida (Alaska Native) (0)	1	<0.01
Tohono O'Odham (0)	0	<0.01
Tsimshian (Alaska Native) (0)	0	<0.01
Ute (0)	0	<0.01
Yakama (0)	0	<0.01
Yaqui (0)	0	<0.01
Yuman (0)	0	<0.01
Yup'ik (Alaska Native) (0)	0	<0.01
Asian (785)	1,019	1.56
Not Hispanic (780)	991	1.52
Hispanic (5)	28	0.04
Bangladeshi (1)	1	<0.01
Bhutanese (0)	0	<0.01
Burmese (7)	7	0.01
Cambodian (7)	9	0.01
Chinese, ex. Taiwanese (207)	254	0.39
Filipino (77)	127	0.19
Hmong (1)	1	<0.01
Indian (84)	115	0.18
Indonesian (0)	2	<0.01
Japanese (47)	71	0.11
Korean (170)	226	0.35
Laotian (16)	31	0.05
Malaysian (1)	4	0.01
Nepalese (3)	4	0.01
Pakistani (41)	53	0.08
Sri Lankan (9)	9	0.01
Taiwanese (6)	7	0.01
Thai (5)	6	0.01
Vietnamese (56)	71	0.11
Hawaii Native/Pacific Islander (18)	53	0.08
Not Hispanic (11)	37	0.06
Hispanic (7)	16	0.02
Fijian (1)	1	<0.01
Guamanian/Chamorro (4)	9	0.01
Marshallese (0)	0	<0.01
Native Hawaiian (7)	25	0.04
Samoan (0)	3	<0.01
Tongan (0)	0	<0.01
White (61,363)	62,245	95.19
Not Hispanic (60,296)	61,067	93.38
Hispanic (1,067)	1,178	1.80

Notes: † The Census 2010 population figure is used to calculate the percentages in the Hispanic Origin and Race categories. Ancestry percentages are based on the 2006-2010 American Community Survey population (not shown); ‡ Numbers in parentheses indicate the number of people reporting a single ancestry; * Numbers in parentheses indicate the number of persons reporting this race alone, not in combination with any other race; Please refer to the Explanation of Data for more information.

Madison County

Population: 73,442

Ancestry	Population	%
Afghan (9)	27	0.04
African, Sub-Saharan (154)	214	0.29
African (65)	89	0.12
Cape Verdean (0)	0	<0.01
Ethiopian (0)	0	<0.01
Ghanaian (12)	22	0.03
Kenyan (10)	10	0.01
Liberian (0)	0	<0.01
Nigerian (33)	48	0.07
Senegalese (0)	0	<0.01
Sierra Leonean (12)	12	0.02
Somalian (0)	0	<0.01
South African (0)	11	0.02
Sudanese (11)	11	0.02
Ugandan (11)	11	0.02
Zimbabwean (0)	0	<0.01
Other Sub-Saharan African (0)	0	<0.01
Albanian (0)	28	0.04
Alsatian (0)	0	<0.01
American (10,024)	10,024	13.75
Arab (98)	173	0.24
Arab (70)	88	0.12
Egyptian (0)	0	<0.01
Iraqi (0)	0	<0.01
Jordanian (0)	0	<0.01
Lebanese (15)	49	0.07
Moroccan (0)	0	<0.01
Palestinian (0)	0	<0.01
Syrian (13)	28	0.04
Other Arab (0)	8	0.01
Armenian (12)	28	0.04
Assyrian/Chaldean/Syriac (0)	0	<0.01
Australian (8)	19	0.03
Austrian (10)	266	0.36
Basque (0)	0	<0.01
Belgian (42)	106	0.15
Brazilian (0)	0	<0.01
British (169)	338	0.46
Bulgarian (0)	0	<0.01
Cajun (0)	0	<0.01
Canadian (234)	460	0.63
Carpatho Rusyn (0)	0	<0.01
Celtic (0)	3	<0.01
Croatian (7)	70	0.10
Cypriot (0)	0	<0.01
Czech (7)	221	0.30
Czechoslovakian (19)	106	0.15
Danish (57)	298	0.41
Dutch (520)	2,648	3.63
Eastern European (82)	89	0.12
English (3,594)	11,718	16.08
Estonian (9)	9	0.01
European (647)	668	0.92
Finnish (4)	48	0.07
French, ex. Basque (628)	4,501	6.18
French Canadian (573)	1,461	2.00
German (3,834)	15,853	21.75
German Russian (0)	0	<0.01
Greek (78)	260	0.36
Guyanese (0)	0	<0.01
Hungarian (117)	282	0.39
Icelander (0)	0	<0.01
Iranian (0)	0	<0.01
Irish (3,752)	13,797	18.93
Israeli (0)	0	<0.01
Italian (3,492)	8,141	11.17
Latvian (9)	20	0.03
Lithuanian (64)	201	0.28
Luxemburger (9)	27	0.04
Macedonian (12)	12	0.02
Maltese (0)	0	<0.01
New Zealander (0)	0	<0.01
Northern European (69)	69	0.09
Norwegian (80)	305	0.42
Pennsylvania German (112)	126	0.17

Ancestry	Population	%
Polish (1,425)	4,350	5.97
Portuguese (26)	137	0.19
Romanian (3)	43	0.06
Russian (181)	521	0.71
Scandinavian (27)	99	0.14
Scotch-Irish (372)	1,148	1.58
Scottish (549)	1,988	2.73
Serbian (0)	0	<0.01
Slavic (33)	113	0.16
Slovak (21)	110	0.15
Slovene (13)	29	0.04
Soviet Union (0)	0	<0.01
Swedish (103)	512	0.70
Swiss (14)	368	0.50
Turkish (0)	0	<0.01
Ukrainian (160)	482	0.66
Welsh (500)	1,628	2.23
West Indian, ex. Hispanic (248)	371	0.51
Bahamian (0)	0	<0.01
Barbadian (0)	0	<0.01
Belizean (0)	0	<0.01
Bermudan (0)	0	<0.01
British West Indian (8)	8	0.01
Dutch West Indian (0)	0	<0.01
Haitian (74)	90	0.12
Jamaican (148)	212	0.29
Trinidadian/Tobagonian (0)	43	0.06
U.S. Virgin Islander (0)	0	<0.01
West Indian (18)	18	0.02
Other West Indian (0)	0	<0.01
Yugoslavian (116)	192	0.26

Hispanic Origin	Population	%
Hispanic or Latino (of any race)	1,316	1.79
Central American, ex. Mexican	90	0.12
Costa Rican	11	0.01
Guatemalan	44	0.06
Honduran	1	<0.01
Nicaraguan	4	0.01
Panamanian	6	0.01
Salvadoran	24	0.03
Other Central American	0	<0.01
Cuban	92	0.13
Dominican Republic	88	0.12
Mexican	279	0.38
Puerto Rican	469	0.64
South American	132	0.18
Argentinean	12	0.02
Bolivian	1	<0.01
Chilean	16	0.02
Colombian	42	0.06
Ecuadorian	16	0.02
Paraguayan	1	<0.01
Peruvian	30	0.04
Uruguayan	2	<0.01
Venezuelan	11	0.01
Other South American	1	<0.01
Other Hispanic or Latino	166	0.23

Race*	Population	%
African-American/Black (1,350)	1,763	2.40
Not Hispanic (1,260)	1,624	2.21
Hispanic (90)	139	0.19
American Indian/Alaska Native (524)	878	1.20
Not Hispanic (473)	800	1.09
Hispanic (51)	78	0.11
Alaska Athabascan (Ala. Nat.) (1)	1	<0.01
Aleut (Alaska Native) (0)	0	<0.01
Apache (0)	0	<0.01
Arapaho (0)	0	<0.01
Blackfeet (4)	5	0.01
Canadian/French Am. Ind. (4)	5	0.01
Central American Ind. (1)	1	<0.01
Cherokee (13)	55	0.07
Cheyenne (0)	2	<0.01
Chickasaw (0)	0	<0.01
Chippewa (8)	11	0.01
Choctaw (1)	4	0.01
Colville (2)	3	<0.01

Race*	Population	%
Comanche (0)	0	<0.01
Cree (0)	1	<0.01
Creek (0)	0	<0.01
Crow (0)	0	<0.01
Delaware (0)	3	<0.01
Hopi (0)	0	<0.01
Houma (1)	1	<0.01
Inupiat (Alaska Native) (0)	0	<0.01
Iroquois (298)	414	0.56
Kiowa (0)	1	<0.01
Lumbee (0)	0	<0.01
Menominee (0)	0	<0.01
Mexican American Ind. (2)	6	0.01
Navajo (0)	4	0.01
Osage (0)	2	<0.01
Ottawa (0)	0	<0.01
Paiute (1)	1	<0.01
Pima (0)	0	<0.01
Potawatomi (0)	1	<0.01
Pueblo (0)	1	<0.01
Puget Sound Salish (0)	0	<0.01
Seminole (0)	0	<0.01
Shoshone (0)	0	<0.01
Sioux (10)	15	0.02
South American Ind. (12)	14	0.02
Spanish American Ind. (4)	4	0.01
Tlingit-Haida (Alaska Native) (2)	2	<0.01
Tohono O'Odham (0)	0	<0.01
Tsimshian (Alaska Native) (0)	0	<0.01
Ute (0)	0	<0.01
Yakama (0)	0	<0.01
Yaqui (0)	0	<0.01
Yuman (0)	1	<0.01
Yup'ik (Alaska Native) (3)	3	<0.01
Asian (583)	793	1.08
Not Hispanic (576)	779	1.06
Hispanic (7)	14	0.02
Bangladeshi (6)	6	0.01
Bhutanese (7)	7	0.01
Burmese (5)	5	0.01
Cambodian (6)	9	0.01
Chinese, ex. Taiwanese (178)	224	0.31
Filipino (48)	90	0.12
Hmong (1)	1	<0.01
Indian (105)	138	0.19
Indonesian (1)	2	<0.01
Japanese (38)	83	0.11
Korean (72)	95	0.13
Laotian (7)	7	0.01
Malaysian (0)	1	<0.01
Nepalese (6)	6	0.01
Pakistani (5)	8	0.01
Sri Lankan (12)	12	0.02
Taiwanese (7)	9	0.01
Thai (8)	15	0.02
Vietnamese (34)	45	0.06
Hawaii Native/Pacific Islander (17)	43	0.06
Not Hispanic (11)	32	0.04
Hispanic (6)	11	0.01
Fijian (0)	0	<0.01
Guamanian/Chamorro (7)	12	0.02
Marshallese (0)	0	<0.01
Native Hawaiian (9)	23	0.03
Samoan (0)	2	<0.01
Tongan (0)	1	<0.01
White (69,740)	70,644	96.19
Not Hispanic (68,916)	69,724	94.94
Hispanic (824)	920	1.25

Notes: † The Census 2010 population figure is used to calculate the percentages in the Hispanic Origin and Race categories. Ancestry percentages are based on the 2006-2010 American Community Survey population (not shown); ‡ Numbers in parentheses indicate the number of people reporting a single ancestry; * Numbers in parentheses indicate the number of persons reporting this race alone, not in combination with any other race; Please refer to the Explanation of Data for more information.

Monroe County

Population: 744,344

Ancestry	Population	%
Afghan (593)	593	0.08
African, Sub-Saharan (9,510)	10,853	1.46
African (6,140)	7,288	0.98
Cape Verdean (0)	0	<0.01
Ethiopian (734)	734	0.10
Ghanaian (49)	49	0.01
Kenyan (9)	9	<0.01
Liberian (89)	109	0.01
Nigerian (503)	603	0.08
Senegalese (26)	26	<0.01
Sierra Leonean (0)	0	<0.01
Somalian (1,018)	1,018	0.14
South African (156)	179	0.02
Sudanese (181)	205	0.03
Ugandan (0)	0	<0.01
Zimbabwean (76)	76	0.01
Other Sub-Saharan African (529)	557	0.08
Albanian (375)	445	0.06
Alsatian (3)	34	<0.01
American (20,394)	20,394	2.75
Arab (2,460)	3,916	0.53
Arab (591)	865	0.12
Egyptian (314)	339	0.05
Iraqi (111)	167	0.02
Jordanian (0)	0	<0.01
Lebanese (539)	1,243	0.17
Moroccan (171)	221	0.03
Palestinian (80)	140	0.02
Syrian (126)	231	0.03
Other Arab (528)	710	0.10
Armenian (338)	695	0.09
Assyrian/Chaldean/Syriac (0)	0	<0.01
Australian (161)	304	0.04
Austrian (484)	2,334	0.31
Basque (13)	13	<0.01
Belgian (346)	1,318	0.18
Brazilian (223)	312	0.04
British (1,603)	3,430	0.46
Bulgarian (95)	224	0.03
Cajun (0)	0	<0.01
Canadian (1,638)	3,828	0.52
Carpatho Rusyn (0)	16	<0.01
Celtic (69)	119	0.02
Croatian (67)	308	0.04
Cypriot (0)	0	<0.01
Czech (445)	2,461	0.33
Czechoslovakian (230)	589	0.08
Danish (406)	1,719	0.23
Dutch (3,397)	19,639	2.65
Eastern European (1,085)	1,267	0.17
English (25,417)	94,030	12.68
Estonian (26)	186	0.03
European (5,777)	6,513	0.88
Finnish (177)	774	0.10
French, ex. Basque (2,904)	23,189	3.13
French Canadian (2,803)	8,059	1.09
German (37,495)	156,984	21.18
German Russian (7)	35	<0.01
Greek (2,336)	4,548	0.61
Guyanese (586)	694	0.09
Hungarian (1,031)	3,581	0.48
Icelander (75)	75	0.01
Iranian (234)	257	0.03
Irish (28,758)	123,123	16.61
Israeli (254)	436	0.06
Italian (71,014)	140,596	18.97
Latvian (208)	456	0.06
Lithuanian (1,049)	2,950	0.40
Luxemburger (43)	101	0.01
Macedonian (564)	754	0.10
Maltese (37)	123	0.02
New Zealander (0)	0	<0.01
Northern European (328)	433	0.06
Norwegian (662)	2,890	0.39
Pennsylvania German (218)	469	0.06
Polish (11,957)	40,211	5.42
Portuguese (453)	1,455	0.20
Romanian (555)	1,117	0.15
Russian (3,981)	8,944	1.21
Scandinavian (166)	486	0.07
Scotch-Irish (3,160)	9,722	1.31
Scottish (3,214)	15,779	2.13
Serbian (52)	164	0.02
Slavic (236)	599	0.08
Slovak (329)	893	0.12
Slovene (86)	226	0.03
Soviet Union (0)	0	<0.01
Swedish (1,498)	6,462	0.87
Swiss (294)	2,029	0.27
Turkish (2,064)	2,586	0.35
Ukrainian (5,827)	10,628	1.43
Welsh (841)	5,288	0.71
West Indian, ex. Hispanic (5,376)	8,191	1.10
Bahamian (58)	218	0.03
Barbadian (318)	379	0.05
Belizean (185)	275	0.04
Bermudan (0)	0	<0.01
British West Indian (99)	223	0.03
Dutch West Indian (0)	13	<0.01
Haitian (917)	1,040	0.14
Jamaican (2,942)	4,448	0.60
Trinidadian/Tobagonian (268)	413	0.06
U.S. Virgin Islander (0)	0	<0.01
West Indian (589)	1,182	0.16
Other West Indian (0)	0	<0.01
Yugoslavian (551)	813	0.11

Hispanic Origin	Population	%
Hispanic or Latino (of any race)	54,005	7.26
Central American, ex. Mexican	1,513	0.20
Costa Rican	156	0.02
Guatemalan	353	0.05
Honduran	242	0.03
Nicaraguan	192	0.03
Panamanian	241	0.03
Salvadoran	320	0.04
Other Central American	9	<0.01
Cuban	2,913	0.39
Dominican Republic	2,160	0.29
Mexican	3,364	0.45
Puerto Rican	38,907	5.23
South American	2,258	0.30
Argentinean	225	0.03
Bolivian	62	0.01
Chilean	321	0.04
Colombian	753	0.10
Ecuadorian	267	0.04
Paraguayan	55	0.01
Peruvian	358	0.05
Uruguayan	29	<0.01
Venezuelan	153	0.02
Other South American	35	<0.01
Other Hispanic or Latino	2,890	0.39

Race*	Population	%
African-American/Black (113,171)	124,305	16.70
Not Hispanic (107,448)	115,820	15.56
Hispanic (5,723)	8,485	1.14
American Indian/Alaska Native (2,136)	6,360	0.85
Not Hispanic (1,589)	4,952	0.67
Hispanic (547)	1,408	0.19
Alaska Athabascan (Ala. Nat.) (2)	7	<0.01
Aleut (Alaska Native) (1)	2	<0.01
Apache (11)	34	<0.01
Arapaho (0)	4	<0.01
Blackfeet (21)	184	0.02
Canadian/French Am. Ind. (27)	52	0.01
Central American Ind. (23)	41	0.01
Cherokee (88)	754	0.10
Cheyenne (3)	4	<0.01
Chickasaw (4)	12	<0.01
Chippewa (46)	70	0.01
Choctaw (8)	57	0.01
Colville (0)	2	<0.01
Comanche (0)	3	<0.01
Cree (6)	15	<0.01
Creek (7)	28	<0.01
Crow (1)	5	<0.01
Delaware (8)	28	<0.01
Hopi (1)	1	<0.01
Houma (2)	2	<0.01
Inupiat (Alaska Native) (4)	7	<0.01
Iroquois (686)	1,325	0.18
Kiowa (0)	0	<0.01
Lumbee (1)	5	<0.01
Menominee (0)	0	<0.01
Mexican American Ind. (53)	95	0.01
Navajo (20)	49	<0.01
Osage (1)	5	<0.01
Ottawa (1)	1	<0.01
Paiute (1)	2	<0.01
Pima (0)	3	<0.01
Potawatomi (11)	17	<0.01
Pueblo (1)	6	<0.01
Puget Sound Salish (1)	1	<0.01
Seminole (3)	63	0.01
Shoshone (3)	3	<0.01
Sioux (26)	72	0.01
South American Ind. (70)	235	0.03
Spanish American Ind. (18)	22	<0.01
Tlingit-Haida (Alaska Native) (4)	12	<0.01
Tohono O'Odham (1)	1	<0.01
Tsimshian (Alaska Native) (0)	0	<0.01
Ute (1)	6	<0.01
Yakama (0)	0	<0.01
Yaqui (0)	0	<0.01
Yuman (3)	3	<0.01
Yup'ik (Alaska Native) (0)	0	<0.01
Asian (24,281)	28,675	3.85
Not Hispanic (24,023)	28,047	3.77
Hispanic (258)	628	0.08
Bangladeshi (79)	98	0.01
Bhutanese (369)	411	0.06
Burmese (559)	599	0.08
Cambodian (485)	580	0.08
Chinese, ex. Taiwanese (5,587)	6,499	0.87
Filipino (954)	1,567	0.21
Hmong (2)	3	<0.01
Indian (6,146)	6,938	0.93
Indonesian (45)	106	0.01
Japanese (586)	1,157	0.16
Korean (2,387)	2,997	0.40
Laotian (1,301)	1,551	0.21
Malaysian (98)	108	0.01
Nepalese (196)	246	0.03
Pakistani (845)	951	0.13
Sri Lankan (149)	173	0.02
Taiwanese (340)	438	0.06
Thai (196)	296	0.04
Vietnamese (2,824)	3,205	0.43
Hawaii Native/Pacific Islander (227)	874	0.12
Not Hispanic (182)	622	0.08
Hispanic (45)	252	0.03
Fijian (5)	9	<0.01
Guamanian/Chamorro (45)	77	0.01
Marshallese (0)	1	<0.01
Native Hawaiian (62)	208	0.03
Samoan (44)	88	0.01
Tongan (5)	6	<0.01
White (566,535)	582,035	78.19
Not Hispanic (542,034)	553,986	74.43
Hispanic (24,501)	28,049	3.77

Notes: † The Census 2010 population figure is used to calculate the percentages in the Hispanic Origin and Race categories. Ancestry percentages are based on the 2006-2010 American Community Survey population (not shown); ‡ Numbers in parentheses indicate the number of people reporting a single ancestry; * Numbers in parentheses indicate the number of persons reporting this race alone, not in combination with any other race; Please refer to the Explanation of Data for more information.

Montgomery County
Population: 50,219

Ancestry	Population	%
Afghan (0)	0	<0.01
African, Sub-Saharan (64)	64	0.13
African (49)	49	0.10
Cape Verdean (0)	0	<0.01
Ethiopian (0)	0	<0.01
Ghanaian (0)	0	<0.01
Kenyan (0)	0	<0.01
Liberian (0)	0	<0.01
Nigerian (4)	4	0.01
Senegalese (0)	0	<0.01
Sierra Leonean (0)	0	<0.01
Somalian (0)	0	<0.01
South African (11)	11	0.02
Sudanese (0)	0	<0.01
Ugandan (0)	0	<0.01
Zimbabwean (0)	0	<0.01
Other Sub-Saharan African (0)	0	<0.01
Albanian (11)	25	0.05
Alsatian (0)	0	<0.01
American (4,301)	4,301	8.61
Arab (22)	105	0.21
Arab (0)	18	0.04
Egyptian (0)	0	<0.01
Iraqi (0)	0	<0.01
Jordanian (0)	0	<0.01
Lebanese (22)	67	0.13
Moroccan (0)	0	<0.01
Palestinian (0)	9	0.02
Syrian (0)	11	0.02
Other Arab (0)	0	<0.01
Armenian (0)	66	0.13
Assyrian/Chaldean/Syriac (0)	0	<0.01
Australian (0)	11	0.02
Austrian (55)	127	0.25
Basque (0)	0	<0.01
Belgian (0)	21	0.04
Brazilian (5)	5	0.01
British (65)	85	0.17
Bulgarian (0)	0	<0.01
Cajun (0)	0	<0.01
Canadian (60)	136	0.27
Carpatho Rusyn (0)	0	<0.01
Celtic (0)	0	<0.01
Croatian (2)	12	0.02
Cypriot (0)	0	<0.01
Czech (54)	168	0.34
Czechoslovakian (0)	15	0.03
Danish (32)	199	0.40
Dutch (296)	2,858	5.72
Eastern European (98)	98	0.20
English (2,674)	6,458	12.93
Estonian (0)	0	<0.01
European (188)	207	0.41
Finnish (0)	13	0.03
French, ex. Basque (218)	2,400	4.81
French Canadian (155)	753	1.51
German (2,515)	8,912	17.84
German Russian (0)	0	<0.01
Greek (41)	218	0.44
Guyanese (0)	0	<0.01
Hungarian (30)	95	0.19
Icelander (0)	0	<0.01
Iranian (0)	0	<0.01
Irish (1,526)	8,038	16.09
Israeli (0)	0	<0.01
Italian (4,249)	9,234	18.49
Latvian (18)	32	0.06
Lithuanian (336)	636	1.27
Luxemburger (0)	0	<0.01
Macedonian (0)	0	<0.01
Maltese (0)	0	<0.01
New Zealander (0)	0	<0.01
Northern European (13)	13	0.03
Norwegian (25)	86	0.17
Pennsylvania German (283)	293	0.59

Ancestry	Population	%
Polish (2,668)	5,283	10.58
Portuguese (8)	40	0.08
Romanian (8)	22	0.04
Russian (25)	172	0.34
Scandinavian (12)	12	0.02
Scotch-Irish (173)	422	0.84
Scottish (192)	772	1.55
Serbian (2)	2	<0.01
Slavic (0)	4	0.01
Slovak (58)	129	0.26
Slovene (4)	11	0.02
Soviet Union (0)	0	<0.01
Swedish (28)	252	0.50
Swiss (17)	86	0.17
Turkish (0)	0	<0.01
Ukrainian (103)	376	0.75
Welsh (16)	108	0.22
West Indian, ex. Hispanic (65)	149	0.30
Bahamian (0)	0	<0.01
Barbadian (0)	0	<0.01
Belizean (0)	0	<0.01
Bermudan (0)	0	<0.01
British West Indian (0)	0	<0.01
Dutch West Indian (0)	0	<0.01
Haitian (5)	5	0.01
Jamaican (56)	140	0.28
Trinidadian/Tobagonian (4)	4	0.01
U.S. Virgin Islander (0)	0	<0.01
West Indian (0)	0	<0.01
Other West Indian (0)	0	<0.01
Yugoslavian (10)	10	0.02

Hispanic Origin	Population	%
Hispanic or Latino (of any race)	5,654	11.26
Central American, ex. Mexican	245	0.49
Costa Rican	131	0.26
Guatemalan	47	0.09
Honduran	11	0.02
Nicaraguan	11	0.02
Panamanian	10	0.02
Salvadoran	35	0.07
Other Central American	0	<0.01
Cuban	90	0.18
Dominican Republic	259	0.52
Mexican	218	0.43
Puerto Rican	4,330	8.62
South American	160	0.32
Argentinean	6	0.01
Bolivian	1	<0.01
Chilean	12	0.02
Colombian	41	0.08
Ecuadorian	76	0.15
Paraguayan	0	<0.01
Peruvian	19	0.04
Uruguayan	1	<0.01
Venezuelan	3	0.01
Other South American	1	<0.01
Other Hispanic or Latino	352	0.70

Race*	Population	%
African-American/Black (951)	1,447	2.88
Not Hispanic (712)	1,067	2.12
Hispanic (239)	380	0.76
American Indian/Alaska Native (169)	408	0.81
Not Hispanic (103)	298	0.59
Hispanic (66)	110	0.22
Alaska Athabascan (Ala. Nat.) (0)	0	<0.01
Aleut (Alaska Native) (0)	0	<0.01
Apache (0)	3	0.01
Arapaho (0)	0	<0.01
Blackfeet (1)	13	0.03
Canadian/French Am. Ind. (0)	1	<0.01
Central American Ind. (2)	4	0.01
Cherokee (7)	37	0.07
Cheyenne (1)	1	<0.01
Chickasaw (0)	0	<0.01
Chippewa (1)	1	<0.01
Choctaw (2)	4	0.01
Colville (0)	0	<0.01

Race*	Population	%
Comanche (0)	0	<0.01
Cree (1)	3	0.01
Creek (0)	0	<0.01
Crow (0)	0	<0.01
Delaware (4)	8	0.02
Hopi (0)	0	<0.01
Houma (0)	0	<0.01
Inupiat (Alaska Native) (0)	0	<0.01
Iroquois (22)	89	0.18
Kiowa (0)	0	<0.01
Lumbee (1)	3	0.01
Menominee (0)	0	<0.01
Mexican American Ind. (3)	6	0.01
Navajo (0)	2	<0.01
Osage (0)	1	<0.01
Ottawa (0)	1	<0.01
Paiute (0)	0	<0.01
Pima (0)	0	<0.01
Potawatomi (0)	0	<0.01
Pueblo (0)	0	<0.01
Puget Sound Salish (0)	0	<0.01
Seminole (0)	1	<0.01
Shoshone (0)	0	<0.01
Sioux (2)	7	0.01
South American Ind. (12)	20	0.04
Spanish American Ind. (2)	5	0.01
Tlingit-Haida (Alaska Native) (2)	3	0.01
Tohono O'Odham (0)	0	<0.01
Tsimshian (Alaska Native) (0)	0	<0.01
Ute (0)	0	<0.01
Yakama (0)	0	<0.01
Yaqui (0)	0	<0.01
Yuman (0)	0	<0.01
Yup'ik (Alaska Native) (0)	0	<0.01
Asian (369)	468	0.93
Not Hispanic (356)	435	0.87
Hispanic (13)	33	0.07
Bangladeshi (0)	0	<0.01
Bhutanese (0)	0	<0.01
Burmese (0)	0	<0.01
Cambodian (0)	0	<0.01
Chinese, ex. Taiwanese (65)	84	0.17
Filipino (42)	58	0.12
Hmong (0)	0	<0.01
Indian (136)	149	0.30
Indonesian (4)	4	<0.01
Japanese (12)	30	0.06
Korean (45)	61	0.12
Laotian (0)	0	<0.01
Malaysian (0)	0	<0.01
Nepalese (1)	2	<0.01
Pakistani (16)	21	0.04
Sri Lankan (0)	0	<0.01
Taiwanese (1)	1	<0.01
Thai (7)	15	0.03
Vietnamese (4)	13	0.03
Hawaii Native/Pacific Islander (19)	56	0.11
Not Hispanic (11)	23	0.05
Hispanic (8)	33	0.07
Fijian (0)	0	<0.01
Guamanian/Chamorro (9)	12	0.02
Marshallese (0)	0	<0.01
Native Hawaiian (4)	9	0.02
Samoan (3)	3	0.01
Tongan (2)	2	<0.01
White (45,519)	46,382	92.36
Not Hispanic (42,732)	43,292	86.21
Hispanic (2,787)	3,090	6.15

Notes: † The Census 2010 population figure is used to calculate the percentages in the Hispanic Origin and Race categories. Ancestry percentages are based on the 2006-2010 American Community Survey population (not shown); ‡ Numbers in parentheses indicate the number of people reporting a single ancestry; * Numbers in parentheses indicate the number of persons reporting this race alone, not in combination with any other race; Please refer to the Explanation of Data for more information.

Nassau County

Population: 1,339,532

Ancestry	Population	%
Afghan (938)	1,420	0.11
African, Sub-Saharan (5,338)	7,241	0.54
African (3,221)	4,618	0.35
Cape Verdean (12)	12	<0.01
Ethiopian (87)	155	0.01
Ghanaian (356)	423	0.03
Kenyan (0)	0	<0.01
Liberian (0)	3	<0.01
Nigerian (1,144)	1,356	0.10
Senegalese (0)	0	<0.01
Sierra Leonean (24)	24	<0.01
Somalian (15)	15	<0.01
South African (190)	225	0.02
Sudanese (33)	50	<0.01
Ugandan (0)	0	<0.01
Zimbabwean (0)	0	<0.01
Other Sub-Saharan African (256)	360	0.03
Albanian (1,157)	1,726	0.13
Alsatian (9)	46	<0.01
American (42,503)	42,503	3.20
Arab (4,560)	7,635	0.57
Arab (502)	692	0.05
Egyptian (1,361)	1,995	0.15
Iraqi (528)	793	0.06
Jordanian (66)	66	<0.01
Lebanese (426)	995	0.07
Moroccan (244)	618	0.05
Palestinian (154)	232	0.02
Syrian (165)	754	0.06
Other Arab (1,114)	1,490	0.11
Armenian (2,406)	3,535	0.27
Assyrian/Chaldean/Syriac (7)	40	<0.01
Australian (154)	388	0.03
Austrian (3,200)	11,903	0.90
Basque (2)	167	0.01
Belgian (311)	821	0.06
Brazilian (1,025)	1,516	0.11
British (1,099)	2,526	0.19
Bulgarian (230)	299	0.02
Cajun (0)	59	<0.01
Canadian (632)	1,951	0.15
Carpatho Rusyn (4)	36	<0.01
Celtic (84)	143	0.01
Croatian (1,742)	2,842	0.21
Cypriot (306)	381	0.03
Czech (1,112)	4,825	0.36
Czechoslovakian (735)	2,195	0.17
Danish (453)	2,201	0.17
Dutch (815)	5,539	0.42
Eastern European (13,083)	13,843	1.04
English (6,821)	42,066	3.17
Estonian (213)	360	0.03
European (10,190)	11,073	0.83
Finnish (197)	1,079	0.08
French, ex. Basque (1,972)	15,598	1.17
French Canadian (907)	3,222	0.24
German (29,737)	143,597	10.80
German Russian (0)	43	<0.01
Greek (13,704)	21,516	1.62
Guyanese (3,463)	4,442	0.33
Hungarian (4,774)	13,637	1.03
Icelander (50)	144	0.01
Iranian (10,076)	11,333	0.85
Irish (73,529)	224,843	16.92
Israeli (4,093)	5,327	0.40
Italian (170,115)	305,805	23.01
Latvian (463)	965	0.07
Lithuanian (1,501)	4,623	0.35
Luxemburger (0)	16	<0.01
Macedonian (41)	51	<0.01
Maltese (496)	1,367	0.10
New Zealander (0)	0	<0.01
Northern European (619)	717	0.05
Norwegian (1,502)	6,174	0.46
Pennsylvania German (121)	182	0.01

Ancestry (cont.)	Population	%
Polish (24,310)	72,081	5.42
Portuguese (5,557)	7,340	0.55
Romanian (2,430)	5,933	0.45
Russian (26,109)	59,061	4.44
Scandinavian (274)	647	0.05
Scotch-Irish (3,219)	8,938	0.67
Scottish (1,993)	8,512	0.64
Serbian (144)	294	0.02
Slavic (100)	549	0.04
Slovak (491)	1,528	0.11
Slovene (98)	277	0.02
Soviet Union (0)	10	<0.01
Swedish (1,026)	7,946	0.60
Swiss (395)	2,316	0.17
Turkish (1,731)	2,980	0.22
Ukrainian (2,820)	5,868	0.44
Welsh (224)	1,755	0.13
West Indian, ex. Hispanic (43,896)	52,648	3.96
Bahamian (5)	51	<0.01
Barbadian (1,197)	1,489	0.11
Belizean (145)	228	0.02
Bermudan (52)	65	<0.01
British West Indian (813)	1,182	0.09
Dutch West Indian (217)	285	0.02
Haitian (18,556)	20,810	1.57
Jamaican (16,745)	19,674	1.48
Trinidadian/Tobagonian (2,369)	3,518	0.26
U.S. Virgin Islander (15)	45	<0.01
West Indian (3,765)	5,269	0.40
Other West Indian (17)	32	<0.01
Yugoslavian (357)	1,166	0.09

Hispanic Origin	Population	%
Hispanic or Latino (of any race)	195,355	14.58
Central American, ex. Mexican	69,816	5.21
Costa Rican	992	0.07
Guatemalan	7,853	0.59
Honduran	11,051	0.82
Nicaraguan	925	0.07
Panamanian	1,360	0.10
Salvadoran	47,180	3.52
Other Central American	455	0.03
Cuban	5,430	0.41
Dominican Republic	20,216	1.51
Mexican	10,535	0.79
Puerto Rican	29,965	2.24
South American	38,719	2.89
Argentinean	2,533	0.19
Bolivian	696	0.05
Chilean	2,945	0.22
Colombian	13,257	0.99
Ecuadorian	9,239	0.69
Paraguayan	406	0.03
Peruvian	7,853	0.59
Uruguayan	628	0.05
Venezuelan	825	0.06
Other South American	337	0.03
Other Hispanic or Latino	20,674	1.54

Race*	Population	%
African-American/Black (149,049)	159,230	11.89
Not Hispanic (141,305)	148,211	11.06
Hispanic (7,744)	11,019	0.82
American Indian/Alaska Native (3,185)	8,027	0.60
Not Hispanic (1,379)	4,240	0.32
Hispanic (1,806)	3,787	0.28
Alaska Athabascan (Ala. Nat.) (0)	1	<0.01
Aleut (Alaska Native) (2)	3	<0.01
Apache (8)	26	<0.01
Arapaho (0)	0	<0.01
Blackfeet (17)	151	0.01
Canadian/French Am. Ind. (10)	18	<0.01
Central American Ind. (73)	138	0.01
Cherokee (83)	783	0.06
Cheyenne (5)	7	<0.01
Chickasaw (0)	7	<0.01
Chippewa (14)	28	<0.01
Choctaw (15)	49	<0.01
Colville (1)	1	<0.01

Race* (cont.)	Population	%
Comanche (7)	11	<0.01
Cree (0)	5	<0.01
Creek (7)	37	<0.01
Crow (0)	3	<0.01
Delaware (9)	24	<0.01
Hopi (1)	5	<0.01
Houma (0)	0	<0.01
Inupiat (Alaska Native) (2)	5	<0.01
Iroquois (102)	240	0.02
Kiowa (1)	1	<0.01
Lumbee (9)	23	<0.01
Menominee (0)	0	<0.01
Mexican American Ind. (157)	239	0.02
Navajo (4)	16	<0.01
Osage (0)	3	<0.01
Ottawa (1)	1	<0.01
Paiute (0)	0	<0.01
Pima (0)	0	<0.01
Potawatomi (2)	4	<0.01
Pueblo (13)	18	<0.01
Puget Sound Salish (0)	0	<0.01
Seminole (2)	29	<0.01
Shoshone (2)	5	<0.01
Sioux (22)	57	<0.01
South American Ind. (210)	450	0.03
Spanish American Ind. (178)	217	0.02
Tlingit-Haida (Alaska Native) (3)	6	<0.01
Tohono O'Odham (7)	7	<0.01
Tsimshian (Alaska Native) (0)	0	<0.01
Ute (2)	2	<0.01
Yakama (0)	0	<0.01
Yaqui (1)	1	<0.01
Yuman (0)	0	<0.01
Yup'ik (Alaska Native) (0)	0	<0.01
Asian (102,266)	113,831	8.50
Not Hispanic (101,558)	111,861	8.35
Hispanic (708)	1,970	0.15
Bangladeshi (1,269)	1,408	0.11
Bhutanese (1)	1	<0.01
Burmese (147)	179	0.01
Cambodian (89)	120	0.01
Chinese, ex. Taiwanese (23,026)	25,716	1.92
Filipino (9,881)	11,622	0.87
Hmong (0)	2	<0.01
Indian (39,572)	43,171	3.22
Indonesian (93)	157	0.01
Japanese (1,967)	2,587	0.19
Korean (13,558)	14,338	1.07
Laotian (30)	42	<0.01
Malaysian (60)	97	0.01
Nepalese (106)	111	0.01
Pakistani (6,737)	7,382	0.55
Sri Lankan (281)	330	0.02
Taiwanese (1,448)	1,673	0.12
Thai (436)	555	0.04
Vietnamese (809)	1,071	0.08
Hawaii Native/Pacific Islander (336)	1,557	0.12
Not Hispanic (197)	1,015	0.08
Hispanic (139)	542	0.04
Fijian (10)	13	<0.01
Guamanian/Chamorro (128)	164	0.01
Marshallese (2)	2	<0.01
Native Hawaiian (48)	193	0.01
Samoan (27)	71	0.01
Tongan (2)	2	<0.01
White (977,577)	1,000,818	74.71
Not Hispanic (877,309)	889,240	66.38
Hispanic (100,268)	111,578	8.33

Notes: † The Census 2010 population figure is used to calculate the percentages in the Hispanic Origin and Race categories. Ancestry percentages are based on the 2006-2010 American Community Survey population (not shown); ‡ Numbers in parentheses indicate the number of people reporting a single ancestry; * Numbers in parentheses indicate the number of persons reporting this race alone, not in combination with any other race; Please refer to the Explanation of Data for more information.

New York County

Population: 1,585,873

Ancestry	Population	%
Afghan (59)	85	0.01
African, Sub-Saharan (19,667)	24,146	1.52
African (10,054)	12,839	0.81
Cape Verdean (81)	206	0.01
Ethiopian (932)	1,043	0.07
Ghanaian (714)	818	0.05
Kenyan (43)	69	<0.01
Liberian (169)	176	0.01
Nigerian (1,650)	1,953	0.12
Senegalese (1,118)	1,216	0.08
Sierra Leonean (422)	422	0.03
Somalian (125)	125	0.01
South African (991)	1,372	0.09
Sudanese (137)	137	0.01
Ugandan (95)	125	0.01
Zimbabwean (80)	100	0.01
Other Sub-Saharan African (3,056)	3,545	0.22
Albanian (1,385)	1,618	0.10
Alsatian (5)	129	0.01
American (54,694)	54,694	3.45
Arab (8,584)	13,828	0.87
Arab (1,250)	1,720	0.11
Egyptian (1,374)	1,906	0.12
Iraqi (275)	583	0.04
Jordanian (0)	48	<0.01
Lebanese (1,838)	3,331	0.21
Moroccan (914)	1,592	0.10
Palestinian (626)	794	0.05
Syrian (518)	1,112	0.07
Other Arab (1,789)	2,742	0.17
Armenian (1,520)	2,653	0.17
Assyrian/Chaldean/Syriac (94)	137	0.01
Australian (1,965)	2,719	0.17
Austrian (4,202)	14,656	0.93
Basque (191)	428	0.03
Belgian (928)	2,470	0.16
Brazilian (2,870)	4,541	0.29
British (6,950)	12,129	0.77
Bulgarian (927)	1,272	0.08
Cajun (22)	224	0.01
Canadian (3,037)	5,646	0.36
Carpatho Rusyn (89)	112	0.01
Celtic (129)	304	0.02
Croatian (1,299)	2,164	0.14
Cypriot (139)	216	0.01
Czech (1,439)	4,820	0.30
Czechoslovakian (619)	1,256	0.08
Danish (1,444)	4,095	0.26
Dutch (2,847)	10,414	0.66
Eastern European (23,269)	25,277	1.60
English (22,270)	77,799	4.91
Estonian (190)	424	0.03
European (25,127)	27,846	1.76
Finnish (666)	1,658	0.10
French, ex. Basque (10,278)	31,783	2.01
French Canadian (1,692)	5,246	0.33
German (27,493)	107,666	6.80
German Russian (0)	41	<0.01
Greek (7,557)	13,078	0.83
Guyanese (1,802)	2,259	0.14
Hungarian (4,686)	14,667	0.93
Icelander (246)	382	0.02
Iranian (3,458)	4,256	0.27
Irish (40,008)	117,355	7.41
Israeli (4,839)	6,624	0.42
Italian (44,498)	98,563	6.22
Latvian (713)	1,822	0.12
Lithuanian (1,597)	5,775	0.36
Luxemburger (23)	68	<0.01
Macedonian (973)	1,086	0.07
Maltese (548)	840	0.05
New Zealander (243)	405	0.03
Northern European (1,296)	1,485	0.09
Norwegian (1,552)	7,445	0.47
Pennsylvania German (123)	327	0.02

Ancestry	Population	%
Polish (20,565)	64,078	4.05
Portuguese (1,436)	3,862	0.24
Romanian (3,035)	7,692	0.49
Russian (36,296)	82,983	5.24
Scandinavian (753)	1,731	0.11
Scotch-Irish (4,283)	13,158	0.83
Scottish (4,846)	19,553	1.23
Serbian (1,160)	1,526	0.10
Slavic (177)	400	0.03
Slovak (812)	2,298	0.15
Slovene (271)	695	0.04
Soviet Union (28)	54	<0.01
Swedish (3,045)	10,408	0.66
Swiss (1,381)	4,962	0.31
Turkish (2,708)	3,703	0.23
Ukrainian (4,361)	8,849	0.56
Welsh (944)	6,000	0.38
West Indian, ex. Hispanic (22,411)	30,009	1.90
Bahamian (303)	457	0.03
Barbadian (738)	907	0.06
Belizean (654)	735	0.05
Bermudan (86)	127	0.01
British West Indian (1,308)	1,658	0.10
Dutch West Indian (212)	276	0.02
Haitian (5,308)	6,500	0.41
Jamaican (7,099)	9,242	0.58
Trinidadian/Tobagonian (3,010)	3,877	0.24
U.S. Virgin Islander (343)	487	0.03
West Indian (3,296)	5,618	0.35
Other West Indian (54)	125	0.01
Yugoslavian (1,478)	1,876	0.12

Hispanic Origin	Population	%
Hispanic or Latino (of any race)	403,577	25.45
Central American, ex. Mexican	13,948	0.88
Costa Rican	987	0.06
Guatemalan	2,051	0.13
Honduran	4,058	0.26
Nicaraguan	1,556	0.10
Panamanian	1,716	0.11
Salvadoran	3,419	0.22
Other Central American	161	0.01
Cuban	11,623	0.73
Dominican Republic	155,971	9.84
Mexican	41,965	2.65
Puerto Rican	107,774	6.80
South American	36,748	2.32
Argentinean	4,339	0.27
Bolivian	522	0.03
Chilean	1,824	0.12
Colombian	8,411	0.53
Ecuadorian	14,132	0.89
Paraguayan	268	0.02
Peruvian	3,852	0.24
Uruguayan	549	0.03
Venezuelan	2,573	0.16
Other South American	278	0.02
Other Hispanic or Latino	35,548	2.24

Race*	Population	%
African-American/Black (246,687)	272,993	17.21
Not Hispanic (205,340)	217,102	13.69
Hispanic (41,347)	55,891	3.52
American Indian/Alaska Native (8,669)	19,415	1.22
Not Hispanic (2,144)	7,395	0.47
Hispanic (6,525)	12,020	0.76
Alaska Athabascan (Ala. Nat.) (11)	18	<0.01
Aleut (Alaska Native) (4)	7	<0.01
Apache (28)	92	0.01
Arapaho (3)	5	<0.01
Blackfeet (41)	356	0.02
Canadian/French Am. Ind. (29)	62	<0.01
Central American Ind. (610)	1,090	0.07
Cherokee (288)	1,845	0.12
Cheyenne (4)	9	<0.01
Chickasaw (15)	43	<0.01
Chippewa (36)	99	0.01
Choctaw (41)	179	0.01
Colville (4)	5	<0.01

	Population	%
Comanche (13)	22	<0.01
Cree (4)	22	<0.01
Creek (12)	61	<0.01
Crow (4)	11	<0.01
Delaware (14)	54	<0.01
Hopi (8)	15	<0.01
Houma (0)	3	<0.01
Inupiat (Alaska Native) (2)	8	<0.01
Iroquois (97)	265	0.02
Kiowa (9)	11	<0.01
Lumbee (10)	21	<0.01
Menominee (2)	3	<0.01
Mexican American Ind. (479)	752	0.05
Navajo (38)	83	0.01
Osage (7)	12	<0.01
Ottawa (0)	3	<0.01
Paiute (2)	8	<0.01
Pima (2)	4	<0.01
Potawatomi (10)	20	<0.01
Pueblo (70)	175	0.01
Puget Sound Salish (2)	5	<0.01
Seminole (6)	110	0.01
Shoshone (3)	6	<0.01
Sioux (38)	133	0.01
South American Ind. (813)	1,935	0.12
Spanish American Ind. (373)	514	0.03
Tlingit-Haida (Alaska Native) (2)	15	<0.01
Tohono O'Odham (11)	15	<0.01
Tsimshian (Alaska Native) (3)	3	<0.01
Ute (1)	2	<0.01
Yakama (1)	2	<0.01
Yaqui (8)	22	<0.01
Yuman (4)	6	<0.01
Yup'ik (Alaska Native) (0)	2	<0.01
Asian (179,552)	199,722	12.59
Not Hispanic (177,624)	194,929	12.29
Hispanic (1,928)	4,793	0.30
Bangladeshi (1,672)	2,029	0.13
Bhutanese (26)	26	<0.01
Burmese (240)	317	0.02
Cambodian (168)	220	0.01
Chinese, ex. Taiwanese (92,088)	99,287	6.26
Filipino (10,399)	13,388	0.84
Hmong (16)	20	<0.01
Indian (25,857)	29,979	1.89
Indonesian (470)	693	0.04
Japanese (13,201)	16,600	1.05
Korean (19,683)	21,996	1.39
Laotian (109)	157	0.01
Malaysian (524)	766	0.05
Nepalese (240)	281	0.02
Pakistani (2,482)	2,940	0.19
Sri Lankan (450)	563	0.04
Taiwanese (2,789)	3,318	0.21
Thai (1,282)	1,657	0.10
Vietnamese (2,194)	2,919	0.18
Hawaii Native/Pacific Islander (873)	3,727	0.24
Not Hispanic (533)	1,776	0.11
Hispanic (340)	1,951	0.12
Fijian (29)	73	<0.01
Guamanian/Chamorro (132)	242	0.02
Marshallese (3)	4	<0.01
Native Hawaiian (185)	608	0.04
Samoan (87)	183	0.01
Tongan (18)	33	<0.01
White (911,073)	956,864	60.34
Not Hispanic (761,493)	785,299	49.52
Hispanic (149,580)	171,565	10.82

Notes: † The Census 2010 population figure is used to calculate the percentages in the Hispanic Origin and Race categories. Ancestry percentages are based on the 2006-2010 American Community Survey population (not shown); ‡ Numbers in parentheses indicate the number of people reporting a single ancestry; * Numbers in parentheses indicate the number of persons reporting this race alone, not in combination with any other race; Please refer to the Explanation of Data for more information.

Niagara County
Population: 216,469

Ancestry	Population	%
Afghan (0)	0	<0.01
African, Sub-Saharan (371)	625	0.29
African (339)	577	0.27
Cape Verdean (0)	0	<0.01
Ethiopian (24)	32	0.01
Ghanaian (0)	0	<0.01
Kenyan (0)	8	<0.01
Liberian (0)	0	<0.01
Nigerian (0)	0	<0.01
Senegalese (0)	0	<0.01
Sierra Leonean (0)	0	<0.01
Somalian (0)	0	<0.01
South African (8)	8	<0.01
Sudanese (0)	0	<0.01
Ugandan (0)	0	<0.01
Zimbabwean (0)	0	<0.01
Other Sub-Saharan African (0)	0	<0.01
Albanian (0)	0	<0.01
Alsatian (0)	14	0.01
American (7,216)	7,216	3.34
Arab (916)	1,832	0.85
Arab (144)	175	0.08
Egyptian (24)	61	0.03
Iraqi (0)	13	0.01
Jordanian (282)	282	0.13
Lebanese (388)	1,098	0.51
Moroccan (0)	0	<0.01
Palestinian (28)	28	0.01
Syrian (9)	83	0.04
Other Arab (41)	92	0.04
Armenian (164)	269	0.12
Assyrian/Chaldean/Syriac (0)	0	<0.01
Australian (31)	60	0.03
Austrian (255)	1,001	0.46
Basque (0)	0	<0.01
Belgian (38)	97	0.04
Brazilian (18)	18	0.01
British (270)	512	0.24
Bulgarian (0)	10	<0.01
Cajun (0)	0	<0.01
Canadian (707)	1,755	0.81
Carpatho Rusyn (14)	14	0.01
Celtic (0)	27	0.01
Croatian (196)	353	0.16
Cypriot (0)	0	<0.01
Czech (63)	422	0.20
Czechoslovakian (86)	245	0.11
Danish (77)	408	0.19
Dutch (548)	3,738	1.73
Eastern European (60)	60	0.03
English (9,005)	29,036	13.44
Estonian (8)	8	<0.01
European (960)	978	0.45
Finnish (0)	44	0.02
French, ex. Basque (1,222)	9,233	4.27
French Canadian (898)	2,590	1.20
German (18,960)	62,469	28.91
German Russian (16)	16	0.01
Greek (348)	969	0.45
Guyanese (43)	43	0.02
Hungarian (708)	2,506	1.16
Icelander (10)	68	0.03
Iranian (15)	24	0.01
Irish (9,618)	39,511	18.29
Israeli (12)	12	0.01
Italian (19,116)	41,083	19.01
Latvian (12)	28	0.01
Lithuanian (191)	455	0.21
Luxemburger (0)	0	<0.01
Macedonian (0)	0	<0.01
Maltese (0)	0	<0.01
New Zealander (0)	0	<0.01
Northern European (50)	50	0.02
Norwegian (257)	1,008	0.47
Pennsylvania German (178)	315	0.15

Ancestry (cont.)	Population	%
Polish (10,633)	26,701	12.36
Portuguese (135)	258	0.12
Romanian (15)	107	0.05
Russian (777)	1,533	0.71
Scandinavian (86)	178	0.08
Scotch-Irish (964)	2,795	1.29
Scottish (1,335)	4,977	2.30
Serbian (0)	27	0.01
Slavic (129)	382	0.18
Slovak (142)	461	0.21
Slovene (28)	65	0.03
Soviet Union (0)	0	<0.01
Swedish (250)	1,940	0.90
Swiss (67)	236	0.11
Turkish (10)	41	0.02
Ukrainian (438)	1,138	0.53
Welsh (301)	1,779	0.82
West Indian, ex. Hispanic (431)	666	0.31
Bahamian (0)	0	<0.01
Barbadian (0)	0	<0.01
Belizean (29)	29	0.01
Bermudan (0)	0	<0.01
British West Indian (9)	9	<0.01
Dutch West Indian (0)	0	<0.01
Haitian (9)	9	<0.01
Jamaican (346)	409	0.19
Trinidadian/Tobagonian (15)	15	<0.01
U.S. Virgin Islander (0)	0	<0.01
West Indian (23)	195	0.09
Other West Indian (0)	0	<0.01
Yugoslavian (28)	123	0.06

Hispanic Origin	Population	%
Hispanic or Latino (of any race)	4,694	2.17
Central American, ex. Mexican	165	0.08
Costa Rican	19	0.01
Guatemalan	50	0.02
Honduran	25	0.01
Nicaraguan	4	<0.01
Panamanian	47	0.02
Salvadoran	19	0.01
Other Central American	1	<0.01
Cuban	164	0.08
Dominican Republic	118	0.05
Mexican	1,107	0.51
Puerto Rican	2,263	1.05
South American	230	0.11
Argentinean	22	0.01
Bolivian	1	<0.01
Chilean	11	0.01
Colombian	104	0.05
Ecuadorian	33	0.02
Paraguayan	6	<0.01
Peruvian	31	0.01
Uruguayan	0	<0.01
Venezuelan	18	0.01
Other South American	4	<0.01
Other Hispanic or Latino	647	0.30

Race*	Population	%
African-American/Black (14,851)	17,632	8.15
Not Hispanic (14,511)	17,058	7.88
Hispanic (340)	574	0.27
American Indian/Alaska Native (2,285)	3,859	1.78
Not Hispanic (2,135)	3,589	1.66
Hispanic (150)	270	0.12
Alaska Athabascan (Ala. Nat.) (0)	1	<0.01
Aleut (Alaska Native) (0)	0	<0.01
Apache (2)	5	<0.01
Arapaho (0)	0	<0.01
Blackfeet (6)	49	0.02
Canadian/French Am. Ind. (39)	53	0.02
Central American Ind. (9)	13	0.01
Cherokee (34)	165	0.08
Cheyenne (1)	3	<0.01
Chickasaw (1)	1	<0.01
Chippewa (39)	64	0.03
Choctaw (1)	13	0.01
Colville (0)	0	<0.01

Race* (cont.)	Population	%
Comanche (1)	1	<0.01
Cree (2)	5	<0.01
Creek (0)	6	<0.01
Crow (2)	2	<0.01
Delaware (5)	7	<0.01
Hopi (0)	0	<0.01
Houma (0)	0	<0.01
Inupiat (Alaska Native) (1)	2	<0.01
Iroquois (1,163)	1,751	0.81
Kiowa (1)	1	<0.01
Lumbee (4)	8	<0.01
Menominee (0)	2	<0.01
Mexican American Ind. (20)	21	0.01
Navajo (9)	9	<0.01
Osage (3)	4	<0.01
Ottawa (1)	2	<0.01
Paiute (0)	0	<0.01
Pima (0)	0	<0.01
Potawatomi (0)	0	<0.01
Pueblo (0)	0	<0.01
Puget Sound Salish (0)	0	<0.01
Seminole (0)	11	0.01
Shoshone (0)	0	<0.01
Sioux (13)	36	0.02
South American Ind. (10)	18	0.01
Spanish American Ind. (5)	5	<0.01
Tlingit-Haida (Alaska Native) (0)	1	<0.01
Tohono O'Odham (0)	0	<0.01
Tsimshian (Alaska Native) (0)	0	<0.01
Ute (1)	1	<0.01
Yakama (0)	1	<0.01
Yaqui (2)	2	<0.01
Yuman (0)	0	<0.01
Yup'ik (Alaska Native) (0)	0	<0.01
Asian (1,823)	2,407	1.11
Not Hispanic (1,807)	2,354	1.09
Hispanic (16)	53	0.02
Bangladeshi (2)	2	<0.01
Bhutanese (0)	0	<0.01
Burmese (13)	13	0.01
Cambodian (3)	8	<0.01
Chinese, ex. Taiwanese (347)	425	0.20
Filipino (133)	262	0.12
Hmong (4)	10	<0.01
Indian (671)	789	0.36
Indonesian (14)	18	0.01
Japanese (66)	135	0.06
Korean (210)	295	0.14
Laotian (18)	25	0.01
Malaysian (2)	2	<0.01
Nepalese (0)	0	<0.01
Pakistani (113)	127	0.06
Sri Lankan (6)	16	0.01
Taiwanese (19)	20	0.01
Thai (21)	38	0.02
Vietnamese (107)	135	0.06
Hawaii Native/Pacific Islander (62)	158	0.07
Not Hispanic (55)	141	0.07
Hispanic (7)	17	0.01
Fijian (1)	2	<0.01
Guamanian/Chamorro (8)	12	0.01
Marshallese (1)	1	<0.01
Native Hawaiian (14)	39	0.02
Samoan (5)	17	0.01
Tongan (4)	4	<0.01
White (191,673)	195,911	90.50
Not Hispanic (188,907)	192,737	89.04
Hispanic (2,766)	3,174	1.47

Notes: † The Census 2010 population figure is used to calculate the percentages in the Hispanic Origin and Race categories. Ancestry percentages are based on the 2006-2010 American Community Survey population (not shown); ‡ Numbers in parentheses indicate the number of people reporting a single ancestry; * Numbers in parentheses indicate the number of persons reporting this race alone, not in combination with any other race; Please refer to the Explanation of Data for more information.

Oneida County

Population: 234,878

Ancestry	Population	%
Afghan (42)	42	0.02
African, Sub-Saharan (699)	998	0.43
African (446)	671	0.29
Cape Verdean (0)	0	<0.01
Ethiopian (20)	79	0.03
Ghanaian (14)	14	0.01
Kenyan (12)	27	0.01
Liberian (88)	88	0.04
Nigerian (2)	2	<0.01
Senegalese (0)	0	<0.01
Sierra Leonean (0)	0	<0.01
Somalian (99)	99	0.04
South African (0)	0	<0.01
Sudanese (0)	0	<0.01
Ugandan (0)	0	<0.01
Zimbabwean (0)	0	<0.01
Other Sub-Saharan African (18)	18	0.01
Albanian (22)	55	0.02
Alsatian (0)	29	0.01
American (9,419)	9,419	4.02
Arab (2,006)	4,287	1.83
Arab (181)	267	0.11
Egyptian (149)	189	0.08
Iraqi (0)	6	<0.01
Jordanian (28)	28	0.01
Lebanese (1,246)	2,742	1.17
Moroccan (41)	50	0.02
Palestinian (10)	10	<0.01
Syrian (155)	742	0.32
Other Arab (196)	253	0.11
Armenian (130)	196	0.08
Assyrian/Chaldean/Syriac (0)	0	<0.01
Australian (32)	92	0.04
Austrian (69)	587	0.25
Basque (0)	0	<0.01
Belgian (8)	75	0.03
Brazilian (33)	86	0.04
British (394)	620	0.26
Bulgarian (0)	5	<0.01
Cajun (0)	0	<0.01
Canadian (288)	644	0.27
Carpatho Rusyn (8)	15	0.01
Celtic (8)	16	0.01
Croatian (24)	106	0.05
Cypriot (0)	0	<0.01
Czech (45)	576	0.25
Czechoslovakian (91)	233	0.10
Danish (99)	560	0.24
Dutch (908)	6,105	2.60
Eastern European (180)	200	0.09
English (6,403)	26,141	11.15
Estonian (0)	9	<0.01
European (1,134)	1,173	0.50
Finnish (30)	198	0.08
French, ex. Basque (1,786)	13,375	5.70
French Canadian (1,392)	3,834	1.63
German (9,284)	44,884	19.14
German Russian (0)	0	<0.01
Greek (145)	490	0.21
Guyanese (54)	68	0.03
Hungarian (203)	964	0.41
Icelander (0)	14	0.01
Iranian (35)	35	0.01
Irish (11,623)	45,802	19.53
Israeli (0)	0	<0.01
Italian (24,027)	47,602	20.30
Latvian (11)	14	0.01
Lithuanian (145)	683	0.29
Luxemburger (0)	0	<0.01
Macedonian (21)	21	0.01
Maltese (0)	0	<0.01
New Zealander (4)	4	<0.01
Northern European (195)	198	0.08
Norwegian (169)	709	0.30
Pennsylvania German (63)	159	0.07

Ancestry (cont.)	Population	%
Polish (10,228)	26,014	11.09
Portuguese (110)	488	0.21
Romanian (148)	239	0.10
Russian (1,169)	2,226	0.95
Scandinavian (32)	161	0.07
Scotch-Irish (737)	2,747	1.17
Scottish (732)	3,742	1.60
Serbian (0)	82	0.03
Slavic (13)	30	0.01
Slovak (135)	249	0.11
Slovene (9)	11	<0.01
Soviet Union (0)	0	<0.01
Swedish (266)	1,098	0.47
Swiss (294)	1,595	0.68
Turkish (0)	7	<0.01
Ukrainian (1,187)	2,419	1.03
Welsh (1,540)	7,279	3.10
West Indian, ex. Hispanic (1,119)	1,537	0.66
Bahamian (0)	0	<0.01
Barbadian (30)	34	0.01
Belizean (0)	10	<0.01
Bermudan (0)	0	<0.01
British West Indian (68)	96	0.04
Dutch West Indian (0)	0	<0.01
Haitian (241)	376	0.16
Jamaican (504)	675	0.29
Trinidadian/Tobagonian (139)	169	0.07
U.S. Virgin Islander (9)	9	<0.01
West Indian (128)	168	0.07
Other West Indian (0)	0	<0.01
Yugoslavian (3,270)	3,482	1.48

Hispanic Origin	Population	%
Hispanic or Latino (of any race)	10,819	4.61
Central American, ex. Mexican	551	0.23
Costa Rican	19	0.01
Guatemalan	88	0.04
Honduran	88	0.04
Nicaraguan	38	0.02
Panamanian	87	0.04
Salvadoran	221	0.09
Other Central American	10	<0.01
Cuban	187	0.08
Dominican Republic	1,211	0.52
Mexican	872	0.37
Puerto Rican	6,538	2.78
South American	448	0.19
Argentinean	25	0.01
Bolivian	12	0.01
Chilean	20	0.01
Colombian	109	0.05
Ecuadorian	154	0.07
Paraguayan	3	<0.01
Peruvian	66	0.03
Uruguayan	4	<0.01
Venezuelan	49	0.02
Other South American	6	<0.01
Other Hispanic or Latino	1,012	0.43

Race*	Population	%
African-American/Black (14,688)	17,445	7.43
Not Hispanic (13,682)	15,969	6.80
Hispanic (1,006)	1,476	0.63
American Indian/Alaska Native (605)	1,692	0.72
Not Hispanic (499)	1,393	0.59
Hispanic (106)	299	0.13
Alaska Athabascan (Ala. Nat.) (0)	0	<0.01
Aleut (Alaska Native) (3)	3	<0.01
Apache (9)	20	0.01
Arapaho (2)	2	<0.01
Blackfeet (3)	41	0.02
Canadian/French Am. Ind. (3)	17	0.01
Central American Ind. (9)	13	0.01
Cherokee (24)	158	0.07
Cheyenne (1)	10	<0.01
Chickasaw (1)	5	<0.01
Chippewa (12)	25	0.01
Choctaw (0)	7	<0.01
Colville (0)	0	<0.01

Race* (cont.)	Population	%
Comanche (0)	0	<0.01
Cree (2)	8	<0.01
Creek (0)	3	<0.01
Crow (0)	3	<0.01
Delaware (2)	4	<0.01
Hopi (0)	1	<0.01
Houma (0)	0	<0.01
Inupiat (Alaska Native) (1)	2	<0.01
Iroquois (190)	419	0.18
Kiowa (1)	3	<0.01
Lumbee (4)	4	<0.01
Menominee (0)	0	<0.01
Mexican American Ind. (6)	12	0.01
Navajo (4)	12	0.01
Osage (0)	0	<0.01
Ottawa (1)	1	<0.01
Paiute (1)	1	<0.01
Pima (0)	1	<0.01
Potawatomi (5)	5	<0.01
Pueblo (3)	5	<0.01
Puget Sound Salish (0)	0	<0.01
Seminole (0)	4	<0.01
Shoshone (0)	1	<0.01
Sioux (22)	60	0.03
South American Ind. (8)	28	0.01
Spanish American Ind. (0)	1	<0.01
Tlingit-Haida (Alaska Native) (1)	4	<0.01
Tohono O'Odham (1)	1	<0.01
Tsimshian (Alaska Native) (0)	0	<0.01
Ute (0)	0	<0.01
Yakama (0)	0	<0.01
Yaqui (0)	5	<0.01
Yuman (0)	0	<0.01
Yup'ik (Alaska Native) (0)	0	<0.01
Asian (6,565)	7,434	3.17
Not Hispanic (6,522)	7,310	3.11
Hispanic (43)	124	0.05
Bangladeshi (18)	18	0.01
Bhutanese (30)	36	0.02
Burmese (2,270)	2,394	1.02
Cambodian (435)	513	0.22
Chinese, ex. Taiwanese (537)	672	0.29
Filipino (219)	379	0.16
Hmong (2)	2	<0.01
Indian (806)	975	0.42
Indonesian (7)	7	<0.01
Japanese (106)	181	0.08
Korean (311)	386	0.16
Laotian (77)	117	0.05
Malaysian (6)	20	0.01
Nepalese (11)	17	0.01
Pakistani (137)	152	0.06
Sri Lankan (18)	23	0.01
Taiwanese (19)	26	0.01
Thai (104)	149	0.06
Vietnamese (1,032)	1,147	0.49
Hawaii Native/Pacific Islander (69)	258	0.11
Not Hispanic (49)	194	0.08
Hispanic (20)	64	0.03
Fijian (0)	0	<0.01
Guamanian/Chamorro (12)	30	0.01
Marshallese (0)	0	<0.01
Native Hawaiian (30)	69	0.03
Samoan (12)	26	0.01
Tongan (2)	4	<0.01
White (204,679)	208,959	88.96
Not Hispanic (199,254)	202,734	86.31
Hispanic (5,425)	6,225	2.65

*Notes: † The Census 2010 population figure is used to calculate the percentages in the Hispanic Origin and Race categories. Ancestry percentages are based on the 2006-2010 American Community Survey population (not shown); ‡ Numbers in parentheses indicate the number of people reporting a single ancestry; * Numbers in parentheses indicate the number of persons reporting this race alone, not in combination with any other race; Please refer to the Explanation of Data for more information.*

Onondaga County

Population: 467,026

Ancestry	Population	%
Afghan (19)	19	<0.01
African, Sub-Saharan (2,607)	3,016	0.65
African (1,156)	1,474	0.32
Cape Verdean (0)	23	<0.01
Ethiopian (12)	12	<0.01
Ghanaian (187)	187	0.04
Kenyan (0)	17	<0.01
Liberian (246)	246	0.05
Nigerian (246)	280	0.06
Senegalese (0)	0	<0.01
Sierra Leonean (13)	13	<0.01
Somalian (478)	478	0.10
South African (10)	10	<0.01
Sudanese (160)	177	0.04
Ugandan (26)	26	0.01
Zimbabwean (0)	0	<0.01
Other Sub-Saharan African (73)	73	0.02
Albanian (472)	537	0.12
Alsatian (39)	39	0.01
American (14,013)	14,013	3.02
Arab (1,701)	3,500	0.75
Arab (580)	951	0.21
Egyptian (164)	228	0.05
Iraqi (0)	0	<0.01
Jordanian (28)	28	0.01
Lebanese (430)	1,493	0.32
Moroccan (60)	86	0.02
Palestinian (154)	184	0.04
Syrian (126)	343	0.07
Other Arab (159)	187	0.04
Armenian (254)	861	0.19
Assyrian/Chaldean/Syriac (19)	29	0.01
Australian (42)	96	0.02
Austrian (469)	2,236	0.48
Basque (0)	0	<0.01
Belgian (130)	347	0.07
Brazilian (103)	120	0.03
British (664)	1,397	0.30
Bulgarian (34)	56	0.01
Cajun (24)	34	0.01
Canadian (872)	1,837	0.40
Carpatho Rusyn (0)	0	<0.01
Celtic (18)	91	0.02
Croatian (60)	239	0.05
Cypriot (0)	0	<0.01
Czech (311)	1,294	0.28
Czechoslovakian (208)	456	0.10
Danish (258)	914	0.20
Dutch (1,303)	10,861	2.34
Eastern European (523)	644	0.14
English (14,320)	60,136	12.97
Estonian (7)	26	0.01
European (2,482)	2,761	0.60
Finnish (235)	699	0.15
French, ex. Basque (3,327)	25,406	5.48
French Canadian (2,708)	8,589	1.85
German (17,906)	90,839	19.59
German Russian (0)	0	<0.01
Greek (1,634)	3,322	0.72
Guyanese (151)	209	0.05
Hungarian (627)	2,113	0.46
Icelander (13)	32	0.01
Iranian (303)	364	0.08
Irish (28,391)	107,847	23.26
Israeli (145)	184	0.04
Italian (35,847)	82,484	17.79
Latvian (116)	280	0.06
Lithuanian (317)	1,064	0.23
Luxemburger (0)	40	0.01
Macedonian (375)	498	0.11
Maltese (33)	53	0.01
New Zealander (2)	17	<0.01
Northern European (315)	333	0.07
Norwegian (417)	1,540	0.33
Pennsylvania German (85)	173	0.04

Ancestry (cont.)	Population	%
Polish (11,929)	35,362	7.63
Portuguese (374)	943	0.20
Romanian (118)	408	0.09
Russian (2,120)	5,700	1.23
Scandinavian (175)	394	0.08
Scotch-Irish (2,597)	7,595	1.64
Scottish (2,048)	9,589	2.07
Serbian (76)	144	0.03
Slavic (64)	322	0.07
Slovak (287)	948	0.20
Slovene (53)	229	0.05
Soviet Union (0)	0	<0.01
Swedish (822)	3,763	0.81
Swiss (401)	1,724	0.37
Turkish (377)	537	0.12
Ukrainian (3,319)	6,832	1.47
Welsh (699)	4,566	0.98
West Indian, ex. Hispanic (2,495)	3,224	0.70
Bahamian (0)	0	<0.01
Barbadian (105)	136	0.03
Belizean (9)	9	<0.01
Bermudan (0)	0	<0.01
British West Indian (39)	67	0.01
Dutch West Indian (0)	0	<0.01
Haitian (351)	415	0.09
Jamaican (1,406)	1,928	0.42
Trinidadian/Tobagonian (187)	187	0.04
U.S. Virgin Islander (0)	0	<0.01
West Indian (398)	482	0.10
Other West Indian (0)	0	<0.01
Yugoslavian (1,565)	1,698	0.37

Hispanic Origin	Population	%
Hispanic or Latino (of any race)	18,829	4.03
Central American, ex. Mexican	802	0.17
Costa Rican	64	0.01
Guatemalan	346	0.07
Honduran	106	0.02
Nicaraguan	53	0.01
Panamanian	126	0.03
Salvadoran	102	0.02
Other Central American	5	<0.01
Cuban	1,766	0.38
Dominican Republic	944	0.20
Mexican	2,338	0.50
Puerto Rican	10,246	2.19
South American	1,190	0.25
Argentinean	108	0.02
Bolivian	26	0.01
Chilean	89	0.02
Colombian	398	0.09
Ecuadorian	195	0.04
Paraguayan	19	<0.01
Peruvian	204	0.04
Uruguayan	33	0.01
Venezuelan	103	0.02
Other South American	15	<0.01
Other Hispanic or Latino	1,543	0.33

Race*	Population	%
African-American/Black (51,220)	58,984	12.63
Not Hispanic (48,696)	55,309	11.84
Hispanic (2,524)	3,675	0.79
American Indian/Alaska Native (3,818)	7,490	1.60
Not Hispanic (3,432)	6,695	1.43
Hispanic (386)	795	0.17
Alaska Athabascan (Ala. Nat.) (0)	5	<0.01
Aleut (Alaska Native) (1)	2	<0.01
Apache (16)	42	0.01
Arapaho (2)	2	<0.01
Blackfeet (10)	156	0.03
Canadian/French Am. Ind. (59)	102	0.02
Central American Ind. (5)	18	<0.01
Cherokee (49)	434	0.09
Cheyenne (0)	3	<0.01
Chickasaw (0)	5	<0.01
Chippewa (32)	53	0.01
Choctaw (9)	49	0.01
Colville (0)	1	<0.01

Race* (cont.)	Population	%
Comanche (7)	14	<0.01
Cree (3)	11	<0.01
Creek (4)	15	<0.01
Crow (0)	2	<0.01
Delaware (8)	14	<0.01
Hopi (0)	5	<0.01
Houma (1)	1	<0.01
Inupiat (Alaska Native) (5)	9	<0.01
Iroquois (1,942)	3,255	0.70
Kiowa (1)	2	<0.01
Lumbee (5)	9	<0.01
Menominee (1)	1	<0.01
Mexican American Ind. (53)	75	0.02
Navajo (8)	12	<0.01
Osage (2)	6	<0.01
Ottawa (1)	4	<0.01
Paiute (0)	0	<0.01
Pima (1)	2	<0.01
Potawatomi (6)	9	<0.01
Pueblo (0)	0	<0.01
Puget Sound Salish (0)	0	<0.01
Seminole (5)	27	0.01
Shoshone (1)	3	<0.01
Sioux (29)	64	0.01
South American Ind. (50)	94	0.02
Spanish American Ind. (9)	9	<0.01
Tlingit-Haida (Alaska Native) (1)	2	<0.01
Tohono O'Odham (1)	1	<0.01
Tsimshian (Alaska Native) (0)	0	<0.01
Ute (0)	0	<0.01
Yakama (0)	0	<0.01
Yaqui (0)	1	<0.01
Yuman (1)	4	<0.01
Yup'ik (Alaska Native) (0)	1	<0.01
Asian (14,454)	16,875	3.61
Not Hispanic (14,370)	16,607	3.56
Hispanic (84)	268	0.06
Bangladeshi (86)	101	0.02
Bhutanese (392)	516	0.11
Burmese (1,202)	1,242	0.27
Cambodian (204)	255	0.05
Chinese, ex. Taiwanese (2,955)	3,411	0.73
Filipino (703)	1,094	0.23
Hmong (112)	134	0.03
Indian (2,910)	3,295	0.71
Indonesian (30)	58	0.01
Japanese (251)	559	0.12
Korean (1,788)	2,125	0.46
Laotian (133)	169	0.04
Malaysian (8)	18	<0.01
Nepalese (177)	280	0.06
Pakistani (343)	388	0.08
Sri Lankan (51)	62	0.01
Taiwanese (144)	178	0.04
Thai (134)	195	0.04
Vietnamese (2,133)	2,393	0.51
Hawaii Native/Pacific Islander (148)	534	0.11
Not Hispanic (120)	432	0.09
Hispanic (28)	102	0.02
Fijian (5)	4	<0.01
Guamanian/Chamorro (41)	53	0.01
Marshallese (0)	1	<0.01
Native Hawaiian (42)	156	0.03
Samoan (14)	44	0.01
Tongan (1)	2	<0.01
White (378,885)	390,050	83.52
Not Hispanic (370,040)	379,663	81.29
Hispanic (8,845)	10,387	2.22

*Notes: † The Census 2010 population figure is used to calculate the percentages in the Hispanic Origin and Race categories. Ancestry percentages are based on the 2006-2010 American Community Survey population (not shown); ‡ Numbers in parentheses indicate the number of people reporting a single ancestry; * Numbers in parentheses indicate the number of persons reporting this race alone, not in combination with any other race; Please refer to the Explanation of Data for more information.*

Ontario County

Population: 107,931

Ancestry	Population	%
Afghan (0)	0	<0.01
African, Sub-Saharan (31)	105	0.10
African (31)	105	0.10
Cape Verdean (0)	0	<0.01
Ethiopian (0)	0	<0.01
Ghanaian (0)	0	<0.01
Kenyan (0)	0	<0.01
Liberian (0)	0	<0.01
Nigerian (0)	0	<0.01
Senegalese (0)	0	<0.01
Sierra Leonean (0)	0	<0.01
Somalian (0)	0	<0.01
South African (0)	0	<0.01
Sudanese (0)	0	<0.01
Ugandan (0)	0	<0.01
Zimbabwean (0)	0	<0.01
Other Sub-Saharan African (0)	0	<0.01
Albanian (436)	436	0.41
Alsatian (0)	0	<0.01
American (5,011)	5,011	4.71
Arab (106)	390	0.37
Arab (6)	6	0.01
Egyptian (0)	0	<0.01
Iraqi (0)	0	<0.01
Jordanian (0)	0	<0.01
Lebanese (23)	63	0.06
Moroccan (0)	3	<0.01
Palestinian (0)	14	0.01
Syrian (77)	304	0.29
Other Arab (0)	0	<0.01
Armenian (14)	24	0.02
Assyrian/Chaldean/Syriac (0)	0	<0.01
Australian (0)	5	<0.01
Austrian (78)	251	0.24
Basque (0)	0	<0.01
Belgian (54)	160	0.15
Brazilian (0)	11	0.01
British (275)	630	0.59
Bulgarian (11)	83	0.08
Cajun (0)	0	<0.01
Canadian (312)	525	0.49
Carpatho Rusyn (0)	0	<0.01
Celtic (3)	6	0.01
Croatian (13)	13	0.01
Cypriot (0)	0	<0.01
Czech (44)	381	0.36
Czechoslovakian (67)	147	0.14
Danish (237)	1,121	1.05
Dutch (1,459)	7,090	6.67
Eastern European (95)	135	0.13
English (5,898)	22,292	20.97
Estonian (0)	0	<0.01
European (1,060)	1,131	1.06
Finnish (85)	136	0.13
French, ex. Basque (635)	4,770	4.49
French Canadian (419)	1,770	1.67
German (6,907)	29,630	27.87
German Russian (0)	0	<0.01
Greek (115)	382	0.36
Guyanese (102)	102	0.10
Hungarian (213)	399	0.38
Icelander (0)	10	0.01
Iranian (0)	0	<0.01
Irish (5,165)	22,198	20.88
Israeli (0)	0	<0.01
Italian (6,590)	16,105	15.15
Latvian (0)	0	<0.01
Lithuanian (109)	270	0.25
Luxemburger (0)	0	<0.01
Macedonian (10)	35	0.03
Maltese (20)	20	0.02
New Zealander (0)	0	<0.01
Northern European (92)	98	0.09
Norwegian (168)	644	0.61
Pennsylvania German (263)	366	0.34

Ancestry (cont.)	Population	%
Polish (1,315)	5,470	5.15
Portuguese (40)	117	0.11
Romanian (87)	142	0.13
Russian (121)	465	0.44
Scandinavian (145)	381	0.36
Scotch-Irish (620)	1,768	1.66
Scottish (735)	2,962	2.79
Serbian (21)	66	0.06
Slavic (0)	51	0.05
Slovak (101)	273	0.26
Slovene (0)	5	<0.01
Soviet Union (0)	0	<0.01
Swedish (453)	1,399	1.32
Swiss (105)	371	0.35
Turkish (3)	20	0.02
Ukrainian (180)	827	0.78
Welsh (251)	1,231	1.16
West Indian, ex. Hispanic (374)	459	0.43
Bahamian (0)	0	<0.01
Barbadian (0)	0	<0.01
Belizean (0)	0	<0.01
Bermudan (0)	0	<0.01
British West Indian (0)	27	0.03
Dutch West Indian (0)	0	<0.01
Haitian (0)	28	0.03
Jamaican (311)	324	0.30
Trinidadian/Tobagonian (29)	46	0.04
U.S. Virgin Islander (0)	0	<0.01
West Indian (34)	34	0.03
Other West Indian (0)	0	<0.01
Yugoslavian (57)	133	0.13

Hispanic Origin	Population	%
Hispanic or Latino (of any race)	3,679	3.41
Central American, ex. Mexican	180	0.17
Costa Rican	22	0.02
Guatemalan	60	0.06
Honduran	30	0.03
Nicaraguan	15	0.01
Panamanian	33	0.03
Salvadoran	20	0.02
Other Central American	0	<0.01
Cuban	105	0.10
Dominican Republic	110	0.10
Mexican	837	0.78
Puerto Rican	2,078	1.93
South American	182	0.17
Argentinean	27	0.03
Bolivian	4	<0.01
Chilean	8	0.01
Colombian	63	0.06
Ecuadorian	26	0.02
Paraguayan	0	<0.01
Peruvian	35	0.03
Uruguayan	0	<0.01
Venezuelan	19	0.02
Other South American	0	<0.01
Other Hispanic or Latino	187	0.17

Race*	Population	%
African-American/Black (2,432)	3,342	3.10
Not Hispanic (2,226)	3,001	2.78
Hispanic (206)	341	0.32
American Indian/Alaska Native (276)	776	0.72
Not Hispanic (244)	688	0.64
Hispanic (32)	88	0.08
Alaska Athabascan (Ala. Nat.) (1)	1	<0.01
Aleut (Alaska Native) (0)	1	<0.01
Apache (5)	14	0.01
Arapaho (0)	0	<0.01
Blackfeet (3)	19	0.02
Canadian/French Am. Ind. (4)	7	0.01
Central American Ind. (1)	1	<0.01
Cherokee (19)	105	0.10
Cheyenne (0)	5	<0.01
Chickasaw (1)	2	<0.01
Chippewa (16)	20	0.02
Choctaw (2)	8	0.01
Colville (0)	0	<0.01

Race* (cont.)	Population	%
Comanche (0)	1	<0.01
Cree (0)	1	<0.01
Creek (0)	0	<0.01
Crow (0)	7	0.01
Delaware (5)	6	0.01
Hopi (2)	2	<0.01
Houma (1)	1	<0.01
Inupiat (Alaska Native) (0)	1	<0.01
Iroquois (84)	190	0.18
Kiowa (1)	1	<0.01
Lumbee (1)	1	<0.01
Menominee (0)	0	<0.01
Mexican American Ind. (2)	2	<0.01
Navajo (1)	2	<0.01
Osage (0)	0	<0.01
Ottawa (1)	1	<0.01
Paiute (0)	0	<0.01
Pima (0)	0	<0.01
Potawatomi (0)	0	<0.01
Pueblo (0)	3	<0.01
Puget Sound Salish (0)	0	<0.01
Seminole (0)	6	0.01
Shoshone (0)	0	<0.01
Sioux (9)	25	0.02
South American Ind. (2)	8	0.01
Spanish American Ind. (0)	0	<0.01
Tlingit-Haida (Alaska Native) (0)	0	<0.01
Tohono O'Odham (0)	0	<0.01
Tsimshian (Alaska Native) (0)	0	<0.01
Ute (0)	2	<0.01
Yakama (0)	0	<0.01
Yaqui (0)	0	<0.01
Yuman (0)	0	<0.01
Yup'ik (Alaska Native) (1)	1	<0.01
Asian (1,126)	1,486	1.38
Not Hispanic (1,111)	1,455	1.35
Hispanic (15)	31	0.03
Bangladeshi (3)	3	<0.01
Bhutanese (0)	0	<0.01
Burmese (7)	7	0.01
Cambodian (18)	18	0.02
Chinese, ex. Taiwanese (318)	391	0.36
Filipino (113)	202	0.19
Hmong (0)	0	<0.01
Indian (231)	271	0.25
Indonesian (7)	16	0.01
Japanese (53)	95	0.09
Korean (144)	205	0.19
Laotian (35)	42	0.04
Malaysian (3)	4	<0.01
Nepalese (3)	4	<0.01
Pakistani (29)	33	0.03
Sri Lankan (5)	5	<0.01
Taiwanese (14)	16	0.01
Thai (23)	27	0.03
Vietnamese (70)	86	0.08
Hawaii Native/Pacific Islander (24)	83	0.08
Not Hispanic (16)	65	0.06
Hispanic (8)	18	0.02
Fijian (0)	0	<0.01
Guamanian/Chamorro (6)	23	0.02
Marshallese (0)	0	<0.01
Native Hawaiian (11)	25	0.02
Samoan (0)	0	<0.01
Tongan (0)	0	<0.01
White (101,078)	102,741	95.19
Not Hispanic (99,119)	100,508	93.12
Hispanic (1,959)	2,233	2.07

*Notes: † The Census 2010 population figure is used to calculate the percentages in the Hispanic Origin and Race categories. Ancestry percentages are based on the 2006-2010 American Community Survey population (not shown); ‡ Numbers in parentheses indicate the number of people reporting a single ancestry; * Numbers in parentheses indicate the number of persons reporting this race alone, not in combination with any other race; Please refer to the Explanation of Data for more information.*

Orange County
Population: 372,813

Ancestry	Population	%
Afghan (25)	25	0.01
African, Sub-Saharan (2,270)	2,998	0.81
African (1,369)	1,938	0.52
Cape Verdean (0)	0	<0.01
Ethiopian (23)	23	0.01
Ghanaian (140)	140	0.04
Kenyan (0)	0	<0.01
Liberian (0)	22	0.01
Nigerian (581)	647	0.17
Senegalese (0)	12	<0.01
Sierra Leonean (0)	0	<0.01
Somalian (20)	61	0.02
South African (14)	22	0.01
Sudanese (0)	0	<0.01
Ugandan (0)	0	<0.01
Zimbabwean (0)	0	<0.01
Other Sub-Saharan African (123)	133	0.04
Albanian (231)	545	0.15
Alsatian (0)	8	<0.01
American (23,068)	23,068	6.23
Arab (828)	1,606	0.43
Arab (16)	38	0.01
Egyptian (387)	508	0.14
Iraqi (0)	15	<0.01
Jordanian (156)	156	0.04
Lebanese (82)	315	0.09
Moroccan (19)	66	0.02
Palestinian (0)	0	<0.01
Syrian (20)	330	0.09
Other Arab (148)	178	0.05
Armenian (177)	407	0.11
Assyrian/Chaldean/Syriac (3)	3	<0.01
Australian (42)	182	0.05
Austrian (528)	2,246	0.61
Basque (0)	40	0.01
Belgian (49)	272	0.07
Brazilian (86)	151	0.04
British (591)	1,408	0.38
Bulgarian (190)	198	0.05
Cajun (52)	67	0.02
Canadian (394)	1,325	0.36
Carpatho Rusyn (0)	0	<0.01
Celtic (59)	82	0.02
Croatian (128)	430	0.12
Cypriot (13)	13	<0.01
Czech (306)	1,641	0.44
Czechoslovakian (325)	773	0.21
Danish (89)	596	0.16
Dutch (2,181)	9,116	2.46
Eastern European (906)	925	0.25
English (4,565)	24,564	6.64
Estonian (58)	125	0.03
European (3,404)	3,842	1.04
Finnish (154)	546	0.15
French, ex. Basque (821)	6,903	1.86
French Canadian (540)	2,032	0.55
German (11,282)	54,956	14.84
German Russian (0)	0	<0.01
Greek (825)	2,583	0.70
Guyanese (206)	432	0.12
Hungarian (3,947)	8,222	2.22
Icelander (23)	124	0.03
Iranian (50)	108	0.03
Irish (23,448)	75,052	20.27
Israeli (302)	1,042	0.28
Italian (26,639)	67,312	18.18
Latvian (107)	332	0.09
Lithuanian (300)	1,081	0.29
Luxemburger (0)	0	<0.01
Macedonian (0)	0	<0.01
Maltese (203)	302	0.08
New Zealander (0)	35	0.01
Northern European (67)	95	0.03
Norwegian (783)	3,015	0.81
Pennsylvania German (31)	128	0.03

Ancestry	Population	%
Polish (6,061)	20,649	5.58
Portuguese (473)	1,228	0.33
Romanian (758)	3,000	0.81
Russian (2,107)	6,133	1.66
Scandinavian (132)	412	0.11
Scotch-Irish (1,373)	4,366	1.18
Scottish (1,032)	4,871	1.32
Serbian (62)	96	0.03
Slavic (59)	201	0.05
Slovak (396)	1,031	0.28
Slovene (33)	103	0.03
Soviet Union (0)	0	<0.01
Swedish (599)	3,116	0.84
Swiss (270)	900	0.24
Turkish (126)	255	0.07
Ukrainian (1,049)	2,847	0.77
Welsh (264)	1,567	0.42
West Indian, ex. Hispanic (4,550)	6,861	1.85
Bahamian (0)	13	<0.01
Barbadian (69)	191	0.05
Belizean (0)	80	0.02
Bermudan (0)	0	<0.01
British West Indian (395)	708	0.19
Dutch West Indian (10)	48	0.01
Haitian (1,324)	1,665	0.45
Jamaican (1,855)	2,353	0.64
Trinidadian/Tobagonian (291)	585	0.16
U.S. Virgin Islander (0)	48	0.01
West Indian (566)	1,128	0.30
Other West Indian (40)	42	0.01
Yugoslavian (75)	369	0.10

Hispanic Origin	Population	%
Hispanic or Latino (of any race)	67,185	18.02
Central American, ex. Mexican	5,302	1.42
Costa Rican	159	0.04
Guatemalan	988	0.27
Honduran	2,659	0.71
Nicaraguan	112	0.03
Panamanian	376	0.10
Salvadoran	965	0.26
Other Central American	43	0.01
Cuban	1,489	0.40
Dominican Republic	4,293	1.15
Mexican	16,480	4.42
Puerto Rican	29,210	7.84
South American	6,144	1.65
Argentinean	654	0.18
Bolivian	81	0.02
Chilean	223	0.06
Colombian	1,772	0.48
Ecuadorian	1,426	0.38
Paraguayan	28	0.01
Peruvian	1,662	0.45
Uruguayan	91	0.02
Venezuelan	152	0.04
Other South American	55	0.01
Other Hispanic or Latino	4,267	1.14

Race*	Population	%
African-American/Black (37,946)	44,056	11.82
Not Hispanic (33,895)	37,986	10.19
Hispanic (4,051)	6,070	1.63
American Indian/Alaska Native (1,748)	4,451	1.19
Not Hispanic (908)	2,843	0.76
Hispanic (840)	1,608	0.43
Alaska Athabascan (Ala. Nat.) (0)	0	<0.01
Aleut (Alaska Native) (1)	2	<0.01
Apache (1)	31	0.01
Arapaho (1)	3	<0.01
Blackfeet (13)	113	0.03
Canadian/French Am. Ind. (3)	9	<0.01
Central American Ind. (23)	38	0.01
Cherokee (65)	477	0.13
Cheyenne (1)	3	<0.01
Chickasaw (0)	3	<0.01
Chippewa (14)	33	0.01
Choctaw (8)	13	<0.01
Colville (0)	0	<0.01

	Population	%
Comanche (2)	3	<0.01
Cree (1)	7	<0.01
Creek (2)	10	<0.01
Crow (1)	7	<0.01
Delaware (214)	428	0.11
Hopi (0)	3	<0.01
Houma (2)	2	<0.01
Inupiat (Alaska Native) (3)	7	<0.01
Iroquois (144)	302	0.08
Kiowa (1)	2	<0.01
Lumbee (4)	7	<0.01
Menominee (0)	0	<0.01
Mexican American Ind. (116)	156	0.04
Navajo (9)	28	0.01
Osage (0)	1	<0.01
Ottawa (1)	1	<0.01
Paiute (0)	0	<0.01
Pima (0)	4	<0.01
Potawatomi (2)	6	<0.01
Pueblo (1)	5	<0.01
Puget Sound Salish (0)	2	<0.01
Seminole (0)	21	0.01
Shoshone (5)	7	<0.01
Sioux (9)	55	0.01
South American Ind. (136)	291	0.08
Spanish American Ind. (101)	113	0.03
Tlingit-Haida (Alaska Native) (2)	2	<0.01
Tohono O'Odham (1)	15	<0.01
Tsimshian (Alaska Native) (0)	0	<0.01
Ute (0)	0	<0.01
Yakama (0)	0	<0.01
Yaqui (0)	0	<0.01
Yuman (1)	5	<0.01
Yup'ik (Alaska Native) (1)	1	<0.01
Asian (8,895)	11,280	3.03
Not Hispanic (8,685)	10,687	2.87
Hispanic (210)	593	0.16
Bangladeshi (136)	154	0.04
Bhutanese (2)	2	<0.01
Burmese (26)	28	0.01
Cambodian (83)	106	0.03
Chinese, ex. Taiwanese (1,718)	2,206	0.59
Filipino (1,601)	2,144	0.58
Hmong (1)	1	<0.01
Indian (2,621)	3,050	0.82
Indonesian (40)	62	0.02
Japanese (196)	486	0.13
Korean (1,005)	1,333	0.36
Laotian (7)	14	<0.01
Malaysian (3)	4	<0.01
Nepalese (7)	10	<0.01
Pakistani (542)	614	0.16
Sri Lankan (47)	56	0.02
Taiwanese (44)	51	0.01
Thai (91)	152	0.04
Vietnamese (374)	481	0.13
Hawaii Native/Pacific Islander (125)	434	0.12
Not Hispanic (80)	266	0.07
Hispanic (45)	168	0.05
Fijian (1)	2	<0.01
Guamanian/Chamorro (44)	63	0.02
Marshallese (0)	0	<0.01
Native Hawaiian (15)	93	0.02
Samoan (13)	29	0.01
Tongan (1)	1	<0.01
White (287,802)	297,221	79.72
Not Hispanic (254,259)	260,102	69.77
Hispanic (33,543)	37,119	9.96

Notes: † The Census 2010 population figure is used to calculate the percentages in the Hispanic Origin and Race categories. Ancestry percentages are based on the 2006-2010 American Community Survey population (not shown); ‡ Numbers in parentheses indicate the number of people reporting a single ancestry; * Numbers in parentheses indicate the number of persons reporting this race alone, not in combination with any other race; Please refer to the Explanation of Data for more information.

Orleans County

Population: 42,883

Ancestry	Population	%
Afghan (0)	0	<0.01
African, Sub-Saharan (8)	37	0.09
African (0)	29	0.07
Cape Verdean (0)	0	<0.01
Ethiopian (0)	0	<0.01
Ghanaian (0)	0	<0.01
Kenyan (0)	0	<0.01
Liberian (0)	0	<0.01
Nigerian (8)	8	0.02
Senegalese (0)	0	<0.01
Sierra Leonean (0)	0	<0.01
Somalian (0)	0	<0.01
South African (0)	0	<0.01
Sudanese (0)	0	<0.01
Ugandan (0)	0	<0.01
Zimbabwean (0)	0	<0.01
Other Sub-Saharan African (0)	0	<0.01
Albanian (0)	9	0.02
Alsatian (0)	0	<0.01
American (2,445)	2,445	5.66
Arab (15)	47	0.11
Arab (0)	0	<0.01
Egyptian (0)	11	0.03
Iraqi (0)	0	<0.01
Jordanian (0)	0	<0.01
Lebanese (15)	36	0.08
Moroccan (0)	0	<0.01
Palestinian (0)	0	<0.01
Syrian (0)	0	<0.01
Other Arab (0)	0	<0.01
Armenian (0)	0	<0.01
Assyrian/Chaldean/Syriac (0)	0	<0.01
Australian (0)	0	<0.01
Austrian (0)	18	0.04
Basque (0)	0	<0.01
Belgian (0)	18	0.04
Brazilian (15)	15	0.03
British (59)	114	0.26
Bulgarian (0)	0	<0.01
Cajun (0)	0	<0.01
Canadian (92)	211	0.49
Carpatho Rusyn (0)	0	<0.01
Celtic (0)	0	<0.01
Croatian (0)	69	0.16
Cypriot (0)	0	<0.01
Czech (4)	52	0.12
Czechoslovakian (0)	0	<0.01
Danish (0)	32	0.07
Dutch (129)	1,314	3.04
Eastern European (39)	39	0.09
English (2,770)	9,383	21.74
Estonian (0)	0	<0.01
European (123)	128	0.30
Finnish (0)	0	<0.01
French, ex. Basque (198)	2,092	4.85
French Canadian (140)	489	1.13
German (3,260)	11,665	27.02
German Russian (0)	0	<0.01
Greek (33)	71	0.16
Guyanese (0)	0	<0.01
Hungarian (13)	144	0.33
Icelander (0)	0	<0.01
Iranian (0)	0	<0.01
Irish (1,230)	7,575	17.55
Israeli (0)	0	<0.01
Italian (2,135)	5,503	12.75
Latvian (0)	0	<0.01
Lithuanian (64)	99	0.23
Luxemburger (0)	0	<0.01
Macedonian (0)	0	<0.01
Maltese (0)	0	<0.01
New Zealander (0)	0	<0.01
Northern European (6)	6	0.01
Norwegian (50)	82	0.19
Pennsylvania German (42)	86	0.20

Ancestry	Population	%
Polish (1,595)	3,934	9.11
Portuguese (0)	29	0.07
Romanian (0)	0	<0.01
Russian (57)	150	0.35
Scandinavian (0)	0	<0.01
Scotch-Irish (158)	509	1.18
Scottish (103)	950	2.20
Serbian (0)	0	<0.01
Slavic (0)	17	0.04
Slovak (8)	28	0.06
Slovene (19)	19	0.04
Soviet Union (0)	0	<0.01
Swedish (56)	157	0.36
Swiss (11)	62	0.14
Turkish (0)	0	<0.01
Ukrainian (101)	573	1.33
Welsh (61)	357	0.83
West Indian, ex. Hispanic (158)	207	0.48
Bahamian (0)	0	<0.01
Barbadian (5)	5	0.01
Belizean (0)	0	<0.01
Bermudan (0)	0	<0.01
British West Indian (0)	0	<0.01
Dutch West Indian (0)	0	<0.01
Haitian (13)	19	0.04
Jamaican (120)	163	0.38
Trinidadian/Tobagonian (14)	14	0.03
U.S. Virgin Islander (0)	0	<0.01
West Indian (6)	6	0.01
Other West Indian (0)	0	<0.01
Yugoslavian (21)	29	0.07

Hispanic Origin	Population	%
Hispanic or Latino (of any race)	1,757	4.10
Central American, ex. Mexican	79	0.18
Costa Rican	1	<0.01
Guatemalan	21	0.05
Honduran	7	0.02
Nicaraguan	4	0.01
Panamanian	31	0.07
Salvadoran	15	0.03
Other Central American	0	<0.01
Cuban	53	0.12
Dominican Republic	46	0.11
Mexican	741	1.73
Puerto Rican	663	1.55
South American	38	0.09
Argentinean	0	<0.01
Bolivian	0	<0.01
Chilean	1	<0.01
Colombian	19	0.04
Ecuadorian	8	0.02
Paraguayan	0	<0.01
Peruvian	8	0.02
Uruguayan	1	<0.01
Venezuelan	1	<0.01
Other South American	0	<0.01
Other Hispanic or Latino	137	0.32

Race*	Population	%
African-American/Black (2,523)	2,965	6.91
Not Hispanic (2,368)	2,771	6.46
Hispanic (155)	194	0.45
American Indian/Alaska Native (247)	527	1.23
Not Hispanic (199)	449	1.05
Hispanic (48)	78	0.18
Alaska Athabascan (Ala. Nat.) (0)	1	<0.01
Aleut (Alaska Native) (1)	3	0.01
Apache (6)	17	0.04
Arapaho (0)	0	<0.01
Blackfeet (1)	17	0.04
Canadian/French Am. Ind. (1)	3	0.01
Central American Ind. (5)	5	0.01
Cherokee (8)	48	0.11
Cheyenne (0)	1	<0.01
Chickasaw (0)	0	<0.01
Chippewa (0)	11	0.03
Choctaw (1)	5	0.01
Colville (0)	0	<0.01

Race*	Population	%
Comanche (0)	0	<0.01
Cree (0)	0	<0.01
Creek (0)	1	<0.01
Crow (0)	1	<0.01
Delaware (10)	14	0.03
Hopi (0)	0	<0.01
Houma (1)	1	<0.01
Inupiat (Alaska Native) (0)	0	<0.01
Iroquois (87)	134	0.31
Kiowa (0)	0	<0.01
Lumbee (0)	0	<0.01
Menominee (0)	0	<0.01
Mexican American Ind. (9)	21	0.05
Navajo (1)	2	<0.01
Osage (0)	0	<0.01
Ottawa (0)	0	<0.01
Paiute (0)	0	<0.01
Pima (0)	0	<0.01
Potawatomi (0)	0	<0.01
Pueblo (0)	1	<0.01
Puget Sound Salish (0)	0	<0.01
Seminole (0)	0	<0.01
Shoshone (0)	8	0.02
Sioux (2)	4	0.01
South American Ind. (3)	5	0.01
Spanish American Ind. (3)	3	0.01
Tlingit-Haida (Alaska Native) (0)	0	<0.01
Tohono O'Odham (0)	0	<0.01
Tsimshian (Alaska Native) (0)	0	<0.01
Ute (0)	0	<0.01
Yakama (0)	0	<0.01
Yaqui (0)	0	<0.01
Yuman (0)	0	<0.01
Yup'ik (Alaska Native) (0)	0	<0.01
Asian (179)	259	0.60
Not Hispanic (173)	250	0.58
Hispanic (6)	9	0.02
Bangladeshi (0)	0	<0.01
Bhutanese (0)	0	<0.01
Burmese (1)	1	<0.01
Cambodian (0)	0	<0.01
Chinese, ex. Taiwanese (31)	41	0.10
Filipino (39)	63	0.15
Hmong (0)	0	<0.01
Indian (17)	40	0.09
Indonesian (0)	0	<0.01
Japanese (6)	17	0.04
Korean (21)	23	0.05
Laotian (0)	0	<0.01
Malaysian (0)	0	<0.01
Nepalese (0)	0	<0.01
Pakistani (15)	15	0.03
Sri Lankan (1)	3	0.01
Taiwanese (0)	5	0.01
Thai (5)	8	0.02
Vietnamese (2)	5	0.01
Hawaii Native/Pacific Islander (9)	35	0.08
Not Hispanic (7)	25	0.06
Hispanic (2)	10	0.02
Fijian (0)	0	<0.01
Guamanian/Chamorro (1)	2	<0.01
Marshallese (0)	0	<0.01
Native Hawaiian (6)	11	0.03
Samoan (2)	3	0.01
Tongan (0)	0	<0.01
White (38,528)	39,297	91.64
Not Hispanic (37,658)	38,305	89.32
Hispanic (870)	992	2.31

*Notes: † The Census 2010 population figure is used to calculate the percentages in the Hispanic Origin and Race categories. Ancestry percentages are based on the 2006-2010 American Community Survey population (not shown); ‡ Numbers in parentheses indicate the number of people reporting a single ancestry; * Numbers in parentheses indicate the number of persons reporting this race alone, not in combination with any other race; Please refer to the Explanation of Data for more information.*

Oswego County

Population: 122,109

Ancestry	Population	%
Afghan (50)	50	0.04
African, Sub-Saharan (105)	109	0.09
African (22)	26	0.02
Cape Verdean (0)	0	<0.01
Ethiopian (0)	0	<0.01
Ghanaian (30)	30	0.02
Kenyan (6)	6	<0.01
Liberian (0)	0	<0.01
Nigerian (0)	0	<0.01
Senegalese (19)	19	0.02
Sierra Leonean (0)	0	<0.01
Somalian (0)	0	<0.01
South African (16)	16	0.01
Sudanese (0)	0	<0.01
Ugandan (0)	0	<0.01
Zimbabwean (0)	0	<0.01
Other Sub-Saharan African (12)	12	0.01
Albanian (0)	3	<0.01
Alsatian (0)	0	<0.01
American (6,704)	6,704	5.49
Arab (63)	291	0.24
Arab (0)	0	<0.01
Egyptian (10)	10	0.01
Iraqi (0)	0	<0.01
Jordanian (0)	0	<0.01
Lebanese (40)	195	0.16
Moroccan (0)	0	<0.01
Palestinian (0)	0	<0.01
Syrian (13)	74	0.06
Other Arab (0)	12	0.01
Armenian (34)	92	0.08
Assyrian/Chaldean/Syriac (0)	0	<0.01
Australian (0)	0	<0.01
Austrian (62)	235	0.19
Basque (0)	0	<0.01
Belgian (12)	94	0.08
Brazilian (17)	17	0.01
British (200)	394	0.32
Bulgarian (0)	0	<0.01
Cajun (0)	15	0.01
Canadian (347)	837	0.68
Carpatho Rusyn (0)	28	0.02
Celtic (15)	15	0.01
Croatian (31)	254	0.21
Cypriot (0)	0	<0.01
Czech (72)	356	0.29
Czechoslovakian (62)	112	0.09
Danish (82)	255	0.21
Dutch (661)	4,758	3.89
Eastern European (42)	65	0.05
English (5,611)	18,945	15.50
Estonian (0)	0	<0.01
European (840)	848	0.69
Finnish (65)	315	0.26
French, ex. Basque (2,417)	12,503	10.23
French Canadian (1,857)	4,004	3.28
German (5,985)	25,630	20.97
German Russian (0)	0	<0.01
Greek (152)	437	0.36
Guyanese (0)	0	<0.01
Hungarian (139)	441	0.36
Icelander (20)	20	0.02
Iranian (0)	0	<0.01
Irish (8,045)	27,954	22.87
Israeli (39)	39	0.03
Italian (6,436)	17,452	14.28
Latvian (0)	10	0.01
Lithuanian (148)	359	0.29
Luxemburger (0)	0	<0.01
Macedonian (19)	40	0.03
Maltese (12)	27	0.02
New Zealander (0)	0	<0.01
Northern European (94)	94	0.08
Norwegian (179)	506	0.41
Pennsylvania German (36)	83	0.07
Polish (2,367)	7,803	6.38
Portuguese (79)	149	0.12
Romanian (0)	39	0.03
Russian (323)	984	0.81
Scandinavian (20)	46	0.04
Scotch-Irish (714)	1,948	1.59
Scottish (710)	2,653	2.17
Serbian (0)	22	0.02
Slavic (2)	13	0.01
Slovak (50)	114	0.09
Slovene (0)	24	0.02
Soviet Union (0)	0	<0.01
Swedish (164)	837	0.68
Swiss (92)	340	0.28
Turkish (0)	23	0.02
Ukrainian (393)	1,111	0.91
Welsh (167)	1,232	1.01
West Indian, ex. Hispanic (98)	226	0.18
Bahamian (0)	0	<0.01
Barbadian (12)	12	0.01
Belizean (0)	12	0.01
Bermudan (0)	0	<0.01
British West Indian (0)	15	0.01
Dutch West Indian (0)	0	<0.01
Haitian (73)	73	0.06
Jamaican (13)	72	0.06
Trinidadian/Tobagonian (0)	42	0.03
U.S. Virgin Islander (0)	0	<0.01
West Indian (0)	0	<0.01
Other West Indian (0)	0	<0.01
Yugoslavian (0)	42	0.03

Hispanic Origin	Population	%
Hispanic or Latino (of any race)	2,552	2.09
Central American, ex. Mexican	140	0.11
Costa Rican	8	0.01
Guatemalan	66	0.05
Honduran	17	0.01
Nicaraguan	4	<0.01
Panamanian	18	0.01
Salvadoran	27	0.02
Other Central American	0	<0.01
Cuban	65	0.05
Dominican Republic	97	0.08
Mexican	641	0.52
Puerto Rican	1,193	0.98
South American	155	0.13
Argentinean	19	0.02
Bolivian	3	<0.01
Chilean	11	0.01
Colombian	49	0.04
Ecuadorian	37	0.03
Paraguayan	2	<0.01
Peruvian	25	0.02
Uruguayan	2	<0.01
Venezuelan	5	<0.01
Other South American	2	<0.01
Other Hispanic or Latino	261	0.21

Race*	Population	%
African-American/Black (972)	1,531	1.25
Not Hispanic (862)	1,367	1.12
Hispanic (110)	164	0.13
American Indian/Alaska Native (520)	1,200	0.98
Not Hispanic (465)	1,097	0.90
Hispanic (55)	103	0.08
Alaska Athabascan (Ala. Nat.) (1)	1	<0.01
Aleut (Alaska Native) (0)	0	<0.01
Apache (1)	9	0.01
Arapaho (0)	0	<0.01
Blackfeet (14)	41	0.03
Canadian/French Am. Ind. (18)	26	0.02
Central American Ind. (2)	4	<0.01
Cherokee (19)	77	0.06
Cheyenne (2)	5	<0.01
Chickasaw (1)	2	<0.01
Chippewa (5)	12	0.01
Choctaw (2)	6	<0.01
Colville (0)	0	<0.01
Comanche (0)	0	<0.01
Cree (0)	3	<0.01
Creek (1)	2	<0.01
Crow (1)	2	<0.01
Delaware (1)	5	<0.01
Hopi (0)	0	<0.01
Houma (0)	0	<0.01
Inupiat (Alaska Native) (0)	0	<0.01
Iroquois (212)	430	0.35
Kiowa (0)	0	<0.01
Lumbee (0)	0	<0.01
Menominee (0)	0	<0.01
Mexican American Ind. (6)	9	0.01
Navajo (2)	5	<0.01
Osage (0)	0	<0.01
Ottawa (0)	0	<0.01
Paiute (0)	0	<0.01
Pima (0)	0	<0.01
Potawatomi (0)	0	<0.01
Pueblo (0)	1	<0.01
Puget Sound Salish (0)	0	<0.01
Seminole (0)	2	<0.01
Shoshone (0)	0	<0.01
Sioux (13)	31	0.03
South American Ind. (6)	16	0.01
Spanish American Ind. (2)	2	<0.01
Tlingit-Haida (Alaska Native) (0)	0	<0.01
Tohono O'Odham (0)	0	<0.01
Tsimshian (Alaska Native) (0)	0	<0.01
Ute (0)	1	<0.01
Yakama (0)	1	<0.01
Yaqui (0)	0	<0.01
Yuman (0)	0	<0.01
Yup'ik (Alaska Native) (0)	0	<0.01
Asian (723)	986	0.81
Not Hispanic (709)	947	0.78
Hispanic (14)	39	0.03
Bangladeshi (2)	2	<0.01
Bhutanese (0)	0	<0.01
Burmese (1)	1	<0.01
Cambodian (0)	1	<0.01
Chinese, ex. Taiwanese (234)	269	0.22
Filipino (139)	222	0.18
Hmong (0)	0	<0.01
Indian (100)	137	0.11
Indonesian (1)	4	<0.01
Japanese (46)	82	0.07
Korean (104)	134	0.11
Laotian (0)	0	<0.01
Malaysian (1)	1	<0.01
Nepalese (0)	0	<0.01
Pakistani (16)	16	0.01
Sri Lankan (4)	4	<0.01
Taiwanese (1)	6	<0.01
Thai (14)	32	0.03
Vietnamese (38)	52	0.04
Hawaii Native/Pacific Islander (16)	65	0.05
Not Hispanic (14)	51	0.04
Hispanic (2)	14	0.01
Fijian (0)	0	<0.01
Guamanian/Chamorro (3)	7	0.01
Marshallese (0)	0	<0.01
Native Hawaiian (5)	18	0.01
Samoan (0)	4	<0.01
Tongan (0)	0	<0.01
White (117,632)	119,116	97.55
Not Hispanic (116,091)	117,378	96.13
Hispanic (1,541)	1,738	1.42

Notes: † The Census 2010 population figure is used to calculate the percentages in the Hispanic Origin and Race categories. Ancestry percentages are based on the 2006-2010 American Community Survey population (not shown); ‡ Numbers in parentheses indicate the number of people reporting a single ancestry; * Numbers in parentheses indicate the number of persons reporting this race alone, not in combination with any other race; Please refer to the Explanation of Data for more information.

Otsego County

Population: 62,259

Ancestry	Population	%
Afghan (0)	0	<0.01
African, Sub-Saharan (131)	151	0.24
African (24)	24	0.04
Cape Verdean (0)	0	<0.01
Ethiopian (0)	0	<0.01
Ghanaian (0)	0	<0.01
Kenyan (81)	81	0.13
Liberian (0)	0	<0.01
Nigerian (0)	0	<0.01
Senegalese (0)	0	<0.01
Sierra Leonean (0)	0	<0.01
Somalian (0)	0	<0.01
South African (0)	20	0.03
Sudanese (0)	0	<0.01
Ugandan (0)	0	<0.01
Zimbabwean (26)	26	0.04
Other Sub-Saharan African (0)	0	<0.01
Albanian (6)	60	0.10
Alsatian (0)	0	<0.01
American (6,461)	6,461	10.32
Arab (110)	207	0.33
Arab (10)	10	0.02
Egyptian (0)	0	<0.01
Iraqi (0)	0	<0.01
Jordanian (0)	0	<0.01
Lebanese (78)	155	0.25
Moroccan (0)	0	<0.01
Palestinian (5)	5	0.01
Syrian (17)	37	0.06
Other Arab (0)	0	<0.01
Armenian (59)	62	0.10
Assyrian/Chaldean/Syriac (0)	0	<0.01
Australian (0)	0	<0.01
Austrian (52)	414	0.66
Basque (0)	0	<0.01
Belgian (0)	33	0.05
Brazilian (0)	0	<0.01
British (163)	234	0.37
Bulgarian (0)	0	<0.01
Cajun (0)	0	<0.01
Canadian (100)	297	0.47
Carpatho Rusyn (0)	0	<0.01
Celtic (0)	5	0.01
Croatian (27)	82	0.13
Cypriot (0)	0	<0.01
Czech (31)	230	0.37
Czechoslovakian (31)	37	0.06
Danish (133)	376	0.60
Dutch (610)	3,421	5.46
Eastern European (109)	157	0.25
English (2,928)	9,969	15.92
Estonian (3)	5	0.01
European (511)	543	0.87
Finnish (32)	94	0.15
French, ex. Basque (345)	3,084	4.93
French Canadian (314)	842	1.34
German (2,872)	13,660	21.82
German Russian (0)	0	<0.01
Greek (84)	239	0.38
Guyanese (12)	12	0.02
Hungarian (165)	678	1.08
Icelander (0)	7	0.01
Iranian (0)	19	0.03
Irish (3,032)	11,787	18.83
Israeli (13)	13	0.02
Italian (2,804)	7,612	12.16
Latvian (16)	22	0.04
Lithuanian (12)	154	0.25
Luxemburger (0)	0	<0.01
Macedonian (0)	0	<0.01
Maltese (0)	0	<0.01
New Zealander (0)	5	0.01
Northern European (42)	42	0.07
Norwegian (243)	784	1.25
Pennsylvania German (79)	144	0.23
Polish (784)	2,833	4.53
Portuguese (56)	95	0.15
Romanian (21)	41	0.07
Russian (299)	1,047	1.67
Scandinavian (51)	115	0.18
Scotch-Irish (366)	1,232	1.97
Scottish (492)	2,493	3.98
Serbian (11)	15	0.02
Slavic (55)	118	0.19
Slovak (78)	143	0.23
Slovene (57)	146	0.23
Soviet Union (0)	0	<0.01
Swedish (153)	1,004	1.60
Swiss (30)	206	0.33
Turkish (0)	0	<0.01
Ukrainian (116)	249	0.40
Welsh (237)	1,116	1.78
West Indian, ex. Hispanic (283)	321	0.51
Bahamian (0)	0	<0.01
Barbadian (0)	0	<0.01
Belizean (0)	0	<0.01
Bermudan (0)	0	<0.01
British West Indian (12)	12	0.02
Dutch West Indian (20)	20	0.03
Haitian (75)	79	0.13
Jamaican (160)	194	0.31
Trinidadian/Tobagonian (15)	15	0.02
U.S. Virgin Islander (0)	0	<0.01
West Indian (1)	1	<0.01
Other West Indian (0)	0	<0.01
Yugoslavian (36)	107	0.17

Hispanic Origin	Population	%
Hispanic or Latino (of any race)	1,921	3.09
Central American, ex. Mexican	122	0.20
Costa Rican	7	0.01
Guatemalan	29	0.05
Honduran	12	0.02
Nicaraguan	2	<0.01
Panamanian	18	0.03
Salvadoran	53	0.09
Other Central American	1	<0.01
Cuban	90	0.14
Dominican Republic	86	0.14
Mexican	306	0.49
Puerto Rican	798	1.28
South American	216	0.35
Argentinean	14	0.02
Bolivian	6	0.01
Chilean	22	0.04
Colombian	67	0.11
Ecuadorian	45	0.07
Paraguayan	1	<0.01
Peruvian	42	0.07
Uruguayan	11	0.02
Venezuelan	6	0.01
Other South American	2	<0.01
Other Hispanic or Latino	303	0.49

Race*	Population	%
African-American/Black (1,066)	1,506	2.42
Not Hispanic (958)	1,309	2.10
Hispanic (108)	197	0.32
American Indian/Alaska Native (121)	497	0.80
Not Hispanic (103)	429	0.69
Hispanic (18)	68	0.11
Alaska Athabascan (Ala. Nat.) (0)	0	<0.01
Aleut (Alaska Native) (0)	0	<0.01
Apache (0)	2	<0.01
Arapaho (0)	0	<0.01
Blackfeet (1)	16	0.03
Canadian/French Am. Ind. (1)	3	<0.01
Central American Ind. (0)	0	<0.01
Cherokee (13)	57	0.09
Cheyenne (0)	0	<0.01
Chickasaw (0)	2	<0.01
Chippewa (3)	11	0.02
Choctaw (1)	11	0.02
Colville (0)	0	<0.01
Comanche (0)	0	<0.01
Cree (0)	0	<0.01
Creek (0)	1	<0.01
Crow (0)	0	<0.01
Delaware (8)	13	0.02
Hopi (0)	1	<0.01
Houma (0)	0	<0.01
Inupiat (Alaska Native) (0)	1	<0.01
Iroquois (14)	63	0.10
Kiowa (0)	2	<0.01
Lumbee (1)	1	<0.01
Menominee (0)	0	<0.01
Mexican American Ind. (1)	6	<0.01
Navajo (2)	3	<0.01
Osage (0)	0	<0.01
Ottawa (0)	0	<0.01
Paiute (0)	0	<0.01
Pima (0)	0	<0.01
Potawatomi (0)	0	<0.01
Pueblo (0)	0	<0.01
Puget Sound Salish (0)	0	<0.01
Seminole (0)	0	<0.01
Shoshone (0)	0	<0.01
Sioux (2)	10	0.02
South American Ind. (3)	8	0.01
Spanish American Ind. (1)	2	<0.01
Tlingit-Haida (Alaska Native) (0)	0	<0.01
Tohono O'Odham (0)	0	<0.01
Tsimshian (Alaska Native) (0)	0	<0.01
Ute (0)	0	<0.01
Yakama (0)	0	<0.01
Yaqui (0)	0	<0.01
Yuman (0)	0	<0.01
Yup'ik (Alaska Native) (0)	0	<0.01
Asian (674)	894	1.44
Not Hispanic (660)	856	1.37
Hispanic (14)	38	0.06
Bangladeshi (0)	0	<0.01
Bhutanese (0)	0	<0.01
Burmese (0)	0	<0.01
Cambodian (0)	0	<0.01
Chinese, ex. Taiwanese (196)	240	0.39
Filipino (59)	122	0.20
Hmong (0)	0	<0.01
Indian (134)	162	0.26
Indonesian (1)	5	0.01
Japanese (56)	87	0.14
Korean (120)	159	0.26
Laotian (1)	1	<0.01
Malaysian (0)	0	<0.01
Nepalese (5)	5	0.01
Pakistani (31)	34	0.05
Sri Lankan (3)	3	<0.01
Taiwanese (12)	16	0.03
Thai (15)	21	0.03
Vietnamese (15)	21	0.03
Hawaii Native/Pacific Islander (18)	50	0.08
Not Hispanic (16)	40	0.06
Hispanic (2)	10	0.02
Fijian (1)	1	<0.01
Guamanian/Chamorro (2)	3	<0.01
Marshallese (0)	0	<0.01
Native Hawaiian (7)	18	0.03
Samoan (4)	5	0.01
Tongan (0)	0	<0.01
White (58,935)	59,860	96.15
Not Hispanic (57,734)	58,502	93.97
Hispanic (1,201)	1,358	2.18

Notes: † The Census 2010 population figure is used to calculate the percentages in the Hispanic Origin and Race categories. Ancestry percentages are based on the 2006-2010 American Community Survey population (not shown); ‡ Numbers in parentheses indicate the number of people reporting a single ancestry; * Numbers in parentheses indicate the number of persons reporting this race alone, not in combination with any other race; Please refer to the Explanation of Data for more information.

Putnam County

Population: 99,710

Ancestry	Population	%
Afghan (0)	0	<0.01
African, Sub-Saharan (180)	263	0.26
African (90)	137	0.14
Cape Verdean (0)	0	<0.01
Ethiopian (26)	26	0.03
Ghanaian (0)	0	<0.01
Kenyan (0)	0	<0.01
Liberian (0)	0	<0.01
Nigerian (0)	20	0.02
Senegalese (64)	64	0.06
Sierra Leonean (0)	0	<0.01
Somalian (0)	0	<0.01
South African (0)	16	0.02
Sudanese (0)	0	<0.01
Ugandan (0)	0	<0.01
Zimbabwean (0)	0	<0.01
Other Sub-Saharan African (0)	0	<0.01
Albanian (924)	980	0.98
Alsatian (0)	0	<0.01
American (2,598)	2,598	2.61
Arab (212)	448	0.45
Arab (0)	61	0.06
Egyptian (103)	117	0.12
Iraqi (0)	0	<0.01
Jordanian (71)	71	0.07
Lebanese (38)	138	0.14
Moroccan (0)	0	<0.01
Palestinian (0)	21	0.02
Syrian (0)	33	0.03
Other Arab (0)	7	0.01
Armenian (10)	42	0.04
Assyrian/Chaldean/Syriac (0)	0	<0.01
Australian (54)	144	0.14
Austrian (174)	879	0.88
Basque (0)	14	0.01
Belgian (21)	135	0.14
Brazilian (49)	143	0.14
British (185)	301	0.30
Bulgarian (35)	35	0.04
Cajun (0)	0	<0.01
Canadian (191)	392	0.39
Carpatho Rusyn (0)	0	<0.01
Celtic (0)	6	0.01
Croatian (140)	200	0.20
Cypriot (0)	0	<0.01
Czech (119)	541	0.54
Czechoslovakian (134)	263	0.26
Danish (114)	298	0.30
Dutch (288)	1,529	1.54
Eastern European (154)	186	0.19
English (1,140)	7,439	7.47
Estonian (0)	64	0.06
European (710)	787	0.79
Finnish (82)	197	0.20
French, ex. Basque (282)	2,532	2.54
French Canadian (251)	680	0.68
German (2,967)	17,556	17.64
German Russian (0)	0	<0.01
Greek (382)	1,015	1.02
Guyanese (0)	0	<0.01
Hungarian (311)	1,309	1.31
Icelander (0)	0	<0.01
Iranian (125)	125	0.13
Irish (8,053)	27,534	27.66
Israeli (0)	32	0.03
Italian (14,946)	31,433	31.58
Latvian (9)	32	0.03
Lithuanian (57)	546	0.55
Luxemburger (0)	0	<0.01
Macedonian (0)	0	<0.01
Maltese (38)	50	0.05
New Zealander (0)	0	<0.01
Northern European (85)	125	0.13
Norwegian (159)	677	0.68
Pennsylvania German (11)	11	0.01

Ancestry	Population	%
Polish (1,827)	5,597	5.62
Portuguese (415)	830	0.83
Romanian (115)	324	0.33
Russian (793)	2,712	2.72
Scandinavian (107)	193	0.19
Scotch-Irish (506)	1,769	1.78
Scottish (297)	1,829	1.84
Serbian (0)	13	0.01
Slavic (27)	66	0.07
Slovak (183)	439	0.44
Slovene (13)	45	0.05
Soviet Union (0)	0	<0.01
Swedish (133)	1,061	1.07
Swiss (16)	140	0.14
Turkish (16)	31	0.03
Ukrainian (368)	959	0.96
Welsh (73)	490	0.49
West Indian, ex. Hispanic (280)	467	0.47
Bahamian (0)	0	<0.01
Barbadian (0)	0	<0.01
Belizean (0)	0	<0.01
Bermudan (0)	0	<0.01
British West Indian (0)	0	<0.01
Dutch West Indian (0)	0	<0.01
Haitian (50)	84	0.08
Jamaican (56)	160	0.16
Trinidadian/Tobagonian (165)	205	0.21
U.S. Virgin Islander (0)	0	<0.01
West Indian (9)	18	0.02
Other West Indian (0)	0	<0.01
Yugoslavian (99)	198	0.20

Hispanic Origin	Population	%
Hispanic or Latino (of any race)	11,661	11.69
Central American, ex. Mexican	2,565	2.57
Costa Rican	62	0.06
Guatemalan	1,909	1.91
Honduran	125	0.13
Nicaraguan	43	0.04
Panamanian	43	0.04
Salvadoran	374	0.38
Other Central American	9	0.01
Cuban	349	0.35
Dominican Republic	605	0.61
Mexican	1,023	1.03
Puerto Rican	3,850	3.86
South American	2,106	2.11
Argentinean	158	0.16
Bolivian	34	0.03
Chilean	89	0.09
Colombian	457	0.46
Ecuadorian	897	0.90
Paraguayan	53	0.05
Peruvian	301	0.30
Uruguayan	63	0.06
Venezuelan	43	0.04
Other South American	11	0.01
Other Hispanic or Latino	1,163	1.17

Race*	Population	%
African-American/Black (2,350)	2,967	2.98
Not Hispanic (2,047)	2,437	2.44
Hispanic (303)	530	0.53
American Indian/Alaska Native (175)	607	0.61
Not Hispanic (121)	452	0.45
Hispanic (54)	155	0.16
Alaska Athabascan (Ala. Nat.) (0)	0	<0.01
Aleut (Alaska Native) (1)	1	<0.01
Apache (1)	3	<0.01
Arapaho (2)	2	<0.01
Blackfeet (2)	31	0.03
Canadian/French Am. Ind. (6)	12	0.01
Central American Ind. (14)	19	0.02
Cherokee (7)	75	0.08
Cheyenne (0)	6	0.01
Chickasaw (0)	0	<0.01
Chippewa (2)	10	0.01
Choctaw (2)	9	0.01
Colville (0)	0	<0.01

	Population	%
Comanche (0)	0	<0.01
Cree (0)	0	<0.01
Creek (1)	5	0.01
Crow (0)	0	<0.01
Delaware (0)	0	<0.01
Hopi (0)	0	<0.01
Houma (0)	0	<0.01
Inupiat (Alaska Native) (1)	1	<0.01
Iroquois (18)	37	0.04
Kiowa (0)	1	<0.01
Lumbee (0)	0	<0.01
Menominee (0)	0	<0.01
Mexican American Ind. (7)	25	0.03
Navajo (1)	1	<0.01
Osage (0)	0	<0.01
Ottawa (0)	0	<0.01
Paiute (0)	0	<0.01
Pima (0)	0	<0.01
Potawatomi (0)	1	<0.01
Pueblo (0)	0	<0.01
Puget Sound Salish (0)	0	<0.01
Seminole (0)	8	0.01
Shoshone (0)	0	<0.01
Sioux (4)	16	0.02
South American Ind. (13)	25	0.03
Spanish American Ind. (2)	3	<0.01
Tlingit-Haida (Alaska Native) (0)	0	<0.01
Tohono O'Odham (0)	0	<0.01
Tsimshian (Alaska Native) (0)	0	<0.01
Ute (0)	0	<0.01
Yakama (0)	0	<0.01
Yaqui (0)	0	<0.01
Yuman (1)	1	<0.01
Yup'ik (Alaska Native) (0)	0	<0.01
Asian (1,882)	2,442	2.45
Not Hispanic (1,832)	2,324	2.33
Hispanic (50)	118	0.12
Bangladeshi (12)	13	0.01
Bhutanese (0)	0	<0.01
Burmese (1)	1	<0.01
Cambodian (6)	7	0.01
Chinese, ex. Taiwanese (530)	691	0.69
Filipino (259)	377	0.38
Hmong (0)	0	<0.01
Indian (573)	666	0.67
Indonesian (6)	3	<0.01
Japanese (122)	189	0.19
Korean (184)	228	0.23
Laotian (1)	5	0.01
Malaysian (6)	12	0.01
Nepalese (13)	16	0.02
Pakistani (35)	45	0.05
Sri Lankan (4)	6	0.01
Taiwanese (11)	15	0.02
Thai (21)	33	0.03
Vietnamese (38)	55	0.06
Hawaii Native/Pacific Islander (35)	118	0.12
Not Hispanic (14)	61	0.06
Hispanic (21)	57	0.06
Fijian (0)	0	<0.01
Guamanian/Chamorro (19)	40	0.04
Marshallese (0)	0	<0.01
Native Hawaiian (2)	18	0.02
Samoan (3)	5	0.01
Tongan (0)	0	<0.01
White (90,470)	92,223	92.49
Not Hispanic (82,709)	83,747	83.99
Hispanic (7,761)	8,476	8.50

Notes: † The Census 2010 population figure is used to calculate the percentages in the Hispanic Origin and Race categories. Ancestry percentages are based on the 2006-2010 American Community Survey population (not shown); ‡ Numbers in parentheses indicate the number of people reporting a single ancestry; * Numbers in parentheses indicate the number of persons reporting this race alone, not in combination with any other race; Please refer to the Explanation of Data for more information.

Queens County
Population: 2,230,722

Ancestry	Population	%
Afghan (5,842)	6,027	0.27
African, Sub-Saharan (19,754)	25,166	1.14
African (9,764)	14,083	0.64
Cape Verdean (46)	117	0.01
Ethiopian (478)	505	0.02
Ghanaian (1,269)	1,326	0.06
Kenyan (96)	96	<0.01
Liberian (297)	381	0.02
Nigerian (5,989)	6,304	0.29
Senegalese (84)	84	<0.01
Sierra Leonean (127)	127	0.01
Somalian (52)	98	<0.01
South African (230)	356	0.02
Sudanese (161)	286	0.01
Ugandan (65)	77	<0.01
Zimbabwean (107)	107	<0.01
Other Sub-Saharan African (989)	1,219	0.06
Albanian (6,264)	6,624	0.30
Alsatian (26)	37	<0.01
American (45,604)	45,604	2.07
Arab (16,286)	19,669	0.89
Arab (1,921)	2,283	0.10
Egyptian (5,905)	6,551	0.30
Iraqi (224)	315	0.01
Jordanian (260)	307	0.01
Lebanese (1,548)	2,228	0.10
Moroccan (2,945)	3,459	0.16
Palestinian (582)	638	0.03
Syrian (193)	420	0.02
Other Arab (2,708)	3,468	0.16
Armenian (4,083)	4,658	0.21
Assyrian/Chaldean/Syriac (13)	13	<0.01
Australian (163)	285	0.01
Austrian (2,702)	7,523	0.34
Basque (29)	159	0.01
Belgian (289)	593	0.03
Brazilian (4,871)	6,175	0.28
British (1,346)	2,457	0.11
Bulgarian (1,928)	2,090	0.10
Cajun (0)	33	<0.01
Canadian (604)	1,308	0.06
Carpatho Rusyn (0)	9	<0.01
Celtic (92)	169	0.01
Croatian (5,621)	7,054	0.32
Cypriot (556)	644	0.03
Czech (1,116)	3,464	0.16
Czechoslovakian (816)	1,467	0.07
Danish (171)	792	0.04
Dutch (727)	3,516	0.16
Eastern European (4,442)	4,673	0.21
English (4,389)	20,267	0.92
Estonian (164)	198	0.01
European (5,335)	6,584	0.30
Finnish (269)	693	0.03
French, ex. Basque (3,945)	12,532	0.57
French Canadian (552)	2,020	0.09
German (20,566)	70,399	3.20
German Russian (33)	78	<0.01
Greek (35,368)	41,654	1.89
Guyanese (47,132)	53,961	2.45
Hungarian (4,718)	9,470	0.43
Icelander (10)	26	<0.01
Iranian (3,162)	3,707	0.17
Irish (43,033)	105,348	4.79
Israeli (3,355)	4,164	0.19
Italian (104,251)	159,812	7.27
Latvian (342)	568	0.03
Lithuanian (1,463)	3,131	0.14
Luxemburger (0)	13	<0.01
Macedonian (938)	1,109	0.05
Maltese (952)	1,565	0.07
New Zealander (0)	16	<0.01
Northern European (370)	512	0.02
Norwegian (670)	2,559	0.12
Pennsylvania German (9)	38	<0.01
Polish (37,726)	59,757	2.72
Portuguese (2,784)	4,727	0.21
Romanian (9,232)	11,686	0.53
Russian (29,779)	44,676	2.03
Scandinavian (131)	545	0.02
Scotch-Irish (2,079)	4,602	0.21
Scottish (1,567)	5,718	0.26
Serbian (2,176)	2,438	0.11
Slavic (370)	765	0.03
Slovak (1,161)	1,882	0.09
Slovene (171)	468	0.02
Soviet Union (12)	71	<0.01
Swedish (511)	2,862	0.13
Swiss (381)	1,260	0.06
Turkish (3,054)	3,767	0.17
Ukrainian (5,770)	8,375	0.38
Welsh (201)	1,666	0.08
West Indian, ex. Hispanic (131,014)	147,460	6.71
Bahamian (134)	185	0.01
Barbadian (4,074)	5,021	0.23
Belizean (1,106)	1,344	0.06
Bermudan (142)	177	0.01
British West Indian (3,765)	4,689	0.21
Dutch West Indian (122)	206	0.01
Haitian (35,439)	38,368	1.74
Jamaican (55,278)	59,999	2.73
Trinidadian/Tobagonian (16,227)	19,255	0.88
U.S. Virgin Islander (234)	364	0.02
West Indian (14,052)	17,400	0.79
Other West Indian (441)	452	0.02
Yugoslavian (3,824)	4,516	0.21

Hispanic Origin	Population	%
Hispanic or Latino (of any race)	613,750	27.51
Central American, ex. Mexican	52,509	2.35
Costa Rican	1,749	0.08
Guatemalan	13,700	0.61
Honduran	8,546	0.38
Nicaraguan	2,842	0.13
Panamanian	3,977	0.18
Salvadoran	21,342	0.96
Other Central American	353	0.02
Cuban	11,020	0.49
Dominican Republic	88,061	3.95
Mexican	92,835	4.16
Puerto Rican	102,881	4.61
South American	214,022	9.59
Argentinean	6,345	0.28
Bolivian	3,268	0.15
Chilean	3,184	0.14
Colombian	70,290	3.15
Ecuadorian	98,512	4.42
Paraguayan	2,775	0.12
Peruvian	22,886	1.03
Uruguayan	1,743	0.08
Venezuelan	3,580	0.16
Other South American	1,439	0.06
Other Hispanic or Latino	52,422	2.35

Race*	Population	%
African-American/Black (426,683)	462,351	20.73
Not Hispanic (395,881)	419,695	18.81
Hispanic (30,802)	42,656	1.91
American Indian/Alaska Native (15,364)	30,033	1.35
Not Hispanic (6,490)	15,412	0.69
Hispanic (8,874)	14,621	0.66
Alaska Athabascan (Ala. Nat.) (2)	3	<0.01
Aleut (Alaska Native) (4)	6	<0.01
Apache (15)	53	<0.01
Arapaho (0)	2	<0.01
Blackfeet (45)	342	0.02
Canadian/French Am. Ind. (20)	38	<0.01
Central American Ind. (419)	733	0.03
Cherokee (267)	1,425	0.06
Cheyenne (13)	20	<0.01
Chickasaw (9)	21	<0.01
Chippewa (14)	37	<0.01
Choctaw (16)	68	<0.01
Colville (1)	1	<0.01
Comanche (3)	6	<0.01
Cree (6)	24	<0.01
Creek (23)	73	<0.01
Crow (1)	4	<0.01
Delaware (14)	35	<0.01
Hopi (1)	15	<0.01
Houma (0)	4	<0.01
Inupiat (Alaska Native) (6)	13	<0.01
Iroquois (140)	308	0.01
Kiowa (0)	0	<0.01
Lumbee (7)	30	<0.01
Menominee (0)	0	<0.01
Mexican American Ind. (1,270)	1,640	0.07
Navajo (13)	37	<0.01
Osage (0)	5	<0.01
Ottawa (0)	2	<0.01
Paiute (3)	4	<0.01
Pima (0)	0	<0.01
Potawatomi (6)	7	<0.01
Pueblo (102)	161	0.01
Puget Sound Salish (2)	5	<0.01
Seminole (15)	79	<0.01
Shoshone (0)	6	<0.01
Sioux (35)	104	<0.01
South American Ind. (1,281)	2,448	0.11
Spanish American Ind. (468)	659	0.03
Tlingit-Haida (Alaska Native) (8)	20	<0.01
Tohono O'Odham (4)	6	<0.01
Tsimshian (Alaska Native) (0)	1	<0.01
Ute (4)	5	<0.01
Yakama (0)	0	<0.01
Yaqui (3)	7	<0.01
Yuman (2)	5	<0.01
Yup'ik (Alaska Native) (1)	1	<0.01
Asian (511,787)	552,867	24.78
Not Hispanic (508,334)	545,389	24.45
Hispanic (3,453)	7,478	0.34
Bangladeshi (33,152)	38,341	1.72
Bhutanese (240)	250	0.01
Burmese (2,132)	2,344	0.11
Cambodian (230)	303	0.01
Chinese, ex. Taiwanese (191,693)	200,714	9.00
Filipino (38,163)	41,773	1.87
Hmong (24)	30	<0.01
Indian (117,550)	141,147	6.33
Indonesian (2,860)	3,386	0.15
Japanese (6,375)	7,790	0.35
Korean (64,107)	66,124	2.96
Laotian (137)	210	0.01
Malaysian (1,029)	1,620	0.07
Nepalese (4,930)	5,319	0.24
Pakistani (16,215)	18,084	0.81
Sri Lankan (1,293)	1,536	0.07
Taiwanese (7,776)	8,962	0.40
Thai (3,677)	4,124	0.18
Vietnamese (3,566)	4,322	0.19
Hawaii Native/Pacific Islander (1,530)	7,691	0.34
Not Hispanic (1,094)	5,685	0.25
Hispanic (436)	2,006	0.09
Fijian (36)	76	<0.01
Guamanian/Chamorro (337)	483	0.02
Marshallese (0)	0	<0.01
Native Hawaiian (191)	486	0.02
Samoan (62)	179	0.01
Tongan (7)	14	<0.01
White (886,053)	941,608	42.21
Not Hispanic (616,727)	638,051	28.60
Hispanic (269,326)	303,557	13.61

Notes: † The Census 2010 population figure is used to calculate the percentages in the Hispanic Origin and Race categories. Ancestry percentages are based on the 2006-2010 American Community Survey population (not shown); ‡ Numbers in parentheses indicate the number of people reporting a single ancestry; * Numbers in parentheses indicate the number of persons reporting this race alone, not in combination with any other race; Please refer to the Explanation of Data for more information.

Rensselaer County

Population: 159,429

Ancestry	Population	%
Afghan (0)	0	<0.01
African, Sub-Saharan (697)	883	0.56
African (405)	565	0.36
Cape Verdean (0)	11	0.01
Ethiopian (0)	0	<0.01
Ghanaian (103)	103	0.06
Kenyan (0)	0	<0.01
Liberian (0)	0	<0.01
Nigerian (8)	8	0.01
Senegalese (0)	0	<0.01
Sierra Leonean (0)	0	<0.01
Somalian (0)	0	<0.01
South African (0)	0	<0.01
Sudanese (28)	28	0.02
Ugandan (0)	0	<0.01
Zimbabwean (0)	0	<0.01
Other Sub-Saharan African (153)	168	0.11
Albanian (80)	82	0.05
Alsatian (13)	13	0.01
American (6,888)	6,888	4.34
Arab (537)	1,052	0.66
Arab (72)	91	0.06
Egyptian (90)	210	0.13
Iraqi (0)	0	<0.01
Jordanian (0)	0	<0.01
Lebanese (284)	572	0.36
Moroccan (0)	0	<0.01
Palestinian (0)	0	<0.01
Syrian (16)	65	0.04
Other Arab (75)	114	0.07
Armenian (412)	992	0.63
Assyrian/Chaldean/Syriac (0)	0	<0.01
Australian (17)	17	0.01
Austrian (117)	580	0.37
Basque (0)	0	<0.01
Belgian (0)	125	0.08
Brazilian (126)	143	0.09
British (258)	500	0.32
Bulgarian (0)	0	<0.01
Cajun (0)	0	<0.01
Canadian (317)	787	0.50
Carpatho Rusyn (0)	0	<0.01
Celtic (0)	40	0.03
Croatian (89)	113	0.07
Cypriot (0)	0	<0.01
Czech (115)	607	0.38
Czechoslovakian (116)	305	0.19
Danish (172)	977	0.62
Dutch (850)	7,465	4.71
Eastern European (126)	171	0.11
English (3,787)	18,308	11.54
Estonian (15)	32	0.02
European (1,054)	1,508	0.95
Finnish (32)	195	0.12
French, ex. Basque (2,073)	16,113	10.16
French Canadian (1,505)	4,489	2.83
German (6,342)	31,702	19.98
German Russian (0)	65	0.04
Greek (301)	959	0.60
Guyanese (138)	217	0.14
Hungarian (161)	744	0.47
Icelander (0)	0	<0.01
Iranian (57)	57	0.04
Irish (11,871)	43,414	27.37
Israeli (13)	13	0.01
Italian (7,939)	24,089	15.19
Latvian (29)	77	0.05
Lithuanian (214)	1,079	0.68
Luxemburger (0)	0	<0.01
Macedonian (0)	0	<0.01
Maltese (0)	3	<0.01
New Zealander (0)	0	<0.01
Northern European (88)	88	0.06
Norwegian (140)	672	0.42
Pennsylvania German (40)	53	0.03

Ancestry (cont.)	Population	%
Polish (2,632)	10,494	6.62
Portuguese (135)	465	0.29
Romanian (11)	88	0.06
Russian (484)	1,724	1.09
Scandinavian (41)	180	0.11
Scotch-Irish (754)	2,400	1.51
Scottish (872)	3,489	2.20
Serbian (0)	10	0.01
Slavic (18)	107	0.07
Slovak (44)	188	0.12
Slovene (8)	23	0.01
Soviet Union (0)	0	<0.01
Swedish (342)	1,747	1.10
Swiss (37)	467	0.29
Turkish (170)	223	0.14
Ukrainian (746)	2,107	1.33
Welsh (289)	1,378	0.87
West Indian, ex. Hispanic (954)	1,304	0.82
Bahamian (0)	0	<0.01
Barbadian (15)	55	0.03
Belizean (0)	10	0.01
Bermudan (0)	0	<0.01
British West Indian (23)	30	0.02
Dutch West Indian (0)	0	<0.01
Haitian (176)	232	0.15
Jamaican (316)	440	0.28
Trinidadian/Tobagonian (274)	320	0.20
U.S. Virgin Islander (0)	0	<0.01
West Indian (150)	204	0.13
Other West Indian (0)	13	0.01
Yugoslavian (21)	51	0.03

Hispanic Origin	Population	%
Hispanic or Latino (of any race)	6,080	3.81
Central American, ex. Mexican	275	0.17
Costa Rican	37	0.02
Guatemalan	58	0.04
Honduran	21	0.01
Nicaraguan	20	0.01
Panamanian	73	0.05
Salvadoran	63	0.04
Other Central American	3	<0.01
Cuban	179	0.11
Dominican Republic	312	0.20
Mexican	806	0.51
Puerto Rican	3,498	2.19
South American	362	0.23
Argentinean	40	0.03
Bolivian	6	<0.01
Chilean	31	0.02
Colombian	104	0.07
Ecuadorian	79	0.05
Paraguayan	7	<0.01
Peruvian	47	0.03
Uruguayan	4	<0.01
Venezuelan	39	0.02
Other South American	5	<0.01
Other Hispanic or Latino	648	0.41

Race*	Population	%
African-American/Black (10,338)	12,620	7.92
Not Hispanic (9,592)	11,487	7.21
Hispanic (746)	1,133	0.71
American Indian/Alaska Native (385)	1,273	0.80
Not Hispanic (283)	1,058	0.66
Hispanic (102)	215	0.13
Alaska Athabascan (Ala. Nat.) (0)	0	<0.01
Aleut (Alaska Native) (0)	0	<0.01
Apache (4)	14	0.01
Arapaho (0)	0	<0.01
Blackfeet (5)	74	0.05
Canadian/French Am. Ind. (6)	26	0.02
Central American Ind. (1)	3	<0.01
Cherokee (29)	149	0.09
Cheyenne (0)	1	<0.01
Chickasaw (0)	0	<0.01
Chippewa (2)	12	0.01
Choctaw (4)	7	<0.01
Colville (0)	0	<0.01

Race* (cont.)	Population	%
Comanche (0)	2	<0.01
Cree (2)	4	<0.01
Creek (0)	3	<0.01
Crow (0)	3	<0.01
Delaware (3)	6	<0.01
Hopi (0)	0	<0.01
Houma (0)	0	<0.01
Inupiat (Alaska Native) (0)	2	<0.01
Iroquois (51)	173	0.11
Kiowa (0)	0	<0.01
Lumbee (2)	5	<0.01
Menominee (3)	3	<0.01
Mexican American Ind. (4)	7	<0.01
Navajo (2)	6	<0.01
Osage (0)	0	<0.01
Ottawa (0)	1	<0.01
Paiute (0)	0	<0.01
Pima (1)	1	<0.01
Potawatomi (0)	0	<0.01
Pueblo (0)	0	<0.01
Puget Sound Salish (0)	0	<0.01
Seminole (1)	4	<0.01
Shoshone (0)	0	<0.01
Sioux (4)	13	0.01
South American Ind. (19)	30	0.02
Spanish American Ind. (4)	5	<0.01
Tlingit-Haida (Alaska Native) (1)	2	<0.01
Tohono O'Odham (0)	0	<0.01
Tsimshian (Alaska Native) (0)	0	<0.01
Ute (0)	0	<0.01
Yakama (0)	0	<0.01
Yaqui (0)	0	<0.01
Yuman (0)	0	<0.01
Yup'ik (Alaska Native) (0)	2	<0.01
Asian (3,517)	4,293	2.69
Not Hispanic (3,469)	4,205	2.64
Hispanic (48)	88	0.06
Bangladeshi (43)	52	0.03
Bhutanese (0)	0	<0.01
Burmese (327)	348	0.22
Cambodian (6)	19	0.01
Chinese, ex. Taiwanese (976)	1,120	0.70
Filipino (228)	380	0.24
Hmong (2)	5	<0.01
Indian (924)	1,075	0.67
Indonesian (9)	15	0.01
Japanese (99)	207	0.13
Korean (315)	413	0.26
Laotian (2)	6	<0.01
Malaysian (12)	14	0.01
Nepalese (16)	22	0.01
Pakistani (193)	217	0.14
Sri Lankan (4)	8	0.01
Taiwanese (46)	52	0.03
Thai (32)	49	0.03
Vietnamese (121)	160	0.10
Hawaii Native/Pacific Islander (34)	123	0.08
Not Hispanic (25)	100	0.06
Hispanic (9)	23	0.01
Fijian (1)	1	<0.01
Guamanian/Chamorro (7)	13	0.01
Marshallese (0)	0	<0.01
Native Hawaiian (12)	43	0.03
Samoan (0)	6	<0.01
Tongan (0)	0	<0.01
White (139,529)	143,012	89.70
Not Hispanic (136,555)	139,499	87.50
Hispanic (2,974)	3,513	2.20

Notes: † The Census 2010 population figure is used to calculate the percentages in the Hispanic Origin and Race categories. Ancestry percentages are based on the 2006-2010 American Community Survey population (not shown); ‡ Numbers in parentheses indicate the number of people reporting a single ancestry; * Numbers in parentheses indicate the number of persons reporting this race alone, not in combination with any other race; Please refer to the Explanation of Data for more information.

Richmond County

Population: 468,730

Ancestry	Population	%
Afghan (0)	0	<0.01
African, Sub-Saharan (6,533)	7,234	1.56
African (3,732)	4,164	0.90
Cape Verdean (0)	11	<0.01
Ethiopian (41)	46	0.01
Ghanaian (239)	250	0.05
Kenyan (78)	78	0.02
Liberian (515)	532	0.11
Nigerian (1,509)	1,679	0.36
Senegalese (126)	126	0.03
Sierra Leonean (90)	117	0.03
Somalian (0)	0	<0.01
South African (0)	0	<0.01
Sudanese (0)	0	<0.01
Ugandan (0)	0	<0.01
Zimbabwean (0)	0	<0.01
Other Sub-Saharan African (203)	231	0.05
Albanian (7,700)	8,108	1.75
Alsatian (0)	24	0.01
American (13,977)	13,977	3.02
Arab (7,711)	8,820	1.90
Arab (1,694)	1,829	0.39
Egyptian (3,200)	3,292	0.71
Iraqi (11)	32	0.01
Jordanian (159)	183	0.04
Lebanese (784)	1,019	0.22
Moroccan (502)	621	0.13
Palestinian (443)	479	0.10
Syrian (209)	584	0.13
Other Arab (709)	781	0.17
Armenian (83)	311	0.07
Assyrian/Chaldean/Syriac (15)	15	<0.01
Australian (24)	49	0.01
Austrian (343)	1,542	0.33
Basque (15)	77	0.02
Belgian (36)	266	0.06
Brazilian (183)	287	0.06
British (231)	615	0.13
Bulgarian (0)	0	<0.01
Cajun (0)	0	<0.01
Canadian (290)	544	0.12
Carpatho Rusyn (63)	63	0.01
Celtic (37)	46	0.01
Croatian (598)	869	0.19
Cypriot (0)	0	<0.01
Czech (146)	735	0.16
Czechoslovakian (93)	237	0.05
Danish (90)	479	0.10
Dutch (137)	1,637	0.35
Eastern European (433)	433	0.09
English (1,973)	9,014	1.94
Estonian (10)	10	<0.01
European (1,914)	2,068	0.45
Finnish (48)	185	0.04
French, ex. Basque (800)	3,772	0.81
French Canadian (248)	750	0.16
German (4,111)	25,477	5.50
German Russian (0)	0	<0.01
Greek (2,403)	4,183	0.90
Guyanese (767)	952	0.21
Hungarian (1,024)	2,288	0.49
Icelander (55)	55	0.01
Iranian (121)	171	0.04
Irish (20,064)	64,762	13.97
Israeli (542)	759	0.16
Italian (107,263)	156,288	33.72
Latvian (98)	142	0.03
Lithuanian (178)	645	0.14
Luxemburger (12)	54	0.01
Macedonian (1,368)	1,590	0.34
Maltese (104)	290	0.06
New Zealander (0)	0	<0.01
Northern European (60)	60	0.01
Norwegian (1,617)	5,135	1.11
Pennsylvania German (9)	41	0.01

Ancestry (cont.)	Population	%
Polish (9,167)	18,430	3.98
Portuguese (180)	617	0.13
Romanian (530)	964	0.21
Russian (11,315)	16,388	3.54
Scandinavian (35)	121	0.03
Scotch-Irish (759)	1,886	0.41
Scottish (718)	2,350	0.51
Serbian (219)	240	0.05
Slavic (68)	143	0.03
Slovak (233)	553	0.12
Slovene (86)	108	0.02
Soviet Union (51)	63	0.01
Swedish (253)	1,936	0.42
Swiss (76)	256	0.06
Turkish (1,267)	1,607	0.35
Ukrainian (3,759)	4,836	1.04
Welsh (68)	417	0.09
West Indian, ex. Hispanic (5,348)	6,967	1.50
Bahamian (31)	31	0.01
Barbadian (94)	94	0.02
Belizean (76)	76	0.02
Bermudan (0)	0	<0.01
British West Indian (113)	236	0.05
Dutch West Indian (39)	89	0.02
Haitian (676)	791	0.17
Jamaican (1,463)	2,033	0.44
Trinidadian/Tobagonian (1,412)	1,807	0.39
U.S. Virgin Islander (22)	22	<0.01
West Indian (1,392)	1,745	0.38
Other West Indian (30)	43	0.01
Yugoslavian (1,237)	1,738	0.38

Hispanic Origin	Population	%
Hispanic or Latino (of any race)	81,051	17.29
Central American, ex. Mexican	4,310	0.92
Costa Rican	266	0.06
Guatemalan	864	0.18
Honduran	1,735	0.37
Nicaraguan	199	0.04
Panamanian	607	0.13
Salvadoran	592	0.13
Other Central American	47	0.01
Cuban	1,831	0.39
Dominican Republic	4,918	1.05
Mexican	18,684	3.99
Puerto Rican	37,517	8.00
South American	8,232	1.76
Argentinean	608	0.13
Bolivian	161	0.03
Chilean	346	0.07
Colombian	2,526	0.54
Ecuadorian	2,675	0.57
Paraguayan	38	0.01
Peruvian	1,462	0.31
Uruguayan	76	0.02
Venezuelan	254	0.05
Other South American	86	0.02
Other Hispanic or Latino	5,559	1.19

Race*	Population	%
African-American/Black (49,857)	55,014	11.74
Not Hispanic (44,313)	47,521	10.14
Hispanic (5,544)	7,493	1.60
American Indian/Alaska Native (1,695)	3,719	0.79
Not Hispanic (695)	2,034	0.43
Hispanic (1,000)	1,685	0.36
Alaska Athabascan (Ala. Nat.) (1)	3	<0.01
Aleut (Alaska Native) (0)	2	<0.01
Apache (16)	35	0.01
Arapaho (1)	1	<0.01
Blackfeet (17)	88	0.02
Canadian/French Am. Ind. (7)	10	<0.01
Central American Ind. (29)	56	0.01
Cherokee (104)	467	0.10
Cheyenne (0)	2	<0.01
Chickasaw (1)	3	<0.01
Chippewa (7)	13	<0.01
Choctaw (3)	11	<0.01
Colville (0)	0	<0.01

Race* (cont.)	Population	%
Comanche (2)	3	<0.01
Cree (0)	4	<0.01
Creek (3)	29	0.01
Crow (0)	0	<0.01
Delaware (16)	43	0.01
Hopi (1)	5	<0.01
Houma (1)	1	<0.01
Inupiat (Alaska Native) (0)	1	<0.01
Iroquois (61)	152	0.03
Kiowa (0)	1	<0.01
Lumbee (1)	8	<0.01
Menominee (0)	0	<0.01
Mexican American Ind. (161)	204	0.04
Navajo (10)	17	<0.01
Osage (0)	0	<0.01
Ottawa (0)	0	<0.01
Paiute (0)	0	<0.01
Pima (2)	2	<0.01
Potawatomi (0)	0	<0.01
Pueblo (4)	5	<0.01
Puget Sound Salish (0)	0	<0.01
Seminole (7)	26	0.01
Shoshone (1)	3	<0.01
Sioux (11)	24	0.01
South American Ind. (146)	288	0.06
Spanish American Ind. (31)	47	0.01
Tlingit-Haida (Alaska Native) (0)	1	<0.01
Tohono O'Odham (4)	8	<0.01
Tsimshian (Alaska Native) (0)	0	<0.01
Ute (1)	1	<0.01
Yakama (0)	0	<0.01
Yaqui (1)	1	<0.01
Yuman (0)	1	<0.01
Yup'ik (Alaska Native) (0)	0	<0.01
Asian (35,164)	38,756	8.27
Not Hispanic (34,697)	37,689	8.04
Hispanic (467)	1,067	0.23
Bangladeshi (360)	387	0.08
Bhutanese (0)	0	<0.01
Burmese (116)	130	0.03
Cambodian (100)	129	0.03
Chinese, ex. Taiwanese (13,144)	14,107	3.01
Filipino (5,224)	6,205	1.32
Hmong (4)	8	<0.01
Indian (6,793)	7,723	1.65
Indonesian (22)	52	0.01
Japanese (201)	408	0.09
Korean (3,207)	3,398	0.72
Laotian (13)	18	<0.01
Malaysian (58)	96	0.02
Nepalese (27)	35	0.01
Pakistani (2,495)	2,777	0.59
Sri Lankan (1,560)	1,766	0.38
Taiwanese (160)	197	0.04
Thai (135)	166	0.04
Vietnamese (468)	570	0.12
Hawaii Native/Pacific Islander (213)	683	0.15
Not Hispanic (137)	439	0.09
Hispanic (76)	244	0.05
Fijian (6)	6	<0.01
Guamanian/Chamorro (88)	115	0.02
Marshallese (1)	1	<0.01
Native Hawaiian (46)	121	0.03
Samoan (5)	26	0.01
Tongan (2)	2	<0.01
White (341,677)	350,679	74.81
Not Hispanic (300,169)	305,118	65.09
Hispanic (41,508)	45,561	9.72

Notes: † The Census 2010 population figure is used to calculate the percentages in the Hispanic Origin and Race categories. Ancestry percentages are based on the 2006-2010 American Community Survey population (not shown); ‡ Numbers in parentheses indicate the number of people reporting a single ancestry; * Numbers in parentheses indicate the number of persons reporting this race alone, not in combination with any other race; Please refer to the Explanation of Data for more information.

Rockland County

Population: 311,687

Ancestry	Population	%
Afghan (172)	172	0.06
African, Sub-Saharan (1,590)	2,071	0.68
African (567)	971	0.32
Cape Verdean (0)	0	<0.01
Ethiopian (27)	44	0.01
Ghanaian (339)	339	0.11
Kenyan (92)	92	0.03
Liberian (0)	0	<0.01
Nigerian (207)	262	0.09
Senegalese (52)	52	0.02
Sierra Leonean (0)	0	<0.01
Somalian (0)	0	<0.01
South African (89)	89	0.03
Sudanese (0)	0	<0.01
Ugandan (86)	86	0.03
Zimbabwean (0)	0	<0.01
Other Sub-Saharan African (131)	136	0.04
Albanian (501)	569	0.19
Alsatian (0)	3	<0.01
American (13,566)	13,566	4.44
Arab (1,299)	1,848	0.60
Arab (330)	351	0.11
Egyptian (344)	377	0.12
Iraqi (19)	72	0.02
Jordanian (87)	87	0.03
Lebanese (161)	338	0.11
Moroccan (216)	301	0.10
Palestinian (0)	25	0.01
Syrian (24)	156	0.05
Other Arab (118)	141	0.05
Armenian (239)	332	0.11
Assyrian/Chaldean/Syriac (11)	51	0.02
Australian (40)	125	0.04
Austrian (667)	2,856	0.93
Basque (0)	0	<0.01
Belgian (270)	922	0.30
Brazilian (215)	476	0.16
British (457)	879	0.29
Bulgarian (8)	24	0.01
Cajun (0)	0	<0.01
Canadian (470)	1,139	0.37
Carpatho Rusyn (4)	4	<0.01
Celtic (19)	19	0.01
Croatian (78)	264	0.09
Cypriot (0)	0	<0.01
Czech (310)	1,346	0.44
Czechoslovakian (489)	955	0.31
Danish (107)	402	0.13
Dutch (469)	2,665	0.87
Eastern European (2,769)	3,036	0.99
English (2,442)	10,647	3.49
Estonian (24)	50	0.02
European (9,157)	10,292	3.37
Finnish (50)	191	0.06
French, ex. Basque (590)	3,512	1.15
French Canadian (318)	795	0.26
German (5,904)	24,634	8.06
German Russian (12)	12	<0.01
Greek (1,370)	2,748	0.90
Guyanese (387)	482	0.16
Hungarian (4,329)	8,874	2.91
Icelander (0)	0	<0.01
Iranian (381)	626	0.20
Irish (22,489)	47,471	15.54
Israeli (1,696)	3,753	1.23
Italian (22,741)	44,310	14.51
Latvian (227)	349	0.11
Lithuanian (439)	1,258	0.41
Luxemburger (0)	0	<0.01
Macedonian (24)	24	0.01
Maltese (38)	85	0.03
New Zealander (0)	58	0.02
Northern European (20)	71	0.02
Norwegian (405)	962	0.31
Pennsylvania German (20)	38	0.01

Ancestry	Population	%
Polish (5,690)	16,940	5.55
Portuguese (692)	1,011	0.33
Romanian (800)	2,551	0.84
Russian (6,114)	13,933	4.56
Scandinavian (38)	88	0.03
Scotch-Irish (611)	1,605	0.53
Scottish (672)	2,422	0.79
Serbian (51)	76	0.02
Slavic (29)	159	0.05
Slovak (362)	801	0.26
Slovene (31)	54	0.02
Soviet Union (0)	0	<0.01
Swedish (298)	1,500	0.49
Swiss (73)	267	0.09
Turkish (139)	282	0.09
Ukrainian (1,524)	2,602	0.85
Welsh (78)	620	0.20
West Indian, ex. Hispanic (17,509)	18,661	6.11
Bahamian (0)	0	<0.01
Barbadian (125)	149	0.05
Belizean (141)	164	0.05
Bermudan (0)	3	<0.01
British West Indian (323)	347	0.11
Dutch West Indian (0)	0	<0.01
Haitian (12,516)	13,086	4.28
Jamaican (3,254)	3,514	1.15
Trinidadian/Tobagonian (738)	819	0.27
U.S. Virgin Islander (0)	19	0.01
West Indian (412)	560	0.18
Other West Indian (0)	0	<0.01
Yugoslavian (110)	207	0.07

Hispanic Origin	Population	%
Hispanic or Latino (of any race)	48,783	15.65
Central American, ex. Mexican	9,272	2.97
Costa Rican	205	0.07
Guatemalan	5,356	1.72
Honduran	383	0.12
Nicaraguan	101	0.03
Panamanian	145	0.05
Salvadoran	3,012	0.97
Other Central American	70	0.02
Cuban	1,191	0.38
Dominican Republic	9,105	2.92
Mexican	5,358	1.72
Puerto Rican	12,650	4.06
South American	7,348	2.36
Argentinean	379	0.12
Bolivian	55	0.02
Chilean	203	0.07
Colombian	982	0.32
Ecuadorian	4,926	1.58
Paraguayan	26	0.01
Peruvian	562	0.18
Uruguayan	63	0.02
Venezuelan	119	0.04
Other South American	33	0.01
Other Hispanic or Latino	3,859	1.24

Race*	Population	%
African-American/Black (37,058)	40,486	12.99
Not Hispanic (34,623)	36,893	11.84
Hispanic (2,435)	3,593	1.15
American Indian/Alaska Native (911)	2,250	0.72
Not Hispanic (487)	1,366	0.44
Hispanic (424)	884	0.28
Alaska Athabascan (Ala. Nat.) (1)	1	<0.01
Aleut (Alaska Native) (1)	1	<0.01
Apache (3)	8	<0.01
Arapaho (0)	0	<0.01
Blackfeet (3)	34	0.01
Canadian/French Am. Ind. (0)	3	<0.01
Central American Ind. (28)	46	0.01
Cherokee (18)	192	0.06
Cheyenne (0)	2	<0.01
Chickasaw (0)	0	<0.01
Chippewa (1)	2	<0.01
Choctaw (3)	12	<0.01
Colville (0)	0	<0.01

Race*	Population	%
Comanche (3)	7	<0.01
Cree (0)	2	<0.01
Creek (0)	3	<0.01
Crow (1)	1	<0.01
Delaware (113)	236	0.08
Hopi (0)	0	<0.01
Houma (0)	0	<0.01
Inupiat (Alaska Native) (0)	0	<0.01
Iroquois (44)	85	0.03
Kiowa (0)	0	<0.01
Lumbee (4)	7	<0.01
Menominee (0)	0	<0.01
Mexican American Ind. (72)	107	0.03
Navajo (0)	5	<0.01
Osage (0)	1	<0.01
Ottawa (0)	0	<0.01
Paiute (1)	1	<0.01
Pima (0)	0	<0.01
Potawatomi (1)	1	<0.01
Pueblo (5)	9	<0.01
Puget Sound Salish (0)	0	<0.01
Seminole (0)	8	<0.01
Shoshone (0)	0	<0.01
Sioux (4)	18	0.01
South American Ind. (62)	185	0.06
Spanish American Ind. (9)	16	0.01
Tlingit-Haida (Alaska Native) (2)	8	<0.01
Tohono O'Odham (2)	4	<0.01
Tsimshian (Alaska Native) (0)	0	<0.01
Ute (0)	0	<0.01
Yakama (1)	1	<0.01
Yaqui (1)	1	<0.01
Yuman (0)	0	<0.01
Yup'ik (Alaska Native) (0)	0	<0.01
Asian (19,293)	21,506	6.90
Not Hispanic (19,099)	21,015	6.74
Hispanic (194)	491	0.16
Bangladeshi (144)	166	0.05
Bhutanese (0)	0	<0.01
Burmese (10)	14	<0.01
Cambodian (147)	166	0.05
Chinese, ex. Taiwanese (2,686)	3,154	1.01
Filipino (4,482)	5,049	1.62
Hmong (30)	32	0.01
Indian (7,028)	7,759	2.49
Indonesian (30)	52	0.02
Japanese (277)	410	0.13
Korean (2,199)	2,340	0.75
Laotian (9)	14	<0.01
Malaysian (5)	16	0.01
Nepalese (14)	16	0.01
Pakistani (961)	1,080	0.35
Sri Lankan (78)	93	0.03
Taiwanese (86)	101	0.03
Thai (185)	220	0.07
Vietnamese (402)	503	0.16
Hawaii Native/Pacific Islander (130)	538	0.17
Not Hispanic (43)	295	0.09
Hispanic (87)	243	0.08
Fijian (0)	2	<0.01
Guamanian/Chamorro (48)	65	0.02
Marshallese (0)	0	<0.01
Native Hawaiian (15)	42	0.01
Samoan (10)	17	0.01
Tongan (2)	2	<0.01
White (228,295)	234,099	75.11
Not Hispanic (203,670)	206,768	66.34
Hispanic (24,625)	27,331	8.77

Notes: † The Census 2010 population figure is used to calculate the percentages in the Hispanic Origin and Race categories. Ancestry percentages are based on the 2006-2010 American Community Survey population (not shown); ‡ Numbers in parentheses indicate the number of people reporting a single ancestry; * Numbers in parentheses indicate the number of persons reporting this race alone, not in combination with any other race; Please refer to the Explanation of Data for more information.

Saratoga County

Population: 219,607

Ancestry	Population	%
Afghan (215)	256	0.12
African, Sub-Saharan (91)	164	0.08
African (5)	78	0.04
Cape Verdean (0)	0	<0.01
Ethiopian (0)	0	<0.01
Ghanaian (61)	61	0.03
Kenyan (0)	0	<0.01
Liberian (0)	0	<0.01
Nigerian (25)	25	0.01
Senegalese (0)	0	<0.01
Sierra Leonean (0)	0	<0.01
Somalian (0)	0	<0.01
South African (0)	0	<0.01
Sudanese (0)	0	<0.01
Ugandan (0)	0	<0.01
Zimbabwean (0)	0	<0.01
Other Sub-Saharan African (0)	0	<0.01
Albanian (101)	148	0.07
Alsatian (0)	0	<0.01
American (26,948)	26,948	12.40
Arab (305)	939	0.43
Arab (0)	13	0.01
Egyptian (146)	156	0.07
Iraqi (0)	10	<0.01
Jordanian (0)	0	<0.01
Lebanese (71)	460	0.21
Moroccan (60)	72	0.03
Palestinian (0)	0	<0.01
Syrian (22)	205	0.09
Other Arab (6)	23	0.01
Armenian (142)	458	0.21
Assyrian/Chaldean/Syriac (13)	13	0.01
Australian (55)	115	0.05
Austrian (318)	966	0.44
Basque (7)	11	0.01
Belgian (46)	222	0.10
Brazilian (179)	214	0.10
British (535)	886	0.41
Bulgarian (20)	39	0.02
Cajun (0)	0	<0.01
Canadian (422)	937	0.43
Carpatho Rusyn (0)	0	<0.01
Celtic (11)	19	0.01
Croatian (112)	198	0.09
Cypriot (0)	0	<0.01
Czech (190)	848	0.39
Czechoslovakian (167)	387	0.18
Danish (117)	964	0.44
Dutch (1,294)	6,872	3.16
Eastern European (261)	287	0.13
English (7,312)	27,103	12.47
Estonian (20)	71	0.03
European (1,477)	1,634	0.75
Finnish (154)	433	0.20
French, ex. Basque (3,190)	21,115	9.72
French Canadian (2,301)	5,476	2.52
German (7,897)	35,201	16.20
German Russian (0)	26	0.01
Greek (552)	1,127	0.52
Guyanese (193)	200	0.09
Hungarian (249)	1,427	0.66
Icelander (0)	14	0.01
Iranian (85)	113	0.05
Irish (15,092)	52,194	24.02
Israeli (113)	127	0.06
Italian (13,634)	34,416	15.84
Latvian (59)	189	0.09
Lithuanian (325)	1,033	0.48
Luxemburger (0)	0	<0.01
Macedonian (11)	11	0.01
Maltese (12)	78	0.04
New Zealander (0)	0	<0.01
Northern European (63)	106	0.05
Norwegian (591)	1,971	0.91
Pennsylvania German (32)	45	0.02

Ancestry	Population	%
Polish (4,777)	16,507	7.60
Portuguese (106)	360	0.17
Romanian (49)	227	0.10
Russian (1,235)	3,548	1.63
Scandinavian (100)	250	0.12
Scotch-Irish (1,288)	3,641	1.68
Scottish (1,088)	4,810	2.21
Serbian (42)	63	0.03
Slavic (72)	236	0.11
Slovak (219)	911	0.42
Slovene (44)	63	0.03
Soviet Union (0)	0	<0.01
Swedish (319)	1,884	0.87
Swiss (95)	442	0.20
Turkish (99)	113	0.05
Ukrainian (697)	1,955	0.90
Welsh (285)	1,941	0.89
West Indian, ex. Hispanic (265)	558	0.26
Bahamian (0)	13	0.01
Barbadian (24)	24	0.01
Belizean (0)	0	<0.01
Bermudan (0)	0	<0.01
British West Indian (0)	0	<0.01
Dutch West Indian (0)	0	<0.01
Haitian (2)	25	0.01
Jamaican (132)	353	0.16
Trinidadian/Tobagonian (40)	40	0.02
U.S. Virgin Islander (9)	9	<0.01
West Indian (58)	94	0.04
Other West Indian (0)	0	<0.01
Yugoslavian (116)	216	0.10

Hispanic Origin	Population	%
Hispanic or Latino (of any race)	5,279	2.40
Central American, ex. Mexican	336	0.15
Costa Rican	32	0.01
Guatemalan	90	0.04
Honduran	46	0.02
Nicaraguan	14	0.01
Panamanian	41	0.02
Salvadoran	110	0.05
Other Central American	3	<0.01
Cuban	225	0.10
Dominican Republic	271	0.12
Mexican	1,331	0.61
Puerto Rican	1,920	0.87
South American	540	0.25
Argentinean	57	0.03
Bolivian	18	0.01
Chilean	61	0.03
Colombian	159	0.07
Ecuadorian	84	0.04
Paraguayan	6	<0.01
Peruvian	80	0.04
Uruguayan	9	<0.01
Venezuelan	54	0.02
Other South American	12	0.01
Other Hispanic or Latino	656	0.30

Race*	Population	%
African-American/Black (3,269)	4,700	2.14
Not Hispanic (3,053)	4,314	1.96
Hispanic (216)	386	0.18
American Indian/Alaska Native (388)	1,377	0.63
Not Hispanic (325)	1,211	0.55
Hispanic (63)	166	0.08
Alaska Athabascan (Ala. Nat.) (1)	1	<0.01
Aleut (Alaska Native) (1)	5	<0.01
Apache (7)	20	0.01
Arapaho (0)	3	<0.01
Blackfeet (8)	56	0.03
Canadian/French Am. Ind. (3)	13	0.01
Central American Ind. (2)	7	<0.01
Cherokee (23)	168	0.08
Cheyenne (0)	1	<0.01
Chickasaw (3)	3	<0.01
Chippewa (3)	13	0.01
Choctaw (4)	9	<0.01
Colville (0)	0	<0.01

Race (cont.)	Population	%
Comanche (2)	5	<0.01
Cree (1)	8	<0.01
Creek (0)	2	<0.01
Crow (1)	1	<0.01
Delaware (2)	6	<0.01
Hopi (0)	0	<0.01
Houma (0)	0	<0.01
Inupiat (Alaska Native) (0)	1	<0.01
Iroquois (64)	186	0.08
Kiowa (0)	1	<0.01
Lumbee (1)	4	<0.01
Menominee (1)	3	<0.01
Mexican American Ind. (17)	22	0.01
Navajo (16)	28	0.01
Osage (0)	0	<0.01
Ottawa (0)	0	<0.01
Paiute (0)	0	<0.01
Pima (0)	0	<0.01
Potawatomi (0)	5	<0.01
Pueblo (2)	3	<0.01
Puget Sound Salish (0)	0	<0.01
Seminole (1)	6	<0.01
Shoshone (0)	0	<0.01
Sioux (4)	20	0.01
South American Ind. (8)	23	0.01
Spanish American Ind. (0)	0	<0.01
Tlingit-Haida (Alaska Native) (0)	2	<0.01
Tohono O'Odham (0)	0	<0.01
Tsimshian (Alaska Native) (0)	0	<0.01
Ute (0)	0	<0.01
Yakama (0)	0	<0.01
Yaqui (2)	2	<0.01
Yuman (0)	0	<0.01
Yup'ik (Alaska Native) (0)	0	<0.01
Asian (3,919)	5,079	2.31
Not Hispanic (3,880)	4,981	2.27
Hispanic (39)	98	0.04
Bangladeshi (24)	24	0.01
Bhutanese (0)	0	<0.01
Burmese (2)	3	<0.01
Cambodian (12)	13	0.01
Chinese, ex. Taiwanese (1,059)	1,280	0.58
Filipino (275)	500	0.23
Hmong (0)	0	<0.01
Indian (1,164)	1,338	0.61
Indonesian (6)	20	0.01
Japanese (184)	346	0.16
Korean (430)	605	0.28
Laotian (5)	13	0.01
Malaysian (7)	9	<0.01
Nepalese (11)	11	0.01
Pakistani (276)	319	0.15
Sri Lankan (12)	17	0.01
Taiwanese (45)	53	0.02
Thai (54)	97	0.04
Vietnamese (187)	223	0.10
Hawaii Native/Pacific Islander (44)	162	0.07
Not Hispanic (35)	132	0.06
Hispanic (9)	30	0.01
Fijian (0)	0	<0.01
Guamanian/Chamorro (10)	16	0.01
Marshallese (0)	0	<0.01
Native Hawaiian (18)	75	0.03
Samoan (4)	16	0.01
Tongan (0)	0	<0.01
White (207,181)	210,587	95.89
Not Hispanic (203,647)	206,635	94.09
Hispanic (3,534)	3,952	1.80

Notes: † The Census 2010 population figure is used to calculate the percentages in the Hispanic Origin and Race categories. Ancestry percentages are based on the 2006-2010 American Community Survey population (not shown); ‡ Numbers in parentheses indicate the number of people reporting a single ancestry; * Numbers in parentheses indicate the number of persons reporting this race alone, not in combination with any other race; Please refer to the Explanation of Data for more information.

Schenectady County

Population: 154,727

Ancestry	Population	%
Afghan (318)	318	0.21
African, Sub-Saharan (639)	860	0.56
African (286)	424	0.28
Cape Verdean (0)	0	<0.01
Ethiopian (0)	0	<0.01
Ghanaian (24)	24	0.02
Kenyan (69)	69	0.05
Liberian (24)	24	0.02
Nigerian (131)	186	0.12
Senegalese (0)	0	<0.01
Sierra Leonean (0)	0	<0.01
Somalian (0)	0	<0.01
South African (0)	0	<0.01
Sudanese (0)	0	<0.01
Ugandan (0)	0	<0.01
Zimbabwean (0)	0	<0.01
Other Sub-Saharan African (105)	133	0.09
Albanian (38)	80	0.05
Alsatian (0)	0	<0.01
American (8,939)	8,939	5.83
Arab (231)	473	0.31
Arab (81)	131	0.09
Egyptian (13)	13	0.01
Iraqi (0)	0	<0.01
Jordanian (0)	0	<0.01
Lebanese (106)	213	0.14
Moroccan (0)	0	<0.01
Palestinian (0)	0	<0.01
Syrian (0)	58	0.04
Other Arab (31)	58	0.04
Armenian (70)	92	0.06
Assyrian/Chaldean/Syriac (0)	0	<0.01
Australian (0)	51	0.03
Austrian (111)	467	0.30
Basque (0)	0	<0.01
Belgian (7)	28	0.02
Brazilian (156)	206	0.13
British (292)	611	0.40
Bulgarian (0)	0	<0.01
Cajun (0)	6	<0.01
Canadian (206)	511	0.33
Carpatho Rusyn (0)	0	<0.01
Celtic (35)	35	0.02
Croatian (15)	40	0.03
Cypriot (54)	54	0.04
Czech (130)	778	0.51
Czechoslovakian (174)	314	0.20
Danish (244)	681	0.44
Dutch (1,069)	5,702	3.72
Eastern European (326)	338	0.22
English (3,915)	14,772	9.64
Estonian (39)	39	0.03
European (1,101)	1,173	0.77
Finnish (15)	32	0.02
French, ex. Basque (1,638)	9,023	5.89
French Canadian (964)	2,716	1.77
German (4,964)	22,454	14.65
German Russian (0)	0	<0.01
Greek (305)	613	0.40
Guyanese (1,867)	1,999	1.30
Hungarian (286)	1,109	0.72
Icelander (0)	0	<0.01
Iranian (8)	8	0.01
Irish (8,174)	26,759	17.46
Israeli (0)	9	0.01
Italian (16,081)	30,411	19.84
Latvian (15)	94	0.06
Lithuanian (210)	708	0.46
Luxemburger (0)	0	<0.01
Macedonian (0)	0	<0.01
Maltese (0)	9	0.01
New Zealander (0)	18	0.01
Northern European (283)	297	0.19
Norwegian (149)	570	0.37
Pennsylvania German (10)	35	0.02

Ancestry	Population	%
Polish (5,392)	12,827	8.37
Portuguese (125)	198	0.13
Romanian (25)	127	0.08
Russian (561)	1,487	0.97
Scandinavian (35)	108	0.07
Scotch-Irish (666)	1,949	1.27
Scottish (906)	3,064	2.00
Serbian (0)	24	0.02
Slavic (54)	84	0.05
Slovak (198)	543	0.35
Slovene (0)	9	0.01
Soviet Union (0)	0	<0.01
Swedish (273)	1,002	0.65
Swiss (204)	517	0.34
Turkish (94)	123	0.08
Ukrainian (335)	808	0.53
Welsh (237)	989	0.65
West Indian, ex. Hispanic (1,560)	1,804	1.18
Bahamian (0)	0	<0.01
Barbadian (43)	94	0.06
Belizean (0)	0	<0.01
Bermudan (0)	0	<0.01
British West Indian (75)	75	0.05
Dutch West Indian (0)	10	0.01
Haitian (24)	61	0.04
Jamaican (766)	817	0.53
Trinidadian/Tobagonian (24)	106	0.07
U.S. Virgin Islander (0)	0	<0.01
West Indian (628)	641	0.42
Other West Indian (0)	0	<0.01
Yugoslavian (48)	73	0.05

Hispanic Origin	Population	%
Hispanic or Latino (of any race)	8,827	5.70
Central American, ex. Mexican	481	0.31
Costa Rican	52	0.03
Guatemalan	101	0.07
Honduran	64	0.04
Nicaraguan	30	0.02
Panamanian	49	0.03
Salvadoran	170	0.11
Other Central American	15	0.01
Cuban	229	0.15
Dominican Republic	582	0.38
Mexican	702	0.45
Puerto Rican	5,442	3.52
South American	661	0.43
Argentinean	65	0.04
Bolivian	21	0.01
Chilean	35	0.02
Colombian	184	0.12
Ecuadorian	115	0.07
Paraguayan	10	0.01
Peruvian	118	0.08
Uruguayan	15	0.01
Venezuelan	55	0.04
Other South American	43	0.03
Other Hispanic or Latino	730	0.47

Race*	Population	%
African-American/Black (14,710)	17,992	11.63
Not Hispanic (13,528)	16,273	10.52
Hispanic (1,182)	1,719	1.11
American Indian/Alaska Native (575)	1,769	1.14
Not Hispanic (445)	1,465	0.95
Hispanic (130)	304	0.20
Alaska Athabascan (Ala. Nat.) (1)	1	<0.01
Aleut (Alaska Native) (0)	0	<0.01
Apache (6)	9	0.01
Arapaho (1)	1	<0.01
Blackfeet (3)	65	0.04
Canadian/French Am. Ind. (5)	12	0.01
Central American Ind. (6)	7	<0.01
Cherokee (14)	174	0.11
Cheyenne (1)	2	<0.01
Chickasaw (0)	1	<0.01
Chippewa (6)	17	0.01
Choctaw (1)	2	<0.01
Colville (0)	0	<0.01

Race*	Population	%
Comanche (0)	0	<0.01
Cree (0)	5	<0.01
Creek (1)	5	<0.01
Crow (0)	6	<0.01
Delaware (4)	12	0.01
Hopi (0)	1	<0.01
Houma (0)	0	<0.01
Inupiat (Alaska Native) (4)	4	<0.01
Iroquois (37)	159	0.10
Kiowa (0)	1	<0.01
Lumbee (2)	4	<0.01
Menominee (0)	0	<0.01
Mexican American Ind. (16)	20	0.01
Navajo (1)	4	<0.01
Osage (0)	0	<0.01
Ottawa (0)	0	<0.01
Paiute (0)	0	<0.01
Pima (1)	5	<0.01
Potawatomi (2)	7	<0.01
Pueblo (0)	1	<0.01
Puget Sound Salish (0)	0	<0.01
Seminole (2)	11	0.01
Shoshone (0)	0	<0.01
Sioux (6)	24	0.02
South American Ind. (18)	39	0.03
Spanish American Ind. (1)	7	<0.01
Tlingit-Haida (Alaska Native) (0)	0	<0.01
Tohono O'Odham (0)	0	<0.01
Tsimshian (Alaska Native) (0)	0	<0.01
Ute (0)	0	<0.01
Yakama (0)	0	<0.01
Yaqui (0)	0	<0.01
Yuman (0)	0	<0.01
Yup'ik (Alaska Native) (0)	0	<0.01
Asian (4,960)	6,587	4.26
Not Hispanic (4,917)	6,436	4.16
Hispanic (43)	151	0.10
Bangladeshi (13)	20	0.01
Bhutanese (1)	1	<0.01
Burmese (6)	9	0.01
Cambodian (9)	13	0.01
Chinese, ex. Taiwanese (938)	1,093	0.71
Filipino (257)	368	0.24
Hmong (0)	0	<0.01
Indian (2,597)	3,182	2.06
Indonesian (16)	22	0.01
Japanese (76)	160	0.10
Korean (325)	451	0.29
Laotian (2)	12	0.01
Malaysian (3)	9	0.01
Nepalese (12)	17	0.01
Pakistani (279)	316	0.20
Sri Lankan (21)	26	0.02
Taiwanese (25)	33	0.02
Thai (31)	53	0.03
Vietnamese (181)	214	0.14
Hawaii Native/Pacific Islander (105)	391	0.25
Not Hispanic (81)	327	0.21
Hispanic (24)	64	0.04
Fijian (1)	1	<0.01
Guamanian/Chamorro (6)	14	0.01
Marshallese (0)	0	<0.01
Native Hawaiian (19)	48	0.03
Samoan (4)	10	0.01
Tongan (1)	1	<0.01
White (123,211)	127,516	82.41
Not Hispanic (119,409)	123,004	79.50
Hispanic (3,802)	4,512	2.92

Notes: † The Census 2010 population figure is used to calculate the percentages in the Hispanic Origin and Race categories. Ancestry percentages are based on the 2006-2010 American Community Survey population (not shown); ‡ Numbers in parentheses indicate the number of people reporting a single ancestry; * Numbers in parentheses indicate the number of persons reporting this race alone, not in combination with any other race; Please refer to the Explanation of Data for more information.

Schoharie County

Population: 32,749

Ancestry	Population	%
Afghan (0)	0	<0.01
African, Sub-Saharan (66)	102	0.31
African (51)	87	0.27
Cape Verdean (0)	0	<0.01
Ethiopian (5)	5	0.02
Ghanaian (0)	0	<0.01
Kenyan (0)	0	<0.01
Liberian (0)	0	<0.01
Nigerian (10)	10	0.03
Senegalese (0)	0	<0.01
Sierra Leonean (0)	0	<0.01
Somalian (0)	0	<0.01
South African (0)	0	<0.01
Sudanese (0)	0	<0.01
Ugandan (0)	0	<0.01
Zimbabwean (0)	0	<0.01
Other Sub-Saharan African (0)	0	<0.01
Albanian (0)	0	<0.01
Alsatian (0)	0	<0.01
American (3,401)	3,401	10.37
Arab (73)	143	0.44
Arab (0)	0	<0.01
Egyptian (0)	40	0.12
Iraqi (46)	46	0.14
Jordanian (0)	0	<0.01
Lebanese (15)	36	0.11
Moroccan (0)	0	<0.01
Palestinian (0)	0	<0.01
Syrian (12)	21	0.06
Other Arab (0)	0	<0.01
Armenian (0)	30	0.09
Assyrian/Chaldean/Syriac (0)	0	<0.01
Australian (0)	20	0.06
Austrian (31)	187	0.57
Basque (0)	0	<0.01
Belgian (5)	33	0.10
Brazilian (0)	10	0.03
British (53)	135	0.41
Bulgarian (3)	3	0.01
Cajun (0)	0	<0.01
Canadian (72)	127	0.39
Carpatho Rusyn (0)	0	<0.01
Celtic (0)	3	0.01
Croatian (21)	34	0.10
Cypriot (0)	0	<0.01
Czech (21)	169	0.52
Czechoslovakian (44)	83	0.25
Danish (29)	118	0.36
Dutch (510)	2,676	8.16
Eastern European (30)	30	0.09
English (1,129)	4,576	13.96
Estonian (0)	24	0.07
European (402)	442	1.35
Finnish (7)	50	0.15
French, ex. Basque (194)	1,670	5.09
French Canadian (152)	546	1.67
German (2,500)	10,082	30.75
German Russian (0)	0	<0.01
Greek (44)	95	0.29
Guyanese (0)	0	<0.01
Hungarian (37)	242	0.74
Icelander (0)	0	<0.01
Iranian (3)	3	0.01
Irish (1,597)	7,351	22.42
Israeli (0)	0	<0.01
Italian (1,592)	4,233	12.91
Latvian (6)	6	0.02
Lithuanian (6)	46	0.14
Luxemburger (0)	0	<0.01
Macedonian (0)	0	<0.01
Maltese (0)	21	0.06
New Zealander (0)	0	<0.01
Northern European (4)	8	0.02
Norwegian (180)	461	1.41
Pennsylvania German (8)	11	0.03

	Population	%
Polish (442)	1,690	5.15
Portuguese (0)	50	0.15
Romanian (20)	26	0.08
Russian (72)	336	1.02
Scandinavian (17)	63	0.19
Scotch-Irish (199)	464	1.42
Scottish (146)	1,033	3.15
Serbian (0)	0	<0.01
Slavic (0)	20	0.06
Slovak (13)	34	0.10
Slovene (0)	4	0.01
Soviet Union (0)	0	<0.01
Swedish (29)	271	0.83
Swiss (14)	158	0.48
Turkish (0)	0	<0.01
Ukrainian (53)	151	0.46
Welsh (55)	384	1.17
West Indian, ex. Hispanic (92)	115	0.35
Bahamian (0)	0	<0.01
Barbadian (0)	0	<0.01
Belizean (0)	0	<0.01
Bermudan (0)	0	<0.01
British West Indian (0)	0	<0.01
Dutch West Indian (0)	0	<0.01
Haitian (19)	22	0.07
Jamaican (47)	67	0.20
Trinidadian/Tobagonian (14)	14	0.04
U.S. Virgin Islander (0)	0	<0.01
West Indian (12)	12	0.04
Other West Indian (0)	0	<0.01
Yugoslavian (0)	13	0.04

Hispanic Origin	Population	%
Hispanic or Latino (of any race)	924	2.82
Central American, ex. Mexican	58	0.18
Costa Rican	2	0.01
Guatemalan	26	0.08
Honduran	6	0.02
Nicaraguan	9	0.03
Panamanian	5	0.02
Salvadoran	10	0.03
Other Central American	0	<0.01
Cuban	60	0.18
Dominican Republic	37	0.11
Mexican	87	0.27
Puerto Rican	449	1.37
South American	96	0.29
Argentinean	9	0.03
Bolivian	0	<0.01
Chilean	3	0.01
Colombian	38	0.12
Ecuadorian	20	0.06
Paraguayan	2	0.01
Peruvian	19	0.06
Uruguayan	1	<0.01
Venezuelan	4	0.01
Other South American	0	<0.01
Other Hispanic or Latino	137	0.42

Race*	Population	%
African-American/Black (435)	603	1.84
Not Hispanic (394)	541	1.65
Hispanic (41)	62	0.19
American Indian/Alaska Native (70)	273	0.83
Not Hispanic (54)	238	0.73
Hispanic (16)	35	0.11
Alaska Athabascan (Ala. Nat.) (0)	0	<0.01
Aleut (Alaska Native) (2)	2	0.01
Apache (2)	7	0.02
Arapaho (1)	2	0.01
Blackfeet (0)	4	0.01
Canadian/French Am. Ind. (0)	0	<0.01
Central American Ind. (0)	1	<0.01
Cherokee (4)	32	0.10
Cheyenne (0)	1	<0.01
Chickasaw (0)	0	<0.01
Chippewa (1)	2	0.01
Choctaw (0)	0	<0.01
Colville (0)	0	<0.01

	Population	%
Comanche (0)	0	<0.01
Cree (0)	0	<0.01
Creek (0)	0	<0.01
Crow (0)	1	<0.01
Delaware (3)	3	0.01
Hopi (0)	0	<0.01
Houma (0)	0	<0.01
Inupiat (Alaska Native) (0)	0	<0.01
Iroquois (11)	42	0.13
Kiowa (1)	1	<0.01
Lumbee (0)	0	<0.01
Menominee (0)	0	<0.01
Mexican American Ind. (0)	0	<0.01
Navajo (1)	1	<0.01
Osage (0)	1	<0.01
Ottawa (0)	0	<0.01
Paiute (0)	0	<0.01
Pima (0)	0	<0.01
Potawatomi (0)	0	<0.01
Pueblo (0)	0	<0.01
Puget Sound Salish (0)	0	<0.01
Seminole (0)	1	<0.01
Shoshone (0)	0	<0.01
Sioux (1)	3	0.01
South American Ind. (5)	9	0.03
Spanish American Ind. (0)	0	<0.01
Tlingit-Haida (Alaska Native) (0)	0	<0.01
Tohono O'Odham (0)	0	<0.01
Tsimshian (Alaska Native) (0)	0	<0.01
Ute (0)	1	<0.01
Yakama (0)	0	<0.01
Yaqui (0)	0	<0.01
Yuman (0)	0	<0.01
Yup'ik (Alaska Native) (0)	0	<0.01
Asian (217)	288	0.88
Not Hispanic (217)	279	0.85
Hispanic (0)	9	0.03
Bangladeshi (0)	0	<0.01
Bhutanese (0)	0	<0.01
Burmese (0)	0	<0.01
Cambodian (0)	0	<0.01
Chinese, ex. Taiwanese (40)	48	0.15
Filipino (26)	45	0.14
Hmong (0)	0	<0.01
Indian (52)	64	0.20
Indonesian (0)	0	<0.01
Japanese (32)	37	0.11
Korean (26)	42	0.13
Laotian (0)	0	<0.01
Malaysian (0)	1	<0.01
Nepalese (3)	4	0.01
Pakistani (17)	17	0.05
Sri Lankan (3)	4	0.01
Taiwanese (0)	0	<0.01
Thai (3)	4	0.01
Vietnamese (7)	9	0.03
Hawaii Native/Pacific Islander (6)	27	0.08
Not Hispanic (3)	21	0.06
Hispanic (3)	6	0.02
Fijian (0)	0	<0.01
Guamanian/Chamorro (3)	4	0.01
Marshallese (0)	0	<0.01
Native Hawaiian (1)	10	0.03
Samoan (0)	2	0.01
Tongan (0)	0	<0.01
White (31,402)	31,818	97.16
Not Hispanic (30,742)	31,106	94.98
Hispanic (660)	712	2.17

Notes: † The Census 2010 population figure is used to calculate the percentages in the Hispanic Origin and Race categories. Ancestry percentages are based on the 2006-2010 American Community Survey population (not shown); ‡ Numbers in parentheses indicate the number of people reporting a single ancestry; * Numbers in parentheses indicate the number of persons reporting this race alone, not in combination with any other race; Please refer to the Explanation of Data for more information.

Schuyler County
Population: 18,343

Ancestry	Population	%
Afghan (0)	0	<0.01
African, Sub-Saharan (0)	0	<0.01
African (0)	0	<0.01
Cape Verdean (0)	0	<0.01
Ethiopian (0)	0	<0.01
Ghanaian (0)	0	<0.01
Kenyan (0)	0	<0.01
Liberian (0)	0	<0.01
Nigerian (0)	0	<0.01
Senegalese (0)	0	<0.01
Sierra Leonean (0)	0	<0.01
Somalian (0)	0	<0.01
South African (0)	0	<0.01
Sudanese (0)	0	<0.01
Ugandan (0)	0	<0.01
Zimbabwean (0)	0	<0.01
Other Sub-Saharan African (0)	0	<0.01
Albanian (107)	126	0.68
Alsatian (0)	0	<0.01
American (2,366)	2,366	12.74
Arab (43)	45	0.24
Arab (43)	43	0.23
Egyptian (0)	0	<0.01
Iraqi (0)	0	<0.01
Jordanian (0)	0	<0.01
Lebanese (0)	2	0.01
Moroccan (0)	0	<0.01
Palestinian (0)	0	<0.01
Syrian (0)	0	<0.01
Other Arab (0)	0	<0.01
Armenian (0)	0	<0.01
Assyrian/Chaldean/Syriac (0)	0	<0.01
Australian (7)	7	0.04
Austrian (11)	34	0.18
Basque (0)	0	<0.01
Belgian (10)	39	0.21
Brazilian (0)	0	<0.01
British (87)	122	0.66
Bulgarian (0)	0	<0.01
Cajun (0)	0	<0.01
Canadian (33)	50	0.27
Carpatho Rusyn (0)	0	<0.01
Celtic (0)	3	0.02
Croatian (0)	0	<0.01
Cypriot (0)	0	<0.01
Czech (95)	183	0.99
Czechoslovakian (7)	42	0.23
Danish (6)	43	0.23
Dutch (178)	942	5.07
Eastern European (11)	46	0.25
English (1,136)	3,077	16.57
Estonian (0)	0	<0.01
European (74)	85	0.46
Finnish (12)	101	0.54
French, ex. Basque (110)	694	3.74
French Canadian (64)	134	0.72
German (1,125)	3,444	18.55
German Russian (0)	0	<0.01
Greek (6)	21	0.11
Guyanese (0)	0	<0.01
Hungarian (7)	47	0.25
Icelander (0)	0	<0.01
Iranian (0)	0	<0.01
Irish (981)	3,340	17.99
Israeli (0)	0	<0.01
Italian (864)	1,984	10.69
Latvian (0)	0	<0.01
Lithuanian (16)	20	0.11
Luxemburger (0)	0	<0.01
Macedonian (0)	19	0.10
Maltese (0)	0	<0.01
New Zealander (0)	0	<0.01
Northern European (0)	0	<0.01
Norwegian (50)	119	0.64
Pennsylvania German (38)	83	0.45

Ancestry	Population	%
Polish (337)	1,027	5.53
Portuguese (0)	19	0.10
Romanian (0)	11	0.06
Russian (11)	130	0.70
Scandinavian (0)	0	<0.01
Scotch-Irish (192)	314	1.69
Scottish (198)	699	3.76
Serbian (0)	0	<0.01
Slavic (0)	3	0.02
Slovak (11)	17	0.09
Slovene (3)	3	0.02
Soviet Union (0)	0	<0.01
Swedish (51)	216	1.16
Swiss (76)	148	0.80
Turkish (0)	0	<0.01
Ukrainian (29)	85	0.46
Welsh (74)	205	1.10
West Indian, ex. Hispanic (39)	39	0.21
Bahamian (0)	0	<0.01
Barbadian (0)	0	<0.01
Belizean (0)	0	<0.01
Bermudan (0)	0	<0.01
British West Indian (0)	0	<0.01
Dutch West Indian (0)	0	<0.01
Haitian (28)	28	0.15
Jamaican (11)	11	0.06
Trinidadian/Tobagonian (0)	0	<0.01
U.S. Virgin Islander (0)	0	<0.01
West Indian (0)	0	<0.01
Other West Indian (0)	0	<0.01
Yugoslavian (0)	7	0.04

Hispanic Origin	Population	%
Hispanic or Latino (of any race)	234	1.28
Central American, ex. Mexican	10	0.05
Costa Rican	1	0.01
Guatemalan	3	0.02
Honduran	1	0.01
Nicaraguan	2	0.01
Panamanian	0	<0.01
Salvadoran	3	0.02
Other Central American	0	<0.01
Cuban	2	0.01
Dominican Republic	14	0.08
Mexican	64	0.35
Puerto Rican	99	0.54
South American	17	0.09
Argentinean	5	0.03
Bolivian	0	<0.01
Chilean	0	<0.01
Colombian	3	0.02
Ecuadorian	1	0.01
Paraguayan	1	0.01
Peruvian	5	0.03
Uruguayan	0	<0.01
Venezuelan	2	0.01
Other South American	0	<0.01
Other Hispanic or Latino	28	0.15

Race*	Population	%
African-American/Black (159)	244	1.33
Not Hispanic (143)	216	1.18
Hispanic (16)	28	0.15
American Indian/Alaska Native (47)	161	0.88
Not Hispanic (44)	152	0.83
Hispanic (3)	9	0.05
Alaska Athabascan (Ala. Nat.) (1)	1	0.01
Aleut (Alaska Native) (0)	0	<0.01
Apache (0)	0	<0.01
Arapaho (0)	0	<0.01
Blackfeet (2)	11	0.06
Canadian/French Am. Ind. (1)	2	0.01
Central American Ind. (0)	0	<0.01
Cherokee (3)	23	0.13
Cheyenne (0)	0	<0.01
Chickasaw (0)	0	<0.01
Chippewa (0)	0	<0.01
Choctaw (0)	2	0.01
Colville (0)	1	0.01

Race*	Population	%
Comanche (0)	0	<0.01
Cree (1)	1	0.01
Creek (0)	0	<0.01
Crow (0)	0	<0.01
Delaware (1)	2	0.01
Hopi (1)	2	0.01
Houma (0)	0	<0.01
Inupiat (Alaska Native) (0)	0	<0.01
Iroquois (12)	41	0.22
Kiowa (0)	0	<0.01
Lumbee (0)	0	<0.01
Menominee (0)	0	<0.01
Mexican American Ind. (0)	0	<0.01
Navajo (0)	4	0.02
Osage (0)	0	<0.01
Ottawa (0)	0	<0.01
Paiute (0)	0	<0.01
Pima (0)	0	<0.01
Potawatomi (0)	0	<0.01
Pueblo (1)	1	0.01
Puget Sound Salish (0)	0	<0.01
Seminole (0)	3	0.02
Shoshone (0)	0	<0.01
Sioux (1)	2	0.01
South American Ind. (0)	1	0.01
Spanish American Ind. (0)	0	<0.01
Tlingit-Haida (Alaska Native) (0)	0	<0.01
Tohono O'Odham (0)	0	<0.01
Tsimshian (Alaska Native) (0)	0	<0.01
Ute (0)	0	<0.01
Yakama (0)	0	<0.01
Yaqui (0)	0	<0.01
Yuman (0)	0	<0.01
Yup'ik (Alaska Native) (0)	0	<0.01
Asian (53)	88	0.48
Not Hispanic (51)	82	0.45
Hispanic (2)	6	0.03
Bangladeshi (0)	0	<0.01
Bhutanese (0)	0	<0.01
Burmese (0)	0	<0.01
Cambodian (1)	1	0.01
Chinese, ex. Taiwanese (9)	12	0.07
Filipino (6)	15	0.08
Hmong (0)	0	<0.01
Indian (14)	23	0.13
Indonesian (1)	2	0.01
Japanese (7)	11	0.06
Korean (5)	8	0.04
Laotian (1)	3	0.02
Malaysian (0)	0	<0.01
Nepalese (0)	0	<0.01
Pakistani (1)	1	0.01
Sri Lankan (0)	0	<0.01
Taiwanese (1)	3	0.02
Thai (3)	6	0.03
Vietnamese (0)	1	0.01
Hawaii Native/Pacific Islander (4)	5	0.03
Not Hispanic (4)	5	0.03
Hispanic (0)	0	<0.01
Fijian (0)	0	<0.01
Guamanian/Chamorro (1)	1	0.01
Marshallese (0)	0	<0.01
Native Hawaiian (0)	0	<0.01
Samoan (1)	1	0.01
Tongan (0)	0	<0.01
White (17,803)	18,035	98.32
Not Hispanic (17,646)	17,851	97.32
Hispanic (157)	184	1.00

Notes: † The Census 2010 population figure is used to calculate the percentages in the Hispanic Origin and Race categories. Ancestry percentages are based on the 2006-2010 American Community Survey population (not shown); ‡ Numbers in parentheses indicate the number of people reporting a single ancestry; * Numbers in parentheses indicate the number of persons reporting this race alone, not in combination with any other race; Please refer to the Explanation of Data for more information.

Seneca County

Population: 35,251

Ancestry	Population	%
Afghan (0)	0	<0.01
African, Sub-Saharan (54)	82	0.23
African (54)	82	0.23
Cape Verdean (0)	0	<0.01
Ethiopian (0)	0	<0.01
Ghanaian (0)	0	<0.01
Kenyan (0)	0	<0.01
Liberian (0)	0	<0.01
Nigerian (0)	0	<0.01
Senegalese (0)	0	<0.01
Sierra Leonean (0)	0	<0.01
Somalian (0)	0	<0.01
South African (0)	0	<0.01
Sudanese (0)	0	<0.01
Ugandan (0)	0	<0.01
Zimbabwean (0)	0	<0.01
Other Sub-Saharan African (0)	0	<0.01
Albanian (9)	9	0.03
Alsatian (2)	6	0.02
American (2,242)	2,242	6.35
Arab (13)	31	0.09
Arab (0)	0	<0.01
Egyptian (0)	0	<0.01
Iraqi (0)	0	<0.01
Jordanian (0)	0	<0.01
Lebanese (13)	31	0.09
Moroccan (0)	0	<0.01
Palestinian (0)	0	<0.01
Syrian (0)	0	<0.01
Other Arab (0)	0	<0.01
Armenian (0)	0	<0.01
Assyrian/Chaldean/Syriac (0)	0	<0.01
Australian (3)	7	0.02
Austrian (10)	76	0.22
Basque (0)	0	<0.01
Belgian (2)	8	0.02
Brazilian (18)	18	0.05
British (43)	121	0.34
Bulgarian (0)	0	<0.01
Cajun (0)	0	<0.01
Canadian (19)	49	0.14
Carpatho Rusyn (0)	0	<0.01
Celtic (0)	0	<0.01
Croatian (39)	43	0.12
Cypriot (0)	0	<0.01
Czech (10)	99	0.28
Czechoslovakian (28)	53	0.15
Danish (44)	170	0.48
Dutch (390)	1,725	4.89
Eastern European (9)	9	0.03
English (2,254)	6,403	18.13
Estonian (0)	0	<0.01
European (129)	155	0.44
Finnish (49)	65	0.18
French, ex. Basque (391)	1,487	4.21
French Canadian (139)	348	0.99
German (2,464)	8,012	22.69
German Russian (0)	0	<0.01
Greek (21)	44	0.12
Guyanese (8)	8	0.02
Hungarian (37)	149	0.42
Icelander (0)	0	<0.01
Iranian (3)	3	0.01
Irish (1,800)	6,509	18.43
Israeli (0)	0	<0.01
Italian (2,972)	6,175	17.49
Latvian (0)	0	<0.01
Lithuanian (21)	100	0.28
Luxemburger (0)	0	<0.01
Macedonian (0)	0	<0.01
Maltese (0)	0	<0.01
New Zealander (0)	0	<0.01
Northern European (0)	0	<0.01
Norwegian (29)	131	0.37
Pennsylvania German (299)	353	1.00
Polish (330)	1,065	3.02
Portuguese (7)	12	0.03
Romanian (11)	46	0.13
Russian (84)	155	0.44
Scandinavian (0)	13	0.04
Scotch-Irish (128)	496	1.40
Scottish (232)	782	2.21
Serbian (0)	0	<0.01
Slavic (2)	6	0.02
Slovak (14)	35	0.10
Slovene (2)	2	0.01
Soviet Union (0)	0	<0.01
Swedish (79)	213	0.60
Swiss (151)	371	1.05
Turkish (0)	0	<0.01
Ukrainian (84)	208	0.59
Welsh (42)	242	0.69
West Indian, ex. Hispanic (50)	97	0.27
Bahamian (0)	0	<0.01
Barbadian (0)	0	<0.01
Belizean (0)	0	<0.01
Bermudan (0)	0	<0.01
British West Indian (0)	0	<0.01
Dutch West Indian (0)	0	<0.01
Haitian (8)	17	0.05
Jamaican (25)	55	0.16
Trinidadian/Tobagonian (9)	17	0.05
U.S. Virgin Islander (0)	0	<0.01
West Indian (8)	8	0.02
Other West Indian (0)	0	<0.01
Yugoslavian (0)	0	<0.01

Hispanic Origin	Population	%
Hispanic or Latino (of any race)	952	2.70
Central American, ex. Mexican	68	0.19
Costa Rican	2	0.01
Guatemalan	13	0.04
Honduran	13	0.04
Nicaraguan	1	<0.01
Panamanian	15	0.04
Salvadoran	21	0.06
Other Central American	3	0.01
Cuban	30	0.09
Dominican Republic	61	0.17
Mexican	154	0.44
Puerto Rican	527	1.49
South American	24	0.07
Argentinean	1	<0.01
Bolivian	0	<0.01
Chilean	0	<0.01
Colombian	14	0.04
Ecuadorian	0	<0.01
Paraguayan	1	<0.01
Peruvian	6	0.02
Uruguayan	0	<0.01
Venezuelan	2	0.01
Other South American	0	<0.01
Other Hispanic or Latino	88	0.25

Race*	Population	%
African-American/Black (1,607)	1,812	5.14
Not Hispanic (1,513)	1,705	4.84
Hispanic (94)	107	0.30
American Indian/Alaska Native (104)	281	0.80
Not Hispanic (96)	269	0.76
Hispanic (8)	12	0.03
Alaska Athabascan (Ala. Nat.) (0)	0	<0.01
Aleut (Alaska Native) (0)	0	<0.01
Apache (0)	1	<0.01
Arapaho (0)	2	0.01
Blackfeet (0)	17	0.05
Canadian/French Am. Ind. (0)	0	<0.01
Central American Ind. (0)	0	<0.01
Cherokee (7)	34	0.10
Cheyenne (0)	0	<0.01
Chickasaw (0)	0	<0.01
Chippewa (2)	5	0.01
Choctaw (0)	0	<0.01
Colville (0)	0	<0.01
Comanche (0)	1	<0.01
Cree (1)	1	<0.01
Creek (0)	2	0.01
Crow (0)	0	<0.01
Delaware (0)	3	0.01
Hopi (0)	0	<0.01
Houma (0)	0	<0.01
Inupiat (Alaska Native) (0)	0	<0.01
Iroquois (12)	53	0.15
Kiowa (0)	0	<0.01
Lumbee (3)	3	0.01
Menominee (0)	1	<0.01
Mexican American Ind. (5)	7	0.02
Navajo (0)	0	<0.01
Osage (0)	0	<0.01
Ottawa (0)	2	0.01
Paiute (0)	0	<0.01
Pima (0)	0	<0.01
Potawatomi (0)	0	<0.01
Pueblo (0)	0	<0.01
Puget Sound Salish (0)	0	<0.01
Seminole (0)	0	<0.01
Shoshone (0)	1	<0.01
Sioux (7)	9	0.03
South American Ind. (1)	2	0.01
Spanish American Ind. (0)	0	<0.01
Tlingit-Haida (Alaska Native) (0)	0	<0.01
Tohono O'Odham (0)	0	<0.01
Tsimshian (Alaska Native) (0)	0	<0.01
Ute (0)	0	<0.01
Yakama (0)	0	<0.01
Yaqui (0)	0	<0.01
Yuman (0)	0	<0.01
Yup'ik (Alaska Native) (0)	0	<0.01
Asian (244)	291	0.83
Not Hispanic (238)	285	0.81
Hispanic (6)	6	0.02
Bangladeshi (0)	0	<0.01
Bhutanese (0)	0	<0.01
Burmese (0)	0	<0.01
Cambodian (0)	0	<0.01
Chinese, ex. Taiwanese (42)	49	0.14
Filipino (20)	31	0.09
Hmong (0)	0	<0.01
Indian (49)	67	0.19
Indonesian (0)	0	<0.01
Japanese (12)	19	0.05
Korean (38)	44	0.12
Laotian (18)	20	0.06
Malaysian (0)	0	<0.01
Nepalese (0)	0	<0.01
Pakistani (11)	14	0.04
Sri Lankan (6)	6	0.02
Taiwanese (7)	7	0.02
Thai (5)	5	0.01
Vietnamese (15)	15	0.04
Hawaii Native/Pacific Islander (2)	8	0.02
Not Hispanic (2)	8	0.02
Hispanic (0)	0	<0.01
Fijian (0)	0	<0.01
Guamanian/Chamorro (1)	1	<0.01
Marshallese (0)	0	<0.01
Native Hawaiian (0)	3	0.01
Samoan (1)	3	0.01
Tongan (0)	0	<0.01
White (32,591)	33,034	93.71
Not Hispanic (31,999)	32,386	91.87
Hispanic (592)	648	1.84

*Notes: † The Census 2010 population figure is used to calculate the percentages in the Hispanic Origin and Race categories. Ancestry percentages are based on the 2006-2010 American Community Survey population (not shown); ‡ Numbers in parentheses indicate the number of people reporting a single ancestry; * Numbers in parentheses indicate the number of persons reporting this race alone, not in combination with any other race; Please refer to the Explanation of Data for more information.*

St. Lawrence County

Population: 111,944

Ancestry	Population	%
Afghan (13)	13	0.01
African, Sub-Saharan (105)	182	0.16
African (54)	113	0.10
Cape Verdean (0)	0	<0.01
Ethiopian (4)	13	0.01
Ghanaian (0)	0	<0.01
Kenyan (15)	15	0.01
Liberian (0)	0	<0.01
Nigerian (17)	26	0.02
Senegalese (0)	0	<0.01
Sierra Leonean (0)	0	<0.01
Somalian (0)	0	<0.01
South African (0)	0	<0.01
Sudanese (2)	2	<0.01
Ugandan (0)	0	<0.01
Zimbabwean (13)	13	0.01
Other Sub-Saharan African (0)	0	<0.01
Albanian (43)	43	0.04
Alsatian (0)	0	<0.01
American (10,121)	10,121	9.05
Arab (162)	284	0.25
Arab (81)	100	0.09
Egyptian (11)	13	0.01
Iraqi (0)	0	<0.01
Jordanian (21)	21	0.02
Lebanese (44)	75	0.07
Moroccan (5)	44	0.04
Palestinian (0)	0	<0.01
Syrian (0)	0	<0.01
Other Arab (0)	31	0.03
Armenian (13)	22	0.02
Assyrian/Chaldean/Syriac (0)	0	<0.01
Australian (17)	17	0.02
Austrian (41)	114	0.10
Basque (0)	0	<0.01
Belgian (3)	64	0.06
Brazilian (4)	5	<0.01
British (289)	476	0.43
Bulgarian (73)	85	0.08
Cajun (0)	6	0.01
Canadian (862)	1,468	1.31
Carpatho Rusyn (0)	0	<0.01
Celtic (0)	0	<0.01
Croatian (23)	35	0.03
Cypriot (0)	0	<0.01
Czech (26)	167	0.15
Czechoslovakian (16)	54	0.05
Danish (22)	147	0.13
Dutch (594)	3,189	2.85
Eastern European (26)	71	0.06
English (7,608)	16,754	14.99
Estonian (13)	13	0.01
European (654)	676	0.60
Finnish (37)	158	0.14
French, ex. Basque (6,347)	18,278	16.35
French Canadian (3,623)	6,370	5.70
German (2,911)	11,355	10.16
German Russian (0)	0	<0.01
Greek (126)	286	0.26
Guyanese (19)	19	0.02
Hungarian (420)	956	0.86
Icelander (0)	13	0.01
Iranian (24)	49	0.04
Irish (6,686)	19,743	17.66
Israeli (30)	34	0.03
Italian (2,977)	8,006	7.16
Latvian (0)	14	0.01
Lithuanian (43)	175	0.16
Luxemburger (0)	9	0.01
Macedonian (0)	7	0.01
Maltese (0)	14	0.01
New Zealander (0)	0	<0.01
Northern European (15)	15	0.01
Norwegian (102)	470	0.42
Pennsylvania German (967)	994	0.89

	Population	%
Polish (980)	3,024	2.71
Portuguese (40)	126	0.11
Romanian (63)	108	0.10
Russian (285)	713	0.64
Scandinavian (52)	184	0.16
Scotch-Irish (932)	2,320	2.08
Scottish (1,251)	4,260	3.81
Serbian (0)	0	<0.01
Slavic (0)	10	0.01
Slovak (69)	117	0.10
Slovene (4)	4	<0.01
Soviet Union (0)	0	<0.01
Swedish (93)	651	0.58
Swiss (42)	138	0.12
Turkish (49)	58	0.05
Ukrainian (139)	464	0.42
Welsh (212)	802	0.72
West Indian, ex. Hispanic (319)	387	0.35
Bahamian (14)	20	0.02
Barbadian (7)	13	0.01
Belizean (0)	0	<0.01
Bermudan (0)	0	<0.01
British West Indian (0)	14	0.01
Dutch West Indian (0)	0	<0.01
Haitian (88)	91	0.08
Jamaican (169)	207	0.19
Trinidadian/Tobagonian (0)	0	<0.01
U.S. Virgin Islander (0)	0	<0.01
West Indian (41)	42	0.04
Other West Indian (0)	0	<0.01
Yugoslavian (24)	83	0.07

Hispanic Origin	Population	%
Hispanic or Latino (of any race)	2,146	1.92
Central American, ex. Mexican	199	0.18
Costa Rican	21	0.02
Guatemalan	65	0.06
Honduran	27	0.02
Nicaraguan	3	<0.01
Panamanian	32	0.03
Salvadoran	49	0.04
Other Central American	2	<0.01
Cuban	67	0.06
Dominican Republic	205	0.18
Mexican	437	0.39
Puerto Rican	845	0.75
South American	137	0.12
Argentinean	13	0.01
Bolivian	2	<0.01
Chilean	6	0.01
Colombian	39	0.03
Ecuadorian	39	0.03
Paraguayan	4	<0.01
Peruvian	16	0.01
Uruguayan	9	0.01
Venezuelan	6	0.01
Other South American	3	<0.01
Other Hispanic or Latino	256	0.23

Race*	Population	%
African-American/Black (2,420)	2,895	2.59
Not Hispanic (2,259)	2,688	2.40
Hispanic (161)	207	0.18
American Indian/Alaska Native (1,135)	1,901	1.70
Not Hispanic (1,051)	1,756	1.57
Hispanic (84)	145	0.13
Alaska Athabascan (Ala. Nat.) (0)	3	<0.01
Aleut (Alaska Native) (0)	0	<0.01
Apache (2)	3	<0.01
Arapaho (1)	1	<0.01
Blackfeet (5)	25	0.02
Canadian/French Am. Ind. (12)	32	0.03
Central American Ind. (4)	4	<0.01
Cherokee (15)	88	0.08
Cheyenne (0)	0	<0.01
Chickasaw (0)	1	<0.01
Chippewa (8)	10	0.01
Choctaw (3)	13	0.01
Colville (0)	0	<0.01

	Population	%
Comanche (0)	0	<0.01
Cree (0)	3	<0.01
Creek (2)	2	<0.01
Crow (0)	1	<0.01
Delaware (14)	19	0.02
Hopi (2)	4	<0.01
Houma (0)	0	<0.01
Inupiat (Alaska Native) (0)	1	<0.01
Iroquois (694)	979	0.87
Kiowa (1)	1	<0.01
Lumbee (1)	1	<0.01
Menominee (0)	0	<0.01
Mexican American Ind. (9)	11	0.01
Navajo (4)	7	0.01
Osage (0)	0	<0.01
Ottawa (1)	1	<0.01
Paiute (0)	0	<0.01
Pima (0)	0	<0.01
Potawatomi (0)	0	<0.01
Pueblo (0)	4	<0.01
Puget Sound Salish (0)	0	<0.01
Seminole (0)	4	<0.01
Shoshone (0)	0	<0.01
Sioux (4)	10	0.01
South American Ind. (13)	19	0.02
Spanish American Ind. (0)	1	<0.01
Tlingit-Haida (Alaska Native) (0)	0	<0.01
Tohono O'Odham (0)	0	<0.01
Tsimshian (Alaska Native) (0)	0	<0.01
Ute (0)	0	<0.01
Yakama (0)	0	<0.01
Yaqui (0)	0	<0.01
Yuman (0)	0	<0.01
Yup'ik (Alaska Native) (0)	3	<0.01
Asian (1,085)	1,366	1.22
Not Hispanic (1,074)	1,343	1.20
Hispanic (11)	23	0.02
Bangladeshi (6)	11	0.01
Bhutanese (0)	0	<0.01
Burmese (0)	1	<0.01
Cambodian (5)	5	<0.01
Chinese, ex. Taiwanese (331)	391	0.35
Filipino (89)	163	0.15
Hmong (2)	3	<0.01
Indian (283)	336	0.30
Indonesian (4)	10	0.01
Japanese (33)	62	0.06
Korean (152)	176	0.16
Laotian (4)	7	0.01
Malaysian (1)	7	0.01
Nepalese (5)	5	<0.01
Pakistani (39)	42	0.04
Sri Lankan (14)	14	0.01
Taiwanese (12)	19	0.02
Thai (13)	15	0.01
Vietnamese (42)	60	0.05
Hawaii Native/Pacific Islander (36)	95	0.08
Not Hispanic (26)	65	0.06
Hispanic (10)	30	0.03
Fijian (0)	0	<0.01
Guamanian/Chamorro (4)	8	0.01
Marshallese (0)	0	<0.01
Native Hawaiian (26)	50	0.04
Samoan (1)	5	<0.01
Tongan (0)	0	<0.01
White (105,064)	106,470	95.11
Not Hispanic (103,943)	105,195	93.97
Hispanic (1,121)	1,275	1.14

Notes: † The Census 2010 population figure is used to calculate the percentages in the Hispanic Origin and Race categories. Ancestry percentages are based on the 2006-2010 American Community Survey population (not shown); ‡ Numbers in parentheses indicate the number of people reporting a single ancestry; * Numbers in parentheses indicate the number of persons reporting this race alone, not in combination with any other race; Please refer to the Explanation of Data for more information.

Steuben County

Population: 98,990

Ancestry	Population	%
Afghan (0)	0	<0.01
African, Sub-Saharan (102)	115	0.12
African (79)	92	0.09
Cape Verdean (0)	0	<0.01
Ethiopian (23)	23	0.02
Ghanaian (0)	0	<0.01
Kenyan (0)	0	<0.01
Liberian (0)	0	<0.01
Nigerian (0)	0	<0.01
Senegalese (0)	0	<0.01
Sierra Leonean (0)	0	<0.01
Somalian (0)	0	<0.01
South African (0)	0	<0.01
Sudanese (0)	0	<0.01
Ugandan (0)	0	<0.01
Zimbabwean (0)	0	<0.01
Other Sub-Saharan African (0)	0	<0.01
Albanian (0)	0	<0.01
Alsatian (0)	12	0.01
American (8,840)	8,840	8.95
Arab (73)	105	0.11
Arab (0)	0	<0.01
Egyptian (0)	0	<0.01
Iraqi (0)	0	<0.01
Jordanian (0)	0	<0.01
Lebanese (41)	61	0.06
Moroccan (14)	14	0.01
Palestinian (0)	0	<0.01
Syrian (18)	30	0.03
Other Arab (0)	0	<0.01
Armenian (7)	19	0.02
Assyrian/Chaldean/Syriac (0)	0	<0.01
Australian (0)	4	<0.01
Austrian (28)	211	0.21
Basque (0)	13	0.01
Belgian (17)	74	0.07
Brazilian (11)	19	0.02
British (250)	488	0.49
Bulgarian (5)	9	0.01
Cajun (0)	0	<0.01
Canadian (81)	184	0.19
Carpatho Rusyn (23)	23	0.02
Celtic (0)	102	0.10
Croatian (0)	31	0.03
Cypriot (0)	0	<0.01
Czech (95)	366	0.37
Czechoslovakian (62)	83	0.08
Danish (106)	229	0.23
Dutch (886)	4,824	4.89
Eastern European (94)	96	0.10
English (5,831)	17,210	17.43
Estonian (5)	5	0.01
European (685)	701	0.71
Finnish (30)	118	0.12
French, ex. Basque (745)	3,810	3.86
French Canadian (323)	859	0.87
German (6,305)	22,942	23.24
German Russian (0)	0	<0.01
Greek (115)	200	0.20
Guyanese (31)	31	0.03
Hungarian (119)	343	0.35
Icelander (0)	0	<0.01
Iranian (0)	0	<0.01
Irish (6,137)	19,859	20.12
Israeli (23)	30	0.03
Italian (2,932)	8,609	8.72
Latvian (6)	42	0.04
Lithuanian (22)	94	0.10
Luxemburger (5)	5	0.01
Macedonian (0)	0	<0.01
Maltese (0)	0	<0.01
New Zealander (0)	0	<0.01
Northern European (70)	80	0.08
Norwegian (184)	541	0.55
Pennsylvania German (772)	1,134	1.15

Ancestry (cont.)	Population	%
Polish (1,810)	5,161	5.23
Portuguese (54)	165	0.17
Romanian (24)	79	0.08
Russian (120)	456	0.46
Scandinavian (37)	82	0.08
Scotch-Irish (681)	1,744	1.77
Scottish (550)	2,433	2.46
Serbian (3)	13	0.01
Slavic (9)	21	0.02
Slovak (60)	161	0.16
Slovene (0)	18	0.02
Soviet Union (12)	12	0.01
Swedish (423)	1,367	1.38
Swiss (122)	317	0.32
Turkish (25)	46	0.05
Ukrainian (194)	456	0.46
Welsh (262)	1,328	1.35
West Indian, ex. Hispanic (120)	142	0.14
Bahamian (0)	0	<0.01
Barbadian (93)	93	0.09
Belizean (0)	0	<0.01
Bermudan (0)	0	<0.01
British West Indian (0)	0	<0.01
Dutch West Indian (0)	0	<0.01
Haitian (6)	6	0.01
Jamaican (21)	32	0.03
Trinidadian/Tobagonian (0)	0	<0.01
U.S. Virgin Islander (0)	0	<0.01
West Indian (0)	11	0.01
Other West Indian (0)	0	<0.01
Yugoslavian (0)	7	0.01

Hispanic Origin	Population	%
Hispanic or Latino (of any race)	1,371	1.38
Central American, ex. Mexican	109	0.11
Costa Rican	1	<0.01
Guatemalan	14	0.01
Honduran	43	0.04
Nicaraguan	10	0.01
Panamanian	13	0.01
Salvadoran	28	0.03
Other Central American	0	<0.01
Cuban	31	0.03
Dominican Republic	44	0.04
Mexican	432	0.44
Puerto Rican	500	0.51
South American	89	0.09
Argentinean	1	<0.01
Bolivian	3	<0.01
Chilean	8	0.01
Colombian	21	0.02
Ecuadorian	19	0.02
Paraguayan	7	0.01
Peruvian	20	0.02
Uruguayan	1	<0.01
Venezuelan	5	0.01
Other South American	4	<0.01
Other Hispanic or Latino	166	0.17

Race*	Population	%
African-American/Black (1,540)	2,158	2.18
Not Hispanic (1,487)	2,074	2.10
Hispanic (53)	84	0.08
American Indian/Alaska Native (230)	765	0.77
Not Hispanic (193)	683	0.69
Hispanic (37)	82	0.08
Alaska Athabascan (Ala. Nat.) (0)	0	<0.01
Aleut (Alaska Native) (0)	0	<0.01
Apache (1)	6	0.01
Arapaho (0)	0	<0.01
Blackfeet (11)	60	0.06
Canadian/French Am. Ind. (1)	4	<0.01
Central American Ind. (0)	0	<0.01
Cherokee (20)	100	0.10
Cheyenne (0)	2	<0.01
Chickasaw (0)	0	<0.01
Chippewa (2)	4	<0.01
Choctaw (3)	10	0.01
Colville (0)	0	<0.01

Race* (cont.)	Population	%
Comanche (0)	0	<0.01
Cree (0)	1	<0.01
Creek (0)	4	<0.01
Crow (3)	4	<0.01
Delaware (1)	9	0.01
Hopi (0)	0	<0.01
Houma (0)	0	<0.01
Inupiat (Alaska Native) (3)	5	0.01
Iroquois (48)	144	0.15
Kiowa (0)	0	<0.01
Lumbee (0)	0	<0.01
Menominee (0)	0	<0.01
Mexican American Ind. (7)	7	0.01
Navajo (1)	3	<0.01
Osage (0)	0	<0.01
Ottawa (0)	0	<0.01
Paiute (0)	0	<0.01
Pima (0)	0	<0.01
Potawatomi (0)	0	<0.01
Pueblo (1)	1	<0.01
Puget Sound Salish (0)	0	<0.01
Seminole (0)	3	<0.01
Shoshone (0)	1	<0.01
Sioux (4)	19	0.02
South American Ind. (2)	7	0.01
Spanish American Ind. (1)	4	<0.01
Tlingit-Haida (Alaska Native) (5)	5	0.01
Tohono O'Odham (0)	0	<0.01
Tsimshian (Alaska Native) (0)	0	<0.01
Ute (0)	0	<0.01
Yakama (0)	0	<0.01
Yaqui (0)	0	<0.01
Yuman (0)	0	<0.01
Yup'ik (Alaska Native) (2)	2	<0.01
Asian (1,161)	1,352	1.37
Not Hispanic (1,151)	1,332	1.35
Hispanic (10)	20	0.02
Bangladeshi (12)	12	0.01
Bhutanese (0)	0	<0.01
Burmese (1)	1	<0.01
Cambodian (5)	5	0.01
Chinese, ex. Taiwanese (336)	382	0.39
Filipino (111)	161	0.16
Hmong (0)	0	<0.01
Indian (392)	438	0.44
Indonesian (6)	6	0.01
Japanese (43)	70	0.07
Korean (82)	108	0.11
Laotian (12)	14	0.01
Malaysian (2)	2	<0.01
Nepalese (12)	12	0.01
Pakistani (45)	49	0.05
Sri Lankan (4)	4	<0.01
Taiwanese (28)	28	0.03
Thai (12)	15	0.02
Vietnamese (25)	30	0.03
Hawaii Native/Pacific Islander (17)	48	0.05
Not Hispanic (14)	42	0.04
Hispanic (3)	6	0.01
Fijian (2)	2	<0.01
Guamanian/Chamorro (3)	6	0.01
Marshallese (2)	2	<0.01
Native Hawaiian (8)	24	0.02
Samoan (0)	1	<0.01
Tongan (0)	0	<0.01
White (94,315)	95,643	96.62
Not Hispanic (93,476)	94,659	95.62
Hispanic (839)	984	0.99

Notes: † The Census 2010 population figure is used to calculate the percentages in the Hispanic Origin and Race categories. Ancestry percentages are based on the 2006-2010 American Community Survey population (not shown); ‡ Numbers in parentheses indicate the number of people reporting a single ancestry; * Numbers in parentheses indicate the number of persons reporting this race alone, not in combination with any other race; Please refer to the Explanation of Data for more information.

Suffolk County

Population: 1,493,350

Ancestry	Population	%
Afghan (742)	823	0.06
African, Sub-Saharan (5,702)	7,192	0.49
African (3,798)	4,984	0.34
Cape Verdean (0)	9	<0.01
Ethiopian (21)	136	0.01
Ghanaian (192)	192	0.01
Kenyan (0)	0	<0.01
Liberian (309)	318	0.02
Nigerian (1,092)	1,220	0.08
Senegalese (0)	0	<0.01
Sierra Leonean (0)	0	<0.01
Somalian (0)	0	<0.01
South African (84)	102	0.01
Sudanese (0)	14	<0.01
Ugandan (0)	0	<0.01
Zimbabwean (0)	0	<0.01
Other Sub-Saharan African (206)	217	0.01
Albanian (614)	824	0.06
Alsatian (0)	39	<0.01
American (31,772)	31,772	2.14
Arab (3,411)	5,631	0.38
Arab (547)	751	0.05
Egyptian (1,042)	1,355	0.09
Iraqi (94)	283	0.02
Jordanian (233)	365	0.02
Lebanese (210)	787	0.05
Moroccan (426)	579	0.04
Palestinian (280)	302	0.02
Syrian (151)	574	0.04
Other Arab (428)	635	0.04
Armenian (1,000)	2,005	0.14
Assyrian/Chaldean/Syriac (0)	0	<0.01
Australian (165)	361	0.02
Austrian (1,961)	9,897	0.67
Basque (48)	76	0.01
Belgian (219)	1,025	0.07
Brazilian (1,446)	2,033	0.14
British (1,885)	3,939	0.27
Bulgarian (199)	296	0.02
Cajun (0)	42	<0.01
Canadian (1,220)	3,384	0.23
Carpatho Rusyn (46)	46	<0.01
Celtic (126)	220	0.01
Croatian (1,176)	2,492	0.17
Cypriot (146)	158	0.01
Czech (1,747)	8,389	0.57
Czechoslovakian (1,155)	2,893	0.20
Danish (865)	3,979	0.27
Dutch (2,110)	12,986	0.88
Eastern European (4,046)	4,484	0.30
English (15,317)	86,937	5.86
Estonian (193)	470	0.03
European (6,998)	7,658	0.52
Finnish (437)	1,833	0.12
French, ex. Basque (2,763)	25,117	1.69
French Canadian (2,013)	6,822	0.46
German (45,404)	248,603	16.77
German Russian (0)	40	<0.01
Greek (8,977)	19,268	1.30
Guyanese (1,567)	1,875	0.13
Hungarian (2,826)	12,736	0.86
Icelander (54)	150	0.01
Iranian (1,181)	1,367	0.09
Irish (87,385)	340,599	22.97
Israeli (740)	1,266	0.09
Italian (202,824)	427,711	28.85
Latvian (251)	567	0.04
Lithuanian (1,966)	5,680	0.38
Luxemburger (0)	36	<0.01
Macedonian (22)	44	<0.01
Maltese (405)	1,698	0.11
New Zealander (44)	57	<0.01
Northern European (525)	590	0.04
Norwegian (3,647)	14,773	1.00
Pennsylvania German (69)	107	0.01

	Population	%
Polish (28,723)	89,379	6.03
Portuguese (4,698)	7,670	0.52
Romanian (1,746)	4,330	0.29
Russian (12,970)	39,198	2.64
Scandinavian (395)	1,115	0.08
Scotch-Irish (5,695)	15,856	1.07
Scottish (2,865)	16,692	1.13
Serbian (64)	237	0.02
Slavic (137)	601	0.04
Slovak (803)	1,936	0.13
Slovene (220)	324	0.02
Soviet Union (3)	3	<0.01
Swedish (1,863)	13,486	0.91
Swiss (672)	3,707	0.25
Turkish (3,736)	4,401	0.30
Ukrainian (2,645)	7,707	0.52
Welsh (687)	3,742	0.25
West Indian, ex. Hispanic (25,884)	31,391	2.12
Bahamian (66)	188	0.01
Barbadian (189)	308	0.02
Belizean (35)	47	<0.01
Bermudan (0)	34	<0.01
British West Indian (378)	665	0.04
Dutch West Indian (49)	49	<0.01
Haitian (11,652)	12,903	0.87
Jamaican (8,020)	10,122	0.68
Trinidadian/Tobagonian (2,485)	2,971	0.20
U.S. Virgin Islander (91)	154	0.01
West Indian (2,912)	3,916	0.26
Other West Indian (7)	34	<0.01
Yugoslavian (475)	1,653	0.11

Hispanic Origin	Population	%
Hispanic or Latino (of any race)	246,239	16.49
Central American, ex. Mexican	77,117	5.16
Costa Rican	1,656	0.11
Guatemalan	11,229	0.75
Honduran	9,563	0.64
Nicaraguan	683	0.05
Panamanian	1,203	0.08
Salvadoran	52,315	3.50
Other Central American	468	0.03
Cuban	4,310	0.29
Dominican Republic	21,751	1.46
Mexican	15,663	1.05
Puerto Rican	58,549	3.92
South American	44,731	3.00
Argentinean	2,260	0.15
Bolivian	565	0.04
Chilean	1,507	0.10
Colombian	13,846	0.93
Ecuadorian	17,638	1.18
Paraguayan	282	0.02
Peruvian	6,962	0.47
Uruguayan	474	0.03
Venezuelan	919	0.06
Other South American	278	0.02
Other Hispanic or Latino	24,118	1.62

Race*	Population	%
African-American/Black (111,224)	125,571	8.41
Not Hispanic (102,117)	112,207	7.51
Hispanic (9,107)	13,364	0.89
American Indian/Alaska Native (5,366)	12,535	0.84
Not Hispanic (2,906)	7,986	0.53
Hispanic (2,460)	4,549	0.30
Alaska Athabascan (Ala. Nat.) (1)	6	<0.01
Aleut (Alaska Native) (5)	7	<0.01
Apache (24)	65	<0.01
Arapaho (0)	3	<0.01
Blackfeet (44)	364	0.02
Canadian/French Am. Ind. (20)	43	<0.01
Central American Ind. (128)	195	0.01
Cherokee (246)	1,501	0.10
Cheyenne (2)	12	<0.01
Chickasaw (2)	11	<0.01
Chippewa (31)	63	<0.01
Choctaw (13)	90	0.01
Colville (0)	0	<0.01

	Population	%
Comanche (6)	24	<0.01
Cree (2)	9	<0.01
Creek (5)	58	<0.01
Crow (13)	23	<0.01
Delaware (7)	35	<0.01
Hopi (5)	11	<0.01
Houma (1)	3	<0.01
Inupiat (Alaska Native) (2)	5	<0.01
Iroquois (160)	388	0.03
Kiowa (1)	1	<0.01
Lumbee (14)	40	<0.01
Menominee (0)	0	<0.01
Mexican American Ind. (264)	376	0.03
Navajo (15)	45	<0.01
Osage (0)	5	<0.01
Ottawa (0)	5	<0.01
Paiute (2)	4	<0.01
Pima (1)	1	<0.01
Potawatomi (9)	13	<0.01
Pueblo (20)	29	<0.01
Puget Sound Salish (5)	7	<0.01
Seminole (12)	63	<0.01
Shoshone (7)	7	<0.01
Sioux (36)	109	0.01
South American Ind. (332)	629	0.04
Spanish American Ind. (133)	182	0.01
Tlingit-Haida (Alaska Native) (5)	14	<0.01
Tohono O'Odham (0)	1	<0.01
Tsimshian (Alaska Native) (0)	0	<0.01
Ute (0)	2	<0.01
Yakama (0)	1	<0.01
Yaqui (2)	7	<0.01
Yuman (1)	2	<0.01
Yup'ik (Alaska Native) (0)	0	<0.01
Asian (50,972)	59,859	4.01
Not Hispanic (50,295)	57,980	3.88
Hispanic (677)	1,879	0.13
Bangladeshi (1,243)	1,469	0.10
Bhutanese (3)	3	<0.01
Burmese (61)	80	0.01
Cambodian (53)	71	<0.01
Chinese, ex. Taiwanese (11,537)	13,502	0.90
Filipino (5,202)	6,881	0.46
Hmong (1)	4	<0.01
Indian (15,975)	18,167	1.22
Indonesian (117)	174	0.01
Japanese (904)	1,673	0.11
Korean (5,627)	6,461	0.43
Laotian (84)	107	0.01
Malaysian (25)	55	<0.01
Nepalese (69)	72	<0.01
Pakistani (5,426)	5,997	0.40
Sri Lankan (149)	183	0.01
Taiwanese (470)	550	0.04
Thai (401)	553	0.04
Vietnamese (1,565)	1,835	0.12
Hawaii Native/Pacific Islander (495)	1,606	0.11
Not Hispanic (275)	939	0.06
Hispanic (220)	667	0.04
Fijian (3)	16	<0.01
Guamanian/Chamorro (208)	263	0.02
Marshallese (1)	1	<0.01
Native Hawaiian (105)	331	0.02
Samoan (25)	59	<0.01
Tongan (1)	5	<0.01
White (1,206,297)	1,234,863	82.69
Not Hispanic (1,068,728)	1,083,973	72.59
Hispanic (137,569)	150,890	10.10

Notes: † The Census 2010 population figure is used to calculate the percentages in the Hispanic Origin and Race categories. Ancestry percentages are based on the 2006-2010 American Community Survey population (not shown); ‡ Numbers in parentheses indicate the number of people reporting a single ancestry; * Numbers in parentheses indicate the number of persons reporting this race alone, not in combination with any other race; Please refer to the Explanation of Data for more information.

Sullivan County

Population: 77,547

Ancestry	Population	%
Afghan (0)	0	<0.01
African, Sub-Saharan (208)	232	0.30
African (84)	108	0.14
Cape Verdean (0)	0	<0.01
Ethiopian (0)	0	<0.01
Ghanaian (16)	16	0.02
Kenyan (9)	9	0.01
Liberian (18)	18	0.02
Nigerian (34)	34	0.04
Senegalese (0)	0	<0.01
Sierra Leonean (0)	0	<0.01
Somalian (0)	0	<0.01
South African (0)	0	<0.01
Sudanese (0)	0	<0.01
Ugandan (0)	0	<0.01
Zimbabwean (40)	40	0.05
Other Sub-Saharan African (7)	7	0.01
Albanian (59)	71	0.09
Alsatian (0)	0	<0.01
American (4,050)	4,050	5.22
Arab (251)	350	0.45
Arab (5)	9	0.01
Egyptian (102)	145	0.19
Iraqi (0)	0	<0.01
Jordanian (117)	137	0.18
Lebanese (2)	21	0.03
Moroccan (0)	0	<0.01
Palestinian (0)	0	<0.01
Syrian (12)	25	0.03
Other Arab (13)	13	0.02
Armenian (24)	26	0.03
Assyrian/Chaldean/Syriac (0)	0	<0.01
Australian (17)	81	0.10
Austrian (130)	374	0.48
Basque (0)	0	<0.01
Belgian (18)	18	0.02
Brazilian (53)	86	0.11
British (84)	183	0.24
Bulgarian (0)	0	<0.01
Cajun (0)	0	<0.01
Canadian (131)	386	0.50
Carpatho Rusyn (0)	0	<0.01
Celtic (14)	38	0.05
Croatian (65)	154	0.20
Cypriot (0)	0	<0.01
Czech (84)	390	0.50
Czechoslovakian (127)	308	0.40
Danish (65)	251	0.32
Dutch (428)	2,234	2.88
Eastern European (227)	299	0.39
English (1,413)	5,957	7.67
Estonian (8)	16	0.02
European (325)	410	0.53
Finnish (35)	64	0.08
French, ex. Basque (450)	2,130	2.74
French Canadian (120)	393	0.51
German (4,582)	14,760	19.01
German Russian (0)	0	<0.01
Greek (285)	449	0.58
Guyanese (35)	35	0.05
Hungarian (318)	1,183	1.52
Icelander (0)	0	<0.01
Iranian (94)	100	0.13
Irish (4,513)	15,183	19.56
Israeli (30)	58	0.07
Italian (4,173)	10,325	13.30
Latvian (34)	60	0.08
Lithuanian (158)	381	0.49
Luxemburger (0)	0	<0.01
Macedonian (53)	64	0.08
Maltese (0)	0	<0.01
New Zealander (0)	18	0.02
Northern European (33)	66	0.09
Norwegian (355)	918	1.18
Pennsylvania German (26)	35	0.05

Ancestry (cont.)	Population	%
Polish (1,384)	4,248	5.47
Portuguese (100)	280	0.36
Romanian (110)	221	0.28
Russian (1,015)	2,172	2.80
Scandinavian (49)	115	0.15
Scotch-Irish (296)	812	1.05
Scottish (291)	1,158	1.49
Serbian (24)	24	0.03
Slavic (0)	22	0.03
Slovak (92)	181	0.23
Slovene (0)	10	0.01
Soviet Union (0)	0	<0.01
Swedish (219)	595	0.77
Swiss (186)	430	0.55
Turkish (39)	86	0.11
Ukrainian (453)	989	1.27
Welsh (128)	600	0.77
West Indian, ex. Hispanic (723)	1,131	1.46
Bahamian (0)	0	<0.01
Barbadian (77)	149	0.19
Belizean (0)	0	<0.01
Bermudan (0)	0	<0.01
British West Indian (16)	16	0.02
Dutch West Indian (0)	55	0.07
Haitian (73)	73	0.09
Jamaican (298)	415	0.53
Trinidadian/Tobagonian (176)	287	0.37
U.S. Virgin Islander (0)	0	<0.01
West Indian (83)	136	0.18
Other West Indian (0)	0	<0.01
Yugoslavian (107)	152	0.20

Hispanic Origin	Population	%
Hispanic or Latino (of any race)	10,554	13.61
Central American, ex. Mexican	1,461	1.88
Costa Rican	46	0.06
Guatemalan	223	0.29
Honduran	575	0.74
Nicaraguan	45	0.06
Panamanian	50	0.06
Salvadoran	516	0.67
Other Central American	6	0.01
Cuban	297	0.38
Dominican Republic	448	0.58
Mexican	1,385	1.79
Puerto Rican	5,309	6.85
South American	866	1.12
Argentinean	68	0.09
Bolivian	9	0.01
Chilean	46	0.06
Colombian	398	0.51
Ecuadorian	144	0.19
Paraguayan	8	0.01
Peruvian	153	0.20
Uruguayan	14	0.02
Venezuelan	13	0.02
Other South American	13	0.02
Other Hispanic or Latino	788	1.02

Race*	Population	%
African-American/Black (7,039)	8,207	10.58
Not Hispanic (6,349)	7,180	9.26
Hispanic (690)	1,027	1.32
American Indian/Alaska Native (354)	950	1.23
Not Hispanic (228)	653	0.84
Hispanic (126)	297	0.38
Alaska Athabascan (Ala. Nat.) (0)	0	<0.01
Aleut (Alaska Native) (0)	0	<0.01
Apache (5)	12	0.02
Arapaho (0)	0	<0.01
Blackfeet (10)	51	0.07
Canadian/French Am. Ind. (1)	3	<0.01
Central American Ind. (3)	4	0.01
Cherokee (24)	147	0.19
Cheyenne (0)	0	<0.01
Chickasaw (0)	0	<0.01
Chippewa (3)	8	0.01
Choctaw (1)	7	0.01
Colville (0)	0	<0.01

Race* (cont.)	Population	%
Comanche (0)	0	<0.01
Cree (0)	3	<0.01
Creek (3)	4	0.01
Crow (1)	3	<0.01
Delaware (30)	60	0.08
Hopi (0)	0	<0.01
Houma (2)	2	<0.01
Inupiat (Alaska Native) (1)	1	<0.01
Iroquois (21)	47	0.06
Kiowa (0)	0	<0.01
Lumbee (0)	0	<0.01
Menominee (0)	0	<0.01
Mexican American Ind. (24)	35	0.05
Navajo (2)	4	0.01
Osage (0)	0	<0.01
Ottawa (0)	0	<0.01
Paiute (0)	0	<0.01
Pima (0)	2	<0.01
Potawatomi (0)	0	<0.01
Pueblo (0)	0	<0.01
Puget Sound Salish (0)	0	<0.01
Seminole (1)	1	<0.01
Shoshone (0)	0	<0.01
Sioux (1)	4	0.01
South American Ind. (16)	25	0.03
Spanish American Ind. (5)	11	0.01
Tlingit-Haida (Alaska Native) (0)	0	<0.01
Tohono O'Odham (1)	2	<0.01
Tsimshian (Alaska Native) (0)	0	<0.01
Ute (0)	0	<0.01
Yakama (0)	0	<0.01
Yaqui (0)	0	<0.01
Yuman (0)	0	<0.01
Yup'ik (Alaska Native) (0)	0	<0.01
Asian (1,075)	1,395	1.80
Not Hispanic (1,033)	1,311	1.69
Hispanic (42)	84	0.11
Bangladeshi (10)	16	0.02
Bhutanese (0)	0	<0.01
Burmese (3)	3	<0.01
Cambodian (3)	3	<0.01
Chinese, ex. Taiwanese (223)	278	0.36
Filipino (142)	212	0.27
Hmong (0)	0	<0.01
Indian (346)	409	0.53
Indonesian (5)	8	<0.01
Japanese (34)	66	0.09
Korean (166)	207	0.27
Laotian (4)	5	0.01
Malaysian (0)	0	<0.01
Nepalese (1)	1	<0.01
Pakistani (48)	58	0.07
Sri Lankan (1)	3	<0.01
Taiwanese (6)	8	0.01
Thai (3)	9	0.01
Vietnamese (24)	35	0.05
Hawaii Native/Pacific Islander (24)	87	0.11
Not Hispanic (14)	55	0.07
Hispanic (10)	32	0.04
Fijian (0)	0	<0.01
Guamanian/Chamorro (13)	19	0.02
Marshallese (0)	0	<0.01
Native Hawaiian (2)	11	0.01
Samoan (6)	15	0.02
Tongan (0)	0	<0.01
White (63,560)	65,476	84.43
Not Hispanic (57,780)	59,010	76.10
Hispanic (5,780)	6,466	8.34

Tioga County

Population: 51,125

Ancestry	Population	%
Afghan (0)	0	<0.01
African, Sub-Saharan (36)	40	0.08
African (11)	15	0.03
Cape Verdean (0)	0	<0.01
Ethiopian (0)	0	<0.01
Ghanaian (0)	0	<0.01
Kenyan (0)	0	<0.01
Liberian (0)	0	<0.01
Nigerian (0)	0	<0.01
Senegalese (0)	0	<0.01
Sierra Leonean (0)	0	<0.01
Somalian (0)	0	<0.01
South African (25)	25	0.05
Sudanese (0)	0	<0.01
Ugandan (0)	0	<0.01
Zimbabwean (0)	0	<0.01
Other Sub-Saharan African (0)	0	<0.01
Albanian (0)	0	<0.01
Alsatian (19)	22	0.04
American (4,114)	4,114	8.01
Arab (76)	115	0.22
Arab (0)	0	<0.01
Egyptian (16)	16	0.03
Iraqi (0)	0	<0.01
Jordanian (0)	0	<0.01
Lebanese (60)	99	0.19
Moroccan (0)	0	<0.01
Palestinian (0)	0	<0.01
Syrian (0)	0	<0.01
Other Arab (0)	0	<0.01
Armenian (0)	28	0.05
Assyrian/Chaldean/Syriac (0)	0	<0.01
Australian (0)	0	<0.01
Austrian (43)	129	0.25
Basque (0)	34	0.07
Belgian (0)	20	0.04
Brazilian (34)	34	0.07
British (86)	123	0.24
Bulgarian (0)	0	<0.01
Cajun (0)	0	<0.01
Canadian (72)	170	0.33
Carpatho Rusyn (0)	0	<0.01
Celtic (0)	16	0.03
Croatian (20)	20	0.04
Cypriot (0)	0	<0.01
Czech (148)	382	0.74
Czechoslovakian (27)	122	0.24
Danish (31)	123	0.24
Dutch (419)	2,091	4.07
Eastern European (0)	0	<0.01
English (3,529)	9,618	18.72
Estonian (0)	0	<0.01
European (598)	624	1.21
Finnish (208)	305	0.59
French, ex. Basque (306)	1,803	3.51
French Canadian (143)	395	0.77
German (3,822)	12,009	23.37
German Russian (0)	0	<0.01
Greek (67)	198	0.39
Guyanese (0)	0	<0.01
Hungarian (241)	430	0.84
Icelander (0)	0	<0.01
Iranian (0)	0	<0.01
Irish (2,587)	9,130	17.77
Israeli (0)	0	<0.01
Italian (1,844)	4,941	9.62
Latvian (28)	61	0.12
Lithuanian (35)	235	0.46
Luxemburger (0)	0	<0.01
Macedonian (0)	0	<0.01
Maltese (0)	16	0.03
New Zealander (0)	0	<0.01
Northern European (110)	110	0.21
Norwegian (120)	344	0.67
Pennsylvania German (242)	441	0.86

Ancestry	Population	%
Polish (881)	2,677	5.21
Portuguese (26)	67	0.13
Romanian (20)	50	0.10
Russian (365)	838	1.63
Scandinavian (17)	45	0.09
Scotch-Irish (338)	858	1.67
Scottish (304)	1,298	2.53
Serbian (0)	0	<0.01
Slavic (22)	81	0.16
Slovak (202)	549	1.07
Slovene (47)	50	0.10
Soviet Union (0)	0	<0.01
Swedish (196)	882	1.72
Swiss (56)	163	0.32
Turkish (10)	18	0.04
Ukrainian (203)	422	0.82
Welsh (156)	1,226	2.39
West Indian, ex. Hispanic (8)	17	0.03
Bahamian (0)	0	<0.01
Barbadian (0)	0	<0.01
Belizean (0)	0	<0.01
Bermudan (0)	0	<0.01
British West Indian (0)	0	<0.01
Dutch West Indian (0)	0	<0.01
Haitian (0)	0	<0.01
Jamaican (8)	8	0.02
Trinidadian/Tobagonian (0)	0	<0.01
U.S. Virgin Islander (0)	0	<0.01
West Indian (0)	9	0.02
Other West Indian (0)	0	<0.01
Yugoslavian (0)	13	0.03

Hispanic Origin	Population	%
Hispanic or Latino (of any race)	694	1.36
Central American, ex. Mexican	53	0.10
Costa Rican	3	0.01
Guatemalan	7	0.01
Honduran	1	<0.01
Nicaraguan	4	0.01
Panamanian	11	0.02
Salvadoran	27	0.05
Other Central American	0	<0.01
Cuban	28	0.05
Dominican Republic	22	0.04
Mexican	169	0.33
Puerto Rican	271	0.53
South American	73	0.14
Argentinean	4	0.01
Bolivian	1	<0.01
Chilean	6	0.01
Colombian	19	0.04
Ecuadorian	24	0.05
Paraguayan	1	<0.01
Peruvian	8	0.02
Uruguayan	4	0.01
Venezuelan	3	0.01
Other South American	3	0.01
Other Hispanic or Latino	78	0.15

Race*	Population	%
African-American/Black (375)	581	1.14
Not Hispanic (349)	532	1.04
Hispanic (26)	49	0.10
American Indian/Alaska Native (86)	306	0.60
Not Hispanic (73)	274	0.54
Hispanic (13)	32	0.06
Alaska Athabascan (Ala. Nat.) (0)	0	<0.01
Aleut (Alaska Native) (0)	0	<0.01
Apache (0)	0	<0.01
Arapaho (0)	0	<0.01
Blackfeet (2)	16	0.03
Canadian/French Am. Ind. (1)	5	0.01
Central American Ind. (0)	0	<0.01
Cherokee (5)	42	0.08
Cheyenne (0)	2	<0.01
Chickasaw (0)	0	<0.01
Chippewa (0)	1	<0.01
Choctaw (0)	1	<0.01
Colville (0)	0	<0.01

Race*	Population	%
Comanche (1)	1	<0.01
Cree (0)	0	<0.01
Creek (0)	4	0.01
Crow (1)	1	<0.01
Delaware (3)	7	0.01
Hopi (1)	1	<0.01
Houma (0)	0	<0.01
Inupiat (Alaska Native) (0)	0	<0.01
Iroquois (15)	61	0.12
Kiowa (0)	0	<0.01
Lumbee (0)	1	<0.01
Menominee (0)	0	<0.01
Mexican American Ind. (3)	5	0.01
Navajo (6)	15	0.03
Osage (0)	0	<0.01
Ottawa (0)	0	<0.01
Paiute (0)	0	<0.01
Pima (0)	0	<0.01
Potawatomi (0)	0	<0.01
Pueblo (0)	0	<0.01
Puget Sound Salish (0)	0	<0.01
Seminole (0)	0	<0.01
Shoshone (0)	0	<0.01
Sioux (2)	11	0.02
South American Ind. (1)	3	0.01
Spanish American Ind. (0)	0	<0.01
Tlingit-Haida (Alaska Native) (0)	0	<0.01
Tohono O'Odham (1)	1	<0.01
Tsimshian (Alaska Native) (0)	0	<0.01
Ute (0)	0	<0.01
Yakama (0)	0	<0.01
Yaqui (0)	0	<0.01
Yuman (0)	0	<0.01
Yup'ik (Alaska Native) (0)	0	<0.01
Asian (372)	475	0.93
Not Hispanic (371)	465	0.91
Hispanic (1)	10	0.02
Bangladeshi (0)	0	<0.01
Bhutanese (0)	0	<0.01
Burmese (0)	0	<0.01
Cambodian (0)	0	<0.01
Chinese, ex. Taiwanese (107)	119	0.23
Filipino (35)	67	0.13
Hmong (0)	0	<0.01
Indian (83)	93	0.18
Indonesian (0)	0	<0.01
Japanese (25)	47	0.09
Korean (35)	46	0.09
Laotian (0)	2	<0.01
Malaysian (0)	0	<0.01
Nepalese (0)	0	<0.01
Pakistani (33)	33	0.06
Sri Lankan (0)	0	<0.01
Taiwanese (9)	11	0.02
Thai (3)	4	0.01
Vietnamese (35)	43	0.08
Hawaii Native/Pacific Islander (15)	40	0.08
Not Hispanic (12)	35	0.07
Hispanic (3)	5	0.01
Fijian (1)	1	<0.01
Guamanian/Chamorro (6)	9	0.02
Marshallese (0)	0	<0.01
Native Hawaiian (6)	11	0.02
Samoan (0)	1	<0.01
Tongan (0)	0	<0.01
White (49,556)	50,101	98.00
Not Hispanic (49,105)	49,578	96.97
Hispanic (451)	523	1.02

Notes: † The Census 2010 population figure is used to calculate the percentages in the Hispanic Origin and Race categories. Ancestry percentages are based on the 2006-2010 American Community Survey population (not shown); ‡ Numbers in parentheses indicate the number of people reporting a single ancestry; * Numbers in parentheses indicate the number of persons reporting this race alone, not in combination with any other race; Please refer to the Explanation of Data for more information.

Tompkins County

Population: 101,564

Ancestry	Population	%
Afghan (15)	15	0.01
African, Sub-Saharan (546)	631	0.63
African (254)	301	0.30
Cape Verdean (0)	0	<0.01
Ethiopian (0)	0	<0.01
Ghanaian (59)	59	0.06
Kenyan (20)	20	0.02
Liberian (44)	44	0.04
Nigerian (56)	56	0.06
Senegalese (0)	0	<0.01
Sierra Leonean (22)	22	0.02
Somalian (0)	0	<0.01
South African (31)	35	0.03
Sudanese (0)	13	0.01
Ugandan (24)	24	0.02
Zimbabwean (13)	24	0.02
Other Sub-Saharan African (23)	33	0.03
Albanian (0)	0	<0.01
Alsatian (0)	0	<0.01
American (4,786)	4,786	4.76
Arab (429)	571	0.57
Arab (85)	85	0.08
Egyptian (88)	88	0.09
Iraqi (0)	0	<0.01
Jordanian (14)	14	0.01
Lebanese (39)	113	0.11
Moroccan (79)	79	0.08
Palestinian (72)	72	0.07
Syrian (52)	92	0.09
Other Arab (0)	28	0.03
Armenian (138)	280	0.28
Assyrian/Chaldean/Syriac (0)	0	<0.01
Australian (24)	30	0.03
Austrian (53)	496	0.49
Basque (0)	0	<0.01
Belgian (41)	81	0.08
Brazilian (58)	116	0.12
British (381)	1,040	1.03
Bulgarian (81)	129	0.13
Cajun (14)	14	0.01
Canadian (309)	594	0.59
Carpatho Rusyn (0)	0	<0.01
Celtic (6)	22	0.02
Croatian (77)	205	0.20
Cypriot (0)	16	0.02
Czech (206)	714	0.71
Czechoslovakian (83)	191	0.19
Danish (43)	266	0.26
Dutch (586)	2,655	2.64
Eastern European (429)	525	0.52
English (3,791)	13,741	13.66
Estonian (36)	50	0.05
European (1,537)	1,682	1.67
Finnish (248)	687	0.68
French, ex. Basque (512)	3,128	3.11
French Canadian (330)	799	0.79
German (3,464)	16,093	16.00
German Russian (0)	0	<0.01
Greek (211)	512	0.51
Guyanese (97)	119	0.12
Hungarian (383)	1,004	1.00
Icelander (14)	29	0.03
Iranian (99)	216	0.21
Irish (3,221)	14,348	14.26
Israeli (145)	194	0.19
Italian (3,055)	8,635	8.58
Latvian (0)	70	0.07
Lithuanian (202)	486	0.48
Luxemburger (10)	24	0.02
Macedonian (0)	0	<0.01
Maltese (0)	0	<0.01
New Zealander (0)	45	0.04
Northern European (163)	210	0.21
Norwegian (215)	873	0.87
Pennsylvania German (124)	377	0.37
Polish (1,003)	3,827	3.80
Portuguese (0)	103	0.10
Romanian (43)	148	0.15
Russian (1,015)	2,382	2.37
Scandinavian (88)	225	0.22
Scotch-Irish (635)	1,729	1.72
Scottish (505)	2,480	2.46
Serbian (16)	71	0.07
Slavic (55)	106	0.11
Slovak (94)	252	0.25
Slovene (6)	24	0.02
Soviet Union (0)	0	<0.01
Swedish (245)	1,517	1.51
Swiss (159)	559	0.56
Turkish (98)	137	0.14
Ukrainian (291)	595	0.59
Welsh (183)	1,158	1.15
West Indian, ex. Hispanic (211)	328	0.33
Bahamian (0)	0	<0.01
Barbadian (0)	10	0.01
Belizean (0)	0	<0.01
Bermudan (0)	0	<0.01
British West Indian (12)	21	0.02
Dutch West Indian (32)	32	0.03
Haitian (103)	135	0.13
Jamaican (27)	72	0.07
Trinidadian/Tobagonian (0)	9	0.01
U.S. Virgin Islander (0)	0	<0.01
West Indian (37)	49	0.05
Other West Indian (0)	0	<0.01
Yugoslavian (64)	87	0.09

Hispanic Origin	Population	%
Hispanic or Latino (of any race)	4,264	4.20
Central American, ex. Mexican	314	0.31
Costa Rican	43	0.04
Guatemalan	115	0.11
Honduran	27	0.03
Nicaraguan	40	0.04
Panamanian	27	0.03
Salvadoran	61	0.06
Other Central American	1	<0.01
Cuban	253	0.25
Dominican Republic	264	0.26
Mexican	909	0.90
Puerto Rican	1,167	1.15
South American	824	0.81
Argentinean	105	0.10
Bolivian	29	0.03
Chilean	88	0.09
Colombian	230	0.23
Ecuadorian	98	0.10
Paraguayan	8	0.01
Peruvian	144	0.14
Uruguayan	17	0.02
Venezuelan	94	0.09
Other South American	11	0.01
Other Hispanic or Latino	533	0.52

Race*	Population	%
African-American/Black (4,020)	5,411	5.33
Not Hispanic (3,773)	4,969	4.89
Hispanic (247)	442	0.44
American Indian/Alaska Native (360)	1,159	1.14
Not Hispanic (270)	952	0.94
Hispanic (90)	207	0.20
Alaska Athabascan (Ala. Nat.) (1)	2	<0.01
Aleut (Alaska Native) (0)	0	<0.01
Apache (6)	16	0.02
Arapaho (0)	0	<0.01
Blackfeet (7)	53	0.05
Canadian/French Am. Ind. (2)	8	0.01
Central American Ind. (4)	9	0.01
Cherokee (37)	167	0.16
Cheyenne (0)	2	<0.01
Chickasaw (0)	4	<0.01
Chippewa (5)	20	0.02
Choctaw (1)	15	0.01
Colville (0)	0	<0.01
Comanche (0)	1	<0.01
Cree (0)	3	<0.01
Creek (3)	11	0.01
Crow (1)	1	<0.01
Delaware (5)	20	0.02
Hopi (0)	1	<0.01
Houma (0)	0	<0.01
Inupiat (Alaska Native) (0)	0	<0.01
Iroquois (52)	159	0.16
Kiowa (0)	1	<0.01
Lumbee (5)	5	<0.01
Menominee (0)	1	<0.01
Mexican American Ind. (18)	30	0.03
Navajo (4)	14	0.01
Osage (1)	2	<0.01
Ottawa (4)	4	<0.01
Paiute (0)	0	<0.01
Pima (0)	1	<0.01
Potawatomi (1)	1	<0.01
Pueblo (1)	1	<0.01
Puget Sound Salish (2)	2	<0.01
Seminole (7)	15	0.01
Shoshone (0)	0	<0.01
Sioux (14)	28	0.03
South American Ind. (29)	51	0.05
Spanish American Ind. (0)	1	<0.01
Tlingit-Haida (Alaska Native) (0)	0	<0.01
Tohono O'Odham (0)	0	<0.01
Tsimshian (Alaska Native) (0)	0	<0.01
Ute (0)	0	<0.01
Yakama (0)	0	<0.01
Yaqui (2)	7	0.01
Yuman (0)	0	<0.01
Yup'ik (Alaska Native) (0)	1	<0.01
Asian (8,737)	9,963	9.81
Not Hispanic (8,680)	9,848	9.70
Hispanic (57)	115	0.11
Bangladeshi (32)	34	0.03
Bhutanese (0)	0	<0.01
Burmese (126)	133	0.13
Cambodian (120)	137	0.13
Chinese, ex. Taiwanese (3,581)	4,058	4.00
Filipino (154)	314	0.31
Hmong (0)	0	<0.01
Indian (1,435)	1,610	1.59
Indonesian (54)	81	0.08
Japanese (285)	535	0.53
Korean (1,722)	1,861	1.83
Laotian (52)	80	0.08
Malaysian (17)	34	0.03
Nepalese (34)	39	0.04
Pakistani (117)	135	0.13
Sri Lankan (24)	32	0.03
Taiwanese (319)	382	0.38
Thai (123)	158	0.16
Vietnamese (236)	297	0.29
Hawaii Native/Pacific Islander (45)	160	0.16
Not Hispanic (40)	141	0.14
Hispanic (5)	19	0.02
Fijian (1)	7	0.01
Guamanian/Chamorro (8)	23	0.02
Marshallese (0)	0	<0.01
Native Hawaiian (14)	43	0.04
Samoan (9)	28	0.03
Tongan (3)	3	<0.01
White (83,941)	86,872	85.53
Not Hispanic (81,490)	84,038	82.74
Hispanic (2,451)	2,834	2.79

Ulster County

Population: 182,493

Ancestry	Population	%
Afghan (29)	29	0.02
African, Sub-Saharan (309)	450	0.25
African (186)	291	0.16
Cape Verdean (0)	0	<0.01
Ethiopian (37)	73	0.04
Ghanaian (0)	0	<0.01
Kenyan (0)	0	<0.01
Liberian (0)	0	<0.01
Nigerian (75)	75	0.04
Senegalese (0)	0	<0.01
Sierra Leonean (0)	0	<0.01
Somalian (0)	0	<0.01
South African (0)	0	<0.01
Sudanese (0)	0	<0.01
Ugandan (0)	0	<0.01
Zimbabwean (0)	0	<0.01
Other Sub-Saharan African (11)	11	0.01
Albanian (180)	180	0.10
Alsatian (0)	20	0.01
American (12,589)	12,589	6.89
Arab (209)	460	0.25
Arab (0)	22	0.01
Egyptian (96)	165	0.09
Iraqi (0)	0	<0.01
Jordanian (0)	0	<0.01
Lebanese (75)	180	0.10
Moroccan (0)	0	<0.01
Palestinian (11)	41	0.02
Syrian (0)	25	0.01
Other Arab (27)	27	0.01
Armenian (71)	127	0.07
Assyrian/Chaldean/Syriac (8)	8	<0.01
Australian (18)	87	0.05
Austrian (169)	1,512	0.83
Basque (27)	50	0.03
Belgian (62)	279	0.15
Brazilian (178)	263	0.14
British (319)	898	0.49
Bulgarian (0)	78	0.04
Cajun (0)	0	<0.01
Canadian (192)	523	0.29
Carpatho Rusyn (0)	10	0.01
Celtic (25)	50	0.03
Croatian (147)	234	0.13
Cypriot (8)	8	<0.01
Czech (213)	801	0.44
Czechoslovakian (98)	286	0.16
Danish (119)	734	0.40
Dutch (1,775)	9,680	5.30
Eastern European (808)	877	0.48
English (3,859)	18,135	9.92
Estonian (0)	0	<0.01
European (3,396)	3,517	1.92
Finnish (112)	409	0.22
French, ex. Basque (1,080)	7,193	3.94
French Canadian (413)	1,291	0.71
German (7,795)	35,911	19.65
German Russian (0)	0	<0.01
Greek (429)	1,460	0.80
Guyanese (185)	185	0.10
Hungarian (486)	1,824	1.00
Icelander (0)	15	0.01
Iranian (58)	70	0.04
Irish (9,720)	38,535	21.08
Israeli (53)	114	0.06
Italian (14,757)	35,905	19.64
Latvian (40)	123	0.07
Lithuanian (59)	527	0.29
Luxemburger (0)	0	<0.01
Macedonian (0)	0	<0.01
Maltese (9)	39	0.02
New Zealander (0)	0	<0.01
Northern European (281)	291	0.16
Norwegian (683)	2,848	1.56
Pennsylvania German (67)	148	0.08

Ancestry (cont.)	Population	%
Polish (2,603)	9,470	5.18
Portuguese (145)	604	0.33
Romanian (259)	440	0.24
Russian (1,337)	4,045	2.21
Scandinavian (89)	248	0.14
Scotch-Irish (907)	2,805	1.53
Scottish (759)	3,592	1.97
Serbian (10)	10	0.01
Slavic (100)	224	0.12
Slovak (145)	540	0.30
Slovene (0)	12	0.01
Soviet Union (0)	0	<0.01
Swedish (539)	2,391	1.31
Swiss (63)	283	0.15
Turkish (109)	156	0.09
Ukrainian (806)	1,416	0.77
Welsh (317)	1,117	0.61
West Indian, ex. Hispanic (1,151)	1,576	0.86
Bahamian (0)	0	<0.01
Barbadian (61)	99	0.05
Belizean (0)	0	<0.01
Bermudan (0)	0	<0.01
British West Indian (30)	62	0.03
Dutch West Indian (0)	0	<0.01
Haitian (69)	219	0.12
Jamaican (666)	738	0.40
Trinidadian/Tobagonian (85)	111	0.06
U.S. Virgin Islander (0)	0	<0.01
West Indian (240)	347	0.19
Other West Indian (0)	0	<0.01
Yugoslavian (162)	237	0.13

Hispanic Origin	Population	%
Hispanic or Latino (of any race)	15,909	8.72
Central American, ex. Mexican	1,464	0.80
Costa Rican	34	0.02
Guatemalan	331	0.18
Honduran	228	0.12
Nicaraguan	17	0.01
Panamanian	106	0.06
Salvadoran	735	0.40
Other Central American	13	0.01
Cuban	438	0.24
Dominican Republic	813	0.45
Mexican	2,945	1.61
Puerto Rican	7,191	3.94
South American	1,449	0.79
Argentinean	142	0.08
Bolivian	13	0.01
Chilean	124	0.07
Colombian	520	0.28
Ecuadorian	267	0.15
Paraguayan	16	0.01
Peruvian	263	0.14
Uruguayan	34	0.02
Venezuelan	46	0.03
Other South American	24	0.01
Other Hispanic or Latino	1,609	0.88

Race*	Population	%
African-American/Black (10,982)	13,644	7.48
Not Hispanic (9,982)	12,055	6.61
Hispanic (1,000)	1,589	0.87
American Indian/Alaska Native (597)	1,975	1.08
Not Hispanic (414)	1,572	0.86
Hispanic (183)	403	0.22
Alaska Athabascan (Ala. Nat.) (0)	0	<0.01
Aleut (Alaska Native) (0)	0	<0.01
Apache (6)	26	0.01
Arapaho (3)	6	<0.01
Blackfeet (6)	61	0.03
Canadian/French Am. Ind. (5)	13	0.01
Central American Ind. (12)	19	0.01
Cherokee (59)	321	0.18
Cheyenne (1)	2	<0.01
Chickasaw (1)	2	<0.01
Chippewa (4)	12	0.01
Choctaw (2)	10	0.01
Colville (0)	0	<0.01

Race* (cont.)	Population	%
Comanche (1)	3	<0.01
Cree (0)	5	<0.01
Creek (12)	22	0.01
Crow (1)	1	<0.01
Delaware (27)	62	0.03
Hopi (1)	2	<0.01
Houma (0)	0	<0.01
Inupiat (Alaska Native) (1)	4	<0.01
Iroquois (52)	188	0.10
Kiowa (0)	0	<0.01
Lumbee (5)	13	0.01
Menominee (0)	1	<0.01
Mexican American Ind. (28)	44	0.02
Navajo (1)	11	<0.01
Osage (0)	3	<0.01
Ottawa (0)	0	<0.01
Paiute (0)	0	<0.01
Pima (0)	1	<0.01
Potawatomi (1)	1	<0.01
Pueblo (6)	6	<0.01
Puget Sound Salish (0)	1	<0.01
Seminole (1)	13	0.01
Shoshone (0)	0	<0.01
Sioux (27)	49	0.03
South American Ind. (26)	57	0.03
Spanish American Ind. (1)	7	<0.01
Tlingit-Haida (Alaska Native) (0)	0	<0.01
Tohono O'Odham (0)	0	<0.01
Tsimshian (Alaska Native) (1)	1	<0.01
Ute (0)	0	<0.01
Yakama (0)	0	<0.01
Yaqui (0)	0	<0.01
Yuman (0)	0	<0.01
Yup'ik (Alaska Native) (2)	2	<0.01
Asian (3,106)	4,029	2.21
Not Hispanic (3,060)	3,892	2.13
Hispanic (46)	137	0.08
Bangladeshi (85)	95	0.05
Bhutanese (1)	1	<0.01
Burmese (6)	8	<0.01
Cambodian (10)	16	0.01
Chinese, ex. Taiwanese (838)	1,039	0.57
Filipino (277)	456	0.25
Hmong (0)	0	<0.01
Indian (709)	926	0.51
Indonesian (15)	27	0.01
Japanese (197)	344	0.19
Korean (302)	402	0.22
Laotian (2)	4	<0.01
Malaysian (5)	16	0.01
Nepalese (19)	24	0.01
Pakistani (175)	211	0.12
Sri Lankan (21)	30	0.02
Taiwanese (41)	45	0.02
Thai (52)	78	0.04
Vietnamese (118)	163	0.09
Hawaii Native/Pacific Islander (34)	165	0.09
Not Hispanic (29)	122	0.07
Hispanic (5)	43	0.02
Fijian (2)	3	<0.01
Guamanian/Chamorro (7)	21	0.01
Marshallese (0)	0	<0.01
Native Hawaiian (8)	40	0.02
Samoan (3)	16	0.01
Tongan (2)	5	<0.01
White (158,184)	162,629	89.12
Not Hispanic (149,099)	152,405	83.51
Hispanic (9,085)	10,224	5.60

Notes: † The Census 2010 population figure is used to calculate the percentages in the Hispanic Origin and Race categories. Ancestry percentages are based on the 2006-2010 American Community Survey population (not shown); ‡ Numbers in parentheses indicate the number of people reporting a single ancestry; * Numbers in parentheses indicate the number of persons reporting this race alone, not in combination with any other race; Please refer to the Explanation of Data for more information.

Warren County

Population: 65,707

Ancestry	Population	%
Afghan (0)	9	0.01
African, Sub-Saharan (9)	36	0.05
African (9)	36	0.05
Cape Verdean (0)	0	<0.01
Ethiopian (0)	0	<0.01
Ghanaian (0)	0	<0.01
Kenyan (0)	0	<0.01
Liberian (0)	0	<0.01
Nigerian (0)	0	<0.01
Senegalese (0)	0	<0.01
Sierra Leonean (0)	0	<0.01
Somalian (0)	0	<0.01
South African (0)	0	<0.01
Sudanese (0)	0	<0.01
Ugandan (0)	0	<0.01
Zimbabwean (0)	0	<0.01
Other Sub-Saharan African (0)	0	<0.01
Albanian (0)	0	<0.01
Alsatian (0)	0	<0.01
American (5,380)	5,380	8.19
Arab (174)	318	0.48
Arab (0)	16	0.02
Egyptian (0)	0	<0.01
Iraqi (0)	0	<0.01
Jordanian (0)	0	<0.01
Lebanese (17)	61	0.09
Moroccan (0)	0	<0.01
Palestinian (0)	0	<0.01
Syrian (150)	230	0.35
Other Arab (7)	11	0.02
Armenian (23)	70	0.11
Assyrian/Chaldean/Syriac (0)	0	<0.01
Australian (9)	9	0.01
Austrian (41)	199	0.30
Basque (0)	0	<0.01
Belgian (7)	24	0.04
Brazilian (8)	8	0.01
British (82)	183	0.28
Bulgarian (20)	32	0.05
Cajun (0)	0	<0.01
Canadian (419)	607	0.92
Carpatho Rusyn (0)	0	<0.01
Celtic (14)	43	0.07
Croatian (0)	9	0.01
Cypriot (0)	0	<0.01
Czech (45)	195	0.30
Czechoslovakian (12)	54	0.08
Danish (31)	142	0.22
Dutch (259)	2,232	3.40
Eastern European (149)	149	0.23
English (2,731)	9,825	14.95
Estonian (18)	18	0.03
European (357)	379	0.58
Finnish (0)	43	0.07
French, ex. Basque (1,964)	8,502	12.94
French Canadian (1,045)	2,407	3.66
German (2,352)	9,279	14.12
German Russian (0)	16	0.02
Greek (34)	92	0.14
Guyanese (17)	17	0.03
Hungarian (93)	439	0.67
Icelander (0)	7	0.01
Iranian (5)	30	0.05
Irish (4,734)	15,493	23.58
Israeli (0)	15	0.02
Italian (3,791)	8,622	13.12
Latvian (28)	59	0.09
Lithuanian (54)	314	0.48
Luxemburger (0)	0	<0.01
Macedonian (0)	0	<0.01
Maltese (0)	0	<0.01
New Zealander (0)	0	<0.01
Northern European (42)	42	0.06
Norwegian (75)	324	0.49
Pennsylvania German (14)	48	0.07

Ancestry	Population	%
Polish (718)	2,771	4.22
Portuguese (17)	113	0.17
Romanian (51)	51	0.08
Russian (212)	669	1.02
Scandinavian (58)	66	0.10
Scotch-Irish (752)	1,489	2.27
Scottish (585)	1,966	2.99
Serbian (17)	17	0.03
Slavic (14)	55	0.08
Slovak (39)	148	0.23
Slovene (0)	0	<0.01
Soviet Union (0)	0	<0.01
Swedish (258)	910	1.38
Swiss (19)	137	0.21
Turkish (0)	4	0.01
Ukrainian (137)	315	0.48
Welsh (206)	986	1.50
West Indian, ex. Hispanic (80)	97	0.15
Bahamian (0)	0	<0.01
Barbadian (0)	0	<0.01
Belizean (0)	0	<0.01
Bermudan (0)	0	<0.01
British West Indian (5)	5	0.01
Dutch West Indian (0)	0	<0.01
Haitian (0)	0	<0.01
Jamaican (70)	70	0.11
Trinidadian/Tobagonian (0)	0	<0.01
U.S. Virgin Islander (0)	0	<0.01
West Indian (5)	22	0.03
Other West Indian (0)	0	<0.01
Yugoslavian (15)	24	0.04

Hispanic Origin	Population	%
Hispanic or Latino (of any race)	1,178	1.79
Central American, ex. Mexican	66	0.10
Costa Rican	5	0.01
Guatemalan	15	0.02
Honduran	9	0.01
Nicaraguan	5	0.01
Panamanian	12	0.02
Salvadoran	20	0.03
Other Central American	0	<0.01
Cuban	45	0.07
Dominican Republic	32	0.05
Mexican	239	0.36
Puerto Rican	528	0.80
South American	92	0.14
Argentinean	9	0.01
Bolivian	3	<0.01
Chilean	5	0.01
Colombian	31	0.05
Ecuadorian	7	0.01
Paraguayan	1	<0.01
Peruvian	23	0.04
Uruguayan	3	<0.01
Venezuelan	10	0.02
Other South American	0	<0.01
Other Hispanic or Latino	176	0.27

Race*	Population	%
African-American/Black (590)	949	1.44
Not Hispanic (556)	861	1.31
Hispanic (34)	88	0.13
American Indian/Alaska Native (144)	531	0.81
Not Hispanic (117)	470	0.72
Hispanic (27)	61	0.09
Alaska Athabascan (Ala. Nat.) (1)	1	<0.01
Aleut (Alaska Native) (0)	0	<0.01
Apache (2)	6	0.01
Arapaho (0)	0	<0.01
Blackfeet (6)	26	0.04
Canadian/French Am. Ind. (6)	8	0.01
Central American Ind. (1)	1	<0.01
Cherokee (16)	45	0.07
Cheyenne (0)	2	<0.01
Chickasaw (0)	0	<0.01
Chippewa (3)	6	0.01
Choctaw (0)	1	<0.01
Colville (0)	0	<0.01

Race*	Population	%
Comanche (0)	0	<0.01
Cree (0)	2	<0.01
Creek (0)	0	<0.01
Crow (0)	1	<0.01
Delaware (1)	1	<0.01
Hopi (0)	0	<0.01
Houma (0)	0	<0.01
Inupiat (Alaska Native) (0)	0	<0.01
Iroquois (17)	77	0.12
Kiowa (0)	0	<0.01
Lumbee (0)	0	<0.01
Menominee (0)	3	<0.01
Mexican American Ind. (5)	6	0.01
Navajo (0)	0	<0.01
Osage (0)	0	<0.01
Ottawa (1)	1	<0.01
Paiute (0)	0	<0.01
Pima (0)	0	<0.01
Potawatomi (0)	1	<0.01
Pueblo (0)	0	<0.01
Puget Sound Salish (0)	0	<0.01
Seminole (1)	5	0.01
Shoshone (0)	0	<0.01
Sioux (2)	15	0.02
South American Ind. (4)	5	0.01
Spanish American Ind. (1)	2	<0.01
Tlingit-Haida (Alaska Native) (1)	4	0.01
Tohono O'Odham (0)	0	<0.01
Tsimshian (Alaska Native) (0)	0	<0.01
Ute (0)	0	<0.01
Yakama (0)	0	<0.01
Yaqui (0)	2	<0.01
Yuman (0)	0	<0.01
Yup'ik (Alaska Native) (0)	0	<0.01
Asian (456)	615	0.94
Not Hispanic (449)	596	0.91
Hispanic (7)	19	0.03
Bangladeshi (1)	2	<0.01
Bhutanese (0)	0	<0.01
Burmese (0)	0	<0.01
Cambodian (0)	1	<0.01
Chinese, ex. Taiwanese (116)	140	0.21
Filipino (75)	118	0.18
Hmong (0)	1	<0.01
Indian (69)	97	0.15
Indonesian (2)	2	<0.01
Japanese (15)	30	0.05
Korean (65)	101	0.15
Laotian (3)	4	0.01
Malaysian (1)	2	<0.01
Nepalese (0)	0	<0.01
Pakistani (27)	34	0.05
Sri Lankan (1)	1	<0.01
Taiwanese (7)	7	0.01
Thai (13)	16	0.02
Vietnamese (41)	47	0.07
Hawaii Native/Pacific Islander (8)	34	0.05
Not Hispanic (5)	25	0.04
Hispanic (3)	9	0.01
Fijian (0)	0	<0.01
Guamanian/Chamorro (1)	6	0.01
Marshallese (0)	0	<0.01
Native Hawaiian (4)	10	0.02
Samoan (2)	3	<0.01
Tongan (0)	0	<0.01
White (63,391)	64,255	97.79
Not Hispanic (62,585)	63,331	96.38
Hispanic (806)	924	1.41

Notes: † The Census 2010 population figure is used to calculate the percentages in the Hispanic Origin and Race categories. Ancestry percentages are based on the 2006-2010 American Community Survey population (not shown); ‡ Numbers in parentheses indicate the number of people reporting a single ancestry; * Numbers in parentheses indicate the number of persons reporting this race alone, not in combination with any other race; Please refer to the Explanation of Data for more information.

Washington County
Population: 63,216

Ancestry	Population	%
Afghan (0)	0	<0.01
African, Sub-Saharan (40)	66	0.10
African (28)	54	0.09
Cape Verdean (0)	0	<0.01
Ethiopian (0)	0	<0.01
Ghanaian (0)	0	<0.01
Kenyan (0)	0	<0.01
Liberian (0)	0	<0.01
Nigerian (8)	8	0.01
Senegalese (0)	0	<0.01
Sierra Leonean (0)	0	<0.01
Somalian (0)	0	<0.01
South African (0)	0	<0.01
Sudanese (0)	0	<0.01
Ugandan (0)	0	<0.01
Zimbabwean (0)	0	<0.01
Other Sub-Saharan African (4)	4	0.01
Albanian (17)	17	0.03
Alsatian (0)	4	0.01
American (6,527)	6,527	10.35
Arab (40)	175	0.28
Arab (0)	0	<0.01
Egyptian (0)	0	<0.01
Iraqi (0)	0	<0.01
Jordanian (0)	0	<0.01
Lebanese (13)	83	0.13
Moroccan (0)	0	<0.01
Palestinian (0)	0	<0.01
Syrian (18)	83	0.13
Other Arab (9)	9	0.01
Armenian (29)	113	0.18
Assyrian/Chaldean/Syriac (0)	0	<0.01
Australian (9)	14	0.02
Austrian (59)	200	0.32
Basque (0)	13	0.02
Belgian (0)	23	0.04
Brazilian (0)	19	0.03
British (106)	174	0.28
Bulgarian (0)	4	0.01
Cajun (0)	0	<0.01
Canadian (204)	341	0.54
Carpatho Rusyn (0)	0	<0.01
Celtic (7)	7	0.01
Croatian (0)	0	<0.01
Cypriot (0)	0	<0.01
Czech (65)	117	0.19
Czechoslovakian (118)	258	0.41
Danish (34)	183	0.29
Dutch (254)	1,822	2.89
Eastern European (84)	84	0.13
English (2,389)	9,121	14.46
Estonian (0)	0	<0.01
European (209)	209	0.33
Finnish (25)	47	0.07
French, ex. Basque (1,714)	9,148	14.50
French Canadian (1,192)	2,416	3.83
German (1,476)	7,658	12.14
German Russian (0)	0	<0.01
Greek (35)	117	0.19
Guyanese (31)	47	0.07
Hungarian (205)	325	0.52
Icelander (0)	0	<0.01
Iranian (0)	0	<0.01
Irish (4,128)	13,852	21.96
Israeli (39)	39	0.06
Italian (1,842)	5,717	9.06
Latvian (23)	42	0.07
Lithuanian (95)	300	0.48
Luxemburger (0)	0	<0.01
Macedonian (0)	0	<0.01
Maltese (5)	9	0.01
New Zealander (5)	5	0.01
Northern European (7)	29	0.05
Norwegian (79)	279	0.44
Pennsylvania German (5)	8	0.01

Ancestry	Population	%
Polish (811)	2,342	3.71
Portuguese (93)	251	0.40
Romanian (12)	69	0.11
Russian (144)	686	1.09
Scandinavian (15)	21	0.03
Scotch-Irish (983)	1,767	2.80
Scottish (694)	2,905	4.60
Serbian (0)	13	0.02
Slavic (8)	20	0.03
Slovak (74)	201	0.32
Slovene (9)	18	0.03
Soviet Union (0)	0	<0.01
Swedish (289)	843	1.34
Swiss (12)	132	0.21
Turkish (0)	0	<0.01
Ukrainian (88)	299	0.47
Welsh (336)	1,157	1.83
West Indian, ex. Hispanic (218)	272	0.43
Bahamian (9)	9	0.01
Barbadian (16)	16	0.03
Belizean (0)	0	<0.01
Bermudan (0)	0	<0.01
British West Indian (9)	9	0.01
Dutch West Indian (0)	0	<0.01
Haitian (87)	110	0.17
Jamaican (33)	60	0.10
Trinidadian/Tobagonian (26)	26	0.04
U.S. Virgin Islander (0)	0	<0.01
West Indian (38)	42	0.07
Other West Indian (0)	0	<0.01
Yugoslavian (0)	0	<0.01

Hispanic Origin	Population	%
Hispanic or Latino (of any race)	1,446	2.29
Central American, ex. Mexican	115	0.18
Costa Rican	2	<0.01
Guatemalan	53	0.08
Honduran	7	0.01
Nicaraguan	2	<0.01
Panamanian	19	0.03
Salvadoran	32	0.05
Other Central American	0	<0.01
Cuban	55	0.09
Dominican Republic	112	0.18
Mexican	452	0.72
Puerto Rican	522	0.83
South American	75	0.12
Argentinean	3	<0.01
Bolivian	6	0.01
Chilean	6	0.01
Colombian	18	0.03
Ecuadorian	18	0.03
Paraguayan	0	<0.01
Peruvian	12	0.02
Uruguayan	6	0.01
Venezuelan	5	0.01
Other South American	1	<0.01
Other Hispanic or Latino	115	0.18

Race*	Population	%
African-American/Black (1,893)	2,149	3.40
Not Hispanic (1,734)	1,966	3.11
Hispanic (159)	183	0.29
American Indian/Alaska Native (128)	420	0.66
Not Hispanic (109)	375	0.59
Hispanic (19)	45	0.07
Alaska Athabascan (Ala. Nat.) (0)	0	<0.01
Aleut (Alaska Native) (1)	1	<0.01
Apache (2)	5	0.01
Arapaho (0)	0	<0.01
Blackfeet (2)	29	0.05
Canadian/French Am. Ind. (2)	3	<0.01
Central American Ind. (1)	1	<0.01
Cherokee (7)	39	0.06
Cheyenne (0)	0	<0.01
Chickasaw (0)	0	<0.01
Chippewa (0)	0	<0.01
Choctaw (1)	2	<0.01
Colville (0)	0	<0.01

Race*	Population	%
Comanche (0)	1	<0.01
Cree (0)	3	<0.01
Creek (0)	0	<0.01
Crow (0)	1	<0.01
Delaware (0)	1	<0.01
Hopi (1)	3	<0.01
Houma (0)	0	<0.01
Inupiat (Alaska Native) (1)	1	<0.01
Iroquois (11)	39	0.06
Kiowa (0)	0	<0.01
Lumbee (0)	0	<0.01
Menominee (0)	0	<0.01
Mexican American Ind. (4)	12	0.02
Navajo (1)	1	<0.01
Osage (0)	0	<0.01
Ottawa (0)	0	<0.01
Paiute (0)	0	<0.01
Pima (0)	0	<0.01
Potawatomi (0)	0	<0.01
Pueblo (0)	0	<0.01
Puget Sound Salish (0)	0	<0.01
Seminole (0)	2	<0.01
Shoshone (0)	0	<0.01
Sioux (2)	4	0.01
South American Ind. (0)	0	<0.01
Spanish American Ind. (0)	0	<0.01
Tlingit-Haida (Alaska Native) (1)	1	<0.01
Tohono O'Odham (0)	0	<0.01
Tsimshian (Alaska Native) (0)	0	<0.01
Ute (0)	0	<0.01
Yakama (0)	0	<0.01
Yaqui (0)	0	<0.01
Yuman (1)	1	<0.01
Yup'ik (Alaska Native) (0)	0	<0.01
Asian (266)	371	0.59
Not Hispanic (260)	359	0.57
Hispanic (6)	12	0.02
Bangladeshi (0)	0	<0.01
Bhutanese (0)	0	<0.01
Burmese (0)	0	<0.01
Cambodian (11)	14	0.02
Chinese, ex. Taiwanese (67)	83	0.13
Filipino (60)	96	0.15
Hmong (0)	0	<0.01
Indian (29)	44	0.07
Indonesian (0)	1	<0.01
Japanese (14)	30	0.05
Korean (46)	62	0.10
Laotian (0)	0	<0.01
Malaysian (1)	1	<0.01
Nepalese (1)	3	<0.01
Pakistani (0)	1	<0.01
Sri Lankan (0)	0	<0.01
Taiwanese (4)	4	0.01
Thai (7)	10	0.02
Vietnamese (5)	6	0.01
Hawaii Native/Pacific Islander (13)	37	0.06
Not Hispanic (11)	32	0.05
Hispanic (2)	5	0.01
Fijian (0)	0	<0.01
Guamanian/Chamorro (0)	4	0.01
Marshallese (0)	0	<0.01
Native Hawaiian (2)	20	0.03
Samoan (2)	2	<0.01
Tongan (0)	0	<0.01
White (59,815)	60,458	95.64
Not Hispanic (58,996)	59,556	94.21
Hispanic (819)	902	1.43

*Notes: † The Census 2010 population figure is used to calculate the percentages in the Hispanic Origin and Race categories. Ancestry percentages are based on the 2006-2010 American Community Survey population (not shown); ‡ Numbers in parentheses indicate the number of people reporting a single ancestry; * Numbers in parentheses indicate the number of persons reporting this race alone, not in combination with any other race; Please refer to the Explanation of Data for more information.*

Wayne County

Population: 93,772

Ancestry	Population	%
Afghan (0)	0	<0.01
African, Sub-Saharan (145)	156	0.17
African (124)	135	0.14
Cape Verdean (0)	0	<0.01
Ethiopian (0)	0	<0.01
Ghanaian (0)	0	<0.01
Kenyan (0)	0	<0.01
Liberian (0)	0	<0.01
Nigerian (0)	0	<0.01
Senegalese (0)	0	<0.01
Sierra Leonean (0)	0	<0.01
Somalian (0)	0	<0.01
South African (0)	0	<0.01
Sudanese (21)	21	0.02
Ugandan (0)	0	<0.01
Zimbabwean (0)	0	<0.01
Other Sub-Saharan African (0)	0	<0.01
Albanian (155)	202	0.22
Alsatian (0)	0	<0.01
American (5,150)	5,150	5.50
Arab (64)	115	0.12
Arab (0)	0	<0.01
Egyptian (0)	0	<0.01
Iraqi (0)	0	<0.01
Jordanian (0)	0	<0.01
Lebanese (45)	87	0.09
Moroccan (19)	19	0.02
Palestinian (0)	0	<0.01
Syrian (0)	0	<0.01
Other Arab (0)	9	0.01
Armenian (0)	13	0.01
Assyrian/Chaldean/Syriac (0)	0	<0.01
Australian (0)	57	0.06
Austrian (52)	174	0.19
Basque (0)	0	<0.01
Belgian (86)	225	0.24
Brazilian (0)	24	0.03
British (161)	396	0.42
Bulgarian (0)	6	0.01
Cajun (3)	3	<0.01
Canadian (231)	527	0.56
Carpatho Rusyn (0)	0	<0.01
Celtic (0)	0	<0.01
Croatian (35)	44	0.05
Cypriot (0)	0	<0.01
Czech (83)	274	0.29
Czechoslovakian (25)	69	0.07
Danish (133)	267	0.29
Dutch (3,364)	12,028	12.84
Eastern European (21)	21	0.02
English (3,997)	15,284	16.32
Estonian (0)	0	<0.01
European (556)	652	0.70
Finnish (68)	167	0.18
French, ex. Basque (462)	4,569	4.88
French Canadian (553)	1,649	1.76
German (6,047)	24,173	25.81
German Russian (0)	0	<0.01
Greek (350)	402	0.43
Guyanese (33)	33	0.04
Hungarian (88)	331	0.35
Icelander (3)	3	<0.01
Iranian (0)	0	<0.01
Irish (2,837)	15,277	16.31
Israeli (0)	0	<0.01
Italian (5,298)	13,414	14.32
Latvian (7)	81	0.09
Lithuanian (121)	258	0.28
Luxemburger (0)	0	<0.01
Macedonian (11)	28	0.03
Maltese (0)	58	0.06
New Zealander (0)	0	<0.01
Northern European (12)	15	0.02
Norwegian (81)	387	0.41
Pennsylvania German (183)	213	0.23
Polish (1,063)	4,302	4.59
Portuguese (62)	149	0.16
Romanian (24)	43	0.05
Russian (113)	392	0.42
Scandinavian (14)	68	0.07
Scotch-Irish (626)	1,703	1.82
Scottish (528)	2,308	2.46
Serbian (0)	0	<0.01
Slavic (47)	72	0.08
Slovak (16)	99	0.11
Slovene (0)	73	0.08
Soviet Union (0)	0	<0.01
Swedish (112)	536	0.57
Swiss (387)	863	0.92
Turkish (0)	0	<0.01
Ukrainian (335)	978	1.04
Welsh (173)	996	1.06
West Indian, ex. Hispanic (248)	285	0.30
Bahamian (0)	0	<0.01
Barbadian (0)	0	<0.01
Belizean (0)	0	<0.01
Bermudan (0)	0	<0.01
British West Indian (0)	0	<0.01
Dutch West Indian (7)	7	0.01
Haitian (124)	156	0.17
Jamaican (68)	68	0.07
Trinidadian/Tobagonian (0)	0	<0.01
U.S. Virgin Islander (0)	0	<0.01
West Indian (49)	49	0.05
Other West Indian (0)	5	0.01
Yugoslavian (45)	96	0.10

Hispanic Origin	Population	%
Hispanic or Latino (of any race)	3,476	3.71
Central American, ex. Mexican	144	0.15
Costa Rican	5	0.01
Guatemalan	53	0.06
Honduran	57	0.06
Nicaraguan	3	<0.01
Panamanian	10	0.01
Salvadoran	16	0.02
Other Central American	0	<0.01
Cuban	51	0.05
Dominican Republic	85	0.09
Mexican	1,219	1.30
Puerto Rican	1,729	1.84
South American	64	0.07
Argentinean	10	0.01
Bolivian	4	<0.01
Chilean	1	<0.01
Colombian	22	0.02
Ecuadorian	10	0.01
Paraguayan	0	<0.01
Peruvian	11	0.01
Uruguayan	0	<0.01
Venezuelan	6	0.01
Other South American	0	<0.01
Other Hispanic or Latino	184	0.20

Race*	Population	%
African-American/Black (2,887)	3,853	4.11
Not Hispanic (2,743)	3,600	3.84
Hispanic (144)	253	0.27
American Indian/Alaska Native (258)	770	0.82
Not Hispanic (201)	661	0.70
Hispanic (57)	109	0.12
Alaska Athabascan (Ala. Nat.) (0)	0	<0.01
Aleut (Alaska Native) (0)	0	<0.01
Apache (2)	6	0.01
Arapaho (0)	0	<0.01
Blackfeet (4)	12	0.01
Canadian/French Am. Ind. (3)	9	0.01
Central American Ind. (3)	3	<0.01
Cherokee (16)	102	0.11
Cheyenne (0)	0	<0.01
Chickasaw (0)	0	<0.01
Chippewa (16)	18	0.02
Choctaw (6)	12	0.01
Colville (0)	0	<0.01

	Population	%
Comanche (2)	2	<0.01
Cree (0)	5	0.01
Creek (1)	1	<0.01
Crow (0)	0	<0.01
Delaware (1)	1	<0.01
Hopi (0)	0	<0.01
Houma (0)	0	<0.01
Inupiat (Alaska Native) (0)	0	<0.01
Iroquois (60)	164	0.17
Kiowa (0)	0	<0.01
Lumbee (1)	8	0.01
Menominee (0)	0	<0.01
Mexican American Ind. (12)	15	0.02
Navajo (1)	2	<0.01
Osage (0)	1	<0.01
Ottawa (0)	0	<0.01
Paiute (0)	0	<0.01
Pima (2)	2	<0.01
Potawatomi (0)	0	<0.01
Pueblo (0)	1	<0.01
Puget Sound Salish (0)	0	<0.01
Seminole (0)	7	0.01
Shoshone (0)	0	<0.01
Sioux (2)	11	0.01
South American Ind. (4)	5	0.01
Spanish American Ind. (1)	2	<0.01
Tlingit-Haida (Alaska Native) (0)	0	<0.01
Tohono O'Odham (0)	0	<0.01
Tsimshian (Alaska Native) (0)	0	<0.01
Ute (0)	0	<0.01
Yakama (0)	0	<0.01
Yaqui (0)	0	<0.01
Yuman (0)	0	<0.01
Yup'ik (Alaska Native) (0)	0	<0.01
Asian (473)	704	0.75
Not Hispanic (465)	685	0.73
Hispanic (8)	19	0.02
Bangladeshi (1)	1	<0.01
Bhutanese (0)	0	<0.01
Burmese (0)	0	<0.01
Cambodian (16)	20	0.02
Chinese, ex. Taiwanese (104)	142	0.15
Filipino (60)	97	0.10
Hmong (0)	0	<0.01
Indian (51)	93	0.10
Indonesian (2)	5	0.01
Japanese (25)	57	0.06
Korean (74)	110	0.12
Laotian (47)	53	0.06
Malaysian (1)	1	<0.01
Nepalese (0)	0	<0.01
Pakistani (6)	6	0.01
Sri Lankan (1)	1	<0.01
Taiwanese (0)	0	<0.01
Thai (12)	25	0.03
Vietnamese (50)	71	0.08
Hawaii Native/Pacific Islander (24)	59	0.06
Not Hispanic (24)	54	0.06
Hispanic (0)	5	0.01
Fijian (0)	0	<0.01
Guamanian/Chamorro (4)	7	0.01
Marshallese (1)	1	<0.01
Native Hawaiian (3)	25	0.03
Samoan (1)	4	<0.01
Tongan (0)	1	<0.01
White (87,148)	88,857	94.76
Not Hispanic (85,318)	86,736	92.50
Hispanic (1,830)	2,121	2.26

*Notes: † The Census 2010 population figure is used to calculate the percentages in the Hispanic Origin and Race categories. Ancestry percentages are based on the 2006-2010 American Community Survey population (not shown); ‡ Numbers in parentheses indicate the number of people reporting a single ancestry; * Numbers in parentheses indicate the number of persons reporting this race alone, not in combination with any other race; Please refer to the Explanation of Data for more information.*

Westchester County

Population: 949,113

Ancestry	Population	%
Afghan (12)	12	<0.01
African, Sub-Saharan (7,149)	9,172	0.98
African (3,123)	4,390	0.47
Cape Verdean (41)	52	0.01
Ethiopian (391)	470	0.05
Ghanaian (952)	1,063	0.11
Kenyan (237)	271	0.03
Liberian (7)	16	<0.01
Nigerian (1,135)	1,280	0.14
Senegalese (21)	33	<0.01
Sierra Leonean (39)	51	0.01
Somalian (6)	6	<0.01
South African (500)	750	0.08
Sudanese (13)	13	<0.01
Ugandan (28)	28	<0.01
Zimbabwean (0)	0	<0.01
Other Sub-Saharan African (656)	749	0.08
Albanian (4,494)	4,876	0.52
Alsatian (0)	0	<0.01
American (41,120)	41,120	4.38
Arab (5,524)	7,908	0.84
Arab (1,268)	1,569	0.17
Egyptian (636)	827	0.09
Iraqi (111)	141	0.02
Jordanian (971)	1,058	0.11
Lebanese (1,105)	2,033	0.22
Moroccan (407)	657	0.07
Palestinian (229)	251	0.03
Syrian (118)	418	0.04
Other Arab (679)	954	0.10
Armenian (879)	1,450	0.15
Assyrian/Chaldean/Syriac (176)	265	0.03
Australian (283)	472	0.05
Austrian (1,636)	7,685	0.82
Basque (75)	94	0.01
Belgian (202)	717	0.08
Brazilian (5,072)	5,979	0.64
British (2,417)	4,054	0.43
Bulgarian (306)	425	0.05
Cajun (0)	0	<0.01
Canadian (723)	1,750	0.19
Carpatho Rusyn (60)	78	0.01
Celtic (66)	120	0.01
Croatian (1,470)	2,181	0.23
Cypriot (105)	105	0.01
Czech (857)	3,626	0.39
Czechoslovakian (610)	1,412	0.15
Danish (413)	1,707	0.18
Dutch (1,314)	5,907	0.63
Eastern European (11,389)	12,279	1.31
English (8,923)	38,197	4.07
Estonian (92)	278	0.03
European (8,977)	10,052	1.07
Finnish (346)	849	0.09
French, ex. Basque (3,407)	15,245	1.62
French Canadian (1,046)	3,477	0.37
German (15,113)	70,010	7.45
German Russian (14)	27	<0.01
Greek (4,560)	7,851	0.84
Guyanese (1,434)	1,848	0.20
Hungarian (3,232)	8,762	0.93
Icelander (0)	52	0.01
Iranian (986)	1,275	0.14
Irish (46,713)	124,206	13.22
Israeli (965)	1,392	0.15
Italian (112,477)	183,819	19.57
Latvian (344)	723	0.08
Lithuanian (778)	2,739	0.29
Luxemburger (0)	33	<0.01
Macedonian (443)	563	0.06
Maltese (164)	263	0.03
New Zealander (60)	60	0.01
Northern European (525)	637	0.07
Norwegian (1,179)	3,840	0.41
Pennsylvania German (33)	67	0.01

Ancestry	Population	%
Polish (12,575)	37,394	3.98
Portuguese (6,819)	9,618	1.02
Romanian (1,381)	3,301	0.35
Russian (14,440)	35,555	3.78
Scandinavian (290)	778	0.08
Scotch-Irish (2,663)	6,751	0.72
Scottish (2,357)	10,201	1.09
Serbian (32)	82	0.01
Slavic (440)	806	0.09
Slovak (899)	2,547	0.27
Slovene (64)	250	0.03
Soviet Union (14)	14	<0.01
Swedish (863)	5,211	0.55
Swiss (576)	2,042	0.22
Turkish (779)	1,198	0.13
Ukrainian (2,421)	4,931	0.52
Welsh (384)	2,296	0.24
West Indian, ex. Hispanic (31,329)	36,267	3.86
Bahamian (65)	72	0.01
Barbadian (718)	979	0.10
Belizean (267)	306	0.03
Bermudan (0)	0	<0.01
British West Indian (935)	1,296	0.14
Dutch West Indian (3)	3	<0.01
Haitian (3,480)	3,878	0.41
Jamaican (21,122)	23,768	2.53
Trinidadian/Tobagonian (1,606)	1,812	0.19
U.S. Virgin Islander (55)	106	0.01
West Indian (3,078)	4,037	0.43
Other West Indian (0)	10	<0.01
Yugoslavian (717)	977	0.10

Hispanic Origin	Population	%
Hispanic or Latino (of any race)	207,032	21.81
Central American, ex. Mexican	22,365	2.36
Costa Rican	584	0.06
Guatemalan	11,337	1.19
Honduran	3,055	0.32
Nicaraguan	885	0.09
Panamanian	686	0.07
Salvadoran	5,658	0.60
Other Central American	160	0.02
Cuban	5,287	0.56
Dominican Republic	26,573	2.80
Mexican	44,060	4.64
Puerto Rican	41,836	4.41
South American	50,521	5.32
Argentinean	1,922	0.20
Bolivian	749	0.08
Chilean	1,551	0.16
Colombian	10,245	1.08
Ecuadorian	22,460	2.37
Paraguayan	1,328	0.14
Peruvian	9,774	1.03
Uruguayan	1,251	0.13
Venezuelan	971	0.10
Other South American	270	0.03
Other Hispanic or Latino	16,390	1.73

Race*	Population	%
African-American/Black (138,118)	149,710	15.77
Not Hispanic (126,585)	133,406	14.06
Hispanic (11,533)	16,304	1.72
American Indian/Alaska Native (3,965)	8,854	0.93
Not Hispanic (1,141)	3,720	0.39
Hispanic (2,824)	5,134	0.54
Alaska Athabascan (Ala. Nat.) (3)	3	<0.01
Aleut (Alaska Native) (0)	5	<0.01
Apache (17)	56	0.01
Arapaho (0)	2	<0.01
Blackfeet (36)	196	0.02
Canadian/French Am. Ind. (11)	19	<0.01
Central American Ind. (106)	232	0.02
Cherokee (104)	742	0.08
Cheyenne (4)	15	<0.01
Chickasaw (2)	15	<0.01
Chippewa (16)	38	<0.01
Choctaw (11)	45	<0.01
Colville (0)	1	<0.01

Race*	Population	%
Comanche (0)	7	<0.01
Cree (0)	6	<0.01
Creek (3)	17	<0.01
Crow (2)	5	<0.01
Delaware (8)	28	<0.01
Hopi (1)	8	<0.01
Houma (4)	4	<0.01
Inupiat (Alaska Native) (8)	11	<0.01
Iroquois (68)	178	0.02
Kiowa (0)	1	<0.01
Lumbee (3)	5	<0.01
Menominee (0)	0	<0.01
Mexican American Ind. (396)	619	0.07
Navajo (11)	28	<0.01
Osage (5)	7	<0.01
Ottawa (1)	3	<0.01
Paiute (0)	0	<0.01
Pima (2)	2	<0.01
Potawatomi (1)	10	<0.01
Pueblo (31)	58	0.01
Puget Sound Salish (0)	3	<0.01
Seminole (4)	43	<0.01
Shoshone (0)	1	<0.01
Sioux (24)	75	0.01
South American Ind. (315)	820	0.09
Spanish American Ind. (162)	216	0.02
Tlingit-Haida (Alaska Native) (1)	2	<0.01
Tohono O'Odham (1)	5	<0.01
Tsimshian (Alaska Native) (0)	0	<0.01
Ute (0)	0	<0.01
Yakama (0)	0	<0.01
Yaqui (0)	2	<0.01
Yuman (2)	4	<0.01
Yup'ik (Alaska Native) (0)	0	<0.01
Asian (51,716)	59,734	6.29
Not Hispanic (51,123)	57,958	6.11
Hispanic (593)	1,776	0.19
Bangladeshi (349)	408	0.04
Bhutanese (19)	19	<0.01
Burmese (106)	116	0.01
Cambodian (104)	135	0.01
Chinese, ex. Taiwanese (10,224)	12,423	1.31
Filipino (6,441)	7,629	0.80
Hmong (1)	1	<0.01
Indian (17,798)	19,819	2.09
Indonesian (92)	146	0.02
Japanese (5,719)	6,828	0.72
Korean (5,440)	6,184	0.65
Laotian (60)	115	0.01
Malaysian (44)	67	0.01
Nepalese (137)	153	0.02
Pakistani (1,868)	2,111	0.22
Sri Lankan (206)	232	0.02
Taiwanese (496)	613	0.06
Thai (633)	796	0.08
Vietnamese (501)	646	0.07
Hawaii Native/Pacific Islander (387)	1,501	0.16
Not Hispanic (218)	825	0.09
Hispanic (169)	676	0.07
Fijian (12)	16	<0.01
Guamanian/Chamorro (121)	196	0.02
Marshallese (1)	1	<0.01
Native Hawaiian (64)	173	0.02
Samoan (15)	43	<0.01
Tongan (0)	0	<0.01
White (646,471)	669,460	70.54
Not Hispanic (544,563)	555,692	58.55
Hispanic (101,908)	113,768	11.99

Notes: † The Census 2010 population figure is used to calculate the percentages in the Hispanic Origin and Race categories. Ancestry percentages are based on the 2006-2010 American Community Survey population (not shown); ‡ Numbers in parentheses indicate the number of people reporting a single ancestry; * Numbers in parentheses indicate the number of persons reporting this race alone, not in combination with any other race; Please refer to the Explanation of Data for more information.

Wyoming County

Population: 42,155

Ancestry	Population	%
Afghan (0)	0	<0.01
African, Sub-Saharan (135)	145	0.34
African (126)	135	0.32
Cape Verdean (0)	0	<0.01
Ethiopian (0)	0	<0.01
Ghanaian (0)	0	<0.01
Kenyan (0)	0	<0.01
Liberian (0)	0	<0.01
Nigerian (9)	10	0.02
Senegalese (0)	0	<0.01
Sierra Leonean (0)	0	<0.01
Somalian (0)	0	<0.01
South African (0)	0	<0.01
Sudanese (0)	0	<0.01
Ugandan (0)	0	<0.01
Zimbabwean (0)	0	<0.01
Other Sub-Saharan African (0)	0	<0.01
Albanian (0)	0	<0.01
Alsatian (0)	2	<0.01
American (1,695)	1,695	4.00
Arab (20)	53	0.13
Arab (0)	0	<0.01
Egyptian (0)	9	0.02
Iraqi (0)	0	<0.01
Jordanian (0)	0	<0.01
Lebanese (20)	44	0.10
Moroccan (0)	0	<0.01
Palestinian (0)	0	<0.01
Syrian (0)	0	<0.01
Other Arab (0)	0	<0.01
Armenian (0)	0	<0.01
Assyrian/Chaldean/Syriac (0)	0	<0.01
Australian (32)	32	0.08
Austrian (37)	102	0.24
Basque (0)	0	<0.01
Belgian (29)	174	0.41
Brazilian (4)	4	0.01
British (65)	125	0.30
Bulgarian (0)	16	0.04
Cajun (0)	9	0.02
Canadian (18)	144	0.34
Carpatho Rusyn (0)	0	<0.01
Celtic (16)	32	0.08
Croatian (6)	43	0.10
Cypriot (0)	0	<0.01
Czech (15)	61	0.14
Czechoslovakian (23)	87	0.21
Danish (22)	62	0.15
Dutch (203)	1,260	2.97
Eastern European (0)	0	<0.01
English (1,993)	7,557	17.84
Estonian (0)	0	<0.01
European (351)	383	0.90
Finnish (0)	12	0.03
French, ex. Basque (177)	1,615	3.81
French Canadian (133)	389	0.92
German (5,087)	14,749	34.81
German Russian (0)	0	<0.01
Greek (14)	96	0.23
Guyanese (8)	8	0.02
Hungarian (56)	163	0.38
Icelander (0)	0	<0.01
Iranian (0)	0	<0.01
Irish (1,451)	6,765	15.97
Israeli (0)	0	<0.01
Italian (1,447)	3,971	9.37
Latvian (0)	0	<0.01
Lithuanian (0)	59	0.14
Luxemburger (0)	12	0.03
Macedonian (0)	0	<0.01
Maltese (0)	0	<0.01
New Zealander (0)	0	<0.01
Northern European (0)	0	<0.01
Norwegian (32)	138	0.33
Pennsylvania German (106)	163	0.38
Polish (1,672)	4,223	9.97
Portuguese (151)	173	0.41
Romanian (31)	31	0.07
Russian (138)	232	0.55
Scandinavian (28)	48	0.11
Scotch-Irish (226)	617	1.46
Scottish (187)	922	2.18
Serbian (0)	19	0.04
Slavic (0)	8	0.02
Slovak (8)	66	0.16
Slovene (8)	32	0.08
Soviet Union (0)	0	<0.01
Swedish (38)	411	0.97
Swiss (57)	271	0.64
Turkish (0)	0	<0.01
Ukrainian (129)	198	0.47
Welsh (45)	486	1.15
West Indian, ex. Hispanic (108)	139	0.33
Bahamian (0)	0	<0.01
Barbadian (0)	0	<0.01
Belizean (9)	9	0.02
Bermudan (0)	0	<0.01
British West Indian (0)	0	<0.01
Dutch West Indian (0)	0	<0.01
Haitian (26)	35	0.08
Jamaican (47)	52	0.12
Trinidadian/Tobagonian (8)	16	0.04
U.S. Virgin Islander (10)	10	0.02
West Indian (8)	17	0.04
Other West Indian (0)	0	<0.01
Yugoslavian (19)	79	0.19

Hispanic Origin	Population	%
Hispanic or Latino (of any race)	1,244	2.95
Central American, ex. Mexican	69	0.16
Costa Rican	1	<0.01
Guatemalan	29	0.07
Honduran	9	0.02
Nicaraguan	3	0.01
Panamanian	14	0.03
Salvadoran	13	0.03
Other Central American	0	<0.01
Cuban	40	0.09
Dominican Republic	94	0.22
Mexican	342	0.81
Puerto Rican	526	1.25
South American	65	0.15
Argentinean	2	<0.01
Bolivian	0	<0.01
Chilean	2	<0.01
Colombian	24	0.06
Ecuadorian	27	0.06
Paraguayan	0	<0.01
Peruvian	7	0.02
Uruguayan	1	<0.01
Venezuelan	2	<0.01
Other South American	0	<0.01
Other Hispanic or Latino	108	0.26

Race*	Population	%
African-American/Black (2,375)	2,492	5.91
Not Hispanic (2,233)	2,337	5.54
Hispanic (142)	155	0.37
American Indian/Alaska Native (126)	272	0.65
Not Hispanic (103)	222	0.53
Hispanic (23)	50	0.12
Alaska Athabascan (Ala. Nat.) (1)	1	<0.01
Aleut (Alaska Native) (0)	0	<0.01
Apache (0)	1	<0.01
Arapaho (0)	0	<0.01
Blackfeet (0)	5	0.01
Canadian/French Am. Ind. (1)	1	<0.01
Central American Ind. (1)	1	<0.01
Cherokee (5)	15	0.04
Cheyenne (0)	0	<0.01
Chickasaw (0)	0	<0.01
Chippewa (5)	5	0.01
Choctaw (0)	1	<0.01
Colville (0)	0	<0.01
Comanche (0)	0	<0.01
Cree (0)	0	<0.01
Creek (0)	0	<0.01
Crow (0)	0	<0.01
Delaware (0)	1	<0.01
Hopi (0)	0	<0.01
Houma (0)	0	<0.01
Inupiat (Alaska Native) (1)	1	<0.01
Iroquois (35)	75	0.18
Kiowa (0)	0	<0.01
Lumbee (0)	0	<0.01
Menominee (0)	0	<0.01
Mexican American Ind. (4)	7	0.02
Navajo (0)	2	<0.01
Osage (0)	0	<0.01
Ottawa (0)	0	<0.01
Paiute (0)	0	<0.01
Pima (0)	0	<0.01
Potawatomi (0)	0	<0.01
Pueblo (0)	0	<0.01
Puget Sound Salish (0)	0	<0.01
Seminole (0)	0	<0.01
Shoshone (0)	0	<0.01
Sioux (1)	3	0.01
South American Ind. (6)	6	0.01
Spanish American Ind. (1)	1	<0.01
Tlingit-Haida (Alaska Native) (0)	0	<0.01
Tohono O'Odham (3)	3	0.01
Tsimshian (Alaska Native) (0)	0	<0.01
Ute (0)	0	<0.01
Yakama (0)	0	<0.01
Yaqui (0)	0	<0.01
Yuman (0)	0	<0.01
Yup'ik (Alaska Native) (0)	0	<0.01
Asian (160)	229	0.54
Not Hispanic (156)	217	0.51
Hispanic (4)	12	0.03
Bangladeshi (3)	3	0.01
Bhutanese (0)	0	<0.01
Burmese (0)	0	<0.01
Cambodian (1)	1	<0.01
Chinese, ex. Taiwanese (39)	52	0.12
Filipino (21)	41	0.10
Hmong (0)	0	<0.01
Indian (24)	32	0.08
Indonesian (0)	1	<0.01
Japanese (7)	16	0.04
Korean (21)	27	0.06
Laotian (10)	14	0.03
Malaysian (0)	0	<0.01
Nepalese (0)	0	<0.01
Pakistani (7)	8	0.02
Sri Lankan (0)	0	<0.01
Taiwanese (1)	1	<0.01
Thai (2)	5	0.01
Vietnamese (7)	11	0.03
Hawaii Native/Pacific Islander (7)	14	0.03
Not Hispanic (7)	12	0.03
Hispanic (0)	2	<0.01
Fijian (0)	0	<0.01
Guamanian/Chamorro (0)	0	<0.01
Marshallese (0)	0	<0.01
Native Hawaiian (1)	3	0.01
Samoan (0)	0	<0.01
Tongan (0)	0	<0.01
White (38,602)	38,955	92.41
Not Hispanic (38,042)	38,323	90.91
Hispanic (560)	632	1.50

*Notes: † The Census 2010 population figure is used to calculate the percentages in the Hispanic Origin and Race categories. Ancestry percentages are based on the 2006-2010 American Community Survey population (not shown); ‡ Numbers in parentheses indicate the number of people reporting a single ancestry; * Numbers in parentheses indicate the number of persons reporting this race alone, not in combination with any other race; Please refer to the Explanation of Data for more information.*

Yates County

Population: 25,348

Ancestry	Population	%
Afghan (0)	0	<0.01
African, Sub-Saharan (10)	14	0.06
African (0)	4	0.02
Cape Verdean (0)	0	<0.01
Ethiopian (0)	0	<0.01
Ghanaian (0)	0	<0.01
Kenyan (10)	10	0.04
Liberian (0)	0	<0.01
Nigerian (0)	0	<0.01
Senegalese (0)	0	<0.01
Sierra Leonean (0)	0	<0.01
Somalian (0)	0	<0.01
South African (0)	0	<0.01
Sudanese (0)	0	<0.01
Ugandan (0)	0	<0.01
Zimbabwean (0)	0	<0.01
Other Sub-Saharan African (0)	0	<0.01
Albanian (0)	0	<0.01
Alsatian (0)	0	<0.01
American (2,456)	2,456	9.73
Arab (3)	17	0.07
Arab (0)	0	<0.01
Egyptian (0)	0	<0.01
Iraqi (0)	0	<0.01
Jordanian (0)	0	<0.01
Lebanese (0)	8	0.03
Moroccan (0)	0	<0.01
Palestinian (0)	0	<0.01
Syrian (3)	9	0.04
Other Arab (0)	0	<0.01
Armenian (0)	28	0.11
Assyrian/Chaldean/Syriac (0)	0	<0.01
Australian (4)	8	0.03
Austrian (12)	56	0.22
Basque (0)	0	<0.01
Belgian (3)	15	0.06
Brazilian (0)	0	<0.01
British (52)	151	0.60
Bulgarian (0)	0	<0.01
Cajun (0)	0	<0.01
Canadian (29)	88	0.35
Carpatho Rusyn (0)	0	<0.01
Celtic (0)	0	<0.01
Croatian (0)	0	<0.01
Cypriot (0)	0	<0.01
Czech (3)	66	0.26
Czechoslovakian (3)	3	0.01
Danish (393)	801	3.17
Dutch (200)	1,287	5.10
Eastern European (19)	19	0.08
English (1,552)	4,563	18.07
Estonian (0)	0	<0.01
European (75)	82	0.32
Finnish (0)	75	0.30
French, ex. Basque (105)	778	3.08
French Canadian (56)	224	0.89
German (2,782)	6,401	25.35
German Russian (0)	0	<0.01
Greek (27)	121	0.48
Guyanese (0)	0	<0.01
Hungarian (48)	128	0.51
Icelander (0)	0	<0.01
Iranian (9)	21	0.08
Irish (1,496)	5,291	20.95
Israeli (0)	6	0.02
Italian (794)	2,160	8.55
Latvian (0)	0	<0.01
Lithuanian (0)	16	0.06
Luxemburger (0)	0	<0.01
Macedonian (0)	0	<0.01
Maltese (0)	0	<0.01
New Zealander (0)	0	<0.01
Northern European (10)	10	0.04
Norwegian (19)	106	0.42
Pennsylvania German (408)	471	1.87

Ancestry (cont.)	Population	%
Polish (256)	915	3.62
Portuguese (13)	13	0.05
Romanian (4)	4	0.02
Russian (50)	123	0.49
Scandinavian (0)	39	0.15
Scotch-Irish (174)	418	1.66
Scottish (219)	770	3.05
Serbian (0)	0	<0.01
Slavic (0)	3	0.01
Slovak (42)	66	0.26
Slovene (10)	13	0.05
Soviet Union (0)	0	<0.01
Swedish (58)	207	0.82
Swiss (501)	719	2.85
Turkish (0)	0	<0.01
Ukrainian (29)	99	0.39
Welsh (59)	266	1.05
West Indian, ex. Hispanic (52)	52	0.21
Bahamian (0)	0	<0.01
Barbadian (0)	0	<0.01
Belizean (0)	0	<0.01
Bermudan (0)	0	<0.01
British West Indian (0)	0	<0.01
Dutch West Indian (0)	0	<0.01
Haitian (0)	0	<0.01
Jamaican (8)	8	0.03
Trinidadian/Tobagonian (0)	0	<0.01
U.S. Virgin Islander (0)	0	<0.01
West Indian (44)	44	0.17
Other West Indian (0)	0	<0.01
Yugoslavian (10)	21	0.08

Hispanic Origin	Population	%
Hispanic or Latino (of any race)	421	1.66
Central American, ex. Mexican	15	0.06
Costa Rican	0	<0.01
Guatemalan	7	0.03
Honduran	5	0.02
Nicaraguan	0	<0.01
Panamanian	3	0.01
Salvadoran	0	<0.01
Other Central American	0	<0.01
Cuban	10	0.04
Dominican Republic	7	0.03
Mexican	152	0.60
Puerto Rican	159	0.63
South American	23	0.09
Argentinean	1	<0.01
Bolivian	0	<0.01
Chilean	3	0.01
Colombian	8	0.03
Ecuadorian	7	0.03
Paraguayan	3	0.01
Peruvian	1	<0.01
Uruguayan	0	<0.01
Venezuelan	0	<0.01
Other South American	0	<0.01
Other Hispanic or Latino	55	0.22

Race*	Population	%
African-American/Black (203)	316	1.25
Not Hispanic (196)	295	1.16
Hispanic (7)	21	0.08
American Indian/Alaska Native (38)	144	0.57
Not Hispanic (35)	127	0.50
Hispanic (3)	17	0.07
Alaska Athabascan (Ala. Nat.) (0)	0	<0.01
Aleut (Alaska Native) (0)	0	<0.01
Apache (0)	1	<0.01
Arapaho (0)	1	<0.01
Blackfeet (0)	6	0.02
Canadian/French Am. Ind. (1)	2	0.01
Central American Ind. (0)	0	<0.01
Cherokee (1)	14	0.06
Cheyenne (0)	0	<0.01
Chickasaw (0)	0	<0.01
Chippewa (0)	4	0.02
Choctaw (0)	0	<0.01
Colville (0)	0	<0.01

Race* (cont.)	Population	%
Comanche (0)	0	<0.01
Cree (0)	0	<0.01
Creek (0)	0	<0.01
Crow (0)	0	<0.01
Delaware (0)	0	<0.01
Hopi (0)	0	<0.01
Houma (0)	0	<0.01
Inupiat (Alaska Native) (0)	0	<0.01
Iroquois (8)	32	0.13
Kiowa (0)	0	<0.01
Lumbee (0)	0	<0.01
Menominee (0)	0	<0.01
Mexican American Ind. (0)	0	<0.01
Navajo (0)	0	<0.01
Osage (0)	0	<0.01
Ottawa (0)	0	<0.01
Paiute (0)	0	<0.01
Pima (0)	1	<0.01
Potawatomi (0)	0	<0.01
Pueblo (1)	1	<0.01
Puget Sound Salish (0)	0	<0.01
Seminole (0)	0	<0.01
Shoshone (0)	0	<0.01
Sioux (1)	5	0.02
South American Ind. (1)	4	0.02
Spanish American Ind. (0)	0	<0.01
Tlingit-Haida (Alaska Native) (0)	0	<0.01
Tohono O'Odham (0)	0	<0.01
Tsimshian (Alaska Native) (0)	0	<0.01
Ute (0)	0	<0.01
Yakama (0)	0	<0.01
Yaqui (0)	1	<0.01
Yuman (0)	0	<0.01
Yup'ik (Alaska Native) (0)	0	<0.01
Asian (97)	124	0.49
Not Hispanic (96)	120	0.47
Hispanic (1)	4	0.02
Bangladeshi (0)	0	<0.01
Bhutanese (0)	0	<0.01
Burmese (0)	0	<0.01
Cambodian (3)	3	0.01
Chinese, ex. Taiwanese (30)	42	0.17
Filipino (8)	10	0.04
Hmong (0)	0	<0.01
Indian (11)	16	0.06
Indonesian (0)	0	<0.01
Japanese (9)	26	0.10
Korean (22)	25	0.10
Laotian (4)	6	0.02
Malaysian (0)	0	<0.01
Nepalese (0)	0	<0.01
Pakistani (0)	0	<0.01
Sri Lankan (0)	0	<0.01
Taiwanese (0)	0	<0.01
Thai (0)	0	<0.01
Vietnamese (1)	2	0.01
Hawaii Native/Pacific Islander (4)	16	0.06
Not Hispanic (1)	11	0.04
Hispanic (3)	5	0.02
Fijian (0)	0	<0.01
Guamanian/Chamorro (1)	7	0.03
Marshallese (0)	0	<0.01
Native Hawaiian (0)	3	0.01
Samoan (3)	3	0.01
Tongan (0)	0	<0.01
White (24,647)	24,903	98.24
Not Hispanic (24,371)	24,577	96.96
Hispanic (276)	326	1.29

Notes: † The Census 2010 population figure is used to calculate the percentages in the Hispanic Origin and Race categories. Ancestry percentages are based on the 2006-2010 American Community Survey population (not shown); ‡ Numbers in parentheses indicate the number of people reporting a single ancestry; * Numbers in parentheses indicate the number of persons reporting this race alone, not in combination with any other race; Please refer to the Explanation of Data for more information.

Place Profiles

Albany

Place Type: City
County: Albany
Population: 97,856

Ancestry	Population	%
Afghan (0)	0	<0.01
African, Sub-Saharan (1,142)	1,533	1.57
African (656)	975	1.00
Cape Verdean (0)	13	0.01
Ethiopian (21)	21	0.02
Ghanaian (143)	143	0.15
Kenyan (101)	101	0.10
Liberian (0)	0	<0.01
Nigerian (132)	191	0.19
Senegalese (0)	0	<0.01
Sierra Leonean (0)	0	<0.01
Somalian (0)	0	<0.01
South African (0)	0	<0.01
Sudanese (25)	25	0.03
Ugandan (0)	0	<0.01
Zimbabwean (0)	0	<0.01
Other Sub-Saharan African (64)	64	0.07
Albanian (318)	384	0.39
Alsatian (19)	51	0.05
American (1,531)	1,531	1.56
Arab (181)	525	0.54
Arab (105)	116	0.12
Egyptian (41)	124	0.13
Iraqi (0)	0	<0.01
Jordanian (0)	0	<0.01
Lebanese (23)	138	0.14
Moroccan (0)	0	<0.01
Palestinian (12)	25	0.03
Syrian (0)	104	0.11
Other Arab (0)	18	0.02
Armenian (26)	75	0.08
Assyrian/Chaldean/Syriac (0)	0	<0.01
Australian (30)	88	0.09
Austrian (31)	247	0.25
Basque (0)	0	<0.01
Belgian (53)	78	0.08
Brazilian (45)	45	0.05
British (132)	255	0.26
Bulgarian (0)	9	0.01
Cajun (0)	0	<0.01
Canadian (80)	128	0.13
Carpatho Rusyn (12)	12	0.01
Celtic (0)	0	<0.01
Croatian (32)	54	0.06
Cypriot (0)	0	<0.01
Czech (153)	392	0.40
Czechoslovakian (11)	35	0.04
Danish (89)	303	0.31
Dutch (321)	1,664	1.70
Eastern European (220)	253	0.26
English (1,100)	5,315	5.43
Estonian (0)	0	<0.01
European (1,163)	1,362	1.39
Finnish (0)	35	0.04
French, ex. Basque (458)	3,690	3.77
French Canadian (329)	1,061	1.08
German (1,888)	10,150	10.36
German Russian (0)	0	<0.01
Greek (368)	755	0.77
Guyanese (466)	483	0.49
Hungarian (183)	405	0.41
Icelander (0)	0	<0.01
Iranian (50)	60	0.06
Irish (5,251)	17,818	18.19
Israeli (0)	0	<0.01
Italian (4,932)	12,860	13.13
Latvian (15)	24	0.02
Lithuanian (38)	217	0.22
Luxemburger (9)	9	0.01
Macedonian (0)	0	<0.01

Ancestry	Population	%
Maltese (11)	24	0.02
New Zealander (0)	0	<0.01
Northern European (56)	160	0.16
Norwegian (146)	406	0.41
Pennsylvania German (0)	12	0.01
Polish (1,282)	4,476	4.57
Portuguese (116)	266	0.27
Romanian (0)	182	0.19
Russian (483)	1,487	1.52
Scandinavian (31)	313	0.32
Scotch-Irish (229)	842	0.86
Scottish (311)	1,162	1.19
Serbian (19)	19	0.02
Slavic (28)	94	0.10
Slovak (110)	351	0.36
Slovene (12)	70	0.07
Soviet Union (0)	0	<0.01
Swedish (57)	444	0.45
Swiss (15)	125	0.13
Turkish (14)	39	0.04
Ukrainian (85)	496	0.51
Welsh (103)	597	0.61
West Indian, ex. Hispanic (2,407)	3,298	3.37
Bahamian (0)	0	<0.01
Barbadian (14)	29	0.03
Belizean (0)	0	<0.01
Bermudan (36)	36	0.04
British West Indian (133)	210	0.21
Dutch West Indian (39)	79	0.08
Haitian (421)	446	0.46
Jamaican (1,228)	1,636	1.67
Trinidadian/Tobagonian (193)	219	0.22
U.S. Virgin Islander (0)	0	<0.01
West Indian (276)	576	0.59
Other West Indian (67)	67	0.07
Yugoslavian (36)	48	0.05

Hispanic Origin	Population	%
Hispanic or Latino (of any race)	8,396	8.58
Central American, ex. Mexican	343	0.35
Costa Rican	35	0.04
Guatemalan	54	0.06
Honduran	70	0.07
Nicaraguan	28	0.03
Panamanian	81	0.08
Salvadoran	65	0.07
Other Central American	10	0.01
Cuban	298	0.30
Dominican Republic	1,095	1.12
Mexican	616	0.63
Puerto Rican	4,654	4.76
South American	626	0.64
Argentinean	38	0.04
Bolivian	5	0.01
Chilean	38	0.04
Colombian	196	0.20
Ecuadorian	184	0.19
Paraguayan	6	0.01
Peruvian	89	0.09
Uruguayan	15	0.02
Venezuelan	39	0.04
Other South American	16	0.02
Other Hispanic or Latino	764	0.78

Race*	Population	%
African-American/Black (30,110)	32,569	33.28
Not Hispanic (28,479)	30,376	31.04
Hispanic (1,631)	2,193	2.24
American Indian/Alaska Native (295)	1,120	1.14
Not Hispanic (191)	856	0.87
Hispanic (104)	264	0.27
Alaska Athabascan (Ala. Nat.) (0)	1	<0.01
Aleut (Alaska Native) (0)	0	<0.01
Apache (0)	5	0.01
Arapaho (0)	0	<0.01
Blackfeet (6)	57	0.06

Race*	Population	%
Canadian/French Am. Ind. (0)	5	0.01
Central American Ind. (5)	10	0.01
Cherokee (23)	205	0.21
Cheyenne (0)	0	<0.01
Chickasaw (2)	2	<0.01
Chippewa (0)	3	<0.01
Choctaw (2)	8	0.01
Colville (0)	0	<0.01
Comanche (0)	0	<0.01
Cree (1)	4	<0.01
Creek (0)	6	0.01
Crow (0)	0	<0.01
Delaware (2)	11	0.01
Hopi (0)	0	<0.01
Houma (0)	0	<0.01
Inupiat (Alaska Native) (1)	1	<0.01
Iroquois (26)	102	0.10
Kiowa (0)	0	<0.01
Lumbee (0)	0	<0.01
Menominee (0)	0	<0.01
Mexican American Ind. (10)	13	0.01
Navajo (1)	2	<0.01
Osage (0)	0	<0.01
Ottawa (0)	1	<0.01
Paiute (0)	0	<0.01
Pima (0)	0	<0.01
Potawatomi (1)	2	<0.01
Pueblo (1)	1	<0.01
Puget Sound Salish (0)	0	<0.01
Seminole (1)	7	0.01
Shoshone (0)	1	<0.01
Sioux (5)	11	0.01
South American Ind. (24)	49	0.05
Spanish American Ind. (6)	10	0.01
Tlingit-Haida (Alaska Native) (1)	3	<0.01
Tohono O'Odham (0)	0	<0.01
Tsimshian (Alaska Native) (0)	0	<0.01
Ute (0)	0	<0.01
Yakama (1)	1	<0.01
Yaqui (0)	0	<0.01
Yuman (0)	0	<0.01
Yup'ik (Alaska Native) (1)	1	<0.01
Asian (4,890)	5,588	5.71
Not Hispanic (4,850)	5,482	5.60
Hispanic (40)	106	0.11
Bangladeshi (148)	171	0.17
Bhutanese (62)	62	0.06
Burmese (294)	322	0.33
Cambodian (8)	12	0.01
Chinese, ex. Taiwanese (1,219)	1,349	1.38
Filipino (645)	746	0.76
Hmong (0)	0	<0.01
Indian (1,009)	1,198	1.22
Indonesian (10)	12	0.01
Japanese (109)	200	0.20
Korean (368)	426	0.44
Laotian (0)	3	<0.01
Malaysian (2)	8	0.01
Nepalese (48)	55	0.06
Pakistani (425)	483	0.49
Sri Lankan (13)	13	0.01
Taiwanese (61)	69	0.07
Thai (35)	46	0.05
Vietnamese (197)	231	0.24
Hawaii Native/Pacific Islander (55)	180	0.18
Not Hispanic (47)	158	0.16
Hispanic (8)	22	0.02
Fijian (0)	1	<0.01
Guamanian/Chamorro (7)	15	0.02
Marshallese (0)	0	<0.01
Native Hawaiian (8)	38	0.04
Samoan (9)	15	0.02
Tongan (0)	1	<0.01
White (55,783)	58,605	59.89
Not Hispanic (52,857)	55,044	56.25
Hispanic (2,926)	3,561	3.64

*Notes: † The Census 2010 population figure is used to calculate the percentages in the Hispanic Origin and Race categories. Ancestry percentages are based on the 2006-2010 American Community Survey population (not shown); ‡ Numbers in parentheses indicate the number of people reporting a single ancestry; * Numbers in parentheses indicate the number of persons reporting this race alone, not in combination with any other race; Please refer to the Explanation of Data for more information.*

Amherst

Place Type: Town
County: Erie
Population: 122,366

Ancestry	Population	%
Afghan (144)	144	0.12
African, Sub-Saharan (897)	1,095	0.91
African (481)	625	0.52
Cape Verdean (0)	0	<0.01
Ethiopian (71)	71	0.06
Ghanaian (15)	15	0.01
Kenyan (12)	12	0.01
Liberian (0)	0	<0.01
Nigerian (167)	167	0.14
Senegalese (0)	0	<0.01
Sierra Leonean (0)	0	<0.01
Somalian (0)	0	<0.01
South African (22)	35	0.03
Sudanese (0)	0	<0.01
Ugandan (0)	0	<0.01
Zimbabwean (0)	0	<0.01
Other Sub-Saharan African (129)	170	0.14
Albanian (26)	114	0.09
Alsatian (9)	32	0.03
American (3,077)	3,077	2.54
Arab (818)	1,530	1.27
Arab (46)	90	0.07
Egyptian (8)	8	0.01
Iraqi (0)	0	<0.01
Jordanian (84)	84	0.07
Lebanese (342)	985	0.81
Moroccan (13)	13	0.01
Palestinian (18)	18	0.01
Syrian (48)	62	0.05
Other Arab (259)	270	0.22
Armenian (157)	203	0.17
Assyrian/Chaldean/Syriac (0)	0	<0.01
Australian (29)	47	0.04
Austrian (367)	1,014	0.84
Basque (0)	0	<0.01
Belgian (11)	38	0.03
Brazilian (223)	223	0.18
British (194)	438	0.36
Bulgarian (68)	98	0.08
Cajun (0)	0	<0.01
Canadian (282)	589	0.49
Carpatho Rusyn (0)	0	<0.01
Celtic (10)	10	0.01
Croatian (114)	393	0.32
Cypriot (0)	0	<0.01
Czech (105)	255	0.21
Czechoslovakian (46)	82	0.07
Danish (55)	199	0.16
Dutch (148)	1,690	1.40
Eastern European (507)	575	0.48
English (3,188)	11,840	9.79
Estonian (10)	25	0.02
European (915)	981	0.81
Finnish (35)	196	0.16
French, ex. Basque (438)	3,549	2.93
French Canadian (283)	983	0.81
German (8,678)	30,579	25.28
German Russian (0)	0	<0.01
Greek (323)	802	0.66
Guyanese (43)	43	0.04
Hungarian (420)	1,194	0.99
Icelander (0)	0	<0.01
Iranian (174)	188	0.16
Irish (5,285)	22,106	18.28
Israeli (75)	122	0.10
Italian (11,256)	23,615	19.53
Latvian (26)	64	0.05
Lithuanian (82)	182	0.15
Luxemburger (0)	0	<0.01
Macedonian (0)	14	0.01
Maltese (0)	0	<0.01
New Zealander (0)	26	0.02
Northern European (29)	101	0.08

Ancestry	Population	%
Norwegian (114)	400	0.33
Pennsylvania German (0)	43	0.04
Polish (6,777)	17,104	14.14
Portuguese (90)	144	0.12
Romanian (169)	324	0.27
Russian (1,684)	3,468	2.87
Scandinavian (11)	116	0.10
Scotch-Irish (504)	1,527	1.26
Scottish (333)	1,736	1.44
Serbian (81)	158	0.13
Slavic (25)	153	0.13
Slovak (40)	141	0.12
Slovene (40)	53	0.04
Soviet Union (0)	0	<0.01
Swedish (139)	902	0.75
Swiss (67)	222	0.18
Turkish (138)	164	0.14
Ukrainian (545)	1,074	0.89
Welsh (218)	798	0.66
West Indian, ex. Hispanic (282)	440	0.36
Bahamian (0)	0	<0.01
Barbadian (12)	12	0.01
Belizean (0)	0	<0.01
Bermudan (0)	0	<0.01
British West Indian (13)	13	0.01
Dutch West Indian (0)	0	<0.01
Haitian (45)	45	0.04
Jamaican (169)	226	0.19
Trinidadian/Tobagonian (5)	19	0.02
U.S. Virgin Islander (0)	0	<0.01
West Indian (38)	125	0.10
Other West Indian (0)	0	<0.01
Yugoslavian (52)	52	0.04

Hispanic Origin	Population	%
Hispanic or Latino (of any race)	2,870	2.35
Central American, ex. Mexican	189	0.15
Costa Rican	20	0.02
Guatemalan	49	0.04
Honduran	23	0.02
Nicaraguan	8	0.01
Panamanian	39	0.03
Salvadoran	49	0.04
Other Central American	1	<0.01
Cuban	120	0.10
Dominican Republic	194	0.16
Mexican	478	0.39
Puerto Rican	1,108	0.91
South American	436	0.36
Argentinean	57	0.05
Bolivian	14	0.01
Chilean	40	0.03
Colombian	163	0.13
Ecuadorian	63	0.05
Paraguayan	5	<0.01
Peruvian	52	0.04
Uruguayan	7	0.01
Venezuelan	33	0.03
Other South American	2	<0.01
Other Hispanic or Latino	345	0.28

Race*	Population	%
African-American/Black (7,009)	7,946	6.49
Not Hispanic (6,765)	7,563	6.18
Hispanic (244)	383	0.31
American Indian/Alaska Native (220)	616	0.50
Not Hispanic (196)	531	0.43
Hispanic (24)	85	0.07
Alaska Athabascan (Ala. Nat.) (0)	1	<0.01
Aleut (Alaska Native) (0)	0	<0.01
Apache (0)	0	<0.01
Arapaho (0)	0	<0.01
Blackfeet (2)	14	0.01
Canadian/French Am. Ind. (9)	11	0.01
Central American Ind. (0)	1	<0.01
Cherokee (7)	67	0.05
Cheyenne (0)	0	<0.01
Chickasaw (0)	0	<0.01
Chippewa (1)	7	0.01

Race*	Population	%
Choctaw (1)	3	<0.01
Colville (0)	0	<0.01
Comanche (0)	0	<0.01
Cree (0)	0	<0.01
Creek (0)	2	<0.01
Crow (2)	2	<0.01
Delaware (1)	2	<0.01
Hopi (0)	0	<0.01
Houma (0)	0	<0.01
Inupiat (Alaska Native) (0)	3	<0.01
Iroquois (84)	155	0.13
Kiowa (0)	0	<0.01
Lumbee (1)	1	<0.01
Menominee (0)	0	<0.01
Mexican American Ind. (11)	22	0.02
Navajo (0)	1	<0.01
Osage (1)	1	<0.01
Ottawa (0)	0	<0.01
Paiute (0)	0	<0.01
Pima (0)	0	<0.01
Potawatomi (0)	0	<0.01
Pueblo (2)	5	<0.01
Puget Sound Salish (0)	0	<0.01
Seminole (0)	10	0.01
Shoshone (0)	0	<0.01
Sioux (0)	1	<0.01
South American Ind. (4)	13	0.01
Spanish American Ind. (0)	0	<0.01
Tlingit-Haida (Alaska Native) (0)	1	<0.01
Tohono O'Odham (1)	1	<0.01
Tsimshian (Alaska Native) (0)	0	<0.01
Ute (0)	0	<0.01
Yakama (0)	0	<0.01
Yaqui (0)	0	<0.01
Yuman (0)	0	<0.01
Yup'ik (Alaska Native) (0)	1	<0.01
Asian (9,675)	10,683	8.73
Not Hispanic (9,643)	10,590	8.65
Hispanic (32)	93	0.08
Bangladeshi (42)	45	0.04
Bhutanese (0)	0	<0.01
Burmese (28)	32	0.03
Cambodian (16)	17	0.01
Chinese, ex. Taiwanese (2,925)	3,146	2.57
Filipino (273)	396	0.32
Hmong (0)	0	<0.01
Indian (3,263)	3,491	2.85
Indonesian (26)	42	0.03
Japanese (215)	294	0.24
Korean (1,377)	1,493	1.22
Laotian (19)	25	0.02
Malaysian (41)	47	0.04
Nepalese (12)	12	0.01
Pakistani (515)	592	0.48
Sri Lankan (122)	130	0.11
Taiwanese (180)	202	0.17
Thai (36)	52	0.04
Vietnamese (307)	362	0.30
Hawaii Native/Pacific Islander (26)	94	0.08
Not Hispanic (26)	86	0.07
Hispanic (0)	8	0.01
Fijian (3)	3	<0.01
Guamanian/Chamorro (8)	10	0.01
Marshallese (1)	1	<0.01
Native Hawaiian (9)	24	0.02
Samoan (3)	12	0.01
Tongan (0)	0	<0.01
White (102,558)	104,439	85.35
Not Hispanic (100,778)	102,429	83.71
Hispanic (1,780)	2,010	1.64

Notes: † The Census 2010 population figure is used to calculate the percentages in the Hispanic Origin and Race categories. Ancestry percentages are based on the 2006-2010 American Community Survey population (not shown); ‡ Numbers in parentheses indicate the number of people reporting a single ancestry; * Numbers in parentheses indicate the number of persons reporting this race alone, not in combination with any other race; Please refer to the Explanation of Data for more information.

Babylon

Place Type: Town
County: Suffolk
Population: 213,603

Ancestry	Population	%
Afghan (219)	219	0.10
African, Sub-Saharan (1,803)	2,217	1.04
African (734)	1,071	0.50
Cape Verdean (0)	9	<0.01
Ethiopian (0)	11	0.01
Ghanaian (64)	64	0.03
Kenyan (0)	0	<0.01
Liberian (300)	309	0.14
Nigerian (670)	707	0.33
Senegalese (0)	0	<0.01
Sierra Leonean (0)	0	<0.01
Somalian (0)	0	<0.01
South African (0)	0	<0.01
Sudanese (0)	0	<0.01
Ugandan (0)	0	<0.01
Zimbabwean (0)	0	<0.01
Other Sub-Saharan African (35)	46	0.02
Albanian (139)	210	0.10
Alsatian (0)	0	<0.01
American (3,343)	3,343	1.56
Arab (595)	842	0.39
Arab (236)	259	0.12
Egyptian (30)	79	0.04
Iraqi (0)	0	<0.01
Jordanian (0)	0	<0.01
Lebanese (20)	79	0.04
Moroccan (142)	209	0.10
Palestinian (114)	114	0.05
Syrian (0)	49	0.02
Other Arab (53)	53	0.02
Armenian (69)	188	0.09
Assyrian/Chaldean/Syriac (0)	0	<0.01
Australian (0)	20	0.01
Austrian (149)	808	0.38
Basque (15)	15	0.01
Belgian (22)	41	0.02
Brazilian (30)	166	0.08
British (149)	348	0.16
Bulgarian (8)	20	0.01
Cajun (0)	0	<0.01
Canadian (80)	581	0.27
Carpatho Rusyn (0)	0	<0.01
Celtic (33)	64	0.03
Croatian (144)	207	0.10
Cypriot (0)	0	<0.01
Czech (61)	578	0.27
Czechoslovakian (296)	438	0.21
Danish (107)	384	0.18
Dutch (218)	1,653	0.77
Eastern European (253)	270	0.13
English (1,368)	8,596	4.02
Estonian (10)	33	0.02
European (342)	416	0.19
Finnish (26)	190	0.09
French, ex. Basque (203)	2,679	1.25
French Canadian (445)	939	0.44
German (5,375)	31,578	14.78
German Russian (0)	0	<0.01
Greek (964)	2,182	1.02
Guyanese (602)	747	0.35
Hungarian (188)	989	0.46
Icelander (22)	22	0.01
Iranian (53)	69	0.03
Irish (10,079)	42,364	19.83
Israeli (28)	172	0.08
Italian (32,274)	61,852	28.95
Latvian (11)	35	0.02
Lithuanian (287)	642	0.30
Luxemburger (0)	0	<0.01
Macedonian (11)	33	0.02
Maltese (61)	378	0.18
New Zealander (0)	0	<0.01
Northern European (45)	61	0.03

Ancestry	Population	%
Norwegian (303)	1,701	0.80
Pennsylvania German (18)	18	0.01
Polish (5,564)	12,444	5.82
Portuguese (168)	676	0.32
Romanian (230)	316	0.15
Russian (845)	3,774	1.77
Scandinavian (17)	48	0.02
Scotch-Irish (570)	1,863	0.87
Scottish (225)	1,548	0.72
Serbian (16)	19	0.01
Slavic (6)	64	0.03
Slovak (134)	367	0.17
Slovene (14)	14	0.01
Soviet Union (0)	0	<0.01
Swedish (205)	1,400	0.66
Swiss (57)	361	0.17
Turkish (826)	939	0.44
Ukrainian (329)	905	0.42
Welsh (103)	423	0.20
West Indian, ex. Hispanic (9,910)	11,187	5.24
Bahamian (35)	88	0.04
Barbadian (105)	183	0.09
Belizean (0)	12	0.01
Bermudan (0)	0	<0.01
British West Indian (64)	119	0.06
Dutch West Indian (6)	6	<0.01
Haitian (3,585)	3,789	1.77
Jamaican (4,141)	4,758	2.23
Trinidadian/Tobagonian (842)	854	0.40
U.S. Virgin Islander (0)	0	<0.01
West Indian (1,132)	1,378	0.64
Other West Indian (0)	0	<0.01
Yugoslavian (14)	156	0.07

Hispanic Origin	Population	%
Hispanic or Latino (of any race)	35,793	16.76
Central American, ex. Mexican	11,096	5.19
Costa Rican	146	0.07
Guatemalan	884	0.41
Honduran	1,756	0.82
Nicaraguan	112	0.05
Panamanian	305	0.14
Salvadoran	7,805	3.65
Other Central American	88	0.04
Cuban	550	0.26
Dominican Republic	6,543	3.06
Mexican	1,145	0.54
Puerto Rican	7,562	3.54
South American	5,576	2.61
Argentinean	336	0.16
Bolivian	78	0.04
Chilean	226	0.11
Colombian	2,036	0.95
Ecuadorian	1,348	0.63
Paraguayan	37	0.02
Peruvian	1,313	0.61
Uruguayan	64	0.03
Venezuelan	104	0.05
Other South American	34	0.02
Other Hispanic or Latino	3,321	1.55

Race*	Population	%
African-American/Black (34,881)	37,421	17.52
Not Hispanic (33,147)	34,993	16.38
Hispanic (1,734)	2,428	1.14
American Indian/Alaska Native (719)	1,894	0.89
Not Hispanic (447)	1,351	0.63
Hispanic (272)	543	0.25
Alaska Athabascan (Ala. Nat.) (0)	0	<0.01
Aleut (Alaska Native) (2)	2	<0.01
Apache (1)	11	0.01
Arapaho (0)	0	<0.01
Blackfeet (4)	44	0.02
Canadian/French Am. Ind. (7)	10	<0.01
Central American Ind. (14)	22	0.01
Cherokee (51)	250	0.12
Cheyenne (1)	1	<0.01
Chickasaw (0)	0	<0.01
Chippewa (6)	7	<0.01

Race*	Population	%
Choctaw (1)	5	<0.01
Colville (0)	0	<0.01
Comanche (1)	2	<0.01
Cree (1)	2	<0.01
Creek (0)	13	0.01
Crow (0)	1	<0.01
Delaware (2)	2	<0.01
Hopi (3)	5	<0.01
Houma (0)	0	<0.01
Inupiat (Alaska Native) (0)	1	<0.01
Iroquois (34)	65	0.03
Kiowa (0)	0	<0.01
Lumbee (3)	12	0.01
Menominee (0)	0	<0.01
Mexican American Ind. (15)	25	0.01
Navajo (1)	6	<0.01
Osage (0)	0	<0.01
Ottawa (0)	0	<0.01
Paiute (0)	0	<0.01
Pima (0)	0	<0.01
Potawatomi (0)	0	<0.01
Pueblo (9)	9	<0.01
Puget Sound Salish (0)	0	<0.01
Seminole (2)	13	0.01
Shoshone (0)	0	<0.01
Sioux (8)	16	0.01
South American Ind. (47)	82	0.04
Spanish American Ind. (8)	17	0.01
Tlingit-Haida (Alaska Native) (0)	1	<0.01
Tohono O'Odham (0)	1	<0.01
Tsimshian (Alaska Native) (0)	0	<0.01
Ute (0)	0	<0.01
Yakama (0)	0	<0.01
Yaqui (0)	0	<0.01
Yuman (0)	0	<0.01
Yup'ik (Alaska Native) (0)	0	<0.01
Asian (6,524)	7,919	3.71
Not Hispanic (6,411)	7,577	3.55
Hispanic (113)	342	0.16
Bangladeshi (271)	341	0.16
Bhutanese (0)	0	<0.01
Burmese (4)	7	<0.01
Cambodian (3)	5	<0.01
Chinese, ex. Taiwanese (1,108)	1,357	0.64
Filipino (765)	1,046	0.49
Hmong (0)	0	<0.01
Indian (2,582)	2,940	1.38
Indonesian (16)	22	0.01
Japanese (88)	186	0.09
Korean (388)	477	0.22
Laotian (6)	9	<0.01
Malaysian (2)	3	<0.01
Nepalese (4)	4	<0.01
Pakistani (678)	739	0.35
Sri Lankan (25)	32	0.01
Taiwanese (24)	26	0.01
Thai (41)	67	0.03
Vietnamese (257)	297	0.14
Hawaii Native/Pacific Islander (51)	272	0.13
Not Hispanic (31)	153	0.07
Hispanic (20)	119	0.06
Fijian (0)	0	<0.01
Guamanian/Chamorro (11)	22	0.01
Marshallese (0)	0	<0.01
Native Hawaiian (13)	45	0.02
Samoan (3)	10	<0.01
Tongan (0)	0	<0.01
White (153,067)	157,336	73.66
Not Hispanic (133,961)	136,259	63.79
Hispanic (19,106)	21,077	9.87

Notes: † The Census 2010 population figure is used to calculate the percentages in the Hispanic Origin and Race categories. Ancestry percentages are based on the 2006-2010 American Community Survey population (not shown); ‡ Numbers in parentheses indicate the number of people reporting a single ancestry; * Numbers in parentheses indicate the number of persons reporting this race alone, not in combination with any other race; Please refer to the Explanation of Data for more information.

Brentwood

Place Type: CDP
County: Suffolk
Population: 60,664

Ancestry	Population	%
Afghan (50)	68	0.12
African, Sub-Saharan (301)	336	0.61
African (86)	106	0.19
Cape Verdean (0)	0	<0.01
Ethiopian (0)	0	<0.01
Ghanaian (45)	45	0.08
Kenyan (0)	0	<0.01
Liberian (0)	0	<0.01
Nigerian (90)	105	0.19
Senegalese (0)	0	<0.01
Sierra Leonean (0)	0	<0.01
Somalian (0)	0	<0.01
South African (0)	0	<0.01
Sudanese (0)	0	<0.01
Ugandan (0)	0	<0.01
Zimbabwean (0)	0	<0.01
Other Sub-Saharan African (80)	80	0.15
Albanian (0)	0	<0.01
Alsatian (0)	0	<0.01
American (588)	588	1.07
Arab (82)	92	0.17
Arab (25)	25	0.05
Egyptian (20)	20	0.04
Iraqi (0)	0	<0.01
Jordanian (0)	0	<0.01
Lebanese (0)	10	0.02
Moroccan (0)	0	<0.01
Palestinian (0)	0	<0.01
Syrian (0)	0	<0.01
Other Arab (37)	37	0.07
Armenian (0)	0	<0.01
Assyrian/Chaldean/Syriac (0)	0	<0.01
Australian (0)	8	0.01
Austrian (19)	80	0.15
Basque (0)	0	<0.01
Belgian (0)	9	0.02
Brazilian (418)	418	0.76
British (46)	78	0.14
Bulgarian (0)	0	<0.01
Cajun (0)	0	<0.01
Canadian (0)	8	0.01
Carpatho Rusyn (0)	0	<0.01
Celtic (0)	0	<0.01
Croatian (0)	0	<0.01
Cypriot (0)	0	<0.01
Czech (0)	38	0.07
Czechoslovakian (8)	25	0.05
Danish (0)	0	<0.01
Dutch (0)	96	0.18
Eastern European (0)	0	<0.01
English (338)	850	1.55
Estonian (0)	17	0.03
European (32)	43	0.08
Finnish (8)	11	0.02
French, ex. Basque (57)	181	0.33
French Canadian (10)	48	0.09
German (310)	1,994	3.64
German Russian (0)	0	<0.01
Greek (37)	59	0.11
Guyanese (126)	138	0.25
Hungarian (16)	42	0.08
Icelander (0)	0	<0.01
Iranian (0)	0	<0.01
Irish (934)	2,578	4.70
Israeli (0)	0	<0.01
Italian (1,517)	3,236	5.90
Latvian (0)	0	<0.01
Lithuanian (9)	25	0.05
Luxemburger (0)	0	<0.01
Macedonian (0)	0	<0.01
Maltese (17)	17	0.03
New Zealander (0)	0	<0.01
Northern European (0)	0	<0.01

Ancestry (cont.)	Population	%
Norwegian (24)	72	0.13
Pennsylvania German (0)	0	<0.01
Polish (164)	623	1.14
Portuguese (504)	524	0.96
Romanian (0)	0	<0.01
Russian (61)	180	0.33
Scandinavian (7)	29	0.05
Scotch-Irish (39)	161	0.29
Scottish (20)	92	0.17
Serbian (0)	10	0.02
Slavic (0)	0	<0.01
Slovak (8)	8	0.01
Slovene (0)	0	<0.01
Soviet Union (0)	0	<0.01
Swedish (39)	210	0.38
Swiss (0)	14	0.03
Turkish (0)	5	0.01
Ukrainian (0)	10	0.02
Welsh (0)	0	<0.01
West Indian, ex. Hispanic (3,143)	3,472	6.33
Bahamian (0)	0	<0.01
Barbadian (5)	5	0.01
Belizean (0)	0	<0.01
Bermudan (0)	0	<0.01
British West Indian (37)	58	0.11
Dutch West Indian (0)	0	<0.01
Haitian (2,072)	2,162	3.94
Jamaican (622)	771	1.41
Trinidadian/Tobagonian (104)	152	0.28
U.S. Virgin Islander (0)	0	<0.01
West Indian (303)	324	0.59
Other West Indian (0)	0	<0.01
Yugoslavian (0)	10	0.02

Hispanic Origin	Population	%
Hispanic or Latino (of any race)	41,529	68.46
Central American, ex. Mexican	19,957	32.90
Costa Rican	85	0.14
Guatemalan	1,553	2.56
Honduran	2,062	3.40
Nicaraguan	87	0.14
Panamanian	148	0.24
Salvadoran	15,946	26.29
Other Central American	76	0.13
Cuban	223	0.37
Dominican Republic	4,205	6.93
Mexican	1,193	1.97
Puerto Rican	6,125	10.10
South American	6,350	10.47
Argentinean	203	0.33
Bolivian	79	0.13
Chilean	153	0.25
Colombian	2,083	3.43
Ecuadorian	1,985	3.27
Paraguayan	36	0.06
Peruvian	1,610	2.65
Uruguayan	80	0.13
Venezuelan	113	0.19
Other South American	8	0.01
Other Hispanic or Latino	3,476	5.73

Race*	Population	%
African-American/Black (9,934)	11,026	18.18
Not Hispanic (8,344)	8,888	14.65
Hispanic (1,590)	2,138	3.52
American Indian/Alaska Native (710)	1,135	1.87
Not Hispanic (132)	326	0.54
Hispanic (578)	809	1.33
Alaska Athabascan (Ala. Nat.) (0)	1	<0.01
Aleut (Alaska Native) (0)	0	<0.01
Apache (0)	0	<0.01
Arapaho (0)	0	<0.01
Blackfeet (5)	6	0.01
Canadian/French Am. Ind. (0)	0	<0.01
Central American Ind. (27)	36	0.06
Cherokee (16)	76	0.13
Cheyenne (0)	0	<0.01
Chickasaw (0)	0	<0.01
Chippewa (4)	5	0.01

Race* (cont.)	Population	%
Choctaw (0)	0	<0.01
Colville (0)	0	<0.01
Comanche (0)	7	0.01
Cree (0)	0	<0.01
Creek (0)	0	<0.01
Crow (11)	11	0.02
Delaware (0)	0	<0.01
Hopi (0)	0	<0.01
Houma (0)	0	<0.01
Inupiat (Alaska Native) (0)	0	<0.01
Iroquois (14)	17	0.03
Kiowa (0)	0	<0.01
Lumbee (2)	2	<0.01
Menominee (0)	0	<0.01
Mexican American Ind. (48)	72	0.12
Navajo (3)	4	0.01
Osage (0)	1	<0.01
Ottawa (0)	0	<0.01
Paiute (0)	0	<0.01
Pima (1)	1	<0.01
Potawatomi (0)	0	<0.01
Pueblo (4)	5	0.01
Puget Sound Salish (0)	0	<0.01
Seminole (0)	0	<0.01
Shoshone (0)	0	<0.01
Sioux (2)	2	<0.01
South American Ind. (63)	87	0.14
Spanish American Ind. (41)	52	0.09
Tlingit-Haida (Alaska Native) (3)	3	<0.01
Tohono O'Odham (0)	0	<0.01
Tsimshian (Alaska Native) (0)	0	<0.01
Ute (0)	0	<0.01
Yakama (0)	0	<0.01
Yaqui (1)	1	<0.01
Yuman (0)	0	<0.01
Yup'ik (Alaska Native) (0)	0	<0.01
Asian (1,193)	1,544	2.55
Not Hispanic (1,101)	1,349	2.22
Hispanic (92)	195	0.32
Bangladeshi (33)	37	0.06
Bhutanese (0)	0	<0.01
Burmese (1)	1	<0.01
Cambodian (5)	5	0.01
Chinese, ex. Taiwanese (95)	141	0.23
Filipino (120)	163	0.27
Hmong (0)	0	<0.01
Indian (516)	647	1.07
Indonesian (10)	12	0.02
Japanese (3)	15	0.02
Korean (11)	17	0.03
Laotian (8)	8	0.01
Malaysian (1)	3	<0.01
Nepalese (0)	0	<0.01
Pakistani (246)	268	0.44
Sri Lankan (6)	10	0.02
Taiwanese (4)	4	0.01
Thai (30)	38	0.06
Vietnamese (47)	57	0.09
Hawaii Native/Pacific Islander (29)	134	0.22
Not Hispanic (11)	59	0.10
Hispanic (18)	75	0.12
Fijian (0)	1	<0.01
Guamanian/Chamorro (8)	8	0.01
Marshallese (0)	0	<0.01
Native Hawaiian (8)	17	0.03
Samoan (1)	4	0.01
Tongan (0)	2	<0.01
White (29,344)	31,986	52.73
Not Hispanic (8,554)	8,973	14.79
Hispanic (20,790)	23,013	37.94

Notes: † The Census 2010 population figure is used to calculate the percentages in the Hispanic Origin and Race categories. Ancestry percentages are based on the 2006-2010 American Community Survey population (not shown); ‡ Numbers in parentheses indicate the number of people reporting a single ancestry; * Numbers in parentheses indicate the number of persons reporting this race alone, not in combination with any other race; Please refer to the Explanation of Data for more information.

Bronx

Place Type: Borough
County: Bronx
Population: 1,385,108

Ancestry	Population	%
Afghan (14)	14	<0.01
African, Sub-Saharan (50,131)	55,928	4.10
African (19,345)	22,647	1.66
Cape Verdean (49)	108	0.01
Ethiopian (790)	945	0.07
Ghanaian (13,163)	13,490	0.99
Kenyan (12)	24	<0.01
Liberian (365)	450	0.03
Nigerian (4,896)	5,538	0.41
Senegalese (956)	1,068	0.08
Sierra Leonean (759)	759	0.06
Somalian (11)	35	<0.01
South African (29)	68	<0.01
Sudanese (88)	149	0.01
Ugandan (0)	0	<0.01
Zimbabwean (108)	108	0.01
Other Sub-Saharan African (9,560)	10,539	0.77
Albanian (7,460)	7,835	0.57
Alsatian (0)	0	<0.01
American (16,297)	16,297	1.19
Arab (4,063)	5,008	0.37
Arab (1,481)	1,719	0.13
Egyptian (495)	718	0.05
Iraqi (64)	73	0.01
Jordanian (8)	8	<0.01
Lebanese (229)	347	0.03
Moroccan (526)	667	0.05
Palestinian (28)	28	<0.01
Syrian (44)	192	0.01
Other Arab (1,188)	1,256	0.09
Armenian (128)	237	0.02
Assyrian/Chaldean/Syriac (0)	18	<0.01
Australian (8)	21	<0.01
Austrian (539)	1,868	0.14
Basque (66)	109	0.01
Belgian (52)	131	0.01
Brazilian (276)	397	0.03
British (517)	1,115	0.08
Bulgarian (506)	521	0.04
Cajun (0)	0	<0.01
Canadian (197)	375	0.03
Carpatho Rusyn (0)	12	<0.01
Celtic (1)	13	<0.01
Croatian (91)	219	0.02
Cypriot (12)	38	<0.01
Czech (99)	388	0.03
Czechoslovakian (90)	226	0.02
Danish (17)	385	0.03
Dutch (314)	1,920	0.14
Eastern European (1,425)	1,646	0.12
English (1,821)	7,038	0.52
Estonian (70)	85	0.01
European (1,845)	2,270	0.17
Finnish (89)	291	0.02
French, ex. Basque (909)	4,971	0.36
French Canadian (102)	403	0.03
German (3,729)	16,487	1.21
German Russian (7)	30	<0.01
Greek (2,499)	3,607	0.26
Guyanese (10,276)	11,837	0.87
Hungarian (966)	2,427	0.18
Icelander (6)	6	<0.01
Iranian (187)	248	0.02
Irish (18,712)	38,479	2.82
Israeli (427)	618	0.05
Italian (38,592)	57,527	4.21
Latvian (92)	103	0.01
Lithuanian (167)	547	0.04
Luxemburger (0)	0	<0.01
Macedonian (628)	628	0.05
Maltese (16)	45	<0.01
New Zealander (23)	23	<0.01
Northern European (25)	25	<0.01

Ancestry	Population	%
Norwegian (260)	773	0.06
Pennsylvania German (0)	0	<0.01
Polish (3,429)	7,834	0.57
Portuguese (474)	1,113	0.08
Romanian (691)	1,164	0.09
Russian (4,351)	8,064	0.59
Scandinavian (102)	155	0.01
Scotch-Irish (516)	1,601	0.12
Scottish (388)	1,570	0.11
Serbian (154)	187	0.01
Slavic (15)	90	0.01
Slovak (87)	226	0.02
Slovene (10)	45	<0.01
Soviet Union (12)	12	<0.01
Swedish (119)	549	0.04
Swiss (24)	166	0.01
Turkish (589)	686	0.05
Ukrainian (970)	1,608	0.12
Welsh (101)	530	0.04
West Indian, ex. Hispanic (93,323)	107,527	7.87
Bahamian (165)	208	0.02
Barbadian (1,285)	1,612	0.12
Belizean (1,253)	1,493	0.11
Bermudan (101)	198	0.01
British West Indian (5,959)	7,136	0.52
Dutch West Indian (127)	172	0.01
Haitian (3,891)	4,652	0.34
Jamaican (58,387)	64,222	4.70
Trinidadian/Tobagonian (3,695)	4,811	0.35
U.S. Virgin Islander (737)	952	0.07
West Indian (17,683)	21,941	1.61
Other West Indian (40)	130	0.01
Yugoslavian (1,275)	1,480	0.11

Hispanic Origin	Population	%
Hispanic or Latino (of any race)	741,413	53.53
Central American, ex. Mexican	34,492	2.49
Costa Rican	1,095	0.08
Guatemalan	4,645	0.34
Honduran	17,990	1.30
Nicaraguan	2,342	0.17
Panamanian	2,372	0.17
Salvadoran	5,469	0.39
Other Central American	579	0.04
Cuban	8,785	0.63
Dominican Republic	240,987	17.40
Mexican	71,194	5.14
Puerto Rican	298,921	21.58
South American	35,463	2.56
Argentinean	1,117	0.08
Bolivian	227	0.02
Chilean	646	0.05
Colombian	4,635	0.33
Ecuadorian	23,206	1.68
Paraguayan	223	0.02
Peruvian	3,596	0.26
Uruguayan	148	0.01
Venezuelan	1,296	0.09
Other South American	369	0.03
Other Hispanic or Latino	51,571	3.72

Race*	Population	%
African-American/Black (505,200)	541,622	39.10
Not Hispanic (416,695)	427,134	30.84
Hispanic (88,505)	114,488	8.27
American Indian/Alaska Native (18,260)	32,011	2.31
Not Hispanic (3,460)	7,638	0.55
Hispanic (14,800)	24,373	1.76
Alaska Athabascan (Ala. Nat.) (4)	8	<0.01
Aleut (Alaska Native) (0)	3	<0.01
Apache (30)	99	0.01
Arapaho (2)	3	<0.01
Blackfeet (43)	310	0.02
Canadian/French Am. Ind. (13)	25	<0.01
Central American Ind. (2,274)	4,520	0.33
Cherokee (247)	1,312	0.09
Cheyenne (2)	5	<0.01
Chickasaw (6)	16	<0.01
Chippewa (25)	38	<0.01

Race*	Population	%
Choctaw (4)	43	<0.01
Colville (0)	2	<0.01
Comanche (8)	26	<0.01
Cree (1)	16	<0.01
Creek (7)	47	<0.01
Crow (1)	16	<0.01
Delaware (1)	10	<0.01
Hopi (0)	2	<0.01
Houma (12)	12	<0.01
Inupiat (Alaska Native) (11)	15	<0.01
Iroquois (81)	170	0.01
Kiowa (1)	1	<0.01
Lumbee (3)	6	<0.01
Menominee (1)	3	<0.01
Mexican American Ind. (714)	963	0.07
Navajo (24)	42	<0.01
Osage (2)	3	<0.01
Ottawa (0)	1	<0.01
Paiute (0)	5	<0.01
Pima (0)	1	<0.01
Potawatomi (1)	2	<0.01
Pueblo (177)	382	0.03
Puget Sound Salish (0)	0	<0.01
Seminole (6)	50	<0.01
Shoshone (0)	8	<0.01
Sioux (46)	82	0.01
South American Ind. (1,568)	2,938	0.21
Spanish American Ind. (709)	992	0.07
Tlingit-Haida (Alaska Native) (1)	11	<0.01
Tohono O'Odham (4)	9	<0.01
Tsimshian (Alaska Native) (0)	0	<0.01
Ute (2)	5	<0.01
Yakama (3)	3	<0.01
Yaqui (4)	5	<0.01
Yuman (1)	2	<0.01
Yup'ik (Alaska Native) (1)	6	<0.01
Asian (49,609)	59,085	4.27
Not Hispanic (47,335)	53,458	3.86
Hispanic (2,274)	5,627	0.41
Bangladeshi (7,323)	8,623	0.62
Bhutanese (74)	104	0.01
Burmese (71)	81	0.01
Cambodian (1,055)	1,188	0.09
Chinese, ex. Taiwanese (6,644)	8,112	0.59
Filipino (5,576)	6,456	0.47
Hmong (1)	3	<0.01
Indian (15,865)	20,357	1.47
Indonesian (50)	96	0.01
Japanese (562)	1,027	0.07
Korean (2,840)	3,101	0.22
Laotian (99)	148	0.01
Malaysian (11)	30	<0.01
Nepalese (129)	159	0.01
Pakistani (2,399)	2,728	0.20
Sri Lankan (174)	234	0.02
Taiwanese (98)	130	0.01
Thai (326)	414	0.03
Vietnamese (3,215)	3,526	0.25
Hawaii Native/Pacific Islander (1,288)	6,213	0.45
Not Hispanic (398)	1,854	0.13
Hispanic (890)	4,359	0.31
Fijian (13)	13	<0.01
Guamanian/Chamorro (251)	376	0.03
Marshallese (3)	3	<0.01
Native Hawaiian (371)	669	0.05
Samoan (70)	160	0.01
Tongan (5)	7	<0.01
White (386,497)	427,659	30.88
Not Hispanic (151,209)	158,245	11.42
Hispanic (235,288)	269,414	19.45

*Notes: † The Census 2010 population figure is used to calculate the percentages in the Hispanic Origin and Race categories. Ancestry percentages are based on the 2006-2010 American Community Survey population (not shown); ‡ Numbers in parentheses indicate the number of people reporting a single ancestry; * Numbers in parentheses indicate the number of persons reporting this race alone, not in combination with any other race; Please refer to the Explanation of Data for more information.*

Brookhaven

Place Type: Town
County: Suffolk
Population: 486,040

Ancestry	Population	%
Afghan (0)	0	<0.01
African, Sub-Saharan (2,475)	2,832	0.59
African (2,224)	2,533	0.53
Cape Verdean (0)	0	<0.01
Ethiopian (0)	0	<0.01
Ghanaian (57)	57	0.01
Kenyan (0)	0	<0.01
Liberian (9)	9	<0.01
Nigerian (163)	179	0.04
Senegalese (0)	0	<0.01
Sierra Leonean (0)	0	<0.01
Somalian (0)	0	<0.01
South African (6)	24	<0.01
Sudanese (0)	14	<0.01
Ugandan (0)	0	<0.01
Zimbabwean (0)	0	<0.01
Other Sub-Saharan African (16)	16	<0.01
Albanian (59)	133	0.03
Alsatian (0)	12	<0.01
American (10,016)	10,016	2.09
Arab (797)	1,321	0.28
Arab (164)	191	0.04
Egyptian (317)	435	0.09
Iraqi (0)	0	<0.01
Jordanian (100)	178	0.04
Lebanese (29)	98	0.02
Moroccan (15)	15	<0.01
Palestinian (0)	13	<0.01
Syrian (12)	220	0.05
Other Arab (160)	171	0.04
Armenian (254)	643	0.13
Assyrian/Chaldean/Syriac (0)	0	<0.01
Australian (31)	79	0.02
Austrian (603)	2,867	0.60
Basque (9)	23	<0.01
Belgian (61)	401	0.08
Brazilian (314)	436	0.09
British (605)	1,235	0.26
Bulgarian (101)	128	0.03
Cajun (0)	0	<0.01
Canadian (432)	999	0.21
Carpatho Rusyn (0)	0	<0.01
Celtic (0)	31	0.01
Croatian (317)	588	0.12
Cypriot (51)	51	0.01
Czech (697)	3,121	0.65
Czechoslovakian (344)	917	0.19
Danish (180)	1,229	0.26
Dutch (554)	4,038	0.84
Eastern European (604)	728	0.15
English (4,862)	30,089	6.27
Estonian (14)	102	0.02
European (1,893)	2,098	0.44
Finnish (144)	706	0.15
French, ex. Basque (933)	8,961	1.87
French Canadian (665)	2,478	0.52
German (16,000)	89,711	18.69
German Russian (0)	40	0.01
Greek (2,196)	5,703	1.19
Guyanese (373)	441	0.09
Hungarian (814)	4,390	0.91
Icelander (18)	45	0.01
Iranian (353)	398	0.08
Irish (29,544)	122,200	25.45
Israeli (355)	545	0.11
Italian (72,814)	155,749	32.44
Latvian (120)	182	0.04
Lithuanian (674)	1,898	0.40
Luxemburger (0)	36	0.01
Macedonian (0)	0	<0.01
Maltese (235)	686	0.14
New Zealander (10)	23	<0.01
Northern European (233)	249	0.05

	Population	%
Norwegian (1,381)	5,078	1.06
Pennsylvania German (45)	66	0.01
Polish (7,478)	27,233	5.67
Portuguese (2,684)	3,802	0.79
Romanian (472)	1,216	0.25
Russian (4,331)	12,073	2.51
Scandinavian (127)	388	0.08
Scotch-Irish (1,789)	5,102	1.06
Scottish (1,051)	5,703	1.19
Serbian (0)	0	<0.01
Slavic (22)	91	0.02
Slovak (304)	690	0.14
Slovene (5)	76	0.02
Soviet Union (0)	0	<0.01
Swedish (519)	4,045	0.84
Swiss (319)	1,356	0.28
Turkish (1,572)	1,935	0.40
Ukrainian (779)	2,350	0.49
Welsh (195)	1,189	0.25
West Indian, ex. Hispanic (4,567)	6,377	1.33
Bahamian (0)	47	0.01
Barbadian (44)	44	0.01
Belizean (0)	0	<0.01
Bermudan (0)	34	0.01
British West Indian (59)	59	0.01
Dutch West Indian (20)	20	<0.01
Haitian (1,544)	2,077	0.43
Jamaican (998)	1,546	0.32
Trinidadian/Tobagonian (922)	1,200	0.25
U.S. Virgin Islander (0)	0	<0.01
West Indian (980)	1,323	0.28
Other West Indian (0)	27	0.01
Yugoslavian (145)	518	0.11

Hispanic Origin	Population	%
Hispanic or Latino (of any race)	60,270	12.40
Central American, ex. Mexican	9,259	1.90
Costa Rican	198	0.04
Guatemalan	1,411	0.29
Honduran	1,195	0.25
Nicaraguan	159	0.03
Panamanian	291	0.06
Salvadoran	5,899	1.21
Other Central American	106	0.02
Cuban	1,500	0.31
Dominican Republic	4,781	0.98
Mexican	4,926	1.01
Puerto Rican	21,429	4.41
South American	12,182	2.51
Argentinean	653	0.13
Bolivian	148	0.03
Chilean	363	0.07
Colombian	2,970	0.61
Ecuadorian	6,437	1.32
Paraguayan	50	0.01
Peruvian	1,074	0.22
Uruguayan	87	0.02
Venezuelan	302	0.06
Other South American	98	0.02
Other Hispanic or Latino	6,193	1.27

Race*	Population	%
African-American/Black (26,639)	31,615	6.50
Not Hispanic (24,428)	28,098	5.78
Hispanic (2,211)	3,517	0.72
American Indian/Alaska Native (1,368)	3,782	0.78
Not Hispanic (847)	2,586	0.53
Hispanic (521)	1,196	0.25
Alaska Athabascan (Ala. Nat.) (1)	4	<0.01
Aleut (Alaska Native) (2)	3	<0.01
Apache (4)	18	<0.01
Arapaho (0)	1	<0.01
Blackfeet (12)	164	0.03
Canadian/French Am. Ind. (4)	15	<0.01
Central American Ind. (27)	53	0.01
Cherokee (82)	546	0.11
Cheyenne (1)	6	<0.01
Chickasaw (0)	3	<0.01
Chippewa (8)	19	<0.01

	Population	%
Choctaw (7)	34	0.01
Colville (0)	0	<0.01
Comanche (0)	4	<0.01
Cree (1)	4	<0.01
Creek (1)	12	<0.01
Crow (0)	1	<0.01
Delaware (3)	12	<0.01
Hopi (0)	1	<0.01
Houma (0)	0	<0.01
Inupiat (Alaska Native) (1)	2	<0.01
Iroquois (39)	116	0.02
Kiowa (0)	0	<0.01
Lumbee (2)	7	<0.01
Menominee (0)	0	<0.01
Mexican American Ind. (37)	64	0.01
Navajo (3)	15	<0.01
Osage (0)	2	<0.01
Ottawa (0)	3	<0.01
Paiute (2)	4	<0.01
Pima (0)	0	<0.01
Potawatomi (6)	6	<0.01
Pueblo (2)	2	<0.01
Puget Sound Salish (5)	6	<0.01
Seminole (7)	33	0.01
Shoshone (0)	4	<0.01
Sioux (16)	42	0.01
South American Ind. (47)	136	0.03
Spanish American Ind. (26)	34	0.01
Tlingit-Haida (Alaska Native) (0)	5	<0.01
Tohono O'Odham (0)	0	<0.01
Tsimshian (Alaska Native) (0)	0	<0.01
Ute (0)	1	<0.01
Yakama (0)	1	<0.01
Yaqui (1)	5	<0.01
Yuman (1)	1	<0.01
Yup'ik (Alaska Native) (0)	0	<0.01
Asian (19,082)	21,849	4.50
Not Hispanic (18,880)	21,257	4.37
Hispanic (202)	592	0.12
Bangladeshi (528)	621	0.13
Bhutanese (0)	0	<0.01
Burmese (36)	40	0.01
Cambodian (14)	29	0.01
Chinese, ex. Taiwanese (5,433)	6,107	1.26
Filipino (2,117)	2,705	0.56
Hmong (1)	4	<0.01
Indian (5,078)	5,745	1.18
Indonesian (38)	63	0.01
Japanese (339)	605	0.12
Korean (1,728)	2,025	0.42
Laotian (42)	54	0.01
Malaysian (9)	18	<0.01
Nepalese (43)	44	0.01
Pakistani (1,867)	2,081	0.43
Sri Lankan (85)	100	0.02
Taiwanese (181)	213	0.04
Thai (150)	211	0.04
Vietnamese (544)	620	0.13
Hawaii Native/Pacific Islander (152)	447	0.09
Not Hispanic (98)	306	0.06
Hispanic (54)	141	0.03
Fijian (3)	10	<0.01
Guamanian/Chamorro (40)	51	0.01
Marshallese (0)	0	<0.01
Native Hawaiian (31)	100	0.02
Samoan (6)	15	<0.01
Tongan (0)	2	<0.01
White (410,649)	419,725	86.36
Not Hispanic (373,782)	379,158	78.01
Hispanic (36,867)	40,567	8.35

Notes: † The Census 2010 population figure is used to calculate the percentages in the Hispanic Origin and Race categories. Ancestry percentages are based on the 2006-2010 American Community Survey population (not shown); ‡ Numbers in parentheses indicate the number of people reporting a single ancestry; * Numbers in parentheses indicate the number of persons reporting this race alone, not in combination with any other race; Please refer to the Explanation of Data for more information.

Brooklyn

Place Type: Borough
County: Kings
Population: 2,504,700

Ancestry	Population	%
Afghan (335)	344	0.01
African, Sub-Saharan (30,768)	63,004	2.55
African (17,256)	48,168	1.95
Cape Verdean (106)	153	0.01
Ethiopian (283)	330	0.01
Ghanaian (3,692)	3,898	0.16
Kenyan (65)	77	<0.01
Liberian (392)	452	0.02
Nigerian (5,499)	6,033	0.24
Senegalese (401)	401	0.02
Sierra Leonean (147)	147	0.01
Somalian (234)	260	0.01
South African (204)	320	0.01
Sudanese (693)	731	0.03
Ugandan (29)	54	<0.01
Zimbabwean (99)	99	<0.01
Other Sub-Saharan African (1,668)	1,881	0.08
Albanian (6,490)	6,871	0.28
Alsatian (0)	27	<0.01
American (78,858)	78,858	3.20
Arab (29,346)	34,840	1.41
Arab (6,779)	7,609	0.31
Egyptian (4,705)	5,231	0.21
Iraqi (71)	134	0.01
Jordanian (714)	752	0.03
Lebanese (3,425)	4,757	0.19
Moroccan (2,156)	2,648	0.11
Palestinian (1,372)	1,482	0.06
Syrian (4,854)	5,890	0.24
Other Arab (5,270)	6,337	0.26
Armenian (1,798)	2,300	0.09
Assyrian/Chaldean/Syriac (22)	44	<0.01
Australian (539)	832	0.03
Austrian (1,677)	5,123	0.21
Basque (69)	129	0.01
Belgian (498)	1,012	0.04
Brazilian (1,257)	1,719	0.07
British (2,002)	4,749	0.19
Bulgarian (970)	1,128	0.05
Cajun (99)	175	0.01
Canadian (1,814)	3,116	0.13
Carpatho Rusyn (46)	53	<0.01
Celtic (16)	32	<0.01
Croatian (488)	998	0.04
Cypriot (37)	62	<0.01
Czech (759)	3,393	0.14
Czechoslovakian (793)	1,684	0.07
Danish (380)	1,267	0.05
Dutch (1,616)	5,664	0.23
Eastern European (11,912)	12,941	0.52
English (9,927)	32,407	1.31
Estonian (209)	340	0.01
European (25,194)	27,499	1.11
Finnish (303)	692	0.03
French, ex. Basque (3,484)	14,137	0.57
French Canadian (1,082)	2,974	0.12
German (12,299)	52,798	2.14
German Russian (29)	55	<0.01
Greek (10,688)	14,075	0.57
Guyanese (36,322)	38,963	1.58
Hungarian (17,858)	26,607	1.08
Icelander (69)	103	<0.01
Iranian (1,520)	1,822	0.07
Irish (32,255)	84,945	3.44
Israeli (7,062)	9,707	0.39
Italian (108,743)	152,814	6.19
Latvian (418)	667	0.03
Lithuanian (938)	2,676	0.11
Luxemburger (41)	58	<0.01
Macedonian (389)	498	0.02
Maltese (197)	362	0.01
New Zealander (71)	140	0.01
Northern European (905)	961	0.04

Norwegian (2,042)	5,982	0.24
Pennsylvania German (19)	59	<0.01
Polish (41,882)	66,792	2.71
Portuguese (1,106)	2,882	0.12
Romanian (4,537)	8,046	0.33
Russian (69,188)	88,579	3.59
Scandinavian (512)	882	0.04
Scotch-Irish (1,997)	6,090	0.25
Scottish (2,407)	8,809	0.36
Serbian (288)	520	0.02
Slavic (289)	564	0.02
Slovak (1,164)	1,826	0.07
Slovene (55)	160	0.01
Soviet Union (185)	219	0.01
Swedish (1,240)	5,185	0.21
Swiss (473)	1,491	0.06
Turkish (4,449)	5,164	0.21
Ukrainian (21,703)	25,046	1.02
Welsh (345)	2,606	0.11
West Indian, ex. Hispanic (257,579)	306,541	12.43
Bahamian (195)	266	0.01
Barbadian (13,358)	14,916	0.60
Belizean (1,610)	2,026	0.08
Bermudan (16)	16	<0.01
British West Indian (28,123)	30,607	1.24
Dutch West Indian (289)	424	0.02
Haitian (67,083)	69,941	2.84
Jamaican (74,216)	80,999	3.28
Trinidadian/Tobagonian (42,450)	46,490	1.88
U.S. Virgin Islander (470)	558	0.02
West Indian (29,404)	59,844	2.43
Other West Indian (365)	454	0.02
Yugoslavian (2,305)	2,800	0.11

Hispanic Origin	Population	%
Hispanic or Latino (of any race)	496,285	19.81
Central American, ex. Mexican	46,119	1.84
Costa Rican	2,576	0.10
Guatemalan	9,160	0.37
Honduran	10,071	0.40
Nicaraguan	2,407	0.10
Panamanian	13,681	0.55
Salvadoran	7,737	0.31
Other Central American	487	0.02
Cuban	7,581	0.30
Dominican Republic	86,764	3.46
Mexican	94,585	3.78
Puerto Rican	176,528	7.05
South American	49,003	1.96
Argentinean	2,760	0.11
Bolivian	310	0.01
Chilean	1,026	0.04
Colombian	8,861	0.35
Ecuadorian	28,684	1.15
Paraguayan	230	0.01
Peruvian	4,222	0.17
Uruguayan	488	0.02
Venezuelan	1,916	0.08
Other South American	506	0.02
Other Hispanic or Latino	35,705	1.43

Race*	Population	%
African-American/Black (860,083)	896,165	35.78
Not Hispanic (799,066)	820,437	32.76
Hispanic (61,017)	75,728	3.02
American Indian/Alaska Native (13,524)	26,571	1.06
Not Hispanic (4,638)	12,062	0.48
Hispanic (8,886)	14,509	0.58
Alaska Athabascan (Ala. Nat.) (1)	5	<0.01
Aleut (Alaska Native) (4)	8	<0.01
Apache (46)	122	<0.01
Arapaho (2)	10	<0.01
Blackfeet (89)	531	0.02
Canadian/French Am. Ind. (42)	62	<0.01
Central American Ind. (616)	1,263	0.05
Cherokee (289)	1,903	0.08
Cheyenne (0)	10	<0.01
Chickasaw (9)	30	<0.01
Chippewa (23)	65	<0.01

Choctaw (30)	104	<0.01
Colville (1)	1	<0.01
Comanche (5)	19	<0.01
Cree (3)	15	<0.01
Creek (20)	81	<0.01
Crow (5)	19	<0.01
Delaware (5)	35	<0.01
Hopi (7)	12	<0.01
Houma (1)	3	<0.01
Inupiat (Alaska Native) (7)	21	<0.01
Iroquois (194)	381	0.02
Kiowa (1)	2	<0.01
Lumbee (6)	24	<0.01
Menominee (1)	4	<0.01
Mexican American Ind. (1,022)	1,363	0.05
Navajo (41)	93	<0.01
Osage (1)	3	<0.01
Ottawa (2)	5	<0.01
Paiute (0)	1	<0.01
Pima (0)	2	<0.01
Potawatomi (3)	11	<0.01
Pueblo (93)	169	0.01
Puget Sound Salish (1)	1	<0.01
Seminole (18)	92	<0.01
Shoshone (6)	23	<0.01
Sioux (29)	121	<0.01
South American Ind. (874)	1,855	0.07
Spanish American Ind. (290)	382	0.02
Tlingit-Haida (Alaska Native) (4)	28	<0.01
Tohono O'Odham (9)	10	<0.01
Tsimshian (Alaska Native) (0)	0	<0.01
Ute (0)	4	<0.01
Yakama (1)	3	<0.01
Yaqui (11)	19	<0.01
Yuman (5)	8	<0.01
Yup'ik (Alaska Native) (0)	1	<0.01
Asian (262,276)	284,489	11.36
Not Hispanic (260,129)	279,499	11.16
Hispanic (2,147)	4,990	0.20
Bangladeshi (10,667)	12,408	0.50
Bhutanese (5)	8	<0.01
Burmese (1,055)	1,260	0.05
Cambodian (613)	751	0.03
Chinese, ex. Taiwanese (171,214)	178,214	7.12
Filipino (7,930)	10,208	0.41
Hmong (14)	22	<0.01
Indian (26,144)	33,490	1.34
Indonesian (383)	564	0.02
Japanese (3,938)	5,917	0.24
Korean (6,904)	8,201	0.33
Laotian (82)	131	0.01
Malaysian (478)	708	0.03
Nepalese (355)	393	0.02
Pakistani (18,296)	19,840	0.79
Sri Lankan (219)	270	0.01
Taiwanese (857)	1,075	0.04
Thai (636)	883	0.04
Vietnamese (3,944)	5,041	0.20
Hawaii Native/Pacific Islander (1,243)	5,784	0.23
Not Hispanic (633)	3,463	0.14
Hispanic (610)	2,321	0.09
Fijian (20)	45	<0.01
Guamanian/Chamorro (386)	568	0.02
Marshallese (1)	2	<0.01
Native Hawaiian (208)	564	0.02
Samoan (72)	216	0.01
Tongan (5)	10	<0.01
White (1,072,041)	1,120,592	44.74
Not Hispanic (893,306)	917,717	36.64
Hispanic (178,735)	202,875	8.10

*Notes: † The Census 2010 population figure is used to calculate the percentages in the Hispanic Origin and Race categories. Ancestry percentages are based on the 2006-2010 American Community Survey population (not shown); ‡ Numbers in parentheses indicate the number of people reporting a single ancestry; * Numbers in parentheses indicate the number of persons reporting this race alone, not in combination with any other race; Please refer to the Explanation of Data for more information.*

Buffalo

Place Type: City
County: Erie
Population: 261,310

Ancestry	Population	%
Afghan (178)	178	0.07
African, Sub-Saharan (5,618)	6,085	2.29
African (3,925)	4,177	1.57
Cape Verdean (95)	95	0.04
Ethiopian (223)	223	0.08
Ghanaian (43)	43	0.02
Kenyan (38)	38	0.01
Liberian (74)	74	0.03
Nigerian (94)	105	0.04
Senegalese (0)	0	<0.01
Sierra Leonean (17)	17	0.01
Somalian (706)	858	0.32
South African (0)	0	<0.01
Sudanese (259)	268	0.10
Ugandan (24)	33	0.01
Zimbabwean (45)	45	0.02
Other Sub-Saharan African (75)	109	0.04
Albanian (360)	369	0.14
Alsatian (12)	12	<0.01
American (6,386)	6,386	2.40
Arab (1,374)	1,815	0.68
Arab (586)	644	0.24
Egyptian (27)	39	0.01
Iraqi (286)	288	0.11
Jordanian (2)	4	<0.01
Lebanese (165)	481	0.18
Moroccan (21)	57	0.02
Palestinian (0)	0	<0.01
Syrian (17)	32	0.01
Other Arab (270)	270	0.10
Armenian (39)	67	0.03
Assyrian/Chaldean/Syriac (0)	0	<0.01
Australian (0)	14	0.01
Austrian (244)	799	0.30
Basque (9)	9	<0.01
Belgian (21)	21	0.01
Brazilian (25)	25	0.01
British (306)	722	0.27
Bulgarian (114)	201	0.08
Cajun (0)	11	<0.01
Canadian (264)	558	0.21
Carpatho Rusyn (0)	0	<0.01
Celtic (0)	13	<0.01
Croatian (249)	487	0.18
Cypriot (0)	0	<0.01
Czech (13)	310	0.12
Czechoslovakian (76)	231	0.09
Danish (41)	152	0.06
Dutch (224)	1,451	0.55
Eastern European (189)	198	0.07
English (2,703)	11,203	4.21
Estonian (0)	11	<0.01
European (884)	1,016	0.38
Finnish (56)	248	0.09
French, ex. Basque (446)	4,110	1.55
French Canadian (420)	1,376	0.52
German (7,601)	35,760	13.44
German Russian (16)	41	0.02
Greek (305)	769	0.29
Guyanese (517)	529	0.20
Hungarian (748)	2,201	0.83
Icelander (0)	0	<0.01
Iranian (82)	125	0.05
Irish (9,009)	34,103	12.82
Israeli (104)	180	0.07
Italian (13,524)	30,606	11.51
Latvian (13)	22	0.01
Lithuanian (121)	358	0.13
Luxemburger (0)	24	0.01
Macedonian (40)	52	0.02
Maltese (0)	8	<0.01
New Zealander (0)	0	<0.01
Northern European (31)	31	0.01

Ancestry (cont.)	Population	%
Norwegian (78)	586	0.22
Pennsylvania German (0)	159	0.06
Polish (12,089)	28,108	10.57
Portuguese (169)	474	0.18
Romanian (30)	122	0.05
Russian (616)	1,883	0.71
Scandinavian (0)	76	0.03
Scotch-Irish (902)	2,324	0.87
Scottish (437)	2,816	1.06
Serbian (115)	291	0.11
Slavic (15)	35	0.01
Slovak (27)	174	0.07
Slovene (23)	100	0.04
Soviet Union (0)	0	<0.01
Swedish (309)	1,596	0.60
Swiss (41)	308	0.12
Turkish (251)	350	0.13
Ukrainian (899)	1,739	0.65
Welsh (90)	729	0.27
West Indian, ex. Hispanic (2,330)	2,773	1.04
Bahamian (13)	13	<0.01
Barbadian (18)	44	0.02
Belizean (0)	0	<0.01
Bermudan (0)	0	<0.01
British West Indian (102)	115	0.04
Dutch West Indian (0)	17	0.01
Haitian (480)	626	0.24
Jamaican (1,260)	1,420	0.53
Trinidadian/Tobagonian (196)	200	0.08
U.S. Virgin Islander (0)	0	<0.01
West Indian (261)	338	0.13
Other West Indian (0)	0	<0.01
Yugoslavian (187)	282	0.11

Hispanic Origin	Population	%
Hispanic or Latino (of any race)	27,519	10.53
Central American, ex. Mexican	386	0.15
Costa Rican	27	0.01
Guatemalan	72	0.03
Honduran	76	0.03
Nicaraguan	25	0.01
Panamanian	89	0.03
Salvadoran	92	0.04
Other Central American	5	<0.01
Cuban	795	0.30
Dominican Republic	707	0.27
Mexican	1,382	0.53
Puerto Rican	22,076	8.45
South American	679	0.26
Argentinean	117	0.04
Bolivian	35	0.01
Chilean	35	0.01
Colombian	215	0.08
Ecuadorian	106	0.04
Paraguayan	8	<0.01
Peruvian	105	0.04
Uruguayan	2	<0.01
Venezuelan	44	0.02
Other South American	12	<0.01
Other Hispanic or Latino	1,494	0.57

Race*	Population	%
African-American/Black (100,774)	106,107	40.61
Not Hispanic (97,637)	101,817	38.96
Hispanic (3,137)	4,290	1.64
American Indian/Alaska Native (2,009)	4,019	1.54
Not Hispanic (1,597)	3,229	1.24
Hispanic (412)	790	0.30
Alaska Athabascan (Ala. Nat.) (1)	1	<0.01
Aleut (Alaska Native) (0)	0	<0.01
Apache (5)	11	<0.01
Arapaho (0)	1	<0.01
Blackfeet (10)	104	0.04
Canadian/French Am. Ind. (29)	57	0.02
Central American Ind. (9)	17	0.01
Cherokee (37)	294	0.11
Cheyenne (0)	0	<0.01
Chickasaw (2)	2	<0.01
Chippewa (24)	42	0.02

Race* (cont.)	Population	%
Choctaw (3)	21	0.01
Colville (0)	0	<0.01
Comanche (1)	4	<0.01
Cree (1)	4	<0.01
Creek (0)	7	<0.01
Crow (0)	1	<0.01
Delaware (6)	10	<0.01
Hopi (5)	5	<0.01
Houma (1)	2	<0.01
Inupiat (Alaska Native) (2)	4	<0.01
Iroquois (935)	1,316	0.50
Kiowa (1)	1	<0.01
Lumbee (1)	1	<0.01
Menominee (2)	2	<0.01
Mexican American Ind. (19)	27	0.01
Navajo (8)	16	0.01
Osage (0)	0	<0.01
Ottawa (0)	0	<0.01
Paiute (0)	0	<0.01
Pima (1)	1	<0.01
Potawatomi (0)	0	<0.01
Pueblo (3)	4	<0.01
Puget Sound Salish (0)	0	<0.01
Seminole (3)	23	0.01
Shoshone (0)	0	<0.01
Sioux (24)	46	0.02
South American Ind. (24)	60	0.02
Spanish American Ind. (11)	14	0.01
Tlingit-Haida (Alaska Native) (2)	3	<0.01
Tohono O'Odham (1)	3	<0.01
Tsimshian (Alaska Native) (0)	0	<0.01
Ute (0)	0	<0.01
Yakama (0)	0	<0.01
Yaqui (2)	2	<0.01
Yuman (1)	1	<0.01
Yup'ik (Alaska Native) (0)	0	<0.01
Asian (8,409)	9,698	3.71
Not Hispanic (8,313)	9,459	3.62
Hispanic (96)	239	0.09
Bangladeshi (167)	206	0.08
Bhutanese (298)	370	0.14
Burmese (2,267)	2,361	0.90
Cambodian (43)	48	0.02
Chinese, ex. Taiwanese (919)	1,065	0.41
Filipino (214)	417	0.16
Hmong (5)	6	<0.01
Indian (1,576)	1,889	0.72
Indonesian (17)	22	0.01
Japanese (128)	243	0.09
Korean (350)	447	0.17
Laotian (248)	288	0.11
Malaysian (19)	21	0.01
Nepalese (115)	160	0.06
Pakistani (320)	362	0.14
Sri Lankan (45)	54	0.02
Taiwanese (31)	43	0.02
Thai (59)	107	0.04
Vietnamese (1,128)	1,220	0.47
Hawaii Native/Pacific Islander (119)	357	0.14
Not Hispanic (79)	252	0.10
Hispanic (40)	105	0.04
Fijian (0)	0	<0.01
Guamanian/Chamorro (10)	30	0.01
Marshallese (0)	0	<0.01
Native Hawaiian (21)	75	0.03
Samoan (32)	63	0.02
Tongan (3)	3	<0.01
White (131,753)	138,013	52.82
Not Hispanic (119,801)	124,612	47.69
Hispanic (11,952)	13,401	5.13

Notes: † The Census 2010 population figure is used to calculate the percentages in the Hispanic Origin and Race categories. Ancestry percentages are based on the 2006-2010 American Community Survey population (not shown); ‡ Numbers in parentheses indicate the number of people reporting a single ancestry; * Numbers in parentheses indicate the number of persons reporting this race alone, not in combination with any other race; Please refer to the Explanation of Data for more information.

Cheektowaga

Place Type: CDP
County: Erie
Population: 75,178

Ancestry	Population	%
Afghan (0)	0	<0.01
African, Sub-Saharan (178)	178	0.23
African (145)	145	0.19
Cape Verdean (0)	0	<0.01
Ethiopian (0)	0	<0.01
Ghanaian (0)	0	<0.01
Kenyan (0)	0	<0.01
Liberian (0)	0	<0.01
Nigerian (0)	0	<0.01
Senegalese (0)	0	<0.01
Sierra Leonean (0)	0	<0.01
Somalian (0)	0	<0.01
South African (0)	0	<0.01
Sudanese (0)	0	<0.01
Ugandan (0)	0	<0.01
Zimbabwean (0)	0	<0.01
Other Sub-Saharan African (33)	33	0.04
Albanian (15)	21	0.03
Alsatian (0)	0	<0.01
American (1,642)	1,642	2.17
Arab (498)	611	0.81
Arab (208)	224	0.30
Egyptian (0)	0	<0.01
Iraqi (30)	30	0.04
Jordanian (0)	0	<0.01
Lebanese (260)	338	0.45
Moroccan (0)	0	<0.01
Palestinian (0)	0	<0.01
Syrian (0)	13	0.02
Other Arab (0)	6	0.01
Armenian (0)	13	0.02
Assyrian/Chaldean/Syriac (0)	0	<0.01
Australian (0)	0	<0.01
Austrian (33)	202	0.27
Basque (0)	0	<0.01
Belgian (0)	29	0.04
Brazilian (0)	0	<0.01
British (51)	217	0.29
Bulgarian (30)	30	0.04
Cajun (0)	0	<0.01
Canadian (63)	193	0.25
Carpatho Rusyn (6)	6	0.01
Celtic (0)	0	<0.01
Croatian (21)	90	0.12
Cypriot (0)	0	<0.01
Czech (0)	249	0.33
Czechoslovakian (10)	10	0.01
Danish (0)	53	0.07
Dutch (59)	763	1.01
Eastern European (0)	0	<0.01
English (753)	4,258	5.62
Estonian (78)	78	0.10
European (101)	122	0.16
Finnish (12)	28	0.04
French, ex. Basque (123)	2,246	2.96
French Canadian (122)	608	0.80
German (6,860)	21,843	28.83
German Russian (12)	12	0.02
Greek (116)	188	0.25
Guyanese (23)	23	0.03
Hungarian (132)	542	0.72
Icelander (0)	0	<0.01
Iranian (0)	0	<0.01
Irish (2,376)	11,306	14.92
Israeli (0)	0	<0.01
Italian (5,350)	12,314	16.26
Latvian (16)	16	0.02
Lithuanian (12)	84	0.11
Luxemburger (0)	0	<0.01
Macedonian (21)	35	0.05
Maltese (0)	0	<0.01
New Zealander (11)	11	0.01
Northern European (0)	0	<0.01
Norwegian (15)	247	0.33
Pennsylvania German (15)	24	0.03
Polish (15,029)	26,237	34.63
Portuguese (11)	75	0.10
Romanian (38)	51	0.07
Russian (173)	411	0.54
Scandinavian (0)	15	0.02
Scotch-Irish (268)	861	1.14
Scottish (183)	788	1.04
Serbian (82)	100	0.13
Slavic (11)	45	0.06
Slovak (71)	229	0.30
Slovene (0)	16	0.02
Soviet Union (0)	0	<0.01
Swedish (143)	418	0.55
Swiss (14)	63	0.08
Turkish (0)	42	0.06
Ukrainian (268)	499	0.66
Welsh (8)	327	0.43
West Indian, ex. Hispanic (240)	315	0.42
Bahamian (0)	0	<0.01
Barbadian (8)	8	0.01
Belizean (0)	0	<0.01
Bermudan (0)	0	<0.01
British West Indian (13)	13	0.02
Dutch West Indian (0)	0	<0.01
Haitian (7)	7	0.01
Jamaican (129)	182	0.24
Trinidadian/Tobagonian (33)	55	0.07
U.S. Virgin Islander (0)	0	<0.01
West Indian (50)	50	0.07
Other West Indian (0)	0	<0.01
Yugoslavian (69)	69	0.09

Hispanic Origin	Population	%
Hispanic or Latino (of any race)	1,672	2.22
Central American, ex. Mexican	55	0.07
Costa Rican	5	0.01
Guatemalan	11	0.01
Honduran	6	0.01
Nicaraguan	1	<0.01
Panamanian	13	0.02
Salvadoran	14	0.02
Other Central American	5	0.01
Cuban	47	0.06
Dominican Republic	55	0.07
Mexican	244	0.32
Puerto Rican	1,011	1.34
South American	105	0.14
Argentinean	7	0.01
Bolivian	6	0.01
Chilean	4	0.01
Colombian	39	0.05
Ecuadorian	22	0.03
Paraguayan	2	<0.01
Peruvian	10	0.01
Uruguayan	2	<0.01
Venezuelan	11	0.01
Other South American	2	<0.01
Other Hispanic or Latino	155	0.21

Race*	Population	%
African-American/Black (6,881)	7,619	10.13
Not Hispanic (6,716)	7,368	9.80
Hispanic (165)	251	0.33
American Indian/Alaska Native (189)	469	0.62
Not Hispanic (171)	416	0.55
Hispanic (18)	53	0.07
Alaska Athabascan (Ala. Nat.) (0)	0	<0.01
Aleut (Alaska Native) (0)	0	<0.01
Apache (1)	6	0.01
Arapaho (0)	0	<0.01
Blackfeet (0)	12	0.02
Canadian/French Am. Ind. (5)	5	0.01
Central American Ind. (1)	1	<0.01
Cherokee (6)	45	0.06
Cheyenne (0)	1	<0.01
Chickasaw (0)	0	<0.01
Chippewa (5)	6	0.01

Race (cont.)	Population	%
Choctaw (2)	3	<0.01
Colville (0)	0	<0.01
Comanche (0)	0	<0.01
Cree (0)	1	<0.01
Creek (1)	1	<0.01
Crow (0)	0	<0.01
Delaware (2)	2	<0.01
Hopi (2)	2	<0.01
Houma (0)	0	<0.01
Inupiat (Alaska Native) (0)	0	<0.01
Iroquois (95)	179	0.24
Kiowa (0)	0	<0.01
Lumbee (0)	0	<0.01
Menominee (0)	0	<0.01
Mexican American Ind. (5)	7	0.01
Navajo (1)	3	<0.01
Osage (0)	0	<0.01
Ottawa (0)	0	<0.01
Paiute (0)	0	<0.01
Pima (0)	0	<0.01
Potawatomi (0)	0	<0.01
Pueblo (0)	3	<0.01
Puget Sound Salish (0)	0	<0.01
Seminole (0)	0	<0.01
Shoshone (0)	0	<0.01
Sioux (1)	6	0.01
South American Ind. (0)	4	0.01
Spanish American Ind. (0)	0	<0.01
Tlingit-Haida (Alaska Native) (0)	0	<0.01
Tohono O'Odham (0)	0	<0.01
Tsimshian (Alaska Native) (0)	0	<0.01
Ute (0)	0	<0.01
Yakama (0)	0	<0.01
Yaqui (0)	0	<0.01
Yuman (0)	0	<0.01
Yup'ik (Alaska Native) (0)	0	<0.01
Asian (1,252)	1,476	1.96
Not Hispanic (1,249)	1,455	1.94
Hispanic (3)	21	0.03
Bangladeshi (2)	2	<0.01
Bhutanese (0)	0	<0.01
Burmese (6)	8	0.01
Cambodian (9)	11	0.01
Chinese, ex. Taiwanese (100)	134	0.18
Filipino (68)	112	0.15
Hmong (1)	1	<0.01
Indian (499)	529	0.70
Indonesian (6)	10	0.01
Japanese (16)	37	0.05
Korean (61)	89	0.12
Laotian (58)	65	0.09
Malaysian (12)	12	0.02
Nepalese (5)	5	0.01
Pakistani (37)	52	0.07
Sri Lankan (0)	2	<0.01
Taiwanese (4)	4	0.01
Thai (5)	10	0.01
Vietnamese (297)	326	0.43
Hawaii Native/Pacific Islander (12)	39	0.05
Not Hispanic (9)	30	0.04
Hispanic (3)	9	0.01
Fijian (2)	2	<0.01
Guamanian/Chamorro (2)	7	0.01
Marshallese (0)	0	<0.01
Native Hawaiian (5)	14	0.02
Samoan (1)	2	<0.01
Tongan (0)	0	<0.01
White (65,225)	66,265	88.14
Not Hispanic (64,288)	65,180	86.70
Hispanic (937)	1,085	1.44

Notes: † The Census 2010 population figure is used to calculate the percentages in the Hispanic Origin and Race categories. Ancestry percentages are based on the 2006-2010 American Community Survey population (not shown); ‡ Numbers in parentheses indicate the number of people reporting a single ancestry; * Numbers in parentheses indicate the number of persons reporting this race alone, not in combination with any other race; Please refer to the Explanation of Data for more information.

Cheektowaga

Place Type: Town
County: Erie
Population: 88,226

Ancestry	Population	%
Afghan (0)	0	<0.01
African, Sub-Saharan (178)	178	0.20
African (145)	145	0.16
Cape Verdean (0)	0	<0.01
Ethiopian (0)	0	<0.01
Ghanaian (0)	0	<0.01
Kenyan (0)	0	<0.01
Liberian (0)	0	<0.01
Nigerian (0)	0	<0.01
Senegalese (0)	0	<0.01
Sierra Leonean (0)	0	<0.01
Somalian (0)	0	<0.01
South African (0)	0	<0.01
Sudanese (0)	0	<0.01
Ugandan (0)	0	<0.01
Zimbabwean (0)	0	<0.01
Other Sub-Saharan African (33)	33	0.04
Albanian (15)	30	0.03
Alsatian (0)	0	<0.01
American (1,927)	1,927	2.17
Arab (768)	905	1.02
Arab (231)	247	0.28
Egyptian (0)	0	<0.01
Iraqi (30)	30	0.03
Jordanian (0)	0	<0.01
Lebanese (260)	350	0.39
Moroccan (0)	0	<0.01
Palestinian (9)	9	0.01
Syrian (25)	25	0.03
Other Arab (238)	244	0.27
Armenian (0)	13	0.01
Assyrian/Chaldean/Syriac (0)	0	<0.01
Australian (0)	0	<0.01
Austrian (33)	225	0.25
Basque (0)	0	<0.01
Belgian (0)	29	0.03
Brazilian (0)	0	<0.01
British (84)	277	0.31
Bulgarian (73)	73	0.08
Cajun (0)	0	<0.01
Canadian (72)	202	0.23
Carpatho Rusyn (6)	6	0.01
Celtic (0)	0	<0.01
Croatian (21)	90	0.10
Cypriot (0)	0	<0.01
Czech (29)	312	0.35
Czechoslovakian (48)	60	0.07
Danish (0)	53	0.06
Dutch (125)	935	1.05
Eastern European (0)	0	<0.01
English (852)	4,818	5.42
Estonian (78)	78	0.09
European (123)	144	0.16
Finnish (12)	28	0.03
French, ex. Basque (132)	2,577	2.90
French Canadian (122)	701	0.79
German (7,899)	26,125	29.39
German Russian (12)	12	0.01
Greek (169)	249	0.28
Guyanese (23)	23	0.03
Hungarian (132)	575	0.65
Icelander (0)	0	<0.01
Iranian (0)	0	<0.01
Irish (2,677)	13,325	14.99
Israeli (0)	0	<0.01
Italian (6,376)	14,630	16.46
Latvian (16)	16	0.02
Lithuanian (12)	99	0.11
Luxemburger (0)	0	<0.01
Macedonian (21)	35	0.04
Maltese (0)	0	<0.01
New Zealander (11)	11	0.01
Northern European (130)	130	0.15
Norwegian (15)	256	0.29
Pennsylvania German (24)	33	0.04
Polish (18,227)	31,456	35.39
Portuguese (11)	84	0.09
Romanian (38)	61	0.07
Russian (182)	430	0.48
Scandinavian (0)	44	0.05
Scotch-Irish (291)	969	1.09
Scottish (232)	954	1.07
Serbian (82)	100	0.11
Slavic (11)	45	0.05
Slovak (71)	229	0.26
Slovene (0)	16	0.02
Soviet Union (0)	0	<0.01
Swedish (228)	542	0.61
Swiss (26)	85	0.10
Turkish (0)	42	0.05
Ukrainian (295)	556	0.63
Welsh (8)	383	0.43
West Indian, ex. Hispanic (240)	315	0.35
Bahamian (0)	0	<0.01
Barbadian (8)	8	0.01
Belizean (0)	0	<0.01
Bermudan (0)	0	<0.01
British West Indian (13)	13	0.01
Dutch West Indian (0)	0	<0.01
Haitian (7)	7	0.01
Jamaican (129)	182	0.20
Trinidadian/Tobagonian (33)	55	0.06
U.S. Virgin Islander (0)	0	<0.01
West Indian (50)	50	0.06
Other West Indian (0)	0	<0.01
Yugoslavian (69)	69	0.08

Hispanic Origin	Population	%
Hispanic or Latino (of any race)	1,900	2.15
Central American, ex. Mexican	78	0.09
Costa Rican	5	0.01
Guatemalan	21	0.02
Honduran	6	0.01
Nicaraguan	4	<0.01
Panamanian	13	0.01
Salvadoran	21	0.02
Other Central American	8	0.01
Cuban	51	0.06
Dominican Republic	59	0.07
Mexican	285	0.32
Puerto Rican	1,138	1.29
South American	112	0.13
Argentinean	7	0.01
Bolivian	6	0.01
Chilean	4	<0.01
Colombian	41	0.05
Ecuadorian	26	0.03
Paraguayan	2	<0.01
Peruvian	10	0.01
Uruguayan	2	<0.01
Venezuelan	12	0.01
Other South American	2	<0.01
Other Hispanic or Latino	177	0.20

Race*	Population	%
African-American/Black (7,069)	7,879	8.93
Not Hispanic (6,898)	7,611	8.63
Hispanic (171)	268	0.30
American Indian/Alaska Native (223)	546	0.62
Not Hispanic (200)	482	0.55
Hispanic (23)	64	0.07
Alaska Athabascan (Ala. Nat.) (0)	0	<0.01
Aleut (Alaska Native) (0)	0	<0.01
Apache (1)	6	0.01
Arapaho (1)	1	<0.01
Blackfeet (0)	15	0.02
Canadian/French Am. Ind. (5)	5	0.01
Central American Ind. (3)	4	<0.01
Cherokee (6)	52	0.06
Cheyenne (0)	1	<0.01
Chickasaw (0)	0	<0.01
Chippewa (5)	6	0.01

	Population	%
Choctaw (2)	3	<0.01
Colville (0)	0	<0.01
Comanche (0)	0	<0.01
Cree (0)	1	<0.01
Creek (1)	2	<0.01
Crow (0)	0	<0.01
Delaware (2)	2	<0.01
Hopi (2)	2	<0.01
Houma (0)	0	<0.01
Inupiat (Alaska Native) (0)	0	<0.01
Iroquois (110)	194	0.22
Kiowa (0)	0	<0.01
Lumbee (0)	4	<0.01
Menominee (0)	0	<0.01
Mexican American Ind. (7)	9	0.01
Navajo (1)	3	<0.01
Osage (0)	0	<0.01
Ottawa (0)	0	<0.01
Paiute (0)	0	<0.01
Pima (0)	0	<0.01
Potawatomi (0)	0	<0.01
Pueblo (0)	3	<0.01
Puget Sound Salish (0)	0	<0.01
Seminole (0)	0	<0.01
Shoshone (0)	0	<0.01
Sioux (1)	6	0.01
South American Ind. (0)	4	<0.01
Spanish American Ind. (0)	0	<0.01
Tlingit-Haida (Alaska Native) (0)	0	<0.01
Tohono O'Odham (0)	0	<0.01
Tsimshian (Alaska Native) (0)	0	<0.01
Ute (0)	0	<0.01
Yakama (0)	0	<0.01
Yaqui (0)	0	<0.01
Yuman (0)	0	<0.01
Yup'ik (Alaska Native) (0)	0	<0.01
Asian (1,336)	1,598	1.81
Not Hispanic (1,333)	1,576	1.79
Hispanic (3)	22	0.02
Bangladeshi (4)	4	<0.01
Bhutanese (0)	0	<0.01
Burmese (6)	8	0.01
Cambodian (10)	15	0.02
Chinese, ex. Taiwanese (111)	146	0.17
Filipino (77)	128	0.15
Hmong (0)	1	<0.01
Indian (530)	568	0.64
Indonesian (6)	10	0.01
Japanese (17)	38	0.04
Korean (69)	106	0.12
Laotian (58)	65	0.07
Malaysian (13)	13	0.01
Nepalese (5)	5	0.01
Pakistani (37)	52	0.06
Sri Lankan (0)	2	<0.01
Taiwanese (4)	4	<0.01
Thai (5)	10	0.01
Vietnamese (315)	344	0.39
Hawaii Native/Pacific Islander (14)	43	0.05
Not Hispanic (10)	33	0.04
Hispanic (4)	10	0.01
Fijian (2)	2	<0.01
Guamanian/Chamorro (3)	8	0.01
Marshallese (0)	0	<0.01
Native Hawaiian (5)	16	0.02
Samoan (1)	5	0.01
Tongan (0)	0	<0.01
White (77,769)	78,958	89.50
Not Hispanic (76,673)	77,687	88.05
Hispanic (1,096)	1,271	1.44

Notes: † The Census 2010 population figure is used to calculate the percentages in the Hispanic Origin and Race categories. Ancestry percentages are based on the 2006-2010 American Community Survey population (not shown); ‡ Numbers in parentheses indicate the number of people reporting a single ancestry; * Numbers in parentheses indicate the number of persons reporting this race alone, not in combination with any other race; Please refer to the Explanation of Data for more information.

Clarkstown

Place Type: Town
County: Rockland
Population: 84,187

Ancestry	Population	%
Afghan (0)	0	<0.01
African, Sub-Saharan (248)	283	0.34
African (149)	184	0.22
Cape Verdean (0)	0	<0.01
Ethiopian (0)	0	<0.01
Ghanaian (99)	99	0.12
Kenyan (0)	0	<0.01
Liberian (0)	0	<0.01
Nigerian (0)	0	<0.01
Senegalese (0)	0	<0.01
Sierra Leonean (0)	0	<0.01
Somalian (0)	0	<0.01
South African (0)	0	<0.01
Sudanese (0)	0	<0.01
Ugandan (0)	0	<0.01
Zimbabwean (0)	0	<0.01
Other Sub-Saharan African (0)	0	<0.01
Albanian (317)	328	0.39
Alsatian (0)	3	<0.01
American (4,138)	4,138	4.96
Arab (440)	705	0.85
Arab (8)	29	0.03
Egyptian (229)	254	0.30
Iraqi (7)	24	0.03
Jordanian (9)	9	0.01
Lebanese (138)	252	0.30
Moroccan (0)	0	<0.01
Palestinian (0)	0	<0.01
Syrian (0)	88	0.11
Other Arab (49)	49	0.06
Armenian (84)	99	0.12
Assyrian/Chaldean/Syriac (11)	51	0.06
Australian (12)	18	0.02
Austrian (199)	827	0.99
Basque (0)	0	<0.01
Belgian (0)	42	0.05
Brazilian (69)	203	0.24
British (105)	190	0.23
Bulgarian (0)	0	<0.01
Cajun (0)	0	<0.01
Canadian (78)	112	0.13
Carpatho Rusyn (0)	0	<0.01
Celtic (0)	0	<0.01
Croatian (54)	111	0.13
Cypriot (0)	0	<0.01
Czech (65)	292	0.35
Czechoslovakian (75)	123	0.15
Danish (20)	91	0.11
Dutch (130)	487	0.58
Eastern European (1,163)	1,282	1.54
English (620)	2,751	3.30
Estonian (0)	0	<0.01
European (659)	690	0.83
Finnish (50)	119	0.14
French, ex. Basque (154)	874	1.05
French Canadian (98)	288	0.35
German (1,752)	7,742	9.28
German Russian (0)	0	<0.01
Greek (204)	613	0.74
Guyanese (77)	95	0.11
Hungarian (301)	1,008	1.21
Icelander (0)	0	<0.01
Iranian (100)	146	0.18
Irish (7,258)	15,823	18.97
Israeli (99)	247	0.30
Italian (9,086)	16,766	20.10
Latvian (64)	87	0.10
Lithuanian (129)	286	0.34
Luxemburger (0)	0	<0.01
Macedonian (24)	24	0.03
Maltese (0)	8	0.01
New Zealander (0)	3	<0.01
Northern European (15)	28	0.03

Ancestry	Population	%
Norwegian (214)	464	0.56
Pennsylvania German (0)	0	<0.01
Polish (1,491)	4,159	4.99
Portuguese (165)	216	0.26
Romanian (167)	544	0.65
Russian (2,652)	5,317	6.38
Scandinavian (12)	16	0.02
Scotch-Irish (228)	499	0.60
Scottish (102)	591	0.71
Serbian (11)	19	0.02
Slavic (11)	40	0.05
Slovak (179)	310	0.37
Slovene (0)	0	<0.01
Soviet Union (0)	0	<0.01
Swedish (65)	359	0.43
Swiss (39)	85	0.10
Turkish (66)	72	0.09
Ukrainian (387)	690	0.83
Welsh (212)	212	0.25
West Indian, ex. Hispanic (2,635)	2,834	3.40
Bahamian (0)	0	<0.01
Barbadian (10)	10	0.01
Belizean (9)	9	0.01
Bermudan (0)	3	<0.01
British West Indian (21)	45	0.05
Dutch West Indian (0)	0	<0.01
Haitian (2,003)	2,077	2.49
Jamaican (382)	432	0.52
Trinidadian/Tobagonian (90)	117	0.14
U.S. Virgin Islander (0)	0	<0.01
West Indian (120)	141	0.17
Other West Indian (0)	0	<0.01
Yugoslavian (43)	53	0.06

Hispanic Origin	Population	%
Hispanic or Latino (of any race)	9,831	11.68
Central American, ex. Mexican	1,656	1.97
Costa Rican	40	0.05
Guatemalan	802	0.95
Honduran	80	0.10
Nicaraguan	10	0.01
Panamanian	41	0.05
Salvadoran	662	0.79
Other Central American	21	0.02
Cuban	421	0.50
Dominican Republic	939	1.12
Mexican	897	1.07
Puerto Rican	3,427	4.07
South American	1,708	2.03
Argentinean	113	0.13
Bolivian	31	0.04
Chilean	73	0.09
Colombian	281	0.33
Ecuadorian	1,051	1.25
Paraguayan	5	0.01
Peruvian	119	0.14
Uruguayan	14	0.02
Venezuelan	14	0.02
Other South American	7	0.01
Other Hispanic or Latino	783	0.93

Race*	Population	%
African-American/Black (8,091)	8,965	10.65
Not Hispanic (7,598)	8,194	9.73
Hispanic (493)	771	0.92
American Indian/Alaska Native (193)	459	0.55
Not Hispanic (111)	308	0.37
Hispanic (82)	151	0.18
Alaska Athabascan (Ala. Nat.) (0)	0	<0.01
Aleut (Alaska Native) (0)	0	<0.01
Apache (0)	2	<0.01
Arapaho (0)	0	<0.01
Blackfeet (1)	8	0.01
Canadian/French Am. Ind. (0)	0	<0.01
Central American Ind. (1)	2	<0.01
Cherokee (1)	42	0.05
Cheyenne (0)	0	<0.01
Chickasaw (0)	0	<0.01
Chippewa (1)	1	<0.01

Race*	Population	%
Choctaw (1)	6	0.01
Colville (0)	0	<0.01
Comanche (0)	0	<0.01
Cree (0)	1	<0.01
Creek (0)	3	<0.01
Crow (0)	0	<0.01
Delaware (12)	16	0.02
Hopi (0)	0	<0.01
Houma (0)	0	<0.01
Inupiat (Alaska Native) (0)	0	<0.01
Iroquois (8)	13	0.02
Kiowa (0)	0	<0.01
Lumbee (2)	2	<0.01
Menominee (0)	0	<0.01
Mexican American Ind. (6)	8	0.01
Navajo (0)	1	<0.01
Osage (0)	0	<0.01
Ottawa (0)	0	<0.01
Paiute (1)	1	<0.01
Pima (0)	0	<0.01
Potawatomi (1)	1	<0.01
Pueblo (1)	4	<0.01
Puget Sound Salish (0)	0	<0.01
Seminole (0)	4	<0.01
Shoshone (0)	0	<0.01
Sioux (1)	2	<0.01
South American Ind. (22)	38	0.05
Spanish American Ind. (0)	0	<0.01
Tlingit-Haida (Alaska Native) (0)	1	<0.01
Tohono O'Odham (0)	0	<0.01
Tsimshian (Alaska Native) (0)	0	<0.01
Ute (0)	0	<0.01
Yakama (0)	0	<0.01
Yaqui (0)	0	<0.01
Yuman (0)	0	<0.01
Yup'ik (Alaska Native) (0)	0	<0.01
Asian (8,800)	9,614	11.42
Not Hispanic (8,748)	9,462	11.24
Hispanic (52)	152	0.18
Bangladeshi (73)	85	0.10
Bhutanese (0)	0	<0.01
Burmese (4)	8	0.01
Cambodian (59)	68	0.08
Chinese, ex. Taiwanese (1,132)	1,326	1.58
Filipino (2,079)	2,320	2.76
Hmong (0)	0	<0.01
Indian (3,576)	3,874	4.60
Indonesian (5)	14	0.02
Japanese (73)	110	0.13
Korean (994)	1,026	1.22
Laotian (0)	0	<0.01
Malaysian (3)	6	0.01
Nepalese (2)	2	<0.01
Pakistani (322)	346	0.41
Sri Lankan (43)	55	0.07
Taiwanese (49)	58	0.07
Thai (109)	121	0.14
Vietnamese (129)	164	0.19
Hawaii Native/Pacific Islander (22)	106	0.13
Not Hispanic (5)	77	0.09
Hispanic (17)	29	0.03
Fijian (0)	0	<0.01
Guamanian/Chamorro (13)	21	0.02
Marshallese (0)	0	<0.01
Native Hawaiian (1)	5	0.01
Samoan (1)	2	<0.01
Tongan (0)	0	<0.01
White (62,210)	63,664	75.62
Not Hispanic (56,369)	57,290	68.05
Hispanic (5,841)	6,374	7.57

*Notes: † The Census 2010 population figure is used to calculate the percentages in the Hispanic Origin and Race categories. Ancestry percentages are based on the 2006-2010 American Community Survey population (not shown); ‡ Numbers in parentheses indicate the number of people reporting a single ancestry; * Numbers in parentheses indicate the number of persons reporting this race alone, not in combination with any other race; Please refer to the Explanation of Data for more information.*

Clay

Place Type: Town
County: Onondaga
Population: 58,206

Ancestry	Population	%
Afghan (0)	0	<0.01
African, Sub-Saharan (172)	216	0.37
African (107)	145	0.25
Cape Verdean (0)	6	0.01
Ethiopian (0)	0	<0.01
Ghanaian (65)	65	0.11
Kenyan (0)	0	<0.01
Liberian (0)	0	<0.01
Nigerian (0)	0	<0.01
Senegalese (0)	0	<0.01
Sierra Leonean (0)	0	<0.01
Somalian (0)	0	<0.01
South African (0)	0	<0.01
Sudanese (0)	0	<0.01
Ugandan (0)	0	<0.01
Zimbabwean (0)	0	<0.01
Other Sub-Saharan African (0)	0	<0.01
Albanian (10)	31	0.05
Alsatian (0)	0	<0.01
American (1,975)	1,975	3.40
Arab (153)	417	0.72
Arab (58)	136	0.23
Egyptian (7)	7	0.01
Iraqi (0)	0	<0.01
Jordanian (0)	0	<0.01
Lebanese (47)	213	0.37
Moroccan (0)	0	<0.01
Palestinian (0)	13	0.02
Syrian (0)	7	0.01
Other Arab (41)	41	0.07
Armenian (0)	0	<0.01
Assyrian/Chaldean/Syriac (0)	0	<0.01
Australian (0)	0	<0.01
Austrian (49)	113	0.19
Basque (0)	0	<0.01
Belgian (57)	68	0.12
Brazilian (43)	43	0.07
British (33)	118	0.20
Bulgarian (0)	0	<0.01
Cajun (0)	0	<0.01
Canadian (176)	345	0.59
Carpatho Rusyn (0)	0	<0.01
Celtic (0)	47	0.08
Croatian (0)	0	<0.01
Cypriot (0)	0	<0.01
Czech (35)	312	0.54
Czechoslovakian (0)	34	0.06
Danish (0)	68	0.12
Dutch (106)	1,704	2.93
Eastern European (25)	40	0.07
English (1,748)	8,266	14.23
Estonian (0)	0	<0.01
European (505)	550	0.95
Finnish (20)	55	0.09
French, ex. Basque (420)	3,175	5.47
French Canadian (432)	1,241	2.14
German (2,624)	14,237	24.51
German Russian (0)	0	<0.01
Greek (203)	475	0.82
Guyanese (17)	17	0.03
Hungarian (170)	353	0.61
Icelander (0)	0	<0.01
Iranian (78)	99	0.17
Irish (3,324)	14,197	24.44
Israeli (0)	0	<0.01
Italian (5,434)	13,235	22.78
Latvian (0)	0	<0.01
Lithuanian (78)	143	0.25
Luxemburger (0)	26	0.04
Macedonian (177)	185	0.32
Maltese (0)	0	<0.01
New Zealander (0)	0	<0.01
Northern European (35)	35	0.06

Ancestry (cont.)	Population	%
Norwegian (55)	221	0.38
Pennsylvania German (20)	38	0.07
Polish (1,694)	4,728	8.14
Portuguese (0)	37	0.06
Romanian (0)	29	0.05
Russian (60)	276	0.48
Scandinavian (8)	8	0.01
Scotch-Irish (380)	1,162	2.00
Scottish (302)	1,377	2.37
Serbian (0)	9	0.02
Slavic (8)	93	0.16
Slovak (78)	150	0.26
Slovene (0)	9	0.02
Soviet Union (0)	0	<0.01
Swedish (114)	625	1.08
Swiss (22)	175	0.30
Turkish (11)	11	0.02
Ukrainian (136)	650	1.12
Welsh (52)	496	0.85
West Indian, ex. Hispanic (380)	494	0.85
Bahamian (0)	0	<0.01
Barbadian (9)	40	0.07
Belizean (0)	0	<0.01
Bermudan (0)	0	<0.01
British West Indian (0)	0	<0.01
Dutch West Indian (0)	0	<0.01
Haitian (157)	157	0.27
Jamaican (162)	245	0.42
Trinidadian/Tobagonian (40)	40	0.07
U.S. Virgin Islander (0)	0	<0.01
West Indian (12)	12	0.02
Other West Indian (0)	0	<0.01
Yugoslavian (108)	132	0.23

Hispanic Origin	Population	%
Hispanic or Latino (of any race)	1,472	2.53
Central American, ex. Mexican	94	0.16
Costa Rican	3	0.01
Guatemalan	35	0.06
Honduran	16	0.03
Nicaraguan	12	0.02
Panamanian	21	0.04
Salvadoran	7	0.01
Other Central American	0	<0.01
Cuban	91	0.16
Dominican Republic	61	0.10
Mexican	283	0.49
Puerto Rican	633	1.09
South American	161	0.28
Argentinean	7	0.01
Bolivian	8	0.01
Chilean	16	0.03
Colombian	65	0.11
Ecuadorian	10	0.02
Paraguayan	6	0.01
Peruvian	29	0.05
Uruguayan	2	<0.01
Venezuelan	16	0.03
Other South American	2	<0.01
Other Hispanic or Latino	149	0.26

Race*	Population	%
African-American/Black (2,524)	3,202	5.50
Not Hispanic (2,398)	3,014	5.18
Hispanic (126)	188	0.32
American Indian/Alaska Native (266)	627	1.08
Not Hispanic (228)	557	0.96
Hispanic (38)	70	0.12
Alaska Athabascan (Ala. Nat.) (0)	0	<0.01
Aleut (Alaska Native) (0)	0	<0.01
Apache (1)	3	0.01
Arapaho (0)	0	<0.01
Blackfeet (0)	11	0.02
Canadian/French Am. Ind. (9)	16	0.03
Central American Ind. (0)	0	<0.01
Cherokee (8)	42	0.07
Cheyenne (0)	0	<0.01
Chickasaw (0)	0	<0.01
Chippewa (5)	11	0.02

Race* (cont.)	Population	%
Choctaw (1)	5	0.01
Colville (0)	0	<0.01
Comanche (1)	1	<0.01
Cree (1)	1	<0.01
Creek (0)	1	<0.01
Crow (0)	0	<0.01
Delaware (0)	1	<0.01
Hopi (0)	2	<0.01
Houma (1)	1	<0.01
Inupiat (Alaska Native) (0)	1	<0.01
Iroquois (130)	252	0.43
Kiowa (0)	0	<0.01
Lumbee (0)	3	0.01
Menominee (0)	0	<0.01
Mexican American Ind. (5)	9	0.02
Navajo (3)	4	0.01
Osage (1)	1	<0.01
Ottawa (1)	1	<0.01
Paiute (0)	0	<0.01
Pima (0)	0	<0.01
Potawatomi (0)	1	<0.01
Pueblo (0)	0	<0.01
Puget Sound Salish (0)	0	<0.01
Seminole (0)	3	0.01
Shoshone (0)	0	<0.01
Sioux (2)	4	0.01
South American Ind. (1)	4	0.01
Spanish American Ind. (8)	8	0.01
Tlingit-Haida (Alaska Native) (0)	0	<0.01
Tohono O'Odham (0)	0	<0.01
Tsimshian (Alaska Native) (0)	0	<0.01
Ute (0)	0	<0.01
Yakama (0)	0	<0.01
Yaqui (0)	0	<0.01
Yuman (0)	0	<0.01
Yup'ik (Alaska Native) (0)	0	<0.01
Asian (1,430)	1,754	3.01
Not Hispanic (1,426)	1,733	2.98
Hispanic (4)	21	0.04
Bangladeshi (0)	1	<0.01
Bhutanese (0)	0	<0.01
Burmese (5)	5	0.01
Cambodian (28)	29	0.05
Chinese, ex. Taiwanese (259)	299	0.51
Filipino (123)	192	0.33
Hmong (61)	75	0.13
Indian (367)	398	0.68
Indonesian (1)	2	<0.01
Japanese (21)	66	0.11
Korean (130)	190	0.33
Laotian (47)	52	0.09
Malaysian (0)	1	<0.01
Nepalese (4)	4	0.01
Pakistani (47)	52	0.09
Sri Lankan (2)	2	<0.01
Taiwanese (11)	12	0.02
Thai (14)	18	0.03
Vietnamese (246)	265	0.46
Hawaii Native/Pacific Islander (20)	44	0.08
Not Hispanic (17)	40	0.07
Hispanic (3)	4	0.01
Fijian (0)	0	<0.01
Guamanian/Chamorro (6)	7	0.01
Marshallese (0)	0	<0.01
Native Hawaiian (7)	18	0.03
Samoan (0)	1	<0.01
Tongan (0)	0	<0.01
White (52,324)	53,514	91.94
Not Hispanic (51,459)	52,515	90.22
Hispanic (865)	999	1.72

Notes: † The Census 2010 population figure is used to calculate the percentages in the Hispanic Origin and Race categories. Ancestry percentages are based on the 2006-2010 American Community Survey population (not shown); ‡ Numbers in parentheses indicate the number of people reporting a single ancestry; * Numbers in parentheses indicate the number of persons reporting this race alone, not in combination with any other race; Please refer to the Explanation of Data for more information.

Colonie

Place Type: Town
County: Albany
Population: 81,591

Ancestry	Population	%
Afghan (0)	0	<0.01
African, Sub-Saharan (408)	482	0.59
African (259)	310	0.38
Cape Verdean (0)	0	<0.01
Ethiopian (13)	13	0.02
Ghanaian (11)	11	0.01
Kenyan (0)	0	<0.01
Liberian (0)	0	<0.01
Nigerian (80)	80	0.10
Senegalese (0)	0	<0.01
Sierra Leonean (0)	0	<0.01
Somalian (0)	0	<0.01
South African (9)	32	0.04
Sudanese (0)	0	<0.01
Ugandan (0)	0	<0.01
Zimbabwean (0)	0	<0.01
Other Sub-Saharan African (36)	36	0.04
Albanian (405)	405	0.50
Alsatian (0)	0	<0.01
American (2,133)	2,133	2.62
Arab (561)	863	1.06
Arab (0)	17	0.02
Egyptian (125)	125	0.15
Iraqi (0)	0	<0.01
Jordanian (0)	0	<0.01
Lebanese (144)	267	0.33
Moroccan (64)	111	0.14
Palestinian (72)	72	0.09
Syrian (27)	116	0.14
Other Arab (129)	155	0.19
Armenian (142)	244	0.30
Assyrian/Chaldean/Syriac (0)	0	<0.01
Australian (10)	10	0.01
Austrian (112)	470	0.58
Basque (0)	0	<0.01
Belgian (0)	25	0.03
Brazilian (13)	13	0.02
British (140)	240	0.29
Bulgarian (9)	9	0.01
Cajun (0)	0	<0.01
Canadian (114)	321	0.39
Carpatho Rusyn (0)	0	<0.01
Celtic (11)	11	0.01
Croatian (16)	74	0.09
Cypriot (0)	0	<0.01
Czech (134)	453	0.56
Czechoslovakian (26)	124	0.15
Danish (35)	195	0.24
Dutch (627)	3,334	4.09
Eastern European (46)	83	0.10
English (1,400)	8,332	10.22
Estonian (0)	0	<0.01
European (492)	544	0.67
Finnish (6)	68	0.08
French, ex. Basque (786)	5,795	7.11
French Canadian (545)	1,591	1.95
German (2,908)	14,495	17.78
German Russian (0)	0	<0.01
Greek (238)	563	0.69
Guyanese (116)	137	0.17
Hungarian (124)	542	0.66
Icelander (0)	0	<0.01
Iranian (0)	9	0.01
Irish (6,490)	23,049	28.27
Israeli (42)	42	0.05
Italian (6,582)	16,393	20.11
Latvian (34)	34	0.04
Lithuanian (55)	377	0.46
Luxemburger (0)	13	0.02
Macedonian (0)	0	<0.01
Maltese (0)	0	<0.01
New Zealander (0)	0	<0.01
Northern European (39)	39	0.05

Ancestry	Population	%
Norwegian (159)	598	0.73
Pennsylvania German (17)	25	0.03
Polish (2,206)	6,915	8.48
Portuguese (0)	80	0.10
Romanian (55)	228	0.28
Russian (690)	1,626	1.99
Scandinavian (27)	39	0.05
Scotch-Irish (468)	1,261	1.55
Scottish (263)	1,526	1.87
Serbian (0)	0	<0.01
Slavic (18)	28	0.03
Slovak (72)	185	0.23
Slovene (0)	0	<0.01
Soviet Union (0)	0	<0.01
Swedish (217)	944	1.16
Swiss (17)	145	0.18
Turkish (10)	10	0.01
Ukrainian (212)	860	1.05
Welsh (41)	704	0.86
West Indian, ex. Hispanic (372)	580	0.71
Bahamian (0)	0	<0.01
Barbadian (0)	0	<0.01
Belizean (0)	0	<0.01
Bermudan (0)	0	<0.01
British West Indian (0)	0	<0.01
Dutch West Indian (0)	0	<0.01
Haitian (60)	83	0.10
Jamaican (235)	373	0.46
Trinidadian/Tobagonian (0)	4	<0.01
U.S. Virgin Islander (0)	0	<0.01
West Indian (77)	120	0.15
Other West Indian (0)	0	<0.01
Yugoslavian (143)	143	0.18

Hispanic Origin	Population	%
Hispanic or Latino (of any race)	2,526	3.10
Central American, ex. Mexican	159	0.19
Costa Rican	24	0.03
Guatemalan	25	0.03
Honduran	20	0.02
Nicaraguan	17	0.02
Panamanian	13	0.02
Salvadoran	59	0.07
Other Central American	1	<0.01
Cuban	114	0.14
Dominican Republic	224	0.27
Mexican	462	0.57
Puerto Rican	1,001	1.23
South American	278	0.34
Argentinean	26	0.03
Bolivian	9	0.01
Chilean	12	0.01
Colombian	94	0.12
Ecuadorian	35	0.04
Paraguayan	3	<0.01
Peruvian	76	0.09
Uruguayan	1	<0.01
Venezuelan	19	0.02
Other South American	3	<0.01
Other Hispanic or Latino	288	0.35

Race*	Population	%
African-American/Black (4,288)	5,091	6.24
Not Hispanic (4,061)	4,752	5.82
Hispanic (227)	339	0.42
American Indian/Alaska Native (121)	397	0.49
Not Hispanic (79)	318	0.39
Hispanic (42)	79	0.10
Alaska Athabascan (Ala. Nat.) (1)	1	<0.01
Aleut (Alaska Native) (0)	0	<0.01
Apache (0)	0	<0.01
Arapaho (0)	0	<0.01
Blackfeet (1)	11	0.01
Canadian/French Am. Ind. (6)	10	0.01
Central American Ind. (3)	3	<0.01
Cherokee (6)	32	0.04
Cheyenne (0)	0	<0.01
Chickasaw (0)	0	<0.01
Chippewa (0)	1	<0.01

Race*	Population	%
Choctaw (0)	1	<0.01
Colville (0)	0	<0.01
Comanche (0)	0	<0.01
Cree (0)	2	<0.01
Creek (0)	0	<0.01
Crow (1)	1	<0.01
Delaware (0)	0	<0.01
Hopi (0)	0	<0.01
Houma (0)	0	<0.01
Inupiat (Alaska Native) (0)	0	<0.01
Iroquois (15)	50	0.06
Kiowa (0)	0	<0.01
Lumbee (0)	0	<0.01
Menominee (0)	0	<0.01
Mexican American Ind. (28)	29	0.04
Navajo (0)	1	<0.01
Osage (0)	1	<0.01
Ottawa (0)	0	<0.01
Paiute (0)	0	<0.01
Pima (0)	0	<0.01
Potawatomi (0)	1	<0.01
Pueblo (0)	0	<0.01
Puget Sound Salish (0)	0	<0.01
Seminole (0)	3	<0.01
Shoshone (0)	0	<0.01
Sioux (3)	7	0.01
South American Ind. (5)	10	0.01
Spanish American Ind. (0)	2	<0.01
Tlingit-Haida (Alaska Native) (1)	1	<0.01
Tohono O'Odham (0)	0	<0.01
Tsimshian (Alaska Native) (0)	0	<0.01
Ute (0)	0	<0.01
Yakama (0)	0	<0.01
Yaqui (0)	0	<0.01
Yuman (0)	0	<0.01
Yup'ik (Alaska Native) (0)	0	<0.01
Asian (5,353)	5,892	7.22
Not Hispanic (5,342)	5,866	7.19
Hispanic (11)	26	0.03
Bangladeshi (78)	80	0.10
Bhutanese (0)	0	<0.01
Burmese (3)	4	<0.01
Cambodian (2)	3	<0.01
Chinese, ex. Taiwanese (1,186)	1,284	1.57
Filipino (306)	397	0.49
Hmong (0)	0	<0.01
Indian (1,969)	2,099	2.57
Indonesian (11)	13	0.02
Japanese (58)	90	0.11
Korean (471)	531	0.65
Laotian (2)	4	<0.01
Malaysian (3)	5	0.01
Nepalese (13)	13	0.02
Pakistani (680)	736	0.90
Sri Lankan (24)	30	0.04
Taiwanese (48)	60	0.07
Thai (30)	40	0.05
Vietnamese (313)	360	0.44
Hawaii Native/Pacific Islander (15)	66	0.08
Not Hispanic (14)	47	0.06
Hispanic (1)	19	0.02
Fijian (1)	1	<0.01
Guamanian/Chamorro (2)	6	0.01
Marshallese (0)	0	<0.01
Native Hawaiian (2)	10	0.01
Samoan (4)	9	0.01
Tongan (1)	5	0.01
White (69,541)	70,917	86.92
Not Hispanic (68,088)	69,290	84.92
Hispanic (1,453)	1,627	1.99

*Notes: † The Census 2010 population figure is used to calculate the percentages in the Hispanic Origin and Race categories. Ancestry percentages are based on the 2006-2010 American Community Survey population (not shown); ‡ Numbers in parentheses indicate the number of people reporting a single ancestry; * Numbers in parentheses indicate the number of persons reporting this race alone, not in combination with any other race; Please refer to the Explanation of Data for more information.*

Greece

Place Type: Town
County: Monroe
Population: 96,095

Ancestry	Population	%
Afghan (0)	0	<0.01
African, Sub-Saharan (373)	434	0.45
African (217)	244	0.26
Cape Verdean (0)	0	<0.01
Ethiopian (49)	49	0.05
Ghanaian (0)	0	<0.01
Kenyan (0)	0	<0.01
Liberian (0)	0	<0.01
Nigerian (0)	0	<0.01
Senegalese (0)	0	<0.01
Sierra Leonean (0)	0	<0.01
Somalian (0)	0	<0.01
South African (38)	48	0.05
Sudanese (27)	51	0.05
Ugandan (0)	0	<0.01
Zimbabwean (0)	0	<0.01
Other Sub-Saharan African (42)	42	0.04
Albanian (113)	113	0.12
Alsatian (0)	0	<0.01
American (2,361)	2,361	2.47
Arab (161)	384	0.40
Arab (0)	42	0.04
Egyptian (0)	0	<0.01
Iraqi (0)	0	<0.01
Jordanian (0)	0	<0.01
Lebanese (98)	214	0.22
Moroccan (0)	0	<0.01
Palestinian (0)	31	0.03
Syrian (63)	97	0.10
Other Arab (0)	0	<0.01
Armenian (0)	0	<0.01
Assyrian/Chaldean/Syriac (0)	0	<0.01
Australian (29)	87	0.09
Austrian (36)	225	0.24
Basque (0)	0	<0.01
Belgian (57)	254	0.27
Brazilian (23)	23	0.02
British (178)	387	0.41
Bulgarian (25)	25	0.03
Cajun (0)	0	<0.01
Canadian (228)	525	0.55
Carpatho Rusyn (0)	0	<0.01
Celtic (12)	12	0.01
Croatian (0)	13	0.01
Cypriot (0)	0	<0.01
Czech (77)	507	0.53
Czechoslovakian (55)	151	0.16
Danish (40)	144	0.15
Dutch (571)	2,890	3.03
Eastern European (81)	115	0.12
English (3,011)	12,568	13.17
Estonian (0)	40	0.04
European (406)	451	0.47
Finnish (15)	62	0.06
French, ex. Basque (553)	3,655	3.83
French Canadian (346)	1,220	1.28
German (6,357)	25,631	26.85
German Russian (0)	0	<0.01
Greek (153)	610	0.64
Guyanese (40)	40	0.04
Hungarian (85)	397	0.42
Icelander (0)	0	<0.01
Iranian (14)	14	0.01
Irish (4,177)	19,015	19.92
Israeli (0)	0	<0.01
Italian (15,156)	26,121	27.36
Latvian (12)	71	0.07
Lithuanian (183)	543	0.57
Luxemburger (0)	15	0.02
Macedonian (92)	119	0.12
Maltese (0)	0	<0.01
New Zealander (0)	0	<0.01
Northern European (0)	0	<0.01
Norwegian (139)	434	0.45
Pennsylvania German (46)	145	0.15
Polish (1,797)	5,879	6.16
Portuguese (111)	314	0.33
Romanian (16)	60	0.06
Russian (229)	654	0.69
Scandinavian (10)	88	0.09
Scotch-Irish (524)	1,469	1.54
Scottish (452)	1,843	1.93
Serbian (10)	10	0.01
Slavic (156)	240	0.25
Slovak (81)	236	0.25
Slovene (31)	31	0.03
Soviet Union (0)	0	<0.01
Swedish (31)	447	0.47
Swiss (16)	116	0.12
Turkish (489)	561	0.59
Ukrainian (993)	1,758	1.84
Welsh (36)	564	0.59
West Indian, ex. Hispanic (285)	447	0.47
Bahamian (0)	0	<0.01
Barbadian (16)	16	0.02
Belizean (0)	0	<0.01
Bermudan (0)	0	<0.01
British West Indian (0)	0	<0.01
Dutch West Indian (0)	0	<0.01
Haitian (114)	114	0.12
Jamaican (144)	243	0.25
Trinidadian/Tobagonian (11)	27	0.03
U.S. Virgin Islander (0)	0	<0.01
West Indian (0)	47	0.05
Other West Indian (0)	0	<0.01
Yugoslavian (77)	91	0.10

Hispanic Origin	Population	%
Hispanic or Latino (of any race)	4,625	4.81
Central American, ex. Mexican	159	0.17
Costa Rican	11	0.01
Guatemalan	27	0.03
Honduran	12	0.01
Nicaraguan	22	0.02
Panamanian	18	0.02
Salvadoran	68	0.07
Other Central American	1	<0.01
Cuban	312	0.32
Dominican Republic	194	0.20
Mexican	338	0.35
Puerto Rican	3,072	3.20
South American	257	0.27
Argentinean	7	0.01
Bolivian	1	<0.01
Chilean	63	0.07
Colombian	89	0.09
Ecuadorian	21	0.02
Paraguayan	4	<0.01
Peruvian	33	0.03
Uruguayan	4	<0.01
Venezuelan	27	0.03
Other South American	8	0.01
Other Hispanic or Latino	293	0.30

Race*	Population	%
African-American/Black (5,743)	6,728	7.00
Not Hispanic (5,446)	6,227	6.48
Hispanic (297)	501	0.52
American Indian/Alaska Native (263)	658	0.68
Not Hispanic (212)	545	0.57
Hispanic (51)	113	0.12
Alaska Athabascan (Ala. Nat.) (0)	0	<0.01
Aleut (Alaska Native) (0)	0	<0.01
Apache (1)	3	<0.01
Arapaho (0)	4	<0.01
Blackfeet (1)	9	0.01
Canadian/French Am. Ind. (8)	14	0.01
Central American Ind. (5)	6	0.01
Cherokee (7)	75	0.08
Cheyenne (0)	0	<0.01
Chickasaw (0)	0	<0.01
Chippewa (10)	13	0.01

	Population	%
Choctaw (3)	8	0.01
Colville (0)	0	<0.01
Comanche (0)	1	<0.01
Cree (3)	4	<0.01
Creek (2)	2	<0.01
Crow (0)	0	<0.01
Delaware (0)	1	<0.01
Hopi (0)	0	<0.01
Houma (2)	2	<0.01
Inupiat (Alaska Native) (0)	1	<0.01
Iroquois (114)	181	0.19
Kiowa (0)	0	<0.01
Lumbee (0)	0	<0.01
Menominee (0)	0	<0.01
Mexican American Ind. (4)	7	0.01
Navajo (2)	2	<0.01
Osage (0)	0	<0.01
Ottawa (0)	0	<0.01
Paiute (0)	0	<0.01
Pima (0)	0	<0.01
Potawatomi (0)	0	<0.01
Pueblo (0)	0	<0.01
Puget Sound Salish (0)	0	<0.01
Seminole (1)	4	<0.01
Shoshone (0)	1	<0.01
Sioux (3)	11	0.01
South American Ind. (7)	16	0.02
Spanish American Ind. (1)	5	0.01
Tlingit-Haida (Alaska Native) (0)	1	<0.01
Tohono O'Odham (0)	0	<0.01
Tsimshian (Alaska Native) (0)	0	<0.01
Ute (0)	0	<0.01
Yakama (0)	0	<0.01
Yaqui (0)	0	<0.01
Yuman (1)	1	<0.01
Yup'ik (Alaska Native) (0)	0	<0.01
Asian (1,664)	2,054	2.14
Not Hispanic (1,643)	2,014	2.10
Hispanic (21)	40	0.04
Bangladeshi (6)	9	0.01
Bhutanese (0)	0	<0.01
Burmese (0)	0	<0.01
Cambodian (33)	47	0.05
Chinese, ex. Taiwanese (294)	351	0.37
Filipino (141)	213	0.22
Hmong (0)	0	<0.01
Indian (283)	330	0.34
Indonesian (3)	5	0.01
Japanese (28)	71	0.07
Korean (209)	261	0.27
Laotian (112)	139	0.14
Malaysian (0)	0	<0.01
Nepalese (3)	3	<0.01
Pakistani (25)	32	0.03
Sri Lankan (5)	5	<0.01
Taiwanese (10)	11	0.01
Thai (21)	24	0.02
Vietnamese (433)	473	0.49
Hawaii Native/Pacific Islander (14)	59	0.06
Not Hispanic (12)	40	0.04
Hispanic (2)	19	0.02
Fijian (0)	0	<0.01
Guamanian/Chamorro (4)	7	0.01
Marshallese (0)	0	<0.01
Native Hawaiian (5)	18	0.02
Samoan (2)	5	0.01
Tongan (0)	0	<0.01
White (85,220)	86,829	90.36
Not Hispanic (82,634)	83,902	87.31
Hispanic (2,586)	2,927	3.05

Notes: † The Census 2010 population figure is used to calculate the percentages in the Hispanic Origin and Race categories. Ancestry percentages are based on the 2006-2010 American Community Survey population (not shown); ‡ Numbers in parentheses indicate the number of people reporting a single ancestry; * Numbers in parentheses indicate the number of persons reporting this race alone, not in combination with any other race; Please refer to the Explanation of Data for more information.

Greenburgh

Place Type: Town
County: Westchester
Population: 88,400

Ancestry	Population	%
Afghan (0)	0	<0.01
African, Sub-Saharan (642)	914	1.04
African (287)	536	0.61
Cape Verdean (0)	0	<0.01
Ethiopian (39)	39	0.04
Ghanaian (16)	16	0.02
Kenyan (55)	55	0.06
Liberian (0)	0	<0.01
Nigerian (231)	231	0.26
Senegalese (0)	0	<0.01
Sierra Leonean (14)	14	0.02
Somalian (0)	0	<0.01
South African (0)	23	0.03
Sudanese (0)	0	<0.01
Ugandan (0)	0	<0.01
Zimbabwean (0)	0	<0.01
Other Sub-Saharan African (0)	0	<0.01
Albanian (80)	80	0.09
Alsatian (0)	0	<0.01
American (3,324)	3,324	3.79
Arab (306)	485	0.55
Arab (0)	22	0.03
Egyptian (9)	37	0.04
Iraqi (0)	0	<0.01
Jordanian (45)	45	0.05
Lebanese (213)	224	0.26
Moroccan (0)	35	0.04
Palestinian (0)	8	0.01
Syrian (32)	107	0.12
Other Arab (7)	7	0.01
Armenian (109)	175	0.20
Assyrian/Chaldean/Syriac (15)	29	0.03
Australian (0)	24	0.03
Austrian (267)	1,117	1.27
Basque (0)	8	0.01
Belgian (21)	93	0.11
Brazilian (74)	123	0.14
British (358)	519	0.59
Bulgarian (54)	54	0.06
Cajun (0)	0	<0.01
Canadian (53)	282	0.32
Carpatho Rusyn (0)	0	<0.01
Celtic (0)	7	0.01
Croatian (384)	609	0.69
Cypriot (0)	0	<0.01
Czech (40)	415	0.47
Czechoslovakian (72)	172	0.20
Danish (10)	130	0.15
Dutch (174)	580	0.66
Eastern European (1,840)	2,009	2.29
English (1,185)	4,118	4.70
Estonian (15)	57	0.07
European (1,275)	1,360	1.55
Finnish (34)	85	0.10
French, ex. Basque (225)	1,496	1.71
French Canadian (166)	483	0.55
German (1,568)	7,526	8.58
German Russian (0)	13	0.01
Greek (762)	1,202	1.37
Guyanese (52)	226	0.26
Hungarian (520)	1,242	1.42
Icelander (0)	0	<0.01
Iranian (248)	267	0.30
Irish (4,736)	11,358	12.95
Israeli (172)	225	0.26
Italian (9,180)	16,339	18.64
Latvian (48)	153	0.17
Lithuanian (51)	328	0.37
Luxemburger (0)	0	<0.01
Macedonian (24)	24	0.03
Maltese (0)	11	0.01
New Zealander (0)	0	<0.01
Northern European (47)	65	0.07
Norwegian (204)	530	0.60
Pennsylvania German (0)	0	<0.01
Polish (1,541)	4,636	5.29
Portuguese (534)	718	0.82
Romanian (234)	489	0.56
Russian (2,209)	5,042	5.75
Scandinavian (46)	79	0.09
Scotch-Irish (336)	741	0.85
Scottish (258)	987	1.13
Serbian (8)	8	0.01
Slavic (6)	6	0.01
Slovak (117)	388	0.44
Slovene (0)	0	<0.01
Soviet Union (0)	0	<0.01
Swedish (33)	374	0.43
Swiss (46)	211	0.24
Turkish (85)	172	0.20
Ukrainian (263)	652	0.74
Welsh (0)	81	0.09
West Indian, ex. Hispanic (2,889)	3,562	4.06
Bahamian (0)	0	<0.01
Barbadian (143)	155	0.18
Belizean (10)	19	0.02
Bermudan (0)	0	<0.01
British West Indian (65)	76	0.09
Dutch West Indian (0)	0	<0.01
Haitian (469)	516	0.59
Jamaican (1,753)	2,150	2.45
Trinidadian/Tobagonian (159)	201	0.23
U.S. Virgin Islander (0)	0	<0.01
West Indian (290)	445	0.51
Other West Indian (0)	0	<0.01
Yugoslavian (123)	130	0.15

Hispanic Origin	Population	%
Hispanic or Latino (of any race)	12,366	13.99
Central American, ex. Mexican	878	0.99
Costa Rican	34	0.04
Guatemalan	434	0.49
Honduran	90	0.10
Nicaraguan	50	0.06
Panamanian	73	0.08
Salvadoran	185	0.21
Other Central American	12	0.01
Cuban	565	0.64
Dominican Republic	1,400	1.58
Mexican	1,711	1.94
Puerto Rican	2,629	2.97
South American	4,004	4.53
Argentinean	188	0.21
Bolivian	48	0.05
Chilean	192	0.22
Colombian	845	0.96
Ecuadorian	1,434	1.62
Paraguayan	144	0.16
Peruvian	962	1.09
Uruguayan	65	0.07
Venezuelan	94	0.11
Other South American	32	0.04
Other Hispanic or Latino	1,179	1.33

Race*	Population	%
African-American/Black (11,103)	12,045	13.63
Not Hispanic (10,377)	11,022	12.47
Hispanic (726)	1,023	1.16
American Indian/Alaska Native (201)	630	0.71
Not Hispanic (64)	334	0.38
Hispanic (137)	296	0.33
Alaska Athabascan (Ala. Nat.) (0)	0	<0.01
Aleut (Alaska Native) (0)	1	<0.01
Apache (1)	6	0.01
Arapaho (0)	0	<0.01
Blackfeet (0)	7	0.01
Canadian/French Am. Ind. (0)	2	<0.01
Central American Ind. (1)	4	<0.01
Cherokee (5)	90	0.10
Cheyenne (0)	5	0.01
Chickasaw (0)	1	<0.01
Chippewa (0)	4	<0.01

	Population	%
Choctaw (0)	3	<0.01
Colville (0)	0	<0.01
Comanche (0)	5	<0.01
Cree (0)	3	<0.01
Creek (0)	0	<0.01
Crow (0)	0	<0.01
Delaware (3)	5	0.01
Hopi (0)	0	<0.01
Houma (0)	0	<0.01
Inupiat (Alaska Native) (1)	1	<0.01
Iroquois (6)	19	0.02
Kiowa (0)	0	<0.01
Lumbee (1)	1	<0.01
Menominee (0)	0	<0.01
Mexican American Ind. (10)	25	0.03
Navajo (0)	3	<0.01
Osage (0)	0	<0.01
Ottawa (0)	0	<0.01
Paiute (0)	0	<0.01
Pima (0)	0	<0.01
Potawatomi (0)	0	<0.01
Pueblo (0)	0	<0.01
Puget Sound Salish (0)	0	<0.01
Seminole (0)	3	<0.01
Shoshone (0)	0	<0.01
Sioux (1)	8	0.01
South American Ind. (30)	72	0.08
Spanish American Ind. (14)	23	0.03
Tlingit-Haida (Alaska Native) (0)	0	<0.01
Tohono O'Odham (0)	0	<0.01
Tsimshian (Alaska Native) (0)	0	<0.01
Ute (0)	0	<0.01
Yakama (0)	0	<0.01
Yaqui (0)	0	<0.01
Yuman (0)	0	<0.01
Yup'ik (Alaska Native) (0)	0	<0.01
Asian (9,210)	10,180	11.52
Not Hispanic (9,155)	10,025	11.34
Hispanic (55)	155	0.18
Bangladeshi (37)	44	0.05
Bhutanese (8)	8	0.01
Burmese (28)	28	0.03
Cambodian (4)	4	<0.01
Chinese, ex. Taiwanese (1,910)	2,225	2.52
Filipino (826)	959	1.08
Hmong (0)	0	<0.01
Indian (3,241)	3,518	3.98
Indonesian (18)	24	0.03
Japanese (1,018)	1,230	1.39
Korean (1,328)	1,452	1.64
Laotian (3)	5	0.01
Malaysian (6)	11	0.01
Nepalese (48)	55	0.06
Pakistani (212)	244	0.28
Sri Lankan (14)	20	0.02
Taiwanese (113)	142	0.16
Thai (62)	77	0.09
Vietnamese (81)	95	0.11
Hawaii Native/Pacific Islander (33)	116	0.13
Not Hispanic (23)	88	0.10
Hispanic (10)	28	0.03
Fijian (0)	0	<0.01
Guamanian/Chamorro (11)	16	0.02
Marshallese (1)	1	<0.01
Native Hawaiian (1)	10	0.01
Samoan (1)	5	0.01
Tongan (0)	0	<0.01
White (61,185)	63,005	71.27
Not Hispanic (54,539)	55,731	63.04
Hispanic (6,646)	7,274	8.23

*Notes: † The Census 2010 population figure is used to calculate the percentages in the Hispanic Origin and Race categories. Ancestry percentages are based on the 2006-2010 American Community Survey population (not shown); ‡ Numbers in parentheses indicate the number of people reporting a single ancestry; * Numbers in parentheses indicate the number of persons reporting this race alone, not in combination with any other race; Please refer to the Explanation of Data for more information.*

Hamburg

Place Type: Town
County: Erie
Population: 56,936

Ancestry	Population	%
Afghan (0)	0	<0.01
African, Sub-Saharan (57)	57	0.10
African (0)	0	<0.01
Cape Verdean (0)	0	<0.01
Ethiopian (0)	0	<0.01
Ghanaian (0)	0	<0.01
Kenyan (0)	0	<0.01
Liberian (0)	0	<0.01
Nigerian (0)	0	<0.01
Senegalese (0)	0	<0.01
Sierra Leonean (0)	0	<0.01
Somalian (0)	0	<0.01
South African (57)	57	0.10
Sudanese (0)	0	<0.01
Ugandan (0)	0	<0.01
Zimbabwean (0)	0	<0.01
Other Sub-Saharan African (0)	0	<0.01
Albanian (0)	0	<0.01
Alsatian (9)	27	0.05
American (1,835)	1,835	3.24
Arab (93)	325	0.57
Arab (23)	70	0.12
Egyptian (38)	38	0.07
Iraqi (0)	0	<0.01
Jordanian (0)	11	0.02
Lebanese (17)	136	0.24
Moroccan (0)	26	0.05
Palestinian (15)	15	0.03
Syrian (0)	0	<0.01
Other Arab (0)	29	0.05
Armenian (0)	0	<0.01
Assyrian/Chaldean/Syriac (0)	0	<0.01
Australian (0)	0	<0.01
Austrian (35)	216	0.38
Basque (0)	0	<0.01
Belgian (0)	25	0.04
Brazilian (0)	0	<0.01
British (66)	154	0.27
Bulgarian (183)	192	0.34
Cajun (0)	0	<0.01
Canadian (180)	368	0.65
Carpatho Rusyn (0)	0	<0.01
Celtic (43)	43	0.08
Croatian (37)	246	0.43
Cypriot (0)	0	<0.01
Czech (45)	144	0.25
Czechoslovakian (27)	57	0.10
Danish (32)	66	0.12
Dutch (69)	660	1.17
Eastern European (37)	45	0.08
English (1,093)	5,284	9.34
Estonian (0)	0	<0.01
European (223)	250	0.44
Finnish (0)	9	0.02
French, ex. Basque (199)	2,079	3.67
French Canadian (153)	586	1.04
German (5,209)	19,590	34.62
German Russian (0)	0	<0.01
Greek (61)	186	0.33
Guyanese (33)	33	0.06
Hungarian (200)	761	1.34
Icelander (0)	0	<0.01
Iranian (44)	44	0.08
Irish (3,944)	15,679	27.71
Israeli (0)	0	<0.01
Italian (3,775)	10,185	18.00
Latvian (0)	11	0.02
Lithuanian (26)	63	0.11
Luxemburger (0)	0	<0.01
Macedonian (119)	149	0.26
Maltese (0)	0	<0.01
New Zealander (0)	0	<0.01
Northern European (0)	0	<0.01

Ancestry	Population	%
Norwegian (9)	52	0.09
Pennsylvania German (39)	103	0.18
Polish (5,175)	13,189	23.31
Portuguese (0)	45	0.08
Romanian (0)	0	<0.01
Russian (39)	385	0.68
Scandinavian (0)	8	0.01
Scotch-Irish (164)	542	0.96
Scottish (159)	836	1.48
Serbian (55)	279	0.49
Slavic (0)	57	0.10
Slovak (24)	182	0.32
Slovene (0)	16	0.03
Soviet Union (0)	0	<0.01
Swedish (188)	948	1.68
Swiss (17)	57	0.10
Turkish (0)	0	<0.01
Ukrainian (185)	664	1.17
Welsh (105)	292	0.52
West Indian, ex. Hispanic (200)	230	0.41
Bahamian (21)	21	0.04
Barbadian (0)	0	<0.01
Belizean (0)	30	0.05
Bermudan (0)	0	<0.01
British West Indian (0)	0	<0.01
Dutch West Indian (0)	0	<0.01
Haitian (0)	0	<0.01
Jamaican (144)	144	0.25
Trinidadian/Tobagonian (13)	13	0.02
U.S. Virgin Islander (0)	0	<0.01
West Indian (22)	22	0.04
Other West Indian (0)	0	<0.01
Yugoslavian (43)	70	0.12

Hispanic Origin	Population	%
Hispanic or Latino (of any race)	1,214	2.13
Central American, ex. Mexican	38	0.07
Costa Rican	7	0.01
Guatemalan	20	0.04
Honduran	2	<0.01
Nicaraguan	4	0.01
Panamanian	0	<0.01
Salvadoran	5	0.01
Other Central American	0	<0.01
Cuban	29	0.05
Dominican Republic	32	0.06
Mexican	296	0.52
Puerto Rican	551	0.97
South American	72	0.13
Argentinean	4	0.01
Bolivian	7	0.01
Chilean	8	0.01
Colombian	37	0.06
Ecuadorian	2	<0.01
Paraguayan	2	<0.01
Peruvian	10	0.02
Uruguayan	0	<0.01
Venezuelan	2	<0.01
Other South American	0	<0.01
Other Hispanic or Latino	196	0.34

Race*	Population	%
African-American/Black (433)	664	1.17
Not Hispanic (404)	608	1.07
Hispanic (29)	56	0.10
American Indian/Alaska Native (179)	319	0.56
Not Hispanic (158)	290	0.51
Hispanic (21)	29	0.05
Alaska Athabascan (Ala. Nat.) (0)	0	<0.01
Aleut (Alaska Native) (0)	0	<0.01
Apache (1)	1	<0.01
Arapaho (0)	0	<0.01
Blackfeet (1)	2	<0.01
Canadian/French Am. Ind. (8)	12	0.02
Central American Ind. (0)	0	<0.01
Cherokee (9)	19	0.03
Cheyenne (0)	0	<0.01
Chickasaw (0)	0	<0.01
Chippewa (2)	7	0.01

	Population	%
Choctaw (0)	0	<0.01
Colville (0)	0	<0.01
Comanche (1)	1	<0.01
Cree (0)	0	<0.01
Creek (0)	0	<0.01
Crow (0)	2	<0.01
Delaware (1)	1	<0.01
Hopi (0)	0	<0.01
Houma (0)	0	<0.01
Inupiat (Alaska Native) (0)	0	<0.01
Iroquois (100)	159	0.28
Kiowa (0)	0	<0.01
Lumbee (0)	1	<0.01
Menominee (0)	0	<0.01
Mexican American Ind. (4)	5	0.01
Navajo (0)	0	<0.01
Osage (0)	0	<0.01
Ottawa (0)	0	<0.01
Paiute (0)	2	<0.01
Pima (0)	0	<0.01
Potawatomi (0)	0	<0.01
Pueblo (0)	0	<0.01
Puget Sound Salish (0)	0	<0.01
Seminole (0)	1	<0.01
Shoshone (0)	0	<0.01
Sioux (1)	3	0.01
South American Ind. (1)	1	<0.01
Spanish American Ind. (2)	2	<0.01
Tlingit-Haida (Alaska Native) (0)	0	<0.01
Tohono O'Odham (0)	0	<0.01
Tsimshian (Alaska Native) (0)	0	<0.01
Ute (0)	0	<0.01
Yakama (0)	0	<0.01
Yaqui (0)	0	<0.01
Yuman (0)	0	<0.01
Yup'ik (Alaska Native) (0)	0	<0.01
Asian (325)	431	0.76
Not Hispanic (322)	423	0.74
Hispanic (3)	8	0.01
Bangladeshi (0)	0	<0.01
Bhutanese (0)	0	<0.01
Burmese (0)	0	<0.01
Cambodian (3)	3	0.01
Chinese, ex. Taiwanese (63)	80	0.14
Filipino (31)	52	0.09
Hmong (0)	0	<0.01
Indian (72)	85	0.15
Indonesian (3)	5	0.01
Japanese (7)	19	0.03
Korean (43)	61	0.11
Laotian (3)	9	0.02
Malaysian (0)	0	<0.01
Nepalese (0)	0	<0.01
Pakistani (11)	11	0.02
Sri Lankan (0)	0	<0.01
Taiwanese (2)	2	<0.01
Thai (26)	32	0.06
Vietnamese (31)	35	0.06
Hawaii Native/Pacific Islander (6)	18	0.03
Not Hispanic (4)	14	0.02
Hispanic (2)	4	0.01
Fijian (0)	0	<0.01
Guamanian/Chamorro (4)	8	0.01
Marshallese (0)	0	<0.01
Native Hawaiian (0)	4	0.01
Samoan (0)	0	<0.01
Tongan (0)	0	<0.01
White (55,242)	55,749	97.92
Not Hispanic (54,366)	54,789	96.23
Hispanic (876)	960	1.69

Notes: † The Census 2010 population figure is used to calculate the percentages in the Hispanic Origin and Race categories. Ancestry percentages are based on the 2006-2010 American Community Survey population (not shown); ‡ Numbers in parentheses indicate the number of people reporting a single ancestry; * Numbers in parentheses indicate the number of persons reporting this race alone, not in combination with any other race; Please refer to the Explanation of Data for more information.

Hempstead

Place Type: Town
County: Nassau
Population: 759,757

Ancestry	Population	%
Afghan (260)	399	0.05
African, Sub-Saharan (4,323)	5,844	0.78
African (2,716)	3,879	0.51
Cape Verdean (0)	0	<0.01
Ethiopian (38)	106	0.01
Ghanaian (239)	306	0.04
Kenyan (0)	0	<0.01
Liberian (0)	0	<0.01
Nigerian (952)	1,115	0.15
Senegalese (0)	0	<0.01
Sierra Leonean (11)	11	<0.01
Somalian (15)	15	<0.01
South African (72)	104	0.01
Sudanese (33)	33	<0.01
Ugandan (0)	0	<0.01
Zimbabwean (0)	0	<0.01
Other Sub-Saharan African (247)	275	0.04
Albanian (733)	1,052	0.14
Alsatian (0)	30	<0.01
American (23,869)	23,869	3.17
Arab (2,403)	4,218	0.56
Arab (232)	319	0.04
Egyptian (787)	1,227	0.16
Iraqi (149)	284	0.04
Jordanian (66)	66	0.01
Lebanese (270)	657	0.09
Moroccan (163)	376	0.05
Palestinian (64)	113	0.01
Syrian (103)	512	0.07
Other Arab (569)	664	0.09
Armenian (922)	1,451	0.19
Assyrian/Chaldean/Syriac (3)	19	<0.01
Australian (98)	236	0.03
Austrian (1,518)	4,963	0.66
Basque (2)	43	0.01
Belgian (136)	405	0.05
Brazilian (208)	479	0.06
British (540)	1,197	0.16
Bulgarian (158)	181	0.02
Cajun (0)	0	<0.01
Canadian (321)	1,084	0.14
Carpatho Rusyn (4)	36	<0.01
Celtic (13)	24	<0.01
Croatian (536)	1,033	0.14
Cypriot (197)	254	0.03
Czech (615)	2,447	0.32
Czechoslovakian (357)	1,054	0.14
Danish (150)	1,023	0.14
Dutch (387)	3,142	0.42
Eastern European (5,468)	5,775	0.77
English (3,407)	21,808	2.89
Estonian (120)	175	0.02
European (5,191)	5,650	0.75
Finnish (105)	647	0.09
French, ex. Basque (1,119)	8,239	1.09
French Canadian (440)	1,779	0.24
German (15,495)	78,518	10.42
German Russian (0)	17	<0.01
Greek (6,061)	10,033	1.33
Guyanese (2,705)	3,520	0.47
Hungarian (2,954)	6,992	0.93
Icelander (19)	92	0.01
Iranian (290)	539	0.07
Irish (41,161)	125,911	16.71
Israeli (1,902)	2,558	0.34
Italian (90,988)	164,467	21.82
Latvian (193)	438	0.06
Lithuanian (826)	2,538	0.34
Luxemburger (0)	0	<0.01
Macedonian (41)	51	0.01
Maltese (254)	540	0.07
New Zealander (0)	0	<0.01
Northern European (433)	514	0.07
Norwegian (826)	3,371	0.45
Pennsylvania German (82)	143	0.02
Polish (11,210)	35,774	4.75
Portuguese (1,774)	2,805	0.37
Romanian (1,090)	2,811	0.37
Russian (11,619)	26,754	3.55
Scandinavian (171)	360	0.05
Scotch-Irish (1,797)	4,788	0.64
Scottish (822)	3,831	0.51
Serbian (23)	38	0.01
Slavic (62)	166	0.02
Slovak (182)	702	0.09
Slovene (6)	89	0.01
Soviet Union (0)	10	<0.01
Swedish (601)	3,930	0.52
Swiss (173)	1,183	0.16
Turkish (820)	1,202	0.16
Ukrainian (1,249)	2,806	0.37
Welsh (84)	865	0.11
West Indian, ex. Hispanic (37,978)	45,733	6.07
Bahamian (5)	51	0.01
Barbadian (1,031)	1,279	0.17
Belizean (85)	118	0.02
Bermudan (52)	52	0.01
British West Indian (635)	972	0.13
Dutch West Indian (165)	199	0.03
Haitian (15,396)	17,422	2.31
Jamaican (15,060)	17,690	2.35
Trinidadian/Tobagonian (2,092)	3,155	0.42
U.S. Virgin Islander (0)	30	<0.01
West Indian (3,440)	4,748	0.63
Other West Indian (17)	17	<0.01
Yugoslavian (227)	649	0.09

Hispanic Origin	Population	%
Hispanic or Latino (of any race)	132,154	17.39
Central American, ex. Mexican	49,236	6.48
Costa Rican	664	0.09
Guatemalan	5,948	0.78
Honduran	7,842	1.03
Nicaraguan	656	0.09
Panamanian	1,163	0.15
Salvadoran	32,681	4.30
Other Central American	282	0.04
Cuban	3,597	0.47
Dominican Republic	16,914	2.23
Mexican	5,000	0.66
Puerto Rican	20,508	2.70
South American	23,626	3.11
Argentinean	1,500	0.20
Bolivian	494	0.07
Chilean	1,415	0.19
Colombian	8,522	1.12
Ecuadorian	5,881	0.77
Paraguayan	185	0.02
Peruvian	4,510	0.59
Uruguayan	359	0.05
Venezuelan	517	0.07
Other South American	243	0.03
Other Hispanic or Latino	13,273	1.75

Race*	Population	%
African-American/Black (125,724)	133,280	17.54
Not Hispanic (119,480)	124,525	16.39
Hispanic (6,244)	8,755	1.15
American Indian/Alaska Native (2,092)	5,363	0.71
Not Hispanic (913)	2,835	0.37
Hispanic (1,179)	2,528	0.33
Alaska Athabascan (Ala. Nat.) (0)	0	<0.01
Aleut (Alaska Native) (1)	2	<0.01
Apache (5)	21	<0.01
Arapaho (0)	0	<0.01
Blackfeet (16)	117	0.02
Canadian/French Am. Ind. (5)	9	<0.01
Central American Ind. (36)	87	0.01
Cherokee (59)	572	0.08
Cheyenne (0)	2	<0.01
Chickasaw (0)	5	<0.01
Chippewa (4)	7	<0.01
Choctaw (10)	36	<0.01
Colville (1)	1	<0.01
Comanche (7)	11	<0.01
Cree (0)	2	<0.01
Creek (6)	29	<0.01
Crow (0)	2	<0.01
Delaware (4)	11	<0.01
Hopi (2)	2	<0.01
Houma (0)	0	<0.01
Inupiat (Alaska Native) (0)	3	<0.01
Iroquois (66)	145	0.02
Kiowa (0)	0	<0.01
Lumbee (9)	22	<0.01
Menominee (0)	0	<0.01
Mexican American Ind. (85)	143	0.02
Navajo (2)	13	<0.01
Osage (0)	2	<0.01
Ottawa (1)	1	<0.01
Paiute (0)	0	<0.01
Pima (0)	0	<0.01
Potawatomi (0)	0	<0.01
Pueblo (9)	13	<0.01
Puget Sound Salish (0)	0	<0.01
Seminole (2)	28	<0.01
Shoshone (1)	3	<0.01
Sioux (12)	33	<0.01
South American Ind. (147)	294	0.04
Spanish American Ind. (111)	137	0.02
Tlingit-Haida (Alaska Native) (3)	6	<0.01
Tohono O'Odham (7)	7	<0.01
Tsimshian (Alaska Native) (0)	0	<0.01
Ute (1)	1	<0.01
Yakama (0)	0	<0.01
Yaqui (0)	0	<0.01
Yuman (0)	0	<0.01
Yup'ik (Alaska Native) (0)	0	<0.01
Asian (39,495)	45,112	5.94
Not Hispanic (39,084)	43,880	5.78
Hispanic (411)	1,232	0.16
Bangladeshi (530)	582	0.08
Bhutanese (0)	0	<0.01
Burmese (37)	61	0.01
Cambodian (46)	65	0.01
Chinese, ex. Taiwanese (6,491)	7,849	1.03
Filipino (6,252)	7,212	0.95
Hmong (0)	2	<0.01
Indian (15,861)	17,802	2.34
Indonesian (37)	66	0.01
Japanese (360)	657	0.09
Korean (2,720)	3,074	0.40
Laotian (21)	32	<0.01
Malaysian (12)	29	<0.01
Nepalese (41)	45	0.01
Pakistani (4,581)	4,976	0.65
Sri Lankan (180)	201	0.03
Taiwanese (367)	438	0.06
Thai (213)	278	0.04
Vietnamese (492)	617	0.08
Hawaii Native/Pacific Islander (229)	1,001	0.13
Not Hispanic (117)	599	0.08
Hispanic (112)	402	0.05
Fijian (9)	10	<0.01
Guamanian/Chamorro (88)	110	0.01
Marshallese (1)	1	<0.01
Native Hawaiian (34)	114	0.02
Samoan (12)	36	<0.01
Tongan (0)	0	<0.01
White (518,756)	532,650	70.11
Not Hispanic (454,883)	460,994	60.68
Hispanic (63,873)	71,656	9.43

*Notes: † The Census 2010 population figure is used to calculate the percentages in the Hispanic Origin and Race categories. Ancestry percentages are based on the 2006-2010 American Community Survey population (not shown); ‡ Numbers in parentheses indicate the number of people reporting a single ancestry; * Numbers in parentheses indicate the number of persons reporting this race alone, not in combination with any other race; Please refer to the Explanation of Data for more information.*

Hempstead

Place Type: Village
County: Nassau
Population: 53,891

Ancestry	Population	%
Afghan (0)	0	<0.01
African, Sub-Saharan (1,102)	1,285	2.41
African (682)	850	1.59
Cape Verdean (0)	0	<0.01
Ethiopian (0)	0	<0.01
Ghanaian (8)	8	0.01
Kenyan (0)	0	<0.01
Liberian (0)	0	<0.01
Nigerian (412)	427	0.80
Senegalese (0)	0	<0.01
Sierra Leonean (0)	0	<0.01
Somalian (0)	0	<0.01
South African (0)	0	<0.01
Sudanese (0)	0	<0.01
Ugandan (0)	0	<0.01
Zimbabwean (0)	0	<0.01
Other Sub-Saharan African (0)	0	<0.01
Albanian (0)	0	<0.01
Alsatian (0)	0	<0.01
American (471)	471	0.88
Arab (54)	54	0.10
Arab (12)	12	0.02
Egyptian (0)	0	<0.01
Iraqi (0)	0	<0.01
Jordanian (0)	0	<0.01
Lebanese (0)	0	<0.01
Moroccan (42)	42	0.08
Palestinian (0)	0	<0.01
Syrian (0)	0	<0.01
Other Arab (0)	0	<0.01
Armenian (0)	0	<0.01
Assyrian/Chaldean/Syriac (0)	0	<0.01
Australian (9)	9	0.02
Austrian (28)	64	0.12
Basque (0)	0	<0.01
Belgian (0)	0	<0.01
Brazilian (0)	41	0.08
British (0)	90	0.17
Bulgarian (0)	0	<0.01
Cajun (0)	0	<0.01
Canadian (0)	143	0.27
Carpatho Rusyn (0)	0	<0.01
Celtic (0)	0	<0.01
Croatian (0)	0	<0.01
Cypriot (0)	9	0.02
Czech (7)	7	0.01
Czechoslovakian (0)	0	<0.01
Danish (0)	0	<0.01
Dutch (6)	6	0.01
Eastern European (34)	34	0.06
English (47)	124	0.23
Estonian (0)	0	<0.01
European (0)	0	<0.01
Finnish (0)	0	<0.01
French, ex. Basque (0)	82	0.15
French Canadian (0)	9	0.02
German (130)	594	1.11
German Russian (0)	0	<0.01
Greek (203)	231	0.43
Guyanese (259)	307	0.58
Hungarian (32)	41	0.08
Icelander (0)	0	<0.01
Iranian (0)	0	<0.01
Irish (278)	659	1.23
Israeli (0)	0	<0.01
Italian (333)	641	1.20
Latvian (0)	6	0.01
Lithuanian (28)	36	0.07
Luxemburger (0)	0	<0.01
Macedonian (0)	0	<0.01
Maltese (0)	0	<0.01
New Zealander (0)	0	<0.01
Northern European (0)	0	<0.01
Norwegian (0)	0	<0.01
Pennsylvania German (0)	0	<0.01
Polish (203)	351	0.66
Portuguese (13)	69	0.13
Romanian (0)	0	<0.01
Russian (44)	129	0.24
Scandinavian (0)	0	<0.01
Scotch-Irish (17)	47	0.09
Scottish (21)	103	0.19
Serbian (0)	0	<0.01
Slavic (0)	0	<0.01
Slovak (0)	9	0.02
Slovene (0)	0	<0.01
Soviet Union (0)	0	<0.01
Swedish (23)	102	0.19
Swiss (9)	47	0.09
Turkish (0)	0	<0.01
Ukrainian (62)	90	0.17
Welsh (0)	71	0.13
West Indian, ex. Hispanic (5,489)	6,463	12.11
Bahamian (0)	0	<0.01
Barbadian (153)	153	0.29
Belizean (0)	0	<0.01
Bermudan (9)	9	0.02
British West Indian (228)	250	0.47
Dutch West Indian (31)	31	0.06
Haitian (1,796)	2,104	3.94
Jamaican (2,500)	2,809	5.26
Trinidadian/Tobagonian (203)	322	0.60
U.S. Virgin Islander (0)	0	<0.01
West Indian (569)	785	1.47
Other West Indian (0)	0	<0.01
Yugoslavian (0)	0	<0.01

Hispanic Origin	Population	%
Hispanic or Latino (of any race)	23,823	44.21
Central American, ex. Mexican	16,171	30.01
Costa Rican	44	0.08
Guatemalan	1,402	2.60
Honduran	3,758	6.97
Nicaraguan	56	0.10
Panamanian	138	0.26
Salvadoran	10,707	19.87
Other Central American	66	0.12
Cuban	174	0.32
Dominican Republic	1,398	2.59
Mexican	752	1.40
Puerto Rican	1,144	2.12
South American	1,575	2.92
Argentinean	25	0.05
Bolivian	23	0.04
Chilean	21	0.04
Colombian	506	0.94
Ecuadorian	641	1.19
Paraguayan	16	0.03
Peruvian	279	0.52
Uruguayan	4	0.01
Venezuelan	37	0.07
Other South American	23	0.04
Other Hispanic or Latino	2,609	4.84

Race*	Population	%
African-American/Black (26,016)	27,076	50.24
Not Hispanic (24,724)	25,388	47.11
Hispanic (1,292)	1,688	3.13
American Indian/Alaska Native (316)	997	1.85
Not Hispanic (96)	404	0.75
Hispanic (220)	593	1.10
Alaska Athabascan (Ala. Nat.) (0)	0	<0.01
Aleut (Alaska Native) (0)	0	<0.01
Apache (2)	5	0.01
Arapaho (0)	0	<0.01
Blackfeet (1)	27	0.05
Canadian/French Am. Ind. (0)	0	<0.01
Central American Ind. (5)	15	0.03
Cherokee (17)	109	0.20
Cheyenne (0)	1	<0.01
Chickasaw (0)	0	<0.01
Chippewa (1)	1	<0.01
Choctaw (0)	3	0.01
Colville (0)	0	<0.01
Comanche (0)	1	<0.01
Cree (0)	0	<0.01
Creek (1)	2	<0.01
Crow (0)	0	<0.01
Delaware (0)	4	0.01
Hopi (0)	2	<0.01
Houma (0)	0	<0.01
Inupiat (Alaska Native) (0)	0	<0.01
Iroquois (13)	19	0.04
Kiowa (0)	0	<0.01
Lumbee (0)	1	<0.01
Menominee (0)	0	<0.01
Mexican American Ind. (17)	27	0.05
Navajo (1)	2	<0.01
Osage (0)	0	<0.01
Ottawa (0)	0	<0.01
Paiute (0)	0	<0.01
Pima (0)	0	<0.01
Potawatomi (0)	0	<0.01
Pueblo (4)	6	0.01
Puget Sound Salish (0)	0	<0.01
Seminole (0)	5	0.01
Shoshone (0)	0	<0.01
Sioux (1)	6	0.01
South American Ind. (9)	18	0.03
Spanish American Ind. (42)	47	0.09
Tlingit-Haida (Alaska Native) (0)	2	<0.01
Tohono O'Odham (0)	0	<0.01
Tsimshian (Alaska Native) (0)	0	<0.01
Ute (0)	0	<0.01
Yakama (0)	0	<0.01
Yaqui (0)	0	<0.01
Yuman (0)	0	<0.01
Yup'ik (Alaska Native) (0)	0	<0.01
Asian (751)	977	1.81
Not Hispanic (704)	842	1.56
Hispanic (47)	135	0.25
Bangladeshi (11)	11	0.02
Bhutanese (0)	0	<0.01
Burmese (0)	0	<0.01
Cambodian (0)	0	<0.01
Chinese, ex. Taiwanese (135)	177	0.33
Filipino (150)	171	0.32
Hmong (0)	0	<0.01
Indian (282)	383	0.71
Indonesian (3)	5	0.01
Japanese (6)	14	0.03
Korean (24)	29	0.05
Laotian (3)	4	0.01
Malaysian (1)	1	<0.01
Nepalese (7)	9	0.02
Pakistani (48)	60	0.11
Sri Lankan (15)	15	0.03
Taiwanese (1)	1	<0.01
Thai (5)	10	0.02
Vietnamese (6)	9	0.02
Hawaii Native/Pacific Islander (23)	117	0.22
Not Hispanic (13)	57	0.11
Hispanic (10)	60	0.11
Fijian (1)	1	<0.01
Guamanian/Chamorro (9)	13	0.02
Marshallese (0)	0	<0.01
Native Hawaiian (1)	9	0.02
Samoan (0)	3	0.01
Tongan (0)	0	<0.01
White (11,788)	13,665	25.36
Not Hispanic (3,548)	3,892	7.22
Hispanic (8,240)	9,773	18.13

Huntington

Place Type: Town
County: Suffolk
Population: 203,264

Ancestry	Population	%
Afghan (314)	314	0.16
African, Sub-Saharan (317)	481	0.24
African (146)	206	0.10
Cape Verdean (0)	0	<0.01
Ethiopian (21)	125	0.06
Ghanaian (0)	0	<0.01
Kenyan (0)	0	<0.01
Liberian (0)	0	<0.01
Nigerian (87)	87	0.04
Senegalese (0)	0	<0.01
Sierra Leonean (0)	0	<0.01
Somalian (0)	0	<0.01
South African (63)	63	0.03
Sudanese (0)	0	<0.01
Ugandan (0)	0	<0.01
Zimbabwean (0)	0	<0.01
Other Sub-Saharan African (0)	0	<0.01
Albanian (216)	237	0.12
Alsatian (0)	9	<0.01
American (5,873)	5,873	2.90
Arab (721)	1,231	0.61
Arab (65)	73	0.04
Egyptian (318)	425	0.21
Iraqi (42)	166	0.08
Jordanian (11)	11	0.01
Lebanese (46)	184	0.09
Moroccan (142)	192	0.09
Palestinian (0)	9	<0.01
Syrian (15)	35	0.02
Other Arab (82)	136	0.07
Armenian (368)	525	0.26
Assyrian/Chaldean/Syriac (0)	0	<0.01
Australian (59)	101	0.05
Austrian (454)	2,004	0.99
Basque (6)	20	0.01
Belgian (30)	115	0.06
Brazilian (142)	195	0.10
British (515)	840	0.42
Bulgarian (44)	65	0.03
Cajun (0)	19	0.01
Canadian (356)	743	0.37
Carpatho Rusyn (20)	20	0.01
Celtic (65)	65	0.03
Croatian (337)	781	0.39
Cypriot (70)	82	0.04
Czech (275)	1,271	0.63
Czechoslovakian (89)	435	0.22
Danish (359)	809	0.40
Dutch (427)	2,168	1.07
Eastern European (1,918)	2,012	1.00
English (2,429)	13,038	6.45
Estonian (77)	140	0.07
European (1,982)	2,177	1.08
Finnish (21)	178	0.09
French, ex. Basque (400)	3,023	1.50
French Canadian (214)	772	0.38
German (6,140)	33,758	16.70
German Russian (0)	0	<0.01
Greek (1,839)	3,284	1.62
Guyanese (124)	180	0.09
Hungarian (784)	3,005	1.49
Icelander (9)	38	0.02
Iranian (443)	471	0.23
Irish (12,700)	45,750	22.63
Israeli (217)	285	0.14
Italian (26,684)	56,013	27.70
Latvian (75)	193	0.10
Lithuanian (269)	956	0.47
Luxemburger (0)	0	<0.01
Macedonian (0)	0	<0.01
Maltese (30)	88	0.04
New Zealander (26)	26	0.01
Northern European (57)	63	0.03

Ancestry	Population	%
Norwegian (538)	1,833	0.91
Pennsylvania German (0)	17	0.01
Polish (3,447)	13,208	6.53
Portuguese (198)	526	0.26
Romanian (503)	1,364	0.67
Russian (3,393)	9,499	4.70
Scandinavian (107)	292	0.14
Scotch-Irish (1,045)	2,325	1.15
Scottish (588)	2,306	1.14
Serbian (17)	80	0.04
Slavic (28)	97	0.05
Slovak (109)	225	0.11
Slovene (27)	37	0.02
Soviet Union (0)	0	<0.01
Swedish (322)	2,237	1.11
Swiss (118)	632	0.31
Turkish (438)	502	0.25
Ukrainian (668)	1,742	0.86
Welsh (126)	533	0.26
West Indian, ex. Hispanic (2,499)	2,882	1.43
Bahamian (31)	31	0.02
Barbadian (18)	18	0.01
Belizean (0)	0	<0.01
Bermudan (0)	0	<0.01
British West Indian (0)	0	<0.01
Dutch West Indian (7)	7	<0.01
Haitian (1,223)	1,277	0.63
Jamaican (733)	893	0.44
Trinidadian/Tobagonian (128)	170	0.08
U.S. Virgin Islander (91)	147	0.07
West Indian (261)	332	0.16
Other West Indian (7)	7	<0.01
Yugoslavian (161)	467	0.23

Hispanic Origin	Population	%
Hispanic or Latino (of any race)	22,362	11.00
Central American, ex. Mexican	9,599	4.72
Costa Rican	118	0.06
Guatemalan	1,080	0.53
Honduran	1,651	0.81
Nicaraguan	58	0.03
Panamanian	77	0.04
Salvadoran	6,563	3.23
Other Central American	52	0.03
Cuban	603	0.30
Dominican Republic	1,011	0.50
Mexican	1,440	0.71
Puerto Rican	4,187	2.06
South American	3,043	1.50
Argentinean	329	0.16
Bolivian	60	0.03
Chilean	252	0.12
Colombian	957	0.47
Ecuadorian	637	0.31
Paraguayan	91	0.04
Peruvian	538	0.26
Uruguayan	57	0.03
Venezuelan	87	0.04
Other South American	35	0.02
Other Hispanic or Latino	2,479	1.22

Race*	Population	%
African-American/Black (9,515)	10,864	5.34
Not Hispanic (8,933)	9,917	4.88
Hispanic (582)	947	0.47
American Indian/Alaska Native (398)	1,197	0.59
Not Hispanic (187)	785	0.39
Hispanic (211)	412	0.20
Alaska Athabascan (Ala. Nat.) (0)	0	<0.01
Aleut (Alaska Native) (0)	0	<0.01
Apache (10)	14	0.01
Arapaho (0)	0	<0.01
Blackfeet (2)	36	0.02
Canadian/French Am. Ind. (6)	10	<0.01
Central American Ind. (11)	20	0.01
Cherokee (15)	150	0.07
Cheyenne (0)	4	<0.01
Chickasaw (0)	3	<0.01
Chippewa (2)	10	<0.01

Race (cont.)	Population	%
Choctaw (0)	13	0.01
Colville (0)	0	<0.01
Comanche (5)	8	<0.01
Cree (0)	3	<0.01
Creek (1)	15	0.01
Crow (2)	5	<0.01
Delaware (1)	12	0.01
Hopi (0)	0	<0.01
Houma (0)	0	<0.01
Inupiat (Alaska Native) (0)	0	<0.01
Iroquois (18)	42	0.02
Kiowa (0)	0	<0.01
Lumbee (2)	5	<0.01
Menominee (0)	0	<0.01
Mexican American Ind. (18)	26	0.01
Navajo (3)	8	<0.01
Osage (1)	1	<0.01
Ottawa (0)	2	<0.01
Paiute (0)	0	<0.01
Pima (0)	0	<0.01
Potawatomi (0)	0	<0.01
Pueblo (0)	0	<0.01
Puget Sound Salish (0)	0	<0.01
Seminole (1)	4	<0.01
Shoshone (0)	0	<0.01
Sioux (1)	9	<0.01
South American Ind. (22)	69	0.03
Spanish American Ind. (8)	16	0.01
Tlingit-Haida (Alaska Native) (0)	1	<0.01
Tohono O'Odham (0)	0	<0.01
Tsimshian (Alaska Native) (0)	0	<0.01
Ute (0)	0	<0.01
Yakama (0)	0	<0.01
Yaqui (0)	0	<0.01
Yuman (0)	0	<0.01
Yup'ik (Alaska Native) (0)	0	<0.01
Asian (10,089)	11,684	5.75
Not Hispanic (10,009)	11,463	5.64
Hispanic (80)	221	0.11
Bangladeshi (108)	120	0.06
Bhutanese (1)	1	<0.01
Burmese (8)	13	0.01
Cambodian (10)	10	<0.01
Chinese, ex. Taiwanese (2,144)	2,546	1.25
Filipino (637)	905	0.45
Hmong (0)	0	<0.01
Indian (3,166)	3,529	1.74
Indonesian (11)	18	0.01
Japanese (218)	338	0.17
Korean (1,952)	2,122	1.04
Laotian (5)	5	<0.01
Malaysian (6)	13	0.01
Nepalese (3)	3	<0.01
Pakistani (1,149)	1,264	0.62
Sri Lankan (20)	22	0.01
Taiwanese (140)	157	0.08
Thai (58)	75	0.04
Vietnamese (151)	186	0.09
Hawaii Native/Pacific Islander (48)	159	0.08
Not Hispanic (32)	93	0.05
Hispanic (16)	66	0.03
Fijian (0)	0	<0.01
Guamanian/Chamorro (18)	25	0.01
Marshallese (0)	0	<0.01
Native Hawaiian (16)	40	0.02
Samoan (6)	7	<0.01
Tongan (0)	0	<0.01
White (171,048)	174,612	85.90
Not Hispanic (158,690)	160,914	79.17
Hispanic (12,358)	13,698	6.74

*Notes: † The Census 2010 population figure is used to calculate the percentages in the Hispanic Origin and Race categories. Ancestry percentages are based on the 2006-2010 American Community Survey population (not shown); ‡ Numbers in parentheses indicate the number of people reporting a single ancestry; * Numbers in parentheses indicate the number of persons reporting this race alone, not in combination with any other race; Please refer to the Explanation of Data for more information.*

Irondequoit

Place Type: CDP/Town
County: Monroe
Population: 51,692

Ancestry	Population	%
Afghan (145)	145	0.28
African, Sub-Saharan (653)	763	1.48
African (344)	454	0.88
Cape Verdean (0)	0	<0.01
Ethiopian (192)	192	0.37
Ghanaian (0)	0	<0.01
Kenyan (0)	0	<0.01
Liberian (0)	0	<0.01
Nigerian (85)	85	0.16
Senegalese (0)	0	<0.01
Sierra Leonean (0)	0	<0.01
Somalian (0)	0	<0.01
South African (0)	0	<0.01
Sudanese (0)	0	<0.01
Ugandan (0)	0	<0.01
Zimbabwean (0)	0	<0.01
Other Sub-Saharan African (32)	32	0.06
Albanian (41)	41	0.08
Alsatian (0)	0	<0.01
American (1,362)	1,362	2.64
Arab (107)	120	0.23
Arab (59)	59	0.11
Egyptian (11)	11	0.02
Iraqi (0)	0	<0.01
Jordanian (0)	0	<0.01
Lebanese (37)	50	0.10
Moroccan (0)	0	<0.01
Palestinian (0)	0	<0.01
Syrian (0)	0	<0.01
Other Arab (0)	0	<0.01
Armenian (54)	72	0.14
Assyrian/Chaldean/Syriac (0)	0	<0.01
Australian (0)	12	0.02
Austrian (25)	176	0.34
Basque (0)	0	<0.01
Belgian (23)	93	0.18
Brazilian (52)	71	0.14
British (94)	189	0.37
Bulgarian (0)	0	<0.01
Cajun (0)	0	<0.01
Canadian (208)	419	0.81
Carpatho Rusyn (0)	0	<0.01
Celtic (14)	14	0.03
Croatian (0)	43	0.08
Cypriot (0)	0	<0.01
Czech (32)	153	0.30
Czechoslovakian (23)	42	0.08
Danish (14)	111	0.22
Dutch (161)	1,310	2.54
Eastern European (35)	35	0.07
English (2,071)	7,215	13.98
Estonian (0)	0	<0.01
European (385)	424	0.82
Finnish (22)	30	0.06
French, ex. Basque (121)	1,636	3.17
French Canadian (191)	465	0.90
German (2,967)	11,815	22.89
German Russian (0)	28	0.05
Greek (199)	335	0.65
Guyanese (0)	0	<0.01
Hungarian (74)	172	0.33
Icelander (0)	0	<0.01
Iranian (12)	12	0.02
Irish (1,901)	9,070	17.57
Israeli (0)	0	<0.01
Italian (8,322)	14,566	28.22
Latvian (12)	26	0.05
Lithuanian (142)	267	0.52
Luxemburger (24)	24	0.05
Macedonian (212)	266	0.52
Maltese (0)	0	<0.01
New Zealander (0)	0	<0.01
Northern European (0)	10	0.02

Ancestry	Population	%
Norwegian (33)	157	0.30
Pennsylvania German (7)	32	0.06
Polish (1,257)	3,828	7.42
Portuguese (34)	113	0.22
Romanian (59)	71	0.14
Russian (120)	491	0.95
Scandinavian (0)	7	0.01
Scotch-Irish (132)	396	0.77
Scottish (153)	935	1.81
Serbian (0)	16	0.03
Slavic (17)	24	0.05
Slovak (10)	43	0.08
Slovene (13)	13	0.03
Soviet Union (0)	0	<0.01
Swedish (86)	482	0.93
Swiss (34)	255	0.49
Turkish (238)	245	0.47
Ukrainian (617)	1,169	2.27
Welsh (21)	352	0.68
West Indian, ex. Hispanic (97)	143	0.28
Bahamian (0)	0	<0.01
Barbadian (29)	29	0.06
Belizean (0)	0	<0.01
Bermudan (0)	0	<0.01
British West Indian (0)	0	<0.01
Dutch West Indian (0)	0	<0.01
Haitian (58)	58	0.11
Jamaican (10)	56	0.11
Trinidadian/Tobagonian (0)	0	<0.01
U.S. Virgin Islander (0)	0	<0.01
West Indian (0)	0	<0.01
Other West Indian (0)	0	<0.01
Yugoslavian (58)	69	0.13

Hispanic Origin	Population	%
Hispanic or Latino (of any race)	3,220	6.23
Central American, ex. Mexican	88	0.17
Costa Rican	19	0.04
Guatemalan	28	0.05
Honduran	4	0.01
Nicaraguan	11	0.02
Panamanian	7	0.01
Salvadoran	19	0.04
Other Central American	0	<0.01
Cuban	167	0.32
Dominican Republic	94	0.18
Mexican	145	0.28
Puerto Rican	2,436	4.71
South American	146	0.28
Argentinean	20	0.04
Bolivian	0	<0.01
Chilean	23	0.04
Colombian	53	0.10
Ecuadorian	18	0.03
Paraguayan	3	0.01
Peruvian	10	0.02
Uruguayan	0	<0.01
Venezuelan	15	0.03
Other South American	4	0.01
Other Hispanic or Latino	144	0.28

Race*	Population	%
African-American/Black (3,996)	4,577	8.85
Not Hispanic (3,741)	4,168	8.06
Hispanic (255)	409	0.79
American Indian/Alaska Native (112)	313	0.61
Not Hispanic (81)	240	0.46
Hispanic (31)	73	0.14
Alaska Athabascan (Ala. Nat.) (0)	0	<0.01
Aleut (Alaska Native) (0)	0	<0.01
Apache (1)	3	0.01
Arapaho (0)	0	<0.01
Blackfeet (3)	4	0.01
Canadian/French Am. Ind. (2)	6	0.01
Central American Ind. (1)	1	<0.01
Cherokee (0)	16	0.03
Cheyenne (0)	0	<0.01
Chickasaw (0)	0	<0.01
Chippewa (6)	7	0.01

Race*	Population	%
Choctaw (0)	0	<0.01
Colville (0)	1	<0.01
Comanche (0)	0	<0.01
Cree (0)	0	<0.01
Creek (0)	1	<0.01
Crow (0)	0	<0.01
Delaware (3)	7	0.01
Hopi (0)	0	<0.01
Houma (0)	0	<0.01
Inupiat (Alaska Native) (0)	0	<0.01
Iroquois (36)	98	0.19
Kiowa (0)	0	<0.01
Lumbee (0)	0	<0.01
Menominee (0)	0	<0.01
Mexican American Ind. (5)	5	0.01
Navajo (0)	0	<0.01
Osage (0)	0	<0.01
Ottawa (0)	0	<0.01
Paiute (0)	0	<0.01
Pima (0)	1	<0.01
Potawatomi (0)	0	<0.01
Pueblo (0)	1	<0.01
Puget Sound Salish (0)	0	<0.01
Seminole (0)	2	<0.01
Shoshone (0)	0	<0.01
Sioux (0)	0	<0.01
South American Ind. (2)	6	0.01
Spanish American Ind. (7)	7	0.01
Tlingit-Haida (Alaska Native) (0)	0	<0.01
Tohono O'Odham (0)	0	<0.01
Tsimshian (Alaska Native) (0)	0	<0.01
Ute (0)	0	<0.01
Yakama (0)	0	<0.01
Yaqui (0)	0	<0.01
Yuman (0)	0	<0.01
Yup'ik (Alaska Native) (0)	0	<0.01
Asian (662)	888	1.72
Not Hispanic (648)	851	1.65
Hispanic (14)	37	0.07
Bangladeshi (0)	1	<0.01
Bhutanese (0)	0	<0.01
Burmese (3)	3	0.01
Cambodian (29)	31	0.06
Chinese, ex. Taiwanese (120)	146	0.28
Filipino (101)	155	0.30
Hmong (0)	0	<0.01
Indian (78)	100	0.19
Indonesian (1)	5	0.01
Japanese (12)	37	0.07
Korean (73)	107	0.21
Laotian (94)	109	0.21
Malaysian (0)	1	<0.01
Nepalese (1)	1	<0.01
Pakistani (28)	30	0.06
Sri Lankan (0)	0	<0.01
Taiwanese (3)	3	0.01
Thai (7)	15	0.03
Vietnamese (88)	98	0.19
Hawaii Native/Pacific Islander (12)	42	0.08
Not Hispanic (10)	34	0.07
Hispanic (2)	8	0.02
Fijian (1)	1	<0.01
Guamanian/Chamorro (2)	2	<0.01
Marshallese (0)	0	<0.01
Native Hawaiian (5)	11	0.02
Samoan (0)	0	<0.01
Tongan (1)	1	<0.01
White (44,883)	45,826	88.65
Not Hispanic (43,125)	43,832	84.79
Hispanic (1,758)	1,994	3.86

*Notes: † The Census 2010 population figure is used to calculate the percentages in the Hispanic Origin and Race categories. Ancestry percentages are based on the 2006-2010 American Community Survey population (not shown); ‡ Numbers in parentheses indicate the number of people reporting a single ancestry; * Numbers in parentheses indicate the number of persons reporting this race alone, not in combination with any other race; Please refer to the Explanation of Data for more information.*

Islip

Place Type: Town
County: Suffolk
Population: 335,543

Ancestry	Population	%
Afghan (182)	263	0.08
African, Sub-Saharan (854)	1,222	0.37
African (464)	793	0.24
Cape Verdean (0)	0	<0.01
Ethiopian (0)	0	<0.01
Ghanaian (71)	71	0.02
Kenyan (0)	0	<0.01
Liberian (0)	0	<0.01
Nigerian (164)	203	0.06
Senegalese (0)	0	<0.01
Sierra Leonean (0)	0	<0.01
Somalian (0)	0	<0.01
South African (0)	0	<0.01
Sudanese (0)	0	<0.01
Ugandan (0)	0	<0.01
Zimbabwean (0)	0	<0.01
Other Sub-Saharan African (155)	155	0.05
Albanian (16)	51	0.02
Alsatian (0)	18	0.01
American (5,894)	5,894	1.77
Arab (986)	1,453	0.44
Arab (51)	177	0.05
Egyptian (339)	364	0.11
Iraqi (0)	0	<0.01
Jordanian (68)	122	0.04
Lebanese (86)	185	0.06
Moroccan (123)	141	0.04
Palestinian (166)	166	0.05
Syrian (69)	144	0.04
Other Arab (84)	154	0.05
Armenian (174)	272	0.08
Assyrian/Chaldean/Syriac (0)	0	<0.01
Australian (32)	100	0.03
Austrian (335)	2,019	0.61
Basque (18)	18	0.01
Belgian (68)	328	0.10
Brazilian (683)	895	0.27
British (132)	453	0.14
Bulgarian (0)	0	<0.01
Cajun (0)	23	0.01
Canadian (111)	405	0.12
Carpatho Rusyn (0)	0	<0.01
Celtic (28)	53	0.02
Croatian (88)	291	0.09
Cypriot (25)	25	0.01
Czech (409)	2,026	0.61
Czechoslovakian (224)	596	0.18
Danish (39)	761	0.23
Dutch (310)	2,191	0.66
Eastern European (337)	433	0.13
English (2,211)	13,963	4.18
Estonian (86)	175	0.05
European (772)	811	0.24
Finnish (59)	271	0.08
French, ex. Basque (403)	4,451	1.33
French Canadian (223)	1,160	0.35
German (7,849)	48,335	14.48
German Russian (0)	0	<0.01
Greek (1,129)	3,126	0.94
Guyanese (460)	499	0.15
Hungarian (433)	2,067	0.62
Icelander (0)	29	0.01
Iranian (111)	170	0.05
Irish (17,586)	68,763	20.61
Israeli (36)	56	0.02
Italian (38,447)	84,360	25.28
Latvian (21)	49	0.01
Lithuanian (294)	799	0.24
Luxemburger (0)	0	<0.01
Macedonian (0)	0	<0.01
Maltese (54)	292	0.09
New Zealander (8)	8	<0.01
Northern European (63)	63	0.02
Norwegian (661)	2,978	0.89
Pennsylvania German (0)	0	<0.01
Polish (3,602)	14,896	4.46
Portuguese (1,434)	1,977	0.59
Romanian (213)	467	0.14
Russian (1,589)	5,019	1.50
Scandinavian (55)	183	0.05
Scotch-Irish (960)	3,159	0.95
Scottish (329)	2,852	0.85
Serbian (0)	46	0.01
Slavic (29)	109	0.03
Slovak (46)	280	0.08
Slovene (27)	27	0.01
Soviet Union (0)	0	<0.01
Swedish (401)	2,528	0.76
Swiss (81)	619	0.19
Turkish (281)	384	0.12
Ukrainian (343)	1,272	0.38
Welsh (102)	552	0.17
West Indian, ex. Hispanic (8,546)	10,274	3.08
Bahamian (0)	22	0.01
Barbadian (22)	63	0.02
Belizean (35)	35	0.01
Bermudan (0)	0	<0.01
British West Indian (255)	470	0.14
Dutch West Indian (16)	16	<0.01
Haitian (5,195)	5,636	1.69
Jamaican (1,961)	2,690	0.81
Trinidadian/Tobagonian (530)	665	0.20
U.S. Virgin Islander (0)	0	<0.01
West Indian (532)	677	0.20
Other West Indian (0)	0	<0.01
Yugoslavian (70)	202	0.06

Hispanic Origin	Population	%
Hispanic or Latino (of any race)	97,371	29.02
Central American, ex. Mexican	38,530	11.48
Costa Rican	297	0.09
Guatemalan	3,256	0.97
Honduran	4,232	1.26
Nicaraguan	253	0.08
Panamanian	466	0.14
Salvadoran	29,849	8.90
Other Central American	177	0.05
Cuban	1,113	0.33
Dominican Republic	8,547	2.55
Mexican	3,139	0.94
Puerto Rican	21,506	6.41
South American	16,012	4.77
Argentinean	616	0.18
Bolivian	220	0.07
Chilean	448	0.13
Colombian	5,156	1.54
Ecuadorian	5,323	1.59
Paraguayan	58	0.02
Peruvian	3,599	1.07
Uruguayan	216	0.06
Venezuelan	322	0.10
Other South American	54	0.02
Other Hispanic or Latino	8,524	2.54

Race*	Population	%
African-American/Black (32,024)	35,995	10.73
Not Hispanic (27,898)	30,295	9.03
Hispanic (4,126)	5,700	1.70
American Indian/Alaska Native (1,586)	3,396	1.01
Not Hispanic (520)	1,565	0.47
Hispanic (1,066)	1,831	0.55
Alaska Athabascan (Ala. Nat.) (0)	1	<0.01
Aleut (Alaska Native) (1)	1	<0.01
Apache (5)	12	<0.01
Arapaho (0)	1	<0.01
Blackfeet (12)	77	0.02
Canadian/French Am. Ind. (0)	0	<0.01
Central American Ind. (52)	73	0.02
Cherokee (44)	316	0.09
Cheyenne (0)	1	<0.01
Chickasaw (1)	3	<0.01
Chippewa (6)	13	<0.01

Choctaw (3)	17	0.01
Colville (0)	0	<0.01
Comanche (0)	8	<0.01
Cree (0)	0	<0.01
Creek (1)	7	<0.01
Crow (11)	16	<0.01
Delaware (1)	7	<0.01
Hopi (1)	3	<0.01
Houma (1)	3	<0.01
Inupiat (Alaska Native) (1)	2	<0.01
Iroquois (36)	92	0.03
Kiowa (0)	0	<0.01
Lumbee (6)	8	<0.01
Menominee (0)	0	<0.01
Mexican American Ind. (83)	135	0.04
Navajo (7)	14	<0.01
Osage (0)	1	<0.01
Ottawa (0)	0	<0.01
Paiute (0)	0	<0.01
Pima (1)	1	<0.01
Potawatomi (1)	1	<0.01
Pueblo (4)	7	<0.01
Puget Sound Salish (0)	0	<0.01
Seminole (2)	4	<0.01
Shoshone (0)	3	<0.01
Sioux (6)	27	0.01
South American Ind. (143)	249	0.07
Spanish American Ind. (67)	91	0.03
Tlingit-Haida (Alaska Native) (5)	6	<0.01
Tohono O'Odham (0)	0	<0.01
Tsimshian (Alaska Native) (0)	0	<0.01
Ute (0)	0	<0.01
Yakama (0)	0	<0.01
Yaqui (1)	1	<0.01
Yuman (0)	1	<0.01
Yup'ik (Alaska Native) (0)	0	<0.01
Asian (9,572)	11,510	3.43
Not Hispanic (9,358)	10,957	3.27
Hispanic (214)	553	0.16
Bangladeshi (305)	356	0.11
Bhutanese (0)	0	<0.01
Burmese (9)	15	<0.01
Cambodian (23)	24	0.01
Chinese, ex. Taiwanese (1,424)	1,766	0.53
Filipino (1,012)	1,301	0.39
Hmong (0)	0	<0.01
Indian (3,680)	4,276	1.27
Indonesian (29)	37	0.01
Japanese (91)	216	0.06
Korean (573)	700	0.21
Laotian (21)	25	0.01
Malaysian (5)	12	<0.01
Nepalese (13)	13	<0.01
Pakistani (1,368)	1,520	0.45
Sri Lankan (13)	21	0.01
Taiwanese (49)	54	0.02
Thai (80)	106	0.03
Vietnamese (433)	518	0.15
Hawaii Native/Pacific Islander (101)	471	0.14
Not Hispanic (52)	244	0.07
Hispanic (49)	227	0.07
Fijian (0)	4	<0.01
Guamanian/Chamorro (28)	44	0.01
Marshallese (1)	1	<0.01
Native Hawaiian (26)	75	0.02
Samoan (6)	15	<0.01
Tongan (0)	2	<0.01
White (245,918)	254,235	75.77
Not Hispanic (195,283)	198,326	59.11
Hispanic (50,635)	55,909	16.66

Notes: † The Census 2010 population figure is used to calculate the percentages in the Hispanic Origin and Race categories. Ancestry percentages are based on the 2006-2010 American Community Survey population (not shown); ‡ Numbers in parentheses indicate the number of people reporting a single ancestry; * Numbers in parentheses indicate the number of persons reporting this race alone, not in combination with any other race; Please refer to the Explanation of Data for more information.

Levittown

Place Type: CDP
County: Nassau
Population: 51,881

Ancestry	Population	%
Afghan (0)	0	<0.01
African, Sub-Saharan (0)	20	0.04
African (0)	20	0.04
Cape Verdean (0)	0	<0.01
Ethiopian (0)	0	<0.01
Ghanaian (0)	0	<0.01
Kenyan (0)	0	<0.01
Liberian (0)	0	<0.01
Nigerian (0)	0	<0.01
Senegalese (0)	0	<0.01
Sierra Leonean (0)	0	<0.01
Somalian (0)	0	<0.01
South African (0)	0	<0.01
Sudanese (0)	0	<0.01
Ugandan (0)	0	<0.01
Zimbabwean (0)	0	<0.01
Other Sub-Saharan African (0)	0	<0.01
Albanian (49)	49	0.09
Alsatian (0)	0	<0.01
American (1,347)	1,347	2.52
Arab (190)	271	0.51
Arab (0)	0	<0.01
Egyptian (136)	136	0.25
Iraqi (0)	0	<0.01
Jordanian (0)	0	<0.01
Lebanese (22)	68	0.13
Moroccan (10)	10	0.02
Palestinian (0)	0	<0.01
Syrian (0)	35	0.07
Other Arab (22)	22	0.04
Armenian (21)	80	0.15
Assyrian/Chaldean/Syriac (0)	0	<0.01
Australian (14)	14	0.03
Austrian (66)	307	0.57
Basque (0)	16	0.03
Belgian (10)	18	0.03
Brazilian (8)	8	0.01
British (92)	121	0.23
Bulgarian (0)	0	<0.01
Cajun (0)	0	<0.01
Canadian (11)	74	0.14
Carpatho Rusyn (0)	0	<0.01
Celtic (0)	0	<0.01
Croatian (24)	67	0.13
Cypriot (0)	0	<0.01
Czech (44)	215	0.40
Czechoslovakian (25)	47	0.09
Danish (10)	110	0.21
Dutch (11)	340	0.64
Eastern European (107)	107	0.20
English (316)	2,076	3.88
Estonian (0)	0	<0.01
European (276)	321	0.60
Finnish (0)	36	0.07
French, ex. Basque (239)	1,242	2.32
French Canadian (74)	206	0.39
German (1,428)	9,190	17.18
German Russian (0)	0	<0.01
Greek (630)	1,100	2.06
Guyanese (0)	0	<0.01
Hungarian (158)	781	1.46
Icelander (9)	52	0.10
Iranian (23)	79	0.15
Irish (4,151)	14,886	27.84
Israeli (32)	72	0.13
Italian (8,524)	17,446	32.62
Latvian (0)	31	0.06
Lithuanian (73)	314	0.59
Luxemburger (0)	0	<0.01
Macedonian (0)	0	<0.01
Maltese (45)	96	0.18
New Zealander (0)	0	<0.01
Northern European (0)	0	<0.01

Ancestry (cont.)	Population	%
Norwegian (49)	274	0.51
Pennsylvania German (0)	54	0.10
Polish (535)	2,652	4.96
Portuguese (189)	243	0.45
Romanian (27)	98	0.18
Russian (640)	1,993	3.73
Scandinavian (0)	33	0.06
Scotch-Irish (261)	722	1.35
Scottish (53)	303	0.57
Serbian (0)	0	<0.01
Slavic (0)	0	<0.01
Slovak (6)	6	0.01
Slovene (0)	0	<0.01
Soviet Union (0)	0	<0.01
Swedish (13)	287	0.54
Swiss (55)	105	0.20
Turkish (112)	181	0.34
Ukrainian (83)	249	0.47
Welsh (0)	43	0.08
West Indian, ex. Hispanic (89)	117	0.22
Bahamian (0)	0	<0.01
Barbadian (0)	0	<0.01
Belizean (0)	0	<0.01
Bermudan (0)	0	<0.01
British West Indian (0)	0	<0.01
Dutch West Indian (0)	0	<0.01
Haitian (0)	0	<0.01
Jamaican (20)	36	0.07
Trinidadian/Tobagonian (69)	69	0.13
U.S. Virgin Islander (0)	0	<0.01
West Indian (0)	12	0.02
Other West Indian (0)	0	<0.01
Yugoslavian (41)	52	0.10

Hispanic Origin	Population	%
Hispanic or Latino (of any race)	5,979	11.52
Central American, ex. Mexican	1,200	2.31
Costa Rican	41	0.08
Guatemalan	132	0.25
Honduran	103	0.20
Nicaraguan	26	0.05
Panamanian	12	0.02
Salvadoran	876	1.69
Other Central American	10	0.02
Cuban	274	0.53
Dominican Republic	260	0.50
Mexican	214	0.41
Puerto Rican	1,716	3.31
South American	1,746	3.37
Argentinean	82	0.16
Bolivian	18	0.03
Chilean	112	0.22
Colombian	733	1.41
Ecuadorian	400	0.77
Paraguayan	19	0.04
Peruvian	285	0.55
Uruguayan	47	0.09
Venezuelan	23	0.04
Other South American	27	0.05
Other Hispanic or Latino	569	1.10

Race*	Population	%
African-American/Black (470)	667	1.29
Not Hispanic (403)	539	1.04
Hispanic (67)	128	0.25
American Indian/Alaska Native (55)	185	0.36
Not Hispanic (43)	134	0.26
Hispanic (12)	51	0.10
Alaska Athabascan (Ala. Nat.) (0)	0	<0.01
Aleut (Alaska Native) (0)	0	<0.01
Apache (0)	0	<0.01
Arapaho (0)	0	<0.01
Blackfeet (0)	4	0.01
Canadian/French Am. Ind. (0)	0	<0.01
Central American Ind. (0)	0	<0.01
Cherokee (2)	26	0.05
Cheyenne (0)	0	<0.01
Chickasaw (0)	0	<0.01
Chippewa (1)	1	<0.01

Race* (cont.)	Population	%
Choctaw (0)	1	<0.01
Colville (0)	0	<0.01
Comanche (7)	7	0.01
Cree (0)	0	<0.01
Creek (0)	1	<0.01
Crow (0)	0	<0.01
Delaware (0)	0	<0.01
Hopi (0)	0	<0.01
Houma (0)	0	<0.01
Inupiat (Alaska Native) (0)	0	<0.01
Iroquois (4)	13	0.03
Kiowa (0)	0	<0.01
Lumbee (3)	6	0.01
Menominee (0)	0	<0.01
Mexican American Ind. (0)	5	0.01
Navajo (0)	0	<0.01
Osage (0)	1	<0.01
Ottawa (0)	0	<0.01
Paiute (0)	0	<0.01
Pima (0)	0	<0.01
Potawatomi (0)	0	<0.01
Pueblo (0)	0	<0.01
Puget Sound Salish (0)	0	<0.01
Seminole (1)	3	0.01
Shoshone (1)	1	<0.01
Sioux (0)	1	<0.01
South American Ind. (9)	12	0.02
Spanish American Ind. (0)	1	<0.01
Tlingit-Haida (Alaska Native) (0)	0	<0.01
Tohono O'Odham (0)	0	<0.01
Tsimshian (Alaska Native) (0)	0	<0.01
Ute (0)	0	<0.01
Yakama (0)	0	<0.01
Yaqui (0)	0	<0.01
Yuman (0)	0	<0.01
Yup'ik (Alaska Native) (0)	0	<0.01
Asian (2,956)	3,352	6.46
Not Hispanic (2,937)	3,298	6.36
Hispanic (19)	54	0.10
Bangladeshi (65)	70	0.13
Bhutanese (0)	0	<0.01
Burmese (1)	6	0.01
Cambodian (10)	14	0.03
Chinese, ex. Taiwanese (467)	589	1.14
Filipino (446)	525	1.01
Hmong (0)	0	<0.01
Indian (1,110)	1,212	2.34
Indonesian (4)	6	0.01
Japanese (26)	44	0.08
Korean (358)	380	0.73
Laotian (3)	3	0.01
Malaysian (0)	7	0.01
Nepalese (2)	2	<0.01
Pakistani (226)	239	0.46
Sri Lankan (1)	1	<0.01
Taiwanese (22)	25	0.05
Thai (26)	40	0.08
Vietnamese (103)	107	0.21
Hawaii Native/Pacific Islander (10)	47	0.09
Not Hispanic (6)	21	0.04
Hispanic (4)	26	0.05
Fijian (0)	0	<0.01
Guamanian/Chamorro (2)	3	0.01
Marshallese (0)	0	<0.01
Native Hawaiian (0)	3	0.01
Samoan (5)	7	0.01
Tongan (0)	0	<0.01
White (46,137)	46,970	90.53
Not Hispanic (41,814)	42,268	81.47
Hispanic (4,323)	4,702	9.06

Notes: † The Census 2010 population figure is used to calculate the percentages in the Hispanic Origin and Race categories. Ancestry percentages are based on the 2006-2010 American Community Survey population (not shown); ‡ Numbers in parentheses indicate the number of people reporting a single ancestry; * Numbers in parentheses indicate the number of persons reporting this race alone, not in combination with any other race; Please refer to the Explanation of Data for more information.

Manhattan

Place Type: Borough
County: New York
Population: 1,585,873

Ancestry	Population	%
Afghan (59)	85	0.01
African, Sub-Saharan (19,667)	24,146	1.52
African (10,054)	12,839	0.81
Cape Verdean (81)	206	0.01
Ethiopian (932)	1,043	0.07
Ghanaian (714)	818	0.05
Kenyan (43)	69	<0.01
Liberian (169)	176	0.01
Nigerian (1,650)	1,953	0.12
Senegalese (1,118)	1,216	0.08
Sierra Leonean (422)	422	0.03
Somalian (125)	125	0.01
South African (991)	1,372	0.09
Sudanese (137)	137	0.01
Ugandan (95)	125	0.01
Zimbabwean (80)	100	0.01
Other Sub-Saharan African (3,056)	3,545	0.22
Albanian (1,385)	1,618	0.10
Alsatian (5)	129	0.01
American (54,694)	54,694	3.45
Arab (8,584)	13,828	0.87
Arab (1,250)	1,720	0.11
Egyptian (1,374)	1,906	0.12
Iraqi (275)	583	0.04
Jordanian (0)	48	<0.01
Lebanese (1,838)	3,331	0.21
Moroccan (914)	1,592	0.10
Palestinian (626)	794	0.05
Syrian (518)	1,112	0.07
Other Arab (1,789)	2,742	0.17
Armenian (1,520)	2,653	0.17
Assyrian/Chaldean/Syriac (94)	137	0.01
Australian (1,965)	2,719	0.17
Austrian (4,202)	14,656	0.93
Basque (191)	428	0.03
Belgian (928)	2,470	0.16
Brazilian (2,870)	4,541	0.29
British (6,950)	12,129	0.77
Bulgarian (927)	1,272	0.08
Cajun (22)	224	0.01
Canadian (3,037)	5,646	0.36
Carpatho Rusyn (89)	112	0.01
Celtic (129)	304	0.02
Croatian (1,299)	2,164	0.14
Cypriot (139)	216	0.01
Czech (1,439)	4,820	0.30
Czechoslovakian (619)	1,256	0.08
Danish (1,444)	4,095	0.26
Dutch (2,847)	10,414	0.66
Eastern European (23,269)	25,277	1.60
English (22,270)	77,799	4.91
Estonian (190)	424	0.03
European (25,127)	27,846	1.76
Finnish (666)	1,658	0.10
French, ex. Basque (10,278)	31,783	2.01
French Canadian (1,692)	5,246	0.33
German (27,493)	107,666	6.80
German Russian (0)	41	<0.01
Greek (7,557)	13,078	0.83
Guyanese (1,802)	2,259	0.14
Hungarian (4,686)	14,667	0.93
Icelander (246)	382	0.02
Iranian (3,458)	4,256	0.27
Irish (40,008)	117,355	7.41
Israeli (4,839)	6,624	0.42
Italian (44,498)	98,563	6.22
Latvian (713)	1,822	0.12
Lithuanian (1,597)	5,775	0.36
Luxemburger (23)	68	<0.01
Macedonian (973)	1,086	0.07
Maltese (548)	840	0.05
New Zealander (243)	405	0.03
Northern European (1,296)	1,485	0.09
Norwegian (1,552)	7,445	0.47
Pennsylvania German (123)	327	0.02
Polish (20,565)	64,078	4.05
Portuguese (1,436)	3,862	0.24
Romanian (3,035)	7,692	0.49
Russian (36,296)	82,983	5.24
Scandinavian (753)	1,731	0.11
Scotch-Irish (4,283)	13,158	0.83
Scottish (4,846)	19,553	1.23
Serbian (1,160)	1,526	0.10
Slavic (177)	400	0.03
Slovak (812)	2,298	0.15
Slovene (271)	695	0.04
Soviet Union (28)	54	<0.01
Swedish (3,045)	10,408	0.66
Swiss (1,381)	4,962	0.31
Turkish (2,708)	3,703	0.23
Ukrainian (4,361)	8,849	0.56
Welsh (944)	6,000	0.38
West Indian, ex. Hispanic (22,411)	30,009	1.90
Bahamian (303)	457	0.03
Barbadian (738)	907	0.06
Belizean (654)	735	0.05
Bermudan (86)	127	0.01
British West Indian (1,308)	1,658	0.10
Dutch West Indian (212)	276	0.02
Haitian (5,308)	6,500	0.41
Jamaican (7,099)	9,242	0.58
Trinidadian/Tobagonian (3,010)	3,877	0.24
U.S. Virgin Islander (343)	487	0.03
West Indian (3,296)	5,618	0.35
Other West Indian (54)	125	0.01
Yugoslavian (1,478)	1,876	0.12

Hispanic Origin	Population	%
Hispanic or Latino (of any race)	403,577	25.45
Central American, ex. Mexican	13,948	0.88
Costa Rican	987	0.06
Guatemalan	2,051	0.13
Honduran	4,058	0.26
Nicaraguan	1,556	0.10
Panamanian	1,716	0.11
Salvadoran	3,419	0.22
Other Central American	161	0.01
Cuban	11,623	0.73
Dominican Republic	155,971	9.84
Mexican	41,965	2.65
Puerto Rican	107,774	6.80
South American	36,748	2.32
Argentinean	4,339	0.27
Bolivian	522	0.03
Chilean	1,824	0.12
Colombian	8,411	0.53
Ecuadorian	14,132	0.89
Paraguayan	268	0.02
Peruvian	3,852	0.24
Uruguayan	549	0.03
Venezuelan	2,573	0.16
Other South American	278	0.02
Other Hispanic or Latino	35,548	2.24

Race*	Population	%
African-American/Black (246,687)	272,993	17.21
Not Hispanic (205,340)	217,102	13.69
Hispanic (41,347)	55,891	3.52
American Indian/Alaska Native (8,669)	19,415	1.22
Not Hispanic (2,144)	7,395	0.47
Hispanic (6,525)	12,020	0.76
Alaska Athabascan (Ala. Nat.) (11)	18	<0.01
Aleut (Alaska Native) (4)	7	<0.01
Apache (28)	92	0.01
Arapaho (3)	5	<0.01
Blackfeet (41)	356	0.02
Canadian/French Am. Ind. (29)	62	<0.01
Central American Ind. (610)	1,090	0.07
Cherokee (288)	1,845	0.12
Cheyenne (4)	9	<0.01
Chickasaw (15)	43	<0.01
Chippewa (36)	99	0.01
Choctaw (41)	179	0.01
Colville (4)	5	<0.01
Comanche (13)	22	<0.01
Cree (4)	22	<0.01
Creek (12)	61	<0.01
Crow (4)	11	<0.01
Delaware (14)	54	<0.01
Hopi (8)	15	<0.01
Houma (0)	3	<0.01
Inupiat (Alaska Native) (2)	8	<0.01
Iroquois (97)	265	0.02
Kiowa (9)	11	<0.01
Lumbee (10)	21	<0.01
Menominee (2)	3	<0.01
Mexican American Ind. (479)	752	0.05
Navajo (38)	83	0.01
Osage (7)	12	<0.01
Ottawa (0)	3	<0.01
Paiute (2)	8	<0.01
Pima (2)	4	<0.01
Potawatomi (10)	20	<0.01
Pueblo (70)	175	0.01
Puget Sound Salish (2)	5	<0.01
Seminole (6)	110	0.01
Shoshone (3)	6	<0.01
Sioux (38)	133	0.01
South American Ind. (813)	1,935	0.12
Spanish American Ind. (373)	514	0.03
Tlingit-Haida (Alaska Native) (2)	15	<0.01
Tohono O'Odham (11)	15	<0.01
Tsimshian (Alaska Native) (3)	3	<0.01
Ute (1)	2	<0.01
Yakama (1)	2	<0.01
Yaqui (8)	22	<0.01
Yuman (4)	6	<0.01
Yup'ik (Alaska Native) (0)	2	<0.01
Asian (179,552)	199,722	12.59
Not Hispanic (177,624)	194,929	12.29
Hispanic (1,928)	4,793	0.30
Bangladeshi (1,672)	2,029	0.13
Bhutanese (26)	26	<0.01
Burmese (240)	317	0.02
Cambodian (168)	220	0.01
Chinese, ex. Taiwanese (92,088)	99,287	6.26
Filipino (10,399)	13,388	0.84
Hmong (16)	20	<0.01
Indian (25,857)	29,979	1.89
Indonesian (470)	693	0.04
Japanese (13,201)	16,600	1.05
Korean (19,683)	21,996	1.39
Laotian (109)	157	0.01
Malaysian (524)	766	0.05
Nepalese (240)	281	0.02
Pakistani (2,482)	2,940	0.19
Sri Lankan (450)	563	0.04
Taiwanese (2,789)	3,318	0.21
Thai (1,282)	1,657	0.10
Vietnamese (2,194)	2,919	0.18
Hawaii Native/Pacific Islander (873)	3,727	0.24
Not Hispanic (533)	1,776	0.11
Hispanic (340)	1,951	0.12
Fijian (29)	73	<0.01
Guamanian/Chamorro (132)	242	0.02
Marshallese (3)	4	<0.01
Native Hawaiian (185)	608	0.04
Samoan (87)	183	0.01
Tongan (18)	33	<0.01
White (911,073)	956,864	60.34
Not Hispanic (761,493)	785,299	49.52
Hispanic (149,580)	171,565	10.82

Mount Vernon

Place Type: City
County: Westchester
Population: 67,292

Ancestry	Population	%
Afghan (0)	0	<0.01
African, Sub-Saharan (1,490)	1,910	2.85
African (786)	1,162	1.73
Cape Verdean (0)	11	0.02
Ethiopian (0)	0	<0.01
Ghanaian (347)	347	0.52
Kenyan (0)	0	<0.01
Liberian (0)	9	0.01
Nigerian (148)	148	0.22
Senegalese (0)	12	0.02
Sierra Leonean (10)	22	0.03
Somalian (0)	0	<0.01
South African (0)	0	<0.01
Sudanese (0)	0	<0.01
Ugandan (19)	19	0.03
Zimbabwean (0)	0	<0.01
Other Sub-Saharan African (180)	180	0.27
Albanian (303)	303	0.45
Alsatian (0)	0	<0.01
American (2,069)	2,069	3.08
Arab (217)	305	0.45
Arab (0)	0	<0.01
Egyptian (56)	68	0.10
Iraqi (0)	0	<0.01
Jordanian (0)	0	<0.01
Lebanese (0)	12	0.02
Moroccan (0)	64	0.10
Palestinian (13)	13	0.02
Syrian (0)	0	<0.01
Other Arab (148)	148	0.22
Armenian (0)	0	<0.01
Assyrian/Chaldean/Syriac (0)	0	<0.01
Australian (0)	13	0.02
Austrian (60)	150	0.22
Basque (0)	0	<0.01
Belgian (0)	0	<0.01
Brazilian (1,938)	2,013	3.00
British (45)	146	0.22
Bulgarian (0)	0	<0.01
Cajun (0)	0	<0.01
Canadian (0)	61	0.09
Carpatho Rusyn (0)	0	<0.01
Celtic (0)	0	<0.01
Croatian (0)	0	<0.01
Cypriot (0)	0	<0.01
Czech (47)	70	0.10
Czechoslovakian (11)	11	0.02
Danish (10)	21	0.03
Dutch (22)	191	0.28
Eastern European (93)	127	0.19
English (260)	843	1.26
Estonian (21)	45	0.07
European (145)	145	0.22
Finnish (12)	12	0.02
French, ex. Basque (129)	377	0.56
French Canadian (14)	62	0.09
German (373)	1,326	1.98
German Russian (0)	0	<0.01
Greek (100)	185	0.28
Guyanese (326)	360	0.54
Hungarian (74)	129	0.19
Icelander (0)	0	<0.01
Iranian (0)	21	0.03
Irish (950)	2,889	4.31
Israeli (116)	174	0.26
Italian (3,462)	5,281	7.87
Latvian (0)	10	0.01
Lithuanian (13)	57	0.08
Luxemburger (0)	0	<0.01
Macedonian (0)	0	<0.01
Maltese (24)	24	0.04
New Zealander (0)	0	<0.01
Northern European (0)	0	<0.01

	Population	%
Norwegian (10)	21	0.03
Pennsylvania German (0)	0	<0.01
Polish (283)	651	0.97
Portuguese (979)	1,149	1.71
Romanian (123)	123	0.18
Russian (143)	433	0.65
Scandinavian (15)	15	0.02
Scotch-Irish (60)	127	0.19
Scottish (46)	150	0.22
Serbian (8)	8	0.01
Slavic (9)	9	0.01
Slovak (0)	0	<0.01
Slovene (0)	0	<0.01
Soviet Union (0)	0	<0.01
Swedish (0)	46	0.07
Swiss (0)	0	<0.01
Turkish (0)	0	<0.01
Ukrainian (0)	69	0.10
Welsh (0)	63	0.09
West Indian, ex. Hispanic (12,148)	13,279	19.80
Bahamian (11)	11	0.02
Barbadian (190)	208	0.31
Belizean (118)	118	0.18
Bermudan (0)	0	<0.01
British West Indian (315)	348	0.52
Dutch West Indian (0)	0	<0.01
Haitian (324)	465	0.69
Jamaican (9,769)	10,445	15.57
Trinidadian/Tobagonian (370)	397	0.59
U.S. Virgin Islander (0)	0	<0.01
West Indian (1,051)	1,287	1.92
Other West Indian (0)	0	<0.01
Yugoslavian (9)	9	0.01

Hispanic Origin	Population	%
Hispanic or Latino (of any race)	9,592	14.25
Central American, ex. Mexican	754	1.12
Costa Rican	64	0.10
Guatemalan	141	0.21
Honduran	233	0.35
Nicaraguan	35	0.05
Panamanian	131	0.19
Salvadoran	137	0.20
Other Central American	13	0.02
Cuban	231	0.34
Dominican Republic	1,611	2.39
Mexican	2,454	3.65
Puerto Rican	2,582	3.84
South American	1,205	1.79
Argentinean	91	0.14
Bolivian	18	0.03
Chilean	29	0.04
Colombian	407	0.60
Ecuadorian	268	0.40
Paraguayan	68	0.10
Peruvian	219	0.33
Uruguayan	16	0.02
Venezuelan	56	0.08
Other South American	33	0.05
Other Hispanic or Latino	755	1.12

Race*	Population	%
African-American/Black (42,667)	44,244	65.75
Not Hispanic (41,226)	42,361	62.95
Hispanic (1,441)	1,883	2.80
American Indian/Alaska Native (312)	820	1.22
Not Hispanic (200)	585	0.87
Hispanic (112)	235	0.35
Alaska Athabascan (Ala. Nat.) (0)	0	<0.01
Aleut (Alaska Native) (0)	0	<0.01
Apache (0)	0	<0.01
Arapaho (0)	0	<0.01
Blackfeet (1)	38	0.06
Canadian/French Am. Ind. (0)	0	<0.01
Central American Ind. (7)	19	0.03
Cherokee (27)	116	0.17
Cheyenne (0)	0	<0.01
Chickasaw (2)	4	0.01
Chippewa (0)	0	<0.01

	Population	%
Choctaw (4)	4	0.01
Colville (0)	0	<0.01
Comanche (0)	0	<0.01
Cree (0)	2	<0.01
Creek (0)	0	<0.01
Crow (0)	0	<0.01
Delaware (1)	1	<0.01
Hopi (0)	0	<0.01
Houma (0)	0	<0.01
Inupiat (Alaska Native) (0)	0	<0.01
Iroquois (2)	8	0.01
Kiowa (0)	0	<0.01
Lumbee (0)	0	<0.01
Menominee (0)	0	<0.01
Mexican American Ind. (13)	14	0.02
Navajo (1)	2	<0.01
Osage (0)	0	<0.01
Ottawa (0)	0	<0.01
Paiute (0)	0	<0.01
Pima (0)	0	<0.01
Potawatomi (0)	0	<0.01
Pueblo (4)	7	0.01
Puget Sound Salish (0)	0	<0.01
Seminole (0)	9	0.01
Shoshone (0)	0	<0.01
Sioux (1)	6	0.01
South American Ind. (15)	36	0.05
Spanish American Ind. (0)	4	0.01
Tlingit-Haida (Alaska Native) (0)	0	<0.01
Tohono O'Odham (0)	0	<0.01
Tsimshian (Alaska Native) (0)	0	<0.01
Ute (0)	0	<0.01
Yakama (0)	0	<0.01
Yaqui (0)	0	<0.01
Yuman (0)	0	<0.01
Yup'ik (Alaska Native) (0)	0	<0.01
Asian (1,236)	1,672	2.48
Not Hispanic (1,206)	1,587	2.36
Hispanic (30)	85	0.13
Bangladeshi (7)	11	0.02
Bhutanese (0)	0	<0.01
Burmese (2)	2	<0.01
Cambodian (7)	9	0.01
Chinese, ex. Taiwanese (187)	264	0.39
Filipino (220)	281	0.42
Hmong (0)	0	<0.01
Indian (529)	711	1.06
Indonesian (0)	11	0.02
Japanese (55)	88	0.13
Korean (72)	92	0.14
Laotian (5)	12	0.02
Malaysian (0)	1	<0.01
Nepalese (4)	4	0.01
Pakistani (26)	38	0.06
Sri Lankan (1)	1	<0.01
Taiwanese (10)	10	0.01
Thai (67)	73	0.11
Vietnamese (7)	12	0.02
Hawaii Native/Pacific Islander (36)	156	0.23
Not Hispanic (27)	130	0.19
Hispanic (9)	26	0.04
Fijian (0)	1	<0.01
Guamanian/Chamorro (1)	4	0.01
Marshallese (0)	0	<0.01
Native Hawaiian (5)	13	0.02
Samoan (1)	3	<0.01
Tongan (0)	0	<0.01
White (16,371)	17,846	26.52
Not Hispanic (12,449)	13,354	19.84
Hispanic (3,922)	4,492	6.68

Notes: † The Census 2010 population figure is used to calculate the percentages in the Hispanic Origin and Race categories. Ancestry percentages are based on the 2006-2010 American Community Survey population (not shown); ‡ Numbers in parentheses indicate the number of people reporting a single ancestry; * Numbers in parentheses indicate the number of persons reporting this race alone, not in combination with any other race; Please refer to the Explanation of Data for more information.

New Rochelle

Place Type: City
County: Westchester
Population: 77,062

Ancestry	Population	%
Afghan (0)	0	<0.01
African, Sub-Saharan (850)	1,030	1.36
African (253)	309	0.41
Cape Verdean (0)	0	<0.01
Ethiopian (0)	0	<0.01
Ghanaian (18)	18	0.02
Kenyan (19)	19	0.03
Liberian (0)	0	<0.01
Nigerian (125)	125	0.16
Senegalese (0)	0	<0.01
Sierra Leonean (15)	15	0.02
Somalian (0)	0	<0.01
South African (92)	179	0.24
Sudanese (0)	0	<0.01
Ugandan (0)	0	<0.01
Zimbabwean (0)	0	<0.01
Other Sub-Saharan African (328)	365	0.48
Albanian (324)	370	0.49
Alsatian (0)	0	<0.01
American (2,542)	2,542	3.35
Arab (338)	413	0.54
Arab (177)	187	0.25
Egyptian (13)	13	0.02
Iraqi (0)	0	<0.01
Jordanian (11)	46	0.06
Lebanese (102)	132	0.17
Moroccan (8)	8	0.01
Palestinian (0)	0	<0.01
Syrian (0)	0	<0.01
Other Arab (27)	27	0.04
Armenian (31)	75	0.10
Assyrian/Chaldean/Syriac (0)	0	<0.01
Australian (33)	33	0.04
Austrian (104)	547	0.72
Basque (12)	12	0.02
Belgian (27)	118	0.16
Brazilian (580)	728	0.96
British (145)	208	0.27
Bulgarian (9)	9	0.01
Cajun (0)	0	<0.01
Canadian (13)	41	0.05
Carpatho Rusyn (0)	0	<0.01
Celtic (0)	0	<0.01
Croatian (103)	167	0.22
Cypriot (0)	0	<0.01
Czech (78)	402	0.53
Czechoslovakian (32)	108	0.14
Danish (0)	55	0.07
Dutch (38)	257	0.34
Eastern European (870)	870	1.15
English (493)	1,832	2.42
Estonian (9)	16	0.02
European (773)	808	1.07
Finnish (36)	60	0.08
French, ex. Basque (342)	1,322	1.74
French Canadian (62)	152	0.20
German (734)	3,942	5.20
German Russian (0)	0	<0.01
Greek (377)	573	0.76
Guyanese (104)	125	0.16
Hungarian (231)	684	0.90
Icelander (0)	0	<0.01
Iranian (12)	33	0.04
Irish (2,797)	7,400	9.76
Israeli (26)	93	0.12
Italian (9,697)	14,355	18.93
Latvian (28)	74	0.10
Lithuanian (130)	228	0.30
Luxemburger (0)	9	0.01
Macedonian (154)	177	0.23
Maltese (0)	16	0.02
New Zealander (0)	0	<0.01
Northern European (25)	25	0.03

	Population	%
Norwegian (18)	72	0.09
Pennsylvania German (0)	0	<0.01
Polish (1,042)	2,744	3.62
Portuguese (615)	830	1.09
Romanian (83)	272	0.36
Russian (917)	3,102	4.09
Scandinavian (0)	0	<0.01
Scotch-Irish (92)	326	0.43
Scottish (166)	563	0.74
Serbian (0)	0	<0.01
Slavic (116)	171	0.23
Slovak (0)	116	0.15
Slovene (0)	0	<0.01
Soviet Union (0)	0	<0.01
Swedish (84)	428	0.56
Swiss (35)	56	0.07
Turkish (48)	137	0.18
Ukrainian (13)	146	0.19
Welsh (17)	129	0.17
West Indian, ex. Hispanic (3,998)	4,597	6.06
Bahamian (0)	0	<0.01
Barbadian (241)	316	0.42
Belizean (0)	0	<0.01
Bermudan (0)	0	<0.01
British West Indian (80)	153	0.20
Dutch West Indian (0)	0	<0.01
Haitian (926)	951	1.25
Jamaican (2,245)	2,635	3.48
Trinidadian/Tobagonian (295)	317	0.42
U.S. Virgin Islander (0)	0	<0.01
West Indian (211)	225	0.30
Other West Indian (0)	0	<0.01
Yugoslavian (23)	47	0.06

Hispanic Origin	Population	%
Hispanic or Latino (of any race)	21,452	27.84
Central American, ex. Mexican	2,017	2.62
Costa Rican	65	0.08
Guatemalan	1,232	1.60
Honduran	242	0.31
Nicaraguan	74	0.10
Panamanian	67	0.09
Salvadoran	330	0.43
Other Central American	7	0.01
Cuban	371	0.48
Dominican Republic	960	1.25
Mexican	10,363	13.45
Puerto Rican	2,779	3.61
South American	3,697	4.80
Argentinean	170	0.22
Bolivian	50	0.06
Chilean	76	0.10
Colombian	1,451	1.88
Ecuadorian	378	0.49
Paraguayan	49	0.06
Peruvian	1,297	1.68
Uruguayan	88	0.11
Venezuelan	131	0.17
Other South American	7	0.01
Other Hispanic or Latino	1,265	1.64

Race*	Population	%
African-American/Black (14,847)	15,858	20.58
Not Hispanic (13,956)	14,611	18.96
Hispanic (891)	1,247	1.62
American Indian/Alaska Native (398)	770	1.00
Not Hispanic (94)	308	0.40
Hispanic (304)	462	0.60
Alaska Athabascan (Ala. Nat.) (0)	0	<0.01
Aleut (Alaska Native) (0)	0	<0.01
Apache (0)	6	0.01
Arapaho (0)	0	<0.01
Blackfeet (5)	25	0.03
Canadian/French Am. Ind. (0)	2	<0.01
Central American Ind. (7)	20	0.03
Cherokee (5)	65	0.08
Cheyenne (1)	1	<0.01
Chickasaw (0)	1	<0.01
Chippewa (0)	3	<0.01

	Population	%
Choctaw (0)	2	<0.01
Colville (0)	0	<0.01
Comanche (0)	0	<0.01
Cree (0)	0	<0.01
Creek (0)	1	<0.01
Crow (0)	0	<0.01
Delaware (0)	2	<0.01
Hopi (0)	0	<0.01
Houma (0)	0	<0.01
Inupiat (Alaska Native) (0)	0	<0.01
Iroquois (5)	11	0.01
Kiowa (0)	0	<0.01
Lumbee (0)	0	<0.01
Menominee (0)	0	<0.01
Mexican American Ind. (47)	72	0.09
Navajo (0)	1	<0.01
Osage (0)	0	<0.01
Ottawa (0)	0	<0.01
Paiute (0)	0	<0.01
Pima (0)	0	<0.01
Potawatomi (0)	0	<0.01
Pueblo (0)	0	<0.01
Puget Sound Salish (0)	0	<0.01
Seminole (0)	1	<0.01
Shoshone (0)	0	<0.01
Sioux (1)	2	<0.01
South American Ind. (29)	56	0.07
Spanish American Ind. (1)	1	<0.01
Tlingit-Haida (Alaska Native) (0)	0	<0.01
Tohono O'Odham (0)	0	<0.01
Tsimshian (Alaska Native) (0)	0	<0.01
Ute (0)	0	<0.01
Yakama (0)	0	<0.01
Yaqui (0)	0	<0.01
Yuman (0)	0	<0.01
Yup'ik (Alaska Native) (0)	0	<0.01
Asian (3,262)	3,798	4.93
Not Hispanic (3,212)	3,631	4.71
Hispanic (50)	167	0.22
Bangladeshi (48)	55	0.07
Bhutanese (2)	2	<0.01
Burmese (6)	8	0.01
Cambodian (8)	9	0.01
Chinese, ex. Taiwanese (547)	715	0.93
Filipino (471)	543	0.70
Hmong (0)	0	<0.01
Indian (1,352)	1,508	1.96
Indonesian (6)	6	0.01
Japanese (106)	158	0.21
Korean (276)	319	0.41
Laotian (2)	14	0.02
Malaysian (5)	5	0.01
Nepalese (5)	5	0.01
Pakistani (147)	164	0.21
Sri Lankan (75)	83	0.11
Taiwanese (18)	32	0.04
Thai (25)	39	0.05
Vietnamese (19)	31	0.04
Hawaii Native/Pacific Islander (48)	123	0.16
Not Hispanic (20)	65	0.08
Hispanic (28)	58	0.08
Fijian (0)	0	<0.01
Guamanian/Chamorro (32)	43	0.06
Marshallese (0)	0	<0.01
Native Hawaiian (1)	12	0.02
Samoan (5)	7	0.01
Tongan (0)	0	<0.01
White (50,231)	52,208	67.75
Not Hispanic (36,948)	37,786	49.03
Hispanic (13,283)	14,422	18.71

*Notes: † The Census 2010 population figure is used to calculate the percentages in the Hispanic Origin and Race categories. Ancestry percentages are based on the 2006-2010 American Community Survey population (not shown); ‡ Numbers in parentheses indicate the number of people reporting a single ancestry; * Numbers in parentheses indicate the number of persons reporting this race alone, not in combination with any other race; Please refer to the Explanation of Data for more information.*

New York

Place Type: City
Counties: Bronx, Kings, New York, Queens, and Richmond
Population: 8,175,133

Ancestry	Population	%
Afghan (6,250)	6,470	0.08
African, Sub-Saharan (126,853)	175,478	2.17
African (60,151)	101,901	1.26
Cape Verdean (282)	595	0.01
Ethiopian (2,524)	2,869	0.04
Ghanaian (19,077)	19,782	0.24
Kenyan (294)	344	<0.01
Liberian (1,738)	1,991	0.02
Nigerian (19,543)	21,507	0.27
Senegalese (2,685)	2,895	0.04
Sierra Leonean (1,545)	1,572	0.02
Somalian (422)	518	0.01
South African (1,454)	2,116	0.03
Sudanese (1,079)	1,303	0.02
Ugandan (189)	256	<0.01
Zimbabwean (394)	414	0.01
Other Sub-Saharan African (15,476)	17,415	0.22
Albanian (29,299)	31,056	0.38
Alsatian (31)	217	<0.01
American (209,430)	209,430	2.59
Arab (65,990)	82,165	1.02
Arab (13,125)	15,160	0.19
Egyptian (15,679)	17,698	0.22
Iraqi (645)	1,137	0.01
Jordanian (1,141)	1,298	0.02
Lebanese (7,824)	11,682	0.14
Moroccan (7,043)	8,987	0.11
Palestinian (3,051)	3,421	0.04
Syrian (5,818)	8,198	0.10
Other Arab (11,664)	14,584	0.18
Armenian (7,612)	10,159	0.13
Assyrian/Chaldean/Syriac (144)	227	<0.01
Australian (2,699)	3,906	0.05
Austrian (9,463)	30,712	0.38
Basque (370)	902	0.01
Belgian (1,803)	4,472	0.06
Brazilian (9,457)	13,119	0.16
British (11,046)	21,065	0.26
Bulgarian (4,331)	5,011	0.06
Cajun (121)	432	0.01
Canadian (5,942)	10,989	0.14
Carpatho Rusyn (198)	249	<0.01
Celtic (275)	564	0.01
Croatian (8,097)	11,304	0.14
Cypriot (744)	960	0.01
Czech (3,559)	12,800	0.16
Czechoslovakian (2,411)	4,870	0.06
Danish (2,102)	7,018	0.09
Dutch (5,641)	23,151	0.29
Eastern European (41,481)	44,970	0.56
English (40,380)	146,525	1.81
Estonian (643)	1,057	0.01
European (59,415)	66,267	0.82
Finnish (1,375)	3,519	0.04
French, ex. Basque (19,416)	67,195	0.83
French Canadian (3,676)	11,393	0.14
German (68,198)	272,827	3.38
German Russian (69)	204	<0.01
Greek (58,515)	76,597	0.95
Guyanese (96,299)	107,972	1.34
Hungarian (29,252)	55,459	0.69
Icelander (386)	572	0.01
Iranian (8,448)	10,204	0.13
Irish (154,072)	410,889	5.09
Israeli (16,225)	21,872	0.27
Italian (403,347)	625,004	7.74
Latvian (1,663)	3,302	0.04
Lithuanian (4,343)	12,774	0.16
Luxemburger (76)	193	<0.01
Macedonian (4,296)	4,911	0.06
Maltese (1,817)	3,102	0.04
New Zealander (337)	584	0.01
Northern European (2,656)	3,043	0.04

Ancestry	Population	%
Norwegian (6,141)	21,894	0.27
Pennsylvania German (160)	465	0.01
Polish (112,769)	216,891	2.68
Portuguese (5,980)	13,201	0.16
Romanian (18,025)	29,552	0.37
Russian (150,929)	240,690	2.98
Scandinavian (1,533)	3,434	0.04
Scotch-Irish (9,634)	27,337	0.34
Scottish (9,926)	38,000	0.47
Serbian (3,997)	4,911	0.06
Slavic (919)	1,962	0.02
Slovak (3,457)	6,785	0.08
Slovene (593)	1,476	0.02
Soviet Union (288)	419	0.01
Swedish (5,168)	20,940	0.26
Swiss (2,335)	8,135	0.10
Turkish (12,067)	14,927	0.18
Ukrainian (36,563)	48,714	0.60
Welsh (1,659)	11,219	0.14
West Indian, ex. Hispanic (509,675)	598,504	7.41
Bahamian (828)	1,147	0.01
Barbadian (19,549)	22,550	0.28
Belizean (4,699)	5,674	0.07
Bermudan (345)	518	0.01
British West Indian (39,268)	44,326	0.55
Dutch West Indian (789)	1,167	0.01
Haitian (112,397)	120,252	1.49
Jamaican (196,443)	216,495	2.68
Trinidadian/Tobagonian (66,794)	76,240	0.94
U.S. Virgin Islander (1,806)	2,383	0.03
West Indian (65,827)	106,548	1.32
Other West Indian (930)	1,204	0.01
Yugoslavian (10,119)	12,410	0.15

Hispanic Origin	Population	%
Hispanic or Latino (of any race)	2,336,076	28.58
Central American, ex. Mexican	151,378	1.85
Costa Rican	6,673	0.08
Guatemalan	30,420	0.37
Honduran	42,400	0.52
Nicaraguan	9,346	0.11
Panamanian	22,353	0.27
Salvadoran	38,559	0.47
Other Central American	1,627	0.02
Cuban	40,840	0.50
Dominican Republic	576,701	7.05
Mexican	319,263	3.91
Puerto Rican	723,621	8.85
South American	343,468	4.20
Argentinean	15,169	0.19
Bolivian	4,488	0.05
Chilean	7,026	0.09
Colombian	94,723	1.16
Ecuadorian	167,209	2.05
Paraguayan	3,534	0.04
Peruvian	36,018	0.44
Uruguayan	3,004	0.04
Venezuelan	9,619	0.12
Other South American	2,678	0.03
Other Hispanic or Latino	180,805	2.21

Race*	Population	%
African-American/Black (2,088,510)	2,228,145	27.26
Not Hispanic (1,861,295)	1,931,889	23.63
Hispanic (227,215)	296,256	3.62
American Indian/Alaska Native (57,512)	111,749	1.37
Not Hispanic (17,427)	44,541	0.54
Hispanic (40,085)	67,208	0.82
Alaska Athabascan (Ala. Nat.) (19)	37	<0.01
Aleut (Alaska Native) (12)	26	<0.01
Apache (135)	401	<0.01
Arapaho (8)	21	<0.01
Blackfeet (235)	1,627	0.02
Canadian/French Am. Ind. (111)	197	<0.01
Central American Ind. (3,948)	7,662	0.09
Cherokee (1,195)	6,952	0.09
Cheyenne (19)	46	<0.01
Chickasaw (40)	113	<0.01
Chippewa (105)	252	<0.01

Race*	Population	%
Choctaw (94)	405	<0.01
Colville (6)	9	<0.01
Comanche (31)	76	<0.01
Cree (14)	81	<0.01
Creek (65)	291	<0.01
Crow (11)	50	<0.01
Delaware (50)	177	<0.01
Hopi (17)	49	<0.01
Houma (14)	23	<0.01
Inupiat (Alaska Native) (26)	58	<0.01
Iroquois (573)	1,276	0.02
Kiowa (11)	15	<0.01
Lumbee (27)	89	<0.01
Menominee (4)	10	<0.01
Mexican American Ind. (3,646)	4,922	0.06
Navajo (126)	272	<0.01
Osage (10)	23	<0.01
Ottawa (2)	11	<0.01
Paiute (5)	18	<0.01
Pima (4)	9	<0.01
Potawatomi (20)	40	<0.01
Pueblo (446)	892	0.01
Puget Sound Salish (5)	11	<0.01
Seminole (52)	357	<0.01
Shoshone (10)	46	<0.01
Sioux (159)	464	0.01
South American Ind. (4,682)	9,464	0.12
Spanish American Ind. (1,871)	2,594	0.03
Tlingit-Haida (Alaska Native) (15)	75	<0.01
Tohono O'Odham (32)	48	<0.01
Tsimshian (Alaska Native) (3)	4	<0.01
Ute (8)	17	<0.01
Yakama (5)	8	<0.01
Yaqui (27)	54	<0.01
Yuman (12)	22	<0.01
Yup'ik (Alaska Native) (2)	10	<0.01
Asian (1,038,388)	1,134,919	13.88
Not Hispanic (1,028,119)	1,110,964	13.59
Hispanic (10,269)	23,955	0.29
Bangladeshi (53,174)	61,788	0.76
Bhutanese (345)	388	<0.01
Burmese (3,614)	4,132	0.05
Cambodian (2,166)	2,591	0.03
Chinese, ex. Taiwanese (474,783)	500,434	6.12
Filipino (67,292)	78,030	0.95
Hmong (59)	83	<0.01
Indian (192,209)	232,696	2.85
Indonesian (3,785)	4,791	0.06
Japanese (24,277)	31,742	0.39
Korean (96,741)	102,820	1.26
Laotian (440)	664	0.01
Malaysian (2,100)	3,220	0.04
Nepalese (5,681)	6,187	0.08
Pakistani (41,887)	46,369	0.57
Sri Lankan (3,696)	4,369	0.05
Taiwanese (11,680)	13,682	0.17
Thai (6,056)	7,244	0.09
Vietnamese (13,387)	16,378	0.20
Hawaii Native/Pacific Islander (5,147)	24,098	0.29
Not Hispanic (2,795)	13,217	0.16
Hispanic (2,352)	10,881	0.13
Fijian (104)	213	<0.01
Guamanian/Chamorro (1,194)	1,784	0.02
Marshallese (8)	10	<0.01
Native Hawaiian (1,001)	2,448	0.03
Samoan (296)	764	0.01
Tongan (37)	66	<0.01
White (3,597,341)	3,797,402	46.45
Not Hispanic (2,722,904)	2,804,430	34.30
Hispanic (874,437)	992,972	12.15

Notes: † The Census 2010 population figure is used to calculate the percentages in the Hispanic Origin and Race categories. Ancestry percentages are based on the 2006-2010 American Community Survey population (not shown); ‡ Numbers in parentheses indicate the number of people reporting a single ancestry; * Numbers in parentheses indicate the number of persons reporting this race alone, not in combination with any other race; Please refer to the Explanation of Data for more information.

Niagara Falls

Place Type: City
County: Niagara
Population: 50,193

Ancestry	Population	%
Afghan (0)	0	<0.01
African, Sub-Saharan (318)	520	1.02
African (286)	488	0.96
Cape Verdean (0)	0	<0.01
Ethiopian (24)	24	0.05
Ghanaian (0)	0	<0.01
Kenyan (0)	0	<0.01
Liberian (0)	0	<0.01
Nigerian (0)	0	<0.01
Senegalese (0)	0	<0.01
Sierra Leonean (0)	0	<0.01
Somalian (0)	0	<0.01
South African (8)	8	0.02
Sudanese (0)	0	<0.01
Ugandan (0)	0	<0.01
Zimbabwean (0)	0	<0.01
Other Sub-Saharan African (0)	0	<0.01
Albanian (0)	0	<0.01
Alsatian (0)	0	<0.01
American (1,655)	1,655	3.25
Arab (204)	411	0.81
Arab (72)	103	0.20
Egyptian (0)	29	0.06
Iraqi (0)	0	<0.01
Jordanian (0)	0	<0.01
Lebanese (116)	228	0.45
Moroccan (0)	0	<0.01
Palestinian (0)	0	<0.01
Syrian (9)	44	0.09
Other Arab (7)	7	0.01
Armenian (96)	156	0.31
Assyrian/Chaldean/Syriac (0)	0	<0.01
Australian (31)	49	0.10
Austrian (38)	115	0.23
Basque (0)	0	<0.01
Belgian (0)	0	<0.01
Brazilian (0)	0	<0.01
British (29)	64	0.13
Bulgarian (0)	0	<0.01
Cajun (0)	0	<0.01
Canadian (210)	442	0.87
Carpatho Rusyn (14)	14	0.03
Celtic (0)	0	<0.01
Croatian (73)	85	0.17
Cypriot (0)	0	<0.01
Czech (37)	92	0.18
Czechoslovakian (0)	6	0.01
Danish (12)	134	0.26
Dutch (62)	498	0.98
Eastern European (0)	0	<0.01
English (2,722)	6,055	11.90
Estonian (0)	0	<0.01
European (44)	44	0.09
Finnish (0)	31	0.06
French, ex. Basque (256)	1,555	3.06
French Canadian (125)	493	0.97
German (2,324)	8,658	17.01
German Russian (16)	16	0.03
Greek (121)	318	0.62
Guyanese (0)	0	<0.01
Hungarian (68)	191	0.38
Icelander (0)	0	<0.01
Iranian (0)	0	<0.01
Irish (1,933)	7,048	13.85
Israeli (12)	12	0.02
Italian (6,763)	11,524	22.64
Latvian (0)	0	<0.01
Lithuanian (71)	128	0.25
Luxemburger (0)	0	<0.01
Macedonian (0)	0	<0.01
Maltese (0)	0	<0.01
New Zealander (0)	0	<0.01
Northern European (11)	11	0.02

Ancestry (cont.)	Population	%
Norwegian (9)	72	0.14
Pennsylvania German (61)	130	0.26
Polish (1,934)	4,962	9.75
Portuguese (135)	151	0.30
Romanian (15)	44	0.09
Russian (140)	312	0.61
Scandinavian (0)	9	0.02
Scotch-Irish (163)	522	1.03
Scottish (257)	747	1.47
Serbian (0)	0	<0.01
Slavic (28)	33	0.06
Slovak (39)	88	0.17
Slovene (0)	0	<0.01
Soviet Union (0)	0	<0.01
Swedish (51)	395	0.78
Swiss (6)	19	0.04
Turkish (0)	18	0.04
Ukrainian (59)	114	0.22
Welsh (93)	346	0.68
West Indian, ex. Hispanic (174)	366	0.72
Bahamian (0)	0	<0.01
Barbadian (0)	0	<0.01
Belizean (29)	29	0.06
Bermudan (0)	0	<0.01
British West Indian (9)	9	0.02
Dutch West Indian (0)	0	<0.01
Haitian (0)	0	<0.01
Jamaican (121)	167	0.33
Trinidadian/Tobagonian (15)	15	0.03
U.S. Virgin Islander (0)	0	<0.01
West Indian (0)	146	0.29
Other West Indian (0)	0	<0.01
Yugoslavian (0)	33	0.06

Hispanic Origin	Population	%
Hispanic or Latino (of any race)	1,508	3.00
Central American, ex. Mexican	39	0.08
Costa Rican	3	0.01
Guatemalan	15	0.03
Honduran	9	0.02
Nicaraguan	0	<0.01
Panamanian	8	0.02
Salvadoran	4	0.01
Other Central American	0	<0.01
Cuban	61	0.12
Dominican Republic	35	0.07
Mexican	228	0.45
Puerto Rican	797	1.59
South American	50	0.10
Argentinean	8	0.02
Bolivian	0	<0.01
Chilean	5	0.01
Colombian	23	0.05
Ecuadorian	3	0.01
Paraguayan	0	<0.01
Peruvian	4	0.01
Uruguayan	0	<0.01
Venezuelan	7	0.01
Other South American	0	<0.01
Other Hispanic or Latino	298	0.59

Race*	Population	%
African-American/Black (10,835)	12,203	24.31
Not Hispanic (10,643)	11,905	23.72
Hispanic (192)	298	0.59
American Indian/Alaska Native (977)	1,624	3.24
Not Hispanic (930)	1,524	3.04
Hispanic (47)	100	0.20
Alaska Athabascan (Ala. Nat.) (0)	0	<0.01
Aleut (Alaska Native) (0)	0	<0.01
Apache (0)	2	<0.01
Arapaho (0)	0	<0.01
Blackfeet (1)	16	0.03
Canadian/French Am. Ind. (18)	20	0.04
Central American Ind. (8)	11	0.02
Cherokee (8)	48	0.10
Cheyenne (1)	1	<0.01
Chickasaw (0)	0	<0.01
Chippewa (16)	23	0.05

Race* (cont.)	Population	%
Choctaw (1)	1	<0.01
Colville (0)	0	<0.01
Comanche (0)	0	<0.01
Cree (2)	3	0.01
Creek (0)	0	<0.01
Crow (0)	0	<0.01
Delaware (0)	0	<0.01
Hopi (0)	0	<0.01
Houma (0)	0	<0.01
Inupiat (Alaska Native) (0)	0	<0.01
Iroquois (542)	801	1.60
Kiowa (0)	0	<0.01
Lumbee (4)	6	0.01
Menominee (0)	2	<0.01
Mexican American Ind. (4)	4	0.01
Navajo (1)	1	<0.01
Osage (0)	0	<0.01
Ottawa (1)	1	<0.01
Paiute (0)	0	<0.01
Pima (0)	0	<0.01
Potawatomi (0)	0	<0.01
Pueblo (0)	0	<0.01
Puget Sound Salish (0)	0	<0.01
Seminole (0)	5	0.01
Shoshone (0)	0	<0.01
Sioux (5)	8	0.02
South American Ind. (1)	2	<0.01
Spanish American Ind. (0)	0	<0.01
Tlingit-Haida (Alaska Native) (0)	0	<0.01
Tohono O'Odham (0)	0	<0.01
Tsimshian (Alaska Native) (0)	0	<0.01
Ute (0)	0	<0.01
Yakama (0)	1	<0.01
Yaqui (1)	1	<0.01
Yuman (0)	0	<0.01
Yup'ik (Alaska Native) (0)	0	<0.01
Asian (609)	751	1.50
Not Hispanic (599)	732	1.46
Hispanic (10)	19	0.04
Bangladeshi (0)	0	<0.01
Bhutanese (0)	0	<0.01
Burmese (1)	1	<0.01
Cambodian (1)	1	<0.01
Chinese, ex. Taiwanese (97)	106	0.21
Filipino (45)	81	0.16
Hmong (0)	0	<0.01
Indian (286)	327	0.65
Indonesian (0)	0	<0.01
Japanese (14)	26	0.05
Korean (36)	48	0.10
Laotian (12)	16	0.03
Malaysian (0)	0	<0.01
Nepalese (0)	0	<0.01
Pakistani (58)	64	0.13
Sri Lankan (0)	5	0.01
Taiwanese (5)	5	0.01
Thai (4)	15	0.03
Vietnamese (19)	22	0.04
Hawaii Native/Pacific Islander (15)	51	0.10
Not Hispanic (10)	43	0.09
Hispanic (5)	8	0.02
Fijian (0)	1	<0.01
Guamanian/Chamorro (5)	5	0.01
Marshallese (0)	0	<0.01
Native Hawaiian (6)	10	0.02
Samoan (2)	2	<0.01
Tongan (0)	0	<0.01
White (35,394)	37,102	73.92
Not Hispanic (34,663)	36,227	72.18
Hispanic (731)	875	1.74

*Notes: † The Census 2010 population figure is used to calculate the percentages in the Hispanic Origin and Race categories. Ancestry percentages are based on the 2006-2010 American Community Survey population (not shown); ‡ Numbers in parentheses indicate the number of people reporting a single ancestry; * Numbers in parentheses indicate the number of persons reporting this race alone, not in combination with any other race; Please refer to the Explanation of Data for more information.*

North Hempstead

Place Type: Town
County: Nassau
Population: 226,322

Ancestry	Population	%
Afghan (88)	203	0.09
African, Sub-Saharan (670)	862	0.39
African (277)	437	0.20
Cape Verdean (0)	0	<0.01
Ethiopian (49)	49	0.02
Ghanaian (117)	117	0.05
Kenyan (0)	0	<0.01
Liberian (0)	3	<0.01
Nigerian (145)	154	0.07
Senegalese (0)	0	<0.01
Sierra Leonean (13)	13	0.01
Somalian (0)	0	<0.01
South African (60)	63	0.03
Sudanese (0)	17	0.01
Ugandan (0)	0	<0.01
Zimbabwean (0)	0	<0.01
Other Sub-Saharan African (9)	9	<0.01
Albanian (156)	296	0.13
Alsatian (9)	9	<0.01
American (7,110)	7,110	3.18
Arab (1,529)	2,078	0.93
Arab (82)	103	0.05
Egyptian (404)	529	0.24
Iraqi (370)	500	0.22
Jordanian (0)	0	<0.01
Lebanese (105)	147	0.07
Moroccan (34)	85	0.04
Palestinian (59)	59	0.03
Syrian (10)	84	0.04
Other Arab (465)	571	0.26
Armenian (391)	631	0.28
Assyrian/Chaldean/Syriac (4)	21	0.01
Australian (22)	80	0.04
Austrian (661)	2,782	1.24
Basque (0)	121	0.05
Belgian (93)	166	0.07
Brazilian (489)	613	0.27
British (233)	705	0.32
Bulgarian (56)	73	0.03
Cajun (0)	22	0.01
Canadian (182)	307	0.14
Carpatho Rusyn (0)	0	<0.01
Celtic (0)	48	0.02
Croatian (478)	672	0.30
Cypriot (46)	64	0.03
Czech (150)	636	0.28
Czechoslovakian (205)	493	0.22
Danish (141)	419	0.19
Dutch (110)	784	0.35
Eastern European (3,518)	3,769	1.69
English (1,073)	6,017	2.69
Estonian (18)	48	0.02
European (1,809)	2,051	0.92
Finnish (38)	128	0.06
French, ex. Basque (273)	2,191	0.98
French Canadian (207)	490	0.22
German (4,524)	18,322	8.19
German Russian (0)	26	0.01
Greek (2,635)	3,568	1.60
Guyanese (324)	405	0.18
Hungarian (894)	2,628	1.18
Icelander (0)	0	<0.01
Iranian (8,611)	9,262	4.14
Irish (10,304)	27,339	12.22
Israeli (1,537)	1,853	0.83
Italian (23,753)	40,182	17.97
Latvian (122)	254	0.11
Lithuanian (197)	718	0.32
Luxemburger (0)	16	0.01
Macedonian (0)	0	<0.01
Maltese (125)	248	0.11
New Zealander (0)	0	<0.01
Northern European (82)	91	0.04

Ancestry	Population	%
Norwegian (129)	715	0.32
Pennsylvania German (15)	15	0.01
Polish (5,076)	13,352	5.97
Portuguese (3,596)	3,978	1.78
Romanian (662)	1,434	0.64
Russian (6,882)	14,712	6.58
Scandinavian (67)	122	0.05
Scotch-Irish (405)	1,188	0.53
Scottish (369)	1,567	0.70
Serbian (109)	153	0.07
Slavic (11)	195	0.09
Slovak (122)	312	0.14
Slovene (59)	79	0.04
Soviet Union (0)	0	<0.01
Swedish (179)	1,391	0.62
Swiss (77)	362	0.16
Turkish (308)	408	0.18
Ukrainian (488)	1,005	0.45
Welsh (46)	328	0.15
West Indian, ex. Hispanic (3,572)	4,095	1.83
Bahamian (0)	0	<0.01
Barbadian (152)	184	0.08
Belizean (44)	81	0.04
Bermudan (0)	0	<0.01
British West Indian (46)	46	0.02
Dutch West Indian (45)	65	0.03
Haitian (2,247)	2,394	1.07
Jamaican (723)	868	0.39
Trinidadian/Tobagonian (87)	94	0.04
U.S. Virgin Islander (0)	0	<0.01
West Indian (228)	363	0.16
Other West Indian (0)	0	<0.01
Yugoslavian (65)	170	0.08

Hispanic Origin	Population	%
Hispanic or Latino (of any race)	29,074	12.85
Central American, ex. Mexican	11,455	5.06
Costa Rican	124	0.05
Guatemalan	1,193	0.53
Honduran	1,572	0.69
Nicaraguan	110	0.05
Panamanian	84	0.04
Salvadoran	8,262	3.65
Other Central American	110	0.05
Cuban	660	0.29
Dominican Republic	1,362	0.60
Mexican	3,488	1.54
Puerto Rican	2,705	1.20
South American	6,333	2.80
Argentinean	435	0.19
Bolivian	62	0.03
Chilean	664	0.29
Colombian	1,914	0.85
Ecuadorian	1,966	0.87
Paraguayan	140	0.06
Peruvian	925	0.41
Uruguayan	84	0.04
Venezuelan	97	0.04
Other South American	46	0.02
Other Hispanic or Latino	3,071	1.36

Race*	Population	%
African-American/Black (12,587)	13,593	6.01
Not Hispanic (11,971)	12,707	5.61
Hispanic (616)	886	0.39
American Indian/Alaska Native (461)	1,149	0.51
Not Hispanic (183)	566	0.25
Hispanic (278)	583	0.26
Alaska Athabascan (Ala. Nat.) (0)	0	<0.01
Aleut (Alaska Native) (0)	0	<0.01
Apache (1)	3	<0.01
Arapaho (0)	0	<0.01
Blackfeet (0)	0	<0.01
Canadian/French Am. Ind. (0)	0	<0.01
Central American Ind. (9)	16	0.01
Cherokee (14)	86	0.04
Cheyenne (3)	3	<0.01
Chickasaw (0)	0	<0.01
Chippewa (0)	4	<0.01

Race*	Population	%
Choctaw (3)	8	<0.01
Colville (0)	0	<0.01
Comanche (0)	0	<0.01
Cree (0)	0	<0.01
Creek (0)	3	<0.01
Crow (0)	0	<0.01
Delaware (2)	5	<0.01
Hopi (1)	3	<0.01
Houma (0)	0	<0.01
Inupiat (Alaska Native) (2)	2	<0.01
Iroquois (17)	37	0.02
Kiowa (0)	0	<0.01
Lumbee (0)	1	<0.01
Menominee (0)	0	<0.01
Mexican American Ind. (36)	48	0.02
Navajo (0)	0	<0.01
Osage (0)	0	<0.01
Ottawa (0)	0	<0.01
Paiute (0)	0	<0.01
Pima (0)	0	<0.01
Potawatomi (1)	1	<0.01
Pueblo (0)	0	<0.01
Puget Sound Salish (0)	0	<0.01
Seminole (0)	0	<0.01
Shoshone (0)	0	<0.01
Sioux (8)	17	0.01
South American Ind. (32)	79	0.03
Spanish American Ind. (39)	40	0.02
Tlingit-Haida (Alaska Native) (0)	0	<0.01
Tohono O'Odham (0)	0	<0.01
Tsimshian (Alaska Native) (0)	0	<0.01
Ute (0)	0	<0.01
Yakama (0)	0	<0.01
Yaqui (1)	1	<0.01
Yuman (0)	0	<0.01
Yup'ik (Alaska Native) (0)	0	<0.01
Asian (33,889)	36,973	16.34
Not Hispanic (33,747)	36,641	16.19
Hispanic (142)	332	0.15
Bangladeshi (392)	441	0.19
Bhutanese (1)	1	<0.01
Burmese (83)	88	0.04
Cambodian (11)	14	0.01
Chinese, ex. Taiwanese (9,631)	10,292	4.55
Filipino (1,567)	1,899	0.84
Hmong (0)	0	<0.01
Indian (12,549)	13,427	5.93
Indonesian (30)	53	0.02
Japanese (1,094)	1,266	0.56
Korean (5,820)	6,015	2.66
Laotian (7)	8	<0.01
Malaysian (24)	35	0.02
Nepalese (17)	17	0.01
Pakistani (904)	1,029	0.45
Sri Lankan (52)	59	0.03
Taiwanese (717)	809	0.36
Thai (103)	126	0.06
Vietnamese (132)	186	0.08
Hawaii Native/Pacific Islander (31)	275	0.12
Not Hispanic (24)	224	0.10
Hispanic (7)	51	0.02
Fijian (0)	0	<0.01
Guamanian/Chamorro (14)	20	0.01
Marshallese (0)	0	<0.01
Native Hawaiian (0)	34	0.02
Samoan (7)	14	0.01
Tongan (0)	0	<0.01
White (161,955)	166,538	73.58
Not Hispanic (146,760)	149,607	66.10
Hispanic (15,195)	16,931	7.48

*Notes: † The Census 2010 population figure is used to calculate the percentages in the Hispanic Origin and Race categories. Ancestry percentages are based on the 2006-2010 American Community Survey population (not shown); ‡ Numbers in parentheses indicate the number of people reporting a single ancestry; * Numbers in parentheses indicate the number of persons reporting this race alone, not in combination with any other race; Please refer to the Explanation of Data for more information.*

Oyster Bay

Place Type: Town
County: Nassau
Population: 293,214

Ancestry	Population	%
Afghan (580)	808	0.28
African, Sub-Saharan (294)	484	0.17
African (215)	289	0.10
Cape Verdean (12)	12	<0.01
Ethiopian (0)	0	<0.01
Ghanaian (0)	0	<0.01
Kenyan (0)	0	<0.01
Liberian (0)	0	<0.01
Nigerian (37)	77	0.03
Senegalese (0)	0	<0.01
Sierra Leonean (0)	0	<0.01
Somalian (0)	0	<0.01
South African (30)	30	0.01
Sudanese (0)	0	<0.01
Ugandan (0)	0	<0.01
Zimbabwean (0)	0	<0.01
Other Sub-Saharan African (0)	76	0.03
Albanian (268)	368	0.13
Alsatian (0)	0	<0.01
American (9,798)	9,798	3.36
Arab (597)	1,227	0.42
Arab (177)	245	0.08
Egyptian (153)	222	0.08
Iraqi (9)	9	<0.01
Jordanian (0)	0	<0.01
Lebanese (51)	191	0.07
Moroccan (47)	131	0.04
Palestinian (31)	60	0.02
Syrian (49)	114	0.04
Other Arab (80)	255	0.09
Armenian (1,034)	1,383	0.47
Assyrian/Chaldean/Syriac (0)	0	<0.01
Australian (3)	41	0.01
Austrian (879)	3,412	1.17
Basque (0)	3	<0.01
Belgian (53)	201	0.07
Brazilian (328)	370	0.13
British (208)	476	0.16
Bulgarian (16)	45	0.02
Cajun (0)	37	0.01
Canadian (107)	441	0.15
Carpatho Rusyn (0)	0	<0.01
Celtic (55)	55	0.02
Croatian (623)	1,002	0.34
Cypriot (63)	63	0.02
Czech (223)	1,379	0.47
Czechoslovakian (163)	618	0.21
Danish (126)	573	0.20
Dutch (288)	1,343	0.46
Eastern European (3,693)	3,841	1.32
English (1,832)	11,799	4.05
Estonian (68)	130	0.04
European (2,787)	2,919	1.00
Finnish (39)	265	0.09
French, ex. Basque (422)	4,302	1.48
French Canadian (238)	807	0.28
German (8,307)	41,381	14.19
German Russian (0)	0	<0.01
Greek (4,277)	6,908	2.37
Guyanese (134)	187	0.06
Hungarian (705)	3,138	1.08
Icelander (31)	52	0.02
Iranian (1,115)	1,464	0.50
Irish (17,041)	59,765	20.49
Israeli (422)	663	0.23
Italian (48,450)	88,723	30.43
Latvian (110)	235	0.08
Lithuanian (378)	1,079	0.37
Luxemburger (0)	0	<0.01
Macedonian (0)	0	<0.01
Maltese (117)	579	0.20
New Zealander (0)	0	<0.01
Northern European (97)	105	0.04

Ancestry (cont.)	Population	%
Norwegian (469)	1,882	0.65
Pennsylvania German (24)	24	0.01
Polish (6,380)	19,395	6.65
Portuguese (145)	445	0.15
Romanian (609)	1,492	0.51
Russian (5,986)	14,554	4.99
Scandinavian (24)	144	0.05
Scotch-Irish (832)	2,523	0.87
Scottish (646)	2,493	0.85
Serbian (12)	103	0.04
Slavic (27)	173	0.06
Slovak (164)	442	0.15
Slovene (10)	55	0.02
Soviet Union (0)	0	<0.01
Swedish (191)	2,325	0.80
Swiss (114)	686	0.24
Turkish (520)	1,232	0.42
Ukrainian (859)	1,774	0.61
Welsh (83)	515	0.18
West Indian, ex. Hispanic (1,924)	2,311	0.79
Bahamian (0)	0	<0.01
Barbadian (14)	26	0.01
Belizean (16)	29	0.01
Bermudan (0)	13	<0.01
British West Indian (125)	157	0.05
Dutch West Indian (7)	21	0.01
Haitian (732)	813	0.28
Jamaican (818)	972	0.33
Trinidadian/Tobagonian (111)	148	0.05
U.S. Virgin Islander (15)	15	0.01
West Indian (86)	102	0.03
Other West Indian (0)	15	0.01
Yugoslavian (65)	334	0.11

Hispanic Origin	Population	%
Hispanic or Latino (of any race)	21,923	7.48
Central American, ex. Mexican	4,958	1.69
Costa Rican	101	0.03
Guatemalan	397	0.14
Honduran	952	0.32
Nicaraguan	78	0.03
Panamanian	88	0.03
Salvadoran	3,297	1.12
Other Central American	45	0.02
Cuban	906	0.31
Dominican Republic	1,429	0.49
Mexican	1,550	0.53
Puerto Rican	4,810	1.64
South American	5,752	1.96
Argentinean	441	0.15
Bolivian	110	0.04
Chilean	569	0.19
Colombian	2,035	0.69
Ecuadorian	1,082	0.37
Paraguayan	64	0.02
Peruvian	1,156	0.39
Uruguayan	134	0.05
Venezuelan	129	0.04
Other South American	32	0.01
Other Hispanic or Latino	2,518	0.86

Race*	Population	%
African-American/Black (6,657)	7,671	2.62
Not Hispanic (6,168)	6,908	2.36
Hispanic (489)	763	0.26
American Indian/Alaska Native (442)	1,035	0.35
Not Hispanic (210)	646	0.22
Hispanic (232)	389	0.13
Alaska Athabascan (Ala. Nat.) (0)	1	<0.01
Aleut (Alaska Native) (1)	1	<0.01
Apache (2)	2	<0.01
Arapaho (0)	0	<0.01
Blackfeet (0)	17	0.01
Canadian/French Am. Ind. (4)	6	<0.01
Central American Ind. (13)	16	0.01
Cherokee (6)	86	0.03
Cheyenne (0)	0	<0.01
Chickasaw (0)	2	<0.01
Chippewa (9)	14	<0.01

Race* (cont.)	Population	%
Choctaw (2)	5	<0.01
Colville (0)	0	<0.01
Comanche (0)	0	<0.01
Cree (0)	3	<0.01
Creek (1)	5	<0.01
Crow (0)	1	<0.01
Delaware (3)	6	<0.01
Hopi (0)	0	<0.01
Houma (0)	0	<0.01
Inupiat (Alaska Native) (0)	0	<0.01
Iroquois (13)	47	0.02
Kiowa (1)	1	<0.01
Lumbee (0)	0	<0.01
Menominee (0)	0	<0.01
Mexican American Ind. (26)	34	0.01
Navajo (2)	3	<0.01
Osage (0)	1	<0.01
Ottawa (0)	0	<0.01
Paiute (0)	0	<0.01
Pima (0)	0	<0.01
Potawatomi (1)	2	<0.01
Pueblo (2)	3	<0.01
Puget Sound Salish (0)	0	<0.01
Seminole (0)	0	<0.01
Shoshone (1)	1	<0.01
Sioux (2)	7	<0.01
South American Ind. (24)	57	0.02
Spanish American Ind. (21)	25	0.01
Tlingit-Haida (Alaska Native) (0)	0	<0.01
Tohono O'Odham (0)	0	<0.01
Tsimshian (Alaska Native) (0)	0	<0.01
Ute (0)	0	<0.01
Yakama (0)	0	<0.01
Yaqui (0)	0	<0.01
Yuman (0)	0	<0.01
Yup'ik (Alaska Native) (0)	0	<0.01
Asian (26,723)	29,203	9.96
Not Hispanic (26,611)	28,910	9.86
Hispanic (112)	293	0.10
Bangladeshi (331)	365	0.12
Bhutanese (0)	0	<0.01
Burmese (23)	26	0.01
Cambodian (29)	38	0.01
Chinese, ex. Taiwanese (6,454)	7,054	2.41
Filipino (1,445)	1,803	0.61
Hmong (0)	0	<0.01
Indian (10,593)	11,289	3.85
Indonesian (24)	33	0.01
Japanese (431)	554	0.19
Korean (4,774)	4,977	1.70
Laotian (2)	2	<0.01
Malaysian (21)	30	0.01
Nepalese (48)	49	0.02
Pakistani (1,212)	1,330	0.45
Sri Lankan (39)	59	0.02
Taiwanese (346)	401	0.14
Thai (90)	110	0.04
Vietnamese (165)	237	0.08
Hawaii Native/Pacific Islander (34)	174	0.06
Not Hispanic (24)	124	0.04
Hispanic (10)	50	0.02
Fijian (0)	2	<0.01
Guamanian/Chamorro (7)	15	0.01
Marshallese (0)	0	<0.01
Native Hawaiian (9)	29	0.01
Samoan (3)	10	<0.01
Tongan (1)	1	<0.01
White (249,159)	252,713	86.19
Not Hispanic (234,536)	236,944	80.81
Hispanic (14,623)	15,769	5.38

Notes: † The Census 2010 population figure is used to calculate the percentages in the Hispanic Origin and Race categories. Ancestry percentages are based on the 2006-2010 American Community Survey population (not shown); ‡ Numbers in parentheses indicate the number of people reporting a single ancestry; * Numbers in parentheses indicate the number of persons reporting this race alone, not in combination with any other race; Please refer to the Explanation of Data for more information.

Queens

Place Type: Borough
County: Queens
Population: 2,230,722

Ancestry	Population	%
Afghan (5,842)	6,027	0.27
African, Sub-Saharan (19,754)	25,166	1.14
African (9,764)	14,083	0.64
Cape Verdean (46)	117	0.01
Ethiopian (478)	505	0.02
Ghanaian (1,269)	1,326	0.06
Kenyan (96)	96	<0.01
Liberian (297)	381	0.02
Nigerian (5,989)	6,304	0.29
Senegalese (84)	84	<0.01
Sierra Leonean (127)	127	<0.01
Somalian (52)	98	<0.01
South African (230)	356	0.02
Sudanese (161)	286	0.01
Ugandan (65)	77	<0.01
Zimbabwean (107)	107	<0.01
Other Sub-Saharan African (989)	1,219	0.06
Albanian (6,264)	6,624	0.30
Alsatian (26)	37	<0.01
American (45,604)	45,604	2.07
Arab (16,286)	19,669	0.89
Arab (1,921)	2,283	0.10
Egyptian (5,905)	6,551	0.30
Iraqi (224)	315	0.01
Jordanian (260)	307	0.01
Lebanese (1,548)	2,228	0.10
Moroccan (2,945)	3,459	0.16
Palestinian (582)	638	0.03
Syrian (193)	420	0.02
Other Arab (2,708)	3,468	0.16
Armenian (4,083)	4,658	0.21
Assyrian/Chaldean/Syriac (13)	13	<0.01
Australian (163)	285	0.01
Austrian (2,702)	7,523	0.34
Basque (29)	159	0.01
Belgian (289)	593	0.03
Brazilian (4,871)	6,175	0.28
British (1,346)	2,457	0.11
Bulgarian (1,928)	2,090	0.10
Cajun (0)	33	<0.01
Canadian (604)	1,308	0.06
Carpatho Rusyn (0)	9	<0.01
Celtic (92)	169	0.01
Croatian (5,621)	7,054	0.32
Cypriot (556)	644	0.03
Czech (1,116)	3,464	0.16
Czechoslovakian (816)	1,467	0.07
Danish (171)	792	0.04
Dutch (727)	3,516	0.16
Eastern European (4,442)	4,673	0.21
English (4,389)	20,267	0.92
Estonian (164)	198	0.01
European (5,335)	6,584	0.30
Finnish (269)	693	0.03
French, ex. Basque (3,945)	12,532	0.57
French Canadian (552)	2,020	0.09
German (20,566)	70,399	3.20
German Russian (33)	78	<0.01
Greek (35,368)	41,654	1.89
Guyanese (47,132)	53,961	2.45
Hungarian (4,718)	9,470	0.43
Icelander (10)	26	<0.01
Iranian (3,162)	3,707	0.17
Irish (43,033)	105,348	4.79
Israeli (3,355)	4,164	0.19
Italian (104,251)	159,812	7.27
Latvian (342)	568	0.03
Lithuanian (1,463)	3,131	0.14
Luxemburger (0)	13	<0.01
Macedonian (938)	1,109	0.05
Maltese (952)	1,565	0.07
New Zealander (0)	16	<0.01
Northern European (370)	512	0.02

Ancestry (cont.)	Population	%
Norwegian (670)	2,559	0.12
Pennsylvania German (9)	38	<0.01
Polish (37,726)	59,757	2.72
Portuguese (2,784)	4,727	0.21
Romanian (9,232)	11,686	0.53
Russian (29,779)	44,676	2.03
Scandinavian (131)	545	0.02
Scotch-Irish (2,079)	4,602	0.21
Scottish (1,567)	5,718	0.26
Serbian (2,176)	2,438	0.11
Slavic (370)	765	0.03
Slovak (1,161)	1,882	0.09
Slovene (171)	468	0.02
Soviet Union (12)	71	<0.01
Swedish (511)	2,862	0.13
Swiss (381)	1,260	0.06
Turkish (3,054)	3,767	0.17
Ukrainian (5,770)	8,375	0.38
Welsh (201)	1,666	0.08
West Indian, ex. Hispanic (131,014)	147,460	6.71
Bahamian (134)	185	0.01
Barbadian (4,074)	5,021	0.23
Belizean (1,106)	1,344	0.06
Bermudan (142)	177	0.01
British West Indian (3,765)	4,689	0.21
Dutch West Indian (122)	206	0.01
Haitian (35,439)	38,368	1.74
Jamaican (55,278)	59,999	2.73
Trinidadian/Tobagonian (16,227)	19,255	0.88
U.S. Virgin Islander (234)	364	0.02
West Indian (14,052)	17,400	0.79
Other West Indian (441)	452	0.02
Yugoslavian (3,824)	4,516	0.21

Hispanic Origin	Population	%
Hispanic or Latino (of any race)	613,750	27.51
Central American, ex. Mexican	52,509	2.35
Costa Rican	1,749	0.08
Guatemalan	13,700	0.61
Honduran	8,546	0.38
Nicaraguan	2,842	0.13
Panamanian	3,977	0.18
Salvadoran	21,342	0.96
Other Central American	353	0.02
Cuban	11,020	0.49
Dominican Republic	88,061	3.95
Mexican	92,835	4.16
Puerto Rican	102,881	4.61
South American	214,022	9.59
Argentinean	6,345	0.28
Bolivian	3,268	0.15
Chilean	3,184	0.14
Colombian	70,290	3.15
Ecuadorian	98,512	4.42
Paraguayan	2,775	0.12
Peruvian	22,886	1.03
Uruguayan	1,743	0.08
Venezuelan	3,580	0.16
Other South American	1,439	0.06
Other Hispanic or Latino	52,422	2.35

Race*	Population	%
African-American/Black (426,683)	462,351	20.73
Not Hispanic (395,881)	419,695	18.81
Hispanic (30,802)	42,656	1.91
American Indian/Alaska Native (15,364)	30,033	1.35
Not Hispanic (6,490)	15,412	0.69
Hispanic (8,874)	14,621	0.66
Alaska Athabascan (Ala. Nat.) (2)	3	<0.01
Aleut (Alaska Native) (4)	6	<0.01
Apache (15)	53	<0.01
Arapaho (0)	2	<0.01
Blackfeet (45)	342	0.02
Canadian/French Am. Ind. (20)	38	<0.01
Central American Ind. (419)	733	0.03
Cherokee (267)	1,425	0.06
Cheyenne (13)	20	<0.01
Chickasaw (9)	21	<0.01
Chippewa (14)	37	<0.01

Race* (cont.)	Population	%
Choctaw (16)	68	<0.01
Colville (1)	1	<0.01
Comanche (3)	6	<0.01
Cree (6)	24	<0.01
Creek (23)	73	<0.01
Crow (1)	4	<0.01
Delaware (14)	35	<0.01
Hopi (1)	15	<0.01
Houma (0)	4	<0.01
Inupiat (Alaska Native) (6)	13	<0.01
Iroquois (140)	308	0.01
Kiowa (0)	0	<0.01
Lumbee (7)	30	<0.01
Menominee (0)	0	<0.01
Mexican American Ind. (1,270)	1,640	0.07
Navajo (13)	37	<0.01
Osage (0)	5	<0.01
Ottawa (0)	2	<0.01
Paiute (3)	4	<0.01
Pima (0)	0	<0.01
Potawatomi (6)	7	<0.01
Pueblo (102)	161	0.01
Puget Sound Salish (2)	5	<0.01
Seminole (15)	79	<0.01
Shoshone (0)	6	<0.01
Sioux (35)	104	<0.01
South American Ind. (1,281)	2,448	0.11
Spanish American Ind. (468)	659	0.03
Tlingit-Haida (Alaska Native) (8)	20	<0.01
Tohono O'Odham (4)	6	<0.01
Tsimshian (Alaska Native) (0)	1	<0.01
Ute (4)	5	<0.01
Yakama (0)	0	<0.01
Yaqui (3)	7	<0.01
Yuman (2)	5	<0.01
Yup'ik (Alaska Native) (1)	1	<0.01
Asian (511,787)	552,867	24.78
Not Hispanic (508,334)	545,389	24.45
Hispanic (3,453)	7,478	0.34
Bangladeshi (33,152)	38,341	1.72
Bhutanese (240)	250	0.01
Burmese (2,132)	2,344	0.11
Cambodian (230)	303	0.01
Chinese, ex. Taiwanese (191,693)	200,714	9.00
Filipino (38,163)	41,773	1.87
Hmong (24)	30	<0.01
Indian (117,550)	141,147	6.33
Indonesian (2,860)	3,386	0.15
Japanese (6,375)	7,790	0.35
Korean (64,107)	66,124	2.96
Laotian (137)	210	0.01
Malaysian (1,029)	1,620	0.07
Nepalese (4,930)	5,319	0.24
Pakistani (16,215)	18,084	0.81
Sri Lankan (1,293)	1,536	0.07
Taiwanese (7,776)	8,962	0.40
Thai (3,677)	4,124	0.18
Vietnamese (3,566)	4,322	0.19
Hawaii Native/Pacific Islander (1,530)	7,691	0.34
Not Hispanic (1,094)	5,685	0.25
Hispanic (436)	2,006	0.09
Fijian (36)	76	<0.01
Guamanian/Chamorro (337)	483	0.02
Marshallese (0)	0	<0.01
Native Hawaiian (191)	486	0.02
Samoan (62)	179	0.01
Tongan (7)	14	<0.01
White (886,053)	941,608	42.21
Not Hispanic (616,727)	638,051	28.60
Hispanic (269,326)	303,557	13.61

Notes: † The Census 2010 population figure is used to calculate the percentages in the Hispanic Origin and Race categories. Ancestry percentages are based on the 2006-2010 American Community Survey population (not shown); ‡ Numbers in parentheses indicate the number of people reporting a single ancestry; * Numbers in parentheses indicate the number of persons reporting this race alone, not in combination with any other race; Please refer to the Explanation of Data for more information.

Ramapo

Place Type: Town
County: Rockland
Population: 126,595

Ancestry	Population	%
Afghan (111)	111	0.09
African, Sub-Saharan (718)	858	0.70
African (292)	427	0.35
Cape Verdean (0)	0	<0.01
Ethiopian (0)	0	<0.01
Ghanaian (77)	77	0.06
Kenyan (0)	0	<0.01
Liberian (0)	0	<0.01
Nigerian (207)	207	0.17
Senegalese (0)	0	<0.01
Sierra Leonean (0)	0	<0.01
Somalian (0)	0	<0.01
South African (56)	56	0.05
Sudanese (0)	0	<0.01
Ugandan (86)	86	0.07
Zimbabwean (0)	0	<0.01
Other Sub-Saharan African (0)	5	<0.01
Albanian (0)	0	<0.01
Alsatian (0)	0	<0.01
American (5,092)	5,092	4.15
Arab (608)	781	0.64
Arab (245)	245	0.20
Egyptian (16)	24	0.02
Iraqi (12)	48	0.04
Jordanian (10)	10	0.01
Lebanese (23)	37	0.03
Moroccan (216)	291	0.24
Palestinian (0)	25	0.02
Syrian (17)	17	0.01
Other Arab (69)	84	0.07
Armenian (33)	63	0.05
Assyrian/Chaldean/Syriac (0)	0	<0.01
Australian (19)	86	0.07
Austrian (328)	1,328	1.08
Basque (0)	0	<0.01
Belgian (218)	751	0.61
Brazilian (101)	228	0.19
British (179)	396	0.32
Bulgarian (8)	24	0.02
Cajun (0)	0	<0.01
Canadian (309)	680	0.55
Carpatho Rusyn (0)	0	<0.01
Celtic (19)	19	0.02
Croatian (0)	16	0.01
Cypriot (0)	0	<0.01
Czech (174)	565	0.46
Czechoslovakian (355)	654	0.53
Danish (56)	129	0.11
Dutch (208)	772	0.63
Eastern European (1,057)	1,144	0.93
English (863)	3,171	2.58
Estonian (24)	48	0.04
European (7,822)	8,814	7.18
Finnish (0)	17	0.01
French, ex. Basque (183)	954	0.78
French Canadian (53)	174	0.14
German (2,191)	7,630	6.22
German Russian (0)	0	<0.01
Greek (402)	653	0.53
Guyanese (294)	371	0.30
Hungarian (3,672)	6,804	5.54
Icelander (0)	0	<0.01
Iranian (181)	314	0.26
Irish (3,209)	8,081	6.59
Israeli (1,511)	3,342	2.72
Italian (4,569)	8,664	7.06
Latvian (87)	174	0.14
Lithuanian (98)	538	0.44
Luxemburger (0)	0	<0.01
Macedonian (0)	0	<0.01
Maltese (0)	0	<0.01
New Zealander (0)	55	0.04
Northern European (0)	38	0.03

Ancestry	Population	%
Norwegian (64)	140	0.11
Pennsylvania German (10)	17	0.01
Polish (3,146)	9,453	7.70
Portuguese (120)	252	0.21
Romanian (524)	1,695	1.38
Russian (2,367)	6,069	4.95
Scandinavian (15)	52	0.04
Scotch-Irish (119)	424	0.35
Scottish (193)	640	0.52
Serbian (0)	0	<0.01
Slavic (18)	63	0.05
Slovak (69)	114	0.09
Slovene (31)	46	0.04
Soviet Union (0)	0	<0.01
Swedish (28)	316	0.26
Swiss (34)	85	0.07
Turkish (28)	114	0.09
Ukrainian (949)	1,403	1.14
Welsh (10)	182	0.15
West Indian, ex. Hispanic (12,117)	12,710	10.36
Bahamian (0)	0	<0.01
Barbadian (10)	34	0.03
Belizean (12)	35	0.03
Bermudan (0)	0	<0.01
British West Indian (253)	253	0.21
Dutch West Indian (0)	0	<0.01
Haitian (8,747)	8,948	7.29
Jamaican (2,336)	2,509	2.04
Trinidadian/Tobagonian (550)	604	0.49
U.S. Virgin Islander (0)	19	0.02
West Indian (209)	308	0.25
Other West Indian (0)	0	<0.01
Yugoslavian (42)	78	0.06

Hispanic Origin	Population	%
Hispanic or Latino (of any race)	17,223	13.60
Central American, ex. Mexican	5,319	4.20
Costa Rican	103	0.08
Guatemalan	4,050	3.20
Honduran	182	0.14
Nicaraguan	29	0.02
Panamanian	54	0.04
Salvadoran	872	0.69
Other Central American	29	0.02
Cuban	279	0.22
Dominican Republic	1,021	0.81
Mexican	2,433	1.92
Puerto Rican	2,904	2.29
South American	3,759	2.97
Argentinean	166	0.13
Bolivian	9	0.01
Chilean	66	0.05
Colombian	308	0.24
Ecuadorian	2,915	2.30
Paraguayan	8	0.01
Peruvian	204	0.16
Uruguayan	16	0.01
Venezuelan	59	0.05
Other South American	8	0.01
Other Hispanic or Latino	1,508	1.19

Race*	Population	%
African-American/Black (20,056)	21,297	16.82
Not Hispanic (19,173)	20,078	15.86
Hispanic (883)	1,219	0.96
American Indian/Alaska Native (430)	963	0.76
Not Hispanic (253)	613	0.48
Hispanic (177)	350	0.28
Alaska Athabascan (Ala. Nat.) (0)	0	<0.01
Aleut (Alaska Native) (1)	1	<0.01
Apache (2)	3	<0.01
Arapaho (0)	0	<0.01
Blackfeet (1)	11	0.01
Canadian/French Am. Ind. (0)	0	<0.01
Central American Ind. (10)	22	0.02
Cherokee (9)	69	0.05
Cheyenne (0)	1	<0.01
Chickasaw (0)	0	<0.01
Chippewa (0)	1	<0.01

Race*	Population	%
Choctaw (1)	1	<0.01
Colville (0)	0	<0.01
Comanche (0)	2	<0.01
Cree (0)	0	<0.01
Creek (0)	0	<0.01
Crow (0)	0	<0.01
Delaware (93)	167	0.13
Hopi (0)	0	<0.01
Houma (0)	0	<0.01
Inupiat (Alaska Native) (0)	0	<0.01
Iroquois (21)	36	0.03
Kiowa (0)	0	<0.01
Lumbee (0)	2	<0.01
Menominee (0)	0	<0.01
Mexican American Ind. (52)	74	0.06
Navajo (0)	4	<0.01
Osage (0)	0	<0.01
Ottawa (0)	0	<0.01
Paiute (0)	0	<0.01
Pima (0)	0	<0.01
Potawatomi (0)	0	<0.01
Pueblo (1)	1	<0.01
Puget Sound Salish (0)	0	<0.01
Seminole (0)	2	<0.01
Shoshone (0)	0	<0.01
Sioux (0)	2	<0.01
South American Ind. (20)	68	0.05
Spanish American Ind. (3)	7	0.01
Tlingit-Haida (Alaska Native) (2)	7	0.01
Tohono O'Odham (2)	4	<0.01
Tsimshian (Alaska Native) (0)	0	<0.01
Ute (0)	0	<0.01
Yakama (0)	1	<0.01
Yaqui (0)	0	<0.01
Yuman (0)	0	<0.01
Yup'ik (Alaska Native) (0)	0	<0.01
Asian (5,082)	5,750	4.54
Not Hispanic (5,013)	5,609	4.43
Hispanic (69)	141	0.11
Bangladeshi (56)	63	0.05
Bhutanese (0)	0	<0.01
Burmese (1)	1	<0.01
Cambodian (48)	52	0.04
Chinese, ex. Taiwanese (606)	730	0.58
Filipino (1,338)	1,472	1.16
Hmong (0)	0	<0.01
Indian (1,751)	1,962	1.55
Indonesian (18)	23	0.02
Japanese (98)	136	0.11
Korean (300)	339	0.27
Laotian (4)	6	<0.01
Malaysian (2)	8	0.01
Nepalese (11)	11	0.01
Pakistani (461)	524	0.41
Sri Lankan (23)	26	0.02
Taiwanese (19)	21	0.02
Thai (30)	37	0.03
Vietnamese (112)	148	0.12
Hawaii Native/Pacific Islander (45)	237	0.19
Not Hispanic (18)	156	0.12
Hispanic (27)	81	0.06
Fijian (0)	2	<0.01
Guamanian/Chamorro (16)	19	0.02
Marshallese (0)	0	<0.01
Native Hawaiian (8)	17	0.01
Samoan (4)	9	<0.01
Tongan (0)	2	<0.01
White (90,924)	92,843	73.34
Not Hispanic (83,094)	84,071	66.41
Hispanic (7,830)	8,772	6.93

*Notes: † The Census 2010 population figure is used to calculate the percentages in the Hispanic Origin and Race categories. Ancestry percentages are based on the 2006-2010 American Community Survey population (not shown); ‡ Numbers in parentheses indicate the number of people reporting a single ancestry; * Numbers in parentheses indicate the number of persons reporting this race alone, not in combination with any other race; Please refer to the Explanation of Data for more information.*

Rochester

Place Type: City
County: Monroe
Population: 210,565

Ancestry	Population	%
Afghan (0)	0	<0.01
African, Sub-Saharan (7,095)	7,909	3.73
African (5,087)	5,828	2.75
Cape Verdean (0)	0	<0.01
Ethiopian (227)	227	0.11
Ghanaian (49)	49	0.02
Kenyan (9)	9	<0.01
Liberian (89)	89	0.04
Nigerian (151)	203	0.10
Senegalese (0)	0	<0.01
Sierra Leonean (0)	0	<0.01
Somalian (980)	980	0.46
South African (19)	32	0.02
Sudanese (107)	107	0.05
Ugandan (0)	0	<0.01
Zimbabwean (76)	76	0.04
Other Sub-Saharan African (301)	309	0.15
Albanian (31)	42	0.02
Alsatian (0)	0	<0.01
American (3,617)	3,617	1.71
Arab (785)	1,077	0.51
Arab (245)	263	0.12
Egyptian (81)	81	0.04
Iraqi (36)	36	0.02
Jordanian (0)	0	<0.01
Lebanese (136)	196	0.09
Moroccan (17)	48	0.02
Palestinian (30)	30	0.01
Syrian (11)	33	0.02
Other Arab (229)	390	0.18
Armenian (84)	105	0.05
Assyrian/Chaldean/Syriac (0)	0	<0.01
Australian (0)	69	0.03
Austrian (103)	450	0.21
Basque (0)	0	<0.01
Belgian (27)	185	0.09
Brazilian (35)	90	0.04
British (259)	606	0.29
Bulgarian (0)	33	0.02
Cajun (0)	0	<0.01
Canadian (227)	550	0.26
Carpatho Rusyn (0)	0	<0.01
Celtic (13)	40	0.02
Croatian (12)	61	0.03
Cypriot (0)	0	<0.01
Czech (77)	484	0.23
Czechoslovakian (30)	44	0.02
Danish (51)	275	0.13
Dutch (406)	2,898	1.37
Eastern European (200)	237	0.11
English (3,972)	13,510	6.37
Estonian (0)	38	0.02
European (893)	1,150	0.54
Finnish (11)	160	0.08
French, ex. Basque (683)	4,083	1.93
French Canadian (652)	1,474	0.70
German (5,802)	22,972	10.84
German Russian (0)	0	<0.01
Greek (337)	623	0.29
Guyanese (348)	381	0.18
Hungarian (246)	783	0.37
Icelander (0)	0	<0.01
Iranian (97)	120	0.06
Irish (5,531)	19,595	9.24
Israeli (37)	57	0.03
Italian (8,976)	19,728	9.31
Latvian (33)	55	0.03
Lithuanian (236)	466	0.22
Luxemburger (19)	62	0.03
Macedonian (0)	10	<0.01
Maltese (34)	100	0.05
New Zealander (0)	0	<0.01
Northern European (23)	23	0.01

Norwegian (135)	444	0.21
Pennsylvania German (8)	70	0.03
Polish (1,583)	5,614	2.65
Portuguese (47)	199	0.09
Romanian (96)	186	0.09
Russian (498)	1,342	0.63
Scandinavian (34)	111	0.05
Scotch-Irish (433)	1,614	0.76
Scottish (526)	3,002	1.42
Serbian (0)	49	0.02
Slavic (32)	78	0.04
Slovak (24)	157	0.07
Slovene (24)	37	0.02
Soviet Union (0)	0	<0.01
Swedish (403)	1,156	0.55
Swiss (36)	271	0.13
Turkish (486)	612	0.29
Ukrainian (727)	1,325	0.63
Welsh (141)	992	0.47
West Indian, ex. Hispanic (3,129)	5,230	2.47
Bahamian (58)	218	0.10
Barbadian (169)	230	0.11
Belizean (119)	171	0.08
Bermudan (0)	0	<0.01
British West Indian (99)	223	0.11
Dutch West Indian (0)	13	0.01
Haitian (352)	383	0.18
Jamaican (1,743)	2,834	1.34
Trinidadian/Tobagonian (199)	288	0.14
U.S. Virgin Islander (0)	0	<0.01
West Indian (390)	870	0.41
Other West Indian (0)	0	<0.01
Yugoslavian (117)	138	0.07

Hispanic Origin	Population	%
Hispanic or Latino (of any race)	34,456	16.36
Central American, ex. Mexican	569	0.27
Costa Rican	72	0.03
Guatemalan	85	0.04
Honduran	129	0.06
Nicaraguan	56	0.03
Panamanian	123	0.06
Salvadoran	96	0.05
Other Central American	8	<0.01
Cuban	1,616	0.77
Dominican Republic	1,373	0.65
Mexican	1,168	0.55
Puerto Rican	27,734	13.17
South American	517	0.25
Argentinean	49	0.02
Bolivian	18	0.01
Chilean	82	0.04
Colombian	182	0.09
Ecuadorian	72	0.03
Paraguayan	10	<0.01
Peruvian	68	0.03
Uruguayan	7	<0.01
Venezuelan	22	0.01
Other South American	7	<0.01
Other Hispanic or Latino	1,479	0.70

Race*	Population	%
African-American/Black (87,897)	94,587	44.92
Not Hispanic (83,346)	88,052	41.82
Hispanic (4,551)	6,535	3.10
American Indian/Alaska Native (1,013)	3,202	1.52
Not Hispanic (666)	2,330	1.11
Hispanic (347)	872	0.41
Alaska Athabascan (Ala. Nat.) (0)	1	<0.01
Aleut (Alaska Native) (1)	2	<0.01
Apache (8)	20	0.01
Arapaho (0)	0	<0.01
Blackfeet (16)	134	0.06
Canadian/French Am. Ind. (3)	9	<0.01
Central American Ind. (15)	29	0.01
Cherokee (51)	411	0.20
Cheyenne (2)	3	<0.01
Chickasaw (0)	2	<0.01
Chippewa (9)	18	0.01

Choctaw (1)	28	0.01
Colville (0)	1	<0.01
Comanche (0)	2	<0.01
Cree (1)	2	<0.01
Creek (2)	9	<0.01
Crow (0)	1	<0.01
Delaware (1)	10	<0.01
Hopi (1)	1	<0.01
Houma (0)	0	<0.01
Inupiat (Alaska Native) (3)	4	<0.01
Iroquois (265)	483	0.23
Kiowa (0)	0	<0.01
Lumbee (0)	0	<0.01
Menominee (0)	0	<0.01
Mexican American Ind. (20)	38	0.02
Navajo (11)	30	0.01
Osage (1)	3	<0.01
Ottawa (0)	0	<0.01
Paiute (1)	1	<0.01
Pima (0)	2	<0.01
Potawatomi (3)	5	<0.01
Pueblo (0)	2	<0.01
Puget Sound Salish (0)	0	<0.01
Seminole (1)	44	0.02
Shoshone (0)	1	<0.01
Sioux (2)	22	0.01
South American Ind. (45)	144	0.07
Spanish American Ind. (9)	9	<0.01
Tlingit-Haida (Alaska Native) (0)	0	<0.01
Tohono O'Odham (1)	1	<0.01
Tsimshian (Alaska Native) (0)	0	<0.01
Ute (0)	4	<0.01
Yakama (0)	0	<0.01
Yaqui (0)	0	<0.01
Yuman (0)	0	<0.01
Yup'ik (Alaska Native) (0)	0	<0.01
Asian (6,493)	7,752	3.68
Not Hispanic (6,350)	7,397	3.51
Hispanic (143)	355	0.17
Bangladeshi (25)	27	0.01
Bhutanese (369)	411	0.20
Burmese (527)	565	0.27
Cambodian (342)	381	0.18
Chinese, ex. Taiwanese (1,195)	1,456	0.69
Filipino (215)	378	0.18
Hmong (2)	3	<0.01
Indian (780)	1,006	0.48
Indonesian (13)	27	0.01
Japanese (127)	301	0.14
Korean (578)	741	0.35
Laotian (564)	668	0.32
Malaysian (8)	10	<0.01
Nepalese (118)	165	0.08
Pakistani (53)	75	0.04
Sri Lankan (23)	27	0.01
Taiwanese (104)	132	0.06
Thai (67)	103	0.05
Vietnamese (942)	1,050	0.50
Hawaii Native/Pacific Islander (101)	449	0.21
Not Hispanic (77)	284	0.13
Hispanic (24)	165	0.08
Fijian (0)	4	<0.01
Guamanian/Chamorro (12)	26	0.01
Marshallese (0)	0	<0.01
Native Hawaiian (30)	77	0.04
Samoan (31)	63	0.03
Tongan (2)	3	<0.01
White (91,951)	98,814	46.93
Not Hispanic (79,178)	84,019	39.90
Hispanic (12,773)	14,795	7.03

Notes: † The Census 2010 population figure is used to calculate the percentages in the Hispanic Origin and Race categories. Ancestry percentages are based on the 2006-2010 American Community Survey population (not shown); ‡ Numbers in parentheses indicate the number of people reporting a single ancestry; * Numbers in parentheses indicate the number of persons reporting this race alone, not in combination with any other race; Please refer to the Explanation of Data for more information.

Schenectady

Place Type: City
County: Schenectady
Population: 66,135

Ancestry	Population	%
Afghan (318)	318	0.49
African, Sub-Saharan (554)	770	1.18
African (201)	334	0.51
Cape Verdean (0)	0	<0.01
Ethiopian (0)	0	<0.01
Ghanaian (24)	24	0.04
Kenyan (69)	69	0.11
Liberian (24)	24	0.04
Nigerian (131)	186	0.28
Senegalese (0)	0	<0.01
Sierra Leonean (0)	0	<0.01
Somalian (0)	0	<0.01
South African (0)	0	<0.01
Sudanese (0)	0	<0.01
Ugandan (0)	0	<0.01
Zimbabwean (0)	0	<0.01
Other Sub-Saharan African (105)	133	0.20
Albanian (28)	39	0.06
Alsatian (0)	0	<0.01
American (3,124)	3,124	4.78
Arab (140)	191	0.29
Arab (81)	113	0.17
Egyptian (0)	0	<0.01
Iraqi (0)	0	<0.01
Jordanian (0)	0	<0.01
Lebanese (59)	78	0.12
Moroccan (0)	0	<0.01
Palestinian (0)	0	<0.01
Syrian (0)	0	<0.01
Other Arab (0)	0	<0.01
Armenian (19)	19	0.03
Assyrian/Chaldean/Syriac (0)	0	<0.01
Australian (0)	0	<0.01
Austrian (11)	77	0.12
Basque (0)	0	<0.01
Belgian (0)	0	<0.01
Brazilian (144)	194	0.30
British (100)	187	0.29
Bulgarian (0)	0	<0.01
Cajun (0)	0	<0.01
Canadian (44)	72	0.11
Carpatho Rusyn (0)	0	<0.01
Celtic (20)	20	0.03
Croatian (0)	0	<0.01
Cypriot (0)	0	<0.01
Czech (50)	236	0.36
Czechoslovakian (68)	167	0.26
Danish (97)	121	0.19
Dutch (393)	1,521	2.33
Eastern European (76)	76	0.12
English (1,339)	3,998	6.12
Estonian (0)	0	<0.01
European (205)	263	0.40
Finnish (15)	26	0.04
French, ex. Basque (658)	2,862	4.38
French Canadian (193)	902	1.38
German (1,915)	6,846	10.47
German Russian (0)	0	<0.01
Greek (147)	224	0.34
Guyanese (1,783)	1,915	2.93
Hungarian (128)	341	0.52
Icelander (0)	0	<0.01
Iranian (0)	0	<0.01
Irish (2,754)	8,655	13.24
Israeli (0)	9	0.01
Italian (5,680)	9,882	15.12
Latvian (0)	0	<0.01
Lithuanian (42)	240	0.37
Luxemburger (0)	0	<0.01
Macedonian (0)	0	<0.01
Maltese (0)	0	<0.01
New Zealander (0)	0	<0.01
Northern European (83)	97	0.15
Norwegian (0)	63	0.10
Pennsylvania German (0)	11	0.02
Polish (1,904)	3,977	6.08
Portuguese (20)	70	0.11
Romanian (10)	10	0.02
Russian (98)	430	0.66
Scandinavian (13)	13	0.02
Scotch-Irish (186)	509	0.78
Scottish (248)	656	1.00
Serbian (0)	12	0.02
Slavic (40)	40	0.06
Slovak (32)	93	0.14
Slovene (0)	0	<0.01
Soviet Union (0)	0	<0.01
Swedish (52)	177	0.27
Swiss (57)	171	0.26
Turkish (10)	10	0.02
Ukrainian (91)	236	0.36
Welsh (65)	320	0.49
West Indian, ex. Hispanic (1,255)	1,477	2.26
Bahamian (0)	0	<0.01
Barbadian (43)	94	0.14
Belizean (0)	0	<0.01
Bermudan (0)	0	<0.01
British West Indian (7)	7	0.01
Dutch West Indian (0)	10	0.02
Haitian (24)	61	0.09
Jamaican (730)	781	1.19
Trinidadian/Tobagonian (18)	78	0.12
U.S. Virgin Islander (0)	0	<0.01
West Indian (433)	446	0.68
Other West Indian (0)	0	<0.01
Yugoslavian (0)	1	<0.01

Hispanic Origin	Population	%
Hispanic or Latino (of any race)	6,922	10.47
Central American, ex. Mexican	321	0.49
Costa Rican	34	0.05
Guatemalan	61	0.09
Honduran	41	0.06
Nicaraguan	17	0.03
Panamanian	31	0.05
Salvadoran	126	0.19
Other Central American	11	0.02
Cuban	150	0.23
Dominican Republic	478	0.72
Mexican	430	0.65
Puerto Rican	4,677	7.07
South American	346	0.52
Argentinean	18	0.03
Bolivian	5	0.01
Chilean	13	0.02
Colombian	86	0.13
Ecuadorian	62	0.09
Paraguayan	9	0.01
Peruvian	74	0.11
Uruguayan	9	0.01
Venezuelan	27	0.04
Other South American	43	0.07
Other Hispanic or Latino	520	0.79

Race*	Population	%
African-American/Black (13,354)	16,103	24.35
Not Hispanic (12,258)	14,556	22.01
Hispanic (1,096)	1,547	2.34
American Indian/Alaska Native (458)	1,372	2.07
Not Hispanic (343)	1,126	1.70
Hispanic (115)	246	0.37
Alaska Athabascan (Ala. Nat.) (0)	0	<0.01
Aleut (Alaska Native) (0)	0	<0.01
Apache (2)	5	0.01
Arapaho (1)	1	<0.01
Blackfeet (2)	58	0.09
Canadian/French Am. Ind. (3)	9	0.01
Central American Ind. (5)	6	0.01
Cherokee (9)	145	0.22
Cheyenne (1)	2	<0.01
Chickasaw (0)	0	<0.01
Chippewa (2)	11	0.02

Choctaw (0)	1	<0.01
Colville (0)	0	<0.01
Comanche (0)	0	<0.01
Cree (0)	4	0.01
Creek (1)	5	0.01
Crow (0)	6	0.01
Delaware (4)	12	0.02
Hopi (0)	0	<0.01
Houma (0)	0	<0.01
Inupiat (Alaska Native) (3)	3	<0.01
Iroquois (17)	88	0.13
Kiowa (0)	1	<0.01
Lumbee (2)	4	0.01
Menominee (0)	0	<0.01
Mexican American Ind. (16)	17	0.03
Navajo (1)	2	<0.01
Osage (0)	0	<0.01
Ottawa (0)	0	<0.01
Paiute (0)	0	<0.01
Pima (1)	5	0.01
Potawatomi (0)	5	0.01
Pueblo (0)	1	<0.01
Puget Sound Salish (0)	0	<0.01
Seminole (1)	4	0.01
Shoshone (0)	0	<0.01
Sioux (3)	14	0.02
South American Ind. (17)	33	0.05
Spanish American Ind. (1)	7	0.01
Tlingit-Haida (Alaska Native) (0)	0	<0.01
Tohono O'Odham (0)	0	<0.01
Tsimshian (Alaska Native) (0)	0	<0.01
Ute (0)	0	<0.01
Yakama (0)	0	<0.01
Yaqui (0)	0	<0.01
Yuman (0)	0	<0.01
Yup'ik (Alaska Native) (0)	0	<0.01
Asian (2,396)	3,522	5.33
Not Hispanic (2,360)	3,400	5.14
Hispanic (36)	122	0.18
Bangladeshi (12)	15	0.02
Bhutanese (1)	1	<0.01
Burmese (0)	0	<0.01
Cambodian (7)	8	0.01
Chinese, ex. Taiwanese (291)	361	0.55
Filipino (116)	157	0.24
Hmong (0)	0	<0.01
Indian (1,571)	2,050	3.10
Indonesian (4)	9	0.01
Japanese (21)	70	0.11
Korean (87)	141	0.21
Laotian (2)	6	0.01
Malaysian (0)	5	0.01
Nepalese (5)	8	0.01
Pakistani (80)	86	0.13
Sri Lankan (4)	6	0.01
Taiwanese (7)	8	0.01
Thai (6)	15	0.02
Vietnamese (75)	87	0.13
Hawaii Native/Pacific Islander (92)	333	0.50
Not Hispanic (68)	272	0.41
Hispanic (24)	61	0.09
Fijian (1)	1	<0.01
Guamanian/Chamorro (6)	14	0.02
Marshallese (0)	0	<0.01
Native Hawaiian (14)	33	0.05
Samoan (4)	10	0.02
Tongan (0)	0	<0.01
White (40,592)	43,710	66.09
Not Hispanic (38,006)	40,587	61.37
Hispanic (2,586)	3,123	4.72

Notes: † The Census 2010 population figure is used to calculate the percentages in the Hispanic Origin and Race categories. Ancestry percentages are based on the 2006-2010 American Community Survey population (not shown); ‡ Numbers in parentheses indicate the number of people reporting a single ancestry; * Numbers in parentheses indicate the number of persons reporting this race alone, not in combination with any other race; Please refer to the Explanation of Data for more information.

Smithtown

Place Type: Town
County: Suffolk
Population: 117,801

Ancestry	Population	%
Afghan (27)	27	0.02
African, Sub-Saharan (8)	150	0.13
African (0)	106	0.09
Cape Verdean (0)	0	<0.01
Ethiopian (0)	0	<0.01
Ghanaian (0)	0	<0.01
Kenyan (0)	0	<0.01
Liberian (0)	0	<0.01
Nigerian (8)	44	0.04
Senegalese (0)	0	<0.01
Sierra Leonean (0)	0	<0.01
Somalian (0)	0	<0.01
South African (0)	0	<0.01
Sudanese (0)	0	<0.01
Ugandan (0)	0	<0.01
Zimbabwean (0)	0	<0.01
Other Sub-Saharan African (0)	0	<0.01
Albanian (121)	130	0.11
Alsatian (0)	0	<0.01
American (3,187)	3,187	2.71
Arab (248)	537	0.46
Arab (11)	16	0.01
Egyptian (38)	52	0.04
Iraqi (52)	89	0.08
Jordanian (54)	54	0.05
Lebanese (24)	150	0.13
Moroccan (4)	4	<0.01
Palestinian (0)	0	<0.01
Syrian (39)	89	0.08
Other Arab (26)	83	0.07
Armenian (69)	210	0.18
Assyrian/Chaldean/Syriac (0)	0	<0.01
Australian (19)	23	0.02
Austrian (205)	930	0.79
Basque (0)	0	<0.01
Belgian (4)	88	0.07
Brazilian (22)	32	0.03
British (94)	242	0.21
Bulgarian (0)	22	0.02
Cajun (0)	0	<0.01
Canadian (85)	315	0.27
Carpatho Rusyn (26)	26	0.02
Celtic (0)	3	<0.01
Croatian (53)	247	0.21
Cypriot (0)	0	<0.01
Czech (151)	692	0.59
Czechoslovakian (88)	310	0.26
Danish (76)	314	0.27
Dutch (199)	983	0.84
Eastern European (651)	651	0.55
English (852)	6,551	5.57
Estonian (0)	0	<0.01
European (936)	997	0.85
Finnish (26)	120	0.10
French, ex. Basque (122)	2,352	2.00
French Canadian (233)	648	0.55
German (4,715)	23,592	20.06
German Russian (0)	0	<0.01
Greek (1,657)	3,078	2.62
Guyanese (8)	8	0.01
Hungarian (307)	1,257	1.07
Icelander (5)	16	0.01
Iranian (199)	237	0.20
Irish (8,107)	31,963	27.18
Israeli (104)	180	0.15
Italian (21,409)	45,388	38.60
Latvian (24)	81	0.07
Lithuanian (141)	627	0.53
Luxemburger (0)	0	<0.01
Macedonian (0)	0	<0.01
Maltese (10)	206	0.18
New Zealander (0)	0	<0.01
Northern European (4)	4	<0.01

Ancestry	Population	%
Norwegian (397)	1,686	1.43
Pennsylvania German (6)	6	0.01
Polish (2,350)	8,707	7.40
Portuguese (47)	247	0.21
Romanian (196)	707	0.60
Russian (1,686)	5,319	4.52
Scandinavian (26)	64	0.05
Scotch-Irish (579)	1,732	1.47
Scottish (148)	1,517	1.29
Serbian (31)	92	0.08
Slavic (9)	116	0.10
Slovak (82)	163	0.14
Slovene (140)	147	0.13
Soviet Union (0)	0	<0.01
Swedish (160)	1,304	1.11
Swiss (34)	217	0.18
Turkish (182)	204	0.17
Ukrainian (145)	452	0.38
Welsh (8)	259	0.22
West Indian, ex. Hispanic (160)	341	0.29
Bahamian (0)	0	<0.01
Barbadian (0)	0	<0.01
Belizean (0)	0	<0.01
Bermudan (0)	0	<0.01
British West Indian (0)	0	<0.01
Dutch West Indian (0)	0	<0.01
Haitian (100)	100	0.09
Jamaican (44)	92	0.08
Trinidadian/Tobagonian (9)	28	0.02
U.S. Virgin Islander (0)	0	<0.01
West Indian (7)	121	0.10
Other West Indian (0)	0	<0.01
Yugoslavian (68)	216	0.18

Hispanic Origin	Population	%
Hispanic or Latino (of any race)	6,272	5.32
Central American, ex. Mexican	768	0.65
Costa Rican	22	0.02
Guatemalan	95	0.08
Honduran	161	0.14
Nicaraguan	9	0.01
Panamanian	37	0.03
Salvadoran	428	0.36
Other Central American	16	0.01
Cuban	298	0.25
Dominican Republic	349	0.30
Mexican	524	0.44
Puerto Rican	2,200	1.87
South American	1,376	1.17
Argentinean	159	0.13
Bolivian	41	0.03
Chilean	96	0.08
Colombian	503	0.43
Ecuadorian	258	0.22
Paraguayan	17	0.01
Peruvian	227	0.19
Uruguayan	28	0.02
Venezuelan	37	0.03
Other South American	10	0.01
Other Hispanic or Latino	757	0.64

Race*	Population	%
African-American/Black (1,238)	1,546	1.31
Not Hispanic (1,122)	1,350	1.15
Hispanic (116)	196	0.17
American Indian/Alaska Native (91)	317	0.27
Not Hispanic (53)	224	0.19
Hispanic (38)	93	0.08
Alaska Athabascan (Ala. Nat.) (0)	0	<0.01
Aleut (Alaska Native) (0)	0	<0.01
Apache (0)	0	<0.01
Arapaho (0)	0	<0.01
Blackfeet (3)	7	0.01
Canadian/French Am. Ind. (0)	2	<0.01
Central American Ind. (1)	1	<0.01
Cherokee (3)	44	0.04
Cheyenne (0)	0	<0.01
Chickasaw (0)	0	<0.01
Chippewa (0)	2	<0.01

Race*	Population	%
Choctaw (0)	2	<0.01
Colville (0)	0	<0.01
Comanche (0)	0	<0.01
Cree (0)	0	<0.01
Creek (0)	7	0.01
Crow (0)	0	<0.01
Delaware (0)	1	<0.01
Hopi (0)	0	<0.01
Houma (0)	0	<0.01
Inupiat (Alaska Native) (0)	0	<0.01
Iroquois (19)	36	0.03
Kiowa (1)	1	<0.01
Lumbee (0)	5	<0.01
Menominee (0)	0	<0.01
Mexican American Ind. (2)	6	0.01
Navajo (0)	1	<0.01
Osage (0)	0	<0.01
Ottawa (0)	0	<0.01
Paiute (0)	0	<0.01
Pima (0)	0	<0.01
Potawatomi (0)	0	<0.01
Pueblo (0)	1	<0.01
Puget Sound Salish (0)	0	<0.01
Seminole (0)	0	<0.01
Shoshone (0)	0	<0.01
Sioux (1)	2	<0.01
South American Ind. (13)	23	0.02
Spanish American Ind. (0)	0	<0.01
Tlingit-Haida (Alaska Native) (0)	1	<0.01
Tohono O'Odham (0)	0	<0.01
Tsimshian (Alaska Native) (0)	0	<0.01
Ute (0)	1	<0.01
Yakama (0)	0	<0.01
Yaqui (0)	1	<0.01
Yuman (0)	0	<0.01
Yup'ik (Alaska Native) (0)	0	<0.01
Asian (4,224)	4,865	4.13
Not Hispanic (4,197)	4,788	4.06
Hispanic (27)	77	0.07
Bangladeshi (24)	24	0.02
Bhutanese (2)	2	<0.01
Burmese (2)	2	<0.01
Cambodian (0)	0	<0.01
Chinese, ex. Taiwanese (1,070)	1,262	1.07
Filipino (414)	562	0.48
Hmong (0)	0	<0.01
Indian (1,206)	1,322	1.12
Indonesian (14)	18	0.02
Japanese (68)	119	0.10
Korean (842)	918	0.78
Laotian (3)	3	<0.01
Malaysian (1)	2	<0.01
Nepalese (4)	4	<0.01
Pakistani (280)	299	0.25
Sri Lankan (5)	6	0.01
Taiwanese (66)	90	0.08
Thai (28)	34	0.03
Vietnamese (59)	70	0.06
Hawaii Native/Pacific Islander (10)	58	0.05
Not Hispanic (7)	41	0.03
Hispanic (3)	17	0.01
Fijian (0)	2	<0.01
Guamanian/Chamorro (3)	5	<0.01
Marshallese (0)	0	<0.01
Native Hawaiian (6)	30	0.03
Samoan (0)	0	<0.01
Tongan (0)	0	<0.01
White (109,790)	111,000	94.23
Not Hispanic (104,976)	105,870	89.87
Hispanic (4,814)	5,130	4.35

Notes: † The Census 2010 population figure is used to calculate the percentages in the Hispanic Origin and Race categories. Ancestry percentages are based on the 2006-2010 American Community Survey population (not shown); ‡ Numbers in parentheses indicate the number of people reporting a single ancestry; * Numbers in parentheses indicate the number of persons reporting this race alone, not in combination with any other race; Please refer to the Explanation of Data for more information.

Southampton

Place Type: Town
County: Suffolk
Population: 56,790

Ancestry	Population	%
Afghan (0)	0	<0.01
African, Sub-Saharan (64)	64	0.11
African (64)	64	0.11
Cape Verdean (0)	0	<0.01
Ethiopian (0)	0	<0.01
Ghanaian (0)	0	<0.01
Kenyan (0)	0	<0.01
Liberian (0)	0	<0.01
Nigerian (0)	0	<0.01
Senegalese (0)	0	<0.01
Sierra Leonean (0)	0	<0.01
Somalian (0)	0	<0.01
South African (0)	0	<0.01
Sudanese (0)	0	<0.01
Ugandan (0)	0	<0.01
Zimbabwean (0)	0	<0.01
Other Sub-Saharan African (0)	0	<0.01
Albanian (63)	63	0.11
Alsatian (0)	0	<0.01
American (1,540)	1,540	2.72
Arab (52)	130	0.23
Arab (20)	35	0.06
Egyptian (0)	0	<0.01
Iraqi (0)	28	0.05
Jordanian (0)	0	<0.01
Lebanese (5)	16	0.03
Moroccan (0)	18	0.03
Palestinian (0)	0	<0.01
Syrian (13)	13	0.02
Other Arab (14)	20	0.04
Armenian (23)	42	0.07
Assyrian/Chaldean/Syriac (0)	0	<0.01
Australian (24)	38	0.07
Austrian (113)	621	1.10
Basque (0)	0	<0.01
Belgian (34)	34	0.06
Brazilian (242)	289	0.51
British (224)	404	0.71
Bulgarian (29)	29	0.05
Cajun (0)	0	<0.01
Canadian (96)	153	0.27
Carpatho Rusyn (0)	0	<0.01
Celtic (0)	4	0.01
Croatian (174)	227	0.40
Cypriot (0)	0	<0.01
Czech (80)	198	0.35
Czechoslovakian (51)	97	0.17
Danish (54)	135	0.24
Dutch (91)	743	1.31
Eastern European (55)	118	0.21
English (1,413)	5,792	10.24
Estonian (6)	6	0.01
European (518)	523	0.93
Finnish (53)	206	0.36
French, ex. Basque (250)	1,438	2.54
French Canadian (49)	352	0.62
German (1,998)	8,313	14.70
German Russian (0)	0	<0.01
Greek (583)	995	1.76
Guyanese (0)	0	<0.01
Hungarian (164)	529	0.94
Icelander (0)	0	<0.01
Iranian (0)	0	<0.01
Irish (4,208)	12,998	22.99
Israeli (0)	28	0.05
Italian (4,376)	9,808	17.35
Latvian (0)	7	0.01
Lithuanian (137)	267	0.47
Luxemburger (0)	0	<0.01
Macedonian (11)	11	0.02
Maltese (15)	33	0.06
New Zealander (0)	0	<0.01
Northern European (42)	42	0.07

Ancestry	Population	%
Norwegian (172)	498	0.88
Pennsylvania German (0)	0	<0.01
Polish (1,918)	4,196	7.42
Portuguese (59)	145	0.26
Romanian (57)	102	0.18
Russian (514)	1,517	2.68
Scandinavian (31)	57	0.10
Scotch-Irish (251)	701	1.24
Scottish (225)	966	1.71
Serbian (0)	0	<0.01
Slavic (0)	53	0.09
Slovak (92)	134	0.24
Slovene (7)	7	0.01
Soviet Union (0)	0	<0.01
Swedish (152)	598	1.06
Swiss (37)	231	0.41
Turkish (75)	75	0.13
Ukrainian (198)	419	0.74
Welsh (43)	132	0.23
West Indian, ex. Hispanic (0)	24	0.04
Bahamian (0)	0	<0.01
Barbadian (0)	0	<0.01
Belizean (0)	0	<0.01
Bermudan (0)	0	<0.01
British West Indian (0)	0	<0.01
Dutch West Indian (0)	0	<0.01
Haitian (0)	16	0.03
Jamaican (0)	0	<0.01
Trinidadian/Tobagonian (0)	0	<0.01
U.S. Virgin Islander (0)	0	<0.01
West Indian (0)	8	0.01
Other West Indian (0)	0	<0.01
Yugoslavian (0)	0	<0.01

Hispanic Origin	Population	%
Hispanic or Latino (of any race)	11,295	19.89
Central American, ex. Mexican	3,715	6.54
Costa Rican	618	1.09
Guatemalan	2,081	3.66
Honduran	246	0.43
Nicaraguan	50	0.09
Panamanian	14	0.02
Salvadoran	689	1.21
Other Central American	17	0.03
Cuban	93	0.16
Dominican Republic	124	0.22
Mexican	2,856	5.03
Puerto Rican	593	1.04
South American	2,446	4.31
Argentinean	89	0.16
Bolivian	9	0.02
Chilean	44	0.08
Colombian	1,024	1.80
Ecuadorian	1,102	1.94
Paraguayan	26	0.05
Peruvian	97	0.17
Uruguayan	7	0.01
Venezuelan	36	0.06
Other South American	12	0.02
Other Hispanic or Latino	1,468	2.58

Race*	Population	%
African-American/Black (2,929)	3,353	5.90
Not Hispanic (2,776)	3,108	5.47
Hispanic (153)	245	0.43
American Indian/Alaska Native (292)	546	0.96
Not Hispanic (136)	344	0.61
Hispanic (156)	202	0.36
Alaska Athabascan (Ala. Nat.) (0)	0	<0.01
Aleut (Alaska Native) (0)	0	<0.01
Apache (0)	0	<0.01
Arapaho (0)	0	<0.01
Blackfeet (6)	14	0.02
Canadian/French Am. Ind. (0)	3	0.01
Central American Ind. (3)	3	0.01
Cherokee (13)	68	0.12
Cheyenne (0)	0	<0.01
Chickasaw (0)	0	<0.01
Chippewa (7)	7	0.01

Race*	Population	%
Choctaw (1)	2	<0.01
Colville (0)	0	<0.01
Comanche (0)	0	<0.01
Cree (0)	0	<0.01
Creek (2)	2	<0.01
Crow (0)	0	<0.01
Delaware (0)	0	<0.01
Hopi (0)	1	<0.01
Houma (0)	0	<0.01
Inupiat (Alaska Native) (0)	0	<0.01
Iroquois (5)	11	0.02
Kiowa (0)	0	<0.01
Lumbee (0)	0	<0.01
Menominee (0)	0	<0.01
Mexican American Ind. (76)	83	0.15
Navajo (0)	0	<0.01
Osage (0)	0	<0.01
Ottawa (0)	0	<0.01
Paiute (0)	0	<0.01
Pima (0)	0	<0.01
Potawatomi (0)	0	<0.01
Pueblo (0)	5	0.01
Puget Sound Salish (0)	0	<0.01
Seminole (0)	1	<0.01
Shoshone (0)	0	<0.01
Sioux (2)	3	0.01
South American Ind. (23)	28	0.05
Spanish American Ind. (7)	7	0.01
Tlingit-Haida (Alaska Native) (0)	0	<0.01
Tohono O'Odham (0)	0	<0.01
Tsimshian (Alaska Native) (0)	0	<0.01
Ute (0)	0	<0.01
Yakama (0)	0	<0.01
Yaqui (0)	0	<0.01
Yuman (0)	0	<0.01
Yup'ik (Alaska Native) (0)	0	<0.01
Asian (633)	869	1.53
Not Hispanic (618)	834	1.47
Hispanic (15)	35	0.06
Bangladeshi (0)	0	<0.01
Bhutanese (0)	0	<0.01
Burmese (0)	0	<0.01
Cambodian (1)	1	<0.01
Chinese, ex. Taiwanese (133)	177	0.31
Filipino (146)	197	0.35
Hmong (0)	0	<0.01
Indian (123)	151	0.27
Indonesian (5)	6	0.01
Japanese (40)	97	0.17
Korean (69)	102	0.18
Laotian (1)	2	<0.01
Malaysian (1)	2	<0.01
Nepalese (1)	1	<0.01
Pakistani (8)	10	0.02
Sri Lankan (0)	0	<0.01
Taiwanese (3)	3	0.01
Thai (30)	37	0.07
Vietnamese (38)	51	0.09
Hawaii Native/Pacific Islander (62)	103	0.18
Not Hispanic (36)	61	0.11
Hispanic (26)	42	0.07
Fijian (0)	0	<0.01
Guamanian/Chamorro (48)	55	0.10
Marshallese (0)	0	<0.01
Native Hawaiian (10)	27	0.05
Samoan (2)	7	0.01
Tongan (0)	0	<0.01
White (47,795)	48,682	85.72
Not Hispanic (41,156)	41,727	73.48
Hispanic (6,639)	6,955	12.25

*Notes: † The Census 2010 population figure is used to calculate the percentages in the Hispanic Origin and Race categories. Ancestry percentages are based on the 2006-2010 American Community Survey population (not shown); ‡ Numbers in parentheses indicate the number of people reporting a single ancestry; * Numbers in parentheses indicate the number of persons reporting this race alone, not in combination with any other race; Please refer to the Explanation of Data for more information.*

Staten Island

Place Type: Borough
County: Richmond
Population: 468,730

Ancestry	Population	%
Afghan (0)	0	<0.01
African, Sub-Saharan (6,533)	7,234	1.56
African (3,732)	4,164	0.90
Cape Verdean (0)	11	<0.01
Ethiopian (41)	46	0.01
Ghanaian (239)	250	0.05
Kenyan (78)	78	0.02
Liberian (515)	532	0.11
Nigerian (1,509)	1,679	0.36
Senegalese (126)	126	0.03
Sierra Leonean (90)	117	0.03
Somalian (0)	0	<0.01
South African (0)	0	<0.01
Sudanese (0)	0	<0.01
Ugandan (0)	0	<0.01
Zimbabwean (0)	0	<0.01
Other Sub-Saharan African (203)	231	0.05
Albanian (7,700)	8,108	1.75
Alsatian (0)	24	0.01
American (13,977)	13,977	3.02
Arab (7,711)	8,820	1.90
Arab (1,694)	1,829	0.39
Egyptian (3,200)	3,292	0.71
Iraqi (11)	32	0.01
Jordanian (159)	183	0.04
Lebanese (784)	1,019	0.22
Moroccan (502)	621	0.13
Palestinian (443)	479	0.10
Syrian (209)	584	0.13
Other Arab (709)	781	0.17
Armenian (83)	311	0.07
Assyrian/Chaldean/Syriac (15)	15	<0.01
Australian (24)	49	0.01
Austrian (343)	1,542	0.33
Basque (15)	77	0.02
Belgian (36)	266	0.06
Brazilian (183)	287	0.06
British (231)	615	0.13
Bulgarian (0)	0	<0.01
Cajun (0)	0	<0.01
Canadian (290)	544	0.12
Carpatho Rusyn (63)	63	0.01
Celtic (37)	46	0.01
Croatian (598)	869	0.19
Cypriot (0)	0	<0.01
Czech (146)	735	0.16
Czechoslovakian (93)	237	0.05
Danish (90)	479	0.10
Dutch (137)	1,637	0.35
Eastern European (433)	433	0.09
English (1,973)	9,014	1.94
Estonian (10)	10	<0.01
European (1,914)	2,068	0.45
Finnish (48)	185	0.04
French, ex. Basque (800)	3,772	0.81
French Canadian (248)	750	0.16
German (4,111)	25,477	5.50
German Russian (0)	0	<0.01
Greek (2,403)	4,183	0.90
Guyanese (767)	952	0.21
Hungarian (1,024)	2,288	0.49
Icelander (55)	55	0.01
Iranian (121)	171	0.04
Irish (20,064)	64,762	13.97
Israeli (542)	759	0.16
Italian (107,263)	156,288	33.72
Latvian (98)	142	0.03
Lithuanian (178)	645	0.14
Luxemburger (12)	54	0.01
Macedonian (1,368)	1,590	0.34
Maltese (104)	290	0.06
New Zealander (0)	0	<0.01
Northern European (60)	60	0.01

Ancestry (cont.)	Population	%
Norwegian (1,617)	5,135	1.11
Pennsylvania German (9)	41	0.01
Polish (9,167)	18,430	3.98
Portuguese (180)	617	0.13
Romanian (530)	964	0.21
Russian (11,315)	16,388	3.54
Scandinavian (35)	121	0.03
Scotch-Irish (759)	1,886	0.41
Scottish (718)	2,350	0.51
Serbian (219)	240	0.05
Slavic (68)	143	0.03
Slovak (233)	553	0.12
Slovene (86)	108	0.02
Soviet Union (51)	63	0.01
Swedish (253)	1,936	0.42
Swiss (76)	256	0.06
Turkish (1,267)	1,607	0.35
Ukrainian (3,759)	4,836	1.04
Welsh (68)	417	0.09
West Indian, ex. Hispanic (5,348)	6,967	1.50
Bahamian (31)	31	0.01
Barbadian (94)	94	0.02
Belizean (76)	76	0.02
Bermudan (0)	0	<0.01
British West Indian (113)	236	0.05
Dutch West Indian (39)	89	0.02
Haitian (676)	791	0.17
Jamaican (1,463)	2,033	0.44
Trinidadian/Tobagonian (1,412)	1,807	0.39
U.S. Virgin Islander (22)	22	<0.01
West Indian (1,392)	1,745	0.38
Other West Indian (30)	43	0.01
Yugoslavian (1,237)	1,738	0.38

Hispanic Origin	Population	%
Hispanic or Latino (of any race)	81,051	17.29
Central American, ex. Mexican	4,310	0.92
Costa Rican	266	0.06
Guatemalan	864	0.18
Honduran	1,735	0.37
Nicaraguan	199	0.04
Panamanian	607	0.13
Salvadoran	592	0.13
Other Central American	47	0.01
Cuban	1,831	0.39
Dominican Republic	4,918	1.05
Mexican	18,684	3.99
Puerto Rican	37,517	8.00
South American	8,232	1.76
Argentinean	608	0.13
Bolivian	161	0.03
Chilean	346	0.07
Colombian	2,526	0.54
Ecuadorian	2,675	0.57
Paraguayan	38	0.01
Peruvian	1,462	0.31
Uruguayan	76	0.02
Venezuelan	254	0.05
Other South American	86	0.02
Other Hispanic or Latino	5,559	1.19

Race*	Population	%
African-American/Black (49,857)	55,014	11.74
Not Hispanic (44,313)	47,521	10.14
Hispanic (5,544)	7,493	1.60
American Indian/Alaska Native (1,695)	3,719	0.79
Not Hispanic (695)	2,034	0.43
Hispanic (1,000)	1,685	0.36
Alaska Athabascan (Ala. Nat.) (1)	3	<0.01
Aleut (Alaska Native) (0)	2	<0.01
Apache (16)	35	0.01
Arapaho (1)	1	<0.01
Blackfeet (17)	88	0.02
Canadian/French Am. Ind. (7)	10	<0.01
Central American Ind. (29)	56	0.01
Cherokee (104)	467	0.10
Cheyenne (0)	2	<0.01
Chickasaw (1)	3	<0.01
Chippewa (7)	13	<0.01

Race* (cont.)	Population	%
Choctaw (3)	11	<0.01
Colville (0)	0	<0.01
Comanche (2)	3	<0.01
Cree (0)	4	<0.01
Creek (3)	29	0.01
Crow (0)	0	<0.01
Delaware (16)	43	0.01
Hopi (1)	5	<0.01
Houma (1)	1	<0.01
Inupiat (Alaska Native) (0)	1	<0.01
Iroquois (61)	152	0.03
Kiowa (0)	1	<0.01
Lumbee (1)	8	<0.01
Menominee (0)	0	<0.01
Mexican American Ind. (161)	204	0.04
Navajo (10)	17	<0.01
Osage (0)	0	<0.01
Ottawa (0)	0	<0.01
Paiute (0)	0	<0.01
Pima (2)	2	<0.01
Potawatomi (0)	0	<0.01
Pueblo (4)	5	<0.01
Puget Sound Salish (0)	0	<0.01
Seminole (7)	26	0.01
Shoshone (1)	3	<0.01
Sioux (11)	24	0.01
South American Ind. (146)	288	0.06
Spanish American Ind. (31)	47	0.01
Tlingit-Haida (Alaska Native) (0)	1	<0.01
Tohono O'Odham (4)	8	<0.01
Tsimshian (Alaska Native) (0)	0	<0.01
Ute (1)	1	<0.01
Yakama (0)	0	<0.01
Yaqui (1)	1	<0.01
Yuman (0)	1	<0.01
Yup'ik (Alaska Native) (0)	0	<0.01
Asian (35,164)	38,756	8.27
Not Hispanic (34,697)	37,689	8.04
Hispanic (467)	1,067	0.23
Bangladeshi (360)	387	0.08
Bhutanese (0)	0	<0.01
Burmese (116)	130	0.03
Cambodian (100)	129	0.03
Chinese, ex. Taiwanese (13,144)	14,107	3.01
Filipino (5,224)	6,205	1.32
Hmong (4)	8	<0.01
Indian (6,793)	7,723	1.65
Indonesian (22)	52	0.01
Japanese (201)	408	0.09
Korean (3,207)	3,398	0.72
Laotian (13)	18	<0.01
Malaysian (58)	96	0.02
Nepalese (27)	35	0.01
Pakistani (2,495)	2,777	0.59
Sri Lankan (1,560)	1,766	0.38
Taiwanese (160)	197	0.04
Thai (135)	166	0.04
Vietnamese (468)	570	0.12
Hawaii Native/Pacific Islander (213)	683	0.15
Not Hispanic (137)	439	0.09
Hispanic (76)	244	0.05
Fijian (6)	6	<0.01
Guamanian/Chamorro (88)	115	0.02
Marshallese (1)	1	<0.01
Native Hawaiian (46)	121	0.03
Samoan (5)	26	0.01
Tongan (2)	2	<0.01
White (341,677)	350,679	74.81
Not Hispanic (300,169)	305,118	65.09
Hispanic (41,508)	45,561	9.72

Notes: † The Census 2010 population figure is used to calculate the percentages in the Hispanic Origin and Race categories. Ancestry percentages are based on the 2006-2010 American Community Survey population (not shown); ‡ Numbers in parentheses indicate the number of people reporting a single ancestry; * Numbers in parentheses indicate the number of persons reporting this race alone, not in combination with any other race; Please refer to the Explanation of Data for more information.

Syracuse

Place Type: City
County: Onondaga
Population: 145,170

Ancestry	Population	%
Afghan (19)	19	0.01
African, Sub-Saharan (2,165)	2,470	1.71
African (898)	1,142	0.79
Cape Verdean (0)	8	0.01
Ethiopian (0)	0	<0.01
Ghanaian (113)	113	0.08
Kenyan (0)	17	0.01
Liberian (246)	246	0.17
Nigerian (148)	167	0.12
Senegalese (0)	0	<0.01
Sierra Leonean (13)	13	0.01
Somalian (478)	478	0.33
South African (10)	10	0.01
Sudanese (160)	177	0.12
Ugandan (26)	26	0.02
Zimbabwean (0)	0	<0.01
Other Sub-Saharan African (73)	73	0.05
Albanian (429)	455	0.31
Alsatian (0)	0	<0.01
American (3,220)	3,220	2.22
Arab (571)	900	0.62
Arab (226)	267	0.18
Egyptian (13)	13	0.01
Iraqi (0)	0	<0.01
Jordanian (0)	0	<0.01
Lebanese (100)	269	0.19
Moroccan (60)	86	0.06
Palestinian (58)	66	0.05
Syrian (57)	114	0.08
Other Arab (57)	85	0.06
Armenian (24)	229	0.16
Assyrian/Chaldean/Syriac (0)	0	<0.01
Australian (42)	54	0.04
Austrian (81)	372	0.26
Basque (0)	0	<0.01
Belgian (53)	81	0.06
Brazilian (30)	42	0.03
British (199)	418	0.29
Bulgarian (18)	18	0.01
Cajun (24)	24	0.02
Canadian (96)	350	0.24
Carpatho Rusyn (0)	0	<0.01
Celtic (12)	12	0.01
Croatian (0)	46	0.03
Cypriot (0)	0	<0.01
Czech (36)	163	0.11
Czechoslovakian (44)	77	0.05
Danish (36)	109	0.08
Dutch (174)	2,128	1.47
Eastern European (153)	178	0.12
English (2,028)	10,153	7.01
Estonian (0)	12	0.01
European (440)	487	0.34
Finnish (14)	52	0.04
French, ex. Basque (735)	6,182	4.27
French Canadian (804)	1,782	1.23
German (3,496)	17,038	11.77
German Russian (0)	0	<0.01
Greek (339)	678	0.47
Guyanese (100)	158	0.11
Hungarian (88)	540	0.37
Icelander (0)	10	0.01
Iranian (65)	105	0.07
Irish (6,064)	22,387	15.47
Israeli (133)	146	0.10
Italian (8,625)	18,571	12.83
Latvian (28)	41	0.03
Lithuanian (72)	309	0.21
Luxemburger (0)	14	0.01
Macedonian (46)	67	0.05
Maltese (0)	0	<0.01
New Zealander (0)	13	0.01
Northern European (71)	71	0.05

Ancestry	Population	%
Norwegian (107)	366	0.25
Pennsylvania German (14)	33	0.02
Polish (2,445)	7,273	5.03
Portuguese (34)	330	0.23
Romanian (38)	113	0.08
Russian (596)	1,831	1.27
Scandinavian (49)	98	0.07
Scotch-Irish (639)	1,546	1.07
Scottish (505)	2,233	1.54
Serbian (0)	26	0.02
Slavic (12)	45	0.03
Slovak (46)	158	0.11
Slovene (15)	85	0.06
Soviet Union (0)	0	<0.01
Swedish (288)	1,044	0.72
Swiss (91)	286	0.20
Turkish (169)	279	0.19
Ukrainian (589)	1,095	0.76
Welsh (155)	1,060	0.73
West Indian, ex. Hispanic (1,588)	1,931	1.33
Bahamian (0)	0	<0.01
Barbadian (96)	96	0.07
Belizean (0)	0	<0.01
Bermudan (0)	0	<0.01
British West Indian (22)	50	0.03
Dutch West Indian (0)	0	<0.01
Haitian (145)	145	0.10
Jamaican (908)	1,181	0.82
Trinidadian/Tobagonian (95)	95	0.07
U.S. Virgin Islander (0)	0	<0.01
West Indian (322)	364	0.25
Other West Indian (0)	0	<0.01
Yugoslavian (765)	774	0.53

Hispanic Origin	Population	%
Hispanic or Latino (of any race)	12,036	8.29
Central American, ex. Mexican	348	0.24
Costa Rican	29	0.02
Guatemalan	133	0.09
Honduran	40	0.03
Nicaraguan	30	0.02
Panamanian	54	0.04
Salvadoran	59	0.04
Other Central American	3	<0.01
Cuban	1,192	0.82
Dominican Republic	689	0.47
Mexican	958	0.66
Puerto Rican	7,594	5.23
South American	530	0.37
Argentinean	49	0.03
Bolivian	11	0.01
Chilean	35	0.02
Colombian	173	0.12
Ecuadorian	101	0.07
Paraguayan	3	<0.01
Peruvian	89	0.06
Uruguayan	27	0.02
Venezuelan	39	0.03
Other South American	3	<0.01
Other Hispanic or Latino	725	0.50

Race*	Population	%
African-American/Black (42,770)	48,029	33.08
Not Hispanic (40,672)	45,084	31.06
Hispanic (2,098)	2,945	2.03
American Indian/Alaska Native (1,606)	3,537	2.44
Not Hispanic (1,390)	3,067	2.11
Hispanic (216)	470	0.32
Alaska Athabascan (Ala. Nat.) (0)	3	<0.01
Aleut (Alaska Native) (0)	1	<0.01
Apache (8)	25	0.02
Arapaho (2)	2	<0.01
Blackfeet (7)	111	0.08
Canadian/French Am. Ind. (35)	51	0.04
Central American Ind. (4)	9	0.01
Cherokee (20)	258	0.18
Cheyenne (0)	2	<0.01
Chickasaw (0)	4	<0.01
Chippewa (11)	18	0.01

Race*	Population	%
Choctaw (1)	28	0.02
Colville (0)	0	<0.01
Comanche (6)	12	<0.01
Cree (1)	6	<0.01
Creek (4)	9	0.01
Crow (0)	1	<0.01
Delaware (3)	5	<0.01
Hopi (0)	0	<0.01
Houma (0)	0	<0.01
Inupiat (Alaska Native) (3)	6	<0.01
Iroquois (790)	1,373	0.95
Kiowa (0)	1	<0.01
Lumbee (4)	4	<0.01
Menominee (1)	1	<0.01
Mexican American Ind. (24)	34	0.02
Navajo (2)	5	<0.01
Osage (1)	1	<0.01
Ottawa (0)	2	<0.01
Paiute (0)	0	<0.01
Pima (1)	2	<0.01
Potawatomi (1)	2	<0.01
Pueblo (0)	0	<0.01
Puget Sound Salish (0)	0	<0.01
Seminole (4)	16	0.01
Shoshone (0)	0	<0.01
Sioux (13)	38	0.03
South American Ind. (25)	49	0.03
Spanish American Ind. (0)	0	<0.01
Tlingit-Haida (Alaska Native) (0)	1	<0.01
Tohono O'Odham (1)	1	<0.01
Tsimshian (Alaska Native) (0)	0	<0.01
Ute (0)	0	<0.01
Yakama (0)	0	<0.01
Yaqui (0)	0	<0.01
Yuman (0)	0	<0.01
Yup'ik (Alaska Native) (0)	1	<0.01
Asian (8,021)	9,073	6.25
Not Hispanic (7,971)	8,924	6.15
Hispanic (50)	149	0.10
Bangladeshi (47)	57	0.04
Bhutanese (392)	516	0.36
Burmese (1,178)	1,218	0.84
Cambodian (114)	149	0.10
Chinese, ex. Taiwanese (1,543)	1,749	1.20
Filipino (218)	388	0.27
Hmong (26)	34	0.02
Indian (1,216)	1,397	0.96
Indonesian (14)	26	0.02
Japanese (109)	243	0.17
Korean (861)	937	0.65
Laotian (71)	89	0.06
Malaysian (5)	13	0.01
Nepalese (160)	262	0.18
Pakistani (107)	121	0.08
Sri Lankan (13)	17	0.01
Taiwanese (80)	93	0.06
Thai (64)	89	0.06
Vietnamese (1,414)	1,554	1.07
Hawaii Native/Pacific Islander (44)	279	0.19
Not Hispanic (37)	218	0.15
Hispanic (7)	61	0.04
Fijian (0)	1	<0.01
Guamanian/Chamorro (5)	12	0.01
Marshallese (0)	1	<0.01
Native Hawaiian (15)	65	0.04
Samoan (8)	21	0.01
Tongan (0)	1	<0.01
White (81,319)	87,414	60.21
Not Hispanic (76,653)	81,787	56.34
Hispanic (4,666)	5,627	3.88

Notes: † The Census 2010 population figure is used to calculate the percentages in the Hispanic Origin and Race categories. Ancestry percentages are based on the 2006-2010 American Community Survey population (not shown); ‡ Numbers in parentheses indicate the number of people reporting a single ancestry; * Numbers in parentheses indicate the number of persons reporting this race alone, not in combination with any other race; Please refer to the Explanation of Data for more information.

Tonawanda

Place Type: CDP
County: Erie
Population: 58,144

Ancestry	Population	%
Afghan (108)	108	0.18
African, Sub-Saharan (59)	194	0.33
African (16)	89	0.15
Cape Verdean (0)	0	<0.01
Ethiopian (0)	0	<0.01
Ghanaian (19)	19	0.03
Kenyan (24)	86	0.15
Liberian (0)	0	<0.01
Nigerian (0)	0	<0.01
Senegalese (0)	0	<0.01
Sierra Leonean (0)	0	<0.01
Somalian (0)	0	<0.01
South African (0)	0	<0.01
Sudanese (0)	0	<0.01
Ugandan (0)	0	<0.01
Zimbabwean (0)	0	<0.01
Other Sub-Saharan African (0)	0	<0.01
Albanian (48)	59	0.10
Alsatian (0)	24	0.04
American (1,226)	1,226	2.09
Arab (293)	502	0.86
Arab (21)	34	0.06
Egyptian (0)	8	0.01
Iraqi (0)	0	<0.01
Jordanian (9)	9	0.02
Lebanese (223)	401	0.68
Moroccan (0)	0	<0.01
Palestinian (0)	0	<0.01
Syrian (0)	10	0.02
Other Arab (40)	40	0.07
Armenian (43)	43	0.07
Assyrian/Chaldean/Syriac (0)	0	<0.01
Australian (0)	29	0.05
Austrian (54)	415	0.71
Basque (0)	0	<0.01
Belgian (0)	13	0.02
Brazilian (0)	13	0.02
British (33)	97	0.17
Bulgarian (0)	0	<0.01
Cajun (0)	0	<0.01
Canadian (144)	288	0.49
Carpatho Rusyn (0)	0	<0.01
Celtic (0)	0	<0.01
Croatian (84)	219	0.37
Cypriot (0)	0	<0.01
Czech (22)	168	0.29
Czechoslovakian (32)	177	0.30
Danish (47)	151	0.26
Dutch (89)	716	1.22
Eastern European (23)	23	0.04
English (1,484)	6,115	10.44
Estonian (0)	0	<0.01
European (354)	354	0.60
Finnish (49)	95	0.16
French, ex. Basque (188)	2,149	3.67
French Canadian (128)	537	0.92
German (4,626)	19,292	32.95
German Russian (0)	0	<0.01
Greek (260)	424	0.72
Guyanese (0)	0	<0.01
Hungarian (220)	976	1.67
Icelander (11)	11	0.02
Iranian (0)	0	<0.01
Irish (2,820)	11,980	20.46
Israeli (0)	0	<0.01
Italian (6,780)	14,269	24.37
Latvian (0)	13	0.02
Lithuanian (29)	162	0.28
Luxemburger (0)	0	<0.01
Macedonian (0)	18	0.03
Maltese (8)	26	0.04
New Zealander (0)	0	<0.01
Northern European (18)	18	0.03
Norwegian (60)	150	0.26
Pennsylvania German (40)	85	0.15
Polish (3,451)	9,014	15.40
Portuguese (10)	24	0.04
Romanian (77)	158	0.27
Russian (337)	688	1.18
Scandinavian (15)	15	0.03
Scotch-Irish (309)	989	1.69
Scottish (328)	1,430	2.44
Serbian (54)	73	0.12
Slavic (30)	59	0.10
Slovak (62)	112	0.19
Slovene (0)	0	<0.01
Soviet Union (0)	0	<0.01
Swedish (77)	584	1.00
Swiss (44)	109	0.19
Turkish (0)	0	<0.01
Ukrainian (239)	422	0.72
Welsh (57)	332	0.57
West Indian, ex. Hispanic (29)	29	0.05
Bahamian (0)	0	<0.01
Barbadian (0)	0	<0.01
Belizean (0)	0	<0.01
Bermudan (0)	0	<0.01
British West Indian (0)	0	<0.01
Dutch West Indian (0)	0	<0.01
Haitian (0)	0	<0.01
Jamaican (12)	12	0.02
Trinidadian/Tobagonian (17)	17	0.03
U.S. Virgin Islander (0)	0	<0.01
West Indian (0)	0	<0.01
Other West Indian (0)	0	<0.01
Yugoslavian (66)	124	0.21

Hispanic Origin	Population	%
Hispanic or Latino (of any race)	1,485	2.55
Central American, ex. Mexican	32	0.06
Costa Rican	2	<0.01
Guatemalan	19	0.03
Honduran	4	0.01
Nicaraguan	0	<0.01
Panamanian	5	0.01
Salvadoran	2	<0.01
Other Central American	0	<0.01
Cuban	31	0.05
Dominican Republic	43	0.07
Mexican	210	0.36
Puerto Rican	942	1.62
South American	89	0.15
Argentinean	7	0.01
Bolivian	7	0.01
Chilean	1	<0.01
Colombian	37	0.06
Ecuadorian	18	0.03
Paraguayan	0	<0.01
Peruvian	14	0.02
Uruguayan	0	<0.01
Venezuelan	1	<0.01
Other South American	4	0.01
Other Hispanic or Latino	138	0.24

Race*	Population	%
African-American/Black (1,773)	2,226	3.83
Not Hispanic (1,678)	2,088	3.59
Hispanic (95)	138	0.24
American Indian/Alaska Native (220)	409	0.70
Not Hispanic (183)	354	0.61
Hispanic (37)	55	0.09
Alaska Athabascan (Ala. Nat.) (0)	0	<0.01
Aleut (Alaska Native) (0)	0	<0.01
Apache (0)	4	0.01
Arapaho (0)	0	<0.01
Blackfeet (2)	5	0.01
Canadian/French Am. Ind. (3)	4	0.01
Central American Ind. (0)	0	<0.01
Cherokee (2)	31	0.05
Cheyenne (0)	0	<0.01
Chickasaw (0)	0	<0.01
Chippewa (2)	3	0.01

	Population	%
Choctaw (0)	5	0.01
Colville (0)	0	<0.01
Comanche (0)	0	<0.01
Cree (0)	0	<0.01
Creek (0)	1	<0.01
Crow (0)	0	<0.01
Delaware (1)	1	<0.01
Hopi (0)	0	<0.01
Houma (0)	0	<0.01
Inupiat (Alaska Native) (0)	0	<0.01
Iroquois (113)	165	0.28
Kiowa (0)	0	<0.01
Lumbee (0)	0	<0.01
Menominee (0)	0	<0.01
Mexican American Ind. (2)	2	<0.01
Navajo (1)	1	<0.01
Osage (0)	0	<0.01
Ottawa (0)	0	<0.01
Paiute (0)	0	<0.01
Pima (0)	0	<0.01
Potawatomi (5)	9	0.02
Pueblo (0)	0	<0.01
Puget Sound Salish (0)	1	<0.01
Seminole (0)	1	<0.01
Shoshone (0)	0	<0.01
Sioux (1)	2	<0.01
South American Ind. (8)	14	0.02
Spanish American Ind. (2)	2	<0.01
Tlingit-Haida (Alaska Native) (0)	0	<0.01
Tohono O'Odham (0)	0	<0.01
Tsimshian (Alaska Native) (0)	0	<0.01
Ute (0)	0	<0.01
Yakama (0)	0	<0.01
Yaqui (1)	1	<0.01
Yuman (0)	0	<0.01
Yup'ik (Alaska Native) (0)	0	<0.01
Asian (831)	1,029	1.77
Not Hispanic (823)	1,011	1.74
Hispanic (8)	18	0.03
Bangladeshi (3)	4	0.01
Bhutanese (0)	0	<0.01
Burmese (2)	3	0.01
Cambodian (1)	1	<0.01
Chinese, ex. Taiwanese (210)	239	0.41
Filipino (57)	93	0.16
Hmong (0)	0	<0.01
Indian (266)	284	0.49
Indonesian (3)	8	0.01
Japanese (16)	33	0.06
Korean (135)	160	0.28
Laotian (11)	17	0.03
Malaysian (3)	4	0.01
Nepalese (1)	1	<0.01
Pakistani (5)	7	0.01
Sri Lankan (8)	8	0.01
Taiwanese (10)	16	0.03
Thai (11)	23	0.04
Vietnamese (64)	77	0.13
Hawaii Native/Pacific Islander (1)	31	0.05
Not Hispanic (1)	21	0.04
Hispanic (0)	10	0.02
Fijian (0)	0	<0.01
Guamanian/Chamorro (0)	3	0.01
Marshallese (0)	0	<0.01
Native Hawaiian (0)	12	0.02
Samoan (1)	2	<0.01
Tongan (0)	1	<0.01
White (54,151)	54,936	94.48
Not Hispanic (53,210)	53,890	92.68
Hispanic (941)	1,046	1.80

Notes: † The Census 2010 population figure is used to calculate the percentages in the Hispanic Origin and Race categories. Ancestry percentages are based on the 2006-2010 American Community Survey population (not shown); ‡ Numbers in parentheses indicate the number of people reporting a single ancestry; * Numbers in parentheses indicate the number of persons reporting this race alone, not in combination with any other race; Please refer to the Explanation of Data for more information.

Tonawanda

Place Type: Town
County: Erie
Population: 73,567

Ancestry	Population	%
Afghan (108)	108	0.15
African, Sub-Saharan (85)	220	0.30
African (16)	89	0.12
Cape Verdean (0)	0	<0.01
Ethiopian (13)	13	0.02
Ghanaian (19)	19	0.03
Kenyan (24)	86	0.12
Liberian (0)	0	<0.01
Nigerian (0)	0	<0.01
Senegalese (0)	0	<0.01
Sierra Leonean (0)	0	<0.01
Somalian (0)	0	<0.01
South African (0)	0	<0.01
Sudanese (0)	0	<0.01
Ugandan (0)	0	<0.01
Zimbabwean (0)	0	<0.01
Other Sub-Saharan African (13)	13	0.02
Albanian (48)	59	0.08
Alsatian (0)	24	0.03
American (1,511)	1,511	2.04
Arab (344)	592	0.80
Arab (21)	46	0.06
Egyptian (0)	8	0.01
Iraqi (0)	0	<0.01
Jordanian (9)	9	0.01
Lebanese (223)	428	0.58
Moroccan (0)	0	<0.01
Palestinian (0)	0	<0.01
Syrian (12)	22	0.03
Other Arab (79)	79	0.11
Armenian (68)	96	0.13
Assyrian/Chaldean/Syriac (0)	0	<0.01
Australian (0)	29	0.04
Austrian (54)	459	0.62
Basque (0)	0	<0.01
Belgian (0)	13	0.02
Brazilian (0)	13	0.02
British (33)	104	0.14
Bulgarian (0)	0	<0.01
Cajun (0)	0	<0.01
Canadian (144)	312	0.42
Carpatho Rusyn (0)	13	0.02
Celtic (0)	0	<0.01
Croatian (132)	326	0.44
Cypriot (0)	0	<0.01
Czech (42)	223	0.30
Czechoslovakian (32)	179	0.24
Danish (60)	179	0.24
Dutch (104)	872	1.18
Eastern European (44)	44	0.06
English (1,746)	7,240	9.77
Estonian (0)	0	<0.01
European (439)	439	0.59
Finnish (49)	95	0.13
French, ex. Basque (254)	2,508	3.39
French Canadian (188)	881	1.19
German (5,590)	24,085	32.51
German Russian (0)	0	<0.01
Greek (260)	493	0.67
Guyanese (0)	0	<0.01
Hungarian (294)	1,188	1.60
Icelander (11)	11	0.01
Iranian (0)	0	<0.01
Irish (3,462)	15,685	21.17
Israeli (0)	0	<0.01
Italian (9,140)	19,213	25.93
Latvian (15)	28	0.04
Lithuanian (41)	174	0.23
Luxemburger (0)	0	<0.01
Macedonian (0)	18	0.02
Maltese (8)	26	0.04
New Zealander (0)	0	<0.01
Northern European (18)	18	0.02

Ancestry (cont.)	Population	%
Norwegian (60)	150	0.20
Pennsylvania German (53)	98	0.13
Polish (4,057)	11,479	15.49
Portuguese (10)	24	0.03
Romanian (77)	158	0.21
Russian (347)	745	1.01
Scandinavian (15)	15	0.02
Scotch-Irish (370)	1,170	1.58
Scottish (448)	1,915	2.58
Serbian (66)	85	0.11
Slavic (62)	123	0.17
Slovak (74)	124	0.17
Slovene (0)	0	<0.01
Soviet Union (0)	0	<0.01
Swedish (144)	758	1.02
Swiss (44)	131	0.18
Turkish (0)	0	<0.01
Ukrainian (295)	535	0.72
Welsh (57)	429	0.58
West Indian, ex. Hispanic (49)	63	0.09
Bahamian (0)	0	<0.01
Barbadian (0)	0	<0.01
Belizean (0)	0	<0.01
Bermudan (0)	0	<0.01
British West Indian (0)	0	<0.01
Dutch West Indian (0)	0	<0.01
Haitian (0)	0	<0.01
Jamaican (32)	46	0.06
Trinidadian/Tobagonian (17)	17	0.02
U.S. Virgin Islander (0)	0	<0.01
West Indian (0)	0	<0.01
Other West Indian (0)	0	<0.01
Yugoslavian (75)	133	0.18

Hispanic Origin	Population	%
Hispanic or Latino (of any race)	2,003	2.72
Central American, ex. Mexican	63	0.09
Costa Rican	9	0.01
Guatemalan	33	0.04
Honduran	5	0.01
Nicaraguan	3	<0.01
Panamanian	9	0.01
Salvadoran	4	0.01
Other Central American	0	<0.01
Cuban	39	0.05
Dominican Republic	51	0.07
Mexican	261	0.35
Puerto Rican	1,277	1.74
South American	130	0.18
Argentinean	12	0.02
Bolivian	8	0.01
Chilean	1	<0.01
Colombian	49	0.07
Ecuadorian	27	0.04
Paraguayan	0	<0.01
Peruvian	20	0.03
Uruguayan	1	<0.01
Venezuelan	8	0.01
Other South American	4	0.01
Other Hispanic or Latino	182	0.25

Race*	Population	%
African-American/Black (2,234)	2,842	3.86
Not Hispanic (2,114)	2,658	3.61
Hispanic (120)	184	0.25
American Indian/Alaska Native (312)	575	0.78
Not Hispanic (266)	510	0.69
Hispanic (46)	65	0.09
Alaska Athabascan (Ala. Nat.) (0)	0	<0.01
Aleut (Alaska Native) (0)	0	<0.01
Apache (0)	4	0.01
Arapaho (0)	0	<0.01
Blackfeet (2)	6	0.01
Canadian/French Am. Ind. (7)	8	0.01
Central American Ind. (0)	0	<0.01
Cherokee (3)	38	0.05
Cheyenne (0)	0	<0.01
Chickasaw (0)	0	<0.01
Chippewa (4)	5	0.01

Race* (cont.)	Population	%
Choctaw (0)	8	0.01
Colville (0)	0	<0.01
Comanche (0)	0	<0.01
Cree (0)	3	<0.01
Creek (0)	1	<0.01
Crow (0)	2	<0.01
Delaware (1)	1	<0.01
Hopi (0)	0	<0.01
Houma (0)	0	<0.01
Inupiat (Alaska Native) (0)	0	<0.01
Iroquois (164)	256	0.35
Kiowa (0)	0	<0.01
Lumbee (0)	1	<0.01
Menominee (0)	0	<0.01
Mexican American Ind. (2)	2	<0.01
Navajo (1)	1	<0.01
Osage (0)	0	<0.01
Ottawa (0)	0	<0.01
Paiute (0)	0	<0.01
Pima (0)	0	<0.01
Potawatomi (5)	9	0.01
Pueblo (0)	0	<0.01
Puget Sound Salish (0)	1	<0.01
Seminole (0)	1	<0.01
Shoshone (0)	0	<0.01
Sioux (2)	5	0.01
South American Ind. (8)	14	0.02
Spanish American Ind. (2)	2	<0.01
Tlingit-Haida (Alaska Native) (0)	0	<0.01
Tohono O'Odham (0)	0	<0.01
Tsimshian (Alaska Native) (0)	0	<0.01
Ute (0)	0	<0.01
Yakama (0)	0	<0.01
Yaqui (1)	1	<0.01
Yuman (0)	0	<0.01
Yup'ik (Alaska Native) (0)	0	<0.01
Asian (981)	1,234	1.68
Not Hispanic (972)	1,209	1.64
Hispanic (9)	25	0.03
Bangladeshi (3)	4	0.01
Bhutanese (0)	0	<0.01
Burmese (2)	3	<0.01
Cambodian (6)	6	0.01
Chinese, ex. Taiwanese (251)	290	0.39
Filipino (68)	114	0.15
Hmong (0)	0	<0.01
Indian (287)	312	0.42
Indonesian (3)	9	0.01
Japanese (27)	59	0.08
Korean (166)	198	0.27
Laotian (13)	19	0.03
Malaysian (5)	6	0.01
Nepalese (2)	2	<0.01
Pakistani (7)	10	0.01
Sri Lankan (8)	8	0.01
Taiwanese (12)	18	0.02
Thai (13)	25	0.03
Vietnamese (68)	81	0.11
Hawaii Native/Pacific Islander (2)	38	0.05
Not Hispanic (2)	25	0.03
Hispanic (0)	13	0.02
Fijian (0)	0	<0.01
Guamanian/Chamorro (0)	3	<0.01
Marshallese (0)	0	<0.01
Native Hawaiian (0)	16	0.02
Samoan (1)	2	<0.01
Tongan (0)	1	<0.01
White (68,462)	69,534	94.52
Not Hispanic (67,172)	68,098	92.57
Hispanic (1,290)	1,436	1.95

*Notes: † The Census 2010 population figure is used to calculate the percentages in the Hispanic Origin and Race categories. Ancestry percentages are based on the 2006-2010 American Community Survey population (not shown); ‡ Numbers in parentheses indicate the number of people reporting a single ancestry; * Numbers in parentheses indicate the number of persons reporting this race alone, not in combination with any other race; Please refer to the Explanation of Data for more information.*

Troy

Place Type: City
County: Rensselaer
Population: 50,129

Ancestry	Population	%
Afghan (0)	0	<0.01
African, Sub-Saharan (643)	773	1.55
African (372)	476	0.95
Cape Verdean (0)	11	0.02
Ethiopian (0)	0	<0.01
Ghanaian (91)	91	0.18
Kenyan (0)	0	<0.01
Liberian (0)	0	<0.01
Nigerian (8)	8	0.02
Senegalese (0)	0	<0.01
Sierra Leonean (0)	0	<0.01
Somalian (0)	0	<0.01
South African (0)	0	<0.01
Sudanese (28)	28	0.06
Ugandan (0)	0	<0.01
Zimbabwean (0)	0	<0.01
Other Sub-Saharan African (144)	159	0.32
Albanian (55)	55	0.11
Alsatian (0)	0	<0.01
American (1,657)	1,657	3.31
Arab (304)	439	0.88
Arab (72)	72	0.14
Egyptian (7)	44	0.09
Iraqi (0)	0	<0.01
Jordanian (0)	0	<0.01
Lebanese (204)	270	0.54
Moroccan (0)	0	<0.01
Palestinian (0)	0	<0.01
Syrian (0)	0	<0.01
Other Arab (21)	53	0.11
Armenian (270)	418	0.84
Assyrian/Chaldean/Syriac (0)	0	<0.01
Australian (11)	11	0.02
Austrian (42)	124	0.25
Basque (0)	0	<0.01
Belgian (0)	19	0.04
Brazilian (25)	42	0.08
British (97)	207	0.41
Bulgarian (0)	0	<0.01
Cajun (0)	0	<0.01
Canadian (60)	177	0.35
Carpatho Rusyn (0)	0	<0.01
Celtic (0)	23	0.05
Croatian (0)	0	<0.01
Cypriot (0)	0	<0.01
Czech (9)	182	0.36
Czechoslovakian (20)	38	0.08
Danish (37)	223	0.45
Dutch (117)	1,379	2.76
Eastern European (11)	24	0.05
English (888)	4,004	8.01
Estonian (15)	15	0.03
European (257)	529	1.06
Finnish (0)	74	0.15
French, ex. Basque (679)	4,862	9.72
French Canadian (445)	1,245	2.49
German (926)	6,417	12.83
German Russian (0)	65	0.13
Greek (161)	358	0.72
Guyanese (79)	79	0.16
Hungarian (14)	129	0.26
Icelander (0)	0	<0.01
Iranian (0)	0	<0.01
Irish (3,757)	12,384	24.76
Israeli (13)	13	0.03
Italian (2,238)	6,644	13.29
Latvian (19)	32	0.06
Lithuanian (30)	141	0.28
Luxemburger (0)	0	<0.01
Macedonian (0)	0	<0.01
Maltese (0)	0	<0.01
New Zealander (0)	0	<0.01
Northern European (10)	10	0.02

Ancestry	Population	%
Norwegian (12)	134	0.27
Pennsylvania German (40)	50	0.10
Polish (733)	2,521	5.04
Portuguese (42)	81	0.16
Romanian (11)	37	0.07
Russian (74)	287	0.57
Scandinavian (8)	8	0.02
Scotch-Irish (239)	784	1.57
Scottish (304)	848	1.70
Serbian (0)	0	<0.01
Slavic (0)	38	0.08
Slovak (0)	52	0.10
Slovene (0)	0	<0.01
Soviet Union (0)	0	<0.01
Swedish (30)	279	0.56
Swiss (0)	79	0.16
Turkish (170)	207	0.41
Ukrainian (299)	819	1.64
Welsh (67)	432	0.86
West Indian, ex. Hispanic (582)	797	1.59
Bahamian (0)	0	<0.01
Barbadian (15)	55	0.11
Belizean (0)	10	0.02
Bermudan (0)	0	<0.01
British West Indian (10)	17	0.03
Dutch West Indian (0)	0	<0.01
Haitian (96)	109	0.22
Jamaican (230)	288	0.58
Trinidadian/Tobagonian (214)	243	0.49
U.S. Virgin Islander (0)	0	<0.01
West Indian (17)	62	0.12
Other West Indian (0)	13	0.03
Yugoslavian (21)	34	0.07

Hispanic Origin	Population	%
Hispanic or Latino (of any race)	3,984	7.95
Central American, ex. Mexican	153	0.31
Costa Rican	16	0.03
Guatemalan	16	0.03
Honduran	12	0.02
Nicaraguan	15	0.03
Panamanian	57	0.11
Salvadoran	37	0.07
Other Central American	0	<0.01
Cuban	96	0.19
Dominican Republic	218	0.43
Mexican	400	0.80
Puerto Rican	2,598	5.18
South American	189	0.38
Argentinean	22	0.04
Bolivian	4	0.01
Chilean	6	0.01
Colombian	61	0.12
Ecuadorian	40	0.08
Paraguayan	3	0.01
Peruvian	29	0.06
Uruguayan	3	0.01
Venezuelan	20	0.04
Other South American	1	<0.01
Other Hispanic or Latino	330	0.66

Race*	Population	%
African-American/Black (8,211)	9,646	19.24
Not Hispanic (7,587)	8,756	17.47
Hispanic (624)	890	1.78
American Indian/Alaska Native (163)	531	1.06
Not Hispanic (104)	407	0.81
Hispanic (59)	124	0.25
Alaska Athabascan (Ala. Nat.) (0)	0	<0.01
Aleut (Alaska Native) (0)	0	<0.01
Apache (4)	10	0.02
Arapaho (0)	0	<0.01
Blackfeet (3)	22	0.04
Canadian/French Am. Ind. (1)	2	<0.01
Central American Ind. (0)	1	<0.01
Cherokee (8)	80	0.16
Cheyenne (0)	1	<0.01
Chickasaw (0)	0	<0.01
Chippewa (0)	5	0.01

Race*	Population	%
Choctaw (0)	1	<0.01
Colville (0)	0	<0.01
Comanche (0)	2	<0.01
Cree (0)	0	<0.01
Creek (0)	2	<0.01
Crow (0)	0	<0.01
Delaware (3)	6	0.01
Hopi (0)	0	<0.01
Houma (0)	0	<0.01
Inupiat (Alaska Native) (0)	0	<0.01
Iroquois (10)	55	0.11
Kiowa (0)	0	<0.01
Lumbee (1)	4	0.01
Menominee (3)	3	0.01
Mexican American Ind. (1)	3	0.01
Navajo (2)	5	0.01
Osage (0)	0	<0.01
Ottawa (0)	1	<0.01
Paiute (0)	0	<0.01
Pima (1)	1	<0.01
Potawatomi (0)	0	<0.01
Pueblo (0)	0	<0.01
Puget Sound Salish (0)	0	<0.01
Seminole (0)	0	<0.01
Shoshone (0)	0	<0.01
Sioux (0)	6	0.01
South American Ind. (8)	16	0.03
Spanish American Ind. (4)	5	0.01
Tlingit-Haida (Alaska Native) (0)	1	<0.01
Tohono O'Odham (0)	0	<0.01
Tsimshian (Alaska Native) (0)	0	<0.01
Ute (0)	0	<0.01
Yakama (0)	0	<0.01
Yaqui (0)	0	<0.01
Yuman (0)	0	<0.01
Yup'ik (Alaska Native) (0)	0	<0.01
Asian (1,721)	2,066	4.12
Not Hispanic (1,687)	2,012	4.01
Hispanic (34)	54	0.11
Bangladeshi (19)	23	0.05
Bhutanese (0)	0	<0.01
Burmese (28)	28	0.06
Cambodian (3)	7	0.01
Chinese, ex. Taiwanese (674)	759	1.51
Filipino (92)	157	0.31
Hmong (0)	0	<0.01
Indian (480)	546	1.09
Indonesian (4)	5	0.01
Japanese (21)	63	0.13
Korean (127)	174	0.35
Laotian (0)	1	<0.01
Malaysian (12)	14	0.03
Nepalese (12)	12	0.02
Pakistani (72)	81	0.16
Sri Lankan (2)	6	0.01
Taiwanese (34)	39	0.08
Thai (10)	15	0.03
Vietnamese (59)	78	0.16
Hawaii Native/Pacific Islander (20)	64	0.13
Not Hispanic (15)	50	0.10
Hispanic (5)	14	0.03
Fijian (0)	0	<0.01
Guamanian/Chamorro (4)	5	0.01
Marshallese (0)	0	<0.01
Native Hawaiian (9)	24	0.05
Samoan (0)	2	<0.01
Tongan (0)	0	<0.01
White (36,555)	38,385	76.57
Not Hispanic (34,953)	36,446	72.70
Hispanic (1,602)	1,939	3.87

*Notes: † The Census 2010 population figure is used to calculate the percentages in the Hispanic Origin and Race categories. Ancestry percentages are based on the 2006-2010 American Community Survey population (not shown); ‡ Numbers in parentheses indicate the number of people reporting a single ancestry; * Numbers in parentheses indicate the number of persons reporting this race alone, not in combination with any other race; Please refer to the Explanation of Data for more information.*

Union

Place Type: Town
County: Broome
Population: 56,346

Ancestry	Population	%
Afghan (0)	0	<0.01
African, Sub-Saharan (117)	208	0.37
African (63)	154	0.27
Cape Verdean (11)	11	0.02
Ethiopian (0)	0	<0.01
Ghanaian (30)	30	0.05
Kenyan (0)	0	<0.01
Liberian (0)	0	<0.01
Nigerian (13)	13	0.02
Senegalese (0)	0	<0.01
Sierra Leonean (0)	0	<0.01
Somalian (0)	0	<0.01
South African (0)	0	<0.01
Sudanese (0)	0	<0.01
Ugandan (0)	0	<0.01
Zimbabwean (0)	0	<0.01
Other Sub-Saharan African (0)	0	<0.01
Albanian (0)	7	0.01
Alsatian (0)	0	<0.01
American (2,180)	2,180	3.87
Arab (175)	231	0.41
Arab (73)	73	0.13
Egyptian (57)	69	0.12
Iraqi (6)	6	0.01
Jordanian (0)	0	<0.01
Lebanese (18)	38	0.07
Moroccan (0)	0	<0.01
Palestinian (13)	25	0.04
Syrian (0)	0	<0.01
Other Arab (8)	20	0.04
Armenian (0)	16	0.03
Assyrian/Chaldean/Syriac (0)	0	<0.01
Australian (0)	0	<0.01
Austrian (36)	297	0.53
Basque (0)	0	<0.01
Belgian (0)	31	0.06
Brazilian (0)	0	<0.01
British (82)	250	0.44
Bulgarian (0)	0	<0.01
Cajun (3)	12	0.02
Canadian (46)	153	0.27
Carpatho Rusyn (46)	101	0.18
Celtic (0)	27	0.05
Croatian (0)	21	0.04
Cypriot (0)	0	<0.01
Czech (289)	929	1.65
Czechoslovakian (221)	364	0.65
Danish (26)	119	0.21
Dutch (410)	1,823	3.24
Eastern European (61)	83	0.15
English (2,117)	7,072	12.56
Estonian (0)	0	<0.01
European (596)	660	1.17
Finnish (0)	10	0.02
French, ex. Basque (304)	2,044	3.63
French Canadian (268)	520	0.92
German (2,612)	10,592	18.81
German Russian (0)	0	<0.01
Greek (128)	417	0.74
Guyanese (136)	191	0.34
Hungarian (61)	266	0.47
Icelander (0)	0	<0.01
Iranian (0)	11	0.02
Irish (3,292)	12,320	21.88
Israeli (0)	0	<0.01
Italian (4,117)	9,710	17.24
Latvian (12)	12	0.02
Lithuanian (124)	452	0.80
Luxemburger (0)	0	<0.01
Macedonian (0)	0	<0.01
Maltese (0)	0	<0.01
New Zealander (0)	0	<0.01
Northern European (0)	0	<0.01

Ancestry	Population	%
Norwegian (127)	291	0.52
Pennsylvania German (148)	197	0.35
Polish (1,489)	4,619	8.20
Portuguese (33)	59	0.10
Romanian (8)	68	0.12
Russian (582)	1,778	3.16
Scandinavian (9)	18	0.03
Scotch-Irish (171)	712	1.26
Scottish (158)	1,114	1.98
Serbian (10)	65	0.12
Slavic (250)	291	0.52
Slovak (1,272)	3,003	5.33
Slovene (18)	67	0.12
Soviet Union (0)	0	<0.01
Swedish (158)	406	0.72
Swiss (12)	76	0.13
Turkish (92)	103	0.18
Ukrainian (317)	666	1.18
Welsh (184)	1,372	2.44
West Indian, ex. Hispanic (92)	189	0.34
Bahamian (0)	0	<0.01
Barbadian (0)	0	<0.01
Belizean (0)	0	<0.01
Bermudan (0)	0	<0.01
British West Indian (0)	0	<0.01
Dutch West Indian (0)	0	<0.01
Haitian (31)	31	0.06
Jamaican (14)	60	0.11
Trinidadian/Tobagonian (0)	0	<0.01
U.S. Virgin Islander (0)	0	<0.01
West Indian (47)	98	0.17
Other West Indian (0)	0	<0.01
Yugoslavian (63)	83	0.15

Hispanic Origin	Population	%
Hispanic or Latino (of any race)	1,802	3.20
Central American, ex. Mexican	120	0.21
Costa Rican	15	0.03
Guatemalan	46	0.08
Honduran	22	0.04
Nicaraguan	15	0.03
Panamanian	11	0.02
Salvadoran	11	0.02
Other Central American	0	<0.01
Cuban	64	0.11
Dominican Republic	108	0.19
Mexican	247	0.44
Puerto Rican	928	1.65
South American	126	0.22
Argentinean	25	0.04
Bolivian	2	<0.01
Chilean	4	0.01
Colombian	48	0.09
Ecuadorian	22	0.04
Paraguayan	0	<0.01
Peruvian	10	0.02
Uruguayan	5	0.01
Venezuelan	9	0.02
Other South American	1	<0.01
Other Hispanic or Latino	209	0.37

Race*	Population	%
African-American/Black (2,499)	3,402	6.04
Not Hispanic (2,338)	3,092	5.49
Hispanic (161)	310	0.55
American Indian/Alaska Native (96)	425	0.75
Not Hispanic (75)	363	0.64
Hispanic (21)	62	0.11
Alaska Athabascan (Ala. Nat.) (0)	0	<0.01
Aleut (Alaska Native) (0)	0	<0.01
Apache (5)	11	0.02
Arapaho (0)	0	<0.01
Blackfeet (0)	13	0.02
Canadian/French Am. Ind. (3)	4	0.01
Central American Ind. (0)	0	<0.01
Cherokee (10)	56	0.10
Cheyenne (0)	0	<0.01
Chickasaw (0)	0	<0.01
Chippewa (2)	2	<0.01

Race*	Population	%
Choctaw (1)	4	0.01
Colville (0)	0	<0.01
Comanche (0)	0	<0.01
Cree (0)	0	<0.01
Creek (0)	0	<0.01
Crow (1)	1	<0.01
Delaware (1)	5	0.01
Hopi (0)	0	<0.01
Houma (0)	1	<0.01
Inupiat (Alaska Native) (0)	0	<0.01
Iroquois (14)	53	0.09
Kiowa (0)	0	<0.01
Lumbee (0)	0	<0.01
Menominee (0)	0	<0.01
Mexican American Ind. (2)	6	0.01
Navajo (0)	2	<0.01
Osage (0)	0	<0.01
Ottawa (0)	0	<0.01
Paiute (0)	0	<0.01
Pima (0)	1	<0.01
Potawatomi (0)	2	<0.01
Pueblo (0)	0	<0.01
Puget Sound Salish (0)	0	<0.01
Seminole (0)	3	0.01
Shoshone (0)	0	<0.01
Sioux (3)	8	0.01
South American Ind. (1)	1	<0.01
Spanish American Ind. (3)	4	0.01
Tlingit-Haida (Alaska Native) (0)	0	<0.01
Tohono O'Odham (0)	0	<0.01
Tsimshian (Alaska Native) (0)	0	<0.01
Ute (0)	0	<0.01
Yakama (0)	0	<0.01
Yaqui (1)	1	<0.01
Yuman (0)	0	<0.01
Yup'ik (Alaska Native) (0)	0	<0.01
Asian (1,625)	1,958	3.47
Not Hispanic (1,619)	1,933	3.43
Hispanic (6)	25	0.04
Bangladeshi (3)	3	0.01
Bhutanese (0)	0	<0.01
Burmese (4)	4	0.01
Cambodian (4)	5	0.01
Chinese, ex. Taiwanese (333)	405	0.72
Filipino (90)	143	0.25
Hmong (0)	0	<0.01
Indian (291)	342	0.61
Indonesian (10)	12	0.02
Japanese (22)	55	0.10
Korean (118)	161	0.29
Laotian (355)	406	0.72
Malaysian (2)	7	0.01
Nepalese (9)	9	0.02
Pakistani (66)	68	0.12
Sri Lankan (2)	2	<0.01
Taiwanese (11)	13	0.02
Thai (14)	19	0.03
Vietnamese (215)	248	0.44
Hawaii Native/Pacific Islander (41)	77	0.14
Not Hispanic (29)	55	0.10
Hispanic (12)	22	0.04
Fijian (0)	1	<0.01
Guamanian/Chamorro (13)	16	0.03
Marshallese (0)	0	<0.01
Native Hawaiian (4)	17	0.03
Samoan (2)	5	0.01
Tongan (0)	0	<0.01
White (50,181)	51,487	91.38
Not Hispanic (49,190)	50,317	89.30
Hispanic (991)	1,170	2.08

Notes: † The Census 2010 population figure is used to calculate the percentages in the Hispanic Origin and Race categories. Ancestry percentages are based on the 2006-2010 American Community Survey population (not shown); ‡ Numbers in parentheses indicate the number of people reporting a single ancestry; * Numbers in parentheses indicate the number of persons reporting this race alone, not in combination with any other race; Please refer to the Explanation of Data for more information.

Utica

Place Type: City
County: Oneida
Population: 62,235

Ancestry	Population	%
Afghan (42)	42	0.07
African, Sub-Saharan (477)	594	0.96
African (272)	374	0.60
Cape Verdean (0)	0	<0.01
Ethiopian (0)	0	<0.01
Ghanaian (0)	0	<0.01
Kenyan (0)	15	0.02
Liberian (88)	88	0.14
Nigerian (0)	0	<0.01
Senegalese (0)	0	<0.01
Sierra Leonean (0)	0	<0.01
Somalian (99)	99	0.16
South African (0)	0	<0.01
Sudanese (0)	0	<0.01
Ugandan (0)	0	<0.01
Zimbabwean (0)	0	<0.01
Other Sub-Saharan African (18)	18	0.03
Albanian (22)	55	0.09
Alsatian (0)	0	<0.01
American (1,237)	1,237	2.00
Arab (875)	1,558	2.52
Arab (170)	198	0.32
Egyptian (22)	37	0.06
Iraqi (0)	0	<0.01
Jordanian (0)	0	<0.01
Lebanese (506)	947	1.53
Moroccan (11)	20	0.03
Palestinian (10)	10	0.02
Syrian (58)	248	0.40
Other Arab (98)	98	0.16
Armenian (18)	29	0.05
Assyrian/Chaldean/Syriac (0)	0	<0.01
Australian (13)	13	0.02
Austrian (0)	79	0.13
Basque (0)	0	<0.01
Belgian (8)	8	0.01
Brazilian (10)	32	0.05
British (9)	31	0.05
Bulgarian (0)	0	<0.01
Cajun (0)	0	<0.01
Canadian (32)	61	0.10
Carpatho Rusyn (0)	0	<0.01
Celtic (8)	16	0.03
Croatian (12)	86	0.14
Cypriot (0)	0	<0.01
Czech (0)	79	0.13
Czechoslovakian (22)	22	0.04
Danish (12)	45	0.07
Dutch (149)	884	1.43
Eastern European (11)	20	0.03
English (812)	3,140	5.08
Estonian (0)	0	<0.01
European (98)	108	0.17
Finnish (17)	17	0.03
French, ex. Basque (167)	2,016	3.26
French Canadian (219)	620	1.00
German (1,489)	7,355	11.89
German Russian (0)	0	<0.01
Greek (57)	225	0.36
Guyanese (8)	8	0.01
Hungarian (37)	118	0.19
Icelander (0)	14	0.02
Iranian (23)	23	0.04
Irish (2,616)	9,380	15.17
Israeli (0)	0	<0.01
Italian (7,837)	14,163	22.90
Latvian (0)	0	<0.01
Lithuanian (43)	76	0.12
Luxemburger (0)	0	<0.01
Macedonian (21)	21	0.03
Maltese (0)	0	<0.01
New Zealander (0)	0	<0.01
Northern European (0)	0	<0.01

Ancestry (cont.)	Population	%
Norwegian (9)	50	0.08
Pennsylvania German (13)	13	0.02
Polish (2,611)	5,408	8.75
Portuguese (27)	114	0.18
Romanian (51)	103	0.17
Russian (655)	862	1.39
Scandinavian (0)	48	0.08
Scotch-Irish (110)	254	0.41
Scottish (68)	351	0.57
Serbian (0)	82	0.13
Slavic (0)	0	<0.01
Slovak (51)	59	0.10
Slovene (0)	0	<0.01
Soviet Union (0)	0	<0.01
Swedish (0)	89	0.14
Swiss (32)	74	0.12
Turkish (0)	0	<0.01
Ukrainian (359)	505	0.82
Welsh (120)	775	1.25
West Indian, ex. Hispanic (681)	952	1.54
Bahamian (0)	0	<0.01
Barbadian (21)	21	0.03
Belizean (0)	0	<0.01
Bermudan (0)	0	<0.01
British West Indian (0)	28	0.05
Dutch West Indian (0)	0	<0.01
Haitian (168)	286	0.46
Jamaican (325)	420	0.68
Trinidadian/Tobagonian (81)	111	0.18
U.S. Virgin Islander (0)	0	<0.01
West Indian (86)	86	0.14
Other West Indian (0)	0	<0.01
Yugoslavian (3,075)	3,231	5.23

Hispanic Origin	Population	%
Hispanic or Latino (of any race)	6,555	10.53
Central American, ex. Mexican	272	0.44
Costa Rican	9	0.01
Guatemalan	8	0.01
Honduran	46	0.07
Nicaraguan	11	0.02
Panamanian	25	0.04
Salvadoran	163	0.26
Other Central American	10	0.02
Cuban	89	0.14
Dominican Republic	940	1.51
Mexican	243	0.39
Puerto Rican	4,220	6.78
South American	231	0.37
Argentinean	7	0.01
Bolivian	2	<0.01
Chilean	7	0.01
Colombian	43	0.07
Ecuadorian	100	0.16
Paraguayan	1	<0.01
Peruvian	35	0.06
Uruguayan	3	<0.01
Venezuelan	31	0.05
Other South American	2	<0.01
Other Hispanic or Latino	560	0.90

Race*	Population	%
African-American/Black (9,501)	11,107	17.85
Not Hispanic (8,851)	10,139	16.29
Hispanic (650)	968	1.56
American Indian/Alaska Native (180)	581	0.93
Not Hispanic (123)	432	0.69
Hispanic (57)	149	0.24
Alaska Athabascan (Ala. Nat.) (0)	0	<0.01
Aleut (Alaska Native) (1)	1	<0.01
Apache (4)	7	0.01
Arapaho (0)	0	<0.01
Blackfeet (0)	17	0.03
Canadian/French Am. Ind. (0)	6	0.01
Central American Ind. (8)	8	0.01
Cherokee (5)	56	0.09
Cheyenne (0)	4	0.01
Chickasaw (0)	1	<0.01
Chippewa (2)	8	0.01

Race* (cont.)	Population	%
Choctaw (0)	3	<0.01
Colville (0)	0	<0.01
Comanche (0)	0	<0.01
Cree (0)	0	<0.01
Creek (0)	1	<0.01
Crow (0)	3	<0.01
Delaware (0)	1	<0.01
Hopi (0)	0	<0.01
Houma (0)	0	<0.01
Inupiat (Alaska Native) (0)	0	<0.01
Iroquois (42)	94	0.15
Kiowa (0)	2	<0.01
Lumbee (1)	1	<0.01
Menominee (0)	0	<0.01
Mexican American Ind. (0)	2	<0.01
Navajo (1)	1	<0.01
Osage (0)	0	<0.01
Ottawa (0)	0	<0.01
Paiute (1)	1	<0.01
Pima (0)	1	<0.01
Potawatomi (0)	0	<0.01
Pueblo (0)	1	<0.01
Puget Sound Salish (0)	0	<0.01
Seminole (0)	0	<0.01
Shoshone (0)	1	<0.01
Sioux (10)	29	0.05
South American Ind. (4)	15	0.02
Spanish American Ind. (0)	0	<0.01
Tlingit-Haida (Alaska Native) (1)	4	0.01
Tohono O'Odham (0)	0	<0.01
Tsimshian (Alaska Native) (0)	0	<0.01
Ute (0)	0	<0.01
Yakama (0)	0	<0.01
Yaqui (0)	0	<0.01
Yuman (0)	0	<0.01
Yup'ik (Alaska Native) (0)	0	<0.01
Asian (4,626)	5,009	8.05
Not Hispanic (4,594)	4,936	7.93
Hispanic (32)	73	0.12
Bangladeshi (0)	0	<0.01
Bhutanese (30)	36	0.06
Burmese (2,198)	2,317	3.72
Cambodian (412)	480	0.77
Chinese, ex. Taiwanese (140)	200	0.32
Filipino (37)	83	0.13
Hmong (0)	0	<0.01
Indian (273)	368	0.59
Indonesian (0)	0	<0.01
Japanese (44)	66	0.11
Korean (107)	133	0.21
Laotian (42)	72	0.12
Malaysian (2)	2	<0.01
Nepalese (6)	12	0.02
Pakistani (41)	46	0.07
Sri Lankan (2)	2	<0.01
Taiwanese (1)	2	<0.01
Thai (34)	50	0.08
Vietnamese (932)	1,022	1.64
Hawaii Native/Pacific Islander (36)	137	0.22
Not Hispanic (16)	95	0.15
Hispanic (20)	42	0.07
Fijian (0)	0	<0.01
Guamanian/Chamorro (10)	18	0.03
Marshallese (0)	0	<0.01
Native Hawaiian (12)	20	0.03
Samoan (9)	18	0.03
Tongan (1)	1	<0.01
White (42,945)	45,066	72.41
Not Hispanic (40,164)	41,788	67.15
Hispanic (2,781)	3,278	5.27

Notes: † The Census 2010 population figure is used to calculate the percentages in the Hispanic Origin and Race categories. Ancestry percentages are based on the 2006-2010 American Community Survey population (not shown); ‡ Numbers in parentheses indicate the number of people reporting a single ancestry; * Numbers in parentheses indicate the number of persons reporting this race alone, not in combination with any other race; Please refer to the Explanation of Data for more information.

White Plains

Place Type: City
County: Westchester
Population: 56,853

Ancestry	Population	%
Afghan (0)	0	<0.01
African, Sub-Saharan (230)	331	0.59
African (97)	97	0.17
Cape Verdean (0)	0	<0.01
Ethiopian (0)	0	<0.01
Ghanaian (0)	0	<0.01
Kenyan (0)	0	<0.01
Liberian (0)	0	<0.01
Nigerian (66)	97	0.17
Senegalese (0)	0	<0.01
Sierra Leonean (0)	0	<0.01
Somalian (0)	0	<0.01
South African (43)	78	0.14
Sudanese (0)	0	<0.01
Ugandan (9)	9	0.02
Zimbabwean (0)	0	<0.01
Other Sub-Saharan African (15)	50	0.09
Albanian (58)	73	0.13
Alsatian (0)	0	<0.01
American (2,743)	2,743	4.91
Arab (162)	307	0.55
Arab (10)	64	0.11
Egyptian (44)	44	0.08
Iraqi (0)	0	<0.01
Jordanian (21)	21	0.04
Lebanese (46)	56	0.10
Moroccan (24)	71	0.13
Palestinian (7)	7	0.01
Syrian (0)	7	0.01
Other Arab (10)	37	0.07
Armenian (44)	60	0.11
Assyrian/Chaldean/Syriac (0)	8	0.01
Australian (0)	0	<0.01
Austrian (201)	572	1.02
Basque (0)	0	<0.01
Belgian (47)	94	0.17
Brazilian (409)	440	0.79
British (34)	126	0.23
Bulgarian (40)	62	0.11
Cajun (0)	0	<0.01
Canadian (69)	128	0.23
Carpatho Rusyn (0)	0	<0.01
Celtic (0)	0	<0.01
Croatian (61)	61	0.11
Cypriot (0)	0	<0.01
Czech (41)	115	0.21
Czechoslovakian (0)	20	0.04
Danish (9)	48	0.09
Dutch (64)	313	0.56
Eastern European (542)	557	1.00
English (489)	1,818	3.25
Estonian (0)	0	<0.01
European (593)	684	1.22
Finnish (15)	25	0.04
French, ex. Basque (101)	696	1.25
French Canadian (30)	155	0.28
German (754)	3,324	5.95
German Russian (0)	0	<0.01
Greek (102)	279	0.50
Guyanese (130)	175	0.31
Hungarian (148)	401	0.72
Icelander (0)	0	<0.01
Iranian (28)	48	0.09
Irish (2,251)	5,662	10.13
Israeli (153)	181	0.32
Italian (5,382)	9,116	16.31
Latvian (7)	7	0.01
Lithuanian (94)	226	0.40
Luxemburger (0)	0	<0.01
Macedonian (14)	54	0.10
Maltese (0)	0	<0.01
New Zealander (29)	29	0.05
Northern European (31)	54	0.10

Ancestry	Population	%
Norwegian (42)	134	0.24
Pennsylvania German (0)	0	<0.01
Polish (765)	2,000	3.58
Portuguese (198)	325	0.58
Romanian (61)	183	0.33
Russian (1,095)	2,307	4.13
Scandinavian (0)	0	<0.01
Scotch-Irish (100)	241	0.43
Scottish (116)	435	0.78
Serbian (16)	16	0.03
Slavic (0)	0	<0.01
Slovak (18)	85	0.15
Slovene (0)	0	<0.01
Soviet Union (0)	0	<0.01
Swedish (30)	282	0.50
Swiss (46)	129	0.23
Turkish (96)	120	0.21
Ukrainian (228)	290	0.52
Welsh (6)	89	0.16
West Indian, ex. Hispanic (1,351)	1,555	2.78
Bahamian (26)	26	0.05
Barbadian (25)	25	0.04
Belizean (125)	155	0.28
Bermudan (0)	0	<0.01
British West Indian (34)	57	0.10
Dutch West Indian (0)	0	<0.01
Haitian (386)	397	0.71
Jamaican (596)	702	1.26
Trinidadian/Tobagonian (49)	49	0.09
U.S. Virgin Islander (23)	23	0.04
West Indian (87)	121	0.22
Other West Indian (0)	0	<0.01
Yugoslavian (24)	24	0.04

Hispanic Origin	Population	%
Hispanic or Latino (of any race)	16,839	29.62
Central American, ex. Mexican	968	1.70
Costa Rican	35	0.06
Guatemalan	551	0.97
Honduran	75	0.13
Nicaraguan	35	0.06
Panamanian	56	0.10
Salvadoran	204	0.36
Other Central American	12	0.02
Cuban	321	0.56
Dominican Republic	1,177	2.07
Mexican	5,773	10.15
Puerto Rican	1,541	2.71
South American	5,850	10.29
Argentinean	189	0.33
Bolivian	72	0.13
Chilean	67	0.12
Colombian	1,838	3.23
Ecuadorian	1,001	1.76
Paraguayan	260	0.46
Peruvian	2,260	3.98
Uruguayan	63	0.11
Venezuelan	77	0.14
Other South American	23	0.04
Other Hispanic or Latino	1,209	2.13

Race*	Population	%
African-American/Black (8,070)	8,768	15.42
Not Hispanic (7,502)	7,918	13.93
Hispanic (568)	850	1.50
American Indian/Alaska Native (394)	890	1.57
Not Hispanic (47)	193	0.34
Hispanic (347)	697	1.23
Alaska Athabascan (Ala. Nat.) (0)	0	<0.01
Aleut (Alaska Native) (0)	0	<0.01
Apache (0)	6	0.01
Arapaho (0)	0	<0.01
Blackfeet (3)	16	0.03
Canadian/French Am. Ind. (0)	0	<0.01
Central American Ind. (1)	6	0.01
Cherokee (2)	36	0.06
Cheyenne (0)	0	<0.01
Chickasaw (0)	0	<0.01
Chippewa (4)	4	0.01

Race*	Population	%
Choctaw (0)	0	<0.01
Colville (0)	0	<0.01
Comanche (0)	0	<0.01
Cree (0)	0	<0.01
Creek (2)	3	0.01
Crow (0)	1	<0.01
Delaware (1)	1	<0.01
Hopi (0)	1	<0.01
Houma (3)	3	0.01
Inupiat (Alaska Native) (0)	0	<0.01
Iroquois (1)	12	0.02
Kiowa (0)	0	<0.01
Lumbee (1)	1	<0.01
Menominee (0)	0	<0.01
Mexican American Ind. (95)	162	0.28
Navajo (0)	1	<0.01
Osage (1)	2	<0.01
Ottawa (0)	0	<0.01
Paiute (0)	0	<0.01
Pima (0)	0	<0.01
Potawatomi (0)	0	<0.01
Pueblo (13)	19	0.03
Puget Sound Salish (0)	0	<0.01
Seminole (0)	1	<0.01
Shoshone (0)	1	<0.01
Sioux (0)	7	0.01
South American Ind. (42)	116	0.20
Spanish American Ind. (12)	15	0.03
Tlingit-Haida (Alaska Native) (0)	0	<0.01
Tohono O'Odham (0)	0	<0.01
Tsimshian (Alaska Native) (0)	0	<0.01
Ute (0)	0	<0.01
Yakama (0)	0	<0.01
Yaqui (0)	1	<0.01
Yuman (0)	0	<0.01
Yup'ik (Alaska Native) (0)	0	<0.01
Asian (3,623)	4,080	7.18
Not Hispanic (3,587)	3,959	6.96
Hispanic (36)	121	0.21
Bangladeshi (35)	37	0.07
Bhutanese (0)	0	<0.01
Burmese (9)	9	0.02
Cambodian (13)	13	0.02
Chinese, ex. Taiwanese (813)	934	1.64
Filipino (373)	451	0.79
Hmong (0)	0	<0.01
Indian (1,281)	1,397	2.46
Indonesian (6)	10	0.02
Japanese (372)	441	0.78
Korean (384)	431	0.76
Laotian (1)	3	0.01
Malaysian (8)	11	0.02
Nepalese (7)	7	0.01
Pakistani (70)	79	0.14
Sri Lankan (10)	17	0.03
Taiwanese (35)	44	0.08
Thai (31)	42	0.07
Vietnamese (73)	82	0.14
Hawaii Native/Pacific Islander (20)	180	0.32
Not Hispanic (14)	71	0.12
Hispanic (6)	109	0.19
Fijian (6)	6	0.01
Guamanian/Chamorro (2)	7	0.01
Marshallese (0)	0	<0.01
Native Hawaiian (4)	7	0.01
Samoan (0)	0	<0.01
Tongan (0)	0	<0.01
White (36,178)	37,846	66.57
Not Hispanic (27,805)	28,446	50.03
Hispanic (8,373)	9,400	16.53

*Notes: † The Census 2010 population figure is used to calculate the percentages in the Hispanic Origin and Race categories. Ancestry percentages are based on the 2006-2010 American Community Survey population (not shown); ‡ Numbers in parentheses indicate the number of people reporting a single ancestry; * Numbers in parentheses indicate the number of persons reporting this race alone, not in combination with any other race; Please refer to the Explanation of Data for more information.*

Yonkers

Place Type: City
County: Westchester
Population: 195,976

Ancestry	Population	%
Afghan (0)	0	<0.01
African, Sub-Saharan (2,404)	2,939	1.51
African (1,162)	1,496	0.77
Cape Verdean (41)	41	0.02
Ethiopian (159)	159	0.08
Ghanaian (489)	585	0.30
Kenyan (73)	107	0.05
Liberian (7)	7	<0.01
Nigerian (371)	442	0.23
Senegalese (21)	21	0.01
Sierra Leonean (0)	0	<0.01
Somalian (6)	6	<0.01
South African (59)	59	0.03
Sudanese (0)	0	<0.01
Ugandan (0)	0	<0.01
Zimbabwean (0)	0	<0.01
Other Sub-Saharan African (16)	16	0.01
Albanian (2,122)	2,270	1.16
Alsatian (0)	0	<0.01
American (5,127)	5,127	2.63
Arab (2,696)	3,210	1.65
Arab (899)	1,036	0.53
Egyptian (243)	243	0.12
Iraqi (103)	103	0.05
Jordanian (855)	907	0.47
Lebanese (44)	327	0.17
Moroccan (103)	110	0.06
Palestinian (139)	139	0.07
Syrian (13)	33	0.02
Other Arab (297)	312	0.16
Armenian (338)	411	0.21
Assyrian/Chaldean/Syriac (135)	157	0.08
Australian (0)	17	0.01
Austrian (121)	618	0.32
Basque (0)	0	<0.01
Belgian (0)	12	0.01
Brazilian (334)	422	0.22
British (168)	297	0.15
Bulgarian (10)	10	0.01
Cajun (0)	0	<0.01
Canadian (111)	182	0.09
Carpatho Rusyn (40)	40	0.02
Celtic (11)	15	0.01
Croatian (65)	121	0.06
Cypriot (0)	0	<0.01
Czech (152)	478	0.25
Czechoslovakian (185)	354	0.18
Danish (0)	62	0.03
Dutch (50)	468	0.24
Eastern European (441)	458	0.24
English (1,054)	3,968	2.04
Estonian (0)	53	0.03
European (325)	391	0.20
Finnish (50)	84	0.04
French, ex. Basque (245)	1,367	0.70
French Canadian (53)	284	0.15
German (1,666)	8,502	4.36
German Russian (14)	14	0.01
Greek (949)	1,272	0.65
Guyanese (410)	526	0.27
Hungarian (410)	920	0.47
Icelander (0)	0	<0.01
Iranian (137)	173	0.09
Irish (10,811)	22,187	11.38
Israeli (38)	77	0.04
Italian (21,697)	32,142	16.49
Latvian (33)	71	0.04
Lithuanian (111)	327	0.17
Luxemburger (0)	13	0.01
Macedonian (236)	236	0.12
Maltese (73)	73	0.04
New Zealander (8)	8	<0.01
Northern European (13)	13	0.01

Ancestry	Population	%
Norwegian (79)	370	0.19
Pennsylvania German (0)	0	<0.01
Polish (2,602)	5,453	2.80
Portuguese (1,947)	2,670	1.37
Romanian (170)	278	0.14
Russian (1,453)	2,804	1.44
Scandinavian (10)	21	0.01
Scotch-Irish (274)	562	0.29
Scottish (293)	1,047	0.54
Serbian (0)	11	0.01
Slavic (185)	237	0.12
Slovak (274)	590	0.30
Slovene (10)	10	0.01
Soviet Union (14)	14	0.01
Swedish (115)	574	0.29
Swiss (12)	83	0.04
Turkish (112)	112	0.06
Ukrainian (943)	1,494	0.77
Welsh (20)	140	0.07
West Indian, ex. Hispanic (7,179)	8,578	4.40
Bahamian (0)	0	<0.01
Barbadian (47)	157	0.08
Belizean (0)	0	<0.01
Bermudan (0)	0	<0.01
British West Indian (313)	497	0.26
Dutch West Indian (3)	3	<0.01
Haitian (897)	1,026	0.53
Jamaican (4,479)	5,051	2.59
Trinidadian/Tobagonian (650)	689	0.35
U.S. Virgin Islander (32)	83	0.04
West Indian (758)	1,072	0.55
Other West Indian (0)	0	<0.01
Yugoslavian (38)	46	0.02

Hispanic Origin	Population	%
Hispanic or Latino (of any race)	67,927	34.66
Central American, ex. Mexican	5,822	2.97
Costa Rican	156	0.08
Guatemalan	765	0.39
Honduran	1,451	0.74
Nicaraguan	534	0.27
Panamanian	185	0.09
Salvadoran	2,691	1.37
Other Central American	40	0.02
Cuban	1,501	0.77
Dominican Republic	15,903	8.11
Mexican	13,761	7.02
Puerto Rican	19,875	10.14
South American	6,622	3.38
Argentinean	273	0.14
Bolivian	30	0.02
Chilean	215	0.11
Colombian	1,493	0.76
Ecuadorian	3,271	1.67
Paraguayan	79	0.04
Peruvian	946	0.48
Uruguayan	45	0.02
Venezuelan	207	0.11
Other South American	63	0.03
Other Hispanic or Latino	4,443	2.27

Race*	Population	%
African-American/Black (36,572)	40,198	20.51
Not Hispanic (31,297)	32,873	16.77
Hispanic (5,275)	7,325	3.74
American Indian/Alaska Native (1,463)	2,801	1.43
Not Hispanic (382)	995	0.51
Hispanic (1,081)	1,806	0.92
Alaska Athabascan (Ala. Nat.) (1)	1	<0.01
Aleut (Alaska Native) (0)	0	<0.01
Apache (3)	10	0.01
Arapaho (0)	0	<0.01
Blackfeet (17)	58	0.03
Canadian/French Am. Ind. (3)	4	<0.01
Central American Ind. (46)	103	0.05
Cherokee (28)	151	0.08
Cheyenne (1)	3	<0.01
Chickasaw (0)	1	<0.01
Chippewa (6)	8	<0.01

Race* (cont.)	Population	%
Choctaw (1)	12	0.01
Colville (1)	1	<0.01
Comanche (0)	1	<0.01
Cree (0)	0	<0.01
Creek (1)	3	<0.01
Crow (1)	2	<0.01
Delaware (2)	6	<0.01
Hopi (1)	5	<0.01
Houma (1)	1	<0.01
Inupiat (Alaska Native) (3)	5	<0.01
Iroquois (16)	41	0.02
Kiowa (0)	0	<0.01
Lumbee (1)	2	<0.01
Menominee (0)	0	<0.01
Mexican American Ind. (99)	171	0.09
Navajo (7)	7	<0.01
Osage (1)	1	<0.01
Ottawa (0)	0	<0.01
Paiute (0)	0	<0.01
Pima (0)	0	<0.01
Potawatomi (0)	0	<0.01
Pueblo (8)	20	0.01
Puget Sound Salish (0)	0	<0.01
Seminole (1)	11	0.01
Shoshone (0)	0	<0.01
Sioux (5)	13	0.01
South American Ind. (95)	270	0.14
Spanish American Ind. (104)	132	0.07
Tlingit-Haida (Alaska Native) (0)	1	<0.01
Tohono O'Odham (0)	3	<0.01
Tsimshian (Alaska Native) (0)	0	<0.01
Ute (0)	0	<0.01
Yakama (0)	0	<0.01
Yaqui (0)	0	<0.01
Yuman (2)	2	<0.01
Yup'ik (Alaska Native) (0)	0	<0.01
Asian (11,556)	13,253	6.76
Not Hispanic (11,370)	12,736	6.50
Hispanic (186)	517	0.26
Bangladeshi (148)	167	0.09
Bhutanese (1)	1	<0.01
Burmese (11)	11	0.01
Cambodian (26)	36	0.02
Chinese, ex. Taiwanese (872)	1,149	0.59
Filipino (2,584)	2,819	1.44
Hmong (0)	0	<0.01
Indian (5,313)	5,818	2.97
Indonesian (20)	28	0.01
Japanese (155)	251	0.13
Korean (906)	977	0.50
Laotian (16)	18	0.01
Malaysian (3)	7	<0.01
Nepalese (8)	9	<0.01
Pakistani (783)	874	0.45
Sri Lankan (36)	39	0.02
Taiwanese (41)	49	0.03
Thai (248)	268	0.14
Vietnamese (79)	95	0.05
Hawaii Native/Pacific Islander (122)	483	0.25
Not Hispanic (58)	211	0.11
Hispanic (64)	272	0.14
Fijian (5)	6	<0.01
Guamanian/Chamorro (27)	52	0.03
Marshallese (0)	0	<0.01
Native Hawaiian (35)	57	0.03
Samoan (4)	8	<0.01
Tongan (0)	0	<0.01
White (109,351)	114,948	58.65
Not Hispanic (81,163)	83,170	42.44
Hispanic (28,188)	31,778	16.22

Notes: † The Census 2010 population figure is used to calculate the percentages in the Hispanic Origin and Race categories. Ancestry percentages are based on the 2006-2010 American Community Survey population (not shown); ‡ Numbers in parentheses indicate the number of people reporting a single ancestry; * Numbers in parentheses indicate the number of persons reporting this race alone, not in combination with any other race; Please refer to the Explanation of Data for more information.

Ancestry Group Rankings

Afghan

Top 10 Places Sorted by Population
Based on all places, regardless of total population

Place	Population	%
New York (city)	6,470	0.08
Queens (borough) Queens County	6,027	0.27
Oyster Bay (town) Nassau County	808	0.28
Hempstead (town) Nassau County	399	0.05
Brooklyn (borough) Kings County	344	0.01
Hicksville (cdp) Nassau County	323	0.77
Schenectady (city) Schenectady County	318	0.49
Huntington (town) Suffolk County	314	0.16
Huntington Station (cdp) Suffolk County	268	0.85
Islip (town) Suffolk County	263	0.08

Top 10 Places Sorted by Percent of Total Population
Based on all places, regardless of total population

Place	Population	%
DeRuyter (town) Madison County	27	2.14
Pomona (village) Rockland County	61	1.73
Malverne (village) Nassau County	139	1.63
Viola (cdp) Rockland County	111	1.57
Huntington Bay (village) Suffolk County	21	1.47
Woodbury (cdp) Nassau County	125	1.38
Wyandanch (cdp) Suffolk County	123	1.13
Jericho (cdp) Nassau County	129	0.99
New Hyde Park (village) Nassau County	89	0.93
Upper Brookville (village) Nassau County	13	0.87

Top 10 Places Sorted by Percent of Total Population
Based on places with total population of 50,000 or more

Place	Population	%
Schenectady (city) Schenectady County	318	0.49
Oyster Bay (town) Nassau County	808	0.28
Irondequoit (cdp/town) Monroe County	145	0.28
Queens (borough) Queens County	6,027	0.27
Tonawanda (cdp) Erie County	108	0.18
Huntington (town) Suffolk County	314	0.16
Tonawanda (town) Erie County	108	0.15
Amherst (town) Erie County	144	0.12
Brentwood (cdp) Suffolk County	68	0.12
Babylon (town) Suffolk County	219	0.10

African, Sub-Saharan

Top 10 Places Sorted by Population
Based on all places, regardless of total population

Place	Population	%
New York (city)	175,478	2.17
Brooklyn (borough) Kings County	63,004	2.55
Bronx (borough) Bronx County	55,928	4.10
Queens (borough) Queens County	25,166	1.14
Manhattan (borough) New York County	24,146	1.52
Rochester (city) Monroe County	7,909	3.73
Staten Island (borough) Richmond County	7,234	1.56
Buffalo (city) Erie County	6,085	2.29
Hempstead (town) Nassau County	5,844	0.78
Yonkers (city) Westchester County	2,939	1.51

Top 10 Places Sorted by Percent of Total Population
Based on all places, regardless of total population

Place	Population	%
Linwood (cdp) Livingston County	64	48.85
Wheatley Heights (cdp) Suffolk County	896	14.46
North Bellport (cdp) Suffolk County	737	6.54
Gordon Heights (cdp) Suffolk County	199	6.10
Hobart (village) Delaware County	29	5.99
Pomona (village) Rockland County	207	5.86
South Blooming Grove (village) Orange County	192	5.83
Aurora (village) Cayuga County	64	5.72
Deferiet (village) Jefferson County	26	5.53
West End (cdp) Otsego County	86	5.50

Top 10 Places Sorted by Percent of Total Population
Based on places with total population of 50,000 or more

Place	Population	%
Bronx (borough) Bronx County	55,928	4.10
Rochester (city) Monroe County	7,909	3.73
Mount Vernon (city) Westchester County	1,910	2.85
Brooklyn (borough) Kings County	63,004	2.55
Hempstead (village) Nassau County	1,285	2.41
Buffalo (city) Erie County	6,085	2.29
New York (city)	175,478	2.17
Syracuse (city) Onondaga County	2,470	1.71
Albany (city) Albany County	1,533	1.57
Staten Island (borough) Richmond County	7,234	1.56

African, Sub-Saharan: African

Top 10 Places Sorted by Population
Based on all places, regardless of total population

Place	Population	%
New York (city)	101,901	1.26
Brooklyn (borough) Kings County	48,168	1.95
Bronx (borough) Bronx County	22,647	1.66
Queens (borough) Queens County	14,083	0.64
Manhattan (borough) New York County	12,839	0.81
Rochester (city) Monroe County	5,828	2.75
Buffalo (city) Erie County	4,177	1.57
Staten Island (borough) Richmond County	4,164	0.90
Hempstead (town) Nassau County	3,879	0.51
Brookhaven (town) Suffolk County	2,533	0.53

Top 10 Places Sorted by Percent of Total Population
Based on all places, regardless of total population

Place	Population	%
North Bellport (cdp) Suffolk County	728	6.46
Gordon Heights (cdp) Suffolk County	199	6.10
Hobart (village) Delaware County	29	5.99
Wheatley Heights (cdp) Suffolk County	368	5.94
Aurora (village) Cayuga County	64	5.72
Great River (cdp) Suffolk County	80	4.86
St. Regis Mohawk Reservation Franklin County	134	4.28
South Blooming Grove (village) Orange County	135	4.10
Deferiet (village) Jefferson County	19	4.04
Groveland (town) Livingston County	132	3.90

Top 10 Places Sorted by Percent of Total Population
Based on places with total population of 50,000 or more

Place	Population	%
Rochester (city) Monroe County	5,828	2.75
Brooklyn (borough) Kings County	48,168	1.95
Mount Vernon (city) Westchester County	1,162	1.73
Bronx (borough) Bronx County	22,647	1.66
Hempstead (village) Nassau County	850	1.59
Buffalo (city) Erie County	4,177	1.57
New York (city)	101,901	1.26
Albany (city) Albany County	975	1.00
Niagara Falls (city) Niagara County	488	0.96
Troy (city) Rensselaer County	476	0.95

African, Sub-Saharan: Cape Verdean

Top 10 Places Sorted by Population
Based on all places, regardless of total population

Place	Population	%
New York (city)	595	0.01
Manhattan (borough) New York County	206	0.01
Brooklyn (borough) Kings County	153	0.01
Queens (borough) Queens County	117	0.01
Bronx (borough) Bronx County	108	0.01
Buffalo (city) Erie County	95	0.04
Yonkers (city) Westchester County	41	0.02
North Elba (town) Essex County	17	0.19
Albany (city) Albany County	13	0.01
Plainview (cdp) Nassau County	12	0.05

Top 10 Places Sorted by Percent of Total Population
Based on all places, regardless of total population

Place	Population	%
Liverpool (village) Onondaga County	9	0.38
North Elba (town) Essex County	17	0.19
New Baltimore (town) Greene County	5	0.15
Endwell (cdp) Broome County	11	0.09
Plainview (cdp) Nassau County	12	0.05
Buffalo (city) Erie County	95	0.04
Copiague (cdp) Suffolk County	9	0.04
Jay (town) Essex County	1	0.04
Salina (town) Onondaga County	9	0.03
Yonkers (city) Westchester County	41	0.02

Top 10 Places Sorted by Percent of Total Population
Based on places with total population of 50,000 or more

Place	Population	%
Buffalo (city) Erie County	95	0.04
Yonkers (city) Westchester County	41	0.02
Mount Vernon (city) Westchester County	11	0.02
Troy (city) Rensselaer County	11	0.02
Union (town) Broome County	11	0.02
New York (city)	595	0.01
Manhattan (borough) New York County	206	0.01
Brooklyn (borough) Kings County	153	0.01
Queens (borough) Queens County	117	0.01
Bronx (borough) Bronx County	108	0.01

African, Sub-Saharan: Ethiopian

Top 10 Places Sorted by Population
Based on all places, regardless of total population

Place	Population	%
New York (city)	2,869	0.04
Manhattan (borough) New York County	1,043	0.07
Bronx (borough) Bronx County	945	0.07
Queens (borough) Queens County	505	0.02
Brooklyn (borough) Kings County	330	0.01
Rochester (city) Monroe County	227	0.11
Buffalo (city) Erie County	223	0.08
Irondequoit (cdp/town) Monroe County	192	0.37
Henrietta (town) Monroe County	177	0.42
Yonkers (city) Westchester County	159	0.08

Top 10 Places Sorted by Percent of Total Population
Based on all places, regardless of total population

Place	Population	%
Lloyd Harbor (village) Suffolk County	110	3.00
Jasper (town) Steuben County	23	1.84
Sparta (town) Livingston County	27	1.62
Deferiet (village) Jefferson County	7	1.49
North Salem (town) Westchester County	75	1.47
Manhasset Hills (cdp) Nassau County	38	1.03
Pomona (village) Rockland County	31	0.88
Elmsford (village) Westchester County	39	0.84
Bedford (town) Westchester County	117	0.67
Athens (village) Greene County	8	0.48

Top 10 Places Sorted by Percent of Total Population
Based on places with total population of 50,000 or more

Place	Population	%
Irondequoit (cdp/town) Monroe County	192	0.37
Rochester (city) Monroe County	227	0.11
Buffalo (city) Erie County	223	0.08
Yonkers (city) Westchester County	159	0.08
Manhattan (borough) New York County	1,043	0.07
Bronx (borough) Bronx County	945	0.07
Huntington (town) Suffolk County	125	0.06
Amherst (town) Erie County	71	0.06
Greece (town) Monroe County	49	0.05
Niagara Falls (city) Niagara County	24	0.05

Please refer to the Explanation of Data in the front of the book for more detailed information.

African, Sub-Saharan: Ghanaian

Top 10 Places Sorted by Population
Based on all places, regardless of total population

Place	Population	%
New York (city)	19,782	0.24
Bronx (borough) Bronx County	13,490	0.99
Brooklyn (borough) Kings County	3,898	0.16
Queens (borough) Queens County	1,326	0.06
Manhattan (borough) New York County	818	0.05
Yonkers (city) Westchester County	585	0.30
Mount Vernon (city) Westchester County	347	0.52
Hempstead (town) Nassau County	306	0.04
Staten Island (borough) Richmond County	250	0.05
Lakeview (cdp) Nassau County	169	3.03

Top 10 Places Sorted by Percent of Total Population
Based on all places, regardless of total population

Place	Population	%
Lakeview (cdp) Nassau County	169	3.03
South Blooming Grove (village) Orange County	57	1.73
Coxsackie (village) Greene County	44	1.54
Katonah (cdp) Westchester County	20	1.36
West Haverstraw (village) Rockland County	108	1.07
Wheatley Heights (cdp) Suffolk County	64	1.03
Bronx (borough) Bronx County	13,490	0.99
Hillcrest (cdp) Rockland County	77	0.94
Flower Hill (village) Nassau County	39	0.85
SUNY Oswego (cdp) Oswego County	30	0.67

Top 10 Places Sorted by Percent of Total Population
Based on places with total population of 50,000 or more

Place	Population	%
Bronx (borough) Bronx County	13,490	0.99
Mount Vernon (city) Westchester County	347	0.52
Yonkers (city) Westchester County	585	0.30
New York (city)	19,782	0.24
Troy (city) Rensselaer County	91	0.18
Brooklyn (borough) Kings County	3,898	0.16
Albany (city) Albany County	143	0.15
Clarkstown (town) Rockland County	99	0.12
Clay (town) Onondaga County	65	0.11
Syracuse (city) Onondaga County	113	0.08

African, Sub-Saharan: Kenyan

Top 10 Places Sorted by Population
Based on all places, regardless of total population

Place	Population	%
New York (city)	344	<0.01
Yonkers (city) Westchester County	107	<0.05
Albany (city) Albany County	101	0.10
Queens (borough) Queens County	96	<0.01
Tonawanda (cdp) Erie County	86	0.15
Tonawanda (town) Erie County	86	0.12
West End (cdp) Otsego County	81	5.18
Oneonta (town) Otsego County	81	1.56
Staten Island (borough) Richmond County	78	0.02
Brooklyn (borough) Kings County	77	<0.01

Top 10 Places Sorted by Percent of Total Population
Based on all places, regardless of total population

Place	Population	%
West End (cdp) Otsego County	81	5.18
Oneonta (town) Otsego County	81	1.56
Houghton (cdp) Allegany County	22	1.29
Piermont (village) Rockland County	32	1.27
Caneadea (town) Allegany County	22	0.86
Mount Ivy (cdp) Rockland County	50	0.76
Horseheads (village) Chemung County	39	0.61
Youngstown (village) Niagara County	8	0.42
Hamilton (village) Madison County	10	0.28
Ossining (village) Westchester County	66	0.27

Top 10 Places Sorted by Percent of Total Population
Based on places with total population of 50,000 or more

Place	Population	%
Tonawanda (cdp) Erie County	86	0.15
Tonawanda (town) Erie County	86	0.12
Schenectady (city) Schenectady County	69	0.11
Albany (city) Albany County	101	0.10

Greenburgh (town) Westchester County	55	0.06
Yonkers (city) Westchester County	107	0.05
New Rochelle (city) Westchester County	19	0.03
Staten Island (borough) Richmond County	78	0.02
Utica (city) Oneida County	15	0.02
Buffalo (city) Erie County	38	0.01

African, Sub-Saharan: Liberian

Top 10 Places Sorted by Population
Based on all places, regardless of total population

Place	Population	%
New York (city)	1,991	0.02
Staten Island (borough) Richmond County	532	0.11
Brooklyn (borough) Kings County	452	0.02
Bronx (borough) Bronx County	450	0.03
Queens (borough) Queens County	381	0.02
Babylon (town) Suffolk County	309	0.14
Wheatley Heights (cdp) Suffolk County	251	4.05
Syracuse (city) Onondaga County	246	0.17
Manhattan (borough) New York County	176	0.01
Rochester (city) Monroe County	89	0.04

Top 10 Places Sorted by Percent of Total Population
Based on all places, regardless of total population

Place	Population	%
Wheatley Heights (cdp) Suffolk County	251	4.05
Copake (town) Columbia County	16	0.45
Wyandanch (cdp) Suffolk County	33	0.30
Smithville (town) Chenango County	4	0.29
Saddle Rock (village) Nassau County	3	0.29
Danby (town) Tompkins County	9	0.28
Port Jervis (city) Orange County	22	0.25
Syracuse (city) Onondaga County	246	0.17
Babylon (town) Suffolk County	309	0.14
Utica (city) Oneida County	88	0.14

Top 10 Places Sorted by Percent of Total Population
Based on places with total population of 50,000 or more

Place	Population	%
Syracuse (city) Onondaga County	246	0.17
Babylon (town) Suffolk County	309	0.14
Utica (city) Oneida County	88	0.14
Staten Island (borough) Richmond County	532	0.11
Rochester (city) Monroe County	89	0.04
Schenectady (city) Schenectady County	24	0.04
Bronx (borough) Bronx County	450	0.03
Buffalo (city) Erie County	74	0.03
New York (city)	1,991	0.02
Brooklyn (borough) Kings County	452	0.02

African, Sub-Saharan: Nigerian

Top 10 Places Sorted by Population
Based on all places, regardless of total population

Place	Population	%
New York (city)	21,507	0.27
Queens (borough) Queens County	6,304	0.29
Brooklyn (borough) Kings County	6,033	0.24
Bronx (borough) Bronx County	5,538	0.41
Manhattan (borough) New York County	1,953	0.12
Staten Island (borough) Richmond County	1,679	0.36
Hempstead (town) Nassau County	1,115	0.15
Babylon (town) Suffolk County	707	0.33
Yonkers (city) Westchester County	442	0.23
Hempstead (village) Nassau County	427	0.80

Top 10 Places Sorted by Percent of Total Population
Based on all places, regardless of total population

Place	Population	%
Wesley Hills (village) Rockland County	180	3.30
Wheatley Heights (cdp) Suffolk County	167	2.70
Deerpark (town) Orange County	196	2.47
Myers Corner (cdp) Dutchess County	134	2.10
Chester (village) Orange County	66	1.67
Wyandanch (cdp) Suffolk County	172	1.57
North Valley Stream (cdp) Nassau County	212	1.28
Orchard Park (village) Erie County	41	1.26
Rock Hill (cdp) Sullivan County	20	1.21
New Lebanon (town) Columbia County	29	1.17

Top 10 Places Sorted by Percent of Total Population
Based on places with total population of 50,000 or more

Place	Population	%
Hempstead (village) Nassau County	427	0.80
Bronx (borough) Bronx County	5,538	0.41
Staten Island (borough) Richmond County	1,679	0.36
Babylon (town) Suffolk County	707	0.33
Queens (borough) Queens County	6,304	0.29
Schenectady (city) Schenectady County	186	0.28
New York (city)	21,507	0.27
Greenburgh (town) Westchester County	231	0.26
Brooklyn (borough) Kings County	6,033	0.24
Yonkers (city) Westchester County	442	0.23

African, Sub-Saharan: Senegalese

Top 10 Places Sorted by Population
Based on all places, regardless of total population

Place	Population	%
New York (city)	2,895	0.04
Manhattan (borough) New York County	1,216	0.08
Bronx (borough) Bronx County	1,068	0.08
Brooklyn (borough) Kings County	401	0.02
Staten Island (borough) Richmond County	126	0.03
Queens (borough) Queens County	84	<0.01
Mahopac (cdp) Putnam County	64	0.84
Carmel (town) Putnam County	64	0.19
Haverstraw (village) Rockland County	52	0.45
Haverstraw (town) Rockland County	52	0.14

Top 10 Places Sorted by Percent of Total Population
Based on all places, regardless of total population

Place	Population	%
Cattaraugus Reservation Erie County	18	0.96
Mahopac (cdp) Putnam County	64	0.84
Clayton (village) Jefferson County	17	0.83
Haverstraw (village) Rockland County	52	0.45
Sackets Harbor (village) Jefferson County	6	0.44
SUNY Oswego (cdp) Oswego County	19	0.43
Crown Heights (cdp) Dutchess County	12	0.42
Clayton (town) Jefferson County	17	0.34
Oswego (town) Oswego County	19	0.24
Carmel (town) Putnam County	64	0.19

Top 10 Places Sorted by Percent of Total Population
Based on places with total population of 50,000 or more

Place	Population	%
Manhattan (borough) New York County	1,216	0.08
Bronx (borough) Bronx County	1,068	0.08
New York (city)	2,895	0.04
Staten Island (borough) Richmond County	126	0.03
Brooklyn (borough) Kings County	401	0.02
Mount Vernon (city) Westchester County	12	0.02
Yonkers (city) Westchester County	21	0.01
Queens (borough) Queens County	84	<0.01
Albany (city) Albany County	0	0.00
Amherst (town) Erie County	0	0.00

African, Sub-Saharan: Sierra Leonean

Top 10 Places Sorted by Population
Based on all places, regardless of total population

Place	Population	%
New York (city)	1,572	0.02
Bronx (borough) Bronx County	759	0.06
Manhattan (borough) New York County	422	0.03
Brooklyn (borough) Kings County	147	0.01
Queens (borough) Queens County	127	0.01
Staten Island (borough) Richmond County	117	0.03
Dryden (town) Tompkins County	22	0.15
Mount Vernon (city) Westchester County	22	0.03
Buffalo (city) Erie County	17	0.01
New Rochelle (city) Westchester County	15	0.02

Top 10 Places Sorted by Percent of Total Population
Based on all places, regardless of total population

Place	Population	%
Hamilton (village) Madison County	12	0.34
Hamilton (town) Madison County	12	0.18
Manhasset (cdp) Nassau County	13	0.16

Place	Population	%
Dryden (town) Tompkins County	22	0.15
Bronx (borough) Bronx County	759	0.06
Baldwin (cdp) Nassau County	11	0.05
Manhattan (borough) New York County	422	0.03
Staten Island (borough) Richmond County	117	0.03
Mount Vernon (city) Westchester County	22	0.03
New York (city)	1,572	0.02

Top 10 Places Sorted by Percent of Total Population
Based on places with total population of 50,000 or more

Place	Population	%
Bronx (borough) Bronx County	759	0.06
Manhattan (borough) New York County	422	0.03
Staten Island (borough) Richmond County	117	0.03
Mount Vernon (city) Westchester County	22	0.03
New York (city)	1,572	0.02
New Rochelle (city) Westchester County	15	0.02
Greenburgh (town) Westchester County	14	0.02
Brooklyn (borough) Kings County	147	0.01
Queens (borough) Queens County	127	0.01
Buffalo (city) Erie County	17	0.01

African, Sub-Saharan: Somalian

Top 10 Places Sorted by Population
Based on all places, regardless of total population

Place	Population	%
Rochester (city) Monroe County	980	0.46
Buffalo (city) Erie County	858	0.32
New York (city)	518	0.01
Syracuse (city) Onondaga County	478	0.33
Brooklyn (borough) Kings County	260	0.01
Manhattan (borough) New York County	125	0.01
Utica (city) Oneida County	99	0.16
Queens (borough) Queens County	98	<0.01
Perinton (town) Monroe County	38	0.08
Newburgh (city) Orange County	35	0.12

Top 10 Places Sorted by Percent of Total Population
Based on all places, regardless of total population

Place	Population	%
Rochester (city) Monroe County	980	0.46
Syracuse (city) Onondaga County	478	0.33
Buffalo (city) Erie County	858	0.32
Port Jervis (city) Orange County	26	0.29
Utica (city) Oneida County	99	0.16
Newburgh (city) Orange County	35	0.12
Perinton (town) Monroe County	38	0.08
Uniondale (cdp) Nassau County	15	0.06
New York (city)	518	0.01
Brooklyn (borough) Kings County	260	0.01

Top 10 Places Sorted by Percent of Total Population
Based on places with total population of 50,000 or more

Place	Population	%
Rochester (city) Monroe County	980	0.46
Syracuse (city) Onondaga County	478	0.33
Buffalo (city) Erie County	858	0.32
Utica (city) Oneida County	99	0.16
New York (city)	518	0.01
Brooklyn (borough) Kings County	260	0.01
Manhattan (borough) New York County	125	0.01
Queens (borough) Queens County	98	<0.01
Bronx (borough) Bronx County	35	<0.01
Hempstead (town) Nassau County	15	<0.01

African, Sub-Saharan: South African

Top 10 Places Sorted by Population
Based on all places, regardless of total population

Place	Population	%
New York (city)	2,116	0.03
Manhattan (borough) New York County	1,372	0.09
Queens (borough) Queens County	356	0.02
Brooklyn (borough) Kings County	320	0.01
New Rochelle (city) Westchester County	179	0.24
Hempstead (town) Nassau County	104	0.01
Scarsdale (town/village) Westchester County	80	0.47
Cortlandt (town) Westchester County	80	0.20
White Plains (city) Westchester County	78	0.14
Mount Pleasant (town) Westchester County	77	0.18

Top 10 Places Sorted by Percent of Total Population
Based on all places, regardless of total population

Place	Population	%
Linwood (cdp) Livingston County	64	48.85
Cape Vincent (village) Jefferson County	15	2.21
York (town) Livingston County	64	1.89
Kinderhook (village) Columbia County	24	1.71
Woodsburgh (village) Nassau County	10	1.34
Rhinebeck (village) Dutchess County	29	1.05
Great Neck Estates (village) Nassau County	25	0.92
Pomona (village) Rockland County	30	0.85
Pelham Manor (village) Westchester County	43	0.79
Orangeburg (cdp) Rockland County	33	0.76

Top 10 Places Sorted by Percent of Total Population
Based on places with total population of 50,000 or more

Place	Population	%
New Rochelle (city) Westchester County	179	0.24
White Plains (city) Westchester County	78	0.14
Hamburg (town) Erie County	57	0.10
Manhattan (borough) New York County	1,372	0.09
Ramapo (town) Rockland County	56	0.05
Greece (town) Monroe County	48	0.05
Colonie (town) Albany County	32	0.04
New York (city)	2,116	0.03
Huntington (town) Suffolk County	63	0.03
North Hempstead (town) Nassau County	63	0.03

African, Sub-Saharan: Sudanese

Top 10 Places Sorted by Population
Based on all places, regardless of total population

Place	Population	%
New York (city)	1,303	0.02
Brooklyn (borough) Kings County	731	0.03
Queens (borough) Queens County	286	0.01
Buffalo (city) Erie County	268	0.10
Syracuse (city) Onondaga County	177	0.12
Bronx (borough) Bronx County	149	0.01
Manhattan (borough) New York County	137	0.01
Rochester (city) Monroe County	107	0.05
Greece (town) Monroe County	51	0.05
Brighton (cdp/town) Monroe County	47	0.13

Top 10 Places Sorted by Percent of Total Population
Based on all places, regardless of total population

Place	Population	%
Northeast Ithaca (cdp) Tompkins County	13	0.49
Morrisville (village) Madison County	11	0.43
Williamson (town) Wayne County	21	0.30
Eaton (town) Madison County	11	0.21
Portland (town) Chautauqua County	7	0.14
Brighton (cdp/town) Monroe County	47	0.13
Syracuse (city) Onondaga County	177	0.12
Russell (town) St. Lawrence County	2	0.12
Port Washington (cdp) Nassau County	17	0.11
Buffalo (city) Erie County	268	0.10

Top 10 Places Sorted by Percent of Total Population
Based on places with total population of 50,000 or more

Place	Population	%
Syracuse (city) Onondaga County	177	0.12
Buffalo (city) Erie County	268	0.10
Troy (city) Rensselaer County	28	0.06
Rochester (city) Monroe County	107	0.05
Greece (town) Monroe County	51	0.05
Brooklyn (borough) Kings County	731	0.03
Albany (city) Albany County	25	0.03
New York (city)	1,303	0.02
Queens (borough) Queens County	286	0.01
Bronx (borough) Bronx County	149	0.01

African, Sub-Saharan: Ugandan

Top 10 Places Sorted by Population
Based on all places, regardless of total population

Place	Population	%
New York (city)	256	<0.01
Manhattan (borough) New York County	125	0.01
Spring Valley (village) Rockland County	86	0.28

Place	Population	%
Ramapo (town) Rockland County	86	0.07
Queens (borough) Queens County	77	<0.01
Brooklyn (borough) Kings County	54	<0.01
Buffalo (city) Erie County	33	0.01
Syracuse (city) Onondaga County	26	0.02
Ithaca (town) Tompkins County	24	0.12
Mount Vernon (city) Westchester County	19	0.03

Top 10 Places Sorted by Percent of Total Population
Based on all places, regardless of total population

Place	Population	%
Hamilton (village) Madison County	11	0.31
Spring Valley (village) Rockland County	86	0.28
Hamilton (town) Madison County	11	0.17
Ithaca (town) Tompkins County	24	0.12
Ramapo (town) Rockland County	86	0.07
Mount Vernon (city) Westchester County	19	0.03
Syracuse (city) Onondaga County	26	0.02
White Plains (city) Westchester County	9	0.02
Manhattan (borough) New York County	125	0.01
Buffalo (city) Erie County	33	0.01

Top 10 Places Sorted by Percent of Total Population
Based on places with total population of 50,000 or more

Place	Population	%
Ramapo (town) Rockland County	86	0.07
Mount Vernon (city) Westchester County	19	0.03
Syracuse (city) Onondaga County	26	0.02
White Plains (city) Westchester County	9	0.02
Manhattan (borough) New York County	125	0.01
Buffalo (city) Erie County	33	0.01
New York (city)	256	<0.01
Queens (borough) Queens County	77	<0.01
Brooklyn (borough) Kings County	54	<0.01
Albany (city) Albany County	0	0.00

African, Sub-Saharan: Zimbabwean

Top 10 Places Sorted by Population
Based on all places, regardless of total population

Place	Population	%
New York (city)	414	0.01
Bronx (borough) Bronx County	108	0.01
Queens (borough) Queens County	107	<0.01
Manhattan (borough) New York County	100	0.01
Brooklyn (borough) Kings County	99	<0.01
Rochester (city) Monroe County	76	0.04
Buffalo (city) Erie County	45	0.02
Callicoon (town) Sullivan County	40	1.30
Oneonta (city) Otsego County	26	0.19
East Ithaca (cdp) Tompkins County	24	1.20

Top 10 Places Sorted by Percent of Total Population
Based on all places, regardless of total population

Place	Population	%
Callicoon (town) Sullivan County	40	1.30
East Ithaca (cdp) Tompkins County	24	1.20
Canton (village) St. Lawrence County	13	0.21
Oneonta (city) Otsego County	26	0.19
Ithaca (town) Tompkins County	24	0.12
Canton (town) St. Lawrence County	13	0.12
Rochester (city) Monroe County	76	0.04
Buffalo (city) Erie County	45	0.02
Bethlehem (town) Albany County	8	0.02
New York (city)	414	0.01

Top 10 Places Sorted by Percent of Total Population
Based on places with total population of 50,000 or more

Place	Population	%
Rochester (city) Monroe County	76	0.04
Buffalo (city) Erie County	45	0.02
New York (city)	414	0.01
Bronx (borough) Bronx County	108	0.01
Manhattan (borough) New York County	100	0.01
Queens (borough) Queens County	107	<0.01
Brooklyn (borough) Kings County	99	<0.01
Albany (city) Albany County	0	0.00
Amherst (town) Erie County	0	0.00
Babylon (town) Suffolk County	0	0.00

African, Sub-Saharan: Other

Top 10 Places Sorted by Population
Based on all places, regardless of total population

Place	Population	%
New York (city)	17,415	0.22
Bronx (borough) Bronx County	10,539	0.77
Manhattan (borough) New York County	3,545	0.22
Brooklyn (borough) Kings County	1,881	0.08
Queens (borough) Queens County	1,219	0.06
New Rochelle (city) Westchester County	365	0.48
Rochester (city) Monroe County	309	0.15
Hempstead (town) Nassau County	275	0.04
Staten Island (borough) Richmond County	231	0.05
Mount Vernon (city) Westchester County	180	0.27

Top 10 Places Sorted by Percent of Total Population
Based on all places, regardless of total population

Place	Population	%
South Nyack (village) Rockland County	105	1.89
Pelham (village) Westchester County	68	1.00
Menands (village) Albany County	36	0.90
Woodbury (cdp) Nassau County	76	0.84
West Hempstead (cdp) Nassau County	143	0.78
Bronx (borough) Bronx County	10,539	0.77
Wheatley Heights (cdp) Suffolk County	46	0.74
Pomona (village) Rockland County	26	0.74
Ravena (village) Albany County	23	0.69
Pelham (town) Westchester County	76	0.62

Top 10 Places Sorted by Percent of Total Population
Based on places with total population of 50,000 or more

Place	Population	%
Bronx (borough) Bronx County	10,539	0.77
New Rochelle (city) Westchester County	365	0.48
Troy (city) Rensselaer County	159	0.32
Mount Vernon (city) Westchester County	180	0.27
New York (city)	17,415	0.22
Manhattan (borough) New York County	3,545	0.22
Schenectady (city) Schenectady County	133	0.20
Rochester (city) Monroe County	309	0.15
Brentwood (cdp) Suffolk County	80	0.15
Amherst (town) Erie County	170	0.14

Albanian

Top 10 Places Sorted by Population
Based on all places, regardless of total population

Place	Population	%
New York (city)	31,056	0.38
Staten Island (borough) Richmond County	8,108	1.75
Bronx (borough) Bronx County	7,835	0.57
Brooklyn (borough) Kings County	6,871	0.28
Queens (borough) Queens County	6,624	0.30
Yonkers (city) Westchester County	2,270	1.16
Manhattan (borough) New York County	1,618	0.10
Hempstead (town) Nassau County	1,052	0.14
Yorktown (town) Westchester County	628	1.75
Syracuse (city) Onondaga County	455	0.31

Top 10 Places Sorted by Percent of Total Population
Based on all places, regardless of total population

Place	Population	%
Yorktown Heights (cdp) Westchester County	170	10.19
Milton (cdp) Ulster County	101	8.68
Shrub Oak (cdp) Westchester County	134	7.40
Brewster Hill (cdp) Putnam County	91	3.78
Monroe (village) Orange County	310	3.73
Saltaire (village) Suffolk County	2	3.45
Farmington (town) Ontario County	388	3.35
Dix (town) Schuyler County	126	3.20
Tivoli (village) Dutchess County	30	3.02
Keene (town) Essex County	23	2.63

Top 10 Places Sorted by Percent of Total Population
Based on places with total population of 50,000 or more

Place	Population	%
Staten Island (borough) Richmond County	8,108	1.75
Yonkers (city) Westchester County	2,270	1.16
Bronx (borough) Bronx County	7,835	0.57
Colonie (town) Albany County	405	0.50

New Rochelle (city) Westchester County	370	0.49
Mount Vernon (city) Westchester County	303	0.45
Albany (city) Albany County	384	0.39
Clarkstown (town) Rockland County	328	0.39
New York (city)	31,056	0.38
Syracuse (city) Onondaga County	455	0.31

Alsatian

Top 10 Places Sorted by Population
Based on all places, regardless of total population

Place	Population	%
New York (city)	217	<0.01
Manhattan (borough) New York County	129	0.01
Albany (city) Albany County	51	0.05
New Bremen (town) Lewis County	50	1.85
Orchard Park (town) Erie County	40	0.14
De Witt (town) Onondaga County	39	0.15
Queens (borough) Queens County	37	<0.01
Amherst (town) Erie County	32	0.03
Hempstead (town) Nassau County	30	<0.01
Hamburg (town) Erie County	27	0.05

Top 10 Places Sorted by Percent of Total Population
Based on all places, regardless of total population

Place	Population	%
Rifton (cdp) Ulster County	20	3.31
New Bremen (town) Lewis County	50	1.85
Pittsford (village) Monroe County	12	0.85
Gainesville (village) Wyoming County	2	0.75
Wayne (town) Steuben County	4	0.41
Tioga (town) Tioga County	19	0.39
Berne (town) Albany County	10	0.36
East Aurora (village) Erie County	21	0.33
Great Neck Estates (village) Nassau County	9	0.33
Varick (town) Seneca County	6	0.33

Top 10 Places Sorted by Percent of Total Population
Based on places with total population of 50,000 or more

Place	Population	%
Albany (city) Albany County	51	0.05
Hamburg (town) Erie County	27	0.05
Tonawanda (cdp) Erie County	24	0.04
Amherst (town) Erie County	32	0.03
Tonawanda (town) Erie County	24	0.03
Manhattan (borough) New York County	129	0.01
Staten Island (borough) Richmond County	24	0.01
Islip (town) Suffolk County	18	0.01
New York (city)	217	<0.01
Queens (borough) Queens County	37	<0.01

American

Top 10 Places Sorted by Population
Based on all places, regardless of total population

Place	Population	%
New York (city)	209,430	2.59
Brooklyn (borough) Kings County	78,858	3.20
Manhattan (borough) New York County	54,694	3.45
Queens (borough) Queens County	45,604	2.07
Hempstead (town) Nassau County	23,869	3.17
Bronx (borough) Bronx County	16,297	1.19
Staten Island (borough) Richmond County	13,977	3.02
Brookhaven (town) Suffolk County	10,016	2.09
Oyster Bay (town) Nassau County	9,798	3.36
North Hempstead (town) Nassau County	7,110	3.18

Top 10 Places Sorted by Percent of Total Population
Based on all places, regardless of total population

Place	Population	%
Cumminsville (cdp) Livingston County	59	50.86
Northumberland (town) Saratoga County	1,519	30.31
Durham (town) Greene County	815	29.96
Ashland (town) Greene County	182	29.74
Schuylerville (village) Saratoga County	441	29.72
Hadley (cdp) Saratoga County	284	29.04
Lodi (village) Seneca County	137	28.84
Victory (village) Saratoga County	154	27.21
Cranberry Lake (cdp) St. Lawrence County	51	26.84
Hadley (town) Saratoga County	462	26.81

Top 10 Places Sorted by Percent of Total Population
Based on places with total population of 50,000 or more

Place	Population	%
Clarkstown (town) Rockland County	4,138	4.96
White Plains (city) Westchester County	2,743	4.91
Schenectady (city) Schenectady County	3,124	4.78
Ramapo (town) Rockland County	5,092	4.15
Union (town) Broome County	2,180	3.87
Greenburgh (town) Westchester County	3,324	3.79
Manhattan (borough) New York County	54,694	3.45
Clay (town) Onondaga County	1,975	3.40
Oyster Bay (town) Nassau County	9,798	3.36
New Rochelle (city) Westchester County	2,542	3.35

Arab: Total

Top 10 Places Sorted by Population
Based on all places, regardless of total population

Place	Population	%
New York (city)	82,165	1.02
Brooklyn (borough) Kings County	34,840	1.41
Queens (borough) Queens County	19,669	0.89
Manhattan (borough) New York County	13,828	0.87
Staten Island (borough) Richmond County	8,820	1.90
Bronx (borough) Bronx County	5,008	0.37
Hempstead (town) Nassau County	4,218	0.56
Yonkers (city) Westchester County	3,210	1.65
North Hempstead (town) Nassau County	2,078	0.93
Buffalo (city) Erie County	1,815	0.68

Top 10 Places Sorted by Percent of Total Population
Based on all places, regardless of total population

Place	Population	%
Clark Mills (cdp) Oneida County	109	9.71
Lackawanna (city) Erie County	1,753	9.61
Crown Point (town) Essex County	167	8.06
Saddle Rock (village) Nassau County	74	7.06
Hewlett Bay Park (village) Nassau County	33	6.36
Ravena (village) Albany County	200	6.03
Deerfield (town) Oneida County	230	5.48
Tannersville (village) Greene County	22	5.07
Northwest Ithaca (cdp) Tompkins County	56	4.85
New York Mills (village) Oneida County	161	4.77

Top 10 Places Sorted by Percent of Total Population
Based on places with total population of 50,000 or more

Place	Population	%
Utica (city) Oneida County	1,558	2.52
Staten Island (borough) Richmond County	8,820	1.90
Yonkers (city) Westchester County	3,210	1.65
Brooklyn (borough) Kings County	34,840	1.41
Amherst (town) Erie County	1,530	1.27
Colonie (town) Albany County	863	1.06
New York (city)	82,165	1.02
Cheektowaga (town) Erie County	905	1.02
North Hempstead (town) Nassau County	2,078	0.93
Queens (borough) Queens County	19,669	0.89

Arab: Arab

Top 10 Places Sorted by Population
Based on all places, regardless of total population

Place	Population	%
New York (city)	15,160	0.19
Brooklyn (borough) Kings County	7,609	0.31
Queens (borough) Queens County	2,283	0.10
Staten Island (borough) Richmond County	1,829	0.39
Manhattan (borough) New York County	1,720	0.11
Bronx (borough) Bronx County	1,719	0.13
Lackawanna (city) Erie County	1,331	7.30
Yonkers (city) Westchester County	1,036	0.53
Buffalo (city) Erie County	644	0.24
Henrietta (town) Monroe County	321	0.76

Top 10 Places Sorted by Percent of Total Population
Based on all places, regardless of total population

Place	Population	%
Lackawanna (city) Erie County	1,331	7.30
Brinckerhoff (cdp) Dutchess County	101	3.13
Millbrook (village) Dutchess County	48	2.94

Place	Population	%
Clark Mills (cdp) Oneida County	32	2.85
Morristown (town) St. Lawrence County	71	2.59
New Scotland (town) Albany County	209	2.41
Orange (town) Schuyler County	43	2.41
Cherry Valley (village) Otsego County	10	2.27
Spencerport (village) Monroe County	72	2.02
Hudson (city) Columbia County	127	1.85

Top 10 Places Sorted by Percent of Total Population
Based on places with total population of 50,000 or more

Place	Population	%
Yonkers (city) Westchester County	1,036	0.53
Staten Island (borough) Richmond County	1,829	0.39
Utica (city) Oneida County	198	0.32
Brooklyn (borough) Kings County	7,609	0.31
Cheektowaga (cdp) Erie County	224	0.30
Cheektowaga (town) Erie County	247	0.28
New Rochelle (city) Westchester County	187	0.25
Buffalo (city) Erie County	644	0.24
Clay (town) Onondaga County	136	0.23
Ramapo (town) Rockland County	245	0.20

Arab: Egyptian

Top 10 Places Sorted by Population
Based on all places, regardless of total population

Place	Population	%
New York (city)	17,698	0.22
Queens (borough) Queens County	6,551	0.30
Brooklyn (borough) Kings County	5,231	0.21
Staten Island (borough) Richmond County	3,292	0.71
Manhattan (borough) New York County	1,906	0.12
Hempstead (town) Nassau County	1,227	0.16
Bronx (borough) Bronx County	718	0.05
North Hempstead (town) Nassau County	529	0.24
Brookhaven (town) Suffolk County	435	0.09
Huntington (town) Suffolk County	425	0.21

Top 10 Places Sorted by Percent of Total Population
Based on all places, regardless of total population

Place	Population	%
Callicoon (town) Sullivan County	125	4.05
Oakdale (cdp) Suffolk County	220	2.87
Orange Lake (cdp) Orange County	183	2.68
Deerfield (town) Oneida County	110	2.62
Northwest Ithaca (cdp) Tompkins County	28	2.43
Woodmere (cdp) Nassau County	418	2.39
Gordon Heights (cdp) Suffolk County	76	2.33
Woodridge (village) Sullivan County	20	2.23
Carlisle (town) Schoharie County	40	2.15
Herricks (cdp) Nassau County	75	1.91

Top 10 Places Sorted by Percent of Total Population
Based on places with total population of 50,000 or more

Place	Population	%
Staten Island (borough) Richmond County	3,292	0.71
Queens (borough) Queens County	6,551	0.30
Clarkstown (town) Rockland County	254	0.30
Levittown (cdp) Nassau County	136	0.25
North Hempstead (town) Nassau County	529	0.24
New York (city)	17,698	0.22
Brooklyn (borough) Kings County	5,231	0.21
Huntington (town) Suffolk County	425	0.21
Hempstead (town) Nassau County	1,227	0.16
Colonie (town) Albany County	125	0.15

Arab: Iraqi

Top 10 Places Sorted by Population
Based on all places, regardless of total population

Place	Population	%
New York (city)	1,137	0.01
Manhattan (borough) New York County	583	0.04
North Hempstead (town) Nassau County	500	0.22
Queens (borough) Queens County	315	0.01
Buffalo (city) Erie County	288	0.11
Hempstead (town) Nassau County	284	0.04
Dix Hills (cdp) Suffolk County	166	0.63
Huntington (town) Suffolk County	166	0.08
Brooklyn (borough) Kings County	134	0.01
West Hempstead (cdp) Nassau County	112	0.61

Top 10 Places Sorted by Percent of Total Population
Based on all places, regardless of total population

Place	Population	%
Saddle Rock (village) Nassau County	46	4.39
Kensington (village) Nassau County	28	2.32
Herricks (cdp) Nassau County	86	2.18
Water Mill (cdp) Suffolk County	28	1.83
Great Neck Gardens (cdp) Nassau County	16	1.76
Hewlett (cdp) Nassau County	94	1.40
Sands Point (village) Nassau County	33	1.24
Middleburgh (town) Schoharie County	46	1.23
Atlantic Beach (village) Nassau County	21	1.13
East Hills (village) Nassau County	71	1.04

Top 10 Places Sorted by Percent of Total Population
Based on places with total population of 50,000 or more

Place	Population	%
North Hempstead (town) Nassau County	500	0.22
Buffalo (city) Erie County	288	0.11
Huntington (town) Suffolk County	166	0.08
Smithtown (town) Suffolk County	89	0.08
Yonkers (city) Westchester County	103	0.05
Southampton (town) Suffolk County	28	0.05
Manhattan (borough) New York County	583	0.04
Hempstead (town) Nassau County	284	0.04
Ramapo (town) Rockland County	48	0.04
Cheektowaga (cdp) Erie County	30	0.04

Arab: Jordanian

Top 10 Places Sorted by Population
Based on all places, regardless of total population

Place	Population	%
New York (city)	1,298	0.02
Yonkers (city) Westchester County	907	0.47
Brooklyn (borough) Kings County	752	0.03
Queens (borough) Queens County	307	0.01
Poughkeepsie (town) Dutchess County	223	0.51
Hyde Park (town) Dutchess County	204	0.94
Staten Island (borough) Richmond County	183	0.04
Brookhaven (town) Suffolk County	178	0.04
Niagara (town) Niagara County	149	1.77

Top 10 Places Sorted by Percent of Total Population
Based on all places, regardless of total population

Place	Population	%
Fairview (cdp) Dutchess County	108	2.32
Niagara (town) Niagara County	149	1.77
Fremont (town) Sullivan County	20	1.62
Putnam Lake (cdp) Putnam County	52	1.42
Woodbury (village) Orange County	126	1.20
Liberty (town) Sullivan County	117	1.18
Woodbury (town) Orange County	126	1.14
La Grange (town) Dutchess County	175	1.12
Baywood (cdp) Suffolk County	82	1.04
Hyde Park (town) Dutchess County	204	0.94

Top 10 Places Sorted by Percent of Total Population
Based on places with total population of 50,000 or more

Place	Population	%
Yonkers (city) Westchester County	907	0.47
Amherst (town) Erie County	84	0.07
New Rochelle (city) Westchester County	46	0.06
Smithtown (town) Suffolk County	54	0.05
Greenburgh (town) Westchester County	45	0.05
Staten Island (borough) Richmond County	183	0.04
Brookhaven (town) Suffolk County	178	0.04
Islip (town) Suffolk County	122	0.04
White Plains (city) Westchester County	21	0.04
Brooklyn (borough) Kings County	752	0.03

Arab: Lebanese

Top 10 Places Sorted by Population
Based on all places, regardless of total population

Place	Population	%
New York (city)	11,682	0.14
Brooklyn (borough) Kings County	4,757	0.19
Manhattan (borough) New York County	3,331	0.21

Place	Population	%
Queens (borough) Queens County	2,228	0.10
Staten Island (borough) Richmond County	1,019	0.22
Amherst (town) Erie County	985	0.81
Utica (city) Oneida County	947	1.53
Hempstead (town) Nassau County	657	0.09
Whitestown (town) Oneida County	495	2.66
Buffalo (city) Erie County	481	0.18

Top 10 Places Sorted by Percent of Total Population
Based on all places, regardless of total population

Place	Population	%
Clark Mills (cdp) Oneida County	65	5.79
Crown Point (town) Essex County	94	4.54
New York Mills (village) Oneida County	145	4.30
Lewiston (village) Niagara County	105	3.88
Williamsville (village) Erie County	177	3.33
Yorkville (village) Oneida County	76	2.83
Vernon (town) Oneida County	144	2.68
Whitestown (town) Oneida County	495	2.66
Lacona (village) Oswego County	16	2.63
Pultneyville (cdp) Wayne County	20	2.61

Top 10 Places Sorted by Percent of Total Population
Based on places with total population of 50,000 or more

Place	Population	%
Utica (city) Oneida County	947	1.53
Amherst (town) Erie County	985	0.81
Tonawanda (cdp) Erie County	401	0.68
Tonawanda (town) Erie County	428	0.58
Troy (city) Rensselaer County	270	0.54
Cheektowaga (cdp) Erie County	338	0.45
Niagara Falls (city) Niagara County	228	0.45
Cheektowaga (town) Erie County	350	0.39
Clay (town) Onondaga County	213	0.37
Colonie (town) Albany County	267	0.33

Arab: Moroccan

Top 10 Places Sorted by Population
Based on all places, regardless of total population

Place	Population	%
New York (city)	8,987	0.11
Queens (borough) Queens County	3,459	0.16
Brooklyn (borough) Kings County	2,648	0.11
Manhattan (borough) New York County	1,592	0.11
Bronx (borough) Bronx County	667	0.05
Staten Island (borough) Richmond County	621	0.13
Hempstead (town) Nassau County	376	0.05
Ramapo (town) Rockland County	291	0.24
Lindenhurst (village) Suffolk County	209	0.76
Babylon (town) Suffolk County	209	0.10

Top 10 Places Sorted by Percent of Total Population
Based on all places, regardless of total population

Place	Population	%
Northwest Ithaca (cdp) Tompkins County	28	2.43
Philmont (village) Columbia County	24	2.07
Tupper Lake (village) Franklin County	68	1.77
South Valley Stream (cdp) Nassau County	76	1.44
Airmont (village) Rockland County	109	1.29
Brookville (village) Nassau County	43	1.24
Wheeler (town) Steuben County	14	1.19
Tupper Lake (town) Franklin County	68	1.13
Mechanicville (city) Saratoga County	58	1.12
Gouverneur (village) St. Lawrence County	44	1.10

Top 10 Places Sorted by Percent of Total Population
Based on places with total population of 50,000 or more

Place	Population	%
Ramapo (town) Rockland County	291	0.24
Queens (borough) Queens County	3,459	0.16
Colonie (town) Albany County	111	0.14
Staten Island (borough) Richmond County	621	0.13
White Plains (city) Westchester County	71	0.13
New York (city)	8,987	0.11
Brooklyn (borough) Kings County	2,648	0.11
Manhattan (borough) New York County	1,592	0.10
Babylon (town) Suffolk County	209	0.10
Mount Vernon (city) Westchester County	64	0.10

Arab: Palestinian

Top 10 Places Sorted by Population
Based on all places, regardless of total population

Place	Population	%
New York (city)	3,421	0.04
Brooklyn (borough) Kings County	1,482	0.06
Manhattan (borough) New York County	794	0.05
Queens (borough) Queens County	638	0.03
Staten Island (borough) Richmond County	479	0.10
Ravena (village) Albany County	200	6.03
Coeymans (town) Albany County	200	2.63
Poughkeepsie (town) Dutchess County	183	0.42
Islip (town) Suffolk County	166	0.05
Yonkers (city) Westchester County	139	0.07

Top 10 Places Sorted by Percent of Total Population
Based on all places, regardless of total population

Place	Population	%
Ravena (village) Albany County	200	6.03
Crown Point (town) Essex County	70	3.38
Coeymans (town) Albany County	200	2.63
Van Etten (town) Chemung County	18	1.43
Roslyn (village) Nassau County	35	1.28
Stuyvesant (town) Columbia County	24	1.19
Oakfield (village) Genesee County	22	1.07
Silver Creek (village) Chautauqua County	23	0.86
Farmingdale (village) Nassau County	58	0.71
Oakfield (town) Genesee County	22	0.68

Top 10 Places Sorted by Percent of Total Population
Based on places with total population of 50,000 or more

Place	Population	%
Staten Island (borough) Richmond County	479	0.10
Colonie (town) Albany County	72	0.09
Yonkers (city) Westchester County	139	0.07
Brooklyn (borough) Kings County	1,482	0.06
Manhattan (borough) New York County	794	0.05
Islip (town) Suffolk County	166	0.05
Babylon (town) Suffolk County	114	0.05
Syracuse (city) Onondaga County	66	0.05
New York (city)	3,421	0.04
Union (town) Broome County	25	0.04

Arab: Syrian

Top 10 Places Sorted by Population
Based on all places, regardless of total population

Place	Population	%
New York (city)	8,198	0.10
Brooklyn (borough) Kings County	5,890	0.24
Manhattan (borough) New York County	1,112	0.07
Staten Island (borough) Richmond County	584	0.13
Hempstead (town) Nassau County	512	0.07
Queens (borough) Queens County	420	0.02
New Hartford (town) Oneida County	351	1.60
Utica (city) Oneida County	248	0.40
Brookhaven (town) Suffolk County	220	0.05
Bronx (borough) Bronx County	192	0.01

Top 10 Places Sorted by Percent of Total Population
Based on all places, regardless of total population

Place	Population	%
Tannersville (village) Greene County	22	5.07
Chautauqua (cdp) Chautauqua County	12	4.55
Mountain Lodge Park (cdp) Orange County	74	3.98
Manchester (village) Ontario County	46	2.86
Beaver Dam Lake (cdp) Orange County	55	2.01
Fort Montgomery (cdp) Orange County	17	1.99
Taylor (town) Cortland County	11	1.98
West Glens Falls (cdp) Warren County	126	1.90
Chadwicks (cdp) Oneida County	22	1.84
Fillmore (cdp) Allegany County	10	1.63

Top 10 Places Sorted by Percent of Total Population
Based on places with total population of 50,000 or more

Place	Population	%
Utica (city) Oneida County	248	0.40
Brooklyn (borough) Kings County	5,890	0.24
Colonie (town) Albany County	116	0.14
Staten Island (borough) Richmond County	584	0.13

Place	Population	%
Greenburgh (town) Westchester County	107	0.12
Albany (city) Albany County	104	0.11
Clarkstown (town) Rockland County	88	0.11
New York (city)	8,198	0.10
Greece (town) Monroe County	97	0.10
Niagara Falls (city) Niagara County	44	0.09

Arab: Other

Top 10 Places Sorted by Population
Based on all places, regardless of total population

Place	Population	%
New York (city)	14,584	0.18
Brooklyn (borough) Kings County	6,337	0.26
Queens (borough) Queens County	3,468	0.16
Manhattan (borough) New York County	2,742	0.17
Bronx (borough) Bronx County	1,256	0.09
Staten Island (borough) Richmond County	781	0.17
Hempstead (town) Nassau County	664	0.09
North Hempstead (town) Nassau County	571	0.26
Binghamton (city) Broome County	521	1.10
Lackawanna (city) Erie County	402	2.20

Top 10 Places Sorted by Percent of Total Population
Based on all places, regardless of total population

Place	Population	%
Hewlett Bay Park (village) Nassau County	26	5.01
Gates (cdp) Monroe County	256	4.76
Saddle Rock (village) Nassau County	28	2.67
Lackawanna (city) Erie County	402	2.20
St. Regis Mohawk Reservation Franklin County	65	2.07
Depew (village) Erie County	303	1.96
Kings Point (village) Nassau County	92	1.85
Roslyn Heights (cdp) Nassau County	107	1.65
Mill Neck (village) Nassau County	13	1.61
Sands Point (village) Nassau County	41	1.54

Top 10 Places Sorted by Percent of Total Population
Based on places with total population of 50,000 or more

Place	Population	%
Cheektowaga (town) Erie County	244	0.27
Brooklyn (borough) Kings County	6,337	0.26
North Hempstead (town) Nassau County	571	0.26
Amherst (town) Erie County	270	0.22
Mount Vernon (city) Westchester County	148	0.22
Colonie (town) Albany County	155	0.19
New York (city)	14,584	0.18
Rochester (city) Monroe County	390	0.18
Manhattan (borough) New York County	2,742	0.17
Staten Island (borough) Richmond County	781	0.17

Armenian

Top 10 Places Sorted by Population
Based on all places, regardless of total population

Place	Population	%
New York (city)	10,159	0.13
Queens (borough) Queens County	4,658	0.21
Manhattan (borough) New York County	2,653	0.17
Brooklyn (borough) Kings County	2,300	0.09
Hempstead (town) Nassau County	1,451	0.19
Oyster Bay (town) Nassau County	1,383	0.47
Brookhaven (town) Suffolk County	643	0.13
North Hempstead (town) Nassau County	631	0.28
Huntington (town) Suffolk County	525	0.26
Troy (city) Rensselaer County	418	0.84

Top 10 Places Sorted by Percent of Total Population
Based on all places, regardless of total population

Place	Population	%
Harbor Hills (cdp) Nassau County	67	13.54
Tannersville (village) Greene County	34	7.83
Duane Lake (cdp) Schenectady County	16	6.61
Pine Hill (cdp) Ulster County	13	5.06
Pleasant Valley (cdp) Dutchess County	41	4.95
Boylston (town) Oswego County	19	3.98
Hewlett (cdp) Nassau County	264	3.92
Munsey Park (village) Nassau County	103	3.87
Pittsford (village) Monroe County	52	3.70
Chenango Bridge (cdp) Broome County	106	3.48

Top 10 Places Sorted by Percent of Total Population
Based on places with total population of 50,000 or more

Place	Population	%
Troy (city) Rensselaer County	418	0.84
Oyster Bay (town) Nassau County	1,383	0.47
Niagara Falls (city) Niagara County	156	0.31
Colonie (town) Albany County	244	0.30
North Hempstead (town) Nassau County	631	0.28
Huntington (town) Suffolk County	525	0.26
Queens (borough) Queens County	4,658	0.21
Yonkers (city) Westchester County	411	0.21
Greenburgh (town) Westchester County	175	0.20
Hempstead (town) Nassau County	1,451	0.19

Assyrian/Chaldean/Syriac

Top 10 Places Sorted by Population
Based on all places, regardless of total population

Place	Population	%
New York (city)	227	<0.01
Yonkers (city) Westchester County	157	0.08
Manhattan (borough) New York County	137	0.01
Clarkstown (town) Rockland County	51	0.06
Cortlandt (town) Westchester County	45	0.11
Brooklyn (borough) Kings County	44	<0.01
Congers (cdp) Rockland County	34	0.43
Greenburgh (town) Westchester County	29	0.03
Peekskill (city) Westchester County	26	0.11
North Hempstead (town) Nassau County	21	0.01

Top 10 Places Sorted by Percent of Total Population
Based on all places, regardless of total population

Place	Population	%
Tuxedo Park (village) Orange County	3	0.50
Congers (cdp) Rockland County	34	0.43
Plandome Heights (village) Nassau County	4	0.38
Cuyler (town) Cortland County	3	0.33
Fairfield (town) Herkimer County	5	0.30
New Paltz (village) Ulster County	8	0.12
East Williston (village) Nassau County	3	0.12
Cortlandt (town) Westchester County	45	0.11
Peekskill (city) Westchester County	26	0.11
Yonkers (city) Westchester County	157	0.08

Top 10 Places Sorted by Percent of Total Population
Based on places with total population of 50,000 or more

Place	Population	%
Yonkers (city) Westchester County	157	0.08
Clarkstown (town) Rockland County	51	0.06
Greenburgh (town) Westchester County	29	0.03
Manhattan (borough) New York County	137	0.01
North Hempstead (town) Nassau County	21	0.01
White Plains (city) Westchester County	8	0.01
New York (city)	227	<0.01
Brooklyn (borough) Kings County	44	<0.01
Hempstead (town) Nassau County	19	<0.01
Bronx (borough) Bronx County	18	<0.01

Australian

Top 10 Places Sorted by Population
Based on all places, regardless of total population

Place	Population	%
New York (city)	3,906	0.05
Manhattan (borough) New York County	2,719	0.17
Brooklyn (borough) Kings County	832	0.03
Queens (borough) Queens County	285	0.01
Hempstead (town) Nassau County	236	0.03
Huntington (town) Suffolk County	101	0.05
Islip (town) Suffolk County	100	0.03
Scarsdale (town/village) Westchester County	96	0.56
Putnam Valley (town) Putnam County	90	0.77
Albany (city) Albany County	88	0.09

Top 10 Places Sorted by Percent of Total Population
Based on all places, regardless of total population

Place	Population	%
Cape Vincent (village) Jefferson County	13	1.91
Galway (village) Saratoga County	2	1.85
Newport (village) Herkimer County	9	1.84

Place	Population	%
Andes (cdp) Delaware County	5	1.80
Bovina (town) Delaware County	9	1.76
Marlboro (cdp) Ulster County	63	1.57
Windham (town) Greene County	25	1.50
Ovid (village) Seneca County	7	1.47
Alexandria Bay (village) Jefferson County	14	1.28
Hagaman (village) Montgomery County	11	1.04

Top 10 Places Sorted by Percent of Total Population
Based on places with total population of 50,000 or more

Place	Population	%
Manhattan (borough) New York County	2,719	0.17
Niagara Falls (city) Niagara County	49	0.10
Albany (city) Albany County	88	0.09
Greece (town) Monroe County	87	0.09
Ramapo (town) Rockland County	86	0.07
Southampton (town) Suffolk County	38	0.07
New York (city)	3,906	0.05
Huntington (town) Suffolk County	101	0.05
Tonawanda (cdp) Erie County	29	0.05
North Hempstead (town) Nassau County	80	0.04

Austrian

Top 10 Places Sorted by Population
Based on all places, regardless of total population

Place	Population	%
New York (city)	30,712	0.38
Manhattan (borough) New York County	14,656	0.93
Queens (borough) Queens County	7,523	0.34
Brooklyn (borough) Kings County	5,123	0.21
Hempstead (town) Nassau County	4,963	0.66
Oyster Bay (town) Nassau County	3,412	1.17
Brookhaven (town) Suffolk County	2,867	0.60
North Hempstead (town) Nassau County	2,782	1.24
Islip (town) Suffolk County	2,019	0.61
Huntington (town) Suffolk County	2,004	0.99

Top 10 Places Sorted by Percent of Total Population
Based on all places, regardless of total population

Place	Population	%
West Hampton Dunes (village) Suffolk County	8	18.60
Harbor Hills (cdp) Nassau County	50	10.10
Great Neck Gardens (cdp) Nassau County	64	7.05
Saltaire (village) Suffolk County	4	6.90
Palenville (cdp) Greene County	70	6.17
Islip Terrace (cdp) Suffolk County	353	6.15
Cuylerville (cdp) Livingston County	25	5.76
High Falls (cdp) Ulster County	45	5.23
Ocean Beach (village) Suffolk County	6	5.22
Golden's Bridge (cdp) Westchester County	86	4.81

Top 10 Places Sorted by Percent of Total Population
Based on places with total population of 50,000 or more

Place	Population	%
Greenburgh (town) Westchester County	1,117	1.27
North Hempstead (town) Nassau County	2,782	1.24
Oyster Bay (town) Nassau County	3,412	1.17
Southampton (town) Suffolk County	621	1.10
Ramapo (town) Rockland County	1,328	1.08
White Plains (city) Westchester County	572	1.02
Huntington (town) Suffolk County	2,004	0.99
Clarkstown (town) Rockland County	827	0.99
Manhattan (borough) New York County	14,656	0.93
Amherst (town) Erie County	1,014	0.84

Basque

Top 10 Places Sorted by Population
Based on all places, regardless of total population

Place	Population	%
New York (city)	902	0.01
Manhattan (borough) New York County	428	0.03
Queens (borough) Queens County	159	0.01
Brooklyn (borough) Kings County	129	0.01
North Hempstead (town) Nassau County	121	0.05
Bronx (borough) Bronx County	109	0.01
Staten Island (borough) Richmond County	77	0.02
Mineola (village) Nassau County	54	0.29
Hempstead (town) Nassau County	43	0.01
Croton-on-Hudson (village) Westchester County	42	0.53

Top 10 Places Sorted by Percent of Total Population
Based on all places, regardless of total population

Place	Population	%
Plattekill (cdp) Ulster County	15	1.09
East Williston (village) Nassau County	17	0.67
Gardiner (town) Ulster County	35	0.62
Williston Park (village) Nassau County	39	0.54
Croton-on-Hudson (village) Westchester County	42	0.53
Fort Edward (village) Washington County	13	0.39
Mill Neck (village) Nassau County	3	0.37
Waterford (village) Saratoga County	7	0.34
Arlington (cdp) Dutchess County	13	0.31
Austerlitz (town) Columbia County	4	0.31

Top 10 Places Sorted by Percent of Total Population
Based on places with total population of 50,000 or more

Place	Population	%
North Hempstead (town) Nassau County	121	0.05
Manhattan (borough) New York County	428	0.03
Levittown (cdp) Nassau County	16	0.02
Staten Island (borough) Richmond County	77	0.02
New Rochelle (city) Westchester County	12	0.02
New York (city)	902	0.01
Queens (borough) Queens County	159	0.01
Brooklyn (borough) Kings County	129	0.01
Bronx (borough) Bronx County	109	0.01
Hempstead (town) Nassau County	43	0.01

Belgian

Top 10 Places Sorted by Population
Based on all places, regardless of total population

Place	Population	%
New York (city)	4,472	0.06
Manhattan (borough) New York County	2,470	0.16
Brooklyn (borough) Kings County	1,012	0.04
Ramapo (town) Rockland County	751	0.61
Queens (borough) Queens County	593	0.03
Hempstead (town) Nassau County	405	0.05
Brookhaven (town) Suffolk County	401	0.08
Monsey (cdp) Rockland County	400	2.66
Islip (town) Suffolk County	328	0.10
Staten Island (borough) Richmond County	266	0.06

Top 10 Places Sorted by Percent of Total Population
Based on all places, regardless of total population

Place	Population	%
DeKalb Junction (cdp) St. Lawrence County	41	12.58
Sheldon (town) Wyoming County	82	3.77
New Square (village) Rockland County	225	3.48
Odessa (village) Schuyler County	18	3.43
Wallkill (cdp) Ulster County	75	3.18
Westport (cdp) Essex County	14	3.11
Strykersville (cdp) Wyoming County	14	2.78
Cold Spring (village) Putnam County	47	2.77
Tuscarora Nation Reservation Niagara County	27	2.68
Monsey (cdp) Rockland County	400	2.66

Top 10 Places Sorted by Percent of Total Population
Based on places with total population of 50,000 or more

Place	Population	%
Ramapo (town) Rockland County	751	0.61
Greece (town) Monroe County	254	0.27
Irondequoit (cdp/town) Monroe County	93	0.18
White Plains (city) Westchester County	94	0.17
Manhattan (borough) New York County	2,470	0.16
New Rochelle (city) Westchester County	118	0.16
Clay (town) Onondaga County	68	0.12
Greenburgh (town) Westchester County	93	0.11
Islip (town) Suffolk County	328	0.10
Rochester (city) Monroe County	185	0.09

Brazilian

Top 10 Places Sorted by Population
Based on all places, regardless of total population

Place	Population	%
New York (city)	13,119	0.16
Queens (borough) Queens County	6,175	0.28
Manhattan (borough) New York County	4,541	0.29

Place	Population	%
Mount Vernon (city) Westchester County	2,013	3.00
Brooklyn (borough) Kings County	1,719	0.07
Rye (town) Westchester County	929	2.05
Islip (town) Suffolk County	895	0.27
Port Chester (village) Westchester County	803	2.81
New Rochelle (city) Westchester County	728	0.96
North Hempstead (town) Nassau County	613	0.27

Top 10 Places Sorted by Percent of Total Population
Based on all places, regardless of total population

Place	Population	%
Three Mile Bay (cdp) Jefferson County	21	9.95
Saddle Rock Estates (cdp) Nassau County	33	6.30
Sagaponack (village) Suffolk County	11	4.30
West Sand Lake (cdp) Rensselaer County	101	3.85
Mount Vernon (city) Westchester County	2,013	3.00
Port Chester (village) Westchester County	803	2.81
University at Buffalo (cdp) Erie County	156	2.77
Flanders (cdp) Suffolk County	120	2.66
Napanoch (cdp) Ulster County	24	2.26
Cragsmoor (cdp) Ulster County	8	2.22

Top 10 Places Sorted by Percent of Total Population
Based on places with total population of 50,000 or more

Place	Population	%
Mount Vernon (city) Westchester County	2,013	3.00
New Rochelle (city) Westchester County	728	0.96
White Plains (city) Westchester County	440	0.79
Brentwood (cdp) Suffolk County	418	0.76
Southampton (town) Suffolk County	289	0.51
Schenectady (city) Schenectady County	194	0.30
Manhattan (borough) New York County	4,541	0.29
Queens (borough) Queens County	6,175	0.28
Islip (town) Suffolk County	895	0.27
North Hempstead (town) Nassau County	613	0.27

British

Top 10 Places Sorted by Population
Based on all places, regardless of total population

Place	Population	%
New York (city)	21,065	0.26
Manhattan (borough) New York County	12,129	0.77
Brooklyn (borough) Kings County	4,749	0.19
Queens (borough) Queens County	2,457	0.11
Brookhaven (town) Suffolk County	1,235	0.26
Hempstead (town) Nassau County	1,197	0.16
Bronx (borough) Bronx County	1,115	0.08
Huntington (town) Suffolk County	840	0.42
Buffalo (city) Erie County	722	0.27
North Hempstead (town) Nassau County	705	0.32

Top 10 Places Sorted by Percent of Total Population
Based on all places, regardless of total population

Place	Population	%
Pierrepont Manor (cdp) Jefferson County	28	22.95
Salisbury Mills (cdp) Orange County	36	12.33
Gorham (cdp) Ontario County	47	8.08
Chazy (cdp) Clinton County	34	6.71
Montague (town) Lewis County	6	6.12
New Suffolk (cdp) Suffolk County	10	5.32
Prattsburgh (cdp) Steuben County	29	4.07
Old Forge (cdp) Herkimer County	20	3.88
Poquott (village) Suffolk County	45	3.85
Burke (village) Franklin County	7	3.85

Top 10 Places Sorted by Percent of Total Population
Based on places with total population of 50,000 or more

Place	Population	%
Manhattan (borough) New York County	12,129	0.77
Southampton (town) Suffolk County	404	0.71
Greenburgh (town) Westchester County	519	0.59
Union (town) Broome County	250	0.44
Huntington (town) Suffolk County	840	0.42
Greece (town) Monroe County	387	0.41
Troy (city) Rensselaer County	207	0.41
Irondequoit (cdp/town) Monroe County	189	0.37
Amherst (town) Erie County	438	0.36
North Hempstead (town) Nassau County	705	0.32

Bulgarian

Top 10 Places Sorted by Population
Based on all places, regardless of total population

Place	Population	%
New York (city)	5,011	0.06
Queens (borough) Queens County	2,090	0.10
Manhattan (borough) New York County	1,272	0.08
Brooklyn (borough) Kings County	1,128	0.05
Bronx (borough) Bronx County	521	0.04
Buffalo (city) Erie County	201	0.08
Hamburg (town) Erie County	192	0.34
Hempstead (town) Nassau County	181	0.02
West Hempstead (cdp) Nassau County	142	0.77
Brookhaven (town) Suffolk County	128	0.03

Top 10 Places Sorted by Percent of Total Population
Based on all places, regardless of total population

Place	Population	%
Bedford Hills (cdp) Westchester County	99	3.04
Wales (town) Erie County	81	2.72
Fairfield (town) Herkimer County	42	2.49
Pembroke (town) Genesee County	83	1.92
Maybrook (village) Orange County	44	1.48
Crompond (cdp) Westchester County	26	1.27
Walden (village) Orange County	82	1.19
Hilton (village) Monroe County	69	1.18
Glasco (cdp) Ulster County	22	0.95
Mayfield (village) Fulton County	8	0.92

Top 10 Places Sorted by Percent of Total Population
Based on places with total population of 50,000 or more

Place	Population	%
Hamburg (town) Erie County	192	0.34
White Plains (city) Westchester County	62	0.11
Queens (borough) Queens County	2,090	0.10
Manhattan (borough) New York County	1,272	0.08
Buffalo (city) Erie County	201	0.08
Amherst (town) Erie County	98	0.08
Cheektowaga (town) Erie County	73	0.08
New York (city)	5,011	0.06
Greenburgh (town) Westchester County	54	0.06
Brooklyn (borough) Kings County	1,128	0.05

Cajun

Top 10 Places Sorted by Population
Based on all places, regardless of total population

Place	Population	%
New York (city)	432	0.01
Manhattan (borough) New York County	224	0.01
Brooklyn (borough) Kings County	175	0.01
Catskill (village) Greene County	62	1.50
Catskill (town) Greene County	62	0.52
West Point (cdp) Orange County	54	0.57
Highlands (town) Orange County	54	0.43
Poughkeepsie (city) Dutchess County	41	0.13
Oyster Bay (town) Nassau County	37	0.01
Queens (borough) Queens County	33	<0.01

Top 10 Places Sorted by Percent of Total Population
Based on all places, regardless of total population

Place	Population	%
Catskill (village) Greene County	62	1.50
Madrid (cdp) St. Lawrence County	6	0.82
Brownville (village) Jefferson County	8	0.76
West Point (cdp) Orange County	54	0.57
Elma Center (cdp) Erie County	15	0.55
East Ithaca (cdp) Tompkins County	11	0.55
Catskill (town) Greene County	62	0.52
Chazy (town) Clinton County	21	0.49
West Sayville (cdp) Suffolk County	23	0.44
Kings Point (village) Nassau County	22	0.44

Top 10 Places Sorted by Percent of Total Population
Based on places with total population of 50,000 or more

Place	Population	%
Syracuse (city) Onondaga County	24	0.02
Union (town) Broome County	12	0.02
New York (city)	432	0.01
Manhattan (borough) New York County	224	0.01

Place	Population	%
Brooklyn (borough) Kings County	175	0.01
Oyster Bay (town) Nassau County	37	0.01
Islip (town) Suffolk County	23	0.01
North Hempstead (town) Nassau County	22	0.01
Huntington (town) Suffolk County	19	0.01
Queens (borough) Queens County	33	<0.01

Canadian

Top 10 Places Sorted by Population
Based on all places, regardless of total population

Place	Population	%
New York (city)	10,989	0.14
Manhattan (borough) New York County	5,646	0.36
Brooklyn (borough) Kings County	3,116	0.13
Queens (borough) Queens County	1,308	0.06
Hempstead (town) Nassau County	1,084	0.14
Brookhaven (town) Suffolk County	999	0.21
Huntington (town) Suffolk County	743	0.37
Ramapo (town) Rockland County	680	0.55
Amherst (town) Erie County	589	0.49
Babylon (town) Suffolk County	581	0.27

Top 10 Places Sorted by Percent of Total Population
Based on all places, regardless of total population

Place	Population	%
Fishers Landing (cdp) Jefferson County	10	18.87
Natural Bridge (cdp) Jefferson County	58	14.36
La Fargeville (cdp) Jefferson County	99	14.14
Cumminsville (cdp) Livingston County	9	7.76
Orleans (town) Jefferson County	164	6.09
Chateaugay (village) Franklin County	31	5.54
Birdsall (town) Allegany County	17	5.54
Waddington (village) St. Lawrence County	37	5.13
Richville (village) St. Lawrence County	15	5.12
Machias (cdp) Cattaraugus County	37	5.08

Top 10 Places Sorted by Percent of Total Population
Based on places with total population of 50,000 or more

Place	Population	%
Niagara Falls (city) Niagara County	442	0.87
Irondequoit (cdp/town) Monroe County	419	0.81
Hamburg (town) Erie County	368	0.65
Clay (town) Onondaga County	345	0.59
Ramapo (town) Rockland County	680	0.55
Greece (town) Monroe County	525	0.55
Amherst (town) Erie County	589	0.49
Tonawanda (cdp) Erie County	288	0.49
Tonawanda (town) Erie County	312	0.42
Colonie (town) Albany County	321	0.39

Carpatho Rusyn

Top 10 Places Sorted by Population
Based on all places, regardless of total population

Place	Population	%
New York (city)	249	<0.01
Manhattan (borough) New York County	112	0.01
Union (town) Broome County	101	0.18
Staten Island (borough) Richmond County	63	0.01
Brooklyn (borough) Kings County	53	<0.01
Yonkers (city) Westchester County	40	0.02
Johnson City (village) Broome County	39	0.26
Hempstead (town) Nassau County	36	<0.01
Oswego (town) Oswego County	28	0.35
Hauppauge (cdp) Suffolk County	26	0.12

Top 10 Places Sorted by Percent of Total Population
Based on all places, regardless of total population

Place	Population	%
Shenorock (cdp) Westchester County	20	1.02
New Hartford (village) Oneida County	15	0.78
Stewart Manor (village) Nassau County	13	0.60
Gang Mills (cdp) Steuben County	23	0.55
Oswego (town) Oswego County	28	0.35
North Salem (town) Westchester County	18	0.35
Erwin (town) Steuben County	23	0.29
Johnson City (village) Broome County	39	0.26
Fairview (cdp) Dutchess County	10	0.22
Persia (town) Cattaraugus County	5	0.20

(Canadian – Percent of Total Population, 50,000+)

Top 10 Places Sorted by Percent of Total Population
Based on places with total population of 50,000 or more

Place	Population	%
Union (town) Broome County	101	0.18
Niagara Falls (city) Niagara County	14	0.03
Yonkers (city) Westchester County	40	0.02
Smithtown (town) Suffolk County	26	0.02
Tonawanda (town) Erie County	13	0.02
Manhattan (borough) New York County	112	0.01
Staten Island (borough) Richmond County	63	0.01
Huntington (town) Suffolk County	20	0.01
Albany (city) Albany County	12	0.01
Cheektowaga (cdp) Erie County	6	0.01

Celtic

Top 10 Places Sorted by Population
Based on all places, regardless of total population

Place	Population	%
New York (city)	564	0.01
Manhattan (borough) New York County	304	0.02
Queens (borough) Queens County	169	0.01
Hornell (city) Steuben County	102	1.18
Huntington (town) Suffolk County	65	0.03
Babylon (town) Suffolk County	64	0.03
Oyster Bay (town) Nassau County	55	0.02
Islip (town) Suffolk County	53	0.02
Williston Park (village) Nassau County	48	0.66
North Hempstead (town) Nassau County	48	0.02

Top 10 Places Sorted by Percent of Total Population
Based on all places, regardless of total population

Place	Population	%
Napanoch (cdp) Ulster County	25	2.35
North Lynbrook (cdp) Nassau County	13	1.75
Katonah (cdp) Westchester County	22	1.50
Lewis (town) Essex County	18	1.41
St. Armand (town) Essex County	17	1.33
Cayuga (village) Cayuga County	6	1.32
Hornell (city) Steuben County	102	1.18
Clinton (town) Dutchess County	45	1.05
Chesterfield (town) Essex County	25	1.04
Delanson (village) Schenectady County	3	1.02

Top 10 Places Sorted by Percent of Total Population
Based on places with total population of 50,000 or more

Place	Population	%
Clay (town) Onondaga County	47	0.08
Hamburg (town) Erie County	43	0.08
Union (town) Broome County	27	0.05
Troy (city) Rensselaer County	23	0.05
Huntington (town) Suffolk County	65	0.03
Babylon (town) Suffolk County	64	0.03
Schenectady (city) Schenectady County	20	0.03
Utica (city) Oneida County	16	0.03
Irondequoit (cdp/town) Monroe County	14	0.03
Manhattan (borough) New York County	304	0.02

Croatian

Top 10 Places Sorted by Population
Based on all places, regardless of total population

Place	Population	%
New York (city)	11,304	0.14
Queens (borough) Queens County	7,054	0.32
Manhattan (borough) New York County	2,164	0.14
Hempstead (town) Nassau County	1,033	0.14
Oyster Bay (town) Nassau County	1,002	0.34
Brooklyn (borough) Kings County	998	0.04
Staten Island (borough) Richmond County	869	0.19
Huntington (town) Suffolk County	781	0.39
North Hempstead (town) Nassau County	672	0.30
Greenburgh (town) Westchester County	609	0.69

Top 10 Places Sorted by Percent of Total Population
Based on all places, regardless of total population

Place	Population	%
Castorland (village) Lewis County	21	5.44
North Lynbrook (cdp) Nassau County	30	4.04
Pleasantville (village) Westchester County	276	3.93

Place	Population	%
Irvington (village) Westchester County	245	3.82
Halesite (cdp) Suffolk County	78	3.70
Rockland (town) Sullivan County	124	3.22
Herricks (cdp) Nassau County	126	3.20
Palenville (cdp) Greene County	31	2.73
Strykersville (cdp) Wyoming County	13	2.58
North Sea (cdp) Suffolk County	133	2.57

Top 10 Places Sorted by Percent of Total Population
Based on places with total population of 50,000 or more

Place	Population	%
Greenburgh (town) Westchester County	609	0.69
Tonawanda (town) Erie County	326	0.44
Hamburg (town) Erie County	246	0.43
Southampton (town) Suffolk County	227	0.40
Huntington (town) Suffolk County	781	0.39
Tonawanda (cdp) Erie County	219	0.37
Oyster Bay (town) Nassau County	1,002	0.34
Queens (borough) Queens County	7,054	0.32
Amherst (town) Erie County	393	0.32
North Hempstead (town) Nassau County	672	0.30

Cypriot

Top 10 Places Sorted by Population
Based on all places, regardless of total population

Place	Population	%
New York (city)	960	0.01
Queens (borough) Queens County	644	0.03
Hempstead (town) Nassau County	254	0.03
Manhattan (borough) New York County	216	0.01
Oceanside (cdp) Nassau County	90	0.29
Huntington (town) Suffolk County	82	0.04
Valley Stream (village) Nassau County	68	0.18
Franklin Square (cdp) Nassau County	67	0.23
Yorktown (town) Westchester County	65	0.18
North Hempstead (town) Nassau County	64	0.03

Top 10 Places Sorted by Percent of Total Population
Based on all places, regardless of total population

Place	Population	%
Hillside (cdp) Ulster County	8	1.06
Eatons Neck (cdp) Suffolk County	12	0.89
Clarence Center (cdp) Erie County	17	0.79
Hewlett Harbor (village) Nassau County	7	0.60
Greenlawn (cdp) Suffolk County	56	0.43
Laurel Hollow (village) Nassau County	8	0.42
Balmville (cdp) Orange County	13	0.39
Muttontown (village) Nassau County	13	0.38
Lake Grove (village) Suffolk County	39	0.35
Roslyn (village) Nassau County	9	0.33

Top 10 Places Sorted by Percent of Total Population
Based on places with total population of 50,000 or more

Place	Population	%
Huntington (town) Suffolk County	82	0.04
Queens (borough) Queens County	644	0.03
Hempstead (town) Nassau County	254	0.03
North Hempstead (town) Nassau County	64	0.03
Oyster Bay (town) Nassau County	63	0.02
Hempstead (village) Nassau County	9	0.02
New York (city)	960	0.01
Manhattan (borough) New York County	216	0.01
Brookhaven (town) Suffolk County	51	0.01
Islip (town) Suffolk County	25	0.01

Czech

Top 10 Places Sorted by Population
Based on all places, regardless of total population

Place	Population	%
New York (city)	12,800	0.16
Manhattan (borough) New York County	4,820	0.30
Queens (borough) Queens County	3,464	0.16
Brooklyn (borough) Kings County	3,393	0.14
Brookhaven (town) Suffolk County	3,121	0.65
Hempstead (town) Nassau County	2,447	0.32
Islip (town) Suffolk County	2,026	0.61
Oyster Bay (town) Nassau County	1,379	0.47
Huntington (town) Suffolk County	1,271	0.63
Union (town) Broome County	929	1.65

Top 10 Places Sorted by Percent of Total Population
Based on all places, regardless of total population

Place	Population	%
West Hampton Dunes (village) Suffolk County	6	13.95
Durhamville (cdp) Oneida County	61	10.61
Pleasant Valley (cdp) Dutchess County	83	10.01
Lakeville (cdp) Livingston County	42	6.98
Shoreham (village) Suffolk County	45	6.73
Andes (cdp) Delaware County	16	5.76
Summerhill (town) Cayuga County	59	5.20
Boylston (town) Oswego County	24	5.03
Constantia (cdp) Oswego County	72	4.77
Williamson (cdp) Wayne County	103	4.33

Top 10 Places Sorted by Percent of Total Population
Based on places with total population of 50,000 or more

Place	Population	%
Union (town) Broome County	929	1.65
Brookhaven (town) Suffolk County	3,121	0.65
Huntington (town) Suffolk County	1,271	0.63
Islip (town) Suffolk County	2,026	0.61
Smithtown (town) Suffolk County	692	0.59
Colonie (town) Albany County	453	0.56
Clay (town) Onondaga County	312	0.54
Greece (town) Monroe County	507	0.53
New Rochelle (city) Westchester County	402	0.53
Oyster Bay (town) Nassau County	1,379	0.47

Czechoslovakian

Top 10 Places Sorted by Population
Based on all places, regardless of total population

Place	Population	%
New York (city)	4,870	0.06
Brooklyn (borough) Kings County	1,684	0.07
Queens (borough) Queens County	1,467	0.07
Manhattan (borough) New York County	1,256	0.08
Hempstead (town) Nassau County	1,054	0.14
Brookhaven (town) Suffolk County	917	0.19
Ramapo (town) Rockland County	654	0.53
Oyster Bay (town) Nassau County	618	0.21
Islip (town) Suffolk County	596	0.18
North Hempstead (town) Nassau County	493	0.22

Top 10 Places Sorted by Percent of Total Population
Based on all places, regardless of total population

Place	Population	%
Smallwood (cdp) Sullivan County	145	21.08
Ellisburg (village) Jefferson County	17	6.75
Yorkshire (cdp) Cattaraugus County	75	5.96
Walker Valley (cdp) Ulster County	28	5.22
Kensington (village) Nassau County	56	4.65
Greenville (cdp) Greene County	34	3.91
Bethel (town) Sullivan County	156	3.62
Preston-Potter Hollow (cdp) Albany County	9	3.30
Freedom (town) Cattaraugus County	75	3.18
Pleasant Valley (cdp) Dutchess County	26	3.14

Top 10 Places Sorted by Percent of Total Population
Based on places with total population of 50,000 or more

Place	Population	%
Union (town) Broome County	364	0.65
Ramapo (town) Rockland County	654	0.53
Tonawanda (cdp) Erie County	177	0.30
Smithtown (town) Suffolk County	310	0.26
Schenectady (city) Schenectady County	167	0.26
Tonawanda (town) Erie County	179	0.24
North Hempstead (town) Nassau County	493	0.22
Huntington (town) Suffolk County	435	0.22
Oyster Bay (town) Nassau County	618	0.21
Babylon (town) Suffolk County	438	0.21

Danish

Top 10 Places Sorted by Population
Based on all places, regardless of total population

Place	Population	%
New York (city)	7,018	0.09
Manhattan (borough) New York County	4,095	0.26
Brooklyn (borough) Kings County	1,267	0.05

Place	Population	%
Brookhaven (town) Suffolk County	1,229	0.26
Hempstead (town) Nassau County	1,023	0.14
Huntington (town) Suffolk County	809	0.40
Queens (borough) Queens County	792	0.04
Islip (town) Suffolk County	761	0.23
Oyster Bay (town) Nassau County	573	0.20
Staten Island (borough) Richmond County	479	0.10

Top 10 Places Sorted by Percent of Total Population
Based on all places, regardless of total population

Place	Population	%
Thousand Island Park (cdp) Jefferson County	16	14.41
Pine Hill (cdp) Ulster County	23	8.95
Windham (cdp) Greene County	37	8.53
Benton (town) Yates County	224	7.99
Hall (cdp) Ontario County	15	7.77
Dresden (village) Yates County	18	7.53
Shokan (cdp) Ulster County	53	6.85
Shrub Oak (cdp) Westchester County	111	6.13
Duane (town) Franklin County	10	5.65
Birdsall (town) Allegany County	17	5.54

Top 10 Places Sorted by Percent of Total Population
Based on places with total population of 50,000 or more

Place	Population	%
Troy (city) Rensselaer County	223	0.45
Huntington (town) Suffolk County	809	0.40
Albany (city) Albany County	303	0.31
Smithtown (town) Suffolk County	314	0.27
Manhattan (borough) New York County	4,095	0.26
Brookhaven (town) Suffolk County	1,229	0.26
Tonawanda (cdp) Erie County	151	0.26
Niagara Falls (city) Niagara County	134	0.26
Colonie (town) Albany County	195	0.24
Tonawanda (town) Erie County	179	0.24

Dutch

Top 10 Places Sorted by Population
Based on all places, regardless of total population

Place	Population	%
New York (city)	23,151	0.29
Manhattan (borough) New York County	10,414	0.66
Brooklyn (borough) Kings County	5,664	0.23
Brookhaven (town) Suffolk County	4,038	0.84
Queens (borough) Queens County	3,516	0.16
Colonie (town) Albany County	3,334	4.09
Hempstead (town) Nassau County	3,142	0.42
Rochester (city) Monroe County	2,898	1.37
Greece (town) Monroe County	2,890	3.03
Arcadia (town) Wayne County	2,484	17.31

Top 10 Places Sorted by Percent of Total Population
Based on all places, regardless of total population

Place	Population	%
Tuscarora (cdp) Livingston County	36	46.75
Malden-on-Hudson (cdp) Ulster County	104	32.20
Livonia Center (cdp) Livingston County	141	28.89
Hall (cdp) Ontario County	55	28.50
Clymer (town) Chautauqua County	431	24.83
Galway (village) Saratoga County	26	24.07
Pultneyville (cdp) Wayne County	183	23.92
Pierrepont Manor (cdp) Jefferson County	27	22.13
Blenheim (town) Schoharie County	64	19.39
Cattaraugus Reservation Chautauqua County	3	18.75

Top 10 Places Sorted by Percent of Total Population
Based on places with total population of 50,000 or more

Place	Population	%
Colonie (town) Albany County	3,334	4.09
Union (town) Broome County	1,823	3.24
Greece (town) Monroe County	2,890	3.03
Clay (town) Onondaga County	1,704	2.93
Troy (city) Rensselaer County	1,379	2.76
Irondequoit (cdp/town) Monroe County	1,310	2.54
Schenectady (city) Schenectady County	1,521	2.33
Albany (city) Albany County	1,664	1.70
Syracuse (city) Onondaga County	2,128	1.47
Utica (city) Oneida County	884	1.43

Eastern European

Top 10 Places Sorted by Population
Based on all places, regardless of total population

Place	Population	%
New York (city)	44,970	0.56
Manhattan (borough) New York County	25,277	1.60
Brooklyn (borough) Kings County	12,941	0.52
Hempstead (town) Nassau County	5,775	0.77
Queens (borough) Queens County	4,673	0.21
Oyster Bay (town) Nassau County	3,841	1.32
North Hempstead (town) Nassau County	3,769	1.69
Huntington (town) Suffolk County	2,012	1.00
Greenburgh (town) Westchester County	2,009	2.29
Bronx (borough) Bronx County	1,646	0.12

Top 10 Places Sorted by Percent of Total Population
Based on all places, regardless of total population

Place	Population	%
Great Neck Gardens (cdp) Nassau County	106	11.67
Saddle Rock Estates (cdp) Nassau County	60	11.45
Hewlett Harbor (village) Nassau County	109	9.29
Harbor Hills (cdp) Nassau County	44	8.89
East Hills (village) Nassau County	523	7.63
Old Westbury (village) Nassau County	297	7.54
Greenvale (cdp) Nassau County	33	7.35
Hewlett Neck (village) Nassau County	34	7.26
Scarsdale (town/village) Westchester County	1,208	7.06
Matinecock (village) Nassau County	54	7.05

Top 10 Places Sorted by Percent of Total Population
Based on places with total population of 50,000 or more

Place	Population	%
Greenburgh (town) Westchester County	2,009	2.29
North Hempstead (town) Nassau County	3,769	1.69
Manhattan (borough) New York County	25,277	1.60
Clarkstown (town) Rockland County	1,282	1.54
Oyster Bay (town) Nassau County	3,841	1.32
New Rochelle (city) Westchester County	870	1.15
Huntington (town) Suffolk County	2,012	1.00
White Plains (city) Westchester County	557	1.00
Ramapo (town) Rockland County	1,144	0.93
Hempstead (town) Nassau County	5,775	0.77

English

Top 10 Places Sorted by Population
Based on all places, regardless of total population

Place	Population	%
New York (city)	146,525	1.81
Manhattan (borough) New York County	77,799	4.91
Brooklyn (borough) Kings County	32,407	1.31
Brookhaven (town) Suffolk County	30,089	6.27
Hempstead (town) Nassau County	21,808	2.89
Queens (borough) Queens County	20,267	0.92
Islip (town) Suffolk County	13,963	4.18
Rochester (city) Monroe County	13,510	6.37
Huntington (town) Suffolk County	13,038	6.45
Greece (town) Monroe County	12,568	13.17

Top 10 Places Sorted by Percent of Total Population
Based on all places, regardless of total population

Place	Population	%
Thousand Island Park (cdp) Jefferson County	58	52.25
Dalton (cdp) Livingston County	165	51.24
Dering Harbor (village) Suffolk County	8	50.00
Redwood (cdp) Jefferson County	152	49.19
Denning (town) Ulster County	202	38.70
Davenport Center (cdp) Delaware County	113	38.18
Honeoye (cdp) Ontario County	266	37.62
Piffard (cdp) Livingston County	21	35.00
Central Bridge (cdp) Schoharie County	208	34.61
Saltaire (village) Suffolk County	20	34.48

Top 10 Places Sorted by Percent of Total Population
Based on places with total population of 50,000 or more

Place	Population	%
Clay (town) Onondaga County	8,266	14.23
Irondequoit (cdp/town) Monroe County	7,215	13.98
Greece (town) Monroe County	12,568	13.17
Union (town) Broome County	7,072	12.56

Niagara Falls (city) Niagara County	6,055	11.90
Tonawanda (cdp) Erie County	6,115	10.44
Southampton (town) Suffolk County	5,792	10.24
Colonie (town) Albany County	8,332	10.22
Amherst (town) Erie County	11,840	9.79
Tonawanda (town) Erie County	7,240	9.77

Estonian

Top 10 Places Sorted by Population
Based on all places, regardless of total population

Place	Population	%
New York (city)	1,057	0.01
Manhattan (borough) New York County	424	0.03
Brooklyn (borough) Kings County	340	0.01
Queens (borough) Queens County	198	0.01
Islip (town) Suffolk County	175	0.05
Hempstead (town) Nassau County	175	0.02
Huntington (town) Suffolk County	140	0.07
Oyster Bay (town) Nassau County	130	0.04
Brookhaven (town) Suffolk County	102	0.02
Bronx (borough) Bronx County	85	0.01

Top 10 Places Sorted by Percent of Total Population
Based on all places, regardless of total population

Place	Population	%
Redford (cdp) Clinton County	31	6.47
Fort Montgomery (cdp) Orange County	55	6.44
Warren (town) Herkimer County	36	3.18
Clarence (cdp) Erie County	78	2.64
Chenango Bridge (cdp) Broome County	32	1.05
Red Hook (village) Dutchess County	18	0.96
Preston (town) Chenango County	9	0.93
Orient (cdp) Suffolk County	5	0.83
Saranac (town) Clinton County	31	0.77
Yaphank (cdp) Suffolk County	47	0.76

Top 10 Places Sorted by Percent of Total Population
Based on places with total population of 50,000 or more

Place	Population	%
Cheektowaga (cdp) Erie County	78	0.10
Cheektowaga (town) Erie County	78	0.09
Huntington (town) Suffolk County	140	0.07
Greenburgh (town) Westchester County	57	0.07
Mount Vernon (city) Westchester County	45	0.07
Islip (town) Suffolk County	175	0.05
Oyster Bay (town) Nassau County	130	0.04
Ramapo (town) Rockland County	48	0.04
Greece (town) Monroe County	40	0.04
Manhattan (borough) New York County	424	0.03

European

Top 10 Places Sorted by Population
Based on all places, regardless of total population

Place	Population	%
New York (city)	66,267	0.82
Manhattan (borough) New York County	27,846	1.76
Brooklyn (borough) Kings County	27,499	1.11
Ramapo (town) Rockland County	8,814	7.18
Queens (borough) Queens County	6,584	0.30
Hempstead (town) Nassau County	5,650	0.75
Monsey (cdp) Rockland County	3,363	22.35
Oyster Bay (town) Nassau County	2,919	1.00
Bronx (borough) Bronx County	2,270	0.17
Huntington (town) Suffolk County	2,177	1.08

Top 10 Places Sorted by Percent of Total Population
Based on all places, regardless of total population

Place	Population	%
Kaser (village) Rockland County	1,293	29.15
Monsey (cdp) Rockland County	3,363	22.35
New Square (village) Rockland County	1,147	17.76
West Hampton Dunes (village) Suffolk County	6	13.95
Ghent (cdp) Columbia County	70	11.02
Adams Center (cdp) Jefferson County	179	10.45
Wesley Hills (village) Rockland County	551	10.11
Covington (town) Wyoming County	111	8.80
Claverack-Red Mills (cdp) Columbia County	72	8.56
Accord (cdp) Ulster County	50	8.40

Top 10 Places Sorted by Percent of Total Population
Based on places with total population of 50,000 or more

Place	Population	%
Ramapo (town) Rockland County	8,814	7.18
Manhattan (borough) New York County	27,846	1.76
Greenburgh (town) Westchester County	1,360	1.55
Albany (city) Albany County	1,362	1.39
White Plains (city) Westchester County	684	1.22
Union (town) Broome County	660	1.17
Brooklyn (borough) Kings County	27,499	1.11
Huntington (town) Suffolk County	2,177	1.08
New Rochelle (city) Westchester County	808	1.07
Troy (city) Rensselaer County	529	1.06

Finnish

Top 10 Places Sorted by Population
Based on all places, regardless of total population

Place	Population	%
New York (city)	3,519	0.04
Manhattan (borough) New York County	1,658	0.10
Brookhaven (town) Suffolk County	706	0.15
Queens (borough) Queens County	693	0.03
Brooklyn (borough) Kings County	692	0.03
Hempstead (town) Nassau County	647	0.09
Bronx (borough) Bronx County	291	0.02
Islip (town) Suffolk County	271	0.08
Oyster Bay (town) Nassau County	265	0.09
Dryden (town) Tompkins County	254	1.78

Top 10 Places Sorted by Percent of Total Population
Based on all places, regardless of total population

Place	Population	%
Van Etten (village) Chemung County	39	8.71
Van Etten (town) Chemung County	109	8.68
Freeville (village) Tompkins County	29	5.80
Ward (town) Allegany County	18	5.34
Spencer (town) Tioga County	151	4.80
Preston-Potter Hollow (cdp) Albany County	12	4.40
Hunter (village) Greene County	21	4.25
East Randolph (village) Cattaraugus County	21	4.07
Smyrna (village) Chenango County	6	3.51
Shelter Island (cdp) Suffolk County	45	3.45

Top 10 Places Sorted by Percent of Total Population
Based on places with total population of 50,000 or more

Place	Population	%
Southampton (town) Suffolk County	206	0.36
Amherst (town) Erie County	196	0.16
Tonawanda (cdp) Erie County	95	0.16
Brookhaven (town) Suffolk County	706	0.15
Troy (city) Rensselaer County	74	0.15
Clarkstown (town) Rockland County	119	0.14
Tonawanda (town) Erie County	95	0.13
Manhattan (borough) New York County	1,658	0.10
Smithtown (town) Suffolk County	120	0.10
Greenburgh (town) Westchester County	85	0.10

French, except Basque

Top 10 Places Sorted by Population
Based on all places, regardless of total population

Place	Population	%
New York (city)	67,195	0.83
Manhattan (borough) New York County	31,783	2.01
Brooklyn (borough) Kings County	14,137	0.57
Queens (borough) Queens County	12,532	0.57
Brookhaven (town) Suffolk County	8,961	1.87
Hempstead (town) Nassau County	8,239	1.09
Syracuse (city) Onondaga County	6,182	4.27
Colonie (town) Albany County	5,795	7.11
Bronx (borough) Bronx County	4,971	0.36
Troy (city) Rensselaer County	4,862	9.72

Top 10 Places Sorted by Percent of Total Population
Based on all places, regardless of total population

Place	Population	%
Witherbee (cdp) Essex County	175	70.56
Chazy (cdp) Clinton County	293	57.79
Redford (cdp) Clinton County	255	53.24

Redwood (cdp) Jefferson County		158	51.13
Saranac (town) Clinton County		1,685	41.73
Bellmont (town) Franklin County		720	39.80
Mooers (cdp) Clinton County		218	38.86
Three Mile Bay (cdp) Jefferson County		80	37.91
Byersville (cdp) Livingston County		23	37.70
Norfolk (cdp) St. Lawrence County		461	37.12

Top 10 Places Sorted by Percent of Total Population
Based on places with total population of 50,000 or more

Place	Population	%
Troy (city) Rensselaer County	4,862	9.72
Colonie (town) Albany County	5,795	7.11
Clay (town) Onondaga County	3,175	5.47
Schenectady (city) Schenectady County	2,862	4.38
Syracuse (city) Onondaga County	6,182	4.27
Greece (town) Monroe County	3,655	3.83
Albany (city) Albany County	3,690	3.77
Tonawanda (cdp) Erie County	2,149	3.67
Hamburg (town) Erie County	2,079	3.67
Union (town) Broome County	2,044	3.63

French Canadian

Top 10 Places Sorted by Population
Based on all places, regardless of total population

Place	Population	%
New York (city)	11,393	0.14
Manhattan (borough) New York County	5,246	0.33
Brooklyn (borough) Kings County	2,974	0.12
Brookhaven (town) Suffolk County	2,478	0.52
Queens (borough) Queens County	2,020	0.09
Syracuse (city) Onondaga County	1,782	1.23
Hempstead (town) Nassau County	1,779	0.24
Colonie (town) Albany County	1,591	1.95
Rochester (city) Monroe County	1,474	0.70
Buffalo (city) Erie County	1,376	0.52

Top 10 Places Sorted by Percent of Total Population
Based on all places, regardless of total population

Place	Population	%
Mooers (cdp) Clinton County	124	22.10
Champlain (town) Clinton County	1,079	18.59
Mooers (town) Clinton County	614	17.16
Rensselaer Falls (village) St. Lawrence County	75	15.56
Waverly (town) Franklin County	157	15.23
Tupper Lake (village) Franklin County	581	15.11
St. Regis Falls (cdp) Franklin County	57	14.73
Clinton (town) Clinton County	114	14.36
Schenevus (cdp) Otsego County	39	14.18
Salt Point (cdp) Dutchess County	46	14.11

Top 10 Places Sorted by Percent of Total Population
Based on places with total population of 50,000 or more

Place	Population	%
Troy (city) Rensselaer County	1,245	2.49
Clay (town) Onondaga County	1,241	2.14
Colonie (town) Albany County	1,591	1.95
Schenectady (city) Schenectady County	902	1.38
Greece (town) Monroe County	1,220	1.28
Syracuse (city) Onondaga County	1,782	1.23
Tonawanda (town) Erie County	881	1.19
Albany (city) Albany County	1,061	1.08
Hamburg (town) Erie County	586	1.04
Utica (city) Oneida County	620	1.00

German

Top 10 Places Sorted by Population
Based on all places, regardless of total population

Place	Population	%
New York (city)	272,827	3.38
Manhattan (borough) New York County	107,666	6.80
Brookhaven (town) Suffolk County	89,711	18.69
Hempstead (town) Nassau County	78,518	10.42
Queens (borough) Queens County	70,399	3.20
Brooklyn (borough) Kings County	52,798	2.14
Islip (town) Suffolk County	48,335	14.48
Oyster Bay (town) Nassau County	41,381	14.19
Buffalo (city) Erie County	35,760	13.44
Huntington (town) Suffolk County	33,758	16.70

Top 10 Places Sorted by Percent of Total Population
Based on all places, regardless of total population

Place	Population	%
Websters Crossing (cdp) Livingston County	42	100.00
Belleville (cdp) Jefferson County	78	66.67
South Lima (cdp) Livingston County	132	65.02
Farnham (village) Erie County	148	62.45
Corfu (village) Genesee County	453	58.83
Livonia Center (cdp) Livingston County	276	56.56
Allen (town) Allegany County	273	55.38
Java (town) Wyoming County	1,212	54.69
Machias (cdp) Cattaraugus County	393	53.91
Alexander (village) Genesee County	330	53.23

Top 10 Places Sorted by Percent of Total Population
Based on places with total population of 50,000 or more

Place	Population	%
Hamburg (town) Erie County	19,590	34.62
Tonawanda (cdp) Erie County	19,292	32.95
Tonawanda (town) Erie County	24,085	32.51
Cheektowaga (town) Erie County	26,125	29.39
Cheektowaga (cdp) Erie County	21,843	28.83
Greece (town) Monroe County	25,631	26.85
Amherst (town) Erie County	30,579	25.28
Clay (town) Onondaga County	14,237	24.51
Irondequoit (cdp/town) Monroe County	11,815	22.89
Smithtown (town) Suffolk County	23,592	20.06

German Russian

Top 10 Places Sorted by Population
Based on all places, regardless of total population

Place	Population	%
New York (city)	204	<0.01
Queens (borough) Queens County	78	<0.01
Troy (city) Rensselaer County	65	0.13
Brooklyn (borough) Kings County	55	<0.01
Buffalo (city) Erie County	41	0.02
Manhattan (borough) New York County	41	<0.01
Mastic (cdp) Suffolk County	40	0.28
Brookhaven (town) Suffolk County	40	0.01
Tonawanda (city) Erie County	33	0.22
Bronx (borough) Bronx County	30	<0.01

Top 10 Places Sorted by Percent of Total Population
Based on all places, regardless of total population

Place	Population	%
Lake George (town) Warren County	16	0.45
Garden City Park (cdp) Nassau County	26	0.33
Mastic (cdp) Suffolk County	40	0.28
Tonawanda (city) Erie County	33	0.22
Fort Drum (cdp) Jefferson County	17	0.14
Troy (city) Rensselaer County	65	0.13
Dobbs Ferry (village) Westchester County	13	0.12
Haverstraw (village) Rockland County	12	0.10
Wantagh (cdp) Nassau County	17	0.09
Le Ray (town) Jefferson County	17	0.08

Top 10 Places Sorted by Percent of Total Population
Based on places with total population of 50,000 or more

Place	Population	%
Troy (city) Rensselaer County	65	0.13
Irondequoit (cdp/town) Monroe County	28	0.05
Niagara Falls (city) Niagara County	16	0.03
Buffalo (city) Erie County	41	0.02
Cheektowaga (cdp) Erie County	12	0.02
Brookhaven (town) Suffolk County	40	0.01
North Hempstead (town) Nassau County	26	0.01
Yonkers (city) Westchester County	14	0.01
Greenburgh (town) Westchester County	13	0.01
Cheektowaga (town) Erie County	12	0.01

Greek

Top 10 Places Sorted by Population
Based on all places, regardless of total population

Place	Population	%
New York (city)	76,597	0.95
Queens (borough) Queens County	41,654	1.89
Brooklyn (borough) Kings County	14,075	0.57

Manhattan (borough) New York County		13,078	0.83
Hempstead (town) Nassau County		10,033	1.33
Oyster Bay (town) Nassau County		6,908	2.37
Brookhaven (town) Suffolk County		5,703	1.19
Staten Island (borough) Richmond County		4,183	0.90
Bronx (borough) Bronx County		3,607	0.26
North Hempstead (town) Nassau County		3,568	1.60

Top 10 Places Sorted by Percent of Total Population
Based on all places, regardless of total population

Place	Population	%
Harbor Hills (cdp) Nassau County	94	18.99
Plandome Manor (village) Nassau County	97	11.02
Manhasset Hills (cdp) Nassau County	328	8.90
Old Brookville (village) Nassau County	189	8.49
Sparkill (cdp) Rockland County	114	8.25
Halcott (town) Greene County	20	7.52
Shinnecock Hills (cdp) Suffolk County	133	7.25
High Falls (cdp) Ulster County	62	7.20
Bellerose (village) Nassau County	84	6.75
Mattituck (cdp) Suffolk County	279	6.73

Top 10 Places Sorted by Percent of Total Population
Based on places with total population of 50,000 or more

Place	Population	%
Smithtown (town) Suffolk County	3,078	2.62
Oyster Bay (town) Nassau County	6,908	2.37
Levittown (cdp) Nassau County	1,100	2.06
Queens (borough) Queens County	41,654	1.89
Southampton (town) Suffolk County	995	1.76
Huntington (town) Suffolk County	3,284	1.62
North Hempstead (town) Nassau County	3,568	1.60
Greenburgh (town) Westchester County	1,202	1.37
Hempstead (town) Nassau County	10,033	1.33
Brookhaven (town) Suffolk County	5,703	1.19

Guyanese

Top 10 Places Sorted by Population
Based on all places, regardless of total population

Place	Population	%
New York (city)	107,972	1.34
Queens (borough) Queens County	53,961	2.45
Brooklyn (borough) Kings County	38,963	1.58
Bronx (borough) Bronx County	11,837	0.87
Hempstead (town) Nassau County	3,520	0.47
Manhattan (borough) New York County	2,259	0.14
Schenectady (city) Schenectady County	1,915	2.93
Staten Island (borough) Richmond County	952	0.21
Valley Stream (village) Nassau County	840	2.27
Babylon (town) Suffolk County	747	0.35

Top 10 Places Sorted by Percent of Total Population
Based on all places, regardless of total population

Place	Population	%
St. Regis Mohawk Reservation Franklin County	162	5.17
Greenville (town) Orange County	161	3.57
Hillcrest (cdp) Rockland County	280	3.42
Schenectady (city) Schenectady County	1,915	2.93
Manhasset Hills (cdp) Nassau County	102	2.77
Highland (cdp) Ulster County	149	2.62
Batavia (town) Genesee County	172	2.60
Queens (borough) Queens County	53,961	2.45
Menands (village) Albany County	97	2.43
Valley Stream (village) Nassau County	840	2.27

Top 10 Places Sorted by Percent of Total Population
Based on places with total population of 50,000 or more

Place	Population	%
Schenectady (city) Schenectady County	1,915	2.93
Queens (borough) Queens County	53,961	2.45
Brooklyn (borough) Kings County	38,963	1.58
New York (city)	107,972	1.34
Bronx (borough) Bronx County	11,837	0.87
Hempstead (village) Nassau County	307	0.58
Mount Vernon (city) Westchester County	360	0.54
Albany (city) Albany County	483	0.49
Hempstead (town) Nassau County	3,520	0.47
Babylon (town) Suffolk County	747	0.35

Hungarian

Top 10 Places Sorted by Population
Based on all places, regardless of total population

Place	Population	%
New York (city)	55,459	0.69
Brooklyn (borough) Kings County	26,607	1.08
Manhattan (borough) New York County	14,667	0.93
Queens (borough) Queens County	9,470	0.43
Hempstead (town) Nassau County	6,992	0.93
Ramapo (town) Rockland County	6,804	5.54
Monroe (town) Orange County	5,591	14.45
Kiryas Joel (village) Orange County	5,471	28.66
Brookhaven (town) Suffolk County	4,390	0.91
Oyster Bay (town) Nassau County	3,138	1.08

Top 10 Places Sorted by Percent of Total Population
Based on all places, regardless of total population

Place	Population	%
South Lima (cdp) Livingston County	72	35.47
Natural Bridge (cdp) Jefferson County	137	33.91
Kiryas Joel (village) Orange County	5,471	28.66
New Square (village) Rockland County	1,787	27.67
Kaser (village) Rockland County	1,034	23.31
Monroe (town) Orange County	5,591	14.45
Prattsville (cdp) Greene County	41	12.85
Lawrence (village) Nassau County	746	11.57
Monsey (cdp) Rockland County	1,483	9.85
Saddle Rock Estates (cdp) Nassau County	48	9.16

Top 10 Places Sorted by Percent of Total Population
Based on places with total population of 50,000 or more

Place	Population	%
Ramapo (town) Rockland County	6,804	5.54
Tonawanda (cdp) Erie County	976	1.67
Tonawanda (town) Erie County	1,188	1.60
Huntington (town) Suffolk County	3,005	1.49
Levittown (cdp) Nassau County	781	1.46
Greenburgh (town) Westchester County	1,242	1.42
Hamburg (town) Erie County	761	1.34
Clarkstown (town) Rockland County	1,008	1.21
North Hempstead (town) Nassau County	2,628	1.18
Brooklyn (borough) Kings County	26,607	1.08

Icelander

Top 10 Places Sorted by Population
Based on all places, regardless of total population

Place	Population	%
New York (city)	572	0.01
Manhattan (borough) New York County	382	0.02
Brooklyn (borough) Kings County	103	<0.01
Hempstead (town) Nassau County	92	0.01
Pittsford (town) Monroe County	63	0.22
Blooming Grove (town) Orange County	62	0.34
Wawayanda (town) Orange County	55	0.77
Staten Island (borough) Richmond County	55	0.01
Lockport (town) Niagara County	52	0.26
Levittown (cdp) Nassau County	52	0.10

Top 10 Places Sorted by Percent of Total Population
Based on all places, regardless of total population

Place	Population	%
Northwest Ithaca (cdp) Tompkins County	14	1.21
Brewerton (cdp) Onondaga County	33	0.81
Wawayanda (town) Orange County	55	0.77
Meredith (town) Delaware County	8	0.51
West Monroe (town) Oswego County	20	0.47
Port Ewen (cdp) Ulster County	15	0.40
Sempronius (town) Cayuga County	3	0.36
Blooming Grove (town) Orange County	62	0.34
Dannemora (town) Clinton County	16	0.32
Homer (village) Cortland County	10	0.30

Top 10 Places Sorted by Percent of Total Population
Based on places with total population of 50,000 or more

Place	Population	%
Levittown (cdp) Nassau County	52	0.10
Manhattan (borough) New York County	382	0.02
Oyster Bay (town) Nassau County	52	0.02
Huntington (town) Suffolk County	38	0.02

Place	Population	%
Utica (city) Oneida County	14	0.02
Tonawanda (cdp) Erie County	11	0.02
New York (city)	572	0.01
Hempstead (town) Nassau County	92	0.01
Staten Island (borough) Richmond County	55	0.01
Brookhaven (town) Suffolk County	45	0.01

Iranian

Top 10 Places Sorted by Population
Based on all places, regardless of total population

Place	Population	%
New York (city)	10,204	0.13
North Hempstead (town) Nassau County	9,262	4.14
Manhattan (borough) New York County	4,256	0.27
Queens (borough) Queens County	3,707	0.17
Great Neck (village) Nassau County	2,382	24.20
Kings Point (village) Nassau County	2,070	41.62
Brooklyn (borough) Kings County	1,822	0.07
Oyster Bay (town) Nassau County	1,464	0.50
Great Neck Plaza (village) Nassau County	673	10.18
Great Neck Estates (village) Nassau County	566	20.72

Top 10 Places Sorted by Percent of Total Population
Based on all places, regardless of total population

Place	Population	%
Kings Point (village) Nassau County	2,070	41.62
Saddle Rock (village) Nassau County	380	36.26
Great Neck (village) Nassau County	2,382	24.20
Great Neck Estates (village) Nassau County	566	20.72
Saddle Rock Estates (cdp) Nassau County	90	17.18
Kensington (village) Nassau County	180	14.94
Great Neck Plaza (village) Nassau County	673	10.18
Roslyn Heights (cdp) Nassau County	452	6.97
North Hills (village) Nassau County	316	6.40
Flower Hill (village) Nassau County	294	6.38

Top 10 Places Sorted by Percent of Total Population
Based on places with total population of 50,000 or more

Place	Population	%
North Hempstead (town) Nassau County	9,262	4.14
Oyster Bay (town) Nassau County	1,464	0.50
Greenburgh (town) Westchester County	267	0.30
Manhattan (borough) New York County	4,256	0.27
Ramapo (town) Rockland County	314	0.26
Huntington (town) Suffolk County	471	0.23
Smithtown (town) Suffolk County	237	0.20
Clarkstown (town) Rockland County	146	0.18
Queens (borough) Queens County	3,707	0.17
Clay (town) Onondaga County	99	0.17

Irish

Top 10 Places Sorted by Population
Based on all places, regardless of total population

Place	Population	%
New York (city)	410,889	5.09
Hempstead (town) Nassau County	125,911	16.71
Brookhaven (town) Suffolk County	122,200	25.45
Manhattan (borough) New York County	117,355	7.41
Queens (borough) Queens County	105,348	4.79
Brooklyn (borough) Kings County	84,945	3.44
Islip (town) Suffolk County	68,763	20.61
Staten Island (borough) Richmond County	64,762	13.97
Oyster Bay (town) Nassau County	59,765	20.49
Huntington (town) Suffolk County	45,750	22.63

Top 10 Places Sorted by Percent of Total Population
Based on all places, regardless of total population

Place	Population	%
Oak Beach-Captree (cdp) Suffolk County	348	73.26
Hopewell Junction (cdp) Dutchess County	290	61.97
Point Lookout (cdp) Nassau County	763	59.98
Walker Valley (cdp) Ulster County	319	59.51
Pearl River (cdp) Rockland County	7,647	52.46
Staatsburg (cdp) Dutchess County	274	52.29
Bellerose (village) Nassau County	648	52.09
Palenville (cdp) Greene County	584	51.45
Winthrop (cdp) St. Lawrence County	236	50.97
Parc (cdp) Clinton County	20	47.62

Top 10 Places Sorted by Percent of Total Population
Based on places with total population of 50,000 or more

Place	Population	%
Colonie (town) Albany County	23,049	28.27
Levittown (cdp) Nassau County	14,886	27.84
Hamburg (town) Erie County	15,679	27.71
Smithtown (town) Suffolk County	31,963	27.18
Brookhaven (town) Suffolk County	122,200	25.45
Troy (city) Rensselaer County	12,384	24.76
Clay (town) Onondaga County	14,197	24.44
Southampton (town) Suffolk County	12,998	22.99
Huntington (town) Suffolk County	45,750	22.63
Union (town) Broome County	12,320	21.88

Israeli

Top 10 Places Sorted by Population
Based on all places, regardless of total population

Place	Population	%
New York (city)	21,872	0.27
Brooklyn (borough) Kings County	9,707	0.39
Manhattan (borough) New York County	6,624	0.42
Queens (borough) Queens County	4,164	0.19
Ramapo (town) Rockland County	3,342	2.72
Hempstead (town) Nassau County	2,558	0.34
North Hempstead (town) Nassau County	1,853	0.83
Kiryas Joel (village) Orange County	949	4.97
Monroe (town) Orange County	949	2.45
Woodmere (cdp) Nassau County	879	5.04

Top 10 Places Sorted by Percent of Total Population
Based on all places, regardless of total population

Place	Population	%
Saddle Rock (village) Nassau County	153	14.60
Kaser (village) Rockland County	540	12.17
Viola (cdp) Rockland County	792	11.23
Greenvale (cdp) Nassau County	32	7.13
Lake Success (village) Nassau County	172	5.94
South Valley Stream (cdp) Nassau County	268	5.09
Woodmere (cdp) Nassau County	879	5.04
Kiryas Joel (village) Orange County	949	4.97
Wesley Hills (village) Rockland County	231	4.24
Monsey (cdp) Rockland County	608	4.04

Top 10 Places Sorted by Percent of Total Population
Based on places with total population of 50,000 or more

Place	Population	%
Ramapo (town) Rockland County	3,342	2.72
North Hempstead (town) Nassau County	1,853	0.83
Manhattan (borough) New York County	6,624	0.42
Brooklyn (borough) Kings County	9,707	0.39
Hempstead (town) Nassau County	2,558	0.34
White Plains (city) Westchester County	181	0.32
Clarkstown (town) Rockland County	247	0.30
New York (city)	21,872	0.27
Greenburgh (town) Westchester County	225	0.26
Mount Vernon (city) Westchester County	174	0.26

Italian

Top 10 Places Sorted by Population
Based on all places, regardless of total population

Place	Population	%
New York (city)	625,004	7.74
Hempstead (town) Nassau County	164,467	21.82
Queens (borough) Queens County	159,812	7.27
Staten Island (borough) Richmond County	156,288	33.72
Brookhaven (town) Suffolk County	155,749	32.44
Brooklyn (borough) Kings County	152,814	6.19
Manhattan (borough) New York County	98,563	6.22
Oyster Bay (town) Nassau County	88,723	30.43
Islip (town) Suffolk County	84,360	25.28
Babylon (town) Suffolk County	61,852	28.95

Top 10 Places Sorted by Percent of Total Population
Based on all places, regardless of total population

Place	Population	%
Witherbee (cdp) Essex County	149	60.08
Hillside Lake (cdp) Dutchess County	350	51.32
North Massapequa (cdp) Nassau County	9,384	50.28

Place	Population	%
Frankfort (village) Herkimer County	1,299	50.17
East Kingston (cdp) Ulster County	170	49.56
Great River (cdp) Suffolk County	803	48.78
Leeds (cdp) Greene County	151	47.19
Fowlerville (cdp) Livingston County	116	46.96
Moriches (cdp) Suffolk County	1,413	46.85
Franklin Square (cdp) Nassau County	13,514	45.54

Top 10 Places Sorted by Percent of Total Population
Based on places with total population of 50,000 or more

Place	Population	%
Smithtown (town) Suffolk County	45,388	38.60
Staten Island (borough) Richmond County	156,288	33.72
Levittown (cdp) Nassau County	17,446	32.62
Brookhaven (town) Suffolk County	155,749	32.44
Oyster Bay (town) Nassau County	88,723	30.43
Babylon (town) Suffolk County	61,852	28.95
Irondequoit (cdp/town) Monroe County	14,566	28.22
Huntington (town) Suffolk County	56,013	27.70
Greece (town) Monroe County	26,121	27.36
Tonawanda (town) Erie County	19,213	25.93

Latvian

Top 10 Places Sorted by Population
Based on all places, regardless of total population

Place	Population	%
New York (city)	3,302	0.04
Manhattan (borough) New York County	1,822	0.12
Brooklyn (borough) Kings County	667	0.03
Queens (borough) Queens County	568	0.03
Hempstead (town) Nassau County	438	0.06
North Hempstead (town) Nassau County	254	0.11
Oyster Bay (town) Nassau County	235	0.08
Huntington (town) Suffolk County	193	0.10
Brookhaven (town) Suffolk County	182	0.04
Ramapo (town) Rockland County	174	0.14

Top 10 Places Sorted by Percent of Total Population
Based on all places, regardless of total population

Place	Population	%
Williamson (cdp) Wayne County	62	2.61
Halesite (cdp) Suffolk County	55	2.61
Stony Creek (town) Warren County	24	2.61
Bemus Point (village) Chautauqua County	6	2.05
Airmont (village) Rockland County	132	1.57
Pleasant Valley (cdp) Dutchess County	13	1.57
Tully (village) Onondaga County	13	1.52
Esperance (village) Schoharie County	6	1.34
LaFayette (town) Onondaga County	65	1.32
North Hills (village) Nassau County	59	1.19

Top 10 Places Sorted by Percent of Total Population
Based on places with total population of 50,000 or more

Place	Population	%
Greenburgh (town) Westchester County	153	0.17
Ramapo (town) Rockland County	174	0.14
Manhattan (borough) New York County	1,822	0.12
North Hempstead (town) Nassau County	254	0.11
Huntington (town) Suffolk County	193	0.10
Clarkstown (town) Rockland County	87	0.10
New Rochelle (city) Westchester County	74	0.10
Oyster Bay (town) Nassau County	235	0.08
Smithtown (town) Suffolk County	81	0.07
Greece (town) Monroe County	71	0.07

Lithuanian

Top 10 Places Sorted by Population
Based on all places, regardless of total population

Place	Population	%
New York (city)	12,774	0.16
Manhattan (borough) New York County	5,775	0.36
Queens (borough) Queens County	3,131	0.14
Brooklyn (borough) Kings County	2,676	0.11
Hempstead (town) Nassau County	2,538	0.34
Brookhaven (town) Suffolk County	1,898	0.40
Oyster Bay (town) Nassau County	1,079	0.37
Huntington (town) Suffolk County	956	0.47
Islip (town) Suffolk County	799	0.24
North Hempstead (town) Nassau County	718	0.32

Top 10 Places Sorted by Percent of Total Population
Based on all places, regardless of total population

Place	Population	%
Lyon Mountain (cdp) Clinton County	61	16.05
Wynantskill (cdp) Rensselaer County	256	7.24
Marion (cdp) Wayne County	102	5.38
Santa Clara (town) Franklin County	21	5.33
Leeds (cdp) Greene County	16	5.00
Hagaman (village) Montgomery County	48	4.52
Webb (town) Herkimer County	68	4.38
Durhamville (cdp) Oneida County	25	4.35
Napeague (cdp) Suffolk County	9	4.31
Old Forge (cdp) Herkimer County	22	4.27

Top 10 Places Sorted by Percent of Total Population
Based on places with total population of 50,000 or more

Place	Population	%
Union (town) Broome County	452	0.80
Levittown (cdp) Nassau County	314	0.59
Greece (town) Monroe County	543	0.57
Smithtown (town) Suffolk County	627	0.53
Irondequoit (cdp/town) Monroe County	267	0.52
Huntington (town) Suffolk County	956	0.47
Southampton (town) Suffolk County	267	0.47
Colonie (town) Albany County	377	0.46
Ramapo (town) Rockland County	538	0.44
Brookhaven (town) Suffolk County	1,898	0.40

Luxemburger

Top 10 Places Sorted by Population
Based on all places, regardless of total population

Place	Population	%
New York (city)	193	<0.01
Manhattan (borough) New York County	68	<0.01
Rochester (city) Monroe County	62	0.03
Brooklyn (borough) Kings County	58	<0.01
Staten Island (borough) Richmond County	54	0.01
Brookhaven (town) Suffolk County	36	0.01
Lenox (town) Madison County	27	0.30
Clay (town) Onondaga County	26	0.04
Ithaca (city) Tompkins County	24	0.08
Irondequoit (cdp/town) Monroe County	24	0.05

Top 10 Places Sorted by Percent of Total Population
Based on all places, regardless of total population

Place	Population	%
Lyndon (town) Cattaraugus County	4	0.70
Dickinson (town) Franklin County	6	0.56
Sheldon (town) Wyoming County	7	0.32
Lenox (town) Madison County	27	0.30
Roslyn Heights (cdp) Nassau County	16	0.25
Virgil (town) Cortland County	6	0.25
Java (town) Wyoming County	5	0.23
Athens (village) Greene County	3	0.18
Caton (town) Steuben County	5	0.17
Terryville (cdp) Suffolk County	18	0.15

Top 10 Places Sorted by Percent of Total Population
Based on places with total population of 50,000 or more

Place	Population	%
Irondequoit (cdp/town) Monroe County	24	0.05
Clay (town) Onondaga County	26	0.04
Rochester (city) Monroe County	62	0.03
Greece (town) Monroe County	15	0.02
Colonie (town) Albany County	13	0.02
Staten Island (borough) Richmond County	54	0.01
Brookhaven (town) Suffolk County	36	0.01
Buffalo (city) Erie County	24	0.01
North Hempstead (town) Nassau County	16	0.01
Syracuse (city) Onondaga County	14	0.01

Macedonian

Top 10 Places Sorted by Population
Based on all places, regardless of total population

Place	Population	%
New York (city)	4,911	0.06
Staten Island (borough) Richmond County	1,590	0.34
Queens (borough) Queens County	1,109	0.05

Place	Population	%
Manhattan (borough) New York County	1,086	0.07
Bronx (borough) Bronx County	628	0.05
Brooklyn (borough) Kings County	498	0.02
Irondequoit (cdp/town) Monroe County	266	0.52
Yonkers (city) Westchester County	236	0.12
Clay (town) Onondaga County	185	0.32
New Rochelle (city) Westchester County	177	0.23

Top 10 Places Sorted by Percent of Total Population
Based on all places, regardless of total population

Place	Population	%
Sunset Bay (cdp) Chautauqua County	50	5.55
Hannibal (village) Oswego County	15	2.65
Cold Brook (village) Herkimer County	6	1.59
Village Green (cdp) Onondaga County	56	1.25
Chappaqua (cdp) Westchester County	13	1.25
Union Vale (town) Dutchess County	57	1.18
Riga (town) Monroe County	61	1.10
Angola on the Lake (cdp) Erie County	12	0.86
Pulaski (village) Oswego County	19	0.78
Hanover (town) Chautauqua County	50	0.70

Top 10 Places Sorted by Percent of Total Population
Based on places with total population of 50,000 or more

Place	Population	%
Irondequoit (cdp/town) Monroe County	266	0.52
Staten Island (borough) Richmond County	1,590	0.34
Clay (town) Onondaga County	185	0.32
Hamburg (town) Erie County	149	0.26
New Rochelle (city) Westchester County	177	0.23
Yonkers (city) Westchester County	236	0.12
Greece (town) Monroe County	119	0.12
White Plains (city) Westchester County	54	0.10
Manhattan (borough) New York County	1,086	0.07
New York (city)	4,911	0.06

Maltese

Top 10 Places Sorted by Population
Based on all places, regardless of total population

Place	Population	%
New York (city)	3,102	0.04
Queens (borough) Queens County	1,565	0.07
Manhattan (borough) New York County	840	0.05
Brookhaven (town) Suffolk County	686	0.14
Oyster Bay (town) Nassau County	579	0.20
Hempstead (town) Nassau County	540	0.07
Babylon (town) Suffolk County	378	0.18
Brooklyn (borough) Kings County	362	0.01
Islip (town) Suffolk County	292	0.09
Staten Island (borough) Richmond County	290	0.06

Top 10 Places Sorted by Percent of Total Population
Based on all places, regardless of total population

Place	Population	%
Tuxedo (town) Orange County	93	2.59
Hamptonburgh (town) Orange County	103	1.89
Plandome Heights (village) Nassau County	15	1.42
Carle Place (cdp) Nassau County	77	1.38
Hillside Lake (cdp) Dutchess County	8	1.17
Wright (town) Schoharie County	21	1.11
East Patchogue (cdp) Suffolk County	220	1.04
Milton (cdp) Ulster County	12	1.03
Sparkill (cdp) Rockland County	13	0.94
Brewerton (cdp) Onondaga County	36	0.89

Top 10 Places Sorted by Percent of Total Population
Based on places with total population of 50,000 or more

Place	Population	%
Oyster Bay (town) Nassau County	579	0.20
Babylon (town) Suffolk County	378	0.18
Smithtown (town) Suffolk County	206	0.18
Levittown (cdp) Nassau County	96	0.18
Brookhaven (town) Suffolk County	686	0.14
North Hempstead (town) Nassau County	248	0.11
Islip (town) Suffolk County	292	0.09
Queens (borough) Queens County	1,565	0.07
Hempstead (town) Nassau County	540	0.07
Staten Island (borough) Richmond County	290	0.06

Please refer to the Explanation of Data in the front of the book for more detailed information.

New Zealander

Top 10 Places Sorted by Population
Based on all places, regardless of total population

Place	Population	%
New York (city)	584	0.01
Manhattan (borough) New York County	405	0.03
Brooklyn (borough) Kings County	140	0.01
Monsey (cdp) Rockland County	55	0.37
Ramapo (town) Rockland County	55	0.04
Ithaca (city) Tompkins County	45	0.15
Milan (town) Dutchess County	35	1.38
Deerpark (town) Orange County	35	0.44
White Plains (city) Westchester County	29	0.05
Eggertsville (cdp) Erie County	26	0.17

Top 10 Places Sorted by Percent of Total Population
Based on all places, regardless of total population

Place	Population	%
Milan (town) Dutchess County	35	1.38
Oriskany Falls (village) Oneida County	4	0.53
Deerpark (town) Orange County	35	0.44
Niskayuna (cdp) Schenectady County	18	0.39
Monsey (cdp) Rockland County	55	0.37
North Harmony (town) Chautauqua County	6	0.28
Cooperstown (village) Otsego County	5	0.28
Hartford (town) Washington County	5	0.22
Spafford (town) Onondaga County	4	0.20
Augusta (town) Oneida County	4	0.19

Top 10 Places Sorted by Percent of Total Population
Based on places with total population of 50,000 or more

Place	Population	%
White Plains (city) Westchester County	29	0.05
Ramapo (town) Rockland County	55	0.04
Manhattan (borough) New York County	405	0.03
Amherst (town) Erie County	26	0.02
New York (city)	584	0.01
Brooklyn (borough) Kings County	140	0.01
Huntington (town) Suffolk County	26	0.01
Syracuse (city) Onondaga County	13	0.01
Cheektowaga (cdp) Erie County	11	0.01
Cheektowaga (town) Erie County	11	0.01

Northern European

Top 10 Places Sorted by Population
Based on all places, regardless of total population

Place	Population	%
New York (city)	3,043	0.04
Manhattan (borough) New York County	1,485	0.09
Brooklyn (borough) Kings County	961	0.04
Hempstead (town) Nassau County	514	0.07
Queens (borough) Queens County	512	0.02
Brookhaven (town) Suffolk County	249	0.05
Oceanside (cdp) Nassau County	161	0.52
Albany (city) Albany County	160	0.16
Depew (village) Erie County	130	0.84
Cheektowaga (town) Erie County	130	0.15

Top 10 Places Sorted by Percent of Total Population
Based on all places, regardless of total population

Place	Population	%
Duanesburg (cdp) Schenectady County	21	12.00
Schenevus (cdp) Otsego County	32	11.64
West Valley (cdp) Cattaraugus County	33	7.37
Newfield Hamlet (cdp) Tompkins County	30	4.48
Long Lake (cdp) Hamilton County	21	3.92
Guilford (town) Chenango County	97	3.27
New Suffolk (cdp) Suffolk County	6	3.19
Scott (town) Cortland County	36	2.85
Long Lake (town) Hamilton County	21	2.80
Laurel (cdp) Suffolk County	30	2.79

Top 10 Places Sorted by Percent of Total Population
Based on places with total population of 50,000 or more

Place	Population	%
Albany (city) Albany County	160	0.16
Cheektowaga (town) Erie County	130	0.15
Schenectady (city) Schenectady County	97	0.15
White Plains (city) Westchester County	54	0.10

Manhattan (borough) New York County	1,485	0.09
Amherst (town) Erie County	101	0.08
Hempstead (town) Nassau County	514	0.07
Greenburgh (town) Westchester County	65	0.07
Southampton (town) Suffolk County	42	0.07
Clay (town) Onondaga County	35	0.06

Norwegian

Top 10 Places Sorted by Population
Based on all places, regardless of total population

Place	Population	%
New York (city)	21,894	0.27
Manhattan (borough) New York County	7,445	0.47
Brooklyn (borough) Kings County	5,982	0.24
Staten Island (borough) Richmond County	5,135	1.11
Brookhaven (town) Suffolk County	5,078	1.06
Hempstead (town) Nassau County	3,371	0.45
Islip (town) Suffolk County	2,978	0.89
Queens (borough) Queens County	2,559	0.12
Oyster Bay (town) Nassau County	1,882	0.65
Huntington (town) Suffolk County	1,833	0.91

Top 10 Places Sorted by Percent of Total Population
Based on all places, regardless of total population

Place	Population	%
Saltaire (village) Suffolk County	8	13.79
Stone Ridge (cdp) Ulster County	91	10.48
Margaretville (village) Delaware County	52	9.83
Great Bend (cdp) Jefferson County	86	9.50
Fishers Island (cdp) Suffolk County	21	8.40
Red House (town) Cattaraugus County	2	7.69
Northville (cdp) Suffolk County	88	7.39
Benson (town) Hamilton County	11	7.24
Pitcher (town) Chenango County	48	7.08
Shokan (cdp) Ulster County	44	5.68

Top 10 Places Sorted by Percent of Total Population
Based on places with total population of 50,000 or more

Place	Population	%
Smithtown (town) Suffolk County	1,686	1.43
Staten Island (borough) Richmond County	5,135	1.11
Brookhaven (town) Suffolk County	5,078	1.06
Huntington (town) Suffolk County	1,833	0.91
Islip (town) Suffolk County	2,978	0.89
Southampton (town) Suffolk County	498	0.88
Babylon (town) Suffolk County	1,701	0.80
Colonie (town) Albany County	598	0.73
Oyster Bay (town) Nassau County	1,882	0.65
Greenburgh (town) Westchester County	530	0.60

Pennsylvania German

Top 10 Places Sorted by Population
Based on all places, regardless of total population

Place	Population	%
New York (city)	465	0.01
Morristown (town) St. Lawrence County	433	15.79
Troupsburg (town) Steuben County	341	23.32
Manhattan (borough) New York County	327	0.02
Conewango (town) Cattaraugus County	262	18.04
Jamestown (city) Chautauqua County	245	0.79
Colesville (town) Broome County	220	4.18
Hume (town) Allegany County	219	10.74
Lisbon (town) St. Lawrence County	215	5.28
St. Johnsville (town) Montgomery County	209	7.99

Top 10 Places Sorted by Percent of Total Population
Based on all places, regardless of total population

Place	Population	%
Troupsburg (town) Steuben County	341	23.32
Conewango (town) Cattaraugus County	262	18.04
Morristown (town) St. Lawrence County	433	15.79
De Peyster (town) St. Lawrence County	147	15.34
Napoli (town) Cattaraugus County	181	11.95
Hume (town) Allegany County	219	10.74
Junius (town) Seneca County	160	10.12
Leon (town) Cattaraugus County	148	10.12
Sherman (town) Chautauqua County	166	8.96
Cherry Creek (town) Chautauqua County	108	8.52

Top 10 Places Sorted by Percent of Total Population
Based on places with total population of 50,000 or more

Place	Population	%
Union (town) Broome County	197	0.35
Niagara Falls (city) Niagara County	130	0.26
Hamburg (town) Erie County	103	0.18
Greece (town) Monroe County	145	0.15
Tonawanda (cdp) Erie County	85	0.15
Tonawanda (town) Erie County	98	0.13
Levittown (cdp) Nassau County	54	0.10
Troy (city) Rensselaer County	50	0.10
Clay (town) Onondaga County	38	0.07
Buffalo (city) Erie County	159	0.06

Polish

Top 10 Places Sorted by Population
Based on all places, regardless of total population

Place	Population	%
New York (city)	216,891	2.68
Brooklyn (borough) Kings County	66,792	2.71
Manhattan (borough) New York County	64,078	4.05
Queens (borough) Queens County	59,757	2.72
Hempstead (town) Nassau County	35,774	4.75
Cheektowaga (town) Erie County	31,456	35.39
Buffalo (city) Erie County	28,108	10.57
Brookhaven (town) Suffolk County	27,233	5.67
Cheektowaga (cdp) Erie County	26,237	34.63
Oyster Bay (town) Nassau County	19,395	6.65

Top 10 Places Sorted by Percent of Total Population
Based on all places, regardless of total population

Place	Population	%
Sloan (village) Erie County	1,831	49.88
Depew (village) Erie County	5,979	38.69
Piffard (cdp) Livingston County	22	36.67
Lancaster (town) Erie County	15,025	36.65
Cheektowaga (town) Erie County	31,456	35.39
Marilla (town) Erie County	1,884	35.06
Cheektowaga (cdp) Erie County	26,237	34.63
Darien (town) Genesee County	946	30.30
Duane Lake (cdp) Schenectady County	73	30.17
Lancaster (village) Erie County	3,134	29.99

Top 10 Places Sorted by Percent of Total Population
Based on places with total population of 50,000 or more

Place	Population	%
Cheektowaga (town) Erie County	31,456	35.39
Cheektowaga (cdp) Erie County	26,237	34.63
Hamburg (town) Erie County	13,189	23.31
Tonawanda (town) Erie County	11,479	15.49
Tonawanda (cdp) Erie County	9,014	15.40
Amherst (town) Erie County	17,104	14.14
Buffalo (city) Erie County	28,108	10.57
Niagara Falls (city) Niagara County	4,962	9.75
Utica (city) Oneida County	5,408	8.75
Colonie (town) Albany County	6,915	8.48

Portuguese

Top 10 Places Sorted by Population
Based on all places, regardless of total population

Place	Population	%
New York (city)	13,201	0.16
Queens (borough) Queens County	4,727	0.21
North Hempstead (town) Nassau County	3,978	1.78
Manhattan (borough) New York County	3,862	0.24
Brookhaven (town) Suffolk County	3,802	0.79
Brooklyn (borough) Kings County	2,882	0.12
Hempstead (town) Nassau County	2,805	0.37
Yonkers (city) Westchester County	2,670	1.37
Mineola (village) Nassau County	2,368	12.67
Islip (town) Suffolk County	1,977	0.59

Top 10 Places Sorted by Percent of Total Population
Based on all places, regardless of total population

Place	Population	%
Freedom Plains (cdp) Dutchess County	134	19.06
Mineola (village) Nassau County	2,368	12.67
Fishers Landing (cdp) Jefferson County	5	9.43

Place	Population	%
Farmingville (cdp) Suffolk County	1,109	6.92
Fishers Island (cdp) Suffolk County	16	6.40
Carle Place (cdp) Nassau County	318	5.69
Fishkill (village) Dutchess County	111	5.34
Decatur (town) Otsego County	15	4.78
Davenport Center (cdp) Delaware County	14	4.73
Phoenicia (cdp) Ulster County	17	4.66

Top 10 Places Sorted by Percent of Total Population
Based on places with total population of 50,000 or more

Place	Population	%
North Hempstead (town) Nassau County	3,978	1.78
Mount Vernon (city) Westchester County	1,149	1.71
Yonkers (city) Westchester County	2,670	1.37
New Rochelle (city) Westchester County	830	1.09
Brentwood (cdp) Suffolk County	524	0.96
Greenburgh (town) Westchester County	718	0.82
Brookhaven (town) Suffolk County	3,802	0.79
Islip (town) Suffolk County	1,977	0.59
White Plains (city) Westchester County	325	0.58
Levittown (cdp) Nassau County	243	0.45

Romanian

Top 10 Places Sorted by Population
Based on all places, regardless of total population

Place	Population	%
New York (city)	29,552	0.37
Queens (borough) Queens County	11,686	0.53
Brooklyn (borough) Kings County	8,046	0.33
Manhattan (borough) New York County	7,692	0.49
Hempstead (town) Nassau County	2,811	0.37
Monroe (town) Orange County	2,439	6.31
Kiryas Joel (village) Orange County	2,293	12.01
Ramapo (town) Rockland County	1,695	1.38
Oyster Bay (town) Nassau County	1,492	0.51
North Hempstead (town) Nassau County	1,434	0.64

Top 10 Places Sorted by Percent of Total Population
Based on all places, regardless of total population

Place	Population	%
Kiryas Joel (village) Orange County	2,293	12.01
Kaser (village) Rockland County	497	11.20
Monroe (town) Orange County	2,439	6.31
Harbor Hills (cdp) Nassau County	27	5.45
University Gardens (cdp) Nassau County	217	5.44
Smallwood (cdp) Sullivan County	32	4.65
Milford (village) Otsego County	21	4.12
Port Henry (village) Essex County	74	4.11
East Norwich (cdp) Nassau County	95	3.67
Barker (town) Broome County	95	3.48

Top 10 Places Sorted by Percent of Total Population
Based on places with total population of 50,000 or more

Place	Population	%
Ramapo (town) Rockland County	1,695	1.38
Huntington (town) Suffolk County	1,364	0.67
Clarkstown (town) Rockland County	544	0.65
North Hempstead (town) Nassau County	1,434	0.64
Smithtown (town) Suffolk County	707	0.60
Greenburgh (town) Westchester County	489	0.56
Queens (borough) Queens County	11,686	0.53
Oyster Bay (town) Nassau County	1,492	0.51
Manhattan (borough) New York County	7,692	0.49
New York (city)	29,552	0.37

Russian

Top 10 Places Sorted by Population
Based on all places, regardless of total population

Place	Population	%
New York (city)	240,690	2.98
Brooklyn (borough) Kings County	88,579	3.59
Manhattan (borough) New York County	82,983	5.24
Queens (borough) Queens County	44,676	2.03
Hempstead (town) Nassau County	26,754	3.55
Staten Island (borough) Richmond County	16,388	3.54
North Hempstead (town) Nassau County	14,712	6.58
Oyster Bay (town) Nassau County	14,554	4.99
Brookhaven (town) Suffolk County	12,073	2.51
Huntington (town) Suffolk County	9,499	4.70

Top 10 Places Sorted by Percent of Total Population
Based on all places, regardless of total population

Place	Population	%
Piffard (cdp) Livingston County	22	36.67
Hewlett Bay Park (village) Nassau County	155	29.87
Great Neck Gardens (cdp) Nassau County	258	28.41
Hewlett Harbor (village) Nassau County	331	28.22
Roslyn Estates (village) Nassau County	327	26.48
Woodsburgh (village) Nassau County	178	23.89
Grand View-on-Hudson (village) Rockland County	62	21.83
Hewlett Neck (village) Nassau County	97	20.73
Russell Gardens (village) Nassau County	199	20.66
Scotts Corners (cdp) Westchester County	102	20.28

Top 10 Places Sorted by Percent of Total Population
Based on places with total population of 50,000 or more

Place	Population	%
North Hempstead (town) Nassau County	14,712	6.58
Clarkstown (town) Rockland County	5,317	6.38
Greenburgh (town) Westchester County	5,042	5.75
Manhattan (borough) New York County	82,983	5.24
Oyster Bay (town) Nassau County	14,554	4.99
Ramapo (town) Rockland County	6,069	4.95
Huntington (town) Suffolk County	9,499	4.70
Smithtown (town) Suffolk County	5,319	4.52
White Plains (city) Westchester County	2,307	4.13
New Rochelle (city) Westchester County	3,102	4.09

Scandinavian

Top 10 Places Sorted by Population
Based on all places, regardless of total population

Place	Population	%
New York (city)	3,434	0.04
Manhattan (borough) New York County	1,731	0.11
Brooklyn (borough) Kings County	882	0.04
Queens (borough) Queens County	545	0.02
Brookhaven (town) Suffolk County	388	0.08
Hempstead (town) Nassau County	360	0.05
Albany (city) Albany County	313	0.32
Huntington (town) Suffolk County	292	0.14
Islip (town) Suffolk County	183	0.05
Bronx (borough) Bronx County	155	0.01

Top 10 Places Sorted by Percent of Total Population
Based on all places, regardless of total population

Place	Population	%
Norfolk (cdp) St. Lawrence County	85	6.84
Pine Hill (cdp) Ulster County	15	5.84
Afton (village) Chenango County	39	4.00
Gardiner (cdp) Ulster County	40	3.82
Clifton (town) St. Lawrence County	27	3.35
Shortsville (village) Ontario County	39	3.08
Cairo (cdp) Greene County	54	2.89
Springfield (town) Otsego County	41	2.85
Limestone (village) Cattaraugus County	9	2.85
Sharon Springs (village) Schoharie County	10	2.77

Top 10 Places Sorted by Percent of Total Population
Based on places with total population of 50,000 or more

Place	Population	%
Albany (city) Albany County	313	0.32
Huntington (town) Suffolk County	292	0.14
Manhattan (borough) New York County	1,731	0.11
Amherst (town) Erie County	116	0.10
Southampton (town) Suffolk County	57	0.10
Greece (town) Monroe County	88	0.09
Greenburgh (town) Westchester County	79	0.09
Brookhaven (town) Suffolk County	388	0.08
Utica (city) Oneida County	48	0.08
Syracuse (city) Onondaga County	98	0.07

Scotch-Irish

Top 10 Places Sorted by Population
Based on all places, regardless of total population

Place	Population	%
New York (city)	27,337	0.34
Manhattan (borough) New York County	13,158	0.83
Brooklyn (borough) Kings County	6,090	0.25

Place	Population	%
Brookhaven (town) Suffolk County	5,102	1.06
Hempstead (town) Nassau County	4,788	0.64
Queens (borough) Queens County	4,602	0.21
Islip (town) Suffolk County	3,159	0.95
Oyster Bay (town) Nassau County	2,523	0.87
Huntington (town) Suffolk County	2,325	1.15
Buffalo (city) Erie County	2,324	0.87

Top 10 Places Sorted by Percent of Total Population
Based on all places, regardless of total population

Place	Population	%
Onondaga Nation Reservation Onondaga County	8	53.33
Laurens (village) Otsego County	35	17.33
Port Gibson (cdp) Ontario County	80	14.98
Argyle (village) Washington County	49	13.61
Parish (village) Oswego County	63	12.91
Claverack-Red Mills (cdp) Columbia County	108	12.84
Oxbow (cdp) Jefferson County	9	12.50
Piffard (cdp) Livingston County	7	11.67
Breesport (cdp) Chemung County	85	10.81
Windham (cdp) Greene County	41	9.45

Top 10 Places Sorted by Percent of Total Population
Based on places with total population of 50,000 or more

Place	Population	%
Clay (town) Onondaga County	1,162	2.00
Tonawanda (cdp) Erie County	989	1.69
Tonawanda (town) Erie County	1,170	1.58
Troy (city) Rensselaer County	784	1.57
Colonie (town) Albany County	1,261	1.55
Greece (town) Monroe County	1,469	1.54
Smithtown (town) Suffolk County	1,732	1.47
Levittown (cdp) Nassau County	722	1.35
Amherst (town) Erie County	1,527	1.26
Union (town) Broome County	712	1.26

Scottish

Top 10 Places Sorted by Population
Based on all places, regardless of total population

Place	Population	%
New York (city)	38,000	0.47
Manhattan (borough) New York County	19,553	1.23
Brooklyn (borough) Kings County	8,809	0.36
Queens (borough) Queens County	5,718	0.26
Brookhaven (town) Suffolk County	5,703	1.19
Hempstead (town) Nassau County	3,831	0.51
Rochester (city) Monroe County	3,002	1.42
Islip (town) Suffolk County	2,852	0.85
Buffalo (city) Erie County	2,816	1.06
Oyster Bay (town) Nassau County	2,493	0.85

Top 10 Places Sorted by Percent of Total Population
Based on all places, regardless of total population

Place	Population	%
Dering Harbor (village) Suffolk County	5	31.25
Rhinecliff (cdp) Dutchess County	86	23.18
Callicoon (cdp) Sullivan County	21	18.75
Colton (cdp) St. Lawrence County	64	16.75
Andes (town) Delaware County	149	15.63
Tuscarora (cdp) Livingston County	12	15.58
Salt Point (cdp) Dutchess County	47	14.42
Thousand Island Park (cdp) Jefferson County	16	14.41
Laurel (cdp) Suffolk County	152	14.14
Walton (village) Delaware County	372	14.06

Top 10 Places Sorted by Percent of Total Population
Based on places with total population of 50,000 or more

Place	Population	%
Tonawanda (town) Erie County	1,915	2.58
Tonawanda (cdp) Erie County	1,430	2.44
Clay (town) Onondaga County	1,377	2.37
Union (town) Broome County	1,114	1.98
Greece (town) Monroe County	1,843	1.93
Colonie (town) Albany County	1,526	1.87
Irondequoit (cdp/town) Monroe County	935	1.81
Southampton (town) Suffolk County	966	1.71
Troy (city) Rensselaer County	848	1.70
Syracuse (city) Onondaga County	2,233	1.54

Serbian

Top 10 Places Sorted by Population
Based on all places, regardless of total population

Place	Population	%
New York (city)	4,911	0.06
Queens (borough) Queens County	2,438	0.11
Manhattan (borough) New York County	1,526	0.10
Brooklyn (borough) Kings County	520	0.02
Buffalo (city) Erie County	291	0.11
Hamburg (town) Erie County	279	0.49
Orchard Park (town) Erie County	247	0.86
Staten Island (borough) Richmond County	240	0.05
Bronx (borough) Bronx County	187	0.01
Amherst (town) Erie County	158	0.13

Top 10 Places Sorted by Percent of Total Population
Based on all places, regardless of total population

Place	Population	%
West Almond (town) Allegany County	6	2.08
Port Henry (village) Essex County	29	1.61
Ames (village) Montgomery County	2	1.24
Roslyn (village) Nassau County	30	1.10
South Nyack (village) Rockland County	57	1.03
Cairo (town) Greene County	68	1.02
Scottsville (village) Monroe County	20	0.96
New Albion (town) Cattaraugus County	19	0.96
Arcade (village) Wyoming County	19	0.87
Orchard Park (town) Erie County	247	0.86

Top 10 Places Sorted by Percent of Total Population
Based on places with total population of 50,000 or more

Place	Population	%
Hamburg (town) Erie County	279	0.49
Amherst (town) Erie County	158	0.13
Cheektowaga (cdp) Erie County	100	0.13
Utica (city) Oneida County	82	0.13
Tonawanda (cdp) Erie County	73	0.12
Union (town) Broome County	65	0.12
Queens (borough) Queens County	2,438	0.11
Buffalo (city) Erie County	291	0.11
Cheektowaga (town) Erie County	100	0.11
Tonawanda (town) Erie County	85	0.11

Slavic

Top 10 Places Sorted by Population
Based on all places, regardless of total population

Place	Population	%
New York (city)	1,962	0.02
Queens (borough) Queens County	765	0.03
Brooklyn (borough) Kings County	564	0.02
Manhattan (borough) New York County	400	0.03
Union (town) Broome County	291	0.52
Greece (town) Monroe County	240	0.25
Yonkers (city) Westchester County	237	0.12
North Tonawanda (city) Niagara County	209	0.66
North Hempstead (town) Nassau County	195	0.09
Oyster Bay (town) Nassau County	173	0.06

Top 10 Places Sorted by Percent of Total Population
Based on all places, regardless of total population

Place	Population	%
Tannersville (village) Greene County	15	3.46
Rhinecliff (cdp) Dutchess County	12	3.23
Depauville (cdp) Jefferson County	12	2.70
Jefferson Heights (cdp) Greene County	40	2.51
Harmony (town) Chautauqua County	44	1.96
Apalachin (cdp) Tioga County	22	1.96
Riverside (cdp) Suffolk County	53	1.89
Corfu (village) Genesee County	13	1.69
Hawthorne (cdp) Westchester County	76	1.68
Ripley (town) Chautauqua County	35	1.64

Top 10 Places Sorted by Percent of Total Population
Based on places with total population of 50,000 or more

Place	Population	%
Union (town) Broome County	291	0.52
Greece (town) Monroe County	240	0.25
New Rochelle (city) Westchester County	171	0.23
Tonawanda (town) Erie County	123	0.17

Place	Population	%
Clay (town) Onondaga County	93	0.16
Amherst (town) Erie County	153	0.13
Yonkers (city) Westchester County	237	0.12
Smithtown (town) Suffolk County	116	0.10
Albany (city) Albany County	94	0.10
Tonawanda (cdp) Erie County	59	0.10

Slovak

Top 10 Places Sorted by Population
Based on all places, regardless of total population

Place	Population	%
New York (city)	6,785	0.08
Union (town) Broome County	3,003	5.33
Manhattan (borough) New York County	2,298	0.15
Queens (borough) Queens County	1,882	0.09
Brooklyn (borough) Kings County	1,826	0.07
Binghamton (city) Broome County	1,334	2.81
Johnson City (village) Broome County	908	5.96
Endwell (cdp) Broome County	740	6.33
Hempstead (town) Nassau County	702	0.09
Brookhaven (town) Suffolk County	690	0.14

Top 10 Places Sorted by Percent of Total Population
Based on all places, regardless of total population

Place	Population	%
Fowlerville (cdp) Livingston County	42	17.00
Port Dickinson (village) Broome County	109	7.68
Endwell (cdp) Broome County	740	6.33
Maine (town) Broome County	334	6.20
Johnson City (village) Broome County	908	5.96
Apalachin (cdp) Tioga County	60	5.36
Union (town) Broome County	3,003	5.33
Endicott (village) Broome County	634	4.76
Hemlock (cdp) Livingston County	11	4.35
Lincolndale (cdp) Westchester County	58	4.33

Top 10 Places Sorted by Percent of Total Population
Based on places with total population of 50,000 or more

Place	Population	%
Union (town) Broome County	3,003	5.33
Greenburgh (town) Westchester County	388	0.44
Clarkstown (town) Rockland County	310	0.37
Albany (city) Albany County	351	0.36
Hamburg (town) Erie County	182	0.32
Yonkers (city) Westchester County	590	0.30
Cheektowaga (cdp) Erie County	229	0.30
Cheektowaga (town) Erie County	229	0.26
Clay (town) Onondaga County	150	0.26
Greece (town) Monroe County	236	0.25

Slovene

Top 10 Places Sorted by Population
Based on all places, regardless of total population

Place	Population	%
New York (city)	1,476	0.02
Manhattan (borough) New York County	695	0.04
Queens (borough) Queens County	468	0.02
Brooklyn (borough) Kings County	160	0.01
Commack (cdp) Suffolk County	150	0.41
Smithtown (town) Suffolk County	147	0.13
Staten Island (borough) Richmond County	108	0.02
Buffalo (city) Erie County	100	0.04
Bedford (town) Westchester County	96	0.55
Hempstead (town) Nassau County	89	0.01

Top 10 Places Sorted by Percent of Total Population
Based on all places, regardless of total population

Place	Population	%
Decatur (town) Otsego County	15	4.78
Bedford (cdp) Westchester County	86	4.73
Bovina (town) Delaware County	20	3.92
Worcester (cdp) Otsego County	51	3.24
Little Falls (town) Herkimer County	41	2.88
Titusville (cdp) Dutchess County	13	2.72
Worcester (town) Otsego County	57	2.22
Pavilion (cdp) Genesee County	9	1.86
Laurel Hollow (village) Nassau County	32	1.70
Horseheads North (cdp) Chemung County	41	1.56

Top 10 Places Sorted by Percent of Total Population
Based on places with total population of 50,000 or more

Place	Population	%
Smithtown (town) Suffolk County	147	0.13
Union (town) Broome County	67	0.12
Albany (city) Albany County	70	0.07
Syracuse (city) Onondaga County	85	0.06
Manhattan (borough) New York County	695	0.04
Buffalo (city) Erie County	100	0.04
North Hempstead (town) Nassau County	79	0.04
Amherst (town) Erie County	53	0.04
Ramapo (town) Rockland County	46	0.04
Greece (town) Monroe County	31	0.03

Soviet Union

Top 10 Places Sorted by Population
Based on all places, regardless of total population

Place	Population	%
New York (city)	419	0.01
Brooklyn (borough) Kings County	219	0.01
Queens (borough) Queens County	71	<0.01
Staten Island (borough) Richmond County	63	0.01
Manhattan (borough) New York County	54	0.01
Yonkers (city) Westchester County	14	0.01
Hornell (city) Steuben County	12	0.14
Bronx (borough) Bronx County	12	<0.01
Oceanside (cdp) Nassau County	10	0.03
Hempstead (town) Nassau County	10	<0.01

Top 10 Places Sorted by Percent of Total Population
Based on all places, regardless of total population

Place	Population	%
Wainscott (cdp) Suffolk County	3	0.69
Hornell (city) Steuben County	12	0.14
Oceanside (cdp) Nassau County	10	0.03
New York (city)	419	0.01
Brooklyn (borough) Kings County	219	0.01
Staten Island (borough) Richmond County	63	0.01
Yonkers (city) Westchester County	14	0.01
East Hampton (town) Suffolk County	3	0.01
Queens (borough) Queens County	71	<0.01
Manhattan (borough) New York County	54	<0.01

Top 10 Places Sorted by Percent of Total Population
Based on places with total population of 50,000 or more

Place	Population	%
New York (city)	419	0.01
Brooklyn (borough) Kings County	219	0.01
Staten Island (borough) Richmond County	63	0.01
Yonkers (city) Westchester County	14	0.01
Queens (borough) Queens County	71	<0.01
Manhattan (borough) New York County	54	<0.01
Bronx (borough) Bronx County	12	<0.01
Hempstead (town) Nassau County	10	<0.01
Albany (city) Albany County	0	0.00
Amherst (town) Erie County	0	0.00

Swedish

Top 10 Places Sorted by Population
Based on all places, regardless of total population

Place	Population	%
New York (city)	20,940	0.26
Manhattan (borough) New York County	10,408	0.66
Jamestown (city) Chautauqua County	5,809	18.63
Brooklyn (borough) Kings County	5,185	0.21
Brookhaven (town) Suffolk County	4,045	0.84
Hempstead (town) Nassau County	3,930	0.52
Queens (borough) Queens County	2,862	0.13
Islip (town) Suffolk County	2,528	0.76
Oyster Bay (town) Nassau County	2,325	0.80
Busti (town) Chautauqua County	2,252	30.51

Top 10 Places Sorted by Percent of Total Population
Based on all places, regardless of total population

Place	Population	%
Chautauqua (cdp) Chautauqua County	119	45.08
Kiantone (town) Chautauqua County	482	32.44
Busti (town) Chautauqua County	2,252	30.51

Celoron (village) Chautauqua County	345	30.45
Busti (cdp) Chautauqua County	158	29.81
Poland (town) Chautauqua County	614	27.47
Frewsburg (cdp) Chautauqua County	531	26.14
Carroll (town) Chautauqua County	903	25.67
Ellicott (town) Chautauqua County	2,238	25.52
Lakewood (village) Chautauqua County	773	25.44

Top 10 Places Sorted by Percent of Total Population
Based on places with total population of 50,000 or more

Place	Population	%
Hamburg (town) Erie County	948	1.68
Colonie (town) Albany County	944	1.16
Huntington (town) Suffolk County	2,237	1.11
Smithtown (town) Suffolk County	1,304	1.11
Clay (town) Onondaga County	625	1.08
Southampton (town) Suffolk County	598	1.06
Tonawanda (town) Erie County	758	1.02
Tonawanda (cdp) Erie County	584	1.00
Irondequoit (cdp/town) Monroe County	482	0.93
Brookhaven (town) Suffolk County	4,045	0.84

Swiss

Top 10 Places Sorted by Population
Based on all places, regardless of total population

Place	Population	%
New York (city)	8,135	0.10
Manhattan (borough) New York County	4,962	0.31
Brooklyn (borough) Kings County	1,491	0.06
Brookhaven (town) Suffolk County	1,356	0.28
Queens (borough) Queens County	1,260	0.06
Hempstead (town) Nassau County	1,183	0.16
Oyster Bay (town) Nassau County	686	0.24
Huntington (town) Suffolk County	632	0.31
Islip (town) Suffolk County	619	0.19
Galen (town) Wayne County	390	9.04

Top 10 Places Sorted by Percent of Total Population
Based on all places, regardless of total population

Place	Population	%
Belleville (cdp) Jefferson County	79	67.52
Constableville (village) Lewis County	36	11.65
Barrington (town) Yates County	184	10.73
Jeffersonville (village) Sullivan County	31	9.63
Galen (town) Wayne County	390	9.04
Castorland (village) Lewis County	34	8.81
Leon (town) Cattaraugus County	116	7.93
Torrey (town) Yates County	100	7.69
Red House (town) Cattaraugus County	2	7.69
Benton (town) Yates County	190	6.78

Top 10 Places Sorted by Percent of Total Population
Based on places with total population of 50,000 or more

Place	Population	%
Irondequoit (cdp/town) Monroe County	255	0.49
Southampton (town) Suffolk County	231	0.41
Manhattan (borough) New York County	4,962	0.31
Huntington (town) Suffolk County	632	0.31
Clay (town) Onondaga County	175	0.30
Brookhaven (town) Suffolk County	1,356	0.28
Schenectady (city) Schenectady County	171	0.26
Oyster Bay (town) Nassau County	686	0.24
Greenburgh (town) Westchester County	211	0.24
White Plains (city) Westchester County	129	0.23

Turkish

Top 10 Places Sorted by Population
Based on all places, regardless of total population

Place	Population	%
New York (city)	14,927	0.18
Brooklyn (borough) Kings County	5,164	0.21
Queens (borough) Queens County	3,767	0.17
Manhattan (borough) New York County	3,703	0.23
Brookhaven (town) Suffolk County	1,935	0.40
Staten Island (borough) Richmond County	1,607	0.35
Oyster Bay (town) Nassau County	1,232	0.42
Hempstead (town) Nassau County	1,202	0.16
Babylon (town) Suffolk County	939	0.44
Bronx (borough) Bronx County	686	0.05

Top 10 Places Sorted by Percent of Total Population
Based on all places, regardless of total population

Place	Population	%
Dering Harbor (village) Suffolk County	5	31.25
Jeffersonville (village) Sullivan County	15	4.66
Orient (cdp) Suffolk County	20	3.33
Port Washington North (village) Nassau County	100	3.29
Walton (village) Delaware County	61	2.31
Wading River (cdp) Suffolk County	178	2.18
Northport (village) Suffolk County	161	2.16
Piermont (village) Rockland County	50	1.99
Bayville (village) Nassau County	128	1.91
East Patchogue (cdp) Suffolk County	388	1.84

Top 10 Places Sorted by Percent of Total Population
Based on places with total population of 50,000 or more

Place	Population	%
Greece (town) Monroe County	561	0.59
Irondequoit (cdp/town) Monroe County	245	0.47
Babylon (town) Suffolk County	939	0.44
Oyster Bay (town) Nassau County	1,232	0.42
Troy (city) Rensselaer County	207	0.41
Brookhaven (town) Suffolk County	1,935	0.40
Staten Island (borough) Richmond County	1,607	0.35
Levittown (cdp) Nassau County	181	0.34
Rochester (city) Monroe County	612	0.29
Huntington (town) Suffolk County	502	0.25

Ukrainian

Top 10 Places Sorted by Population
Based on all places, regardless of total population

Place	Population	%
New York (city)	48,714	0.60
Brooklyn (borough) Kings County	25,046	1.02
Manhattan (borough) New York County	8,849	0.56
Queens (borough) Queens County	8,375	0.38
Staten Island (borough) Richmond County	4,836	1.04
Hempstead (town) Nassau County	2,806	0.37
Brookhaven (town) Suffolk County	2,350	0.49
Oyster Bay (town) Nassau County	1,774	0.61
Greece (town) Monroe County	1,758	1.84
Huntington (town) Suffolk County	1,742	0.86

Top 10 Places Sorted by Percent of Total Population
Based on all places, regardless of total population

Place	Population	%
Washington Mills (cdp) Oneida County	186	17.30
Kerhonkson (cdp) Ulster County	202	15.97
Cragsmoor (cdp) Ulster County	43	11.94
Clarendon (town) Orleans County	374	10.35
Webster (village) Monroe County	531	9.90
Redwood (cdp) Jefferson County	30	9.71
Schuyler (town) Herkimer County	321	9.46
Mountain Lodge Park (cdp) Orange County	175	9.41
Cayuga (village) Cayuga County	36	7.93
Walker Valley (cdp) Ulster County	41	7.65

Top 10 Places Sorted by Percent of Total Population
Based on places with total population of 50,000 or more

Place	Population	%
Irondequoit (cdp/town) Monroe County	1,169	2.27
Greece (town) Monroe County	1,758	1.84
Troy (city) Rensselaer County	819	1.64
Union (town) Broome County	666	1.18
Hamburg (town) Erie County	664	1.17
Ramapo (town) Rockland County	1,403	1.14
Clay (town) Onondaga County	650	1.12
Colonie (town) Albany County	860	1.05
Staten Island (borough) Richmond County	4,836	1.04
Brooklyn (borough) Kings County	25,046	1.02

Welsh

Top 10 Places Sorted by Population
Based on all places, regardless of total population

Place	Population	%
New York (city)	11,219	0.14
Manhattan (borough) New York County	6,000	0.38
Brooklyn (borough) Kings County	2,606	0.11

Queens (borough) Queens County	1,666	0.08
Union (town) Broome County	1,372	2.44
Brookhaven (town) Suffolk County	1,189	0.25
Syracuse (city) Onondaga County	1,060	0.73
Rochester (city) Monroe County	992	0.47
Rome (city) Oneida County	891	2.63
Hempstead (town) Nassau County	865	0.11

Top 10 Places Sorted by Percent of Total Population
Based on all places, regardless of total population

Place	Population	%
Parc (cdp) Clinton County	22	52.38
Barneveld (village) Oneida County	74	24.10
Duanesburg (cdp) Schenectady County	28	16.00
Remsen (town) Oneida County	274	14.13
West Winfield (village) Herkimer County	112	14.11
Winfield (town) Herkimer County	268	13.96
Remsen (village) Oneida County	76	13.89
Holland Patent (village) Oneida County	75	13.54
Madison (village) Madison County	49	12.47
Thousand Island Park (cdp) Jefferson County	13	11.71

Top 10 Places Sorted by Percent of Total Population
Based on places with total population of 50,000 or more

Place	Population	%
Union (town) Broome County	1,372	2.44
Utica (city) Oneida County	775	1.25
Colonie (town) Albany County	704	0.86
Troy (city) Rensselaer County	432	0.86
Clay (town) Onondaga County	496	0.85
Syracuse (city) Onondaga County	1,060	0.73
Irondequoit (cdp/town) Monroe County	352	0.68
Niagara Falls (city) Niagara County	346	0.68
Amherst (town) Erie County	798	0.66
Albany (city) Albany County	597	0.61

West Indian, excluding Hispanic

Top 10 Places Sorted by Population
Based on all places, regardless of total population

Place	Population	%
New York (city)	598,504	7.41
Brooklyn (borough) Kings County	306,541	12.43
Queens (borough) Queens County	147,460	6.71
Bronx (borough) Bronx County	107,527	7.87
Hempstead (town) Nassau County	45,733	6.07
Manhattan (borough) New York County	30,009	1.90
Mount Vernon (city) Westchester County	13,279	19.80
Ramapo (town) Rockland County	12,710	10.36
Babylon (town) Suffolk County	11,187	5.24
Islip (town) Suffolk County	10,274	3.08

Top 10 Places Sorted by Percent of Total Population
Based on all places, regardless of total population

Place	Population	%
Hillcrest (cdp) Rockland County	2,791	34.04
Elmont (cdp) Nassau County	9,499	27.54
Spring Valley (village) Rockland County	7,957	26.24
North Valley Stream (cdp) Nassau County	4,249	25.74
North Amityville (cdp) Suffolk County	3,825	21.47
Uniondale (cdp) Nassau County	5,218	21.30
Mount Vernon (city) Westchester County	13,279	19.80
Lakeview (cdp) Nassau County	1,015	18.22
South Floral Park (village) Nassau County	271	17.35
Wheatley Heights (cdp) Suffolk County	1,036	16.72

Top 10 Places Sorted by Percent of Total Population
Based on places with total population of 50,000 or more

Place	Population	%
Mount Vernon (city) Westchester County	13,279	19.80
Brooklyn (borough) Kings County	306,541	12.43
Hempstead (village) Nassau County	6,463	12.11
Ramapo (town) Rockland County	12,710	10.36
Bronx (borough) Bronx County	107,527	7.87
New York (city)	598,504	7.41
Queens (borough) Queens County	147,460	6.71
Brentwood (cdp) Suffolk County	3,472	6.33
Hempstead (town) Nassau County	45,733	6.07
New Rochelle (city) Westchester County	4,597	6.06

West Indian: Bahamian, excluding Hispanic

Top 10 Places Sorted by Population
Based on all places, regardless of total population

Place	Population	%
New York (city)	1,147	0.01
Manhattan (borough) New York County	457	0.03
Brooklyn (borough) Kings County	266	0.01
Rochester (city) Monroe County	218	0.10
Bronx (borough) Bronx County	208	0.02
Queens (borough) Queens County	185	0.01
North Amityville (cdp) Suffolk County	88	0.49
Babylon (town) Suffolk County	88	0.04
Hempstead (town) Nassau County	51	0.01
Miller Place (cdp) Suffolk County	47	0.38

Top 10 Places Sorted by Percent of Total Population
Based on all places, regardless of total population

Place	Population	%
North Amityville (cdp) Suffolk County	88	0.49
Miller Place (cdp) Suffolk County	47	0.38
South Floral Park (village) Nassau County	5	0.32
Fowler (town) St. Lawrence County	6	0.24
Melville (cdp) Suffolk County	31	0.16
West Hempstead (cdp) Nassau County	28	0.15
Potsdam (village) St. Lawrence County	14	0.15
Fort Ann (town) Washington County	9	0.14
Peekskill (city) Westchester County	28	0.12
Elmira (city) Chemung County	31	0.11

Top 10 Places Sorted by Percent of Total Population
Based on places with total population of 50,000 or more

Place	Population	%
Rochester (city) Monroe County	218	0.10
White Plains (city) Westchester County	26	0.05
Babylon (town) Suffolk County	88	0.04
Hamburg (town) Erie County	21	0.04
Manhattan (borough) New York County	457	0.03
Bronx (borough) Bronx County	208	0.02
Huntington (town) Suffolk County	31	0.02
Mount Vernon (city) Westchester County	11	0.02
New York (city)	1,147	0.01
Brooklyn (borough) Kings County	266	0.01

West Indian: Barbadian, excluding Hispanic

Top 10 Places Sorted by Population
Based on all places, regardless of total population

Place	Population	%
New York (city)	22,550	0.28
Brooklyn (borough) Kings County	14,916	0.60
Queens (borough) Queens County	5,021	0.23
Bronx (borough) Bronx County	1,612	0.12
Hempstead (town) Nassau County	1,279	0.17
Manhattan (borough) New York County	907	0.06
Freeport (village) Nassau County	447	1.05
New Rochelle (city) Westchester County	316	0.42
Rochester (city) Monroe County	230	0.11
Mount Vernon (city) Westchester County	208	0.31

Top 10 Places Sorted by Percent of Total Population
Based on all places, regardless of total population

Place	Population	%
Carthage (village) Jefferson County	183	4.92
Wilna (town) Jefferson County	183	2.87
South Nyack (village) Rockland County	105	1.89
Harriman (village) Orange County	44	1.86
Lakeview (cdp) Nassau County	89	1.60
South Valley Stream (cdp) Nassau County	73	1.39
Hornell (city) Steuben County	93	1.08
Freeport (village) Nassau County	447	1.05
Monticello (village) Sullivan County	68	1.01
Westbury (village) Nassau County	129	0.87

Top 10 Places Sorted by Percent of Total Population
Based on places with total population of 50,000 or more

Place	Population	%
Brooklyn (borough) Kings County	14,916	0.60

New Rochelle (city) Westchester County	316	0.42
Mount Vernon (city) Westchester County	208	0.31
Hempstead (village) Nassau County	153	0.29
New York (city)	22,550	0.28
Queens (borough) Queens County	5,021	0.23
Greenburgh (town) Westchester County	155	0.18
Hempstead (town) Nassau County	1,279	0.17
Schenectady (city) Schenectady County	94	0.14
Bronx (borough) Bronx County	1,612	0.12

West Indian: Belizean, excluding Hispanic

Top 10 Places Sorted by Population
Based on all places, regardless of total population

Place	Population	%
New York (city)	5,674	0.07
Brooklyn (borough) Kings County	2,026	0.08
Bronx (borough) Bronx County	1,493	0.11
Queens (borough) Queens County	1,344	0.06
Manhattan (borough) New York County	735	0.05
Rochester (city) Monroe County	171	0.08
White Plains (city) Westchester County	155	0.28
South Nyack (village) Rockland County	120	2.16
Orangetown (town) Rockland County	120	0.25
Mount Vernon (city) Westchester County	118	0.18

Top 10 Places Sorted by Percent of Total Population
Based on all places, regardless of total population

Place	Population	%
South Nyack (village) Rockland County	120	2.16
Black River (village) Jefferson County	22	1.41
Panama (village) Chautauqua County	6	1.26
Herricks (cdp) Nassau County	37	0.94
Rutland (town) Jefferson County	22	0.73
Cattaraugus Reservation Erie County	12	0.64
Carthage (village) Jefferson County	17	0.46
Chestnut Ridge (village) Rockland County	35	0.45
Brookville (village) Nassau County	13	0.38
Chili (town) Monroe County	85	0.30

Top 10 Places Sorted by Percent of Total Population
Based on places with total population of 50,000 or more

Place	Population	%
White Plains (city) Westchester County	155	0.28
Mount Vernon (city) Westchester County	118	0.18
Bronx (borough) Bronx County	1,493	0.11
Brooklyn (borough) Kings County	2,026	0.08
Rochester (city) Monroe County	171	0.08
New York (city)	5,674	0.07
Queens (borough) Queens County	1,344	0.06
Niagara Falls (city) Niagara County	29	0.06
Manhattan (borough) New York County	735	0.05
Hamburg (town) Erie County	30	0.05

West Indian: Bermudan, excluding Hispanic

Top 10 Places Sorted by Population
Based on all places, regardless of total population

Place	Population	%
New York (city)	518	0.01
Bronx (borough) Bronx County	198	0.01
Queens (borough) Queens County	177	0.01
Manhattan (borough) New York County	127	0.01
Hempstead (town) Nassau County	52	0.01
Roosevelt (cdp) Nassau County	43	0.29
Albany (city) Albany County	36	0.04
Centereach (cdp) Suffolk County	34	0.11
Brookhaven (town) Suffolk County	34	0.01
Brooklyn (borough) Kings County	16	<0.01

Top 10 Places Sorted by Percent of Total Population
Based on all places, regardless of total population

Place	Population	%
Green Island (town/village) Albany County	13	0.51
Old Westbury (village) Nassau County	13	0.33
Roosevelt (cdp) Nassau County	43	0.29
Clermont (town) Columbia County	3	0.15
Upper Nyack (village) Rockland County	3	0.15
Centereach (cdp) Suffolk County	34	0.11
Albany (city) Albany County	36	0.04

Hempstead (village) Nassau County	9	0.02
New York (city)	518	0.01
Bronx (borough) Bronx County	198	0.01

Top 10 Places Sorted by Percent of Total Population
Based on places with total population of 50,000 or more

Place	Population	%
Albany (city) Albany County	36	0.04
Hempstead (village) Nassau County	9	0.02
New York (city)	518	0.01
Bronx (borough) Bronx County	198	0.01
Queens (borough) Queens County	177	0.01
Manhattan (borough) New York County	127	0.01
Hempstead (town) Nassau County	52	0.01
Brookhaven (town) Suffolk County	34	0.01
Brooklyn (borough) Kings County	16	<0.01
Oyster Bay (town) Nassau County	13	<0.01

West Indian: British West Indian, excluding Hispanic

Top 10 Places Sorted by Population
Based on all places, regardless of total population

Place	Population	%
New York (city)	44,326	0.55
Brooklyn (borough) Kings County	30,607	1.24
Bronx (borough) Bronx County	7,136	0.52
Queens (borough) Queens County	4,689	0.21
Manhattan (borough) New York County	1,658	0.10
Hempstead (town) Nassau County	972	0.13
Yonkers (city) Westchester County	497	0.26
Islip (town) Suffolk County	470	0.14
Mount Vernon (city) Westchester County	348	0.52
Wallkill (town) Orange County	296	1.09

Top 10 Places Sorted by Percent of Total Population
Based on all places, regardless of total population

Place	Population	%
Wawayanda (town) Orange County	271	3.79
Scotchtown (cdp) Orange County	222	2.28
Amagansett (cdp) Suffolk County	17	1.90
Cumberland Head (cdp) Clinton County	25	1.51
Brooklyn (borough) Kings County	30,607	1.24
Hillcrest (cdp) Rockland County	93	1.13
Wallkill (town) Orange County	296	1.09
Bay Shore (cdp) Suffolk County	253	0.91
Highland (cdp) Ulster County	49	0.86
Mechanicstown (cdp) Orange County	63	0.84

Top 10 Places Sorted by Percent of Total Population
Based on places with total population of 50,000 or more

Place	Population	%
Brooklyn (borough) Kings County	30,607	1.24
New York (city)	44,326	0.55
Bronx (borough) Bronx County	7,136	0.52
Mount Vernon (city) Westchester County	348	0.52
Hempstead (village) Nassau County	250	0.47
Yonkers (city) Westchester County	497	0.26
Queens (borough) Queens County	4,689	0.21
Ramapo (town) Rockland County	253	0.21
Albany (city) Albany County	210	0.21
New Rochelle (city) Westchester County	153	0.20

West Indian: Dutch West Indian, excluding Hispanic

Top 10 Places Sorted by Population
Based on all places, regardless of total population

Place	Population	%
New York (city)	1,167	0.01
Brooklyn (borough) Kings County	424	0.02
Manhattan (borough) New York County	276	0.02
Queens (borough) Queens County	206	0.01
Hempstead (town) Nassau County	199	0.03
Bronx (borough) Bronx County	172	0.01
North Valley Stream (cdp) Nassau County	134	0.81
Staten Island (borough) Richmond County	89	0.02
Albany (city) Albany County	79	0.08
Brownville (town) Jefferson County	71	1.16

Top 10 Places Sorted by Percent of Total Population
Based on all places, regardless of total population

Place	Population	%
Brownville (town) Jefferson County	71	1.16
Barnum Island (cdp) Nassau County	25	0.95
German (town) Chenango County	3	0.95
Hartwick (town) Otsego County	20	0.83
North Valley Stream (cdp) Nassau County	134	0.81
Mamakating (town) Sullivan County	55	0.46
Westbury (village) Nassau County	65	0.44
Lansing (village) Tompkins County	14	0.40
Preston (town) Chenango County	3	0.31
Lansing (town) Tompkins County	32	0.29

Top 10 Places Sorted by Percent of Total Population
Based on places with total population of 50,000 or more

Place	Population	%
Albany (city) Albany County	79	0.08
Hempstead (village) Nassau County	31	0.06
Hempstead (town) Nassau County	199	0.03
North Hempstead (town) Nassau County	65	0.03
Brooklyn (borough) Kings County	424	0.02
Manhattan (borough) New York County	276	0.02
Staten Island (borough) Richmond County	89	0.02
Schenectady (city) Schenectady County	10	0.02
New York (city)	1,167	0.01
Queens (borough) Queens County	206	0.01

West Indian: Haitian, excluding Hispanic

Top 10 Places Sorted by Population
Based on all places, regardless of total population

Place	Population	%
New York (city)	120,252	1.49
Brooklyn (borough) Kings County	69,941	2.84
Queens (borough) Queens County	38,368	1.74
Hempstead (town) Nassau County	17,422	2.31
Ramapo (town) Rockland County	8,948	7.29
Spring Valley (village) Rockland County	6,665	21.98
Manhattan (borough) New York County	6,500	0.41
Islip (town) Suffolk County	5,636	1.69
Elmont (cdp) Nassau County	5,587	16.20
Bronx (borough) Bronx County	4,652	0.34

Top 10 Places Sorted by Percent of Total Population
Based on all places, regardless of total population

Place	Population	%
Spring Valley (village) Rockland County	6,665	21.98
Elmont (cdp) Nassau County	5,587	16.20
Hillcrest (cdp) Rockland County	1,310	15.98
North Valley Stream (cdp) Nassau County	1,827	11.07
Hillburn (village) Rockland County	88	9.27
Wheatley Heights (cdp) Suffolk County	545	8.80
New Cassel (cdp) Nassau County	1,053	8.38
Nyack (village) Rockland County	577	8.29
Deferiet (village) Jefferson County	38	8.09
Uniondale (cdp) Nassau County	1,927	7.87

Top 10 Places Sorted by Percent of Total Population
Based on places with total population of 50,000 or more

Place	Population	%
Ramapo (town) Rockland County	8,948	7.29
Brentwood (cdp) Suffolk County	2,162	3.94
Hempstead (village) Nassau County	2,104	3.94
Brooklyn (borough) Kings County	69,941	2.84
Clarkstown (town) Rockland County	2,077	2.49
Hempstead (town) Nassau County	17,422	2.31
Babylon (town) Suffolk County	3,789	1.77
Queens (borough) Queens County	38,368	1.74
Islip (town) Suffolk County	5,636	1.69
New York (city)	120,252	1.49

West Indian: Jamaican, excluding Hispanic

Top 10 Places Sorted by Population
Based on all places, regardless of total population

Place	Population	%
New York (city)	216,495	2.68
Brooklyn (borough) Kings County	80,999	3.28

Place	Population	%
Bronx (borough) Bronx County	64,222	4.70
Queens (borough) Queens County	59,999	2.73
Hempstead (town) Nassau County	17,690	2.35
Mount Vernon (city) Westchester County	10,445	15.57
Manhattan (borough) New York County	9,242	0.58
Yonkers (city) Westchester County	5,051	2.59
Babylon (town) Suffolk County	4,758	2.23
Poughkeepsie (city) Dutchess County	3,093	9.53

Top 10 Places Sorted by Percent of Total Population
Based on all places, regardless of total population

Place	Population	%
Mount Vernon (city) Westchester County	10,445	15.57
Lakeview (cdp) Nassau County	791	14.20
North Amityville (cdp) Suffolk County	2,248	12.62
Hillcrest (cdp) Rockland County	854	10.42
Poughkeepsie (city) Dutchess County	3,093	9.53
South Floral Park (village) Nassau County	141	9.03
Elmont (cdp) Nassau County	2,968	8.61
Uniondale (cdp) Nassau County	1,905	7.78
North Valley Stream (cdp) Nassau County	1,257	7.62
Morrisville (village) Madison County	173	6.83

Top 10 Places Sorted by Percent of Total Population
Based on places with total population of 50,000 or more

Place	Population	%
Mount Vernon (city) Westchester County	10,445	15.57
Hempstead (village) Nassau County	2,809	5.26
Bronx (borough) Bronx County	64,222	4.70
New Rochelle (city) Westchester County	2,635	3.48
Brooklyn (borough) Kings County	80,999	3.28
Queens (borough) Queens County	59,999	2.73
New York (city)	216,495	2.68
Yonkers (city) Westchester County	5,051	2.59
Greenburgh (town) Westchester County	2,150	2.45
Hempstead (town) Nassau County	17,690	2.35

West Indian: Trinidadian and Tobagonian, excluding Hispanic

Top 10 Places Sorted by Population
Based on all places, regardless of total population

Place	Population	%
New York (city)	76,240	0.94
Brooklyn (borough) Kings County	46,490	1.88
Queens (borough) Queens County	19,255	0.88
Bronx (borough) Bronx County	4,811	0.35
Manhattan (borough) New York County	3,877	0.24
Hempstead (town) Nassau County	3,155	0.42
Staten Island (borough) Richmond County	1,807	0.39
Brookhaven (town) Suffolk County	1,200	0.25
Babylon (town) Suffolk County	854	0.40
Yonkers (city) Westchester County	689	0.35

Top 10 Places Sorted by Percent of Total Population
Based on all places, regardless of total population

Place	Population	%
Brewster (village) Putnam County	131	6.53
Hillcrest (cdp) Rockland County	367	4.48
East Marion (cdp) Suffolk County	54	4.04
South Floral Park (village) Nassau County	53	3.39
North Valley Stream (cdp) Nassau County	551	3.34
Rockland (town) Sullivan County	106	2.75
South Valley Stream (cdp) Nassau County	110	2.09
Greenwood Lake (village) Orange County	67	2.07
Goshen (village) Orange County	111	2.00
Brooklyn (borough) Kings County	46,490	1.88

Top 10 Places Sorted by Percent of Total Population
Based on places with total population of 50,000 or more

Place	Population	%
Brooklyn (borough) Kings County	46,490	1.88
New York (city)	76,240	0.94
Queens (borough) Queens County	19,255	0.88
Hempstead (village) Nassau County	322	0.60
Mount Vernon (city) Westchester County	397	0.59
Ramapo (town) Rockland County	604	0.49
Troy (city) Rensselaer County	243	0.49
Hempstead (town) Nassau County	3,155	0.42
New Rochelle (city) Westchester County	317	0.42
Babylon (town) Suffolk County	854	0.40

West Indian: U.S. Virgin Islander, excluding Hispanic

Top 10 Places Sorted by Population
Based on all places, regardless of total population

Place	Population	%
New York (city)	2,383	0.03
Bronx (borough) Bronx County	952	0.07
Brooklyn (borough) Kings County	558	0.02
Manhattan (borough) New York County	487	0.03
Queens (borough) Queens County	364	0.02
South Huntington (cdp) Suffolk County	147	1.49
Huntington (town) Suffolk County	147	0.07
Yonkers (city) Westchester County	83	0.04
Poughkeepsie (city) Dutchess County	42	0.13
Middletown (city) Orange County	33	0.12

Top 10 Places Sorted by Percent of Total Population
Based on all places, regardless of total population

Place	Population	%
South Huntington (cdp) Suffolk County	147	1.49
Roxbury (town) Delaware County	28	1.12
Brownville (village) Jefferson County	7	0.67
Brookville (village) Nassau County	15	0.43
Otisville (village) Orange County	4	0.36
New Hyde Park (village) Nassau County	30	0.31
Washingtonville (village) Orange County	11	0.18
Poughkeepsie (city) Dutchess County	42	0.13
Attica (town) Wyoming County	10	0.13
Middletown (city) Orange County	33	0.12

Top 10 Places Sorted by Percent of Total Population
Based on places with total population of 50,000 or more

Place	Population	%
Bronx (borough) Bronx County	952	0.07
Huntington (town) Suffolk County	147	0.07
Yonkers (city) Westchester County	83	0.04
White Plains (city) Westchester County	23	0.04
New York (city)	2,383	0.03
Manhattan (borough) New York County	487	0.03
Brooklyn (borough) Kings County	558	0.02
Queens (borough) Queens County	364	0.02
Ramapo (town) Rockland County	19	0.02
Oyster Bay (town) Nassau County	15	0.01

West Indian: West Indian, excluding Hispanic

Top 10 Places Sorted by Population
Based on all places, regardless of total population

Place	Population	%
New York (city)	106,548	1.32
Brooklyn (borough) Kings County	59,844	2.43
Bronx (borough) Bronx County	21,941	1.61
Queens (borough) Queens County	17,400	0.79
Manhattan (borough) New York County	5,618	0.35
Hempstead (town) Nassau County	4,748	0.63
Staten Island (borough) Richmond County	1,745	0.38
Babylon (town) Suffolk County	1,378	0.64
Brookhaven (town) Suffolk County	1,323	0.28
Mount Vernon (city) Westchester County	1,287	1.92

Top 10 Places Sorted by Percent of Total Population
Based on all places, regardless of total population

Place	Population	%
Aurora (village) Cayuga County	76	6.79
Rushville (village) Yates County	44	6.48
Fairview (cdp) Westchester County	103	4.32
Hillburn (village) Rockland County	38	4.00
Ledyard (town) Cayuga County	76	3.41
South Blooming Grove (village) Orange County	105	3.19
South Hempstead (cdp) Nassau County	90	2.82
Moravia (town) Cayuga County	102	2.75
Calcium (cdp) Jefferson County	91	2.57
North Valley Stream (cdp) Nassau County	422	2.56

Top 10 Places Sorted by Percent of Total Population
Based on places with total population of 50,000 or more

Place	Population	%
Brooklyn (borough) Kings County	59,844	2.43

Mount Vernon (city) Westchester County	1,287	1.92
Bronx (borough) Bronx County	21,941	1.61
Hempstead (village) Nassau County	785	1.47
New York (city)	106,548	1.32
Queens (borough) Queens County	17,400	0.79
Schenectady (city) Schenectady County	446	0.68
Babylon (town) Suffolk County	1,378	0.64
Hempstead (town) Nassau County	4,748	0.63
Albany (city) Albany County	576	0.59

West Indian: Other, excluding Hispanic

Top 10 Places Sorted by Population
Based on all places, regardless of total population

Place	Population	%
New York (city)	1,204	0.01
Brooklyn (borough) Kings County	454	0.02
Queens (borough) Queens County	452	0.02
Bronx (borough) Bronx County	130	0.01
Manhattan (borough) New York County	125	0.01
Albany (city) Albany County	67	0.07
Staten Island (borough) Richmond County	43	0.01
Monroe (village) Orange County	40	0.48
Monroe (town) Orange County	40	0.10
Brookhaven (town) Suffolk County	27	0.01

Top 10 Places Sorted by Percent of Total Population
Based on all places, regardless of total population

Place	Population	%
Unionville (village) Orange County	2	0.52
Monroe (village) Orange County	40	0.48
Horseheads (village) Chemung County	11	0.17
Monroe (town) Orange County	40	0.10

Stony Brook (cdp) Suffolk County	12	0.09
Albany (city) Albany County	67	0.07
Massapequa (cdp) Nassau County	15	0.07
Williamson (town) Wayne County	5	0.07
Horseheads (town) Chemung County	11	0.06
Centereach (cdp) Suffolk County	15	0.05

Top 10 Places Sorted by Percent of Total Population
Based on places with total population of 50,000 or more

Place	Population	%
Albany (city) Albany County	67	0.07
Troy (city) Rensselaer County	13	0.03
Brooklyn (borough) Kings County	454	0.02
Queens (borough) Queens County	452	0.02
New York (city)	1,204	0.01
Bronx (borough) Bronx County	130	0.01
Manhattan (borough) New York County	125	0.01
Staten Island (borough) Richmond County	43	0.01
Brookhaven (town) Suffolk County	27	0.01
Oyster Bay (town) Nassau County	15	0.01

Yugoslavian

Top 10 Places Sorted by Population
Based on all places, regardless of total population

Place	Population	%
New York (city)	12,410	0.15
Queens (borough) Queens County	4,516	0.21
Utica (city) Oneida County	3,231	5.23
Brooklyn (borough) Kings County	2,800	0.11
Manhattan (borough) New York County	1,876	0.12
Staten Island (borough) Richmond County	1,738	0.38
Bronx (borough) Bronx County	1,480	0.11

Syracuse (city) Onondaga County	774	0.53
Hempstead (town) Nassau County	649	0.09
Brookhaven (town) Suffolk County	518	0.11

Top 10 Places Sorted by Percent of Total Population
Based on all places, regardless of total population

Place	Population	%
Napeague (cdp) Suffolk County	51	24.40
Pinckney (town) Lewis County	15	6.33
Utica (city) Oneida County	3,231	5.23
Lebanon (town) Madison County	73	4.93
Hawthorne (cdp) Westchester County	211	4.66
Angola on the Lake (cdp) Erie County	55	3.92
Exeter (town) Otsego County	27	3.11
Fleischmanns (village) Delaware County	6	2.91
Masonville (town) Delaware County	38	2.81
Milan (town) Dutchess County	71	2.80

Top 10 Places Sorted by Percent of Total Population
Based on places with total population of 50,000 or more

Place	Population	%
Utica (city) Oneida County	3,231	5.23
Syracuse (city) Onondaga County	774	0.53
Staten Island (borough) Richmond County	1,738	0.38
Huntington (town) Suffolk County	467	0.23
Clay (town) Onondaga County	132	0.23
Queens (borough) Queens County	4,516	0.21
Tonawanda (cdp) Erie County	124	0.21
Smithtown (town) Suffolk County	216	0.18
Colonie (town) Albany County	143	0.18
Tonawanda (town) Erie County	133	0.18

Hispanic Origin Rankings

Hispanic or Latino (of any race)

Top 10 Places Sorted by Population
Based on all places, regardless of total population

Place	Population	%
New York (city)	2,336,076	28.58
Bronx (borough) Bronx County	741,413	53.53
Queens (borough) Queens County	613,750	27.51
Brooklyn (borough) Kings County	496,285	19.81
Manhattan (borough) New York County	403,577	25.45
Hempstead (town) Nassau County	132,154	17.39
Islip (town) Suffolk County	97,371	29.02
Staten Island (borough) Richmond County	81,051	17.29
Yonkers (city) Westchester County	67,927	34.66
Brookhaven (town) Suffolk County	60,270	12.40

Top 10 Places Sorted by Percent of Total Population
Based on all places, regardless of total population

Place	Population	%
Brentwood (cdp) Suffolk County	41,529	68.46
Haverstraw (village) Rockland County	7,993	67.11
North Bay Shore (cdp) Suffolk County	12,310	64.98
Port Chester (village) Westchester County	17,193	59.35
Brewster (village) Putnam County	1,338	55.98
New Cassel (cdp) Nassau County	7,577	53.89
Bronx (borough) Bronx County	741,413	53.53
Central Islip (cdp) Suffolk County	17,938	52.07
Sleepy Hollow (village) Westchester County	5,038	51.04
Newburgh (city) Orange County	13,814	47.86

Top 10 Places Sorted by Percent of Total Population
Based on places with total population of 50,000 or more

Place	Population	%
Brentwood (cdp) Suffolk County	41,529	68.46
Bronx (borough) Bronx County	741,413	53.53
Hempstead (village) Nassau County	23,823	44.21
Yonkers (city) Westchester County	67,927	34.66
White Plains (city) Westchester County	16,839	29.62
Islip (town) Suffolk County	97,371	29.02
New York (city)	2,336,076	28.58
New Rochelle (city) Westchester County	21,452	27.84
Queens (borough) Queens County	613,750	27.51
Manhattan (borough) New York County	403,577	25.45

Central American, excluding Mexican

Top 10 Places Sorted by Population
Based on all places, regardless of total population

Place	Population	%
New York (city)	151,378	1.85
Queens (borough) Queens County	52,509	2.35
Hempstead (town) Nassau County	49,236	6.48
Brooklyn (borough) Kings County	46,119	1.84
Islip (town) Suffolk County	38,530	11.48
Bronx (borough) Bronx County	34,492	2.49
Brentwood (cdp) Suffolk County	19,957	32.90
Hempstead (village) Nassau County	16,171	30.01
Manhattan (borough) New York County	13,948	0.88
North Hempstead (town) Nassau County	11,455	5.06

Top 10 Places Sorted by Percent of Total Population
Based on all places, regardless of total population

Place	Population	%
Brewster (village) Putnam County	967	40.46
Brentwood (cdp) Suffolk County	19,957	32.90
New Cassel (cdp) Nassau County	4,455	31.69
North Bay Shore (cdp) Suffolk County	5,763	30.42
Hempstead (village) Nassau County	16,171	30.01
Inwood (cdp) Nassau County	2,509	25.62
Uniondale (cdp) Nassau County	6,264	25.30
Central Islip (cdp) Suffolk County	8,487	24.64
Flanders (cdp) Suffolk County	1,034	23.12
Roosevelt (cdp) Nassau County	3,748	23.05

Top 10 Places Sorted by Percent of Total Population
Based on places with total population of 50,000 or more

Place	Population	%
Brentwood (cdp) Suffolk County	19,957	32.90
Hempstead (village) Nassau County	16,171	30.01
Islip (town) Suffolk County	38,530	11.48
Southampton (town) Suffolk County	3,715	6.54
Hempstead (town) Nassau County	49,236	6.48
Babylon (town) Suffolk County	11,096	5.19
North Hempstead (town) Nassau County	11,455	5.06
Huntington (town) Suffolk County	9,599	4.72
Ramapo (town) Rockland County	5,319	4.20
Yonkers (city) Westchester County	5,822	2.97

Central American: Costa Rican

Top 10 Places Sorted by Population
Based on all places, regardless of total population

Place	Population	%
New York (city)	6,673	0.08
Brooklyn (borough) Kings County	2,576	0.10
Queens (borough) Queens County	1,749	0.08
Bronx (borough) Bronx County	1,095	0.08
Manhattan (borough) New York County	987	0.06
Hempstead (town) Nassau County	664	0.09
Southampton (town) Suffolk County	618	1.09
Hampton Bays (cdp) Suffolk County	406	2.98
Islip (town) Suffolk County	297	0.09
Staten Island (borough) Richmond County	266	0.06

Top 10 Places Sorted by Percent of Total Population
Based on all places, regardless of total population

Place	Population	%
Hampton Bays (cdp) Suffolk County	406	2.98
Tuckahoe (cdp) Suffolk County	23	1.68
Springs (cdp) Suffolk County	103	1.56
East Hampton North (cdp) Suffolk County	53	1.28
Bridgehampton (cdp) Suffolk County	21	1.20
Peconic (cdp) Suffolk County	8	1.17
Southampton (town) Suffolk County	618	1.09
East Hampton (town) Suffolk County	216	1.01
Shinnecock Hills (cdp) Suffolk County	22	1.01
Woodridge (village) Sullivan County	8	0.94

Top 10 Places Sorted by Percent of Total Population
Based on places with total population of 50,000 or more

Place	Population	%
Southampton (town) Suffolk County	618	1.09
Brentwood (cdp) Suffolk County	85	0.14
Brooklyn (borough) Kings County	2,576	0.10
Mount Vernon (city) Westchester County	64	0.10
Hempstead (town) Nassau County	664	0.09
Islip (town) Suffolk County	297	0.09
New York (city)	6,673	0.08
Queens (borough) Queens County	1,749	0.08
Bronx (borough) Bronx County	1,095	0.08
Yonkers (city) Westchester County	156	0.08

Central American: Guatemalan

Top 10 Places Sorted by Population
Based on all places, regardless of total population

Place	Population	%
New York (city)	30,420	0.37
Queens (borough) Queens County	13,700	0.61
Brooklyn (borough) Kings County	9,160	0.37
Hempstead (town) Nassau County	5,948	0.78
Bronx (borough) Bronx County	4,645	0.34
Ramapo (town) Rockland County	4,050	3.20
Spring Valley (village) Rockland County	3,265	10.42
Islip (town) Suffolk County	3,256	0.97
Rye (town) Westchester County	2,654	5.78
Port Chester (village) Westchester County	2,433	8.40

Top 10 Places Sorted by Percent of Total Population
Based on all places, regardless of total population

Place	Population	%
Brewster (village) Putnam County	912	38.16
Mount Kisco (town/village) Westchester County	1,782	16.38
Flanders (cdp) Suffolk County	678	15.16
Cattaraugus Reservation Chautauqua County	5	13.16
Greenport (village) Suffolk County	287	13.06
Quiogue (cdp) Suffolk County	103	12.62
Bedford Hills (cdp) Westchester County	317	10.56
Spring Valley (village) Rockland County	3,265	10.42
Westhampton Beach (village) Suffolk County	178	10.34
Riverside (cdp) Suffolk County	273	9.38

Top 10 Places Sorted by Percent of Total Population
Based on places with total population of 50,000 or more

Place	Population	%
Southampton (town) Suffolk County	2,081	3.66
Ramapo (town) Rockland County	4,050	3.20
Hempstead (village) Nassau County	1,402	2.60
Brentwood (cdp) Suffolk County	1,553	2.56
New Rochelle (city) Westchester County	1,232	1.60
Islip (town) Suffolk County	3,256	0.97
White Plains (city) Westchester County	551	0.97
Clarkstown (town) Rockland County	802	0.95
Hempstead (town) Nassau County	5,948	0.78
Queens (borough) Queens County	13,700	0.61

Central American: Honduran

Top 10 Places Sorted by Population
Based on all places, regardless of total population

Place	Population	%
New York (city)	42,400	0.52
Bronx (borough) Bronx County	17,990	1.30
Brooklyn (borough) Kings County	10,071	0.40
Queens (borough) Queens County	8,546	0.38
Hempstead (town) Nassau County	7,842	1.03
Islip (town) Suffolk County	4,232	1.26
Manhattan (borough) New York County	4,058	0.26
Hempstead (village) Nassau County	3,758	6.97
Brentwood (cdp) Suffolk County	2,062	3.40
Babylon (town) Suffolk County	1,756	0.82

Top 10 Places Sorted by Percent of Total Population
Based on all places, regardless of total population

Place	Population	%
Woodridge (village) Sullivan County	60	7.08
Hempstead (village) Nassau County	3,758	6.97
South Fallsburg (cdp) Sullivan County	200	6.97
New Cassel (cdp) Nassau County	812	5.78
Newburgh (city) Orange County	1,545	5.35
Huntington Station (cdp) Suffolk County	1,260	3.81
Brentwood (cdp) Suffolk County	2,062	3.40
Uniondale (cdp) Nassau County	806	3.26
Central Islip (cdp) Suffolk County	1,118	3.25
Oyster Bay (cdp) Nassau County	212	3.16

Top 10 Places Sorted by Percent of Total Population
Based on places with total population of 50,000 or more

Place	Population	%
Hempstead (village) Nassau County	3,758	6.97
Brentwood (cdp) Suffolk County	2,062	3.40
Bronx (borough) Bronx County	17,990	1.30
Islip (town) Suffolk County	4,232	1.26
Hempstead (town) Nassau County	7,842	1.03
Babylon (town) Suffolk County	1,756	0.82
Huntington (town) Suffolk County	1,651	0.81
Yonkers (city) Westchester County	1,451	0.74
North Hempstead (town) Nassau County	1,572	0.69
New York (city)	42,400	0.52

Central American: Nicaraguan

Top 10 Places Sorted by Population
Based on all places, regardless of total population

Place	Population	%
New York (city)	9,346	0.11
Queens (borough) Queens County	2,842	0.13
Brooklyn (borough) Kings County	2,407	0.10
Bronx (borough) Bronx County	2,342	0.17
Manhattan (borough) New York County	1,556	0.10
Hempstead (town) Nassau County	656	0.09
Yonkers (city) Westchester County	534	0.27
Islip (town) Suffolk County	253	0.08
Staten Island (borough) Richmond County	199	0.04
Brookhaven (town) Suffolk County	159	0.03

Top 10 Places Sorted by Percent of Total Population
Based on all places, regardless of total population

Place	Population	%
Quiogue (cdp) Suffolk County	8	0.98
Inwood (cdp) Nassau County	79	0.81
Cove Neck (village) Nassau County	2	0.70
Hewlett (cdp) Nassau County	36	0.53
North Hornell (village) Steuben County	4	0.51
Woodmere (cdp) Nassau County	73	0.43
Bellerose Terrace (cdp) Nassau County	9	0.41
South Fallsburg (cdp) Sullivan County	11	0.38
Greenport (village) Suffolk County	8	0.36
Cedarhurst (village) Nassau County	23	0.35

Top 10 Places Sorted by Percent of Total Population
Based on places with total population of 50,000 or more

Place	Population	%
Yonkers (city) Westchester County	534	0.27
Bronx (borough) Bronx County	2,342	0.17
Brentwood (cdp) Suffolk County	87	0.14
Queens (borough) Queens County	2,842	0.13
New York (city)	9,346	0.11
Brooklyn (borough) Kings County	2,407	0.10
Manhattan (borough) New York County	1,556	0.10
New Rochelle (city) Westchester County	74	0.10
Hempstead (village) Nassau County	56	0.10
Hempstead (town) Nassau County	656	0.09

Central American: Panamanian

Top 10 Places Sorted by Population
Based on all places, regardless of total population

Place	Population	%
New York (city)	22,353	0.27
Brooklyn (borough) Kings County	13,681	0.55
Queens (borough) Queens County	3,977	0.18
Bronx (borough) Bronx County	2,372	0.17
Manhattan (borough) New York County	1,716	0.11
Hempstead (town) Nassau County	1,163	0.15
Staten Island (borough) Richmond County	607	0.13
Islip (town) Suffolk County	466	0.14
Babylon (town) Suffolk County	305	0.14
Brookhaven (town) Suffolk County	291	0.06

Top 10 Places Sorted by Percent of Total Population
Based on all places, regardless of total population

Place	Population	%
Lakeview (cdp) Nassau County	53	0.94
Northampton (cdp) Suffolk County	5	0.88
Evans Mills (village) Jefferson County	5	0.81
Parc (cdp) Clinton County	2	0.79
Washington Heights (cdp) Orange County	11	0.65
Otego (village) Otsego County	6	0.59
North Valley Stream (cdp) Nassau County	93	0.56
Corfu (village) Genesee County	4	0.56
Brooklyn (borough) Kings County	13,681	0.55
Wyandanch (cdp) Suffolk County	57	0.49

Top 10 Places Sorted by Percent of Total Population
Based on places with total population of 50,000 or more

Place	Population	%
Brooklyn (borough) Kings County	13,681	0.55
New York (city)	22,353	0.27
Hempstead (village) Nassau County	138	0.26
Brentwood (cdp) Suffolk County	148	0.24

Mount Vernon (city) Westchester County	131	0.19
Queens (borough) Queens County	3,977	0.18
Bronx (borough) Bronx County	2,372	0.17
Hempstead (town) Nassau County	1,163	0.15
Islip (town) Suffolk County	466	0.14
Babylon (town) Suffolk County	305	0.14

Central American: Salvadoran

Top 10 Places Sorted by Population
Based on all places, regardless of total population

Place	Population	%
New York (city)	38,559	0.47
Hempstead (town) Nassau County	32,681	4.30
Islip (town) Suffolk County	29,849	8.90
Queens (borough) Queens County	21,342	0.96
Brentwood (cdp) Suffolk County	15,946	26.29
Hempstead (village) Nassau County	10,707	19.87
North Hempstead (town) Nassau County	8,262	3.65
Babylon (town) Suffolk County	7,805	3.65
Brooklyn (borough) Kings County	7,737	0.31
Huntington (town) Suffolk County	6,563	3.23

Top 10 Places Sorted by Percent of Total Population
Based on all places, regardless of total population

Place	Population	%
Brentwood (cdp) Suffolk County	15,946	26.29
New Cassel (cdp) Nassau County	3,477	24.73
North Bay Shore (cdp) Suffolk County	4,530	23.91
Uniondale (cdp) Nassau County	4,998	20.19
Hempstead (village) Nassau County	10,707	19.87
Central Islip (cdp) Suffolk County	6,381	18.52
Roosevelt (cdp) Nassau County	2,891	17.78
Huntington Station (cdp) Suffolk County	5,233	15.84
Inwood (cdp) Nassau County	1,523	15.55
Wyandanch (cdp) Suffolk County	1,485	12.75

Top 10 Places Sorted by Percent of Total Population
Based on places with total population of 50,000 or more

Place	Population	%
Brentwood (cdp) Suffolk County	15,946	26.29
Hempstead (village) Nassau County	10,707	19.87
Islip (town) Suffolk County	29,849	8.90
Hempstead (town) Nassau County	32,681	4.30
North Hempstead (town) Nassau County	8,262	3.65
Babylon (town) Suffolk County	7,805	3.65
Huntington (town) Suffolk County	6,563	3.23
Levittown (cdp) Nassau County	876	1.69
Yonkers (city) Westchester County	2,691	1.37
Brookhaven (town) Suffolk County	5,899	1.21

Central American: Other Central American

Top 10 Places Sorted by Population
Based on all places, regardless of total population

Place	Population	%
New York (city)	1,627	0.02
Bronx (borough) Bronx County	579	0.04
Brooklyn (borough) Kings County	487	0.02
Queens (borough) Queens County	353	0.02
Hempstead (town) Nassau County	282	0.04
Islip (town) Suffolk County	177	0.05
Manhattan (borough) New York County	161	0.01
North Hempstead (town) Nassau County	110	0.05
Brookhaven (town) Suffolk County	106	0.02
Babylon (town) Suffolk County	88	0.04

Top 10 Places Sorted by Percent of Total Population
Based on all places, regardless of total population

Place	Population	%
Mount Kisco (town/village) Westchester County	31	0.29
New Cassel (cdp) Nassau County	37	0.26
Flanders (cdp) Suffolk County	10	0.22
Pawling (village) Dutchess County	5	0.21
Amityville (village) Suffolk County	19	0.20
West Nyack (cdp) Rockland County	7	0.20
Central Islip (cdp) Suffolk County	65	0.19
Berne (town) Albany County	5	0.18
Greenvale (cdp) Nassau County	2	0.18
Mattituck (cdp) Suffolk County	7	0.17

Top 10 Places Sorted by Percent of Total Population
Based on places with total population of 50,000 or more

Place	Population	%
Brentwood (cdp) Suffolk County	76	0.13
Hempstead (village) Nassau County	66	0.12
Islip (town) Suffolk County	177	0.05
North Hempstead (town) Nassau County	110	0.05
Bronx (borough) Bronx County	579	0.04
Hempstead (town) Nassau County	282	0.04
Babylon (town) Suffolk County	88	0.04
Huntington (town) Suffolk County	52	0.03
Southampton (town) Suffolk County	17	0.03
New York (city)	1,627	0.02

Cuban

Top 10 Places Sorted by Population
Based on all places, regardless of total population

Place	Population	%
New York (city)	40,840	0.50
Manhattan (borough) New York County	11,623	0.73
Queens (borough) Queens County	11,020	0.49
Bronx (borough) Bronx County	8,785	0.63
Brooklyn (borough) Kings County	7,581	0.30
Hempstead (town) Nassau County	3,597	0.47
Staten Island (borough) Richmond County	1,831	0.39
Rochester (city) Monroe County	1,616	0.77
Yonkers (city) Westchester County	1,501	0.77
Brookhaven (town) Suffolk County	1,500	0.31

Top 10 Places Sorted by Percent of Total Population
Based on all places, regardless of total population

Place	Population	%
Hunt (cdp) Livingston County	2	2.56
Hewlett Bay Park (village) Nassau County	10	2.48
East Kingston (cdp) Ulster County	6	2.17
Tarrytown (village) Westchester County	205	1.82
Bellerose (village) Nassau County	20	1.68
South Floral Park (village) Nassau County	23	1.30
Sleepy Hollow (village) Westchester County	123	1.25
North Hudson (town) Essex County	3	1.25
Port Chester (village) Westchester County	359	1.24
Plattekill (cdp) Ulster County	14	1.11

Top 10 Places Sorted by Percent of Total Population
Based on places with total population of 50,000 or more

Place	Population	%
Syracuse (city) Onondaga County	1,192	0.82
Rochester (city) Monroe County	1,616	0.77
Yonkers (city) Westchester County	1,501	0.77
Manhattan (borough) New York County	11,623	0.73
Greenburgh (town) Westchester County	565	0.64
Bronx (borough) Bronx County	8,785	0.63
White Plains (city) Westchester County	321	0.56
Levittown (cdp) Nassau County	274	0.53
New York (city)	40,840	0.50
Clarkstown (town) Rockland County	421	0.50

Dominican Republic

Top 10 Places Sorted by Population
Based on all places, regardless of total population

Place	Population	%
New York (city)	576,701	7.05
Bronx (borough) Bronx County	240,987	17.40
Manhattan (borough) New York County	155,971	9.84
Queens (borough) Queens County	88,061	3.95
Brooklyn (borough) Kings County	86,764	3.46
Hempstead (town) Nassau County	16,914	2.23
Yonkers (city) Westchester County	15,903	8.11
Islip (town) Suffolk County	8,547	2.55
Babylon (town) Suffolk County	6,543	3.06
Haverstraw (town) Rockland County	6,277	17.13

Top 10 Places Sorted by Percent of Total Population
Based on all places, regardless of total population

Place	Population	%
Haverstraw (village) Rockland County	3,847	32.30
Sleepy Hollow (village) Westchester County	1,831	18.55
Bronx (borough) Bronx County	240,987	17.40

Place	Population	%
Haverstraw (town) Rockland County	6,277	17.13
West Haverstraw (village) Rockland County	1,667	16.40
Freeport (village) Nassau County	5,539	12.92
Copiague (cdp) Suffolk County	2,846	12.38
Manhattan (borough) New York County	155,971	9.84
Yonkers (city) Westchester County	15,903	8.11
New York (city)	576,701	7.05

Top 10 Places Sorted by Percent of Total Population
Based on places with total population of 50,000 or more

Place	Population	%
Bronx (borough) Bronx County	240,987	17.40
Manhattan (borough) New York County	155,971	9.84
Yonkers (city) Westchester County	15,903	8.11
New York (city)	576,701	7.05
Brentwood (cdp) Suffolk County	4,205	6.93
Queens (borough) Queens County	88,061	3.95
Brooklyn (borough) Kings County	86,764	3.46
Babylon (town) Suffolk County	6,543	3.06
Hempstead (village) Nassau County	1,398	2.59
Islip (town) Suffolk County	8,547	2.55

Mexican

Top 10 Places Sorted by Population
Based on all places, regardless of total population

Place	Population	%
New York (city)	319,263	3.91
Brooklyn (borough) Kings County	94,585	3.78
Queens (borough) Queens County	92,835	4.16
Bronx (borough) Bronx County	71,194	5.14
Manhattan (borough) New York County	41,965	2.65
Staten Island (borough) Richmond County	18,684	3.99
Yonkers (city) Westchester County	13,761	7.02
New Rochelle (city) Westchester County	10,363	13.45
Newburgh (city) Orange County	6,181	21.41
White Plains (city) Westchester County	5,773	10.15

Top 10 Places Sorted by Percent of Total Population
Based on all places, regardless of total population

Place	Population	%
Fleischmanns (village) Delaware County	117	33.33
Newburgh (city) Orange County	6,181	21.41
Port Chester (village) Westchester County	4,864	16.79
Middletown (city) Orange County	4,208	14.98
New Rochelle (city) Westchester County	10,363	13.45
Tuckahoe (cdp) Suffolk County	181	13.18
Shinnecock Hills (cdp) Suffolk County	282	12.89
New Cassel (cdp) Nassau County	1,739	12.37
Rye (town) Westchester County	5,313	11.57
Dresden (village) Yates County	34	11.04

Top 10 Places Sorted by Percent of Total Population
Based on places with total population of 50,000 or more

Place	Population	%
New Rochelle (city) Westchester County	10,363	13.45
White Plains (city) Westchester County	5,773	10.15
Yonkers (city) Westchester County	13,761	7.02
Bronx (borough) Bronx County	71,194	5.14
Southampton (town) Suffolk County	2,856	5.03
Queens (borough) Queens County	92,835	4.16
Staten Island (borough) Richmond County	18,684	3.99
New York (city)	319,263	3.91
Brooklyn (borough) Kings County	94,585	3.78
Mount Vernon (city) Westchester County	2,454	3.65

Puerto Rican

Top 10 Places Sorted by Population
Based on all places, regardless of total population

Place	Population	%
New York (city)	723,621	8.85
Bronx (borough) Bronx County	298,921	21.58
Brooklyn (borough) Kings County	176,528	7.05
Manhattan (borough) New York County	107,774	6.80
Queens (borough) Queens County	102,881	4.61
Staten Island (borough) Richmond County	37,517	8.00
Rochester (city) Monroe County	27,734	13.17
Buffalo (city) Erie County	22,076	8.45
Islip (town) Suffolk County	21,506	6.41
Brookhaven (town) Suffolk County	21,429	4.41

Top 10 Places Sorted by Percent of Total Population
Based on all places, regardless of total population

Place	Population	%
Plattekill (cdp) Ulster County	328	26.03
Dunkirk (city) Chautauqua County	2,782	22.14
Bronx (borough) Bronx County	298,921	21.58
Amsterdam (city) Montgomery County	3,923	21.07
Ellenville (village) Ulster County	832	20.12
Middletown (city) Orange County	4,533	16.14
Monticello (village) Sullivan County	1,073	15.95
Washington Heights (cdp) Orange County	261	15.45
Scotchtown (cdp) Orange County	1,410	15.31
Mechanicstown (cdp) Orange County	996	14.52

Top 10 Places Sorted by Percent of Total Population
Based on places with total population of 50,000 or more

Place	Population	%
Bronx (borough) Bronx County	298,921	21.58
Rochester (city) Monroe County	27,734	13.17
Yonkers (city) Westchester County	19,875	10.14
Brentwood (cdp) Suffolk County	6,125	10.10
New York (city)	723,621	8.85
Buffalo (city) Erie County	22,076	8.45
Staten Island (borough) Richmond County	37,517	8.00
Schenectady (city) Schenectady County	4,677	7.07
Brooklyn (borough) Kings County	176,528	7.05
Manhattan (borough) New York County	107,774	6.80

South American

Top 10 Places Sorted by Population
Based on all places, regardless of total population

Place	Population	%
New York (city)	343,468	4.20
Queens (borough) Queens County	214,022	9.59
Brooklyn (borough) Kings County	49,003	1.96
Manhattan (borough) New York County	36,748	2.32
Bronx (borough) Bronx County	35,463	2.56
Hempstead (town) Nassau County	23,626	3.11
Islip (town) Suffolk County	16,012	4.77
Brookhaven (town) Suffolk County	12,182	2.51
Staten Island (borough) Richmond County	8,232	1.76
Ossining (town) Westchester County	6,825	18.12

Top 10 Places Sorted by Percent of Total Population
Based on all places, regardless of total population

Place	Population	%
East Hampton North (cdp) Suffolk County	1,076	25.98
Ossining (village) Westchester County	6,440	25.70
Springs (cdp) Suffolk County	1,623	24.62
Sleepy Hollow (village) Westchester County	2,098	21.26
Port Chester (village) Westchester County	5,769	19.92
Ossining (town) Westchester County	6,825	18.12
Elmsford (village) Westchester County	812	17.41
Peekskill (city) Westchester County	4,041	17.14
East Hampton (town) Suffolk County	3,513	16.37
Patchogue (village) Suffolk County	1,777	15.06

Top 10 Places Sorted by Percent of Total Population
Based on places with total population of 50,000 or more

Place	Population	%
Brentwood (cdp) Suffolk County	6,350	10.47
White Plains (city) Westchester County	5,850	10.29
Queens (borough) Queens County	214,022	9.59
New Rochelle (city) Westchester County	3,697	4.80
Islip (town) Suffolk County	16,012	4.77
Greenburgh (town) Westchester County	4,004	4.53
Southampton (town) Suffolk County	2,446	4.31
New York (city)	343,468	4.20
Yonkers (city) Westchester County	6,622	3.38
Levittown (cdp) Nassau County	1,746	3.37

South American: Argentinean

Top 10 Places Sorted by Population
Based on all places, regardless of total population

Place	Population	%
New York (city)	15,169	0.19
Queens (borough) Queens County	6,345	0.28
Manhattan (borough) New York County	4,339	0.27

Place	Population	%
Brooklyn (borough) Kings County	2,760	0.11
Hempstead (town) Nassau County	1,500	0.20
Bronx (borough) Bronx County	1,117	0.08
Brookhaven (town) Suffolk County	653	0.13
Islip (town) Suffolk County	616	0.18
Staten Island (borough) Richmond County	608	0.13
Oyster Bay (town) Nassau County	441	0.15

Top 10 Places Sorted by Percent of Total Population
Based on all places, regardless of total population

Place	Population	%
Russell Gardens (village) Nassau County	9	0.95
Kiryas Joel (village) Orange County	186	0.92
Hobart (village) Delaware County	4	0.91
Northville (cdp) Suffolk County	9	0.67
Woodsburgh (village) Nassau County	5	0.64
Asharoken (village) Suffolk County	4	0.61
Lynbrook (village) Nassau County	110	0.57
Salisbury Mills (cdp) Orange County	3	0.56
Monroe (town) Orange County	217	0.54
Harbor Hills (cdp) Nassau County	3	0.52

Top 10 Places Sorted by Percent of Total Population
Based on places with total population of 50,000 or more

Place	Population	%
Brentwood (cdp) Suffolk County	203	0.33
White Plains (city) Westchester County	189	0.33
Queens (borough) Queens County	6,345	0.28
Manhattan (borough) New York County	4,339	0.27
New Rochelle (city) Westchester County	170	0.22
Greenburgh (town) Westchester County	188	0.21
Hempstead (town) Nassau County	1,500	0.20
New York (city)	15,169	0.19
North Hempstead (town) Nassau County	435	0.19
Islip (town) Suffolk County	616	0.18

South American: Bolivian

Top 10 Places Sorted by Population
Based on all places, regardless of total population

Place	Population	%
New York (city)	4,488	0.05
Queens (borough) Queens County	3,268	0.15
Manhattan (borough) New York County	522	0.03
Hempstead (town) Nassau County	494	0.07
Rye (town) Westchester County	375	0.82
Port Chester (village) Westchester County	350	1.21
Brooklyn (borough) Kings County	310	0.01
Bronx (borough) Bronx County	227	0.02
Islip (town) Suffolk County	220	0.07
Staten Island (borough) Richmond County	161	0.03

Top 10 Places Sorted by Percent of Total Population
Based on all places, regardless of total population

Place	Population	%
Poospatuck Reservation Suffolk County	4	1.23
Port Chester (village) Westchester County	350	1.21
Rye (town) Westchester County	375	0.82
Merritt Park (cdp) Dutchess County	6	0.48
Inwood (cdp) Nassau County	43	0.44
Matinecock (village) Nassau County	3	0.37
Friendship (cdp) Allegany County	4	0.33
East Rockaway (village) Nassau County	31	0.32
Islandia (village) Suffolk County	10	0.30
Cedarhurst (village) Nassau County	18	0.27

Top 10 Places Sorted by Percent of Total Population
Based on places with total population of 50,000 or more

Place	Population	%
Queens (borough) Queens County	3,268	0.15
Brentwood (cdp) Suffolk County	79	0.13
White Plains (city) Westchester County	72	0.13
Hempstead (town) Nassau County	494	0.07
Islip (town) Suffolk County	220	0.07
New Rochelle (city) Westchester County	50	0.06
New York (city)	4,488	0.05
Greenburgh (town) Westchester County	48	0.05
Oyster Bay (town) Nassau County	110	0.04
Babylon (town) Suffolk County	78	0.04

Please refer to the Explanation of Data in the front of the book for more detailed information.

South American: Chilean

Top 10 Places Sorted by Population
Based on all places, regardless of total population

Place	Population	%
New York (city)	7,026	0.09
Queens (borough) Queens County	3,184	0.14
Manhattan (borough) New York County	1,824	0.12
Hempstead (town) Nassau County	1,415	0.19
Brooklyn (borough) Kings County	1,026	0.04
North Hempstead (town) Nassau County	664	0.29
Bronx (borough) Bronx County	646	0.05
Oyster Bay (town) Nassau County	569	0.19
Islip (town) Suffolk County	448	0.13
Brookhaven (town) Suffolk County	363	0.07

Top 10 Places Sorted by Percent of Total Population
Based on all places, regardless of total population

Place	Population	%
Manorhaven (village) Nassau County	234	3.57
Oyster Bay (cdp) Nassau County	179	2.67
Windham (cdp) Greene County	6	1.63
Sleepy Hollow (village) Westchester County	146	1.48
Forest Home (cdp) Tompkins County	8	1.40
Ames (village) Montgomery County	2	1.38
Inwood (cdp) Nassau County	108	1.10
North Lynbrook (cdp) Nassau County	8	1.01
Cedarhurst (village) Nassau County	65	0.99
Port Washington (cdp) Nassau County	149	0.94

Top 10 Places Sorted by Percent of Total Population
Based on places with total population of 50,000 or more

Place	Population	%
North Hempstead (town) Nassau County	664	0.29
Brentwood (cdp) Suffolk County	153	0.25
Greenburgh (town) Westchester County	192	0.22
Levittown (cdp) Nassau County	112	0.22
Hempstead (town) Nassau County	1,415	0.19
Oyster Bay (town) Nassau County	569	0.19
Queens (borough) Queens County	3,184	0.14
Islip (town) Suffolk County	448	0.13
Manhattan (borough) New York County	1,824	0.12
Huntington (town) Suffolk County	252	0.12

South American: Colombian

Top 10 Places Sorted by Population
Based on all places, regardless of total population

Place	Population	%
New York (city)	94,723	1.16
Queens (borough) Queens County	70,290	3.15
Brooklyn (borough) Kings County	8,861	0.35
Hempstead (town) Nassau County	8,522	1.12
Manhattan (borough) New York County	8,411	0.53
Islip (town) Suffolk County	5,156	1.54
Bronx (borough) Bronx County	4,635	0.33
Brookhaven (town) Suffolk County	2,970	0.61
Staten Island (borough) Richmond County	2,526	0.54
Brentwood (cdp) Suffolk County	2,083	3.43

Top 10 Places Sorted by Percent of Total Population
Based on all places, regardless of total population

Place	Population	%
East Hampton North (cdp) Suffolk County	284	6.86
Springs (cdp) Suffolk County	430	6.52
Bellerose Terrace (cdp) Nassau County	124	5.64
East Hampton (town) Suffolk County	987	4.60
Hampton Bays (cdp) Suffolk County	614	4.51
Elmsford (village) Westchester County	186	3.99
Shinnecock Hills (cdp) Suffolk County	84	3.84
Montauk (cdp) Suffolk County	119	3.58
Brentwood (cdp) Suffolk County	2,083	3.43
White Plains (city) Westchester County	1,838	3.23

Top 10 Places Sorted by Percent of Total Population
Based on places with total population of 50,000 or more

Place	Population	%
Brentwood (cdp) Suffolk County	2,083	3.43
White Plains (city) Westchester County	1,838	3.23
Queens (borough) Queens County	70,290	3.15
New Rochelle (city) Westchester County	1,451	1.88

Southampton (town) Suffolk County	1,024	1.80
Islip (town) Suffolk County	5,156	1.54
Levittown (cdp) Nassau County	733	1.41
New York (city)	94,723	1.16
Hempstead (town) Nassau County	8,522	1.12
Greenburgh (town) Westchester County	845	0.96

South American: Ecuadorian

Top 10 Places Sorted by Population
Based on all places, regardless of total population

Place	Population	%
New York (city)	167,209	2.05
Queens (borough) Queens County	98,512	4.42
Brooklyn (borough) Kings County	28,684	1.15
Bronx (borough) Bronx County	23,206	1.68
Manhattan (borough) New York County	14,132	0.89
Brookhaven (town) Suffolk County	6,437	1.32
Hempstead (town) Nassau County	5,881	0.77
Islip (town) Suffolk County	5,323	1.59
Ossining (town) Westchester County	4,988	13.24
Ossining (village) Westchester County	4,840	19.31

Top 10 Places Sorted by Percent of Total Population
Based on all places, regardless of total population

Place	Population	%
Ossining (village) Westchester County	4,840	19.31
Sleepy Hollow (village) Westchester County	1,731	17.54
East Hampton North (cdp) Suffolk County	717	17.31
Springs (cdp) Suffolk County	1,137	17.25
Peekskill (city) Westchester County	3,490	14.80
Patchogue (village) Suffolk County	1,616	13.70
Ossining (town) Westchester County	4,988	13.24
East Hampton (town) Suffolk County	2,319	10.81
Port Chester (village) Westchester County	2,774	9.58
Spring Valley (village) Rockland County	2,681	8.55

Top 10 Places Sorted by Percent of Total Population
Based on places with total population of 50,000 or more

Place	Population	%
Queens (borough) Queens County	98,512	4.42
Brentwood (cdp) Suffolk County	1,985	3.27
Ramapo (town) Rockland County	2,915	2.30
New York (city)	167,209	2.05
Southampton (town) Suffolk County	1,102	1.94
White Plains (city) Westchester County	1,001	1.76
Bronx (borough) Bronx County	23,206	1.68
Yonkers (city) Westchester County	3,271	1.67
Greenburgh (town) Westchester County	1,434	1.62
Islip (town) Suffolk County	5,323	1.59

South American: Paraguayan

Top 10 Places Sorted by Population
Based on all places, regardless of total population

Place	Population	%
New York (city)	3,534	0.04
Queens (borough) Queens County	2,775	0.12
Manhattan (borough) New York County	268	0.02
White Plains (city) Westchester County	260	0.46
Harrison (town/village) Westchester County	235	0.86
Brooklyn (borough) Kings County	230	0.01
Bronx (borough) Bronx County	223	0.02
Hempstead (town) Nassau County	185	0.02
Greenburgh (town) Westchester County	144	0.16
North Hempstead (town) Nassau County	140	0.06

Top 10 Places Sorted by Percent of Total Population
Based on all places, regardless of total population

Place	Population	%
Bedford (cdp) Westchester County	28	1.53
Scotts Corners (cdp) Westchester County	10	1.41
Cove Neck (village) Nassau County	3	1.05
Fairview (cdp) Westchester County	28	0.90
Harrison (town/village) Westchester County	235	0.86
Elmsford (village) Westchester County	35	0.75
Mamaroneck (village) Westchester County	130	0.69
Hewlett Bay Park (village) Nassau County	2	0.50
Bedford Hills (cdp) Westchester County	14	0.47
White Plains (city) Westchester County	260	0.46

Top 10 Places Sorted by Percent of Total Population
Based on places with total population of 50,000 or more

Place	Population	%
White Plains (city) Westchester County	260	0.46
Greenburgh (town) Westchester County	144	0.16
Queens (borough) Queens County	2,775	0.12
Mount Vernon (city) Westchester County	68	0.10
North Hempstead (town) Nassau County	140	0.06
New Rochelle (city) Westchester County	49	0.06
Brentwood (cdp) Suffolk County	36	0.06
Southampton (town) Suffolk County	26	0.05
New York (city)	3,534	0.04
Huntington (town) Suffolk County	91	0.04

South American: Peruvian

Top 10 Places Sorted by Population
Based on all places, regardless of total population

Place	Population	%
New York (city)	36,018	0.44
Queens (borough) Queens County	22,886	1.03
Hempstead (town) Nassau County	4,510	0.59
Brooklyn (borough) Kings County	4,222	0.17
Manhattan (borough) New York County	3,852	0.24
Islip (town) Suffolk County	3,599	1.07
Bronx (borough) Bronx County	3,596	0.26
White Plains (city) Westchester County	2,260	3.98
Rye (town) Westchester County	1,734	3.78
Brentwood (cdp) Suffolk County	1,610	2.65

Top 10 Places Sorted by Percent of Total Population
Based on all places, regardless of total population

Place	Population	%
Port Chester (village) Westchester County	1,485	5.13
Island Park (village) Nassau County	234	5.03
Elmsford (village) Westchester County	189	4.05
White Plains (city) Westchester County	2,260	3.98
Rye (town) Westchester County	1,734	3.78
Glen Cove (city) Nassau County	883	3.27
Baywood (cdp) Suffolk County	222	3.02
Barnum Island (cdp) Nassau County	73	3.02
Fairview (cdp) Westchester County	89	2.87
Bellerose Terrace (cdp) Nassau County	60	2.73

Top 10 Places Sorted by Percent of Total Population
Based on places with total population of 50,000 or more

Place	Population	%
White Plains (city) Westchester County	2,260	3.98
Brentwood (cdp) Suffolk County	1,610	2.65
New Rochelle (city) Westchester County	1,297	1.68
Greenburgh (town) Westchester County	962	1.09
Islip (town) Suffolk County	3,599	1.07
Queens (borough) Queens County	22,886	1.03
Babylon (town) Suffolk County	1,313	0.61
Hempstead (town) Nassau County	4,510	0.59
Levittown (cdp) Nassau County	285	0.55
Hempstead (village) Nassau County	279	0.52

South American: Uruguayan

Top 10 Places Sorted by Population
Based on all places, regardless of total population

Place	Population	%
New York (city)	3,004	0.04
Queens (borough) Queens County	1,743	0.08
Manhattan (borough) New York County	549	0.03
Brooklyn (borough) Kings County	488	0.02
Hempstead (town) Nassau County	359	0.05
Ossining (town) Westchester County	273	0.72
Ossining (village) Westchester County	230	0.92
Islip (town) Suffolk County	216	0.06
Rye (town) Westchester County	211	0.46
Port Chester (village) Westchester County	159	0.55

Top 10 Places Sorted by Percent of Total Population
Based on all places, regardless of total population

Place	Population	%
Ossining (village) Westchester County	230	0.92
Ossining (town) Westchester County	273	0.72
Cove Neck (village) Nassau County	2	0.70

Place	Population	%
Buchanan (village) Westchester County	13	0.58
Port Chester (village) Westchester County	159	0.55
Hillside Lake (cdp) Dutchess County	6	0.55
Crugers (cdp) Westchester County	8	0.52
Rye (town) Westchester County	211	0.46
Islandia (village) Suffolk County	15	0.45
Chappaqua (cdp) Westchester County	6	0.42

Top 10 Places Sorted by Percent of Total Population
Based on places with total population of 50,000 or more

Place	Population	%
Brentwood (cdp) Suffolk County	80	0.13
New Rochelle (city) Westchester County	88	0.11
White Plains (city) Westchester County	63	0.11
Levittown (cdp) Nassau County	47	0.09
Queens (borough) Queens County	1,743	0.08
Greenburgh (town) Westchester County	65	0.07
Islip (town) Suffolk County	216	0.06
Hempstead (town) Nassau County	359	0.05
Oyster Bay (town) Nassau County	134	0.05
New York (city)	3,004	0.04

South American: Venezuelan

Top 10 Places Sorted by Population
Based on all places, regardless of total population

Place	Population	%
New York (city)	9,619	0.12
Queens (borough) Queens County	3,580	0.16
Manhattan (borough) New York County	2,573	0.16
Brooklyn (borough) Kings County	1,916	0.08
Bronx (borough) Bronx County	1,296	0.09
Hempstead (town) Nassau County	517	0.07
Islip (town) Suffolk County	322	0.10
Brookhaven (town) Suffolk County	302	0.06
Staten Island (borough) Richmond County	254	0.05
Yonkers (city) Westchester County	207	0.11

Top 10 Places Sorted by Percent of Total Population
Based on all places, regardless of total population

Place	Population	%
Westport (cdp) Essex County	6	1.16
Ward (town) Allegany County	4	1.09
Shinnecock Reservation Suffolk County	4	0.60
Scotts Corners (cdp) Westchester County	4	0.56
Shoreham (village) Suffolk County	3	0.56
Merritt Park (cdp) Dutchess County	6	0.48
Westport (town) Essex County	6	0.46
Mountain Lodge Park (cdp) Orange County	7	0.44
Jewett (town) Greene County	4	0.42
Washington Mills (cdp) Oneida County	4	0.34

Top 10 Places Sorted by Percent of Total Population
Based on places with total population of 50,000 or more

Place	Population	%
Brentwood (cdp) Suffolk County	113	0.19
New Rochelle (city) Westchester County	131	0.17
Queens (borough) Queens County	3,580	0.16
Manhattan (borough) New York County	2,573	0.16
White Plains (city) Westchester County	77	0.14
New York (city)	9,619	0.12
Yonkers (city) Westchester County	207	0.11
Greenburgh (town) Westchester County	94	0.11
Islip (town) Suffolk County	322	0.10
Bronx (borough) Bronx County	1,296	0.09

South American: Other South American

Top 10 Places Sorted by Population
Based on all places, regardless of total population

Place	Population	%
New York (city)	2,678	0.03
Queens (borough) Queens County	1,439	0.06
Brooklyn (borough) Kings County	506	0.02
Bronx (borough) Bronx County	369	0.03
Manhattan (borough) New York County	278	0.02
Hempstead (town) Nassau County	243	0.03
Brookhaven (town) Suffolk County	98	0.02
Staten Island (borough) Richmond County	86	0.02
Yonkers (city) Westchester County	63	0.03
Islip (town) Suffolk County	54	0.02

Top 10 Places Sorted by Percent of Total Population
Based on all places, regardless of total population

Place	Population	%
Woodsburgh (village) Nassau County	8	1.03
Quiogue (cdp) Suffolk County	4	0.49
East Hampton North (cdp) Suffolk County	19	0.46
Plattekill (cdp) Ulster County	5	0.40
Scio (town) Allegany County	5	0.27
Northwest Harbor (cdp) Suffolk County	8	0.24
Dolgeville (village) Herkimer County	5	0.23
Lakeview (cdp) Nassau County	12	0.21
Harriman (village) Orange County	5	0.21
Cold Spring (village) Putnam County	4	0.20

Top 10 Places Sorted by Percent of Total Population
Based on places with total population of 50,000 or more

Place	Population	%
Schenectady (city) Schenectady County	43	0.07
Queens (borough) Queens County	1,439	0.06
Mount Vernon (city) Westchester County	33	0.05

Place	Population	%
Levittown (cdp) Nassau County	27	0.05
Greenburgh (town) Westchester County	32	0.04
Hempstead (village) Nassau County	23	0.04
White Plains (city) Westchester County	23	0.04
New York (city)	2,678	0.03
Bronx (borough) Bronx County	369	0.03
Hempstead (town) Nassau County	243	0.03

Other Hispanic or Latino

Top 10 Places Sorted by Population
Based on all places, regardless of total population

Place	Population	%
New York (city)	180,805	2.21
Queens (borough) Queens County	52,422	2.35
Bronx (borough) Bronx County	51,571	3.72
Brooklyn (borough) Kings County	35,705	1.43
Manhattan (borough) New York County	35,548	2.24
Hempstead (town) Nassau County	13,273	1.75
Islip (town) Suffolk County	8,524	2.54
Brookhaven (town) Suffolk County	6,193	1.27
Staten Island (borough) Richmond County	5,559	1.19
Yonkers (city) Westchester County	4,443	2.27

Top 10 Places Sorted by Percent of Total Population
Based on all places, regardless of total population

Place	Population	%
Riverside (cdp) Suffolk County	348	11.95
Watchtower (cdp) Ulster County	171	7.18
Brentwood (cdp) Suffolk County	3,476	5.73
North Bay Shore (cdp) Suffolk County	967	5.10
Northwest Harbor (cdp) Suffolk County	168	5.06
New Cassel (cdp) Nassau County	699	4.97
Hempstead (village) Nassau County	2,609	4.84
Central Islip (cdp) Suffolk County	1,667	4.84
Inwood (cdp) Nassau County	467	4.77
Brewster (village) Putnam County	113	4.73

Top 10 Places Sorted by Percent of Total Population
Based on places with total population of 50,000 or more

Place	Population	%
Brentwood (cdp) Suffolk County	3,476	5.73
Hempstead (village) Nassau County	2,609	4.84
Bronx (borough) Bronx County	51,571	3.72
Southampton (town) Suffolk County	1,468	2.58
Islip (town) Suffolk County	8,524	2.54
Queens (borough) Queens County	52,422	2.35
Yonkers (city) Westchester County	4,443	2.27
Manhattan (borough) New York County	35,548	2.24
New York (city)	180,805	2.21
White Plains (city) Westchester County	1,209	2.13

Racial Group Rankings

African-American/Black

Top 10 Places Sorted by Population
Based on all places, regardless of total population

Place	Population	%
New York (city)	2,228,145	27.26
Brooklyn (borough) Kings County	896,165	35.78
Bronx (borough) Bronx County	541,622	39.10
Queens (borough) Queens County	462,351	20.73
Manhattan (borough) New York County	272,993	17.21
Hempstead (town) Nassau County	133,280	17.54
Buffalo (city) Erie County	106,107	40.61
Rochester (city) Monroe County	94,587	44.92
Staten Island (borough) Richmond County	55,014	11.74
Syracuse (city) Onondaga County	48,029	33.08

Top 10 Places Sorted by Percent of Total Population
Based on all places, regardless of total population

Place	Population	%
Lakeview (cdp) Nassau County	4,757	84.72
Wyandanch (cdp) Suffolk County	7,865	67.53
Mount Vernon (city) Westchester County	44,244	65.75
Roosevelt (cdp) Nassau County	10,657	65.55
North Amityville (cdp) Suffolk County	10,971	61.42
Fairview (cdp) Westchester County	1,895	61.15
South Floral Park (village) Nassau County	1,075	60.94
Wheatley Heights (cdp) Suffolk County	2,960	57.70
Hillcrest (cdp) Rockland County	4,328	57.26
Gordon Heights (cdp) Suffolk County	2,294	56.75

Top 10 Places Sorted by Percent of Total Population
Based on places with total population of 50,000 or more

Place	Population	%
Mount Vernon (city) Westchester County	44,244	65.75
Hempstead (village) Nassau County	27,076	50.24
Rochester (city) Monroe County	94,587	44.92
Buffalo (city) Erie County	106,107	40.61
Bronx (borough) Bronx County	541,622	39.10
Brooklyn (borough) Kings County	896,165	35.78
Albany (city) Albany County	32,569	33.28
Syracuse (city) Onondaga County	48,029	33.08
New York (city)	2,228,145	27.26
Schenectady (city) Schenectady County	16,103	24.35

African-American/Black: Not Hispanic

Top 10 Places Sorted by Population
Based on all places, regardless of total population

Place	Population	%
New York (city)	1,931,889	23.63
Brooklyn (borough) Kings County	820,437	32.76
Bronx (borough) Bronx County	427,134	30.84
Queens (borough) Queens County	419,695	18.81
Manhattan (borough) New York County	217,102	13.69
Hempstead (town) Nassau County	124,525	16.39
Buffalo (city) Erie County	101,817	38.96
Rochester (city) Monroe County	88,052	41.82
Staten Island (borough) Richmond County	47,521	10.14
Syracuse (city) Onondaga County	45,084	31.06

Top 10 Places Sorted by Percent of Total Population
Based on all places, regardless of total population

Place	Population	%
Lakeview (cdp) Nassau County	4,534	80.75
Wyandanch (cdp) Suffolk County	7,550	64.82
Mount Vernon (city) Westchester County	42,361	62.95
Roosevelt (cdp) Nassau County	10,138	62.36
North Amityville (cdp) Suffolk County	10,434	58.41
Fairview (cdp) Westchester County	1,800	58.08
South Floral Park (village) Nassau County	1,024	58.05
Wheatley Heights (cdp) Suffolk County	2,821	54.99
Hillcrest (cdp) Rockland County	4,140	54.78
Gordon Heights (cdp) Suffolk County	2,073	51.29

Top 10 Places Sorted by Percent of Total Population
Based on places with total population of 50,000 or more

Place	Population	%
Mount Vernon (city) Westchester County	42,361	62.95
Hempstead (village) Nassau County	25,388	47.11
Rochester (city) Monroe County	88,052	41.82
Buffalo (city) Erie County	101,817	38.96
Brooklyn (borough) Kings County	820,437	32.76
Syracuse (city) Onondaga County	45,084	31.06
Albany (city) Albany County	30,376	31.04
Bronx (borough) Bronx County	427,134	30.84
Niagara Falls (city) Niagara County	11,905	23.72
New York (city)	1,931,889	23.63

African-American/Black: Hispanic

Top 10 Places Sorted by Population
Based on all places, regardless of total population

Place	Population	%
New York (city)	296,256	3.62
Bronx (borough) Bronx County	114,488	8.27
Brooklyn (borough) Kings County	75,728	3.02
Manhattan (borough) New York County	55,891	3.52
Queens (borough) Queens County	42,656	1.91
Hempstead (town) Nassau County	8,755	1.15
Staten Island (borough) Richmond County	7,493	1.60
Yonkers (city) Westchester County	7,325	3.74
Rochester (city) Monroe County	6,535	3.10
Islip (town) Suffolk County	5,700	1.70

Top 10 Places Sorted by Percent of Total Population
Based on all places, regardless of total population

Place	Population	%
Bronx (borough) Bronx County	114,488	8.27
Gordon Heights (cdp) Suffolk County	221	5.47
Haverstraw (village) Rockland County	574	4.82
Middletown (city) Orange County	1,209	4.30
Monticello (village) Sullivan County	283	4.21
Washington Heights (cdp) Orange County	68	4.03
North Bay Shore (cdp) Suffolk County	756	3.99
Lakeview (cdp) Nassau County	223	3.97
Parc (cdp) Clinton County	10	3.94
Yonkers (city) Westchester County	7,325	3.74

Top 10 Places Sorted by Percent of Total Population
Based on places with total population of 50,000 or more

Place	Population	%
Bronx (borough) Bronx County	114,488	8.27
Yonkers (city) Westchester County	7,325	3.74
New York (city)	296,256	3.62
Manhattan (borough) New York County	55,891	3.52
Brentwood (cdp) Suffolk County	2,138	3.52
Hempstead (village) Nassau County	1,688	3.13
Rochester (city) Monroe County	6,535	3.10
Brooklyn (borough) Kings County	75,728	3.02
Mount Vernon (city) Westchester County	1,883	2.80
Schenectady (city) Schenectady County	1,547	2.34

American Indian/Alaska Native

Top 10 Places Sorted by Population
Based on all places, regardless of total population

Place	Population	%
New York (city)	111,749	1.37
Bronx (borough) Bronx County	32,011	2.31
Queens (borough) Queens County	30,033	1.35
Brooklyn (borough) Kings County	26,571	1.06
Manhattan (borough) New York County	19,415	1.22
Hempstead (town) Nassau County	5,363	0.71
Buffalo (city) Erie County	4,019	1.54
Brookhaven (town) Suffolk County	3,782	0.78
Staten Island (borough) Richmond County	3,719	0.79
Syracuse (city) Onondaga County	3,537	2.44

Top 10 Places Sorted by Percent of Total Population
Based on all places, regardless of total population

Place	Population	%
Tonawanda Reservation Erie County	34	100.00
Oil Springs Reservation Allegany County	1	100.00
Onondaga Nation Reservation Onondaga County	457	97.65
St. Regis Mohawk Reservation Franklin County	3,131	97.00
Tonawanda Reservation Genesee County	463	95.86
Cattaraugus Reservation Cattaraugus County	294	93.63
Cattaraugus Reservation Erie County	1,672	91.22
Shinnecock Reservation Suffolk County	584	88.22
Cattaraugus Reservation Chautauqua County	29	76.32
Allegany Reservation Cattaraugus County	670	65.69

Top 10 Places Sorted by Percent of Total Population
Based on places with total population of 50,000 or more

Place	Population	%
Niagara Falls (city) Niagara County	1,624	3.24
Syracuse (city) Onondaga County	3,537	2.44
Bronx (borough) Bronx County	32,011	2.31
Schenectady (city) Schenectady County	1,372	2.07
Brentwood (cdp) Suffolk County	1,135	1.87
Hempstead (village) Nassau County	997	1.85
White Plains (city) Westchester County	890	1.57
Buffalo (city) Erie County	4,019	1.54
Rochester (city) Monroe County	3,202	1.52
Yonkers (city) Westchester County	2,801	1.43

American Indian/Alaska Native: Not Hispanic

Top 10 Places Sorted by Population
Based on all places, regardless of total population

Place	Population	%
New York (city)	44,541	0.54
Queens (borough) Queens County	15,412	0.69
Brooklyn (borough) Kings County	12,062	0.48
Bronx (borough) Bronx County	7,638	0.55
Manhattan (borough) New York County	7,395	0.47
Buffalo (city) Erie County	3,229	1.24
St. Regis Mohawk Reservation Franklin County	3,116	96.53
Syracuse (city) Onondaga County	3,067	2.11
Hempstead (town) Nassau County	2,835	0.37
Brookhaven (town) Suffolk County	2,586	0.53

Top 10 Places Sorted by Percent of Total Population
Based on all places, regardless of total population

Place	Population	%
Tonawanda Reservation Erie County	34	100.00
Oil Springs Reservation Allegany County	1	100.00
St. Regis Mohawk Reservation Franklin County	3,116	96.53
Onondaga Nation Reservation Onondaga County	447	95.51
Tonawanda Reservation Genesee County	447	92.55
Cattaraugus Reservation Cattaraugus County	283	90.13
Cattaraugus Reservation Erie County	1,613	88.00
Shinnecock Reservation Suffolk County	554	83.69
Allegany Reservation Cattaraugus County	645	63.24
Cattaraugus Reservation Chautauqua County	24	63.16

Top 10 Places Sorted by Percent of Total Population
Based on places with total population of 50,000 or more

Place	Population	%
Niagara Falls (city) Niagara County	1,524	3.04
Syracuse (city) Onondaga County	3,067	2.11
Schenectady (city) Schenectady County	1,126	1.70
Buffalo (city) Erie County	3,229	1.24
Rochester (city) Monroe County	2,330	1.11
Clay (town) Onondaga County	557	0.96
Albany (city) Albany County	856	0.87
Mount Vernon (city) Westchester County	585	0.87
Troy (city) Rensselaer County	407	0.81
Hempstead (village) Nassau County	404	0.75

American Indian/Alaska Native: Hispanic

Top 10 Places Sorted by Population
Based on all places, regardless of total population

Place	Population	%
New York (city)	67,208	0.82
Bronx (borough) Bronx County	24,373	1.76
Queens (borough) Queens County	14,621	0.66
Brooklyn (borough) Kings County	14,509	0.58
Manhattan (borough) New York County	12,020	0.76
Hempstead (town) Nassau County	2,528	0.33
Islip (town) Suffolk County	1,831	0.55
Yonkers (city) Westchester County	1,806	0.92
Staten Island (borough) Richmond County	1,685	0.36
Brookhaven (town) Suffolk County	1,196	0.25

Top 10 Places Sorted by Percent of Total Population
Based on all places, regardless of total population

Place	Population	%
Cattaraugus Reservation Chautauqua County	5	13.16
Baxter Estates (village) Nassau County	51	5.11
Shinnecock Reservation Suffolk County	30	4.53
Poospatuck Reservation Suffolk County	14	4.32
Cattaraugus Reservation Cattaraugus County	11	3.50
Tonawanda Reservation Genesee County	16	3.31
Cattaraugus Reservation Erie County	59	3.22
Allegany Reservation Cattaraugus County	25	2.45
Onondaga Nation Reservation Onondaga County	10	2.14
Shinnecock Hills (cdp) Suffolk County	46	2.10

Top 10 Places Sorted by Percent of Total Population
Based on places with total population of 50,000 or more

Place	Population	%
Bronx (borough) Bronx County	24,373	1.76
Brentwood (cdp) Suffolk County	809	1.33
White Plains (city) Westchester County	697	1.23
Hempstead (village) Nassau County	593	1.10
Yonkers (city) Westchester County	1,806	0.92
New York (city)	67,208	0.82
Manhattan (borough) New York County	12,020	0.76
Queens (borough) Queens County	14,621	0.66
New Rochelle (city) Westchester County	462	0.60
Brooklyn (borough) Kings County	14,509	0.58

Alaska Native: Alaska Athabascan

Top 10 Places Sorted by Population
Based on all places, regardless of total population

Place	Population	%
New York (city)	37	<0.01
Manhattan (borough) New York County	18	<0.01
Salamanca (city) Cattaraugus County	9	0.15
Watertown (city) Jefferson County	8	0.03
Bronx (borough) Bronx County	8	0.01
Brighton (cdp/town) Monroe County	5	0.01
Brooklyn (borough) Kings County	5	<0.01
Brookhaven (town) Suffolk County	4	<0.01
Schroon (town) Essex County	3	0.18
Gouverneur (town) St. Lawrence County	3	0.04

Top 10 Places Sorted by Percent of Total Population
Based on all places, regardless of total population

Place	Population	%
Burdett (village) Schuyler County	1	0.29
Schroon (town) Essex County	3	0.18
Salamanca (city) Cattaraugus County	9	0.15
Little Valley (town) Cattaraugus County	2	0.11
Orwell (town) Oswego County	1	0.09
Randolph (town) Cattaraugus County	2	0.08
Napoli (town) Cattaraugus County	1	0.08
Randolph (village) Cattaraugus County	1	0.08
Orleans (town) Jefferson County	2	0.07
Lattingtown (village) Nassau County	1	0.06

Top 10 Places Sorted by Percent of Total Population
Based on places with total population of 50,000 or more

Place	Population	%
New York (city)	37	<0.01
Manhattan (borough) New York County	18	<0.01
Bronx (borough) Bronx County	8	<0.01
Brooklyn (borough) Kings County	5	<0.01

Brookhaven (town) Suffolk County	4	<0.01
Queens (borough) Queens County	3	<0.01
Staten Island (borough) Richmond County	3	<0.01
Syracuse (city) Onondaga County	3	<0.01
Albany (city) Albany County	1	<0.01
Amherst (town) Erie County	1	<0.01

Alaska Native: Aleut

Top 10 Places Sorted by Population
Based on all places, regardless of total population

Place	Population	%
New York (city)	26	<0.01
Brooklyn (borough) Kings County	8	<0.01
Manhattan (borough) New York County	7	<0.01
Queens (borough) Queens County	6	<0.01
Wilton (town) Saratoga County	5	0.03
Denmark (town) Lewis County	4	0.14
Mamaroneck (town) Westchester County	4	<0.01
Carlton (town) Orleans County	3	0.10
Champion (town) Jefferson County	3	0.07
Bronx (borough) Bronx County	3	<0.01

Top 10 Places Sorted by Percent of Total Population
Based on all places, regardless of total population

Place	Population	%
Denmark (town) Lewis County	4	0.14
Sempronius (town) Cayuga County	1	0.11
Carlton (town) Orleans County	3	0.10
Richmondville (town) Schoharie County	2	0.08
Champion (town) Jefferson County	3	0.07
Little Valley (town) Cattaraugus County	1	0.06
Morrisonville (cdp) Clinton County	1	0.06
Beaver Dam Lake (cdp) Orange County	1	0.04
Rhinebeck (village) Dutchess County	1	0.04
Salem (town) Washington County	1	0.04

Top 10 Places Sorted by Percent of Total Population
Based on places with total population of 50,000 or more

Place	Population	%
New York (city)	26	<0.01
Brooklyn (borough) Kings County	8	<0.01
Manhattan (borough) New York County	7	<0.01
Queens (borough) Queens County	6	<0.01
Bronx (borough) Bronx County	3	<0.01
Brookhaven (town) Suffolk County	3	<0.01
Babylon (town) Suffolk County	2	<0.01
Hempstead (town) Nassau County	2	<0.01
Rochester (city) Monroe County	2	<0.01
Staten Island (borough) Richmond County	2	<0.01

American Indian: Apache

Top 10 Places Sorted by Population
Based on all places, regardless of total population

Place	Population	%
New York (city)	401	<0.01
Brooklyn (borough) Kings County	122	<0.01
Bronx (borough) Bronx County	99	0.01
Manhattan (borough) New York County	92	0.01
Queens (borough) Queens County	53	<0.01
Staten Island (borough) Richmond County	35	0.01
Syracuse (city) Onondaga County	25	0.02
Hempstead (town) Nassau County	21	<0.01
Rochester (city) Monroe County	20	0.01
Brookhaven (town) Suffolk County	18	<0.01

Top 10 Places Sorted by Percent of Total Population
Based on all places, regardless of total population

Place	Population	%
Breesport (cdp) Chemung County	5	0.80
Smithville Flats (cdp) Chenango County	2	0.57
Benson (town) Hamilton County	1	0.52
Waterville (village) Oneida County	6	0.38
Lyndonville (village) Orleans County	3	0.36
Ellenburg (town) Clinton County	6	0.34
Stone Ridge (cdp) Ulster County	4	0.34
Windsor (village) Broome County	3	0.33
Carlton (town) Orleans County	9	0.30
German (town) Chenango County	1	0.27

Top 10 Places Sorted by Percent of Total Population
Based on places with total population of 50,000 or more

Place	Population	%
Syracuse (city) Onondaga County	25	0.02
Union (town) Broome County	11	0.02
Troy (city) Rensselaer County	10	0.02
Bronx (borough) Bronx County	99	0.01
Manhattan (borough) New York County	92	0.01
Staten Island (borough) Richmond County	35	0.01
Rochester (city) Monroe County	20	0.01
Huntington (town) Suffolk County	14	0.01
Babylon (town) Suffolk County	11	0.01
Yonkers (city) Westchester County	10	0.01

American Indian: Arapaho

Top 10 Places Sorted by Population
Based on all places, regardless of total population

Place	Population	%
New York (city)	21	<0.01
Brooklyn (borough) Kings County	10	<0.01
Manhattan (borough) New York County	5	<0.01
Greece (town) Monroe County	4	<0.01
Malta (town) Saratoga County	3	0.02
Bronx (borough) Bronx County	3	<0.01
New Baltimore (town) Greene County	2	0.06
Waterloo (town) Seneca County	2	0.03
Philipstown (town) Putnam County	2	0.01
Kingston (city) Ulster County	2	0.01

Top 10 Places Sorted by Percent of Total Population
Based on all places, regardless of total population

Place	Population	%
Rifton (cdp) Ulster County	1	0.22
New Baltimore (town) Greene County	2	0.06
Victory (town) Cayuga County	1	0.06
Boonville (village) Oneida County	1	0.05
Carlisle (town) Schoharie County	1	0.05
Berne (town) Albany County	1	0.04
Machias (town) Cattaraugus County	1	0.04
Waterloo (town) Seneca County	2	0.03
Montauk (cdp) Suffolk County	1	0.03
Saugerties (village) Ulster County	1	0.03

Top 10 Places Sorted by Percent of Total Population
Based on places with total population of 50,000 or more

Place	Population	%
New York (city)	21	<0.01
Brooklyn (borough) Kings County	10	<0.01
Manhattan (borough) New York County	5	<0.01
Greece (town) Monroe County	4	<0.01
Bronx (borough) Bronx County	3	<0.01
Queens (borough) Queens County	2	<0.01
Syracuse (city) Onondaga County	2	<0.01
Brookhaven (town) Suffolk County	1	<0.01
Buffalo (city) Erie County	1	<0.01
Cheektowaga (town) Erie County	1	<0.01

American Indian: Blackfeet

Top 10 Places Sorted by Population
Based on all places, regardless of total population

Place	Population	%
New York (city)	1,627	0.02
Brooklyn (borough) Kings County	531	0.02
Manhattan (borough) New York County	356	0.02
Queens (borough) Queens County	342	0.02
Bronx (borough) Bronx County	310	0.02
Brookhaven (town) Suffolk County	164	0.03
Rochester (city) Monroe County	134	0.06
Hempstead (town) Nassau County	117	0.02
Syracuse (city) Onondaga County	111	0.08
Buffalo (city) Erie County	104	0.04

Top 10 Places Sorted by Percent of Total Population
Based on all places, regardless of total population

Place	Population	%
Ellisburg (village) Jefferson County	6	2.46
Cohocton (village) Steuben County	7	0.84
Nassau (village) Rensselaer County	9	0.79

Place	Population	%
Cameron (town) Steuben County	7	0.74
Cayuta (town) Schuyler County	4	0.72
Dresden (village) Yates County	2	0.65
Theresa (village) Jefferson County	5	0.58
Hemlock (cdp) Livingston County	3	0.54
Lyons Falls (village) Lewis County	3	0.53
East Avon (cdp) Livingston County	3	0.49

Top 10 Places Sorted by Percent of Total Population
Based on places with total population of 50,000 or more

Place	Population	%
Schenectady (city) Schenectady County	58	0.09
Syracuse (city) Onondaga County	111	0.08
Rochester (city) Monroe County	134	0.06
Albany (city) Albany County	57	0.06
Mount Vernon (city) Westchester County	38	0.06
Hempstead (village) Nassau County	27	0.05
Buffalo (city) Erie County	104	0.04
Troy (city) Rensselaer County	22	0.04
Brookhaven (town) Suffolk County	164	0.03
Yonkers (city) Westchester County	58	0.03

American Indian: Canadian/French American Indian

Top 10 Places Sorted by Population
Based on all places, regardless of total population

Place	Population	%
New York (city)	197	<0.01
Brooklyn (borough) Kings County	62	<0.01
Manhattan (borough) New York County	62	<0.01
Buffalo (city) Erie County	57	0.02
Syracuse (city) Onondaga County	51	0.04
Queens (borough) Queens County	38	<0.01
Bronx (borough) Bronx County	25	<0.01
Niagara Falls (city) Niagara County	20	0.04
Clay (town) Onondaga County	16	0.03
Grand Island (town) Erie County	15	0.07

Top 10 Places Sorted by Percent of Total Population
Based on all places, regardless of total population

Place	Population	%
Tonawanda Reservation Genesee County	5	1.04
Clare (town) St. Lawrence County	1	0.95
Farnham (village) Erie County	3	0.79
Orwell (town) Oswego County	6	0.51
Rifton (cdp) Ulster County	2	0.44
Verona (cdp) Oneida County	3	0.35
Sinclairville (village) Chautauqua County	2	0.34
East Avon (cdp) Livingston County	2	0.33
Bellmont (town) Franklin County	4	0.28
Decatur (town) Otsego County	1	0.28

Top 10 Places Sorted by Percent of Total Population
Based on places with total population of 50,000 or more

Place	Population	%
Syracuse (city) Onondaga County	51	0.04
Niagara Falls (city) Niagara County	20	0.04
Clay (town) Onondaga County	16	0.03
Buffalo (city) Erie County	57	0.02
Hamburg (town) Erie County	12	0.02
Greece (town) Monroe County	14	0.01
Amherst (town) Erie County	11	0.01
Colonie (town) Albany County	10	0.01
Schenectady (city) Schenectady County	9	0.01
Tonawanda (town) Erie County	8	0.01

American Indian: Central American Indian

Top 10 Places Sorted by Population
Based on all places, regardless of total population

Place	Population	%
New York (city)	7,662	0.09
Bronx (borough) Bronx County	4,520	0.33
Brooklyn (borough) Kings County	1,263	0.05
Manhattan (borough) New York County	1,090	0.07
Queens (borough) Queens County	733	0.03
Yonkers (city) Westchester County	103	0.05
Hempstead (town) Nassau County	87	0.01
Islip (town) Suffolk County	73	0.02
Staten Island (borough) Richmond County	56	0.01

Place	Population	%
Brookhaven (town) Suffolk County	53	0.01

Top 10 Places Sorted by Percent of Total Population
Based on all places, regardless of total population

Place	Population	%
Shelter Island (cdp) Suffolk County	14	1.05
Shelter Island (town) Suffolk County	16	0.67
Nelliston (village) Montgomery County	3	0.50
Mount Kisco (town/village) Westchester County	43	0.40
Washington Heights (cdp) Orange County	6	0.36
Bronx (borough) Bronx County	4,520	0.33
Copenhagen (village) Lewis County	2	0.25
Columbus (town) Chenango County	2	0.21
Shelter Island Heights (cdp) Suffolk County	2	0.19
Bolton Landing (cdp) Warren County	1	0.19

Top 10 Places Sorted by Percent of Total Population
Based on places with total population of 50,000 or more

Place	Population	%
Bronx (borough) Bronx County	4,520	0.33
New York (city)	7,662	0.09
Manhattan (borough) New York County	1,090	0.07
Brentwood (cdp) Suffolk County	36	0.06
Brooklyn (borough) Kings County	1,263	0.05
Yonkers (city) Westchester County	103	0.05
Queens (borough) Queens County	733	0.03
New Rochelle (city) Westchester County	20	0.03
Mount Vernon (city) Westchester County	19	0.03
Hempstead (village) Nassau County	15	0.03

American Indian: Cherokee

Top 10 Places Sorted by Population
Based on all places, regardless of total population

Place	Population	%
New York (city)	6,952	0.09
Brooklyn (borough) Kings County	1,903	0.08
Manhattan (borough) New York County	1,845	0.12
Queens (borough) Queens County	1,425	0.06
Bronx (borough) Bronx County	1,312	0.09
Hempstead (town) Nassau County	572	0.08
Brookhaven (town) Suffolk County	546	0.11
Staten Island (borough) Richmond County	467	0.10
Rochester (city) Monroe County	411	0.20
Islip (town) Suffolk County	316	0.09

Top 10 Places Sorted by Percent of Total Population
Based on all places, regardless of total population

Place	Population	%
Poospatuck Reservation Suffolk County	11	3.40
Shinnecock Reservation Suffolk County	16	2.42
Winthrop (cdp) St. Lawrence County	11	2.16
Bloomingburg (village) Sullivan County	9	2.14
North Rose (cdp) Wayne County	11	1.73
Phoenicia (cdp) Ulster County	5	1.62
Wainscott (cdp) Suffolk County	9	1.38
Hopewell Junction (cdp) Dutchess County	5	1.33
Morehouse (town) Hamilton County	1	1.16
Natural Bridge (cdp) Jefferson County	4	1.10

Top 10 Places Sorted by Percent of Total Population
Based on places with total population of 50,000 or more

Place	Population	%
Schenectady (city) Schenectady County	145	0.22
Albany (city) Albany County	205	0.21
Rochester (city) Monroe County	411	0.20
Hempstead (village) Nassau County	109	0.20
Syracuse (city) Onondaga County	258	0.18
Mount Vernon (city) Westchester County	116	0.17
Troy (city) Rensselaer County	80	0.16
Brentwood (cdp) Suffolk County	76	0.13
Manhattan (borough) New York County	1,845	0.12
Babylon (town) Suffolk County	250	0.12

American Indian: Cheyenne

Top 10 Places Sorted by Population
Based on all places, regardless of total population

Place	Population	%
New York (city)	46	<0.01

Place	Population	%
Queens (borough) Queens County	20	<0.01
Brooklyn (borough) Kings County	10	<0.01
Manhattan (borough) New York County	9	<0.01
Kent (town) Putnam County	6	0.04
Brookhaven (town) Suffolk County	6	<0.01
Greenburgh (town) Westchester County	5	0.01
Bronx (borough) Bronx County	5	<0.01
Whitestown (town) Oneida County	4	0.02
Utica (city) Oneida County	4	0.01

Top 10 Places Sorted by Percent of Total Population
Based on all places, regardless of total population

Place	Population	%
Bloomville (cdp) Delaware County	1	0.47
Celoron (village) Chautauqua County	2	0.18
Hannibal (village) Oswego County	1	0.18
Conewango (town) Cattaraugus County	3	0.16
Crompond (cdp) Westchester County	3	0.13
Willsboro (cdp) Essex County	1	0.13
Yorkville (village) Oneida County	3	0.11
Cameron (town) Steuben County	1	0.11
Nelson (town) Madison County	2	0.10
Allegany Reservation Cattaraugus County	1	0.10

Top 10 Places Sorted by Percent of Total Population
Based on places with total population of 50,000 or more

Place	Population	%
Greenburgh (town) Westchester County	5	0.01
Utica (city) Oneida County	4	0.01
New York (city)	46	<0.01
Queens (borough) Queens County	20	<0.01
Brooklyn (borough) Kings County	10	<0.01
Manhattan (borough) New York County	9	<0.01
Brookhaven (town) Suffolk County	6	<0.01
Bronx (borough) Bronx County	5	<0.01
Huntington (town) Suffolk County	4	<0.01
North Hempstead (town) Nassau County	3	<0.01

American Indian: Chickasaw

Top 10 Places Sorted by Population
Based on all places, regardless of total population

Place	Population	%
New York (city)	113	<0.01
Manhattan (borough) New York County	43	<0.01
Brooklyn (borough) Kings County	30	<0.01
Queens (borough) Queens County	21	<0.01
Bronx (borough) Bronx County	16	<0.01
Mount Kisco (town/village) Westchester County	5	0.05
Hempstead (town) Nassau County	5	<0.01
Chatham (village) Columbia County	4	0.23
Chatham (town) Columbia County	4	0.10
Rockville Centre (village) Nassau County	4	0.02

Top 10 Places Sorted by Percent of Total Population
Based on all places, regardless of total population

Place	Population	%
Chatham (village) Columbia County	4	0.23
Port Gibson (cdp) Ontario County	1	0.22
Chatham (town) Columbia County	4	0.10
Gasport (cdp) Niagara County	1	0.08
Philadelphia (village) Jefferson County	1	0.08
West Sparta (town) Livingston County	1	0.08
Pittsfield (town) Otsego County	1	0.07
Austerlitz (town) Columbia County	1	0.06
Cumberland Head (cdp) Clinton County	1	0.06
Mount Kisco (town/village) Westchester County	5	0.05

Top 10 Places Sorted by Percent of Total Population
Based on places with total population of 50,000 or more

Place	Population	%
Mount Vernon (city) Westchester County	4	0.01
New York (city)	113	<0.01
Manhattan (borough) New York County	43	<0.01
Brooklyn (borough) Kings County	30	<0.01
Queens (borough) Queens County	21	<0.01
Bronx (borough) Bronx County	16	<0.01
Hempstead (town) Nassau County	5	<0.01
Syracuse (city) Onondaga County	4	<0.01
Brookhaven (town) Suffolk County	3	<0.01
Huntington (town) Suffolk County	3	<0.01

American Indian: Chippewa

Top 10 Places Sorted by Population
Based on all places, regardless of total population

Place	Population	%
New York (city)	252	<0.01
Manhattan (borough) New York County	99	<0.01
Brooklyn (borough) Kings County	65	<0.01
Buffalo (city) Erie County	42	0.02
Bronx (borough) Bronx County	38	<0.01
Queens (borough) Queens County	37	<0.01
Niagara Falls (city) Niagara County	23	0.05
Brookhaven (town) Suffolk County	19	<0.01
Rochester (city) Monroe County	18	0.01
Syracuse (city) Onondaga County	18	0.01

Top 10 Places Sorted by Percent of Total Population
Based on all places, regardless of total population

Place	Population	%
Barneveld (village) Oneida County	3	1.06
Milford (village) Otsego County	3	0.72
Poospatuck Reservation Suffolk County	2	0.62
Amenia (cdp) Dutchess County	5	0.52
Morristown (village) St. Lawrence County	2	0.51
Dickinson (town) Franklin County	4	0.49
Piffard (cdp) Livingston County	1	0.45
French Creek (town) Chautauqua County	4	0.44
Greenville (cdp) Greene County	3	0.44
Wampsville (village) Madison County	2	0.37

Top 10 Places Sorted by Percent of Total Population
Based on places with total population of 50,000 or more

Place	Population	%
Niagara Falls (city) Niagara County	23	0.05
Buffalo (city) Erie County	42	0.02
Clay (town) Onondaga County	11	0.02
Schenectady (city) Schenectady County	11	0.02
Manhattan (borough) New York County	99	0.01
Rochester (city) Monroe County	18	0.01
Syracuse (city) Onondaga County	18	0.01
Greece (town) Monroe County	13	0.01
Utica (city) Oneida County	8	0.01
Amherst (town) Erie County	7	0.01

American Indian: Choctaw

Top 10 Places Sorted by Population
Based on all places, regardless of total population

Place	Population	%
New York (city)	405	<0.01
Manhattan (borough) New York County	179	0.01
Brooklyn (borough) Kings County	104	<0.01
Queens (borough) Queens County	68	<0.01
Bronx (borough) Bronx County	43	<0.01
Hempstead (town) Nassau County	36	<0.01
Brookhaven (town) Suffolk County	34	0.01
Syracuse (city) Onondaga County	28	0.02
Rochester (city) Monroe County	28	0.01
Buffalo (city) Erie County	21	0.01

Top 10 Places Sorted by Percent of Total Population
Based on all places, regardless of total population

Place	Population	%
Winthrop (cdp) St. Lawrence County	5	0.98
Smallwood (cdp) Sullivan County	5	0.86
Schaghticoke (village) Rensselaer County	4	0.68
Cattaraugus Reservation Cattaraugus County	2	0.64
Theresa (village) Jefferson County	3	0.35
Old Field (village) Suffolk County	3	0.33
Rose (town) Wayne County	7	0.30
Worcester (cdp) Otsego County	3	0.27
Leeds (cdp) Greene County	1	0.27
Marcellus (village) Onondaga County	4	0.22

Top 10 Places Sorted by Percent of Total Population
Based on places with total population of 50,000 or more

Place	Population	%
Syracuse (city) Onondaga County	28	0.02
Manhattan (borough) New York County	179	0.01
Brookhaven (town) Suffolk County	34	0.01
Rochester (city) Monroe County	28	0.01

Buffalo (city) Erie County	21	0.01
Islip (town) Suffolk County	17	0.01
Huntington (town) Suffolk County	13	0.01
Yonkers (city) Westchester County	12	0.01
Albany (city) Albany County	8	0.01
Greece (town) Monroe County	8	0.01

American Indian: Colville

Top 10 Places Sorted by Population
Based on all places, regardless of total population

Place	Population	%
New York (city)	9	<0.01
Manhattan (borough) New York County	5	<0.01
Brookfield (town) Madison County	3	0.12
Bronx (borough) Bronx County	2	<0.01
Sidney (village) Delaware County	1	0.03
St. Regis Mohawk Reservation Franklin County	1	0.03
Triangle (town) Broome County	1	0.03
Hector (town) Schuyler County	1	0.02
LaFayette (town) Onondaga County	1	0.02
Sidney (town) Delaware County	1	0.02

Top 10 Places Sorted by Percent of Total Population
Based on all places, regardless of total population

Place	Population	%
Brookfield (town) Madison County	3	0.12
Sidney (village) Delaware County	1	0.03
St. Regis Mohawk Reservation Franklin County	1	0.03
Triangle (town) Broome County	1	0.03
Hector (town) Schuyler County	1	0.02
LaFayette (town) Onondaga County	1	0.02
Sidney (town) Delaware County	1	0.02
New York (city)	9	<0.01
Manhattan (borough) New York County	5	<0.01
Bronx (borough) Bronx County	2	<0.01

Top 10 Places Sorted by Percent of Total Population
Based on places with total population of 50,000 or more

Place	Population	%
New York (city)	9	<0.01
Manhattan (borough) New York County	5	<0.01
Bronx (borough) Bronx County	2	<0.01
Brooklyn (borough) Kings County	1	<0.01
Hempstead (town) Nassau County	1	<0.01
Irondequoit (cdp/town) Monroe County	1	<0.01
Queens (borough) Queens County	1	<0.01
Rochester (city) Monroe County	1	<0.01
Yonkers (city) Westchester County	1	<0.01
Albany (city) Albany County	0	0.00

American Indian: Comanche

Top 10 Places Sorted by Population
Based on all places, regardless of total population

Place	Population	%
New York (city)	76	<0.01
Bronx (borough) Bronx County	26	<0.01
Manhattan (borough) New York County	22	<0.01
Brooklyn (borough) Kings County	19	<0.01
Syracuse (city) Onondaga County	12	0.01
Hempstead (town) Nassau County	11	<0.01
Huntington (town) Suffolk County	8	<0.01
Islip (town) Suffolk County	8	<0.01
Brentwood (cdp) Suffolk County	7	0.01
Levittown (cdp) Nassau County	7	0.01

Top 10 Places Sorted by Percent of Total Population
Based on all places, regardless of total population

Place	Population	%
Westport (cdp) Essex County	3	0.58
Cato (village) Cayuga County	3	0.56
Westport (town) Essex County	3	0.23
Schroon (town) Essex County	3	0.18
Accord (cdp) Ulster County	1	0.18
Ira (town) Cayuga County	3	0.14
Elmsford (village) Westchester County	5	0.11
Amenia (cdp) Dutchess County	1	0.10
Tyre (town) Seneca County	1	0.10
North Dansville (town) Livingston County	3	0.05

Top 10 Places Sorted by Percent of Total Population
Based on places with total population of 50,000 or more

Place	Population	%
Syracuse (city) Onondaga County	12	0.01
Brentwood (cdp) Suffolk County	7	0.01
Levittown (cdp) Nassau County	7	0.01
Greenburgh (town) Westchester County	5	0.01
New York (city)	76	<0.01
Bronx (borough) Bronx County	26	<0.01
Manhattan (borough) New York County	22	<0.01
Brooklyn (borough) Kings County	19	<0.01
Hempstead (town) Nassau County	11	<0.01
Huntington (town) Suffolk County	8	<0.01

American Indian: Cree

Top 10 Places Sorted by Population
Based on all places, regardless of total population

Place	Population	%
New York (city)	81	<0.01
Queens (borough) Queens County	24	<0.01
Manhattan (borough) New York County	22	<0.01
Bronx (borough) Bronx County	16	<0.01
Brooklyn (borough) Kings County	15	<0.01
Syracuse (city) Onondaga County	6	<0.01
Elizabethtown (cdp) Essex County	5	0.66
Elizabethtown (town) Essex County	5	0.43
Pembroke (town) Genesee County	5	0.12
Brownville (town) Jefferson County	5	0.08

Top 10 Places Sorted by Percent of Total Population
Based on all places, regardless of total population

Place	Population	%
Elizabethtown (cdp) Essex County	5	0.66
Elizabethtown (town) Essex County	5	0.43
Fonda (village) Montgomery County	2	0.25
Germantown (cdp) Columbia County	2	0.24
Port Gibson (cdp) Ontario County	1	0.22
Denning (town) Ulster County	1	0.18
Margaretville (village) Delaware County	1	0.17
Pembroke (town) Genesee County	5	0.12
St. Regis Mohawk Reservation Franklin County	4	0.12
Triangle (town) Broome County	3	0.10

Top 10 Places Sorted by Percent of Total Population
Based on places with total population of 50,000 or more

Place	Population	%
Schenectady (city) Schenectady County	4	0.01
Niagara Falls (city) Niagara County	3	0.01
New York (city)	81	<0.01
Queens (borough) Queens County	24	<0.01
Manhattan (borough) New York County	22	<0.01
Bronx (borough) Bronx County	16	<0.01
Brooklyn (borough) Kings County	15	<0.01
Syracuse (city) Onondaga County	6	<0.01
Albany (city) Albany County	4	<0.01
Brookhaven (town) Suffolk County	4	<0.01

American Indian: Creek

Top 10 Places Sorted by Population
Based on all places, regardless of total population

Place	Population	%
New York (city)	291	<0.01
Brooklyn (borough) Kings County	81	<0.01
Queens (borough) Queens County	73	<0.01
Manhattan (borough) New York County	61	<0.01
Bronx (borough) Bronx County	47	<0.01
Staten Island (borough) Richmond County	29	0.01
Hempstead (town) Nassau County	29	<0.01
Huntington (town) Suffolk County	15	0.01
Babylon (town) Suffolk County	13	0.01
Brookhaven (town) Suffolk County	12	<0.01

Top 10 Places Sorted by Percent of Total Population
Based on all places, regardless of total population

Place	Population	%
Cattaraugus Reservation Cattaraugus County	6	1.91
Tonawanda Reservation Genesee County	4	0.83
Pamelia Center (cdp) Jefferson County	1	0.38

Place	Population	%
Milton (cdp) Ulster County	5	0.36
Apalachin (cdp) Tioga County	4	0.35
Plandome Manor (village) Nassau County	3	0.34
Avoca (village) Steuben County	3	0.32
Cattaraugus Reservation Erie County	5	0.27
Rapids (cdp) Niagara County	3	0.18
Rock Hill (cdp) Sullivan County	3	0.17

Top 10 Places Sorted by Percent of Total Population
Based on places with total population of 50,000 or more

Place	Population	%
Staten Island (borough) Richmond County	29	0.01
Huntington (town) Suffolk County	15	0.01
Babylon (town) Suffolk County	13	0.01
Syracuse (city) Onondaga County	9	0.01
Smithtown (town) Suffolk County	7	0.01
Albany (city) Albany County	6	0.01
Schenectady (city) Schenectady County	5	0.01
White Plains (city) Westchester County	3	0.01
New York (city)	291	<0.01
Brooklyn (borough) Kings County	81	<0.01

American Indian: Crow

Top 10 Places Sorted by Population
Based on all places, regardless of total population

Place	Population	%
New York (city)	50	<0.01
Brooklyn (borough) Kings County	19	<0.01
Bronx (borough) Bronx County	16	<0.01
Islip (town) Suffolk County	16	<0.01
Brentwood (cdp) Suffolk County	11	0.02
Manhattan (borough) New York County	11	<0.01
Schenectady (city) Schenectady County	6	0.01
Bombay (town) Franklin County	5	0.37
Huntington (town) Suffolk County	5	<0.01
Crown Heights (cdp) Dutchess County	4	0.14

Top 10 Places Sorted by Percent of Total Population
Based on all places, regardless of total population

Place	Population	%
Benson (town) Hamilton County	1	0.52
Bombay (town) Franklin County	5	0.37
Santa Clara (town) Franklin County	1	0.29
Valley Falls (village) Rensselaer County	1	0.21
East Avon (cdp) Livingston County	1	0.16
Crown Heights (cdp) Dutchess County	4	0.14
Cumberland Head (cdp) Clinton County	2	0.12
Manchester (village) Ontario County	2	0.12
Portville (village) Cattaraugus County	1	0.10
Gilboa (town) Schoharie County	1	0.08

Top 10 Places Sorted by Percent of Total Population
Based on places with total population of 50,000 or more

Place	Population	%
Brentwood (cdp) Suffolk County	11	0.02
Schenectady (city) Schenectady County	6	0.01
New York (city)	50	<0.01
Brooklyn (borough) Kings County	19	<0.01
Bronx (borough) Bronx County	16	<0.01
Islip (town) Suffolk County	16	<0.01
Manhattan (borough) New York County	11	<0.01
Huntington (town) Suffolk County	5	<0.01
Queens (borough) Queens County	4	<0.01
Utica (city) Oneida County	3	<0.01

American Indian: Delaware

Top 10 Places Sorted by Population
Based on all places, regardless of total population

Place	Population	%
New York (city)	177	<0.01
Ramapo (town) Rockland County	167	0.13
Hillburn (village) Rockland County	120	12.62
Warwick (town) Orange County	58	0.18
Wallkill (town) Orange County	57	0.21
Manhattan (borough) New York County	54	<0.01
Blooming Grove (town) Orange County	51	0.28
Middletown (city) Orange County	43	0.15
Staten Island (borough) Richmond County	43	0.01
Port Jervis (city) Orange County	39	0.44

Top 10 Places Sorted by Percent of Total Population
Based on all places, regardless of total population

Place	Population	%
Hillburn (village) Rockland County	120	12.62
Mountain Lodge Park (cdp) Orange County	25	1.57
Brushton (village) Franklin County	4	0.84
La Fargeville (cdp) Jefferson County	5	0.82
Wurtsboro (village) Sullivan County	8	0.64
Brandon (town) Franklin County	3	0.52
Greenwood Lake (village) Orange County	15	0.48
Port Jervis (city) Orange County	39	0.44
Chester (village) Orange County	17	0.43
Roseboom (town) Otsego County	3	0.42

Top 10 Places Sorted by Percent of Total Population
Based on places with total population of 50,000 or more

Place	Population	%
Ramapo (town) Rockland County	167	0.13
Clarkstown (town) Rockland County	16	0.02
Schenectady (city) Schenectady County	12	0.02
Staten Island (borough) Richmond County	43	0.01
Huntington (town) Suffolk County	12	0.01
Albany (city) Albany County	11	0.01
Irondequoit (cdp/town) Monroe County	7	0.01
Troy (city) Rensselaer County	6	0.01
Greenburgh (town) Westchester County	5	0.01
Union (town) Broome County	5	0.01

American Indian: Hopi

Top 10 Places Sorted by Population
Based on all places, regardless of total population

Place	Population	%
New York (city)	49	<0.01
Manhattan (borough) New York County	15	<0.01
Queens (borough) Queens County	15	<0.01
Brooklyn (borough) Kings County	12	<0.01
Babylon (town) Suffolk County	5	<0.01
Buffalo (city) Erie County	5	<0.01
Staten Island (borough) Richmond County	5	<0.01
Yonkers (city) Westchester County	5	<0.01
Village Green (cdp) Onondaga County	3	0.08
Massena (village) St. Lawrence County	3	0.03

Top 10 Places Sorted by Percent of Total Population
Based on all places, regardless of total population

Place	Population	%
Tonawanda Reservation Genesee County	1	0.21
Cayuta (town) Schuyler County	1	0.18
Shinnecock Reservation Suffolk County	1	0.15
Village Green (cdp) Onondaga County	3	0.08
North Collins (town) Erie County	2	0.06
Massena (village) St. Lawrence County	3	0.03
Shandaken (town) Ulster County	1	0.03
Theresa (town) Jefferson County	1	0.03
Cornwall (town) Orange County	3	0.02
Kingsbury (town) Washington County	3	0.02

Top 10 Places Sorted by Percent of Total Population
Based on places with total population of 50,000 or more

Place	Population	%
New York (city)	49	<0.01
Manhattan (borough) New York County	15	<0.01
Queens (borough) Queens County	15	<0.01
Brooklyn (borough) Kings County	12	<0.01
Babylon (town) Suffolk County	5	<0.01
Buffalo (city) Erie County	5	<0.01
Staten Island (borough) Richmond County	5	<0.01
Yonkers (city) Westchester County	5	<0.01
Islip (town) Suffolk County	3	<0.01
North Hempstead (town) Nassau County	3	<0.01

American Indian: Houma

Top 10 Places Sorted by Population
Based on all places, regardless of total population

Place	Population	%
New York (city)	23	<0.01
Bronx (borough) Bronx County	12	<0.01
Queens (borough) Queens County	4	<0.01

Place	Population	%
White Plains (city) Westchester County	3	0.01
Brooklyn (borough) Kings County	3	<0.01
Islip (town) Suffolk County	3	<0.01
Manhattan (borough) New York County	3	<0.01
Liberty (village) Sullivan County	2	0.05
Firthcliffe (cdp) Orange County	2	0.04
West Bay Shore (cdp) Suffolk County	2	0.04

Top 10 Places Sorted by Percent of Total Population
Based on all places, regardless of total population

Place	Population	%
Willing (town) Allegany County	1	0.08
Coventry (town) Chenango County	1	0.06
Liberty (village) Sullivan County	2	0.05
Firthcliffe (cdp) Orange County	2	0.04
West Bay Shore (cdp) Suffolk County	2	0.04
Kendall (town) Orleans County	1	0.04
Cornwall (town) Orange County	2	0.02
Liberty (town) Sullivan County	2	0.02
Elmira Heights (village) Chemung County	1	0.02
White Plains (city) Westchester County	3	0.01

Top 10 Places Sorted by Percent of Total Population
Based on places with total population of 50,000 or more

Place	Population	%
White Plains (city) Westchester County	3	0.01
New York (city)	23	<0.01
Bronx (borough) Bronx County	12	<0.01
Queens (borough) Queens County	4	<0.01
Brooklyn (borough) Kings County	3	<0.01
Islip (town) Suffolk County	3	<0.01
Manhattan (borough) New York County	3	<0.01
Buffalo (city) Erie County	2	<0.01
Greece (town) Monroe County	2	<0.01
Clay (town) Onondaga County	1	<0.01

Alaska Native: Inupiat (Eskimo)

Top 10 Places Sorted by Population
Based on all places, regardless of total population

Place	Population	%
New York (city)	58	<0.01
Brooklyn (borough) Kings County	21	<0.01
Bronx (borough) Bronx County	15	<0.01
Queens (borough) Queens County	13	<0.01
Manhattan (borough) New York County	8	<0.01
Syracuse (city) Onondaga County	6	<0.01
Port Chester (village) Westchester County	5	0.02
Rye (town) Westchester County	5	0.01
Yonkers (city) Westchester County	5	<0.01
Frewsburg (cdp) Chautauqua County	4	0.21

Top 10 Places Sorted by Percent of Total Population
Based on all places, regardless of total population

Place	Population	%
West Winfield (village) Herkimer County	3	0.36
Frewsburg (cdp) Chautauqua County	4	0.21
Winfield (town) Herkimer County	3	0.14
Mountain Lodge Park (cdp) Orange County	2	0.13
North Hornell (village) Steuben County	1	0.13
Pine Plains (town) Dutchess County	3	0.12
Schroon Lake (cdp) Essex County	1	0.12
Carroll (town) Chautauqua County	4	0.11
Dexter (village) Jefferson County	1	0.10
Rathbone (town) Steuben County	1	0.09

Top 10 Places Sorted by Percent of Total Population
Based on places with total population of 50,000 or more

Place	Population	%
New York (city)	58	<0.01
Brooklyn (borough) Kings County	21	<0.01
Bronx (borough) Bronx County	15	<0.01
Queens (borough) Queens County	13	<0.01
Manhattan (borough) New York County	8	<0.01
Syracuse (city) Onondaga County	6	<0.01
Yonkers (city) Westchester County	5	<0.01
Buffalo (city) Erie County	4	<0.01
Rochester (city) Monroe County	4	<0.01
Amherst (town) Erie County	3	<0.01

American Indian: Iroquois

Top 10 Places Sorted by Population
Based on all places, regardless of total population

Place	Population	%
St. Regis Mohawk Reservation Franklin County	2,493	77.23
Syracuse (city) Onondaga County	1,373	0.95
Buffalo (city) Erie County	1,316	0.50
Cattaraugus Reservation Erie County	1,295	70.65
New York (city)	1,276	0.02
Salamanca (city) Cattaraugus County	951	16.35
Niagara Falls (city) Niagara County	801	1.60
Allegany Reservation Cattaraugus County	610	59.80
Rochester (city) Monroe County	483	0.23
Massena (town) St. Lawrence County	442	3.43

Top 10 Places Sorted by Percent of Total Population
Based on all places, regardless of total population

Place	Population	%
St. Regis Mohawk Reservation Franklin County	2,493	77.23
Tonawanda Reservation Erie County	26	76.47
Cattaraugus Reservation Cattaraugus County	227	72.29
Cattaraugus Reservation Erie County	1,295	70.65
Allegany Reservation Cattaraugus County	610	59.80
Cattaraugus Reservation Chautauqua County	20	52.63
Tonawanda Reservation Genesee County	168	34.78
Onondaga Nation Reservation Onondaga County	93	19.87
Salamanca (city) Cattaraugus County	951	16.35
Bombay (town) Franklin County	206	15.18

Top 10 Places Sorted by Percent of Total Population
Based on places with total population of 50,000 or more

Place	Population	%
Niagara Falls (city) Niagara County	801	1.60
Syracuse (city) Onondaga County	1,373	0.95
Buffalo (city) Erie County	1,316	0.50
Clay (town) Onondaga County	252	0.43
Tonawanda (town) Erie County	256	0.35
Tonawanda (cdp) Erie County	165	0.28
Hamburg (town) Erie County	159	0.28
Cheektowaga (cdp) Erie County	179	0.24
Rochester (city) Monroe County	483	0.23
Cheektowaga (town) Erie County	194	0.22

American Indian: Kiowa

Top 10 Places Sorted by Population
Based on all places, regardless of total population

Place	Population	%
New York (city)	15	<0.01
Manhattan (borough) New York County	11	<0.01
Middlefield (town) Otsego County	2	0.09
Roxbury (town) Delaware County	2	0.08
Brooklyn (borough) Kings County	2	<0.01
Utica (city) Oneida County	2	<0.01
Old Forge (cdp) Herkimer County	1	0.13
Tuscarora Nation Reservation Niagara County	1	0.09
Webb (town) Herkimer County	1	0.06
Carlisle (town) Schoharie County	1	0.05

Top 10 Places Sorted by Percent of Total Population
Based on all places, regardless of total population

Place	Population	%
Old Forge (cdp) Herkimer County	1	0.13
Middlefield (town) Otsego County	2	0.09
Tuscarora Nation Reservation Niagara County	1	0.09
Roxbury (town) Delaware County	2	0.08
Webb (town) Herkimer County	1	0.06
Carlisle (town) Schoharie County	1	0.05
New Hartford (village) Oneida County	1	0.05
Triangle (town) Broome County	1	0.03
Elmira Heights (village) Chemung County	1	0.02
Old Bethpage (cdp) Nassau County	1	0.02

Top 10 Places Sorted by Percent of Total Population
Based on places with total population of 50,000 or more

Place	Population	%
New York (city)	15	<0.01
Manhattan (borough) New York County	11	<0.01
Brooklyn (borough) Kings County	2	<0.01
Utica (city) Oneida County	2	<0.01

Bronx (borough) Bronx County	1	<0.01
Buffalo (city) Erie County	1	<0.01
Oyster Bay (town) Nassau County	1	<0.01
Schenectady (city) Schenectady County	1	<0.01
Smithtown (town) Suffolk County	1	<0.01
Staten Island (borough) Richmond County	1	<0.01

American Indian: Lumbee

Top 10 Places Sorted by Population
Based on all places, regardless of total population

Place	Population	%
New York (city)	89	<0.01
Queens (borough) Queens County	30	<0.01
Brooklyn (borough) Kings County	24	<0.01
Hempstead (town) Nassau County	22	<0.01
Manhattan (borough) New York County	21	<0.01
Babylon (town) Suffolk County	12	0.01
Islip (town) Suffolk County	8	<0.01
Staten Island (borough) Richmond County	8	<0.01
Rose (town) Wayne County	7	0.30
Brookhaven (town) Suffolk County	7	<0.01

Top 10 Places Sorted by Percent of Total Population
Based on all places, regardless of total population

Place	Population	%
Limestone (village) Cattaraugus County	3	0.77
Shinnecock Reservation Suffolk County	3	0.45
Newfield Hamlet (cdp) Tompkins County	3	0.40
Farmersville (town) Cattaraugus County	4	0.37
St. Armand (town) Essex County	5	0.32
Rose (town) Wayne County	7	0.30
Hermon (village) St. Lawrence County	1	0.24
Carrollton (town) Cattaraugus County	3	0.23
Brushton (village) Franklin County	1	0.21
Shandaken (town) Ulster County	6	0.19

Top 10 Places Sorted by Percent of Total Population
Based on places with total population of 50,000 or more

Place	Population	%
Babylon (town) Suffolk County	12	0.01
Levittown (cdp) Nassau County	6	0.01
Niagara Falls (city) Niagara County	6	0.01
Schenectady (city) Schenectady County	4	0.01
Troy (city) Rensselaer County	4	0.01
Clay (town) Onondaga County	3	0.01
New York (city)	89	<0.01
Queens (borough) Queens County	30	<0.01
Brooklyn (borough) Kings County	24	<0.01
Hempstead (town) Nassau County	22	<0.01

American Indian: Menominee

Top 10 Places Sorted by Population
Based on all places, regardless of total population

Place	Population	%
New York (city)	10	<0.01
Cattaraugus Reservation Erie County	5	0.27
Brooklyn (borough) Kings County	4	<0.01
Crown Heights (cdp) Dutchess County	3	0.11
Northumberland (town) Saratoga County	3	0.06
Glens Falls (city) Warren County	3	0.02
Poughkeepsie (town) Dutchess County	3	0.01
Troy (city) Rensselaer County	3	0.01
Bronx (borough) Bronx County	3	<0.01
Manhattan (borough) New York County	3	<0.01

Top 10 Places Sorted by Percent of Total Population
Based on all places, regardless of total population

Place	Population	%
Cattaraugus Reservation Erie County	5	0.27
Fillmore (cdp) Allegany County	1	0.17
Crown Heights (cdp) Dutchess County	3	0.11
Pine Plains (cdp) Dutchess County	1	0.07
Northumberland (town) Saratoga County	3	0.06
Trumansburg (village) Tompkins County	1	0.06
Angola (village) Erie County	1	0.05
Hume (town) Allegany County	1	0.05
Pine Plains (town) Dutchess County	1	0.04
Glens Falls (city) Warren County	3	0.02

Top 10 Places Sorted by Percent of Total Population
Based on places with total population of 50,000 or more

Place	Population	%
Troy (city) Rensselaer County	3	0.01
New York (city)	10	<0.01
Brooklyn (borough) Kings County	4	<0.01
Bronx (borough) Bronx County	3	<0.01
Manhattan (borough) New York County	3	<0.01
Buffalo (city) Erie County	2	<0.01
Niagara Falls (city) Niagara County	2	<0.01
Syracuse (city) Onondaga County	1	<0.01
Albany (city) Albany County	0	0.00
Amherst (town) Erie County	0	0.00

American Indian: Mexican American Indian

Top 10 Places Sorted by Population
Based on all places, regardless of total population

Place	Population	%
New York (city)	4,922	0.06
Queens (borough) Queens County	1,640	0.07
Brooklyn (borough) Kings County	1,363	0.05
Bronx (borough) Bronx County	963	0.07
Manhattan (borough) New York County	752	0.05
Staten Island (borough) Richmond County	204	0.04
Yonkers (city) Westchester County	171	0.09
White Plains (city) Westchester County	162	0.28
Poughkeepsie (city) Dutchess County	160	0.49
Hempstead (town) Nassau County	143	0.02

Top 10 Places Sorted by Percent of Total Population
Based on all places, regardless of total population

Place	Population	%
Cattaraugus Reservation Chautauqua County	5	13.16
Shinnecock Hills (cdp) Suffolk County	27	1.23
Westhampton Beach (village) Suffolk County	13	0.76
Flanders (cdp) Suffolk County	29	0.65
Phoenicia (cdp) Ulster County	2	0.65
Rensselaer Falls (village) St. Lawrence County	2	0.60
Lorraine (cdp) Jefferson County	1	0.57
Poughkeepsie (city) Dutchess County	160	0.49
Palatine Bridge (village) Montgomery County	3	0.41
Woodstock (cdp) Ulster County	8	0.38

Top 10 Places Sorted by Percent of Total Population
Based on places with total population of 50,000 or more

Place	Population	%
White Plains (city) Westchester County	162	0.28
Southampton (town) Suffolk County	83	0.15
Brentwood (cdp) Suffolk County	72	0.12
Yonkers (city) Westchester County	171	0.09
New Rochelle (city) Westchester County	72	0.09
Queens (borough) Queens County	1,640	0.07
Bronx (borough) Bronx County	963	0.07
New York (city)	4,922	0.06
Ramapo (town) Rockland County	74	0.06
Brooklyn (borough) Kings County	1,363	0.05

American Indian: Navajo

Top 10 Places Sorted by Population
Based on all places, regardless of total population

Place	Population	%
New York (city)	272	<0.01
Brooklyn (borough) Kings County	93	<0.01
Manhattan (borough) New York County	83	0.01
Bronx (borough) Bronx County	42	<0.01
Queens (borough) Queens County	37	<0.01
Rochester (city) Monroe County	30	0.01
Le Ray (town) Jefferson County	24	0.11
Fort Drum (cdp) Jefferson County	23	0.18
Staten Island (borough) Richmond County	17	<0.01
Buffalo (city) Erie County	16	0.01

Top 10 Places Sorted by Percent of Total Population
Based on all places, regardless of total population

Place	Population	%
Rodman (cdp) Jefferson County	1	0.65
Tonawanda Reservation Genesee County	3	0.62

Place	Population	%
Margaretville (village) Delaware County	3	0.50
Lakeville (cdp) Livingston County	3	0.40
Allegany Reservation Cattaraugus County	4	0.39
Baldwin (town) Chemung County	3	0.36
East Avon (cdp) Livingston County	2	0.33
Strykersville (cdp) Wyoming County	2	0.31
Brant (town) Erie County	5	0.24
Owego (village) Tioga County	9	0.23

Top 10 Places Sorted by Percent of Total Population
Based on places with total population of 50,000 or more

Place	Population	%
Manhattan (borough) New York County	83	0.01
Rochester (city) Monroe County	30	0.01
Buffalo (city) Erie County	16	0.01
Troy (city) Rensselaer County	5	0.01
Brentwood (cdp) Suffolk County	4	0.01
Clay (town) Onondaga County	4	0.01
New York (city)	272	<0.01
Brooklyn (borough) Kings County	93	<0.01
Bronx (borough) Bronx County	42	<0.01
Queens (borough) Queens County	37	<0.01

American Indian: Osage

Top 10 Places Sorted by Population
Based on all places, regardless of total population

Place	Population	%
New York (city)	23	<0.01
Manhattan (borough) New York County	12	<0.01
Queens (borough) Queens County	5	<0.01
Oakfield (village) Genesee County	4	0.22
Oakfield (town) Genesee County	4	0.12
Manlius (town) Onondaga County	4	0.01
Moravia (village) Cayuga County	3	0.23
Moravia (town) Cayuga County	3	0.08
Wheatfield (town) Niagara County	3	0.02
Le Ray (town) Jefferson County	3	0.01

Top 10 Places Sorted by Percent of Total Population
Based on all places, regardless of total population

Place	Population	%
Poospatuck Reservation Suffolk County	1	0.31
Moravia (village) Cayuga County	3	0.23
Oakfield (village) Genesee County	4	0.22
Oakfield (town) Genesee County	4	0.12
Moravia (town) Cayuga County	3	0.08
North Collins (town) Erie County	2	0.06
Wolcott (village) Wayne County	1	0.06
Woodstock (cdp) Ulster County	1	0.05
Florida (town) Montgomery County	1	0.04
Cazenovia (town) Madison County	2	0.03

Top 10 Places Sorted by Percent of Total Population
Based on places with total population of 50,000 or more

Place	Population	%
New York (city)	23	<0.01
Manhattan (borough) New York County	12	<0.01
Queens (borough) Queens County	5	<0.01
Bronx (borough) Bronx County	3	<0.01
Brooklyn (borough) Kings County	3	<0.01
Rochester (city) Monroe County	3	<0.01
Brookhaven (town) Suffolk County	2	<0.01
Hempstead (town) Nassau County	2	<0.01
White Plains (city) Westchester County	2	<0.01
Amherst (town) Erie County	1	<0.01

American Indian: Ottawa

Top 10 Places Sorted by Population
Based on all places, regardless of total population

Place	Population	%
New York (city)	11	<0.01
Auburn (city) Cayuga County	5	0.02
Brooklyn (borough) Kings County	5	<0.01
Newfield Hamlet (cdp) Tompkins County	4	0.53
Newfield (town) Tompkins County	4	0.08
East Aurora (village) Erie County	3	0.05
Aurora (town) Erie County	3	0.02
Setauket-East Setauket (cdp) Suffolk County	3	0.02
Brookhaven (town) Suffolk County	3	<0.01

| Manhattan (borough) New York County | 3 | <0.01 |

Top 10 Places Sorted by Percent of Total Population
Based on all places, regardless of total population

Place	Population	%
Newfield Hamlet (cdp) Tompkins County	4	0.53
Newfield (town) Tompkins County	4	0.08
East Aurora (village) Erie County	3	0.05
Cattaraugus Reservation Erie County	1	0.05
Seneca Falls (village) Seneca County	2	0.03
Mohawk (town) Montgomery County	1	0.03
Auburn (city) Cayuga County	5	0.02
Aurora (town) Erie County	3	0.02
Setauket-East Setauket (cdp) Suffolk County	3	0.02
Lewisboro (town) Westchester County	2	0.02

Top 10 Places Sorted by Percent of Total Population
Based on places with total population of 50,000 or more

Place	Population	%
New York (city)	11	<0.01
Brooklyn (borough) Kings County	5	<0.01
Brookhaven (town) Suffolk County	3	<0.01
Manhattan (borough) New York County	3	<0.01
Huntington (town) Suffolk County	2	<0.01
Queens (borough) Queens County	2	<0.01
Syracuse (city) Onondaga County	2	<0.01
Albany (city) Albany County	1	<0.01
Bronx (borough) Bronx County	1	<0.01
Clay (town) Onondaga County	1	<0.01

American Indian: Paiute

Top 10 Places Sorted by Population
Based on all places, regardless of total population

Place	Population	%
New York (city)	18	<0.01
Manhattan (borough) New York County	8	<0.01
Perrysburg (town) Cattaraugus County	6	0.37
Cattaraugus Reservation Erie County	6	0.33
Bronx (borough) Bronx County	5	<0.01
Brookhaven (town) Suffolk County	4	<0.01
Queens (borough) Queens County	4	<0.01
Olean (city) Cattaraugus County	3	0.02
Conklin (town) Broome County	2	0.04
Manorville (cdp) Suffolk County	2	0.01

Top 10 Places Sorted by Percent of Total Population
Based on all places, regardless of total population

Place	Population	%
Perrysburg (town) Cattaraugus County	6	0.37
Cattaraugus Reservation Erie County	6	0.33
Upper Nyack (village) Rockland County	1	0.05
Conklin (town) Broome County	2	0.04
Gowanda (village) Cattaraugus County	1	0.04
St. Regis Mohawk Reservation Franklin County	1	0.03
Olean (city) Cattaraugus County	3	0.02
Collins (town) Erie County	1	0.02
Manorville (cdp) Suffolk County	2	0.01
Miller Place (cdp) Suffolk County	1	0.01

Top 10 Places Sorted by Percent of Total Population
Based on places with total population of 50,000 or more

Place	Population	%
New York (city)	18	<0.01
Manhattan (borough) New York County	8	<0.01
Bronx (borough) Bronx County	5	<0.01
Brookhaven (town) Suffolk County	4	<0.01
Queens (borough) Queens County	4	<0.01
Hamburg (town) Erie County	2	<0.01
Brooklyn (borough) Kings County	1	<0.01
Clarkstown (town) Rockland County	1	<0.01
Rochester (city) Monroe County	1	<0.01
Utica (city) Oneida County	1	<0.01

American Indian: Pima

Top 10 Places Sorted by Population
Based on all places, regardless of total population

Place	Population	%
New York (city)	9	<0.01

Schenectady (city) Schenectady County	5	0.01
Manhattan (borough) New York County	4	<0.01
Fort Montgomery (cdp) Orange County	3	0.19
Gowanda (village) Cattaraugus County	3	0.11
Collins (town) Erie County	3	0.05
Highlands (town) Orange County	3	0.02
Fallsburg (town) Sullivan County	2	0.02
Ontario (town) Wayne County	2	0.02
Harrison (town/village) Westchester County	2	0.01

Top 10 Places Sorted by Percent of Total Population
Based on all places, regardless of total population

Place	Population	%
Fort Montgomery (cdp) Orange County	3	0.19
Rushville (village) Yates County	1	0.15
Gowanda (village) Cattaraugus County	3	0.11
Collins (town) Erie County	3	0.05
Potter (town) Yates County	1	0.05
Highlands (town) Orange County	3	0.02
Fallsburg (town) Sullivan County	2	0.02
Ontario (town) Wayne County	2	0.02
Minisink (town) Orange County	1	0.02
Ulysses (town) Tompkins County	1	0.02

Top 10 Places Sorted by Percent of Total Population
Based on places with total population of 50,000 or more

Place	Population	%
Schenectady (city) Schenectady County	5	0.01
New York (city)	9	<0.01
Manhattan (borough) New York County	4	<0.01
Brooklyn (borough) Kings County	2	<0.01
Rochester (city) Monroe County	2	<0.01
Staten Island (borough) Richmond County	2	<0.01
Syracuse (city) Onondaga County	2	<0.01
Brentwood (cdp) Suffolk County	1	<0.01
Bronx (borough) Bronx County	1	<0.01
Buffalo (city) Erie County	1	<0.01

American Indian: Potawatomi

Top 10 Places Sorted by Population
Based on all places, regardless of total population

Place	Population	%
New York (city)	40	<0.01
Manhattan (borough) New York County	20	<0.01
Brooklyn (borough) Kings County	11	<0.01
Tonawanda (cdp) Erie County	9	0.02
Tonawanda (town) Erie County	9	0.01
Queens (borough) Queens County	7	<0.01
Brookhaven (town) Suffolk County	6	<0.01
Fort Drum (cdp) Jefferson County	5	0.04
Le Ray (town) Jefferson County	5	0.02
Schenectady (city) Schenectady County	5	0.01

Top 10 Places Sorted by Percent of Total Population
Based on all places, regardless of total population

Place	Population	%
Onondaga Nation Reservation Onondaga County	4	0.85
Mina (town) Chautauqua County	2	0.18
Denning (town) Ulster County	1	0.18
Merritt Park (cdp) Dutchess County	2	0.16
Russia (town) Herkimer County	3	0.12
Cuyler (town) Cortland County	1	0.10
Greenport West (cdp) Suffolk County	2	0.09
Truxton (town) Cortland County	1	0.09
Lake Erie Beach (cdp) Erie County	3	0.08
Vernon (town) Oneida County	3	0.06

Top 10 Places Sorted by Percent of Total Population
Based on places with total population of 50,000 or more

Place	Population	%
Tonawanda (cdp) Erie County	9	0.02
Tonawanda (town) Erie County	9	0.01
Schenectady (city) Schenectady County	5	0.01
New York (city)	40	<0.01
Manhattan (borough) New York County	20	<0.01
Brooklyn (borough) Kings County	11	<0.01
Queens (borough) Queens County	7	<0.01
Brookhaven (town) Suffolk County	6	<0.01
Rochester (city) Monroe County	5	<0.01
Albany (city) Albany County	2	<0.01

American Indian: Pueblo

Top 10 Places Sorted by Population
Based on all places, regardless of total population

Place	Population	%
New York (city)	892	0.01
Bronx (borough) Bronx County	382	0.03
Manhattan (borough) New York County	175	0.01
Brooklyn (borough) Kings County	169	0.01
Queens (borough) Queens County	161	0.01
Yonkers (city) Westchester County	20	0.01
White Plains (city) Westchester County	19	0.03
Hempstead (town) Nassau County	13	<0.01
Le Ray (town) Jefferson County	11	0.05
Fort Drum (cdp) Jefferson County	10	0.08

Top 10 Places Sorted by Percent of Total Population
Based on all places, regardless of total population

Place	Population	%
DeKalb Junction (cdp) St. Lawrence County	4	0.77
Denning (town) Ulster County	2	0.36
Pine Hill (cdp) Ulster County	1	0.36
Natural Bridge (cdp) Jefferson County	1	0.27
De Kalb (town) St. Lawrence County	4	0.16
Northwest Harbor (cdp) Suffolk County	4	0.12
Ripley (cdp) Chautauqua County	1	0.11
Stone Ridge (cdp) Ulster County	1	0.09
Fort Drum (cdp) Jefferson County	10	0.08
Ripley (town) Chautauqua County	2	0.08

Top 10 Places Sorted by Percent of Total Population
Based on places with total population of 50,000 or more

Place	Population	%
Bronx (borough) Bronx County	382	0.03
White Plains (city) Westchester County	19	0.03
New York (city)	892	0.01
Manhattan (borough) New York County	175	0.01
Brooklyn (borough) Kings County	169	0.01
Queens (borough) Queens County	161	0.01
Yonkers (city) Westchester County	20	0.01
Mount Vernon (city) Westchester County	7	0.01
Hempstead (village) Nassau County	6	0.01
Brentwood (cdp) Suffolk County	5	0.01

American Indian: Puget Sound Salish

Top 10 Places Sorted by Population
Based on all places, regardless of total population

Place	Population	%
New York (city)	11	<0.01
Brookhaven (town) Suffolk County	6	<0.01
Gordon Heights (cdp) Suffolk County	5	0.12
Manhattan (borough) New York County	5	<0.01
Queens (borough) Queens County	5	<0.01
Bronxville (village) Westchester County	3	0.05
Eastchester (town) Westchester County	3	0.01
East Ithaca (cdp) Tompkins County	2	0.09
Horseheads (village) Chemung County	2	0.03
Orange Lake (cdp) Orange County	2	0.03

Top 10 Places Sorted by Percent of Total Population
Based on all places, regardless of total population

Place	Population	%
Gordon Heights (cdp) Suffolk County	5	0.12
East Ithaca (cdp) Tompkins County	2	0.09
Bronxville (village) Westchester County	3	0.05
Bellport (village) Suffolk County	1	0.05
Cattaraugus Reservation Erie County	1	0.05
Horseheads (village) Chemung County	2	0.03
Orange Lake (cdp) Orange County	2	0.03
Calcium (cdp) Jefferson County	1	0.03
Southold (cdp) Suffolk County	1	0.02
Eastchester (town) Westchester County	3	0.01

Top 10 Places Sorted by Percent of Total Population
Based on places with total population of 50,000 or more

Place	Population	%
New York (city)	11	<0.01
Brookhaven (town) Suffolk County	6	<0.01
Manhattan (borough) New York County	5	<0.01
Queens (borough) Queens County	5	<0.01

Place	Population	%
Brooklyn (borough) Kings County	1	<0.01
Tonawanda (cdp) Erie County	1	<0.01
Tonawanda (town) Erie County	1	<0.01
Albany (city) Albany County	0	0.00
Amherst (town) Erie County	0	0.00
Babylon (town) Suffolk County	0	0.00

American Indian: Seminole

Top 10 Places Sorted by Population
Based on all places, regardless of total population

Place	Population	%
New York (city)	357	<0.01
Manhattan (borough) New York County	110	<0.01
Brooklyn (borough) Kings County	92	<0.01
Queens (borough) Queens County	79	<0.01
Bronx (borough) Bronx County	50	<0.01
Rochester (city) Monroe County	44	0.02
Brookhaven (town) Suffolk County	33	0.01
Hempstead (town) Nassau County	28	<0.01
Staten Island (borough) Richmond County	26	0.01
Buffalo (city) Erie County	23	0.01

Top 10 Places Sorted by Percent of Total Population
Based on all places, regardless of total population

Place	Population	%
Randolph (village) Cattaraugus County	5	0.39
Cuylerville (cdp) Livingston County	1	0.34
Wainscott (cdp) Suffolk County	2	0.31
Poospatuck Reservation Suffolk County	1	0.31
West Sparta (town) Livingston County	3	0.24
Randolph (town) Cattaraugus County	5	0.19
Haviland (cdp) Dutchess County	5	0.14
Greenport (village) Suffolk County	3	0.14
Veteran (town) Chemung County	4	0.12
De Kalb (town) St. Lawrence County	3	0.12

Top 10 Places Sorted by Percent of Total Population
Based on places with total population of 50,000 or more

Place	Population	%
Rochester (city) Monroe County	44	0.02
Manhattan (borough) New York County	110	0.01
Brookhaven (town) Suffolk County	33	0.01
Staten Island (borough) Richmond County	26	0.01
Buffalo (city) Erie County	23	0.01
Syracuse (city) Onondaga County	16	0.01
Babylon (town) Suffolk County	13	0.01
Yonkers (city) Westchester County	11	0.01
Amherst (town) Erie County	10	0.01
Mount Vernon (city) Westchester County	9	0.01

American Indian: Shoshone

Top 10 Places Sorted by Population
Based on all places, regardless of total population

Place	Population	%
New York (city)	46	<0.01
Brooklyn (borough) Kings County	23	<0.01
Yates (town) Orleans County	8	0.31
Bronx (borough) Bronx County	8	<0.01
Manhattan (borough) New York County	6	<0.01
Queens (borough) Queens County	6	<0.01
Middletown (city) Orange County	4	0.01
Brookhaven (town) Suffolk County	4	<0.01
Bay Shore (cdp) Suffolk County	3	0.01
Hempstead (town) Nassau County	3	<0.01

Top 10 Places Sorted by Percent of Total Population
Based on all places, regardless of total population

Place	Population	%
Rhinecliff (cdp) Dutchess County	2	0.47
Hobart (village) Delaware County	2	0.45
Yates (town) Orleans County	8	0.31
St. Regis Falls (cdp) Franklin County	1	0.22
Waverly (town) Franklin County	1	0.10
Stamford (town) Delaware County	2	0.09
Covert (town) Seneca County	1	0.05
Minisink (town) Orange County	2	0.04
Afton (town) Chenango County	1	0.04
Rhinebeck (town) Dutchess County	2	0.03

American Indian: South American Indian

Top 10 Places Sorted by Percent of Total Population
Based on places with total population of 50,000 or more

Place	Population	%
New York (city)	46	<0.01
Brooklyn (borough) Kings County	23	<0.01
Bronx (borough) Bronx County	8	<0.01
Manhattan (borough) New York County	6	<0.01
Queens (borough) Queens County	6	<0.01
Brookhaven (town) Suffolk County	4	<0.01
Hempstead (town) Nassau County	3	<0.01
Islip (town) Suffolk County	3	<0.01
Staten Island (borough) Richmond County	3	<0.01
Albany (city) Albany County	1	<0.01

American Indian: Sioux

Top 10 Places Sorted by Population
Based on all places, regardless of total population

Place	Population	%
New York (city)	464	0.01
Manhattan (borough) New York County	133	0.01
Brooklyn (borough) Kings County	121	<0.01
Queens (borough) Queens County	104	<0.01
Bronx (borough) Bronx County	82	0.01
Buffalo (city) Erie County	46	0.02
Brookhaven (town) Suffolk County	42	0.01
Syracuse (city) Onondaga County	38	0.03
Hempstead (town) Nassau County	33	<0.01
Utica (city) Oneida County	29	0.05

Top 10 Places Sorted by Percent of Total Population
Based on all places, regardless of total population

Place	Population	%
Hardenburgh (town) Ulster County	10	4.20
Napeague (cdp) Suffolk County	3	1.50
Poospatuck Reservation Suffolk County	3	0.93
Windham (cdp) Greene County	3	0.82
Redfield (town) Oswego County	4	0.73
Plessis (cdp) Jefferson County	1	0.61
Allegany Reservation Cattaraugus County	6	0.59
Perrysburg (village) Cattaraugus County	2	0.50
Ashland (town) Chemung County	7	0.41
Calcium (cdp) Jefferson County	14	0.40

Top 10 Places Sorted by Percent of Total Population
Based on places with total population of 50,000 or more

Place	Population	%
Utica (city) Oneida County	29	0.05
Syracuse (city) Onondaga County	38	0.03
Buffalo (city) Erie County	46	0.02
Schenectady (city) Schenectady County	14	0.02
Niagara Falls (city) Niagara County	8	0.02
New York (city)	464	0.01
Manhattan (borough) New York County	133	0.01
Bronx (borough) Bronx County	82	0.01
Brookhaven (town) Suffolk County	42	0.01
Islip (town) Suffolk County	27	0.01

American Indian: South American Indian

Top 10 Places Sorted by Population
Based on all places, regardless of total population

Place	Population	%
New York (city)	9,464	0.12
Bronx (borough) Bronx County	2,938	0.21
Queens (borough) Queens County	2,448	0.11
Manhattan (borough) New York County	1,935	0.12
Brooklyn (borough) Kings County	1,855	0.07
Hempstead (town) Nassau County	294	0.04
Staten Island (borough) Richmond County	288	0.06
Yonkers (city) Westchester County	270	0.14
Islip (town) Suffolk County	249	0.07
Rochester (city) Monroe County	144	0.07

Top 10 Places Sorted by Percent of Total Population
Based on all places, regardless of total population

Place	Population	%
Onondaga Nation Reservation Onondaga County	9	1.92
Cattaraugus Reservation Cattaraugus County	5	1.59
Allegany Reservation Cattaraugus County	9	0.88

Shinnecock Hills (cdp) Suffolk County	18	0.82
Poospatuck Reservation Suffolk County	2	0.62
Roslyn Harbor (village) Nassau County	4	0.38
Fairview (cdp) Westchester County	11	0.35
East Hampton North (cdp) Suffolk County	13	0.31
St. Regis Mohawk Reservation Franklin County	10	0.31
Haverstraw (village) Rockland County	32	0.27

Top 10 Places Sorted by Percent of Total Population
Based on places with total population of 50,000 or more

Place	Population	%
Bronx (borough) Bronx County	2,938	0.21
White Plains (city) Westchester County	116	0.20
Yonkers (city) Westchester County	270	0.14
Brentwood (cdp) Suffolk County	87	0.14
New York (city)	9,464	0.12
Manhattan (borough) New York County	1,935	0.12
Queens (borough) Queens County	2,448	0.11
Greenburgh (town) Westchester County	72	0.08
Brooklyn (borough) Kings County	1,855	0.07
Islip (town) Suffolk County	249	0.07

American Indian: Spanish American Indian

Top 10 Places Sorted by Population
Based on all places, regardless of total population

Place	Population	%
New York (city)	2,594	0.03
Bronx (borough) Bronx County	992	0.07
Queens (borough) Queens County	659	0.03
Manhattan (borough) New York County	514	0.03
Brooklyn (borough) Kings County	382	0.02
Hempstead (town) Nassau County	137	0.02
Yonkers (city) Westchester County	132	0.07
Newburgh (city) Orange County	92	0.32
Islip (town) Suffolk County	91	0.03
Brentwood (cdp) Suffolk County	52	0.09

Top 10 Places Sorted by Percent of Total Population
Based on all places, regardless of total population

Place	Population	%
Shinnecock Reservation Suffolk County	4	0.60
Fort Covington Hamlet (cdp) Franklin County	7	0.54
Fort Covington (town) Franklin County	7	0.42
Newburgh (city) Orange County	92	0.32
Lebanon (town) Madison County	4	0.30
Westhampton Beach (village) Suffolk County	5	0.29
Greenport West (cdp) Suffolk County	6	0.28
South Floral Park (village) Nassau County	4	0.23
Woodstock (cdp) Ulster County	4	0.19
Canisteo (village) Steuben County	4	0.18

Top 10 Places Sorted by Percent of Total Population
Based on places with total population of 50,000 or more

Place	Population	%
Brentwood (cdp) Suffolk County	52	0.09
Hempstead (village) Nassau County	47	0.09
Bronx (borough) Bronx County	992	0.07
Yonkers (city) Westchester County	132	0.07
New York (city)	2,594	0.03
Queens (borough) Queens County	659	0.03
Manhattan (borough) New York County	514	0.03
Islip (town) Suffolk County	91	0.03
Greenburgh (town) Westchester County	23	0.03
White Plains (city) Westchester County	15	0.03

Alaska Native: Tlingit-Haida

Top 10 Places Sorted by Population
Based on all places, regardless of total population

Place	Population	%
New York (city)	75	<0.01
Brooklyn (borough) Kings County	28	<0.01
Queens (borough) Queens County	20	<0.01
Manhattan (borough) New York County	15	<0.01
Bronx (borough) Bronx County	11	<0.01
Ramapo (town) Rockland County	7	0.01
Hempstead (town) Nassau County	6	<0.01
Islip (town) Suffolk County	6	<0.01
Hilton (village) Monroe County	5	0.08

Parma (town) Monroe County	5	0.03

Top 10 Places Sorted by Percent of Total Population
Based on all places, regardless of total population

Place	Population	%
Wampsville (village) Madison County	1	0.18
Lake George (town) Warren County	4	0.11
Dolgeville (village) Herkimer County	2	0.09
Poestenkill (cdp) Rensselaer County	1	0.09
Hilton (village) Monroe County	5	0.08
Gordon Heights (cdp) Suffolk County	3	0.07
Bellmont (town) Franklin County	1	0.07
Manheim (town) Herkimer County	2	0.06
Hornell (city) Steuben County	4	0.05
Hillcrest (cdp) Rockland County	3	0.04

Top 10 Places Sorted by Percent of Total Population
Based on places with total population of 50,000 or more

Place	Population	%
Ramapo (town) Rockland County	7	0.01
Utica (city) Oneida County	4	0.01
New York (city)	75	<0.01
Brooklyn (borough) Kings County	28	<0.01
Queens (borough) Queens County	20	<0.01
Manhattan (borough) New York County	15	<0.01
Bronx (borough) Bronx County	11	<0.01
Hempstead (town) Nassau County	6	<0.01
Islip (town) Suffolk County	6	<0.01
Brookhaven (town) Suffolk County	5	<0.01

American Indian: Tohono O'Odham

Top 10 Places Sorted by Population
Based on all places, regardless of total population

Place	Population	%
New York (city)	48	<0.01
Manhattan (borough) New York County	15	<0.01
Brooklyn (borough) Kings County	10	<0.01
Bronx (borough) Bronx County	9	<0.01
Staten Island (borough) Richmond County	8	<0.01
Hempstead (town) Nassau County	7	<0.01
Middletown (city) Orange County	6	0.02
New Windsor (town) Orange County	6	0.02
Uniondale (cdp) Nassau County	6	0.02
Queens (borough) Queens County	6	<0.01

Top 10 Places Sorted by Percent of Total Population
Based on all places, regardless of total population

Place	Population	%
Hillburn (village) Rockland County	4	0.42
Covington (town) Wyoming County	3	0.24
Allegany Reservation Cattaraugus County	1	0.10
Chester (village) Orange County	3	0.08
Durham (town) Greene County	1	0.04
Chester (town) Orange County	3	0.03
Middletown (city) Orange County	6	0.02
New Windsor (town) Orange County	6	0.02
Uniondale (cdp) Nassau County	6	0.02
Poughkeepsie (city) Dutchess County	3	0.01

Top 10 Places Sorted by Percent of Total Population
Based on places with total population of 50,000 or more

Place	Population	%
New York (city)	48	<0.01
Manhattan (borough) New York County	15	<0.01
Brooklyn (borough) Kings County	10	<0.01
Bronx (borough) Bronx County	9	<0.01
Staten Island (borough) Richmond County	8	<0.01
Hempstead (town) Nassau County	7	<0.01
Queens (borough) Queens County	6	<0.01
Ramapo (town) Rockland County	4	<0.01
Buffalo (city) Erie County	3	<0.01
Yonkers (city) Westchester County	3	<0.01

Alaska Native: Tsimshian

Top 10 Places Sorted by Population
Based on all places, regardless of total population

Place	Population	%
New York (city)	4	<0.01

Manhattan (borough) New York County	3	<0.01
Rochester (town) Ulster County	1	0.01
Queens (borough) Queens County	1	<0.01
Accord (cdp) Ulster County	0	0.00
Adams (village) Jefferson County	0	0.00
Adams (town) Jefferson County	0	0.00
Adams Center (cdp) Jefferson County	0	0.00
Addison (village) Steuben County	0	0.00
Addison (town) Steuben County	0	0.00

Top 10 Places Sorted by Percent of Total Population
Based on all places, regardless of total population

Place	Population	%
Rochester (town) Ulster County	1	0.01
New York (city)	4	<0.01
Manhattan (borough) New York County	3	<0.01
Queens (borough) Queens County	1	<0.01
Accord (cdp) Ulster County	0	0.00
Adams (village) Jefferson County	0	0.00
Adams (town) Jefferson County	0	0.00
Adams Center (cdp) Jefferson County	0	0.00
Addison (village) Steuben County	0	0.00
Addison (town) Steuben County	0	0.00

Top 10 Places Sorted by Percent of Total Population
Based on places with total population of 50,000 or more

Place	Population	%
New York (city)	4	<0.01
Manhattan (borough) New York County	3	<0.01
Queens (borough) Queens County	1	<0.01
Albany (city) Albany County	0	0.00
Amherst (town) Erie County	0	0.00
Babylon (town) Suffolk County	0	0.00
Brentwood (cdp) Suffolk County	0	0.00
Bronx (borough) Bronx County	0	0.00
Brookhaven (town) Suffolk County	0	0.00
Brooklyn (borough) Kings County	0	0.00

American Indian: Ute

Top 10 Places Sorted by Population
Based on all places, regardless of total population

Place	Population	%
New York (city)	17	<0.01
Bronx (borough) Bronx County	5	<0.01
Queens (borough) Queens County	5	<0.01
Brooklyn (borough) Kings County	4	<0.01
Rochester (city) Monroe County	4	<0.01
Farmington (town) Ontario County	2	0.02
Manhattan (borough) New York County	2	<0.01
Jefferson (town) Schoharie County	1	0.07
Calcium (cdp) Jefferson County	1	0.03
Amenia (town) Dutchess County	1	0.02

Top 10 Places Sorted by Percent of Total Population
Based on all places, regardless of total population

Place	Population	%
Jefferson (town) Schoharie County	1	0.07
Calcium (cdp) Jefferson County	1	0.03
Farmington (town) Ontario County	2	0.02
Amenia (town) Dutchess County	1	0.02
Little Falls (city) Herkimer County	1	0.02
Wilson (town) Niagara County	1	0.02
Center Moriches (cdp) Suffolk County	1	0.01
Hastings (town) Oswego County	1	0.01
Kings Park (cdp) Suffolk County	1	0.01
Lynbrook (village) Nassau County	1	0.01

Top 10 Places Sorted by Percent of Total Population
Based on places with total population of 50,000 or more

Place	Population	%
New York (city)	17	<0.01
Bronx (borough) Bronx County	5	<0.01
Queens (borough) Queens County	5	<0.01
Brooklyn (borough) Kings County	4	<0.01
Rochester (city) Monroe County	4	<0.01
Manhattan (borough) New York County	2	<0.01
Brookhaven (town) Suffolk County	1	<0.01
Hempstead (town) Nassau County	1	<0.01
Smithtown (town) Suffolk County	1	<0.01
Staten Island (borough) Richmond County	1	<0.01

American Indian: Yakama

Top 10 Places Sorted by Population
Based on all places, regardless of total population

Place	Population	%
New York (city)	8	<0.01
Bronx (borough) Bronx County	3	<0.01
Brooklyn (borough) Kings County	3	<0.01
Poughkeepsie (city) Dutchess County	2	0.01
Manhattan (borough) New York County	2	<0.01
Austerlitz (town) Columbia County	1	0.06
Coxsackie (village) Greene County	1	0.04
Gordon Heights (cdp) Suffolk County	1	0.02
Coxsackie (town) Greene County	1	0.01
Oswego (city) Oswego County	1	0.01

Top 10 Places Sorted by Percent of Total Population
Based on all places, regardless of total population

Place	Population	%
Austerlitz (town) Columbia County	1	0.06
Coxsackie (village) Greene County	1	0.04
Gordon Heights (cdp) Suffolk County	1	0.02
Poughkeepsie (city) Dutchess County	2	0.01
Coxsackie (town) Greene County	1	0.01
Oswego (city) Oswego County	1	0.01
New York (city)	8	<0.01
Bronx (borough) Bronx County	3	<0.01
Brooklyn (borough) Kings County	3	<0.01
Manhattan (borough) New York County	2	<0.01

Top 10 Places Sorted by Percent of Total Population
Based on places with total population of 50,000 or more

Place	Population	%
New York (city)	8	<0.01
Bronx (borough) Bronx County	3	<0.01
Brooklyn (borough) Kings County	3	<0.01
Manhattan (borough) New York County	2	<0.01
Albany (city) Albany County	1	<0.01
Brookhaven (town) Suffolk County	1	<0.01
Niagara Falls (city) Niagara County	1	<0.01
Ramapo (town) Rockland County	1	<0.01
Amherst (town) Erie County	0	0.00
Babylon (town) Suffolk County	0	0.00

American Indian: Yaqui

Top 10 Places Sorted by Population
Based on all places, regardless of total population

Place	Population	%
New York (city)	54	<0.01
Manhattan (borough) New York County	22	<0.01
Brooklyn (borough) Kings County	19	<0.01
Queens (borough) Queens County	7	<0.01
Groton (village) Tompkins County	5	0.21
Pembroke (town) Genesee County	5	0.12
Groton (town) Tompkins County	5	0.08
Kirkland (town) Oneida County	5	0.05
Bronx (borough) Bronx County	5	<0.01
Brookhaven (town) Suffolk County	5	<0.01

Top 10 Places Sorted by Percent of Total Population
Based on all places, regardless of total population

Place	Population	%
Groton (village) Tompkins County	5	0.21
Lake Luzerne (cdp) Warren County	2	0.16
Rushville (village) Yates County	1	0.15
Pembroke (town) Genesee County	5	0.12
Schuyler (town) Herkimer County	4	0.12
Chateaugay (village) Franklin County	1	0.12
Allegany Reservation Cattaraugus County	1	0.10
Groton (town) Tompkins County	5	0.08
Lake Luzerne (town) Warren County	2	0.06
Kortright (town) Delaware County	1	0.06

Top 10 Places Sorted by Percent of Total Population
Based on places with total population of 50,000 or more

Place	Population	%
New York (city)	54	<0.01
Manhattan (borough) New York County	22	<0.01
Brooklyn (borough) Kings County	19	<0.01
Queens (borough) Queens County	7	<0.01

Place	Population	%
Bronx (borough) Bronx County	5	<0.01
Brookhaven (town) Suffolk County	5	<0.01
Buffalo (city) Erie County	2	<0.01
Brentwood (cdp) Suffolk County	1	<0.01
Islip (town) Suffolk County	1	<0.01
Niagara Falls (city) Niagara County	1	<0.01

American Indian: Yuman

Top 10 Places Sorted by Population
Based on all places, regardless of total population

Place	Population	%
New York (city)	22	<0.01
Brooklyn (borough) Kings County	8	<0.01
Manhattan (borough) New York County	6	<0.01
Queens (borough) Queens County	5	<0.01
Deerpark (town) Orange County	4	0.05
De Witt (town) Onondaga County	4	0.02
Webster (village) Monroe County	2	0.04
Bronx (borough) Bronx County	2	<0.01
Webster (town) Monroe County	2	<0.01
Yonkers (city) Westchester County	2	<0.01

Top 10 Places Sorted by Percent of Total Population
Based on all places, regardless of total population

Place	Population	%
Deerpark (town) Orange County	4	0.05
Webster (village) Monroe County	2	0.04
Brewster (village) Putnam County	1	0.04
De Witt (town) Onondaga County	4	0.02
Lyncourt (cdp) Onondaga County	1	0.02
Eastchester (cdp) Westchester County	1	0.01
Granville (town) Washington County	1	0.01
Greece (cdp) Monroe County	1	0.01
Highlands (town) Orange County	1	0.01
Southeast (town) Putnam County	1	0.01

Top 10 Places Sorted by Percent of Total Population
Based on places with total population of 50,000 or more

Place	Population	%
New York (city)	22	<0.01
Brooklyn (borough) Kings County	8	<0.01
Manhattan (borough) New York County	6	<0.01
Queens (borough) Queens County	5	<0.01
Bronx (borough) Bronx County	2	<0.01
Yonkers (city) Westchester County	2	<0.01
Brookhaven (town) Suffolk County	1	<0.01
Buffalo (city) Erie County	1	<0.01
Greece (town) Monroe County	1	<0.01
Islip (town) Suffolk County	1	<0.01

Alaska Native: Yup'ik

Top 10 Places Sorted by Population
Based on all places, regardless of total population

Place	Population	%
New York (city)	10	<0.01
Bronx (borough) Bronx County	6	<0.01
Cazenovia (town) Madison County	3	0.04
Canton (town) St. Lawrence County	3	0.03
Fort Drum (cdp) Jefferson County	3	0.02
Le Ray (town) Jefferson County	3	0.01
Stephentown (town) Rensselaer County	2	0.07
Colden (town) Erie County	2	0.06
New Paltz (village) Ulster County	2	0.03
New Paltz (town) Ulster County	2	0.01

Top 10 Places Sorted by Percent of Total Population
Based on all places, regardless of total population

Place	Population	%
Forest Home (cdp) Tompkins County	1	0.17
Savona (village) Steuben County	1	0.12
Ripley (cdp) Chautauqua County	1	0.11
Rathbone (town) Steuben County	1	0.09
Stephentown (town) Rensselaer County	2	0.07
Colden (town) Erie County	2	0.06
Cazenovia (town) Madison County	3	0.04
Franklin (town) Delaware County	1	0.04
Green Island (town/village) Albany County	1	0.04
Orleans (town) Jefferson County	1	0.04

Top 10 Places Sorted by Percent of Total Population
Based on places with total population of 50,000 or more

Place	Population	%
New York (city)	10	<0.01
Bronx (borough) Bronx County	6	<0.01
Manhattan (borough) New York County	2	<0.01
Albany (city) Albany County	1	<0.01
Amherst (town) Erie County	1	<0.01
Brooklyn (borough) Kings County	1	<0.01
Queens (borough) Queens County	1	<0.01
Syracuse (city) Onondaga County	1	<0.01
Babylon (town) Suffolk County	0	0.00
Brentwood (cdp) Suffolk County	0	0.00

Asian

Top 10 Places Sorted by Population
Based on all places, regardless of total population

Place	Population	%
New York (city)	1,134,919	13.88
Queens (borough) Queens County	552,867	24.78
Brooklyn (borough) Kings County	284,489	11.36
Manhattan (borough) New York County	199,722	12.59
Bronx (borough) Bronx County	59,085	4.27
Hempstead (town) Nassau County	45,112	5.94
Staten Island (borough) Richmond County	38,756	8.27
North Hempstead (town) Nassau County	36,973	16.34
Oyster Bay (town) Nassau County	29,203	9.96
Brookhaven (town) Suffolk County	21,849	4.50

Top 10 Places Sorted by Percent of Total Population
Based on all places, regardless of total population

Place	Population	%
Herricks (cdp) Nassau County	1,943	45.24
Manhasset Hills (cdp) Nassau County	1,483	41.29
Searingtown (cdp) Nassau County	2,008	40.85
Forest Home (cdp) Tompkins County	210	36.71
Merritt Park (cdp) Dutchess County	442	35.19
Garden City Park (cdp) Nassau County	2,698	34.56
University Gardens (cdp) Nassau County	1,316	31.14
North New Hyde Park (cdp) Nassau County	4,585	30.77
Bellerose Terrace (cdp) Nassau County	663	30.16
Thomaston (village) Nassau County	783	29.92

Top 10 Places Sorted by Percent of Total Population
Based on places with total population of 50,000 or more

Place	Population	%
Queens (borough) Queens County	552,867	24.78
North Hempstead (town) Nassau County	36,973	16.34
New York (city)	1,134,919	13.88
Manhattan (borough) New York County	199,722	12.59
Greenburgh (town) Westchester County	10,180	11.52
Clarkstown (town) Rockland County	9,614	11.42
Brooklyn (borough) Kings County	284,489	11.36
Oyster Bay (town) Nassau County	29,203	9.96
Amherst (town) Erie County	10,683	8.73
Staten Island (borough) Richmond County	38,756	8.27

Asian: Not Hispanic

Top 10 Places Sorted by Population
Based on all places, regardless of total population

Place	Population	%
New York (city)	1,110,964	13.59
Queens (borough) Queens County	545,389	24.45
Brooklyn (borough) Kings County	279,499	11.16
Manhattan (borough) New York County	194,929	12.29
Bronx (borough) Bronx County	53,458	3.86
Hempstead (town) Nassau County	43,880	5.78
Staten Island (borough) Richmond County	37,689	8.04
North Hempstead (town) Nassau County	36,641	16.19
Oyster Bay (town) Nassau County	28,910	9.86
Brookhaven (town) Suffolk County	21,257	4.37

Top 10 Places Sorted by Percent of Total Population
Based on all places, regardless of total population

Place	Population	%
Herricks (cdp) Nassau County	1,931	44.96
Manhasset Hills (cdp) Nassau County	1,476	41.09
Searingtown (cdp) Nassau County	2,000	40.69

Place	Population	%
Forest Home (cdp) Tompkins County	210	36.71
Merritt Park (cdp) Dutchess County	442	35.19
Garden City Park (cdp) Nassau County	2,670	34.20
University Gardens (cdp) Nassau County	1,309	30.97
North New Hyde Park (cdp) Nassau County	4,558	30.59
Bellerose Terrace (cdp) Nassau County	652	29.66
Thomaston (village) Nassau County	772	29.50

Top 10 Places Sorted by Percent of Total Population
Based on places with total population of 50,000 or more

Place	Population	%
Queens (borough) Queens County	545,389	24.45
North Hempstead (town) Nassau County	36,641	16.19
New York (city)	1,110,964	13.59
Manhattan (borough) New York County	194,929	12.29
Greenburgh (town) Westchester County	10,025	11.34
Clarkstown (town) Rockland County	9,462	11.24
Brooklyn (borough) Kings County	279,499	11.16
Oyster Bay (town) Nassau County	28,910	9.86
Amherst (town) Erie County	10,590	8.65
Staten Island (borough) Richmond County	37,689	8.04

Asian: Hispanic

Top 10 Places Sorted by Population
Based on all places, regardless of total population

Place	Population	%
New York (city)	23,955	0.29
Queens (borough) Queens County	7,478	0.34
Bronx (borough) Bronx County	5,627	0.41
Brooklyn (borough) Kings County	4,990	0.20
Manhattan (borough) New York County	4,793	0.30
Hempstead (town) Nassau County	1,232	0.16
Staten Island (borough) Richmond County	1,067	0.23
Brookhaven (town) Suffolk County	592	0.12
Islip (town) Suffolk County	553	0.16
Yonkers (city) Westchester County	517	0.26

Top 10 Places Sorted by Percent of Total Population
Based on all places, regardless of total population

Place	Population	%
Salamanca (town) Cattaraugus County	4	0.83
Nelsonville (village) Putnam County	5	0.80
North Lynbrook (cdp) Nassau County	6	0.76
Grove (town) Allegany County	4	0.73
La Fargeville (cdp) Jefferson County	4	0.66
Tonawanda Reservation Genesee County	3	0.62
Rensselaer Falls (village) St. Lawrence County	2	0.60
Tannersville (village) Greene County	3	0.56
Waterford (village) Saratoga County	11	0.55
Chautauqua (cdp) Chautauqua County	1	0.52

Top 10 Places Sorted by Percent of Total Population
Based on places with total population of 50,000 or more

Place	Population	%
Bronx (borough) Bronx County	5,627	0.41
Queens (borough) Queens County	7,478	0.34
Brentwood (cdp) Suffolk County	195	0.32
Manhattan (borough) New York County	4,793	0.30
New York (city)	23,955	0.29
Yonkers (city) Westchester County	517	0.26
Hempstead (village) Nassau County	135	0.25
Staten Island (borough) Richmond County	1,067	0.23
New Rochelle (city) Westchester County	167	0.22
White Plains (city) Westchester County	121	0.21

Asian: Bangladeshi

Top 10 Places Sorted by Population
Based on all places, regardless of total population

Place	Population	%
New York (city)	61,788	0.76
Queens (borough) Queens County	38,341	1.72
Brooklyn (borough) Kings County	12,408	0.50
Bronx (borough) Bronx County	8,623	0.62
Manhattan (borough) New York County	2,029	0.13
Brookhaven (town) Suffolk County	621	0.13
Hempstead (town) Nassau County	582	0.08
North Hempstead (town) Nassau County	441	0.19
Staten Island (borough) Richmond County	387	0.08
Oyster Bay (town) Nassau County	365	0.12

Top 10 Places Sorted by Percent of Total Population
Based on all places, regardless of total population

Place	Population	%
Hudson (city) Columbia County	271	4.04
Bellerose Terrace (cdp) Nassau County	44	2.00
Queens (borough) Queens County	38,341	1.72
Harriman (village) Orange County	40	1.65
Clintondale (cdp) Ulster County	22	1.52
Manhasset Hills (cdp) Nassau County	33	0.92
Greenvale (cdp) Nassau County	9	0.82
Deer Park (cdp) Suffolk County	224	0.81
Herricks (cdp) Nassau County	35	0.81
New York (city)	61,788	0.76

Top 10 Places Sorted by Percent of Total Population
Based on places with total population of 50,000 or more

Place	Population	%
Queens (borough) Queens County	38,341	1.72
New York (city)	61,788	0.76
Bronx (borough) Bronx County	8,623	0.62
Brooklyn (borough) Kings County	12,408	0.50
North Hempstead (town) Nassau County	441	0.19
Albany (city) Albany County	171	0.17
Babylon (town) Suffolk County	341	0.16
Manhattan (borough) New York County	2,029	0.13
Brookhaven (town) Suffolk County	621	0.13
Levittown (cdp) Nassau County	70	0.13

Asian: Bhutanese

Top 10 Places Sorted by Population
Based on all places, regardless of total population

Place	Population	%
Syracuse (city) Onondaga County	516	0.36
Rochester (city) Monroe County	411	0.20
New York (city)	388	<0.01
Buffalo (city) Erie County	370	0.14
Queens (borough) Queens County	250	0.01
Bronx (borough) Bronx County	104	0.01
Albany (city) Albany County	62	0.06
Utica (city) Oneida County	36	0.06
Manhattan (borough) New York County	26	<0.01
Greenville (cdp) Westchester County	8	0.11

Top 10 Places Sorted by Percent of Total Population
Based on all places, regardless of total population

Place	Population	%
Syracuse (city) Onondaga County	516	0.36
Rochester (city) Monroe County	411	0.20
Meredith (town) Delaware County	3	0.20
Buffalo (city) Erie County	370	0.14
Greenville (cdp) Westchester County	8	0.11
Albany (city) Albany County	62	0.06
Utica (city) Oneida County	36	0.06
Kerhonkson (cdp) Ulster County	1	0.06
Sullivan (town) Madison County	7	0.05
Harrison (town/village) Westchester County	8	0.03

Top 10 Places Sorted by Percent of Total Population
Based on places with total population of 50,000 or more

Place	Population	%
Syracuse (city) Onondaga County	516	0.36
Rochester (city) Monroe County	411	0.20
Buffalo (city) Erie County	370	0.14
Albany (city) Albany County	62	0.06
Utica (city) Oneida County	36	0.06
Queens (borough) Queens County	250	0.01
Bronx (borough) Bronx County	104	0.01
Greenburgh (town) Westchester County	8	0.01
New York (city)	388	<0.01
Manhattan (borough) New York County	26	<0.01

Asian: Burmese

Top 10 Places Sorted by Population
Based on all places, regardless of total population

Place	Population	%
New York (city)	4,132	0.05
Buffalo (city) Erie County	2,361	0.90
Queens (borough) Queens County	2,344	0.11

Place	Population	%
Utica (city) Oneida County	2,317	3.72
Brooklyn (borough) Kings County	1,260	0.05
Syracuse (city) Onondaga County	1,218	0.84
Rochester (city) Monroe County	565	0.27
Albany (city) Albany County	322	0.33
Manhattan (borough) New York County	317	0.02
Rensselaer (city) Rensselaer County	316	3.36

Top 10 Places Sorted by Percent of Total Population
Based on all places, regardless of total population

Place	Population	%
Utica (city) Oneida County	2,317	3.72
Rensselaer (city) Rensselaer County	316	3.36
East Ithaca (cdp) Tompkins County	46	2.06
Buffalo (city) Erie County	2,361	0.90
Syracuse (city) Onondaga County	1,218	0.84
Lakeville (cdp) Livingston County	4	0.53
Union Springs (village) Cayuga County	6	0.50
Northeast Ithaca (cdp) Tompkins County	12	0.45
Green Island (town/village) Albany County	11	0.42
Albany (city) Albany County	322	0.33

Top 10 Places Sorted by Percent of Total Population
Based on places with total population of 50,000 or more

Place	Population	%
Utica (city) Oneida County	2,317	3.72
Buffalo (city) Erie County	2,361	0.90
Syracuse (city) Onondaga County	1,218	0.84
Albany (city) Albany County	322	0.33
Rochester (city) Monroe County	565	0.27
Queens (borough) Queens County	2,344	0.11
Troy (city) Rensselaer County	28	0.06
New York (city)	4,132	0.05
Brooklyn (borough) Kings County	1,260	0.05
North Hempstead (town) Nassau County	88	0.04

Asian: Cambodian

Top 10 Places Sorted by Population
Based on all places, regardless of total population

Place	Population	%
New York (city)	2,591	0.03
Bronx (borough) Bronx County	1,188	0.09
Brooklyn (borough) Kings County	751	0.03
Utica (city) Oneida County	480	0.77
Rochester (city) Monroe County	381	0.18
Queens (borough) Queens County	303	0.01
Manhattan (borough) New York County	220	0.01
Syracuse (city) Onondaga County	149	0.10
Staten Island (borough) Richmond County	129	0.03
Ithaca (city) Tompkins County	68	0.23

Top 10 Places Sorted by Percent of Total Population
Based on all places, regardless of total population

Place	Population	%
Fowlerville (cdp) Livingston County	2	0.88
Utica (city) Oneida County	480	0.77
East Ithaca (cdp) Tompkins County	13	0.58
York Hamlet (cdp) Livingston County	3	0.55
East Nassau (village) Rensselaer County	3	0.51
Bloomingburg (village) Sullivan County	2	0.48
Lansing (village) Tompkins County	16	0.45
Andes (cdp) Delaware County	1	0.40
Parc (cdp) Clinton County	1	0.39
Argyle (town) Washington County	12	0.32

Top 10 Places Sorted by Percent of Total Population
Based on all places with total population of 50,000 or more

Place	Population	%
Utica (city) Oneida County	480	0.77
Rochester (city) Monroe County	381	0.18
Syracuse (city) Onondaga County	149	0.10
Bronx (borough) Bronx County	1,188	0.09
Clarkstown (town) Rockland County	68	0.08
Irondequoit (cdp/town) Monroe County	31	0.06
Greece (town) Monroe County	47	0.05
Clay (town) Onondaga County	29	0.05
Ramapo (town) Rockland County	52	0.04
New York (city)	2,591	0.03

Asian: Chinese, except Taiwanese

Top 10 Places Sorted by Population
Based on all places, regardless of total population

Place	Population	%
New York (city)	500,434	6.12
Queens (borough) Queens County	200,714	9.00
Brooklyn (borough) Kings County	178,214	7.12
Manhattan (borough) New York County	99,287	6.26
Staten Island (borough) Richmond County	14,107	3.01
North Hempstead (town) Nassau County	10,292	4.55
Bronx (borough) Bronx County	8,112	0.59
Hempstead (town) Nassau County	7,849	1.03
Oyster Bay (town) Nassau County	7,054	2.41
Brookhaven (town) Suffolk County	6,107	1.26

Top 10 Places Sorted by Percent of Total Population
Based on all places, regardless of total population

Place	Population	%
University Gardens (cdp) Nassau County	711	16.82
Thomaston (village) Nassau County	398	15.21
Lake Success (village) Nassau County	382	13.02
Russell Gardens (village) Nassau County	119	12.59
Forest Home (cdp) Tompkins County	68	11.89
Manhasset Hills (cdp) Nassau County	417	11.61
Binghamton University (cdp) Broome County	694	11.24
Lansing (village) Tompkins County	375	10.63
North Hills (village) Nassau County	516	10.17
University at Buffalo (cdp) Erie County	589	9.71

Top 10 Places Sorted by Percent of Total Population
Based on places with total population of 50,000 or more

Place	Population	%
Queens (borough) Queens County	200,714	9.00
Brooklyn (borough) Kings County	178,214	7.12
Manhattan (borough) New York County	99,287	6.26
New York (city)	500,434	6.12
North Hempstead (town) Nassau County	10,292	4.55
Staten Island (borough) Richmond County	14,107	3.01
Amherst (town) Erie County	3,146	2.57
Greenburgh (town) Westchester County	2,225	2.52
Oyster Bay (town) Nassau County	7,054	2.41
White Plains (city) Westchester County	934	1.64

Asian: Filipino

Top 10 Places Sorted by Population
Based on all places, regardless of total population

Place	Population	%
New York (city)	78,030	0.95
Queens (borough) Queens County	41,773	1.87
Manhattan (borough) New York County	13,388	0.84
Brooklyn (borough) Kings County	10,208	0.41
Hempstead (town) Nassau County	7,212	0.95
Bronx (borough) Bronx County	6,456	0.47
Staten Island (borough) Richmond County	6,205	1.32
Yonkers (city) Westchester County	2,819	1.44
Brookhaven (town) Suffolk County	2,705	0.56
Clarkstown (town) Rockland County	2,320	2.76

Top 10 Places Sorted by Percent of Total Population
Based on all places, regardless of total population

Place	Population	%
Hillcrest (cdp) Rockland County	441	5.83
Bellerose Terrace (cdp) Nassau County	119	5.41
Valley Cottage (cdp) Rockland County	485	5.33
Orangeburg (cdp) Rockland County	237	5.19
Sparkill (cdp) Rockland County	56	3.58
Nanuet (cdp) Rockland County	574	3.21
Merritt Park (cdp) Dutchess County	37	2.95
South Valley Stream (cdp) Nassau County	174	2.92
New Hempstead (village) Rockland County	150	2.92
Clarkstown (town) Rockland County	2,320	2.76

Top 10 Places Sorted by Percent of Total Population
Based on places with total population of 50,000 or more

Place	Population	%
Clarkstown (town) Rockland County	2,320	2.76
Queens (borough) Queens County	41,773	1.87
Yonkers (city) Westchester County	2,819	1.44
Staten Island (borough) Richmond County	6,205	1.32

Place	Population	%
Ramapo (town) Rockland County	1,472	1.16
Greenburgh (town) Westchester County	959	1.08
Levittown (cdp) Nassau County	525	1.01
New York (city)	78,030	0.95
Hempstead (town) Nassau County	7,212	0.95
Manhattan (borough) New York County	13,388	0.84

Asian: Hmong

Top 10 Places Sorted by Population
Based on all places, regardless of total population

Place	Population	%
New York (city)	83	<0.01
Clay (town) Onondaga County	75	0.13
Syracuse (city) Onondaga County	34	0.02
Orangetown (town) Rockland County	32	0.07
South Nyack (village) Rockland County	31	0.88
Queens (borough) Queens County	30	<0.01
Brooklyn (borough) Kings County	22	<0.01
Manhattan (borough) New York County	20	<0.01
Cicero (town) Onondaga County	12	0.04
Salina (town) Onondaga County	11	0.03

Top 10 Places Sorted by Percent of Total Population
Based on all places, regardless of total population

Place	Population	%
South Nyack (village) Rockland County	31	0.88
Newfane (cdp) Niagara County	10	0.26
Clay (town) Onondaga County	75	0.13
Newfane (town) Niagara County	10	0.10
Orangetown (town) Rockland County	32	0.07
Spafford (town) Onondaga County	1	0.06
Nelson (town) Madison County	1	0.05
Cicero (town) Onondaga County	12	0.04
Galeville (cdp) Onondaga County	2	0.04
Johnsburg (town) Warren County	1	0.04

Top 10 Places Sorted by Percent of Total Population
Based on places with total population of 50,000 or more

Place	Population	%
Clay (town) Onondaga County	75	0.13
Syracuse (city) Onondaga County	34	0.02
New York (city)	83	<0.01
Queens (borough) Queens County	30	<0.01
Brooklyn (borough) Kings County	22	<0.01
Manhattan (borough) New York County	20	<0.01
Staten Island (borough) Richmond County	8	<0.01
Buffalo (city) Erie County	6	<0.01
Brookhaven (town) Suffolk County	4	<0.01
Bronx (borough) Bronx County	3	<0.01

Asian: Indian

Top 10 Places Sorted by Population
Based on all places, regardless of total population

Place	Population	%
New York (city)	232,696	2.85
Queens (borough) Queens County	141,147	6.33
Brooklyn (borough) Kings County	33,490	1.34
Manhattan (borough) New York County	29,979	1.89
Bronx (borough) Bronx County	20,357	1.47
Hempstead (town) Nassau County	17,802	2.34
North Hempstead (town) Nassau County	13,427	5.93
Oyster Bay (town) Nassau County	11,289	3.85
Staten Island (borough) Richmond County	7,723	1.65
Yonkers (city) Westchester County	5,818	2.97

Top 10 Places Sorted by Percent of Total Population
Based on all places, regardless of total population

Place	Population	%
Herricks (cdp) Nassau County	1,036	24.12
Manhasset Hills (cdp) Nassau County	690	19.21
Garden City Park (cdp) Nassau County	1,487	19.05
Searingtown (cdp) Nassau County	935	19.02
New Hyde Park (village) Nassau County	1,682	17.32
North New Hyde Park (cdp) Nassau County	2,547	17.10
Merritt Park (cdp) Dutchess County	208	16.56
Muttontown (village) Nassau County	569	16.27
Albertson (cdp) Nassau County	690	13.32
Bellerose Terrace (cdp) Nassau County	277	12.60

Top 10 Places Sorted by Percent of Total Population
Based on places with total population of 50,000 or more

Place	Population	%
Queens (borough) Queens County	141,147	6.33
North Hempstead (town) Nassau County	13,427	5.93
Clarkstown (town) Rockland County	3,874	4.60
Greenburgh (town) Westchester County	3,518	3.98
Oyster Bay (town) Nassau County	11,289	3.85
Schenectady (city) Schenectady County	2,050	3.10
Yonkers (city) Westchester County	5,818	2.97
New York (city)	232,696	2.85
Amherst (town) Erie County	3,491	2.85
Colonie (town) Albany County	2,099	2.57

Asian: Indonesian

Top 10 Places Sorted by Population
Based on all places, regardless of total population

Place	Population	%
New York (city)	4,791	0.06
Queens (borough) Queens County	3,386	0.15
Manhattan (borough) New York County	693	0.04
Brooklyn (borough) Kings County	564	0.02
Bronx (borough) Bronx County	96	0.01
Hempstead (town) Nassau County	66	0.01
Brookhaven (town) Suffolk County	63	0.01
North Hempstead (town) Nassau County	53	0.02
Staten Island (borough) Richmond County	52	0.01
Amherst (town) Erie County	42	0.03

Top 10 Places Sorted by Percent of Total Population
Based on all places, regardless of total population

Place	Population	%
Forest Home (cdp) Tompkins County	11	1.92
Grand View-on-Hudson (village) Rockland County	2	0.70
Colton (cdp) St. Lawrence County	2	0.58
Lyndon (town) Cattaraugus County	4	0.57
Lansing (village) Tompkins County	11	0.31
Adams Center (cdp) Jefferson County	4	0.26
Kensington (village) Nassau County	3	0.26
South Hempstead (cdp) Nassau County	7	0.22
Port Gibson (cdp) Ontario County	1	0.22
Hillburn (village) Rockland County	2	0.21

Top 10 Places Sorted by Percent of Total Population
Based on places with total population of 50,000 or more

Place	Population	%
Queens (borough) Queens County	3,386	0.15
New York (city)	4,791	0.06
Manhattan (borough) New York County	693	0.04
Amherst (town) Erie County	42	0.03
Greenburgh (town) Westchester County	24	0.03
Brooklyn (borough) Kings County	564	0.02
North Hempstead (town) Nassau County	53	0.02
Syracuse (city) Onondaga County	26	0.02
Ramapo (town) Rockland County	23	0.02
Smithtown (town) Suffolk County	18	0.02

Asian: Japanese

Top 10 Places Sorted by Population
Based on all places, regardless of total population

Place	Population	%
New York (city)	31,742	0.39
Manhattan (borough) New York County	16,600	1.05
Queens (borough) Queens County	7,790	0.35
Brooklyn (borough) Kings County	5,917	0.24
North Hempstead (town) Nassau County	1,266	0.56
Harrison (town/village) Westchester County	1,239	4.51
Greenburgh (town) Westchester County	1,230	1.39
Bronx (borough) Bronx County	1,027	0.07
Eastchester (town) Westchester County	903	2.79
Hempstead (town) Nassau County	657	0.09

Top 10 Places Sorted by Percent of Total Population
Based on all places, regardless of total population

Place	Population	%
Manorhaven (village) Nassau County	368	5.61
Hartsdale (cdp) Westchester County	246	4.65
Harrison (town/village) Westchester County	1,239	4.51

Place	Population	%
Tuckahoe (village) Westchester County	210	3.24
Greenville (cdp) Westchester County	223	3.13
Eastchester (cdp) Westchester County	610	3.12
Rye (city) Westchester County	482	3.07
Eastchester (town) Westchester County	903	2.79
Scarsdale (town/village) Westchester County	428	2.49
Fishkill (village) Dutchess County	52	2.40

Top 10 Places Sorted by Percent of Total Population
Based on places with total population of 50,000 or more

Place	Population	%
Greenburgh (town) Westchester County	1,230	1.39
Manhattan (borough) New York County	16,600	1.05
White Plains (city) Westchester County	441	0.78
North Hempstead (town) Nassau County	1,266	0.56
New York (city)	31,742	0.39
Queens (borough) Queens County	7,790	0.35
Brooklyn (borough) Kings County	5,917	0.24
Amherst (town) Erie County	294	0.24
New Rochelle (city) Westchester County	158	0.21
Albany (city) Albany County	200	0.20

Asian: Korean

Top 10 Places Sorted by Population
Based on all places, regardless of total population

Place	Population	%
New York (city)	102,820	1.26
Queens (borough) Queens County	66,124	2.96
Manhattan (borough) New York County	21,996	1.39
Brooklyn (borough) Kings County	8,201	0.33
North Hempstead (town) Nassau County	6,015	2.66
Oyster Bay (town) Nassau County	4,977	1.70
Staten Island (borough) Richmond County	3,398	0.72
Bronx (borough) Bronx County	3,101	0.22
Hempstead (town) Nassau County	3,074	0.40
Huntington (town) Suffolk County	2,122	1.04

Top 10 Places Sorted by Percent of Total Population
Based on all places, regardless of total population

Place	Population	%
Lake Success (village) Nassau County	290	9.88
Forest Home (cdp) Tompkins County	54	9.44
University Gardens (cdp) Nassau County	383	9.06
Fishkill (village) Dutchess County	179	8.25
Thomaston (village) Nassau County	209	7.99
Jericho (cdp) Nassau County	1,078	7.95
Searingtown (cdp) Nassau County	380	7.73
North Hills (village) Nassau County	383	7.55
Manorhaven (village) Nassau County	457	6.97
Lansing (village) Tompkins County	237	6.72

Top 10 Places Sorted by Percent of Total Population
Based on places with total population of 50,000 or more

Place	Population	%
Queens (borough) Queens County	66,124	2.96
North Hempstead (town) Nassau County	6,015	2.66
Oyster Bay (town) Nassau County	4,977	1.70
Greenburgh (town) Westchester County	1,452	1.64
Manhattan (borough) New York County	21,996	1.39
New York (city)	102,820	1.26
Amherst (town) Erie County	1,493	1.22
Clarkstown (town) Rockland County	1,026	1.22
Huntington (town) Suffolk County	2,122	1.04
Smithtown (town) Suffolk County	918	0.78

Asian: Laotian

Top 10 Places Sorted by Population
Based on all places, regardless of total population

Place	Population	%
Rochester (city) Monroe County	668	0.32
New York (city)	664	0.01
Union (town) Broome County	406	0.72
Buffalo (city) Erie County	288	0.11
Johnson City (village) Broome County	278	1.83
Henrietta (town) Monroe County	235	0.55
Binghamton (city) Broome County	211	0.45
Queens (borough) Queens County	210	0.01
Manhattan (borough) New York County	157	0.01
Bronx (borough) Bronx County	148	0.01

Top 10 Places Sorted by Percent of Total Population
Based on all places, regardless of total population

Place	Population	%
Fowlerville (cdp) Livingston County	5	2.20
Johnson City (village) Broome County	278	1.83
Union (town) Broome County	406	0.72
Interlaken (village) Seneca County	4	0.66
Henrietta (town) Monroe County	235	0.55
Smithfield (town) Madison County	7	0.54
Chautauqua (cdp) Chautauqua County	1	0.52
York (town) Livingston County	16	0.47
Binghamton (city) Broome County	211	0.45
Endicott (village) Broome County	54	0.40

Top 10 Places Sorted by Percent of Total Population
Based on places with total population of 50,000 or more

Place	Population	%
Union (town) Broome County	406	0.72
Rochester (city) Monroe County	668	0.32
Irondequoit (cdp/town) Monroe County	109	0.21
Greece (town) Monroe County	139	0.14
Utica (city) Oneida County	72	0.12
Buffalo (city) Erie County	288	0.11
Cheektowaga (cdp) Erie County	65	0.09
Clay (town) Onondaga County	52	0.09
Cheektowaga (town) Erie County	65	0.07
Syracuse (city) Onondaga County	89	0.06

Asian: Malaysian

Top 10 Places Sorted by Population
Based on all places, regardless of total population

Place	Population	%
New York (city)	3,220	0.04
Queens (borough) Queens County	1,620	0.07
Manhattan (borough) New York County	766	0.05
Brooklyn (borough) Kings County	708	0.03
Staten Island (borough) Richmond County	96	0.02
Henrietta (town) Monroe County	70	0.16
Amherst (town) Erie County	47	0.04
North Hempstead (town) Nassau County	35	0.02
Oyster Bay (town) Nassau County	30	0.01
Bronx (borough) Bronx County	30	<0.01

Top 10 Places Sorted by Percent of Total Population
Based on all places, regardless of total population

Place	Population	%
Forest Home (cdp) Tompkins County	5	0.87
Grand View-on-Hudson (village) Rockland County	1	0.35
Portage (town) Livingston County	3	0.34
University at Buffalo (cdp) Erie County	15	0.25
Brocton (village) Chautauqua County	3	0.20
Washington Mills (cdp) Oneida County	2	0.17
Henrietta (town) Monroe County	70	0.16
Breesport (cdp) Chemung County	1	0.16
New Berlin (town) Chenango County	4	0.15
Wainscott (cdp) Suffolk County	1	0.15

Top 10 Places Sorted by Percent of Total Population
Based on places with total population of 50,000 or more

Place	Population	%
Queens (borough) Queens County	1,620	0.07
Manhattan (borough) New York County	766	0.05
New York (city)	3,220	0.04
Amherst (town) Erie County	47	0.04
Brooklyn (borough) Kings County	708	0.03
Troy (city) Rensselaer County	14	0.03
Staten Island (borough) Richmond County	96	0.02
North Hempstead (town) Nassau County	35	0.02
Cheektowaga (cdp) Erie County	12	0.02
White Plains (city) Westchester County	11	0.02

Asian: Nepalese

Top 10 Places Sorted by Population
Based on all places, regardless of total population

Place	Population	%
New York (city)	6,187	0.08
Queens (borough) Queens County	5,319	0.24
Brooklyn (borough) Kings County	393	0.02

Place	Population	%
Manhattan (borough) New York County	281	0.02
Syracuse (city) Onondaga County	262	0.18
Rochester (city) Monroe County	165	0.08
Buffalo (city) Erie County	160	0.06
Bronx (borough) Bronx County	159	0.01
Albany (city) Albany County	55	0.06
Greenburgh (town) Westchester County	55	0.06

Top 10 Places Sorted by Percent of Total Population
Based on all places, regardless of total population

Place	Population	%
Windham (cdp) Greene County	6	1.63
Forest Home (cdp) Tompkins County	3	0.52
Merritt Park (cdp) Dutchess County	6	0.48
Windham (town) Greene County	6	0.35
Nelliston (village) Montgomery County	2	0.34
Argyle (village) Washington County	1	0.33
Northeast Ithaca (cdp) Tompkins County	8	0.30
Brewster (village) Putnam County	7	0.29
Elmsford (village) Westchester County	12	0.26
Queens (borough) Queens County	5,319	0.24

Top 10 Places Sorted by Percent of Total Population
Based on places with total population of 50,000 or more

Place	Population	%
Queens (borough) Queens County	5,319	0.24
Syracuse (city) Onondaga County	262	0.18
New York (city)	6,187	0.08
Rochester (city) Monroe County	165	0.08
Buffalo (city) Erie County	160	0.06
Albany (city) Albany County	55	0.06
Greenburgh (town) Westchester County	55	0.06
Brooklyn (borough) Kings County	393	0.02
Manhattan (borough) New York County	281	0.02
Oyster Bay (town) Nassau County	49	0.02

Asian: Pakistani

Top 10 Places Sorted by Population
Based on all places, regardless of total population

Place	Population	%
New York (city)	46,369	0.57
Brooklyn (borough) Kings County	19,840	0.79
Queens (borough) Queens County	18,084	0.81
Hempstead (town) Nassau County	4,976	0.65
Manhattan (borough) New York County	2,940	0.19
Staten Island (borough) Richmond County	2,777	0.59
Bronx (borough) Bronx County	2,728	0.20
Brookhaven (town) Suffolk County	2,081	0.43
Islip (town) Suffolk County	1,520	0.45
Oyster Bay (town) Nassau County	1,330	0.45

Top 10 Places Sorted by Percent of Total Population
Based on all places, regardless of total population

Place	Population	%
Bellerose Terrace (cdp) Nassau County	103	4.69
South Valley Stream (cdp) Nassau County	249	4.18
North Valley Stream (cdp) Nassau County	425	2.56
Herricks (cdp) Nassau County	85	1.98
Elmont (cdp) Nassau County	650	1.96
Valley Stream (village) Nassau County	733	1.95
East Meadow (cdp) Nassau County	708	1.86
Garden City Park (cdp) Nassau County	124	1.59
Muttontown (village) Nassau County	50	1.43
North Bellmore (cdp) Nassau County	278	1.39

Top 10 Places Sorted by Percent of Total Population
Based on places with total population of 50,000 or more

Place	Population	%
Colonie (town) Albany County	736	0.90
Queens (borough) Queens County	18,084	0.81
Brooklyn (borough) Kings County	19,840	0.79
Hempstead (town) Nassau County	4,976	0.65
Huntington (town) Suffolk County	1,264	0.62
Staten Island (borough) Richmond County	2,777	0.59
New York (city)	46,369	0.57
Albany (city) Albany County	483	0.49
Amherst (town) Erie County	592	0.48
Levittown (cdp) Nassau County	239	0.46

Asian: Sri Lankan

Top 10 Places Sorted by Population
Based on all places, regardless of total population

Place	Population	%
New York (city)	4,369	0.05
Staten Island (borough) Richmond County	1,766	0.38
Queens (borough) Queens County	1,536	0.07
Manhattan (borough) New York County	563	0.04
Brooklyn (borough) Kings County	270	0.01
Bronx (borough) Bronx County	234	0.02
Hempstead (town) Nassau County	201	0.03
Amherst (town) Erie County	130	0.11
Brookhaven (town) Suffolk County	100	0.02
New Rochelle (city) Westchester County	83	0.11

Top 10 Places Sorted by Percent of Total Population
Based on all places, regardless of total population

Place	Population	%
Poquott (village) Suffolk County	6	0.63
Bellerose Terrace (cdp) Nassau County	10	0.45
Watchtower (cdp) Ulster County	10	0.42
Fishers Island (cdp) Suffolk County	1	0.42
Staten Island (borough) Richmond County	1,766	0.38
Forestburgh (town) Sullivan County	3	0.37
South Floral Park (village) Nassau County	6	0.34
Bedford (cdp) Westchester County	6	0.33
Harbor Isle (cdp) Nassau County	4	0.31
Garden City Park (cdp) Nassau County	22	0.28

Top 10 Places Sorted by Percent of Total Population
Based on places with total population of 50,000 or more

Place	Population	%
Staten Island (borough) Richmond County	1,766	0.38
Amherst (town) Erie County	130	0.11
New Rochelle (city) Westchester County	83	0.11
Queens (borough) Queens County	1,536	0.07
Clarkstown (town) Rockland County	55	0.07
New York (city)	4,369	0.05
Manhattan (borough) New York County	563	0.04
Colonie (town) Albany County	30	0.04
Hempstead (town) Nassau County	201	0.03
North Hempstead (town) Nassau County	59	0.03

Asian: Taiwanese

Top 10 Places Sorted by Population
Based on all places, regardless of total population

Place	Population	%
New York (city)	13,682	0.17
Queens (borough) Queens County	8,962	0.40
Manhattan (borough) New York County	3,318	0.21
Brooklyn (borough) Kings County	1,075	0.04
North Hempstead (town) Nassau County	809	0.36
Hempstead (town) Nassau County	438	0.06
Oyster Bay (town) Nassau County	401	0.14
Ithaca (city) Tompkins County	214	0.71
Brookhaven (town) Suffolk County	213	0.04
Amherst (town) Erie County	202	0.17

Top 10 Places Sorted by Percent of Total Population
Based on all places, regardless of total population

Place	Population	%
Russell Gardens (village) Nassau County	23	2.43
Forest Home (cdp) Tompkins County	13	2.27
Thomaston (village) Nassau County	47	1.80
University Gardens (cdp) Nassau County	63	1.49
East Ithaca (cdp) Tompkins County	33	1.48
North Hills (village) Nassau County	56	1.10
Lansing (village) Tompkins County	36	1.02
Harbor Hills (cdp) Nassau County	5	0.87
Lake Success (village) Nassau County	25	0.85
Saddle Rock (village) Nassau County	7	0.84

Top 10 Places Sorted by Percent of Total Population
Based on places with total population of 50,000 or more

Place	Population	%
Queens (borough) Queens County	8,962	0.40
North Hempstead (town) Nassau County	809	0.36
Manhattan (borough) New York County	3,318	0.21
New York (city)	13,682	0.17

Amherst (town) Erie County	202	0.17
Greenburgh (town) Westchester County	142	0.16
Oyster Bay (town) Nassau County	401	0.14
Huntington (town) Suffolk County	157	0.08
Smithtown (town) Suffolk County	90	0.08
White Plains (city) Westchester County	44	0.08

Asian: Thai

Top 10 Places Sorted by Population
Based on all places, regardless of total population

Place	Population	%
New York (city)	7,244	0.09
Queens (borough) Queens County	4,124	0.18
Manhattan (borough) New York County	1,657	0.10
Brooklyn (borough) Kings County	883	0.04
Bronx (borough) Bronx County	414	0.03
Hempstead (town) Nassau County	278	0.04
Yonkers (city) Westchester County	268	0.14
Brookhaven (town) Suffolk County	211	0.04
Staten Island (borough) Richmond County	166	0.04
North Hempstead (town) Nassau County	126	0.06

Top 10 Places Sorted by Percent of Total Population
Based on all places, regardless of total population

Place	Population	%
Forest Home (cdp) Tompkins County	8	1.40
Watchtower (cdp) Ulster County	20	0.84
Greenvale (cdp) Nassau County	9	0.82
Lyon Mountain (cdp) Clinton County	3	0.71
Tribes Hill (cdp) Montgomery County	7	0.70
Quiogue (cdp) Suffolk County	5	0.61
Cooperstown (village) Otsego County	11	0.59
West Nyack (cdp) Rockland County	18	0.52
Middlefield (town) Otsego County	11	0.52
Lansing (village) Tompkins County	16	0.45

Top 10 Places Sorted by Percent of Total Population
Based on places with total population of 50,000 or more

Place	Population	%
Queens (borough) Queens County	4,124	0.18
Yonkers (city) Westchester County	268	0.14
Clarkstown (town) Rockland County	121	0.14
Mount Vernon (city) Westchester County	73	0.11
Manhattan (borough) New York County	1,657	0.10
New York (city)	7,244	0.09
Greenburgh (town) Westchester County	77	0.09
Utica (city) Oneida County	50	0.08
Levittown (cdp) Nassau County	40	0.08
White Plains (city) Westchester County	42	0.07

Asian: Vietnamese

Top 10 Places Sorted by Population
Based on all places, regardless of total population

Place	Population	%
New York (city)	16,378	0.20
Brooklyn (borough) Kings County	5,041	0.20
Queens (borough) Queens County	4,322	0.19
Bronx (borough) Bronx County	3,526	0.25
Manhattan (borough) New York County	2,919	0.18
Syracuse (city) Onondaga County	1,554	1.07
Buffalo (city) Erie County	1,220	0.47
Rochester (city) Monroe County	1,050	0.50
Utica (city) Oneida County	1,022	1.64
Brookhaven (town) Suffolk County	620	0.13

Top 10 Places Sorted by Percent of Total Population
Based on all places, regardless of total population

Place	Population	%
Byersville (cdp) Livingston County	2	4.26
North Gates (cdp) Monroe County	183	1.92
Utica (city) Oneida County	1,022	1.64
Salt Point (cdp) Dutchess County	3	1.58
Gates (town) Monroe County	411	1.45
Gates (cdp) Monroe County	71	1.45
Websters Crossing (cdp) Livingston County	1	1.45
Galeville (cdp) Onondaga County	62	1.34
Pamelia Center (cdp) Jefferson County	3	1.14
Syracuse (city) Onondaga County	1,554	1.07

Top 10 Places Sorted by Percent of Total Population
Based on places with total population of 50,000 or more

Place	Population	%
Utica (city) Oneida County	1,022	1.64
Syracuse (city) Onondaga County	1,554	1.07
Rochester (city) Monroe County	1,050	0.50
Greece (town) Monroe County	473	0.49
Buffalo (city) Erie County	1,220	0.47
Clay (town) Onondaga County	265	0.46
Colonie (town) Albany County	360	0.44
Union (town) Broome County	248	0.44
Cheektowaga (cdp) Erie County	326	0.43
Cheektowaga (town) Erie County	344	0.39

Hawaii Native/Pacific Islander

Top 10 Places Sorted by Population
Based on all places, regardless of total population

Place	Population	%
New York (city)	24,098	0.29
Queens (borough) Queens County	7,691	0.34
Bronx (borough) Bronx County	6,213	0.45
Brooklyn (borough) Kings County	5,784	0.23
Manhattan (borough) New York County	3,727	0.24
Hempstead (town) Nassau County	1,001	0.13
Staten Island (borough) Richmond County	683	0.15
Yonkers (city) Westchester County	483	0.25
Islip (town) Suffolk County	471	0.14
Rochester (city) Monroe County	449	0.21

Top 10 Places Sorted by Percent of Total Population
Based on all places, regardless of total population

Place	Population	%
Philadelphia (village) Jefferson County	25	2.00
Fort Drum (cdp) Jefferson County	226	1.74
Quiogue (cdp) Suffolk County	13	1.59
Burke (village) Franklin County	3	1.42
Le Ray (town) Jefferson County	286	1.31
Philadelphia (town) Jefferson County	25	1.28
Herrings (village) Jefferson County	1	1.11
Brewster (village) Putnam County	24	1.00
Speculator (village) Hamilton County	3	0.93
Calcium (cdp) Jefferson County	32	0.92

Top 10 Places Sorted by Percent of Total Population
Based on places with total population of 50,000 or more

Place	Population	%
Schenectady (city) Schenectady County	333	0.50
Bronx (borough) Bronx County	6,213	0.45
Queens (borough) Queens County	7,691	0.34
White Plains (city) Westchester County	180	0.32
New York (city)	24,098	0.29
Yonkers (city) Westchester County	483	0.25
Manhattan (borough) New York County	3,727	0.24
Brooklyn (borough) Kings County	5,784	0.23
Mount Vernon (city) Westchester County	156	0.23
Utica (city) Oneida County	137	0.22

Hawaii Native/Pacific Islander: Not Hispanic

Top 10 Places Sorted by Population
Based on all places, regardless of total population

Place	Population	%
New York (city)	13,217	0.16
Queens (borough) Queens County	5,685	0.25
Brooklyn (borough) Kings County	3,463	0.14
Bronx (borough) Bronx County	1,854	0.13
Manhattan (borough) New York County	1,776	0.11
Hempstead (town) Nassau County	599	0.08
Staten Island (borough) Richmond County	439	0.09
Brookhaven (town) Suffolk County	306	0.06
Rochester (city) Monroe County	284	0.13
Schenectady (city) Schenectady County	272	0.41

Top 10 Places Sorted by Percent of Total Population
Based on all places, regardless of total population

Place	Population	%
Quiogue (cdp) Suffolk County	13	1.59
Fort Drum (cdp) Jefferson County	196	1.51

Philadelphia (village) Jefferson County	18	1.44
Le Ray (town) Jefferson County	244	1.12
Herrings (village) Jefferson County	1	1.11
Burke (village) Franklin County	2	0.95
Speculator (village) Hamilton County	3	0.93
Philadelphia (town) Jefferson County	18	0.92
Constableville (village) Lewis County	2	0.83
La Fargeville (cdp) Jefferson County	5	0.82

Top 10 Places Sorted by Percent of Total Population
Based on places with total population of 50,000 or more

Place	Population	%
Schenectady (city) Schenectady County	272	0.41
Queens (borough) Queens County	5,685	0.25
Mount Vernon (city) Westchester County	130	0.19
New York (city)	13,217	0.16
Albany (city) Albany County	158	0.16
Syracuse (city) Onondaga County	218	0.15
Utica (city) Oneida County	95	0.15
Brooklyn (borough) Kings County	3,463	0.14
Bronx (borough) Bronx County	1,854	0.13
Rochester (city) Monroe County	284	0.13

Hawaii Native/Pacific Islander: Hispanic

Top 10 Places Sorted by Population
Based on all places, regardless of total population

Place	Population	%
New York (city)	10,881	0.13
Bronx (borough) Bronx County	4,359	0.31
Brooklyn (borough) Kings County	2,321	0.09
Queens (borough) Queens County	2,006	0.09
Manhattan (borough) New York County	1,951	0.12
Hempstead (town) Nassau County	402	0.05
Yonkers (city) Westchester County	272	0.14
Staten Island (borough) Richmond County	244	0.05
Islip (town) Suffolk County	227	0.07
Rochester (city) Monroe County	165	0.08

Top 10 Places Sorted by Percent of Total Population
Based on all places, regardless of total population

Place	Population	%
Brewster (village) Putnam County	23	0.96
Philadelphia (village) Jefferson County	7	0.56
Haverstraw (village) Rockland County	66	0.55
Aquebogue (cdp) Suffolk County	13	0.53
Woodridge (village) Sullivan County	4	0.47
Burke (village) Franklin County	1	0.47
Philadelphia (town) Jefferson County	7	0.36
Tivoli (village) Dutchess County	4	0.36
Bronx (borough) Bronx County	4,359	0.31
Sleepy Hollow (village) Westchester County	31	0.31

Top 10 Places Sorted by Percent of Total Population
Based on places with total population of 50,000 or more

Place	Population	%
Bronx (borough) Bronx County	4,359	0.31
White Plains (city) Westchester County	109	0.19
Yonkers (city) Westchester County	272	0.14
New York (city)	10,881	0.13
Manhattan (borough) New York County	1,951	0.12
Brentwood (cdp) Suffolk County	75	0.12
Hempstead (village) Nassau County	60	0.11
Brooklyn (borough) Kings County	2,321	0.09
Queens (borough) Queens County	2,006	0.09
Schenectady (city) Schenectady County	61	0.09

Hawaii Native/Pacific Islander: Fijian

Top 10 Places Sorted by Population
Based on all places, regardless of total population

Place	Population	%
New York (city)	213	<0.01
Queens (borough) Queens County	76	<0.01
Manhattan (borough) New York County	73	<0.01
Brooklyn (borough) Kings County	45	<0.01
Bronx (borough) Bronx County	13	<0.01
Brookhaven (town) Suffolk County	10	<0.01
Hempstead (town) Nassau County	10	<0.01
Sound Beach (cdp) Suffolk County	6	0.08
Woodmere (cdp) Nassau County	6	0.04

White Plains (city) Westchester County	6	0.01

Top 10 Places Sorted by Percent of Total Population
Based on all places, regardless of total population

Place	Population	%
Salamanca (city) Cattaraugus County	5	0.09
Sound Beach (cdp) Suffolk County	6	0.08
Woodmere (cdp) Nassau County	6	0.04
Florida (village) Orange County	1	0.04
Fairmount (cdp) Onondaga County	3	0.03
Pelham (village) Westchester County	2	0.03
South Hill (cdp) Tompkins County	2	0.03
Westmere (cdp) Albany County	2	0.03
Lansing (village) Tompkins County	1	0.03
Spencer (town) Tioga County	1	0.03

Top 10 Places Sorted by Percent of Total Population
Based on places with total population of 50,000 or more

Place	Population	%
White Plains (city) Westchester County	6	0.01
New York (city)	213	<0.01
Queens (borough) Queens County	76	<0.01
Manhattan (borough) New York County	73	<0.01
Brooklyn (borough) Kings County	45	<0.01
Bronx (borough) Bronx County	13	<0.01
Brookhaven (town) Suffolk County	10	<0.01
Hempstead (town) Nassau County	10	<0.01
Staten Island (borough) Richmond County	6	<0.01
Yonkers (city) Westchester County	6	<0.01

Hawaii Native/Pacific Islander: Guamanian or Chamorro

Top 10 Places Sorted by Population
Based on all places, regardless of total population

Place	Population	%
New York (city)	1,784	0.02
Brooklyn (borough) Kings County	568	0.02
Queens (borough) Queens County	483	0.02
Bronx (borough) Bronx County	376	0.03
Manhattan (borough) New York County	242	0.02
Staten Island (borough) Richmond County	115	0.02
Hempstead (town) Nassau County	110	0.01
Le Ray (town) Jefferson County	88	0.40
Fort Drum (cdp) Jefferson County	70	0.54
Southampton (town) Suffolk County	55	0.10

Top 10 Places Sorted by Percent of Total Population
Based on all places, regardless of total population

Place	Population	%
Quiogue (cdp) Suffolk County	13	1.59
Burke (village) Franklin County	2	0.95
Brewster (village) Putnam County	22	0.92
Fort Drum (cdp) Jefferson County	70	0.54
Aquebogue (cdp) Suffolk County	13	0.53
Port Gibson (cdp) Ontario County	2	0.44
Le Ray (town) Jefferson County	88	0.40
Southold (cdp) Suffolk County	22	0.38
Adams Center (cdp) Jefferson County	6	0.38
Pamelia Center (cdp) Jefferson County	1	0.38

Top 10 Places Sorted by Percent of Total Population
Based on places with total population of 50,000 or more

Place	Population	%
Southampton (town) Suffolk County	55	0.10
New Rochelle (city) Westchester County	43	0.06
Bronx (borough) Bronx County	376	0.03
Yonkers (city) Westchester County	52	0.03
Utica (city) Oneida County	18	0.03
Union (town) Broome County	16	0.03
New York (city)	1,784	0.02
Brooklyn (borough) Kings County	568	0.02
Queens (borough) Queens County	483	0.02
Manhattan (borough) New York County	242	0.02

Hawaii Native/Pacific Islander: Marshallese

Top 10 Places Sorted by Population
Based on all places, regardless of total population

Place	Population	%
New York (city)	10	<0.01
Le Ray (town) Jefferson County	6	0.03
Carthage (village) Jefferson County	5	0.13
Wilna (town) Jefferson County	5	0.08
Fort Drum (cdp) Jefferson County	5	0.04
Philadelphia (village) Jefferson County	4	0.32
Philadelphia (town) Jefferson County	4	0.21
Manhattan (borough) New York County	4	<0.01
Bronx (borough) Bronx County	3	<0.01
Hornell (city) Steuben County	2	0.02

Top 10 Places Sorted by Percent of Total Population
Based on all places, regardless of total population

Place	Population	%
Philadelphia (village) Jefferson County	4	0.32
Philadelphia (town) Jefferson County	4	0.21
Carthage (village) Jefferson County	5	0.13
Wilna (town) Jefferson County	5	0.08
Huron (town) Wayne County	1	0.05
Fort Drum (cdp) Jefferson County	5	0.04
Le Ray (town) Jefferson County	6	0.03
Hornell (city) Steuben County	2	0.02
Hartland (town) Niagara County	1	0.02
Hartsdale (cdp) Westchester County	1	0.02

Top 10 Places Sorted by Percent of Total Population
Based on places with total population of 50,000 or more

Place	Population	%
New York (city)	10	<0.01
Manhattan (borough) New York County	4	<0.01
Bronx (borough) Bronx County	3	<0.01
Brooklyn (borough) Kings County	2	<0.01
Amherst (town) Erie County	1	<0.01
Greenburgh (town) Westchester County	1	<0.01
Hempstead (town) Nassau County	1	<0.01
Islip (town) Suffolk County	1	<0.01
Staten Island (borough) Richmond County	1	<0.01
Syracuse (city) Onondaga County	1	<0.01

Hawaii Native/Pacific Islander: Native Hawaiian

Top 10 Places Sorted by Population
Based on all places, regardless of total population

Place	Population	%
New York (city)	2,448	0.03
Bronx (borough) Bronx County	669	0.05
Manhattan (borough) New York County	608	0.04
Brooklyn (borough) Kings County	564	0.02
Queens (borough) Queens County	486	0.02
Staten Island (borough) Richmond County	121	0.03
Hempstead (town) Nassau County	114	0.02
Brookhaven (town) Suffolk County	100	0.02
Rochester (city) Monroe County	77	0.04
Buffalo (city) Erie County	75	0.03

Top 10 Places Sorted by Percent of Total Population
Based on all places, regardless of total population

Place	Population	%
Speculator (village) Hamilton County	3	0.93
Felts Mills (cdp) Jefferson County	3	0.81
Hemlock (cdp) Livingston County	4	0.72
Waterville (village) Oneida County	8	0.51
Philadelphia (village) Jefferson County	6	0.48
Ischua (town) Cattaraugus County	4	0.47
Tivoli (village) Dutchess County	5	0.45
Calcium (cdp) Jefferson County	15	0.43
Plandome Heights (village) Nassau County	4	0.40
Fort Drum (cdp) Jefferson County	49	0.38

Top 10 Places Sorted by Percent of Total Population
Based on places with total population of 50,000 or more

Place	Population	%
Bronx (borough) Bronx County	669	0.05

Place	Population	%
Schenectady (city) Schenectady County	33	0.05
Southampton (town) Suffolk County	27	0.05
Troy (city) Rensselaer County	24	0.05
Manhattan (borough) New York County	608	0.04
Rochester (city) Monroe County	77	0.04
Syracuse (city) Onondaga County	65	0.04
Albany (city) Albany County	38	0.04
New York (city)	2,448	0.03
Staten Island (borough) Richmond County	121	0.03

Hawaii Native/Pacific Islander: Samoan

Top 10 Places Sorted by Population
Based on all places, regardless of total population

Place	Population	%
New York (city)	764	0.01
Brooklyn (borough) Kings County	216	0.01
Manhattan (borough) New York County	183	0.01
Queens (borough) Queens County	179	0.01
Bronx (borough) Bronx County	160	0.01
Rochester (city) Monroe County	63	0.03
Buffalo (city) Erie County	63	0.02
Le Ray (town) Jefferson County	53	0.24
Fort Drum (cdp) Jefferson County	49	0.38
Hempstead (town) Nassau County	36	<0.01

Top 10 Places Sorted by Percent of Total Population
Based on all places, regardless of total population

Place	Population	%
Philadelphia (village) Jefferson County	12	0.96
Constableville (village) Lewis County	2	0.83
La Fargeville (cdp) Jefferson County	4	0.66
Philadelphia (town) Jefferson County	12	0.62
Staatsburg (cdp) Dutchess County	2	0.53
Fremont (town) Sullivan County	6	0.43
Fort Drum (cdp) Jefferson County	49	0.38
Caroline (town) Tompkins County	12	0.37
Sagaponack (village) Suffolk County	1	0.32
Worcester (cdp) Otsego County	3	0.27

Top 10 Places Sorted by Percent of Total Population
Based on places with total population of 50,000 or more

Place	Population	%
Rochester (city) Monroe County	63	0.03
Utica (city) Oneida County	18	0.03
Buffalo (city) Erie County	63	0.02
Albany (city) Albany County	15	0.02
Schenectady (city) Schenectady County	10	0.02
New York (city)	764	0.01
Brooklyn (borough) Kings County	216	0.01
Manhattan (borough) New York County	183	0.01
Queens (borough) Queens County	179	0.01
Bronx (borough) Bronx County	160	0.01

Hawaii Native/Pacific Islander: Tongan

Top 10 Places Sorted by Population
Based on all places, regardless of total population

Place	Population	%
New York (city)	66	<0.01
Manhattan (borough) New York County	33	<0.01
Queens (borough) Queens County	14	<0.01
Brooklyn (borough) Kings County	10	<0.01
Bronx (borough) Bronx County	7	<0.01
Chateaugay (village) Franklin County	6	0.72
Chateaugay (town) Franklin County	6	0.28
Colonie (town) Albany County	5	0.01
Stone Ridge (cdp) Ulster County	4	0.34
Cambria (town) Niagara County	4	0.07

Top 10 Places Sorted by Percent of Total Population
Based on all places, regardless of total population

Place	Population	%
Chateaugay (village) Franklin County	6	0.72
Staatsburg (cdp) Dutchess County	2	0.53
Elizabethtown (cdp) Essex County	3	0.40
Stone Ridge (cdp) Ulster County	4	0.34

Place	Population	%
Chateaugay (town) Franklin County	6	0.28
Elizabethtown (town) Essex County	3	0.26
Fort Plain (village) Montgomery County	2	0.09
Franklin (town) Franklin County	1	0.09
Washington Mills (cdp) Oneida County	1	0.08
Cambria (town) Niagara County	4	0.07

Top 10 Places Sorted by Percent of Total Population
Based on places with total population of 50,000 or more

Place	Population	%
Colonie (town) Albany County	5	0.01
New York (city)	66	<0.01
Manhattan (borough) New York County	33	<0.01
Queens (borough) Queens County	14	<0.01
Brooklyn (borough) Kings County	10	<0.01
Bronx (borough) Bronx County	7	<0.01
Buffalo (city) Erie County	3	<0.01
Rochester (city) Monroe County	3	<0.01
Brentwood (cdp) Suffolk County	2	<0.01
Brookhaven (town) Suffolk County	2	<0.01

White

Top 10 Places Sorted by Population
Based on all places, regardless of total population

Place	Population	%
New York (city)	3,797,402	46.45
Brooklyn (borough) Kings County	1,120,592	44.74
Manhattan (borough) New York County	956,864	60.34
Queens (borough) Queens County	941,608	42.21
Hempstead (town) Nassau County	532,650	70.11
Bronx (borough) Bronx County	427,659	30.88
Brookhaven (town) Suffolk County	419,725	86.36
Staten Island (borough) Richmond County	350,679	74.81
Islip (town) Suffolk County	254,235	75.77
Oyster Bay (town) Nassau County	252,713	86.19

Top 10 Places Sorted by Percent of Total Population
Based on all places, regardless of total population

Place	Population	%
Putnam (town) Washington County	609	100.00
Odessa (village) Schuyler County	591	100.00
DeKalb Junction (cdp) St. Lawrence County	519	100.00
Cold Brook (village) Herkimer County	329	100.00
Pinckney (town) Lewis County	329	100.00
West Union (town) Steuben County	312	100.00
Madison (village) Madison County	305	100.00
Gainesville (village) Wyoming County	229	100.00
Osceola (town) Lewis County	229	100.00
Pierrepont Manor (cdp) Jefferson County	228	100.00

Top 10 Places Sorted by Percent of Total Population
Based on places with total population of 50,000 or more

Place	Population	%
Hamburg (town) Erie County	55,749	97.92
Tonawanda (town) Erie County	69,534	94.52
Tonawanda (cdp) Erie County	54,936	94.48
Smithtown (town) Suffolk County	111,000	94.23
Clay (town) Onondaga County	53,514	91.94
Union (town) Broome County	51,487	91.38
Levittown (cdp) Nassau County	46,970	90.53
Greece (town) Monroe County	86,829	90.36
Cheektowaga (town) Erie County	78,958	89.50
Irondequoit (cdp/town) Monroe County	45,826	88.65

White: Not Hispanic

Top 10 Places Sorted by Population
Based on all places, regardless of total population

Place	Population	%
New York (city)	2,804,430	34.30
Brooklyn (borough) Kings County	917,717	36.64
Manhattan (borough) New York County	785,299	49.52
Queens (borough) Queens County	638,051	28.60
Hempstead (town) Nassau County	460,994	60.68
Brookhaven (town) Suffolk County	379,158	78.01
Staten Island (borough) Richmond County	305,118	65.09

Place	Population	%
Oyster Bay (town) Nassau County	236,944	80.81
Islip (town) Suffolk County	198,326	59.11
Huntington (town) Suffolk County	160,914	79.17

Top 10 Places Sorted by Percent of Total Population
Based on all places, regardless of total population

Place	Population	%
Osceola (town) Lewis County	229	100.00
Birdsall (town) Allegany County	221	100.00
Oxbow (cdp) Jefferson County	108	100.00
Morehouse (town) Hamilton County	86	100.00
Woodsville (cdp) Livingston County	80	100.00
Linwood (cdp) Livingston County	74	100.00
Tuscarora (cdp) Livingston County	74	100.00
Red House (town) Cattaraugus County	38	100.00
Saltaire (village) Suffolk County	37	100.00
Thousand Island Park (cdp) Jefferson County	31	100.00

Top 10 Places Sorted by Percent of Total Population
Based on places with total population of 50,000 or more

Place	Population	%
Hamburg (town) Erie County	54,789	96.23
Tonawanda (cdp) Erie County	53,890	92.68
Tonawanda (town) Erie County	68,098	92.57
Clay (town) Onondaga County	52,515	90.22
Smithtown (town) Suffolk County	105,870	89.87
Union (town) Broome County	50,317	89.30
Cheektowaga (town) Erie County	77,687	88.05
Greece (town) Monroe County	83,902	87.31
Cheektowaga (cdp) Erie County	65,180	86.70
Colonie (town) Albany County	69,290	84.92

White: Hispanic

Top 10 Places Sorted by Population
Based on all places, regardless of total population

Place	Population	%
New York (city)	992,972	12.15
Queens (borough) Queens County	303,557	13.61
Bronx (borough) Bronx County	269,414	19.45
Brooklyn (borough) Kings County	202,875	8.10
Manhattan (borough) New York County	171,565	10.82
Hempstead (town) Nassau County	71,656	9.43
Islip (town) Suffolk County	55,909	16.66
Staten Island (borough) Richmond County	45,561	9.72
Brookhaven (town) Suffolk County	40,567	8.35
Yonkers (city) Westchester County	31,778	16.22

Top 10 Places Sorted by Percent of Total Population
Based on all places, regardless of total population

Place	Population	%
Brewster (village) Putnam County	993	41.55
Brentwood (cdp) Suffolk County	23,013	37.94
North Bay Shore (cdp) Suffolk County	6,358	33.56
Haverstraw (village) Rockland County	3,914	32.86
Port Chester (village) Westchester County	9,507	32.82
Central Islip (cdp) Suffolk County	9,372	27.20
Springs (cdp) Suffolk County	1,608	24.39
Sleepy Hollow (village) Westchester County	2,406	24.38
East Hampton North (cdp) Suffolk County	999	24.12
Rye (town) Westchester County	11,021	24.00

Top 10 Places Sorted by Percent of Total Population
Based on places with total population of 50,000 or more

Place	Population	%
Brentwood (cdp) Suffolk County	23,013	37.94
Bronx (borough) Bronx County	269,414	19.45
New Rochelle (city) Westchester County	14,422	18.71
Hempstead (village) Nassau County	9,773	18.13
Islip (town) Suffolk County	55,909	16.66
White Plains (city) Westchester County	9,400	16.53
Yonkers (city) Westchester County	31,778	16.22
Queens (borough) Queens County	303,557	13.61
Southampton (town) Suffolk County	6,955	12.25
New York (city)	992,972	12.15

Climate

New York State Physical Features and Climate Narrative

PHYSICAL FEATURES. New York State contains 49,576 square miles, inclusive of 1,637 square miles of inland water, but exclusive of the boundary-water areas of Long Island Sound, New York Harbor, Lake Ontario, and Lake Erie. The major portion of the State lies generally between latitudes 42° and 45° N. and between longitudes 73° 30' and 79° 45' W. However, in the extreme southeast, a triangular portion extends southward to about latitude 40° 30' N., while Long Island lies eastward to about longitude 72° W.

The principal highland regions of the State are the Adirondacks in the northeast and the Appalachian Plateau (Southern Plateau) in the south. A minor highland region occurs in southeastern New York where the Hudson River has cut a valley between the Palisades on the west, near the New Jersey border, and the Taconic Mountains on the east, along the Connecticut and Massachusetts border. Just west of the Adirondacks and the upper Black River Valley in Lewis County is another minor highland known as Tug Hill. Much of the eastern border of the State consists of a long, narrow lowland region which is occupied by Lake Champlain, Lake George, and the middle and lower portions of the Hudson Valley.

Approximately 40 percent of New York State has an elevation of more than 1,000 feet above sea level. In northwestern Essex County are a number of peaks with an elevation of between 4,000 to 5,000 feet. The highest point, Mount Marcy, reaches a height of 5,344 feet above sea level. The Appalachian Plateau merges variously into the Great Lakes Plain of western New York with gradual- to steep-sloping terrain. This Plateau is penetrated by the valleys of the Finger Lakes which extend southward from the Great Lakes Plain. Other prominent lakes plus innumerable smaller lakes and ponds dot the landscape, with more than 1,500 in the Adirondack region alone.

GENERAL CLIMATE. The climate of New York State is broadly representative of the humid continental type which prevails in the Northeastern United States, but its diversity is not usually encountered within an area of comparable size. The geographical position of the State and the usual course of air masses, governed by the large-scale patterns of atmospheric circulation, provide general climatic controls. Differences in latitude, character of the topography, and proximity to large bodies of water have pronounced effects on the climate.

Lengthy periods of either abnormally cold or warm weather result from the movement of great high pressure (anticyclonic) systems into and through the Eastern United States. Cold winter temperatures prevail over New York whenever Arctic air masses, under high barometric pressure, flow southward from central Canada or from Hudson Bay. High pressure systems often move just off the Atlantic coast, become more or less stagnant for several days, and then a persistent air flow from the southwest or south affects the State. This circulation brings the very warm, often humid weather of the summer season and the mild, more pleasant temperatures during the fall, winter, and spring seasons.

TEMPERATURE. Many atmospheric and physiographic controls on the climate result in a considerable variation of temperature conditions over New York State. The average annual mean temperature ranges from about 40°F. in the Adirondacks to near 55°F. in the New York City area. The winters are long and cold in the Plateau Divisions of the State. Winter temperatures are moderated considerably in the Great Lakes Plain of western New York. The moderating influence of Lakes Erie and Ontario is comparable to that produced by the Atlantic Ocean in the southern portion of the Hudson Valley.

The summer climate is cool in the Adirondacks, Catskills, and higher elevations of the Southern Plateau. The New York City area and lower portions of the Hudson Valley have rather warm summers by comparison, with some periods of high, uncomfortable humidity. The remainder of New York State enjoys pleasantly warm summers, marred by only occasional, brief intervals of sultry conditions. Summer daytime temperatures usually range from the upper 70s to mid-80s over much of the State. The moderating effect of Lakes Erie and Ontario on temperatures assumes practical importance during the spring and fall seasons. The lake waters warm slowly in the spring, the effect of which is to reduce the warming of the atmosphere over adjacent land areas. In the fall season, the lake waters cool more slowly than the land areas and thus serve as a heat source.

PRECIPITATION. Moisture for precipitation in New York State is transported primarily from the Gulf of Mexico and Atlantic Ocean through circulation patterns and storm systems of the atmosphere. Distribution of precipitation within the State is greatly influenced by topography and proximity to the Great Lakes or Atlantic Ocean. Average annual amounts in excess of 50 inches occur in the western Adirondacks, Tug Hill area, and the Catskills, while slightly less than that amount is noted in the higher elevations of the Western Plateau southeast of Lake Erie. Areas of least rainfall, with average accumulations of about 30 inches, occur near Lake Ontario in the extreme western counties, in the lower half of the Genesee River Valley, and in the vicinity of Lake Champlain.

New York State has a fairly uniform distribution of precipitation during the year. There are no distinctly dry or wet seasons which are regularly repeated on an annual basis. Minimum precipitation occurs in the winter season. Maximum amounts are noted in the summer season throughout the State except along the Great Lakes where slight peaks of similar magnitude occur in both the spring and fall seasons.

SNOWFALL. The climate of New York State is marked by abundant snowfall. With the exception of the Coastal Division, the State receives an average seasonal amount of 40 inches or more. The average snowfall is greater than 70 inches over some 60 percent of New York's area. The moderating influence of the Atlantic Ocean reduces the snow accumulation to 25 to 35 inches in the New York City area and on Long Island. About one-third of the winter season precipitation in the Coastal Division occurs from storms which also yield at least one inch of snow. The great bulk of the winter precipitation in upstate New York comes as snow.

A durable snow cover generally begins to develop in the Adirondacks and northern lowlands by late November and remains on the ground until various times in April, depending upon late winter snowfall and early spring temperatures. The Southern Plateau, Great Lakes Plain in southern portions of western upstate New York, and the Hudson Valley experience a continuous snow cover from about mid-December to mid-March, with maximum depths usually occurring in February. Bare ground may occur briefly in the lower elevations of these regions during some winters. From late December or early January through February, the Atlantic coastal region of the State experiences alternating periods of measurable snow cover and bare ground.

FLOODS. Although major floods are relatively infrequent, the greatest potential and frequency for floods occur in the early spring when substantial rains combine with rapid snowmelting to produce a heavy runoff. Damaging floods are caused at other times of the year by prolonged periods of heavy rainfall.

WINDS AND STORMS. The prevailing wind is generally from the west in New York State. A southwest component becomes evident in winds during the warmer months while a northwest component is characteristic of the colder one-half of the year. Thunderstorms occur on an average of about 30 days in a year throughout the State. Destructive winds and lightning strikes in local areas are common with the more vigorous warm-season thunderstorms. Locally, hail occurs with more severe thunderstorms. Tornadoes are not common. About 3 or 4 of these storms strike limited, localized areas of New York State in most years. Tornadoes occur generally between late May and late August. Storms of freezing rain occur on one or more occasions during the winter season and often affect a wide area of the State in any one incident. Such storms are usually limited to a thin but dangerous coating of ice on exposed surfaces. Hurricanes and tropical storms periodically cause serious and heavy losses in the vicinity of Long Island and southeastern upstate New York. The greatest storm hazard in terms of area affected is heavy snow. Coastal northeaster storms occur with some frequency in most winters. Blizzard conditions of heavy snow, high winds, and rapidly falling temperature occur occasionally, but are much less characteristic of New York's climate than in the plains of Midwestern United States.

OTHER CLIMATIC ELEMENTS. The climate of the State features much cloudy weather during the months of November, December, and January in upstate New York. From June through September, however, about 60 to 70 percent of the possible sunshine hours is received. In the Atlantic coastal region, the sunshine hours increases from 50 percent of possible in the winter to about 65 percent of possible in the summer. The occurrence of heavy dense fog is variable over the State. The valleys and ridges of the Southern Plateau are most subject to periods of fog, with occurrences averaging about 50 days in a year. In the Great Lakes Plain and northern valleys, the frequency decreases to only 10 to 20 days annually. In those portions of the State with greater maritime influence, the frequency of dense fog in a year ranges from about 35 days on the south shore of Long Island to 25 days in the Hudson Valley.

nationalatlas.gov™
Where We Are

POPULATED PLACES

- ● **New York**   1,000,000 and over
- ● **Syracuse**   100,000 – 499,999
- ● Binghamton   25,000 – 99,999
- • Saranac Lake   24,999 and less
- ★ Albany   State capital
-   Urban areas

TRANSPORTATION

- ══ Interstate; limited access highway
-   Other principal highway
-   Railroad
-   Ferry

PHYSICAL FEATURES

- Streams
- Lakes
- Highest elevation in state (feet)   +5344
- Other elevations (feet)   +4180

The lowest elevation in New York is sea level (Atlantic Ocean).

MILES
0   20   40   60   80

Albers equal area projection

U.S. Department of the Interior
U.S. Geological Survey

80° 49' 45" West
Lambert Azimuthal Equal-Area
Projection

72° 01' 07" West
http://nationalatlas.gov
02-Dec-10 01:29PM

nationalatlas.gov™

Miles   25   50   75

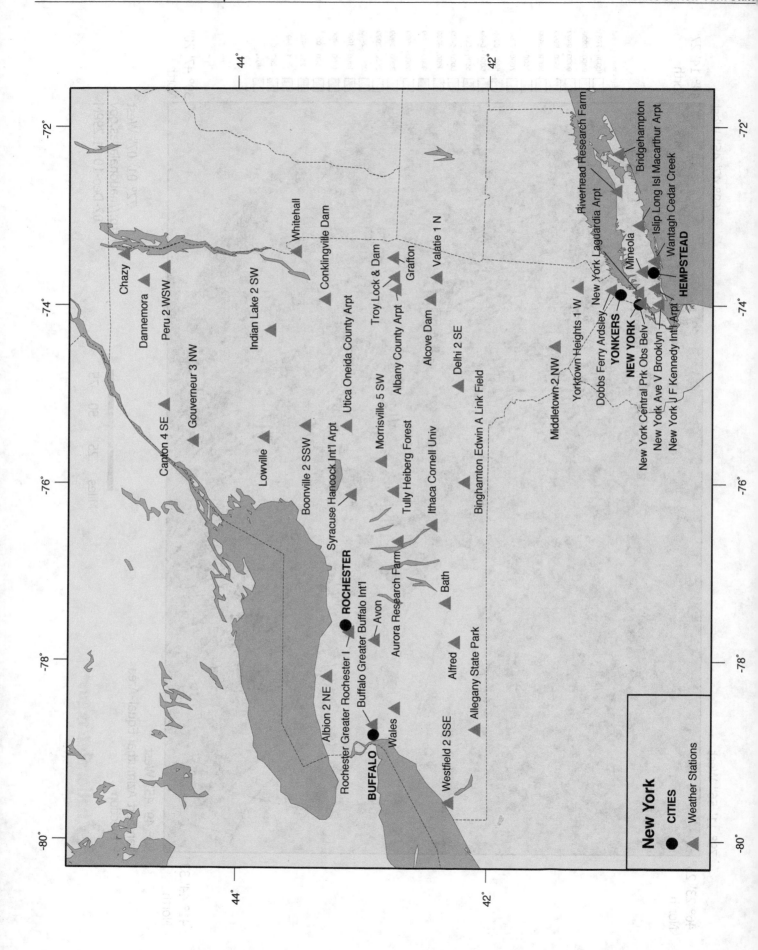

New York Weather Stations by County

County	Station Name
Albany	Albany County Arpt
	Alcove Dam
Allegany	Alfred
Broome	Binghamton Edwin A Link Field
Cattaraugus	Allegany State Park
Cayuga	Aurora Research Farm
Chautauqua	Westfield 2 SSE
Clinton	Chazy
	Dannemora
	Peru 2 WSW
Columbia	Valatie 1 N
Cortland	Tully Heiberg Forest
Delaware	Delhi 2 SE
Erie	Buffalo Greater Buffalo Int'l
	Wales
Hamilton	Indian Lake 2 SW
Kings	New York Ave V Brooklyn
Lewis	Lowville
Livingston	Avon
Madison	Morrisville 5 SW
Monroe	Rochester Intl Arpt
Nassau	Mineola
	Wantagh Cedar Creek
New York	New York Central Park Observ
Oneida	Boonville 2 SSW
	Utica Oneida County Arpt
Onondaga	Syracuse Hancock Int'l Arpt
Orange	Middletown 2 NW
Orleans	Albion 2 NE
Queens	New York J F Kennedy Int'l Arpt
	New York Laguardia Arpt
Rensselaer	Grafton
	Troy Lock and Dam
Saratoga	Conklingville Dam
St. Lawrence	Canton 4 SE
	Gouverneur 3 NW
Steuben	Bath

County	Station Name
Suffolk	Bridgehampton
	Islip-Macarthur Arpt
	Riverhead Research Farm
Tompkins	Ithaca Cornell Univ
Washington	Whitehall
Westchester	Dobbs Ferry Ardsley
	Yorktown Heights 1 W

See User Guide for station inclusion criteria.

New York Weather Stations by City

City	Station Name	Miles
Albany	Albany County Arpt	6.2
	Alcove Dam	15.4
	Grafton	18.3
	Troy Lock and Dam	8.1
	Valatie 1 N	16.5
Amherst	Buffalo Greater Buffalo Int'l	4.5
	Wales	21.1
Babylon	Islip-Macarthur Arpt	14.7
	Mineola	13.2
	New York J F Kennedy Int'l Arpt	23.2
	Wantagh Cedar Creek	8.3
Brentwood	Islip-Macarthur Arpt	7.5
	Mineola	19.8
	Wantagh Cedar Creek	16.2
Bronx	Essex Fells Serv Bldg, NJ	21.0
	Newark Intl Arpt, NJ	18.3
	Dobbs Ferry Ardsley	10.7
	Mineola	16.1
	New York Ave V Brooklyn	18.1
	New York Central Park Observ	6.4
	New York J F Kennedy Int'l Arpt	14.5
	New York Laguardia Arpt	4.6
	Wantagh Cedar Creek	24.3
Brookhaven	Bridgeport Sikorsky Memorial, CT	24.2
	Islip-Macarthur Arpt	7.6
	Riverhead Research Farm	16.3
Brooklyn	Canoe Brook, NJ	21.8
	Cranford, NJ	18.1
	Essex Fells Serv Bldg, NJ	21.4
	Newark Intl Arpt, NJ	12.8
	Plainfield, NJ	23.6
	Mineola	18.6
	New York Ave V Brooklyn	3.8
	New York Central Park Observ	9.2
	New York J F Kennedy Int'l Arpt	8.1
	New York Laguardia Arpt	9.9
	Wantagh Cedar Creek	23.8
Buffalo	Buffalo Greater Buffalo Int'l	6.0
	Wales	20.1
Cheektowaga	Buffalo Greater Buffalo Int'l	2.1
	Wales	16.1
Clarkstown	Stamford 5 N, CT	22.6
	Charlotteburg Reservoir, NJ	24.3
	Dobbs Ferry Ardsley	11.7
	New York Central Park Observ	23.7
	New York Laguardia Arpt	24.3
	Yorktown Heights 1 W	13.6
Clay	Syracuse Hancock Int'l Arpt	5.2
Colonie	Albany County Arpt	1.5
	Alcove Dam	19.7
	Grafton	16.7
	Troy Lock and Dam	5.4
	Valatie 1 N	21.2

City	Station Name	Miles
Greece	Albion 2 NE	24.6
	Avon	22.3
	Rochester Intl Arpt	8.2
Greenburgh	Stamford 5 N, CT	16.0
	Dobbs Ferry Ardsley	2.1
	Mineola	23.5
	New York Central Park Observ	18.4
	New York Laguardia Arpt	17.3
	Yorktown Heights 1 W	16.4
Hamburg	Buffalo Greater Buffalo Int'l	14.0
	Wales	16.8
Hempstead	Dobbs Ferry Ardsley	24.8
	Mineola	3.6
	New York Ave V Brooklyn	19.9
	New York Central Park Observ	19.6
	New York J F Kennedy Int'l Arpt	9.7
	New York Laguardia Arpt	15.6
	Wantagh Cedar Creek	6.6
Huntington	Stamford 5 N, CT	20.7
	Islip-Macarthur Arpt	14.9
	Mineola	15.1
	Wantagh Cedar Creek	15.4
Islip	Islip-Macarthur Arpt	5.2
	Mineola	22.1
	Wantagh Cedar Creek	17.7
Levittown	Islip-Macarthur Arpt	22.0
	Mineola	5.5
	New York Central Park Observ	24.1
	New York J F Kennedy Int'l Arpt	15.9
	New York Laguardia Arpt	19.8
	Wantagh Cedar Creek	5.2
Manhattan	Canoe Brook, NJ	20.3
	Cranford, NJ	19.7
	Essex Fells Serv Bldg, NJ	17.1
	Newark Intl Arpt, NJ	12.2
	Dobbs Ferry Ardsley	16.7
	Mineola	18.5
	New York Ave V Brooklyn	12.5
	New York Central Park Observ	0.2
	New York J F Kennedy Int'l Arpt	12.5
	New York Laguardia Arpt	4.3
Mount Vernon	Stamford 5 N, CT	20.4
	Essex Fells Serv Bldg, NJ	24.2
	Newark Intl Arpt, NJ	22.8
	Dobbs Ferry Ardsley	6.0
	Mineola	16.7
	New York Ave V Brooklyn	23.0
	New York Central Park Observ	11.4
	New York J F Kennedy Int'l Arpt	18.2
	New York Laguardia Arpt	9.3
	Yorktown Heights 1 W	24.5
New Rochelle	Stamford 5 N, CT	18.2
	Dobbs Ferry Ardsley	6.0
	Mineola	15.7

See User Guide for station inclusion criteria.

City	Station Name	Miles
New Rochelle (cont.)	New York Ave V Brooklyn	24.5
	New York Central Park Observ	13.5
	New York J F Kennedy Int'l Arpt	18.8
	New York Laguardia Arpt	10.8
	Wantagh Cedar Creek	24.0
	Yorktown Heights 1 W	23.9
New York	Canoe Brook, NJ	22.5
	Cranford, NJ	20.5
	Essex Fells Serv Bldg, NJ	20.4
	Newark Intl Arpt, NJ	13.7
	Dobbs Ferry Ardsley	19.6
	Mineola	15.9
	New York Ave V Brooklyn	9.2
	New York Central Park Observ	4.7
	New York J F Kennedy Int'l Arpt	8.2
	New York Laguardia Arpt	4.5
	Wantagh Cedar Creek	22.7
Niagara Falls	Buffalo Greater Buffalo Int'l	18.2
North Hempstead	Stamford 5 N, CT	24.1
	Dobbs Ferry Ardsley	17.6
	Mineola	4.1
	New York Ave V Brooklyn	20.7
	New York Central Park Observ	15.7
	New York J F Kennedy Int'l Arpt	11.3
	New York Laguardia Arpt	11.4
	Wantagh Cedar Creek	12.5
Oyster Bay	Stamford 5 N, CT	24.8
	Dobbs Ferry Ardsley	24.1
	Islip-Macarthur Arpt	20.8
	Mineola	6.5
	New York Central Park Observ	24.6
	New York J F Kennedy Int'l Arpt	17.6
	New York Laguardia Arpt	20.3
	Wantagh Cedar Creek	7.6
Queens	Cranford, NJ	24.9
	Essex Fells Serv Bldg, NJ	24.8
	Newark Intl Arpt, NJ	18.3
	Dobbs Ferry Ardsley	19.2
	Mineola	11.4
	New York Ave V Brooklyn	11.5
	New York Central Park Observ	8.2
	New York J F Kennedy Int'l Arpt	5.3
	New York Laguardia Arpt	5.0
	Wantagh Cedar Creek	18.2
Ramapo	Charlotteburg Reservoir, NJ	19.7
	Essex Fells Serv Bldg, NJ	22.7
	Dobbs Ferry Ardsley	15.1
	New York Central Park Observ	24.1
	Yorktown Heights 1 W	17.4
Rochester	Avon	18.5
	Rochester Intl Arpt	4.9
Schenectady	Albany County Arpt	7.5
	Alcove Dam	23.3
	Grafton	23.5
	Troy Lock and Dam	13.0
Smithtown	Bridgeport Sikorsky Memorial, CT	22.7

City	Station Name	Miles
Smithtown (cont.)	Stamford 5 N, CT	24.9
	Islip-Macarthur Arpt	8.0
	Mineola	22.7
	Wantagh Cedar Creek	20.8
Southampton	Bridgehampton	11.7
	Riverhead Research Farm	12.1
Staten Island	Canoe Brook, NJ	15.8
	Cranford, NJ	9.6
	Essex Fells Serv Bldg, NJ	18.6
	Newark Intl Arpt, NJ	9.2
	New Brunswick 3 SE, NJ	17.7
	Plainfield, NJ	13.8
	New York Ave V Brooklyn	8.1
	New York Central Park Observ	16.1
	New York J F Kennedy Int'l Arpt	18.2
	New York Laguardia Arpt	18.9
Syracuse	Syracuse Hancock Int'l Arpt	5.5
	Tully Heiberg Forest	19.3
Tonawanda	Buffalo Greater Buffalo Int'l	7.0
	Wales	23.4
Union	Binghamton Edwin A Link Field	6.2
	Montrose, PA	19.3
Utica	Utica Oneida County Arpt	8.5
White Plains	Stamford 5 N, CT	12.8
	Dobbs Ferry Ardsley	4.0
	Mineola	21.6
	New York Central Park Observ	19.8
	New York Laguardia Arpt	17.9
	Yorktown Heights 1 W	16.7
Yonkers	Stamford 5 N, CT	20.9
	Essex Fells Serv Bldg, NJ	22.6
	Newark Intl Arpt, NJ	22.2
	Dobbs Ferry Ardsley	4.8
	Mineola	19.5
	New York Ave V Brooklyn	24.0
	New York Central Park Observ	11.7
	New York J F Kennedy Int'l Arpt	20.2
	New York Laguardia Arpt	10.7
	Yorktown Heights 1 W	23.1

Note: Miles is the distance between the geographic center of the city and the weather station.

New York Weather Stations by Elevation

Feet	Station Name
1,898	Tully Heiberg Forest
1,770	Alfred
1,660	Indian Lake 2 SW
1,600	Binghamton Edwin A Link Field
1,580	Boonville 2 SSW
1,560	Grafton
1,500	Allegany State Park
1,439	Delhi 2 SE
1,339	Dannemora
1,299	Morrisville 5 SW
1,120	Bath
1,089	Wales
959	Ithaca Cornell Univ
859	Lowville
830	Aurora Research Farm
808	Conklingville Dam
711	Utica Oneida County Arpt
707	Westfield 2 SSE
705	Buffalo Greater Buffalo Int'l
700	Middletown 2 NW
669	Yorktown Heights 1 W
606	Alcove Dam
600	Rochester Intl Arpt
544	Avon
509	Peru 2 WSW
439	Albion 2 NE
439	Canton 4 SE
419	Gouverneur 3 NW
410	Syracuse Hancock Int'l Arpt
299	Valatie 1 N
274	Albany County Arpt
200	Dobbs Ferry Ardsley
169	Chazy
131	New York Central Park Observ
119	Whitehall
100	Riverhead Research Farm
96	Mineola
83	Islip-Macarthur Arpt
60	Bridgehampton
23	Troy Lock and Dam
20	New York Ave V Brooklyn
16	New York J F Kennedy Int'l Arpt
11	New York Laguardia Arpt
9	Wantagh Cedar Creek

Albany County Airport

Albany is located on the west bank of the Hudson River some 150 miles north of New York City, and 8 miles south of the confluence of the Mohawk and Hudson Rivers. The river-front portion of the city is only a few feet above sea level, and there is a tidal effect upstream to Troy. Eleven miles west of Albany the Helderberg hill range rises to 1,800 feet. Between it and the Hudson River the valley floor is gently rolling, ranging some 200 to 500 feet above sea level. East of the city there is more rugged terrain 5 or 6 miles wide with elevations of 300 to 600 feet. Farther to the east the terrain rises more sharply. It reaches a north-south range of hills 12 miles east of Albany with elevations ranging to 2,000 feet.

The climate at Albany is primarily continental in character, but is subjected to some modification by the Atlantic Ocean. The moderating effect on temperatures is more pronounced during the warmer months than in winter when outbursts of cold air sweep down from Canada. In the warmer seasons, temperatures rise rapidly in the daytime. However, temperatures also fall rapidly after sunset so that the nights are relatively cool. Occasionally there are extended periods of oppressive heat up to a week or more in duration.

Winters are usually cold and sometimes fairly severe. Maximum temperatures during the colder winters are often below freezing and nighttime lows are frequently below 10 degrees. Sub-zero readings occur about 12 times a year. Snowfall throughout the area is quite variable and snow flurries are quite frequent during the winter. Precipitation is sufficient to serve the economy of the region in most years, and only occasionally do periods of drought exist. Most of the rainfall in the summer is from thunderstorms. Tornadoes are quite rare and hail is not usually of any consequence.

Wind velocities are moderate. The north-south Hudson River Valley has a marked effect on the lighter winds and in the warm months, average wind direction is usually southerly. Destructive winds rarely occur.

The area enjoys one of the highest percentages of sunshine in the entire state. Seldom does the area experience long periods of cloudy days and long periods of smog are rare.

Based on the 1951-1980 period, the average first occurrence of 32 degrees Fahrenheit in the fall is September 29 and the average last occurrence in the spring is May 7.

Albany County Airport *Albany County*   Elevation: 274 ft.   Latitude: 42° 45' N   Longitude: 73° 48' W

	JAN	FEB	MAR	APR	MAY	JUN	JUL	AUG	SEP	OCT	NOV	DEC	YEAR
Mean Maximum Temp. (°F)	31.1	34.9	44.3	58.3	69.6	77.9	82.3	80.5	72.4	60.0	48.2	36.1	58.0
Mean Temp. (°F)	22.8	25.9	34.8	47.6	58.2	67.0	71.6	70.0	61.8	49.8	39.8	28.4	48.2
Mean Minimum Temp. (°F)	14.5	16.8	25.2	36.9	46.8	56.1	60.9	59.5	51.2	39.4	31.3	20.8	38.3
Extreme Maximum Temp. (°F)	71	68	89	92	94	96	99	97	92	86	81	71	99
Extreme Minimum Temp. (°F)	-23	-18	-6	13	28	36	44	34	28	18	6	-20	-23
Days Maximum Temp. ≥ 90°F	0	0	0	0	0	2	4	2	0	0	0	0	8
Days Maximum Temp. ≤ 32°F	17	11	4	0	0	0	0	0	0	0	1	10	43
Days Minimum Temp. ≤ 32°F	29	26	24	9	1	0	0	0	0	7	18	27	141
Days Minimum Temp. ≤ 0°F	5	2	1	0	0	0	0	0	0	0	0	1	9
Heating Degree Days (base 65°F)	1,301	1,099	929	519	231	51	6	19	138	469	749	1,127	6,638
Cooling Degree Days (base 65°F)	0	0	1	4	27	117	217	183	50	4	0	0	603
Mean Precipitation (in.)	2.54	2.09	3.26	3.22	3.58	3.80	4.11	3.62	3.26	3.52	3.27	2.87	39.14
Maximum Precipitation (in.)*	6.4	5.0	5.9	7.9	9.0	7.4	7.0	7.3	7.9	8.8	8.1	6.7	47.2
Minimum Precipitation (in.)*	0.4	0.2	0.3	1.1	1.0	0.6	0.5	0.7	0.4	0.2	0.6	0.6	21.5
Extreme Maximum Daily Precip. (in.)	1.78	1.60	2.02	2.26	2.16	3.30	3.49	2.78	5.60	2.82	2.21	2.79	5.60
Days With ≥ 0.1" Precipitation	6	5	7	7	8	8	7	7	6	6	7	7	81
Days With ≥ 0.5" Precipitation	2	1	2	2	3	3	3	2	2	2	2	2	26
Days With ≥ 1.0" Precipitation	0	0	1	1	0	1	1	1	1	1	1	0	8
Mean Snowfall (in.)	17.7	11.5	11.4	2.3	0.1	trace	trace	0.0	trace	0.3	3.2	13.7	60.2
Maximum Snowfall (in.)*	48	35	35	18	2	0	0	0	0	7	25	58	107
Maximum 24-hr. Snowfall (in.)*	13	17	22	17	2	0	0	0	0	7	22	14	22
Maximum Snow Depth (in.)	24	20	28	13	trace	trace	trace	0	trace	2	10	16	28
Days With ≥ 1.0" Snow Depth	19	16	9	1	0	0	0	0	0	0	2	12	59
Thunderstorm Days*	< 1	< 1	1	1	3	5	6	5	2	1	< 1	< 1	24
Foggy Days*	10	9	11	9	12	13	14	17	17	15	13	12	152
Predominant Sky Cover*	OVR	OVR	OVR	OVR	OVR	OVR	OVR	OVR	OVR	OVR	OVR	OVR	OVR
Mean Relative Humidity 7am (%)*	77	77	76	72	74	77	80	85	88	86	82	80	80
Mean Relative Humidity 4pm (%)*	64	59	54	48	50	53	53	55	57	56	64	67	57
Mean Dewpoint (°F)*	14	15	23	33	45	55	60	59	52	41	31	20	38
Prevailing Wind Direction*	WNW	WNW	WNW	WNW	S	S	S	S	S	S	WNW	WNW	S
Prevailing Wind Speed (mph)*	15	15	15	15	10	9	8	8	9	9	14	14	12
Maximum Wind Gust (mph)*	62	67	61	58	67	59	77	62	64	60	67	63	77

Note: (*) Period of record is 1946-1995

Binghamton Edwin A. Link Field

Binghamton, in south central New York lies in a comparatively narrow valley at the confluence of the Susquehanna and Chenango Rivers. Within a radius of 5 miles, hills rise to elevations of 1,400-1,600 feet above mean sea level. In the spring, melting snow, sometimes supplemented by rainfall, occasionally causes flooding in the city and along the streams.

The climate of Binghamton is representative of the humid area of the north-eastern United States and is primarily continental in type. The area, being adjacent to the so-called St. Lawrence Valley storm track, and also subject to cold air masses approaching from the west and north, has a variable climate, characterized by frequent and rapid changes. Furthermore, diurnal and seasonal changes assist in the production of an invigorating climate. As a rule, the temperature rises rapidly to moderate daytime levels with readings of 90 degrees or above only a few days in any month summer nights provide favorable sleeping conditions.

Winters are usually cold, but not commonly severe. Highest daytime temperatures average in the high 20s to low 30s, while the lowest nighttime readings average from the mid-teens to low 20s. Ordinarily a few sub-zero readings may be expected in January and February, with a lesser number in November, December, and March. The transitional seasons, spring and autumn, are the most variable of the year.

Most of the precipitation in the Binghamton area derives from moisture laden air transported from the Gulf of Mexico and cyclonic systems moving northward along the Atlantic coast. The annual rainfall is rather evenly distributed over the year. However, the greatest average monthly amounts occur during the growing season, April through September. As a rule, rainfall is ample for good crop growth and comes mostly in the form of thunderstorms. Annual snowfall is around 50 inches in Binghamton and above 85 inches at Edwin A. Link Field, some 10 miles to the NNW, and about 700 feet higher in elevation. Most of the snow falls during the normal winter months. However, heavy snows can occur as early as November and as late as April. Being adjacent to the track of storms that move through the St. Lawrence Valley, and being under the influence of winds that sweep across Lakes Erie and Ontario to the interior of the state, the area is subject to much cloudiness and winter snow flurries.

For the most part, the winds at Binghamton have northerly and westerly components. Tornadoes, although rare, have struck in the Binghamton area.

Based on the 1951-1980 period, the growing season averages 150 to 160 days. Usually the last spring frost occurs during early May, and the first frost in autumn during early October.

Binghamton Edwin A. Link Field *Broome County*   Elevation: 1,600 ft.   Latitude: 42° 12' N   Longitude: 75° 59' W

	JAN	FEB	MAR	APR	MAY	JUN	JUL	AUG	SEP	OCT	NOV	DEC	YEAR
Mean Maximum Temp. (°F)	29.4	32.5	41.3	54.6	66.0	74.2	78.3	77.0	69.1	57.2	45.4	33.8	54.9
Mean Temp. (°F)	22.6	25.0	33.0	45.3	56.2	64.7	69.0	67.8	59.9	48.7	38.5	27.5	46.5
Mean Minimum Temp. (°F)	15.8	17.4	24.6	36.0	46.2	55.1	59.7	58.4	50.8	40.2	31.5	21.2	38.1
Extreme Maximum Temp. (°F)	63	63	82	89	89	92	98	95	91	82	77	65	98
Extreme Minimum Temp. (°F)	-15	-10	-7	9	28	33	44	38	27	19	8	-18	-18
Days Maximum Temp. ≥ 90°F	0	0	0	0	0	0	1	1	0	0	0	0	2
Days Maximum Temp. ≤ 32°F	19	15	7	0	0	0	0	0	0	0	3	14	58
Days Minimum Temp. ≤ 32°F	29	26	24	11	1	0	0	0	0	6	18	27	142
Days Minimum Temp. ≤ 0°F	3	1	0	0	0	0	0	0	0	0	0	1	5
Heating Degree Days (base 65°F)	1,307	1,124	987	588	290	85	20	35	180	500	790	1,154	7,060
Cooling Degree Days (base 65°F)	0	0	1	4	22	82	152	128	35	2	0	0	426
Mean Precipitation (in.)	2.38	2.29	3.09	3.53	3.53	4.33	3.67	3.37	3.55	3.30	3.29	2.81	39.14
Maximum Precipitation (in.)*	6.4	4.4	6.0	8.6	6.5	9.5	7.4	7.5	9.7	9.4	7.5	6.1	48.0
Minimum Precipitation (in.)*	0.8	0.4	0.7	1.0	0.8	1.0	0.8	0.6	0.6	0.3	1.0	0.9	29.9
Extreme Maximum Daily Precip. (in.)	1.64	1.80	1.83	2.86	2.91	4.05	1.70	2.73	3.50	2.94	2.35	2.66	4.05
Days With ≥ 0.1" Precipitation	6	6	7	8	8	8	7	7	7	6	7	7	84
Days With ≥ 0.5" Precipitation	1	1	2	2	2	3	3	2	2	2	2	2	24
Days With ≥ 1.0" Precipitation	0	0	0	1	1	1	1	1	1	1	1	0	8
Mean Snowfall (in.)	21.7	15.9	15.5	4.3	0.1	trace	0.0	trace	trace	1.1	7.0	17.2	82.8
Maximum Snowfall (in.)*	44	44	38	23	3	0	0	0	trace	12	29	60	138
Maximum 24-hr. Snowfall (in.)*	18	21	19	12	3	0	0	0	trace	7	11	14	21
Maximum Snow Depth (in.)	32	19	35	9	1	trace	0	trace	trace	3	13	15	35
Days With ≥ 1.0" Snow Depth	23	20	13	2	0	0	0	0	0	0	5	16	79
Thunderstorm Days*	< 1	< 1	1	2	4	6	7	5	3	1	< 1	< 1	29
Foggy Days*	11	10	13	12	14	15	16	19	17	15	14	13	169
Predominant Sky Cover*	OVR	OVR	OVR	OVR	OVR	OVR	OVR	OVR	OVR	OVR	OVR	OVR	OVR
Mean Relative Humidity 7am (%)*	80	79	79	76	78	83	85	89	90	85	82	82	82
Mean Relative Humidity 4pm (%)*	69	65	60	54	54	57	57	59	62	60	68	72	61
Mean Dewpoint (°F)*	15	16	23	32	44	54	59	58	51	40	31	20	37
Prevailing Wind Direction*	WNW	NW	NW	NW	NW	SW	SW	SW	SW	S	SW	WNW	NW
Prevailing Wind Speed (mph)*	14	14	14	13	12	9	8	8	9	9	10	14	12
Maximum Wind Gust (mph)*	61	56	58	64	54	60	74	63	48	51	58	54	74

Note: (*) Period of record is 1948-1995

Buffalo Int'l Airport

The country surrounding Buffalo is comparatively low and level to the west. To the east and south the land is gently rolling, rising to pronounced hills within 12 to 18 miles, and to 1,000 feet above the level of Lake Erie about 35 miles south-southeast of the city. A steep slope of 50 to 100 feet lies east-west one and a half miles to the north. The eastern end of Lake Erie is nine miles to the west-southwest, while Lake Ontario lies 25 miles to the north, the two being connected by the Niagara River, which flows north-northwestward from the end of Lake Erie.

Buffalo is located near the mean position of the polar front. Its weather is varied and changeable, characteristic of the latitude. Wide seasonal swings of temperature from hot to cold are tempered appreciably by the proximity of Lakes Erie and Ontario. Lake Erie lies to the southwest, the direction of the prevailing wind. Wind flow throughout the year is somewhat higher due to this exposure. The vigorous interplay of warm and cold air masses during the winter and early spring months causes one or more windstorms. Precipitation is moderate and fairly evenly divided throughout the twelve months.

The spring season is more cloudy and cooler than points not affected by the cold lake. Spring growth of vegetation is retarded, protecting it from late spring frosts. With heavy winter ice accumulations in the lake, typical spring conditions are delayed until late May or early June.

Summer comes suddenly in mid-June. Lake breezes temper the extreme heat of the summer season. Temperatures of 90 degrees and above are infrequent. There is more summer sunshine here than in any other section of the state. Due to the stabilizing effects of Lake Erie, thunderstorms are relatively infrequent. Most of them are caused by frontal action. To the north and south of the city thunderstorms occur more often.

Autumn has long, dry periods and is frost free usually until mid-October. Cloudiness increases in November, continuing mostly cloudy throughout the winter and early spring. Snow flurries off the lake begin in mid-November or early December. Outbreaks of Arctic air in December and throughout the winter months produce locally heavy snowfalls from the lake. At the same time, temperatures of well below zero over Canada and the midwest are raised 10 to 30 degrees in crossing the lakes. Only on rare occasions do polar air masses drop southward from eastern Hudson Bay across Lake Ontario without appreciable warming.

Buffalo Int'l Airport *Erie County*   Elevation: 705 ft.   Latitude: 42° 56' N   Longitude: 78° 44' W

	JAN	FEB	MAR	APR	MAY	JUN	JUL	AUG	SEP	OCT	NOV	DEC	YEAR
Mean Maximum Temp. (°F)	31.8	33.6	42.1	55.2	66.7	75.5	80.1	78.7	71.4	59.3	47.8	36.5	56.6
Mean Temp. (°F)	25.3	26.5	34.0	46.0	57.1	66.4	71.3	69.9	62.5	51.1	41.0	30.3	48.5
Mean Minimum Temp. (°F)	18.8	19.3	25.9	36.9	47.5	57.2	62.4	61.0	53.5	42.9	34.2	24.1	40.3
Extreme Maximum Temp. (°F)	68	71	79	94	91	96	97	96	92	86	73	74	97
Extreme Minimum Temp. (°F)	-16	-6	-7	12	31	38	46	38	32	25	11	-10	-16
Days Maximum Temp. ≥ 90°F	0	0	0	0	0	1	1	1	0	0	0	0	3
Days Maximum Temp. ≤ 32°F	16	14	7	1	0	0	0	0	0	0	2	11	51
Days Minimum Temp. ≤ 32°F	27	25	23	9	0	0	0	0	0	3	13	25	125
Days Minimum Temp. ≤ 0°F	2	1	0	0	0	0	0	0	0	0	0	1	4
Heating Degree Days (base 65°F)	1,223	1,083	953	566	261	61	7	16	126	430	713	1,069	6,508
Cooling Degree Days (base 65°F)	0	0	0	3	25	109	208	175	57	5	0	0	582
Mean Precipitation (in.)	3.13	2.47	2.94	3.03	3.41	3.58	3.24	3.32	3.95	3.57	3.97	3.88	40.49
Maximum Precipitation (in.)*	6.9	5.9	6.0	5.9	7.2	8.4	8.9	10.7	9.0	9.1	9.8	8.7	53.5
Minimum Precipitation (in.)*	1.0	0.8	1.2	1.3	1.2	0.1	0.9	1.1	0.8	0.3	1.5	1.7	28.5
Extreme Maximum Daily Precip. (in.)	1.83	1.74	1.39	1.66	3.41	5.01	2.19	2.41	3.55	2.42	2.31	1.66	5.01
Days With ≥ 0.1" Precipitation	9	7	8	8	8	8	6	7	7	8	9	10	95
Days With ≥ 0.5" Precipitation	1	1	2	2	2	2	2	2	3	3	2	2	24
Days With ≥ 1.0" Precipitation	0	0	0	0	1	1	1	1	1	1	1	0	7
Mean Snowfall (in.)	24.4	17.2	13.4	2.8	0.3	trace	trace	trace	trace	0.9	8.1	26.9	94.0
Maximum Snowfall (in.)*	68	54	29	15	8	0	0	0	trace	3	31	68	176
Maximum 24-hr. Snowfall (in.)*	18	18	15	6	8	0	0	0	trace	3	19	34	34
Maximum Snow Depth (in.)	30	20	20	6	4	trace	trace	trace	trace	22	25	44	44
Days With ≥ 1.0" Snow Depth	21	19	11	1	0	0	0	0	0	0	4	15	71
Thunderstorm Days*	< 1	< 1	1	2	3	5	6	6	4	2	1	< 1	30
Foggy Days*	12	12	14	13	14	13	13	15	13	13	13	13	158
Predominant Sky Cover*	OVR	OVR	OVR	OVR	OVR	OVR	SCT	OVR	OVR	OVR	OVR	OVR	OVR
Mean Relative Humidity 7am (%)*	79	80	80	77	76	77	79	83	83	81	80	80	79
Mean Relative Humidity 4pm (%)*	73	70	65	57	55	54	54	56	59	60	69	73	62
Mean Dewpoint (°F)*	18	18	25	34	44	54	59	59	52	42	33	23	39
Prevailing Wind Direction*	WSW	WSW	SW	SW	SW	SW	SW	SW	SW	SW	W	W	SW
Prevailing Wind Speed (mph)*	18	17	16	15	14	14	13	13	13	15	15	15	15
Maximum Wind Gust (mph)*	71	82	73	74	64	79	59	81	62	63	73	69	82

Note: (*) Period of record is 1946-1995

Islip Macarthur Airport

Long Island is the terminal moraine marking the southernmost advance of the ice sheet along the Atlantic Coast during the last ice age. The terrain is generally flat, with only a gradual rise in elevation from Long Island Sound on the northern shore and from the Atlantic Ocean on the southern shore toward the middle of the island. Islip is located about half-way out Long Island on the southern coast. The airport is located about seven miles to the northeast of the city. Islip is protected from flooding during periods of high tides by Fire Island, a natural barrier located about three miles offshore. Most of the air masses affecting Islip are continental in origin, however the ocean has a pronounced influence on the climate of the area.

A cool sea breeze blowing off the ocean during the summer months helps to alleviate the afternoon heat. There are an average of 7 days between June and September when the afternoon temperature exceeds 90 degrees, while farther inland there are 10 to 15 such days.

It is uncommon for the eye of a tropical storm to pass directly over Long Island. Tropical weather systems moving along the Atlantic Coast, however, are capable of producing episodes of heavy rain and strong winds in the late summer or fall.

The winter season is relatively mild. Below zero temperatures are reported on only one or two days in about half the winters. Temperatures of 10 degrees below zero or colder are extremely rare. The seasonal snowfall averages about 29 inches. Almost all of this snow falls between December and March. Coastal low pressure systems, Northeasters, are the principle source of this snow. These weather systems will occasionally produce a heavy snowfall. There are usually extended periods during the winter when the ground is bare of snow.

Based on the 1951-1980 period, the average date of the last spring temperature of 32 degrees is April 27 and the average first fall occurrence is October 21. Inland locations would expect a shorter freeze-free season.

Islip Macarthur Airport *Suffolk County*　Elevation: 83 ft.　Latitude: 40° 47' N　Longitude: 73° 06' W

	JAN	FEB	MAR	APR	MAY	JUN	JUL	AUG	SEP	OCT	NOV	DEC	YEAR
Mean Maximum Temp. (°F)	39.5	41.0	47.8	58.0	67.9	77.2	82.0	81.1	74.2	63.5	53.8	43.9	60.8
Mean Temp. (°F)	31.9	33.0	39.5	49.3	58.8	68.7	74.1	73.3	65.9	54.6	45.5	36.2	52.6
Mean Minimum Temp. (°F)	24.4	24.9	31.2	40.6	49.6	60.2	66.1	65.4	57.6	45.5	37.2	28.5	44.3
Extreme Maximum Temp. (°F)	69	67	82	94	98	96	102	100	92	88	78	77	102
Extreme Minimum Temp. (°F)	-7	2	5	23	32	42	50	50	38	29	11	5	-7
Days Maximum Temp. ≥ 90°F	0	0	0	0	1	2	3	2	0	0	0	0	8
Days Maximum Temp. ≤ 32°F	7	5	1	0	0	0	0	0	0	0	0	4	17
Days Minimum Temp. ≤ 32°F	25	23	18	3	0	0	0	0	0	1	10	21	101
Days Minimum Temp. ≤ 0°F	0	0	0	0	0	0	0	0	0	0	0	0	0
Heating Degree Days (base 65°F)	1,017	898	782	467	211	32	1	2	59	327	579	886	5,261
Cooling Degree Days (base 65°F)	0	0	0	3	24	151	290	266	94	11	0	0	839
Mean Precipitation (in.)	3.79	2.99	4.37	4.25	3.80	4.08	3.29	4.34	3.83	4.01	3.59	4.19	46.53
Maximum Precipitation (in.)*	6.3	5.5	5.5	5.1	10.1	7.9	8.4	13.8	5.1	8.7	8.0	6.1	65.3
Minimum Precipitation (in.)*	1.3	1.1	1.3	1.3	0.7	0.6	1.2	0.5	0.8	0.3	1.3	0.9	34.4
Extreme Maximum Daily Precip. (in.)	3.61	2.32	3.25	4.63	4.01	4.87	3.34	6.74	2.85	5.38	2.63	2.65	6.74
Days With ≥ 0.1" Precipitation	7	6	7	7	7	6	6	6	6	6	6	7	77
Days With ≥ 0.5" Precipitation	3	2	3	3	2	2	2	3	3	3	3	3	32
Days With ≥ 1.0" Precipitation	1	1	1	1	1	1	1	1	1	1	1	1	12
Mean Snowfall (in.)	na	na	na	na	na	na	na	na	na	na	na	na	na
Maximum Snowfall (in.)*	14	20	13	3	0	0	0	0	0	0	8	10	34
Maximum 24-hr. Snowfall (in.)*	6	7	8	3	0	0	0	0	0	0	8	9	9
Maximum Snow Depth (in.)	na	na	na	na	na	na	na	na	na	na	na	na	na
Days With ≥ 1.0" Snow Depth	na	na	na	na	na	na	na	na	na	na	na	na	na
Thunderstorm Days*	< 1	< 1	1	2	3	5	6	4	2	1	1	< 1	25
Foggy Days*	15	14	16	16	18	16	22	19	17	15	14	14	196
Predominant Sky Cover*	OVR	OVR	OVR	OVR	OVR	SCT	OVR	SCT	OVR	CLR	OVR	OVR	OVR
Mean Relative Humidity 7am (%)*	76	76	77	76	76	77	81	84	85	85	80	76	79
Mean Relative Humidity 4pm (%)*	62	59	57	58	59	59	63	63	63	62	62	60	61
Mean Dewpoint (°F)*	22	22	28	38	48	58	65	64	57	46	36	26	43
Prevailing Wind Direction*	WNW	NW	NW	SW	SW	SW	SW	SW	SW	SW	SW	WNW	SW
Prevailing Wind Speed (mph)*	13	13	13	10	10	10	10	9	10	10	10	12	12
Maximum Wind Gust (mph)*	na	na	na	na	na	na	na	na	na	na	na	na	na

Note: (*) Period of record is 1984-1995

New York Central Park Observatory

New York City, in area exceeding 300 square miles, is located on the Atlantic coastal plain at the mouth of the Hudson River. The terrain is laced with numerous waterways, all but one of the five boroughs in the city are situated on islands. Elevations range from less than 50 feet over most of Manhattan, Brooklyn, and Queens to almost 300 feet in northern Manhattan and the Bronx, and over 400 feet in Staten Island.

The New York Metropolitan area is close to the path of most storm and frontal systems which move across the North American continent. Therefore, weather conditions affecting the city most often approach from a westerly direction, resulting in higher temperatures in summer and lower ones in winter than would otherwise be expected in a coastal area. However, the frequent passage of weather systems often helps reduce the length of extremes.

Although continental influence predominates, oceanic influence is by no means absent. During the summer local sea breezes, winds blowing onshore from the cool water surface, often moderate the afternoon heat. The effect of the sea breeze diminishes inland. On winter mornings, ocean temperatures which are warm relative to the land reinforce the effect of the city heat island and low temperatures are often 10-20 degrees lower in the inland suburbs than in the central city. The relatively warm water temperatures also delay the advent of winter snows. Conversely, the lag in warming of water temperatures keeps spring temperatures relatively cool.

Precipitation is moderate and distributed fairly evenly throughout the year. Most of the rainfall from May through October comes from thunderstorms, usually of brief duration and sometimes intense. Heavy rains of long duration associated with tropical storms occur infrequently in late summer or fall. For the other seasons precipitation is associated with widespread storm areas, producing day-long rain or snow. Coastal storms, occurring most often in the fall and winter months, produce on occasion considerable amounts of precipitation, record rains, snows, and high winds.

The average annual precipitation is reasonably uniform within the city but higher in the suburbs and less on eastern Long Island. Annual snowfall totals also show a consistent increase to the north and west of the city with lesser amounts along the south shores and the eastern end of Long Island.

Local Climatological Data is published for three locations in New York City, Central Park, La Guardia Airport, and John F. Kennedy International Airport.

Based on the 1951-1980 period, the average first occurrence of 32 degrees Fahrenheit in the fall is November 11 and the average last occurrence in the spring is April 1.

New York Central Park Observatory *New York County* Elevation: 131 ft. Latitude: 40° 47' N Longitude: 73° 58' W

	JAN	FEB	MAR	APR	MAY	JUN	JUL	AUG	SEP	OCT	NOV	DEC	YEAR
Mean Maximum Temp. (°F)	39.2	42.2	50.3	61.9	71.6	79.9	84.8	83.5	76.0	64.5	54.5	43.8	62.7
Mean Temp. (°F)	33.1	35.5	42.7	53.3	62.8	71.7	76.8	75.8	68.4	57.2	48.0	37.9	55.3
Mean Minimum Temp. (°F)	26.9	28.7	35.0	44.8	54.0	63.5	68.8	68.0	60.8	49.9	41.4	31.9	47.8
Extreme Maximum Temp. (°F)	72	75	86	96	97	98	102	103	99	87	80	75	103
Extreme Minimum Temp. (°F)	-2	4	10	21	40	47	53	50	43	31	18	-1	-2
Days Maximum Temp. ≥ 90°F	0	0	0	0	1	3	7	5	1	0	0	0	17
Days Maximum Temp. ≤ 32°F	8	4	1	0	0	0	0	0	0	0	0	4	17
Days Minimum Temp. ≤ 32°F	21	19	11	1	0	0	0	0	0	0	3	15	70
Days Minimum Temp. ≤ 0°F	0	0	0	0	0	0	0	0	0	0	0	0	0
Heating Degree Days (base 65°F)	983	829	687	355	124	15	0	1	36	254	505	833	4,622
Cooling Degree Days (base 65°F)	0	0	2	12	64	223	374	343	145	20	1	0	1,184
Mean Precipitation (in.)	3.59	2.92	4.13	4.35	4.16	4.51	4.73	4.24	4.21	4.36	4.00	3.88	49.08
Maximum Precipitation (in.)*	10.5	6.0	10.4	8.3	10.2	9.3	11.8	12.4	9.3	7.8	12.4	10.0	67.0
Minimum Precipitation (in.)*	0.6	0.5	0.9	1.3	0.6	1.2	1.3	0.2	1.3	0.1	0.3	0.6	26.1
Extreme Maximum Daily Precip. (in.)	2.73	1.94	3.10	7.56	2.40	3.07	3.75	4.64	5.02	4.35	3.60	2.41	7.56
Days With ≥ 0.1" Precipitation	6	6	7	7	7	7	7	6	6	6	6	7	78
Days With ≥ 0.5" Precipitation	3	2	3	3	3	3	3	3	3	3	3	3	35
Days With ≥ 1.0" Precipitation	1	1	1	1	1	1	1	1	1	1	1	1	12
Mean Snowfall (in.)	7.0	7.6	3.8	0.6	trace	0.0	trace	0.0	0.0	trace	0.3	4.3	23.6
Maximum Snowfall (in.)*	20	26	17	10	trace	0	0	0	0	trace	5	12	53
Maximum 24-hr. Snowfall (in.)*	12	16	10	10	trace	0	0	0	0	trace	4	7	16
Maximum Snow Depth (in.)	14	na	9	9	trace	0	trace	0	0	0	5	10	na
Days With ≥ 1.0" Snow Depth	8	na	3	0	0	0	0	0	0	0	0	2	na
Thunderstorm Days*	< 1	< 1	1	1	3	4	5	4	1	1	< 1	< 1	20
Foggy Days*	0	0	0	0	0	0	0	0	0	0	1	< 1	1
Predominant Sky Cover*	OVR	OVR	OVR	OVR	OVR	SCT	SCT	SCT	OVR	CLR	OVR	OVR	OVR
Mean Relative Humidity 7am (%)*	67	67	66	64	72	74	74	76	78	75	72	69	71
Mean Relative Humidity 4pm (%)*	55	53	50	45	52	55	53	54	56	55	58	59	54
Mean Dewpoint (°F)*	18	19	26	34	47	57	62	62	56	44	34	25	40
Prevailing Wind Direction*	NW	NW	NW	NW	NE	SW	SW	SW	SW	W	W	NW	NW
Prevailing Wind Speed (mph)*	12	12	13	12	10	8	8	8	8	9	9	12	10
Maximum Wind Gust (mph)*	52	51	63	46	44	41	46	43	52	46	58	64	64

Note: (*) Period of record is 1965-1995

New York JFK Int'l Airport

New York City, in area exceeding 300 square miles, is located on the Atlantic coastal plain at the mouth of the Hudson River. The terrain is laced with numerous waterways, all but one of the five boroughs in the city are situated on islands. Elevations range from less than 50 feet over most of Manhattan, Brooklyn, and Queens to almost 300 feet in northern Manhattan and the Bronx, and over 400 feet in Staten Island.

The New York Metropolitan area is close to the path of most storm and frontal systems which move across the North American continent. Therefore, weather conditions affecting the city most often approach from a westerly direction, resulting in higher temperatures in summer and lower ones in winter than would otherwise be expected in a coastal area. However, the frequent passage of weather systems often helps reduce the length of extremes.

Although continental influence predominates, oceanic influence is by no means absent. During the summer local sea breezes, winds blowing onshore from the cool water surface, often moderate the afternoon heat. The effect of the sea breeze diminishes inland. On winter mornings, ocean temperatures which are warm relative to the land reinforce the effect of the city heat island and low temperatures are often 10-20 degrees lower in the inland suburbs than in the central city. The relatively warm water temperatures also delay the advent of winter snows. Conversely, the lag in warming of water temperatures keeps spring temperatures relatively cool.

Precipitation is moderate and distributed fairly evenly throughout the year. Most of the rainfall from May through October comes from thunderstorms, usually of brief duration and sometimes intense. Heavy rains of long duration associated with tropical storms occur infrequently in late summer or fall. For the other seasons precipitation is associated with widespread storm areas, producing day-long rain or snow. Coastal storms, occurring most often in the fall and winter months, produce on occasion considerable amounts of precipitation, record rains, snows, and high winds.

The average annual precipitation is reasonably uniform within the city but higher in the suburbs and less on eastern Long Island. Annual snowfall totals also show a consistent increase to the north and west of the city with lesser amounts along the south shores and the eastern end of Long Island.

Local Climatological Data is published for three locations in New York City, Central Park, La Guardia Airport, and John°F. Kennedy International Airport.

Based on the 1951-1980 period, the average first occurrence of 32 degrees Fahrenheit in the fall is November 11 and the average last occurrence in the spring is April 1.

New York JFK Int'l Airport *Queens County*   Elevation: 16 ft.   Latitude: 40° 39' N   Longitude: 73° 48' W

	JAN	FEB	MAR	APR	MAY	JUN	JUL	AUG	SEP	OCT	NOV	DEC	YEAR
Mean Maximum Temp. (°F)	39.1	41.7	48.8	58.8	68.4	77.7	82.9	82.0	75.4	64.4	54.3	44.1	61.5
Mean Temp. (°F)	32.8	34.8	41.4	51.2	60.6	70.2	75.7	75.0	68.2	57.1	47.5	37.9	54.4
Mean Minimum Temp. (°F)	26.3	27.9	34.0	43.6	52.8	62.5	68.5	68.0	60.9	49.7	40.8	31.5	47.2
Extreme Maximum Temp. (°F)	71	71	85	90	95	98	102	100	98	90	77	75	102
Extreme Minimum Temp. (°F)	-2	7	8	20	37	48	56	51	43	31	19	2	-2
Days Maximum Temp. ≥ 90°F	0	0	0	0	0	2	4	3	1	0	0	0	10
Days Maximum Temp. ≤ 32°F	7	4	1	0	0	0	0	0	0	0	0	3	15
Days Minimum Temp. ≤ 32°F	22	20	12	1	0	0	0	0	0	0	3	16	74
Days Minimum Temp. ≤ 0°F	0	0	0	0	0	0	0	0	0	0	0	0	0
Heating Degree Days (base 65°F)	993	846	725	410	162	19	0	1	33	255	518	834	4,796
Cooling Degree Days (base 65°F)	0	0	0	3	33	180	341	319	135	15	0	0	1,026
Mean Precipitation (in.)	3.15	2.42	3.77	4.01	3.97	3.93	4.13	3.61	3.39	3.57	3.37	3.32	42.64
Maximum Precipitation (in.)*	8.3	4.9	8.2	9.5	10.7	8.1	8.5	8.3	9.6	6.6	9.5	6.7	59.1
Minimum Precipitation (in.)*	0.5	1.0	0.9	1.4	0.6	trace	0.5	0.2	1.0	0.9	0.3	0.6	25.4
Extreme Maximum Daily Precip. (in.)	3.78	1.62	2.56	3.15	2.70	6.27	3.51	4.10	3.42	4.66	2.45	2.55	6.27
Days With ≥ 0.1" Precipitation	6	5	7	7	7	6	6	6	5	5	6	6	72
Days With ≥ 0.5" Precipitation	2	2	3	3	3	3	3	2	2	3	3	2	31
Days With ≥ 1.0" Precipitation	1	1	1	1	1	1	1	1	1	1	1	1	12
Mean Snowfall (in.)	6.4	7.4	3.6	0.8	trace	0.0	trace	0.0	0.0	trace	0.3	4.2	22.7
Maximum Snowfall (in.)*	20	25	16	8	0	0	0	0	0	trace	4	22	49
Maximum 24-hr. Snowfall (in.)*	13	20	9	8	0	0	0	0	0	trace	3	18	20
Maximum Snow Depth (in.)	22	28	8	8	trace	0	trace	0	0	trace	4	14	28
Days With ≥ 1.0" Snow Depth	7	5	3	0	0	0	0	0	0	0	0	3	18
Thunderstorm Days*	< 1	< 1	1	2	3	4	5	5	2	1	1	< 1	24
Foggy Days*	10	9	11	11	13	12	13	12	11	10	11	10	133
Predominant Sky Cover*	OVR	OVR	OVR	OVR	OVR	OVR	SCT	SCT	OVR	CLR	OVR	OVR	OVR
Mean Relative Humidity 7am (%)*	71	71	71	70	73	74	75	78	79	78	76	73	74
Mean Relative Humidity 4pm (%)*	61	59	57	58	61	63	63	63	62	60	61	62	61
Mean Dewpoint (°F)*	21	22	28	37	48	58	64	63	57	46	36	26	42
Prevailing Wind Direction*	NW	NW	NW	S	S	S	S	S	S	WSW	NW	NW	S
Prevailing Wind Speed (mph)*	16	17	17	13	13	12	12	12	12	10	15	16	14
Maximum Wind Gust (mph)*	59	60	68	61	71	56	54	68	60	62	67	61	71

Note: (*) Period of record is 1948-1995

New York Laguardia Airport

New York City, in area exceeding 300 square miles, is located on the Atlantic coastal plain at the mouth of the Hudson River. The terrain is laced with numerous waterways, all but one of the five boroughs in the city are situated on islands. Elevations range from less than 50 feet over most of Manhattan, Brooklyn, and Queens to almost 300 feet in northern Manhattan and the Bronx, and over 400 feet in Staten Island.

The New York Metropolitan area is close to the path of most storm and frontal systems which move across the North American continent. Therefore, weather conditions affecting the city most often approach from a westerly direction, resulting in higher temperatures in summer and lower ones in winter than would otherwise be expected in a coastal area. However, the frequent passage of weather systems often helps reduce the length of extremes.

Although continental influence predominates, oceanic influence is by no means absent. During the summer local sea breezes, winds blowing onshore from the cool water surface, often moderate the afternoon heat. The effect of the sea breeze diminishes inland. On winter mornings, ocean temperatures which are warm relative to the land reinforce the effect of the city heat island and low temperatures are often 10-20 degrees lower in the inland suburbs than in the central city. The relatively warm water temperatures also delay the advent of winter snows. Conversely, the lag in warming of water temperatures keeps spring temperatures relatively cool.

Precipitation is moderate and distributed fairly evenly throughout the year. Most of the rainfall from May through October comes from thunderstorms, usually of brief duration and sometimes intense. Heavy rains of long duration associated with tropical storms occur infrequently in late summer or fall. For the other seasons precipitation is associated with widespread storm areas, producing day-long rain or snow. Coastal storms, occurring most often in the fall and winter months, produce on occasion considerable amounts of precipitation, record rains, snows, and high winds.

The average annual precipitation is reasonably uniform within the city but higher in the suburbs and less on eastern Long Island. Annual snowfall totals also show a consistent increase to the north and west of the city with lesser amounts along the south shores and the eastern end of Long Island.

Local Climatological Data is published for three locations in New York City, Central Park, La Guardia Airport, and John°F. Kennedy International Airport.

Based on the 1951-1980 period, the average first occurrence of 32 degrees Fahrenheit in the fall is November 11 and the average last occurrence in the spring is April 1.

New York Laguardia Airport *Queens County*   Elevation: 11 ft.   Latitude: 40° 47' N   Longitude: 73° 53' W

	JAN	FEB	MAR	APR	MAY	JUN	JUL	AUG	SEP	OCT	NOV	DEC	YEAR
Mean Maximum Temp. (°F)	39.1	42.0	49.4	60.5	71.0	80.1	85.0	83.5	76.1	64.9	54.4	44.2	62.5
Mean Temp. (°F)	33.3	35.6	42.3	52.8	62.8	72.3	77.6	76.6	69.4	58.3	48.4	38.4	55.6
Mean Minimum Temp. (°F)	27.4	29.1	35.1	45.1	54.6	64.4	70.1	69.6	62.6	51.6	42.4	32.6	48.7
Extreme Maximum Temp. (°F)	72	73	83	94	97	100	103	104	96	89	80	75	104
Extreme Minimum Temp. (°F)	-3	4	8	22	38	49	56	51	45	34	20	-1	-3
Days Maximum Temp. ≥ 90°F	0	0	0	0	1	4	7	5	1	0	0	0	18
Days Maximum Temp. ≤ 32°F	8	5	1	0	0	0	0	0	0	0	0	4	18
Days Minimum Temp. ≤ 32°F	21	18	10	1	0	0	0	0	0	0	3	14	67
Days Minimum Temp. ≤ 0°F	0	0	0	0	0	0	0	0	0	0	0	0	0
Heating Degree Days (base 65°F)	976	825	698	366	124	13	0	1	29	227	491	816	4,566
Cooling Degree Days (base 65°F)	0	0	1	8	62	238	395	366	166	25	1	0	1,262
Mean Precipitation (in.)	3.18	2.62	3.94	4.13	3.77	4.00	4.57	4.09	3.67	3.73	3.49	3.47	44.66
Maximum Precipitation (in.)*	8.7	5.7	8.7	11.5	9.3	8.1	12.3	16.0	9.6	7.3	9.9	7.7	60.8
Minimum Precipitation (in.)*	0.5	0.7	0.9	1.0	0.4	trace	0.7	0.1	1.0	0.1	0.3	0.3	22.2
Extreme Maximum Daily Precip. (in.)	2.60	1.63	2.83	6.69	2.57	4.00	3.53	3.54	4.63	4.39	2.91	2.74	6.69
Days With ≥ 0.1" Precipitation	6	5	7	7	7	7	7	6	5	5	6	7	75
Days With ≥ 0.5" Precipitation	2	2	3	2	3	3	3	3	2	3	3	3	32
Days With ≥ 1.0" Precipitation	1	1	1	1	1	1	1	1	1	1	1	1	12
Mean Snowfall (in.)	7.5	8.2	4.5	0.6	trace	0.0	trace	trace	0.0	trace	0.3	4.8	25.9
Maximum Snowfall (in.)*	18	26	19	8	trace	0	0	0	0	1	6	22	60
Maximum 24-hr. Snowfall (in.)*	11	17	14	8	trace	0	0	0	0	1	6	16	17
Maximum Snow Depth (in.)	25	22	9	8	trace	0	trace	trace	0	trace	6	15	25
Days With ≥ 1.0" Snow Depth	7	6	3	0	0	0	0	0	0	0	0	3	19
Thunderstorm Days*	< 1	< 1	1	2	3	4	5	5	2	1	< 1	< 1	23
Foggy Days*	10	9	10	10	11	9	8	8	8	8	9	10	110
Predominant Sky Cover*	OVR	OVR	OVR	OVR	OVR	OVR	SCT	SCT	OVR	OVR	OVR	OVR	OVR
Mean Relative Humidity 7am (%)*	67	67	67	67	71	71	73	75	76	74	71	68	71
Mean Relative Humidity 4pm (%)*	57	55	52	51	53	53	54	56	56	55	57	59	55
Mean Dewpoint (°F)*	20	21	27	36	48	57	63	62	56	45	35	25	41
Prevailing Wind Direction*	NW	WNW	NW	NW	S	S	S	S	S	SW	WNW	WNW	NW
Prevailing Wind Speed (mph)*	17	17	17	16	12	12	12	12	10	12	15	16	14
Maximum Wind Gust (mph)*	61	67	71	63	56	56	59	73	64	71	76	77	77

Note: (*) Period of record is 1947-1995

Rochester Int'l Airport

Rochester is located at the mouth of the Genesee River at about the mid point of the south shore of Lake Ontario. The river flows northward from northwest Pennsylvania and empties into Lake Ontario. The land slopes from a lakeshore elevation of 246 feet to over 1,000 feet some 20 miles south. The airport is located just south of the city.

Lake Ontario plays a major role in the Rochester weather. In the summer its cooling effect inhibits the temperature from rising much above the low to mid 90s. In the winter the modifying temperature effect prevents temperatures from falling below -15 degrees most of the time, although temperatures at locations more than 15 miles inland do drop below -30 degrees.

The lake plays a major role in winter snowfall distribution. Well inland from the lake and toward the airport, the seasonal snowfall is usually less than in the area north of the airport and toward the lakeshore where wide variations occur. This is due to what is called the lake effect. Snowfalls of one to two feet or more in 24 hours are common near the lake in winter due the lake effect alone. The lake rarely freezes over because of its depth. The area is also prone to other heavy snowstorms and blizzards because of its proximity to the paths of low pressure systems coming up the east coast, out of the Ohio Valley.

Precipitation is rather evenly distributed throughout the year. Excessive rains occur infrequently but may be caused by slowly moving thunderstorms, slowly moving or stalled major low pressure systems, or by hurricanes and tropical storms that move inland. Hail occurs occasionally and heavy fog is rare.

The growing season averages 150 to 180 days. The years first frost usually occurs in late September and the last frost typically occurs in mid-May.

Rochester Int'l Airport *Monroe County* Elevation: 600 ft. Latitude: 43° 07' N Longitude: 77° 41' W

	JAN	FEB	MAR	APR	MAY	JUN	JUL	AUG	SEP	OCT	NOV	DEC	YEAR
Mean Maximum Temp. (°F)	32.0	34.2	42.8	56.0	67.8	76.8	81.2	79.4	72.0	59.8	48.2	36.8	57.3
Mean Temp. (°F)	24.9	26.4	34.2	46.4	57.2	66.4	71.0	69.6	62.1	50.8	40.7	30.2	48.3
Mean Minimum Temp. (°F)	17.8	18.6	25.6	36.7	46.5	55.9	60.8	59.7	52.1	41.7	33.2	23.5	39.3
Extreme Maximum Temp. (°F)	68	73	83	93	94	95	98	97	95	85	75	72	98
Extreme Minimum Temp. (°F)	-17	-8	-7	13	30	36	45	38	30	21	9	-12	-17
Days Maximum Temp. ≥ 90°F	0	0	0	0	0	1	3	2	0	0	0	0	6
Days Maximum Temp. ≤ 32°F	16	13	6	0	0	0	0	0	0	0	1	10	46
Days Minimum Temp. ≤ 32°F	28	25	23	10	1	0	0	0	0	4	15	25	131
Days Minimum Temp. ≤ 0°F	3	1	0	0	0	0	0	0	0	0	0	0	4
Heating Degree Days (base 65°F)	1,236	1,084	948	556	265	64	10	20	135	440	723	1,072	6,553
Cooling Degree Days (base 65°F)	0	0	0	5	29	112	204	170	55	6	0	0	581
Mean Precipitation (in.)	2.37	1.90	2.55	2.76	2.83	3.36	3.20	3.49	3.39	2.73	2.92	2.62	34.12
Maximum Precipitation (in.)*	5.8	5.1	5.0	4.1	6.6	6.8	6.0	6.0	6.3	7.8	7.0	4.6	40.5
Minimum Precipitation (in.)*	0.7	0.7	0.5	1.2	0.4	0.2	0.6	0.8	0.3	0.2	0.4	0.6	22.4
Extreme Maximum Daily Precip. (in.)	1.77	1.59	1.44	1.79	2.12	2.19	3.33	2.51	3.08	2.94	1.83	1.46	3.33
Days With ≥ 0.1" Precipitation	7	6	7	7	6	7	6	6	7	6	7	8	80
Days With ≥ 0.5" Precipitation	1	1	1	2	2	2	2	2	2	2	2	1	20
Days With ≥ 1.0" Precipitation	0	0	0	0	0	1	1	1	1	0	0	0	4
Mean Snowfall (in.)	27.0	21.3	17.0	3.9	0.4	trace	trace	0.0	trace	0.1	7.6	22.1	99.4
Maximum Snowfall (in.)*	60	65	40	20	11	0	0	0	trace	3	23	46	152
Maximum 24-hr. Snowfall (in.)*	18	18	18	10	11	0	0	0	trace	3	12	18	18
Maximum Snow Depth (in.)	28	17	34	7	4	trace	trace	0	trace	trace	10	13	34
Days With ≥ 1.0" Snow Depth	21	20	12	1	0	0	0	0	0	0	4	15	73
Thunderstorm Days*	< 1	< 1	1	2	3	5	6	6	3	1	< 1	< 1	27
Foggy Days*	8	9	10	10	10	10	11	13	12	11	11	10	125
Predominant Sky Cover*	OVR	OVR	OVR	OVR	OVR	OVR	SCT	OVR	OVR	OVR	OVR	OVR	OVR
Mean Relative Humidity 7am (%)*	79	80	80	78	77	79	82	86	88	85	82	81	81
Mean Relative Humidity 4pm (%)*	71	69	63	56	53	53	52	55	59	60	69	73	61
Mean Dewpoint (°F)*	18	18	25	35	45	55	60	59	53	42	33	23	39
Prevailing Wind Direction*	WSW	WSW	WSW	WSW	WSW	WSW	SW	SW	SW	WSW	WSW	WSW	WSW
Prevailing Wind Speed (mph)*	16	15	15	14	13	12	8	8	8	12	14	14	13
Maximum Wind Gust (mph)*	63	70	68	71	64	52	56	62	51	60	67	55	71

Note: (*) Period of record is 1948-1995

Syracuse Hancock Int'l Airport

Syracuse is located approximately at the geographical center of the state. Gently rolling terrain stretches northward for about 30 miles to the eastern end of Lake Ontario. Oneida Lake is about 8 miles northeast of Syracuse. Approximately five miles south of the city, hills rise to 1,500 feet. Immediately to the west, the terrain is gently rolling with elevations 500 to 800 feet above sea level.

The climate of Syracuse is primarily continental in character and comparatively humid. Nearly all cyclonic systems moving from the interior of the country through the St. Lawrence Valley will affect the Syracuse area. Seasonal and diurnal changes are marked and produce an invigorating climate.

In the summer and in portions of the transitional seasons, temperatures usually rise rapidly during the daytime to moderate levels and as a rule fall rapidly after sunset. The nights are relatively cool and comfortable. There are only a few days in a year when atmospheric humidity causes great personal discomfort.

Winters are usually cold and are sometimes severe in part. Daytime temperatures average in the low 30s with nighttime lows in the teens. Low winter temperatures below -25 degrees have been recorded. The autumn, winter, and spring seasons display marked variability.

Based on the 1951-1980 period, the average first occurrence of 32 degrees Fahrenheit in the fall is October 16 and the average last occurrence in the spring is April 28.

Precipitation in the Syracuse area is derived principally from cyclonic storms which pass from the interior of the country through the St. Lawrence Valley. Lake Ontario provides the source of significant winter precipitation. The lake is quite deep and never freezes so cold air flowing over the lake is quickly saturated and produces the cloudiness and snow squalls which are a well-known feature of winter weather in the Syracuse area.

The precipitation is uncommonly well distributed, averaging about 3 inches per month throughout the year. Snowfall is moderately heavy with an average just over 100 inches. There are about 30 days per year with thunderstorms.

Wind velocities are moderate, but during the winter months there are numerous days with sufficient winds to cause blowing and drifting snow.

During December, January, and February there is much cloudiness. Syracuse receives only about one-third of possible sunshine during winter months. Approximately two-thirds of possible sunshine is received during the warm months.

Syracuse Hancock Int'l Airport *Onondaga County*   Elevation: 410 ft.   Latitude: 43° 07' N   Longitude: 76° 06' W

	JAN	FEB	MAR	APR	MAY	JUN	JUL	AUG	SEP	OCT	NOV	DEC	YEAR
Mean Maximum Temp. (°F)	31.7	34.2	43.0	57.1	68.9	77.5	81.7	80.2	72.3	59.9	48.2	36.5	57.6
Mean Temp. (°F)	23.8	25.7	33.9	46.8	57.6	66.6	71.3	69.9	62.1	50.5	40.5	29.3	48.2
Mean Minimum Temp. (°F)	15.8	17.3	24.8	36.5	46.3	55.7	60.9	59.5	51.8	41.0	32.7	22.0	38.7
Extreme Maximum Temp. (°F)	70	69	87	92	93	97	98	101	95	85	76	72	101
Extreme Minimum Temp. (°F)	-25	-15	-15	12	27	36	46	42	28	22	6	-22	-25
Days Maximum Temp. ≥ 90°F	0	0	0	0	0	2	4	2	0	0	0	0	8
Days Maximum Temp. ≤ 32°F	16	13	6	0	0	0	0	0	0	0	2	11	48
Days Minimum Temp. ≤ 32°F	28	26	24	10	0	0	0	0	0	5	15	26	134
Days Minimum Temp. ≤ 0°F	4	2	1	0	0	0	0	0	0	0	0	1	8
Heating Degree Days (base 65°F)	1,272	1,103	957	543	249	59	7	19	134	446	729	1,100	6,618
Cooling Degree Days (base 65°F)	0	0	0	1	5	114	209	177	53	4	0	0	590
Mean Precipitation (in.)	2.46	2.04	3.00	3.27	3.17	3.24	3.72	3.40	3.62	3.40	3.52	3.06	37.90
Maximum Precipitation (in.)*	5.8	5.4	6.8	8.1	7.4	12.3	9.5	8.4	8.8	8.3	6.8	5.5	57.9
Minimum Precipitation (in.)*	1.0	0.6	1.0	1.2	0.8	1.0	0.9	1.3	0.8	0.2	1.3	0.8	27.1
Extreme Maximum Daily Precip. (in.)	1.41	1.62	1.33	1.60	1.69	2.86	4.29	2.98	2.59	2.98	3.56	1.48	4.29
Days With ≥ 0.1" Precipitation	7	6	8	8	8	7	7	7	7	8	9	8	90
Days With ≥ 0.5" Precipitation	1	1	2	2	2	2	3	2	2	2	2	2	23
Days With ≥ 1.0" Precipitation	0	0	0	0	0	0	1	1	1	1	0	0	4
Mean Snowfall (in.)	34.9	26.2	18.7	3.8	0.1	trace	trace	trace	trace	0.4	9.7	30.7	124.5
Maximum Snowfall (in.)*	72	73	54	16	2	0	0	trace	trace	6	34	65	208
Maximum 24-hr. Snowfall (in.)*	22	21	22	7	2	0	0	trace	trace	3	12	16	22
Maximum Snow Depth (in.)	26	33	35	6	1	trace	trace	trace	trace	trace	10	20	35
Days With ≥ 1.0" Snow Depth	23	21	13	1	0	0	0	0	0	0	4	16	78
Thunderstorm Days*	< 1	< 1	1	2	3	5	6	5	3	1	1	< 1	27
Foggy Days*	10	9	11	10	11	11	12	13	14	12	12	11	136
Predominant Sky Cover*	OVR	OVR	OVR	OVR	OVR	OVR	OVR	OVR	OVR	OVR	OVR	OVR	OVR
Mean Relative Humidity 7am (%)*	77	78	78	76	76	77	79	85	86	84	80	79	80
Mean Relative Humidity 4pm (%)*	69	67	60	52	53	54	54	57	60	60	68	72	60
Mean Dewpoint (°F)*	16	17	24	34	45	55	60	59	53	42	32	22	38
Prevailing Wind Direction*	WSW	WSW	WNW	WNW	WNW	WNW	WSW	WSW	WSW	WSW	WSW	WSW	WSW
Prevailing Wind Speed (mph)*	15	14	14	14	12	12	9	9	9	10	13	14	12
Maximum Wind Gust (mph)*	58	56	61	63	76	67	66	49	48	60	58	63	76

Note: (*) Period of record is 1945-1995

Albion 2 NE *Orleans County* Elevation: 439 ft. Latitude: 43° 17' N Longitude: 78° 10' W

	JAN	FEB	MAR	APR	MAY	JUN	JUL	AUG	SEP	OCT	NOV	DEC	YEAR
Mean Maximum Temp. (°F)	32.3	34.6	43.5	57.1	68.9	78.0	82.1	80.4	73.2	60.7	48.5	37.1	58.0
Mean Temp. (°F)	25.4	26.9	34.8	47.1	57.9	67.4	72.0	70.5	63.5	51.8	41.3	30.6	49.1
Mean Minimum Temp. (°F)	18.4	19.2	26.0	36.9	46.9	56.8	61.8	60.5	53.7	42.9	33.9	24.0	40.1
Extreme Maximum Temp. (°F)	67	74	80	87	91	96	101	98	93	84	74	75	101
Extreme Minimum Temp. (°F)	-15	-6	-5	13	28	35	45	39	32	22	11	-10	-15
Days Maximum Temp. ≥ 90°F	0	0	0	0	0	2	4	2	0	0	0	0	8
Days Maximum Temp. ≤ 32°F	16	13	6	0	0	0	0	0	0	0	1	10	46
Days Minimum Temp. ≤ 32°F	28	25	23	10	1	0	0	0	0	3	14	25	129
Days Minimum Temp. ≤ 0°F	2	1	0	0	0	0	0	0	0	0	0	0	3
Heating Degree Days (base 65°F)	1,222	1,070	931	537	245	53	6	15	110	409	706	1,061	6,365
Cooling Degree Days (base 65°F)	0	0	0	1	5	32	132	229	192	71	7	0	669
Mean Precipitation (in.)	2.68	2.04	2.77	3.01	2.99	3.14	3.01	3.04	3.57	3.13	3.22	2.95	35.55
Extreme Maximum Daily Precip. (in.)	2.00	1.36	1.90	1.85	2.15	3.79	2.31	3.06	3.28	2.28	2.16	1.96	3.79
Days With ≥ 0.1" Precipitation	8	6	7	8	7	7	6	7	7	7	9	8	87
Days With ≥ 0.5" Precipitation	1	1	2	2	2	2	2	2	2	2	2	1	21
Days With ≥ 1.0" Precipitation	0	0	0	0	0	1	1	1	1	1	0	0	5
Mean Snowfall (in.)	19.5	13.6	11.1	2.1	0.3	0.0	0.0	0.0	0.0	0.2	4.5	15.1	66.4
Maximum Snow Depth (in.)	30	25	19	5	6	0	0	0	0	2	9	12	30
Days With ≥ 1.0" Snow Depth	15	11	6	1	0	0	0	0	0	0	0	3	47

Alcove Dam *Albany County* Elevation: 606 ft. Latitude: 42° 28' N Longitude: 73° 56' W

	JAN	FEB	MAR	APR	MAY	JUN	JUL	AUG	SEP	OCT	NOV	DEC	YEAR
Mean Maximum Temp. (°F)	31.3	34.6	42.4	56.3	67.7	75.8	80.0	78.9	71.0	58.9	47.3	35.9	56.7
Mean Temp. (°F)	21.5	24.1	32.0	45.1	55.9	64.6	69.1	67.9	59.8	48.0	38.3	27.2	46.1
Mean Minimum Temp. (°F)	11.6	13.6	21.6	33.9	44.1	53.4	58.1	56.8	48.6	37.1	29.2	18.6	35.5
Extreme Maximum Temp. (°F)	71	70	86	91	90	96	100	96	98	83	81	73	100
Extreme Minimum Temp. (°F)	-29	-16	-13	10	26	32	39	35	28	18	6	-24	-29
Days Maximum Temp. ≥ 90°F	0	0	0	0	0	1	2	2	0	0	0	0	5
Days Maximum Temp. ≤ 32°F	16	12	6	0	0	0	0	0	0	0	2	11	47
Days Minimum Temp. ≤ 32°F	30	27	27	14	2	0	0	0	1	10	21	28	160
Days Minimum Temp. ≤ 0°F	6	3	1	0	0	0	0	0	0	0	0	2	12
Heating Degree Days (base 65°F)	1,343	1,150	1,017	592	291	83	20	36	180	521	794	1,163	7,190
Cooling Degree Days (base 65°F)	0	0	0	2	16	78	153	131	31	1	0	0	412
Mean Precipitation (in.)	2.43	2.05	3.54	3.77	3.48	4.46	3.84	3.54	3.71	3.45	3.48	2.81	40.56
Extreme Maximum Daily Precip. (in.)	2.15	1.80	5.38	3.95	2.25	4.28	3.42	2.84	6.89	3.51	3.38	2.05	6.89
Days With ≥ 0.1" Precipitation	5	5	6	7	7	8	7	7	6	6	6	6	76
Days With ≥ 0.5" Precipitation	2	1	3	3	2	3	3	2	2	2	3	2	28
Days With ≥ 1.0" Precipitation	0	0	1	1	1	1	1	1	1	1	1	1	10
Mean Snowfall (in.)	na	na	na	0.4	trace	0.0	0.0	0.0	0.0	0.1	0.4	na	na
Maximum Snow Depth (in.)	na	na	na	na	na	na	na	na	na	na	na	na	na
Days With ≥ 1.0" Snow Depth	na	na	na	0	0	0	0	0	0	0	0	na	na

Alfred *Allegany County* Elevation: 1,770 ft. Latitude: 42° 16' N Longitude: 77° 47' W

	JAN	FEB	MAR	APR	MAY	JUN	JUL	AUG	SEP	OCT	NOV	DEC	YEAR
Mean Maximum Temp. (°F)	31.4	34.8	43.6	56.7	68.2	76.3	80.1	78.5	70.7	59.1	47.0	36.1	56.9
Mean Temp. (°F)	22.0	24.1	31.9	44.0	54.3	63.0	67.1	65.5	58.2	47.2	37.4	27.3	45.2
Mean Minimum Temp. (°F)	12.6	13.4	20.4	31.3	40.3	49.8	54.1	52.5	45.7	35.3	27.8	18.6	33.5
Extreme Maximum Temp. (°F)	63	65	83	91	93	93	96	98	94	84	77	68	98
Extreme Minimum Temp. (°F)	-25	-15	-16	5	22	28	37	27	20	15	4	-21	-25
Days Maximum Temp. ≥ 90°F	0	0	0	0	0	1	2	1	0	0	0	0	4
Days Maximum Temp. ≤ 32°F	17	13	5	0	0	0	0	0	0	0	2	11	48
Days Minimum Temp. ≤ 32°F	29	27	27	17	7	0	0	0	2	12	21	28	170
Days Minimum Temp. ≤ 0°F	6	5	2	0	0	0	0	0	0	0	0	2	15
Heating Degree Days (base 65°F)	1,325	1,151	1,019	624	339	114	38	60	219	545	821	1,161	7,416
Cooling Degree Days (base 65°F)	0	0	0	2	14	62	110	83	22	1	0	0	294
Mean Precipitation (in.)	2.15	1.71	2.66	2.99	3.32	4.25	3.91	3.63	3.73	3.30	3.29	2.55	37.49
Extreme Maximum Daily Precip. (in.)	1.75	1.29	1.62	1.70	2.23	3.33	2.46	1.96	2.43	2.92	2.10	1.10	3.33
Days With ≥ 0.1" Precipitation	6	6	7	8	8	8	8	7	7	8	8	7	88
Days With ≥ 0.5" Precipitation	1	1	2	2	2	3	3	2	2	2	2	1	23
Days With ≥ 1.0" Precipitation	0	0	0	0	0	1	1	1	1	1	1	0	6
Mean Snowfall (in.)	20.8	16.7	17.1	4.0	0.3	0.0	0.0	0.0	0.0	0.5	8.6	19.6	87.6
Maximum Snow Depth (in.)	na	na	na	8	trace	0	0	0	0	2	8	na	na
Days With ≥ 1.0" Snow Depth	na	na	na	1	0	0	0	0	0	0	2	na	na

Allegany State Park *Cattaraugus County* Elevation: 1,500 ft. Latitude: 42° 06' N Longitude: 78° 45' W

	JAN	FEB	MAR	APR	MAY	JUN	JUL	AUG	SEP	OCT	NOV	DEC	YEAR
Mean Maximum Temp. (°F)	30.3	32.9	41.8	54.7	66.7	74.6	77.9	76.3	*69.0*	57.2	46.1	34.6	*55.2*
Mean Temp. (°F)	21.8	23.4	31.1	43.2	53.8	62.2	66.0	64.9	*57.9*	46.6	37.6	27.1	*44.6*
Mean Minimum Temp. (°F)	13.3	13.9	20.4	31.5	40.9	49.8	54.0	53.4	*46.7*	36.0	29.1	19.5	*34.0*
Extreme Maximum Temp. (°F)	63	68	80	89	90	92	97	93	*89*	80	75	70	*97*
Extreme Minimum Temp. (°F)	-22	-18	-17	11	21	24	29	31	*26*	14	-1	-16	*-22*
Days Maximum Temp. ≥ 90°F	0	0	0	0	0	0	1	0	0	0	0	0	1
Days Maximum Temp. ≤ 32°F	18	14	7	1	0	0	0	0	0	0	3	13	56
Days Minimum Temp. ≤ 32°F	28	26	26	17	6	1	0	0	1	11	20	27	163
Days Minimum Temp. ≤ 0°F	5	4	2	0	0	0	0	0	0	0	0	2	13
Heating Degree Days (base 65°F)	1,330	1,169	1,045	651	351	127	52	70	*226*	562	816	1,168	*7,567*
Cooling Degree Days (base 65°F)	0	0	0	1	11	50	89	73	*19*	1	0	0	*244*
Mean Precipitation (in.)	3.03	2.34	3.05	3.53	3.78	4.92	4.55	4.08	4.07	3.81	3.88	3.43	44.47
Extreme Maximum Daily Precip. (in.)	2.08	1.64	1.84	2.15	2.30	4.00	2.62	3.38	3.75	2.55	2.05	1.45	4.00
Days With ≥ 0.1" Precipitation	9	7	8	9	8	9	9	7	8	10	9	10	103
Days With ≥ 0.5" Precipitation	1	1	2	2	3	3	3	2	3	2	2	2	26
Days With ≥ 1.0" Precipitation	0	0	0	0	1	1	1	1	1	0	0	0	5
Mean Snowfall (in.)	na	na	*10.5*	2.1	trace	0.0	0.0	0.0	0.0	0.1	*4.3*	na	na
Maximum Snow Depth (in.)	24	21	25	9	trace	0	0	0	0	5	16	24	25
Days With ≥ 1.0" Snow Depth	26	24	18	2	0	0	0	0	0	5	6	19	95

The period of record for all cooperative weather station data is 1980 – 2009. See User Guide for detailed explanation of data.

Aurora Research Farm *Cayuga County*   Elevation: 830 ft.   Latitude: 42° 44' N   Longitude: 76° 39' W

	JAN	FEB	MAR	APR	MAY	JUN	JUL	AUG	SEP	OCT	NOV	DEC	YEAR
Mean Maximum Temp. (°F)	31.9	34.4	42.1	55.8	67.7	76.9	81.3	80.1	72.7	59.9	48.2	36.8	57.3
Mean Temp. (°F)	24.4	26.2	33.5	46.1	57.1	66.6	71.0	69.6	62.5	50.7	40.7	30.0	48.2
Mean Minimum Temp. (°F)	16.9	18.0	24.9	36.4	46.5	56.3	60.6	59.1	52.2	41.5	33.2	23.1	39.0
Extreme Maximum Temp. (°F)	67	67	85	93	94	96	101	97	98	87	81	69	101
Extreme Minimum Temp. (°F)	-21	-15	-11	10	28	34	45	40	27	23	10	-15	-21
Days Maximum Temp. ≥ 90°F	0	0	0	0	0	2	4	2	1	0	0	0	9
Days Maximum Temp. ≤ 32°F	16	12	7	0	0	0	0	0	0	0	1	10	46
Days Minimum Temp. ≤ 32°F	28	25	24	11	1	0	0	0	0	4	14	25	132
Days Minimum Temp. ≤ 0°F	3	1	0	0	0	0	0	0	0	0	0	1	5
Heating Degree Days (base 65°F)	1,252	1,091	970	566	270	70	15	24	132	442	722	1,079	6,633
Cooling Degree Days (base 65°F)	0	0	1	7	32	125	207	174	63	6	0	0	615
Mean Precipitation (in.)	1.85	1.68	2.57	3.26	3.18	3.83	3.53	3.12	4.10	3.36	3.22	2.31	36.01
Extreme Maximum Daily Precip. (in.)	1.75	1.44	1.83	1.91	1.36	*1.91*	2.85	2.98	3.03	1.85	2.73	1.34	*3.03*
Days With ≥ 0.1" Precipitation	5	5	7	8	8	8	8	6	7	7	7	6	82
Days With ≥ 0.5" Precipitation	1	1	1	2	2	2	2	2	3	2	2	1	21
Days With ≥ 1.0" Precipitation	0	0	0	0	0	1	1	1	1	1	0	0	5
Mean Snowfall (in.)	14.5	11.8	12.1	3.9	0.2	0.0	0.0	0.0	0.0	0.2	4.9	11.3	58.9
Maximum Snow Depth (in.)	25	28	43	16	4	0	0	0	0	3	17	17	43
Days With ≥ 1.0" Snow Depth	21	19	12	2	0	0	0	0	0	0	4	13	71

Avon *Livingston County*   Elevation: 544 ft.   Latitude: 42° 55' N   Longitude: 77° 45' W

	JAN	FEB	MAR	APR	MAY	JUN	JUL	AUG	SEP	OCT	NOV	DEC	YEAR
Mean Maximum Temp. (°F)	32.5	34.5	42.6	55.9	68.1	77.3	81.3	79.7	72.5	60.6	48.8	37.0	57.6
Mean Temp. (°F)	24.6	25.8	33.1	45.3	56.5	66.3	70.4	68.7	61.4	50.2	40.4	29.8	47.7
Mean Minimum Temp. (°F)	16.7	17.0	23.5	34.7	44.8	55.2	59.4	57.6	50.2	39.7	31.9	22.6	37.8
Extreme Maximum Temp. (°F)	67	72	84	91	93	95	99	97	93	87	77	71	99
Extreme Minimum Temp. (°F)	-24	-13	-9	11	28	35	45	37	28	21	9	-7	-24
Days Maximum Temp. ≥ 90°F	0	0	0	0	0	2	3	2	0	0	0	0	7
Days Maximum Temp. ≤ 32°F	16	12	7	0	0	0	0	0	0	0	1	10	46
Days Minimum Temp. ≤ 32°F	28	26	25	14	1	0	0	0	0	6	17	26	143
Days Minimum Temp. ≤ 0°F	4	2	1	0	0	0	0	0	0	0	0	1	8
Heating Degree Days (base 65°F)	1,246	1,102	982	587	284	67	13	29	150	456	733	1,083	6,732
Cooling Degree Days (base 65°F)	0	0	0	4	26	113	187	150	48	5	0	0	533
Mean Precipitation (in.)	1.79	1.56	2.42	2.72	2.78	3.25	3.31	3.35	3.35	2.65	2.72	2.09	31.99
Extreme Maximum Daily Precip. (in.)	3.04	1.91	1.95	1.35	1.71	1.85	1.92	5.20	3.12	2.60	1.57	1.23	5.20
Days With ≥ 0.1" Precipitation	5	4	5	6	7	7	7	7	7	7	7	6	75
Days With ≥ 0.5" Precipitation	1	1	1	2	2	2	2	2	2	1	2	1	19
Days With ≥ 1.0" Precipitation	0	0	0	0	0	1	1	1	1	0	0	0	4
Mean Snowfall (in.)	13.3	10.5	10.7	2.1	0.2	0.0	0.0	0.0	0.0	trace	3.7	11.4	51.9
Maximum Snow Depth (in.)	18	14	27	7	4	0	0	0	0	1	10	10	27
Days With ≥ 1.0" Snow Depth	21	19	11	1	0	0	0	0	0	0	3	15	70

Bath *Steuben County*   Elevation: 1,120 ft.   Latitude: 42° 21' N   Longitude: 77° 21' W

	JAN	FEB	MAR	APR	MAY	JUN	JUL	AUG	SEP	OCT	NOV	DEC	YEAR
Mean Maximum Temp. (°F)	31.5	*34.9*	42.7	55.9	68.2	76.6	80.7	79.3	72.2	59.7	47.4	36.4	57.1
Mean Temp. (°F)	22.1	*24.6*	31.7	44.0	54.7	63.5	67.8	66.5	59.2	47.6	38.0	27.8	45.6
Mean Minimum Temp. (°F)	12.7	*14.2*	20.6	32.0	41.3	50.5	54.9	53.7	46.1	35.3	28.6	19.2	34.1
Extreme Maximum Temp. (°F)	*64*	69	84	92	94	*93*	*101*	100	94	85	77	70	*101*
Extreme Minimum Temp. (°F)	*-24*	*-13*	-18	8	24	28	39	28	25	16	1	-16	*-24*
Days Maximum Temp. ≥ 90°F	0	*0*	0	0	0	*1*	*3*	2	0	*0*	*0*	0	*6*
Days Maximum Temp. ≤ 32°F	*16*	12	6	0	0	*0*	*0*	0	0	*0*	2	10	*46*
Days Minimum Temp. ≤ 32°F	29	*27*	27	17	5	*0*	*0*	0	2	13	21	28	*169*
Days Minimum Temp. ≤ 0°F	*5*	*4*	1	0	0	*0*	*0*	0	0	*0*	0	2	*12*
Heating Degree Days (base 65°F)	*1,314*	*1,137*	1,026	626	325	*106*	*33*	50	200	534	804	1,146	*7,301*
Cooling Degree Days (base 65°F)	0	*0*	0	3	14	*68*	*127*	104	30	1	0	0	*347*
Mean Precipitation (in.)	1.69	*1.48*	2.09	2.79	2.86	*3.75*	*3.19*	2.84	3.37	2.46	2.67	2.05	*31.24*
Extreme Maximum Daily Precip. (in.)	*3.00*	*1.25*	*1.55*	1.73	*2.20*	*4.67*	*2.30*	2.90	2.40	2.05	2.06	*1.30*	*4.67*
Days With ≥ 0.1" Precipitation	4	*4*	6	7	7	*7*	7	6	6	6	6	5	*71*
Days With ≥ 0.5" Precipitation	1	*1*	1	2	2	*2*	2	2	2	1	1	1	*18*
Days With ≥ 1.0" Precipitation	0	*0*	0	0	0	*1*	0	1	1	0	0	0	*3*
Mean Snowfall (in.)	*11.1*	*9.1*	*10.3*	1.5	trace	*trace*	0.0	0.0	0.0	*trace*	3.6	9.2	*44.8*
Maximum Snow Depth (in.)	23	*28*	36	9	trace	*trace*	0	0	0	*trace*	*14*	14	*36*
Days With ≥ 1.0" Snow Depth	*19*	*18*	12	1	0	*0*	0	0	0	*0*	4	13	*67*

Boonville 2 SSW *Oneida County*   Elevation: 1,580 ft.   Latitude: 43° 27' N   Longitude: 75° 21' W

	JAN	FEB	MAR	APR	MAY	JUN	JUL	AUG	SEP	OCT	NOV	DEC	YEAR
Mean Maximum Temp. (°F)	24.7	27.9	36.1	50.5	63.0	71.3	74.9	73.9	65.9	53.9	41.4	29.8	51.1
Mean Temp. (°F)	16.5	19.1	27.5	41.2	53.1	61.6	65.8	64.7	56.9	45.3	34.4	22.6	42.4
Mean Minimum Temp. (°F)	8.3	10.2	18.8	31.9	43.0	52.0	56.7	55.4	47.8	36.6	27.4	15.3	33.6
Extreme Maximum Temp. (°F)	57	55	77	86	88	89	94	90	89	79	68	62	94
Extreme Minimum Temp. (°F)	-31	-22	-18	0	22	29	33	38	25	17	0	-33	-33
Days Maximum Temp. ≥ 90°F	0	0	0	0	0	0	0	0	0	0	0	0	0
Days Maximum Temp. ≤ 32°F	24	19	12	2	0	0	0	0	0	0	6	19	82
Days Minimum Temp. ≤ 32°F	30	27	28	17	3	0	0	0	1	11	22	29	168
Days Minimum Temp. ≤ 0°F	9	7	3	0	0	0	0	0	0	0	0	4	23
Heating Degree Days (base 65°F)	1,498	1,291	1,157	709	373	140	53	74	253	604	910	1,307	8,369
Cooling Degree Days (base 65°F)	0	0	0	1	10	46	86	71	16	0	0	0	230
Mean Precipitation (in.)	4.99	3.95	4.48	4.49	4.52	4.69	4.37	4.69	5.50	5.57	5.37	5.46	58.08
Extreme Maximum Daily Precip. (in.)	3.11	2.65	1.90	3.18	2.66	3.11	3.67	3.01	4.86	3.08	3.15	1.97	4.86
Days With ≥ 0.1" Precipitation	12	10	10	9	9	9	8	8	10	11	12	11	116
Days With ≥ 0.5" Precipitation	3	2	3	3	3	3	3	3	4	4	3	3	37
Days With ≥ 1.0" Precipitation	1	1	1	1	1	1	1	1	2	1	1	1	13
Mean Snowfall (in.)	52.9	39.8	31.4	8.5	0.2	trace	0.0	0.0	trace	2.2	17.8	44.7	197.5
Maximum Snow Depth (in.)	51	48	57	48	2	trace	0	0	trace	9	21	35	57
Days With ≥ 1.0" Snow Depth	29	28	29	10	0	0	0	0	0	1	11	26	134

The period of record for all cooperative weather station data is 1980 – 2009. See User Guide for detailed explanation of data.

Bridgehampton *Suffolk County*   Elevation: 60 ft.   Latitude: 40° 57' N   Longitude: 72° 18' W

	JAN	FEB	MAR	APR	MAY	JUN	JUL	AUG	SEP	OCT	NOV	DEC	YEAR
Mean Maximum Temp. (°F)	38.7	40.4	46.6	56.1	65.9	75.1	80.9	80.2	73.6	63.2	53.5	43.8	59.8
Mean Temp. (°F)	31.0	32.6	38.5	47.6	56.8	66.3	72.1	71.4	64.4	53.8	45.2	35.9	51.3
Mean Minimum Temp. (°F)	23.2	24.8	30.3	39.0	47.6	57.4	63.3	62.7	55.2	44.4	36.8	27.9	42.7
Extreme Maximum Temp. (°F)	67	63	79	92	93	95	102	98	93	83	75	70	102
Extreme Minimum Temp. (°F)	-11	0	6	14	29	39	48	41	35	24	10	-5	-11
Days Maximum Temp. ≥ 90°F	0	0	0	0	0	1	2	2	0	0	0	0	5
Days Maximum Temp. ≤ 32°F	8	5	1	0	0	0	0	0	0	0	0	3	17
Days Minimum Temp. ≤ 32°F	26	23	19	5	0	0	0	0	0	3	11	22	109
Days Minimum Temp. ≤ 0°F	0	0	0	0	0	0	0	0	0	0	0	0	0
Heating Degree Days (base 65°F)	1,047	908	815	518	260	51	4	7	80	347	589	897	5,523
Cooling Degree Days (base 65°F)	0	0	0	1	11	97	232	214	70	7	0	0	632
Mean Precipitation (in.)	3.99	3.52	4.86	4.65	3.73	4.18	3.41	3.95	4.44	4.19	4.41	4.32	49.65
Extreme Maximum Daily Precip. (in.)	2.35	2.49	3.96	3.46	3.25	6.61	3.55	7.04	5.87	5.69	3.19	3.27	7.04
Days With ≥ 0.1" Precipitation	7	6	7	8	7	6	5	5	6	6	7	8	78
Days With ≥ 0.5" Precipitation	3	2	3	3	2	3	2	2	3	3	3	3	32
Days With ≥ 1.0" Precipitation	1	1	1	1	1	1	1	1	1	1	1	1	12
Mean Snowfall (in.)	7.7	7.9	5.3	0.9	0.0	0.0	0.0	0.0	0.0	trace	0.7	4.0	26.5
Maximum Snow Depth (in.)	27	24	13	8	0	0	0	0	0	trace	7	18	27
Days With ≥ 1.0" Snow Depth	8	6	3	0	0	0	0	0	0	0	0	3	20

Canton 4 SE *St. Lawrence County*   Elevation: 439 ft.   Latitude: 44° 34' N   Longitude: 75° 07' W

	JAN	FEB	MAR	APR	MAY	JUN	JUL	AUG	SEP	OCT	NOV	DEC	YEAR
Mean Maximum Temp. (°F)	26.2	29.4	38.7	53.3	65.7	74.4	79.0	77.5	69.4	56.8	44.8	32.3	54.0
Mean Temp. (°F)	15.8	18.6	28.5	43.1	54.9	64.0	68.7	66.8	58.6	46.8	36.4	23.2	43.8
Mean Minimum Temp. (°F)	5.3	7.7	18.4	32.8	44.1	53.6	58.4	56.1	47.7	36.7	27.9	14.1	33.6
Extreme Maximum Temp. (°F)	66	65	92	89	90	93	93	97	93	82	76	69	97
Extreme Minimum Temp. (°F)	-40	-37	-26	6	23	29	35	33	22	15	-5	-37	-40
Days Maximum Temp. ≥ 90°F	0	0	0	0	0	0	1	1	0	0	0	0	2
Days Maximum Temp. ≤ 32°F	20	17	10	1	0	0	0	0	0	0	3	15	66
Days Minimum Temp. ≤ 32°F	30	26	27	15	3	0	0	0	2	11	20	28	162
Days Minimum Temp. ≤ 0°F	12	10	3	0	0	0	0	0	0	0	0	6	31
Heating Degree Days (base 65°F)	1,521	1,308	1,124	653	323	102	30	59	218	559	851	1,287	8,035
Cooling Degree Days (base 65°F)	0	0	0	2	17	80	153	122	33	3	0	0	410
Mean Precipitation (in.)	2.10	1.79	2.13	2.90	3.11	3.26	3.86	3.67	4.03	3.86	3.37	2.56	36.64
Extreme Maximum Daily Precip. (in.)	1.30	1.58	1.17	1.43	1.86	1.75	4.10	2.85	3.20	2.35	2.68	1.46	4.10
Days With ≥ 0.1" Precipitation	6	5	6	7	8	7	7	7	8	8	8	6	83
Days With ≥ 0.5" Precipitation	1	1	1	2	2	2	2	2	3	2	2	1	21
Days With ≥ 1.0" Precipitation	0	0	0	0	0	0	1	1	1	1	0	0	4
Mean Snowfall (in.)	20.1	16.9	12.4	3.6	trace	0.0	0.0	0.0	trace	0.6	5.8	18.5	77.9
Maximum Snow Depth (in.)	30	33	38	11	1	0	0	0	trace	8	8	24	38
Days With ≥ 1.0" Snow Depth	25	23	17	2	0	0	0	0	0	0	6	19	92

Chazy *Clinton County*   Elevation: 169 ft.   Latitude: 44° 53' N   Longitude: 73° 26' W

	JAN	FEB	MAR	APR	MAY	JUN	JUL	AUG	SEP	OCT	NOV	DEC	YEAR
Mean Maximum Temp. (°F)	27.4	30.4	40.1	55.4	67.8	76.3	80.4	78.7	70.1	57.2	44.8	32.9	55.1
Mean Temp. (°F)	17.7	20.2	30.1	44.7	56.3	65.2	69.8	68.0	59.8	48.0	37.0	24.5	45.1
Mean Minimum Temp. (°F)	8.0	10.0	20.2	34.0	44.8	54.1	59.1	57.3	49.5	38.6	29.2	16.1	35.1
Extreme Maximum Temp. (°F)	61	60	79	91	91	97	96	100	95	85	74	66	100
Extreme Minimum Temp. (°F)	-44	-41	-28	6	27	30	38	36	22	17	-2	-26	-44
Days Maximum Temp. ≥ 90°F	0	0	0	0	0	1	1	1	0	0	0	0	3
Days Maximum Temp. ≤ 32°F	20	16	7	0	0	0	0	0	0	0	3	14	60
Days Minimum Temp. ≤ 32°F	29	26	26	14	2	0	0	0	1	9	19	27	153
Days Minimum Temp. ≤ 0°F	10	8	3	0	0	0	0	0	0	0	0	4	25
Heating Degree Days (base 65°F)	1,460	1,260	1,074	604	275	73	16	36	181	523	833	1,249	7,584
Cooling Degree Days (base 65°F)	0	0	0	3	14	84	170	136	32	2	0	0	441
Mean Precipitation (in.)	*0.78*	na	*0.85*	2.25	2.94	3.46	3.53	3.81	3.23	3.05	*2.21*	*0.81*	na
Extreme Maximum Daily Precip. (in.)	*1.30*	na	*1.80*	2.10	1.65	*2.66*	1.76	2.98	2.80	*2.85*	*4.27*	*1.30*	na
Days With ≥ 0.1" Precipitation	*2*	*2*	2	5	7	7	7	7	6	6	*4*	*2*	*57*
Days With ≥ 0.5" Precipitation	*0*	*0*	0	2	2	2	3	3	2	2	*1*	*1*	*18*
Days With ≥ 1.0" Precipitation	*0*	*0*	0	0	0	1	1	1	1	1	*0*	*0*	*5*
Mean Snowfall (in.)	13.7	*12.7*	11.1	2.9	0.1	0.0	0.0	0.0	0.0	0.3	*4.6*	11.2	*56.6*
Maximum Snow Depth (in.)	30	31	50	15	0	0	0	0	0	0	*12*	20	*50*
Days With ≥ 1.0" Snow Depth	22	21	16	2	0	0	0	0	0	0	*4*	16	*81*

Conklingville Dam *Saratoga County*   Elevation: 808 ft.   Latitude: 43° 19' N   Longitude: 73° 56' W

	JAN	FEB	MAR	APR	MAY	JUN	JUL	AUG	SEP	OCT	NOV	DEC	YEAR
Mean Maximum Temp. (°F)	29.4	*33.1*	*41.1*	54.3	*66.3*	*74.1*	*78.3*	76.6	69.1	57.8	*45.8*	*33.4*	*54.9*
Mean Temp. (°F)	19.4	*22.3*	*31.1*	43.7	*55.4*	64.0	*68.4*	66.9	59.3	48.1	*37.8*	*25.2*	*45.1*
Mean Minimum Temp. (°F)	9.4	11.5	*20.9*	33.1	*44.6*	53.7	*58.4*	57.2	49.4	38.3	*29.7*	*17.0*	*35.3*
Extreme Maximum Temp. (°F)	60	61	80	87	89	92	95	91	88	80	75	67	95
Extreme Minimum Temp. (°F)	-29	-22	-13	7	27	30	44	35	28	22	8	-22	-29
Days Maximum Temp. ≥ 90°F	0	0	0	0	0	0	1	0	0	0	0	0	1
Days Maximum Temp. ≤ 32°F	18	12	5	0	0	0	0	0	0	0	1	12	48
Days Minimum Temp. ≤ 32°F	29	25	26	14	1	0	0	0	0	7	18	27	147
Days Minimum Temp. ≤ 0°F	8	5	1	0	0	0	0	0	0	0	0	3	17
Heating Degree Days (base 65°F)	1,408	*1,202*	*1,046*	633	*302*	*89*	*19*	*39*	189	519	*809*	*1,228*	*7,483*
Cooling Degree Days (base 65°F)	0	*0*	*0*	0	*13*	64	*131*	105	24	0	*0*	*0*	*339*
Mean Precipitation (in.)	3.35	2.77	3.96	3.69	4.06	4.06	4.19	4.02	3.76	3.71	3.84	3.75	45.16
Extreme Maximum Daily Precip. (in.)	2.53	1.71	2.70	2.97	*2.67*	2.25	2.85	2.25	4.01	2.83	2.90	*2.38*	*4.01*
Days With ≥ 0.1" Precipitation	7	6	7	7	8	8	7	6	6	7	7	7	83
Days With ≥ 0.5" Precipitation	2	2	3	2	3	3	3	3	2	2	2	2	29
Days With ≥ 1.0" Precipitation	1	1	1	1	1	1	1	1	1	1	1	1	12
Mean Snowfall (in.)	19.9	13.8	13.8	2.6	trace	0.0	0.0	0.0	0.0	0.1	3.7	16.5	70.4
Maximum Snow Depth (in.)	39	37	45	20	1	0	0	0	0	trace	16	23	45
Days With ≥ 1.0" Snow Depth	24	25	20	3	0	0	0	0	0	0	3	19	94

The period of record for all cooperative weather station data is 1980 – 2009. See User Guide for detailed explanation of data.

Dannemora *Clinton County*   Elevation: 1,339 ft.   Latitude: 44° 43' N   Longitude: 73° 43' W

	JAN	FEB	MAR	APR	MAY	JUN	JUL	AUG	SEP	OCT	NOV	DEC	YEAR
Mean Maximum Temp. (°F)	25.7	29.5	38.4	52.6	65.4	74.0	78.0	76.1	68.5	55.7	42.5	31.0	53.1
Mean Temp. (°F)	16.9	20.4	29.3	43.0	55.0	64.0	68.2	66.4	58.6	46.9	35.1	23.1	43.9
Mean Minimum Temp. (°F)	8.1	11.3	20.2	33.3	44.5	53.9	58.5	56.7	48.8	38.0	27.7	15.1	34.7
Extreme Maximum Temp. (°F)	64	62	77	87	88	94	96	93	93	79	70	65	96
Extreme Minimum Temp. (°F)	-34	-23	-22	2	18	32	42	33	25	17	0	-28	-34
Days Maximum Temp. ≥ 90°F	0	0	0	0	0	1	1	0	0	0	0	0	2
Days Maximum Temp. ≤ 32°F	22	18	10	1	0	0	0	0	0	0	5	17	73
Days Minimum Temp. ≤ 32°F	30	27	27	14	2	0	0	0	1	9	21	29	160
Days Minimum Temp. ≤ 0°F	9	6	2	0	0	0	0	0	0	0	0	4	21
Heating Degree Days (base 65°F)	1,485	1,255	1,098	657	319	97	23	49	210	556	890	1,294	7,933
Cooling Degree Days (base 65°F)	0	0	0	0	15	73	131	100	25	1	0	0	347
Mean Precipitation (in.)	2.45	2.12	2.53	3.32	3.63	3.98	4.18	4.40	3.85	3.94	3.61	2.92	40.93
Extreme Maximum Daily Precip. (in.)	2.79	2.10	1.78	2.30	1.62	1.95	3.01	2.80	4.55	3.09	3.64	2.41	4.55
Days With ≥ 0.1" Precipitation	6	6	8	8	9	9	9	9	8	9	8	8	97
Days With ≥ 0.5" Precipitation	2	1	1	2	2	3	3	3	3	3	2	2	27
Days With ≥ 1.0" Precipitation	0	0	0	0	0	1	1	1	1	1	1	0	6
Mean Snowfall (in.)	na	na	na	*trace*	0.0	0.0	0.0	0.0	0.0	trace	*1.0*	na	na
Maximum Snow Depth (in.)	na	na	na	na	na	na	na	na	na	na	na	na	na
Days With ≥ 1.0" Snow Depth	na	na	na	0	0	0	0	0	0	0	0	na	na

Delhi 2 SE *Delaware County*   Elevation: 1,439 ft.   Latitude: 42° 15' N   Longitude: 74° 54' W

	JAN	FEB	MAR	APR	MAY	JUN	JUL	AUG	SEP	OCT	NOV	DEC	YEAR
Mean Maximum Temp. (°F)	31.1	34.3	42.3	55.4	66.7	75.1	79.2	78.3	70.7	59.4	47.3	35.7	56.3
Mean Temp. (°F)	20.9	23.4	31.4	43.6	53.9	62.7	66.7	65.7	58.3	47.1	37.8	26.7	44.8
Mean Minimum Temp. (°F)	10.6	12.4	20.5	31.8	41.0	50.3	54.2	53.1	45.8	34.7	28.2	17.7	33.3
Extreme Maximum Temp. (°F)	65	64	83	91	91	91	97	96	90	83	77	66	97
Extreme Minimum Temp. (°F)	-32	-24	-18	8	20	26	33	32	23	11	-1	-25	-32
Days Maximum Temp. ≥ 90°F	0	0	0	0	0	1	1	1	0	0	0	0	3
Days Maximum Temp. ≤ 32°F	16	12	6	0	0	0	0	0	0	0	2	12	48
Days Minimum Temp. ≤ 32°F	29	27	26	17	6	0	0	0	2	14	21	28	170
Days Minimum Temp. ≤ 0°F	8	5	2	0	0	0	0	0	0	0	0	3	18
Heating Degree Days (base 65°F)	1,362	1,170	1,035	637	349	121	48	60	218	551	811	1,180	7,542
Cooling Degree Days (base 65°F)	0	0	0	2	11	60	106	89	24	1	0	0	293
Mean Precipitation (in.)	3.23	2.49	3.54	3.94	4.24	4.60	4.55	3.64	4.38	4.02	3.90	3.45	45.98
Extreme Maximum Daily Precip. (in.)	2.05	2.00	2.17	2.46	2.77	4.31	2.91	3.40	4.49	3.15	3.62	2.54	4.49
Days With ≥ 0.1" Precipitation	8	6	8	8	9	9	8	7	7	8	8	8	94
Days With ≥ 0.5" Precipitation	2	1	2	2	3	3	3	3	3	3	3	2	30
Days With ≥ 1.0" Precipitation	0	0	0	1	1	1	1	1	1	1	1	0	8
Mean Snowfall (in.)	18.2	12.4	11.2	3.8	0.1	0.0	0.0	0.0	0.0	0.6	4.3	14.8	65.4
Maximum Snow Depth (in.)	25	23	28	17	3	0	0	0	0	0	7	9	31	31
Days With ≥ 1.0" Snow Depth	23	20	13	2	0	0	0	0	0	0	0	4	16	78

Dobbs Ferry Ardsley *Westchester County*   Elevation: 200 ft.   Latitude: 41° 00' N   Longitude: 73° 50' W

	JAN	FEB	MAR	APR	MAY	JUN	JUL	AUG	SEP	OCT	NOV	DEC	YEAR
Mean Maximum Temp. (°F)	38.7	42.3	50.5	62.4	72.4	80.6	85.2	83.6	76.4	65.3	54.3	43.3	62.9
Mean Temp. (°F)	30.9	33.5	40.7	51.4	61.1	69.8	74.8	73.6	66.2	55.1	45.4	35.6	53.2
Mean Minimum Temp. (°F)	23.1	24.6	30.8	40.4	49.6	58.9	64.3	63.5	55.9	44.9	36.4	27.8	43.4
Extreme Maximum Temp. (°F)	72	75	86	96	97	98	104	100	98	88	81	77	104
Extreme Minimum Temp. (°F)	-10	-2	2	17	29	38	49	44	34	27	12	-4	-10
Days Maximum Temp. ≥ 90°F	0	0	0	0	1	4	7	5	1	0	0	0	18
Days Maximum Temp. ≤ 32°F	8	4	1	0	0	0	0	0	0	0	0	4	17
Days Minimum Temp. ≤ 32°F	26	23	18	5	0	0	0	0	0	2	10	22	106
Days Minimum Temp. ≤ 0°F	1	0	0	0	0	0	0	0	0	0	0	0	1
Heating Degree Days (base 65°F)	1,049	884	748	408	160	24	1	3	64	312	582	905	5,140
Cooling Degree Days (base 65°F)	0	0	1	6	45	175	312	277	106	13	0	0	935
Mean Precipitation (in.)	3.78	3.03	4.45	4.74	4.47	4.39	4.64	4.23	4.64	4.48	4.39	4.25	51.49
Extreme Maximum Daily Precip. (in.)	3.11	2.85	2.97	5.34	2.80	4.49	3.22	3.30	7.62	3.27	3.25	3.07	7.62
Days With ≥ 0.1" Precipitation	7	6	7	8	7	7	7	6	6	6	7	7	81
Days With ≥ 0.5" Precipitation	3	2	3	3	3	3	3	3	3	3	3	3	35
Days With ≥ 1.0" Precipitation	1	1	1	1	1	1	2	1	1	1	1	1	13
Mean Snowfall (in.)	9.0	8.4	5.7	0.9	trace	0.0	0.0	0.0	0.0	0.1	0.7	5.8	30.6
Maximum Snow Depth (in.)	26	20	17	10	trace	0	0	0	0	0	2	4	14	26
Days With ≥ 1.0" Snow Depth	12	11	5	0	0	0	0	0	0	0	0	6	34

Gouverneur 3 NW *St. Lawrence County*   Elevation: 419 ft.   Latitude: 44° 21' N   Longitude: 75° 31' W

	JAN	FEB	MAR	APR	MAY	JUN	JUL	AUG	SEP	OCT	NOV	DEC	YEAR
Mean Maximum Temp. (°F)	27.3	30.6	39.8	54.8	66.9	75.8	80.1	78.8	71.0	57.7	45.4	32.9	55.1
Mean Temp. (°F)	16.5	19.3	28.9	43.6	54.6	64.0	68.3	66.7	58.8	46.9	36.6	23.6	44.0
Mean Minimum Temp. (°F)	5.7	7.9	17.9	32.3	42.1	52.1	56.5	54.6	46.5	36.0	27.7	14.2	32.8
Extreme Maximum Temp. (°F)	65	64	81	87	88	96	95	98	94	81	73	70	98
Extreme Minimum Temp. (°F)	-45	-37	-27	4	23	29	36	32	22	15	-10	-37	-45
Days Maximum Temp. ≥ 90°F	0	0	0	0	0	1	1	1	0	0	0	0	3
Days Maximum Temp. ≤ 32°F	19	16	8	1	0	0	0	0	0	0	3	14	61
Days Minimum Temp. ≤ 32°F	30	27	27	16	4	0	0	0	2	11	20	29	166
Days Minimum Temp. ≤ 0°F	12	10	4	0	0	0	0	0	0	0	0	6	32
Heating Degree Days (base 65°F)	1,498	1,288	1,114	638	327	96	29	51	209	556	846	1,278	7,930
Cooling Degree Days (base 65°F)	0	0	0	0	2	72	138	111	29	2	0	0	364
Mean Precipitation (in.)	2.30	1.97	2.24	3.00	3.09	3.26	3.60	3.44	3.94	4.04	3.72	2.72	37.32
Extreme Maximum Daily Precip. (in.)	1.56	1.45	1.68	1.95	1.72	2.48	4.18	2.50	4.51	2.06	2.70	1.72	4.51
Days With ≥ 0.1" Precipitation	6	5	6	7	7	7	7	7	8	8	9	7	84
Days With ≥ 0.5" Precipitation	1	1	1	2	2	2	3	2	3	3	2	1	22
Days With ≥ 1.0" Precipitation	0	0	0	0	0	1	1	1	1	1	1	0	6
Mean Snowfall (in.)	21.9	18.2	13.6	3.9	trace	trace	0.0	0.0	trace	1.0	6.8	19.2	84.6
Maximum Snow Depth (in.)	30	30	30	8	trace	0	0	0	trace	12	12	19	30
Days With ≥ 1.0" Snow Depth	26	25	19	2	0	0	0	0	0	0	5	20	97

The period of record for all cooperative weather station data is 1980 – 2009. See User Guide for detailed explanation of data.

Grafton *Rensselaer County*   Elevation: 1,560 ft.   Latitude: 42° 47' N   Longitude: 73° 28' W

	JAN	FEB	MAR	APR	MAY	JUN	JUL	AUG	SEP	OCT	NOV	DEC	YEAR
Mean Maximum Temp. (°F)	28.2	32.5	41.0	54.4	66.4	73.6	77.9	75.9	68.1	56.7	44.5	33.3	54.4
Mean Temp. (°F)	20.2	23.8	31.9	44.4	55.8	63.5	68.1	66.5	58.9	47.9	36.9	25.9	45.3
Mean Minimum Temp. (°F)	12.1	15.0	22.7	34.3	45.2	53.4	58.2	57.1	49.8	39.1	29.3	18.5	36.2
Extreme Maximum Temp. (°F)	61	62	83	88	86	90	93	94	89	79	76	65	94
Extreme Minimum Temp. (°F)	-26	-21	-11	5	26	32	40	32	27	18	4	-23	-26
Days Maximum Temp. ≥ 90°F	0	0	0	0	0	0	0	0	0	0	0	0	0
Days Maximum Temp. ≤ 32°F	21	15	7	0	0	0	0	0	0	0	4	15	62
Days Minimum Temp. ≤ 32°F	30	26	26	14	1	0	0	0	0	8	20	28	153
Days Minimum Temp. ≤ 0°F	6	4	1	0	0	0	0	0	0	0	0	2	13
Heating Degree Days (base 65°F)	1,383	1,161	1,020	613	293	100	24	47	201	524	835	1,205	7,406
Cooling Degree Days (base 65°F)	0	0	0	0	2	14	62	128	102	26	1	0	335
Mean Precipitation (in.)	2.88	2.57	3.56	3.87	4.53	4.15	4.51	4.46	4.19	3.98	4.00	3.21	45.91
Extreme Maximum Daily Precip. (in.)	1.50	2.60	1.95	2.14	2.06	2.52	3.75	3.50	3.58	4.75	2.65	2.56	4.75
Days With ≥ 0.1" Precipitation	7	6	9	9	9	8	8	8	7	8	9	8	96
Days With ≥ 0.5" Precipitation	2	2	3	3	3	3	3	3	3	3	3	2	33
Days With ≥ 1.0" Precipitation	0	0	1	1	1	1	1	1	1	1	1	1	10
Mean Snowfall (in.)	20.6	14.9	15.4	5.9	0.2	0.0	0.0	0.0	trace	1.2	7.2	17.8	83.2
Maximum Snow Depth (in.)	37	31	32	23	trace	0	0	0	trace	22	14	23	37
Days With ≥ 1.0" Snow Depth	24	24	18	3	0	0	0	0	0	0	5	20	94

Indian Lake 2 SW *Hamilton County*   Elevation: 1,660 ft.   Latitude: 43° 45' N   Longitude: 74° 17' W

	JAN	FEB	MAR	APR	MAY	JUN	JUL	AUG	SEP	OCT	NOV	DEC	YEAR
Mean Maximum Temp. (°F)	25.5	28.7	36.6	49.8	62.5	70.7	74.2	73.1	65.8	53.7	41.6	30.3	51.0
Mean Temp. (°F)	15.3	17.5	25.7	39.1	50.8	59.8	63.8	62.6	55.3	43.7	33.5	21.4	40.7
Mean Minimum Temp. (°F)	5.0	6.3	14.8	28.4	39.0	48.8	53.4	52.1	44.7	33.6	25.4	12.6	30.3
Extreme Maximum Temp. (°F)	55	57	74	85	85	90	91	90	89	78	68	64	91
Extreme Minimum Temp. (°F)	-35	-30	-25	-1	21	29	35	31	23	15	-2	-27	-35
Days Maximum Temp. ≥ 90°F	0	0	0	0	0	0	0	0	0	0	0	0	0
Days Maximum Temp. ≤ 32°F	22	18	11	1	0	0	0	0	0	0	5	18	75
Days Minimum Temp. ≤ 32°F	30	28	29	21	8	0	0	0	2	15	23	30	186
Days Minimum Temp. ≤ 0°F	12	11	5	0	0	0	0	0	0	0	0	6	34
Heating Degree Days (base 65°F)	1,537	1,338	1,211	770	437	178	85	111	295	653	938	1,343	8,896
Cooling Degree Days (base 65°F)	0	0	0	0	4	28	55	44	9	0	0	0	140
Mean Precipitation (in.)	2.83	2.34	2.92	3.20	3.59	3.70	3.85	3.62	3.73	4.22	3.33	2.86	40.19
Extreme Maximum Daily Precip. (in.)	1.70	2.10	2.40	2.09	2.03	3.00	2.42	2.58	3.43	3.34	2.90	1.70	3.43
Days With ≥ 0.1" Precipitation	7	6	7	7	8	8	8	8	7	8	7	7	88
Days With ≥ 0.5" Precipitation	2	1	2	2	2	2	2	3	3	2	2	2	25
Days With ≥ 1.0" Precipitation	0	0	1	1	1	1	1	1	1	1	1	0	9
Mean Snowfall (in.)	na	na	na	3.0	0.1	0.0	0.0	0.0	0.0	0.7	na	na	na
Maximum Snow Depth (in.)	na	na	na	na	na	na	na	na	na	na	na	na	na
Days With ≥ 1.0" Snow Depth	na	na	na	4	0	0	0	0	0	1	na	na	na

Ithaca Cornell Univ *Tompkins County*   Elevation: 959 ft.   Latitude: 42° 27' N   Longitude: 76° 27' W

	JAN	FEB	MAR	APR	MAY	JUN	JUL	AUG	SEP	OCT	NOV	DEC	YEAR
Mean Maximum Temp. (°F)	31.2	33.6	41.4	54.8	67.0	75.5	79.5	78.6	71.2	58.9	47.3	35.8	56.2
Mean Temp. (°F)	23.0	24.7	32.2	44.6	55.4	64.4	68.7	67.7	60.3	48.8	39.3	28.5	46.5
Mean Minimum Temp. (°F)	14.7	15.7	22.9	34.3	43.8	53.4	57.7	56.7	49.3	38.6	31.4	21.1	36.6
Extreme Maximum Temp. (°F)	66	67	83	91	93	94	98	97	92	84	78	69	98
Extreme Minimum Temp. (°F)	-24	-18	-17	11	25	31	40	34	24	18	2	-19	-24
Days Maximum Temp. ≥ 90°F	0	0	0	0	0	1	2	1	0	0	0	0	4
Days Maximum Temp. ≤ 32°F	17	13	7	1	0	0	0	0	0	0	2	12	52
Days Minimum Temp. ≤ 32°F	29	26	25	13	4	0	0	0	1	8	17	27	150
Days Minimum Temp. ≤ 0°F	5	3	1	0	0	0	0	0	0	0	0	2	11
Heating Degree Days (base 65°F)	1,297	1,132	1,011	609	309	96	30	42	175	500	763	1,126	7,090
Cooling Degree Days (base 65°F)	0	0	1	4	20	86	150	133	41	3	0	0	438
Mean Precipitation (in.)	1.99	1.83	2.76	3.27	3.16	3.91	3.86	3.54	3.69	3.29	3.16	2.32	36.78
Extreme Maximum Daily Precip. (in.)	1.87	1.52	2.06	2.13	2.25	2.04	2.08	3.30	3.90	5.08	4.02	1.87	5.08
Days With ≥ 0.1" Precipitation	6	5	6	8	8	9	8	7	7	7	7	6	84
Days With ≥ 0.5" Precipitation	1	1	1	2	2	2	3	2	2	2	2	1	21
Days With ≥ 1.0" Precipitation	0	0	0	0	0	1	1	1	1	1	0	0	5
Mean Snowfall (in.)	17.3	12.7	12.2	3.6	0.0	0.0	0.0	0.0	0.0	0.4	4.8	12.9	63.9
Maximum Snow Depth (in.)	19	20	28	14	0	0	0	0	0	5	12	11	28
Days With ≥ 1.0" Snow Depth	21	20	12	2	0	0	0	0	0	0	4	15	74

Lowville *Lewis County*   Elevation: 859 ft.   Latitude: 43° 48' N   Longitude: 75° 29' W

	JAN	FEB	MAR	APR	MAY	JUN	JUL	AUG	SEP	OCT	NOV	DEC	YEAR
Mean Maximum Temp. (°F)	26.2	29.1	37.5	52.4	65.0	73.6	77.9	76.7	68.7	56.1	43.7	31.6	53.2
Mean Temp. (°F)	16.7	19.1	28.1	42.4	53.9	62.9	67.2	65.8	57.7	46.3	35.7	23.4	43.3
Mean Minimum Temp. (°F)	7.2	9.1	18.6	32.4	42.7	52.2	56.5	54.8	46.7	36.5	27.6	15.0	33.3
Extreme Maximum Temp. (°F)	62	59	80	87	88	97	94	96	92	81	72	67	97
Extreme Minimum Temp. (°F)	-35	-28	-25	5	23	28	39	32	24	18	-1	-29	-35
Days Maximum Temp. ≥ 90°F	0	0	0	0	0	1	1	1	0	0	0	0	3
Days Maximum Temp. ≤ 32°F	21	17	10	1	0	0	0	0	0	0	4	15	68
Days Minimum Temp. ≤ 32°F	30	27	27	17	3	0	0	0	2	11	21	29	167
Days Minimum Temp. ≤ 0°F	10	9	3	0	0	0	0	0	0	0	0	5	27
Heating Degree Days (base 65°F)	1,491	1,292	1,138	673	349	119	40	65	235	573	873	1,285	8,133
Cooling Degree Days (base 65°F)	0	0	0	2	11	63	116	95	23	1	0	0	311
Mean Precipitation (in.)	3.16	2.49	2.73	3.23	3.34	3.35	3.63	3.70	3.96	4.09	3.92	3.64	41.24
Extreme Maximum Daily Precip. (in.)	2.35	2.03	2.12	2.27	2.45	2.10	2.25	3.05	4.78	2.60	3.30	2.02	4.78
Days With ≥ 0.1" Precipitation	8	7	7	7	8	7	7	7	8	9	9	10	94
Days With ≥ 0.5" Precipitation	2	1	2	2	2	2	2	2	3	3	2	2	25
Days With ≥ 1.0" Precipitation	0	0	0	1	1	1	1	1	1	1	1	0	8
Mean Snowfall (in.)	33.0	25.7	14.9	4.7	0.1	0.0	0.0	0.0	trace	0.8	9.3	32.9	121.4
Maximum Snow Depth (in.)	33	26	27	16	1	0	0	0	trace	8	11	28	33
Days With ≥ 1.0" Snow Depth	27	26	20	4	0	0	0	0	0	1	7	23	107

The period of record for all cooperative weather station data is 1980 – 2009. See User Guide for detailed explanation of data.

Middletown 2 NW *Orange County*   Elevation: 700 ft.   Latitude: 41° 28' N   Longitude: 74° 27' W

	JAN	FEB	MAR	APR	MAY	JUN	JUL	AUG	SEP	OCT	NOV	DEC	YEAR
Mean Maximum Temp. (°F)	35.4	39.2	48.1	61.1	71.5	79.4	83.4	82.1	74.9	63.4	51.4	39.7	60.8
Mean Temp. (°F)	27.0	29.8	37.9	50.2	60.4	68.9	73.2	71.9	64.6	53.2	42.9	32.1	51.0
Mean Minimum Temp. (°F)	18.5	20.4	27.7	39.3	49.2	58.3	63.0	61.6	54.3	43.0	34.3	24.5	41.2
Extreme Maximum Temp. (°F)	66	71	85	91	92	93	101	97	94	87	78	71	101
Extreme Minimum Temp. (°F)	-23	-8	-7	17	26	40	47	41	27	19	12	-10	-23
Days Maximum Temp. ≥ 90°F	0	0	0	0	0	2	4	3	1	0	0	0	10
Days Maximum Temp. ≤ 32°F	12	7	2	0	0	0	0	0	0	0	0	7	28
Days Minimum Temp. ≤ 32°F	28	25	21	5	0	0	0	0	0	3	14	25	121
Days Minimum Temp. ≤ 0°F	2	1	0	0	0	0	0	0	0	0	0	0	3
Heating Degree Days (base 65°F)	1,172	990	832	443	177	30	3	7	85	364	658	1,012	5,773
Cooling Degree Days (base 65°F)	0	0	0	0	6	40	153	265	227	80	7	0	778
Mean Precipitation (in.)	2.66	2.34	3.14	4.03	4.13	4.47	3.98	3.98	4.15	3.76	3.58	3.14	43.36
Extreme Maximum Daily Precip. (in.)	2.00	2.52	2.45	3.46	2.51	2.95	2.49	5.00	3.00	4.12	1.94	2.87	5.00
Days With ≥ 0.1" Precipitation	6	5	6	7	8	8	7	6	6	6	6	6	77
Days With ≥ 0.5" Precipitation	2	2	2	3	3	3	3	3	3	3	3	2	32
Days With ≥ 1.0" Precipitation	0	0	1	1	1	1	1	1	1	1	1	1	10
Mean Snowfall (in.)	na	na	na	trace	0.0	0.0	0.0	0.0	0.0	0.0	0.2	na	na
Maximum Snow Depth (in.)	na	na	na	na	na	na	na	na	na	na	na	na	na
Days With ≥ 1.0" Snow Depth	na	na	na	0	0	0	0	0	0	0	0	na	na

Mineola *Nassau County*   Elevation: 96 ft.   Latitude: 40° 44' N   Longitude: 73° 37' W

	JAN	FEB	MAR	APR	MAY	JUN	JUL	AUG	SEP	OCT	NOV	DEC	YEAR
Mean Maximum Temp. (°F)	39.1	42.2	49.4	59.4	69.2	78.8	83.7	82.4	75.1	64.4	55.1	44.3	61.9
Mean Temp. (°F)	32.4	34.7	41.4	50.6	59.7	69.5	74.8	73.7	66.5	56.0	47.5	37.6	53.7
Mean Minimum Temp. (°F)	25.7	27.3	33.2	41.8	50.2	60.2	65.9	64.9	57.8	47.3	39.8	30.8	45.4
Extreme Maximum Temp. (°F)	71	73	85	94	97	101	103	105	95	89	79	76	105
Extreme Minimum Temp. (°F)	-4	3	5	13	34	43	50	46	38	29	18	-1	-4
Days Maximum Temp. ≥ 90°F	0	0	0	0	1	3	6	4	1	0	0	0	15
Days Maximum Temp. ≤ 32°F	8	4	1	0	0	0	0	0	0	0	0	3	16
Days Minimum Temp. ≤ 32°F	23	20	14	2	0	0	0	0	0	0	5	18	82
Days Minimum Temp. ≤ 0°F	0	0	0	0	0	0	0	0	0	0	0	0	0
Heating Degree Days (base 65°F)	1,002	850	725	430	190	23	1	4	56	287	519	844	4,931
Cooling Degree Days (base 65°F)	0	0	0	4	34	167	313	279	107	14	0	0	918
Mean Precipitation (in.)	3.49	2.72	4.28	4.37	3.99	3.90	4.36	3.65	3.81	4.01	3.78	3.72	46.08
Extreme Maximum Daily Precip. (in.)	4.05	2.05	3.11	3.72	2.87	4.30	3.82	4.04	3.52	4.02	2.92	2.95	4.30
Days With ≥ 0.1" Precipitation	6	5	7	7	7	6	6	6	5	6	6	7	74
Days With ≥ 0.5" Precipitation	2	2	3	3	3	3	3	2	3	3	3	3	33
Days With ≥ 1.0" Precipitation	1	1	1	1	1	1	1	1	1	1	1	1	12
Mean Snowfall (in.)	4.9	6.4	3.6	0.6	0.0	0.0	0.0	0.0	0.0	0.0	0.1	4.2	19.8
Maximum Snow Depth (in.)	12	20	8	9	0	0	0	0	0	0	3	14	20
Days With ≥ 1.0" Snow Depth	7	6	2	0	0	0	0	0	0	0	0	3	18

Morrisville 5 SW *Madison County*   Elevation: 1,299 ft.   Latitude: 42° 50' N   Longitude: 75° 44' W

	JAN	FEB	MAR	APR	MAY	JUN	JUL	AUG	SEP	OCT	NOV	DEC	YEAR
Mean Maximum Temp. (°F)	28.7	32.0	39.9	53.9	65.8	73.8	77.5	76.0	69.1	56.6	44.8	33.6	54.3
Mean Temp. (°F)	20.0	22.6	30.2	43.5	54.6	63.0	67.0	65.6	58.8	47.0	37.1	26.2	44.6
Mean Minimum Temp. (°F)	11.4	13.1	20.4	33.1	43.4	52.2	56.3	55.3	48.5	37.3	29.3	18.7	34.9
Extreme Maximum Temp. (°F)	60	60	82	87	87	89	92	90	89	80	75	64	92
Extreme Minimum Temp. (°F)	-27	-25	-21	4	24	30	36	35	24	16	1	-30	-30
Days Maximum Temp. ≥ 90°F	0	0	0	0	0	0	0	0	0	0	0	0	0
Days Maximum Temp. ≤ 32°F	19	15	9	1	0	0	0	0	0	0	3	15	62
Days Minimum Temp. ≤ 32°F	29	26	26	15	3	0	0	0	1	9	20	28	157
Days Minimum Temp. ≤ 0°F	7	5	2	0	0	0	0	0	0	0	0	2	16
Heating Degree Days (base 65°F)	1,388	1,192	1,074	641	325	108	36	57	203	551	830	1,196	7,601
Cooling Degree Days (base 65°F)	0	0	0	2	10	57	104	84	25	1	0	0	283
Mean Precipitation (in.)	3.15	2.99	3.38	3.66	4.09	4.48	4.02	3.57	4.32	4.08	3.94	3.88	45.56
Extreme Maximum Daily Precip. (in.)	1.65	2.39	1.55	2.15	3.39	2.80	2.08	2.36	4.11	2.10	2.89	1.67	4.11
Days With ≥ 0.1" Precipitation	10	8	9	8	9	8	7	7	8	9	9	11	103
Days With ≥ 0.5" Precipitation	1	2	2	2	3	3	3	2	3	3	2	2	28
Days With ≥ 1.0" Precipitation	0	0	0	0	1	1	1	1	1	1	1	0	7
Mean Snowfall (in.)	30.5	25.7	21.1	5.6	0.2	0.0	0.0	0.0	trace	1.5	12.0	27.5	124.1
Maximum Snow Depth (in.)	45	51	44	29	4	0	0	0	trace	17	16	30	51
Days With ≥ 1.0" Snow Depth	27	27	22	5	0	0	0	0	0	1	9	24	115

New York Ave V Brooklyn *Kings County*   Elevation: 20 ft.   Latitude: 40° 36' N   Longitude: 73° 59' W

	JAN	FEB	MAR	APR	MAY	JUN	JUL	AUG	SEP	OCT	NOV	DEC	YEAR
Mean Maximum Temp. (°F)	39.5	42.3	49.6	60.2	70.4	79.5	84.5	83.3	76.1	64.8	54.6	43.6	62.4
Mean Temp. (°F)	33.4	35.7	42.3	52.4	62.3	71.7	77.1	76.1	68.9	57.6	48.1	37.8	55.3
Mean Minimum Temp. (°F)	27.2	29.0	34.9	44.5	54.2	63.8	69.7	68.9	61.7	50.3	41.5	31.9	48.2
Extreme Maximum Temp. (°F)	70	73	83	91	96	97	103	101	98	86	79	75	103
Extreme Minimum Temp. (°F)	-4	6	10	19	40	48	57	51	44	36	23	-1	-4
Days Maximum Temp. ≥ 90°F	0	0	0	0	1	3	6	4	1	0	0	0	15
Days Maximum Temp. ≤ 32°F	7	4	1	0	0	0	0	0	0	0	0	4	16
Days Minimum Temp. ≤ 32°F	21	18	11	1	0	0	0	0	0	0	3	15	69
Days Minimum Temp. ≤ 0°F	0	0	0	0	0	0	0	0	0	0	0	0	0
Heating Degree Days (base 65°F)	973	822	697	378	130	13	0	1	29	241	501	836	4,621
Cooling Degree Days (base 65°F)	0	0	0	6	54	220	382	353	153	18	1	0	1,187
Mean Precipitation (in.)	3.54	2.66	4.22	4.36	4.19	3.92	4.83	3.68	3.73	3.73	3.78	3.32	45.96
Extreme Maximum Daily Precip. (in.)	3.13	1.68	2.92	5.46	2.36	2.91	4.62	2.85	4.44	4.29	2.68	2.49	5.46
Days With ≥ 0.1" Precipitation	7	6	7	7	7	7	7	6	6	5	6	6	77
Days With ≥ 0.5" Precipitation	3	2	3	2	3	3	3	3	2	2	3	3	32
Days With ≥ 1.0" Precipitation	1	1	1	1	1	1	2	1	1	1	1	1	13
Mean Snowfall (in.)	6.6	7.3	3.9	0.7	0.0	0.0	0.0	0.0	0.0	0.0	trace	0.3	3.5	22.3
Maximum Snow Depth (in.)	23	20	10	9	0	0	0	0	0	0	trace	4	12	23
Days With ≥ 1.0" Snow Depth	7	6	3	0	0	0	0	0	0	0	0	0	2	18

The period of record for all cooperative weather station data is 1980 – 2009. See User Guide for detailed explanation of data.

Peru 2 WSW *Clinton County*   Elevation: 509 ft.   Latitude: 44° 34' N   Longitude: 73° 34' W

	JAN	FEB	MAR	APR	MAY	JUN	JUL	AUG	SEP	OCT	NOV	DEC	YEAR
Mean Maximum Temp. (°F)	27.9	31.7	41.0	55.7	68.4	77.2	81.4	79.4	71.0	57.9	45.4	33.3	55.8
Mean Temp. (°F)	18.6	21.9	31.1	44.7	56.5	65.7	70.2	68.0	59.9	48.0	37.3	25.1	45.6
Mean Minimum Temp. (°F)	9.2	12.1	21.2	33.8	44.6	54.2	58.9	56.5	48.7	37.9	29.1	16.8	35.3
Extreme Maximum Temp. (°F)	65	63	83	92	93	98	98	98	95	84	75	69	98
Extreme Minimum Temp. (°F)	-34	-30	-17	5	25	29	40	37	24	18	1	-26	-34
Days Maximum Temp. ≥ 90°F	0	0	0	0	0	1	3	2	0	0	0	0	6
Days Maximum Temp. ≤ 32°F	20	15	7	0	0	0	0	0	0	0	3	14	59
Days Minimum Temp. ≤ 32°F	29	26	26	14	2	0	0	0	1	9	19	28	154
Days Minimum Temp. ≤ 0°F	8	6	2	0	0	0	0	0	0	0	0	4	20
Heating Degree Days (base 65°F)	1,434	1,212	1,043	604	276	70	13	37	182	523	825	1,231	7,450
Cooling Degree Days (base 65°F)	0	0	0	3	21	98	180	136	35	2	0	0	475
Mean Precipitation (in.)	1.37	1.29	1.71	2.56	2.73	3.62	3.49	3.51	2.81	3.00	2.67	1.96	30.72
Extreme Maximum Daily Precip. (in.)	1.12	1.26	1.50	1.85	2.40	4.10	3.27	3.11	4.08	2.41	4.80	1.85	4.80
Days With ≥ 0.1" Precipitation	4	3	4	6	7	7	7	7	5	6	6	4	66
Days With ≥ 0.5" Precipitation	1	1	1	2	2	2	3	2	2	2	2	1	21
Days With ≥ 1.0" Precipitation	0	0	0	0	0	1	1	1	1	1	1	0	6
Mean Snowfall (in.)	11.3	10.4	11.1	2.9	0.0	0.0	0.0	0.0	0.0	0.5	3.2	12.6	52.0
Maximum Snow Depth (in.)	na	na	na	na	na	na	na	na	na	na	na	na	na
Days With ≥ 1.0" Snow Depth	na	na	na	0	0	0	0	0	0	0	0	0	na

Riverhead Research Farm *Suffolk County*   Elevation: 100 ft.   Latitude: 40° 58' N   Longitude: 72° 43' W

	JAN	FEB	MAR	APR	MAY	JUN	JUL	AUG	SEP	OCT	NOV	DEC	YEAR
Mean Maximum Temp. (°F)	39.6	41.5	48.6	59.8	70.5	79.3	84.0	82.5	75.7	64.8	54.5	44.5	62.1
Mean Temp. (°F)	32.3	34.0	40.3	50.3	60.3	69.5	74.8	73.7	67.1	56.3	47.1	37.3	53.6
Mean Minimum Temp. (°F)	25.0	26.4	32.0	40.8	50.0	59.7	65.5	64.8	58.4	47.8	39.5	30.1	45.0
Extreme Maximum Temp. (°F)	68	67	80	92	96	97	100	99	97	85	78	76	100
Extreme Minimum Temp. (°F)	-8	4	9	18	32	42	47	45	37	28	17	0	-8
Days Maximum Temp. ≥ 90°F	0	0	0	0	1	2	5	3	0	0	0	0	11
Days Maximum Temp. ≤ 32°F	7	4	1	0	0	0	0	0	0	0	0	3	15
Days Minimum Temp. ≤ 32°F	25	21	17	3	0	0	0	0	0	1	6	19	92
Days Minimum Temp. ≤ 0°F	0	0	0	0	0	0	0	0	0	0	0	0	0
Heating Degree Days (base 65°F)	1,006	870	758	436	172	22	0	2	42	274	532	851	4,965
Cooling Degree Days (base 65°F)	0	0	0	3	33	165	310	280	111	12	0	0	914
Mean Precipitation (in.)	3.71	3.14	4.48	4.49	3.86	4.12	3.21	3.90	3.84	4.22	4.27	4.01	47.25
Extreme Maximum Daily Precip. (in.)	3.10	2.34	3.06	3.18	3.01	5.27	3.38	6.34	3.84	5.58	2.90	3.62	6.34
Days With ≥ 0.1" Precipitation	7	6	7	7	7	7	5	6	6	6	7	7	78
Days With ≥ 0.5" Precipitation	3	2	3	3	3	3	2	3	3	3	3	3	34
Days With ≥ 1.0" Precipitation	1	1	1	1	1	1	1	1	1	1	1	1	12
Mean Snowfall (in.)	8.4	7.6	5.1	0.7	0.0	0.0	0.0	0.0	0.0	0.0	0.5	4.7	27.0
Maximum Snow Depth (in.)	20	16	14	6	0	0	0	0	0	0	7	20	20
Days With ≥ 1.0" Snow Depth	9	6	3	0	0	0	0	0	0	0	0	3	21

Troy Lock and Dam *Rensselaer County*   Elevation: 23 ft.   Latitude: 42° 45' N   Longitude: 73° 41' W

	JAN	FEB	MAR	APR	MAY	JUN	JUL	AUG	SEP	OCT	NOV	DEC	YEAR
Mean Maximum Temp. (°F)	31.7	35.3	44.3	58.6	70.4	78.7	83.5	82.2	74.3	61.6	49.4	37.1	58.9
Mean Temp. (°F)	23.2	25.9	34.7	48.0	59.2	68.2	73.1	71.6	63.5	51.3	40.9	29.6	49.1
Mean Minimum Temp. (°F)	14.6	16.5	25.0	37.4	47.9	57.7	62.6	60.9	52.6	40.9	32.4	22.1	39.2
Extreme Maximum Temp. (°F)	66	67	84	92	92	96	101	99	93	86	81	69	101
Extreme Minimum Temp. (°F)	-23	-14	-7	15	27	39	48	40	31	23	10	-15	-23
Days Maximum Temp. ≥ 90°F	0	0	0	0	0	3	5	4	1	0	0	0	13
Days Maximum Temp. ≤ 32°F	15	11	4	0	0	0	0	0	0	0	1	9	40
Days Minimum Temp. ≤ 32°F	28	26	24	8	0	0	0	0	0	5	16	26	133
Days Minimum Temp. ≤ 0°F	5	2	1	0	0	0	0	0	0	0	0	1	9
Heating Degree Days (base 65°F)	1,290	1,098	933	506	204	40	3	12	107	423	716	1,090	6,422
Cooling Degree Days (base 65°F)	0	0	0	4	30	142	260	224	68	5	0	0	733
Mean Precipitation (in.)	2.23	1.88	2.98	3.26	3.74	4.22	4.42	4.09	3.32	3.65	3.09	2.58	39.46
Extreme Maximum Daily Precip. (in.)	1.80	1.71	3.00	2.20	2.40	2.68	2.70	2.71	3.00	2.22	2.62	2.50	3.00
Days With ≥ 0.1" Precipitation	5	5	6	7	8	7	7	8	6	7	6	6	78
Days With ≥ 0.5" Precipitation	1	1	2	2	3	3	3	3	2	3	2	2	27
Days With ≥ 1.0" Precipitation	0	0	1	1	1	1	1	1	1	1	1	0	9
Mean Snowfall (in.)	12.7	8.0	7.5	1.3	0.0	0.0	0.0	0.0	0.0	0.1	1.8	7.2	38.6
Maximum Snow Depth (in.)	38	39	30	16	0	0	0	0	0	0	10	19	39
Days With ≥ 1.0" Snow Depth	19	16	8	1	0	0	0	0	0	0	1	10	55

Tully Heiberg Forest *Cortland County*   Elevation: 1,898 ft.   Latitude: 42° 46' N   Longitude: 76° 05' W

	JAN	FEB	MAR	APR	MAY	JUN	JUL	AUG	SEP	OCT	NOV	DEC	YEAR
Mean Maximum Temp. (°F)	27.2	29.8	37.5	50.6	63.0	71.6	75.9	74.7	66.9	54.9	43.1	31.9	52.3
Mean Temp. (°F)	19.5	21.3	28.9	41.5	53.1	61.9	66.4	65.2	57.6	46.1	35.7	24.7	43.5
Mean Minimum Temp. (°F)	11.6	12.8	20.3	32.2	43.2	52.2	56.9	55.7	48.2	37.2	28.2	17.5	34.7
Extreme Maximum Temp. (°F)	61	58	80	85	88	89	93	92	89	80	74	65	93
Extreme Minimum Temp. (°F)	-21	-19	-11	5	24	30	41	33	25	17	3	-29	-29
Days Maximum Temp. ≥ 90°F	0	0	0	0	0	0	0	0	0	0	0	0	0
Days Maximum Temp. ≤ 32°F	21	17	11	2	0	0	0	0	0	0	5	16	72
Days Minimum Temp. ≤ 32°F	30	27	27	16	3	0	0	0	1	10	21	29	164
Days Minimum Temp. ≤ 0°F	6	5	1	0	0	0	0	0	0	0	0	2	14
Heating Degree Days (base 65°F)	1,406	1,228	1,113	702	374	141	50	69	238	580	872	1,241	8,014
Cooling Degree Days (base 65°F)	0	0	0	2	11	53	101	83	21	1	0	0	272
Mean Precipitation (in.)	2.85	2.67	3.33	3.96	3.99	4.85	4.00	4.04	4.80	3.97	4.00	3.28	45.74
Extreme Maximum Daily Precip. (in.)	1.91	1.30	2.22	2.23	1.85	3.22	2.30	4.24	4.98	3.56	3.56	2.68	4.98
Days With ≥ 0.1" Precipitation	9	7	9	9	9	10	8	8	8	9	9	8	103
Days With ≥ 0.5" Precipitation	1	1	2	2	2	3	2	3	3	2	3	2	27
Days With ≥ 1.0" Precipitation	0	0	0	1	1	1	1	1	1	1	1	0	8
Mean Snowfall (in.)	26.3	23.3	21.1	7.6	0.4	trace	0.0	0.0	trace	1.8	11.9	23.4	115.8
Maximum Snow Depth (in.)	47	43	60	36	5	0	0	0	trace	9	17	34	60
Days With ≥ 1.0" Snow Depth	28	27	26	8	0	0	0	0	0	1	10	24	124

The period of record for all cooperative weather station data is 1980 – 2009. See User Guide for detailed explanation of data.

Utica Oneida County Arpt *Oneida County*   Elevation: 711 ft.   Latitude: 43° 09' N   Longitude: 75° 23' W

	JAN	FEB	MAR	APR	MAY	JUN	JUL	AUG	SEP	OCT	NOV	DEC	YEAR
Mean Maximum Temp. (°F)	29.4	32.3	40.9	55.0	67.6	75.9	80.4	78.7	70.6	58.1	46.0	34.0	55.7
Mean Temp. (°F)	21.9	24.1	32.4	45.3	56.8	65.4	70.2	68.6	60.8	49.0	38.8	27.0	46.7
Mean Minimum Temp. (°F)	14.3	15.9	23.9	35.6	46.0	54.9	59.9	58.4	50.9	39.9	31.5	20.1	37.6
Extreme Maximum Temp. (°F)	65	63	85	91	91	94	96	97	92	82	79	69	97
Extreme Minimum Temp. (°F)	-27	-17	-12	9	27	33	45	40	25	21	1	-23	-27
Days Maximum Temp. ≥ 90°F	0	0	0	0	0	1	2	1	0	0	0	0	4
Days Maximum Temp. ≤ 32°F	18	15	7	0	0	0	0	0	0	0	2	13	55
Days Minimum Temp. ≤ 32°F	28	26	24	11	1	0	0	0	0	6	17	27	140
Days Minimum Temp. ≤ 0°F	5	3	1	0	0	0	0	0	0	0	0	2	11
Heating Degree Days (base 65°F)	1,328	1,149	1,005	586	269	77	12	29	162	492	780	1,170	7,059
Cooling Degree Days (base 65°F)	0	0	1	3	22	95	181	148	42	2	0	0	494
Mean Precipitation (in.)	2.94	2.38	3.15	3.47	3.90	4.28	3.86	3.88	4.10	3.66	3.91	3.37	42.90
Extreme Maximum Daily Precip. (in.)	1.64	1.88	2.31	1.96	2.75	2.98	3.24	2.80	4.14	1.88	2.35	2.11	4.14
Days With ≥ 0.1" Precipitation	8	7	8	9	9	8	7	7	7	8	10	9	97
Days With ≥ 0.5" Precipitation	1	1	2	2	2	3	3	3	3	2	2	1	25
Days With ≥ 1.0" Precipitation	0	0	1	0	1	1	1	1	1	1	1	0	8
Mean Snowfall (in.)	na	na	na	na	na	na	na	na	na	na	na	na	na
Maximum Snow Depth (in.)	33	na	na	na	na	na	na	na	na	na	na	na	na
Days With ≥ 1.0" Snow Depth	24	na	na	na	na	na	na	na	na	na	na	na	na

Valatie 1 N *Columbia County*   Elevation: 299 ft.   Latitude: 42° 26' N   Longitude: 73° 41' W

	JAN	FEB	MAR	APR	MAY	JUN	JUL	AUG	SEP	OCT	NOV	DEC	YEAR
Mean Maximum Temp. (°F)	32.2	35.9	44.2	57.7	69.4	77.5	82.2	80.9	73.4	61.1	49.2	37.2	58.4
Mean Temp. (°F)	22.6	26.1	34.2	46.6	57.6	66.2	70.7	69.6	61.7	49.6	39.9	28.3	47.8
Mean Minimum Temp. (°F)	13.0	16.2	24.0	35.3	45.7	54.9	59.2	58.2	49.9	38.1	30.6	19.5	37.1
Extreme Maximum Temp. (°F)	71	69	86	93	92	97	100	97	94	87	81	69	100
Extreme Minimum Temp. (°F)	-25	-13	-9	10	27	34	43	35	28	19	2	-20	-25
Days Maximum Temp. ≥ 90°F	0	0	0	0	0	2	4	3	1	0	0	0	10
Days Maximum Temp. ≤ 32°F	15	11	4	0	0	0	0	0	0	0	1	9	40
Days Minimum Temp. ≤ 32°F	29	26	25	12	2	0	0	0	0	9	18	27	148
Days Minimum Temp. ≤ 0°F	6	2	1	0	0	0	0	0	0	0	0	2	11
Heating Degree Days (base 65°F)	1,308	1,094	950	550	250	65	13	25	142	474	747	1,129	6,747
Cooling Degree Days (base 65°F)	0	0	1	3	27	109	197	173	48	3	0	0	561
Mean Precipitation (in.)	2.05	1.90	2.82	3.74	4.07	4.50	4.06	4.14	3.96	3.91	3.29	2.55	40.99
Extreme Maximum Daily Precip. (in.)	1.28	1.15	3.89	3.65	3.00	2.68	3.87	3.51	5.10	2.94	2.16	2.25	5.10
Days With ≥ 0.1" Precipitation	5	5	6	8	8	8	7	7	7	7	6	6	80
Days With ≥ 0.5" Precipitation	2	1	2	2	3	3	3	3	3	3	2	2	29
Days With ≥ 1.0" Precipitation	0	0	1	1	1	1	1	1	1	1	1	0	9
Mean Snowfall (in.)	10.8	8.2	6.4	2.2	0.0	0.0	0.0	0.0	0.0	0.3	2.4	11.1	41.4
Maximum Snow Depth (in.)	33	24	18	14	0	0	0	0	0	6	9	17	33
Days With ≥ 1.0" Snow Depth	18	15	8	1	0	0	0	0	0	0	1	10	53

Wales *Erie County*   Elevation: 1,089 ft.   Latitude: 42° 45' N   Longitude: 78° 31' W

	JAN	FEB	MAR	APR	MAY	JUN	JUL	AUG	SEP	OCT	NOV	DEC	YEAR
Mean Maximum Temp. (°F)	31.3	32.5	41.2	54.6	65.5	74.0	77.4	76.3	69.5	57.9	46.9	35.2	55.2
Mean Temp. (°F)	23.6	23.6	31.6	44.0	54.4	63.8	67.4	66.1	59.3	48.4	38.9	28.2	45.8
Mean Minimum Temp. (°F)	15.9	14.7	22.0	33.4	43.3	53.7	57.4	55.9	48.9	38.8	30.9	21.1	36.3
Extreme Maximum Temp. (°F)	65	71	82	89	88	92	95	94	90	83	73	68	95
Extreme Minimum Temp. (°F)	-18	-14	-12	12	27	31	40	35	26	21	7	-19	-19
Days Maximum Temp. ≥ 90°F	0	0	0	0	0	0	0	0	0	0	0	0	0
Days Maximum Temp. ≤ 32°F	17	14	9	1	0	0	0	0	0	0	3	12	56
Days Minimum Temp. ≤ 32°F	28	26	26	16	3	0	0	0	1	8	18	27	153
Days Minimum Temp. ≤ 0°F	4	4	1	0	0	0	0	0	0	0	0	1	10
Heating Degree Days (base 65°F)	1,275	1,163	1,027	625	337	103	38	55	195	513	776	1,135	7,242
Cooling Degree Days (base 65°F)	0	0	1	3	17	75	120	96	29	4	0	0	345
Mean Precipitation (in.)	3.49	2.55	3.00	3.35	3.36	4.17	3.90	3.71	4.26	3.72	3.68	3.80	42.99
Extreme Maximum Daily Precip. (in.)	2.47	2.30	1.76	1.64	1.54	5.33	2.97	3.22	3.09	1.89	2.35	1.43	5.33
Days With ≥ 0.1" Precipitation	11	8	8	8	8	8	8	8	8	8	9	11	103
Days With ≥ 0.5" Precipitation	2	1	2	2	2	3	3	3	3	3	3	2	29
Days With ≥ 1.0" Precipitation	0	0	0	0	0	1	1	1	1	1	0	0	5
Mean Snowfall (in.)	32.7	19.0	15.9	4.8	0.3	0.0	0.0	0.0	0.0	0.3	10.1	27.7	110.8
Maximum Snow Depth (in.)	34	28	29	11	6	0	0	0	0	2	20	19	34
Days With ≥ 1.0" Snow Depth	25	23	16	3	0	0	0	0	0	0	6	20	93

Wantagh Cedar Creek *Nassau County*   Elevation: 9 ft.   Latitude: 40° 39' N   Longitude: 73° 30' W

	JAN	FEB	MAR	APR	MAY	JUN	JUL	AUG	SEP	OCT	NOV	DEC	YEAR
Mean Maximum Temp. (°F)	38.3	40.2	47.1	56.4	65.9	76.1	81.4	81.2	74.4	64.0	54.0	43.4	60.2
Mean Temp. (°F)	32.3	33.8	40.3	49.3	58.4	68.7	74.0	73.8	66.7	56.3	47.0	37.4	53.2
Mean Minimum Temp. (°F)	26.2	27.3	33.4	41.9	50.9	61.2	66.7	66.4	59.0	48.5	40.0	31.3	46.1
Extreme Maximum Temp. (°F)	69	67	81	89	95	97	103	103	92	90	78	77	103
Extreme Minimum Temp. (°F)	-3	0	5	19	29	34	45	48	38	28	15	3	-3
Days Maximum Temp. ≥ 90°F	0	0	0	0	0	1	3	2	0	0	0	0	6
Days Maximum Temp. ≤ 32°F	8	5	1	0	0	0	0	0	0	0	0	4	18
Days Minimum Temp. ≤ 32°F	22	21	14	2	0	0	0	0	0	0	6	18	83
Days Minimum Temp. ≤ 0°F	0	0	0	0	0	0	0	0	0	0	0	0	0
Heating Degree Days (base 65°F)	1,008	876	760	466	220	32	7	3	51	279	534	847	5,083
Cooling Degree Days (base 65°F)	0	0	0	2	23	149	295	283	109	16	1	0	878
Mean Precipitation (in.)	3.32	2.62	4.00	4.22	3.60	3.57	3.60	3.29	3.50	3.67	3.46	3.55	42.40
Extreme Maximum Daily Precip. (in.)	4.91	2.19	2.47	4.64	2.44	3.32	3.90	3.89	3.73	5.43	2.21	2.36	5.43
Days With ≥ 0.1" Precipitation	6	5	7	7	6	6	6	5	5	5	6	7	71
Days With ≥ 0.5" Precipitation	2	1	3	3	2	2	3	2	2	2	3	3	28
Days With ≥ 1.0" Precipitation	1	0	1	1	1	1	1	1	1	1	1	1	11
Mean Snowfall (in.)	na	na	na	0.0	na	0.0	0.0	0.0	0.0	0.0	0.0	0.0	na
Maximum Snow Depth (in.)	na	na	na	na	na	na	na	na	na	na	na	na	na
Days With ≥ 1.0" Snow Depth	na	na	na	0	0	0	0	0	0	0	0	0	na

The period of record for all cooperative weather station data is 1980 – 2009. See User Guide for detailed explanation of data.

Westfield 2 SSE *Chautauqua County*   Elevation: 707 ft.   Latitude: 42° 18' N   Longitude: 79° 35' W

	JAN	FEB	MAR	APR	MAY	JUN	JUL	AUG	SEP	OCT	NOV	DEC	YEAR
Mean Maximum Temp. (°F)	32.8	35.3	43.1	55.6	67.3	76.1	80.3	78.2	71.0	59.7	48.2	37.4	57.1
Mean Temp. (°F)	26.4	28.0	35.0	46.8	58.3	67.2	71.8	70.1	63.1	52.2	41.8	31.5	49.3
Mean Minimum Temp. (°F)	19.9	20.5	26.9	37.9	49.2	58.1	63.3	62.0	55.2	44.6	35.4	25.6	41.6
Extreme Maximum Temp. (°F)	66	70	82	90	91	97	96	99	92	83	74	72	99
Extreme Minimum Temp. (°F)	-16	-7	-13	14	29	37	49	41	36	27	16	-8	-16
Days Maximum Temp. ≥ 90°F	0	0	0	0	0	2	2	1	0	0	0	0	5
Days Maximum Temp. ≤ 32°F	15	12	6	0	0	0	0	0	0	0	1	10	44
Days Minimum Temp. ≤ 32°F	27	25	23	9	0	0	0	0	0	1	11	24	120
Days Minimum Temp. ≤ 0°F	1	1	0	0	0	0	0	0	0	0	0	0	2
Heating Degree Days (base 65°F)	1,191	1,041	924	546	241	60	7	14	119	398	690	1,032	6,263
Cooling Degree Days (base 65°F)	0	0	1	7	40	131	226	180	70	7	0	0	662
Mean Precipitation (in.)	2.50	2.20	2.90	3.40	3.82	4.14	4.16	3.96	4.89	4.88	4.32	3.42	44.59
Extreme Maximum Daily Precip. (in.)	1.38	2.09	1.11	1.76	2.17	4.29	3.36	2.41	2.85	2.52	3.38	1.65	4.29
Days With ≥ 0.1" Precipitation	7	7	8	8	8	8	7	7	9	10	10	9	98
Days With ≥ 0.5" Precipitation	1	1	2	2	2	2	3	3	4	4	3	2	29
Days With ≥ 1.0" Precipitation	0	0	0	0	1	1	1	1	1	1	1	0	7
Mean Snowfall (in.)	21.2	14.0	12.7	2.7	0.4	0.0	0.0	0.0	trace	0.4	8.7	24.4	84.5
Maximum Snow Depth (in.)	23	22	17	9	na	0	0	0	trace	na	11	25	na
Days With ≥ 1.0" Snow Depth	25	20	12	1	0	0	0	0	0	0	5	17	80

Whitehall *Washington County*   Elevation: 119 ft.   Latitude: 43° 33' N   Longitude: 73° 24' W

	JAN	FEB	MAR	APR	MAY	JUN	JUL	AUG	SEP	OCT	NOV	DEC	YEAR
Mean Maximum Temp. (°F)	30.1	34.4	44.3	58.6	70.8	79.7	84.0	81.8	73.1	60.6	47.5	35.1	58.3
Mean Temp. (°F)	21.0	24.1	34.1	47.5	59.1	68.2	72.6	70.9	62.4	50.6	39.7	27.4	48.1
Mean Minimum Temp. (°F)	11.8	13.7	23.9	36.2	47.0	56.6	61.2	60.1	51.7	40.6	31.8	19.7	37.9
Extreme Maximum Temp. (°F)	64	63	84	94	92	102	100	96	94	83	75	68	102
Extreme Minimum Temp. (°F)	-36	-33	-14	13	23	36	45	37	28	19	4	-25	-36
Days Maximum Temp. ≥ 90°F	0	0	0	0	0	3	4	3	0	0	0	0	10
Days Maximum Temp. ≤ 32°F	17	11	4	0	0	0	0	0	0	0	1	12	45
Days Minimum Temp. ≤ 32°F	29	26	24	11	1	0	0	0	0	6	17	27	141
Days Minimum Temp. ≤ 0°F	7	5	1	0	0	0	0	0	0	0	0	2	15
Heating Degree Days (base 65°F)	1,360	1,150	952	523	204	38	3	13	132	442	755	1,158	6,730
Cooling Degree Days (base 65°F)	0	0	0	5	29	141	246	204	62	3	0	0	690
Mean Precipitation (in.)	3.01	2.52	2.95	3.22	3.67	3.89	4.46	4.16	3.68	3.72	3.55	3.22	42.05
Extreme Maximum Daily Precip. (in.)	1.96	2.40	2.02	2.23	1.85	2.96	3.45	4.01	4.25	2.62	2.59	2.89	4.25
Days With ≥ 0.1" Precipitation	6	5	6	7	8	7	7	7	6	7	7	6	79
Days With ≥ 0.5" Precipitation	2	2	2	2	2	3	3	3	2	2	3	2	28
Days With ≥ 1.0" Precipitation	1	0	1	1	1	1	1	1	1	1	1	1	11
Mean Snowfall (in.)	16.6	12.0	12.5	2.1	0.0	0.0	0.0	0.0	0.0	trace	2.7	13.6	59.5
Maximum Snow Depth (in.)	na	na	na	2	0	0	0	0	0	0	na	na	na
Days With ≥ 1.0" Snow Depth	na	na	na	0	0	0	0	0	0	0	0	na	na

Yorktown Heights 1 W *Westchester County*   Elevation: 669 ft.   Latitude: 41° 16' N   Longitude: 73° 48' W

	JAN	FEB	MAR	APR	MAY	JUN	JUL	AUG	SEP	OCT	NOV	DEC	YEAR
Mean Maximum Temp. (°F)	34.5	38.4	46.8	59.1	69.4	77.5	82.0	80.7	73.5	62.1	51.2	39.6	59.6
Mean Temp. (°F)	26.6	29.7	37.5	49.2	59.2	67.9	72.7	71.4	63.9	52.6	43.1	32.3	50.5
Mean Minimum Temp. (°F)	18.7	21.0	28.2	39.2	48.8	58.2	63.3	62.1	54.4	43.1	35.0	24.9	41.4
Extreme Maximum Temp. (°F)	67	73	85	95	94	95	100	100	95	87	78	73	100
Extreme Minimum Temp. (°F)	-15	-5	0	14	33	39	49	39	32	25	13	-9	-15
Days Maximum Temp. ≥ 90°F	0	0	0	0	0	2	3	2	1	0	0	0	8
Days Maximum Temp. ≤ 32°F	13	8	3	0	0	0	0	0	0	0	1	7	32
Days Minimum Temp. ≤ 32°F	28	25	21	5	0	0	0	0	0	3	12	25	119
Days Minimum Temp. ≤ 0°F	2	0	0	0	0	0	0	0	0	0	0	0	2
Heating Degree Days (base 65°F)	1,183	991	846	474	208	43	4	11	96	385	650	1,008	5,899
Cooling Degree Days (base 65°F)	0	0	1	6	33	136	249	217	71	7	0	0	720
Mean Precipitation (in.)	3.59	2.97	3.96	4.60	4.35	4.76	4.82	4.41	4.53	4.53	4.39	3.88	50.79
Extreme Maximum Daily Precip. (in.)	2.48	2.22	4.60	5.15	3.35	2.82	3.44	4.04	10.95	4.64	2.97	3.00	10.95
Days With ≥ 0.1" Precipitation	7	6	7	8	8	8	7	7	6	6	7	6	83
Days With ≥ 0.5" Precipitation	3	2	3	3	3	3	3	3	3	3	3	3	35
Days With ≥ 1.0" Precipitation	1	1	1	1	1	1	2	1	1	1	1	1	13
Mean Snowfall (in.)	11.0	10.3	7.7	2.1	0.0	0.0	0.0	0.0	0.0	trace	1.3	7.6	40.0
Maximum Snow Depth (in.)	29	29	19	17	0	0	0	0	0	trace	5	15	29
Days With ≥ 1.0" Snow Depth	18	15	9	1	0	0	0	0	0	0	1	10	54

The period of record for all cooperative weather station data is 1980 – 2009. See User Guide for detailed explanation of data.

New York Weather Station Rankings

Annual Extreme Maximum Temperature

Highest			Lowest		
Rank	**Station Name**	**°F**	**Rank**	**Station Name**	**°F**
1	Mineola	105	1	Indian Lake 2 SW	91
2	Dobbs Ferry Ardsley	104	2	Morrisville 5 SW	92
2	New York Laguardia Arpt	104	3	Tully Heiberg Forest	93
4	New York Central Park Observ	103	4	Boonville 2 SSW	94
4	New York Ave V Brooklyn	103	4	Grafton	94
4	Wantagh Cedar Creek	103	6	Conklingville Dam	95
7	Bridgehampton	102	6	Wales	95
7	Islip-Macarthur Arpt	102	8	Dannemora	96
7	New York J F Kennedy Int'l Arpt	102	9	Allegany State Park	97
7	Whitehall	102	9	Buffalo Greater Buffalo Int'l	97
11	Albion 2 NE	101	9	Canton 4 SE	97
11	Aurora Research Farm	101	9	Delhi 2 SE	97
11	Bath	101	9	Lowville	97
11	Middletown 2 NW	101	9	Utica Oneida County Arpt	97
11	Syracuse Hancock Int'l Arpt	101	15	Alfred	98
11	Troy Lock and Dam	101	15	Binghamton Edwin A Link Field	98
17	Alcove Dam	100	15	Gouverneur 3 NW	98
17	Chazy	100	15	Ithaca Cornell Univ	98
17	Riverhead Research Farm	100	15	Peru 2 WSW	98
17	Valatie 1 N	100	15	Rochester Intl Arpt	98
17	Yorktown Heights 1 W	100	21	Albany County Arpt	99
22	Albany County Arpt	99	21	Avon	99
22	Avon	99	21	Westfield 2 SSE	99
22	Westfield 2 SSE	99	24	Alcove Dam	100
25	Alfred	98	24	Chazy	100

Annual Mean Maximum Temperature

Highest			Lowest		
Rank	**Station Name**	**°F**	**Rank**	**Station Name**	**°F**
1	Dobbs Ferry Ardsley	62.9	1	Indian Lake 2 SW	51.0
2	New York Central Park Observ	62.7	2	Boonville 2 SSW	51.1
3	New York Laguardia Arpt	62.5	3	Tully Heiberg Forest	52.3
4	New York Ave V Brooklyn	62.4	4	Dannemora	53.1
5	Riverhead Research Farm	62.1	5	Lowville	53.2
6	Mineola	61.9	6	Canton 4 SE	54.0
7	New York J F Kennedy Int'l Arpt	61.5	7	Morrisville 5 SW	54.3
8	Islip-Macarthur Arpt	60.8	8	Grafton	54.4
8	Middletown 2 NW	60.8	9	Binghamton Edwin A Link Field	54.9
10	Wantagh Cedar Creek	60.2	9	Conklingville Dam	54.9
11	Bridgehampton	59.8	11	Chazy	55.1
12	Yorktown Heights 1 W	59.6	11	Gouverneur 3 NW	55.1
13	Troy Lock and Dam	58.9	13	Allegany State Park	55.2
14	Valatie 1 N	58.4	13	Wales	55.2
15	Whitehall	58.3	15	Utica Oneida County Arpt	55.7
16	Albion 2 NE	58.1	16	Peru 2 WSW	55.9
17	Albany County Arpt	58.0	17	Ithaca Cornell Univ	56.2
18	Avon	57.6	18	Delhi 2 SE	56.3
18	Syracuse Hancock Int'l Arpt	57.6	19	Buffalo Greater Buffalo Int'l	56.6
20	Aurora Research Farm	57.3	20	Alcove Dam	56.7
20	Rochester Intl Arpt	57.3	21	Alfred	56.9
22	Bath	57.1	22	Bath	57.1
22	Westfield 2 SSE	57.1	22	Westfield 2 SSE	57.1
24	Alfred	56.9	24	Aurora Research Farm	57.3
25	Alcove Dam	56.7	24	Rochester Intl Arpt	57.3

Rankings include 25 highest/lowest stations. If state has less than 25 stations, all stations are included. The period of record is 1980–2009. See User Guide for detailed explanation of data.

Annual Mean Temperature

Highest			Lowest		
Rank	Station Name	°F	Rank	Station Name	°F
1	New York Laguardia Arpt	55.6	1	Indian Lake 2 SW	40.7
2	New York Central Park Observ	55.3	2	Boonville 2 SSW	42.4
2	New York Ave V Brooklyn	55.3	3	Lowville	43.3
4	New York J F Kennedy Int'l Arpt	54.4	4	Tully Heiberg Forest	43.5
5	Mineola	53.7	5	Canton 4 SE	43.8
6	Riverhead Research Farm	53.6	6	Dannemora	43.9
7	Dobbs Ferry Ardsley	53.2	7	Gouverneur 3 NW	44.0
7	Wantagh Cedar Creek	53.2	8	Allegany State Park	44.6
9	Islip-Macarthur Arpt	52.6	8	Morrisville 5 SW	44.6
10	Bridgehampton	51.3	10	Delhi 2 SE	44.8
11	Middletown 2 NW	51.0	11	Chazy	45.1
12	Yorktown Heights 1 W	50.5	11	Conklingville Dam	45.1
13	Westfield 2 SSE	49.4	13	Alfred	45.2
14	Albion 2 NE	49.1	14	Grafton	45.3
14	Troy Lock and Dam	49.1	15	Bath	45.6
16	Buffalo Greater Buffalo Int'l	48.5	15	Peru 2 WSW	45.6
17	Rochester Intl Arpt	48.3	17	Wales	45.8
18	Albany County Arpt	48.2	18	Alcove Dam	46.1
18	Aurora Research Farm	48.2	19	Binghamton Edwin A Link Field	46.5
18	Syracuse Hancock Int'l Arpt	48.2	19	Ithaca Cornell Univ	46.5
21	Whitehall	48.1	21	Utica Oneida County Arpt	46.7
22	Valatie 1 N	47.8	22	Avon	47.7
23	Avon	47.7	23	Valatie 1 N	47.8
24	Utica Oneida County Arpt	46.7	24	Whitehall	48.1
25	Binghamton Edwin A Link Field	46.5	25	Albany County Arpt	48.2

Annual Mean Minimum Temperature

Highest			Lowest		
Rank	Station Name	°F	Rank	Station Name	°F
1	New York Laguardia Arpt	48.7	1	Indian Lake 2 SW	30.3
2	New York Ave V Brooklyn	48.2	2	Gouverneur 3 NW	32.8
3	New York Central Park Observ	47.8	3	Lowville	33.3
4	New York J F Kennedy Int'l Arpt	47.2	4	Delhi 2 SE	33.4
5	Wantagh Cedar Creek	46.1	5	Alfred	33.5
6	Mineola	45.4	6	Boonville 2 SSW	33.6
7	Riverhead Research Farm	45.0	6	Canton 4 SE	33.6
8	Islip-Macarthur Arpt	44.3	8	Allegany State Park	34.0
9	Dobbs Ferry Ardsley	43.4	9	Bath	34.1
10	Bridgehampton	42.7	10	Dannemora	34.7
11	Westfield 2 SSE	41.6	10	Tully Heiberg Forest	34.7
12	Yorktown Heights 1 W	41.4	12	Morrisville 5 SW	34.9
13	Middletown 2 NW	41.2	13	Chazy	35.1
14	Buffalo Greater Buffalo Int'l	40.3	14	Conklingville Dam	35.3
15	Albion 2 NE	40.1	14	Peru 2 WSW	35.3
16	Rochester Intl Arpt	39.3	16	Alcove Dam	35.5
17	Troy Lock and Dam	39.2	17	Grafton	36.2
18	Aurora Research Farm	39.1	18	Wales	36.3
19	Syracuse Hancock Int'l Arpt	38.7	19	Ithaca Cornell Univ	36.6
20	Albany County Arpt	38.3	20	Valatie 1 N	37.1
21	Binghamton Edwin A Link Field	38.1	21	Utica Oneida County Arpt	37.6
22	Whitehall	37.9	22	Avon	37.8
23	Avon	37.8	23	Whitehall	37.9
24	Utica Oneida County Arpt	37.6	24	Binghamton Edwin A Link Field	38.1
25	Valatie 1 N	37.1	25	Albany County Arpt	38.3

Rankings include 25 highest/lowest stations. If state has less than 25 stations, all stations are included. The period of record is 1980–2009. See User Guide for detailed explanation of data.

Annual Extreme Minimum Temperature

	Highest				Lowest	
Rank	Station Name	°F		Rank	Station Name	°F
1	New York Central Park Observ	-2		1	Gouverneur 3 NW	-45
1	New York J F Kennedy Int'l Arpt	-2		2	Chazy	-44
3	New York Laguardia Arpt	-3		3	Canton 4 SE	-40
3	Wantagh Cedar Creek	-3		4	Whitehall	-36
5	Mineola	-4		5	Indian Lake 2 SW	-35
5	New York Ave V Brooklyn	*-4*		5	Lowville	-35
7	Islip-Macarthur Arpt	*-7*		7	Dannemora	-34
8	Riverhead Research Farm	-8		7	Peru 2 WSW	-34
9	Dobbs Ferry Ardsley	-10		9	Boonville 2 SSW	-33
10	Bridgehampton	-11		10	Delhi 2 SE	-32
11	Albion 2 NE	-15		11	Morrisville 5 SW	*-30*
11	Yorktown Heights 1 W	-15		12	Alcove Dam	-29
13	Buffalo Greater Buffalo Int'l	-16		12	Conklingville Dam	-29
13	Westfield 2 SSE	*-16*		12	Tully Heiberg Forest	*-29*
15	Rochester Intl Arpt	-17		15	Utica Oneida County Arpt	*-27*
16	Binghamton Edwin A Link Field	-18		16	Grafton	*-26*
17	Wales	*-19*		17	Alfred	-25
18	Aurora Research Farm	-21		17	Syracuse Hancock Int'l Arpt	-25
19	Allegany State Park	*-22*		17	Valatie 1 N	*-25*
20	Albany County Arpt	-23		20	Avon	-24
20	Middletown 2 NW	-23		20	Bath	*-24*
20	Troy Lock and Dam	-23		20	Ithaca Cornell Univ	-24
23	Avon	-24		23	Albany County Arpt	-23
23	Bath	*-24*		23	Middletown 2 NW	-23
23	Ithaca Cornell Univ	-24		23	Troy Lock and Dam	-23

July Mean Maximum Temperature

	Highest				Lowest	
Rank	Station Name	°F		Rank	Station Name	°F
1	Dobbs Ferry Ardsley	85.2		1	Indian Lake 2 SW	74.2
2	New York Laguardia Arpt	85.0		2	Boonville 2 SSW	74.9
3	New York Central Park Observ	84.8		3	Tully Heiberg Forest	75.9
4	New York Ave V Brooklyn	84.5		4	Wales	*77.4*
5	Riverhead Research Farm	84.0		5	Morrisville 5 SW	*77.5*
5	Whitehall	84.0		6	Allegany State Park	77.9
7	Mineola	83.7		6	Grafton	*77.9*
8	Troy Lock and Dam	83.5		6	Lowville	77.9
9	Middletown 2 NW	83.4		9	Dannemora	78.0
10	New York J F Kennedy Int'l Arpt	82.9		10	Conklingville Dam	*78.3*
11	Albany County Arpt	82.3		11	Binghamton Edwin A Link Field	78.4
12	Valatie 1 N	*82.2*		12	Canton 4 SE	79.0
13	Albion 2 NE	82.1		13	Delhi 2 SE	79.2
14	Islip-Macarthur Arpt	*82.0*		14	Ithaca Cornell Univ	79.5
14	Yorktown Heights 1 W	82.0		15	Alcove Dam	80.0
16	Syracuse Hancock Int'l Arpt	81.7		16	Alfred	80.1
17	Peru 2 WSW	81.4		16	Buffalo Greater Buffalo Int'l	80.1
17	Wantagh Cedar Creek	81.4		16	Gouverneur 3 NW	80.1
19	Aurora Research Farm	81.3		19	Westfield 2 SSE	*80.3*
19	Avon	81.3		20	Chazy	80.4
21	Rochester Intl Arpt	81.2		20	Utica Oneida County Arpt	80.4
22	Bridgehampton	80.9		22	Bath	*80.7*
23	Bath	*80.7*		23	Bridgehampton	80.9
24	Chazy	80.4		24	Rochester Intl Arpt	81.2
24	Utica Oneida County Arpt	80.4		25	Aurora Research Farm	81.3

Rankings include 25 highest/lowest stations. If state has less than 25 stations, all stations are included. The period of record is 1980–2009. See User Guide for detailed explanation of data.

January Mean Minimum Temperature

	Highest				Lowest	
Rank	Station Name	°F		Rank	Station Name	°F
1	New York Laguardia Arpt	27.4		1	Indian Lake 2 SW	5.0
2	New York Ave V Brooklyn	27.2		2	Canton 4 SE	5.3
3	New York Central Park Observ	26.9		3	Gouverneur 3 NW	5.7
4	New York J F Kennedy Int'l Arpt	26.3		4	Lowville	7.2
5	Wantagh Cedar Creek	26.2		5	Chazy	8.0
6	Mineola	25.7		6	Dannemora	8.1
7	Riverhead Research Farm	25.0		7	Boonville 2 SSW	8.3
8	Islip-Macarthur Arpt	24.4		8	Peru 2 WSW	9.2
9	Bridgehampton	23.2		9	Conklingville Dam	9.4
10	Dobbs Ferry Ardsley	23.1		10	Delhi 2 SE	10.6
11	Westfield 2 SSE	19.9		11	Morrisville 5 SW	11.4
12	Buffalo Greater Buffalo Int'l	18.8		12	Alcove Dam	11.6
13	Yorktown Heights 1 W	18.7		13	Tully Heiberg Forest	11.7
14	Middletown 2 NW	18.5		14	Whitehall	11.8
15	Albion 2 NE	18.4		15	Grafton	12.1
16	Rochester Intl Arpt	17.8		16	Alfred	12.7
17	Aurora Research Farm	16.9		16	Bath	12.7
18	Avon	16.7		18	Valatie 1 N	13.0
19	Wales	15.9		19	Allegany State Park	13.4
20	Binghamton Edwin A Link Field	15.8		20	Utica Oneida County Arpt	14.3
20	Syracuse Hancock Int'l Arpt	15.8		21	Albany County Arpt	14.5
22	Ithaca Cornell Univ	14.7		22	Troy Lock and Dam	14.6
23	Troy Lock and Dam	14.6		23	Ithaca Cornell Univ	14.7
24	Albany County Arpt	14.5		24	Binghamton Edwin A Link Field	15.8
25	Utica Oneida County Arpt	14.3		24	Syracuse Hancock Int'l Arpt	15.8

Number of Days Annually Maximum Temperature ≥ 90°F

	Highest				Lowest	
Rank	Station Name	Days		Rank	Station Name	Days
1	Dobbs Ferry Ardsley	18		1	Boonville 2 SSW	0
1	New York Laguardia Arpt	18		1	Grafton	0
3	New York Central Park Observ	17		1	Indian Lake 2 SW	0
4	Mineola	15		1	Morrisville 5 SW	0
4	New York Ave V Brooklyn	15		1	Tully Heiberg Forest	0
6	Troy Lock and Dam	13		1	Wales	0
7	Riverhead Research Farm	11		7	Allegany State Park	1
8	Middletown 2 NW	10		7	Conklingville Dam	1
8	New York J F Kennedy Int'l Arpt	10		9	Binghamton Edwin A Link Field	2
8	Valatie 1 N	10		9	Canton 4 SE	2
8	Whitehall	10		9	Dannemora	2
12	Aurora Research Farm	9		12	Buffalo Greater Buffalo Int'l	3
13	Albany County Arpt	8		12	Chazy	3
13	Albion 2 NE	8		12	Delhi 2 SE	3
13	Islip-Macarthur Arpt	8		12	Gouverneur 3 NW	3
13	Syracuse Hancock Int'l Arpt	8		12	Lowville	3
13	Yorktown Heights 1 W	8		17	Alfred	4
18	Avon	7		17	Ithaca Cornell Univ	4
19	Bath	6		17	Utica Oneida County Arpt	4
19	Peru 2 WSW	6		20	Alcove Dam	5
19	Rochester Intl Arpt	6		20	Bridgehampton	5
19	Wantagh Cedar Creek	6		20	Westfield 2 SSE	5
23	Alcove Dam	5		23	Bath	6
23	Bridgehampton	5		23	Peru 2 WSW	6
23	Westfield 2 SSE	5		23	Rochester Intl Arpt	6

Rankings include 25 highest/lowest stations. If state has less than 25 stations, all stations are included. The period of record is 1980–2009. See User Guide for detailed explanation of data.

Number of Days Annually Maximum Temperature ≤ 32°F

Highest			Lowest		
Rank	Station Name	Days	Rank	Station Name	Days
1	Boonville 2 SSW	82	1	New York J F Kennedy Int'l Arpt	15
2	Indian Lake 2 SW	75	1	Riverhead Research Farm	15
3	Dannemora	73	3	Mineola	16
4	Tully Heiberg Forest	72	3	New York Ave V Brooklyn	16
5	Lowville	68	5	Bridgehampton	17
6	Canton 4 SE	66	5	Dobbs Ferry Ardsley	17
7	Grafton	62	5	Islip-Macarthur Arpt	17
7	Morrisville 5 SW	62	5	New York Central Park Observ	17
9	Gouverneur 3 NW	61	9	New York Laguardia Arpt	18
10	Chazy	60	9	Wantagh Cedar Creek	18
11	Peru 2 WSW	59	11	Middletown 2 NW	28
12	Binghamton Edwin A Link Field	58	12	Yorktown Heights 1 W	32
13	Allegany State Park	56	13	Troy Lock and Dam	40
13	Wales	56	13	Valatie 1 N	40
15	Utica Oneida County Arpt	55	15	Albany County Arpt	43
16	Ithaca Cornell Univ	52	16	Westfield 2 SSE	44
17	Buffalo Greater Buffalo Int'l	51	17	Whitehall	45
18	Alfred	48	18	Albion 2 NE	46
18	Conklingville Dam	48	18	Aurora Research Farm	46
18	Delhi 2 SE	48	18	Avon	46
18	Syracuse Hancock Int'l Arpt	48	18	Bath	46
22	Alcove Dam	47	18	Rochester Intl Arpt	46
23	Albion 2 NE	46	23	Alcove Dam	47
23	Aurora Research Farm	46	24	Alfred	48
23	Avon	46	24	Conklingville Dam	48

Number of Days Annually Minimum Temperature ≤ 32°F

Highest			Lowest		
Rank	Station Name	Days	Rank	Station Name	Days
1	Indian Lake 2 SW	186	1	New York Laguardia Arpt	67
2	Alfred	170	2	New York Ave V Brooklyn	69
2	Delhi 2 SE	170	3	New York Central Park Observ	70
4	Bath	169	4	New York J F Kennedy Int'l Arpt	74
5	Boonville 2 SSW	168	5	Mineola	82
6	Lowville	167	6	Wantagh Cedar Creek	83
7	Gouverneur 3 NW	166	7	Riverhead Research Farm	92
8	Tully Heiberg Forest	164	8	Islip-Macarthur Arpt	101
9	Allegany State Park	163	9	Dobbs Ferry Ardsley	106
10	Canton 4 SE	162	10	Bridgehampton	109
11	Alcove Dam	160	11	Yorktown Heights 1 W	119
11	Dannemora	160	12	Westfield 2 SSE	120
13	Morrisville 5 SW	157	13	Middletown 2 NW	121
14	Peru 2 WSW	154	14	Buffalo Greater Buffalo Int'l	125
15	Chazy	153	15	Albion 2 NE	129
15	Grafton	153	16	Rochester Intl Arpt	131
15	Wales	153	17	Aurora Research Farm	132
18	Ithaca Cornell Univ	150	18	Troy Lock and Dam	133
19	Valatie 1 N	148	19	Syracuse Hancock Int'l Arpt	134
20	Conklingville Dam	147	20	Utica Oneida County Arpt	140
21	Avon	143	21	Albany County Arpt	141
22	Binghamton Edwin A Link Field	142	21	Whitehall	141
23	Albany County Arpt	141	23	Binghamton Edwin A Link Field	142
23	Whitehall	141	24	Avon	143
25	Utica Oneida County Arpt	140	25	Conklingville Dam	147

Rankings include 25 highest/lowest stations. If state has less than 25 stations, all stations are included. The period of record is 1980–2009. See User Guide for detailed explanation of data.

Number of Days Annually Minimum Temperature ≤ 0°F

	Highest				Lowest	
Rank	Station Name	Days		Rank	Station Name	Days
1	Indian Lake 2 SW	34		1	Bridgehampton	0
2	Gouverneur 3 NW	32		1	Islip-Macarthur Arpt	0
3	Canton 4 SE	31		1	Mineola	0
4	Lowville	27		1	New York Central Park Observ	0
5	Chazy	25		1	New York J F Kennedy Int'l Arpt	0
6	Boonville 2 SSW	23		1	New York Laguardia Arpt	0
7	Dannemora	21		1	New York Ave V Brooklyn	0
8	Peru 2 WSW	20		1	Riverhead Research Farm	0
9	Delhi 2 SE	18		1	Wantagh Cedar Creek	0
10	Conklingville Dam	17		10	Dobbs Ferry Ardsley	1
11	Morrisville 5 SW	16		11	Westfield 2 SSE	2
12	Alfred	15		11	Yorktown Heights 1 W	2
12	Whitehall	15		13	Albion 2 NE	3
14	Tully Heiberg Forest	14		13	Middletown 2 NW	3
15	Allegany State Park	13		15	Buffalo Greater Buffalo Int'l	4
15	Grafton	13		15	Rochester Intl Arpt	4
17	Alcove Dam	12		17	Aurora Research Farm	5
17	Bath	12		17	Binghamton Edwin A Link Field	5
19	Ithaca Cornell Univ	11		19	Avon	8
19	Utica Oneida County Arpt	11		19	Syracuse Hancock Int'l Arpt	8
19	Valatie 1 N	11		21	Albany County Arpt	9
22	Wales	10		21	Troy Lock and Dam	9
23	Albany County Arpt	9		23	Wales	10
23	Troy Lock and Dam	9		24	Ithaca Cornell Univ	11
25	Avon	8		24	Utica Oneida County Arpt	11

Number of Annual Heating Degree Days

	Highest				Lowest	
Rank	Station Name	Num.		Rank	Station Name	Num.
1	Indian Lake 2 SW	8,896		1	New York Laguardia Arpt	4,566
2	Boonville 2 SSW	8,369		2	New York Ave V Brooklyn	4,621
3	Lowville	8,133		3	New York Central Park Observ	4,622
4	Canton 4 SE	8,035		4	New York J F Kennedy Int'l Arpt	4,796
5	Tully Heiberg Forest	8,014		5	Mineola	4,931
6	Dannemora	7,933		6	Riverhead Research Farm	4,965
7	Gouverneur 3 NW	7,930		7	Wantagh Cedar Creek	5,083
8	Morrisville 5 SW	7,601		8	Dobbs Ferry Ardsley	5,140
9	Chazy	7,584		9	Islip-Macarthur Arpt	5,261
10	Allegany State Park	7,567		10	Bridgehampton	5,523
11	Delhi 2 SE	7,542		11	Middletown 2 NW	5,773
12	Conklingville Dam	7,483		12	Yorktown Heights 1 W	5,899
13	Peru 2 WSW	7,450		13	Westfield 2 SSE	6,263
14	Alfred	7,416		14	Albion 2 NE	6,365
15	Grafton	7,406		15	Troy Lock and Dam	6,422
16	Bath	7,301		16	Buffalo Greater Buffalo Int'l	6,508
17	Wales	7,242		17	Rochester Intl Arpt	6,553
18	Alcove Dam	7,190		18	Syracuse Hancock Int'l Arpt	6,618
19	Ithaca Cornell Univ	7,090		19	Aurora Research Farm	6,633
20	Binghamton Edwin A Link Field	7,060		20	Albany County Arpt	6,638
21	Utica Oneida County Arpt	7,059		21	Whitehall	6,730
22	Valatie 1 N	6,747		22	Avon	6,732
23	Avon	6,732		23	Valatie 1 N	6,747
24	Whitehall	6,730		24	Utica Oneida County Arpt	7,059
25	Albany County Arpt	6,638		25	Binghamton Edwin A Link Field	7,060

Rankings include 25 highest/lowest stations. If state has less than 25 stations, all stations are included. The period of record is 1980–2009. See User Guide for detailed explanation of data.

Number of Annual Cooling Degree Days

	Highest			Lowest	
Rank	Station Name	Num.	Rank	Station Name	Num.
1	New York Laguardia Arpt	1,262	1	Indian Lake 2 SW	140
2	New York Ave V Brooklyn	1,187	2	Boonville 2 SSW	230
3	New York Central Park Observ	1,184	3	Allegany State Park	244
4	New York J F Kennedy Int'l Arpt	1,026	4	Tully Heiberg Forest	272
5	Dobbs Ferry Ardsley	935	5	Morrisville 5 SW	283
6	Mineola	918	6	Delhi 2 SE	293
7	Riverhead Research Farm	914	7	Alfred	294
8	Wantagh Cedar Creek	878	8	Lowville	311
9	Islip-Macarthur Arpt	839	9	Grafton	335
10	Middletown 2 NW	778	10	Conklingville Dam	339
11	Troy Lock and Dam	733	11	Wales	345
12	Yorktown Heights 1 W	720	12	Bath	347
13	Whitehall	690	12	Dannemora	347
14	Albion 2 NE	669	14	Gouverneur 3 NW	364
15	Westfield 2 SSE	662	15	Canton 4 SE	410
16	Bridgehampton	632	16	Alcove Dam	412
17	Aurora Research Farm	615	17	Binghamton Edwin A Link Field	426
18	Albany County Arpt	603	18	Ithaca Cornell Univ	438
19	Syracuse Hancock Int'l Arpt	590	19	Chazy	441
20	Buffalo Greater Buffalo Int'l	582	20	Peru 2 WSW	475
21	Rochester Intl Arpt	581	21	Utica Oneida County Arpt	494
22	Valatie 1 N	561	22	Avon	533
23	Avon	533	23	Valatie 1 N	561
24	Utica Oneida County Arpt	494	24	Rochester Intl Arpt	581
25	Peru 2 WSW	475	25	Buffalo Greater Buffalo Int'l	582

Annual Precipitation

	Highest			Lowest	
Rank	Station Name	Inches	Rank	Station Name	Inches
1	Boonville 2 SSW	58.08	1	Peru 2 WSW	30.72
2	Dobbs Ferry Ardsley	51.49	2	Bath	31.24
3	Yorktown Heights 1 W	50.79	3	Avon	31.99
4	Bridgehampton	49.65	4	Rochester Intl Arpt	34.12
5	New York Central Park Observ	49.08	5	Albion 2 NE	35.55
6	Riverhead Research Farm	47.25	6	Aurora Research Farm	36.01
7	Islip-Macarthur Arpt	46.53	7	Canton 4 SE	36.64
8	Mineola	46.08	8	Ithaca Cornell Univ	36.78
9	Delhi 2 SE	45.98	9	Gouverneur 3 NW	37.32
10	New York Ave V Brooklyn	45.96	10	Alfred	37.49
11	Grafton	45.91	11	Syracuse Hancock Int'l Arpt	37.90
12	Tully Heiberg Forest	45.74	12	Albany County Arpt	39.14
13	Morrisville 5 SW	45.56	12	Binghamton Edwin A Link Field	39.14
14	Conklingville Dam	45.16	14	Troy Lock and Dam	39.46
15	New York Laguardia Arpt	44.66	15	Indian Lake 2 SW	40.19
16	Westfield 2 SSE	44.59	16	Buffalo Greater Buffalo Int'l	40.49
17	Allegany State Park	44.47	17	Alcove Dam	40.56
18	Middletown 2 NW	43.36	18	Dannemora	40.93
19	Wales	42.99	19	Valatie 1 N	40.99
20	Utica Oneida County Arpt	42.90	20	Lowville	41.24
21	New York J F Kennedy Int'l Arpt	42.64	21	Whitehall	42.05
22	Wantagh Cedar Creek	42.40	22	Wantagh Cedar Creek	42.40
23	Whitehall	42.05	23	New York J F Kennedy Int'l Arpt	42.64
24	Lowville	41.24	24	Utica Oneida County Arpt	42.90
25	Valatie 1 N	40.99	25	Wales	42.99

Rankings include 25 highest/lowest stations. If state has less than 25 stations, all stations are included. The period of record is 1980–2009. See User Guide for detailed explanation of data.

Annual Extreme Maximum Daily Precipitation

	Highest			Lowest	
Rank	Station Name	Inches	Rank	Station Name	Inches
1	Yorktown Heights 1 W	10.95	1	Troy Lock and Dam	3.00
2	Dobbs Ferry Ardsley	7.62	2	Aurora Research Farm	3.03
3	New York Central Park Observ	7.56	3	Alfred	3.33
4	Bridgehampton	7.04	3	Rochester Intl Arpt	3.33
5	Alcove Dam	6.89	5	Indian Lake 2 SW	3.43
6	Islip-Macarthur Arpt	6.74	6	Albion 2 NE	3.79
7	New York Laguardia Arpt	6.69	7	Allegany State Park	4.00
8	Riverhead Research Farm	6.34	8	Conklingville Dam	4.01
9	New York J F Kennedy Int'l Arpt	6.27	9	Binghamton Edwin A Link Field	4.05
10	Albany County Arpt	5.60	10	Canton 4 SE	4.10
11	New York Ave V Brooklyn	5.46	11	Morrisville 5 SW	4.11
12	Wantagh Cedar Creek	5.43	12	Utica Oneida County Arpt	4.14
13	Wales	5.33	13	Whitehall	4.25
14	Avon	5.20	14	Syracuse Hancock Int'l Arpt	4.29
15	Valatie 1 N	5.10	14	Westfield 2 SSE	4.29
16	Ithaca Cornell Univ	5.08	16	Mineola	4.30
17	Buffalo Greater Buffalo Int'l	5.01	17	Delhi 2 SE	4.49
18	Middletown 2 NW	5.00	18	Gouverneur 3 NW	4.51
19	Tully Heiberg Forest	4.98	19	Dannemora	4.55
20	Boonville 2 SSW	4.86	20	Bath	4.67
21	Peru 2 WSW	4.80	21	Grafton	4.75
22	Lowville	4.78	22	Lowville	4.78
23	Grafton	4.75	23	Peru 2 WSW	4.80
24	Bath	4.67	24	Boonville 2 SSW	4.86
25	Dannemora	4.55	25	Tully Heiberg Forest	4.98

Number of Days Annually With ≥ 0.1 Inches of Precipitation

	Highest			Lowest	
Rank	Station Name	Days	Rank	Station Name	Days
1	Boonville 2 SSW	116	1	Chazy	57
2	Allegany State Park	103	2	Peru 2 WSW	66
2	Morrisville 5 SW	103	3	Bath	71
2	Tully Heiberg Forest	103	3	Wantagh Cedar Creek	71
2	Wales	103	5	New York J F Kennedy Int'l Arpt	72
6	Westfield 2 SSE	98	6	Mineola	74
7	Dannemora	97	7	Avon	75
7	Utica Oneida County Arpt	97	7	New York Laguardia Arpt	75
9	Grafton	96	9	Alcove Dam	76
10	Buffalo Greater Buffalo Int'l	95	10	Islip-Macarthur Arpt	77
11	Delhi 2 SE	94	10	Middletown 2 NW	77
11	Lowville	94	10	New York Ave V Brooklyn	77
13	Syracuse Hancock Int'l Arpt	90	13	Bridgehampton	78
14	Alfred	88	13	New York Central Park Observ	78
14	Indian Lake 2 SW	88	13	Riverhead Research Farm	78
16	Albion 2 NE	87	13	Troy Lock and Dam	78
17	Binghamton Edwin A Link Field	84	17	Whitehall	79
17	Gouverneur 3 NW	84	18	Rochester Intl Arpt	80
17	Ithaca Cornell Univ	84	18	Valatie 1 N	80
20	Canton 4 SE	83	20	Albany County Arpt	81
20	Conklingville Dam	83	20	Dobbs Ferry Ardsley	81
20	Yorktown Heights 1 W	83	22	Aurora Research Farm	82
23	Aurora Research Farm	82	23	Canton 4 SE	83
24	Albany County Arpt	81	23	Conklingville Dam	83
24	Dobbs Ferry Ardsley	81	23	Yorktown Heights 1 W	83

Rankings include 25 highest/lowest stations. If state has less than 25 stations, all stations are included. The period of record is 1980–2009. See User Guide for detailed explanation of data.

Number of Days Annually With ≥ 0.5 Inches of Precipitation

Highest			Lowest		
Rank	Station Name	Days	Rank	Station Name	Days
1	Boonville 2 SSW	37	1	Bath	18
2	Dobbs Ferry Ardsley	35	1	Chazy	18
2	New York Central Park Observ	35	3	Avon	19
2	Yorktown Heights 1 W	35	4	Rochester Intl Arpt	20
5	Riverhead Research Farm	34	5	Albion 2 NE	21
6	Grafton	33	5	Aurora Research Farm	21
6	Mineola	33	5	Canton 4 SE	21
8	Bridgehampton	32	5	Ithaca Cornell Univ	21
8	Islip-Macarthur Arpt	32	5	Peru 2 WSW	21
8	Middletown 2 NW	32	10	Gouverneur 3 NW	22
8	New York Laguardia Arpt	32	11	Alfred	23
8	New York Ave V Brooklyn	32	11	Syracuse Hancock Int'l Arpt	23
13	New York J F Kennedy Int'l Arpt	31	13	Binghamton Edwin A Link Field	24
14	Delhi 2 SE	30	13	Buffalo Greater Buffalo Int'l	24
15	Conklingville Dam	29	15	Indian Lake 2 SW	25
15	Valatie 1 N	29	15	Lowville	25
15	Wales	29	15	Utica Oneida County Arpt	25
15	Westfield 2 SSE	29	18	Albany County Arpt	26
19	Alcove Dam	28	18	Allegany State Park	26
19	Morrisville 5 SW	28	20	Dannemora	27
19	Wantagh Cedar Creek	28	20	Troy Lock and Dam	27
19	Whitehall	28	20	Tully Heiberg Forest	27
23	Dannemora	27	23	Alcove Dam	28
23	Troy Lock and Dam	27	23	Morrisville 5 SW	28
23	Tully Heiberg Forest	27	23	Wantagh Cedar Creek	28

Number of Days Annually With ≥ 1.0 Inches of Precipitation

Highest			Lowest		
Rank	Station Name	Days	Rank	Station Name	Days
1	Boonville 2 SSW	13	1	Bath	3
1	Dobbs Ferry Ardsley	13	2	Avon	4
1	New York Ave V Brooklyn	13	2	Canton 4 SE	4
1	Yorktown Heights 1 W	13	2	Rochester Intl Arpt	4
5	Bridgehampton	12	2	Syracuse Hancock Int'l Arpt	4
5	Conklingville Dam	12	6	Albion 2 NE	5
5	Islip-Macarthur Arpt	12	6	Allegany State Park	5
5	Mineola	12	6	Aurora Research Farm	5
5	New York Central Park Observ	12	6	Chazy	5
5	New York J F Kennedy Int'l Arpt	12	6	Ithaca Cornell Univ	5
5	New York Laguardia Arpt	12	6	Wales	5
5	Riverhead Research Farm	12	12	Alfred	6
13	Wantagh Cedar Creek	11	12	Dannemora	6
13	Whitehall	11	12	Gouverneur 3 NW	6
15	Alcove Dam	10	12	Peru 2 WSW	6
15	Grafton	10	16	Buffalo Greater Buffalo Int'l	7
15	Middletown 2 NW	10	16	Morrisville 5 SW	7
18	Indian Lake 2 SW	9	16	Westfield 2 SSE	7
18	Troy Lock and Dam	9	19	Albany County Arpt	8
18	Valatie 1 N	9	19	Binghamton Edwin A Link Field	8
21	Albany County Arpt	8	19	Delhi 2 SE	8
21	Binghamton Edwin A Link Field	8	19	Lowville	8
21	Delhi 2 SE	8	19	Tully Heiberg Forest	8
21	Lowville	8	19	Utica Oneida County Arpt	8
21	Tully Heiberg Forest	8	25	Indian Lake 2 SW	9

Rankings include 25 highest/lowest stations. If state has less than 25 stations, all stations are included. The period of record is 1980–2009. See User Guide for detailed explanation of data.

Annual Snowfall

	Highest			Lowest	
Rank	Station Name	Inches	Rank	Station Name	Inches
1	Boonville 2 SSW	197.5	1	Mineola	19.8
2	Syracuse Hancock Int'l Arpt	124.5	2	New York Ave V Brooklyn	22.3
3	Morrisville 5 SW	124.1	3	New York J F Kennedy Int'l Arpt	22.7
4	Lowville	121.4	4	New York Central Park Observ	23.6
5	Tully Heiberg Forest	115.8	5	New York Laguardia Arpt	25.9
6	Wales	110.8	6	Bridgehampton	26.5
7	Rochester Intl Arpt	99.4	7	Riverhead Research Farm	27.0
8	Buffalo Greater Buffalo Int'l	94.0	8	Dobbs Ferry Ardsley	30.6
9	Alfred	87.6	9	Troy Lock and Dam	38.6
10	Gouverneur 3 NW	84.6	10	Yorktown Heights 1 W	40.0
11	Westfield 2 SSE	84.5	11	Valatie 1 N	41.4
12	Grafton	83.2	12	Bath	44.8
13	Binghamton Edwin A Link Field	82.8	13	Avon	51.9
14	Canton 4 SE	77.9	14	Peru 2 WSW	52.0
15	Conklingville Dam	70.4	15	Chazy	56.6
16	Albion 2 NE	66.4	16	Aurora Research Farm	58.9
17	Delhi 2 SE	65.4	17	Whitehall	59.5
18	Ithaca Cornell Univ	63.9	18	Albany County Arpt	60.2
19	Albany County Arpt	60.2	19	Ithaca Cornell Univ	63.9
20	Whitehall	59.5	20	Delhi 2 SE	65.4
21	Aurora Research Farm	58.9	21	Albion 2 NE	66.4
22	Chazy	56.6	22	Conklingville Dam	70.4
23	Peru 2 WSW	52.0	23	Canton 4 SE	77.9
24	Avon	51.9	24	Binghamton Edwin A Link Field	82.8
25	Bath	44.8	25	Grafton	83.2

Annual Maximum Snow Depth

	Highest			Lowest	
Rank	Station Name	Inches	Rank	Station Name	Inches
1	Tully Heiberg Forest	60	1	Mineola	20
2	Boonville 2 SSW	57	1	Riverhead Research Farm	20
3	Morrisville 5 SW	51	3	New York Ave V Brooklyn	23
4	Chazy	50	4	Allegany State Park	25
5	Conklingville Dam	45	4	New York Laguardia Arpt	25
6	Buffalo Greater Buffalo Int'l	44	6	Dobbs Ferry Ardsley	26
7	Aurora Research Farm	43	7	Avon	27
8	Troy Lock and Dam	39	7	Bridgehampton	27
9	Canton 4 SE	38	9	Albany County Arpt	28
10	Grafton	37	9	Ithaca Cornell Univ	28
11	Bath	36	9	New York J F Kennedy Int'l Arpt	28
12	Binghamton Edwin A Link Field	35	12	Yorktown Heights 1 W	29
12	Syracuse Hancock Int'l Arpt	35	13	Albion 2 NE	30
14	Rochester Intl Arpt	34	13	Gouverneur 3 NW	30
14	Wales	34	15	Delhi 2 SE	31
16	Lowville	33	16	Lowville	33
16	Valatie 1 N	33	16	Valatie 1 N	33
18	Delhi 2 SE	31	18	Rochester Intl Arpt	34
19	Albion 2 NE	30	18	Wales	34
19	Gouverneur 3 NW	30	20	Binghamton Edwin A Link Field	35
21	Yorktown Heights 1 W	29	20	Syracuse Hancock Int'l Arpt	35
22	Albany County Arpt	28	22	Bath	36
22	Ithaca Cornell Univ	28	23	Grafton	37
22	New York J F Kennedy Int'l Arpt	28	24	Canton 4 SE	38
25	Avon	27	25	Troy Lock and Dam	39

Rankings include 25 highest/lowest stations. If state has less than 25 stations, all stations are included. The period of record is 1980–2009. See User Guide for detailed explanation of data.

Number of Days Annually With ≥ 1.0 Inch Snow Depth

	Highest			Lowest	
Rank	Station Name	Days	Rank	Station Name	Days
1	Boonville 2 SSW	134	1	Mineola	18
2	Tully Heiberg Forest	*124*	1	New York J F Kennedy Int'l Arpt	18
3	Morrisville 5 SW	115	1	New York Ave V Brooklyn	*18*
4	Lowville	107	4	New York Laguardia Arpt	19
5	Gouverneur 3 NW	97	5	Bridgehampton	20
6	Allegany State Park	95	6	Riverhead Research Farm	21
7	Conklingville Dam	94	7	Dobbs Ferry Ardsley	34
7	Grafton	*94*	8	Albion 2 NE	47
9	Wales	*93*	9	Valatie 1 N	*53*
10	Canton 4 SE	92	10	Yorktown Heights 1 W	54
11	Chazy	*81*	11	Troy Lock and Dam	55
12	Westfield 2 SSE	*80*	12	Albany County Arpt	59
13	Binghamton Edwin A Link Field	79	13	Bath	*67*
14	Delhi 2 SE	78	14	Avon	70
14	Syracuse Hancock Int'l Arpt	78	15	Aurora Research Farm	71
16	Ithaca Cornell Univ	74	15	Buffalo Greater Buffalo Int'l	71
17	Rochester Intl Arpt	73	17	Rochester Intl Arpt	73
18	Aurora Research Farm	71	18	Ithaca Cornell Univ	74
18	Buffalo Greater Buffalo Int'l	71	19	Delhi 2 SE	78
20	Avon	70	19	Syracuse Hancock Int'l Arpt	78
21	Bath	*67*	21	Binghamton Edwin A Link Field	79
22	Albany County Arpt	59	22	Westfield 2 SSE	*80*
23	Troy Lock and Dam	55	23	Chazy	*81*
24	Yorktown Heights 1 W	54	24	Canton 4 SE	92
25	Valatie 1 N	*53*	25	Wales	*93*

Rankings include 25 highest/lowest stations. If state has less than 25 stations, all stations are included. The period of record is 1980–2009. See User Guide for detailed explanation of data.

Significant Storm Events in New York: 2000 – 2009

Location or County	Date	Type	Mag.	Deaths	Injuries	Property Damage ($mil.)	Crop Damage ($mil.)
Buffalo Metro Area, Western Southern Tier	11/20/00	Heavy Snow	na	0	0	46.5	0.0
New York City Metro Area	02/17/03	Heavy Snow	na	0	0	20.0	0.0
Northwest New York	04/04/03	Ice Storm	na	1	0	28.5	8.5
Northwestern Central New York	04/04/03	Ice Storm	na	0	0	28.5	0.0
Broome	06/13/03	Flash Flood	na	5	0	0.1	0.0
Sullivan	08/30/04	Flash Flood	na	0	0	20.0	0.0
Delaware	06/27/06	Flash Flood	na	2	0	250.0	0.0
Broome	06/27/06	Flash Flood	na	0	0	200.0	0.0
Tioga	06/27/06	Flash Flood	na	0	0	100.0	0.0
Sullivan	06/27/06	Flash Flood	na	1	0	100.0	0.0
Oneida	06/27/06	Flash Flood	na	0	0	50.0	0.0
Chenango	06/27/06	Flood	na	0	0	50.0	0.0
Otsego	06/27/06	Flash Flood	na	0	0	50.0	0.0
Broome	06/27/06	Flood	na	0	0	50.0	0.0
Chenango	06/27/06	Flash Flood	na	1	0	50.0	0.0
Madison	06/27/06	Flash Flood	na	0	0	25.0	0.0
Southeast New York	08/01/06	Excessive Heat	na	42	0	0.0	0.0
Southwest Suffolk County	04/16/07	Coastal Flood	na	0	0	26.0	0.0
Delaware	06/19/07	Flash Flood	na	4	0	30.0	0.0
Cattaraugus	08/09/09	Flash Flood	na	1	1	45.0	0.0
Chautauqua	08/09/09	Flash Flood	na	0	0	30.0	0.0
Jefferson and Lewis Counties	12/09/09	High Wind	58 mph	0	0	100.0	0.0

Note: Deaths, injuries, and damages are date and location specific.

REFERENCE